S0-AIJ-860

Who's Who in American Art™

Who'sWho in American Art™

2016

36th Edition

MARQUIS
Who'sWho®
430 Mountain Avenue, Suite 400
New Providence, NJ 07974 U.S.A.
www.marquiswhoswho.com

Who'sWho in American Art™

Marquis Who's Who

For information, contact: Marquis Who's Who, 430 Mountain Avenue, Suite 400
New Providence, New Jersey 07974
1-800-473-7020; www.marquiswhoswho.com

WHO'S WHO IN AMERICAN ART ® is a registered trademark of Marquis Who's Who LLC.

Library of Congress Catalog Number 36-27014
International Standard Book Number 978-0-8379-6316-7
International Standard Serial Number 0000-0191

Manufactured in the United States of America.

Table of Contents

Preface

Marquis Who's Who is proud to present the 36th edition of *Who's Who in American Art*. This annual directory, first published in 1953, profiles more than 10,530 contributors to the visual arts. Within this publication, you will find all segments of the art world including artists, gallery/museum administrators, consultants, writers, critics, curators, dealers, historians, educators, lecturers, collectors, exhibitors, association/organization executives, award/grant recipients, librarians, scholars and publishers.

As in all Marquis Who's Who biographical volumes, the individuals profiled in *Who's Who in American Art* are selected on the basis of current reference value. Factors such as position, noteworthy accomplishments, visibility, and prominence in a field are all taken into account. While the vast majority of the individuals profiled on the following pages are American, *Who's Who in American Art* also includes the biographies of select individuals from around the world whose lives have had considerable impact and influence in America.

Biographical information is gathered in a variety of manners. In most cases, we invite our biographees to submit their biographical details. Otherwise, the information is collected independently by our research/editorial staff members, who use a wide assortment of tools to gather the most complete, accurate, and up-to-date information available.

As a complement to the biographical profiles, this publication contains 3 Indexes. A Geographic Index breaks down listings by state/province/city within the United States and Canada. For entrants who reside outside North America, a breakdown by country is included. A Professional Classifications Index locates entrants by area of expertise. Also, a Necrology Index profiles deceased individuals cumulative from 1953.

While the Marquis Who's Who editors exercise the utmost care in preparing each biographical sketch for publication, it is inevitable in a publication involving so many profiles that occasional errors will appear. Users of this publication are urged to notify the publisher of any issues so that adjustments can be made, which will not only be reflected in all subsequent editions of the book but which can now be immediately displayed via *Marquis Biographies Online*.

All of the profiles featured in *Who's Who in American Art* are available on www.marquiswhoswho.com through a subscription. At the present time, subscribers to *Marquis Biographies Online* have access to all of the names included in all of the Marquis Who's Who publications, as well as many new biographies that will appear in upcoming publications.

We sincerely hope that this volume will be an indispensable reference tool for you. We are always looking for ways to better serve you and welcome your ideas for improvements. In addition, we continue to welcome your Marquis Who's Who nominations.

Key to Information

[1] SCOTT, ISSAC M
[2] PHOTOGRAPHER, EDUCATOR

[3] b Honolulu, Hawaii, Apr 25, 1978. **[4]** *Study*: Yale Univ, BA, 99; Sch Art Inst, Chicago, MFA, 2002. **[5]** *Work*: Mus Mod Art, New York.; Metrop Mus Art, New York; Hammer Mus, Los Angeles, Calif.; Smithsonian Nat Mus Am Hist. **[6]** *Comn*: 3D Photo, City Univ NY, 97. **[7]** *Exhib*: Solo exhibs, Moore Gallery, Pa, 2000, 2004; Mint Mus Art, Charlotte, NC, 2002; Sheldon Gallery, Univ Nebr, 2003; Micaëla Gallery, San Francisco, 2003, 2004, 2006, 2009; group exhib, Artists of the Book, Boston Craft Mus, 98; Munson Gallery, Santa Fe, 98; Whitney Mus Am Art, New York, 2000, 2002; Mus Contemp Arts, Chicago, 2004; Mus Mod Art, New York, 2006; San Francisco Mus Mod Art, Calif, 2007, 2009; PS 1 Contemp Art Ctr, Long Island, NY, 2008, 2009. **[8]** *Collections Arranged*: dir & cur, People & Time, San Francisco Mus Mod Art, 2005; Exploring Nature (auth, catalog), Mus Fine Arts, NMex, 2006. **[9]** *Pos*: Founder/dir, People Photography, San Francisco, 2007-. **[10]** *Teaching*: instr photog, Corcoran Sch Art, DC, 2000-2002, San Francisco State Univ, 2002-2005, Univ Calif Berkeley, 2005-. **[11]** *Awards*: Artist Fel, Nat Endowment Arts, 99; Guggenheim Fel, 2002; Prof Award of Merit, Am Asn Univ Prof, 2005. **[12]** *Bibliog*: Thomas McMahon (auth), Picture California, Phoenix, New York, 2000; Photographers of the decade, Los Angeles Times, 5/3/2002; Scenes of Nature, New York Times, 7/11/2006; Victoria Tran (auth), Picture This, Univ Cailf Press, 2006. **[13]** *Mem*: Soc Photog Educ; Prof Photogrs Am; Nat Press Photogr Asn. **[14]** *Media*: Digital **[15]** *Publ*: Patricia Cooper (auth), Beauty and Photography, Yale Univ Press, 2008; coauth, Art and Photography, Univ Calif Press, 2005; auth, People & Pictures, Univ Calif Press, 2009. **[16]** *Dealer*: Micaëla Gallery 49 Geary St No 234 San Francisco CA 94108. **[17]** *Mailing Add*: 10 Orchard Dr San Francisco CA 94129

KEY

[1] Name
[2] Classification
[3] Vital Statistics
[4] Education
[5] Public Works
[6] Commissions
[7] Exhibitions
[8] Collections Arranged
[9] Professional Positions
[10] Teaching Positions
[11] Honors & Awards
[12] Bibliography
[13] Memberships
[14] Media
[15] Publications
[16] Dealer
[17] Address

Table of Abbreviations

The following is a list of some of the most frequently used Marquis abbreviations:

A

abstr—abstract(s)
acad—academia, academic, academica, academie, academique, academy, accademia
acoust—acoustic(s), acoustical
actg—acting
addn—addition, additional
adj—adjunct
Adm—Admiral
admin—administration, administrative
adminr—administrator
admis(s)—admission(s)
adv—adviser(s), advisory
advan—advance(d), advancement
advert—advertisement, advertising
aesthet—aesthetics
affil—affiliate, affiliation
agr—agricultural, agriculture
akad—akedemi, akademia
Ala—Alabama
Alta—Alberta
Am—America, American
anal—analysis, analytic, analytical
analog—analogue
anat—anatomic, anatomical, anatomy
ann—annual
anthrop—anthropological, anthropology
antiq—antiquary, antiquities, antiquity
antiqn—antiquarian
app—appoint, appointed
appl—applied
approx—approximate, approximately
Apr—April
apt—apartment(s)
arch—archive, archiva, archives, archivio, archivo
archeol—archeological, archeologie, archeologique, archeology
archit—architectural, architecture
Arg—Argentina
Ariz—Arizona
Ark—Arkansas
asn—association
asoc—asociacion
assoc(s)—associate(s), associated
asst(s)—assistant(s)
atty—attorney
Aug—August
auth—author
AV—audiovisual
Ave—Avenue

B

b—born
BC—British Columbia
bd—board
Belg—Belgian, Belgium
bibliog—bibliografia, bibliographic, bibliographical, bibliography(ies)
bibliot—biblioteca, bibliotek, bibliotheca, bibliothek, bibliotheque
biog—biographical, biography
bk(s)—book(s)
Bldg—Building(s)
Blvd—Boulevard
br—branch(es)
bro(s)—brother(s)
Brit—Britain, British
bull—bulletin
bur—bureau
bus—business
BWI—British West Indies

C

Calif—California
Can—Canada, Canadian, Canadien, Canadienne
Capt—Captain
Cath—Catholic
CBS—Columbia Broadcasting System
cent—central
Cent Am—Central America
cert—certificate(s), certification, certified
chap—chapter
chmn—chairman
c/o—care of
co—companies, company
Co—County
coauth—coauthor
co-chmn—co-chairman
co-dir—co-director
co-ed—co-editor
co-educ—co-educational
CofC—Chamber of Commerce
Col—Colonel
coll(s)—college(s), collegiate
collab—collaboration, collaborative
collabr—collaborator
Colo—Colorado
com—commerce, commercial
comdr—commander
commun—communication(s)
comn(s)—commission(s), commissioned
comnr—commissioner
compos—composition
comt(s)—committee(s)
conf—conference
Cong—Congress, Congressional
Conn—Connecticut
conserv—conservacion, conservation, conservatiore, conservatory
construct—construction
consult—consult, consultant, consultantship, consultation, consulting
contemp—contemporary
contrib—contribute, contributing, contribution
contribr—contributor
conv—convention
coop—cooperating, cooperation, cooperative
coord—coordinate, coordinating, coordination
coordr—coordinator
corp—corporate, corporation
corresp—correspondent, corresponding
coun—council, counsel, counseling
counr—councilor, counselor
CPA—Certified Public Accountant
Ct—Court
ctr—center
cult—cultural, culture
cur—curator
curric—curriculum
Czech—Czechoslovakia

D

DC—District of Columbia
Dec—December
Del—Delaware
deleg—delegate, delegation
demonstr—demonstrator
dept—department, departmental
develop—development, developmental
dict—dictionaries, dictionary
dig—digest
dipl—diplom, diploma, diplomate, diplome
dir(s)—director(s), directory
dist—district
distribr—distributor
div—division, divisional, divorced
doc—document(s), documentary, documentation
Dom—Dominion
Dr—Doctor, Drive

E

E—East
econ—economic(s), economical, economist, economy
ed—edicion, edit, edited, editing, edition, editor(s), editorial, edizione
educ—educate, educated, educating, education, educational
elec—electric, electrical, electricity
elem—elementary
emer—emeriti, emeritus

encyl—encyclopedia
eng—engineering
Eng—England, English
environ—environment(s), environmental
equip—equipment
estab—established, establishment
estud—estudante, estudas, estudiante, estudio, estudo
Europ—European
exam—examination
exec(s)—executive(s)
exhib(s)—exhibit(s), exhibition
exped(s)—expedition(s)
explor—exploration(s), exploratory
expos—exposition
exten—extention

F

fac—faculty
Feb—February
fed—federal
fedn—federation
fel(s)—fellow(s), fellowship(s)
Fla—Florida
for—foreign
found—foundation
Fr—France, French
Ft—Fort
ft—feet, foot

G

Ga—Georgia
gen—general, generale
Ger—German, Germany
Ges—Gesellschaft
gov—governing, governor
govt—government, governmental
grad—graduate, graduated
Gt Brit—Great Britain
gym—gymnasium

H

handbk(s)—handbook(s)
hist—historia, historic, historica, historical, historique, historisch(e), history
HM—Her Majesty
hochsch—hochschule
hon(s)—honor(s), honorable, honorary
hosp(s)—hospital(s), hospitalization
hq—headquarters
Hwy—Highway

I

Ill—Illinois
illum—illuminating, illumination
illus—illustrate, illustrated, illustration
illusr—illustrator
Inc—Incorporated
incl—include, included, includes, including
Ind—Indiana
indust(s)—industrial, industries, industry
info—information
inst—institut, instituto
inst(s)—institute(s), institution(s)
instnl—institutional, institutionalized
instr(s)—instruct, instruction, instructors
instrnl—instructional
int—internacional, international, internazionale
introd—introduction
ist—istituto
Ital—Italia, Italian, Italiana, Italiano, Italica, Italien, Italienisch, Italienne(s)

J

J—Journal (title)
Jan—January
jour—journal (descriptive)
jr—junior
juv—juvenile(s)

K

Kans—Kansas
Ky—Kentucky

L

La—Louisiana
lab(s)—laboratories, laboratory
lang—language(s)
lect—lecture(s)
lectr—lecturer(s)
lett—letter(s)
lib—liberal
libr—libraries, library, librerio
librn—librarian
lit—literary, literaure, literatura, literature, littera, litterature
Lt—Lieutenant
ltd—limited

M

mag—magazine
maj—major
Man—Manitoba
Mar—March
Mass—Massachusetts
mat—material(s)
Md—Maryland
med—medical, medicine, medicinal
mem—member(s), membership(s), memoirs
Mem—Memorial
metrop—metropolitan
Mex—Mexican, Mexicano, Mexico
mgr—manager
mgt—management
Mich—Michigan
Minn—Minnesota
Miss—Mississippi
Mo—Missouri
mo—month
mod—modern, moderna, moderne, moderno
monogr—monograph
Mont—Montana
Mt—Mount
munic—municipal, municipalities
mus—musee, museo, museum(s)

N

N—North
nac—nacional
nat—nationaal, national, nationale, nationalis
naz—nazionale
NB—New Brunswick
NC—North Carolina
NDak—North Dakota
Nebr—Nebraska
Neth—Netherlands
Nev—Nevada
New Eng—New England
Nfld—Newfoundland
NH—New Hampshire
NJ—New Jersey
NMex—New Mexico
Norweg—Norwegian
Nov—November
NS—Nova Scotia
NSW—New South Wales
NY—New York
NZ—New Zealand

O

Oct—October
off—office, official
Okla—Oklahoma
Ont—Ontario
oper(s)—operation(s), operational, operative
Ore—Oregon
orgn—organization, organizational

P

Pa—Pennsylvania
Pac—Pacific
Pan-Am—Pan-American
partic—participant, participating
PEI—Prince Edward Island
philos—philosophic, philosophical, philosophy
photog—photographic, photography
photogr—photographer(s)
Pkwy—Parkway
Pl—Place
PO Box—Post Office Box
polytech—polytechnic, polytechnical
Port—Portugal, Portuguese
PQ—Province of Quebec
PR—Puerto Rico

prehist—prehistoric, prehistory
pres—president
Presby—Presbyterian
preserv—preservation
prof—profession, professional, professor, professorial
prog(s)—program(s), programmed, programming
proj(s)—project(s), projection(s), projectional, projective
prom—promotion
prov—province, provincial
pub—public
publ—publication(s), published, publisher(s), publishing
pvt—private

Q

Quart—Quarterly
Que—Quebec

R

Rd—Road
RD—Rural Delivery
rec—record(s), recording
regist—register, registered, registration
registr—registrar
relig—religion, religious
rep—represent, representative
Repub—Republic
res—research
ret—retired
rev—review, revised, revision
RFD—Rural Free Delivery
RI—Rhode Island
Rm—Room
RR—Rural Route
Rte—Route
Russ—Russia, Russian

S

S—South
S Africa—South Africa, South African
S Am—South America, South American
Sask—Saskatchewan
SC—South Carolina
Scand—Scandinavia, Scandinavian
sch(s)—school(s)
scholar—scholarship
sci—science(s), scientific
SDak—South Dakota
sec—secondary
sect—section
secy—secretary
sem—seminar, seminary
Sen—Senator, Senatorial
Sept—September
ser—series
serv—service(s), serving
soc(s)—sociedad, societa, societas, societate, societe, societet, societies, society
Span—Spanish
spec—special
Sq—Square
sr—senior
St—Saint, Street
sta(s)—station(s)
Ste—Sainte
struct—structural, structure(s)
super—superieur, superior, superiore
suppl—supplement, supplemental, supplementary
supt—superintendent
supv—supervising, supervision
Swed—Swedish
Switz—Switzerland
symp—symposium(s)

T

tech—technical, technique
technol—technologic, technological, technology
tel—telegraph(y), telephone
Tenn—Tennessee
Terr—Terrace
Tex—Texas
transp—transparent, transportation
transl—tranlation(s)
translr—translator
treas—treasurer, treasury
Twp—Township

U

UN—United Nations
undergrad—undergraduate
UNESCO— United Nations Educational, Scientific and Cultural Organization
univ(s)—universidad, universite, universities, university
US—United States
USA—United States Army
USAF—United States Air Force
USMC—United States Marine Corps
USN—United States Navy

V

Va—Virginia
var—various
vchmn—vice chairman
Vet—Veteran(s)
VI—Virgin Islands
vis—visiting
voc—vocational
vol(s)—volume(s)
vpres—vice president
Vt—Vermont

W

W—West
Wash—Washington
Wis—Wisconsin
wk—week
WVa—West Virginia
Wyo—Wyoming

Y

yearbk—yearbook
YMCA—Young Men's Christian Association
YMHA—Young Men's Hebrew Association
yr(s)—year(s)
YWCA—Young Women's Christian Association
YWHA—Young Women's Hebrew Association

Alphabetical Practices

Names are arranged alphabetically according to the surnames, and under identical surnames according to the first given name. If both surname and first given name are identical, names are arranged alphabetically according to the second given name.

Surnames beginning with De, Des, Du, however capitalized or spaced, are recorded with the prefix preceding the surname and arranged alphabetically under the letter D.

Surnames beginning with Mac and Mc are arranged alphabetically under M.

Surnames beginning with Saint or St. appear after names that begin Sains, and are arranged according to the second part of the name, e.g., St. Clair before Saint Dennis.

Surnames beginning with Van, Von, or von are arranged alphabetically under the letter V.

Compound surnames are arranged according to the first member of the compound.

Many hyphenated Arabic names begin Al-, El-, or al-. These names are alphabetized according to each biographee's designation of last name. Thus Al-Bahar, Neta may be listed either under Al- or under Bahar, depending on the preference of the listee.

Also, Arabic names have a variety of possible spellings when transposed to English. Spelling of these names is always based on the practice of the biographee. Some biographees use a Western form of word order, while others prefer the Arabic word sequence.

Similarly, Asian names may have no comma between family and given names, but some biographees have chosen to add the comma. In each case, punctuation follows the preference of the biographee.

Parentheses used in connection with a name indicate which part of the full name is usually omitted in common usage. Hence, Chambers, E(lizabeth) Anne indicates that the first name, Elizabeth, is generally recorded as an initial. In such a case, the parentheses are ignored in alphabetizing and the name would be arranged as Chambers, Elizabeth Anne.

However, if the entire first name appears in parentheses, for example, Chambers, (Elizabeth) Anne, the first name is not commonly used, and the alphabetizing is therefore arranged as though the name were Chambers, Anne.

If the entire middle name is in parentheses, it is still used in alphabetical sorting. Hence, Belamy, Katherine (Lucille) would sort as Belamy, Katherine Lucille. The same occurs if the entire last name is in parentheses, e.g., (Brandenberg), Howard Keith would sort as Brandenberg, Howard Keith.

For visual clarification:

Smith, H(enry) George: Sorts as Smith, Henry George
Smith, (Henry) George: Sorts as Smith, George
Smith, Henry (George): Sorts as Smith, Henry George
(Smith), Henry George: Sorts as Smith, Henry George

Who'sWho in American Art™

Biographies

A

AADLAND, DALE LYNN
PRINTMAKER, PAINTER
b Sisseton, SDak, Mar 21, 1962. *Study:* Minn State Univ, BFA, 1997. *Comn:* print etching, Dakota Fine Art, Fargo, NDak, 95. *Exhib:* Northern Plains Int Printmaking Exhib, Fifth St Gallery, Bismarck, NDak, 97; Tekakwitha Fine Art Ctr, Sisseton, 99. *Teaching:* mentor, Wilmot Pub Sch, SDak, 99-. *Awards:* Artists Grant, SDak Arts Coun, 2000; Career Opportunity Grant, Minn Arts Coun, 96. *Media:* Etching. *Dealer:* Harold Moore PO Box 147 Browns Valley MN 56219

ABANY, ALBERT CHARLES
PAINTER, PRINTMAKER
b Boston, Mass, Mar 30, 1921. *Study:* Sch Mus Fine Arts, Boston, M O H Longstreth scholar, 42, dipl, 48; Tufts Univ, BS (educ), 49. *Exhib:* Solo exhib, Carl Siembab Gallery, Boston, 56; Clark Univ, 63; Northeastern Univ, 67; Wessell Libr, Tufts Univ, 71; Art Inst Boston, 72. *Teaching:* Instr drawing & painting, Boston Ctr Adult Educ, 49-51, Danforth Mus Sch, Framingham, 75-77 & S Shore Art Ctr, Cohasset, Mass, 83-; instr drawing, painting, printmaking & art hist, Art Inst Boston, 65-73; instr drawing, painting & hist art, Quincy Jr Coll, 75-76; instr oil & acrylic painting, Brockton Art Mus, Mass, 75-77. *Media:* Oil, Graphics, Mixed Media. *Mailing Add:* 42 MacArthur Rd Natick MA 01760-2938

ABBE, ELFRIEDE MARTHA
SCULPTOR, PRINTMAKER
b Washington, DC. *Study:* Coll Archit, Cornell Univ, BFA, 40. *Work:* Rosenwald Collection, Nat Gallery Art; Mus Fine Arts, Boston; Houghton Libr, Harvard Univ; Sloniker Collection, Cincinnati Art Mus; Mus Fine Arts, Venice, Italy. *Comn:* The Hunter (large statue), NY World's Fair, 39; oak frieze, Mann Libr, Cornell Univ, 55 & bronze sculptures, Clive McCay Mem, 67; Napoleon (bronze head), McGill Univ Libr; The Illuminator (walnut carving), Sterling Mem Hunt Libr, Carnegie-Mellon Univ, 69. *Exhib:* Nat Acad Design, New York; San Diego Fine Arts Gallery, 60; Printing in the USA & United Kingdom, London Chapel Exhib, Eng, 63; Int Botanical Artists, Hunt Libr, Carnegie-Mellon Univ, 68; Nat Arts Club, New York, 69 & 70. *Awards:* Gold Medal, Nat Arts Club, 70 & Acad Artists Asn, Springfield, Mass, 76; Elliot Liskin Cash Award, Salmagundi Club, 79. *Bibliog:* Norman Kent (auth), The Book Art of Elfriede Abbe, Am Artist Mag, 60. *Mem:* Fel Nat Sculpture Soc; Nat Soc Mural Painters. *Media:* Wood; Woodcut. *Publ:* Designed, illus & printed, Garden Spice & Wild Pot-Herbs, Cornell Univ, 55, The American Scholar, 56, Seven Irish Tales, 57 & Significance of the Frontier, 58

ABBETT, ROBERT KENNEDY
PAINTER, WRITER
b Hammond, Ind, Jan 5, 1926. *Study:* Purdue Univ, BS, 46; Univ Mo, BA (art), 48; Chicago Acad Fine Art, 48-50; Am Acad Art, Chicago, 49. *Work:* Cowboy Hall Fame & Western Heritage Ctr, Oklahoma City; Diamond M Mus, Snyder, Tex; Genesee Country Mus, Rochester, NY; Dog Mus Am, St Louis; Nat Bird Dog Mus, Grand Junction, Tenn. *Comn:* Portrait of Mrs Roy Larsen, Audubon Soc, Fairfield, Conn, 73; portrait of Jimmy Stewart, Cowboy Hall Fame, Oklahoma City, 75; portrait of Luther Burbank, Burbank Ctr Arts, Santa Rosa, Calif, 75; portrait of Silver comn by Ann Cox Chambers, US Embassy, Brussels, Belgium, 77; Generals Jackson and Lee, Am Military Collection, 84. *Exhib:* Nat Cowboy Western Heritage Mus, Oklahoma City, 74, 75, 86, 95, 2000, 01, 02 & 03; Artists of Am, Denver Rotary, 82-85 & 90-93; miniature show, Thomas Gilcrease Mus, Tulsa, 84, 85, 88, 95 & 96; Cheyenne Frontier Days, Old West Mus, 85-90; Wildlife & Sporting Art, Legacy Gallery, Jackson, Wyo, 1995-2004. *Teaching:* Instr media, Silvermine Col, New Canaan, Conn, 59-61; instr drawing, Sisters Notre Dame, Wilton, Conn, 70 & Washington Art Asn, Conn, 77; workshop, Scottsdale Artists Sch, Ariz, 86-96; coun, Private Career Counseling, 1992-2005. *Awards:* Outstanding Work, Artists & Books, Soc Illusr, 65; First Prize, Salmagundi Club, New York, 73; Artist Year, Nat Wildlife Art Collectors Soc, Minneapolis, 84. *Bibliog:* Nick Meglin (auth), Robert Abbett, Am Artist, 7/77; Michael McIntosh (auth), Robert Abbett, Southwest Art, 11/88; Tom Davis (auth), The Magic Show of Robert Abbett, Wildlife Art News, 9-10/88. *Mem:* Soc Illusr; Westport Artists (pres, 67); Soc Animal Artists. *Media:* Oil. *Res:* Writing and researching art subjects for my column, Abbett on Art, For Sporting Classics Magazines. *Interests:* Sporting art, dogs, horses, hunting scenes and fishing. *Publ:* Coauth, Outdoor Paintings of Robert K Abbett, Peacock/Bantam, 76; coauth with Michael McIntosh, Abbett Briar Patch Pubs, 89; auth, From behind the easel, column, Wildlife Art News, 85-; Wings from Cover, The Upland Images of Robert K Abbett and Ed Gray, Willow Creek Press, 96; auth, A Season for Painting the Outdoor Art of Robert K Abbett, Collectors Covey, 2001. *Dealer:* Russell Fink Box 250 Lorton VA 22199; Legacy Gallery Scottsdale AZ & Jackson WY; Collectors Covey Gallery Dallas. *Mailing Add:* 168 Henry Sanford Rd Bridgewater CT 06752

ABBOTT, LINDA J
STAINED GLASS ARTIST, INSTRUCTOR
b Hempstead, NY, Oct 10, 1943. *Study:* Queensboro Soc Allied Arts & Crafts, 55-59; Fashion Inst Technol, State Univ NY, AAS (design), 63; Art Inst Ft Lauderdale, cert, 97. *Work:* Holocaust Mus, Copper City, Fla. *Comn:* Entry restoration of glass, Paiewonsky Mansion-Govt Hill, Charlotte Amalie, Virgin Islands, 85; etched & carved glass, Vanderbilt Estate, Manalapan, Fla, 88; 16 windows, entry & creche, St Matthews Catholic Church, Hallandale, Fla 96; 14 windows, Temple Israel, W Palm Beach, Fla, 97; 45 ft skylight dome, Wind Jammer Cruises, Miami Beach, Fla, 98. *Exhib:* Glass in the Garden, Denver Colo Gardens, 81; Art Glass Symposium, Salt Lake City Mus Art, Utah, 82; Art Glass Expo, Art Barn Mus, Salt Lake City, Utah, 83-84; Retrospective, Art Serve, Mus Art, Ft Lauderdale, Fla, 97; Designer's Invitational, Miami Conv Ctr, Fla, 98. *Pos:* Coordr, Art Glass Expo, Salt Lake City, 81-83 & Art Glass Am, Tampa, 98; educ seminar coordr, Art Glass Supplies Asn, Chicago, 94-95; freelance consult various manufacturers & art orgns, 93-; instr, Educ Comn, Int Art Glass Supplies Asn, Long Beach, 99. *Teaching:* Instr, Crystal Rainbow Inc, Dania, Fla, 89- & Art Glass Expo, Las Vegas, 94-. *Awards:* Best of Show, Cal City Art Asn, 78. *Bibliog:* Al Lewis (auth), Beautiful entryways, Prof Stained Glass Mag, 94; Staff writer (auth), Clearly Beautiful, Palm Beach Illus, 97; Kay Bain Weiner (auth), Stained Glass - The Tiffany Style, Watkins Guptil, 97. *Mem:* Int Stained Glass Designers Asn (pres, 95-98); Art Glass Guild Artisans (founder & bd mem, 96-); Art Glass Supplies Asn (educ sem comn, 2001). *Media:* Stained & Carved Glass; Painted Glass. *Publ:* Auth, bi-monthly articles on various art glass subjects, Glass Craftsman Mag, 95-; coauth, Hot & Wired (with instrnl video), 93, Something's Fishy, 94, Rainforest, 95 & Image is Everything, 96, Stained Glass Images

ABBOTT, REBECCA PHILLIPS
CURATOR, PHOTOGRAPHER
b Giessen, Ger, Jan 10, 1950; US citizen. *Study:* Emory & Henry Col, Va, BA, 73. *Exhib:* C & O Canal, Anton Gallery, Washington, DC, 92, The Wind, 94 & Shadows at 18th & K, 98. *Pos:* Dir, Nat Mus Women Arts, Washington, DC, 89-98. *Mem:* Am Asn Mus; Art Table. *Res:* Picturing Time: Self-Portraits of Andy Warhol; Remedios Varo: A Feminist Vision for a New Metaphysics. *Dealer:* Burton Marinkovich Fine Art 1506 21st St NW Washington DC 20036. *Mailing Add:* 1250 New York Ave NW Washington DC 20005

ABELES, KIM VICTORIA
SCULPTOR
b Richmond Heights, Mo, Aug 28, 1952. *Study:* Ohio Univ, BFA (painting), 74; Univ Calif, Irvine, MFA (studio art), 80. *Work:* Washington & Jefferson Col, Washington, Pa; Fashion Inst, Los Angeles, Calif; Cal State Univ; Long Beach Art Mus, Long Beach, Calif; City of Santa Monica, Calif; Mus Contemp Art, Los Angeles, Los Angeles Co Mus of Art; Calif Science Ctr, Berkeley Art Mus; African Am Mus; US Info Agency. *Comn:* Artistic enhancements for the new Secretary of State/State Archives Building, Sacramento, Calif, 90; Panorama City Pub Libr, 92-93; Los Angeles Hill St Pedestrian Corridor, 94; Marvin Braude San Fernando Constituency Ctr, Van Nuys, Calif. *Exhib:* Solo exhibs, Munic Art Gallery, 81, Karl Bornstein Gallery, 81-83, 85 & 87, Los Angeles City Hall, 82, Phyllis Kind Gallery, Chicago & NY, 83, AIR Gallery, NY, 86, Mt St Mary's Col, Los Angeles, 87, Calif Mus Sci & Indust, Los Angeles, 90, Atlanta Pavilion, Atlanta, GA, 90, Santa Monica Art Mus, Calif, 93, The Forum, St Louis, 94 & Fresno Art Mus, 94, Torranc Art Mus, 2009, Harvard-Westlake, 2009, Univ Colo Mus Nat History, 2011, Nat Ctr Atmosphere Rsch, 2012, Syu Gallery, 2012, John Simon Guggenheim Meml Found, 2013; ART Inc, NY, 89; Nat Mus Fine Arts, Santiago, Chile, 96; Mus Mod Art, Rio de Janeiro, Brazil, 96; CEPA Gallery, Buffalo, 98; Contemp Art Ctr, Cincinnati, Ohio, 2000; Intersection, San Francisco, 2001; Arts Resource Transfer, NY, 2001; Calif Sci Ctr, Los Angeles Calif, 2001, 2003; El Camino Coll, Torrance, Calif, 2003; Ignite! The Art of Sustainability, Univ Calif Davis Design Mus, Davis, Calif, 2012; Green Acres: Artists Farming Fields, Greenhouses and Abandoned Lots, Contemporary Arts Ctr, Cincinnati, Oh, 2012; Do Not Destroy: Art, Trees, and Jewish Though, The Contemporary Jewish Mus, 2012; Swept Away: Dust, Ashes, and Dirt in Contemporary Art and Design, Mus Arts and Design, NY, 2012. *Teaching:* Distinguished vis artist, Calif State Univ, Fullerton, 85-87; vis artist, Claremont Grad Sch, 86, 87, 90 & 93 & Univ Calif, Irvine, 87-89; Prof, Calif State Univ Northridge,

98-2009. *Awards:* Fel, J Paul Getty Trust Fund Visual Arts, 93; Grant, Pollock-Krasner Found, 90 & US Info Agency, 96; Richard Neutra Award for Professional Excellence, 2001; Durfee Found grant, 2010; grant, Calif Community Found, 2010; fellowship, John Simon Guggenheim Meml Found, 2013. *Bibliog:* Patterson Sims (essayist), Kim Abeles, ART Press, 89; Andrea Liss (auth), The Insistent Voice, After Image, 3/90; Kim Abeles: Encyclopedia Persona, A 15-Year Survey, Fel Contemp Art, 93; Brandon LaBelle, Ken Ehrlich and Stephen Vitiello (editors) Problematics of Site-Surface Tension. Errant Bodies Press, 2003; Peter Selz (auth), Art of Engagement: Political Art in California 1945-Present, University of California Press, 2005; Karen Jacobson (auth), See/Hear-Museums and Imagination, California Natural History Museum, 2006; Lucinda Barnes (auth), Measure of Time, University of California, Berkeley Art Museum and Pacific Film Archive, 2007; Robert Hirsch (auth), Photographic Possibilities-The Expressive Use of Equipment, Ideas, Materials, and Processes, Focal Press, Boston, 2009, Exploring the Color Photography: From Film to Pixels, Focal Press, Boston, 2009. *Mem:* Coll Art Asn; Womens Caucus for the Arts. *Media:* Miscellaneous. *Publ:* Contribr, Fiction International, San Diego State Univ, 85; The Image of St Bernadette, pvt publ, 87; High Performance, spring/summer 88; Camerawork, San Francisco Camerawork Inc, 94; Twelve Artists, Art Press, 97; Lewis MacAdams (poetry) and Kim Abeles (images), The Family Trees, Blue Press, 2001. *Mailing Add:* 821 Traction Ave #110 Los Angeles CA 90013

ABELES, SIGMUND
PRINTMAKER, PAINTER, SCULPTOR

b New York, NY, Nov 6, 1934. *Study:* Pratt Inst; Univ SC, BA, 55; Art Student League; Skowhegan Sch Painting & Sculpture; Brooklyn Mus Sch; Columbia Univ, MFA, 57; Coastal Carolina Univ, DA (hon), 2000. *Hon Degrees:* Hon DFA, Coastal Carolina Univ, Conway, SC, 99. *Work:* Mus Mod Art, NY; Mus Arte, Ponce, PR; Philadelphia Mus Art; Boston Mus Fine Arts; Brit Mus; Albert & Victoria Mus, London; Smithsonian Inst, Washington, DC; Metrop Mus Art, NY; Nat Acad Design, NY; Whitney Mus Am Art; Butler Inst Am Art, Legacy Pastel Coll. *Comn:* Illustrations, Maggie Girl of the Streets, Limited Editions Club, 74. *Exhib:* Solo exhibs, Mary Ryan Gallery, NY, 83, Isis Gallery, Notre Dame Univ, South Bend, Ind, 88, Brattleboro Mus, Vt, 88, Yeshiva Univ Mus, NY, 88-89, Shaare Zedek Med Ctr, Jerusalem, Israel, 89, Univ WVa Art Galleries, Charlottesville, Starr Gallery, Leventhal-Sidman Jewish Community Ctr, Newton Ctr, 89, Barridoff Galleries, Portland, Maine, 90, The Cult Ctr, New York, 2009; With Nothing On, New Orleans Mus Art, La, 90; Am Drawing Invitational, Hastings Col, Nebr, 90; Solo retrospectives, New Eng Col, Henniker, NH, Art & Sci Ctr, Manchester, NH, McKissick Mus, Univ SC, Columbia, Cheekwood Mus, Nashville, Tenn & Fitchburg, Mass, 92-93; Abeles Drawings, Boston Pub Lib, 93; Thomas Williams Fine Arts, London, Eng, 2000; Group exhibs, Pinkard Gallery, Bunting Ctr, Md, Coll Art, Baltimore, 2001, Randall Bryan Art Gallery, 2001; Art 2003, London; Memorials of War, Whitney Mus Am Art, Summer, 2004; Drawings by Sigmund Abeles & Philip Growsman, Union Col, Schenectady, NY, 2004. *Pos:* bd dir, Artist Fel, New York City. *Teaching:* Instr, Swain Sch Design, New Bedford, Mass, 61-64, Wellesley Col, 64-69, Boston Univ, 69-70, Univ NH, 70-87; prof emer dept Am Art, Univ NH, 87-; instr, Acad Realist Art, Seattle, Wash, 95 & Art Student League, NY, 97-01. *Awards:* Grant for Graphics, Louis Comfort Tiffany Found, 67; Academic Seminar to Israel, Am Jewish Comt, 81; Summer Sr Fac Fel, Univ NH, 84; Chateau Rochfort en Terra, Britany, France, 2000; Hall of Fame Honoree, Pastel Soc Am Nat Arts Club, 2004; Degas Pastel Soc Award, Nat Arts Club, 2006. *Bibliog:* Philip Isaacson (auth), Fine Artists Turn Talented Hands to Applied Art (review), Maine Sunday Telegram, 3/25; Louise Dunn Yochim (auth), Michael Weinberg (ed), The Harvest Freedom, Jewish Artists in America, 1930-80's, Am References, Chicago, IL, 90; Sigmund Abeles (monogr), New Eng Coll Gallery, 92. *Mem:* Soc Am Graphic Artists (Hall of Fame Hon, 2004); Assoc Nat Acad Design (Leo Meisner prize 1983, acad 1990, mem coun, corresponding sec, 1991-); Pastel Soc Am; Artists Fel. *Media:* Etching, Lithography; Oil, Pastel. *Publ:* Illusr, Maggie, A Girl of the Streets, Limited Ed Press, 75; The Max Drawings, Tom Bolt (auth), Am Artist Mag, 11/87; collaborated with Nora Lavori, Toward Sixty, 2010; Art is...The Permanent Revolution (film), 2012. *Dealer:* Thomas Williams Fine Arts London Eng; Cheryl Newby Fine Arts Pawley's Island SC; The Old Print Shop New York NY; Hampton III Gallery Greenville SC. *Mailing Add:* Box 433 57th Concourse Niverville NY 12130

ABELLO, JUAN
COLLECTOR

Pos: Pres, AirTel (acquired by Vodafone), formerly; chmn, Grupo Torreal, SA, Nueva Compania de Inversiones, SA & Inversiones Naira SIMCAVF, SA; chmn & bd dirs, RTL Group, 2000-04; bd dirs, Grupo Televisa, SA, 2000-, Banco Santander Central Hispano, 2002-, Sacyr-Vallehermoso, SA & Compania Vinmcola del Norte de Espana, SA. *Awards:* Named one of 200 Top Collectors, ArtNews Magazine, 2004, 2008-11. *Collection:* Spanish Old Masters & modern and contemporary art. *Mailing Add:* c/o Banco Santander Central Hispano Edificio Pereda Piso 1 Ave de Cantabria Madrid 28669 Spain

ABER, ITA
ARTIST, HISTORIAN

b Montreal, Que, Mar 27, 1932; US citizen. *Study:* Empire State Col, MA; Jewish Theological Sem, NY grad courses. *Work:* Smithsonian Inst, Washington, DC; B'nai B'rith Klutznick Nat Jewish Mus, Washington, DC; Israel Mus, Jerusalem; Brooklyn Mus; Mobile Mus Art, Ala; Ark Art Ctr, Little Rock; Mus of Art & Design, NY; Newark Mus, NJ; Hudson River Mus, NY; World Trade Ctr Mem Mus; Cooper Hewitt Mus, NY; The Jewish Mus, NY; The Doerfner Mus, Riverdale, NY; Helen Hayes Rehab Hospital. *Comn:* Wall hangings (outdoor/indoor), Holy Scroll Covers, Park Ave Synagogue, NY, 74-2008; Ark Curtains, Bnai Israel, Millburn, NJ, 1974-1998; Hebrew Union Coll, NY, Cincinnati, Ohio, 9/00-6/01; S.A.R. Acad, Riverdale, NY; Hebrew Home, Riverdale, NY. *Exhib:* Solo exhib, Seltzer Gallery, 88, Empire State Col, 90; traveling exhib, Yeshiva Univ Mus, NY, 93-98; CORE Exhib, Jewish Mus, NY, 93-; Israel Mus, Jerusalem, Israel, 95, 2011-2012; B'Nai Brith Nat Jewish Mus, Washington, 95; Hudson River Mus, NY, 97; 55 yr retrospective exhib, Broome St Gallery, NY, 1/01; 60 Yr Retrospective, Yeshiva Univ Mus, NY, 2007. *Pos:* Cur hist, Hudson River Mus, Yonkers, 1969-70; cur, The Jewish Mus, NY, 72-74; cur collection, Park Ave Synagogue, NY, 83-2004; cur, Hebrew Home for Aged, Riverdale, NY, 89-93; bd mem, Judaica Mus, Riverdale, NY, 89-; Int Soc Jewish Art, 90-95; comnr, Yonkers Landmark Bd, 91-94, 95; bd mem, Glenview Mansion com Hudson River Mus, 00. *Teaching:* Lecturer at many museums & institutions. *Awards:* Cert Honors, Valentine Mus, 75; Hudson River Philip Morris Mus Grant, N, 97; and many pvt & anonymous grants. *Bibliog:* Video, Yeshiva Univ Mus, 93; Outlook Mag, 93 & 97; Riverdale Press, 96 & 97, 2007; Am Craft 2007. *Mem:* Int Soc Jewish Art (bd mem, 90-, treas, 92-95); Surface Design Pomegranate Guilds, US & Can; Bead Soc of Greater NY; Am Asn Mus; Archives of Am Art, DC. *Media:* Textiles, mixed media, paint, applique, embroidery. *Res:* Ancient & pre Christian art. *Interests:* Teaching handwork to senior citizens, beading, knitting, curved, surgical needles. *Collection:* over 100. *Publ:* The Art of Judaic Needlework, Charles Scribner's Sons, NY, 79; Textile Study Guide, Ind Univ, 85; Woman's Art J, 87; Jewish Art, 87; Jewish Art, Sepharad, 92; monograph, 55 Yrs, 00; Yeshiva Univ Mus Pub, 2007. *Mailing Add:* 2600 Netherland Ave Apt 704 Bronx NY 10463

ABERNETHY-BALDWIN, JUDITH ANN
PAINTER

b Cincinnati, Ohio, May 15, 1942. *Study:* With Philip Pearlstein, Dan'l Greene & Robert Natkin; Cincinnati Art Acad, 70-74; Univ Cincinnati, 75-78. *Work:* Sun Bank NA & Orlando Regional Med Ctr, Orlando, Fla; Scripps-Howard Newspapers, Cincinnati, Ohio; Feldman Group Inc, West Chester, NY; Kennedy Capital Management Inc, St Louis, Mo; Keep Fla Beautiful Inc. *Exhib:* 34th Ann Knickerbocker and Grand Nat Exhib, Salmagundi Club, NY, 84; 48th Ann Nat Midyear, Butler Inst Am Art, Youngstown, Ohio, 84; Invitational Exhib, High Mus, Atlanta, Ga, 88; Abernethy At-Large, Brest Mus, Jacksonville Univ, 86; 37th Ann All Fla, Boca Raton Mus, 88; Places Revisited, Brevard Art Mus, Melbourne, Fla, 88; Atlantic Ctr Arts, New Smyrna, Fla, 88; Judith Abernethy, Boca Raton Mus Art, 91; one-person exhib, Hospitality Gallery, Orlando, Fla, 93 & TK Enterprises, Longwood, Fla, 94; Scott Laurent Gallery, Winter Park, Fla, 95; 34th Ann Fine Arts Competition & Exhib, Ridge Art Asn, Winter Haven, Fla, 96; Ryals Gallery, Boca Raton, Fla, 96. *Teaching:* Seminole Community Col, 87. *Awards:* Second Prize, 83 & 88, Judges Award, 84, Ridge Art Asn. *Bibliog:* Chris Schneider (auth), Judith Abernathy, Ctr Stage Mag, 6/86; Jim Runnels (auth), Artist depicts, Lake Sentinel, 11/88; Sally Henderson (auth), Light taking possession, Zelo Mag, 2/89; Keep Fla Beautiful Mag, Cover Spring, 91. *Mem:* Nat Asn Women Artists; Int Women Artists Archive; Women's Caucus Art; Women Artists of West. *Media:* Acrylic. *Dealer:* Albertson-Peterson 329 Park Ave S Winter Park FL 32789. *Mailing Add:* PO Box 4061 Enterprise FL 32725

ABID, ANN B
LIBRARIAN

b St Louis, Mo, Mar 17, 1942. *Pos:* Asst librn, St Louis Art Mus, 63-68, librn, 68-85; head librn, Cleveland Mus Art, 85-. *Mem:* Mus, Arts, & Humanities Div, Spec Libr Asn; Art Libr Soc NAm; Soc Am Archivists; Int Fedn Libr Asns & Insts; Am Libr Asn; Coll Art Asn. *Publ:* Auth, Documents of Surrealism: 1918-1942, St Louis Art Mus, 81; ed, Roy Lichtenstein, 81; Max Beckmann Retrospective, 84; auth, Loss liability: risk, responsibility, recovery, Art Doc, winter 91; coauth, Planning for automation of the slide and photograph collections at the Cleveland Mus of Art: a Draft MARC/Visual materials record, VRA Visual Resources Asn Bulletin, summer 92. *Mailing Add:* Cleveland Mus Art 11150 East Blvd Cleveland OH 44106

ABISH, CECILE
ENVIRONMENTAL ARTIST, PHOTOGRAPHER

b New York, NY. *Study:* Brooklyn Coll, BFA. *Comn:* Boxed Monuments-3, Multiples, Inc, NY, 69, Field Quartering, Lakeview Ctr Arts, Peoria, Ill, 72; Renaissance Fix, Independent Curators, Inc, NY, 79; Atlanta Arts Festival, Piedmont Park, Ga, 80; Land Marks, Bard Coll, NY, 84. *Exhib:* Inst Contemp Art, Boston, Mass, 74; Hudson River Mus, Yonkers, NY, 79; The New Mus, NY, 80; Kunstgebaude, Stuttgart, Ger, 81; Fine Arts Ctr, State Univ NY, Stony Brook, 82; Long Beach Mus, Calif, 83; Ctr Creative Photog, Tucson, Ariz, 84; Mus Mod Kunst, Vienna, Austria, 85; Architektur Zentrum, Vienna, Austria, 93; Artists Space, NY, 94; Islip Art Mus, NY, 95; Books & Co, NY, 96; PSI Contemp Art Ctr, NY, 99; and others. *Teaching:* Instr art, Queens Coll, NY; vis artist, Univ Mass, Amherst, Cooper Union, NY & Harvard Univ, Mass. *Awards:* Creative Artists Pub Service Fel, 75; Nat Endowments Arts Fel, 77 & 80; Deutscher Akademischer Austavschdienst, Berlin, 87. *Bibliog:* Lawrence Alloway (auth), article, Arts Mag, 2/77; Jeffrey Keeffe (auth), article, Artforum, 10/78; Donald B Kuspit (auth), article, Art in Am, 1/82. *Mem:* Coll Art Asn. *Media:* Varied Media. *Publ:* Firsthand, Photo/work, Wright State Univ, Dayton, Ohio, 78; Situation esthetics, Artforum, 1/80; Greek Gifts, LAICA J, winter 86; Chinese Crossing Photo/work, Conjunctions 9, 86; 99: The New Meaning, Photo/work, Burning Deck, 90

ABLOW, ROSELYN KAROL (ROZ KAROL ABLOW)
PAINTER, INSTRUCTOR

b Allentown, Pa. *Study:* Bennington Coll, BA, 54; Boston Univ Sch Arts, with Walter Murch, 59-61; studied in Europe, 59-60 & 68-69. *Work:* Mobil Corp, Chemical Bank, NY; New Eng Mutual Life Insurance Co, Boston; Conn Gen Life, Hartford; Sears, Roebuck & Co, Chicago; Wiggin Collection, Boston Pub Libr. *Comn:* Diptych mixed media on paper, Broadway Crown Plaza Hotel, NY, 89. *Exhib:* New Am Monotypes, Smithsonian Inst Traveling Exhib, 78-80; Three Grant Recipients, The Bunting Inst, Radcliffe Coll, 88; David Brown Gallery, Provincetown, Mass, 88; Contemp Monotypes, Gallery 30, Burlingame, Calif, 93; fac exhib, New Art Ctr, Newton, Mass, 94; solo exhibs, Works on Paper, Lee Gallery, Miami Univ, Oxford, Ohio, 95, Image and Abstraction, Rosenau Gallery Arts Ctr, Old Forge, NY, 2002; New Artists, New Works, Pucker Gallery, 2004; Together, Pucker Gallery, 2007. *Collection Arranged:* Four Sculptors: Pub Comns-Pvt Works, 85, Watercolor in the 1980s, 86, & Volume and Plane, Wall Sculpture, 91, Newton Arts Ctr; Legacy: Nine Artists Who Studied with Philip Guston, New Art Ctr, Newton, Mass, 94; Paper & Color, Vineyard Studio, 96; Unique Print, Star Gallery, Newton, Mass, 97. *Teaching:* Monotype workshops, Bunting Inst, 88, Newton Arts Ctr, 89-92, New Arts Ctr, 93-95 & 96-97. *Awards:* Fel, Bunting Inst, Radcliffe Coll, 88; Mass Arts Lottery Coun Grant, 90-91. *Bibliog:* Robert Taylor (auth), article, Boston Sunday Globe, 6/10/79; Kenneth Baker (auth), Lasting impressions, Boston Phoenix, 2/9/81; Christine Temin (auth), The Work of the Superiors, Boston Globe, 4/24/91. *Media:* Mixed Water Media, Collage on Paper. *Dealer:* Pucker Gallery Boston. *Mailing Add:* 16 Monmouth Ct Brookline MA 02446

ABOU-ISSA, ISSA
PAINTER, SCULPTOR
b New York, NY, Jan 3, 1966. *Study:* New Orleans Acad Fine Arts; Acad Art Univ; studied with Kinzey Branham, New Orleans Acad Fine Arts. *Comn:* Figure paintings, Dr Mark Peters, Houma, La, 2006; abstract works, Craig J Landry, Houma, La, 2008; abstract paintings, Ellendale Country Club, Houma, La, 2010. *Exhib:* Postcards on the Edge, Robert Miller Gallery, New York, 2005, Metro Pictures, New York, 2008. *Awards:* People to watch, Renaissance Publ, New Orleans Mag, 9/2010. *Bibliog:* Dunbier Lonnie Pierson(ed), Artists Bluebook: 34000 N Am Artists, Askart.com, Inc, 2005. *Mem:* Arts Coun New Orleans; Nat Women's Caucus Art; Am for the Arts; NY Found Arts. *Publ:* art, New Orleans Homes & Lifestyle: Artist Profile, Renaissance Publ, 2005; art, Art with a New York Flair, Houma Courier, 2004; Interpecting the Abstract, La Homes & Gardens, 2007; art, Scene Louisiana, 8/2010; People to Watch, New Orleans Mag, 9/2010

ABRAHAM, CAROL JEANNE
ASSEMBLAGE ARTIST, CERAMIST
b Philadelphia, Pa, 1949. *Study:* Tyler Sch Art, Philadelphia, 64-67; Boston Mus Sch Fine Arts, 67-71; Tufts Univ, Medford, Mass, BS, 67-71; Rochester Inst Technol, Sch Am Craftsmen, MFA, 73; Penland Sch Crafts, NC, 75, Brooks Inst Photog, dipl, 88. *Work:* Rochester Inst Technol, NY; Mus Ceramics, Bassano Del Grappa, Italy; Renwick Gallery, Smithsonian Inst, Washington, DC; Brigham Young Univ, Provo, Utah; Int Acad Ceramics, Canada; Brooks Inst Photog. *Comn:* Mural, sculpture, Romerbad Hotel, Ger, 84. *Exhib:* Renwick Gallery, Smithsonian Inst, Washington, DC, 75; Tweed Mus Art, Duluth, Minn, 81; Celebration 81, Spokane, Wash; Interfaith Forum Relig, Art & Archit, 81; State Univ Mus Art, University Park, Pa, 81; Fletcher Brownbuilt Pottery Exhib, Auckland, NZ, 81; and many others. *Pos:* Cur, Western States Mus Photog, Santa Barbara, Calif, 85-89. *Teaching:* Silk screening, Boston Pub Sch System (Pilot Sch), 70; instr ceramics, Rochester Inst Technology, NY, 72-73; asst prof ceramics & sculpture, Southern Utah State Col, Cedar City, 75-77; ceramics, El Camino Col, Torrance, Calif, 80-81; ceramics, Ventura Community Col, 82-84; design, Brooks Inst Photog, 89-. *Awards:* Third Prize, Ceramics International 1973, Canada; Grant, Burbank Fine Arts Fedn, 81; Purchase Award, Second Crossing Gallery, 81. *Bibliog:* Hildegard Storr-Britz (auth), Contemp Int Ceramics, 80; Jan Axel & Karen McCready (coauths), Porcelain: Traditions and New Visions, 81; Glen C Nelson (auth), Ceramics, A Potters Handbook, 4th & 5th eds, 78-84. *Media:* Photography, Fiber; Porcelain, Thixotropic Porcelain. *Publ:* Auth, The Mirror Book, Jay & Lee Newman, 78; Crafts Horizons, 8/73, 12/73, 2/76; Ceramics Monthly, 9/73, 5/75, 5/76, 10/76; Decorazione - Ceramica, Nino Caruso, Italy, 88; Egypt: Land of Adventures, 89

ABRAM, RUTH J
WRITER
b Calif, Sept 19, 1945. *Study:* Sarah Lawrence Coll, BA, 67; Florence Hellar Sch, Brandeis Univ, MSW, 70; NY Univ, MA, 83. *Hon Degrees:* Russell Sage Coll, Hon D Pub Serv, 99. *Work:* Lower E Side Tenement Mus. *Exhib:* Send Us A Lady Physician: Women Doctors in Am, 1835-1920, Med Coll Pa, 85. *Pos:* Prog dir, Am Civil Liberties Union Found, 72-74; exec dir, Women's Action Alliance, 74-79; founder & dir, Lower East Historic Conservancy; founder, Lower East Side Tenement Mus; pres, Paraphrase, Inc. *Awards:* Alvin Brown Fel, Aspen Inst Humanistic Studies; Kenan Fel, NY Univ, 81-82; Camille Mermod Award, Am Med Women's Asn, 87. *Mem:* Am Asn Hist Med; Am Asn State & Local Hist; Am Mus Asn; Organization Am Hist; Independent Sector; Archives Med Coll Pa; MAZON; Nat Conf Soviet Jewry; New Israel Fund; Telecommun Coop Network. *Publ:* Auth, Send Us a Lady Physician: Women Doctors in America; Women's Section, Information Please Almanac, 78-79; Poetry in Midwest Poetry Review, Poetry Mag, 81; In Recognition of Sara A Cohen, MD, Women in Health, 82; To Do Something and To Be Something, Philadelphia Co Med Soc J, 85. *Mailing Add:* 110 Riverside Dr No 11B New York NY 10024

ABRAMOVIC, MARINA
PERFORMANCE ARTIST
b Belgrade, Yugoslavia, 1946. *Study:* Acad Fine Arts, Belgrade, 1965-70; Acad Fine Arts, Zagreb, 1970-73. *Hon Degrees:* Art Inst Chicago, PhD, 2004; Hon DFA, U Plymouth, 2009, Instituto Superior de Arte, 2012. *Work:* Brooklyn Mus, European Performance Series, NY, 1978, Mus Contemp Art, Chicago, 1982, Artist Body-Pub Body, Mus Contemp Art, Valencia, Spain, 1998, The House with the Ocean View, 2003 (NY Dance & Performance Award, 2003), Directions, Hirschhorn Mus & Sculpture Garden, 2001, Moving Pictures, Solomon R Guggenheim Mus, NY, 2002, exhib in group shows at Whitney Biennial Exhib, Whitney Mus Am Art, 2004. *Exhib:* Solo exhibs, Art must be Beautiful Artist must be Beautiful, Art Festival, Copenhagen, Denmark, 1975, Breathing out/Breathing in (with Ulay), Studenski Kulturni Ctr, Belgrade, 1977, Charged Space (with Ulay), Rest Energy (with Ulay), ROSC 80, Dublin, 1990, Nightsea Crossing (with Ulay), Die Mond der Sonne (with Ulay), The House, Santa Monica, 1987, The Lovers: The Great Wall Walk (with Ulay), The Great Wall China, 1988, Dragon Heads, Kunstmuseum, Bonn, Ger, 1994, Cleaning the Mirror, Sean Kelly Gallery, NY, 1995, Luminosity, 1997, The House with the Ocean View, 2002 & Balkan Erotic Epic, 2005, The Biography, Schouwburg, Groningen, 1996, Balkan Baroque, Biennale di Venezia, Venice, Italy, 1997, Mus Contemp Art, Sydney, 1998, Expiring Body, Fabric Workshop & Mus, Philadelphia, 1998 & 1999, Mus Art Contemp (with Ulay), Lyon, France, 1999, Cleaning the House, Kiasma Mus Contemp Art, Helsinki, 1999 & 2000, Soup Operations Room, Kappatos Gallery, Athens, 2000, Galerie Cent8, Paris, 2000 & 2002, Energy Clothes, Atelier Calder, Saché, France, 2001, Marking the Territory, Irish Mus Modern Art, Dublin, 2001, The Star, Contemp Art Mus, Kumamoto, Japan, 2003, Loop Performance, PS1 Contemp Art Ctr, NY, 2004, Biography Remix, Fond Roma Europa, 2004, Guggenheim Mus, NY, 2005, Avignon Theatre Festival, France, 2005, Seven Easy Pieces, Guggenheim Mus, 2005, The Artist is Present, MoMA, 2010, 512 Hours, 2014; Biennial, Whitney Mus Am Art, NY, 2004. *Pos:* Bd mem, Contemp Art Mus, Kitakyushu, Japan, 1998; creator, Marina Abramovic Inst, NY, 2013-. *Teaching:* Instr, Acad Fine Arts, Novi Sad, 1973-75; vis prof, Académie des Beaux-Arts, Paris, 1983, 1990-91; vis prof, Hochschule der Kunst, Berlin, 1990-91; prof, Hochschule fur Bildende Kunst, Hamburg, 1992-96; prof, Hochschule fur Bildende Kunst, Braunschweig, 1997; artist-in-residence, Atelier Calder, Saché, 2001. *Awards:* Recipient Niedersächsicher Kunstpreis, 2003; NY Dance & Performance Award, 2004; Austrian Decoration for Science & Art, 2008; Cultural Leadership award, Am Federation Arts, 2011; Berliner Bear, 2012; Named one of The 100 Most Influential People in the World, TIME Mag, 2014. *Dealer:* Sean Kelly Gallery 528 W 29th St New York NY 10001

ABRAMOVICH, ROMAN ARKADYEVICH
COLLECTOR
b Saratov, Soviet Union, Oct 24, 1966. *Study:* Moscow State Law Acad, law degree. *Pos:* Head of Moscow office, Runicom SA, Switz, 1993-96; controlling stock holder, Sibneft Oil, Moscow, 1995-2005; founder, dir-gen, Runicom Ltd Gibraltar, 1997-99; mem, lower house, Russian Parliament (Duma), 1999-2000; gov, Chukotka Autonomous District, Russia, 2000-08; owner, Millhouse Capital, England, Chelsea Football Club, England, 2003-. *Awards:* Named one of World's Richest People, Forbes mag, 2001-; Person of Yr, Expert mag, Russia, 2003; named one of World's 100 Most Influential People, Time mag, 2005; Order of Honor, Russia, 2006; named one of Top 200 Collectors, ARTnews mag, 2008-2013. *Collection:* Modern and contemporary art. *Mailing Add:* Chelsea Football Club Fulham Rd London United Kingdom SW6 1HS

ABRAMOWICZ, JANET
PAINTER, PRINTMAKER
b New York, NY. *Study:* Art Students League, Columbia Univ, Acad delle Belle Arti, Bologna, Italy, BFA & MFA, with Giorgio Morandi. *Work:* Mus Mod Art, Kyoto; Dept of Prints, NY Pub Libr & Metrop Mus Art, NY; Ohara Mus, Kurashiki; Contemp Art, Mus d'Arte Mod, Bologna; Mus d'Arte Mod, La Spezia, Italy; Yale Univ Art Gallery. *Exhib:* Works on Paper, Harvard Sch Design, 74; Abstract Art (sculpture), Boston City Hall, 75; solo exhib, Susan Caldwell Gallery, NY, 80, Nantenshi Gallery, Tokyo, 81 & Galleria del Milione, Milano, Italy, 81; Prints Recently Acquired, RI Sch Design & Metrop Mus Art, NY, 85; 24th Nat Print Exhib, Brooklyn Mus, 86; British 11th Int Print Biennale (invitational), 90-91; Synthetic Century, Yale Univ Art Gallery, (Int catalog), 2002. *Collection Arranged:* Giorgio Morandi (with catalog), Busch-Reisinger Mus, Harvard Univ, 68, Pace Univ, NY; L'Opera Grafica di Giorgio Morandi, Rome, 90. *Pos:* Critic, Asahi Evening News, Tokyo & Print Collector's Newsletter; vis artist, Am Acad Rome, 84-85. *Teaching:* Instr, Radcliffe Col, Worcester Art Mus, Acad delle Belle Arti & Univ Ill; lectr art hist, Div Educ, Boston Mus Fine Arts, 58-70; sr lectr painting, printmaking & drawing, Fine Arts Dept, Fogg Art Mus, Harvard Univ, 71-91. *Awards:* McDowell Colony Fel, 75 & 76; Fulbright Fel, 79 & 89; Rockefeller Found, Bellagio, 89; Am Coun Learned Soc Fel, 90-91; Guggenheim Fel, 92. *Mem:* Am Acad Rome; hon mem Accademia Clementina, Bologna, Italy; vis fel, Am Acad, Rome, Italy; PEN. *Media:* Oil, Etching. *Publ:* Auth, Vision and Technique, The Etchings of Giorgio Morandi, 9/10/82 & A European Sensibility: The Photographs of Andre Kertesz, 9/10/83, Print Collector's Newsletter; Milan: The Liberation of the Object, Art Am, 83; auth, Technique of the Graphic Works of Giorgio Morandi; In memoriam: Kasuo Shimizu, Ahsahi Evening News, Tokyo; La tecnia dell 'arte incisonia di Giorgio Morandi, exhib catalog, Rome, 90; Yale Univ Press, Giorgio-Morandi, The Art of Silence; A World in Black and White The Imagery and Technique of Morandi's Etchings, Metropolitan Mus Art, NY, 2008. *Dealer:* Tokyo Nanten Shi Gallery Kyo-Bashi Tokyo. *Mailing Add:* 30 W 15th St New York NY 10011-6816

ABRAMS, EDITH LILLIAN
INSTRUCTOR, SCULPTOR
b New York, NY. *Study:* Brooklyn Col, BA, 74; Pratt Inst, MFA, 78. *Work:* Evansville Mus Arts & Science, Ind; Brookdale Hosp, NY. *Comn:* Many pvt portrait sculptures. *Exhib:* Int Sculpture Fair, Sheraton Hotel, NY, 79; 4th & 6th Ann Exhib Painting & Sculpture; Brooklyn Mus, 79-81; Catharine Lorillard Wolfe Art Club, Nat Arts Club, NY, 79-88; Audubon Artists 38th Ann Exhib, NY, 80; ArtExpo, NY Coliseum, NY, 80; Providence Art Club Centennial Exhib Sculpture, RI, 80; Brooklyn Mem Am Soc Contemp Artists, 15th Ann Exhib, 84, Brooklyn Mus; Nat Acad Design, 86-88. *Teaching:* Instr sculpture & ceramics, Sephardic Community Ctr, New York, 82-85. *Awards:* Purchase Award, 1st Prize, Schulman Rehabilitation Inst, Brookdale Hosp, NY, 76; Margaret Hirsch Levine Mem Prize, Audubon Artists 38th Ann, 80; Ann Hyatt Huntington Bronze Medal, Catharine Lorillard Wolfe Art Club 84th Ann, 80 & 89th Ann, Helen McCahill Slottman Mem Award, 85; Charles D Murphy Award, Nat Asn Women Artists, 82. *Mem:* Metrop Painters & Sculptors; New York Artists Equity Asn; Am Soc Contemp Artists (pres, 83-85); Nat Asn Women Artists; Catharine Lorillard Wolf Art Club. *Media:* All. *Mailing Add:* 2820 Ave J Brooklyn NY 11210

ABRAMS, JANE ELDORA
PAINTER
b Eau Claire, Wis, Jan 2, 1940. *Study:* Univ Wis-Stout, Menomonie, BS, 62, MS, 67; Ind Univ, Bloomington, with Pozzath & Lowe, MFA (with distinction), 71. *Work:* Ind Univ Mus Fine Arts; Univ Dallas, Tex; Tex Tech Univ; Tamarind Inst; Mus NMex; and others. *Exhib:* Works on Paper traveling exhib, Univ Utah, Salt Lake City, Univ Tex, Houston & Los Angeles Co Mus of Art, Calif, 77; Works on Paper: Southwest

1978, Dallas Mus Fine Arts, 78; Art Inst Chicago, 81; New Mexico Impressions, Mus Fine Arts, Santa Fe; Modes of Expression, State Univ Mus, Potsdam; Common Ground-New Acquisitions, Albuquerque Mus; Retrospective, Fine Arts Gallery, Ind Univ; and many others. *Teaching:* Instr art, Univ Wis-Stout, Menomonie, 67-69; from asst prof to regents prof art, painting, drawing & grad studies, Univ NMex, 71-; guest artist, Ind Univ, Bloomington, 76 & Univ Tex, Austin, 83; and others. *Awards:* Artist-in-Residence Grant, Roswell Mus, 85-86; Distinguished Alumni Award, Ind Univ, Bloomington, 91 & Univ Wisc, 92; Pollock-Krasner Found Grant, 2009. *Mem:* Coll Art Asn Am; Women's Caucus Art; Los Angeles Print Soc; Soc Am Graphic Artists. *Media:* All Media. *Publ:* Contribr, Colorprints, USA (slide series), 71-72; Two Decades of Change (exhib catalog), Ind Univ, 91; contribr, Clinton Adams, Printmaking in New Mexico. *Mailing Add:* 7811 Guadalupe Tr NW Albuquerque NM 87107

ABRAMS, JOYCE DIANA
PAINTER, SCULPTOR
b New York, NY, Dec 8, 1945. *Study:* Cooper Union, New York, BFA, 66; Columbia Univ, MFA, 72. *Work:* Gannett Ctr Media Studies, New York Pub Libr & Franklin Furnace Archives Mus Mod Art, NY; Atlantic Richfield Co, Anchorage, Alaska; Burlington Northern, Inc, Seattle, Wash; Anaconda Co, Denver, Colo; Alberta Gas Trunk Line, Ltd, Calgary, Alta, Can; Citrus Ctr, Orlando, Fla; UCLA, Los Angeles, Calif; Wilshire Carlyle, Los Angeles, Calif. *Exhib:* Newscapes Land & City-States of Mind, One Penn Plaza, NY, 84; Painted Constructions-Constructed Paintings, Rockland Ctr Arts, Nyack, NY, 85; Mid Am Biennial, Owensboro Mus Fine Art, Ky, 88; one-person show, Edward Williams Gallery, Fairleigh Dickinson Univ, Hackensack, NJ, 88; Works on Paper, Knoxville Mus Fine Art, Tenn, 89; Spirit of the Object, Humphrey Fine Art, NY, 92; Women of the Book, 98-05, 2011; Stephen F Austin State, Tex Nat, 2010; In Search of A Copper Book, Paintings by Joyce Abrams, NY Public Libr, Bloomingdale Brance, 2013. *Pos:* Art consult, Neville Lewis & Assoc, New York, NY, 80-82 & Tokyo Cent Mus, 83, 89-; cur, Orgn Int Artists, New York, 82 & Rockland Ctr Arts, West Nyack, New York, 91. *Teaching:* Instr painting, City Univ New York, 78-81; Univ South Maine, 87; Parsons Sch Design, 89-92; Art Instr Older Adults & Intergenerational wkshps, West Side NORC, NY, 2009-2012; NY Public Libr, Lifetime Arts, Coll, 2014. *Awards:* MacDowell Colony Fel, 85 & 87; Fel, Corp Yaddo, 88; Creative Artist Fel, The Japan Found, 99-2000. *Bibliog:* Diana Morris (auth), Summer group show, Arts Mag, 10/83; Steve Bush (auth), See here, now-back to the present, Artspeak, 2/16/86; Rick Delaney (auth), Women of the Book; Hedwig Brenner (auth), Jewish Women in Visual Arts, Vol. 4. *Mem:* New York Artists Equity Asn. *Media:* Paint; Wood. *Res:* Then and Now Japan; Fifty Years of Tradition and Change; Comparison Between Japan in the 1950's; Japan at the Turn of the 21st Century, a Visual Essay. *Publ:* Auth, A personal view of the MacDowell experience, Artist's Proof, 4/88; Discarded, Rockland Ctr Arts; Born in a Fire, 94. *Mailing Add:* 100 W 94th St New York NY 10025

ABRAMSON, ELAINE SANDRA
CARTOONIST, DESIGNER, ART LICENSOR, AUTHOR, SPEAKER
b Cleveland, Ohio, Aug 27, 1942. *Study:* NY Univ, Cert, 90; Kent State Univ, Ohio, BS (art); Cleveland Inst Art, Ohio; Hayim Greenberg Inst, Scholar, Jerusalem, Israel. *Work:* State Capitol, Austin, Tex; Cleveland Mus Art, Ohio; Maryland Pub Television, Baltimore; Kent State, traveling exhibs, Ohio; Times Newspapers, Baltimore, Md. *Comn:* Rapco Inc, Chicago, Ill; Ann Richards Gov Campaign, Austin & Ft Worth, Tex; Paragon Neddle Craft, NY; General Crafts Corp, Baltimore; plus many others. *Exhib:* Invitational Maryland Artists, Baltimore Harbor, 71-75; PCM Hall of Fame, PCM Exhibit, Dallas, Tex, 85; Texas State Artist, 88-90 & Tex Woman's Hall of Fame, 89, State Capitol, Austin; Composers, Authors & Artists of Am, NY & FTW, 91-92; Artists Christmas, 91-92; Solo Shows: Palace Art Gallery, Baltimore; Levendale Art Gallery, Graphic Arts Show, Baltimore; Portfolio Gallery, Mt Wash, Md; Loyola Fed Savings & Loan, Baltimore; Calvert Savings & Loan Asn, Reisterstown, Md; Design House, Stevenson, Md & Kent State Univ Gallery, Ohio; New Eng Fine Arts Inst, Boston, Mass; Lincoln Center Art Gallery, NY; Butler Inst Art, Youngstown, Ohio; The Temple, Cleveland, Ohio; Temple Emanuel, Baltimore, Maryland; Clifton Bank, Baltimore, Maryland; Park Arts Festival, Cleveland, Ohio; Shaker Square Arts Sale, Shaker Heights, Ohio; Foundry Christmas Show, 2010; Artsravaganza, St Louis, 2012. *Pos:* Owner, Toy & Craft Design, 67-; syndicated columnist, Appraisals by Abramson, currently; Bd Dir, Nat League Am Pen Women; Nat Bd Dir, Graphic Artists Guild; Founding Artist, Sassy Cat Art Gallery; featured presenter, Southwest Book Fiesta & Moonlight Magnolias, Romance Writers of America. *Teaching:* Art, Cleveland Pub Sch, 65-67; lectr, workshops for artists and authors. *Awards:* All-expense scholar, Govt Israel/Hayim Greenberg Inst, Jerusalem, Israel, 60-61; First American Art/Craft Instr to train Israeli pub sch teachers, Israel, 64; Tex Women's Hall of Fame, 91-94; Nobel Prize and Guinness Book of Records Nominee, 91-93; First Woman State Artist, Tex, 93-94; Int Women of Yr in Art, Eng, 93, 95, 96 & 98; Am Express aaart.com licensing, NY, 2000-2002; Outstanding Artist and Designer of 20th Cent, Int Biog Ctr; First Woman/First Cartoonist, State of Tex, 93-94; Editors Choice Award, Int Libr Photog; Nomination, Nat Assembly Local Arts Agencies (bd Dir 1994); Hon Mention, Nat Park Acad of Fine Arts; Outstanding Woman of the 21st Century, Am Biog Inst, 2001; Int Commendation of Success, Am Biog Inst; Int Women of the Milennium, IBC, UK, 1999; Woman of the Year, ABI, 1994-2001; Int Cultural Diploma of Honor, 1996-1998; Pen Women People's Choice award, Nat League Am, 2009-2011. *Bibliog:* B J Hennersdorph, article, Tex Woman, fall 89; Campaigning characters, Greetings Mag, winter/spring 90; Dallas Times Herald, 92; St Louis Post Dispatch, 2010, 2012; Riverfront Times, 2012. *Mem:* Metrop Mus Art; Soc Craft Designers; Nat Enamelists Guild; Am Crafts Coun; Nat League Am Pen Women (pres, 95-); Graphic Artists Guild; Cartoonists Guild; Cleveland Int of Art Alumni Assoc; Tex Asn Film/Tape Prof (legal chair); Maryland Art League (Vice Pres); St. Louis Writer's Guild (advisor); Best of Missouri Hands; Greater St. Louis Artists Asn; St. Louis Artists Guild; Society of Childrens Writers & Illusrs; Nat League Am; Pen Women (Mo state asn pres); Sisters-in-Crime; Romance Writers Am. *Media:* Pen and Ink, Mixed Media Painting. *Specialty:* Create-a-Craft Paintings. *Interests:* Writing and illusr children's picture books, creating children's plush toys, painting and rug making. *Publ:* Auth, Animation, First Tex Co Camp Fire; SW Art Review, Tarrant Bus, Tex Source Bk; contribr, Baltimore Sun; Creative Entrepreneur Legal & Business Series of Workshops for Artists & Writers; St Louis Post Dispatch; Riverfront Times; Dallas Times Herald; St Louis Writers Guild; founding editor, GAG Art Forum, NLAPW Forum; St Louis Post, Dispatch, Riverfront Times; Books in the St Louis Jewish Book Festival, 2012; From Fat to Fabulous: A Diet Guide for Restaurant Lovers, on ABC, CBS, NBS, and PBS TV, on the radio, and in major newspapers

ABT, JEFFREY
PAINTER, WRITER
b Kansas City, Mo, Feb 27, 1949. *Study:* Drake Univ, Des Moines, BFA, 71; MFA, 77; Jewish Inst of Religion, Hebrew Union Coll, Jerusalem, Fel, 71-72. *Work:* Des Moines Art Ctr, Iowa; Minn Mus Art, St Paul; Nelson-Atkins, Mus Art, Kansas City, Mo; Washington & Jefferson Coll, Pa; Wichita Art Mus, Kans; Dow Automotive, Mich; Polk Technologies, Mich; Federal Reserve Bank, Detroit. *Comn:* Bas relief, Iowa Jewish Guild, Des Moines, 74; sculpture, Waldinger Found, Des Moines, 75; Detroit Contemp, 2002. *Exhib:* Dobrick Gallery, Ltd, Chicago, 82; Art/Work, Art Inst Chicago Gallery, 87; Egg Tempera, Contemp Art Workshop, Chicago, 88; Exquisite Visions, Meadowbrook Gallery, Oakland Univ, Rochester, Mich, 92; Jeffrey Abt: Paintings and Drawings, The Cliff Dwellers, Chicago, 97 & Cary Gallery, Rochester, Mich, 98; Washington Arts Coun Gallery, Worthington, Ohio, 2000; Jeffrey Abt, Recent Work, Wayne State Univ, Detroit, Mich, 2003; Cafritz Found Arts Ctr, Montgomery Coll, Silver Spring, Md, 2013; Bruce Gallery, Edinboro Univ, 2014; 1912 Gallery, Emory and Harry Coll, 2015. *Pos:* Exhibs coordr, Dept Spec Collections, Univ Chicago Libr, 80-86; asst dir, Smart Mus Art, Univ Chicago, 86-87, acting dir, 87-89. *Teaching:* prof drawing, painting, mus studies, James Pearson Duffy Dept Art & Art History, Wayne State Univ, Detroit, 89-. *Awards:* Var grants, Nat Endowment Humanities, Nat Endowment Arts & Inst Mus Servs; Polk Tech Purchase Award; Pub award Hist Soc of Mich; Bd Governors Fac Achievement Award, Wayne State Univ, 2003, 2013; Benard L. Maas Prize; Marilyn Williamson Distinguished Faculty Fellowship, Wayne State Univ, 2014. *Bibliog:* Andy Argy (auth), Art/Work, New Art Examiner, 87; Frank Provenzano (auth), Abt depicts an orderly world, Birmingham Observer & Eccentric, 98; Keri Guten Cohen (auth), Exhib Celebrates Prolific Prof, Detroit Free Press, 88; Jeanne C Fryer-Kohles (auth), Dislocations: Recent Work by Jeffrey Abt, Dialogue: Voicing the Arts, 2000. *Mem:* Coll Art Asn; Ragdale Found, Artists Colony (trustee, 85-2001); Detroit Artists Market (bd dir, 94-); Am Asn Mus, 86-; Wayne State Univ Press (ed bd, 90-2014 & chmn, 96-2001); Asn Mus Hist, (cofounder, 2003-); Mus Hist J (ed bd, 2006-2014, co-editor 2014-). *Media:* Oil, Drawing. *Res:* The history of museums and exhibitions; artists and museums. *Publ:* Auth, The Printers Craft, 82 & The Book Made Art, 86, Univ Chicago Libr; contribr, Guide to the Collections, Smart Mus Art, 90; Dictionary of Art, MacMillan, 95; article, Art Hist, 96; auth, A Museum on the Verge: a Socioeconomic History of the Detroit Institute of Arts, 1882-2000, Wayne State Univ Press, 2001; article, Blackwells Companion to Museum Studies, 2006; auth, Am Egyptologist: The Life of James Henry Breasted & The Creation of His Oriental Inst, Univ Chicago Press, 2011. *Mailing Add:* 26881 York Rd Huntington Woods MI 48070

ABTS, TOMMA
PAINTER
b Kiel, Germany, 1967. *Study:* Hochschule der Kunst, Berlin, 1989-95. *Exhib:* Solo exhibs include Habitat, London, 1998, Greengrassi, London, 1999, 2002, 2005, Galerie Giti Nourbakhsch, Berlin, 2001, 2004, Galerie Daniel Buchholz, Cologne, 2003, 2006, Wrong Gallery, New York, 2003, Kunsthalle Basel, 2005, Douglas Hyde Gallery, Dublin, 2005, Tate Britain, London, 2006, New Mus Contemp Art, New York, 2008; two-person exhib with Vincent Fecteau, Marc Foxx, LA, 2002; group exhibs include The Origins of Parties, Greengrassi, London, 1998, Honey I Rearranged the Collection, 2003; The Devil is in the Details, Allston Skirt Gallery, Boston, 2001; Galerie Daneil Buchholz, Cologne, 2002, 2004; Frankfurter Kunstverein, Germany, 2003; Black Rainbow, Lucky Tackle, Oakland, Calif, 2003; Carnegie Int, Carnegie Mus Art, Pittsburgh, 2004; Brit Art Show 6, Hayward Gallery, London, 2005; Turner Prize, Tate Britain, London, 2006, Turner Prize: A Retrospective, 2007; Axis of Praxis, Midway Contemp Art, Minneapolis, 2006. *Awards:* Turner Prize, Tate Britain, 2006. *Dealer:* Greengrassi 1a Kempsford Rd London SE11 4NU England UK. *Mailing Add:* c/o David Zwirner 525 W 19th St New York NY 10011

ABULARACH, RODOLFO MARCO
PAINTER, PRINTMAKER
b Guatemala City, Guatemala, Jan 7, 1933. *Study:* Nat Sch Plastic Arts, Guatemala City; Art Students League; Pratt Graphic Art Ctr, NY. *Work:* Mus Mod Art, New York Pub Libr & Metrop Mus Art, NY; World Print Council, San Francisco; Philadelphia Mus Art, Pa; and others. *Comn:* Print-engraving-etching, Hommage Aux Prix Nobel, Malmo, Sweden, 77; print edition, etching & engraving, World Print Coun, San Francisco, 80. *Exhib:* Mus Mod Art, NY, 60, 63, 64, 69 & 70; 100 Contemp Graphics, Pratt Graphic Art Ctr at Jewish Mus, NY, 64; 17th Nat Exhib Graphics, Brooklyn Mus, NY, 70; 12 Latin-Am Artists, Ringling Mus, Fla, 71; Biennial PanAm Graphic Arts, Mus Mod Art, La Tertulia, Columbia, 73; Biennial, Firenze, Italy, 74; Biennial Prints, Mus Mod Art, Tokyo, Japan, 79; and others. *Teaching:* Instr graphic workshop, Univ Costa Rica, 76; taller nove arte, Bogota, Columbia, 82 & 83. *Awards:* First Prize in Drawing, Pan-Am Exhib Graphic Arts, Columbia, 70; Special Ed Prize & Award of Merit, World Print Council, San Francisco, 80; Silver Medal, Buenos Aires, Argentina, 87. *Bibliog:* Stuart Preston (auth), 20th century sense & sensibility, New York Times, 5/7/61; John Canaday (auth), New talent in printmaking, New York Times, 5/27/67; Elisabeth Perez Luna (auth), The eyes of Abularach, Hombre Mag, 7/79. *Media:* Oil; Pen & Ink. *Publ:* Tamarind: Homage to Lithography, Mus Mod Art, New York, 69; Biblioteca Luis Angel, Mus Plastic Arts, Bogota, Columbia, 79; The Council House, The Art Collection by Lee Nordness, Perimeter Press Inc, 80; Modern Masters, Galerie Borjeson, Malmo, Sweden, 80; Artists of Am, Rafael Squirru, Art Editions,

Gaglione, 84; Mus Mod Art Latin Am, selections from the permanent collection, Orgn Am States, Washington, DC, 85; Mus Mod Art, La Tertulia, Carvajal, Colombia, 86; The Latin Am Spirit, 1920-1970, Bronx Mus, N Abrams Inc, 88. *Mailing Add:* c/o Anita Shaplsky Gallery 152 E 65 St New York NY 10021

ACCETTA, SUZANNE RUSCONI
PAINTER, INSTRUCTOR
b Cincinnati, Ohio, June 26, 1953. *Study:* Univ Cincinnati, BFA, 75, and with Everet Raymond Kinstler, 87, 88 & 89; Otterbein Col, 94-96. *Work:* Vanderbilt Univ Hosp & Northern Telcom Inc, Nashville, Tenn; Cincinnati Bell Tel, Scioto Mem Hosp, Ohio; Franklin Park Conserv, Columbus, Ohio. *Comn:* Portrait of Reggie Williams, NFL Man of the Year, Van Levnans Co, Cincinnati, Ohio; painting, Franklin Park Conserv, Columbus, Ohio,. *Exhib:* Midwest Watercolor Soc, Madison, Wis, 89; Elyria Ohio Art Ctr, 90; Middletown Ohio Art Ctr, 91; Allied Artists Am, NY, 90; Rocky Mountain Nat, Denver, Colo, 89; and others. *Pos:* Chmn bd, Okla Artist Guild, Oklahoma City, Okla, 83-84; dir, Ohio Realist Group, Columbus, Ohio, 87-90, show dir, 87-; pres, Bexley Art Guild, 90-91; vpres, bd dir, Columbus Children's Theatre. *Teaching:* Instr drawing, Cheekwood Fine Art Ctr, Nashville, Tenn, 81-82, Okla Art Guild, Okla City, 83-85, North Light Art Sch, Cincinnati, Ohio, 86-87, Immaculate Conception Sch, Columbus, Ohio, 86-89, Gahanna Art League, 99; Delaware Art Ctr, Oh, 89-91, Westerville Art League, 89-92 & Dublin Art League, 91; guest artist, Marietta Col, 89-91; Instr drawing & painting, Otterbein Col, 2003-. *Awards:* Jurors Merit Award, Tenn All State Exhib, 81; Best of Show, Oklahoma City Artist Guild, 84; Best of Show, 86-88 & Awards, 89-94, Central Ohio Watercolor Soc. *Bibliog:* Calvin J Goodman (auth), Supplementing Gallery Sales, Am Artist, 6/89; Suzanne Rusconi Accetta (auth), Putting emotion into your art, Am Artist, 91; Bernard Poulin (auth), The Complete Colored Pencil Book, 92. *Mem:* Bexley Area Artist Guild (vpres); Ohio Realist Group (dir, 87-); Cent Ohio Watercolor Soc (chmn com, 96-97); Ohio Watercolor Soc Signature (chmn com, 97-2001); The Artists Fel; Am Watercolor Soc; Allied Artists Am. *Media:* Watercolor, Colored Pencil. *Publ:* Auth, Capturing emotion, Gallery J Ohio Realist Group, 87. *Dealer:* Madison Rd Gallery 1991 Madison Rd Cincinnati OH 45208; Columbia Portraits 291 S Columbia Ave Columbus OH 43209. *Mailing Add:* 4787 Rustic Bridge Dr Columbus OH 43214

ACCONCI, VITO
SCULPTOR
b New York, NY, Jan 24, 1940. *Study:* Holy Cross Col, AB; Univ Iowa, MFA. *Work:* Mus Mod Art, Paris; Mus Mod Art, Whitney Mus Am Art, NY; Los Angeles Co Mus; Williams Coll Mus Art, Williamstown, Mass. *Comn:* Coca Cola Co, Atlanta; Lloma Station, Scottsdale, Ariz.; Indoor Park for Departures Terminal, Philadelphia Airport; Billboards for Breda (Neth) Garbage Dump; Store Windows for Saks Fifth Ave, New York City; Shibuya Subway Station Entrance, Tokyo. *Exhib:* Sonnabend Gallery, NY, 72-73, 76-77, 79-80; Eight Contemp Artists, Mus Mod Art, NY, 74; Venice Biennale, 76, 78 & 80; Whitney Biennial, 77, 81 & 91; Stedelijk Mus, Amsterdam, 78; Kunstmuseum Luzern, 78; Mus Contemp Art, Chicago, 80; Kunstverein Koln, 81; Brooklyn Mus, 85; Vienna Festival, 86; La Jolla Mus, Calif, 87; Committed to Print, Mus Mod Art, NY, 88; 15th Ann Exhib, Rhona Hoffman Gallery, Chicago, Ill, 92; solo exhibs, L'Usine, Le consortium, Dijon, France, 94, La Criee Centre d'Art Contemporain, Rennes, France, 95, Dia Ctr Arts, Brooklyn Acad Music, NY, 95, Monika Spruth Gallery, Koln, Ger, 96, Centro Gellego de Art Contemporanea, Santiago de Campostela, Spain, 96, Stroom, The Hague, The Neth, 97 & Barbara Gladstone Gallery, NY, 98 Univ of Arts, Philadelphia, 99, Inst Francais d'Architecture, Paris, 2000, Arnolfini Gallery, Bristol, Eng, Acts of Archit, Milwaukee Art Mus, Wis and Aspen Art Mus, Colo, 2002; group exhibs, Passenger: the Viewer as Participant, Astrup Fearnley Mus of Mod Art, 2002, En Route, Serpentine Gallery, London, Eng, 2002. *Teaching:* Instr art, Sch Visual Arts, NY, 68-71, Nova Scotia Col Art, 71 & 78, Calif Inst Art, 76, Cooper Union, NY, 82 & 86, Chicago Art Inst, 83, Minn Col Art, 84, Univ NC Sch Art, 85, Tyler Sch Arts, Philadelphia, 90, Yale Univ, 91-94 & Bard Col, NY, 94. *Awards:* Nat Endowment Arts Fel, 76, 80 & 83; Guggenheim Fel, 79; Sculpture Ctr Award for Lifetime Achievement, 1997; Excellence in Design award, ID Mag, 1998; Spe Citation NY Chap AIAA, 99; Recipient Archit Fel NY Found for Arts, 2000; Nancy Graves grant for Visual Artists, 2001. *Bibliog:* R Pincus-Witten (auth), Vito Acconci & the conceptual performance, Artforum, 4/72; Alan Sondheim (auth), Vito Acconci: Work 1973-74, Arts, 3/75; Mario Diacono (auth), Vito Acconci: Dal Testo-Azione Al Corpo Come Testo, Out-of-London Press, 76; G Celant (auth), Dirty Acconci, Artforum, 11/80; S Platt (auth), Vito Acconci: The sheltering city, Artweek, 9/83; P Phillips (auth), Vito Acconci at Nature Morte, Artforum, 2/85. *Media:* All. *Publ:* Contribr, Conceptual Art, Dutton, 72; Vito Acconci Issue, Avalanche Mag, 72; auth, Pulse: From my mother, Multiplicata, 72; Ten-Point Plan for Video, Video Art, Harcourt-Brace, 76; Think-Leap-Rethink-Fall, Wright State Univ Press, 77; Television, Furniture and Sculpture: The Room with an American View, Stedelijk Mus, Amsterdam, 84; Notes on Vienna, Wienfluss, Austria, 86. *Dealer:* Barbara Gladstone Gallery 515 W 24th New York NY 10011. *Mailing Add:* 20 J St Ste 215 Brooklyn NY 11201

ACEBO, DAVIS TERRY
PRINTMAKER
b Oakland, Calif. *Study:* Calif State Univ, Hayward, BS (nursing), 76; Univ Calif, San Francisco, D (pediatric oncology), 83; San Jose State Univ, BFA (printmaking), 91, MFA (printmaking), 93. *Exhib:* Nat Acad Mus, NY City, 2006. *Pos:* Pediatric transport nurse Lucile Packard Children's Hosp, Stanford, Calif, 76-; principal artist DIWA artists' collective. *Awards:* James D Phelan Award in Printmaking, 97; Radius Award, Palo Alto, Calif, 97. *Mem:* LA Printmaking Soc; Asian Americans Artists Asn. *Mailing Add:* 169 Bryant St Palo Alto CA 94301

ACHEPOHL, KEITH ANDEN
PRINTMAKER, PAINTER
b Chicago, Ill, Apr 11, 1934. *Study:* Knox Col, BA, 56; Univ Iowa, MFA, 60. *Hon Degrees:* Pac Lutheran Univ, DFA, 89; Knox College, DFA, 96. *Work:* Nat Gallery Art & Pennell Collection, Libr Cong, Washington, DC; Los Angeles Co Mus, Calif; Art Inst Chicago; Bibliot Nac, Madrid, Spain; Whitney Mus Am Art; Smithsonian Am Art Mus; Seattle Art Mus. *Comn:* Garden of Stone & Light, paintings, Atrium Durham Ctr, Iowa State Univ, 89. *Exhib:* Nat Print Exhib, Libr Cong, 60-61, 63 & 69; Brooklyn Mus, 68-74; Utah Mus Fine Arts, 80; Art Inst Chicago, 81; Honolulu Acad Art Exhib, Japan, 90; Egyptian Nat Mus, 90; Gonzaga Univ, 96; Western Ill Univ, 97; Washburn Univ, 97; Davenport Art Mus, 97; Percival Gallery, Des Moines, 97; Printworks Chicago, 2003; Premio Leonardo Sciascia Invitational, Milano, Italy, 2006. *Pos:* Dir, Univ Iowa Summer in Venice Prog, 96-. *Teaching:* Instr printmaking, Univ Iowa, 64-67; asst prof, Hope Coll, 67-69; vis artist printmaking, Univ Wash, summer 69 & Scuola Int di Grafica, Venezia, summer, 92-93 & 95; vis artist printmaking, Univ Iowa, 72-73, assoc prof, 73-78 & prof, 78-. *Awards:* Tiffany Found Award, 66; Fulbright Sr Lectureship Award, Cairo, Egypt, 79-80 & Ankara, Turkey, 84; Gold Medal Printmaking, Mediterranean Biennale, Alexandria, Egypt, 82; Edmondson Award, Des Moines Art Ctr, 90. *Media:* All Media. *Res:* Turkish nomad weaving. *Interests:* African Art. *Publ:* Auth, Yield from the Sea, Transformations with Ink on Paper, 2003; Gardens of Earth and Water, Prints and Watercolors, 2005. *Dealer:* Printworks Chicago 311 W Superior Chicago IL. *Mailing Add:* 1375 Olive St Apt 302 Eugene OR 97401-7933

ACKERMAN, ANDY
MUSEUM DIRECTOR
Study: Herbert H Lehman Col, BA; Univ Mich, MA (Near Eastern Studies), 1976. *Pos:* Dir educ, The Jewish Mus, 1977-1985, asst dir, 1985-86; supervisor, field supervisor, Emeq Hefer Regional Project, 1982-83; dir, Arts Educ Program, NY State Coun on the Arts, 1986-90; exec dir, Children's Mus of Manhattan, 1990-. *Teaching:* Instr, The Exhibit Mus, Ann Arbor, Mich, 1975-77. *Mem:* Asn of Children's Mus (pres, 1998-2000); NYC Arts Coalition (exec com). *Mailing Add:* Children's Mus of Manhattan The Tisch Building 212 W 83rd St New York NY 10024

ACKERMAN, GERALD MARTIN
HISTORIAN, EDUCATOR
b Alameda, Calif, Aug 21, 1928. *Study:* Univ Calif, BA, 52; Munich Univ, 56-58, with Prof Sedlmayr; Princeton Univ, MFA, 60, PhD, 64, with Prof Lee & Panofsky. *Work:* Life and Work of JL Gerome, 86; American Orientalists, 94; The Barque-Gerome Drawing Course, 2003. *Collection Arranged:* Thiebaud Figures, Stanford Univ Mus, 65; Gerome, Dayton Art Inst, Minneapolis Art Inst, Walters Art Gallery, Baltimore, 72-73; Gerome and Goupil/Art & Industry, Dahesh Mus, NY City, 2000; Charles Barque, Dahesh Mus, NY City, 2003. *Teaching:* Instr art hist, Bryn Mawr Col, 60-64; asst prof, Stanford Univ, 65-70; assoc prof, Pomona Col, 71-76, prof, 76-89, emer prof, 89- chmn art dept, 72-81; Fulbright prof, Univ Leningrad, USSR, 79; Appleton Eminent Scholar, Fla State Univ, 94. *Media:* Printed, Bound Books. *Res:* Am, French & British Orientalist painters, in particular academic artists such as Jean Leon Gerome, & Charles Bargue; art theory. *Publ:* Lomazzo's treatise on painting, Art Bull, 59; Thomas Eakins and His Parisian Masters, Gerome and Bonnat, Gazette des Beaux Arts, 72; The Life and Works of JL Gerome, New York, 86; American Orientalist, Paris, 94; La Vie et l'Oeuvre de j-l Gerome, 3rd edit, Paris, 2000; The Barque-Gerome Drawing Course, 2003. *Mailing Add:* 360 S Mills Ave Claremont CA 91711-5331

ACKERMAN, JAMES S
HISTORIAN, EDUCATOR
b San Francisco, Calif, Nov 8, 1919. *Study:* Yale Univ, BA, 41; NY Univ, MA, 47, PhD, 52. *Hon Degrees:* Kenyon Coll, LHD, 61; Md Inst Art, Hon DFA, 72; Univ Md, Baltimore Co, LHD, 76; Univ Venice, D'Arch, 84; Mass Coll Art, DFA, 84; D Arch, Politecnico, Milan, 2009. *Pos:* Ed-in-chief, Art Bull, 56-60; co-founder & pres, Univ Film Study Ctr, 67-75; trustee, Am Acad in Rome, 67-84, resident scholar, 74-75; trustee, Artists Found, 77-87, pres, 77-79; coun scholars, Libr Cong, 80-82; art hist panel, Sr Fulbright fels, 89-92; ed, Annali di Architettura, 92-94, ed bd, 92-. *Teaching:* Lectr, Yale Univ, 46 & 49; asst prof hist art & archit, Univ Calif, 52-56, assoc prof, 56-60; Fel, Coun Humanities, Princeton Univ, 60-61; prof fine arts, Harvard Univ, 61-90, chmn dept, 63-66 & 82-84, Arthur Kingsley Porter prof, emer, 90-; Slade prof fine art, Univ Cambridge, 69-70; Mellon lectr, Nat Gallery Art, 85; Meyer Schapiro vis prof art hist, Columbia Univ, 88, vis prof, 91; vis prof fine arts, New York Univ, 92; vis prof archit, Mass Inst Tech, 96 & Harvard Univ Sch Design, 97 & 99. *Awards:* Grand Officer in the Order of Merit of the Italian Republic, 78; Am Inst of Architects Award in History & Theory, 92; Fel, Guggenheim Found, 93; Premio Daria Borghese, 95; Paul Oskar Kristeller Lifetime Achievement Award, Renaissance Soc Am, 98; Int Balzan Prize for career achievement in the history of archit and urban planning, 2001; Leone d'oro Award, Architecture Biennale, Venice, 2008; Hon Citizen, Padua, Italy; Presidential medal Distinguished Services to Educ in Art, 66; Lifetime Achievement Award, Inst Italiano di Cult, Los Angeles, 2008. *Mem:* Corresp fel Accademia Olimpica Vicenza; corresp fel Brit Acad; corresp fel Royal Acad Uppsala; corresp fel Ateneo Veneto; hon fel Bavarian Acad Sci; Am Philosophical Soc; Am Acad of Arts & Sci; Accademia di San Luca, Rome; Royal Acad Arts; Fel, Soc Arch Hist. *Res:* History of architecture; critical and historical theory; interaction of art and science in the period of 1200-1700. *Publ:* The Cortile del Belvedere, Vatican City, 54; The Archit of Michelangelo, London/NY, 61; Art and Archaeology (with Rhys Carpenter), Englewood Cliffs, 62; Auth, Palladio, Penguin, England, 66; auth, Palladio the Architect and his Influence in America (film), 80; The Villa: Form & Ideology of Country Houses, Princeton Univ Press, Thames & Hudson, London, 90; Distance Points: Studies in Theory and Renaissance Art and Architecture, Cambridge, Mass, 91; Osservazioni sui progetti di chiese di Leonardo da Vinci, pvt publ, 98; co-ed, Conventions of Architectural Drawing: Representation and Misrepresentation, Harvard Univ, 2000; Origins, Imitation, Conventions, Cambridge, Mass, 2002. *Mailing Add:* Sackler Mus Harvard Univ 485 Broadway Cambridge MA 02138

ACKERMAN, RUDY SCHLEGEL
PAINTER, EDUCATOR
b Allentown, Pa, Mar 30, 1933. *Study:* Kutztown State Col, BS (art educ), 58; Temple Univ, MS (educ), 63; Pa State Univ EdD, 67. *Work:* Allentown Art Mus, Pa; Pa State Col; Lehigh Univ; Moravian Col, Pa; The Fossil Wall, DaVinci Science Center, Allentown, Pa, 2010. *Comn:* 14 ft metal sculpture, Pa Power & Light Co, Allentown,

67; tunnel mural, Allentown-Bethlehem-Easton Airport, Pa, 76; murals, The Marketplace, Bethlehem Mall, 78, Civic Ctr, Bethlehem, Pa, 84; Children's Sculpture Park, Trexlerton, Pa; sculpture, Community Service for Children, Allentown, Pa, 1990-2009; 14 ft Fountain, Lederach, Pa, 2002. *Exhib:* The Circle, Allentown Art Mus, 74; Works on Paper, Studio Proposte, Florence, Italy, 79; Solo exhibs: Gallery Doshi, Harrisburg, 79, Lehigh Univ, 80 & Monotypes 81; Alain Bilham Gallery, NY, 81; Allenton Art Mus, 83; Moravian Col, 85, 87, 89, 91, 93, 95, 97, 2008; Muhlenberg Col, 88. *Pos:* Chmn art dept, Moravian Col, 63-2002; exec dir, Baum Sch Art, Allentown, 65-2006, dir exhibs and collections, 2006-. *Teaching:* Prof studio art & art hist, Moravian Col, 63-2002; Emeritus prof Arts & Humanities, 2002-. *Awards:* Distinguished Prof Achievement Award, Kutztown State Univ Alumni, 94; Excellence in Environment award, Bethlehem Steel, 95; Sculpture Award, Community Service for Children, Allentown, Pa, 1990-2008. *Mem:* Coll Art Asn. *Media:* Oil Paint, Sculpture. *Publ:* Moravian Coll Mag, fall 91, spring 93, spring 2009. *Mailing Add:* 2708 W Washington Allentown PA 18104-9839

ACORD, JAMES See Shie & Acord, Susan & James

ACTON, ARLO C
SCULPTOR
b Knoxville, Iowa, May 11, 1933. *Study:* Wash State Univ, BA, 58; Calif Inst Arts, MFA, 59. *Work:* San Francisco Mus Art. *Exhib:* Some Points of View for '62, Stanford Univ, 62; The Artist's Environment: The West Coast, Ft Worth, Tex, 62; Fifty California Artists, Whitney Mus Am Art, NY, 62-63; California Sculpture, Kaiser Ctr, Oakland, Calif, 63; 3rd Paris Biennial, 63; and many others. *Teaching:* Univ Calif, Berkeley, 63. *Awards:* Edgar Walter Mem Prize, San Francisco Mus Art, 61; Second Prize, Richmond Art Asn Ann, 61; Award, San Francisco Art Asn, 64; plus others. *Bibliog:* Peter Selz (auth), Funk, Univ Calif, Berkeley, 67; Maurice Tuchman (auth), American Sculpture of the Sixties, Los Angeles Co Mus Art, 67. *Mailing Add:* PO Box 75 North San Juan CA 95960

ADAIR, JIM R
PAINTER, DESIGNER
b May 18, 1927. *Study:* Univ Mich, BS (design), 1952. *Comn:* painting, Cara & John Boyce, 2005; painting, Katherine Lombardo, 2007; painting, Art Storin, 2009. *Exhib:* Solo Exhib, Woodstock Artists Asn & Mus, Woodstock, NY, 2005; 78th Grand Nat Exhib, Am Artists Prof League, NYC, 2006; 30th Ann Open Exhib, North East Watercolor Soc, Kent, Conn, 2006; 65th Ann Juried Exhib, Salmagundi Art Club (Audubon), NYC, 2007; 2008 Ann Open Exhib 32, Northeast Watercolor Soc, Kent Conn, 2008, Exhib 33, 2009; Salmagundi Art Club, Nwe York, 2009; Woodstock Sch Art, NY, 2009. *Pos:* 1st Vpres, North East Watercolor Soc, 2006-. *Teaching:* intr, Red Pump Studio/Gallery, New Paltz, NY. *Awards:* Art Student League, Audubon Artists 59th, 2001; Rose Yeni Mem, Am Artists Prof League (AAPL) Grand Nat, 2003; Award for Excellence, Juried Mem Show,North East Watercolor Soc, 2009. *Bibliog:* Steve Doherty, (ed in chief, auth), Testing the Waters, Watercolor Mag, fall 2004. *Mem:* North East Watercolor Soc News (vpres, 2006-); Am Artists Prof League (AAPL); Audubon Artists Soc (AA). *Media:* Watercolor. *Dealer:* Red Pump Studio/Gallery 75 Allhusen Rd New Paltz, NY 12561. *Mailing Add:* 75 Allhusen Rd New Paltz NY 12561

ADAMO, DAVID
INSTALLATION SCULPTOR
b Rochester, NY, 1979. *Exhib:* Solo exhibs, Dispatch, New York, 2007, Part of Performa 07, New York, 2007, Dispatch for Les Urbaines, Lausanne, CH, 2007, Fruit & Flower Deli, New York, 2008, IBID Proj, London, 2008, Berlin, 2008, Le Confort Mod, Poitiers, France, 2009, Ghent, Belgium, 2009, Basel, Ch, 2009, NO Gallery, Milan, Italy, 2009, Galerie Nelson Freeman, Paris, 2010; group exhibs, None of The Above, Swiss Inst, New York, 2004; On the Beach, Printed Matter, New York, 2005; Re-Make/Re-Model, D'Amelio Terras Gallery, New York, 2006; Elizabeth Found Gallery, New York, 2006; Art in General, New York, 2007; Peres Proj, Athens, Greece, 2007; Miami Beach Cinematheque, Miami Beach, 2007; Andrea Rosen Gallery, New York, 2009; Galleria Comunale d'Arte Contemp Monfalcone, Italy, 2010; Greater New York, PS1, New York, 2010; Whitney Biennal, Whitney Mus Am Art, New York, 2010; Untitled, New York, 2010. *Mailing Add:* Galerie Nelson Freeman 59 rue Quincampoix Paris 75004 France

ADAMS, ALICE
SCULPTOR
b New York, NY, Nov 16, 1930. *Study:* Columbia Univ, BFA, 53; Fulbright travel grant, 53-54; French govt fel, 53-54; L'Ecole Nat d'Art Decoratif, Aubusson, France. *Work:* Haags Gemeentemuseum, The Hague, Neth; Univ Nebr, Lincoln; Hertz Corp, NY; Mus Art and Design, NY; Chase Manhattan Bank, NY; Edwin I Ulrich Mus, Wichita, Kans; NJ State Mus, Trenton; City of Denver, Colo; Broward Co, Fla; The State Conn; Univ Del, Newark, Del; Herbert F Johnson Mus, Ithaca, NY; Weatherspoon Gallery; Univ NC, Greensboro; Brooklyn Mus, NY; Brooklyn Mus, NY; Whitney Mus, NY; Metropolitan Mus Art, NY. *Comn:* Small Park with Arches, Toledo Botanical Garden, Ohio, 83; Glider Park, Bronx, NY, 90; The Roundabout, Philadelphia, Pa, 92; African Garden, Brooklyn, NY, 93; The River, Middletown, Conn, 93; Beaded Circle Crossing, Denver Int Airport, Colo, 94; Healer's Spring, Univ Tex, San Antonio, 97; Scroll Circle, Univ Del, 2001; Habitat, Little Falls, NJ, 2004; Wall of the Tides, Vineland, NJ, 2006; and others. *Exhib:* Contemp Am Sculpture, Whitney Mus Am Art, 70-71 & 73; Am Women Artists, Kunsthaus, Hamburg, Ger, 72; An Int Survey of Painting and Sculpture, Mus Mod Art, NY, 84; Builtwork, Sarah Lawrence Coll Gallery, Bronxville, NY, 85; Am Abstract Artists 1936-1986, Brox Mus Arts, NY, 86; House and Garden, Nassau Co Mus Fine Arts, Roslyn, NY, 86; Fiber-Five Decades, Selections from the Permanent Collection, Am Craft Mus, NY, 95; Alice Adams: Pub Projects, Lehman Coll Art Gallery, Bronx, NY, 2000; Solo exhibs, 55 Mercer, NY, 70, 72-73 & 75, Hal Bromm Gallery, 78-79 & 81, Artemisia Gallery, Chicago, 80 & Dag Hammarskjold Plaza, NY, 83; Materializing Six Years: Lucy Lippard and the Emergence of Conceptual Art, Brooklyn Mus, NY, 2012; Artparks 40th Anniv Exhib, Buffalo, NY, 2013. *Collection Arranged:* Haags Gemete Mus, The Hague, Neth; Univ Nebr; Everson Mus, Syracuse, NY; Edwin Ulrich Mus, Wichita, Kans; Rosenquist Collection, East Hampton, NY; Ryman Collection, NY City; Columbia Univ, NY City; Whitney Mus, NY City; Mus Art & Design, New York City. *Pos:* Design Team Artist, Downtown Seattle Transit Project, 88-90, St Louis Metrolink Rail, 92-93, Centro Transit Syst, Birmingham, Eng, 93, NJ Transit, NJ, 2002-2003, Charlotte Area Transit Syst, NC, 2002-2003. *Teaching:* Instr sculpture, Manhattanville Col, 61-79; instr, Pratt Inst, 79-80; instr, Sch Visual Arts, 80-85. *Awards:* MacDowell Colony, MacDowell Found, 67; Nat Endowment Arts Grant, 79 & 84-85; Princeton Univ Fel, 80; Fel, Guggenheim Found, 81-82; Award Sculpture, Am Acad & Inst Arts & Letts, 84; Prize winning entry, Westside Competition, Munic Art Soc, NY; Rockefeller Study and Conference Center, Bellagio, Italy, 2002; and others. *Bibliog:* Barbara Kafka (auth), The Woven Structures of Alice Adams, Craft Horizons, 3/67; Lucy Lippard (auth), The Abstract Realism of Alice Adams, Art Am, 9/79; Jonathan Goodman (auth), Alice Adams, Susan Boettger Excavating Land Art by Women in the 1970's, Susan Hoeltzel, Alice Adams. *Mem:* Am Abstr Artists (secy, 67). *Media:* Wood, Metal, Concrete, Landscape. *Publ:* auth (exhib catalog), Alice Adams: Public Projects, Lehman Coll Art Gallery. *Mailing Add:* 3370 Ft Independence St Bronx NY 10463

ADAMS, BOBBI
COLLAGE ARTIST, PAINTER
b Plainfield, NJ, July 30, 1939. *Study:* Wheaton Coll, Ill, BS (high honors), 61; Art Students League, with R Brackman, R Philipp, M Cooper & V Vytlacil, 70-74; Nat Acad Design, New York, 73-74, New York Univ, MA, 98. *Work:* State SC Art Collection; Nat Bank SC; Munic Collection, Brescia, Italy; Florence Mus, SC; Morris Mus, Augusta, Ga. *Comn:* Two murals, William S Hall Psychiatric Inst, 88; mural, Calhoun Co High Sch, St Matthews, 89; mural, Redcliffe Elem, Aiken, 90; mural, Govs Sch Math & Sci, 93 & 96; mural, Mayo Magnet High Sch, Darlington, 97; mural, Lee County Pub Libr, 2006. *Exhib:* Guild SC Artists, Columbia Mus Art, 82; Gallery Exhib, Jimmy Milling, Sumter Daily Item, 86; SC Arts Comn Retrospective, 88; Oil Painters Invitational, 92 & 97; Centennial Exhib, SC State Mus, 94; Fausto Lorenzi Contemporanea, Brescia, Italy, 97; Washington Sq E Galleries, New York, 98; Mus St Paul de Vance, Nice, 2000; Frances Marion Univ, 2002; Winthrop Univ, 2003; Biennale Int del L'arte Contemporanea, 2003; Oils Painter' Invitational, 2004 & 2006; Milestones, Burroughs-Chapin Mus, Myrtle Beach, SC, 2010; Solo exhib: Ephemera, Sumter Gallery of Art, Sumter, SC, 2011. *Pos:* SC artist-in-residence, 80-2006. *Teaching:* adj, Central Carolina Comm Col, Sumter, Sc. *Awards:* Purchase Award, State SC, 80; Westvaco Award, Gibbes Gallery, 80. *Bibliog:* The Adams Papers, NJ Music-Arts, 75; Sumter Daily Item, 4/14/86; Contemporanea 8, Brescia, Italy, 97; The ITEM, 1, 20, 2011. *Mem:* Art Students League (life mem). *Media:* Oil, Pigment, Paper. *Interests:* Gardening, nature. *Publ:* auth, Gatherings from the Garden, 2013 (volume 1). *Mailing Add:* 215 S Heyward St Bishopville SC 29010

ADAMS, CELESTE MARIE
MUSEUM DIRECTOR, CURATOR
b Cleveland, Ohio, July 4, 1947. *Study:* Univ Mich, Ann Arbor, BA, 1969; Univ Pa, Philadelphia, AM (art hist), 1970; Harvard Univ, AM, 1978. *Work:* Cleveland Mus Art, Ohio; Mus Fine Arts, Houston, Tex; Grand Rapids Art Mus, Mich. *Collection Arranged:* Japanese Landscape and Figure Painting (auth, catalog), Am Australian Found Arts, 1983 & Visions of the Am West (auth, catalog), 1986; Mattuas Alter: Journey of an Am Painter, Mus Fine Arts, Houston, 1997; Quiet Grandeur: Four Centuries of Dutch Art, 1998. *Pos:* Asst dir & cur, Mus Fine Arts, Houston, Tex, 1980-93; dir, Grand Rapids Art Mus, 1997-. *Mailing Add:* Grand Rapids Art museum 101 Monroe Center St NW Grand Rapids MI 49503-2801

ADAMS, DENNIS PAUL
SCULPTOR, CONCEPTUAL ARTIST
b Des Moines, Iowa, Nov 15, 1948. *Study:* Drake Univ, BFA, 69; Tyler Sch Art, Philadelphia, Pa, MFA, 71. *Work:* Etablissement Public pour L'Amanagement de la Defense & Centre Nat d'Art Contemporain, Paris, France; Mus Mod Art, NY; Gemäldegalerie Staatliche Museen Preussischer Kulturbesitz, Ger; Israel Mus, Jerusalem; Lenbachhaus Städtische Galerie, Munich; Whitney Mus Am Art, NY; Neue Galerie am Landesmuseum, Joanneum, Graz, Austria; Walker Art Ctr, Minneapolis; Westfalisches Landesmuseum fur Kunst und Kulturgeschichte, Munster, Ger; Denver Art Mus; Mus Contemp Art, Chicago; New Mus, NY; Israel Mus, Jerusalem; Queens Mus Art, NY; plus many others. *Comn:* Bus Shelter IV, Skulptur Projekte Münster, WGer, 87; Fallen Angels, Steirischer Herbst, Graz, Austria, 88; Pedestrian Tunnels, Villa Merkel, Esslingen, Ger, 89; Terminus II, de Achterstraat, Hoorn, Holland, 90; Siege, TSWA Four Cities Proj, Derry, Northern Ireland, 90; Emancipation, Boston, 91; Arcadian Blind, Floriadepark, Holland, 92; Réservoir, Musée d'Art Contemporain de Montreal, 92; Port View, Marseille, France, 92. *Exhib:* Solo exhib, Alternative Mus, NY, 87, Portikus, Frankfurt, 93 & Mus Van Hedendaagse Antwerpen, 94; Images Critiques, Musee d'Art Mod de La Ville de Paris, 89 & Passages de L'Image, 90, Magiciens de la Terre, 89, Musee Nat d'Art Mod, Centre Pompidou, Paris, France; Image World: Art & Media Cult, Whitney Mus, NY, 89; Photog of Invention, Nat Mus Am Art, Smithsonian Inst, 89 & Works: The Archive, Hirshhorn Mus, 90, Washington, DC; Images in Transition, Nat Mus Mod Art, Kyoto, Japan, 90; Mus Mod Art, NY, 91; Sala Montcado de la Fundacío "la caixa", Barcelona, 92; plus others. *Pos:* Bd govs, NY Found for Arts, 89-92. *Teaching:* Vis artist sculpture, Tyler Sch Art, Philadelphia, Pa, 87, Cooper Union Sch Art, 88, Parsons Sch, 90-99, NY, Ecole Nationale Superieure des Beaux-Arts, Paris, 92, Rijkakademi, Amsterdam, 92-, Akademie der Bildenden Kuenste, Munich, 93-94 & prof and dir visual arts prog Mass Inst Technol, Boston, 94-2001, NY Found for the Arts, 2004; prof, Cooper Union, 2001-, acting dean, 2004-. *Awards:* Nat Endowment Arts Fel, 84, 88 & 95; Deutscher Akademischer Austauschdienst, WGer, 89. *Bibliog:* Eleanor Heartney (auth), Dennis Adams, Flash Art, summer 89; Daniella Goldmann (auth), Interview with Dennis Adams, Noema Art J, 10-11/91; Lynne Cooke (auth), Dennis Adams, Galeries Mag, 2-3/91. *Media:* All

Media. *Publ:* Works--Hirshhorn Mus--Dennis Adams, Hirshhorn Mus, 90; Architecture of Amnesia--Dennis Adams, Kent Fine Art, 90; Dennis Adams: El Pavelló de l'Est, Sala Montcado de la Fundacio "la Caixa", Barcelona, 92; Port of view, L'observatoire/Marseille; Trans/Actions, Mus Van Hedendaagse Kunst Antwerpen. *Dealer:* Kent Gallery 541 W 25th St New York NY 10001. *Mailing Add:* 42 Walker St New York NY 10013

ADAMS, DERRICK
CONCEPTUAL ARTIST
Study: Pratt Inst, BFA, 1996; Columbia Univ, MFA, 2003. *Exhib:* Greater New York, PS1 Contemp Art; Wall Streets Risins, Deutsche Bank, New York; Sampson Projects, Boston; Brooklyn Mus Art; Contemp Art Centre, Vilnius, Lithuania; Roebling Hall, NY; Studio Mus in Harlem, New York; Centenary Gallery, Camberwell Coll Arts, London, UK; LC Bates Mus, Hinckley, Maine. *Pos:* Founding dir, Rush Arts Gallery, 1996; founder, Bingeonline.com, 2009. *Awards:* Space Program, Marie Walsh Sharpe Art Found, 2003; Louis Comfort Tiffany Found Grant, 2009

ADAMS, HANK M
CRAFTSMAN
b Philadelphia, Pa, 1956. *Study:* RI Sch Design, BFA (painting), 78; Penland Sch, Spruce Pine, NC, 80; Pilchuck Sch, Stanwood, Wash, 81; Tenn Technol Univ, Cookeville, Tenn, 81-84. *Work:* Detroit Inst Art, Mich; Brooks Mus, Memphis, Tenn; Oberglas Mus, Barnbach, Austria; JB Speed Art Mus, Louisville, Ky; Contemp Arts Ctr, Honolulu, Hawaii. *Exhib:* Solo exhibs, Traver Sutton Gallery, Seattle, Wash, 86, Mich Gallery, Detroit, 87, Great Am Gallery, Atlanta, Ga, 87, Dorothy Weiss Gallery, San Francisco, Calif, 87, 89, 92 & 93, Kohler Arts Ctr, Sheboygan, Wis, 88 & Heller Gallery, NY, 88, 90 & 94, The Arts Ctr of the Capital Region, NY, 2001, Elliot Brown Gallery, Wash, 2001, Marx-Saunders Gallery, Chicago, Ill, 2002; Maximizing the Minimum: Small Glass Sculpture, Mus Am, Millville, NJ, 93; Contemp Crafts & the Saxe Collection, Toledo Mus Art, 93; The Art of Contemp Glass, JB Speed Art Mus, 93; Tiffany to Ben Tre, A Century of Glass, Milwaukee Art Mus, 93; The Forest, Elliott Brown Gallery, Seattle, 95; Hokkaido Mus of Modern Art, Sapporo, Japan (traveling to other city museums in Japan and on to Dusseldorf, Ger), 97; Bumbershoot, 2000, Seattle Ctr, 2000, SeaTac Airport, 2001; group exhibs, Primary Colors, Elliot Brown Gallery, Seattle, Wash, 2001, Glass Am, Heller Gallery, 2001, 02, Fire and Form, Norton Mus of Art, W Palm Beach, Fl, 2003. *Pos:* Designer, Benko Glass Co, Milton, WVa, 88-94. *Teaching:* Appalachian Ctr, Smithville, Tenn, 81-85; Pilchuck Sch, Stanwood, Wash, 81; Ctr Creative Studies, Detroit, Mich, 87, 96, 97; vis artist, Univ Hawaii, Honolulu, 82, Toledo Mus Sch, 84, At Park, Lewiston, NY, 85, Univ Ill, Urbana, 86, Univ Ala, Tuscaloosa, 88, Oberglas Barnbach, Austria, 89 & 90 & Cranbrook Educ Community, Bloomfield Hills, Mich, 91, Corning Mus, NY, 2002, Mass Col of Art, Boston, 2002, Calif State Univ at Fullerton, Calif, 2003, San Jose State Univ, Calif, 2003, Calif Col of Arts and Crafts, Oakland, Calif, 2003. *Awards:* Fel, Nat Endowment Arts, 86, 88 & 90; Prize, Simonoseki City Art Mus, 92; Grant, Empire State Crafts Alliance, 93; Wheaton Fel, Creative Glass Ctr of Am, 2001; NY State Arts Fel, 2003. *Bibliog:* Warmus, William (auth) Castings: Hank Murta Adams, Glass Mag, 97. *Dealer:* Elliott Brown Gallery 619 N 35th St Seattle WA 98103. *Mailing Add:* 16 117th St Troy NY 12182-2436

ADAMS, HENRY
EDUCATOR, CURATOR
b Boston, Mass, May 12, 1949. *Study:* Harvard Univ, BA, 71; Yale Univ, MA, 77, PhD (art hist), 80. *Pos:* Cur fine arts, Carnegie Inst Mus Art, Pittsburgh, Pa, 82-84; Samuel Sosland cur Am art, Nelson-Atkins Mus Art, Kansas City, 84-93; dir, Cummer Mus Art & Gardens, Jacksonville, Fla, 94-95; interim dir, Kemper Mus Art, Kans City, Mo, 96; cur am art, Cleveland Mus Art, 97. *Teaching:* Asst, Yale Univ, 77; vis lectr, Wesleyan Univ, 77-78; asst prof art hist, Univ Ill, Urbana-Champaign, 81-82; adj prof fine arts, Univ Pittsburgh, 82-84; adj prof art hist, Univ Kansas, Lawrence, 84-93 & Univ Mo, 89-93; vis prof, Colo Coll, Colorado Springs, 96; prof am art, Case Western Reserve Univ, 97-. *Awards:* Frances Blanshard Prize, Yale Univ; Arthur Kingsley Porter Prize, Coll Art Asn, 1985; Distinguished Serv Medallion, William Jewell Coll, 1989. *Mem:* Coll Art Asn; Asn Historians Am Art; Mass Hist Soc. *Publ:* Auth, A Fish by John LaFarge, Art Bulletin, 80; Mortal themes: Winslow Homer, Art Am, 83; The Development of William Morris Hunt's the Flight of Night, Am Art J, 83; New books on Japonisme, 83 A new interpretation of Bingham's Fur Traders Descending the Missouri, 83, Art Bull; contribr (essay), John La Farge, Abbeville Press, 87; Thomas Hart Benton: An American Original, Alfred Knopf, 89; Thomas Hart Benton: Drawing from Life, Abbeville Press, 90; Victor Schreckengost and 20th Century Design, Cleveland Mus Art, 2000; Eakins Revealed, Oxford Univ Press, NY, 2005; Andrew Wyeth: Master Drawings from the Artist's Collection, Brandywine River Mus, Chadds Ford, Pa, 2006; Whats American About American Art? Hudson Hills Press, 2009; Tom and Jack: The Intertwined Lives of Thomas Hart Benton and Jackson Pollack, Bloomsbury Press, NY, 2009; Out of the Kokoon: Cleveland's Festival of Art and Dance, 1911-1938, Cleveland Artists Found, 2011; The Wyeths: Three Generations of American Art, Mona Bismark Found, Paris, 2011; Abe Frajndlich: Penelope's Hungry Eyes: Portraits of Famous Photographers, Schirmer/Mosel, Munich, 2011; Painting in Pure Color: Modernism in Cleveland, 1908-1913, Cleveland Artist's Found, 2013. *Mailing Add:* Case Western Univ Dept Art History and Art 10900 Euclid Ave Cleveland OH 44106-7110

ADAMS, KIM HASTINGS
SCULPTOR
b Dec 17, 1951; Can citizen. *Study:* Univ Victoria, BFA, 80. *Work:* Nat Gallery Can, Ottawa, Ont; Art Gallery Ont, Ydessa Hendeles Art Found, Toronto; Art Gallery Windsor, Winnipeg, Man; Winnipeg Art Gallery, Windsor, Ont; Concordia Art Gallery, Musee d' art Contemporain, Montreal; Canada Coun Art Bank, Ottawa; Centraal Mus, Holland; London Regional Art and Hist Mus; Macdonald Stewart Art Ctr; MacKenzie Art Gallery. *Comn:* Crab legs (outdoor sculpture), Macdonald Stewart Art Ctr, Guelph, Can, 94; The Studio, Toronto Sculpture Garden, Can, 94. *Exhib:* On Track, Olympic Arts Festival, Calgary, Alta, 88; Can Biennial of Contemp Art, Nat Gallery Can, Ottawa, Ont, 89; Solo exhibs, Shedhalle Zurich, Switz, 90, Winnipeg Art Gallery, Man, 91 & The Power Plant, Toronto, Ont, 92; Unnatural Acts: Contemp Art, Barbican Art Gallery, London, Eng, 91; Mus d'Art Contemp (auth, catalog), Montreal, Quebec, 96; Sculpture Projects (auth, catalog), Munster, Ger, 97; In Site 97, San Diego, Calif, 97; Mus Civilization, Hull, Que, 97; Winnipeg Art Gallery, Manitoba, 98; Dunlop Art Gallery, Regina, 98; Mendel Art Gallery, Saskatoon, 99; Edmonton Art Gallery, 99; Art Gallery of Hamilton, 99; Charles H Scott Gallery, Vancouver, 99; Vancouver Art Gallery, 2000; Art Grandeur Nature, Paris, 2000. *Bibliog:* Bruce Ferguson (auth), Northern Noises, Winnipeg Art Gallery, 87; Nancy Tousley (auth), Worlds within worlds, Can Art Mag, 88; Gary Garnels & Jack Reynolds (auths), Sculpture at the Point, 88; Madill (auth), Kim Adams, Winnipeg Art Gallery, 91; Sandra Grant Marchand (auth), Kim Adams, 96; Klaus Bussman, Kasper Konig & Florian Matzner (ed), Sculpture Projects, 97; Sara Milroy (auth), Kim Adams, Artnews, 98; Joan Murray (auth), Canadian Art in the Twentieth Century, 99. *Media:* All Media. *Dealer:* Galerie Christine Chassay 372 St Catherine W Montreal PQ H3B 1A2 Canada; Genereux/Grünwald Gallery 21 Morrow Ave Toronto ON M6R 2H9 Canada. *Mailing Add:* RR 2 Grand Valley ON L0N 1G0 Canada

ADAMS, LAURIE SCHNEIDER
HISTORIAN, EDITOR
b New York, NY, Sept 29, 1941. *Study:* Tulane Univ, BA, 62; Columbia Univ, MA (art hist), 63, MA (psychology), 64, PhD (art hist), 67. *Pos:* Ed, Source: Notes in the History of Art J, 84-. *Teaching:* Prof art hist, John Jay Col, City Univ New York, 67-2011, CUNY Grad Ctr, 90-2011, prof emer 2011-. *Mem:* Coll Art Asn. *Res:* Renaissance art, art and psychoanalysis, iconography, psychobiography, psychoiconography. *Publ:* auth, The Methodologies of Art, Westview Press, 2010; Federico da Montefeltro and Sigismondo Malatesta: The Eagle and the Elephant (with Maria G Pernis), Peter Lang, 96; Art Across Time, McGraw-Hill, 2011; A History of Western Art, McGraw-Hill, 2011; Key Monuments of the Italian Renaissance, Westview Press, 2000; Key Monuments of the Baroque, Westview Press, 2000; Italian Renaissance Art, Westview Press, 2001; Looking at Art, Prentice Hall, 2002; Lucrezia Tornabuoni De'Medici and the Medici Family in the Fifteenth Century (with Maria G. Pernis), Peter Lang, 2006; auth, Art: A Beginner's Guide, Oneworld Publs, 2012. *Mailing Add:* 224 E 68th St New York NY 10065

ADAMS, LISA KAY
PAINTER
b Bristol, Pa, Aug 3, 1955. *Study:* Univ Heidelberg, Ger, 75; Scripps Col, BA, 77; Claremont Grad Univ, MFA, 80. *Work:* Edward Albee Found, Montauk, NY; Weisman Mus, Malibu, Calif; Laguna Mus Art, Laguna Beach, Calif; Nippon Steel, USA Inc & Eli Broad Corp Collection, Los Angeles; San Jose Mus Art. *Comn:* BMW N Am, ArtCar, 93; West Valley Branch Lib, Resenda, Calif, 2008; Fire Station 64, Watts, LA, Calif, 2008; Chatsworth Station, METRO, Ca, 2012. *Exhib:* Solo Exhibs: Recent Paintings, William Turner Gallery, Venice, Calif, 94, Coll Southern Nev, 95, Miller Fine Art, Los Angeles, 97 & Gallery Paradise, Costa Mesa, Calif, 98, New Image Art, Los Angeles, Apocalypse Twins, Santa Monica, Calif, 2000, The Living room, Santa Monica, Calif, 2001, Patricia Correia Gallery, Santa Monica, Calif, 2002, Sandbox, Venice, Calif, 2003, The Office, Huntington Beach, Calif, 2004, White Box Gallery, Marina del Rey, Calif, 2005, Lawrence Asher Gallery, Los Angeles, Calif, 2007; Lawrence Asher Gallery, Los Angeles, Calif, 2009, Offramp Gallery, Pasadena, Calif, 2011, CBI Gallery, Los Angeles, Calif, 2011, 2013, 2014, 2015; AB Strak Shun, William Turner Gallery, Venice, Calif, 94; Others Among Others, Wierzbowski Gallery, Houston, 94; Smoggy Abstraction, Haggerty Mus, Milwaukee, 96; New Image Art, Los Angeles, 98; Patricia Correia Gallery, Santa Monica, 99 & 2002; The Living Room 2000, Sandberg Inst, The Neth, 2000; The Sandbox, Venice, 2003; The Office, 2004; White Box Gallery, 2005; Lawrence Asher Gallery, Los Angeles, 2007 & 2009; Riverside Art Mus, 2009; Green Gallery, Milwaukee, 2009; Pederson Proj, Pomona, Calif, 2010; Angel's Gate, San Pedro, Calif, 2010; Unfinished Paintings, LACE, Calif, 2011; Calif State Northridge, 2012; Descanso Gardens, 2013. *Pos:* Instr painting, Art Ctr Col, Pasadena, Calif, 94 & Claremont Grad Univ, Calif, 94. *Teaching:* Instr drawing, Univ Calif Los Angeles Extension, 88-98; instr painting, Santa Monica Col Design, Art & Archit, 90-09; instr drawing, Univ Southern Calif, Los Angeles, 96; instr painting & drawing, Univ Calif Riverside, 99-2000 & Otis Col Art & Design, 2001-02. *Awards:* Fulbright Senior Award, 96; Artist in Residence, Nordic Inst Contemp Art, Helsinki, 99; Artist in Residence, Gifu Design, 2000; White Residency, Costa Rica, 2002; Andy Warhol Grant for Curating, 2004. *Bibliog:* James Scarborough (auth), Smoggy Abstraction (catalogue essay) & The Future of Paradise Past (catalogue essay); Betty Brown (auth), Muses (catalog); A. Moret (auth), Installation Mag, 2011; James Scarborough (auth), Huffington Post, 2011; Lisa Adams (auth), Vicissitude of Circumstance (monograph), 2011; Holly Myers (auth), LA Times, 2013; Tibby Rothman (auth), LA Weekly, 2013. *Media:* Oil, Painting

ADAMS, LOREN DEAN, JR
PAINTER, SCULPTOR
b Linton, Ind, Sept 28, 1945. *Study:* Famous Artist Sch, Westport, Conn, 65; Univ Hawaii Maui Coll, 2013. *Work:* Vancouver Centenial Maritime Mus, Vancouver; RW Norton Art Gallery, Shreveport, La; Cummins Fannin Hall Mus, Edmonton, Alberta. *Comn:* Naacal Temple Mural, Sammy Hager, Mill Valley, Calif, 86, Telos-Mu Mural, 96, Cabo Wabo Cantina Mural, 96; Ode to John Stabile, Mr & Mrs Walter Ennis, El Cajon, Calif, 2005; Northwest Passage, Mr & Mrs Bob Allen Lee, La Porte, Tex, 2013. *Exhib:* Group exhibs, Roseville Municipal Mus, Calif, 67, Vancouver Centenial Maratime Mus, Vancouver, BC, Can, 77, Founders of the Western Art Cir, Nat Archives Mus, Victoria, BC, 80; Solo retrospective, RW Norton Art Gallery, Shreveport, La, 79; Solo exhib, Cummins Fannin Hall Mus, Edmonton, Alberta, Can, 80. *Pos:* artist in res emeritus, Loren Adams Mus Fine Art, Makawao, Hawaii, 96-. *Teaching:* instr oil painting, Acad Ocean Art Graphy, Vancouver, 74-81; guest teacher oil painting, Fugere Sch Art, Denver, Colo, 78-83. *Awards:* Marine Artist of the Yr, Palmer Art Tours, Dol Palmer, 69; 1st Pl Grand prize, Internat Art Biennial, World of

Art Publications, Stockholm, Sweden, 2006-2007. *Bibliog:* Cash Edwards (auth), Accelerated Evolution, Kicking Horse Productions, 86; Lonnie Anderson (auth), Get Wet, TV Documentary, 92. *Mem:* Wester Artists Assn British Columbia; Art Collectors Rsch Assn, Carmel by the Sea; Lahaina Art Soc; Hui Owa'a Kaulua, Canoe Club. *Media:* All Media. *Specialty:* local, regional, national & international fine art. *Collection:* classic & contemporary Western Art; Bob A Lee, Joe Grandee, Dalhart Windberg, Roger Arndt, Robert Moak, Alfredo Rodrigues. *Publ:* contbr, Contemporary Western Artists (book), Samuels, Peggy, & Harold, 82; contbr, Artists in Hawaii (book), Vogelsberger Paul, Francis, 94; auth, Confessions of an Art Appraiser, End of the Storm, 2005. *Dealer:* Lahaina Galleries 828 Front St Lahaina Maui Hawaii 96761. *Mailing Add:* PO Box 1496 Makawao HI 96768

ADAMS, MAC
SCULPTOR, PHOTOGRAPHER
b South Wales, Gt Brit, 1943. *Study:* Cardiff Coll Art (nat dipl design), 61-66, ATD, 66-67; Rutgers Univ, MFA, 67-69. *Work:* Brooklyn Mus & Guggenheim Mus, New York; Wallraf Richartz Mus, Cologne, Ger; Univ Iowa Mus; Victoria & Albert Mus, London, Eng; Musee De Toulon, France; Los Angeles Co Mus, Calif; Ga Mus Art, Athens; La Jolla Mus Contemp Art, Calif; Microsoft Corp; Maison Europeenne de la Photographie, Paris; Getty Mus Art, Los Angeles; Harvard Univ; Mus Mod Art, New York; Zimmerli Art Mus, Rutgers Univ, NJ; and others. *Comn:* NY Korean War Mem, Battery Park, New York, 91; Mustangs at Noon, Henry Gonzalez Conv Ctr, San Antonio, Tex, 98; Wings and Wheels, Solar Pavilion, Dept Transportation, Cherry Hill, NJ, 2002; Apparitions, Castle Blois, France, 2002; Wetlands (two photo mosaics), New Secaucus Transfer Sta Concourse, NJ Dept Transportation, 2003. *Exhib:* Solo exhibs, Hammerskjold Plaza Sculpture Garden, New York, 84, Galerie Maier-Hahn, Dusseldorf, Fed Repub Ger, 87, Montclair State Coll, NJ, 88, La Jolla Mus Contemp Art, Calif, 88-89, Gracie Mansion Gallery, New York, 90, Silence of Shadows, Cardiff Arts Trust, Touring Exhib, Eng, 98, Printemps de Cahors, Extraordinaire Cahors, France, 99, Serge Aboukrat Gallery, Paris, 2000, Centre Photographique D'ile-De-France, Pontault-Combault, France, 2001, G/B Agency, Paris, 2002-03, Musees de Chateauroux, France, 2004 & CEAAC, Strasbourg, France, 2006, GB Agency, Paris, 2007, Art Premiere (with Dominique Petitgand, Basel Art Fair 39, 2008, Musee NIcephone-Niepce, Chalon-sur Soane, 2010, Mudam Musee D'Art Moderne, Luxembourg, 2011, GB Agency Paris, 2011, Lianzhou Int Photo Festival, Narrative and Narrative Forms, 2012, Blackmail GB Agency, The Independent Art Fair, NY, 2012, The Bathroom, GB Agency, FIAC, Paris, 2012, Illuminated Perception State Univ Iowa, Ames Christian Peterson Art Mus, 2013, Crimes of Perception, Elizabeth Dee Gallery, NY, 2013, Dialogues & Erasure, GB Agency, Paris, France, 2014; New York Diary: Almost 25 Different Things, PS 1 Mus, Inst Contemp Art, 91; The Seventies, John Gibson Gallery, New York, 92; The Order of Things: Toward a Politic of Still Life, Widner Gallery, Trinity Coll & Real Art Ways, Conn, 92; Quotations, The Second Hist of Art, Aldrich Mus Contemp Art & Mus Contemp Art, Wright State Univ, 92; Eclipses, CEAC, Strasbourg, France, 99; plus others. *Pos:* Chmn, State Univ NY, 88-. *Teaching:* Prof photog, State Univ NY Coll, Old Westbury, 88-. *Awards:* Nat Endowment Fel Arts, 76, 80, 82; Berlin Artist-in-residence Prog, 81; NY State Fel Arts (sculpture), 88; Chancellors Award Res Arts & Humanities, State Univ NY, 2002, Distinguished Teaching Professor, State Univ NY, Coll at Old Westbury, 2009; Pollack/Krasner Found award, 2013. *Bibliog:* Shoichiro Higuchi (auth), Water as Environmental Art, p 148, Kashiwashobo Publ Co, 91; Julia Ballerini (auth), The Surrogate Figure: Intercepted Identities in Contemporary Photography, Ctr Photog, 91; Charles Hagen (auth), NY Times Reviews, 3/92; David Campany (ed), Art & Photography, 94-95, Phaidon Publ, 2003; Nancy Princethal (auth), Shadow of a Doubt, JOCA SERA, 2004; and many others. *Media:* All. *Dealer:* GB Agency Paris France

ADAMS, PAT
PAINTER, EDUCATOR
b Stockton, Calif, July 8, 1928. *Study:* Univ Calif, Berkeley, BA, 49; Brooklyn Mus Art Sch, with Max Beckmann & John Ferren, 50-51. *Work:* Whitney Mus; Joseph Hirshhorn Mus; Yale Gallery Art; Brooklyn Mus; Jane Voorhees Zimmerli Mus, Rutgers Univ; Corcoran Gallery Art; Palm Springs Desert Mus; Nat Acad Mus, NY; Berkshire Mus, Mass; Brooks Mus, Memphis, Tenn; and others. *Comn:* TRW Hq, Lyndhurst, Ohio. *Exhib:* One person shows, Zabriskie Gallery Biennial, 54-2006, Survey 1954-79, Cincinnati Contemp Art Ctr, 79, MModA traveling Exh to France, 56-57, Stable Gallery, NY, 56, Zabruskie Gallery, Paris, 80, Columbia Mus Art & Sci, SC, 82, Va Commonwealth, 82, Haggin Mus, Stockton, Calif, 86, NY Acad Sci, 88, Addison-Ripley, Washington, 88, Survey, 68-88, Berkshire Mus, Pittsfield, Mass, 88-89 & Jaffe-Friede Strauss Galleries, Dartmouth Col, 94, Torrant Gallery, Flynn Informing Arts Ctr, Burlington, Vt; Yale Sch Art Fac 1950-1990, Marilyn Pearl, NY, 90; Traditional Sources: Contemp Visions, Webb & Parsons Gallery, Burlington in collaboration with Shelburne Mus, Vt, 91; Bennington Coll Collects, Williams Coll Mus Art, 91; Nat Acad Mus, 92-95, 2001; Late Modern Drawings 1960-70's, Corcoran Gallery Art, 93; A View of Ones Own: Nat Asn Women Artists Collection, Zimmerli Mus, Rutgers, NJ, 94; Urdang Gallery, Boston, 97; Rider Univ, Lawrenceville, NJ, 97; Silvermine Guild, 98; Helen Day Art Ctr, Stowe, Vt, 98 & 2006; Middlebury Coll Art Mus, 2000; Univ Rhode Island, 2000; Decordova Mus, Lincoln, Mass; Block Mus, Northwestern Univ, 2001, Fleming Mus Univ Vt, Burlington, 2002; Nat Acad Mus, Challenging Tradition, 2003; Galeria Nat/Museo de Los Ninos, 2004; Vermont Arts Council, Wood Gallery, Montpelier, Vt, 2005; Zabruskie Gallery, NY, Paris Season, 2005. *Pos:* Bd dir, Vt Coun Arts, 77-81, Yaddo Corp, 81-, vchmn, 85-88, Williamstown Regional Art Conserv Lab, 85-86 & Col Art Asn, 86-90; artist-in-residence, Dartmouth Col, 94. *Teaching:* Art fac painting, Bennington Col, 64-93; vis critic painting, Yale Univ, 71-72; grad sem, Queens Col, 72, RI Sch Design, 81; vis prof, Grad Sch Art, Yale Univ, 83; vis artist, Univ Iowa, Univ NMex, Western Ky Univ, Columbia Univ, Kent State Univ & Cornell Univ, Mills Col; lectr & critic, RI Sch Design, 89, Univ Mass, Amherst, 89 & Skidmore Col, summer 92; lectr, The Not as Yet, Nat Asn Women Artists, NY; sr critic, Grad Prog, Yale Sch Art, 90-95; lectr critique, Vt Studios Ctr, 93, 94, 97, 99, 2000 & 2001, Am Univ, Washington, DC, 2002. *Awards:* Nat Endowment Arts, 68,76 & 87; Hassam Purchase Award, Am Acad Arts & Letters, 83, 85 & 89; Distinguished Teaching Art Award, 84; Govs Award Excellence Arts, Vt Coun Arts, 95; Andrew Carnegie Prize for Painting, Nat Acad Design Exhib, 95; Jimmy Ernst Award for painting, Am Acad Arts & Letters, 96; Ranger Purchase Award, 2005. *Bibliog:* Emmy Donadio (auth), Nightflight to Byzantium: Pat Adams' new work, Arts, summer 86; Debra Bricker Balken (auth), Pat Adams, Paintings, 68-88, Berkshire Mus Pittsfield, Mass, 88; Jed Perl (auth), Gallery Going, 91; Ruth Meyer (auth), Pat Adams Paintings 1954-1979, Cincinnati Art Center; and others. *Mem:* Vt Acad Arts & Sci (elections Fel, 90); Nat Acad Design (assoc, 92, acad, 93); Coll Art Asn; Vt Coun Arts; Phi Beta Kappa. *Media:* Oil-Isobutyl Methacrylate, Acrylic, Monoprint, Etching. *Publ:* Auth, Art Now, 6/72; On working, Quadrille, fall 77; Subject and being, Art J (Coll Art Asn Am), 82; The Making of Art & the Making of Artists Colloquium, Atlanta Coll Art, 87; Zabruskie 50th Anniversary, Ruden Finn, 2005. *Dealer:* Virginia Zabriskie Gallery 41 E 57th New York NY 10019. *Mailing Add:* 370 Elm St Bennington VT 05201

ADAMS, PETER
PAINTER
b Los Angeles, Calif, Aug 27, 1950. *Study:* Otis Art Inst, Los Angeles, 70; Art Ctr Coll Design, Los Angeles, 70; Lukits Acad Fine Art, Los Angeles, 77. *Work:* Forbes Magazine Coll, New York, NY; Carnegie Art Mus, Oxnard, Calif; Calif Club, Los Angeles; Stephen's Col, Columbia, Mo; Southern Alleghenies Mus Art, Loretto, Pa. *Comn:* 50th Anniversary (painting), Chadwick Sch, Palos Verdes, Calif, 87; Headmaster (portrait), Curtis Sch, Los Angeles, 88; family portrait, comn by Eric & Ronna Hoffman, Portland, Ore, 93; family portrait, comn by Mr & Mrs Robert Warren, Portland, Ore, 94; book cover, Caroline Hudson Firestone, Afghan Story Teller. *Exhib:* The Mystical Paintings of Peter Adams, Carnegie Art Mus, Oxnard, Calif, 98; On Location Malibu, Frederick R Weisman Mus Art, Malibu, Calif, 99 & 2003; Drawn to Yellowstone, Mus Am West, Autry National Ctr, Los Angeles, Calif, 2004. *Pos:* Mem bd trustees, Pac Asia Mus, Pasadena, Calif; coauth, Calif Art Club News, 93-2006; bd dir, Acad Art Univ, San Francisco, currently; pres, California Art Club, 93-; adv bd member, Am Soc Portrait Artists, 2000-. *Awards:* Challacombe Award, Oil Painters of Am, 93; Art Calif Discovery Award, 94-95; Gold Crown Award, vis art, Pasadena Arts Council, 97. *Bibliog:* Berkley Hudson (auth), Art of War, Los Angeles Times, 2/23/89; B Eric Rhoads (auth), Imagination at Work, Plein Air Magazine, 9/04; Paul Soderberg (auth), Peter and Elaine Adams: The Art Bridge Builders of California, Art-Talk, 3/04. *Mem:* Calif Art Club (pres, 93-); signature mem Pastel Soc Am; signature mem Oil Painters Am; signature mem Plain Air Painters Am; hon emer assoc guild mem Am Soc Classical Realism. *Media:* Oil, Pastel. *Publ:* Auth, Moods of the Pacific, Pac Asia Mus, 93; Peter Adams: Eastern Exposure, Southwest Art Mag, 96; auth, Afghanistan Evolving, Caroline Hudson Firestone Publ, 2004; auth, From Sea to Shining Sea: A Reflection of America, Thomas Haggin Mus Publ, CA, 2004. *Dealer:* American Legacy Fine Arts LLC PO Box 92345 Pasadena CA 91109. *Mailing Add:* 949 Linda Vista Ave Pasadena CA 91103

ADAMS, PHOEBE
SCULPTOR
b Greenwich, Conn, 1953. *Study:* Philadelphia Coll Art, Pa, BFA, 76; Skowhegan Sch Painting & Sculpture, Maine, 77; State Univ NY, Albany, MFA, 78. *Work:* Solomon R Guggenheim, Metrop Mus Art, NY; Brooklyn Mus, NY; AT&T, Chicago, Ill; Pa Acad Fine Arts, Philadelphia, Pa Convention Ctr & Philadelphia Mus Art, Pa; Storm King Art Ctr, Mountainville, NY; Prudential Insurance Co; Walker Art Ctr, Minneapolis, Minn; Harn Mus, Fla; others. *Comn:* Sculpture for outdoor garden, Walker Art Ctr, Minneapolis, Minn, 88; Intaglio print, Friends of the Philadelphia Mus Art, Pa, 91; Sculpture, Pa Convention Ctr, Philadelphia, 93. *Exhib:* Solo exhibs, Lawrence Oliver Gallery, Philadelphia, 84, 86 & 90, Curt Marcus Gallery, NY, 87, 90, & 95, Pence Gallery, Santa Monica, Calif, 88 & 91, Locks Gallery (with catalog), Philadelphia, 93 & Anna Leonouens Gallery, NS Coll Art & Design, 94, Bellas Artes Gallery, Santa Fe, NMex, 99, 2000 & 2001, Nesbit Gallery, Drexel Univ, Philadelphia, 2000; Sculpture Inside/Out (with catalog), Walker Art Ctr, Minneapolis, Minn, traveling, 88; The Material Imagination, Guggenheim Mus Soho, 95; Subjective Vision, Kipp Gallery, Ind Univ Pa, 96; Contemp Art Ctr of Va, Va Beach, 97; San Francisco Mus Mod Art, 2000; Univ Colo, Denver, 2001. *Teaching:* Asst prof, Kutztown Univ, Pa, 91-; Artist in residence, Kent State Univ, Ohio, Pilchuck Glass Sch Stanwood, Wash, 2001. *Awards:* Pa Coun Arts, 82 & 84; Guggenheim Sculptor in Residence, Chesterwood, Stockbridge, Mass, 86; Nat Endowment Arts Fel Grant, 86. *Bibliog:* Kimberly Davenport (auth), Impossible liberties: contemporary artists on the life of their work, Art J, summer 95; Pepe Karmel (auth), Art in review: Phoebe Adams, NY Times, 2/3/95; Tom Csaszar (auth), In the studio, Phoebe Adams, Sculpture, 1/96; and others. *Mailing Add:* c/o Bellas Artes 653 Canyon Rd Santa Fe NM 87501

ADAMS, ROBERT MCCORMICK
ADMINISTRATOR, WRITER
b Chicago, Ill, July 23, 1926. *Study:* Univ Chicago, PhD, 47 AM, 52, PhD, 56; Univ Pittsburgh, Dr Sci, 85; Hunter Col, City Univ New York, LHD, 86; Ill Univ, Edwardsville, LHD, Coll William and Mary, LHD, 89; Dartmouth Col, Dr Sci, 89. *Pos:* Trustee, Nat Opinion Res Ctr, 70-95, Russell Sage Found, 78-92, Santa Fe Inst, 84- & George Washington Univ, 86-92; auth, column, Smithsonian Horizons, Smithsonian Mag, 84-94; chief exec, Smithsonian Inst, 84-94. *Teaching:* Instr, Univ Chicago, 55-63, dir Oriental Inst, 62-68 & 81-83, prof, 64-84, dean Social Sci, 70-74 & 79-80, Harold Swift Distinguished Serv Prof, 75-84, provost, 83-84, res assoc dept anthropology, 84-; adj prof, dept anthropology & Near Eastern studies, John Hopkins Univ, formerly. *Mem:* Am Oriental Soc; assoc mem Iraqi Acad; fel Am Acad Arts & Sci; Soc Antiquaries London. *Publ:* Auth, Heartland of Cities: Surveys of Ancient Settlement and Land Use on the Central Floodplain of the Euphrates, Univ Chicago Press, 81; co-ed, Behavioral and Social Science Research: A National Resource, Vol 1 & 2, Nat Acad Press, 82; auth, Change and continuity in faculty, student body and research support: A decade-long perspective, Chicago Chronicle, 5/10/84; approx 100 articles & reviews. *Mailing Add:* 9753 Keeneland Row La Jolla CA 92037

ADAMS, SHELBY LEE
PHOTOGRAPHER
b Hazard, Ky, Oct 24, 1950. *Study:* Cleveland Inst Art, BFA (photog), 74; Univ Iowa, MA (photog), 75; Mass Coll Art, Boston, MFA (photog), 89. *Work:* Art Inst Chicago; Los Angeles Co Mus Art; San Francisco Mus Mod Art; Mus Fine Arts, Houston; Mus Mod Art, NY; Whitney Mus Am Art; and others. *Exhib:* Solo exhibs, Southern Light Gallery, Amarillo, Tex, 84, Harvard Fogg Mus, Cambridge, 89, OK Harris Works of Art, NY, 93 & 95, Robert Koch Gallery, San Francisco, 93, Northern Ill Univ, 94, Etherton Gallery, Tucson, Ariz, 94, Catherine Edelman Gallery, Chicago, 94, Int Ctr Photog, Midtown, NY, 94, FotoGalerie, Amsterdam, The Neth, 95 & Cleveland Mus Art, 95; Devotion, Faith and Fervor - The Faithful and the Damned, 292 Gallery, NY, 94; Workshop Instructor, Anderson Ranch Arts Ctr, Aspen, Colo, 94; A Photog Bestiary, Robert Koch Gallery, San Francisco, 94; Photog Exhib-Three, Cinti Art Acad, 95; Appalachian Legacy (with catalog), Arles Int Photog Festival, France, 99; Stephen Bulger Gallery, Toronto, 2002; Yossi Milo Gallery, NY, 2002. *Pos:* Freelance photogr, 80-87 & 92-98. *Teaching:* Instr photog hist, Northern Ky Univ, Highland Heights, 79; instr camera & studio lighting, Cincinnati Art Acad, 79; head instr photog, Ill Cent Col, East Peoria, 81-84; asst prof & head photog prog, Salem State Col, Salem, Mass, 85-92; instr nat & int workshops, 92-; artist-in-residence, Bennington Coll, Vt, 96-97; lectr, Cincinnati Art Mus, Ohio, 98, Dallas Mus Art, Tex, 98. *Awards:* Nat Endowment Arts Fel, 78 & 92; Artist Support Grant, Polaroid Corp, Cambridge, Mass, 89-92; Artist Support Grant, Elizabeth Firestone Graham Found, Akron, Ohio, 1990, Peter S Reed Found, NY, 2000; Guggenheim Found Fel, 2010. *Publ:* Illusr, Photographer's Forum (by Gretje Ferguson), 93; View Camera (Elizabeth A Johnson, ed), 93; Appalachian Portraits, Univ Press Miss, Jackson, 93; Camera and Darkroom (by Dean Brierly), 94; Amerika (Frans Zerhagen, ed), Amsterdam, Holland, 94; auth introduction, 80 photogs, Appalachian Legacy, Univ Press Miss, 1998; 80 photogs, Appalachian Lives, Univ Press Miss, introduction by Vicki Goldberg, 2003; Lens Work, (by Brooks Jensen), 2000; ARTForum (by Bob Nickas), 2002; Photovision (by Ellen Rennard), 2001; Documentary film on work & life, New Release (70 mins); True Meaning of Pictures, (film, dir Jennifer Baichwal), Mercury Films, Inc, 2002. *Dealer:* Yossi Milo Gallery New York; David Fahey/Klein Gallery Los Angeles. *Mailing Add:* 3 S Church St Pittsfield MA 01201-6103

ADAMSON, GLENN
MUSEUM DIRECTOR
b Boston, Mass. *Study:* Cornell Univ, BA in Art History, 1994; Yale Univ, PhD in Art History, 2001. *Collection Arranged:* curator, Gord Peteran: Furniture Meets its Maker, 2009; co-curator, Postmodernism: Style and Subversion 1970 to 1990, 2011. *Pos:* adj curator, Milwaukee Art Mus, formerly; chair bd trustees, Crafts Study Ctr, Farnham, currently; curator, Chipstone Found, 2000-2005; head rsch dept, Victoria & Albert Mus, London, 2005-2013; Nanette L Laitman dir, Mus Art & Design, NY, 2013-; co-editor, Journal of Modern Craft. *Awards:* Iris award. *Publ:* auth, Thinking Through Craft, 2007; The Craft Reader, 2010; The Invention of Craft, 2013. *Mailing Add:* Museum of Art and Design 2 Columbus Cir New York NY 10019

ADAMSON, JEROME D
ART DEALER, GALLERY DIRECTOR
b Glendale, Calif, July 14, 1944. *Study:* Whittier Coll, BA, 67. *Pos:* Dir, Adamson-Duvannes Galleries, 80-. *Mem:* Art Dealers Asn Calif (pres). *Specialty:* 19th and 20th-century American and European painting. *Interests:* paintings that focus on grandeur and beauty of the West, its hist, settlement and develop. *Publ:* Auth, With an Eye Toward Collecting California Painting (exhib catalog), 85; American Art 1830-1940: A Century Observed (exhib catalog), 89; The California Vision: Watercolors in the California Style (exhib catalog), 90. *Dealer:* Adamson-Duvannes Galleries. *Mailing Add:* Adamson/Duvannes Galleries 484 S San Vicente Blvd Los Angeles CA 90048

ADAMSON, LINNY J
CURATOR, WEAVER
b Portland, Ore, Jan 4, 1952. *Study:* Ore State Univ, 70-73; Portland State Univ, 74; special studies with Britt Warsinki, Norway & Peter Collingwood, Eng. *Work:* Timberline Lodge, Nat Hist Landmark, Ore. *Comn:* Wall hanging (woven), Rankin, McMurry & Osborn Attys, Portland, Ore, 76; office dividers (woven), Willamette Dental Group, Portland, 77; International Kings Table (wall woven pieces), Eugene, Ore, 78; (wall piece), Clatskanie Ore Savings & Loan, 78. *Exhib:* Ore Artists Under 35, Portland Art Mus, Ore, 74. *Collection Arranged:* LACE Collection, Portland Art Mus, 81; Mountain High IV-Glass, 83; Mountain High V-Metal, Northwest Blacksmiths, 85; Timberline Textiles, Ore Hist Soc, 86; Rachael Griffin Hist Exhib Ctr, 86. *Pos:* Dir, Fibres Gallery, Portland, Ore, 75-77; weaver, Friends of Timberline, 75-78; dir, Timberline Textile Workshop, 78-80 & 40 volunteer rug hookers, 83-86; cur, Timberline Lodge, 78-86; bd mem, Ore Sch Arts & Crafts, 84-86. *Teaching:* Instr sales & weaving, Wildflowers Fibres, Portland, Ore, 73-76; instr weaving, Portland Parks Bureau, 74-79. *Awards:* First Place, Valley Invitational, Corvallis Art Ctr, 74. *Bibliog:* Portraits in Art, Linda Adamson, Handweaver, Curator (film), Rogers Cable Systems, 84. *Media:* Textiles. *Res:* 1930's Works Progress Administration arts and crafts. *Mailing Add:* c/o Friends Timberline Lodge PO Box 69544 Portland OR 97240

ADAN, SUZANNE
PAINTER
b Woodland, Calif, Feb 12, 1946. *Study:* Calif State Univ, Sacramento, BA, 69, MA, 71. *Work:* Crocker Art Mus, Sacramento; Continental Bank, Houston; Lexecon Inc, Chicago; Impact Commun, Bloomington, Ill; Livingston & Mattesich, Sacramento. *Comn:* Ceramic Tile Mural, Univ Calif Med Ctr, Sacramento, 90; Ceramic Tile Murals, Nat Sta, Folsom, Calif, 90. *Exhib:* San Francisco Art Institute Centennial Exhibition, San Francisco Mus Mod Art, 71; Extraordinary Realities, Whitney Mus Art, NY, 73-74; one-person exhibs, Womanspace, Los Angeles, 74, Betsy Rosenfield Gallery, Chicago, 83 & 85, Himovitz-Salomon Gallery, Sacramento, 84, 86 & 93, John Berggruen Gallery, San Francisco, 87 & Susan Cummins Gallery, Mill Valley, 97; two-person show, A Survey, Mem Union Gallery, Univ Calif, Davis, 90; Tribute Exhib: Works on Paper & Sculpture By Crocker Kingsley Artists, Crocker Art Mus, Sacramento, 91; Black & White in Color, Spectrum/Himovitz Gallery, San Francisco, 91; Discovery Contemp Calif Narrations, Am Cult Ctr, Brussels, 92; Ink & Clay, Holmes Fine Art Gallery, San Jose, Calif, 93; The Michael Himovitz Gallery, Crocker Art Mus, Sacramento, 94; Art of Collecting: The Artist as Collector, Mem Union Gallery, Univ Calif, Davis, 94; plus many others. *Teaching:* Instr drawing, Am River Col, Sacramento, Calif, 75-76; artist-in-residence, Calif Arts Coun. *Awards:* Hardison, Komatsu, Ivelich & Tucker Award, Richmond Art Ctr, 80; New Works Grant, Sacramento Metrop Arts Comn, 90 & 96; James D Phelan Art Award, San Francisco Found Kala Inst, Berkeley, 91. *Bibliog:* Ruth Holland & Susan Willoughby (auths), Fifty Years of Crocker Kingsley, Crocker Art Mus, Sacramento, 75; Roger Clisby (auth), Welcome to the Candy Store, Crocker Art Mus, Sacramento, 81; Janice T Dreisbach & Barbara K Gibbs (auths), Michael Himovitz Gallery: An Exhibition at the Crocker Art Mus, Sacremento, 94. *Mem:* Coll Art Asn. *Media:* Oil on Canvas. *Mailing Add:* 3977 Rosemary Cir Sacramento CA 95821

ADATO, LINDA JOY
PRINTMAKER, INSTRUCTOR
b Edgware, England, Oct 24, 1942; US citizen. *Study:* Hornsey Coll Art, Eng, 60-61; Univ Calif, Los Angeles, BA, 66, MA, 67. *Work:* Fine Arts Mus San Francisco; Corcoran Gallery, Washington DC; DeCordova Mus, Lincoln, Mass; Brit Mus, London; NY Pub Libr; Miss Mus Art, Jackson; Detroit Inst Arts, Detroit, Mich. *Comn:* presentation print, Print Club of Albany, 2009; editions of 25 prints, West Shore Graphic Arts Soc, Muskegon, Mich, 2010. *Exhib:* British Int Miniature Prints, City Gallery, London, 97, 2000; New York City Centennial Portfolio, The Old Print Shop, NY, 98 & 2002; Int Print Biennial, Silvermine Guild Galleries, New Canaan, Conn, 94, 96, 98; City Views, DeCordova Mus, Lincoln, Mass, 98-99; 5th British Int Miniature Prints, 2003-05, 6th British Int Miniature Prints, 2006, 7th British Int Miniature Prints, 2008; NY Soc Etchers & Gallery, Australia Exchange Exhib, 2004; Boston Printmakers N Am Print Biennial, Boston Univ, Mass, 2005, 2007, 2009; Hollar Soc Gallery, Prague, Czech Repub, 2006; solo exhib, Silvermine Guild Galleries, New Canaan, Conn, 2007; Delta Nat Small Prints Exhib, Bradbury Gallery, Art State Univ, 2008, 2012, 2015; 183rd Ann: An Invitational Exhib Contemp Am Art, Nat Acad Mus, New York, 2008; Old Print Shop (two person exhib), New York, 2009; Int Miniature Print Exhib Ctr for Contemp Printmaking, Norwalk, Conn, 2009, 2011; 77th Soc Am Graphic Artists Mem Show, Fyre Gallery, Braidwood, Australia, 2010; 14th Ann Nat Small Works Exhib, Wash Printmakers Gallery, Silver Spring, MD, 2011; Footprint, Ctr Contemporary Printmaking, Norwalk, Conn, 2012; NY Soc Etchers, 3rd Nat Exhib of Intaglio Prints, Nat Arts Club, NY, 2013. *Teaching:* Adj lectr printmaking, Manhattanville Col, Purchase, NY, 87-2000; instr printmaking, Silvermine Sch Art, New Canaan, Conn, 95-2009. *Awards:* Gold Medal of Honor, Audubon Artists, NY, 2000; Ralph Fabri Medal of Merit, Audubon Artists, 2002; Art Students League NY Award, Audubon Artists, 2003; Marquis Who's Who in Am Art References Award, Audubon Artists, 2007-2008; The Old Print Shop Graphics Award, Audubon Artists, 68th Exhib, NY, 2010; Silver Medal of Honor, Audubon Artists, NY, 2012; Legion Paper Purchase Award, 10th Biennial Miniprint Int Exhib, Ctr for Contemporary Printmaking, Norwalk, Conn. *Mem:* Soc Am Graphic Artists (treas, 95-2002); Boston Printmakers; Silvermine Guild Arts Ctr (hon life mem); Audubon Artists; Soc Am Graphic Artists (pres 2007-2010). *Media:* Etching. *Dealer:* The Old Print Shop 150 Lexington Ave New York NY 10016; Platt Fine Art LLC 561 West Diversey Parkway Suite 204A Chicago IL 60614. *Mailing Add:* 494 President St #1 Brooklyn NY 11215

ADDISON, BYRON KENT
PAINTER, EDUCATOR
b St Louis, Mo, July 12, 1937. *Study:* Washington Univ, St Louis, Mo, BFA, 59; Univ Notre Dame, South Bend, Ind, MA, 60. *Work:* Univ Tulsa Libr, Okla; Maryville Univ Libr, St Louis, Mo; Springfield Art Mus, Springfield, Mo; Neville Pub Mus, Green Bay, Wis; The Evansville Mus Arts & Sci, Ind; Dunnegan Gallery of Art (Mus), Bolivar, Mo; Am Embassy, Bamako, Mali, Negelan; Islip Mus, East Islip, NY; Most of Us Are Immigrants; The Granary, Assoc Segou Laben, Segou, Mali; many other private collections. *Comn:* Forest Park sculpture, St Louis Award Comt, Mo, 65; entrance wall sculpture, Continental Tel Co, Wentzville, Mo, 67; wall sculpture, Westinghouse Elec Corp, Abington, Va, 71; fountain & sculpture, United Methodist Church, Sun City, Ariz, 74; religious sculpture, St Joseph Church, Manchester, Mo, 80. *Exhib:* Nat Competition, Nat Watercolor Soc, Muckenthaler Cult Ctr, Fullerton, Calif, 1992, 1999; Nat Exhib Transparent Watercolors, Midwest Watercolor Soc, Neville Pub Mus, Green Bay, Wis, 92; Five State Exhib, Wichita Art Mus, Kans, 92; Rocky Mountain Nat Watermedia Exhib, Foothills Art Ctr, Colo, 92, 94, 96, 97, 99, 2002, 2007, 2009, 2010, 2011, 2012, 2013; Watercolor USA, Springfield Art Mus, MO, 81, 82, 84-87, 89-93, 97-99, 2001, 2002, 2004-2013; Ga Watercolor Soc 18th Nat Exhib, Mus Art & Sci, Macon, Ga, 97; Kans Watercolor Soc 26th Ann 7 State Exhib, Wichita Art Mus, Kans, 97, 2010; Rocky Mountain Nat Watermedia Exhib, The Foothills Art Ctr, Golden, Colo, 1997, 1999, 2007, 2010; Watercolor USA, Springfield Art Mus, Mo, 1998, 1999, 2001, 2004, 2005, 2007, 2008, 2009, 2010, 2011, 2012; 24th Exhib Nat Watercolor Okla, Kirkpatrick Galleries, Oklahoma City, 98; Midwest Nat Exhib, The Rahr-West Art Mus, Wis, 99; Watercolor USA Hon Soc Exhib, Huntsville (Ala) Mus Art, 2000; Midwest Nat Exhib, The Canton (Ohio) Mus Art, 2000; Kans Watercolor Soc Honor Show, Wichita Ctr Arts, 2000 & 06; MOAK 4 State Exhib, Springfield Art Mus, 2000; Western Colo Watercolor Soc Ann Nat Exhib, Western Colo Ctr Arts, Colo, 2000, 2001; Watercolor USA Honor Soc, 9th Biennial Exhib, Springfield Art Mus, MO, 2004-2007, 2011; Ann Kans Watercolor Soc Competition, Wichita Art Mus, Kans, 2004 & 06; Winston Churchhill Mem, Fulton, Mo, 2006; Univ Art & Design Gallery, Springfield, Mo, 2006; Transparent Watercolor Soc Am, Elmhurst Art Mus, 2007; Mo Watercolor Soc, 2004-2006; Winston Churchill Mem, Fulton, Mo, 2007, 2008, 2009, 2012, 2013; Transparent Watercolor Soc Am, Bloomington Art Ctr, Bloomington, Minn, 2009; Transparent Watercolor Soc Am, Kenosha Pub Mus, Kenosha, Wis, 2009, 2010, 2011; Rocky Mountain Nat

Watermedia, Foothills Art Ctr, Colo, 2009, 2010, 2011; Celebrating St Louis Artists Over 70, Sheldon Art Galleries, Mo, 2010; Adirondack Nat Exhib Am Watercolor, Arts Guild of Old Forge, NY, 82, 83, 84, 85, 89, 90, 91, 92, 93, 95, 96, 99, 2000, 2009, 2010, 2011; Faculty and Alumni Show, Morton J. May Foundation Gallery, Maryville Univ, St. Louis, Mo, 2010; Watercolor USA Japan Show, Nat Art Center, Tokyo, Japan, 2010. *Teaching:* Emer prof art, Maryville Univ, St Louis, Mo, 61-95, chmn, Art Dept, 65-79 & prof drawing, watercolor & sculpture, 80-95; Pillsbury chair of Fine Arts, 73-95. *Awards:* Springfield Art Mus Cash Award, 92; Purchase, Neville Pub Mus, 92; Winsor & Newton Art Award, Adirondack Exhib, 92; Southern Watercolor Soc Award of Distinction, 97, Award of Citation, 97; Watercolor USA Cash Award, 97, John and Beth Raidel Patorn Purchase Award, 98; Kans Watercolor Soc Charles & Ruth Sanderson Cash Award, 97; Context Mo Collection Award, St Louis Artists' Guild, 97; Special Merit Award, Midwest Watercolor Soc, 99, Prof Packers & Shippers Award, 99; Ecus Paper Award, Ky Watercolor Soc, 2000, Airfloat Award, 2000; Robert E Goodier Memorial Cash Award, Watercolor USA, Springfield Art Mus, Springfield, Mo, 2001; Southwest Mo Mus Asn Purchase for Springfield Art Mus Permanent Col, Springfield, Mo, 2002; Beaver Bend Prairie Naturals Award, Annual Kans Watercolor Soc Competition, Wichita Art Mus, Wichita, Kans, 2004; Springfield Art Mus Purchase Award for Watercolor for the Mus Permanent Collection, 2007; Mo Artists Award, Watercolor Mo Nat 7th Ann Exhib, Winston Churchill Mem, Fulton, Mo, 2007; Artists Mag 23rd Ann Art Competition (hon mention); Watercolor USA, Springfield Art Mus, 2008; Potomac Valley Watercolorist Award; Mo Artist's Award, Watercolor Mo Nat 8th Ann Exhib, Winston Churchill Mem, Mo, 2008; 28th Ann Adirondacks Nat exhib of Am Watercolors, Judith & A Richard Cohen Mem Prize, the Arts Guild of Old Forge, NY; Purchase Award for Museum Collection & the Robert E Goodier Mem Award, Watercolor USA, Springfield Art Mus, 2010; Exhib Award in Memorial, 30th Ann Adirondacks Nat Exhib Am Watercolors, Art Center of Old Forge, NY, 2011; Potomac Valley Award, Watercolor USA, Springfield Art Mus, 2011; Kkyledge Award, 35th Nat Exhib Transparent Watercolors Am, Kenosha Public Mus, Kenosha, Wisc; Ardren Dodge award, Rocky Mt Nat Watermedia, Goothills Art Ctr, Golden, Colo, 2011; Emprise Bank Purchase award, Kansas Watercolor Soc Nat, Wichita Ctr Arts, Kans, 2011; Artists Merit award, Watercolor Miss Nat 12th Ann Open Exhib, Nat Churchill Mus, Anson Cutts Gallery, Fulton, Mo, 2012; Cash award, Watercolor USA, Springfield Art Mus, Springfield, Mo, 2012; Rocky Mt Nat Watermedia Soc award, Best of Show, 2012; Cash award, Kans Watercolor Soc Nat Exhib, 2012; Merit award, Watercolor Mo International, 2013. *Bibliog:* Herbert Gralnick (auth), Alone with His God, St Louis Mag, 3/84; M Stephen Doherty (auth), Recent Images Recent Concerns, Watercolor 90, Am Artist Publ, fall 90; Bebe Raupe (auth), Award Winning Watercolors: The Regional Showcase, Artists Mag, 9/91; Betsy Schein Goldman (auth), Kent & Sharon's Place, Watercolor 95, Am Artist Publ, Premiere issue, winter 95; Bebe Raupe (auth), Award Winning Watercolors, Artists' Mag, 8/98; Watercolor Magic Winter 2002, Maureen Bloomfield (auth), In the Spotlight: Center Stage, 2001. *Mem:* Watercolor USA Honor Soc; Transparent Watercolor Soc Am; Nat Watercolor Soc, Rocky Mountain Nat Watermedia Soc. *Media:* Welded Steel, Watercolor. *Mailing Add:* 17775 Orville Rd Wildwood MO 63005

ADELMAN, BUNNY
SCULPTOR

b New York, NY, May 7, 1935. *Study:* Mt Holyoke Coll, Columbia Univ, BA, 56; Nat Acad Sch Fine Arts, with Stephen Csoka & Evangelos Frudakis, scholar, 76. *Comn:* Figure, comn by A Petaccio, Clifton, NJ, 77; B'Nai Brith Medal, comn by Roger Williams Mint, 78; presidential relief, M H Lamston Inc, New York, 78; Manager of Year Award, M H Lamston Inc, New York, 79; mem relief, W R Thomas Co, Warsaw, Ind, 80. *Exhib:* Allied Artists Am, Nat Acad Design, New York, 74-79 & 81; Nat Acad Ann, Nat Acad Design, New York, 76-78; Salmagundi Club Ann, New York, 78; solo exhib, Bergen Community Mus, Paramus, NJ, 79; Pen & Brush Soc, New York, 81. *Awards:* Gold Medal, Catharine Lorillard Wolfe Ann Show, 74; Coun Am Artists Soc Award, Nat Sculpture Soc, 75; Bronze Casting Award, Pen & Brush Ann, Joel Meisner Foundry, 81. *Mem:* Nat Sculpture Soc (fel); Catharine Lorillard Wolfe Club; Allied Artists Am. *Media:* Bronze. *Mailing Add:* 68 Homestead Rd Tenafly NJ 07670-1109

ADIBI, ELISE
PAINTER, PHOTOGRAPHER

Study: Swarthmore Coll, BA (Lucretia Mott Fel, 1991), 1988; Univ Pa, MArch, 1994; Columbia Univ, MFA (Agnes Martin Fel, 2005 & Hayman Trust Fel, 2006), 2007. *Exhib:* Etherington Fine Art, Vineyard Haven, Mass, 1999; In their Midst, Wallach Gallery, 2006 & Rockefeller Ctr, 2007, Columbia Univ; Musee d'Art Americain, Terra Found, Giverny, France, 2007; Pattern vs Decoration, Hosfelt Gallery, New York, 2007; Recess!, Recess Gallery, New York, 2009; Gold in Braddock, UnSmoke Systems Artspace, Braddock, PA, 2010. *Teaching:* Teaching asst, Univ Pa, 1993 & Columbia Univ, 2006-2007; adj lectr, Brooklyn Coll, 2008; guest lectr, Parsons New Sch for Design, 2008; adj asst prof, Columbia Univ, 2008; instr, Old Sculpin Gallery, Edgartown, Mass, 2009. *Awards:* Terra Found for Am Art Award, 2007; Pollock-Krasner Found Grant, 2008

ADICKES, DAVID (PRYOR)
PAINTER, SCULPTOR

b Huntsville, Tex, Jan 19, 1927. *Study:* Kansas City Art Inst, 48; Sam Houston Univ, Huntsville, Tex, BS, 48; Atelier Fernand Leger, Paris, 48-50. *Work:* Houston Mus Fine Art, Tex; Pa Acad Fine Art, Philadelphia; James A Michener Found Mus, Univ Tex, Austin; Witte Mus Art, San Antonio; World Bank, NY. *Comn:* Permian Basin (tapestry), Petroleum Club, Houston, 61; Spring Trees (tapestry), Hyatt Regency Hotel, Houston, 69; Virtuoso (sculpture monument), Lyric Ctr Bldg, Houston, 83; Pres George Bush (bronze sculpture); Sam Houston Monument, Huntsville, Tex, 94; George Bush Int Airport, Houston, Tex, 92. *Exhib:* Solo exhibs, Mus Fine Art, Houston, 51, New Works, Witte Mus Art, San Antonio, 57 & Laguna Gloria Art Mus, Austin, 57; retrospective, Ft Worth Art Ctr, 66. *Teaching:* Instr painting, Univ Tex, Austin, 55-57. *Awards:* First Purchase Prize, Houston Artists, Contemp Arts Asn, 54; First Purchase Prize, Houston Artists Ann, Mus Fine Arts, Houston, 55; Purchase Prize, Texas Art, DD Feldman, Dallas, 57. *Bibliog:* Campbell Geeslin (auth), Adickes (monograph), James Bute Co, 57; A Cantey (auth), Adickes (monograph), 62 & James A Michener (auth), Adickes, 68, Seix y Barral, Barcelona; Dr Linda Wiley (auth), Making It Happen, Wiley Publ, Huntsville, Tex. *Media:* Oil, Bronze, Portland Cement. *Publ:* Illusr, El Centauro, Seix Barral, 67 & illusr, Ingenioso Caballero Don Quixote de la Mancha: Cervantes, 68. *Dealer:* David Adickes Sculpture Works 2500 Summer St Houston TX 77007. *Mailing Add:* 2409 Kingston St Houston TX 77019

ADKISON, KATHLEEN (GEMBERLING)
PAINTER

b Beatrice, Nebr. *Study:* With Mark Tobey. *Work:* Seattle Art Mus; Seattle First Nat Bank; Bank Wash, Tacoma & Spokane; Butler Inst Am Art, Youngstown, Ohio; Cheney Cowles Mus, Spokane; Northwest Bell & Boeing, Seattle. *Exhib:* Butler Inst Am Art Ann, 61-69; World's Fair Northwest Artists, Seattle, 62 & 74; Pa Acad Fine Arts 159th Ann, 64; one-person shows, Univ Wash Mus Art, Pullman, 76, Univ Ore Mus Art, Eugene, 77, Wash State Art Mus, Olympia, 77 & Bellevue Art Mus, Wash, 81; Spokane World's Fair Expo 74 Northwest Art, Wash; and others. *Teaching:* Instr painting, Wash State Univ Exten, 55-67. *Awards:* Sun Carnival First Prize, El Paso Mus, 61; Dr Fuller Purchase Award, Northwest Ann, 61; Prize for Winter Retreat, Friends Am Art, 69. *Bibliog:* Twenty five years painting, Bellevue Art Mus, Wash, 81. *Media:* Oil. *Dealer:* Gordon Woodside Gallery 1101 Howell Seattle WA 98101. *Mailing Add:* c/o Woodside & Braseth Gallery 2101 Ninth Ave Seattle WA 98121

ADLER, MYRIL
PAINTER, PRINTMAKER

b Vitebsk, Belarus, Sept 22, 1920; US citizen. *Study:* Brooklyn Mus Art Sch; Art Students League; Theatre Arts Workshop, NY, with Moi Solotaroff; Pratt Graphics Ctr, 60-64; Mobile Puppet Theatre Social Commentary, NYC, 60-64; Yale Joel Photog Workshop, 65, Computer Generated Imagery via Printmaking, Pratt Ctr, 82. *Work:* NY Pub Libr, Hudson River Mus, Yonkers, NY; Mus Mod Art, Caracas, Venezuela; Univ Calif, Berkeley; Univ RI, Providence; and others. *Comn:* 50 Yrs/50 Faces: 50 Yr Portrait Retrospective (painting, drawing, printmaking), Fine Art Gallery, Westchester Community Col, 91. *Exhib:* Gallerie Berneim Jeune, Paris, 50; Csa Municipale, Merano, Italy, 52; One-person shows, West Broadway Gallery, NY, 72, 74 & 76, Hudson River Mus, Yonkers, 72 & 74, Katonah Mus Art Gallery, NY, 72, 76 & 80, Ossining Pub Libr, Ossining, NY, 90 & Royal Athena Gallery, NY; High Tech/High Touch: Computer Graphics Printmaking, Pratt Manhattan Gallery, NY, 87; Rubelle & Norman Schafer Gallery, Pratt Inst, Brooklyn, 89; Javitz Ctr, NY, 90; Myths & Mysteries, Temple Israel Northern Westchester, Croton, NY, 93; 30 yr retrospective printmaking, Katonah Libr Gallery, NY, 94; all media, incl puppets, Ossining Arts Coun Gallery 60-Yr Retrospective, 1996; monotype portraits of NY homeless, Articoli Fine Arts, 1999; Ava Fine Arts, White Plains, NY, 2000; Working with Technol, Gallery on the Hudson, Irvington, NY, 2001; Mus Gallery, Univ Colo, Boulder, 44. *Pos:* Dir, Myril Adler Arts Workshop, Briarcliff Manor, NY, 56-; artist-in-residence, Pratt Graphics Ctr, NY, 82-86. *Teaching:* Myril Adler Arts Workshop, 56-; printmaking, Pratt Graphics Ctr, NY, 82-86; various comprehensive art programs. *Awards:* Purchase Award, Hudson River Mus, Yonkers, NY; 100th Ann Award, Nat Asn Women Artists; Abel Silvan Mem Award for Printmaking, 83; Hortense Ferne Mem Award, 89. *Bibliog:* Norman Lalibert & Alex Mogelon (coauths), The Reinhold Book of Art Ideas, Van Nostrand Reinhold, 77; coauth, The Complete Printmaker, Ross, Romand & Ross, Free Press-Macmillan, 90; Jules Heller (auth), Encyclopedia of American Woman Artists, 95; collage, montage assemblage, Laliberte & Mogelon (auths), Demonstrations, Van Nostrand Reinhold. *Mem:* Artists Equity, NY; Nat Asn Women Artists; Abraxas Artists Group (secy, treas). *Media:* Oil; Mixed Media; Intaglio Etching, Monoprinting; Xerox Collages; Multimedia Computer-Generated Works. *Res:* Computer-generated images via photography, etching, silk screen, lithography. *Specialty:* Visual arts in all media from classical to contemporary. *Interests:* Reading, cooking, world travel, gardening. *Publ:* Illusr, Dances of Palestine, B'Nai B'Rith Hillel Foundations, New York, 47. *Dealer:* Images Art Gallery Inc 1157 Pleasantville Rd Briarcliff Manor NY 10510; artsnet.net. *Mailing Add:* 266 Dalmeny Rd Briarcliff Manor NY 10510

ADLER, TRACY L
CURATOR, EDUCATOR

b New York, NY, Apr 5, 1968. *Study:* Skidmore Col, BA (art hist) with Prof Harry Gaugh, 90; Hunter Col, CUNY, MA (art hist) with Prof William C Agee, 96. *Collection Arranged:* After Rabin: New Art from Israel, 99; Giulio Romano: Master Designer, 99; Remnant, 2001; Exotic Representation, 2002; Strange Worlds, 2003; Off the Wall, 2005; New History, 2007; Mixing It Up, 2009; and others. *Pos:* dept asst, Dept Prints & Photogs, Metrop Mus Art, NY, 91-92; admin asst, BlumHelman Gallery, NY, 92-93; studio mgr, Shonna Valeska Photog, NY, 94-97; exhib asst, The Jewish Mus, NY, 97-98; cur, Hunter Col Art Galleries, NY, 98-; consultant, Adler Arts, 2003-. *Bibliog:* Sari Carel (auth), Critic's Picks, Off the Wall, Artforum, 2005; Tania Dudina (auth), The Secret Treasure of Hunter College, Hunter Envoy, 2005; John Ewing (auth), Off the Wall, Modern Painters, 2005. *Mem:* Arttable; Am Asn Mus. *Res:* Contemporary art. *Publ:* auth, I wanna tell you something: Omer Fast, Gb Agency, Paris, 2002; auth, Strange Worlds, Hunter Col, NY, 2003; ed, Tracing Tony Smith's Tau, Hunter Col, NY, 2004; contribr, Seeing Red: On Nonobjective Painting & Color Theory, Salon Verlag, Cologne, Ger, 2004; auth, Off the Wall, Hunter Col, NY, 2005; contribr, New History, 2007

ADOUR, COLLEEN
SCULPTOR, EDUCATOR

Study: Syracuse Univ (Dept Visual Arts), BFA (studio arts), 1980-1984; Alfred Univ, Grad Level (ceramics/Glaze Chemistry), summer 1994; Binghamton Univ, MA (art hist), 2002; Binghamton Univ, Post-Masters Study (art hist), 2005. *Work:* Syracuse Univ, Univ Col Mus, Syracuse, NY. *Comn:* 10 commandments, clay tablets, produced at Roberson Mus Clayworks Studio for Broome Co Bar Asn for ethics video, 2008.

Exhib: Group Exhibs: Women's Issues: A Commentary, Avenue Art Gallery, Endicott, NY, 2003; Alumni Art Exhib, Binghamton Univ Art Mus, Binghamton, NY, 2003; Greater Binghamton - El Charcon (El Salvador) Sister Cities Project, Roberson Mus, Binghamton, NY, 2004; Staats & His Students at the Dog House, Dog House Gallery, Woodstock-Saugerties, NY, 2005; 2008 Earth Fest at Roberson Mus with Clayworks Potters, Binghamton, NY, 2008; Adour at the Wall (two woman show), Cooperative Gallery, Binghamton, NY, 2004; Faculty Art Exhib, Dept Fine & Media Arts, Broome Co Coll, NY, 2011; Mentor and Student Art Exhib, Broom Community Coll, Broome Co Arts Council, Binghamton, NY, 2012. *Pos:* instr, Children's Pottery, Roberson Mus, Binghamton, 1996-1997; Art instr, lectr, Broome Community Col, SUNY Broome, 2003-2007; State Univ NY Broome. *Teaching:* Adj prof, art & art hist, Broome State Univ NY, 2011-. *Awards:* First Place (ceramics art student exhib), Syracuse, Univ, 1981. *Mem:* Fine Arts Soc Southern Tier (FASST), (guest artist, sculpture demonstration, 2005-11). *Media:* Clay. *Publ:* Auth, C R Ashbee's Writings on Arts & Crafts, Binghamton Univ Press, 2002; auth, Ashbee: Dawn of the Modern Movemont, NY, 2010; auth, Ashbee, 2014 (2nd ed), published under auspices of SUNY-Broome Bookstore, BGM, NY. *Mailing Add:* Adour Art & Pottery PO Box 1196 Vestal NY 13850-1196

ADRIAN, BARBARA TRAMUTOLA
PAINTER, COLLECTOR
b New York, NY, July 25, 1931. *Study:* Art Students League, with Reginald Marsh, 47-54; Hunter Coll, 51; Columbia Univ, 52-54. *Work:* City Hall, San Juan, PR; Nat Acad Design; Ark Arts Ctr; So Alleghenies Mus Art, Lorreto, Pa; Philharmonic Ctr Arts, Naples, Fla; The Century Asn, New York. *Exhib:* Butler Inst Am Art, 70; Suffolk Mus, Stony Brook, NY, 71; Whitney Mus, 75; Ranger Fund Exhib, Nat Acad Design, 81; Women in the Making of Art Hist, Art Students League, NY, 82; Seventh Ann Nat Invitational Drawing Exhib, Norman Eprink Gallery, Emporia State Univ, & Univ Kans; Art and the Law, five locations, 86; Nat Acad Design, New York, 90, 2003-2004; Century Asn, New York, 2003-2004. *Pos:* Art consult, R H Macy, NY, 60-61; Saks Fifth Ave, NY, 60; Doyle Dane & Bernbach, NY, 60. *Teaching:* Art instr painting & drawing, Art Student League, 68-. *Awards:* Dorothy Haphman Ferriss Award, Pen & Brush, 83 & Walker Award, 85; Forbes Award, 90; Cert Merit, Nat Acad Design, 95; Richard H Recchia Meml Prize, 2001; Nat Acad Design, New York, 2002. *Bibliog:* Painting Techniques, Comprehensive Treatise, 81; Am Artists, 9/90; Maine Bar J Cover, 9/90. *Mem:* Life mem Art Students League; Nat Acad Design; Century Asn. *Media:* Oil, Egg Tempera. *Collection:* Reginald Marsh, John Sloan, Will Barnet, Henry Pearson, Rouault, Versalius, Goya, Martin Lewis. *Publ:* Auth, Art as Image and Ideas, Feldman Publ. *Dealer:* Harmon-Meek Gallery 386 Broad Ave S Naples FL 34102; Gerald Peters Gallery Santa Fe NM. *Mailing Add:* 420 E 64th St New York NY 10021

AEBI, ERNST WALTER
ILLUSTRATOR, PAINTER
b Zurich, Switz, Mar 25, 1938; US citizen. *Study:* Zurich Univ, lic oec publ, 65. *Work:* Montclair Mus & Kasser Found, Montclair, NJ; Adriance Mus, Westchester, NY; Klimastation, Gais, Switz. *Comn:* Roosevelt Raceway (mural in lobby), NY Racing Comn, Long Island, 70; sculpture, Swiss Am Soc, NY, 70; sculpture, Sandoz Inc, Hanover NJ, 74. *Exhib:* NY Artists, Southampton Parrish Mus, 66; Community Art, Brooklyn Mus, 68; Contemp Swiss Art, Prague State Mus, Czech, 69; Biennale Europeenne, Berheim-Jeune, Paris, 69; solo exhib, NY Univ, 76. *Collection Arranged:* One Trillion People Falling Off the Edge of the Earth, James Yu, NY, 77. *Pos:* Illusr, New York Times & Harpers Mag, 76-79, Harvard Bus Rev & Times Mag, 77. *Teaching:* Illusr, New York Times & Harpers Mag, 76-79, Harvard Bus Rev & Times Mag, 77. *Bibliog:* Henry J Seldis (auth), Phantasmagoria, Los Angeles Times, 66; Malcolm Preston (auth), The world of Ernst Aebi, Newsday, 70; Stuart Murray (auth), The restless artist, New York Times, 74. *Media:* Pen and Ink; Concrete. *Publ:* Auth, Seasons of Sand, Simon & Schuster, 93. *Dealer:* James Yu 393 W Broadway New York NY 10012. *Mailing Add:* 231 Kent Ave #3 Brooklyn NY 11211-4112

AFSARY, CYRUS
PAINTER
b Middle East, Oct 18, 1940; US citizen. *Study:* Liberal Arts Col, BA (fine arts) & BA (interior design), 70. *Comn:* Murals & portraits, MGM Grand Hotel, Las Vegas, Nev, 81. *Exhib:* C M Russell Show & Auction, C M Russell Mus, Great Falls, Mont, 84-86; Gilcrease Mus Show, Tulsa, Okla, 85; Southwest Fine Art Competition, Mus Fine Arts, Santa Fe, NMex, 85; Northwest Rendezvous Show, Helena, Mont, 85-88; Nat Acad Western Art, Cowboy Hall Fame, Oklahoma City, Okla, 86-88. *Awards:* Nat Arts Club Award Exceptional Merit, Pastel Soc Am, 86; Gold Medal in Oil, 87 & Robert Lougheed Mem Award, 88; Gold Medal Oil Painting & Silver Medal Drawing, Nat Accad Western Art, 86; and others. *Mem:* Nat Acad Western Art Northwest Rendezvous. *Media:* Oil, Pastel. *Publ:* Southwest Art, 1/87; Art of the West, 11-12/88; Int Fine Arts Collectors Mag, 3/92. *Mailing Add:* PO Box 3217 Scottsdale AZ 85271

AGAR, EUNICE JANE
PAINTER, WRITER
b Great Barrington, Mass, May 14, 1934. *Study:* Wellesley Coll Mass, BA (art hist), 56; Art Students League, 58-60 & 69, study under Jean Liberte, 57-63, Robert Beverly Hale, 69. *Work:* Columbia-Greene Community Coll, Hudson, NY; Le Moyne Art Found, Tallahassee, Fla; Bates Coll Mus Art; Univ Maine, Machias. *Comn:* Many pvt comns. *Exhib:* Solo exhibs, Le Moyne Art Ctr, Tallahassee, Fla, 66, 91 & 96, Albany Inst Hist & Art, NY, 67, Ainilian Gallery, Washington, DC, 85, 87, & 90, Windham Gallery, New York, 86 & Columbia-Greene Community Coll, Hudson, NY, 88; Dunedin Fine Arts Ctr, Fla, 91; Denise Bibro Fine Art, New York, 95, 98-99, 2002 & 2004; Univ Maine, Machias, 99-2004; Becket Art Ctr, Mass, 2000; Rensselaerville Inst, Rensselaerville, NY, 2009; Gallery at the Goldsmith, Great Barrington, Ma, 2011; Agraforestry Resource Ctr, Acra, NY, 2012. *Collection Arranged:* Cur, Monotypes, The Painterly Print, Catskill Gallery, Catskill, NY, NY State Coun Arts, 86. *Pos:* Asst ed, Am Artist, NY, 58-60, managing ed, 60-63, writer, 80-, contrib ed, 83-; Writer for the Artful Mind, Barrington, Mass, 2012-. *Teaching:* Instr painting, drawing & printmaking, Simon's Rock Early Coll, 69-78, chmn studio arts, 74-78, chmn arts div & studio arts, 75-78. *Bibliog:* Article, Am Artist, 2/84; article, Tallahassee Mag, 4/91; articles, The Artful Mind, 3/2000, 6/2011. *Mem:* Life mem Art Students League New York. *Media:* Oil, Casein, Watercolor, All drawing Media, Block prints. *Publ:* Interview articles, Am Artist, The Artful Mind. *Mailing Add:* 20 Egremont Plain Rd Great Barrington MA 01230

AGEE, ANN G
SCULPTOR, PAINTER
b Philadelphia, Pa, Apr 19, 1959. *Study:* Cooper Union Sch Art, New York, BFA (painting), 81; Yale Sch Art, Yale Univ, MFA, 86. *Comn:* men's room, John Micheal Kohler Arts Ctr, Sheboygan, Wis, 98; lobby, Pub Sch 137, Queens, NY, in process. *Exhib:* Solo exhibs, Ann Nathan Gallery, Chicago, 91, John Michael Kohler Art Ctr, Sheboygan, Wis, 93, Arena Gallery, Brooklyn, NY, 94 & Yoshii Gallery, NY, 96 & Rena Bransten Gallery, San Francisco, 98, 2000, PPOW, New York City, 2001; Domestic Exceptions, Elsa Mott Ives Gallery, NY, 96; Douglas Udell Gallery, Vancouver, 96; Millennium Eve Dress, Fabric Workshop, Philadelphia, 96; Eccentricities, Judy Ann Goldman Fine Art at Beth Urdang Gallery, Boston, Mass, 96; Working in the 90's, Coll Mainland, Tex City, 96; Domestic Exceptions, Elsa Mott Ives Gallery, NY, 96; Group exhib, Douglas Udell Gallery, Vancouver, 96; Codpiece, Griffin Linton, Contemp Exhib, Los Angeles, Calif, 97; Ornament and Landscape: on the Nature of Artifice, Apex Gallery, NY, 97; Felissimo NYFA Design Award Show, Felissimo, NY, 97; The Art Exchange Show, Arena Gallery, NY, 97; Figuring Women's Lives, Kingsborough Community Coll Art Gallery, Brooklyn, NY, 97; Pool, Rena Bransten Gallery, San Francisco, Calif, 97; Ordinary/Extraordinary, Johnson Co Community Coll Art, Kansas City, Mo, 98; Domestic Transformations/Working in Brooklyn, Brooklyn Mus Art, NY, 98-99; Portrait of Our Time II, Revolution, Ferndale, Mich, 99; Pattern, James Graham and Sons, New York City, 99; The Erotic Life of Clay: Sex Pots, Fine Arts Gallery, San Francisco State Univ, 02. *Awards:* Fel, Nat Endowment Arts, 89, 92 & 93; Design Award, Felissimo, NY Found Arts, 97; Tiffany Found Grant, 98; John Simon Guggenheim Memorial Foundation Fine Arts Fel, 2011. *Bibliog:* Shawn Hill (auth), The body as battlefield, Bay Windows, 2/29/96; Cate McQuaid (auth), Eccentricities' nicely mixes it up, Boston Globe, 3/14/96; Roger Green (auth), Chicago Expo's world acclaim grows, Ann Arbor News, 5/26/96. *Publ:* Auth, Art in a factory, Ceramics Monthly, 10/92; Welcome to the Doll House, NY Times Mag, 12/26/99. *Dealer:* Rena Bransten Gallery 77 Geary St San Francisco CA. *Mailing Add:* 373 DeGraw St Brooklyn NY 11231

AGEE, WILLIAM C
EDUCATOR, HISTORIAN
b New York, NY, Sept 26, 1936. *Study:* Princeton Univ, AB, 60; Yale Univ, MA, 63. *Collection Arranged:* Synchronism & Am Painting (auth, catalog), 65; Donald Judd (auth, catalog), 68; Modern Am Painting: Toward a New Perspective (auth, catalog), 77; Patrick Henry Bruce (auth, catalog), 79; Morton Livingston Schamberg (auth, catalog), 82. *Pos:* Dir, Mus Fine Arts, Houston, 74-82; sr vis scholar, Arch Am Art, Smithsonian Inst, 83-85; ed, Stuart Davis Catalogue Raisonné, 85-; prof art hist, Hunter Col, 90-. *Teaching:* Am Modernism, Hurto Col, 87 & 89. *Mem:* Am Asn Mus; Coll Art Asn. *Res:* Modern American and European art. *Publ:* Auth, Ralston Crawford, Twelve Trees Press, 83; Herbert Ferber, Mus Fine Arts, Houston, 83; The Advent of Modernism, High Mus, Atlanta, 86. *Mailing Add:* 157 Alta Ave Yonkers NY 10705-1414

AGID, LUCY BRADANOVIC
SCULPTOR
b San Pedro, Calif, May 5, 1929. *Study:* Otis Art, 55. *Work:* Mus Deio Bozzetti, Pietrasanta, Italy; Mus Storico della Resistenza Sant'Anna, Italy; Braille Inst, Los Angeles, Calif; City of Torrance, Calif; Warner Brothers; Univ of Loyola; Marymount Col; and others. *Exhib:* Loyola Marymount Univ, Laband Gallery, Los Angeles, 89; Woman Artist of West, Visalia, Calif, 91; Hands on Exhib, Braille Inst, Los Angeles, 93; Rise & Fall of Man, Fed Bldg, NY, 93; Dance of Life, Mus Deio Bozzetti, Italy, 94; Calif Art Gallery, 99; Marymount Univ, 2000; Univ of Loyola, 2002; many others. *Teaching:* lectr on sculpture, Palos Verdes Art. *Awards:* Madonna Festival, Nat Competition, Wilshire Ebel; Susman Award, Pen & Brush, NY, 1st Place Sculpture Award; First Place, Palos Verdes Art Show, 96; Millard Sheets Gallery award; LA Co Fair Award, 2002. *Bibliog:* Marcia Forsberg (auth), Inspired by Italian Marble, Quadrifoglia; Day with the Artist (film), Torrance Cable, City of Torrance. *Mem:* Nowa NY. *Media:* Marble, Granite, Bronze. *Dealer:* Starry Sheets 1590 S Coast Hwy Laguna Beach CA 92651; Herb Agid Gallery; Leica Art@Verizon.net. *Mailing Add:* 60 Portuguese Bend Rd Rolling Hills CA 90274

AGUILERA, ALEJANDRO
SCULPTOR
b Holguin, Cuba, May 3, 1964. *Study:* Escuela Provincial de Arte, Holguin, Cuba, BA, 83; Inst Superior de Arte, La Habana, higher educ, 88; Mass Coll Art, MA, 90. *Work:* Mus Nac de Bellas Artes & Centro de DeSarrollo de las Artes Visuales, Havana, Cuba; Peter Ludwig Museo de Aachen, Ger; Marco & Ramis Barquet, Monterrey, Mex. *Exhib:* Colonizacion y Descolonizacion, Mus Nac de Bellas Artes, Havana, Cuba, 91; 15 Artistas Cubanos, Ninart, Centro de Cultura, Mex, 91; Nuevas Adquisiciones Contemporaneas, Mus Nac de Bellas Artes, Havana, Cuba, 91; Forum Int Arte, Colecion Peter Ludwig, Cologne, 91; Cuba Construye, Euskal Fonda Bilbao, 91; Solo exhib, Los buenos y los malos, Galería Ramos Barquet, Monterrey, Mex. *Teaching:* Prof sculpture, Inst Superior del Arte, 89-91. *Awards:* Critics Award, Sci Student Journey, High Inst Art, 89. *Bibliog:* Antonio E Tonel (auth), Cuba OK, Stadische Kunstalle, 90; Edward Sullivan (auth), Los Buenos y Los Malos, Galeria Ramis Barquet, 92; Luis Camnitzer (auth), New Art of Cuba, Univ Tex Press, 94. *Media:* All Media. *Dealer:* Ave Real San Agustin No 304 L-2B Residencial San Agustin Garza Garcia N L Mexico 66260. *Mailing Add:* E/T Guarez y Morelos Ave Vasconcelos No 116-10 San Pedro Garza Garcia Monterrey 66200 Mexico

AGUSTIN, HERNANDEZ
ARCHITECT, SCULPTOR
b Mexico City, Mex, Feb 29, 1924. *Study:* Escuela Nac De Arquitectura UNAM, Archit, 54; Modern Art Cult Ctr, with hons & thesis, 54. *Hon Degrees:* Professor International Academy of Architecture, 2001; National Prize of Science and Art, 2004. *Exhib:* Pratt Inst NY, 83; Int Bauausstellung, Berlin, Ger, 84; Miami Univ, 92; Houston Univ, 93; solo exhib, Mus De Monterrey, Nuevo Leon, Mex, 94; Archit Mus, Inst Nat de Bellas Artes, Mex, 97; Ctr de Arte Mod, Guadalajara Jalisco, 98; Casa Lamm, Escultura Simbolica, 2002. *Pos:* Chief design comt, Fed Prog Sch Construction, 54-55; dir, Praxis Interdisciplinary Group Design, Mexico City, Mex, 78-. *Teaching:* Prof, Nat Sch Archit, UNAM, 57-68 & dir design, Atelier Sch Archit, 65-68; Design Atelier Chief at the Northern Anahuac Univ, Mex, 1994-. *Awards:* First Prize Gold Medal, II Biennial De Mex, 92; First Prize, Lifetime Prof Achievement Award Fedn Mex Repub, Archit Coll, 96; Silver Medal, Int Triennial of Archit, Sophia Bulgary, 97; Nat Prize of Archit, 98; Emeritus creator of educ secretary, Conaculta, Mex 94; Archit Nat Prize, 99; IAA Prof Int Acad Archit, 2001; Nat Prize Arts, Mex, 2004; Gold medal, Interarch, Triennial Archit Int Acad Archit, 2006; IAA Ann Prix, 2007; Special prize, Mayor of The Saloniki, Stilver Interarch Medal & diploma Proj, 2009. *Bibliog:* Ministerio de la Vivienda Arquitect, Actual de las Am, 65; Archit Record, 90; Antonio Toca (auth), Mex Nueva Arquitetura, G Dgili, 91. *Mem:* Mex Soc Archits SAM, 64-; Mex Acad Archit; acad emer mem Nat Acad Archit, 79-; hon mem Nat Coll Engineers & Archit, 90-; Arts Acad Mex, 91-; Am Inst Archit, 93-. *Publ:* Contribr, Search for identity, Pratt Inst, 83; auth, Gravedad, Geometria Y Simbolismo, UNAM, 89; coauth, Agustin Hernandez, Arquitectura Y Pensamiento, Louise Noelle, UNAM, 89; Archit Dig, 90; Arquitectura De Agustin Fernandez, Noriega Editores, 94. *Mailing Add:* Bosque de Acacias 61 Bosques De Las Lomas Mexico 117 00 Mexico

AHEARN, JOHN
SCULPTOR
b Binghamton, NY, 1951. *Study:* Cornell Univ, Ithaca, NY, BFA, 73. *Work:* Australian Nat Gallery, Canberra; Metrop Mus, NY; Wallrat-Richartz Mus, Mus Ludwig, Cologne; Lannan Found, Lake Worth, Fla; Eli Broad Family Found, Los Angeles; Greenville Co Art Mus. *Exhib:* Solo exhibs, Contemp Arts Mus, Houston, 91-92, Honolulu Adv Gallery, 92, Washington Proj Arts, 92, Baltimore Mus Art, 93-94 & Douglas F Cooley Mem Art Gallery, Reed Col, Portland, Ore, 93-94, Univ Art Gallery, Univ Calif, San Diego, 95 & Alexander & Bonin, NY, 98, Sculpture from East 100th Street, part II, Alexander and Bonin, NY, 2000, Pan Chiao, Alexander Bonin, NY, 2001; After Street Art, Boca Raton Mus Art, 88; The Future Now, Bass Mus Art, Miami, 89; Personae: Contemp Portraiture & Self-Portraiture, Islip Art Mus, NY, 89; The Blues Aesthetic: Black Cult-Modernism, Traveling, 89. *Awards:* Sculpture Fel, 80 & Art in Pub Places, 82, Nat Endowment Arts; Block Grant, Housing & Urban Develop, 81; Joan Mitchell Found Grant, 2009. *Bibliog:* Brigitte Engler (auth), Behind the Mask, Paper, 11/89; Jonathan Phillips (auth), Ahearn at Alexander, Art World, 89; Robert C Morgan (auth), John Ahearn, Arts, 1/89; Suzanne Muchnic (auth), Family Puts Art on a Firm Foundation, Los Angeles Times, 12/5/89. *Mailing Add:* c/o Alexander & Bonin 132 10th Ave New York NY 10011

AHERN, MAUREEN J
MUSEUM DIRECTOR, CURATOR
b Salem, Mass, Oct 7, 1947. *Study:* Univ Mass, Amherst, BFA, 69; Metrop Mus Art, courses in museology; Univ Albany, MA Painting, 74. *Exhib:* Currier Gallery Art, Manchester, NH, 2000; Northfield Mt Herman, Bolger Gallery, Northfield, Mass; The McIninch Art Gallery, Southern New Hampshire Univ, 2002; McQuade Gallery, Merrimack Coll, North Andover, Mass; Library Arts Ctr, 2006; Jaffrey Civic Ctr, 2006; InSight: Visions and Reflections, Jeffrey Civic Center, Jeffrey, NH, 2011; Visions and Reflections, Diverse Journeys, Millbrook Gallery and Sculpture Garden, Concord, NH, 2011; Ahoon Pollock, Occular Rythm, The Gettyfield Sch, Concord, NH, 2012. *Collection Arranged:* Native Am Neighbors (print, paintings & sculpture), 97; Worldviews (photog), 98; Technics: Bauble of Ballast, 2001; New Hampshire: The State of Art, 2005; Art = Body & Mind, 2006. *Pos:* Art dir, Jewish Community Ctr, Boston, 69-70; cur, Albany Inst Hist & Art, 71-81; dir, Thorne-Sagendorph Art Gallery, Keene State Coll, 81-. *Awards:* Grant, Int Partnership. *Mem:* NH Visual Arts Coalition (pres, 87-92); Am Asn Mus; New Eng Mus Asn. *Media:* Acrylic, Silver, Pastel. *Res:* Development of traveling exhibition on the Dublin Art Colony. *Specialty:* Hist & contemp art. *Interests:* Travel. *Collection:* 19th century work by artists from the Dublin Art Colony, paintings & prints, European & Am, African objects, contemp sculpture. *Publ:* coauth & producer, Land of Legacies & Legend: The Art of Georgia (film); New Hampshire Summer Colonies, Dublin and Cornish, Blue Tree, Portsmouth, Me, 2007; and others. *Mailing Add:* Thorne-Sagendorph Art Gallery Keene State Col-Wyman Way Keene NH 03535-3501

AHLANDER, LESLIE JUDD
CRITIC, CONSULTANT
b New York, NY. *Study:* Acad Mod, Paris, with Fernand Leger; Pa Acad Fine Arts, with Henry MacCarter, PAFA; Cresson traveling scholar to Eur. *Collection Arranged:* Women Contemp Art (with catalog), Duke Univ, 63; After Surrealism (with catalog), Ringling Mus, 72; Contemp Religious Imagery (with catalog), 74; Latin Am Contemp Artists (with catalog), Brickely Gallery, Miami, Fla, 74; Syd Solomon (with catalog), 75; Doris Leeper (with catalog), 75; Continuing Surrealism (with catalog), 76; Latin Am Horizons (with catalog), 76; The Circus in Art (with catalog), 77; Contemp Condemned Art (with catalog), Ringling Mus, 80; Wash Color Sch Revisited (with catalog), Frederick Gallery, Washington, DC, 80; Through Haitian Eyes (with catalog), Bacardi Gallery, Miami, 84; Haitian Art (with catalog), 86. *Pos:* Asst to dir, Mus Mod Art, New York, 41-43; asst to US State Dept, coord Inter Am - Can Affairs, Nelson Rockafeller, 42-44; dir exhibs, US Off Educ, Washington, DC, 43-44; chief div visual arts, Pan-Am Union, Washington, DC, 44-45; art critic, Washington Post, Washington, DC, 50-63; cur educ, Corcoran Gallery, Washington, DC, 69-70; from dir educ to cur contemp art, John & Mabel Ringling Mus Art, Sarasota, Fla, 71-78; dir Art in Pub Places, Dade Co, Miami, Fla, 78-83; art critic, Miami News, 83-88; Arte en Colombia, Art Nexus, Art News, 88-; cur contemp art, Ringling Mus. *Teaching:* Cur educ, Corcoran Gallery, Ringling Mus & Sarasota Art Ctr. *Awards:* Cresson Traveling Scholar fel, Pa Acad Fine Arts, Philadelphia, 38; Art Critics Award, Coll Art Asn Am, 52 & 53; Lifetime Achievement Award, Fla Art Mus Dirs Asn, 93. *Res:* Latin Am art. *Interests:* Contemp art. *Publ:* Auth, Lynn Gelfman, 85, Trevor Bell, 86 & Hal Kaye, 86; Six Cuban painters, 85; Connie Lloveras (auth), Cuba-USA - The First Generation, 90; Century Mexican Art, Naples Mus, 2007. *Mailing Add:* 730 S Osprey Ave #4113 Sarasota FL 34236-7778

AHLSTED, DAVID R
PAINTER
b Minneapolis, Minn, 1943. *Study:* Minneapolis Coll Art, BFA, 65; Indiana Univ, MFA, 68. *Work:* Whitney Mus Am Art, Mus Mod Art, New York; Aldrich Mus Contemp Art, Ridgefield, Conn; PepsiCo Inc, Purchase, NY; State Univ NY, Cortland, NY. *Comn:* 6 murals, NJ State Capitol, Trenton, 95; 7 murals, Rutgers Univ, NJ, 95. *Exhib:* Solo exhibs, Hawthorn Gallery, Skidmore Coll, Saratoga, NY, 71, Art Gallery, State Univ NY, Cortland, 75, SoHo Ctr Visual Arts, New York, 76, Art Gallery, Stockton State Coll, Pomona, NJ, 84, Marian Locks Gallery, Philadelphia, Pa, 86 & 89 & Perlow Gallery, New York, 92; Art Gallery, State Univ Cortland, NY, 75; Contemp Reflections, Aldrich Mus Art, Ridgefield, Conn, 76; SoHo Ctr Visual Arts, New York, 76; Art Gallery, Stockton State Coll, Pomona, NJ, 84; Nature Morte, Southern Alleghenies Mus Art, Loretto, Pa, 86; Marian Locks Gallery, Philadelphia, PA, 86, 89; Fel Exhib, Morris Mus, Morristown, NJ, 87; Philadelphia Mus Art, Pa, 90; Katharina Rich Perlow Gallery, 92, 94, 97 & 2000; Gross McCleaf Gallery, 2003 & 2006. *Teaching:* Asst prof painting, Skidmore Coll, 69-75; assoc prof painting, State Univ NY, Cortland, 75-76; prof painting, Stockton State Coll, 76-. *Awards:* Painting Fel, NJ State Coun Arts, 81 & 85. *Bibliog:* Anne Fabbri (auth), Celebration of NJ Artists The NOYES Mus Art, 83; Anne d'Harnoncourt (auth), Contemp Philadelphia Artists, Philadelphia Mus Art; Gerrit Henry (auth), Art in America, New York, 140-141, 2/2001; John Parks (auth), Am Artist, New York, 48-57, 4/2007. *Media:* Oil on Canvas, Oil on Gessoed Paper. *Dealer:* Gross McCleaf Gallery 127 S Sixteenth St Philadelphia PA 19102. *Mailing Add:* 840 W Clarks Landing Rd Egg Harbor City NJ 08215-3900

AHLSTROM, RONALD GUSTIN
COLLAGE ARTIST, PAINTER
b Chicago, Ill, Jan 17, 1922. *Study:* Art Inst Chicago, BFA, with Paul Weighart; Univ Chicago; DePaul Univ. *Work:* Art Inst Chicago, Blue Cross Collection & Ill Bell Tel, Chicago; Tacoma Art Mus, Wash; Philbrook Art Ctr, Tulsa. *Exhib:* 27th Corcoran Biennial, Washington, DC, 61; Chicago & Vicinity Exhib, Art Inst Chicago, 62; 12 Chicago Artists, McCormick Pl Gallery, 62; 50th Northwest Ann, Seattle Art Mus, 64; 6 American Artists, Touchstone Gallery, New York, 73; Zriny-Hayes Gallery, Chicago, 78; Collection Container Corp, Smithsonian Inst, Washington, DC, 88; traveling exhib, Suitcase Painting-Small Scale, Abstract, Expressionism. *Pos:* Asst dir, McCormick Place Art Gallery, Chicago; dir, Tacoma Art Mus, Wash. *Awards:* Clyde Carr Prize, 55 & William H Bartels Prize, 58, Art Inst Chicago; Purchase Prize, 50th Northwest Ann, Ford Found, 64. *Bibliog:* Meilach & Ten Hoor (auth), Collage and Found Art, 64 & Collage, Trends and Technique, 73, Reinholt Publ; Gerald F Brommer (auth), The Art of Collage, Davis Publ, 78; Gerald Brommer (auth), Collage Techniques, A Guide for Artists & Illustrators, Watson-Guptill, New York, 94. *Media:* Collage & Acrylic; Mixed Media. *Dealer:* Corbett Vs Dempszy 1120 N Ashland Ave Chicago IL 60622. *Mailing Add:* 121 W Park St Lombard IL 60148

AHO, PAUL RICHARD
PAINTER
b Milwaukee, Wis, Sept 3, 1954. *Study:* Fla State Univ, BFA, 77; Univ South Fla, MFA, 79. *Work:* Sioux City Art Ctr; New Orleans Pub Libr; Boca Raton Mus of Art; Univ South Fla, Tampa; Miami Univ, Oxford, Ohio; Palm Beach Int Airport; Fla Atlantic Univ, Boca Raton, Fla; Scripps Fla, Scripps Rsch Inst, Jupiter, Fla. *Comn:* Ruth Among the Rushes, Set Design for Dau Raku Productions, Lake Worth, Fla, 92; Jah Music, Set Design for Ballet Fla, West Palm Beach, 2001; Rio de Ais, Fla Art in State Buildings, Fla Atlantic Univ, 2009. *Exhib:* Ann All Fla Juried Exhib, Boca Raton Mus Art, 2002; Painting Abstraction, NY Studio Sch, 2000; Manif, Seoul 97, Seoul Arts Ctr, 97; New Am Talent, Laguna Gloria Mus, 93, 2004; Tampa Triennial, Fla, 85; Cool Intentions, Somerhill Gallery, Chapel Hill, NC; Select, Schmidt Coll of Arts & Humanities, Fla; Atlantic Univ, Norte Americanos, Arch Arte Contemporaneo, San Pedro Garza Farcia, Mex; Undertow: A survey of South Florida Contemp Art, Mimar Sinan Univ, Istanbul, Turkey; Here & Now, Recent Works by Paul Aho, Present Global Art Gallery, W Palm Beach, Fla, 2009. *Collection Arranged:* Janet Fish - A Sea of Color, Armory Act Ctr, 2003; Thought Through My Eyes, Graham Nickson, 2001; A Sense of Urgency - Sidney Goodman, 85; Armort Art, Conn, 2000; Nelson Shanks, Armory Art Ctr, 2002. *Pos:* chief prog officer, Palm Beach Photog Ctr, Delray Beach, Fla, 03; dir visual arts, Palm Beach Co Cult Coun. *Teaching:* Dean Armory Art Ctr, West Palm Beach, 96-; adj fac, Palm Beach Com Coll, 80-99; adj fac, Fla Atlantic Univ, 2004-; dean, Paducah Sch Art & Design, Ky, 2012. *Awards:* S Fla Cult Consortium Fel, Boca Mus Art, 1995 & 2008; Jurors Award, Laguna Gloria Mus, 93; Ubertelli Mem award, 87; Santo Found Fel, 2010. *Bibliog:* New Am Paintings, Opon Studios Press, #45, 03; Digital Realms, Fla; Atlantic Univ, 97; Culture Mag, 6/87. *Mem:* Nat Asn Schs Art and Design; Coll Art Asn. *Media:* Painting. *Interests:* Surfing. *Publ:* Surfing Florida: A Photographic History, Univ Press Fla, 2014. *Dealer:* Gallery Biba Palm Beach FL 33408; Boston Art MA 02210; Collectors Corner Naples Fla

AHRENDT, MARY E
CONCEPTUAL ARTIST
b Chicago, Ill, Oct 19, 1940. *Study:* Univ Ill, Chicago, BA (sculpture hons), 78; Art Inst Chicago, Ill, MFA (painting & performance), 80. *Work:* Mus Contemp Art, Chicago, Ill. *Exhib:* Seven Artists, 81 & Alternative Spaces, 84, Mus Contemp Art, Chicago, Ill; Sculpture Today, 1982, Indianapolis Mus Art, Ind; Recent Color, San Francisco Mus Mod Art, Calif, 82; Construction Works, Inst Contemp Art, Va Mus,

Richmond, 84; Drawings, Chicago & Vicinity, Art Inst Chicago, Ill, 85; Self-Portraits by Women Artists, Collage Arts Asn, Los Angeles, Calif, 85; Nude, Naked Stripped, Albert & Vera List Visual Ctr, Mass Inst Technol, Boston, 86; Images for Human Conduct (catalog), Mus Contemp Art, Chicago, 86, First Person Singular: Self-Portrait Photog (catalog), High Mus Art, Atlanta, 88, Toward the Future: Contemp Art in Context (catalog), Mus Contemp Art, Chicago, 90. *Pos:* Bd mem, Artemisia Gallery, 78-79 & NAME Gallery, 81-86, Chicago, Ill. *Teaching:* Vis artist painting, Univ Ind, Terre Haute, 83 & Univ Ill, Champaign, 85; vis artist painting & photogr, Minneapolis Col Art & Design, Minn, 83. *Awards:* Ill Artists Grant, 83-87. *Bibliog:* David Elliott (auth), Chicago enjoys it's own eclecticism, Art News, 5/82; Catherine Reeve (auth), The New Photography, Prentice-Hall, 83; Alan G Artner (auth), Arts, Chicago Tribune, 6/15/84. *Media:* Photography, Film

AHRENS, HANNO D
SCULPTOR
b Ft Worth, Tex, 1954. *Exhib:* Solo exhibs, Santa Cruz Art Ctr, 77, Dan McHenrey Libr, Santa Cruz, 79, Deborah Sharpe Gallery, NY, 87-88, Kim Foster Gallery, 97 & 98 & Boulder Mus Contemp Art, Colo; Univ Art Gallery, Albany, 89; Farnsworth Art Mus, Rockport, Maine, 90; David Beitzel Gallery, NY, 90; Frumkin/Adams Gallery, NY, 91; The Returns of the Cadavre Exquis, Drawing Ctr, NY, 93; The Edward R Broida Collection: A Selection of Works, Orlando Mus Art, Fla, 98. *Awards:* Pollock-Krasner Found Grant, 86, 91 & 97; Nat Endowment Arts Grant, 86 & 90; New York Found Arts Grant, 89. *Bibliog:* Corrine Robbins (auth), Hanno Ahrens, Sculpture, 7/8/88; Dan Rubey, Hanno Ahrens, Studio, 2/89; AFC, Mass appeal, Vanity Fair, 1/90. *Mailing Add:* c/o Kim Foster Gallery 529 W 20th St New York NY 10011

AHRENS, KENT
HISTORIAN
b Martinsburg, WV. *Study:* Dartmouth Col, AB, 61; Univ Md, MA, 66; Univ Del, PhD, 72. *Collection Arranged:* Painting from the Netherlands & German-speaking Countries, Wadsworth Atheneum, 78; The Drawings and Watercolors by Truman Seymour (1824-1891) (auth, catalog), Everhart, 86; Frederic C Knight (1898-1979), Everhart, 87; Edward D Boit (auth, catalog), Oils & Watercolors, Everhart, 90; Cyrus E Dallin: His Small Bronzes and Plasters (auth, catalog), Rockwell Mus, 95; Currier and Ives: Selection from the Nationwide Collection (auth catalog), Kennedy Mus Art, 2000; Small Bronzes by Harriett W Frishmuth (auth, catalog), Kennedy Mus Art, 2001. *Pos:* Assoc cur paintings, Wadsworth Atheneum, 77-78; dir, Everhart Mus, 82-90, Rockwell Mus, 90-95, Civic Fine Arts Ctr, SDak, 96-97 & Kennedy Mus Am Art, Ohio Univ, 97-2000; mus cons, 2000-; dir, Southern Allegheries Mus Art, 2006-2007. *Teaching:* Fac mem, Fla State Univ, 71-74 & Georgetown Univ, 79-82; fac mem & cur, Randolph-Macon Woman's Coll, 74-77; lectr, Smithsonian Assoc, DC, 80; adj prof, Ohio Univ, 97-2000. *Awards:* Kress Fel, 68 & Dale Fel, 70, Nat Gallery Art. *Mem:* Mus Asn Pa (chmn, 84-90); Williamstown Regional Art Conserv Lab Inc (trustee, 84-92); Mus West (bd dir, 90-95); Bosnia-Herzeqovinra Heritage Rescue, trustee 2001-2003. *Res:* American art. *Publ:* auth, Variations on a Theme by Edward Forbes, Wadsworth Atheneum Bulletin, spring/fall 72; Robert Weir's Embarkation of the Pilgrims, Capitol Studies, Fall 72; Contribr, Allqemeines Kunstlerlexikon, 99-2012; Auth, The portraits by Robert W Weir, 74 & Henry R Newman (1843-1917), 76, Am Art J; Constantino Brumidi's Apotheosis of Washington, 76 & Nineteenth Century History Painting in the United States Capitol, 80, Rec Columbia Hist Soc; American paintings before 1900 at the Wadsworth Atheneum, Antiques, 78; Jennie Brownscombe, 81 & Priscilla Longshore Garrett, 85, Woman's Art J; Cyrus E Dallin: American Sculptor (1861-1944), American Art Review, 95; and others. *Mailing Add:* 7207 Radford Rd Athens OH 45701

AHUJA, MEQUITTA
PAINTER
Study: Hampshire Coll, BA, 1998; Univ Ill, MFA, 2003. *Work:* Blanton Mus Art, Austin; Cleveland Clinic, Ohio; Mus Fine Arts Houston; Philadelphia Mus Art; Ulrich Mus, Wichita; US State Dept, Mumbai. *Exhib:* Solo exhibs, Mus Contemp Art, Chicago, 2005, BravinLee Programs, New York, 2007, Lawndale Art Ctr, Houston, 2008, Obadia Gallery, Paris, France, 2010; d'Afrique d'Asie, Ethan Cohen Fine Arts, 2005; New Art Event, Ulrich Mus, Wichita, 2006; Global Feminisms, Brooklyn Mus, 2007; Houston Collects, Mus Fine Arts, Houston, 2008; Undercover, Spelman Coll Mus Fine Arts, Atlanta, 2009. *Pos:* Pres, Blue Sky Project, Dayton Univ, Ohio, 2004-, Artist Pension Trust, New York, 2008-; artist-in-residence, Mus Fine Arts, Houston, 2006-08, Studio Mus, Harlem, 2009-. *Awards:* First Place, Chicago Civic Arts Found Visual Arts Competition, 2003; Artadia Award, 2008; Joan Mitchell Found Grant, 2009. *Bibliog:* Holland Cotter (auth), Last Chance, NY Times, 6/1/2007; Douglas Britt (auth), Artwork is a Reflection of its Audience, Houston Chronicle, 1/8/2009. *Media:* Acrylic, Oil

AIKEN, WILLIAM A
PAINTER, DESIGNER
b Pittsburgh, Pa, May 26, 1934. *Study:* Carnegie-Mellon Univ, BFA, 55. *Work:* City of San Francisco & Embarcadero Ctr, Calif; Carnegie Mellon Univ; ABC, Washington, DC; Univ Santa Clara, Calif; Delaware Mus of Art, Wilmington, Del. *Comn:* Oil painting, Shaklee Corp, Emeryville, Calif, 74. *Exhib:* Paintings, USA, Mus Mod Art, NY, 61; Allied Artists Am, Nat Acad, NY, 74, 80, 82, 2004, 2005, 2006, 2009; 39th Ann Midyear Show, Butler Inst Am Art, Youngstown, Ohio, 75; Sun Carnival Nat Art Exhib, El Paso Mus Art, Tex, 77; solo exhibs, San Francisco Art Comn Gallery, 78; The New Realists, Mongerson Gallery, Chicago, 82; Nature Interpreted, Cincinnati Mus Nat Hist, 82; and others. *Awards:* Charles F Romans Award for Oil Painting, Allied Artists Am Ann Exhib, 80; John Young-Hunter Mem Award for Oil Painting, 92; Second Place Award for Oil Painting, Yosemite Renaissance Ann Exhib, 2001, Elmhurt Artists' Guild 2011 Annual Exhib, Elmhurt Mus of Art, Elmhurt, Ill. *Bibliog:* Paul Perry (auth), View from the Rorschach Canvas, Southwest Art, 12/77. *Mem:* Allied Artists of Am. *Media:* Oil Paint; Oil Glaze. *Mailing Add:* 1587 35th Ave San Francisco CA 94122

AINSLIE, SOPHIA
PAINTER, INSTALLATION SCULPTOR
b Johannesburg, South Africa. *Study:* Univ S Africa, BFA; Tufts, Sch Mus Fine Arts, MFA, 2001; Skowhegan Sch Painting & Sculpture, Maine, 2001. *Work:* Medicade, Westborough, MA; Northeastern Univ, Boston, MA; Fidelity, Boston, MA; Natixis Global Associates, Boston, MA; Hebrew Rehabilitation Ctr for Aged, Boston, MA; Andrea Mgmt Corp, Lawrence, Ma; and others. *Exhib:* Solo exhibs include Kingston Gallery, Boston, 2007, HallSpace, Boston, Gasworks Gallery, London, Goodman Gallery, Johannesburg, S Africa, Snuggle, Tide & All, St Botolph Club, Boston, Ma, 2008, Landmarks, Kingston Gallery, Boston, MA, 2009, Fragments, St Botolph Club, Boston, Ma, 2010, Inside Out, Kingston Gallery, Boston, Ma, 2011, Sophia Ainslie, Kingston Members Gallery, Boston, Ma, 2012, Inside Out 2, Grillo Gallery, Endicott Coll, Beverly, Ma, 2012, in person, Kingston Gallery, Boston, Ma, 2013, Instersitial, Carol Schlosberg Gallery, Montserrat Coll Art, Beverly, Ma, 2013; Group exhibs include Trace Elements, Ainslie & Anderson, New Eng Sch Art and Design, Boston, MA, 2006, Back to Work, Northeastern Univ, Boston, Ma, 2007, Paper Quilts, Essex Art Ctr, Lawrence, Ma, 2008, From Taboo to Icon-Africanist Turnabout, Ice Box Project Space, Crane Arts, PA, 2008, On the Wall, NU Art & Design, Northeastern Univ, Boston, Ma, 2010, The Drawing Show, New Eng Sch Art & Design, Boston, Ma, 2010, Sting! IX, The Real World, The Beehive, Boston, Ma, 2010, Projected Image, ArtStrand, Provincetown, Ma, 2011, Still, Kingston Gallery, Boston, Ma, 2011, Then and Now, Spoke Gallery, Medicine Wheel, Boston, Ma, 2012, Skowhegan Alumni, Whitney Mus Am Art, NY, 2012, Deconstruct/Reconstruct, Blanc Gallery, 2012, Resident: The Gift of Time, Bannister Gallery, Rhode Island Coll, RI, 2012, Pigment: Color and Metaphor, Brant Gallery, MassArt, Boston, Ma, 2012, Faculty Focus, Gallery 360, Northeastern Univ, Boston, Ma, 2013. *Pos:* visiting artist, Endicott Coll, Sch Visual & Performing Arts, Beverley, Ma, 2012, MassArt, Brant Gallery, Boston, Ma, 2013. *Teaching:* lectr, Sch Mus Fine Arts, Boston, Ma, 2001-2004, Tufts Univ, Medford, Ma, 2001-2008, New Eng Sch Art and Design, Boston, Ma, 2002-2012, Northeastern Univ, Boston, Ma, 2001-, study abroad program, 2010, 2010. *Awards:* Hamlyn Found Grant, United Kingdom; African Arts Trust, United Kingdom; Oppenheimer Trust, S Africa; George Sugarman Found Grant, 2007; Grant, Artists Resource Trust, Ma, 2012. *Bibliog:* Brenda Maguire (auth), The Huntington News-Inside Arts & Entertainment, 2011; Franklin W Liu (auth), Artscope, New England's Culture Mag, 2011; Cate McQuaid (auth), The Boston Globe, Weekend Arts and Performance, 2012; Lindsey Davis (auth), Artscope, New England's Culture Mag, 2013; Celine Browning (auth), ArtFetch, 2013. *Dealer:* Kingston Gallery 450 Harrison Ave. #43 Boston Mass 02118. *Mailing Add:* 46 Rawson Rd Arlington MA 02474

AINSWORTH, DIANE
PAINTER
Study: Univ Okla & Univ Tulsa. *Comn:* Evergreen Hosp Med Center, Kirkland, Wash; Providence Everett Med Center, Everett, Wash. *Pos:* Las Cruces Art Guild demo & judging, 1995; Demonstrations & workshops for Daniel Smith, Seattle, Wash, 1995-2001; Sequim arts demo, 2000; Judge for Jefferson Art Alliance Small Expressions show, 2002; Judge for Northwest Pastel Society, 2004. *Mem:* Oil Painter of Am; Northwest Watercolor Society; Taos Art Asn; Society of Taos Watercolorists; Wash Plein Air Painters; Okla Society of Impressionists. *Media:* Watercolor, Oil. *Publ:* Southwest Art Mag, Best of the West, Feb 2001; Artists to Watch, Dec 2001; Rivers & Lakes, Vol I, Int Artist Pub, 2004; Cover story, Peninsula Lifestyle mag, Feb 2006; Gathering Place calendar cover, 2006. *Mailing Add:* 410 S Jacob Miller Rd Port Townsend WA 98368

AISTARS, JOHN
PAINTER, EDUCATOR
b Riga, Latvia, Jun 9, 1938; US citizen. *Study:* Sch Art Inst Chicago, BFA, 61; Syracuse Univ, MFA, 65. *Work:* Syracuse Univ, Marine Midland Bank & Crouse-Irving Hosp, Syracuse, NY; Ohio Dominican Coll, Columbus; First City Nat Bank, Binghamton, NY. *Exhib:* Sch Art Inst Chicago, Ill, 57 & 59-61; Everson Regional Exhib, Everson Mus, Syracuse; Regional Exhib, Mem Art Gallery, Rochester, NY, Munson-Williams-Proctor Inst, Utica, NY, Robeson Ctr Arts & Sci, Binghamton, NY; Cooperstown Nat, Cooperstown Art Asn, NY; Art & Comm Ctr, Rome, NY, 99-2011. *Collection Arranged:* Various exhibs for Chapman Art Ctr Gallery, Cazenovia Coll; Marine Midland Bank, Syracuse, NY; Crouse-Irving Mem Hosp, Syracuse, NY; First City Nat Bank, Binghamton, NY; Syracuse Univ, Syracuse, NY; Ohio Dominican Coll, Columbus, OH. *Pos:* Dir, Chapman Art Ctr Gallery, Cazenovia Coll & Studio Art Prog, Cazenovia Coll. *Teaching:* Grad asst color & lettering, Syracuse Univ, 64-65; prof painting & drawing, Cazenovia Coll, NY, 65-2003. *Awards:* First City National Award, Susquehanna Regional, 75; First Prize, Central NY Regional Exhib, 89; M Bevier Prize, Cooperstown Nat, 89; Distinguished Fac Achievement Award, Cazenovia Col, 91; First Prize for Painting, Art & Community Ctr, Rome, NY, 99; 2nd Place, Art & Community Ctr, Rome, NY, 2005; Special Award, RACC Gallery Comt, Art & Community Ctr, Rome, NY, 2008. *Bibliog:* Articles in numerous publ. *Mem:* Cooperstown Art Asn. *Media:* Oil. *Interests:* Literature; Music; Hiking. *Publ:* auth & illusr of 70 articles, Laiks, Brooklyn, 81-98; auth & illusr, 2 novels, short stories, & 40 articles, Latvija Amerika, Toronto, 99-2011. *Dealer:* Steuben Park Gallery 25 Hopper St Utica NY 13501. *Mailing Add:* 3999 Oran Delphi Rd Manlius NY 13104

AKAWIE, THOMAS FRANK
EDUCATOR, PAINTER
b New York, NY, Feb 22, 1935. *Study:* Los Angeles City Col, 53-56; Univ Calif, Berkeley, BA (art hist), 59, MA (painting), 63. *Work:* Milwaukee Art Ctr, Wis; Ithaca Coll Art Mus, NY; Oakland Mus, Calif; Williams Coll Mus, Williamstown, Mass; San Francisco Mus Mod Art; San Antonio Mus Art; Sheldon Mem Art Mus, Lincoln, Neb. *Exhib:* Solo exhibs, La Jolla Mus Art, Calif, 67, Calif Palace Legion Hon, San Francisco, 72 & San Jose Mus Art, Calif, 77, Terry Delapp Gallery, Los Angeles, Calif, 86, Steven Wolf Fine Arts, 2008; Ann Exhib, Whitney Mus Am Art, NY, 69;

Painting & Sculpture in Calif, San Francisco Mus Mod Art, 76 & Nat Collection Fine Arts, Smithsonian Inst, Washington, DC, 77; 4th Triennial-India 78 Inc, Thailand & Iran, 78; Calif Visionary Painting, Japan, 78; and others. *Teaching:* Asst prof painting & drawing, Calif State Univ, Los Angeles, 65-66; lectr painting & drawing, Univ Calif, Berkeley, 72-73; prof, spray-painting & drawing, San Francisco Art Inst, 66-99. *Awards:* Los Angeles All-City Exhib Award, City of Los Angeles, Calif, 65; First Prize, Ann Downey Mus Invitational, Calif, 66; First Prize, Jack London Art Exhib, Oakland, Calif, 69; Ann Bremer Prize in art, Univ Calif, Berkeley, 63. *Bibliog:* Charles Shere & John Coney (auths), Art of Tom Akawie, KQED-TV, 71. *Media:* Acrylic. *Interests:* Woodworking, film-making. *Publ:* Contribr, Visions, Pomegranate Publ, 77; California Art 450 Years of Painting & Other Media, Dustin Publ, 98; Circe Star, The Painting of Thomas Akawie, Steven Wolf Fine Art Publ, 2008. *Dealer:* Thomas Akawie Studios. *Mailing Add:* 1740 University Ave Berkeley CA 94703-1514

AKERS, ADELA
WEAVER, CRAFTSMAN

b Santiago de Compostela, Spain, 1933. *Study:* Univ Havana, 55; Sch Art Inst Chicago, 57-60; Cranbrook Acad Art, 60,-61 & 62-63. *Work:* W B Saunders Publs, Philadelphia, Pa; Sumitono Bank, NY; Manchester Community Col, Conn; Olympia-York, Toronto, Ont; Chase Manhattan Bank, NY. *Exhib:* Solo exhibs, Bloomsburg State Col, Pa, 77, Fiberworks Gallery, Berkeley, Calif, 80, Triangle Gallery, San Francisco, 81, Mandell Gallery, Los Angeles, 81, Modern Master Tapestries, NY, 84, Pa Acad Fine Arts, Philadelphia, 86 & Patrick King Contemp Art, Indianapolis, Ind, 87; Multiplicity in Clay-Metal-Fiber, Skidmore Col, Saratoga Springs, NY, 84; Inaugural Exhib, Am Crafts Mus, NY, 86; Fiber: The Next Generation, Ill State Univ, Normal, 87; Maple Hill Gallery, Portland, Maine, 88; Pa Acad Fine Arts, 86; Helen Drutt Gallery, New York City, 90; Brown/Gratta Arts, Wilton, Conn, 00; Triangle Gallery, San Francisco, 01; Solomon Dubrick Gallery, San Francisco, 01; Snyderman-Works Galleries, Philadelphia, 98, 02. *Collection Arranged:* Metrop Mus Art, NYC, Renwick Gallery, Washington, DC, Bell Atlantic, Hewlett Packard, and others. *Pos:* Lectr, Ctr for Textile Arts, Berkeley, Calif, 84, NC Weaver's Guild, Charlotte, 86, Philadelphia Textile Soc, Pa, 86, Philadelphia Weaver's Guild, Pa, 88; designer for Oaxaca Loom, cottage industry in Diaz Ordas, Oaxaca, Mex, 87; Seminar leader, Nat Conference Handweaver's Guild of Am, Chicago, 88. *Teaching:* Inst, crafts prog, City of Chicago, 65-67; Penland Sch Crafts, NC, summers 68, 69, & 70; New Sch Social Res, 70-71; Cooper Square Art Ctr, New York, 71; San Francisco State Univ, 81; prof, Tyler Sch Art, Temple Univ, Philadelphia, Pa, 72-. *Awards:* Artist in Residence Penland Sch, 69 & 71, Craftsman's Fel, 74 & 80, Nat Endowment Arts; NJ State Coun Arts Grants, 71; Research Grants, Temple Univ, 75, 79, 84 & 88; Pa Coun Arts Grants, 83; Pollock-Krasner Found Grant, 2008. *Bibliog:* Articles in Crafts Horizons Mag, 2/77 & Fiberarts Mag, 3/4/81, 2001; Weaving: A Handbook for Fiber Artists, 80. *Mailing Add:* c/o Snyderman Gallery 303 Cherry St Philadelphia PA 19106

AKERS, GARY
PAINTER, WRITER

b Pikeville, Ky, Feb 22, 1951. *Study:* Morehead State Univ, BA (Greenshields Found Grant), 72, MA, 74. *Work:* Boone Co Pub Libr & Art Gallery & St Luke Hosp, Florence, Ky; Mus Art Ogunquit, Maine; Ky Fried Chicken Corp & Brown/Foreman Corp, Louisville, Ky; Coca Cola Bottling Co, Zaring Nat Corp, Cincinnati Financial Corp & Proctor & Gamble Corp, Cincinnati, Ohio; USF&G Co, Baltimore, Md; Claypool-Young Art Gallery, Morehead State Univ, Ky; Kemper Mus of Contemp Art, Kansas City, Mo; Ross Collection; McGraw Hill Publications. *Comn:* Egg tempera, comn by pvt collector, Maine; Cincinnati Financial Corp, Ohio; watercolor, Brown-Forman Corp, Louisville, Ky; 3 watercolors, Eastern Ky Univ, Richmond; watercolor for President Reagan, Republican Party, Cincinnati, Ohio; painting for President Reagan, Republican Party, Cincinnati, Ohio. *Exhib:* Ky Art Exhib, JB Speed Art Mus, Louisville, Ky, 86; Asheville Art Mus, NC, 86; Ogunquit Mus Am Art, Maine; Nat Acad Design, NY, 94; Am Watercolor Soc Ann Exhib, NY; Owensboro Mus Fine Art, Ky, 96; Artists of Am, Colo Hist Mus, Denver, 97 & 98; Great Am Artists Exhib, Cincinnati Mus Ctr, Ohio, 98; Haynes Galleries, Me, 2011, Tenn, 2012; Borders of Change, Behringer Crawford Mus, Ky, 2012; By the Sea, Me, 2012. *Teaching:* instr private classes, Egg Tempura & Watercolor. *Awards:* Friends Ky Watercolor Soc Award, 78; Dale Meyers Cooper Medal Hon, Southern Watercolor Soc Award, 83, Lee Printing Co Award, 84; Top Merit Award, Aqueous, Ky Watercolor Soc, 83, Ky Artist Award, 85; Mario Cooper Award, Am Watercolor Soc, 84. *Bibliog:* Bill R Booth (auth), Painting: Border Brothers Farm, Am Artist, 82 & Pages from a passing scene, Southwest Art, 82; Artist's Mag, 10/84 & 2/88. *Mem:* Ky Watercolor Soc; Am Watercolor Soc; Southern Watercolor Soc. *Media:* Egg Tempera, Watercolor. *Publ:* Kentucky: Land of Beauty, Paintings by Gary Akers, pvt publ, 98; Memories of Maine, 03; Kemper Mus Art: The First Ten Years, Am Art Collecotr, 2007, Fine Art Connoisseur, 2007; Borders of Change, Behringer-Crawford Mus, KY, 2012. *Dealer:* Gary-Lynn Galleries 10100 Meiman Dr Union Ky; The Gary Akers Gallery Green Schoolhouse South 131 South Thomaston ME; Tree's Place Gallery Rt 6A Orleans MA; Haynes Galleries 91 Main St Thomaston ME & 3021 Flagstone Dr Franklin TN. *Mailing Add:* PO Box 100 Union KY 41091

AKIN, GWEN
PHOTOGRAPHER

b New York, NY, July 26, 1950. *Study:* Boston Mus Sch; Tufts Univ. *Work:* San Francisco Mus Mod Art; Los Angeles Co Mus Art; Mus Fine Arts, Houston; New Orleans Mus Art; Kiyosato Mus Photog Arts, Japan; Espace Photographique de Paris; Chrysler Mus, Norfolk, VA; Tokyo Inst Technol, Tokyo; Mus Photog Arts, San Diego; Los Angeles Co Mus Art, Los Angeles; Ctr Creative Photog, Tucson, Ariz. *Exhib:* Mirror Mirror, Wadsworth Atheneum, Hartford, Conn, 93; Bad Girls, New Mus, NY; Addison Gallery Am Art, Andover, Mass, 94; Solo exhibs, Twining Gallery, New York City, 87-, Sha Idai Gallery, Tokyo, 87, Cepa Gallery, Buffalo, 87-, White Columns, New York City, 88-, XYZ Gallery, Ghent, Belgium, 89, Farideh Cadot Gallery, NYC, 88, 90, Pamela Auchincloss Gallery, NY, 94, Gallery 954, Chicago, 94, Gallery at 777, Los Angeles, 94, Cepa Gallery, Buffalo, 95, Chrysler Mus, Norfolk, 95, Hudson River Mus Westchester, Yonkers, NY, 95 & Houston Ctr Photog, Tex, 95; Within Memory, Montage, Rochester, NY, 93; Parko Gallery, Tokyo, 93; Natural Hist Formaldehyde Photog, The Ctr Photog at Woodstock, NY, 93; Narcissism, Thread Waxing Space, NY, Beyond Ars Medica (catalog), Calif Ctr Arts Mus, Escondido, Calif, 95; Ricco/Maresca Gallery, New York City, 99-2001; In Visible Light, Mus Photog Helsinki, Finland, 99; Extra Ordinary Bodies from the Muter Mus, List Gallery, Swarthmore Col, PA, 2005. *Awards:* Materials grant, Polaroid Corp, 86 & 87; Materials grant, AGFA Corp, 90; Nat Endowment Arts, 91; and others. *Bibliog:* Newspaper article in De Cenbenaar, Ghent, Belg, 5/5/89; Kate McQuaid (auth), Photo surrealism, South End News, Boston, 2/15/90; articles in numerous other newspapers, mags & J's; Photography Speaks, 150 Photographers Speak on their Art, Brooks Johnson, ed, Aperture Foundation & Chrysler Mus, 2004, pp 304-305. *Media:* Photography. *Publ:* Fine Art Photog 95, Graphis Press Corp, Zurich; Contemporary Photography from Chicago Collections, by Nadine Wasserman, Mus Contemp Art, Chicago, Ill, 3/95; Beyond Ars Medica, Charles Hagen, NY Times, 12/95; Ars Medica by John Strausbaugh, New York Press, Vol 8, No 47, 95; A Gallery of Women, by William Zimmer, NY Times, 5/95; and others. *Dealer:* Galerie Farideh Cadot 77 Rue Des Archives 75003 Paris France; Ricco/Maresca Gallery NYC, 529 E 20th St, New York, NY 10011. *Mailing Add:* 55 Prince St New York NY 10012

AKINS, FUTURE RENE
PRINTMAKER, SCULPTOR

b Hampton, Va, Feb 5, 1950. *Study:* Tex Tech Univ, Lubbock, BA (art hist), 72, MFA (printmaking), 77. *Work:* Sch of Art Inst Chicago, Ill; World Bank Am, San Francisco; Red River Mus, Moorhead, Minn; Valley Nat Bank, Phoenix, Ariz; Mus Southwest, Midland, Tex. *Comn:* Print ed, Tex Fine Arts Asn, Austin, 81 & The Mus, Tex Tech Univ, Lubbock, 83. *Exhib:* World Print Competition III, Smithsonian Inst, Washington, DC, 76-78; Breaking the Bindings: Am Book Art Now, Univ Wis, Madison, 83; Artists Books, San Antonio Art Inst, Tex, 83; Women Artists of Tex, Nat Mus for Women in the Arts, Washington, DC; solo exhibs, New Paintings & New Prints, James Harris Gallery, Seattle, Wash, 2000, Material Handling, Stephen Wirtz Gallery, 2001 & Deborah Oropallo, San Jose Mus Art, 2001. *Collection Arranged:* Nothin Else to Do (auth, catalog), Music Heritage W Tex, 84; Con Dios, Retabloes, 85; Peter Hurd in Lubbock, Drawings Mural, 86; Honky Tonk Visions (auth, catalog), Art & Music W Tex, 86. *Pos:* Asst to dir, The Mus, Tex Tech Univ, 83-85, cur art, 85-88. *Awards:* Cash Awards, Los Angeles Printmaking Soc, 77 & Brand Gallery, 78; Jurors Award, Objects in Transition, Temari-Book Art, Honolulu, Hawaii, 84. *Mem:* Nat Orgn Women; World Print Coun; Tex Asn Mus. *Dealer:* Charles Adams Gallery Kingsgate North Lubbock TX 79401; Stephen Wirtz Gallery San Francisco CA. *Mailing Add:* 4715 27th St Lubbock TX 79410-2323

AKSEL, ERDAG
SCULPTOR, INSTRUCTOR

b. Izmir, Turkey, Aug 13, 1953. *Study:* W Va Univ, BFA, 77, MA, 79; Dokuz Eylul Univ, DA, 84. *Work:* Istanbul Mod; Santral Istanbul. *Exhib:* 2nd Istanbul Int Biennial, Haigha Eirene, Turkey, 89; In & Out of Istanbul, Slought Found Gallery, Philadelphia, Pa, 2009; 45th Venice Int Biennial, Italian Pavillion, Giardini, Venice, 93; I am Another, Charlottenborg Udstillingsbygning, Copenhagen, Denmark, 95; Dialogues, The Lost Idea of Order of Things, Kunstpalast, Dusseldorf, Germany, 96; Du Bosphore a la Moine, Mus d'Art et d'Histoire, Cholet, France, 2004; Quiet Time/Love's Labour, Katherine E Nash Gallery, Minn, 2007; Seriously Ironic, Kunsthaus CentrePasquArt, Cetre d'Art, Biel/Biene, Switzerland, 2009. *Teaching:* vis Fulbright fel, San Jose State univ, Calif, 91-92; vis prof art, Ecole Nat d'Art de Bourges, France, 2006-2007; prof art, Sabanci Univ, Istanbul, Turkey, 98-. *Bibliog:* Edward Lucie-Smith (auth), Artoday, Phaidon, 95; Baumgartner von Luise (auth), Leichtfussige Ironie oder bleierner Ernst, Artensuite bern, Switzerland, Aug 2009; Hossein Amirsadegh (ed), Unleashed, Thames & Hudson, 2010; David Ebony, Erdag Aksel, Art in Am, New York, 2010; Deborah Root, Erdag Aksel & Phantoms, Artpapers, Atlanta, Ga, 2010. *Media:* Mixed Media. *Dealer:* Gallery Nev Macka Cad33 Macka Istanbul Turkey 34367

AKUTSU, SHOICHI
PAINTER, INSTRUCTOR

b Japan, Jan 18, 1956; Japanese citizen. *Study:* Musashino Art Univ, BFA, 80; The Art Students League, New York, 98. *Work:* The Art Students League, New York. *Exhib:* Key West Biennial Contemp Fla Art, Key West Mus Art, Key West, Fla, 2000; NY Classicism Now, Hirschl & Adler Gallery, New York, 2000; The Arts Students League New York Highlights from the Permanent Collection, Owensboro Mus Fine Art, Owensboro, Ky, 2006. *Awards:* Gold Medal, 85th Ann Exhib, The Allied Artists Am, 98; Silver Medal, 59th Ann Exhib, The Audubon Artists, 2001; Juror Award, Small Works, New York Univ, 80 & Wash Sq Gallery, 2002-2003. *Mem:* Allied Artists Am. *Media:* Oil. *Publ:* Auth, Art in rev, NY Times, 2000; Hodgepodge exhibition is classicism - not, New York Observer, 2000. *Dealer:* Allen Sheppard 530 W 25 St New York NY 10001. *Mailing Add:* 215 W 109th St New York NY 10025

AL-HADID, DIANA
SCULPTOR

b Aleepo, Syria, 1981. *Study:* Kent State Univ, BFA (sculpture & art hist), 2003; Va Commonwealth Univ, MFA (sculpture), 2005; Skowhegan Sch Painting & Sculpture, Maine, 2007. *Work:* C-Collection, Vaduz, Liechtenstein; Judith Rothschild Found, New York; Saatchi Collection, London; Mus Fine Arts, Houston, TX; Whitney Mus American Art, NY. *Exhib:* Solo exhibs, Pangaea's Blanket, Peeler Galleries, DePauw Univ, Greencastle, Ind, 2006, Immodest Mountain, Arlington Art Ctr, Washington, DC, 2006, The Gradual Approach of My Disintegration, Priska C Juschka Fine Art, New York, 2006, The Fourth Room, Vox Populi, Philadelphia, 2006, Record of a Mortal Universe, 2007 & Reverse Collider, 2008, Perry Rubenstien Gallery, New York, Water Thief, Hammer Mus, 2010, Nev Mus Art, 2011, Play the Wolf Fifth, Centro de Arte Contemporáneo, La Conservera, Spain, 2011, Sightings: Diana

Al-Hadid, Nasher Sculpture Ctr, 2011, The Vanishing Point, Marianne Boesky Gallery, 2012, Weatherspoon Art Mus, Greensboro, NC, 2013, SCAD Mus Art, Ga, 2013, Akron Mus Art, 2013; Sanctuary and the Scrum, Black and White Gallery, New York, 2006; Mutiny, The Happy Lion, Los Angeles, 2006; AIM 26, Bronx Mus, 2006; Blood Meridian, Galerie Michael Janssen, Berlin, Ger, 2007; Agitation and Repose, Tanya Bonakdar Gallery, New York, 2007; Black Bile, Red Humour: Aspects of Melancholy, b-05 Art & Design Ctr, Montbaur, Ger, 2008; Anthology, Otero Plassart, Los Angeles, 2008; Unveiled: New Art from the Middle East, Saatchi Gallery, London, 2009; Next Wave Art, Brooklyn Acad Music, 2009; New Weather, Univ S Fla Contemp Art Mus, Tampa, 2009; Am Acad Arts & Letts Invitational, New York, 2009. *Teaching:* visiting faculty, Installation Art, Bard Coll, Annandale-on-Hudson, NY, 2012; visiting critic, MFA Fine Arts Workshop, Sch Visual Arts, NY, 2012. *Awards:* Vt Studio Ctr Fel, Johnson, NY, 2006; Grant, Pollock Krasner Found, New York, 2007; NY Found Arts Fel, 2009; US Artists Rockefeller Fel, 2009; Louis Comfort Tiffany Found Grant, 2009; Grant for Painters & Sculptors, Joan Mitchell Found, 2011. *Bibliog:* Michael O'Sullivan (auth), New Sensations, Washington Post, 8/19/205; Steve Rockwell (auth), A Stir in Richmond, D'Art Int, winter & spring 2006; Billy Stone (auth), Going Down to Chinatown, Los Angeles Entertainment Today, 11/10-16/2006; Sophia Powers (auth), Citadel of Fancy, rev, ArtSlant, 10/28/2007; Seth Curcio (auth), rev, Daily Serving, 11/19/2007; David Grosz (auth), rev, Artinfo, 9/5/2008; David Cohen (auth), Painting's Post-Feminist Form & Sculpture's Matron Saint, The New York Sun, 9/17/2008; Vanessa Thorpe (auth), Record crowds for China art show, The Observer, 12/14/2008; Anna Tomforde (auth), Islamic art a taboo buster, The Brunei Times, 1/31/2009; Alexander Barakat (auth), Baring the Middle East, Canvas, 178-181, 3-4/2009; Sarah Trigg (auth), Studio Check: Diana Al-Hadid, Modern Painters, 2011; Barbara Pollack (auth), Diana Al-Hadid Makes a Sculpture: The Birth of a A Multihued Venus, ARTnews, 2012; Amy Michael (auth), Ghosts of Things: A Conversation with Diana Al-Hadid, Sculpture, pp 20-77, 4/2013. *Dealer:* Marianne Boesky Gallery 509 W 24th St New York NY 10011. *Mailing Add:* Marianne Boesky Gallery 509 W 24th St New York NY 10001

ALBA, ELIA
PHOTOGRAPHER
b New York, New York. *Study:* Hunter Coll, New York, BA (Philos & Lit), 1989-1994; Whitney Mus Am Art Independent Study Prog, New York, 200-01. *Exhib:* Solo exhibs include Jersey City Mus, NJ, 2003, Generous Miracles, New York, 2003, Bernice Steinbaum Gallery, Miami, 2003, Atlantica TransArt & Universidad Austral de Chile, Santiago, Chile, 2005; group exhibs include Artists in Marketplace, Bronx Mus Arts, New York, 1998; Open Studios, Whitney Mus Independent Study Prog, New York, 2001; Island Nation, RI Sch Design Mus, 2004; Tropicalisms, Jersey City Mus, NJ, 2006; Everything all at once, Queens Mus Art, NY, 2006; Field, Jamaica Ctr Arts & Learning, 2007; Agua, Cuarto Espacio Cultural, Diputación de Zaragoza, Spain, 2007. *Awards:* Whitney Museum Van Lier Found Fel, 2001; New York Found Arts Fel, 2002, 2008; Joan Mitchell Found Grant, 2003; Pollack-Krasner Found Grant, 2004. *Mailing Add:* 4333 46th St Apt F9 Long Island City NY 11104

ALBANESE, ROSE ANN
PAINTER, INSTRUCTOR
b New York, NY, Jan, 8, 1942. *Study:* studied with, Joseph Peller, Burton Silverman, Timothy Clark, Phyllis George, & Peter Homitsky, Art Students League, 2000-. *Work:* Siben & Siben Law Office, Bay Shore, NY; Littler Mendelson, PC, Melville, NY. *Comn:* portrait, librarian, Sloatsburg, NY; landscape, Tuscany, Va; portrait, pet, Sloatsburg, NY; landscape, bldg, Bay Shore, NY; landscape, portrait, Islip, NY. *Exhib:* Oils Competition, Art Students League Gallery, NY, 2000-2012; Audubon Artists Exhib, Salmagundi Art Club, NY, 2002-2012; Landscape Competition, Huntington Arts Coun, NY, 2003; Weill Cornell Univ Libr, NY, 2004; Islip Art Mus, NY, 2006; Eros Agape, Canvas Paper & Stone Gallery, NY, 2007; Phoenix Art Gallery, Bellport, NY, 2009. *Pos:* treas, Wet Paints Studio Group, W Sayville, NY, 2000-2009; recording secy, Audubon Artists Soc, NY, 2003-2012; exec bd, Islip Art Coun, Islip, NY, 2011-2012. *Teaching:* instr oil, watercolor, acrylic, Pvt Studio, Bayshore, NY, 2002-2012; demo teacher oils, watercolor, Wet Paints Studio Group, W Sayville, NY, 2005-2010. *Awards:* First Place, Townwide Art Show, BACA Art Group, Babylon, NY, 2001; First Place, Portraits, Suburban Art League, 2004; First Place, Wet Paints Studio Group, NY, 2004; Winsor Newton Painting, Suburban Art League, NY, 2005; Hon Mention, Portraits/Figures, W/C Magic Mag, 2006; Top Honors, Portrait and Still Life, Art Students League, NY, 2008, 2010. *Bibliog:* Derrick J Lang (auth), The Business of Art, Am Artist Mag, 2004; Dave Willinger (auth), Review of Blue Monday, The South Shore Press, 2006; Kelly Kane (auth), Watermedia Showcase Online, Watercolor Magic Mag, 2007; Tina Marie Caputo (auth), Landscape Review, Islip Art Bulletin, 2008. *Mem:* Audubon Artists Inc (recording secy); Wet Paints Artists Asn (treas); Southampton Artists Asn; East Hampton Art Guild; Islip Art Council. *Media:* Oil, Watercolor. *Dealer:* Armands Gallery 97 W Main St Bayshore NY 11706. *Mailing Add:* 1391 Pine Acres Blvd Bay Shore NY 11706

ALBANO, PATRICK LOUIS
ART DEALER
b St Louis, Mo, June 19, 1947. *Study:* Univ Miss, BA, 69; Univ Iowa, MA, 71. *Pos:* Dir, Aaron Galleries, Chicago, Ill, currently. *Mem:* Int Fine Print Dealers; Am Hist Print Collectors Soc. *Specialty:* American masters of the 19th and 20th centuries. *Publ:* Auth, articles in: Antique Market Report, Bales Publ, 1/86 & 9/86

ALBERTI, DONALD WESLEY
PAINTER
b Ft Eustis, Va, Dec 25, 1950. *Study:* Coll William & Mary, BA, 71. *Work:* Zaragoza Highway, 82; Mus des Beaux-Arts, La Chaux de Fonds, Switzerland. *Exhib:* Condeso/Lawler Gallery, New York City, 84, 86, Kunsthalle Bielefeld, Ger, 86, G Brownstone & Co, Paris, 88, La Couleur Seule L'Experience De Monochrome, Mus St Pierre, Lyon, France, 88; Mediterranean Abstraction, Fr Inst Naples, Italy, 92; F NY, Mus Modernerkunst, Ottendorf, Ger, 92; F NY, Am House, Berlin, Ger, 93; Konkret Konstruktiv Mus, St Ingbert, Saarland, 96; Pardo View Gallery, New York City, 96; Molloy Coll Art Gallery, NY, 2000; Estrada Fine Art, Los Angeles, Calif, 2007; Ctr Nat d'Art Contemp de Grenoble, France, 2009; Estrada Fine Arts, PYO Gallery, Los Angeles, 2010; Mus des Beaux-Arts, Ville de la Chaux de Fonds, Switzerland, 2010. *Teaching:* Guest lectr, Sch Visual Arts, NY, 83-84; vis artist lectr ser, Hartwick Col, Oneonta, NY, 87. *Awards:* Fel, NY Found Arts, 87; Fel, Igor Found, 90. *Bibliog:* Clio Mitchell (auth), Instant myth, Art Int, winter 88; Peter Bellamy (auth), The Artist Project, 91. *Media:* All Media. *Publ:* Dir, Pollock/Beaubourg: 1982 (16mm Film Doc), 86; Martin Hentschel (ed), Alan Uglow, Kerber, 2010. *Dealer:* Estrada Fine Art Los Angeles CA. *Mailing Add:* 93 Crosby St New York NY 10012

ALBRECHT, DONALD
CURATOR, EDUCATOR
Study: Ill Inst Tech, BArch. *Collection Arranged:* The Green House, New Directions in Sustainable Architecture & Design, Nat Bldg Mus; Eero Saarinen Retrospective, Finnish Cult Inst; Samuel H Gottscho, Mus City New York; Dorothy Draper, Mus City New York; The Work of Charles & Ray Eames, Vitra Design Mus. *Pos:* Founding cur, Am Mus Moving Image; adj cur archit & Design, Mus City New York. *Teaching:* Adj prof decorative arts master program, Cooper Hewitt. *Mem:* Fellow, Am Acad Rome, 2003-. *Publ:* Auth, Designing Dreams: Modern Architecture in the Movies, Harper & Row; contribr, NY Times, House & Garden, Architectural Digest, Interiors & Architectural Record. *Mailing Add:* 1220 Fifth Ave New York NY 10029

ALDANA, CARL
PAINTER
b Guatemala City, Guatemala; US citizen. *Study:* Self taught. *Work:* USAF, Washington DC; City of Hockaichi Collection, Japan; US Embassy, El Salvador; Auto Club of Calif, Los Angeles; Long Beach Mus Art, Calif; Galleria Nacional Costa Rica; US Navy Automobile; AAA; Calif Hist Soc; Calif State libr Poster Collection; Petersen Automotive Mus, Los Angeles. *Comn:* Portrait of Margaret Mead, 69, portrait Dr Jean Mayer, 68, portrait BF Skinner, 73, Psychology Today, San Diego, Calif; portrait Richard Nixon, Los Angeles Times, Calif, 72; painting, CRM Books, San Diego, Calif, 68. *Exhib:* Arco Ctr for Visual Arts, Los Angeles, 77, Rio Hondo Col, Whittier, 88, Wilding Mus, Los Olivos, Calif; Los Angeles As Seen By Los Angeles Artists, Los Angeles Munic Art Gallery, 81; San Diego Mus Art; Solo exhibs: San Bernardino Co Mus, 94; FACES Gallery, Long Beach & Golden W Col, Calif, 98; Galeria Nacional, Costa Rica; La Sierra Univ; Texas Tech Univ; 70 Yrs of Westways Covers, Petersen Mus, Los Angeles, 95; Portrait Exhib, Barnsdall Munic Art Gallery, Los Angeles, 96; Los Angeles Skyline, Los Angeles Conservancy Invitational Auction, 97; Archangels, Mus Latin Am Art, 97; Mirate Galleria, Costa Rica, 2007; Munic Art Gallery, 2007; George Krevsky Gallery; Calif State Univ, Dominguez Hills. *Collection Arranged:* Long Beach Mus of Art; US Naval Art; Calif Hist Soc, AAA; Wilding Art Mus. *Teaching:* instr painting, Calif State Univ, Long Beach, 67-68, 80-81; instr drawing & painting, Fullerton Col, Calif, 72-77, Santa Monica, 75-78. *Bibliog:* article in Cinema Mag, Ger, 7/94; article in Anthem, Eureka/Humbolt Co Calif, 8/94; TV interview with Maria Hall Brown, KOCE-PBS, Channel 50, 2/28/98. *Mem:* Acad Motion Pictures Arts & Sciences (bd mem, currently). *Media:* Oil, Watercolor. *Specialty:* Easel Painting. *Publ:* art dir, Air Force One (film), Columbia Pictures, 96. *Mailing Add:* 386 Ultimo Long Beach CA 90814

ALDEN, RICHARD
PAINTER
US citizen. *Study:* Pratt Inst, Brooklyn, BA (archit), 66, MA (archit), 68; Archit Asn, Fulbright Grant, 67. *Work:* Milford Fine Arts Coun, Conn; Trenton State Col, NJ. *Exhib:* Salmagundi Club 3rd Ann, NY, 80; Audubon Artists 38th Ann Nat, NY, 80; Springfield Art League 61st Nat, Mass, 80; Nat Print Exhib, Holman Art Gallery, Trenton, NJ, 80; Mamaroneck Artists Guild, Larchmont, NY, 81; and others. *Teaching:* Asst prof design, Pa State Univ, 68-. *Awards:* Third Prizes, 8th Ann, York Art Asn, 78 & Cent Pa Festival Arts, 78; First Prize, 21st Three Rivers Arts Festival, 80. *Media:* Colored Pencil. *Publ:* Fragments of a Total Picture: Beyond Style & Fashion, Alden Publ, 86. *Dealer:* Capricorn Gallery 4849 Rugby Ave Bethesda MD 20014

ALDEN, TODD
CRITIC, CONCEPTUAL ARTIST
b Oct 7, 1963. *Study:* Grad Ctr, City Univ New York, MA (art hist), 91. *Mem:* Coll Art Asn; Conceptual Clearinghouse Ltd (dir, 92-). *Publ:* Ed & auth, The Library of Babel (exhib catalog), Hallwalls Cont Arts Ctr, Buffalo, NY, 91; auth, Sophie Calle & the Aesthetics of the Uncanny Arts, 91, Louise Lawler: Love for Sale, 91 & coauth, Total Metal, 91, Arts; auth, Marcel Broodthaers: On the tautology of art & merchandise, Print Collector's Newsletter, 92. *Mailing Add:* 225 W 14th St Apt 3E New York NY 10011-7135

ALDERDICE, CYNTHIA LOU
PAINTER, JEWELER
b Des Moines, Iowa, Mar 16, 1932. *Study:* Univ Tex, BA, 57; New York Univ, 81; Acad Jewelry, New York, 75-95. *Work:* Robert C Williams Am Mus Papermaking, Atlanta; Musee d'Art Contemp, France; Ga Tech Univ, Atlanta; Int Monetary Fund Collection, Washington, DC; Fisher Coll Bus, Ohio State Univ, Columbus; Fed Home Loan Mortgage Corp, Washington, DC; Jane Voorhees Zimmerli Art Mus, New Brunswick, NJ; Fisher Coll Bus, Ohio State Univ, Columbus. *Exhib:* World Wide Triennial Exhib, Musee d'Art Contemp, Chamalieres, France, 91; Prints '97, Corcoran Mus Art, Washington, DC, 97; A Cult Language, Robert First Ctr Arts, Ga Tech, Atlanta, 98; Frequencies Nature, Tallahassee Mus Hist Natural Sci, Fla, 98; A Cult Language, Robert C Williams Am Mus Papermaking, Atlanta, Ga, 98; Beyond Words, Ellen Noel Art Mus, Odessa, Tex, 99; Printer's Identity, Am Swedish Hist Mus, Philadelphia, 2000; An Exhib of Am Vietnamese Artists, Hanoi Coll Fine Art,

Vietnam, 2000; Surfacetension, Rep River Valley Mus, Vernon, Tex, 2000, Kirkpatric Galleries at Omniplex, Oklahoma City, 2001; Pass Through It, Mill River Gallery, Ellicott City, Md, 2001; Cross Currents, Art Gallery Univ Md, Coll Park, 2001; solo exhibs, Touchstone Gallery, Washington, DC, 2002, Morris Mechanic Theater, Baltimore, 2002 & Touchstone Gallery, 2004; Impressions-Printmaking, Carla Massoni Gallery, Chestertown, Md, 2002; Pushing Paper, Hand Workshop Art Ctr, Richmond, Va, 2002; group exhibs, Invitational, past & present bd dirs, Md Fedn Art, Annapolis, Md, 2004 & Pulp Painting Exhib, Sandy Spring Mus, Sandy Spring, Md, 2005; Jewelry Fair Invitational, Walters Art Mus, 2005, Baltimore, 2007, 2008, 2009, Richmond, Va, 2007,; Creative Craft Coun Exhib, Rockville, Md, 2009. *Awards:* Individual Artist Award, Visual Arts, Md State Arts Coun, 92; Annie Award Vis Arts Recipient, Cult Arts Found Anne Arundel Co, 2004. *Bibliog:* Lynne Allen/Phyllis McGibbon, The Best of Printmaking, Rockport Publ, 97. *Mem:* Md Fedn Art (pres, 85-87); Md Printmakers; Pyramid Atlantic (treas, 96-2000). *Media:* Oil on canvas, jewelry. *Mailing Add:* Annapolis Bus Park 2104 Renard Ct Annapolis MD 21401

ALDRICH, LYNN (BARRON)
SCULPTOR, CONCEPTUAL ARTIST

b Bryan, Tex, Dec 16, 1944. *Study:* Univ NC, Chapel Hill, BA, 66; Calif State Univ, Northridge, BA, 84; Art Cent Coll Design, MFA, 86. *Work:* Los Angeles Co Mus Art; Mus Contemp Art, Los Angeles; Neuberger Berman, Inc, NYC; Neiman Marcus, Inc, Dallas; Calder Found, New York. *Comn:* permanent structural installation, Metro, Los Angeles, Calif, 96. *Exhib:* Flying Lessons, Santa Monica Mus Art, 93; Forms of Address, San Francisco Art Inst, 94; Intersections: Personal & Social, MOCA, Los Angeles, 95, Altered States, 93; The Garden Show, PICA, Portland, Ore, 97; COLA 2000, UCLA Hammer Mus Art, Los Angeles, 2000; Made in Calif, Los Angeles Co Mus Art, 2000; Liquid Art, Long Beach Mus Art, Long Beach, Calif, 2001; The Permanent Collection, 1970-2000, Los Angeles Co Mus Art, 2001; New Works, New Spaces, Armory Ctr for the Arts, Pasadena, 2002; Los Angeles Post-Cool, San Jose Mus Art, Calif, 2002; Certain Traces, Kampa Mus, Prague, 2004; Contemporaries, Gallery at REDCAT, Disney Concert Hall, Los Angeles, 2004; The Next Generation, Mus of Biblical Art, New York, 2005; Extreme Materials, Rochester Mem Art Mus, NY, 2006; Observe, Williamson Gallery, Art Ctr Coll Design, Pasadena, 2008; 3 Solo Projects, Ben Maltz Gallery, Otis Coll Art Design, Los Angeles, 2009. *Teaching:* Instr fine arts, Art Ctr Coll Design, Pasadena, Calif, 86-98. *Awards:* Purchase Award, Los Angeles Co Mus, 99; Individual Artist Fel Award, City Los Angeles, 99; Individual Artist Fel Award, J Paul Getty Trust Fund, 2000. *Bibliog:* M A Greenstein (auth) Meeting of Disciplines, World Sculpture News, 98; Michael Duncan (auth) Review, Art in America, 2000; Doug Harvey (auth), Stuff: The Sculptures of Lynn Aldrich, LA Weekly, 2003; Leah Ollmann (auth), Aldrich is Such a Natural at Fakery, Los Angeles Times, 1/18/2008. *Media:* Miscellaneous Media, Plastic, Construction Materials. *Publ:* Auth, What's the Matter with Matter, In: Beholding the Glory: Incarnation Through the Arts, Cambridge Univ, 2000. *Dealer:* Carl Berg Gallery, Los Angeles; Art Affairs Gallery, Amsterdam. *Mailing Add:* 2020 N Main St #238 Los Angeles CA 90031

ALEJO, MAURICIO
PHOTOGRAPHER

b Mexico City, Mexico, 1969. *Study:* Univ Intercontinental Mexico City, Commun Sci, 1988-92; NY Univ, New York, MA, 2000-02. *Exhib:* Solo exhibs include Espacio Cult El Juglar, Mexico, 1999, Galeria Occurrence, Montreal, Canada, 2000, Ississ Gallery, Kyoto, Japan, 2002, Lee-Ka sing Gallery, Toronto, Canada, 2004, Mus Arte Contemp Rufino Tamayo, Mexico, 2004, Galeria Ramis Barquet, New York, 2004, 2006, Monterrey, Mexico, 2005; group exhibs include Expo Foto, Univ Intercontinental, México, 1993; Int Biennial Photog, Mus Alejandro Otero, Caracas, Venezuela, 2000; Parallel Zone, Miami, 2002; ARCO, Galeria OMR, Madrid, Spain, 2004; Come Closer Sept Back Up, Isola Art Ctr, Milan, Italy, 2005; El equilibrio & sus derivados, Casa del Lago Juan José Arreola, Mexico City, 2006; Objects of Desire, NUS Ctr Arts, Singapore, 2007; Puntos de Vista, Bochum Mus, Germany, 2007. *Awards:* New York Found Art Fel, 2008

ALEXANDER, ANTHONY K
SCULPTOR

b Granite City, Ill, May 21, 1951. *Comn:* Tribal Totem Pole, 88 & Tribal Symbols, 89, Greater Albany Sch Dist, Ore; Caduceus Sculptor, comn by Dr Roger P Setera, Portland, Ore, 90; Northwest Coast Art, Larry Day Assoc, Portland, Ore, 90; sculpture (life-size female Deputy Sheriff), Linn Co, Albany, Ore, 93. *Exhib:* Wildlife & Western Wildlife Exhib, Minneapolis, 90; Roughrider Art Show, Williston, NDak, 91; Jazzed About Art, Newberg, Ore, 91, 92, 93 & 94. *Media:* Bronze, Wood; Silver

ALEXANDER, EDMUND BROOKE
ART DEALER, PUBLISHER

b Los Angeles, Calif, Apr 26, 1937. *Study:* Yale Univ, BA, 60. *Pos:* Dir Editions Alecto, New York, 67 & Brooke Alexander, Inc, 68-; owner, Brooke Alexander Gallery & Brooke Alexander Editions Inc, 75-; partner, Galeria Weber, Alexander y Cobo, Madrid, 90; mem gov bd, Yale Univ Art Gallery; bd mem, Chinati Foundation. *Mem:* Art Dealers Asn Am. *Specialty:* Contemp Am prints; contemp paintings, drawings and sculpture. *Publ:* Ed, Robert Motherwell-Selected Prints 1961-1974, 74, Jasper Johns-Screenprints, 77 & Sam Francis--The Litho Shop 1970-1979, 79, pvt publ; Jasper Johns: The Season, 91. *Mailing Add:* c/o Brooke Alexander Gallery 59 Wooster St New York NY 10012

ALEXANDER, PETER
SCULPTOR

b Los Angeles, Calif, Feb 27, 1939. *Study:* Univ Pa, Univ Park, 57-60; Univ London, Eng, 60-62; Univ Calif, Berkeley, 62-63; Univ Southern Calif, Los Angeles, 63-64; Univ Calif, Los Angeles, BA, 65, MFA, 68. *Work:* Walker Art Ctr, Minneapolis, Minn; Mus Mod Art, Brooklyn Mus, Guggenheim Mus, Metrop Mus Art, NY; Corcoran Gallery Art, Washington, DC; Los Angeles Co Mus Art; San Francisco Mus Mod Art, Calif; Fogg Mus, Harvard Univ, Cambridge, Mass; and others. *Comn:* Blue, painting, Walt Disney Concert Hall, Los Angeles, 2003. *Exhib:* Whitney Mus Am Art Ann, 69; Highlights: 1968-1969, Aldrich Mus Contemp Art; Painting & Sculpture in Calif: The Modern Era, San Francisco Mus Mod Art, 76; solo exhibs, James Corcoran Gallery, Los Angeles, Calif, 81, 85-92, Van Straaten Gallery, Chicago, Ill, 84, Fuller Goldeen Gallery, San Francisco, Calif, 84, Gallery 454 North, West Hollywood, Calif, 88, Work Gallery, Costa Mesa, Calif, 91, Brian Gross Fine Art, San Francisco, 91 & 94, Laguna Art Mus, Calif, 92, Charles Whitchurch Gallery, Huntington Beach, Calif, 92, Barbara Mathes Gallery, (catalogue), NY, 94, Craig Krull Gallery, Santa Monica, 94 & Gallery at 777 (catalogue), Los Angeles, 95; Brooklyn Mus, 83; Mus Mod Art, NY, 84; Best of the West, Zero One Gallery, Los Angeles, 94; City Art, Millard Sheets Gallery, Pomona, Calif, 94; Shoes or No Shoes, Provincial Mus Mod Art, Oostende, Belg, 94; Paper Presence, Jan Abrams Gallery, Los Angeles, 94; Dennis Ochi Gallery, Ketchum, Idaho, 95; retrospective, Orange Co Mus Art, Newport Beach, Calif, 99; Los Angeles Co Mus Art, 2000; Primary Atmospheres, David Zwirner Gallery, NY, 2010; Pacific Standard Time, J Paul Getty Mus, Los Angeles, Calif, 2011; Overdrive, J Paul Getty Mus, Los Angeles, Calif, 2013. *Pos:* Artist-in-residence, Calif Inst Technol, Pasadena, 70-71, Calif State Univ, Long Beach, 76, Fullerton Col, Calif, 76, Univ Colo, Boulder, 81, Centrum Found, Wash, 82 & Cirrus Publ, Los Angeles, 83. *Awards:* Nat Endowment Arts Fel, 80. *Bibliog:* Monroe Hodder (auth), Unto Caesar: Peter Alexander at Brian Gross Art, Artweek, 10/20/94; Edith Newhall (auth), Peter Alexander at Barbara Mathes, Art News, 12/94; Naomi Vine and Dave Hickey (coauth), Peter Alexander: In This Light, OCMA, 99. *Mailing Add:* 1811 16th St Santa Monica CA 90404-4403

ALEXANDER, VIKKY M
CONCEPTUAL ARTIST

b Jan 30, 1959. *Study:* NS Coll Art & Design, BFA, 79. *Work:* Vancouver Art Gallery; Winnipeg Art Gallery; Household Finance Corp; Prudential Insurance Co; Progressive Corp; Nat Gallery Can; Mackenzie Art Gallery; Edmonton Art Gallery; Art Gallery Surrey; Art Bank Can; Goldman Sachs Ltd, Toronto; Kenderine Art Gallery, Univ Saskatoon, Can. *Comn:* Camera, lobby mural for intracorp developers, Vancouver. *Exhib:* Window Installation, New Mus Contemp Art, New York, 85; The Castle, Documenta, Kassel, Fed Repub Ger, 87; Art of the Real, De Appel, Amsterdam, The Neth, 87; New Territories in Art: Europe-Am, Fondabione Michetti, Rome, Italy, 87; Past/Future/Tense, Winnipeg Art Gallery, Winnipeg & Vancouver Art Gallery, British Columbia, 90-91; James Welling & Vikky Alexander, Kunsthalle Bern, Switz, 90; Nat Gallery Can, Ottawa, 2000; Intertidal, Mukha, Antwarp, Belgium, 2005; Houses of Glass, Massey Univ, New Zealand, 2010. *Teaching:* prof photog, New York Univ, 89-92 & Univ Victoria, 92-, full prof, currently. *Awards:* Visual Arts Grants; Can Coun Visual Arts Grant, 83-84, 87, 89, 91 & 2004; Can Coun Projects Grant, 85; London Life Young Contemporaries Purchase Award, 90; Univ Victoria Fac Res Grant, 92, 94-98, 2001-2002 & 2004-2007. *Bibliog:* Nancy Tousley (auth), Vikky Alexander, Canadian Arts, 88; Brian Wallis (auth), Vikky Alexander (catalog), Stride Gallery, 89; Bruce Ferguson (auth), Glass Sculpture (catalog), 90; Ian Wallace, Contemp Art Gallery, 2000. *Mem:* AAUW; Coll Art Asn; BC Photog & Media Arts Soc; Ctr Experimental & Photog Arts (aesthetic adv bd 97-). *Media:* Mixed Media. *Res:* Landscape & architecture. *Publ:* Contribr, Tropical codes, Kunstforum, 86; Thought Objects, JAA, 87; Contemporary photography, Art & Auction, 87; Fabrications, Abbeville Press, 88. *Dealer:* Trepanier Baer Gallery Calgary AB Canada; Wildin Cran Gallery Los Angeles. *Mailing Add:* 1445 Marpole Apt 410 Vancouver BC V6H 1S5 Canada

ALEXANDER, WICK
PAINTER

b San Diego, Calif, Apr 10, 1955. *Study:* San Diego State Univ, 73-75; Univ Calif, San Diego, BA, 79, MFA, 83. *Work:* Mission Bay Pump Station, San Diego, Calif; Sushi Gallery, San Diego, Calif; Tijuana River Estuary, Imperial Beach, Calif; Banff Ctr Arts, Alta, Can; Mus Contemp Art, San Diego. *Comn:* Pillars of the Community, South Escondido Blvd, Calif, 96 & 99; Work in Progress, San Diego, Calif, 96; Light is Life (mural), San Diego, Calif, 98; Bird Park, Balboa Park, 99; Banner Project, City of San Diego, 98; Moving Pictures, Culver City, Calif, 2000. *Exhib:* Solo exhibs, Java Art Space, San Diego, Calif, 92, Simay Space, San Diego, 93 & Quint Gallery, San Diego, 94, SW Coll Art Gallery, Tulla Vista, Calif, 96, Robin Brailsford Gallery, San Diego, 97, San Diego Mesa Coll Gallery, 98 & Calif Ctr Arts, 99, RB Stevenson Gallery, San Diego, 2000; retrospective, Installation Gallery, 91; La Calle, Tijuana River Estuary, 91; Orange Co Ctr Contemp Art, 92; Transcending Borders, Centro Cult Tijuana, Mex, 92; San Diego Mus Contemp Art, 95, 96 & 97; Santa Fe Mus Fine Arts, 96; Mus Contemp Art, San Diego, 97; San Diego State Univ, 97; Irvine Art Ctr, 98; Calif Ctr for the Arts, Escondido, 99; Cannon Gallery, Carlsbad, Calif, 2000; RB Stevenson Gallery, San Diego, 2000. *Teaching:* Instr art, Metrop Correctional Ctr, US Dept Justice, San Diego, 83-87 & San Diego State Univ, 89; artist-in-residence, Young at Art, San Diego City Sch, 91-92; instr painting & drawing, Univ Calif, San Diego, presently. *Awards:* Ford Found Grant, 82; Nat Endowment Arts Fel, 89; CAC Artist Fel Painting, 90; Orchid Award, City San Diego, 96; Artist-in-Residence, Banff Ctr for the Arts, Alberta, Can, 96; Project of the Yr Landscape Design Award, Am Pub Works Asn, 97

ALEXANDER-GREENE, GRACE GEORGE
EDUCATOR, MUSEUM DIRECTOR

b Cleveland, Ohio, Sept 18, 1918. *Study:* NJ State Teachers Col, with Sybil Browne, BS, 40; Hunter Col; NY Univ; Queens Col; Univ PR; Columbia Univ. *Exhib:* Lever House, 86. *Pos:* TV producer-broadcaster art, New York City Bd Educ, 65-73, supervisor art, 73-77, dir art, 77-79; bd mem, Inst Study Art in Educ, 78 & 79; freelance TV producer art, 79-; consult, Am Mus Moving Image, 85. *Teaching:* Instr visual literacy, Am Festival in Britain, 73; instr art educ, Queens Col, 71-72; instr art educ, Sch Visual Arts, New York, 79-. *Awards:* Ohio State Award, 63 & 73; Outstanding Alumni Award, Kean Col, 80; Monitor Award, Video Production Asn, 84. *Bibliog:* Barbara Y Newsom (auth), The Art Museum as Educator, Univ Calif, Press,

78; Potell Herbert (ed), Rationale for Art Education in the Eighties, High Points, 80. *Mem:* Nat Art Educ Asn; Univ Coun Art Educ; Am Women Radio & TV; New York City Art Teachers Asn. *Publ:* Auth, Artists in New York, 66 & The Moving Image, 70, New York City Bd Educ; From the Teachers Corner, Am Educ US Dept Health Educ & Welfare, 78

ALEXENBERG, MEL
CONCEPTUAL ARTIST, EDUCATOR
b Brooklyn, NY, Feb 24, 1937. *Study:* Queens Coll, City Univ New York, BS, 58; Yeshiva Univ, MS, 59; Art Students League; New York Univ, EdD, 69. *Work:* Metrop Mus Art, New York; Baltimore Mus Art, Md; Israel Mus, Jerusalem; Haags Gemeente Mus, The Hague, Neth; Victoria & Albert Mus, London, Eng; Mus Modern Art; Everson Mus Art, Syracuse, NY; Birmingham Mus Art, Birmingham, Ala; Nat Mus Am History, Smithsonian Inst, Wash DC; Nelson-Atkins Mus Art, Kansas City, MI; Jewish Mus, Prague. *Comn:* Mem to Six Million, Dachau Death Camp, Fed Repub Ger, 83; Torah Spectrogram, Ramat Hanegev Coll, Yeroham, Israel, 84; Pinim/Panim: Biofeedback-computer graphics interactive system, Yeshiva Univ Mus, New York, 87; Faxart Homage to Rembrandt, AT&T, NY, Amsterdam, Jerusalem, Tokyo & Los Angeles, 89; Four Wings of America (environment art work), Miami, San Diego, Seattle & Portland, 96. *Exhib:* Crash: Computer Assisted Hardcopy, Wright Mus Art, Beloit, Wis, 88; Golem, Jewish Mus, New York, 88; Lights/Orot, Yeshiva Univ Mus, New York, 88; Faxart Mem, Mus Het Rembrandthuis, Amsterdam, The Neth, 89; High Tech/High Touch, Miami Univ Art Mus, Oxford, Ohio, 90; Imagenes Norteamericanas, Instituto Chileno Nortamericano de Cultura, Santiago, Chile, 92 & 98; Aesthetic Peace Plan, Nat Jewish Mus, Washington, DC, 94; Four Corners of Am, ArtMiami, 96; Cyberangels, Jewish Mus, Prague, 2004; Hidden Gardens, Jerusalem Botanical Gardens, Israel, 2007-2008; Photograph God, Kuhn Fine Arts Gallery, Ohio State Univ, 2010; Torah Tweets: A Postdigital Biblical Commentary as Blogart Narrative, 2011; Bar Mitzvah in a Brooklyn Mosque, Detroit, 2012. *Pos:* Res fel, MIT Ctr Advan Vis Studies, 84-88; dean, vis arts, New World Sch Arts, Miami, Fla, 90-2000; Council mem, Wolf Found, 2002-; head, Sch Arts, Emunah Coll, Jerusalem, Israel, 2006-2013. *Teaching:* Sr lectr, Tel Aviv Univ, Israel, 69-73; assoc prof art, Columbia Univ, New York, 73-77; assoc prof aesthetic educ, Bar-Ilan Univ, Ramat Gan, Israel, 77-84; prof & chmn fine arts, Pratt Inst, Brooklyn, New York, 85-90; prof art & Jewish thought, Ariel Univ, Israel, 2000-2007; prof art, Emunah Coll, Jerusalem, Israel, 2001-. *Bibliog:* Elizabeth Hayt-Atkins (auth), Lights Orot, Art News, 9/88; John Ross, Clare Romano & Tim Ross (auths), The Complete Printmaker, Macmillan, 90; Ori Z Soltis (auth), Fixing the world: Jewish American painters in the twentieth century, Brandeis Univ Press, Univ Press New Eng, 2003; Michaela Hajkova (auth), Mel Alexenberg: Cyberangels-Aesthetic peace plan for the Middle East, Jewish Mus, Prague, 2004; Tsipi Luria (auth), Thoughtful craft, computer angel, Makor Rishon, 2006; David Sperber (auth), Visa Versa, Bar-Illan Univ, Isreal, 2008. *Media:* Multimedia, Systems Art. *Res:* Art in Jewish thought; art in a digital age; art educ in a networked world; creativity. *Interests:* Blogging, wikiart. *Publ:* Auth, Jewish consciousness and art of the digital age, J Judaism & Civilization, 2003; Semiotic redefinition of art in a digital age, Semiotics & Visual Cult: Sights, Signs & Significance, 2004; From science to art: Integral structure and ecological perspective in a digital age, Interdisciplinary Art Educ: Building Bridges to Connect Disciplines & Cult, 2005; Cyberangels: Aesthetic Peace Plan for the Middle East, Leonardo: Journal of the International Society for the Arts, Sciences, and Technology, 2006; Ancient Schema and Technoetic Art, Technoetic Arts: Journal of Speculative Research, 2006; The future of art in a digital age: 2006; Educating artists for the future: Learning at the intersections of art, science, technology & culture, 2008, Intellect Bks; Dialogic Art in a Digital World: Judaism and Contemporary Art, Jerusalem: Rubin Mass House, 2008; Space-Time Structures of Digital Visual Culture: Paradigm Shift from Hellenistic to Hebraic Roots of Western Civilization, Inter/Sections/Inter/actions: Art Education in a Digital Visual Culture, 2010; The Future of Art in a Postdigital Age: From Hellenistic to Hebraic Consciousness, Univ Chgo Press, 2011; Eruv as Conceptual and Kinetic Art, Images, 2011; Fringed Sukkah, Architectural Inventions: Visionary Drawings, 2012; Postdigital Consciousness, Archithese, 2012

ALEXICK, DAVID FRANCIS
EDUCATOR, PAINTER
b Philadelphia, Pa, 1942. *Study:* Richmond Prof Inst, BFA, 64; Va Commonwealth Univ, MFA, 66; Pa State Univ, PhD, 76. *Work:* private collections. *Exhib:* Va Artists Biennial, Va Mus Fine Arts, Richmond, 64; Solo Exhib: Robinson House, Va Mus Fine Arts, Richmond, 65; Longwood Coll Fac Show, Bedford Gallery, Farmville, Va, 71-78; James River Show, Mariners Mus, Newport News, Va, 73; various fac shows, Falk Gallery, Christopher Newport Univ; Solo retrospective, 1960-20007, Christopher Newport Univ, 2008; Hamton Rds Convention Ctr, Hampton, Va, 2010-2013; Charles Taylor Art Ctr, 2013. *Teaching:* Instr art, York Col Pa, 66-68; asst prof art, Longwood Col, Farmville, Va, 71-78; instr art educ, Col William & Mary, Williamsburg, Va, 79-80; asst prof art, Christopher Newport Col, VA, 79-82, dir art, Dept Arts & Communications, 82-88, assoc prof, 82-2003, prof, 2003-2007, 2008 (retired). *Awards:* Cert Distinction, Va Mus Fine Arts, 64; 1st Prize, South Eastern Regional, Lynchburg Fine Arts Ctr, 67; Patron Arts Award, Lynchburg Art Festival, 78; Art Educator of the Yr, Southeastern Region, 2003. *Mem:* Coll Art Asn; Nat Art Educ Asn; Va Art Educ Asn. *Media:* Oil, Acrylic, Bronze. *Res:* Programs of art and perceptual awareness for institutionalized retarded children. *Interests:* currency trading, futures and options. *Collection:* Robert Nelson Roane. *Mailing Add:* 220 Crittenden Ln Newport News VA 23606

ALEXIS, MICHAEL
PAINTER
b 1950. *Exhib:* Solo exhibs, Frail Monument, Ruth Bachofner Gallery, Santa Monica, 90, 92, 95, 97, Hide-Seek, 99, 2001, New Paintings, 2006; Fragments, Espace Malraux, Maison de la Culture, France, 93; Dahn Gallery, NY, 95; The Birthday Book, Elga Wimmer Gallery, 97; Heriard-Cimino Gallery, New Orleans, 99, 2001, 2005; Stephen Haller Gallery, NY City, 2001, Alphabets, 2002, Subtracted World, 2003, 2004, Synesthesia, 2005, Epigrams, 2006; Stolen Diaries, Galerie Isabelle Gounod, Paris, 2006; Group exhibs, Elga Wimmer Gallery, NY City, 94, 98, 2001, 2002; The Outside Inside Gertrude Stein, Dortmunder Kunstverein, Dortmund, Ger, 95; World, Image, Gesture, Irvine Fine Arts Ctr, Calif, 96; World View, Rosenberg + Kaufman Fine Art, NY, 97; Surface Tension, Part I, Stephen Haller Gallery, NY City, 2000, Simple Truths, 2000, Constant Aesthetic, 2001, Surface Fragments, 2002, Narrative Abstraction, 2003, Coda, 2003, Focal Point, 2005, Solstice, 2006; Unlocking the Grid, Univ RI, 99; Robert McCain & Co, Houston, Tex, 2002; Werner Bommer Gallery, Zurich, 2003; Abstraction with a Twist, RVS Fine Art, Southampton, NY, 2004; Labyrinth, Holland Tunnel Gallery, Paros, Greece, 2005; Eye on Art, 54 Greenwich Avenue, Conn, 2006. *Awards:* French Ministry of Culture Grant, 92; Pollock-Krasner Found, 94; Elizabeth Found for Arts Grant, 2003. *Mailing Add:* c/o Stephen Haller Gallery 542 W 26 St New York NY 10001

ALF, MARTHA JOANNE
PAINTER, WRITER
b Berkeley, Calif, Aug 13, 1930. *Study:* San Diego State Univ, with Everett Gee Jackson, BA, MA (painting), 63; Univ Calif, Los Angeles, with James Weeks, William Brice & Richard Diebenkorn, MFA (pictorial arts), 70. *Work:* Los Angeles Co Mus Art; San Diego Mus Art; Santa Barbara Mus Art; Newport Harbor Art Mus, Newport Beach, Calif; Israel Mus Art, Jerusalem; Chemical Bank & Metrop Mus Art, NY. *Exhib:* Whitney Biennial Contemp Art, Whitney Mus Am Art, 75; Contemp Am Luminism, Henry Gallery, Univ Wash, 80-85; The Michael and Dorothy Blankfort Collection, Los Angeles Co Mus Art, Calif, 82; Solo retrospective, Los Angeles Munic Art Gallery & San Francisco Art Inst, 84; Martha Alf-Helen Ludenberg: Two Views: 1970-1987, Palos Verdes Art Ctr, Calif, 87; Martha Alf: Survey 1965-1990, Art Inst Southern Calif, Laguna Beach, 91; Recent Drawings, Fresno Art Mus, Calif, 92; Internal Interface: 25 yrs survey, Mt San Antonio Col, Walnut, Calif, 93; Generation of Mentors, Nat Mus of Women in the Arts, Washington, DC, 94 & traveling, 94-95; and many other solo & group exhibs. *Pos:* Guest cur, Painting: Color Form & Surface (17 Los Angeles Painters), Lang Art Gallery, Scripps Col, Claremont, Calif. *Teaching:* Instr drawing & painting, Los Angeles Harbor Col, Wilmington, Calif, 71-75; instr, current art in Los Angeles, Univ Calif Exten, Los Angeles, 71-78, inside the art world, 73-79. *Awards:* Nat Endowment Arts Visual Artist Grant for Drawing, 89; Nat Endowment Arts Grant, 79; Kay Nielsen Mem Purchase Award, Los Angeles Co Mus Art, 79; and others. *Bibliog:* Merle Schipper (auth), Martha Alf (Tortue Gallery), Art News, 24, 27, 2/87; Wendy Beckett (auth), Martha Alf, 18, 19, Contemporary Woman Artists, Phaidon, Oxford, 88; Peter Clothier (auth), Martha Alf: Red Pulse, Artspace, 7/8/92. *Media:* Painting, Photography. *Publ:* Auth, My interest in women artists of the past, Womanspace J, Vol 1, No 2; The psychological world of Joyce Treiman, 3/76, The structural language of Claire Falkenstein, 4/76 & Women artists throughout history, 1/77, Artweek. *Dealer:* Newspace Gallery 5241 Melrose Ave Los Angeles CA 90038. *Mailing Add:* 822 Pacific Ave Venice CA 90291

ALFANO, ANGEL
PAINTER
b Cosenza, Italy, Oct 6, 1940. *Study:* Liceo Artistico, Rome, Italy. *Work:* Garibaldi-Meucci Mus, NY; Current Art Boston; W Broadway Gallery, NY; Alternate Space Gallery, NY. *Exhib:* Salon Int De L'Art Libre, Paris, France, 68; 10th Art Exhib, NY, 75; Contemp Art Show, Santa Fe, NMex, 78; Fine Art Gallery, Westchester Community Coll, Valhalla, NY, 86; Garibaldi-Meucci Mus, NY, 91; Int Art Show, Rio De Janeiro, Brazil, 98; Contemp Art Show, Sharjah Art Mus, United Arab Emirates, 99; Int Art Show, Toledo Univ, Toledo, Ohio, 2000; The 6th Int Ann Miniature Art, Stockholm, Sweden, 2001; and others. *Awards:* Gold Medal Award, Miami, Fla, 65; Prize Special Au Salon Int De L'Art Libre, Paris, France, 65; First Place, Nat Art Show, Naples, Italy, 70. *Media:* Oil, Watercolor. *Publ:* Illusr, Concoa de Amor, Kim Sam Young, 88; Poesie, Teresinka Pereira, 89. *Mailing Add:* 44 Merritt Ave Eastchester NY 10707-3110

ALFANO, EDWARD C
PHOTOGRAPHER, EDUCATOR, ADMINISTRATOR
Study: Shimer Col, Chgo, Ill, AB, 1971; Northeastern Univ, Boston, Mass, MS, 1976; attended U NC, Chapel Hill, 1972-1973, Art Inst Boston, 1977-1979. *Comn:* Client list includes: Amtrak, Anne Kline, Arthur D. Little, Cornell Medical Ctr, Gendarme, Hewlett-Packard, Hollywood Arts Council, Houghton-Mifflin Inc Magazine, Metropolitan Hotel Hollywood, NYC District Attorney's Office, Parents Magazine, Ramada Inn, Rockport, Sheraton Hotels, Solvanf Tourist Bureau, Sonesta Hotels, UCLA Medical Ctr, Westways Magazine, Xerox, and others. *Exhib:* Group Exhibitions include: Mystic River One, CN, 1979, Second Sight Carpenter Ctr, Harvard Univ, 1981, Art Gallery, Univ NY New Paltz, 1982, Cameraworks Gallery, San Francisco, 1983, Selected Works, Fort Point Channel Artists Show, Boston, Mass, 1989, California Still Lifes, Disting Artists Forum, Calif State Univ, East Bay, 1991, Berlin-Los Angeles, Backstreet Galleries, Los Angeles, 2001, Mysterious Light, Orlando Gallery, Encino, Calif, 2004, Faculty Exhibition, Calif State Univ, Northridge, 2012, Freestyle Photography, Hollywood, Calif, 2013 and others; Two person exhibitions include: Travel & Trivial, Orlando Gallery, 2008, Pacific Univ, 2011; Solo exhibitions include: Radiance, Seoul Inst of the Arts, Korea, 2010, Transformations, Shanghai Normal Univ, 2010, Luzy Sombra Art Galerry Universidad Iberoamericana, Mexico City, 210, East China Normal Univ, 2014, Nanjing Univ of Arts, China, 2014. *Collection Arranged:* Inst for Arts and Media, Calif State Univ, Northridge, Pacific Univ, Forest Grove, Oregon, Seoul Inst for the Arts, Korea, Shanghai Normal Univ, China, and private collectors. *Pos:* Asst-studio manager, Van-S Studio, Boston, Mass, 1979-1981; freelance asst, Los Angeles, 1981-1983; Professional photographer, 1982-. *Teaching:* Asst prof, Art Inst Boston, 1987-1989; assoc prof art, Calif State Univ, Northridge, 1989-1993, prof art, 1993-,dept chair, currently. *Mailing Add:* California State University Office SG 231 18111 Nordhoff St Northridge CA 91330

ALFORD, GLORIA K
PAINTER, SCULPTOR
b Chicago, Ill, Oct 3, 1928. *Study:* Univ Calif, Berkeley, AB; Art Inst Chicago; Penland Sch Crafts, NC; Columbia Univ; Pratt Graphics Ctr. *Work:* Elvehjem Mus, Univ Wis-Madison; CUNA Art Collection, Madison, Wis; Prudential Art Collection, Monterey Mus Art, Calif; Paper construction, Silicon Graphics, Mountain View, Calif; Mus Art & Hist, Santa Cruz. *Comn:* Four paper sculptures, Ask Computer Systems, Inc, 88, TGV Inc Santa Cruz, 94. *Exhib:* In Her Own Image, Philadelphia Mus Art, 74; 19th Ann Print Exhib, Brooklyn Mus, 74; Wis Directions, Milwaukee Art Ctr, 75; Solo exhibs, Monterey Peninsula Mus Art, 80; The Neth Inst Advan Study, Wassenar, 82; Djurovich Gallery, Sacramento, Calif, 86; Jofi Gallery, Santa Cruz, Calif, 2006; Placement-Displacement Sculpture Show, Cabrillo Col, 83; Content Contemp Issues, Euphrat Gallery, 86; The Chaminade Artists Series, Santa Cruz, Calif, 90-94; Computer Technology in the Arts, Sesnon Art Gallery, Univ Calif, 90, Galerie Reve, Los Angeles, Calif, 90; Woven Wonders, Pajaro Valley Arts Coun, 94; Oriental Influences, Pope Gallery, 95; Biennale Int dell'Arte Contemp, Florence, Italy; Arte Studio, Via Guelfa. *Pos:* Vis artist, Cult Exchange Prog, France, 76; bd mem & chairperson exhib Comt, Santa Cruz Ctr Arts, 91-94. *Teaching:* Instr monoprints, Univ Calif Extension at Santa Cruz, 91; guest lectr, Printmaking, Univ Calif Santa Cruz, summer 92-94. *Awards:* Top Honors, Univ Wis Art Show, Richland Ctr, 72. *Bibliog:* Donna Maurillo (auth), Gloria Alford of Santa Cruz, Monterey Life Mag, 11/84; Robert Sward (auth), Autobiography Contemporary Authors Autobiography Series (CAAS), Vol 13, 91. *Mem:* Santa Cruz Art League (bd mem, 91); founding Santa Cruz Mus Art and History. *Media:* All Media. *Interests:* Paper making, sculpture art hist, innovating comuter artitifacts. *Dealer:* American Art Gallery Carmel CA. *Mailing Add:* 435 Meder St Santa Cruz CA 95060

ALHILALI, NEDA
ENVIRONMENTAL ARTIST, PAINTER
b Cheb, Czech, Nov 26, 1938. *Study:* St Martin's Sch Art, London, Eng; Kunst Akademie, Munich, WGer; Univ Calif, Los Angeles, BA, 65, MA, 68. *Work:* Banff Art Ctr, Canada; Crocker Art Mus, Sacramento, Calif; Albright Col, Pa; ARAMCO, Houston; Central Mus Textiles, Lodz, Poland; and others. *Comn:* Blue Cross Hq, Los Angeles, 77; Hyatt Regency Hotels, Chicago, 77, also Los Angeles, Columbus, Maui & Palm Beach; Tishman Corp, Los Angeles, 78; Prince Kuhio Hotel, Hawaii, 80; Sheraton Hotel, Crystal City, Va; and others. *Exhib:* Mus Contemp Art, Chicago, Pac Design Ctr, Los Angeles & Mus of Sci & Indust, Los Angeles, 76; Fiberworks, Cleveland Mus of Art, Ohio, 77; The Americas & Japan--Fiberworks, Nat Mus Mod Art, Tokyo & Kyoto, Japan, 77; Solo exhibs, Allrich Gallery, San Francisco, Vanguard Gallery, Los Angeles, 77, Hunsaker Gallery, Los Angeles, Calif, 80 & 82 & Renwick Gallery, Washington, DC; Art Fabric: Mainstream, Am Fedn Arts: Mus Mod Art, San Francisco, Calif. *Collection Arranged:* Fiberworks (auth, catalog), Lang Art Gallery, Scripps Col, Claremont, Calif, 73; Inaugural Exhib, Mano Gallery, Chicago, 76; Paper Art (coauth, catalog), Galleries of the Claremont Cols, 77. *Teaching:* Asst prof art, Univ Calif, Los Angeles Exten, 70-77; from asst prof to assoc prof, Scripps Col & Claremont Grad Sch, 71-, chmn dept art, Scripps Col, 82-. *Awards:* Nat Endowment for the Arts Grants, 74 & 79; First Scripps Coll Fac Recognition Award, 81. *Bibliog:* Betty Pawk (auth), Interview with N Al-Hilali, Fiberarts Mag, 7/8/79; Scott Miller (auth), Cassiopeia's Court, Images & Issues, Vol 3, No 1; Nan Hackett (auth), Opposites, Seattle Post Intelligencer, 7/2/82. *Mem:* Artists Equity Asn; Am Crafts Coun; World Crafts Coun. *Media:* Mixed. *Res:* Historic textiles. *Dealer:* Allrich Gallery San Francisco CA; Joyce Munsaker Gallery 812 N La Cienega Blvd Los Angeles CA 90069. *Mailing Add:* 3114 Halm Ave Los Angeles CA 90034

ALICEA, JOSE
PRINTMAKER
b Ponce, PR, Jan 12, 1928. *Study:* Acad Pov, Ponce; Inst PR Cult, with Lorenzo Homar. *Work:* Philadelphia Mus Art; Mus Mod Art, NY; Libr of Cong, Washington, DC; Boston Pub Libr; Mus Arte Ponce. *Comn:* Woodcut mural, Inst PR Cult for Guayanilla High Sch, 70. *Exhib:* 4th Int Exhib of Drawing, Yugoslavia; 10th & 11th Biennale Int d'Art, Menton, France; 12th Biennale de Sao Paulo, Brazil; 2nd & 3rd Biennale Int de Grafica, Frechen, Ger; and others. *Pos:* Asst to dir, Inst PR Cult Workshop, 58-62, instr, currently. *Teaching:* Instr printmaking, Escuela Artes Plasticas, San Juan, 67-. *Awards:* Prize for Graphic, Ateneo Puertorriqueno, 65; Mildred Boerike Prize, Print Club Philadelphia, 67; Travel Grant, Casa Del Arte, San Juan, 68. *Bibliog:* E Ruiz de la Mata (auth), The art of Jose R Alicea, San Juan Rev Mag, 7/66 & Graphics by Alicea, San Juan Star, 8/9/70; Gloria Borras (auth), El grabado en la vida de Jose R Alicea, El Mundo, 69. *Media:* Miscellaneous. *Publ:* Illusr, Trovas larenas, 68; auth, Rio grande de Loiza (portfolio of prints), 68; Cancion de Baquine (portfolio of prints), 70; En las manos del pueblo, 72; Calambrenas

ALIKI, LIACOURAS BRANDENBERG
ILLUSTRATOR, WRITER
b Philadelphia, Pa, 1929. *Study:* Philadelphia Mus Coll Art, grad. *Work:* Kerlan Collection, Walter Libr, Univ Minn, Minneapolis; de Grummond Collection, Univ Southern Miss, Hattiesburg; Seattle Pub Libr, Wash; Falvey Mem Libr, Villanova Univ, Pa; Rutgers Univ Children's Literature Collection, New Brunswick, NJ; Free Libr Philadelphia; Mazza Collection, Ohio; Arne Nixon Ctr, Study of Children's Books. *Exhib:* Children's Bk Coun Showcase Exhib; Biennale of Illus, Bratislava, Czech, 75; Soc Illusr Exhib, NY; Am Inst Graphic Arts Bk Exhib. *Awards:* Children's Sci Book Award, NY Acad Scis, 77; Zilveren Griffel, Netherlands, 81; Garden State Children's Book Award, 82, 96; Omar's Book Award, 86; Prix del Libre, Switz, 87; Drexel Univ Free Libr Philadelphia Citation, 91; Pa Sch Librns Asn Award, 91; Jane Addams Picture Book Award, New York, 99. *Bibliog:* Grace Hogarth (auth), Illustrators of Children's Books, Horn Bk Inc, 78; Iris M Tiedt (auth), Exploring Books with Children, Houghton Mifflin, 79; Monson & Sutherlan (auths), Children & Books, Scott, Foresman, 81. *Media:* Watercolor, Crayon. *Res:* Research varies according to current book project. *Interests:* Gardening, cooking, traveling & reading. *Publ:* A Medieval Feast, 83, Digging Up Dinosaurs, 88, Harper/Collins; Feelings, Greenwillow, 84; Marianthe's Story, Greenwillow, 98; William Shakespeare and the Globe, Harper Collins, 99; Ah, Music!, 2003; A Play's the Thing, 2005; and many others. *Mailing Add:* 17 Regent's Park Terr London NW1 7ED United Kingdom

ALINDER, JAMES GILBERT
GALLERY OWNER, PHOTOGRAPHER
b Glendale, Calif, Mar 31, 1941. *Study:* Macalester Col, BA, 62; Univ Minn, 62-64; Univ NMex, MFA, 68. *Work:* Mus Mod Art, NY; Bibliotheque Nat, Paris; Art Inst Chicago & Mus Contemp Photog, Chicago; Int Mus Photog, George Eastman House, Rochester, NY; Nat Gallery Can, Ottawa; San Francisco Mus Mod Art; Victoria & Albert Mus, London, Eng; Stanford Univ, Ctr for Creative Photog; and others. *Comn:* Markets of Province, Mattson & Co. *Exhib:* Light, Hayden Gallery, Mass Inst Technol, 68; Solo exhibs, Sheldon Gallery, Univ Nebr, 69, Camerawork Gallery, San Francisco, 79 & Spiva Art Ctr, Joplin, Mo, 80; Be-Ing Without Clothes, Hayden Art Gallery, Mass Inst Technol, 70; The Diana Show, Wynn Bullock Gallery, Carmel, Calif, 80; Am Photog Today: Univ Colo, 82; Exposed & Developed, Nat Mus Am Art, Washington, 84; Family Portraits, Wright State Univ, 87; Photog Truth: Bruce Mus, 88; Retrospective, Int Photog Hall Fame, 92; Image and Text, Ctr Creative Photog, Univ Ariz, Tucson, 93; Somalia, As it Was, Alinder Gallery, Gualala, 93; Selections from the Permanent Collection, Mus Contemp Art, Los Angeles, 93; On the Road, Mus Fine Arts, Houston, 94; EvenColor, Ctr Arts, Vero Beach, Fla, 94; The Discerning Eye, Santa Cruz Mus Art, 94; The Enduring Illusion, Stanford Univ Mus Art, 95; The Family, Spencer Mus Art, Univ Kans, 97; Looking Back, Clear Sky Gallery, Lincoln, 98; 20/20 Mus NMex, Santa Fe, 2000; Classic Images, Ctr Creative Photog, Tucson, 2002; Edges and Intersections, Nat Steinbeck Ctr, Salinas, 2003; Reality Revisited, Monerna Museet, Stockholm, 2009; Altered Land, Sheldon Mus Art, Lincoln, Nebr, 2009. *Collection Arranged:* Wright Morris: Structures & Artifacts, Sheldon Mem Art Gallery, Lincoln, Nebr, 75; Crying for a Vision, 76; Twelve Photographers: A Mid-Am Contemporary Document, 78; Jerome Liebling: Retrospective, 78; New Color Work: Divola, Fitch, North, Ollman & Pfahl, 78; Ruth Bernhard Retrospective (with catalog), 79; The Contact Print (with catalog), 82; Ansel Adams Classic Images (with catalog), 86; Light Years, 87. *Pos:* Exec dir, Friends of Photog, Carmel, Calif, 77-87, bd trustees, 87, actg exec dir, 88-89 & juror Ferguson Grant, 92; bd trustees, Monterey Pen Mus Art, 86-, vpres, 87, pres, 88; vis artist, Sheldon Mus Univ Nebr, Lincoln, 1997. *Teaching:* Assoc prof photog & photog hist, Univ Nebr, Lincoln, 68-77; instr, Ansel Adams Yosemite Workshop, 79-81 & workshop, Jackson Hole, Wyo, 2003; lectr, Calif Hist Soc, San Francisco, 94, Stanford Univ Mus Art, 2002 & Joslyn Mus Art, Omaha, 2002. *Awards:* Nat Endowment Arts Fel, 73 & 80; Woods Found Fel, 74. *Bibliog:* N Geske (ed), Photographs, Univ Nebr Press, 77; J Enyeart (ed), Kansas Album, Kans Bankers Asn, 77; J Green (auth), Am Photog, Abrams, 84. *Mem:* Soc Photog Educ (ed Exposure, 73-77, secy, 73-75, vchmn, 75-77, chmn, 77-79); Photog Arts & Sci Found (pres, 85); Monterey Co Cult Coun (chmn, 81-82); Am Asn Mus. *Media:* Photography. *Specialty:* Ansel Adams . *Publ:* Coauth, Ansel Adams: Classic Images, 85 & The Sea Ranch, 2004; intro, Quiet Light, 90; contribr, ViewCamera Mag, 94; ed, Solomon's Temple, 96; auth, Sparkling Harvest, Abrams, 97; coauth, Houses Made of Wood and Light, UT Press, 2012; The Sea Ranch, PAP, 2013. *Mailing Add:* Alinder Gallery PO Box 449 Gualala CA 95445

ALINDER, MARY STREET
WRITER, CURATOR
b Bowling Green, Ohio, Sept 23, 1946. *Study:* Univ Mich; Univ NMex; Univ Nebr, BA, 76. *Comn:* Authentication of the work of Ansel Adams for mus, auction houses, insurance co and pvt individuals. *Collection Arranged:* Ansel Adams: 80th Birthday Retrospective - 150 Prints (auth, catalog), Monterey Mus Art & Calif Acad Sci, 82; Ansel Adams - 200 prints (auth, catalog), Denver Mus Natural Hist, 83; Ansel Adams - A 125 Print Exhib, Nat Mus Art, Beijing & People's Cult Palace, Shanghai, People's Repub China; One with Beauty - A 168 print Exhib retrospective of Ansel Adams (auth, catalog), The MH de Young Mem Mus, San Francisco, 87; Ansel Adams: Am Artist, The Ansel Adams Ctr, San Francisco, 89; Ansel Adams: Native Californian, State Capitol Bldg, Sacramento, Calif, 2001; Ansel Adams 100th Birthday Celebration (auth catalog), Green Ctr Music and Arts. *Pos:* Mgr, Weston Gallery, Carmel, Calif, 78-79; exec asst to Ansel Adams, Carmel, Calif, 79-84; exec ed & bus mgr, Ansel Adams Publ Rights Trust, 84-87; freelance, & co-owner Alinder Gallery, Gualala, Calif, 90-. *Teaching:* Lectr & instr workshops in US, France, Eng & People's Rep China, 82-86; Nat Gallery Art, Washington, DC, 85; Los Angeles Co Mus; MH de Young Mus; Univ Calif, Berkeley; Univ Mich; Univ Cincinnati; Cleveland Mus Natural Hist; Stanford Univ; High Mus Art; Calif Wilderness Collection; visiting artist & lectr, Univ Nebr, 97; speaker, Wallace Stegner Mem Lect, 98; team teacher, Lured to Taos: Artist Pilgrims in the Southwest, Stanford Univ, 2000. *Mem:* Ctr Creative Photog. *Res:* Work and life of Ansel Adams; Group f/64; creative photography. *Publ:* Ansel Adams: An Autobiography, 85; Ansel Adam: Letters and Images, 88; coauth, Seeing Straight: The F-64 Revolution in Photography, Oakland Mus, 92; selector & auth, all biographies, The Focal Encyclopedia of Photography, 3rd ed, Boston & London, 93; coauth, Beaumont Newhall: Colleagues and Friends, Mus NMex, 93; Ansel Adams, A Biography, Henry Holt, 96; auth, Motel Mabel: Mabel Dodge Luhan and Photography, View Camera, 98; Ansel Adams and Manzanar, Civilization, 99; coauth, Remembering Virginia, Anne Adams Helms, 2000. *Mailing Add:* PO Box 449 Gualala CA 95445-1146

ALLAIN, RENE PIERRE
PAINTER, SCULPTOR
b Montreal, Que, Dec 28, 1951. *Study:* Loyola Montreal, Que, CEGEP, 71; Univ Ottawa, Ont, BA (fine arts), 81; Hunter Col, City Univ New York, MFA, 86. *Work:* Brooklyn Mus, NY; Nat Gallery Can & Can Coun Art Bank, Ottawa, Ont; London Regional Art & Historical Mus, Ont; Wadsworth Atheneum, Hartford,Conn; Art Gallery Hamilton, Ont; and others. *Comn:* Pub sculpture, City of Ottawa, 82. *Exhib:* Mus Contemp Art, Montreal, Que, 84; selected NY Found Arts Artists, Univ Art Gallery, State Univ NY, Albany, 90; Open Mind: The Lewitt Collection, Wadsworth

Atheneum, Hartford, Conn, 91-92; Slow Art: Painting in New York Now, PS 1 Mus, 92; Presence, Ctr Int D'Art Contemporain Montreal (exhib catalog), 93-; The Steel Paintings (traveling), Univ Waterloo Art Gallery, Ont, 96; Steelwork, Littlejohn Contemp, NY, 96; New Paintings, Stefan Stux Gallery, NY, 98; One-woman shows, Galerie de Bellefeuille, Montreal, 98 & 2000, Stefan Stux Gallery, NY, 99, Winchester Galleries, Victoria, Can, 2001 & Roger Ramsay Gallery, Chicago, 2001. *Teaching:* Instr drawing, Sch Visual Arts, New York, 90-. *Awards:* B Grants, Can Coun, 84, 88 & 94; New York Found Arts Fel, 90; Nat Endowment Arts Fel, 91. *Bibliog:* Laurel Berger (auth), In their sights, ARTnews, 3/97; Jean-Jacques Bernier (auth), Aux limites de l'abstraction, Vie des Arts, Spring, 98; Tom McDonough (auth), Review, Art in Am, 4/2000. *Media:* Plaster, Pigments; Steel. *Publ:* Coauth, The Core Island Complex (exhib cat), London Regional Art & Historical Mus, 84. *Dealer:* Stux Gallery 529 W 20th St 9th Flr New York City, NY 10011; Roger Ramsay Gallery Ste 207 325 W Huron St Chicago Il 60610. *Mailing Add:* Ricco Maresca Gallery 529 W 20th St, 3rd Fl New York NY 10011

ALLARA, PAMELA EDWARDS
EDUCATOR
b Scarsdale, NY, Sept 11, 1943. *Study:* Brown Univ, BA, 65; Johns Hopkins Univ, PhD, 71. *Exhib:* Co-existence: Contemp Cult Production in South Africa (Waltham: Rose Art Mus and Cape Town: South African Nat Gallery, 2003). *Pos:* Bd trustees, Inst Contemp Art, Photog Resource Ctr, Boston & Rose Art Mus, Brandeis Univ. *Teaching:* Assoc dean, Mus Sch progs & sr lectr art hist, Fine Arts Dept, Tufts Univ, 73-90; asst prof, Fine Art Dept, Brandeis Univ, Waltham, Mass, 90-. *Awards:* 1998 Choice Outstanding Academic Book Award. *Mem:* Coll Art Asn. *Res:* Contemporary art; history of photography; film & women artists. *Publ:* Auth, Expressionism in Boston, de Cordova Mus, 86; Cross Currents/Cross Country, Photog Resource Ctr, Boston, 88; Exterior/Interior: Alice Neel, Tufts Univ Art Gallery, 90; Matter of Fact: Alice Neel's Pregnant Nudes, Am Art, 8/2/94; Pictures of People: Alice Neel's American Portrait Gallery, 98. *Mailing Add:* Brandeis Univ Dept Fine Arts Waltham MA 02254

ALLEN, BRIAN
MUSEUM DIRECTOR
Study: Wesleyan Univ, BA; Williams Coll, MA (Art History); Univ Conn Sch Law, JD; Yale Univ, Doctorate (Art History), 1998. *Pos:* Atty, Day, Berry & Howard, formerly; chief of staff for pres, Conn Gen Assembly, formerly; dir collections & exhibs, cur Am art, Sterling & Francine Clark Art Inst, Williamstown, Mass, 1997-2004; dir, Addison Gallery Art, Andover, Mass, 2004-. *Mailing Add:* Addison Gallery of American Art 180 Main St Andover MA 01810

ALLEN, BRUCE WAYNE
EDUCATOR, SCULPTOR
b Columbia, Mo, Feb 27, 1953. *Study:* Centenary Col, La, with Willard Cooper, BA, 75, BS, 77; Acad Der Bildenden Kunst, Stuttgart, WGer, 80-81; Univ Wyo, with David Reif & John van Alstein, MFA, 81. *Work:* Wyo State Mus, Cheyenne; Horizons Gallery, Ft Collins, Colo. *Comn:* Sculpture, Glory Bound, Univ Wyo, Laramie, 82; sculpture, Building Blocks, Red Devil Corp, Cincinnati, Ohio, 86. *Exhib:* Solo Exhib, Wyo State Mus, Cheyenne, 81. *Pos:* cur, Meadows Mus Art, currently. *Teaching:* prof studio & art history, Centenary Col La, 83-90. *Mem:* Art in Action (co-founder, 86); La Artists Inc (pres, 88-90); Int Sculpture Conf; Coll Art Asn; Women's Caucus for Arts; Shreveport Regional Arts Coun (vp). *Media:* All Media. *Mailing Add:* Centenary College Dept Art and Visual Culture Turner Art Ctr Rm 104 2911 Centenary Blvd Shreveport LA 71104

ALLEN, CONSTANCE OLLEEN WEBB
PAINTER, JEWELRY DESIGNER
b Camphill, Ala, June 10, 1923. *Study:* George Washington Univ; Inst Allende, San Miguel de Allende, Mex; also with Richard Goetz, Oklahoma City & Roy Swanson, Green Valley, Ariz. *Work:* Jane Brooks Sch Deaf; Chickasha Pub Libr. *Comn:* 20 Indian Portraits, AC Leftwich, Duncan, Okla, 72; Landscapes of Southwest Okla, comn by Susan Johnston, Oklahoma City, 78. *Exhib:* 39th & 41st Ann Miniature Painters, Sculptors & Gravers Soc of Washington, Art Club Washington, 72 & 74; Ann Festival of the Arts, Tubac, Ariz, 85, 87, 88, 89, 90, 92, 93 & 94; Ariz State Exhib, Nat League Am Pen Women, Sedona, 87, Phoenix, 89, Ariz; Mont Miniature Art Soc Ninth Ann Int Show, Billings, Mont, 87. *Teaching:* Instr drawing & painting, Univ Sci & Arts of Okla, Chickasha, 74-76. *Awards:* First Place for Pastel, Chickasha Art Guild, Okla, 73; Merit Award Graphic, Fla Nat Miniature Art Show, Okla, 76; First Place Watercolor, Santa Rita Art League Show, Nogales, Ariz, 87; Hon Mention, Santa Cruz Valley Art Asn, Tubac, Ariz, 86; and others. *Bibliog:* AC Leftwich (auth), Indian Hall of Fame, painted by Mrs Webb, 72 & Mrs NH Welch (auth), Mrs Webb has exhib, 74 Chickasha Daily Express; Dale Parish (auth), Artist paints favorite subjects, Green Valley News, 84. *Mem:* Santa Rita Art League, Ariz (pres, 83-84); Nat League Am Pen Women (pres, Sonora Desert Br, 88-90); Arts & Crafts Asn, Green Valley, Ariz, (vpres, 86-87); Santa Cruz Valley Art Asn, Tubac, Ariz. *Media:* Watercolor, Pastels, Precious Metals, Gemstones

ALLEN, E DOUGLAS
PAINTER, WRITER, SCULPTOR
b Jersey City, NJ, Mar 18, 1935. *Study:* Ford Sch, Jersey City, NJ, 45-51; Newark Sch of Fine Indust Arts, 53-55; WJ Aylward (Howard Pyle pupil), John Graback, Charles Waterhouse, Paul Bransom (summer classes Wyoming), 60-61. *Work:* Nat Mus Wildlife Art, Jackson, Wyo; Glenbow Mus, Calgary, Can; Hiram Blauvelt Art Mus, Oradell, NJ; Johnson & Johnson Collection, New Brunswick, NJ; PNC Bank Corp Collection, Philadelphia, Pa; Brandywine River Mus, Chadds Ford, Pa. *Comn:* Leather Stocking Tales (mural), Lincoln High Sch, Jersey City, NJ, 52-53. *Exhib:* Western Vision, Ann Nat Mus Wildlife Art, Jackson Hole Wyo, 91-2008; DA, A Retrospective Exhib 1945-1995, Hiram Blauvelt Art Mus, Oradel, NJ, 95; Reflections of Nature, Newington Cropsey Art Found, Hastings, NY, 98; Wildlife for a New Century, Nat Mus Wildlife Art, Jackson, Wyo, 2005; Prix de West, Nat Cowboy & Western Heritage Mus, Okla City, 2005-2008. *Collection Arranged:* Animal Art (assembled), Brandywine River Mus, 74; Charles Livingston Bull Exhib (co-cur exhibits & wrote artists bio & bibliog for catalog), Hiram Blauvelt Art Mus, Oradel, NJ, 94. *Pos:* Jury chmn, exec bd, Soc Animal Artists, NY, 90-2008. *Teaching:* Instr, private classes, Somerville, NJ, 68-74. *Awards:* Nat Wildlife Fedn, Washington, DC, 52; Small Exhib Award, Salmagundi Club, 62; Award of Excellence, Soc Animal Artists, 85; Bott Borghi-Brnasom, Animal Artist Legacy Award, Soc Animal Artists, 2006. *Bibliog:* Bonnie Silverstein (auth), Douglas Allen: Echoes of the Brandywine, Am Artist, 77; Zack Taylor (auth), Outdoor Art of Doug Allen, Sports Afield, 84; Terry Wieland (auth), Painting Animals Inside Out, Sporting Classics, 90. *Mem:* Salmagundi Club, NY, 60-2006; Soc Animal Artists (jury chmn & exec bd), 61-; Du Cret Art Sch (bd mem), Plainfield, NJ, 90-. *Media:* Oil, Metal, Cast. *Specialty:* Hist western art, Taos Painters & contemp sporting art. *Interests:* Spend at least one mo per yr in West, Can Rockies & Africa painting, drawing & photographing animals & landscapes; Continually collect, write & res the publ works of artist NC Wyeth. *Collection:* Works of NC Wyeth, Howard Pyle, Carl Rungius, Fredric Remington & 19th century animal artists. *Publ:* Illusr, The Big Game Animals of North America, Dutton Outdoor Life, 61; Complete Book of Hunting, Harper Brothers, 62; coauth, NC Wyeth: Paintings, Illus & Murals, Crown Publ Co, 72; illusr, Game Birds of North America, Harpers Outdoor Life, 73; Game Animals of North America, Crown Outdoor Life, 78. *Dealer:* JN Bartfield Galleries Michael Frost 30 W 57th St NY 10019. *Mailing Add:* 9 Craig Rd Neshanic Station NJ 08853

ALLEN, EDDA LYNNE
PAINTER, ART DEALER
b Big Spring, Tex, July 29, 1932. *Study:* With Randall Davey, Will Schuster & William Longley, 57-62; Southern Methodist Univ; Tex Tech Univ; Univ NMex; Coll Santa Fe, BA (summa cum laude), 68. *Work:* Santa Fe Co Munic Ct, NMex State Capitol, Mayors Off, Santa Fe; NMex State Police Off. *Exhib:* Joslyn Art Mus, Omaha, Nebr, 72; Artist Alpine Holiday, Ouray Arts Asn, Colo, 72; Arts Festival, NMex Art League, Albuquerque, 72-74; Roswell Mus & Art Ctr, NMex, 73; Solo exhib, NMex State Fair, 75. *Teaching:* Instr tech, Col of Santa Fe, 67-68; lectr Alla Prima tech, Univ NMex, 70-71. *Awards:* Award of Merit, Am Arthritis Found, 75; First in Show, Rio Grande Arts & Crafts, 77-78. *Mem:* Santa Fe Soc Art. *Media:* Oil, Watercolor

ALLEN, HENRY SOUTHWORTH
CRITIC
b Summit, NJ, May 23, 1941. *Study:* Hamilton Col, BA, 67. *Pos:* Copy ed, New Haven (Conn) Register, 66; reporter, New York News, New York City, 67-70; reporter, ed, critic, The Wash Post, 70-; Teacher in cult and meaning, Univ Md Honors Prog. *Awards:* Nat Endowment of the Humanities fel for journalists, Univ Mich, 75-76; Recipient Am Soc Newspaper Editors award for commentary, 92; Am Soc of Sunday and Feature Editors prize for creative writing, finalist Pulitzer prize, 94; Pulitzer prize Journalism for Criticism, 2000; Sherwood Media award, Blinded Ams Veterans Found, 2000. *Mem:* Marine Corps Hist Asn. *Publ:* Auth, Fool's Mercy, 1982; auth, Glare, 1991; auth, Going Too Far Enough, 1994; What It Felt Like Living in the Am Century, 2000; auth, articles in, NY Review of Books, New Yorker, Forbes, Paris Review, Smithsonian, Vogue, Wilson Quarterly.

ALLEN, JERE HARDY
PAINTER, EDUCATOR
b Selma, Ala, Aug 15, 1944. *Study:* Ringling Sch Art, Sarasota, Fla, four yr cert, 69, BFA, 70; Univ Tenn, Knoxville, MFA, 72. *Work:* Mobile Mus Art, Ala; Coos Art Mus, Ore; Liberty Corp, Greenville, SC; R I Kahn Gallery, Houston; Meridian Mus Art, Miss; City of Hameln, WGer; Huntsville Mus Art, Ala ; La State Univ Mus Art, Baton Rouge. *Exhib:* West 79 and 80/The Law, Minn Mus Art, 79 & 80; Der Kunstkreis Hameln, 89; Oldenburger Kunstuerein, 89; Stadtische Galerie, Paderborn, WGer, 90; Brenau Coll, Gainesville, Ga, 92; Carol Robinson Gallery, New Orleans, La, 92; Outward Bound, Am Art at the Brink of the Twenty-First Century, Meridian Int Ctr, Washington; plus others; Solo Exhibs: Peoria Contemp Arts Center. *Teaching:* Instr drawing, Carson-Newman Col, 71-72; prof painting, Univ Miss, 72-2000. *Awards:* Award of Distinction, Mainstreams of Marietta Col, 75; Award, Shreveport Nat, Barnwell Art Ctr, La, 75; Visual Arts Award, Miss Inst Arts & Letts, 93. *Media:* Oil, Mixed Media. *Mailing Add:* c/o Carol Robinson Gallery 840 Napoleon Blvd New Orleans LA 70115

ALLEN, JONATHAN
PAINTER, COLLAGE ARTIST
b New York, NY, 1975. *Study:* Columbia Univ, New York, BA, 1997. *Work:* Microsoft Corp. *Exhib:* At Issue, Queens Theatre in the Park, New York, 2001; In Response, Savannah Coll Art & Design, Ga, 2002; Founders Day, Spencertown Acad, NY, 2003; The Presidency, Exit Art, New York, 2004; Sub-version, PS 122, New York, 2005; Evolve Dissovle, Go North Gallery, Beacon, New York, 2007; A Wrinkle in Time, Rotunda Gallery, Brooklyn, 2008; Human Nature Machine, Wonderland Art Space, Copenhagen, 2009. *Awards:* Louise Sudler Prize, Columbia Univ, 1997; Puffin Found Grant, 2003; George Sugarman Found Grant, 2004; Pollock-Krasner Found Grant, 2008. *Bibliog:* Holland Cotter (auth), Critical Consumption, NYTimes, 3/7/2003; Kim Levin, (auth), The Presidency, Village Voice, 10/2004; Dan Bischoff (auth), The Art of War, The Star Ledger, 5/11/2006; Anita Tan (auth), Tips and Picks, NY Arts Mag, 9-10/2008

ALLEN, JUDITH S
PHOTOGRAPHER, EDUCATOR
b New York, NY, Jan 21, 1956. *Study:* Oberlin Col, BA, 77; Mills Col, MFA, 90. *Exhib:* San Francisco Arts Comn Gallery, 91; Bellevue Art Mus, Wash, 94; Ctr Contemp Art, Seattle, Wash, 94; Photographic Ctr NW, Seattle, Wash, 2002; Tacoma Art Mus, 2004; Ctr Contemp Art, Seattle, Wash, 2006. *Teaching:* lectr photog, San

Francisco State Univ, 91-92; assoc prof art, Cornish Col Arts, 92-. *Awards:* Trefethen Award, Mills Col, 89; Visual Artist Fel, Nat Endowment Arts, 90-91; Betty Bowen Memorial-Spec Recognition Award, Seattle Art Mus, 94; Cornish Excellence in Teaching Award, Cornish Coll Arts, 2000. *Mem:* Coll Art Asn; Soc Photog Educ. *Media:* Mixed Media. *Mailing Add:* Cornish Col Arts 1000 Lenora St Seattle WA 98121

ALLEN, KAOLA See Phoenix, Kaola Allen

ALLEN, PAUL
COLLECTOR
b Seattle, Jan 21, 1953. *Study:* Wash State Univ, 1971-73. *Pos:* Co-founder, Traf-O-Data Co, Seattle, 1972-73; programmer, Honeywell Int Inc, Waltham, 1974-75; co-founder, Microsoft Corp (formerly Micro-Soft), Albuquerque, 1975, general partner, 1975-77, vpres, 1977-81, exec vpres res & new product develop, 1981-83, bd dir, 1983-2000, sr strategy adv, 2000-; founder, Asymetrix Corp, Bellevue, Wash, 1985, Starwave Corp, Bellevue, 1992, Experience Music Project, Allen Institute Brain Sci, 2003, Experience Sci Fiction Mus, 2004, Allen Telescope Array & SETI Inst Univ Calif Berkeley, 2004; chief exec officer, Vulcan Ventures, Bellevue, 1987-; co-founder, Interval Research Corp, Palo Alto, Calif, 1992; owner & chmn, Portland Trail Blazers, Ore, 1988-, Seattle Seahawks, 1997-; chmn, Charter Communications Inc, 1998-, Charter Investment, Inc, 1998-; sponsor & founder, SpaceShipOne Venture, Mojave, Calif, 2003; owner, TechTV; bd dir, Egghead Discount Software, Darwin Molecular, Inc; partner, DreamWorks SKG; founder & chmn, Vulcan Inc, Seattle. *Awards:* Named one of Top 15 Philanthropists in America; named one of Top 200 Collectors, ARTnews mag, 2004-13; named to Computer Mus Hall of Fame; Ansari X Prize, 2004. *Bibliog:* auth, Idea Man: A Memoir by the Co-Founder of Microsoft, Penguin, NY, 2011. *Collection:* Impressionism, Old Masters, modern & contemporary art, tribal art. *Mailing Add:* Vulcan Inc 505 5th Ave S Ste 900 Seattle WA 98104

ALLEN, ROBERTA
CONCEPTUAL ARTIST, PHOTOGRAPHER
b New York, NY, Oct 6, 1945. *Work:* Metrop Mus Art, NY; Cooper-Hewitt Mus, NY; Cincinnati Art Mus; Univ Wis-Milwaukee; Stadtische Galerie im Lenbachhaus, Munich; Bibliotheque du France, Paris; Yale Univ Coll, Wadsworth, Atheneum, Conn; Art Gallery of Western Australia, Perth. *Exhib:* Solo exhibs, John Weber Gallery, NY, 74, 75, 77 & 79, Kunstforum, Staadtische Gallerie im Lenbachhaus, Munich, 81, Galerie Walter Storms, Munich, 81, Galeria Primo Piano, Rome, 81, Perth Inst Contemp Arts, Australia, 89 & Art Resources Transfer Inc, 2001, Minus Space, 2014; Contemp Abstract Art: Works on Paper, Baltimore Mus Art, 76; Abstract Drawings, Albright-Knox Art Gallery, Buffalo, NY, 76; MTL Galerie, Brussels, Belg, 78; and others. *Collection Arranged:* Metrop Mus Art, NY; Bibliotheque Nat, Paris; Cincinnati Art Mus; Yale Univ Collection; Wadsworth Atheneum, Conn. *Teaching:* Guest lectr, Corcoran Sch Art, Washington, DC, 75, CW Post Coll, Glenville, NY, 79, Kutztown Univ, 79 & Ctr Fine Arts, Univ W Australia, 89; vis fel, Curtin Univ, Perth, Australia, 89. *Awards:* Residence Fel Yaddo, 83; Fel, Va Ctr for Creative Arts, 85; Artist-in-Residence Fel, Art Gallery W Australia, Perth, 89. *Bibliog:* Jeff Deitch (auth), Roberta Allen, Arts Mag, 2/78; Judith Lopez Cardozo (auth), Roberta Allen, Artforum, 2/78; Holly O'Grady (auth), The paradoxical arrow: Roberta Allen's installations and books, Arts Mag, 2/79. *Media:* Photography, drawing, collage, digital prints. *Publ:* Auth, Pointless Arrows, pvt publ, 76; Pointless Acts, Collation Ctr, 77; Possibilities, John Weber Gallery & Parasol Press, 77; Everything in the World There is to Know by Somebody, But Not by the Same Knower, Ottenhausen Verlag, Munich, 81; The Traveling Woman, Vehicle Ed, 86. *Dealer:* Matthew Deleget Minus Space 111 Front St Ste 200 Brooklyn NY 11201. *Mailing Add:* 5 W 16th St New York NY 10011

ALLEN, STAN
ARCHITECT, EDUCATOR
Study: Brown Univ, BA; Cooper Union Sch Archit, B Arch; Princeton Univ, MArch. *Pos:* Richard Meier and Partners, NYC, formerly; architect, with Rafael Moreno, Spain, formerly; architect, prin, SAA/Stan Allen Archit, NYC, 90-. *Teaching:* prof, dir advanced design program, Columbia Univ Grad Sch Archit, Planning, & Preservation, 89-2002; dean, George Dutton '27 prof archit design, Princeton Univ Sch Archit, NJ, 2002-. *Awards:* President's Citation, The Cooper Union, 2002; Fel, NY Found Arts, 86; NY State Coun Arts, Design Arts Grant, NEA, 90; Grand Found fel, 93. *Mem:* AIA (fel); Nat Acad. *Publ:* contbr, Points and Lines: Diagrams and Projects for the City, Princeton Archit Press, NY, 99, reissued, 2004; Practice, Architecture, Technique and Representation, Routledge, 2008; Landform Building: Architecture's New Terrain, Lars Muller, 2011. *Mailing Add:* SAA 274 Water St No 3 New York NY 10038

ALLEN, TERRY
MULTI-MEDIA ARTIST
b Wichita, Kans, May 7, 1943. *Study:* Chouinard Art Inst, Los Angeles, BFA, 66. *Work:* Mus Mod Art & Metrop Mus Art, NY; Los Angeles Co Mus Art & Mus Contemp Art, Los Angeles; San Francisco Mus Mod Art, Calif; Dallas Mus Art, Tex; Oakland Mus Art, Calif; plus many others. *Exhib:* Extraordinary Realities (with catalog) & 1973 Biennial Exhib (with catalog), 73 & Whitney Biennial, Whitney Mus, NY, 77; Selections from Cirrus Editions (with catalog), Los Angeles Co Mus Art, Calif, 74; Eight from Calif (with catalog), Nat Collection Fine Arts, Smithsonian Inst, Washington, DC, 75; The Small Scale in Contemp Art (with catalog), Chicago Art Inst, Ill, 75; Painting & Sculpture in California: The Modern Era (with catalog), San Francisco Mus Mod Art, Calif, traveling, 76; The Modern Era: Bay Area Update, Huntsville Mus Art, Ala, 77; The Record as Artwork (with catalog), Fort Worth Art Mus, Tex, traveling, 77; New Acquisitions Exhib (Prints), Mus Mod Art, NY, 77; Aesthetics of Graffiti, San Francisco Mus Mod Art, Calif, 78; The Southern Voice (with catalog), Ft Worth Art Mus, Tex, 81; Exchange Between Artists 1931-82, Poland-USA (with catalog), Mus Mod Art, Paris, France, 82; Awards in Visual Arts (with catalog), Nat Gallery, Washington, DC, traveling, 82; Site Strategies (with catalog), Oakland Mus, Calif, 83; Boston Collects: Contemp Painting & Sculpture (with catalog), Boston Mus Fine Arts, Mass, 86; Avant Garde in the Eighties (with catalog), Los Angeles Co Mus Art, Calif, 87; Lost & Found in California: Four Decades of Assemblage Art, James Corcoran Gallery, traveling, 88; Centenary Print Exhib, Mod Mus Ft Worth, Tex, 92; Profiles II: On Paper (with catalog), Adair Margo Gallery, El Paso, Tex, traveling, 92; Printmaking in Tex: The 1980's, Laguna Gloria Mus, Austin, Tex, 92; La Frontera-The Border (with catalog), Mus Contemp Art, San Diego, Calif, traveling, 93-94; Mapping, UTSA Art Gallery, Univ Tex, San Antonio, traveling, 94; solo shows, Moody Gallery, Houston, Tex, 94 & 96, Blaffer Gallery, Univ Houston, Tex, 94, Blue Star Art Space, San Antonio, Tex, 94, Univ Mo Kansas City Gallery Art, 95, LA Louver Gallery, Venice, Calif, 96, Barry Whistler Gallery, Dallas, Tex, 97 & Michael Solway Gallery, Cincinnati, Ohio, 97; The Prints of Cirrus Edition, Los Angeles Co Mus, Calif, 95; Temporarily Possessed, New Mus, NY, 95; Am Kaleidoscope, Nat Mus Am Art, Washington, DC, 96; Scene of the Crime, Univ Calif Los Angeles, Armand Hammer Mus Art & Cult Ctr, 97; Stephen F Austin State Univ Dept Art, Griffith Gallery, Nacogdoches, Tex, 98; plus many other group & solo shows. *Teaching:* Instr drawing, Chouinard Art Inst, Los Angeles, 68-69; guest artist & lectr, numerous univ, mus & institutions, 71-84; assoc prof, 74-77, Calif State Univ, Fresno, prof, 78-79. *Awards:* Nat Endowment Arts Fel, 70, 78 & 85; Bessie Award, NY, 86; Guggenheim Fel, 96; US Artists Oliver Fel, 2009. *Bibliog:* Jody Zellen (auth), Terry Allen, Arts Mag, 10/91; Joan Smith (auth), He'll Take it and Make Art, San Francisco Examiner, 10/91; Benjamin Weissman (auth), Terry Allen, Artforum, 11/91. *Publ:* Auth & coauth, numerous theatre & music performance recordings, 68-94; featured on numerous radio progs, 71-93; auth & coauth, numerous videos, 76-94; coauth, A Simple Story (juarez), Wexner Ctr Arts, Columbus, Ohio, 92; Poison Armor, Blue Star Art Space, San Antonio, Tex, 94; and many more. *Dealer:* Moody Gallery 2815 Colquitt Houston TX 77098

ALLEN, TOM
PAINTER
b Westfield, Mass, 1975. *Study:* Univ Southern Calif, BFA, 1998; Art Ctr Coll Design, Pasadena, Calif, MFA, 2001. *Exhib:* Solo exhibs include Richard Telles Fine Art, Los Angeles, 2002, 2003, 2006, Galerie Michael Janssen, Cologne, Germany, 2005, 2008; Group exhibs include Morbid Curiosity, Acme, Los Angeles, 2001, I-20 Gallery, New York, 2002; What a Painting Can Do, Hayworth, Los Angeles, 2002 ; Emergent Behavior, At the Brewery Projs, Los Angeles, 2002; Crisp, Marianne Boesky Gallery, New York, 2002 ; Now Is a Good Time, Andrea Rosen Gallery, New York, 2004; Follow Me: A Fantasy, Arena Gallery, Santa Monica, 2005; The Great Outdoors, Angles Gallery, Santa Monica, 2005; Plip, Plip, Plippity, Richard Telles Fine Art, Los Angeles, 2005 ; Alle-Gory, Mandarin, Los Angeles, 2005; LA Trash & Treasure, Milliken Gallery, Stockholm, 2006 ; Against the Grain, Los Angeles Contemp Exhibs, 2008. *Mailing Add:* Richard Telles Gallery 7380 Beverly Blvd Los Angeles CA 90036

ALLEN, WILLIAM J
HISTORIAN, EDUCATOR
b Tuscaloosa, Ala, Nov 8, 1945. *Study:* Univ Ala, BA, 68; Johns Hopkins Univ, MA, 73, PhD (Kress Fel, Am Res Inst Turkey Fel), 81. *Teaching:* Vis asst prof, Okla State Univ, 77-79; assoc prof art hist, Ark State Univ, Jonesboro, 79-, chmn art dept, 83-87, dean Col Fine Arts, 87-91, prof art hist, 91- & dir Ctr Learning Technol, 97-2005. *Mem:* Coll Art Asn Am; Hist Photog Group (nat coordr 87-). *Res:* history of photography. *Publ:* Auth, The Spirit of fact in court: Southworth's testimony in Marcy vs Barnes, In: History of Photography, 83 & The Abdul Hamid II collection, 83, Legal Tests of Photography-as-Art: Sarony and Others, 86, History of Photography; Sixty-Nine Istanbul Photographers in Shadow and Substance: Essays on the History of Photography in Honor of Heinz K Henisch, 90; coauth, The McGraw-Hill Guide to Electronic Research in Art, 99 & Teaching Composition Digitally, Visual Resources XV, 99. *Mailing Add:* 1224 S Madison St Jonesboro AR 72401

ALLGOOD, CHARLES HENRY
ART HISTORIAN, PAINTER
b Augusta, Ga, Apr 24, 1923. *Study:* Univ Ga, with Lamar Dodd, Carl Holty, Yasuo Kunyoshi, BFA, MFA; Ecole du Louvre, Paris. *Exhib:* Painting of the Yr, Atlanta, Ga, 63 & 65; Southeastern Art Exhib, Atlanta, 65; Miss Nat Exhib, Jackson, 66; Mid-South Exhib, Memphis, Tenn, 71. *Collection Arranged:* African Art & Artifacts, 74; Egyptian Art & Artifacts, 75. *Pos:* Dir, EH Little Gallery, Memphis State Univ; illusr children's bks, 89. *Teaching:* Prof painting, Judson Col, Marion, Ala, 51-55 & Memphis State Univ, 55-89. *Media:* Oil, Transparent Watercolor. *Mailing Add:* 1929 Brooksedge Dr Germantown TN 38138

ALLING, JANET D
PAINTER
b New York, NY Dec 19, 1939. *Study:* Skidmore Coll, 57-60; Yale Univ Sch Art, MFA, 64; studied with Alex Katz, Neil Welliver, Philip Pearlstein. *Work:* Univ Va Art Mus, Charlottesville; The Tang Teaching Mus, Skidmore Coll, Saratoga Springs, NY; York Coll, City Univ NY & Brooklyn City Tech Coll; Florists Transworld Deliveries Art Collection, Mich; Newport Art Mus, Newport, RI. *Comn:* Cape Primrose (painting), comn by Hugh Hardy, NY, 81; Garvins Restaurant, comn by Richard Garvin, NY, 82; Lobelia, comn by Virginia Stein, Somerville, NJ, 88. *Exhib:* Solo exhibs, St Mary's Coll Md, 90, Vassar Coll, Poughkeepsie, NY, 90, Komblee Gallery, 74, 79, 55 Mercer St, Coop Gallery, 72, Princeton Day Sch, 87, Trinity Coll, Vt, 94, Newport Art Mus, Newport, RI, 2010; group exhibs: Painterly Realists, Art Sch, Art Inst Chicago, 72; Color Light Image Exhib for United Nations, NY, 75; York Coll, City Univ NY, 95; Gallery at 17 Peck, Providence, RI, 2006; The Essence of Flowers: Redefining Flower Painting, Arsenal Gallery, Central Park, NY Parks and Recreation, 2011; Mem Show, Newport Art Mus, 2012; A Coastal Living Gallery, 2013. *Teaching:* Instr, oil & watercolor painting, Brooklyn Mus Art Sch, 73-77; instr, oil painting, Bronxville Adult School, Bronxville, NY, 89-2005. *Awards:* CAPS Award, NY State

Coun Arts, 73; Support Grant, Adolph Gottlieb Found, 88; Fel Grant, Nat Endowment Arts, 89. *Bibliog:* Cindy Nemser (auth), The Close Up Vision-Representative Art, Arts Mag, 72; Bob Stone (auth), Janet Alling's Passionate Eye, Am Artist Mag, 10/94. *Media:* Oil, Watercolor. *Interests:* Art hist, literature, music, physics. *Publ:* Flora: Paintings by Janet Alling, Beaufort Books Inc, June 2010. *Mailing Add:* 88 Orange St Unit 2B Providence RI 02903

ALLMAN, MARGO
PAINTER, SCULPTOR

b New York, NY, Feb 23, 1933. *Study:* Smith Coll; Moore Coll Art; Univ Pa; Univ Del; with Leonard Nelson, Reginald Marsh & Hans Hofmann. *Work:* Del Art Mus, Wilmington; Philadelphia Mus Art. *Comn:* Travertine sculpture, comn by Mrs Werner Hutz & family, Kennett Square, Pa, 73; cor-ten steel sculpture, comn by Richard Vanderbilt, Chadds Ford, Pa, 74; ferro-cement sculpture, Tidewater Publ co, Centerville, Md, 75; bronze sculpture, comn by Wesley & Harriet Memeger Jr, Wilmington, Del, 90. *Exhib:* Del Art Mus, 56-81, 93, 2000, 2010; Univ Del, 65-72 & 76; solo exhibs, Haas Gallery Art, Bloomsburg State Coll, Pa, 76-77, Moore Coll Art, 79 & Del State Art Coun, 81; West Chester Univ, Pa, 94, 2008-2012, & 2014; Del Ctr Contemp Art, 2002 & 05; Parallel Visions, Vonderau Mus, Fulda, Ger, 2007 & Towson Univ, Towson, MD, Coral Spring Mus Art, Fla, 2009, Villanova Univ, Pa, 2011; Serpentine Gallery, West Chester, Pa, 2011; Blue Streak Gallery, Wilmington, Del, 2012; The Delaplaine Visual Arts Edn Ctr, Frederick, Md, 2013; Affinities Regional Ctr for Women in the Arts, Widener Univ, Chester, PA, 2014. *Teaching:* Instr, Del Inst Arts Educ, 84-85. *Awards:* Drawing Prize, 51st Ann Show, Del Art Mus, 65; Best Landscape, Wilmington Trust Bank Prize, Del Art Mus, 69; Distinguished Alumnae Award, Moore Coll Art & Design, 98. *Bibliog:* Linnette Maxson (auth), Space, Time and Something to Say, Chester Co Press, 10/14/98; Renee Paquin (auth), West Grove woman to exhibit in Biennial 2000, The Kennett Paper, 5/25/2000; Victoria Donohoe (auth), Contemplative Works Examine Structure of Life, The Philadelphia Inquirer, 6/2/2002; JD Samuel (auth), Local artist masters the oval shape, The Avon Grove Sun, Pa, 11/16-22/2006; Victoria Donohoe (auth), Allman's Abstracts, the Philadelphia Inquirer, 10/03/2008; Catherine Quillman (auth), Artists of the Brandywine Valley, pp 214-215, Schiffer, 2010; Virginia M daCosta (auth), Serpentine Gallery Features Abstract Work from Two Locals, Daily Local News, West Chester, Pa, 10/28/2011; Victoria Donohoe (auth), Artists and Art, Are in Contrast, The Philadelphia Inquirer, 11/25/2011. *Mem:* Del Ctr Contemp Arts; Del Art Mus; Nat Mus Women Arts; Syne, a Delaware Valley Consortium of Nine Professional Artists; Regional Ctr for Women in the Arts; Woodmere Art Mus, Pa; Phila Art Mus. *Media:* Acrylic, Miscellaneous Media; Carved Concrete, Miscellaneous Media. *Mailing Add:* 202 State Rd West Grove PA 19390

ALLMOND, CHARLES
SCULPTOR

b Wilmington, Del, Apr 25, 1931. *Study:* Univ Del, BS, 53, MS, 57; Sch Law, Temple Univ, JD, 63. *Work:* Hercules Inc, NY; Hiram Blauvelt Art Mus, Oradell, NJ; Leigh Yawkey Woodson Art Mus, Wausau, Wis; Biggs Mus of Am Art, Dover, Del; Morris Libr Univ of Del, Newark, Del; Del State Bar Asn; Grace Episcopal Church, Wilmington, Del; Salmagundi Club, NY. *Comn:* Madonna and Child, Christ in Christmas Comt, Wilmington, 89; Ode to Joy, Class of 1953, Morris Libr, Univ Del, 93; Cantilevers, Frank Lloyd Wright House, Wilmington, 96 & 2002; State of Del for Ambassador of Arts Award, 2004. *Exhib:* Nat Acad Design Ann, NY, 88; Salmagundi Club Ann, NY, 89-93, 95-2008; Art and the Animal, Ann, 87-2013 & Touring, 90-2010; Woodmere Art Mus, Philadelphia, 94, 95 & 98-2003, 2006; Birds in Art Ann 94-97, 99, 2001-2003, 2008, 2010, 2011 & Touring, 94-95, 96-99, 2001-2003, 2008, 2010, & 2011; The Am Coll, Bryn Mawr, Pa, 94 & 98; Hiram Blauvelt Art Mus, Oradell, NJ, 98; Ira Spanierman Gallery, NY, 98; Ward Mus Wildfowl Art, Salisbury, Md, 99-2001, 2009; Del Div Arts, Wilmington, 2000; Audubon Artists, NY, 2000-2007, 2011-2013; outdoor sculpture exhib, Leigh Yawkey Woodson Art Mus, 2002-2003; Biggs Mus Am Art, Dover, Del, 2003, 2012; Toad Hall Gallery, Grounds for Sculpture, Hamilton, NJ, 2003-2004; Aerie Art Gallery, Rehoboth Beach, Del, 2005-2007, 2011; Shidoni Galleries, Tesuque, NMex, 2006; Am Swedish Hist Mus, 2008; Int Game Fish Asn, 2011. *Pos:* Pres, Soc of Animal Artists, 95-2001. *Teaching:* Guest lectr enrichment ser, Acad Lifelong Learning, Univ Del, 88, Gloucester Co Coll, Sewell, NJ, 99, World Wild Life Art Brought to Life Symp, Bjorklunden, Lawrence Univ, Wis, 2000 & It's Wild Out There confs, West Valley Art Mus, Surprise, Ariz, 2001. *Awards:* Soc of Animal Artists Award of Excellence, 87, 98-2000, 2002 & 2010; Salmagundi: Club Sculpture Awards, 89, 90, 92, 96, 99-2004, 2006-2008; Woodmere Art Mus Sculpture Awards, 94, 2002; Audubon Artists Sculpture Awards, 2001, 2002, 2004, 2005, & 2012; Governor's Award for the Arts, Del, 2004; Alumni Wall of Fame, Univ Del, 2007; Bott-Borghi Bransom Legacy Award, 2008; Best in Show, Ward Wildlife Sculpture Competition, 2013. *Bibliog:* Fine Woodworking Design Book Seven, Taunton Press, 96; The Edge of Abstraction, Wildlife Art/Sculpture Forum, 7-8/97; Natural Habitat: Contemporary Wildlife Artists of North America, Spanierman Gallery, LLC, NY; Artistic Elements that Create a Sense of Style; J Brown, Wildlife Art, 2003; dir (film), Charles Allmond, Sculptor, Del Div Arts, 2004. *Mem:* Soc Animal Artists (master signature mem 2008); Salmagundi Club (hon mem, 2011); Rehoboth Art League; Audubon Artists; Delaware By Hand (master, 2011). *Media:* Stone, Bronze, Wood. *Publ:* Cover illusr, Rehoboth Art League Members Fine Art Show Catalog, 89; contribr, Del Today Mag, 7/91; cover for invitation, Beebe Hosp Dinner & Auction, 94; cover, Rehoboth Art League Calendar, 96; illus, Jeffery Whiting's Owls of North America, Heliconia Press, Clayton, Ontario, 97; poster, Soc of Animal Artists Ann Exhib, 2002. *Dealer:* Shidoni Galleries 1508 Bishops Lodge Rd Tesuque NM 87574; Somerville Manning Gallery Breck's Mill 101 Stone Block Rd Greenville DE 19807; Aeric Art Gallery 451/2 Lake St Rehoboth Beach DE 19971; Hardcastle Gallery 5714 Kennett Pike Centreville DE 19807. *Mailing Add:* 104 Rowland Park Blvd Wilmington DE 19803

ALLRICH, M LOUISE BARCO
ART DEALER, ART CONSULTANT

b Ft Monroe, Va, Feb 16, 1947. *Study:* Univ Calif, Davis, BA, 68; Univ Calif, Berkeley, post-grad work art hist & theory; Univ Calif, Irvine, Appraisal Studies in Fine & Decorative Art. *Pos:* Pres, Allrich Gallery, San Francisco, 71-95; trustee, Fiberworks Ctr for Textile Arts, Berkeley, 72-81; trustee, Old Pueblo Mus, Tucson, Ariz, 88-90. *Teaching:* Lectr, Alta Col Art, 73, Wash State Univ, Pullman, 78, Los Angeles Co Mus, 79, Oakland Mus, 82, Art Inst Chicago, 82 & Portland Art Mus, 83, Sch Art Inst, Chicago, 83, San Jose State Univ, MH de Young Mus, Calif, 97. *Bibliog:* Kuniko Lucy Kato (auth), Tangible Eternity - Magdalena Abakanowicz, Int Art Research, Sapporo, Japan, 91; Jessica Scarborough (auth), From a Gallery Owner's Perspective, an interview with Louise Allrich, Fiberarts Mag, 94; Barbara Mayer (auth), Contemp Am Craft Art, Gibbs M Smith, Inc Peregrine, Smith Books, Salt Lake City, 98. *Mem:* Art Table. *Specialty:* Contemp textile art, painting and sculpture. *Publ:* Auth, Center for the Arts, pvt publ, 74; contribr, A Look at Fiber, Currant Mag, 76. *Mailing Add:* 236 W Portal Ave Suite 406 San Francisco CA 94127

ALLUMBAUGH, JAMES
SCULPTOR, EDUCATOR

b Dallas, Tex, Jan 27, 1941. *Study:* E Tex State Univ, BS, 63 & MS, 65; N Tex State Univ, EdD, 68. *Work:* Richardson Pub Libr, Tex; Beaumont Art Mus, Tex; Houston Ctr 2, Tex; Tyler Art Mus, Tex; Seaman Collection, Corpus Christi, Tex; MADI Mus, Dallas, Tex; Bonomi Collection, Contemp Art Ctr, Brescia, Italy. *Exhib:* Solo exhibs, E Tex State Univ, Commerce, Tex, 92, N Lake Coll, Irving, Tex, 92, Del Mar Coll, Corpus Christi, Tex, 93, MADI Mus, Dallas, Tex, 2005 & Bath House Cult Ctr, Dallas, 2009; Critics Choice, Dallas Visual Art Ctr, Tex, 96; Americas 2000, Northwest Art Ctr, Minot State Univ, 96; Celebration Am Crafts, Creative Arts Workshop, New Haven, Conn, 97-99; Crafts Nat, Zoller Gallery, The Penn State Univ, 98; LaGrange Nat Biennial, Lamar Dodd Art Ctr, LaGrange, Ga, 98; Meyerson Symphony Ctr, Dallas, Tex, 2000; Black and Blue, MAC Arts Ctr, Dallas, Tex, 2000; La Petite, Alder Gallery, Eugene Ore, 2001-2002; Oct Int Armory Art Ctr, W Palm Beach, Fla, 2001; Nat Small Works, Schoharie Co Art Gallery, Cobleskill, NY, 2001 & 2003-2004; Vision Int, Art Ctr Waco, Waco, Tex, 2002; Am MADI Artists, MADI Mus, Dallas Tex, 2004; Celebration of Geometric Art Salon Barbonico, Naples, Italy, 2004; MADI Mus, Dallas Tex, 2005-2006; Art on the Streets, US Bank, Colorado Springs, Colo, 2006; Bath House Cult Ctr, Dallas, Tex, 2006; Art MADI Inst, Spazio Lattuada, Milan, Italy, 2006; Int Madi, Fondazione Toniolo, Verona, Italy, 2008. *Pos:* Dir, Tex Coll Sculpture Symposium, Dallas, 77-; photogr and consult, Cent Time Zone Sculpture Symposium, Fermilab, Batavia, Ill, 91; photographic liaison, Tex Sculpture Asn, Dallas, 90-2000. *Teaching:* Fel design, N Tex State Univ, 66-68; assoc prof 3-D design, E Tex State Univ, 68-81, prof, 81-99 (now Tex A&M); instr & consult, MADI Mus, 2004-2007. *Awards:* Spanish & Art Mex, Cemanahuac Inst, Cuernavaca; Ice House Cult Ctr, Dallas, 2001; Tex Sculpture Asn, Dallas, 2001-. *Bibliog:* American Madi Artists, MADI Mus & Gallery, 2004; 2 Southwestern Artists, MADI Mus & Gallery, 2005. *Mem:* Int Sculpture Ctr. *Media:* Metal, Digital Imagery. *Publ:* Illusr (cover illus), 16th Ann Invitational Exhib, Longview Arts Ctr, 74 & 45th Ann Exhib, Springfield Art Mus, 75; auth, Cubes Space and Light, Spiral Enterprises, 77; Basic Techniques for Photographing Sculpture, Tex Sculpture Asn, fall journal, 92; Now and Then, Bath House Cult Ctr, 2009. *Dealer:* Mus Geometric & MADI Art Dallas TX. *Mailing Add:* 2009 St Francis Dallas TX 75228

ALLYN, JERRI
CONCEPTUAL ARTIST, EDUCATOR

b Paterson, NJ, Feb 21, 1952. *Study:* Goddard Col, Vt, MA (art & society), 80. *Comn:* Pub Art Fund, NY; MTA Arts for Transit & Creative Time, NY; 3 - New Am Radio, NY. *Exhib:* Sisters of Survival, Nat & European Tour, 82-84; Love Novellas, Franklin Furnace, NY, 83, West Coast Tour, 84; Rape, Univ Gallery, Ohio State Univ, Columbus, 85, Nat Tour, 86-87; Committed to Print, Mus Mod Art, NY, 88, Nat Tour; Am Dining: A Working Woman's Moment, New Mus Contemp Art, NY, 85, Nat Tour, 86-88; Art in the Anchorage, Creative Time, NY, 90; Angels Have Been Sent to Me, Creative Time, NY, 91; Six Moons Over Oaxaca, Bicultural Exchange - Galerie Arte de Oaxaca, Mex & Artists Space, NY, 94-95; High Performance: The First 5 Yrs 1978-1982, Bard Col, NY & LACE Contemp Art Exhibs, Calif, 02-03; A Chair is, Lower Manhattan Cult Coun, NY, 02. *Collection Arranged:* Mus Mod Art; JP Getty Mus, Calif; Wesleyan Univ; Mus Fine Arts, Mass; Smithsonian Inst; pvt collections include Gerardo Barbara, Zebra Davis, David Ehrich III, Aurora Fox, Bill Gordh, Donna Henes, Patricia Spears Jones, Jerry Kearns, Nancy & Alfonso Mayagoitia, Peter McCracken, Dierdre & Fran Resch, Ester Smith & Dikko Faust, Cheryl Swannack. *Pos:* Panelist, NY Coun Arts, Visual Arts, 85-86 & Theatre/Solo Performance, 92, Wash State Arts Comn, 89, NY Found Arts, 90, Pittsburgh Filmmakers & Pa Coun Arts, 96, Arts Link Residencies/CEC Int Partners, NY, 98; policy & guideline develop, Nat Endowment Arts, Interarts, 88, Vis Arts & Challenge Prog, Washington, DC, 93; consult, Performance Studies Prog, Syracuse Univ, NY, 86 & Franklin & Marshall Col, Pa, 89; Dir Educ & Pub prog, Bronx Mus Arts, NY, 94-98; mem, Bessies Dance & Performance Art Awards Comn, NY, 87-; entrance examiner, LaGuardia HS of Music, Art & Performing Arts, NY, 97-. *Teaching:* Prof, New Sch Social Res, NY, 87-92; prof, Western Wash Univ, Bellingham, 87-90; artist-in-residence, Univ Ill, Champagne/Urbana, 87, Cal Col Arts & Crafts, 88, Humboldt Univ, Oakland, Calif, 88, Kutztown Univ, Pa, 89, 90; staff develop, New York City Bd Educ, 98-02. *Awards:* Nat Endowment for the Arts, 81, 85, 87, 89, 90; NY State Coun Arts - Radio, New Tech & Artist Project Grants, 83, 86, 89, 91, 01; Am Int Lila Wallace Readers Digest Residency, Mex, 93-94; Project Arts, Bronx, 99, 00, 01, 02; NY Found Arts/Arts in Educ, 00-01, World Views Studio Spec Project Residency, Lower Manhattan Cult Coun, NY, 00-01; Fund for Creative Communities, NY State Coun Arts, 01-02; Ctr for Arts Educ, NY, 02; Manhattan Graphics Ctr Residency, NY, 02; Rockefeller Fund, Bellagio Conf and Study Ctr, Italy, 02; Joan Mitchell Fund, NY, 02-03. *Bibliog:* Pink Glass Swan, Feminist Essays Art, 95; Mapping the Terrain, New Genre Pub Art, 95; El Guia/Arts Mediterranea (Spain), 96, Pub Art Review, 98; Performance Artists Talking in the Eighties, 00; Parallels &

Intersections: A Remarkable History of Woman Artists in California, 1950-2000, 02; Moravic, M, Woman's Building Oral History Project, Smithsonian Archives, 02, Faxen (Austria), 99; High Performance: First 5 Years, 1978-1982, 01; City Folk Morning Prog, Arts Feature, WFUV Radio, 02; Sunday Arts, Staten Island Advance, 02; Sunday Arts & Leisure, NY Times, 02; Cat Radio Café/Arts Mag, WBAI Radio, 02. *Media:* new art forms, Interdisciplinary. *Publ:* Role Confusion, 77; Love Novellas, 84; American Dining Part 1 & 2, 85, 87; Angels Have Been Sent to Me, 90; Six Moons Over Oaxaca, 94; A Chair is a Throne is a Freedom Fighter's Camp Stool, 03

ALMOND, JOAN
PHOTOGRAPHER
b Los Angeles, Calif, June 3, 1935. *Work:* Can Mus Contemp Photog, Ottawa; Brookings Inst, Washington, DC; Santa Barbara Mus Art, Calif. *Exhib:* Solo exhibs, Saiyde Bronfman Ctr, Montreal, 87, Tekeyan Cult Ctr, Montreal, 88, St John's Armenian Church, Southfield, Mich, 89, Soc Contemp Photog, Kansas City, 92, Nile Gallery, Cairo, 92, Schatten Gallery, Emory Univ, Atlanta, Ga, 93, Brooks Inst Photog, Santa Barbara, 94 & Gallery Contemp Photog, Santa Monica, 97, Staton Greenberg Gallery, Santa Barbara, 2004, Cumberland Gallery, Nashville, TN, 2005, June Batehan Gallery, NYC 2003; Dimensions in Art, Int Design Ctr, Montreal, 88; Visual Concepts, Univ Judaism, Los Angeles, Calif, 90; Celebrating Children, Jacob Javits Conv Ctr, NY, 91. *Collection Arranged:* Canadian Mus Contemp Photography, Ottawa,; Brookings Inst, Washington, DC; Santa Barbara Mus Art, Calif. *Bibliog:* Roberto Tejada (auth), The Past in the Present (monograph) 2002; B & W Magazine, 2004. *Mem:* Women in Photography Int. *Media:* Platinum. *Specialty:* Photographic. *Publ:* Armenians in Jerusalem, Ararat, winter 89; C comme cinema, Art Global, 91; Best of photography, Photographer's Forum, 91; Collector Print Program, Friends of Photography, 98; The Past in the Present, a Catalog of Photographs, 97; The Harvard Jerusalem Studio, MIT Press, 86. *Dealer:* Halted Gallery, Bloomfield Hills, MI; Cumberlano Gallery Nashville, TN; Staton Greenberg Gallery, Santa Barbara, CA; Hochelber Fine Arts, Montreal, Quebec, CDA. *Mailing Add:* 54 Malibu Colony Dr Malibu CA 90265-4637

ALMOND, PAUL
FILMMAKER, WRITER
b Montreal, Que, Apr 26, 1931. *Study:* Bishop's Coll Sch, 44-48; McGill Univ; Balliol Col, Oxford, BA & MA. *Pos:* Dir & producer, Can Broadcasting Corp, 53-65, BBC, 57, Granada TV, 63; Quest Films, 64-91. *Awards:* Special Award of Merit for Seven Up, Prague, 63; Canadian Film Awards, Best Motion Picture Dir, 70; Best Television Drama Dir, 79; Officer of the Order of Can, 2001; Lifetime Achievement Award, Dir Guild Canada. *Bibliog:* Janet Edsforth (auth), The Flame Within (a study of Paul Almond's Films), Can Film Inst, 71. *Mem:* Dir Guild Am; hon life mem Dir Guild Can; Acad Can Cinema & TV, Royal Can Acad; Acad Motion Picture Arts & Sci. *Interests:* birding. *Publ:* Auth, La Vengence des Dieux (Novel); co-auth, High Hopes (memoirs); writer, producer & dir, Isabel (film), 68, Act of the Heart (film), 70, Journey (film), 72, Ups & Downs (film), 82 the Dance Goes On, (film), 91. *Mailing Add:* 54 Malibu Colony Dr Malibu CA 90265-4637

ALONSO, EUGENIO LOPEZ
COLLECTOR
b Mexico City, 1968. *Pos:* Dir mktg, Grupo Jumex, Ecatepec, Mex; owner and founder, Chac Mool Gallery, Los Angeles, 1994-, Jumex Collection, Escatepec, Mex, 2001-; trustee, Los Angeles Mus Contemp Art, New Mus Contemp Art, New York. *Awards:* Named one of Top 200 Collectors, ARTNews mag, 2006-13. *Collection:* Contemporary art. *Mailing Add:* Jumex Antigua Carretera Mex Pachuca Xalostoc Mexico 55340

ALPERN, MERRY B
PHOTOGRAPHER
b New York, NY, Mar, 15, 1955. *Study:* Grinnell Coll, Iowa, 73-77. *Work:* Mus Mod Art, NY; Houston Mus of Fine Arts; Los Angeles Co Mus of Art; Baltimore Mus of Art; Whitney Mus of Am Art, NY. *Exhib:* One-woman shows, Camera Club of NY, 89, Bonni Benrubi Gallery, NY, 95, 99; group Exhib, Mus Mod Art, NY, 91, 92 & 95; The Montreal Mus of Fine Arts, 2000. *Pos:* Photo lab technician, Exposure/Effects, NY, 77-78; staff photogr & studio mgr, LGI Photo Agency, 78-80; asst photog ed, Rolling Stone Mag, 80-81; freelance photogr, 81-. *Teaching:* Guest instr, Int Ctr Photog, NY, 89; guest lectr, New Sch, NY, 90; instr, Int Ctr Photog, NY, 94. *Awards:* Second Place, Pictures Yr, Mag Picture Story, 88; Leica Medal Excellence Photojournalism Award, 88; Nat Endowment Arts, Visual Artists Fel Grant, 90. *Bibliog:* Gerri Hershey (auth), Return to Spender, Mirabella, Sept 99; Julie Caniglia (auth), Merry Alpern (review), Artforum, Oct 99; Daphne Merkin (auth), The Last Taboo, NY Times Mag, Dec 2000. *Publ:* Many credits in var newspapers & mags. *Dealer:* Bonni Benrubi 52 E 76th New York NY 10021. *Mailing Add:* 1 Plaza St W Apt 7C Brooklyn NY 11217

ALPERT, BILL (WILLIAM) H
PAINTER, SCULPTOR
b Bronx, NY, Dec 21, 1934. *Study:* Univ Calif, Los Angeles, Pharm D, 58, BA, 63, grad sch, 63-65. *Work:* Power Gallery Contemp Art, Sydney, Australia. *Exhib:* Orgn Independent Artists, Group exhib, US Courthouse, 77; Art in Pub Places, 26 Fed Plaza, New York, 77; Postcard Show, Bologna Art Fair, Italy, 78; Albright-Knox Mus, 78-79; Six Artists View Develop, New York Acad Sci, 78; Current NY, Joe & Emily Lowe Art Gallery, Syracuse Univ, 80; Color on Structure, W Paterson Coll NJ, Wayne, 81; Coll Charleston, SC, 86 & 89; Artists in Paradise, New York Botanical Gardens, Bronx, New York, 93; Dactyl Found Arts & Humanities, New York, 2005; b2 Art, WMF Gallery, NY, 2011. *Teaching:* Adj prof painting, Cooper Union Sch Art, New York, 79-82; adj instr drawing, Parsons Sch Design, New York, 81-82 & Pratt Inst, Summer Prog, 81; instr watercolor, Sch Visual Arts, New York, 89-; Yunnan Inst Fine Arts, Kunming, China, 93; Cent Accad Fine Arts, Beijing, China, 93; The Green Horse, Ulaanbaatar, Mongolia, 98. *Awards:* Creative Artist Pub Serv Prog Finalist, 77-78 & 80-82; Tiffany Found Finalist, 79. *Bibliog:* Peter Frank (auth), New York Revs, Art News, 11/77; Ellen Lubell (auth), Arts Mag, 11/77; JoAnn Lewis (auth), Sculpture room, Washington Post, 5/27/78; Gregory Battcock (auth), Art Info, 5/81; Nancy S Smith (auth), articles, The News & Courier/The Evening Post, Charleston SC, 2/23/86. *Mem:* NY Artists Equity Asn; Orgn Independent Artists (mem exhib comt, 77-78). *Media:* Watercolor, All Media; Photographs, Chinese Ink. *Publ:* Contribr, New York Art Yearbook, 75-76; Re-View, Vol I, Issue 1, Vered Lieb, 77; The Whitney Counterweight Catalog, 77; Sciences, New York Acad Sci, 3/78; NY Art Rev, 88. *Mailing Add:* 64 Grand St Apt 5 New York NY 10013

ALPERT, GEORGE
PHOTOGRAPHER, PAINTER
b New York, NY, Apr 3, 1922. *Study:* NY Univ; NC State Col; Stanford Univ; Univ Calif, Berkeley; Inst Seven Arts, NY. *Work:* Il Diaframma, Milan, Italy; Miller-Plummer Collection, Philadelphia. *Exhib:* Solo exhibs, Alfred Stieglitz Gallery, Neikrug Gallery, Light Gallery, NY, Period Gallery West, Scottsdale, Ariz, Everson Mus, Heard Mus, Udinotti Gallery & O'Brien Art Emporium, Ariz, C G Rein. *Pos:* Chmn, pres & dir gallery, Sohophoto Found, 70-. *Teaching:* Mem fac creative photog, New Sch Social Res, NY, 74-79. *Bibliog:* George Alpert: paintings, sculpture; George Albert photographs women. *Media:* Acrylic. *Specialty:* Photography, paintings, sculpture. *Publ:* Auth, The Queens, 75 & co-auth, Second Chance to Live: The Suicide Syndrome, 75, Da Capo Press; Taos Pueblo, Paradise House, 83

ALPERT, HERB
PAINTER, SCULPTOR
b Los Angeles, Calif, Mar 31, 1935. *Study:* Study with Rufino Tamayo & Calvin J Goodman, Univ Southern Calif. *Hon Degrees:* Berk Lee Sch, Hon DMusic, 2000. *Work:* Calif Inst Arts, Valencia; Indian Wells Country Club, Palm Springs, Calif; Vanderbilt Univ Med Ctr, Nashville, Tenn. *Exhib:* Basel Art Fair, Switz, 93; World Contemp Art 98, Los Angeles, 98; Miami Int Art Fair, Fla, 99; MB Modern, NY, 11/2000; Retrospective, Tenn St Mus, 8/2000. *Pos:* Co-chair, Found Communities in Schs, 91; spokesperson, Nat Found Advan Arts, 91. *Awards:* A V Call Achievement Award, Univ Southern Calif, 94. *Bibliog:* Tango Nuevo, The Paintings and Sculpture of Herb Alpert (catalogue), M Barnes Gallery, 98; Peter Frank (auth), Entertainment Today, 11/99. *Media:* Acrylic, Oil; Miscellaneous Media. *Dealer:* Galerie Van der Planken NV Steehouwersvest 13 2000 Antwerp Belgium; MB Modern 41 E 57th New York NY 10022. *Mailing Add:* c/o Molly Barnes Gallery 1414 6th St Santa Monica CA 90401

ALPERT, RICHARD HENRY
VIDEO ARTIST
b Apr 11, 1947. *Study:* Univ Pittsburgh, BA, 70; San Francisco Art Inst, MFA (sculpture), 73. *Work:* Mus Conceptual Art, San Francisco; J H Cohn & Co, NY; Va Mus Fine Art, Richmond. *Exhib:* Projekt '74, Kolnischer Kunstverein, Koln, Ger, 74; solo exhibs, La Mamelle Art Ctr, San Francisco, 76 & 80, Los Angeles Inst Contemp Art, 79 & Washington Proj Arts, Washington, DC, 81; Space Time Sound 1970's: A Decade in the Bay Area, San Francisco Mus Mod Art, 79; California Performance Now and Then, Mus Contemp Art, Chicago, 81. *Teaching:* Instr, San Francisco Art Inst, 72-73 & 77 & Calif Col Arts & Crafts, Oakland, 78-79. *Awards:* Artist's Fel Grant, Nat Endowment Arts, 79-80. *Mailing Add:* 2123 Castro St San Francisco CA 94131-2224

ALQUILAR, MARIA
PAINTER, CERAMIST
b Brooklyn, NY, May 25, 1938. *Study:* Hunter Col, New York, AB, 59. *Work:* Chase Manhattan Bank, NY & Phoenix; Nat Gallery Am Art, Int Finance Corp-World Bank, Washington; Sacramento Metrop Arts Comn; Redding Mus Art; Dante Mus, Ravenua, Italy; Mus Civico, Padova, Italy; and many others. *Comn:* Light Rail Sta, Sacramento, 84; ceramic and metal altar, US Border Sta, San Luis, Ariz, 85; ceramic mural, fountain & waterfall, Water & Sewer Admin Bldg, Sacramento, 86; ceramic mural, Los Viajeros Vienen a San Jose, San Jose Int Airport, Calif, 90; Livermore Cent Libr, Livermore, Calif, 2002-2003; 16th St Viaduet Mod Proj, Denver, Colo, 92; Fairbairn Water Treatment Plant, Sacramento, Calif, 93; paintings, Int Finance Corp (aka World Bank), 96; ceramic mural, World Bank, Washington, DC, 97; Dept Environ Protection, Tallahassee, Fla, 98; Valley Med Ctr, San Jose, 99. *Exhib:* Inedible Renwick Birthday Cake, Smithsonian Inst, 82; Out of the Fire, Betty Rhymer Gallery, Art Inst Chicago, Ill; retrospective exhib, Redding Mus Art, Redding, Calif, 92; The World's Women on Line, Beijing China, Ariz State Univ; Art Mus Santa Cruz Co, Calif; Seventh Ann, John Natsoulis Gallery, Davis, Calif; La Galeria La Mano Magica, Oaxaca, Mex; John Pence Gallery, San Francisco; Mus Civico, Padova, Italy; Latin Am Art Mus, Miami, 2001; Virginia Miller Gallery, Miami, Fla, 2002; Pence Gallery and Cultural Mus, Davis, Calif, 2005; Miami Int Univ Art, Miami, Fla, 2005, 2006; Bibliotec, Mt Temblant Ctr, Quebec, Can, 2008. *Pos:* Dir, Jennifer Pauls Gallery, Sacramento, Calif, 70-85. *Awards:* Residency, John Michael Kohler Art Ctr, Sheboygan, Wis; Hon Award, US Gen Serv Admin, 90. *Bibliog:* Ellen Schlesinger (auth), Sunday woman-artist in residence, Sacramento Bee, 8/83; article, Ceramics Monthly, 5/88. *Media:* Acrylic, Clay. *Interests:* Narrative art and ceramics. *Publ:* Perspective on public art, Ceramics Monthly, 96; Pottery and Ceramics, New Holland, London; Sculpture, Technique, Form, Content, Arthur Williams; Art in Architecture, Our Hispanic Heritage, US Gen Serv Admin; 50 Yrs of Santa Cruz Studio Ceramics, Art Mus Santa Cruz Co, SC, 97. *Dealer:* Guild.com. *Mailing Add:* 90 NE 46th St Miami FL 33137-3422

ALSWANG, HOPE
MUSEUM DIRECTOR
Study: Goddard Coll, BA (Am History), 1971; Attingham Summer Sch, 1976; Columbia Univ, Sch Architecture & Planning, Historic Preservation Prog, 1975-77; Winterthur Mus Summer Inst, 1982. *Pos:* Dir, mus prog, NY State Coun on Arts, formerly; exec dir, NJ Hist Soc, 1992-97; pres & CEO, Shelburne Mus, Vt,

1997-2005; dir, Mus Art, RI Sch Design, 2005-2010; dir & CEO, Norton Mus Art, West Palm Beach, Fla, 2010-. *Teaching:* Prof, History of Decorative Arts grad prog, Cooper-Hewitt Mus, Parson Sch Design, Sch Architecture & Planning, Columbia Univ. *Mailing Add:* Museum of Art Rhode Island School of Design 224 Benefit St Providence RI 02903

ALTAFFER, LAWRENCE F, III
PAINTER
b Richmond, Va, Jan 7, 1947. *Study:* Univ Va, BA, 69; MD, 74. *Work:* McGraw Hill Publ, New York; Media Gen, Richmond, Va; Galen Capital Group, McLean, Va. *Exhib:* Show Time - Palisades Lake, Oil Painters Am, Carmel, Calif, 2000; Old Rag Mountain, Arts for the Parks, Jackson Hole, Wyo, 2001; Taggart Lake, Oil Painters Am, Chicago, Ill, 2002; Morning on the Potomac, Salmagundi Club, New York, 2002; Slipping Away, Salon Int, San Antonio, Tex, 2006. *Pos:* Physician urologist, pvt practice; retired. *Awards:* Risser Award, Art League, Alexandria, Va. *Mem:* Wash Soc Landscape Painters (Am Artist Mar 2002); Salmagundi Club, New York; Oil Painter Am; Allied Artists Am; Am Society of Marine Artists; Am Impressionist Society. *Media:* Oil. *Interests:* Gardening, hunting, fishing, home. *Dealer:* Carspecken Scott Gallery Wilmington DE. *Mailing Add:* General Delivery Syria VA 22743

ALTEN, JERRY
DIRECTOR, DESIGNER
b Philadelphia, Pa. *Study:* Philadelphia Coll Art; Temple Univ, BA (fine arts). *Comn:* SI, NY. *Exhib:* Society of Illustrators. *Pos:* art dir, TV Guide Mag, 67; mem staff, Triangle Publ Inc, Radnor, Pa, currently; corp art dir News Corp, 95; art dir, CRR Mag, Egiving Mag, Coventry Health Care; bd dir, Antonelli Col of Art/Photography; creative dir, Girina Mag, 04-. *Teaching:* Lectr, Syracuse Univ, Temple Univ, Univ Arts, Royal Coll Art, Antonelli's Coll Art, Harvard Univ. *Awards:* Awards of Excellence & Gold & Silver Medals, NY Art Dirs Club, Soc Publ Designers & Soc Illusr, graphics. *Mem:* Soc Publ Designers; Art Alliance Philadelphia; NY Art Dirs Club; Philadelphia Art Dirs; Philadelphia Coll Art Alumni Asn; Soc Illusrs. *Interests:* Western art, cosmology. *Publ:* auth, The Art of TV Guide, 2009; auth, The Art of TV Guide Expanded, 2012. *Mailing Add:* 10 Wynnedale Cir Narberth PA 19072-1723

ALTERMANN, TONY
ART DEALER
b Dallas, Tex, Aug 10, 1940. *Study:* Univ NTex, BA & MS. *Pos:* Dir publicity & pub relations, MGM, Dallas, Tex, 70-72; vpres, Tex Art Gallery, Dallas, 72-78; owner & pres, Altermann Art Gallery, Dallas, Tex, 78- & Altermann & Morris Galleries, Houston, Dallas, Santa Fe & Hilton Head SC; bd dir, Dallas Visual Arts Ctr, Currently. *Mem:* Dallas Art Dealers Asn; Dallas Visual Arts Ctr; Cowboy Artists of Am Mus (life, bd dir); Prix de West Soc of Nat Cowboy Hall of Fame; Western Heritage Ctr; Coll of Arts & Scis/Univ N Tex (chmn adv bd). *Specialty:* Western, wildlife and Americana subjects in all media. *Mailing Add:* Altermann Galleries & Auctioneers 225 Canyon Rd Santa Fe NM 87501

ALTFEST, ELLEN
PAINTER
b NYC, New York, 1970. *Study:* Cornell Univ, BFA; Yale Univ, MFA; attended, Skowhegan Sch Painting and Sculpture. *Exhib:* Solo exhibs, White Cube, London, 2007; Group exhibs, USA Today, curated from Saatchi Collection, Royal Acad, London, The Leg, Chinati Found, Marfa, Tex, 2010, 55th Int Art Exhib Biennale, Venice, 2013. *Bibliog:* Roberta Smith (auth), Ellen Altfest, Still Lives, NY Times, 12/23/2005; Randy Kennedy (auth), Warming to Painting in the Cold, New York Times, 6/6/2013. *Dealer:* White Cube London; Saatchi Gallery London. *Mailing Add:* Saatchi Gallery Duke of Yorks HQ Kings Rd London United Kingdom SW3 4RY

ALTHOFF, KAI
PAINTER, INSTALLATION SCULPTOR
b Cologne, Germany, 1966. *Exhib:* Solo exhibs include Anton Kern Gallery, New York, 2001, Mus Contemp Art, Chicago, 2004, ACME, Los Angeles, 2005, We Are Better Friends for IT, Gladstone Gallery, NY, 2007, Vancouver Art Gallery, 2008, Punkt, Absatz, Bluemli, Gladstone Gallery, NY, 2011; Group exhibs include Oldnewtown, Casey Caplan, New York, 1999; Drawing 2000, Gladstone Gallery, New York, 2000; Drawing Now, Mus Mod Art, New York, 2002; Nature Boy, Elizabeth Dee, New York, 2003; Venice Biennale, Museo Correr, Venice, 2003; Heart of Darkness: Kai Althoff, Ellen Gallagher & Edgar Cleijne, Thomas Hirschhorn", The Walker Art Ctr, Minneapolis, 2006, 2007; Genesis I'm Sorry, Greene Naftali, New York, 2007; Make Your Own Life: Artists In & Out of Cologne, Mus Contemp Art, Miami, 2007; Makers and Modelers, Gladstone Gallery, New York, 2007, Nick Z & Kai Althoff: We Are Better Friends For It, 2007; Life on Mars: Carnegie Int Exhib, Carnegie Mus Art, Pittsburgh, 2008; Between Art and Life: The Painting and Sculpture Collection, San Francisco Mus Modern Art, Calif, 2009; Mapping the Studio: Artists from the Francois Pinault Collection, Palazzo Grazzi, Venice, Italy, 2009; Mirror Me, DISPATCH Projects, NY, 2009; Video Journeys, Sister Gallery, Los Angeles, Calif, 2009; At Home/Not at Home, Hessel Mus Art, Hudson, NY, 2010; Beyond/In WNY, Alternating Currents, Albright Knox Triennial, Buffalo, NY, 2010; The Summer Bazaar, Tanya Bonakdar Gallery, NY, 2010; Whitney Biennial, Whitney Mus Am Art, 2012. *Mailing Add:* Gladstone Gallery 515 West 24th Street New York NY 10011

ALTMAN, EDITH
SCULPTOR, CONCEPTUAL ARTIST
b Altenberg, Ger, May 5, 1931; US citizen. *Study:* Wayne State Univ, Detroit, Mich, 49; Marygrove Coll, with Paul Weigardt (from the Bauhaus), 56-57. *Work:* Standard Oil Co, Mus Contemp Art, Chicago; State of Ill; Yale Univ Mus; Holocaust Mus; Peace Mus. *Exhib:* Art Inst Chicago Vicinity Exhib, 75, 79, 81 & 85; Mus Contemp Art, Chicago, 76, 81 & 83; Solo exhibs, Spertus Mus Gallery Contemp Art (with catalog), 88, Reclaiming The Symbol/The Art of Memory (with catalog), Rockford Art Mus, 89, State of Ill Mus Gallery, Chicago, 92 & Topography of Terror (with catalog), Loyola Univ Fine Arts Gallery, 93; Light Weight Works, Mitchell Mus, Ill, 95; Legacy, Minn Mus Am Art, 95; Drawing in Chicago Now, Columbia Coll, Chicago, 96; The Spiritual in Contemp Art Today, Hope Col, Mich, 96; Art Chicago 1945-1995, Mus Contemp Art, Chicago, 96-97; Political Vision, Fassbender Gallery, Chicago, Ill, 99; Knoxville Mus Art, Tenn, 98; Spiritual Passport and Transformative Journeys, State Ill Art Gallery, Springfield, Ill, 98; Edith Altman Retrospective, Lindenau Mus, Altenburg, Ger, 2001; group exhibs Witness and Legacy, Knowville Mus Art, 98, Polit Visions, Fassbender Gallery, Chicago, 99, Witness and Legacy, Tucson Mus Fine Art, Huntsville Mus, Ala, Decordova Mus, Mass, 2000, Text Cult Ctr, Chicago, 2000, Pedagogy: Beyond Reeling, Writhing, Uglification & Derision, Book & Paper Ctr, Columbia Col, Chicago, 2000, Transcultural Visions: Polish-Am Contemp Art, Hyde Park Art Ctr, Chicago, 2001. *Teaching:* Vis artists & print proj, Univ Omaha, Neb, 84; asst prof painting & grad advisor, Univ Chicago, 84-85; vis asst prof painting, Sch Art Inst Chicago, 85-86; lectr painting, Univ Ill, Columbia Col & Oakton Col, Chicago; lectr, Loyola Univ, 93, Columbus Mus, 93, Notre Dame, 96, Spartus Mus, Chicago, Ill, 98, DePaul Univ, Chicago, Ill & Univ Houston, Tex, 98. *Awards:* Individual Artist Fel, Ill Arts Coun, 84 & 95; Nat Endowment Arts Individual Artist Fel Grant, 90-91; Art Matters, 94. *Bibliog:* V W Jones (auth), Edith Altman at the NAME Gallery, Contemporary American Women Sculptors, The New Art Examiner, ORYK Press, 87; Gloria Feman Orenstein (auth), The Reflowering of the Goddess, Pergamon Press, 90; Claire Krantz (auth), Questions as Model, New Art Examiner, 6/92. *Mem:* Chicago Artist Coalition; founding mem, Comt Artists Rights, 88; hon mem, State of Ill, 92. *Media:* Multimedia. *Publ:* Auth, articles in Art in Am, 79 & 87, Artforum, 83, Chicago Tribune, Chicago Sun-Times & New Art Examiner, 92; Positions, NYFAI/Women's Ctr for Learning, 89; Allemenines Lexikon Der Bilden Kunstler, Themel Baecker Publ, Ger, 90. *Mailing Add:* 819 Foster #3 South Evanston IL 60201

ALTMANN, HENRY S
PAINTER, EDUCATOR
b New York, NY, Dec 4, 1946. *Study:* Pratt Inst, Brooklyn, BFA (art educ), 68; Queens Col, Flushing, NY, MFA (painting), 70; Fulbright Fel painting, 70-71, Fine Arts Acad, Munich, Ger. *Work:* First Nat Bank New York; Skowhegan Sch Painting & Sculpture, NY; Shawmut Bank Boston, Mass. *Comn:* Three stained glass windows & paintings for rear portal (with Maxine Ann Sorokin), Kehillath Jakob Synagogue, Newton, Mass, 73. *Exhib:* Solo exhibs, First St Gallery, New York, Meetinghouse Gallery, Boston, 73 & Framed-In Time Gallery, Framingham, Mass, Feb, 2004; Young Realist Show, Harbor Gallery, Cold Spring Harbor, Long Island, NY, 72; two-person exhib, Goethe Inst, Boston, 80, Young Adult Ctr, Boston, 84 & Univ Cincinnati, Rose Warner Gallery, 86; Jewish Community Ctr, Southern NJ Gallery, Cherry Hill, 80; group exhib, Shore Road Gallery, Ogunquit, Maine, 2005-; 2 Person Show, Weston, Mass, 2014; Wells Maine, 2014. *Pos:* Exhib chmn, West Roxbury Art Asn, 77-; res comt arch, West Roxbury Hist Soc, 77-, dir visual arts, Jewish Community Ctr, Newton, Mass, 83-. *Teaching:* Instr art, Boston Univ, 71-75; adj assoc prof, Art Inst Boston, 75-; Framingham State Coll, Mass, 72-80; visual arts dir, art dept, Leventhal-Sidman JCC, 83-2006; Mass Bay Community Coll, 90-91; instr drawing & painting, Fisher College, Boston, Mass, 2004-. *Awards:* Finalist, Mass Found Arts Fel Competition, 83. *Bibliog:* W Rox (auth), Boston Globe article, 5/81; Norman Keyes (auth), Transcript Newspaper article, 81; article, Boston Globe, 96; Making it At Home, Journal Tribune, 2014. *Mem:* Boston Vis Artists Union. *Media:* Oil, Pastel, Watercolor. *Res:* Fine Arts. *Interests:* old books. *Collection:* USA, European. *Dealer:* Whitney Galleries Wells ME. *Mailing Add:* 61 Perham St West Roxbury MA 02132

ALTSCHUL, CHARLES
ADMINISTRATOR
Study: Yale Univ, BA, MFA. *Pos:* Dir educ, Eastman Kodak Ctr for Creative Writing, Camden, Maine, 1991-97; chair, Am Ctr for Design Conf, 1996; pres, Maine Media Col, 2006-11; dir design and book arts program, Maine Media Workshops and Col, 2011-. *Teaching:* Sr lectr, Yale Univ, formerly; founder, BFA program in multimedia, Univ of Arts, Phildelphia, 1997. *Mem:* Int Acad Digital Arts and Scis. *Mailing Add:* Maine Media College 70 Camden St PO Box 200 Rockport ME 04856

ALTSHULER, BRUCE J
EDUCATOR, WRITER
b Newark, NJ, Apr 2, 1949. *Study:* Princeton Univ, BA, 71; Harvard Univ, MA, 74, PhD, 77. *Collection Arranged:* Isamu Noguchi: Early Abstraction, Whitney Mus Am Art, 94; Isamu Noguchi, Juan March Found, Madrid, Spain, 94. *Pos:* Asst to dir, NY Hist Soc, 83-85; assoc dir, Zabriskie Gallery, New York, 85-89; dir, Isamu Noguchi Garden Mus, Long Island City, NY, 92-98; dir studies, Christie's Educ, NY, 98-2000; dir, Mus Studies Prog, New York Univ, 2001-. *Teaching:* Asst prof philos, Univ Puget Sound, Tacoma, Wash, 77-82; grad fac cur studies, Black Ctr Cur Studies, Bard Coll, Annandale on Hudson, NY, 94-2010; adj prof mus studies & art hist, New York Univ, 2001-2010, prof mus studies, 2009. *Mem:* Int Asn Art Critics USA (bd dir, 94-2000); Coll Art Asn; Am Asn Mus. *Res:* Twentieth century art; contemporary art. *Publ:* (Auth), The Avant-Garde in Exhibition, Harry N Abrams, 94; Isamu Noguchi, Abbeville Press, 94; coauth, Isamu Noguchi: Essays and Conversations, Harry N Abrams, 94; ed, Collecting the New: Museums & Contemporary Art, Princeton Univ Press, 2005; auth, Salon to Biennial Vol 1 (1863-1960), Phaidon Press, 2008; auth, Biennials and Beyond, Exhibition that Made History, 1962-2002, Phaidon Press, 2013. *Mailing Add:* New York Univ Museum Studies Program 240 Greene St Suite 400 New York NY 10003

ALVARADO-JUÁREZ, FRANCISCO
PAINTER, PHOTOGRAPHER
b Honduras, Dec 18, 1950. *Study:* Stony Brook Univ, BA, 1974; Int Ctr Photog, 1975; Md Inst, MFA, 1993. *Work:* Brooklyn Mus of Art, NY; The Bronx Mus of Art, NY; Everson Mus of Art, Syracuse, NY; Museo Pablo Serrano, Zaragoza, Spain; Smithsonian Am Art Mus, Washington, DC; Museo de Arte de Querétaro, Mex;

Museo Universitario del Chopo, Mex City; Islip Art Mus, New York; Museo de Arte Contemporáneo, Ateneo de Yucatán, Mex; Mus TV & Radio, New York; Noyes Mus Art, NJ; San Antonio Mus Art, Tex; Studio Mus in Harlem, NY; Art Gallery, Univ Md; Galería Nacional de Arte, Tegucigalpa, Honduras; Housatonic Mus Art, Bridgeport, Conn; Bibliothéque Nationale (Cabinet des Estampes), Paris, France; Museo de Arte Contemporáneo, Caracas, Venezuela. *Comn:* Painting, Wash State Art in Pub Places, Wash, 1995; Serigraph print, Cartón de Venezuela, Caracas, 1985; Serigraph print, United Nations Children's Fund, NY, 1990. *Exhib:* Solo exhibs, New York, Int Ctr of Photography, New York, 76; Faces, Cayman Gallery, New York, 80; Photos by Alvarado-Juárez, Art Mus Am, Wash DC, 80; Francisco Alvarado-Juárez: Paintings/Constructions, Arlington Arts Ctr, Arlington, Va, 85; Native/Stranger, El Museo del Barrio, New York, 86; Native/Stranger: 1983-1988, The Art Gallery, Univ Md, College Park, Md, 88; Trophies, BACA Downtown, Brooklyn, NY, 89; Fractured Spaces, InterAmerican Art Gallery, Miami-Dade Comm. Coll, Miami, Fla, 90; Reefs: Song of the Ocean, Islip Art Mus, Oakdale, New York, 92; The North American Trophy Room, The Bronx Mus Art, The Bronx, NY, 92; Selected Work: 1978-1993, Portales Galería de Arte, Tegucigalpa, Honduras, 93; Border to Border: Across Lines, Contemp Arts Ctr, Cincinnati, Ohio, 94; Mex en el Corazón: Para Lucas, Museo Univ del Chopo, Mex City, 95; Mythological Dreams: Recent Paintings, Galería Nina Menocal, Mexico City, 95; Natura-Frágil, Sala de Arte Los Lavaderos, Santa Cruz de Tenerife, Spain, 99; Endangered, The Noyes Mus of Art, Oceanville, NJ, 98; The Mythology of the Flora and the Fauna, Museo Pablo Serrano, Zaragoza, Spain, 2000; Canto a la Fauna: NY Trophies & NY Fauve, Everson Mus of Art, Syracuse, NY, 2001; Canto a la fauna Am, Museo de Arte Contemp de Oaxaca, Mex, 2002; Nature of Love/Love of Nature, Museo de Arte de Querétaro, Mex, 2005; Gates to the Sea, 9th Int Festival-Hist District Campeche, Mex, 2005; Secrets of Flora & Fauna, Jardín Borda, Cuernavaca, Mex, 2006; Two Worlds of my New York, Museo de los Pintores Oaxaqueños, Oaxaca, Mex, 2006; From Manhattan to Oaxaca, CSV Cult Ctr, New York, 2007; The Topography of Love, Museo de Arte Contemporáneo, Ateneo de Yucatán, Mex, 2007; Between Light & Shadow, Inst Veracruzano de la Cultura, Veracruz, Mex, 2008; Visible & Unseen, Taller Boricua, New York, 2008; Llamas y ofrendas: Oaxaca 2006-2007, Museo de Antropología de Xalapa, Mex, 2009; Mirrors of Light, Galería Nacional de Arte, Tegucigalpa, Honduras, 2011; Group exhibs, Artes gráficas panamericanas; Museo de Arte Contemporáneo, Caracas, Venezuela, 84; Recent Am works on paper, Int tour, Smithsonian Inst Traveling Exhib Serve, 85; The Second Biennial of Havana, Museo Nat de Bellas Artes, Cuba, 1986, 19th São Paulo Int Biennial, Fundaçao Bienal de São Paolo, Brazil, 87; Working in Brooklyn-Painting, Brooklyn Mus Art, New York, 87; Día de los muertos, Alternative Mus, NY, 88; Artists-in-Residence, 1987-88, The Studio Mus in Harlem, NY, 88; The Awakening, The Discovery Mus, Bridgeport, Conn, 90; China: June 4, 1989, PS 1, Mus Mod Art, New York, 90; Selections from the Permanent Collection, The Bronx Mus Arts, NY, 93; Reclaiming Hist, El Museo del Barrio, New York, 94; Paper Visions 5, Housatonic Mus Art, Bridgeport, Conn, 94; The First Ten Yrs of the Permanent Collection, Islip Art Mus, East Islip, NY, 96; Selected Works from the Permanent Collection, The Studio Mus in Harlem, NY, 99; Buying Time: Nourishing Excellence, NYFA Painting Fellowship Recipients, Sotheby's, NY, 2001; Object Lessons: Additions to the Collection, 97-2002; Everson Mus of Art, Syracuse, NY, 2003; Encore, The Noyes Mus Art, Oceanville, NJ, 2005; Masters of Graphic Arts 8th Int Biennial, Municipal Mus Art, Györ, Hungary, 2005; Black Now, Longwood Art Gallery, The Bronx, NY, 2006; Idearte: Subasta Internacional de Arte, Museo de la Identidad Nacional, Tegucigalpa, Honduras, 2010; Illusive Abstractions, Andre Zarre Gallery, NY, 2011; Biennial, Instítuto Hondureño de Cultura Interamericana, Tegucigalpa, Honduras, 2012; Environs, Biennial of the Americas, Museo de las Américas, Denver, Colo, 2013; La Placita, Islip Art Mus, East Islip, NY, 2013, III Cumbre de Arte Latinoamericana, Museo Karura Art Centre, Spain, 2013, Rumbo 5: Hacia el cuerpo, Centro de Arte y Cultura, UNAH, Tegucigalpa, Honduras, 2015, Now Biennial of the Americas, Biennial Pavilion, Denver, 2015. *Awards:* Artist in Residence Fel, Mid Atlantic Arts Found, 93, 98; Pollock-Krasner Found, Fel, 91, 2000; Grant, Gottlieb Found, 2004; fel, DC Comn on the Arts, 82, 85; Artist in Residence, Studio Mus in Harlem, 87; fel, Nat Endowment Arts, 85, 89; fel, NY Found Arts, 2000; Artist in Residence, Fel, Fundación, Valparaíso, Almería, Spain, 2004; Res fel, Fulbright Scholar Prog, 2005. *Bibliog:* Michael Welzenbach, Painting From Memories of Another Land, The Washington Post, 9/17/84; Susan Stamberg, interviewer, All Things Considered, Nat Public Radio, Wash DC, 11/8/84; Jane Addams Allen, Alvarado in the vanguard of Hispanic art, The Washington Times, 9/27/84; Edward Lucie-Smith (auth), American Art Now, William Morrow & Co., New York, 85; Pablo Sánchez, dir, Native/Stranger (video), ICS Productions, Wash DC, 86; David Tannous, The Story So Far, El Museo del Barrio, NY, 10/86; Carter Ratcliff, Native/Stranger, El Museo del Barrio, NY, 10/86; Eleanor Heartney, Francisco Alvarado-Juárez, ARTnews, Vol 88 #4, New York, 89; Eleanor Heartney, Fractured Spaces, Inter-American Art Gallery, Miami, Fla, 4/90; Filadelfo Suazo, El Más Grande Pintor Hondureño de nuestra era en "Galería Portales," La Tribuna, Tegucigalpa, Honduras, 8/14/93; Elaine A King (auth), Border to Boarder: Across Lines, Horizons, Vol 1 #6, The Contemp Arts Ctr, Cincinnati, Ohio, 94; Merry Mac Masters (auth), Mito, magia y fantasía en la pintura de Alvarado-Juárez, La Jornada, Mex City, 8/9/95; Vera Milarka, Comentario a la ecología, El País, Mex City, 7/25/95; Mario del Valle, Obra reciente de Alvarado-Juárez, El Financiero, Mex City, 7/18/95; Edward J Sozanski, You can add a phrase to an ecology statement, Philadelphia Inquirer, Pa, 8/21/98; Robert Baxter, Brown-paper beach, Courier Post, NJ, 8/21/98; Sergio del Molino, Alvarado-Juárez, Heraldo de Aragón, Spain, 8/24/2000; Maria Lozano (auth), Francisco Alvarado-Juárez un artista transatlántico: Mus Pablo Serrano, Zaragoza, Spain, 2000; Carl Mellor, Wild Thing, Syracuse New Times, NY, 3/14/2001; Mireya Ballesteros, Nature of Love/Love of Nature, Noticias, Querétaro, Mex, 7/20/2005; Margarita Ladrón de Guevara Heresmann, Francisco Alvarado-Juárez, Diario de Querétaro, Mex, 7/31/2005; Gisela Blas Piñón, Francisco Alvarado-Juárez Artista en todos los sentidos, El Imparcial, Oaxaca, Mex, 3/19/2006; Candelaria López, Rinde Alvarado tributo a la flora y a la fauna, Tiempo, Oaxaca, Mex, 2/4/2006; Jorge Sifuentes Cañas, Mi obra es un homenaje al amor: Francisco Alvarado, La Jornada -Morelos, Mex, 5/31/2006; Jonathan Cohen (auth), About Francisco Alvarado-Juárez & His Secrets, Fondo Editorial Borda Cult, Inst de Cult de Morelos, Mex, 2006; Elaine A King (auth), Passion Puzzles of Francisco Alvarado-Juárez, Fondo Editorial Borda Cult, Mex, 2006; María Teresa Mézquita Méndez, Goza La Topografía del amor, Diario de Yucatán, Mex, 8/8/2007; Jorge A. González, Busca otra lectura de la fotografía, Imagen, Veracruz, Mex, 7/10/2008; José Ángel Gonzalo, Entre Muñecas y peces de colores, El Diario / La Prensa, New York, 11/30/2008; Talina Ramírez, Interviewer, Televisión Universitaria, Xalapa, Veracruz, Mex, 1/21/2009; Marcelo Sánchez Cruz, Llamas y Ofrendas: el arte viendo el conflicto de Oaxaca, Universo, Xalapa, Veracruz, Mex, 2/16/2009; Rigoberto Paredes, Interviewer, Retrato Hablado del Pintor Francisco Alvarado-Juárez, Letra Libre, Tegucigalpa, Honduras, 7/16/2010; Gustavo Banegas, Francisco Alvarado-Juarez, Poeta de la Pintura y el Dibujo, El Heraldo, Tegucigalpa, Honduras, 7/23/2010; Fernando Neda, (auth), Espejos de Luz, Cromos, Vol. 12, no. 8, 139, Tegucigalpa, Honduras, 8/2011; Gustavo Banegas (auth), "Espejos de luz" estará mañana en la Galería Nacional, El Heraldo, Tegucigalpa, Honduras, 7/11/2011; Yenny Hernández (auth), Los espejos de luz de Francisco Alvarado, La Tribuna, Tegucigalpa, Honduras, 7/11/2011; Aileen Jacobson (auth), Celebrating Heritage, and Drawing Others In, The New York Times, Long Island, NY, 12/30/2012. *Mem:* Bronx Mus of Arts; Brooklyn Mus of Art; Everson Mus of Art; Noyes Mus of Art. *Media:* Painting, installation & video art, photography. *Publ:* Ruth Bass (auth), Francisco Alvarado-Juárez, Art News, Vol 91, # 9, New York, 1992; Helen A. Harrison (auth), A Close Look at the Fragile Beauty & Perils of Ocean Reefs, NY Times, 10/25/92; Jorge Luis Berdeja, Mitología Fantástica que rompe los marcos, El Univérsal, Mex City, 7/12/95; Helen A Harrison, Emerging Artists and Irish Works, NY Times, Long Island, NY, 7/21/96; Thomas Piché Jr, Canto a la Fauna, Everson Mus Art, Syracuse, NY 3/3/2001; Elaine A King, An Eloquent Hybrid of Nature & Culture, Museo de Arte Contemporáneo de Oaxaca, Mex, 2/2002; Ronald DeFeo, A Conversation with Francisco Alvarado-Juárez, Review-Latin American Literature and Arts, Fall, #67, NY, 2003; Janet Sassi (auth), Crossing Landscapes, The Bear Deluxe, Vol 20, Portland, Ore, Fall 2003; Mireya Ballesteros, Secretos de Flora y Fauna, Libro de Francisco Alvarado-Juárez, Noticias, Querétaro, Mex 10/6/2006; Leticia González Ortiz (auth), Secretos de flora y fauna, Diario de Morelos, Cuernavaca, México, 5/27/2006; María Acosta Aragón (auth), Brilla, la topografía del amor, Diario de Yucatán, Mérida, México, 7/7/2007; Yenny Hernández, Los Espejos de Luz de Francisco Alvarado, La Tribuna, Tegucigalpa, Honduras, 7/21/2011; Gustavo Banegas, Espejos hacia otra dimensión, El Heraldo, Tegucigalpa, Honduras, 7/22/2011; Samai Torres, Conciencia ecologica desde el pincel Francisco Alvarado, entre la tierra y el mar, Revistas El Heraldo, Tegucigalpa, Honduras, 5/31/15; Francisco Miraval, Museo de Arte presenta la magia de artista visual hondureno, La Prensa de Colorado, Denver, Colo, 5/15/15; Ana Flores, Francisco Alvarado Juarez: Arte desde el tropico hondureno hasta las metropolis del mundo, La Tribuna, Tegucigalpa, Honduras, 2/26/15; Arte, CAC-UNAH inaugura hoy la exposicion Rumbo 5 Hacia el Cuerpo, La Tribuna, Tegucigalpa, Honduras, 2/18/15. *Mailing Add:* 3647 Broadway Apt 2F New York NY 10031-2506

ALVAREZ, CANDIDA
PAINTER, EDUCATOR

b Brooklyn, NY, Feb 2, 1955. *Study:* Fordham Univ, BA, 77, Skowhegan Sch Painting and Sculpture, 81, Yale Univ, MFA, 97. *Work:* Studio Mus Harlem, Whitney Mus Am Art, El Museo Del Barrio & Readers Digest, NY; Univ Del, Newark; German Consulate & Brandywine Workshop, Philadelphia; and many pvt collections. *Comn:* Selected Works by Langston Hughes (mural), CETA Artists proj, NY, 79; drawings, Children's Psychiatric Div, Bellevue Hosp, NY, 84; percent for art, New York, Stained Glass Windows for IS 206A South Bronx, 92. *Exhib:* Recollections, Brooklyn Mus, NY, 79; Books Alive, Met Mus Art, NY, 83; solo exhibs, Paintings and Drawings, June Kelly Gallery, NY, 89 & 93, John Street Series, Galerie Schniderei, Cologne, Ger, 90, Paintings and Works on Paper, Queens Mus, Flushing, NY, 91 & Recent Paintings, Bronx Mus Art, NY, 92, Paintings: 1990-1992, Kenyon Col, Ohio, 93, New/Now: Candida Alvarez, New Britain Mus Am Art, Conn, 92; Working on Paper: Contemp Am Drawing, High Mus Art, Atlanta, Ga, 90; Polyptychs, June Kelly Gallery, NY, 93; Contemp Pub Art in the Bronx, Lehman Coll Art Gallery, Bronx, NY, 93; Paintings: 1989-92, Olin Art Gallery, Kenyon Col, Gambier, Ohio, 93; Artists Talk Back: Visual Conversations with El Museo; Part 3: Reaffirming Spirituality, El Museo Del Barrio, NY, 95; Creative Artists Network: Selections 1984-96 (with Catalog), Woodmere Art Mus, Philadelphia, 96; Community of Creativity: A Century of MacDowell Colony Artists (with catalog), The Currier Gallery Art, Manchester, NH, 96; Heaven-Private View, PS1 Contemp Art Ctr, Long Island City, NY, 97; Exit Art, New York City-Choice 99, Studio Mus, Harlem, NY; Out of Line: Drawings by Illinois Artists, Chicago Cult Ctr, Ill, 2000. *Pos:* juror, Art Kauai, Hawaii. *Teaching:* Vis artist, Hamilton Col, NY, 91, Sch Mus Fine Arts, Boston, 92-93, Trinity Col, Conn, 93, Univ Wis, Oshkosh, 94, Art Inst Chicago, Ill, 95; artist-in-residence, Addison Gallery Am Art, Phillips Acad, Mass, 93, Pilchuck Glass Sch, Wash, 98; vis asst prof art, Kenyon Col, Ohio, 94; instr drawing, Penland Sch Arts & Crafts, 96; teaching asst, Yale Univ Sch Art, 97; part time lectr, Mason Gross Sch Arts, Rutgers Univ, New Brunswick, 97-98; asst prof drawing & painting, Sch Art Inst Chicago, 98-; Int artists studio prog, Stockholm, Sweden, 99; dept art, Univ Wis, Madison, 2000 & Vt Studio Ctr, Johnson, 2000; educ adv comt, Smart Mus, Univ Chicago, Chicago, Pub Art Prog, 99-. *Awards:* NY Found Arts Fel, 86; Mid-Atlantic Nat Endowment Arts Reg Fel, 88; Artist Fel, Art Matters, NY, 89; Pollach-Krasner Found Grant, 95. *Bibliog:* Debra Bricker Balken (auth), rev, Art in Am, 4/94; Holland Cotler (auth), NY Times, 4/95; article, The Herald, 5/96; and others. *Mem:* Coll Art Asn. *Mailing Add:* 5300 S Shore Dr Apt 22 Chicago IL 60615-5719

ALVAREZ-CERVELA, JOSE MARIA
EDUCATOR, HISTORIAN

b La Guardia, Spain, Sept 21, 1922. *Study:* Univ Santiago, Spain, BA, 48, Lic en Derecho, 56, PhD (law & artistic works), 68; Middlebury Col, Vt, MA, 65. *Pos:* Dir, Fine Arts Mus, Univ PR, Mayaguez, 58-64. *Teaching:* Prof art & humanities, Univ PR, Mayaguez, 57-. *Awards:* 1983 Citizen of the Year in Mayaguez in Education, 84. *Mem:* PR Acad Arts, Hist & Archaeol. *Res:* Woodcarving of saints in Puerto Rico;

mural paintings on ceilings and vaults; funerary art in Puerto Rico. *Publ:* Auth, Signos y Firmas Reales, La Comercial, Santiago, Spain, 57; A Pintura Mitologica e Alegorica nos Tectos e Abobadas do Escorial e do Palacio Real, Ed Imperio, Lisbon, 68; Los Contratos de Obra Artistica de la Catedral de Santiago de Compostela en Siglo XVII, Industrias Graficas Noroeste, Spain, 68; La Arquitectura Clasica Actual en Mayaguez, Antillian Coll Press, Mayaguez, 83; El Portico Federico Degetau en UPR Mayaguez, Universidad de Puerto Rico en Mayaguez, 88

ALYS, FRANCIS
CONCEPTUAL ARTIST, PERFORMANCE ARTIST, PAINTER
b Antwerp, Belgium, 1959. *Study:* Inst Archit de Tournai, Belgium, 78-83; Inst Univ Archit di Venezia, Italy, 83-86. *Work:* Nat Mus Mod Art, Centre George Pompidou & ARC, Mus de la Ville de Paris; Art Inst Chicago; Carnegie Mus Art, Pittsburgh; Nat Center Contemp Art, Rome; Guggenheim Mus & Mus Mod Art, New York; Kunsthaus Zurich; Israel Mus, Jerusalem; LA County Mus Art & LA Mus Contemp Art; Tate Collection, Great Britain; Wadsworth Atheneum, Conn; Walker Center Arts, Minneapolis. *Exhib:* Solo exhibs include Galeria Art Contemp, Mex City, 1992, Jack Tilton Gallery, New York, 1995 & 1996, Boulder Mus Contemp Art, Colo, 1996, ACME, Santa Monica, Calif, 1996 & 1999, Mus Art Mod, Mex City, 1997, DIA Center Arts, New York, 1998 & 1999, Portland Inst Contemp Art, Oreg, 1998, Galerie Peter Kilchmann, Zurich, 1999 & 2001, Lisson Gallery, London, 1999 & 2001, Fundacio la Caixa, Barcelona, 2000, Wadsworth Atheneum Mus Art, Hartford, Conn, 2001, The Project, LA, 2002, Mus Mod Art, New York, 2002, Mus Art Mod, Paris, 2003, Centro Nat Art Contemp, Rome, 2003, Mus Art Contemp, Avignon, France, 2004, Kunstmuseum Wolfsburg, Ger, 2004, Nat Portrait Gallery, London, 2005, Israel Mus, Jerusalem, 2005, Hirshhorn Mus & Sculpture Garden, Washington, 2006, David Zwirner, New York, 2007, Hammer Mus, LA, 2007, Univ Chicago Renaissance Soc, 2008; group exhibs include Galeria Art Contemp, Mex City, 1991; Lesa Natura, Mus Art Mod, Mex City, 1993; Havana Bienal, Cuba, 1994, 2000; Interiors, LACE, 1996; Antechamber, Whitechapel Art Gallery, London, 1997, Faces in the crowd, 2004; inSITE 1997, San Diego Mus Art & Centro Cult, Tijuana, Mex, 1997; Mexcellente, Yerba Buena Center Arts, San Francisco, 1998; Loose Threads, Serpentine Gallery, London, 1999, En Route, 2002; go away - Artists & Travel, Royal Coll Art Galleries, London, 1999; Venice Biennial, 1999, 2001, 2007; Versiones del Sur, Mus Nat Reina Sofia, Madrid, 2000, Latin America, 2000; Age of Influence, Mus Contemp Art, Chicago, 2000; Making Time, Hammer Mus, LA, 2001; Painting at the Edge of the World, Walker Art Center, Minneapolis, 2001; Axis Mexico, San Diego Mus Art, 2002, Farsites, 2005; Hello There!, Galerie Peter Kilchmann, Zurich, 2002; Imagenes en movimiento/Moving picture, Guggenheim Bilbao, Spain, 2003-04; Mexico City, PS1 Contemp Art Center, New York, 2003; Structures of Difference, Wadsworth Athenaeum Mus Art, Hartford, Conn, 2003; Extra Art, Inst Contemp Arts, London, 2003; Shanghai Biennial, 2002; Elsewhere, here, Mus Art Mod de la Ville de Paris, 2004; Treble, Sculpture Center, Long Island City, NY, 2004; Made in Mexico, Inst Contemp Art, Boston, 2004; Point of View, New Mus Contemp Art, New York, 2004; Carnegie Int, Carnegie Mus Art, Pittsburgh, 2004; Time Zones, Tate Modern, London, 2004, Acquisitions of the Collection, 2007, Street & Studio, 2008; What's New Pussycat? Mus Mod Kunst, Frankfurt, 2005; Odd Lots, White Columns, New York & Queens Mus Art, 2005; Ecstasy, Geffen Contemp, LA, 2005; Early Work, David Zwirner, New York, 2005; Version Animée, Centre Image Contemp, Geneva, 2006; Satellite of Love, Witte de With, Rotterdam, The Netherlands, 2006; I Am As You Will Be: The Skeleton in Art, Cheim & Read, New York, 2007; Viva la Muerte, Kunsthale Wien, Vienna, 2007; This is Not to be Looked At, Mus Contemp Art, LA, 2008, Collecting Collections, 2008. *Awards:* Named one of 10 Most Important Artists of Today, Newsweek mag, 2011. *Mailing Add:* c/o David Zwirner Gallery 525 W 19th St New York NY 10011

AMADO, JESSE V
SCULPTOR
b San Antonio, Tex, 1951. *Study:* Univ Tex, Austin BA (Eng), 1977, Univ Tex, San Antonio, BFA (studio art), 1987, MFA (studio art), 1990. *Work:* Michael Tracy, pvt collection, San Ygnacio, Tex; Ken Bentley, AIA, pvt collection, San Antonio, Tex; Matthews & Branscomb, Attorneys, corp collection, San Antonio, Tex; Sunbelt Corp, corp collection, San Antonio, Tex. *Exhib:* Solo exhibs, Davis McClain Gallery, Houston, 93, 95, Bemis Ctr Contemp Art, Omaha, Nebr, 94, Milagros Contemp Art Gallery, San Antonio, 94, San Antonio Mus Art, 95, Carla Stellwig Gallery, NY, 95 & Contemp Art Mus, Houston, 96, McNay Mus Art, San Antonio, Tex, 2003; Group exhibs, Commissioners Exhib, Tex Comn Arts, Tobin Estates, San Antonio, 94; Putting it on Paper, McNay Art Inst, San Antonio, 94; Low Tech, Ctr Res Contemp Art, Univ Tex, Arlington, 94; Pace Roberts Found Contemp Art, San Antonio, 95; Tres Proyectos Latinos, Austin Mus Art, Tex, 96; Schemata: Drawings by Sculptors, Glassell Sch Art & Mus Fine Art, Houston, Tex, 96-97; Barbara Davis Gallery, Pennzoil Gallery, Kwanglu, S Korea, 97; Art on Paper: Thirty Third Ann Exhib, Weatherspoon Art Gallery, Univ NC, Greensboro; Linc Real Art, San Francisco, 2001; Univ Tex, San Antonio, 2002; San Antonio Mus Art, 2002; San Francisco Arts Comn Gallery, 2002; Finesilver Gallery, San Antonio, Tex, 2000, 2001; Barbara Davis Gallery, Houston, 2004. *Pos:* Artist-in-residence, Philadelphia Fabric Workshop, 1990-91, Bemis Ctr Contemp Arts, Bemis Found, Omaha, Nebr, 1994, Pace Roberts Found Contemp Art, San Antonio, Tex, 1994-95. *Teaching:* Guest lectr sculpture, Univ Tex, Austin, spring 1996. *Awards:* Visual Arts Orgn Grant Artist-in-residence, 1990 & Visual Artists Fel Grant (sculpture), Nat Endowment Arts, 1990; Visual Arts Fel Grant, Art Matters Inc, NY, 1992; Int Artist in Res Prog, City Gallery Kwanglu, S Korea, 1997. *Bibliog:* Patricia Johnson (auth), Contemporary Art in Texas, Craftsman House, 1994; New Works for a New Space (forward by Robert Storr), Art Pace, San Antonio, 1995; Dana Fries-Hansen (auth), Perspectives Series, Contemp Art Mus, Houston, 1996; Dan Goddard (auth), Reflecting on Beauty, San Antonio Express News, 2/26/2003. *Dealer:* Davis McClain Gallery 2627 Colquitt Houston TX 77098. *Mailing Add:* 816 Camaron St Ste 105 San Antonio TX 78212-5106

AMALFITANO, LELIA
CURATOR, GALLERY DIRECTOR
b New York, NY. *Study:* Calif Inst Arts, Valencia, BFA, 74; Sch Art Inst Chicago, MFA, 78. *Collection Arranged:* New Territory: Art from East Germany, traveling exhib of work by seventeen contemp artists from East Germany (ed & intro, catalog), 90; Between Intuition and Reason (ed, catalog), exhib of work by Jonathan Lasker & St Clair Cemin, 91, Private Visions selected works from pvt collections by Nayland Blake, Cady Noland & Gary Hume, 93, Closed Environments, exhib of work by Jon Cook & Luke Dohner, 94, Self/Conscious Self/Made: Janine Antoni & Bruce Nauman (auth, catalog), selected works, 94, Grossman Gallery, Boston. *Pos:* Vis artist, Art Resources Open to Women, Schenectady, NY, 78; dir & cur, Rathbone Gallery, Russell Sage Jr Col Albany, NY, 83-86; cur, Stux Gallery, Boston & New York, 86-87; cur & dir Exhibs & Vis Artists Progs, Sch Mus Fine Arts, Boston, 86-. *Teaching:* Instr, Women in Art, an art hist survey, Albany Inst Hist & Art, NY, 79; adj prof, Fine Arts Div, Russell Sage Junior Col, Albany, NY, 80-86; instr, Coun Int Educ, Italy, 84. *Bibliog:* Reviews in many publ including, Art New Eng, Boston Globe, Art Am, Boston Phoenix & Albany Times Union. *Publ:* Auth, Self/Made Self/Conscious: Janine Antoni & Bruce Nauman (essay, exhib catalog), Sch Mus Fine Arts, Boston, 94; Carroll Dunhan: Selected Paintings 1990-1995 (essay, exhib catalog), Sch Mus Fine Arts, Boston, 95; Boston School (essay, exhib catalog), Inst Contemp Art, Boston, 95; Social Fictions: Lari Pittman and Andrea Zittel (essay, exhib catalog), Sch Mus Fine Arts, Boston, 96; Lucy Gunning: Persistence of Vision (essay, exhib catalog), Sch Mus Fine Arts, Boston, 96. *Mailing Add:* 441 Shawmut Ave Boston MA 02118-3832

AMANO, TAKA
PAINTER
b Toyama, Japan, Apr 24, 1950. *Study:* Ikvei Col, Tokyo, BA, 71; Sch Visual Arts, New York, BFA, 77. *Work:* Solomon R Guggenheim Mus, NY; NY State Univ, Albany; Bronx Mus Arts, NY. *Exhib:* Five-person show, Artists Space, NY, 84; Curators Choice, Bronx Mus Arts, 85; Selections 30, Drawing Ctr, NY, 85; Ten from the Drawing Ctr, NY, 85; Four-person show, Soho Ctr Visual Artists, NY, 87; New Acquisitions, Guggenheim Mus, NY, 87; Group Show, Jilian Pretto Gallery, NY, 89; solo shows, Jilian Pretto Gallery, NY, 89 & 90. *Awards:* Working Space Prog PS 1, Inst for Art & Urban Resources, 77-79; Nat Endowment Arts Regional Fel, Mid-Atlantic Arts Found, 88; Individual Artist Fel, Nat Endowment Arts, 89. *Bibliog:* Kay Larson (auth), article, New York Mag, 10/20/86; Marc Furstenberg (auth), article, Downtown Mag, 4/8/87. *Media:* Watercolor. *Mailing Add:* 6 Greene St New York NY 10013-5814

AMASON, ALVIN ELI
PAINTER
b McKenny, Tex, Apr 6, 1948. *Study:* Cent Wash Univ, BA, 73, MA, 74; Ariz State Univ, MFA, 76. *Work:* Nat Collection Fine Arts, Smithsonian Inst, Washington, DC; Nordjyllands Kunstmuseum, Aalborg, Denmark; Alaska State Mus, Juneau; Anchorage Hist & Fine Arts Mus, Alaska; Am Embassy, Brasilia, Brazil. *Comn:* Painting (with Robert Hudson, Sam Francis & Dan Flavin), Govt Serv Admin, Anchorage, 79. *Exhib:* Nat Collection Fine Arts, Washington, DC, 80. *Awards:* Jurors Award, Phoenix Mus Art, 75; Purchase Award, Alaska State Coun Arts, 80. *Bibliog:* Jamake Highwater (auth), The Sweet Grass Lives On, Harper & Row, 80; Sculpture out in the open, Newsweek, 8/18/80; Sandra B Betz (auth), Alvin Eli Amason, Arts & Cult N, 81. *Mem:* Alaska State Coun Arts (councilman, 79-80). *Media:* Oil, Mixed. *Dealer:* Decker Morris Gallery 621 W 6th Ave Anchorage AK 99501-2200. *Mailing Add:* c/o University of Alaska Mus PO Box 756960 Fairbanks AK 99775-1200

AMATO, MICHELE (MICAELA)
PAINTER, SCULPTOR
b New York, NY, July 29, 1945. *Study:* Boston Univ, BFA, 68; Univ Colo, Boulder, MFA, 73. *Work:* Chase Manhattan Bank, NY; Nat Mus Women Artists, Washington, DC; Marie Luise Hessel Riverdall Collection, Bard Col, NY; Denver Art Mus, Colo; Rose Art Mus, Brandeis Univ; Palmer Mus Art, Pa; and others. *Exhib:* Solo Exhibs: Minneapolis Coll Art & Design, Minn, 80 & Marianne Deson Gallery, Chicago, 82-84; The Jewish Mus, NY, 94; Yeshiva Univ, NY, 95; Davidson Coll Gallery, NC, 99; Mary Washington Coll Mus, Va, 99; 55 Mercer St Gallery, NY, 98, 99 & 2000; Flatfile Gallery, Chicago, Ill, 2000 & 01; Acme Gallery, Los Angeles, 2005; Forum Gallery, NY, 2007; Riverside Art Mus and Paintings, Edge, Calif, 2008; Kornblee Gallery, New York, 74, 75, 76, 78, 79, 85, 86; Nancy Hoffman Gallery, New York, 2000; Bertha Urdang Gallery, New York, 80; Heather James Gallery, Palm Desert, Calif, 2009; Angles Gallery, Los Angeles, 2010. *Collection Arranged:* Couples Discourse, Palmer Mus Art, Pa, 2006. *Pos:* Interviewer & reviewer art & dance, Straight Creek J, Denver, 73-75 & Boulder Daily Camera, Colo, 76-77, Ocular Mag 76-79 & Pa State Univ, 88-; cur, Patrick Gallery, Austin, Tex, 83-85. *Teaching:* Grad painting & drawing dept head, Wichita State Univ, Kans, 77-78; vis artist, Minneapolis Col Art & Design, 79-80, Univ Tex, San Antonio, 81-82, Univ Tex, Austin, 84, Univ Colo, 84-85 & E Carolina Univ, NC, 86; Tenured prof art & women's studies, Penn State Univ, 88-. *Awards:* Painting Award, Nat Endowment Art, 87, 88 & 92, New Forms Regional Award, 92; Pollock Krasner Fel, 98-99; Research Award, Inst Arts and Humanities, 2007. *Bibliog:* Lucy Lippard (auth), Tijuana Tavolettas, Lafayette Coll Press, Pa, 98; William Zimmer (auth), NY Times, 10/6/99; Robert Saltonstall Mattison (auth), Women's Art Jour, 5/2001; Sarah Rich (auth), Through the Looking Glass: Women and Self Representation, Palmer Mus Art, 2005. *Mem:* Nat Orgn Women Artists; Women's Caucus Art; founding mem Front Range Women, Colo; Coll Art Asn. *Media:* All. *Publ:* Auth, In Praise of Paradox & Contradiction, Westminster Col, Pa; co-cur/auth, Couples Discourse, Penn State Univ Press. *Dealer:* Angles Gallery Los Angeles. *Mailing Add:* 1721 Linden Hall Rd Boalsburg PA 16827

AMAYA, ARMANDO
SCULPTOR
b Puebla, Pue, Mex, Nov 29, 1935. *Study:* Escuela Nac Pintura & Escultura La Esmeralda, with Francisco Zuniga. *Work:* Mex Mus, San Francisco, Calif. *Comn:* Benito Juarez (bronze mask), Mex Govt, Santa Ursula, 69. *Exhib:* Pasquale Iannetti Gallery, San Francisco Mus; Mus Contemp Art, Israel; Museo de Arte Latino Americano, Chile; Galeria Tasende, Mex. *Teaching:* Prof art, Escuela Nac Pintura & Escultura La Esmeralda, 69-. *Bibliog:* Mexican Studies, Univ Calif Press, Vol 3, No 2, 87; Diccionario de escultura mexicana del siglo XX, Universidad Nacional Autonoma de Mex, 83. *Media:* Bronze. *Mailing Add:* Cuauh Temoc 168 Col Deo Carmen Coyoacan CP #04100 Mexico

AMBE, NORIKO
SCULPTOR
b Saitama, Japan, 1967. *Study:* Musashino Art Univ, Tokyo, BFA, 1990. *Work:* Whitney Mus Am Art, New York; Flag Art Found, NY; K.K. Kravis Col, NY & Tokyo; Urawa Mus, Saitama, Japan; Francis J. Greenburger Collection, NY. *Exhib:* Solo exhibs include Gallery Q, Tokyo, 1992, Gallery Natsuka, Tokyo, 1993, 2002 & 2003, J2 Gallery, Tokyo, 1994 & 1995, Makii Masaru Fine Arts, Tokyo, 2001, Pierogi, Brooklyn, 2003, Vt Studio Ctr, 2003, Snug Harbor Cult Ctr, Staten Island, NY, 2004, Josee Bienvenu Gallery, New York, 2006, DEN Contemp Gallery, Culver City, Calif, 2007; group exhibs include Contemp Art Exhib Japan, Tokyo Metrop Art Mus, 1993; Biennale Int Miniature Exhib, Vancouver, Can, 2000; Hudson River Mural, Hudson River Gallery, Dobbs Ferry, NY, 2001; Looking East Looking West: Asian Artists at the Vt Studio Ctr, Brattleboro Mus, Vt, 2002; Line Dancing, Islip Art Mus, NY, 2003; Take Out, Zabriskie Gallery, New York, 2003; Talespinning-Selection Fall 2004, Drawing Ctr, New York, 2004; New World Orders, Experimental Space, New York, 2006; Art on Paper Biannual 2006, Weatherspoon Art Mus, Greensboro, NC, 2006; Making a Home: Japanese Contemp Artists in New York, Japan Soc, New York, 2007. *Awards:* Freeman Fel, 2002-03; Pollock-Krasner Found Grant, 2007. *Bibliog:* Merrily Kerr (auth), New Paper Sculpture, Art on Paper, 2005; Kunie Sugiura (auth), Around the World from NY Report, BT, 2006; Jonathan Goodman (auth), Flat Globe, Sculpture, 2006; Karen Rosemberg (auth), Willingly or Unwillingly, Calling New York Their Home, New York Times, 2007; Eric Bryant (auth), On the Cutting Edge, Art News, 2008. *Media:* Paper; Plastic Film. *Publ:* R. Klanten & M. Hubner (eds), Fully Booked: Cover Art and Design for Books, 5/2008. *Mailing Add:* Noriko Ambe Studio 44-02 23rd St #415 Long Island City NY 11101

AMBROSE, ANDY
MUSEUM DIRECTOR
Study: Univ Tenn, BA, MA (Hist); Emory Univ, PhD (Am Studies). *Pos:* Historic Res Coordr, dir, Mus Exhibs, COO Atlanta Hist Ctr, formerly; exec dir, Tubman African Am Mus, Macon, Ga, 2006-. *Mailing Add:* Tubman African American Museum PO Box 6671 Macon GA 31208

AMBROSE, CHARLES EDWARD
PAINTER, EDUCATOR
b Memphis, Tenn, Jan 6, 1922. *Study:* Univ Ala, BFA, 49, MA, 50. *Work:* Univ Southern Miss; Carey Col; Biloxi Art Asn; First Nat Bank, Hattiesburg, Miss. *Comn:* Portrait reliefs, 58 & portraits, 60, Univ Southern Miss; Pat Harrison Waterways Bldg, 65; Carey Col; Miss Archives Bldg, 72. *Exhib:* Mid-Continent Exhib, Mo, 71; Watercolor USA, Springfield, Mo, 73; 1st Ann Bi-State, Meridian, Miss, 73; Central South, Nashville, Tenn, 75; 17th Dixie Ann, Montgomery, Ala, 75. *Teaching:* Assoc prof drawing & painting, Univ Southern Miss, 50-70; head art dept, Miss Univ for Women, 70-82. *Awards:* First Place Watercolor, Miss Art Asn, 68; First Place Drawing, Edgewater Ann, 70; Purchase Award/Drawing, 1st Ann Bi-State, 73. *Mem:* Southeastern Coll Arts Conf; Nat Coun Art Adminr; Southern Asn Sculptors; Coll Art Asn; Miss Art Asn. *Media:* Watercolor, Oil. *Mailing Add:* 1125 Seventh St N Columbus MS 39701-3409

AMBROSE, KIRK
EDUCATOR, ADMINISTRATOR
Study: Oberlin Col, Ohio, BA (Art History), 1990; McGill Univ, Canada, Studied French Literature, 1991-92; Univ of Mich, Ann Arbor, MA (History in Art), 1994, PhD (History of Art), 1999. *Teaching:* Instructor, Univ Colo, Boulder, 1999-2001, asst prof. 2001-09, assoc prof, 2009-, assoc chair for undergraduate studies, department of art and art history, 2008-10, assoc chair for art history, department of art and art history, 2011-12, chair, department of art and art history, 2012-. *Awards:* Recipient of several awards and fellowships. *Mem:* Col Art Asn (editor designate, The Art Bulletin, 2012-2013, editor-in-chief 2013-); International Center of Medieval Art; International Medieval Soc; Medieval Acad of America; Societe Francaise d'Archeologic. *Publ:* Contributor of articles to several publications and book chapters; (auth) The Nave Sculpture of Vezelay: The Art of Monastic Viewing, 2006; (co-ed) Current Directions in Eleventh- and Twelfth-Century Sculpture Studies, 2010. *Mailing Add:* Department of Art and Art History UCB 318 University of Colorado Boulder CO 80309-0318

AMBROSE, RICHARD MICHAEL
DIRECTOR, CURATOR
b Feb 23, 1954. *Study:* Univ Ore, BFA, 79; Colo State Univ, MFA, 81. *Collection Arranged:* Ansel Adams: Classic Images, 89; Frank Lloyd Wright: California Architecture, 90; The Am Cowboy: From Saddle to the Silverscreen, 92; Stuart Davis and His Contemporaries, 95; Rodin and His Contemporaries, 98; Am Accents, Masterpieces from the San Francisco Mus Fine Arts, 2004; Pop Art and its Legacy, 2004. *Pos:* Cur visual art, Sandre de Cristo Arts Ctr, Pueblo, Colo, 84-88; prog dir, Fresno Metrop Mus, Calif, 88-92; deputy dir, Sunrise Mus Inc, Charleston, WVa, 93-; bd mem, Governor's Mansion Historic Preserv, 97-; deputy dir/cur art, Arampato Discovery Mus, Charleston, WV, 2003-. *Teaching:* Drawing instr, WV State Univ, 2005. *Mem:* Pueblo Arts Coun (vpres, 84-88); Fresno Arts Coun (bd mem, 89-91); WVa Arts Advocacy (vpres). *Publ:* Auth, Contemporary Visions of New Mexico (exhib catalog), 85; Shaman of the Prairie: Orlin Helgoe Retrospective (exhib catalog), 85; coauth, Marc Chagall: Les Ames Mortes (exhib catalog), 94; Lee Savage: A Retrospective (exhib catalog), 95; (auth), Color & Light: Selections from Vincent Melzac Collection (exhib catalog), 97; auth, Where Are They Now? (exhib catalog), 98; auth, Appalachian Corridors Juried Exhib (catalog), 2003. *Mailing Add:* Avampato Discovery Museum 300 Leon Sullivan Way Charleston WV 25301

AMELCHENKO, ALISON M
PAINTER, INSTRUCTOR
b Summit, NJ, Nov 30, 1947. *Study:* Pratt Inst, BFA, 69; Studied with Jochen Seidel. *Comn:* murals, Rohallion Estate, Rumson, NJ, 2000. *Exhib:* Solo exhibs, Ocean Co Col, Toms River, NJ, 85 & Georgian Ct Col, Lakewood, NJ, 90; Noyes Mus, Oceanville, NJ, 2001; Georgian Ct Col, Lakewood, NJ, 2001. *Pos:* Chmn, Ocean Co Cult & Heritage Comn, 91-99, vice-chair, 2000-2001 & commissioner, 2001-. *Teaching:* Dir, instr, Kids Art Studio, Sea Girt, NJ, 90-. *Awards:* Best in Show, Ocean Co Artists Guild, 82, 2000. *Mem:* Ocean Co Artist Guild (pres, 87-89). *Media:* Oils. *Dealer:* Thistledown Gallery 1405-1 Third Ave Spring Lake NJ 07762. *Mailing Add:* Ocean Co Cultural & Heritage Comn 126 Osborne Ave Point Pleasant Beach NJ 08742

AMEND, EUGENE MICHAEL
HISTORIAN, ADVISOR
b Jefferson City, Mo, Oct 31, 1950. *Study:* Univ Mo, Columbia, BA, 75, MA, 77; studied with Dr Saul Weinberg, Dr Edzard Baumann, Dr Osmond Overby & Dr Vera Townsend. *Collection Arranged:* Nathan Jones: Works on Paper, Univ Tex, Dallas, 79; Arie Van Selm: Recent Works, Tex Woman's Univ, Denton, 79; Charles Campbell: Retrospective, Longview Mus & Art Ctr, Tex, 79; Auguste Ravier, 1814-1895, Univ Tex, Dallas, 81; Rob Pepper: Biblical Interpretation, Northway Church, Dallas, Tex, 2008. *Pos:* Cur & art historian, Stewart Gallery, Dallas, 78-80; art adv & freelance cur, EM Amend & Assoc, Dallas, 80-; dir, Omni Art, Dallas, 84-; consult, Tex Instruments Inc, 87-, Achievement Video Network Inc, 88-89 & Art Alley, 95-98; Raytheon Tech Inst, 98-. *Teaching:* Instr art hist & humanities, Univ Mo, Columbia, 75-76; instr art hist, Richland Coll, 80-93; instr humanities, Brookhaven Coll, Dallas, Tex, 2002-2011. *Awards:* Excellence in Teaching award, Sch Arts, Brookhaven Coll, Dallas, Tex, 2011, 2012. *Mem:* Coll Art Asn; Artist Coalition Tex (pres, 79-80); Tex Asn Art Dealers (pres, 93-); candidate mem Am Soc Appraisers. *Res:* American artists and current art patrons and patronage in regional localities; Australian artist, Norman Lloyd (1895-1983). *Mailing Add:* 3130 Chatsworth Dr Dallas TX 75234

AMENOFF, GREGORY
PAINTER
b St Charles, Ill, 1948. *Study:* Beloit Coll, BA, 1970; Mass Coll Arts, DFA (hon) 1994. *Hon Degrees:* Mass Coll Art, D, 94. *Work:* Albright-Knox Art Gallery, Buffalo, NY; Art Inst of Chicago; Metrop Mus Art, NY; Mus Mod Art, NY; Whitney Mus Am Art; Brooklyn Mus Art; Butler Inst Am Art, Youngstown, Ohio; Currier Gallery Art, Manchester, NH; and others. *Exhib:* Solo exhibs, Thirty Views, Lyman Allyn Art Mus, New London, Conn, Lowe Art Gallery, Syracuse Univ, NY, Univ Art Gallery, SUNY, Oswego & Maier Art Mus, Randolph-Macon Women's Col, Lynchburg, Va, 98-2000, Silvermine Guild Arts Ctr, New Canaan, Conn, 99, Paintings, Galerie Vidal St Phalle, Paris, 99, Gregory Amenoff Thirty Views, Nielsen Gallery, Boston, Gregory Amenoff Paintings, Salander O'Reilly Galleries, NY 99, & Gregory Amenoff, Selected Paintings, Drawings and Prints 1987-99, Wright Mus Art, Beloit (Wis) Col, 2000, Facing North, Alexandre Gallery, NY, 2007; group exhibs include Works on Paper, Hayden Corridor, Mass Inst Technol, 76; Stephen Wirtz Gallery, San Francisco, 83; Texas Gallery, Houston, 84; The Monotypes, Butler Inst Am Art, Columbus, Ohio, 89; Hirschl & Adler Modern, NY, 90; The Symphony of Trees Project, Art & Cult Ctr Hollywood, Fla, 98; Green Woods and Crystal Water: The Am Landscape Tradition Since 1950, Philbrook Mus Art, Tulsa, 99; Mark Makers: Painterly Abstraction from the Colo Collection, Univ Coll Art Galleries, Boulder, 99; Invitational Exhib of Painting and Sculpture, Am Acad Arts & Letters, NY, 99; Green Woods and Crystal Water: The Am Landscape Tradition Since 1950, the Philbrook Mus Art, Tulsa, 99; Mark Makers: Painterly Abstraction from the Colorado Collection, Univ Colo Art Galleries,Boulder, 99; After Nature II, Herter Art Gallery, Univ Mass, Amherst, 99; Beyond the Mountains: The Contemp Am Landscape, Lyman Allyn Mus Art, New London, Conn, Ft Wayne (Ind) Mus Art, Boise Art Mus, Polk art Mus, Landeland, Fla, Muskegon Mus Art & Newcomb Art Gallery Tulane U, New Orleans, 99; The Contemp Landscape, Mira Mar Gallery, Sarasota, Fla, 2000; The Poetry of the Earth is Never Dead, 55 Mercer St, NY, 2000; An Homage to Albert Pinkham Ryder, The State of Art Gallery, Brooklyn, 2000; over 65 group exhibs, 74-90. *Pos:* Pres, Nat Accad Design Sch Fine Arts, New York City, 2000-. *Teaching:* Grad painting, Sch Visual Arts, 87; prof art, Columbia Univ, NY, 94-. *Awards:* Mass Bicentennial Painting Award, 76; Nat Endowment Arts, 80, 81 & 89; Tiffany, 80; Recipient Purchase award, Am Acad of Arts and Letters, 1993, 1995, 1996; John Simon Guggenheim Memorial Foundation 2011 Fine Arts Fellowship. *Bibliog:* Ed Hallahan (auth), Gregory Amenoff: The Monotypes, Dialogue, 3/4/89; Donald Kuspit (auth), Gregory Amenoff Hirschl Aldler Modern, Art Forum, summer, 93; Eleanor Heartney (auth), Gregory Amenoff at Salander O'Reilly, Art in America, 10/2000; William Zimmer (auth), Foray into the big forms of land, sea and sky, New York Times, 10/24/99. *Mem:* Nat Accad Design (assoc, 1991; acad, 1994). *Media:* Oil. *Collection:* Moma, The Metropolitan Museum of Art; The Whitney Museum of American Art; and many others. *Publ:* Notes on identity a look at the landscape in American painting, Napa Contemp Arts Found J, Vol 1, 92; cover art, (Donald Kuspit, auth), The Rebirth of Painting in the Late Twentieth Century, Cambridge U Press, 2000; cover art, Full Moon Boat, Graywolf Press, St Paul, Minn, 2000. *Mailing Add:* c/o Nielsen Gallery 128 Eastbrook Rd Carlisle MA 01741-1755

AMES, LEE JUDAH
ILLUSTRATOR, WRITER
b New York, NY, Jan 8, 1921. *Study:* Columbia Univ, with Carnahan. *Work:* Many pieces, layouts & finished illus in Univ Ore & Univ Southern Miss permanent collections. *Pos:* Art dir, Weber Assocs, New York, 47-52; pres, Ames Advert, New York, 53-54, Lee Ames & Zak Ltd, 75- & Lee J Ames Enterprises; artist-in-residence, Doubleday Publ Co, New York, 55-60. *Teaching:* Instr comic art, Sch Visual Arts, New York, 48-49; lectr advert art, Dowling Coll, 70-72. *Awards:* Garden State Children's Book Award, 86. *Mem:* Nat Cartoonists Soc; Berndt Toast Gang. *Media:* Mixed Media. *Publ:* City Street Games (co-auth with Jocelyn Ames), New York: Holt, Rinehart and Winston, 1963; The Draw 50 series (27 titles), New York, 1974-2000; Make 25 Crayon Drawings of the Circus, 1st ed, Garden City, NY: Doubleday, 1980; Make 25 Felt-Tip Drawings Out West, 1st ed, Garden City, NY: Doubleday, 1980 ; Draw, Draw, Draw, 1st ed. Garden City, NY: Doubleday, 1962; Drawing with Lee Ames: From the Bestselling, Award-Winning Creator of the Draw 50 Series, A Proven Step-by-Step Guide to the Fundamentals of Drawing for All Ages, 1st ed, New York: Doubleday, 1990 ; The Dot, Line, and Shape Connection, or, How to Be Driven to Abstraction, 1st ed. Garden City, NY: Doubleday, 1982 ; illusr, Isaac Asimmov (auth) Great Ideas of Science, Houghton Mifflin, Boston, 1969; illustr, Mary Blocksma (auth), Amazing Mouths and Menus, Prentice-Hall, Englewood Cliffs, NJ, 1986 ; illustr, Shannon Garst (auth), Big Foot Wallace of the Texas Rangers, New York, 1951.; illustr, Adelaide Holl (auth). Hide-and-Seek ABC, New York, 1971; illustr, David Knight (auth), The Battle of the Dinosaurs, NJ, 1982. ; illustr, Jerome Edward Leavitt (auth), By Land, By Sea, By Air, The Story of Transportation, New York, 1969. ; illustr, Alvin Harold Urey Silverstein (auth), The Man Who Explored from Earth to Moon, New York, 1970; illustr, Herbert Spencer Zim, Commercial Fishing, New York, 1973; and many more. *Mailing Add:* 41 Hemlock Ave Huntington NY 11743

AMICO, DAVID MICHAEL
PAINTER, INSTRUCTOR
b Rochester, NY, Sept 24, 1951. *Study:* Calif State Univ, Fullerton, BA, 74; Hunter Col, New York, 75. *Exhib:* New Figuration in Am, Milwaukee Art Mus, Wis, 82; Sonata, Newport Harbor Art Mus, Newport Beach, Calif, 82; Circus Boy, 87 & Profound Visions, 88, Ace Contemp Exhibs, Los Angeles; Ace Gallery, Los Angeles, 89 & 90, Mexico City, 99, NY, 2000; Los Angeles Munic Gallery, Sociedade Cult Arte Brazil, 90; Solo exhibs: Marc Jancou Galerie, Zurich, Switz, 91; Physical Abstraction in Los Angeles, Ace Gallery, Los Angeles, 92 & 94, Douglas Lawing Gallery, 94; Ace Gallery, 98; Ace Gallery, Los Angeles, Calif, 2000-04; Claremont Graduate Univ, Claremont, Calif, 2002; Toy District, Ace Gallery, 2003; Drift Trace Paintings, Ace Gallery, 2007-2008; Factory/Park Series, Gallery Reis, Singapore, 2011; Factory Park, Ace Gallery, 2012. *Teaching:* full prof, Claremont Grad Univ, Claremont, Calif. *Awards:* Guest Honorarium Cartier Found, Juey es Josas France, 90; Pellack Krasner Found Award, 94, 97; Pres Scholars Distinguished Teacher Award. *Bibliog:* Christopher Knight (auth), Amico's paintings portray private mystery, Los Angeles Herald Examiner, 81; Ralph Rugoff (auth), Hottest new artists, Los Angeles Mag, 85; Lee Wohlfert-Wihldorg (auth), LA's electric, eclectic artists, Town & Country, 86; Margaret Lazzari (auth), Parameters of Meaning, Artweek, 6/90; Lisa Zeitz (auth), The Last Cry in Abstractionism, Kunstmarkt, 2000; Christopher Knight (auth), Accidental Art that Transforms, LA Times, 7/2008; Alice Hutchison (auth), A Conversation with David Amico, (exhib catalog), Gallery Reis, Singapore. *Media:* Oil, Drawing. *Dealer:* Douglas Chrismas 5514 Wilshire Blvd Los Angeles CA 90036; Ace Gallery 9430 Wilshire Blvd Los Angeles CA 90036. *Mailing Add:* 443 S San Pedro No 601 Los Angeles CA 90013

AMOROS, GRIMANESA
PAINTER, SCULPTOR, VIDEO ARTIST
b July 21, 1962. *Study:* The Art Students League, MY, 85-88. *Work:* Univ Vt, Burlington; Doro Productions, Vienna, Austria; Poncidi Press, Rhinebeck, NY; Latin Am Mag, Coltsdale, Ariz; Jack Lowe Visual Arts, NY. *Comn:* Lighting Sculpture Installation, Int Corporate Art, The Art Advisors of Royal Caribbean International Cruise Lines, Racimo, 2010; Lighting Sculpture Installation, 54th Venice Biennale Collateral Event, Uros Island, 2011; Lighting Sculpture Installation, Times Square Public Arts Program in Collab with Armory Show, Uros House, 2011. *Exhib:* Solo exhibs, Mus Nahin Isaias, Ecuador, 91, Mus Mod Art, Ecuador, 92, Javier Lumbreras Fine Art, Fla, 93, Porter Troupe Gallery, San Diego, 93, Carolyn J Roy Gallery, NY, 94, Mus Mod Art, Sto Domingo Rep Dominican, 95 & Art Renaca Gallery, Chile, 97, Egizio's Project, Timeless Terracotta, NY, 99, Artco Gallery, Installations of Drawings, Lima, Peru, 03; The Body Electric, Spruill Ctr Gallery, Atlanta, 97; K & A Gallery, France, 97. *Awards:* Art Student League, painting fel, 85 & merit scholar, 86; Nat Endowment Arts, 93 & 94; Fel Va Ctr for Creative Arts Residency, 02; Art In Embassies Prog, US State Dept, Lima, Peru, 03. *Bibliog:* Pamela Blume Leonard (auth), Fashion speaks volumes, J Constitution, Art Leisure, 9/97; Michael Carravagio (auth), Body electric, Dunwood Crier, Atlanta, 9/3/97; Pat Worrell (auth), The body electric, Am Style Mag, Atlanta, 8-9/97; Castro, Juan El Universo, Guayaquil, Ecuador, 2001; Trowbridge, Tom KUNM Radio, Santa Fe Art Series, 2002; and others. *Mem:* Art in Gen (bd dirs); Inst for Women and Art Advisory Council; Adarsh Alphons Projects (bd dirs). *Media:* Installation Sculpture, Plastic, Lexan Diffusion Material, Custom Lighting Sequence, Electrical Hardware. *Dealer:* Porter Troupe Gallery 301 Spruce St San Diego CA 92103; Itturalde Gallery 154 La Brea Ave Los Angeles CA 90069. *Mailing Add:* 117 Hudson St 6th fl New York NY 10013

AMOROSO, NICOLAS ALBERTO AMOROSO BOELCKE
PAINTER, FILMMAKER
b San Miguel de Tucuman, Arg, May 15, 1944. *Study:* Facultad de Artes Univ Nac de Tucuman, Artes Plast, 68; Faculted de Bellas Aftes Univ Nac La Plata, Lic Cinematography, 72 & Prof Sup Cinematography, 74 Ar; PhD, Universidad Autonoma Metrop de Mex. *Work:* Mus de Arte Contemp Latinoamericano, Punta del Este, Uruguay; Mus de Artes y Ciencias, Univ Nac Autonaoma, Mus de Arte Jose Luis Cuevas, Mexico City; Mus Nac de Arte, Managua, Nicaragua; Mus Prov de Bellas Artes, Buenos Aires, Arg. *Comn:* Pintura mural sobre una cupula, comn by Ing Alfredo Sliapnic, Mexico City, 92. *Exhib:* La Seriegrafia en el Arte, Mus de Artes y Ciencias, Mexico City, 84; De su Album Inciertas, Mus de Arte Mod, Mexico City, 85; Las Horas que Pasan, Mus de Arte Mod, Mexico City, 87; Conociendo a Victoria, Mus de Bellas Artes, Tucuman, 91; Carpeta Universitaria, Mus de la Estampa, Mexico City, 93; La ciudad de la imagen, pinturas, Galeria Parish, Washington, DC, 2006. *Teaching:* Prof & investigador diseno & grafico, Univ Autonoma Metrop de Mex, 82-2007, dir de tesis de doctorado en diseno, 2006-2007. *Awards:* Mencion de Honor, XIII Salon de Artes, 76 & Primer Premio, XV Salon de Artes, 77, Mus de Buenos Aires. *Bibliog:* Silvestre Byron (auth), La Optica Descarnada, Pajaro de Fuego, 78; Santiago Espinosa (auth), Historia de Vida, Revista Universitaria, 87; Raquel Tibol (auth), Memoria y Olivido, Proceso, 91. *Mem:* Asociacion Mex de Estudios en Estetica. *Media:* Acrylic, Oil; Video. *Publ:* Auth, La imagen como discurso, Artes Visuales, 79; Tata Dios, Univ Autonoma Metrop de Mex, 88; coauth, Las Artes Plasticas y el Disneo, Trece Ensayos Univ Autonoma Metrop de Mex, 88; Creacion: Contexto de la Idea, Teoria/Arte Univ Autonoma Metrop de Mex, 91; auth, El Acto de Crear, Univ Autonoma Metrop de Mex, 93; auth, La gran pizarra, la ciudad de la imagen, Significacao, Revista Brasileira de Semiotica, 2003; auth, El cine latinoamericano, Revista de Occidente, Fundacion Jose Ortega y Gasset, Madrid, 2005; auth, Nombrar la historia, el cine como instrumento, Fuentes Humanisticas, UAM, 2006. *Dealer:* Galeria Juan Martin Dickens 33B Colonia Polanco Mex DF 11560 Mexico. *Mailing Add:* Av Centenario 300 Ed 6 Dpto 503 Lomas de Tarango Mexico DF 01620 Mexico

AMOS, EMMA
PAINTER, PRINTMAKER
b Atlanta, Ga, Mar 16, 1938. *Study:* Antioch Coll, Yellow Springs, Ohio, BA, 1958; London Cent Sch Art, Eng, BFA, 1960; New York Univ, MA, 1965. *Work:* Mus Mod Art, NY; Wadsworth, Atheneum, Conn; Newark Mus, NJ; NJ State Mus, Trenton; Minn Mus Art, Minn. *Comn:* Mosaic Ceiling, NY Bd Educ, 94; Mosaics, bronzes, landscaping, Ralph David Abernathy Mem, Atlanta, 96. *Exhib:* Solo exhibs, Art Resources Transfer (ART), New to NY, recent retrospective exhib, Oct 6-Nov, 2002; Emma Amos, Works on Paper, The Nat Afro-Am Mus and Cult Ctr, Wilberforce, Ohio, 2004; K Caraccio Printmaking Studio, NY, Print Retrospective, April-Oct 2004, Online at www.kcaraccio.com; Emma Amos Works on Paper, Middle Collegiate Church, NY, Jan-Feb, 2005; Flomenhaft Gallery, Emma Amos, Paintings and Prints, Chelsea, NY, 2006, Headfirst Flomenhaft Gallery, 2008, Heroes & Folk, Lamont Gallery, Exeter, NH, 2010, Spiral: A Perspective on African Am Coll, Birmingham Mus, Ala, 2010-2011, Studio Mus, Harlem, NY, 2011; group shows incl Committed to Print, Mus Mod Art, NY, 1988-90; The Decade Show, Mus Contemp Hispanic Art, NY, 1990; Bronx Mus, McIntosh Gallery, Ga; Changing the Subject (traveling exhib), Art in Gen, NY, 1994-95; Emma Amos Paintings & Prints 1982-1992 retrospective, Coll Wooster Art Mus, 1994-95; Bearing Witness, Contemp Works by African Am Women Artists (traveling exhib), Spelman Col, 1996; Academy of Arts and Letters, Ceremonial Exhib, New York City, May, 2003; Crosscurrents in the Mainstream: Transcultural NJ, catalogue, The Jane Voorhees Zimmerli Mus of Art, Rutgers, The State Univ of NJ, April-July, 2004; On Their Own: Transcultural New Jersey, Mason Gross Sch of Arts Galleries, with Melvin Edwards, Fausto Sevila, Hughie Lee Smith, Tashiko Takaezu 2004; and many others. *Pos:* prof, chair, Mason Gross Sch Arts, Rutgers Univ, retired; trustee, Richard A Florsheim Art Fund, currently; co-chair bd govs, Skowhegan Sch Painting & Sculpting, Maine, currently. *Teaching:* Prof fine art, Mason Gross Sch Arts, Rutgers Univ, NJ, 1980-2008; gov, Skowhegan Sch Painting & Sculpture, 1987. *Awards:* Nat Endowment Fel-Drawing, 1983; NY Found Fel--Painting, 1989; The Jame Van Derzee Award, Kimmel Ctr, PA, 2002; Purchase Award, American Acad of Arts & Letters, NY, 2003; Lifetime Achievement Award, Women 's Caucus for Art, CAA, Seattle, 2004; Pollock-Krasner Found, 2010; Civitella Ranieri Found Fel, 2012-2013. *Bibliog:* Peter Erickson (auth), Seeing White, Vol 5, No 3, Transition Mag, Oxford Univ Press, NC, fall 1995; Art on my mind-visual politics, New Press, New York, 1995; Subject: Action Lines, L&M Video, 1996; City Paper, Darkness Visible: The BMA Exhib the Sights of Blackness, Lee Gardner, Feb 13, 2002; Nka: Journal of Contemp African Art, Emma Amos, Art Matters, Dr Sharon Patton, pp42-47, Fall-Winter, 2002-2003; Creating their Own Image: African- AM Women Artist, Lisa Farrington, PhD, Amos, Cover Art, Tightrope, Nov Pub, 2004; Creating Black AM, Nell Irvin Painter, Oxford Univ Press, Illustration, Paul Robeson Frieze, 2005. *Mem:* Coll Art Asn; Nat Acad Design. *Media:* Acrylic; Mosaic. *Collection:* AZ State Univ Art Mus, Tempe, AZ; Bellevue Hospital Fine Arts Collection, New York, NY; Birmingham Mus of Fine Art, AL; Colgate-Palmolive Collection, NY; The College Board Collection of Prints by AM Artist, New York City; The Columbia Mus, Columbia, SC; Dade County Mus of Art, FL; The Ford Fountain; Mus Modern Art, NY; Morris Mus, Augusta, Ga; Phila Mus Art, Pa; Nat Gallery, Wash DC; Schomberg Coll, NYPL, NY; Spellman Coll Mus, Atlanta, Ga. *Publ:* Coauth, Racism is the issue, Issue 15, 82, & The Art of Education, Issue 25, 90, Heresies Collective; illusr, IKON--Creativity and Change, No 5/6, Ikon Inc, 1986; auth & co-host, Show of Hands (ser), WGBH Educ TV, Boston, Mass, 1987-88; coauth, M/E/A/N/I/N/G Magazine, Mira Schor & Susan Bee, 1990. *Dealer:* Flomenhaft Gallery NY. *Mailing Add:* 21 Bond St New York NY 10012-2451

AMOSS, BERTHE
ILLUSTRATOR, PAINTER
b New Orleans, La, Sept 26, 1925. *Study:* Newcomb Col, BA; Univ Hawaii; Kunsthalle Bremen, Ger, three yrs; Acad des Beaux Arts, Antwerp, Belg, one yr; Tulane Univ, MA (literature & art). *Work:* La State Libr; De Grummond Collection, Univ Southern Miss, Kerlan; Town of Kerlan, Minn; Tulane Univ. *Exhib:* One person show, Exhib of Illustrators, Howard Tilton Libr, Tulane Univ, 82. *Pos:* Children's bk rev ed, New Orleans Times Picayune, currently; pres, More Than a Card Inc, currently; pres, Cocodrie Press, currently. *Teaching:* Instr, writing & illustrating children's books, Tulane Univ, 76-82, children's literature & folklore, 82-. *Bibliog:* Selma Lanes (auth), Down the Rabbit Hole, Children's Literature, Stewig. *Media:*

Watercolor. *Publ:* Auth & illusr, The Marvelous Catch of Old Hannibal, 70, Old Hasdrubal and the Pirates, 71, Parents Publ; Secret Lives, Atlantic-Little-Brown, 79; The Loup Garou, Pelican, 79; auth, Mockingbird Song, Tom in the Middle, What did you lose Santa, Harper & Row, 87 & 88; auth, More Than a Card, private publ, 88; auth, Draw Yourself into the Ark, WAU Press, 03; auth, Draw Yourself into a Starlit Journey, WAU Press, 03; co-auth rev ed, Writing & Illustrating Children's Books, Writers Digest Books, 05. *Mailing Add:* 3723 Carondelet St New Orleans LA 70115

ANACKER, JOHN WILLIAM
GALLERY DIRECTOR, PAINTER
b Bozeman, Mont, June 22, 1960. *Study:* Mont State Univ, BAA, 83; Univ NC, Chapel Hill, MFA, 86. *Exhib:* 29th Ann Nat Exhib Am Art, Chautauqua Art Asn Galleries, NY, 86; Celebrating Paper, Yellowstone Art Ctr, Billings, Mont, 88. *Pos:* Gallery dir, Haynes Fine Arts Gallery, Bozeman, Mont, 86-. *Teaching:* Instr painting, Mont State Univ Sch Art, 86-. *Mem:* Mont Art Gallery Dirs Asn (treas, 89-90 & pres, 90-). *Media:* Watercolor. *Mailing Add:* 11 Flathead Ave Bozeman MT 59718-6335

ANASTASI, WILLIAM (JOSEPH)
PAINTER, SCULPTOR
b Philadelphia, Pa, Aug 11, 1933. *Study:* Univ Pa, 53-61. *Work:* Mus Contemp Art, Los Angeles, Calif; Contemp Mus, Honolulu, Hawaii; Moderna Museet, Stockholm, Sweden; Chrysler Mus, Norfolk, Va; Oklahoma City Art Mus. *Comn:* Viewing a Film of the Period (film), 78, Collapse (photo installation), 81 & Terminus II (photo installation), 81, Whitney Mus Am Art; photo installation, Kunstmus, Dusseldorf, Ger, 79; Terminus I (photo installation), Hudson River Mus, NY, 79. *Exhib:* Menil Collection, Houston, Tex, 94; Mito Tower, Japan, 94; Philadelphia Mus Art, Pa, 95; Niels Borch Jensen Gallery, Berlin, Ger, 2000; Stalke Gallery, Copenhagen, 2000; Anastasi Bradshaw and Cage 2001, Museet for Samtidskunst, Roskelde, Denmark, 2001; Anastasi Bradshaw, Cage and Cunningham, Bayly Art Mus, Univ Va, 2005; Bjorn Ressle Fine Art, 2006. *Pos:* Artistic co-adv, Merce Cunningham Dance Co, NY, 84-; artist-in-residence, Sirius Art Ctr, Cork, Ireland, 2000 & Statens Vaerkstedes for Kunst, Copenhagen, 2000. *Teaching:* Painting, Sch Visual Arts, NY, 71-86; lectr, Art After Duchamp, Chicago Art Fair, 88, Yale Univ, 91; Alfred Jarry & James Joyce, The Sorbonne, Paris, 95. *Bibliog:* Gregory Battcock (auth), Minimal Art (Introduction), Dutton, 68; Lucy R Lippard (auth), Six Years: The De-materialization of the Art Object, Praeger, 73; Brian O'Doharty, Inside the white cube: Notes on the Gallery Space, Artforum, 3/76; Thomas McEvilley (auth), The Triumph of Anti-Art, McPherson & Co, 2005. *Media:* All Media. *Interests:* Chess. *Publ:* Duchamp on the Jarry Road, Artforum, 9/91; Me Innerman Monophone & Even Haha, Notes on Jarry & Duchamp with Joyce, Anders Tornberg Gallery, Lund, Sweden, 5/92; Jarry, Joyce, Duchamp & Cage, Venice Biennale, 93; Jarry in Joyce, Joyce Studies Ann, 95; Marcel Duchamp in Finnegan's Wake Tout Fait, 2003; Aaron Levy & Jean-Michel Rabate (eds), William Anastasi's Pataphysical Society, Jarry, Joyce, Duchamp & Cage, Slought Found, Philadelphia, Pa, 2005. *Dealer:* Anders Tornberg Gallery Lund Sweden; Sandra Gering Gallery New York; Nicholas von Bartha Gallery London Great Britian; Thomas Rehbein Gallery Cologne Germany; Art Agents Gallery Hamburg Germany; Stalke Gallery Copenhagen; Ressle Fine Art New York NY; Baumgartner Gallery New York NY; 360 Degrees Gallery Tokyo Japan; Peter Blum Gallery New York NY

ANASTASIA, SUSANNA
PAINTER, INSTRUCTOR
b Elizabeth, NJ, July 26, 1945. *Study:* Newark Sch Fine & Indust Art, 66; studied with noted artists. *Work:* Prudential Bache, NY; Wall Twp Bd Educ, NJ; Sea Girt Libr, NJ; Capital Contracting & Design, Plainfield, NJ; Trenton-Mercer Campus Capital Health Syst, Trenton, NJ; Techiemedia, NJ. *Comn:* Painting for Christine Todd Whitman/NJ Gov's Mansion, John R Whitman, Island Beach State Park, 98; guest house watercolor for company postcard, Conover Guest House, Bay Head, NJ, 99; burro portrait Weidel's Boxwood Farm, Pennington, NJ, 2000; design-graphic collage Brielle Riverview Seniors, Brielle, NJ, 2000; Bohler Eng, Pa; NY Hosp Bldg. *Exhib:* Monmouth Co Arts Coun Monmouth Mus, Lincroft, NJ, 88, 93, 96, 98, 2001-2006; Millburn/Short Hills Art Asn, Walsh Libr Gallery, Seton Hall Univ, NJ, 98; NJ Watercolor Soc, Renee Fossner Gallery Paper Mill Play House, Millburn, NJ, 98, 2005-2009; NJ Watercolor Soc Ann, Monmouth Mus, Lincroft, NJ, 99, 2005-2006; Am Artists Profl League, Salmagundi Club, New York, 2000; Johnson & Johnson Pharmaceutical Inc, 2013; Seton Hall Univ, Walsh Libr Gallery, 2005; Pa Watercolor Soc Open, 2005-2006, 2009; 72nd Nat, Cooperstown, NY, 2007, 2009, 2010; Baltimore Watercolor Soc Mansion at Strathmore, Bethesda, Md, 2007; Summer Invitational Watercolor & Oil students, Ocean Co Coll, Toms River, NJ; Solo exhib, Branches-Blossoms & Butterflies, Ocean County Artists Guild, NJ, 2009; Garden State Watercolor Society, Der Greenway, Princeton, NJ, 2011; 32nd Ann Int Exhib, Pa Watercolor Soc, 2011; 115th Ann Exhib, Nat Arts Club, Catherine Lorillard Wolfe Arts Club, NY, 2011; 69th Ann Exhib, Salmagundi Club, Audubon Artists, NY, 2011; Millburn/Short Hills Art Asn, Atlantic Health Systems Corp Hq, 2012; Essex Water Color Soc, Celebration 80th at Morris Mus, 2012; Int Exhib, Pa Watercolor Soc, 2012; Essex Water Color Club, Chatham Libr, 2012, 2013; Dabbling in the Arts, Manalapan Libr, NJ, 2013; solo exhib, Carol Simon Building Gallery, Morristown, NJ; NJ Water Color Soc Ann Juried Exhib, 2014. *Pos:* Judge, 31st Ann Senior Citizens Art Exhib, Ocean Co, NJ, 2006-2008 & 2013; Juror of selection, Audubon Art Soc, New York, 2009; chair, Ocean Co Arts Guild Mem Juried Exhibs, NJ, 2011; panel juror, NJNC Soc, 2013; 2015 Critique: Ocean County Teen Arts & 2015 Juror for Awards: Ocean County Senior Citizens Art & Crafts State Wide Exhib. *Teaching:* Demonstrator/lectr watercolor, Ocean Co Teen Arts Festival Ann, 90 & 2005-2006, Judge, 2007-2009, 2012, critic, 2009, 2010; watercolor demonstrator, NJ Div of the Aging, 99; lectr Wall HS Nat Art Honor Soc Induction, 2000; workshops, Watercolor, Visual Arts Ctr NJ, Summit; juror, Bloomfield Art League, NJ, 2010; demonstrator, Clifton Art Asn, 2009; juror, NJ State Fed of Women's Club of GFWC, 2009; instr, Marlboro Township senior citizen watercolor, 2009-2013; workshop, Belmar Art Council, 2012. *Awards:* Best Design award NJ Watercolor Soc Ann, Harry & Ruth Kalish, 93; Grumbacher Gold Medal, Essex WC Club, Grumbacher Corp, 96; Nat Am Artists Prof League Juried award, NY Am Artists Prof League, 96; Watercolor Award, Winsor Newton Grand Nat Am Artist Prof League, New York, 2004; Oil and Acrylic Award, Summer Boardwalk Show, Ocean City, NJ, 2004; Alice Berhle Award, Essex Watercolor Club, 2005; awards of excellence, 75th Ann Essex Watercolor Club & NJWCS Exhib Assoc, Morris Co Libr Gallery, Whippany, NJ, 2007; Best in Show, Millburn-Short Hills Art Asn, NJ, 2008; 1st Watercolor, Ocean County Artists Guild, NJ, 2008; Award of Excellence, Essex Watercolor Club, NJ, 2008, 2009; Joan & John W Ewan Award, Perkins Ctr for the Arts, 2009; Award of Excellence, Millburn/Short Hills Art Asn, NJ, 2010; Award of Excellence, Clifton Ctr Arts, NJWES, 2010; Nummie Warga Award, Garden State Watercolor Soc, 2011; Brielle McDonald Award, Manasquan River Group of Artists Awards Exhib, 2011; Catherine Lorillard Wolfe Art Club Ann Open, Edgar Whitney Mem Award, 2011; Audubon Artists Inc 72 Ann Exhib, The Hon John M Angelini award Watercolor, 2014; NJ Boarcwalk Show, Best In Show, Ocean City, 2014; Ridgewood Art Assoc Ann Juried, The Winsor & Newton award, 2014; Alfa Gallery, Second Prize, New Brunswick, NJ, 2014; Bouras Building Gallery, Honorable Mention, Summit, NJ, 2014; Artsbridge Art Asn Juried Art Exhib, The Jerry's Artarama of Lawrenceville Watercolor award, Stockton, NJ, 2015. *Bibliog:* Tova Novarra (auth), The Nature of Art, Asbury Park Press, NJ, 90; Francis Molinaro (auth), Susanna Anastasia's Flowers in Watercolor, Asbury Park Press, NJ, 98; Desiree A DiCorcia (auth), Into the Woods, The Coast Star, NJ, 2000; Stephen Bove (auth), Artistic vision, Asbury Park Press, 2005; Dabble Vision, 2013. *Mem:* Essex Watercolor Club NJ (1st vpres, 98-2003, 2012, 2013, pres, 2005-2011); Manasquan River Group of Artists/NJ (pres, 85-87, 2011-2013); Garden State Watercolor Soc (2011-2012); Allied Artists Am, New York (2011-2012); Audubon Art Soc, New York (sig mem, 2006-2012); Am Artist Prof League, New York; Pa Watercolor So (sig mem, 2006-2012); NJ Watercolor Soc (elected mem, 2007, board member, 2007-2008, 2009-2012); Audubon Art Soc, NY (signature mem, 2006-2011); Catherine Lorillard Wolfe Club (2011-); Am Watercolor Soc, 2011; NJWCS (bd, 2011-2013); Catharine Lorillard Wolfe Art Club, NYC, 2014-. *Media:* Watercolor, Oil. *Publ:* Contrib artist, Long Beach Island Rhapsody. *Mailing Add:* 4141 W 18th Ave Farmingdale NJ 07727

ANATSUI, EL
SCULPTOR
b Anyako, Ghana, 1944. *Study:* Kwane Nkrumah Univ Sci & Technol, Kumasi, Ghana, BA (Art), Post-grad degree (Art Educ). *Work:* Brit Mus, London; Ctr George Pompidou, Paris; Metrop Mus Art, New York; Smithsonian Inst, Washington; Nigeria Nat Art Gallery. *Exhib:* Solo exhibs include Asele Art Gallery, Nsukka, Nigeria, 1976, Brit Coun & Inst African Studies, Univ Nigeria, 1979, Nat Mus, Lagos, Nigeria, 1991, October Gallery, London, 1995, 1998, 2002, Skoto Gallery, New York, 2005, Contemp African Gallery, New York, 2005, David Krut Projects, New York, 2006, Hood Mus, Dartmouth Coll, NH, 2006, Jack Shainman Gallery, New York, 2008, El Anatsui, Belger Arts Ctr, Kans City, Mo, 2009, Jack Shainman Gallery, NY, 2010, A Fateful Journey: Africa in the Works of El Anatsui, Nat Mus Ethnology, Osaka, 2010, Mus Modern Art, Hayama, 2011, Stitch in Time, Axel Vervoordt Gallery, Antrwerp, 2012, Broken Bridge II, Friends of the High Line, 2013, Pot of Wisdom, Jack Shainman Gallery, NY, 2013; two-person exhibs include Thoughts & Processes, with Ndubisi Ohan, Italian Cult Inst, Lagos, Nigeria, 1988; Walls & Gates, with Liz Willis, Avante-Garde Gallery, Kaduna, Nigeria, 1988; with Sol LeWitt, Skoto Gallery, New York, 1996; with Tesfaye Tessema, Contemp African Gallery, New York, 1996; group exhibs include Contemp African Artists: A Changing Tradition, Studio Mus Harlem, New York, 1990; Venice Biennale, 1990 & 2007; Six African Artists, October Gallery, London, 1993, Transforms, 1996, Transvangarde, 1996, New Colours from Old Worlds, 1999, News from the Front, 2001, Africa Informs, 2003; Art in the Shadow, Johannesburg Biennale, South Africa, 1995; Seven Stories About Mod Art in Africa, Whitechapel Art Gallery, London, 1995; The Poetics of Line, Nat Mus African Art, Smithsonian Inst, Washington, 1997 & Encounters with the Contemp, 2001; Osaka Sculpture Triennale, Japan, 1999; Riddle of the Spirits, Skoto Gallery, New York, 1999; The Independent, Liverpool Biennial Contemp Art, 1999 & 2002; Altered, Stitched & Gathered, PS1 Contemp Art Ctr, Long Island City, NY, 2007; Tapping Currents: Contemp African Art & Diaspora, Nelson-Atkins Mus Art, Kans City, 2008; Transvangarde, October Gallery, London, 2009; Extreme Frontiers, Urban Frontiers, Inst Valencia d'Art Modern, 2009; Who Knows Tomorrow, Nationalgalerie, Berlin, 2010; The World Belongs to You, Palazzo Grassi, Venice, Italy, 2011; Hunters and Gatherers: The Art of Assemblage, Sotheby's, NY, 2011; Mus Contemporary Art Kiasma, Helsinki, Finland, 2011; 1st Montevideo Biennial, Montevideo, Uruguay, 2012; African Cosmos: Stellar Art, Nat Mus African Art, Smithsonian Inst, Wash DC, 2012; Earth Matters: Land as Material and Metaphor in the Arts of Africa, Nat Mus African Art, Smithsonian Inst, Wash DC, 2013. *Pos:* Founding mem, fel, Forum African Arts, 2000-. *Teaching:* Lectr, Specialist Training Coll (now Univ Winneba), Winneba, Ghana, 1969-75; lectr, Univ Nigeria, Nsukka, 1975-1982, sr lectr, 1982-96, prof sculpture, 1996-, head of fine & applied arts dept, 1998-2000. *Mem:* Fel, Pan-African Circle Artists. *Media:* Miscellaneous Media. *Dealer:* October Gallery 24 Old Gloucester St Bloomsbury London WC1N 3AL England UK. *Mailing Add:* c/o Jack Shainman Gallery 513 W 20th St New York NY 10011

ANDELL, NANCY
PAINTER
b Boston, Mass, Nov 14, 1953. *Study:* Sch Mus Fine Arts, Boston, Mass, dipl, 74, 5th yr certif, 76; Tufts Univ, Medford, Mass, 75. *Exhib:* Solo exhibs, Flag Gallery, Boston, Mass, 78, Impressions Gallery, Boston, Mass, 79, Impressions Gallery, Boston, Mass, 80, Shaker Mus, Old Chatham, NY, 91 & Vt Coll, Montpelier, 94; Water/Clay/Stone, Smithy Pioneer Gallery, Cooperstown, NY, 92; 20th Anniversary Traveling Exhib; Luminous Emanations, Simon's Rock Coll, Great Barrington, Mass, 95; Metrop Mus Art, New Mus Contemp Art, NY; Brooklyn Mus, NY; Worcester Art Mus, Mass; Provincetown Mus Art, Mass; Danforth Mus, Framingham, Mass. *Teaching:* Fac, Experimental Etching Studio, Boston, Mass, 79-80, McDowell Colony, 1980, Albany Inst Hist & Art, NY, 89-90, Berkshire Mus, Pittsfield, Mass, 89, Rensselaer Co Coun for Arts, Troy, NY, 89-92, Taconic Hills HS, 1990-. *Awards:* Spec

Opportunity Stipend: NY Found Arts & Rensselaer Co Coun Arts, 91; Face to Face with the Arts, Columbia Co Initiative Prog, 91; Skidmore Coll Fel, Saratoga Springs, NY, 91; Arad Arts Project, Arad, Israel, 1998. *Bibliog:* Lois Tarlow (auth), Profile: Ten Years Later, Art New Eng, 12/89; Lael Locke (auth), Idealized Landscapes, The Paper, 10/91; Meredith Fife Day (auth), Review: Luminous Emanations, paintings on wood, New Eng Art J, 6/96. *Media:* Oil, Mixed Media. *Mailing Add:* PO Box 46 Chatham NY 12037

ANDERSEN, DAVID R L
PAINTER, CURATOR
b Logan, Utah, Sept 30, 1957. *Study:* Brigham Young Univ, Provo, Utah, MFA, 88. *Work:* Dartmouth Coll, Hanover, NH; Ohio Univ; Utah State Collection; Mauritian Embassy, Washington, DC. *Exhib:* Solo exhibs, Calculations for Future Events, Darthmouth Col, Hanover, NH, 90 & Spiritus Mundi, Grossmont Col, San Diego, Calif, 91; two-person shows, Midland Col, Tex, 90 & Diverse Works Gallery, Houston, Tex, 90; Nat Draw Exhib, Brigham Young Univ, Provo, Utah, 89; Nat Juried Exhib, Natsoulas/Novelozo Gallery, Davis, Calif, 90; Animals, Centennial Mus, El Paso, Tex, 90. *Collection Arranged:* Robert Colescott (paintings), 89; Sera Siempre Asi? (prints; catalog); Sleeping Mutations (sculpture), 89; Cont Graphic Design, 90; Prints From Life, 90. *Pos:* Preparator, Brigham Young Univ, Provo, Utah, 85-88; dir galleries, Univ Tex at El Paso, 88-91; Instr painting/drawing, Brigham Young Univ, Provo, Utah, 85- 88; drawing/design, Univ Tex, El Paso, 88-91. *Awards:* URI Grant, Tex Comn on the Arts. *Media:* Mixed media. *Mailing Add:* c/o Gremillion & Co Fine Art Inc 2501 Sunset Blvd Houston TX 77005

ANDERSEN, JEFFREY W
MUSEUM DIRECTOR
Study: Lewis & Clark Coll, BA (History); State Univ New York, Cooperstown, MA (Mus Studies). *Pos:* Dir, Florence Giswold Mus, 1976-; Art Consult, Hartford Steam boiler Instpection & Inc Co, 1983-1992. *Mem:* mem, adv bd, Weir Farm; Am Asn Mus; treas, New England Mus Asn, 1998-2000. *Mailing Add:* Florence Griswold Mus 96 Lyme St Old Lyme CT 06371

ANDERSEN, LEIF (WERNER)
PAINTER
b Baltimore, Md, Mar 6, 1925. *Study:* Art Students League, with Reginald Marsh & Louis Bouche, 46-48. *Work:* Bordighera Mus, Italy. *Exhib:* Am Group Show, Venice, Italy, 52; Nat Accad Design Ann, NY, 57 & 62; Allied Artist Am Ann, Nat Accad Design, 58 & 61; and numerous solo exhibs. *Awards:* S J Wallace Truman Award, Nat Acad Design Ann, 57; Margaret Cooper Prize, Allied Artist Am, Nat Acad Design, 61. *Media:* Oil, Acrylic. *Mailing Add:* 300 E 51st St Apt 2f New York NY 10022

ANDERSON, ALEXANDRA C See Anderson-Spivy, C Alexandra

ANDERSON, BILL (WILLIAM) MAXWELL
PAINTER, PRINTMAKER
b Mankato, Minn, July 31, 1941. *Study:* Mankato State Univ, BS, 59-63; grad studies, 74; Calif State Univ Long Beach, grad studies, 64-68. *Work:* Carnegie Mus Art, Oxnard, Calif; Nat Mus Prints, Mexico City, Mex; Conejo Valley Mus, Thousand Oaks, Calif; Mus Nat De La Acuarela, Mexico City; Bowers Mus, Santa Ana, Calif; Cora Mus, Mexico; The Union Inst, Cincinnati, Ohio; Chaffey Art Mus, Rancho Cucamonga, Calif; Ontario Mus History and Art; Vincent Price Mus, East Los Angeles Coll. *Comn:* Murals, Mankato State Univ, 90; Painted Mural, Raul Anguiano, East Los Angeles Col, 2002; Heritage Series (series of 75 paintings), Joint Forces Military Training Base, Los Alamitos, Calif. *Exhib:* Solo exhibs: Galeria Coyoacan, Mexico City, 80; Geometry & Line, Carnegie Art Mus, Oxnard, Calif, 88; Europe, Univ Calif, Los Angeles, 90; Homecoming, Mankato State Univ, 90; Meeuwis Art Gallery, Oirschot, The Neth, 92; Lodi Art Gallery, Pasadena, Calif, 93; Sunset Beach, Calif, 96; Retrospective, Chaffey Art Mus, Rancho Cucamonga, Calif, 2007; Joint Forces Training Base, Heritage Series, Los Alamitos, Calif, 2007; Paintings of Crete, Malia, Crete, Greece, 2008, Graber Olive Historic House, Ontario, 2012, 50 Yrs of Printmaking and Sculpture, Anderson Art Gallery, Sunset Beach, Calif, 2012-2013, 50 Years of Printmaking and Sculpture, Anderson Art Gallery, Sunset Beach, Calif, 2013, Paintings of Sunset Beach, Sunset Beach Community Fire House Gallery, Sunset Beach, Calif, 2014; The Yr of the Horse, Conejo Valley Art Mus, Thousand Oaks, Calif, 90; The Figure and the Horse, Calif State Univ, Los Angeles, 91; 5 Calif Artists in Mex, Museo Nac De La Acuarela, Mexico City, 93; Primera Bienal Int De La Acuarela At Mus Nat De La Acuarela, Mexico City, 94; Generations, Six California Artists, Luckman Fine Arts Complex, Calif State Univ, Los Angeles, 96; Southern Exposure-Six Southern Calif Artists, King Co Art Ctr, Hanford, Calif, 97; 4 Maestros, Raul Anguiano, Vladimir Cora, Felipe Casteneda, Bill Anderson, Cruz Gallery, Santa Ana, Calif, 99; Sculpture by Casteneda, Paintings by Anderson, Sunset Beach, Calif, 2000; group exhib: Manzanar Nat Mus, 2005-2006; Vincent Price Permanent Collection Exhib, E Los Angeles Col, 2006; Two-person exhib, Bill Anderson & Milford Zornes, Ontario Mus Hist & Art, Ontario, Calif, 2006; Two Artists from Minn, Bill Anderson & John Salminen, Views of Calif & New York, 19th St Gallery, Coasta Mesa, Calif, 2008; 100th Ann Huntington Beach, Anderson At Gallery, Sunset Beach, Calif, 2009; 3 people exhib, Bill Anderson, Ron Liborecht, Milford Zornes, APC Fine Arts & Graphics Gallery, Calif, 2010; California Geometric Abstractionism from 1945-1965, John Wayne Airport, 2010; Dynamic Duos, Anderson/Zornes and Setton/Fuknhara, Schroeder Gallery, Orange, Calif, 2011; Portraits, Anguiano, Anderson Librecht, Zornes, APC Gallery, Torrance, Calif, 2011; Realism and Abstraction, Bill Anderson, Raul Anguiano, Gerald Brommer, Henry Fuknhara, Howard Hitchcock, George Post, Bea Riley, Milford Zornes, Anderson Art Gallery, Sunset Beach, Calif, 2011; Millard Sheets Ctr Arts, Pomona, Calif, 2012; Solo exhib and book presentation, Greece, island of Crete, Greece, 2014; group exhib, Chaffey Community Mus of Art, Calif Watercolorists, Ontario, Calif, 2014, Millard Sheets Art Center, Inland Empire Art Mus, Pomona, Calif, 2015. *Collection Arranged:* Milford Zornes in Greenland, Vincent Price Mus, E Los Angeles, Calif; Milford Zornes 100th Birthday Exhibs, Chaffey Art Mus, 2008; Henry Fukuhara's Life Work, Vincent Price Mus,. *Pos:* Art Comn Huntington Beach Calif, 80-94; art curric chmn, Los Alamitos Unified Sch Dist, 84-88; gallery dir, Los Alamitos Unified Sch Dist Gallery, 84-92; owner, Anderson Art Gallery, Sunset Beach, Calif, 95-2000. *Teaching:* Art teacher, gen visual art, Long Beach Unified Sch Dist, Calif, 63-69 & Anaheim & Los Alamitos Sch Dist, Calif, 72-2000, Orange Co High Sch for Arts, 85-94; art teacher printmaking, drawing & painting, Appleton Unified Sch Dist, Wis, 69-72. *Awards:* Teacher of Yr, Anaheim Union HS Dist, 78-79; Huntington Beach, First Outstanding Artist of Yr, 86; Art Mentor, Los Alamitos Unified Sch Dist, 87-88. *Bibliog:* Luis Bruno Ruiz (auth), Estampas Romanticas Caballos en la Pintora Bill Anderson, Excelsior, Mexico City, 80; auth, Anderson, George Zada Publishing, 85; Elaine Craft, The Art of Bill Anderson, cable channel 3, Huntington Beach, 92; James Figmoa (auth) Bill Anderson & Felipe Casteneda, Harbor Sun, 2000; Bill Andersons Line, Kennedy Libr, Calif State Univ at Los Angeles (book/catalog), 98; California Watercolors 1850-1970, Hillcrest Press, 2002; Craig McDonald (auth), Old West Christmas, 2011. *Mem:* Arts Comn Huntington Beach (pres 81-87); Arts Assoc Huntington Beach; Studio Artists Huntington Beach (founder, 83, pres, 83-87); Cult Task Force Huntington Beach Calif, (94). *Media:* Oils, Watercolor. *Publ:* Illus, Creative Experience, Kendall/Hunt Pub, 89; Raul Anguiano's 75th Anniversary, Excelsior, 90; illus, El Completo de Circe, Eda Mex Pub, 91; Portfolio of Linoleum Cuts, 5 Engravers From USA & Mexico, 94; Primera Biennal Int De La Acuarela, Mus Nat De La Acuarela, 94; co-auth with Milford Zornes, Nine Decades with a Master Painter (bk), Earthen Vessel Productions, 2005; auth, The Work of Bill Anderson (bk), Havana Graphics, 1985; California Watercolors 1850-1970 (bk), Gordon McClelland & Jay Last, 2002; Sierra Heritage (mag, feature article, Endless Expression: Art of Bill Anderson), Apr 2008; Illustr, Sierra Heritage mag; Craig McDonald (auth), illustr book, Gold Rush Glimpses III, 2009; illusr, Old West, Sierra Heritage Mag, 2008-2011; auth, The Heritage Series, Watercolors & Pastels, Joint Forces Military Base, Mesa Art, 2011; Artist Bill Anderson Paints Surf City Huntington Beach, Mesa Art, 2011; illusr, Yosemite's Unsung Hero; auth, The Fantastic Horse Through the Eyes of Artist Bill Anderson, 2013; auth, Sunset Beach and The Views From Through The Eyes of Artist Bill Anderson, 2014; auth, Greece Through The Eyes of Artist Bill Anderson. *Dealer:* Anderson Art Gallery 16812 Pacific Coast Hwy Sunset Beach CA 90742; Mesa Art 789 W 19th St Ste D Costa Mesa CA 92627. *Mailing Add:* 17831 San Leandro Lane Huntington Beach CA 92647

ANDERSON, BRUCE A
GOLDSMITH, SCULPTOR
b Spokane, Wash, Sept 14, 1948. *Study:* Western Wash State Univ, BA, 73; Syracuse Univ, with Michael Jerry, MFA (metalsmithing), 79. *Exhib:* Young Americans Exhib, Am Craft Mus, NY, 77; Ger-Am Blacksmithing Exhib, Goethe Inst, Atlanta, Ga, 81-82; The First Int Shoebox Sculpture Exhib, Univ Hawaii, Manoa, 82; Jewelry USA, 84 & Am Jewelry, 85, Am Craft Mus, NY. *Mem:* Soc NAm Goldsmiths. *Media:* Metal. *Dealer:* Quadrum Gallery The Mall at Chestnut Hill Chestnut Hill MA

ANDERSON, CRAIG
PAINTER, SCULPTOR
b Minneapolis, Minn, Aug 22, 1946. *Study:* Hamline Univ, BFA, 69; Univ Colo, Boulder, 79. *Exhib:* Small Works, Aspen Art Ctr, Colo, 83; 4th Tex Sculpture Symp, Univ Tex Mus, Austin, 85; Exhib Installation, Southwest Tex Univ, San Marcos, 91; IAIA Fac, Univ Colo, Boulder, 94; IAIA Fac, Inst Am Indian Arts, Santa Fe, 95. *Pos:* Preparator, Minneapolis Art Inst, 69-70; mus tech, Walker Art Ctr, 70-71. *Teaching:* Instr drawing, Univ Colo, Boulder, 78-79, drawing, design, video, Southwest Tex State Univ, 79-82; prof painting, Inst Am Indian Arts, Santa Fe, 89-96. *Awards:* Top 10 Selection, Video Meaning Use, Univ Chicago, 78. *Mem:* Coll Art Asn. *Media:* Painting everything. *Mailing Add:* 669 NE 60th St Miami FL 33137-2350

ANDERSON, CURTIS LESLIE
CONCEPTUAL ARTIST, PAINTER
b Minneapolis, Minn, Oct 5, 1956. *Study:* Cooper Union for Advan Sci & Art, BFA, 79. *Work:* Libr Cong, Washington, DC; New York Pub Libr; Mus Atlantico, Tenerife Canary Islands, Spain; Mus des Beaux-Arts de Nantes, France; Toledo Art Mus, Ohio. *Exhib:* Excess in the Techno-Mediacratic Society, Mus Sarret de Grozon Arbois, France, 92; Drawn in the Nineties, Katonah Mus Art, NY, 92; The Return of the Cadavre Exquis, Drawing Ctr, NY, 93; Recent Acquisitions, NY Pub Libr, 93; Drawing the Line Against Aids, Peggy Guggenheim Collection, Venice, Italy, 93. *Bibliog:* Martijn van Nieuwenhuyzen (auth), Curtis Anderson/t'Venster, Flashart, 86; Dore Ashton (auth), Curtis Anderson/Catalogue, Galerie Jule Kewenig, 90; Noel Frackman (auth), Curtis Anderson, Arts, 91. *Mem:* Berufsverband bildender kunstler. *Dealer:* Baron/Boisante 421 Hudson St #419 New York NY 10014. *Mailing Add:* Am Neuen Forst 34 Koeln-Hahnwald Germany 50996

ANDERSON, DANIEL J
CERAMIST, EDUCATOR
b St Paul, Minn, Nov 2, 1945. *Study:* Studied with Renato Bassoli, Milan, Ital 1967-68; Univ Wis-River Falls, BS (art ed, Nat Asn Tobacco Distribrs Scholar), 68; Cranbrook Accad Art, Bloomfield Hills, Mich, MFA (ceramics, Rocco DiMarco Scholar, Sponsored Scholar), 70. *Work:* Carnegie Mus Art, Pittsburgh, Pa, Boise Art Mus, Idaho; Philadelphia Mus Art, Pa; Weisman Art Mus, Minneapolis, MN; Wustum Mus Art, Racine, Wis. *Exhib:* One-man shows, Gail Severn Gallery Sun Valley, 10 Manchester Craftsmen's Guild, Pittsburgh, Pa & Garth Clark Gallery, NY; 52nd Scripps Ceramic Exhib, Claremont, Calif; Ceramics USA 1996, Univ NTex, Denton; SOFA, Navy Pier, Chicago, Ill; Clay/Wood/Fire, Northern Clay Ctr, St Paul, Minn; Clay Ariz Art, N Ariz Univ, Flagstaff, Ariz; Third St Louis Art Fair, Clayton, Mo. *Teaching:* Prof & area head ceramic dept, Southern Ill Univ, Edwardsville, 70-2002; prof emeritus, S Ill Univ; vis instr, Ewha Woman's Univ, Seoul, Korea, 83 & Sch Art Inst, Chicago, Ill, 91; instr, Univ Ga, Cortona, Italy, 90. *Awards:* various grants & awards, Southern Ill Univ, Edwardsville, 70-83, 86, 87, 91, 93, 94, 96 & 99; Ill Arts Coun Grants, 75, 79, 81, 84, 85, 87-89, 91, 96 & 99; Artist Fel, Nat Endowment Arts, 91; and others. *Mem:* NCECA. *Publ:* Ceramics: Art & Perception, Vol 11 & 12. *Mailing Add:* 5519 Old Poag Rd Edwardsville IL 62025

ANDERSON, DAVID KIMBALL
SCULPTOR
b Los Angeles, Calif, Feb 3, 1946. *Study:* San Francisco Art Inst, 67-71. *Work:* Mus Mod Art, San Francisco; Mus Fine Arts, Santa Fe; Sheldon Mem Art Mus, Lincoln, Nebr; San Antonio Mus Art, Tex; Art Bank Program, Dept State, Washington, DC. *Comn:* City of Albuquerque. *Exhib:* Solo Exhibs: San Francisco Art Inst, 79; Braunstein Gallery, San Francisco, 75, 78, 80, 83, 85, 87, 90, 94 & 96; Linda Durham Gallery, Santa Fe, 79, 81, 83, 85, 87, 89, 91, 94, 96, 06, 08, 2010; Christopher Grimes Gallery, Santa Monica, Calif, 91; Hokin/Kaufman Gallery, Chicago, 91, Bellas Artes Gallery, Santa Fe, NMex, 2012, Morris Graves Mus Art, Eureka, Calif, 2013, Robischon Gallery, Denver, Colo, 2013; Pub Sculpture/Urban Environ, Oakland Mus, Calif, 74; 1975 Biennial Exhib Contemp Art, Whitney Mus, NY, 75; Linda Durham Contemp Art, NY, 2003; Lemmons Contemp, NY, 2005. *Pos:* San Jose State Univ, 97-2011; Anderson Ranch Art Ctr, 2005-2010, 2014; Vt Studio Ctr, 2008, 2010. *Teaching:* Sculpture, San Francisco Art Inst, 76-79, Calif Col Arts & Crafts, Oakland, 79 & Univ NMex, 84-94. *Awards:* Nat Endowment Arts Fel Grant, 74, 81 & 88; Pollock-Krasner Found Grant, 86; Artists Found Grant, 94. *Bibliog:* Art News, 3/86; Artspace, 3-4/90; Art News, 5/94; NY Times, 10/04; Sculpture, 2008; Art News, 2012. *Media:* Bronze, Steel. *Dealer:* Linda Durham Contemp Art New York; Santa Fe NMex. *Mailing Add:* 235 Surfside Ave Cruz CA 95060

ANDERSON, DAWOLU JABARI
ILLUSTRATOR
Study: Tex S Univ, Houston, BFA, 1995. *Exhib:* Changing Perspective Mus, 1995; Preventions Collective, Project RowHouse & Commun Arts, 1996; Breaking Into the Mainstream, Irving Arts Ctr, 1996; Artist Board Chooses, Diverse Works, 1997; Bound Books, Brazos, 1998; Sixth Ann African Am Advisory Assn, Mus Fine Arts, 2002; Soul Sonic LustraSilk, Houston Com Coll NE, 2002; Symmetrical Patterns of Def/Collaborative Group Installation, Lawndale Art Ctr, 2004; Who Goliards? Artists at the Turn of the Century, Univ Tex S Univ, 2004; Whitney Biennial, Whitney Mus Am Art, 2006; solo exhib: Birth of a Nation: Yo! Bumrush the Show, Art League Houston, 2006; Negro Week, Ingalls & Assocs, Miami, 2007. *Pos:* Asst Coord, Project RowHouses, 1995-97; illusr, 1997-. *Awards:* First Prize, Houston Area Exhib, Blaffer Gallery, 2004; grant, Skowhegan Sch Paint & Sculpture, 2006; Louis Comfort Tiffany Found Grant, 2009

ANDERSON, GAIL KANA
MUSEUM DIRECTOR
b Baytown, Tex. *Study:* Univ Tex, BA (Fine Arts), 1971, MA (Art History), 1979. *Pos:* Slide Librn, Univ Tex, 1973-1978; cur of visual resources, Coll of Design, Iowa State Univ, 1979-1982 ; Registrar, Univ Ky Art Mus, 1986-1988, Fred Jones Jr Mus Art, 1991-1995 ; Photography cur, Austin Hist Ctr, 1988-1989; cur, asst dir, interim dir, deputy dir, Fred Jones Jr Mus Art, 1995-. *Teaching:* adj fac, dept of Art, Iowa State Univ, 1980-1982; instr mus studies, Univ Okla, 2005-, adj prof art history, 1998-. *Mem:* Am Asn Mus; Mountain-Plains Mus Asn Registrar's Comt; Firehouse Art Ctr Gallery Comt, 1992-2003; Okla Visual Artists Coalition Bd, 1999-2003 . *Mailing Add:* Fred Jones Jr Museum of Art 555 Elm Ave Norman OK 73019

ANDERSON, GUNNAR DONALD
PAINTER, ILLUSTRATOR
b Berkeley, Calif, 1927. *Study:* Calif Sch Fine Arts, with Clyfford Still; Art Ctr Coll Design, BFA, with Lorser Feitelson. *Work:* Brown-Forman Distillers, Louisville, Ky. *Comn:* Gov Lamar Alexander, Tenn; Mr & Mrs Meredith Long, Houston, Tex, 71; Mr & Mrs George Weyerhauser, Tacoma, Wash, 72; Mr & Mrs Charlie Rich, Memphis, Tenn; Mr & Mrs Charles Schulz, Calif. *Exhib:* 5th Winter Invitational, Calif Palace Legion Hon, San Francisco, 64; MH de Young Mem Mus, San Francisco, 25th Ann, Soc Western Artists, 68; Charles & Emma Frye Mus, Seattle, 71; Calif State Fair, Sacramento, 71; Mainstream 72, Grover M Hermann Fine Arts Ctr, Marietta Coll, Ohio, 72. *Pos:* Bd trustees, Soc Western Artists. *Teaching:* Instr, Acad Art Coll, San Francisco, Calif. *Awards:* Best figure or portrait, 29th Ann, Soc Western Artists, 71 & first place, Ann, 85 & 90-91; Best Fine Art, Exhib One, Soc Art Ctr, Alumni, 72; Grumbacher Gold Medallion, 86; Best of Show, 53rd Ann Exhib Soc Western Art, 2003. *Bibliog:* Mrs Linda Hardwick (auth), Collage, educational TV, Memphis Community TV Found, 71-72; TV interview, Memphis, Tenn, 71; Don J Anderson (auth), Paintings of children, Chicago Today, 72. *Mem:* Soc Western Artists; Soc Art Ctr Alumni; Bohemian Club. *Media:* Oil. *Interests:* Soaring, flying. *Publ:* Illusr, Oscar Lincoln Busby Stokes, Harcourt, Brace & World Inc, 70. *Dealer:* Mrs Robert W Sanderson 475 N Highland #4C Memphis TN; Mrs Laura Healy 4335 Alla Rd #6 Marina Del Ray CA 90292. *Mailing Add:* 4583 Belmont Ct Sonoma CA 95476

ANDERSON, LAURA (GRANT)
PAINTER
b Hartford, Conn, Dec 15, 1943. *Study:* Lasell Jr Col, Mass, 63-64; Hartford Art Sch, Univ Hartford, 64-66; RI Sch Design, 88-89. *Work:* Decordova Mus, Lincoln, Mass; Fuller Mus, Brockton, Mass; Mass Mutual Life Insurance Co, Springfield, Mass; Cabot Corp, Boston, Mass; Fleet Nat Bank, RI. *Exhib:* Annual Show, Springfield Mus Art, 89; Realism 94, Parkersburg Art Mus, WVa, 94; In the Grand Tradition, Fairfield Univ Mus, Conn, 94; Get Real: Representational Paintings from the Permanent Collection, DeCordova Mus, Lincoln, Mass, 99. *Awards:* First Prize, Am Artists Golden Ann Exhib, 87; Salzman Award, Nat Arts Club, 93; First Prize, Nat Arts Club, 94. *Bibliog:* Earl Killeen (auth), Acrylic Painting Techniques, North Light Books, 95; Best of Acrylic Painting, Rockport Publs, 96; New American Paintings, A Resource for Collectors, 93. *Mem:* Nat Arts Club, NY; Audubon Artists, NY; Allied Artists of Am, NY; Marion Art Ctr, Mass. *Media:* Acrylic. *Publ:* Contribr, Yankee Mag, 8/81, Graphic deFrance & Artists, 6/91

ANDERSON, LAURIE
CONCEPTUAL ARTIST
b Chicago, Ill, 1947. *Study:* Barnard Coll, BA (art hist, magna cum laude, 1969); Columbia Univ, MFA, 1972. *Hon Degrees:* San Francisco Art Inst, Hon Inst, Hon Dr, 1980; Philadelphia Coll Arts, Hon Dr, 1987; Art Inst Chicago, Hon Dr, 1990; Cal Arts, Hon Dr, 1996; Pratt Inst, Hon Dr, 1996. *Comn:* Carmen (video), Expo '92, 1992; Bridge of Dreams (score), Deutsche Opera, Berlin, 1993; New York City for Encyl Brittanica, 2000; Far Side of the Moon (music for Rober LePage theater piece), 2000; Who Am I?, Swiss Expo '02 pavilion, 2001. *Exhib:* Solo shows incl Whirlwind, Artists Space, 1998; group shows incl Sydney Festival, Australia, 1997; Handphone Table, Musee Art Contemporain, France, 1998; Duets on Ice 1974-75, MOCA Mus, Los Angeles, 1998; AE (Amelia Earhart), Am Composers Orch, 1999. *Pos:* Art critic, Art Forum, Art News, Art in Am. *Teaching:* Instr art hist, City Coll New York, 1973-75. *Awards:* Nat Endowment Arts Grant 1974-75, 1977 & 1979; Guggenheim Found Fel, 1982; Marlene Award for Performing Arts, Munich, Ger, 1996; Dorothy & Lillian Gish Prize, 2007. *Bibliog:* Rose Lee (auth), Laurie Anderson, Abrams, 2000. *Media:* Records; Film & Video. *Publ:* Auth, Empty Places, Harper Collins, 1991; Monster in a Box (score), Spalding Gray, 1991; Faraway So Close (score), 1993; co-producer, Bright Red (record), Warner Brothers, 1994; auth, Stories from the Nerve Bible (a retrospective), Harper Perennial, 1994; Talk Normal, anthology, Rhino Records, 2000; Life on a String, Nonesuch Records, 2001. *Mailing Add:* Canal Street Communications 530 Canal St New York NY 10013

ANDERSON, MARGARET POMEROY
APPRAISER, COLLECTION MANAGER
b San Francisco, Calif, 1943. *Study:* Univ Calif, Berkeley, BA, 65. *Pos:* Researcher, Pomeroy Galleries, San Francisco, 65-69; archivist, Hoover Gallery, San Francisco, 69-81, consult, 78-; owner, Pomeroy-Anderson, 82, Accredited Senior Appraiser, 81-. *Teaching:* Lectr art, Westport Arts Ctr, 85-91, Fairfield Univ, Conn, 86-92, Wadsworth Atheneum, Hartford, 91 & Univ Hartford, 2008. *Awards:* Conn Press Club, 89-91. *Mem:* Arch Am Art; West Coast Area Support Comt (chmn, 78-80); Am Soc Appraisers (accredited sr appraiser, 81-, regional gov 93-95); Archives Am Art (NY Area Comt, 83-90); Fairfield Hist Soc (pres, 89-92); Fairfield Mus & Hist Ctr. *Res:* Life of Marie Laurencin; nineteenth and twentieth century American and European provenance searches; Paul Manship. *Publ:* Contribr, Antiques & the Arts Weekly; Maine Antique Digest; Antiques West Newspaper, New York Correspondent; Antique Monthly; Art & Auction. *Mailing Add:* 9B Marion Ave Sausalito CA 94965

ANDERSON, MARK ROBERT
STAINED GLASS ARTIST, SCULPTOR
b Iola, Kans, Aug 14, 1948. *Study:* Am Craft Coun, 75-79; Art League Sch, Alexandria, Va, 79-82; Pilchuck Glass Sch, Stanwood, Wash, 79 & 85. *Comn:* Solar Collectors with Stained glass, Brandon Residence, Cabin John, Md, 81-83; Spiral Staircase (sculpture), Torpedo Factory Art Ctr, Alexandria, Va, 84; Stained Glass Window, Bolling Air Force Base Officers Club, Washington, DC, 85; Stained Glass Window, Montgomery Co Pub Schs, Woodlin-Silver Spring, 86; Glass & Neon wall panels, May Ctrs Inc, Ballston Common Ctr, Arlington, Va, 86. *Exhib:* Virginia Craftsmen, Va Mus Fine Arts, Richmond, 80; Studio Glass-Contemp Am Survey, Redding Mus, Calif, 85; Spotlight: Southeast Crafts, Longwood Col, Farmville, Va, 85; Spotlight: Southeast Crafts, Univ Gainesville, Fla, 86; Solo exhib, Jackie Chalkley Fine Crafts, Washington, DC, 86; New Art Forms I & II: Virginia, Hand Workshop, Richmond Va, 88 & 89; Beyond Function: New Directions in Decorative Arts, Wash Sq Bldg, Washington, DC, 88; Breaking Boundaries: Craft Now, Va Mus Fine Arts, Richmond, 88-91; Creative Craft Coun Winners, Renwick Gallery, Smithsonian, Washington, DC, 89; Rhapsody in Neon, Zenith Gallery, Washington, DC, 89. *Collection Arranged:* High Style, Tomlinson Craft Collection, 83. *Pos:* Exec dir, Friends of Torpedo Factory Art Ctr, Alexandria, Va, 82-84. *Teaching:* Instr stained glass, Art League Sch, Alexandria, Va, 80-. *Awards:* First Prize for Glass, Arlington Arts Ctr, Va, 78; Schwarzschild Award, Schwarzschild Jewelers, 85; First Prize for Glass, Creative Craft Coun, Washington, DC, 86. *Bibliog:* Karen M E Alexis (auth), Washington's fragile world of glass art, Washington Post, 81; Clare Fiore (auth), Which Are Jewels?, Reston Connection, 85; Joseph Porcelli (auth), Profile, Prof Stained Glass, 87; Patricia Dane Rogers (coauth with Cristina Del Sesto), The Move From Down Home to Uptown, Wash Post, 88. *Mem:* Torpedo Factory Artists Asn (vpres, 82-83); Coalition Wash Artists, (steering comt, 86-87); Am Craft Coun. *Media:* Glass. *Dealer:* Glass Arts Collaborative 31 Norfolk Rd Arlington MA 02174. *Mailing Add:* 827 S Quincy St Arlington VA 22204

ANDERSON, MAXWELL L
MUSEUM DIRECTOR, EDUCATOR
b New York, NY, May 1, 1956. *Study:* Dartmouth Col, AB, 77; Harvard Univ, AM (hist), 78, PhD (art hist), 81. *Collection Arranged:* The Vatican Collections: The Papacy and Art, 82; Treasures of the Holy Land, 86; Roman Portraits in Context, 88; Radiance in Stone, 89; The Courtauld Collection at the AGO, Art Gallery Ont, 98; Art in the Age of Van Gogh: Dutch Paintings from the Rijksmuseum, Amsterdam, Arm Gallery of Ont, 98-99; Biennial Exhib, Whitney Mus Am Art, 2000, 2004 & 2006; Tony Oursler: The Darkest Color Infinitely Applied, Whitney Mus Am Art, 2000. *Pos:* Asst cur, Metrop Mus Art, 82-87; dir, Emory Univ Mus, Atlanta, 87-95, Michael C Carlos Mus, 98, Art Gallery Ont, Toronto, 95-98 & Whitney Mus Amer Art, 98-2003; Melvin & Ben Simon dir & CEO, Indianapolis Mus Art, 2006-2011; mem adv bd NYC 2012 (pvt org seeking to bring Olympic games to New York), 2000; principal, AEA Consulting; Eugene McDermott dir, Dallas Mus Art, 2011-. *Teaching:* Lectr Roman art, Princeton Univ, 85; vis prof, Univ di Roma, 87; adj assoc prof, Emory Univ, 89-95. *Awards:* Commendatore Order Merit, Republic of Italy, 90; Cult Laureate New York City Historic Landmarks Preservation Ctr, 99; Insignia of the Chevalier of the Order of Arts and Letters, 2011. *Mem:* Am Asn Mus; Coll Art Asn; Asn Art Mus Dirs (pres 2002-03); Am Fedn Art (trustee). *Publ:* Coauth, Greece and Rome, Metrop Mus, 87; Pompeian Frescoes in the Metropolitan Museum of Art, Metrop Mus, 87; Roman Portraits in Context, De Luca, 88; Radiance in Stone, De

Luca, 89; Intro to The Wired Mus, 97; auth, Preserving the perishable art of the digital age, Arts and Leisure sect, NY Times, 9/24/2000; preface, Whitney Museum of American Art, Building Blocks series, Princeton Archtl Press, 2000; Online museum coordination, Museum Int, Vol 51, No 4, 10-12/99; and numerous other articles. *Mailing Add:* Indianapolis Mus Art 4000 Michigan Rd Indianapolis IN 46208-3326

ANDERSON, ROBERT ALEXANDER
PAINTER, ILLUSTRATOR
b Wyandotte, Mich, Jan 26, 1946. *Study:* Yale Univ, BA, 64-68, drawing with Bernard Chaet, portrait painting with Deane Keller; Wayne State Univ, 66; Sch Mus Fine Arts, Boston, dipl, 72-75, with Henry Schwartz & John Clift. *Work:* Phillips Exeter Acad, NH; Harvard Univ, Cambridge, Mass; Yale Univ, New Haven, Conn; Fed Reserve, DC; Nat Portrait Gallery, Smithsonian Inst, DC. *Comn:* Portraits, Sidney Farber & Charles A Dana, Md, Dana Farber Cancer Inst, Boston, Mass, 84, Andrew G DeRocco, Pres Denison Univ, Granville, Ohio & Hon Edward J King, Hon William F Weld, Gov Mass, Boston, Mass, 90, Rev William Sloane Coffin, Yale Univ, New Haven, Conn, 90 & George W Bush, comn by Yale Club, New York, 93 & 2002, former Pres George W Bush, Nat Gallery of Smithsonian Inst, Washington, DC, 2008; Eleven drawings & portraits, US Postage Stamps, US Postal Serv, Washington, DC, 84-86; Former Fed Res Chairman Alan Greenspan, comm by Fed Res Bd, DC, 2010; Former Homeland Securities Secretaries, Tom Ridge & Michael Chertoff, 2013. *Exhib:* Boston Symphony, John F Kennedy Pres Libr & Mus, Dorchester, 81 & Symphony Hall, Boston, 82, Mass; Francesca Anderson Gallery, Boston, Mass, 84-88; Soc Illusrs, NY, 87; St Botolph Club, Boston, Mass, 88; Boston Atheneum, Mass, 89. *Bibliog:* Laura White (auth), A Letter Will Take Two of These, Boston Globe, 2/10/85; Valerie Cruice (auth), The Painter & the President, New York Times, 11/9/2003; Christopher Brooks (auth), Robert Anderson-Picture Perfect, New Canaan Darien Mag, 10/2005. *Mem:* Yale Club, New York; Conn Soc Portrait Artists (sen adv). *Media:* Oil, Pastel. *Publ:* Illusr advertising, (TV & print), Breck Shampoo, 76- & Coca Cola USA, 80; Heath Sci Textbks, DC Heath, 79 & 81; album cover, Karen Kayen: You Don't Have to Take What You Get, Rooster Records, 81. *Dealer:* Portraits Inc 2801 6th Ave Birmingham AL 35233. *Mailing Add:* 160 Horseneck Rd Dartmouth MA 02748

ANDERSON, ROBERT DALE
PAINTER, DRAFTSMAN, PRINTMAKER
b Glendale, Calif, Mar 12, 1949. *Study:* Pasadena City Coll, AA, 70; Calif State Coll Long Beach, BA, 72, MFA, 76. *Work:* Blanton Mus Art, Austin, Tex; Albuquerque Mus, NMex; De Young Mus, San Francisco. *Exhib:* Anderson / Dill, Acro Ctr Visual Arts, Los Angeles, 77; Anderson / Alderette, Fine Arts Gallery, Long Beach, Calif, 86; Print Exhib of 6 Calif Artist, Am Center, Uagoya, Japan, 87; 40 Yrs of Calif Assemblage, Wight Gallery, Los Angeles, 89; Obsessed By Magic, ACA Galleries, New York, 97; Crossed Lines, Conduit Gallery, Dallas, Tex, 2000; Dark Ages, Conduit Gallery, Dallas, Tex, 2001; Robert Dale Anderson/Sydney Yeager, D Berman Gallery, Austin, Tex, 2002. *Collection Arranged:* Small World Drawings, Conduit Gallery, Dallas, Tex, 2005. *Teaching:* Instr, Univ Southern Calif, 76-77 & Pasadena City Coll, 77; sr lectr, Univ Tex Austin, 88-. *Bibliog:* Artweek, 2/28/81; Marnie Weber (auth), 40 Years of Calif Assemblage Catalog: Robert Anderson; Robbie Conal (auth), Figural Obsessions. *Mem:* Southern Graphics Coun. *Media:* Graphite, Ink; Lithography; Oil. *Dealer:* Conduit Gallery 1626C Hi Line Dr Dallas TX 75207; d berman Gallery 1701 Guadalupe St Austin TX 78701; ACA Gallery 529 W 20th St 5th Fl New York NY 10011. *Mailing Add:* 19611 Wiersma Ave Cerritos CA 90703-6556

ANDERSON, ROSS CORNELIUS
MUSEUM DIRECTOR, HISTORIAN
b Washington, DC, May 2, 1951. *Study:* Princeton Univ, AB, 73; Harvard Univ, MA, 77. *Pos:* Chief cur, Everson Mus Art, Syracuse, NY, 79-83; dir, Montgomery Mus Fine Arts, Ala, 83-87; Riverside Art Mus, Calif, 87-90, art consult, 91-. *Teaching:* Instr, Syracuse Univ, 81-83. *Res:* 19th and 20th century American painting and sculpture. *Publ:* Contribr, Grueby Pottery, 81, Abbott Handerson Thayer, 82 & American Clay Sculpture 1925-1950, 83, Everson Mus Art; Maurice and Charles Prendergast Raisonne (exhib catalog), Williams Coll Mus Art, Prestel, 90. *Mailing Add:* 419 N Larchmont Blvd # 50 Los Angeles CA 90004-3013

ANDERSON, SALLY J
PAINTER, PRINTMAKER
b Rockford, Ill, Feb 5, 1942. *Study:* Inst Allende, San Miguel Allende, Mex, 62; Beloit Col, BA, 64; Univ Wis, 67. *Work:* Fed Bldg, Vickers Corp, Oklahoma City; Sunwest Bank, Albuquerque; Saks Fifth Ave, NY; Marriott Hotel Corp, Washington, DC; Product design, Swan/Dolphin Hotel, Orlando, Fla, Connie Chung set, CBS Network, NY, 90. *Exhib:* Solo exhib, Roswell Art Mus, NMex, 70; Southwest Fine Arts Biennial, Mus NMex, Santa Fe, 75 & 79; Convergence 76, Carnegie Inst Mus Art, Pittsburgh, Pa, 76; Ariz Biennial, Phoenix Art Mus, 79; One Space, Three Visions, Albuquerque Mus, 80; and others. *Awards:* First Prize, NMex Crafts Biennial, Mus NMex, Santa Fe, 75; Nat Endowment Arts Grants, 76 & 77. *Bibliog:* Donald Locke (auth), article, Arts Mag, 9/83. *Media:* Acrylic, Oil; Lithography, Product Design. *Dealer:* C G Rein Galleries Edina MN; C G Rein Galleries Scottsdale AZ. *Mailing Add:* 7522 Bear Canyon Albuquerque NM 87109-4464

ANDERSON, SCOTT
PAINTER, GRAPHIC ARTIST
Study: Kans State Univ, BFA, 1997; Univ Ill, Urbana-Champaign, MFA, 2001. *Exhib:* Solo exhibs include Peter Miller Gallery, Chicago, 2001, Mus Contemp Art, Chicago, 2003, Galerie Jean-Luc & Takako Richard, Paris, 2004, Mark Moore Gallery, Santa Monica, Calif, 2005, Kavi Gupta Gallery, Chicago, 2005 & 2008 Kavi Gupta Gallery, Leipzig, Germany, 2007; two-person exhib with Aaron Baker, Community Coll Southern Nev, Las Vegas, 2004; group exhibs include Apocalypse Next Week, I-Space, Chicago, 2001; Social Landscape, PPOW Gallery, New York, 2002; Post-Digital Painting, Cranbrook Art Mus, Bloomfield Hills, Mich, 2003; New Works, Kavi Gupta Gallery, Chicago, 2006; Mutiny, The Happy Lion, Los Angeles, 2006; Future Tense: Reshaping the Landscape, Neuburger Mus, Purchase, NY, 2008. *Awards:* Kate Neal Mem Fel, 2001; William & Dorothy Yeck Award, 2003; Pollock-Krasner Found Grant, 2006. *Mailing Add:* c/o Kavi Gupta Gallery 835 W Washington Chicago IL 60607

ANDERSON, SUSAN MARY
PAINTER
b Evanston, Ill. *Study:* St Mary's Col, Notre Dame, Ind, with Norman La Liberté, 60; Marquette Univ, Milwaukee, Wis, BA (english & painting), 65; Art Students League, with Barbara Adrian, Hillary Holmes & Robert Hale, 70-80. *Work:* Housatonic Mus. *Comn:* Lower East Side #1, Am Jewish Comt, 98. *Exhib:* Le Livre dans tous see États, Bibliotheque Nat, Argenteuil, France, 87 & Beauvais, France, 88; Le Livre Object, Bibliot Nat, Orgeval, France, 88; League at the Cape, Provincetown Mus, Mass, 93; solo exhib, Sound Shore Gallery, Cross River, NY, 96-97 & Stamford Ctr Arts, 99. *Awards:* First & Second Prize, Art Students League, New York, 83. *Bibliog:* Vivien Raynor (auth), Visions in an arcade, NY Times, 8/28/94; Linda Matys O'Connell (auth), Hot tickets: quadruple vision, Advocate & Village Times, 9/9/94. *Mem:* Life mem, Art Students League. *Media:* Oil. *Dealer:* Mary Udell Sound Shore Gallery 6 Landmark Sq Stamford Ct 06901. *Mailing Add:* 142 Minuteman Cir Allentown NJ 08501

ANDERSON, TROY
PAINTER, SCULPTOR
b Siloam Springs, Ark, Aug 23, 1948. *Study:* WTex State Univ, Canyon, BS (art), 70. *Work:* Ark State Bank, Siloam Springs; Bur Indian Affairs, Washington, DC; Five Civilized Tribes Mus, Muskogee, Okla; Capital, State of Ark, Little Rock, Ark. *Comn:* Cherokee Sesquicentennial Trail of Tears Commemorative Gold Medallion, 89. *Exhib:* Denver Mus Natural Hist, 80; Am Indian & Cowboy Artists, San Dimas, Calif, 80-83; Five Civilized Tribes Mus, Muskogee, Okla, 81; Cherokee National History Museum; and others. *Pos:* pres, Am Indian & Cowboy Artist, Inc, formerly. *Awards:* Ambassador of the Year Award, Ctr Am Indian, Kirkpatrick Ctr, Oklahoma City; Grand Award Master Artists, Five Civilized Tribes Mus, 82-88; First Place Painting, Cherokee Nat Hist Mus, Tahlequah, Okla, 83-90; Heritage Grand Award, 89; Am Indian & Cowboy Artist Indian Heritage Award, 90. *Bibliog:* Southwest Art, 2/90. *Mem:* Am Indian & Cowboy Artists Inc (vpres, 84-85, pres, 86-87). *Media:* Acrylic, Oil; Mixed Media, Bronze. *Specialty:* Native Am & wildlife. *Publ:* Contrib, Southwest Art, 2/90. *Dealer:* ArtMarket, 9515-D E 51st St, Tulsa, Okla, 74145. *Mailing Add:* c/o Studio of Troy Anderson 23450 Quicks Loop Siloam Springs AR 72761

ANDERSON, VALERIE B
PAINTER, ILLUSTRATOR
b Boston, MA, Jan 4, 61. *Study:* Cornell Univ (advanced placement student), 78. *Work:* Pvt collection of Dr Alfonz Lengyel (art historian & critic), Sarasota, Fla. *Exhib:* Group exhib, 67th Ann Members Exhib, Main Line Art Ctr, Haverford, Pa, 2004-2005; Non Representational Exhib (electronic), juried, art-exchange.com, inc, Hot Springs, Ark, 2006; New York Art Expo 2007, Jacob K Javits Convention Ctr, NY, 2007; 11th Ann Faces Int Juried Online Art Exhib, Upstream People Gallery, 2009, 14th Ann Faces Int Juried Online Art Exhib, 2012; NY Art Expo, 2014; Southern Nev Mus Fine Arts Show; International Contemporary Masters, Worldwide Art Los Angeles, Los Angeles, 2014. *Awards:* Special Recognition award, 14th Ann Faces Juried Online Int Art Exhib, Upstream People Gallery, 2012. *Bibliog:* Trendsetters (Emerging Artists), Art Business News (Vol 32, 138, 3/2005); International Contemporary Masters Vol 9, Vol 10. *Media:* Acrylic & Oil. *Publ:* (A, I, B), Reflections on the Word in Black and White, Dry Bones Press, 2002; (I, B), Boogaloo: a dandy collection of star-spangled masques, Edwin Mellen Poetry Press, 2003; (A, I, B), ROXAN. REM Press Inc, 2007 (in manuscript); (I,B), Angels of the Bible (in manuscript); (A, I, B), Archetypes: Christina's Lotus Dream Book (in manuscript); The Dream of Emerald Blue (images), Lighthouse Christian Publishing, 2014. *Dealer:* art-exchange.com inc 804 Central Ave Hot Springs AR 71901. *Mailing Add:* PO Box 12 Abington PA 19001

ANDERSON, WARREN HAROLD
GRAPHIC ARTIST, PAINTER
b Moline, Ill, Sept 27, 1925. *Study:* Western Ill Univ, BS, 50; Univ Iowa, MA, 51; Stanford Univ, PhD, 61. *Work:* Joseph H Hirshhorn Collection, Washington; Phoenix Art Mus; Tucson Mus Art; Univ Ariz Mus Art; Western Ill Univ Art Gallery Solo-exhibs. *Exhib:* solo-exhibs, Highway Drawings/Video, Phoenix Art Mus, Ariz, 79, US 80, Drawings, El Paso Mus Art, Tex, 79 & 99, Vanishing Roadside Am (prismacolor drawings), Tucson Mus Art, 82, Tohono Chul Gallery, Tucson, Ariz, 89, Univ NMex, AE Gallery, 91 & Western Ill Univ Gallery, 94; 30 year retrospective, Univ Ariz Mus Art, 86; See the USA, Nat Bldg Mus, Washington, DC, 99, 2000. *Teaching:* Prof art, Univ Ariz, Tucson, 56-86, prof emer, currently. *Awards:* Several state and Southwest regional awards, 58-90; Creative Teaching Award in Art, Ariz Found, 82. *Bibliog:* Vanishing roadside America, Mod Maturity, 9/84; Signs of our Times, Signs of the Times, 5/97 & 5/98; Jesse Greenberg (auth), Art of Warren Anderson: Past Intertwining With Present, Tucson Guide Quart, spring 2001. *Mem:* Soc Com Archeol. *Media:* Prismatic Pencil, Floated Montages. *Res:* Environmental aesthetics; vernacular roadside art forms; cartifacts--artifacts that exist because of cars; vestiges west; ghost town objects and textures. *Specialty:* Realistic Prismatic Pencil; Paintings & Retro ERA; Floated Montages. *Interests:* American & Southwest History. *Publ:* Vanishing Roadside America, Univ Ariz Press, 81. *Dealer:* Vanished Roadside America & Vestiges West Art 6802 N Longfellow Tucson AZ 85718. *Mailing Add:* c/o Univ Ariz Art Dept 108 PO Box 210002 Tucson AZ 85721

ANDERSON, WILLIAM THOMAS
PAINTER, PRINTMAKER
b Minneapolis, Minn, Dec 13, 1936. *Study:* Calif State Univ, Los Angeles, with Leonard Edmondson, Bob Fiedler & Walter Askin; Chaffey Col; El Camino Col, with Charles Blusk. *Work:* Downey Mus Art; Civil Air Patrol, Calif Wing; Humboldt Cult Ctr; Humboldt State Univ; and others. *Comn:* Mural, CAP, Calif Wing; drawing, Kinnebrew Mem. *Exhib:* 18th Ann Nat Printmaking Show, Brooklyn Mus, NY, 73; World Print Competition, San Francisco Mus of Mod Art, 77; Invitational, Univ Puget Sound, 79; Stages/Four Printmakers, Mt St Mary's Col, Los Angeles, 79; Works on a Transparent Support, John Kohler Arts Ctr, Sheboygan, Wis, 79; Invitational, C N Gorman Mus, Univ Calif, Davis, 81; Nat Screenprint Show, Old Dominion Univ, Norfolk, Va, 85-86; and many others. *Pos:* Chief reader, ETS, AP Studio Art; chmn, Art Dept, Humboldt State Univ. *Teaching:* Prof art, Humboldt State Univ, 67-. *Media:* Miscellaneous; Silkscreen. *Mailing Add:* Humboldt State Univ Dept Art Arcata CA 95521

ANDERSON, WILMER (LOUIS)
PAINTER, WRITER
b Houston, Tex, Dec 24, 1933. *Study:* Rice Univ, BA, 56; Harvard Univ, AM, 57, PhD, 60. *Work:* Univ Wis Physics dept, Madison. *Exhib:* Aqueous 2000, Houston, 2000; Nat Arts Club, NY, 2000; Salmagundi Club, NY, 2000; Watercolor West Exhib; New Eng Watercolor Soc; Audubon Artists; Transparent Watercolor Soc Am; Nat Soc Painter; Am Watercolor Soc, 2008, 2009, 2010, 2011, 2013; Nat Watercolor Soc, 2007. *Pos:* co-founder Madison Watercolor Soc, 83 & pres, 83-89. *Awards:* Edmund A Steinbock Purchase Award, Ky Watercolor Soc, 98; Winsor Newton Award, Audubon Artists, Inc, 99; Maria M Naimir Award, San Diego Watercolor Soc, 2000; Second Prize, Pittsburgh Watercolor Soc, 2004; Second Prize, Harrisburg Art Asn, 2004; First Prize, New Eng Watercolor Soc, Biennial Exhib, 2007; Michael Engle Founder's Award, Audubon Artists, 2008; Judy & Elias Neuman Award, NSPCA, 2009; Signature Mem Award, Alabama Watercolor Soc, 2009; Hardy Gramaky Award, Am Watercolor Soc, 2010; Watercolor West, 2012; Mgraham award, Phila Watercolor Soc, 2012; Silver Medal of Honor, Allied Artists, 2013. *Mem:* Audubon Artists, Inc; Nat Painters Casein and Acrylic; Western Fedn Watercolor Socs; Transparent Watercolor Soc Am; Watercolor West; Acad Artists Asn; Allied Artists; Am Watercolor Soc. *Media:* Acrylic, Watercolor, Gouache. *Publ:* coauth, illusr, Electric Circuits and Modern Electronics, Holt Rinehart Winston, 73; auth, Light and Color, Raintree, 78. *Dealer:* Stony Hill Antiques 2140 Regent St Madison WI 53705. *Mailing Add:* 1818 Chadbourne Ave Madison WI 53726-4045

ANDERSON, WINSLOW
DESIGNER, PAINTER
b Plymouth, Mass, May 17, 1917. *Study:* State Univ NY Coll Ceramics, Alfred Univ, BFA; Plymouth Pottery, Mass; Hans Hofmann Sch Art, Provincetown, Mass; Pa Acad Fine Arts, Philadelphia; Pratt Graphics Ctr, NY. *Comn:* Triptych mural, Church of St Mary the Virgin Concert Hall, NY. *Exhib:* 5th & 11th Ceramic Exhibs, Syracuse Mus Fine Arts, NY, 40 & 46; Guggenheim Mus Ann, NY, 43-46; Kanawha Artists Asn, Charleston, WVa, 50. *Pos:* Glass designer, Blenko Glass Co, Milton, Va, 46-53; design dir, Lenox China Inc, Trenton, NJ, 53-64, dir dimensional design, 64-80. *Awards:* First Prize for African Mask (sculpture), Nat USA Contest, 44; First Prize for Fish (stained glass), Stained Glass Soc Washington, DC, 53. *Bibliog:* Don Wallace (auth), Shaping America's Products, Reinhold Publ Co, 56. *Media:* Clay, Glass; Pastel, Oil. *Collection:* Haitian primitives. *Publ:* Auth, Offhand design for offhand glass, Am Ceramic Soc J, 4/49. *Mailing Add:* PO Box 1700 Huntington WV 25717-1700

ANDERSON, ZULIA GOTAY
PAINTER, ILLUSTRATOR
b San Juan, Puerto Rico, Jan 5, 1953. *Study:* Coll Sacred Heart, San Turce, PR, BA, 75; Univ New Mex, MA, 92; studied with Myrna Baez, Coll Sacred Heart, 75. *Exhib:* Solo exhibs, Wirtz Gallery, Miami, 2002, Art Divas Gallery, Taos, NMex, 2007, Hispanic Mus Art, Miami, 2004, Kucera Gallery, Corpus Christi, Tex, 2010; Group exhibs, Los Nuevos Artistas, S Tex Inst Arts, Corpus Christi, Tex, 2006; Paint the Town, Buffalo Hist Mus, Buffalo, NY, 2006; Los Artistas, Art Mus S Tex, 2008; Artrageous Too, Art Mus S Tex, Corpus Christi, Tex, 2008. *Awards:* First prize in oil, NMex State Fair, NMex, 93; Award of Exellence, NMex State Fair, NMex, 94; Grumbacher Gold, Artist of the Campus, Grumbacher, 2000; First prize, Impact Gallery, Buffalo, NY, 2006. *Bibliog:* Bob Seetoo (auth), Hispanic Art Show, Poughkeepsie Joun, 9/1/2001; Painting by Zulia Gotay, Profesa Informa, Summer 2003; Much Planned, Rockport Pilot, 12/7/2002; Beth Reese (auth), Immersion, Caller Times, 3/19/2010; The Figure, Southwest Art Mag, Jan 2010. *Media:* Acrylic, Oil. *Dealer:* Act One Gallery 218 Paseo Del Norte Taos NM 87571; Jane Hamilton Fine Art 2890 East Skyline Dr Tucson AZ 87571; St Charles Gallery 414 S Austin St Rockport TX 78382; Art of the Island 323 N Alister Port Arkansas TX 78375. *Mailing Add:* PO Box 18300 Corpus Christi TX 78480

ANDERSON-SPIVY, C ALEXANDRA
CRITIC, WRITER, EDITOR
b Boston, Mass, May 14, 1942. *Study:* Sarah Lawrence Coll, BA, 61; Sorbonne, France, 63. *Pos:* Art ed, Paris Rev, 73-78 & Village Voice, 74-77; sr ed, Portfolio Mag, 79-83; ed in chief, Art & Antiques, 83-84; exec ed, Am Photogr, 85-87; arts ed & exec ed, Smart Mag, 88-89; contrib art ed, Esquire Mag, 90-94; revs ed, Art J, 95-2001; ed, Interactive Bureau, 96-2000; ed dir, Circle.com, 2000-02; featured writer, artnet.com, 2003-2013; contbr, artcritical.com, 2010-. *Awards:* Japan Found grant, 76; Nat Endowment Arts Critic Grant, 78; Prof Fel, Morgan Libr. *Mem:* Int Asn Art Critics (pres, US sect); Am Soc Mag Ed; Art Table; Colby Coll Art Mus (bd govs, currently); Contemp Arts Coun, Mus Mod Art (vpres); Exhib Int (chair adv bd, 98-2005); Mus Modern Art (libr trustee comt); Columbia Co Historical Soc (trustee); AWA (bd dirs, 2014). *Res:* Contemporary art and artist's publications; 20th century art. *Interests:* Decorative & fine arts. *Publ:* Coauth, Anderson and Archer's Soho: The Essential Guide to Art and Life in Lower Manhattan, Simon & Schuster, 79; Living with Art, Rizzoli, 88; auth, Passions & Tenderness: Portraits of Olga by the Baron de Meyer, Graystone Books, 92; Gardens of Earthly Delight: The Art of Robert Kushner, Hudson Hills Press, 97; Foleage, The Art of Harold Finestein, 99; Facing India, Photographs of Marcus Leatherdale, 2009; James Havend, John Molloy Galley, 2014. *Mailing Add:* PO Box 771 Kinderhook NY 12106

ANDERSON-STALEY, KELIY
PHOTOGRAPHER
b 1937. *Study:* Hampshire Coll, Amherst, Mass, BA, 2001; Hunter Coll, New York, MFA (Photog), 2006. *Work:* Mod Museet, Stockholm, Sweeden. *Exhib:* group exhibs include Hampshire Coll Photog Gallery, Amherst, Mass, 2000; Home Away from Home, Walker Space, New York, 2003; Hunter Coll Times Square Gallery, New York, 2005, Off the Grid, 2006; How Women Look, Safe-T-Gallery, Brooklyn, NY, 2007; Space Stories, Chashama Gallery, New York, 2007; Want, Dana Warp Mill Gallery, Westbrook, Maine, 2008; Found at Fotofest, John Cleary Gallery, Houston, 2008; How Soon is Now?, Bronx Mus Arts, NY, 2008. *Awards:* New York Found Arts Fel, 2008

ANDRADE, BRUNO
PAINTER
b San Antonio, Tex, Nov 3, 1947. *Study:* Tex A & I Univ, BS, 70; Univ Mich, MFA, 77. *Work:* Mus Contemp Hispanic Art, NY; Art Mus South Tex, Corpus Christi; Sondra & Charles Gilman Jr Found, NY; McAllen Int Mus, Tex; Mexican Mus, San Francisco, Calif. *Comn:* A H Belo Corp, Dallas, Tex; Pepsi Co Foods Int, Plano, Tex; Compaq Computer, Houston, Tex; Tex Instrument Inc, Houston; B D Holt Co, San Antonio, Tex. *Exhib:* Solo exhibs, Lynn Goode Gallery, Houston, Tex, 89, 91, 93 & 94 & Edith Baker Gallery, Dallas, Tex, 90 & 98; Abstract Visions (with catalog), Mus Contemp Hispanic Art, NY, 87; Confrontacion, Mexico-Arte Mus, Austin, Tex, 92; Bruno Andrade and Michael Lathrop, Barbara Gillman Gallery, Miami Beach, Fla, 93; The Good Earth, Edith Baker Gallery, Dallas, 94; Gallery Artists, Lynn Goode Gallery, Houston, Tex, 95; MB Mod, NY, 96 & 98; MB in LA, Jerry Solomon Gallery, Los Angeles, 97; Art Patterns, Austin Mus Art at Laguna, Gloria, Tex, 97; and others. *Teaching:* Instr painting, Stephens Col, Columbia, Mo, 77-80; prof art painting, Corpus Christi State Univ, Tex, 81-. *Awards:* Artist Fel Grant, Nat Endowment Arts, 80 & 89. *Bibliog:* Diane Armitage (auth), Rediscovering the Landscape of the Americas, The Mag, 9/96; Peter Dellolio (auth), Reviews/New York/Bruno Andrade, NY Arts Mag, Issue No 11, 6/97; Elizabeth B Reese (auth), Mind Mapping Texas Landscapes: Postmodern Pedagogy with or without Computers, Art Educ, Vol 50, No 6, 11/97. *Media:* Oil on Canvas. *Publ:* Contribr, spec issue cover, Contemp Art, Art & Antiques, summer 97. *Dealer:* Edith Baker Gallery Dallas TX; Barbara Gillman Gallery Miami Beach FL

ANDRE, CARL
SCULPTOR
b Quincy, Mass, Sept 16, 1935. *Study:* Phillips Acad, 51-53; With Patrick & Maud Morgan, Hollis Frampton; Michael Chapman, Frank Stella. *Work:* Nat Gallery Can, Ottawa; Tate Gallery, London; Mus Mod Art, NY; Albright-Knox Art Gallery, Buffalo; Art Inst Chicago; and others. *Comn:* Found Pub Giving, Hartford, Conn. *Exhib:* Solo Exhibs: Solomon R Guggenheim Mus, 70; Mus Mod Art, NY, 73; Paula Cooper Gallery, 93, 95, 97-98, 2000, 2002, 2004, 2006, 2007, 2008; Gagosian Gallery, NY, 95; Syningarsalur Exhib Space, Reykjavik, Iceland, 96; Mus Mod Art, Oxford, Eng, 96; Royal Botanic Garden, Edinburgh, 98; Konrad Fischer Galerie, Dusseldorf, Ger, 99, 2003-2004, 2006; Galerie Tschudi, Glarus, Switz, 2002-2004, 2006; Sadie Coles HQ, London, 2006, 2009, 2011; Andrea Rosen, NY City, 2007; Konrad Fischer Galerie, Dusseldorf, Germany, 2008; Yon Lambert Galerie, Paris, 2008, Sadie Coles HQ, London, Eng, 2009, Carl Andre, Paula Cooper Gallery, New York, 2009, Carl Andre, Tin Works, Galerie Tschudi, 2002, 2009; Konrad Fischer Galerie, Dusseldorf, Ger, 2009, 2011; Alfronso Artiaco, Naples, Italy, 2010; The Chinati Found, Marfa, Tex, 2010; Mus Kurhaus Kleve, Ger, 2011; Galeria Cayon, Madrid, Spain, 2011; Group Exhibs: Multiplicity, Inst Contemp Art, Boston, 66; Cool Art, Aldrich Mus Contemp Art, 68; Art of the Real: USA 1948-88 Traveling Exhib, Mus Mod Art, NY, 68; Directions 1: Options, Milwaukee Art Ctr, 68; Anti-Illusion: Procedures/Materials, Whitney Mus Am Art, 69; 555,087, Seattle Art Mus, 69; Information, Mus Mod Art, NY, 70; 1970 Ann Exhib: Contemp Am Sculpture, Whitney Mus Am Art, 70; Guggenheim Int Exhib, Solomon R Guggenheim Mus, 72; 1973 Biennial Exhib: Contemp Am Art, Whitney Mus Am Art, 73; 10th Anniversary Exhib, Aldrich Mus Contemp Art, 74; Drawing Now, Mus Mod Art, NY, 76; 72nd Am Exhib Traveling Show, Art Inst Chicago, 76; 200 Yrs Am Exhib, Whitney Mus Am Art, 76; 20th Century Am Drawings: Five Yrs of Acquisition, Whitney Mus Am Art, 78; American Art 1950 to the Present, Whitney Mus Am Art, 78; The Reductive Object, Inst Contemp Art Boston, 79; The Minimal Tradition, Aldrich Mus Contemp Art, 79; Contemp Sculpture: Selections from the Collection of the Mus of Modern Art, Mus Mod Art, NY, 79; Surveying the Seventies, Whitney Mus Am Art, 82; postMINIMALISM, Aldrich Mus Contemp Art, 82; Minimalism x 4, Whitney Mus Am Art, 82; The NY Sch: Four Decades, Solomon R Guggenheim Mus, 82; Contrasts of Form: Geometric Abstract Art, Mus Mod Art, NY, 85; Transformations in Sculpture, Solomon R Guggenheim Mus, 85; Contemp Installation, Mus Mod Art, NY, 86; Immaterial Objects, Whitney Mus Am Art, 91; Manifeste, Mus d'Art Mod, Paris, 92; Mus Fridericianum, Kassel, Germany, 93; Mus Contemp Art, Tokyo, 95; Tel Aviv Art Mus, Israel, 95; Solomon R Guggenheim Mus, 96; Tate Gallery, London, 96; Mus Mod Art, NY City, 97; Sydney Biennale, 98; Whitney Mus Am Art, NY City, 99, 2004, 2005; Oriel Mostyn Gallery, 2000; Kunsthalle Bielefeld, Ger, 2001; Walker Art Ctr, Minneapolis, 2002, 2003; Mus Contemp Art San Diego, 2004; Stedelijk Mus, Amsterdam, 2005; L&M Arts, NY City, 2006; Arnaud Lefebvre, Paris, 2006, 2007; Cultureel Centrum Strombeek, Mechelen, Belgium, 2007; Risd Mus Art, Providence, RI, 2008; Gallery Yamaguchi, Kunst-Bau, Tokyo, 2009; Kunst Mus Wlsburg, Germany, 2009; Compass in Hand, Selections from the Judith Rothschild Found Contemp Drawings Collection, Mus Mod Art, New York, 2009; 1969 PS1 Contemp

Art Ctr, Long Island City, New York, 2009; Collection: Mus Contemp Art's First 30 Years, Mus Contemp Art, Los Angeles, 2010; Radical Conceptual, MMK, Frankfurt, Germany, 2010; John Kaldor Family Collection, Art Gallery of New South Wales, Sydney, Australia, 2011; Personal Structures: Time-Space-Existence, Palazzo Bembo, Venice, Italy, 2011; 55th Int Art Exhib Biennale, Venice, 2013. *Bibliog:* Carl Andre, Cuts: Text 1959-2004, James Meyer (edi), Cambridge, Mass:MIT Press, 2005; 560 Broadway: A New York Drawing Collection at Work 1991-2006, Amy Eshoo (ed), Yale Univ Press, New Haven, Conn, 2008; Klaus Biesenbach (auth), Political/Minimal, KW Inst for Contemp Arts, Berlin, 2009; Alistair Rider (auth) Carl Andre: Things in their Elements, London, Phaidon Press, 2011. *Media:* All. *Publ:* 12 Dialogues 1962-1963, with Hollis Frampton, New York Univ Press, 80. *Dealer:* Konrad Fischer Galerie Platanenstrasse 1 40233 Dusseldorf Germany; Galerie Tschudi Eichenstrasse 26 CH-8750 Glarus Switzerland; Sadie Coles HQ 35 Heddon St London W1B 4BP; Galerie Arnaud Lefebvre 30 rue Mazarine 75006 Paris France; Paula Cooper Gallery 534 W 21st St New York NY 10011. *Mailing Add:* c/o Paula Cooper Gallery 534 W 21st St New York NY 10011

ANDREASON, LEE
SCULPTURE

b Lebanon, Ore, Mar 20, 1937. *Study:* Santa Barbara City Col, pvt study with Anthony Priolo, 80; Pierce Jr Col, 80; UCLA Art Hist, France, 85-86. *Work:* US Congressman Sam Farr House of Rep, Washington, DC; Mus of the Horse Ky Horse Park, Lexington, Ky; pvt collection, Ambassador Patricia Gates Lynch, Fort Bellvoir, Va, Mr & Mrs Nicolas Hahn, Zurich, Switz; Ascott Racetrack, Eng; Gold Cup Ascot, Liz Woods, Mr & Mrs Clinton Bonavia. *Comn:* Man & Horse, Monterey Co Mus of Art, Monterey, 84; Bust of Client, Colleen Colins, Pebble Beach, Calif, 93; 5' Bronze Horse Gallery 444 Post, San Francisco, Calif, 94; 10' Bronze Horse, Reflections Gallery, Santa Fe, NMex, 2000; Hercules II Task Douglas White, San Antonio Tex, 2003. *Exhib:* Solo Exhibs: Highlands Sculpture Gallery Carmel Calif, 85; Pacific Grove Art Ctr, Pacific Grove Calif, 1984; Smith Crosby Gallery, Carmel, Calif, 1988; Gallery Brisomar, Marbella, Spain, 1988, 1995; Highlands Sculpture Gallery, Carmel, Calif, 1989; Marin Price Gallery, Chevy Chase, Md, 1994; Galeria Sculptures, Paris, France, 99; Amsteleen Gallery, Amsterdam, 2001; Solo Show sponsored by Spainish Government, Antequara, Spain, 2007; Major Retrospect, Jimena de la Frontera, Spain, 2005; Studio Exhib, Jimena de la Frontera; Group exhibs: Galerie Leidel, Munich Ger, 2011; Sammer Gallery, Puerto Banus, Spain, 2006; Horses Ponies & Unicorns (juried), Nat Sculpture Soc, NY, 2004; (juried), Cravens Arts Council & Gallery, NC, 2007; Oh Well Orwell, Monterey Co Mus of Art, Monterey, Calif, 84; Pacific Grove Art Ctr Mus, Pacific Grove, Calif, 83; Mus of the Horse, Ky, Horse Park, Lexington, Ky, 93, 94, 95; Am Acad of Equine Art (juried), 94-95; Gallery Brisomar, Marbella, Spain, 96; Ky Horse Park, Lexington, Ky, 95; Annual Art Show (juried), Churchill Downs Mus, Louisville, Ky, 95. *Pos:* Mus & gallery exhib & sales for 40 yrs & prof invitations; teaching sculpture techniques with clay. *Teaching:* Instr, Sculpture pvt lessons, Spain, currently; Instr of sculpture, working in clay, Spain, currently. *Awards:* Quendoline May award, Monterey Co, Calif, 97. *Bibliog:* Susan Lee Hubbard (auth), Alta Vista Mag, Monterey, Calif, 93, Monterey Herald Tribune; Beth Bueher (auth), Equine Mag, Susan Badger, 94; Vanesa Mingorance (auth) Prestige Mag, Sam Benaby, Spain, Vol X, 2001; Briony Flectcher, Andalusan Mag, 2007-2008. *Mem:* Nat Sculpture Soc, NY; Am Women Artists, Washington, DC; Hirshhorn Mus, Washington, DC; Int Sculpture Soc, Chicago; NDFAS Cultural Soc, England. *Media:* Bronze, Terracotta, Glazed Ceramic Sculpture. *Res:* Workshops, UCLA travel study France, International Sculpture Society Conference, Int Sculptture Soc Conf Chicago, 2001, Nat Sculpture Conf, 2005, Trinity College, Dublin. *Specialty:* Sculpture, Fine Art. *Interests:* Fine Art Paintings & Sculpture, horsemanship, sailing, foreign culture travel, art study, ancient culture- art & hist. *Dealer:* Gallery 444 Post San Francisco Ca; Reflection Gallery Santa Fe NM. *Mailing Add:* Lee Andreason Correos Apt #35 Jimena de La Frontera Cadiz 11330 Spain

ANDRES, GLENN MERLE
HISTORIAN, EDUCATOR

b Chicago, Ill, July 15, 1941. *Study:* Cornell Univ, BArch, 64; Princeton Univ, MFA, 67, PhD, 71; Am Acad Rome, fel, 67-69. *Collection Arranged:* Builders and Humanists, Univ St Thomas, Houston, 66; Hardy Holzman Pfeiffer Associates: Twenty-Five Years, Middlebury Col, Vt, 93; Hardy Holzman Pfeiffer Associates: Creating Special Places, San Angelo, Mus Art, 99-2000; Tex Tech Univ, 99-2000; Del Mus Art, 99-2000. *Pos:* Assoc dir, Johnson Gallery, Middlebury Col, 76-78. *Teaching:* Asst prof art hist, Middlebury Col, Vt, 70-78, assoc prof, 78-83, prof, 83-, Christian A Johnson prof art, 84-87, 2000-; Fulbright lectr in Am visual cult, Univ Exeter, United Kingdom, 87-88. *Mem:* Sheldon Mus, Middlebury, Vt (trustee, 75-84, 92- & vpres, 78-82); Vt Adv Council for Hist Preservation, 86-; Soc of Architectural Historians; Soc of Fels; Am Acad in Rome. *Res:* 16th century Italian architecture; 19th century American architecture. *Publ:* Auth, A Walking History of Middlebury, Vermont, Addison Press, 75; auth, The Villa Medici in Rome, Garland Press, 76; coauth (with J M Hunisak & A R Turner), The Art of Florence, Abbeville Press, 88; contribr La Villa Medicis, Ecole Francaise de Rome, 91; contribr Hardy Holzman Pfeiffer Associates, Buildings and Projects II, Rizzoli, 99. *Mailing Add:* Dept of History of Art/Arch Middlebury VT 05753

ANDRES, HOLLY
PHOTOGRAPHER, FILMMAKER

b Missoula, Mont, 1977. *Study:* Univ Mont, Missoula, BFA, 2002; Portland State Univ, Ore, MFA (summa cum laude), 2004. *Exhib:* Solo exhibs, Second Thought, Missoula, 2000, Eating Cake Gallery, Missoula, 2001, Art Annex Gallery, Univ Mont, 2002, MK Gallery, Portland State Univ, 2004, Missoula Art Mus, 2008, Quality Pictures Contemp Art, Portland, 2008, Robert Mann Gallery, New York, 2008 & DNJ Gallery, Los Angeles, 2009; 32nd Ann NW Film and Video Festival, Portland, 2005; Affair at the Jupiter Hotel, Jupiter Hotel, Portland, 2005; Portland Documentary & Experimental Film Festival, 2006 & 2009; Portland Art Mus Ore Biennial, Portland, 2006; 29th Portland Int Film Festival, 2006; Current Photography: New Directions, Archer Gallery, Clark Coll, Vancouver, Wash, 2006; Experimental Film & Narratology Symposium, 2007; Private Contemplations/Private Conversations, Salem Art Asn, 2007; Girl Machine, Honfluer Gallery, Washington, DC, 2007; Deep Play: Joyful Revelry and Subversive Whimsy in the MAM Collections, Missoula Art Mus, Mont, 2007; Portland Women's Film Festival, 2008; Pulse Miami, Fla, 2008; Urban Nomad Film Fest, Taipei Biennial, Taiwan, 2008; Baltimore Women's Film Festival, Baltimore, Md, 2008. *Pos:* Camera asst, Mal, 2003; art dir, Disconnected, 2006; art dir & camera asst, Static, 2006; camera operator, Love Me Do, 2007; dir photog, Eldorado, 2007 & Future Series, 2008. *Teaching:* Adj prof, Fine Art Dept, Portland State Univ, Pacific Northwest Coll Art. *Awards:* Viewer's Choice Award for Best Film, WIT Film Festival, Portland, 2005; Profl Devel Grant, Regional Arts & Cult Coun, Portland, 2006; Gearhead Filmmaker's Grant, The Portland Experimental Film Festival, 2006. *Bibliog:* John Maynard (auth), Oregon: Time of the Biennial, The Washington Post, 7/14/2006; Skylar Browning (auth), Up Close and Personal, The Independent, Missoula, 11/11/2006; Ron Cowan (auth), Delivering the Message, Statesman J, 1/27/2007; Mark Jenkins (auth), At Area Galleries: Singularly Focused Groups, Washington Post, 8/24/2007; Leah Olman (auth), Not Your Usual Kid Pictures, Los Angeles Times, 3/7/2008; John Coakley (auth), Sparrow Lane at Robert Mann Gallery, SoHo J, 11/3/2008; Martha Langford (auth), Down the Rabbit-Hole Redux, Exit Mag, No 33, 12/2009. *Publ:* Dir & writer, Getting to Know Suzy Rose (film), 2003; co-writer & dir, Brave New Girl (film) & Dandelion (film), 2005; co-writer & dir photog, Nora (film), 2007; co-writer & dir, Eye of the Tiger (film), 2008. *Dealer:* Robert Mann Gallery New York NY; Jackson Fine Art Gallery Atlanta GA; DNJ Gallery Los Angeles CA. *Mailing Add:* c/o Robert Mann Gallery 210 11th Ave Fl 10 New York NY 10001

ANDREWS, CHARLEEN KOHL
SCULPTOR

b New York, NY, July 27, 1925. *Study:* Univ Southern Calif, BA, 54; Scottsdale Artist Sch with Bruno Luchesi & Ken Bunn, 87 & 89. *Work:* Descanso Gardens, La Canada, Calif; Carnegie Cult Arts Mus, Oxnard, Calif; Los Angeles Arboretum; Whittier City Hall, Calif; Brand Art Gallery. *Comn:* Pelicans, wood sculpture, State Farm Insurance, Los Angeles, 87; Bronze Indian, McDonalds Franchises, Glendora, Calif, 89. *Exhib:* Artists Soc Int, San Francisco, 86; Burbank City Art Competition, Burbank Libr, 87; Anniversary Show, Los Angeles Arboretum, 87; Glendale Arts Coun, Glendale Galleria, 88; Winners Circle, Alhambra City Hall, 88; and others. *Bibliog:* Mary Forgione (auth), For arts sake, Glendale Star, 86; Art highlights, W Art, 89; Bill Youngs (auth), Sculpture in wood, Star/News Herald, 89. *Mem:* Pasadena Soc Artists; Burbank Art Asn; San Gabriel Fine Arts; Int Sculptors Asn & Calif Sculptors Asn. *Media:* Wood. *Mailing Add:* 1278 Upton Pl Eagle Rock CA 90041

ANDREWS, GAIL
MUSEUM DIRECTOR

b Calif. *Study:* Coll William & Mary, BA (History), 1974; Cooperstown Grand Progs, NY, MA (Am Folk Culture), 1975; Winterthur Summer Inst, Postgrad Study, 1997; Attingham Summer Sch, further studies in decorative arts, 1981. *Pos:* Mus dir, Birmingham Mus Art. *Awards:* Women Making a Difference Award, Birmingham Bus Journ, 1998; Women of Distinction Award, Girl Scout Coun, Ala, 1999; Ala Acad of Honor, 2005. *Mem:* Member, Ala State Coun Arts, 1988-92; Birmingham Arts Comn, 1986-88; Univ Ala Birmingham Leadership Cabinet; co-chair, Region 20/20 Arts & Culture Task Force; member of first class, Leadership Birmingham, 1983-94, 1997-98; Treas, Asn Art Mus Dir, 2002-07, Pres, 2007-. *Mailing Add:* Birmingham Museum of Art 2000 8th Ave N Birmingham AL 35203

ANDREWS, KIM
PAINTER

b Aug 4, 1939. *Study:* Univ Alberta, Dipl Art, 61, BFA, 63, Brooklyn Col, City Univ NY, MFA, 68. *Work:* Can Coun Art Bank; Owens Art Gallery, Sackville, NB; Westburne Industries, Montreal; Art Gallery Hamilton, Ont; Art Gallery North York, Ont. *Exhib:* Solo exhibs, Nightingale Gallery, Toronto, 70, Owens Art Gallery, Mt Alison Univ, Sackville, NB, 72, The Gallery, Scarborough Col, Univ Toronto, Olga Korper Gallery, Toronto, 82, 84, 86, 87 & 96, Gallery Wack, Ger, 87 & 92 & Galerie Dr Luise Krohn, Ger, 89; Art Gallery Ont, Traveling Exhib: Owens Art Gallery, Mt Alison Univ, Sackville, NB, 73; Cologne Int Art Fair, Ger, 86 & 87; 15 Anniversary Group Show, Olga Korper Gallery, Toronto, 88; 49th Parallel, NY, 89; Entschieden & Konsequent, Galerie Dr Luise Krohn, Ger, 91. *Pos:* Course dir, drawing, York Univ, Toronto, 73-74 & 76-77. *Teaching:* spec lectr, Univ Toronto, 75-80, asst prof, drawing & painting, 80-82, assoc prof, 82-. *Dealer:* Olga Korper Gallery 17 Morrow Ave Toronto Ont M6R 2H9. *Mailing Add:* c/o Olga Korper Gallery 17 Morrow Ave Toronto ON M6R 2H9 Canada

ANDREWS, LAWRENCE
VIDEO ARTIST, SCULPTOR

b May 7, 1964. *Study:* San Francisco Art Inst, Sobel Scholar, 85, BFA, 87; Corcoran Sch Art, Washington, DC, 82. *Exhib:* Solo exhibs, Western Addition Cult Ctr, San Francisco, 87, New Langton Arts, San Francisco, Calif, 89, Rene Coelho Gallery Monte Video, Amsterdam, 90, The Kitchen, 92 & Washington Project for Arts, 92, Capp ST Proj, San Francisco, Calif, 94 & San Francisco Exploratorium, 95; An I for An I, San Francisco Mus Mod Art, 88; Strategies for the develop of NY, Whitney Biennial, 91; Enlightenment, Revolution Gallery, Ferndale, Mich, 93; The Final Frontier, New Mus Contemp Art, NY, 93; When Worlds Collide, Mus Mod Art, NY, 94; Walker Art Ctr, 94; Flagging the 21st Century, Capp St Proj, 94; Post Colonial Strategies, San Francisco State Univ, Calif, 95; Whitney Biennial, 95; and others. *Pos:* Freelance ed, Bay Area Video Coalition, Video Free Am; bd dir, New Am Makers, 89 & New Langton Arts, 90-; fel panelist visual arts, Nat Endowment Arts, 90; lectr, San Francisco Film Festival, 90, 92 & 93, Mill Valley Film Festival, 92, Pub Art Works, Mill Valley, 92; adv bd, secession Gallery, San Francisco, Calif, 92-; selection panelist, Film Arts Found Grants prog, 92, Seattle Arts Comn Coliseum Proj, 94 & Wash State Pub Schs Video Art Collection; juror, Girbaud Peace Movement Art

Exhib; panelist, Creating Democracy: Technology, Pedagogy & the Arts, San Francisco State Univ, 94, Free Media/Accessing Audiences Through Electronic Commons, Capp St Proj, 94. *Teaching:* Asst prof film & electronic media, Univ Calif, Santa Cruz, bd studies theater arts, 91-; artist-in-residence, Rijksacademie Amsterdam, Holland, 89-90; guest lectr & artist-in-residence, Univ Indust Arts, Helsinki, Finland. *Awards:* Fulbright Grant, 89; Visual Arts Fel, Nat Endowment Arts, 89 & 93; Intercultural Media Arts Fel, Rockefeller Found, 93. *Bibliog:* Articles in San Francisco Mag, 1/89, Artweek, 7/1/89, Los Angeles Times, 7/29/89 & High Performance Mag, summer 89; Human Attention/Regaining Control of our senses, Village Voice, 2/4/92; The Body and technology, New York Times, 7/30/93. *Mem:* Bay Area Video Coalition (bd dir, 93-); Acad Standing Comt, 92-93 & 96-97. *Publ:* Shift Mag, Vol 2, No 4, 40-41; Art Week, 2/22/90 & 11/8/90. *Mailing Add:* 376 Capricorn Ave Oakland CA 94611-2058

ANDRUS, BARBARA
SCULPTOR
b 50. *Study:* Sarah Lawrence Coll, BA, Bronxville, NY, 75; Sch Mus Fine Arts, Diploma, Boston, 80. *Exhib:* Solo shows incl New Eng Sch Art and Design, Boston, 86, Broomfield Gallery, Boston, 92, 94, Milton Acad, Nesto Gallery, Mass, 94, Hudson T Walker Gallery, Provincetown, Mass, 95, Lionheart Gallery, Boston, 98, The Art Lot, Brooklyn, 99, 125 Maiden Lane, New York, 2000, AOH, Yonkers, NY, 2003, DM Contemp, Mill Neck, NY, 2004; Group exhibs: Madeleine Carter Gallery, Brookline, Mass, 79; Art in General, New York, 83; New Eng Sch Art and Design, Boston, 87; Soc Arts and Crafts, Boston, 88; Arts Lottery Prog Mass Cult Coun, 90; Korean Cult Serv, New York, 91; Cambridge Art Asn, Mass, 92; Bronx Mus Art, NY, 94; Attleboro Mus, Mass, 95; Women's Caucus for Arts Nat Juried Exhib, Boston, 96; DeCordova Mus and Sculpture Park, Lincoln, Mass, 99; Islip Art Mus, Carriage House, NY, 2000; Queens Botanical Garden, NY, 2001; Ace Gallery, 2002; Dolan Ctr Gallery, Locust Valley, NY, 2003. *Awards:* Arts Lottery Grant, Somerville Arts Coun, 90; Myron Stout Fel, Fine Arts Work Ctr, Provincetown, Mass, 94, Ione and Hudson D Walker Fel, 95; Visual Arts Fel, Edward F Albee Found, 99. *Media:* Wood, String. *Mailing Add:* DM Contemp PO Box 263 Mill Neck NY 11765

ANDRY, KEITH ANTHONY
PAINTER, INSTRUCTOR
b Thibodaux, La, June 28, 1960. *Study:* Special instruction with Ed Whitney, Robert E Wood, Millard Sheets & Milford Zornes, 73-84; Calif Sch of Art, with Rex Brandt, 86; Nicholls State Univ, AB, 86. *Work:* Fine Arts Mus S, Mobile, Ala; Zigler Mus Art, Jennings, La; Baton Rouge Waterworks, Baton Rouge, La; George's Inc, Springdale, Ark; Andry Interior's, Thibodaux, La. *Comn:* Three paintings, Disney World Dixie Landings Resort, 92. *Exhib:* Georgia Watercolor Soc 3rd Ann, Mus Arts & Sci, Macon, Ga, 82; Georgia Watercolor Soc 6th Ann, Madison-Morgan Cult Ctr, Madison Ga, 85; Rocky Mountain Nat Watermedia Exhib, Foothills Art Ctr, Golden, Colo, 86-87; Nat Watercolor Soc 66th Ann Muckenthaler Cult Ctr, Fullerton, Calif, 87; and others. *Pos:* Chmn Arts, 1984 World's Fair, New Orleans, La, 84. *Awards:* Grumbacher Art Award, Grumbacher, 80; Foothills Art Ctr Award, Foothills Art Ctr, 86; Muckenthaler Cult Found, Muckenthaler Cult Ctr, 87. *Bibliog:* Trent Angers (auth), Keith Andry: Watercolorist on a winning streak, Anger's Publ Corp, 83; Sheila Elliot (auth), Keith Andry: Rocky Mountain Watermedia Asn, F & W Publ Corp, 87; Stephen Doherty (auth), Painting on Location - Special Feature, Am Artist Mag, 89. *Mem:* Nat Watercolor Soc signature mem; Ky Watercolor Soc; La Watercolor Soc life mem; Midwest Watercolor Soc life mem; Ga Watercolor Soc signature mem. *Media:* Watercolor. *Publ:* Illusr, The Longest Street, 82; Keith Andry: Watercolorist on a Winning Streak, Anger's Publ Corp, 83; contrib, Louisiana Men are Dinamight, Elm Publ, 84; illusr, Keith Andry: Rocky Mountain National Watermedia Exhibition, F & W Publ Inc, 87; Painting on Location, Stephen Doherty, 89. *Mailing Add:* 16410 Jefferson Hwy Baton Rouge LA 70817

ANGELINI, JOHN MICHAEL
PAINTER, WRITER
b New York, NY, Nov 18, 1921. *Study:* Newark Sch Fine & Indust Art; spec studies in Europe, 61; Fla State Univ, Cert Fla Master Gardener, 98. *Work:* David L Yunich Collection, Bambergers, NJ; Morris Mus of Art, Morristown, NJ; Paterson Main Libr, NJ; Longlines Div, Am Tel & Tel; Morgan Guarantee Trust Co, NY; Lady Laura, Fla; Boy Scouts of Am; Bloomfield Coll, NJ. *Comn:* EVA mural, 2009. *Exhib:* Nat Arts Club Watercolor Ann, NY, 64; NJ Pavilion, NY World's Fair, 65; Watercolor USA, Nat Ann & Traveling Exhib, Springfield Mus, Mo, 66; NJ Watercolor Soc Ann, 74-11; Int Exhib, Nabisco World Hq; Miniature Artists Am Traveling Exhib, 86-11; 1998 Winter Olympics, Nagano, Japan, 98; 2000 Summer Olympics, Sydney; Smithsonian, Wash, DC, 2003; and solo exhibs in NY, NJ, Fla; 50 Year Retrospective, Pasco Hernando Community Coll, Fla, 2004; Moscow, Russia, 2012. *Collection Arranged:* O'Connor Law Group, Fla. *Pos:* Art dir, Berles Carton Co Inc, Paterson, NJ, 50-79; adv bd, NJ Music & Arts, Chatham, 72-78. *Teaching:* Instr, watercolor, private students. *Awards:* Silver Medal for Watercolor, NJ Watercolor Soc, 63; Medal of Honor for Watercolor, Audubon Artists, Nat Acad, 63 & Nat Arts Club, 64; Artist of the Year, Hudson Artists, Inc, NJ, 74; and many other state, regional & nat exhibs. *Bibliog:* L Pessolano (auth), John Angelini--a profile, 70 & R Williams (auth), John Angelini--A W S, 71, NJ Music & Arts; interview & watercolor demonstration, cable TV networks, NY & NJ. *Mem:* Am Watercolor Soc; hon mem Audubon Artists; Fla & NJ Miniature Art Soc; Miniature Artists of Am; Allied Artists Am; Miniature Art Soc Fla Inc. *Media:* Watercolor, Pencil Rendering. *Res:* Renaissance art studies, Italy. *Interests:* Photography, Bonsai, travel. *Publ:* Contribr, NJ Music & Arts, 70-77; auth, articles in Am Artist, 72; The North Light Art Competition Handbook, North Light Books, 86; Watercolor 86, Am Artist, 86; contribr, 59 More Studio Secrets, North Light Bks, 90; Images, ltd ed bound print portfolio, 2000, Images II, 2005; St Petersburg Times, Fla, 99-2011; Just Trees, 2012. *Mailing Add:* 18211 Autumn Lake Blvd Hudson FL 34667-8436

ANGELL, TONY
SCULPTOR, PAINTER
b Los Angeles, Calif, Nov 15, 1940. *Study:* Univ Wash, BA, 62. *Work:* Safeco Plaza, Seattle; Tacoma Art Mus, Wash; Gilcrease Mus, Tulsa, Okla; Frye Art Mus, Seattle, Wash; Lywam Art Mus, Wausau, Wis; Sleeping Lady Conf Ctr, Leavenworth, Wash; Emergence of NW Art Show, Mus of NW Art, La Conner, Wash. *Comn:* Ascending Eagles, Offices of Qwest, Seattle, Wash; Trumpeter Swans, Lywam Art Mus, Wausau, Wis; Animal Forms in Stone, Woodland Park Zoo, City Seattle, Wash, 94; Parliament of Owls, Whatcom Coll, Wash, 97; Wisdom Seekers, Redmond Pub Libr, Wash, 99; Raven Greet, City of Shoreline, Wash; Emissaries, Sleeping Lady Conference Center, 2006; Raven Pair, Mt Baker, Wash, 2007. *Exhib:* Northwest Collection (with catalog), Rainier Bank Bldg, Seattle, 78; Nat Acad Western Art, Oklahoma City, 81-2007; Artists of Am Show, Denver, 81-2008; Wash State Mus, 82; Silcrease Mus, Tulsa, Okla, 84; Tony Angell Retrospective, Gilcrease Mus, Tulsa, Okla, 86; Animals in Art, Leigh Yawkey Woodson Art Mus, Wasau, Wis, 86-2005; Wildlife Art Am, Univ Minneapolis, Minn, 94; The Artful Animal, Minneapolis Inst Art, 98; Emergence of Northwest Art, Mus North West Art, Laconner, Wash, 2002; From Wild Skies, Gerald Peters Gallery, 2004; Wild at Heart, Nat Mus Wildlife Art, 2005; In the Company of Crows & Ravens, Victoria & Albert Mus, 2006; Victoria Albert Mus, 2007; Mus Northwest Art, 2009-; Sculpture exhib, City of Redmano, Wash 2009-2010. *Pos:* Comnr & chair, Visual Arts Comt, King Co Arts Comn, 78-82; adj fac sci illus, Univ Wash Sch Art. *Teaching:* Guest lectr, City of Seattle, 83 & Artists of Am, Denver, 83-88; lectr, Nat Acad Western Art, 93; adj lectr art, Univ Wash. *Awards:* 50 Best Books Design Award, 86; Blodel Lectr Fel, 94; Master Artist Award, Leigh Yawkey Woodson Art Mus, 2001; Overall Award, Victoria & Albert Mus, London; Illus Award, Victoria & Albert Mus, 2006. *Bibliog:* Evening Edition (T Angell), KCTS TV, Seattle, Wash, 87; New York Art Rev, 89; Todd Wilkenson (auth), Spirits from stone, Seattle Mag, 11/96 & Touch stones, Orion Mag, winter 97; Don Hagerty (auth), Leading the West, Northland Publ, 97; A Life in Stone, Pacific Northwest Magazine, Seattle Times, Wash, 99; Iridescent Light: The Emergence of NW Art, Univ Wash Press, 2002; Western Art Collector, 7/2008; Humans, Nature & Birds, Wehey & Kennedy, Yale Univ Press, 2008. *Mem:* Fel Nat Acad Western Artists; fel Nat Sculpture Soc; Artists Am (designated master). *Media:* Marble, Bronze; Oils, Ink. *Interests:* Natural history & its influence on culture. *Publ:* Auth-illusr, Owls, 74 & Ravens, Crows, Magpies and Jays, 78, Univ Wash; co-auth-illusr, Marine Birds and Mammals of Puget Sound, Nat Oceanic & Atmospheric Admin, 82; illusr, Blackbirds of the Americas, Univ Wash Press, 84; Sea Brothers, 88 & Descent of Love, 95, Univ Pa Press; The Pinyon Jay, TA Poyser, London, 92; In the Company of Crows & Ravens, Yale Univ, 2005; Contemporary Animal Sculptors, Art West Magazine, 7-8/2006; Puget Sound Through an Artist's Eye: Tony Angell, Univ Wash Press, Seattle, Wash, London, Eng, 2009; and others. *Dealer:* Foster/White Gallery; Gerald Peters Gallery Santa Fe NM. *Mailing Add:* 18237 40th Ave NE Seattle WA 98155

ANGELO, SANDRA MCFALL
WRITER, INSTRUCTOR
b St Louis, Mo, Apr 24, 1950. *Study:* Seattle Pac Univ, BA, 72; Nat Univ, MBA, 85. *Comn:* Scripps Womens Birthing Ctr, Scripps Hospital, La Jolla, Calif. *Pos:* Nat dir, Discover Art, San Diego, Calif, prod & dir; dir, Int Colored Pencil Symp, 89; contrib ed, Art Mat Today, 93; producer, video/TV. *Teaching:* Teacher art, La Jolla Country Day Sch, 81-86; prof art, US Int Univ, 86-89, Palomar Col, 86-. *Awards:* Fel Award, RI Sch Design, 86; WAVE Award, 95; Award of Excellence, Videographer, 97. *Bibliog:* Tiffany Windsor (dir), Everyone Can Draw, Creative Living TV-TNN, 94; Tiffany Windsor (dir), Fun with Colored Pencil, Creative Living; docs, HGTV (5 shows), summer 98, Discovery Channel, spring 98 & ABC-Good Morning Texas, 2/98. *Mem:* Hobby Indust Am; Soc Decorative Painters; Nat Speakers Asn; Publ Marketing Asn. *Media:* Graphite, Oil, Pastels. *Res:* Drawing methods for new artists lacking natural talent. *Publ:* Auth, Using colored pencil on a colored ground, Am Artist, 93; Colored Pencil Basics, Walter Foster, 94; So You Thought You Couldn't Draw, Discover Art, 94; Combining oil pastels with colored pencils, Drawing Highlights, 94; Painting with colored pencils, Artists Mag, 94; plus many others

ANGELOCH, ROBERT
PAINTER, PRINTMAKER
b Richmond Hill, NY, Apr 8, 1922. *Study:* Art Student League; Acad Fine Arts, Florence, Italy; also with Fiske Boyd, Martin Lewis & Y Kuniyoshi. *Work:* Art Student League; Munson-Williams-Proctor Inst, Utica, NY; Russell Sage Col; Western Ky Univ. *Comn:* Murals, NY Bd Educ, Kellogg Corp, Brunswick, NJ & Queensboro Pub Libr. *Exhib:* Metrop Mus; Nat Acad; Libr Congress. *Pos:* Supvr, Woodstock Summer Sch, Art Students League, 60-68; artist-in-residence, Western Ky Univ, 74; dir, Woodstock Sch Art Inc, 80-86, pres, 80-. *Teaching:* Instr, Art Students League, Woodstock Summer Sch, 64-79; instr, Woodstock Sch Art, 68-; instr, Russell Sage Col, 71-72. *Awards:* McDowell Traveling Scholar, Art Students League, 51; Artist in Residence Grant, Nat Endowment Arts, 74; Pollack-Krasner Found Grant, 95. *Bibliog:* S R Day (auth), Creative Woodstock, Mead Mt Press, 66; Fridolf Johnson (auth), Robert Angeloch, Am Artists Mag, 85. *Mem:* Art Student League; Woodstock Artists Asn. *Media:* Oil; Etching. *Publ:* Auth, Basic Oil Painting Techniques, Pitman, 70; Outdoor sketching, Am Artist Mag, 70; contribr, Angeloch: Color Prints, 80. *Dealer:* Paradox Gallery Woodstock NY 12498

ANGULO, CHAPPIE
PAINTER, ILLUSTRATOR
b Mar 3, 1928; US citizen. *Study:* Los Angeles City Coll, 49; Univ Calif, Los Angeles; Kahn Art Sch; Esmeralda, Inst Nac Bellas Artes, Mexico City, 55; Fort Mason Ctr, San Francisco, 60. *Work:* Mus Cult, Mexico City; Univ Mus Art, Mexico City. *Comn:* Reproduction pre-Columbian murals, Bonampak, 57, Chichen Itza & Tomb 7 Oaxaca, 58, Nat Mus Anthrop; reproduction mural, Teotihuacan, Museo Beatriz de la Fuente; pintura mural, Teotihuacana, Teotihuacan, Mex. *Exhib:* Solo exhibs, Mus Fronterizo, Juarez, Mex, 71; Age Aquarius, Univ Las Americas, Cholula, 73, Gentes y Lugares Mus de las Cult, Mex, Exploraciones, ISSSTE, Cuernavaca, Mor, Mex, 96,

Abstracciones, Centro Cult Univ, Morelos, Mex, 97, Iconografias, Museo Carmen, Mex DF, 98, Caminos, SPM, 98, Aspetos Diversos, Mus Jalapa, Mex, 99, Centro Cult Coyoacan, Mex, 2000, Song of Joy, Salon de la Plastica, Mex, 2006, Iconogramas, Museo del Carmen, Mex City, 2007; 3 decades of Plastic Art-UNAM, Mex, DF, 90; Artistas del Mundo (UNESCO), Tlaxcala, Mex, 96; US Artists in Mexico, Mex DF, 96; Exhib Int Artistas Plasticas, Honduras, 97; Coll Cristo, 98; Diversidades, Bellas Artes, 2002; Mus Salon de la Plastica San Carlos, Salon de la Plastica Siglo XXI, 2003; Cantos de Alegria, Salon de la Plastica, Mexico, 2006; Para Frida con Amor, Ctr Cult Otumba, Edo Mex, 2007; 60 anos de Arte del SLP Ciudadela, Mex, 2009; Maga-Exposicion, Mus Arte de Tlaxcala, 2010; 100 Años de Circo, 2010; Imagenes Museo Arte, Puebla, 2010; Salon Pintura, Mencion Honorifica, 2010; Centro Fox Guanajuato, 2011; S Anual Pintura SPM, 2012; Majueres en el Arte: Encuentro INternacional Bellas Artes, Politecnico, 2012; Encuentro International Mujeres en el Arte Bellas Artes, 2013, 2014; Reencuentros, Fundacion Pascual, 2013; Salon Plastica Mexicana, 2014; Mus Arte Contemporaneo. *Collection Arranged:* Salon Plastica Mexicana, 99-2000; Collectivas, 96-2006; Mujeres en la Plástica: 60 años, Mus UPAEP, Puebla, Mex. *Teaching:* Pvt instr, currently. *Bibliog:* M Vazquez (auth), Museo de las Culturas, Inst Nat Antropologia, 65; A Pastrana (auth), El concreto, Arquitectura Arte & Urbanism Mag, 68; Cirulo de Arte, Mex, 97. *Mem:* Salon de la Plastica, Mex; Comoarte. *Media:* Acrylic, Monotype. *Specialty:* Diverse. *Interests:* Art. *Publ:* Illusr, A Guide to Coatetelco; Iconographic Analysis of Ancient Chalcatzingo, 87; El Axayotl--Un sistema de drenaje aljibe--,Agricultura Indigena, Ciesas, Mex, 90; Aspects of a Culture thru its Pictoric Expression--Section Teotihuacan--Prehispanic Mural Painting in Mexico, Inst Esthetic Investigation, UNAM, Mex, 92; illus, Water Control & Communal Labor, Research in Economic Anthropology, JAI Press, 93; Mujeres in SPM, 2015. *Dealer:* Salon Plastica Mexicana. *Mailing Add:* Cda A Zamora 11 Coyoacan Mexico CP 04000

ANKER, SUZANNE C
SCULPTOR, PAINTER
b Brooklyn, NY, Aug 6, 1946. *Study:* Brooklyn Col, BA; Univ Colo, MFA. *Work:* St Louis Art Mus, Mo; Denver Art Mus, Colo; Williams Coll Mus Art. *Comn:* Cleveland Art Mus. *Exhib:* New Ways With Paper, Nat Collection Fine Arts, Smithsonian Inst, Washington, DC, 77 & Paper as Medium, 78; Walker Art Ctr, Minneapolis, 79; Richard Gray Gallery, Chicago, 79; Greenberg Wilson Gallery, NY, 88 & 90. *Teaching:* Asst prof experimental printmaking, Washington Univ, St Louis, 76-78. *Awards:* NY Found Grant in Sculpture, 89. *Bibliog:* Meyer Raphael Rubinstein (auth), Suzanne Anker, Arts, 12/88; Carter Ratcliff (auth), Swamp things, Vogue, 4/89; rev, Howard Risatti, Artforum, summer 90. *Mem:* Coll Art Asn. *Media:* Paper, Stone. *Mailing Add:* 101 Wooster St Apt 7F New York NY 10012-3895

ANNIS, NORMAN L
EDUCATOR, SCULPTOR
b Des Moines, Iowa, May 26, 1931. *Study:* Univ Northern Iowa, BA, 53; Drake Univ; Univ Iowa, MFA, 59. *Work:* Cent Coll, Pella, Iowa; Corcoran Gallery Art, Washington, DC; Washington & Lee Univ, Lexington, Va. *Comn:* Life-size bronze figure, Gettysburg Coll, Pa, 70; life-size welded steel figure, Frey Village, Middletown, 76; life-size cor-ten steel figure, Gettysburg Sr High Sch, 77. *Exhib:* Fourth Dulin Nat Prints, Dulin Gallery, Knoxville, 61; 4th Nat Drawing Exhib, Okla Art Ctr, Oklahoma City, 61; Drawings USA, St Paul Art Ctr, Minn, 61 & 63; 4th Nat Ultimate Concerns, Ohio Univ, Athens, 65; Washington Area Artists Series, Corcoran Gallery Art, DC, 65; Living Am Artists & Human Figure, Pa State Univ Mus Art, State Col, 74. *Teaching:* Instr sculpture, Univ Ill, Champaign, 59-60; prof sculpture, Gettysburg Col, 60-78; prof & head dept art, Southwest Mo State Univ, Springfield, 78-. *Awards:* First Sculpture Award, Fifth Ann Pennational, 62; Purchase Award, St Paul Art Ctr, 63; Anna Hyatt Huntington Award, Corcoran Gallery Art, 63. *Media:* Bronze, Welded Steel. *Dealer:* Michelson Gallery 707 G St NE Washington DC 20002. *Mailing Add:* 108 Round Ridge Rd Mechanicsburg PA 17055-9201

ANREUS, ALEJANDRO
EDUCATOR, ADMINISTRATOR
Study: Kean Col, BA (art history), 1984; City Univ of NY, MA (art history), 1995, PhD (art history), 1997. *Pos:* Critic in residence, Latino Ctr for Art and Culture, Rutgers Univ, 1999-2000; curator, Montclair Art Mus, 1986-93, Jersey City Mus, 1993-2001; nat adv bd mem, A Ver, 2003-. *Teaching:* Taught art history, New Jersey City Univ, Seton Hall Univ, & Kean Univ; prof and chair, art dept, William Paterson Univ, NJ, currently. *Publ:* (auth) Ben Shahn and The Passion of Sacco and Vanzetti, 2001, Orozco in Gringoland: The Years in New York, 2001, The Social and The Real: Political Art of the 1930's in the Western Hemisphere, 2006; articles have appeared in Art Journal, Third Text, Art Nexus and Encuentro de la Cultura Cubana; (co-auth) Mexican Muralism, A Critical History. *Mailing Add:* William Paterson University Office Ben Shahn 128 300 Pompton Rd Wayne NJ 07470

ANTHONISEN, GEORGE RIOCH
SCULPTOR, PAINTER
b Boston, Mass, July 31, 1936. *Study:* Univ Vt, BA, 61; Nat Acad Design, with Douglas Gorsline, 61-62; Art Students League, with Jose De Creeft & John Hovannes, 62-64; Dartmouth Coll Med Sch, 67. *Hon Degrees:* Doc of Humane Letters, Ursinus Coll, Collegeville, Penn, 2009. *Work:* World Health Orgn, Geneva, Switz; James A Michener Art Mus, Doylestown, Pa; Berman Mus Art, Collegeville, Pa; US Capitol, Hall of Columns, Washington, DC; Carnegie Hall, New York; Ctr for Interfaith Relations, Louisville, Ky; Woodmere Art Mus, Philadelphia, Pa; Curtis Inst Music, Philadelphia, Pa. *Comn:* Sculpture, Germantown Hosp & Med Ctr, Philadelphia, Pa, 93; sculpture, Philadelphia Coll Osteopathic Med, Pa, 94; fresco, Doylestown Hosp, Pa; Relief sculpture, Ursinus Coll, Collegeville, Pa, 98; sculpture, Please Touch Mus, Philadelphia, Pa, 99. *Exhib:* I Set Before You This Day, Rotunda, Cannon House Off Bldg, US Capitol, Washington, DC, 89; Anthonisen, Woodmere Art Mus, Philadelphia, Pa, 92; The Compassionate Spirit: Sculpture and Fresco, Berman Mus Art, Collegeville, Pa, 96; The Second Century, Contemp Works Exhib, Nat Sculpture Soc, New York, 93; Caring-Humanity's Hope for Survival, Monuments Conservancy, New York, 97; Reflections on the Human Condition: Nine Sculptures, Center for Interfaith Relations, Festival of Faiths Gardens of Louisville, Ky, 99; The Sculpture of George R Anthonisen, Jonathan Edwards Coll, Yale Univ, New Haven, Conn, 2006; Life in Bronze, Cooley Gallery, Old Lyme, Conn, 2007; Fellows Exhib, Nat Sculpture Soc, 2007. *Awards:* Alaska State Coun Arts, 76; Sculptor in Residence, Augustus St Gaudens Nat Hist Site, US Dept Interior, 71; Exemplary Achievement in Arts Award, Bucks Co CofC, 85. *Bibliog:* I Set Before You This Day (sculpture), James A Michener Art Mus, 90; George Anthonisen: Sculptor, Quest Series, Cable Television Network NJ, Trenton State Coll, 93; The visual vocabulary of George R. Anthonisen, Nouveau, Fine Arts Issue, 92-96, 9/2001; Doris Brandes (auth), Artists of the River Towns: Their works and their stories, River Arts Press, 2002; Valerie Reed (auth), Showing Humanity's Extremes, Philadelphia Inquirer, 6/22/2003; Sally Friedman (auth), A Space Enlivened, Home and Design, Sect E1, Philadelphia Inquirer, 1/7/2011. *Mem:* Nat Sculpture Soc; Allied Art Am; Audubon Artists. *Media:* Metal, Cast, Miscellaneous Media. *Interests:* Fishing & baseball. *Publ:* Ernest Gruening, Statue Dedication, US Govt Patent Office, 79; The Compassionate Spirit: Sculpture and Fresco by George Authonisen, Berman Mus Art, 96; Anthonisen, Woodmere Art Mus, Philadelphia, Pa, 92; Dedication WWII Mem, Promise/Anthem, Berman Mus Art, Collegeville, Pa, 98; The Sculpture of George R Anthonisen, Jonathan Edwards Coll, Yale Univ, Cannelli Printing Inc, New Haven, Conn, 2006. *Dealer:* Cooley Gallery Old Lyme CT 06371; Travis Gallery New Hope PA 18938. *Mailing Add:* Box 147 Solebury PA 18963

ANTHONY, AMY ELLEN
CRAFTSMAN, JEWELER
b Concord, Mass, May 11, 1955. *Study:* Syracuse Univ, New York, BFA, 77; Sch Am Craftsmen, Rochester Inst Technol, NY, MFA, 85. *Work:* Temple Emmanuel, Woodcliff, NJ; pvt collections, Malcom & Sue Knapp; Leta Stathalos. *Exhib:* Table Top, 80, Young Americans, 80 & Approaches to Collecting, 82, Am Craft Mus, New York; Four Jewelry Artists from the States, V&V Gallery, Vienna, Austria, 83; Contemp Metals II, Downey Mus Art, Calif, 87; SNAG 88 Earring Competition, Jean Michilin Collection, New York, 88; One of a Kind: Am Art Jewelry, JoAnne Rapp Gallery, Scottsdale, Ariz, 95. *Teaching:* Lectr, Sch Am Craftsmen, Rochester, NY, 88. *Bibliog:* Susan Grant Lewin (auth), One of a Kind: American Jewelry Today; Deborah Krupenia (auth), The Art of Jewelry Design. *Mem:* Am Crafts Coun. *Media:* Metals. *Publ:* Contribr, Amy Anthony: Studies in aluminum, J Soc NAm Goldsmiths, 85. *Mailing Add:* 9 Tulip Ln Greenfield MA 01301-2718

ANTHONY, LAWRENCE KENNETH
SCULPTOR, PAINTER
b Hartsville, SC, May 27, 1934. *Study:* Washington & Lee Univ, BA; Univ Ga, MFA; study with Lamar Dodd & Howard Thomas. *Work:* Memphis Brooks Mus, Tenn; Vanderbilt Univ, Nashville, Tenn; Ark State Univ, Jonesboro; Gibbes Art Gallery, Charleston, SC; SC Art Comn, Columbia; Audubon Park & Rhodes Col, Memphis. *Comn:* Menorah sculpture, Jewish Community Ctr, Memphis, 67; sculpture, Corinthian Broadcasting Co, NY, 71; wall sculpture, CBS-TV, Sacramento, Calif, 72; Audubon Park, Memphis; Vanderbilt Univ, Nashville. *Exhib:* Solo exhibs, Columbia Mus Art, 66, Memphis Brooks Mus, 68, Vanderbilt Univ, 72, 74 & Terre Des Hommes, Pavilion, Montreal, 79. *Teaching:* Prof sculpture & drawing, Rhodes Col, Memphis, currently. *Media:* Metal, Plastic. *Mailing Add:* 1111 Ocean Dr Summerland Key FL 33042-4507

ANTHONY, WILLIAM GRAHAM
PAINTER, DRAFTSMAN
b Ft Monmouth, NJ, Sept 25, 1934. *Study:* Yale Univ, BA, 58, with Josef Albers; San Francisco Art Inst, 59-60; Art Student League. *Work:* Whitney Mus Am Art, Metrop Mus Art & Guggenheim Mus, New York; Art Inst Chicago; Corcoran Gallery Art, Washington, DC; Mus Mod Art, NY; Hermitage Mus, St Petersburg, Russia; Ludwig Mus, Cologne; Yale Art Gallery, New Haven; plus others. *Comn:* Museum Exhibitions (humorous page), Artforum, 1990; Edvard & Andy (humorous page), Art in Am, 2008. *Exhib:* Solo exhibs, Calif Palace Legion Hon, San Francisco, 62, Frank Marino Gallery, New York, 81, Jane Baum Gallery, New York, 86, Berland-Hall Gallery, New York, 91, Stuart Katz Gallery, Laguna Beach, Calif, 92, Cokkie Snoei Gallery, Rotterdam, The Neth, 95 & Robert Berman Gallery, Santa Monica, 98; Cokkie Snoei Gallery, Rotterdam, The Neth, 99; Dorfman Gallery, New York, 2002 & 2004; Stalke Gallery, Kirke Sonnerup, Denmark, 2004, 2007, 2010, & 2013; Christopher Henry Gallery, NY, 2007, 2009, 2010, & 2012. *Teaching:* Instr figure drawing, San Francisco Acad Art, 62-63. *Bibliog:* Barry Schwabsky (auth), Bill Anthony, Arts Mag, 1/92; Ken Johnson (auth), William Anthony, NY Times, 10/11/02; Robert Rosenblum (auth), Hilarious Shockers, Art News, 9/2004; Roberta Smith (auth), NY Times, 1/11/08; Sam Jedig (auth), Ironic Icons: The Art of William Anthony, Stalke Gallery, Denmark, 2013. *Media:* Pencil, Oil. *Interests:* Satire. *Publ:* Auth, A New Approach to Figure Drawing, Crown Publ, 65, Odhams, Ltd, Eng, 67 & Bonanza Publ; auth & illusr, Bible Stories, 78 & Bill Anthony's Greatest Hits, 88, Jargon Soc; War is Swell, Smart Art Press, 2000. *Dealer:* Stalke Gallery Kirke Sonnerup Denmark; Stalke Gallery Englerupveg 62 Kirke Sonnerup 4060 Saby Denmark. *Mailing Add:* 903 Westbeth 463 West St New York NY 10014

ANTIC, MIROSLAV
PAINTER, ILLUSTRATOR
b Belgrade, Yugoslavia, June 11, 1947. *Study:* Acad of Fine Arts, MFA, 73. *Work:* Rose Art Mus, Brandies Univ, Waltham, Mass; Wellesley Coll Art Mus, Mass; De Cordova Mus, Lincoln, Mass; Boca Raton Art Mus, Fla; Chase Manhattan Bank; ITET Corp; Mc Donald Corp; Fidelity Investments; Boston Pub Libr. *Exhib:* Cult Commentaries, Berkshire Mus, Pittsfield, Mass, 85; The Object Found and Perceived, Fitchburg Art Mus, Mass, 91; Shrines, Symbols & Cherished Objects, Fuller Mus Art, Brockton, Mass, 94; Boston Now, Inst Contemp Art, Boston, 94; New Paintings, 511

Gallery, NY City, 2007; New Paintings, Kidder Smith Gallery, Boston, 2007. *Teaching:* Instr, Sch of the Mus of Fine Art, Boston, 80-2000. *Awards:* NEA Fel, 96; Pollock-Krasner Found Grant, 97; Fla Visual Art Fel, 00. *Publ:* Charles Giuliano, Miroslav Antic, New Paintings, Arts Media Mag, 00; Cate McQuaid, Miroslav Antic, The Boston Globe, 00; Mary Sherman, Miroslav Antic, Boston Herald, 00. *Dealer:* Caesarea Gallery 608 Banyan Tr Boca Raton FL 33431

ANTIN, DAVID A
ART CRITIC, WRITER
b New York, NY, Feb 1, 1932. *Study:* Coll City New York, BA, 55; NY Univ, MA, 66. *Teaching:* Prof visual arts, Univ Calif, San Diego, 68-, chmn dept, 70-72, 80-81 & 87-89. *Awards:* Guggenheim Fel, 76-77; Nat Endowment Humanities Fel, 82-83. *Bibliog:* Sherman Paul (auth), In Search of the Primitive, LS Univ Press, 86; Henry Sayre (auth), The Object of Performance, Chicago, 89; William G Doty (ed), Picturing Cultural Values in Postmodern America, Univ Ala, 95; The Beggar and the King, Pacific Coast Philology, Vol 30, No 2, 95; C Carr (auth), review of On the Edge: Performance at the End of the 20th Century, Modernism and Modernity, U Chicago, Vol 2, No 3, 95; Larry McCaffery & Marjorie Perloff (auth), Interview of David Antin, Some Other Frequency, U Pa, 96; Wittgenstein Among the Poets, Modernism and Modernity, Winter 98; I Never Knew What Time It Was, 108, 107, Atlanta, 99; California--the nervous camel, Review of Contemp Fiction, Vol XXI, No 1, Normal, Ill, Spring 2001; An Interview with David Antin, Review of Contemp Fiction, Vol XXI, No 1, Normal, Spring, 2001; The Noise of Time, Boston Rev, MIT, Cambridge, Vol 26, No 2, Apr/May 2001; Fred Garber (auth), Repositionings, Pa State Press, 95; Michael Davidson (auth), Ghostlier Demarcations, U Calif Press, 97; The Poetry Reading, ed Stephen Vincent & Ellen Zweig, Momo's Press, San Francisco, 81; The Poetics of Indeterminacy, Marjorie Perloff, Princeton Univ, 81; Chrales O Hartman (auth), Jazz Text, Princeton Univ Press, 91. *Mem:* Int Asn Art Critics. *Res:* Studies in modernism and post modernism; history of art criticism and theory; sociology of art; interpretation and meaning in culture and language; theory of narrative. *Publ:* Biography: Representations 16, fall 86; The Stranger at the Door, Genre, Vol XX, No 3-4, fall, winter 87; Selected Poems 1963-1973, Sun & Moon, 89; The real thing, Art Am, 5/81; Tuning, New Directions, 84; What it Means to be Avant-Garde, New Directions, 93; Selected Essays, A Conversation with David Antin, U Chicago, Granary Press, 2001; auth, I never knew what time it was, Univ Cailf Berkeley, 2005; auth, John Cage uncaged is still cagey, Singing Horse Press, San Diego, 2005. *Mailing Add:* PO Box 1147 Del Mar CA 92014

ANTIN, ELEANOR
CONCEPTUAL ARTIST, PHOTOGRAPHER
b New York, NY, Feb 27, 1935. *Study:* City Coll NY, BA; Tamara Daykarhanove Sch for the Stage. *Work:* Whitney Mus Am Art, NY; San Francisco Mus Modern Art; Mus Mod Art, NY; Art Inst Chicago; Los Angeles Co Mus Art. *Exhib:* Solo exhibs, Mus Mod Art, NY, 73, Everson Mus, Syracuse, NY, 74, Clocktower, NY, 76, M L D'Arc Gallery, NY, 77, Wadsworth Atheneum, Hartford, Conn, 77, Whitney Mus Am Art, NY, 78 & Long Beach Mus Art, Calif, 79; Nurse & the Hijackers, 77, Before the Revolution, 79, Recollections of My Life with Diaghilev, 80, El Desdichado, 83 & Loves of a Ballerina, 86, Ronald Feldman Fine Arts Gallery, NY; Venice Biennale, Contemp Art Mus, Calif, 76; Last Night of Rasputin, Whitney Mus Biennial, 89 & Hirshhorn Mus, Washington, DC, 89; From the Inside Out: Contemp Artists, Jewish Mus, NY, 93; Minetta Lane, A Ghost Story, Ronald Feldman Gallery, NY, 95 & Santa Monica Mus Art, Los Angeles, Calif, 95; Minetta Lane, Ghosts, SE Ctr Contemp Art, Winston-Salem, NC, 96; Eleanor Antin: Selections from the Angel of Mercy, Whitney Mus, NY, 97; Eleanor Antin: An Anthology (retrospective), Los Angeles Co Mus Art, 99; Meade Gallery, Univ Warrwick, UK, 2001; plus others. *Teaching:* Prof visual arts, Univ Calif, San Diego, 75-. *Awards:* Dorothy Arzner Spec Recognition Award, 16th Ann Crystal Awards, Women in Film, 91; Guggenheim Fel, 97; Nat Found Jewish Culture Media Achievement Award, 98; and others. *Bibliog:* Eleanor Munro (auth), Originals: American Women Artists, Simon & Schuster, 79; Frantisck Deak (auth), Eleanor Antin: Before the revolution: Acting as an art paradigm, Images & Issues, 1-2/84; Henry Sayre (auth), The Object of Performance: The American Avant-Garde Since 1970, Univ Chicago Press, 89; Howard Fox (auth) Desire and destiny in the art of Eleanor Antin, Eleanor Antin, Los Angeles Co Mus Art, 99; Leah Ollman (auth) Art in Am, 2/2000. *Media:* Performance; Video & Film, Installation Photography. *Publ:* Auth, Autobiography of the artist as an autobiographer, J Los Angeles Inst Contemp Art, 10/74; Some thoughts on autobiography & Olga Feodorova's story, winter 78-79 & A romantic interlude from: Recollections of My Life with Diaghilev, summer 80, Sun & Moon; Being Antinova, Astro Artz Press, 83; Eleanora Antinova Plays, Sun & Moon, 94; 100 Boots, Running Press, 99. *Dealer:* Ronald Feldman Fine Arts 31 Mercer St New York NY 10013; Electronic Arts Intermix New York NY; Milestone Film and Video Harrington Park NJ. *Mailing Add:* PO Box 1147 Del Mar CA 92014

ANTOL, JOSEPH (JAY) JAMES
SCULPTOR, CONCEPTUAL ARTIST
b Rexis, Pa, May 2, 1947. *Study:* Old Dominion Univ, BFA, 78, MFA, 84; Tamarind Inst, 81. *Work:* Old Dominion Univ, Norfolk, Va. *Exhib:* Still Alive in 85, LAS, Modesto, Calif, 85; Now That We're Home, Art Consortium, Art Ctr, Cincinnati, Ohio, 86; Bookworks, WPA, Washington, DC, 86; Les Hommes, TAG Gallery, D'art Ctr, 87, Va Artists, 88, Peninsula Fine Arts Ctr, 88, Va Comn Arts, 1708 Gallery, 88 & Irene Leach Mem, Chrysler Mus, Va, 88; Visual Arts Home, Ctr UNICEF, Atlanta, Ga, 88. *Teaching:* instr printing drawing, Old Dominion Univ, 81-84; instr lithography, Hampton Univ, 86; instr drawing, Governor's Sch Arts, 88-89. *Awards:* Old Dominion Univ fel, 84; D'art Ctr Fel, 86-87; Va Commission/Arts, State Va, 88. *Bibliog:* Joseph Perrin (auth), Visual Arts for the Home, Southern Homes, 88. *Mem:* Peninsula Fine Art Ctr; Artist Against Hunger; Va Beach Arts Ctr. *Media:* Installation, All Media. *Mailing Add:* 2260 London St Virginia Beach VA 23454-4440

ANTONI, JANINE
SCULPTOR
b Freeport, Bahamas, Jan 19, 1964. *Study:* Sarah Lawrence Col, Bronxville, NY, BA, 86; RI Sch Design, Providence, MFA (sculpture, hons), 89. *Exhib:* Israel Mus, Jerusalem, 92; Whitney Mus Am Art Biennial, 93; Aldrich Mus Contemp Art, 93; Mus Contemp Art, Seoul, Korea, 93; Kunsthaus Zurich, Switz, 94; Joslyn Art Mus, 94; Mus Fine Arts, Boston, 94; solo exhibs, Irish Mus Mod Art, Dublin, 95, Ctr Contemp Arts, Glasgow, Scotland, 95, High Mus Art, 96, Wadsworth Atheneum, 96, Sala Monicada de Fundacio "la Calxa", Barcelona, 96, Whitney Mus Am Art, NY, 98, Luhring Augustine, NY, 99, Aldrich Mus, 01, Woldenberg Art Ctr, Tulane Univ, New Orleans, 02, Site Santa Fe, NMex, 02-03; Glen Dimplex Award Exhib, Irish Mus Mod Art, Dublin, 96; Nowhere, La Mus, Denmark, 96; Hugo Boss Price, Solomon R Guggenheim Mus, 96; Three Legged Race, Harlem Fire House, NY, 96; Rrose is a Rrose is a Rrose, Guggenheim Mus, NY & Andy Warhol Mus, Pittsburgh, Pa, 97; On Life, Beauty, Translations and other Difficulties, 5th Int Istanbul Biennial, Turkey, 97; Looking at Ourselves: Works by Women Artist from the Logan Collection, San Francisco Mus Mod Art, 99; The Am Century: Art & Cult 1950-2000, Whitney Mus Am Art, 99; Open Ends: Minimalism and After, Art at MoMA since 1980, Mus of Modern Art, NY, 2000; Inst Contemp Art, 02-03; Portland Inst Contemp Art, 02, 03; James Cohan Gallery, NY, 03. *Awards:* MacArthur Found Fel, 98; Joan Mitchell Found Painting & Sculptor Grant, 98; New Media Award, ICA, Boston, 99; John Simon Guggenheim Memorial Foundation Fine Arts Fel, 2011. *Bibliog:* Kay Larson (auth), Women's work (or is it art?) is never done, NY Times, 1/7/96; Holland Cotter (auth), 3 legged race, Janine Antoni, Marcel Odenbach, Nari Ward, NY Times, 9/27/96; Holland Cotter (auth), A Soho sampler: Short list for prize, NY Times, 11/22/96. *Mem:* Nat Acad. *Dealer:* Luhring Augustine 531 W 24th St New York NY 10011. *Mailing Add:* Luhring Augustine Gallery 531 W 24th St New York NY 10011

ANTREASIAN, GARO ZAREH
PAINTER, EDUCATOR
b Indianapolis, Ind, Feb 16, 1922. *Study:* Herron Sch Art, BFA, 48; studied with Stanley William Hayter & Will Barnet. *Hon Degrees:* DFA Indiana/Perdue Univ, Indianapolis, 72. *Work:* Metrop Mus Art, Mus Mod Art, Guggenheim Mus, NY; Art Inst Chicago; Los Angeles Co Mus Art, Calif; Brooklyn Mus; Boston Mus; Albuquerque Mus; NY Public Lib; Mus Modern Art Phila. *Comn:* History of Indiana University, Bloomington, Ind, 54; Lincoln in Indiana (with Ralph Peck), Ind State Off Bldg, Indianapolis, 63. *Exhib:* Tamarind: Homage to Lithography, Mus Mod Art, NY, 69; Rettig/Martinez Gallery, 81, 91 & 92; Pace Gallery, NY, 91; Albuquerque Mus, 91; Worcester Art Mus, 91; Garo Antreasian, written on stone catalogue raisonne print, 94-95; Retrospective, Indianapolis Mus Art, 94 & 95; Gerald Peters Gallery, Santa Fe, 2006; Fresno Mus Art, 2006; Works on Paper - 50 Yrs, Gerald Peters Gallery, Santa Fe, 2008; Peters Gallery, 2009-2012; David Findlay Jr Gallery, NY, 2012; Am Acad Arts & Letters, NY, 2013. *Pos:* Tech dir lithography, Tamarind Lithography Workshop, Inc, Los Angeles, 60-61, Tamarind Inst, Univ NMex, 70-72; dir, Coll Art Asn Am, 73-80 & World Print Coun, 80-87; bd dir, Albuquerque Mus, 80-90; printmaker, emer Southern Graphics Coun, 94. *Teaching:* Instr, Herron Sch Art, 48-64; prof art, Univ NMex, 64-87, chmn, Dept Art, 81-84; vis lectr, artist numerous univs; Fulbright vis lectr, Univ São Paulo and Found Armando Alvares Penteado, Brazil, 85. *Awards:* Visual Artists Grant, Nat Endowment Arts, 82-83; Fulbright lectr, Brazil, 85; NMex Gov's Award, 87; fel Nat Acad Design, New York, 93. *Bibliog:* James Waterous (auth), A Century of American Printmaking, 84; Riva Castleman (auth), American Impressions: Prints Since Pollock, 85; Printmaking in New Mexico 1980-1990, Clinton Adams, 91. *Mem:* World Print Coun (bd dir 80-87); Nat Print Coun Am (co-pres, 80-82); Coll Art Asn Am (bd dir 77-80); Nat Acad Design (assoc, 93, acad, 94). *Media:* Painting, Lithography. *Res:* Fundamental res, stone & metal plate lithography, 1950-1986. *Specialty:* Paintings, Drawings, Prints, Sculpture. *Interests:* Literature, History, Philately. *Publ:* Coauth, The Tamarind Book of Lithography: Art & Techniques, 71; Some thoughts about printmaking & print publications, Art J, Coll Art Asn, spring 80; Garo Z Antreasian: A Retrospective 1942-1987, Albuquerque Mus, 88; Garo Z Antreasian: A Retrospective Exhibition of Lithographs, Univ NMex Press, 93; Abstract Art: The New Mexico Artists Series, Stuart Ashman, Fresco Fine Art Publ, 2003; Garo Z Antreasian: Continuum, Gerald Peters Gallery, Santa Fe, NM, 2006; Proof: The Rise of Print Making in Southern California, Norton Simon Mus, 2012. *Dealer:* Gerald Peters Gallery 1011 Paseo De Peralta Santa Fe NM 87501; David Findlay Jr Fine Art 724 Fifth Ave NY 10019. *Mailing Add:* 11105 Malaguena Ln NE Albuquerque NM 87111-6827

ANTRIM, CRAIG KEITH
PAINTER, DRAFTSMAN
b Pasadena, Calif, Sept 6, 1942. *Study:* Univ Calif, Santa Barbara, Ford Found Experimental Prog Instrs Col, Europ study, 63-65, hons prog, 63-65, BA (art, with hons), 65; Claremont Grad Sch, Calif State Fel, 69-70 & MFA (painting & drawing), 70. *Work:* Mus Mod Art & Whitney Mus Am Art, NY; San Francisco Mus Mod Art; Corcoran Gallery Art, Washington; Los Angeles Co Mus Art, Calif; Palm Springs Desert Mus. *Comn:* Float Light (canvas), Los Angeles Co/Univ Southern Calif Med Credit Union, Los Angeles, 77; Painting, Fairmont Hotel, San Jose, Calif; Painting, Emerald Schaffer Ctr, San Diego, Calif; Los Angeles Co Univ S Calif Med Credit Union, Los Angeles, Calif. *Exhib:* Spiritual in Art/Abstract Painting 1890-1985 (catalog), Los Angeles Co Mus Art, traveling to Haags Gemeentemus, The Neth, 87; solo exhibs, Works Gallery, Long Beach, Calif, 90 & 92, Restaurant Lozano, Sierra Madre, Calif, 93, LACA Gallery, Los Angeles, 93, Pasadena City Col, Calif, 93, Gallery 317, Venice, Calif, 94 & Phoenix Gallery, Santa Monica, Calif, 95; Shape of Abstraction, Luckman Fine Arts Ctr, Los Angeles, 95; Nature Finds/Abstraction, Korean Cult Ctr, Los Angeles, 95; Celebrating New Beginnings, Artworks, Riverside, Calif, 96; Calif Painters, Ash Kenazy Gallery, Los Angeles, 96; Blessings & Beginnings, Skirball Cult Ctr, Los Angeles, 96. *Pos:* Studio Asst, Dockum Mobil-Color Proj System, Altadena, Calif, 68-70. *Teaching:* Instr, Univ Fla, Gainesville, 70-72; asst prof color & design, Scripps Col, Claremont, Calif, 74-76; instr painting & myth, Univ S Cal, Los Angeles, 89-90, instr painting, 91; instr

painting, drawing, design & art apprec, El Camino Col, Torrance, Calif, 74-92; instr painting & drawing, Harbor Col, Wilmington, Calif, 75-92; instr adv painting workshop, Otis/Parsons Sch Art, Los Angeles, Calif, 86-92; vis artist/grad supv, Claremont Grad Sch, Claremont, Calif, 75-76, 88 & 92; vis asst prof painting & drawing, Loyola Marymount Univ, Los Angeles, Calif, 92-93. *Bibliog:* Mario Cutajar (auth), The slow growth alternative, Artweek, Vol 22, No 32, 91; Nancy Kapitanoff (auth), Up close & personal, Los Angeles Times, Valley ed, 2/18/94; Edward Lucie-Smith (auth), Artoday, Phaidon, Oxford, Gt Brit, 96; Kinney Littlefield (auth), Meaningful mystery in spiritual objects, Long Beach Press Telegram, 8/25/91. *Media:* Acrylic, Oil. *Publ:* Auth, Color Consciousness: Seven Los Angeles Artists (catalog), Lang Art Galleries, 78. *Dealer:* John Thomas Gallery 1831 Colorado Ave Santa Monica CA 90404; 317 Gallery 1208 Abbot Kinney Blvd Venice CA 90291. *Mailing Add:* 1129 N LaBrea Ave Inglewood CA 90302

ANZIL, DORIS
PAINTER, SCULPTOR
b Colchester, Vt. *Study:* City Univ New York, BA & MA, 68; NY Univ-Columbia Univ, 68-69; studies in Switz, France & Ger, 70-80. *Work:* Am Cult Inst Gallery in Amerika Haus, Siemens Gallery (Siemens Corp), Haus der Kunst (Mus Contemp Art), Munich, Ger; Brooklyn Mus, NY; Philadelphia Mus Art, Pa. *Comn:* Mural, comn by Dr F Occhionero, Munich, Ger, 81; mural, comn by Dr Von Heusinger, CEO, Siemens Corp, Munich, Ger, 82; mural, Rennert Sch Lang, NY, 84; large painting, comn by RC Archdiocese, Brooklyn, NY, 90; large scale painting, Waverly Sch, Brooklyn, NY, 91; large painting, comn by RC Archdiocese, Brooklyn, 2000. *Exhib:* Solo exhibs, Regensburg Mus, Ger, 80, Maryland Univ Annex, Ger, 81, Am Inst, Munich, Ger, 82, Volker Kundes Mus, Munich, Ger, 84, Wisteria Artspace, Brooklyn, 95, Wisteria Artspace, 2001, 2003, Galeria via Roma, Italy, 2005, 2007, 2008, 2009, Treppo Grande, Galeria via Roma, Italy, 2010-2012; Brooklyn Artists, Brooklyn Mus, NY, 85; Artist Teacher, Lincoln Ctr, Avery Fisher Hall, 94, Cork Gallery, 96; Third Independents Biennial, NY, 96; Art in the Park, Queens Mus, Flushing, 96; Ct St Gallery, Brooklyn, NY, 97; Broom St Gallery, Soho, NY, 97; Avery Fisher Hall, Lincoln Ctr, NY, 97; Growanus Community Arts, Brooklyn, NY, 98; Grand St Gallery, Soho, NY, 98; Independents Biennial IV, NY, 98; Cork Gallery, Lincoln Ctr, NY, 98; Grand St Gallery, New York, 2001; Broome St Gallery, New York, 2000, 2003, 2004, 2005, 2006, 2007; St Saviour Church, Brooklyn, 2005. *Bibliog:* Dianne Copelon (auth), Doris Anzil: An American artist, Ger Television Film, 81; Doris Schmidt (auth), Review-Doris Anzil, Suddentsche Zeitung, 81; Ingo Glass (auth), Haidhausen Artists, Munich Cultural Affairs Municipality, Lenbach Mus Art-Art Forum, 82. *Mem:* Artists Equity; New York City Artists Teacher Asn. *Media:* All Media. *Mailing Add:* 943 President St Brooklyn NY 11215

AOKI, CAROLE I
CERAMIST
b Salt Lake City, Utah. *Study:* Univ Utah, Salt Lake City, 69-71; Calif Coll Arts & Crafts, Oakland, BFA, 77. *Work:* Munic Anchorage Capital Projs, Performing Arts Ctr, Alaska; Everson Mus, Syracuse, NY; Upjohn, Kalamazoo, Mich; IBM, Raleigh, NC; Franklin Mint, Pa; numerous pvt & corp collections. *Exhib:* Solo shows, Joyce Petter Gallery, Sangatuck, Minn, 87, Andrea Schwartz Gallery, San Francisco, Calif, 89, Works Gallery, Philadelphia, Pa, 90 & Worth Gallery, Taos, NMex, 92 & 95; Charles A Wustum Mus Fine Arts, Racine, Wis, 93; Int Ceramics Exhib Ceramic, Czech Repub, 94; NY, NY: Clay, Oslo, Norway, 96; Japanese Ceramics, Arlington Mus Arts, Tex, 96. *Pos:* Dir ceramic dept, Berkeley Parks & Recreation & Ctr Blind, Oakland, Calif, 72-74. *Teaching:* Lect/workshop, var art ctrs, art coun, univ & col, 85-89; instr ceramics, 92nd St Y, 90 & 91; guest lectr, Teacher's Col, Columbia Univ, 91; prof ceramics, Marymount Manhattan Col, NY, 94 & adj prof, 94. *Awards:* Ceramic Art Award, Calif Mus Art, Luther Burbank Ctr Arts, Santa Rosa, 89; Artist-in-residence, Lakeside Studio, Lakeside Group, Mich; Visual Arts Fel, Nat Endowment Arts, 90-91. *Bibliog:* American Craft, Gallery, Vol 52, No 4, 8-9/92; Judy Rowland (auth), The Craftsperson Speaks, Greenwood Press, 92; American Craft Gallery, Vol 53, 12/93-1/94. *Media:* Clay, Mixed. *Mailing Add:* 2231 Broadway New York NY 10024

APESOS, ANTHONY
PAINTER, CRITIC
b Newark, NJ, Jan 6, 1953. *Study:* Vassar Coll, BA, 75; Pa Acad Fine Arts, cert, 79; Bard Coll, MFA, 91. *Work:* Summit Art Ctr, NJ; Sacred Heart Hosp, Chester, Pa; Mt Alvernia Coll, Reading, Pa; Emerson Coll, Boston, Mass; Tufts Univ Med Sch, Boston. *Comn:* Employee's Cafeteria (mural), Meridian Hotel, Boston, 96; numerous portrait comns. *Exhib:* Solo exhibs: More Gallery, Philadelphia, 83, 85, 86 & 91, M Dunev Gallery, San Francisco, 87 & Fan Gallery, Philadelphia, 92, 94, 95, 97, 2001, Andrea Marquit, 97 & Univ Mass, Boston, 98; Figure in Landscape, Artists Choice Mus, NY, 85; Myth & Symbol, Pa State Univ, 86; Ann Exhib, Nat Acad Design, NY, 86; Four Contemp Artists, Allentown Art Mus, Pa, 87. *Teaching:* Lectr painting & drawing, Univ of the Arts, 83-86; asst prof, Moore Coll Art, 86-92; assoc prof painting, Art Inst Boston, Lesley Univ, 92-, chair fine arts, 92-98, prof painting, 2006, prof fine arts, currently, dir MFA prog in visual arts, Art Inst Boston, 2002-2004. *Awards:* Purchase Prize, Art Quest, 87; New Eng Found Arts Fel, 96; Faculty Dev Grant, Lesley Univ, 99, 2003 & 2009. *Bibliog:* Victoria Donahue (auth), review, Philadelphia Inquirer, 2/4/89; Tom Cezar (auth), review, New Art Examiner, 3-4/93; Edward Sozanski (auth), review, Philadelphia Inquirer, 7/24/94. *Mem:* Coll Art Asn. *Media:* Oil. *Res:* history of artists' techniques. *Interests:* anatomy, botany. *Publ:* Auth, Re-affirming values through the depiction of space, New Art Examiner, 80; The Parkway Madonna, New Art Examiner, 83; Contemporary realist drawing, New Art Examiner, 83; coauth, Raising the reserve: PMA hosts J Johns Show, New Art Examiner, 89; Anatomy for Artists, North Light Books, 2007; Caravaggw Taking of Chart: The Artist as Evangelist, Aurora, 2010. *Dealer:* FAN Gallery Philadelphia. *Mailing Add:* 366 Arborway Jamaica Plain MA 02130

APFELBAUM, POLLY
ARTIST
Study: Tyler Sch Art, Elkins Park, Pa, BFA, 1978. *Work:* Austin Mus Art, Tex; Bowdoin Coll Mus Art, Brunswick, Maine; Brooklyn Mus Art, NY; Dallas Mus Art, Tex; Des Moines Art Ctr, Iowa; FRAC Nord-Pas de Calais, Dunkerque, France; Henry Art Gallery, Seattle; Israel Mus, Jerusalem; Magasin 3, Stockholm; Mus d'Art Moderne de la Ville de Paris; Mus Mod Art, NY; Mus Contemp Art, Chicago; Whitney Mus Am Art, NY; Yale Univ Art Gallery. *Exhib:* Solo exhibs, Wood Work, Paulo Salvador Gallery, NY, 1986, Still Lives, Hallwalls, Buffalo, NY, 1986, The Somnambulist, Loughelton Gallery, NY, 1989 & The Daisy Chain, 1989, The Language of Flowers, PS1, NY, 1990, Wives' Tales, Amy Lipton Gallery, NY, 1990 & The Blot on my Bonnet, 1992, The Constellation of the Dart, Sue Spaid Fine Art, Los Angeles, 1991, Level World, Hilly Sea, Galerie Etienne Ficheroulle, Brussels, 1991 & Wonderbread, 1993, Wallworks & Drawings, Hirschl & Adler Mod, NY, 1995, Eclipse, Boesky & Callery Fine Arts, NY, 1996, The Night, Walter & McBean Galleries, 1997, Ice, D'Amelio Terras, 1998, Powerpuff, 2000 & Cartoon Garden, 2005, Crazy Green, Karyn Lovegrove Gallery, Los Angeles, 2000 & Gun Club, 2002, Today I Love Everybody, Triple Candie, Harlem, 2003, Crazy Love, Love Crazy, 2004, Contemp Art Mus, St Louis, 2004, Flags of Revolt & Defiance, Columbia Univ, 2006, Love Street, Angles Gallery, Santa Monica, Calif, 2007, Love Sculpture, Frith Street, London, 2007, D'Amelio Terras, New York, 2010; Group exhibs, New Uses, White Columns, NY, 1986, Fragments, Parts, Wholes, 1990, DIY, 1994; The Level of Volume, Carl Soloway Gallery, Cincinnati, 1987, 30 Ways to Make a Painting, 2005; The Double Bind, Loughelton Gallery, NY, 1987, Fabricated Not Found, 1988; Containers, Shoshana Wayne Gallery, Santa Monica, Calif, 1989, The Milky Way, 1989, The Kingdom of Flora, 1996; Snug Harbor Sculpture Festival, Snug Harbor Cult Ctr, Staten Island, NY, 1990, 1991, After the Fall, 1997; Shape Shifters, Amy Lipton Gallery, NY, 1992, There Is a Light That Never Goes Out, 1992; Sense & Sensibility, Mus Mod Art, NY, 1994, Comic Abstraction, 2007, Lines, Grids, Stains, Words, 2007; Untitled, Postmasters Gallery, NY, 1994, Raw, 1995; Painting, The Extended Field, Magasin 3, Stockholm, 1996, Spatiotemporal, 1998, Plingeling, 2003; Simple Form, Henry Art Gallery, Univ Wash, Seattle, 1997, Hover, 2003, Viewfinder, 2007; Other, 4th Contemp Art Biennial, Lyon, France, 1997; Hindsight, Whitney Mus Am Art, NY, 1998; Humble County, D'Amelio Terras, NY, 1998, 2001, 2002, Stacked, 2003, One-Armed Bandit, 2005; Everyday, 11th Sydney Biennale, 1998; Painting Pushed to Extremes, Worcester Art Mus, Mass, 2001, Frontiers, 2005; The Return of the Real, Tel Aviv Mus Art, Israel, 2001; Drawings, Frith Street Gallery, London, 2001, Print Run, 2006, Resonance, 2006; Abstract Painting, Once Removed, Contemp Arts Mus, Houston, 2001, Splat, Boom, Pow, 2003; The Eye of the Beholder, Dundee Contemp Arts, Scotland, 2002; Valencia Bienal, Spain, 2003; Lodz Biennale, Poland, 2004; Flowers Observed, Flowers Transformed, Andy Warhol Mus, Pittsburgh, 2004; Ann Invitational Exhib, Nat Acad Mus, NY, 2004; Galerie Nächst St Stephan, Vienna, 2005, 2006; Contemp Masterworks, Contemp Art Mus St Louis, 2006; Like Color in Pictures, Aspen Art Mus, Colo, 2007. *Awards:* Artists Space Grant, 1986; Pollock-Krasner Found Grant, 1987; Guggenheim Fel in Sculpture, 1993; NY Found for the Arts Fel, 1995; Anonymous Was a Woman Grant, 1998; Joan Mitchell Grant, 1999; Acad Award, Am Acad Arts & Letts, 2002; Gallery of Success Seasoned Alumni Award, Temple Univ, 2003. *Mailing Add:* 274 Water St Apt 3F New York NY 10038

APGAR, JEAN E
PAINTER
b Rockford, Ill, 1949. *Study:* Northern Ill Univ, BFA, 71, MA, 78. *Work:* Swed Am Hosp, Rockford, Ill; Crusader Clinic, Rockford, Ill; Kishwaukee Coll, Malta, Ill; Winn Co Title Co, Rockford, Ill; US Ambassadorial Residence, Niamey, Niger & Rangoon, Burma. *Comn:* Rose Day (serigraph), Rockford Breakfast Lions, Ill, 80 & 92. *Exhib:* All on Paper Nat, Columbia Green Coll, Palenville, NY, 82; Nat Asn Women Artists Traveling Print Exhib, USA, 84-86; Nat Drawing Exhib, Bergen Community Mus, Paramus, NJ, 84; Naturally, Earth, Sea & Sky, Adelphi Univ, NY, 91; Prairie Ctr Arts, Schaumburg, Ill, 92; Int Exhib Animals Art, La State Univ, Baton Rouge, 96; Silk Painters Int, Fairfax, Va, 98; solo exhibs, Gallery 451, Rockford, Ill, 94-95 & N Suburban Dist Libr, Loves Park, Ill, 2001; Realism or Not, UIC Community Gallery, Rockford, Ill, 2000 & Animal Imagery, 2000; group exhibs, Womanspace Traveling Exhib, 2000-2001, Animal Imagery, Burpee Nat Hist Mus, Rockford, 2002 & Animals, Wild and Otherwise, Sinsinawa Mounds Ctr, Wis, 2003; juried exhibs, Silk Painters Int, Fairfax, Va, 2000, 26th Ann Fiber and Textile Exhib, Whitewater, Wis, 2002, Masterpieces of Maturity, Lexington, Ky, 2002, Bead Int '06, Athens, Ohio, 2006 & Silk Painters Int, Santa Fe, NMex, 2006; Bead Expo '07, Sacramento, Calif, 2007; Monroe Arts Ctr, Monroe, Wis, 2007; Fine Arts Incubator, Beloit, Wis, 2007, 2009; Bead Int, 2008; Next Picture Show, 2009; Byron Hist Mus, 2009; Animal in Art, 2010; Wings, Tails, Hooves, Scales, 2011; ArtSpace West, 2011; Int Exhib on Animals in Art, 2012; Midwest Folk & Fiber, 2012; Seasons on the Land, 2012; Regional Juried Exhib, 2012; Nat Art Premiere, 2013; Skip Watts Memorial Watercolor, 2013; Wings, Tails, and Scales, 2013. *Pos:* Chmn, spec events, Beattie Is Festival, Rockford, Ill, 79-80; pres, Images/4, Rockford, Ill, 80-84; partner/publicist, Gallery Ten, Rockford, Ill, 90-94; juror, Rockford Area Artists Fair, 2005, 2007, 2008. *Teaching:* Instr drawing painting, Rock Valley Coll, Rockford, Ill, 72-79. *Bibliog:* Tuckman & Janus, The Best of Silk Painting, 97; Art Rockford, 2004; Beadwork Mag, 6-7/2007. *Mem:* Nat Watercolor Soc (assoc mem); Rockford Area Arts Coun; Silk Painters Int; Womanspace. *Media:* Watercolor, Silk, Bead Embroidery. *Publ:* Approaching Galleries, Art Calendar, 4/92; coauth, Now What? This Art Business (artists' business manual), Jester Publ, 94. *Dealer:* Artisan Gallery Paoli WI; Ravens Wish Vanesville WI. *Mailing Add:* 2513 Knight Ave Rockford IL 61101

APP, TIMOTHY
PAINTER, EDUCATOR
b Akron, Ohio, July 5, 1947. *Study:* Kent State Univ, BFA, 70; Tyler Sch Art, MFA, 74. *Work:* Mus Albuquerque, NMex; Roswell Mus & Art Ctr, NMex; Mus Fine Arts, Santa Fe, NMex; Albright-Knox Art Gallery, Buffalo; Baltimore Mus Art; Long Beach Mus Art, Calif; Joslyn Art Mus, Omaha, NB; Tucson Art Mus, Ark. *Exhib:* Linda Durham Gallery, 83-92, 20-Year Survey, 89, Santa Fe, NMex; Anthony Ralph Gallery, NY, 87-92; Five New Painters, John Davis Gallery, NY, 89; Am Embasy, Sarajevo, Bosnia, 2005-2007; Am Univ, DC, 2005; Denise Bibro Gallery, New York, 2005; Goya Contemp, Baltomore, 2001, 2003, 2005, 2009; Albright-Knox Gallery Art, 2005, 2008; Nat Acad Design, New York, 2010. *Teaching:* Asst prof painting, Pomona Col, 74-78; assoc prof, Univ NMex, Albuquerque, 78-90; prof art, Md Inst Col Art, 90-. *Awards:* Nat Endowment Arts Fel, 87-88; Md State Arts Grant, 99-2000; McLean Proj Arts, Va, 2000, 2007. *Bibliog:* Kathleen Sheild (auth), Timothy App at Linda Durham, Art Am, 89; John Dorssey (auth), Art Rev, Baltimore Sun, 94, 97 & 98; & others. *Media:* Acrylic. *Dealer:* Goya Contemporary Baltimore MD

APPEL, ERIC A
SCULPTOR, PAINTER
b Brooklyn, NY, Dec 26, 1945. *Study:* Pratt Inst, 63-67, BID, 67; Tyler Sch Art, Rome, 67-68; Tyler Sch Art, Temple Univ, Philadelphia, Pa, MFA (painting), 70. *Exhib:* Garden of Delight, Cooper-Hewitt Mus, NY, 81; Spring Garden, Yves Arman Gallery, NY, 81; solo exhibs, Winter Garden, Queens Mus, NY, 81, Joy Horwich Gallery, Chicago, Ill, 83, Field Mus Nat Hist & Chicago Sculpture Int Navy Pier, 83-84 & Windows on Broadway, NY Univ, 85, OK Harris, NY, 91. *Bibliog:* Beth Fallow (auth), Make yourself at home in the mansion gardens, Daily News, 7/24/81; Robin Brentano & Mark Savitt (auth), 112 Workshop, 112 Green St, NY Univ Press, 81. *Media:* Mixed. *Mailing Add:* 102 Christopher St New York NY 10014

APPEL, KEITH KENNETH
SCULPTOR, MURALIST
b Bricelyn, Minn, May 21, 1934. *Study:* Mankato State Col, BA, BS & MS; Ohio State Univ, PhD. *Comn:* Sculpture, Alaska Art in Public Places, 81-2002; sculpture, Anchorage C of C, 81; sculpture, Anchorage Art in Public Places; sculpture, Fairbanks Art in Public Places; sculpture, State Courthouse, Fairbanks, 2001; Mural, Lathrop High School, Fairbanks, 99; sculpture, Eilson Air Force Base, Fairbanks, 98; sculpture, Chugiak/Eagle River Middle School, 97. *Exhib:* All Alaska Exhib, 64-80; Alaska Centennial, 67; Solo exhibs, Stonington Gallery, Anchorage, 85, Volcano Nat Park, Hawaii, 85, Anchorage Historical & Fine Arts Mus, 70, 75, The Gathering, Ketchikan, Alaska, 80, 82; Alaskan Smithsonian Exhib, 78; Earth, Fire & Fiber Exhib, Anchorage, 97-99. *Pos:* Chmn art dept, Univ Alaska, Anchorage, 78-81. *Teaching:* Assoc prof art, Univ Alaska, Anchorage, 70-78; retired. *Awards:* Alaska Centennial, 67; All Alaska Juried Exhibition Awards, var times, 67-77. *Mem:* Alaska Artists Guild; Alaska State Arts Coun (mem bd); Nat Art Educ Asn. *Media:* Miscellaneous. *Interests:* architectural scales sculpture, murals. *Mailing Add:* 4705 Malibu Dr Anchorage AK 99517-3273

APPEL, THELMA
PAINTER, INSTRUCTOR
b Tel Aviv, Israel, Jan 6, 1940; US citizen. *Study:* St Martins Sch Art, London, dipl art & design, 61; Hornsey Coll Art, London, art teacher's dipl, 62. *Work:* Milwaukee Arts Ctr, Wis; Am Tel & Tel Co, NY & Summit, NJ; Chase-Manhattan Bank & Metrop Life Co, NY; Vt State Legislature, Montpelier; Port Authority, NY; IBM Corp, Lawrence, NJ; Bank of Tokyo, NY; Xerox Corp, NY; Cabot Corp, Boston, Mass; Hale & Dore Assocs, Boston; Prudential Collection, NY; Police Academy Mus, NY. *Comn:* Five paintings, Western Corp Bldg, Dallas, Tex, 80; two paintings, Hospital Insurance Co, Grand Prairie, Tex, 85; two paintings, Farm Credit Bank, Austin, Tex, 85. *Exhib:* Solo exhibs, Adelle M Gallery Fine Art, Dallas, Tex, Fischbach Gallery, NY, 79, 82 & Westchester Co Ctr, White Plains, NY, 92, Sacred Spaces, JCC of Greater New Haven, 99, Cabrini Art Gallery Cabrini Hospital, Hastings on Hudson, 2000, Daniels Art Gallery, HRCA, Boston, 2000, 2001, Warner Atrium Gallery, Torrington, Conn, 2012, Bruce Kerschner Gallery, Fairfield Public Libr, Conn, 2013; Realism Today, Clary Miner Gallery, Buffalo, NY, 87; Int Art Competition, Pyramid Gallery, NY, 90; Current River View, Hastings Creative Arts Coun, NY, 91; Neighbors, Krasdale Foods Art Gallery in conjunction with Lehman Coll Art Gallery, 92; Face to Face, Paramount Ctr Arts, Peekskill, NY, 98; History of Woman, Regina Quick Ctr for the Arts, Fairfield Univ, 2012; Fabrications, Artwell Gallery, Torrington, Conn, 2012; and others. *Teaching:* Instr, Southern Vermont Col, 75-76 & Parsons Sch Art, 76-77; Summer Painting Workshop, Bennington Col, 76-83; Northern Westchester Ctr Arts, 89-95; Putnam Arts Coun, 90-96. *Awards:* Vt Coun Arts Award, 73; Yaddo Residency fel, 74; State of Vt Purchase Award, Vt Coun Arts & Nat Endowment Arts, 78; Jury Award, JCC Greater New Haven, 99. *Bibliog:* Gabrielle V Arnhem (auth), American Romantic Painting, Art Ger, 80; Sunday Times (Westchester Sect), 10/4/92; Judy Birke (auth), New Haven Regist, 5/10/98; Hedwig Brenner (auth), Jewish Women in Visual Arts, 2008. *Mem:* Minneapolis Art Inst, Minn, IBM Corp (NJ), Metropolitan Life Corp, MCI Telecommun, GTE Corp, Chase Manhattan Bank, Bank of Tokyo, Nynex Corp, Xerox Corp, Fed Reserve Bank, Boston, RJR Industries, Winston-Salem, NC, Cabot Corp, Ziff-Davis Publishing, NY, Hale & Dorr Attorneys, Police Academy Mus, NY. *Media:* Oil, Acrylic, Fabric Collage. *Interests:* History, Music, Literature

APPELHOF, RUTH A
CURATOR
b Washington, DC, Feb 14, 1945. *Study:* Syracuse Univ, BFA (painting & art hist), 65, MFA (art hist), 75; PhD, 88. *Collection Arranged:* Outside New York City: From Drawing to Sculpture (auth, catalog), 82; Margaret Bourke-White: The Humanitarian Vision (auth, catalog), Syracuse Univ, 83; The New Figure, Birmingham Mus, 85; The Expressionist Landscape, Birmingham Mus, Ala, 87 & Looking South, 88; The Common Wealth: Twentieth Century American Masterpieces, Va Collections, 90; and others; Voices Rising, Mus Women Arts, DC, 99-. *Pos:* Lectr, Whitney Mus Am Art, 80-; cur exhib, Syracuse Univ, 81-85; cur paintings & sculpture, Birmingham Mus, 84-89; exec dir, Art Mus Western, Va, 89-94; exec dir, Hill-Stead Mus, Farmington, Conn, 1997-1998; dir, Minn Mus Am Art, St Paul, 1997-1997; exec dir, Guild Hall Mus and John Drew Theater, East Hampton, NY, 1999-. *Teaching:* Assoc prof art, Cayuga Co Community Col, 74-79, gallery dir, 78-79; asst prof museology, Syracuse Univ, 81-85; adj prof, Univ Ala, Birmingham, 85. *Mem:* Col Art Asn; Women's Caucus Art; Nat Women's Studies Asn; Women in the Arts; Art Table. *Res:* Modern and contemporary women in art; iconography and historical context. *Publ:* Auth, Beth Ames Schwartz: Israel Revisited, Whitney Mus, 81; Recent Developments in Landscape Painting, Whitney Mus, 81; Nature as Image and Metaphor, Women's Caucus Arts, 82; The Expressionist Landscape, 87 & Looking South, 88. *Mailing Add:* Guild Hall Museum and John Drew Theater 158 Main St East Hampton NY 11937

APPELSON, HERBERT J
EDUCATOR, PRINTMAKER
b Brooklyn, NY, Dec, 31, 1937. *Study:* Brooklyn Coll, NY, BA, 59; Univ Wis, Madison, MS, 60, MFA, 61; Columbia Univ, NY, EDD, 72. *Work:* Fairmount Inst, Philadelphia; Atlantic City Office of Cult Affairs, NJ; Columbia Univ, NY; Luther Coll, Iowa; Edgewood Coll, Madison, Wis; Univ Wisc; Kansas State Univ; NJ Dept Treas, Trenton; Noyes Mus, Oceanville, NJ; Camden Co Cult & Heritage Comns Art Bank, NJ; Auburn Univ, Ala. *Exhib:* Solo exhibs, ETS Conant Gallery, Princeton, 85 & Artists' House, Philadelphia, Pa, 95; Malaspina Gallery, Granville Island, Vancouver, BC, Can, 98; Int Miniature Print Competition, Graphic Arts Ctr, Noralle, Conn, 99; Am Color Print Soc Ann, Revsin Gallery, Philadelphia, Pa, 2000; Am Coll, Bryn Manor, Pa, 2001; Noyes Mus, Oceanville, NJ, 2001; Am Color Print Soc Exhib, 2004 & 05. *Collection Arranged:* Images of Southern New Jersey from the Heartland to the Seashore (with catalog), Hollybush Invitation Art Exhib, 86; Am Artists/Russian Roots (with catalog), Hollybush Arts Festival, 87; Light-Chemistry and a Creative Vision (with catalog), Hollybush Arts Festival, 88; Forms to Figure (with catalog), Hollybush Arts Festival, 89; Abstract Art, Intuition-Invention-Expressionism (with catalog), Hollybush Arts Festival, 90. *Teaching:* Prof printmaking & drawing, Rowan Univ, NJ, 67-. *Awards:* Exhib Award, Ann Water Color Exhib, Camden Co Cult & Heritage Comn, 2000; Juror Award, Camden Co Cult & Heritage Comn, 2001; First Prize, Philadelphia Plastic Club, 2002. *Bibliog:* Burton Wasserman (auth), Exploring the visual arts, Davis, Worchester, Mass, 76. *Mem:* Philadelphia Watercolor Club; Am Color Print Soc; Cheltenham Printmakers Guild. *Media:* Relief, Mixed Media. *Mailing Add:* 17 Highgate Ln Cherry Hill NJ 08003-1824

APPLE, JACKI
VISUAL, MEDIA AND PERFORMANCE ARTIST, WRITER, PRODUCER
b New York, NY. *Study:* Syracuse Univ; Parsons Sch Design, BFA. *Work:* Martin Luther King Rehabilitation Ctr, Los Angeles, CA; Little Tokyo Branch Pub Libr, Los Angeles, Calif, 97-2005; Pub Arts Comn, City of Los Angeles, 97-99; Oakwood Community Ctr, Venice, Calif. *Comn:* Urban Suite (soundtrack), Rudy Perez Performance Ensemble, Los Angeles, 84; Swan Lake (a film noir "ballet" for radio), New Am Radio, 88-89; Palisade 1987, Fluctuations of the Field (performance), Santa Monica Arts Comn, 89; Redefining Democracy in America, Parts 1-6 (radio art), New Am Radio, NY, 91, 92; and many others. *Exhib:* Story Art: Recent Am Narrative Traveling Exhib, Contemp Arts Mus, Houston, 77-78; Mus Mod Art, NY, 78; Schemes: A Decade of Installation Drawings Traveling Exhib, Elise Meyer Gallery, NY, 81-82; Sydney Biennale, Australia, 82; Live to Air, Tate Gallery, London, 82; Sonorita Prospettiche Traveling Exhib, Contemp Art Gallery, Rimini, Italy, 82-83; Whitney Mus Philip Morris, NY, 90; Transit Art, ORL Television, Innsbruck, Austria, 93; Outside the Frame: Performance, Object, Cleveland Ctr Contemp Art, Ohio, 94; Sound Culture, Auckland, NZ, 99; Gloria: Another Leek at Feminist Art of the 1970's, White Columns, NYC, 2002-03; Birdspace, New Orleans Contemp Art Ctr, Norton Mus Art, West Palm Beach Fla, 2004; Women Artists of S Calif: Then & Now, Track 16 Gallery, Santa Monica, 2007; On the Trail of..., Newton Art, 2009; Materializing Six Years: Lucy Lippard & the Emergence of Conceptual Art, Brooklyn Mus, NY, 2012. *Collection Arranged:* Visual and Sculptural Bookworks, Montclair Mus, NJ & Seibu Mus, Tokyo, 79; Artists Bookworks: Alterations and Transformations, Nelson Gallery, Kansas City, Mo, 80; Alternatives in Retrospect: An Historical Overview 1969-1975, New Mus, NY, 81; Art Lobby, Lower Manhattan Cult Coun, NY, 82. *Pos:* Cur exhibs & performances, Franklin Furnace, 77-80; guest cur, New Mus, NY, 81; producer/host, KPFK-FM, Pacifica Radio, Los Angeles, 82-95; freelance writer, 82-; contrib ed, Artweek, 83-90, Los Angeles Wkly, 85-89, High Performance Mag, 84-95 & Media Arts, 83-90; producer/writer, US EAR, 87-88; co-producer, EARJAM new Music Festival, Los Angeles, Calif, 2000-2004. *Teaching:* Instr, Concordia Univ, Montreal, fall 80, Calif State Univ, Long Beach, spring 83 & Otis Art Inst, Los Angeles, 84-85, 90 & Univ Calif, San Diego, 95-99; prof, Art Ctr Coll of Design, Pasadena, CA, 1983-, fac coun repr, 2001-2006, dir, office of fac affairs, 2007/2008. *Awards:* Individual Artist Fel, Nat Endowment Arts, 79 & 81, Inter Arts Prog Grant, 84 & 91-92; Vesta Award, Los Angeles, 90; Artists Fel, California Arts Council, 96; Fac Enrichment Grant, Art Ctr Coll Design, 2001 & 2007; Durfee Found, 2002 & 2007; Distinguished Teaching of Art award, Coll Art Asn, 2012. *Bibliog:* Steven Durland (auth), Sound Philosophies: The audio art of Jacki Apple, High Performance, 84; Douglas Sadownick (auth), Palisade: exploring love as a high art form, Los Angeles Times, 7/28/87; Colin Gardner (auth), Colonialism and postmodernism, Artweek, 9/7/85; and others. *Mem:* Int Asn Art Critics; Coll Art Asn. *Media:* Performance, Installation, Photography; Audio, Radio. *Collection:* Anthony Lumsden (Los Angeles); Stanley Goldberg (NY). *Publ:* Auth, The Life & Times of Lin Hixson: The LA Years, Drama Rev, winter 91; Voices in the Dark (CD) Aerial, 92; Thank You for Flying American, Stories and Songs 80-91 & 95 (CD); One Word at a Time, Errant Bodies, 95; Ghost Dances/on the Event Horizon (CD), 96; A (auth), A Different World: A Personal History of Franklin Furnace; The Drama Review, Spring 2005; Resurrecting the Disappeared, Art Journal, 97; Alternatives Reconsidered, Alternative Histories, MIT Press, 2012; and others. *Mailing Add:* 3532 Jasmine Ave Apt 2 Los Angeles CA 90034-4947

APPLEBAUM, LEON
GLASS BLOWER, SCULPTOR
b Toledo, Ohio, Dec 19, 1945. *Study:* Peabody Coll Vanderbilt, MA, 73; Akrahallskollan Orrefors, Sweden, 74; Rochester Inst Technol, MFA, 75-76. *Work:* Wheaton Mus Glass, Millville, NJ; Smithsonian Nat Air Space Mus, Washington, DC; Corning Mus Glass, NY; McDonauch Collection Am Art, Youngstown, Ohio; Patrick Lannen Art Found, Palm Beach. *Comn:* Seventy wine decanters with state seal of Tenn, Tenn Arts Comn, Nashville, 73. *Exhib:* Saenger Nat Sculpture Exhib; Am Contemp Art Glass, Galerie Verrd Art, Montreal, Can; Butler Inst Am Art, Youngstown, Ohio; Crafts Int, Kanazawa, Japan; Glass Int, Kyoto, Japan; NY Craftsman Show, Smithsonian Inst, Washington, DC; Creative Glass Chap Am Fel Exhib, Snyderman Gallery, Philadelphia; Nat Glass Show, Habitat Gallery, Southfield, Mich. *Pos:* Specialty glass blower, Sonaland, Sweden. *Teaching:* Instr glass, Peabody Col Vanderbilt, Nashville & Rochester Inst Technol, NY. *Awards:* Best of Crafts Gold Medal, Toledo Mus Art, Ohio; Best of Show, Miami Beach Art Festival; Creative Glass Chap Am Fel, Millville, NJ. *Bibliog:* Jacquelin Hall (auth), Hawk Gallery Bedazzling (catalog), Columbus Dispatch, 88; Dan Goddard (auth), Breaking into glass, San Antonio Express News, 5/11/96; article in Ceskolipsko, Czech Repub, 5/28/98. *Mem:* Am Craft Asn. *Media:* Glass. *Mailing Add:* c/o Fanny Garver Gallery 230 State St Madison WI 53703

APPLEBY, ANNE L
PAINTER, PRINTMAKER
b Pa, Aug 22, 1954. *Study:* Univ Mont, BFA, 77; San Francisco Art Inst, MFA, 89. *Work:* San Francisco Mus Mod Art; Berkeley Art Mus, Calif; Holter Mus Art, Helena, Mont; Yellowstone Art Mus; MH de Young Meml Mus, San Francisco, Calif; San Jose Mus of Art, Calif. *Comn:* Palazzo Ducale, Sassoulo, Italy. *Exhib:* SECA, 1996, San Francisco Mus Mod Art, 96; Towards a New Millennium, Berkeley Mus Art, Calif, 97; Like a Prayer (with catalog), Holter Mus Art, Helena, Mont, 98; Littlejohn Contemp, NY, 98; Greg Kucera Gallery, Seattle, 98; Yellowstone Art Mus, 99; San Jose Mus Art, 2000; Am Acad in Rome, Italy, 2000; Nora Eccles Harrison Mus Art, Logan, Utah, 2000; Berkeley Art Mus, Berkeley, Calif, 2000; and others. *Pos:* bd dir, Mont Artist Refuge, Basin. *Teaching:* Instr, San Francisco Art Inst, 93-96. *Awards:* Pollock Krasner Found Award, 91; Southeastern Ctr Contemp Art Award, San Francisco Mus Mod Art, 96; Western States Arts Found Grant, 96; Louis Tiffany Found Biennale Award, 99. *Bibliog:* David Mabscott (auth), Minimalist Mandelas, World Art, 97; Rick Newby (auth), Like a Prayer: Recent Prints and Paintings Catalogue Essay, Holter Mus Art, 98; Robin Updike (auth), The Color of Memory, The Seattle Times, 98; Kenneth Baker (auth), Memory Fields Catalogue Essay, Greg Kuleva Gallery and Paule Anglim Gallery, 2000; The Panza di Biumo Collection: Works from the 80's and 90's, Am Acad in Rome, 2000; Profs Lester K Little, Linda Blumberg, Marlo Franciolli (auth), Giuseppe Panza Di Biumo, 2000. *Media:* Oil. *Dealer:* Gallery Paul Anglim 14 Geary St San Francisco CA 94108; Greg Kucera Gallery Seattle WA. *Mailing Add:* PO Box 116 Clancy MT 59634-0116

APT, CHARLES
PAINTER, DESIGNER
b New York, NY, Dec 10, 1933. *Study:* Pratt Inst, BFA, 56. *Work:* Chem Bank; Bowery Bank; Celanese Corp; Paine, Webber, NY; Principality of Monaco, France; Am Stock Exchange. *Comn:* Painting, Am Stock Exchange, 68; Loring Gallery, Springfield, Mass, 2001. *Exhib:* Allied Artists Am, NY, 64, 65, 67 & 69; Am Watercolor Soc, NY, 65, 66, 68 & 69; Nat Acad Design, NY, 65, 68, 73-81, 83, 85, 87 & 99, 2001, 2003, 2005, 2007; Exposition Intercontinentale, Monaco, France, 66 & 68; Mus Fine Art, Springfield, Mass, 66; Nat Mus Racing Ann, Saratoga, NY, 67; solo exhibs, Loring Gallery, Cedarhurst, NY, 85, 87 & 92; Loring Gallery, Sheffield, Mass, 2007; and many others. *Teaching:* Instr painting & drawing, Nat Acad Design, 77-81 & Art Students League. *Awards:* Best in Show, Saratoga Mus Racing, 67; 2nd Benjamin Altman Award, Nat Acad Design, 68; Le Prix Prince Souverain, Prince Rainier, Monaco, 68. *Bibliog:* Joan Hess Michael (auth), Charles Apt in Portugal, Am Artist Mag, 4/70; Leonard Kriegel (auth), Charles Apt, Arts Mag, 10/78. *Mem:* Nat Acad Design (assoc, 72, acad, 79); Artists Equity Asn, NY. *Media:* All Media. *Interests:* music, woodworking. *Publ:* Auth, article, House Beautiful, Hearst Publ, 2/85. *Dealer:* Dassin Gallery Los Angeles CA; Loring Gallery Sheffield MA. *Mailing Add:* Studio 152 S Almont Dr Los Angeles CA 90048

APTEKAR, KEN
PAINTER
b Detroit, Mich, May 13, 1950. *Study:* Univ Mich, BFA, 73, Pratt Inst, MFA, 75. *Work:* Corcoran Gallery Art; Denver Mus Art; Progressive Corp; Jewish Mus, NY; Bell Atlantic Corp, Philadelphia; Meml Art Gallery, Rochester, NY; Kemper Mus Contemp Art; Nat Mus of American Art, Washington, DC; Contemp Art Soc, London, 2003; Victoria & Albert Mus, London; Harvard Univ Sch of Bus, Boston; Huntington Mus Art, Va. *Comn:* Conrad Hilton, Hong Kong; Victoria and Albert Mus and Serpentine Gallery, London, 2001; Meml Art Gallery, Rochester, 2002. *Exhib:* Corcoran Biennial of Am Painting, Corcoran Gallery Art, Washington, 93-94; Solo exhibs, Jack Shainman Gallery, NY, 94 & 96, Corcoran Gallery Art, Washington, DC, 97-98, Steinbaum Krauss Gallery, NY, 99 Bernice Steinbaum Gallery, Miami, 2001, Huntington (WVa) Mus of Art, 2001, Kemper Mus Contemp Art & Design, Kansas City, Mo, 2001; Rembrandt Redux: The Paintings of Ken Aptekar, Palmer Mus Art, Pa State Univ, 95; Going for Baroque, Walters Art Gallery, Baltimore, 95; Too Jewish? traveling exhib, 96; Masculine Measures, Kohler Art Ctr, Wis, 96; Asheville Art Mus (NC) and traveling, 98-2000; Skirball Mus and Cult Ctr, Los Angeles, 2000; Metrop Mus, Tokyo, Shizuoka Prefectural Mus, Hiroshima Prefectural Mus, 2000; James Graham & Sons/JG Contemp, NY, 2006, 2010; Rubin Mus, New York, 2007; Musée Robert Dubois-Corneau, Burnoy, France, 2007; Beard & Weil Gallery, Wheaton Coll, Norton, Mass, 2012. *Awards:* Fel, Nat Endowment Arts, 87 & 95; Rockefeller Found, Bellagio Residency, 92; Fel, Mid Atlantic Arts Found, 98; and others. *Bibliog:* JoAnn Lewis (auth), The Washington Post, 11/8/97; Scott Heller (auth), Art News, 4/98; Helen Harrison (auth.) N.Y. Times, 98; Mieke Bal (auth), Quoting Caravaggio, Univ Chicago Press, 99; Stuart Jeffries (auth) The Guardian, London, 2001; and others. *Dealer:* James Graham & Sons/JG Contemp NY. *Mailing Add:* 35-16 85th St Apt 3E Jackson Heights NY 11372-5517

AQUINO, EDMUNDO
PAINTER, SCULPTOR
b Zimatlan Oaxaca, Mex, June 30, 1939. *Study:* Nat Sch Plastics Art, Nat Univ Mex, cert (teacher fine arts), 62; Ecole Nat Superieure Beaux-Arts, Paris, Fr Govt Scholar, 67-69; Slade Sch Fine Arts, London, Brit Coun Scholar, 69. *Work:* Nat Libr Paris; Univ Mass Collection; Mus Mod Art Latin Am, Washington; Nat Inst Fine Arts, Mexico City, Mex; AGPA (Panamerican Graphic Art), Mus Mod Art, NY; and others. *Exhib:* Mus Mod Art, Mexico City, 77-78; Mus Mod Art Latin Am, OAS, Washington, 80; Picasso Mus, Antibes, France, 80; Contemp Latin Am Art and Japan, Nat Mus Art, Osaka, 81; Olympic Mus, Lausanne, Switz, 94; Mus Mural Diego Rivera, 95-96; Inst Cervantes, Bremen, Ger, 96; Ger Fed Parliament, Bonn, Ger, 97; Museo de las Americas, Denver, Colo, 2000; Sogn og Fjordane Art Mus, Forde, Norway, 03; Museo Chihuahuense de Arte Contemporaneo, Mex, 2013-2014. *Teaching:* Instr drawing & painting & head plastic arts sect, Sch Fine Arts, Oaxaca, Mex, 64-67. *Awards:* First Prize Painting & Drawing, French Gov Scholars, Paris, 69; Nat Prize, 6th Int Festival Painting, Cagnes-Sur-Mer, France, 74; Third Prize, First Iberoamerican Biennial of Painting, Mexico City, 78; DAAD Fel, Artists in Berlin Prog, Berlin, 86. *Bibliog:* Mariana Frenk-Westheim (auth), article in Unomasuno, Mexico City, 11/83; Antonio Rodriguez (auth), article Excelsior, Mexico City, 7/88; Dr Hans Haufe (auth), article, Albatros viajero-Revista Mexicana de Cultura, 1-3/96; Marcela Cauduro (auth) Ecuaciones inesperadas, Collages de Edmundo Aquino (book), 2013. *Media:* All. *Publ:* Zimatlan Lugar de la raiz del frijolan, Edmundo Aquino, Ediciones Guielachi, 2005; Leonard Brooks (auth), My Watercolor World, Coor. Edmundo Aquino, Ediciones Guielachi, 2006; Tierra de Flores Guielachi (auth), Edmundo Aquino, Ediciones Guielachi, 2012. *Mailing Add:* Calle Ave Maria 60-1 Coyoacan 04000 Mexico DF Mexico

AQUINO, HUMBERTO
PAINTER
b Lima, Peru, Oct 20, 1947. *Study:* Nat Sch Fine Arts Lima, Peru, with Alberto Davila, 70; Cardiff Coll Art, Wales, Great Britain, 73; Pratt Inst, Brooklyn, NY, 78. *Work:* Smithsonian Inst, Washington, DC; Art Inst Chicago, Ill; Univ Tex Art Mus, Austin; Mus Mod Art Latin Am, Washington, DC; Biblioteca Lvis Angel Arango, Bogota, Columbia. *Exhib:* Latin Am Drawings, Indianapolis Mus Art, 76; Drawings of the 70's, Art Inst Chicago, 77; Solo exhib, Mus Mod Art Latin Am, Washington, DC, 78; Latin Am Artists in NY Since 1970, Univ Tex Art Mus, 87; Latin Am Drawings Today, San Diego Mus Art, Calif, 4/91. *Pos:* Lectr, Soc of the Americas, NY, 85, Mus of the City of NY, 86. *Awards:* Fulbright Fel, 77; Artist's Fel, NY Found Arts, 85; Mid-Atlantic Regional, Nat Endowment Arts, 88. *Bibliog:* Sebastian Dominguez (auth), Six Artists Working in New York, Visiones - NBC Television, Channel 4, 5/87; Jacqueline Barnitz (auth), Latin Am Artists in New York, Archer M Huntington Art Gallery, 9/87; Framing the Past: essays on art education, Nat Art Educ Asn, 90. *Media:* Oils, Mixed Media. *Dealer:* Odon Wagner 194 Daveport Rd Toronto ON M5R 1J2. *Mailing Add:* c/o Odon Wagner Gallery 196 Davenport Rd Toronto ON M5R 1J2 Canada

ARAI, TOMIE
PRINTMAKER, MURALIST
b New York, NY, Aug 16, 1949. *Study:* Philadelphia Coll Art, 68. *Work:* Library of Congress Pennel Print Coll; Bronx Mus Arts; Mus Modern Art Lib; Whitney Mus Am Art; Williams Coll Mus Art. *Comn:* silkscreen prints, Wash State Arts Comn, Seattle; terrazzo floor design, Percent for Art Prog, NY Sch Construction Authority, 93; ceramic tile mural, NY Sch Construction Authority, 94; mural, Int Memorialization African Burial Ground, Fed Off Bldg, NY; pub art comn, Morse Sch, Cambridge Arts Coun, Mass, 97-98; glass mural, Riverside Ch, NY, 2000; glass wall syst, Filmore St Bridge, Pub Art Comn, San Francisco Art Comn, San Francisco Redevelop Agency, 2000; etched glass mural, Martin Luther King Jr Wing, Riverside Ch, NY, 2000-01; Public Art/Faceted Glass Windows, MTA Arts for Transit Program, 2006. *Exhib:* Committed to Print, Mus Modern Art, NY, 88; Decade Show, New Mus Contemp Art, NY, 91; Framing an Am Identity, Alternative Mus, NY, 92; Breda Fotographica '93, de Beyerd Mus, The Neth, 93; Fables, Fantasies & Everyday Things, Whitney Mus Am Art at Champion, Stamford, 94; Evidence of Memory: Work by Tomie Arai & Lynne Yamamoto, Whitney Mus Am Art; Is it Art? Transgressions in Contemp Art, Katonah Mus, NY; (dis)Oriented: Shifting Identities of Asian Women in Am, Steinbaum Krauss Gallery, NY, 95; Cult Economies: Histories from the Alternative Arts Movement-New York City Drawing Ctr, 96; Precious Objects, Painted Bride Gallery, Philadelphia, Pa, 97; Transferring Cult, LaMama La Galleria, NY, 97; Eye of the Beholder: Photographs From the Avon Collection, Int Ctr Photog, NY, 97; Album: 30 Years at the Lower East Side Printshop, W Chelsea Arts Bldg, NY, 98; Solo shows, Double Happiness, Bronx Mus Arts, NY, 98, Momotaro/Peach Boy, Asian Pacific Am Studies Inst, NY Univ, 98, Tomie Arai/New Work, Cheryl Mcginnis Gallery, NY, 99 & Selected Work, Galeria Otra Vez, Self-Help Graphics & Art, Los Angeles, 2000; Les Reves: Tomie Arai, Nashormeh Lindo, Bomani Gallery, San Francisco, 99; Familiarity, Bronx River Art Ctr and Gallery, NY, 99; Recent Acquisitions from the Permanent Collections, The Bronx Mus Arts, 99; LAtitutudes: A Collaborative Installation, Self Help Graphics and Arts, Los Angeles, 2000; Good Art is the Best Business, Bronx Mus Arts, 2000; A Plurality of Truths, Schick Gallery, Skidmore Col, NY, 2000; Fifteen Asian Am Artists, Staller Arts Ctr, Stonybrook Univ, NY, 2001; Faces Seen, Hearts Unknown, Snite Mus Art, IN, 2007; Treasures from the Library of Congress, Wash DC, 2008; Out of the Incubator, Islip Mus, NY, 2009. *Pos:* Artist in residence art, NY Found Arts, 92-93, Asian Pacific Am Studies Program, NY, 98-99; artist/instr murals, Sites for Students Prog, NY Sch Construction Authority, 94-95; bd dir, Printed Matter Inc, 93-; pres, bd trustees, Chinatown Hist Mus, 94-; cur, Mus

Chinese Ams, NY, 98-99; residency, Artists & Communities, Am Creates for the Millennium Artist Residency, 99-2000; Longwood Cyber residency, Bronx Coun Arts, 2000; advisor, artist adv com, NY Found Arts, 97-2001; Guest Speaker, Whitney Mus Am Art, 99; Advisory Panel for SmART Power, US Dept of State's Bureau of Educational & Cultural Affairs Int Residency Program, 2011. *Teaching:* teaching artist residency, Lower East Side Tenement Mus, 2006; artist residency, Mid Atlantic Arts Found, Asian Arts Initiative, Philadelphia, Pa, 2006. *Awards:* New York Found Arts Fel in Printmaking, 91 & 95; Nat Endowment Arts Visual Arts Fel for Works on Paper, 93-94; Anonymous Was a Woman Award, 97; Phoenix award, New York Asian Women's Ctr, NY, 98; Women's Studio Workshop 21 for 25 Visual Arts Grant, 99; Urban Artists Initiative Grant, 2007; Asian Arts Alliance Honoree, 2009. *Bibliog:* Lucy Lippard (auth), Mixed blessings, Pantheon Bks, 90; Kerri Sakamoto (auth), Tomie Arai: Face to face encounters, Alternative Mus, 92; Margo Machida (auth), New feminist criticism: Art identity action, Harper Collins, 94; The Power of Feminist Art, Harry N Abrams Inc, 94; Screenprinting: Water Based Techniques, Watson-Guptill Publ, 94; Edward Wong (auth), Walls stop talking: Political murals are vanishing, The New York Times, 11/26/99; James Prigoff & Robin Dunitz (auths), Walls of Heritage/Walls of Pride African American Murals, Pomegranate Communications, Inc, 2000; Across the color lines, Amerasia Jour, Vol 6, No 3, 2000/2001; Andrea Frohne, Commemorating the Africanburial ground in New York City: Spirituality of space in contemporary art works, Ijele: Art e-Jour of the African World, vol 1,1, 2000; Rebecca Brown and Deborah Hutton (auths), Blackwell's Companion to Asian Art and Architecture, Wiley Blackwell Pub, 2011. *Mem:* Joan Mitchell Found (bd dirs); Women's Studio Workshop (bd dirs); Center for Book Arts; Asian Arts Alliance; Diasporic Asian Art Network. *Media:* All Media. *Interests:* public art, community art. *Publ:* Illusr, Sachiko Means Happiness, Children's Book Press, 92; China's Bravest Girl, Children's Book Press, 93; The NuyorAsian Anthology, Asian American Writings About New York City, 99; Foodculture: Tasting Identities and Geographies in Art, XYZ Books, Toronto, 2000. *Mailing Add:* 245 W 107th St Apt 12H New York NY 10025

ARAKAWA, EI
SCULPTOR, DIRECTOR
b Iwaka, Japan, 1977. *Study:* Sch Vis Arts, New York, BFA, 2004; Whitney Mus Am Art Independent Study Prog, New York, 2005-06; Bard Coll, Annandale-on-Hudson, NY, MFA, 2006. *Exhib:* Solo exhibs include Front Room Contemp Art Mus, St Louis, 2008; two-person exhibs include Continuous Proj 8, Ctr Nat L'estampe et L'art Imprimé, Paris/Chatou, France, (with Simon Baier), 2006; group exhibs include Diversity + Self-Identity, Vis Arts Gallery, New York, 2004; Succeeding Where Hippies Failed, LeRoy Neiman Gallery, Columbia Univ, New York, 2004; Whitney Independent Study Studio Prog Exhib, Chelsea Art Mus, New York, 2006; Various Small Fires, Royal Coll Art, London, 2007; Performa07, Japan Soci Lobby, New York, 2007; Schattenspiel/Shadow Play (I), Studio Sassa Trülzsch, Berlin, 2008; Egypted, Kunsthalle Exnergasse, Vienna, Austria, 2008. *Awards:* Hon Mention, Galleria Civica di Arte Contemp, Trento, Italy, 2007; Altoids Award, Altioids & New Mus, 2008; New York Found Arts Fel, 2009. *Mailing Add:* Reena Spaulings Fine Art 165 E Broadway New York NY 10002

ARALUCE, RICK
SCULPTOR
Exhib: The Mens' Show, Michael Ivy Gallery, Los Angeles, 1987; solo exhibs, Onyx Sequel, Los Angeles, 1988, La Luz de Jesus, Los Angeles, 1991-93, 98,, Rachelle Lozzi Gallery, 1993, Orange County Ctr for Contemp Art, Santa Ana, 1994, Louis Newman Gallery, Los Angeles, 1994, Horwich/Newman Gallery, Scottsdale, 1995, William Traver Gallery, Seattle, 1996, 2000, 2002-03, 2005, 2007, 2009, Ok Harris, New York, 2004, 2006, 2008, Marion Oliver McCaw Hall, Seattle, 2006, Offramp Gallery, Pasadena, 2009, Watson McRae Gallery, Sanibel, Fla, 2009; China: June 4 1989, Los Angeles Contemp Exhibs, 1990; California Perspetives, Mod Mus Art, Santa Ana, Calif, 1991; Dark Suburban Fantasies, Art Inst Southern Calif, Laguna Beach, 1993; Assemblages, William Traver Gallery, Seattle, 2000; The Box Show, Mark Woolley Gallery, Portland, Ore, 2002; Actor! Actor!, Palo Alto Art Ctr, Calif, 2007; 9th Northwest Biennial, Tacoma Art Mus, 2009. *Awards:* Seattle City Artist Projects Grant, 2006; Artist Trust Gap Award, 2008; Pollock-Krasner Found Grant, 2008; Adolph & Esther Gottlieb Award, 2009; People's Choice Award, 9th Northwest Biennial, Tacoma Art Mus, 2009. *Bibliog:* Tom McTaggart (auth), Paranoid Dollhouse, The Stranger, 9/19/1996; Regina Hackett (auth), Doug Jeck and Assemblages, The Seattle Post Intelligencer, 4/14/2000; Michael S Gant (auth), Floater, San Jose Metro, 3/7/2007; Adriana Grant (auth), A Study in Small, The Seattle Weekly, 10/15/2008. *Mailing Add:* c/o Traver Gallery 110 Union St #200 Seattle WA 98101

ARAM, KAMROOZ
PAINTER
b Shiraz, Iran, 1978. *Study:* Md Inst, Coll Art, Baltimore, BFA; Columbia Univ, MFA, 2003. *Exhib:* Solo exhibs, Beyond the Borders, Between the Trees, Oliver Kamm/5BE Gallery, NY, 2004 & Night Visions & Revolutionary Dreams, 2007, Realms & Reveries, Mass Mus Contemp Art, North Adams, Mass, 2006, Lightning, Thunder, Brimstone & Fire, Wilkinson Gallery, London, 2006; Group exhibs, Mirror of the Invisible, Robert V Fullerton Art Mus, San Bernardino, Calif, 2000; November, H Lewis Gallery, Baltimore, 2000; Calligraphic Legacy, Transamerica Bldg Lobby, San Francisco, 2001; Multitude, Artists Space, NY, 2002; Process/ion, Columbia Univ, NY, 2002, The Broken Mirror, 2003; Studebaker Bldg, NY, 2003; Prague Biennale I, 2003; Oliver Kamm/5BE Gallery, NY, 2003, KA/VH:RA/AG, 2005, Bricks in the Hood, 2006; Greater New York, PS1, NY, 2005; The Common Room, Wilkinson Gallery, London, 2005; The Most Splendid Apocalypse, PPOW Gallery, NY, 2005; Time's Arrow, Rotunda, Brooklyn, NY, 2005; Contemp Art Exhib, Busan, Korea, 2006; A Tale of Two Cities, Busan Biennale, Korea, 2006; Cosmologies, James Cohan Gallery, NY, 2007. *Dealer:* Perry Rubenstein Gallery 527 W 23rd St New York, NY 10011

ARANGO, PLACIDO G, JR
COLLECTOR
Study: Tufts Univ, MA. *Pos:* Pres, Grupo Vips, Madrid, Sigla, SA, Arango Group; bd trustees, Tufts Univ, 1987-96. *Awards:* Named one of 200 Top Collectors, ARTnews mag, 2004-12. *Collection:* Old Masters, primitive Spanish paintings, modern and contemporary art, Chinese ceramics. *Mailing Add:* Sigla, SA Calle Edison 4 Madrid Spain 28036

ARBEITER, JOAN
ARTIST, EDUCATOR
Study: CUNY, BA, 1959; Pratt Inst, MFA, 1982. *Work:* Noyes Mus, Oceanville, MS Found, NYC, Fairmount Chem, Newark, CSR Group Archs and Builders-Leon Cohen, Nutley, NJ, JFK Med Ctr, Edison, NJ, 1st Presbyn Church, Metuchen, NJ, Rutgers Inst for Health, New Brunswick, NJ. *Exhib:* Solo shows include Ceres Gallery, NYC, 1985, 1987, 1989, 1993, 1997, 2000, 2001, Columbia Univ, 1986, Stony Brook-Millstone Watershead Assn Gallery, Pennington, NJ, 1991, Wagner Coll, SI, NY, 1992, Douglas Coll Ctr, New Brunswick, NJ, 1992, 1996, Union County Coll, Cranford, NJ, 1999, Elizabeth Found, NYC, 2001, Cedar Crest Coll, Allentown, Pa, 2004, Du Cret Sch, Plainfield, NJ, 2006, Rutgers Univ Art Libr, 2008, Raconteur, Metuchen, NJ, 2009, Drake House Mus, Plainfield, NJ, 2010; Group shows include Ramapo Coll, Mahwah, NJ, 1980, Brookdale Coll, Lincroft, NJ, 1980, Westbeth Gallery, NYC, 1980, Douglas Coll Libr, NB, NJ, 1982, 1999, Douglas Coll Ctr, NB, 2009, Ceres Gallery, 1983-2013, NY Feminist Art Inst, NYC, 1985, 1988, Ednl Testing Svc, Princeton, NJ, 1986, Appalachian State U, Boone, NC, 1989, Soho 20 Gallery, NYC, 1990, 1998, Noyes Mus, Oceanville, NJ, 1995, 1998, 2005, 2008, Krasdale Corp Gallery, Bronx, NY, 1995, 2006, Monmouth Mus, Lincroft, 1996, Kingsbourgh CC, Bklyn, 1999, Kunstler Forum, Bonn, Germany, 1999, EPA, Washington, 2001-02, Solaris Gallery, Califon, NJ, 2004, Pratt Inst, Bklyn., 2006, Woman Made Gallery, Chgo., 2006, 2011, Univ Wisc, Madison, 2007, Long Beach Island Arts Found, NJ, 2007, South Brunswick Municipal Galleries, 2008, 2009, 2011, 2013, Int House, Phila, 2011, 2012, AIR Gallery, NYC, 2007, 2010, Tuckerton, NJ, 2007, 2009, St Francis Coll, Bklyn, Auburn Univ, St Francis, Montgomery, Ala, 2011, Fairleigh Dickinson Univ, Teaneck, NJ, 2010, Arts Guild, Rahway, NJ, 2010, Suffolk Cmty Coll, Brentwood, NY, 2010, Alexander Libr, Rutgers Univ, New Brunswick, NJ, 2009-10, Holy Family, Phila, 2009, Boricua Coll, NYC, 2012, Sandy Spring Mus, MD, 2012, Riverside Libr, NYC, 2013, Mongomery Guild Prof Art, 2013, Hadas Gallery, Brooklyn, NY, 2013. *Pos:* Juror various art orgns, NJ, 1981-; cons Ednl Testing Svc, Princeton, NJ, 1988; curator travelling art exhibit Age As a Work of Art, Plainfield, Boston, NYC, 1985-86, Lives and Works, NYC, 2000; presenter paper, slides Coll Art Assn Conf, San Antonio, 1995, NYC, 2003; presenter, moderator Nat Mus Women in Arts, Wash, 1997, Artists Talk on Art, NYC, 1997, 2000, 2005, Sackler Ctr, Brooklyn Mus Art, 2008; lectr art appreciation South Brunswick Libr, 2006-07, Gt Neck Pub Libr, 2008, Metuchen Pub Libr, 2009. *Teaching:* Lic art tchr NY, NJ Tchr, NYC Sch Sys Bd Edn, 1959-63; dir Joan Arbeiter Studio Sch, Metuchen, NJ, 1976-90; instr art, coord founds Ducret Sch Art, Plainfield, NJ, 1978-, instr color and design, 1978-2006, instr art history, 1981-2001, instr art appreciation, 1983-; workshop instr, NJ Teen Arts Festival, 1998-2003; artist in residence NJ Sch Arts, 1995-2002. *Awards:* 1st Place Mixed Media, Westfield Art Assn, 1978; 1st Place All Media award, Metuchen Cultural Arts Commn Art Exhib, 1988; Best in Show award, Middlesex County Mus, New Brunswick, NJ, 1989; AIA award, Hunterdon Arts Ctr, NJ, 1996; People's Choice award, Watchung Arts Ctr, NJ, 1998; Excellence award, Manhattan Arts Mag, 2000, 2007; Elan award for Mentoring Women's Studio Ctr, 2004; grantee, Vt Studio Colony, 1987. *Mem:* Varo Registry, Art Table, Women's Caucus Art, Coll Art Assn, Alpha Beta Kappa. *Publ:* co-author: Lives & Works Talks With Women Artist Vol 2, 1996, 1999. *Mailing Add:* 41 Victory Ct Metuchen NJ 08840

ARBITMAN, KAHREN JONES
DIRECTOR, HISTORIAN
b Pittsburgh, Pa, May 16, 1948. *Study:* Penn State Univ, BA, 69; Univ Pittsburgh, MA, 71; PhD, 80. *Collection Arranged:* Rembrandt Etchings from the Charles J Rosenbloom Collection, 83; Pre-Rembrandt Etchers from the Boymans-van Beuningen Mus, 85; An Englishman Abroad: Watercolors of Edward Lear, 86; Gardens of Earthly Delight: 16th and 17th Century Netherlandish Gardens, 86; At Home in Pittsburgh: Art and Furnishings of Henry Clay Frick, 88; Rembrandt Etchings from Carnegie Mus Art, 94; Rembrandt Redux: Paintings of Ken Aptekar, 94; Etchings of Leonard Leibowitz, 94. *Pos:* Cur, Frick Art Mus, 85-89; dir, Palmer Mus Art, Pa State, 90-95 & Cummer Mus Art & Gardens, Jacksonville, Fla, 96-. *Teaching:* Asst prof art history, West Va Univ, Morgantown, 84-5; adj assoc prof art history, Univ Pittsburgh, 85-; vis prof art history, Carnegie Mellon Univ, Pittsburgh, 89-90. *Mem:* Historians of Netherlandish Art (board of dir, 85-88, Pres, 91-93); Am Asn Netherlandish Studies; Am Asn Mus; Coll Art Asn. *Res:* 16th and 17th century Netherlandish Art and Iconography. *Publ:* Auth, From These Slopes & Flats: The Paintings of Lee Dittley, PA Council on Humanities, 76; contribr, Landscape Painting in Rome, 1595-1675, Richard Feigen & Co, 85; co-auth, Pre-Rembrandt Etchers (illustrated Bartsch Vol 53) Abaris Books, 85; auth, Gardens of Earthly Delight; co-auth, Clayton, The Pittsburgh Home of Henry Clay Frick, Univ Pittsburgh Press, 88. *Mailing Add:* 829 Riverside Ave Jacksonville FL 32204

ARBUCKLE, LINDA J
CERAMIST, EDUCATOR
b Cleveland, Ohio, Nov 16, 1950. *Study:* Cleveland Inst Art, BFA, 81; RI Sch Design, MFA, 83. *Work:* Detroit Inst Art; Stetson Univ; Arrowmont Sch Arts & Crafts; Lamar Dodd Art Ctr; Weisman Mus, Univ Minn; Charles A Wustrum Mus Fine Arts, Racine, Wis; Nations Bank Corporate Hq, Charlotte, NC; Archie Bray Found; Mus Decorative Arts, Ark Art Ctr, Little Rock; Racine Art Mus, Racine, Wis; City of Orlando, Orlando, Fla; var pvt collection incl Caroline & Dan Anderson, Edwardsville, Iowa &

David Demming, Pres, Cleveland Inst Art, Cleveland, Ohio; Jingdezhen Cermaics Mus, Jingdezhen, China; Margaret Harlow Collection, Bemidji Univ, Minn; Rudy Turk Cup Collection, Ariz State Univ Art Mus, Tempe; Stetson Univ, Deland, Fla; World Ceramics Exposition Korea Int Collection, Inchon. *Exhib:* A Tea Party, Nat Mus Ceramic Art, Baltimore, 93; Nat Coun Educ Ceramic Art Clay Nat, Frederick R Weisman Mus, Minneapolis, 95; 4th Ann Strictly Functional Pottery Nat, Market House, Ephrata, Pa, 96; Clay Cup V, Univ Mus, Southern Ill Univ, Carbondale, 96; Madcap Teaparty, Renwick Gallery, Nat Mus Am Art, Washington, 96; Robert Archambeau: Artist, Teacher and Collector, Winnipeg, Manitoba, Canada, 2003; Art to Use: Functional Clay, Thirteen Moons Gallery, Santa Fe, NM, 2004; From Hands to Lips, Canadian Clay and Glass Gallery, Waterloo, ON, Canada, 2004; The Informed Surface, Baltimore Clayworks, Md, 2005; Am Masters Invitational, Santa Fe Clay, NMex, 2005; Contemp Functional Ceramics: Transcending Utilitarian Concerns, Fort Wayne Mus Art, Ill, 2005; Treasure Hunt: Teapots, Racine Art Mus, Wustrum Campus, Racine, Wis, 2006; Cup, the Intimate Object V, Charlie Cummings Gallery, 2006; Ala Clay Conf Exhib, Univ of Northern Ala, Florence, Ala, 2007; Hand Held Drinking Vessels, Main St Art Gallery, Edwardsville, Ill, 2007; Simple Cup Invitational, KOBO Gallery, Seattle, Wash, 2007; Ahead of the Need, Clay West, Red Lodge, Mont, 2008; Contemp Clay Biennial, The Art Ctr, Western Colo Ctr for the Arts, Grand Junction, 2008; Shared Journeys: American Art in China, Jingdezhen, China, 2008; Am Pottery Festival, Northern Clay Ctr, Minneapolis, Minn, 2011; Cup: The Intimate Object, Charlie Cummings Gallery, 2011; For Tea, Dubhe Carreno Gallery, Chicago, Ill, 2011. *Pos:* juror, Gulf State Coll, Fla, 2011; advisory bd mem, Ceramics Monthy, Studio Potter, Ceramics: Art & Perception, Baltimore Clayworks. *Teaching:* Asst prof ceramics, La State Univ, Baton Rouge, 85-90; asst prof, Univ Fla, 93-96, assoc prof ceramics, 96-2002, prof 2002-; vis prof & res fel, Univ Wales Inst Cardiff, fall 2000; instr lectures, La Grange Coll, LaGrange, Ga, Ceramic League of Dallas, Tex, Northern Clay Ctr, Minneapolis, Mn, C and R Ceramics, Ocala, Fla, 2011. *Awards:* Individual Artist Fel, State of Fla, 92; Nat Endowment Arts Fel, 94; Skutt Award, 95; Cups of Merit Award, NCECA, 2004; Doctoral Dissertation Advisor/Mentor Award, Univ Fla, 2008; NCECA Lifetime Honors, Svc to Field, 2010. *Bibliog:* Best of Pottery, Rockport Publ, 96; Mathias Ostermann (auth), The New Majolica: Contemporary Approaches to Color & Technique, Tinglaze, A&C Black, London. 2000; Kevin Hluch (auth), Beautiful Use, 2001; Matthias Osterman (auth, Ceramic Surface Decoration: Contemporary Approaches and Techniques, A & C Black, London, Univ Pa Press, Philadelphia, 2002; Robin Hopper (auth), Making Marks: Discovering the Ceramic Surface, Krause Publ, Iola, WI, 2004; 500 Cups, Lark Boosk, Asheville, NC, 2005; 500 Pitchers, Lark Books, Asheville, NC, 2006; Harn Mus, Univ Fla, Gainsville, Fla, 2006; Studio Potter Mag, 2006; Portcard from Penland; An Introduction to Penland Sch Crafts, DVD, Work pictured, 2007; 500 Plates, Platters, & Chargers, Lark Books, Asheville, NC, 2008; Maureen Mills (auth), Surface Design for Ceramics, Lark Books, Asheville, NC, 2008; China Ceramic Artist, Beijing, 2008; Nat Coun on Educ Ceramic Arts Journ, 2008; Susan & Jan Peterson, Working with Clay, Pearson Educ, Prentice Hall, Inc, Upper Saddle River, NJ, 2009; La ceramica in italia e nel mondo, 2010; Masters: Earthenware: Major Works by Leading Artists, Lark Boosk, 2010; Angelica Pozo (auth), Ceramics for Beginners: Surfaces, Glazes & Firing, Lark Books, 2010; Craig Adcock (auth), Linda Arbuckle, Clary Illian, Doug Hanson, and Chuck Hindes, pp 58-9, Ceramics Art and Perception, 2011; Jake Allee (auth), Messing with Majolica, Vol 14, No 3, pp 40-42, Pottery Making Illustrated, 2011; Caroline Cheng (auth), The Pottery Workshop: 25 Years (pictured, cited), p. 13, 2011; and many others. *Mem:* Nat Coun Educ Ceramic Arts; Am Crafts Coun; Clayart; Fla Craftsmen; Am Coun Arts; Int Acad Ceramics, Geneva, Switz. *Media:* Ceramics, Majolica Glaze on Terracotta. *Specialty:* ceramics. *Publ:* Contribr, The dynamics of useful objects, Ceramics Monthly, Vol 41, No 1, 93; ed, Majolica: Essays, Studio Potter Mag, Vol 24, No 2, 96; contrib, Creative Pottery, Rockport Publ, 98; contribr, 500 Cups, 107 & 194, Lark Bks, 2005; contribr, Learning to use color, Studio Potter Mag, Vol 35, No 1, 58-59, images of work, 4-5, 59, 60, 61 & 88, 2006; illus, Glen R Brown (auth), Teaching Ceramic History, Ceramics Technical, No 23, 41, 2006; contribr, 2 works incl, Maureen Mills (auth), Surface Design for Ceramics, Lark Bks, Asheville, NC, 2008; auth, The Colorful World of Majolica, Vol 59, No 6, pp 56-9, Ceramics Monthly, 2011. *Dealer:* Sante Fe Clay Santa Fe NM; Northern Clay Ctr Minneapolis Mn. *Mailing Add:* 14716 SE 9th Terrace Micanopy FL 32667-5276

ARCANGEL, CORY
GRAPHIC ARTIST
Study: Oberlin Col, BA in Technol in Music & Related Arts. *Work:* Am Mus Moving Image, NY, Royal Acad, London, Guggenheim, New Mus Contemp Art, Mus Modern Art, NY, Lothringer 13, Make-World Festival, Munich, Migros Mus, Zurich, 2004, exhib in group shows at Whitney Biennial Am Art, Whitney Mus Am Art, 2004. *Exhib:* Cur (distrib on floppy disk, group shows) 1.44 Megs, with Moving Image Gallery & Rhizome.org, (web exhib) Low Level All Stars, Kingdom of Piracy; exhibs incl, NY Underground Film Festival, Fassbender Gallery, Chicago, Deadtech Gallery, Chicago, Foxy Production, Eye Beam, Lothringer 13, Make-World Festival, Munich, Leroy Neiman Gallery, Columbia Univ, 2004; exhibs incl, Deitch Projs, 2005. *Pos:* Founding mem, BIEGE Program Ensemble, The 8-bit Construct Set. *Awards:* Grantee, turbulence.org, NY State Coun Arts. *Media:* All Media. *Mailing Add:* c/o Team Gallery 83 Grand St New York NY 10013

ARCENEAUX, EDGAR
INSTALLATION SCULPTOR
b Los Angeles, 1972. *Study:* Art Ctr Coll Design, Pasadena, Calif, BFA, 1996; Project Row Houses, Houston, 1998; Banff Ctr Arts, Atla, Can, 1998; Skowhegan Sch Painting, Maine, 1999; Fachhochschule Aachen, Ger, 2000-01; Calif Inst Arts, MFA, 2001. *Work:* Mus am Ostwall, Dortmund, Ger; New York Pub Libr; San Francisco Mus Mod Art, San Francisco; Univ Calif Los Angeles Armand Hammer Mus, Westwood, Calif; Los Angeles County Mus Art; Walker Art Ctr, Minneapolis; Mus Contemp Art, La Jolla, Calif; Carnegie Mus Art, Pittsburgh, Pa. *Exhib:* Solo exhibs, Remnants Project, Armory Ctr Arts, Pasadena, Calif, 1998, The Project, New York, 1999, The Trivium, Pomona Coll, Calif, 2001 & Gallery Kamm, Berlin, 2002, Drawings of Removal, Studio Mus Harlem, New York, 2002 & Univ Calif Los Angeles Hammer Mus, 2003, Rootlessness, Susanne Vilemetter Los Angeles Projects, 2002, 107th St, Watts, Revolver Verlag, Frankfurt, 2003, Library as Chaos, Frehrking Wiesehoefer, Ger, 2003, Library as Cosmos, Kunstverein Ulm, Ger, 2003, An Arrangement Without Tormentors, Witte de With Mus, Rotterdam, 2004 & Mus Contemp Art, Austria, 2006, Negative Capability, Galerie Kamm, Berlin, 2004, Borrowed Sun, Susanne Vilemetter Los Angeles Projects, 2004, San Francisco Mus Contemp Art, 2005 & The Kitchen, New York, 2005, Kunstwerke Mus, Berlin, 2005, Adamski Gallery Contemp Art, Aachen, Ger, 2005, Alchemy of Comedy, Gallery 400, Chicago, 2005, Alchemy of Comedy...Stupid, ArtPace, San Antonio, 2006 & Susanne Vielmetter Los Angeles Projects, 2006, Snake River, REDCAT Gallery, Los Angeles, 2006, The Agitation of Expansion, Galerie Kamm, Berlin, 2007 & Contemp Art Ctr Va, 2008, Miracles and Jokes, Circle Disk Rotation and 22 Lost Signs of the Zodiac, Mus. Contemporary Art Detroit, 2011, Blind Pig City, Praz-Delavallade, 2011, Hopelessness Freezes Time 1967 Detroit Riots, Detroit Techno and Michael Heizner's Dragged Mass, Mus. fur Gegenwartskunst, 2011, and many others; Group exhibs, 9 Hours at Bliss, Bliss Gallery, Pasadena, Calif, 1996; Fantasy, Desire & Memory, Porter Troupe Gallery, San Diego, 1997, Sitegeist, 2000; Kwangju Biannale, Kwangju, Korea, 1997; Uncommon Sense, Mus Contemp Art Geffen Contemp, Los Angeles, 1997; Ann exhib, Los Angeles Contemp Exhibs, 1997; Round 9, Project Row Houses, Houston, 1998; Triangle of Nice, Book of Lies, Vol II, Los Angeles & Fullerton, Calif, 1998; Warming, The Project, New York, 1998; I, Me, Mine, Luckman Fine Arts Gallery, Los Angeles, 1999, Fade, 2004; Permanent Collection of 1999, San Diego Mus Contemp Art, 1999, Lateral Thinking, 2002; Spaceship Earth, Art in General, New York, 1999; Paradise 8, Exit Art, New York, 1999; Veni, Vidi, Video, Kunstfaktor, Berlin, 2000; Pierogi Flat Files, Post Gallery, Los Angeles, 2000; Hers, Video as Female Terrain, Landesmuseum Joanneum, Graz, Austria, 2000; Rappers Delight, Yerba Buena Ctr Arts, San Francisco, 2001; Superman in Bed, Museum Am Ostwall, Dortmund, Ger, 2001; Prosthetics, Camouflage & War, Adamski Frehrking Wiesehoefer Gallery, Koln, Ger, 2001; Profiler, Kunstlerhaus Bethanien, Berlin, 2001; One Planet Under a Groove, Bronx Mus, New York, 2001; Unjustified, Apex Art, New York, 2002; Prophets of Boom, Kunsthalle Baden Baden, Ger, 2002; Mass Appeal: The Art Object and Hip Hop Culture, Gallery 101, Ottawa, Can, 2002; Persoenliche Plaene, Kunsthalle Basel, Ger, 2002; Urban Aesthetics, African Am Mus Art, Los Angeles, 2003; 5th Ann Altoids Curiously Strong Collection, traveling, 2003; Social Strategies: Redefining Social Realism, Univ Art Mus Santa Barbara, Calif, 2003; True Stories, Witte de With Mus, Rotterdam, 2003; Summer of 2003, Galerie Paul Andriesse, Amsterdam, 2003; Korrekturen, Galerie Kamm, Berlin, 2003; The Michael Jackson Project, Susanne Vielmetter Los Angeles Projects, 2004, Cut, 2006; Remembering, Sweeny Art Gallery, Univ Calif Riverside, 2004; Upside Down, Ludwigforum Aachen, Ger, 2004; Art and the Afterall Effect, PlaySpace, Calif Coll Arts, San Francisco, 2004; Double Consciousness, Contemp Arts Mus, Houston, 2005; Monuments for the USA, CCA Wattis Inst Contemp Arts, San Francisco, 2005; Mixed Doubles, Forum Gallery, Carnegie Mus Art, 2005; The Imaginary Number, KW Inst Contemp Art, Berlin, 2005; Uncertain States of America, Astrup Fearnley Mus Art, Oslo, 2005; Philosophy of Time Travel, Studio Mus Harlem, New York, 2006; Symmetry, MAK Ctr Art & Archit, Schindler House, Los Angeles, 2006; Tomorrowland, Mus Mod Art, New York, 2006; Materialization of Sensibility, Leslie Tonkonow Artworks + Projects, New York, 2006; Whitney Biennial, Whitney Mus Am Art, New York, 2008; California Biennial, Orange County Mus. Art, 2008; The Artist's Museum: Los Angeles Artists 1980-2010, Mus. Contemporary Art, Los Angeles, 2010; Bearden Project, Studio Mus, NY, 2011; Making Time, Mus. Contemporary Art Sydney, 2012; Pairings, The Collection at 50, Orange County Mus. Art, 2012; my.LA, Sammlung-Haubrok, Berlin, 2012; and many others. *Awards:* Creative Capital Grant, 2005; Joyce Award, 2005; William H Johnson Prize, 2006; Broad Fel, US Artists, 2007; REDCAT award, Roy and Edna Disney/CalArts Theater, 2012

ARCHBOLD, ANN M
EDUCATOR, ADMINISTRATOR
Study: Univ Mich, BGS; San Diego State Univ, MFA (design and technical production). *Teaching:* Assoc prof, chair, Dept Theatre and Drama, Univ Wisconsin-Madison, currently, head MFA program in lighting design, currently. *Mailing Add:* University of Wisconsin Theatre and Drama 6008 Vilas Communication Hall 821 University Ave Madison WI 53706

ARCHER, CYNTHIA
PRINTMAKER, PAINTER
b New Martinsville, WVa, Mar 28, 1953. *Study:* Goucher Col, BA, 75; WVa Univ, MFA, 78. *Work:* Nat Art Gallery, Wellington, New Zealand; Portland Art Mus, Ore; Ill State Mus, Springfield; MacDonald's Corp Hq, Oakbrook, Ill; Danforth Mus, Framingham, Mass; Block Gallery, Northwestern Univ; Benedictine Univ; and others. *Comn:* Chicago Pub Libr, Westlawn Br; Color Lithograph Editions, Lakeside Studio, Lakeside, Mich; edition of hand-painted ceramic plates, Jane Meyer Fine Art, Elburn, Ill, 92; 3D art bench, The Chicago Children's Mus; stained glass window design, Wheller Hall, Southern Ill Univ, Carbondale. *Exhib:* Solo exhibs, Malton Gallery, Cincinnati, Ohio, 87 & 90 & Marcus Gordon Gallery, Pittsburgh, 91; Provenance Inc, Chicago & Kenilworth, Ill, 91-92; New Acquisitions, Coll Lake Co, Grayslake, Ill, 92; Open Spectrum, David Adler Cult Ctr, Libertyville, Ill, 92; Art in Mythology, Wood St Gallery, Chicago, 94; Jane Meyer Fine Art, 05; and others. *Pos:* Workshop S, Lakeside Studios, Mich, 77-79; workshops, Shepherd Col, Shepherdstown, WVa, 78; master lithographer, Plucked Chicken Press, Evanston, Ill, 84-96; vis artist, Southern Ill Univ, Edwardsville, Ill, 84 & Univ Nevada, Reno, 87; artist-in-residence, Benedictine Univ, Lisle, Ill, 96, 2006. *Teaching:* Forum in printmaking, Bradley Univ, Peoria, Ill, 87; lithography class, Benedictine Univ, Lisle Ill, 2007. *Awards:*

Governor's Award, WVa Exhib, Charleston, 79; Merit Award, 6th Baer Art Competition, Beverly Art Ctr, Chicago, 82; Pres Purchase Award, Bradley Univ, 87. *Media:* Lithography; Acrylic. *Dealer:* Jane Meyer Fine Arts 3 N 692 Highpoint Elburn IL 60119; Jane Meyer Fine Arts 205 1/2 State St Geneva Il. *Mailing Add:* 1604 Greenleaf Evanston IL 60202-1159

ARCILESI, VINCENT J
PAINTER, DRAFTSMAN
b St Louis, Mo, May 5, 1932. *Study:* Furman Univ, 49-50; Univ Okla, BFA (design), 53; Art Inst Chicago, BFA (painting), 56, MFA, 61. *Work:* Art Inst Chicago Mus; Ill State Mus, Springfield; Fashion Inst Technol, NY; Hirshhorn Mus, Washington, DC; Mus Contemp Art, Chicago; plus pvt collections. *Exhib:* 70th Ann, Art Inst Chicago, 67; Visions/Painting & Sculpture, Distinguished Alumni 1945-Present, Art Inst Chicago Gallery, 76; America 1976 Traveling Exhib, Corcoran Gallery, 76-78; New Art, FIT Galleries, NY, 90; Vincent Arcilesi & Don Perlis, Garrison Art Ctr, NY, 91; Contemp Realism, Farrington-Keith Creative Arts Ctr, Dexter, Mich, 92; Triplex Gallery, Borough of Manhattan City Col, NY, 94; Galleries at FIT, NY, 93-98, 2001-2004 & 08; Ox-Bow Spring Benefit, Sch Art Inst Chicago, 98; The City, Feldman Ctr Gallery, FIT, 98; 5th Ann Small Works Invitational, Blue Mountain Gallery, NY, 98, 2000, 2001, 2002, 2004, 2007; Media Madness, Westbeth Gallery, NY, 98; Small Works, Wall-to-Wall at Gallery 402, Org Ind Artists, 99; The 4th Ann Loft Pioneer Show, The Puffin Room, NY, 99; Holiday Invitational Exhib (yearly exhib), Broome St Gallery, 99-2008; Y2K - Aotic: Uncensored All-Media Salon Show, Org Ind Artists, 2000; Artists of the Ideal, Mus Modern & Contemp Art, Palazzo Forti, Verona, Ital, 2002; Whitney Biennial, Whitney Mus Art, NY, 2006; Figurative Phases, Walter Wickiser Gallery, NY, 2003; Watercurrents 2006: The Figure, Lori Bookstein Fine Art, NY, 2006; People, Jim Kempnar Fine Art, 2008; Musing AHA Arcilesi Homberg Fine Art, 2011, 2012, 2013 & 2014; Scope Art Fair, NY, AHA Arcilesi Homberg Fine Art, NY, 2013, FIT Facility, Albany State Mus, NY; Scope Art Fair, Miami/Basel, AHA Arcilesi Homberg Fine Art, NY, 2014; Solo shows: Noho Gallery, NY, 81, 85 & 88; Z Gallery, NY, 91; 148 Gallery, NYart, 93,; Broome St Gallery, NY, 95, 97, 99, 2010; AHA Arcilesi Homberg Fine Art, NY, 2013, & 2015; paintings; Carmichael & Carmichael Fine Art, St Paul, Minn, 95; Garden City, NY, Broome St Gallery, NY, 2001, 2003 & 2005, 2008; 2/20 Gallery, NY, 96, 2000, 2002, 2004 & 2006. *Teaching:* Asst prof art, Fashion Inst Tech, NY, 74-95, assoc prof, 95-99, prof fine art, 99-2015. *Awards:* American 1976 Grant, US Dept Interior, Washington, 74-75; Creative Artists Pub Serv Prog Fel, 81-82; Nat Endowment Arts Grant, 82. *Bibliog:* Pat Van Gelder (auth), Vincent Arcilesi, Am Artist, 10/83; John Arthur (auth), Spirit of Place, Contemporary Landscape Painting & the American Tradition, Bulfinch Press, Little Brown & Co, 89; Edward Lucie-Smith (auth), American Realism, Harry Abrams, 94; Edward Lucie-Smith (auth), Artist of the Ideal, Palazzo Forti, Verona, Italy, 02. *Mem:* NY Artists' Equity, (bd dir, 86-90 & 2002-2015). *Media:* Oil, Pastel. *Dealer:* AHA Arcilesi Homeberg Fine Art, NY. *Mailing Add:* 116 Duane St New York NY 10007

ARCURI, FRANK
PAINTER
b Brooklyn, NY, 1946. *Study:* Sch Visual Arts, NY; Art Students League, NY. *Exhib:* Solo exhibs at Eleanor Ettinger Gallery, NY, 1997, 1999, 2001, 2003, 2005, 2007, Catto Gallery, London, England, 2000, 2003, Travis Gallery, Pa, 2006; group exhibs include US Artists 97, Philadelphia, 1997; The Figure in American Art, Eleanor Ettinger Gallery, NY, 1998, 2002, New Masters of Realism, 1998, Third Annual Int Summer Salon Exhib, 2000, The Art of Still Life, 2001, Int Winter Salon, 2004, Int Summer Salon, 2004, Int Autumn Salon, 2005, Summer Salon, 2006; 75th Anniversary Retrospective Exhib, Phillip's Mill Gallery, 2005. *Teaching:* Teacher, Art Students Laegue, NY, formerly, Arcuri Atelier, Pa, formerly. *Awards:* Jesse B McReynolds Memorial Award, Salmagundi Gallery, 88; Spec Patrons Award for Painting, Phillip's Mill Gallery, Pa, 89, Renee B McNeely Award for Painting, 94; Larson-Juhl Award for Painting, Bianco Gallery, Pa, 94, Nancy Wiener Award for Painting, 95. *Mailing Add:* c/o Eleaner Ettinger Inc 24 W 57th St Ste 609 New York NY 10019

ARDAY, DONALD K
EDUCATOR, GRAPHIC ARTIST, ILLUSTRATOR
Study: Cleveland Inst Art, BFA, 1978; Syracuse Univ, MFA, 1980. *Exhib:* Solo exhib, Geisel Gallery, Bausch & Lomb World Headquarters. *Pos:* Art dir, Eisenberg Inc, Dallas, 1983-88. *Teaching:* Asst prof, Univ Mo, St Louis, 1980-81, Univ Tex, Arlington, 1981-83, assoc prof, 1988; prof, Sch of Art, Rochester Inst Technol, currently. *Mailing Add:* Rochester Institute of Technology College of Imaging Arts and Sciences 60 Lomb Memorial Dr Rochester NY 14623-5604

ARENDT, MARY See DeLoyht-Arendt, Mary

ARGENT, PHILIP
PAINTER
b Essex, Eng, 1962. *Study:* Cheltenham Sch of Art, Eng, BA, 1985; Univ Idaho, MA, 1990; Univ Las Vegas, MFA, 1994. *Exhib:* Solo exhibs include Post, Los Angeles, 1999, Tate, New York City, 1999, Shoshana Wayne Gallery, Santa Monica, Calif, 2001, 2002, Galerie Jette Rudolph, Berlin, 2002; group exhibs include Level One Gallery, Southend-on-Sea, Essex, Eng, 1991; Donna Beam Fine Art Gallery, Las Vegas, 1994, 1996; Nev State Coun on Arts, Carson City, 1995; Small Works Gallery, Las Vegas, 1998; Under the Influence - New Art from LA, H&R Block Artspace, Kans City, Mo, 2000; Phoenix Triennial, 2001; red: The 7th Ann Valentines Benefit and Exhib, Santa Barbara Contemp Arts Forum, 2003; Stop & Stor, Luxe Gallery, NY City, 2004; Populence, Blaffer Gallery, Houston, 2005, Mus Contemp Art Cleveland, 2005, Southeastern Ctr Contemp Art, Winston-Salem, NC, 2006. *Media:* Acrylic. *Dealer:* Galeria Leyendecker Rambla General Franco 86 Spain 38004

ARGUE, DOUGLAS
PAINTER
b St Paul, Minn, Jan 21, 1962. *Study:* Bemidji State Univ, Minn, 80-82; Univ Minn, 83. *Work:* Walker Art Ctr, Minneapolis; Weismann Art Mus, Minneapolis; Minn Inst Arts, Minneapolis; General Mills; and others. *Comn:* Target Corp; Weisman Art Mus. *Exhib:* Viewpoints: Doug Argue & Jim Lutes, Walker Art Ctr, Minneapolis, 85-86; Bockley Gallery, 87-90; The Persistent Figure, Walker Art Ctr, 90; Katherine Nash Gallery, Univ Minn, 92; McKnight Found Exhib, MCAD Gallery, Minneapolis, Minn, 93; Minneapolis Inst Arts, 94; Minn Hist Soc, 94; Asn Am Artists, New York, 96; Threadwaxing Space, New York, 96; Libr of Babel, Assoc Am Artists, New York, 97; Ann exhib, Am Acad, Rome, Italy, 98; Post Gallery, Los Angeles, 2002; Pepperdine Univ, Malibu, Calif, 2003; Scope LA, Calif, 2004; Gallery Co Minneapolis, 2004; Sherry Leedy Gallery, Kansas City, 2005. *Awards:* McKnight Found Fel, 92; Pollack Krasner Found, 95; Prix de Rome, vis Arts, 97-98. *Bibliog:* Melissa Stang (auth), Doug Argue at Bockley Artpaper, 7/88; Mary Abee (auth), Minneapolis Star Tribune, 4/15/93; Michael Amy (auth), Art in Am, 4/98. *Media:* All. *Dealer:* Sherry Leedy Contemp Art Kansas City MO 64108

ARGUIMBAU, PETER L
PAINTER, LECTURER
b Stamford, Conn, Oct 22, 1951. *Study:* The Loomis Sch, 67-70; Vassar Col, 1970-71; Art Students League, 1973-1981; Classical Study in Venice, Rome and Naples, Italy. *Work:* The Lawrenceville Sch, Bund Libr, Princeton, NJ; Union League (permanent collection), New York, NY; Cheese Borough Ponds Collection, Greenwich, Conn. *Comn:* Greenwich Panorama (mural), Putnam Trust Bank, Greenwich, Conn, 1989; Chateau Mont Rozier, comn by Claude Cochin, Mt. Rozier, France, 1997; Revelation (ceiling mural), comn by Louis Karcher, New Canaan, Conn, 2000; Hon Gerald Heaney (portrait), 5th Dist Court Bldg, St Paul, MN; Drawing Room, Palace of Prince d' Avalos, Naples, Ital. *Exhib:* Nat Acad Design Show Biannual, New York, NY, 1986; Silvermine Guild New Eng Invitational, Silvermine Guild, New Canaan, Conn, 1987-; 350 years of Greenwich, Greenwich, Conn, 1990; Art's for the Parks Top 100 US Artists, Jackson Hole, Wyo, 1991-93; Mystic Int Exhib, Mystic Maritime Gallery, Mystic, Conn, 1994, 96-98, 2001-02. *Collection Arranged:* Retrospective, The Metrop Club, 1987; Italian Monument Drawing Show, 1992; Retrospective, Union League Club, 1994; NY Harbor Tallship 2000, Wally Findlay Gallery, 2000; Yachting Events of the Present, Harbour Court, Newport, 2005; Nantucket, Gallery Four India Street, 2005. *Teaching:* Oil painting, Darien, Conn, 1985-91; oil painting, Meadows Mus, Dallas, Tex, 1987; oil painting, Omega Inst, Rhinebeck, NY, 1989. *Awards:* Newington Coopsey Award, Hudson River Valley Art Assoc, 1969; Award of Merit, Mystic Intl Competition, 1991. *Bibliog:* Artist brings cause against Michelangelo Restoration, Eden Prairie Sailor, 1984; There is a young Old Master in Darien, Darien News Review, Sept 1993; Nancy Helle (auth), Classicism in a Modern Age, Greenwich Mag, Sept 2003. *Mem:* Nat Soc Mural Painters (vpres, 1996-2000); Art Students League, NY. *Media:* Oil, Flemish Technique. *Specialty:* Marine Art; Classic Yachts; Animal Paintings. *Interests:* oily-resinous techniques of the Flemish Masters from 1450-1650; classic yachts & workboats of Am waterfront 1850-. *Publ:* Art, The Artist Returns to Art Restoration, Am Art's Quart, Vol XIII No 3, 1996; art, The Sistine Chapel: Science versus Art, Am Art's Quart, Vol XV No 23, 1998; art, Impressionism and the Loss of Transparency, Am Art's Quart, Vol XVIII No 3, 2001. *Dealer:* Linda Lyons PO Box 7674 Greenwich CT 06830; Harbor Gallery 151 Rowayton Ave Rowayton CT 06853; Gallery 4 India St Nantucket MA 02554; Wally Findlay Galleries 165 Worth Ave Palm Beach FL; Mystic Seaport Gallery Mystic CT 06355; Tilly Pad Gallery Watch Hill RI. *Mailing Add:* 121 E Middle Patent Rd Greenwich CT 06831

ARIAS, SOLEDAD M
CURATOR
b Buenos Aires, Arg. *Study:* Fine Arts, Buenos Aires; Art Students League (Reginald Marsh scholar), NY. *Exhib:* Salon Provincial, Mus De Lujan, Buenos Aires, 90; Small Works, Mus Sivori, Buenos Aires, 91; Nat Show of Fine Arts, Mus Sivori, Buenos Aires, 92. *Awards:* Hommage A Van Gogh Award, Nacion, Buenos Aires; Aim Prog, Bronx Mus Arts, New York, 94. *Bibliog:* Ed McCormick (auth), Art Speak, 4/11/93; Holland Cotter (auth), New York Times, 8/19/94. *Mem:* Art Initiatives. *Media:* Painting. *Mailing Add:* 200 W 70th St New York NY 10023-4323

ARIAS-MISSON, ALAIN
VISUAL POET, GRAPHIC ARTIST
b Brussels, Belg, Dec 11, 39; US citizen. *Study:* Harvard Univ, BA (Greek lit; magna cum laude), 59. *Work:* State Mus (Stedelijk), Amsterdam, Holland; Archive H Sohm, State Gallery, Stuttgart, Ger; Galleria Schwarz, Milan; Cabinet d'Estampes, Bibliotheque Nat, Paris; Dresden Mus; Mus Casabianca, Vicenza, Italy; Mus de Senigallia; Liublin Mus, Poland; Jean Brown Collection, Getty Mus, Calif. *Comn:* Public Poem-Beethoven Bicentennial, Bonn, WGer; Public Art, City of Bielefeld, 91. *Exhib:* Galerie Donguy, Paris, 88; Poesia Visiva & Group Art-Documenta 8 Mus Santos Rocha, Portugal, 88; Le Mois de La photographie, Paris, Oct 88; Visual Poetry, Otis Art Inst, Los Angeles, 90; Domus Jani, Int Inst Total Art, Verona, 92, The Lyon Biennale, 93; Emily Harvey Gallery, NY, 98, 01; Galleria Caterina Gualco, Genoa, 99; Leonardo da Vinci, Last Supper, Vinci Mus, Italy, 2001; Emily Harvey Archive, Venice, Italy, 02; Lara Vincy Gallery, Paris, 03. *Teaching:* Creative writing, Columbia Univ, 81-82. *Awards:* NJ State Coun Arts, 85-86; Artists Liaison, 88. *Bibliog:* S H Anderson (auth), When reality becomes superfiction, Int Herald Tribune, 5/75; M Dachy (auth), New York art, Critique, 81, & L'espace Amerique, Change, Paris; and others in Art Vivant, Flashart & Artpress; Infinite, Paris, France, 99. *Mem:* Poets & Writers. *Media:* Shaped Plexiglas and Illumination. *Res:* Shamanic Culture, exp. Maya. *Specialty:* Fluxus. *Publ:* Co-ed, 5 anthologies in Europe & America, 74, Poesia Visiva, Chicago Rev, 76 & Visual poetry, Paris Rev; auth, Confessions of a Murderer, Bomber, Fascist, Rapist, Thief, Chicago Rev Press & Swallow, 75; The Public Poem Book, Arias-Misson, Factotum Press, Italy, 78-79; Verbo-visual Sins of a Literary Saint, Rara Bks, Italy, 92; The Mind Crime of August Saint, Fiction Coll 2. *Dealer:* Emily Harvey Gallery 50 Battery Place 5J New York NY 10280

ARIKE, MICHAEL WHITAKER
PRINTMAKER, PAINTER
b Oklahoma City, Okla, Oct 15. 1933. *Study:* Okla Stat Univ, with Doel Reed, BFA, 1955; Art Inst Chic, 1956-57; New School with John Ross, New York City. *Work:* British Mus, London, Eng; Portland, Mus, Seattle, Wash; Mus of City of New York, NYC; Fed Reserve Bank, New York City; Nelson-Atkins Mus, Kansas City, Mo. *Comn:* presentation print 2003, Print Club of Albany, 2003; limited edition print, Print Soc of Nelson-Atkins Mus, Kansas City, Mo, 2005. *Awards:* The Wm H Leavin Prize, Nat Acad Design Ann, 2000; Silver Medal in Graphics, Audubon Artist's Ann, 2002; Gold Medal in Graphics, Audubon Artist's Ann, 2004. *Mem:* council mem, Soc Am Graphic Artists (1996-); Audubon Artists; Print Club of Albany; Artist's Fel. *Media:* Miscellaneous Media. *Dealer:* The Old Print Shop 150 Lexington Ave at 30th St New York NY 10016. *Mailing Add:* 331 Prospect Ave Mamaroneck NY 10543

ARISS, HERBERT JOSHUA
PAINTER, ILLUSTRATOR
b Guelph, Ont, Sept 19, 1918. *Study:* Ont Coll Art. *Work:* Nat Gallery Can; Art Gallery Ont; Winnipeg Art Gallery; Vancouver Art Gallery; London Art Gallery, Ont; and others. *Comn:* Casein, Huron & Erie Co, Chatham, 58; ceramic, John Labatt Brewery, London, 59; multimedia, Sir Adam Beck Sec Sch, London, 67; multimedia, Ont Govt Bldg, Toronto, 68; mural, Sch Med, Univ Western Ont, London. *Exhib:* 2nd & 3rd Can Biennial, Ottawa, 64-66; Can Soc Graphic Arts, 70; Can Printmakers, Nat Gallery, Can Int Show, 71; Can Soc Painters in Watercolour, London & NY, 72. *Collection Arranged:* Nat Gallery Can, Ont; Vancouver Arts; Calgary Art Gallery Mus, London. *Pos:* Pres, Western Art League, 57-60; mem, London Art Gallery Bd, 68-71; dir, London Art Gallery Asn, 69-72; chmn acquisition comt, London Pub Libr & Art Mus, 70-71. *Teaching:* Instr drawing & painting, Doon Sch Fine Arts, 55-58; head dept art, H B Beal Art Sch, London, Ont, from 65. *Awards:* Can Coun Senior Fel, 60-61; Can Soc Painters in Watercolor Hon Award, 65; Mayor's Hon Award, London, 80. *Bibliog:* Bright lights of London, Time, 68; Barry Lord (auth), How Beal has made London an art centre, Toronto Star, 70; J Bryce (auth), Herb Ariss retrospective, Arts Can, 71. *Mem:* Royal Can Acad Arts; Can Soc Painters in Watercolor. *Media:* Acrylic, Watercolor, Pastel. *Publ:* Illusr, Lectures variees, 58; La double mort de Frederic Belot, 58; Contes d'Aujour d'hui, 63; War, 71; auth, Encounters, London Regional Art Gallery, 82. *Dealer:* Michael Gibson Gallery. *Mailing Add:* 770 Leroy Crescent London ON N5Y 4G7 Canada

ARISS, MARGOT JOAN PHILLIPS
PAINTER, SCULPTOR
b Belleville, Ont, Sept 14, 1929. *Study:* London Cent Col, Ont; H B Beal Sec Sch, London, Ont. *Work:* Can Coun Art Bank, Ottawa; London Regional Art Gallery, Ont; London Free Press Newspaper, Ont; Vancouver Art Gallery, BC; McIntosh Art Gallery, London, Ont. *Comn:* Ceramic mural, City of London, Ont; ceramic & fibre mural, City of Kingston, Ont; and many other pvt commissions. *Exhib:* Ceramic Objects, Art Gallery Ontario, 73, Ariss-Hogbin-Hunt, York Univ, 78, Toronto; McIntosh Gallery, Univ Western Ont, 75; Words & Images, Trent Univ, McKenzie Art Gallery, 76; London & Area Artists Part I, 80, Clay & Fibre Show, 86, 40th Ann Western Ontario Exhib, 87, London Regional Art Gallery; Univ Western Ont Collection, Art Gallery, Windsor, 82; one-person show, Univ Waterloo, Ont, 83; Ten Yrs After, Spectrum Art Gallery, London, Ont, 85; Yellow Show, 87, Box Art (touring) 87, Red Show, 88, Blue Show, 89, Book Show, 94, Durham Art Gallery; retrospective, Zen Song, London Regional Art Gallery, 89. *Bibliog:* Articles, Arts Can, 8/69 & Craft Horizons, 10/73 & 6/74; cover & article, Craftsman, 8/78. *Mem:* Royal Can Acad. *Media:* Mixed Media. *Mailing Add:* 770 Leroy Crescent London ON N5Y 4G7 Canada

ARMAJANI, SIAH
SCULPTOR
b Teheran, Iran, 1939; US citizen. *Study:* Macalester Col, St Paul, Minn, BA, 63. *Work:* MoMA; Guggenheim Mus; British Mus; Stedelijk Mus; Mus für Moderne Kunst; Walker Art Ctr. *Comn:* Gazebo for two architects, Gabriella & Arberto Antolini, Storm King Art Park, Mountainville, NY; The Gazebo for the Irene Hixon Whitney Bridge, Loring Park, Minneapolis, Minn, 93; Bridge/Ramp, City Ctr-Sudwest LB Lautenschlagerstrasse, Stuttgart, Ger, 94; Garden, Villa Arson Mus, Nice, France, 94; The Lighthouse and Bridge, Staten Island, NY, 95; and others. *Exhib:* Archit Analogues (with catalog), Whitney Mus Am Art, 78; Archit Sculpture (with catalog), Inst Contemp Art, Los Angeles, 80; Metaphor: New Projects by Contemp Sculptors, Hirshhorn Mus & Sculpture Garden, Smithsonian Inst, 81; Body Language: Figurative Aspects of Recent Art (with catalog), Hayden Gallery, Mass Inst Technol, 81; Biennial (with catalog), Whitney Mus Am Art, 81; Artists' Gardens & Parks, Hayden Gallery, Mass Inst Technol, 81; 74th Ann Am Exhib (with catalog), Art Inst Chicago, 82; Postminimalism (with catalog), Aldrich Mus Contemp Art, 82; Form and Function: Proposals for Pub Art in Philadelphia (with catalog), Pa Acad Fine Arts, 82; New Art (with catalog), Tate Gallery, London, Eng, 83; Directions 1983 (with catalog), Hirshhorn Mus & Sculpture Garden, Smithsonian Inst, 83; Beyond the Monument (with catalog), Hayden Gallery, Mass Inst Technol, 83; An Int Survey of Recent Painting and Sculpture (with catalog), Mus Mod Art, NY 84; Content: A Contemp Focus, 1974-1984, Hirshhorn Mus & Sculpture Garden, Smithsonian Inst, 84; The Artist as Social Designer: Aspects of Public Urban Life Today, Los Angeles Co Mus Art, 86; Second Sight: Biennial IV (with catalog), San Francisco Mus Art, 86; Solo exhibs, Stedelijk Mus, Amsterdam, 87, Kunsthalle Basel, Switz, List Visual Arts Ctr, Mass Inst Technol, 88, Lannan Found, Los Angeles, 92, Storm King Art Ctr, 93, Swiss Inst, NY, 93 & Wright Mus, Beloit Coll, Wis, 93; Emerging Artists 1978-1986: Selections from the Exxon Series (with catalog), Solomon R Guggenheim Mus, 87; Avant-Garde in the Eighties, Los Angeles Co Mus Art, 87; View Points: Post-War Painting and Sculpture, Solomon R Guggenheim Mus, 88; Carnegie Int (with catalog), Carnegie Mus Art, Pittsburgh, 88; Cult and Commentary: An Eighties Perspective (with catalog), Hirshhorn Mus & Sculpture Garden, Smithsonian Inst, 90; Enclosures and Encounters (with catalog), Storm King Sculpture Ctr, Mountainville, NY, 91; 20th Century Art, Mus Mod Art, Frankfurt, 91; Century of Sculpture, Stedelijk Mus Amsterdam & Nieuwe Kerk Found, 92; The Open Work, John Good Gallery, NY, 92; Differentes Natures: Visions de l'Art Contemporain (with catalog), Place de la Defense, France, 93; Unpainted to the Last: Moby Dick and the Visual Arts, Spencer Art Mus, Univ Kans, Lawrence, 93; Inside and Out, Roanoke Coll, Salem, Va 93; Muelensteen Gallery, 2011 . *Awards:* Fellow award, United States Artists, 2010; Chevalier de L'Ordre des Arts et des Lettres, 2010; McKnight Found Distinguished Artist award, 2010. *Bibliog:* Howard Pousner (auth), The olympic cauldron, Atlanta J, 3/25/94; Howard Pousner (auth), Sculpture for olympic flame unveiled, Atlanta J, 3/21/94; Catherine Fox (auth), Armajani's art speaks to American democracy, Atlanta J, 3/24/94. *Mem:* Nat Acad. *Mailing Add:* c/o Max Protech Gallery 245 8th Ave New York NY 10011

ARMSTRONG, BILL HOWARD
PAINTER, EDUCATOR
b Horton, Kans, Dec 13, 1926. *Study:* Bradley Univ, Peoria, Ill, BFA (cum laude), 49; Univ Ill, Urbana, MFA, 55, with Abraham Rattner. *Work:* Brooklyn Mus, NY; San Francisco Mus of Art, Calif; Springfield Art Mus, Mo; Albrecht Gallery, St Joseph, Mo; Art and the Law, West Publ Co, St Paul, Minn. *Comn:* Hist mural, Am Bank, Irving, Tex, 75. *Exhib:* 20th & 24th Print Exhib, San Francisco Mus Art, 56 & 59; Butler Inst Am Art, Youngstown, Ohio, 56-67; Pa Acad Fine Art, Philadelphia, 56-67; 10th Ann Print Exhib, Brooklyn Mus, 59; Soc Am Graphic Artist Int Traveling Exhib, 60; Watercolor USA Nat Exhib, Springfield, Mo, 65-76; Calif Nat Watercolor Soc, Los Angeles, 69-71; Art and the Law, 82-83; Watercolor mural, Hammons Hall for the Performing Arts, Springfield, Mo, 92. *Collection Arranged:* Watercolor USA Nat Invitational Exhib, 76. *Pos:* Art adv, Burma Transl Soc, Rangoon, Ford Found, 57-58; co-founder & past pres, Watercolor USA Hon Soc, 85-86. *Teaching:* Asst prof painting, Univ Wis, Madison, 56-63; prof watercolor & graphic design, Southwest Mo State Univ, Springfield, 63-88, emer prof, 88-. *Awards:* Purchase Awards, Watercolor USA, 62-71 & Calif Nat Watercolor Soc, 69 & 70; Purchase Awards, West Publ Co Art & the Law Exhib, 82 & 83; Lifetime Achievement in & Contrib Arts Award, Mo Arts Coun Award, 90. *Media:* Watercolor. *Mailing Add:* 3029 E Wilshire Dr Springfield MO 65804-4149

ARMSTRONG, CAROL
PAINTER
Study: Cent State Univ, Edmond, Okla, BA, 78. *Comn:* Sir William W Talley II, Wes Lane, OKC DA, David Thompson, Mark Funke, Dr and Mrs Lynn Jurasak, Dr and Mrs William Banousky, Gene Rainbolt, Mr and Mrs Randy Cassimus, Frank Eskridge, Emily Eskridge, Dr and Mrs Eric Wollman, Mrs Lynn Talley, Pat and Don Allen, OU Mewbourne Coll Earth and Energy, Dr and Mrs Christianson, Mr and Mrs Carl Melton. *Exhib:* Okla Art Guild Juried Exhib, 82, 85, 86 & 87; Lawton Jr Serv League 15th, 17th & 18th Ann Exhibs, 84, 85 & 87; Nat Watercolor Okla, 86; Tex and Neighbors Art Competition, 86; Art in the Woods, Fifth Juried Exhib, 88; Bricktown Gallery, 2000-2002; Dodson Gallery, 2002-2012; Aunt Gertrudes House Gallery, 2005-2012; Framemasters Art Gallery, 2008-2010; Heritage Gallery, Scottsdale, Ariz, 2009-2012; Brick Town Marketplace, 2010-2011; Reining in the Arts, 2011; Okla Friendly Nat Show, 2012. *Teaching:* Painting instr, Norman Woodward's Art & Crafts, Oklahoma City Tabco Hobbies, 80-88 & Firehouse Art Ctr, 89-90. *Awards:* Equal Merit OAG Juried Exhib, 85, 86, Second place, 97; Special Merit, Patrons Watercolor Gala, 86; Best of Show, Lawton Junior Svc League, 86; Hon Mention, NOW Juried Exhib, 97. *Bibliog:* Best of Show, Lawton Jr Serv League 18th Ann Exhib, 86. *Mem:* Okla Watercolor Asn; Okla Art Guild

ARMSTRONG, ELIZABETH NEILSON
CURATOR
b Winchester, Mass, June 30, 1952. *Study:* Hampshire Col, BA (am studies), 74; Univ Calif, Berkeley, MA (history art), 82. *Collection Arranged:* Jasper Johns: Printed Symbols (auth, catalog), 90; Viewpoints: Hachivie Edgar Heap of Birds, Walker Art Ctr, Minneapolis, 90; Ann Hamilton/David Ireland, Walker Art Ctr, Minneapolis, 92; Claes Oldenburg: In the Studio, Walker Art Ctr, Minneapolis, 92; Robert Motherwell: The Spanish Elegies, Walker Art Ctr, Minneapolis, 92; In the Spirit of Fluxus (auth, catalog), Walker Art Ctr, Minneapolis, 93; Michael Sommers/Susah Haas: The Question of How, Walker Art Ctr, Minneapolis, 93; Duchamp's Leg, Walker Art Ctr, Minneapolis, 94; Paul Shambroom: Hidden Places of Power, Walker Art Ctr, Minneapolis, 95; Robert Motherwell: Reality and Abstraction, Walker Art Ctr, Minneapolis, 96; Peter Fishcli and David Weiss: In a Restless World, Walker Art Ctr, Minneapolis, 96; Recent Additions to Collection, Mus Contemp Art, San Diego, 96; Primarily Paint, Mus Contemp Art, San Diego, 97; Armando Rascón, Mus Contemp Art, San Diego, 97; Geoffrey James: Running Fences, Mus Contemp Art, San Diego, 97; Jay Johnson, Mus Contemp Art, San Diego, 97; Silvia Gruner, Mus Contemp Art, San Diego, 98; Double Trouble: The Patchett Collection, Mus Contemp Art, San Diego, 98; David Reed Paintings: Motion Pictures, Mus Contemp Art, San Diego, 98; Recent Acquisitions from the Lannan Found, Mus Contemp Art, San Diego, 99; Marcos Ramirez ERRE: Amor Como Primer Idioma (Love as First Language), Mus Contemp Art, San Diego, 99; Bertrand Lavier: Walt Disney Productions: Mus Contemp Art, San Diego, 99; Jean Lowe: The Evolutionary Cul-de-Sac, Mus Contemp Art, San Diego, 2000; Ultrabaroque: Aspects of Post-Latin Am Art, Mus Contemp Art, San Diego, 2000. *Pos:* Grants adminr, Nat Endowment Humanities, 76-79; asst cur, Walker Art Ctr, 83-86, assoc cur, 86-89 & cur, 89-96; sr cur, Mus Contemp Art, San Diego, 96-2001; dep dir art, chief cur, Orange Co Mus Art, Newport Beach, Calif, 2001-2008; cur contemp art, Minneapolis Inst Arts, 2008-. *Awards:* Govt Merit Award, Nat Endowment Humanities, 79; Humanities Grad Res Grant, Univ Calif, Berkeley, 81; Mus Profs Fel, Nat Endowment Arts, 89; Int Asn Art Critics award, 1994-95; Spec Exhib Award, Int Asn Art Critics Ger, 98. *Mem:* Coll Art Asn; Print Coun Am. *Res:* Contemporary art; American art. *Publ:* Coauth, First Impressions, Walker/Hudson Hills Press, 89; Double trouble: The Patchett Collection, Mus Contemp Art, 98. *Mailing Add:* Orange County Mus Art 850 San Clemente Dr Newport Beach CA 92660

ARMSTRONG, GEOFFREY
PAINTER, ARCHITECT
b Toronto, Ont, May 27, 1928. *Study:* Univ Toronto, BArch, 52. *Work:* Art Gallery Windsor, Ont; Univ Nebr, Fredericton; City North Bay, Ont; Esso Resources, Calgary, Alta; Royal Bank, Toronto. *Exhib:* Art Gallery Hamilton; Montreal Mus Fine Arts; Art Gallery Ont; Trent Univ; Queens Univ, Kingston; Ont Soc Artists Traveling Exhib; Soc Can Artists Traveling Exhib. *Mem:* Royal Archit Inst Can; Soc Can Artists; Ont Soc Artists; Royal Can Acad. *Media:* Acrylic. *Publ:* Contribr, Art Mag, 68-70. *Dealer:* Roberts Gallery 641 Yonge St Toronto ON M4Y 1Z9. *Mailing Add:* 78 B Crescent Rd Toronto ON M4W 1T5 Canada

ARMSTRONG, L C
PAINTER
b Humboldt, Tenn, Dec 18, 1954. *Study:* Art Ctr Coll Design, BFA, 82; San Francisco Art Inst, BFA, 87. *Work:* Corcoran Gallery Art, Washington, DC; Sony Corp; Univ S Fla, Tampa. *Exhib:* 42nd Biennial, Contemp Am Painters, Corcoran Gallery Art, Washington, DC, 91; Biennial of Sydney, 92; Making & Unmaking, Univ S Fla Contemp Mus, Tampa, 95; Pittura Immedia, Neue Galerie/Landesmuseum, Graz, Austria, 95; L C Armstrong Paintings, Bravin Post Lee, NY, 97; The Corcoran Collects, Corcoran Gallery Art, Washington, DC, 98; Maul Flower, Gallerie Ausstellungspraum Hubner, Frankfurt, Ger, 98; Life is Beautiful, Laing Art Gallery, Newcastle-Upon-Tyne, Eng, 2002; Flowe Power, Musee des Beaux Arts, Lille, France, 2004; POPulace, Blaffer Gallery, The Art Mus Univ Houston, Tex, 2005; Solo Exhibs: Galerie Sophia Ungers, Cologne, Ger, 91, 92; White Columns, New York City, 92; Marsha Mateyka Gallery, Washington, DC, 93, 97; Bravin Post Lee, New York City, 94; USF Contemp Mus, Tampa, Fla, 95; Hofstra Univ, Hempstead, NY, 98; Angeles Gallery, Santa Monica, Calif, 99; Galerie Huebner, Frankfurt, Ger, 2000; Postmasters Gallery, NY, 2001; Marsha Mateyka Gallery, Washington, DC, 2003; Marlborough Gallery, New York, NY, 2007; and others; Group Exhib: Cornell Fine Arts Mus, Winter Park, Fla, 2006. *Awards:* Pollock Krasner Found Grant, 92. *Bibliog:* Faye Hirsch (auth), L C Armstrong at John Post Lee, Art Am, 94; Ferdinand Protzman (auth), Business is Booming, Washington Post, 3/22/97; Barry Schwabsky (auth), The Widening Circle Consequences of Modernism in Contemporary Art, Cambridge Univ Press, 97. *Media:* Acrylic, Bombfuse. *Dealer:* Angles Gallery 2230 Main St Santa Monica CA 90405. *Mailing Add:* 33 Harrison St New York NY 10013

ARMSTRONG, MARTHA (ALLEN)
PAINTER, PHOTOGRAPHER
b Brunswick, Ga, 1935. *Study:* Converse Col, under August Cook, 53-56; Heatherly Sch Fine Art, London, Eng, advan painting, 67-69. *Work:* C G Jung Educ Ctr, Rovi Tex Corp, Rapada Corp & Apple Computers, Dallas, Tex; United Energy Resources, Dresdner Bank, Texaco USA, Houston, Tex; Smithsonian Inst, Washington, DC; Lowell Early Childhood Ctr, Fresh Meadows, NY; Enpro Int, Jeddah, Saudi Arabia; and others. *Comn:* Cover art, Performing Arts Mag, 81; cover art, spring brochure, C G Jung Educ Ctr, Houston, 84; cover art, inaugural brochure, Tex Inst Arts Educ, 84; cover art, Houston on Stage Mag, 85. *Exhib:* Houston Mus Fine Arts, Glassell Sch, 78; McMurtrey Gallery, Houston, Tex, 91; Inman Gallery, Houston, Tex, 91; Visual Arts Alliance, 93; Galveston Arts Ctr, 94; Hooks Epstein, Houston, Tex, 94. *Collection Arranged:* 34 Houston Artists Working in their Studios, 77. *Pos:* Visual arts panelist, La State Coun for the Arts, Baton Rouge, 86. *Teaching:* Instr art, All Saints Aids Ctr, Pasadena, Calif, 90-91. *Bibliog:* Patricia Johnson (auth), Martha Armstrong's photography is softly personal, Houston Chronicle, 82; Carol Everingham (auth), New York exhibit features Armstrong photos, Art News, Houston Post, 84; Essays on Texas Women in the Arts, Moore, Sylvia, Midmarch Arts, 88. *Mem:* Cult Arts Coun Houston (bd dir 79-85, vpres, 81, pres, 82, chmn bd, 83); Houston Ctr Photog (trustee, 83-94); Contemp Arts Mus (trustee, 78-80); Fel of Contemp Art, Los Angeles. *Media:* Acrylic, Oil. *Dealer:* McMurtrey Gallery 3508 Lake St Houston TX 77006. *Mailing Add:* 14 Sutton Pl S New York NY 10022

ARMSTRONG, RICHARD
CURATOR, MUSEUM DIRECTOR
b Kansas City, Mo, May 1, 1949. *Study:* Universite de Dijon, cert, 1969; Universite de Paris IV, Sorbonne, dipl, 1970; Lake Forest Col, Ill, BA (art hist), 1971; Whitney Mus Am Art, Independent Study Prog (Helena Rubinstein Fel), 1973-74. *Collection Arranged:* Kim Mac Connel, 1976, Manny Farber, 1977, The Modern Chair: Its Origins and Evolution, 1978 & Richard Art Schwager's Theme(s), 1979, La Jolla Mus Contemp Art, Calif; Five Painters in NY, 1984, The Sculpture of RM Fischer, 1984, Biennial Exhib, 1985, 1987, 1989 & 1991, Mechanical Illusions by Robert Cumming, 1986, Guy Pene du Bois: The 1920s, 88, Recent Drawings, 1988 & Richard Artschwager, 1988, Whitney Mus Am Art, NY; David Park: Paintings and Drawings of the 1950s, 89, Craig Kauffman, 89, The New Sculpture 1965-75: Between Geometry and Gesture, 90, Hunt Diederich, 91, Gifts and Acquisitions, 91 & Alexis Smith, 91, Whitney Mus Am Art, NY; Alexis Rockman, 93, Pittsburgh Collects, 93, Andrew Lord, 93, Craigie Horsfield, 93, Andrea Zittel, 94, The Modern Chair, 94, Manny Farber, 94 & Carnegie Int, 95, Carnegie Mus Art. *Pos:* From assoc cur to cur, La Jolla Mus Contemp Art, Calif, 1975-80; sr instr, Independent Study Prog, Whitney Mus Am Art, 1981-85, adj cur, 1984-87, assoc cur, 1988-89 & cur, 1989-92; cur contemp art, Carnegie Mus Art, Pittsburgh, 1992-96, chief cur, 1995-96, Henry J Heinz II dir, 1996-2008; dir, Solomon R Guggenheim Mus, NY, 2008-. *Mem:* Russell Found, La Jolla, Calif (bd mem, 1983-91); Artists Space, New York (bd mem, 1985-92); White Columns, New York (bd mem, 1986-92). *Publ:* Contribr, Artforum, 1979-84. *Mailing Add:* Solomon R Guggenheim Mus 1071 5th Ave New York NY 10128

ARNAULT, HELENE & BERNARD JEAN ETIENNE
COLLECTOR
b Roubaix, France, Mar 5, 1959. *Study:* Ecole Poly, Paris, BA, 1971. *Pos:* With Ferret Savinel SA, Roubaix, France, 1972-76, gen mgr, 1976-78; pres, Ferret Savinel-Ferinel Group, 1978-1984, FS of America (subsidiary of Ferinel Group), Roubaix, 1978-1984; pres, chmn & chief exec officer, LVMH (Louis Vuitton Moet Hennessy), Paris, 1989- & Christian Dior, Paris, 1984-; pres, Group Arnault SAS, France, currently; owner, Phillips de Pury & Co, 1999-2003. *Awards:* Officier, Nat Order Merit, France; Grand Officier de la Legion d'Honneur, France; named one of World's Richest People, Forbes mag, 1999-; named one of Top 200 Collectors, ARTnews mag, 2006-13; named one of World's Most Influential People, Time mag, 2007; named one of 25 Most Powerful People in Business, Fortune mag, 2007. *Collection:* Contemporary art. *Mailing Add:* LVMH 22 Ave Montaigne Paris 75008 France

ARNESON, WENDELL H
PAINTER
b Madison, Wis, Sept 10, 1946. *Study:* Luther Col, BA, 68; Bowling Green State Univ, MA, 77, MFA, 78. *Work:* Miller Mus Art, Sturgeon Bay, Wis. *Comn:* Univ Wis Hosp, Madison, 82; watercolor triptych, Prudential Life Insurance Corp, Minneapolis, 83; watercolor triptych, Benson Optical Corp, 84; watercolor triptych, 3M Corp, 84; watercolor triptych, IBM Corp, 85. *Exhib:* Minn State Competition Exhib, Rochester Art Ctr, 79; Nat Watercolor Invitational, Clarks Art Ctr, Rockford, Ill, 84. *Teaching:* Prof painting & drawing, St Olaf Coll, Northfield, Minn, 78-, chmn dept, 84-91, 94-98. *Awards:* Drawing Award, Toledo Mus Art, 78; Painting Award, Watercolor USA, Springfield Art Mus, 84. *Mem:* Coll Art Asn. *Media:* Watercolor, Oil Painting. *Mailing Add:* St Olaf Col Dept Art Northfield MN 55057

ARNETT, JOE ANNA
PAINTER, SCULPTOR
b Jacksonville, Tex, May 9, 1950. *Study:* Univ Tex, BFA, 72; Art Students League, New York, 78-82. *Work:* Norwest Bank, Santa Fe, NMex; Blount Corp Collection, Montgomery, Ala; Franklin Mint Corp Collection, Pa; also pvt collections, Mr & Mrs Brian Dennehy, Mr & Mrs Don Meredith, Mr & Mrs Gary Biszantz, Mr & Mrs John Dobbs, Mr & Mrs Luther Hodges & Mr Roger Ebert. *Comn:* Still Life of Memorable Objects, comn by Sen John Warner, Washington, 92; peppers & brass, comn by James Robinson, NY, 94. *Exhib:* solo exhib, Flowers: A Celebration of Life, 93 & From the Artist's Garden, 95, Zaplin-Lambert Gallery, Santa Fe, NMex; Artists of Am, Denver Hist Soc Mus, Colo, 88-2000; two person show, Catto Gallery, London, 89-92; Albuquerque Art in Miniature, Albuquerque Mus Fine Art, NMex, 89-96; Art Asia, Exhib Ctr, Hong Kong, 94; Prix de West, Nat Cowboy Hall of Fame, 96-2000; Great Am Artists, Cincinnati, Ohio, 97-2000. *Pos:* Art Dir, Young & Rubicam Advert, 76-80. *Teaching:* Inst still life, Scottsdale Artists Sch, Ariz, 91-2000 & La Villa Arrigo, Atelier, Florence, Italy, 98; Fredericksburg Artists' Sch, 98-2000. *Awards:* Master Artist, Artist's Am Show; Katherine A Lovell meml Award, Catharine Lorillard Wolfe Art Club, Inc, 84. *Bibliog:* Claire Frankle (auth), Article in Int Herald Tribune, 2/89; Carole Katchen (auth), Painting with Passion, North Light, 94; Vicki Stavice, Art of the west, Art West, fall, 95. *Mem:* Kappa Pi. *Media:* Oil. *Publ:* Auth, The painted flower, Promethena, 95; auth, The Best of Fresh Flowers, 96, Painting Sumptuous Vegetables, Fruits, and Flowers in Oil, 98 & The Best of Flower Painting II, 99, North Light. *Dealer:* Zaplin-Lampert Gallery 651 Canyon Rd Santa Fe NM 87501. *Mailing Add:* PO Box 8022 Santa Fe NM 87504

ARNHOLM, RONALD FISHER
DESIGNER, EDUCATOR
b Barre, Vt, Jan 4, 1939. *Study:* RI Sch Design, BFA (graphic design), 61; Yale Univ, MFA (graphic design), 63. *Work:* Ga Comn Arts Traveling Exhib. *Comn:* Corp design prog (with Jack MacDonald), Am Tube & Controls, West Warwick, RI, 62; typeface: Jenson Roman, Mergenthaler Linotype Co, Plainview, NY, 64; wall mural, Mead Corp, Atlanta, Ga, 65; typefaces: Aquarius series, 70-74, Fovea series, 77-79, Visual Graphics Corp, Tamarac, Fla, Veritas series, 89, World Typeface Ctr, NY, Headline series, 80, Financial & Classified Types, 88, Los Angeles Times, Legacy Series, Int Typeface Corp, NY, 93. *Exhib:* Composing Rm Award Typography Exhib, Gallery 303, NY, 63; Solo exhibs, Ga Mus Art, Athens, 65; 45th Ann Art Dir Club NY Ann Exhib, 66; Southeastern Ann, High Mus Art, Atlanta, 67; Typomundus 20/2 Int Typography Exhib, Stuttgart, Ger, 70. *Pos:* Art dir, The Moderator Mag, New Haven, Conn, 62-63. *Teaching:* From instr to asst prof art, Univ Ga, 63-71, assoc prof, 71-82, prof, 82-. *Awards:* Award of Distinctive Merit, Art Dir Club, New York, 66; Cert of Merit, Typomundus 20/2, 70; Albert Christ-Janer Award, Univ Ga, 94. *Bibliog:* Eugene Ettenberg (auth), The Word Paintings of Ronald Arnholm, Am Artist, 11/70; Edward M Gottschall (auth), The Word Paintings of Ronald Arnholm, Typographic, Vol 3, No 3. *Mailing Add:* Univ Ga Dept Art Athens GA 30602

ARNING, BILL A
CURATOR, ADMINISTRATOR
b New York, NY, Sept 16, 1960. *Study:* New York Univ, BA, 84. *Exhib:* Stux Boston, Stux Gallery, NY; The Second Second at Althea Viafora Gallery; The Anti-Masculine, Kimlight Gallery, Los Angeles, 92; Faggots: A Communique From North Am Gay & Lesbian Artists, F Rojas BA, Arg. *Pos:* Asst dir, White Columns, 84-85, exec dir & chief cur, 85-96; art ed, Bomb Mag, 91; dir, Contemp Arts Mus, Houston, 2009-. *Teaching:* Guest lectr, Pace Univ, 85, Art Inst Chicago, 88, Sch Visual Arts, NY Univ, 90, Snug Harbor, 92, Toronto Coll Art, 91, Tyler Sch Art, Philadelphia, 92, Tama Art Univ, Japan, 91, Yale, 94 & Forum Gallery, St Louis. *Publ:* Auth, Update 86, Update 87, Update 88, Update 89, Update 90 & Update 91 & 92 (catalogs), White Columns; Tom Brazelton's fickle abstractions, In: USA Pavilion Catalog, 87; Glittering Prize, 87, Ecuadorian Biennial, 88 & Russel Floersche, 88, Stux Gallery; auth, catalog, Peter Scott, Riverside Studios, London; Jeffrey Jenkins (catalog), Stux Gallery, 89; contribr (with Kirby Gookin), A Naming of the Colors, 93. *Mailing Add:* Contemporary Arts Mus Houston 5216 Montrose Blvd Houston TX 77006

ARNOLD, ANN
ILLUSTRATOR
b San Francisco, 1952. *Study:* Univ Calif Santa Cruz, BA, 75. *Exhib:* numerous exhib in London and the US. *Mem:* Nat Acad. *Media:* Oil on wood; Watercolor on paper. *Interests:* Still Life painting. *Publ:* Illusr (books) Fanny at Chez Panisse, 1992; Stop Smelling My Rose, 1997; The Children's Kitchen Garden: A Book of Gardening,

Cooking, and Learning, 1997; Firehouse Max, 1997; auth & illusr, The Adventurous Chef: Alexis Soyer, 2002; auth & illusr, Sea Cows, Sharmans, & Scurvy: Alaska's First Naturalists: Georg Wilhelm Steller, 2008. *Dealer:* North Point Gallery, Jackson St, San Francisco, Calif. *Mailing Add:* c/o Pippin Properties Inc 155 E 38th St Ste 2H New York NY 10016

ARNOLD, GLORIA MALCOLM
PAINTER, INSTRUCTOR

b Covington, Ga, July 16, 1945. *Study:* Univ Ga, BS (educ), 66; study with John Gould, 71-78, Jack Flynn, 78-83, & Gunter Korus, 84-98. *Work:* General Electric & Berkshire Bank, Pittsfield, Mass; Beloit Corp, Dalton, Mass; Red Lion Inn/Country Curtains, Stockbridge, Mass; Sweet Brook Care Ctr Inc, Williamstown, Mass; Bennington Ctr Arts, Vt. *Comn:* Mt Greylock (painting), Berkshire Bank, Pittsfield, Mass, 87; Water Garden (mural), Sweet Brook Care Ctrs, Williamstown, Mass, 90; Autumn (painting), Beloit Corp, Dalton, Mass, 91. *Exhib:* Copley Soc Boston, Mass, 90-98; Springfield Art League Nat, Mus Fine Art, Springfield, Mass, 91-92; Am Artists Professional League, Salmagundi, Club, NY, 91; Academic Artists, First Church Gallery, Springfield, Mass, 91-93, 95-96 & 98; Oil Painters of Am, Quast Galleries, Taos, NMex & others, 93, 94, 96-98, 99-2002; one-man shows, Western New Eng Col, Springfield, Mass, 94 & Southern Vt Art Ctr, Manchester, Vt, 95, Bethlehem Art Gallery, NY, 99; Arts for the Parks Nat Tour, Jackson, Wyo, 96, 99 & 2006; Made in Massachusetts Exhib, The Norman Rockwell Mus, Stockbridge, Mass, 99; Art of the Animal Kingdom V, Bennington Ctr for Arts, Vt, 2000, 2013; Colonie Art League Nat Exhib, Latham, NY, 2000; Oxford Coll of Emory Univ, 2002; Int Exhib Animals in Art, 2003; Exhib Large Works, Workshop Live, Pittsfield, Mass, 2006; Paint the Parks Nat Tour, Topeka, Kans, 2007; Acad Artists Asn Nat Exhib, 2008; Impressions of New England Exhib, Ctr for the Arts, Bennington, Vt, 2008; Variety is the Spice of Life, Main St Books, Lee, Mass, 2011-2012. *Pos:* Vpres, Pittsfield Art League, Mass, 87-89; mem, Lee Cult Coun, Lee, Mass, 90-98 & 2000; vpres, Kent Art Asn, Conn, 94-96, bd mem, 94-99; bd mem, Academic Artists, 2002-2010. *Teaching:* Oil & watercolor, Gloria Malcolm Arnold Studio, 84-2012; watercolor, Berkshire Mus, Pittsfield, Mass, 90-92. *Awards:* First in Oils, Intl Nature Fine Arts Competition, 98; Finalist, The Artist's Mag Competition, 96-98 & 2000; Jane Peterson Still life Award, Hudson Valley Art Asn, 99; Women Artists of the West, Wildlife Art Magazine Award, 2003. *Bibliog:* Timothy Q Cebula (auth), Lee Woman's oil painting receives national honor, Berkshire Eagle, 10/96; Kristin Mally (ed), Showtime, US Art Mag, 12/96; Cristina Adams (auth), Oil Painters America, Southwest Art Mag, 5/98. *Mem:* Acad Artists (bd mem, 2002-10); Oil Painters Am (signature mem). *Media:* Oil, Watercolor. *Specialty:* Realism, multi-media, scratchboard, oil, watercolor, photos. *Interests:* Hiking, reading, travel . *Collection:* Oil and watercolor paintings of local and national landscapes; flowers and wildlife. *Publ:* Auth, Creating a mood, No 71, Palette Talk Mag, 87; contrib, Best of Flower Painting 2, 99, Painting More Creatively: Tips and Techniques From North Light Book Club, 2000, Best of Wildlife Art 2, 99, N Light Bks. *Dealer:* The Landmark Gallery 31 Ocean Ave Kennebunkport ME; Gloria Malcolm Arnold Fine Art Gallery 69 Church St Lenox Ma 01240. *Mailing Add:* Studio Fine Art 301 E Center St Lee MA 01238

ARNOLD, JACK
ART DEALER, PUBLISHER

b New York, NY. *Study:* Syracuse Univ, BS, 50. *Pos:* Pres, Collector's Workshop, NY, 76-78; vpres, Gallery Hawaii, Honolulu, 78-80; pres, Falcon Fine Art, NY, 80-82; owner, Jack Arnold Fine Arts, NY, 83-. *Teaching:* Dir lithography, Shorewood Atelier, NY, 72-75. *Specialty:* Contemp paintings, drawings, watercolors & graphics. *Publ:* Contribr, The Contemporary Lithographic Workshop Around the World, Van Nostrand Reinhold Co, 74. *Mailing Add:* 3293 Esplanade Cir SE Rio Rancho NM 87124-7625

ARNOLD, JOHN DOUGLAS
COLLECTOR

b 1974. *Study:* Vanderbilt Univ, BS (economics), 1996. *Pos:* Stock trader, Enron Corp, 1996-2001; founder & mng dir, Centaurus Energy LP (formerly Centaurus Advisors, LLC), Houston, 2002-. *Awards:* Named one of The 400 Richest Americans, Forbes mag, 2008 & 2009; named one of 40 Under 40 Rising Stars, Fortune mag, 2009; named one of 200 Top Collectors, ARTnews mag, 2010-2013. *Collection:* Impressionism, postwar & contemp art. *Mailing Add:* Centaurus Energy, LLC 2800 Post Oak Blvd, Suite 225 Houston TX 77056

ARNOLD, JOSEPH PATTERSON
PAINTER

b Los Angeles, Calif, May 17, 1954. *Study:* Univ Wyo, pre Coll art courses, 1972; Philadelphia Coll Art, BFA, 1977. *Work:* Univ Wyo Art Mus; Wyo State Mus, Cheyenne; Rock Springs (Wyo) Fine Art Ctr. *Comn:* outdoor mural, Town of Wheatland, Wyo. *Exhib:* Creative Process, Dahl Art Mus, Rapid City, SD, 1997; Western Visions, Nat Mus Wildlife Art, Jackson, Wyo, 2002; Wild Water, Bradford Brinton Mus, Sheridan, Wyo, 2002; Expanded Horizons, Yellowstone Art Mus, Billings, Mont, 2003; Wyoming, High & Wide, Ucross Found Gallery, Clearmont, Wyo, 2004; Painting the American West, Univ Wyo Art Mus, Laramie, Wyo, 2005. *Pos:* cur, Artmobile, Univ Wyo Art Mus, 96-98; roster artist, Wyo Arts Coun, 95-. *Awards:* Purchase award, Defining Line, cur Denver Art Mus, 1994; Best of Show, Int Platform Asn, cur Denver Art Mus, 1994; Fine Arts award, Wheatland Pocket Park, Wyo State Hist Soc, 2000. *Bibliog:* Artist celebrates Wyoming, Am Artist, 90; Bob Budd (auth) Wyoming ranches, Southwest Art, 90; Chase Reynolds (auth) J Arnold, Southwest Art, 93. *Mem:* Alpine Club, London. *Media:* Oil, Pastel. *Publ:* auth, Pattie Layser, Southwest Art Reaching Great Heights, 6/2007. *Mailing Add:* 701 S 4th St Laramie WY 82070

ARNOLD, NANCY ANN
CURATOR, EDUCATOR

b Pasadena, Calif, Mar 3, 1967. *Study:* Univ Calif, Santa Barbara, MA (art hist and archit), 98, doctoral studies with Bruce Robertson, 2000. *Collection Arranged:* Obsessions I and II, 97, 99; In the Mood: Early California Photography, 99; Illuminating Pamela Benham, 2000. *Pos:* asst to registr, Univ Art Mus, Santa Barbara, Calif, 97-99; asst to photog cur, Santa Barbara Mus Art, 99; cur, Univ Calif Women's Ctr Art Gallery, Santa Barbara, 97-2000. *Teaching:* teaching asst art hist, Univ Calif, Santa Barbara, 98-2000. *Mem:* Coll Art Asn. *Publ:* Auth, Communal Material: The AIDS Memorial Quilt, Univ Calif Santa Barbara, 99. *Mailing Add:* Women's Ctr Art Gallery U Calif Women's Ctr Bldg 434 Santa Barbara CA 93106

ARNOLD, PAUL BEAVER
EDUCATOR, PRINTMAKER

b Taiyuanfu, China, Nov 24, 1918; US citizen. *Study:* Oberlin Col, AB, 40, MA, 41; Cleveland Inst Art; Univ Minn, MFA, 55. *Work:* Libr Cong, Washington, DC; Seattle Art Mus, Wash; Baltimore Mus, Md; Dayton Art Inst, Ohio; Cleveland Mus Art, Ohio; Cleveland Mus Print Club (2 print editions), 2001. *Comn:* Pheasant (color intaglio), Int Graphic Arts Soc, NY, 56; White Peacock (color woodcut), Int Graphic Arts Soc, NY, 57; mural, Gilford Instrument Co, Oberlin, Ohio, 71; Martin Luther King Monument, Oberlin, Ohio, 87; Wellington Rescue Monument, Oberlin, Ohio, 88; John Frederick Oberlin Monument, Oberlin, Ohio, 92. *Exhib:* May Show, Cleveland Mus, 61, 63, 66, 74 & 76; Solo exhibs: Jersey City State Coll, NJ, 66, 78, 86 & 97; Miami Univ, Oxford, Ohio, 68; Univ Kans, Manhattan, 70; Firelands Asn Visual Arts, Oberlin, 85;95; Allen Art Mus, Oberlin, 85; Lorain Co Community Coll, 2000; Kendal Gallery, Oberlin, Ohio, 2002, 2007; Contemp Prints for Collectors, Columbus Gallery Art, Ohio, 75; Two-person exhib, US Info Serv, US Embassy, Ankara, Turkey, 75; Jane Haslem Gallery, Wash, DC, 90; Intown Club Gallery, Cleveland, 93; Atrium Gallery, Boulder, Colo, 96; Group exhibs, Cleveland Playhouse Gallery, 96, 98, 2001; Firelands Asn Visual Arts, 2008. *Teaching:* From instr to prof art & chmn dept, Oberlin Col, 41-86, John Young-Hunter prof, 82-85, prof emer (retired); guest prof, Tunghai Univ, Taiwan, 72, Sarah Lawrence Col, Lacoste, France, 79 & 80 & Lacoste Cleveland Inst Art, 85. *Awards:* Ford Found Fac Fel Prog, 51-52; Audubon Artists Medal of Honor, 57; Great Lakes Cols Asn Res Grant, 65-66; Oberlin Alumni Medal, 85. *Mem:* Nat Asn Schs Art (bd dir, 70-81, vpres, 72-75, pres, 75-78); Coll Art Asn (bd dir, 79-, secy, 82-, vpres, 84-86, pres, 86-88); Mid-Am Coll Art Asn (bd dir, 89-91); Firelands Asn Visual Arts (bd dirs, 2003-2009). *Media:* Woodcut, Intaglio. *Interests:* Japanese woodblock technique. *Publ:* Illusr, General chemistry & laboratory experiments in general chemistry, Campbell & Steiner, 55; coauth, The Humanities at Oberlin, 57; auth, Printmaking today, 4/70 & Silkscreen printing, 12/74, Lalit Kala Contemp, New Delhi, India; contribr, Terra cotta army of Quin Shihuangdi, Ceramics Monthly, 11/80; Prism 1981 Wood's Latent Image; illus (bk design), Oberlin in Asia, Ellsworth Carlson, 1983; Edward Munch's Graphic Techniques (catalogue), Allen Art Mus, Oberlin Col, 1983; Print Making Collaboration Review (5 bks), Art Jour, Col Art Asn, 1988

ARNOLD, ROBERT LLOYD
PAINTER, EDUCATOR

b Buffalo, NY, June 28, 1940. *Study:* NY State Univ Coll, Buffalo, BS, 66; Fla State Univ, MS, 68; Ind Univ, EdD, 72. *Work:* NY Coll Ceramics, Alfred; Nat Art Gallery NZ, Wellington; Fla State Univ, Tallahassee; Ind Univ. *Exhib:* Sign/Symbol, Nat Art Gallery NZ, 77; Artwords & Bookworks, Los Angeles Inst Contemp Art, 78; solo exhibs, Ind Univ, Bloomington, 78, Ohio State Univ, 78, Ashland Coll, Ohio, 79, Bowling Green State Univ, 80 & Ohio State Univ, Newark, 82; Spangler Cummings Gallery, 86. *Pos:* Assoc provost, Ohio State Univ, 90-94 & vprovost, 94-97. *Teaching:* Prof art & art educ, Ohio State Univ, 70-2005, prof emer, 2005-. *Awards:* Mem Award, Lester C Bush, 74; Battelle Exhib Award, Dollar Savings, 76; Columbus Mus Award, 79. *Bibliog:* Gina Franz (auth), Six in Ohio, New Art Examiner, 78; Robert Pincus-Witten (auth), Six in Ohio, Ohio State Univ/Ohio Arts Coun, 78; Donald Kuspit (auth), Columbus, Art in Am, 79. *Mem:* Ohio Art Educ Asn; Nat Art Educ Asn; Columbus Art League (pres, 79 & 80). *Media:* Acrylic Paint; Canvas. *Res:* Contemporary art; art education. *Publ:* Auth, An analysis of selected teacher preparation programs: 1975, Art Educ, 76; The spoken retrospective: Chris Burden at 30, Midwest Art, 76; The development of a pluralistic avant-garde, Art Educ, 76; An interview with Lawrence Alloway, Midwest Art, 77; Studies in art education (invited ed), 95. *Mailing Add:* 5860 Dunheath Loop Dublin OH 43016

ARNOLD, SKIP
VIDEO ARTIST, PERFORMANCE ARTIST

b Binghamton, NY. *Study:* State Univ Col, Buffalo, NY, BFA, 80; Univ Calif, Los Angeles, MFA, 84. *Exhib:* One-artist exhibs, Punch (video), Laguna Art Mus, Laguna Beach, Calif, 92, Statue (performance), Kim Light Gallery, Los Angeles, Calif, 93, Living Quarters/Conducting Business, Unfair, Cologne, Ger, 93, Spin (performance), Jack Tilton Gallery, NY, 94, Roger Merians Gallery, NY, 95, 35 rue des Bains, Geneva, 96, Spencer Brownstone Gallery, NY, 97, 99, Galerie Montenay-Giroux, Paris, 99, Aeroplastics, Brussels, Belg, 2000, Shoshana Wayne Gallery, Santa Monica, Calif, 2000, Galerie MXM, Prague, 2000, Roberts and Tilton, Los Angeles, 2000; Let the Artist Live, Exit Art, NY, 94; Courage, New Mus Contemp Art, NY, 94; Persistent Dispositions - Technetronic Identities, Calif Inst Arts, Valencia, 95; Cadeaux Paquets, Galerie Satellite, Paris, 95; Skip Arnold - Sigrid Hackenberg, Roger Merians Gallery, NY, 95; Menu du Jour, Silverstein Gallery, NY, 96; Angel Hair: Ex LA, Dogenhaus Galerie, Leipzig, Ger, 97; The Road Show, Bronwyn Keenan Gallery, NY, 97; Sunshine & Noir: Art from La, 1960-1997, La Mus Art, Humlebaek, Denmark, 97; Identity Crisis, Spencer Brownstone Gallery, New York City, 98; Venus, ARC Galerie, Wien, Austria, 99; Recontre, Int d'Art Performance de Que, Le Lieu, Que, Can, 00; Exit Festival, Helsinki, Finland, 01; Art Unlimited, Art 33 Basel, Switz, 02; and many others. *Teaching:* Vis fac, VUT Acad Art, Brno, Czech, 00; adj fac, Grad Studio Fine Arts and Liberal Arts and Scis, Art Ctr Col Design, Pasadena, Calif, 97-. *Awards:* Brody Arts Found Fel, 92; Art Matters Inc Fel, 92; Nat Endowment Arts Visual Arts

Fel Grant, 93; John Simon Guggenheim Mem Found Fel, 95. *Bibliog:* Steve Mikulan (auth), Like a little boy in his fort, Visions, winter 93; Unfair - Art Cologne - Saatchi Collection, Flash Art, Vol XXVII, No 174, 1-2/94; Kateri Butler (auth), Long gone train, LA Weekly, 2/4-10/94; Grady T Turner (auth), Skip Arnold at Spencer Brownstone, 118-119, Art in America, 10/1997; Charlene Roth, Abject Edge: Recent American Figurative Art, 40-45, 12/1999; Shana Nys Dambrot (auth), Pushed to an Abject Edge, 27, d'Art Int, 2000. *Dealer:* Spencer Brownstone Gallery New York NY; Aeroplastics Brussels Belgium

ARNOLDI, CHARLES ARTHUR
SCULPTOR, PAINTER
b Dayton, Ohio, April 10, 1946. *Study:* Chouinard Art Inst, Los Angeles, 68. *Work:* Los Angeles Co Mus Art; Mus Mod Art, New York; Chicago Art Inst; Metrop Mus Art, New York; San Francisco Mus Mod Art; Guggenheim Bilbao, Bilbao, Spain. *Comn:* Wood relief paintings, Continental Nat Bank, Ft Worth, 81 & First Int Bank, Houston, 82; Hughes Corp, Los Angeles, 85; State of Calif, State Office Bldg, San Francisco, 88; bronze sculpture, City Beverly Hills, Calif; canvas paintings, 101 2nd St, San Francisco, 99 & Hollywood Renaissance Hotel, Calif, 2001. *Exhib:* Solo exhibs, Nicholas Wilder Gallery, 74-75, 77-78 & 79, Seattle Art Mus, 76, Robert Elkon Gallery, New York, 78 & 79, James Corcoran Gallery, Los Angeles, 80-85, Charles Arnoldi: Unique Prints, Los Angeles Co Mus Art, 84, Fuller Goldeen Gallery, San Francisco, 85 & 87, Charles Cowles Gallery, New York, 85-87 & 93-94, Arts Club Chicago, 86, Univ Mo-Kansas City Gallery Art, 86, Univ Art Mus, Calif State Univ, Long Beach, 87, Mus Italo Am, San Francisco, 88, Fred Hoffman Fine Art, Santa Monica, 91 & 96, Tony Shafrazi Gallery, New York, Imago Galleries, Palm Desert, Calif, 96 & 2004, Charles Cowles Gallery, New York, 99-2001, 2003, 2005-2006, Ochi Fine Art, Ketchum Idaho, 99, Modernism, San Francisco, 2001, 2003, 2005 & 2007, Busan Metrop Art Mus, South Korea, 2002, Bobbie Greenfield Gallery, Santa Monica, 2003-2005 & 2007 & Charlotte Jackson Fine Art, Santa Fe, 2006 & 2007; group exhibs, Whitney Biennial, 81; Am: The Landscape, Contemp Arts Mus, Houston, 81; 38th Biennial, Corcoran Gallery Art, Washington, DC, 83; Am Prints Today, Brooklyn Mus, 86; 70's in 80's: Printmaking Now, Mus Fine Arts, Boston, 86; Prints by Los Angeles Artists, Asahi Shimbun Gallery, Tokyo, 87; The 1980's: A New Generation, Metrop Mus Art, New York, 88; The Unique Print: 70s into 90s, Mus Fine Arts, Boston, 90; Visions/Revisions, Denver Art Mus, 91; The Contemp Mus Collects the First Five Yrs 1988-1993, Contemp Mus, Honolulu, 93; Between Reality & Abstraction: Calif Art at the End of the Century, Art Mus S Tex, Corpus Christi, 95; Calif Color, Univ Nebr, Lincoln, 96; The View from Denver, Mus Mod Art, Vienna, Austria, 97; Radical Past: Contemp Art and Music in Pasadena 1960-74, Armory Ctr Arts, 99; Celebrating Modern Art: The Anderson Collection, San Francisco Mus Mod Art, 2000; Lost but Found: Assemblage, Collage & Sculpture, 1920-2002, Norton Simon Mus, Pasadena, Calif, 2004; Paint on Metal, Theson Mus Art, 2005; Driven to Abstraction: Southern Calif & the Non-Objective World, 1950-1980, Riverside Art Mus, Riverside, Calif, 2006. *Awards:* Young Talent Award, LA County Mus Art, 69; Wittkowsky Award, Art Inst Chicago, 72; Fels, Nat Endowment Arts, 74 & 82 & John Simon Guggenheim Found, 75; Maestro Fel, Calif Arts Coun, 82. *Bibliog:* Fredericka Hunter (auth), Charles Arnoldi: Paintings & Sculpture 1971-1988, Mus Italo Americano, 88; Sam Hunter (auth), Charles Arnoldi, A Mid-Career Survey: 1970-1996, Fred Hoffman Fine Arts, 96; Suzanne Muchnic (auth), Charles Arnoldi at Fred Hoffman, Artnews, 9/96; Fred Hoffman (auth), The Pictorial Journey of Charles Arnoldi, Busan Metrop Art Mus, 2002. *Media:* Bronze; Acrylic, Canvas. *Dealer:* Modernism San Francisco; Charlotte Jackson Fine Art Santa Fe; OCHI Gallery Ketchum ID; Greenfield Sacks Gallery Santa Monica CA. *Mailing Add:* Charles Arnoldi Studio 721 Hampton Dr Venice CA 90291

ARNOT, ANDREW H
GALLERY DIRECTOR
b Detroit, Mich, Nov 28, 60. *Study:* Mich State Univ, BA (art hist), 84; Ball State Univ, Postgrad, 86. *Pos:* Grad asst, Ball State Univ Art Gallery, Muncie, Ind, 85-86; slide librn, Fogg Art Mus, Harvard Univ, Cambridge, Mass, 87-89; admin asst, PSG Framing, Boston, 87-89; asst dir, Tibor de Nagy Gallery, New York, 89-90, co-owner, co-dir, 93-. *Mailing Add:* Tibor de Nagy Gallery 724 5th Ave New York NY 10019

ARON, MARLENE
INSTALLATION SCULPTOR
b 1943. *Study:* Youngstown State Univ, Youngstown, Ohio, BFA (Art), 1966; Calif Coll Arts & Crafts, MFA, 1992. *Exhib:* Solo exhibs include McDonough Mus Art, Youngstown State Univ, 1996, Catham Coll, Pittsburgh, 1997, Butler Inst Am Art, Howland, Ohio, 1998, Bowman Gallery, Allegheny Coll, Meadville, Pa, 1998, Hewlett Gallery, Carnegie Mellon Univ, Pittsburgh, 1998, Trumbull Art Gallery, Warren, Ohio, 1999, Kipp Gallery, Indiana Univ, Indiana, Pa, 2001; Group exhibs include My Country, Right or Left: Artists Respond to the State of the Union, LH Horton Jr Gallery, San Joaquin Delta Coll, Stockton, Calif, 2005; Ann Members' Showcase, Berkeley Art Ctr, Berkeley, Calif, 2006. *Awards:* George Sugarman Found Grant, 2007

ARONSON, BENJAMIN
PAINTER, ILLUSTRATOR
b Boston, Mass, Oct 4, 1958. *Study:* Boston Univ Sch Fine Arts, BFA, 80, MFA, 82; studies in painting with Philip Guston, David Aronson, James Weeks & John Wilson. *Work:* Reading Pub Mus, Pa; Boston Mus Fine Arts; Dayton Art Inst, Ohio; Ga Mus Art; Flint Inst Arts, Mich; Mus Arts & Scic, Daytona Beach, Fla; Nat Mus Fine Arts, Houston; Va Mus Fine Arts; Utah Mus Fine Arts. *Comn:* Photo portrait of Justice Sandra Day O'Connor, US Supreme Court, comn by New Eng Sch Law, Boston, Mass, 91; undersea technical illustration, Woodshole Oceanographic Inst, Mass, 91; mural (painting), RI State Coun Arts, Providence, 91; mural (painting), ITT Sheraton Corp, Boston, Mass, 92; photo portrait of Justice H Blackmun, US Supreme Court, comn by New Eng Sch Law, Boston, Mass, 93. *Exhib:* Solo exhibs include Louis Newman Galleries, Beverly Hills, 1994, Jerry Solomon Gallery, Hollywood, 1996, Horwitch Newman Gallery, Scottsdale, Ariz, 1996, MB Modern, NY, 1997, Sydne Bernard Fine Art, Hollywood, 1998, Scott White Contemp, La Jolla, 1999, Alpha Gallery, Boston, 2000, 2002, DFN Gallery, NY, 2003, Jenkins Johnson Gallery, San Francisco, 2003, 2007, 2008, Tibor de Nagy Gallery, NY, 2005, Alpha Gallery, 2009, Ogunquit Mus Am Art, Ogunquit, Maine, 2009; group exhibs include New England Regional, Blanche Coleman Found, Boston, Mass, 1988; Nat Exhib & Competition of Am Painting & Sculpture, Nat Acad Design, NY, 1990 & 1992; Int Sixth Ann Exhib & Competition of Archit & Illus, Urban Ctr Munic Art Soc, NY, 1991; Recent Acquisitions to the Permanent Collection, Reading Pub Mus, Pa, 1994; Only in America, Koplin Gallery, Santa Monica, 1995; Jerry Solomon Gallery, Hollywood, Calif, 1997; Urban Suburban, Sydne Bernard Fine Arts, Hollywood, 1998; Town & Country, MB Modern, NY, 1998; Works on Paper, Spheris Gallery, NY, 2001; The Burbs, DFN Gallery, 2003; Dualities, LewAllen Contemp, Santa Fe, 2004, Cities Different, 2006; Looking Back, Moving Forward, Campbell Gallery, San Francisco, 2005; Beyond Representation, Jenkins Johnson gallery, San Francisco, 2008; Winter Haiku, Jenkins Johnson Gallery, San Francisco, 2009; Urban Perspectives, Mark Gallery, Englewood, NJ, 2009; Art Miami, Jenkin Johnson Gallery, Miami, Fla, 2009; People, Places & Things, The Art of Aronson, Babb, & Soth, Naples Mus Art, Fla, 2010; Summertime, Jenkins Johnson Gallery, San Francisco, Calif, 2010. *Pos:* Cur & dir, Nancy Lincoln Gallery, Brookline, Mass, 1984-90; Computer graphic artist, Security Computer Systems, Sudbury, Mass, 1987-90; freelance illusr, 1988-93. *Teaching:* Instr fine art, Beaver Co Day School, Chestnut Hill, Mass, 1983-90. *Awards:* William P & Gertrude Schweitzer Painting Prize, Nat Acad Design 165th Ann Nat Exhib Am Painting, 1990; Thomas Fisher Award, Sixth Ann Int Exhib & Competition of Archit Illus, 1991; Ogden M Pleissner Award Painting, Nat Acad Design 167th Ann Nat Exhib Am Painting, 1992. *Bibliog:* B Raupe (auth), Award winning watercolorist Benjamin Aronson, The Artist Mag, 8/1990; T Fisher (auth), International awards 1991, Architecture in Perspective IV, 10/1991; Margaret Lee (auth), 5th Ann Realism Int, ARTnews, Sept 2003; Kenneth Baker, Bubbling Over in Talent, ARTnews, Sept 2004; Daniel Grant (auth), Ben Aronson: Urban Geometries, Am Artist, Jun 2006; James F Cooper (auth), Contemporary Realism, The View from San Francisco, Am Ats Quarterly, Fall 2007; RC Baker (auth), Review: Ben Aronson, The Village Voice, 4/29/2008; James Foritano (auth), ArtScope Mag, May/June 2009; Donald Miller (auth), People, Places, & Things, Naples Mus Art, ARTnews, June 2010. *Mem:* Nat Acad. *Media:* Oil, Water Based Media & Collage. *Publ:* Contribr (illus), Human Anatomy and Figure Drawing, 1984. *Dealer:* Alpha Gallery 38 Newbury St Boston MA 02116; LewAllen Contemp 129 W Palace Ave Santa Fe NM 87501; Tibor de Nagy Gallery 724 Fifth Ave NY City NY 10019. *Mailing Add:* Jenkins Johnson Gallery 464 Sutter St San Francisco CA 94108

ARONSON, GEORGIANNA B See Nyman, Georgianna Beatrice

ARONSON, SANDA
ASSEMBLAGE ARTIST, SCULPTOR
b New York, NY, Feb 29, 1940. *Study:* Oswego State Coll, BS, 60; study with J De Creeft & Paul Pollaro at New Sch for Social Res, New York, 64; Tulane Univ, New Orleans, 65; Art Students League. *Work:* NC Print & Drawing Soc. *Comn:* Handprint Clem Hauper's Woodcut, comn by Dr Marvin Oleshanky, 82. *Exhib:* Solo exhibs, Bloomingdale Regional Branch, NY Pub Libr, 74,75, 95, 96, Barnard Coll, NY, McIntosh Ctr, 85; Artists' Soc Int Exhib, ASI Galleries, San Francisco, 87; Tenth Am NDak, Nat Exhib, Minot Art Gallery, 87; Tenth Ann US Print & Drawing Exhib, NC Print & Drawing Soc, 87; Nat Small Works Exhib, Schoharie City Art Coun, Cobleskill, NY, 87; Winter Solstice Invitational, Ceres Gallery, NY, 87; Am Herstory, Atlanta Coll Art Gallery, 88-90; Third Am Int Juried Exhib of Minis, Del Bello Gallery, Toronto, 88; Three Artists, Matrix Gallery, Sacramento, Calif, 88; Assembled Object, Atlanta Coll, Art Gallery, 89; West Side Art Coalition, Broadway Mall, 99. *Teaching:* Original artist-in-residence Studio in a Sch, NY Found Arts, 77-79. *Awards:* Purchase Award, NC Print & Drawing Soc, 87; 2 Pollock-Krasner Found Grants, 86-88; First Place, Sculpture, Emerald City Classic VI, Nepthe Mundi Soc Int Competition, 87; Hon Mention Sculpture, Emerald City Classic V, 86; Hon Mention, Bodyparts Contest, Lee S McDonald Inc, 88. *Bibliog:* Dr Eleanor Tufts (auth), American Women Artists: A Biblioguide, Vol II, Garland, 89. *Mem:* Disabled Artists' Network (founder & exec dir, 85-); NY Artists Equity Asn; Women in the Arts Found (bd-mem-at-large, 75-76); Artist Lightbox. *Media:* Assemblage, Xerographics. *Interests:* Sculpture jewelry. *Publ:* Contribr frontpiece, John Beecher (auth), Hear the Wind Blow, Int Publ, 68. *Mailing Add:* PO Box 20781 New York NY 10025-1523

ARSENAULT, KATE WHITMAN See Whitman-Arsenault, Kate

ARTEAGA, AGUSTÍN
MUSEUM DIRECTOR
b Tierra Blanca, Mex, Feb 14, 1958. *Study:* Univ Metropolitana, Mex City; Univ Autónoma, Mex, PhD History of Art. *Pos:* Dept dir, cur, Mus Mod Art, Mex City, 1990-94; nat dir, Visual Arts Inst, Nat Bellas Artes, Mex, 1994-98; dir & chief cur, Mus Palacio Belles Artes, Mex City, 1994-99; founding dir & chief cur, Malba-Constantini Collection, Argentina, 2000-02; cur, Gallery Nat Jeu du Paume, Paris, 2002-04, Bienal de Mercosur, Porto Alegre, Brazil, 2002-04, Mus Nat Art, Mex City, 2002-04; dir & chief exec officer, Mus Art Ponce, PR, 2004-. *Teaching:* Prof, Univ Autónoma, Mex, 1983-89, Univ Nuevo Mundo, 1993-96. *Awards:* Chevalier, Ordre des Arts Lettres, France. *Mem:* AAM; AAMD. *Publ:* Auth, Cuerpos Terrenales, 2003. *Mailing Add:* Museo de Arte de Ponce 2325 Ave Las Americas Ponce PR 00732-9027

ARTEMIS, MARIA
SCULPTOR, EDUCATOR
b Greensboro, NC, April 21, 1945. *Study:* Agnes Scott Col, Decatur, Ga, BA, 69; Univ Ga, Athens, MFA, 77; Ga Inst Technol, Coll Archit, MS, 91. *Work:* High Mus Art, Atlanta; Huntsville Mus Art, Ala; Columbia Mus Art & Sci, SC; City of Atlanta; Mus Contemp Art of Ga. *Comn:* Ctr for Disease Control and Prevention, Environ Health

Lab, Gen Serv Admin Art-in Archit, Chamblee, Ga, 99-2001; Mem Proj, Atlanta Detention Ctr, 94; Ex-static (site sculpture), Corp Olympic Develop Atlanta, 95-96; Unknown Remembered Gate (site-specific sculpture), Agnes Scott Col, 96; interfaith chapel, Hartsfield Int Airport, Atlanta, 99-2003; Hist 4th Ward Park Atlanta, 2010; Hamilton Mill Libr, Gqinnett Co, Ga, 2009. *Exhib:* Avant-Garde/12 in Atlanta, High Mus Art, Ga, 79; Earth Art: Sand & Clay Southeastern Ctr Contemp Art, Winston-Salem, NC, 80; Solo exhibs, Nexus Inc 3rd floor Gallery, Atlanta, Ga, 80, Fine Art Gallery, Univ Tenn, Chattanooga, Upstairs Gallery, Tryon, NC, 84, Works on Paper, Univ Cent Fla Gallery, Orlando, 87 & Labyrinths: Event, Distillation Artifact, Tulla Found Gallery, Atlanta, 94; Atlanta Women's Art Collective, AIR Gallery, NY, 80; Origins and Evolutions, Part II, Atlanta Coll Art Gallery, Mem Art Ctr, Ga, 84; First Atlanta Biennial, Nexus Gallery, Ga, 84; Avant Garde/12 in Atlanta-Five Yrs Later, Heath Gallery, Ga, 84; Analemma, On Site Work, Atlanta Arts Fest, Piedmont Park, Ga, 85; Contemp Artists in Ga, High Mus Art, Atlanta, 88; New South Group: Installations and Drawings, 112 Greene St, NY, 89; The Women's Path, Permenent Installation, Nexus Art Ctr, 94; Event that Rhyme, Mus Contemp Art of Ga, 2009; Heavy Leavity, Sandler Hudson Gallery, Atlanta, 2000; Georgia Masterpieces, Ga Mus, 2009. *Pos:* Vis artist slides, Univ Wis, Superior, 79; artist-in-residence, Cortona, Italy, 79 & Southeastern Ctr Contemp Art, Winston-Salem, NC, 80; artist fel, Va Ctr Creative Arts, 84 & 91; bd dir, treas, artists initiated projs, New South Group, 89; panel moderator, S Arts Fedn Nat Endowment Arts Regional Fel in Sculpture, 90. *Teaching:* Fac mem sculpture & visual studies, Atlanta Col Art, 79-81; lectr, Atlanta Col Art, spring 83; guest lectr, Ga Inst Technol, Col Archit, Atlanta, Ga, 84; vis prof, Dept Art, Agnes Scott Col, Decatur, Ga, 87-90; adj prof, Atlanta Col Art, 82-2006. *Awards:* Ga Women in the Visual Arts Award, 97; Mayor's Fel in the Arts Award in Visual Arts, Atlanta, 96; Fulton Co Grant; Working Artist Award, Ga, 2009. *Bibliog:* Ann Glenn Crowe (auth), New South Group, Art Papers, 89; Cathy Byrd (auth), Rev of Exhib: Heavy Levity, Sculpture mag, 2000; Anna Bloomfield (auth) 1997 Engaging the Site, Sculpture Mag, Jan/Feb/99; 1997 Comms, Ex-Static, 1/97. *Mem:* Int Sculpture Ctr. *Media:* Mixed. *Publ:* Andy Nasisse: Works off the Wall, Craft Horizon, 78; Art and the Sacred, Art Papers, 11-12/86; auth, Rethinking the Sacred Image, Artpapers, vol IV & V, 90; Public Art in Review, Art in America, 2002; Ga Masterpieces, 2009. *Dealer:* Sandler Hudson Gallery Atlanta GA. *Mailing Add:* 675 Drewry St Studio 9 Atlanta GA 30306

ARTNER, ALAN GUSTAV
CRITIC
b Chicago, Il, May 14, 1947. *Study:* Northwestern Univ, BA 68, MA, 69. *Pos:* Apprentice music critic, Chicago Tribune, 72-73, art critic, 73—; contributing editor, The Art Gallery Mag, 75-76; corr, Artnews Mag, 77-80. *Awards:* Decorated Chevalier de l'ordre des Arts et des Lettres; Rockefeller Found grantee, 71-72. *Publ:* Contribr to Playbill, 1994—. *Mailing Add:* Chgo Tribune Co 435 N Mich Ave Chicago IL 60611-4066

ARUM, BARBARA
SCULPTOR
b Des Moines, Iowa, Oct 9, 1937. *Study:* With Raymond Rocklin, Vincent Leggiadro, Chaim Gross & Philip Listengart. *Work:* Alan Towers, Inc. *Comn:* Courthouse Annex, Des Moines, Iowa. *Exhib:* Hudson River Mus, 82-90; Andre Zarre Gallery, 86; Elaine Benson Gallery, 87; Monmouth Mus Fine Arts, 87; Hammond Mus, 92; and others. *Awards:* Bus Community Award, North Am Sculpture Exhib, Golden, Colo, 87; Dir Max Ellenberg Mem Award, 89 & Gretchen Richardson Freelander Mem Award, 90 & 91, Nat Asn Women Artists, NY; Salvatore Maida Mem Award, Am Soc Contemp Artists, NY, 91. *Bibliog:* Reporters Dispatch, 11/12/82; articles, NY Times, 83, 85 & 87; article, Art World, 10/15/83. *Mem:* Nat Asn Women Artists (sculptor juror, 86-88); Allied Artists (treas, 86); NY Soc Women Artists (pres 90-93); Am Soc Contemp Artists (treas, 92-94); and others. *Media:* Steel; Wood, Bronze. *Publ:* The Guild 9. *Mailing Add:* 20 Hill Rd Accord NY 12404

ARVIDSON, BETSY
PRINTMAKER
b Boston, Mass. *Study:* Kean Univ, BA, NJ; Art Students League, New York; Nat Acad Design Sch Fine Arts, New York; Ringling Sch Art, Sarasota, Fla. *Work:* Calfee, Halter & Griswold, LLP, Columbus, Oh; Ohio Dominican Univ, Columbus, Oh; Upper Arlington Cultural Arts Comn, Upper Arlington, Oh; Mr & Mrs Will Barnet; Dr & Mrs William H Gerdts; Everett Raymond Kinstler, NA; pvt collections in the US, Canada, Ireland, Japan. *Comn:* portrait, Leslie Anne Williams, Ariz; paintings, Judith Anderson Christensen, Ohio & Fla; Prints & Drawings, Terry Kane & Martin Grissom, Fla. *Exhib:* Solo exhibs: Tonalist Landscape, Wehrle Gallery, Ohio Dominican Univ, Columbus, Oh, 2003-2004, Intimate Landscapes, Wehrle Gallery, Ohio Dominican Univ, Columbus, OH, 2007, Landscapes from Within, Sharon Weiss Gallery, Columbus, Oh, 2008; Group exhibs: NJ State Mus, Trenton, NJ, NY Acad Sch Figurative Art Benefit Auction, NY, Morningstar Gallery, NY, Susan Conway Carroll Gallery, Wash DC, Gallery on Second, NY, Bradshaw House Gallery, Birmingham, AL, Roy G Biv Gallery, Columbus, Oh, High Rd Gallery, Worthington, Oh, Columbus Cultural Arts Ctr, Columbus, Oh,, The Parker Gallery, Wash DC, 2004, 2005, 2006, DSPS Printmakers Show, Dayton, Oh, 2006, 2007, All Paintings Great and Small, The Cooley Gallery, Old Lyme, Conn, 2006, 2006, 2007, 2008, Art for Life, Aids Task Force, Columbus, Oh, 2004, 2006, 2008, Ten Years Soaring, Wehrle Gallery, Ohio Dominican Univ, Columbus, Oh, 2008, Sharon Weiss Gallery, Columbus, OH, 2006-2008, My View Gallery, Conway, SC, 2007-2008, Pen and Brush, Six on Tenth, NY, 2008, Wash Sq East Galleries, NYU Steinhardt Sch, 32nd Small Works Exhib, NY, 2009, Salmagundi CLub Fall Auction Exhib, NY, 2009, Salmagundi Club Thumb Box Exhib, NY, 2009, Audubon Artists Soc, 68th Exhib, NY, 2010, Ctr Contemporary Printmaking, International Miniature Print Biennial, Norwalk, Conn, 2009, 2011, Wash Printmakers Gallery, Nat Small Works Exhib, Wash DC, 2011, Katonah Mus Art, Art to the Point, Katonah, NY, 2012, Bennington Ctr Arts, Laumeister Art Competition, Bennington, Vt, 2012, AIR Gallery, Wish You Were Here, Brooklyn, NY, 2011, 2012, 2013, 2014, Ctr Contemporary Printmaking, Portraits in Print, Norwalk, Conn, 2013, NY Soc Etchers Inc, Nat Exhib Intaglio Prints, NY, 2013, Salmagundi Club, Am Masters Exhib, NY, 2014. *Pos:* Coordr, Artist Mem & Dir Special Events, Nat Acad Design Mus, New York, 82-96; admin coordr, Ohio Physicians Health Prog, Columbus, Ohio, 97-2008. *Awards:* Lieser Memorial award, 2009. *Mem:* The Salmagundi Club, NY; Art Students League, NY; Phoenix Rising Printmaking Cooperative, Columbus, Oh

ASANTE, MAYA FREELON
COLLAGE ARTIST
b NC, 1982. *Study:* Am Univ Paris, 2004; Lafayette Coll, Easton, Pa, BA (art, cum laude), 2005; Skowhegan Sch Painting & Sculpture, Skowhegan, Maine, 2006; Sch Mus Fine Arts, Boston, MFA, 2007. *Exhib:* Solo exhibs include Grubbs Gallery, Easthampton, Mass, 2001, 2005, Durham, NC, 2003, Lyda Moore Merrick Gallery, Durham, NC, 2006, Cheikh Anta Diop Int Conf, Philadelphia, 2006, Mus Nat Ctr Afro-Am Artists, Boston, 2007, Mary Lou Williams Ctr Black Cult, Duke Univ, Durham, NC, 2008, Stagville Hist Found, Durham, NC, 2008; group exhibs include The Body Show, Craven Allen Gallery, Durham, NC, 2004; What is Freedom?, Gallery Social & Political Art, Boston, 2005; Blurring Racial Barriers, Diggs Gallery, Winston-Salem, NC, 2006; Blurring Racial Barrieres II, Delta Fine Arts Gallery, Winston-Salem, NC, 2006; Access: A Feminist Perspective, Rhonda Schaller Studio, New York, 2007; Seeds, Piano Factory Gallery, Boston, 2007; She's So Articulate, Arlington Art Ctr, Va, 2008; Double Exposure, Mus African Diaspora, San Francisco, 2008. *Pos:* Founder & instr, Make Your Mark Art, Philadelphia, 2005-; Asst dir, African Am Visual Artists Database, Boston, 2005-07; coord, 2nd African & African Am Art & Film Conf, New York, 2007. *Teaching:* Teaching asst, Lafayette Coll, Easton, Pa, 2002, Sch Mus Fine Art, Boston, 2005; artist in residence, Int Printmaking Workshop, Kokrobitey Inst, Ghana, 2007; instr, Community Coll Baltimore County, 2007-08; adj faculty, Morgan State Univ & Towson Univ, Baltimore, 2007-08. *Publ:* Dir, writer, prodr, White Privilege (film), Easton, Pa, 2003; assoc prodr, 500 Years Later (film), London, 2005; dir photog, Conversation Between Elizabeth Catlett & Maya Angelou (film), Delta Fine Arts Ctr, Winston-Salem, NC, 2008. *Mailing Add:* 702 Cobb St Durham NC 27707-1336

ASARO, JOHN
PAINTER, ILLUSTRATOR
b San Diego, Calif, Feb 28, 1937. *Study:* Apprentice to Donal Hord (sculptor), San Diego, Calif, 52-55; Art Ctr Sch Design, Pasadena, Calif, 55-59; Los Angeles Inst Archit, 79. *Exhib:* Ann Am Watercolor Soc, NY, 83 & 84. *Pos:* Illusr, New Ctr Studios, Detroit, Mich, 60-65; freelance illusr, NY, 65-68 & Los Angeles, 68-70. *Teaching:* Teacher painting, Art Ctr-Col Design, Pasadena, Calif, 74-81, Laguna Beach Sch Art & Design, Calif, 82 & Palomar Col, San Marcos, Calif, 82-85. *Awards:* Excellence Award, NY Art Dirs Club, 68; Cash Award, Ann Am Watercolor Soc, NY, 85. *Bibliog:* J Mathew Fabris (auth), Innocent light, Stepping Out Arts Mag, 11/90; Robert Perine (auth), Asaro, A New Romanticism, Astra Publ, 12/91. *Mem:* Art Students League, NY. *Media:* Oil, Watercolor & Charcoal Drawing. *Publ:* Auth, Painting with Light, Artra Publ, 90. *Dealer:* Marco Fine Arts 201 Nevada St El Segundo CA 90245. *Mailing Add:* 7711 Quitasol St Carlsbad CA 92009-8036

ASCALON, DAVID
SCULPTOR, STAINED GLASS ARTIST
b Tel Aviv, Israel, Mar 8, 1945; US citizen. *Study:* Calif State Univ, San Fernando Valley, 65; Pratt Inst, BS (archit), 74; Bernard Baruch Coll, 74. *Work:* Simon Wiesenthal Ctr, Los Angeles, Calif; Appel Gallery, Jewish Fed Southern NJ, Cherry Hill; Sci Fiction Mus & Hall of Fame, Seattle, Wash. *Comn:* Holocaust Mem for Buffalo, Temple Beth El, NY, 86; Holocaust Mem for Pa, Jewish Community Greater Harrisburg, Pa, 94; Tree of Life Monolith, Jewish Fed Broward Co, Davies, Fla, 99; Light Monument, Beth Synagogue, Montgomery, Ala, 99; Holocaust Mem monument, Suburban Torah Ctr, Livingston, NJ, 2000; Totem (sculpture), Cherry Hill Public Libr, Cherry Hill, NJ; Kinetic Mobile Sculpture, Temple Israel, Memphis, Tenn; Holocaust Mem, Temple Sinai, Cinnaminson, NJ; Stained glass windows, Robert Wood Johnson Univ Hospital, New Brunswick, NJ; Light of Our People, Menorah Sculpture, Cornerstone Church, San Antonio, Tex. *Exhib:* Art of the Menorah, The Mus Am Jewish Hist, Philadelphia, Pa, 87; Sculpture Retrospective, The Appel Gallery Jewish Fed Southern NJ, 2004; Holocaust Mem, Congregation Beth El, Voorhees, NJ, 2009; Windows, Temple Bat Yahm, Newport Beach, Calif, 2008; Stained Glass Windows, the Frisch Sch, Paramus, NJ, 2010. *Pos:* Designer, Ari El-Hannani Archit, Tel Aviv, Israel, 67-68; pres, Ascalon Studios Inc, W Berlin, NJ, 82-. *Teaching:* Lectr, Judaic Art & Holocaust Mems. *Awards:* Liturgical Art award, Am Inst Archit, IFRAA, 86-89; Artists-in-residence award, Jewish Fedn Festival Art, Music & Cult, 2004. *Bibliog:* Tom Haydon (auth), Message in a Mural, Star Ledger, 4/28/91; Simon Bronner (auth), Inventing and Invoking Tradition in Holocaust Memorials, Penn State Univ, 10/2000; Jan Heffler (auth), Inside & Outside Sculptor, Philadelphia Inquirer, 10/31/2004; Public Art: A World's Eye View, Integrating Art into the Environment, I.C.O. Publ, Japan, 2008; Daniel Grant (auth), When Creator and Owner Clash, The Wall St Jour, 2010; Martha Lufkin (auth), What is the Meaning of This, Art Newspaper, 10/2010; Gary McGray & Carrie Crow (auth), Stained Glass Appraisal Guide, Presidential Press, 2010-2011; E Ashley Rooney (auth), 100 Mid Atlantic Artists, Schiffer Publ, 2011; Daniel Grant (auth), The Visual Artists Rights Act at 20, Huffington Post, 2/7/2011. *Mem:* Am Guild Judaic Art (pres, 2004-2009); Interfaith Forum Religion Art Archit; Am Inst Archit; Philadelphia Sculptors; Int Sculpture Ctr. *Media:* Sculpture - metal, Stained Glass. *Interests:* Judaica, flying (private pilot); Artists Rights. *Publ:* Contribr, Synagogues of Am Art Calendar, United Synagogue, 97-98 & 2000-2003. *Dealer:* Eric J. Ascalon, Esq. *Mailing Add:* Ascalon Studios 430 Cooper Rd West Berlin NJ 08091-3843

ASCALON, ERIC J
DIRECTOR, ADMINISTRATOR
b NY, Nov 10, 1971. *Study:* Rutgers Univ, BA, 93; Am Univ, JD (cum laude), 96. *Comn:* Founders Circle, Sci Fiction Mus Hall of Fame, Seattle, Wash; Kinetic mobile sculpture, Temple Israel, Memphis, Tenn. *Collection Arranged:* Metal Crafts of Pal-Bell co 1939-1956 (traveling exhib). *Pos:* Atty, Eric J Ascalon, Atty at Law, 97-;

gen mgr, Ascalon Studios, West Berlin, NJ, 2001-. *Bibliog:* Aaron Ha'Tell and Yanin Ben Or (authors), Lighting the Way to Freedom, Devora Publ Co, NY, 2006; Gary McGray and Carrie Crow, The Stained Glass Appraisal Guide, 1st ed, 2008-09, Presidential Press, Edmond, Okla; Gary McGray & Carrie Crow (auth), Stained Glass Appraisac Guide, Presidential Press, 2010-2011; Daniel Grant (auth), The Visual Artists Rights Act at 20, The Huffington Post, 2/7/2011. *Mem:* Am Guild Judaic art, (treas, 2002-2004); Hist Comn, Cherry Hill, NJ, (voting mem, 2004-2008); Arts Adv Bd, Cherry Hill, NJ (2006-2008); Mem Am Glass Guild. *Media:* Sculpture. *Interests:* Lawyer specializing in visual arts issues, representation of artists; flying (private pilot); Artists Rights Advocacy. *Collection:* Mid-Century Mod Design. *Mailing Add:* Ascalon Studios Inc 430 Cooper Rd West Berlin NJ 08091-3843

ASCHHEIM, EVE MICHELE
PAINTER
b New York, NY, Aug 30, 1958. *Study:* Univ Calif, Berkeley, BA, 83; Univ Calif, Davis, MFA, 87. *Work:* Nat Gallery Art, Washington, DC; Brooklyn Union Gas Co, NY; Ark Art Ctr; Boise Art Mus; Fogg Art Mus, Harvard Univ; Colo Spring Fine Art Ctr; Hamburger Bahnhof, Berlin, Germany; Hood Mus, Dartmouth Coll, NH; Kunst Mus, Bonn, Germany; Mus Contemp Art, N Miami; Mus Mod Art, New York; Univ Ala; San Diego Mus Art; Yale Univ Art Mus; Pierpont Morgan Lib, NY; Kupferstichkabinett, Nationalgalerie, Berlin; and many more. *Exhib:* Solo exhibs include Saron Truax Fine Art, Venice, Calif, 90, Snug Harbor Cultural Ctr, Staten Island, 92, Stefan Stux Gallery, NY, 97, Larry Becker Contemp Art, Philadelphia, 98, 2004, Galerie Benden and Klimczak, Germany, 99, Galerie Magnus Aklundh, Sweden, 99, Galerie Rainer Borgemeister, Berlin, Germany, 99, 2001, Univ Gallery, Univ Mass, Amherst, 2003, Patrick Verelst Gallery, Belgium, 2004, Lori Bookstein Fine Art, NY, 2006, 2007; group exhibs include Intimate Universe (Revisited), Noyes Mus, NJ, 79; Selections 42, Drawing Ctr, New York, 88; The Eidetic Image, Kranneut Mus, Champagne-Urbana, Ill, 91; American Abstract Artists, Noyes Mus, NJ, 94 & Ulrich Mus, Wichita, Kans, 94; American Academy Invitational, Am Acad Arts & Letters, New York, 97; Recent American Drawing Traveling Exhib, Arthur M Sackler Mus, Harvard Univ, Cambridge, Mass, 97; Art on Paper, Weatherspoon Gallery, Greensboro, NC, 98; DNA Gallery, Provincetown, Mass, 2004; Tang Mus, Saratoga, NY, 2004, 2006; Lohin/Geduld Gallery, NY, 2005; Stuhltrager Gallery, Brooklyn, 2006; Von Lintel Gallery, NY, 2007; Shick Gallery, Skidmore Coll, 2007; traveling, Drawn by NY, NY Historical Soc, Loeb Ctr, Vassar Coll, Taft Mus, Cincinatti, Oh, 2007-10; Weatherspoon Mus, Greensboro, NC, 2008; Gallen Inga Kondeyne, Berlin, 2009; Galleri Magnus Aklundh, Sweden, 2010. *Teaching:* Asst prof drawing, Occidental Coll, 90; visiting lectr, Princeton Univ, 91-93 & 1998-2000, sr lectr, 2001-, dir visual arts program, 2003-2007; asst prof drawing & painting, Sarah Lawrence Col, 94-97; vis artist, Atlantic Ctr Arts, Fla, 98; guest critic, sr painting seminar, Md Inst Col Art, 1998-2000. *Awards:* Richard and Hinda Rosenthal Award, Am Acad Arts & Letters, 87, Purchase Award, 2005; Nat Endowment Arts Grant, 88; Pollock Krasner Found Grant, 90, 2001; NY Found Arts, 91; Elizabeth Found Arts, 97; Joan Mitchell Found Grant, 2008; Guggenheim Found Fel, 2012. *Bibliog:* Dieter Schwarz & Christine Mehring (auths), Drawing is Another, Harvard Univ Press, 97; Lilly Wei (auth), Eve Aschheim at Stefan Stux, Art in Am, 6/98; Carter Ratcliff (auth), Eve Aschheim: Berlin/Lund/Koin (exhib catalog), Weidle Verlag, 1/99. *Mem:* Am Abstract Artists. *Media:* Oil, Drawing. *Dealer:* Rainer Borgemeister Muskauer Str 24 Berlin D10997 Germany; Lori Bookstein Fine Art New York; Larry Becker Contemp Art Philadelphia; Galleri Inga Kondeyne Berlin Germany; Galleri Magnus Aklundh Sweden. *Mailing Add:* c/o Lori Bookstein Fine Art 138 10th Ave New York NY 10011-4727

ASCIAN See Meader, Jonathan (Ascian)

ASHBAUGH, DENNIS JOHN
PAINTER
b Red Oak, Iowa, Oct 25, 1946. *Study:* Orange Coast Col, Costa Mesa, Calif, AA, 66; Calif State Univ, Fullerton, BA, 68, MA, 69. *Work:* Rolls Royce Inc, Owens Corning, Inc, Metrop Mus Art, Mus Mod Art, NY; Miami Art Ctr, Fla; Toledo Art Mus, Ohio; Seattle Art Mus, Wash. *Exhib:* Solo exhibs, Whitney Mus Am Art, 75, Seattle, Art Mus, Wash, 76, Kasmin Gallery, 89 & 90, Margulies-Taplin, Miami, Fla, 91, The Kitchen, NY, 92, Metrop Mus Art Print Gallery, NY, 92, Americas Soc, NY, 92, Goode, Crowley Gallery, Houston, Tex, 93, Marisa del Re Gallery, NY, 93 & Ralls Collection, Washington, DC, 93 Margulies-Taplan Gallery, Miami, 94, Galeri Antoninina Zaru, Capri, Italy, Gallery Twenty Two Eleven, Los Angeles, 2001, The Ralls Collection, Washington, 2001, and many others; The Painter & His Occasion, Marta Cervera Gallery, NY, 90; Abstraction, Margulies-Taplan Gallery, Boca Raton, Fla, 91; Invisible Body, Empire Fine Art Gallery, NY, 91; Abstract Painting the '90's, Andre Emmerich, NY; Behind Bars, Thread Waxing Space, NY, 92. *Awards:* Newport Harbor Art Patron's Award, 66; Creative Artists Pub Serv Grant, NY Coun Arts, 75; John Simon Guggenheim Found Fel, 76. *Bibliog:* Guy Martin (auth), Read it Once, Esquire, 5/92; Garvin Edwards (auth), Details, 6/92; Rhonda Lieberman, Artforum, 6/92; and others. *Media:* Oil. *Dealer:* Margulies Taplin Gallery Inc 3310 Ponce De Leon Blvd Coral Gables FL 33134. *Mailing Add:* PO Box 499 Wainscott NY 11975

ASHCRAFT, EVE
PAINTER
b Pontiac, Mich, Mar 1, 1963. *Study:* RI Sch Design, BFA, 85. *Pos:* Owner, Eve Ashcraft Studio, 87; freelance painter, commercial-decorative murals. *Awards:* Nat Endowment Arts Fel, 87. *Mailing Add:* 247 Centre St 7th Fl New York NY 10013

ASHER, FREDERICK M
HISTORIAN, EDUCATOR
b Chicago, Ill, May 25, 1941. *Study:* Dartmouth Col, BA; Univ Chicago, MA & PhD. *Pos:* Actg dir, Univ Gallery, Univ Minn, 71-72, chair, dept art hist, 78-81; assoc dean, Col Lib Arts, 85-91, chair, dept art hist, 91-. *Teaching:* Instr art hist, Lake Forest Col, 67-70; assoc prof art hist, Univ Minn, Minneapolis, 70-81, prof, 81. *Mem:* Am Comt S Asian Art (treas, 72-74); Am Inst Indian Studies (treas, 87-). *Res:* South Asian art. *Publ:* Various publications pertaining to the art of India

ASHER, LILA OLIVER
PRINTMAKER, PAINTER
b Philadelphia, Pa. *Study:* With Gonippo Raggi, Joseph Grossman & Frank B A Linton; Univ Arts, Philadelphia, grad. *Work:* Corcoran Gallery Art, Georgetown Univ, Howard Univ & Nat Mus Am Art, Washington, DC; Fisk Univ, Nashville; Univ Va, Charlottesville; Nat Mus Women Arts; Gallaudet Univ, Wash, DC; Nat Mus History, Taipei, Taiwan; Kastrupgårdsamlingen Kunst Mus, Denmark; Sweet Briar Coll, Va; City Wolfsbang, Ger; David Lloyd Kreeger Coll, Washington, DC; Ctr Res & Educ, Jerusalem; Embassy of Israel, Tel Aviv; Embassy of US, Mexico City; Montgomery Community Coll Contemp Prints, Md; Jundt Art Mus; Gonzaga Univ, Spokane, Wash; Driskell Collection, Univ Md; Cosmos Club, Wash DC; Univ Maryland; Art Club Wash DC. *Comn:* Oil paintings, two panels, Congregation Rodeph Shalom, Philadelphia, 1940; murals, two rooms, Indian Spring Country Club, Glenmont, Md. *Exhib:* Retrospective Exhib, Howard Univ, 78 & 91; over 50 solo exhibs In: US, Japan, India, Taiwan, Denmark, Turkey & Pakistan, var times, 51-85; Univ Calif Los Angeles; Rockville Art Mansion, Md; Cosmos Club, Washington, DC; Franz Bader, Washington, DC, 72; Fisk Univ, Nashville, Tenn, 74; Strathmore Arts Ctr, Rockville, Md, 2002; Washington Printmakers Gallery, 2013; Strathmore Hall Arts Ctr, North Bethesda, MD; Stimson Inst Internat Peace, Wash DC; Montgomery County Art Coll. *Pos:* prof emer. *Teaching:* Instr art, Howard Univ, 47-51, prof emer, currently; instr art, Wilson Teachers Coll, 53-54; from lectr to prof art, Howard Univ, 61-91; prof emer. *Awards:* Printmaker of the Year, High Sch Graphics Prog, Nat Mus Am Art, 81. *Bibliog:* American Prints from Wood, Smithsonian Inst; Catalogues, Kastrugårdsamlingen Kunst Mus, Denmark & Howard Univ, Washington, DC; Barnett-Adan Gallery (film); Eric J Sundquist (auth), Strangers in the Land; Andrew Carroll (auth), War Letters; Milly Heyd (auth), Mutual Reflections, Rutgers Univ Press; Eric Sundquist (auth), Strangers in the Land, Bellknap Press, Harvard Univ; Andrew Carroll (auth), Behind the Lines, Scribner; Haus der Verwandlung (video), Deutsches Theatre Mus. *Mem:* Artist Equity Asn (treas, DC Chap, 71-74); Cosmos Club Washington, DC; Washington Print Club; Md Printmakers; Washington Printmakers Gallery; and many others. *Media:* Wood & Linoleum Block; Oil. *Res:* study in Japan & India, teaching methods & printmaking. *Specialty:* hand pulled prints. *Interests:* figurative work. *Publ:* Auth, Men I Have Met in Bed, Heritage Press, 2002. *Dealer:* Washington Printmakers Gallery 1641 Wisconsin Ave NW Wash DC. *Mailing Add:* 4100 Thornapple St Chevy Chase MD 20815

ASHKIN, MICHAEL
SCULPTOR
b Morristown, NJ, 1955. *Study:* Univ Pa, Philadelphia, BA, 77; Columbia Univ, New York, MA, 80; Sch Art Inst Chicago, MFA (painting & drawing), 93. *Exhib:* Five Different, 1800 N Clybourne, Chicago, 90; Dome Room, Chicago, Ill, 91; Response to War, Artemisia Gallery, Chicago, 91; Migration, Dome Room, Chicago, 92; Ashkin, Fujiwara, Gouch, Levin, Starbuck, Tikka, Gallery 2, Sch Art Inst Chicago, 92; Ambient Spaces/Virtual Reality, Peter Miller Gallery, Chicago, 92; Solo exhibs, Peter Miller Gallery, Chicago, 92 & 94, Bronwyn Keenan Gallery, NY, 96, Feigen Inc, Chicago, 96, Galerie Jousse Sequin, Paris, France 97 & 99, Andrea Rosen Gallery, NY, 98 & 2000, Emily Tsingou Gallery, London, 99; MFA Thesis Show, Sch Art Inst Chicago, 93; The New Pier Show Sculpture Garden, Cityfront Ctr Plaza, Chicago, 93; Investigations into the Physical and Metaphorical Hole, Gallery 2, Sch Art Inst Chicago, 94; Mini-Mindus (with catalog), White Columns, NY, 95; Lookin' Good, Feelin' Good, 450 Broadway Gallery, NY, 95; Ooze, Black & Herron Space, NY, 95; Constructions, Michael Klein Gallery, NY, 96; Open Skies, SPAS Gallery, Rochester Inst Technol, NY, 96; Site Specifics, Carriage House Proj Space (with catalog), Islip Art Mus, NY, 96; Space, Mind, Place, Andrea Rosen Gallery, NY, 96; Currents in Contemp Art, Christie's E, NY, 96; The Lie of the Land (brochure), Univ Art Mus, Univ Calif, Santa Barbara, 96; At the Edge of the Landscape, Galeria Estrany - de la Mota, Barcelona, Spain, 97; Picturing, Ctr Curatorial Studies, Annandale-on-Hudson, NY, 97; Across Lines, Rosenberg Gallery, Hofstra Univ, Hempstead, NY, 97; 20th Ann Benefit Gala & Art Auction, New Mus Contemp Art, NY, 97; 1997 Biennial Exhib (with catalog), Whitney Mus Am Art, NY, 97; Tableaux (with catalog), Mus Contemp Art, Miami, Fla, 97; 24Seven, Galerie Klaus-Peter Goebel, Stuttgart, Ger, 97; Elsewhere: Works by Michael Ashkin, Julie Becker, James Casebere, Miles Coolidge, and Thomas Demand (with catalog), Carnegie Mus Art, 97-98; New Found Landscape, Kerlin Gallery, Dublin, Ireland, 97-98; Where: Allegories of Site in Contemp Art, Whitney Mus Am Art Champion, Stamford, Conn, 98; Sliding Scale, SE Ctr Contemp Art, Winston-Salem, NC, 99; Souvenirs/Documents: 20 Yrs, PS 122 Gallery, NY, 99; Contemp Collections XIV, Mus Contemp Art, San Diego, La Jolla, 99; Landworks Studio, Inc, Salem, Mass, 99; Small World: Dioramas in Contemp Art, Mus Contemp Art, San Diego, 2000; Berardo Collection, Centro Cult de Belem, Lisbon, 2000; 2000 Benefit and Silent Auction, White Columns, NY, 2000, Gallery Patrick Seguin, Paris, 2000; Human/Nature, Caren Golden Gallery, NY, 2000; Piqued Land, Barbara Krakow Gallery, Boston, 2001; Andrea Rosen Gallery, NY, 2000 & 2002. *Pos:* Bd trustees, Ft Worth Country Day Sch, 82-94; bd adv, art dept, Univ North Tex, 90-; mem, Bush Presidential Libr steering com, Tex A&M Univ, 90-91; mem gov bd, Yale Univ Art Gallery, 91-98; mem vis com, Sherman Fairchild Paintings Conservation Ctr, Metrop Mus Art, NY, 82-; chmn, int bd adv, State Hermitage Mus, 95-2000; vp, Chinati Found, Marfa, Tex, 96-; bd trustees various orgs. *Awards:* Pahlavi Found, 78 Hon Pres Fel, Columbia Univ, 78; Full Merit Scholar, Sch Art Inst Chicago, 91-93; Pollock-Krasner Found, 97; Lily Auchincloss Found Fel Grant, NY Found for the Arts, 99. *Bibliog:* Maia Damianovic (auth), article, Tema Celeste, 9/98; Jennifer Dalton (auth), shake, Rev, Summer 98; Martin Coomer (auth), Time after time, Time Out London, 1/20-27/99. *Mem:* Am Fedn Arts (bd trustees 82-88); Am Friends Hermitage (co-chmn 98-); Asn Art Mus Dirs (bd trustees 89-90); Villa I Tatti Coun (mem adv com 88). *Dealer:* Andrea Rosen Gallery 525 W 24th St New York NY 10011

ASHTON, DORE
ART CRITIC, WRITER, EDUCATOR
b Newark, NJ, 1928. *Study:* Univ Wis, BA; Harvard Univ, MA; Phi Beta Kappa. *Hon Degrees:* Moore Coll, PhD, 75; Hamline Univ, 82; Minneapolis Coll Art, 2002. *Pos:* Assoc ed, Art Digest, NY, 52-54; art critic, NY Times, 55-60; contrib ed, Opus Int, Paris, 65-75 & Arts Mag, 74-90; lectr, Pratt Inst, 62-63, head humanities dept Sch Visual Arts, 65-68; mem adv bd John Simon Guggenheim Found, Dedalus Found. *Teaching:* Prof art hist, Cooper Union, 69-; adj prof, Yale Univ. *Awards:* Mather Award Art Criticism, Coll Art Asn, 63; Guggenheim Fels, 64 & 69; Ford Found Award, 65; Nat Endowment for Humanities Grant, 80; Lawrence A Fleischman Award for Scholarly Excellence, Smithsonian Inst, 2011. *Mem:* Int Asn Art Critics; Pen Club. *Res:* Modern art. *Publ:* Auth, Out of the Whirlwind, 87; Fragonard in the Universe of Painting, 88; Noguchi East and West, 92; Terence La Noue, 92; The Delicate Thread: Hiroshi Teshigahara's Life in Art, 97; The Black Rainbow: The Work of Fernando de Szyszlo, 2000; and 20 others. *Mailing Add:* 217 E 11th St New York NY 10003

ASHVIL-BIBI, SIGALIT
PAINTER
b Kutaissi, Georgia, Apr 29, 1952; US citizen. *Study:* Acad Music Tbillissi, USSR, BA, 69-73; study with Mordechai-Misha Dzanashvilli, 73-83; NY Acad Art, cert, 91-93. *Work:* Mus Beit Ha'Omamin, Jerusalem, Israel; Mus Yad Le Banim, Hulon, Israel; Yeshiva Univ Mus, NY; White House, Washington, DC. *Exhib:* Solo exhibs, White House, Washington, DC, 81 & 96, Queens "Y", NY, 96, 97 & 98 & Chassidic Art Inst, Brooklyn, NY, 2000; Father Daughter Team, Brooklyn Mus, 89; The Sephardic Journey, Yeshiva Univ Mus, Manhattan, 91-92; Group exhib, San Francisco, 91; Brooklyn-Queens Conservatory, 2000 & 2001; Family Group exhib, Jerusalem, Israel. *Teaching:* Art & music, currently. *Awards:* Gold Medal, 6th Int Festival between Musicians in USSR, 68. *Bibliog:* Cindy Garfinkel Blaustein (auth), An Investigation, Twentieth Century Observant Jewish Fine Arts, Fla Int Univ, 93; Shivuh Woolfson (auth), Capturing the inner spirit, Chai Mag, 93; Itzhak Atanelov (auth), Jewish-Georgian Spirit, 99; article in Druzhba Mag, 2000. *Mem:* Asn Israeli Artists (bd dir, 79); Am Artist Prof League; Judaic Art. *Media:* Oil, Acrylic & Pastel. *Publ:* Spiritual Leaders (35 portrait exhib), Ben-Raphael, 84; numerous articles in newspapers & mags. *Mailing Add:* 110-01 62nd Dr Apt 2C Forest Hills NY 11375

ASKIN, WALTER MILLER
PAINTER, PRINTMAKER
b Pasadena, Calif, Sept 12, 1929. *Study:* Univ Calif, Berkeley, BA & MA; Ruskin Sch Drawing & Fine Art, Oxford Univ. *Hon Degrees:* 75th Anniversary Honoree, Pasadena City College. *Work:* Mus Contemp Art, Chicago; Nat Gallery Art, Washington, DC; San Francisco Mus Art; Los Angeles Co Mus Art; Albright-Knox Gallery, Buffalo; Calif State Univ, Los Angeles; Franco-Am Union, Rennes, France; Norton Simon Mus Art, Pasadena, Calif; Whitney Mus, New York; Mus Mod Art, New York; Univ Calif, Berkeley; Hawaiian State Found on Cult & the Arts. *Comn:* Pasadena, Gold Line Inaugural Art Work, Los Angeles Metro Transportation Authority, Calif; Pasadena Playhouse, 2003; Los Angeles City Coll, 2005. *Exhib:* Solo exhibs, La Jolla Mus Art, Calif, 67, Abraxas Gallery, Calif, 79-81, Univ Southern Calif, 80 & Kunstlerhaus, Vienna, Austria, 81, Kauai Mus, Hawaii, 2009; Prints by Seven, Whitney Mus Am Art, 70; Int Biennial Graphic Art, Mus Mod Art, Ljubljana, Yugoslavia, 83; Lizardi/Harp Gallery, Pasadena, 88, 90 & 95; Lightside Gallery, Santa Fe, NMex, 95; Univ Kans, Lawrence (traveling), 97; 15th Int Biennial Prints & Drawings, Taipei Art Mus, Taiwan, Repub China, 97-98 & 2000-2001; Riverside Art Mus, Calif, 2000; From Paris to Pasadena Norton Simon Mus, 2000-2001; Calif State Univ, Channel Islands, 2002 & 10th Ann Exhib; Brigham Young Univ, 2002; Kimball Art Ctr, Park City, Utah, 2002; Painting Ctr, New York, 2006; Int Print Ctr, New York, 2007; Los Angeles City Col, da Vinci Gallery, 2007; Exceptionally Gifted, Norton Simon Mus, Calif, 2009; Ariz State Univ Alumni Portfolio, Southern Graphics Coun, Chicago, 2008; Palm Desert El Paseo Sculpture Show, 2007-2009; San Fran Contemp Art Fair, Thomas Paul Gallery, Los Angeles, 2011; Burbank Creative Art Ctr, 2011; Los Angeles Printmaking Soc, City of Brea Art Gallery, 2011; Flights of Pancy, Folk Tree, Pasadena, 2011; Trio of Four, Kavai Mus, Hawaii; New Hot Five CD & Jazz for Cows; Monster Truck Gallery, Dublin, Ireland; LA and Beyond, LA Print Space, Pacific Design Ctr, 2013; OK, Play That Thing; The Joint is Jumping, Steve Call and His Big Horns. *Pos:* Bd trustees, Pasadena Art Mus, 63-68; bd dir, Los Angeles Inst Contemp Art, Los Angeles, 77-81; bd gov, Baxter Art Gallery, Calif Inst Technol, 80-90; artist rep, Graphic Arts Coun, Los Angeles Co Mus Art, 80-89; chmn visual arts panel, Nat Art Awards, 81-82; advan placement, studio art exam comt, The Coll Bd, 85-, chmn arts adv comt, 86-93; coll bd comn, Future of the Advan Placement Prog, 98-2000; Taskforce, Col Bd (on the future of the arts in educ), 2008. *Teaching:* Prof art, Calif State Univ, Los Angeles, 56-92, prof emer, 92-; vis prof art, Univ Calif, Berkeley, 68-69, Calif State Univ, Long Beach, 74-75 & Univ Hawaii, 83; vis artist, Kelpra Studio, London, 69 & 73, Tamarind Inst, Univ NMex, 72 & 90, Athens Sch Fine Arts, 73, Cranbrook Acad Art, 79, Ariz State Univ, 80 & 83, Ossabaw Island Found, Ga, 82, Va Ctr Creative Arts, 83 & 86, Vt Studio Colony, 88 & John Michael Kohler Arts Indust Prog, 89; Hambridge Ctr Arts & Sci, Rabun Gap, Georgia, 91; Brigham Young Univ, Provo, Utah, 92; Univ Dallas, 2002. *Awards:* Artist Award, Pasadena Arts Coun, 70; Outstanding Prof Award, Calif State Univ, Los Angeles, 73; First Award Painting, Calif State Fair, 76; Past Presidents' Award, 80th Annual Nat Watercolor Soc, 2000. *Bibliog:* Violante (auth), American Printmakers 74, Graphics Group, 74; Newman (auth), Innovative Printmaking, Crown, 77; Walter Askin 1970-1980, Univ Southern Calif, 80; Roukes (auth), Humor in Art, Davis 97; Roukes (auth), Artful Jesters, Ten Speed Pub, 2003. *Mem:* Coll Art Asn Am; Los Angeles Printmaking Soc (pres, 2002-2004); Nat Watercolor Soc; Am Print Alliance; Alumni Art Asn Univ Calif Berkeley (hist, 2002-). *Media:* screen prints, lithographs, oil, watercolor, bronze, steel. *Res:* Image making in British colleges of art, bureau of research, US office of education. *Specialty:* Contemporary Art. *Interests:* Critical theory, modes of discourse. *Collection:* Java Wayang Klittiks, Dogon, Baule, Nepal & India, New Guinea, Feininger, Durer, Steinberg, Kimball, Britton, Loran, Crown, Wonner, Fuller, Ellis, Hansen, Wilson. *Publ:* Auth, Another Art Book To Cross Off Your List, 84; A Briefer History of the Greeks, 85; The Modern Manifesto Match Game, 98; Contemporary Impressions, Vol 8 #1; J Am Print Alliance, 2000; Womsters & Fooglers, 98; How to Become and Artist, 99; The Artists' Man, Dog, Bone Calendar for the Year 2000. *Dealer:* Floating Rock. *Mailing Add:* PO Box D South Pasadena CA 91031-0120

ASKMAN, TOM K
PAINTER, EDUCATOR
b Leadville, Colo, Oct 27, 1941. *Study:* Calif Coll Arts & Crafts, BFA; Univ Colo, MFA. *Work:* City Seattle, Wash; Cheney Cowles Art Mus, Spokane, Wash; Ft Worth Art Mus, Tex; Mus Art, Univ Okla, Norman; Mus Art, Univ Colo, Boulder. *Comn:* Columbia River Correctional Inst, Ore Arts Comn, Portland, 94; Tukwilla Park & Ride, Metro Arts Comn, Seattle, Wash, 94; Turnagain Elem Sch, Anchorage, Alaska, 95 & 97; Camino Real Proj, Las Cruces, NMex, 96 & 97; Raccoon River Park, West Des Moines, Iowa, 97. *Exhib:* New Orleans Mus Art, La, 71; Addison Gallery Am Art, Andover, Mass, 71; Minneapolis Art Inst, Minn, 71; Va Mus Fine Arts, Richmond, 72; Extraordinary Realities, Whitney Mus Am Art, NY, 73; Springfield Art Mus, Mo, 73-74; Contemp Arts Ctr, Cincinnati, Ohio, 74; Seattle Art Mus, Wash, 74; Private Views, Henry Gallery, Univ Wash, 80. *Teaching:* Instr, Univ Minn, Minneapolis, 68-70; assoc prof, Nicholls State Univ, Thibodaux, La, 70-72 & Eastern Wash Univ, Cheney, 72-. *Awards:* Cheney Cowles Art Mus, Spokane, 74, 76, 80 & 81; Painting Award, 60th Ann NW Artists, Seattle Art Mus, Wash, 74; State Wash Commissions, 79

ASMAN, ROBERT JOSEPH
PHOTOGRAPHER, PRINTMAKER
b Washington, DC, June 16, 1951. *Study:* Cath Univ Am, BA, 73; Rochester Inst Tech, MFA, 76. *Work:* Libr Cong & Nat Gallery Art, Washington, DC; Philadelphia Mus Art; Mus Fine Arts, Houston; Pa State Mus, Harrisburg. *Exhib:* Virginia Collects, Chrysler Mus, Norfolk, 88; photogs, Allentown Art Mus, Pa, 89; Art 21 90 (photo-1980's), Basel, Switz, 90; Artists select Artists, Inst Contemp Art, Philadelphia, 92; Cologne Int Arts Festival, Ger, 96; Basel Int Arts Festival, Switz, 96; Roger LaPelle Gallery, Philadelphia, 02; Philadelphia Mus Art, 02. *Teaching:* Sr lectr photog, Univ Arts, Philadelphia, 97-98, Drexel Univ, 2000; Adj Prof Grad Sch Fine Arts, Univ Pa, 2002. *Awards:* Pa Coun Arts Award, State of Pa, 93; Pew Found Fel, 97. *Media:* Photography. *Publ:* Contribr, Vietnam Veterans Memorial, Crown, 92; Sisters, Mothers, Daughters, Best Friends, Doubleday, 92-94 & 98; Bass Line, Overtime: Photos of Milt Hinton, Temple Univ, 92-96; In Search of Robert E Lee, Combined Books, 96; Excavating Voices & Listening to Voices of Native Americans, Univ Pa Mus, 98. *Dealer:* Galerie Francoise et Alain Paviot 57 Rue Sainte-Anne Paris France 75002. *Mailing Add:* 610 Kimball St Philadelphia PA 19147

ASMAR, ALICE
PAINTER, PRINTMAKER
b Flint, Mich. *Study:* Lewis & Clark Col, BA (magna cum laude); with Edward Melcarth & Archipenko, Univ Wash, MFA; Woolley Fel, Ecole Nat Super des Beaux-Arts, Paris, with M Souverbie; Huntington Hartford Found residence Fels, 61-64; Mac Dowell Colony, Peterboro, NH. *Work:* Nat Mus Am Hist Smithsonian Inst, Washington; Pub Int Mus, Gabrova, Bulgaria; Roswell Mus & Art Ctr, NMex; Metro Med Mall, Los Angeles; Kaiser-Permanente, Panorama City, Calif. *Comn:* Painting of doves, Bangs Manufacturing Co, Burbank, 92; paintings of Indian dancers, Navarro's, Hillsboro, Ore, 92; 45 ink drawings for educ brochures & posters, Small Wilderness Area Preserv, 92; paintings of Calif quail, Maples, San Marino, 93; Los Angeles City-Scape at Sunset (mural), comn by Dr Walter Jayasinghe, 96; Ocean Scenes, comn by Danner Corp, Ore, 2000; Malibu Scenes, comn by Alena Konkol, Malibu, Calif, 2001; Saint Joseph Medical Ctr, Burbank, Calif, 2003. *Exhib:* Seattle Art Mus, 52; Drawings USA, Minn Mus Art Nat Travel Show, 71-73; West 79/The Law, Minn Mus Art, 79-80; Solo exhibs, Mus of Sci & Indust, Los Angeles, 81, Sr Eye Art Gallery, Long Beach, 77 & 82, Circle Gallery Ltd, Houston, 83, Hilton Hotel, 91, Abbott Hall Gallery, William Temple House, Portland, Ore, 92, Descanso Gardens, La Canada Flintridge, Calif, 96 & Gloria Lee Gallery, 96; Sun Cities Art Mus, Ariz, 94; Audubon Art Exhib, Portland, Ore, 94; Walt Disney Sch Art Auction, Burbank, Calif, 94-96; Pasadena Showcase, 96; McGroarty Cult Arts Ctr, 96; Rainforest Art Auction, 96; Descanso Gardens Art Gallery, 97; Media Ctr, Burbank Mall, Burbank, Calif, 98; Christmas Exhibit, Domazale, Slovenia, 2001; Solo exhib, Burbank Media Ctr, 2002; Dorothy Chandler Pavilion, Los Angeles, 2003; Aztech Gallery, 2004; Hollenbeck 4th July exhibit, 2005; Future Photo Gallery, Toluca Lake, Calif, 2006. *Collection Arranged:* Millennium Art Collection, The Neth, 2000; Burbank Libr, Buena Vista branch, 2002. *Pos:* Eng draftsman, Boeing Aircraft, 52-54; engraver, Nambe Mills, Santa Fe, NMex, 68-; free-lance illusr, Los Angeles Times, 77-81; free-lance illusr for publs, 83-87; art consult, art judging, lectr & demos, var art groups, 88-92; mem, Burbank City Coun, Art in Pub Places, 91-; mem, Site Specific Comt, City of Burbank. *Teaching:* Asst prof painting & drawing, Lewis & Clark Col, 55-58; instr painting, Lennox Adult Educ, Calif, 63-65; part-time, Woodbury Col & Santa Monica City Col, 65-66; watercolor, Descanso Gardens, 88; art instr with admin duties, McGroarty Arts Ctr, Los Angeles Cult Affairs, 88-90; pvt teaching, 90-95, 98-2006 & McGroarty Cult Arts Ctr, 96-97. *Awards:* Sale Cent Purchase Award, NBC, 88; 2000 Notable Am Women, 89; Hon mem, Nat League Am Pen Women, Washington, 91; Phi Beta Kappa, Gamma Chapter, Lewis & Clark Coll, Portland, Ore, 2000. *Bibliog:* David Howard (dir), Alice Asmar Documentary (video), Visual Studies, San Francisco, 91; Le-Ann Jolakian (interviewer), Creating World Peace (video), United Artists Production, 91; feature articles, Flowerlover Mag, 95; Edmund Penny & Assoc (video), Alice Asmar, Descanso, 98. *Mem:* Visual Artists & Galleries Asn; Calif Lawyers for Arts; Artists Equity; League of Americas; Int Mus & Artist Registration; Los Angeles co Art Mus; and others. *Media:* Casein, Oil; India Ink, Lithographs. *Publ:* Southwest Arts Mag, 11/78; Los Angeles Times Home Mag, 3/26/78 & 12/3/78; Lewis & Clark J, fall 86; Tolucan, 1/15/92; Flowerlover Mag, 95. *Dealer:* Sachs Gallery Pacific Design Ctr 8687 Melrose Ave Los Angeles CA 90069; Dora Haslett 735 SW St Clair Portland OR 97205. *Mailing Add:* Asmar Studios PO Box 1963 Burbank CA 91507

ASOMA, TADASHI
PAINTER
b Iwatsuki, Japan, Apr 28, 1923. *Study:* Saitama Teachers Col, Urawa, MS; Bijitsu Gakko, Tokyo, govt scholar; Grande Chaumiere, Paris, govt scholar; Art Students League. *Work:* Nelson Gallery, Kansas City; Am Express Co, NY; 3M Co, St Paul; Andrew Dickson White Mus, Ithaca, NY; San Diego Mus Art. *Exhib:* Solo exhibs, David Findlay Galleries, NY, biennially 65-97, Dubins Gallery, Los Angeles, 79 & 85, Foundry Sch Mus NY, 79 & Steckler-Haller Galleries, Scottsdale, Ariz; Tokyo Central Mus, 81 & 84. *Teaching:* Instr art educ, Iwatsuki Jr High Sch, 50-64. *Awards:* Second Prize, Saitama Bijitsu Ten, 55; Second Prize, Nat Exhib Prof Art, 68; People's Westchester Savings Bank Award Best in Show, 20th, 22nd & 24th Ann Fine Art Shows, Putnam Art Coun, Mahopac, NY, 82. *Bibliog:* Articles in Art News, NY Times & NY Post, 65, 67, 69, 79 & 83; and others. *Media:* Oil. *Dealer:* David Findlay Galleries 984 Madison Ave New York NY 10021; John Szoke Graphics Inc 164 Mercer St New York NY 10012. *Mailing Add:* 2 Pondfield Dr N Chappaqua NY 10514-1308

ASPELL, AMY SUZANNE
DIRECTOR, WEAVER
b Chicago, Ill, June 28, 1942. *Study:* Knox Col, Galesburg, Ill, BA (art), 63, Univ SFla, Tampa, MA (art educ), 76, Ordained in Centers for Spiritual Living, 2011. *Comn:* Woven relief wall hanging, Bay Waves, Carter Corp, Caspers Inc, Tampa, Fla, 80. *Collection Arranged:* Touching Art Corner, Hillsborough Co Arts Council Gallery, Tampa, Fla. *Pos:* Dir, Tampa Community Design Ctr, 79-81, Ark Arts Coun, 84-87 & Irvine Fine Arts Ctr, 87-99, Minister, Centers for Spiritual Living, 1999-2012, Vista Volunteer, Housing Resources Board, 2011-2012. *Teaching:* Univ Calif, Irvine; Arts Advocacy. *Bibliog:* Cookbook Weaving I (book). *Mem:* Centers for Spiritual Living. *Media:* Fiber Art. *Interests:* Ecology, earth building. *Publ:* Auth, Cookbook Weaving I, Craft Publications Inc, 77; Arts & Crafts for the Blind, Educational Gerontology: An International Quarterly, a portion of Masters Thesis. *Mailing Add:* 11469 Kallgren Rd NE Bainbridge Island WA 98110

ASTMAN, BARBARA ANNE
PHOTOGRAPHER, VISUAL ARTIST
b Rochester, NY, July 12, 1950. *Study:* Sch Am Craftsmen, with Albert Paley; Rochester Inst Technol, AA, 70; Ont Coll Art, Toronto, Assoc, 73. *Hon Degrees:* Royal Canadian Art. *Work:* Victoria & Albert Mus, London, Eng; Art Gallery Ont, Toronto; Winnipeg Art Gallery; Bibliotheque Nat, Paris, France; Nat Gallery Can, Ottawa; George Eastman House, Rochester, NY; and others. *Comn:* CIL Corp, Toronto, Can; Calgary Winter Olympics, 88; City of Ottawa, Art in Public Places Programme; Cadillac Fairview, Simcoe Place, Toronto, 94; Baycrest Geriatric Ctr, Toronto, 2001; Wolfond Ctr for Jewish Studies, Univ Toronto, 2004; Murano On Bay, Toronto, 2010; Can Embassy in Berlin, 2004; Loblaws Corp Hq, Brampton, Ont, 2006. *Exhib:* Xerography, Art Gallery Ont, Toronto, 77; Contemp Can Photog Portrait, Edmonton Art Gallery, Alta, 78; Winnipeg Perspectives, Winnipeg Art Gallery, 79; Alternative Imaging Systems, Everson Mus, Syracuse, NY, 79; Electroworks, George Eastman House, Rochester, NY, 79-80; Solo exhibs, Centre Cult, Paris, France, 82, Sable-Castelli Gallery, Ltd, Toronto, Can, 77-90, Jane Corking Gallery, Toronto, 97, 99, Modern Fuel Gallery, Kingston, Ont, 98, plus others; Generation Polaroid, Forum des Halles, Paris, France, 85; Visual Facts, Third Eye Ctr, Glasgow, Scotland & Mus du Que, Quebec City, 86; Porkkanna Collection, Pro Mus Contemp Art, Helsinki, Finland, 89; Thunder Bay Art Gallery, Ont, 92; 20 Yr Survey Touring Exhib, Art Gallery Hamilton, 95; Corkin Gallery, Toronto, 97, 2000-2001 & 2004-2009; Windsor Art Gallery, ON, 2005; Koffler Art Gallery, Toronto, 2006; plus others. *Pos:* Coordr, Color Xerox Prog, Visual Arts Ont, 77-83; mem, Pub Art Comn, Toronto; bd dir, Toronto Arts Awards Found, 92; bd trustees, Art Gallery Ontario, Toronto, currently. *Teaching:* Fac, camera art, Ont Col Art, 75-; Prof, fac art, Ont Col Art & Design, Toronto, 75-. *Awards:* Can Coun Arts Awards Grants, 76, 77, 80, 81, 83, 84, 86 & 88; Prov Ont Coun Arts Grants, 74-82, 84, 92 & 94; Can Coun Sr Arts Awards Grant, 93-94. *Bibliog:* Barbara Astman (catalog), Centre Cult Can, Paris, 82; Astman Places, Nickel Arts Mus, Univ Calgary, Can, 83; Barbara Astman: Personal/Persona, A 20-Year Survey, 95. *Mem:* Univ Art Asn Can; Visual Arts Asn Ont; Royal Can Arts. *Media:* Mixed Media, Camera Art. *Res:* Pop culture, history, memory. *Interests:* Art & literature. *Dealer:* Corkin Gallery 55 Mill St Toronto Bldg 61. *Mailing Add:* 23 Alcina Ave Toronto ON M6G 2E7 Canada

ASTRUP, HANS RASMUS
COLLECTOR, MUSEUM FOUNDER
Pos: Founder, Astrup Fearnley Art Mus, Oslo, 1993. *Awards:* Named one of Top 200 Collectors, ARTnews mag, 2004-13. *Collection:* Contemporary art. *Mailing Add:* Astrup Fearnley Mus PO Box 1158 Dronningens Gate Oslo 4 0107 Norway

ATKINS, ROBERT
CRITIC, EDUCATOR, EDITOR
b Cleveland, Ohio. *Study:* Univ Calif, Berkeley, MA (art hist), 76; Univ Calif, Riverside, BA 72, Hon Dr, Phi Beta Kappa, 72. *Collection Arranged:* David Ireland (auth, catalog), New Mus Contemp Art, 84; Between Science & Fiction (auth, catalog), Sao Paulo Biennial, 85; Decoding Gender (auth, catalog), 92; From Media to Metaphor: Art About AIDS (auth, catalog), traveling, 92-94. *Pos:* Art columnist, Village Voice, New York, 88-; Founder, Visual AIDS, New York, 89; Founder, Artists' Survival Workshop, New York, 84; Vpres/ed in chief, Arts Tech entertainment network 96-98; ed: artery The Aids Arts forum, 2000-01; arts ed media channel, 2000-02. *Teaching:* San Francisco State Univ, summers, 84-. *Awards:* Art Critics Fel, Nat Endowment Arts, 81 & Summer Seminar Coll Teachers, 81; Manufacturers Hanover Art/World Award Distinguished Art Criticism, 85; Penny McCall Found award in the Visual Arts, for an independent writer/cur, 2001; Penny Mc Call Award for Outstanding Arts Achievement, 2001. *Mem:* Coll Art Asn; Visual AIDS. *Publ:* Auth, Artspeak: A Guide To Contemp Ideas, Movements and Buzzwords, 1945-Present, 90 & Artspoke: A Guide to Modern Ideas, Movements and Buzzwords, 1848-1944, 93, Abbeville; co-auth (exhib catalog and book for travelling mus exhib): From Media to Metaphor: Art About AIDS, 1991; "Critic's Choice" Eaton/Shoen Gallery, San Francisco, 1981(also cur); "Apologia" Union Gallery, San Jose State Univ, 1981(also cur); "About TV" Just Above Midtown, NY, 1983 (also cur); "Intro: Alan Shepp" Stephen Wirtz Gallery, San Francisco, 1982; "Currents: David Ireland" New Mus of Contemp Art, NY, 1984 (also cur) "; "San Francisco/Science Fiction" San Francisco Art Commission Gallery, Otis-Parsons Gallery (LA), Clocktower Gallery, New York, 1984 (also curator); "Between Science and Fiction" for the 18th Sao Paulo Bienal, Brazil, 1985 (also curator); "What's Happening: Contemporary Art from California, Washington, and Oregon" Alternative Museum, New York, 1984; "Art Against AIDS: Washington, DC" American Foundation for AIDS Research, New York, 1990; "Of Luminosity, Accident and Power Sanders" (for the exhibition Stephen Hannock), James Graham & Sons, New York, 1996; "Rinaldo Hopf: Golden Queers" (for the exhibition of the same name), Wessel + O'Connor Gallery, New York, 1998; "Interactivity and Intervention: Peter D'Agostino's Art of Ideas" (for the exhibition, Peter D'Agostino: Interactivity and Intervention, 1978-99); Lehman College Art Gallery, Bronx, New York, 1999; "Fusion! Artists in a Research Setting" (for the exhibition of the same name), Carnegie Mellon University, Pittsburgh, 2001 (also curator); contribr articles to Advocate, Aperture, Arena (Spain), art + architecture, Art + Text (Australia), Art and Auction, Art Aurea (Ger), Art in America, Art J (Coll Art Assoc), Art Paper, ArtByte, Artery: The AIDS-Arts Forum (online), Artforum, ArtLook (CD-Rom), ArtNews, ARTS BT (Japan), Cahier/Witte de With (Neth), Calif, Calif Monthly, Contemporanea, Elle, Esquire (Japan), Flash Art (Italy), Glass Art J, High Performance, Images & Issues, Le Millennium (Japan), Live LA Institute of Contemp Art J, The Media Channel (online), New Art Examiner, Newsday, New West, NY Mag, NY Times, Poz, Print News, San Francisco Bay Guardian, 7 Days, Studio Inter, TalkBack! A Forum for Critical Discourse (online), Vogue, Wired (Japan), Wolkenkrazer (Ger), World Art; cur N.O. Show, South of Market Cultural Ctr (San Francisco), Fashion Moda (the Bronx), 1982; Positive Actions: The Visual AIDS Competition, Clocktower Gallery, DC 37 Union Headquarters, Longwood Gallery (all NY), 1990; From Media to Metaphor: Art About AIDS, (with Thomas Sokolowski), Independent Curs, NY, 1991-1994 (9 mus tour); Decoding Gender, School 33 Art Center, Baltimore, 1992; Peter D'Agostino: Interactivity and Intervention, 1978-99; Lehman Coll Art Gallery, Bronx, NY, 1999; Censorship in Camouflage The New Press, Feb. 2006; and several others

ATKINS, ROSALIE MARKS
PAINTER
b Charleston, WVa, July 21, 1921. *Study:* Mason Coll Music & Fine Arts, Charleston, WVa; Morris Harvey Col, Charleston; workshops with Leo Manso & Victor Candell, Provincetown, Mass; also with Bud Hopkins, Truro, Mass. *Work:* WVa Arts & Humanities Permanent Collection; Erma Byrd Gallery, Univ Charleston, 2007. *Exhib:* Nat League Am Pen Women Ann Show, Washington, DC, 72, Univ Charleston, 90, 92 & 94; 39th Ann Exhib Contemp Am Paintings, Four Arts, Palm Beach, Fla, 77; Lighthouse Gallery, Tequesta, Fla, 78-79; Nat League Am Pen Women, Wash, 87; WVa Tech, 98; Univ Charleston, 98; WVa State Col, WVa Juried Exhib; WVa Artists on the Move (traveling); Am Drawing Biennial, Portsmouth, Va; Tirca Carlis Gallery, Provincetown, Mass; Provincetown Art Center, Provincetown, Mass; Soc of Four Arts, Palm Beach, Fla; and others. *Collection Arranged:* WVa Div Culture & Hist; Univ Charleston; Rep in many pvt collections. *Awards:* Selected for traveling show, Art in the Embassies Prog, 70 & Nat League Am Pen Women, 72 & 77; Purchase Awards, WVa Arts & Humanities, Allied Artists Award, 72; Purchase Award, Lighthouse Gallery, Jupiter, Fla; and others. *Bibliog:* Dorothy Seckler (auth), article in Provincetown Painters; article in Artists/USA, 79-80; article, Focus, 5/83. *Mem:* Allied Artists of WVa (vpres, 67); Am Pen Women (pres, Charleston Br, 73-74). *Media:* Acrylic, Oil. *Specialty:* Gallery Eleven, Charleston, WVa. *Publ:* article, Provincetown Painters, Everson Mus Art Syracuse, NY. *Mailing Add:* 1518 Quarrier St Charleston WV 25311

ATKINSON, CONRAD
SCULPTOR, PAINTER
b Cumbria, Eng, June 15, 1940. *Study:* Liverpool Coll Art, NDD, ATD, 61; Royal Acad Sch, London, Cert, RAS, Hons, 65; Manchester Coll Art, AFD, 67. *Work:* Brooklyn Mus, NY; Pushkin Mus, Moscow; Tate Gallery, Victoria & Albert Mus & Brit Mus, London; Mus Mod Art, NY; Australian Nat Gallery, Canberra. *Comn:* Arts Coun Northern Ireland/Irish Trades Union, Belfast, 75; banners, Gen & Munic Workers Union, Newcastle, Eng, 77; record/sound, comn by Geoff Gordon/Ronald Feldman, NY, 83; painting, Lewisham Borough Coun, London, 85. *Exhib:* Manchester City Art Gallery, Eng, 67; Royal Acad Bicentenary, London, 68; Biennale de Paris, Mus d'Art Mod, Paris, 75; Art for Soc, Whitechapel Art Gallery, London, 78; Messages, Albright-Knox Art Gallery, Buffalo, 80; Victoria & Albert Mus, London, 80, 84, 85 & 87; Tate Gallery, London, 81, 82 & 95; Australian Prints, Nat Gallery, Canberra, 84; Laing Art Gallery, Newcastle, Eng, 86; solo exhibs, Victoria & Albert Mus, London, 89, ICA, Moscow, 93, Ruth Bloom Gallery, Los Angeles, 93, Paule Anglim Gallery, San Francisco, 95 & Univ Art Gallery & Mus, Berkeley, Calif, 95, Tullie House Mus & Art Gallery, Carlisle, Eng, 96, Ronald Feldman Fine Arts, NY, 97, The Atlanta Coll of Art Gallery, Atlanta, Ga, 98, Intersection for the Arts, San Francisco, Calif, 2000, Abbot Hall Art Gallery, Kendal Cumbria, 2000; Fractured Fairy Tales (with catalogue), Duke Univ Fine Art Gallery, 96; Ronald Feldman Gallery, NY, 96; Face a l'Histoire, Ctr Georges Pompidou, Paris, France, 96; Campaign to Ban Land Mines, The Very Special Art Gallery, Washington, DC, 97; The Liverpool Biennial of Contemp Art, St Georges Hall, Liverpool, Eng, 99. *Pos:* Vis arts adv, Greater London Coun, 81-86 & Inner London Educ Authority, 86-; chair art & art hist, Univ Calif, Davis. *Teaching:* Lectr fine art, Slade Sch Fine Art, 75-78; artist-in-residence, London Borough of Lewisham, 85; vis prof, Carnegie Melon Univ, Pittsburgh, 89-90; chmn, Univ Calif, Davis, 92-. *Awards:* Churchill Fel, 72; Henry Moore Found Residency, 91-92; Official Artist Award, US Campaign to Ban Landmines, 97. *Bibliog:* Cumbrias, Greatest Living Artist, Cumbria Life Mag, 96; An Interview with Conrad Atkinson: From the Political to the Popular, Sculpture 17, 9/98;

Conrad Atkinson at Intersection for the Arts, Artweek 31, 6/2000; Secondhand second thoughts, Guardian 34, 5/2000. *Mem:* Arts Coun Gt Brit; Percent for Art, Nat Steering Comt. *Media:* Multi. *Publ:* Auth, Passive Action/Active Passion, Artforum, 9/80; 1984 in the Light of Guernica, Ronald Feldman Fine Arts, 84; On Practice, Artists on Art, Rudulf Baranik Publ, 86; Desires of Permanence: Dreams of Transience, Huddersfield Art Gallery, 91; Challenging the status quo, The Year of the Visual Arts, Eng, 96. *Mailing Add:* c/o Ronald Feldman Fine Arts 31 Mercer St New York NY 10013

ATKINSON, ERIC NEWTON
PAINTER, EDUCATOR
b Hartlepool, Durham, Eng, July, 23, 1928; Brit & Can Citizen. *Study:* Hartlepool Coll Art, Eng, NDD (hons), 52; Royal Acad Sch, London, Eng, 55. *Hon Degrees:* Fanshawe Coll, Hon degree. *Work:* Contemp Art Soc; Leeds City Art Gallery; Arts Coun, Gt Brit, London; Univ Marburg, Ger; London Regional Art Gallery, Ont; and others. *Exhib:* Figures in their Settings, Tate Gallery, London, Eng, 53; Four Northern Artists, Hatton Gallery, Newcastle, 59; Art from Yorkshire, Stadhausgalerie Mus, Dortmund, Ger, 65; Edinburgh 100, Demarco Gallery, Edinburgh, Scotland, 67; British Painting, Corcoran Gallery, Washington, DC, 70; retrospectives, Mendel Art Gallery, Saskatoon, Sask, 80 & London Regional Art Gallery, Ont, 94; Lewis Collection, Carnegie Mus Art, Pittsburgh, 80; Wallace Gallery, Calgary, Alberta, Can, 97; Tate Gallery, St Ives, Eng, 98; Modigliani Ctr, Florence, 2002; McMaster Univ Gallery, Hamilton, 2010; Drawings 1944-2010, Mus London, 2010; Beaverbrook Gallery, Fredericton, NB, 2014. *Teaching:* Lectr fine arts, Leeds Coll Art, Yorkshire, 56-65, dept head, fine arts, 62-69; dean fac applied arts, Fanshawe Coll, London, Ont, 73-82. *Awards:* David Murray Travel Scholar, Royal Acad, London, 52-54; J M Turner, Landscape Bursary, Royal Acad, London, 54. *Bibliog:* Atkinson-Pollock (auth), Artists proof (film), 82; Univ Western Ont, Canadian Art Collection, 84. *Mem:* Royal Can Acad Arts. *Media:* Mixed. *Interests:* History. *Publ:* Auth, Alfred Wallis Cornish Primitive, Accent, Leeds, 64; coauth, Art Education at Leeds, Studio Int, 69; auth, Art Education, MASH, Chicago Art Inst, 70; exhib rev, Arts, Can, 76; Forum: Imaginative Use of Space for Arts, London, Ont, 81; Visual education on the back burner, Bulletin Mag, 86; The Incomplete Circle, A Scholar Press Bk, Eng, 2000; plus others. *Dealer:* Mendelson Gallery 5874 Ellsworth Ave Pittsburgh PA 15232; Thielsen Galleries Inc 1038 Adelaide St London ON; Wallace Galleries 500 5th Ave SW Calgary Alberta Can; Moore Gallery LTD 80 Spadina Ave Toronto Ontario. *Mailing Add:* 69 Paddock Green Crescent London ON N6J 3P6 Canada

ATKINSON, LESLIE JANE See Temple, Leslie Alcott (Leslie Jane Atkinson)

ATKINSON, TRACY
CONSULTANT, MUSEOLOGIST
b Middletown, Ohio, Aug 10, 1928. *Study:* Ohio State Univ, BFA (summa cum laude), 50; Univ of the Americas, 50; Univ Pa, MA, 51; Bryn Mawr Col, 53. *Collection Arranged:* Pop Art and the Am Tradition, 65; The Inner Circle, 66; Botero, 67; Options & The Bradley Collection, 68; Seymour Lipton & A Plastic Presence, 69; Aspects of a New Realism, 70; Portraits Exhibition, 71; Six Painters, 72; The Urban River, 73, Milwaukee Art Mus; Tremaine Collection; Sol Lewitt Wall Drawings; JP Morgan Collector; The Great River, David Bermant Collection, Hartford, Conn. *Pos:* Curatorial asst, Albright-Knox Art Gallery, 55-59; asst dir, Columbus Gallery Fine Arts, 59-61, actg dir, 61-62; dir, Milwaukee Art Ctr, 62-76; dir, Wadsworth Atheneum Mus Art, 77-88, emer dir, 88-; pvt consultant, 88. *Publ:* Articles in prof journals, nat art news mags & newspapers. *Mailing Add:* 117 Ciderbrook Rd Avon CT 06001

ATLAS, CHARLES
FILMMAKER
b St Louis, Mo, 1958. *Exhib:* The Hanged One; Television Dance Atlas, Hail the New Puritan, 87; Superhoney, 94; Merce Cunningham: A Lifetime of Dance, 2000; consulting dir, Art in the 21st Century, 2001; The Legend of Leigh Bowery, 2002; William Kentridge: Anything is Possible, 2010; Whitney Biennial, Whitney Mus Am Art, 2012. *Pos:* filmmaker in res, Merce Cunningham Dance Co, NY. *Awards:* recipient of multiple Bessie Awards, NY. *Mailing Add:* Merce Cunningham Dance Co 55 Bethune St New York NY 10014

ATLAS, NAVA
WRITER, BOOK ARTS
b Jaffa, Israel, Apr 29, 1955; US citizen. *Study:* Univ Mich, BFA, 77; State Univ NY, New Paltz, MA, 2007. *Work:* Wichita Art Mus, Kans; New York Pub Libr Print Collection; Samuel Dorsky Mus, State Univ NY, New Paltz; Nat Mus Women Arts; Weatherspoon Art Gallery; MoMa Art Libr, Collection Artist's books; Victoria & Albert Mus, Nat Art Libr; Yale Univ, Arts of the Bk Collection; Sallie Bingham Ctr Women's History and Culture; Duke Univ Lib. *Exhib:* The Radwaste & Stonehenge Series, traveling exhib, collab with Chaim Tabak, 85-89; Recent Acquisitions, State Univ NY, New Paltz, 93; Wash Pavilion Arts & Sci, SDak, 2006; Iona Coll, NY, 2007; Suffolk Mus, Va, 2008; Calif State Univ, 2008; Purdue Univ, 2008; Oakland Comm Coll, 2008; ARC Gallery, Chicago, 2008; Pyramid Atlantic Art Ctr, 2009; Everson Mus, Syracuse, 2010; Duke Univ, Perkins Lib, Durham, 2010; Ctr for Book Art, NY, 2011; Delaware Ctr for Contemporary Art, Wilmington, 2011; Manhattanville Coll, Purchase, NY, 2012; Retrospective Traveling, 2010-2012; Abecedarian Gallery, Denver; Hope Coll, Holland, Mich; SUNY Ulster, Stone Ridge, NY; Lafayette Coll, Easton, Pa; Visual Studies Wkshp, Rochester, NY; Wells Coll, Aurora, NY; Coll New Rochelle, NY. *Bibliog:* Howard Dalee Spencer (auth), A Collaborative Exhibition: The Radwaste & Stonehenge Series, Wichita Art Mus, 85; Maureen Cummins, Ann Lovett, Nava Atlas (co-auths), Artists Books and Works on Paper (catalog). *Media:* Digital Media; Book Arts. *Publ:* Vegetariana, 84; auth, Secret Recipes for the Modern Wife, 2009; Secret Recipes for the Mod Wife, ltd ed, 2007, Simon & Schuster, 2009; Love & Marriage, ltd ed; Dear Literary Ladies, Ltd Ed, 2010; Literary Ladies Guide to the Writing Life, Sellers Pub, 2011. *Mailing Add:* 509 Albany Post Rd New Paltz NY 12561

ATLEE, EMILIE DES
PAINTER, INSTRUCTOR
b Bethlehem, Pa, July 6, 1915. *Study:* Spring Garden Inst, Philadelphia; also with Roswell Weidner & Joseph & Gertrude Capolino. *Work:* United Airlines, Philadelphia Airport; Palisades High Sch, Bucks Co, Pa; La Salle Coll & Franklin Inst, Philadelphia; Cult Arts Ctr Ocean City, NJ. *Comn:* Portraits, Libr Univ Del & Berks Co Ct House, Pa. *Exhib:* Solo exhibs, Little Gallery, 63, Newman's Gallery, Philadelphia, 70 & Arrowroot Natural Foods II, Paoli, Pa, 96; Knickerbocker Artists Ann, NY, 64; Philadelphia Art Teachers Asn, 69-71; Harrisburg Mus, Pa, 71. *Pos:* Critic, 78-. *Teaching:* Instr, 53-69; instr, Main Line Ctr Arts, Bryn Mawr, Pa, 69-77. *Awards:* Hon mention, Nat, Ogunquit Art Ctr, 59 & Nat Benedictine Art Awards, 69; First Prize, Main Line Ctr Arts Members Show, 85. *Bibliog:* Dorothy Grafly (ed), The changing moods of art, Art in Focus, 71. *Mem:* Artists Equity Asn. *Media:* Oil, Pastel. *Dealer:* Newman Galleries 1624 Walnut St Philadelphia PA 19103. *Mailing Add:* 27 Fairview Rd Narberth PA 19072

ATTAL, M GEORGE
ART DEALER, CONSULTANT
b Austin, Tex, Dec 12, 1934. *Pos:* Owner, Gen Store Gallery, Austin, Tex, 64-68, Int Fine Arts, HI, 68-79, Austin Galleries, Tex, 79-86 & 89-. *Specialty:* US Agent for the Estate of Joaquin Torrents Llado; 19th and 20th century artists; national and international artists. *Collection:* Modern impressionists paintings

ATTIE, SHIMON
PHOTOGRAPHER, VIDEO INSTALLATION
b Los Angeles, Calif, 1957. *Study:* Univ Calif Berkeley, BA, 1980; Antioch Univ, San Francisco, MA, 1982; San Francisco State Univ, MFA, 1991. *Work:* Los Angeles County Mus Art; San Francisco Mus Mod Art; Mus Mod Art, New York; High Mus Art, Atlanta; Mus Fine Arts, Houston; Int Ctr Photography, New York; Mus Photographic Art, San Diego; Jewish Mus, New York; Mus Contemp Photography, Chicago. *Comn:* Between Dreams and History, comn by Creative Time, NY, 1998; An Unusually Bad Lot, comn by Inst Contemp Art ICA, Boston, Mass, 1999-00; White Nights, Sugar Dreams (prog of Mus Am Art at RI Sch Design) comn by ArtConText, Providence, RI, 2000; Re-Collecting: Centennial Artwork (year long new media installation), comn by Jewish Mus NY with Norma Ballard, NY, 2004; Light Under Night (3-channel video installation), comn by Norsk Hydro, Oslo Symphony Hall, 12/2005. *Exhib:* Solo Exhibs: Camerawork Gallery, San Francisco, 1992; Ruth Bloom Gallery, Los Angeles, 1995; Nicole Klagsbrun Gallery, New York, 1995; Cleveland Mus Art, 1996; Jack Shainman Gallery, New York, 1998, 2002, 2004; Inst Contemp Art, Boston, 1998; Gallery Paule Anglim, San Francisco, 2001; Numark Gallery, Washington, 2002, 2005; Mus Contemp Photography, Chicago, 2004; Jewish Mus, New York, 2004; Miami Art Mus, Miami, 2006; DeYoung Mus, Fine Arts Mus San Francisco, CA, 2008; Group Exhibs: Recent Acquisitions, Mus Photographic Arts, San Diego, 1993; After Images: Art as Social Memory, Neues Mus Weserberg, Bremen Germany, 2004; Common Ground: Discovering Community in 150 Years of Art, Corcoran Gallery Art, Wash DC, 2004-2005; Recent Acquisitions to the Permanent Collection, Mus Contemp Photog, Chicago, Il, 2006; Beautiful Suffering: Photog and the Traffic in Pain, Williams Coll Mus Art, Williamstown, Mass, 2006; New Acquisitions, Miami Art Mus, Miami Fl, 2007; Art of Memory, Jewish Mus, New York, 1994; After Art: Rethinking 150 Years of Photography, Henry Art Gallery, Seattle, 1994; New Photography 10, Mus Mod Art, New York, 1994, Seeing Double, 2000, Open Ends, 2000; Human/Nature, New Mus Contemp Art, New York, 1995; Recent Acquisitions, High Mus Art, Atlanta, 1996; Inaugural Exhib, Henry Art Gallery, Seattle, 1997; Mus Photographic Arts, San Diego, 2000; Cultural Crossing, Numark Gallery, Washington, 2002; San Francisco Mus Mod Art, San Francisco, 2003; Monument Recall, Camerawork Gallery, San Francisco, 2004; Common Ground: Discovering Community in 150 Years of Art, Selections from the Collection of Julia J Norrell, Corcoran Mus Art, Washington, 2004; Beautiful Suffering: Photography & the Traffic in Pain, Williams Coll Mus Art, Williamstown, Mass, 2006. *Teaching:* adj prof art, Accad Art (Hochschule der Kuenste), Berlin, Germ, 1995; full time vis prof, Dept Art, Univ Calif Santa Cruz, Santa Cruz, Calif, 1997; vis prof, Parson's Sch Design, NY, 1998; vis prof, Sarah Lawrence College, Bronxville, NY, 2000-1; instr, Bard/ICP MFA prog, NY, 2004. *Awards:* Vis Artist Fel, NY Found Arts, NY, 2005; Cultural Achievement Award in Visual Arts, Nat Found Jewish Culture, NY, 2006; Vis Artist Fel, Pollock-Krasner Foundation, NY, 2006; Vis Artist Fel, Radcliffe Inst Advanced Study, Harvard Univ, Cambridge, Mass, 2006-7. *Publ:* auth, Finstere Medine, Gallerie im Scheunenviertel, Berlin, Germ, 1992; photog & installations, The Writing on the Wall: Projections in Berlin's Jewish Quarter, Heidelberg, Germany, 1993; auth, Sites Unseen, Edition Braus, Heidelberg, Germany, 1998; auth, The History of Another: Projections in Rome, Twim Palms Press, Santa Fe, NMex, 2004; auth, Attraction of Onlookers: Aberfan-Anatomy of a Welsh Village, Parthian Books, UK, 2007. *Dealer:* Numark Gallery 625-27 E St NW Washington DC 20004; Jack Shainman Gallery 513 W 20th St New York NY 10011

ATWOOD PINARDI, BRENDA
PAINTER, INSTRUCTOR
b 1936. *Study:* Am Acad Art, Chicago, cert, 56. *Comn:* Dr Raymond Carhart portrait, Northwestern Univ, Evanston, Ill, 73; Nicholas Santucci portrait, comn by Santucci family, Skokie, Ill, 75. *Exhib:* Classic Am Art Show, Beverly Hills, Calif, 85-89; solo exhib, Mus SW, Midland, Tex, 86; Ann Plein Art Show, Catalina Island, Calif, 87-89; Northwest Rendezvous, Holter Mus, Helena, Mont, 88 & 92; Four Am Impressionists, Cincinnati, 91; Am Collectors Invitational, Scottsdale, Ariz, 92; CM Russell Show & Auction, 1993-2003; Artists for Open Space, 1999, 2001, 2003; Miniatures, Albuquerque Mus, 2000-03; Treasure State Invitational, 2000, 02; and others. *Pos:* Dir, founder, Village Art Sch, 66-76, consult, 76-. *Teaching:* instr, Scottsdale Artists' Sch, 1991-2004; instr, Pocatello Art Ctr, 1997, 98; instr, Abbrescia Fine Art & Pottery Studios. *Awards:* Best of Show, Eighth Ann NW Art Show, 78; Artist of Yr, Am Royal Asn, 84; Ashton & Louise Smith Artists' Choice, 94, 2004; Best of Show, CM Russell Mus Show, 1998, 2002, 04; Best Painting, CM Russell Mus Show, 1997; People's

Choice award Artists for Open Space, 2001; Artist-in-Residence, Glacier Nat Park, 1998. *Bibliog:* Scott E Dial (auth), Montana's special light, SW Art Mag, 1/77; Susan Hallsten McGarry (auth), Joe Abbrescia, SW Art Mag, 9/86; Lewis Barrett Lehrman (auth), Energize Your Paintings with Color and Freshen Your Paintings With New Ideas, SW Art Mag, 8/95. *Media:* Oil. *Interests:* conservation & restoration, fine art. *Mailing Add:* c/o Abbrescia Inc 12 1st Ave W Kalispell MT 59901-4440

AUBIN, BARBARA
PAINTER, COLLAGE ARTIST
b Chicago, Ill, Jan 12, 1928. *Study:* Carleton Col, BA, 49; Art Inst Chicago, BAE, 54, MAE, 55, George D Brown foreign travel fel, France & Italy, 55-56; Buenos Aires Conv Act grant, Haiti, 58-60. *Work:* Ill State Mus; Art Inst Chicago; Ball State Univ; Centre d'Art, Port-au-Prince, Haiti. *Comn:* Collage, 100th Anniversary of the First Exhib of Seurat's Sunday Afternoon on the Island of Grand Jatte, Roy Boyd Gallery, Chicago, 86. *Exhib:* Mid-Year Shows, Butler Inst Am Art, Ohio, 61 & 62; 10th Ann Nat Prints & Drawings Exhib, Okla Art Ctr, 68; Clocktower, NY, 86; Am Hist: Women & the US Constitution, Atlanta, Ga & traveling, 88; Survey of Contemp Ill Watercolor, Springfield Art Asn & Tarble Art Ctr, Charleston, Ill, 91, 93, 95, 2000, 2001; Women & Surrealism, Women's Caucus Nat Art, Chicago, 92; Three Rivers Arts Festival, Pittsburgh, Pa, 94; Fulbright Nat, Washington, DC, 97; Chicago Women's Caucus Art Ann Show, 98. *Collection Arranged:* Print & Drawing Dept, Art Institute Chicago; Shomer Col, Waukegan, Ill; Kemper Group Collection, Long Grove, Ill; State of Ill Bldg, Chicago. *Pos:* Reporter, Women Artists News, 77-78 & 83-90; critic for var publ; cur, Send a Postcard to Barbara, Loyola Univ & traveling, 79-80; co-cur, Kimo Theatre, Albuquerque, NMex, 97. *Teaching:* Asst prof painting, drawing & watercolor, Sch Art Inst Chicago, 60-68; asst prof painting, drawing & design, Loyola Univ (Chicago), 68-71; lectr painting, drawing & design, St Joseph's Col, 71-74; prof painting, drawing & visual fundamentals, Chicago State Univ, 71-91. *Awards:* Hon Mention for Dana Medal, Pa Acad Fine Arts, 53; Mich Watercolor Soc Award, 65 & 70; Ill Arts Coun Proj Completion grant, 77 & 78; Patron Purchase award, Springfield Art Mus, Mo, 1999; Community Arts Ass Prog Grant, Chicago Dept Current Affairs; SE Ill Arts Coun Access Program. *Mem:* Arts Club Chicago; Chicago Artists Coalition; Women's Caucus Art (vpres, Midwest, 82-85, bd mem, Chicago chap); Albuquerque United Artists. *Media:* Water-based Media, Mixed Media. *Mailing Add:* The Hallmark 2960 N Lake Shore Dr Chicago IL 60657

AUDEAN
PAINTER, ILLUSTRATOR
b Reading, Pa, June 2, 1929. *Study:* Philadelphia Mus Sch Industrial Art, 51. *Bibliog:* Article, Am Artist Mag, 5/87; Victoria Mag, 10/90; posters, Frontline Graphics, San Diego. *Media:* Watercolor. *Publ:* Illusr, Soft as a Kitten, Fuzzy as a Puppy, & A B C, Random House. *Dealer:* Craft Haus Vermont. *Mailing Add:* c/o Eleanor Ettinger Gallery 24 W 57th St Ste 609 New York NY 10019

AUERBACH, LISA ANNE
PHOTOGRAPHER
Study: Boston Univ, Sch Comm, 1985-88; Rochester Inst Technol, BFA (photog), 1990; Art Ctr Coll Design, Pasadena, MFA, 1994. *Exhib:* Solo exhibs, Univ Rochester Gallery, NY, 1991, Art Ctr Coll Design, Pasadena, 1994, Thomas Solomon's Garage, LA, 1995, CPK Kunsthal, Copenhagen, 2006, Gavlak, West Palm Beach, Fla, 2006, Daric Patton, LA, 2007, Art Basel Miami Beach, 2007; Gorgeous Politics: 8th Ann, LACE, 1994; PLAN: Photog Los Angeles Now, LA County Mus Art, 1995; Opening Group Show, Gavlak Projects, West Palm Beach, Fla, 2005; Interstat, Socrates Sculpture Park, NY, 2006; Locale, Margo Leavin Gallery, LA, 2006; Open Walls 2, White Columns, New York, 2006; Words Fail Me, Mus Contemp Art Detroit, 2007; The Way That We Rhyme, Yerba Buena Ctr Arts, San Francisco, 2008. *Awards:* Louis Comfort Tiffany Found Grant, 2009

AUERBACH, TAUBA
PRINTMAKER
b San Francisco, 1981. *Study:* Stanford Univ, Calif, BA (visual art), 2003. *Exhib:* ING, Luggage Store Gallery, San Francisco, 2001, No War, 2002, Writing Letters, 2005; The San Francisco Show, New Image Art Gallery, Los Angeles, 2004; Signs of the Real & Infinite, New Image Art Gallery, 2005; Dreamland Artist's Club, Coney Island, New York, 2005; solo exhibs, New Image Art Gallery, Los Angeles, 2005, San Francisco Art Comn, 2005, Deitch Projects, New York, 2006, Jack Hanley Gallery, San Francisco, 2007, Wattis Inst Contemp Art, San Francisco, 2008, Standard, Oslo, 2008; New Prints, Int Print Ctr, New York, 2006; Calli/Graffi, Fine Arts Gallery, San Francisco State Univ, 2006; Almost Home, Jack Hanley Gallery, San Francisco, 2007; Beneath the Underdog, Gagosian Gallery, New York, 2007; Warhol And...Kantor Feuer Gallery, Los Angeles, 2007; Words Fail Me, Mus Contemp Art Detroit, 2007; Successive Approximation, Perry Rubenstein Gallery, New York, 2008; Whitney Biennial, Whitney Mus Am Art, 2010. *Awards:* Seven Young Artists to Watch, Art News, 2010. *Dealer:* Deitch Projects 76 Grand St New York NY 10013; New Image Art 7908 Santa Monica Blvd West Hollywood CA 90046; Paulson Press 1318 10th St Berkeley CA 94710

AUGUSTINE, SETH
SCULPTOR
Study: Cornell Univ, BFA, 2000; Univ Calif San Diego, MFA, 2008. *Exhib:* Cent Park, Marbella, Spain, 1996; Sibley Gallery, Ithaca, NY, 1997 & 2000; Palazzo Lazzaroni, Rome, 1998; Tjaden Fine Arts Gallery, Ithaca, NY, 2000; solo exhibs, Franconia Sculpture Park, Shafer, Minn, 2000-01, Tjaden Hall Experimental Studios, 2000 & 2001, Utrecht Art Gallery, Sacramento, 2002, Fuller Projects, Bloomington, 2004 & Marcuse Gallery, La Jolla, 2006; Calif State Fair Art Gallery, Sacramento, 2002; Jim Ferry's 20th St Art Gallery, 2002 & 2003; SoFA Gallery, Bloomington, Ind, 2003; McCalla Sch, Bloomington, 2004; Marcuse Gallery, La Jolla, Calif, 2006; CSULB art dept. galleries, Long Beach, Calif, 2006; 16:One Gallery, Santa Monica, Calif, 2006. *Awards:* Art Matters Foundation Grant, 2008

AUNE-HINKEL, ALISON J
EDUCATOR
Teaching: Asst prof art educ, Univ Minn, Duluth; assoc prof comparative art, Ohio State Univ. *Awards:* Fulbright Grant, 2009-2010. *Mailing Add:* University of Minnesota Dept Art & Design 317 Humanities Bldg 1201 Ordean Ct Duluth MN 55812-2496

AUNIO, IRENE
PAINTER
b Finland; US citizen. *Study:* Art Students League; Brooklyn Mus, studies with John Costigno. *Work:* Evansville Mus Fine Arts, IN; Reading Mus Fine Arts, PA; Art Students League, Dag Hammarskjold Plaza, NY; Katz Commun New York & Int. *Exhib:* Solo exhibs, Brooklyn Mus, NY, 66, Suffolk Mus, NY, 74, Gallery Machias, Maine, Grist Mill Gallery, Vt, Jeanne Taylor Gallery, NY, Miriam Perlman Gallery, Ill & Belanthi Gallery, NY. *Teaching:* Instr, watercolor, Prospect Harbor, Maine, 93-; workshops watercolor, Rocky Point, Long Island, NY, currently, Nat Asn Women Artists, NY, Am Watercolor Soc; instr, Elderhostel Program. *Awards:* First Award of Excellence, Independent Art Soc, 92; Best in Show, Nat League Am Pen Women, 98; Ranger Fund Purchase Prize. *Mem:* Am Watercolor Soc, NY; Nat Asn Women Artists; Allied Artists Am; Nat League Am Pen Women. *Media:* Watercolor, Acrylic, Oil. *Specialty:* watercolor, oil. *Interests:* Landscapes, flowers, portraits, painting, dancing. *Publ:* NY Art, Rev, Les Krantz, 88. *Mailing Add:* Aunio Art Gallery 43 Prospect St Huntington NY 11743

AUPING, MICHAEL GRAHAM
CURATOR, HISTORIAN
b Portland, Ore, Oct 17, 1949. *Study:* Santa Ana Coll, AA, 69; Calif State Univ, Fullerton, BA (art hist), 71; Calif State Univ, Long Beach, MA (art hist), 75. *Exhib:* Matrix: A Changing Exhib Contemp Art, Univ Art Mus, Berkeley, Calif, 78-80; Francesco Clemente, Walker Art Ctr, Minneapolis, Minn, Dallas Mus Art, Albright-Knox Art Gallery, Buffalo, NY, 85; Hamish Fulton: Selected Walks 1969-1989 (traveling show), Nat Gallery, Ottawa; Jenny Holzer: The Venice Installation, Albright-Knox Art Gallery, Buffalo, NY, Walker Art Ctr, Minneapolis, Minn, traveling, 92; Selected Geometric Abstract Painting in America Since 1945 (traveling show), Milwaukee Art Mus, Wis; Structure to Resemblance: Work by Eight American Sculptors; Drawing Rooms: Jonathan Borofsky, Sol Lewitt, Richard Serra, 94; Arshile Gorky: The Breakthrough Yrs, 95; Tatsuo Miyajima, Big Time, 96; Georg Baselitz: Portraits of Elke, 97; Agnes Martin/Richard Tuttle, 98; House of Sculpture, 99; Natural Deceits, 2000; Modern Art Mus of Ft Worth 2000, 2002; Philip Guston Retrospective, 2003; Anselm Kiefer: Heaven & Earth (traveling), Mus d'art contemp de Montreal, Hirshhorn Mus, San Francisco Mus Mod Art, 2005-2007; Declaring Space: Mark Rothko, Barnett Newman, Lucio Fontana, Yves Klein, 2007; Susan Rothenberg: Moving in Place (traveling), Georgia O'Keeffe Mus, Miami Art Mus, 2009. *Collection Arranged:* Richard Serra Collection; Robert Irwin Collection; John Chamberlain Collection; Francesco Clemente Collection. *Pos:* Var consults, 73-95; ed, Los Angeles Inst Contemp Art J, 76-78; assoc cur, Univ Art Mus, Berkeley, 78-80; cur 20th century art, John & Mable Ringling Mus Art, Sarasota, Fla, 80-84; prof adv comt, Art Pub Places, Metro-Dade Area, Miami, 84-; chief cur, Albright-Knox Art Gallery, Buffalo, NY, 84-93 & Mod Art Mus, Ft Worth, Tex, 93-. *Teaching:* Adj lectr art hist, Univ Calif, Santa Barbara, fall 77 & Univ Buffalo, 88-89; lectr, Inst Contemp Art, Boston, Baltimore Mus Art, St Louis Art Mus, Nelson-Atkins Mus Art, Kansas City, Milwaukee Art Mus, Hirshhorn Mus & Sculpture Garden, 89-92, Int Conf, Univ York, Toronto, Can, 91, NC Mus Art, Seattle Art Mus, San Francisco Mus Mod Art, Dallas Mus Art & Boston Mus Fine Arts, 93-94. *Awards:* Comnr, American Pavilion 1990 Venice Biennale, Italy. *Res:* Post-War American and European Art. *Publ:* Auth, Clyfford Still in New York: The Buffalo Project, In: Clyfford Still, Munich: Prestel Verlag, 92; Chuck Close: Face to Face, Artforum, 10/93; Drawing Rooms: Jonathan Borofsky, Sol LeWit, Richard Serra, 94; Arshile Gurky: The Breakthrough Years, 95; Tatsuo Miyajima Big Time, 96. *Mailing Add:* c/o Mod Art Mus Ft Worth 3200 Darnell St Fort Worth TX 76107

AURBACH, MICHAEL LAWRENCE
SCULPTOR, EDUCATOR
b Wichita, Kans, Dec 13, 1952. *Study:* Univ Kans, Lawrence, BA, 74, BSJ, 76, MA (art hist), 79, BFA (studio art), 81; Southern Methodist Univ, Dallas, MFA (sculpture), 83. *Work:* Nat Civil Rights Mus, Memphis; Loyola Univ New Orleans; Univ of NDak, Grand Forks. *Exhib:* Southwest 85, NMex Mus Fine Arts, 85; solo exhibs, Artemisia Gallery, Chicago, 87, Macon Mus, Ga, 89, Bernice Steinbaum Gallery, NY, 91 & Univ Notre Dame, Southbend, 91, Southern Methodist Univ, Dallas, 93, WVa Univ, Morgantown, 94, ARC/RAW Space, Chicago, 95,N Dakota Mus Art, Grand Forks, NDak, 96, Univ Ga, Athens, 97, Indianapolis Art Ctr, 97, Alexandria (La) Mus Art, 99, Frist Ctr Visual Arts, Nashville, Tenn, 2001, Spartanburg Mus Art, SC, 2003, Del Center Contemp Arts, Wilmington, Del, 2007; Birmingham Biennial IV & V, Birmingham Mus Art, Ala, 87 & 89; Sculpture Tour Nat Invitational, Univ Tenn, 89-90; The Edge of Childhood Nat Invitational, Heckscher Mus, Huntington, NY, 92; Coll Art Asn Members Exhib, Atlanta Ctr Contemp Art, Ga, 2005; Tenn Arts Comn, Nashville, Tenn, 2008; Univ Tenn-Knoxville, 2009; Wichita Art Mus, Kans, 2010; Jacksonville Mus Contemporary Art, Jacksonville, Fla, 2013; Tarble Arts Center, Eastern Ill Univ. Charleston, 2015. *Teaching:* prof Art, Vanderbilt Univ. *Awards:* NEA/Southern Arts Fedn Fel, 87; Art Matters Inc Grant, 89, 92; Tenn Arts Comn Grant, 90, 2003; NEA Art in Pub Places Grant, 93; Outstanding Artistic Achievement, Southeastern Coll Art Conf, 95; Puffin Found Grant, 2002; Ga Exhib Grant, Mus Contemp Art, 2005; Joan S Beren Found Grant, 2010; Southeastern Coll Art Conf Award for Outstanding Exhib and Catalogue of Contemp Materials, 2011; Barbara Ritzman Devereux Grant, 2013; Professional Development Grant, Tenn Arts Comn, 2015. *Bibliog:* Glen Brown (auth), Secrecy and Institutional Power, World Sculpture News, autumn 2000; Dorothy Joiner (auth), rev, Metalsmith, spring 2006; Dorothy Joiner (auth), rev, Sculpture, 2005; Joseph Whitt (auth), rev, Art Papers, March/Apr 2002; Dorothy Joiner (auth), Art Papers, Nov/Dec/2008; Dorothy Joiner (auth), rev

World Sculpture News, autumn, 2009; Dorothy Joiner (auth), Michael Aurbach: Secrecy, the Promethean Weapon, Sculpture Mag, Vol 29, No 7, 58-9, 9/2010; Dorothy Joiner (auth), Academic Vanitas: Michael Aurbach and Critical Theory, Leonardo Electronic Almanac, Vol. 17, No. 1, pp. 8-13, MIT Press, 8/2011; Dorothy Joiner (auth), Morality, Secrecy, Wit, and Satire, World Sculpture News, pp 36-42, Vol 18, No 4, 2012; Dorothy Joiner (auth), rev, Show at Northwest Fla State Col, No 76, autumn, 2013, p 14. *Mem:* Coll Art Asn (bd dir, 99-, vpres, external affairs 99-2000, vpres, coms 2000-01, pres 2002-2004); Southeast Coll Art Conf; Int Sculpture Ctr; Founds in Art: Theory and Educ; SECAC (bd mem 98-2004); Mid-Am Coll Asn (bd dirs 2005-2008); Tenn Volunteer Lawyers for the Arts (bd mem 2006-2007); Number, Inc (bd mem, 2009-11). *Media:* Mixed-Media. *Publ:* Auth, Ten in Tennessee review, 12/87 & Jim Poag review, 2/87, New Art Examiner; Primitive elegance: sculpture by D Hall & C Michael, Vol 12, 88 & The Don Evans Case, Vol 17, 93, Art Papers. *Mailing Add:* Vanderbilt Univ Dept Art Box 351660B Nashville TN 37235

AUSTIN, BARBARA JEAN See Adams, Bobbi

AUSTIN, PAT
PAINTER, PRINTMAKER
b Detroit, Mich, Mar 17, 1937. *Study:* Univ Mich, AB, 59; Univ Wash, BFA (art), 71; Univ Alaska, Anchorage, MFA, 77. *Work:* Evergreen State Col, Olympia; Anchorage Hist & Fine Arts Mus, Alaska; Alaska State Coun Arts, Printmakers Alaska Permanent Collection, Anchorage; Anchorage Borough Sch Dist Permanent Print Collection; Visual Arts Ctr, Permanent Print Collection. *Comn:* Providence Hospital Print Project, 86; mural, Family Resource Ctr, 87; mural, Chugach Sr Ctr, Munic Anchorage, 94; 14 series from the Resurrection paintings, St Paul's Episcopal Church, Port Townsend, Wash, 2002; Video of this 30 minute documentary for PT TV (publ television) Glen Paris-Stamm Productions. *Exhib:* All Alaska Juried Exhib, Anchorage, 66-69 & 72-86; 20 Printmakers Touring Invitational, Wash State Artmobile, 71-72; Solo exhibs, Anchorage Hist & Fine Arts Mus, 75 & 83 & Stonington Gallery, Anchorage, 86; Northwest Print Coun, group exhib, 84-86; Silverwater, Port Townsend, Wash, 98; Taylor St Coffee House, Port Townsend, Wash, 2000; group exhib, Quimper Universal Unitarian Church, 2004. *Teaching:* Instr art & Eng, Anchorage Borough Sch Dist, 65-69; instr printmaking & painting, Univ Alaska, 71-87 & Peninsula Col, Wash, 95-97; ret, Univ Alaska, 87; lect, Art of the Print, lect series, Northwind Gallery, 2004; Guy Anderson: Northwest Mystic, lect with his exhib, 2005. *Awards:* Printmaking Award, All Alaska Juried Exhib, 69-74; Mel Kohler Painting Award, 75; Artist Fel, Alaska State Coun Arts, 85. *Bibliog:* Connie Godwin (auth), Pat's art is exploring world, Anchorage Daily Times, 11/3/75; Virginia McKinney (auth), Pat Austin: Printmaker and more, Alaska J, winter 83; Kesler E Woodward (auth), Painting in the North, 93; Painting Alaska, Alaska Geographic, vol 27 no 3, 2000; Anne Chandonnet (auth), Alaska's Arts, Crafts, & Collectibles, 98. *Mem:* Anchorage Hist & Fine Arts Mus Asn; Northwest Print Coun (found, bd mem); Northwind Arts Alliance; Quimper Arts (guild); Corvidae Press (found, mem). *Media:* Watermedia, Etching. *Interests:* artists books, writing poetry & memoirs, non-toxic printmaking. *Publ:* Auth, National Collection of Fine Arts (catalog), Washington, DC, 78; Passing off reproductions as real art, Alaska J, winter 80; auth, Love, Loss, Lust, publ by Knightsmove; auth, poetry, Northwind Readers; auth, poetry, Poetry at Lahani's; auth, poetry, Minotaur

AUTEN, GERALD
PAINTER, EDUCATOR
Study: Univ Iowa, BFA (drawing and painting); Washington Univ, St Louis, MFA (painting); Univ Wis, Milwaukee, (MA archit). *Exhib:* in Teheran, Mexico City, NY and Vancouver; Am Acad Arts and Letters, 2002, 2004; Nat Acad, 2006; represented in permanent collections of Albright Knox Gallery Art, Booz Allen Hamilton, The Hood Mus Art; Inaugural Exhib, Lori Bookstein Fine Art, NY, 2004, In Black and White, 2005. *Teaching:* Sr lectr studio art Dartmouth Col, currently. *Mailing Add:* Dartmouth Coll Dept Studio Art Hinman Box 6081 Hanover NH 03755-3599

AUTH, SUSAN HANDLER
CURATOR, EDUCATOR
b New York, NY, June 25, 1939. *Study:* Swarthmore Col, BA; Univ London; Univ Mich, MA; Am Sch Classical Studies, Athens, Fulbright Scholar, 64-65; Bryn Mawr Col, PhD, 68. *Work:* Toledo Mus of Art Ohio; Newark Mus NJ. *Collection Arranged:* Myth & Gospel: Art of Coptic Egypt, Newark Mus, 77, Ancient Greece: Life and Art, 80; The Classical Collection, 81 & 89; Coptic Art of Ancient Egypt, Nadler Collection & Newark Mus, NJ, 86; Stepping Into Ancient Egypt: House of the Artist Pashed, 91; The Roman Banquet, 1994; Ancient Adornment, 1997; Artisans of Ancient Rome, 1997; Ancient Galleries 1999-2001; Garden of Remembrance, 2002. *Pos:* Curatorial asst, Toledo Mus Art, Ohio, 67; cur classical collection, Newark Mus, 71-. *Teaching:* Asst prof ancient art & archaeol, Dept Art, Rutgers Univ, Newark, 68-71. *Awards:* Am Numismatic Soc Summer Fel, 63; Travel Grants, Smithsonian Inst, Washington, DC, summer 71, Ford Found Publ, 75, Nat Endowment Arts, Mellon, 91-93, Dodge Found, 97, Mus Loan Network, 2001 & 2003. *Mem:* Archaeol Inst Am; Int Asn Hist Glass; Am Research Ctr, Egypt; Int Asn Egyptologists. *Res:* Ancient glass; Greek, Roman, Egyptian & Coptic art & archaeology. *Publ:* Auth, Ancient Glass at the Newark Mus, from the Eugene Schaefer Collection of Ancient Glass, Newark Mus, 76; var articles, Am J Archaeol, J Glass Studies, Archaeol & Annales Int d'Etude Hist du Verre, Brunildes Ridgway Festschrift, 98, Annales of Int Asn Coptic Studies, 2003; Coptic Glass, The Coptic Encyclopedia, 91; Pottery & Glass, Beyond the Pharaohs, 89. *Mailing Add:* Newark Mus 49 Washington St Newark NJ 07102-3176

AVAKIAN, JOHN
PRINTMAKER, INSTRUCTOR
b Worcester, Mass. *Study:* Yale Univ Sch Art & Archit, BFA & MFA. *Work:* Fed Reserve Bank, Boston; Western Mich Univ; Bucknell Univ; Tulsa Civic Ctr, Okla; Boston Pub Libr & Print Dept. *Exhib:* 20th Nat Exhib Prints, Libr Cong, Washington, DC; 38th Int Printmakers Exhib, Seattle Art Mus; Solo exhib, Higgins Wing, Worcester Art Mus, Mass; 21st Ann Int Exhib, Beaumont Art Mus, Tex, 72; Erector Sq Gallery, New Haven, Conn, 94. *Teaching:* Instr color & design, Northeastern Univ, Mass, 89 & Mt Ida Jr Col, 69-, chmn art dept, 69-83. *Awards:* Blanche E Colman Found Award, 70; Art Patrons League of Mobile Award, 72; Commendation Award, Boston Printmakers NAm Exhib, 93. *Mem:* Coll Art Asn Am. *Media:* Monotype, Monoprint. *Mailing Add:* 43 Morse St Sharon MA 02067-2729

AVANT, TRACY WRIGHT
PAINTER, GRAPHIC ARTIST
b Ft Dix, NJ, Dec 15, 1960. *Study:* McNay Art Inst, 69; Southwest Tex State Univ, BS, 83; Warren Hunter Acad Art, 90; Coppini Acad Fine Art, 94-95. *Work:* Phil Isley Inc, Tex; Normangee State Bank, Tex; Ocean Wash, USA, Tex. *Comn:* Landscape painting, Minton Oil Co, Tex, 88; bldg painting, Dilley Flower & Gift Shop, Tex, 90; portrait, comn by Dr & Mrs H I Garfield, Tex, 94. *Exhib:* Am Art in Miniature, Thomas Gilcrease, Tulsa, Okla, 94; Oil Painters Am, San Antonio, Tex, 94; Nat Soc Artists, Santa Fe, Tex, 94; Fifth Ann Wildlife Exhib, Colo, 94; Debut '94 Jr Mooney, San Antonio, Tex, 94; Salon Int, Miss, 94; Bridge Nat Juried Expos, NY, 94. *Awards:* Judge's Choice, Oil Painters Am, Heritage Gallery, 94; First Place, Colo Wildlife Expos, Gwendolyn's Gallery, 94; Second Place, Coppini May Garden Show, Coppini Gallery, 94. *Bibliog:* Review, The Current, 94; review, Pleasanton Express, 94; review, The Eagle, 94. *Mem:* Oil Painters Am; Nat Soc Artists; assoc mem Allied Artists Am; Palette & Chisel Acad Fine Art; New Braunfels Art League. *Media:* Oil, Acrylic. *Mailing Add:* PO Box 4 1120 Hwy 81 N Dilley TX 78017-0009

AVEDON, BARRY
PAINTER, EDUCATOR
b Brooklyn, NY, Jan 2, 1941. *Study:* Rochester Inst Technol Sch Art, BFA, 62, MFA, 64. *Work:* Eastern Mich Univ, Ypsilanti; Rochester Inst Technol, NY; Bank of Com, Hamtramck, Mich. *Exhib:* Ann Exhib, Albright-Knox Mus Art, 64; Butler Inst Am Art Mid-Year Show, 66; Ball State Nat Drawing Ann, Ball State Univ Gallery, 79; Mich Artists 80/81, Flint Inst Arts, Mich, 81; The Corporation Collects Art, Muskegon Mus Art, Mich, 83; Focus Gallery, Detroit, 85; Battle Creek Art Ctr, 86; Water Street Gallery, Saugatuck, Mich, 96. *Teaching:* Prof painting & drawing, Eastern Mich Univ, 66-. *Awards:* Julius Hallgarten Award, Nat Acad Design Ann, 64; Purchase Award, Ethno-Art '81, Bank of Commerce, Hamtramck, Mich, 81; All Media State Juried Award, Mt Clemens Art Ctr, Mich, 92. *Bibliog:* A Scaglione & B Parker (auth), Detroit Summer III, Park West Galleries, Inc, 82; Robert Iglehart (auth), article, Ann Arbor News, 83. *Mem:* Artists Equity Asn, Mich. *Media:* Oil; Pencil. *Dealer:* Water Street Art Gallery, Saugatuck MI. *Mailing Add:* Dept Art 114 Ford Hall Eastern Mich Univ Ypsilanti MI 48197

AVERBUCH, ILAN
SCULPTOR
b Tel Aviv, Israel, 1953. *Study:* Wimbledon Sch Art, London, Eng, 77-78, Sch Visual Arts, BFA, 79-81, Hunter Col, NY, MFA, 83-84. *Work:* Israel Mus, Jerusalem; Martin Margulies, Coconut Grove, Fla; Vera List, Bryam, Conn; Michael Haas, Toytlof, Berlin, Ger; Ashley D Hoffman, Kings Point, NY. *Exhib:* Solo exhibs, Kunstlerhaus Bethanien, Berlin, Ger, 85, Daadgalerie, Berlin, Ger, 86, Mabat Gallery, Tel Aviv, Israel, 86, Jewish Mus, NY, 86, O K Harris Works of Art, NY, 87, Nancy Hoffman, NY, 89; Peace Biennale, Hamburg, WGer, 85; Sculpture in the Square, Lincoln Ctr, NY, 85-86; Mythos Berlin Concept Show (with catalog), 86; 49th Parallel, NY, 89; Int Contemp Art, Art Gallery Ont, Toronto, 89. *Pos:* Steel instr & coordr sculpture dept, Sch Visual Arts, New York, 80-82; lectr, Brown Univ, Providence, RI, 83, Berlin Technical Univ, 86. *Awards:* DAAD Award, Berlin, WGER. *Bibliog:* Gil Goldfine (auth), Averbuch Sculpture, Jerusalem Post, 10/11/86; Thomas Wulfen (auth), Donald Judd, Carlm Andre, Ilan Averbuch, Tages Spiegel, 6/87; Beatrice V Bismark (auth), Reviews: Ilan Averbuch, Daad Galene, Berlin, Flash Art, winter 86, 87. *Mailing Add:* 1015 48th Ave Long Island City NY 11101-5693

AVLON-DAPHNIS, HELEN BASILEA
PAINTER, SCULPTOR
b New York, NY, June 18, 1932. *Study:* Hunter Col, New York, BA, 59, MA, 72; Aspen Mus Sch, 70; Provincetown Sch Fine Arts, Mass, 70-75. *Work:* Gallery I, Westbeth, NY; Cook Gallery, NY. *Comn:* Mural, 250 W 57th Street, NY; The Sea, Provincetown Art Asn Mus. *Exhib:* Solo exhib, Gallery I Mus, Westbeth, NY, 84; Bertha Schaeffer Gallery, NY, 60-65; Provincetown Art Mus, Show of the 60's, 82; Forum Gallery, NY; Baltimore Art Mus. *Bibliog:* Articles in New York Daily News, Art News, Art Digest, Art Speaks and others. *Mem:* Westbeth Workshop Graphics Int. *Media:* Watercolor, Acrylic. *Mailing Add:* 463 W St New York NY 10014-2010

AWALT, ELIZABETH GRACE
PAINTER
b Baltimore, Md, 1956. *Study:* Skowhegan Sch Painting, ME, 77; Boston Col, BA, 78; Univ Pa, MA (painting), MFA, 81. *Work:* Boston Pub Libr, Bank Boston, Boston Coll Mus Art; Snite Mus Art, Notre Dame, Ind; Prudential Ins Co; Rose Art Mus; AT&T. *Exhib:* Brave New Works, Mus Fine Arts, Boston, 84; solo exhibs, Thomas Segal Gallery, Boston, 85, GW Einstein Co, NY, 88, 90 & 95, Samuelis Baumgarte Galerie, Ger, 93, Seasonal Meditations, GW Einstein, NY, 95 & Salute to Boston, Boston Pub Libr, 98; The Watercolor Show, Loise Ross Gallery, NY, 91; Celebration, GW Einstein Co Inc, 93; Beyond Description: Visions of Nature, GW Einstein Co Inc, NY, 93; Inspired by Nature, Boston Coll Mus Art, 95. *Teaching:* Instr painting, drawing, ceramics, Wyncote Acad, Pa, 81; instr art, Boston Col, Newton, Mass, 84-87; instr painting, Waltham Sr Citizen Ctr, Mass, 85-86; instr painting, watercolor, drawing, Danforth Mus Sch, Framingham, Mass, 85-86; instr beginning painting, DeCordova Mus Sch Art, Lincoln, Mass, 86; asst prof, painting & drawing, Boston Col, 85-93, assoc prof, 93-. *Awards:* Mass Artist Fel, Painting, 83; Nat Endowment Arts Grant, Painting, 87; Finalist, Mass Artist Found, 90. *Media:* Oil, Pastel. *Publ:* Contribr, Oil Pastel: Watson-Guptill, 90; Pilgrims & Pioneers: New England Women in the Arts, Faxon & Moore, 87. *Mailing Add:* 40 Hosmer Rd Concord MA 01742-2216

AYASO, MANUEL
PAINTER, SCULPTOR
b Riviera, Spain, Jan 1, 1934; US citizen. *Study:* Newark Sch Fine & Indust Arts, cert. *Work:* Whitney Mus Am Art, NY; Worcester Mus, Mass; Pa Acad Fine Arts, Philadelphia; NJ State Mus, Trenton; Newark Mus, NJ; San Francisco Mus Art, San Francisco, Calif; and others. *Exhib:* 22nd Int Watercolor Biennial, Brooklyn Mus, NY, 63; El Neo-Humanismo en el Dibujo de USA, Ital y Mexico, Univ Mex, 63; American Painting & Sculpture, Pa Acad Fine Arts, 67; Contemp Am Artists, Nat Inst Arts & Lett, 71; Contemp Am Spiritual Art, Mus Contemp Art, Vatican, Rome, 76; The Fine Line: Drawing with Silver in America, circulating exhib, 85 & 86; Objects & Drawings, circulatory exhib, Sanford M & Diane Besser Collection, 92-93; retrospective exhib, Museo del Grabado, Artes-Riveira, Spain, 2002-03; and others. *Collection Arranged:* Whitney Mus Am Art; Newark Mus; NJ State Mus; Butler Inst Am Art; Summer Found for Arts, NJ; St Paul Gallery and Sch of Art, Minn; Norma and John C Marin Jr Coll; Ill Wesleyan Univ; Univ Mass, Amherst; Pa Acad of Fine Arts; Worcester Mus, Mass; Slaten Mem Mus, Norwich Free Acad, Conn; Am Israel Found; Montclair Art Mus, NJ; Univ Ore Mus Art, Eugene; Ark Arts Ctr, Little Rock; Samford M and Diane Besser Collection; Casa da Cultura, Ribeira, Spain; Casa de Galicia, Madrid; Centro de Arte Contemporanea, Santiago de Compostela, Spain; Museo Valle Inclan, Puebla del Caraminal, Spain; Museo del Grabado, Artes-Ribeira, Spain. *Awards:* Tiffany Found Scholar in Painting, 62; Ford Found Purchase Award, 64; Childe Hassam Fund Purchase Award, 71; Paleta de Prata ARGA, Asociacion de Artistas Plasticos Galegos, 2007. *Bibliog:* Brian O'Doherty (auth), New York Times, 5/31/61; John Canaday (auth), New York Times, 12/8/63; Barry Schwartz (auth), The New Humanism, Praeger Publ, 74. *Mem:* Am Fedn Arts. *Media:* Goldpoint, Mixed Media. *Dealer:* Jean Frank 25 E 83rd St New York NY 10021. *Mailing Add:* 12 Vincent Pl Verona NJ 07044

AYERS, CAROL LEE
PAINTER, GALLERY DIRECTOR
b Newark, NJ, Dec 25, 1929. *Study:* Basically self-taught; studied with David Kwo & Allan Eldredge, 75-76. *Work:* Bicentennial Expos, Everson Mus, Syracuse, NY; Am Telephone & Telegraph Corp Hq, Bedminster, NJ; Westinghouse Corp, Bath, NY; Sterling Drug Corp, New York & Athens, Greece; Trenton Mus; Corning Glass, Corning, NY; and others. *Comn:* Acrylic wall panel, Archdiocese of Rochester, Geneva, NY, 70; mural, comn by B Burley, vpres Sterling Drug Corp, NY, 75; Highland Telephone Corp, Warwick, NY, 86; Mr & Mrs George Plimpton Collection, Southampton, NY, 86-88; First Hope Bank, Hope, NJ, 97. *Exhib:* Silvermine Guild Artists, New Canaan, Conn, 75; Northeast Watercolor Soc, Hall Fame Trotter, Goshen, NY, 84-90, 96 & 98; West Point Acad, 85; Connoisseur Gallery, Rhinebeck, NY 87-90; Springhouse Gallery, Philadelphia, Pa, 90; Dutot Mus, Del Water Gap, Pa, 92; NJ Watercolor Soc, Chester, 98; Buck Hills Falls Art Asn, Pa, 99-2000. *Pos:* Dir, Esperanza Gallery, Yates Co, NY, 68-73, Erincourt Gallery, Penn Yan, NY, 73-79, Gallery-in-the-Gap, Delaware Water Gap, Pa, 80-83 & Sunflower Studio, 83-. *Teaching:* Demonstr acrylic painting, Rotring-Koh-I-Noor, Inc; instr, home studio. *Awards:* First Awards, Monroe Co Mus, 83, Chester Art Asn, NJ, 83, Suburban Art League, 83 & Keuka Lake Art Asn, 70, 73-74, 79 & 84-85; Coun Am Artists Soc Award, 93; NE Watercolor Soc Award, 96-97 & 99; First Award, Buckhill Falls Art Asn, Pa, 2000. *Bibliog:* Articles in NJ Music & Art Mag, Ridgewood, NJ, 6/77; T Noverro (auth), Save the gallery, Easton Publ Co, Pa, 9/81; articles in NY Art Review, 88 & Am Artist Mag, 89, Watercolor '92 Spring & Fall Issues, The Artist's Mag, 3/92. *Mem:* Signature mem Northeast Watercolor Soc; assoc mem NJ Watercolor Soc; Hunterdon Co Art Ctr, Clinton, NJ; Pocono Mountains Art Group, Pa; Nat Soc of Painters in case in Acrylic, 2003, Assoc mem. *Media:* Watercolor, Liquid Acrylic, Mixed Media. *Specialty:* Original contemporary paintings. *Publ:* Auth, Manuscript on liquid acrylic, Am Artist Mag, 90-91. *Dealer:* Morgan Gallery Fine Art Blakeslee PA; Gallery 23 Blairstown NJ

AYHENS, OLIVE MADORA
PAINTER
b Oakland, Calif, Nov 2, 1943. *Study:* San Francisco Art Inst, BFA, 68, MFA, 69. *Work:* Oakland Mus, Calif; Mills Col, Oakland, Calif; Evergreen State Col, Olympia, Wash; Univ Northern Iowa, Cedar Falls; Intercontinental Pac Group, San Francisco, Calif; Watkins Collection, Am Univ; West Collection, Pa; also pvt collections. *Comn:* painting for David Rockefeller Jr, comn by Lower Manhattan Cult Coun, 2000. *Exhib:* Survey Show, San Francisco Mus Art, 75; Passages Calif Women 1945 to present, Fresno Art Ctr & Mus, 87; Solo Exhibs: San Francisco Mus Mod Art, 89; Michael Himovitz Gallery, 91 & 94; Beall Park Art Ctr, 94; Extreme Interiors, Frederieke Taylor Gallery, NY, 2007 & Nature/Architecture, 2009, Volta, 2010; Perilous Worlds of Olive Ayhens, Lockhart Gallery, SUNY Geneseo, 2008; Artists Views on Romance, Monterey Peninsula Mus, 91; Lejauu, Frederick Spratt Gallery San Jose, 96; Earth, Water & Air, DC Moore Gallery, NY, 98; Meaning Method Meaning, Rush Art, NY; Solo Exhib Gary Tatintsian Gallery, New York City, 2002, 2003, 2004, 2005; Group Exhib Am Acad of Artist Letters Invitational & Purchase Award, 2004; Frederieke Taylor Gallery, NY, 2006; Rivers of Light, NY Midtown Pub Libr, 2007; New Wave, Brooklyn Acad Music, 2009; Frederieke Taylor, Anniversary invitational, 2010; Volta Art Fair, NY, 2010; Drawing Show, Sue Scott Gallery, 2011; Into the Trees, L'Institut Franco-Am, Rennes, France, 2011; Lorie Bookstein, 2011; New York Drawings, Adam Baumgold Gallery, 2011; Land Use Misuse, Gerald Peters Gallery, Santa Fe, NMex, 2011; State Mus NY City, Albany, NY, 2011-2012; Electronic Labyrinth, Lori Bookstein Gallery, 2012; curated and included in, Enticing Luminosity, Lesley Heller gallery, NYC, 2014; one person show, Interior Wilderness, Lori Bookstein Fine Art, NYC, 2014; one person show, Transformations of Place, Roswell Mus and Art Center, 2015. *Collection Arranged:* Michael Boodro, NY; Anderson Mus, Don Anderson, Roswell, NMex; Mr. & Mrs. Munir Javeri, Greenwich, Conn. *Pos:* Roswell Artist in Residence, 2014-2015; Virginia Center of the Creative Arts (VCCA) residency, 2014; Djerassi Alumni Residency, 2014; Yaddo, 2013. *Teaching:* painting & drawing, Univ Tex, Austin, 80-81; Asst prof painting & drawing, Univ Calif, Berkeley, 84-85, Brown Univ, 89-90 & Mont State Univ, 93-94; drawing, Stanford Univ, 91; watercolor, Sarah Lawrence Col, 99-2000; American University, 2004-2005; Ox-Bow (Chicago Art Inst summer prog), 2006-2007; Anderson Ranch, Colo, 2008; Vt Summer Workshop, Mass Col Art, 2009; Pont-Aven, Britney, Franc Sch Art, 2010; Mass Coll Art, Bennington, 2009-2010; Chautauqua, 2012. *Awards:* Marie Walsh Sharpe Art Found Space Grant, 96; Adolph & Esther Gottlieb Individual Support Grant, 96; Pollock Krasner Found Grant, 98; Lower Manhattan Cult Coun World Trade Ctr Residency, 99; Pollock/Krasner, 2001; Va Ctr Creative Arts, 2001, 2006, 2011; Ucross, 2003, 2010; Guggenheim Fel, 2006; Macdowell, 2007; Joan Mitchell Fellowship, 2013. *Bibliog:* Mary Hull Webster (auth), Perils of the Artist Hero, Art Week, 92; Roberta Smith (auth), Aerial Perspectives: Imagination, Reality and Abstraction, New York Times, c 25, Vol CXLVI, 8/21/97; Robert Mahoney (auth), Aerial Perspectives, Imagination, Reality and Abstraction, Time Out New York, Issue 98, 47, 97; Cathy Lebountz Art in America, 2002; Mario Nares New York Observers, 2003-2004; David Cohey NY Sun, 2004; Cynthia Nadelman Art News, 5/2005; Village Voice, Best in Show, 2006; Light Show, NY Sun, 2007 & 2008; Mario Naves (auth), City Arts, Nature/Archit, 2009; David Cohen (auth), Art Critical Artist Pick. *Mem:* Coll Art Asn; Artist Equity; Siera Club. *Media:* Painting, Oil; Watercolor, Mixed Media. *Res:* aesthetics of pollution, extreme interiors ; Whiskeytown-Calif Gold Rush. *Interests:* aesthetics of pollution; Extreme interiors. *Publ:* DC Moore Gallery, Earth, Water & Air, 98; New York Sun, 2004, 2007 & 2008; Harpers Mag, 2001, 2004, 2007, 2009 & 2011; Art In America, 2004; Art News, 2005; Harpers Mag, 2007, 2009, 2011, 2012, 2013, 2014, 2015; NY Times, 1997, 2003; Art News, by Barbara Pollack, reviews, 2014; Jerry Saltz (auth), TO DO, 4, To See, Un sweet Candy, New York Magazine, 2014; Stephen Maine (auth), Hyperallergic painting-the-wilderness-of-the-artistic-imagination, 2014; William Eckhardt Kohler (auth), A Few Current Shows Downtown, Enticing Luminosity, Lesley Heller Gallery; Rey Berrones (auth), Visions Magazine, The Art of Olive Ayhens, 2015; Vicky Lowry (auth), Elle Decor, Olive Ayhens, art show July/August. *Dealer:* Lori Bookstein, Nev; San Francisco Mus Modern Art Artist Gallery Fort Mason; Bucheon Gallery San Francisco; Frederieke Taylor Gallery NYC; Adam Baungold Gallery. *Mailing Add:* 85 Devoe St # 2c Brooklyn NY 11211

AYLON, HELÈNE
PAINTER, CONCEPTUAL ARTIST
b Brooklyn, NY. *Study:* Dept Art, Brooklyn Coll, BA (cum laude), 60; Antioch Coll W, MA (performance art). *Work:* Whitney Mus Am Art; Mass Inst Technol, Cambridge; San Francisco Mus Mod Art; Mus Mod Art, NY; SFMMA; Hudson Valley Ctr Contemporary Art; MoMA; Whitney; Jewish Mus. *Comn:* Chapel Libr, John F Kennedy Airport, 66; Lobby, NY Univ Med Ctr, 68; The Earth Ambulance, Hudson Valley Center for Contemp Arts, Peekskill, NY, 2002; The Digital Liberation of C-d, The Swig Beit Midrash, JCC, SF, 2004. *Exhib:* Lyrical Abstraction, Whitney Mus Am Art, Aldrich Mus Contemp Art & traveling, 69; Season's Highlights, Aldrich Mus Am Art, Ridgefield, Conn, 71; Stretchers, Cleveland Ctr Contemp Art, 89; Paintings in Transition (with Dove Bradshaw), Aldrich Mus, Conn, 94; two sacs en route, Sony Jumbotron, Times Sq, 95; The Liberation of G-d, Jewish Mus, New York, San Francisco Jewish Mus, Armand Hammer Mus, Los Angeles, Contemp Baltimore & Nat Mus Am Jewish History, 1997 & Jewish Mus, New York, 2000; Bridge of Knots, facade installation, Am Univ, Mus Art, 2006; Warhol Mus, Pittsburgh, Liberation of God; El Harod Mus, Israel, Matronita. *Teaching:* Instr painting, Brooklyn Mus & Hunter Coll, 72-73; instr, San Francisco State Univ, 73-76; instr painting, Lone Mountain Coll, San Francisco, 77; interdisciplinary instr, Women's Ctr Learning, NY, 89. *Awards:* New Genre, NY Found Arts, 88 & 93; Installation, two sacs for 1995, NY State Coun Arts, 95; Pollock/Krasner Found Award, 95-96, 2003 & 2007; Yaddo-Philip Morris Award, 99; Yaddo-MacArthur Ann Award, 2000; NY State Coun Arts Award, 2001; Nat Found Jewish Cult Award for Visual Art, 2002; Pollock Krasner, 2007. *Bibliog:* Peter Schjeldahl (auth), Art in America, 11/75; Leslie Camhi (auth), Village Voice, 4/2/96; Michael Kimmelman (auth), NY Times, 3/8/96; Benjamin Genuchio (auth), NY Times, 1/15/2006; Mary Thomas, Pittsburgh Gazette, 6/22/2011. *Mem:* Coll Art Asn; Women's Caucus for Art. *Media:* Installation, Environmental Land Art. *Interests:* Feminist Judaism, Ecofeminism. *Publ:* Too Jewish? Challenging Traditional Identities (exhib catalog), Norman Kleeblat; The SF Jewish Bulletin, 9/96; The Liberation of G-d, Lilith Mag, fall 96; Art in America, 10/99; Bridges Mag, vol 8, 2000; Peter Selz, Art of Engagement, 2006; A Complex Weave: Identity and Women in Contemporary Art, 2011; Whatever is Contained Must be Released: My Jewish Orthodox Girlhood, My Life as a Feminist Artist (memoir). *Mailing Add:* 463 West St A808 New York NY 10014-2037

AYOUB, ROULA
PAINTER
b Monrovia, Liberia, West Africa, 1964. *Study:* Univ Nebr, BA (interior design), 1985; Fla State Univ, MS (interior design and fine art), 1988. *Work:* Appleton Mus of Art, Ocala, Fla; Mus of Fine Arts, Fla State Univ, Tallahassee, Fla; Sharjah Art Mus, Sharjah, UAE; Istanbul Contemp Art Mus, Istanbul, Turkey; Jordan Nat Gallery of Fine Arts, Amman, Jordan. *Exhib:* Art From the Heartland, Coutts Mem Mus of Art, El Dorado, Kans, 2003; Jordan Nat Gallery of Fine Arts, Amman, Jordan, 2003; Anniversary Invitational, Louisville Art Gallery, Nebr, 2003; Gov's Mansion, Lincoln, Nebr, 2003; Women's Invitational, Louisville Art Gallery, Nebr, 2003; Sharjah Art Mus, Sharjah, UAE, 2004; State of the Art Gallery, Beirut, 2004; Arte Las Americas Galleria, Houston, 2004; Kulturzentrum, Jounieh, Lebanon, 2005; Galerie Espace Lucrece, Paris, 2005; Noah's Ark Art Gallery, Beirut, 2005 ; Galerie Farra, Beirut, 2006; JHS Gallery, Taos, NMex, 2006; Norfolk Arts Ctr, Nebr, 2006. *Awards:* Third place award, Watercolor Juried Exhib, Union Col, 1986; Special Recognition award, Abstraction VI, Period Gallery, 2003. *Bibliog:* Andrea Cranford (auth), Ayoub Paints a Free World on Canvas, Nebr Mag, 2004. *Mem:* Berkeley Art Ctr; Kansas City Artists coalition; Audubon Artists Inc; Nat Oil & Acrylic Painters Soc. *Media:* Acrylic, Oil. *Dealer:* Chasen Galleries of Fine Art 3554 West Cary St Richmond VA 23221; Galerie Espace Lucrece 16 Rue Salneuve Paris 75017 France; D Pierre McClenaghan 1029 West 35th St Chicago IL 60609; Alexander Corporate Art PO Box 4704 Honolulu HI 96812; Galerie Farra 155 Main St Mkalles 2701 2115 Beirut Lebanon. *Mailing Add:* c/o Chasen Galleries of Fine Art 3554 West Cary St Richmond VA 23221

AYRES, JULIA SPENCER
WRITER, PRINTMAKER
b Havana, Cuba, Aug 16, 1931; US citizen. *Study:* Boston Mus Fine Art Sch, Mass Coll Art, 48-49; Art Inst Chicago, 50-52; pvt study with William Maynard, Frederic Taubes & Ralph Love. *Work:* Home Savings Am; Marriott Corp; Unocal Corp, Calif; First Interstate Bank, San Diego; Hilton Corp, Daytona Beach, Fla; Toyota Corp, Calif. *Comn:* Landscapes, seascapes, monotypes & suite of 18 watercolors, Marriott Corp, var locations. *Exhib:* Nat Arts Club Watercolor Ann, New York, 85; Am Artist Prof League Grand Nationals, New York, 85 & 86; Nat Watercolor Soc 64th Ann, Calif; Nat Watercolor Okla, Okla Art Ctr Mus, Oklahoma City, 87; Los Angeles Audubon Nat Art Exhib, Beverly Hills, Calif, 87; Printzero Exhib, 2003-2007; Okla State Capital, North Gallery, 2012. *Teaching:* Monotype Workshops Nat; Taught Art Methods, Pasadena, CA, 96-2005; plus many other workshops & studio lessons. *Awards:* Winsor & Newton Award, Nat Watercolor Soc 64th Ann. *Bibliog:* Art Marketing Handbook, Gee Tee Bee, 86; Dorothy Hoyal (auth), Taking oneself seriously as an artist, Am Artist, 6/88; Ayers on Making Monotypes, Am Artist, 88. *Publ:* Auth, numerous articles, Watercolor, Am Artist, Southwest Art, others; American Artist & Watercolor Mag, Concerning Printmaking, 86-2006; Paper, the critical support, In: Watercolor 87, 87 & Making watercolor monotypes, In: Watercolor 88, Am Artist Publ, 88; Julia S Ayres on Monotypes (pictures), Am Artist Mag, 88; Francoise Gilot's Monotypes, Am Arts Mag, 1/90; Monotype, Medius and Methods of Painterly Printmaking, 91 & Printmaking, Watson Guptill Pub, 93; Printmaking Techniques, Watson Guptill, 93; Monotype, Medius & Methods of Painterly Printmaking (paperback), Watson Guptill, 2000; coauth (with Gail Ayres), Painterly Printmaking with Monotype (DVD), Creative Catalyst Production Inc, 2007; contribr articles, American Artist & Watercolor. *Mailing Add:* PO Box 667 Chouteau OK 74337

AYRES, LARRY MARSHALL
HISTORIAN
b Nov 15, 1939. *Study:* Dartmouth Col, AB, 64; Univ Oxford, BLitt, 66; Harvard Univ, PhD, 70. *Pos:* Bd dir, Int Ctr Medieval Art, 77-80. *Teaching:* Asst prof art hist, Univ Calif, Santa Barbara, 70-74, assoc prof, 74-79, chmn, 76-88, prof, 79-. *Awards:* Alexander von Humboldt Stiftung Res Fel, 79-80 & 86 & 93; Am Philos Soc Grants, 81 & 82; Prix Rome Res Fel, Am Acad Rome, 83-84. *Mem:* Coll Art Asn Am; Mediaeval Acad Am; Southern Calif Art Historians. *Res:* Medieval art; history of the book. *Publ:* Auth, Sources of the lyre drawings, Speculum, 74; English painting and the Continent, Eleanor of Aquitaine: Patron and Politician, 76; Salzburg affiliations of a Bible fragment in Vienna, Zeitschrift Kunstgeschichte, 82; Parisian Bibles in Berlin Staatsbibliotek, Pantheon, 82; in Dumbarton Oaks Papers, 87; in Studi Gregoriani, 92; Romanesque Manuscript illumination, Braziller (in prep). *Mailing Add:* Dept Art History Univ Calif Santa Barbara Santa Barbara CA 93106

AZACETA, LUIS CRUZ
PAINTER
b Marianao, Cuba, Apr 5, 1942; arrived in US, 1960; US citizen, 1967. *Study:* Sch Visual Arts, New York, with Leon Golub, Frank Roth & Michael Loew, cert, 69. *Work:* Metrop Mus Art, Mus of Mod Art, NY; Va Mus Fine Arts, Richmond; RI Sch Design Mus; Del Art Mus. *Exhib:* Solo exhibs include Univ Art Gallery, San Diego State Univ, Calif, 1996, Fredric Snitzer Gallery, Coral Gables, 1997, 1998, Mary-Anne Martin/Fine Art, NY City, 1998, Arthur Roger Gallery, New Orleans, 2000, Galeria Ramis Barquet, NY, 2000, 2002, Generous Miracles Gallery, NY, 2001, Arthur Roger Gallery, New Orleans, 2002, Univ Ga Lamar Dodd Sch Art, 2006, Pan American Art Projects, Miami, 2010; group exhibs include Contemp Narratives in American Prints, Whitney Mus Am Art, 199-2000; Cuban Art of Three Generations, Ark Arts Ctr, Little Rock, 2000, About Face, 2001, Collector's Show, 2001; La Luz, Nat Hispanic Cultural Ctr, NMex, 2000; Am Embassy, Havana, Cuba, 2000; Artists Respond, George Adams Gallery, NY, 2001, Me, Myself and I, 2002, Multiple Artists, 2003; Real(ist) Men, Selby Gallery, Ringling Sch Art and Design, Sarasota, Fla, 2001-2002; Crisis Response, RI Sch Design, 2002; Ahora es el futuro/The Future is Now, The Durst Organization, NY, 2004. *Teaching:* Vis artist, Univ Calif, Davis, La State Univ, Baton Rouge, Univ Calif, Berkeley & Cooper Union, NY. *Awards:* Nat Endowment Arts, 80-81, 85-86; Guggenheim Mem Found Grant, NY, 85-86; NY Found Arts Grant, 85-86; Joan Mitchell Found Grant, 2009. *Bibliog:* Grace Glueck (auth), article, New York Times, 1/27/84; Ellen Schlesinger (auth), No room for apathy, Artweek, 84; Linda McGreevy (auth), Painting his heart out, Arts Mag, 6/85; Jose Gomez Sicre (auth), Cuban Artist in Exile, 86. *Media:* Acrylic, Watercolor. *Dealer:* Frumkin/Adams Gallery 50 W 57th St New York NY 10019. *Mailing Add:* c/o Adams Gallery 525 W 26th St New York NY 10001

AZANK, ROBERTO
PAINTER
b Buenos Aires, Arg, Nov 3, 1955. *Study:* Sch Archit, Univ Buenos Aires, 74-79. *Comn:* Still Life #34, comn by Ruth & Charles Henri Ford, NY, 97; Still Life #65, comn by Fernando de Martini, NY, 98; Still Life #72, comn by Jorge Quitequi, Buenos Aires, 98; Still Life #73, comn by Beatriz Zobel, Madrid, 98; Still Life #78, comn by Fran Garriguez, Madrid, 98; Still Life #276, Fabrice & Veronique Gikson, 2008. *Exhib:* Solo exhibs, 98, Lizan Tops Gallery, East Hampton, Albers Fine Art Gallery, Memphis, Consulate Argentina, NY, M J Alegria Sch Art, PR, Byron Comen Gallery, Kansas City, 2000 & Eleonore Austerer Gallery, San Francisco, 2001, Eleonore Austerer Gallery, Palm Desert, Calif, 2002-, Addison-Ripley Gallery, Wash, DC, 2003, Eleonore Austerer Gallery, San Francisco, Calif, 2003, Plus-One Plus-Two Gallery, London, Eng, 2004 & 2006, The Simmons Gallery, San Francisco, Calif, Unison Arts Center, Ctr of the Earth Gallery, Charlotte, NC; group exhibs, Brewster Arts Ltd, NY, 98 & Va Miller Gallery, Miami, 98. *Bibliog:* Cypherism and the Age of Computation, Inside Art, 8/99; Still Lifes are Still Effective, Kansas City Star, 11/25/99; Big Names in the Summer, Miami Herald, 8/1/99; The Desert Sun, 2001; New York Arts Mag, 2001; When the Subject is Also an Object, Addison-Ripley Gallery, 2003, 2005; Woodstock Times, Moving Stills, 2005. *Mem:* NY Artists Equity Asn. *Media:* Oil on Canvas. *Interests:* Astronomy, Classical Music, Chess, Chi-Kung Bridge. *Collection:* Wash D.C. Conv Ctr, Am Express Financial Advs, Sprint Telecommunications. *Dealer:* Eleonore Austerer Gallery 73-660 El Paseo Palm Desert CA 92260; Center of The Earth Gallery 3204 N Davidson St Charlotte NC; Plus One Gallery 91 Pimlico Rd London England. *Mailing Add:* 8 Watch Hill Rd New Paltz NY 12561-2705

AZARA, NANCY J
SCULPTOR, PAINTER
b New York, NY, Oct 13, 1939. *Study:* Finch Col, AAS, 59; Art Students League, sculpture with John Hovannes, painting & drawing with Edwin Dickinson, 64-67; Empire State Col, BS (sculpture), 74. *Work:* Sculptors, sound film strip, Harcourt, Brace, Jovanovich; Everson Mus, Syracuse, NY; Univ Southern Ill, Edwardsville; Franklin Furnace, NY; City Coll New York, City Univ NY; Sanyi Mus, Miaoli, Taiwan; Yale Mus, New Haven, Conn; Univ Okla, Fred Jones Mus Art, Norman, Okla; Provincetown Art Asn Mus, Mass; Phila Mus Art, Pa; Nat Gallery of Women in the Art, Wash DC; Mus Modern Art, NY; Milwaukee Mus, Wisc; Metropolitan Mus Art, NY; Grounds for Sculpture, Hamilton, NJ; David Dorsky, Dorsky Projects, NY; Cincinnati Mus, Oh; Brooklyn Mus, NY; Amherst Coll, Mass. *Comn:* About the Goddess KALI (wood sculpture), Pamela Oline, S France, 77; Hand Garden/Doctor's Wall, Robert Wood Johnson Univ Hosp, Hamilton, NJ, March 2004; Hands for Phyllis & Susan (private), 2005; Femage, Collection of prints, Brodsky Ctr, Rutgers Univ; Heart Wall, Lobby of 340 Madison, 2008. *Exhib:* Solo Exhibs: AIR Gallery, NY, 89 & 92; Lannon Gallery, Chicago, 90; James Chapel, Union Seminary, 91; E M Donahue & AIR Gallery, 94; Tweed Mus Art, Duluth, 95 & Donahue/Sosinski Gallery, 97; Gwinnett Fine Arts Ctr, Duluth, Ga, 98; Nancy Azara Sculpture, The Art Studio at Woodstock, NY, 98; SACI Gallery, Florence, Italy, 99; Heart Wall & other works, Donahue/Sosinski Art, New York City, 2000; Changes & Passages, Froelick Gallery of Portland, Ore & Gallery of Univ of Vt, 2001; The Int Church Center, Treas Rm Gallery, NY & Western Wyo Community Coll, 2002; The Inquiring Mind, NY, 2003, Froelick Gallery, Portland, Ore, Firehouse Art Gallery, Nassau Community Gallery, NY, 2004; Comma Gallery, Fla, 2005; Sanyi Mus, Miaoli, Taiwan & AIR Gallery, NY, 2008, Andre Zarre Gallery, New York, 2010, Fairleigh Dickinson Univ, NJ, 2010, Gaga Arts Ctr, Garnerville, NY, 2011, Traffic Zone Gallery, Minn, 2012, Saci Gallery, Florence, 2013; Group exhibs: From Celestial to Earthly, Paterson Mus, NJ, 95; Chips off the Old Block, Luise Ross Gallery, NY; Healing Art, Mus Fine Arts, The Univ Mont, Missoula, 99; Mirror of the Invisible: Contemp Artists Reflecting on Rumi and Islamic Mysticism, RV Fullerton Art Mus, San Bernardino, Ca, 09/28/2000-11/19/2000; Encaustic Palimpsests, Art Link Gallery, Seoul, Korea, 2010; Calandra Show, Calandra Inst, 2011; Conversations, R and F Gallery, Kingston, NY, 2011; Traveling exhib, NYFAI Visual Diaries, Fairleigh Dickinson Univ, Teaneck, NJ, Suffolk Comm Coll, Long Island, NY, 2010; Auburn Univ, Montgomery, Ala, 2011; Soho20 Gallery, NY, 2011; Muroff Kotler Visual Arts Gallery, SUNY Ulster Comm Coll, Stoneridge, NY, 2012; Cornell Cooperative Extension Agroforestry Ctr, Acra, NY, 2012; Katherine Nash Gallery, Univ Mo, Minneapolis, MN, 2013; Sideshow Gallery, Brooklyn, NY, 2013; Soho20 Gallery, NY, 2013; Art Current, Provincetown, Ma; Asya Geisberg Gallery, NY, 2013. *Collection Arranged:* The Lily: Loosely Seen (outdoor sculpture exhib), Woodstock Guild, NY, 2003; Paths: Real & Imagined, Woodstock Guild, NY, 2007; Eccentric Portraits, Kleinert James Art Ctr, Woodstock Guild, NY, 2011. *Teaching:* Lectr art, Sch Contemp Studies, Brooklyn Col, 73-75, lectr sculpture, 75-76; instr sculpture, Brooklyn Mus Sch, 74-77; instr, Col New Rochelle, NY, 79-89; instr, founding mem & mem bd dir, NY Feminist Art Inst, formerly; instr, Coll Art Asn, Los Angeles, Calif, 2012; guest lect numerous schs. *Awards:* Adolph & Esther Gottlieb Found Grant, 85; Bogliasco Found Fel, Genoa, Italy, 2000; Chikraniketan Fel, Kovalam Junction, Kerala, South India, 2001; Elan Lifetime Achievement Award, Womens Studio Center, NYC, 2004; Civitella Ranieri Found Fel, Italy,2010; La Macina di San Cresci, Chianti, Italy, 2013. *Bibliog:* Harriet Senie (auth), Nancy Azara at Donahue/Sosinski Art, Sculpture Mag, July/Aug 2000; Janet Koplos (auth), Nancy Azara at Donahue/Sosinski, Art in America, 6/2000; Holland Cotter (auth), Nancy Azara, Art in Review, NY Times, 2/18/00; Azara, Mattera & Rando, Italian American Women in the Visual Arts, In Our Own Voices, Bordighera Press, 2003; Richard Speer (auth), Going for Gold: Nancy Azara Conjures a Guilded World, Willamette Week, Oct 2004; Harriet Senie (auth) Nancy Azara, Sculpture Mag, 2009; many others; Harreit Senie (auth), Maxi's Wall, AIR Gallery, Sculpture Mag, 2008; Walter Robinson (auth), Nancy Azara at 340 madison, Artnet Mag, 2008; Beverly McFarland (auth), Calyx: A Journal of Art and Literature by Women, Vol 26, 2010; Katie Cercone (auth), The Healing Art of Nancy Azara, Vol 31, Womens Art Jour, 2010; Lissa Rankin (auth), Encaustic Art, Watson Guptill, 2010; Jill Fields (auth), Our Journey to the New York Feminist Art Institute, Entering the Picture: Judy Chicago, the Fresno Feminist Art Program and the Collective Visions of Women Artists, Routledge, 2011; Christine Cote (auth), The Flowering of the Fig Tree, Nancy Azara the Veteran Feminists of America, Stone Voices, 2012; Renee Phillips (auth), Celebrate the Healing Powers of Art: Featured Artist, Manhatten Arts Int, 2013; Mary Abbe (auth), Womens Work and Proud of it, Minneapolis Star Tribune, 2013; Sonia Cosco (auth), Nancy Azara: La Mia Italia, Ancestrale, di legno e foglie, Neura Mag, 2013; Paul Smart (auth) Secular and the Sacred, Woodstock Times, 2013. *Mem:* Art Students League; Womens Caucus Art (adv bd, 80-83); Coll Art Asn; Orgn Independent Artists (adv bd, 91-94); Woodstock Byrdcliffe Guild (bd mem). *Media:* Wood, Oil; Paper, Paint, gold and silver leaf and encaustic. *Publ:* Auth, Artists in their own image, Ms Mag, 73; The Group, A Mandala, Heresies Mag, spring 79; Auth, Spirit Taking Form: Making a Spiritual Practice Out of Making Art, 2002; Auth, Sculpture and the Devine, the Spiritual and Divine in Art, 2002; auth, Spirit Taking Form: a Spiritual Practice of Making Art, Red Wheel/ Weiser, 2002; auth, coauth with Matera & Rando, Italian American Women in the Visual Arts, In Our Own Voices, Bordighera Press, 2003; many others. *Mailing Add:* 91 Franklin St New York NY 10013

B

BAAS, JACQUELYNN
DIRECTOR, WRITER
b Grand Rapids, Mich, Feb 14, 1948. *Study:* Mich State Univ, with Elizabeth G Holt, BA, 71; Univ Mich, with Charles Sawyer & Joel Isaacson, MA, 73, PhD, 82. *Collection Arranged:* The Artistic Revival of the Woodcut in France 1850-1900 (coauth, catalog), Univ Mich, Ann Arbor 83-84; The Dartmouth Collection (coauth, catalog), 85, Encounter in Space: Double Images in the Graphic Art of Edward Munch (auth, catalog), 86, Mills and Factories of New England, 88 & Hood Mus Art, Dartmouth Col, Hanover, NH; The Independent Group: Postwar Britain & the Aesthetics of Plenty (co-auth, catalog), 91; The Here & the Hereafter: Images of Paradise in Islamic Art, 91; Prints from Van Dycks Iconography, 91; Transformation: The Art of Joan Brown (auth, catalog), Univ Calif Berkeley Art Mus, 98; Sixtyslippers: Peter Shelton. *Pos:* Registr, Univ Mich Mus Art, Ann Arbor, 74-78, asst dir, 78-82; chief cur, Hood Mus Art, Dartmouth Col, Hanover, NH, 82-83, acting dir, 84, dir, 85-89; dir, Univ Calif, Berkeley Art Mus & Pac Film Archive, 89-99; dir emeritus, 99-; project dir, Awake: Art and Buddhism in America, 2000-. *Teaching:* Hist print media, Univ Mich, 81. *Awards:* Nat Endowment Arts Fel, 88-89. *Mem:* Coll Art Asn Am; Am Asn Mus. *Res:* Orozco's Dartmouth mural; Relationship between art and Buddhism in America. *Publ:* auth, Peter Shelton: sixtyslippers, Univ Calif Berkeley Art Mus; Citadels of Inclusive Awareness, Conversations at the Castle: Changing Audiences and Contemporary Culture, 128-135, Mass Inst Technol Press, 98; To Know this Place for the First Time, The Art of Joan Brown (preface & essay), xxxi-xxxii, 189-229, Univ Calif Press, 98; The Epic of American Civilization: The Mural at Dartmouth College, 2002; Smile of the Buddha: Influences in Western Art from Monet to the Present

BABCOCK, JO (JOSEPH) WARREN
PHOTOGRAPHER, SCULPTOR
b St Louis, Mo, Feb 24, 1954. *Study:* Univ Calif Los Angeles, with Robert Heinicken, Todd Walker, Bea Nettles, 75; San Francisco Art Inst with, Pirkle Jones, BFA, 76; with Linda Conner & Larry Sultan, MFA, 79. *Work:* Brooklyn Mus; San Francisco Mod Art; George Eastman House, Rochester, NY; Newport Harbor Art Mus, Newport Beach, Calif; Biblioteque, Avignon, France; and others; Smithsonian Nat Gallery Am Art, Wash DC; Palace of the Governor's State Archives, Santa Fe, NMex. *Comn:* Photo installation (site specific), Levi Strauss Mus, San Francisco, 90; hist display, Levi Strauss & Co, San Francisco, 91; photos in bus shelters, Arts Comn, San Francisco, 92. *Exhib:* Solo exhibs, Steven Wolf Fine Arts, Duncan Miller Gallery, Los Angeles, Zwinger Gallery, Berlin, 1987, Chicago Art Inst, 1982, Marcuse Pfeiffer Gallery, New York City, 1988, CEPA, Buffalo, 1988, Artspace, San Francisco, 1989, Visual Studies Workshop, Rochester, NY, 1990, Ctr for Arts, San Francisco, 1995, Oakland Mus, Calif, 1997, Kyle Roberta Gallery, San Francisco, 1992, Addison Gallery Am Art, Andover, Mass, 1997, Bolinas Mus, Calif, 2014, and others; California Color, San Francisco Mus Mod Art, 89; de Young Mus, San Francisco, 93; Victoria Room, 94; Luggage Store, 95; San Francisco Ctr Arts, 96; Addison Gallery, Phillips Acad, Mass, 97; Oakland Mus, Calif; MH De Young Memorial Mus; Contemp Arts Mus, Houston; 1000 Cameras, Rayko Photo Ctr, 2010; Oakland Mus, Oakland Airport, 2011; Haines Gallery, 2011; Calif State Fullerton, 2012; NMex History Mus, Santa Fe, NMex, 2014; Cannon Art Gallery, Carlsbad, Calif, 2014. *Collection Arranged:* The NO Show, San Francisco, Calif, 85; Science Fiction, San Francisco, New York, Los Angeles, 86; Hotel Proj, West Oakland, San Francisoc, Richmond, 87; Monumental Women, San Francisco, 89. *Pos:* exhib designer, Levi Strauss & Co, 1989-. *Teaching:* Assoc prof new genres in photog, San Francisco Art Inst, 1989-93; vis prof pinhole photog, Visual Studies Workshop, Rochester, NY, 1990; assoc prof, Acad Art, San Francisco, 2006-2012. *Awards:* NY State Coun Arts, 88; Art in Transit, Market St Bus Shelter, San Francisco Arts Comn, 92; Fel, Nat Endowment Arts, 90; Fel, San Francisco Arts Comn, 92; Artist in Residence, Rayko Photo Ctr, 2010. *Bibliog:* Kenneth Baker (auth), San Francisco Chronicle, 12/18/2005; Doug Nickel (auth), Low Tech Photography & Sculpture, Invented Camera, 2005; San Francisco Camerawork Quarterly, spring 2006; and others; Poetics of Light, Univ Press, Santa Fe, NMex, 2014; Book of Art, Photographic Processes, Christopher James, 3rd Edition, Focal Press, 2014. *Mem:* Primitive Hunting Soc. *Media:* Alternative Photography. *Res:* Pinhole photog. *Specialty:* Fine art. *Interests:* Tai chi, cycling. *Collection:* Flashlights, Suitcases, Radios. *Publ:* Illusr, Flash Art, 2/88; Low Tech - Camera and Photographs; Newsweek, 8/21/89. *Dealer:* Visual Studies Workshop 31 Prince St Rochester NY 14607; Steven Wolf Fine Arts San Francisco CA 94110. *Mailing Add:* 378 San Jose Ave Apt B San Francisco CA 94110

BACA, JUDITH
MURALIST
b 1946. *Work:* Great Wall of Los Angeles (mural), Tujunga Wash Flood Control Channel. *Exhib:* Traveling installation, World Wall: A Vision of the Future without Fear. *Pos:* Co-founder, Social and Pub Art Resource Ctr, Venice, Calif, 76-, exec dir, 76-84, artistic dir, 84-; founder, City of Los Angeles Mural Prog, Citywide Mural Proj, Dept Recreation and Parks, 74, Great Walls Unlimited: Neighborhood Pride Prog, 88; founding fac mem, Calif State Univ, Monterey Bay. *Teaching:* Prof, studio arts, Univ Calif Irvine, 80-96, world art and cultures, Univ Calif Los Angeles, 96-; vice chair, Cesar Chavez Ctr, Univ Calif Los Angeles, 96-. *Mailing Add:* Social Pub Art Resource Ctr 685 Venice Blvd Venice CA 90291

BACARELLA, FLAVIA
PAINTER
b Brooklyn, NY. *Study:* State Univ of NY, Albany, BA; New Sch Soc Res, MA, 75; Brooklyn Col, MFA, 1983; New York Studio Sch Drawing, 1978-80. *Work:* Arthur Andersen, Minneapolis; Va Ctr Creative Arts, Sweet Briar; Bryn Mawr Col. *Exhib:* Prince St Gallery, 85, 88, 91, 95 & 99; Krasdale Galleries, 94. *Teaching:* Asst prof to assoc prof, Herbert H Lehman Col, 85-, chair currently. *Awards:* Painting Fel, NY Found Arts, 86; Grant, City Univ NY Res Found, 88, 91 & 98. *Mem:* Women's Caucus Art; Coll Art Asn. *Media:* Oils. *Mailing Add:* Lehman College Fine Arts Building 122 250 Bedford Park Blvd W Bronx NY 10468

BACH, DIRK
PAINTER, EDUCATOR
b Grand Rapids, Mich, Nov 27, 1939. *Study:* Univ Denver, BFA (painting), 61, MA (painting), 62; Univ Mich, Ann Arbor, MA (Orient art hist), 64. *Work:* Denver Art Mus, Colo; Hopkins Ctr Art Galleries, Dartmouth Col, Hanover, NH; Lamont Gallery, Phillips Exeter Acad, NH; Loretto-Hilton Gallery, Webster Col, St Louis, Mo; Mus Art, RI Sch Design, Providence; Currier Gallery, Mancester, NH; Webster Univ; Univ NH. *Comn:* Wall reliefs, Denver Art Mus, 62, NH Comn Arts NH Voc Inst, Berlin, 68 & Grad & Music Schs, Univ NH, 68; St Gaudens Nat Hist Site, Cornish, NH, 72. *Exhib:* New Eng Drawing Exhib, Addison Gallery, Andover, Mass, 70; New Eng Drawing Competition, DeCordova Mus, Lincoln, Mass, 74; Phillips-Exeter Acad, 67, 74 & 79; Newport Art Asn, RI, 76, 77-81; RI Sch Design Mus of Art, Providence, 69-91; Seasons Gallery, Den Haag, The Neth, 80-81; Susan Cumming Gallery, Mill Valley, Calif, 90; and many others. *Collection Arranged:* One Hundred Years of Am Art, 66 & The Rose Art Mus Collection at New Hampshire (with catalog), 69, Scudder Gallery, Durham, NH. *Pos:* Dir, Scudder Gallery, Univ NH, 65-69; adv & contribr, Newport Rev, 79-; coun mem, Art Asn Newport, 80-83. *Teaching:* Asst prof painting, Univ NH, 65-69; assoc prof art hist, RI Sch Design, 69-91, prof, formerly, chmn art hist dept, formerly, chmn fac asn, 89-91; assoc & lectr, Asian Studies, Brown Univ, 70-; dir, RI Sch Design, European Honors Program, Rome, 74-75. *Awards:* Univ NH Cent Univ Res Grant Commemorative Stamp Paintings, 68; Nat Endowment Humanities Travel & Res Grant, Japan, 71; Mellon Fel, Egypt, 84. *Mem:* Coll Art Asn Am; Artists Equity Asn; Newport Art Asn; NH Art Asn; NEARI. *Media:* Graphite, Paper, Colored Pencil. *Res:* Development of Ch'an painting in China; production of cosmic diagrams in the Far East. *Publ:* Contribr, The Painting of Tao Chi, Univ Mich Mus Art, 67; auth, The stamp collection of Dirk Bach, Ramparts, 11/68; Selections From the Oriental Collections, RI Sch Design, 72. *Mailing Add:* 243 Spring Garden St Easton PA 18042

BACH, LAURENCE
PHOTOGRAPHER, EDUCATOR
b Philadelphia, Pa, Jan 2, 1947. *Study:* Philadelphia Coll Art, BFA, 68; Allgemeine Gewerbeschule, Basel, Switz, grad, 70. *Work:* Philadelphia Mus Art; Mus Fine Arts, St Petersburg, Fla. *Exhib:* Three Centuries Am Art, Philadelphia Mus Art, 76; solo exhibs, Modernism Gallery, San Francisco, 79, Robert Samuel Gallery, NY, 81, Photo Ctr Athens, Greece, 82 & Wesleyan Univ, Conn, 83; Group Photographs, Inst Contemp Art, Philadelphia, 80; and others. *Teaching:* Asst prof photog & design, Moore Col Art, 70-72, Philadelphia Col Art, 72-74 & State Univ NY, Purchase, 74-86; prof, Univ Arts, Philadelphia Col Art & Design, currently. *Awards:* Photog Grant, Nat Endowment Arts, 80; Photog Study Grant, Polaroid Corp, 81; NY State Coun Arts Grant, Visual Studies Workshop, 82. *Bibliog:* William Stapp (auth), Three Centuries of American Art (exhib catalog), Philadelphia Mus, 76; Don Ernst (auth), Laurence Bach: Paros shards, Aperture, No 82, 2/79; Owen Edwards (auth), Laurence Bach portfolio, Am Photog, 9/81. *Publ:* Auth, The Paros Dream Book, Visual Studies Workshop Press, 83. *Mailing Add:* 502 E Gorgas Ln Philadelphia PA 19119-1321

BACHARDY, DON
PAINTER, DRAFTSMAN
b Los Angeles, Calif, May 18, 1934. *Study:* Chouinard Art Inst, 56-60; Slade Sch Art, London Univ, 61. *Work:* Metrop Mus Art, New York; Nat Portrait Gallery Eng, London; Princeton Univ; Fogg Art Mus; Nat Portrait Gallery, Smithsonian Inst, Washington, DC; Huntington Libr, Calif; Norton Simon Mus, Calif. *Comn:* Off portrait Calif State Capitol Bldg, Former Gov Edmund G Brown Jr. *Exhib:* Solo exhibs, de Young Mem Mus, 64, Los Angeles Munic Art Gallery, 73 & 83 & NY Cult Ctr, 74; Inside-Out: Self Beyond Likeness, Newport Harbor Art Mus, 81; Portland Art Mus, 81; James Corcoran Gallery, Santa Monica, Calif, 87, 91 & 93; Charles Cowles Gallery, New York; de Young Mem Mus, 96; Nat Portrait Gallery, London, Eng, 96; Univ Tex, Austin, 97; Laguna Art Mus, Laguna Beach, 99; Acad Motion Picture Arts & Scis, Beverly Hills, Calif, 2000; Huntington Libr, San Marino, Calif, 2004-2005; White Columns Gallery, NY, Apr-May 2008; Craig Krull Gallery, Santa Monica, Ca, 2008; Cheim and Read, NY, 2009. *Bibliog:* One Hundred Drawings, 83 & Drawings of the male nude, 85, Twelvetrees Press; 70XI, Drawings of Seventy Artists, Illuminati Press, 83; Last Drawings of Christopher Isherwood, Faber & Faber, 91; Stars in My Eyes, Univ Wis Press, 2000. *Mem:* ACLU; Prospect I and Prospect 2: US Biennial Inc (bd dirs, 2009-). *Media:* Ink, Acrylic. *Specialty:* art. *Publ:* Illusr, Michigan Quart Rev, Univ Mich, winter 80; Paris Rev, Vol 23, No 79, 81 & Vol 25, No 89, 83; Ancestors of Congo Square: African Art in the New Orleans Museum of Art, Scala Publishers, 2011. *Dealer:* Craig Krull Gallery 2525 Michigan Ave Bldg B3 Santa Monica CA 90404; Cheim & Read 547 W 25th St New York NY 10001. *Mailing Add:* 145 Adelaide Dr Santa Monica CA 90402

BACHERT, HILDEGARD GINA
ART DEALER
b Mannheim, Ger, Apr 3, 1921; US citizen. *Study:* Hunter Coll, BA (summa cum laude), 54. *Collection Arranged:* Grandma Moses (contribr, catalog), Nat Gallery Art, Washington, DC, 79; Alfred Kubin, 83; Paula Modersohn-Becker, 83; Kollwitz/Modersohn-Becker traveling exhib, 84-86; Grandma Moses traveling exhib, Japan, 90; Käthe Kollwitz Exhib (auth, catalog), Found Neumann, Gingins & Mus Jenisch, Vevey, Switz, 94. *Pos:* Secy & asst, Nierendorf Gallery, New York, 39-40; exec secy, Galerie St Etienne, New York, 40-78, co-dir, 78-. *Awards:* Decorated Cross of Merit, 1st Class, Ger, 99; Inductee, Hunter Coll Hall of Fame, 2004. *Mem:* Art Dealers Asn Am. *Res:* Käthe Kollwitz. *Specialty:* Early 20th century Austrian and German art: Schiele, Klimt, Kokoschka, Kollwitz & Corinth; 19th and 20th century naive art. *Publ:* Contribr, Otto Kallir's Egon Schiele: Oeuvre Catalog of the Paintings,

66 & contribr, Otto Kallir's Egon Schiele: The Graphic Work, 70, Zsolnay, Vienna & Crown; Otto Kallir's Grandma Moses, Crown & Harry N Abrams, 73, Ger transl, DuMont, Cologne, Ger, 79; Jane Kallir's Egon Schiele: The Complete Works, Harry N Abrams, 90 & 98; auth, Collecting the Art of Käthe Kollwitz, Käthe Kollwitz by Elizabeth Prelinger, Nat Gallery Art & Yale Univ Press, 92; auth, Kathie Kollwitz: Dessins, gravures, sculptures, Gingins, Switz, 1994; auth, Hildegard Bachert, A memoir, New York, 2010

BACHINSKI, WALTER JOSEPH
PAINTER, PRINTMAKER
b Ottawa, Ont, Aug 6, 1939; Can citizen. *Study:* Ont Coll Art, AOCA, 65; printmaking with Frederick Hagen; Univ Iowa, with Mauricio Lasansky, MA (printmaking), 67. *Work:* Montreal Mus Fine Arts, Que; Uffizi Gallery, Florence, Italy; Can Coun Art Bank, Ottawa, Ont; Nat Libr of Canada, Nat Gallery of Canada. *Comn:* Three bas-reliefs on a humanitarian theme, Univ Waterloo, Ont, 75; The Sculptor's Studio (bas-relief), MacLean-Hunter Bldg, College Park, Toronto; Mother and Child (bronze relief), Donald Forster Sculpture Park, MacDonald Stewart Art Gallery, Guelph, Ont, 85; Pastoral (pastel), Cineplex-Odean Theatre, Kiochener, Ont; The Four Seasons (pastel), Mine & Minerals Res Ctr, Laurentian Univ, Sudbury, Ont. *Exhib:* Solo exhibs (traveling), Mt St Vincent Univ, 73, Walter Bachinski: Sculpture & Drawing, Art Gallery, Hamilton, 81; Bachinski, A Decade (traveling exhib), Kitchener-Waterloo Art Gallery, 76-77; Approaching Classicism, Selected Works, 1979-89, Kitchener-Waterloo Art Gallery, 91; Still-life, 10 Yrs, McLaren Art Ctr, Barrie, 92. *Teaching:* Prof drawing & printmaking, Dept Fine Arts, Univ Guelph, 67-94. *Awards:* Can Coun Arts Grants, 69, 78, 79 & 82; Arts Coun Ont Grants, 78 & 79; Premio dell Instituto Bancario Si Paolo di Torino, 4th Int Biennale of Graphic Art, Florence, Italy, 74; Can Coun Materials Grant, 78-79; and others. *Bibliog:* Bachinski: A Decade, Kitchener-Waterloo Art Gallery, 76; Walter Bachinski: Sculpture and Drawing, Art Gallery Hamilton, 81; Walter Bachinski: Approaching Classicism, Kiochener-Waterloo Art Gallery, 91. *Mem:* fine Press Book Asn. *Media:* Pastels, All Media. *Publ:* Virgil's The Ecologues, Shanty Bay Press, 99; five poems with pochoir illustrations by Walter Bachinski, Shanty Bay Press, 99; CIRCUS, 5 Poems in the Circus with Pochoirs, Shanty Bay Press, 2002, The Artist as Saltimbanqua, Various authors with Color Linocuts and Pochoirs, Shanty Bay Press, 2011; Virgil, GEORGICS, translated by Robert Wells, with Pochoirs and Woodcuts by Walter Bachinski, Shanty Bay Press, 2007; Ovid, Stories from the Metamorphoses, The Garth Translation, with Photogranures by Walter Bachinski, Shanty Bay Press, 2013. *Dealer:* Wallace Galleries Ltd Calgary Alberta Can. *Mailing Add:* 152 Drury Hill Rd Shanty Bay ON L0L 2L0 Canada

BACHMEIER, BRADLEY JOHN
CERAMIST, EDUCATOR
b Aug 2, 1970, Harvey, ND. *Study:* Minn State Univ, Moorhead, BS, 93; Univ North Dakota, MFA, 2007; studied with Kathryn McCleery. *Work:* Office of the First Lady of the US, Michelle Obama, Wash DC; Microsoft Permanent Collection, Redmond, Washington; South Dakota Mus Art, Aberdeen; Plains Art Mus, Fargo, ND; Rourke Art Mus, Moorhead, MN. *Comn:* brick relief sculpture 8x8, Fargo North High School, ND, 2008; brick relief sculpture 14x6, US Army Base, Camp Grafton, Devils Lake, ND, 2010; ceramic tile relief sculpture 6x12, Sanford Heart Hospital, Sioux Falls, SD, 2012; ceramic tile relief sculpture 8x12, Concordia Coll, Moorhead, MN, 2013. *Exhib:* Two person show, SD Mus Art, Brookings, SD, 2009; Solo exhib, Building a Decade, Rourke Art Mus, Moorhead, MN, 2010; Group exhibs, Visions in Clay, LH Horton Gallery, Stockton, Calif, 2011, 50 States Fire Up, Am Clay Invitational, Margaret Harwell Art Mus, Popular Bluffs, MO, 2012, Red River Reciprocity, Plains Art Mus, Fargo ND, 2014, Contemporary Indigeneity, Great Plains Mus, Univ Nebr, Lincoln, 2014, Arts 64, Buchanan Ctr Arts, Monmouth, Ill, 2014, Potter's Council, Rhode Island, NCECA Convention, Providence, RI, 2015. *Collection Arranged:* Ceramic Community, Rourke Art Gallery, 2011. *Pos:* pres bd dirs, The Arts Partnership, 2012-2013, Rourke Art Mus, 2013-2014, gov appointed bd dirs, ND Council on Arts, 2014-. *Teaching:* visual art dept chair, Fargo North High School, 2001-2008; adj prof ceramics, Minn State Univ Moorhead, 2006-2007, assoc prof art edn, 2008-. *Awards:* Best of Show, RoughRider Internat, City of Williston, ND, 2005; Nat NICE award in Ceramics, NICHE Winners Exhib, Rosen Group, Phila, 2007; 3rd Place in Ceramics, ArtBuzz Internat, Art Buss Book Coll, 2008; Distinguished Creative Exhib, A Ceramic Humanity, Univ ND, 2008; Govs Award in the Arts, Lifetime Achievement, Gov ND, 2009. *Bibliog:* Vol 18 Staff, Artist Feature: Brad Bachmeier, Briar Cliff Review, 2006; HGTV Staff/film crew, Thats Clever, HGTV, 2007; Gaylen Peterson (auth), Interviews with 12 Nat Potters, Becoming a Potter, 2007; Matt O'Lien (auth), A Prairie Mosaic, Prairie Public Television, 2010; MN State Arts Bd Staff, Review: Building a Decade, State of the Arts Publication, 2011. *Mem:* Nat Council on Education for the Ceramic Arts (mem, 2009-); The Arts Partnership (bd mem, 2009-2013, pres, 2012-2013); Rourke Art Mus (bd mem, 2010-2014, pres, 2013-2014); Nat Art Edn Assn (mem, 2008-); North Dakota Council on the Arts (bd dirs, 2013-). *Publ:* Briar Cliff Review (book), 2006, 2008; Alumni Success Feature (Alumnews), MSUM Alumni Found, 2007; Award Winners Feature, NICHE Mag, Rosen Group, 2007; Art Buzz (book), Art Buzz Internat, 2008; Building a Decade, State of the Arts (art), MN State Arts Bd, 2011. *Dealer:* Rourke Art Mus 521 Main Ave Moorhead MN 56560; Uptown Gallery 74 Broadway Fargo ND 58102; Oland Arts Consulting PO Box 116 Sioux Falls SD 57104. *Mailing Add:* 8417 25th ST S Fargo ND 58102

BACHNER, BARBARA L
PAINTER, INSTALLATION SCULPTOR
b Waterville, ME, Sept 14, 1934. *Study:* NY Univ Fine Arts, NY BA Magna Cum Laude, 68; Nat Acad Sch Fine Arts, Art Students League, Merit Awards, 75-80; Johnson State Coll, Vt Studio, MFA, 2000. *Work:* Robert Blackburn Printmaking Workshop Coll, Libr Congress, Washington, DC; Southwest Minn State Univ Coll, Marshall, Minn; Kaatsbaan Intl Dance Ctr, Tivoli, NY; Four Seasons Hotel Corp, Las Vegas, Nev; Texaco Corp, Houston, Tex; Jane Voorhees Zimmerli Art Mus, Rutgers Univ, New Brunswick, NJ. *Comn:* Pvt collection, comn by Gerald & Lola Sherman, Washington, DC. *Exhib:* Solo exhibs, Tai Gallery, New York, 94, 98 & 2003, Fletcher Gallery, Woodstock, NY, 95, Memory into Matter, Studio D'ARS, Milan, Italy, 2001, Roessler Gallery, Rauvensburg, Ger, 2002, Echoes, AIR Gallery, NY, Kleinert/ James Gallery, Woodstock, NY, 2004, Dacia Gallery, NY, 2012; NY State Biennial, NY State Mus, Albany, 98; Biennale d'ELL Arte Contemporanea, Fortezza Da Basso, Florence, Italy, 99; Dream Worlds & Neo-Surrealism, at the Millennium, Attleboro Mus, Attleboro, Mass, 2000; Superhighway, CVB Space, New York & Berlin Kuntsproject, Berlin, Ger, 2000; NY Meets Berlin, Max Planck inst for Human Develop, Berlin, Ger, 2004; Point of View, Poughkeepsie Art Mus, Poughkeepsie, NY, 2004; Depth of the Surface, William Whipple Gallery, SW Minn State Univ, Marshall, Minn, 2004; Recycle/Revisited, Samuel Dorsky Mus Art, State Univ NY, New Paltz, NY, 2005; How we see China Today, NY Arts Beijing Gallery, Lhao Yang Qu, Beijing, China, 2006; Retrograde, Venezuelan Consulate Gen, New York, 2006; Abram's Rib, Eve's Air in her Hair, Soho 20, NY, 2007; Woodstock Biennal, Woodstock, NY, 2007; Paths: Real and Imagined, Woodstock Byrdcliffe Guild, Woodstock, NY, 2007; Chinese Ideas in Am Art, China Gallery, NY, 2007; Gallery 705, Stroudsburg, Pa, 2008; Retrograde, Westbeth Gallery, New York, 2009; The (Un)Real City, Kasia Kay Art Proj Gallery, Chicago, Ill, 2009; Heart, Onishi Gallery, New York, 2009; Eleven Pick Two, Woodstock Artists Asn, NY, 2009; Heart II, Kasia Kay Art Proj Gallery, Chicago, Ill, 2010; Butterfly Show, M.U.S.E.E. Cavour, Bologna, Italy, 2011, Camden Art Gallery, London, England, 2011, Archeological Mus, Pitigliano, Italy, 2011; Eccentric Portraits, Kleinert James Arts Ctr, Woodstock, NY, 2011; Earth, Air, Water, Woodstock, Artists Asn and Mus, Woodstock, NY, 2012. *Pos:* Bd dir, graphics co-chmn, Pen & Brush, New York, 90-95; bd dir, trustee, Woodstock Artists Asn, Woodstock, NY, 90-2002; bd dir, Nat Assn Women Artists, New York, 2000-02; cur, Woodstock Artist Asn & Mus, Woodstock Guild, Arts Soc Kingston, Kingston, NY, 2002-. *Teaching:* Instr, Woodstock Sch Art, Woodstock, NY, 2000-01. *Awards:* Medal Hon, Annual Exhib, Nat Asn Women Artists, 98; Lorenzo Il Magnifico Metal, Biennale D'Ell Arte Contemporanea, Florence, 99; Travel Grant, NY Meets Berlin, US Embassy, Berlin, 2004. *Bibliog:* Bonnie Langston, Terrorist Attacks Ripple Effect, Daily Freeman, Kingston, NY, 12/4/2000; Silvia Venuti, Memory into Matter, Corriere dell Arte, Milan, Italy, 11/24/2001; Ed McCormack (auth), Barbara Bachner at Gallery at 49, Gallery & Studio, 4/5, 2002; Beth Elaine Wilson (auth), Lucid Dreams, Reduce, Reuse, Recycle-Rethink, Chronogram, 6/2002; Paul, Smart (auth), Like Alchemy: Bachners Echoes on Exhibit at Kleinert, Woodstock Times, Woodstock, NY, 4/22/2004; Leanna Valenti (auth), Art & Fashion Salon (online review), 2012; and others. *Mem:* Coll Art Asn; Nat Asn Women Artists, (bd dir, 2000-02); Art Students League (life mem); NY Artists Asn; Woodstock Artists Asn (trustee/dir, juror, cur, painting, printmaking, exhib comt, 90-2002); Los Angeles Printmaking Soc. *Media:* Acrylic, Mixed Media. *Interests:* Collecting found objects to transform as sculptures for installations. *Publ:* Behind Closed Eyes, Artist's Book, K Caraccio Printshop Publ, 98. *Dealer:* TAI Resources 150 West 30th St New York NY. *Mailing Add:* 25 Sutton Pl S Apt 19N New York NY 10022-2455

BACIGALUPI, DON
FORMER MUSEUM DIRECTOR, CURATOR
b New York, NY, Apr 24, 1960. *Study:* Univ Houston, BA (art hist), 83; Univ Tex, MA (art hist), 85, PhD (art hist), 93. *Collection Arranged:* Whatley Collection, 90-93; Am Photography: A History in Pictures, 94; Synesthesia: Sound & Vision in Contemporary Art (auth, catalog), San Antonio Mus Art, 95; Stella in Studio: The Public Art of Frank Stella, 96; Michael Ray Charles, 1989-1993: An Am Artist's Work (auth, catalog), Blaffer Gallery, 97. *Pos:* Cur contemp art, San Antonio Mus Art, Tex 93-95; dir & chief cur, Blaffer Gallery, Univ Houston Art Mus, 95-99; dir, San Diego Mus Art, 99-2003 & Toledo Mus Art, Ohio, 2003-2009, Crystal Bridges Mus Am Art, Bentonville, Ark, 2009-2015, bd. dirs. 2013-. *Teaching:* Lectr art hist, Univ Tex, Austin, 88-93; adj prof, Univ Houston, 96-. *Awards:* Gold Award Best Catalog, Synesthesia: Sound & Vision, Addy Awards, 96; First Prize, Best Catalog, Michael Ray Charles, Am Asn Mus, 98. *Mem:* Tex Asn Mus (co-chmn); Am Asn Mus; Houston Coalition Visual Arts (co-chmn); Asn Art Mus Dirs (bd, 2004). *Res:* Contemporary American and International art. *Mailing Add:* c/o Crystal Bridges Museum of American Art 600 Museum Way Bentonville AR 72712

BACKES, JOAN
PAINTER, ARTIST
b Milwaukee, Wis. *Study:* Univ Iowa, BA, 72; Univ Mo, Kansas City, MA, 83; Northwestern Univ, Evanston, Ill, MFA, 85. *Work:* Aberdeen Art Galleries & Mus, Scotland; Nova Scotia Coll of Art and Design, Halifax, NS, Can; Embassy of USA, Reykjavik, Iceland; Boston Publ Libr, Boston, Mass; Wright Mus Art, Beloit Coll, Wis; Nelson-Atkins Mus Art, Kansas City, Mo; Milwaukee Art Mus, Wis; SAFN Mus, Reykjavik, Iceland; Reykjavik Art Mus, Iceland; Rauma Art Mus, Finland; Silpakorn Univ Collection, Bangkok, Thailand; Linnaeus Garden, Uppsala, Sweden; Racine Art Mus, Racine, Wis; Joslyn Art Mus, Omaha, Neb; Gruenwald, Berlin, Germany; Odenwald, Darmstadt, Germany; Racine Art Mus, Wisc; Hafnarborg Inst Culture & Fine Art, Iceland; Nerman Mus Art, Overland Park, Kans; Spencer Mus Art, Lawrence, Kans; RISD Mus, Providence, RI; Newport Art Mus, Newport, RI; Smith Coll Mus Art, Northampton, Mass. *Exhib:* Primordial Landscape, Hafnarborg Inst Cult & Fine Art, Iceland, 91; Ut Pictora Poesis, Mulvane Art Mus, Topeka, 93; Rocks, Markers, Places, Wustum Mus Fine Art, Racine, Wis, 93; The Landscape Beyond The Landscape, Centro Cult Recoleta, Buenos Aires, Arg, 97; Hafnarborg Inst Cult & Fine Art, 98; Nature Interrupted, New Bedford Art Mus, Mass; Drawing-drawing 2, The Foundry, London Biennial, Eng; Faculty Exhib, Brown Univ, Providence, RI, 2007; Chelsea Art Mus, New York, 2008; Arbores Venerabiles, Glyndor Gallery, Wave Hill, Bronx, NY, 2009; Art Chicago, NEXT, 2009; The Decorata Proj, Bristol Art Mus, Bristol, RI, 2009; Int Forest Path Biennial Darmstadt, Germany, 2010; Gallery Benoit, Boston, Mass, 2010; Hunterdon Art Mus, Clinton, NJ, 2010; Berlin Germany Waldkunst Int Biennial, 2011; Zentrum, Darmstadt, Ger, 2013; Art Ctr, Grand Junction, Colo, 2013; Solo exhibs, Aberdeen Art Galleries & Mus, Scotland, 87 & Museo de Arte Contemporaneo, Santiago, Chile, 96; Nova Scotia Coll Art & Design,

Halifax, 99; Braitmayer Art Ctr, Marion, Mass, 2000; Jan Weiner Gallery, Kansas City, MO, 2001; Dartmouth Col, Hanover, NH, 2002; Hafnarborg Inst Cult & Fine Art, 2003; Wright Mus Art, Beloit Col, Wis, 2004; Rauma Art Mus, Finland, 2005; SAFN Mus, Reykjavik, Iceland, 2006; McCormick Gallery, Chicago, Ill, 2007; Nova Scotia Coll Art & Design, NS, Can, 2007; Silpakorn Univ, Bangkok, Thailand, 2007; Univ Gallery, Salve Regina Univ, Newport, RI, 2007; Dean Jensen Gallery, Milwaukee, Wis; Los Angeles Contemp, Calif; 2008 Linnaeus Garden, Uppsala Univ, Sweden, 2009; Sleeper Gallery, Edinburgh, Scotland, 2010; Dean Jensen Gallery, Milw, Wis, Catalogue, 2011;Dedee Shattuck Gallery, Westpoint, Mass, book, 2012; Newport Art Mus, Newport, RI, 2012; Torrance Art Mus, Calif, brochure, 2013, Francine Seders Gallery, Seattle, Washington, 2013; Beach Mus Art, KSU, one yr mus installation, brochure, Studio 21 Fine Art, Halifax, Nova Scotia, Canada, Cutlog NY, Site Specific installation presented by Yellow Peril Gallery, SCOPE NY International, Special Project, presented by Yellow Peril Gallery, Cardboard Trees and Tree, New England, 2014; Racine Art Mus Installation up for one yr, brochure, Dean Jensen Gallery, Milw, Wis, Joan Backes, Strathnaver, Scotland, Angela MacKay, curator, Joan Backes/Carpets of Leaves, Lessedra Gallery, Sofia, Bulgaria, 2015; Group Exhibs: All You Can See, Wendy Cooper Gallery, Madison, Wis, 2000; Seascapes, Virginia Lynch Gallery, Tiverton, RI, 2001; Natural Selections: New England Artists Interpret Nature, Newport Art Mus, RI, 2002; Artists and the Cultivated Landscape, Racine Art Mus, Wis, 2003; A Forest Somewhere, Dean Jensen Gallery, Milw, 2004; Summarize, Jan Weiner Gallery, Kansas City, 2005; drawing_drawing2, The Foundry, London Biennial, Eng, 2006; Faculty Exhib, Bell Gallery, Brown Univ, Providence, RI, 2007, Nature Interrupted, Chelsea Art Mus, NY, Brochure, 2008; Art Chgo/NEXT, Ill, 2009; Botanica, Hunterdon Art Mus, Clinton, NJ, 2010; Internat Biennial and Symposium: Internationaler Waldkunstpfad, Darmstadt, Germany, 2010, 2011; Highlights, Francine Seders Gallery, Seattle, 2012; New Acquisitions, Smith Col Mus Art, Northampton, Mass, 2013; Branching Out: Trees as Art, Peabody Essex Mus, curator Jane Winchell, Salem, Mass (one year installation), 2014; Jamestown Art Ctr, curated by Robert Stack, Yellow Peril Gallery, RI, 2015 and several others. *Pos:* Cur, New Bedford Art Mus, Mass; vis artist Silpakorn Univ, Bangkok, Thailand, 2007; Salve Regina Univ, Newport, 2009, Hunter Col, NY, 2010; Tyler Sch Art, Temple Univ, Phila, Pa, 2013; Pace Univ, NY, 2014; Ripon Col, Wis, 2015; and many others; curator, Vault Series, NBAM, MA; bd. mem, Sarah Doyle Gallery, Brown Univ. *Teaching:* Adj prof painting, Univ Mo, 85-88; vis artist painting, Kansas City Art Inst, 88-95; adj prof, Brown Univ, 97-; adj prof Coll Art Grad Prog, Portland, Maine, 2000-; prof painting, Rhode Island Sch Design, Providence, 2006; Nova Scotia Coll Art & Design, Halifax, NS, Can, 1999, 2007. *Awards:* Nat Endowment Arts & Kans Arts Comn Award, 86 & 92; Sr Fulbright Scholar, Ctr Intl Exchange Scholars, 94-95; Ragdale Found Fel, 98, 99, 2000; Fulbright Hays Award, 2003; US Embassy Grant, Iceland, 2006; Fac Award, Brown Univ Creative Arts Coun, 2008; Am/Scandinavian Found Proj Grant, 2009; Edwin Austin Abbey Mural Fel, Nat Acad Mus, New York, 2009; Int Biennial & Symposium, Darmstadt, Germany, 2010; Waldkunst Int Biennial, Berlin, Germany, 2011; Zentrum Biennial, Darmstadt, Ger, 2013; Artist residency invitational, Art Source, Fremantle, Western Australia, 2014. *Bibliog:* Eva Grinstein (auth), An Aesthetic View of Inapprehensible Natural Phenomena, Rev El Cronistia, Buenos Aires, Arg, 97; Jon Proppe (auth), Joan Backes Remembering, Hafnarborg Inst, 98; James Yood (auth), Tré, Hafnarborg Inst, 2003; Jon Proppe (auth), Pleasure in the Pathless Wood, Hafnarborg Inst, 2003; Gerald Nordland (auth), Joan Backes, Wright Mus Art, Beloit Coll Press, 2004; Alan Artner (auth), Joan Backes, Paper House, Chicago Tribune, July 13, 2007; Lauren Wienberg (auth), Paper House, Time Out Chicago, 7/12-18/2007; Constance Mallinson (auth), Joan Backes LA Contemporary, Art in America, March 2009; Peter Frank (auth), Joan Backes: Trees & Houses, LA Contemp, 2008; Uppsala Nya Tidning, Sweden, 7/18/2009; Mary Louise Schumacher (auth), Joan Backes..., Milwaukee Jour Sentinel, 5/2011; Peggy Durnigan (auth), Shephard Express, 5/2011; Mark Mack (auth), Newport Mercury, 5/2012; Don Wilkinson (auth), Standard Times, 7/22/12; Stephen Kobasa (auth), Art New England, 7 & 8/2012; Wolfson, Dalia (auth), Lines and Letters, Yale Daily News, New Haven, Conn, 10/18/13; Zimmer, Lori (auth), Culture Grandlife Guide, SCOPE, Review, NY, 3/6/14; and many others. *Mem:* Coll Art Asn. *Media:* Mixed Media, Installation Sculpture. *Publ:* Auth, Letter from the Living, Borderline, Big Blue Prairie Ed, 92; Hafnarborg: 1988-1993, Felagsbokdandid Bokfell, Iceland, 93; Joan Backes Images and Essays, 2004-2012; Seaton, Liz (auth), Beach Mus Art, Where the Heart Belongs, brochure essay, 2013. *Dealer:* Dean Jensen Gallery 759 N Water St Milwaukee WI 53202; Dedee Shattuck Gallery Westport MA. *Mailing Add:* PO Box 100 Seekonk MA 02771

BACKSTRÖM, FIA
CONCEPTUAL ARTIST
b Stockholm, Sweden, 1970. *Study:* Colombia Univ & Univ Stockholm, 88-92; Accad Photog, Konstfack, Stockholm, MFA, 95. *Exhib:* Solo exhibs include Konstfack, Stockholm, 94, Hemma Hos, Stockhom, 95, Atlasmuren Gallery, Stockholm, 96, Index Gallery, Swedish Contemp Art Found, Stockholm, 99, Space Martina Hogland, Stockholm, 2003, Blonde Revolution, New York, 2004, Champion Fine Art, New York, 2004, Lesser New York, 2005, Andrew Kreps Gallery, New York, 2006; group exhibs include Ikonoklasm, Vita Havet Art Space, 94; Everything is Under Control, Konstfack, Stockholm, 95; Under the Influence, Service Gallery, Stockholm, 96; Stockholm Film Festival, 96; Faith, Index Gallery, Stockholm, 97, Kit for People Lost in Space, 98; Stockholm Art Fair, 99; Bevil Goes Iceland, Living Art Mus, Reykjavik, 2001; Whitneybiennial.com, 2002; Pop Rocks, Caren Golden Fine Art, New York, 2003; None of the Above, Swiss Inst, New York, 2004; Basel Art Fair, 2005; Circles, Sculpture Center, 2005, The Happiness of Objects, 2007; Slow Burn, Galerie Edward Mitterrand, Geneva, 2007; Experiment Marathon, Serpentine Gallery, London, 2007; Whitney Biennial, Whitney Mus Am Art, 2008. *Teaching:* Mem faculty, Sch Visual Arts, New York, 2003-. *Dealer:* Galerie Edward Mitterand 52 Rue des Bains 1205 Geneva. *Mailing Add:* Sch Visual Arts 209 E 23rd St New York NY 10010

BACOT, HENRY PARROTT
MUSEUM DIRECTOR, EDUCATOR
b Shreveport, La, Dec 13, 1941. *Study:* Baylor Univ, Waco, Tex, BA, 63; La State Univ, Baton Rouge, 64-65; Attingham Park Summer Sch Study Great English Country Houses, Shropshire, fel, 66; State Univ NY Cooperstown, MA (Scriven Found Fel, Cooperstown Grad Progs), 67. *Collection Arranged:* Am Folk Art 1730-1968, 68; Southern Furniture & Silver: The Federal Period 1788-1830, 68; Louisiana Landscape 1800-1969, 69; Natchez-Made Silver of the 19th Century, 70; Sail & Steam in Louisiana Waters, 71; Louisiana Folk Art, 72; Crescent City Silver, 80; Rhoda Stokes: A Retrospective (with catalog), 84; Louisiana Art from the Roger Houston Ogden Collection, 92; France Folse Rediscovered, 97. *Pos:* Dir, Anglo-Am Art Mus, Baton Rouge, 67-; hist interiors consult, Kings' Tavern, Natchez, Miss, 71-, Kent Plantation House, Alexandria, La, 71- & Magnolia Mound Plantation House, Baton Rouge, 72-; sponsor, Am Friends of Attingham Summer Sch, 77-; exec dir, La State Univ Mus Complex, 82. *Teaching:* Asst prof art hist, La State Univ, 67-84, asst prof hist of interior design, 73, prof art hist, 84-. *Awards:* Ed Bd, J Early Southern Decorative Arts, 97. *Mem:* Soc Archit Historians; Am Victorian Soc; Found Hist La (bd mem, 72-74); Old State Capitol Adv Comt. *Res:* Fine arts, architecture and decorative arts of the Deep South. *Publ:* Coauth, Nineteenth century Natchez-made Silver, 71, Crescent City silver, Historic New Orleans collection, 80; articles, Antiques, 72-97; contribr, Soc Archit Historians J, 74; auth, Nineteenth Century Lighting: Candle-Powered Devices: 1783-1883, Schiffer Pub Ltd, 87; with 4 coauths, Adrien Persac: Louisiana Artist (catalog), 2000; with 4 co-auths, Furnishing Lousisiana, Creole and Arcadian Furniture 1735-1835, 2010

BACZEK, PETER GERARD
PAINTER, PRINTMAKER
b Webster, Mass, June 6, 1945. *Study:* San Jose State Univ, BA (art), 70. *Work:* Achenbach Found Graphic Arts, Calif Palace Legion Hon, San Francisco; Brooklyn Mus; Philadelphia Mus Art; Metrop Mus Art Ctr, Coral Gables, Fla; Cooper-Hewitt Mus, New York & Brooklyn Mus Art. *Exhib:* 21st Nat Print Exhib, Brooklyn Mus, 79; Eighth Int Print Biennial, Crakow, Poland, 80; Subjective Realities (with catalog), Calif Palace Legion Hon, San Francisco, 82; Urban Documents: 20th Century Am Prints, Cooper-Hewitt Mus, NY, 83; Rockford Int, Rockford Col, 83; Boston Printmakers 37th Nat Exhib Art Mus, Brandeis Univ, 85; Crocker-Kingsley Ann, Crocker Mus Art, Sacramento, Calif; Ninth British Int Print Biennale, Bradford, Eng, 86. *Awards:* Patron Award, Print Club, Pa, 82; Jurors Spec Mention, Cabo Frio Int Print Biennial, Brazil, 83; Monotype Award, Northern Calif Print Competition, 86. *Bibliog:* Roberta Loach (auth), Book of Hours: A Portfolio of 21 Prints, Visual Dialog, 79; Julie van der Ryn (auth), Shadows and Patterns in the Everyday, City Arts Monthly Mag, 81. *Media:* Oil; Etchings. *Dealer:* Suzy R Locke & Assocs 201 Estates Dr Piedmont CA 94611. *Mailing Add:* 2433 Scenic Ave Oakland CA 94602

BADALAMENTI, FRED L
PAINTER, EDUCATOR
b Long Island, NY, June 25, 1935. *Study:* Pratt Inst, 53-55; State Univ NY Col, New Paltz, BS, 61; Brooklyn Col, MFA (fel), 67; studied with Philip Pearlstein, Carl Holty & Burgoyne Diller. *Work:* Brooklyn Col, NY; State Univ NY, Stony Brook; DBG Properties Corp, New York City; Torrington Mfg Corp, Torrington, Conn; Bellevue Hosp, NYC; Stony Brook Univ Hosp, Stony Brook, NY, 2012. *Comn:* Bellevue Hosp, NY. *Exhib:* Solo Exhibs: First St Gallery, NY, 76, 80 & 89; Van Loen Gallery, S Huntington, NY, 98; Suffolk Co Community Col, Selden, NY, 2007; Nassau Co Mus Fine Arts, 87; St Joseph's Col, 87; group exhibs incl: City Univ NY Res Foun Univ Art Gallery, State Univ NY, Stony Brook, 94, 89, Contemp Realist Gallery, San Francisco, Calif, 90, Brooklyn Coll Art Gallery, 93, Images Gallery, NY, 95, Gallery N, Setauket, NY, 98, 2003 & 04, First St Gallery, 2009, Gallery North, 2009, 2010, 2011, 2013, 2014, Long Island Mus, 2009, 2010, Delaware County Community Coll, 2012. *Pos:* Dir, First St Gallery, 78-79; art exhib jurist, Drawing and Painting, various LI locations, 2000-06; artist advisory bd, Gallery N, Setauket, NY, 2009-. *Teaching:* Prof drawing & painting, Brooklyn Col, 69-92, deputy chmn grad art, 72-89, dept chmn undergrad art, 89-92, prof emer, 92-; vis prof drawing & painting, State Univ NY, Stony Brook, 77-78 & summers 78, 80, 81 & 83; adj prof, Brooklyn Col, 92-93, State Univ NY, Stony Brook, 93-99. *Awards:* Fel, Brooklyn Col, 65-67. *Mem:* Coll Art Asn; Am Asn Univ Prof; PSC; CUNY. *Media:* Oil, Drawing, Printmaking. *Specialty:* Fine Arts of Long Island. *Interests:* travel abroad, reading, gardening. *Dealer:* Gallery North Setauket NY 11733. *Mailing Add:* 182 Lower Sheep Pasture Rd Setauket NY 11733

BADGETT, STEVEN
ARTIST
b Ill, 1962. *Exhib:* Exhibs incl Highwayscape, Weber State Univ, Ogden, Utah, 1997, An Investigation of Trans-Architecture in Western Am, 1997, Rise Overrun, Plan B Evolving Arts, Santa Fe, 1997, L'Arche, Ecole Nationale d'Art, Cergy, France, 1998, SIMPARCH, Bemis Ctr Contemp Arts, Omaha, 1998, Ship from the Desert, Maschinenhalle, Potsdam, Ger, 1998, Moorings Project, 1998, The Unit, Ctr Land Use Interpretation, Wendover, Utah, 1999, Free Basin, Hyde Park Arts Ctr, Chicago, 2000, Spec, Renaissance Soc, Univ Chicago, 2001, Mood River, Wexner Ctr Arts, Columbus, Ohio, 2002, Documenta XI, Kassel, Ger, 2002, Session the Bowl, Deitch Projects, NY, 2002, Whitney Biennial, Whitney Mus Am Art, NY, 2004, InSITE, San Diego, 2005. *Pos:* Co-found & mem, SIMPARCH, 96-; lectr, Columbus Col Art & Design, Ohio, 2001; Documenta XI, Kassel, Ger, 2002. *Teaching:* lectr, Weber State Univ, Ogden, Utah, 97; resident, Brandenburgischer Kunstverein, Potsdam, Ger, 98; lectr, Univ Utah, Salt Lake City, 99; resident, Ctr Land Use Interpretation, LA, 99, 2003. *Awards:* NMex Arts Coun Grant, 97; Creative Capital Grant, 2002

BAEDER, JOHN
PAINTER
b South Bend, Ind, Dec 24, 1938. *Study:* Auburn Univ, Ala, AB, 60. *Work:* Denver Art Mus; Whitney Mus of Am Art; Mus Mod Art Lending Serv; Cooper-Hewitt Mus; High Mus, Atlanta; and others. *Exhib:* Place, Product, Package, Cooper-Hewitt Mus, Smithsonian Inst, NY, 78; Kunstgewerbemuseum, Zurich, Switz, 79; Danforth Mus,

Framingham, Mass, 80; Philbrook Art Ctr, Tulsa, Okla, 80; Real, Really Real, Super Real, San Antonio Mus, 81; Contemp American Realism Since 1960, Pa Acad Fine Arts, 81; Painting NY, Mus City NY, 83-84; and others. *Bibliog:* Gregory Battcock (auth), Super Realism, Dutton, 75; D Filipacchi (auth), Les Hyper Realists Americans. *Media:* Lithography, Oil. *Publ:* Auth, Diners, Harry N Abrams Inc, New York, 78; Gas, Food and Lodging, Abbeville Press, 82. *Dealer:* O K Harris 383 W Broadway New York NY 10012. *Mailing Add:* 1025 Overton Lea Rd Nashville TN 37220-1413

BAER, ADAM
PHOTOGRAPHER, VIDEO ARTIST
b Mar 16, 1969. *Study:* State Univ NY, BFA (photog), 91. *Work:* Art Mus at Princeton Univ; Calif Mus of Photog, Brooklyn Mus of Art. *Exhib:* Taboo, Woman Made Gallery, Chicago, 97; 7th Ann Showcase Exhib, Alternative Mus, NY, 97; Working/Still, Neuberger Mus, NY, 97; Jones Ctr for Contemp Art, Austin, Tex, 97; Expansion Arts: Artists of Our Times II, Alternative Mus, NY, 98; Nat Exhib, Provincetown Art Asn & Mus, Mass, 98; Bonni Benrubi Gallery, NY, 98; The Alternative Mus, NY, 99; PS1 Contemp Art Ctr, NY, 2000; Akus Gallery, Eastern Conn State Univ, 2001; Calif Mus of Photog, 2001; Fifty One Fine Art Photog, Antwerp, 2001; New Photog by Adam Baer, Antwerp, Belg, 2001, Soho Photo, 97, others; Paris Photo, 2002, The Aldrich Mus of Contemp Art, Ridgefield, Conn, 2002; and others. *Awards:* NY Found Arts Fel, 94; Aaron Siskind Found Fel, 95; JS Guggenheim Mem Found Fel, 98. *Bibliog:* Kim Levin (auth), Short List, Village Voice, 1/98; Stewart Klewans (auth), Critics Choice, NY Daily News, 1/17/98; Vince Aletti (auth), Choices, Village Voice, 4/22-28/98; Chris Macleod (auth), Resident, 8/21-27/98; Nadine S Kibanda (auth), Out There: Adam Baer's Surrealist Photographs, www.ps1.org, 2000; Vince Aletti (auth), Choices, Village Voice, 2/2000; Holland Cotter (auth), NY Contemporary, Defined 150 Ways, NY Times (Art Section), 3/6/2000; JS Irons (auth), A Conversation with Adam Baer, Zingmagazine, 2000; Laurie Hurwitz-Attias (auth), Flash Forward, Art & Auction, p54, Dec 2002; Adam Baer: The Surrealistic Illusion, www.phtography.collecties.com, Jan 3 2002; Phillip Willaert (auth), News, Art Expo Belgium, p23, Dec/Jan 2002; Lieven Sioen, De Fotoroman Herleeft, Antwerp Standard, p 8-11, Mar 18, 2004; Maurites Brands (auth), FotoMuseum Antwerpen heropent na driejaar, Photoq, Mar 24, 2004; Jonathan Green (auth), Being Digital Without Photoshop, Zonezero.com, Jan, 2005; Aeroplastics Contemporary Presents Unspeakable, Newsgrist.net, Feb 3, 2005. *Media:* Photography, Digital Video. *Specialty:* Photography. *Publ:* Adam Baer: Displaced Perspectives, Catalog: Calif Mus of Photog, 2001. *Dealer:* Fifty One Fine Art Photog, Antwerp, Belgium

BAER, JO
PAINTER, WRITER
b Seattle, Wash, Aug 7, 1929. *Study:* Univ Wash; Grad Fac, New Sch Social Res. *Work:* Guggenheim Mus, Mus Mod Art, Whitney Mus Am Art, NY; Stedelijk Mus, Amsterdam; Albright-Knox Art Gallery, Buffalo, NY; Nat Mus, Canberra, Australia; Tate Gallery, London, England; and others. *Exhib:* Solo exhibs, Stedelijk Vanabbe Mus, Eindhoven, The Neth, 1978 & 1986, Galerie Ricke, Cologne, 1978, Lisson Gallery, London, 1980, Riverside Studios, London, 1982, Paley/Levy Gallery, Moore Col, Philadelphia, 1993, Paula Cooper Gallery, NY, 1995 & Stedelijk Mus, Amsterdam, 1998, Paul Andriesse Gallery, Amsterdam, 1999, 2001, Daniel Weinberg Gallery, Los Angeles, 2001, Dia Ctr For Arts, NY City, 2003, Alexander Gray Gallery, NY City, 2007; Group exhibs, Systematic Paintings, Guggenheim Mus, 1966; Whitney Mus Am Art Biennial, NY, 1967, 1969, 1973, 1975; Documenta IV, Mus Friedericianum, Kassel, Ger, 1968; 31st Biennial, Corcoran Gallery Art, Washington, DC, 1969; Ft Worth Mus, Tex, 1977; Indianapolis Mus, Ind, 1977; Chicago Art Inst, 1977; Stadtische Kunsthelle, Dusseldorf, 1982; The Window in 20th Century Art, Neuberger Mus, State Univ NY, Purchase, 1986-87; La Couleur Seule, Musce St Pierre, Lyon, France, 1988; Selected Geometric Abstract Painting in Am since 1945, Albright-Knox Gallery, Buffalo, NY, 1989; From Minimal to Conceptual Art, Nat Gallery Art, Washington, 1994; Abstraction, Pure & Impure, Mus Mod Art, NY, 1996; The Pursuit of Painting, Irish Mus Modern Art, Dublin, 1997; Contemp Drawings, Fogg Mus, Cambridge, 1997; Paula Cooper Gallery, NY City, 1998, 2002, 2007; Mus Contemp Art, Chicago, 1999; Whitney Mus Am Art, NY City, 1999; Mus Ludwig, Cologne, 2000; Paul Andriesse Gallery, Basel, 2001-2006; New Britain Mus Am Art, 2003, 2004; Mus Mod Art, New York, 2005; Mus Mod Kunst, Frankfurt, 2007. *Teaching:* Instr painting, Sch Visual Arts, NY, 1969-70; guest instr painting, Brighton Tech, England, 1982 & Rijksakedemie, Amsterdam, 1987-88. *Awards:* Nat Coun Arts Award, 1968-69. *Bibliog:* Miriam Seidel (auth), Jo Baer at Moore College of Art, Art in Am, New York, 1/1994; Linda Yablonsky, Jo Baer Paintings from the '60s & Early '70s, Time Out, New York, 1/1996; Roberta Smith (auth), Philip Johnson & the modern: a loving Marriage, NY Times, 6/7/1996. *Media:* Oil. *Publ:* Auth, Radical Attitudes to the Gallery: Statement No 2, Studio Int, London, 1980; coauth (with Bruce Robbins), Beyond the pale, Real Life Mag, NY, summer 1983; auth, Jo Baer: I am no longer an abstract artist, Art in Am, NY, 1983; Jo Baer: Red, White & Blue Gelding Falling to its Right (Doublecross Britanicus/Tricolor Hibernicus), Tis Ill Puddling in the Cockatrice Den (La-Bas), The Rod Reversed (Mixing Memory & Desire) (Catalog), Amsterdam, 1990; coauth (with Bruce Robbins), Jo Baer: Four Drawings (catalog), Amsterdam, 1993; auth, When Thou Cometh to Women. *Dealer:* Paul Andriesse Gallery Withoedenveem 8 1019 HE Amsterdam Netherlands; Brooke Alexander Editions 59 Wooster St NY City NY 10012. *Mailing Add:* 534 W 21 St New York NY 10011

BAER, NORBERT S
EDUCATOR
b Brooklyn, NY, June 6, 1938. *Study:* Brooklyn Col, BSc (physical chemistry), 59; Univ Wis, MSc (chemistry), 62; NY Univ, PhD (physical chemistry), 69. *Pos:* Ed adv & assoc ed, Studies in Conservation, J Int Inst for Conserv, 71-; co-chmn, Conserv Ctr, Inst Fine Arts, New York Univ, 75-83, actg dir admin, 78-79; assoc ed, Restaurator, 75-; US exec ed, Conservation in the Arts, Archeol & Archit, Butterworths, 79-; chmn, Adv Comt on Preserv, Nat Archives & Rec Serv, 80-; chmn, Comt Conserv Historic Store Bldgs & Monuments, Nat Mat Adv Bd, Nat Acad Sci, 80-82; mem, Vis Comt Dept Objects Conserv, Metrop Mus Art, 80-. *Teaching:* Instr, Inst Fine Arts, Conserv Ctr, NY Univ, 69-70, asst prof, 70-75, assoc prof, 75-78, prof, 78-86, Hagop Kevorkian prof conserv, 86-. *Awards:* Guggenheim Fel, 83-84. *Mem:* Fel Int Inst Conserv; fel Am Inst Conserv (bd dir, 73-76); fel Am Inst Chemists; Am Chemical Soc; Sigma Xi. *Res:* Application of physicochemical techniques to the preservation & examination of artistic and historic works. *Publ:* Coauth, Chemical Investigations on Ancient Near Eastern Archaeological Ivory Artifacts: III, Fluorine & Nitrogen Composition & Chemical Aspects of the Conservation of Archaeological Materials, Archeological Chemistry II, Advances in Chemistry, 78; Synthetic Blue Pigments: IX-XVI Centuries, I, Literature, Studies in Conservation, 80; Mechanisms of air pollution-induced damage to stone, Sixth World Congress Air Quality, Paris, Vol 3, 83; and others. *Mailing Add:* 194 Ascan Ave Forest Hills NY 11375

BAER, ROD
CONCEPTUAL ARTIST, SCULPTOR
b Los Angeles, Calif. *Study:* San Diego State Univ, BA; Claremont Grad Sch, MFA. *Work:* Skirball Mus, Los Angeles; Airport Plaza, Van Nuys, Calif; Art/Omi, NY; Armand Hammer Mus, Los Angeles, Calif; Principal Financial Group, Des Moines, Iowa; Jewish Mus, NY. *Comn:* Endless Columns, Carnation Co, Los Angeles, 91; Pocketwatch and Others, Metro-link Train Depot/City Claremont, Calif, 92; Precedent, Zelle & Larson, San Francisco, Calif, 94; Dancing Chairs, St Louis Arts in Transit & St Louis Art Fair, 98; Here Is, Robertson Blvd Public Art Project, Dept Transportation & City of Los Angeles, 98 & 99; All Roads Lead to Westwood, Weyburn Ave Streetscape, Dept Transportation, Los Angeles, Calif, 2001; Palm Tree, Water Drop, Vanowen St Bridge, Aliso Creek, City of Los Angeles, San Fernando Valley, Calif, 2005; Flower, Saticoy St Bridge, Aliso Creek, City of Los Angeles, San Fernando Valley, Calif, 2006; Falling Leaves, Strathern St Bridge, Aliso Creek, City of Los Angeles, San Fernando Valley, Calif, 2006. *Exhib:* Art and Archit, Santa Monica Heritage Mus, 88; Solo exhibs, The Cost of Implosion, Meyers/Bloom Gallery, Santa Monica, 89, Armory Ctr Arts, Pasadena, Calif, 94; Three Sculptors/Three Coasts, Blue Star Art Space, San Antonio, Tex, 90; The Book as Art, The Book in Art, Fendrick Gallery, NY, 90; two-man show, Pima Col, Tucson, Ariz, 92 & Pierce Col, Woodland Hills, Calif, 94; Blessings & Beginnings Inaugural Exhib, Skirball Mus, Los Angeles, Calif, 96; Looking Awry, Coleman Gallery, Albuquerque, NMex, 96; The Book of Lies, New York City Libr & Brooke Alexander Gallery, New York, Armand Hammer Mus, Los Angeles & Art Ctr Sch Design Libr, Pasadena, 96; Got Art, Laguna Art Mus, 97; Unbuilt Southern California, Guggenheim Gallery, Chapman Col, Orange, Calif, 97; The Perpetual Well: Contemp Art from the Jewish Mus (traveling), Samuel Harn Mus, Gainesville, Fla, Sheldon Mem Art Gallery, Lincoln, Nebr & Parish Art Mus, Southampton, NY, 2000; Culture & Continuity: the Jewish Journey, Jewish Mus, NY, 2001; 27 Years of Showing Artists, Drudis-Biada Art Gallery, My Saint Mary's Col, Los Angeles, Calif, 2003. *Teaching:* Instr sculpture, Otis Parsons Art Inst, 90-91. *Awards:* Art/Omi Int Residency Fel, New York, 95; Djerassi Found Residency, Calif, 96; Artists Fel Award in New Genre, Calif Arts Coun, 96-97. *Bibliog:* Wesley Pulkka (auth), Sculptors explore, Albuquerque J, 7/28/96; Kathleen Whitney (auth), The body Exhausted, Sculpture, 10/97; Dona Meilach (auth), Direct Metal Sculpture, Schiffer Publ, rev 2nd ed, 2001; Susan Braunstein (auth), Luminous Art, Yale Press, 2004; and others. *Mem:* Int Sculpture Ctr. *Media:* All Media; Text, New Genre. *Mailing Add:* 3803 San Rafael Ave Los Angeles CA 90065

BAGGET, WILLIAM (CARTER), JR
PRINTMAKER, MURALIST
b Montgomery, Ala, Jan 12, 1946. *Study:* Auburn Univ, BFA, 68, MFA, 73. *Work:* US Info Agency Embassy Collections, (worldwide); Montgomery Mus Fine Arts, Ala; Univ Miss Mus, Oxford; Vision Nouvelle, Paris, France; IDL Editions Lecureux-Possot, Paris, France; Lauren Rogers Mus Art, Laurel, Miss. *Comn:* Portraits, William Faulkner, Univ Miss, Oxford, 77, TK Mattingly & HM Hartsfield, Auburn Univ, 82; multicolor lithographs, Vision Nouvelle, Paris, 80 & Nahan Ed, New Orleans, 81 & 86; mural, Libr Hattiesburg, Miss, 95; mural, Winfred Wiser Hosp Women & Infants, Univ Miss, Med Ctr, Jackson, 98. *Exhib:* New Orleans Biennial, New Orleans Mus Art, 73; 107th Ann Exhib Am Watercolor Soc, Nat Acad Design, NY, 74; Rocky Mountain Nat Watermedia Exhib, Foothills Art Ctr, Golden, Colo, 74; East/West Echoes, Mokpo Nat Col, Korea, 85; Echo Returns, Dong Duk Art Gallery, Seoul, Korea, 86; solo exhib, Nahan Galleries (with catalog), NY, 91; Les Mois de L'Estampe a Paris, 97. *Teaching:* Asst prof design, Univ Miss, 73-76; assoc prof & coordr visual commun, Auburn Univ, 76-83; prof & chmn dept art, Univ Southern Miss, 83-86, actg dean, 86-87, prof, 87-. *Awards:* Endowed Professorship, Auburn Univ, 82; Faculty Award of Excellence for Creative Research & Achievement, Univ S Miss, 97; Official Artist of the Sixth USA Int Ballet Competition, Jackson, Miss, 98. *Bibliog:* William Baggett's mural for the New Library of Hattiesburg, Mississippi, Nat Forum Mag, spring 96; Southern Expressions (film), Miss Found Pub Broadcasting, 93-95; P Black (auth), Art in Mississippi, Univ Press Miss, 98. *Mem:* Am Inst Graphic Arts. *Media:* Lithography, Egg Tempera

BAI, LISHA
PAINTER
Study: Washington Univ, St Louis, BA (painting), 2001; Yale Univ, MFA (painting/printmaking), 2004. *Exhib:* Group exhibs include Exposition/Portes-Ouvertes, Mus d'Art Am Giverny, France, 2004; Breaking & Entering, Tyler Estate, New York, 2005; Vt Studio Ctr Benefit & Auction, Sotheby's, New York, 2005; Brooklyn Art Mus Benefit Auction & Exhib, Brooklyn Art Mus, 2006; U Can't Touch Dis: The New Asian Art, Zone Chelsea Ctr Arts, New York, 2007; Muzzle of Bes, 33 Bond Gallery, New York, 2007; Ann Invitational Exhib Contemp Am Art, Nat Acad, New York, 2008. *Teaching:* Teaching asst, Yale Univ, 2003; vis instr fine arts & design educ, Pratt Inst, Brooklyn, NY, 2005-; vis artist, RI Sch Design, 2008. *Awards:* Ruth Hindman Found Scholar, 2003; Terra Summer Residency Fel, 2004; Vt Studio Ctr Fel, 2005; SJ Wallace Truman Fund Award, Nat Acad, 2008. *Media:* Acrylic

BAIBAKOV, OLEG
COLLECTOR
Pos: Former mng dir, GMK Norilsk Nickel; pres, City Co. *Awards:* Named one of Top 200 Collectors, ARTnews mag, 2009-13. *Collection:* Contemporary art including Andy Warhol, Jeff Koons, Damien Hirst, Richard Prince & Andreas Gursk

BAIBAKOVA, MARIA
COLLECTOR
Study: Courtauld Inst Art, London; Columbia Univ, BA. *Pos:* Dir & chief cur, Baibakov Art Projects, 2008-. *Awards:* Named one of Top 200 Collectors, ARTnews mag, 2009-13. *Collection:* Contemporary art

BAILEY, BARRY STONE
SCULPTOR, PAINTER
b High Point, NC, 0ct 21, 1952. *Study:* ECarolina Univ, BS (art educ), 75, studies with Norman Keller, MFA (sculpture), 79; studies at Univ Ga, Cortona, Italy prog, 77. *Work:* New Orleans Mus Art; R J Reynolds World Trade Ctr, Winston-Salem, NC; Westminster Corp. *Comn:* Welded steel kiosk, Pan Am Life, New Orleans, 82; New Orleans Palms, eight paintings on paper, Hotel Intercontinental, New Orleans, 82; Palm Shrine, Pontchartrain Beach, Contemp Arts Ctr, New Orleans, 83; Rain Pavilion, 2 kinetic bronze sculptures, Hist New Orleans collection, 84; 8' wall sculpture, Saratoga Bldg, Westminster Corp, New Orleans, 85; Crucifix, St Ann's Episcopal, 2002; Madona, St Mary of the Assumption, 2009. *Exhib:* Solo exhibs, Louisiana World Expo, New Orleans, 84 & Arthur Roger Gallery, New Orleans, La, 94; Perspectives, Cross Creek Gallery, Malibu, Calif, 87; Seven Sculptors, Alternative Mus, NY, 81; Contemp Arts Ctr, New Orleans, 87; 112 Greene Street, NY, 85; Chicago Int, Navy Pier, 87; Il Via Nazionale, Cortona, Italy, 96; Cole Pratt, New Orleans, 98. *Collection Arranged:* First Louisiana Sculpture Biennial, 81 & The New Louisiana Landscape, 81, Contemp Arts Ctr, New Orleans. *Teaching:* Teaching fel art appreciation & 3D design, ECarolina Univ, Greenville, NC, 75-77; teaching asst sculpture, Univ Ga abroad, Cortona, Italy, 77; instr sculpture, La State Univ, Baton Rouge, 85; instr, Newcomb Sculpture Dept, Tulane Univ, formerly, assoc prof, currently; Assoc prof, Tulane Univ. *Bibliog:* Roger Green (auth), Environmental influence on shape, Times-Picayune, 7/11/82; Marion Orr (auth), article, in: Gambit, Vol 5, No 37, 9/15/84; Roger Green (auth), Barry Bailey, Randy Ernst at Arthur Roger Gallery, Artnews, 12/86. *Mem:* Tri State Sculpture Int Sculpture Conference; Int Conference Contemporary Iron Art. *Media:* Miscellaneous Media. *Interests:* Jong Writing, Acoustic Guitar

BAILEY, CLAYTON GEORGE
SCULPTOR, CERAMIST
b Antigo, Wis, Mar 9, 1939. *Study:* Univ Wis-Madison, BS, 61, MS, 62. *Hon Degrees:* MFA, Fat City Sch Fine Art, 03. *Work:* Oakland Mus, Calif; Mus Contemp Crafts, NY; Addison Gallery Am Art, Andover, Mass; Milwaukee Art Mus; San Francisco Mus Mod Art; San Jose Mus of Art; Crocker Mus Art; City of Sacramento, Calif. *Comn:* Exec Teapot, Kohler Co, Kohler, Wis, 79; Sacramento Metrop Light Rail, 86. *Exhib:* Solo exhibs, Milwaukee Art Ctr, 61, Mus Contemp Crafts, NY, 63, MH DeYoung Mus, San Francisco, 75, Triton Mus, Santa Clara, Calif, 81, Monterey Mus Art, Calif, 84 & Henry Gallery, Seattle; Objects USA, Smithsonian traveling exhib, 69; A Decade of Am Ceramics, San Francisco Mus Mod Art, 73; A Century of Ceramics, Syracuse Mus, 79; Am Porcelain, Renwick Gallery, 80; Humor in Art, Los Angeles Co Mus, 81; Ceramics From the Sixties, Ariz, State Univ, Tempe, 2004; 50 year Retrospective exhib, Crocker Art Mus, Sacramento, Calif, 2011; and others. *Collection Arranged:* Port Costa Jews Harp Mus, 03. *Pos:* webmaster, www.claytonbailey.com. *Teaching:* Prof ceramics, Wis State Univ, Whitewater, 63-66; prof ceramics, Calif State Univ, Hayward, 68-96, chmn art dept, 79-81, prof emer, 96-. *Awards:* Artists Grants, Louis Comfort Tiffany Found, 63, Am Craftsmen Coun, 63 & Nat Endowment Arts, 79 & 90; Nominated for Nobel Prize, 76; and others; Calif Artist of the Year, Calif State Fair, 2009. *Bibliog:* Tom Albright (auth), California Art, 86; Donhauser (auth), Am Ceramics, 78; Speight (auth), Hands in Clay, 94; DePaoli (auth) Happenings in the Circus of Life-The Work of Clayton Bailey, 01; Bay area Figuration, Susan Landauer, San Jose Mus of Art 2004; Diana Daniels (auth), Clayton Bailey's World of Wonders, 2012. *Mem:* Hon Fel Nat Coun Educ in Ceramic Arts (dir at large, 78-80); Calif Nut Art Group (co-founder). *Media:* Clay, Metal. *Res:* Funk Art Practitioner, Experimental Jews Harp Maker. *Specialty:* Ceramic Sculpture. *Interests:* Guns, Jews Harps. *Collection:* San Jose Mus of Art, San Jose, CA; Crocker Art Mus, Sacramento, Calif; SF Mus Modern Art; deYoung Mus, SFCA. *Publ:* Coauth, My father is a sculptor, Jack & Jill Mag, 70; auth, Wonders of the World Catalog of Kaolithic Curiosities, Artist, 75; Clayton Bailey's World of Wonders, Diana Daniels, Crocker Mus, 2011. *Dealer:* Bailey Art Mus 325 Rolph Ave Crockett Ca 94525

BAILEY, COLIN B
MUSEUM DIRECTOR
b London, Oct 20, 1955; arrived in US, 85. *Study:* Brasenose Coll, Oxford, BA, 78; Univ Paris IV, Sorbonne, Dipl (Art Hist), 83; Oxford Univ, MA, 82, PhD, 85. *Pos:* Asst cur Europ painting & sculpture, Philadelphia Mus Art, 85-95; cur Europ painting & sculpture, Kimbell Art Mus, Ft Worth, 89-90, sr cur, 90-94; chief cur, Nat Gallery Can, Ottawa, 95-98, dep dir & chief cur, 1999-2000; chief cur, Frick Collection, New York, 2000-2007, Peter Jay Sharp chief cur, 2007-2013, assoc dir/Peter Jay Sharp chief cur, 2008-2013; dir, Fine Arts Museums San Francisco, Calif, 2013-. *Teaching:* Vis prof, Univ Pa, 88, Bryn Mawr Coll, 89, Columbia Univ, 2005, 2007; The Grad Ctr, City Univ NY, 2009. *Awards:* Chevalier Ordre Arts & Lett, France, 1994; J Paul Getty Mus Fel, 83; Clark Fel, 99; Mitchell Prize, 2004. *Mem:* Assn Art Mus Curs; The Century Asn. *Publ:* coauth with JJ Rishel, Masterpieces of Impressionism & Post-Impressionism (Annenberg Collection), 1989, second ed, 2009; Auth: The Loves of the Gods: Mythological Painting from Watteau to David, 92; Renoir's Portraits: Impressions of an Age, 97; Jean Baptiste Greuze, The Laundress, 2000; Patriotic Taste: Collection Modern Art in Pre-Revolutionary Paris, 2002; The Age of Watteau, Chardin & Fragonard: Masterpieces of French Eighteenth-Century Genre Painting, 2003; Building the Frick Collection: An Introduction to the House & Its Collections, 2006; Renoir's Landscapes 1867-1883, 2007; Gabriel de Saint-Aubin 1724-1780, 2007; Watteau to Degas, French Drawings from the Lugt Collection, 2009; Fragonard's Progress of Love at the Frick Collection, 2011; Rembrandt and His School: Masterworks from the Frick and Lugt Collections, 2011; Renoir, Impressionism, and Full-Length Painting, 2012; Mantegna to Matisse: Master Drawings from the Courtauld Gallery, 2012. *Mailing Add:* Fine Arts Museums of San Francisco 50 Hagiwara Tea Garden Dr San Francisco CA 94118

BAILEY, GAUVIN ALEXANDER
HISTORIAN, EDUCATOR
Study: Univ Toronto, BA, 1989, MA, 1990; Harvard Univ, PhD (fine art hist), 1996. *Collection Arranged:* Hope and Healing: Painting in Italy in a Time of Plague 1500-1800, Worcester Art Mus, 2005. *Teaching:* Assoc prof art hist, Clark Univ, 1997-, prog dir art hist, currently; instr, Boston Coll & Univ Aberdeen, formerly. *Awards:* Bainton Prize Art Hist, 2000; Villa I Tatti Fel, Harvard Univ Ctr for Italian Renaissance Studies, 2001; Guggenheim Found Fel, 2010. *Publ:* Auth, The Jesuits and the Grand Mogul: Renaissance Art at the Imperial Court of India, 1580-1630, Smithsonian Inst, 1998; Art on the Jesuit Missions in Asia and Latin America, 1542-1773, Toronto Univ Press, 2001; Between Renaissance and Baroque: Jesuit Art in Rome, 1565-1610, Univ Toronto Press, 2003; Art of Colonial Latin America, Phaidon Press, 2005. *Mailing Add:* Clark Univ Dept Visual & Performing Art 950 Main St Worcester MA 01610-1477

BAILEY, MARCIA MEAD
PAINTER
b Hartford, Conn, Jan 10, 1947. *Study:* Self-taught. *Exhib:* Henry Ward Ranger Ann Exhib, Nat Acad Design, New York, 80; 39th-45th Ann, Audubon Artists, New York, 81-87 & Lever House, 86; 68th-74th Ann, Allied Artists Am, New York, 81-87; Dr Maury Leibovitz Exhib, New York, 86; Invitational Traveling Exhib, Allied Artists Am, 2003-05. *Awards:* S J Wallace Truman Prize, Nat Acad Design, New York, 80; Binney and Smith Liquitex Award, Audubon Artists, New York, 81; Gold Medal Honor, Allied Artists Am, 81. *Mem:* Audubon Artists; Allied Artists Am (hon mem). *Media:* Oil. *Dealer:* Arts Exclusive Inc 690 Hopmeadow St Simsbury CT 06070. *Mailing Add:* 189 Wickham Rd Glastonbury CT 06033

BAILEY, RICHARD H
SCULPTOR
b Dover, Del, June 24, 1940. *Study:* Del Art Ctr, Wilmington; Art Students League; New Sch Soc Res, New York City; study in Carrara, Italy, Barre, Vt, Goddard Col, Plainfield, Vt; also with Jose DeCreeft, Lorrie Goulet & Leroy Smith. *Work:* Am Mus Natural Hist, NY; Univ Del; Newark Pub Libr; Blue Cross Blue Shield; Bell Tel, Del. *Comn:* Sculpture, comn by Reverend C Jones, 67; sculpture, comn by John Gilbert, 69; sculpture, St Polycarp's Roman Cath Church, 73; medallion, De Trust Co, 76; sculpture, 2nd Baptist Church, 84. *Exhib:* Int Exhib Sculpture, Carrara, Italy; solo exhibs, Springfield Mus Art, 67, Del Art Mus, 74 & 85 & Baltimore Art Mus, 78; Randall Galleries, NY; Nelson Rockefeller Collections; Peel Gallery Fine Art; Annapolis Marina Art Gallery; Wilmington Gallery 119, 2013; Smyrna Mus, 2014; Rehoboth Art League, 2014; Gibby Art Ctr, Middletown, Del, 2014; Dover Libr, 2014. *Teaching:* Monitor, New Sch for Soc Res, 68; Rehoboth Art League, 72; YWCA, Newark, 73. *Awards:* Founders Award, Rehoboth Art League, Del, 71 & 75-80 & 86-87; Silvermine Guild Award Sculpture, 72 & 73. *Bibliog:* Del Today Mag, 77; VCR, Day with Bailey, 87; Television special, 10/86; A Sculptors Miracles, Cherokee Books, 2013. *Mem:* Del Art Mus; Rehoboth Art League. *Media:* Stone; Miscellaneous Media. *Dealer:* Annapolis Marina Gallery Annapolis MD; Carspecken-Scott Gallery Wilmington DE. *Mailing Add:* c/o James Hanna, Mitch Howell Cherokee Books 231 Meadow Ridge Pkwy Dover DE 19904

BAILEY, WILLIAM HARRISON
PAINTER
b Council Bluffs, Iowa, Nov 17, 1930. *Study:* Univ Kans, Sch Fine Arts, 1951; Yale Univ, BFA (Alice Kimball English Traveling Fel), 1955, MFA, 1957; with Josef Albers. *Hon Degrees:* UNW Utah, Hon LHD, 1987; Adelphi Univ, Hon DFA, 1993; Pa Acad Fine Arts, Hon DFA, 2004; Maryland Inst Coll Art, Hon DFA, 2012; Lyme Acad Art, Hon DFA, 2012. *Work:* Joseph Hirshhorn Mus; Mus Mod Art, NY; Hirshhorn Mus, Washington, DC; Chicago Art Inst; Neue Galerie Der Stadt, AA achen; Whitney Mus Am Art, NY; Art Mus San Francisco; Yale Univ Art Gallery; Nat Coll Fine Arts, Washington, DC; St Louis Mus Art; Boston Mus Fine Arts; Phillips Coll, Washington DC; Nat Gallery of Art, Wash DC. *Exhib:* Solo exhibs include Robert Schoelkopf Gallery, New York, 1968, 1971, 1974, 1979, 1982, 1986, 1991, Galerie Claude Bernard, 1978 & 2000, Galleria d'Arte il Gabbiano, Rome, 1980, 1985, 1993 & 1997, Am Acad Rome, 1984, John Berggruen Gallery, San Francisco, Calif, 1988, Donald Morris Gallery, Birmingham, Mich, 1991, Andre Emmerich Gallery, NY, 1992, 1994 & 1996, Betsy Senior Gallery, NY, 1994, Galleria Appiana Arte Trantadue, Milan, 1994, Crown Point Gallery, San Francisco, 1998, Alpha Gallery, Boston, 1998, 2007, Robert Miller Gallery, 1999 & 2003, Calif Palace of the Legion of Honor, San Francisco, 2003, Clark House Gallery, Bangor, Maine, 2005, Betty Cuningham Gallery, NY, 2005, 2007, 2010, 2012, Dunn & Brown Contemp, Dallas, 2006, 2009, Hite Art Inst, Univ Louisville, 2013; group exhibs include 22 Realists, Whitney Mus Am Art, NY, 1970, Am Painting of the 60s & 70s, 1979, Univ Tulsa- Works on Paper, travelled to Philbrook Mus & Wichita Art Mus, The Whitney Mus & the Figurative Tradition, 1980, Biennial, 1981, Live from Conn, 1983, Print Acquisitions, 1984; Childe Hassam Purchase Exhib, Am Acad & Inst Arts & Letts, NY, 1970, 1971, Paintings & Sculpture by Candidates for Art Awards, 1982, Exhib of Work by Newly Elected Mems & Recipients of Awards, 1986; Realism Today, Nat Acad Design, NY, 1987-88; Painting & Works on Paper, John Berggruen Gallery, San Francisco, 1989, Large Scale Works on Paper, 1991, The Painted Canvas, 1999; 35 Yrs of Crown Point Press, Nat Gallery of Art, Washington, 1997-98; Ann Exhib, Nat

Acad Mus, NY, 1998 & 2007, The Acad & Am Art, 1998; Contemp Am Realist Drawings, Art Inst Chicago, 1999-2000; Approach to Scale in the Collection of MOMA, Mus Mod Art, NY, 2003; Strangely Familiar, NY State Mus, Albany, 2003, Extra-Ordinary, 2005; When I Think About You I Touch Myself, NY Acad Art, 2004; The Figure in Am Painting & Drawing, Ogunquit Mus Am Art, Maine, 2006; William Bailey, Works on Paper, Whitney Humanities Ctr, Yale Univ. *Pos:* Vis artist, Am Acad Rome, 1976; mem bd, Smithsonian Archives Am Art, 2000-2010. *Teaching:* Prof fine arts, Ind Univ, 1962-69; vis prof, Univ Pa, 1974; Andrew Carnegie vis prof, The Cooper Union, NY, 1975; Meadows distinguished prof, Southern Methodist Univ, Dallas, 1982-83; prof art, Yale Univ, 1969-78, dean sch art, 1974-75 Kingman Brewster prof, 1978-95, Kingman Brester emer prof, 1995-. *Awards:* Guggenheim Fel, 1965; Ingram Merrill Found Grant, 1975; Yale Arts Medal for Distinguished Contrib in Painting, 1985; Benjamin Altman Award in Painting, Nat Acad Design, 2007; New Criterion Award, Distinguished Contributions to Culture and the Arts. *Bibliog:* Mark Stevens (auth), Art Imitates Life: The Revival of Realism, Newsweek, 6/82; Giuliano Briganti & John Hollander (auths), William Bailey, Rizzoli International, 91; Richard Kalina (auth), William Bailey, Arts Mag, 5/91; Hilton Kramer (auth), Emmerichs Bailey show puts museums to shame, New York Observer, 3/21/94; Roger Kimball (auth), William Bailey Selected Works 1964-94, The New Criterion, 4/94; Robert Hughes (auth), Realist as Corn God, Time, 1/72; Mark Strand (ed), William Bailey, Abrams, 87 & Art of the Real, Clarkson Potter Inc, 83. *Mem:* Am Acad Arts & Letters (vp art 2012-); Nat Coun Arts, 92-96; Tiffany Found (bd dir, currently); Yaddo; Arch Am Art (trustee, 2000-2010); Nat Acad Design (assoc 1983, acad, 1994); Accademia Nazionale di San Luca, Rome; Accademia di Belle Arti Pietro Vanucci, Perugia. *Media:* Oil. *Dealer:* Betty Cuningham Gallery 541 W 25 St New York NY 10001

BAILIN, DAVID
PAINTER, EDUCATOR
b SDak, July 3, 1954. *Study:* Univ Colo, Boulder, BFA; Hunter Col, New York, MA. *Work:* Ark State Univ Jonesboro Ark, Ark Arts Ctr Found Collection, Systematics Inc, Stephens Inc, Mitchell Law Firm, Little Rock, Ark; Klutznick Nat Jewish Mus, Washington DC; Palmer & Dodge Law Firm, Boston, Mass; Total Systems Serv, Columbus, Ga; Bingham, Dana & Gould, Boston, Mass; Verizon, Little Rock; Stephens Inc, Little Rock. *Comn:* Portrait, pvt, 95; portrait, pvt comn, 98; Hot Springs Convention Ctr, Ark, 2000; Hot Springs Nat Park, Ark, 2001; Large scale drawing, pvt collections, Los Angeles, Calif, 2010. *Exhib:* Delta Art competition, Ark Arts Ctr, 86-89, 91-93, 96-2007, 2012; solo exhibs, Alice Bingham Gallery, Memphis, 88, Territorial Restoration, Little Rock, 89, Snow Fine Arts Gallery, Univ Cent Ark, Conway, 89, 96, 97, Chroma Gallery, Little Rock, 92, Strauss Gallery, Ark Arts Ctr, 2000, Rivermarket Arts Place, 2000, Koplin del Rio Gallery, Los Angeles, Calif, 2002, 2004, 2007, 2012, Washington's Profile (with catalog), Washington Pavillion, SDak, 2008; 52nd Ann Competition, Butler Inst Am Art, Youngstown, Ohio, 90; Edith Lambert Gallery, Santa Fe, NMex, 93, 2007, Ark Artists Exhib, Collector Gallery, 93; Hidden Concealed Revealed, Jewish Community Ctr, Pittsburgh, 97; Kuutznick Nat Jewish Mus, Washington, DC, 97; Adair Margo Gallery, El Paso, Tex, 2000; Portfolio One: Arkansas Masters, Ark Territorial Restoration, Little Rock, 2001; Koplan Del Rio, Culver City, 2003-2004, 2007; Gescheidle Gallery, Chicago, 2004; 20th Anniversary Celebration of Fellowship Program, Decorative Arts Mus, Little Rock, 2006; New Am Paintings, Open Studio Press, Boston, 2006; The Reality Show, Peninsula Fine Arts Ctr, VA, 2005; Art Chicago, Navy Pier; San Francisco Internat Art Expo; W Coast Drawings VIII, Davidson Gallery, Seattle, Wash, 2009; Fine Arts Gallery, Univ Ark Fayetteville; Butler Inst Ark Studies Gallery, 2010; Things to Come, Prographic, Seattle, Wash; Cross Sections, Prographica, Seattle, Wash, 2011; Legacy Art Exhib, Winthrop Rockefeller Inst, AR, 2011; Past and Present, Arkansas Arts Ctr, Little Rock, 2011; 54th Ann Delta Art Comp, Ark Arts Ctr, Little Rock, Ark, 2011; Exhib of New Drawings, Koplan Del Rio Gallery, Culver City, 2012; Ark Contemporary Selected Fellows, Ark Arts Coun, Historic Ark Mus, Little Rock, 2012; The Backview, Prographia, Seattle, Wash, 2012; Between Truth & Fiction: Pictoral Narratives, Koplin Del Rio Gallery, 2012; Dreams and Disaster 2, Norman Hall Art Gallery, Ark Tech Univ, Russellville, Ark, 2013; Dreams and Disaster: New Drawings by David Bailin, Kennedy Gallery, Arts & Science Ctr, Pine Bluff, Ark, 2013; Black Beauty: Artists Who Find Beauty in the Uncompromising Prographica Gallery, Seattle, Wash, 2013; The Big Picture, Prographica Gallery, Seattle, Wash, 2013. *Collection Arranged:* Verizon, Little Rock; Ark Arts Ctr Found Coll, Little Rock; Bingham Dana & Gould Law Offices, Boston; Palmer Dodge, Boston; Stephens Inc, Little Rock; Total Sys Servs, Columbus, Ga; Klutznick Nat Jewish Mus, Washington; Allen, McCain & Mahoney, PC, Atlanta, Ga; Ark State Univ, Jonesboro, Ark. *Pos:* Dir, Ark Arts Ctr Mus Sch, Little Rock, 86-96; vis artist, Augstana Coll, SD, 2009, presenter; cur, Legacy Art Exhib, Winthrop Rockefeller, Petit Jean Mtn, Ar, 2011; presenter, Ark League Artists, North Little Rock, Ark, 2012; panelist, MD and NJ Works on Paper, MidAtlantic Arts Found, 2012; juror, Ark League Art Show, Ark Studies Inst Galleries, Little Rock, Ark, 2013; juror, Batesville Area Arts Council, Main St Art Gallery, Batesville, Ark, 2013. *Teaching:* Studio & theory classes in painting, drawing, figure drawing & painting, art history & art appreciation; art hist, Hendrix Coll, 2006-12; drawing, Univ Ctr Ark, Conway, Univ Ark, Littlerock, 97-2005, 2008-14. *Awards:* Mid-Am Arts Alliance/Nat Endowment Arts, 88; Nat Endowment Arts, 89; Mus Educator of the Year, Ark Art Educ Asn, 94. *Bibliog:* Arkansan Wins 41st Delta, Ark Times, 9/11/98; Art rev, Delta Has Attitude, 9/18/98; Lisa Broadwater (auth), Ark Democrat Gazette, 4/9/2000; Leah Olman (auth), LA Times, 7/6/2007; Warner Trieschmann (auth), Ark Democrat Gazette, 12/18/2007; Jay Kirschenmann (auth), Argus Leader, Sidux Falls, SD, 12/2008; Cindy Monuchilou (DVD), An Interview with David Bailin, 2008; Leslie Peacock (auth), Following Paper Trails, Ark Times, Mar 2010; Lea Feinstein (auth), on paper, Art News, Jan 2010; Artists: A Conversation, 30 Arkansas Artists (documentary), 2011; 22 Mag, NY, 2012. *Mem:* Coll Art Asn. *Media:* Charcoal. *Res:* Kafka, Buster, Keaton. *Specialty:* Contemp Am Art. *Publ:* Designer & auth, The Studio Project, Jonsson Found, Dallas, Tex, 91; A Spectrum Reader, Aug House Publ, Little Rock, Ark, 91; Prophets, Parables, Paradoxes, catalog; Washington's Profile, Catalog, 2009; Paper Trails (catalog), 2010; writer, Winthrop Rockefeller Legacy Art Exhib Catalogue; Artists: A Conversation, 60 Min Interview Documentary on Contemp Ark Artists; Drawing Conclusions Newsletter, Bailinstudio.com, 2012-. *Dealer:* Koplin Del Rio Gallery Culver City CA; Erdreich White Boston MA; Photographica, Seattle, Wash. *Mailing Add:* 30 Chimney Sweep Ln Little Rock AR 72212-2083

BAKANOWSKY, LOUIS J
SCULPTOR, ARCHITECT
b Norwich, Conn, Oct 8, 1930. *Study:* Yale Univ with Joseph Albers, 56; Syracuse Univ, BFA, 57; Harvard Univ, MArch, 61. *Work:* Harvard Univ; Syracuse Univ; Trinity Col; Addison Gallery Am Art; and others. *Comn:* Mem structure, Brunswick, Maine, 73; Mstislav Rostropovich residence, NY, 82. *Exhib:* View, 60 & Selection, 61, Inst Contemp Art, Boston, Mass; Solo exhib, Siembab Gallery, Boston, 60; Sculpture, DeCordova Mus, Lincoln, Mass, 64; New Eng Art Today, Boston, 65; Immanent Domains, Boston, NY & Philadelphia, 77; Decordova Mus, 87; Paul Dietrich Gallery, Cambridge, Mass, 2006. *Pos:* Archit, Cambridge Seven Assocs, Inc, 62-97. *Teaching:* Asst prof design, Cornell Univ, 61-62; prof design, Grad Sch Design, Harvard Univ, 63-75, prof visual studies, 75- & chmn, Dept Visual & Environ Studies, 75-85; dir, Carpenter Ctr Visual Arts, Harvard Univ, 83-90, Osgood Hooker prof visual arts emer, 98-. *Awards:* Sculpture Prizes, Boston Arts Festival, 58 & Providence Art Festival, 59. *Bibliog:* Sculpture of Louis J Bakanowsky, Connection Mag, 61; article, Kenchiku Bunka Mag, 71. *Mem:* Fel Am Inst Archit. *Media:* Mixed

BAKER, BLANCHE
SCULPTOR, INSTRUCTOR
b New York, NY. *Study:* Overseas Sch Rome, 1974; Wellesley Coll 1978; Parsons Sch Design, with Bruno Lucchessi, 1980. *Work:* Grants Pass Mus Art, Eugene, Ore; Tibet House Mus & Gallery, New York City; Frederick Douglass Mus, Washington, DC. *Comn:* mural, Westchester Coun Arts, 99; sculpture, Tibet House, New York City, 2000; sculpture, comn by Frederick Douglass Mus, Washington, DC, 2001. *Exhib:* Solo exhibs, Stephen Gang Gallery, New York City, 97, River Gallery, Irvington, NY, 97-98, Gallery at 678, New York City, 98, Westchester Arts Coun, White Palins, NY, 99, Grants Pass Mus Art, Eugene, Ore; group exhibs at Nat Sculpture Soc, New York City, 2000, The Pen & Brush Club, New York City, 2000, Catharine Lorillard Wolfe Foun, New York City, 2000. *Awards:* Leonard Meiselman Award, Pen & Brush Club, New York City, 99; Agop Agopoff Mem Award, Salmagundi Club, New York City, 2000. *Bibliog:* Jenifer Stern (auth), Woman Wins Honorable Mention in War Memorial Design, The Enterprise, 8/18/95; Kirsten A Conover (auth), Art Sparks Dialogue on Race & Religion, The Christian Sci Monitor, 8/14/97; Helaine Chersonsky (auth), Art Show at Museum, Daily Courier, Grants Pass, Ore, 8/7/2000. *Mem:* Hudson Valley Art Asn (sculpture chair, 98-2001); Catharine Lorillard Wolfe Found (chair annual dinner, 99); Pen & Brush Club; Am Artists Prof League. *Media:* Bronze. *Publ:* illustr, Inkwell Mag, winter 99. *Dealer:* Larry Leckerman The Sculpture Showcase 156 S Main St New Hope PA 18938

BAKER, CORNELIA DRAVES
PRINTMAKER, PAINTER
b Woodbury, NJ, Mar 2, 1929. *Study:* Ohio Wesleyan Univ, 47-50; Kunst Stadel Inst, Ger, 50; Univ St Louis, Florence Italy, 92. *Work:* Bergen Mus Art & Sci, Paramus; Berkeley Internat Skiing Fine Arts and Graphics Collection. *Comn:* Oil painting, comn by Paul Nelson, Wyckoff, NJ, 86; gouache work, comn by Jane Gut, Wayne, NJ, 87; monoprint, Stratton Travel Inc, Franklin Lakes, 90. *Exhib:* Solo exhibs, Ramapo Coll Gallery, Mahwah, NJ, 86, Sekaikan Gallery, Tokyo, 90, Shimada Mus, Kumamoto, Japan, 90, Presbyterian Church Gallery, Franklin Lakes, NJ, 92 & Bergen Mus Art & Sci, Paramus, NJ, 93, L'Ateliet Inc Gallery, 94, NY Theological Sem, 96, The Gallery Franklin Lakes, 97, Off Congressman SR Rothman, Hackensack, NJ, 97, Lee Hecht Harrison, Paramus, NJ, 98, Willows Cafe, Ramsey NJ, 2000; Bergen Mus Art & Sci, Paramus, NJ, 88 & 90; Nat Asn Women Artists, traveling exhib, India, 89; 100 Years/100 Works, Nat Asn Women Artists, traveling exhib, USA, 89-90; 14th Ann Small Works, S Washington Sq E Gallery, NY, 90; Barn Gallery, Ringwood State Park, NJ, 92. *Pos:* dir The Gallery Franklin Lakes, NJ, 88-97, Marsella Geltman Gallery, New Milford, NJ, 93-96. *Awards:* Women Making Hist in Arts Award, Bergen Co, NJ, 93; Artist showcase award, Manhattan Art Int 93; Crabbie Award, Art Calendar, 94; Gold Prize, Riso Educ Found, Japan, 97; Artist Profile Award, Manhattan Arts Int Her Story Competition, 2003. *Bibliog:* A clearer picture at Bergen Museum, Bergen Record, 1/3/88; At the Bergen Museum Art Show--less is more, Bergen Record, 12/7/89; Monoprints, Nishinippon Simbum, 6/5/90. *Mem:* Nat Asn Women Artists (nominating vchmn, 90-91, chair, printmaking jury, 92-94); Salute to Women in Arts Inc (pres, 89-90); Ringwood Manor Asn of Arts (dir, Ann exhib, 88 & 89); Community Arts Asn (prog chmn, 87); Printmaking Coun of NJ. *Media:* Printmaker, Mixed Media. *Interests:* Travel, mentor artists, organize fund raisers. *Collection:* Pears monoprint, permanent collection of Bergen Mus of Arts & Science; Rendezvous, gouache painting & limited edition print are a part of the Berkeley International skiing & Fine arts Coll in New Hartford, CT

BAKER, DIANNE ANGELA
ASSEMBLAGE ARTIST, SCULPTOR
b Buffalo, New York, 1944. *Study:* Syracuse Univ, Florence Study, 64; Syracuse Univ, BA, 65; State Univ Buffalo, NY, MS, 69, grad, 73-76. *Work:* Charles Rand Penny Collection, Lockport, NY; The Ashford Hollow Found, East Otto, NY; Roswell Park Cancer Inst, Buffalo, NY; Rigidized Metal Corp, Buffalo, NY; Gilda's Club Western New York, Buffalo; Ross Eye Inst, Buffalo, NY; Accumed, Buffalo, NY. *Comn:* Environmental Weaving, Lancaster Public Sch, Lancaster, NY, 78; Woven/Assemblage Hanging, Econo Lodge Motel, Erie, Pa, 91; Mixed Media Wall Sculptures, Spikes Restaurant, Buffalo, NY, 92; Wall Assembly, Wis Arts Bd, Janesville, Wis, 94; Assemblage, Park Sch, Buffalo, NY, 98. *Exhib:* The Libr, D'Youville Coll, Buffalo, NY, 2000; Jewish Community Ctr Greater Buffalo, Buffalo, NY, 2001; Soc for Contemp Craft, One Mellon Ctr, Pittsburgh, Pa, 2002; Underground Gallery, Ellicottville, NY, 2003; Craft Art Western NY, (Juror: Mark Leach), Burchfield-Penney Art Ctr, Buffalo, NY, 2004; Refuse, Reuse, Redeux, Castellani

Satellite Art Mus, Niagara Univ, NY, 2003 & 2005; Lost & Found, Nicholas School Gallery, Buffalo, NY, 2006; Prima Materia, McMaster Mus Art, Hamilton, Ontario Can, 2006; Dianne Baker: Sculptor Discover Artworks, Mayville, NY, 2006; 50th Chautauqua Nat Exhib; Accorahage: Kouros Gallery, New York, 2008; Textile Miniature Exhib, Zoom, Bratislava, Slovakia, 2009, 2011; Goldesberry Gallery, Houston, Tex; Scene at the Harbor, Nat Harbor, Md; Rethreads, Jewish Community Ctr, Buffalo, NY; 16th Internat Arts in Harmony, Elk River, NY; 3-D Wit, Burcfield-Penney Art Ctr, Buffalo, NY; Triology, Art Dialogue Gallery, Buffalo, NY; 115th Catalog Exhib of Buffalo Society of Artists, UB Anderson Gallery, Buffalo, NY; 2 Person Exhib, Material Ethereal Constructs, Weeks Gallery, Jamestown Community Coll, Jamestown, NY; Artists Among Us, Burchfield Penney Art Ctr; Topspin 10 Retrospective, Castellani Art Mus, Niagara Falls, NY; Past-Present-Perfect Tense, Studio Hart, Buffalo, NY; Arte & Industrie Gallery, Housatonic, Mass. *Teaching:* Artist-in-residence, Buffalo Pub Sch, NY, Lancaster Pub Sch, NY & Park Sch, Amherst, NY. *Awards:* First prize, Tonawanda Art Assoc, Mem Exhib, 85; Pub work in Nat juried quarterly, Art Calendar Mag, 2000; Hon mention, WWY Regional, Art Dialogue Gallery, 2003; Buffalo Big Print Award, BSA 113th Catalog Exhib; First prize, Coll Exhib Art Dialogue Gallery; Second Prize, Emerging, Converging, & Damon Morey, Buffalo, NY. *Mem:* Buffalo Soc of Artists; Western NY Artists Group; Albright Knox Art Gallery; Burchfield: Penney Art Ctr; Castellani Art Mus; Hallwalls. *Publ:* Artist Beat, Arts Coun Buffalo, 89; Windrush Gallery, The Republican, Oakland, MD, 99; Louis Continelli, Unfamiliar Landmarks, The News, Buffalo, NY, 2001; The Buffalo Jewish Rev, 2010. *Mailing Add:* 67 Cleveland Ave Buffalo NY 14222

BAKER, DINA GUSTIN
PAINTER

b Philadelphia, Pa, 1924. *Study:* Philadelphia Col Mus Sch Fine Art; Barnes Found, Merion, Pa, with Dr Albert C Barnes & Violet DeMazia; Temple Univ Tyler Sch Fine Art, Philadelphia; Art Students League; Atelier 17, New York. *Work:* NY Univ; Barnes Found; Philadelphia Art Mus; Butler Mus Am Art, Youngstown, Ohio; Bergen Mus Arts & Sci, Paramus, NJ; Gannet Found, Columbia Univ, New York. *Exhib:* Solo exhibs, Roko Gallery, NY, 60-63, Angeleski Gallery, NY, 65, Southampton East Gallery, Long Island & New York, 68, Amerika House, Hamburg, Munich & Regensburg, Ger, 74 & Ingber Gallery (with catalog), NY, 76, 78, 80, 84 & 87, Gracie Lawrence Gallery, Delray Beach, Fla, 96-99, Ora Sorenson Gallery, Delray Beach, 97-2005, Ezair Gallery, NY, 2006-2010, Walter Wickiser Gallery Retrospective 1940-2012, NY, 2012, Cultural Council of Palm Beach County, Fl, 2013; Group exhibs, Nexus: Science & Art, Scripps Rsch Inst, Jupiter, Fla, 2009-2013, Walter Wickiser Gallery, NY, 2011-2014; and many others. *Teaching:* Instr, Henry St Settlement, 54-55; dir pvt art classes, New York, 60-63. *Awards:* Barnes Found Award, 42-45; Art Students League Award, 46-47; Edward MacDowell Fel, 59. *Bibliog:* Allen Ellenzweig (auth), article, Arts Mag, 79; Laurel Bradley (auth), article, Arts Mag, 1/79; Grace Glueck (auth), article, NY Times, 3/84; Claude Lesver (auth), article in Artspeak, 9/87; IBM-German Brochure, Review of 3 Internat Shows in Ger; Art News Mag, Feature by Walter Wickiser Gallery, NY, 2011; Dominique Nahas at Pratt Inst, NY, 2012; Greg Lindquist (auth), Art News Review of Retrospective Show; Art & Culture Mag, Cultural Council of Palm Beach Co, Opening Show Review, 2013. *Mem:* Women in the Arts. *Media:* Oil, Acrylic. *Dealer:* Ingber Gallery 3 E 78th St New York NY 11004. *Mailing Add:* 11820 Blackwoods Ln West Palm Beach FL 33412

BAKER, ELIZABETH C
ART EDITOR, CRITIC

b Boston, Mass. *Study:* Bryn Mawr Col, BA; Radcliffe Col, MA; Inst Art & Archeology & Ecole du Louvre, Paris, Fulbright Scholar. *Pos:* Assoc ed, Art News, New York, 1963-65, managing ed, 1965-73; ed, Art in America, New York, 1973-2008, editor at large, 2008-. *Teaching:* Instr art hist, Boston Univ, 1958-59, Wheaton Col, Norton, Mass, 1960-61 & Sch of Visual Arts, New York, 1968-74. *Awards:* Mather award for Criticism, Coll Art Asn, 72, Lifetime Achievement Award, 92; AICA/USA Disting Contribution to Criticism, 2011. *Publ:* numerous articles on contemporary art and artists, mostly in ARTnews, 63-74 & Art in America (74-present). *Mailing Add:* 310 E 46th St Apt 25M New York NY 10017

BAKER, JILL WITHROW
PAINTER, WRITER

b Ilion, NY, Oct 12, 1942. *Study:* Baylor Univ, BA, 64; Fla State Univ, with Karl Zerbe; Acad di Belle Arti, Florence, Italy, with Silvio Lofreddo; Pratt Inst, MFA, 81. *Work:* James Milliken Collection; Merton Collection, Bellarmine Col, Louisville, Ky; Am Nat Bank; St Thomas Aquinas Chapel; Western Ky, Univ Educ, Bowling Green; Goethe House, NY; Purdue Univ, Lafayette, Ind; multiple pvt & pub collections; Lee Pennington Collection, Louisville, Ky; Cohen Collection, Sanibel, Fla. *Exhib:* Solo shows, US Info Serv, Seoul, Korea, 77, Ward-Nasse Gallery, NY, 80, Long Island Univ, Brooklyn, 81 & Baylor Univ, Waco, Tex, 81; Pratt Alumni Invitational, 85; SOHO/20, NY, 86; Installations One, Los Angeles, 91; Artists Space, 92; Sumner Reg Med Ctr, 10/98; Plowhouse Gallery, 2004; USL Art Faculty Exhib, Evansville NJ, 2011, 2012; Working Together, Evansville Mus Arts & Sci, 2009, 2010. *Collection Arranged:* Target LA, Pasadena, Calif, 83; Thinking Eye Gallery, Calif, 85; Student Art Show, Calif State Univ, Northridge, 86; SPARC Gallery, Venice, Calif, 86. *Pos:* Mem bd dir, Ward-Nasse Gallery, 76-81; western corresp ed, Women Artists News, 84-88; mem, Graphic Arts Coun, Los Angeles Co Mus Art, 85-89; regional vpres, Artists Equity (nat); proprietor & owner, Winchester Cottage Gallery. *Teaching:* Instr, adult painting community educ prog, Bowling Green, Ky, 76-81; teaching asst, Pratt Inst, Brooklyn, NY, 78-79; instr, Pierce Col, Woodland Hills, Calif, 84-85, Gallatin Civic Ctr, 96-98 & Nossi Col Art, Goodlettesville, Tenn, 98; Art Inst Tenn-Nashville, 2006; prof, Univ Southern Ind Dept Humanities, Dept Art, 2009-; owner, Artists' Studio, Louisville, Ky. *Awards:* Achievement Award, Bank Am, State Calif, 60; Achievement Trophy, 60; scholar, Southern Women's Club, 63; Awards, Coca Cola Art Show, Elizabethtown, NJ, 78, LA'84, Brand Galleries, 84 & Window to the Future, Scottsdale, Ariz, 84 & Pratt Alumni Invitational, 85; 16th Ann Working Together Juried Invitation Award, Evansville mus Arts, 2009; Affiliate Art Award, Arts Coun SW Ind, 2009; Hon Mention, Hoosier Salon Juried Invitational, 2008; Hon Mention, Working Together, Evansville Mus Arts & Sci, 2009, 2010. *Bibliog:* Article, Courier-J, Louisville, Ky, 8/17/80; article, Artspeak, NY, 2/4/82 & Gallatin News Examiner, 10/16/98, 3/5/05; Courier Press, Evansville, NJ, 2008, 2011; Mt Vernon Democrat, 2011; NFocus, Louisville, Ky, 7/28/2012. *Mem:* Women Artists' Coalition; Los Angeles Visual Artists Guild (mem bd dir, 84-); NY Chap Artists Equity (pres, 94-96); founding mem ART-Sumner (pres, 2000-); Gallatin Arts Coun (pres, 2003-04). *Media:* Oil, Collage, Watercolor, Pen and Ink. *Specialty:* Fine arts, paintings, prints, digital art. *Interests:* Dancing, swing, ballroom & hustle, horseback riding. *Collection:* Multiple Private Collections & Public Collections. *Publ:* Illusr, The More Things Change, Whippoorwill Press, 71; Songs of Bloody Harlan, Westburg Asn Press, 75; Spring of Violets, 76, Under the Sign of the Waterbearer, 76 & I Knew A Woman, 77, Love St Bks; Auth, Poems of Accord and Satisfaction, Elba Journal and My Turn, Winchester Cottage Print, LSI. *Dealer:* Gallery Contemporary Art New Harmony IN. *Mailing Add:* 11905 Lilac Way Louisville KY 40243

BAKER, KENNETH
CRITIC, WRITER

b Weymouth, Mass, May 3, 1946. *Study:* Bucknell Univ, BA, 68. *Pos:* Art critic, Boston Phoenix, Mass, 72-85; sr art critic, San Francisco Chronicle, Calif, 85-. *Teaching:* Adj fac art hist, RI Sch Design, Providence, 79-81 & Boston Col, Chestnut Hill, Mass, 79-85. *Awards:* Distinguished Newspaper Art Criticism Award, Manufacturers Hanover Trust & Art-World, 85; Nominated for Non-fiction Award by Bay Area Book Reviewers Assoc, 90. *Mem:* Int Asn Art Critics; Nat Book Critics Circle. *Res:* Studies in aesthetics, history & criticism of Minimal art. *Publ:* Auth, Giorgio Morandi: Redemption through painting, Des Moines Art Ctr, 81; Julian Opie, Kôlnische Kunstverein, 84; Second generation: Mannerism or momentum & Report from London: The Saatchi museum opens, 85, Art Am; Flashes of understatement: Elmer Bischoff, Artforum, 86; auth, Minimalism, Abbeville Press, 89. *Mailing Add:* c/o San Francisco Chronicle San Francisco CA 94119

BAKER, NANCY SCHWARTZ
PAINTER, PRINTMAKER

b Brooklyn, NY, July 30, 1951. *Study:* Sch Visual Arts, New York, BFA, 1975; int study, art residency, Studio Camnitzer, Valdottavo, Italy, 1994-99; art residence, Casa de Mateus, Vila Real, Portugal, 2001. *Work:* NC Mus Art, Raleigh; Bellevue Hosp, NY; Glaxo-Wellcome Corp, Research Triangle Park, NC; TRW Corp, Cleveland; Reynold Industries, Winston Salem, NC. *Exhib:* Solo exhibs, Redemptive Spirit, Artspace, Raleigh, NC, 1996, The Hazards of Living, Raleigh Contemp Gallery, 1997, Fed Up, Artspace, 1998, Covered in Thirty Days, The Tire Shop, Raleigh, 1999, Devolution, The Tire Shop, 1999, Alien Stories, Manbites Dog Theatre, Durham, NC, 2000 & The Tire Shop, 2001, Fenómenos de Natureza, Casa de Mateus, Vila Real, Portugal, 2001, Alien Allegations, Artspace, 2002 & 1708 Gallery, Richmond, Va, 2003; Of the Land, Lowe Gallery, Duke Univ Mus Art, Durham, NC, 1997; Valentines, The Tire Shop, 1998; Rage and Resolution, Denver Jewish Ctr, 1999 & Hebrew Union Col, NY, 1999; Deconstructing Santa, The Tire Shop, 2000; When Toys Bite Back, Lump Gallery, Raleigh, 2000; North Carolina Artists Exhibition, NC Mus Art, Raleigh, 2000; A Sense of Place, East Carolina Univ, Greeneville, NC, 2000; North Carolina Fellowship Exhibition, 2001, Wake Forest Univ, Winston Salem, NC, 2001. *Pos:* art critic, Spectator Mag, 96; artist-in-residence, Cary Acad, NC; owner, dir, The Tire Shop, Raleigh, 97-. *Awards:* Artist Project grant, United Arts Coun, 1997; Visual Arts Fel awrd, NC Arts Coun, 2000; New Works grant, NC Arts Coun, 2001. *Bibliog:* Huston Paschal (auth), NC Mus Artists Exhib (catalog), 2000; Lissa Brennan (auth), Alien invasion, The Independent, Durham, NC, 2002; Luis Camnitzer (auth), Me Alien, You Local (catalog) Alien Allegations, 2003. *Media:* Acrylic, Oil; Miscellaneous Media. *Dealer:* Joe Rowand Somerhill Gallery 3 Eastgate East Franklin St Chapel Hill NC 27514

BAKER, RICHARD
PAINTER

b Baltimore, Md, 1959. *Study:* Md Inst, Coll Art, Baltimore, 1977-79; Sch Mus Fine Arts, Boston, 1979-81. *Exhib:* Solo shows include Joan T Washburn Gallery, NY City, 1996-97, 1998, 1999, 2000, 2001, 2003, Contemp Mus, Honolulu, 2001, Cirrus Gallery, 2001, Tibor de Nagy Gallery, 2007; Exhibs include Boston Ctr for Arts, 1985; East End Gallery, Provincetown, Mass, 1987; Provincetown Group Gallery, 1988, 1990; Cape Mus Fine Arts, Dennis, Mass, 1992; Provincetown Art Asn, Mus Provincetown, 1993; Southeast Ctr Contemp Art, Winston Salem, NC, 1993; L'Ecole des Beaux-Arts, Lorient, France, 1994; Universal Fine Objects, 1996; Whitney Mus Am Art, NY City, 1997; Albert Merola Gallery, 1997. *Pos:* Mem, Ohio Art Coun Grant Review Panel. *Awards:* New Eng Found for Arts Grant; Fine Arts Work Ctr Fel, Providence, RI. *Media:* Oil. *Mailing Add:* c/o Tibor de Nagy Gallery 724 Fifth Ave New York NY 10019

BAKKE, KAREN LEE
ASSEMBLAGE ARTIST, CALLIGRAPHER

b Everett, Wash, Nov 21, 1942. *Study:* Univ Wash; Syracuse Univ, NY, BFA (design), 67, MFA (design), 69. *Work:* Everson Mus, Syracuse. *Comn:* Extensive calligraphy, Syracuse Univ. *Exhib:* Two-person show, Fabric Forms, Kirkland Art Ctr, Clinton, NY, 76; Rubberstamp Invitational, Lightworks Gallery, Syracuse, 81; Calligraphy & Rubberstamps, Everson Mus, 82; Clothing, The Put-On and the Poor Man's Art, Am Home Econ Asn NY State Convention, 82; Suspended in Media, You Are What You See, Cornell Univ, 82; Int Calligraphy Today, Women in Design, 83. *Pos:* Asst cur, Syracuse Univ Art Collection, 67-69; vis artist soft sculpture, NY State Summer Sch of Arts, Fredonia & Chautauqua Inst. *Teaching:* Assoc prof & chairperson dept environ arts, Syracuse Univ, 69-. *Awards:* Hancock Purchase Prize & One-Person Show Award, Cent NY Regional, Everson Mus, 71. *Mem:* Am Crafts Coun; Soc Scribes; Handweavers Guild Am; Women in Design. *Media:* Fabric, Metal. *Publ:* Auth, Sewing Machine as a Creative Tool, Prentice-Hall, 76. *Mailing Add:* 1136 Cumberland Ave Syracuse NY 13210-3413

BAKKER, GABRIELLE
PAINTER
Study: Art Inst Chicago, BA; Yale Univ, MFA (painting), 1984. *Exhib:* Solo exhibs, Earl McGrath Gallery, Los Angeles, John Berggruen Gallery, San Francisco, Dart Gallery, Chicago & Frye Art Mus, Seattle; Am Acad Arts & Letts Invitational, New York, 2010. *Teaching:* Lectr, Yale Univ, Art Inst Chicago, Stanford Univ & San Francisco Sch Arts. *Awards:* Art award, Am Acad Arts and Letts, 2010. *Media:* Oil

BAKOIAN, LAUREN
DIRECTOR
Study: Maine Coll Art, BFA (printmaking), 92; Washington Univ, MFA, 94. *Pos:* Dir Lori Bookstein Fine Art, NY, currently. *Teaching:* Vis artist in various NY City public schools. *Mailing Add:* 50 E 89th St #32F New York NY 10128-1225

BALABAN, DIANE
PAINTER
b Ogden, Utah, Nov 29, 1935. *Study:* With Robert E Wood, Charles Reid, Randal Lake & Valoy Eaton. *Comn:* Painting, St Mary Catholic Church, Park City, Utah, 83; Painting ser, Stein Erikson Lodge, Deer Valley, Utah, 84. *Exhib:* San Diego Art Inst, Calif, 75; Sun Valley Western Art, Idaho, 79; Utah Watercolor Soc, Salt Lake City, 80; Solo exhib, Kimball Art Ctr, Park City, Utah; Eccles Art Ctr Invitational, Ogden, Utah. *Pos:* Pres, Park City Artist Asn, 81-83; dir, Kimball Art Ctr, 83-; lectr & judge various art groups. *Teaching:* Instr watercolor workshops, Kimball Art Ctr, Park City, currently. *Awards:* First Place Watercolor, Kimball Art Centennial Exhib, Park City Gallery Asn, 84. *Mem:* Utah Watercolor Soc; Park City Artist's Asn. *Media:* Watercolor, Oil

BALAHUTRAK, LYDIA BODNAR
PAINTER
b Cleveland, Ohio, May 6, 1951. *Study:* Kent State Univ, BS (art educ), 73; Corcoran Sch Art, 76-77; George Washington Univ, MFA (painting), 77. *Work:* George Washington Univ, Washington, DC; Univ Houston, Transco Energy Co & Baylor Coll Med, Houston; Hoyt Inst Fine Arts, New Castle, Pa. *Exhib:* Nat Small Painting & Drawing Competition, Coll Mainland, Texas City, Tex, 83; Solo exhibs, Univ Houston, 83 & 85, Graham Gallery, Houston, Tex, 88, Galveston Arts Ctr, 93, Dallas Visual Arts Ctr, 95 & Nave Mus Art, 96; Sept Int Competition, Alexandria Mus, La, 84; Hoyt Nat Drawing & Painting Show, Hoyt Inst Fine Arts, 84; 47th Ann Nat Midyear Show, Butler Inst Am Art, 84; Tex Visions Juried traveling show, Transco Art Gallery, Abilene Fine Arts Mus & McAllen Int Mus, 86; Frivolity & Mortality, traveling exhib, 87-89; Int Painters Symp Exhib, Kiev, Ukraine, 93. *Pos:* Art exhibs coordr, Univ Houston, Clear Lake City, 81-82. *Teaching:* Instr drawing & painting, San Jacinto Coll, North City, 77-79; lectr drawing 2-D design, Univ Houston, Clear Lake City, 79-82, 86-87 & 93; guest lectr art, Univ Pittsburgh, 83; vis guest artist, Inst Art, Lviv, Ukraine, 91. *Awards:* La Napoule Art Found Grant, 85; Irex Grant Int Res & Exchange, 90; Cult Arts Coun Houston Visual Art Award, 93. *Bibliog:* Donna Tennant (auth), art rev, Houston Chronicle, 12/14/79; Jill Kyle (auth), Lydia Bodnar-Balahutrak: Portrait of a Figure Painter, In Art, 6/85; Robin Longman (auth), Emerging Artists, Am Artist, 8/85; Susan Chadwick (auth), rev, Houston Post, 6/88; Michael Crespo (auth), Watercolor Day By Day, Watson-Guptill, 87. *Media:* Oil, Paint. *Dealer:* Edith Baker Gallery 2404 Cedar Springs Dallas TX 75201. *Mailing Add:* 2528 Dryden Houston TX 77030

BALANCE, JERRALD CLARK
PAINTER
b Ogden, Utah, July 20, 1944. *Study:* Univ Utah, Salt Lake City; mainly self-taught. *Work:* Chrysler Mus at Norfolk, Va; Atlantic City Fine Arts Ctr & Atlantic City Munic Bldg Collection, NJ; Coopers & Lybrand Corp, Washington, DC; US State Dept, Washington, DC; Sperry Corp, Reston, Va. *Exhib:* 19th Area Exhib, Corcoran Gallery Art, Washington, DC, 74; 14th Md Biennial, Baltimore Mus Art, 74; Five Am Abstract Painters, Northeastern Univ Gallery, Boston, 77; Best of NY--A Survey, Root Art Ctr, Hamilton Col, Clinton, 77; Solo exhibs, Genesis Gallery, NY, 78-79 & US State Dept, Washington, DC; Art in the Embassies Prog, Madrid, Spain & Bangkok, Thailand, 78-80. *Awards:* Nat Endowment Grant, Va Commission Arts & Humanities & Emerson Gallery, 76; Washington Cherry Blossom Festival Nat Art Competition Award in Sculpture, 72. *Bibliog:* Joe Mayer (producer), Beyond Abstract Expressionism: Balance & Chelimsky, Prince Georges Community Col. *Media:* Oil, Enamel; Plastic. *Publ:* Contribr, Washington artists, Artists Equity, 72. *Dealer:* Harriet Lebish Gallery 41 E 57th St New York NY 10022; Jane Hasley Gallery 406 Seventh St Washington DC

BALAS, IRENE
PAINTER
b Budapest, Hungary, Feb 28, 1928; US citizen. *Study:* Acad Fine Arts, Vienna, Austria, MA, 48; studied art therapy with Hans Hoffman & psychiatry with Karl Kaufman. *Work:* Mus Luis Angel Arango, Bogota, Columbia; Mus Vatican, Rome, Italy; Rockefeller Collection, Henry Ford Collection, NY; Mus Atelier; Attila Matyas. *Comn:* Portrait of the Pres, comn by Victor Paz Estenssoro, La Paz, Bolivia, 55; Bolivia Pintoresca, comn by Ger Embassador, La Paz, Bolivia, 55; religious abstracts, Mus el Minuto de Dios, Bogota, Columbia, 67; Birth of Emerald, Banco de Colombia, Bogota, Colombia, 72; Expedition Hungary-USA, Hungarian Air Force, 90; and others. *Exhib:* En Honor del Presidente, Mus Victor Paz, La Paz, Bolivia, 55; solo show, Luis Angel Arango, Bogota, Columbia, 60; South Am, Ed Nacional, Madrid, Spain, 65; The Beauty of Am, Casements, Ormond Beach, Fla, 82; Space, Mus Hist & Art, Palm Beach, Fla, 89; Wings of Ambitions, Art Mus, Budapest, Hungary, 90; and others. *Teaching:* Instr bellas artes, Santiago de Chile, 53-54; Universidad La Javeriana, Bogota, Colombia, 69-71. *Awards:* Nat Prize, Austrian Painters, Kunstlerhaus, 48; Bronze Medal, Salon Oficial, Mus de Bellas Artes, 51; Gold Medal, Concepcion, Univ Medicin, 56. *Bibliog:* Gladys Ostrom (auth), Irene Balas Painter of Presidents, Ann Fabe Isaacs, 77; Tom Elliot (auth), Petit Museum of Irene Balas (film), Fla, 77-78; Lizette Alvarez (auth), Little museum, Miami Herald, 88. *Media:* Oil, Acrylic. *Interests:* Painting. *Publ:* Auth, Exposicion del mes, El Correo; Notas de arte, Aramen Dia, 67; The best exhibition; Irene Balas, Andean Times, 69; Irene Balas communicates through her art, Morning J, 82; Artist profile, Directions, 88. *Mailing Add:* 1621 Collins Ave Apt 907 Miami Beach FL 33139

BALAS, JACK J
PAINTER, PHOTOGRAPHER
Study: Sch Archit, Ill Inst Technol, Chicago, 73-74; Inst Design, Ill Inst Technol, Chicago, 74-75; Salzburg Col, Austria, 76; Northern Ill Univ, DeKalb, BA, BFA (sculpture, studio), 78, MA (sculpture), 80, MFA (sculpture), 81. *Work:* San Francisco Mus Art, Calif; US W Commun, Denver, Colo; Hewlett Packard, Fort Collins, Colo; Brooklyn Mus Art; Nat Mus Wildlife Art, Jackson, Wyo; Tucson Mus Art; Usminas Cult Inst, Brazil. *Exhib:* solo shows, Univ Wyo Art Mus, Laramie, 96, Univ Alaska, Anchorage, 97 & Robinson Gallery, Denver, Colo, 98, Mus of the Southwest, Midland, Tex, Jenkin Johnson Gallery, New York, 2006, Conduit Gallery, Dallas, 2006, Mus Contemp Art, Colo, 2008, Ego llery, Barcelona, Spain, 2009; Personal/Political: Sexuality Self-Defined, Art Inst Chicago, 90; Rodeo in Fact & Fantasy, Philbrook Mus Art, Tulsa, Okla, 91; Out of Bounds: The Word Becomes Art, Scottsdale Ctr Arts, Ariz, 92; Focus on Colorado/The Front Range: Jack Balas, Wes Hempel & Scott Chamberlin, Aspen Art Mus, Colo, 94; The New Narratology - Examining the Narrative in Image/Text Art (traveling exhib), Artspace Annex, San Francisco, Calif, 89; group exhibs, Egypt of the Mind, Denver Colo, 98, Conceptualisticationism, Brooklyn, NY, 99, The Image of Text, Harrisonburg, Va, 2000, London Biennale, London, Eng; Clamp Arts, New York, 2005; Gatov & Merlino Galleries, Calif State Univ, 2006; Form & Content Gallery, Minneapolis, 2007; Istanbul Convention Ctr, Turkey, 2007; Andrea Schwartz Gallery, San Francisco, 2009. *Teaching:* Artist in Residence, Art Dept, Skidmore Col, NY, 2000. *Awards:* First Place Short Fiction Award, WestWord Mag, Denver, Colo, 89; Creative Fel Photog, Colo Coun Arts & Humanities, 91; Individual Fel Painting, Nat Endowment Arts, Washington, 95; Artist Residency, Mus Contemp Art, Denver, 2008. *Bibliog:* Mary Voelz Chandler (auth), Write your own story to go with these pieces, Rocky Mountain News, Denver, Colo, 9/26/93; Hart Hill (auth), Text and texture, WestWord, Denver, Colo, 10/6/93; Marilynne Mason (auth), Not quite on the map: magic & art, Colo Expression, Denver, winter 93; David Leddick (auth), Male Nude Now, Univ Publ, New york, 2001; David Leddick (auth), he Nude Male: 21st Century Visions, Univ Publ, New York, 2008. *Media:* Acrylic, Oil. *Publ:* Contribr, Today I drove along the Rio Grande, The Paris Rev, New York, No 120, 121-129, fall 91; The New Censorship, Denver, Colo, Vol 4, No 1, 4/93; High Performance, No 61, 38-39, spring 93; Art & the Law, 20th Annual Exhibition (exhib catalog), West Publ Corp, Minneapolis, Minn, 95; New American painting, The Open Studios Press, Boston, 2001; Blue #45, Studio Mag, Sydney, Australia, 2003; The Front Range & the Range of Identity, Mus Cotnemp Art, Denver, 2007; Timeless: The Art of Drawing, The Morris Mus, NJ, 2008; Code D'Acces, Factory Ed, Paris, 2008. *Dealer:* Robischon Gallery 1740 Wazee St Denver CO 80202. *Mailing Add:* 825 Fourth St Berthoud CO 80513

BALAS-WHITFIELD, SUSAN
PAINTER, FILMMAKER
b New Jersey, April 29, 1943. *Study:* Rutgers Univ, BA, 64; New York Univ, 61-64; Studied with Dr Elaine Debeauport, Mead Inst, New York, 88. *Work:* Standardbred Breeders & Owners Asn, Freehold, NJ; A Slokker, The Netherlands; Mark Hack, Spain; Bryant Gumbel; Anthony Abatiello, Trotters & Pacers; Herve Fillion, Trotters & Pacers; Ho Chunk Indians, Wisc. *Comn:* Mural of palace, Palace Amusements, Asbury Park, NY, 73; Portrait of Herve Fillion, Standardbred Breeders & Owners Asn, Freehold, NJ, 76; Portrait of Tony Abatiello, cover of Trotters & Pacers Mag, Standardbred Breeders & Owners Asn, Freehold, NJ, 76. *Exhib:* Mem Exhib, Salmagundi Club, New York, 76-; Scholarship Exhib, Salmagundi Club, New York, 76; Pastel Soc NMex, Albuquerque, NMex, 2001; Int Asn Pastel Soc, NMex, 2001; Pastel Soc Am Ann, Nat Arts Club, New York, 2000; Am Artists Prof League Grand Nat, Salmagundi Club, New York, 2004; Pastel Soc Am Invitational, Butler Mus Am Art, Youngstown, Ohio, 2003. *Teaching:* creative arts, William R Satz Sch, Homdel, NJ, 80-89. *Awards:* Hon mention, Salmagundi Club Oil Show, Salmagundi Club, 80; Best of show, Durango Arts Ctr Juried Exhib, Toh-atin Gallery, Durango, Colo, 2001; Artist of the year, Ann Juried Exhib, Colo Chamber of Commerce, 2003; Award for excellence in pastel, 76th Grand Nat Exhib, Pastel Soc Am, 2004. *Bibliog:* Balas paints Anthony Abatiello, Trotters & Pacers Mag, 76; Luscious Pastels, SW Art Mag, 2003; Kathleen Busch (auth), featured Artist of Four Corners, Western Style Mag, 2000; Adam P & Rene Kennedy (auths), Susan Balas-Whitfield PSA, Best of Am Pastel Artists, 2009. *Mem:* Salmagundi Club; Pastel Soc Am/ Nat Arts Club; Pastel Soc Colo. *Media:* Oil, Pastel, Watercolor. *Publ:* auth, Into the Triangle, A Teacher's Trot, Vantage Press, New York, 89; Balas, Prager, & Kuehn (coauths), The Maya Tzol'kin Oracle (film), Charles Kuehn, 2010

BALCIAR, GERALD GEORGE
SCULPTOR
b Medford, Wis, Aug 28, 1942. *Work:* Denver Zoo, Colo; Nat Cowboy Mus, Okla City; Beaver Creek Resort, Avon, Colo; Okla City Zoo; Buffalo Bill Historical Ctr, Cody, Wyo. *Comn:* Challenge (bronze elk monument), Westminster Sculpture Garden, Westminster, Colo; Centennial (bronze moose monument), Loyal Order of Moose, Mooseheart, Ill; In High Places (bald eagle monument), Univ N Tex, Denton, Tex; Bull, Elk, Cow & Two Calves, Beaver Creek Resort, Avon, Colo; Pride (marble cougar), Nat Mus Wildlife Art, Jackson, Wyo; Family Pride (bronze lions), Okla City Zoo, Okla; Sound of Autumn, 12' bronze elk, Leanin Tree Mus, Boulder, Colo. *Exhib:* Nat Acad Design, New York, 77, 86, 90 & 92; Nat Sculpture Soc, New York, 77-96 & 2002; Allied Artists Am, New York, 77-96 & 2002; Nat Acad Western Art, Cowboy Hall Fame, Okla City, 78, 84 & 2008; Artists Am, Denver, 85-98. *Awards:* Prix de

West & Gold Medal, Nat Acad Western Art, 85; Ellin Speyer Prize, Nat Acad Design, 86; People's Choice Award, Silver Medal, Nat Acad Western Art, 90. *Mem:* Nat Sculpture Soc; Soc Animal Artists; Allied Artist Am; Northwest Rendezvous. *Media:* Marble, Bronze. *Mailing Add:* 12501 Roundup Rd Parker CO 80138

BALDAIA, PETER JOSEPH
CURATOR, DIRECTOR

b Providence, RI, Sept 12, 1953. *Study:* RI Coll, Providence, BA, 78; Brown Univ, Providence, grad studies, 79; Grad Sch, Boston Univ, Mass, MA (art hist), 82 & dipl (mus studies), 83. *Collection Arranged:* Bunny Harvey, Fuller Mus Art, Brockton, Mass, 88; Henry Schwartz, Fuller Mus Art, Brockton, Mass, 90; Subjective Intentions, Rockford Art Mus, Ill, 93; Harold Gregor, Rockford Art Mus, Ill, 93; Roland Miller: Abandoned in Place (auth, catalog), Huntsville Mus Art, Ala, 94; Breaking the Mold: New Directions in Glass (auth, catalog), Huntsville Mus Art, Ala, 96; Embracing Beauty: Aesthetic Perfection in Contemporary Art (auth, catalog), Huntsville Mus Art, Ala, 97; Josh Simpson: A Visionary Journey in Glass, Huntsville Mus Art, Huntsville, AL, 2007; A Silver Manageric: The Betty Grisham Collection of Buccallati Silver Animals (auth, catalog), Huntsville Mus Art, Hunstville, AL, 2006. *Pos:* Cur, Fuller Mus Art, Brockton, Mass, 86-91; cur exhibs & collections, Rockford Art Mus, Ill, 92-94; chief cur, Huntsville Mus Art, Ala, 94-2004; cur dir, Huntsville Mus Art, 2004-. *Mem:* Am Asn Mus; Southeastern Mus Conf. *Publ:* Auth, Towards Transcendence: The Works of Nan Tull (exhib catalog), Akin Gallery, Boston, Mass, 91; Wrestling with Hist: Trachtman, Erony and the Theme of the Holocaust (exhib catalog), Newton Arts Ctr, Newtonville, Mass, 92; From Hand to Heart: The art of the American miniature portrait, Am Art Rev, 2-3/96; Breaking the Mold: New Directions in Glass (exhib, catalog), Huntsville Mus Art, Ala, 96; Will Berry: Completely Hatched into Light (exhib catalog essay), Huntsville Mus Art, Ala, 97. *Mailing Add:* c/o Huntsville Mus Art 300 Church St S Huntsville AL 35801

BALDASSANO, VINCENT
PAINTER

b State Island, NY. *Study:* Wagner Coll, BA, 64; Univ of Ore, MFA, 66; State Univ NY, Painting Fel, 69-73. *Work:* Housatonic Mus Art, Bridgeport, Conn; Hammond Mus, North Salem, NY; Savannah Coll Art & Design, Savannah, GA; Sacred Heart Univ Fairfield, Conn; The Children's Mus Arts, New York City; Mattatuck Mus, Waterbury, Conn; Queensboro Community Coll, New York City; Slater Memorial Mus, Norwich, Conn. *Exhib:* Western NY Art Exhib, Albright-Knox Art Gallery, Buffalo, NY, 68, 70, 72; The Flower in Am Art, Butler Art Inst, Youngstown, Ohio, 90; Meditations, Hammond Mus, N Salem, NY, 96 & 2005; Vincent Baldassano, Stamford Mus, Stamford, Conn, 97; The Energists, Mus of Art, Cagnes Sur Mer, France, 98; 40th Anniversary, Housatonic Mus of Art, Bridgeport, Conn, 2007. *Pos:* Managing Dir, Northern Westchester Ctr for the Arts, Mt Kisco, NY, 1995-1996; Dir, Silvermine Guild Art Gallery, New Canaan, Conn, 1996-2000; Exec Dir, Conn Graphic Arts Ctr, Norwalk, Conn, 1999-2000. *Teaching:* Instr, Silvermine Sch of Art, 1991-2001 & Nat Academy of Design, New York, 2002-2013; prof, Gateway Community Col, 2003-; art history, painting & drawing design, Gateway Community Coll, New Haven, Conn, 2004-2006; adj prof art appreciation, Univ Conn, Stamford, Conn, 2002 & 2004, Quinnipiac Univ, Hamden, Conn, 2004 & Western Conn State Univ, 2006-2014. *Awards:* Va Ctr for Creative Arts Fel, 78; S.O.S. Grant, NY State Coun on Arts, 1999; Creative Arts Public Service, 2002-2006; Gateway Found Grant, 2006-2007, 2012, 2014; Conn Community Coll Grant, 2006-2008, 2012; grant, Vermont Studio Ctr, 2011; vis artist, Am Acad in Rome, 2012, 2014. *Bibliog:* Vivien Raynor (auth), Abstract Works to Catch the Adult Eye, NY Times, 1996; Willam Zimmer (auth) Form Color & More, NY Times, 2000; D. Dominick Lombardi (auth), Baldassano, NY Times 2004. *Mem:* New York Artist Equity; Silvermine Guild of Artists; New Haven Art Council; Coll Art Assoc. *Media:* All Media. *Res:* Ancient methods & materials: encaustic, egg tempera, fresco painting. *Dealer:* Artifacts-Lanier Gallery South Salem NY; Buster Levi Gallery Cold Spring NY; Ober Gallery Kent Ct; Reynolds Grove Art New Haven Ct. *Mailing Add:* 190 Maple Tree Hill Rd Oxford CT 06478

BALDERACCHI, ARTHUR EUGENE
SCULPTOR, ADMINISTRATOR

b New York, NY, Mar 25, 1937. *Study:* Duke Univ, BA, 60; Univ Ga, MFA, 65. *Work:* Duke Univ, Durham; St Lawrence Univ; State Univ NY Potsdam; Univ Ga, Athens. *Comn:* Seven ft high mem to Dr Martin Luther King, Roland Gibson Art Found, Potsdam, NY. *Exhib:* Numerous solo & group exhibs in the Northeast. *Pos:* Chmn dept arts, Univ NH, 74-80. *Teaching:* Prof art, Univ NH, Durham, 65-. *Mem:* Coll Art Asn Am; NH Art Asn. *Media:* Welded Metals, Cast Metals. *Publ:* Coauth (with C Pratt), In the Orchard, Tidal Press, 86; Drawings, 1948, Univ Va Press, 90. *Mailing Add:* 321 Sagamore Ave Portsmouth NH 03801-5530

BALDESSARI, JOHN ANTHONY
CONCEPTUAL ARTIST

b National City, Calif, June 17, 1931. *Study:* San Diego State Col, BA, 53, MA, 57; Univ Calif, Berkeley, 54-55; Univ Calif, Los Angeles, 55; Otis Art Inst, Los Angeles, 57-59. *Hon Degrees:* Otis Art Inst, Parsons Sch Design of the New Sch for Social Rsch, D Fine Arts, 2000, San Diego State Univ & Calif State Univ, 2003, Nat Univ Ireland, 2006. *Work:* Mus Mod Art, NY; Basel Mus, Switz; Los Angeles Co Mus Art; Chicago Art Inst; Whitney Mus, NY. *Exhib:* Konzeption-Conception, Stadtischen Mus, Leverkusen, Ger, 69; Information, Mus Mod Art, NY, 70; Prospect, Stadtischen Kunsthalle, Dusseldorf, Ger, 71; Documenta 5 & 7, Kassel, Ger, 72 & 83; Contemporanea, Rome, 73; Carnegie Inst, Pittsburgh, Pa, 86; John Baldessari: Oeuvres Recentes, Palais des Beaux Arts, Brussels, Belgium, 88, Photoarbeiten, Kestner-Gessellschaft (auth, catalog), Hanover WGer, 88-89, Ni Por Esas/Not Even So (auth, catalog), Ctr de Arte Reina Sofia, Madrid, 89; Bilderstiet, Mus Ludwig in den Rheinhallen der KolnerMesse, Cologne, WGer, 89; Magiciens de la Terre, Ctr Georges Pompidou; and Grande Halle-La Villette, Paris, 89; John Baldessari Retrospective, Mus Contemp Art, Los Angeles, San Francisco Mus Mod Art, Hirshhorn Mus and Sculpture Garden, Walker Art Ctr, Whitney Mus Am Art, Mus d'Art Contemp de Montreal, 90; Spengel Mus, Hannover, Ger, 2000; Museu d'Art Contemporania, Barcelona, Spain, 98; Kunstmalle Basel, Switz, 2000; Monika Spruth/Philomene Magers, Cologne, Ger, 2002; Margo Leavin Gallery, Los Angeles, 2002; Nose & Ears, Etc, Marian Goodman Gallery, 2006; Learn to Read, Tate Mod, London, 2007; Arms & Legs (Specif Elbows & Knees), Etc, Marian Goodman Gallery, Paris, 2007; Whitney Biennial, Whitney Mus Am Art, New York, 2008; 53rd Int Art Exhib Biennale, Venice, 2009. *Teaching:* Asst prof art, Univ Calif, San Diego, 68-70; prof art, Calif Inst Arts, Valencia, 70-87; prof art, Univ Calif, Los Angeles, 96-. *Awards:* Nat Endowment Arts Grants, 73-75; Guggenheim Grant, 86; Skowhegan Medal, 88; Oscar Kokoschaka Prize, Austria, 96; Govs Award for Lifetime Achievement in the Visual Arts, Calif, 97; Spectrum Int Award for Photography of the Found of Lower Saxony, Ger, 99; Lifetime Achievement Award, Americans for the Arts, 2005; Archives Am Art Medal, 2007; Biennial Award Contemp Art, Bonnefantenmuseum Maastricht, 2008; Golden Lions for Lifetime Achievement, Venice Biennale, 2009; Distinguished Body of Work Award, Coll Art Asn, 2011. *Bibliog:* James Collins (auth), John Baldessari, Artforum, 10/73; Coosje von Bruggen (auth), John Baldessari, Rizzoli, NY, 90; Meg Granston (coauth) While Something is Happening Here, Something Else is Happening There, Sprengel Mus, Hannover and Staatliche Kunstammlungen, Dresden, Germany, 99; Thomas McEvilley (auth) John Baldessari, Tetrad Series, Marian Goodman Gallery, NY, 99, others. *Mem:* Fel Am Acad Arts & Sci; Am Acad Arts & Lett. *Media:* Photography, Printmaking. *Publ:* Auth, Ingres & Other Parables, 72; Choosing: Green Beans, 72; Throwing Three Balls in the Air to Get a Straight Line (Best of 36 Attempts), 73; Close Cropped Tales, 81; The Telephone Book (with Pearls), 88; coauth The Metaphor Problem Again, Ink Tree Kunsnacht and Mai 36 Galerie, Zurich, Switzerland, 99; A Sentence of Thirteen Parts (with Twelve Alternate Verbs) Ending in Fable, Hamburg, West Germany, 77; Zorro (Two Gestures and One Mark), Octagon Press, 99; plus others. *Dealer:* Marian Goodman Gallery 24 W 57th St New York NY 10019. *Mailing Add:* Baldessari Studio 626 1/2 Vernon Ave Venice CA 90291

BALDRIDGE, MARK S
GOLDSMITH, EDITOR

b Lyons, NY, Dec 7, 1946. *Study:* State Univ NY Col, Buffalo, BS (art educ), 68; Cranbrook Acad Art, Bloomfield Hills, Mich, MFA (metalsmithing), 70. *Exhib:* 10th Piedmont Crafts Exhib, Mint Mus Art, Charlotte, NC, 73; Profiles in US Jewelry, 73, Lubbock, Tex, 73; Va Artists 1973, Va Mus Fine Arts, Richmond, 73; 11th Ann Southern Tier Art & Crafts Show, Corning Glass Ctr, NY, 74; Reprise, Cranbrook Acad Art Mus, Bloomfield Hills, Mich, 75; Objects 75 Designer/Craftsman Show, Grand Junction, Colo, 75; Craft Art & Relig, Vatican Mus, Rome, 76; Marietta Coll Crafts Nat, Ohio, 77; Va Craftsmen Biennial, Va Mus Fine Arts, Richmond, 80; SE Metalsmiths, Mint Mus Art; Metalsmith 81, Univ Kans, Lawrence, 81; US Jewelry Invitational, Walker Hill Art Ctr, Seoul, Korea; LeMoyne Arts Found, Tallahassee, Fla; Pensacola Mus of Art; and others. *Pos:* Ed & creator, Goldsmiths J, 74-; co-ed, Metalsmith Mag, 86. *Teaching:* Instr metal-jewelry, Univ Evansville, 70-72; from asst to prof metal-jewelry, Longwood Col, 72-, chmn art dept, 89-93; conduct numerous workshops in field. *Awards:* First Prize-Metal, 40th Nat Cooperstown, NY, 75; First Prize, Lake Superior Int, 75; Merit Award, Goldsmiths 77, Soc NAm Goldsmiths, Phoenix Art Mus, 77. *Mem:* Va Crafts Coun (bd mem, 78-80); Soc NAm Goldsmiths (bd mem, 79-87); SE Am Craft Coun (Va rep & treas, 82-); Richmond Craftsman's Guild (secy, 97-2004, treas 2005). *Media:* Gold, Stained Glass. *Res:* American metalsmithing in the 1940's and 1950's; Glass Casting. *Publ:* Auth, Bi-metal casting to titanium, Metalsmith, Vol 6, No 2, spring 86; Kenneth Bates: Dean of American Enameling, Metalsmith, Vol 8, No 2, spring 88; creator, ed, SNAG newsletter & Goldsmiths Jour; co-ed, assoc ed, Metalsmith Mag; book reviewer, Jeweler's Circular Keystone. *Mailing Add:* 1600 Otterdale Midlothian VA 23114

BALDWIN, GORDON C
CURATOR

b Cleveland, Ohio, Feb 20, 1939. *Study:* Amherst Col, AB, 60; Harvard Law Sch; Harvard Grad Sch Design, 63-67. *Collection Arranged:* Photography in Nineteenth-Century Egypt, J Paul Getty Mus, 87; Gustave Le Gray, 88; Grave Testimony: Photographs of the Civil War, 92; Fame & Photography, 93; Roger Fenton: The Orientalist Suite, 96; Jean Gabriel Eyhard: A Life in D Aguerreotypes, 98; Nadar/Warhol: Paris/NY, 99; The Man in the Street, Eugene Atget in Paris, 2000; Gustave Le Gray, Photographer, 2002; Recent Acquisitions. 2004 (co-curator); All the Mighty World The Photographs of Roger Fenton, 2005 (co-curator). *Pos:* Study room supervisor, J Paul Getty Mus, 87-90, asst cur, 90-94, assoc cur, 94-. *Awards:* Rome Prize, Am Acad Rome, 77. *Mem:* Europ Soc Hist Photog; fel Am Acad Rome. *Publ:* Auth, Looking at Photographs: A Guide to Technical Terms, J Paul Getty Mus/British Mus, 91; coauth, Phiz 93: The John Kobal Foundation, Cheatle Gallery, 93; auth, Roger Fenton: Pasha and Bayadére, J Paul Getty Mus, 96; co-auth, Nador/Warhol, Paris/New York; Photography and Fame, J Paul Gettty Mus. 99; In Focus; Eugene Atget, J Paul Getty Mus, 2000; ed, Gustave Le Gray, 1820-1884, J Paul Getty Mus, 2002; co-auth, All the Mighty World, The Photographs of Roger Fenton, 1851-1862, Metrop Mus Art, 2004

BALDWIN, RICHARD WOOD
ILLUSTRATOR, SCULPTOR

b Needham, Mass, June 8, 1920. *Study:* Pa Acad Fine Arts, with George Harding; also with Harold Von Schmidt. *Work:* Smithsonian Inst, Washington, DC; Whitney Gallery Western Art; Brown Univ, Libr. *Comn:* Murals, comn by USA, 42-45, now in Smithsonian Inst. *Pos:* Sr master sculptor, Franklin Mint, 70-. *Awards:* Cresson Fel, Pa Acad Fine Arts, 41. *Media:* Oil, Watercolor; Clay, Plaster. *Publ:* Illusr books & periodicals, 46-65

BALDWIN, RUSSELL W
EDUCATOR, GALLERY DIRECTOR
b San Diego, Calif, May 26, 1933. *Study:* San Diego State Univ, BA, 58, MA, 63. *Work:* Joseph Hirshhorn Collection, Washington, DC; San Diego Mus Contemp Art, Calif; Santa Barbara Mus Art; San Francisco Mus Mod Art; Newport Harbor Mus, Calif; Int Paper Co, NY; Kelley Found, Los Angeles. *Exhib:* Solo exhibs, Santa Barbara Mus Art, 64, San Diego Mus Contemp Art, 64, 73 & 81, Jewish Community Ctr, San Diego, 74 & Casat Gallery, La Jolla, 78; Solo retrospective, San Francisco Mus Mod Art, 81; New Works, San Francisco Mus Mod Art, 81; Space Gallery, 82 & 92. *Collection Arranged:* Paintings by John Baldessari, 72; Robert Irwin (installation piece), 75; Photog as a Means, 76; Andy Warhol, 77; Wayne Thiebaud, 78; William Wiley, 78; Masami Tenaoka, 80; Roland Reiss, 81; Star Wars Exhib from Lucas, 86. *Pos:* Dir, Dwight Boehm Gallery. *Teaching:* Assoc prof art, Palomar Col, San Marcos, Calif, 65-. *Awards:* First Painting Award, San Diego Mus Contemp Art, 60; Sculpture Award, Long Beach Mus Art, 73; First Award, Calif-Hawaii Regional, Fine Arts Mus San Diego, 74. *Mem:* San Diego Mus Contemp Art. *Specialty:* Information art. *Publ:* auth, articles in LA Times, San Diego Mag, San Diego Union, Newsweek & Art Week. *Dealer:* Space Gallery Los Angeles CA

BALISLE, JENNY ELLA
PAINTER, EDUCATOR
b Stevens Point, Wis, Jan 17, 1974. *Study:* Univ Wis, Stevens Point, BA, 98; Acad Art Coll, San Francisco, Calif, MFA, 2003. *Work:* Bonneville Int, San Francisco, Calif; Hilton, Tokyo, Japan; Radians Inc, Memphis, Tenn; Westin, Palo Alto, Calif; Group Marketing 3, San Francisco, Calif. *Comn:* Hearts in San Francisco, San Francisco Hospital Found, 2004. *Exhib:* Golda Found 1st Ann Juried Competition, Fresno Art Mus, Calif, 2004; All-In Juried Art Exhib, Torrance Art Mus, Calif, 2007; MOCA Paperworks!, Marin Mus Contemp Art, Novato, Calif, 2008; Gateway to Imagination, Farmington Mus, NMex, 2008; Gallery 555, Oakland Mus, Calif, 2008; Balancing Prespectives: East Asian Influences in Contemp Art, de Young Mus, John F Kennedy Univ, Berkeley, Calif, 2008; In the Abstract, Los Angeles Dept of Cultural Affairs, Los Angeles Int Airport, Calif, 2009; A Book About Death, Mus Brasileiro, Sao Paolo, Brasil, 2010; Deconstructed Applications, Dept Cult Affairs, Los Angeles Munic Art Gallery, Los Angeles, Calif, 2010-2011; Factor XX Art Mus Los Gatos, Los Gatos, Calif, 2010-2011; Triton Mus Statewide Painting Competition, Triton Art Mus, Santa Clara, Calif, 2012; The Delaplaine Visual Arts Educ Ctr, Frederick, Md, 2012; San Luis Obispo Mus Art, San Luis Obispo, Calif, 2013; Ormond Memorial Art Mus, Ormond Beach, Fla, 2013. *Pos:* MFA, Acad Art Univ, San Francisco, 2006-. *Teaching:* MFA, Dir Studies & Critical Thinking, Acad Art Univ, San Francisco, 2006-. *Awards:* Golda Found 1st Ann Juried Painting Exhib, Fresno Art Mus, 2004; Half Page Layout in Issue Winner, Sculptural Pursuits 1st Ann Art/Lit Competition, 2005; Coordinator's Award, Abstract-Sebastopol Ctr for the Arts, 2005; Hon mention, RIC Art Futura, Chicago Cultural Ctr, 2007; Juror's Choice Award, ArtSpan Benefit Art Show & Auction, 2008. *Bibliog:* Amber Rayon-Justin (auth), Eye-catching Art Display an Invigorating Experience, Golden Gate Express, 2005; Hiya Swanhuyser (auth), Wet Paint, SF Weekly, 2011; Susan O'Malley (auth), Jenny E Balisle, Catalogue, 2011; Anne Weltner (auth), Golden Circles, New Times, 2013. *Mem:* Berkeley Art Ctr Asn; Pro Arts Oakland, East Bay Open Studios Comt, 2008; Calif Arts Advocates; Northern Calif Women's Causus for Art. *Media:* Layers of Oil, Paint & Mediums on Wood Panel; Pen & Ink. *Interests:* Curating, reading, writing, internet, nature, walking. *Publ:* Illustr, the Last Word: West Coast Artists & Writers, Zyzzyva, 2007; Sculptural Pursuits 1st Ann Art/Lit Competition, Sculptural Pursuit Mag, 2005; The Renascent, Writing Vol 2, ER Morse & JSB Morse, 2005; Best of America, Mixed Media Artists & Artisans Vol 1, Kennedy Promotions, LLC, 2007; Illustr, The Noe Valley Voice, 2008; Am Art Collector, 2009, 2011; Studio Visit Mag, Vol 15 & 16, 2011. *Dealer:* Wexler Gallery 201 N 3rd St Philadelphia PA 19106; SFMOMA Artist Gallery Building A Fort Mason Ctr San Francisco CA 94123; Hang Art 567 Sutter St San Francisco CA 94102

BALKA, SIGMUND RONELL
GALLERY DIRECTOR, CURATOR
b Aug 8, 1935. *Study:* Williams Coll, BA, 56; Harvard Univ, JD, 59. *Hon Degrees:* Hebrew Union Coll, LHD, 2008. *Collection Arranged:* Cur, major collection of 20th century mod and contemp arts and Am decorative arts. *Pos:* Vpres public & cultural affairs, gen counsel, Krasdale Foods, Inc, Bronx, NY; dir & cur, Krasdale Galleries, Bronx, NY and White Plains, NY; pres, Print Connoisseurs Soc NY, 74; chmn, Hunts Point Sculpture Park Task Force, NY, 88-91; bd dir, Bronx Coun Arts, 80-2004; chmn, fel & mem, Williams Col Mus Art, vis com, 96-99, fel, 2000-; mem adv coun, visual arts, Mason Gross Sch Art, Rutgers Univ; mem exhibs & acquisition comt bd trustees, Queens Mus Art, NY 97-98, chmn, 2001-; bd dir, Jewish Repertory Theatre, co-chmn, 2000-01, chmn, 2001-; bd dir, Coun Arts, Longwood Center, 2005; bd dir, Judaica Mus, 2006; bd dir, Bronx Mus Art, 2007-; numerous community & environ activities. *Awards:* Gala Award, Queens Mus Art, 2002, 2009. *Mem:* Am Bar Found (fel), 98-; ABA (mem com corp gen counsel, 74-, planning chmn, 94-96, mem chmn & sec, 96-98); Met Corp Counsel (corp counsel adv com); Asn Bar City NY; Am Corp Counsel Fedn (bd dir & treas, 92-99); Am Corp Counsel Asn (bd dir & chmn Met NY chap, mem pro-bono com); Greater NY Met Food Coun (bd dir, 86-98); Bronx Art Alliance (founder, 2011-). *Specialty:* Mod and Contemp and Am art from all regions of the Country. *Collection:* 20th century American art; American 18th & 19th Century American decorative arts. *Publ:* Over 130 catalogues. *Mailing Add:* 70-27 Harrow St Forest Hills NY 11375-5153

BALKIN, AMY
CONCEPTUAL ARTIST
Study: Sch Art Inst Chicago, BFA, 1991; Stanford Univ, MFA, 2003. *Exhib:* Exhibs include Mixing Messages, Cooper Heweitt Mus, New York, 1997; Dystopia, Roebling Hall, New York, 1998; The Love Show, San Francisco, 2001; Lite Light Show, Pasadena, Calif, 2001; NO WAR, The Luggage Store, San Francisco, 2002; Lead Poisoning, New Image Art, Los Angeles, 2003; Our Hospitality, Adobe Books, San Francisco, 2003; This Way Please: Tours of the Everyday, Pond, San Francisco, 2004; Invisible-5, Southern Exposure, San Francisco, 2006; Off-Site, Fresno Metrop Mus, Fresno Calif, 2006. *Awards:* Murphy Cadogan Fel, San Francisco Found, 2002; Creative Work Fund Grant, 2004; Louis Comfort Tiffany Found Grant, 2008. *Mailing Add:* 2136 Fell St Apt 301 San Francisco CA 94117

BALL, KEN WESTON
ARTIST
b Denver, Colo, June 2, 1942. *Study:* Univ Colo, BA, 66. *Work:* The Harmsen Collection, Denver Art Mus; The Gene Autry Western Heritage Mus, Los Angeles. *Comn:* Five Bronze Figures of Native Ams, Aurora Art in Public Places, Colo, 97; Six Bronze Bas Relief Sports Figures, Colo Coun on the Arts, Trinidad, 98. *Exhib:* Iron Eyes Cody Tribute, Washington, DC, 82; Western Reg Exhib, Sangre De Christo Fine Art Center, Pueblo, Colo, 85; Western Art Rendezvous, Morrison, Colo, 92; Sculpture Garden Invitational, Hudson Botanic Gardens, Littleton, Colo, 98; Views of the West, Red Rocks Community Col, Lakewood, Colo, 00. *Awards:* Arts & Humanities Award, Nat Recreation & Park Asn, 98; Best of Show, Arvada Harvest Art Show, 82. *Mem:* Am Soc Landscape Architects. *Publ:* Calif Art Rev, American References, 89; Xeriscape Programs for Water Utilities, Am Water Works Asn, 90; Water Saving Gardening-Taylors Guide, Houghton-Mifflin, 90

BALL, LILLIAN
SCULPTOR
b Augusta, Maine, Jan 6, 1955. *Study:* Inst Bellas Artes, San Miguel Allende, Mex, 71; Nordenfjords Verdens Univ, Copenhagen, BA, 72; Harvard Univ, Cambridge, 75-76; Parsons Sch Design, NY, 78; Columbia Univ, NY, 84-85; New Sch Soc Res, NY, 85. *Work:* Mus Contemp Art, MAMCO, Geneva, Switzerland; Progressive Insurance Corp, Cleveland, Ohio; Bingham, Dana & Gould Attorneys, Boston, MA; Andre Emmerich Sculpture Park, Pawling, NY; William Patterson Col, Patterson, NJ. *Exhib:* Sculpture Forms, Aldrich Mus Contemp Art, 80; solo exhibs, Socrates Sculpture Park, Long Island, NY, 89, Snug Harbor Cult Ctr, Staten Island, NY, 89, Hudson River Mus, Yonkers, NY, 90, Rubin Spangle Gallery, New York, 92 & Sculpture Ctr (with catalog), NY, 95, Support systems, Queens Mus/Bulova, 98, On the Waterfront, Liberty State Park, Jersey City, NJ, 99, Joselyn Naef Fine Art, Lillian Ball, Waterworks, Montreal Canada, 2002; Chateau Chazelles, France, 95; The Transformal, Vienna Secession, Austria, 96; Object Art/Art Object, Elga Wimmer Gallery, NY, 96; Abstract/Real, Mus Mod Art, Vienna, 96; Abstracted & Unfixed, Art in General, NY, 97; Formes du simple, MAMCO Genva, Annemasse, France, 97; Real fiction, Wigmore Fine Art, London, 98; Tick, Tick, Tick, Real Art Ways, Hartford, Conn, 98; 22/21 Vsion, Hofstra Univ, Hempstead, NY, 98; Chromaform, Color in Sculpture, Univ Tex Art Gallery, San Antonio, 98; Achieving Failure Gym Cult, Threadwaxing Space, NY, 2000; many others; Archipeligo, Denver Mus Contemp Art, 2002; Hellsapoppin, Sculpture Exhibition from Coll, MAMCO, Geneva, 2002; Allure Electronica, Wood St Galleries, Pittsburgh, Pa, 2004; 100 Artists See God, Independent Cur Int Contemp Jewish Mus, San Francisco, Ca, 2004; Cuttting Edge, Exploratorium, San Francisco, Ca, 2004. *Pos:* Guest lectr, Boston Univ Prog in Arts, 78, NY Univ Sculpture Dept, 92 & Acad der Kunst, Berlin, 92; asst to Jackie Winsor, NY, 79-80; invited artist, Garner Tullis Monoprints, 87, Santa Barbara, Calif, 87, Urdla Print Publ, Villeurbanne, France, 91 & Int Contemp Art Cruise, France, Spain, Italy, 91; adjudicator, Conn State Sculpture Grants, Hartford, 88; panelist, Dooley Cappelaine Gallery, 92 & Arts Link-Citizen Exchange Coun, NY, 93; collabr, Bioinformatica-Blast 4, X Art Found, 95; artist-in-residence, Pilchuck Glass, Stanwood, Ore, 96; vis artist, guest lectr, UCLA Graduate Dept, Los Angeles, Ca, 2001; grad stud advisor, Maine College Art, Portland, ME, 2002-2003. *Teaching:* vis artist RI Sch Design, 87, NY Univ, 92, Sch Visual Arts, 92, Sch Visual Arts grad dept, New York, 93 & Vt Studio Ctr, Johnson, 93; Instr sculpture, NY Feminist Art Inst, 88-91; visiting artist, guest lectr, RISD, Providence, 98, Vt Studio Ctr, Johnson, 98, The Virutal Life of Sculpture, Mt Holyoke Co, 2000; guest lectr, Col Art Asn, NY, 2000. *Awards:* Sculpture Fel, Nat Endowment Arts, 86-87; Artists Space, Visual Arts Comt, Materials Fund Award, 89; NY Found Arts Grant, 91; John Simon Guggenheim Found Fel in Visual Arts, 99. *Bibliog:* William Zimmer (auth), Mirror of the moment, New York Times, 8/8/98; Edie Newhouse (auth), New York Mag, 8/10/98; Alice Winn (auth), The Female Form, Pulp-Pittsburgh, 2/19/04. *Mem:* NY Artists Equity; Orgn Independent Artists. *Media:* Miscellaneous Media. *Publ:* Auth, Phallus control, Promotional Copy, fall 93; contribr, Time Capsule, NY, 95; auth, The Fantastic, Tema Celeste, spring 96

BALL, SUSAN L
ADMINISTRATOR, HISTORIAN
b Altadena, Calif, May 25, 1947. *Study:* Scripps Col, BA, 69; Univ Calif, Riverside, MA, 74; Yale Univ, PhD, 78. *Collection Arranged:* The Impressionists & the Salon (contribr), Univ Calif, Riverside & LACMA, 74; Richard Brown Baker Collects (contribr), Yale Univ, 75; Rossetti & the Double Work of Art (contribr), Yale Univ, 76. *Pos:* Dir govt & found affairs, Art Inst Chicago, Ill, 85-86; exec dir, Col Art Asn NY, pres, 86-. *Teaching:* Asst prof art hist, Univ Delaware, Newark, 78-81. *Mem:* Am Asn Mus; Art Table; bd mem, Nat Cult Alliance & Nat Humanities Alliance; exec comt mem, Conference Admin Officers Am Coun of Learned Soc. *Res:* Late nineteenth and early twentieth century European painting and architecture. *Publ:* Auth, The impressionists and the salon Los Angeles County Mus, 74; auth, Richard Brown Baker collects (essays), Yale, 75; auth, Works before 1962, Dante Gabriel Rossetti, 76; auth, The early figural paintings of Andre Derain, 1905-1910, Zeitschrift für Kunstgeschichte, 80; auth, Ozenfant and Purism: The evolution of a style 1915-1930, UMI Press, 81

BALLARD, JAMES A
PAINTER, ARCHITECT
b Monticello, NY, Apr 9, 1946. *Study:* Pratt Inst Sch Archit, 63-66; Pratt Inst Sch Fine Art, BFA (cum laude), 71; Columbia Univ, grad studies, 91. *Work:* Mus Mod Art, NY. *Comn:* Studio, Lissom Gallery, London, 97; gallery design, Ricco Manesca Gallery, NY, 97; gallery design, Christine Ruse Gallery, NY, 97; gallery design, John Weber

Gallery, NY, 97; renovation, Elizabeth Found Arts, NY, 98. *Exhib:* Untitled V, Mus Mod Art, NY, 72; Art on Paper, Weatherspoon, Univ NC, Greensboro, 72; Jusmetched Paintings, Brockton Art Ctr, Mass, 73; solo exhibs, Fisch Bach Mus, NY, 73, Race Gallery, Philadelphia, 79, Bova Music Club, NY, 86; Untitled Arc, Fed Plaza, NY, 89; Bird as Critic, Barbara Krakow Gallery, Boston, Mass, 91. *Bibliog:* Jane Coller (auth), review, Art News, 3/73; Nancy Staplen (auth), review, Boston Globe, 7/18/91; David Raymond (auth), review, Art New Eng, 10-11/91. *Media:* Acrylic on Canvas. *Mailing Add:* 315 Church St 3rd Fl New York NY 10013

BALLINGER, JAMES K
MUSEUM DIRECTOR, HISTORIAN
b Kansas City, Mo, July 7, 1949. *Study:* Univ Kans, BA, 1972, MA (art hist), 1974. *Collection Arranged:* Painter in Taos, Eiteljorg Collection, 1980; Visitors to Arizona: 1846-80 (auth, catalog), Phoenix Art Mus, 1980; Charles M Russell (auth, catalog), The Renner Collection, 1981; Dale Eldred: Phoenix Project, 1981; Beyond the Endless River Western Am Drawings & Watercolors (auth, catalog), Phoenix Art Mus, 1979; Am in Brittany and Normandy: 1810-1910, 1982; Peter Hurd: Insight to a Painter (auth, catalog), 1983; Diego Rivera: The Cubist Years, 1984; Frank Lloyd Wright Drawings, Frank Lloyd Found, 1990; Lucy Drake Marlow Traveling Exhib, 1991; Frederic Remington's Southwest Traveling Exhib, Memphis Brooks Mus Art & Joslyn Art Mus, Omaha, Nebr, 1992. *Pos:* Gallery coordr, Tucson Art Ctr, 1973; registrar, Univ Kans Mus Art, Lawrence, 1973-74; cur collections, Phoenix Art Mus, Ariz, 1974-81, asst dir & chief cur, 1981-82, actg dir, 1981-82, Sybil Harrington dir & chief cur, 1982-; juror var exhibs, 1977-89; lectr var mus, 1979-92; bd mem, Balboa Art Conservation Ctr, San Diego, 1981-89. *Awards:* Grants, Nat Endowment Arts, 1977, 1980 & 1987; Flinn Found Grant, 1988; Nat Arts Stabilization Fund Grant, 1989; Nonprofit Dir of the Yr, Orgn Nonprofit Execs Am, 2004. *Mem:* Western Asn Art Mus; Central Ariz Mus Asn; Am Asn Mus; Am Art Mus Dirs (bd dirs 2002-); Nat Coun Arts. *Publ:* Auth, American Painting from the Whitney Mus, Phoenix Art Mus, 1976; Biennial 1979, Phoenix Art Mus, 1979; Frederic Remington, Abrams, 1989. *Mailing Add:* Phoenix Art Mus 1625 N Central Ave Phoenix AZ 85004

BALLOU, ANNE MACDOUGALL See MacDougall, Anne

BALMORI, DIANA
LANDSCAPE ARCHITECT
b Gijon, Spain, Jun 4, 1936. *Study:* Univ Tucuman, Argentina, Diploma in Archit, 60; UCLA, BA in Uban Hist, 68; UCLA, PhD, 73; Radcliffe Univ, student in landscaping, 89. *Pos:* assoc, Cesar Pelli & Assoc, New Haven, 77-81; principal, for landscape and urban design, 81-90; principal, Balmori Assoc, 90-; appointed mem, Comn Fine Arts, 2003; Davenport Chair, of Archit Design Yale Sch of Archit, 2004. *Teaching:* Asst prof, State Univ NY, Oswego, 74-78, assoc prof, 78-79. *Awards:* Grantee Ossabaw Found, 80; res fel NYU, 82; judges Award, Harry Chapin Media Awards, 95. *Mem:* Am Soc Landscape Archits, Catalog of Landscape Records (bd dir, currently); Van Alen Inst (mem exec comt, currently); Am Hist Asn. *Publ:* Auth: Beatrix Farrand, Beatrix Jones Ferrand (1872-1959) Fifty Yrs Of Am Landscape Archit, 1982, Beatrix Farrand's Am Landscapes, 1985, Transitory Gardens, Uprooted Lives, 1993, Redesigning the Am Lawn, 1993, Saarinen House and Garden: A Total Work of Art, 1995; contribr Beatrix Farrand At Dumbarton Oaks: The Design Process of a Garden; co-auth: The Land and Nat Development (LAND) Code: Guidelines for Environmentally Sustainable Land Development

BALOSSI, JOHN
SCULPTOR, PAINTER
b Staten Island, NY, May 28, 1931. *Study:* Columbia Univ, BFA & MA. *Work:* Mus Mod Art, Finch Coll Mus & Chase Manhattan, NY; Ponce Mus, PR; Mus Art, Ft Lauderdale, Fla. *Comn:* Mural, Student Union Bldg, Univ PR, 69; aluminum wall relief, Inst Puerto Rican Cult, 71; mural, CRUV Pub Housing, Manati, PR, 72; mural, Pan Am Games, San Juan, 79. *Exhib:* Sculpture in Clay from Puerto Rico, Mus Fine Arts, Springfield, Mass, 80; Art Mus STex, Corpus Christi, 80; Newark Mus, 81; Bacardi Gallery, Miami, Fla, 81; 39th & 40th Int Competition of Artistic Ceramics, Faenza, Italy, 81 & 82; Solo exhib, paintings, Columbian Quincentennary Celebration, Genoa, Italy, 92. *Teaching:* Assoc prof fine arts, Univ PR, Rio Piedras, formerly. *Awards:* Ateneo Puertorriqueno Award, San Juan, 67; UNESCO Salon Award, San Juan, 74 & 79; R J Reynolds Tobacco Co Award, San Juan, 79. *Bibliog:* Gottfried Borrmann (auth), Keramik der Welt, Kunst & Handwerk, Vertagsanstalt, Dusseldorf, 81; Myrna Rodrigues (auth), Balossi: A Selection of His Work from 1960-1982, 82; Charlotte F Speight (auth), Images in Clay Sculpture, Harper & Row, 83. *Media:* Clay fired; Acrylic on Canvas, Paper. *Dealer:* Studio B 865 49 St SE Reparto Metro San Juan PR 00921. *Mailing Add:* 865 49th St SE Reparto Metro San Juan PR 00921

BALSLEY, JOHN GERALD
PAINTER, SCULPTOR
b Cleveland, Ohio, Apr 15, 1944. *Study:* Univ Americas, 65; Ohio Northern Univ, BA, 67; Northern Ill Univ, MFA, 69. *Work:* St Louis Mus Art, Mo; Nelson-Atkins Gallery, Kansas City, Mo; Des Moines Art Ctr, Iowa; Joslyn Mus Art, Omaha, Nebr; Univ Iowa Art Mus, Iowa City. *Exhib:* Allan Stone Gallery, NY, 72, 74, 76, 78; solo exhibs, Madison Art Ctr, Wis, 79, Univ Del, 79, Frumpkin-Struve Gallery, Chicago, Ill, 79 & 80, New Gallery Contemp Art, Cleveland, 80 & Rahr-West Mus, Manitowoc, Wis, 82; Sheldon Mem Art Gallery, Univ Nebr, Lincoln, 82; Yarres Gallery, Scottsdale, Ariz, 83; Birmingham Art Mus, 83, 87 & 88; Painting & Sculpture Today, Indianapolis Mus Art, Ind, 76; Realisms, Ulrich Mus, Wichita State Univ, 76; Chicago Vicinity Show, Art Inst Chicago, 77; Michael Lord Gallery, Milwaukee, Wis, 91; Perimeter Gallery, Chicago, Ill, 91; Morgan Gallery, Kansas City, Mo, 96; SOFA, Chicago, Ill, 99. *Teaching:* Prof sculpture, Univ Wis-Milwaukee, 76-. *Awards:* Louis Comfort Tiffany Found Grant, 72; Nat Endowment Arts Grant, 72 & 80; Univ Wis, Milwaukee Grant, 78; Milwaukee Artists Found Grants, 82 & 87. *Bibliog:* Lou Dunkak (auth), Balsley sculptures explore man and machines, Arts, 12/76; Josh Kind (auth), Model art: The intimate environment, New Art Examr, 1/78; Betty Kaufman (auth), John Balsley at Allan Stone, Art World, 1/78; Article in Artspeak, 97. *Mem:* Coll Art Asn Am. *Media:* Welded Metal, Wood. *Dealer:* Perimeter Gallery Chicago IL; Michael Lord Gallery Milwaukee WI. *Mailing Add:* 8325 N Cedarburg Rd Milwaukee WI 53209-1526

BALTZ, LEWIS
PHOTOGRAPHER
b Newport Beach, Calif, Sept 12, 1945. *Study:* San Francisco Art Inst, BFA, 69; Claremont Grad Sch, MFA, 71. *Work:* Mus Mod Art, Metrop Mus Art, NY; Art Inst Chicago; Los Angeles Mus Contemp Art; Victoria & Albert Mus, London; Nat Gallery Australia, Mod Museet, Stockholm; Palazzo Fortuny, Venice, Italy; Nat Mus Mod Art, Kyoto; and 60 other collections in US, Canada, Australia, Europe & Japan. *Comn:* Courthouse, Joseph E Seagrams Co, 76; American Images, Am Tel & Telgr Co, 78; Nev State Arts Comn, 86; La Mission photographique, Datar, France, 86; Toshiba Project, Japan, 89; Linea di Confine, Reggio Emilia, Italy, 91. *Exhib:* Corcoran Gallery Art, 74-76; Philadelphia Coll Art, 75; Mus Fine Arts, Houston, 76; San Francisco Mus Mod Art, 81; RI Sch Design, 83; Univ Art Mus, Univ Calif, Berkeley, 84; Victoria & Albert Mus, London, 85; Ringling Mus, Sarasota, Fla, 91; Des Moines Art Ctr, Iowa, 91; Los Angeles City Mus Art, Calif, 92; solo exhibs, Centre Pompidou, Paris, 92, Galerie Michelle Chomette, Paris, 93, Mus de Cahors, France, 93, Fotomuseum Winterthur, Switz, 93, Mus Art Mod Paris, 93, Janet Borden, Inc, NY, 93 & La Mus Mod Art, Humlebaek, Denmark, 94. *Teaching:* Vis prof, Univ Calif, Riverside, 90; vis art, Calif Inst Arts, 92; vis artist, Yale Univ, 92; vis artist, Ecole des Beaux Arts, Paris, 92. *Awards:* Nat Endowment Arts Fel, 73 & 77; Guggenheim Mem Found Fel in Photography, 77; Charles Pratt Mem Award, 91. *Bibliog:* Paul Hill (auth), Approaching Photography, Focal Press, London & Boston, 82; Dr Naomi Rosenblum (auth), The World History of Photography, Abbeville Press, NY, 85; Estelle Jussim (coauth Elizabeth Lindquist-Coci), Landscape As Photograph: Reflections on Nature, 85; Ideology, Yale Univ Press, New Haven, 85; Arthur Rothstein (auth), Documentary Photography, p 131, Stoneham, Mass, 86. *Publ:* Auth, Candlestick Point, 89; Giocchi di Simulazione, 91; Rule Without Exception, 91; Ronde de Nuit, 92; Lewis Baltz: 5 Projects, Stedelijk Mus. *Dealer:* Janet Borden Inc 560 Broadway New York NY 10012; Stephen Wirtz Gallery 49 Geary Blvd San Francisco CA 94102. *Mailing Add:* 23 Rue Des Blancs Mantgaux 94966 Paris France 75004

BALZEKAS, STANLEY, JR
MUSEUM DIRECTOR, COLLECTOR
b Chicago, Ill, Oct 8, 1924. *Study:* DePaul Univ, BA, 50, MA, 51. *Pos:* Pres, Balzekas Mus Lithuanian Cult, Chicago, Ill, 66-; advisory bd mem, Chicago Dept of Cult Affairs, 79-. *Collection:* 18th-19th century oils by European masters; contemporary graphics and sculptures. *Mailing Add:* c/o Balzekas Museum Lithuanian Culture 6500 S Pulaski Rd Chicago IL 60629

BANAS, ANNE
PAINTER, EDUCATOR
b Long Beach, Calif, Dec 9, 1948. *Study:* Orange Coast Col, 67-69; Calif State Univ, Fullerton, BA, 71; Claremont Grad Sch, MFA, 74. *Work:* Security Pac Bank, Santa Barbara, Beverly Hills & La Jolla, Calif; Eastern NMex Univ, Roswell; Daytona Beach Int Airport, Barnett Bank, Accordia Corp, Fla; Vistacon, Fla. *Comn:* Profiler's 90 (mural), Daytona Beach Int Airport, Jacksonville, Fla, 92; Jacksonville Jaguars & City of Jacksonville (mural), 94; First Union Bank & Jacksonville Jaguars (mural, 98 x 215), 98. *Exhib:* One woman shows, Grandview Gallery, Los Angeles, 75, Art Rental Gallery, Santa Barbara Mus Art, 78, Alice Benjamin Gallery, Santa Barbara, 80 & Hills Gallery, Santa Fe, 81; Selections from Roswell, Albuquerque Downtown Ctr Arts, 81; Southwest Invitational, Midland Col, Tex, 84; Gallery 88, Jacksonville, Fla, 90; Fla Community Col, Jacksonville, 91; Contemporania Gallery, Jacksonville, Fla, 91 & 93; Orlando Mus Art, 92; Jacksonville Univ, 95 & 97; Fla Community Coll, Kent, 2004. *Pos:* Founding mem, steering comt, Grandview Gallery, Los Angeles, 73-75; founding mem, Double X, educational art orgn, Los Angeles, 75; dir, art in the community, Santa Barbara Mus, Calif, 77-78; art dept coordr, Fla Community Coll, Kent, 90-present. *Teaching:* Instr painting & drawing, West Los Angeles City Col, 75-77; instr painting, drawing, art hist & printmaking, Eastern NMex Univ, Roswell, 82-89; prof art, Fla Community Col, Jacksonville, Fla, 89-. *Awards:* Outstanding Fac, Fla Community Coll, Jacksonville, 2006; Fac Excellence Award, Univ Tex, Austin, 2006. *Bibliog:* Kalliope, Vol XIV, No 2, 5/92. *Media:* Oil. *Mailing Add:* 1775 Forest Blvd Jacksonville FL 32216

BAND, DAVID MOSHE
PAINTER, ART DEALER
b Portland, Maine, Oct 16, 1947. *Study:* Self taught. *Work:* First Texas Savings, Dallas, Tex; The Dunnegan Gallery of Art, Bolivar, Mo; Wichita Falls (Tex) Teacher's Credit Union; Davie Mus and Cult Ctr, Wellesley (Mass) Col; Mus Tex Tech Univ, Lubbock; Springfield Art Mus, Mo; and others. *Exhib:* 169th Ann Exhib, Nat Acad Design, 94, 175th, 2000 & 179th, 2004; 79th Ann Exhib Allied Artists Am, Nat Arts Club, Gramercy Park, NY, 92, 81st, 94, 85th, 98, 86th, 99 & 87th, 2000-2004; retrospective, Wichita Falls (Tex) Mus & Art Ctr, 95; Watercolor USA, Springfield (Mo) Mus Art, 99, 2000, 2002, 2004; 63rd Ann Midyear Exhib, Butler Inst Am Art, Youngstown, Ohio, 99 & 64th, 2000, 65th, 2001, 66th, 2002, 67th, 2003, 68th, 2004; Membership Exhib, Nat Watercolor Soc, Glendale, Calif, 2000; 58th Ann Exhib Audubon Aritsts, Salmagundi Club, NY, 2000. *Pos:* Dir, Eden Gallery, Wichita Falls, Tex. *Teaching:* Instr, Wichita Falls Mus & Art Ctr, 73-74 & N Tex Artists Guild, 84-. *Awards:* Kent Day Coes Mem Award, Watercolor, 91st annual exhib, Allied Artists of Am, 2004; William A Paton Prize for Watercolor, Nat Acad Design, 2004; Audubon Artists Gold Medal of Honor, 63d Ann Exhib, 2005; Genevieve Cain Award for watercolor, 107th Exhib Nat Arts Club, 2006; Ogden Pleissner Mem Award, Salmagundi Club, 2007; D Wu & Elsie Ject Key Mem Award, Salmagundi Club, 2007; Robert L Johnson Mem Award, Watercolor USA, Springfield, MO, 2008; Macowin Tuttle, Memorial Award, Salmagundi Club, NY, 2008; Samuel O King

Award, Watercolor USA, Springfield Mus, Springfield MO, 2009; Samuel O King Award, Prints USA, Springfield Mus, Springfield, MO, 2009; SCNY Purchase Prize, Salmagundi Club, NY, 2009; Martin Hannon Mem Award, Salmagundi Club, 2009; Grumbacher Gold Medallion, Nat Arts Club, NY, 2010; Loring W Coleman Award for Watercolor, 98th Ann Exhib, Allied Artists Am, 2011. *Mem:* Allied Artists Am; Artists' Fel; Watercolor USA Hon Soc; Nat Watercolor Soc (signature mem); Audubon Artists Inc; Salmagundi Club; Nat Arts Club. *Media:* Watercolor, Acrylic, Printmaking. *Specialty:* American prints 1900-1950. *Interests:* restoration of works on paper. *Publ:* Splash II, Americas Best Contemporary Watercolors, North Light & Writer's Dig Bks, 92; auth, Inspirations and Ideas In: Splash II, America's Best Contemporary Watercolors, 93, Splash III, 105 Americas Best Contemporary Watercolors Show and Tell How They Find Their Inspirations and Ideas, North Light & Writer's Dig Bks, 94, Splash IV, America's Best Contemporary Watercolorists, 96; contribr, 10th anniversary issue, Art's Mag, 1/94; Catching the drift of snow, Artists' Mag, 2/95, Landscape basics, Clearing the way to clouds, 10/99, Landscape basics, Shaping realistic rocks, 12/99, Landscape basics, The Laws of Light, 7/2000, Landscape basics, Harnessing Nature's elements, 12/2000. *Mailing Add:* 1903 Eden Ln Wichita Falls TX 76306

BANDES, SUSAN JANE
MUSEUM DIRECTOR, EDUCATOR
b New York, NY, Oct 18, 1951. *Study:* NYU, BA, 71; Bryn Mawr Coll, MA, 73, PhD, 78; Mus Mgmt Inst, Berkeley, Calif, 90. *Collection Arranged:* Affordable Dreams: The Goetsch-Winckler House by Frank Lloyd Wright, 90; Maria de Medici Enters Amsterdam: prints by Pieter Nolpe, 95-96; Abraham Rattner in the Tampa Mus of Art Collection (auth, catalog), Tampa Mus Art, 97; Pursuits & Pleasures: Barogue Painting from Detroit Ins of Arts, 2003-04; Circulating Mich Exhib, 2003-04; Am Modernism, 1920's-1940's, 2010; East Lansing Modern, 1940-1970; MSU Mus, 2013. *Pos:* Proj dir, Am Asn Mus, Washington, DC, 83-84; prog off, J Paul Getty Trust Grant Prog, Los Angeles, 84-86; bd dir, Mich Mus Asn, 87-92; coun, Mich Coun for Humanities, 88-92; dir, Kresge Art Mus, 86-2010. *Teaching:* Asst prof, Sweet Briar Coll, Va, 78-83; prof, Kresge Art Mus, Mich State Univ, E Lansing, 86-, co-dir, mus studies. *Awards:* Whiting Fel, 76-77; Am Philos Soc, 81; Publ Award AIA, 90. *Mem:* Nat Inst for Conserv (treas, 86-90); Mich Mus Asn (bd dir's, 1987-92); Mich Coun for Humanities (coun, 1988-92); Mich Alliance for Conserv (treas, 94-96, pres, 98-2000). *Res:* Baroque Art Am, 1920-40's, Frank Llyd Wright. *Publ:* Ed, The Prints of John S. de Martelly: 1903-1979; auth & ed, Caring for Collections, 84; Affordable Dreams: The Goetsch-Winckler House and Frank Lloyd Wright, 91; Abraham Rattner (auth), The Tampa Mus of Art Collection, 97; auth & cur, Pursuits and Pleasures: Baroque Painting from the Detroit Inst of Arts, 2003; contribr, articles in prof jour; Am Modernism, 1920s-1940s, 2010. *Mailing Add:* Mich State Univ Kresge Art Center Dept Art & Art History 600 Auditorium Rd East Lansing MI 48824

BANDY, GARY
PAINTER, EDUCATOR
b Pontiac, Mich, May 10, 1944. *Study:* Oakland Univ, BA, 65; Columbia Univ, MFA, 68. *Work:* Norton Simon Inc & Muriel Siebert, NY, New Sch Social Res, NY; St Peter's Col, Jersey City, NJ. *Exhib:* Solo exhibs, Herbert H Lehman Coll Gallery, Bronx, NY, 79 & F Marino Gallery, NY, 82, Charles Cowles Gallery, NY, 2007; Group exhib, Artists Market, Detroit, Mich, 64; Aldrich Mus Contemp Art, Ridgefield, Conn, 74; Large Drawings, Independent Curators Inc traveling, 85-86; and others. *Teaching:* Adj instr art hist, St Peter's Col, Jersey City, NJ, 68-72; lectr & workshop instr, Mus Mod Art, NY, 77-. *Awards:* Artist's Fel, Nat Endowment Arts, 83. *Bibliog:* Review, Art News, 9/74; Palmer Poroner (auth), review, Art Speak, 4/80; Susan Filen Yeh (auth), Gary Bandy, Arts Mag, 4/82. *Media:* Acrylic. *Dealer:* Fawbush Gallery New York NY. *Mailing Add:* 118 W 29th St New York NY 10001-5301

BANDY, MARY LEA
EDITOR, ADMINISTRATOR
b Evanston, Ill, June 16, 1943. *Study:* Stanford Univ, BA, 65. *Pos:* Asst ed, Harry N Abrams, New York, 67-73; assoc coordr exhibs, Mus Mod Art, New York, 76-78, dir film dept, 80-2006. *Publ:* Ed, Rediscovering French film (catalog), Mus Mod Art, 83; Michael Balcon (catalog), Mus Mod Art, 84. *Mailing Add:* Museum Modern Art 11 W 53rd St New York NY 10019

BANE, MCDONALD (MACKEY)
PAINTER, CURATOR
b Bland, Va, Mar 1, 1928. *Study:* Va Polytech Inst & State Univ, BS, 49; Univ NC, Greensboro, with Gregory Ivy & John Opper, MFA, 59. *Work:* Mus Mod Art, NY; Weatherspoon Art Gallery, Greensboro, NC; Mint Mus Art, Charlotte, NC; US Dept State, Washington, DC; E Carolina Univ Sch Art. *Comn:* Painting, Philip Morris Co, Salisbury, NC, 82. *Exhib:* Okla Art Ctr, Oklahoma City, 70; Contemp Am Drawings V, Smithsonian Inst, traveling, 71-74; NC Mus Art, Raleigh, NC, 76; Univ Evansville, Ind, 76; solo exhibs, Southeastern Ctr Contemp Art, Winston-Salem, NC, 80 & Univ Ga Art Gallery, Athens, 81; McDonald Dane Retrospective, A Survey of 65 Yrs in Art, 2013. *Collection Arranged:* Collections Arranged Gregory Ivy Watercolors, 1938-1949, Raleigh, Greensboro & Hickory, NC, 96. *Pos:* Cur exhibs, Southeastern Ctr Contemp Art, Winston-Salem, NC, 77-80; exhib coord, The Arts Coun, Winston-Salem, NC, 80-91. *Teaching:* Asst prof, Calif State Univ, Fullerton, 66-68; instr, NC Sch Arts, Winston-Salem, 70-73; asst prof, Southern Ill Univ, Carbondale, 73-76; vis assoc prof, Va Polytech Inst & State Univ, 80. *Awards:* Best Show, Southeastern Ctr Contemp Art 39th Painting & Sculpture Competition, 73. *Media:* Oil. *Publ:* Ed, The Southeast Seven II, 78, Paper Making and Paper Using, 79, Art Patron Art, 79 & Southeast Seven III, 79 (catalogs), Southeastern Ctr Contemp Art, Winston-Salem, NC; auth, Oliver Lee Jackson & The SECCA/WFU/NCSA Prog, Arts J, 80; Corp Art Collections, NC, R J Reynolds Indust, Art J, 83. *Dealer:* Lee Hansley Gallery 225 Glenwood Ave Raleigh NC 27603. *Mailing Add:* 3424 Avent Ferry Rd New Hill NC 27562-9298

BANERJEE, (BIMAL)
PAINTER, SCULPTOR
b Calcutta, India, Sept 4, 1939; US citizen. *Study:* Indian Coll Art, Calcutta, DFA (first class hon), 55-60; Coll Art, New Delhi, Indian Govt Nat Cult Scholar, 65-67; Atelier 17, Paris, Fr Govt Grant, 67-69; Ecole des Beaux Arts, Paris, Fr Govt Grant & cert of grad study, 67-70; Pratt Inst Exten, NY, inst grants & cert of post grad study, 69 & 70-72; NY Univ, with H W Jensen, 76; Columbia Univ MA, 80, EdM, 81, EdD, 88. *Work:* Mus Mod Art, Paris; Mus Fine Arts, Boston; Brooklyn Mus of Art; Nat Gallery Mod Art, New Delhi; Radford Univ Mus, Va; plus many others. *Comn:* Mural with five panels, comn by Mario Manto, Levanto, Italy, 68; mural with three panels, Proj Find Clinton Sr Citizens Ctr, NY, 79; Silk Screen Proj, NY & NJ Port Authority, CCF/CETA Artists Proj, NY, 79; plus others. *Exhib:* Paris Biennale, Mus Mod Art, Paris, 68; Salon de Mayo, Mus Modern Art, Barcelona, 1969; Montreal Mus Fine Art, Montreal, 1971; Tokyo Biennial, Mus Mod Art, Tokyo, 72; Brooklyn Mus Biennial, 72-73 & 81; World Print Competition, San Francisco Mus Mod Art, 77-79; Inter-Grafik Triennale, Berlin, 84; 42 Solo exhibs, incl Galerie du Haut Pavé, Paris, 68, Columbia Univ, 78-79 & 84, Art Heritage Gallery, New Delhi, Chitrakoot Art Gallery, Calcutta, 90 & Bertha Urdang Gallery, NY, 91, Chemould Gallery, Calcutta, 93 & Cité Int des Arts, Paris, 94; Ljubljana Biennial, Mus Mod Art, Ljubljana, Yugoslavia, 87; Kanagawa Biennial, Knagawa, Japan, 90, 92; Cite Int des Art, Paris, 94, 99; Millennium Art Collection Exhib, 2000 Found, Diemen, The Neth, 2000. *Pos:* Therapist, art & educ, St John's Episcopal Hosp, Far Rockaway, NY, 81-83; art consult, New York City Bd Educ, 83-84; founding mem, Bill Clintons presidential Foundation, Little Rock, Ark; founding mem, Wall of Tolerance, Nat Campaign for Tolerance, Montgomery, Ala; founding sponsor mem, Martin Luther King Jr, Nat Mem Found, Nat Mall, Washington, DC. *Teaching:* Vis asst teacher graphics, Nat Acad Fine Arts, NY, 69; guest lectr, Parsons Sch Design, NY, 79; lectr philos educ, Bloomfield Col, NJ, 80-81, New Sch Social Res, Parsons Sch Design, NY, 83-88, New York City Bd Educ, 83-2001; Columbia Univ, Teachers' Col, 88. *Awards:* World Cult Prize, Statue of Victory for Arts, Letters & Sciences, Nat Ctr Study & Res, Salsomaggiore, Italy, 84; Grant Award, Adolph and Esther Gottueb Found, NY, 89-90; Change Inc Grant, Robert Rauschenberg's Found, Captiva, Fla, 2010; Artists' Fellowship Inc grant, NYC, 2010. *Bibliog:* Fumage Works on Paper, catalog for the one-person show of Banerjee, 90, Banerjee's Fumages: Behind the Smoke Screen, Art Heritage Gallery, New Delhi, 90; Arther Jones (auth), Permanent Coll Expo Catalogue, Univ Va, 2000; Basu Chitralekha (auth), Fire & Smoke, Statesman, Calcuta, 8/26/2000; Sebanti Sarkar (auth), Still Smoldering, Statesman, Calcutta, 1/18/2004. *Mem:* Bill Clinton Pres Found (founding mem); Nat Campaign for Tolerance (founding mem); Martin Luther King Jr Nat Memorial Found (founding mem). *Media:* Fumage; Carbontransfer. *Publ:* Coauth, Mine, 64; contribr, Revolutionist Master-Artist Henri Matisse, 70, Painter Sonia Delaunay, 70, Metaphysical Master-Artist de Chirico, 72 & Picasso, 82; Contemporary Artists of New York, 93; Picasso, 82; and many others; and others. *Dealer:* Bertha Urdang Gallery 23 E 74th St New York NY 10021; RoGallery 47-15 36th St Long Island City NJ 11101. *Mailing Add:* Loft 2C 106 Ridge St New York NY 10002-2554

BANGERT, COLETTE STUEBE
PAINTER
b Columbus, Ohio, July 7, 1934. *Study:* John Herron Art Inst, BFA, 57; Boston Univ, MFA, 58; Ind Univ; Kans Univ. *Work:* Mulane Art Mus, Topeka, Kans; Mus Mod Art, NY; Univ Okla Mus Art, Norman; Springfield Art Mus, Mo; Sheldon Mem Art Gallery, Lincoln, Nebr; Spencer Art Mus, Univ Kans, Lawrence; Victoria and Albert Mus, London, Eng; Block Mus of Art, Northwestern Univ, Evanston, Ill; Kunsthalle Bremen, Germany; Muscarelle Mus Art, Coll William & Mary, Williamsburg, Va. *Comn:* Grassland Garden, Topeka Pub Libr, 69 & Landlace: Greening III, Townsite Eatery, 77, Topeka, Kans. *Exhib:* Solo exhibs, HL Liber Gallery, Recent Work, Indianapolis, 57, 58, Sheldon Mem Art Gallery, Lincoln, Nebr, 78 & Albrecht Art Mus, Mo, 84, Krasner Gallery, New York City, 63, 80, The Garden Series: Works on Paper and Thread Pieces, Lawrence Arts Ctr, Kans, 2002 & Kans Governor's Offices, Topeka, 2005, Land Thread Line, Trinity Episcopal Church, Lawrence, Kans, 2008, All.Go.Rhythm, Ukrainian Inst of Modern Art, Chgo, Ill, 2015; Computer Art, Ben Shahn Galleries, Wayne, NJ, 85; ACM Siggraph 86 Art Show: A Twenty Year Computer Art Retrospective, Dallas, Tex & ACM Siggraph 98 Art Show: 25 Year Art Exhib Celebration, Orlando, Fla; Computers and Art, Everson Mus Art, Syracuse, NY & IBM Gallery, NY; Second Emerging Expression Biennial: The Artist and the Computer, Bronx Mus Art, 87; Computer and Video Art, Southern Alleghenies Mus Art, 88; At the Speed of Thought: Two Dimensional Algorithmic Art, Print Club, Philadelphia, Pa, 89; In context: Digital Expressions, Kans State Univ Gallery, Manhattan, 92; A Selection from the Series: The Garden That Was, Kansas City Artists Coalition, Mo, 95; Sumptuous Surfaces/Structured Surfaces, Mulvane Art Mus, Topeka, Kans, 97; Nine Connections, Alice C Sabatini Gallery, & Shawnee Cty Public Libr, Topeka, Kans, 2004; Recent Works on Paper and A Thread Piece, Fields Gallery, Lawrence, Kans, 2006; Imaging by Numbers: A Historical View of the Computer Print, Block Mus of Art, Northwestern Univ, Evanston, Ill, 2008; Cryptograph: An Exhibition for Alan Turing, Spencer Art Mus, Univ Kansas, Lawrence, 2012. *Teaching:* Art instr, Ferry Hall Sch Girls, Lake Forest, Ill, 58-59, Avila Coll, Kansas City, Mo, 69-72; drawing instr Univ Mo, Kansas City, 72-74. *Bibliog:* Allan Millstein (auth), Artist abstracts Kansas terrain, Topeka Capital J, 7/14/79; Patrick White (auth), Colette Bangert, New Art Examiner, 5/83; Carolyn McMaster (auth), Personal Visions, Lawrence J World, 9/14/86; Judy Malloy (ed), Women, Art and Technology, 2003; Patric D Prince (auth, MIT pres), Women and The Search for Visual Intelligence, 2003. *Mem:* Kansas City Artists Coalition (pres, 77-78); Imagination & Place Comt, Lawrence, Kans, 2002-. *Media:* Mixed Painting and Drawing, Computer Algorithmic Drawing, Thread Pieces. *Publ:* Coauth, Experiences in making drawings by computer and by hand, Leonardo, 74; illusr, Appreciating Poetry (ed, R P Sugg), Houghton Mifflin, 75; coauth, Computer grass is natural grass, In: Artist and Computer (ed, Ruth Leavitt), Harmony Bks, 76; A short story, In: The Visual Computer (ed, Herbert Franke), Int J Computer Graphics, 86. *Mailing Add:* 721 Tennessee Lawrence KS 66044

BANKER, MAUREEN
DIRECTOR, PRINTMAKER
b Bayonne, NJ. *Study:* Meredith Col, Raleigh, BA, 79; Grad Sch Fine Art, Villa Schifanoia, Florence, Italy, MA (printmaking), 85. *Work:* Munic Bldg Sansepolcro, Italy, Tuscany; Ill Bisonte Graphic Studio & Gallery, Florence, Italy; Meredith Col, Raleigh. *Exhib:* Triennial Int Print Exhib, Clermont-Ferrand, France, 94. *Pos:* Dir galleries, Meredith Col, Raleigh, 90-. *Teaching:* Instr art, Ravenscroft Sch, Raleigh, 80-85; asst prof art & printmaking, Meredith Col, Raleigh, 90-. *Awards:* City Raleigh Emerging Artist Award, 95. *Mem:* United Arts Coun, Raleigh. *Media:* Multiplate Color, Intaglio Etching. *Mailing Add:* Meredith Col 3800 Hillsborough St Raleigh NC 27607-5298

BANKOWSKY, JACK
CRITIC, CURATOR
Exhib: Pop Life, Tate Modern. *Pos:* Editor-in-chief, Artforum, 1992-2004, art critic, editor-at-large, 2004-; founding editor, Bookforum, 1996-98, now editorial dir; mem adv bd, graduate studies program in criticism and theory, Art Ctr Coll Design; freelance critic and curator. *Teaching:* Vis scholar, Yale Sch Art, 2004, 2005, UCLA, 2008. *Mailing Add:* Artforum 350 Seventh Ave New York NY 10001

BANKS, ALLAN R
PAINTER
b Dearborn, Mich, Feb 15, 1948. *Study:* Sch Fine Arts, Detroit, Mich, 66-68; Atelier of Richard F Lack, Minneapolis, 70-73; R H Ives Gammell Studios, Boston, 76. *Work:* Wadsworth Atheneum, Hartford; Springville Mus Art, Utah; Vixseboxse Galleries, Cleveland Heights, Ohio. *Comn:* Dr James McBride (portrait), Friends of Bowling Green State Univ, Huron, Ohio; two portraits, Hamilton Fish Found, Garrison, NY, 81; five portraits of corporate chairmen, Brush-Wellman Corp, Cleveland, 84; Dr Algalee Adams (portrait), Friends of Bowling Green State Univ, Huron, Ohio, 85. *Exhib:* Butler Inst Am Art, Youngstown, Ohio, 77; Grand Cent Art Founders Show, Grand Cent Galleries, New York, 81; Art Expo, Nat Coun Jewish Women, Teaneck, NJ, 82; Classical Realism, Amarillo Art Ctr, Tex, 82. *Pos:* Dir, Atelier of Plein Air Studies, 91-; pres, Banks Studios LGC. *Awards:* E T Greenshields Award, Greenshields Found, Montreal, 72 & 73; Stacey Award, Stacey Found, NMex, 74; Gold Medal, April Salon, Springville Mus Art, Utah, 82. *Bibliog:* Helen Cullinan (auth) Current day Sargent, Cleveland Plain Dealer, 82; Richard Lack (auth), article, in: Realism in Revolution, Taylor, Dallas, 85; artist subject of film profile, Bowling Green State Univ, Ohio, 85. *Mem:* New Am Acad Art, New York; Soc Classical Realism, Minn; Art Rev Ctr. *Media:* Oil. *Specialty:* Figurative painting. *Publ:* Cover, feature & biog, Am Artist mag, 8/87; publ, Salon Am J. *Dealer:* Vixseboxse Art Galleries 12413 Cedar Rd Cleveland Heights OH 44106; Tree's Place Gallery, Cape Cod, MA; REHS Galleries NY NY. *Mailing Add:* PO Box 145 Safety Harbor FL 34695-0145

BANKS, ANNE JOHNSON
PAINTER, EDUCATOR
b New London, Conn, Aug 10, 1924. *Study:* Wellesley Coll, BA, 46; Honolulu Sch Art, with Willson Stamper, 48-50; George Washington Univ, with Thomas Downing, MFA, 68, sculpture with Jim Sanborn, 78-80. *Work:* Am Soc Advancement Sci; Northern Va Community Coll; Nat Mus Women Arts; George Washington Univ, Acad del Arte, Montecatini, Italy; Va Ctr for Creative Arts; New Brit Mus Am Art. *Exhib:* Solo exhibs, Lyman Allyn Mus, New London Conn, 64, Alexandria Art League, 73, Foundry Gallery, Washington, DC, 78, 81, 83 & 86, Gallery 10 Ltd, Washington, DC, 93-97, 99, 2001-2002 & 2005-2009; Group exhibs, Hyatt Regency Competition, 81; Va Mus, Richmond, 83; Chrysler Mus, Norfolk, Va, 88; Vartai Gallery, Vilnius, Lithuania, 94, Gallery Riva Sinistra, Florence, Italy, 97; Phoenix Gallery, New York, 98; Washington Square, Washington, DC, 2000-2002; Amos Eno Gallery, New York, 2001; Venice Prato, Florence, Italy, 2001-2002 & Pistoia, Montecatini, Italy; Wisconsin Ave Studios, 2011. *Collection Arranged:* The Cabinet, Katzen Studios, Wisconsin Av, Wash DC. *Pos:* Chair visual arts, Northern Va Community Coll, 73-89; retired. *Teaching:* Lectr art, George Washington Univ, summer 68; instr art, George Mason Univ, 68-69, Northern Va Community Coll, 71-72, asst prof, 73-80, chmn dept, 73-89, assoc prof, 80-89, prof emer, 90. *Awards:* Six Merit Awards, Art League, Alexandria, Va, 71-74; Merit Award, Northern Va Fine Arts Asn, 72; Va Ctr Creative Arts Fel, Sweetbriar, 82, 85 & 92; Merit Award Arlington Arts Ctr, 2000. *Mem:* Womens Caucus Art; Alexandria Art League; Coll Art Asn Am (former mem); Design Forum (former mem). *Media:* Drawing, Mixed Media, Painting, Collage, Sculpture. *Res:* History of design. *Specialty:* Contemporary Fine Art. *Interests:* Travel photog, writing on art/memoirs, stories, essays. *Publ:* Numerous articles in Northern Va Rev, NY Art Rev & Washington Rev Arts between 81, 87, 98, 2002 & 2007; Art Criticism: Washington Review of the Arts, Koan, Articulate Mag; Int Sculpture Mag; auth book, What is Design? x-libris, Kirkus Rev, 2005. *Dealer:* Gallery 10 Ltd Washington DC. *Mailing Add:* Avery Apt 506 705 New Britain Ave Hartford CT 06106

BANKS, ELLEN
PAINTER
Work: Addison Gallery Am Art, Andover, Mass; Atlanta Pub Libr, Ga; Boston Pub Libr; Citicorp, NY; Chicago Art Inst. *Exhib:* One-person exhibs, McIntosh Gallery, Atlanta, Ga, 89, Soho 20, NY, 90, Akin Gallery, Boston, Mass, 90, Amerika Haus, Berlin, 91, Fine Arts Ctr, Neubrandenburg, Ger, 92, Spandow Gallery, Berlin, Ger, 96 & Artist Haus, Erfreut, Ger, 97; Espace Riquet, 90, Centre de Documentation, 90, CC Gallery, Paris, France, 92; Kennesaw State Col, Marietta, Ga, 91; Stephen Rosenberg Gallery, NY, 91; Donahue/Sosinski, Soho, NY, 97. *Teaching:* Prof painting, Sch Mus Fine Arts, Boston. *Awards:* Nat Endowment Arts, Visual Artist Grant, 87; Nexus Press Bk Grant, 88; Mass Artists Fel, 91. *Bibliog:* Addison Parks (auth), The Christian Science Monitor, 1/91; Alicia Faxon (auth), Women Artists News, winter 91; Renee Schipp (auth), Berliner Morgenpost, 92. *Dealer:* McIntosh Gallery Atlanta GA. *Mailing Add:* 329 Park Place Brooklyn NY 11238

BANKS, HOLLY HOPE
PAINTER
b Columbus, Ohio, 1957. *Study:* Univ Toledo, BA, 81; Atelier of Plein-Air Studios, 93-96. *Work:* Butler Inst Am Art, Youngstown, Oh. *Exhib:* Hilton Head Art League, 97; Catharine Lorillard Wolfe Art Club, Ann Exhib, Nat Arts Club, NY, 98-2012, 2013; Ann Exhib, Audubon Artists, Salmagundi Club, New York, 99-2006; Ann Midyear Exhib, Butler Inst Am Art, Youngstown, Ohio, 2000-2001, 2010, 2011, & 2012; Small Works Holiday Exhib, Tree's Place Gallery, Cape Cod, Mass, 2003-2006; and others. *Pos:* Registered copyist, Nat Gallery Art, Washington, DC, 82-85. *Awards:* Art Interests Award, 80; J Paul Dorfmuller Pastel Award, 92; Daler-Rowney Award, Audubon Artists 57th Ann Exhib, Salmagundi Club, NY, 99; Tara Fredrix Canvas Award, Audubon Artists 62nd Ann Exhib, Salmagundi Club, New York, 2004; Col George J Morales Mem Award, Catharine Lorillard Wolfe Art Club, Nat Arts Club, New York, 2004; CLWAC Medal of Hon, Nat Arts Club, New York, 2009, Leila Gardin Sawyer award, 2011; Diane B Barnhard Art Spirit Purchase award, 2011. *Mem:* Am Soc of Classical Realism; Am Artist Prof League; Audubon Artists; Portrait Soc of Am, Inc; Nat Mus of Women in the Arts; Catharine Lorillard Wolfe Art Club. *Media:* Oil & Pastels, Oil. *Specialty:* florals, still life, animal, landscape, figure, portrait. *Publ:* Cover artist, Masterpieces, 1/97; article Am Artist Mag, 10/98 & 2001. *Dealer:* Richard Gandy Gallery of Realistic Art Website Gallery; Rehs Galleries NY. *Mailing Add:* PO Box 233 Safety Harbor FL 34695

BANKS, MARCIA GILLMAN
PAINTER, ILLUSTRATOR
b New York, NY, Feb 20, 1934. *Study:* Parsons Sch Design, 55. *Work:* Montclair Art Mus, NJ. *Comn:* Mural, Cotton Entertainment, Dallas, Tex, 93; mural, Melrose Hotel, Dallas, Tex, 94. *Exhib:* Martin Lawrence Gallery, NY. *Awards:* Generoso Pope Award, NY. *Media:* Acrylic on Canvas. *Collection:* Bank of Am

BANKS, ROBERT HARRIS
ART DEALER, PUBLISHER
b New York, NY, Nov 25, 1957. *Study:* Fla State Univ, BFA, 78. *Pos:* Dealer, Banks Fine Art, currently. *Mem:* Appraisers Asn Am. *Specialty:* 19th and 20th century American & European paintings. *Mailing Add:* 1231 Dragon St Dallas TX 75207

BANNARD, WALTER DARBY
PAINTER, ART WRITER
b New Haven, Conn, Sept 23, 1934. *Study:* Phillips Exeter Acad; Princeton Univ. *Work:* Whitney Mus Am Art, Guggenheim Mus Mod Art, Metrop Mus Art, NY; Albright-Knox Art Gallery, Buffalo, NY; Boston Mus Fine Arts; Houston Mus Fine Arts; plus many others; Risks Mus, Amsterdam, Netherlands. *Exhib:* Whitney Mus Ann, NY, 72; Abstract Painting in the 70's, Mus Fine Arts, Boston, 72; Maj retrospective, Baltimore Mus Art, 73; The Great Decade of American Abstraction, Mus Fine Arts, Houston; Art in America after World War II, Guggenheim Mus, 79; Retrospective, Montclair Mus Art, 91; Lowe Art Mus, Miami, 99; Clement Greenberg: A Critics Collection, Portland Art Mus, Ore, 2001; Recent Acrylic Paintings, The 1912 Gallery, Emory & Henry Coll, Va, 2002; Painting Explosion: 1958-1963, Blanton Mus, Univ Tex, Austin, 2003; Color Field Revisited, Haggerty Mus Art, Marquette Univ, Wis, 2004; Moving into Color, Rauschenberg Gallery, Edison Coll, Ft Myers, Fla, 2006; The Scallop Series, Western Mich Univ, Kalamazoo, Mich, 2006; Minimal Paintings, Jacobson/Howard Gallery, New York, 2007; Born in the USA, Nat Gallery Victoria, Melbourne, Aus, 2007; Color into Light, Mus Fine Arts, Houston, 2009; Abstract USA: 58-68, RIJKS Mus, Amsterdam, Netherlands, 2010; Lowe Art Mus, Coral Gables, Fla, 2012. *Pos:* Contrib ed, Artforum Mag, 73-74; deleg, Europ-Am Assembly Art Mus, England, 75; cur, Hans Hofmann, Hirshhorn Mus, Washington, DC, 76; mem, Int Exhib Comt, 78-79; co-chmn, Nat Endowment Arts Int Comt Visual Arts, 79-81. *Teaching:* Lectr at numerous universities; symposium & sem, Princeton Univ, NY Univ, Mus Fine Arts, Boston & others, 66-; grad fac, Sch Visual Arts, NY, 84-89; chmn dept art & art history, Univ Miami, 89-97. *Awards:* Nat Endowment Arts, 68-69; Guggenheim Fel, 68-69; Richard A Florsheim Award, 91. *Bibliog:* K Wilkin (auth), Walter Darby Bannard, Contemporary Artist, St James Press, 89 & Notes on Color Field Painting, The New Criterion, Vol 26, 44, 10/2007. *Media:* Acrylic. *Publ:* Auth, The Art Museum and the Living Artist, Prentice-Hall, 75; Hans Hofmann, Hirshhorn Mus, 76; Painting of the 50s, Duke Univ, 83; Chihuly: Form from Fire, Mus Arts & Sci Daytona Beach, 93; Jules Olitski, catalog essay, New Gallery, Univ Miami, Coral Gables, Fla, 2-3/94; Excellence and Postexcellence, Critical Perspectives in Art History, McEnroe & Pokinski, Prentice Hall, 2001; Future of Abstract Art, The New Criterion, Vol 21, No 10, 89-90, 6/2003; Aphorisms for Artists, New Modern Press, 2011. *Dealer:* Loretta Howard Gallery 525 W 26th St New York NY 10001; Ctr for Visual Commun 541 NW 27th St Miami FL 33127; Daniel Weinberg Gallery 6363 Wilshire Blvd Los Angeles Ca 90048. *Mailing Add:* c/o Univ Miami Art Dept PO Box 248106 Coral Gables FL 33124-4410

BANNING, JACK, JR
ART DEALER
b Mt Vernon, NY, June 12, 1939. *Study:* Brown Univ, AB, 61. *Pos:* Owner, Banning & Assocs Ltd, 74-; partner, Ubu Gallery, NY, 94-. *Mem:* Poster Soc, Inc (founder, treas & bd mem); New Amsterdam Symphony Orchestra (treas & bd mem); Guggenheim Mus Int Asn; Mus Mod Art, NY. *Specialty:* Avant-garde art movements, 20th Century; Original graphic design & vintage modernist photography. *Publ:* Auth, The New Bauhaus, Sch Design Chicago, 93

BANNISTER, PATI (PATRICIA) BROWN BANNISTER
PAINTER, SCULPTOR
b London, Eng, Oct 29, 1929; US citizen. *Study:* Slade Acad, London; Studied with father Harold Brown. *Work:* Daytona Beach Mus Arts & Sci, Fla. *Comn:* portraits, Del Mar Race Track, Turf Paradise Ariz Downs; portrait, Comn by Cambrell Jone. *Exhib:* Solo exhibs: Daytona Beach Mus, Fla, 79; Southwest Arts Found, Houston, Tex, 83; Rotary Club Art Exhib, Amarillo, Tex; portrait, Comn by, Robert Unsell, 87. *Awards:*

Nat Publishing Inst, Award Gold Medal for Color Printing; E Emerson Albright Award. *Bibliog:* Dr Gary Libby (dir), Pati Bannister, SW Art Mag, 4/82; Peggy Samuels (coauth) with Harold Samuels, Pati Bannister, Contemp Western Artists, 82; Dr Gary Libby (dir), Romantic Pati Bannister, Daytona Beach Mus Mag, fall, 84. *Media:* Oil, Acrylic; Bronze. *Publ:* Equestrian illustrations, Riding, London; Various children's books, England. *Dealer:* The Bannister Collection 2301 14th St Gulfport MS 39501. *Mailing Add:* 6518 Mauna Loa Dr Diamondhead MS 39525-3838

BANNON, ANTHONY
MUSEUM DIRECTOR
b Hanover, NH, Dec 6, 1942. *Study:* St Bonaventure Univ, BS, 64; SUNY, Buffalo, MA, 74, PhD, 94. *Work:* Lincoln Center Dance Collection; George Eastman House and Burchfield Penney Art Center. *Comn:* Illuminated Working Man, Experimental Intermedia Found. *Collection Arranged:* Albright-Knox Art Gallery; Buscaglia-Castellani Art Gallery, Niagara Univ, NY; State Mus NY, Albany; Washington DC Project for the Arts; Burchfield-Penney Art Ctr & Rockwell Hall Performing Arts Ctr, SUNY Coll, Buffalo; David Anderson Gallery; George Eastman House; Schweinfurth Mus, Auburn, NY. *Pos:* Dir, Burchfield-Penney Art Ctr, 85-86, 2002-; asst vpres cult affairs, SUNY Coll, Buffalo, 94-96; chmn visual arts program panel, NY State Coun on Arts, New York, 86-88 ; vice chmn, Empire State Craft Alliance, Saratoga Springs, NY, 88-93; co-chmn arts programming comt, World Univ Games, Buffalo, 91-93; chmn adv bd, Quick Fine Arts Ctr, St. Bonaventure Univ, 96-2002; dir, George Eastman House, 96-2012; co-chmn adv coun, ArtsAction, NY, 99-2002. *Teaching:* rsch prof, Buffalo State Univ, 2012-. *Awards:* Merit Award, Am Photog Hist Soc, 82; Excellence in Writing about Deafness Award, Gallaudet Coll, 85; Prof Study Leave Grant, NY State/United Univ Professions, 93; Outstanding Arts Adminr Award, The Buffalo Partnership, 95; Arts Award, St Bonaventure Univ, 2002; Golden Career Award, Palm Beach Photog Ctr, 2007; CEO of the Year, Rochester Chapter of Public Relations, Society of America, 2008; Gaudete award, St Bonaventure Univ; J Dudley Johnson award for Achievement in Photo Criticism & History, Royal Motographic Soc. *Mem:* Mus Asn NY State (counselor 94-2003); Am Asn Mus; Gallery Asn NY State (trustee 97-2000); Buffalo State Coll Found (trustee 85-91); Soc Photog Edn; Asn Art Mus Dirs; Rochester Int Fringe Festival (trustee, 2011-). *Publ:* Auth, Steve McCurry, Phaidon Bks; The Taking of Niagara & The Photo Pictorialist of Buffalo, Media Study Buffalo; other var catalogs; co auth with Estelle Jussim, Arcadia Revisited, Photographs by John Pfahl Univ, NY Press. *Mailing Add:* Burchfield Penney Art Ctr 1300 Elmwood Ave Buffalo NY 14222

BANSEMER, ROGER L
PAINTER, WRITER
b Brockton, Mass, July 25, 1948. *Study:* Ringling Sch Art, Sarasota, Fla, BA, 69. *Work:* Sperry Rand Corp, NY; Clearwater Oaks Bank & Barnett Bank, Clearwater, Fla; Rutgers Univ, New Brunswick, NJ; Pioneer Bank, Fla; Forbes, Chateau Balleroy, France. *Comn:* Wall Mural, Spyglass Hotel, Clearwater, 79; etching for Pres Carter, City of Clearwater, 79; mural, City Clearwater, 8; The Rocks (mural), Sydney, Australia, 82; painting for poster, City of Clearwater, 83; mural (20 ft x 30 ft), Home Shopping Network, St Petersburg, Fla, 88; and others. *Exhib:* Infinite Space & Kinetic Color, Adelphi Univ, 77; 15th Ann Maj Fla Artists, Harmon Gallery, Naples, Fla, 77; Pan-Am Bldg, DC, 79; Adelphi Univ, NY, 80; Byways Gallery, Sarasota, Fla, 81; St Petersburg Mus Fine Arts, Fla, 85 & 86; Voorhees Gallery Sarasota, Fla, 88; Upham Gallery, St Petersburg, Fla, 88 & 90; Mystic Seaport Gallery, Conn, 90. *Pos:* Artist-in-residence, City of Clearwater, 78. *Awards:* Int Award of Excellence, Mystic Mus, Conn, 91. *Bibliog:* Review by Gene Shalit Today Show, 89; review, Forbes Mag, 89 & Playboy Mag, 90; feature story, Artist Mag, 89. *Media:* Acrylics; Etching. *Publ:* Auth, Smithsonian, Air & Space Mag, 88, Am Artist Mag, 88, Tampa Tribune, 88, Tampa Bay Life Mag, 88, Homes Mag, 88; The Art of HotAir Ballooning; Southern Shores; Rachael's Splendifilous Adventure; Art Water's Edge, The Birds of Florida; Mountians in the Mist (with foreword by James A Michener)

BANTEL, LINDA
MUSEUM DIRECTOR
b King City, Calif, May 30, 1943. *Study:* Inst Fine Arts, New York Univ, MA, 71; Wharton Advand Mgt Prog, Univ Pa, cert, 92. *Pos:* Res assoc, Metrop Mus Art, New York 78-80; assoc to chief cur, Pa Acad Fine Arts, 80-85, dir mus, 85-95. *Mem:* Coll Art Asn; Asn Art Mus Dirs; Cosmopolitan Club, Philadelphia. *Publ:* Auth, William Rush, American Sculptor, 82 & introduction, Searching Out the Best, 88, Pa Acad Fine Arts, Philadelphia; coauth, American Paintings in the Metropolitan Museum of Art, Vol II: A Catalog of Works by Artists Born Between 1816-1845, Princeton Univ Press, 85; Raphaelle Peale in Philadelphia, Nat Gallery Art & Pa Acad Fine Arts, 88; The Potamkin collection of American art, Mag Antiques, 8/89; and others. *Mailing Add:* 703 W Phil-Ellena St Philadelphia PA 19119-3513

BAPST, SARAH
ARTIST
b Chicago, Ill, May 21, 1950. *Study:* Ind Univ, Bloomington, with Mary Ellen Solt, BA 73; Cranbrook Acad Art, studied with Richard DeVore, MFA, 77. *Exhib:* Affinities: Am Women Artists, Laura Knotts Gallery, Bradford Coll, Haverhill, Mass, 2000; Works on Paper, South Shore Art Ctr, Cohasset, Mass, 2000; Small Works, Wash Sq East Gallery, NY Univ, 2001; Drawing the New Millennium: The Challenge of Media and Idea to the Nature of Drawing, Danforth Gallery, Portland, Maine, 2001; Hopscotch: Associative Leaps in the Construction of Narrative, Bride Art Ctr, 2002; Artists Under the Influence, Brickbottom Gallery, Somerville, Maine, 2003; group exhibs, Marks, Exhib Contemp Drawing, Target Gallery at Torpedo Factory, Alexandria, Va, 2003, Merry Peace, Sideshow Gallery, Brooklyn, NY, 2004, Second Ann Drawing Faculty Exhib, Brant Gallery, MassArt, 2004, Cambridge Art Asn Nat Prize Show, Mus Contemp Art Chicago, Cambridge Art Asn Gallery, Mass, 2004 & Out of the Blue, Nat Juried Art Exhib, Attleboro Arts Mus, 2008; Selections 10 Artworks by 25 Mass Art Faculty Mem, Bakalar Gallery, Mas Coll Art, Boston, 2009; Foster Exhib, Inst Contemporary Art Boston, Mass, 2013. *Teaching:* prof, Studio Found Dept, Mass Coll Art & Design, Boston, Mass, 84-. *Awards:* Fel Works on Paper, Nat Endowment Arts, 91; Best of Show, Marks Contemp Drawing Exhib, 2003; Second prize, Works on Paper Exhib, South Shore Art Ctr, 2003; Boston Foster prize, Inst Contemporary Art, 2013. *Bibliog:* Ron Jones (auth), The last nat sculpture show, Art Papers, 1-2/83; Mary Sherman (auth), Tenth ann Boston drawing show, Art New Eng, 9/89. *Media:* Paper, Sculpture. *Mailing Add:* 20 Concord Ave No 3 Cambridge MA 02138

BARATZ, ROBIN
PAINTER
b Chicago, IL, July 20, 1951. *Study:* Northwestern Univ, BS, 1973; MA, 1974; Studied privately c artist, Joshua Graham, Boston, Mass, 1977-1999. *Exhib:* Am Artists Prof League (NYC), Ann Juried Exhibs; Catherine Lorillard Wolfe Art Club (NYC), Ann Juried Open Exhibs; Salmagundi Club (NYC), Ann Juried Open Exhibs; Audubon Atists (NYC), Ann Juried Exhibs; Lyme Art Asn (Old Lyme, Conn), Art of New Eng. *Awards:* Guilia Palermo Award, Audubon Artists Ann Exhib, 2000; Allied Artists of Am Award, Conn Acad Fine Arts, 2004; Alfred & Mary Crimi Award for Creative Oil, Audubon Artists, 2005. *Bibliog:* J Sanders Eaton (auth), Isle of Skye limned (luminously in oils by Robin Baratz), Gallery & Studio, 2001; Katie Kresser (auth), Boston Weekly Dig, 2003; Jeannie McCormack (auth), Gallery & Studio, 2003. *Mem:* Am Artists Prof League; Audubon Artists; Catharine Lorillard Wolfe Art Club. *Media:* Oil. *Mailing Add:* 159 Bellevue St Newton MA 02458

BARBEAU, MARCEL (CHRISTIAN)
PAINTER, SCULPTOR
b Montreal, Que, Feb 18, 1925. *Study:* Ecole Meuble, dipl, 47; with Paul-Emile Borduas. *Work:* Nat Gallery, Can & Washington, DC; British Mus, London; Musee des Beaux-Arts de Lyons & Mus d'Art Contemp, Montreal, Que; Stellejk Mus, Amsterdam; Musee d'art moderne et contemporain de Strasbourg, France; Musee Nat des Gezux Arts du Quebec, AGO, Toronto, Ontario. *Comn:* Nadia or Le saut du tremplin (painted welded aluminum sculpture), Societe du Vieux-Port, Montreal, 76; Liberte, liberte cherie (painted welded steel), Lachine-Marina, Que, 86; Laurentians (acrylic on aluminium mural), Via Rail intercontinental train, 89; Les portes du regard (painted welded steel), City Hall Parc, Montreal-Est, 90; Window on Future (painted welded steel sculpture), McLennan Libr Terr, McGill Univ, 92. *Exhib:* Pen House Show, Mus Mod Art, New York, 65; retrospectives, Winnipeg Art Gallery & Mus Art Contemp, Montreal, 69; Borduas er le Automatist, Grand Palais, Paris, 71; Modern Painting in Canada, Edmonton Art Gallery, 78 & The Contemp Art Society: Montreal 1939-1947, 80, Edmonton Art Gallery; Montreal Mus Fine Arts, 91; Mus d'art Contemporain de Montreal, 92; Canadian Abstract Painting & Design in Fifties, Winnipeg Art Gallery, 92; Modern Sculpture in Quebec: 1947-1960, Mus du Que, 93; Second Jeux de la Francophonie, Paris, 94; The Sixties in Canada, Nat Gallery, Can, 2005; Be-bomb, The Transatlantic war of Images and all that jazz in the 1950's, Barcelona Mus Mod & Contemp Art, Spain, 2007; The Autonomist Revolution 1941-1960, Varley Art Gallery, 10/20/2009; Albright Knox Gallery, 3/19-3/30/2010. *Pos:* Pres, Fedn des arts visuels du Que, 77-80; Vpres, Conseil de la peinture du Que, 77-80. *Teaching:* Bishop Univ, 78-80. *Awards:* First Prize Sculpture Competition, McDonalds Restaurant, 85; Gold Medal (painting), Second Jeux de la Francophonie, Paris, 94; 5th Painting Prize, Int Biennale Contemp Art, Florence, Italy, 2001; Officer, Canada Order, 95. *Bibliog:* Carolle Gagnon & Ninon Gauthier, introd by Charles Delloye, Marcel Barbeau: Fugato, CECA Publ, Montreal, 90; Cercle D'Art Paris, 94; Manon Barbeau (film dir, producer), Les Enfants De Refus Global, NFB, 98 & Barbeau Libre comme l'art, NFB, Can & Info film, Mtl, Que, 2000. *Mem:* Conseil artistes peintres (vpres, 78-79); Fedn artistes arts visuels Que; Artist for Peace; Royal Can Acad Arts. *Media:* Acrylic; Welded Metal, Wood. *Interests:* Contemporary Dance & Music, Movies, Poetry. *Publ:* Co-signatory, Re Fus Global Automatist Manifesto, by PE Borduas, Refus Global, Mytra-Mythe, Mtl, 48; auth, Grande probite intellectuelle, Devoir, Que, 60; L'artiste devant son oeuvre, Cahiers, Que, 79; and others. *Dealer:* Windsor Gallery Van Couver BC Canada; 1540 West 2nd Avenue Vancouver BC Canada; Virginia Christopher Fine Art 816 11th Ave Calgary AB T2R 0E5

BARBEE, ROBERT THOMAS
PAINTER, GRAPHIC ARTIST
b Detroit, Mich, Sept 25, 1921. *Study:* Cranbrook Acad Art, BA & MFA; Centenary Col; also in Mex. *Work:* Butler Inst Am Art, Youngstown, Ohio; Cranbrook Acad Art, Bloomfield Hills, Mich. *Exhib:* Five shows, Va Mus Fine Arts, Richmond, 53-65 & Traveling Exhibs, 58 & 62; Birmingham Mus Art, 59; Norfolk Mus Art & Sci, 60; Mus Art of Ogunquit, Maine, 62 & 63; Am Fedn Arts, NY, 65; and others. *Teaching:* Instr painting & drawing, Univ Va, assoc prof art, 70-. *Awards:* Prizes, Irene Leach Mem Exhib, Norfolk Mus Arts & Sci, 62 & 64 & Thalheimer's Exhib, Richmond, 63

BARBER, BRUCE ALISTAIR
ARTIST, ART HISTORIAN
b Auckland, NZ, Dec 11, 1950; Can & NZ citizen. *Study:* Auckland Univ Sch Fine Arts, BFA, 73, MFA, 74; NS Coll Art & Design, Halifax, NS, MFA, 78; European Grad Sch, Leuk-Stadt, Switz, PhD, 2005. *Work:* Ludnizca Centre Poland, AGNS; Halifax & ACAG, Auckland, NZ; Franklin Furnace Archive; Bibliotech Nationale, Paris; Nat Archive Film & Video, NZ; MOMA. *Exhib:* The Art of Memory-The Loss of Hist (with catalog), New Mus, New York, 85-86; A Different War: Vietnam in Art (catalog), Whatcom Mus, Bellingham De Cordova Traveling, 89-92; Interscop Festival (catalog), Warsaw, Poland, 90; Memory Works (catalog), London Regional Art Gallery, traveling, 90-91; Story Telling/Real Time (catalog), Gdansk, Poland, 91; Reading & writing Room Exhibs, 84, 87, 90, 93, 95, 98 & 2003; Photographers, Workshop Gallery, Toronto, 96; The Seventies, Artspace, Auckland, 98; Lopdell Art Gallery, Auckland, 98; Gallery, Newcastle Sch Arts, Australia; Room 103, Auckland, NZ; Govett-Brewster, New Plymouth, NZ; Meaning Making, Artspace, Auckland, 2007; Reading & Writing Rooms, Two Survey exhib, Te Tuhi, Auckland, New Zealand, 2008; Artspace, Sydney, Australia, 2008; Traffic Conceptual Arts in Canada,

2010; Adam Art Gallery, Univ Victoria Wellington, NZ, Duchamp in New Zealand, 2012; Traveling, Traffic: Conceptual Art in Canada 1968-1980, Barnicke Gallery, Vancouver Art Gallery, 2010-2013; Continental Drift: Conceptual Art in Canada: The 1960s and 70s, 2013; Weak Force, Collaborative Art Installation, Surrey Univ Art Gallery, 2013; Te tuhi (the mark) Gallery, Auckland, 2013. *Collection Arranged:* Bruce Barber, Auckland City Gallery Res Libr, Archive; N2, Film Archive, Wellington. *Pos:* ECoast ed, FUSE Mag, Toronto, 84-90; bd mem, Univ Art Asn Can, 89-94, LJB Media Arts Soc, 89-2004 & Can Film Studies Asn, 97-98; Dalhousie rev, 2001; ed bd, NSCAD Press, 2003; Topia J Can Cult Studies; NZ J Art Hist. *Teaching:* Jr lectr sculpture, Auckland Univ, NZ, 74-75; asst prof fine art, Simon Fraser Univ, 79-81; asst prof intermedia-studio & art hist, NS Coll Art & Design, 81-89, assoc prof, 90-95, intermedia coordr & chmn media arts dept, 96-; prof media arts & visual cult studies teaching fel, Univ Kings Coll, Halifax, 98-2003; dir MFA prog, NSCAD, U, 90-94, 98, 2005-2006, 2008-2012, chair media arts, 2013-; hon prof, Sydney Coll Art, Univ Sydney, Australia, 2010-. *Awards:* Queen Elizabeth II Arts Coun, 77 & 79; Social Sci & Humanities Res Coun Can, 82-83, 89, 91-92, 96-99, 2009; Ont Critics Grant, 85. *Bibliog:* M Cheetham (auth), Remembering Postmodernism, Oxford Univ Press, Can; L Hutcheon (auth), Splitting Images, Toronto Oxford Univ Press, 91; A M Richard & C Robertson (auths), Performance in Canada 1970-1990, Que Inter/Editeur, 91; M Dunn (auth), NZ Sulpture: A History, 2003; B French & S Cleland (ed), Bruce Barber Work 1970-2008, Artspace, Te Tuhi, Sydney & Auckland, 2010; TRAFFIC: Conceptual Art in Canada, 1965-1980, Vancouver Art Gallery, 2012; The Last Art College: Nova Scotia Coll Art & Design, 1968-1978, Garry Neill Kennedy, MIT Press, 2012. *Mem:* Univ Art Asn Can; Can Film Studies Asn; Cinema Studies Asn; CAA. *Media:* Interdisciplinary, Video, Installation Performance. *Res:* Popular culture, film, theory & politics, cultural studies. *Publ:* Auth, C Pontbriand (ed), Performance Texts & Documents, Parachute Publ, 81; ed, essays Performance & Cultural Politicization, Open Letter 5: 5 & 6, 83; D Lander & M Lexier (auths), Sound by Artists, Art Metropole Publ, Toronto, 90; auth, Reading Rooms, Halifax, Eyelevel Pub, 92; co-ed (with S Guilbaut & J O'Brian), Voices of Fire: Art, Rage, Power and The State, Toronto, Univ Toronto Press, 96; Conceptual Art: The NSCAD Connection 1967-1973, 2002; auth, Performance and Performers (ed, Mare Leger), YYZ Press, Toronto, 2007; auth, Trans/actions: Art, Film, & Death, Atropos Press, NY, 2008; Littoral Art and Communicative Action, Common Ground Press, Ill, 2013. *Dealer:* Michael Lett Gallery Auckland New Zealand. *Mailing Add:* School of Graduate Studies NSCAD Univ 5163 Duke St Halifax NS B3J 3J6 Canada

BARBER, CYNTHIA
SCULPTOR, PRINTMAKER
b Boston, Mass, Dec 12, 1939. *Study:* Barnard Col, BA, 61; Brandeis Univ, MA, 63; Richmond Col, Eng, 71-73. *Work:* Albuquerque Mus, NMex; Albuquerque Tech-Vocational Inst, NMex; Duke Univ, Raleigh, NC; Grants Mining Mus, Grants, NMex; George Meany Ctr Labor Studies, Silver Springs, MD. *Comn:* Holocaust Memorial, Gaithersburg Hebrew Congregation, Md, 81; outdoor sculpture for office complex, Shell Plaza, Bakersfield, Calif, 86; Hacienda Towers, Los Angeles, Calif, 90; bronze wall sculpture & lamps, Temple Emanuel, Kensington, MD, 96; outdoor sculpture, Albuquerque Tech-Voc Inst, 96-97. *Exhib:* Asn Int de Defense des Artistes, Amsterdam, 81, traveling throughout Europe, 81-82; Nat Coun Art Jewish Life Judaic Art Exhib, Lever House, NY, 83; Festival Arts: Sculpture for Pub Spaces, Albuquerque, NMex, 85; North Am Sculpture Exhib, Golden, Colo, 86; Art of Albuquerque, Albuquerque Mus, 90; Mile of Sculpture, Gov's Gallery, State of NMex, Santa Fe, 91; Johnson Gallery, Univ NMex, Albuquerque, NMex, 95; Outdoor Installation, NMex Mus Natural Hist, Albuquerque, NMex, 95-98. *Pos:* Founding mem & bd dir, Touchstone Gallery, Washington, DC, 76-77 & Association Internationale de Defense des Artistes, US, 81-85; prog coordr, Tamarind Inst, Albuquerque, NMex, 93-; capitol art found bd, Santa Fe, NMex, 93-96. *Teaching:* Instr humanities, Howard Univ, Washington, DC, 66-70. *Awards:* NMex Art in Pub Places Purchase Awards, Harriet B Samons State Office Bldg, Farmington, NMex, 86; Grants, Mus Mining, NMex, 86. *Bibliog:* Commissions, Sculpture Mag, 11-12/87; Myles Nye (auth), Taos Galleries Have Poetry, Controversy, Albuquerque J, 10/25/92; Wesley Pulka (auth) Space Can't Limit Five Sculptors' Potent Images, Albuquerque J, 8/6/95. *Media:* All; Woodcut. *Mailing Add:* 425 Hermosa Dr SE Albuquerque NM 87108

BARBER, PHILIP JUDD
PAINTER, PRINTMAKER
b Cleveland, Ohio, Sept 27, 1951. *Study:* Ohio Univ, BS, 73, BFA, 77. *Work:* Minneapolis Inst Arts; Purdue Univ, Ind; First Banks Systs, Minneapolis; Chemical Bank, NY; Frans Masereel Centrum, Kasterlee, Belg. *Exhib:* Boston Printmakers, DeCordova Mus, Boston, 78; Chautauqua Nat Exhib of Am Art, Chautauqua Art Mus, NY, 83; May Show, Cleveland Mus Art, 83; Small Print Exhib, Purdue Art Mus, Ind, 84; Minn Artists Exhib Prog - 10th Anniversary Exhib, Minneapolis Inst Arts, 86. *Pos:* Studio mgr, Vermillion Ed Ltd, Minn, 78-. *Awards:* First Place, Art Ctr Minn, 85. *Media:* Tempera, Oil; Stick. *Dealer:* Vermillion Ed Ltd 2919 Como Ave SE Minneapolis MN 55414. *Mailing Add:* 2904 Buchanan St NE Minneapolis MN 55418-2209

BARBER, SAM
PAINTER, SCULPTOR
b Naples, Italy, April 9, 1943. *Study:* Art Students League, Nat Acad Fine Art, New York, Cape Sch Art, Provincetown, Mass. *Work:* Miss Mus Art, Jackson; New Orleans Mus Art, La; Midwest Mus Am Art, Elkhart, Ind; Hickory Mus Art, NC; Memphis Brooks Mus Art, Tenn. *Exhib:* eleven one-man exhibs, 83-90. *Awards:* Purchase Prize, La Grange Col, Ga, 74; Philip Eisenberg Award, Salmagundi Club, New York, 81. *Media:* Oil. *Dealer:* Cape Cod Guild Fine Arts 248 Stevens Street Hyannis MA 02601. *Mailing Add:* Studio of Fine Art 10 Hyannis Ave Hyannis Port MA 02647

BARBERA, ROSS WILLIAM
PAINTER
b Brooklyn, NY, Dec 11, 1950. *Study:* St John's Univ, Jamaica, NY, BFA, 73; Pratt Inst, Brooklyn, NY, MFA, 75. *Work:* Harley Sch, Wilson Arts Ctr, Rochester, NY; Univ Wis, Milwaukee; La Grange Col, Ga; Chautauqua Arts Ctr, NY. *Comn:* Landscape painting (oil on canvas), Univ Wis, Milwaukee, 85. *Exhib:* One-man shows, Jean Lumbard Gallery, NY, 83 & Clark Whitney Gallery, Lenox, Mass, 89; And the Living is Easy, Visual Arts Mus, NY, 84; The Razor Show, Jayne Baum & Hudson Ctr Galleries, NY, 85; Six Long Island Artists, Islip Art Mus, NY, 85; The Landscape, Columbus Mus Ohio, 87; and others. *Pos:* cur, St John's Univ Gallery, Jamaica, NY, 94-2000. *Teaching:* Asst Prof Fine Art, St John's Univ, Jamaica, NY, 80-, assoc prof, 96- chairperson, 2010-; adj asst prof fine art, Nassau Community Col, Garden City, NY, 87-. *Awards:* Creative Artist Pub Serv Painting Fel, NY State, 76; Nat Endowment Arts Painting Fel, 85-86; Grant, Hillwood Mt Mus, Long Island Univ, CW Post. *Bibliog:* Ellen Lubell (auth), Rev, Arts Mag, 10/75; Laurie Hurwitz (auth), Airbrush techniques for landscape painters, Am Artist, 10/87; Eunivce Agar (auth), Painting Expressively with an airbrush, Am Artist, 10/94. *Mem:* Organization of Independent Artists. *Media:* Acrylic, Oil. *Dealer:* Art Exchange Gallery 60 E San Francisco St Santa Fe NM 87501. *Mailing Add:* 340 Croaton St Ronkonkoma NY 11779-4917

BARBIER-MUELLER, MONIQUE & JEAN-PAUL
COLLECTOR, MUSEUM FOUNDER
Pos: Pres, bd, Barbier-Mueller Art Mus, Geneva & Barcelona, 1977-; recipient Commandeur de l'Ordee Légion d'Honneur, France, 2002, Commandeur de l'Order des Arts et Lettres, 97. *Awards:* Commandeur de l'Order des Arts et Lettres, 1997, Commandeur de l'Ordre Légion d'Honneur, France, 2002; named one of Top 200 Collectors, ARTnews mag, 2004-09. *Collection:* Tribal art, Pre-Columbian art, Modern and Contemporary art. *Mailing Add:* Barbier-Mueller Museum Rue Jean-Calvin Geneva 10 1204 Switzerland

BARBOZA, ANTHONY
PHOTOGRAPHER, PAINTER
b New Bedford, Mass, May 10, 1944. *Study:* Self taught. *Work:* Mus Mod Art & Studio Mus Harlem, NY; Oberlin Col, Ohio; Newark Art Mus, NJ; Brooklyn Mus, Brooklyn, NY; Cornell Univ. *Exhib:* Mirrors & Windows, Mus Mod Art, NY, 78; Nine Contemp Photographers, Witkin Gallery, NY, 79; Polaroids, Photokina, Cologne Ger, 82 & 84; Nude in Photog, Munchner Stadtmuseum, Munich, WGer, 85; Los Angeles Expression, Los Angeles Co Mus Art, 90; Songs of my People, Time Life Worldwide Tour, 90; Picturing New York, Traveling Exhib and book, Mus Mod Art, New York, 2009. *Pos:* Asst cur photog, 2001 exhib Committed To The Image: Contemporary Black Photog - Brooklyn Mus, NY, 1998-2000. *Teaching:* Lectr, Int Ctr Photog, New York, 75 & 83, Columbia Col, Chicago, 84, Rochester Inst Technol, 91, RI Sch Design, Providence, 2001, Wadsworth Atheneum Gallery, Hartford, Conn, 2002, Tisch Sch of the Arts, NY Univ, 2005 & Columbia Col, 2007. *Awards:* Photog Grants NY State Coun Arts, 74 & 76; Nat Endowment Arts Photog Grant, 80. *Bibliog:* Allen Porter (auth), Portraits, Camera Mag, Switz, 6/80. *Media:* Oil. *Publ:* Auth, Black Borders, pvt publ, 80; Color of Fashion, Stuart, Tabori & Chang/Kodak; African Americans, Viking, 93; Day in the Life of Israel, Viking, 94; Double take, Jazz Portfolio-Duke Univ, fall 95. *Dealer:* Robert Mann Gallery 42 E 76th St New York NY 10021. *Mailing Add:* 915 Gloucester Ct Westburg NY 11590-5301

BARD, GAYLE
PAINTER, SCULPTOR
b Kansas City, Kans. *Study:* DePauw Univ, Univ Chicago, Univ Wis, Milwaukee, Yale Univ, Cornish Coll Arts. *Work:* City of Seattle, var collections; Key Corp, Albany, NY; Howard Hughes Properties, Las Vegas, Nev; Microsoft Corp, Federal Home Loan Bank & Safeco Insurance, Seattle; Management Compensation Group, Portland, Ore; Providence Hospital, Portland, Ore. *Comn:* Univ Hosp, Univ Wash; Seattle Arts Comn; Wash State Arts Comn; Va Mason Hosp. *Exhib:* First Impressions: Northwest Monotypes, Seattle Art Mus, 89; Linda Hodges Gallery, 98-2007; From Here to the Horizon: Artists of the Rural Landscape, Whatcom Mus History & Art, Bellingham, Wash, 99; The View from Here: 100Artists/Centennial of Mount Rainier, Kittredge Gallery/Univ Puget Sound and Tokyo, Japan, 99; Self Images, Art Space, Seattle, Wash, 99; Laura Russo Gallery, Portland, Ore, 2000; and others. *Teaching:* Fac, Cornish Inst Arts, Seattle, Wash, 88-90 & NW Col Art, Poulsbo, Wash, 96-97. *Awards:* Fel, Nat Endowment Arts, 87; Fel Printmaking, Centrum Found, 88; Artist Trust, Nat Endowment Arts, 90. *Media:* Painting, Installation. *Dealer:* Linda Hodges Gallery 316 First Ave S Seattle WA 98104. *Mailing Add:* 11197 Blue Pond Pl NE Bainbridge Island WA 98110

BARD, JOELLEN
INSTRUCTOR, PAINTER
b Brooklyn, NY, June 19, 1942. *Study:* Syracuse Univ Art Sch, 59-62; Brooklyn Col, painting with Philip Pearlstein, MA, 67, adv cert, 87; Brooklyn Mus Art Sch, Max Beckman, scholar class, 70-73; Pratt Inst, Hon BFA; AAS (knitwear design), Fashion Inst Technol, 2001. *Work:* Many pvt & corp collections. *Exhib:* Brooklyn Mus, 73 & 74; solo exhibs, Brooklyn Mus Little Gallery, 73, Gallery 91, Brooklyn, 74-76 & Pleiades Gallery, NY, 75, 77, 79 & 82; Windows of Bergdorf Goodman New York City, 89, Brooklyn Botanic Garden, 89. *Collection Arranged:* Tenth St Days--The Co-ops of the 50s. *Pos:* Dir, Asn Artist Run Galleries, 77-. *Teaching:* Art teacher, New York Bd Educ, 64-69 & 78-, Kingsborough Community Col, 79-83 & 86-94. *Bibliog:* Eileen Blair (auth), Mindscapes, Phoenix, 3/21/75; David Shirey (auth), Artists forming sobro, NY Times, 3/75; Helen Thomas (auth), article in Arts Mag, 3/79. *Mem:* Asn Artist Run Galleries; United Fedn Teachers. *Media:* Acrylic on canvas; Plexiglas, Mixed Media; Knitwear

BARD, PERRY
VIDEO ARTIST, INSTALLATION SCULPTOR
Study: McGill Univ, Montreal, Can, BA, 1966; San Francsico Art Inst, MFA (sculpture), 1980. *Work:* Art Bank of the Can Coun; Southeast Mus Photog, Fla; Fonds Regional d'Art Contemporain des Pays de la Loire, France; Groupe Intervention Video, Can; Heure Exquise Lile, France. *Exhib:* Solo exhibs, ARE Gallery, San Francisco, 1982, Sculpture Ctr Gallery, New York, 1990, Unvi Art Mus, Tallahassee, 1993, Palm Beach Mus Art, Fla, 1995, Centro de Arte Unicef, Seville, Spain, 2003, Newhouse Ctr for Contemp Art, Snug Harbor, NY, 2003; Postmarked New York, Southern Alberta Art Gallery, 1986; Back Seat Foot Arm Lead, PS1 Contemp Art Ctr, New York, 1990; Work from the Margin, Sch Archit Gallery, Fla A&M Univ, 1993; Domestic Unrest, Southeast Mus Photog, Daytona, Fla, 1996; Video 2000, Contemp Mus, Baltimore, 2001; Don't Call it Performance, Reina Sofia Mus, Madrid, Spain, 2003. *Teaching:* Vis artist lectr, Univ Calif, Irvine, Univ Calif, Riverside, 1991-2003, MIT, Cambrdge, 1996-97; instr, Sch Visual Arts, New York, 1993-2005; vis asst prof, Rutgers Univ, 2002-03. *Awards:* Can Arts Coun Project Grant, 1981, 1985-86, 1989-90, 1994; Individual Artist Grant, Nat Endowment for the Arts, 1983; Yaddow Fel, 1988; Pollock-Krasner Found Grant, 1990; New York Found Arts Fel, 2009. *Bibliog:* Richard Huntington (auth), Four Sculptors, Buffalo News, 4/18/1986; Roberta Smith (auth), Social Spaces, NY Times, 2/12/1988; Ruth Dusseault (auth), Works From the Margin, Art Papers, 3-4/1994; Ann Barclay Morgan (auth), Ethereal Images, Sculpture, 56-57, 7-8/1996; Catherine Fox (auth), Shades of Racism, Atlanta J-Constitution, 12/6/2002

BARDAZZI, PETER
PAINTER, FILMMAKER
b New York, NY, Mar 5, 1943. *Study:* Pratt Inst, BFA, 67; Yale Univ, MFA, 69; also study art & archit, Asia; Alias Technology, Toronto, Canada, Power Animator Certificate in 3D Computer Animation, 91; Silicon Studios, Santa Monica, CA, Digital Masters Certificate, 96. *Work:* Mus Mod Art, NY; Purchase Mus, NY; Corcoran Gallery, Washington, DC; Rockefeller Univ; Neuberger Mus, Purchase, NY; Elder Art Gallery, Wesleyan Univ; Weatherspoon Art Mus, Univ NC; Libr Cong, Am Folklife Ctr; Kutztown State Coll, Pa; corp collections, Amstar, NY, Artco Int, Geneva, Chase Manhattan Bank, Crocker Nat Bank, NY, French & co, London, Singer corp, NY, Starwood Corp; pvt collections, Antonino Cusimano, Mariella Allotta, Armand Deutsch, Henry Markus, Jan von Haeften, Leo Castielli, Olivier de la Fouchardiere, Roy Neuberger, Sandra Payson. *Exhib:* Solo exhibs, Cordier & Ekstrom Gallery, 71, 72, 74, 76 & 78 & St Mary's Col, Md, 75, Skylight Gallery, 2012, NY; Whitney Mus Am Art Painting Ann, 72; Indianapolis Mus Art Painting & Sculpture Today, 72; Am Acad Arts & Lett, 73; Cordier & Ekstrom, 76; Corcoran Gallery, 76; Univ Tex, Austin, 76; Shriek if You Know What I Did Last Friday the 13th, 99; Curiosity, 2000; Hollywood Goes Digital, 2001; Digital Printmaking Now, Brooklyn Mus Art, 2001; Independent Film Project, NY, 2002; Projects in Hell, Documentary about Coll student's vision of hell, 2002; DYI Convention, NY; The Exquisite Body (body on the surrealist concept of the Exquisite Corpse), 2003; Scents: Locks: Kisses, Limburg, Belgium, 2005; Collection of a Lifetime, Neuberger Mus Art, Purchase Coll, SUNY, 2006; Zeitgeist, Art-O-Mat Gallery, New York, 2009; Art Zine, 21st Century Mus Contemporary Art, Kanazawa, Japan, 2011; Under 30 Group exhib, Skylight Gallery, NY, 2012; Holy BOS Art and Instillation Show, Brooklyn, NY, 2013. *Pos:* Guest lectr & artist-in-residence, St Mary's Coll, Md, 75; dir & co-founder, Ctr for Advanced Digital Applications, NY Univ, 96-2004; dir & creator, digital imaging & design master's degree prog, NY Univ, 2000-05; dir, New Media Development, New York Univ, 2004-06; MFA Mentoring Prog, The Art Inst Boston, 2006-. *Teaching:* Asst instr, drawing, Yale Univ Undergrad Sch Art, 69; sr asst prof, painting, Pratt Inst, Brooklyn, NY, 70-72; adj prof, computer graphics, Fashion Inst Technol, New York, 87-98; adj prof, computer animation & visual effects, Tisch Sch Arts, NY Univ, 89-96; assoc prof, digital arts, NYU, 96-2006; instr, art of filmmaking & interactive media, Fashion Inst Technol, New York, 2006-10. *Awards:* Fed Work Study Prog Award, 68; Painting Award, New Britain Mus, Conn, 69; Am Accad Arts & Letters Award, painting, 73; Childe Hassam Fund Purchase Award, 73; Digital Masters Award, Silicon Studios & Graphics, 96; and others. *Bibliog:* Hilton Kramer (auth), 10/74 & Vivian Raynor (auth), 5/78, articles, NY Times; Peter Frank (auth), article, Art News Mag, 10/78; Film and Video Mag, Education & Training; Challenge 3, by Iain Blair, Aug 15, 99; Shoot Mag, Second Time Around, by Justine Ellas, Jan, 14, 2000; Millimeter Mag, What CADA Did Last Summer, by Kristinha Mc Cort, May, 1, 2000; Karen W Arenson, Allison Fass, and Jacques Steinberg (auths), When A Film Needs a Good Buzz, NY Times, 11/29/2000; Jennifer Jacobson (auth), Chronicle of Higher Education, Descent Into Darkness, 4/2001; William Porter (auth), Cinematic Silk Purses Hollywood Portrayals of Historical Women, Unlike Men, Turn Even the Homeliest into Glamour Queens, Denver Post, 11/12/2002; Lynn Smith (auth), In Supporting Roles, Los Angeles Times, 3/30/2003; David Halbfinger (auth), Burying Private Ryan, NY Times, 10/2006; James Hebert (auth), Success of Mexican Directions has Deep Roots, San Diego Union-Tribune, 2/2007; Western Revenge, 2009; Why are Vampire Movies Big in Am, 2009. *Media:* paint, video. *Collection:* Albert Petcavage, NY; Amstar Corp, NY; Armand Deutsch, Beverly Hills, CA; Artco International, Geneva, Switzerland; Chase Manhattan Bank; Corcoran Gallery, Washington, DC; Cordier & Ekstrom, Gallery, NY; Crocker National Bank, NY; Elder Art Gallery, Wesleyan, Univ, NE; French & Company, London; Henry Markus, Chicago, IL; Jan von Haeften, Hambury, Germany; Joseph Barber, NY; Kutztown State College, PA; Mus of Modern Art, NY; Neuberger Mus, Purchase, NY; Rockefeller Univ, NY; Roy Neuberger, NY; Sandra Payson, NY; Singer Corp., NY; Starwood Corp; Willis van Devanter, Upperville, VA; Zao Wou-Ki and Francoise Marquet, Paris France; The Weatherspoon Art Mus at The Univ of North Carolina. *Publ:* The Carabaggio Place (auth & dir), film; Handmade Holiday Cards, Smithsonian Books, 2012. *Mailing Add:* 210 E15th St Apt 7K New York NY 10003

BARELLO, JULIA M
ADMINISTRATOR, EDUCATOR
Pos: head dept art, prof metalsmithing & jewelry, NMex State Univ, currently. *Res:* body adornment and the resulting construction of meaning through supplements to the body. *Mailing Add:* New Mexico State University DW Williams Hall PO Box 30001, MSC 3572 Las Cruces NM 88003

BARGER, M SUSAN
CONSULTANT, CONSERVATOR
b Tucson, Ariz, Sept 7, 1949. *Study:* Immaculate Heart Col, BA, 70; Rochester Inst Technol, MST, 75; Pa State Univ, PhD, 82. *Collection Arranged:* Barbara Erdman Estate Inventory, 2008. *Pos:* Mus consult scientist, 82-; res chemist, Libr of Cong Preserv Lab, 84-86; co dir, Barger & Wilson Collection Serv, Santa Fe, NMex, 96-99 & Barger & Lewis Collection Svcs, 2000; prog mgr, Small Mus Develop Prog, NMex, 2001-04, Mus Develop Assoc, 2005-2010, dir, 2008-2010, online comm coordr, Connecting to Collections Care, 2014-. *Teaching:* Textiles, M H de Young Mus Art Sch, San Francisco, 71-73; assoc res prof mat sci, Johns Hopkins Univ, 86-92; adj prof, Univ NMex, 90-2008. *Awards:* fellow, American Inst Conservation. *Bibliog:* NM Brown & Gordon Shed (auths), Scattered Images, Research/Penn State 5, 9/84; Quantum, Australian Broadcasting Corp, 9/3/93 & 10/22/93. *Mem:* Am Inst for Conserv Art & Hist Works; Am Asn Mus; Art Table Asn. *Publ:* Auth, Bibliography of Photographic Processes in NSC Before 1880, Graphic Arts Res Group, 81; coauth, Robert Cornelius: Portraits from the Dawn of Photography, 83, The Daguerreotype: 19th Century Technology & Modern Science, 91, Smithsonian Inst Press, 2d edit, Johns Hopkins Press, 2001. *Mailing Add:* 3 Moya Lane Santa Fe NM 87505

BARKER, AL C
PAINTER, PRINTMAKER
b West Paterson, NJ, June 19, 411. *Study:* WVa Univ, BS, 64; Univ RI, MS, 67; Rutgers Univ, 69-70. *Work:* Sportman's Edge Ltd, NY; Easton Waterfowl, Md; Chesapeake Maritime Mus, Md; NJ Bell Tel; Coun Arts, Easton, Md. *Comn:* NH Ducks Unlimited, 79 & 80; Theodore Gordon Flyfishers, NY, 81-83, 90 & 92; First Nat State Bank, Newark, NJ, 81; NJ State Ducks Unlimited, 81-92 & 95-2004. *Exhib:* Easton Waterfowl Festival, Md, 70-2012; Safari Club Int, Am Fac Dallas-Ft Worth Airport, Tex, 80; Lyme Art Asn, 9/2007-2010; Mystic Maritime Mus, 2007-2012; US Artists, Phila, 2007-2012; Florence Griswold Mus, 9/2008. *Collection Arranged:* White House, Washington, DC, 2001. *Pos:* Instr painting, Montclair Art Mus, NJ, 91. *Teaching:* Instr forestry, wildlife, Essec Agr Inst, Danvers, Mass, 67-69; instr, Univ RI, Kingston, 67 & NJ State Conserv Sch, Branchville, 69; instr biology, Hightstown High Sch, NJ, 71-78. *Awards:* Whisky Painters Am, Akron, Ohio, 86; Best in Show, Fels Point Nat, Md, 91; SCNY Award; Bryam Mem, 2005; Salmagundi Club, NYC; Bruce Crane, 2007; Gordon H Grant, 2008; Mary Fitch Memorial 2009; D.Wv/Elsie Ject-Key, 2009; GW Innes 2010. *Mem:* Salmagundi Club, NY (bd dir, 78-81); Miniature Artists Am; Whisky Painters Am; Miniature Art Socs, NJ, Fla, Washington; Artist Fel. *Media:* Watercolor, Oil; Graphics. *Specialty:* Traditional/Representational. *Interests:* Hunting, Fishing, Collectibles. *Publ:* Illusr, Deer Hunting, 82, The Grizzly Book, 82, The Bear Book, 83, Trout Book, 84 & North Light, 85. *Dealer:* Annapolis Marine Annapolis Md; Mystic Seaport Mus Mystic Conn. *Mailing Add:* 224 Prince St PO Box 703 Bordentown NJ 08505

BARKER, ELIZABETH E
MUSEUM DIRECTOR, CURATOR
Study: Yale Univ, BA (art hist); NYU Inst Fine Arts, MA (art hist), PhD (art hist), 2003. *Hon Degrees:* Cert, Curatorial Studies, NYU. *Pos:* Cur intern, assoc cur drawings & prints, Met Mus Art, New York, formerly; dir, Picker Art Gallery, Colgate Univ, Hamilton, 2005-2007; dir & chief cur, Mead Art Mus, Amherst Coll, 2007-; guest cur, Yale Ctr for Brit Art, 2003-. *Mailing Add:* Mead Art Museum Amherst College PO Box 5000 Amherst MA 01002

BARKER, WALTER WILLIAM, JR
PAINTER, WRITER
b Coblenz, Ger, Aug 8, 1921; US citizen. *Study:* Washington Univ, BFA, 48, with Horst Janson, Phillip Guston & Max Beckmann; Iowa Univ, with Mauricio Lassansky; Univ Ind, with Alton Pickens & Henry Hope, MFA, 50; Florence, Italy, with Dr Frederick Hart, 56. *Work:* Mus Mod Art & Brooklyn Mus, NY; Hirshhorn Collection, Washington; Boston Mus Fine Arts; James Michener Collection, Univ Tex, Austin; Joseph Pulitzer Jr Collection; and others. *Exhib:* Univ Tex, Austin; Int Exhib Mod Graphic Art, Mus Mod Art, NY, 52; Am Painting, Va Mus Fine Arts, Richmond, 62; Painting & Sculpture Today, Herron Inst Art, Indianapolis, Ind, 67; Weatherspoon Gallery, 75; Univ NC, Greensboro, 77 & 94; solo retrospective, 1951-1994, Univ NC, Greensboro. *Pos:* Spec corresp, St Louis Post-Dispatch, 62-78. *Teaching:* Lectr art hist, Salem Col, 49-50; instr painting, Washington Univ, 50-62; instr basic found, Brooklyn Mus Sch, 63-66; assoc prof painting, Univ NC, 66-85; prof painting, Univ NC, 85-92, prof emer, 92 & lectr, 92-97. *Awards:* New Talent USA Award, 56; Spec Citation Art Rev, Coll Art Asn Am, 66; Distinguished Alumnus, Washington Univ, 72. *Bibliog:* Ernest Smith (auth), Walter Barker, 1958-1968, Webster Col, 68; Joseph Pulitzer, Jr (auth), Walter Barker, Fogg Mus Art, Harvard Univ, 71; Patricia Krebs (auth), On the making of an artist, Greensboro Daily News, 77. *Mem:* Max Beckmann Gesellschaft, Munich, Ger; and others. *Media:* All. *Res:* Max Beckmann's last years in the US. *Publ:* Auth introd, Max Beckmann in America (catalog), Viviano Gallery, 69; auth, Lucian Krokowski & Max Beckmann, Joseph Pulitzer Collection, Vol 3, 71; auth, Max Beckmann's advice to his students, Weatherspoon Gallery Asn Bulletin, Univ NC, 79; auth, Max Beckmann as a Teacher (exhib catalog), Prestel-Verlag, Munich, 84. *Mailing Add:* Dept Art Univ NC Greensboro NC 27412

BARKLEY, JAMES
PAINTER, DESIGNER
b New York City, Apr 19, 1941. *Study:* Sch Visual Arts, full scholar recipient, NY; studied with Robert Weaver, Robert Andrew Parker, Phil Hayes, Bernard Hogarth, John Cabor, Jack Potter & Robert Shore. *Work:* US Air Force Permanent Art Collection; US Coast Guard Art Collection for 200th Anniversary; US Bur Info,

Famous Am Quotes Poster Prog, US Embassies, worldwide; US Dept Interior, Nat Parks Art Prog; Mus Am Illus, permanent collection. *Comn:* US Postal Stamp, First Centennial Nat Parks System, Mt McKinley, Alaska; Famous Am Quotes Poster Prog, US Bur of Info; Nat Parks, Artists in the Parks Prog; Prog for Two Hundredth Anniversary, Coast Guard; Art Prog, US Air Force. *Exhib:* The Illustrator and the Environment, Earth Island Inst; Pushing the Envelope, Norman Rockwell Mus, 2000; The Art of the Stamp, Smithsonian Inst, Nat Postal Mus, 2003-04. *Collection Arranged:* US Air Force Permanent Art Collection; US Coast Guard Art Collection for 200th Anniversary; US Bur of Info, Famous Am Quotes Poster Prog, US Embassies, worldwide; US Dept Interior, Nat Parks Art Prog; Mus Am Illus, Permanent Collection. *Pos:* Bd dirs, chmn exhib comt, mem mus comt & permanent collection comt, Soc of Illus; chmn, Nat Scholar Competition & Instnl Category for Ann Show, Soc Illus; guest lectr, Lect Series Prog, Soc Illus; lects, Pratt Inst, NY, pub & private schs & various Galleries, Mus & Orgns. *Teaching:* Prof illus, Bridgeport Univ, Bridgeport, Conn; Prof, Parsons Sch of Design, NY. *Awards:* Gold Medal, Soc Illusr; Award Excellence, Soc Illusr; Designer's Award, Soc Publ. *Bibliog:* The Postal Service Guide to US Stamps 28th Ed, 72; 20 Years of Award Winners, Soc Illusr, Hastings House Publ Inc, 81; Outstanding American Illustrators Today, Graphic Sha Publ Co Ltd, 84; Frieda Gales (auth), How to Write Illustrate & Design Children's Books, Lloyd Simone Publ Co, 86; The Art for Survival, Griphis Press, Zurich Switz, 92. *Mem:* Soc of Illusrs (chmn, mus comt mem); NY Art Dirs Club, New York; Chicago Art Dirs Club. *Media:* Acrylic, Watercolor. *Interests:* Restoration of antique carousel, figures & frames. *Publ:* Illusr, Sounder, Winds, The Drinking Gourd, Why the Wind God Wept, Landis & the Ant, The Minstrel Knight, Cheer the Lonesome Traveler, Silent Night, The Good Earth, Pearl Buck, The India Fan, The Estuary Pilgrim. *Dealer:* The Art Source PO Box 257 Pleasantville NY 10570; DRC Publishing 4 Eagle Road Danbury CT 06810 . *Mailing Add:* 25 Brook Manor Pleasantville NY 10570

BARKUS, MARIONA
GRAPHIC ARTIST, PAINTER

b 1948. *Study:* Art Inst Chicago, Ill, 66; Northwestern Univ, Evanston, Ill, BA, 70; Univ Calif, Los Angeles, 72; Pepperdine Univ, 74. *Work:* Yale Univ Art Gallery; Calif Inst Arts Libr; Mus Mod Art Libr, NY; Art Inst Chicago Libr; Indiana-Purdue Univ; Wexford Arts Center, Ireland; UCLA Medical Center; Getty Res Inst; Whitney Mus Art, Special Collections. *Exhib:* Solo exhibs, Founders Gallery, Knox Col, Ill, 79, Freeport Art Mus, Ill, 80, Eastern Wash Univ, 86, Southern Oregon State Col, 89, Univ Calif Berkeley Extension, San Francisco, 91 & SUSHI, San Diego, 91, Munic Art Gallery, 95, Rogue Community Col, ORE, 99, Sinclair Col, Ohio, 99, Univ Tenn, 2002, Univ Nevada, Reno, 2003, Corridor Gallery, TKLofts, Seattle, Wash, 2012, The Lofts "A" Gallery, Seattle, Wash, 2012; Two Person exhib, In Tandem, Highline Community Coll, Wash, 2012; Group exhibs, Themes: Social & Political, Mt St Mary's Col, Los Angeles, 1991, Art & Advocacy, Am Jewish Univ, Los Angeles, Calif, 2008, In Black and White, El Camino Col, Calif, 2008, Show and Tell: The Art of Language, Zimmer Mus, Los Angeles, 2009, Masterpeaces, Da Vinci Gallery, Los Angeles City Col, 2009, Insight/Inside LA, Mt St Mary's Col, Los Angeles, 2009, Provisional Art, Orange Co Ctr Contemp Art, 2009, Ray Warren Multicultural Symposium, Lewis and Clark Coll, Ore, 2010, Making Change, 18 St Projects, Santa Monica, 2010, By and Far: Democracy and Art, Ave 50 Gallery, Los Angeles, 2011, Subvertisements, Calif State Univ, Dominguez Hills, 2011, April Foods, Space Camp Gallery, Indianapolis, IN, 2011, Plenty, Calif State Univ, Northridge, 2013, Prison Nation, UC Merced, 2013; Speaking out, Univ Judaism, 96; Art & the Law, Kresge Art Mus, Univ Miami, Mich, 96; Fun with Dick & Jane, Univ Toledo, Ohio, 97; Indiana-Purdue, Univ, 99; Art Inst, Chicago, 99; SUNY, Buffalo, 2000; Darkroom & Digital, John Wayne Airport, 2001; Univ Richmond Mus, 2002; Universal Warning Sign, Univ Nev, 2002; Angels Gate Cult Ctr, 2004; Berkeley Arts Ctr, 2004; AIR Gallery, NY, 2005; Politick, Los Angeles Munic Gallery, 2006; Gender and Identity, Arts & Literature Lab, 2006; At Work-Art of Calif Labor, Pico House Gallery, Los Angeles, 2006; 4th Int Triennial, Contemp Arts Ctr, Vilnius, Lithuania; Women Artists Then & Now, Track 16 Gallery, Santa Monica, Calif, 2007; and others. *Awards:* Inserts, NY State Coun Arts, Woodstock Times, 90; Earth Banner, Fullerton Mus, Fullerton Cult & Fine Arts Div, Calif, 91; Individual Artist's Grant, Los Angeles Cult Affairs Dept, 91. *Bibliog:* Paul Von Blum (auth), Other Visions, Other Voices, Univ Press Am, 94; Judy Birke (auth), Old Emblems, New Haven Register, 2/19/95; Artworks fusion technology, Satire, Los Angeles times, 7/18/96; Paul Van Blum (auth), Southern California Artist Challenge America, Journal of Am Studies of Turkey, 2004; Sondra Hale & Terry Wolverton (auth), From Site to Vision, Otis Coll, 2011; Marguerite Elliot & Maria Karras (auth), The Womans Building & Feminist Art Education, Otis Coll, 2011. *Mem:* Womens Caucus for Art. *Media:* Graphics; Acrylic, Collage, Digital Prints. *Publ:* Auth, Illustrated History-1981-2009, Litkus Press; Visual Satire (catalog), Fla State Univ; Of Nature & Nation (catalog), Security Pac, Los Angeles, 90; Multiples (catalog), Chastain Gallery & Nexus Ctr Contemp Art, Atlanta, 90; Reinventing the Emblem, Yale Univ, 95; Women Artists Then & Now (catalog), Track 16 Gallery, Santa Monica, Calif, 2007; Mariona Barkus, Soc Photograhic Educ, vol 34:1/2, 2001; Black & White, Daily Breeze, 9/12/08; Show and Tell (catalog), Zimmer Mus, 2009; Art in Southern California (catalog), Mt St Mary's Col, Los Angeles; Provisional Art (catalogue), 2009; By and Far: Democracy and Art (catalog), Ave 50 Gallery, 2011; These Ads Sending A Different Message, Daily Breeze, 2011. *Mailing Add:* PO Box 34785 Los Angeles CA 90034

BARLETTA, EMILY
WEAVER, FIBER ARTIST

Study: Md Inst Coll Art, BFA (fiber arts), 2003. *Exhib:* Fiber for the Future, AIR Gallery, New York, 2004; 21st Ann Nat Juried Arts Exhib, Barrett Art Ctr, Poughkeepsie, NY, 2005; Fiberart International, Pittsburgh Ctr for the Arts, 2007; Contemporary Repetition, Long Beach Island Ctr for the Arts & Sci, NJ, 2008; Drawing in Thread: Contemporary Embroidery, Mount Ida Coll Gallery, Newton, Mass, 2010. *Awards:* NY Found Arts Fel, 2009. *Bibliog:* Roberta Fallon (auth), Aw-some Art, Philadelphia Weekly, 11/14/2007; Kim Werker (auth), Going Biological Interweave Crochet Mag, 2008; Zoe Buck (auth), In Stitches, Foam Mag, 4-5/2009

BARNES, CAROLE D
PAINTER

b Bellefonte, Pa, Nov 12, 1935. *Study:* Pa State Univ, BA (art ed), 57; also with Edward Betts, Glenn Bradshaw & Alex Nepote. *Work:* IBM, Austin, Tex; Utah State Univ, Logan; United Banks & Midland Savings, Colo. *Exhib:* Rocky Mountain Nat Watermedia Soc, Golden, Colo, 78, 80, 82-84, 86, 87, 89-92; Am Watercolor Soc, NY, 75-78, 83, 86, 89 & 91; Nat Acad Design Ann, NY, 76, 78, 81, 82, 84, 86 & 92; Allied Artists Ann, NY, 76, 77, 81, 83, 85 & 87; Nat Watercolor Soc, Los Angeles, 77, 78, 80, 82, 84 & 87. *Teaching:* Instr, Watercolor Workshops, numerous cities across the US; juror, Nat Watercolor Soc & Am Watercolor Soc. *Awards:* Over 30 Nat Award incl: Ralph Fabri Medal Honor, Nat Soc Painters Casein & Acrylic, 80; Gold Medal, San Diego Nat, Calif, 82; Ford Times Award, Am Watercolor Soc, New York, 83. *Bibliog:* Maxine Masterfield (auth), Painting Spirit of Nature; Marilyn Hughey Phillis (auth), Watercolor Techniques for Releasing the Creative Spirit; Greg Albert (auth), Splash; and others. *Mem:* Am Watercolor Soc; Allied Artists; Nat Watercolor Soc; Nat Soc Painters Casein & Acrylic; Rocky Mountain Nat Watermedia Soc; Audubon Artists. *Media:* Watercolor, Acrylic. *Mailing Add:* 3772 Lakebriar Dr Boulder CO 80304

BARNES, CLIFF (CLIFFORD V)
PAINTER, ILLUSTRATOR

b Bell, Calif, Mar 19, 1940. *Study:* Art Ctr Sch Design, Los Angeles, BFA, 62. *Work:* San Bernardino County Govt Ctr, Redlands, Calif, 84-88; Gilcrease Mus, Tulsa, Okla, 85; Crosbyton Co Mus, Tex, 88; Featured artist at Pomona Fairgrounds, Calif, 87; Festival Western Art, San Dimas, Calif, 81-92. *Comn:* Two 10 by 8 ft oil paintings, San Bernardino Co Govt Ctr, 84; Portrait of Frederic Renner, City of San Dimas, 85; Wells Fargo Stage, 94; Portrait of Martin Grelle for San Dimas Festival, 2016. *Exhib:* One man show at the San Bernardino Co Mus, Redlands, Calif, 88 & 92; Wildlife West Show, San Bernardino Co Mus, Redlands, 86-88 & 2015-16; Nat Western Artists, Lubbock, Tex, 86-88; Watercolor West, Riverside & Brea Art Ctr, Calif, 86-2015; Cliff Barnes, Western Am Art, Los Angeles Co Fair, Pomona, Calif, 87; Arts in the Parks, Jackson, Wyo, 93 & 95; American Indian & Cowboy Artists, Autry Mus Western Heritage, Calif, 94-98, Echos and Visions, 02; Am Impressionists, 2011; Oil Painters Am, 2012-2015; Nat Watercolor Soc Show, 2013; Calif Watercolor Soc, 2014; Western Spirit Show, Cheyenne, Wyo, 2014. *Collection Arranged:* City of San Dimas, San Bernardino County Gov Ctr. *Pos:* LW Davidson Architects, Los Angeles, 66-70; Architectural Illustrator, ITT Gilfillian, Los Angeles, 64-66; juror & demonstr, San Bernardino County Mus, Redlands, Calif, 86-88 & 92. *Teaching:* Sem & workshop, Rocky Mountain Nat Park, 90, Fine Arts Inst, 83-90. *Awards:* City of Paramount Best of Show, 85; Nat Western Artists Golden Spur in Drawing, 88; Am Indian & Cowboy Artists, Gold Medals, 88-01; Masters of the Am West, Silver medal, 98; Echoes & Visions People's Choice, 02; Best of Show, Am Plains Artists, 2012 & Weather Award, 2016; Oil Painters of Am, Animal award, 2012; Wildlife Art San Dimas, Silver Medal, Oil, 2012 & Gold Medal in Landscape, 2016; Fallbrook Art Ctr, Signature Watercolor Show, Lush Expressionism award, 2013; Festival of Art San Dimas, Silver Medal Watercolor, 2014; Featured Artist Wild West Show, Banning, Calif, 2016, Featured Artist Wildlife & the Great Outdoors, San Bernardino Co Mus, 2016. *Bibliog:* Profiling Cliff Barnes, Inland Empire Mag, 10/84; Contemporary Western Artists, 82; Art of the West Mag, 1995. *Mem:* Am Indian & Cowboy Artists (pres, 81-82, bd mem, 82-91); Fine Arts Inst (vpres, 87-91); Watercolor West; Am Impressionists; Oil Painters America; Nat Watercolor Soc; Calif Watercolor Soc; Cattlemens Western Art. *Media:* Oil, Watercolor; Charcoal. *Publ:* Illusr, Palette Pleasers Cookbook, 84 & City of San Dimas, 84; Contemporary Western Artists, 82; Leaning Tree, 90. *Mailing Add:* 1320 N Sparks St Burbank CA 91506-1124

BARNES, CURT (CURTIS) EDWARD
PAINTER, INSTRUCTOR

b Taft, Calif, Jan 17, 1943. *Study:* Univ Calif, Berkeley, BA, 64; Pratt Inst, MFA, 66. *Work:* Mus Contemp Art, Bogota, Columbia; Prudential Insurance Corp Am, Newark, NJ; Franklin Furnace Arch, Mus Mod Art, NY; Whanki Mus, Seoul, Korea. *Exhib:* Chicago Ann, Art Inst of Chicago, 67; O K Harris Gallery, NY, 70, 72, 79, 85, 88, 97 & 2002; Contemp Reflections, Aldrich Mus Contemp Art, Ridgefield, Conn, 75; Terry Dintenfass Gallery, NY, 89; Gray Gallery, East Carolina Univ, Greenville, NC, 90; Physicality Hunter Coll Art Gallery, NY, 91; Defining Spaces, Sigma Gallery, NY, 96; Golden Found Tenth Anniversary Exhib, New Berlin, NY, 2007. *Teaching:* Instr painting & drawing, Univ Wis, Stevens Point, 66-67; instr drawing, Parsons Sch Design, New York, 67-71; assoc prof painting, drawing & 20th century art hist, Fordham Univ, 69-84; vis assoc prof, Hampshire Col, 79-80 & 84-86; vis adj prof, Pratt Inst, 81; lectr art, Princeton Univ, 91. *Awards:* Yaddo Fel, summer 76 & 88; Grant in Painting, Nat Endowment for Arts, 93-94; Abbey Found Award, British Sch, Rome, 98; Golden Found Grant, 2004. *Bibliog:* John Perreault (auth), Catching up, Soho Weekly News, 3/76; Nancy Grove (auth), Curt Barnes (rev), Arts Mag, 4/76; Joseph Wiltsee (auth), Investing in young artists, Bus Wk, 5/76; Donald Goddard (auth), Curt Barnes: Convex Paintings, New York Art World, 2/2002. *Mem:* Coll Art Asn; Am Asn Mus. *Media:* Acrylic, Oil. *Publ:* Auth, Table of Contents, Allesandra Publ, 76; ed & contribr, Coll Art Asn, Art J, spring 91. *Mailing Add:* 114 W Houston St New York NY 10012

BARNES, KITT
PAINTER

US citizen. *Study:* Univ NC, Chapel Hill, BFA, 73, MFA, 75. *Work:* Ackland Mus; Sovereign Am Arts Corp; Fayetteville Arts Coun. *Exhib:* Drawing Presentation of MFA Candidates, Corcoran Gallery, 75; Biennial Exhib Piedmont Painting & Sculpture, Mint Mus, 79; Consideration of Line, 20th Century Works On Paper, Stephan Haller Gallery, NY, 95; Textural Integrity, Stephan Haller Gallery, NY, 95; Hudson Guild Invitational NY, 95; Virtuosity, Int Art Fair, The Armory, NY, 95; Aesthetic Makers, Stephen Haller Gallery, NY, 96; Surface Issues, Stephen Haller

Gallery, NY, 96; Cult Markers, Stephen Haller Gallery, NY, 96. *Awards:* Grant, NC Arts Coun Exhib, 94. *Bibliog:* Valentin Tatransky (auth), Group show, Arts Mag, 3/83; Carl Schiffman (auth), New York galleries, late fall, New England Review, Vol 17 No 4, 95. *Media:* Oil on Canvas. *Mailing Add:* PO Box 1244 Madison Sq Sta New York NY 10159

BARNES, MARGO
PAINTER
b New York, NY, Sept 3, 1947. *Study:* Brooklyn Mus Art Sch, with Isaac Soyer; Boston Univ Sch Fine Arts, BFA, 69. *Exhib:* Solo exhibs, Benson Gallery, Bridgehampton, NY, 76, Meredith Long Contemp Gallery, NY, 78-79, A M Sachs Gallery, NY, 83, Capricorn Galleries, Washington, DC, 84 & Watermill Mus, NY, 85; Waterworks, Heckscher Mus, Huntington, NY, 85; 10 Yr Retrospective (with catalog), Guild Hall Mus, East Hampton, NY, 86; Rease Galleries, NY, 88; Meredith Long Galleries, Houston, 88. *Teaching:* Pvt instruction in studio, NY, 75-. *Awards:* Fulbright Grant, 72; Best in show, Guild Hall Mus Artists Mem Show, East Hampton, NY, 85. *Bibliog:* Gerrit Henry (auth), rev, Art News, 11/79; Nina French-Frazier (auth), rev, Art Int, 12/79; Amei Wallach (auth), Water, water everywhere, Newsday, 10/6/85. *Media:* Oil

BARNES, MOLLY
ART DEALER, WRITER
b London, Eng, May 18, 1936; US citizen. *Study:* Univ Calif, Berkeley, BA, 57. *Pos:* Owner & dir, Molly Barnes Gallery, 67-85; art critic, KFWB Radio, Los Angeles, 74-78, KPKF Radio, Los Angeles, 80-, KPCC, Pasadena & KSCN Radio, Los Angeles, 2005-present; asst, Frank Perls Gallery, 78; writer, Hollywood Reporter, 78-; art consult, Roger Smith Hotel, NY, 91-; own, Molly Barnes Gallery, 96-2000; prog dir, New York City Now, Roger Smith Hotel, NY; prog dir, Artist Talk on Art (ATOA), SVA, NY; host, Molly Barns Art News, KCSN-FM, Los Angeles & cable Art Inquiry, 2008-; artist in res, West Los Angeles Coll Art, Culver City, 2012-. *Teaching:* Otis Art Inst, Los Angeles, Calif, currently. *Awards:* Woman of Yr, Artcore, Los Angeles, 99; Women of the Yr, Marlborough Sch Alumni, 2010. *Mem:* Art Critics Am; Mus Contemp Art Los Angeles; AICA; Art Table, New York & Los Angeles; Century City Arts Com. *Specialty:* Contemp Californians, Robert Cottingham, Don Eddy, John Baldessari, Jack Reilly, Mark Kostabi. *Publ:* Auth, How to Get Hung, Tuttle Publ, 94. *Mailing Add:* Molly Barnes Gallery 474 S Rodeo Dr Beverly Hills CA 90212-4220

BARNES, ROBERT M
PAINTER, EDUCATOR
b Washington, DC, Sept 24, 1934. *Study:* Art Inst Chicago, BFA, 56; Univ Chicago, BFA, 56; Columbia Univ, 56; Hunter Col, 57-61; Univ London Slade Sch, Fulbright Grant, 61-63. *Work:* Mus Mod Art, Whitney Mus Am Art, NY; Art Inst Chicago; Pasadena Art Mus, Calif; Nat Gallery Art, Washington; Mus of contemp art, Chicago; and others. *Comn:* Ed lithographs, NY Hilton Hotel, 62. *Exhib:* Mus Civico, Bologna, 65; Galerie Dragon, Paris, 67; Univ Ill, 67; Kansas City Art Inst, 72; Galeria Fanta Spade, Rome, 72; one person exhib, Allan Frumkin Gallery, NY, 83 & 85, Robert Barnes, Struve Gallery, Chicago, Ill, 86, Watercolors, 89, Sources of Power, 92, Blood & Perfume: New Paintings, Sonia Zaks Gallery, Chicago, Ill, 96, Robert Barnes, New Works, 98 & The Ogham, Sonia Zaks Gallery, Chicago, Ill, 2000; Sonia Zaks, New Work, 2002; Printworks, Chicago, 2008, 2009; Corbett vs. Dempsey, 2010; Am Acad Art & Letts Invitational, New York, 2010; The Dill Pickle Club, Printworks, Chgo, Ill, 2012. *Teaching:* Instr grad painting, Ind Univ, 60-61; vis artist, Kansas City Art Inst, 63-64; asst prof painting & drawing, Ind Univ, Bloomington, 65-70, prof, Dept Fine Arts, 70-2000, Ruth N Hall prof fine art emeritus, retired, 99. *Awards:* Fulbright Grant, 63; Nat Endowment Arts, 82; Ruth N Halls, prof fine art, Endowed Chmn, 96; Acad Award, Am Acad Arts and Scis, 93; Gurie Siever Award, Chicago Art Inst. *Bibliog:* Michael Rooks (auth), Seeking the City of Truth: Robert Barnes' Pastels for the Cantos of Ezra Pound, The Smart Mus of Art Bulletin, 96-97, 8-19; Franz Schulze (auth), Fantastic Images Chicago Art Since 1945, Follet Pub Co, 72; Robert Barnes: Work in Progress, interview by L E McCullough, Arts Indiana, 12/90, 28-32; Rough, Dirty, and Dangerous Pastels, Am Artist, 2005; McSweeny's Quarterly #36, 2010. *Mem:* Nat Acad Design. *Media:* Oil/canvas-panel, Casein. *Collection:* Albrecht-Kemper Mus of Art, St. Joseph, MO; Art Ctr Coll of Design, Pasadena, Calif; The Art Inst of Chicago; Elvehjem Mus of Art, Univ of Wis, Madison; Fla Int Univ Art Gallery; Ind Univ Art Mus, Bloomington. *Dealer:* Corbett vs Dempsey 1120 No Ashland Chicago, IL 60622; Print Works Galery 311 W Superior Chicago IL 60610. *Mailing Add:* PO Box 438 Searsport ME 04974

BARNES, WILLIAM DAVID
PAINTER, PRINTMAKER
b Chicago, Ill, Apr 13, 1946. *Study:* Drake Univ, Des Moines, Iowa, BFA, 69; Univ Ariz, Tucson, MFA, 74. *Work:* Bowery Gallery, NY; Montgomery Mus, Ala; Lamar Dodd Art Ctr, LaGrange, Ga; Portsmouth Art Ctr, Va; CSX Corp; Washington and Lee Univ, Va; Coll William and Mary, Va. *Exhib:* Faculty Show, Muscarelle Mus, Williamsburg, Va, 91, 96 & 2002 (catalog, 2002); solo show, Monotypes, Peninsula Fine Arts Ctr, Newport News, Va, 92, Bowery Gallery, NY, 95 & 98 & John Taylor Art Ctr, Hampton, Va, 96; Paintings and Monotypes, Bowery Gallery, NY, 92; Monotypes, Reynolds Gallery, Richmond, Va, 93; Duo Show, Hermitage Found Mus, Norfolk, Va, 96; Commonwealth Collects, Va Beach Art Ctr, Va, 96; Zenxist-Human Presence, Painting Ctr, NY, 2000. *Teaching:* Instr painting, Univ Ariz, Tucson, 74-75; prof painting, Col William & Mary, Williamsburg, 75-. *Awards:* Cert Distinction, Va Artists, Va Mus, 79; Best in Show, LaGrange Nat, Lamar Dodd Art Ctr, 86; Award of Distinction & Award of Achievement, Peninsula Fine Arts Ctr, 95 & 96. *Bibliog:* PSA Art Showcase Inaugural Exhib Chronicling Time (catalog); Monotypes/William Barnes (catalog), 92. *Mem:* Bowery Gallery, NY; Coll Art Asn. *Media:* Oil Paint & Monotype. *Mailing Add:* 716 Jamestown Rd Williamsburg VA 23185

BARNETT, CHERYL L
SCULPTOR
b Merced, Calif, Feb 24, 1956. *Study:* Univ Calif Santa Cruz, BA (art), 77; Calif State Univ Fresno, MA (sculpture), 85. *Work:* In over 440 art collections in 11 countries. *Comn:* Over 10 private and public art commissions; Mercy / UC Davis Cancer Center, Calif, 2000. *Exhib:* In over 80 misc group shows with over 16 solo shows: Erika Meyerovich Gallery, San Francisco, Calif, 1986-87; Banakar Gallery Walnut Creek, Calif, 1988; Eleonore Austerer Gallery, San Francisco, Calif, 1990-2004; The Simmons Gallery, San Francisco, Calif, 2003-2005, Eleonore Austerer Gallery, Palm Desert, Calif, 2002-2011; Merced Coll Art Gallery, Calif, 82-2012; Bay Area Bronze, Civic Arts Ctr, Walnut Creek, Calif, 88; 250 Women, Artworks Foundry and Gallery, Berkeley, Calif, 89; Salute to Arts & Flowers, Arts Comn of San Francisco, 89; one-women show, Merced Coll Art Gallery, Calif, 82-2012, Phebe Conley Art Gallery, Calif Stat Univ, Fresno, 85, The Art Circle, Visalia, Calif, 86, Erika Myerovich Gallery, San Francisco, 86-87, Banaker Gallery, Walnut Creek, Calif, 88, Eleonore Austerer Gallery, San Francisco, 90-2001, 04 & The Simmons Gallery, San Francisco, 2005; Life Lines, Mendocino Art Center, Calif, 95 & 97; Speaking of Her, Pac Rim Sculpture Group, San Francisco, 96; Brumley Art Gallery, Bass Lake, Calif, 02-05; Studies of the Human Figure-Henry Moore and Cheryl Barnett, E.A. Gallery, Palm Desert, Calif, 2004; Eleonore Austerer Gallery, Palm Desert, Calif, 2002-2011; Gallery of the Square Merced, Calif, 2011-2012; The William and Joseph Gallery, Santa Fe, NMex, 2012; Ekasake Sculpture Garden & Gallery, 2013-2016; 35 Year in Bronze-Retrospective, Calif State Univ Stanislaus, 2015. *Teaching:* prof art, Merced Col, Calif, 88-. *Awards:* Achievement Award in Art, Bank of Am, 74; NISOD Excellence Award for Teaching, Merced Col, Univ Tex, 96; The Frances DeB Henderson Nat Sculpture Prize, Mus Fine Arts, Cambridge, Mass, 98; Nat Prize Show, Cambridge Art Asn, 98; Award of Merit, Santa Clara Biennial Indoor/Outdoor Sculpture Exhib, Calif, 01. *Bibliog:* In Three Dimensions: Women Sculptors of the 90's, New House Cen for Contemp Art & Snug Harbor Cultural Ctr, 95; Virtuosity CD-ROM, Art Commun Int, 96; 2000 Outstanding Women of the 21st Century, Int Biographical Centre, Melrose Press Ltd, Eng, 2000; Two Thousand Notable American Women, Am Biog Inst, Raleigh, NC, 2000; American Art Collector, Annual Alcove Books, Berkeley, Calif, 2006-2016. *Mem:* Int Sculpture Ctr, Washington DC (past mem); Nat Educators Asn (past mem); Am Asn Univ Women (past mem); Pac Rim Sculpture Group, San Francisco (past mem); Nat Mus Women in the Arts, Wash DC (past mem). *Media:* Cast Bronze, Abstract Figurative Sculpture

BARNETT, DAVID J
ART DEALER, PAINTER
b Milwaukee, Wis, Feb 22, 1946. *Study:* Lincoln Coll, Lincoln, Ill; Univ Wis, Milwaukee. *Exhib:* Scottsdale Mus Contemp Art, Ariz. *Pos:* Owner, David Barnett Gallery, currently; pres, Van Go Frame & Art America's Gallery to You, currently. *Teaching:* Lectr & adv art acquisition to prof orgn, pvt individuals & corp. *Bibliog:* Art experts can save money & reputation for the wary dealer, Art Bus News, 2/84; Exclusively Yours, For the Love of Art, 4/96; Milwaukee Dealer puts art on wheels in 'gold coast' area, Milwaukee Art Bus News, 9/86; The Renaissance Man, Lifestyle West, 11/01; 6,000 Sq Foot Home Started as Run-Down Wreck, Milwaukee Jour Sentinel, 10/02. *Mem:* Milwaukee Art Mus; Chicago Art Inst; Milwaukee Pub Mus; Appraisers Asn Am. *Media:* Painting; Watercolor. *Specialty:* Nineteenth and twentieth century European and American masters; leading Wisconsin artists; contemporary American artists; American historical prints; International, African, Indonesian & Latin American Art. *Publ:* Auth, Milton Avery-Retrospective (catalog), pvt publ, 12/8/84-1/31/85; Carol Summers woodcuts 1950-1988 (catalog), pvt publ, 88; Milton Avery-The 1930's Period (catalog), pvt publ, summer, 88; Milton Avery-The 1940's Period (catalog), pvt publ, summer, 89; Lester Johnson-Retrospective The 1940's To The Present (catalog), pvt publ, Nov-Dec/89. *Mailing Add:* David Barnett Gallery 1024 E State St Milwaukee WI 53202

BARNETT, EMILY
PAINTER, PRINTMAKER
b Brooklyn, NY, Oct 23, 1947. *Study:* Queens Coll, NY, BFA, 69, Louisiana State Univ, MFA, 76; cert in interior design, Parsons, New Sch Design. *Work:* Jane Voorhees Zimmerli Art Mus; West Publ co; Adelphi Univ; City of Seattle Portable Works Collection; Siena Coll; Nassau Community Coll. *Exhib:* Nat Acad Design Ann Juried Exhib, NY, 81, 82 & 90; 33rd New Eng Exhib, Silvermine Ctr Arts, Conn, 82; Ann juried exhib, Fine Arts Mus of Long Island, 88 & 93; Gwenda Jay Gallery, Chicago, 95; Fairleigh Dickinson Univ, NJ, 95; Hutchins Gallery, Long Island Univ, 96; African-Am Mus Nassau Co, 97, 98 & 2000; Parrish Art Mus, 99; Watermark Gallery, Greenport, LI, 2002; Jane Voorhees Zimmerli Art Mus, NJ, 2002; NY Soc Etchers, 2003; Solo exhibs, Heckscher Mus, Bryant Libr, NY, 97, Firehouse Gallery, Nassau Community Coll, NY, 2000, Islip Art Mus Store, NY, 2002, Custer Inst Observatory Gallery, Southold, NY, 2002, Jamaica Wildlife Refuge, NY, 2002; The Catskill Center's Erpf Gallery, 2004; Adelphi Univ, 2004; William Paterson Univ, NJ, 2005; Fashion Inst Tech, NY, 2005-2006; NC Mus Natural Sci, NC, 2006; DeCordova Gallery, 2007, 2008; Mack Cali Lobby, NJ, 2007; Nest Interiors, New York, 2009; Heckscher Mus, Long Island Biennial, 2010, 2012; Monmouth Mus, NJ, 2010; Mills Pond House Gallery, Long Island, 2010; Target Gallery, Torpedo Art Ctr, Va, 2011; Red Filter Gallery, NJ, 2012; Maloney Gallery, Coll St Elizabeth, NJ, 2012; Intaglio Prints, NY Soc Etchers, 2013; Victory Hall Drawing Rooms, NJ, 2013; Side Tracks Gallery, PA, 2013; NY Soc Etchers, Intaglio Prints, NY, 2013. *Teaching:* Fac painting, drawing color theory, color & design, Parsons Sch Design, New York, 80-; adj prof, Dowling Coll, Oakdale, NY, 87, Nassau Co Mus Art, 87-, Suffolk Community Coll, 92-2000 & Hofstra Univ, 2000-2011; Fashion Inst Tech, 2005; Adelphi Univ, 2005-2006; Nassau Community Coll, 2006; visiting master artist workshop, Armory Art Ctr, Fla, 2013. *Awards:* Purchase Award, West Publ Corp, 95; Millay Colony Artist Residence Grant, 98; Irwin Zlowe Award, Nat Asn Women Artists, 2000; City of Seattle Purchase Award, 2003; New York Found Arts, 2003; Platte Clove artist-in-residence, 2003; and others. *Bibliog:* The Originals, WLIW-TV, 8-88; Emily Barnett's painting, Life and Art in the Studio (monogr), 88. *Media:* Oil, Prints. *Dealer:* Nest Interiors NY. *Mailing Add:* 222 Carle Pl New York NY 11514

BARNETT, HELMUT
PAINTER, PRINTMAKER
b Stuttgart, Ger, Feb, 16, 1946; US citizen. *Study:* Univ Tex, Austin, BFA (studio art) & BA, 73. *Comn:* Mixed media paintings on canvas, Shefelman & Nix, & IBM, Austin, Tex, 84, Am Security Life Insurance Co, San Antonio, 85, Houston Showroom, Hayworth Inc, 85 & Clann, Bell & Murphy, Houston, 85. *Exhib:* Soc Photogrs & Artist Reps National, Shreveport, La, 76; Western Asn Art Mus Traveling Exhib, 79; Solo exhibs, Amdur Gallery, Austin, Tex, 84 & 86; II Ann Exhib, Art Mus S Tex, Corpus Christi, 83; Soho Invitational Show, Works on Paper, Austin, 85; 11th Int Independents Exhib of Prints, Kanagawa Prefectural Gallery, Japan, 85; New Am Talent, Tex Fine Arts Asn, Laguna Gloria Art Mus, Austin, 86. *Media:* Acrylic, Pastel. *Dealer:* Martin/Rathburn Gallery The Blue Star San Antonio TX. *Mailing Add:* 709 Spofford St Austin TX 78704

BARNETT, VIVIAN ENDICOTT
CURATOR, HISTORIAN
Study: Vassar Coll, AB, 65; Inst Fine Arts, NY Univ, MA, 71; Grad Ctr, City Univ New York. *Collection Arranged:* Kandinsky Watercolors from Solomon R Guggenheim Collection (auth, catalog), 81-82; Vasily Kandinsky (auth, catalog), Art Gallery NSW, 82; Kandinsky in Munich, 82, Kandinsky: Russian and Bauhaus Years, 83, Kandinsky in Paris, 85, Hans Reichel, 88, Guggenheim Mus, Kandinsky Och Sverige, Malmo Kunsthall (auth, catalog), 89; Kandinsky Kleine Freuden, Dusseldorf (auth, catalog), 92. *Pos:* Res asst, Solomon R Guggenheim Mus, 73-77, curatorial asst, 78-79, assoc cur, 80-81, res cur, 81-82, cur, 82-91; dir, Roethel-Benjamin Archive, 91-. *Awards:* John Simon Guggenheim Fel, 90; Inst for Advanced Study, Princeton, 2003-2004; Leon Levy Fellow, Frick, 2010-2011. *Mem:* Coll Art Asn Am; Kandinsky Soc; Int Coun Mus; Int Found Art Rsch. *Res:* Kandinsky; Klee; Arthur Jerome Eddy; Jawlensky. *Publ:* Kandinsky Watercolors: Catalogue Raisonne, Vol I 1900-1921, 92; The Russian Presence in the 1924 Venice Biennale, The Great Utopia, 92; Kandinsky Watercolors: Catalogue Raisonne, Vol II 1922-1944, 94; Vasily Kandinsky: A Colorful Life, 95; The Blue Four: Feininger, Jawlensky, Kandinsky, and Klee in the New World, 97; Exiles and Emigres, 97; Die Brücke in Dresden, 2001; Mies in America, 2001; The Blue Four Collection at the Norton Simon Museum, 2002; Klee & America, 2006; Kandinsky Drawings: Catalogue Raisonne, Vol I, 2006; Kandinsky Drawings: Catalogue Raisonne, Vol II, 2007; Kandinsky: Absolute Abstract, 2008; Der Grosse Widerspruch; Franz Marc Zwischen Delaunay und Rousseau, 2009; Blaues Haus und Gelber Klang; Kandinsky und Jawlensky in Murnau, 2014. *Mailing Add:* Solomon R Guggenheim Mus 1071 Fifth Ave New York NY 10128

BARNEY, MATTHEW
SCULPTOR, FILMMAKER
b San Francisco, Calif, 1967. *Study:* Yale Univ, BA, 1989. *Work:* Whitney Mus Am Art, Mus Mod Art, NY; Mus Boymans-van Beuningen, Rotterdam, Holland; Walker Art Ctr, Minneapolis, Minn; Sammlung Goetz, Munich, Ger. *Exhib:* Solo exhibs include Matthew Barney: The CREMASTER Cycle, Solomon R Guggenheim Mus, NY, 1994-2002, Tate Gallery, London, 1995, San Francisco, 1996, 2000, 2006, Kunsthalle Wien, Austria, 1997, Barbara Gladstone Gallery, New York City, 1997, 2011, Walker Art Ctr, Mpls, 1999, Samsung Mus Art, Seoul, 2005, Serpentine Gallery, London, 2007, Fondazione Merz, Turin, 2008, Sadie Coles HQ, 2010, Subliming Vessel: The Drawings of Matthew Barney, Morgan Library & Mus, NY, 2013, and many others; group exhibs include Foreign Body, Mus Gegenwartskunst, Basel, Switz, 1996; Sydney Biennale, Australia, 1996; Die Rache der Veronika, Fotosammlung Lambert, Deichtorhallen Hamburg, 1998; Global Vision, New Art from the 90's, Dakis Joannou Collection, Desle Found, Athens, 1998; Galerie Rudolfino, Prague, 2001; Imperfect Innocence, Contemp Mus, Baltimore, Md, 2003; Working Editions, Fine Art in Space, Long Island, NY, 2004; Quartet, Walker Art Ctr, Minneapolis, 2005; Figures in the Field, Mus Contemp Art, Chicago, 2006; Narcissus Faces, Cook Fine Art, 2007; Yokohoma Triennial: Time Crevasse, Yokohama, Japan, 2008; Bad Habits, Albright-Knox Art Gallery, Buffalo, NY, 2009; Houdini: Art and Magic, The Jewish Mus, NY, 2010; Black Swan, Regen Projects, Los Angeles, 2011; and many others. *Awards:* Europa 2000, XLV Venice Biennale, 1993; Hugo Boss Award, Guggenheim Mus, NY, 1996; James D Phelan Art award in video, Bay Area Video Coalition, San Francisco Found, 2000; Medal of Honor for Lifetime Achievement in Art, Nat Arts Club, 2008. *Bibliog:* Stuart Morgan (auth), Of goats and men, Frieze, 1/95; Norman Bryson (auth), Matthew Barney's Gonadotrophic Cavaleade, Parkett, 12/95; Jerry Saltz (auth), The next sex, Art in Am, 10/96; Alison Chernik (dir), Matthew Barney: No Restraint, 2006. *Mailing Add:* c/o Barbara Gladstone Gallery 515 W 24th St New York NY 10011

BARNEY, TINA
PHOTOGRAPHER
b New York, NY, 1945. *Study:* Sun Valley Ctr Arts & Humanities, 76-79. *Work:* Baltimore Art Mus; Boise Gallery Art, Idaho; Mus Fine Arts, Boston; Mus Fine Arts, Houston; Nat Mus Am Art, Washington, DC. *Exhib:* Solo shows incl Nederlands Foto Institut, Rotterdam, 99, Columbus Mus of Art, Ohio, 99, Ctr for Photog, Univ de Salamanca, 2000, Mus Ctr Vaprikki, Tampere, Finland, 2000, Galerie der Hochschule fur Grafik and Bruchkunst, Leipzig, 2000, Janet Borden Inc, NY, 2000 & Carol Ehlers Gallery, Chgo, 2001; group shows incl In and Out of Place, Mus Fine Arts, Boston, 93; Living with Contemporary Art, Aldrich Mus, Ridgefield, Conn, 95; Permanent Collection Exhib, Mus of Modern Art, 98; The Nude in Contemporary Art, Aldrich Mus of Contemp Art, Conn, 99; Insites: Interior Spaces in Contemporary Art, Whitney Mus of Am Art, Stamford, Conn, 2000; At Home, Lennon Weinberg Inc, NY, 2001; Portraits, Rena Bransten Gallery, San Francisco, 2001; Portraits, Rena Bransten Gallery, San Francisco, 2001; Settings and Players, Prague City Gallery, Czech Republic, 2001; Double Vision: Photographs from the Strauss Collection, Univ Mus, Calif State Univ, Long Beach, 2001. *Awards:* John Simon Guggenheim Mem Foundation Fel, 91. *Bibliog:* Edith Newhall (auth), Preview, BOMB Mag, 95; Charles Hagen (auth), Review, NY Times, 4/28/95. *Publ:* illusr, The Garden of Eden, Doubletake, 97; Male/Female, Aperture #156, 99; Art on Paper, 5-6/99; Settings and Players, White Cube 2, 2001. *Dealer:* Janet Borden Inc 560 Broadway New York NY 10012. *Mailing Add:* 11 Foster Cove Rd Westerly RI 02891-5505

BARNHILL, GEORGIA BRADY
CURATOR, HISTORIAN
b Mt Kisco, NY, 1944. *Study:* Wellesley Coll, BA (art hist), 66. *Pos:* Am Antiqn Soc, Worcester, Mass, 69-2009; Dir, Ctr for Hist Am Visual Culture, 2007-2012, retired, 2012. *Awards:* Fel, First Pub Humanities Inst, Mass Found Humanities & Pub Policy, 82, Bibliog Soc Am, 86, Am Philos Soc, 86 & Huntington Libr, 93; Maurice Rickards Award, Ephemera Soc Am, 87; and others. *Mem:* Fitchburg Art Mus (pres, bd trustees, 91-96); Am Hist Print Collectors Soc (pres, 96-98); Archives Am Art; Arts Worcester (pres, 97-99); Coll Art Assn. *Res:* Eighteenth & Nineteenth century Am prints; Am literary illustration. *Interests:* Landscape imagery, depictions of national historical events, American lithography, book illustration. *Publ:* Ed, Prints of New England, Am Antiqn Soc, 91; auth, Wild Impressions: The Adirondacks on Paper, Adirondack Mus & David Godine, 95; Cultivation of American Artists, Am Antiquarian Soc, 97; Illustrations of the Adirondacks in the Popular Press, Adirondack Prints & Printmakers, 98; Depictions of the White Mountains in the Popular Press, Hist NH, Vol 24, 99; auth, Markets for Images from 1670 to 1790 in America, Imprint, Vol 25, 2000; ed, Bibliography on American Prints of the Seventeenth to the Nineteenth Centuries, 2006; many others; Written on Stone: Family Registees, Family Trees, & Mem Prints in Picturing Victorian Am: Prints by the Kellog Brothers of Hartford, Conn 1830-1880, 2009; co-editor, New Views of New England: Studies in Material and Visual Culture, 1680-1830, 2012. *Mailing Add:* 54 Larkspur Dr Amherst MA 01002

BARNWELL, JOHN L
PAINTER
b Los Angeles, Calif, Mar 17, 1922. *Study:* Univ Calif, Berkeley, BA; Newark Sch Fine & Indust Art, NJ; Art Students League, with Frank Reilly; watercolor with Ed Whilney & Ferdinand Petrie. *Work:* Blue Cross, Blue Shield, Rochester, NY. *Exhib:* Jersey City Mus, NJ, 77; Bergen Community Mus, NJ, 77; NJ Watercolor Soc Show, 84, 87, 88 & 89; solo exhib, Hamilton, Mass, 87, Bloomfield, NJ 90; West Essex, NJ, 92, 94, 97, 98. *Awards:* Windsor & Newton Award, 90; Community Art Asn Award of Excellence, 93; P Wick Award, Am Artist Prof Soc, 94; NJ State Show, Best in Show, 97, 98. *Mem:* Assoc NJ Watercolor Soc; fel Am Artists Prof League; Miniature Art Soc NJ (pres, 75-80); Art Students League. *Media:* Oil, Watercolor. *Dealer:* Essex Fine Art Gallery 13 S Fullerton St Montclair NJ; Art-on-the-Ave Verona NJ. *Mailing Add:* 11 Kingsland Rd Boonton NJ 07005-9020

BAROFF, JILL (EMILY)
PAINTER, DRAFTSMAN
b Summit, NJ, Mar 10, 1954. *Study:* Antioch Coll, BFA, 76; studied, Hunter Coll, New York, 80-81. *Work:* Fogg Art Mus, Harvard Univ; Werner Kramarsky, NY; Mus of Modern Art, NY; Nat Gallery of Art, Washington, DC; Yale Univ Art Mus; Staatsgalerie Stuttgart; Cleveland Mus Contemp Art; Dayton Art Inst; Progressive Insurance co, Cleveland; Mus Folkwang, Essen, Germany; Kupferstichkabinett, Berlin, Germany. *Awards:* Pollock-Krasner Found Fel, 87-88 & 92-93; Fel Nat Endowment Arts, 93-94, exchange Fel with Japan, 96; NY Found Arts Fel, 95, Lily Auchincloss Fel, 2009; Aaron Siskind Found Grant for Photog, 01; Gottlieb Found Grant; MacDowell Colony Grant. *Bibliog:* Drawing is Another Kind of Language, Fogg Art Mus/Daco Verlag, 97; Josef Helfenstein and Jonathan Fineberg (auths), Drawings of Choice from a New York Collection, Kannert Art Mus, Univ Ill, 2002; Anja Chavez (auth), Infinite Possibilities: Serial Imagery in 20th Century Drawings, Davis Mus and Cult Ctr, Wellesley Coll, Mass, 2004; Infinite Possibilities: Serial Imagery in 20th C. Drawings, Davis Mus, 2004; Anja Chavez (auth), The Invisible Thread: Buddhist Spirit in Contemp Art, Newhouse Ctr for Contemp Art, New York, 2004; The Shape of Time: Jill Baroff & Stefana McClure, Mondo Verlag Freiburg, 2006; Zeichnung als Prozess, Mus Folkwang, Essen, Ger, 2008; Aus Gezeichnet, Kunstverein KISS, Untergroeningen, Ger, 2008; New York New Drawings 1946-2007, Museo de Arte Contemporaneo Esteban Vicente, 2009. *Mem:* Orgn Independent Artists; NY Artists Equity. *Media:* Installation, drawing. *Dealer:* Margarete Roeder Gallery 545 Broadway New York City, NY 10012; Bartha Contemporary London England; Galerie Christian Lethert, Cologne, Germany. *Mailing Add:* 474 Dean St Brooklyn NY 11217

BARON-MALKIN, PHYLLIS
EDUCATOR, PAINTER
b Newark, NJ, Apr 15, 1927. *Study:* Culinary Sch NY, 47; Nat Acad Design, New York, 70-76; Sch Interior Design, Miami, Fla, 78. *Work:* Sher Gallery, Miami Beach, Fla; Rosie the Riveter Park, Richmond, Calif. *Exhib:* Group exhibs, Int Fine Arts Exhib, Calif, Nat Acad Design, 70-76, Newark Pub Libr, Lever House, NY, Bernardsville State Show, Salmagundi Club, Nat Arts Club, Miniature Show NJ, Catherine Larriland Wolfe Club, NY, Cou Jewish Women, Teaneck, NJ, Greenwich Village, NJ State Show, East Orange, Audubon Show, Newark Mus & Jersey City Mus; solo exhibs, South Orange Gallery, NJ, Originique Gallery, Korby Gallery, Bloomfield Gallery, Delaney Gallery, Fort Lauderdale, Tattum Gallery. *Pos:* Owner, designer Kirojada Sugar Creations, 60-70; principal, owner, Dade Co Taxi, 61-78, Jewelers, Fort Lauderdale, Fla; judge, numerous art shows, ran outdoor art shows, currently. *Mem:* Nat Pastel Soc

BARONE, MARK
PAINTER
b Chicago, Ill, Aug 25, 1959. *Study:* Univ Minnesota, BA, 83; Univ Southern Ill, MFA, 89. *Work:* Evansville Mus Arts and Scis, Ind; Univ Southern Ind, Evansville; Bristol-Meyers Permanent Collection; Williams, Williams & Lentz Accountants, Paducah, Ky; Yeiser Art Center, Paducah; Shawnee Community Coll, Shawnee Town,

Ill. *Exhib:* Univ Wis Univ Mus, Madison, 90; Ill Figurative, Bradley Univ, Galesburg, Ill, 90; One-man shows, Northern Ind Arts Asn, Muster, 93, Mercyhurst Coll, Erie, Pa, 94, Murray State Univ, 1995, Ky, Lyons Wier Gallery, Chicago, 97, Van de Griff Gallery, Chicago, 98, Principle Gallery, Alexandria, Va, 2000, numerous others; group shows, Neville Pub Mus, Green Bay, Wis, 94, Eastern Ill Univ, Charleston, Ill, 95, Van de Griff Gallery, Santa Fe, 97, 98, Lyons Wier Gallery, Chicago, 97; Small Works Exhib, Schoharie Arts Coun, Cobleskill, NY, 92; Southeast Ctr Contemp Art, Winston Salem, NC, 94; New Works, Hoyt Nat, New Castle, Pa, 96; Renewal of Spirit, H Lee Moffit Cancer Center, Tampa, Fla, 2000. *Pos:* artist relocation program, Paducah Ky, 2000-. *Teaching:* instr, Galesburg Civic Art Center, Ill, 92; instr, Southern Ill Univ, 86-89. *Awards:* Grumbacher Gold Medallion, Hoyt Inst, 1987; Ill Arts Coun fellow 1991; Wis Arts Bd fellow 1992; Best of Show Award, MPUAG Nat, 1992; Southern Arts Fedn fellow 1994; Ky Arts Coun fellow 1997, 2000; Donors Award, Great Plains Nat, 2000. *Media:* Oil, Panel. *Publ:* artist, New Art Examiner, 94; auth, New American Paintings, Open Studio Press, 97, 99; artist, The Other Side, 11/2000. *Dealer:* Principal Gallery 208 King St Alexandria VA 22314

BARONS, RICHARD IRWIN
MUSEUM DIRECTOR, HISTORIAN
b Bergen, NY, Apr 25, 1946. *Study:* State Univ NY Coll, New Paltz, BA, 70. *Collection Arranged:* Eighteenth and Nineteenth Century Am Folk Pottery (auth, catalog), State Univ NY Coll, New Paltz, 68; The Am Cooking Hearth: Colonial and Post-Colonial Cooking Tools (auth, catalog), Broome Co Hist Soc, 76; The Folk Arts and Crafts of the Susquehanna and Chenango River Valleys, Roberson Ctr Arts & Sci, 78; Multiples: Am Printmaking of the Last Ten Years, 79; Emil Holzhauer: Seventy-Five Years of an Artist's Life (auth, catalog), 80; Severity and Simplicity: The Arts and Crafts Aesthetic in the Northeast 1895-1925 (auth, catalog), Binghamton Univ Mus Art, 94. *Pos:* Cur, Genesee Co Mus, 70-74; cur hist, Roberson Mus & Sci Ctr, 74-79; preservation dir, Bement-Billings House, Newark Valley, NY, 83-89; dir, Preservation Asn of the Southern Tier, 86-91; dir Southampton Hist Mus, 99-2006; exec dir, East Hampton Hist Soc, 2006-; exec dir, Thomas Moran Trust, 2013-. *Teaching:* Prof art hist & archit, Broome Community Coll, Binghamton, NY, 79-99. *Mem:* Am Asn Mus; Asn State & Local Hist; Hist New England. *Res:* Eighteenth and nineteenth century American arts, crafts and architecture. *Publ:* Coauth, Franck Taylor Bowers 1875-1932, 77 & auth, The Folk Tradition: The Early Arts and Crafts of the Susquehanna River Valley, 81, Roberson Ctr Arts & Sci; coauth, The Lost Hamptons, Arcadia Books, 2003; Coauth with John Jonas Gruen, Sag Harbor: Classic Houses Great & Small, Gallery Press, 2007. *Mailing Add:* 94 Church Lane East Hampton NY 11937

BAROOSHIAN, MARTIN
PAINTER, PRINTMAKER
b Chelsea, Mass, Dec 18, 1929. *Study:* Boston Mus Fine Arts Sch, full tuition scholars, dipls with highest hons, 52 & 55; Albert H Whitin Traveling Fel, Europe, 52; Boston Mus Sch Travelling Fel, 52-53; Tufts Univ, BSEd, 53; Boston Univ, MA (art hist), 58; and with Gaston Dorfinant & S W Hayter, Paris. *Work:* Libr & Mus Performing Arts, Lincoln Ctr Mus Mod Art, Metrop Mus Art, NY; Nat Gallery Art, New Delhi, India; Mus Mod Art & Nat Gallery, Yerevan, Armenia; Montreal Art Mus; Boston Pub Libr, Mass. *Exhib:* Boston Printmakers Traveling Exhibs; Soc Am Graphic Artists, NY; First Int Can Graphic Art Exhib, Montreal Mus Fine Art, 71; 1st & 2nd NH Int, 73 & 74; retrospective, Art Complex Mus, Duxbury, Mass, 83 & Firehouse Gallery, Garden City, NY, 93; Julie Heller Gallery, Provincetown, Mass, 2001; Winsor Art Gallery, NY, 2005; multiple group exhibs. *Pos:* Consult, Works on Paper, Swann Galleries, NY; fine arts consult, prints & drawings, 88-95. *Teaching:* Instr lithography Boston Mus Sch, 54-55; instr printmaking workshops, Pratt Inst, NY, 60-69; art instr, Half Hollow Hills Sch, NY, 60-92. *Awards:* Asian Studies Grant, US Dept Educ, 72; Print Prize, Nat Acad Design, 76; USSR Studies Grant, US Dept Educ, 79; and others. *Bibliog:* Helen Terzian (auth), Martin Barooshian, the changing face of art, Ararat, No 21, winter 65; William P Carl (auth), The Inner World of Martin Barooshian, Duxbury Art Complex Mus, Mass, 83; Michael Russo (auth), Discovering the art of Martin Barooshian-surrealist works of the fifties, J of Print World, 2001 & 04. *Mem:* Soc Am Graphic Artists (pres, 72-74); Print Club Albany. *Media:* Oils; Printmaking. *Publ:* Auth, Some Thoughts on Paper & Printmaking, Rising Paper Co, Mass, 86; auth, Reflections on Atelier 17 and Lithography Studios in 1950's, Paris. *Dealer:* Ro Gallery 36th St Long Island City NY 10019; Herbert Halpern Fine Art 1520 St Charles Ave New Orleans LA 70130. *Mailing Add:* c/o Julie Heller Gallery PO Box 915 Provincetown MA 02657

BAROWITZ, ELLIOTT
PAINTER
b Westwood, NJ, Aug 22, 1936. *Study:* Carnegie-Mellon Univ; RI Sch of Design, BFA; San Francisco Art Inst; Univ Cincinnati; Cincinnati Art Acad, MFA. *Work:* NJ State Mus, Trenton; Rose Mus, Brandeis Univ; Cincinnati Art Mus; Paterson Mus, NJ; Main Ctr Contemp Art; RI School of Design; House of Humor and Satire, Bulgaria. *Exhib:* San Francisco Art Asn Mus, 61; Nova Zembla Gallery, Hertogebusch, The Neth, 93; Drexel Univ, 93; Cent Conn State Coll, Forum Gallery, Jamestown, NY, 94; Regard Parole, Elancourt, France, 94; Exchanging Thought, Univ Thailand, Chiangmai, 96; Spil Cult Ctr, Roselare, Belg, 99; Midrash: Memoirs, Art & Art History, Slifka Ctr, Yale Univ, New Haven, Conn, 2000; retrospective, Leonard Perlstein Gallery, Drexel Univ, 2003; Elder Arts, Napa, Calif, Madelyn Jordon Fine Arts, 2004; Ctr Maine Contemporary Art, 2006; de Spil Cultural Ctr, Belgium, 2011; and many others. *Pos:* Exec ed, Art & Artist, 80-89. *Teaching:* Prof painting & art theory, Drexel Univ, Philadelphia, 66-2002, prof emer, 2002; instr painting & design, Maine Coll Art, Maine, summers 76-99; adj prof contemp art & cultural hist, New York Univ, 74-2010. *Awards:* Grant, NY State Coun Arts. *Bibliog:* Articles, Arts Mag, 69, 80 & 84, Art in Am, 64, Art News 69 & Art in America, 88. *Mem:* Artists Tenants Asn; Artists Cert Comt, New York, 71-85; Found Community Artists (pres bd dir, 78-79); US Comt-Int Asn of Art, Inc (vpres); New York City Loft Board. *Media:* Oil, Photocopy Prints, Drawings. *Res:* Student's Guide to Art Schools. *Interests:* Writer on the arts. *Publ:* Rev, Leon Golub: Existential/Activist Painter by Donald Kuspit, Art & Artists, 86; All's Well that Ends Well Perhaps or Something is Rotten in the State of Denmark-Chicago-USA, Art & Artist, 89; What the Art Student Needs By Golly, 1991 Nat Conf Proceedings, Sch Visual Arts, New York, 91; Conservative Echos in Fins-de-Sieole, Paris Art Criticism, (book review) English Literature in Translation, Univ NC, Greensboro, 93; Italian Art Deco Graphic Design Between The Word (book review), Woman Artist News, 94; Dictionary of the avant-gardes (rev), Woman Artist News, 95; and others. *Dealer:* Madelyn Jordon, Fine Arts. *Mailing Add:* 330 Lafayette St New York NY 10012

BARR, DAVID JOHN
SCULPTOR, CONCEPTUAL ARTIST
b Detroit, Mich, Oct 10, 1939. *Study:* Wayne State Univ, BFA & MA. *Work:* Detroit Inst Arts; Portland Art Mus; Mich Hist Mus; Flint Airport; and others. *Comn:* Polaris Ring, Lansing, Mich, 88; Fountain, Detroit Zoo, 95; Revolution, Chrysler World Hq, 96; Revolution II, Brussels, Belgium; Synergy, Dennos Mus, Traverse City, Mich, 99; Galileo, Pisa, Italy, 2002; Liberation, Pfizer Corp, Ann Arbor, Mich, 2002; Transcending, Hart Plaza, Detroit, Mich, 2003; Diversity, Mich Legacy Art Park, 2002; and others. *Exhib:* Solo exhibs: Donald Morris Gallery, 72-96; Richard Gray Gallery, Calif, 78; Dennos Mus, 2000; Vault, Columbus State Community Coll, Ohio, 2006; Dawn, Warren, Mich, 2006; and others. *Pos:* Founder, artistic dir, Mich Legacy Art Park, Thompsonville, Mich. *Teaching:* Prof sculpture, Macomb Co Coll, 64-. *Awards:* Mich Found of the Arts Award, 77; Concerned Citizens Arts Award, 88; Humanity in the Arts Award, Wayne State Univ, 98. *Bibliog:* Realities and Impressions, Brady Production, 88; Arctic Arc, Grace Productions, 88; Tapestry, MCC Prod, 93; Arc of the Umiak, MCC Prod, 93; "Nets", MCC Production, 99; Time is my Window, 2011; Michigan Legacy Art Park, 2011. *Mem:* AIA (hon mem). *Media:* Masonite, Steel, Stone. *Publ:* Auth, Notes, 70; Notes III, 72; Structurist, 76; Notes on Celebration, 80; article, CoEvolution Quart, fall 81; Crossing Lines, 2008, Amercordo, 2010, Sieve, 2010; Time is my Window; Solar, Mich Legacy Art Park, 2012; Villa Barr, 2013; Solar II, 2013; Fragments, 2014. *Mailing Add:* 22600 Napier Novi MI 48374

BARR-SHARRAR, BERYL
ART HISTORIAN, PAINTER
b Richmond, Va. *Study:* Mt Holyoke Col, BA; Univ Calif, Berkeley, MA; Inst Fine Arts, NY Univ, MA, PhD. *Work:* Mt Holyoke Coll Mus; Los Angeles Saving & Loan Asn; Palmer Mus, Pa State Univ. *Exhib:* Maisons Cult Amiens, Bourges, Mus Avignon, Besancon Montpellier, Nancy & Ste-Etienne, 67; Mus Bordeux, Menton & le Havre, 68; Sachs Gallery, NY, 73, Livingstone-Learmonth Gallery, NY, 75; Art Galaxy Gallery, NY, 81; Univ Art Mus, State Univ NY, Binghamton, 94; Palmer Art Mus, Penn State, PA, 96; and others. *Pos:* Co-founder, Col Art Study Abroad, Paris, 61, co-dir, 61-68. *Teaching:* Vis lectr painting, Mt Holyoke Col, 68-69; vis lectr art hist, Pratt Inst, 78-79; adj assoc prof art hist, Fordham Univ, 81-82; vis prof art hist, Vassar Col, 82-83; adj prof, New York Univ, 2002-2007, 2008-; adj prof, Inst Fine Arts, NYU, 2008-2012. *Awards:* Am Philos Soc Grants, 82 & 96; Ctr Advan Study Visual Arts, Nat Gallery, Washington, 85; Kress Joint Scientific Study Grant, 2000; Prof Dev Grants, NYU, 2005-2006; Hazen Alumnae Grant, Mt Holyoke, 2006; Nat Endowment Humanities Grant, 2007-; 2015 John Simon Guggenheim Memorial Foundation Fellow. *Bibliog:* B Guest (auth), Exhibit Review, Art in Amer, 3/95. *Mem:* Am Inst Archaeology; Coll Art Asn; Asn Ancient Historians. *Media:* Acrylic on Canvas, Paper. *Publ:* The Antikythera Fulcrum attachment: A portrait of Arsinöe III, vol 89, No 4, Am J Archaeology, 10/85; The Hellenistic & Early Imperial Bust, 87; How Important is Provenance? Archaeological & Stylistic Questions in the Attribution of Ancient Bronzes in Small Bronze Sculpture from the Ancient World, Los Angeles, 91; Vergina Tomb II: Dating the Objects in Alexander the Great, VII, The Ancient World, Vol 22, No 2, 91; Earth & Water: Early Traditions & Uses of Ancient Greek Clay in Greek Terracottas of the Hellenistic World, Harvard Univ Art Mus Bull, Vol 1, No 3, Spring 93; Four articles in Das Wrack, Der Antike Schiffsfund von Mahdia, Bonn, 94; Hellenistic Bronze Production on Delos, in Regional Schools in Hell, Sculpture, 98; Cast Bronze Ovoid Situla, Kölner JB, Jahrbuch, 99; auth, Derveni Krater: Masterpiece of Classical Metalwork, 2008; A New Proposal for Restoration of the Marble Maerad in Dresden in Skopas of Paros, 2012. *Mailing Add:* 311 E 72nd St New York NY 10021-4684

BARRELL, BILL
PAINTER, COLLECTOR
b London, Eng, Dec 4, 1932. *Study:* Pa Acad Fine Art, 56. *Work:* Columbia Univ; Housatonic Mus Art, Conn; NJ State Mus; Jersey City Mus, NJ; Noyes Mus, Oceanville, NJ; and many others. *Exhib:* Solo exhibs, Dorsky Gallery, NY, Peter Findlay Gallery, NY, David Klein Gallery, Birmingham, Ill, Baghdad Gallery, St Barth, FWI, Shoe-String Gallery, 94, Chamot Gallery, 97, Halle St Pierre, Paris, France, 98; Ingber Gallery, NY; Jupiter Gallery, NJ; Art Banque, Minneapolis, Minn; The Interior Self, Montclair Mus, NJ, 87; Directors Choice, ARTWORKS, Trenton, NJ, 89; NJ Council on Art Ann, Jersey City Mus, 90; NJ Art Ann, NJ State Mus, Trenton, 94, Six Artists - The Nineties, 96; Artist As Curator, Curator As Artist, Bergen Mus, Paramus, NJ, 96; Art + Suitcase Will Travel, DNA Gallery, Provincetown, Mass, 99; Baghdad Gallery, 2000; Perolas Raras, Portuguese Biennial, 2001; Recent Paintings, Chamot Gallery, NJ, 2002. *Pos:* Owner, Sun Gallery, Provincetown, 59-61. *Teaching:* Vis artist, La State Univ, fall 82; artist-in-residence, Colorado Mountain Col, Vail, Colorado. *Awards:* Harry Devlin Award, NJ State Coun Arts, 83; Rutgers Univ Print fel, 94; Pollock-Krasner fel, 95. *Bibliog:* Barry Barrell (dir), Fruits and Vegetables (film), Barrell Productions, 12/6/67; Peter Schjeldahl (auth), Bill Barrell hits the streets & George Preston (auth), The urbanscape as ideal still life, Potholes, 1/3/78; Herbert E. Reichert (auth), Bill Barrell & The Tree of Life (catalogue), Peter Findlay Gallery, 2000. *Mem:* Orgn Independent Artists. *Media:* Oil-Base Paints; Mixed Media. *Collection:* Red Groom's wood sculpture, Oldenburg's paper collage, Bob Beauchamp's drawings, Mimi Gross Groom's watercolors, Bob Thompson's paintings and drawings and Gandy Brody's gouache. *Publ:* Potholes, Custombook Inc, 78. *Dealer:* Peter Findlay New York NY

BARRETT, BILL
SCULPTOR
b Los Angeles, Calif, Dec 21, 1934. *Study:* Univ Mich, Ann Arbor, BS (design), 58, MS (design), 59, MFA, 60. *Work:* Cleveland Mus Art, Ohio; Aldrich Mus Contemp Art; Norfolk Mus Art, Va; Hakone Open Air Mus, Tokyo; Va Mus Fine Arts, Richmond, Va. *Comn:* Sculpture, New Dorp Sch, NY, 82; sculpture, Rockefeller Reality Group, San Francisco, Calif; sculpture, Criminal Courts Bldg, Hartford, Conn, 86; sculpture, West Group Inc, One Bunker Hill, Los Angeles, Calif, 90; sculpture, Neiman-Marcus, King of Prussia, Pa; Univ Mich, Ann Arbor, Mich; Eastern Mich Univ, Lansing, Mich, 2007. *Exhib:* Nat Art Inst Show, San Francisco Mus Art, 64; Whitney Mus Am Art Sculpture Ann, NY, 70; Storm King Art Ctr, NY, 75; Solo exhibs, Sculpture Ctr, NY, 83, Kouros Gallery, NY, 85, 94 & 96, Bellevue Sculpture Garden, 85-86 & Roswitha Benkert Gallery, Zurich, Switz, 86, 90 & 92, De Graaf Gallery, Chicago, 89, Shidoni, Santa Fe, NMex, 90; Cline Gallery, Santa Fe, NMex, 93-96; Mongerson-Wunderlich Gallery, Chicago, Ill, 94; Navy Pier Expo, Sculpture Walk, Chicago, 96; Elaine Baker Gallery, Boca Raton, Fla, 2004; Kouros Gallery, NYC, 2005; LewAllen Contemp, Santa Fe, NMex, 2006. *Pos:* Cur exhib, Sculptors Guild, NY, 90; Cline Fine Art, Santa Fe, 94. *Teaching:* Assoc prof sculpture, Eastern Mich Univ, 60-68; instr, Cleveland Art Inst, 63-64; asst prof, City Col NY, 69-76; lectr, Columbia Univ, 79-; vis artist, Univ Pa, Columbia Univ, & Vt Studio Sch. *Awards:* R S Reynolds Mem Award For Sculpture, 86; Hakone Open Air Mus Award, Japan; Gold Medal of Honor in Sculpture, Audubon Artists, NY. *Bibliog:* Mac McCloud (auth), The Santa Fean, New Mexican, 10/19/90; Guy Cross (auth), article, The Mag, 4/96; Richard Tobin (auth), article, The Mag, 9/96; Philip F Palmedo (auth), Evolution of a Sculptor, Hudson Hills Press. *Mem:* Sculptors Guild NY (pres, formerly); Audubon Artists, NY; Int Sculpture Ctr, Washington, DC; Century Asn. *Media:* Bronze, Stainless Steel. *Mailing Add:* 11 Worth St New York NY 10013-2922

BARRETT, DAWN
ADMINISTRATOR, EDUCATOR
Study: Univ Mass, Amherst, BA (art history); NC State Univ, Raleigh, MA. *Pos:* Head of design, Jan van Eyck Akademie, Netherlands, 1995-2000; dean, Archit and Design Div, RI Sch Design, Providence, 2001-11; pres, Mass Col of Art and Design, 2011-; bd trustees, Penland Sch of Crafts, NC, vis evaluator, Nat Asn of Schs of Art and Design, currently. *Mem:* Am Landscape Asn Accreditation Bd. *Mailing Add:* Massachusetts College of Art and Design 621 Huntington Ave Boston MA 02115

BARRETT, DEBORAH
COLLAGE ARTIST
b Detroit, Mich. *Study:* Wayne State Univ, BA (creative writing), 1972. *Exhib:* Solo exhibs include Liz Blackman Gallery, Los Angeles, 1991 & 1993, Susan Cummins Gallery, Mill Valley, Calif, 1996, 1997 & 1999, Augen Gallery, Portland, Ore, 1998 & 2000, Adam Baumgold Gallery, New York, 1999 & 2000; group exhibs include Great Balls of Art, Palo Alto Cult Ctr, Calif, 1996, Interior Lines, 1996 & Group Exhib, 2000; In the Image of a Woman, Carl Hammer Gallery, Chicago, 1997 & Small Wonders, 1997; Works on Paper, Park Ave Armory, New York, 1999 & 2000; Linda Hodges Gallery, Seattle, 2000. *Awards:* Pollock-Krasner Found Grant, 2007

BARRETT, TERRY M
WRITER, EDUCATOR
b Chicago, Ill, 1945. *Study:* Webster Univ, BA, 67; Ohio State Univ, MA, 74, PhD, 83. *Pos:* Ed, Columbus Art, 81-91; sr ed, Studies in Art Educ, 93-95; vis prof, Art Hist and Art Educ, Univ N Tex, Denton, Tex, Fall, 2008; Artist in Res, Amsterdam Accad Art, Netherlands, 2008-9. *Teaching:* Prof art criticism, aesthetics, photog criticism, & art educ, Ohio State Univ, 83-2009 & prof emeritus, 2009; vis scholar, Getty Educ Inst Educ Arts, Los Angeles, 95-96; vis prof, Univ Ariz, 97; vis scholar educ, Ctr Creative Photog, Tucson, Ariz, 97; invited art critic, Critic & Artist Residence Series, Colo State Univ, Ft Collins, Colo, 98; vis artist/scholar, Lamar Dodd Sch Art Prog, Univ Ga, Athens, 99 & HISK, Antwerp, Belgium, 2002; prof art educ, Univ North Tex, 2009-. *Awards:* Honored Educator, Midwest Soc Photog Educ, 2001; Outstanding Alumnus, Webster Univ, 2003; Distinguished Fel, Nat Art Educ Asn, 2004; Hatcher Mem Award, Ohio State Univ, 2005. *Mem:* Nat Art Educ Asn. *Res:* Teaching art criticism and aesthetics. *Publ:* Auth, Criticizing Photographs, McGraw-Hill, 90, 2nd ed, 95, 3rd ed, 2000, 4th ed, 2006; ed, Lessons for Teaching Art Criticism, ERIC: Univ Ind, 95; auth, Talking About Student Art, Davis, 97; Auth, Criticizing Art, McGraw-Hill, 2nd ed, 2000; auth, Interpreting Art, McGraw Hill, 2003; auth, David Burton, in: Exhibiting Student Art, Teachers College Press, New York, 2005; auth, Teaching Toward Appreciation, in: Handbook of Research of Arts Education, Springer, New York, 2006; auth, Why is That Art?, Oxford, 2008; auth, Making Art: Form & Meaning, McGraw-Hill, 2010; ed, Kunst Werkt: Mensen Reageren op Hedendaagse Kunst, Thieme Art: Armsterdam, 2010

BARRETT, TIMOTHY D
EDUCATOR, CRAFTSMAN
Study: Antioch Coll, BA (art commun), 1973; Twinrocker Handmade Paper, 1973-75; Saitama Prefecture Paper Industry Res Station, Japan, 1975-77; Western Mich Univ, 1982-85. *Exhib:* Twinrocker Retrospective, Univ Ill Gallery, Bloomington, 1990; Iowa Scribes Calligraphy Exhib, Cedar Rapids Mus Art, 1991; solo exhib, Luther Coll Libr, Decorah, Iowa, 1992; PaperBooks, Minn Ctr for Book Arts, 1994; Expanded Text, Penland Sch Crafts, NC, 1995; On Papermaking, Die Donne Papermill, New York, 1996; Book & Paper Art, Marion Arts Coun, Lowe Arts and Enviornment Ctr, 2007. *Pos:* Owner, Kalamazoo Handmade Papers, 1977-85; consult, UN Indust Devel Org, 1995. *Teaching:* Instr, Univ Va Rare Book Sch, 1987-2007; assoc res scientist, Univ Iowa Ctr for the Book, 1986-1996, dir, 1996-2000, res scientist, 1996-, adj assoc prof, 2004-2005, adj prof, 2005-; adj assoc prof, Univ Iowa Sch Art & Art Hist, 1986-2004; vis prof, Univ Mich Sch Art & Design, 2003. *Awards:* Am Printing History Asn Inst Award, 1999; Anita Lynn Forgach Award, 2003; Newberry Library Short Term fel, 2007; MacArthur Found fel, 2009. *Bibliog:* Hillary Gardner (auth), Charting a New Course in Book Studies, Hand Papermaking, Vol 13, No 2, 16-20, winter 1998. *Mem:* Am Inst for Conserv, Book & Paper Group; Friends of Dard Hunter Inc (pres, 1981-83, adv bd, 1986-93); Int Asn of Paper Historians. *Media:* Papermaking. *Publ:* Auth, Nagashizuki-The Japanese Craft of Hand Papermaking, The Bird and Bull Press, 1979; Japanese Papermaking: Traditions, Tools, and Techniques, John Weatherhill Inc, 1983; dir, Papermaking (video), 1994 & Papermaking by Hand in India (video), 1995, Univ Iowa Ctr for the Bk. *Mailing Add:* Univ Iowa 216 North Hall Iowa City IA 52242

BARRETT, WILLIAM O
ADMINISTRATOR
b Hartford, Conn, Sept 1, 1945. *Study:* RI Sch Design, BFA, 67; New York Univ, MA, 78. *Pos:* Asst Dean, Parsons Sch Design, 79-81; dean, Corcoran Sch Art, Washington, DC, 81-87; pres, San Francisco Art Inst, 87-94; exec dir, Asn Independent Col Art & Design, 94-. *Mem:* Life mem & fel Nat Asn Schs Art & Design

BARRIE, DENNIS RAY
MUSEUM DIRECTOR, HISTORIAN
b Cleveland, Ohio, July 9, 1947. *Study:* Oberlin Col, BA, MA, 1970; Wayne State Univ, PhD, 1983. *Comn:* Int Spy Mus, DC; Rock and Roll Hall of Game, Cleveland, Ohio; Bethel Woods Ctr fpr tje Arts, Bethel, NY; Maltz Mus of Jewish Heritage, Beachwood, Ohio; Great Lakes Sci Ctr, Cleveland, Ohio; Steamshup William G Mather Mus, Cleveland, Ohio. *Exhib:* Body & Soul: Recent Figurative Sculpture, 85; Jenny Holzer & Cindy Sherman: Personae, 86; New Art of Italy: Chia, Clemente, Cucchi, Paladino, 86; The Ties That Bind: Folk Art in Contemp Am Cult, 87; Standing Ground: Sculpture by Am Women, 87. *Collection Arranged:* The New British Painting, 1988; Drawings Jim Dine, 1973-87, 1988; Mike & Doug Starn: The Starn Twins, 1990; The Continuous Presence of Organic Archit, 1991; Mechanika, New Kinetic Sculpture, 1991; Int Spy Mus, 2002; Bethel Woods Performing Arts Ctr, 2006. *Pos:* Midwest regional dir & contrib ed Jour, Arch Am Art, Smithsonian Inst, Detroit, 1972-83; dir, Contemp Arts Ctr, Cincinnati, 1983-92, Rock & Roll Hall of Fame & Mus, 1993-98; pres, Dennis Barrie & Assocs, 1992-93; pres, Barrie Consult, Cleveland Heights, Ohio, 1996-98; pres, Malrite Co, 1998-2005; dir cultural planning, Westlake Reed Leskosky Architects, 2005-; prin, Barrie Project, 2005-. *Awards:* Frederick Weisman Art Found Award; Am Soc Newspaper Eds Award; First Amendment Award, Soc Prof Journalists; Distinguished Alumni Award-Oberlin Col, 2004; Distinguished Alumni Award- Wayne State Univ, 2004. *Bibliog:* Peter Plagens (auth), Mixed signals on obscenity, Newsweek, 10/15/90; Jayne Merkel (auth), Art on Trial, Art in Am, 12/90; James R Petersen (auth), Showdown in Cincinnati, Playboy, 3/91. *Mem:* Am Asn Mus. *Res:* American 20th century art. *Publ:* Auth, The school years 1926-1976, In: Arts and Crafts in Detroit 1906-1970, The Movement, The Society, The School, Detroit Inst Arts, 1976; auth & producer TV docs, Artists-in-Residence Portraits of Five Ohio Artists, 1980, Artists in America--Portraits of Roger Brown, Richard Hunt, John Hegarty and Marshall Fredericks, 1983 & Celebration: The Four Corners--Project of David Barr, 1983, Smithsonian Inst; auth, Artists in Michigan in the 20th Century, Wayne State Univ Press, 1988. *Mailing Add:* Westlake Reed Leskosky 1422 Euclid Ave Ste 309 Cleveland OH 44114

BARRIOS, BENNY PEREZ
PAINTER, ART DEALER
b Bisbee, Ariz, Mar 20, 1925. *Study:* Sacramento City Col, AA, 48; Chouinard Art Inst, 53; Calif State Univ, Sacramento, BA, 74. *Work:* Crocker Art Gallery, Sacramento; Oakland Art Mus, Calif; Smithsonian Inst, Washington, DC. *Exhib:* Solo exhibs, Los Angeles Co Mus, 52, San Francisco Mus, 52, De Young Mus, 52, Oakland Mus, 52 & Crocker Art Gallery, 53 & 63; 1st, 2nd & 3rd Invitational, Calif Palace Legion Hon, San Francisco, 56-58; Butler Inst Am Art, Youngstown, Ohio, 58; Gov Brown Invitational Chicano Art Exhib, Sacramento, 75; Group exhib, Instituto Cult Mexicano, Los Angeles, 94. *Pos:* Owner, Barrios Gallery, Sacramento, 59-96. *Teaching:* Instr oils & acrylics, San Juan Unified Sch Dist, Sacramento, 62-77, Sacramento Unified Sch Dist, 68-77 & Sacramento City Col, 77-82. *Awards:* Second in Watercolor, Laguna Art Festival, 56; First in Oil, Northern Calif Arts, 58; Second in Oil, Auburn Art Festival, 62. *Bibliog:* Alfred Frankenstein (auth), Wetbacks, San Francisco Chronicle, 54; Charles Johnson (auth), Farm workers plight inspires artist, Sacramento Bee, 75; Peter Moore (auth), Lynton Kistler: The happy printer, Art News, 78; Bob Sylva (auth), Daring to Dream, Sacramento Bee, 8/6/99. *Media:* Acrylic, Watercolor, Bronze. *Specialty:* All medias; contemporary artists. *Mailing Add:* 4220 Watkins Dr Fair Oaks CA 95628-7534

BARRIS, ROANN
ADMINISTRATOR
Study: Univ Michigan, BA, 1972; Col of Physicians and Surgeons, Columbia Univ, MS (occupational therapy), 1976; Teachers Col, Columbia Univ, EdD, 1983; Univ Ill, MA, 1989; Univ Ill-Urbana-Champaign, PhD, 1994. *Teaching:* teaching and research asst, Univ Ill Art History Department, 1989-94; vis instructor Art History, Bemidji State Univ, 1995-96; vis lecturer Modern Art History, design history, visual studies, Bucharest Acad of Art and the Univ of Bucharest, 1996-97; vis instructor Renaissance, Baroque, American, Medieval Art History, Southern Ill Univ, 1997-98; Instructor Art History, Eastern Ill Univ, Charleston, 1998-99; vis asst prof Art History, Texas Tech Univ, 1999-2000; vis asst prof Art History, Kutztown Univ, Pa, 2000-01; instructor, gallery dir, Casper Col, Wyoming, 2001-03; vis asst prof Art/film history, humanities, St Xavier Univ, Chicago, 2003-05; asst prof Radford Univ 2005-09, assoc prof Art History, 2009-, interim dir Radford Univ Art Mus, 2009-10, chair Art Department, currently. *Publ:* Several articles to peer reviewed journals. *Mailing Add:* Radford University Art Department PO Box 6965 Radford VA 24142

BARRON, ROS
PAINTER, VIDEO ARTIST
b Boston, Mass, July 4, 1933. *Study:* Mass Coll Art, BFA (painting & ceramics); and with Carl Nelson, 48-51; Bunting Inst, Harvard Univ, fel, 66-68. *Work:* Addison Gallery Am Art, Andover, Mass; Worcester Art Mus; Dartmouth Coll Collection; Harvard Univ; Boston Mus Fine Arts; MOMA, NY; and others. *Comn:* Seasons (wall painting), YMCA, Roxbury, Mass, 65; Rainbow, Rocket, Road (wall painting), Lawrence Sch, Brookline, Mass, 67; polarized light painting, comn by SDI, San Francisco, 69; ser wall paintings for Community Ctr, Wilmington, Del, 70; and others. *Exhib:* Solo exhibs, De Cordova Mus, Lincoln, 57, Univ Conn, Storrs, 69, Lenore Gray Gallery, Providence, 72, Portland Mus Art, 74 & Helen Shlien Gallery, Boston, 79 & 82; Whitney Ann Am Painting, Salon, 71-72; Surreal Image, De Cordova Mus, 68; UNESCO Art in Architecture, Rotterdam, The Neth; Am Painting & Sculpture, US Info Agency Exhib, Europe; Montevideo Gallery, The Neth, 78; Carnegie Inst, 78; Mus Mod Art, NY, 80; Video Art of Ros Barron Video Pioneer (retrospective video screening), Remis Auditorium Mus Fine Arts, Boston, 2007. *Pos:* co-dir, founder, Zone, Visual Theater, 68-. *Teaching:* asst prof art, Univ Mass, Boston, 72-76, assoc prof, 76-; vis artist, de Cordova Mus, Lincoln Mass, 55-58, Univ Mass, 71-72, Univ Colo, Boulder, 83, and others. *Awards:* Guggenheim Found Award for Zone's Yellow Sound, 72; Rockefeller Found Grants, 77-79; Nat Endowment Arts Individual Fel, 75-76; Mass Coun Individual Art Fel in Video, 80-81; and others. *Bibliog:* Frames of reference: Ros Barron (film), co-produced by WGBH Educ Found, 80; Ros Barron: An Artist in Profile, Mass Coun Arts & Humanities, 9/81; Linda Furlong (auth), State of the Art Scan: The Ithaca Video Festival, Afterimage, 1/82. *Mem:* Boston Performance Artists; Mobius Artists Group. *Media:* Video, Painting. *Specialty:* Painting, prints. *Dealer:* Gilbert Urbano. *Mailing Add:* PO Box 470394 Brookline Village MA 02147

BARRON, STEPHANIE
CURATOR
b New York, NY. *Study:* Barnard Coll, Columbia Univ, AB, 72; Studied arts admin, Harvard Inst, 73; Columbia Univ, MA, 74; Grad Ctr, City Univ NY, PhD course work, 75-76. *Collection Arranged:* Degenerate Art, 91; Russian Avant-Garde, 80; David Hockney, 88; Ger Expressionist Sculpture, 82; Made in Calif, 2000; Exiles & Emigres, 97; Magritte & Contemp Art, 2006; Art of Two Germanys, 2009; Ken Price Retrospective, 2012. *Pos:* Intern & curatorial asst, Solomon R Guggenheim Mus, 71-72; intern educ, Toledo Mus Art, 73-74; exhib coordr, Jewish Mus, NY, 75-76; assoc cur mod art, LACMA, 76-80, cur twentieth century art, 80-94, coordr curatorial affairs, 93-96, sr cur twentieth century art, 95- & vpres educ & pub progs, 96-2003, sr cur mod art, 2003-. *Awards:* Nat Endowment Arts Fel, 86-87; Best Am Exhib Yr Award, Asn Int Critics Art, 91 & 97; Am Acad Arts & Sci Fel, 97; Alred Barr Award from Coll Art Assoc, 92, 2013; E L Kirchner Prize, 97; Order of Merrit, Ger Govt, 84; Commanders Curse of the Ger Govt, 2000; Frederick Runge Prize, 2011. *Mem:* Coll Art Asn; Am Asn Mus; Int Coun Mus; Bd of Trustees, Scripps, Col; Villa Aurora; US Domestic Indemnity. *Res:* Modern & contemp art, Ger Expressionism. *Publ:* Russian Avant Garde, 1910-1930; New Perspectives, LACMA & MIT Press, 80; Ger Expressionist Sculpture, Prestel, 82; David Hockney Retrospective, LACMA & Abrams, 88; Degenerate Art, Abrams & LACMA, 91; Exiles & Emigre's, 97; Abrams Magritte & Contemp Art, Ludion, 2006; Art of Two Germanys, LACMA & Abrams, 2009; Ken Price Retrospective, Prestel, 2012. *Mailing Add:* Los Angeles Co Mus Art 5905 Wilshire Blvd Los Angeles CA 90036

BARRON, SUSAN
PRINTMAKER, PHOTOGRAPHER
b Lake Forrest, Ill, May 15, 1947. *Study:* MS (Analytical & Clinical Chemistry), 1968. *Work:* Metrop Mus Art, New York; Philadelphia Mus Art; Pierpont Morgan Libr & Mus, New York; Fitzwilliam Mus, Cambridge, United Kingdom; Mus Mod Art, New York; Newberry Libr Chicago; Nat Libr France; Libr Congress, Special Collections; Univ Ill Libr; Wash Univ Libr. *Comn:* Delivre II (illuminated manuscript), 86 & Twisting Silence (unique book), 91, Sackner Arch, Miami Beach, Fla. *Exhib:* Solo exhibs, Philadelphai Mus Art, Victoria & Albert Mus, London, Newberry Libr Cicago, Ctr Contemp Art, St Louis, Smith Coll, Northampton, Mass, Bibliotheque Nat Paris, Univ Ill Mus Art, Univ Iowa Mus Art, Columbia Coll Ctr Books & Paper Art, Chicago, Univ Tex Art Mus, Hochschule der Bildene Kunst, Kassel, Dela Mus Art, Southeastern Mus Photography, Daytona Beach, Fla, Frexel Univ Art Gallery, Philadelphia, Galerie Wilde, Cologne, Die Brucke, Vienna; Groups exhibs, Whitney Mus Am Art, New york; Newberger Mus Art, New York; Wash Univ Mus Art, St Louis; Metrop Mus Art, New York; Dept Photography, Israel Mus, Jerusalem; Chapelle du Bon Pasteur, Montreal; Philadelphia mus Art; Collage as Intimate Art, Brooklyn Mus Art, New York; New Britain Mus Am Art, Conn; Int Writer's Ctr, Wash Univ, St Louis; Artists Books, Brooklyn Mus Art, New York; Israel Mus Art, Jerusalem; Print Club of Philadelphia; Block Gallery, Northwestern Univ; Knox Albright Mus Art, Buffalo; Munson-Williams Proctor Inst, Utica. *Awards:* Artists Grant (photography), NY State Coun on Arts, 81; Dreyfus Award, MacDowell Fel, 85; Artists Grant (Works on Paper), Nat Endowment for Arts, 93-94. *Bibliog:* Nicolas Barker (auth) Labyrinth of Time, The Newberry Libr, Philadelphia Mus Art, Victoria & Albert Mus, 95; Molly Schwartzburg (auth), Reading in Four Dimensions, The Poetics of the Contemporary Experimental Book, Doctoral Dissertation, Comparative Lit, Stanford Univ, 2004; Nicolas Barker (auth), The Book Collector, 97; John Cage (auth), Another Song for Susan Barron, Callaway Ed, New York, 81; Kate Hammer (auth), Contemporary Theatre Review, Amsterdam, 99. *Interests:* Reading, travel, animals, trees. *Publ:* John Cage (coauth), Another Song, Callaway Ed, 81; auth, Labyrinth of Time, 11 Unique Volumes, 87; Twisting Silence, Unique Book, 91; Jamaica Mistake, Unique Book, 94; Mirror, Unique Scroll in Braille, 95; Senza Ancora, Unique Book, 99; Expe, Unique Book, 2004; Casting Memory, Unique Book, 2005; Open Book, Unique Book, 2007; The Writing on the Wall, Unique Book, 2010; Still, Unique Book, 2012; Resorting to Flight, 2011. *Dealer:* Elizabeth Phillips Rare Books 19 East 80th St New York NY 10021; Printworks Gallery 311 West Superior St Chicago IL 60610. *Mailing Add:* 39 Plaza West Apt 8A Brooklyn NY 11217-3906

BARRON, THOMAS
PAINTER
b Newton, Mass, 1949. *Study:* Harvard Univ, 67-70, study painting with Marilyn Powers & Jason Berger, 71-74. *Work:* Boston Mus Fine Arts, Bank Boston; Rose Art Mus, Brandeis Univ, Waltham, Mass; Duxbury Art Complex Mus, Mass; Mills Coll Art Gallery, Oakland, Calif; Currier Gallery Art, Manchester, NH; and others. *Comn:* Portrait, Ms Kevin Kling, Paris, France, 77; Ms Catherine Ventura, New York, 80. *Exhib:* The Direct Vision, Fitchburg Art Mus, Mass, 73, Acad Arts, Easton, Md, 76 & Rose Art Mus, Waltham, Mass, 88; Panorama Symposium, Centre d'Arte, Baie St Paul, Que, Can, 89; The Drawing Show, Boston Ctr Arts, Boston, Mass, 97; Currier Gallery Art, Manchester, NH, 97; Le Cri Muet, Centre D'Art Baiest Paul, Que, Can, 2000; Abstraction Now, Rensselaer Polytechnical Inst, Troy, NY, 2004. *Pos:* Instr painting & drawing, pvt classes, 75-. *Awards:* Grant, Mass Coun Arts & Humanities, 73 & 75. *Bibliog:* Kenworth Moffett (auth), Abstraction offers most exciting possibilities, Vol 6, Art New Eng, 9/85; Nancy Stapen (auth), Thomas Barron at Andrea Marquit, Art News, 11/96; Piri Halasz (auth), Review of Abstraction Now, From the Mayor's Doorstep, New York, 12/2004; Menachem Wecker (auth), The Aesthetic of Mishigaas, Jewish Press Mag, 2004; Amir Aczel (auth), The Artist and the Mathematician, Avalon Publ Group, 2006; Kevin D Murphy (auth), Hudson River: Abstract Revision, Art New Eng, Feb/Mar 2008. *Media:* All. *Res:* Included in book by Vicky Perry. *Specialty:* Abstract Painting, Concepts & Techniques. *Publ:* Contribr, drawings, An empty glass house, New Renaissance Mag, spring 86; book cover drawing, Puncturing Our Illusions, Simon & Schuster Press, 99; cover painting, J Current Res & Practices in Language Minority Educ, Pearson Custom Publ, 2002; contribr, Communication, Making Connections, Pearson Publ, 2003; 2 drawings, The Cave & Cathedral, Amir D. Aczel (auth), John Wily & Sons, Inc, 2009. *Dealer:* Andrea Marquit Fine Arts 71 Pinckney St Boston MA 02114. *Mailing Add:* 25 Parkman St Brookline MA 02146

BARROW, AMANDA MCLAUGHLIN
PRINTMAKER, COLLAGE ARTIST
b Indianapolis, Ind, Nov 15, 1959. *Study:* Colo State Univ, with Richard DeVore & Nilda Getty, BA (humanities), 82. *Work:* Mus Mod Art & Pub Libr, NY; Fine Arts Libr, Harvard Univ; Mus of the Book, The Hague, Neth; Yale Univ, New Haven, Conn. *Exhib:* Modern Tapestries, DeCordora Mus, Lincoln, Maine, 94; Int Kunst Festival, Lokshuppen, Ger, 94; Images of Gotts Island, Wendell Gilley Mus, SW Harbor, Maine, 95; Artist Books, Soc Arts Crafts, Boston, Mass, 97; Look Both Ways, Lawrence Acad, Groton, Mass, 97; Pyramid Atlantic Bk Fair, Corcoran Gallery Art, Washington, DC, 97; Selections Exhib, Univ Mass, Dartmouth, 99; Artist/Author: The Book as Art Since 1980, Am Fedn Arts traveling exhib, USA & Europe, 98-2000. *Awards:* Honorarium, Drawing Ctr, NY, 89; Fulbright Res Grant, India, 92; New England Found Arts Award, 4/98. *Bibliog:* Srimati Lal (auth), Indian art & the big apple, Times India, 94; Judith Hoffberg (auth), Apollo's stage, Umbrella Mag, 97; Clive Phillpot & Cornelia Lauf (auths), Artist/Author: Contemporary Artist's Books, Distributed Art Publ, NY, 98. *Mem:* Womens Caucus Art; Monotype Guild New Eng. *Media:* Artist Books, Works on Paper. *Publ:* Contrib, Tagore Nagar, Dupis Press, 92; Apollo's Stage, Quick Brown Fox, 95. *Mailing Add:* 79 Bridge St Apt 2A Brooklyn NY 11201-7446

BARROW, THOMAS FRANCIS
PHOTOGRAPHER, EDUCATOR
b Kansas City, Mo, Sept 24, 1938. *Study:* Kansas City Art Inst, BFA (graphic design), 63; Northwestern Univ, film courses with Jack Ellis, 65; Inst Design, Ill Inst Technol, photog with Aaron Siskind, MS, 67. *Work:* Nat Gallery Can, Ottawa; Mus Mod Art, NY; San Francisco Mus Mod Art, Calif; Philadelphia Mus Fine Arts; Los Angeles Co Mus Art; Archive housed at CCP, Tucson; plus others. *Exhib:* Sharp Focus Realism: A New Perspective, Pace Gallery, NY, 73; Light & Lens: Methods of Photog, Hudson River Mus, Yonkers, NY, 73; Solo exhibs, Light Gallery, NY, 74, 76 & 79; The Extended Document, Int Mus Photog, Rochester, NY, 75; Am Photog: Past & Present, Seattle Art Mus, 76; Contemp Am Photog Works, Mus Fine Arts, Houston, 77; Solo retrospectives, San Francisco Mus Mod Art, 86, Los Angeles Co Mus Art, 87; A Restless Mind, Joseph Bellows Gallery, 2010; Works: 1974-2010, Derek Eller Gallery, 2012. *Collection Arranged:* Light and substance (with Van Deren Coke), 73 & Self as Subject, 83, Univ NMex Art Mus. *Pos:* Asst dir, George Eastman House, Rochester, NY, 71-72; assoc dir, Univ NMex Art Mus, 73-76, actg dir, 85. *Teaching:* Assoc prof, Univ NMex, 73-81, prof art, 81-2001, Presidential Prof, 85-90. *Awards:* Distinguished Alumnus, City Art Inst, Kans, 2009. *Bibliog:* William Jenkins (auth), The Extended Document, Int Mus Photog, George Eastman House, 74; Inventories and Transformations: The Photographs of Thomas Barrow, Los Angeles Co Mus Art-Univ NMex Press, 86; Geoffrey Batchen (auth), Cancellation in The Last Picture Show, Walker Art Center, 2003. *Media:* Photography, Lithography. *Publ:* The camera fiend, Image, Vol 14, No 4; contribr, Britannica Encycl Am Art, 73; auth, Three photographers and their books, In: A Hundred Years of Photographic History: Essays in Honor of Beaumont Newhall, 75; ed, Reading Into Photography, Univ NMex Press, 82; Perspectives on Photography: Essays in Honor of Beaumont Newhall, 86; Experimental Vision, Denver Art Mus, 94; The Collectible Moment: Photography in the Norton Simon Mus, 2006; cur, Photography: New Mexico, Fresco Fine Art Publ, 2008; Cancellations, Powerhouse, 2012. *Dealer:* Richard Levy Gallery 514 Central Ave Albuquerque NM 87102; Joseph Bellows Gallery 7661 Girard Ave La Jolla Calif 92037; Derek Eller Gallery NY 10001

BARRY, ROBERT E
ILLUSTRATOR, EDUCATOR
b Newport, RI, Oct 7, 1931. *Study:* Kunstgewerbeschule, Zurich, Switz; RI Sch Design, BFA & MAT. *Work:* Kerlan Collection of Children's Literature & Illus, Univ Minn; Klingspor Mus, Frankfurt, Ger; Mus of the Book, San Juan, PR; Mus of the Virgin Islands, St Thomas. *Pos:* Dir, Art Gallery Southeastern Mass Univ, 77-78; originator & owner, Sportcards, 79-. *Teaching:* Instr art, Averett Col, Danville, Va, 67-68; asst prof art, Tex Woman's Univ, Denton, 68-69; assoc prof art-design, Univ

Mass Dartmouth, North Dartmouth, 69-81, prof, 81-97, prof emer, 98. *Awards:* BK Awards, Boys Club Am, 64 & 67; Cert of Merit, Art Dir Club of NY, 64; Award of Merit, NY Soc Illusrs, 65; NY Times Ten Best Illus Books of the Yr, 65. *Mem:* Guild Natural Sci Illusrs. *Publ:* Auth & illusr, Faint George, Houghton Mifflin Co, 63; The Musical Palm Tree, 71 & Ramon and the Pirate Gull, 72, McGraw Hill; auth, Snowman's Secret, MacMillan, 75; auth & illustr, Mr Willowby's Christmas Tree, Doubleday, 92; Muppets television production, CBS, 92

BARRY, STEVE
SCULPTOR
b Jersey City, NJ, June 22, 1956. *Study:* Sch Visual Arts, New York, BFA, 80; Hunter Col, MFA, City Univ New York, 84. *Work:* Albuquerque Mus Art; John Michael Kohler Arts Ctr. *Exhib:* Improbable Machines, Santa Barbara Mus Art, 90; Mechanika, Contemp Arts Ctr, Cincinnati, 91; Visual Arts Awards X, Hirshhorn Mus & Sculpture Garden, Washington, 91; Contemp Art in NMex, Site Santa Fe, 96; Taos, Albuquerque, Santa Fe, Cedar Rapids Mus Art, 98; Stasis, Plan B, Santa Fe, 2000; one-person shows, Contemp Arts Mus, Houston, 92, Ctr Contemp Arts, Santa Fe, 94 & Univ Wyo Art Mus, 95, Albuquerque Contemp Arts Center, 2000; Plan B Santa Fe 2000; Donkey Gallery, Albuquerque, 2004, Univ NMex Art Mus, 2006; SCA Fine Art, 2009. *Collection Arranged:* Ray Grahm, Mead/Penhall Collection, Kohler Arts Center, Albuquerque Art Mus. *Teaching:* Adj instr sculpture, Hunter Col, New York, 84-89; prof sculpture, Univ NMex, 89-, Regents lectr, 2006-, prof emer, 2011-. *Awards:* Fel Nat Endowment Arts, 86, 88 & 90; Awards in the Visual Arts, 90. *Bibliog:* Motion, Motion, Kinetic Art, Perrigrine Press, 89; Contemporary Art in New Mexico, Craftsman House Press, 95; Visual Analogy, MIT Press, 99; Land/Art New Mexico, Radius Book, 2010. *Media:* Steel, Film. *Res:* viewer activated sculpture. *Interests:* white water kayak. *Mailing Add:* PO Box 1046 Corrales NM 87048

BARSANO, RON (RONALD) JAMES
PAINTER, SCULPTOR
b Chicago, Ill, Jan 13, 1945. *Study:* Am Acad Fine Art, William Mosby Scholar, 62-67. *Work:* Harwood Found Mus, Taos, NMex; US Army Hq, Washington, DC. *Exhib:* Allied Artists Am, NY 72; Meadowbrook Hall, Mich, 75; Maxwell Gallery, San Francisco, Calif, 75; The Taos 6, Philbrook Mus, Tulsa, Okla, 77; Western Art, Grand Central Art Galleries, NY 78; Am Western Art, Beijing Exhib Palace, China, 81; Pioneer Mus, Colorado Springs, Colo, 85. *Bibliog:* Steve Parks (auth), articles, Profile Mag, 7/78 & Art Lines, 9/81; Brand Shelton (auth), article, SW Profile Mag, 10/83; Tricia Hurst (auth), article, SW Art Mag, 2/85. *Mem:* Fechin Inst, Taos, NMex; Taos Art Asn, NMex. *Media:* Oil, Conte Crayon; Clay. *Publ:* Contribr, Taos Mag, 10/88, NMex Mag, 2/82, Artists of the Rockies Mag, spring 82, Am Artist, 6/82 & Art Gallery Mag, 12/83. *Dealer:* Collins-Pettit Gallery 1 Ledoux St Taos NM 87571. *Mailing Add:* PO Box 590 Arroyo Hondo NM 87513-0590

BARSCH, WULF ERICH
PAINTER, PRINTMAKER
b Reudnitz, Ger, Aug 27, 1943; US citizen. *Study:* Staatliche Hochschule fur Bildende Kunste, Hamburg, 63; Studienatelier K Kaschak, Hamburg, 62; Werkkunstschule, BFA, 68; Brigham Young Univ, MA, 70, MFA, 71. *Work:* Utah Mus of Fine Arts; Utah State Div of Fine Arts; San Francisco Mus of Art; Calif Coll of Arts & Crafts, Oakland; States Senate, Hamburg, Ger. *Exhib:* Calif Coll Arts & Crafts World Print Competition, San Francisco Mus, 73-76; Mus of Art, Monterey, Calif, 74; Am Acad in Rome, Italy, 76; Smithsonian Inst Traveling Exhib, 77; Corcoran Biennial, 83; 2d Western States Art Found Exhib, Corcoran Gallery Art, Washington, DC, 83; Tamarind, Twenty-five Yrs, 85 & 86; The New West, Colorado Springs Mus Art, 86; solo exhibs, Kimbal Art Ctr, Park City, Utah, 79, Utah Mus Fine Arts, 84, Okla Art Ctr, Scottsdale Ctr Arts, 85, Gremillion Fine Arts, Houston, 86, 87 & 88, Mus Church Hist & Art, Salt Lake City, 86 & River Ctr Gallery, Memphis, Tenn, 88, Dolores Chase Fine Arts, Salt Lake City, 89; 4x4 Western State Printmakers, Nora Eccles Harrison Mus Art, Logan, Utah, 88; Elaine Horwitcz Galleries, Scottsdale, 91; Macon and Co Fine Art, Atlanta, 94, 98, 2000, & 2001; Wyndy Morehead Gallery, New Orleans, 96; Munson Gallery, Santa Fe, 97; 50 Yr Retrospective, Ex Corde Lux, Springville Mus Art, Utah. *Teaching:* Utah Tech Col, 72, Prof printmaking & painting, Brigham Young Univ, 72-. *Awards:* Special Edition Purchase Award, World Print Competition, San Francisco Mus Modern Art, 1973; Prix de Rome Award, Am Acad, Rome, Italy, 75-76; World Culture Prize-Centro Studie Ricerecke Belle Nazioni, Salromaggiore, Italy, 83; Karl Maeser Res & Creative Arts Award, Karl G Maeser Found, 83; Cliff Lodge Inaugural Exhib, Purchase Award, Utah, 87; Springville Mus of the Arts, Purchase Award, Utah, 86. *Media:* Lithography; Oil. *Publ:* In the Desert (exhib catalog), 85; Looking Toward Home (exhib catalog), 86; Susan Fountleroy (auth), Pasatiempo, Santa Fe Weekly Arts Mag, 10/17/97; All things Testify of Him: Latter Day Saint Inspirational Paintings, Bookcraft, 98; Stephen May (auth), The Reign of Cowboy Art: Western Art in the 1980's, Southwest Art, 10/99. *Mailing Add:* c/o Brigham Young Univ Dept Visual Arts C-502 HFAC Provo UT 84602-6402

BARSNESS, JIM
PAINTER, CARTOONIST
b Bozeman, Mont, 1954. *Study:* Boise State Univ, BA, 79; Boise State Univ, MA, 85; San Francisco Art Inst, MFA, 88. *Exhib:* Solo exhib, San Francisco Art Inst, Calif, 87 & 89, Susan Cummins, Mill Valley, Calif, 90, 91 & 93, Caplan, Santa Monica, Calif, 92, Dominican Col, San Rafael, Calif, 93, George Adams Gallery, NY, 95, 97, 98, 99; group exhib, NY Univ, Small Works, NY, 90, Crocker Art Mus, Sacramento, Calif, 91, Caplan, Santa Monica, Calif, 92, Ark Art Ctr, Collector's Forum, Little Rock, 93, Charles More, Figuratively Speaking, Philadelphia, Pa, 94, Monique Knowlton, NY, 97, Luise Rose, NY, 98, Arkansas Arts Ctr, Little Rock, 98, George Adams Gallery, NY, 2000, Cornell Fine Arts Mus, Rollins Col, Winter Park, Fla, 2000, The Art Mus, Fla Int Univ, Miami, 2000. *Awards:* Binney & Smith Nat Art Achievement Award, San Francisco Art Inst, Calif, 88; Juror's Choice Award, Annual Crocker Art Mus, Sacramento, Calif, 89; Elizabeth Found Grant, 96. *Bibliog:* Terri Cohn (auth), Artweek, 11/28/91; Susan Kandel (auth), Los Angeles Times, 11/12/92; Kenneth Baker (auth), Art News, 3/94; Margaret Shearin (auth), Triad, 5/95; Jonathon Goodman (auth), Art in Am, fall, 98. *Media:* Drawing. *Mailing Add:* 189 Fortson Ctr Athens GA 30606

BARTA, DOROTHY WOODS VADALA
PHOTOGRAPHER, WRITER
b Toledo, Ohio, June 23, 1924. *Study:* Tex Women's Univ, Denton, 41; Dallas Mus Fine Arts, with Ed Bearden, Chapman Kelley, Stephen Wilder & Roger Winter, 45-49; Art Students League, with Gustav Rehberger, Ray Goodbred, Thomas Fogarty, Ray Froman, Robert E Wood, Ed Whitney, Joseph Magniani, Jan Herring & Charles Reid, 78-80; study with Everett Raymond Kinstler, William Reese, Henry Caselli. *Work:* Russell Daniel Trust, El Paso, 83; John Herring Newcomb Hall, Univ Va, 85; Univ NTex, Denton. *Comn:* Record cover, comn by Maestro Tino Comini, 78; pvt comns by James Babcock, Dallas, 87 & Harriet Ragland, Dallas, 88, Hilary Nicholas, Dallas, 92, Vicki Hummel, 94, Charles McLaughlin, 94, Graham & Caroline Shelby, 94, Charu Shah, 95 & Tom & Dan Sullivan, 96; portrait, Judge Sarah T Hughes for Willis Library, UNT Denton, Tex, 96. *Exhib:* Dallas Mus Fine Arts Co Ann, 56; Southwestern Watercolor Soc, 78, 82 & 83-93; Tex Fine Arts Citation, Dallas, 80 & 83; Pastel Soc Am, 80, 82-84, 88, 91 & 96; Pastel Soc Southwest, 81-85, 87-88, 90-91, 92-94 & 95-96; Knickerbocker 28th Ann, 81; Copley Pastel Exhib, 81; solo exhibs, Artisan's Studio-Gallery, 81-93, Watercolors, Univ Va, 85 & Images of the Ballet, Sheraton Hotel Gallery, Dallas, 88; Okla Art Ann, 82; El Paso Mus Show, 84; Presenting Nine Dallas Women Artists, 85; Artists & Craftsmen, 86-91; Tex Watercolor Soc, 87; Irving Art Asn, 87; Western Fedn Watercolor Socs, 87 & 90; La Watercolor Soc, 87, 90, 91 & 94; Art Focus XC Group, Longview Mus, Dallas, 96 & Ft Worth, Corpus Christi, Rockport, Tex, 97. *Teaching:* Instr portrait painting, Brookhaven Col, Dallas, Tex; instr life drawing & portrait figure painting, Artisan's Studio-Gallery, Dallas, 81-86; instr, painting workshops nationwide, also international, 90-95. *Awards:* McMurray Grant, 85; Am Artist Achievement Award for pastel artist, 92; Best of Show SWS Signature, 2005; Texas and Nat Mother of the Year Award, American Mothers Inc, 2000; Southwestern Watercolor Best of Show, 2007. *Bibliog:* Article, Am Artist Mag, 6/92; article, Southwest Art, 12/93 & 96; article, Am Artist, 10/94. *Mem:* Pastel Soc Am, NY; Pastel Soc Southwest, Dallas (founder & pres, 79-83 & 94), life member; Tex Fine Arts Asn, Dallas; Southwestern Watercolor Soc, Dallas; Knickerbocker Artists. *Media:* Various and Mixed, Pastel. *Res:* Horticulture and women in art for magazine and newspaper articles, master gardens. *Interests:* writing hist, memoir of the millinery industry, 1940-1967. *Publ:* Today's Dallas Woman, Woman's Publ Group, 8/94 7 4/96; auth, The Best of Watercolor, Rockport Publ, 95; American Mothers Magazine Cover, 98, 2001; Dallas Morning News. *Dealer:* Artisan's Studio-Gallery Dallas TX; Barta Originals 3151 Chapel Downs Dallas TX 75229. *Mailing Add:* 3151 Chapel Downs Dr Dallas TX 75229-5834

BARTEK, TOM
PAINTER, ASSEMBLAGE ARTIST
b Omaha, Nebr, July 25, 1932. *Study:* Creighton Univ, Omaha, 50-53; Cooper Union Art Sch, New York, with Robert Gwathmey, 55-56; and studied with Arnold Blanch, 65 & 68. *Work:* Joslyn Art Mus, Omaha; Inst Mex-N Am Relaciones Cult, Mexico City; Mus Nebraska Art, Kearney, Nebraska; Neville Pub Mus, Green Bay, Wis; Wichita Art Mus, Kans. *Comn:* World Insurance co, Omaha; 10 murals, executed in glass mosaic by Scuola Mosaici, Murano, Italy. *Exhib:* Solo exhibs, Inst Mex-N Am Relaciones Cult, Mexico City, 65, Sheldon Gallery, Univ Nebr, Lincoln, 74, Joslyn Art Mus, Omaha, 78, Wesleyan Univ, Nebr, 81, Peter H Davidson Gallery, New York, 88, Artspace, Omaha, Nebr, 91-92 & Haydon Gallery, Lincoln, Nebr, 94; A Sense of Place, traveling, 73-74; Nebraska Seen, Sheldon Art Gallery, Univ Nebr, Lincoln & traveling, 78; Mid-Four, Nelson-Atkins Mus, Kansas City, Mo, 78; Sylvia White Gallery, New York & Santa Monica, Calif, 97-98; Coll St Mary, Omaha, 98; Kans City Artists' Coalition, 98; Retrospective exhib, Nebraska Arts Council, Fred Simon Gallery, 2012, Univ Nebraska at Omaha Gallery, 2012, Lied Art Gallery, Creighton Univ, 2012. *Pos:* Exhib mgr, Joslyn Art Mus, Omaha, 63-66. *Teaching:* Instr, Coll St Mary, Omaha, 64-66; assoc prof, Creighton Univ, Omaha, 66-74 & 88-89. *Awards:* Hon Mentions, Midwest Biennial, Joslyn Art Mus, 62, 64 & 66 & Mid-Four, Atkins Mus Fine Arts, Kansas City, Mo, 78; Purchase Award, Anderson Winter Show, Anderson Fine Arts Ctr, Ind, 85. *Media:* Assemblage, Painting. *Mailing Add:* 400 Center St Omaha NE 68108

BARTELIK, MAREK
ART HISTORIAN, ART CRITIC
Study: attended, Ecole des Beaux Arts, Paris; Columbia Univ, MS; City Univ NY, PhD. *Pos:* Critic in Res, Md Inst Coll Art, Baltimore, 2006-2011; pres, AICA-USA, currently, XVth pres, AICA-Int. *Teaching:* instr modern & contemp art, Cooper Union for the Advancement of Sci & Art, NY, 96-; visiting prof, Yale Univ & MIT; lectr, MoMA, NY, Boston Mus Art, Polish Acad Sci, Warsaw, Municipal Mus, Hague, Mondrian House, Amersfoort, Holland, Museo Nacional de Bellas Artes, Buenos Aires, Argentina, Pinacoteca, São Paolo, Brazil. *Publ:* contbr, CAA Art Jour, Art in Am, Artforum; auth, The Sculpture of Ursula von Rydingsvard, Hudson Hills Press, NY, 96, Early Polish Modern Art: Unity in Multiplicity, Manchester Univ Press, Eng, 2005, East Sixth St: 50 Poems, 7Letras, Rio de Janiero, Brazil, 2006, Lagodny deszcz, Fundacja Twarda Sztuka, 2010, Gentle Rain (English verson), 2012; co-auth, with Dore Ashton & Matti Megged, To Invent a Garden: The Life and Art of Adja Yunkers, Hudson Hills Press, NY, 2000; editor, POZA: On the Polishness of Contemporary Polish Art, Real Art Ways, Hartford, Conn, 2008, Contemporary German Paintings from Portuguese Collections, ARTing, Lisbon, 2008. *Mailing Add:* AICA-USA London Terrace Station PO Box 20533 New York NY 10011

BARTELS, PHYLLIS ELAINE
PAINTER
b Joliet, Ill, Mar 8, 1930. *Study:* Ray Sch Design, Chicago, 48-49; Gerald Merfeld, 70-92. *Exhib:* Alaskan Wild Life Exhib, Fine Arts Mus, Anchorage, 88-91; Park Forest Art Ctr Show, Ill 80-92; Brookwood Gallery Teachers, New Lenox, Ill, 88-91; Ray Coll Design Invitational, Schaumburg, Ill, 90; Akron Soc Artists Grand Exhib, Sheraton Inn, Cuyahoga Falls, Ohio, 91-92; and others. *Teaching:* Pastel painting, Brookwood Gallery, 89-92, Churchmouse Studio, 92-94 & Young Rembrants, 96. *Awards:* Merit Award, Pastel Soc Am, 82; Town Gallery Award, Acad Artists Asn, 84; Julia Lucille Award, Salmagundi Club, 84. *Mem:* Pastel Soc Am; Midwest Pastel Soc; Oil Painters Am. *Media:* Pastel. *Interests:* landscape and still life. *Publ:* Today's Art, Erwin Feldman, Vol 27, 79. *Mailing Add:* 19555 Noel Rd Elwood IL 60421-9542

BARTER, JUDITH A
CURATOR, HISTORIAN
b Chicago, Ill, May 21, 1951. *Study:* Ind Univ, Bloomington, BA, 73; Attingham Park Summer Sch, Shropshire, Eng, 75; Univ Ill, Urbana, MA, 75; Boston Univ-Yale Univ Summer Inst, 76; Victorian Soc Summer Sch, Univ London, 78; Univ Calif, Berkeley; Getty Mus Mgmt Inst, studied mus mgt, 84; Univ Mass Amherst, PhD, 91. *Collection Arranged:* Currents of Expansion (auth, catalog), St Louis Mus Art, 77; Women Artists 1600-1980: Five College Selections (auth, catalog), 80 & Ideas in Contemporary Papers, Amherst Col, 84; traveling exhibs, Invention and Tradition in Russian Modernist Art (auth, catalog), 81-82 & Am Watercolors & Drawings (auth, catalog), Wadsworth Atheneum, 85-86; Prairie Sch, Art Inst Chicago, 96; Mary Cassatt: Modern Woman (auth, catalog), Art Inst, Chicago, 98; Window on the West: Chicago and the Art of the American West, 1890-1940, Art Inst Chicago, 2003; Edward Hopper (traveling), Mus Fine Arts, Boston, Nat Gallery Art, Washington, DC, Art Inst Chicago, 2007. *Pos:* Cur asst, Krannert Art Mus, Univ Ill, Urbana, 74-75; asst cur, St Louis Art Mus, 75-78; cur collections, Amherst Col, 78-86, assoc dir, 86-92; Field-McCormick cur Am art, Art Inst Chicago, 92-. *Teaching:* Decorative arts, Worcester Art Mus, 80; hist of prints, Amherst Col, 89; Am art & cult, Art Inst Chicago, 94- & Univ Chicago, 98-; adj prof art hist, Univ Chicago, 99; numerous lectures, 77-. *Awards:* Nat Endowment Humanities Grant; Chmn Award, Art Inst Chicago, 95; Getty Trust, 97; Chancellor's Medal, Disting Scholarship, Univ Mass, Amherst, 99. *Mem:* Am Asn Mus; Coll Art Asn; Victorian Soc; Decorative Arts Soc (reviewer Choice mag); Am Ceramic Circle. *Res:* 18th-20th Century American paintings & sculptures; decorative arts, prints, drawings & watercolors, particularly 20th Century; corporate support of art. *Publ:* Ed, Shaping the Modern: American 20th Century Decorative Arts, Art Inst Chicago Mus Studies, Vol 27, 2, 2001; auth, True to the Senses, and False in Its Essence: Still-Life and Trompe l'Oeil Painting in Victorian America, in: Objects of Desire: Victorian Art, Art Inst Chicago Mus Studies, Vol 31, 1, 2005; auth, Nighthawks: Transcending Reality & Travels and Travails: Hopper's Later Pictures, 2007; auth, Apostles of Beauty, Arts and Crafts from Britain to Chicago, Art Inst Chgo, Yale Univ Press, 2009; auth, American Modernism at the Art Inst of Chicago, Vol II, Henry Luce Found, Art Inst Chgo, Yale Univ Press, 2009; auth, Kith and Kin: American Folk Art at the Art Institute of Chicago, Yale Univ Press, 2012; auth, American Art in the Age of Impressionism, Yale Univ Press, 2012. *Mailing Add:* Field-McCormick Chair of Am Arts Art Inst of Chicago 111 S Michigan Ave Chicago IL 60603-6110

BARTH, CHARLES JOHN
EDUCATOR, PRINTMAKER
b Chicago, Ill, Nov 27, 1942. *Study:* Chicago State Univ, BEduc; Inst Design, Ill Inst Technol, MS (art educ); Ill State Univ, EdD. *Work:* Art Inst Chicago; Philadelphia Mus Art; Okla Art Ctr, Oklahoma City; Cedar Rapids Mus Art, Iowa; Ma Bolom, San Cristobal, Chiapas, Mex. *Comn:* Two prints & plates, Okla Christian Col, Oklahoma City, 71; 50 intaglio prints, Des Moines Art Ctr Print Club, 97. *Exhib:* Iowa Artists Exhib, Des Moines Art Ctr, 93, 94, 95, 97, 98, 99; The American Century, Cedar Rapids Mus of Art, Cedar Rapids, Iowa, 2009; Works by Charles Barth, Waterloo Ctr for the Arts, Waterloo, Iowa, 2012; Prints by Charles Barth, La Mano Magica Galeria, Oaxaca, Mex, 2012. *Teaching:* Instr art, Lincoln Univ, Jefferson City, Mo, 69-72; from assoc prof art to prof, Mt Mercy Col, Iowa, 72-2013, retired. *Awards:* Best of Show, 41st Iowa Artists Exhib, Des Moines Art Ctr, 92. *Bibliog:* Michael Beime (auth), Charles Barth Comes Home, pp 14-17, Cedar Rapids SW Life, 11/2012; Loulou Kane (auth), Well-Traveled Talents, Vol 1, No 1, IA Mag, 2012. *Mem:* Boston Printmakers, Mass; The Print Consortium, St Joseph, Mo. *Media:* Etching, Collagraph. *Publ:* Charles Barth: A Kaleidoscope Culture, James Snidle Fine Arts Publs, 2009. *Dealer:* Campbell/State Gallery Marion IA; La Mano Magica Oaxaca Mex; James Snidle Fine Arts, San Francisco & Chico, CA. *Mailing Add:* 1307 Elmhurst Dr NE Cedar Rapids IA 52402-4762

BARTH, JACK ALEXANDER
PAINTER
b Los Angeles, Calif, 1946. *Study:* Calif State Univ, Northridge, BA, 69; Univ Calif, Irvine, MFA, 71. *Work:* Los Angeles Co Mus Art; San Francisco Mus Art; Mus Mod Art, NY; Mead Mus Art; Brown Univ, Providence, RI; and others. *Exhib:* Solo exhibs, Karen Jaen Bernier Gallery, Athens, 83, Peder Bonnier Gallery, NY, 84, Blum Helman Gallery, NY, 89 & Vaughn & Vaughn, Minneapolis, 90; Points of View: Contemp Landscapes, Univ Gallery, Univ Mass, Amherst, 88; Summer Group Exhib: Works on Paper, Blum Helman Gallery, NY, 89; The Observatory, Thomas Soloman's Garage, Los Angeles, Calif, 89; Nocturnal Landscapes in Contemp Painting, Whitney Mus Am Art at Equitable Ctr, NY, 89; Harmony & Discord: Am Landscape Today, VA Mus, Richmond, 90; Waterworks, Edward Thorpe Gallery, NY, 94; Paul Kasmin Gallery, NY, 95 & 96; and others. *Teaching:* Instr art, Cooper Union, 83-; Columbia Univ, 93, 95 & 96. *Awards:* Nat Endowment Arts, 84. *Bibliog:* Susan Lubowsky (auth), Nocturnal Visions (exhib pamphlet), Whitney Mus Am Art, New York, 89; Frederick R Brandt (auth), Harmony & Discord: American Landscape Painting Today (exhib catalog), VA Mus Fine Arts, Richmond, 90; Saul Ostrow (auth), Jack Barth, Arts Mag, 2/90. *Media:* Miscellaneous. *Publ:* Auth, Toughts and Crosses, Sculpture, ed 15, A/D Gallery, NY, 91; String of Nights, Granfel Press, NY, 94; Songbirds, Conjunctions, 30th issue, Bard Col, 98; and others. *Mailing Add:* 472 Broome St New York NY 10013

BARTH, UTA
CONCEPTUAL ARTIST, PHOTOGRAPHER
b Berlin, Ger, Jan 29, 1958. *Study:* Univ Calif, Davis, BA, 82; Univ Calif, Los Angeles, MFA, 85. *Work:* Mus Mod Art, NY; Los Angeles Co Mus Art, Calif; Whitney Mus Am Art, NY; Mus Contemp Art, Los Angeles; San Francisco Mus Mod Art, Calif; Baltimore Mus of Art, Md; Miami Art Mus, Fla; Seattle Art Mus, Wash. *Exhib:* Deliberate Investigations (with catalog), Los Angeles Co Mus Art, Calif, 89; New Acquisitions, Los Angeles Co Mus Art, Calif, 94; one-person exhibs, London Projects, Eng, 96, Tanya Bonakdar Gallery, NY, 96, Philip Nelson Gallery, Paris, 97, ACME, Santa Monica, 97 & 99, Inst Contemp Art, Portland, 97, Presentation House, Ctr for the Visual & Performing Arts, Vancouver, 97, Mus Contemp Art, Chicago, 97 & (catalog) Henry Art Gallery, Seattle, 2000, Kunstmuseum Wolfsburg, Ger, 2000, Lanna Found, Santa Fe NMex, 2000; Plan (with catalog), Los Angeles Co Mus Art, 95; New Photog II, Mus Mod Art, 95; Painting the Extended Field (with catalog), Magasin 3, Stockholm Konsthall, 96; Malmö, Rooseum, Ctr Contemp Art, Sweden, 96; Just: The Contemp in the Permanent Collection, 1975-96, Mus Contemp Art, 96; Scene of the Crime (with catalog), Armand Hammer Mus Art, Los Angeles, 97; Evidence (with catalog), Wexner Ctr Arts, Columbus, 97; Painting into Photog/Photog into Painting (with catalog), Mus Contemp Art, Miami, 97; New to Houston, Mus Fine Arts, Houston, 98; Apposite Opposites, Mus Contemp Art, Chicago, 99; In-sites: Interior Spaces in Contemp Art, Whitney Mus Am Art, NY, 2000; Open Ends: White Spectrum, Mus Mod Art, NY, 2000; Tanya Bonakdar Gallery, New York, 2002, 2005, 2010; Alison Jacques Gallery, London, 2006; ...and to draw a bright, white line with light, 2011. *Teaching:* Assoc prof art, Univ Calif, Riverside, 90-2008, prof emeritus, 2008-. *Awards:* Grant, Nat Arts Asn, 83; Nat Endowment Arts Fellow, 90-91 & 94-95; Named a Visual Artist Fellow, Art Matters, Inc, 92-93 & 95; Guggenheim Fellow, 2004-2005; MacArthur Fellow, John D and Catherine T MacArthur Found, 2012. *Bibliog:* Julia Thrift (auth), Uta Barth, London Time Out, 7/15-24/96; Uta Barth: Nowhere Near, ACME & Tanya Bonakdar Gallery, 99; Uta Barth: And of Time, 2000; Lyle Rexer (auth), The Edge of Vision: The Rise of Abstraction in Photography, Aperture Found, New York, 2009; Roswell Angier (auth), Train Your Gaze: A Practical & Theoretical Introduction to Portrait Photography, AVA Publ, 2007. *Media:* Mixed. *Publ:* Auth, Artist Project: Field 1996, Blind Spot, 96. *Dealer:* ACME 1800 B Berkeley St Santa Monica CA; Tanya Bonakdar Gallery 521 W 21st St New York NY 10011

BARTLETT, BARRY THOMAS
SCULPTOR
b Detroit, Mich, Dec 15, 1952. *Study:* RI Sch Design, Providence (sculpture), 71-73; Kansas City Art Inst, Mo, BFA, 73-75; NY State Coll Ceramics, Alfred, MFA, 75-77. *Exhib:* Kansas City Art Inst, Nelson Atkins Mus Art, Mo, 85; Shaw-Guido Gallery, Mich, 91; Jane Hartsbok Gallery, NY, 94; Sch Arts Inst Chicago, 95; Revolution Gallery, Detroit, Mich, 96. *Teaching:* Vis artist ceramics, Camberwell Sch Arts & Crafts, London, Eng, 78 & Arco Sch, Ctr Arts, Lisbon Port, 90; art fac ceramics, Bennington Col, Vt, 87-. *Awards:* Visual Arts Fel, Nat Endowment Arts, 82 & 90. *Media:* Ceramics. *Publ:* Articles, Ceramics Monthly & Am Ceramics. *Mailing Add:* 1973 County Route 9 Chatham NY 12037-1926

BARTLETT, BO
PAINTER
b Columbus, Ga, 1955. *Study:* Univ of Arts, 75; Pa Acad Fine Arts, 76-81; Philadelphia Coll Osteopathic Med, 77-78; Univ Pa, 80-81; NY Univ (in filmmaking), 86. *Comn:* Director, editor, Andrew Wyeth, Self Portrait: Snow Hill (documentary film), 1995. *Exhib:* Solo exhibs, Columbus Mus Arts, Ga, 83, The Cast Iron Bldg, Philadelphia, 88, Greenville Co Mus Art, SC, 90, Daniel Saxon Gallery, Los Angeles, 92, FAN Gallery, Philadelphia, 93, PPOW, NYC, 96, 1998-2000, 2002, 2006, 2008, 2010, Winston Wachter Fine Art, Seattle, 2006-2007, David Klein Gallery, Mich, 2007, Farnsworth Art Mus, 2007; Group exhibs, Columbus Mus Art, Ga, 79; Midyear Show, Butler Inst Fine Art, Ohio, 83; Centennial Exhib, NC Bradley Collection, 85; NY Inspired: Past and Present, John Szoke Gallery, NYC, 88; Salon Show, NY Acad Arts, 90; Preternatural Worlds, Center for Visual Arts, Metrop State Coll Denver, 93; 25 Years, John Berggruen Gallery, San Francisco, 95; Heroic Painting, Southeastern Center Contemp Arts, Winston-Salem, North Carolina, 96-98; Reality-Bites: Realism in Contemp Art, Kemper Mus Contemp Art and Design, Kansas City, 96; El Paso Art Mus, 98-99; In the Shadow of the Flag, Tippy Stern Fine Art, Charleston, South Carolina, 2000; Transforming the Commonplace, Susquehanna Art Mus, Harrisburg, Pa, 2003; The Art Show, ADAA, NYC, 2004. *Awards:* Packard Prize, Pa Acad Fine Arts, 77; Philadelphia Mus Art Award, 87; Distinguished Artist Award, Ursinus Col, 2005. *Media:* Miscellaneous

BARTLETT, CHRISTOPHER E
GALLERY DIRECTOR, ILLUSTRATOR
b Stratford-on-Avon, Eng, Dec 11, 1944. *Study:* St Paul's Col, Eng, cert educ, 70; Bristol Univ, hon BEd, 71; Syracuse Univ, with James McMullan, Robert Weaver, Tom Allen & Isadore Seltzer, MFA, 78. *Work:* Towson Univ. *Comn:* Illus & design, Van Sant Dugdale Advert, 79, General Electric, 80, Soc Security Admin, Baltimore Sunpapers, Johnson & Higgins, 89. *Exhib:* Int 3-D Illusr Show, NY, 95; Am Soc, Marine Artists Eleventh Ann Juried, Frye Mus, Seattle, 97; Small Sculpture, Gallery Art Club 21, Seoul, Korea; Nat Portrait Gallery, Washington, DC, 93; Illusrs who teach, Soc Illusrs Mus, NY, 98. *Collection Arranged:* Illustrators Invitational, Holtzman Gallery, Towson State Univ, 75, Technol Art Exhib, 76, New Directions in Fabric Design, 77, Function-non-Function, 79 & Low-Fire Clay Sculpture, 81; Clay in the East III, 86. *Pos:* Dean, Md Col Art & Design, 72-74, pres, 73-74; dir, Holtzman

Gallery, Towson State Univ, 74-. *Teaching:* Assoc prof illus, Md Col Art & Design, 71-74; from asst prof illus & design to prof, Towson Univ, Baltimore, 74-. *Awards:* Silver Medal and 4 Merit Awards, Three Dimensional Illus, The Best in 3-D Advert and Publ Worldwide, 91; Award Excellence in Illus, Illus only, NY, 95; Excellence in Design Award, Am Graphic Design Awards, 2001. *Bibliog:* Barbara Tipton (auth), article in Ceramics Mo, 77; Dr D Blum (auth), article, Chesapeake Bay Mag, 85; Inda Schaenen (auth), Watercolors-The Art, Baltimore Messenger, 89. *Mem:* Am Soc Marine Artists. *Media:* Ceramic Sculpture, Acrylic Painting. *Res:* The Geometry of Composition in Painting. *Publ:* article, Royal Coll Art, 11/81; Mixed media, Graphics World, London, 2/83; Fable-ism Ceramics: Art & Perception, Australia, 96; Friendship in clay, Ceramics Monthly, 98; Decoding Fairfield Porter's July Interior, Am Art Joun, 2007. *Mailing Add:* 1316 Ivy Hill Rd Cockeysville MD 21030-1414

BARTLETT, JENNIFER LOSCH
PAINTER, WRITER

b Long Beach, Calif, Mar 14, 1941. *Study:* Mills Col, BA, 1963; Yale Univ, BFA, 1964, MFA, 1965. *Work:* Walker Art Ctr, Minneapolis; Mus Mod Art, Metrop Mus Art, Whitney Mus Am Art, NY; Philadelphia Mus Art; Cleveland Mus Art; Fine Art Mus San Francisco; and others. *Comn:* 9-painting series, oil-painted canvas & baked enamel steel plates, Gen Serv Admin; Volvo Corp; Nat Airport, Washington, DC; Sheraton Grand Hotel, Sacramento, Calif; The Mayo Clinic. *Exhib:* Solo exhibs include Wadsworth Atheneum, 1977, Baltimore Art Mus, Albright-Knox Gallery, 1980, Orlando Mus Art, 1993, Paula Cooper Gallery, NY, 1994, A/D, NY 1994 & Baldwin Gallery, Aspen, Colo, 1994, 2006, Painting the Language of Nature and Painting, Locks Gallery, 2006; group exhibs include Seven Walls, Mus Mod Art, NY, 1971; Painting Ann, Whitney Mus Am Art, NY, 1972; Painting: New Options, Walker Art Ctr, 1972; Contemp Am Drawings, Whitney Mus Am Art, 1973; Works on Paper, Va Mus Fine Art, 1974; Corcoran Biennial, Corcoran Gallery Art, 1975; Private Images: Photographs by Painters, Los Angeles Co Mus Art, 1977; Maps, Mus Mod Art, NY, 1977; 1977 Biennial Exhib, Whitney Mus Am Art, 1977; 20 Century American Art from Friends' Collections, Whitney Mus Am Art, 1977; New Image Painting, Whitney Mus Am Art, 1978; Whitney Biennial, Whitney Mus Am Art, 1979, 1981 & 1991; The Decade in Review, Whitney Mus Am Art, 1979; 20th Century Recent Acquisitions, Metrop Mus Art, NY, 1979; New Dimensions in Drawing, Aldrich Mus Contemp Art, 1981; Summer Light, Mus Mod Art, NY; Art in Our Time, Brooks Mem Art Gallery, 1982; Block Prints, Whitney Mus Am Art, 1982; The American Artists as Printmaker: 23rd National Print Exhib, Brooklyn Mus, 1983; Nine Printmakers & the Working Process, Whitney Mus Am Art, 1985; 20th Anniversary of the National Endowment for the Arts, Mus Mod Art, 1985; Four Printmakers, Whitney Mus Am Art, 1986; The 75th American Exhib, Art Inst Chicago, 1986; 50th National Midyear Exhib, Butler Inst Am Art, 1986; Contemp Diptychs: Divided Visions, Whitney Mus Am Art, 1987; New Art On Paper, Philadelphia Mus Art, 1988; Nocturnal Visions, Whitney Mus Am Art, 1989; Evolutions in Expression: Minimalism & Post-Minimalism From The Permanent Collection of the Whitney Mus of Am Art, Whitney Mus Am Art, 1994; Locks Gallery, Philadelphia, 1994, 1996, 1998, 2000-01; Richard Gray Gallery, Chicago, 1996, 1999-2001; Pace Editions, NY City, 2003, 2005; represented in permanent collections Albright-Knox Art Gallery, Buffalo, NY, Brooklyn Mus, Dallas Mus Fine Arts, Denver Art Mus, Met Mus Art, Mus Contemp Art, Chicago, Tate Gallery, Walker Art Ctr, Minneapolis, Whitney Mus Am Art. *Teaching:* Vis artist, Chicago Art Inst, fall 1972; instr painting, Sch Visual Arts, NY, 1972-77. *Awards:* Am Acad Arts & Letters Award, 1983; Harris Prize, Art Inst Chicago, 76, Harris Prize & M V Kohnstamm Award, 86; Am Inst Architects Award, 1987. *Bibliog:* Many articles & reviews in Am & Europ publ, incl Eric Gibson (auth), New York reviews, Rhapsody, Art Int, 3/1979; Thomas B Hess (auth), Les nouvelle images de la peinture americane, Art Press Int, 5/1979; Roberta Smith (auth), Bartlett's Summers, Art in Am, 11/1979 & others. *Mem:* NY Inst Humanities; Nat Acad (assoc, 1990, acad, 1994). *Publ:* Auth, Cleopatra I-IV, Adventures in Poetry Press, 1971. *Dealer:* Locks Gallery 600 Washington Square S Philadelphia PA 19106; Richard Gray Gallery 875 N Michigan Ave #2503 Chicago IL 60611; Paula Cooper 534 W 21 St NY City NY 10011. *Mailing Add:* 315 Vanderbilt Ave Brooklyn NY 11205-3604

BARTNICK, HARRY WILLIAM
PAINTER, PHOTOGRAPHER, EDUCATOR

b Newark, NJ, July 30, 1950. *Study:* Tyler Sch Art, Temple Univ, BFA, 72; Syracuse Univ, MFA, 74. *Work:* Hyde Collection, Glens Falls, NY; DeCordova Mus, Lincoln, Mass; McMullen Mus Art, Boston Col. *Exhib:* Boston (in dialogue) Now, Inst Contemp Art, Boston, Mass, 94; McMullen Mus Art, Boston Col, 95; Lyman Allyn Mus Art, Conn Col, 98; Fuller Mus Art, 98; Palazzo Sertoli, Sondrio, Italy, 2001; Royal Acad Fine Arts, Madrid, 2004; Shifting Ecologies, The Painting Ctr, NY, 2014; and others. *Teaching:* Instr painting & drawing, Lake Placid Sch Art, 74-78; prof, New Eng Sch Art & Design, Suffolk Univ, 78-2014; instr painting, Montserrat Col Art, 94. *Awards:* Trustee's Prize, Everson Regional, 74; Creative Artists Pub Serv Grant, 77; Mass Artists Found Grant, 81; Nat Endowment Arts Fel, New Eng Found Arts, 92 & 96; John Simon Guggenheim Grant, 01. *Bibliog:* The Boston art party, Art News, 11/80; New Am Paintings, 98, 02; Art in Aviation, Lundwerg Press, Barcelona, 01; Civil Eng and Painting, Royal Acad Fine Arts Press, Madrid, 04; 100 Boston Painters, Schiffer Pub, 2011. *Media:* Oil, Acrylic on Canvas, Digital Printmaking. *Interests:* European travel, Italian history and culture. *Dealer:* Bridgewater Fine Arts. *Mailing Add:* 14 Prospect St Beverly MA 01915

BARTOLINI, MASSIMO
SCULPTOR, PHOTOGRAPHER

b Cecina, Italy, 1962. *Exhib:* Solo exhibs, Galleria Untitled e Artra, Milano, Italy, 1993, Cusano Milanino, Milano, Italy, 1994, Galleria Gentili, Firenze, Italy, 1995, Henry Moore Found, Leeds, 1996, Galleria Massimo De Carlo, Milano, Italy, 1997, Studio Barbieri, Venice, 1998, Forum Kunst Rottweil, 2000, PS1, New York, 2001, Frith St Gallery, London, 2002, Mus Abteiberg, Ger, 2003, Magazzino d'Arte Moderna Roma, 2004, D'Amelio Terras, New York, 2007 & Espais Obets, Caixa Forum, Barcelona, 2007; Domestic Violence, Casa di G. Marconi, Milano, 1994; Moby Dick, I.J. Hansard Gallery, Southampton, 1995; East Int, Sainsbury Ctr for Visual Art, Norwich, 1995; Mutoidi, Maschio Angioino, Napoli, Italy, 1996; Truce, SITE, Santa Fe, 1997; Seamless, De Appel, Amsterdam, 1998; Esca, Milhaud de Nimes, France, 1999; Furturama, Museo L. Pecci, Prato, 2000; Homo Ludens, Museo de Arte Moderno, Buenos Aires, 2000; Squatters, Museu Serralves, Rotterdam, Neth, 2001; Freespace, Provinciaal Centrumvoor Beeldende Kunsten, Begijnhof, Hasselt, Belgium, 2002; Das Lebendige Mus, Mus fur Mod Kunst, Frankfurt, 2003; Aligned, Frith St Gallery, London, 2004; Thrust, 26th Biennial of Graphic Arts, Ljubljana Int Ctr of Graphic Arts, 2005; Art 37 Basel, Art in Pub Space, Basel, Switz, 2006; Rexistros e Habitos, CAGC Santiago de Compostela, 2007; Left Overs, Mariano Pichler Collection, Micamoca, Berlin, 2008; 53rd Int Art Exhib Biennale, Venice, 2009. *Bibliog:* Milovan Farronto (auth), interview, Terna Celeste, 2002; hans Ulrich Obrist (auth), interview, Mus Abteiberg Monchengladbach, 2003; Susanna Saez (auth), Aire De R osa En Caixaforum, El Paris, 2007; Freire Barnes (auth), The Dark Acts, BBC, 2007. *Mailing Add:* Frith Street Gallery 17-18 Golden Sq London W1F 9JJ United Kingdom

BARTON, NANCY
EDUCATOR, PHOTOGRAPHER

Study: Calif Inst of the Arts, BFA, 1982, MFA, 1984. *Work:* Mus Modern Art, Long Beach Mus, Shoshana Wayne Gallery, Los Angeles. *Exhib:* Exhibited internationally, including MoMA, NY, Long Beach Mus, and the Shoshana Wayne Gallery, Los Angeles. *Teaching:* Clin assoc prof art and art educ, Steinhardt Sch Culture, Educ, and Human Develop, NY Univ, chair, Art Dept, formerly, dir of the undergraduate program, currently. *Awards:* Sch Educ Rsch Challenge Fund. *Mailing Add:* New York University Steinhardt School of Culture, Education Barney, 34 Stuyvesant St, 303C New York NY 10003

BARTZ, JAMES ROSS
PAINTER

b Blufton, Ohio, Feb 20, 1942. *Study:* Ohio State Univ, BS, 64, MA (art educ), 70. *Work:* Wichita Art Asn, Wichita Art Mus; Topeka Art Mus, Kans. *Comn:* The Baptism of Christ, Messiah Lutheran Church, Cleveland, Ohio. *Exhib:* Mid-Four, Nelson-Atkins Mus Art, Kansas City, Mo, 83; Smoky Hill Art Exhib, Hays Libr, Kans, 83; Art Ann IV, Okla Art Ctr, Oklahoma City, 83; Fifth Salina Ann, Salina Art Ctr, Kans, 83; Lenox Hill Artists Forum, NY; Regional Artists Biennial, Fort Wayne Mus Art, Ind, 94; Regional Art Ctr, LaCrosse, Wis, 97 & 98; and others. *Teaching:* Asst prof art educ, Wichita State Univ, Kans, 70-78; painting instr figure, Wichita Art Asn, 80-83. *Awards:* Best Show, Second Ann Small Oil Painting, Wichita Art Asn, 82; Best Show, Fifth Salina Ann, Salina Art Ctr, Kans, 83; Best of Show, Smoky Hill Art Exhib, Hays, Kans Art Ctr, 85. *Media:* Acrylic, Oil. *Mailing Add:* 938 Streblow St Onalaska WI 54650-2059

BARUCH, BARBARA
GALLERY DIRECTOR

Study: Univ Calif, Berkeley, BA (art & psychology). *Pos:* Advertising sales, Art in America, Brant Publications, 1996-2001; sales dir, Paulson Bott Press, 2001-2003; dir, Brooke Alexander Gallery, NYC, 2003-. *Mailing Add:* Brooke Alexander Gallery 59 Wooster St New York NY 10012

BASQUIN, KIT (MARY SMYTH)
WRITER, EDUCATOR

b New York, NY, July 3, 1941. *Study:* Goucher Col, BA, 63; Ind Univ, Bloomington, MA (art hist), 70; Bread Loaf Writers Conf, Middlebury Coll, 83 & 85: Yale Summer Sch, 85; Union Inst, PhD, 2009. *Collection Arranged:* Karl Priebe: A Look at African Am (galley guide), 90; Images & Death in Contemporary Art (catalog), 90; Francesco Spicuzza: Wisconsin Impressionist (catalog), 92; Marvin Lowe Retrospective (catalog), 98; The Lunts on Stage in Wisconsin (catalog), 99; Wording the Image/Imaging the Word: The Prints of Pat Steir, Jaune Quick-to-See, Lynn Allen and Lesley Dill (dissertation & brochure), 2010; Wording the Image, Imaging the Word, Sch Visual Arts, Sherman Gallery, Boston Univ, 2010. *Pos:* Owner & dir, Washington Gallery, Indianapolis, 77-79 & Kit Basquin Gallery, Milwaukee, 81-83; Wis ed, New Art Examiner, 80; interim cur, Haggerty Mus Art, Milwaukee, 88-89; asst dir collections & pub progs, Haggerty Mus, Marquette Univ, Milwaukee, 89-90, cur ed, 90-95; dir outreach, Milwaukee, Wis Humanities Coun, 95-98; trustee, Ten Chimney Found Inc, Wis, 1997-99; exhib mgr, Auction House, Doyle, NY, 1999-2000; asst, dept drawings and prints, Met Mus of Art, 2000-2008, assoc, 2008-2014. *Teaching:* Instr art hist, Fine Arts Sch, Addis Ababa, Ethiopia, 67-68; instr art hist, Concordia Univ Mequon, 92; teacher, Marquette Univ Gaza, 96. *Bibliog:* Holly Day (auth), Indianapolis, Cincinnati, Dayton, Art in Am, 7-8/79; Dean Jensen (auth), Basquin Gallery has different air, Milwaukee Sentinel, 10/2/81. *Mem:* Univ Club Milwaukee; Univ Club, NY; Print Forum (pres, 96-97); Milwaukee Art Mus; Jame Joyce Soc, 99-; Coll Art Asn, 2001-2013; Yeats Soc, 2009-; Collegiate Chorale, 2013-. *Res:* Contemporary Prints by Women and by African Americans; Mary Ellen Bute, Filmmaker. *Interests:* writing, music, art. *Collection:* modern prints. *Publ:* published by Brooklyn Mus, 95 artists' biographies in Committed to the Image, 2001; auth, Words Expand Postmodern Prints, ProQuest, 2009; Lynne Allen, Womens Art Jour, 11/2010; Anders Zorn (Swedish 1860-1920), The Illuminator 4, no1, spring/summer, pp 6-7, 2012; The Incomparable Max: Max Beerbohm, (British 1872-1953), The Illuminator 5, no 1, pp 14-16, spring/summer, 2013; illusr, Ulysses, Art in Print 3, No, 11-12, 2013, pp 6-10. *Mailing Add:* 110 East End Ave Apt 14G New York NY 10028-7416

BASS, CLAYTON
DIRECTOR

b Clinton, North Carolina, 1952. *Pos:* Coordr of exhibs, Michael C Carlos Mus, Emory Univ, formerly; dir, Walter Anderson Mus Art, 1996-2003; pres & CEO, Huntsville Mus Art, 2003- . *Mailing Add:* Huntsville Museum of Art 300 Church Street Huntsville AL 35801

BASS, DAVID LOREN
PAINTER
b Conway, Ark, July 19, 1943. *Study:* Univ NC, Greensboro, MFA; Univ NC, Chapel Hill; Aspen Sch Contemp Art; Univ Cent Ark, BSE; study with Peter Agostini, Walter Barker, Andrew Martin & Larry Day. *Work:* Mint Mus, Charlotte, NC; Dillard Collection, Weatherspoon Art Gallery, Greensboro, NC; Duke Univ, Durham, NC; US Dept State, Washington, DC; Washington & Lee Univ, Lexington, Va; Art in Public Places, Santa Fe, NM; Mus of the Big Bend, Alpine, Tex; Yaddo, Saratoga Springs, NY; Maitland Art Ctr, Maitland, Fla. *Exhib:* Biennial Exhib of Piedmont Painting & Sculpture, Mint Mus, Charlotte, 79 & 81; Summer Leisure: Mountains to the Sea, Mint Mus, Charlotte, 82; Selected Works, 1983-1989, Theater Art Galleries, High Point, NC, 90; Santa Fe Contemp Art, 98; Watercolor USA 1993, Springfield Mus Art, Mo, 93; Ten By Ten, Addison and Ripley Fine Art, Washington, DC, 99; High Point Theatre Art Gallery, High Point, NC, 2000; solo exhibs, Morocco Experienced, Bass Fine Art, Santa Fe, NMex, 2001, Paintings of the Big Bend, Mus Big Bend, Alpine, Tex, 2004 & Paintings of Tex and NMex, Bass-Thompson Gallery, Santa Fe, NMex, 2004; Trappings of Tex, Mus Big Bend, Alpine, Tex, 2006-2008; Invitational Western Art Show, Panhandle Plains Hist Mus, Canyon, Tex, 2008; Mostly Marin, San Geronimo, Calif, 2008; Paintings of W Tex, Greasewood Gallery, Marfa, Tex, 2008; 15x15, Lee Hansley Gallery, Raleigh, NC, 2008; Moroccan Memories, 1981-2011, Santa Fe, NMex, 2011; Let There Be Art, Columbus Mus Art, Columbus, Ga, 2011; Far West Texas and Further Afield III, Fort Davis, Tex, Grease-Wood Gallery, 2010-14. *Collection Arranged:* Drawings & Sculpture by Peter Agostini, 76 & Prints, Dept of Fine Arts, 76, Du Pont Art Gallery, Washington & Lee Univ. *Pos:* Artist-in-residence, Brevard Coll, Brevard, NC, Greensboro Day Sch, NC, 89. *Teaching:* Instr art, Kenitra Am HS, 67-73; instr painting, Univ NC, Greensboro, NC, 75, Washington & Lee Univ, Lexington, Va, 76; instr watercolor, Explore Guatemala, 2003. *Awards:* Yaddo Residency, Saratoga Springs, NY, 78, 81 & 84; Va Ctr Creative Arts, Sweetbriar, Va, 78; Ossabaw Island Proj, Ga, 79; Art in Pub Places, Santa Fe, 93-94. *Bibliog:* Tom Dewey (auth), Southern realism, Miss Mus Art, 79. *Media:* Oil, Watercolor. *Collection:* Peter Agostini, sculpture; Andrew Martin, painting; Suzanne Valodon, Lithograph; Maurice Grosser, Painting; Carol Anthony, painting; Rosemarie Beck, Painting; Isabel McElvain, sculpture; Duane Dishta, painting; Jennine Hough, painting; Cavin Gonzales, sculpture, Sally Condon, painting. *Dealer:* Greasewood Gallery Marfa TX; Ortiz Gallery Chimayo NM. *Mailing Add:* 11 Reno Rd Santa Fe NM 87508

BASS, JUDY
PAINTER, COLLAGE ARTIST
b Baltimore, Md, Mar 17, 1946. *Study:* Univ Md, College Park, BA, 67; George Washington Univ, MFA, 74. *Work:* The Phillips Collection, Washington, DC; George Washington Univ, Washington, DC; Dept of Health & Human Servs, Washington, DC; Univ NMex, Albuquerque, NMex; MCI Copr Hq; Charles E Smith Corp, Arlington, Va; Dept Homeland Security, DC. *Exhib:* Emerging Artists, Wash Proj for the Arts, 79; solo exhibs, Phillips Collection (with catalog), 81, Cath Univ of Am Art Gallery, Washington, 81, Univ NMex Teaching Gallery, 81, Marsha Mateyka Gallery, Washington, DC, 84, 86 & 88, Mt Vernon Coll, Washington, DC, 96; Color as Light, Washington Co Mus, Hagerstown, Md, 86; Marymount Univ, Barry Gallery, 86-; Susan Conway Gallery, 95 & 98; Bird in the Hand Gallery, Washington, DC, 2000; Galerie Francoise, Balt, Md, 2006; Phillips pvt collection; Marymount Univ, Barry Gallery Collages and Paintings; Paintings and Collages Marymount Univ Gallery, 2012. *Pos:* Prof Fine Art, Marymount Univ, Arlington, Va, 84-; Dir, Barry Art Gallery, Marymount Univ, Arlington, Va, 86-. *Teaching:* Instr art, Mt Vernon Coll, Washington, 79-85 & Maryland Inst Coll Art, Baltimore, 83-84; vis asst prof painting, Univ NMex, 81-82; prof fine arts, Marymount Univ, Arlington, Va, 84-. *Awards:* Cecile R Hunt Mem Prize Painting, Alumni Show, George Washington Univ, Washington, DC, 86. *Bibliog:* Benjamin Forgery (auth), The uptown downtown insider world of Washington Art, Art News, 9/79; Lee Fleming (auth), Washington Iconoclassicism, 8 Washington Women (catalog), 5/82; Frank Getlein & Joann Lewis (coauths), Washington Review. *Mem:* Coll Art Asn; Smithsonian Asn Prog; Va Asn Mus. *Media:* Acrylic Paint; Color Pencils, Collage. *Res:* Extensive exploration in NMex. *Interests:* Jewelry design, yoga, pets. *Mailing Add:* 3318 St James Pl Falls Church VA 22042

BASS, RUTH
EDUCATOR, CRITIC
b Boston, Mass, 1938. *Study:* Radcliffe Col, BA (magna cum laude), 60; study with Irving Marantz, Victor Candell, Gabriel Laderman & Maurice Golubov, 60-64; Art Students League, 61-74; NY Univ, MA, 62, PhD, 78. *Exhib:* One-person show, Brata Gallery, NY, 73, Portraits of Women, Rotunda Hall Fame for Great Americans, Bronx, NY, 87; Works on Paper--Women Artists, Brooklyn Mus, NY & Fairleigh Dickinson Univ, 75-76; Shreveport Parks & Recreation Dept Nat, Shreveport, La, 76; Artists Choice Traveling Exhib, 76-77; Women in Definition, First Women's Bank, NY, 83. *Collection Arranged:* Portraits: Form and Content, First Women's Bank, NY, 84; Contemporary Images and Universal Images, 86, John Gundelfinger Paintings, 20 Broad Street, NY, 86. *Pos:* Guest cur, First Women's Bank, NY, 84, The Mendik Co, 86. *Teaching:* Lectr, Univ Bridgeport, Conn, 63-64 & Queens Col, NY, 65-66; from instr to assoc prof art, Bronx Community Col, City Univ NY, 65-81, prof, 81-; instr, New York Univ, 80-81. *Awards:* Women's Res and Develop Fund Award, City Univ New York, 86- 88; Fel, Arts & Soc, funded by Andrew W Mellon Found, Community Coll Proj, 82, Humanities, Fel, 90; Borchard Found Grant, 92; and others. *Bibliog:* Lawrence Campbell (auth), review, Art News, 3/73; Michael Brenson (auth), review, NY Times, 6/29/84; Don Gray (auth), article, Art World, 5/87. *Mem:* Am Asn of Univ Prof; Int Asn Art Critics; Art Students League. *Media:* Oil, Charcoal. *Res:* Comedy in Contemporary Art, Contemporary American realist painting, including painterly realism; phenomenological criticism and aesthetics. *Publ:* Auth, The illusion of reality, 12/81 & Bland power, 4/86, Artnews; Minimalism Made Human on Joel Shapiro, Art News, 3/87 & Ordinary People on Ida Applebroog, Art News, 5/88; contribr, Groves Dictionary Art, Vol 34, 96. *Mailing Add:* 125 E 87th St New York NY 10028

BASSET, GENE
POLITICAL CARTOONIST
b Brooklyn, NY, 1927. *Study:* Univ Mo; Brooklyn Col, BA (design); Cooper Union; Art Students League; Pratt Inst. *Work:* Syracuse Univ Libr, NY; Wichita State Univ; Univ Mo; Univ Southern Miss; Gustavus Adolphus Col. *Exhib:* Vietnam Drawings, Hilstrom Arts Mus, Gustavos Adolphus Collection. *Pos:* Polit cartoonist, Honolulu-Star Bull, 61-62, Scripps-Howard Newspapers, Washington, DC, 62-81 & United Features Syndicate, 72-; ed cartoonist, Atlanta J, 82-92, Mankazo Free Press, Minn, 93-. *Teaching:* Instr seminar, Gustavus Adolphus Col, Famous Artist Sch; instr cartoon course, Gustaus Adolphus Col, 94. *Awards:* Best Ed Cartoon, Population Inst, 74. *Mem:* Asn Am Ed Cartoonists (pres, 73-74); Nat Cartoonist Soc. *Media:* Ink. *Mailing Add:* 1308 Pine Pointe Curv Saint Peter MN 56082-9804

BASSIN, JOAN
HISTORIAN, EDUCATOR
b St Louis, Mo, Oct 29, 1938. *Study:* Swarthmore Col, BA; Ind Univ, MA & PhD; fel in residence for Coll teachers, Nat Endowment for Humanities, 78-79; Andrew W Mellon sr fel in humanities, 81. *Exhib:* Curator, GSA Design Awards Exhib, National Building Mus, Washington, DC, 97. *Pos:* Art columnist, City Mag, 78-79; art reviewer, Austin American-Statesman, 82-83; asst to dean, Sch of Archit, New York Inst of Technol, 86-89; exec Dir, Nat Inst Arch Educ, 89-95. *Teaching:* Lectr mod archit, Dartmouth Col, Hanover, NH, 70; instr mod archit & mod sculpture, Kansas City Art Inst, 72-74, asst prof, 74-78, assoc prof, 78-83; assoc prof archit, New York Inst of Technol, 85-89, adj prof, 89-. *Mem:* Landmarks Pres Comm, FT Greene Assoc, Brooklyn, NY, 2005-. *Res:* Nineteenth and twentieth century architecture; Frank Lloyd Wright. *Interests:* NYC Architecture. *Publ:* Auth, The English Landscape Garden in the Eighteenth Century: The Cultural Importance of an English Institution, Albion, Spring 79; Architectural Competitions in 19th Century England, UMI Res Press, 84; Frank Lloyd Wright, BluePrint, 96

BASSLER, ROBERT COVEY
SCULPTOR, PAINTER
b New York, NY, Nov 9, 1935. *Study:* Chouinard Art Inst, 52-53; Bard Coll, New York, BA, 57; Univ Southern Caiif, MFA, 60. *Work:* Chicago Convention Ctr; Bard Coll, Annandale on Hudson, NY; Univ Southern Calif, Los Angeles; Arts Coun Great Britain, London; Ahmanson Collection, Los Angeles; Container Corp Am; Atlantic Richfield Corp, Los Angeles, Calif; Central Savings & Loan, San Diego, Calif; Bank of Am; Calif State Univ, Northridge. *Comn:* 12 ft Wall Relief, Camarillo City Hall, Camarilllo, Calif; Celtic Cross, Kirk O'the Valley, Reseda, Calif, 93; Welded steel logo entry gate, Kirk Sch, Reseda, Calif, 2006; 2 Spirit Water Painting, Kirk O'the Valley, Reseda, 2009. *Exhib:* Solo exhibs include Robert Bassler Sculpture, Comara Gallery, Los Angeles, 61, 63, Robert Bassler, Sculpture, Santa Barbara Mu Art, Santa Barbara, Calif, 68, Robert Bassler, Molly Barnes Gallery, Los Angeles, 69, Bassler Sculptures, Galerie La Demeure, Paris, France, 71, Bassler, Amerika House, W Berlin, Germany, 72, Robert Bassler, Large Scale Sculpture, Security Pac Plaza, Los Angeles, Calif, 89-90, Robert Bassler, The Metamorphosis of an Image, Los Angeles Munic Galleries, Calif, 81, Robert Bassler, Wenger Gallery, Los Angeles, 88, Robert Bassler, Changing Light, Art Dome Gallery, Calif State Univ Northridge, 97, Robert Bassler, Paintings, Orlando Gallery, Sherman Oaks, Calif, 97; Group exhibs include A Plastic Presence, Jewish Mus, New York, 70; Salon de Mai, Mus D'Art Mod, Paris, France, 71; Translucent & Transparent Art, Mus Fine Arts, St Petersburg, Fla, 71; Calif Suite, Los Angeles Co Mus Art, Los Angeles, 77; Private Images, Los Angeles Co Mu Art, Los Angeles, 77; Olympic Proj, Los Angeles Co Mus Art, Los Angeles, 84; Nat Peace Garden Proj, Nat Bldg, Mus, DC, 89. *Pos:* Artist in Residence, Calif Inst Tech, Pasadena, Calif, 70-71; dir, CSUN Sculpture Park Assoc, 84-88; Sculpture edit adv, Int Sculpture Ctr, DC, 85-89; deans cir exec bd, CSUN Coll Arts, Media & Communications, 2012-2013. *Teaching:* instr, Occidental Coll, Los Angeles, Calif, 60-64; prof, Calif State Univ, Northridge, Calif, 64-97; teaching assist, Univ Southern Calif, Los Angeles, 59-60. *Bibliog:* Robert Pincus Witten (auth), Plastic Presence, Artforum VIII #5, 70; Harold Spencer (auth), The Image Maker, Scribners, NY, 74; Nickolas Roukes (auth), Sculpture in Plastics, Watson-Guptil, 78; Marlena Donahue (auth), California, Robert Bassler, Sculpture Mag, 88; Sharon Emanuelli, Robert Bassler, Changing Light, Exhib catalog, CSUN, 97; Josine Ianco Starrels & Louise Lewis (auth), Robert Bassler Cliffwall (exhib catalog), Los Angeles Munic Art Gallery; Lyn Keinholz (auth), LA Rising, SoCal Artists Before 1980, 2010. *Mem:* Int Sculpture Ctr; Mus Contemp Art, Los Angeles; Los Angeles Co Mus Art. *Media:* Mixed Media. *Res:* procedures for casting polyester resin. *Publ:* 16mm film, Variations, 71

BASTIAN, LINDA
PAINTER, EDUCATOR
b Ayer, Mass, Nov 7, 1940. *Study:* Antioch Col, BA, 63; Tufts Univ, Boston Mus Sch, MEd, 65; New York Univ, PhD, 72. *Work:* Art in Embassies Prog, US Dept State; Port Authority NY & NJ; Hosp Corp, Bellevue, NY; Temple Univ, Pa. *Exhib:* Works on Paper, Brooklyn Mus, NY, 75 & Weatherspoon Mus, Univ NC, Greensboro, 79; Solo exhibs, Soho 20 Gallery, 78, 80, 83, 84, & 86 & Birds, Fish & Flowers, Bronx Mus Arts, 85; Animals in Art, Dept Cult Affairs, NY, 81; Home Work, Women Make Art for the Home, Henry St, Syracuse Univ, 81; Translucency/Transparency, Fordham Univ & Coll Art Asn, NY, 82; Artists of Merit, Hudson River Mus, 85. *Teaching:* Chairperson art educ, Sch Visual Arts, New York, 79-. *Awards:* Salamagundi Third Ann Drawing Prize, 80. *Bibliog:* Articles in Arts Mag, 78, Diversion Mag, 82 & House Beautiful, 82. *Media:* Oil, Watercolor. *Dealer:* Soho 20 Gallery 99 Spring St New York NY 10012. *Mailing Add:* 418 Fulton Hill Rd Callicoon NY 12723-4424

BATCHELOR, BETSEY ANN
PAINTER, EDUCATOR
b Wilmington, Del, Dec 12, 1952. *Study:* Philadelphia Coll Art, BFA, 75; RI Sch Design, MFA, 77. *Work:* Continental Ill Bank & Trust, Chicago; Leif Johnson; CIGNA Corp. *Exhib:* Affect, Effect, Philadelphia Coll Art, Pa, 83; solo exhib, Matthews Hamilton Gallery, Philadelphia, Pa, 84, Florence Wilcox Gallery,

Swarthmore, Pa, 85, Munson-Williams-Proctor Inst, Utica, NY, Jessica Berwind Gallery, 89 & 92 & Dartmouth Col, 95; Works on Paper, Beaver Col, 89, 90 & 92; Goldey Paley Gallery, Philadelphia, Pa, 89; Woodmere Art Mus, Philadelphia, Pa, 90; solo exhib, Matthews Hamilton Gallery, Philadelphia, Pa, 84, Florence Wilcox Gallery, Swarthmore, Pa, 85, Munson-Williams-Proctor Inst, Utica, NY, 85, Jessica Berwind Gallery, 89 & 92 & Dartmouth Col, 95. *Teaching:* Instr painting, drawing & design, RI Sch Design, 76-80 & Community Col RI, 77-80; asst prof painting & design, Millersville Univ, 83-; asst prof, Munson-Williams-Proctor Inst, 84-85 & Swarthmore Col, 86, Moore Col Art & Design, 86-89, Swarthmore Col, 89-90, Beaver Col, 90-; assoc prof, Beaver Col, 90-. *Awards:* RI State Coun Arts, 80; Pa State Coun Arts, 84; MacDowell Colony Fel. *Bibliog:* Ronald J Onorato (auth), Gallery, Art Express, 3/82; Sid Sachs (auth), Does Philadelphia have an imagist tradition too?, New Art Examiner, 2/83; Edward Sozanski (auth), Philadelphia Inquirer, 6/85, 10/89. *Mem:* Coll Art Asn. *Dealer:* Jessica Berwind Gallery 301 Cherry St Philadelphia PA. *Mailing Add:* 709 W Carpenter Ln Philadelphia PA 19119-3407

BATEMAN, ROBERT MCLELLAN
PAINTER
b Toronto, Ont, May 24, 1930. *Study:* Univ of Toronto, BA (hon); pvt lessons at Toronto Arts & Lett Club from Gordon Payne; part time studies with Carl Schaeffer; Carlton Univ, Ottawa, hon DSc, 82; Brock Univ, St Catherines, LLD, 82; McMaster Univ, Hamilton, Ont, LHD, Guelph Univ, Ont, DDL, 85. *Work:* Art Gallery of Hamilton, Ont; Toronto Board of Trade; Prince of Wales; Am Artist Col, NY; (The Late) Serene Highness, Princess Grace of Monaco; HRH Prince Philip; Gilcrease Mus, Tulsa, Okla. *Comn:* Polar Bear (silver bowl commemorating endangered species), World Wildlife Fund, 76; Window into Ontario, Toronto Bd Trade, 77; Endangered Species Stamps: Eastern Cougar, 77, Peregrine Falcon, 78, Bowhead Whale, 79 & Prairie Chicken, 80, Can Post Off; Polar Bear, World Wildlife Fund, 85; Mallard Pair--Early Winter, Wildlife Habitat Can, 85; Snowy Blizzard--Red Tailed Hawk, Art Gallery of Hamilton, 86; Royal Can Mint-Platinum Polar Bear Ser, 90. *Exhib:* Queen Elizabeth Jubilee Show, Tryon Gallery, London, 77; Solo exhibs, Endangered Species Show, Tryon Gallery, 75 & 79 & Beckett Gallery, Hamilton, Ont, 78, 86 & 91; Smithsonian Inst, Washington, DC, 80 & 87; Images of the Wild, Nat Mus Natural Sci, Ottawa & traveling, Can, USA and Europ, 81-84; Gilcrease Art Mus, Tulsa, Okla, 86; Natural World, Canadian Embassy, Tokyo, 92; Natural Visions, Calif Acad Sci, Los Angeles Mus Natural Hist, Vancouver Mus, Victoria Art Gallery, 92-93; and others. *Pos:* Art consult, Halton Co Bd of Educ, 68-70; art teacher, Lord Elgin High Sch, Burlington, Ont, 70-76; self-employed artist, 77-. *Teaching:* Head dept art, Nelson High Sch, 59-68 & Lord Elgin High Sch, 70-76, Burlington. *Awards:* Merit Award, Soc Animal Artists, 79, 80, 86 & 90; Artist of the Year, Am Artist Mag, 80; Master Artist, Leigh Yawkey Art Mus, Wausau, Wis, 82. *Bibliog:* Norman Lightfoot (dir), Images of the Wild (film), Nat Film Bd of Can, 78; Ramsay Derry (auth), The Art of Robert Baleman, Penguin-Viking Publ, Madison Press, 81, Donnalu Wigmore (prod), Robert Bateman: Artist & Naturalist (film), Can Broadcasting Syst, 84; Ramsay Derry (auth), The World of Robert Bateman, Random House, 85; Rick Archbold (auth), Robert Bateman: An Artist in Nature, Penguin-Viking Publ, Madison Press, 90. *Mem:* Soc Animal Artists; Royal Can Acad Arts; hon life mem Fedn Can Artists; hon life mem Fedn Ont Artists; Brit Soc Wildlife Artists; and others. *Media:* Acrylic and Oils. *Publ:* Illusr, The Nature of Birds, Natural Hist of Can Series, 74. *Dealer:* Mill Pond Press Inc 310 Center Court Venice FL 33595. *Mailing Add:* c/o Mill Pond Press 310 Center Ct Venice FL 34292-3505

BATEMAN, RONALD C
PAINTER
b Caerphilly, Glamorgan, Wales, July 26, 1947. *Study:* Cardiff Coll of Art, predipl, study with Tom Hudson; Swansea Coll of Art, study with William Price; Tyler Sch of Art, Temple Univ, study with David Pease & J Moore, MFA. *Work:* Philadelphia Mus of Art; AT&T, Basking Ridge, NJ; Museo de Ayuntamiento De Pego, Alicante, Spain. *Comn:* Three murals, Wistar Inst, Univ of Pa, Philadelphia, 77; Creative Walls, Inc, Univ Pa. *Exhib:* Pego Ayuntamiento Mus Group Exhib, Alicante Province, Spain, 76; Contemp Artists in Philadelphia, 77; Solo exhibs, Marian Locks Gallery, 77, 82 & 87; About Face, Squibb Gallery, Princeton, NJ; What's Real, Marian Locks Gallery, 81. *Awards:* Elizabeth Greenshields Mem Found Grant, Can, 73; Primero Premio, Certimen de Pintura, Pascual Hermanos, Spain, 76; Mus Purchase, Cheltenham Art Ann, Philadelphia Mus of Art, 76. *Media:* Oil over Acrylic Underpainting on Canvas. *Mailing Add:* c/o Locks Gallery 600 Washington Sq S Philadelphia PA 19106

BATES, DAVID
PAINTER
b Dallas, Tex, 1952. *Study:* Southern Methodist Univ, Dallas, BFA, 76 MFA, 77. *Work:* Archer M Huntington Art Gallery, Univ Tex, Austin, Dallas Mus Art, Fort Worth Mus, Tex; Contemp Art Ctr, Honolulu, Hawaii; Metrop Mus Art, NY; New Orleans Mus Art, La; San Francisco Mus Mod Art. *Exhib:* Solo exhibs include Charles Cowles Gallery, NY, 84, 85, 86 & 87, Tex Gallery, Houston, 84 & 86, traveling exhib, Fort Worth Mus Art, Tex, 88, DC Moore Gallery, 2006; group exhibs include The Innovative Still Life, Holly Solomon Gallery, NY, 85; 50th Anniversary Acquisitions, San Francisco Mus Mod Art, 85; The Figure in the Landscape, Art Mus, Fla Int Univ, Miami, 86; Contemp Still Life, Rathbone Gallery, Junior Coll Albany, 86; Texas Landscape 1900-1986, Mus Fine Arts, Houston, 86; Sculpture and Works in relief, John Berggruen Gallery, San Francisco, 86; Biennial Exhib, Whitney Mus Am Art, NY, 87. *Awards:* Artist Grant, Dallas Mus Fine Arts, 82; Hassam & Speicher Fund Purchase, Acad & Inst Arts & Letters, 84. *Media:* Oil. *Mailing Add:* 34 Horatio St No 4B New York NY 10014-1622

BATISTA, KENNETH
PAINTER, EDUCATOR
b Pittsburgh, Pa, Oct 1, 1952. *Study:* Columbus Coll Art & Design, BFA, 75; Tyler Sch Art, Temple Univ, MFA, 77. *Work:* Westmoreland Co Mus Art, Greensburg, Pa; Grand Rapids Mus Art, Mich; Curtis Inst, Philadelphia, Pa; Hoyt Inst Fine Arts, New Castle, Pa; Erie Art Ctr, Pa. *Exhib:* Pensacola Nat Watermedia Exhib, Pensacola Jr Col, Fla, 82; Nat Watermedia Biennial, Zauer Gallery, Rochester, NY, 82; Am Drawings IV (traveling exhib), Smithsonian Inst, 83-84; Tyler Sch Art Alumni Exhib, Philadelphia, Pa, 87; Perspectives from Pennsylvania, Carnegie Mellon Art Gallery, Pittsburgh, 88. *Pos:* Chmn admin, Univ Pittsburgh, Pa, 87-93. *Teaching:* Instr drawing, Kendall Sch Design, Grand Rapids, Mich, 77-78; assoc prof drawing, Univ Pittsburgh, Pa, 78-. *Awards:* Chancellor's Distinguished Pub Service Award, 97; Purchase Award, Hoyt Nat Painting Show, 82; Jurors Award, Nat Watermedia Biennial, 82. *Mem:* Coll Art Asn; Nat Asn Sch Art & Design. *Media:* Watermedia; Drawing. *Dealer:* Rosenfeld Gallery 113 Arch St Philadelphia PA 19106; Concept Gallery 1031 S Braddock Ave Pittsburgh PA 15218. *Mailing Add:* 1217 Milton Ave Pittsburgh PA 15218

BATTENFIELD, JACKIE
PAINTER
b Pittsburgh, Pa, May 13, 1950. *Study:* Pa State Univ, BS, 71; Syracuse Univ, MFA, 78. *Work:* Dow Jones & Co, Inc, Princeton, NJ; US Dept State, Washington; Sasaki Collection, Tokyo, Japan; Montclair Art Mus, NJ; Univ Richmond, Va. *Comn:* Painting, The United States Pharmacopeial Convention, Inc, Rockville, Md; Uzu Maki (set painting) for Janis Brenner & Dancers, Danspace, NY, 94. *Exhib:* Del Mus Art, Wilmington, 78; Selections from the Sasaki Collection, Gallerie Saison, Tokyo, 82; Abstraction, Soho Ctr Vis Artists, NY, 87; Mizu: The Sounds of Water (with catalog), Marsh Gallery, Univ Richmond, Va, 93; solo shows, Erickson & Elins, San Francisco, 94, Addison-Ripley, Washington, 95, 98 & Gwenda Jay Gallery, Chicago, 98. *Pos:* Dir, Rotunda Gallery, Brooklyn, 81-89; proj coordr, Artist in the Marketplace Seminar (AIM), Bronx Mus Arts, 92-99. *Teaching:* Vis artist, Syracuse Univ Col Visual & Performing Arts, 80; adj prof, RI Sch Design, 80-81; adj asst prof, Laguardia Community Col, 87-95; Empire State Col, 89-92 & 95-97. *Awards:* Pollock-Krasner Found, 93; Warren Tanner Mem Award for Painting, OIA, 96. *Bibliog:* Richard Waller (auth), Jackie Battenfield: Mizu, The Sounds of Water, Univ Richmond Press, 93. *Mem:* Am Asn Mus. *Media:* All Media. *Publ:* Auth, Ikat Technique, Van Nostrand Reinhold, 78. *Dealer:* Ericson & Elins 345 Sutter San Francisco; Gwenda Jay Gallery Chicago IL

BATTIS, NICHOLAS
PAINTER, GALLERY DIRECTOR
Study: Univ Pitts, BA (Studio Arts, cum laude), 1985; Pratt Inst, MFA (Painting, with distinction), 1989. *Exhib:* CLPH Gallery, Brooklyn, 1989; Three Rivers Art Festival, Pitts, 1990 & 1991; Nat Exhib Am Art, Chautauqua Art Asn Galleries, Chautauqua, NY, 1990 & 1991; Art on the Block, Raintree's, Brooklyn, 1995; Beach Reveries, Pres's Gallery, Pratt Inst, Brooklyn, 1995; Small Works Show, 450 Broadway Gallery, New York, 1995, Assemble #2, 1995; HBO Gallery, Westchester, NY, 1997; Small Works, Cooley Gallery, Old Lyme, Conn, 1997; Grecian Treasures, Internat Images, Pitts, 1997; Surface, George Billis Gallery, New York, 1997, Art Exchange, 1998, Color in Motion, 1998, Additives...On Paper, 1999, Alchemy, 2001, Group Show, 2003, Round, 2003, Fresh Assortment, 2004; Invitational, Prince St Gallery, New York, 1998; Behind the Walls, Lawton Gallery, Univ Wis, 2000; solo exhibs, Paintings, George Billis Gallery, New York, 2001 & 2004, Los Angeles, 2006; Rental Sales Gallery, Albright-Knox Art Gallery, Buffalo, NY, 2003. *Pos:* Asst dir exhibs, Pratt Manhattan Gallery & Rubelle & Norman Schafler Gallery, Pratt Inst, Brooklyn, 2001-06, dir exhibs, 2006-. *Dealer:* George Billis Gallery 511 W 25th St Ground Fl New York NY 10001. *Mailing Add:* Pratt Manhattan Gallery 144 W 14th St 2nd Fl New York NY 10011

BATTLE, LAURA
PAINTER
Study: Kirkland Coll, 1974-76; RI Sch Design, BFA, 1979; Yale Sch art, MFA, 1983. *Exhib:* Solo exhibs, Albany Ctr Galleries, NY, 1996; 45th Anniversary Exhib, Binational Fulbright Commission, Cairo, Egypt, 1995; Lorraine Kessler Gallery, Poughkeepsie, NY, 1997, 1999; Calender 2000, Ctr Curatorial Arts, Bard Coll, 2000; Postcards from the Edge, Visual AIDS, Alexander & Bonin, 2000; Am Acad Arts & Letts Invitational, New York, 2003 & 2010; Ann Invitational Exhib Contemp Am Art, Nat Acad, New York, 2008; Lohin Geduld Gallery, New York, 2010. *Pos:* Cur dir & owner, Kendall Art & Design, Hudson, NY, 1998-2000. *Teaching:* Asst instr, Yale Sch Art, 1983-84; prof studio arts, Bard Coll, Annandale-on-Hudson, NY, 1986-; vis artist, Hampshire Coll, 1986-. *Awards:* Fulbright Fel, 1984-85; Charles Loring Elliot Award & Medal, Nat Acad Design, 2008. *Mailing Add:* Bard Coll Dept Studio Art PO Box 5000 Annandale On Hudson NY 12504-5000

BAUER, BETSY (ELIZABETH)
PAINTER, PRINTMAKER
b Mt Holly, NJ, Jan 18, 1959. *Study:* Mass Inst Techol with Robert Breer, 79; Philadelphia Coll Art, BFA (painting), 76-80; Santa Fe Art Inst with Elizabeth Murray, 95. *Work:* Hallmark Fine Art Collection, Kansas City, Mo; US State Dept, US Embassy, Sarejevo; Nat Acad Sci, Washington, DC; Philadelphia Coll Art, Pa; Rohm & Haas Corp, Pa. *Comn:* Painted banner, St Patrick's Cathedral, NY, 84; animated kitchen angels ad, FOX-TV, Albuquerque, 93; painting, Permaculture Drylands J, Tucson, 95; commission poster & notecard set of paintings, Santa Fe Opera, NMex, 96 & 98; cover, Nat Acad Sci Press. *Exhib:* Spacescapes, Visual Arts Mus, NY, 84; solo exhibs, Ceres Gallery, NY, 86 & 88, Hahn Ross Gallery, Santa Fe, NMex, 95, 96 & 98 & Nat Acad Sci, Washington, DC, 97; Women's Sensibilities, Warm Gallery, Minn, 86; The Political Is Personal, NY Feminist Art Inst, NY, 87; The Inspired Garden, Eidilon Gallery, Santa Fe, NMex, 95; Riparte, Int Prints Exhib, Rome, Italy, 95; Botanica, Hand Graphics Gallery, Santa Fe, NMex, 95; Monothon 10, Site Santa Fe, NMex, 96; Spectrum 1996, Hunter Mus, Chattanooga, Tenn, 96; Intimate Prints, Hand Graphics Gallery, Santa Fe, 96; Betsy Bauer Paintings & Prints, Nat Acad Sci, Washington, DC, 97; Organics, Bridgewater/Lustberg Gallery, NY, 97; Read: Text & the Visual, Gallery A, Chicago, 97; Monothon 12, Site Santa Fe, NMex, 98; Fresh, Addison/Ripley Gallery, Washington, DC, 98. *Awards:* Rohm & Haas Painting Award,

Rohm & Haas Corp, 80. *Bibliog:* Lis Bensley (auth), Awakening Botanica, Nat Acad Sci, 97; Paula Eastwood (auth), Santa Fean Mag, Santa Fe Opera Collectors ed, 98; Craig Smith (auth), A Marriage of Color & Music, New Mex Pasatiempo, 98. *Mem:* Santa Fe Coun for the Arts. *Media:* Oil Paint, All Media. *Dealer:* Hahn Ross Gallery 409 Canyon Rd Santa Fe NM 87501. *Mailing Add:* 66 Two Trails Rd Santa Fe NM 87505-9357

BAUER, RUTH KRUSE
PAINTER
b Dallas, Tex, July 26, 1956. *Study:* RI Sch Design, BFA, 78. *Work:* Mass Inst Technol; Graham Gund Found, Boston; Chase Manhattan Bank, NY; Equitable Life, NY; Chemical Bank, NY; DeCordova Mus, Lincoln, Mass. *Exhib:* Solo exhib, Kathryn Markel Gallery, NY, 84; Art of the State, Rose Art Mus, Waltham, 82; Selections 18, Drawing Ctr, NY, 82; Brave New Works, Boston Mus Fine Arts, 83; New Vistas: Contemp Am Landscapes (with catalog), Hudson River Mus & Tucson Mus Art, 84; Landscape of the Spirit, Bruce Mus, Greenwich, Conn & Maxwell Davidson Gallery, NY, 89. *Pos:* Artist-in-residence, City Arts Prog, Dallas, 79-80. *Bibliog:* In a Quiet Way, Art & Antiques, 9/84; Christine Temin (auth), Bauer's landscapes pull in viewer, Boston Globe, 5/86. *Mem:* Women's Caucus Art. *Media:* Oil, Watercolor. *Dealer:* Hokin-Kaufman 210 W Superior Chicago IL 60610. *Mailing Add:* 14 Aber St Beverly MA 01915

BAUER, WILL N
CONCEPTUAL ARTIST, VIDEO ARTIST
b Edmonton, Alta, Dec 12, 1960. *Study:* Univ Alta, BSC, 83; Univ Victoria, BC, Can, 85-87. *Work:* Telefonica Found, Madrid, Spain. *Comn:* The Trace, Telefonica Found, Madrid, Spain, 95; Displaced Emperors, ARS Electronic Ctr, Linz, Austria, 97; Re: Positioning Fear, Film & Arc, Graz, Austria, 97. *Exhib:* ARS Electronica, Linz, Austria, 93, 95 & 97; Interactive Media Festival, Los Angeles, Calif, 94; 4 Cyber Conf, Banff Ctr, Alta, Can, 94; ARCO Art Biennale, Madrid, Spain, 95; Film & Arc Biennale, Film & Archit Festival, Graz, Austria, 97. *Pos:* dir media res, APR Inc, 92-; residency, Art & Virtual Environs Prog, Banff Ctr, Alta, Can, 93-94. *Teaching:* adj prof Univ Alberta, 2001-; guest lectr Univ Karlstad Media and Comms Dept, 2000. *Awards:* ARS Electronica Golden Nical (Knowbotic Res), ARS Electronica, 93, (Rafael Lozano-Hemmer), 2000; Best Installation Piece, Int Digital Media Awards, 96. *Bibliog:* Mary Anne Moser (ed), Immersed in Technology, Mass Inst Technol Press, 96; Ole Bouman (auth), Quick space in real time, Archis Mag, No 9, 98; Jen Budney (auth) Artful engineering, Univ Alberta Engineer mag, Fall/99. *Mem:* Edmonton Arts Coun; IEEE. *Media:* Integrated Interactive Electronic Media. *Res:* Theory of Integrated-Media Artwork, Hyper-dimensional Virtual Art Objects, Artistic Bandwidth Measurement Techniques, others. *Publ:* Auth, Integrated Media Manifesto, Wayward Press, 90; coauth, GAMS-An integrated media controller system, Computer Music J, Mass Inst Technol Press, 92; auth, Age of the Data Poets, Flash Art Int, 96. *Dealer:* Relational Art Ciudad Rodrigo # 2 4-Izquierda Madrid Spain 28012. *Mailing Add:* 1803 11027-87 Ave Edmonton AB T6G 2P9 Canada

BAUM, ERICA
PHOTOGRAPHER
b New York, New York, 1961. *Study:* Barnard Coll, Columbia Univ, New York, BA (Anthropology), 1984; Hunter Coll, City Univ NY, MA, 1988; Yale Univ Sch Art, MFA (Photog), 1994. *Exhib:* Solo exhibs include Univ Calif Berkeley, San Francisco, 1995, Southern Light Gallery, Amarillo Coll, Tex, 1996, Clementine Gallery, New York, 1997, D'Amelio Terras, New York, 2000, 2003, 2004, HiArt, New York, 2005; group exhibs include Yale Sch Art Gallery, New Haven, Conn, 1994; Snapshot, Contemp Mus, Baltimore, 2001; Face Value, NY Acad Sci, New York, 2005; Silent Auction, Brooklyn Acad Music, NY, 2007; A New Reality, Zimmerli Art Mus, Rutgers Univ, New Brunswick, NJ, 2007; Remembering 9/11, NY Hist Soc, New York, 2007. *Awards:* New York Found Arts Fel, 2008. *Mailing Add:* D'Amelio Terras Gallery 525 W 22nd St New York NY 10011

BAUM, JAYNE H
ART DEALER
b Newark, NJ, Dec 3, 1954. *Study:* Clark Univ, Mass; NY Univ, BS (fine arts). *Pos:* Assoc & cur, Margo Feiden Galleries, New York, 75-77; dir & consult, Dan Greenblat Assoc, New York, 77-82; owner, Jayne Baum Gallery, New York, currently. *Bibliog:* Gallery exhibs reviewed in Arts Mag, Artnews, Artscribe & Village Voice. *Specialty:* Contemporary photography, paintings, drawings, limited edition prints and sculpture. *Publ:* Auth, Interior design, Whitney Comn Mag Div, 83; Facilities Design and Management, Gralla Publ, 83. *Mailing Add:* 26 Grove St Apt 4C New York NY 10014-5329

BAUM, MARILYN RUTH
PAINTER, PRINTMAKER
b Pittsburgh, Pa, May 24, 1939. *Study:* Univ Calif, Los Angeles, BFA, 62, 63-65. *Work:* Mus Mod Art, NY; Nat Mus Am Art; Achenbach Found Graphic Arts, Fine Arts Mus San Francisco; San Jose Mus, Calif; Jacksonville Art Mus, Fla. *Exhib:* Solo exhib, San Jose Mus, 81; California Artists, Oakland Mus, Calif, 81; Recent Acquisitions Part II, Achenbach Found, San Francisco, 83. *Bibliog:* Elise Miller (auth), Marilyn Baum--new paintings, Art Express, 3/82; Jeffrey Weiss (auth), article, Arts, 6/82; Frank Cebulski (auth), The selfish eye, Artweek, 1/83. *Dealer:* Olga Dollar Gallery 126 Post St San Francisco CA 94108. *Mailing Add:* 561 Summit Ave Mill Valley CA 94941-1032

BAUMANN, CAROLINE
MUSEUM DIRECTOR
Study: Bates Coll, Maine, BA (French lit & art hist); New York Univ, MA (medieval art). *Pos:* Artbook ed, George Braziller Inc, 89-91; dir develop, The Calhoun Sch, 91-93; dir develop & membership, Mus Mod Art, NY, 93-2001; dir external affairs, Cooper-Hewitt Nat Design Mus, 2001-2005, dep dir, 2006-2009, acting dir, 2012-2013, dir, 2013-. *Mem:* mem advisory committee, Citizens' Stamp for the US Postal Service, NYC Landmark50; dir Royal Col of Art US Alumni Group Advisory Board; mem Collective mem. steering committee, NYCxDesign. *Mailing Add:* Cooper-Hewitt Nat Design Mus Smithsonian Inst 2 E 91st St New York NY 10128

BAUME, NICHOLAS
CURATOR, DIRECTOR
b Syndey, Australia. *Study:* Univ Sydney, MA (fine arts & philos), 1987. *Collection Arranged:* Sol LeWitt: Incomplete Open Cubes (ed, catalog), 2001; Kai Althoff: Kai Kein Respekt, 2004; Getting Emotional, 2005; Thomas Hirschhorn: Utopia Utopia = One World, One War, One Army, One Dress (with Ralph Rugoff), 2005; Super Vision (ed, catalog), 2006; Anish Kapoor: Past, Present, Future (ed, catalog), 2008; Tara Donovan, 2008; Momentum 14: Rodney McMillian, 2009; Sandra & Gerald Fineberg Art Wall: Ugo Rondinone, 2009. *Pos:* Dir & cur, John Kaldor Art Projects & Collection, 1988-1993; founding cur, Mus Contemp Art, Sydney, 1993-1998; Emily Hall Tremaine cur contemp art, Wadsworth Atheneium Mus Art, Hartford, Conn, 1998-2003; chief cur, Inst Contemp Art, Boston, 2003-2009; dir & chief cur, Pub Art Fund, 2009-. *Mailing Add:* 1 E 53rd St New York NY 10022

BAUMEL-HARWOOD, BERNICE
PAINTER, PRINTMAKER, SCULPTOR
b Brooklyn, NY, Mar 6, 1923. *Study:* 5 Towns Music & Art Asn, NY, with Jacob Lawrence, 57-58; Anthony Toney, Pearl Fine; Hofstra Univ, Hempstead, NY, BS (Art Educ, cum laude with high hon in fine arts), 68-73; Hofstra Univ, MS in Special Educ, 75 Ruth Leaf Graphic Studio, Douglastown, NY, 80-85; Pratt Graphics Ctr, NY, 85-86; Studio Camnitzer, Valdottavo, Italy, with David Finkbeiner, 83-; Frank Varga Sculpture Studio Fla, 99-2001. *Work:* Am Stock Exchange, NY; IBM, Bethlehem, Pa; Chase Manhattan Bank, NY; Arthur Andersen & Co, St Louis, Mo; Sandoz-Nabisco; Arvin Industries, Farmington Hills, Mich Citizen & Southern Mortgage Co, Tampa, Fla; Bertholon & Rowland Corp, NY. *Exhib:* Solo exhib, Etchings & Monoprints, Calkins, Gallery, Hofstra, NY, 85; Nat Asn Women Artists Traveling Print, Greenville Mus Art, NC, 86, Albrecht Mus Art, St Joseph, Mo, 86, & Corcoran Sch Art, Washington, DC, 87; Long Island Artists, Nassau Co Mus, Roslyn, NY, 88; Body Conscious, Elaine Benson Gallery, Bridgehampton, NY, 89; Mari Gallery, Westchester, NY, 90; Gallery 84, NY, Norton Mus Art, West Palm Beach, Fla, 93; Coral Springs Mus of Art, Fla; 6 Person Show, Artists Guild of the Boca Raton Mus of Art, 98; Cornell Mus Art & American Culture, Delray Fla; Boca Raton Mus Art, Fla, 2010; Capital Bldg, Tallahassee, Fla; Armory Art Ctr, W Palm Beach, Fla; Rossetti Gallery, Pompano Beach, Fla, 2011. *Pos:* Nassau Co Mus Fine Arts, NY (bd adv 81-88); Graphic Eye Gallery, Port Washington, NY (pres, 86-88); Nat Asn Women Artists (juror graphics, 88-90); Lectr and Print Demonstrations Nassau Co Mus of Art, NY; Cornel Mus of Art, Delray, Fla; Coral Springs Mus of Art, Fla; Chap pres, Nat Asn Women Artists, 2008-2010, exhib coordr, 2010-2013. *Teaching:* Artist in residence, Monoprints, Syosset High Sch, NY, 86. *Awards:* Leila Sawyer award, NAWA, 83; Award Excellence, Long Beach Mus, Long Beach Art Asn, 85; Sally Carson Award, Norton Mus Art, 93; 3rd prize, NAWA, Northwood Univ W Palm Beach, Fla; Best in Show, Rossetti Gallery, Pompano Beach, Fla, 2012. *Bibliog:* Artspeak, NY, 89; Spotlight, 90; Interview with Artist, Art In the World Radio Program Nassau Community College; Article in the Sun Sentinal FL, 2002, On my Life Experiences; Palm Beach Post, 2008; 9/11 Memorial Artists Registry Sculpture, Group Zero and Rebirth. *Mem:* Nat Asn Women Artists (juror, 88-90, mem, 82-); Nat Mus Women in the Arts, DC (charter mem); Artists Guild of the Boca Raton Mus of Art, Fla (95-); NAWA, Fla Chapter, 95; Cornell Mus Art & American Culture, Fla, 2003; Cultural Council Palm Beach Co, 2012-. *Media:* Etchings, Monoprints, Watercolors. *Interests:* travel, reading, volunteer, art, theatre, music. *Collection:* Queensborough Community College Art Gallery NY; Coral Springs Mus of Art, FL; private collections. *Publ:* Illustrator: Five Towns, 62. *Mailing Add:* 41 Windsor Lane Boynton Beach FL 33436

BAUMGARDNER, MATT (MATTHEW) CLAY
PAINTER
b Columbus, Ohio, Feb 5, 1955. *Study:* Univ NC, Chapel Hill, MFA, 82. *Work:* Gibbs Mus, Charleston; Mint Mus, Charlotte; Spartenburg Arts Ctr. *Exhib:* Biennial Exhib, Mint Mus, Charlotte, 81; Exhibition 280, Huntington Mus, 82; Totem and Taboo, Wessel O'Connor Gallery, NY, 89; solo exhib, Charles Cowles Gallery, NY, 93, Gallery A, Chicago, 95 & 98, Bentley Gallery, Scottsdale, 98, 2000, Md Modern, Houston, 98, Jeffrey Coploff Fine Arts, New York City, 2000, 2001; Visions of Six, Gallery A, Chicago, 94; Pulp Fictions, Gallery A, Chicago, 95; Bentley Gallery, Scottsdale, Ariz, 97; Carrie Secrist Gallery, Chicago, 98; Robert Kidd Gallery, Birmingham, Mich, 99; Jeffrey Coploff Fine Art, New York City, 99; Bemis Ctr, Omaha City, Nebr, 99; Lew Allen Contemp, Santa Fe, 99. *Collection Arranged:* Bear Stearns, Boston; Blank Rome Cominsky & McCauley, Philadelphia; Boston Millennia Partners; Gibbes Mus, Charleston, SC; Hale & Dorr, Boston; Mint Mus, Charlotte, NC; Palmer & Dodge, Boston; Spartenburg Arts Ctr, SC; XL Captial, Pembroke, Bermuda. *Awards:* Visual Artist Fel, Nat Endowment Arts, 93. *Bibliog:* David McCraken (auth), Sampler of Abstraction from New York is down to earth, Chicago Tribune, 2/25/94; interview by Suzy Hendrikx, VTM Belg Television, 97; interview by Richard Hake, WNYC, NPR Radio, 97; Rick Marin (auth), Footloose Where Art Lives, NY Times, 11/21/98. *Media:* Acrylic, Oil. *Mailing Add:* Eckert Fine Art PO Box 649 Millerton NY 12546

BAUTZMANN, CA-OPA (NANCY ANNETTE)
PAINTER
b Morganton, NC. *Study:* Westminster Col, BA (fine art), 74; study with Hans Axel Walleen, 75-76, Gunter Korus, 92-94. *Work:* J P Adams, Dalton, Mass. *Comn:* Oil painting, comn by David Derry, Pittsfield, Mass, 94; oil portrait, comn by Ed Lewis, Worthington, Mass, 94; watercolor, comn by Mrs Michel Leonart, Tucson, Ariz, 97. *Exhib:* Springfield Art League Nat, George Walter Vincent Smith, Mass, 93; Oil Painters of Am Nat, 93, 94, 95, 96 & 98; 18th Ann Art Exhib Nat, Salmagundi Club,

NY, 95; Ariz Aqueous Nat, Tubac Ctr Arts, Ariz, 96; Western Fedn Soc Watercolor, Tucson Mus Art, Ariz, 97. *Collection Arranged:* Portfolio of Realism, Berkshire Botanical Garden Ctr, 93; Paintings by Nancy Bautzmann, Pittsfield Art League Co-op Gallery, 94; El Presidio Gallery, Tucson, Ariz, 1995-2003; Granite Mus Gallery, Prescott, Ariz; J&F Fine Arts Gallery, Scottsdale, Ariz. *Pos:* Jury of selection, Kent Art Asn, 92; judge, Cent Berkshire Chamber Com Poster Contest, 94. *Teaching:* Art, Art-for-Children, Berkshire Mus, 88-94, Becket Arts Coun, 89; drawing & watercolor, Pittsfield, Mass & Tucson, Ariz, 1988-2003. *Awards:* Merit Award, 74th Nat Exhib, Springfield Art League, 93; First in Oil, Kent Art Asn, Conn, 94; Merchandise Award, Oil Painters Am, 98; First Place, Southern Ariz Watercolor Guild's Signature Show, 2003. *Bibliog:* Chamber Showing Bautzmann Works, Cent Berkshire Chamber Com, 1/29/92; Janet Jahn (auth), Visiting artist-Nancy Bautzmann, First Congregational Church, 4/16/93. *Mem:* Signature mem Oil Painters Am; signature mem Copley Soc Boston; artist mem Acad Arts Asn; signature mem Southern Ariz Watercolor Guild (show chmn, 97-); Ariz Watercolor Asn. *Media:* Oil, Watercolor. *Publ:* Contribr, The Best of Flower Painting, Northlight, 97; Villages in the spotlight, Casas Adobes Courier, 1999; contribr article and cover Tea A Mag, fall, 2001

BAXTER, BONNIE JEAN
PRINTMAKER, PAINTER
b Texarkana, Tex, July 30, 1946. *Study:* Monticello Col, AS, 64-66; Kans Univ, 66-67; Cranbrook Art Acad, BFA, 67-69. *Work:* Mus Mod Art, Montreal; Monticello Col, Godfrey, Ill; Maison de la Cult, Montreal; Galleria Fenwick, Forano, Italy; Maison des Metiers, Rennes, France. *Comn:* Mural, Mich High Sch, Bloomfield Hills, 69; mural for tomb, comn by Gen Paciantiani, Forano, Italy, 73. *Exhib:* Que-Boston Exchange, Experimental Etching Studio, Boston, 82; 171 Artistes Quebecoise, Maison de la Cult, Montreal, 82; Quebec Artists, Maison des Metiers, Rennes, France, 83; Artists Book L'lle, Mus Mod Art, Montreal, 83; l'Atelier de L'Ile, Delegation du Que, NY, 83; and others. *Pos:* Owner & dir, Le Scarabee Printing Studio, Val-David, Que, 82-; printer in residence, l'Atelier de L'Ile Asn, 80-82, master printer, 82-. *Teaching:* Instr wood-cut, Les Createurs Assoc, Que, 82-83. *Bibliog:* Jacques Gireldeau (dir), Etoile de Aurainegiea (film), Can Nat Film Bd, 78. *Mem:* Conseil Gravare Que; Am Graphics Soc; Les Createur Asn Val-David (pres, 82-); Conseil Regional Cult Laurentides (exec dir, 83-87). *Media:* All. *Publ:* Auth, Atelier d l'lle a Boston, 81 & Atelier d l'lle a New York, 82, Skis-Dite; illusr, L'Ille, Iconia Ed, 82; auth, Bonnie Baxter: Printmaker--fine arts director, Skis-Dite, 82; contribr, Quebec Artists 1970-1983, Iconia Ed, 83. *Mailing Add:* 3224 Ave du Pins CP 375 Val-David PQ J0T 2N0 Canada

BAXTER, DOUGLAS W
ART DEALER
b Ohio, Nov 8, 1949. *Study:* Oberlin Col, with Ellen Johnson, BA (art hist), 72. *Exhib:* Cy Twombly: Works on Paper 1957-87, 88; Barnett Newman: The Sublime in Now, 94. *Pos:* Art dealer, Fischbach Gallery, 73-74; art dealer, Paula Cooper Gallery, New York, 74-87; vpres, Pace Gallery, 87- 93 & exec dir, 93-96; exec dir, Pace Wildenstein, 93 & pres, 96-; trustee, Independent Cur Inc, New York, 89-, Chinati Found, Marfa, Tex, 94- & Trisha Brown Dance Co, New York, 97-. *Mem:* Feria de Arte Contemporaneo, Madrid, Spain (mem, org comm, 86-89); Robert Kovich Dance Found, New York (bd mem, 89-93); Art Pro-Choice, Benefit for Nat Abortion Rights Action League (mem, exhib comm, 90). *Specialty:* Contemporary and modern art. *Publ:* Ed, catalogs for Twombly and Newman exhibs, Pace Gallery, New York, 88. *Mailing Add:* Pace Gallery 32 E 57th St New York NY 10022

BAXTER, PAULA ADELL
EDUCATOR, WRITER
b Hackensack, NJ, Sept 21, 1954. *Study:* State Univ MY, Binghamton, BA (art hist), 75, MA, 77; Columbia Univ, MSLS, 79. *Collection Arranged:* Victorian Ornament: Excerpts in Design History, Edna Barnes Salomon Gallery, NY Pub Libr, 89-90 & A change of clothes, 93; Artful Interiors: Rooms with a View, 96-97; Decoration in the Age of Napoleon, 2004-05; A Rakish History of Men's Wear, 2006-07; Art Deco Design: Rhythm and Verve, Wachenheim Gallery, 2008-2009. *Pos:* Visual arts libr, State Univ NY, Purchase, 81-83; assoc librn reference, Mus Mod Art, New York, 83-87; cur art & archit collection, New York Pub Libr, 87-09; prof humanities, Berkeley Coll, NY, 2010-. *Teaching:* Instr, Sch Libr and Information Sci, Inst on Art Citations, Pratt Inst, summer 2002; instr interior design history, Purchase Coll, 2010-. *Mem:* Art Librs Soc NAm (exec bd, 87-88); Popular Cult Asn; Am Soc of Journalists and Authors. *Res:* American Indian jewelry design history. *Interests:* British and Native American art, history of decorative arts and design. *Publ:* Navajo and Pueblo Jewelry, 1940-1970, Three Decades of Innovative Design Revisited, Am Indian Art Mag, autumn, 96; Nineteenth-century Navajo and Pueblo silver jewelry, Antiques Mag, 1/98; Encyclopedia of Native American Jewelry, Oryx Pr, 2000; Southwest Silver Jewelry, Schiffer, 2001; The Regency Style's Debt to Napoleon, Antiques Mag, 10/2004; When Rakes Ruled: French Masculine Costume of the Revolutionary Era, Antiques Mag, 2/2007; Auth, articles, The Journal of Antiques and Collectibles; Southwestern Indian Rings, Schiffer, 2011; Southwestern Indian Bracelets, forthcoming, 2014

BAXTER, VIOLET
PAINTER, CALLIGRAPHER
b New York, NY, 1934. *Study:* Hunter Coll, New York, 52-54, Cooper Union Sch Art, New York, Cert, 60, with Morris Kantor, Paul Standard, Robert Gwathmey, Adya Yunkers, Nicholas Carone, 60; Columbia Univ, New York, with Ralph Mayer, 60-62; Pratt Graphic Art Ctr, New York, 81. *Work:* Hon Shunichi Suzuki, Gov Tokyo; Consolidated Edison Co, Oppenheimer Capital Corp, Schroder & Co, NY, Fidelity Investments, Morgan Stanley Trust, Jersey City, NJ; Mus City New York; Savannah Coll Art & Design, Ga; SE Mo State Univ Mus; Council Environ, New York; Jacqueline Casey Hudgens Ctr Arts, Duluth, Ga; pvt collection, Jonathan Fanton, Lucy Liu, Sam Mendes; The Crisp Mus, SE Missouri State U. *Exhib:* solo exhibs, Suffolk Co Community Coll, Riverhead, NY, 86, NY Vista, World Trade Ctr, 91, Gallery Juno, NY, 99-2000 & Nat Arts Club, NY, 99, Southeast Mo State Univ Mus, 2002, Jeffrey Leder Gallery, Long Island City, NY, 2012; Group exhibs, Sharon Creative Arts Found Gallery, Conn, 85-87; Monmouth Mus, NJ, 85; Nexus Found, Philadelphia, 86; 80 Wash Sq E Galleries, NY Univ, 93; GE Corp HQ, Fairfield, Conn, 94; Owen Gallery, NY, 95; Park Ave Atrium, NY, 96; Mus City NY, 96; Staten Island Inst Arts Sci (biennial), 96; Forham Univ Lincoln Ctr, NY, 96 & 2000; Xian Acad Fine Arts Gallery, Xian, China & Badahsenzi Mem Gallery, Nanchang, 97; Md Fedn Art, Annapolis, 97-2000; Boston Ctr Arts, Artcetera Auction, 98 & 2001; Butler Inst Am Art, Youngstown, Ohio, 98, 2001 & 2005; NYC Tech Coll, City Univ NY, 98 & 2000; NY Law Sch, 99; The Gallery, Mercer Co Community Coll, Trenton, NJ, 2001; Southeast Mo State Univ Mus, 2002; David Findlay Jr Fine Art, New York, 2003; Butler Gallery, Marymount Coll, Fordham Univ, NY, 2003; ACA Galleries, New York, 2006; The Painting Ctr, New York, 2007; Lori Bookstein Fine Art, New York, 2008; Smithtown Township Art Coun, Mills Pond House, St James, New York, 2001; Southeast Mo State Univ Mus, 2002; NY Studio Sch Auction, 2005-2007; 185th Ann Invitational, Nat Acad Mus, New York, 2010; Jeffrey Leder Gallery, LIC, NY, 2010-2012. *Pos:* Bd dir, NY Artists Equity, 88-, vpres, 91-2002; dir, Fine Arts Federation, NY, 2004-08. *Teaching:* Mentor, Integrative Studies (calligraphy), Pratt Inst, NY, 74-75; guest lectr, Sch Practical Philosophy, Pastel Soc Am & Parsons Sch Design, 85-; panel, Art Students League, NY, 2003. *Awards:* Gold Medal of Honor, Audubon Artists, NY, 94; Bronze Medal, Audubon Artists, NY, 95-97; Jane Peterson Mem Award, Audubon Artists, 96; Vermont Studio Center, Artist Grant, 96; Richard Florsheim Art Fund Grant, 2002. *Bibliog:* Jed Perl (auth), Gallery Going, Harcourt Brace Jovanovich, 91; Jed Perl (auth), Real Worlds, Art & Antiques, 1/92; Katherine Hobson (auth), The Deal of the Art, The Street.com, 10/99 and The Street's Art Lovers, The New York Observer, 11/99; Elizabeth Wilson (auth): Interview, Violet Baxter, The Pastel Jour, 12-16, 9-10/2001; F.R. Rivers, Art Review: sub(Urban), Princeton Town Topics, 10/2001; Pat Summers (auth), Three Artists, Vision at Mercer, U.S. 1, 10/2001; Tamara Kerr Art Bank/NY Artists Equity, honoring Placide and George A. Schriever, Univ Mus, exhib catalogue with essay by Stanley I. Grand, Cape Girardeau, Mo, Univ Mus, SE Mo State Univ, 2002; Sam Blackwell (auth), Windows on Manhattan, Interview, Arts & Leisure, Southeast Missourian, 10/2002; and others; Steve Mosco (auth), LIC Courier, 2012 (1, 10-11); Patrick Neal (auth), Hyperallergic, 2012. *Mem:* New York Artists Equity Asn; Fedn Mod Painters & Sculptors; Nat Arts Club, New York (hon mem). *Media:* All Media, Oil; Watercolor, Pastel, Drawing. *Specialty:* Contemp Art. *Publ:* Best of Pastel, 96, Landscape Inspirations, 97 & Best of Drawing & Sketching, 99, Rockport Publ; Univ Mus, Violet Baxter: The View from Union Square, exhib catalogue with essay by Stanley I. Grand, Cape Girardeau, Mo Univ Mus, SE Mo State Univ, 2002; Maureen Bloomfield & James Markle (auths), Pure Color: The Best of Pastel, North Light Bks, 2006; Contemporary American Oil Painting, Jilin Fine Arts Publ, China, 2008. *Dealer:* Jeffrey Leder Gallery. *Mailing Add:* 2137 45th Rd Long Island City NY 11101

BAYER, ARLYNE
PAINTER, PRINTMAKER
b Washington, DC. *Study:* State Univ NY, Buffalo, BFA; Hunter Coll, with Tony Smith, John McCracken & Rosalind Krauss, MA (fine arts). *Work:* Herbert F Johnson Mus Art, Ithaca, NY; Chase Manhattan Bank, Equitable Life Assurance, NY; Prudential Insurance Co, Newark, NJ; Housatonic Mus Art, Bridgeport, Conn. *Comn:* Shearman & Sterling, NY. *Exhib:* Contemp Reflections, Aldrich Mus Contemp Art, 75; 15 New Talents, Aldrich Mus Contemp Art, 79; solo exhib, Hudson Gallery, NY, 86; Pastel Anthology II, Grace Borgenicht Gallery, NY, 87; Invitational, Richard Green Gallery, Santa Monica, Calif, 91; Activated Walls, Artists Space, NY, 93; Selections, Adam Baumgold Fine Art, NY, 96; and others. *Awards:* Creative Artists Pub Serv Grant, 76-77; MacDowell Colony Fel, 77. *Bibliog:* Jacqueline Moss (auth), article, Arts Mag, 2/80. *Dealer:* Adam Baumgold Gallery 60 E 66th St New York NY 10065. *Mailing Add:* 903 Park Ave No 16C New York NY 10075

BAYLISS, GEORGE
PAINTER, EDUCATOR
b Washington, DC, Oct 14, 1931. *Study:* Univ Va; Univ Md, with Herman Maril, BA, 55; Cranbrook Acad Art, with Zoltan Sepeshy, MFA, 56; Corcoran Sch Art. *Work:* Akron Art Inst, Ohio; State Univ NY; Corcoran Gallery Art; Univ Mich; Ford Motor Co; Sloan Kettering Found; Telfair Mus. *Comn:* Mural, Rural Elect Transmission, Mus Hist & Technol, Smithsonian Inst, 56-57. *Exhib:* Corcoran Biennial Contemp Am Painters, 55 & 59; New Accessions USA, Colorado Springs Fine Arts Ctr, 58; 12 Washington Painters, Univ Ky, 60; Four Washington Artists, Corcoran Gallery Art, 61; Drawings USA, circulated by Smithsonian Inst, 62. *Teaching:* Instr painting & drawing, Sch Akron Art Inst, Ohio, 57-59 & Flint Jr Col, Mich, 59-62; asst prof painting & drawing, State Univ NY Col Potsdam, 62-63; acting dean, Parsons Sch of Design, New York City, 63-67; chmn dept art, State Univ NY Col, Fredonia, 67-72; chmn dept art, Univ Mich, 72-74, dean, Sch Art, 74-84; dean, Tyler Sch Art, 84-89, prof painting, 89-95, prof emeritus, 95-. *Awards:* Principal Purchase Prize, Corcoran Gallery Art, 55; Award of Merit, South Bend Art Asn, Ind, 56; Bundy Co Prize, Bloomfield Hills Art Asn, 56. *Mem:* Coll Art Asn; Nat Asn Schs Art & Design (bd dir & pres). *Media:* Oil, Watercolor, Acrylic. *Specialty:* Painting, sculpture, prints, crafts. *Dealer:* Turtle Gallery Deer Isle ME. *Mailing Add:* 213 Royal Ave Wyncote PA 19095

BEACHUM, SHARON GARRISON
PHOTOGRAPHER, GRAPHIC ARTIST
b Oklahoma City, Okla, Dec 1, 1953. *Study:* Univ Okla, BFA, 75; Old Dominion Univ & Norfolk State Univ, coop prog, MFA, 86. *Work:* Chrysler Mus, Norfolk, Va; Franklin Furnace, NY. *Exhib:* Why Do Girls Have to Act Like That?, Va Beach Art Ctr, 86; Chromatic Abberations, Washington Ctr Photog, Washington, DC, 88; The Portrait in Am, Chyrsler Mus, Norfolk, Va, 90; solo exhib, Mich State Univ, East Lansing, 90; Light Aberations, Univ Tex, San Antonio, 90; Mid-Atlantic State Photog, James Madison Univ, Harrisonburg, Va, 91. *Pos:* Owner, Swift Graphics, Okla & Va, 77-92; tech illusr, Telemedia, Norfolk, Va, 80-82; graphic designer, Off PR, E Va Med Sch, Norfolk, 82-83. *Teaching:* Assoc prof graphic designs & photog, Hampton Univ, Va, 88-, chmn art dept, 90-94. *Awards:* Mat & Equip Grant, Four Sharp Artists, Copy

Data Group, 87; Communs Excellence, Donor Recruitment, 88 & First Place in Nation, Donor Recruitment Campaign, 90, Nat Red Cross; Fulbright-Hays Travel Simihon Award: China, 98; Artist Residency Award, Va Ctr Creative Arts, 98. *Bibliog:* Stephen Perloff (auth), Photo Review, Pa Coun Arts, 87; Brooks Johnson (auth), The Portrait in America, Chrysler Mus, 90. *Mem:* Va Soc Photog Art; Tidewater Artists Asn (bd & publicity, 86-87); Coll Art Asn. *Media:* Photo; Collage. *Mailing Add:* Dept Art Hampton Univ Box 6205 Hampton VA 23668

BEAL, GRAHAM WILLIAM JOHN
DIRECTOR, CURATOR
b Stratford-on-Avon, Eng, Apr 22, 1947. *Study:* Manchester Univ, BA, 69; Courtauld Inst, London Univ, MA, 72. *Exhib:* Wiley Territory (with catalog), 79; Jim Dine: Five Themes (coauth, catalog), 84; Giacometti: The Last Two Decades (with catalog), 84; Second Sight (with catalog), 86; Recent British Sculpture (with catalog), 87; David Nash: Voyager & Vessels, 94. *Collection Arranged:* Van Gogh: Face to Face, 2000; Degas and the Dance, 2002; On the Edge: Contemporary Art from the DaimlerChrysler Collection, Detroit Inst Arts, 2003; Magnificenza! The Medici, Michelangelo and the Art of Late Renaissance Florence, 2003; American Attitude: Whistler and His Followers, 2003; Camille Claudel and Rodin: Fateful Encounter, 2006. *Pos:* Dir, Wash Univ Art Gallery, 74-77, Sainsbury Ctr, UK, 83-84, Joslyn Art Mus, Omaha, 89-96, Los Angeles Co Mus Art, Calif, 96-99; chief cur, Walker Art Ctr, Minneapolis, 77-83 & San Francisco Mus Mod Art, 84-89; mem Fed Adv, Comt on Int Exhib, 91-94; dir, pres, CEO, Detroit Inst Arts, 99-; bd trustees, Asn Am Mus Dirs, 2002-05 & Am Assn Mus, 2004-2007. *Res:* Contemporary art and the surrealist tradition. *Publ:* Auth, Jim Dine: Five Themes (exhib catalog), 84; co-auth, A Quiet Revolution (exhib catalog), 87, David Nash: Voyages and Vessels, 94, Sainsbury Collection Catalogue, Vol 1, 97, Joslyn Air Mus: Fifty Favorites, 94, Joslyn Art Mus: A Bldg Hist, 98, American Beauty: Am Paintings and Sculpture from the Detroit Inst of Arts, 2002; contrib to Apollo Mag, London, 89-91. *Mailing Add:* Detroit Inst Arts 5200 Woodward Ave Detroit MI 48202

BEAL, MACK
SCULPTOR
b Boston, Mass, Apr 20, 1924. *Study:* Harvard Univ, BS, 46; grad study, Dept of Art, Univ NH, Durham; apprentice to master blacksmith Joe Tucker, Milford, NH. *Work:* Addison Gallery Am Art, Phillips Acad, Andover, Mass; New Eng Ctr, Univ NH, Durham; Worcester Art Mus, Mass; Permanent Exhib, Symp Lindabruun, Bad Voslau, Austria. *Exhib:* Inst Contemp Art, Boston, 70-73; Addison Gallery Am Art, Phillips Acad, Andover, Mass, 74; Norfolk Art Ctr, Nebr, 79; Nat Ornamental Metal Mus, Memphis, 79; Rowe Gallery, Univ NC, 80; Int Conf Exhib, Hereford, Eng, 80; NH Comn Arts, 81; and many others. *Pos:* Dir, The Sculptors Workshop, Somerville, Mass, 70-80, New Eng blacksmith Asn, NH League Craftsmen's Scholar Awards, NH Coun on The Arts Awards Comt. *Teaching:* Pvt classes at MB's Studio in blacksmithing & sculpture in wood & stone. *Awards:* Silver Medals (2) & Gold Medals (2), Int Teaching Ctr for Metal Design, Aachen, Ger, 86 & 91; FIFI Exhib, Cardiff, Wales, 89; HEFAISTON 90, Int Blacksmiths Prerov, Czech, 90, 99, 2002, 2004 & 2006; Abana's Bealer Award, 2005. *Mem:* NH League Craftsmen; Boston Visual Artists Union; Ogunquit Art Asn; Artist Blacksmith Asn N Am (dir, 76-80); and others. *Media:* Installation Sculpture, Metal, Welded, Stone. *Mailing Add:* PO Box One Jackson NH 03846

BEAL, STEPHEN
ACADEMIC ADMINISTRATOR
Study: Occidental Coll, Los Angeles; Sch Art Inst Chicago, MFA; Univ Vt, Burlington, grad prog in hist preservation. *Pos:* Vpres academic planning & assoc vpres academic affairs, Sch of the Art Inst Chicago, 1995-97; provost, Calif Coll Arts, 1997-2008, pres, 2008-; bd dirs, Yerba Beuna Ctr Arts, San Francisco; bd pres, Creative Growth Art Ctr, Oakland, Calif. *Teaching:* Grad asst, Sch of the Art Inst Chicago, 1972-73, instr & technician, 1973-77, chair grad design & assoc prof painting, 1993-95; asst prof art appreciation, collage, photog & design, Elmhurst Coll, Ill, 1980-83. *Mem:* Am Film Inst (advisory bd); Girls Inc (advisory bd); Asian Art Mus (advisory bd). *Mailing Add:* Office of the President Calif College of Arts 1111 Eighth St San Francisco CA 94107-2247

BEALE, ARTHUR C
FILMMAKER, CONSULTANT
b Needham, Mass, Apr 12, 1940. *Study:* Brandeis Univ, BA, 62; Boston Univ Sch Fine & Appl Arts, 62-64; Harvard Univ Fogg Art Mus, apprentice conserv, 66-68. *Pos:* Conserv, Joint Am Exped Idalion, Cyprus, 71; assoc conserv, Fogg Art Mus, Harvard Univ, 71-74, head conserv, Ctr Conserv & Tech Studies, 75-81, dir, 81-86; conserv, Kress Collection Renaissance Bronzes & Medals, Nat Gallery Art, 72-75; dir res, Mus Fine Arts, Boston, 86-93; vis comt, J Paul Getty Conserv Inst, 87-92; Nat Mus Serv Bd, 88-95; dir, Objects Conserv & Scientific Res, 93-98 & Conserv & Scientific Res, 98-99, chair Conserv & Collections Mgt, 99-2005, chair emer Conserv & Collections Mgt, 2005-. *Teaching:* Asst appl arts, Boston Univ, 62-64; lectr fine arts, Harvard Univ, 74-77 & 87-, sr lectr, 77-86. *Awards:* First Univ Products Award for Distinguished Achievement in the Field of Conserv, 95. *Mem:* Fel Am Inst Conserv; Nat Inst Conserv (pres, 81-82, chmn, 82-85); Int Coun Mus. *Media:* High Definition Video. *Interests:* Native American art. *Publ:* Auth, Technical perspectives on Ital medals, surface characteristics and their interpretation, Studies Hist Art, 87; Scientific Approaches to the Question of Authenticity, small bronze sculpture from the Ancient World, J Paul Getty Mus, 90; Understanding, resorting and conserving ancient bronzes with the aid of science, The fire of hephaistos: Large classical bronzes from North American Collections (ed by Carol C Mattusch), Harvard Univ Art Mus, 96; Little Dancer Aged Fourteen: The Search for the Lost Modele, Degas and the Little Dancer, Joslyn Art Mus, 98. *Mailing Add:* 151 Bulrush Farm Rd Scituate MA 02066-1429

BEALE, MARK
PAINTER, DIRECTOR
b Richmond, Va, May 11, 1962. *Study:* Univ Va, BA, 1984; Va workshop, with Barclay Sheiks, 1980; Mentee, with Brent Cotton, 2011-2012. *Work:* Magnolia Gardens and Plantation, Chas, SC. *Exhib:* Salmagundi Club New York, 2014; 57th Ann Members Exhib, Charleston Artist Guild, Charleston, SC, 2011; First Federal People's Choice Exhib, Charleston, SC, 2011; Botanicals exhib, Light Space and Time Gallery, Jupiter, Fla, 2011; Signature exhib, Charleston Visitors Center, Charleston, SC, 2011; Signature Exhib, Charleston Art Guild, 2012; Piccolo Spoleto, Charleston, SC, 2012; Int Fine Arts Exhib, Am Juried Art Salon, 2012; Solo exhib, Tones of the Coastal Landscape, Charleston Artist Guild Gallery, 2012; On the Waterfront, Charleston Artist Guild Gallery, 2013; Magnolia Gardens Nat Landscape Competition, Charleston, SC, 2013; Paint the Parks two-year traveling Exhib (Winners Show), Coutts Mus of Art, El Dorado, Kans, 2013; Wildlife Experience Mus, Denver, Colo, 2013; Gibbes Mus of Art, Chas, SC, 2014. *Pos:* founder & dir, Beale Fine Art, Charleston, SC, 2010-; bd dirs, Charleston Artist Guild, 2012-2013; ed in chief, EASEL, 2012-2013. *Awards:* Special Recognition Award, Botanicals Exhib, 2011; Emerging Artist Award, Art Network News Quarterly, 2011; Exhibiting Member Status, Charleston Artist Guild, 2011; Emerging Artist, Am. Art Salon, 2011; Award of Merit, 12th Fine Arts Int Exhib, 2011; 2nd Pl, First Federal People's Choice Exhib, Charleston, SC, 2011; Hon Mention, 57th Ann Members Exhib, Charleston Artist Guild, SC, 2011; Paint the Parks Top 100 Award, Nat Parks Found, 2012-2013; 2nd Pl, South State Bank People's Choice Exhib, 2013; First Prize, Magnolia Gardens Nat Landscape Competition, 2013; First Place, Charleston Artist Guild Member's Show, 2015. *Bibliog:* Ephemeral Visions: Collecting Landscape Art, Am Art Collector Mag, 2012; Oil Painters of Am Featured Artists; Art Lovers Guide to Charleston, Am Art Collector Mag, 2012, Focus on Representational Art, 2012, Collecting Art In Charleston and the Carolinas, Am Art Collector Mag, 2013. *Mem:* Oil Painters of America; American Impressionist Society; Charleston Artist Guild. *Media:* Oil. *Interests:* Coastal Landscape Painting, Tonalism. *Publ:* contribr, Artist Portfolio Mag, 2011; contribr, Kevin MacPherson's Charleston Demonstration, Easel, 7/2011; Bringing Artists Together, Artist Daily/American Artist Mag, 2011; ed in chief, EASEL, Chas. Artist Guild, 2012-2013. *Dealer:* Reinert Fine Art 179 King St Charleston SC 29401. *Mailing Add:* 669 St. Andrews Blvd Charleston SC 29407

BEALL, DENNIS RAY
PRINTMAKER, EDUCATOR
b Chickasha, Okla, Mar 13, 1929. *Study:* Oklahoma City Univ; San Francisco State Univ. *Work:* Achenbach Found for Graphic Arts, San Francisco; San Francisco Mus Mod Art; Mus Mod Art, NY; Libr Cong, Washington, DC; Philadelphia Mus. *Comn:* Lone Star (ed 20, collagraph), C Troup Gallery-Codex Press, Inc, Dallas, 66; Emblem V (ed 75, relief & etching), Univ Calif, Berkeley Mus, 67; Emblem VI (ed 50, collagraph), San Francisco Mus Mod Art, 67; Miz Am (ed 20, etching), Hansen-Fuller Gallery, 68; Ars Medicus (ed 20, etching & screen print), San Francisco Art Comn, 71. *Exhib:* Original Prints, Calif Palace of Legion of Honor, San Francisco, 64; Art in the Embassies Prog, US Dept State, Oakland Art Mus, Calif, 66; Solo Exhib: Achenbach Found Graphic Arts, 68-69; 1st Bienal Int, Segovia, Spain, 73; 11th Biennial Graphic Art, Ljubljana, Yugoslavia, 75; Collagraph, Univ Mont, touring, 87-93; The Stamp of Impulse, Worcester (Mass) Art Mus, 2001; Cleveland Mus, 2001; Amon Carter Mus, Ft Worth, Tex, 2002; Mary & Leigh Block Mus of Art, Northwestern Univ, 2003; Desert Mus, Palm Springs, Calif, 2003; Int Print Ctr, New York City, 2003; Cummer Mus Art and Gardens, Jacksonville, Fla, 2003; Works on Paper, Tweed Mus Art, Duluth, 2005; Abstract Expressionist Prints, Pollock-Krasner House & Study Ctr, East Hampton, NY, 2006; Eye on the Sixties, De Saisset Mus, Santa Clara Univ, Santa Clara, Calif, 2008; 19th-21st Century Fine Prints Annex Galleries, Santa Rosa, Calif, 2008; Spray, Tape, & Stencil, Quncia Gallery, Duncan Mills, Calif, 2013. *Collection Arranged:* Libr Cong, Wash; Mus Mod Art, NY City; Nat Libr Med, Wash; Cleveland Mus; Whitney Mus; Philadelphia Mus; US Embassy Collections, Tokyo, London and other major cities; Victoria & Albert Mus, London; Achenbach Found for Graphic Arts; Calif Palace Legion Hon, San Francisco; Oakland Art Mus; Philadelphia Free Libr; Roanoke Art Ctr, Va; Worcester Art Mus, Mass; and others. *Pos:* Cur, Achenbach Found Graphic Arts, 58-65. *Teaching:* Prof art, San Francisco State Univ, 65-92, emer prof, 92-. *Awards:* Purchase Awards, Ultimate Concerns, Ohio Univ, Athens, 63, 25th & 26th San Francisco Art Festivals, 71 & 72 & 5th Ann Graphics Competition, De Anza Col, Cupertino, Calif, 76. *Bibliog:* Leonard Edmondson (auth), Etching, Van Nostrand, Reinhold, 73; Ross & Romano (coauth), The Complete Collagraph, MacMillian; Una Johnson (auth), American Printmakers, Doubleday. *Mem:* Calif Soc Printmakers (past chmn). *Media:* All media, Watercolor. *Interests:* Videography, natural history. *Dealer:* Annex Gallery 604 College Ave Santa Rosa CA 95404. *Mailing Add:* 59 Silvia Dr Cazadero CA 95421

BEALL, JOANNA
PAINTER, SCULPTOR
b Chicago, Ill, Aug 17, 1935. *Study:* Yale Sch Fine Art, with Josef Albers, 53-57; Art Inst Chicago, 57. *Comn:* Sculpture (wood), comn by B H Freidman, NY, 63. *Exhib:* Extraordinary Realities, Whitney Mus Am Art, NY, 73; Wadsworth Atheneum Group Exhib, Hartford, Conn, 73; Univ Calif Riverside Group Exhib, 73; Solo exhibs, James Corcoran Gallery, Los Angeles, 74 & Rebecca Cooper Gallery, Washington, DC, 75; Visions, Art Inst Chicago, 76; Reality of Illusion, Denver Art Mus, 79, Univ Southern Calif Art Galleries, 79 & Xavier Fourcade, Inc, NY, 79 & 85; and others. *Pos:* Practicing prof artist. *Teaching:* Vis artist, Univ Colo, Boulder, 79 & 84; Vis artist, Ogden, Utah, 84. *Bibliog:* New Talent USA, Art in Am, New York, 64; Melinda Wortz (auth), The World of Joanna Beall, Art Week, Los Angeles, 74; Dennis Adrian (auth), Visions, Art Inst Chicago, 76. *Mem:* Artists Equity. *Media:* Oil, Watercolor; Wood. *Dealer:* James Corcoran Gallery 8223 Santa Monica Blvd Los Angeles CA 90046. *Mailing Add:* 76 Warren Ave Manchester NH 03102

BEALL, KAREN FRIEDMANN
CURATOR, WRITER
b Washington, DC. *Study:* Am Univ, BA, 59, grad work, 61-62; Johns Hopkins Univ, grad work, 65-66. *Collection Arranged:* Graphic Landscape, 70, Prints from Eastern Europe, 71 & The Pennell Legacy, 82-83, Libr Cong; Eloquence of the Simple: Shaker & Japanese Craft & The Day of the Dead: A Living Tradition in Mexican Folk Art, Carleton Col, 91; Warren Mackenzie and the Functional Tradition in Clay, 95; Connections: Altars and Objects of Personal Devotion, 96. *Pos:* Cur fine prints, Libr Cong, Washington, DC, 68-82; Res assoc, art hist, Carleton Col, Northfield, Minn, 82-97; independent cur, 1997-. *Teaching:* Assoc, Kyoto Prog, Kyoto, Japan, 94. *Awards:* Res Grants, Am Philosophical Soc, 66 & 82. *Mem:* Print Coun Am; Coll Art Asn; Am Asn Mus. *Res:* Specialist in American graphic arts, 20th century prints of Czechoslovakia, Poland, Yugoslavia and research in ceramics and folk crafts of Japan & Greece. *Interests:* ephemeral arts. *Publ:* coauth, Viewpoints, Libr Cong, 75; Spectrum of Innovation: Color In American Printmaking, Worcester Art Mus, 90; Graphic Excursions: American Prints in Black & White, Am Fed Arts, 91; Warren MacKenzie and the Functional Tradition in Clay, 95; Connections: Alters and Objects of Personal Devotion, 96; numerous articles in prof jour. *Mailing Add:* 3101 Old Pecos Trail No 610 Santa Fe NM 87505

BEALLOR, FRAN
PAINTER, PRINTMAKER
b New York, NY, Sept 27, 1957. *Study:* Pvt study with August Mosca, 71-76; Antioch Col, 74-75; Brooklyn Mus Art Sch, 75-76; also with Charles Pfahl, 76-78. *Work:* PPG Indust, Pittsburgh, Pa; Bellevue Hosp, NY; Texaco Corp, NY; Fidelity Investment, Boston, Mass; Bern Israel-Deaconness Med Ctr, Boston, Mass. *Exhib:* solo exhibs, Nicholas Roerich Mus, NY, 88, Grand Cent Art Galleries, NY, 90 & William Carlos Williams Ctr Arts, Rutherford, NJ, 94, Union Co Col, Cranford, NJ, 97,Paris Gallery, 2005, Lotus Fine Arts Gallery, Woodstock, New York, 2008; Am Acad Women Artists, Desert Caballeros Mus, Ariz; group show, Coplan Gallery, Boca Raton, Fla, 98; Midegear Show, Butler Art Inst, Youngstown, Ohio, 97 & 99; Self Reflections, Pfizer, Inc, New York City, 2000; Butler Inst Am, 2001; Lowe Gallery, Hudson Guild, New York, 2002; Gallery Korea, New York, 2003; Paul Mellon Arts Ctr, Conn, 2004; Small Space Gallery, Arts Coun Greater New Haven, Conn, 2006; Art at First Gallery, 2006; NY Mercantile Exchange, New York, 2008; Brattleboro Mus & Art Ctr, Brattleboro, Vt, 2009. *Pos:* Workshop leader, Int Conf Art & Healing, Ibiza, Spain, 85; Painting, MFA Prog, Norwich Univ, Montpelier, Vt, 90-; guest lectr painting & printmaking, NY, NY & NJ, 93-. *Teaching:* Pvt instr painting & drawing, 78-; Instr painting, MFA Prog, Norwich Univ, Montpelier, Vt, 90-. *Awards:* John F & Anna Lee Stacey Grant, Oklahoma City, 93; Funding Grant Exhib, NJ State Coun Arts, 94; Dealers Choice Exhib (one of 13 artists chosen), Leo Castelli, John Weber & K&E Galleries, Art Initiatives, 96; Honorable Mention Award, Butler Inst Am Art, Ohio, 97; Painting chosen for publ in Art Calendar, 2000. *Bibliog:* Stephen Parks (auth), Top of the line, Art Lines, Taos, NMex, 80; articles, Newsday, NY, 6-8/78, Houston Post, 7/15/84, Miami Herald, 12/7/91 & East Side Resident, New York, 11/4/93; Eunice Agar (auth), Mirror images, Am Artist Mag, 11/94; Kristin Godsey (auth), Reflecting on Still Lifes, Artist's Mag, 2002; Alexander Schoenfeld, NYU's arts show, 89.1FM, 2006. *Mem:* Artists Equity. *Media:* Oil; Etching, All Media. *Publ:* cover illus, Happy All the Time, Penguin, 85; cover, Art Calendar, 5/91; Hootenanny Ltd Ed, Lit Art J, issues, 3, 4 & 5, 95-96; cover illus, Manhattan Arts Mag, summer 96; exhib catalogue, Butler Inst, Ohio, 97. *Mailing Add:* 839 W End Ave No 6F New York NY 10025-5350

BEAM, MARY TODD
PAINTER
b Dayton, Ohio, Feb 12, 1931. *Study:* Cent State Univ, 61-65; Univ Dayton, 62-63; studied with Edward Betts, Maxine Masterfield, Homer Hacker, Edgar Whitney & John Pike. *Work:* Zanesville Art Ctr, Ohio; Bank One & Bank Ohio, Cambridge; Goodyear Corp, Akron, Ohio; Dow Chemical Corp; Fisher Sch Bus, Ohio State Univ; Electric Blueprint and Supply, Louisville, Ky; Magna Oil Co, Houston, Tex; Love Realty, Columbus, Ohio; Liberty School, Cambridge, Ohio; Associate Building, Houston, Tex; Nelle Lane Gardner Home, Cambridge, Ohio; IBM, Columbus, Ohio; Quaker City Bank, Cambridge, Ohio; McDonalds Restaurant, Cambridge, Ohio; Bowling Green Bank, Bowling Green, Ohio; Huntington Nat Bank, Columbus, Ohio; AmeriTrust Bank, Columbus, Ohio; Ohio Co, Columbus, Ohio; Eversole Corp, Columbus, Ohio; Liebert and Liebert, Columbus, Ohio; WW Williams Co, Columbus, Ohio; Fairmont Hgh School, Kettering, Ohio; Good Samaritan Hospital, Dayton, Ohio; Bell Laboratories, Columbus, Ohio; Grant Hosp, Columbus, Ohio; Good Samaritan Hosp, Zanesville, Ohio; Columbus Orthopedic Surgeons, Columbus, Ohio; Distribution Ctrs, Inc, Columbus, Ohio; Goal Systems, Columbus, Ohio. *Comn:* Mt Carmel East Hosp, Columbus, Ohio. *Exhib:* San Diego Watercolor Soc Int Exhib, Hyde Gallery, Grossmont Col, 88; Nat Watercolor Soc Ann, Desert Mus, Muckenthaler Cult Ctr, 88; Am Watercolor Soc Ann, NY, 88, 93 & 96; Keynote Exhib, Shrines & Sacred Places, Albuquerque, NMex, 88; Ohio Watercolor Soc Ann, 89, 90, 91, 92, 93 & 94; 1st and 2nd Int Invicational Exhib of watercolor Masters, Nanjing, China, 2010. *Pos:* Juror, Fla Watercolor Soc 28th Ann, 93, Rocky Mountain Nat Exhib, 94 & St Louis Artists Guild, 94, Watercolor Soc Ore & NC Watercolor; juror of awards, Am Watercolor Soc NY; Juror, New Mexico Watercolor Soc. *Teaching:* Instr art, Zanesville Art Ctr, 79-, experimental workshops, nat & worldwide. *Awards:* Ann Experimental Award, Nat Watercolor Soc, Fullerton, Calif, 88; Silver Medal, Ohio Watercolor Soc, 90 & 94; Gold Medal Hon, Am Watercolor Soc, 96, 2002 & Dolphin Fel; and others; Guernsey County Hall of Fame, 2003. *Bibliog:* Jacqueline Hall (auth), Exuberant paintings show both versatility, dynamics, Columbus Dispatch, 10/81; Mary Carroll Nelson (auth), Shrines & Sacred Spaces, 88; Betsy Schein Goldman (auth), Watercolor "90", Am Artist Mag, 90. *Mem:* Nat Watercolor Soc; Am Watercolor Soc; Soc Layerists Multi-Media; Ohio Watercolor Soc. *Media:* Watercolor, Acrylic. *Res:* Collecting antiques. *Publ:* Maxine Masterfieldl (auth), Painting the Spirit of Nature, Marilyn Phillis, Watson-Guptill, 84; Michael Ward (auth), The New Spirit of Painting, 89 & Nita Leland (auth), The Creative Artist, North Light Publ, 90; Watermedia Techniques for Releasing the Creative Spirit (video), Fla Watercolor Soc, 93; The Rounds, Stanford Univ Med Ctr Publ; Celebrate Your Creative Self, F&W Pubs, 2001; From Trash to Treasure (video); auth, The Creative Edge, F&W Pubs; plus others. *Dealer:* F & W Publishers; Cricket Hollow Gallery; Contemporary Watermedia Gallery. *Mailing Add:* 125 Cricket Hollow Way Cosby TN 37722

BEAM, PATRICE K
ADMINISTRATOR, MUSEUM DIRECTOR
b Los Angeles, Calif, Aug 5, 1948. *Study:* Simpson Col, Indianaola, Ind, BA, 78; Iowa State Univ, MA, 88. *Pos:* Asst dir, Davenport Mus Art, 94-96; exec dir, Octagon Ctr Arts, Ames, Iowa, 96-. *Mem:* Victorian Soc Am (v pres, 93-96). *Publ:* Ed, Hope & Glory, IA VSA, 87-93; contribr, Hope & Glory, IA VSA, 92; auth, The last Victorian fair, J West, 94. *Mailing Add:* 2940 Cottage Grove Ave Des Moines IA 50311-3909

BEAMENT, TIB (THOMAS HAROLD)
PAINTER
b Montreal, PQ, Feb 17, 1941. *Study:* Fettes Col, Edinburgh, Scotland, O level cert; Ecole Beaux-Arts, Montreal, dipl; Acad Belle Arti, Rome, Italian Govt grant; Ecole Beaux-Arts, Montreal, postgrad studies & teaching cert; Sir George Williams Univ, MA (art educ); also in graphic studios of Shirly Wales, France; Richard Lacroix, Albert Dumouchel & Atelier 838, Montreal. *Work:* Tate Gallery, London; Mus Mod Art, NY; Mus Rio de Janeiro; Nat Gallery Can, Ottawa; Art Inst Chicago. *Exhib:* 4th Biennial Paris, France, 65; Int Exhib Northwest Printmakers, Seattle, Wash, 65; 1st Biennial Graphics, Crakov, Poland, 66; Int Art Fair, Basel, Switz, 74; Solo exhib, Switz Union Bank, Zurich, 81. *Pos:* Mem exec comt & bd dir, Greenshields Found. *Teaching:* Dir art dept, Edgars & Cramps Sch, Montreal, 66-79; lectr drawing, McGill Univ, 74-82; lectr design & drawing, Concordia Univ, 76-83. *Awards:* Quebec Govt Grant, 66 & 73; Spec Mention, Price Fine Arts Awards, 70; Elizabeth T Greenshields Found Grant, 71 & 75. *Mem:* Royal Can Acad Arts; Print & Drawing Coun Can. *Media:* Acrylic, Lithography. *Dealer:* Walter Klinkhoff Gallery 1200 Sherbrooke St W Montreal PQ Can. *Mailing Add:* RR 1 Ayers Cliff PQ J0B 1C0 Canada

BEARCE, JEANA DALE
PAINTER, PRINTMAKER
b St Louis, Mo. *Study:* St Louis Sch Fine Arts, Washington Univ, with Fred Conway, Fred Becker, Paul Burlin & George Lockwood, BFA, 51; NMex Highlands Univ, MA, 54; Independent study, Italy, France, India. *Work:* St Louis City Art Mus, Mo; Brooklyn Mus Art; Sarasota Art Asn, Fla; Calif Coll Arts & Crafts, Oakland; Cornell Univ; Colby Coll Mus Art; Bates Coll Mus Art; Bowdoin Coll Mus Art; CMCA Ctr Main Contemp Art, Rockport. *Comn:* Indian Sand Paint (mural), NMex Highlands Univ, Las Vegas, 54; Seven Gifts (cross), Good Shepherd Church, Brunswick, Maine, 62; Search for Truth (mural), Bowdoin Coll Libr, Brunswick, Maine, 65; 14 Stations to the Cross, St Charles Borromeo, Brunswick, Maine, 75; Monumental Mary and Bartholomew, St Bartholomew's, Cape Elizabeth, Maine, 77; and others. *Exhib:* Solo exhibs, Univ Maine, 57, 65, 80, 85, 91 & 95; Print Show, Philadelphia Print Club, 58; St Peter's Church Gallery, New York, 74; Maine Printmakers, 80-2005; India Revisited, Ctr Arts, Bath, 88; Maine to India Series, USM Environ Studies Ctr, 96; The Silk Road: Rome to China and Back; Journeys along the Silk Road, 97-2007; and others. *Teaching:* Instr, drawing, painting & printmaking, Univ Maine, Portland, 65-66, asst prof, 66-70, assoc prof, 70-81; prof, Univ Southern Maine, 81-. *Awards:* Purchase Prize, Sarasota Art Asn, 58; Eight Maine Artists, State Maine, 64; Sabbatical & Res Awards, India, 80-81, 85, 88 & 93; and others. *Bibliog:* Pat Boyd Wilson (auth), Paintings of the Taj, Christian Sci Monitor, 68; Milldred Burrage (auth), Five Women Artists, Maine Art Gallery, 75. *Media:* Oil, Encaustic; Intaglio. *Dealer:* Benbow Gallery 515 Thane St Newport RI. *Mailing Add:* 327 Maine St Brunswick ME 04011

BEARD, MARK
PAINTER
b Salt Lake City, 1956. *Exhib:* Solo exhibs include The Harcus Gallery, 85, Galerie Biedermann, Munich, 86, 88, Home for Contemp Theatre and Art, NY, 87, 90, Helio Gallery, NY, 90, Galerie Niel Ewerbeck, Vienna, 91, Here Art, NY, 94, Wessel + O'Connor Gallery, NY, 97, 98, 99, Galerie Wolf, Berlin, 99, John Stevenson Gallery, NY, 2003, 2004, 2005, Jonathan Edwards House Gallery, Yale Univ, 2005; group exhibs include Andy Warhol Mus, Pittsburgh, 97; Art and Culture Ctr, Hollywood, Fla, 2000; Morris-Healy Gallery, NY, 2000; Columbia Univ, 2000; John Stevenson Gallery, NY, 2003; Carrie Haddad Gallery, Hudson, NY, 2005

BEARDSLEY, BARBARA H
CONSERVATOR
b New York, NY, Mar 30, 1945. *Study:* Elmira Col, BA; Europ Study Prog, Univ Wis, cert; Univ NMex; State Univ NY, Cooperstown, study with Kecks, MA(conserv), cert (advan standing); study with Louis Pomerantz; McCrone Res Inst. *Comn:* Cleveland Mus Art; I Tatti, Harvard Univ, Florence, Italy; Currier Gallery, Manchester, NH; William Hayes Fogg Art Mus, Cambridge, Mass. *Collection Arranged:* Mary Lester Field Collection of Santos, Albuquerque, NMex, 70; Harwood Collection, Span Colonial Art, Taos, NMex, 71; Noyes Collection, Portland, Maine. *Pos:* Conservator, Intermus Conserv Assoc Lab, Oberlin, Ohio, 73-75; conserv intern, Newberry Libr, Chicago, 74-75; guest lectr conserv methods, State Univ NY, Cooperstown, 75-77; conservator, New Eng Coun, Am Asn Mus, six locations, 75-76; chief conservator, Art Conserv Lab Inc, 75-. *Teaching:* Univ NH. *Bibliog:* K Schaal (auth), New life for old masters, NH Profiles, 10/77; J Dueland (auth), Barbara Beardsley's barn, Christian Sci Monitor, 1/78; S Goss (auth), The Art Conservation Laboratory, NH Times, 2/82. *Mem:* Int Coun Mus; Fel Am Inst Conserv Hist & Artistic Works; Nat Conserv Adv Coun; Am Inst Conserv (dir, 76-79); Festival Arts, Waterville Valley, NH (mem, exec bd, 84); Cent for Art (co-chmn, 88-). *Res:* Polarizing pigment analysis, material studies, art history research, Spanish Colonial Santos. *Publ:* Auth, The field collection of Santos, Univ NMex Art Mus Bulletin, 70; The adaptation of an examination microscope, Am Inst Conserv Bulletin, 72; Basic Guide to a Healthy Collection, Art Conserv Lab, rev ed 76; A Flexible Back for the Stabilization of a Botticelli Panel Painting, Oxford Wood Conference, Int Inst Conserv, 78

BEASLEY, BRUCE
SCULPTOR
b Los Angeles, Calif, May 20, 1939. *Study:* Dartmouth Col; Univ Calif, Berkeley, BA. *Work:* Mus Mod Art & Solomon R Guggenheim Mus, NY; Los Angeles Co Mus Art; Musee d'Art Moderne, Paris, France; Nat Mus Am Art, Washington, DC; Oakland Mus, Calif; Kunsthalle Mannheim, Mannheim, Ger; Fine Arts Mus & Mus Mod Art, San Francisco; Seattle Art Mus, Wash; Santa Barbara Mus Art, Calif; Crocker Art Mus, Sacramento, Calif; Fresno Art Mus, Calif; Wichita Art Mus, Kans; Nat Gallery, Beijing, China; and many more. *Comn:* metal sculpture, City of Dortmund, Ger, 96; Village of Flossmoor, Ill, 2000; Univ Ore Art Mus, 2002; Miami Univ, Oxford, Ohio, 2002; City of Oakland, 2002; La Jolla Crossroads, San Diego, Calif, 2005; City of South San Francisco, 2006; Beijing Olympics, Sculpture Park, 2008; City of Monterrey, Mexico, 2008; City of Palo Alto, Calif, 2009; City of Wuhu, China, 2011; City of Fremont, Calif, 2013. *Exhib:* City Ctr, Dortmund, Ger, 96; Sculpture Invitational, Bad Homburg, Ger, 97; 7th Int Cairo Biennale, Egypt, 98; Mathematical Sci Res Inst, Berkeley, Calif, 2000; Gail Severn Gallery, Ketchum, Ind, 2001, 2010; Solomon Dubnick Gallery, Sacramento, Calif, 2002; 45 yr retrospective, Oakland Mus Calif, 2005; Shanghai Sculpture Space, China, 2008; Today Art Mus, Beijing, China, 2008; Duolun Art Mus, Beijing, China, 2008; Kouros Gallery, New York, 2009; Smith Anderson Gallery, Palo Alto, Calif, 2011; Pangolin Gallery, London, 2012; Autodesk Gallery, San Francisco, Calif, 2013; Univ Calif, Berkeley Campus, Calif, 2013-2015. *Awards:* Andre Malraux Purchase Award, Biennale de Paris, 63; Frank Lloyd Wright Mem Purchase Award, Marin Mus Asn, 65; Purchase Prize, San Francisco Arts Festival, 67; Ind Artist Award, Oakland Chamber Commerce, 89. *Bibliog:* Donald Thalacker (auth), The Place of Art in the World of Architecture, Chelsea House, 80; Thomas Albright (auth), The Art of the San Francisco Bay Area: 1945 to 1980, Berkeley Univ Calif Press, 85; Artforms, Harper Collins, 5th ed, 94; Peter Selz & Manfred Fath (auths), Bruce Beasley Sculpture, Mannheim Mus Art, 94; Jame McCarthy & Laurily Epstein (auth), Sculpture Parks and Gardens of America, Michael Resend Pub, 96; Brooke Barrie (auth), Contemporary Outdoor Sculpture, Rockport Pub, 99; Sculpture by Bruce Beasley, A 45 Yr Retrospective, Oakland Mus Calif, 2005; Dictionnaire Int De La Sculpture Moderne & Contemporaine, 2008; Gathering Dreams: Beijing 100 Olympic Sculptures Coll, 2008. *Mem:* Int Sculpture Ctr (bd dir). *Media:* Metal, Stone. *Mailing Add:* 322 Lewis St Oakland CA 94607

BEASON, DONALD RAY
EDUCATOR, SCULPTOR
b Camden, Ark, Oct 22, 1943. *Study:* Kilgore Col, 63; Stephen F Austin State Univ, BA, 65; Mich State Univ, MFA, 67. *Work:* Cult Exchange Between Italy & US, Rome; Centro Int Ceramica, Rome; Cameron Univ. *Exhib:* Drawing USA, Minn Mus Art, 71; solo exhib, San Antonio Sun Shine, San Antonio Art Inst, 82, Amarillo Sun Set, Amarillo Art Mus, 83 & Midnight Air, Tyler Mus Art, 83; East Texas Show, Tyler Mus Art, 82; Triennial 1983, New Orleans Mus, 83. *Pos:* Mem, fine arts panel, Tex Comn on the Arts, 85-. *Teaching:* Prof art, Stephen F Austin State Univ, 67-, Regents prof, 83-. *Awards:* Fulbright-Hays Fel, 72; Nat Endowment Arts Fel, 82. *Mailing Add:* Stephen F Austin Univ Art Dept Nacogdoches TX 75962

BEATTIE, ELISE MEREDITH
PAINTER, EDUCATOR
b New York City, NY, Jan 4, 1958. *Study:* Skidmore Coll, 80; Bellingham Tech Coll, 2000; Advan studies with Milford Zornes, Katherine Chang Liu, Glen Bradshaw, Timothy Clarke & Jean Grastorf, 97-2005, Cheng-Khee Chee, 2010; Prof studies with Harold Greigor, 2008. *Work:* Easter Seals Asn, Hemlock Rehabe Ctr, Conn; Ronald McDonald House, Spokane City Bear Necessities Fund Raiser, Wash. *Comn:* Hawaiian Sun Investments, Mr & Mrs Ron Blanset, Hilo, HI, 98; Adich Chiropractic Ctr, Dr & Mrs Adich, Bellingham, Wash, 2002; Palma Realty, Mr & Mrs Jim Palma, Anthem, Ariz, 2004; Casitas Mont, Mr & Mrs Jugenheimer, Anthem, Ariz, 2005; Maui Lani Develop, Mr & Mrs Joe Paci, Maui, HI, 2005; Sam & Pam Ragle, New Burgh, Ind; Sarah O'Donnell, Boston; Alice Beattie, Spokane, Wash. *Exhib:* Solo exhib, Short Stories from the Road Less Traveled by..., Nat Asn Women Artists' Gallery, NY, 2006, Anne P Baker Gallery, Glema Mahr Ctr for the Arts, Madisonville Community Coll, 2009 ; Heart to Heart Invitational, Whatcom Mus of Art, Bellingham, Wash, 2000; Northwest Watercolor Int Exhib, Seattle Conv Ctr, 2002; Women Who Happen to Artist, Tex A&M Univ, 2004; San Diego Int Watermedia Exhib, Showcase Gallery, San Diego, 2005; Catherine Lorillard Wolfe Nat Exhib, Nat Arts Club, NY, 2005; Fla Watercolor Nat Juried Exhib, Dundee Mus, Fla, 99; Personal Landscapes, Longview Mus Art, Tex, 2007; 62nd Ann Watercolor Soc NC Juried Exhib, Hendersonville, 2007; Fla Watercolor Nat Juried Exhib, Cornell Mus Art and Am Culture, 2008; NC Watercolor Nat Juried Exhib, Greenville Mus Art, 2008; Montana Nat Watercolor Exhib, Big Fork Center for the Arts, 2008; Nat Asn Women Artists, Goggle Center for the Arts, 2008; Kentucky Watercolor Soc, 2009; Watercolor Soc of NC, 2009; Montana Watercolor Soc, Big Fork Ctr Arts, 2010; Southern Watercolor CSoc, Glema Mahr Ctr Arst, Ky, 2010; Nat Asn Women Artists, Nat Arts Club, New York, 2010; Yeiser Art Ctr, Paducah, Ky, 2010; Paducah City Hall, Ky; Nat Exhib, Adirondack Nat Exhibs of Am Watercolors, Arts Ctr Old Forge, NY, 2011, Int Soc Acrylic Painters Juried Nat Exhib, Santa Cruz, Calif, 2011, Ky Nat Exhib, Murrey State Univ, Murrey, Ky, 2011; Historical Speaking, Johnson & Johnson World Headquarters, New Brunswick, NJ, 2012; 8th Biennial Nat Arts Exhib, Visual Arts Ctr, Punta Gorda, Fla 2012; Spring, Nat Assn Women Artists, Mid-Day Gallery, Englewood, NJ, 2012; Adirondack Nat Exhib, American Watercolor Art Ctr, Old Forge, 2012; Am Signature Exhib Watercolors, 2013; Sylvia Glessman Floral Exhib, Salmagundi Art Club, NY, 2013. *Pos:* Chairperson Exhibs, Charlotte Co Art Ctr, 97-1998; juror, Mont Watercolor Soc Exhib, 2007; Ky State Rep, Southern Watercolor Society, Vpres; vice pres, Southern Watercolor Soc, 2010; bd dirs, Yeiser Arts Ctr, Paducah, Ky, 2012-2013. *Teaching:* Instr art, Whatcom Community Coll, Wash, 2002-2003; instr, Maricopa Community Coll, Scottsdale, Ariz, 2004-2005; instr workshop, Mont Watercolor Soc; instr, Madisonville Community Coll, Ky; instr, Kentucky Watercolor Soc. *Awards:* Elizabeth Erlanger Mem Award, Nat Asn of Women Artists (family), 2002; Grumbacher Gold Award, Mont Watercolor Soc, Grumbacher co, 2002; Merit Award, Mont Watercolor Soc, St Cuthberts Mill, 2005; 2nd Place Professional Paducah Art Exhib, Paduca, Ky; best of show, Paducah Art Exhib, Ky, 2010; President's Award, Montana Watercolor Soc Nat Juried Exhib, 2010. *Mem:* Nat Watercolor Soc (assoc mem, 99-); Fla Watercolor Soc (life mem, 99-2008, signature life mem 2008); Nat Assoc of Women Artists (signature mem, 2000-); Am Watercolor Soc (assoc mem); Salmagundi Art Club (signature member); Montana Watercolor Soc; Southern Watercolor Soc; Watercolor Soc of NC (signature mem); Northwest Watercolor Soc (signature mem, 2010-); Int Soc Acrylic Painters (signature mem, 2011-); Southern Watercolor Soc (signature mem, 2012). *Media:* Watercolor, Acrylics, Mixed Media & Collage. *Interests:* Great Danes, Nutrition. *Publ:* Contrib, (art), Art Calendar Mag, Carolyn Blakeslee Proeber, 2002; articles, Myamericanartist.com; articles, watercolorartist/artistnetwork.com; Best of Am, Watermedia, Kennedy Publ; Creativity Workshop, Beyond the Ordinary, Artist Network.com; Art World News, Aug 2009; Online Tributes, Bark Mag; Splash 13 - Alternative Approaches, F&W/Northlight Publ, 2011; Incite, Dreams Realized-The Best of Mixed Media, F & W, Northlight PUbs, 2013. *Mailing Add:* PO Box 7829 Paducah KY 42002-7829

BEATTY, FRANCES FIELDING LEWIS
ART DEALER, COLLECTOR
b New York, NY, Nov 23, 1948. *Study:* Vassar Coll, BA; Columbia Univ, with Meyer Schapiro & Theodore Reff, MA (art hist; Noble Found Fel), PhD. *Pos:* Sr ed, Art-World, 76-84; pres, Richard L Feigen & Co, currently; dir, Estate of Ray Johnson, currently. *Teaching:* Instr surrealism, Renaissance & 19th & 20th century art hist & lit, Ramapo Coll, NJ, 74; instr art hist, Columbia Coll, 74-76. *Mem:* The Drawing Ctr (bd dir, chmn bd); Contemp Arts Coun, Mus Mod Art; Frick Cur Visiting Committee; Century Asn; Checkerboard Film Found (bd mem). *Res:* Work of Andre Masson in the 1920s and its relation to surrealist poetry and prose. *Interests:* Renaissance Medals, 16th to 20th century, prints and drawings, contemporary photography. *Publ:* Contribr, Andre Masson (catalog), Mus Mod Art, New York, 76; contribr, Richard Smith (catalog), R L Feigen & Co, NY, 92; introduction, Pierre Roy (catalog), R L Feigen & Co, NY, 93; contribr, Ray Johnson: A Memorial Exhibition (catalog), R L Feigen & Co, NY, 95; co-producer (documentary), How to Draw a Bunny, Ray Johnson, Beckman & Picasso. *Mailing Add:* c/o Richard L Feigen & Co 34 E 69th St New York NY 10065

BEAUDOIN, ANDRE EUGENE
PRESS MANUFACTURER, PHOTOGRAPHER
b Calais, France, Apr 11, 1920; US citizen. *Study:* Ecole des Arts de Metiers, Paris, France, machine design & metallurgy; Brown Univ, photog. *Pos:* Owner, designer & constructor of etching & lithographic presses for artist printmakers, Am-French Tool Co, 69-. *Mailing Add:* PO Box 227 Coventry RI 02816

BEAUMONT, BETTY
ENVIRONMENTAL ARTIST
b Toronto, Can; US citizen. *Study:* Calif State Univ, BA, 1969; Univ Calif Berkeley, MA, 1972. *Exhib:* Pub art projs include Underwater Proj, West Hill Pond, Conn, 1973, Wind Piece, Naples, 1974 & Overlapping Spheres, 1975, Kansas City Drag, Mo, 1974, Cable Piece, Macomb, Ill, 1977, Ocean Landmark Proj, Atlantic Ocean, 1980, Ground Level, Sculpturesites, Amagansett, NY, 1983, River Walk, Rochdale, Eng, 1989, Lower Manhattan Street Sign Proj, New York, 1992, Border Crossing, Austria, Ger & Czech Repub, 1993, Longwood Lake Series, Jefferson Twp, NJ, 1994-98, Stories Garden, Lexington, NY, 1997, Shore/Lines, Ontario, Can, 2002-03. *Teaching:* Instr, Sch Art Inst Chicago, 1972-73, Univ Calif, Berkeley, 1976; asst prof 3-D media, State Univ NY, Purchase, 1985-90; assoc prof art, Hunter Coll, New York, 1989-93; advisor, NY Univ, Gallatin Sch Individualized Study, 1998-. *Awards:* Prof of Yr, State Univ NY Purchase, 1989; Pollock-Krasner Found Grant, 2007. *Mailing Add:* 40 Lispenard St New York NY 10013-3011

BEAUMONT, MONA
PAINTER, GRAPHIC ARTIST
b Paris, France; US citizen. *Study:* Univ Calif, Berkeley, BA & MA; grad study, Fogg Mus, Harvard Univ, Cambridge, Mass; spec study with Hans Hoffman, NY. *Work:* Oakland Mus Art, Calif; City & Co San Francisco; Hoover Found; Bulart Found, San Francisco. *Exhib:* San Francisco Art Inst, 58, 62-66 & 74, traveling exhib, 64 & 65; Calif Painters & Sculptors, Univ Calif, Los Angeles, 59; Regional Painters, De Young Mem Mus Art, San Francisco, 62; one-person shows, Calif Palace of Legion of Honor, San Francisco, 64, San Francisco Mus Art, 68 & Palo Alto Cult Ctr, Calif, 77; San Francisco Gallery Artists, Stanford Univ Art Mus, 66; Print & Drawing Ann, Richmond Art Ctr, Va, 68; Bell Tel Print-Drawing, Chicago, 69; L'Armitire Gallery, Rouen, France, 72; Honolulu Acad Art, Hawaii, 80; Int Biennial Contemp Art, 98; Trevi Flash Art Mus, Italy; Venice Mask 2 Exhib, Italy, 99; Int Florence Biennale III, Florence, Italy, 2001; plus others. *Awards:* Purchase Award, US Artists Tour of Asia, Grey Found, 63; Purchase & One-Person Show Awards, San Francisco Art Festival Ann, 66 & 75; Ackerman Award, San Francisco Woman Artists Ann, 68; Silver Medal Mask 2 Exhibit, Venice, Italy, 99. *Bibliog:* Andrew De Shong (auth), Works on Paper--San Francisco Art Inst, Art Week Mag, 11/74; Thomas Albright (auth), Art in the San Francisco Bay Area, 85. *Mem:* Arch Am Art; Soc Encouragement Contemp Art. *Media:* Acrylic, Mixed. *Publ:* Contribr, articles in Artforum, 5/64 & 12/64; Frankenstein, San Francisco Chronicle, 66 & 67

BECHTLE, ROBERT ALAN
PAINTER
b San Francisco, Calif, May 14, 1932. *Study:* Calif Coll Arts & Crafts, BA, 54 & MFA, 58; Univ Calif, Berkeley, 61. *Work:* Whitney Mus Am Art, Mus Mod Art & Guggenheim Mus, NY; San Francisco Mus Mod Art; Metrop Mus Art, NY. *Exhib:* Image, Form & Color: Recent Paintings by 11 Americans, Toledo Mus of Art, Ohio, 75; Aspects of Realism-Du Realisme, Rothmans of Can Ltd, Montreal, 76-77; Illusion & Reality, Australian Gallery Dirs Coun, 77-78; Representations of Am, Pushkin Fine

Arts Mus, Moscow, USSR, 78; Contemp Am Realism since 1960, Pa Acad Fine Arts, Philadelphia, 81; Am Realism: The Precise Image, Inetan Mus, Tokyo, Japan, 85; Robert Bechtle: New Work, San Francisco Mus Mod Art, 91; Invitational Exhib Painting & Sculpture, Am Acad Arts & Letters, 95; 35 Years at Crown Point Press, Nat Gallery Art, Washington, 97; New American Century: Art & Culture 1950-2000, Whitney Mus Am Art, New York, 99, Full House, 2006, Whitney Biennial, 2008; Made in Calif: Art, Image & Identity 1900-2000, Los Angeles County Mus Art, 2000; Looking at You, Metrop Mus Art, New York, 2001; Les Années Pop, Centre Georges Pompidou, Paris, 2001; Retrospectives; San Francisco Mus Mod Art, Mod Art Mus Ft Worth, 2005; Corcoran Gallery, Washington, 2006; Painting of Mod Life, Hayward Gallery, London, 2007; and many others. *Teaching:* Prof printmaking, Calif Col Arts & Crafts, 57-85; vis artist, Univ Calif, Davis, 66-68; prof art, San Francisco State Univ, 68-99, prof emeritus, 99-. *Awards:* Nat Endowment Arts Grant, 77, 82 & 89; Guggenheim Fel, 86; Nat Acad, Nat Acad Design, 93; Acad award Am Acad Arts and Letters, 95. *Bibliog:* G Battcock (auth), Super Realism, A Critical Anthology, Dutton, 75; L Meisel (auth), Photo Realism, Abrams, 80; R Kalina (auth), Painting Snapshots or the Cursory Spectacle, Art in Am, 6/93; C Lindey (auth), Super Realist Painting and Sculpture, William Morrow & Co, 80; J Bishop (auth), Robert Bechtle: A Retrospective, Univ Calif Press/San Francisco Mus Mod Art, 2005; and others. *Mem:* Nat Acad Design (assoc, 93, acad, 94). *Media:* Oil, Watercolor. *Dealer:* Gladstone Gallery 515 W 24th St New York NY 10011; Gallery Paule Anglim 14 Geary St San Francisco CA 94108. *Mailing Add:* 871 De Haro St San Francisco CA 94107

BECHTLER-LANFRANCONI, CRISTINA & THOMAS W
COLLECTOR
b Switz, 1949. *Study:* Univ Zurich, LLB, 1973, Doctorate, 1976; Harvard Univ, LLM, 1976. *Pos:* Chmn, Swisscontact, 1987-99, Zurich Art Soc, 1987-2002, Schiesser Group AB, Kusnacht, 1992-2008, Zellweger Luwa AG, Uster, 1994-2006 & Zurich comt, Human Rights Watch, 2005-; bd dirs, Bucher Industries, 1987, Conzzetta Holding AG, 1987- & Swiss Reinsurance Co, 1993-2009; bd dirs, Credit Suisse Group ADS, Zurich, 1994-2009, mem audit comt, 1999-2003, compensation comt, 2003-04 & 2006-2009, risk comt, 2003-06; vice-chmn, Hesta AG, 1982-, Hesta Tex AG, 1982-2011, & Sika AG, 1989-. *Awards:* Named one of Top 200 Collectors, ARTnews mag, 2003-13. *Collection:* Contemporary art, Minimalism & photography. *Mailing Add:* Weinrallee 11a Usler 8610 Switzerland

BECK, DOREEN
WRITER, FIBER ARTIST
b Medomsley, Co Durham, Eng; US & UK citizen. *Study:* Leicester Univ Col, Univ London, BA (hons) in French, 57; NY Univ, film prod; NY Sch Visual Arts, screen writing with Andrew Sarris. *Comn:* Long Island Sound (contemp tapestry), Pvt collector, 86; Limited Ed Art Prints, World Fed, UN Asn. *Exhib:* Miller-Jaeger Window Displays, New York, 1985; Metrop Mus Gallery, Lincoln Ctr, New York, 1985; Art in Embassies, US State Dept, Washington, DC, 1986; Soc Illusrs, New York, 1989; Gallery 500, Philadelphia, 1990; Nat Trust Hist Preservation, Decatur House, Washington, DC, 1991-92; October Salon, Pratt Mansion, New York, 2007; 10th Ann & 11th Salon, Williamsburg Art & Hist Soc, New York, 2009, 2010. *Pos:* Writer & producer AV mat, UN; researcher & writer, Med Newsmag; research, ed & writing, BBC, World Bk Enc (int ed), The Observer, Thames & Hudson, Julian Press, Ved Mehta & New Yorker. *Awards:* Industrial Design Excellence Award, Human Well Being Exhib, UN, 94-95. *Bibliog:* From Pen & Paper to Glorious Quilts, Creative Quilting Mag, 90; The Artful Home, Guild Sourcebook of Art, 2000. *Media:* Fiber, Contemporary Tapestries. *Interests:* cello, tennis. *Publ:* Auth, Country & Western Americana, 75; auth & producer, exhibs and related photo books for United Nations offices; auth, Book of American Furniture, 73; Book of Bottle Collecting, 73. *Mailing Add:* 100 W 57th St New York NY 10019

BECK, KEN
PAINTER, INSTRUCTOR
b Salem, Mass, 1943. *Study:* Goddard Coll, BA; Tufts Univ, MFA; Skowhegan Sch Painting & Sculpture, Maine; Union Grad Sch, PhD. *Work:* Mus Fine Arts, Boston; Boston Pub Libr; DeCordova Mus & Sculpture Park, Lincoln, Mass. *Exhib:* Solo exhibs include Mills Gallery, Boston, Newton Free Gallery, Gallery NAGA, Boston; group exhibs include Leo Castelli Gallery, New York; DeCordova Mus, Lincoln, Mass; Mus Fine Art, Boston; Saturated Color, More or Less, Gallery NAGA, Boston, 2006; Ann Invitational Exhib Contemp Am Art, Nat Acad Mus, New York, 2008; Unrapt, Piano Factora, 2010; Hieratics Gallery, NAGA, Boston, 2012. *Teaching:* Adj assoc prof, Art Inst, Leslie Univ, Boston. *Awards:* Pollock-Krasner Found Grant; Mass Cult Coun Award, Painting; Fac Award of Excellence in Teaching, Art Inst Boston, Lesley Univ, 2010. *Bibliog:* Ken Beck: Artist Talk, Boston Pub Libr, Sun Hill Press, 97; West Branch No 57, Autum/Winter/2005; New American Paintings, No 56, March/2005; Art New England: Those Who Paint Teach, Oct/Nov/2007; A Portrait of the Artist, Boston Mag, Summer Issue, 2011; 100 Boston Painters, Schiffer Art Books, 2012. *Media:* Oil, Watercolor. *Specialty:* painting and studio furniture. *Dealer:* NAGA Gallery 67 Newbury St Boston MA 02116. *Mailing Add:* 791 Tremont St Apt W109 Boston MA 02118

BECK, LONNIE LEE
PAINTER, EDUCATOR
b Marion, Ind, Jan 6, 1942. *Study:* Herron Sch Art, Ind Univ, BFA (advan design), 65, BFA (painting), 67; Miami Univ, MFA (painting), 69. *Work:* Herron Sch Art, Ind Univ, Indianapolis. *Exhib:* Indianapolis Mus Art, 68 & 69; Owensboro Mus Fine Arts, Ky, 80; Evansville Mus Art & Sci, Ind, 80; Appalachian State Univ, Boone, NC, 80; Okla Art Ctr, Oklahoma City, 81; Ball State Univ, Muncie, Ind, 82; and many others. *Collection Arranged:* Robert Berkshire Paintings, 75, Rockwell Kent (coauth, catalog), 79, Dean Howell Sculpture, 80, Terrance LaNoue, Jim Sullivan & Frank Owens Paintings, 81 & Dennis Puhalla Paintings, 82, Hiestand Gallery, Miami Univ. *Awards:* Best Show Painting, 500 Festival Arts Comn, 67; Purchase Award, Del Mar Col, 75; Purchase Award, Ball State Univ, 82. *Media:* Oil, Charcoal

BECKER, CAROL
DEAN, EDUCATOR, WRITER
Study: BA, SUNY Buffalo; PhD, Univ Calif, San Diego. *Pos:* Asst prof, Sch of the Art Inst of Chicago, formerly, dean faculty, sr vpres academic affairs, formerly; prof art, dean, Sch of Arts, Columbia Univ, 2007-. *Teaching:* Prof, Ionian Univ, San Diego State Univ, Northeastern Ill Univ, Univ Calif, San Diego, formerly. *Res:* Art and Artists in Society, Social Change, South African Art and Culture, Art in the Public Sphere. *Publ:* Auth, The Invisible Drama: Women and the Anxiety of Change, Zones of Contention: Essays on Art, Institutions and Anxiety, Surpassing the Spectacle: Global Transformations and the Changing Politics of Art; editor, The Subversive Imagination: Essays on Art, Artists, and Social Responsibility; Zones of Contention: Essays on Art, Institutions, Gender and Anxiety; Surpassing the Spectacle: Global Transformations and the Changing Politics of Art; Thinking in Place: Art, Action, and Cultural Production. *Mailing Add:* Columbia University School of the Arts 305 Dodge Hall, MC 1803 2960 Broadway New York NY 10027

BECKER, DAVID
PAINTER, EDUCATOR
b Milwaukee, Wis, Aug 16, 1937. *Study:* Univ Wis-Milwaukee, BS, 61; Univ Ill, Urbana, MFA, 65. *Work:* Libr Cong, Washington, DC; Brooklyn Mus, NY; Mus de Arte Mod, Cali, Colombia; Art Inst Chicago; Detroit Inst Arts, Mich; Nat Mus Am Art, Washington, DC; Chazen Mus Art, Univ Wisc, Madison, Wisc. *Comn:* Print, Detroit Inst Art Drawing & Print Club, 83. *Exhib:* Solo exhib, Jane Haslem Gallery, Washington, DC, 90, Ann Nathan Gallery, Chicago, 2007, 2009; Nat Acad Design Ann Exhib, 76, 87, 93, 99, 03, 09; 30 Yrs of Am Printmaking, Brooklyn Mus, NY, 76; Sapporo Int Print Biennale, Sapporo, Japan, 93; First Int Print Biennial Maastright, The Neth, 93; Integrafia, Katowice, Poland, 94; outside Art Fair, New York City, 2002, Art Chicago, 2002-10; and others. *Teaching:* Prof art, Wayne State Univ, Detroit, Mich, 65-85; vis prof printmaking, Univ Wis-Madison, 78-79; vis artist, Utah State Univ, Logan, summer 81; prof art, Univ Wis-Madison, 85-2006, prof emer, 2006-. *Awards:* Cannon Prize, 165th & 168th Nat Acad Ann, 90 & 93; Sponsors Prize, Sapporo Int Print Biennale, Japan, 93; Nat Endowment Arts Visual Artists Fel, 93-94; and others. *Bibliog:* James Watrous (auth), A Century of American Printmaking, Univ Wis Press, 84; Gene Baro (auth), 30 Yrs of American Printmaking, Brooklyn Mus, NY, 77; Warrington Colescott & Arthur Hove (coauth), Progressive Printmakers: Wisconsin Artists and The Print Renaissance, Univ Wisc Press, 99; David Acton (auth), 60 Years of North American Prints, Boston Printmakers, 1947-2007. *Mem:* Nat Academy (assoc, 83, acad, 91); fel, MacDowell Colony. *Media:* Oil, Charcoal Drawing. *Dealer:* Ann Nathan Gallery 218 W Superior St Chicago IL 60610. *Mailing Add:* 2512 Lunde Lane Mount Horeb WI 53572

BECKER, NATALIE ROSE
PAINTER, INSTRUCTOR
b Philadelphia, Pa. *Study:* Fleisher Art Mem, Philadelphia; Temple Univ, AA; Pa Acad Fine Arts; Art Students League, with Robert Phillip & Henry Gasser; Editon State Coll, BA. *Work:* Fine Arts Galleries, Carnegie Inst; Bloomfield Col; Slide Photo Archives-Juley Collection, Smithsonian Inst, Nat Mus Am Art. *Exhib:* Audubon Artists Am, 73-2004, 2006, 2007; Audubon Artists, 73-2005, 2008, 2009, 2010, 2011, 2012, 2013; Allied Artists Am, 74-2004, 2006, 2007, 2008-2009, 2012, 2013; Allied Artists, 74-2005, 2010, 2011; Nat Arts Club Invitational, 78; Bergen Mus Invitational, 80; Butler Inst Am Art, 2001; Attleboro Mus, 2002; Catherine Lorillard Wolfe Nat Exhib, 2010, 2011; Pioneer Women, First Ladies of Salmagundi Club, 2011. *Teaching:* Instr drawing, Union Col, Cranford, NJ. *Awards:* First Prize & Medal of Honor, Audubon Artists Ann Exhib, 80; Katherine Lowell Mem Award, Allied Artists Am Ann Exhib, 95; Pen & Brush Award, 2000; Paul Puzinas Mem Award, Allied Artists Am Ann Exhib, 2000; Len Everett Mem Award, Audubon Artists Ann Exhib, 2001. *Mem:* Audubon Artists (bd mem 73-2013); Allied Artist Am (74-2014); Pen & Brush Club; Catharine Lorillard Wolfe Art Club; Nat Asn Women Artists; Fedn Mod Painters & Sculptors; Salmagundi Club. *Media:* Oil, Watercolor over Pen & Ink. *Interests:* Painting on location; Plein air painting landscape. *Publ:* Auth, The Best of Oil Painting, 96 & Floral Inspirations, 97, Rockport Publ. *Mailing Add:* 111 Prospect St 1D Westfield NJ 07090

BECKERMAN, NANCY GREYSON
PAINTER, CRAFTSMAN, STUDIO ART QUILTER
b New York, NY. *Study:* Cornell Univ, 60-62; Hunter Coll, BA (magna cum laude & phi beta kappa), 62-64; NY Univ, 65; Boston Univ, 65. *Work:* ABC Collection, New York; numerous pvt collections. *Exhib:* Painted Surfaces, Albany Inst Hist & Art, New York, 86; Out of Time, Art Quilts, San Jose Mus of Textiles, 2000; Threads That Bind, Grants Pass Mus Art, 2002; SAQA Invitational Art Quilts, Manhattanville Coll, Purchase, NY, 2002; Quilts for Change, Cincinnati, Ohio, 2004; Changing Definitions: The Art Quilt, SAQA Ark Art Ctr, 2004; Far Out Fiber, Grants Pass Mus Art, 2005; Sacred Threads, 2005; Nearness of You, Invitational, 2006; Traveling Trunk Show, SAQA, 2006. *Awards:* Marion deSola Mendes Mem Award, 79; Juror's Prize, Washington & Jefferson Painting Exhib, 81; First Prize in Contemporary, Pa Nat Quilt Extravaganza, 94. *Bibliog:* Rev, La Revue Moderne, Paris, 80; Robin Bergstrom (dir), Meet the VIP's: Nancy Beckerman, WVIP (radio, cable-tv), 83; Lauren Otis (auth), A powerful presence of women, Artspeak, 86. *Mem:* Nat Asn Women Artists; Artists Equity NY; Studio Art Quilt Assocs; Women in the Arts. *Media:* Acrylic on Canvas; Fabric. *Mailing Add:* 26 White Birch Rd Pound Ridge NY 10576

BECKHARD, ELLIE (ELEANOR)
PAINTER, PHOTOGRAPHER
b Brooklyn, NY. *Study:* Brooklyn Col, 47-51; studied Hans Hoffman Technique with Shirley Gorelick (student of Hoffman) & studied with Leo Manso & Jerry Okimoto, 78. *Exhib:* Silvermine juried show, Silvermine Mus, New Canaan, Conn, 78; 157th Ann, Nat Acad Design, NY, 82; Long Island Invitational, 83 & juried show, 83 & 89, Islip Mus, NY; Fine Arts juried shows, Fine Arts Mus Long Island, Hempstead, NY,

83, 85, 88, 89 & 91; The Expert Eye, Coun Arts N Shore, Glen Cove, NY, 84; Showcase of Excellence III Invitational, Midge Karr Art Ctr, Brookville, NY, 89. *Awards:* Award, Parsons: Leland Bell & Jane Freilicker, 81 & Award Merit, G McCarthy & Irving Sandler, 87 Huntington Township Art League at Heckscher Mus; Ziuta & Joseph Akston Found Award, Nat Asn Women Artists, 86. *Bibliog:* Helen Harrison (auth), Debut of a museum series, 10/83 & Unusual energy mark juried show, 4/87, NY Times; Karin Lipson (auth), Showcase 100 artists, 4/87 & Four gallery exhibition, 6/87, News Day. *Mem:* Nat Asn Women Artists; Huntington Township Art League. *Media:* Acrylic, Pastel. *Publ:* Contribr, Contract Interiors (cover), Donald J Carroll, 9/77; Process Architecture: The Legacy of Marcel Breuer, no 32, p 5, Bunji Murotani, 82; NY Times: Home, section C1, 7/23/81. *Mailing Add:* Red Springs Rd Glen Cove NY 11542

BECKMAN, ERICKA
FILMMAKER, PHOTOGRAPHER
b Hempstead, NY, July 7, 1951. *Study:* Wash Univ, BFA, 74; Whitney Independent Study Prog, 75; Calif Inst Arts, MFA, 76. *Work:* Inst Contemp Art, London; Am Fedn Arts, NY. *Comn:* DVD, The Walter Art Center, Minneapolis. *Exhib:* Pictures Today, Padligione D'Artes Contemp, Milan, Italy, 80; Whitney Mus Biennial, 83, 85, 89 & 91; Film Screening Cinderella, Walker Art Inst, Minneapolis, Minn, 86; Coeur du Malstrom, Palais Des Beaux Arts, Brussels, 86; Mus Mod Art, Bern, Switz, 92; Mus Mod Art, NY, 93; Wexner Ctr Art, Columbus, Ohio, 94; Gender and Technology, Wexner Ctr Arts, Columbus, Ohio, 95; Cinderella (16mm)-Here and Now Exhib, La Mus Mod Art, 96; Film Retrospective (with catalog), Viper Festival, Lucerne, Switz, 98; We Imitate: We Break-Up (8mm), Big as Life Show, Mus Mod Art, NY, 98; Hiatus (16mm, 40 mins), World Premier, Rotterdam Film Festival, 99; Switch Center, Views from the Avant Garde, NY Film Festival, 2002; Switch Center, Media Scope, MOMA at Gramercy Park Theater, NY, 2003; and others. *Teaching:* asst prof film, Mass Col Art, 83-. *Awards:* Grants, NY State Coun Arts, 88, Jerome Found, 81 & 83 & Nat Endowment Arts, 83 & 94; CAPS Film Grant, Jerome Found Grant, 83; Artist Fel Prog Film Award, NY Found Arts, 87; Experimental Television Ctr projects grant, 99; ArtsLink Collaborative Projects grant, 99; Creative Contact Grant, Harvest Works, NY, 2000. *Bibliog:* J Hoberman (auth), article, 81 & Carrie Rickey (auth), article, 83, Art Forum; Sally Banes (auth), Films by Ericka Beckman, Millennium Film J, 83; J Hoberman (auth), Avant to Live, Village Voice, 6/18/87, Bernice Reynaud (auth), Erika Beckman-Independent America New Film (catalog essay), Am Mus Moving Image, Astoria, Queens, 88. *Publ:* Auth, Chances territory, Effects Mag, 83; The turn-about, Wedge Mag, 83; illusr, The Journal, LAICA, Los Angeles, Calif, 1/85; auth, Polities, Desire & Everyday Life, New Observations, No 45, 87; auth & photogr, The Beanstalk and Jack, Hallwalls Books, Buffalo, NY, 88. *Mailing Add:* 358 Broadway New York NY 10013

BECKMANN, ROBERT OWEN
PAINTER, MURALIST
b Philadelphia, Pa, Mar 20, 1942. *Study:* Coll Wooster, BA, 64; Univ Iowa, with Byron Burford, David Proctor, Herbert Katzman, MA, 66, MFA, 67. *Work:* Denver Art Mus, Colo; Amarillo Mus Art, Tex; Bank of Am, Las Vegas; Ringling Sch Art & Design, Sarasota, Fla; plus others. *Comn:* Symbiosis, Friends of Contemp Art, Denver, 72; murals, Lynn Co Courthouse, Las Vegas & Clark Co, Nev, 76-80. *Exhib:* Monumental Propaganda World Financial Ctr, NY, 93; Inst Contemp Art, Moscow, 93; Int Gallery, Smithsonian Inst, Washington, DC, 95; Dunlop Gallery, Regina Pub Libr, Saskatchewan, Can, 95; Contemp Art Mus, Estonia, 95; Lubiljana, Slovenia, 95; Yale Univ Art Gallery, 95; Terrain Gallery, San Francisco, 96 & 97; Bass Mus Art, Miami Beach, Fla, 96; Lenin Mus, Finland, 97; Uppsala Konstmuseum, Sweden, 97; Solo exhibs, Univ Ala, Tuscaloosa, 97, Bellevue Art Mus, Wash, 97, Ringling Sch Art & Design, Sarasota, Fla, 97, Bowling Green Univ, Ohio, 97 & Sam Francis Gallery, Cross Roads Sch, Santa Monica, Calif, 98; Donna Beam Gallery, Univ Nev, 98; State Mus, The Artists Necropolis, St Petersburg, Russia; and others. *Pos:* Artist, Beckmann Studio, Denver, 71-77 & 92-; pres, Wallternatives Inc, Las Vegas, 79-92. *Teaching:* Instr studio art, Univ Southern Ala, 67-68; instr life drawing, Northern Ill Univ, Dekalb, 68-71; instr art hist, Kendall Col, summer 69; instr art, Univ Nev, Las Vegas, 77-78. *Awards:* Laura Slobe Mem Prize, Art Inst Chicago, 71; Western States Arts Found Fel, 76; Gov Award, State of Nev, 96. *Bibliog:* Patricia Raymer (auth), Climb aboard the Artrain, Am Educ, 12/73; Duncan Pollock (auth), rev in arts now, Rocky Mountain News, Denver, 9/22/74; Jean Morrison (auth), Project murals, Nevadan, 4/24/77; William L Fox (auth) Mapping the Empty, Univ Nev Press, Reno, 99; Scott Dickensheets (auth) Vegas sublime, Las Vegas Life, 7/2000; plus numerous others. *Media:* Latex, Acrylic. *Mailing Add:* Beckmann Studio 1125 Prospect St Ashland OR 97520

BECKNER, JOY KROEGER
SCULPTOR
b St. Louis, MO, Dec 17, 1944. *Study:* Washington Univ Sch of Fine Art (H Rich Duhme), 1962-1964; Fontbonne Univ (Jaye Gregory, Hank Knickmeyer, Rudi Torrini), 1990-1992; Independent workshops (Tuck Langland, Eugene Daub, Tito Gay, Donna Dickson). *Work:* From display stylist to fashion show coord. Famous-Barr, St. Louis, MO, 1964-69; Runway and print model Famous-Barr, Prima, St. Louis, MO, 1969-2004; West Model & Talent, Chesterfield, MO, 2008-; Fund Raising Specialist, Community Projects for Students, 1974-1980; Joy of Youth, 1980-1995. *Comn:* Fourteen Bronze Bas Relief Portraits, Nat Cosmetology Asn, Chicago, IL, 1993-1997; Two Timer, bronze portrait head, Gloria Bahn, Chesterfield, MO, 2004; Pals, two dog bronze composition, Dr. Dennis Birenbaum, Dallas, TX, 2006; Dear to my Heart, gold pin & pendant, Lovaine Coxon, Eng, 2006; Bouvier des Flandres, sterling pendant, Charlotte Peltz, Redway, CA, 2008; Gentle Cloud, Akita Bronze, Deborah Hostetter, Ballwin, MO, 2008; Big Heart, Gordon Setter Bronze, Barbara Waterfall, DC, 2009; Squirrel Season, 2009; Long, Bronze, Sandy Arnold, Bloomington, IN, 2007; Long Haired Dreaming of Tomatoes, Bronze, Sandy Arnold, Bloomington, IN, 2010; Wire Haired So Good to See You, Bronze, Carol Ann Klein, Miami Shores, FL, 2010; Long Haired So Good to See You, Bronze, Carolyn Davenport, Mayfield Heights, OH, 2010; Quarter Life-size Merry Sunshine, Bronze, Taylor Herrick, Beaver Creek, OH, 2011; Bouvier des Flandres, Sterling Belt Buckle, George (Mike) Sloane, Scottsdale, AZ, 2012; Long Haired Deli's Open, Bronze, Sandy Arnold, Bloomington, IN, 2012; Wire Haired Deli's Open Bronze, Dr. Edna (Midge) Martin, Libertyville, IL, 2013; Four Long Haired dachshunds, Anonymous, Laguna Niguel, CA,2013-2014; Life-size Merry Sunshine, Bronze, Michael Trueblood, Cape Girardeau, MO, 2015. *Exhib:* Soc of Animal Artists, Nat Mus Tour, 1999-2001, 2003-2006; The Garden of Eden, Memphis Botanic Garden, Sculpture Works, Memphis, Tenn, 2001; Soc of Animal Artists 2000 Encore, Nat Geographic Mus, Washington, DC, 2002; Animals in Art, Miami Metro Zoo, Miami, Fla, 2004; Night of Artists, Nat Western Art Found, San Antonio, Tex, 2005-2006; Masters in Miniature, CM Russell Mus, Great Falls, Mont, 2006; American Art in Miniature, Gilcrease Mus, Tulsa, Okla, 2006-2008; 21st Ann Conservatory Art Classic, Bosque Conservatory, Clifton, Tex, 2006, 2008, 2011; Nat Sculpture Soc Ann Exhib, 98, 99, 2000, 2002, 2003, 2005, 2008, 2012; Artists for Conservation, Hiram Blauvelt Art, Oradell, NJ, 2009; Art of the Animal Kingdom, Bennington Ctr Arts, Bennington, Vt, 2009, 2012, 2013; Paws & Reflect, Art of Canine, Mus traveling show, 2007-2010; Art on the Aves, Wenachee, Wash, 2010-2016; Fidem XXXI Congress & Exhib, Tampere, Finland, 2010; AMSA with the Am Medallic Art Asn, 2010; 35th Int Miniature Art Shows, The Miniature Art Soc Fla, Tarpon Springs, Fla, 2001; 79th Ann Exhib, Hudson Valley Art Asn, 2010; Margaret Harwell Art Mus, Poplar Bluff Mo, 2012; AKC Mus of the Dog, The Art of the Dachshund, St Louis, Mo, 2013; David A Straz Performing Arts Ctr, Tampa, Fla, 2012-2015; Miniature Painters, Sculptors & Gravers Soc of Wash DC, 2000, 2002, 2004-2006, 2009-2013; All Creatures Great & Small, Naples Botanical Garden, Naples, FL, 2014-2015; Allied Artists 100th Ann Exhib, Canton Art Mus, Canton, OH, 2015; Salmagundi Club, 132nd Ann Mem Exhib, NY, 2015; Artists for Conservation, 8th Ann Virtual Exhib, 2015. *Collection Arranged:* co-cur, It's Reigning Cats & Dogs, St Louis Artists Guild, Mo, 2001; juror/judge: Art Show at the Dog Show, 12th Ann Exhib, Wichita, KS, 1998; Juror of Acceptance for Sculpture: Catharine Lorillard Wolfe Art Club, Ann Juried Open Exhib, Nat Arts Club, NY, 2011, 2013; Am Women Artists, Ann Juried Exhib, 2012. *Teaching:* Instr, dog sculpture (workshop), Loveland Acad, Loveland, Colorado, 2001. *Awards:* Best in Show, Purchase award, Art Show at the Dog Show, Wichita, Kans 97, Best Entry, Golden Retriever, 2012; Lindsey Morris Mem Award, 96th Ann Show, Allied Artists Am, 2009; 1st place metal sculpture, 19th Ann Int Miniature Art Show, Seaside Art Gallery, Nags Head, NC, 2010; The Agop Agropoff Mem Award, 79th Ann Exhib, Hudson Valley Art Asn, 2010; Gold Medal, 68th Ann Audubon Artists, NY, 2010; Barry and Fran Werner award, 46th Ann Central Southern Art Exhib, Tenn Art League, Nashville, Tenn, 2011; Kathryn Thayer Hudson award, 84th Grand Nat Exhib, Am Arts Professional League, 2012; Best Entry Depicting a Golden Retriever, 26th Ann Art Show at the Dog Show, Wichita, Kans, 2012; Anna Hyatt Huntington Horses Head award, Best Sculpture in Show, Members Exhib, Catharine Lorillard Wolfe Art Club, NY, 2012; First Prize, New Members Exhib, Salmagundi Club, NY, 2013; Marilyn Newmark award, Allied Artists 100th Ann Exhib, Salmagundi Club, NY, 2014. *Bibliog:* Michael J. Rosen (auth), 21st Century Dog: A Visionary Compendium, 2000; William Secord (auth), A Breed Apart: The Collections of the Am Kennel Club Mus, 2001; Cindy Billhartz (auth), Dachshunds of Bronze, St Louis Post Dispatch, 2004; Jim Schugal (auth), Dog Gone Good Artist, KSDK Channel 5, 2006; Patricia Leigh Brown (auth), In Death as in Life, New York Times, 2007; Liesl Bradner (auth), Going Out in Style, LA Times, 2008; Lisa Joele (auth), The Daily Republic, 2012; Todd Wilkinson (auth), The Wildlife Art Jour, 2012; St Louis Mag, 2012; Dog Gone Art Mag (cover), 2012; Sirius Newsletter of AKC Mus, Dog, 2013; AKC Judge Dan Harrison (auth) The Dachshund on the Move, The Dachshund History Project, 2013. *Mem:* Nat Sculpture Soc, Fellow Member; Soc of Animal Artists, Signature Member; Allied Artists of Am; Catharine Lorillard Wolfe Art Club; Audubon Artists; Am Medallic Sculpture Assn; Salmagundi Club; Am Artists Profl League; Am Women Artists Master Signature Member, 2000-2013, (treas), 2006-2012; Miniature Painters, Sculptors, and Gravers Soc of Wash DC; Miniature Art Society of Florida. *Media:* Metal, Cast-bronze, gold, sterling, pewter. *Specialty:* Classical realism from hounds to humans. *Interests:* Gardening, yoga, Pilates. *Collection:* Fountain Hills Cultural & Civic Asn Centennial Circle, Fountain Hills, Ariz; Ella Carothers Dunnegan Gallery of Art, Bolivar, MO; Galleries of the Library of Hattiesburg, MS; Am Kennel Club Mus of the Dog, St. Louis, MO; Nat Cosmetology Asn, Chicago, Il; Matrix Essentials, Solon, OH; The Wild Corporation, Englewood Cliffs, NJ; Creative Nail Design, Vista, Calif. *Publ:* Auth, Sixteen Years of Inspiration, Canine Images, 5-6/2000; auth, Clay to Collector, Doxie Digest, summer 2009, DGK Grave Hunden, 2010. *Dealer:* Dog and Horse Fine Art 102 Church St Charleston SC; Gallerie Gabrie 597 E Green St Pasadena CA; Kodner Gallery 9650 Clayton Rd St Louis MO; RS Hanna Gallery 208 S Llano St Fredericksburg TX 78624; Hildt Galleries Drake Hotel Arcade 140 East Walton St Chicago IL 60611; Stockbridge Gallery-Dogs in Art Parsonage Stratford-sub-Castle Salisbury SP1 3LH United Kingdom. *Mailing Add:* 15268 Kingsman Cir Chesterfield MO 63017-7412

BECKWITH, MARY ANN
PAINTER, EDUCATOR
b Philadelphia, Pa, May 17, 1945. *Study:* Marygrove Coll, Detroit, Mich, BFA, 1967; studied with (prof workshops) Glenn Bradshaw, Al Brouilette, Cheng Khee Chee, Virginia Cobb, N Engle, Katherine Liu, Alex Powers, 1979-1998. *Work:* State Mich Gov's Mansion, Lansing, Mich; Mich House Reps, Lansing, Mich; Mich Technol Univ, Van Pelt Libr & pres's office, Houghton, Mich; Repub Nat Bank, Hancock, Mich. *Exhib:* Am Watercolor Soc, Salmagundi Club, NY, 1987, 2007, 2009, 2010; Allied Artists Am, Am Acad Arts & Letters, NY, 1994, 2001, 2006, 2007; Audubon Artists, Salmagundi Club, NY, 2001, 2003, 2005, 2007; Int Soc Experimental Artists (Tex, Mich, Ind), 2005, 2006; Nat Watercolor Soc, 2000, 2008. *Pos:* Prof art, Mich Tech Univ, Houghton, Mich, 1973-. *Teaching:* Instr prof workshop & studio courses (US, Can, Eng, Korea), 1990-. *Awards:* President's Award, Mont Watercolor Soc, 2001; Award of Merit, Int Soc Experimental Artists, 2002; Traveling Show Award, Show Award, Adirondack Watercolor Soc, 2005; Hal P Moore Experimental, Ga Watercolor Soc, 2005; Silver Medal, Audubon Artists, Audubon Soc, 2007. *Bibliog:*

Rockport Publ, Best of Watercolor: Creative Inspirations, 1997; Rachel Wolf (auth), Splash 5, North Light Publ, 1998; Nita Engle (auth), How to Make a Watercolor Paint Itself, Watson-Guptill, 1999; Mary Alice Braukman (auth), Watercolor Mag, winter 2000; Midwest Watercolor Soc, 25 Tips by the Best of MWS, 2001. *Mem:* Transparent Watercolor Soc Am (bd, vpres, pres, 1989-1993); Audubon Artists (full, 2005); Int Soc Experimental Artists (bd, pres, 2005-2006, dir, 2008-); Nat Watercolor Soc (signature mem); Allied Artists Am; Hon Soc Watercolor USA; Nat Watercolor Soc; Am Watercolor Soc. *Media:* Watercolor; Watermedia. *Publ:* Auth (bk), Creative Watercolor: A Step by Step Guide, Rockport Publs, (Japanese ed), MPC (Tokyo), 1997; contrib (bk), Collected Best of Watercolor, Rockport Publs, 2002; Creative Watercolor Workshop, North Light Bks, 2005; auth, Experimenting with Texture & Media, In: Int Artist, Feb, Mar 2006. *Dealer:* Vertin Gallery Calumet MI 49913

BEDFORD, CHRISTOPHER
CURATOR
Study: Oberlin Coll, BA (art hist); Case Western Reserve Univ, MA (art hist); Courtauld Inst Art, Univ London, PhD candidate. *Collection Arranged:* Mixed Signals: Artists Consider Masculinity in Sports, Independent Curators Int; Contemporary Projects 11: Hard Targets--Masculinity & Sport, Los Angeles County Mus Art, 2008. *Pos:* Curatorial asst, consult cur sculpture & decorative arts, Getty Mus, Los Angeles, formerly; asst cur contemp art, Los Angeles County Mus Art, 2006-08; cur, Wexner Ctr Arts, Ohio State Univ, 2008-2012; Henry and Lois Foster Dir, Rose Art Mus, Brandeis Univ, Waltham, Mass, 2012-. *Awards:* Cur's Award, Fellows of Contemp Art, 2007. *Mailing Add:* Brandeis University Rose Art Mus 415 S St Waltham MA 02453

BEDIA, JOSE
PAINTER, SCULPTOR
b Havana, Cuba, 1959; US citizen. *Study:* Sch Art San Alejandro, MA, 1976; Super Inst Art, Havanna, BA, 1981. *Work:* Hirshhorn Mus & Sculpture Garden, Washington, DC; Ludwig Collection, Ger; Philadelphia Mus Art; Phoenix Art Mus; Whitney Mus Am Art, NY. *Exhib:* Solo exhibs, Jose Bedia: De Donde Vengo, Inst Contemp Art, Philadelphia, 1994-95; Mi Esencialismo (with catalog), Hyde Gallery, Trinity Col, Dublin, Ireland, 1995, Pori Art Mus, Finland, 1996 & George Adams Gallery, NY; Jose Bedia: The Island, the Hunter & the Prey, Site Santa Fe, NMex, 1997; Cronicas Americanas: Obra de Jose Bedia (with catalog), Mus Contemp Art, Monterrey, Mex, 1997-98; 20/21: Jose Bedia, Joslyn Art Mus, Omaha, 1998; A Survey of Paintings and Works on Paper 1992-2006, George Adams Gallery, NY, 2007; group exhibs, Latin Am Artists of the 20th Century, Mus Mod Art, NY, 1992-93; Cuba Siglo XX: Modernidad y Sincretismo, Centro Atlantico Moderno, Grand Canary Island, 1996 & Centre d'Art Santa Monica, Barcelona, Spain, 1996; Latin-Am Group Show, George Adams Gallery, NY, 1998, Saints, Sinners & Sacrifices, 1999, Me, Myself & I, 2002; Contemp Narratives in Am Prints, Whitney Mus Am Art at Champion, 1999-2000; Crisis Response, RI Sch Design Mus, 2002, Island Nations, 2004; Ann Invitational Exhib Contemp Am Art, Nat Acad Mus, NY, 2008. *Awards:* Gran Premio del Salon del Paisaje, Havana, 1982; Premio de la Segunda Bienal de la Habana, 1986; Guggenheim Mem Found Int Fel, 1994; Kent Day Coes Prize, Nat Acad Design, 2008. *Bibliog:* Several articles and reviews in New York Times, Art Nexus, Art in Am, ARTnews, Arts Mag and many others. *Mailing Add:* c/o George Adams Gallery 525 W 26th St New York NY 10001

BEDRICK, JEFFREY K
PAINTER, ILLUSTRATOR
b Providence, RI, Oct 4, 1960. *Study:* Studies with Gage Taylor, 77-79; Coll Marn, studies with Bill Martin, 79-80; San Francisco State Univ (cinematography & animation), 83. *Work:* Pacific Telesis Corp; Mazda Corp; Syntex Corp; Proctor & Gamble Corp; GTE Corp. *Comn:* Various decorative murals, Renaissance Mural Co, 83; decorative murals for var hotels & restaurants, Elizabeth Weiner & Assocs, Los Angeles, Calif, 86; decorative interior mural, Pacific Telesis Corp, San Francisco, Calif, 88; Valentine Mus mural restoration, John Canning Co, Richmond, Va, 90; decorative interior mural, Peter & Gabrielle Wais, Ross, Calif, 92. *Exhib:* Vision Quest 78 Invitational, Hall of Flowers, Golden Gate Park, San Francisco, Calif, 78; Interfaith Peace Conference, Grace Cathedral, San Francisco, Calif, 83; 100 Vows of the Sun Invitational, Southern Exposure Gallery, San Francisco, Calif, 85; The Environment Invitational, Toyota Amlux Corp Hq, Japan, 91; Collector's Eds/Lyrical Art Co, Tokyo, Japan. *Pos:* Animation prod artist, Colossal Pictures, San Francisco, Calif, 81-91; trade show display muralist, Giltspar Inc, San Francisco, Calif, 92; ad comp artist, Transphere Int Ad Agency, San Francisco, Calif, 92. *Teaching:* Pvt instr painting, 91. *Bibliog:* Michael Bell (auth), Custodian of light, Magical Blend Mag, 90; Jeff Bedrick-Pop Icons, City Mag, 92. *Mem:* San Francisco Soc Illusr. *Media:* Oil on Canvas. *Publ:* Illusr, Line of Fine Art Gift-Cards, titles, Aquamarin Verlag, Ger, 87, The Queens Cards, 91; var book covers, Inner Traditions, Int, 89; Weather, Doubleday, 90; The Lost Continent of Mo, Brotherhood of Life, 90. *Dealer:* Collectors Editions Canoga Park CA

BEE, SUSAN
PAINTER, BOOK ARTIST
US citizen. *Study:* Barnard Coll, BA, 73; Hunter Coll, MA, 77. *Work:* Bienecke Libr, Yale Univ, New Haven, Conn; Getty Collection, Los Angeles, Calif; NY Pub Libr, Special Collection, New York; Victoria & Albert Mus, London, Eng; Clark Art Inst, Williamstown, Mass. *Exhib:* Solo exhibs, Seeing Double, AIR Gallery, New York, 2006, Eye of the Storm, AIR Gallery, New York, 2009, Recalculating, AIR Gallery, New York, 2011; Group exhibs, Triennial 9, Mus Art & Design, New York, 2003-2004; AIR Gallery: Hist Show, NY Univ Libr, New York, 2008-2009; Too Much Bliss!, Smith Coll Mus Art, Amherst, Mass, 2005-06; Complicit! Univ Va Art Mus, Charlottesville, Va, 2006; Metaphor Taking Shape, Yale Univ, New Haven, Conn, 2008; Criss-Cross Acola Griefen Gallery, 2013; Air Gallery, NY, 2014. *Teaching:* Adj prof, Sch Visual Arts, MFA in art criticism & writing, 2005-. *Awards:* NYSCA Publ Award, 89-97; NEA Publ Award, 92-97; Yaddo Fel, 96, 2001; Fel, Va Ctr for the Arts, 99, 2002; Guggenheim Fellowship, 2014. *Bibliog:* Johanna Drucker (auth), Seeing Double (catalogue), 2006; John Yau (auth), Beware the Lady (catalogue), 2000; Jonathan Goodman (auth), Susan Bee at AIR, Art in Am Rev, 2006; Meredith Mendelsohn (auth), Susan Bee at AIR, Art News Rev, 2009; Craig Olson, Susan Bee at AIR, Brooklyn Rail Rev, 2009. *Mem:* Coll Art Asn. *Media:* Oil painting & Collage; Artist's Book. *Publ:* Little Orphan Anagram (with Charles Bernstein), Granary Books, New York, 97; Bed Hangings (with Susan howe), Granary Books, New York, 2001; A Girl's Life (Artist's book with Johanna Drucker), Granary Books, New York, 2002; The Burning Babe (Artist's book with Jerome Rothenberg), Granary Books, New York, 2005; Entre (Artist book), Global Books, France, 2009. *Dealer:* AIR Gallery 111 Front St #228 Brooklyn NY 11201; Accola Griefen Gallery. *Mailing Add:* 290 President St, Ground Fl Brooklyn NY 11231

BEEBE, MARY LIVINGSTONE
ART ADMINISTRATOR
b Portland, Ore, Nov 5, 1940. *Study:* The Catlin GablinSch, 45-58; Bryn Mawr Coll, Pa, BA, 62; Univ Paris & L'Ecole de Louvre, Paris, 62-63. *Comn:* Commn by Terry Allen, Michael Asher, John Baldessari, Jackie Ferrara, Ian Hamilton Finlay, Richard Fleischner, Tim Hawkinson, Jenny Holzer, Robert Irwin, Barbara Kruger, Elizabeth Murray, Bruce Nauman, Nan June Paik, Niki de Saint Phalle, Alexis Smith, Kiki Smith, William Wegman, Do Ho Suh. *Exhib:* Over 100 exhibs 72-81. *Collection Arranged:* Stuart Coll; UCSF Mission Bay Bishop Collection. *Pos:* Mus apprentice, Portland Art Mus, 63-64; asst to registr & secy, Mus Fine Arts, Boston, 65-66; curatorial asst, Fogg Art Mus, Harvard Univ, 66-68; producer, Am Theater co, Portland, 69-72; exec dir, Portland Ctr Visual Arts, 72-81; dir, Stuart Collection Sculpture, Univ Calif, San Diego, 81-. *Teaching:* Instr, Univ Calif, San Diego. *Awards:* Nat Endowment Arts Fel, 79; AIA Allied Profession Award, 92; Am for the Arts, The Pub Art Network Award, 2011. *Mem:* Art Matters Inc, New York (bd mem, 85-); Russell Found, La Jolla (bd mem); Univ Wash (arts adv comt, 89-94); UCSF Mission Bay Arts (adv bd, 99-). *Interests:* Contemporary art and sculptures, gardening. *Publ:* Landmarks: Sculpture Commissions for the Stuart Collection at the Univ of Calif-San Diego, 2001. *Mailing Add:* Stuart Collection Univ Calif San Diego-0010 9500 Gilman Dr La Jolla CA 92093-0010

BEECH, JOHN
INSTALLATION SCULPTOR
b Winchester, England, 1964. *Study:* Univ Calif, Berkeley, BA, 1986. *Work:* San Francisco Mus Mod Art, CA; Univ Art Mus, Berkeley, CA; Mus Art, Fort Lauderdale; Ctr Contemp Non-Objective Art, Brussels, Belgium. *Exhib:* Solo exhibs include Main Spaces I & II, Ctr for Contemp Non-Objective Art, Brussels, Germany, 1999, main space, 2008, Albright-Knox Art Gallery, Buffalo, NY, 2004, Peter Blum Gallery, New York, 2005, That & This, 2007; two-person exhibs include Peter Blum Gallery, New York, (with Stephanie Brooks), 2003, Galerie Gisèle Linder, Basel, Switzerland, (with Peter Willen), 2007; group exhibs include Into the 21st Century, San Jose Mus Art, CA, 1999, Material Issues, 1999; minimalpop, Florence Lynch Gallery, New York, 2004; Spectrum, Galerie Lelong, New York, 2005; Summertime, Galerie Gisèle Linder, Basel, Switzerland, 2006; Photograph as Canvas, Aldrich Contemp Art Mus, Ridgefield, CT, 2007; Pierogi Flatfiling, Artnews Projs, Berlin, 2007; Der zweite Blick, Stiftung für Konkrete Kunst - Reutlingen, Germany, 2007; Invitational Exhib Visual Arts, AAAL, 2008. *Awards:* Maybelle Toombs Award for Practice of Art, Univ Calif, Berkeley, 1986; Seca Award, San Francisco Mus Mod Art, Calif, 1992; Pollock-Krasner Found Award, 1999. *Dealer:* Peter Blum 99 Wooster St New York NY 10012; Peter Blum Chelsea 526 W 29th New York NY 10001; Gallery Paule Anglim 14 Geary St San Francisco CA 94108; Charlotte Jackson Fine Art 200 W Marcy Suite 101 Santa Fe NM 87501; Gisèle Linder Elisabethentrasse 54 ch-4051 Basel Switzerland; CCNOA Boulevard Barthelemylaans 5 Brussels Belgium 1000

BEECROFT, VANESSA FIONA
PAINTER
b Genoa, Italy, Apr 25, 1969; Brit citizen. *Study:* Civico Liceo Artistico Nicolo Barabino, archit, Genoa, Italy, 83-87; Acad Ligustica Di Belle Arti, painting, Genoa, Italy, 87-88; Acad Di Belle Arti Di Brera, stage design, Milan, Italy, 88-93. *Work:* Castello di Rivoli, Fondazione Sandretto Rerebaudengo, Turin, Italy; Castello di Rivara, Rivara, Italy; Oakis Joannou Collection, Athens, Greece. *Exhib:* Id, Munic Van Abbe Mus Eindhoven, Nfld, 96; Persona, Renaissance Soc, Chicago, 96; Quadriennale d'Arte di Roma, Palazzo Esposizioni, Rome, 96; Traffic, CACP Mus Art Contemp, Bordeaux, France, 96; Conversation Pieces, Inst Contemp Art, Philadelphia, 96; Conversation Pieces, Inst Contemp Art, Boston, 97; Aperto Ital 95, Trevi Flash Art Mus, Italy, 95; Prima Linea (with catalog), Trevi Flash Art Mus, Trevi, Italy, 95; Young and Restless, Mus Mod Art, NY, 96; The Scream (with catalog), Mus Mod Art, Ishoj, Denmark, 96; Fatto in Italia (with catalog), Inst Contemp Art, London, UK, 97; Enterprise (with catalog), Inst Contemp Art, Boston, Mass, 97; Kritische Eleganie, Critical Elegance (with catalog), Musem Dhondt-Dhaenens Deurle, Belgium, 98; Then and Now, Lisson Gallery, London, UK, 98; Helmut Newton, Big Nudes, L'Elac, L'Espace Lausannois d'Art Contemporian, Geneva, Switz, 98; Wounds Between Democracy and Redemption in Contemp Art (with catalog), Modema Museet, Stockholm, Sweden, 98. *Bibliog:* Visual Images of Today, Monthly Art Mag, Bijutsu Techo BT 9, 9/98; H Kontova & G Politi, Arte (auth), Vanessa Beecroft, Intervista No 14, Polita Editore, 7-8/98; Flash Art XXXI Years, Flash Art Int, Politi Editore, 98. *Media:* Oil, Watercolor. *Publ:* Coauth & illusr, Eh No? - Geapoliti, 96 & coauth, Slownet-Flash Art, summer 96, Politi Editore; contribr, Purple Fashion N2, Purple Inst, 96-97. *Dealer:* Jeffrey Deitch 721 Fifth Ave New York NY 10022. *Mailing Add:* 235 Berry St Brooklyn NY 11211

BEER, KENNETH JOHN
EDUCATOR, SCULPTOR
b Ferndale, Mich, May 4, 1932. *Study:* Wayne State Univ, BA & MA. *Work:* Detroit Inst Art; Thalhimers & First Merchants Bank, Richmond & Va Beach Art Ctr, Va. *Comn:* Campus libr relief, Eastern Mennonite Col, Harrisonburg, Va, 69; James Madison Mem (cast bronze), James Madison Univ, Harrisonburg, 77; Arboretum

Gates, James Madison Univ, Harrisonburg, 88. *Exhib:* Ann Mich Artists, Detroit Inst Art, 55-62; Va Artists Biennial, Va Mus, Richmond, 65, 67 & 73; Southern Sculpture, Mint Mus, Charlotte, NC, 65, Birmingham Mus, Ala, 66 & Columbus Mus, Ga, 66; solo exhib, Columbia Mus, SC, 69 & Va Mus, 73; Drawing & Sculpture Ann, Ball State Univ Art Gallery, 74 & 76. *Teaching:* Assoc prof sculpture, James Madison Univ, Harrisonburg, 61-. *Awards:* Whitcomb Prize, Mich Artists Ann, Detroit Inst Arts, 61; Best in Show, Thalhimers Invitational, 66; Distinction Award, Va Artists Biennial, Va Mus, 73. *Media:* Bronze, Steel. *Publ:* Auth, Sanctum, The Emergence of a Form, Studies & Res Bull of Madison Col, 64. *Mailing Add:* James Madison Univ School of Art & Art History MSC 7101 Harrisonburg VA 22807

BEERMAN, JOHN THORNE
PAINTER
b Greensboro, NC, Feb 21, 1958. *Study:* Skowhegan Sch Painting & Sculpture, 1980; RI Sch Design, BFA, 1982. *Work:* Metrop Mus Art, New York; Brooklyn Mus; Mus Fine Arts, Houston; Walker Art Ctr, Minneapolis; NC Mus Art, Raleigh; Whitney Mus Am Art, NY; Neuberger Mus, Purchase, NY; Farnsworth Mus, Rockland, Me; Cleveland Mus Art, Cleveland, Ohio. *Exhib:* Group shows include The New Romantic Landscape, Whitney Mus Am Art, New York, Fairfield Co, Stamford, Conn, 1987; The 1980's: A New Generation, Metrop Mus Art, New York; Harmony & Discord: Am Landscape Today, Va Mus Fine Arts, Richmond, 1990; Am Narrative Painting & Sculpture 80's, Nassau Co Mus Art, Roslyn, New York, 1991; Seeing the Forest Through the Trees, Contemp Arts Mus, Houston, 1993; Inspired by Nature, Newberger Mus, Purchase, NY, 1994; Changing Horizons, Katonah Mus Art, New York, 1996; Divining Nature, Southeastern Mus Contemp Art, Winston-Salem, NC, 1998; Bently Gallery, Scottsdale, Ariz, 1999; David Beitzel Gallery, New York, 2001; Meredith Long Gallery, Houston, 2001; Somerhill Gallery, Chapel Hill, NC, 2002; Tibor de Nagy Gallery, New York, 2003, 2004, 2006, 2011; Mira Mar Gallery, Sarasota, Fla, 2003; Rockland Ctr Arts, 2004. *Teaching:* instr 2D design, Rhode Island Sch Design, 2005-2009. *Awards:* Scholar, Skowhegan Sch Painting & Sculpture, Maine, 1980; Visual Artist Fel Painting, Yaddo, Saratoga Springs, NY, 1984; Subscription Prize, Jane Voorhees Zimmerli Art Mus, Rutgers Univ, New Brunswick, NJ, 1986. *Bibliog:* John W Coffey II (auth), Finding the Forgotten Landscape (exhib catalog), NC Mus Art, 1991; Vivian Raynor (auth), Surveying realism in celebration of Hopper, NY Times, 1996; Ed Bumgardner (auth), Landscape artists tries to capture the magic, Winston-Salem J, 1996; Susan Dominus (auth), LInked to the Hudson by Love, Art, and History, New York Times, 2008; Reynolds Price (auth), Strokes of Genius, 2010. *Media:* Oil on Linen. *Dealer:* Meredith Long Gallery 2323 San Felipe Houston Tex 77019; Tibor de Nagy Gallery 724 5th Ave New York NY 10014; Hudson River Editions 278 Piermont Ave South Nyack NY 10960; Sightlines PO Box 750430 Forest Hills NY 11375-0430

BEERMAN, MIRIAM
PAINTER, PRINTMAKER
b Providence, RI. *Study:* RI Sch Design, BFA; Art Students League, with Yasuo Kuniyoshi; New Sch Social Res, with Adja Yunkers; New York Univ; Atelier 17, Paris, with Wm Hayter. *Work:* Victoria and Albert Mus, London, Whitney Mus Am Art, Metrop Mus Art, New Sch Social Res, Brooklyn Mus, Queens Mus & Jewish Mus, NY; Newark Mus, Newark Pub Libr, NJ; Israel Mus, Jerusalem; NJ State Mus, Trenton; Jersey city Mus, NJ; Allan Meml Mus Fine Art, Oberlin, Ohio; Mus Art; Montclair Art Mus; Zimmerli Mus, NJ; Yale Univ, Sterling Art Libr; Corcoran Mus, Wash DC; Cambridge Univ; Everson Mus, Syracuse, NY; Bass Mus, Miami, Fla; Vasser, Poughkeepsie, NY; Queensborough Comm. Coll, Queens, NY. *Comn:* Mus Art, RI Sch Design, Providence, RI. *Exhib:* Whitney Mus, NY, 58; Brooklyn Mus, NY, 60; Nat Gallery Can, Ottawa, 60; solo exhibs, Am Acad Arts & Letters & Brooklyn Mus, NY, 72, Primal Ground Miriam Beerman: Works from 1983-1987, Montclair, NJ, 87, Works from 1949-1990, NJ State Mus, Trenton, 91, Bergan Mus, Paramus, NJ, 96, Univ Wis, Oshkosh, 2002; solo retrospectives, Pratt Inst, NY, 89 & Miriam Beerman: Artist Books, Jersey City Mus, 98; Chicago Art Expo, Ill, 93; Traveling Exhib, Corcoran Gallery Art, Washington, DC, 94; Drawing Invitational, Jersey City Mus, NJ, 95; Queens Mus, NY, 96; Univ Wisconsin, Oshkosh, WI, 2002; Chautauqua Ctr for Vis Arts, Chautauqua, NY, 2004; Collage Retrospective, Wriston Art Galleries, Lawrence Univ, Appleton, Wis, 2015. *Collection Arranged:* Israel Mus; NJ State Mus; Bklyn Mus; Whitney Mus Am Art; Met Mus Art; RI Sch Design Mus Art; Jersey City Mus; Allen Meml Mus Art; Montclair Mus; Nat Mus Women in the Arts, Washington, DC; Neuberger Mus, Purchase, NY; New Walk Mus, Leicester, England; MEAM, Barcelona, Spain. *Pos:* Artist-in-Residence, Burston Graphic Ctr, Jerusalem, Israel, 80; guest artist, Rutgers Univ, New Brunswick, NJ, 87 & 97. *Awards:* Artists Residency, Va Ctr Creative Arts, 85-96, 2000; Artists Residency, Blue Mtn Ctr, 89-96; Mid Atlantic Grant, 96; Fulbright Grant, 2000; Joan Mitchell Award, 2000; Mid-Atlantic grant, 2000; Pollock-Krasner grant, Women's Studio Workshop, 2000; ED Found grant, Dodge Found, 2000; and many others; RI Sch of Design Lifetime Achievement award, 2015. *Bibliog:* Vivien Raynor (auth), Imaginary Monsters That Dare a Visitor to See the Show, NY Times, 4/14/91; Dimitri Rotov (auth), New Art Examiner, 10/91; John Loughery (auth), Women's Art J, fall 91, winter 92; All Things Considered, Nat Pub Radio, 6/26/94; and many others. *Media:* Oil, Large Drawings. *Interests:* social and political injustice. *Publ:* Ed & illusr, The Enduring Beast, Doubleday, 72

BEERY, ARTHUR O
PAINTER
b Marion, Ohio, Mar 4, 1930. *Study:* Self taught. *Work:* Butler Inst Am Art, Youngstown, Ohio; Lessco Data, NY; JM Katz Collection, Pa; Johnson Art Mus, Cornell Univ; Sweet Briar Mus, Sweet Briar Univ; Springfield Art Mus, Springfield, Mo; and others; Historical Mus, Marion, Ohio. *Comn:* Murals on canvas of Athens, Greece, Monte Carlo, Stromboli, Rock of Gibralter & Charleston, SC for US Navy Minecraft Base, Charleston, 54. *Exhib:* Solo exhibs, Galerie Cernuschi, NY, 77, 80, Gallery DeJanout, Cleveland, Ohio, 98, Mansfield Art Ctr, 2006; Group exhibs, Nat Exhib, Butler Inst Am Art, Youngstown, Ohio, 68, 72, 73, 79; Le Salon De Nations, Paris, France, 83; 28th Ann Chautauga Nat Exhib Am Art, 85; Watercolor USA Hon Soc Biennial Exhib, 87, 89, 91 & 93; Ohio Art League Exhib, Columbus Mus Fine Art, 98 & 2000; Richland Acad, 2000; 23rd Grand Prix, Deauville, France, 72; Contemp Ams, Paris France, 72; New Am Open, Nat Exhib, 2004; Ohio Curated Exhib, Riffle Gallery, 2005; 61st Ann, Mansfield Art Ctr, Ohio, 2006; Rhodes Tower, Columbus, Ohio, 2005; 75th Nat Exhib, Butler Inst Am Art, 2011. *Collection Arranged:* Butler Inst Am Art, Youngstown, OH; J M Katz Collection-P2; Johnson Art Mus, Cornell Univ; Sweet Briar Univ; Sweet Briar Gallery, Sweet Briar, VA. *Awards:* Richard P Stahl Award, Watercolor USA, 71; Purchase Prize, Butler Inst Am Art, 73; Oscar D'Ital Award, Acad Ital, 85; Mansfield Art Ctr Award, 99; Ohio Art League Exhib awarded Mary Lou Chess Award, 2000; Best in Show, Nat New Am Open, 2004; 3rd Award, Ohio State Univ Mansfield Campus, 2009; award, Ohio State Fair, 2009; Professional Award, Ohio State Fair, 2011. *Bibliog:* Int Dir Arts, 11th ed, Berlin Ger 72; BF Goodrich (auth), BFG-Today, vol 1 no 4, 77; Roger Schlueter (auth), Saluto to the master, Belleville New Dem, 91; David Breeding (auth), Am art to remember, Marlon Ohio Star, 98; Renne Phillips (auth), Manhattan Arts Int, 2000; Joel Hochman (auth), The Art Crows, 2000; Bill Mayr (auth), Visual Arts, Coll Ohio Dispatch, 2004. *Mem:* Mansfield Fine Arts Guild, Ohio; Ohio Art League (Award 2000); Watercolor USA Hon Soc. *Media:* Oils, Watercolor. *Interests:* the creation of beauty by the use of the continuous curve, quotes by Americans on the 13 stripes of the flag. *Mailing Add:* 452 E Church St Marion OH 43302

BEGININ, IGOR
PAINTER, EDUCATOR
b Susak, Croatia, Aug 31, 1931; US citizen. *Study:* Wayne State Univ, AB (cum laude), 63, MA, 66. *Work:* Fisher New Ctr, Chrysler Corp, Ford Motor Co, Detroit; Gen Motors, NY; Tung-Hai Univ, Taichong, Taiwan. *Comn:* Detroit Free Press, Mich Med Mag. *Exhib:* Watercolor USA, 68, 73, 93, 98 & 2004; Nat Soc Painters in Casein/Acrylic, New York City, 69, 94; Kentucky Aqueous, Louisville, 86; Flint Inst Art, 86; Int Watercolor, San Diego, Calif, 88; Okla Nat Exhib, 93, 98 & 2001; Tex Watercolor Soc, 93 & 2005. *Pos:* Bd mem, Mich Watercolor Soc, 66-70 & 82-91, chmn, 74-77. *Teaching:* Asst prof watercolor, Eastern Mich Univ, 70-77, assoc prof, 77-83, prof, 83-2001, prof emer art. *Awards:* Soc Illusr Award, 68; Mich Watercolor Soc Ann Award, 67, 71, 83, 89, 91, 95 & 2000; Int Exhib, San Diego Watercolor Soc, 88; Watercolor USA, 2004. *Bibliog:* The Daily Sentinel, 70; Ann Arbor News, 73; Associated Newspapers, 87; Observer-Eccentric, 98. *Mem:* Mich Watercolor Soc; Detroit Inst Arts Founders Soc; Watercolor USA Hon Soc. *Media:* Watercolor, Acrylic. *Publ:* Detroit Mag, Detroit Free Press, 65-69 & Michigan Medicine, 69; The Artistic Touch, 95 & The Artistic Touch 2, 97, Creative Art Press; Creative Watercolor, Rockport Publ, 95, Illustrators 10, New York City. *Mailing Add:* 43524 Bannockburn Dr Canton MI 48187

BEGLEY, J (JOHN) PHILLIP
MUSEUM DIRECTOR
b Akron, Ohio, Mar 21, 1947. *Study:* Univ NMex, BFA (hons), 69; Ind Univ, MFA, 75; Mus Management Inst, Getty Trust, AFA, 89. *Collection Arranged:* Traveling Exhibs, Making it in Crafts (auth, catalog), 78, Fiber: State of the Art, 81, Making it in Paper: Twinrocker, 83, Individual Talent (auth, catalog), 84, Kentucky Guild 25th Anniversary Ceremony (auth, catalog), 86 & Contemporary Directions in Fiber (assembled & arranged), 88; Ladies Lunch (producer), 92. *Pos:* Dir, New Harmony Gallery Contemp Art, 75-83; exec dir, Louisville Visual Art Asn, 83-. *Teaching:* Lectr art, Univ Evansville, 76-83 & Univ Louisville, 88-89, adj assoc prof art, Univ Louisville, 97-. *Awards:* Louis Comfort Tiffany Fel, 78. *Media:* All Media Contemporary. *Mailing Add:* 1506 Hepburn Ave Louisville KY 40204-1618

BEHNKE, LEIGH
PAINTER
b Hartford, Conn, Dec 22, 1946. *Study:* Pratt Inst, BFA, 69; New York Univ, MA, 76. *Work:* H J Heinz Corp, Pittsburgh, Pa; Deloitte, Haskins, Sells, Marsh & McClennan co & Xerox Corp, New York; Southeast Banking Corp, Miami, Fla; Currier Mus, Manchester, NH; and others. *Exhib:* Solo exhibs, Fischbach Gallery, New York, 78, 79, 82, 85, 91, 94, 98, 2003, 2006, Thomas Segal Gallery, Boston, 81, Nat Acad Sci, Wash, DC, 92, Elaine Baker Gallery, Boca Raton, Fla, 2000; group exhibs, Urban Landscape, Wave Hill, NY, 79; New Am Still Life, Westmoreland Mus, Pa, 79; On Paper, Inst Contemp Art, Va Mus, Richmond, 80; Real, Really Real, Super Real, San Antonio Mus, Tex, 81, Carnegie Inst, Pittsburgh, 81 & Indianapolis Mus, Ind, 81; Contemp Am Realist, Univ Art Gallery, Pittsburgh, Pa, 81; Lower Manhattan from Street to Sky, Whitney Mus, 82; Fischbach Gallery, 78-94, 2002, 2004; Flint Inst Arts, 91; Nassau Co Mus, 92; Nat Acad Sci, 92; Boise Art Mus, 93-94; Art Mus Fla Int Univ, Miami, 95; MA Doran Gallery, Tulsa, Okla, 2001; Neuberger Mus Art, Purchase, NY, 2003; Nat Acad Mus, New York, 2004; Exactitude, Plus One Gallery, London, Eng, 2006; Fichbach Gallery, 2009; The Value of Water, Cathedral of St John the Divine, NY. *Pos:* Master teacher & panelist, Nat Foun Adv Arts, 89-93. *Teaching:* Lectr fine art, drawing and painting, Sch Visual Arts, New York, 79-. *Awards:* ED Found grant, 99, 2000; Guggenheim fellow, 2013. *Bibliog:* New Editions: Leigh Behnke, Art News, 4/82; Christopher Finch (auth), Twentieth Century Watercolors, 88; Roni Cohen (auth), Artforum Mag (rev), 91; RH Art Mag (interview), Vol 88, 2012. *Mem:* Coll Art Asn. *Media:* Watercolor, Oil; Silkscreen. *Dealer:* Fischbach Gallery 29 W 57th St New York NY 10019; Plus One Gallery 91 Pimlico Rd London SW1W 8PH. *Mailing Add:* Dept Fine Arts School of Visual Arts 543 Broadway #3 New York NY 10012

BEHNKEN, WILLIAM JOSEPH
PRINTMAKER, EDUCATOR
b New York, NY, Mar 29, 1943. *Study:* City Coll New York, BA, 68, MA, 95. *Work:* British Mus, London; Nat Acad Design Mus, New York; NY Pub Libr Print Collection, New York; Brooklyn Mus, New York; Indianapolis Mus Fine Art, Ind; Metrop Mus Art, New York; Fitzwilliam Mus, Cambridge, Eng; New Orleans Mus, La; Newark Pub Libr Print Div, NJ; Miss Mus, Miss; Boston Athenaeum; Mus City of

NY; NY Historical Soc; Art Students League NY. *Comn:* print ed, Gallery New World, Dusseldorf, Ger, 96; print ed, CECO Corp, New York, 97-99; print ed/portfolio, The Old Print Shop Gallery, New York, 98; print ed, Print Club Albany, 2006. *Exhib:* NY at Night, Auburn Coll, NY, 89; Small Print Invitational, State Gallery, Lodz, Poland, 96; Drawings Int, Wagner Coll, NY, 96; Provincetown Then and Now, St Botolph's Club, Boston, 98; 19th & 20th Century Am Works on Paper, Nat Acad Design, New York, 99; Parkside Nat Small Print Exhib, Univ Wis, Kenosha, 2000; Prints & Drawings, Old Print Shop Gallery, New York, 2003; Century Asn Invitational, New York, 2003; La Biennale Int d'estampe de Trois-Rirvieres, Que, Can, 2005; Impressions on NY, NY Hist Soc, 2005; SAGA, Hollar Soc Gallery, Prague, Czech Rep, 2006; traveling collection, Art Students League NY, 2006-; Visions of New York, Art Students League Printmakers, Manhattan Borough Pres off, 2007; The Print & The Self, Terrain Gallery, NY, 2008; KB Gallery, 2008; Old Print Shop Gallery, 2009; Mem Ann, Nat Acad Design, 2009; Soc Am Graphic Artists, 2011; Bronx Artists, The Interchuch Ctr, NY, 2012; Drawn to NY, Cohen Lib Archives Gallery, City Coll NY, 2012; 80th Members Exhib, Soc Am Graphic Artists, Delind Gallery, Milwaukee, Wisc, 2013. *Teaching:* asst prof art, City Coll New York, 70-; vis lectr hist printmaking, CW Post Coll, Long Island, New York, 96-97; instr printmaking, Art Students League, New York, 98- & Nat Acad Design, 2001-2007. *Awards:* Recipient Louis Lozowick awards Audubon Artists Soc, New York, 91-92; Carl Schrag Award, Soc Am Graphic Artists, 97; Graphics Award, Nat Acad Design, 97; John Taylor Arms Purchase Award Albany Print Club, New York, 98; 1st Anniversary Art Career Achievement award City Coll Art Alumni Asn, 2004; Ralph Fabri Award, Nat Acad Design, 2003; Audubon Artist Gold Medal Graphics Award, 2003; Silver Medal Graphics Award, Audubon Artists, 2005; Emile & Dines Carlsen Graphics Award, Nat Acad Design; Ralph Fabri & Leo Meissner Prizes, Charles Loring Elliot Medal, Nat Acad Design, 2009. *Bibliog:* Trudie A Grace (auth), Paper Trail, Nat Acad Design, 97; Marilyn Symmes (auth), Impressions of New York, New York Hist Soc, 2005; Linda Price (auth), Black and White in New York City, Am Artist Mag, 5/2007; The Visual Language of Drawing Lessons on the Art of Seeing, James McElhinney & Instructors of The Art Students League of NY, 2012. *Mem:* Provincetown Art Asn Mus (sch dir, 84-95); Audubon Artist (dir graphics, 91-92); Soc Am Graphic Artists (pres, 98-2002); Nat Acad Design (mem comt person, 2000-); Boston Printmakers, Phi Beta Kappa (pres, City Coll New York Gamma chap, 2001); Print Coun New York. *Media:* Aquatint, Mezzotint, Lithography. *Dealer:* The Old Print Shop 150 Lexington Ave New York NY 10016; Julie Heller Gallery, Provincetown, Mass; Allan Platt Gallery, Chicago, Ill. *Mailing Add:* 3400 Fort Independence St 9 B Bronx NY 10463

BEHR, MARION RAY
ARTIST, WRITER
b Rochester, NY, Sept 12, 1939. *Study:* Syracuse Univ, BFA, 61, MFA, 62. *Work:* Jane Voorhees Zimmerli Mus, New Brunswick, NJ, 93, 96 & 2002; Social Sci Res Coun Corp Col, NY, 2005; Nat Mus Am Hist, Smithsonian Inst, Washington, DC; Royal Thai Art Collection, 94; Inst Cult Peruano Norteamericano, Lima, Peru, 99; Bethaniem Gallery, Berlin, 2004; Ben Shahn Gallery, 2006; San Agustin Etla, Mex; Johnson Gallery, Bedminster, NJ. *Exhib:* solo exhib, Beamesderfer Gallery, Highland Park, NJ, 92, Hunterton Art Mus, Clinton, NJ, 98, Nat Acad Exhib, NY, 98, Cult Peruano Norteamericano, Lima, Peru, 99, Johnson Gallery, Bedminster, NJ, 2002, 2009, Steeplechase Cancer Ctr, Somerville, NJ, 2008, ISO Corp Gallery, 2010, Nat Asn Women Artists Gallery, New York, 2010, Walter Meade Gallery, Roxbury, NY, 2012; Kanagawa Prefectual Gallery, Yokahama, Japan 89; Miniature Print Biennial, John Szoke Gallery, NY, 89; Small Works, Wash Sq Gallery, NY, 92; Pac Rim Int Exhib, Univ Hilo, Hawaii, 95; Ann Audubon Artists Exhib, Salmagundi Club, NY, 95 & 97; Zimmerli Art Mus, New Brunswick, NJ 99 & 2005; Grounds for Sculpture, Hamilton, NJ, 2001; Bankgesellschaft Gallery, Berlin, Germ, 2001; Pierro Gallery, NJ, 2004; Deutsche Architektur Zentrum, Berlin, Germ, 2004; World of ElectroEtch, Ortho Gallery, 2006; Redbrick Gallery, Beverly, Mass, 2006; NJ Print Council, 2008, 2009, 2012. *Collection Arranged:* The World of ElectroEtch, Print Coun NJ, 2005. *Pos:* Pres, Women Working Home Inc, 79-90; partner, ElectroEtch Enterprises, 91-. *Teaching:* Vis lectr, Parsons Sch Design, NY, 95; lectr, Stanford Univ, Calif, 99, Holman Island Eskimo Coop, Can, 99, Int Cult Moussem, Asilah, Morocco, 2000, Howard Univ, DC, 2001, Syracuse Univ, NY, 2001; prof, Univ Alaska, Fairbanks & Juneau, Alaska, Druckwerkstatt Bethanien, Berlin, Ger, 2001, Christchurch Polytechnic Univ & U Coll, Wanganui, NZ, 2004; prof, printmaking-electroetch, San Agustin Etla, Mex, 2008. *Awards:* Merit Award, Del Bello Gallery, Toronto, Can, 90; Merit Award, Am Artists Prof League, 91; Arts & Humanities Award, Charles A Lindbergh Fund, 93; NY Central Award, Audubon Artists Exhib, 95, Art News Award, 98; NJ Artist of the Month, 8/2005; Purchase Prize, Ben Shahn Gallery, 2006; Grant for Electroetch, US Embassy, Mex, Francisco, Toledo & Conaculta; Ortho grant, Johnson Gallery Show, 2009. *Bibliog:* Edmond Andrews (auth), Patent of the week, NY Times, 5/2/92; Eileen Watkins (auth), Weekend guide of arts, Star Ledger, Newark, 11/6/92; Drew Steis (auth), News of the print world, Art Calendar, 10/93; Michele Le Tourneau (auth), News North- Printmaking Innovation in Holman, 10/4/99; Gabriella Wiener (auth), El-Sol, Lima, Peru, 11/4/99; William Zimmer (auth), New York Times, 1/24/99; Le Matin (The Morning of Sahara and Morocco-Electrical Etching: A New Non-Toxic Artistic Process, 8/15/2000; Ralph J. Bellantoni (auth), Courier News, 9/11/2002. *Mem:* Nat Asn Women Artists; Soc Am Graphic Artists; Southern Graphics Coun; Printmaking Coun NJ; Audubon Artists. *Media:* Acid Free Etching, painting, sculpting. *Res:* Co-inventor (with Omri Behr), ElectroEtch, an acid free, environmentally safe graphic etching process. *Interests:* Drawing, reading, Swimming, Gardening. *Publ:* Illusr, Jewish Holiday Book, Doubleday, 77; illusr & coauth, Women Working Home, WWH Press, 81 & 83; Environmentally safe etching, J Print World, 92; Etching & Tone Creation using Low Voltage etc, Leonardo, 93; illusr & auth, ElectroEtch, Printmaking Today, 94; ElectroEtch II, Printmaking Today, Winter, 95. *Mailing Add:* 377 River Rd Somerville NJ 08876-3554

BEHRENS, MARY SNYDER
PAINTER, ASSEMBLAGE ARTIST
b Milwaukee, Wis, Oct 26, 1957. *Study:* Mt Mary Coll, Milwaukee, 75-77; Minneapolis Coll Art & Design, 78-80; Univ Wis, Milwaukee, BFA, 82. *Work:* Pvt collections of Cinncinnati Bell Info Systems, IBM & Thriftway, Cincinnati, Ohio; Hearst Ctr Arts, Cedar Falls, Iowa; Harper Coll, Palatine, Ill; Univ Northern Iowa, Cedar Falls, Iowa; Dordt Coll, Sioux Center, Iowa. *Comn:* Rivertown Trading Corp, St Paul, Minn; Storey-Kenworthy, DesMoines, Iowa. *Exhib:* Celebrating the Stitch, Textile Arts Ctr, Chicago, 91; Newton Arts Ctr, Boston, 92; Fiber Art Int, Pittsburgh Arts Ctr, 99; New Art, Cedar Rapids Mus of Art, 2002; Visions Int, Art Ctr, Waco, Tex, 2002; solo exhib, Univ Northern Iowa, 2005; Icon Gallery, Fairfield, Iowa, 2009. *Awards:* Individual Artists Grant, Ohio Artists Coun, 88 & 90; Proj Grants, Iowa Arts Coun, 97-99 & 2002; Best of Show, Augustana Coll Art Gallery Exhib, Rock Island, Ill, 2002. *Bibliog:* Kate Mattews (auth), Fiberarts Design Book III, Larkbooks, 87; Barbara L Smith (auth), Celebrating the Stitch, Taunton Press, 91; Robbie Steinbach (auth), Lifework: Portraits of Iowa Women Artists, Lifework Arts Found, 98; NEW WORK, 05, Bobolink Books, 2005. *Mem:* mem, Nat Coll Soc; Internat Soc Assemblage and Collage Artists. *Media:* Miscellaneous Media. *Dealer:* Moberg Gallery Des Moines IA. *Mailing Add:* 2022 X Ave Dysart IA 52224-9767

BEHRENS, ROY R
EDITOR, DESIGNER, CURATOR
b Independence, Iowa, 1946. *Study:* Pond Farm Sch, with Bauhaus Potter, M Wildenhain, 64; Univ Northern Iowa, BA, 68; RI Sch Design, MA (art educ), 72. *Work:* Preuss Libr; Luther Coll; Rod Libr; Univ Northern Iowa; Waterloo Mus Art, Dordt Coll. *Exhib:* 8th Ann Ed Design, NY, 73; Commun Arts Ann, Palo Alto, 90; Print Regional, NY, 90; Soc Am Illusrs, NY, 90. *Collection Arranged:* Walter Hamady: Books, Collages and Assemblages, Univ Northern Iowa, 95; Paintings by William Cook: The Man Who Taught Gertrude Stein to Drive, Univ Northern Iowa, 96; Robert Tabor: Four Seasons on an Iowa Farm, Hearst Ctr for Arts, Cedar Falls, Iowa, 99; Art, Design and Camouflage, Univ Northern Iowa, 2000; Modern Design Icons, Univ Northern Iowa, 2001; The Bauhaus and Beyond: The Shape of Design Education, Univ N Iowa, 2005; Camouflage: Art, Science, and Popular Culture, Univ N Iowa, 2006; Envisioning Design: Education, Culture, Practice, Univ N Iowa, 2013. *Pos:* Design ed, NAm Rev, 72-92, 99-2006; ed, Ballast Quart Rev, 85-2005; chmn, Commun Design, Art Acad Cincinnati, 87-90; contrib ed, Print Mag, 92-2006; corresp ed, Leonardo, 97-; bd adv, Gestalt Theory, 98-. *Teaching:* Assoc prof art design, Univ Northern Iowa, 72-77 & Univ Wis, Milwaukee, 77-87; prof art design, Art Acad Cincinnati, 87-90; prof art design, Univ Northern Iowa, 90-. *Awards:* Res grant, 91, 93, 95, 97, 99, 03 & 05 and Donald McKay Outstanding Res Award, 95, Univ Northern Iowa; Hon Mention Throne/Aldrich Award, State Hist Soc Iowa, 98; Fac Excellence Award, Iowa Bd Regents, 96 & 2005; Fac Excellence Award, Col Humanities and Fine Arts, Univ N. Iowa, 2006; Distinguished Scholar Award, Univ N Iowa, 2009. *Bibliog:* Steve Heller & Marie Finamore (ed), Design Culture, 97, Steve Heller (ed), The Education of a Graphic Designer, 98; Steve Heller (ed), Graphic Design and Sex Appeal, Allworth, 2000; Hardy Blechman (auth), DPM: Disruptive Pattern Material: An Encyl of Camouflage, Maharishi, 2004; Dean and Geraldine Schwarz (eds), Marquerite Wildenhain and the Bauhaus: An Eyewitness Anthology, South Bear Press, 2007; E Bruce Goldstein (ed), Ames Demonstrations in Perception, Encyclopedia of Perception, Sage, 2009; Camouflage, 2009; Color & Camouflage in Ark: The StoJournal for Architects, No 4, 2010; Martin Stevens & Sami Merilaita (eds), Animal Camouflage, Cambridge, 2011; A. Post (ed), Intro in Abbott Thayer: A Beautiful Law of Nature, 2013; H Rothstein & B Whaley (eds) Now You See It, Now You Don't, in the Art and Science of Military Deception, Artech House, 2013; A Elias (ed), Khaki to Khaki (Dust to Dust), in Camouflage Cultures: Beyond the Art of Disappearance, Sidney Univ Press, 2014; Art, Design, & Brain Research, Gestalt Theory, 2013. *Mem:* Art Dirs Asn Iowa; Soc Gestalt Theory & Its Applications. *Media:* collage, digital. *Res:* Camouflage; art and perceptual psychology; history and theory of graphic design. *Interests:* Ventriloquism, Sleight of Hand, Comedy. *Publ:* Adelbert Ames, Fritz Heider and the Chair Demonstration, Gesalt Theory, 99; Revisiting Gottschaldt: Embedded Figures in Art, Architecture and Design, Gestalt Theory, 2000; False Colors: Art, Design and Modern Camouflage, Bobolink Books, 2002; Cook Book: Gertrude Stein, William Cook & Le Corbusier, Bobolink Books, 2005; Camoupedia: A Compendium of Research on Art, Architecture, and Camouflage, Bobolink Books, 2009; Ship Shape: A Dazzle Camouflage Sourcebook, Bobolink Books, 2012; Abbott H Thayers Vanishing Ducks, MAS Context, 2014. *Mailing Add:* Univ Northern Iowa Dept Art Cedar Falls IA 50614-0362

BEILIN, HOWARD
ART DEALER
Pos: Owner & dir, Howard Beilin Inc, currently. *Specialty:* Nineteenth and 20th century art with a special emphasis on European impressionists and post-impressionists; Norman Rockwell. *Mailing Add:* 510 E 85th St New York NY 10028-7430

BEIRNE, BILL
VIDEO ARTIST, CONCEPTUAL ARTIST
b Brooklyn, NY, Oct 25, 1941. *Study:* Pratt Inst, with Louise Bourgeois BFA, 68; Hunter Col, with Robert Morris, MA, 74. *Comn:* Madison Square Trapezoids, Madison Sq Park, New York, 2009. *Exhib:* Video as Attitude, Mus Fine Arts Santa Fe, NMex, 83; The Commuter, Fashion Moda, NY, 89; You Connect the Dots, Whitney Mus Am Art, NY, 91; Grief in an Age of Scientific Advance, Int Ctr of Photog, NY, 92; Something's In The Air, Sculpture Ctr, NY, 94; Frames of Reference, List Visual Arts Ctr, Mass Inst Technol, Cambridge, 97; The Gaze of the Other, Nat Ctr Contemp Art, Moscow, 99; Ru Dima's Homework, Contemp Art Ctr, Odessa, Ukraine; Timeless-Cell, PSI Contemp Art Center, NY, 2001; Tai Chi, Art 3, Valence, France, 2005; Emergency Room, PSI Contemp Art Ctr, 2007; The Parachutist, The Shed, Brooklyn, NY, 2012. *Teaching:* Video, NY Univ, 89-94; instr, Pratt Inst, 2004-. *Awards:* Nat Endowment Arts fellowship, 80; NY State Coun Arts Fell (video), 79.

Bibliog: Ann Sargent-Wooster (auth), Formerly formalists, High Performance 14, 91; John G Hanhardt (auth), Understanding television, TV Mag, 80; Elizabeth Hayt-Atkins (auth), megaloculus, 11/92. *Media:* Video Installation & Performance. *Publ:* Auth, A Pedestrian Blockade, Collation Ctr & Wittenbourn Bks, 76. *Mailing Add:* 157 E 72nd St New York NY 10021

BEKMAN, JEN
GALLERY DIRECTOR
b New York, 1970. *Study:* Hunter Coll. *Pos:* Founder, dir, Jen Bekman Gallery, New York, 2003-, Jen Bekman Projects: Hey, Hot Shot!, 2005- & 20x200, 2007-; founding ed, Unbeige design blog, formerly & Personism photog blog, currently. *Teaching:* Guest lectr, Sch Visual Arts, New York, Photographic Resource Ctr, Boston Univ, Minn Ctr Photog. *Awards:* Innovator of Yr, Am Photo, 2007; Rising Star Award, Griffin Mus Photog, 2008. *Mailing Add:* Jen Bekman Gallery 6 Spring St New York NY 10012

BELAG, ANDREA
PAINTER, GRAPHIC ARTIST
b New York, NY, Nov 21, 1951. *Study:* New York Studio Sch. *Work:* Newark Mus, NJ; Morris Mus Arts & Sci, Morristown, NJ; Jersey City Mus, NJ; Quaker Oats Corp, Chicago; NJ State Mus, Trenton. *Exhib:* Recent Paintings: Andrea Belag, NJ State Mus, Trenton, 84; Realism & Abstraction: 20th Century Art in the Newark Mus, NJ, 87; After the Fall, Aspects of Abstract Painting Since 1970, Snug Harbor Cultural Ctr, Staten Isl, NY; solo exhibs, David Beitzel Gallery, NY, 91 & Richard Anderson Gallery, NY, 92, 93 & 94; Littlejohn Contemp Gallery, NY, 96; Bill Maynes Gallery, NY, 98, 2000, 2002; Galerie Heinz Holtmann, Cologne, Ger, 98, 2000, 2002. *Teaching:* Adj lectr arts, State Univ NY, Purchase, 90-, Maryland Inst, 93, Princeton Univ, 95; instr, Sch Visual Arts, NY, 95-; resident, Bezlagio Study Ctr, Rockefeller Found. *Awards:* Fel, NJ Coun Arts, 84; Individual Fel, Nat Endowment Arts, 87; Guggenheim Fel, 99. *Bibliog:* Robert Edelman (auth), Andrea Belag, Artpress, 9/94; Barry Schwabsky (auth), Andrea Belag, Artforum, 9/94; John Yau (auth), Longing and unbridgable distance, Weidle Verlag, 98; Stephen Westfall (auth), Andrea Belag, Paintings, Calerie Heinz Holtmann, 2000; Sarah Schmerler (auth), Andrea Belag New Paintings and Works on Paper, 2002. *Media:* Oil, Gouache. *Publ:* Auth, Eight Painters, Jersey City Mus, 80; Selected Drawings, Jersey City Mus, 83. *Dealer:* Bill Maynes Gallery New York NY; Galerie Heinz Holtmann Koln. *Mailing Add:* 80 Chambers St Apt 100 New York NY 10007

BELAN, KYRA
ARTIST, WRITER
b China; US citizen. *Study:* Ariz State Univ, BFA; Fla State Univ, MFA; Fla Int Univ, EdD. *Work:* Art & Cult Ctr, Southern Regional Courthouse, Hollywood, Fla; Bass Mus Art, Miami Beach; Metro-Dade Art in Public Places, Miami, Fla; Mus Fine Art, Fla State Univ; Latin Am Art Mus, Coral Gables, Fla; Mus Am, Doral, Fla; and others. *Comn:* Drawing (color pencil), Broward Co Art in PP, Ft Lauderdale, 81; drawing, site specific sculpture, Metro-Dade Art in Pub Places, Fla, 86; and others. *Exhib:* Women's Mus, Lincoln Ctr, New York, 77; solo exhibs, The Magic Circle Series 1978-1985, Nova Univ, 85, Great Am Goddess Coatlicue, 85, In Quest of the Am Goddess Coatlicue, 86 & Sun Goddess: Emergence of Myth, 86, Broward Community Col, Great Goddess Chicomecoatl, Art & Cult Ctr, Hollywood, Fla, 87, Cosmic Goddess Chiocomecoatl/Demeter, Dupont Gallery, Washington & Lee Univ, Va, 88, Great Goddess Rhea, Malia, Crete, Greece, 88, Great Goddess Chicomecoatl/Shakti, Rim Inst, Payson, Ala, 88; Mother Earth, Mother God, The 621 Gallery, Tallahassee, Fla, 93; Mother Earth, Changing Woman, Art Gallery, Broward Col, 94; Goddess of the World, Art & Cult Ctr, Fla, 96; Celebrating Mother Earth, Rochester Inst Technol, Rochester, NY; Digital Art 98, Spirit Circle, Broward Col, 99-2000; Lady Liberty, Broward Col, 2004; Mother Earth, Broward Col, 2009; Art Takes Time Sq, NY, 2012; and others. *Pos:* Coalition Womens Art Org (CWAO); Southeastern Col Art Conference (SECAC); Col Art Asn Am (CAA). *Teaching:* Prof art & art hist, Broward Col. *Awards:* Fla Arts Coun Fel Grant, Tallahassee, 82; Barbara Deming Mem Fund Grant, 86; Int Woman of the Year, Cambridge, Eng, 97-98; Endowed Chair, BCC, 2001; Outstanding Artistic Achievement award, SECAC. *Bibliog:* Patrice Wynn (auth), The Womanspirit Sourcebook, Harper & Row, 88; Gloria Orenstein (auth), The Reflowering of the Goddess, Pergamon Press, 90; Norma Broude & Mary Garrard (auths), The Power of Feminist Art, Harry F Abrams, 94. *Mem:* Coll Art Asn Am; South Eastern Art Conference; CWAO. *Media:* Painting, Drawing Installations, Performance Art; Digital Art, Mixed Media. *Interests:* Mythology; feminist aesthetics. *Publ:* Auth, Art, Myth & Rituals, Bent Tree Press, 2007; Lucid Future, Aegina Press, 99; Madonna: From Medieval to Modern, Parkstone Press, 2001; The Virgin in Art, Barnes & Noble Press, 2006. *Mailing Add:* PO Box 275 Matlacha FL 33993

BELANGER, RON
PAINTER
b Montreal, Que, Apr 13, 1941. *Study:* Three Sch Art, 76-80; Royal Ont Mus, 79-82; Ont Coll Art, 81-88. *Work:* Mus AOAV, Chatham, Can. *Exhib:* Totem, Royal Ont Mus, Toronto, 87; Celestial Phenomenons, Mus AOAV, Chatham, Can, 89; Theodore Mus Contemp Art, 91; Reves, Relais des Epoques, Montreal, 92; Lumiere Du Ciel, Conviv Art Gallery, Vert St Denis, France, 93; Moment in Time, Connoisseur Gallery, Toronto, 93; Bleu Cid-Galleria Arte, Elemental, Cadiz, Spain, 95; Dreams, Castle San Jorge, Lisbon, Port, 97; Colour Seduc, Gallery 1313, Toronto, Can, 98; Galerie 1040, Montreal, 2005; Espace Contemporain Quebec, 2005-2006; Galerie Alternance, Montreal, 2006; Galerie Mile-End, Montreal, 2006. *Awards:* Gold Medal, Biennale de Lutece, 92; Gold Medal, Grand Prix du Soleil Levant, 92; Gold Medal, Grand Prix des Am, 92. *Bibliog:* Sam Aberg (auth), Passages et Abstraction, Dans L'Art Ed Renaissance; Louis Bruens (auth), 101 Peintres, Ed Poly Inter, 92; Guilde International art Contemporain, France, 2005. *Mem:* Cercle des Artistes du Que; Artistes Ontarios Art Visuel; Bureau de Regroupment des Peintres. *Media:* Acrylic, Watercolor. *Publ:* Cotes des Artistes Peintres et Sculpteurs, Jacques de Roussan, 90; International Art Guide, Semadiras, Paris, 92, 94; Guide Vallee, Mr Vallee, 92, 95; Le Marche de L'Art, Louis Bruens, 93; Magazin Art Guide, 96-98 & 2000-2005. *Dealer:* Gallery 1313 1313A Queen St W Toronto Can M6K 1L8; Galerie Mile-End 5345 Ave du Parc Montreal Que H2V 4G9. *Mailing Add:* Galerie Del Bello 788 King St W Toronto ON M5VIN6 Canada

BELCHER, JAQ
CONCEPTUAL ARTIST
b Australia. *Study:* Melbourne Univ, Australia, BEduc (visual arts); Univ NSW, Coll Fine Arts, MA; Nat Acad Sch Fine Arts, New York. *Exhib:* Solo exhibs, Haven Arts, New York; group exhibs include Drawing Revealed, Garrison Art Ctr, NY, 2008; Solos, Haven Arts, New York, 2008; 183rd Ann: Invitational Exhib Contemp Am Art, Nat Acad, New York, 2008. *Awards:* State Prize for Emerging Artists, Craft Victoria; Mary Hinman Carter Prize, Nat Acad Design, Dessie Greer Prize, 2008

BELDNER, LYNN KAREN
SCULPTOR
b Philadelphia, Pa. *Study:* San Francisco Art Inst, BFA, 84. *Work:* Univ Art Mus, Berkeley, Calif; St Mary's Col, Orinda, Calif; Ohio State Univ, Columbus. *Exhib:* Patricia Correia Gallery, Santa Monica, Calif, 97; Pulliam Deffenbaugh, Portland, Ore, 98; Kiddush Cup, Jewish Mus, San Francisco, 98; Graystone, San Francisco, 98; Traywick Gallery, Berkeley, Calif, 98; Traywick Contemporary, 2012. *Collection Arranged:* Microsoft; Berkeley Art Mus; Ohio State Univ; Fine Arts Mus, San Francisco. *Bibliog:* Cheryl Coon (auth), Process and memory, Art Papers, 98; Alicia Miller (auth), Process and memory, Art Week, 98. *Media:* Installation Sculpture. *Dealer:* Traywick Contemporary 895 Colusa Ave Berkeley CA 94707. *Mailing Add:* 5528 Dover St Oakland CA 94609

BELFORT-CHALAT, JACQUELINE
SCULPTOR, PAINTER
b Mt Vernon, NY, Feb 23, 1930. *Study:* With Frederick V Guinzburg, 43, Ruth Nickerson, 44, Columbia Univ, sculpture with Oronzio Maldarelli & casting with Ettore Salvatore, 47; Art Students League, life drawing with Klonis, 48; Univ Chicago, AB, 48; Fashion Inst Technol, 48-50; Royal Acad Fine Arts, Copenhagen, Denmark, 60-62. *Work:* Smithsonian Inst, Washington; Govt of Nigeria; Our Lady of Victory, NY; Everson Mus, Syracuse, NY; Jesuit Curia, Rome, Italy; Le Moyne Coll, Syracuse, NY; Georgetown Law Libr; numerous pvt collections. *Comn:* Dr Eugene J Fisher, Washington, 83; Holy Family (terra cotta relief), St Michael's Church, NY, 83; Mary (life-size mixed media), Cathedral Immaculate Conception, Syracuse, NY, 86; Heroic Size Christ, Mixed Media, Most Holy Rosary Church, NY, 92; Dolphin, life-size, Lemoyne Athletic Ctr, Syracuse, 93; and others. *Exhib:* Nat Collection Fine Arts, Washington, 63; Wash Gallery Art, 66; Everson Mus, Syracuse, NY, 72; solo exhibs, Everson Mus, 79, City Hall, 81 & Wilson Gallery, Le Moyne Coll, 83, Syracuse; Zurich, Switz, 95; and others. *Teaching:* Prof fine arts/visual arts, Founding Chair, Le Moyne Col, Syracuse, NY, 70-2009, prof emer, 2009-. *Bibliog:* P Scala (auth), Begotten not made (film), ABC-TV, Syracuse, NY, 74; Idea to Image (video), R Smith, 89. *Mem:* Int Sculpture Ctr; Am Aesthetic Soc; Soc for Art, Relig & Cult; Coll Art Asn Am; Int Womens Writers Guild; Womens Bus Owners Connection (WBOC). *Media:* All. *Res:* Application of art in a business curriculum; habits for the entrepreneur. *Interests:* Religion, philos, nature, Tai chi, literature. *Collection:* America, Europe, Africa. *Publ:* Open Sesame, City New York Bus J, 92; J Funson (dir), Artist's Dance, Cath TV, 94; Holistic or Hole, 97 & Thats Art, 98, NYSA; Idea to Image (essay), Notre Dame Univ, 2004; Joining in Joy (essay), Notre Dame Univ, 2005; Now or Never, 2006, Journey to Joy, Notre Dame Univ, 2010. *Mailing Add:* 321 Hurlburt Rd Syracuse NY 13224

BELGUM, ROLF HENRIK
FILMMAKER
b Minneapolis, Minn, Apr 1, 1965. *Study:* Univ Minn, BA, 87; Univ Calif San Diego, MFA, 92. *Work:* Driver 23 (film, 72 minutes), 98; The Atlas Moth (video, 75 minutes), 2001. *Exhib:* Pac Film Arch, Berkeley, Calif, 98; Wexner Ctr for Arts, Columbus, Ohio, 99; Nelson Atkin Mus, 2000; Calif Coll Arts & Crafts, 2000; Art Inst Chicago, 2000; Northwest Film Ctr, Portland, Oreg, 2000; Whitney Mus Am Art Biennial, NY, 2000; Showtime's Sundance Channel, Double film DVD released through Image Entertainment. *Teaching:* teacher design Art Insts Int Minn, 97-. *Awards:* Jacob Javits fel, 88; Best Film Award, Minneapolis/St Paul Int Film Festival, 98, Best Documentary feature, 2001; Cinematic Arts Award Whitney Mus Art Biennial, NYC, 2000; Best Documentary, Chicago Underground, 2001; Film Critics Choice, Village Voice, 2000. *Media:* Film, Video. *Res:* Study at The Darwin Archives, Cambridge, England. *Specialty:* The Proposition, NYC. *Collection:* Art Institute Int, Minn. *Dealer:* The Proposition, Ronald Sosinski, New York NY. *Mailing Add:* 4405 Pleasant Ave Minneapolis MN 55409

BELIAN, ISABELLE
ADMINISTRATOR
b Addis Ababa, Ethiopia. *Study:* Beirut Univ Col, BA. *Pos:* Man dir, Belian Art Ctr, Troy, Mich, currently. *Mailing Add:* Belian Art Ctr 5980 Rochester Rd Troy MI 48098

BELL, ANONDA
GALLERY DIRECTOR
b Australia. *Study:* Univ Melbourne, BA (Psychology & English), 1991; RMIT Univ, BFA (painting & printmaking), 1995; Monash Univ, MFA, 2007. *Exhib:* Chaos Theory - No Vacancy Exhibition Space, 1994; Hysteria - Monash Univ Project Space, 2007; Green Spaces - Pub Art Project, East Harlem, 2008. *Pos:* With, Bendigo Art Gallery & Nat Gallery of Victoria, Australia, formerly; dir, curator, Paul Robeson Galleries, Rutgers Univ, currently. *Awards:* Univ Melbourne Post Grad Exhib award, Australia, 97; Community Arts Fund grant, Lower Manhatten Cultural Coun, NY, 2008; Jerome Found, 2013. *Mem:* Art Table; ICOM. *Specialty:* Contemporary Art. *Mailing Add:* Paul Robeson Galleries Rutgers University 350 Dr Martin Luther King Jr Blvd Newark NJ 07102

BELL, DOZIER
PAINTER
b Lewiston, Maine, 1957. *Study:* Smith Col, BA, 81; Skowhegan Sch Painting & Sculpture, 85; Univ Pa, MFA, 86. *Hon Degrees:* Maine Coll of Art, DFA, 97. *Work:* Portland Mus Art, Maine; AT&T, NY; Farnsworth Mus, Rockland, Maine; Arthur Andersen & Co, Minneapolis, Minn; Prudential Insurance Co, Newark, NJ; United Talent Agency, Calif; and many others. *Exhib:* Solo Exhibs: Ogunquit Mus Art, Maine, 91, Bingham Kurts Gallery, Memphis, Tenn, 91, Schmidt Bingham Gallery, NY, 92, 95 & 2000, The Dissonant Heart (with poet, Wesley McNair), Portland Mus Art, Maine, 95, Schmidt Bingham Gallery, NY, 98 & Dozier Bell: Primary Themes, Lyman Allyn Art Mus, New London, Conn, 98, Chase Gallery, Boston, 99, 2000, 2005, June Fitzpatrick Gallery, Portland, 2000, Aucosisco Gallery, Portland, Maine, 98, 2002, 2004, 2005, Univ Maine, 2003, Hudson River Mus, NY, 2003, Nat Acad Sciences, Washington, DC, 2004, Univ Maine Mus Art, Bangor, 2004, DFN Gallery, NY, 2004, 2006, Aucocisco Gallery, Portland, 2007; group exhibs Farnsworth Mus Art, Rockland, Maine, 95; Changing Horizons: Landscape on the Eve of the Millennium, Katonah Mus Art, NY, 96; Secrets, Schmidt Bingham Gallery, NY, 97; group exhibs: 2001 Collectors Show, The Ark Arts Ctr, 2001, Arnot Art Mus, Elmira, NY, 2001, Chase Gallery, Boston, Mass, 2001, From Nature, AVC Contemp Arts Gallery, NY, 2002, 9/11: Prelude to an Apocalypse, Art Gallery, Univ of New Eng, Maine, 2002; Seasons of Change: Maine Women Artists and Nature, Payson Gallery, Westbrook Coll, Portland, 98; After Nature, Herter Gallery, Univ of Mass, Amherst, 99; Different Strokes, Farnsworth Mus, Rockland, Maine, 99; Photographing Maine: 1850-2000, Maine Coast Artists, Rockland, 2000; Re-Presenting Representation V, Arnot Art Mus, NY, 2001-2002; Keenly Observed, Sacred Heart Univ, Conn, 2002; Past, Present and Future: 50th Anniversary Exhibition, Ctr Maine Contemp Art, Rockport, 2002; Prelude to Apocalypse, Art Gallery Univ New England, Westbrook, Maine, 2002; Facing Reality: The Seavest Collection Contemporary Realism, Neuberger Mus Gallery, NY, 2003-2004; Images of Time and Place: Contemporary Views of Landscape, Lehman Gallery, Bronx, 2004; The Environment of Landscape: Works from the Olivia and Ellwood Straub Collection, Bates Coll Mus Art, Maine, 2005; The Figure in American Painting and Drawing 1985-2005, Ogunquit Mus Am Art, Maine, 2006; Introductions II, Stremmel Gallery, Reno, Nev, 2007; Bentley Gallery, Scottsdale, Ariz, 2007. *Awards:* Visual Artist Fel Grant, Nat Endowment Arts Grant, 87; Bellagio Study & Conf Ctr Residency, Rockefeller Found, 93; Pollock-Krasher Found Grant, 93; Fulbright Full Grant, residency, Weiman, Ger, 95; Achievement Award, Maine Coll of Art, Portland, 97; Residency at MacDowell Colony, Peterborough, NH, 2000; Pollock-Krasner Found Grant, 2003-04. *Bibliog:* Edgar Allen Beem (auth), True Native Vision: Celeste Roberge and Dozier Bell, Two of Maine's Most Important Artists, Maine Times, 12/2/88, Laurent and Bell in Black and White, Maine Times, 7/12/91 & Two June Shows in July, Maine Times, 7/16/98. *Dealer:* Aucocisco Gallery 613 Congress St Portland ME 04101; DFN Gallery 210 11th Ave 6th Fl NY 1001. *Mailing Add:* Danese Gallery 525 W 26th St 4th Fl New York NY 10001

BELL, KAREN A
EDUCATOR
b Ithaca, NY, Mar 16, 1951. *Study:* State Univ NY, Potsdam, BA, 73; Sarah Lawrence Col, MFA, 80. *Comn:* Free for All (choreography), Univ Memphis, Tenn, 94; Commadeire (choreography), Cornell Univ, Ithaca, NY, 94; I'll Take Five (choreography), comn by Peggy Gaither, Honolulu, 94; More (choreography), comn by Dori Jenks, Waikoloa, Hawaii, 94. *Pos:* Assoc dean, Col Arts, Ohio State Univ, 92-; Northeast regional coordr, Am Col Dance Festival Asn, 92-; chairperson, Dept Dance, Ohio State Univ, 95; assoc dean, Col Arts. Ohio State Univ, 1995-2001, interim dean, 2001-02, dean, 2002-. *Teaching:* Instr dance, Cornell Univ, 74-78; assoc prof dance, Ohio State Univ, 80-. *Awards:* Ohio State Univ Coll Arts Res Grant, 83 & 84; Ohio Arts Coun Individual Fel, 85. *Mem:* Am Coll Dance Festival Asn. *Media:* Choreography. *Mailing Add:* OSU Col of the Arts Off of the Dean 152 Hopkins Hall 128 No Oval Mall Columbus OH 43210

BELL, LARRY STUART
SCULPTOR
b Chicago, Ill, 1939. *Study:* Chouinard Art Inst, Los Angeles, with Robert Irwin, Richards Ruben, Robert Chuey & Emerson Woelfer, 57-59. *Work:* Nat Collection Fine Arts, Washington, DC; Mus Mod Art, New York; Solomon R Guggenheim Mus, New York; Whitney Mus Am Art, New York; Tate Gallery, London, Eng; Menil Collection, Houston, Tex; Carre d'Art, Musee d'Art Contemporain de Nimes, Fr. *Comn:* Gen Elec Corp, Gen Hg Fairfield, Conn; City of Abilene, Abilene Zoological Gardens, Tex; Myers Develop Co, San Francisco; City of Albquerque; Mus Abteiberg, Ger; The Great Eagle Corp, Hong Kong; Billingsley Co, Dallas, Tex. *Exhib:* Solo exhibs, Tampa Mus Art, Fla, 92, Galerie Rolf Ricke, Cologne, Ger, 93, Art Mus Univ NMex, Taos, 2004, Bernard Jacobson Gallery, London, 2005, Pace Wildenstein Gallery, New York, 2005, Daniel Templon Gallery, Paris, 2006, Annandale Galleries, Sydney, 2006, Frank Lloyd Gallery, Calif, 2006 & Bernard Jacobson Gallery, London, 2007, Seiller-Mosserie-Marlio Galerie, Zurich, 2008, Taos Ctr Arts, NMex, 2009, Carre d'Art Musee d'Art Contemporain de Nimes, France, 2011; Group exhibs, Beyond Geometry, LACMA, Los Angeles, Calif, 2004; The Big Nothing, Univ Pa, Inst Contemp Art, Philadelphia, Pa, 2004; Specific Objects, Mus Contemp Art, San Diego, Calif, 2004; Centro Cult Belem, Lisboa, Portugal, 2005; Las Vegas Art Mus, Nev, 2006; Centre George Pompidou, Paris, 2006; Los Angeles County Mus Art, Calif, 2006; Norton Simon Mus, Los Angeles, 2006; Smithsonian Inst, 2007; Orange Co Mus Art, Calif, 2007; Danese Gallery, NY, 2007; Frederick R Weisman Art Found, Los Angeles, 2007; Ctr Pompidou, Paris, France, 2007; Solomon R Guggenheim Mus, New York, 2007; Milwaukee Art Mus, 2009; Mus Contemp Art, Sydney, 2008; Mod Museet, Stockholm, Sweden, 2008; Walker Art Ctr, Minn, 2009; Santa Barbara Mus Art, Calif, 2009; Zwirner Gallery, New York, 2010; Ferus Gallery, Los Angeles, Calif, 2010; Venice in Venice, Nyehaus, Italy, 2011; Harwood Mus Art/UNM, Taos, NMex, 2011; Smithsonian Inst, Wash DC, 2011; Mus Contemp Art San Diego, Calif, 2011; Frederick R Weisman Art Found, Malibu, Calif, 2011; Pasadena Art Mus, Calif, 2011; Getty Ctr, Los Angeles, Calif, 2011; Carnegie Art Mus, Pittsburgh, Pa, 2012; Martin Gropius-Bau, Berlin, Ger, 2012. *Collection Arranged:* Larry Bell in Persepctive, Carre d'Art, Musee d'Art Contemporain de Nimes, 2011. *Pos:* art dir, Hotel Erwin, Venice, Calif. *Teaching:* Instr sculpture, Univ S Fla, Tampa, Univ Calif, Berkeley, Univ Calif, Irvine, 70-73, Southern Calif Inst Archit, Santa Monica, 88 & Taos Inst Arts, NMex, 89-90; instr, Chouinard, 2004-05. *Awards:* Guggenheim Mus Fel, 70; Nat Endowment for Arts Grant, 75; Gov Award for Excellence & Achievement in Arts, Visual Arts, State of NMex, 90. *Bibliog:* Peter Plagens (auth) Ferus, Art Forum Int Best of 2002, 12/2002; James Meyer (auth), Minimalism, Phaidon, 2003; Anne Goldstein (auth), A Minimal Future, Los Angeles, 2004; Christopher Knight (auth), Max Minimal, LA Times, 2004; Terry Berne (auth), In the Age of Monchrome, Art in Am, 2005; Phoebe Hoban (auth), Larry Bell, Art News, 12/07; David Pagel (auth), Taking Collages to a Dazzling Place, Los Angeles Times, 2/15/08; Douglas Fairfield (auth), Filling a Vacuum, The New Mexican. Santa Fe, NMex, 2009; BIB: Kunsthalle Bielefeld, The Great Innocents 1968, Germany; Hot Spots Rio de Janeiro/Milano/Torino/Los Angeles 1956-1969, Kunsthaus, Zurich, 2009; Kristine McKenna (auth), A Place to Begin, Ferus Gallery, 2009; Peter Schjeldahl (auth), The New Yorker, 1/15/2010; Ken Johnson (auth), NY Times, 1/14/2010; Christian Viveros-Faune (auth), Primary Atmospheres, Village Voice, 2010; Lance Esplund (auth), California Gleaming, Wall St Jour, 1/2010; Peter Plagens (auth), When the West Coast Went Pop, Wall St Jour, 7/2011; Faye Hirsch (auth), Flocked Pink Ladies on Anomaly, Art in Am, 10/2011; Leah Ollman (auth), Sensory Remix, Art in Am, 1/2012; Lynne Cooke (auth), Perfect Fit, Art Forum, 3/2012. *Media:* Light. *Mailing Add:* 4101 NDCBU Taos NM 87571

BELL, LILIAN A
SCULPTOR, CONCEPTUAL ARTIST
b London, Eng, Nov 5, 1943; US citizen. *Study:* William Morris Tech Sch, London; Linfield Coll, McMinnville, Ore, 69-70. *Work:* Portland Art Mus; Visual Art Ctr, Beer Sheva, Israel; Nexus Found Today's Art, Philadelphia; Seattle City Light, Wash; State Ore Pub Art Collection. *Exhib:* Solo exhibs, Blackfish Gallery, Portland, Ore, 90, Nat Mus, San Jose, Costa Rica, 91, Linfield Coll, Ore, 96, DNA Dreams, Georgi Velchev Mus, Varna, Bulgaria, 2004 & Portland Art Inst, Ore, 2005; group exhibs, Medium: paper, Mus Fine Arts, Budapest, 92, Int Fax Art, Int Electrographic Mus, Cuenca, Spain, 92, Outside from Within, Univ Arts, Philadelphia, Pa, 94, Libros de Artistas, Musee Nacional de Bellas Artes, Buenos Aires, Arg, 96, Boundless San Francisco Ctr Bk, 98, 3rd Int Triennial Graphic Art Mus Bitola, Macedonia, 2000 & Mus Contemp Art, Miskoki Gallery, Budapest, Hungary, 2004. *Pos:* Guest lectr, US & abroad, 73-; guest cur, Univ Ore Traveling Exhib, 80-82 & Int Fax Art Events, Enter the Electronic River & Megaliths & Office Machines, Linfield Coll, McMinnville, Ore, 94 & 96. *Awards:* Western States Arts Found Visual Arts Fel, 77; Ore Arts Comn Individual Artist Fel, 89. *Bibliog:* Juan Carlos Flores (auth), The death of the icon: The post modern paper sculpture of Lilian A Bell, Vol 4, No 2, Reflex, 90; L Robin Rice (auth), Outside from within: paper as sculpture, Hand Papermaking, Vol 9, No 1, 94; David Schlater (auth), University of Idaho Book Arts Gallery, 95. *Mem:* Artists Equity Asn (bd mem, Ore chap, 78-79); Digital Art Exchange Global Interconnectivity Initiative, Spokane, Wash; YLEM: Artists Using Sci & Technol. *Media:* Artists Books; Laser Prints. *Publ:* Contribr, The Art of Papermaking, Davis, 83; Sculpture: Technique, Form/Content, Davis, 89; Booth-Clibborn (eds), Urgent Images - The Graphic Image of the Fax, London, 94; Co-Media, Arnyekkotok Electro-Graphic Art, Budapest, Hungary, 92-2003; Arte Telematica, Itau Cultural, Sao Paulo, Brazil, 2003. *Mailing Add:* PO Box 1235 McMinnville OR 97128-1235

BELL, MARIA & WILLIAM J, JR
COLLECTOR
Pos: Pres, Bell-Phillip TV Productions & Bell Dramatic Serial Co, Los Angeles; trustee, Los Angeles County Mus Art, 2005-. *Awards:* Named one of 200 Top Collectors, ArtNews Magazine, 2008-13. *Collection:* Modern & contemporary art. *Mailing Add:* LA County Museum Art 5905 Wilshire Blvd Los Angeles CA 90036

BELL, MARY CATHERINE
ART DEALER
b Richmond, Va, Jan 1, 1946. *Study:* Wayne State Univ, Detroit, BA (art hist), 71. *Pos:* Asst sales dir, Samuel Stein Fine Arts, Chicago, 73-76; owner, Mary Bell Galleries, Chicago, 76-. *Bibliog:* Gladys Riskind (auth), Corporate art up and coming, Avenue M Mag, 6/81. *Specialty:* Contemporary American art; Unique paper paintings, sculpture and graphics; Corporate art collections. *Publ:* Auth, Art in the corporate suite, Commerce Mag, 82

BELL, PHILIP MICHAEL
ADMINISTRATOR, HISTORIAN
b Toronto, Ont, Dec 31, 1942. *Study:* Univ Toronto, BA & MA (fine art). *Collection Arranged:* W H Coverdale Collection of Canadiana, 73, Western Odyssey, Drawings by S P Hall, 74, Ouebec and Its Environs, Drawings by J P Cockburn (with catalog), 75; Goodridge Roberts: Drawings, 76; William Sawyer: Portrait Painter, 79; Life Forces: Photographs by Carol Marino, Agnes Etherington Art Ctr, 87; Pictorial Incidents: Photographs by William Gordon Shields, Agnes Etherington Art Ctr, 89. *Pos:* Cur paintings, drawings & prints, Pub Archives Can, Ottawa, Ont, 68-73; dir, Agnes Etherington Art Ctr, Queen's Univ, 73-78; visual arts officer, Ont Arts Coun, 78-79; asst dir, Pub Programs, Nat Gallery Can, 79-81, actg dir, 81; dir & chief exec officer, McMichael Can Collection, 81-86; assoc cur, Agnes Etherington Art Ctr, 86-92; dir, Carleton Univ Art Gallery, Ottawa, Ont, 92-. *Teaching:* Instr Can art hist, Queen's Univ, Kingston, Ont, 75-76; assoc prof, Carelton Univ. *Awards:* Governor-General's Award for Non-Fiction for Painters in a New Land, Can Coun, 74. *Mem:* Asn Coll & Univ Art Galleries Can (pres, 94-). *Res:* Nineteenth century & Contemp Canadian art. *Publ:* Auth, William Goodridge Roberts 1904-1974: Drawings, 76; The Last Lion, Rambles in Quebec with J P Cockburn, 78; William Sawyer: Portrait Painter, 79; Kanata: Robert Houle's Histories, 93; Colville Being Seen: The Serigraphs, 94. *Mailing Add:* c/o Carleton Univ Art Gallery 1125 Colonel By Dr Ottawa ON K1S 5B6 Canada

BELL, ROBERLEY A
SCULPTOR, EDUCATOR
Study: Univ Mass, Amherst, BFA, 1977; SUNY Alfred Univ, NY, MFA (sculpture), 1982. *Work:* Allentown Sculpture Park, Pa; Munson-Williams-Proctor Inst, Utica; DeCordova Mus; George Eastman House, Rochester; Three Rivers Park, Pittsburgh; Cummer Mus, Jacksonville, Fla; Neuberger Mus Art, Purchase, NY. *Exhib:* Solo exhibs, Southeastern Ctr Contemp Art, NC, 1983, Burchfield Art Ctr, BUffalo, 1987, Pyramid Art Ctr, ROchester, 1989, TOledo Mus ARt, 1992, East Tenn State Univ Slocumb Gallery, 1993, Brown Univ Sarah Doyle Gallery, 1994, Wright State Univ Contemp Art Mus, 1996, Allegheny Coll Meghan Gallery, 1997, Laumeier Sculpture Park, Mo, 2009, Rezan Has Mus, Instanbul, 2010; In Three Dimensions: Women Sculptors of the '90's, Snug Harbor Cult Ctr, 1995; Un/Common, Va Mus Fine Arts, Richmond, 1998; Univ Mass Fine Art Ctr Gallery, Amherst, 1999; The View From Here, State Tretyakov Gallery, Moscow, 2000; Books at Evergreen, Johns Hopkins Univ, Baltimore, 2001; Drawings by Sculptors, Black and White Gallery, Brooklyn, 2004; Beauty, Everson Mus, Syracuse, NY, 2006; Persistent Play, Cohen Fine Art Ctr Gallery, Alfred Univ, 2007; Fantastical Imaginings, Del Ctr for Contemp Arts, 2008. *Teaching:* Prof found studies & art hist, Coll Imaging Arts & Sciences, Rochester Inst Technology, NY. *Awards:* Artist-in-residence grant, NY Coun on the Arts, 1987; Residency award, Sculpture Space, Utica, 1993; Studio residency award, Int Studio Program, New York, 2000; NY Found for the Arts Fel, 2001; Pollock-Krasner Found Grant, 2001; Fulbright Grant, 2010. *Mailing Add:* c/o Pentimenti Gallery 145 N Second St Philadelphia PA 19106

BELL, TREVOR
PAINTER
b Leeds, Eng, Oct 18, 1930. *Study:* Leeds Coll Art, NDD, 49, ATD, 50. *Work:* Tate Gallery, London; Victoria and Albert Mus, London; IBM, Atlanta, NY; Rouse Company, Ohio; Shearson, Lehman, Hutton, NY; Cummer Mus, Fla; Coca-Cola, Atlanta; Arts Coun Great Britain; Contemp Art Soc, London; Balliol, St Annes, St Catherines & Trinity Col, Oxford, Eng; Am Express, Fla. *Comn:* (painting) The Art of Fugue, Phillips Collection, Holland, 64; Southern Light (painting), Lewis State Bank, Fla, 75; Fla Queen (painting), Orlando Aviation Authority, Fla, 81; painting, Tallahassee Civic Ctr, Fla, 82; IBM, NY, 85; Miami Center, Fla, 88. *Exhib:* Retrospective, Demarco, Edinburgh Arts Coun NIreland, Sheffield, Eng, 70; New Work, Corcoran Gallery, Washington & White Chapel Gallery, London, 73; Print Exhib, Tate Gallery, London, 77; Metrop Mus & Gloria Luria Gallery, Miami, 85, 89 & 91; Eves Mannes Gallery, Atlanta, 86 & 90; Cummer Mus, Jacksonville, Fla, 86; New Art Centre, London, 89; Fort Lauderdale Mus, Fla, 89; Lydon Fine Arts, Chicago, 90-92, 93, 94; Gillian Jason Gallery, London, 90; Ctr Arts, Vero Beach, Fla, 90; Ill Ctr, Chicago, 96; Tate Gallery St Ives, 96; Stephen Lacy Gallery, London, 99. *Pos:* Fla Fine Arts Coun Grants Review Panel, 79 & 80. *Teaching:* Head of painting, Winchester Col Art, United Kingdom, 66-70; chairperson art, Fanshawe Col, Ontario, 70-71; prof graduate painting, Fla State Univ, Tallahassee, 72-96, prof emer 96-. *Awards:* Int Painting Prize, Paris Biennale, 59; Gregory Fel, Univ Leeds, United Kingdom, 60-64; Fla Fine Arts Coun Individual Fel, State Fla, 81. *Bibliog:* Patrick Heron (auth), 2 Cultures: Studio Int, 70; John Elderfield (auth), Studio Int, 70; Burlington Mag, 7/2000. *Media:* Acrylic. *Dealer:* Lydon Fine Art 203 W Superior St Chicago IL 60610; Hodgell Gallery Sarasota FL 34236. *Mailing Add:* c/o Fla State Univ Mus Fine Arts Copeland & W Tenn Tallahassee FL 32306

BELL-SMITH, MICHAEL
VIDEO ARTIST
b East Corinth, Maine, 1978. *Study:* Brown Univ, BA (Art Semiotics), 2001. *Work:* Hirshhorn Mus, Washington. *Exhib:* Solo exhibs include Foxy Prod, New York, 2006, 2008, Roslyn Oxley9 Gallery, Sydney, 2007; Group exhibs include Beta Launch: Artists In Residence 02, Eyebeam, New York, 2002; Fresh Meat, CEPA Gallery, Buffalo, 2003; Infinite Fill Show, Fox Production, New York, 2004, Geo, 2005, Solar Set, 2007; EAI Presents: Multiplex 2, Smack Mellon, Brooklyn, 2005; Gif Show, Rx Gallery, San Francisco, 2006; Ghosts & Machines, Rush Arts Gallery, New York, 2006; Peace King Mother Nature: Part 1, Second Gallery, Boston, 2006; A Moving World, Dinaburg Arts, New York, 2007; Reality Bytes, Dallas Ctr Contemp Arts, 2007; Bitten, Kim Light Gallery, Los Angeles, 2008; Dreams, Hirshhorn Mus, Washington, 2008. *Dealer:* Fox Production 617 W 27th St Ground Floor New York NY 10001. *Mailing Add:* 168 Beard St Apt 4 Brooklyn NY 11231

BELLAVANCE, LESLIE
ADMINISTRATOR, EDUCATOR
Study: Tyler Sch of Art, Temple Univ, BFA (summa cum laude); Univ Chicago, MFA. *Exhib:* several solo, group and invitational exhibitions 1981-2005. *Collection Arranged:* Milwaukee Art Mus, Weber State Univ, Sachner Archive of Concrete and Visual Poetry, First Bank, Minneapolis, Madison Art Center, The Sch of the Art Institute of Chgo Library, and Private Collections. *Pos:* Fac mem, Dept Visual Art, Peck Sch of Arts, Univ Wis, 1981-2005, head Photography Program, dir grad studies in art, interim assoc dean, formerly; prof art, dir Sch of Art and Art History, James Madison Univ, Va, 2005-2010; dean, prof Sch of Art and Design, NY State Col of Ceramics, Alfred Univ, 2010-; guest curator and co-curator for a several galleries, art centers and libraries. *Awards:* Nat Endowment for Arts fellowship; Wis Arts Bd fellowship. *Publ:* Auth, analemmic, 1997. *Mailing Add:* School of Art and Design New York State College of Ceramics Alfred University 2 Pine St Alfred NY 14802

BELLOSPIRITO, ROBYN SUZANNE
PAINTER, WRITER
b Glen Cove, NY, Sept 11, 1964. *Study:* CW Post Col, Long Island Univ, BA (art hist), 86. *Work:* Nat Mus Women Arts, Washington; 1-800-FLOWERS. *Exhib:* Solo exhibs, 1-800-Flowers sponsored exhib, NY, 95 & Manhasset Pub Libr, 96, Inter Media Arts Ctr, Huntington, NY, 2002, Michael Peter Hayes Salon, East Norwich, NY, 2005; Pulse Points, Harvard Univ, Cambridge, Mass, 96; The L-Word, Eighth Floor Gallery, NY, 96; Fine Arts Mus, Long Island, NY, 96; Still Life, Islip Art Mus, NY, 96; Watchung Arts Ctr, NJ, 97-98; Barnes & Noble, NY, 98; Mask Project NY, Westbury, NY, 2000; Soc Illustrators, New York City, 2002; Group Show: Lana Santorelli Gallery, Southampton, NY, 2007; ATM Gallery, Oyster Bay, NY, 2008-09. *Pos:* Asst slide libr, Metrop Mus Art, NY, 87-88; asst-classification, Frick Art Ref Libr, NY, 88-89; ed, Exhibitioner Art Mag, 93-96; artistic dir, Sea Cliff Gallery, NY, 94. *Awards:* Award of Merit, NY State Art Teacher's Asn, 82; Puffin Found Grant (multi-media installation), 97. *Bibliog:* Geri Lipschultz (auth), From the personal to the universal, North Shore Woman's Newspaper, 98; Nicole Burdett (auth), Spiritual Reflection, Town Search, 2002; art review, New Island Ear, 2002. *Media:* Oil, Wood, Photography(digital media). *Interests:* Art, writing, photography, nature, drumming, animals, history, spirituality. *Publ:* Cover Illus, Manteia, No 15, 11/95; Creations Mag, fall 98, fall 2003; illus, Pentacle Magazine, Eng, 2/2006; illus & interview, Magickal Light, Italy, 12/2006, cover, 2008

BELL ZAHN, COCA (MARY) CATLETT
PAINTER
b Weleetka, Okla, Sept 26, 1924. *Study:* Univ Okla, BA; painting with Milford Zornes, Edith & Richard Goetz & Charles Reid; drawing with Don Coen & Robert Kaupelis. *Comn:* Oil painting, Gov Mansion, Oklahoma City, 70; three comns, Kerr Conf Ctr, 83; poster, Arts Coun Oklahoma City, 84; watercolor, Omniplex Sci & Arts Ctr, Oklahoma City, 84; Oklahoma City Tree Bank Found, 88; White House, 88. *Exhib:* 14th Ann Eight State Exhib, Okla Art Ctr, 72; 18th Ann Eight State Exhib, 76, four-man show, 77 & two-man shows, 78, 79 & 81, Okla Art Ctr, Oklahoma City; Distinguished Artists of Okla Exhib, Midwestern Gov's Conf, 77; Living Women, Living Art, Gov Gallery, 81; Nat Gov Asn Conf, Okla, 82; Diamond Jubilee Arts Festival, Okla State Capitol, 82; Smithsonian Inst, 88; and others. *Awards:* Fourth Award, 10th Ann Southwestern Watercolor Soc Regional Exhib, 73; Second Award, Watercolor 74, Okla Watercolor Asn, 74. *Bibliog:* Interview, Okla Educ TV, 79. *Mem:* Okla City Mus Art; Okla Art Guild. *Media:* Watercolor, Oil. *Mailing Add:* 6303 Christon Ct Oklahoma City OK 73118

BELOFF, ZOE
VIDEO ARTIST
b Scotland. *Study:* Studied painting & art hist at Edinburg Univ & Coll Art; Columbia Univ, MFA. *Exhib:* Mus Mod Art, NY; Pacific Film Archives; Sundance, Berlin, AFI; NY Film Festival; Beyond, Wexner Ctr Arts, Palais de Beaux Arts, Brussels & Whitney Mus Biennial, 97. *Teaching:* Instr film & digital media, City Col & New York Univ. *Awards:* First Prize, Apple Computer, 97; grant, Found Contemp Performance Art, 97. *Publ:* Contrib, Life Underwater (film) Lost (film); CD-Rom Where There There There Where (film); A Mechanical Medium (film). *Mailing Add:* 504 Grand St A35 New York NY 10002-4182

BELTRAN, ELIO (FRANCISCO)
PAINTER
b Regla Habana, Cuba, Dec 3, 1929; US citizen. *Study:* Ministry Educ, MA, 53; Fernando Aguardo Rico Sch Arts & Trades, Havana, 55; Cuyahoga Coll, Cleveland & Temple Univ, Pa, 60-; studied drawing with Prof Matilde Single, San Alejandro Sch Art, Havana; essentially self-taught. *Work:* Inst Art & Educ, NY; Bergen Mus Art & Sci, Paramus, NJ; Mus Mod Art of the Americas, Washington, DC; Jersey City Mus, NJ; Art Mus Fla Int Univ, Miami; and others. *Comn:* Oil painting, comn by C Abril, Madrid, Spain, 92; oil painting, Ed Am, Miami, 93; tribute to Mex painter Refino Tamayo (pvt comn), Princeton, NJ, 97. *Exhib:* Third Biennial Exhib, Newark Mus, NJ, 83; African Currents, Mus Contemp Hispanic Art, NY, 87; Recent Work, Paterson Mus Art, NJ, 89 & Bergen Mus Art & Sci, Paramus, NJ, 95; Cuba USA The First Generation, Mus Contemp Art, Chicago, 91; Discovery Celebration, City Mus NY, 92; First Generation Honor Guest Artist, Mus Fla Int Univ, Miami, 92; Caribbean Connections, Discovery Mus, Bridgeport, 98-99; solo exhib, Jadite Galleries, NY, 98, ARS Atelier, Gustavo Valdes Studio, 99; Tribute to Cervantes & Goya, Spain, 2005. *Pos:* Judge fel awards, NJ State Coun Art, 85-86. *Teaching:* pvt tutoring. *Awards:* Painting Award, Cinta Found Inst Art & Educ, 83; Priority Winner, NJ State Coun Arts Fel, 83-84; National Outstanding Latino Image Award, NJ Network, 95-96; Silver Medal Award, French Acad Sci, Art & Lett, 2004; Visual Artist of the Yr, Biographical Ctr Cambridge Univ, Eng, 2004; Invitational hon, Tribute to Goya, Zaragoza, Land of the Spanish artist of Spain, 2007. *Bibliog:* Many articles in newspapers & mags, 81-; Judie Dash (auth & critic), Life Style Mag, Bergen Record, 3/86; Eileen Watkins (auth), Art Section, Star Ledger, Newark, NJ, 10/9/89. *Mem:* PanAm Circle Cult. *Media:* Oil. *Publ:* Back to Cuba, Xlibris, Philadelphia, Pa. *Dealer:* xlibris.com. *Mailing Add:* 1865 S Green Dr 4A Hallandale FL 33009

BELTRAN, FELIX
PAINTER, PRINTMAKER
b Havana, Cuba, June 23, 1938; Mex citizen. *Study:* Sch Visual Arts, New York, NY, 60; New Sch, New York, 61; Am Art Sch, 62. *Work:* Stedelijk Mus, Amsterdam; Kunstgewerbemuseum, Zurich; Moderna Musset, Stockholm; Victoria & Albert Mus, Paris; Ermitage Mus, Leningrad. *Comn:* Murals, Cuban Pavilion, Osaka, 69. *Exhib:* The Art of the Book, Mus der Bilden Kunste, Leipzig, 65; The Art in Cuba, Kunstgewerbemuseum, Zurich, 65; The Art in Cuba, Lunds Konsthall, Lunds, 68; New Prints, Nat Mus, Stockholm, 68; The Art of Cuba, Museo de Arte, Chile, 71; The Art of Cuba, Stedelijk Mus, Amsterdam, 71; New Prints, Ermitage Mus, Leningrad, 73; The Art of Cuba, Altes Mus, Berlin-East, 75. *Pos:* Pres, Union de Artistas de Cuba, Havana, 77-81 & Nat Comt Int Asn Art, Havana, 79-82. *Teaching:* Titular prof fine art, Inst Superior de Arte, Havana, 75-81, Univ Autonoma Metrop, 82- & Univ Iberoamericana, 85-. *Awards:* Excellence Award, Am Inst Graphic Art, New York, 61. *Mem:* Alliance Graphic Int (nat pres, 76); Am Inst Graphic Art; Print Club, Philadelphia. *Media:* All. *Dealer:* Marcela Sotelo-Galeria Trazo-Montanas Rocallosas 508 Lomas de Virreyes Mexico 11000 DF. *Mailing Add:* Apartado De Correos M 10733 Mexico DF 06000 Mexico

BELVILLE, SCOTT ROBERT
PAINTER, EDUCATOR
b Jan 8, 1952; US citizen. *Study:* Ohio Univ, Athens, MFA, 77. *Work:* Hirshhorn Mus, Washington, DC; Ga Mus Art, Athens; Greenville Co Mus Art, SC; Chase Manhattan Bank & Walker Art Ctr, Minneapolis, Minn; First Bank Systems, Minneapolis, Minn. *Exhib:* Solo exhibs, Jus de Pomme Gallery, NY, 86, Greenville Co Mus Art, SC, 88, Thomas Barry Fine Arts, Minneapolis, 88, 91, Sandler/Hudson Gallery, Atlanta, 90, 94, 95 & 98, Kavesh Gallery, Idaho, 95 & Opelika Art Asn Gallery, Ala, 98; Thomas Barry Fine Arts, Minneapolis, Minn, 88 & 90; Sandler/Hudson Gallery, Atlanta, Ga, 89 & 91; Exploring the Canvas/Int Landscape, Gwinnett Fine Arts Ctr, Ga, 94; Talent, Alan Stone Gallery, NY, 96; Bridgewater/Lustberg Gallery, NY, 96; SEastern Ctr Contemp Art, NC, 97; Greenville Co Mus Art, SC, 97; and others. *Teaching:* Artist-in-residence, Univ Ga, Athens, 77-78, instr painting, 80-81, asst prof, 84-86; instr painting, Converse Col, Spartanburg, SC, 82-84 & 86-88; assoc prof painting, Univ Ga, Athens, 89. *Awards:* Ford Found Fel, Univ Ga, Athens, 77-78; MacDowell Colony Fel, 79; Nat Endowment Arts Grant, 83-84 & 96-97; South Carolina Individual Artist Grant in Painting, 88-89. *Mem:* Coll Art Asn. *Media:* Oil. *Dealer:* Thomas Barry Fine Art Minneapolis MN; Sandler/Hudson Gallery 1831A Peachtree Rd Atlanta GA 30309

BEMAN, LYNN SUSAN
MUSEUM DIRECTOR, HISTORIAN
b Buffalo, NY, Dec 23, 1942. *Study:* Goucher Coll, 60-62; Briarcliff Coll, BA, 75. *Collection Arranged:* Am Watercolors: 1860-1940, Trisdonn Gallery, 82; 19th Century Painters & Paintings of Rockland Co Hopper House, 84; Julian O Davidson: Am Marine Artist, Hist Soc Rockland Co, 86; Elmer Stanley Hader: The Grand View Years, Hopper House, 88; The Ice Horse-Paintings by Thomas Locker, 93; Silent Soliloquy: Paintings by Susan Reddy, 97. *Pos:* Cur, ADC Fine Art Inc, 73-78; dir, Trisdonn Gallery Ltd, 80-84 & Beman Galleries Inc, 84-89; cur, Hudson River Maritime Mus, 90, actg dir, 90-91 & exec dir, 91-93; exec dir, Amherst Mus, 94-2005; bd dir, Erie & Co Hist Fedn, 94- & WNY Asn Hist Agencies, 95-; comnr, Town Amherst Hist Preserv Comn, Western Erie Canal Heritage Corridor; exec dir, Mus Disability Hist, 2005-08. *Teaching:* Lectr art hist, hist preserv & mus studies, Empire State Coll. *Awards:* Distinguished Historian, Tappantown Hist Soc, 85; Award for Excellence Hist Agencies & Mus, Hist Serv, Lower Hudson Conf, 87; Award of Merit, Western NY Asn Hist Agencies, 98-99 & 2004-2005; Winslow Award for Outstanding Individual Achievement, Western NY Asn Hist Agencies, 2008. *Mem:* Eric Co Hist Fedn; Am Asn Mus; AASLH; MAAM; Western NY Asn Hist Agencies; Mus Asn NY. *Res:* 19th and early 20th-century American art with emphasis on the rediscovery of artists and their work; American marine art. *Publ:* Auth, George Merritt Clark: A Buffalo Bohemian, NY-Pa Collector, 83; 19th-Century Painters & Paintings of Rockland Co, NY, Ed Hopper Found, 84; Julian O Davidson (1853-1894): American Marine Artist, Hist Soc Rockland Co, 86; Julian O Davidson, A Rediscovery in American Marine Art, Sea Hist Mag, 87; Elmer Stanley Hader (1889-1973): Rediscovered American Impressionist, Nyack Publ, 89; The Diverse Career of Raphael Beck, Western NY Heritage Mag, Summer 2009

BEN-HAIM, TSIPI
CRITIC, EXECUTIVE DIRECTOR
b USSR; Am & Israeli Citizen. *Study:* Tel-Aviv Univ, BA, 79; NY Univ, MA, 83; Columbia Univ, 87. *Work:* Founded CITYarts '89 Pub Art '91 Catalog, 2002. *Exhib:* Back to Earth (sculpture; catalog), 87; Creative Process (catalog), 87; MozArt (catalog), 91; CITYarts Pieces for Peace Traveling Exhib, 2005-. *Pos:* Art critic & NY corresp, Sculpture Mag, 82-; exec & creative dir, Cityarts Inc, 89-; Art & Culture Writer Yedioth, 2006-08; Corresp Jewish Business News, 2013-. *Awards:* Am Israel Cult Found, 84; NY Univ, 81-83; Visual Arts Travel Fund, Mid-Atlantic Arts Found; Arts & Business/Partnership, Cityarts, Disney, 2009. *Bibliog:* Nicole Lyn Pesce (auth), Students Mural Dreams are Coming True, Online News, 7/04; Art Bears an Olive Branch, Daily News, 7/14/06; Christopher Casof (auth), Paint for Peace, NY Post, 7/29/06. *Mem:* Int Sculpture Ctr; Int Art Critics Asn Am; Foreign Press Asn; ArtTable. *Interests:* Visual art, traveling, reading. *Publ:* Auth, Cartier Foundation/France/Sculpture Park, 86, Isamu Noguchi - The Cullen Sculpture Park, 86 & Awakening the Brooklyn, 90, Sculpture Mag; The Creative Process (catalog) CITYArts, 89 & Charlotto Kotik, Sculpture Mag, 90; Comets, Poems by Tsipi Ben-Haim, Donna Barrett (illustr), 2009; auth, CITYarts Pieces for Peace Book, 2009

BEN-HAIM, ZIGI
SCULPTOR, PAINTER
b Bagdad, Iraq, Nov 28, 1945; US citizen. *Study:* Avni Inst Fine Arts, Tel Aviv, Israel, 66-70; Calif Coll Arts & Crafts, Oakland, 71; Calif State Univ, San Francisco, MFA, 74. *Work:* Guggenheim Mus, Jewish Mus & Brooklyn Mus, NY; Israel Mus, Jerusalem; Ghent Mus, Belg; Ursinus Col, Pa; Weisman Found. *Comn:* Wind Hunter (sculpture), Israel Mus, Jerusalem, 84; Blooming Stone (sculpture), Frederick Weisman Found, Los Angeles, 86; Rising Path (sculpture), Snug Harbor, Staten Island, NY, 86; Univ Md (sculpture), College Park, 88; Comment in the Green, Tel-Aviv, 93; Splendid Step, Tel Aviv Mus Sculpture Garden; and others. *Exhib:* Solo exhibs, Art Gallery Hamilton, Ont, 82 & Israel Mus, Jerusalem, 84, Jewish Mus Sculpture Court, 87; With Paper about Paper, Albright-Knox Gallery, Buffalo, NY, 80; Brooklyn Mus, NY, 85; Walking Field, PS 1, Long Island City, NY, 86; Am Experience, Bass Mus, Miami Beach, Fla, 86; Chelouch Gallery, Tel Aviv Israel, 93; Ann Harper Gallery, NY, 96; Stux Gallery, NY, 2003, 2005, 2007. *Awards:* Nat Endowment Arts Sculpture Grant, 84; Grant, Pollack Krasner Found, 90 & 95. *Bibliog:* Henry Scarupa (auth), Outdoor Sculpture, 11/13/87; William Zimmer (auth), The importance of imagination, NY Times, 10/9/94; Phyllis Braff (auth), Zigi Ben-Haim at Ann Harper NY, NY Times, 9/8/96. *Mem:* Int Sculpture Ctr, Washington. *Media:* Steel, Wire Mesh, Stainless Steel; Oil, Aluminum, Acrylic, Paper. *Dealer:* Stefan Stux Gallery New York City; Chelouch Gallery Tel-Aviv, Isreal. *Mailing Add:* 94 Mercer St New York NY 10012

BEN-TOR, TAMY
PERFORMANCE ARTIST
b Jerusalem. *Study:* Sch Visual Theatre, Jerusalem; Columbia Univ, MFA, New York, 2006. *Exhib:* Aco Festival, Israel, 2001; Ins Contemp Art, London, 2003; Fritz Bauer Institut, Franfurt am Main, Germany, 2004; PS1/MoMA, Queens, 2005; Mus Contemp Art, Los Angeles, 2006; Sara Meltzer Gallery, New York, 2007; Biennial Sydney, Australia, 2008; Urbis, Manchester, United Kingdom, 2009; solo exhibs, Lutke 3rd Internat Puppet Festival, Ljubljana, Slovenia, 2001, Women's Rights Evening. Tel-Aviv, 2002, Tmuna Theatre, Tel-Aviv, 2002, Zach Feuer Gallery, New York, 2006, Cubitt, London, 2006, Moderna Museet, Stockholm, 2007, Brown Gallery, London, 2008, Kunsthalle Winterthur, Switzerland, 2008 & Atlanta Contemp Art Ctr, 2009. *Awards:* Found Contemp Arts Award, New York; Art Matters Found Grant, 2008. *Mailing Add:* c/o Zach Freur Gallery 548 W 22nd St New York NY 10011

BENARCIK, SUSAN
INSTALLATION SCULPTOR
Study: Rosemont Coll, Pa, BFA; Cranbrook Acad Art, Mich, MFA. *Work:* RI Sch Design; Libr Congress; Madison Art Ctr; Oregon Art Inst; Calif State Univ. *Exhib:* Solo exhibs, Inman Gallery, Houston, 2000, NYU, 2003-04, Storage Art Space, NY, 2004, Del Ctr Contemp Art, Wilmington, 2005, Lyman ALlyn Art Mus, Conn, 2006, Brooklyn Botanic Garden, NY, 2007; Gathering Time, Cranbrook Mus, Mich, 2000; 25th Small Works, Washington Sq E Gallery, New York, 2002; Gallery in The Garden, Hawk Mountain, Pa, 2003; Toy Box, White Box Gallery, New York, 2006; Trifolia, Del Ctr for Horticulture, 2008; Viridis, Hewitt Gallery, Marymount Manhattan Coll, New York, 2009; Introductions, Moore Coll Art, Pa, 2009. *Pos:* Apprentice, Fabric Workshop, Philadelphia, 1989; artist-in-residence, Edward F Albee Found, Montauk, NY, 1994, 2003, 2006, I-Park, East Haddam, CT, 2005, Wave Hill, Bronx, NY, 2009. *Teaching:* Teaching asst, Cranbrook Acad Art, Mich, 1990; instr, Glassell Sch Art, Mus Fine Arts, Houston, 1992. *Awards:* Core Program Fel, Mus Fine Arts, Houston, 1991-92; Draper Award, Del Ctr for Contemp Art, 2006; Ctr for Emerging Visual Artists Fel, 2008; Pollock-Krasner Found Grant, 2009. *Bibliog:* Marissa Cole (auth), Artist Gives Found Materials a New Form, Wilmington News J, 6/9/2005; Caroline Tiger (auth), New Salons: Homes are Where the Art Is, The Philadelphia Inquirer, 10/17/2008. *Mailing Add:* 34 E 23rd St 4th Fl New York NY 10010

BENDER, BILL
PAINTER
b El Segundo, Calif, Jan 5, 1919. *Work:* US Air Force Acad, Colorado Springs, Colo; US Navy, Pensacola, Fla; Pentagon, Washington; Living Desert Asn, Palm Desert, Calif; Visitors Ctr, Death Valley, Calif. *Exhib:* Mountain Oyster Contemp Western Art Show, Tucson, Ariz, 72-97; High Plains Heritage Ctr, Spearfish, SDak. *Awards:* Hon Deputy Sheriff, San Bernardino Co. *Bibliog:* Ed Ainsworth (auth), Painters of the desert, Desert Mag, 60; Ed Ainsworth (auth), The Cowboy in Art, World Publ, 69; Peggy & Harold Samuels (auths), Contemporary Western Artists, 83. *Mem:* Life mem Cowboy Hall Fame, Okla; hon life mem, Mountain Oyster Club, Tucson; Death Valley 49ers Inc (hon dir); life mem, Westerners, San Dimas, Calif. *Media:* Oil, Watercolor. *Publ:* Illusr, Christmas cards, stationery & calendars, Leanin' Tree Publ, 60-98; Beckoning Desert, Prentice-Hall, 62; Day I Climb Down from the Horse, Brand Bk 3m, San Diego Westerners, 73; illusr, Paul Bailey (auth), An Unnatural History of Death Valley, 78; auth & illus, The Death Valley 49ers as I Remember Them, 98; contribr, The Story of Leanin Tree, Ed Trumble (auth), 2008. *Mailing Add:* 24887 Nat Trails Hwy Oro Grande CA 92368

BENDER, LESLIE MARILYN
PAINTER, MURALIST
b Newark, NJ, Jan 30, 1952. *Study:* Art Studies League, 1968-1974; Pratt Inst, BFA, 1975; Cobalt Studies (scenic painting), 1995. *Work:* Mus of Mod Art, NYC; Fairview Art Mus, Springville, UT; Dutchess Community Col, Hyde Park, NY; Fins Grafiske Vaerksted, Odense, Denmark; Woodstock Hist Soc. *Comn:* 3 Pub Art Murals, City Arts Workshop, NYC, 1981-1983; Artwork on Paper: Women Chefs, Culinary Inst of Am, Hyde Park, NY, 1990; Mural, St Mark African Am Episcopal Church, Kingston, NY, 1999; Mural, Vassar PEACE Project, Poughkeepsie, NY, 2001. *Exhib:* Meta Manhattan, Whitney Downtown, NYC, 1984; Committed to Print, Mus Mod Art, NYC, 1988; NY Series IX: Message to the Future, Herbert F Johnson Mus, Ithaca, NY, 1991; Hudson-Mohawk Regional, NY State Mus, Albany, NY, 1995-1996, 1998; Chrysler Mus Art, Norfolk, Va, 1998. *Pos:* Mural Artist, various projects, 1981-2006; Scenic Artist, various theaters, 1995-2006. *Teaching:* Mural project coordr, art-in-educ, various schs, 1985-2006. *Awards:* Barbara Bertoli Award for drawing, Woodstock Artists Asn, 1989; Woodstock Artists Grant to Emerging Artists, Woodstock Artists Asn, 1992; Va Center for the Arts, Artist-in-Residence Program, 2000. *Bibliog:* Deborah Wye (auth), Committed to Print, Mus Mod Art, 1990; Angry Graphics, Peregrine Books, 1991. *Media:* Oil, Oilstick, Acrylic, Pastel, Gouache, Graphite. *Dealer:* Chase-Randall Gallery Andes NY 13731. *Mailing Add:* 64 Plains Rd New Paltz NY 12561

BENDER, MAY
PAINTER
b Newark, NJ, Feb 8, 1921. *Study:* Art Students League, New York, 45-50, 68-74 & 88-90. *Work:* over 450 oils and many works on paper. *Exhib:* solo exhibs, Middlesex Co Coll, Edison, NJ, 93, Temple B'nai Jeshurun, Short Hills, NJ, 93, Tucker Anthony, Princeton, NJ, 94, Johnson & Johnson & Sons Inc, New Brunswick, NJ, 95, Gallery Swan, New York, 96, Georgian Court Coll, Lakewood, NJ, 98, Piscataway Cult Comn, NJ, 98, Northwood Univ, Cedar Hill, Tex, 2002, Full House Productions, New York, 2001-02 & Artsforum, New York, 2003; NJ Performing Arts Ctr, Newark, 2000-05; Red River Valley Mus, Tex, 2001; Omniplex Gallery, Oklahoma City, 2001; Estados Unidos de Am, Seville, Madrid, Barcelona, Spain, 2002-03; New Art Ctr, New York, 2003-05; Amsterdam Whitney Gallery, New York, 2004. *Pos:* Creative dir

& pres, May Bender Design Assocs, NY & NJ, 68-91. *Teaching:* Instr marketing & package design, Parsons, New York, 80; lectr packaging seminars, Rutgers Univ, Pratt Inst, Long Island Univ & others. *Awards:* Clio Award for packaging, Ann Awards, 77-79; Painting Award, Ridgefield Artists Asn. *Mem:* Life mem, NY Art Students League; NY Artists Equity; Visual Artists League, NJ. *Media:* Oil, Ink. *Specialty:* Painting, sculpture and photography. *Interests:* Music, Opera, etc. *Publ:* Auth, Package Design & Social Change, Am Mgt Asn, 75; Package Design in New York, Japanese Publ; numerous articles on package design. *Dealer:* New Art Center New York NY 580 Eigth Ave NYC 10018. *Mailing Add:* 332 Leedom Way Newtown PA 18940

BENEDICT-JONES, LINDA
CURATOR, PHOTOGRAPHER

b Beloit, Wis, Oct 21, 1947. *Study:* Univ Wis-LaCrosse, BA (English), 1969, Univ Lisboa, Portugal, dipl, 1972, Mass Inst Tech, MA (visual studies, Arts Coun Gr Brit Grant), 1982, Alliance Française, Paris, dipl. *Work:* Bibliotheque Nat, Paris; Mus Cantini, Marseilles, France; Mus Art Hist Fribourg, Switz; Dept Environ, London; Polaroid Collection, Cambridge, Mass. *Exhib:* Solo exhib, Madison Art Gallery, Wis, 1976; group exhibs, Imagens de Portugal, Ctr Cult Am, Lisboa, Portugal, 1973; Serpentine Gallery, London, 1978; Quiet Places, Graves Art Gallery, Sheffield, Eng, 1979; Les Autoportraits, Ctr Georges Pompidou, Paris, 1981; Contemp Self Portraiture, Hayden Gallery, Mass Inst Technol, 1983; Latvian Photo Soc, 1991. *Collection Arranged:* Botanical Works by Regional Photogrs, Silver Eye Ctr Photog, Pittsburgh, Assignment: Six Pittsburgh Photogrs, Ansel Adams: Photographs from the Polaroid Collection, Eloquent Eggs & Disintegrating Dice: Photographs by Rosamond Purcell, Luke Swank, Modernist Photogr, Dream Street: W Eugene Smith's Pittsburgh Project, Pittsburgh Revealed, Photographs Since 1850. *Pos:* Dir, Clarence Kennedy Gallery, Polaroid Corp, Cambridge, Mass, 1984-90; cur, Polaroid Collection, Cambridge, 1989-1993; adj cur, Carnegie Mus Art, Pittsburgh, 1994-97, chief cur photog, 2008-; cur, First Pittsburgh Int Youth Film Festival, 1994-95; cur educ, Frick Art & Hist Ctr, Pittsburgh, 1997-99; exec dir, Silver Eye Ctr Photog, Pittsburgh, 1999-2008. *Teaching:* Lectr photog, London Col Printing, Eng, 1977-79; instr, Mass Inst Technol Creative Photo Lab, 1981, DeCordova Mus Sch, Lincoln, Mass, 1982-83 & Northeastern Univ, Mass, 1983; lectr hist photog, Harvard, 1987. *Bibliog:* Au Coeur d'Elle Meme, Le Nouveau Photo-Cinema, Paris, 1976; Roberto Salbitani (auth), Linda Benedict-Jones Progresso Fotografico, Milan, 1978; Women on Women, Aurum Press, London, 1978. *Mem:* Soc Photog Educ. *Publ:* Auth, biography, Print Letter 24, Switz, 1979; Minor White: Contributions & Controversy, Positive, Mass Inst Technol, 1981; Lee Friedlander, Positive, Mass Inst Technol, 1982; Whither documentary? Ten contemporary British photographers, Positive, Mass Inst Technol, 1982; Black British Photographers, Spot, 1992. *Dealer:* Photogr Gallery 8-12 Gt Newport St London England. *Mailing Add:* Carnegie Mus Art 4400 Forbes Ave Pittsburgh PA 15213-4080

BENEZRA, NEAL
MUSEUM DIRECTOR, CURATOR

b Oakland, Calif, Aug 20, 1953. *Study:* Univ Calif, Berkeley, BA, 76; Stanford Univ, MA, 81; Stanford Univ, PhD, 83; Ger Acad Exchange Serv, Postgrad, 83. *Pos:* Coordr Anderson Collection, Atherton, Calif, 80-83; asst cur, Des Moines Art Ctr, 83-84; assoc cur, The Art Inst Chicago, 85-86, cur, 87-91; chief cur, Hirshhorn Mus and Sculpture Garden, Smithsonian Inst, Washington, DC, 91-96; asst dir, art and pub prog, 96; dep dir, Frances and Thomas Dittmer cur modern and contemp art, 2000-2002; dir, San Francisco Mus Modern Art, 2002-; mem, Smithsonian Coun; art adv bd mem, Univ Calif, San Francisco; art adv panel IRS, Dept Treas. *Teaching:* Vis lectr, Univ Ill, Urbana-Champaign, 88; vis assoc prof, Univ Chicago, 90. *Awards:* Grad fel, Stanford Univ, 78-81, McCloy fel in Ger art, 84-85. *Publ:* Cur exhib & auth catalogue, Robert Arneson: A Retrospective, 86, Ed Paschke: Paintings, 89, Affinities and Intuitions: The Gerald S. Elliott Collection of Contemp Art, 90, Martin Puryear, 91, Bruce Nauman, 93-94, Stephen Balkenhol, 95-96. *Mailing Add:* San Francisco Mus Mod Art 151 Third St San Francisco CA 94103

BENGLIS, LYNDA
SCULPTOR, PAINTER

b Lake Charles, La, Oct 25, 1941. *Study:* Yale Norfolk Summer Fel, 63; Newcomb Col, Tulane Univ, with Ida Kohlmeyer, Pat Trivigno, Zolton Buki & Harad Carney, BFA, 64; Brooklyn Mus Art Sch, with Rubin Tam, Max Beckman Scholar, 65. *Hon Degrees:* Hon Dr, Kansas City Art Inst, 2000. *Work:* Whitney Mus Am Art; Solomon R Guggenheim Mus; Am Mus Mod Art, NY; Hokkaido Mus Mod Art, Sapporo, Japan; Gihon Found, Dallas; and others. *Comn:* Adhesive products, Walker Art Ctr, Minneapolis, 71; Hartsfield Int Airport, Atlanta, 80; Leo W O'Brien Fed Bldg, Albany, 81; Fairmont Hotel, Denver, 82; Prudential Life Insurance Co, Parsippany, NJ, 82; Cadillac Fairview, Dallas, Tex, 84; Crocker Bldg, Crocker Properties, San Francisco, 85. *Exhib:* Painting in Relief, Whitney Mus Am Art, 80; With Paper, About Paper, Albright-Knox Art Gallery, 80; 1981 Whitney Biennial, Whitney Mus Am Art, 81; New Dimensions in Drawing, Aldrich Mus Contemp Art, 81; Developments in Recent Sculpture, Whitney Mus Am Art, 81; 74th Am Exhib, Art Inst Chicago, 82; PostMINIMALISM, Aldrich Mus Contemp Art, Ridgefield Conn; 20th Century Sculpture: Process & Presence, Whitney Mus Am Art, NY, 83; Minimalism to Expressionism: Painting & Sculpture Since 1965 from the Permanent Collection, Whitney Mus Am Art, 83; 20th Anniversary of the National Endowment for the Arts, Mus Mod Art, NY, 86; Made in India, Mus Mod Art, NY, 85; Philadelphia Collects: European & Am Art Since 1940, Philadelphia Mus Art, Pa, 86; Contemp Painting & Sculpture Galleries, Mus Mod Art, NY, 86-87; Structure to Resemblance: Work by Eight Am Sculptors, Albright-Knox Art Gallery, Buffalo, NY, 87; From the LeWitt Collection, Wadsworth Atheneum, 87; Contemp Am Collage Traveling Show, Butler Inst Am Art, 88; La Toilette de Venus: Women and Mirrors, CRG, NY, 96; solo exhibs, Gallery Chemould, Jehangir Art Gallery, Mumbai, India, 97, Univ NTex, Sch Visual Arts, Denton, 97, Galerie Michael Janssen, Cologne, Ger, 97, Forum Kunst Rottweil, Ger, 98, Contemp Art Mus, Univ SFla, Tampa, 98, Cheim & Read, NY, 98 & 99, Kappatos Gallery, Athens, Greece, 98, Weatherspoon Gallery, Univ NC at Greensboro, 2000, Toomey Turrell Gallery, San Francisco, 01, Susanne Hilberry Gallery, Ferndale, Mich, Frank Lloyd Gallery, Santa Monica, Calif, 2005, Linda Benglis: Pleated, Knotted, Poured, Locks Gallery, Philadelphia, Pa, 2006; The Edge of Chaos, Fotouhi Cramer Gallery, NY, 97; After the Fall: Aspects of Abstract Painting Since 1980, Newhouse Ctr Contemp Art, Sang Harbor Cult Ctr, NY, 97; Plastik Wurttembergischer Kunstverein, Stuttgart, Ger, 97; Laying Low, Kunstnernes Hus, Oslo, Norway, 97; Cheim & Read, NY, 97; Gravity-Axis of Contemp Art, Nat Mus Art, Osaka, Japan, 97; Hanging By a Thread, Hudson River Mus, Yonkers, NY, 97; MAI 98 Positions in Contemp Art Since the 1960's, Kunsthalle Koln, 98; Maschile Feeminile per esempio Picasso, Newton, Yoko One e, Centro Internazionale Mostre, Rome, 98; Small Paintings, Cheim & Read, NY, 98; Dreams for the Next Century, Parrish Art Mus, NY, 98; Off the Wall: Eight Contemp Am Sculptors, Asheville Art Mus, NC, 98-99; Afterimage, Drawing Through Process, Mus of Contemp Art, Los Angeles, 99; Am Acad Invitational, NY, 2000; The Am Century: Whitney Mus Modern Art, NY, 2000; Matter, Mus of Modern Art, NY, 01; Contemp Woman Artists, Univ Art Gallery, Ind State Univ, Terre Haute, Ind, 2005; Women's Work, Greenberg Van Doren, NY, 2006; The Last Time They Met, Stephen Friedman Gallery, London, UK, 2006. *Teaching:* Asst prof sculpture, Univ Rochester, 70-72; asst prof, Hunter Col, 72-73, prof, 80-81; vis prof, Calif Inst Arts, 74 & 76, Princeton Univ, 75, Dept Art, Univ Ariz, 82, fine arts workshop, Sch Visual Arts, 85-96 & Santa Fe Inst Fine Arts, 93, 94 & 96; vis artist, Kent State Univ, 77 & Skowhegan Sch Painting & Sculpture, 79; Col Santa Fe, 94 & 95; sr critic, Yale Univ, 94. *Awards:* Nat Endowment Arts Grant, 79 & 90; Olympiad Art Sculpture Park, Korea, 88; Award of Distinction, Nat Coun Art Adminr, 89; Jimmy Ernst Award, Am Acad Arts and Letters, 2006; Lifetime Achievement Award, Coll Art Asn, 2011. *Bibliog:* Robert Pincus-Witten (auth), The Frozen Gesture & Benglis, Video Medium to Media, In: Post Minimalism, 77; Doug Davis (auth), article, Art Cult, 77; Lynda Benglis (auth), interview in Ocular, summer 79; Michael Brenson (auth), Art, New York Times, 8/3/86; Lisbet Nelson (auth), Chicago's Art Explosion, Artnews, 5/87; Suzanne Muchnic (auth), Lynda Benglisat Margo Leavin, Los Angeles Times 5/22/87; Holland Cotter (auth), Lynda Benglis at Paula Cooper, Art in Am, 7/87; Phyllis Braff (auth), Faculty Show: Range of Ideas, The New York Times, 9/6/87; Robert C Morgan (auth), American Sculpture & the Search for a Referant, Arts Mag, 11/87; and many others

BENINI
PAINTER, SCULPTOR

b Imola, Bologna, Italy, Apr, 17, 1941. *Study:* Liceo Classico, Cento & Bologna, Italy, 54-57; Enalc, Assisi, Italy, 57-59; also with Morandi, 61-63; Jan Hus Univ (fine art), Hon PhD, 84. *Hon Degrees:* Univ Ark, Hon Dr Art. *Work:* Pensacola Art Ctr & Mus, Fla; Jacksonville Univ, Fla; Brevard Art Ctr & Mus, Melbourne, Fla; Empire Am, Deland, Fla; Thomas Ctr Arts, Gainesville, Fla. *Exhib:* 160 solo exhibs mus, pub insts & univ, Fla State Capitol, 84; Mid-Am Mus, Ark, 91; Ind State Univ, 91; Contemp Art Mus, Rosicrucian Mus, San Jose, 92; Carnegie Art Ctr, Calif, 93; McAllen Int Mus, Tex, 94; Duke Univ, NC, 88; Grace Mus, Abilene, 2000; Michelson Mus, 1999; plus many others. *Media:* Acrylics. *Dealer:* The Benini Galleries and Sculpture Ranch, 377 Shiloh Rd, Johnson City, TX, 78636. *Mailing Add:* 377 Shiloh Rd Johnson City TX 78636

BENJAMIN, ALICE
PAINTER, EDUCATOR

b Minneapolis, Minn, May 2, 1936. *Study:* Wellesley Coll, Mass, 54-56; Univ Minn, Minneapolis, Minn, BA, 58, BS, 63; San Francisco Art Inst, Calif, BFA, 61; State Univ NY, New Paltz, MS, 67; Instituto Allende, San Miguel d'Allende, Mex, 71; Frederic Munoz Workshops, 88-94; Studied with Joanna Coke, pastel sessions, 2010. *Work:* 3MCo, St Paul, Minn; Univ Art Mus, Northrop auditorium, Minneapolis, Minn; East Cent Reg Libr & Cambridge Ctr Anoka-Ramsey Community Col, Cambridge, Minn; Decision Systems Inc, Minneapolis, Minn; Figures, Portraits, Still Life, Spectrum Series, Braden River; Meals on Wheels, Renaissance Ctr, Bradenton, Fla, 2009; Weisman Mus Art, 2012. *Exhib:* two-person exhib, Vern Carver Gallery, Minneapolis, Minn, 93; Local Talent Revealed, Cambridge, Minn, 94; Arts in Harmony, Elk River, Minn, 96; solo exhib, There is Something About France, Iris Gallery, Lindstrom, Minn, 96 & Minn State Fair, 96; Figures, Faces, Unitarian Universalist Church Sarasota, 2006; Meals on Wheels Plus, Unity Gallery, 2007; Dancing Crane Gallery, Village of the Arts, Bradenton, Fla, 2008; Harmony Gallery, Sarasota Symphony, 2008. *Pos:* Illusr zoology dept, Univ Minn, Minneapolis, 58-60. *Teaching:* Instr elem art, Onteora Pub Schs, Boiceville, NY, 63-66; Northrop & Blake Schs, Minneapolis, Minn, 69-75; instr art, drawing, painting & design, Cambridge Ctr, Anoka-Ramsey Community Col, Cambridge, Minn, 78-92; teacher Art League of Manatee Co, Bradenton, Fla. *Awards:* Best of Show, Liberty Studios, White Bear, Minn; First Place, Art League of Manatee Co, 2001; 2nd place Art Center Manatee, 2005. *Bibliog:* Joanne Frank (auth), Alice Benjamin Boudreau, Minn Rural Artists Asn, 6/86. *Mem:* Nat League Am Pen Women; Art Ctr Manatee Art Coun of Manatee Co Graphics; Art Ctr Sarasota; Women Contemporary Artists. *Media:* Acrylic, All Graphic Media. *Res:* Expressionist and post-impressionist figures, plein air. *Interests:* Reading, philosophy, swimming, sailing. *Dealer:* The Dancing Crane Village of the Arts Bradenton Fla

BENJAMIN, BRENT R
MUSEUM DIRECTOR

b 1959. *Study:* St Olaf Coll, BA (cum laude), 1981; Rice Grad Sch Archit, 1981-83; Williams Coll, MA, 1986. *Pos:* Curatorial intern, Mus Fine Arts, Houston; dir, Head of the Charles Regatta, Cambridge, Mass, formerly; with, Mus Fine Arts, Boston, 1987-99, dep dir curatorial affairs, 1994-99; exec dir, St Louis Art Mus, 1999-. *Mem:* Asn Art Mus Dirs. *Mailing Add:* St Louis Art Mus 1 Fine Arts Dr Saint Louis MO 63110

BENJAMIN, LLOYD WILLIAM, III
HISTORIAN, ADMINISTRATOR
b Painesville, Ohio, Sept 2, 1944. *Study:* Emory Univ, BA, 66; Univ NC, Chapel Hill, PhD, 73. *Hon Degrees:* Univ Hassan II, Mohammedia, Moracco, Hon DFA. *Collection Arranged:* The Art of Designed Environments in the Netherlands (auth, catalog), 83-85. *Pos:* Chmn, Southeastern Col Art Conf, 74-76 & 80-83, dean, 83- & vpres, 91-; pres, Ind State Univ, 2000-2008. *Teaching:* Asst prof art hist, E Carolina Univ, 70-76, chmn dept, 74-76; from asst to assoc prof, Univ Ark, Little Rock, 76-82, chmn dept art, 80-, prof, 83-, dean, Col Fine Arts, 83-88, dean, Col Arts, Humanities & Soc Sci, 88-. *Mem:* Ark Endowment Humanities (bd mem & treas, 77-83); Southeastern Coll Art Conf (bd mem, 78-83); Coll Art Asn Am; Medieval Acad Am; Ind Humanities Council, 2005-2009. *Res:* Twentieth century Dutch art and environmental design. *Publ:* Auth, The art of designed environments in the Netherlands, Livability, 82 & Stichting Kunst Bedrijf, 83; coauth, Drawings from the Collection of Herbert and Dorothy Vogel, Univ Ark at Little Rock & Pa State Univ, 86; contribr, Nederlandse opdrachtgebonden kunst in de Verenigde Staten-een primeur: Harmonius Wedding of Art and Technology, Kwartaalblad Kunst en Bedrijf, 87; Public Art in the Netherlands, Dutch Heights: Art and Culture in the Netherlands, 4/88; Painting for the Delectation of the Inner Eye in Sammy Peters: Baser Matter (exhib catalog), 89; and others. *Mailing Add:* Indiana State Univ 107 Fine Arts Terre Haute IN 47809

BENNETT, DON BEMCO
PAINTER, PRINTMAKER
b McGlaughlin, SDak, Jan 8, 1916. *Study:* Univ Wash; Edison Voc Sch, Seattle; also with the late Eliot O'Hara. *Work:* Cheney-Cowles Fine Arts Mus, Spokane, Wash; Ford Motor Co Collection Am Art, Dearborn, Mich; Boise Cascade Corp, Boise, Idaho; Valley Nat Bank, Phoenix, Ariz; ITT Sheraton Corp, Boston, Mass. *Exhib:* Fourth Ann Art Exhib, Merchant Seamen UN, Corcoran Gallery, 46; US Info Agency Exhib Contemp Am Artists Worldwide Traveling Exhib, 60; Craftsman Competition, Pac Northwest Painters, Fry Mus, Seattle, 68; 15th Ann Exhib, Acad Artists Asn, Mus Fine Arts, Springfield, Mass, 64; Am Natural Hist Art Show, James Ford Bell Mus, Univ Minn, Minneapolis, 71. *Awards:* First Place in graphics, Acad Artists Asn, 64; Top Twenty Award, Craftsman Press, Seattle, 68; Second Place Award, Representational Watercolor, 28th Ann Exhib Idaho Artists, Boise Art Asn. *Media:* Watercolor, Oil; Lithography. *Publ:* Auth & illusr, Ford Times Mag, 58. *Mailing Add:* 621 Walnut St Bellevue ID 83313

BENNETT, JOHN M
WRITER, GRAPHIC ARTIST
b Chicago, Ill, Oct 12, 1942. *Study:* Wash Univ, St Louis, BA (cum laude), 64, MS, 66; Univ Calif, Los Angeles, PhD, 70. *Work:* Poetry Collection, State Univ New York, Buffalo; Rare Bks Libr, Washington Univ, St Louis; The Ohio State Univ Libr; Mus Mod Art Libr. *Exhib:* Solo exhibs, Hopkins Gallery, Ohio State Univ, 74 & 75 & Ten Window on 8th Avenue, NY, 80; Ft Hayes Gallery, Columbus, 88; Cult Arts Ctr, Columbus Sch Fine Arts, Willoughby, 90; Art Gallery, Dayton, Ohio, 91; Mus Poste, Paris, 95; Diana Lowenstein Fine Arts, Miami, Fla, 2003; Minn Center for Book Arts, Minneapolis, Minn, 2004; Gallery Oculus, Tokyo, Japan, 2004; Durban Segnini Gallery, Miami, Fla, 2005; Nave Gallery, Somerville, Mass, 2005; Gallery 324, Cleveland, Ohio, 2006; Vortice, Buenos Aires, 2007; Hopkins Gallery, Columbus, Ohio, 2007; Beinecke Rare Bode & Manuscript Libr, Yale Univ, 2008; Centro MEC, Montevideo, Urguay, 2008; Univ Autonoma Metrop, Azcapotzalco, Mexico, 2008; Main Libr, SUNY, Albany, NY, 2009. *Pos:* Cur, An American Avant Garde: First Wave, Ohio State Univ Libr, 2001, Second Wave, 2002 & Avant Writing Coll, Ohio State Univ Libr, 98. *Awards:* Artist Fel, Ohio Arts Coun, 88; Film & Pub Grants, 93-00; Artist fel, Ohio Arts Coun, 97. *Bibliog:* John McClintock (producer), Mail Art Romance (film), 82; Leonard Trawick (auth), John Bennett's Poetry of Beauty and Disgust, The Gamut, 85; Gregory V St Thomasino (auth), Reading John M Bennett, Pudding, 96; Philippe Billè, Rrêves, 2009. *Media:* Wordart. *Interests:* Wordart, concrete, visual, and experimental poetry. *Publ:* Auth, Infused, 94 & Eddy, 95, Luna Bisonte Prods, Columbus, Ohio; Prime Sway, Texture Press, 96; Ridged, Poeta, 96; coauth (with Sheila E Murphy), Milky Floor, Luna Bisonte Prods, Columbus, Ohio, 96; Mailer Leaves Ham, 99; Rolling Combers, 01; The Peel, 04; Glue, 05; Instruction Book, 06; La Mal, 06; Cantar del Huff, 06; Backwords, 07; D Rain B Loom, 07; Visual Poetry in the Avant Writing Collection, 2008; L Entes, 2008; EET, 2008; Duh Hud, 2008; Changdents, 2008; Spitting Dreams, 2008; Voclalo, with Jon cone, 2009; Las Cabezas Mayas, 2010; La Vista Gancha, 2010; Neolipic, 2010; El Humo Letrado, White Sky Books, 2011; auth, Correspondence 1979-1983 with Davi Det Hompson, Luna Bisonte Prods, 2011; Object Objet (video with Nicolas Carras), 2012; over 400 books and chapter books of poetry and other materials; The Gnat's Window, 2012; Caraarac & El Titulo Invisible, 2012; Liber X, 2012; Block, 2012; with Martin Gubbins, Tic Tac T, 2012; Olividos del Peru, 2012; with Byron Smith, Pico Mojado, 2012; Solo Dadas, 2013; Dog Font, 2013; with Nicolas Carras, Parolbjects, 2013; La Chair du Cenote, 2013. *Dealer:* Volatile Peter Huttinger PO Box 3274 Cincinnati OH 45201. *Mailing Add:* c/o Luna Bisonte Prods 137 Leland Ave Columbus OH 43214

BENNETT, PHILOMENE DOSEK
PAINTER, CERAMIST
b Lincoln, Nebr, Jan 2, 1935. *Study:* Univ Nebr, BFA, 56. *Work:* Albrecht Art Mus, St Joseph, Mo; Mushkin Art Mus, Atcheson, Kans; Nelson-Atkins Mus Art, Kansas City, Mo; Mulvane Mus, Washburn Univ, Topeka, Kans; Nat Women's Mus, Washington; Hallmark Collection, Kansas City, Mo; United Mo Bank, Kansas City; Prudential Ins, NY. *Comn:* Paintings, Crown Ctr Hotel, Kansas City, Mo, 74 & Rockhurst Coll Libr, Kansas City, Mo, 75; stained glass windows, St Charles Church, North Kansas City, Mo, 74; 14 Stations of the Cross, Conway Chapel, Rockhurst Col, Kansas City, Mo, 75. *Exhib:* Porcelains, Sheldon Mem Art Gallery, 81; Settings: Inside & Out, Jayne Gallery, Kansas City, Mo, 93, Ann Show, 99, 2000; Myth in the Making, Summerfield Gallery, Santa Fe, NMex, 94; solo show, Walnut St Gallery, Springfield, Mo, 96; Lummiere Gallery, 99; Joyce Petter Gallery, Saugatauck, Mich, 99, 2000; Gallery a, Taos, NMex, 2000. *Pos:* Mem prof bd, Mo Arts Coun, Kansas City, 79-82; art ed, Helicon Nine, 79-; mem bd, Kansas City Arts Council, 82-83. *Teaching:* Artist-in-residence painting, Rockhurst Col, 69-70, Kansas City Art Inst, 83, 84-85 & 90, Univ Ark, 89-; pvt instr painting, Bennett-Marak Studio, Kansas City, Mo, 73-96; instr & lectr, Kans Art Inst, 98. *Awards:* Purchase Award, William Rockhill Nelson Gallery Art, Kansas City, Mo, 62; Award Winner, Univ Mo-Kansas City Women's Caucus for Arts, 77; Eller Outdoor Advert & Kansas City Arts Comn Billboard Award; Alumni award, Univ Nebr; Humanitarian award, Med Missions, Kansas City, Mo, 2003. *Bibliog:* Film-interview, Johnson Co Community Col, 74; Patrick White (auth), article, New Art Examiner, 82; Don Lambert (auth), Images from heaven, Saturday Rev, 1-2/86. *Mem:* Kansas City Artists Coalition (co-founder, vpres, 75, pres, 76, prog chmn, 77); Women's Nat Caucus for Arts; Soc Contemp Photog, Kansas City, Mo; Kansas City Arts Coun (bd mem). *Media:* Acrylic, Oil; Porcelain. *Dealer:* Petter Gallery Sougatuck MI; Hallar Gallery, Kansas City, MO; Gallery Ortiz, San Antonion, TX; Gallery A, Taos, NM. *Mailing Add:* 2400 Red Bridge Terr Kansas City MO 64131

BENSIGNOR, PAULETTE (MRS PHILIP STEINBERG)
PAINTER, PRINTMAKER
b Philadelphia, Pa, Dec 4, 1948. *Study:* Pa Acad Fine Art, 70; Univ Pa, BFA, 71; Temple Univ, Tyler Sch Fine Arts, MEd, 73. *Work:* Bell Atlantic, Dupont Inc, Colonial Penn Insurance, Fidelity Bank, Green Tree Insurance, Hilton, Verizon, Wyeth, McGraw Hill Publ Co, Phila Mus Art; Delaware Mus Art. *Exhib:* Muse Gallery, 2002; Winterthur Mus, 2003; Moore Coll of Art & Design, 2003; Ester Klein Gallery, 2004; Denise Bilbro, 2004-2005; Tyme Gallery, 2006; Qbix Gallery, 2007. *Collection Arranged:* McGraw Hill Pub Co, London & NYC; Del Mus Art; First Union Bank; Verson, Hilton Corp. NYC & S Korea; Colonial Penn Ins Co; McKinsey Co, Chicago, Ill; Bell Atlantic; many others. *Teaching:* Instr fine art, Pa Sch Dist, 72-88, Gratz Col, 89-; instr, Philadelphia Acad Fine Arts, 91. *Awards:* Pacard Prize, Pa Acad Fine Arts, 70; First Prize, 82 & Edith Emerson Prize, 85, Woodmere Art Mus; Harry Rockower Mem Award, Cheltenham Ctr, Pa, 91; PW Club Award Excellence in Prints, 93; Artist Equity Merit Award, 2005. *Bibliog:* PBS Television, Documentary, Artist at Blue Hill, 1996. *Mem:* Fel of Pa Acad Fine Arts (exec bd mem, 79-81); Pa Watercolor Club; Artist Equity; Nat Drawing Soc; Nation Women's Mus, Wash, DC. *Media:* Oil. *Specialty:* fine art. *Interests:* making art. *Publ:* NY Times review, 1973; Auth, Cosmopolitan, Japan Edition, 4/92; An Illustrated Survey of Leading Contemporaries, Am Artist, 91; Phila Inquirer reviews, 2004. *Dealer:* Mary Felton New York NY; Edna Davis Thyme Gallery Havertown PA. *Mailing Add:* 124 Rockland Ave Bala Cynwyd PA 19004-1828

BENSON, MARTHA J
JEWELER, ASSEMBLAGE ARTIST
b Kansas City, Mo, July 30, 1928. *Study:* Univ Kansas City; Baker Univ, BA; spec study Kans Univ, Iowa State Univ, Utrecht, Holland, London, Eng, Glasgow & Scotland. *Comn:* Five wood-assemblage panels, St David's Episcopal Church, Ames, 75; six wood-assemblage panels, Chapel, Mary Greeley Hosp, Ames, 77; wall assemblages for pvt homes, Ames, Iowa & Fairmont, Minn; restoration of village oratorio, Bilek, Czech Repub. *Exhib:* 46th Ann Quad-State Juried Exhib, Quincy, Ill, 96; Art of Women, Iowa State Univ, 96; Refined, Nat Silversmithing Exhib, Nacogdoches, Tex, 98; Int Spice Container Exhib, Spertus Mus, Chicago, 98. *Collection Arranged:* Twelve Dutch Potters, 71; Three Chilean Printmakers, 73; Technol & the Artist-Craftsman-A Nat Crafts Exhib, 73-75; The Artists of San Miguel, 74-75; British Ceramics Today, US Tour (auth, catalog), 79; Hand, Mind & Spirit: Crafts Today (auth, catalog), 83; Women in Clay: The Ongoing Tradition (auth, catalog), 84; Legends in Fiber, 86, Textiles of Indian: A Living History, 89; and over 200 other exhibs. *Pos:* found & dir, Octagon Art Ctr, Ames, 68-91; bd dir, British Am Art Asn, Am Asn Mus, Iowa Designers Crafts Asn. *Teaching:* Prof oil painting, Iowa State Univ, 69, basic design, 72. *Awards:* Metal: Octagon Community Artists Exhib, 93; Metal: Octagon Ann (Nat), 95; First Place Metals, Iowa Crafts, MacNider Mus, 95. *Bibliog:* Annabelle Liu (auth), Martha Benson-A Profile, Craft Connection, 75. *Mem:* Am Craft Coun; Am Asn Mus; Art Mus Asn; Iowa Mus Asn; Soc NAm Goldsmiths. *Media:* Wood, Metal. *Dealer:* Mus Shop Nat Mus Women in Arts Washington DC; Octagon Shop Ames IA

BENTLEY-SCHECK, GRACE MARY
PRINTMAKER
b Troy, NY, Apr 20, 1937. *Study:* NY State Coll Ceramics Alfred Univ, BFA, 59, MFA, 60. *Work:* Knoxville Mus Art, Tenn; Portland Art Mus; Silvermine Guild Artists, New Canaan, Conn; Newport Art Mus, RI; Univ NDak, Grand Forks; Microsoft; Wheaton Coll. *Comn:* Theme: the Celebrated Worker (2 prints), RI, 92. *Exhib:* Int Print Triennial, Cracow, Poland, 94; Int Print Triennial, Bridge to the Future, Cracow, Poland & Nurnberg, Ger, 2000; solo exhibs, Newport Art Mus, RI, 2001 & Arts Exclusive Gallery, Sinsbury, Conn, 2005; At Issue: Prints and Social Commentary, Beard Gallery, Wheaton Coll, Norton, Mass, 2004; Saga Exhib in Prague, Hollar Soc Gallery, Czech Republic, 2006; The Old Print Shop at Graphic Studio, Dublin, Ireland, 2006; Saga, 71st Nat Juried Show, The Old Print Shop, NY; two-person exhib, The Old Print Shop, 2006; 25th Nat Print Biennial, Silvermine Guild Galleries, Conn, 2006; 63rd Nat Open Exhib, Am Color Print Soc, 2007; Hand-pulled prints Int XIII, StoneMetal Press Printmaking Ctr, San Antonio, Tex, 2007; Janet Turner Nat Print Competition & Exhib, Janet Turner Print Mus, California State Univ, 2008; Americas 2000 Paperworks Competition, Minot State Univ, NDak, 2008, 2009; Field Report, Boston Printmakers Members Show, 2008; Nat Juried Exhib 1st Prize, Watermark 2009, Works on Paper, 2009; 69th Mem Exhib, Am Color Print Soc, Philadelphia, 2009; New Prints 2010, Spring, Int Print Ctr, NY, 2010; Micro/Macro, Print Network of Southern New England, Newport Art Mus, 2011; Bradley Int Print and Drawing Exhib, Peoria, Ill, 2011; Place, Clemson Nat Print and Drawing Exhib, Clemson Univ, Ohio, 2011; Ann Members Exhib, Soc Am Graphic Artists, Prince St Gallery, NY, 2011; New Prints Autumn, Int Print Ctr, NY, 2011; Univ Tex Austin; Soc Am Graphic Artists Members Show, Old Print Shop, NY, 2012;

72nd Members Exhib, Am Color Print Soc, 2013; two person show, The Old Print Shop, NY, 2014; Look Again, Duxbury Art Complex, Mass; The Future: The Los Angeles Printmaking Soc Int Exchange Exhib, Scuola Int di Grafica, Venice, Italy. *Collection Arranged:* Cur, 3 Printmakers Consider the Environment, Courthouse Center for the Arts, West Kingston, RI, 2002. *Pos:* Cur, Hera Gallery, 89, 91 & 94; vis artist, Univ S Dak, Vermillion, 90-; juror, Winter Wonderland, Gallery 297, Bristol, RI; vis artist, Colby Coll, Maine, 2008. *Teaching:* N Colonie Cent Schools, 67-73; Jr high art teacher, 67-72; developed ceramics prog, Shaker Sr High Sch, 72-73; Rwerhead Jr High Sch, 63-67; collagraph wkshp, Univ Rhode Island, 2012; Collagraph Printmaking, Coleman Ctr for Creative Study, Newport Art Mus, RI, 2012; Collagraph Paintmaking, Coleman Ctr, 2013. *Awards:* Award, Nat Mem Show, Soc Am Graphic Artists; Juror's Award, 20th Ann Nat Print Exhib, Artlink, Ft Wayne, Ind, 2000; Robert Conover Mem Award, 2003; Coll NJ, Ewing; First Place in Printmaking, Newport Art Mus; Juror's Award, 25th Nat Exhib, Silvermine Guild Galleries, New Canaan, Conn, 2006; Purchase Award, Americas 2000 Paperworks Competition, Minot State Univ, NDak, 2008; 1st prize, Watermark, 2009; Stella Drabkin Mem Award, Am Color Print Society 70th Mem Exhib; Best in Show, Printmaking Newport Mem Exhib, 2011; Honorable Mention, Am Color Print Exhib, 2013. *Bibliog:* Buildings cycle reflect our own (rev), Boston Globe, 90; Ordinary is spectacular in art show (rev), Wichita Eagle, 90; The Art of Printmaking at Spring-Bull Gallery, Jour of the Print World, 2006; rev of 2-person exhib, The Old Print Shop, New York, 2006. *Mem:* Boston Printmakers; Printmaker's Network Southern New Eng; 19 on Paper; Soc Am Graphic Artists; Los Angeles Printmaking Soc; Am Color Print Soc, Art League, RI. *Media:* Collagraph, Collage. *Interests:* Cooking, German sheperds, politics, reading. *Dealer:* Elaine Beckwith Gallery 3923 Vermont Rt 30 Jamaica VT 05343; Button- Petter Gallery 161 Blue Star Saugatuck/Douglas MI 49406; The Old Print Shop 150 Lexington Ave New York NY 10016; Old Print Factory 1220 31st St Wash DC 20009; Ebo Gallery 89 Inningwood Rd Millwood NY 10546. *Mailing Add:* 63 Sassafras Trail Narragansett RI 02882

BENTON, DANIEL C
PATRON
Study: Colgate Univ, AB, 80; Harvard Univ, MBA. *Pos:* Pres, Pequot, formerly; founder, chmn, Chief Exec Officer, Andor Capital Mgt, Stamford, Conn, 2001-; trustee, Colgate Univ, James B Colgate Soc, 2001-; vpres, Whitney Mus Am Art, currently

BENTON, SUZANNE E
SCULPTOR, ART WRITER
b New York, NY, Jan 21, 1936. *Study:* Queens Col, New York, BA (fine arts), 56; studies in New York at Art Students League, Columbia Univ, NY Univ, Brooklyn Col, Brooklyn Mus Art Sch, Mus Mod Art; Silvermine Coll Art, Conn & Ctr Contemp Printmaking, Conn. *Work:* Oakton Community Col, Ill; Fulbright House, Calcutta, India; Tokyo Sch Fine Arts, Japan; Deree Pierce Col, Athens, Greece; Temple Beth-El, Houston; Cent Conn State Univ; Adams House, Harvard Univ; Am Libr, Kathmandu, Nepal; Andover-Harvard Theol Libr, Harvard Divinity Sch, Cambridge, Mass; Nat Women's Hist Park, Seneca Falls, NY; Housatonic Mus, Bridgeport, Conn; Womens Studies Ctr, Univ Conn, Storrs, Conn; St Petersburg Mus Art, Fla; Lyman Allyn Mus, New London, Conn; Oberlin Coll, Oberlin, Ohio; Susan B Anthony House, Rochester, NY; Boehringer Ingelheim Inc, Danbury, Conn; Mattatuck Mus, Waterbury, Conn; Rutgers Univ, New Brunswick, NJ; Queens Col, CUNY, Queens, NY; Allen Mem Art Mus, Oberlin Coll, Ohio; Adirondack Community Coll, Queensbury, NY; Cooper Roberts Res Inc, Calif; Eugene O'Neill Mem Theater Ctr, Waterford, Conn; Field Point Private Banking, Greenwich, Conn; The Fogg Mus, Cambridge, Mass; Allen Memorial Art Mus, Oberlin Coll, Oh; St Petersburg Mus Fine Art, Fla; Fulbright House, New Delhi, India. *Comn:* Sculptured theatre sets, Viveca Lindfor's I Am A Woman Theatre Co, 73; The Sun Queen, large-scale bronze sculpture & Throne of the Sun Queen, bronze & corten steel, Art Park, Lewiston, NY, 75; Constellation (steel & bronze), comn by Wardlaw, 83-84; Ravage: Sun (sheet bronze), 85; Secret Future Work #1, Vivien Leone Collection, 90. *Exhib:* Solo Exhibs: Touching Ritual, Wadsworth Atheneum, Hartford, Conn, 75; Art Park, Lewiston, NY, 75; Hellenic Am Union, Athens, Greece, 76; AB Condon Gallery, NY 81; Korean Cult Ctr, NY, 83; The Great Goddess, Asia Soc, NY, 87; India Int Ctr, New Delhi, 93; Nineteenth-Century Oberlin Women, Oberlin Col, 1998; Metal Masks and Sculpture, Cabot House, Harvard Univ, 2000; Bosnia and Beyond: An Artist's Commentary on Crisis, Gutman Libr, Harvard Univ, 2001; From Painting to Painting, PMW Gallery, Stamford, Conn, 2002; Spirit of Hope: A Retrospective Exhibition (with catalog), Silvermine Guild Arts Ctr, New Canaan, Conn, 2003, Royals & Robots, New Art Lab, Hong Kong, 2009, Monoprints & Encaustics, Picture This, Westport, Conn, 2009, A Bridge Between Cultures, Am Ctr, New Delhi, India, World Piece ARTHAUS, San Fran, Calif, 2011. Passage to India, Nylen Gallery, Westport, Conn, 2012, Chekhov Festival, Theatre at Schlumberger, Ridgefield, Conn, 2012; Mystic Works, Nat Mus Am Jewish Hist, 94; 19th Century Women Writers & Feminist Activities, Schlesinger Libr, 94; Journies Through Diverse Worlds: Masks, Monoprints & Secret Future Works, Gallery Contemp Art, Sacred Heart Univ, 95, Univ Dhaka, Bangladesh, 95 & Indigo Gallery, Kathmando, Nepal, 95; 19th Century Women Writers & Feminist Activists, Women's Rights Nat Hist Park, 95-; Adams House, Harvard Univ; KSI Galleries, NY, 97; Director's Choice, Silvermine Guild Artists, Conn, 98; Spirit of Hope (with catalog), Silvermine Guild Art Ctr, Conn, 2003; Face and Figure (with catalog), Queens Coll Art Ctr, 2005, Eckerd Col, St Petersburg, Fla, 2006; The Sue Eugene Mercy Gallery, Loomis Chaffee Sch, Windsor, Conn, 2007; Keeler Tavern Mus, Ridgefield, Conn, 2007; One World, Art Students League, New York, 2009; Mysterious Forces, Curtis Gallery, New Canaan, Conn, 2010; Passage to India, Nylen Gallery, Conn, 2011; Girl Group, Arthaus, San Francisco, 2011; Crossroads, Silvermine Guild Ctr for Art, New Canaan, Conn, 2011; Continuum, Ridgefield Guild of Art, Ridgefield, Conn, 2011; Threads, Ctr Contemp Printmaking, Norwalk, Conn, 2011; Duras Europos, Jewish Mus, Phila, Pa, 2011; 90th Anniv Exhib, Silvermine Guild Ctr Art, New Canoon, Conn, 2012; Panorama, Ctr Contemporary Printmaking, Norwalk, Conn, 2012; Sculpture Fest, Peter Lawrence Gallery, Gaylodsville, Conn, 2012. *Collection Arranged:* guest cur Facing East: Asian Masks & Artist Inspired By Them, Hammond Mus, North Salem, NY, 99. *Pos:* Convener-coordr, Arts Festival-Metamorphosis I, New Haven, Conn, 69-70 & Conn Feminists in the Arts, 69-72; performance artist, Mask Ritual Tales, 69-; producer-dir, Four Chosen Women, NY, 72; art consult, Xerox, 73-76; Boeringer Ingelheim Ltd, 80-83; vis artist-in-residence, Adams House, Harvard Univ, 97; artistic, managing dir Positive Power: Women Artists of Conn Forums, 99-2000; artist-in-residence Weir Farm Nat Hist Site Trust, Wilton, Conn, 1999, Artist studio, Asilah, Morocco, 2000, Byrdcliffe Artist Colony, Woodstock, NY, 2001; co-chair, Salute to Feminist Artists, Veteran Feminists of Am, held at Nat Arts Club, NY, 2003; Helene Wurlitzer Found Fel, Taos, NM, 2006; artist res, Sanscriti Kendra, New Delhi, India, 2011; Perla Artist Residency, Barcelona, Spain, 2012, Herzilya, Israel, 2012. *Teaching:* Instr welded sculpture, Brookfield Craft Ctr, Brookfield, Conn, 72-73, Norwalk Community Col, fall 80 & various art appreciation workshops, mask & all performances & workshops at cols throughout USA, 71- & 28 countries world-wide; Fulbright lectr India, 92-93; guest artist & vis lectr, Oberlin Col, 96; Mask Workshops for Women & Youth, Sarajevo & Zenica, Bosnia through UMCOR; printmaking Armory Art Ctr, 98, 2000, Ctr Contemp Printmaking, Norwalk, Conn, St Petersburg Art Ctr, 2005 & 2006; guest artist, Eckerd Coll, St Petersburg, Fla, 2005-, Custom House Studios, Westport, Co Mayo, Ireland, 2004; master printer, Monothon, Ctr Contemp Printmaking, S Norwalk, Conn, 2007; lectr, Masks as a Portal to the World, Brooklyn Mus Art, Elizabeth Sackler Ctr Feminist Art, 2009; instr, Silvermine Art Ctr, Art Students League, NY, 2011, 2012; Printmaking without a Press wkshp, Art Students League, NY, 2011, 2012, 2013. *Awards:* Fulbright Lectureship to India, 92; Thanks be to Grandmother Winifred, Travel Grant to Africa, 93; Resident Artist, Foundacion Valparaiso, Spain, 96 & 98; Hon assoc Sr Common Room, Adams House, Harvard Univ, 2003-2006; Pioneer Feminist Award, Veteran Feminists of Am, 1996; US Info Svcs grant to Bulgaria, Bangladesh, Nepal, 76, India, Yugoslavia & Greece, 77, Pakistan, Nepal, Bulgaria, 1995; to Kenya & Tanzania, 1993. *Bibliog:* LP Steitfeld (auth), Suzanne Benton's Spirit of Hope at Silvermine, Advocate & Greenwich Time, 4/12/2003; Foxy Gwynne (auth), Revisiting the High Priestess of Art, Record Rev, 7/2/2004; Adele Annesi (auth), Artist of the Ages Unmasked, Ridgefield Press, 12/22/2005; others. *Mem:* Women's Caucus Art; Silvermine Guild Artists (mem bd, 88-90); hon mem Nat Korean Sculptress Asn; Nat Asn Women Artists; Coll Art Asn; Bd mem Michael Chekhov Theatre Festival, Ridgefield, 2010. *Media:* Welded Metal, Printmaking; Performance Art, Painting. *Interests:* Art, literature, hist, mythology, anthropology, women's studies & others. *Publ:* Auth, Beyond the mask: Crossing cultural boundaries, India Mag, 94; Remembering Rachel, Chosen Tales: Stories Told by Jewish Storytellers, Jason Aronson Inc, 95; Myths, symbols and the artist, Art: A Quart J, 95; Spirit poles and flying pigs: Public art and cultural democracy in American communities (review), Women Artist News, Smithsonian Inst Press, 96; The mask, Art: A Quart J, 96; Myths & Masks, Women, Heritage & Violence, Papyros, India, 97; The Art of Welded Sculpture, Van Nostrand Reinhold, 1975; The Journey Letters of a Traveling Artist, Four Blackbirds Press, 2001; papers acquired by the Schlesinger Lib Women's Archive, Harvard Univ, Mass, 2008; Feminist artist activist papers acquired by the Women Artists Archive, Rutgers Univ, NJ. *Dealer:* Arthaus 1053 Bush St Ste 2 San Francisco CA 94109; Jso Art Assocs 6 Nappa Dr Westport CT 06880. *Mailing Add:* 22 Donnelly Dr Ridgefield CT 06877

BEN TRE, HOWARD B
SCULPTOR, DRAFTSMAN
b Brooklyn, NY, May 13, 1949. *Study:* Portland State Univ, BSA, 78; RI Sch Design, MFA, 80. *Work:* Metrop Mus Art, NY; Nat Mus Mod Art, Tokyo, Japan; Nat Mus Am Hist, Smithsonian Inst; Hirshhorn Mus & Sculpture Garden, Washington, DC; Mus Art, RI Sch Design; Los Angeles Co Mus Art, Calif; Philadelphia Mus Art, Pa. *Comn:* Fountains, Post Office Sq Park Redevelop, 91; sculpture, Toledo Mus Art, 92; plaza design & fountains, BankBoston, 98; sculpture, Hunter Mus Am Art, 98; Pedestrianization of Warrington Town Ctr (sculpture & street scheme), Eng, 98. *Exhib:* New Glass Touring Exhib, Corning Mus Glass, Metrop Mus Art & Renwick Gallery, Nat Collection Art, 78-82; Contemp Glass, Nat Mus Mod Art, Kyoto & Tokyo, Japan; Art Gallery Western Australia, Perth, 82; World Glass Now 82, Hokaido Mus Mod Art, Sapporo, Japan, 82; Four Sculptors, Jesse Besser Mus, Alpena, Mich, 82; Columns, Ornament & Sculpture, Cooper Hewitt Mus, NY, 82; solo exhibs, Hadler Rodriguez Galleries, Houston, Tex, 81, 83 & 85, Interior/Exterior, Palm Springs Desert Mus, Calif, 99-02 (traveling), Sculpting Space in the Pub Realm, The Minneapolis Inst of Arts, Minn, 2001, Charles Cowles Gallery, NY, 2001 & 02; Habatat Galleries, Detroit, 81, 83, 84, 85 & 92; Foster/White Gallery, Seattle, Wash, 81 & 83; Clarke Gallery, Lincoln, Mass, 83 & 91; Charles Cowles Gallery, NY, 85, 86, 88, 89, 91, 93 & 96; John Berggruen Gallery, San Francisco, 86; solo exhibs, Fay Gold Gallery, Atlanta, Ga, 87, Dorothy Goldeen Gallery, Santa Monica, Calif, 89 & 91, The Phillips Collection, Washington, DC, 89-90, Carnegie-Mellon Art Gallery, Pittsburgh, Pa, 90, Toledo Mus Art, 92; Brown Univ Bell Gallery, 93; Musee D'Art Moderne et D'Art Contemporain, Nice, France, 94; Cleveland Ctr Contemp Art, 95; Newport Art Mus, 96; Marsh Art Gallery, Richmond, Va, 96; Univ Art Gallery, San Diego, 98; Palmsprings Desert Mus, 99; San Jose Mus Art, 2000; Scottsdale Mus Contemp Art, 2000. *Awards:* Grant, RI State Coun Arts, 79, 84 & 90; Nat Endowment Arts Fel, 80, 84 & 90; Pell Award, 97. *Bibliog:* 100 Selected Works from the Collection, Hokkaido Mus Mod Art, 97; R Pincus (auth), Glassworks, San Diego Union-Tribune, 98; Danto, Arthur & others (auths), Howard Bentre, Hudson Hills Press, 99. *Media:* Cast Glass, Metal

BENZLE, CURTIS MUNHALL
CERAMIST, EDUCATOR
b Lakewood, Ohio, Apr 20, 1949. *Study:* Ohio State Univ, BFA, 72; Sch Am Craftmen/RIT, 73; Northern Ill Univ, MA, 78. *Work:* Nat Collection Am Art/Smithsonian Inst, White House, Washington; Int Mus Ceramics, Faenza, Italy; Cleveland Mus Art, Ohio; Los Angeles Co Mus Art, Calif; Everson Mus, Syracuse, NY. *Comn:* Governor's Art Award, State Ohio, Columbus, 82, 01. *Exhib:* Ann, Cleveland Mus Art, Ohio, 71 & 73; Int Competition Artist Ceramics, Faenza, Italy, 81

& 82; Featured Artists, Renwick Gallery/Smithsonian Inst, Washington, 83; Am Porcelain, Suntory Art Mus, Tokyo, Japan, 84; solo exhib, Indianapolis Mus Art, Indiana, 84 & Alaska Green Gallery, Tokyo, Japan, 87 & 90; Ceramic National, Everson Mus Art, Syracuse, NY, 87; Limoges Creative Porcelain Invitational, Limoges, France, 88; Contemp Porcelain, Maggie Banner Ceramics, London, Eng; and others. *Pos:* Pres, Ohio Designer Craftsman, 84-86; pres, Japan/USA Exchange Exhib, 87-91; bd dir, Am Craft Retailer Asn, 90-92; chair, Am Craft Asn/Am Craft Coun, 92-96; exec dir, Ohio Designer Craftsman, 96-. *Teaching:* Instr ceramics, Univ SC, 78-79; Savannah Col Art, 79-80; prof ceramics, CCAD, Columbus, 82-. *Awards:* Fel Grant, Nat Endowment Art Craftsmen, 80; Individual Fel Grant, Ohio Arts Coun, 81, 83, 84 & 88; Individual Fel Grant, Greater Columbus Arts Coun, 87. *Bibliog:* Hideto Satonaka (auth), Patterns & Styles, Honoho Geijutsu, 87; Engracia Schuster (auth), Curtis & Suzan Benzle, Ceramica, 1/88; MJ VanDeventer (auth), Benzle Porcelains, Art Gallery Int, 3/88. *Mem:* Ohio Designer Craftsmen; Japan/USA Exchange Exhib (pres, 87); Ohio Citizens Com Arts; Nat Coun Educ Ceramic Arts; Am Crafts Coun. *Media:* Ceramic. *Publ:* Auth, Edible Art, Sch Arts, 80; The Craft Aesthetic, Dialogue, 81; David Leach, Dialogue, 82; Earning Your Worth, Ceramics Monthly, 88; Robert Eckels, Ceramics Monthly, 93. *Dealer:* Martha Schneider Gallery Inc 2055 Green Bay Rd Highland Park IL 60035. *Mailing Add:* c/o Benzle Porcelain Co 6100 Hayden Run Rd Hilliard OH 43026

BERCOWETZ, JESSE
INSTALLATION SCULPTOR
Study: Sch Art Inst Chicago, BFA, 1996. *Exhib:* Solo exhibs, Rice Univ Gallery, Houston, 2003, Zoller Gallery, Pa State Univ, 2004, Jack the Pelican Presents, New York, 2005, Locust Projects, Miami, 2006, Derek Eller Project Space, New York, 2007, Galerie Michael Janssen, New York, 2008, Mus Contemp Art, Mass, 2009; Open House: Working in Brooklyn, Brooklyn Mus, 2004; Set and Drift, Lower Manhattan Cult Coun, New York, 2005; Mr President, Univ Albany Art Mus, NY, 2007; Don't Torture the Rotten Ducklings, Univ Wis, Milwaukee Peck Sch Arts, 2008; Town Hall Meeting, Midland Art Ctr, Ind, 2009. *Awards:* Jerome Found Fel, 2002 & 2009; Contemp Arts Grant, Henry Moore Found, 2004 ; New York Found Arts Fel, 2005 & 2009; Artists & Communities Grant, Mid Atlantic Arts Found, 2007; MacDowel Colony Fel, 2009. *Bibliog:* Jane Ingram Allen (auth), In My Room, Sculpture, 1999; Kim Levin (auth), Relentless Proselytizers, Village Voice, 2004; Roberta Smith (auth), Pent-Up and Under Gone, NY Times, 2005; Merrily Kerr (auth), Things Got Legs, Time Out New York, 2006; Christopher Miles (auth), Opening Week at LA Galleries, Los Angeles Weekly, 2008

BERDING, THOMAS G
PAINTER
b Cincinnati, Ohio, Oct 16, 1962. *Study:* Edgecliff Col, Xavier Univ, BA (fine arts), 84; RI Sch Design, MFA (painting), 87. *Work:* Hoyt Inst Fine Arts, New Castle, Pa; Lincoln Nat Corp, Mich. *Exhib:* Recent Works, In Vivo Gallery, Indianapolis, 92; Faculty Show, Ind Univ Mus, Bloomington, 93; Struct Group Invitational, New Eng Sch Art & Design, Boston, 94; Regional Artists Biennial, Ft Wayne Mus Art, Ind, 94 & 98; Depauw Univ, Greencastle, Ind, 96; Mus Fine Art, Fla State Univ, 97; Rochester Inst Technol, 98. *Pos:* Vis artist/critic, Univ Washington, State Univ of NY-Buffalo, RISD, Alfred Univ, Univ Louisville, Univ Kentucky, Rochester Inst of Technology, DePauw, and the Univ of Dayton and others; practicing studio artist, currently. *Teaching:* Vis asst prof, Dartmouth Col, Hanover, NH, 91 & Ind Univ, Bloomington, 92-93, Southwest Missouri State Univ (now Missouri State Univ), formerly; asst prof painting, Mich State Univ, E Lansing, 93-98 & assoc prof, studio art, 98-, chair Dept Art and Art History, Design, currently. *Awards:* Mid-Am Alliance/Nat Endowment Arts Fel, 90; Pollack-Krasner Found Grant, 92; Nat Endowment Art Fel in Painting, 93; CIC-Academic Leadership Fellow, Office of the Provost, Michigan State Univ, 2010. *Bibliog:* Marc Pally (auth), Winners, mid-America biennial, Nelson-Atkins Mus Art, 91; Steve Mannheimer (auth), Gallery owners aren't hiding local lights under bushels, Indianapolis Star, 9/27/92; Addison Parks (auth), The artist's conviction marked out in oil, Christian Sci Monitor, 1/26/93. *Mem:* Regular Panel Chair, presenter, mem. Services to Artists Comittee, Col Art Asn. *Media:* Oil, Canvas. *Mailing Add:* Michigan State University 113 Kresge Art Center East Lansing MI 48824-1119

BERG, MICHAEL R
PAINTER, PRINTMAKER
b Portland, Ore, May 19, 1948. *Study:* Univ Wash, independent study with Spencer Mosley, BA, 71; Ft Wright Col, Spokane, Wash, scholar prize, BFA, 72; Skowhegan Sch, scholar prize, 72. *Work:* Boulder Mus Contemp Art, Colo; Queens Mus, NY; Neuberger Mus, Purchase, NY. *Comn:* Govt guest house, Peoples Repub China, Fuzhou, 94; 20 Renwick St, comn by Daniel Lazar, NY, 95; PS 3 (wall painting), PS 3, NY, 96; The Days Now Move from Left to Right (wall painting), Denver Found, Boulder, 98; A Walk Across Continents (wall painting), comn by C & A Latham, Seattle, 98. *Exhib:* Painted Light, Reading Mus, Queens Mus, Colby Coll & Butler Inst, 83; Vis Artist Show, Sch Art Gallery, La State Univ, Baton Rouge, 85; Interior/Exterior: Architectured Fantasies, Queens Mus, Flushing Park, 87; Inaugural Exhib, Queens Mus & Bulova Corp Ctr, NY, 87; Vis Artists Show, Cantor Art Gallery, Holy Cross Col, Worchester, Maine, 87; Collaboration/Transformation, Montgomery Gallery, Pomona Coll & Fred Jones Jr Mus, Univ Okla, 97 & 98; LA Current: Armond Hammer Mus, Los Angeles, 98. *Bibliog:* John Ash (auth), A History of Backward Glances, Art Forum, summer 93; Garrit Henry (auth), Mike Berg at Elaine Kaufman, Art News, 4/96; Michael Petry (auth), A Thing of Beauty, Art & Design, Acad Group Limited, 97. *Media:* All Media. *Dealer:* Gina Fiore Salon Fine Arts 9 McDougal Alley New York NY 10012

BERG, MONA LEA
MUSEUM DIRECTOR
b Los Angeles, Calif, Nov 9, 1935. *Study:* Univ Minn, studied with Cameron Booth, BA (art hist & studio), 60; Univ Kans, 69; Univ Okla, MLS (mus studies), 86. *Collection Arranged:* Old Students & Old Masters: The School of Rembrandt, 80, The Geometric Vision: Arts of the Zulu, 83, Renaissance & Baroque Prints, 83, L'Estampe Française, 85, Japanese Packages, 86, Italian Baroque Paintings, 87 & David & Bonnie Ross Collection of Pre-Columbian Art, 88, Purdue Univ Galleries, Ind. *Pos:* Gallery coordr, Purdue Univ Galleries, Ind, 78-80, dir galleries, 80-. *Mem:* Am Asn Mus; Asn Ind Mus; Asn Coll & Univ Mus & Galleries; Midwest Mus Conf. *Res:* 19th & 20th century American art. *Mailing Add:* 231 Tamiami Tr West Lafayette IN 47906-1207

BERG, SIRI
COLLAGE ARTIST, PAINTER
b Stockholm, Sweden; US citizen. *Study:* Inst Art & Archit, Univ Brussels, Belgium, BA; Pratt Graphics Ctr, NY. *Work:* NY Univ, NY; Herbert F Johnson Mus, Cornell Univ; Guggenheim Mus; Jewish Mus, NY; Southwest Minn State Univ Col; Mod Mus, Stockholm, Sweden; others. *Comn:* Kreab-Ann Report Cover, 89-93. *Exhib:* Contemp Reflections, Aldrich Mus, Ridgefield, Conn, 76-77; The Silvia Pizitz Collection, Birmingham Mus, Ala, 80; Yeshiva Univ Mus, NY, 93-98; Thomas Nordenstad Gallery, NY, 95; McLean Gallery, Malibu, Calif, 97; Workspace, NY, 2002; Monique Goldstrom Gallery, NY, 2002; Martin Gallery, NY, 2002; Workspace, NY, 2002; William Whipple Gallery, Southwest State Univ, Marshall, Minn, 2002 & 2003; Swedish Am Mus, Chicago, 2003; Konstnarshuset, Stockholm, 2003; Berlin Kunstproject, Berlin, 2004; Color Elefante, Valencia, Spain, 2004; Pickled Art Gallery, Beijing, 2005; Nat Maritime Mus, Sydney, Australia, 2005; Year of Swedish Design, Gibson Gallery Art Mus, SUNY, Potsdam, 2006; The Grid, Reeves Contemp; Am Abstract Artists Continuum 70th Anniversary, Saint Peters Art Coll, Jersey City, NJ, 2007; Silent Auction Benefit Equality, Franklin 54 Gallery, 2007; New Art Project, NAP Smallworks Invitational, 2007, 2013; OK Harris: No Chlorophobia, NY, 2008; The Painting Center, Am Abstract Artists, 2008; Metaphor Contemp Art, Brooklyn, NY, 2008; Solo Exhibs: Walter Wickiser Gallery, NY, 97 & 99; Am Swedish Mus, Philadelphia, 99-2000; Mus of Southwest, Midland, Tex, 99; Hallwyl Mus, Stockholm, Sweden, 2000; Rutgers Univ, New Brunswick, NJ, 2000; Consul Gen Sweden, NY, 2002; Educ Testing Serv Brodsky Gallery, Princeton, NJ, 2003; Southwest Minnesota State Univ Art Mus, 2008; Gallery Franklin 54 & Projects, New York, 2008 & 09; Gallery 705, Stroudsbury, Pa, 2008, Broadway Gallery, New York,; NY Arts Venice Pavillion, 2009, NAP Small Works Invitational, 2009, 1976-1981: Redux, NY, 2012, Phases, Hionas Gallery, NY, 2013, Galleri Sander in Linkoping and Norrkoping, Sweden, 2015; It's a Wonderful Truth, Sideshow Gallery, Brooklyn, 2010; Continuing Color Abstration, Painting Ctr, New York, 2010; Pelham Art Ctr, New York, 2010; Small Works Invitational, New Art Proj, Kutztown, Pa, 2010; Am Abstract Artists Invitational, Mus Aragonses Castle, Italy, 2010; Structural Madness Virtual Gallery, Siri Berg Works on Paper; Regeneration Project, Its All About Color, The Painting Center, NY, 2012; Group Shows, Visual Play: 5 Contemp Painters, Fine Arts Gallery, Shovecreset Prep Sch, St. Petersburg, Fla, 2010; Splendor of Dynamic Structure, Celebrating 75 Yrs of the Am Abstract Artists, Herbert F Johnson Mus, Cornell U, Ithaca, NY, 2011; Streamline, C2 Fine Art, St Petersburg, Fla, 2011; AAA Celebrating 75 Anniversary, NY, 2011; Works on Paper, C2 Fine Art, St. Petersburg, Fla, 2011; 75th Anniv AAA, Berlin, Germany, 2011; Embrace Vaxjo, Emigrant Mus & Ljungberg Mus, Sweden, 2011; Twist, Southwest Minn State Univ Art Mus, William Whipple Gallery, Marshal, Minn; Sideshow Gallery, Mic Check, Brooklyn, NY; Concrete, Am Abstract Artists International 75th Anniv, Paris; AAA Print Portfolio, Brattleboro Mus and Art Ctr, Vermont, 2013; Working it Out, The Painting Ctr, NY, 2013; Gallery 705, Primarily Black and White, Stroudsburg, Pa, 2013. *Pos:* Mem fac, New Sch - Parsons Sch Design, New York, 77-. *Teaching:* instr color theory, Parson's Sch Design, 77-. *Awards:* Arts Grant, NY State Coun, Artist in Residence, 78; Top Award 8th Ann Works on Paper, Art Gallery City Univ New York, 90; artist in residence, Rutgers Univ, 2000. *Bibliog:* Brandy Schutter (auth), Mater paintings and woodcuts, Impact, 11/2002; Alan Artner (auth), Chicago Tribune, Critics Choice, 9/2003; Chicago Tribune, Visual Logic, Siri Berg, 11/2003; Video of Siri Berg, TV4, Sweden, 2004; Dan Keane (auth), Living History, Nyarts Mag, Nov-Dec/2005; Lina Otterdohl (auth), Datorkonst, PC for Alla, 2/2006; Cynthia Maris Dantzic (auth), Color Theory (bk 100 NY Painters), Schiffer Publ Ltd, 2006; Steven Phyllos (auth), The Artwork of Siri Berg, NY Arts Mag (cover & 4 pages, illus); Brett Baker (auth), Siri Berg: All about Color, Painter's Table; Eva Stenskar (auth), Nordstjernan, In Focus: Siri Berg, 2010; Francis Rothluebber (auth), One-The Mind Aware, New Momentum for Humanity, 2010; Swea Bladet, Ingrid Marie Ericsson, In the City, 2013. *Mem:* Am Scand Found; Am Scand Soc; Swedish Womens Educ Asn, NY; Am Abstract Artists. *Media:* Collage, Oil. *Interests:* film. *Publ:* Contribr, Contemp Graphic Artists, Vol III, 88; illustrator, It's Only a Paper Moon, Atlanta Jewish Times, 1/97, The Tip of the Siri Berg, Poets, Artists & Madmen, 1/97, Paper Museum, Atlanta Jour, 1/97, Tampa Review, fall 98, Summer House, Metro Source, 99, Siri Berg at The Swedish Museum, Art Matters, 11/99; Moderna Museet Nästa för Siri, SWEA; Svenska Dagbladet (largest Swedish daily newspaper), SVD Home Section, 6 pgs, cover, photos, 4/31/2012; Svenska Dagbladet, S.V.D. Homesection (6 pgs & cover/text photos). *Dealer:* Monica Gallery Konstruktiv Tendeng Stockholm Sweden; Gallery 705 Stroudsburg Pa; Gallery Franklin 54 NY 526 West 26th St #403 New York NY 10011; Hionas Gallery 124 Forsyth St New York NY 10013. *Mailing Add:* 93 Mercer Apt 6E New York NY 10012

BERG, TOM
PAINTER
b Aberdeen, SDak, Feb 10, 1943. *Study:* Univ Wyo, BA, 66, MA, 68, MFA, 72; Univ Ore, 69. *Work:* Albuquerque Mus, NMex; Palm Springs Desert Mus, Calif; Okla Arts Inst, Oklahoma City; Whitney Mus Am Art, NY; Phillip Morris Collection, NY; Mus NMex, Santa Fe. *Exhib:* Southwest '85, Mus NMex, Santa Fe; Janus Gallery, Santa Fe, 91; Cacciola Gallery, NY, 92, 94 & 96; Munson Gallery, Santa Fe, 93, 95, 97, 99,

2001 & 2003; Hidell Brooks Gallery, 2002, 2006; Victoria Price Contemp Art & Design, Santa Fe, NMex, 2005, 2007 & 2009; Wade Wilson Art, 2008 & 2011. *Pos:* Vis lectr, Univ Rochester, 71, NMex State Univ, Las Cruces, 89, Univ Okla, Norman, 89 & Okla Arts Inst, Oklahoma City, 89 & 91; artist-in-residence, Univ Maine, Augusta, 72-73 & 87, Wyo Artists in Schs Prog, 73-76 & Delta State Univ, Cleveland, Miss, 76; guest artist, Tamarind Found, Univ NMex, Albuquerque, 88 & 92. *Teaching:* Instr art, Point Park Coll, Pittsburgh, Pa, 69-71; vis lectr painting, Univ Wyo, Laramie, summer 77. *Awards:* Visual Arts Fel Wyo, Western States Arts Found, Denver, 76-77. *Bibliog:* David Bell (auth), Report from Santa Fe, Art in Am, Vol 73, No 9, 9/85; Clinton Adams (auth), New Mexico Impressions: Printmaking from 1880-1990, Univ NMex Press, Albuquerque, 91; Jan Adlman & Barbara McIntyre (auths), Contemporary Art In New Mexico; Joseph Traugott (auth), The Art of New Mexico: How the West is One, Mus NMex Press, Santa Fe, 2007. *Media:* Oil Painting. *Dealer:* Wade Wilson Art Santa Fe 409 Canyon Rd Santa Fe NMex 87501; Hidell Brooks Gallery 1910 S Blvd #130 Charlotte NC 28203; Wade Wilson Art 4411 Montrose Blvd Suite 200 Houston TX 77006. *Mailing Add:* 31 Don Bernardo Santa Fe NM 87506

BERGDOLL, BARRY
HISTORIAN, EDUCATOR
b Apr 16, 1955. *Study:* Columbia Col, BA; Cambridge Univ, Eng, BA, MA; Columbia Univ, PhD (art history), 1986. *Collection Arranged:* Co-cur, Mies in Berlin; cur, Le Panthéon: Symbole des Révolutions, 1989; cur, Les Vaudoyers: une dynastie d'architectes, Paris, 1992; cur, Home Delivery: Fabricating the Modern Dwelling, Mus Mod Art, New York, 2008; cur, Bauhaus 1919-1933 workshops for. *Pos:* Bd dirs, Archit League, NY, 1986-2004; ed bd, Architectura, Berlin and Munich, currently; exhibs ed, Jour Soc Archit Historians, 1996-2000, pres, Soc Archit Historians, 2006-; Philip Johnson chief cur archit and design, Mus Mod Art, New York, 2007-. *Teaching:* Faculty, Columbia Univ, 1986-, prof, chmn dept art hist and archeol, 2004-2006; guest prof Harvard Univ, formerly, Mass Inst Technol, formerly, Univ Canterbury, New Zealand, formerly. *Awards:* JP Morgan Berlin Prize, Am Acad Berlin, 2005; fel, Nat Inst Art Hist, Paris. *Mem:* Soc Archit Historians (pres; journal exhib ed, 1996-2000). *Interests:* mod & contemp archit. *Publ:* Contributes articles to professional journals, chapters to books; co-auth, Friedrich Weinbrenner, 1984; co-auth, Karl Friedrich Schinkel: An Architecture of Prussia, 1994 (AIA Book Award, 1995); co-auth, Mies in Berlin, 2001; co-auth, Mies van der Rohe, 2002; co-auth, The Eiffel Tower, 2002; auth, Léon Vaudoyer: Historicism in the Age of Industry, 1994; European Architecture 1750-1890, 2000; Ed, Fragments: Architecture and the Unfinished, 2006. *Mailing Add:* Dept Architecture Museum Modern Art 11 West 53 St New York NY 10019-5497

BERGE, DOROTHY ALPHENA
SCULPTOR, INSTRUCTOR
b Ottawa, Ill, May 8, 1923. *Study:* St Olaf Col, Northfield, Minn, BA, 45; Minneapolis Sch Art, BFA, 50; Ga State Univ, Atlanta, MVA, 76. *Work:* Minneapolis Inst Art, Walker Art Ctr & Univ Minn Gallery, Minneapolis; High Mus Art, Atlanta, Ga. *Comn:* Copper wall sculpture, Mead Packaging Corp, Atlanta, Ga, 66; corten steel sculptures, Great Southwest Indust Park, Atlanta, 68 & 100 Colony Sq, 69; corten steel sculpture, St Olaf Col, comn by Mrs John Oslund, Northfield, Minn, 75; aluminum wall sculpture, Metrop Atlanta Rapid Transit Authority, 80. *Exhib:* Minn Biennial, Minneapolis Inst Art, 54; Recent Sculpture USA, Mus Mod Art, NY, 57; 16 Younger Minn Artists, Walker Art Ctr, Minneapolis, 58; one-person shows, Walker Art Ctr, 59 & High Mus Art, Atlanta, 68; Ga Artists 1, 2 & 6, High Mus Art, Atlanta, 71, 72 & 79. *Pos:* Registr, Walker Art Ctr, Minneapolis, 54-60; coordr circulating exhibs, Mus Mod Art, NY, 60-63. *Teaching:* Instr sculpture, drawing & ceramics, St Olaf Col, Northfield, Minn, 46-48; artist-in-residence sculpture, Nat Endowment Arts, Ga, 71-72. *Awards:* Purchase Award, Ford Found Prog Humanities & Arts, 60. *Media:* Welded Metal. *Dealer:* Heath Gallery 416 E Paces Ferry Rd NE Atlanta GA 30309

BERGEN, JEFFREY B
ART DEALER, DIRECTOR
b New York, NY, Jan 14, 1953. *Study:* Antioch Coll, Ohio. *Pos:* Owner & dir, ACA Galleries, New York, currently; bd mem, NY Open Ctr. *Mem:* Art Dealers Asn Am; Threshold Found; Social Venture Network. *Specialty:* est 1932, ACA specializes in modern and contemporary, American, and European art. *Interests:* American impressionism, Stieglitz Circle, Ashcan Sch, 14th St Sch, Regionalism, WPA, American Abstraction, Social Realism, Abstract Expressionism. *Mailing Add:* ACA Galleries 529 West 20th St New York NY 10011

BERGER, EMILY
PAINTER
Study: Int Ctr Photog; Skowhegan Sch Painting & Sculpture; Brown Univ, BA (art); Columbia Univ, MFA (painting). *Exhib:* Solo exhibs include Hunt-Cavanagh Gallery, Providence Coll, RI, 1984, The New Prospect, Brooklyn, 1987, Painting Ctr, NY, 2008; two-person show with Iona Kleinhaut, Painting Ctr, NY, 2005; group exhibs include Ann Invitational, AIR Gallery, NY, 1984, 1985; Nature as Image, Org Independent Artists, NY, 1984; Artist in the Marketplace, Bronx Mus Arts, NY, 1985, A Decade in the Marketplace, 1990; Invitational, Soho20 Gallery, NY, 1998, Artists' Choice, 2000; From Postwar to Postmodernism, Columbia Univ, NY, 2006; 183rd Ann: Invitational Exhib Contemp Am Art, Nat Acad, New York, 2008. *Collection Arranged:* Nature Abstract, Painting Ctr, New York, 2004. *Pos:* Prog coord, Children's Art Carnival, New York, 1985-87, prog dir, 1987-89, consultant, 1989-93; educ coord, Lehman Coll Art Gallery, 1989-90. *Teaching:* Asst prof art educ, Pratt Inst, New York, 1990-91; instr, educ dept, Metrop Mus Art, 1993-. *Awards:* John Hultburg Mem Prize, Nat Acad, 2008. *Mem:* Painting Ctr; Am Abstract Artists. *Mailing Add:* c/o Painting Ctr 547 W 27th St Suite 500 New York NY 10001

BERGER, JERRY ALLEN
DIRECTOR, CURATOR
b Buffalo, Wyo, Oct 8, 1943. *Study:* Univ Wyo, BA, 65, BA (art), 71, MA (art hist), 72. *Pos:* Cur collections, Univ Wyo Art Mus, Laramie, 72-88, actg dir, 84-86, asst dir, 80-83 & 87-88; dir, Springfield Art Mus, Springfield, Mo, 88-2011. *Mem:* The Nat Arts Club

BERGER, MAURICE
CULTURAL HISTORIAN, CRITIC
b New York, NY, May 22, 1956. *Study:* Hunter Col, City Univ New York, BA (Thomas Hunter Scholar), 78; City Univ New York Grad Ctr, PhD, 88. *Exhib:* Threshold, Whitney Mus Am Art, 2012. *Pos:* Asst to dir exhibs, City Univ NY Grad Ctr, 81-; cur, Hunter Col Art Gallery, 83-85, cur, spec projects, 85-; jr fel, NY Inst Humanities, 83-85; cur, Univ Md, Baltimore Co, 92-; Res prof, chief cur, Center for Art, Design & Visual Cult, Univ Md, Baltimore Co, 2006-. *Teaching:* Adj lectr art hist, Hunter Col, NY, 80-84; vis lectr, Queens Col, City Univ NY, 81; vis asst prof, Hunter Col, City Univ, NY, 85-91; vis lectr, Yale Univ, 87; vis lectr, State Univ NY, Stony Brook, 89 & Rutgers Univ, 90; sr fel, New Sch Social Res, 94-. *Awards:* Finalist, Horace Mann Bond Book award, Harvard Univ; Hon Mention, Gustavus Myers Book Award, Boston Univ; Alumni Achievement Award, City Univ NY Grad Ctr; Best Thematic Exhib in NY, Int Asn Art Critics, Am Section, 2008; Exhib of the Yr, Asn Art Mus Cur, 2008; nominee, Emmy Award, 2011; Best Exhib in University Art, Asn Art Mus Cur, 2011; Finalist, Benjamin Ilooks Nat Book Award, 2011. *Mem:* PEN Am Ctr. *Res:* Art hist, criticism & critical theory; Am cult hist; race studies. *Publ:* auth, White Lies: Race and the Myths of Whiteness, Farrar Straus Giroux, 99; auth, Fred Wilson: Objects and Installations, Ctr for Art and Visual Cult, 2001; auth, White: Whiteness and Race in Contemporary Art, Ctr for Art and Visual Cult, 2006; auth, For All the World to See: Visual Culture and the Struggle for Civil Rights, Yale, 2010; auth, Masterworks of the Jewish Mus, New York, 2004; and others. *Mailing Add:* 740 W End Ave Apt 22A New York NY 10025

BERGER, PAT (PATRICIA) EVE
PAINTER, EDUCATOR
b New York, NY. *Study:* Art Ctr Coll Design, 48; Univ Calif, Los Angeles, 50-55; studied with Sam Amato, Richard Boyce & John Altoon. *Hon Degrees:* Bravo Award Nominnee-Archievement in the Arts 91-92, 93-94; Nat'l Watercolors Soc, Honorary Life Member, Past Pres, WaterColor USA Honor Soc, Life time Member. *Work:* Long Beach Mus Art; San Diego Mus Art; Palm Springs Desert Mus, Calif; Springfield Art Mus, Mo; Sodertalje Konsthall, Jarnagatan, Sweden; West Publ, St Paul, Minn; and others. *Comn:* Olympic mural, Cent Adult High Sch, Los Angeles, 84; Pac Bell, Exec Floor, Los Angeles, Calif, 89; Northwest Memorial Hospital Chicago, IL, 2000. *Exhib:* Solo exhibs, Light, Illusion & Reality, Riverside Art Ctr & Mus, 83, Paintings of the Homeless, Capitol Bldg, Sacramento & Bridge Gallery, City Hall, 86, Int Contemp Art Fair, Los Angeles, Calif, 86, Jewish Fedn Galleries, Los Angeles, Calif, 88, Univ Judaism, Los Angeles, Calif, 91, Evansville Mus Art & Sci, Ind, 95 & Univ Fairfield, Conn, 96, Bakersfield Mus Art, Calif, 2009-2010, Silvia Plotkin Judaica Mus, Scottsdale, Ariz, 2009, West Valley Art Mus, Surprise, Ariz, 2008-2009, La Art Core, 50 Year Retrospective, Los Angeles, Calif, 2010, Homeless in America, Marshall Lekae Gallery, Scottsdale, Ariz, 2012, Women & Plants of the Bible, Karpeles Manuscript Lib Mus, Santa Barbara, Calif, 2013; Group Exhibs, Am Watercolors, Chateau de Tours, France, 87; Jewish Mus, San Francisco, Calif, 87; travel exhibs, Nat Women Artists Centennial, India, 89, Hunger 1990's, Not by Bread Alone, Carson Sq House Mus, Panhandle, Tex, 90, West Art & The Law, 83, 84, 91, 93 & 96; Inaugural Exhib, Huntington Beach Arts Ctr, 95; Kittakyushn Japan, 2001; Fukuoka Prefectural Mus, Fukyoka, Japan, 2001; Kitakyushu Monicipal Mus, 2005; Pacific Standard Time, So Cal Artists, 1945-1980, Am Jewish Univ, 2011; Long Beach Mus Art, Highlights from Permanent Coll, 1945-1980, 2012. *Collection Arranged:* Pat Berger's Homelss Series (auth, catalog), Karpeles Manuscript Libr Mus, Buffalo, NY; 12 paintings on homeless, Karpeles,. *Pos:* Muralist, Millard Sheets, Claremont, 75-77; keynote speaker, United Way, Kern Co, 2012. *Teaching:* Instr painting & drawing, Los Angeles Unified Sch Dist, Adult Div, 71-2003; instr murals, Cent Adult High Sch, Los Angeles, 82-85. *Awards:* Purchase Awards, Pa Acad Fine Arts, Ford Found, 64, Los Angeles All City Exhib, Ahmanson Collection, 69 & 76 & Art & the Law, West Publ Co, 91, 93 & 96; Fel, Brody Arts Fund, Calif Community Found, 88; Fel, Julia & David White Artists' Colony, Costa Rica. *Bibliog:* Hazel Harrison (auth), Watercolor School, Quatro Publ, 93; Sandra Knipe (auth), article, Evansville Press, 1/26/95; Phyllis Boros (auth), Artist with a Cause, Conn Post, 1/14/96; Bill Laserow (auth), Women of a Certain Age, Art Scene, 2007; LA Story (catalog), Hebrew Union Coll, New York, 2007; Lyn Kienholz (auth), LA Rising So Cal Artists Before 1980, 2010. *Mem:* Hon life mem Nat Watercolor Soc (pres, 73-74); Watercolor USA Honor Soc (secy, 94); Fine Arts Coun, Am Jewish Univ; LA Artcore; life mem Watercolor USA Hon Soc; Jewish Initiative Artist of So CA; Fine Art Coun, Am Jewish Univ. *Media:* Acrylic, Watercolor. *Res:* women in the bible. *Specialty:* Landau 20th Century Art, (traveling), Contemp Painting & Sculpture, LA Artcore, Los Angeles, CA. *Interests:* Painting, curating, photography, community involvement in arts. *Collection:* Karpeles Manuscript Libr Mus, Buffalo, NY; Long Beach Mus, Calif; Northwest Memorial Hosp, Chicago, Ill; Univ Minneapolis Law Sch. *Publ:* Contribr, Museum Opening Exhibit, Desert Sun, Palm Springs, 70; contribr, West '84 Art & the Law, West Publ Co, 83, 84, 91, 93 & 96; auth, California Romantics, Harbingers of Watercolorism, Perine, 86. *Dealer:* Landau 20th Century Art 3615 Moore St Los Angeles Ca 90066; Landau 20th Century Art 1525 Selby Ave Los Angeles CA 90024. *Mailing Add:* 2648 Anchor Ave Los Angeles CA 90064

BERGER, PAUL ERIC
COLLAGE ARTIST, PHOTOGRAPHER
b The Dalles, Ore, Jan 20, 1948. *Study:* Art Ctr Coll Design, Los Angeles, with Tod Walker, 67-69; Univ Calif, Los Angeles, with Robert Heinecken & Robert Fichter, BA, 69-70; Visual Studies Workshop, State Univ NY, Buffalo, with Nathan Lyons, MFA, 70-73. *Work:* Int Mus of Photog/George Eastman House, Rochester, NY; Bibliot

Nat, Paris, France; Art Inst Chicago; San Francisco Mus Mod Art; Los Angeles Co Mus Art, Calif. *Exhib:* Solo exhibs, Photographs, 75-90, Opened Bk, Art Inst Chicago, 75 Mathematics Series, 77, Seattle Subtext, 82, Light Gallery, NY & Cards, USC Altier Gallery, Santa Monica, Calif, Galerie Lichtblick, Cologne, Ger, 96; Works 1976-1989, Seattle Art Mus, Wash; Card Plates, Soho Photo, New York City, 99; Paul Berger: 1973-03, Mus of Contemp Photo, Chicago, 03; Blue Sky Gallery, Portland, Ore. *Pos:* Asst prof art, Univ Wash, Seattle, 78, prof art, currently. *Teaching:* Lectr photog, Univ Ill, Champaign, 74-78; from asst to assoc prof photog, Univ Wash, Seattle, 78-. *Awards:* Young Photogr Award, Int Meeting Photog, Arles, France, 75; Nat Endowment Arts photogr fel, 79; Nat Endowment Arts, Visual Artists Fel, 86. *Bibliog:* Leroy Searle (auth), Paul Berger's mathematics photographs, Afterimage, Rochester, 78; Jim Burns (auth), From Old Images to New, Argus Publ, Seattle, Wash, 79; Rod Slemmons (auth), Paul Berger: Marco Polo in the Land of the Computer, Photo Education (Polaroid Newsletter), 90; Rod Slemmons (auth), Paul Berger: The Machine in the Window, Seattle Art Mus, Wash, 90. *Mem:* Soc Photog Educ (bd dir, 80-84). *Media:* Photography, Digital media. *Collection:* International Museum of Photography, GEH; The Art Institute of Chicago; LA County Museum of Art; San Francisco Museum of Modern Art; Museum of Contemp Photography, Chicago; The Art Museum, Princeton University. *Publ:* Auth, Seattle Subtext, USW and Real Comet Press, 84. *Mailing Add:* Sch of Art Univ Wash Seattle WA 98195

BERGER-KRAEMER, NANCY
ASSEMBLAGE ARTIST
b New York, NY, Aug 15, 1941. *Study:* Adelphi Univ, BA, 63; Queens Coll, MS, 68. *Work:* Fordham Univ, Lowenstein Libr, New York; Johnson & Johnson, NJ; Cali Assocs; AT&T; Nabisco. *Comn:* Large collage mixed media box, comn by Mr & Mrs Sandor Hochheiser, W Orange, NJ, 90; large woven wall hanging, comn by Mr & Mrs S Scatcherd, Summit, NJ, 90; fiber, string, paper collage, comn by Mr & Mrs Syd Corn, Palm Beach, Fla, 95 & 2nd comn, 2002; Dr & Mrs Zacharias, Maplewood, NJ; Mr & Mrs Polon, Tinton Falls, NJ; Mr & Mrs Brunswick, Wynnewood, Pa; and others; Ruth Corn, Whippany, NJ; Jean Kawecki, Sussex Co, NJ; soft sculpture wall art, comn by Tina Berezuk, Maplewood, NJ; Mrs. Syd Corn, Whippany, NJ. *Exhib:* Artists of Cent NJ, Middlesex Co Mus, Piscataway, NJ, 90; NJ Fine Arts Ann, Montclair Art Mus, 91 & Noyes Mus, Oceanville, NJ, 92; Five Chinese Elements, Trenton City Mus, NJ, 96; solo exhibs, Newark Mus, Bergen Mus, Montclair Art Mus, Trenton State Mus & Trenton City Mus; San Diego Art Inst Int; City Without Walls, Newark, NJ, Skylands Arts Ann Exhib, Sparta, NJ, Ceres, New York Invitational & many others, 2001-2003; Jersey City Mus, NJ; Contemp Art, The Mill, Lafayette, NJ; Griffin Gallery, Madison, NJ; Court Gallery, Ben Shahn Ctr, Wayne, NJ; Fifth Ann Pike Co Art Exhib, Milford, Pa; Anyone Can Fly Found Inc, Faith Ringgold Salon Exhib, Englewood, NJ; Small Works Exhib, Maplewood Arts Ctr, NJ; Interweave's Second Ann Art Show, Dynamic Diversity, Summit, NJ; Invitational Ann Art Show, Calvary Church, Summit, NJ; The Puffin Cult Forum, Invitational: Human Nature: Green, Black & Blue, Teaneck, NJ; Artist Salon Exhib, Summit, NJ; Gallery Space, Prana Mandir Yoga Studio, NY; Group exhib: Maplewood Art Ctr, NJ. *Teaching:* Mixed media weavings, Clinton Elem Sch, Maplewood, NJ, 80-89; instr, local workshops. *Awards:* Middlesex Co Mus Best of Show, Artists Cent NJ, 89; Cali Assocs First Place Sculpture, Arts Coun Essex Area Art Exhib, 90; NJ Ctr Visual Art Second Place Award Int Juried Show, 95; and others. *Bibliog:* Dennis C Dougherty (auth), The dichotomy of a creative woman, Essex J-News Rec, NJ, 3/22/90; Nancy Berger-Kraemer fiber sculpture & hangings, Essex J-News Rec, NJ, 2/17/94; Eileen Watkins (auth), Women head field at international show, NJ Star Ledger, 3/15/94; and others. *Mem:* Women's Caucus for Art; Princeton Art Asn; Stamford Art Asn; Studio Montclair Inc, NJ. *Media:* Mixed Media Assemblage & Sculptured Tapestry, Environmental Hangings. *Collection:* Pres Jimmy Carter, Carter Ctr, Atlanta, Ga

BERGGRUEN, JOHN HENRY
ART DEALER
b San Francisco, Calif, June 18, 1943. *Study:* San Francisco State Coll, AB, 67. *Pos:* Pres & owner, John Berggruen Gallery, San Francisco, 70-; mem bd trustees, San Francisco Art Inst. *Mem:* Soc Encouragement Contemp Art; Art Dealers Asn Am. *Specialty:* Paintings, drawings and original prints of the 20th century. *Mailing Add:* 228 Grant Ave 3rd Fl San Francisco CA 94108

BERGHASH, MARK W
PHOTOGRAPHER, PAINTER
b Buffalo, NY, Mar 8, 1935. *Study:* Univ Buffalo, 52-55; Univ Vienna, Austria, 55-56; Art Students League, with George Grosz, 57-60; with George Tice & Philippe Halsman, 76-78. *Work:* Metrop Mus Art, Jewish Mus & Franklin Furnace Archive, NY; Calif Mus Photography, Riverside; Dayton Art Inst, Ohio; Cameraworks, San Francisco, Calif; Int Ctr Photog, NY. *Exhib:* The Portrait Extended, Mus Contemp Art, Chicago, Ill, 80; Counterparts and Affinities, Metrop Mus Art, NY, 82; Indelible Images, The Jewish Mus, NY, 82; Holocaust Survivors Remembered, Jewish Ctr, Buffalo, NY; Solo exhibs, Nudes in Parts, Gallery Photog Art, Tel Aviv, 84, Segmented Photogs, Marcuse Pfeifer Gallery, NY, 84, 87 & 89, San Francisco Cameraworks, Calif, 88, CEPA, Buffalo, NY, 88, Trienrak Int de la Photographis, Fribourg, Switz, 88, Art Inst, Chicago, 89, Hilton Hotel, NY, 89 & Port Washington Libr, NY, 89; Jews and Germans: Aspects of the True Self (with catalog), Calif Mus Photog, Riverside, 85; Two to Tango, Int Ctr Photog, NY; Golem, Danger, Deliverance & Art (with catalog), Jewish Mus, NY, 88; The Photographer of Invention (with catalog), Mus Am Art, Washington, DC, Mus Contemp Art, Chicago & Walker Art Ctr, Minneapolis, 89-90; Laurence Miller Gallery, NY, 89; Phyllis Rothman Gallery, Farleigh Dickenson Univ, Madison, NJ, 89; Portraits of Me Rooted and Uprooted, SF Camerawork, San Francisco, Calif, 92. *Pos:* Pres, Twenty-Twenty Serv, Inc. *Bibliog:* Any Grundberg (auth), Why the holocaust defies pictorialization, New York Times, 5/2/82; Zan Dubin (auth), Jews & Germans, Los Angeles Times, 12/2/85; Carol Stevens (auth), Still performances, Print Mag, 3/88; Richard Woodard (auth), Serving up the Poor as Exotic Fare for Voyeurs?, NY Times, 6/89; Catherine Calhoun (auth), Just How Life Is, New York Press, 6/89. *Mem:* Art Students League. *Media:* Silver Emulsion, Color Coupler Print. *Publ:* Coauth, Jews & Germans, CMP, 85

BERGNER, LANNY MICHAEL
SCULPTOR
b Anacortes, Wash, Dec 4, 1952. *Study:* Univ Wash, Seattle, BFA (sculpture), 81; Tyler Sch Art, Philadelphia, Pa, MFA (sculpture), 83. *Work:* Philadelphia Mus Art, Pa; Delaware Art Mus, Wilmington; Walker Hill Art Ctr, Seoul, Korea; Seattle Art Mus, Whatcom Art Mus, Woodenmere Art Mus. *Comn:* Wall Sculpture, Philadelphia Int Airport, Pa, 93. *Exhib:* Biennial 89 & 91, Del Art Mus, Wilmington, 89 & 91; Contemp Philadelphia Artists, Philadelphia Mus Art, Pa, 90; Artists Choose Artists, Inst Contemp Art, Philadelphia, Pa, 91; A New World View, Nat Craft Gallery, Kilkenny, Ireland, 2006; Natures Matrix, Philadelphia Int Airport, Pa, 2006. *Awards:* Sculpture Prize, Contemp Philadelphia artists, Philadelphia Mus Art, 90; Betty Bowen Mem Award, 95; Artist Trust Craft Fellowship, Seattle, 97; Artist Trust Gap Grant, Seattle, 2000; Gold Prize, 4th Cheongju Int Craft Biennial, 2005. *Mem:* Fiber Art Int; Northwest Designer Craftsmen. *Media:* Mixed. *Interests:* music, gardening. *Publ:* 500 Baskets, Lark Books, 2005; Intertwined, ASU Art Mus, 2005; and others. *Dealer:* Snyderman/Works Gallery 303 Cherry St Philadelphia PA 19106; Mobilia Gallery 385 Huron Ave Cambridge MA 02138; Pacini Lubel Gallery 207 2nd Ave Seattle WA 98104; Duane Reed Gallery 4729 McPherson Ave Saint Louis MO 63108. *Mailing Add:* 7064 Miller Rd Anacortes WA 98221-8321

BERGSTROM, EDITH HARROD
PAINTER
b Denver, Colo. *Study:* Pomona Col, BA, 63; Stanford Univ, MA, 64; Study with Richard Diebenkorn. *Work:* Palm Springs Desert Mus, Calif; San Jose Mus Art, Calif; Utah State Univ, Logan; Achenbach Found for Graphic Arts, Calif, Palace of the Legion of Hon, San Francisco; Claremont Graduate Sch, Calif; Springfield Art Mus, Springfield, Mo; and others. *Comn:* Ten paintings, Hyatt Corp, Houston, Tex. *Exhib:* Am Watercolor Soc,; Rocky Mountain Nat Watermedia Exhib,; Nat Watercolor Soc,; Watercolor USA,; Palm Springs Desert Mus,; Butler Inst Am Art 45th Nat, Youngstown, Ohio, 81 & 86; Solo exhibs, Capricorn Galleries, Bethesda, Md, 86, A Gallery, Palm Desert, Calif, 89; Tropical Topics, Monterey Penninsula Mus Art, 88. *Pos:* jury chmn, Nat Watercolor Soc, 87. *Teaching:* Private. *Awards:* Foothill Art Ctr Award, Rocky Mountain Nat Watermedia Exhib, 87; Southwest Mo Mus Asn Purchase Award, Springfield Art Mus, 87; Oil Painting award, Butler Inst American Art, 2011. *Bibliog:* Mary Carhartt (auth), Watercolor: See for Yourself, Grumbacher, 84; Gerald Brommer (auth), Exploring the Art of Painting, Davis Publ, 87; Michael Ward (auth), The New Spirit of Watercolor, N Light Publ, 89. *Mem:* Rocky Mountain Nat Watermedia Soc; Nat Watercolor Soc; Am Watercolor Soc; W Coast Watercolor Soc (past-pres); Watercolor USA Hon Soc. *Media:* Oil, Watercolor. *Specialty:* A Gallery Fine Art-Painting-all Media. *Interests:* Gardening. *Collection:* Many Corp Collections. *Publ:* Auth, article, Am Artist, 1/82; auth, article, Artist's Mag, 7/87. *Dealer:* A Gallery Fine Art 73-956 El Paseo Dr Palm Desert CA 92261. *Mailing Add:* PO Box 126 Palo Alto CA 94302

BERGUSON, ROBERT JENKINS
DRAFTSMAN, PAINTER
b Blossburg, Pa, Dec 6, 1944. *Study:* Corning Community Col, NY, AA, 64; Univ Iowa, Iowa City, BA, 67, MA, 68, MFA, 70. *Work:* Norfolk Mus Arts & Sci, Va; Univ NDak Art Gallery, Grand Forks; Univ Iowa Sch Art Gallery, Iowa City; Hunter Mus Art, Bluff View, Chattanooga, Tenn; Miss Mus Art, Jackson; La State Univ, Alexandria; New Orleans Mus Art, La; Masur Mus Art, Monroe, La; Concordia Univ, Austin, Tex; Univ Tex at Tyler; Mason Mus Art, Monroe, La; Lessedra Gallery of Contemp Art Projects, Sofia, Bulgaria. *Exhib:* XXIII Am Drawing Biennial, Smithsonian Traveling Exhib Serv, Norfolk Mus Arts & Sci, Va, 69; Louisiana: Major Works 1984, La World Expo, Inc, New Orleans, 84; Louisiana Competition, Baton Rouge, 87 & 90; Fifth Ann Fla Nat, Fla State Univ, Tallahassee, 90; 37th Ann Delta Art Exhib, Little Rock Art Ctr, Ark, 94; Mobile Mus Art Biennial, Ala, 99; Concordia Univ Nat Exhib, Austin, 2001; 27 solo painting & drawing exhibs; and others. *Teaching:* Asst prof painting & drawing, La Tech Univ, Ruston, 70-76, assoc prof, 77-83, prof, 83-07, prof Emeritus, 2007. *Awards:* Louisiana Artist Fel; Louisiana Mini-Grantee, 2001, 2003, 2004, and 2005; Best of Show, 21st Int Exhib, Meadows Gallery, Univ Tex, Tyler, Tex. *Media:* Graphite, Acrylic, Prisma Colors. *Interests:* Travelling and athletics. *Publ:* Auth, article, Art Voices-South, 7-8/79; illusr, Upper & lower case, Int J Typographics, 79. *Dealer:* Cole Pratt Gallery New Orleans, La

BERHANG, MATTIE
SCULPTOR, LECTURER
b Dec 17, 1943, New York, NY. *Study:* Tyler Sch Art, BFA; Art Students League, with R B Hale & J DeCreeft; New York Studio Sch, with G Spaventa, R Nakian & M Matter. *Work:* Lannan Found Mus, Los Angeles, Calif; Reich & Tang Inc, Leukemia Soc Am, New York; Sigal Construction Corp, Washington, DC; Albert & Vera List Gallery, Brown Univ, Providence, RI; David Bermant Found, Harrison, NY. *Comn:* Mobile construct, comn by Cermak Plaza Assocs, Berwyn, Ill, 87; mobile construct, comn by Jane Abrams, Palm Beach, Fla, 89; construct, comn by Dr Joseph & Helene Chazan, Providence, RI, 90; crucifix, comn by Grant Nicolson, New York, 96; restoration, comn by Church St Mary & St Andrew, Ellenville, NY, 2001. *Exhib:* Varfor NY (with catalog), Stockholm Int Art Expos, Sweden, 83; Sculpture: The Tradition in Steel (with catalog), Nassau Co Mus Fine Arts, Roslyn, NY, 83; Am Women Artists Part II: The Recent Generation (with catalog), Sidney Janis Gallery, New York, 84; Discarded (with catalog), Rockland Ctr Arts, West Nyack, NY, 91; The Big Picture (with catalog), O K Harris Works Art, NY, 92; and many others. *Teaching:* Guest lectr, Syracuse Univ, 81 & 85, New Sch Social Res, New York, 81, Univ Wis, Eau Claire, 83 & Univ Cincinnati, 84. *Awards:* Artists Space Individual Artist Grant, Artists Space Inc, New York, 87-89. *Bibliog:* The artist framed, Esquire, 4/86; Harvey Stein (auth), Artists Observed, Harry N Abrams, New York, 86; Majory E Bevlin (auth), Design Through Discovery, Holt, Rinehart and Winston Inc, New York, 89. *Media:* Mixed Materials, Cast Metal. *Publ:* contbr, Atheist to Catholic (book), Rebecca Vitz Cherico, Servant Books, 2011. *Mailing Add:* PO Box 92 Ellenville NY 12428-0092

BERIO, MARINA
DRAFTSMAN, PRINTMAKER
Study: Oberlin Coll, BA (art hist), 1988; Bard Coll, MFA (photog), 2006. *Exhib:* Shy, Artists Space, New York, 1999; Rethinking the Landscape, Photographic Resource Ctr, Boston, 2001; solo exhibs, Acta Int, Rome, Italy, 2003, Italian Inst Advanced Studies, Columbia Univ, 2004; In Focus: 75 Years of Collecting American Photography, Addison Gallery Am Art, Mass, 2006; Aires de Paris, Centre Pompidou, France, 2007; Ça me touche, Les Rencontres d'Arles, Arles, France, 2009. *Pos:* Instr, Int Ctr for Photog, 2001-, chmn Gen Studies in Photog program, 2008-; lectr, Lehman Coll, CUNY, 2006-08. *Awards:* Arron Siskind Found Grant, 1998; Yaddo Fel, 2008; Pollock-Krasner Found Grant, 2008; NY Found Arts Fel, 2009. *Bibliog:* Vince Aletti (auth), Voice Choices, Village Voice, 3/16/1999; Kate McQuaid (auth), Finding Beauty Amid Sadness, in Full Color, Boston Globe, 5/7/2004; Benjamin Genocchio (auth), Love, Without Makeup, NY Times, 4/9/2006

BERK, AMY LYNNE
ARTIST, EDUCATOR
b Brooklyn, NY, Aug 3, 1967. *Study:* Wesleyan Univ, BA, 89; San Francisco Art Inst, MFA, 95. *Work:* Oakland Mus, Calif; Children's Television Workshop, New York; Judah L Magnes Mus, Berkeley, Calif. *Comn:* Architectonic (Goethe wall installaion), Goethe Inst, San Francisco, 98-99; Market St Art, In: Transit Poster Series, San Francisco Art Comn, San Francisco, 99; Mt Bruce, www.neighborhoodfilms.org. *Exhib:* Needles and Pins, Ctr Arts, San Francisco, Calif, 98; Better, San Francisco Arts Comn, San Francisco, Calif, 99; Needle Art, Bedford Gallery, Walnut Creek, 99; Holy Cow! Divine Bovines, Mus da Republica, Rio De Janeiro, 99; Following the Tradition, Kraushaar Gallery, New York, 2003; Revealing Influences, Conversations, Mus Folk & Craft Art, San Francisco, Calif, 2003; Wall Works, Traywick Contemp, Berkeley, 2005; Swell, Ten Yrs Later, Meridian Gallery, San Francisco, 2006; Revisions, Recoverings, Magnes Mus, Berkeley, 2006; Contemp Jewish Mus, San Fran, 2009; Shadow Shop San Fran Mus Modern Art, San Francisco, Calif, 2010; Process and Place, Berkeley Art Center, Calif, 2010, 2011; Capitol Offense: The End of Capitalism, Beacon Arts, Los Angeles, 2011; Near and Far: Meridian Gallery, 2012; Guerilla Cafe as Part of Temporary Structures, Walter and McBean Galleries, San Francisco, 2012. *Pos:* Co-dir, Meridian Interns Prog, San Francisco, Calif, 96-2004; co-publ, www.stretcher.org, San Francisco, Calif, 2000-. *Teaching:* Instr, Contemp Art San Francisco Art Inst Adult Community Educ, 97-2003, San Francisco State, 2000 & UC Berkeley Extension, San Francisco, Calif, 2004-; vis fac, San Francisco Art Inst, 2006-; Program Chair, Contemp Practice, San Francisco Art Inst, 2011-2013. *Awards:* Gerbade Purchase Award, 98; Artist in Residence, New Pacific Studio, 2001. *Bibliog:* Brenda Peyton (auth), Art springs from everyday life, Oakland Tribune, 6/29/2007; Alison Bing (auth), Amy Berk at the Judah L Magnes Mus, Artweek, 10/2007; David Buuck (auth), Swell at Meridian Gallery, Artweek, 10/2008. *Mem:* San Francisco Art Inst Artists Comt Chair, 96-99; Together We Can Defeat Capitalism (TWCDC), 2000-. *Media:* Painting, Sculpture, Drawing, Video. *Publ:* Article, Margaret Harrison & Conrad Atkinson at Refusalon, Art Papers, 2000; Forever on the Move, World Sculpture News, 2000; ed & co-publ, Stretcher.org, 2000-; Artist at work, Sabina, Otto Art Contemp, 2004; Sarah Ratchye, Marjorie Wood Gallery, 2004. *Mailing Add:* 67 29th St San Francisco CA 94110-4910

BERKENBLIT, ELLEN
PAINTER
b Paterson, NJ, 1958. *Study:* Cooper Union, BFA, 80. *Comn:* Two fabric designs for spring couture line, comn by Todd Oldham, 93. *Exhib:* Solo exhibs, Club 57, NY, 82, Limbo Lounge, NY, 83, Semaphore East, NY, 84, 85 & 86, White Columns, NY, 92, Galerie Hubert Klocker, Vienna, 93 & Boesky & Callery, NY, 96; East Village Artists, Va Mus Fine Arts, Richmond, 84; Small Wonders, Barry Whistler Gallery, Dallas, 94; Berkenblit, Nares, Prince, Wool, Galleria Bonomo, Rome, 95; Group Hanging, Griffin Linton Fine Arts, Costa Mesa, Calif, 96; Bronwyn Keenan Gallery, NY, 96; and others. *Awards:* NY Found Arts Painting Fel, 92; Nat Endowment Arts Visual Artist Fel, 93. *Bibliog:* Wendy Goodman (auth), Precious nothings, HG, 9/92; Johanna Hofleipner (auth), Rev, Kureir, Vienna, 6/93; Visiting artist, Paper Mag, 4/96

BERKMAN, LILLIAN
COLLECTOR
Study: Univ Philippines, Hon Dr Humanities; Marquette Univ, Hon Dr Fine Arts. *Pos:* Pres, Rojtman Found Inc; fel, Morgan Libr; fel in perpetuity, Metrop Mus Art, NY; overseer, Univ Pa Mus; trustee, Telfair Mus, Savannah, Ga; mem exec bd adv, Inst Fine Arts, NY Univ; trustee Nat Coun, Mem Acquisition Comt Fine Arts Mus, San Francisco; chmn, Asn Am Artists Inc, currently. *Awards:* Pere Marquett Award; Presidential Award for Cult Interchange, Costa Rica; Kyros Award, Marquette Univ. *Mem:* Asia Soc (president's coun); Drawing Soc; Japan Soc, founding mem; Lotos Club, NY; Univ Club NY. *Collection:* Paintings, prints, drawings, sculpture, porcelains; 18th century French furniture; 18th century Chinese jades, archaic Chinese bronzes

BERKON, MARTIN
PAINTER
b Brooklyn, NY, Jan 30, 1932. *Study:* Brooklyn Col, BA; New York Univ, MA; Pratt Inst. *Work:* Texaco Inc, White Plains, NY; NASA Gallery of Art, Kennedy Space Ctr, Cape Canaveral, Fla; Pepsico Inc, Somers, NY; Vero Beach Mus Art, Vero Beach, Fla; Pfizer Inc, Rye Brook, NY. *Comn:* Painting, NASA, 84 & 87. *Exhib:* solo exhibs, Soho Ctr for Visual Artists, NY, 74, Genesis Gallery, NY, 78, Adelphi Univ, 83 & Blue Hill Cult Ctr, Pearl River, NY, 95, Schering Plough Corp Gallery, Madison, NJ, 2001; Butler Inst Am Art Ann Midyear Show, 65, 67 & 69; Contemp Reflections, 74, A Change of View, 75, A Look Back A Look Forward, 82, Aldrich Mus Contemp Art, Ridgefield, Conn; Brooklyn Mus, 58; Oakland Univ, Rochester, Mich, 75; Am Fedn Arts Traveling Exhib, 75-76; Kennedy Space Center, Cape Canaveral, Fla, 84 & 87; Visions of Flight: Retrospective From NASA Art Collection, Smithsonian Inst Traveling Exhib World Tour, 88-91; The Abstract Image, Vero Beach Mus Art, 96; Interpreting the River, Blue Hill Cult Ctr, Pearl River, NY, 97-98. *Teaching:* Instr elements of design, Fairleigh Dickinson Univ, 66-67; lect art, City Coll NY, 68-69; guest lectr, Middlebury Coll, 77, Nassau Community Coll, 82 & St Thomas Aquinas Coll, 95. *Bibliog:* Grace Glueck (auth), Art notes, New York Times, 12/1/74; Evalyn E Milman (auth), article, in: Bridgeport Sunday Post, 1/24/82; Merle English (auth), article, in: Newsday, 10/5/84; Shirley Romaine (interviewer), Long Island Artscene, Cox Cable TV, 9/86; Robert Schulman & Lori Dempsey (auth), Visions of Flight: A Retrospective from the NASA Art Collection, catalogue, 88; Genie Carr (auth), Review of NASA Retrospective, color reproduction, in: Winston-Salem J, 9/13/90; color reproduction, Internet publ, Alison Wright (auth), Nature Art: Imagine Space, 10/2002; color reproductions, Internet publ, Martin Wattenberg (ed), Art and space, Dome News, 9/2002; Julie Clay (auth) NASA's Hospital Visit, Ft Myers Mag 6/2005. *Media:* Oil, Acrylic, Watercolor. *Mailing Add:* 503 DeVries Ct Piermont NY 10968

BERKOWITZ, HENRY
PAINTER, DESIGNER
b Brooklyn, NY, Feb 5, 1933. *Study:* Brooklyn Mus Art Sch, with Sidney Simon; Workshop Sch Advert & Ed Art; Sch Visual Arts, NY. *Work:* Gutenberg Mus, Main, Ger; Maitland Art Ctr, Fla; Raymond Duncan Mus, Paris. *Exhib:* Berkshire Mus, Pittsfield, Mass, 71; Galleries Raymond Duncan, Paris, 74; Art Festival Tours, France, 74; Parrish Art Mus, 75; Surindependants, Paris, 75; The Brooklyn Mus, NY; The New York Coliseum, NY; The Nat Arts Club, NY; The Wilkes Gallery, NY; The Gutenberg Mus, Mainz, Ger; Orlando Mus Art, Fla; Maitland Art Center, Maitland, Fla; plus others. *Pos:* Art dir, Pyramid Publ, New York, 63-77. *Awards:* Award of Merit, New York Coliseum, 70; Am Vet Soc for Artists Award for an Abstract Work of Art, 72; Prix de Paris, France, 72 & 73; Palmas de Oro, Int Art Festival, Paris, 74; Statue of Victory World Cult Prize, Italy, 84; Oscar D'Italia, 85; Premio D'Italia, 86. *Mem:* Am Vet Soc Artists; Huntington Art League; Berkshire Art Asn; Awixa Pond Art Asn; Shore Arts Asn. *Media:* Oil, Mixed Media. *Publ:* Auth & illusr, Fish, Facts and Fancies, 81 & Amphibians & Reptiles, 85, Banyan Bks; Dinosaurs, 87, Sharks, 88 & Monsters, 94, Henart Bks; Dolphins & Whales, Winner Enterprises, 96. *Dealer:* Ligoa Duncan Gallery 1045 Madison Ave New York NY 10021

BERKOWITZ, TERRY
INSTALLATION ARTIST, PHOTOGRAPHER
b Brooklyn, NY. *Study:* Sch Visual Arts, New York, cert, 71, Art Inst, Chicago, MFA, 73. *Work:* Mus of Modern Art, NY; pvt collections. *Exhib:* Solo exhibs, People Who Live In Glass Houses, Alternative Mus, NY, 80, Contemp Art Mus, Houston, Tex, 90, Whitney Mus Am Art, 92 & Backseat, Sculpture Ctr, NY (auth, catalog), 94, Metronom, Barcelona, 99, Galeria Magda Bellotti, Madrid, 2008, Harvestworks, NY, 2013; Group Exhib: Schemes, Film as Installation, The Clocktower, NY, 83; Galeria Magda Bellotti, Madrid, Spain, 2008; El Sueño Imperativo, Circulo De Bellas Artes, Madrid, Spain, 91; Construction in Process, Kodz, Poland, 91; Transition/Dislocation, Cleveland Ctr Contemp Art, 96; Carcel de Amor, Museo Nacional Centro de Arte, Reina Sofia, Madrid, Spain, 2005; EMAP, Korea, 2005; Diva Video Fair, New York City, 2005 & 06; Loop Video Festival, Barcelona, 2006; Trauma Interrupted, Cul Center Philippines, Manila, 2007; Resonances: Looking for Mr Luhan, Pratt Gallery, NY, 2012; Four Houses, Some Buildings, NY, 2013. *Teaching:* Prof art, Baruch Col/CUNY, 95-; chmn, Dept Fine & Performing Arts, 2007-2010. *Awards:* Fel, Nat Endowment Arts, 74; Fel, Creative Artists in Pub Serv, 74; Macdowell Art Colony Fel, Summer, 89; Jerome Found Film/Video Prod Grant, 90 & 96; Fulbright Scholar, 96; NYSCA, Production Grant, 2007; NYFA, Photography, 2010. *Bibliog:* John Paoletti (auth), At the edge where art becomes media and message becomes polemic: Disinformation at the Alternative Museum, Arts Mag, 5/85; Sue Cramer (auth), Report from Poland: Back to the Future, Art in Am, 3/91; Judy Cantor (auth), El Sueño Imperativo, Art News, 5/91. *Media:* Video, Photography. *Publ:* Auth, Report from behind the scenes, Art Criticism, Vol 2, No 3, 86; Bloodstone, Contemp Arts Mus, Houston, 91. *Dealer:* Galeria Magda Belloti, Madrid, Spain. *Mailing Add:* 38 N Moore St New York NY 10013

BERKSON, BILL
CRITIC, POET
b New York, NY, Aug 30, 1939. *Study:* Brown Univ, 57-59; New Sch, NY, 59-61; Columbia Univ, 59-60. *Pos:* Assoc prod, Art-New York, WNDT-TV, 64-65; film ed, Kulchur, 62-63; guest ed, Mus Mod Art, 65-69; ed & publ, Best & Co, 69 & Big Sky Mag & Bks, 71-78; consult, Coord Coun Lit Mag, 75; ed, The World Record, St Marks Poetry Proj, 80; corresp, Artforum, 85-91; poetry ed, Video & the Arts, 85-86; coord, Bay Area Consortium Visual Arts, 85-87; contrib ed, Zyzzyva, 87-92; corresp ed, Art in Am, 88-; guest cur, San Francisco Mus Mod Art, 91; cur, Susan Cummins Gallery, 92, Mills Coll Art Gallery, 93 & Campbell-Thiebaud Gallery, 97; co-cur, Gallery Paule Anglim, 92; interim dean, San Francisco Art Inst, 92, dir, Letters & Sci, 94-98, prof emer, 2011-; adj cur, Fine Arts Mus, San Francisco, 95; ed bd, Modern Painters, 2002-2006; ed assoc, Artnews, 60-63; contrib ed, artcritical, com 2009-. *Teaching:* Assoc prof art hist, Calif Coll Arts & Crafts, 83-84; prof art hist, San Francisco Art Inst, 84-2008. *Awards:* Artspace Art Criticism Award, 90; Mellon Fel, Skowhegan Sch Painting and Sculpture, 2006; Goldie, in lit, San Francisco Bay Guardian, 2008. *Bibliog:* Irving Sandler (co-ed), Alex Katz, 71; Joe LeSueur (co-ed), Homage to Frank O'Hara, 78; Rackstraw Downes (co-ed), J DeKooning issue, 89; adv ed, Jenni Quiler, NY Sch Painters and Poets: Neon in Daylight, Rizzoli Int, 2014; The Schneeman Touch in A Painter and His Poets: The Art of George Schneeman, Poets House, 2014; Empathy and Sculpture in Joel Shapiro, Craig Starr Gallery, 2014; Hands On/Hands Off, The Art of Collaboration, Cuneiform Press, 2015; New Energies: Philip Guston Among the Poets, in Philip Guston: Drawings for Poets, Sieveking Verlag, 2015; Allen Ruppersberg: Familiar and Engimatic in Allen Ruppersberg, Writing, Christine Burgin, 2014. *Mem:* Int Art Critics Asn. *Res:* Contemporary art. *Publ:* Auth, Report from San Francisco, 6/94, In the Heat of the Rose, 3/96, As Ever, de Kooning, 2/97 & The Pollock Effect (rev), 12/97, The Photographist (on Carleton Watkins), 4/2000, Art in Am; About Ernie Gehr (exhib

catalog), Walter/McBean Gallery, 95; (exhib cat) Changes Like the Weather, De Young Mas, 95; Shaw Business, 10-11/96 & Nagle Wares, 8-9/97, Am Craft; From the Land of Drawers (exhib catalog), Berggruen Gallery, 1/98; Wayne's World, summer, 98 & A New York Beginner, 9/98, The Portraitist (Elaine de Kooning), spring, 99, What Is There, winter, 99-2000, De Kooning, with Attitude, summer, 2000, Mod Painters; Jackson Pollock/Drawings on Colored Papers, Joan Washburn Gallery; Existing Light in Henry Wessel, Rena Branstem Gallery, 2000; Ceremonial Surfaces: California Art in the Anderson Collection, Univ Calif Press, fall, 2000; The Searcher in Elmer Bischoff, Univ Calif Press, 2001; What the ground looks like in Arial Use: The Art of Yvonne Jacquette, Stanford Art Mus, 2001; The Sweet Singer of Modernism & selected art writings 85-03, Qua Books, 2003; auth, Sudden Address: Selected Lectures 1981-2006, Cuneiform Press, 2007; Of Origin and Good Hope in Measure of Time, Berkeley Art Mus; For the Ordinary Artist, BlazeVox, 2010. *Mailing Add:* 25 Grand View Ave San Francisco CA 94114

BERLIND, ROBERT
PAINTER, EDUCATOR
b New York, NY, Aug 20, 1938. *Study:* Columbia Coll, BA, 60; Sch Art & Archit, Yale Univ, BFA, 62, MFA, 63. *Work:* J B Speed Art Mus, Louisville, Ky; Neuberger Mus Art, Purchase, NY; Mus City New York; Ringling Mus Art, Sarasota, Fla, 2000; Nat Acad Design Painting Ctr, New York, 2004. *Exhib:* Solo exhibs, Gallery One, Toronto, 85, Del Valley Arts Asn, 92, Tibor de Nagy Gallery, New York, 94, 96, 98, 2001, & 2005, Reynolds Gallery, Richmond, 96, Univ Art Galleries, Wright State Univ, Dayton, Ohio, 97, Newberger Mus Art, Purchase, NY, 98, Picker Art Gallery, Colgate Univ, Hamilton, NY, 98 & Alexandre Acque Gallery, Univ Tulsa, 2005, David Findlay Jr Fine Art, 2010; group exhibs, Bronx Mus Arts, New York, 87, Three River Arts Festival, Pittsburg, Pa, 89, Art Mus Fla Int Univ, Miami, Fla, 89 & 96, Mem Art Gallery Univ Rochester, NY, 89, Md Inst, Coll Art, Baltimore, Md, 89, Found Mona Bismarck, Paris, France, 91, Neuberger Mus, Purchase, NY, 94, The Police Building, New York, 94 & Kunstrarein in Hamburg, Hamburg, Ger, 94; Maier Mus Art, Lynchburg, Va, 96; Lennon, Weinberg Inc, New York, 98 & Apex Art, 97; Locks Gallery, Philadelphia, 2002. *Teaching:* Asst prof, Minneapolis Sch Art, 64-66 & 69-70; asst prof art hist & humanities, Haarlem, Neth, 66-68; assoc prof & dir grad studies, NS Coll Art & Design, 74-76; assoc prof, State Univ NY at Purchase, full prof, 79-. *Awards:* Am Acad Inst Arts & Lett, 92; Nat Endowment Arts Fel Painting, 93; Pollock-Krasner Found Award, 97; B Altman Award, Painting, 2007. *Bibliog:* Ken Johnson (auth), rev, NY Times, 6/26/98; Roberta Smith (auth), article, NY Times, 7/17/98; Jonathan Goodman (auth), rev, Art in Am, 1/99; Karen Wilkin (auth) article, Partison Rev, 2002 & catalog, Tibor de Nagy Gallery, the First Fifty Years, 1950-2000. *Mem:* Nat Acad Design; Asn Int des Critiques d'Art; Coll Art Asn. *Media:* Oil. *Publ:* Guest ed, Art & Old Age, Art J, spring 94; articles & revs In: Art in Am, Border Crossings, The Brooklyn Rail & var mus catalogs. *Dealer:* Tibor De Nagy Gallery 724 Fifth Ave New York NY 10019. *Mailing Add:* 215 W 20th St New York NY 10011

BERLYN, SHELDON
PAINTER, PRINTMAKER
b Worcester, Mass, Sept 6, 1929. *Study:* Yale Norfolk Summer Art Sch, 49-50; Worcester Art Mus Sch, cert, 51; Art Acad Cincinnati with Herbert Barnett, 54-55; State Univ NY, Buffalo, 59-62. *Work:* Worcester Art Mus, Mass; Dayton Art Inst; Albright-Knox Art Gallery, Buffalo, NY; State Univ NY Brockport Gallery Collection; Burchfield-Penny Art Ctr, Buffalo, NY; State Univ NY at Buffalo, Anderson Gallery, NY; and numerous pvt & corp collections; Portland Art Mus, Ore; Kennedy Art Mus; Ohio Univ, Athens. *Exhib:* Albright-Knox Art Gallery, Buffalo, NY, 76, Castellani Art Mus, Niagara Univ, 97 & Univ Gallery, Ctr for Arts, State Univ NY, Buffalo, 97; Western NY Exhib, Albright-Knox Art Gallery, Buffalo, NY, 58-66 & 77; Drawings Above the Pa Line, Roberson Ctr Arts, Binghamton, NY, 68; Am Drawings, Moore Coll Art, Philadelphia, 68; Begegnung-Mass Inst Technol, Auslands Inst, Dortmund, W Ger, 76; Anderson Gallery, Buffalo, NY 94; 50th & 52nd Chautauqua Nat Exhib Am Art, 2007, 2009; Beyond in Western NY, Alternating Currents, 2010; Albright-Knox Art Gallery, Buffalo, 2010; Abstraction, Nancy Margolis Gallery, NY, 2011; 63rd Fingerlakes Exhib, Mem Art Gallery, Rochester, NY, 2011; Kennedy Art Mus: Sheldon Berlyn Prints, Color: Geometric Variations, 2015. *Teaching:* Assoc prof painting & drawing, State Univ NY Buffalo, 58-, prof emer, 99. *Awards:* Stephen Wilder Traveling Fel, Cincinnati Mus Asn, 55-56; Sattler Award Painting, Western NY Exhib, Albright-Knox Art Gallery, 60 & Reeb Award Drawing, 64; State Univ NY Res Found Fel, 66-70. *Bibliog:* Richard Huntington (auth), In Bright Abstract Paintings, Centuries of Possibility, Buffalo News, 4/24/97; Robert Bertholf, Sheldon Berlyn: Caravaggio in New Colors, Artvoice, 5/7/97; Mark Lavatelli, Abstract Expressionism Without the Angst, Artvoice, 5/13/97. *Media:* Acrylic, Oil; Serigraphy. *Dealer:* 20th Century Finest Dean Brownrout Buffalo NY. *Mailing Add:* 4598 Vine Rd Penn Yan NY 14527

BERMAN, BERNARD
COLLECTOR
b Pennsburg, Pa, Aug 28, 1920. *Mem:* Am Asn Mus, Washington, DC (trustee); Allentown Art Mus, Pa (pres bd trustees, 71-). *Collection:* German Expressionist, Italian sculpture, American artists. *Mailing Add:* 3003 W Turner St Allentown PA 18104-5331

BERMAN, MICHAEL P
PHOTOGRAPHER
b New York, New York, 1956. *Study:* Colorado Coll, Biology, 1979; Arizona State Univ, MFA Photog, 1985. *Work:* Ctr Creative Photog, Univ Arizona, Tucson; Mus des beaux-arts Canada, Ottawa; Metrop Mus Art, New York. *Exhib:* UMC Fine Arts Ctr Univ Colorado, Boulder, 1985; Houston Ctr Photog, Tex, 1986; Stark Gallery, New York, 1988; Mus Fine Arts, Santa Fe, 1997; Magnifico, Albuquerque, NMex, 2002; Nash Ephemeral Gallery, Marfa, Tex, 2002, 2003; Light Factory, Charlotte, NC, 2003; Permanent Collection, New Mexico State Univ Art Mus, Las Cruces, 2004; Creativity, Ohio Wesleyan Univ, Ross Art Mus, Delaware, Ohio, 2004. *Teaching:* Photog Instr, Western New Mexico Univ, Silver City, 1994-95. *Awards:* Vis Artist Fel, Arizona Comn Arts Painting, 1989; Fel, Wurlitzer Found, Taos, NMex, 1991; John Simon Guggenheim Mem Found Fel, 2008. *Dealer:* Scheinbaum & Russek LTD 369 Montezuma #345 Santa Fe NM 87501; Etherton Galleries 135 S 6th Ave Tucson AZ 85701; Joseph Bellows Gallery 7661 Girard Ave La Jolla CA 92037

BERMAN, NINA
PHOTOGRAPHER
Study: Univ Chicago, BA (english), 1982; Columbia Univ Grad Sch Journalism, MS, 1985. *Exhib:* Solo exhibs, Nat Vietnam Veterans Art Mus, Chicago, 2005, Univ Hawaii, Hilo, 2006, Univ Md, Baltimore, 2006, Crumb Libr, SUNY Potsdam, NY, 2007, Columbia Sch Social Work, New York, 2007, Alice Austen House Mus, Ne wYork, 2007, Elon Univ, NC, 2008, Gage Gallery, Roosevelt Univ, Chicago, 2009; The Human Condition, Flint Inst Arts, Mich, 2006; Thy Brother's Keeper, Boca Raton Mus Art, Fla, 2007; New on the Wall, Portland Art Mus, Ore, 2008; The Art of Caring, New Orleans Mus Art, 2009; Whitney Biennial, Whitney Mus Am Art, 2010. *Awards:* Documentary Grant, Open Soc Inst, 2005; NY Found Arts Fel, 2006; PDN Ann Bk Award, 2009. *Bibliog:* Cate McQuaid (auth), The enduring attempt to come to grips with war, Boston Globe, 2/21/2008; Alan G Artner (auth), Homeland rev, Chicago Tribune, 2/27/2009; Richard Lacayo (auth), Stars of the Arts, Time Mag, 3/12/2010. *Mailing Add:* Jen Beckman Gallery 6 Spring St New York NY 10012

BERMAN, VIVIAN
PRINTMAKER, EDUCATOR
b New York, NY, Aug 28, 1928. *Study:* Cooper Union, BFA; Art Students League; Brandeis Univ. *Work:* Libr Cong; Wiggin Collection, Boston Pub Libr, Mass; Pa Acad Art; De Cordova Mus, Lincoln, Mass; Hopkins Art Ctr, Dartmouth Col; United States Information Agency; Fogg Mus, Cambridge, MA. *Exhib:* The Boston Printmakers Ann, 68-2014; Libr Cong Nat Print Exhib, 70; 18th Nat Print Exhib, Brooklyn Mus, 73; Nat Exhib Collagraphs, Pratt Graphic Ctr, NY, 75; British Biennale 1979, Bradford, Eng; The Making of a Print, Delaware Ctr Contemp Art, 90 & Boston Univ, 91. *Pos:* Exec Bd, The Boston Printmakers, Boston, MA. *Teaching:* Instr, DeCordova Mus Sch, Lincoln, Mass. *Awards:* MacDowell Colony Fel, 81; and others. *Bibliog:* Wenniger (auth), Collagraph Printmaking, Macmillan, 78; Ross & Romano (auth), The Complete Collagraph, Free Press, 80. *Mem:* The Boston Printmakers; Concord Art Asn; Monotype Guild of New England. *Media:* Collagraph, Monoprint, Collage. *Dealer:* Flatrock Gallery Gloucester Mass; Depot Square Gallery Lexington Mass; Musaratt Gallery Somerville Mass. *Mailing Add:* 1010 Waltham St #312 Lexington MA 02421

BERMINGHAM, JOHN C
PAINTER
b Wharton, NJ, Jan 12, 1920. *Study:* Univ Notre Dame, Ind, BFA, 42. *Exhib:* Audubon Artists Ann Exhib, Nat Acad Galleries,NY, 73-77 & 81; Allied Artists Ann Exhib, Nat Acad Galleries/Salmagundi Club Galleries, NY, 73-79, 81, 83-87 & 91; Ann Exhib Am Watercolor Soc, Nat Acad Galleries/Salmagundi Club, NY, 73, 74, 76-78, 81, 89, 91, 93, 94 & 95; Am Watercolor Soc Traveling Exhib, 74, 78, 81, 89 & 93; Acad Artists Nat Exhib, Springfield Mus, Mass, 75-82; Ann Exhib Nat Acad Design, Nat Acad Galleries, NY, 76, 80, 82, 84, 88 & 92; Adirondacks Nat Exhib Am Watercolors, 85-87, 92, 95, 96 & 98. *Awards:* Anne Williams Glushien Award, Am Watercolor Soc, 93; Muriel Alvord Award, Hudson Valley Art Assoc, 94; Avery & Nina Johnson Mem Award, NJ Watercolor Soc, 96, Silver Medal of Honor, 97, R & M Price Mem Award, 99, Irving & Frances Phillips Award, 2000; Mary Greca Award, Hudson Valley Art Asn, 99; and others. *Mem:* Allied Artists Am; Am Watercolor Soc; NJ Watercolor Soc (pres, 77-78); Acad Artists; Hudson Valley Art Asn; Salmagundi Club. *Media:* Watercolor

BERMUDEZ, EUGENIA M See Dignac, Geny (Eugenia) M Bermudez

BERNAY, BETTI
PAINTER
b New York, NY, 1926. *Study:* Pratt Inst; Nat Acad Design, New York, with Louis Bouche; Art Students League, with Frank Mason; also with Robert Brackman. *Work:* Circulo Amistad, Cordoba, Spain; Columbus Mus Arts & Crafts, Ga; Columbia Mus Art, SC; Andre Weil Collection, Paris. *Comn:* Painting, pres of Renault, Madrid, Spain, 64; painting, Children Have No Barriers, IOS Found, Geneva, 69; paintings, Macaws, Seacost E Bldg, Miami Beach, Fla, 69 & mural, Sandy Cove, S Bldg, 70. *Exhib:* Mus Mod Art, Paris, 63; Salon Populiste, Mus Mod Art, Paris, 63; Bacardi Gallery, Miami, Fla, 67; Metrop Mus & Art Ctr, Miami, 75; Rosenbaum Gallery, Palm Beach, Fla, 77; Solo exhibs, Columbus Mus, GA & Columbia Mus, SC; and many other solo & group exhibs. *Awards:* Artistic Merit Medal, City of New York, 42; Prix de Paris, 58; Medal of Honor, Mus Bellas Artes, Malaga, 65; inductee, Library of Human Resources, Am Bicentennial Research Inst, 74. *Mem:* Artists Equity Asn; Am Artists Prof League; Nat Asn Painters & Sculptors Spain; Soc Artistes Francais; Prof Artists Guild; and others. *Media:* Oil, Pastel. *Mailing Add:* 10155 Collins Ave Apt 1705 Miami FL 33154

BERNHARD, DIANNE BARBEE
PAINTER, DIRECTOR
Study: studied with, Fernie Parker Taite, Elsie Andrews, & William Henry Earle; attended Univ Houston, Yale Univ. *Pos:* Pres, Conn Classic Artists Assn; adv bd mem, Nat Acad Design; bd govs, Nat Acad Design; bd govs, Nat Arts Club, chair Exhibitions Com, pres, 2011-; founder, Art Spirit. *Awards:* Gold Medal of Excellence, Nat Arts Club, 2003. *Mem:* Pastel Soc of America; Salmagundi Club; Nat Mus of Women in Arts. *Mailing Add:* National Arts Club 15 Gramercy Park S New York NY 10003

BERNHEIM, STEPHANIE HAMMERSCHLAG
PAINTER, PHOTOGRAPHER
b New York, NY. *Study:* Sarah Lawrence Col, BA; NY Univ, MA; studied with AD Reinhardt, Milton Resnik. *Work:* Cincinnati Mus Book Collection, Ohio; Metrop Mus Book Collection, NY; Princeton Univ Art Mus, NJ; Milwaukee Mus Art, Wis; Yale Univ Art Gallery, New Haven, Conn. *Exhib:* One-person exhibs, Inst for Art & Urban Resources, PS1 Mus, Long Island City, NY, 81, Hinterglasmaleri, AIR Gallery, NY, 94, In the Bag, Delaware Ctr for Contemp Art, Wilmington, 94; PS1 Mus, Long Island, NY, 81; Barbara Mathes Gallery, NY, 86 & 87; Primal Forces, Cooper Union, NY, 90; Burning in Hell, Franklin Furnace, NY, 91; Americana, Tricia Collins/Grand Salon, NY, 95 & 97; Milwaukee Mus Art, 97; Art Resource Transfer, NY, 2004; A.I.R. Gallery, Brooklyn, NY, 2011; The Arts Club of Chicago, 4 Artists, Ill, 2012; Group exhibs, Bau Inst Gallery, Hudson, NY, 2006-7, 2010, Puck Bldg/Air Gallery, NY, 2008, Heimhold Visual Arts Ctr, Sarah Lawrence Coll, Bronxville, NY, 2012; The Arts Club of Chgo, 2012; Andre Zarre Gallery, 2013. *Pos:* Created & organized art events/community panels at Air Gallery, NY, 11/91 & Sarah Lawrence Col, Bronxville, NY, 4/92; vis artist, Parsons Sch Design, 97 & Sarah Lawrence Col, 98. *Teaching:* Lectr, Parsons '96, Panel NY Studio Sch, 95. *Bibliog:* Joseph Ruzicka (auth), Stephanie Bernheim at AIR Gallery, Art in Am, 9/91; Raphael Rubenstein (auth), From End to Beginning (catalog), Hinterglasmaleri, AIR Gallery, New York, 94; Reagan Upshaw (auth), Stephanie Bernheim at AIR, Art in Am, 10/94; Steve Mumford (auth), Pine Plains Paintings, 97; The Sam & Adele Golden Fdn for the Arts, Inc, Golden Artists Colors Gallery, New Berlin, NY, 2000; Anne Rorimer (auth), Figures & Grounds: Approaches to Abstraction, Arts Club Chicago, Ill, 2012. *Mem:* Women's Caucus for Arts; AIR Gallery (exec comt 89-92); Women in Arts Found; Women's Action Coalition; Coll Art Asn. *Media:* Photography, Mixed Media. *Specialty:* painting. *Dealer:* Andre Zarre Fine Art Gallery 529 W 20th St New York NY 10011

BERNS, PAMELA KARI
PAINTER, ADMINISTRATOR
b Sturgeon Bay, Wis, Sept 4, 1947. *Study:* Lawrence Univ, Appleton, Wis, BA, 69; Univ Wis, Madison, MFA (painting), 71. *Work:* Bergstrom Art Ctr, Neenah, Wis; Kemper Insurance Co's, Inc, Long Grove, Ill; Miller Art Ctr, Sturgeon Bay, Wis; Andersen Window Corp, Bayport, Minn. *Exhib:* Solo exhib, Bergstrom Art Ctr, Neenah, Wis, 70; Watercolor Wis, Wustum Mus Art, Racine, 72-79 & 81-82; New Horizons, Chicago, 75; Women in the Arts, West Bend Mus Art, Wis, 76; Art Inst Chicago, 83. *Pos:* Coordr educ programs, Chicago Artists' Coalition, 80-83; publ, Chicago Life Mag, 84-. *Awards:* Second Prizes, Artists Guild Chicago, 76 & Watercolor Wis, 81; Best of Show in Painting, Idea Corp, 79. *Bibliog:* M Tourtelot (auth), Resume--A Selective Guide, The Studios, 75; R Dozer (auth), Recording Door County's Singularity, Chicago Tribune, 75; Door County Creations, Strom Channel 10, 77. *Mem:* Chicago Artists' Coalition (int dir, 79); Wis Watercolor Soc; Wis Painters & Sculptors Asn; Peninsula Arts Asn, Fish Creek, Wis. *Media:* Watercolor, Acrylic. *Dealer:* Edgewood Orchard Gallery Peninsula Players Rd Fish Creek WI 54212. *Mailing Add:* PO Box 11311 Chicago IL 60611

BERNSTEIN, JUDITH
PAINTER, EDUCATOR
b Newark, NJ, Oct 14, 1942. *Study:* Pa State Univ, BS & MS, 64; Yale Univ Sch Art, BFA & MFA, 67. *Work:* Mus Mod Art, Brooklyn Mus, New York; Univ Colo Mus, Boulder; Yale Art Gallery, New Haven, Conn; Kronhausen, Lund, Sweden; Colgate Univ Mus, Hamilton, NY; Neuberger Mus Art, Purchase, NY; William Copley; Lawrence Alloway; Warren Benedek; Walter De Maria; John Perreault; John Waters. *Comn:* Two on-site wall installations, William N Copley, 77. *Exhib:* Solo Exhibs: AIR Gallery, 73 & 84; State Univ NY, Stony Brook, 77; Brooks Jackson Iolas Gallery, New York, 78; Univ Ark, Fayetteville, 87; Mitchell Algus Gallery, NY, 2008, The Box, Los Angeles, Calif, 2011; Contemp Women: Consciousness & Content, Brooklyn Mus, New York, 77; Venerezia-Revenice, Titan's Forbidden Fruit, Plazzo Grassi, Venice, Italy, 78; The Great Big Drawing Show, LIC, PS1, New York, 79; Contemp Arte, Hague Gemeente Mus, The Neth, Belg & Ger, 79-81; 100 Drawings by Woman, Hillwood Art Mus, Nat Womens Mus, Yale Univ, Crocker Mus, Sacramento & Blum Helman Mus, New York, USA & Europe, 89-91; Man Revealed, Graham Mod Gallery, New York, 92; Seeing Red, White & Blue-Censored in USA, Visual Arts Ctr, Anchorage, Alaska, 92; Coming to Power, David Zwirner, New York, 93; Phallic Symbols, 24 Hours for Life, New York, 95; Sexual Politics: Rewriting Hist (photo catalog), Armand & Hammer Mus Art, Univ Calif, Los Angeles, 96; New Sch, Mus Mod Art, Apex Gallery, New York, 98; Not For Sale, Video Essay, Laura Cottingham, Mus Mod Art, Apex Gallery, New York, 98; End Papers: 1890-1900 & 1990-2000, Neuberger Mus Art, New York, 2000; Personal & Political: Women's Art Movement, 1969-1975, Guild Hall Mus, East Hampton, NY, 2002; Funky Fall Line, Chelsea Art Mus, New York & Berliner Kunstprojekt, Berlin, 2003; The F Word/Sex & Feminism, Mitchell Algus Gallery, New York, 2004; Upstairs and Matriarches: Jewish Women Artists and the Transformation of Am Art, Mizel Ctr, Denver, Colo, 2005; Eviction, Asian Arts Ctr, New York, 2005; Women's Work, Homage to Feminist Art, Tabla Rosa Gallery, New York, 2007; Claiming Space: The American Feminist Originators, Katzen Art Mus, Am Univ, Washington, DC, 2007-2008; How to Cook a Wolf, Finter Fine Art Gallery, New York, 2008; NY Artists, traveling print exhib, Galeria Gravura Brasileira & Belas Artes Univ Gallery, San Paolo, Brazil, 2009; Naked, Paul Kasmin Gallery, New York, 2009; Frieze Fair, The Box LA Booth, London, 2011; 185th Ann Exhib Contemp Am Art: Nat Acad, 2010. *Pos:* Adj prof, sch visual Arts, New York, 99-2005 & Queens Coll, New York, 97-. *Teaching:* adj prof, Purchase Coll, Suny, 1978; adj prof, Pratt Inst, 2008-; assoc prof fine arts, State Univ NY, Purchase, 78-; adj assoc prof, Queens Coll, CUNY, 1997-; Mason Gross Sch Arts, Rutgers Univ, 96-98. *Awards:* Elizabeth Canfield Hicks Mem Scholar, Yale Univ Sch Art & Archit, 64-67; Nat Endowment Arts Grant, 74-75 & 85-86; NY Found Arts, 88; Adolph and Esther Gottlieb Found Grant, 2000; Anonymous Was a Woman Grant, 2007; Joan Mitchell Found, 2008-2009; Penn State Distinguished Arts & Architecture Alumni Award, Sch Visual Arts, 2011. *Bibliog:* Thomas Lawson (auth), Judith Bernstein, Art Am, 148, 1-2/79; John Russell (auth), Judith Bernstein, NY Times, C2, 4/27/84; Elinor Gadon (auth), The Once and Future Goddess, Phantasmagoria: The Sexual Metaphors of Judith Bernstein, Harper & Row, San Francisco 331-332, 89; No Guts No Glory, Sunday Arts and Leisure, NY Times, 35-36, 2002; Holland Cotter (auth), Judith Bernstein, NY Times, 2008; Robert Berlind (auth), Sticking it, Art in Am, 2008; Emmelyn Butterfield-Rosen (auth), Critics Picks: Judish Bernstein, Artforum.com, 2008; Nick Stillman, Reviews, Artform, 4/2008; Walter Robinson (auth), Weekend Picks: Judith Bernstein, Artnet.com, 2008; The New Yorker, short list, Judith Bernstein, 2011; Time Out New York, Art Listings and Critics Picks, 2011. *Mem:* Coll Art Asn Am; Nat Soc Lit & Arts; Women's Caucus Art. *Media:* Charcoal drawings & oil paintings. *Publ:* centerfold, Guggenheim Panel Drawings, Soho Weekly News, 32, 3/12/80; Dr Judy Collischan Van Wagner (auth), Drawing in Situ (catalog), Hillwood Art Mus, Long Island Univ, New York, 86; N Broude & M Garrard (co-eds), The Power of Feminist Art, Abrams, New York, 105-112, 22 & 207, 94; Amelia Jones (ed, cur), Sexual Politics, photo, UCLA Armand Hammer Mus & Univ Calif Press, Berkeley, Los Angeles & London, 35, 234 & 261, 96; Carey Lovelace (auth), Art and Politics I, Feminism at 40, photo, Art Am, 67-73, 5/2003; Claiming Space: The American Feminist Originators, photo, Katzen Art Mus, Am Univ, Washington, DC & Brooklyn Mus, 2007; Cornelia H Butler (cur, co-ed with Lisa Gabrielle Mark), WACK! Art of the Feminist Revolution (catalog), Los Angeles Co Mus Contemp Art, photo, 367-368, The MIT Press, 2007. *Dealer:* Mitchell Algus Gallery New York; The Box Los Angeles. *Mailing Add:* Knickerbocker Sta PO Box 1045 New York NY 10002-0912

BERNSTEIN, SARALINDA
ART DEALER, HISTORIAN
b New York, NY, Jan 7, 1951. *Study:* Ecole Pratique des Hautes Etudes, Sorbonne, Paris, 70-71; Swarthmore Col, Pa, BA (magna cum laude), 72; NY Univ Sch Arts, 72; New Sch Social Res, New York, 74, Japan Soc, New York, 82-84. *Collection Arranged:* Edvard Munch: Paradox of Woman (auth, catalog), Aldis Browne Fine Arts, NY, 81; Prints about Prints, 81-82; Nineteenth and Twentieth Century Works on Paper (auth, catalog), 82 & Edgar Chahine: Images of Venice and The Belle Epoque (auth, catalog), 83, Picasso 156, Aldis Browne Fine Arts. *Pos:* Asst to dir, Asn Am Artists, NY, 72-78; exec vpres & dir, Aldis Browne Fine Arts, NY, 78-84; own & dir, Saralinda Bernstein Fine Art, 84-. *Teaching:* Lectr, Soc Ethical Cult, NY, 81. *Res:* Form and function of original prints in society; the concept and definition of form in visual arts, particularly in late 19th through early 20th century European works. *Publ:* Contribr, 10 Jahre Galerie Kühl, Galerie Kühl, 77. *Mailing Add:* 265 Massachusetts Ave Haworth NJ 07641-1809

BERNSTEIN, WILLIAM JOSEPH
DESIGNER, GLASSBLOWER
b Newark, NJ, Dec 3, 1945. *Study:* Philadelphia Coll Art, BFA, 68; Penland Sch, NC, 68-70. *Work:* Int Glasmus, Ebeltoft, Denmark; Australian Coun Arts, Sidney; Corning Mus Glass, NY; Renwick Gallery, Nat Mus Am Art, Smithsonian Inst, Washington; Glasmus Frauenau, Bavaria, WGer; Yamaha Corp, Japan; Chrysler Mus, Norfolk, Va; Mint Mus Art, Charlotte, NC. *Exhib:* Baroque '74, Mus Contemp Crafts, NY, 74; In Praise of Hands, 1st World Crafts Exhib, Toronto, Can, 74; Craft Multiples, Renwick Gallery, Smithsonian Inst, Washington, DC, 75; Philadelphia Mus of Art, 77; Am Crafts in the White House, Washington, 77; Victoria & Albert Mus, Eng; USA: Portrait of the South, Palazzo Venezia, Rome, Italy; Am Studio Glass, Isetan Galleries, Japan; Glass from the Corning Collection, Spaso House, Moscow, USSR; Solo exhibs, Somerhill Gallery, Chapel Hill, NC, Grohe Glass Gallery, 91, Marx Gallery, Chicago, Ill, 91; Vessels: From Use to Symbol, Am Craft Mus, NY. *Teaching:* Penland Sch Crafts, NC, Univ Southern Calif, Los Angeles, Pilchuck Glass Ctr, Stanwood, Wash & Naples Mill Sch, NY; Summervail Workshop, Vail, Colo. *Awards:* Nat Endowment Arts Fel, 74 & Grant, 76; Louis Comfort Tiffany Found Grant, 75; NC Arts Coun Fel, 83; Masterworks Fel, Creative Glass Ctr Am, 90. *Bibliog:* RL Grover (auth), Contemporary Art Glass, Crown Publ, 75; F Kulasiewicz (auth), Glassblowing, Watson-Guptill, 75; Design in Modern Interiors, Studio Vista, 75; Dan Klein (auth), Glass, A Contemporary Art, Rizzoli. *Publ:* NY Mag, NY Times; Atlanta Constitution Sunday Mag; State Mag NC; Am Craft (portfolio sect); Crafts Report. *Mailing Add:* 250 Chimney Ridge Rd Burnsville NC 28714

BERRETH, DAVID SCOTT
MUSEUM DIRECTOR
b Portland, Ore, Oct 10, 1949. *Study:* Bowdoin Col, BA, 71; Syracuse Univ, MA, 76. *Pos:* Asst dir, Elvehjem Mus Art, Univ Wis, Madison, 76-79; dir, Miami Univ Art Mus, Oxford, Ohio, 79-88, Madison Art Ctr, Wis, 88-90, Belmont, Gari Melchers Mem Gallery, Fredericksburg, Va, 90-. *Mailing Add:* 224 Washington St Fredericksburg VA 22405

BERRIER, WESLEY DORWIN
PAINTER, CONSERVATOR
b Chicago, Ill, July 24, 1951. *Study:* Apprentice to Joseph Abbrescia, Village Gallery, 70-74; Coll DuPage, AA, 74; George Williams Col, BA (summa cum laude), 80. *Work:* Tesla Mem Soc, Lackawanna, NY. *Comn:* Family portraits, Dr Ned Mandich, HBM Corp, Homewood, Ill, 81-85; restoration of Christ on Mount by Henry Kratzner, First United Methodist Church, Hobart, Ind, 85; portrait, Lou Boudreax (Hall of Fame Baseball Player), 89; restoration 16th century panels, Richard Crowe Collection, Chicago, 92; portrait of Mikola Tesla, Serbian Acad Arts & Sci, Belgrade, 96. *Exhib:* Series of Faust Paintings, Village Art Sch, Skokie, Ill, 90; Serbian-Tesla Mus, Belgrade, 96; Salon Show, Northern Ind Arts Asn, Munster, 97. *Pos:* Own & operator, Berrier Art Studios, Ill, 72-82; restorator, Village Gallery, Skokie, Ill, 74-; judge art exhibs, NIAA, Munster, Ind, 93-. *Teaching:* Instr oil painting, Berrier Art Studios, Ill, 72-82, Northern Ind Arts Asn, Munster, Ind, 91-; instr aesthetics, Col DuPage, Glen Elyn, Ill, 90-91. *Awards:* Fel, DuPaul Univ, 84-85. *Bibliog:* Northern Ind Arts, Artist

at Work Series, Metrovision, 83; This Week in Munster, Munster Cable Studio, Muncab Cable, 92; Berrier, artist & his work, Post Tribune Times, 96. *Mem:* Hogart Arts League; Northern Ind Arts Asn. *Media:* Oil. *Publ:* Auth, Rules for judging, Hogart Arts League, 81. *Mailing Add:* c/o Northern Ind Art Asn 1040 Ridge Rd Hammond IN 46321

BERRY, CAROLYN B
PAINTER, ILLUSTRATOR
b Sweet Springs, Mo, June 27, 1930. *Study:* Univ Mo, BA, 53; Humboldt Univ, 71; Univ Calif, 85-87. *Work:* Sackner Collection, Miami Beach, Fla; Monterey Peninsula Mus Art, Calif; Nat Mus Women Art; Mus Mod Art Libr; Art Inst Chicago; Museo Internacional De Electrografia, Cuenca, Spain; Univ Calif at Los Angeles; St Stephan Mus, Hungary; Stanford Univ, Stanford, Calif. *Exhib:* Women's Artists Series, Rutgers Univ, 88 & 96; Pacific Rim Exhib, 90-93; Monterey Conf Ctr, 93-94; All Our Lives (with catalog), Women's Caucus for Art, Monterey Bay, 95-96; Lisa Parker Fine Art, NY, 96; Claypoole-Freese, 98; Core Gallery, New Paltz, NY, 2002-03; Walter Avery Gallery, Seaside, Calif, 2004; Int Invitational Mail Art Show, Guy Bleus, Wallen, Belgium, 2005. *Collection Arranged:* Gene McComas Exhib, Monterey Mus Art, 80. *Pos:* Artist-in-residence, Calif Arts Coun. *Teaching:* Instr bk art, Monterey Peninsula Col, 87. *Awards:* First Graphic Award, Monterey Peninsula Mus Art, 74 & 3rd Award, 85; Best in Show, Pac Grove Art Ctr, 97; Lifetime Achievement Award, Women's Caucus for Art, 2006. *Bibliog:* Artists & Their Cats, Midmarch, New York, 90; Mary H Dana (auth), Women Artists Series, Rutgers, 96. *Mem:* Women's Caucus for Art; Montery Mus Art; Nat Mus Women Art; Pac Grove Art Ctr. *Media:* Miscellaneous Media. *Res:* Vinnie Ream, Artist; Gene McComas, Artist; Mildred Walker, Artist; Comenha, The Sorrowing One, Northern Cheyenne, Anna Guy, Chickasaw. *Publ:* Contribr, Zoom Mag, France, 89. *Dealer:* Lisa Parker Fine Art 584 Broadway Ste 308 New York NY 10012; ClayPoole-Freese Gallery. *Mailing Add:* 3 Bundy Rd Santa Fe NM 87506-2639

BERRY, GLENN
PAINTER, EDUCATOR
b Glendale, Calif, Feb 27, 1929. *Study:* Pomona Coll, BA (magna cum laude); Art Inst Chicago, BFA & MFA. *Work:* Storm King Art Ctr, Mountainville, NY; Joseph H Hirshhorn Collection, Washington, DC; Kaiser Aluminum & Chem Corp, Oakland, Calif; Palm Springs Desert Mus, Calif; Calif State Univ, Humboldt. *Exhib:* Phelan Awards Exhib & Artists Behind Artists, Calif Palace Legion Hon, San Francisco, 67; solo exhibs, Ankrum Gallery, Los Angeles, 70, Esther Bear Gallery, Santa Barbara, Calif, 71, Coll Redwoods, 89 & Humboldt State Univ, 92 & Morris Graves Mus Art, 2000; Six Northern Calif Artists, Henry Gallery, Univ Wash, 75; two-person exhib, Humboldt Cult Ctr, Eureka, Calif, 77; and others. *Teaching:* Prof painting, Humboldt State Univ, 56-81, prof emer, 81-. *Media:* Acrylic, Oil

BERSHAD, DAVID L
HISTORIAN, EDUCATOR
b San Francisco, Calif, Mar 11, 1942. *Study:* Stanford Univ, AB, 62; Univ Calif, Los Angeles, PhD (with distinction), 70. *Teaching:* Asst prof art hist, Ariz State Univ, 70-72; assoc prof art hist, Univ Calgary, 75-85, prof, 85-. *Awards:* Fulbright Fel, 68; Kress Fel, 69; Distinguished Scholar, Univ Lethbridge, 80. *Mem:* Univ Art Asn Can. *Res:* 17th & 18th century Italian painting & sculpture, with specific emphasis on Roman art. *Publ:* Auth, A series of papal busts by Domenico Guidi, 70, Domenico Guidi and Nicolas Poussin, 71, The cardinal Marco Bragadino tomb in the church of San Marco in Rome, 77 & auth, New documents concerning Michelangelo's deposition in Florence, 78, Burlington Mag; The tapestries of Raphael and their re-acquisition in 1808, 78 & P E Monnot: Newly discovered sculpture and documents, 84, Antologia di Belle Arti. *Mailing Add:* c/o Univ Calgary Dept Art 2500 University Dr NW Calgary AB T2N 1N4 Canada

BERTELLI, PATRIZIO
COLLECTOR
Study: Univ Bologna. *Pos:* Chief exec officer, Prada SPA. *Awards:* Named one of Top 200 Collectors, ARTnews mag, 2009-13. *Collection:* Contemporary art. *Mailing Add:* Prada SPA Via Fogazzaro 28 Milan 20135 Italy

BERTI, MARY VITELLI
PAINTER
b Brooklyn, NY. *Study:* Suffolk Co Com Col, Selden, NY, AA (honors), 1974; LI Univ School of Arts, CW Post Ctr, Brookville, NY, BA (summa cum laude), 1975; MA (summa cum laude), 1979. *Work:* Lou Henry Hoover House at Stanford, Univ, Calif; Jin-Hyun Hwang Coll, Samick Park Mansion, Gil-Dong, Seoul, Korea; Dr Kurt Grimm Coll, Untere Augarter, Vienna, Aus; Mr & Mrs G Vlasic Collection, Bloomfield Hills, Mich; Dr & Mrs John L Hennessy Coll Stanford Univ, Calif. *Exhib:* 48th Ann Juried LI Art Exhib, Heckscher Mus Art, Huntington, NY, 1978-2001, 2003; Pastel Soc of Am Juried Ann, Nat Arts Club, New York City, 1980-2005; 27th Parrish Juried Art Exhibit, Parrish Art Mus, Southampton, NY, 1981; Nat Acad of Design Ann Exhib, New York City, 1981, 1986, 1988, 1992, 1996; Nat League Am Pen Women Juried Exhib, Vanderbilt Mus, Centerport, NY, 1993; Pastel Invitational, Hermitage Mus, Norfolk, Va, 1999; Master Pastelists, Butler Inst Am Art, Youngstown, Ohio, 2003. *Awards:* Best in Show, Nat League Am Pen Women, Winsor Newton Oils, 1993; Am Artist Mag Award, Pastel Soc of Am, Ann Am Artist Mag, 2001; Award of Excellence, Ann Juried Exhib, Heckscher Mus Art, 2003. *Bibliog:* Rachelle DePalma (auth), Family Portrait, Attenzione Mag Adam Pub, New York City, 1985; R. Tenenbaum (dir), Originals (film), Interview Cable WLIW, Long Island, NY, 1989; Judith Baker (dir), For Art's Sake, Interview Cable, Champaign, Il, 1991. *Mem:* Pastel Soc Am, Nat Arts Club, New York City; Heckscher Mus Art, Huntington, NY; Huntington Arts Coun, Huntington, NY; Art League Long Island, Dix Hills, NY; Friends of Gallery, North Setauket, NY. *Media:* Pastel, Oil, Acrylic. *Publ:* auth, Personal Style, Pastelagram, Pastel Soc of Am, 2003. *Mailing Add:* 107 Townsend St Birmingham MI 48009

BERTINE, DOROTHY W
PAINTER
b Madill, Okla, Sep 28, 1916. *Study:* Okla State Univ, BS, 1942; Houston Mus Sch Art, with Frances Skinner, 1960-1963; Tex Woman's Univ, MA, 1975. *Work:* Brownsville Mus & Art League, Tex; Laredo Fine Arts Mus & Art League, Tex; Heard Nature Mus Sci, McKinney, Tex; Women's Collection, MBH Libr, Tex Woman's Univ, Denton, Tex; Print Collection, State Mus of NJ; Charles B Goddard Ctr Visual & Performing Arts, Ardmore, Okla. *Comn:* Painting, comn by Mr. & Mrs. Bennett Wooley, Dallas, 1980; Historic Houses remaining in Denton (map), City of Denton, Tex, 1980; watercolor, Lady Love Cosmetics, Dallas, 1993. *Exhib:* Major retrospectives include Laredo Art Mus, Tex, 2000 & Charles B Goddard Ctr Visual & Performing Arts, Ardmore, Okla, 2007 & 2008; exhibs include Hist Victorian Archit & Lect, Tex Woman's Univ Gallery, Denton, Tex, 1975 & 1982; TWU Diamond Jubilee Exhib, Tex Woman's Univ Gallery, Denton, Tex, 1976; Hist Archit, Ft McIntosh & Nueva Santander Mus Art, Laredo, Tex, 1978; Citation Exhib, Laguna Gloria Art Mus, Austin, Tex, 1979-1981; Southern Watercolor Soc Ann, Columbia Mus Art, Columbia, SC, 1980; Trees and Flowers, Heard Mus of Sci, McKinney, Tex, 1983 & 1989; Charles B Goddard Ctr Visual & Performing Arts, Ardmore, Okla, 1984-1987; Hist Tex Archit, Brownsville Art Mus, Tex1984; Southwestern Watercolor Soc 25th Ann Mem Exhib, Mall Gallery, Dallas, 1988; Retrospective exhib, Goddard Mus, 2013. *Pos:* Dept head and instr watercolor & drawing, City of Denton Parks & Recreation, 1975-1985. *Teaching:* Instr watercolor, Brownsville Art Mus, 1965-1970 & 1984-1988; instr watercolor, Tex Woman's Univ, 1974-1975. *Awards:* Grumbacher Medal, Southwestern Watercolor Soc, 1982; Soc Watercolor Artists, Best of Show & Presidents Award, Ft Worth, 1986; Visual Artist of the Year, Int Biog Ctr, 2004; Casa Editric Alba, Ferrara, Italy, Premio Alba, 2003, 2004, 2005. *Bibliog:* Placing Oak Street homes on canvas, Denton Record Chronicle, 1985; Spotlight on the Artist, Southwestern Watercolor Soc, 1983 & 1985. *Mem:* Southwestern Watercolor Soc (signature mem 1965-); Assoc Creative Artists, Dallas, Tex (signature mem); Soc Watercolor Artists (signature mem), Ft Worth, Tex; La Watercolor Soc (life mem); Brownsville Art League (life mem & instr). *Media:* Acrylic, Oil, Watercolor, All Media. *Res:* Hist of ornament used in high Victorian houses. *Interests:* Painting & teaching. *Collection:* Private collection East coast & Calif painters work. *Publ:* Contribr, Best of Watercolor, Painting Light and Shadow, Schleem & Doherty Rockport publ, 1997; Collected Best of Watercolor, Schlemm & Doherty Rockport publ, 2002; Encyclopedia of Living Artists in America, ArtNetWork, 1990 & 2003; Dizionario Enciclopedia Internazionale d'Arte, Alba, Italy, 2003 & 2005; "Le Mer" Book of Modern & Contemporary Art, Regards d'Arte, Pau, France, 2005, Art, Peintres et Sculpteurs du XVe au XXI Siècle, 2006, Portraits d'Artistes, 2007 & Art: des Mots, des Oeuvres, 2008; Art and Popsie, 2012. *Dealer:* Craig Wilkerson Gallery Rupp Fine Arts 1025 E 15th St Plano TX 75074. *Mailing Add:* d' Bertine Studio PO Box 2965 Denton TX 76202

BERTOLLI, EUGENE EMIL
SCULPTOR, DESIGNER
b Boston, Mass, Feb 19, 1923. *Study:* Boston Coll, AB, 43; Hartford Coll Grad Sch, cert art educ, 49; pvt study with EG Chandler, 78-83. *Comn:* Stained glass windows, Madigan Convalescent Hosp, Ft Lewis, Wash, 45; sculptured gold pectoral cross, Bishop McGurkin, Tanganyika, Africa, 56; commemorative medal, City of Meriden, Conn, 85; also numerous pvt comns in sculpture & precious jewelry. *Exhib:* Solo exhibs, Conn Town & Co Asn, Hartford, 80 & Rockport Art Asn, Mass, 85; Nat Exhib, Hudson Valley Arts Asn, Hudson Valley, NY, 83-88; Ann Nat Exhib, Acad Artists Asn, Springfield, Mass, 84-90; Ann Awards Exhib, Guild Boston Artists, Mass, 85. *Pos:* Dir art & educ, Madigan Convent Hosp, Ft Lewis, Wash, 45-47; sr vpres & chief designer, Napier Co, NY, 47-85; pres, Meriden Community Theatre, formerly; pres, Meriden Curtis Mem Libr Bd, formerly; US Army off in charge of the arts and crafts for wounded soldiers WWII; 23 years, Meriden bd of educ for 6 years for pres of Art & Crafts Asn Meriden Ctr. *Teaching:* Lectr fine arts; Portraits & figure Sculpture; metallic art sculpture; In the Jewelry design & production (The Napier Co); Lectr on jewelry and its design & production in the USA & Int; Traveled to major dept stores as the artist designer of Napier Jewelry: (Stores Lord & Taylor NYC; Lazarus Stores; Marshall Fields, Chicago, Dallas Tex, Disney World Orlando, Hawaii, Eng, Jordan Marsh, Boston, Etc). *Awards:* Coun Am Artists Soc Award, Acad Artists Asn Nat Exhib, 92; Paul Manship Mem Award Excellence Sculpture, North Shore Arts Asn, 92; Elected, Meriden Hall Fame for Achievements in Art, 95; and others. *Bibliog:* Linda Fridy (auth), Bertolli: Dean of American jewelry designers, Accent Mag, 86. *Mem:* Am Artists Prof League; Guild Boston Artist; Acad Artists Asn (mem, exec comt, Springfield, Mass, 83); Hudson Valley Art Asn; Am Medallic Sculpture Asn; Salmagundi Club; New Eng Sculptors Asn; FIDEM; Rockport Art Asn, Rockport Mass; North Shore Art Asn, E Gloucester. *Media:* Metals; All Media. *Publ:* Auth & illusr, Continuity through change: A history of jewelry design, Conn Mag, 60. *Mailing Add:* Bertolli Studios 73 Reynolds Dr Meriden CT 06450

BERTONI, CHRISTINA
CERAMIST, PAINTER
b Ann Arbor, Mich, Jan 15, 1945. *Study:* Univ Mich, BFA (painting), 67; Cranbrook Acad Art, MFA (ceramics), 76. *Work:* Brooklyn Mus, Brooklyn, NY; Victoria & Albert Mus, London; Crocker Art Mus, Sacramento, Calif; Mus Fine Arts, Boston, Mass. *Exhib:* Am Potters Today (with catalog), Victoria & Albert Mus, London, Eng, 86; solo exhib, Victoria Munroe Gallery, NY, 87 & 93; Virginia Lynch Gallery, Tiverton, RI, 95 & 97; Sculptural Ceramics in New Eng, Boston Athenium, Mass, 96-97; Painters & Sculptures of the McDowell Colony, Currier Gallery Art, Manchester, NH, 96-97; Power of the Center, Pewabic Pottery, Detroit, Mich, 97. *Teaching:* Assoc prof art, RI Sch Design, Providence, 77-, dean grad studies, currently. *Awards:* Purchase Prize, Crocker Art Mus, Calif, 77; Nat Endowment Arts Craftsman Fel, 79 & 86; Craftsman Grant, RI State Coun Arts, 83. *Bibliog:* Lois Tarlow (auth), Christina Bertoni, Art New Eng, 4/84; James Cobb (auth), article, Am Ceramics, 88; On the spiritual art, Agni Rev, fall, 88. *Media:* Clay; Paint. *Dealer:* Siparist Gallery Laurel Oak MI

BESANT, DEREK MICHAEL
PAINTER, INSTRUCTOR
b Ft MacLeod, Alta, July 15, 1950. *Study:* Univ Calgary, Alberta Can, BFA, 73. *Work:* De Cordova Mus, Boston, Mass; Metrop Mus, Miami, Fla; Can Coun Art Bank, Ottawa, Ont; Cineplex Odeon Corp, NY; Royal Bank Can. *Comn:* Flatiron mural, A E LePage, Royal Insurance Lavalin Inc, Toronto, Ont, 80; Eau Claire Peel, Bourgeau Developments Sturgets Architects, Calgary, Alta, 82; cardboard windows installation proj, Liberty of London, Eng, 87; paintings, Amoco, Mt Royal Col, Calgary & Bank of Nova Scotia, Toronto. *Exhib:* Boston Printmakers, Boston Ctr Arts, Mass, 78; 8th Int Triennial Color Prints, Grenchen Arts Mus, Switz, 79; Other Realities, Can House London, Eng, Paris, France, 79; Royal Canadian Soc Arts, Mickle Arts Mus, Calgary, Alta, 80; Can Prints, Asn Print Workshops Gt Brit, Edinborough, Scotland, 80; Ten Can Print Artists, Nat Mus Can Japanese Print Coun, Tour Japan Nat Mus, 80-81; Int Print Exhibs Repub China, Taipei, 84; 6th Int Impact Art Festival, Kyoto City Mus, 85; Diagrams, Mira Godard Gallery, Toronto, 86; Asian-Pacific, Univ New Delhi, India, 86; Solo exhib, Woltjen Udell Gallery, Vancouver & Mira Godard Gallery, Toronto, 89, Art Gallery of Hamilton, 90; San Antonio Mus Art, Tex, 92; Sao Paulo, Brazil, 92; Centre de Langues, Brussels, Belg, 92; and others. *Pos:* Exhibs designer, Glenbow Mus, Calgary, 73-77; Alta ed, Artmagazine, Toronto, 74-; drawing chmn, Alta Col Art, 77-; comt mem, Alta Legislature Art Acquisition Comt, 81-82. *Teaching:* Guest artist collaborations, Univ Arts Asn, Univ Alta, 76; guest artist printmaking, Mem Univ, Newfoundland, 77; lectr pub art, Univ Regina, Sask, 81; lectr murals, Red Deer Col, 82 & Southwest Tex State Univ, 89. *Awards:* Canada Coun Grant, 77, 85 & 92; Second Prize, Miami Biennale, Mus Mod Art, 77; Award Winner, Andrew Nelson Wheehead Co, 78; World Cult Prize for Lett, Arts & Sci, 84; Alberta Achievement Award, 84. *Bibliog:* Nancy Tousley (auth), Falls transplanted to Toronto, Calgary Herald, 5/89; Christopher Hume (auth), Huge waterfall graces Scotia Plaza, The Sunday Star, Toronto, 5/89; Patrick McHugh (auth), Toronto Architecture, McClelland & Stewart, Can, 89. *Mem:* Royal Can Acad Arts; Print & Drawing Coun Can (vchmn, 76-78); Can Artists Representation; Visual Arts Ont; World Print Coun. *Media:* Watercolor, Ink. *Res:* Contemporary Canadian. *Publ:* Illusr, The Back Room, Oberon, 80; A Culinary Palette, Merritt, 81; contribr, Artmagazine, 81; Artviews, Visual Arts Ont, 82; Macleans, Maclean Hunter, 82. *Mailing Add:* Dept Art Alberta Col Art 1407 14th Ave NW Calgary AB T2N 1M4 Canada

BESANTE, JOHN L, JR
PAINTER
b Jersey City, NJ, 1951. *Study:* Sch Visual Arts, New York, 74-76; State Teachers Coll, NJ, 80-83; Upstairs Art Sch, Jersey City, 68-. *Exhib:* Group exhibs at Washington Square Park, NY; Tribes Gallery, NY; Bowery Art Gallery, NY; Blvd East Arts, NJ; Art Exchange Gallery, NJ; Bayonne Library, NJ; Jersey City Hall, Rotunda, NJ; Stuyvesant Gallery, NJ; Upstairs Art Gallery, NJ; Mary Benson Gallery; Es Oro Gallery; Annex Gallery, NJ; Women of Color, Sirens Song, Am in Paris, A Night at the Met, Gallery 58, NJ; Jersey City Ann Studio Walking tour, NJ 80-2012; Walking for 2013. *Pos:* Founder, Arts Students League of West Indies & Artists Retreat, Belize; mem bd & adv, Hudson Artists of NJ, currently; copyist, Metrop Mus Art, New York, 2001-; owner, cur, 58 Gallery & Mary Benson Gallery. *Teaching:* Stained glass instr, Snug Harbor Cultural Ctr, Staten Island, 76-80; life drawing, 58 Gallery, 2010-. *Mem:* Hudson Artists; Pro Arts; SAG/AFTRA Union. *Media:* Oil. *Interests:* Nudes and Landscapes. *Collection:* D Hue Bente, SVA, F. Weeks, S Gordon, Michael Francis, Viveen Dormer, James Waddleton, Triscia Henry. *Publ:* SVA Christmas Card 1970. *Dealer:* Gallery 58 58 Coles St Jersey City NJ 07302. *Mailing Add:* 291 Fifth St Jersey City NJ 07302

BESHTY, WALEAD
PHOTOGRAPHER
b London, 1976. *Study:* Bard Coll, BA, 1999; Yale Univ Sch Art, MFA, 2002. *Work:* Whitney Mus Am Art, Neuberger Berman Art Collection, New York; Armand Hammer Mus, LA; Francis Lehmann Loeb Art Center, Poughkeepsie, NY; Orange County Mus Art, Newport, Calif. *Exhib:* Solo exhibs include Wallspace, New York, 2004, 2006 & 2008, PS1 Contemp Art Center, Long Island City, NY, 2004, China Art Objects Galleries, LA, 2005 & 2008, Armand Hammer Mus Art, LA, 2006, Inst Glaspavillon/Galerie Meerrettich, Berlin, 2007, LAXART, LA, 2008; group exhibs include Anti-Social, Wallspace, New York, 2003, Photography for People; For Us, 2003, Bucolica, 2005, From a Distance, 2007; Self-Evidence: Indentity in Contemp Art, DeCordova Mus & Sculpture Park, Lincoln, Mass, 2004; Upstream: Idea Drawings, Hayworth Gallery, LA, 2004; Manufactured Self, Mus Contemp Photog, Chicago, 2005; The ArtReview 25: Emerging US Artists, Phillips, de Pury & Co, New York, 2005; Post No Bills, White Columns, New York, 2005, White Columns Ann, 2006; The New City: Sub/Urbia in Recent Photog, Whitney Mus Am Art, New York, 2005, Whitney Biennial, 2008; Galerie Rodolphe Jannsen, Brussels, 2006; Hammer Contemp Collection, Armand Hammer Mus Art, LA, 2007; The Backroom, Kadist Art Found, Paris, 2007; Meanwhile in Baghdad, Renaissance Soc, Chicago, 2007. *Collection Arranged:* Pictures are the Problem, Pelham Art Center, NY, 2005; Invisible Hands and the Common Good, Champion Fine Art, LA, 2005; 24 Hour Armageddon: A Cold War Slumber Party, Armand Hammer Mus Art, LA, 2006; The Gold Standard, PS1 Contemp Art Center, New York, 2006. *Mailing Add:* care Wallspace Ground Fl 619 W 27th St New York NY 10001

BESSIRE, MARK HC
MUSEUM DIRECTOR
Study: NYU, BA; Hunter Col, MA in art hist; Columbia Univ, MBA. *Pos:* Dir, Inst Contemp Art, Maine Col Art, 1998—2003; Bates Col Mus Art, Lewiston, Maine, 2003—. *Mailing Add:* Bates Col Mus Art Olin Arts Ctr Rm 202 2 Andrews Rd Lewiston ME 04240-6028

BETSKY, AARON
MUSEUM DIRECTOR
b Missoula, Mont, 1958. *Study:* Yale Univ, BA, 79, MArch, 83. *Exhib:* Magnets of Meaning, 97. *Collection Arranged:* Dir, First Int Archit Biennnale Rotterdam, 2002. *Pos:* Designer, Frank O Gehry Assocs Inc, 85-87 & Hodgetts & Fung Design, 87; cur Archit & Design, San Francisco Mus Mod Art, 95-2001; co-founder, San Francisco Prize, 95; founder, first biannual San Francisco Forum, Architecture of Imagination, 97; dir, Netherlands Archit Inst, Rotterdam, 2001-2006 & Cincinnati Art Mus, 2006-2014; archit dir, Venice Biennale, 2008. *Teaching:* Instr, Univ Cincinnati Sch Archit & Interior Design, 83-85; instr & coordr Special Projects, Southern Calif Inst Archit; adj prof, Calif Coll Arts and Crafts; Eero Saarinen chmn in archit, Univ Mich; vis prof, Columbia Univ, Calif Coll Arts, Houston Sch Archit & Southern Calif Inst Santa Monica; Instr, Univ Kentucky, Lexington. *Mem:* British Inst Architects. *Publ:* Auth, Violated Perfection: Architecture and the Fragmentation of the Modern, 90; James Gamble Rogers and the Architecture of Pragmatism, 94; Building Sex: Men, Women, Architecture and the Construction of Sexuality; Queer Space: The Spaces of Same Sex Desire, 97; Architecture Must Burn, 2000; The United Nations Building, Thames & Hudson, 2006; What is Modernism, Phaidon Press, 2008; At Home in Sprawl: Selected Essays on Architecture, RMIT Univ Press, 2011

BETTERIDGE, LOIS ETHERINGTON
LECTURER, SILVERSMITH
b Drummonville, Que, Nov 6, 1928. *Study:* Ont Coll Art, 47-48; Univ Kans, BFA, 51; Cranbrook Acad Art, MFA, 57. *Work:* Royal Scottish Mus, Edinborough; Int Bus Machines, Can; Nat Mus Natural Sci & Nat Mus Man, Ottawa; Cranbrook Acad Art, Mich; R Abramson, Seattle, Wash; Royal Ontario Mus, Toronto, On. *Comn:* Communion set, Christ Church Cathedral, Vancouver, 74; bronze sculptures, IBM Can, 75; desk sets, Provincial Premiers & Prime Minister, Can Pac Railways; bronze sculptures, Imperial Oil Can; ongoing medals, McLuhan Teleglobe Can UNESCO Award; Rings 2010, New Gallery, Toronto, 2010. *Exhib:* Contemp Ont Crafts, Agnes Etherington Gallery, Kingston, Ont, 77; Artisans Touring Exhib, Can, 78; solo-exhibs, Reflections in Silver & Gold Traveling Exhib (catalog), 81-83, Recent Works Traveling Exhib (catalog), 88-90 & New Works, Harbinger Gallery, 96; Remains To Be Seen, John Michael Kohler Arts Ctr, Sheboygan, Wis, 82; Silversmithing-Three and a Half Decades, Cranbrook Acad Art, Mich, 82; The Mich Influence, Eastern Mich Univ, Ypsilanti, 82; Masters of Am Metalsmithing, Nat Ornamental Metal Mus, Memphis, 88; Silver: New Forms and Expressions, USA 1990; RCA Canadian Designers, Budapest, Burgundy Edinburgh, 1995; Raised from Tradition; Holloware Past and Present Seafirst Gallery, Seattle, WA, 1998; Benchmarkers; Women in Metal, National Ornamental Metal Mus, Memphis Tenn, 1999; Contemp Images of Ont Lieutenant-Governor's Suite, Queen's Park, 1999; Arts 2000 RCA Stratford, Ont, May 2000; Tribute Exhib at the Macdonald Stewart Art ctr in Guelph in 2000 and at the Nova Scotia Art Gallery, (catalogue); In Service, Anna Leonowens Gallery, Halifax, NS, 2004; Illingworth Kerr Gallery, Calgary, Alta, 2005; Beyond the Frame, Macdonald Stewart Art Centre, Guelph, Ont, 2006; New Gallery, Toronto, Ont, 2006; Ont Coll Art & Design, 2007; In Celebration: Tribute Exhib, Jonathons, London, 2008; A Table, Lt Governors, Fredericktown, NC, 2012; The Six Inch Disli Art Gallery, Ontario, 2013; Zilbursmit Gallery, 2013; A Table, MacDonald Stewart Art Gallery, 2013; Materia, Quebec City, 2013; Design Exchange Toronto, 2013; Affinity Gallery, Saskatoon, 2013. *Collection Arranged:* Pewter workings, Rails End Gallery, Haliburton, Ont, Can. *Pos:* Studio Silversmith. *Teaching:* Lectr design, metal & weaving, Univ Guelph, Ont, 57-61; vis lectr & workshop leader, worldwide, 69-; Holloware instr, Fleming Col, Haliburton Sch Art, Ont, 82; vis artist to Col & Guilds, USA, Can, Europe & Gt Brit; pvt tutor in studio, 75-. *Awards:* Fel, New Brunswick Craft Sch, 88; Joan M Chalmers 15 Anniversary Award, 91; Hon Fel, Ont Coll Art, 92; Citation for Distinguished Professional Achievement, Univ of Kansas, 1975; Saidye Bronfman Award for Excellence in Crafts, 1978; The YMCA, YWCA Women of Distinction Award for Lifetime Achievement, Guelph, 2002; Order of Canada, 97; Queen's Golden Jubilee Medal, 2002; Queen Elizabeth II, Golden Jubilee award, 2012. *Mem:* Ont Crafts Coun (mem bd, 72-73); distinguished mem Soc Am Goldsmiths (mem bd, 85-88); Royal Acad Arts; fel Royal Can Acad Arts. *Media:* Silver, Gold. *Res:* my designs. *Specialty:* Holloware, silversmithing. *Publ:* Auth, The Smiths Mandate, Introd, Metalsmith, 4/5/86; David Didur Recent Work, Ont Craft, spring 88; Ken Vickerson & Collen Brzezick, Ont Craft, fall 88; Donald Staurt The Challenge of Metals, Metalsmith, summer 94; Gold of Meroe, Royal Ont Mus, Toronto, 94. *Dealer:* Renann Isaacs Gallery Guelph Ont Can. *Mailing Add:* 9 Kirkland St Guelph ON N1H 4X7 Canada

BETTINSON, BRENDA
PAINTER, PRINTMAKER
b King's Lynn, Eng, Aug 17, 1929; US citizen. *Study:* St Martins Sch Art, London, 46-48; Cent Sch Arts & Crafts, London, 48-50, Nat Dipl in Design, 50; Acad de la Grande Chaumiere, Paris, 51; Ecole Pratique des Hautes Etudes, Sorbonne, 51-53, Eleve Titulaire, 52. *Work:* St Anselm's Abbey, Washington, DC; also pvt collections of St Mary's Benedictine Abbey, Morristown, NJ & Dominican House Studies, Washington, DC; Mus Art, Bates Coll, Maine; Ogunquit Mus Am Art, Maine. *Comn:* Murals, Calvary Hosp, Bronx, 78; outdoor installation, etched steel and marble. *Exhib:* Numerous solo and group exhibs in Europe and USA most recently Ogunquit Mus Am Art, 2002; Arcadia & Archetypes, Ctr Maine Contemp Art, 2009; Homage to Brenda Bettinson, Mathias Fine Art, Trevett, Maine, 2009; Larger than Life: Paintings by Brenda Bettinson Mathias Fine Art, Maine, 2011; Archdiocese of Brisbane, Australia, 2013. *Pos:* Art ed, Riverside Radio WRVR-FM, New York, 61-65; consult, Soc for Renewal of Christian Art, 69-87. *Teaching:* Prof art, Pace Univ, New York, 63-90, chairperson art & design, 79-85 & prof emer, 90; lectr art, Katonah Gallery, New York, 72-75, instr Docents' Prog, 88-89. *Awards:* Gold Medal, Nat Arts Club, New York, 66. *Bibliog:* Brenda Bettinson: Dancing with Buoys, Bob Keyes, Maine Sunday Telegram, 2002; Brenda Bettinson: from King's Lynn to Barter's Island, Carl Little, Maine Boats Harbors, 2004; Bob Keyes (auth), Profile: Brenda Bettinson, a new angle, Maine Sunday Telegram, 12/25/2005; Walker, Bettinson & Katz, Change

& Light in Maine, Carl Little, Maine Home & Design, 5/2008; At 80: A Festschrift for Brenda Bettinson, M-Press, Maine, 6/2009; Carl Little (auth), Maine's Veterans of Painting: Brenda Bettinson, Beverly Hallam, and Dahlov Ipcar, Art in New England, 2010. *Mem:* Ctr Maine Contemp Art. *Media:* All Media. *Dealer:* Mathias Fine Art Trevett ME 04571. *Mailing Add:* 10 Mathias Dr Trevett ME 04571

BETTS, JUDI POLIVKA
PAINTER, INSTRUCTOR
b Western Springs, Ill, July 26, 1936. *Study:* Ind U, AB (fine art), 58; La State Univ, MEd, 64; Studied under Barse Miller, Rex Brandt, Millard Sheets & Milford Zornes. *Work:* New Orleans Mus Art, La; Springfield Art Mus, Mo; Loma Linda Univ, Riverside, Calif; State of La Permanent Collection, Baton Rouge; State of Ark Permanent Collection, Little Rock. *Comn:* 10 Hist Bldgs, Commonwealth Mortgage, Houston, Tex, 84; 12 Hist Bldgs, Am Fed Bank, Greenville, SC, 85; religious triptych, DePaul Hosp, New Orleans, La, 85; triptych, dining room, Omni Hotel Chain, Durham, NC, 88; painting, Sen Russell B Long Fed Bldg, Washington, DC, 98. *Exhib:* Nat Acad Design, New York, 90, 92, 94; Signatures Above & Below, Fed Can Artists, Vancouver, 92; In the Grand Tradition, Nat Arts Club, Fairfield, Conn, 94; Nat Taiwan Art Educ Inst, Taipei, 94; Watercolor USA, Springfield Art Mus, Mo; Butler Inst Am Art, Youngstown, Ohio; Art in the Garden, EPCOT Ctr, Orlando, 2000. *Pos:* vpres, La Art & Artists Guild, 65-66, pres, 66-67; owner, Aquarelle Art Sems, 77-. *Teaching:* chair dept art, E Ascension Sr High, Gonzales, La, 66-84; mem watercolor staff, Arrowmont Sch, Univ Tenn, 91-96. *Awards:* Purchase award, Watercolor USA, 80; Mary Pleisner Mem Award, AWS, 86; Obrig Prize, Nat Acad Design, 94. *Bibliog:* George A Magnan (auth), Judi Betts: Watercolors, Today's Art, 79; PJ Gentile (author), Les Ateliers de Judy Betts, Magazin' Art, 90; Randolph Delehanty (auth), Art in the American South, LSU Press, 96. *Mem:* AWS (bd dir 91-); Watercolor USA & Hon Soc; Nat Arts Club; hon mem Fed Can Artists; hon mem Soc Can de l'aquarelle. *Media:* Watercolor. *Publ:* auth, Watercolor...Let's Think About It, Aquarelle Press, 84, The Watercolor Page, Am Artist, 87 & Watercolor Magic-Take It Off!, Artists' Mag, 94; co-auth, Painting...A Quest Toward Xtraord!nary, Aquarelle Press, 99; auth, A Luminous Start, Artists' Mag, 2000. *Dealer:* Taylor Clark Galleries 2623 Government St Baton Rouge LA 70806. *Mailing Add:* PO Box 3676 Baton Rouge LA 70821-3676

BEVERIDGE, KARL J
PHOTOGRAPHER, COLLAGE ARTIST
b Ottawa, Ont, Nov 7, 1945. *Study:* Ont Coll Art, 65-66; New Sch, Toronto, Ont, 66-67. *Hon Degrees:* Ont Coll Art & Design, Hon degree, 2010; Prix Au Merite Artistique, Universite Du Quebec a Montreal. *Work:* Nat Gallery Can & Can Coun Art Bank, Ottawa, Ont; Art Gallery Ont, Toronto; Owens Art Gallery, Sackville, NB; Stedelijk Mus, Amsterdam; Nat Photog Collection, Pub Archives Can. *Exhib:* Social Criticism & Art Practice, San Francisco Art Inst, Calif, 77; solo exhibs, Cepa Gallery, Buffalo, NY, ICA, London, 83, MIA Gallery, Stockholm, 88, Mus Folkswang, Essen, Fed Repub Ger, 88, Hippolyte Gallery, Helsinki, 89, Neue Gesellschaft fur Bildenda Kunst, Berlin, Fed Repub Ger, 89 & Museu de Arte Contemporanea, Sao Paulo, Brazil, 94; group exhibs, Lettering in Photog, Centre Nat de la Photographie, Polais de Tokyo, Paris, 89, 4eme Triennale Int de la Photographie a Charleroi, Musee de la Photographie, Centre d'Art Contemporain, Charleroi, Belg, 90, Fotobiennal 1990 Vigo, Spain, 90, Fotografie Biennale Rotterdam, Wilhelminakade, Rotterdam, 90 & Pub Domain: Santa Monica Art Ctr, Barcelona, 94; Centre Cult Triangle Rennes, France, 91; Museet For Fotokunst Odense, Denmark, 92; Cepa Gallery, Buffalo, NY, 2000; Edmonton Art Gallery, Alberta, Can, 2003; Taxis Palais, Innsbruck, Austria, 2005; Lewis Glucksman Gallery, Cork, Ireland, 2006; Agnes Etherington Art Centre, Kingston, Ontario, 2008; Nooderlicht Festival, Groningen, Netherlands, 2011; and others; Badischer Kunstveren, Karlsrule, Ger, 2013; Museo Reina Sofia, Madrid, Spain, 2014; Manif D'Art, Quebec, Quebec, 2014. *Pos:* Ed, Fox Mag, New York, 76; Red Herring Mag, New York, 77-78; Centerfold/Fuse Mag, Toronto, 79-80. *Teaching:* Instr, NS Coll Art & Design, Halifax, 75-76; Ontario Coll Art & Design, 90-2003. *Bibliog:* Irene Berggren (auth), New Documentary, Bildtidningen, #41, Stockholm, 89; David Evans & Sylvia Gohl (auths), Photomontage: A Political Weapon, Gordon Fraser, London, 86; Dot Tuer (auth), It's still privileged art, in Nina Felshin (ed), "But is it art", Bay Press, Seattle, 94. *Mem:* Can Artists Representation (chmn, 99-2000). *Media:* Digital Photography. *Collection:* It's Still privileged Art, 75, Work in Progress, 80, No Immediate Threat, 85, Free Expression, 89, Non Hábera Nada Para Ninquen, 94, Not a Care, 99, Theatre of Operations, 2000, Calling the Shots, 2002, Cultural Relations, 2005. *Publ:* Auth, Standing Up, Toronto, 86; First Contract, Between the Lines Press, Toronto, 86; Class Work, Communications and Electrical Workers of Canada, Toronto, 90; In the Corporate Shadows, Leonardo, 94; Telling Stories, Questions of Address, Walter Phillips Gallery Publ, Banff Ctr; Condé and Beveridge: Class Works, Bruce Barber (ed), NSCAD Press, Halifax, 2008. *Mailing Add:* 131 Bathurst St Toronto ON M5V 2R2 Canada

BEVERLAND, JACK E
PAINTER
b Idaho Falls, Idaho, May 15, 1939. *Study:* Self taught. *Work:* Oldsmar Arts in Pub Places, Fla; Mus Am Folk Art, OK Harris Gallery, New York; Kennedy Ctr Very Special Arts, Washington, DC & Beverly Hills, Calif; Artists Unlimited, Tampa, Fla; Hillsborough Co, Fla; Mennellon Mus, Orlando, Fla; 5 paintings, Jan Kaminis Platt Regional Libr, Tampa, Fla; Jimmie B Keel Libr, Tampa, Fla, 98-2007; Tampa Int Airport, 2005-2006; St. Petersburg Mus Fine Art; City of Tampa, Fla; VSA Arts, Fla. *Comn:* Painting, City Hall, City of Oldsmar, Fla, 95; painting, Vero Beach Ctr Art, Fla, 96 & 97; painting, Nat Mus Health & Med, Washington, DC, 97; Mennellon Mus, Orlando, Fla; Tampa Mayor's Beautification prog, 2002-2010; poster artist, Art for Life & Project Return, 2006; Polk Co Mus Art, Lakeland, Fla. *Exhib:* African-Am, African Am Mus, Dallas, 95; Minority Enterprises Educ for Tomorrow, Tampa, 95; Juried Exhib, Fla Ctr Contemp Art, Tampa, 95; Benefit, McKee Botanical Garden, Vero Beach, Fla, 96-98; Folk Fest 97, Atlanta, 97; Festival of Arts, Northport, Ala, 97-2013; Challenged Children Art, 97-99; Hillsborough Co, Fla, 98; Mennellon Mus, Orlando, Fla, 2000-2013; Tampa Mus Art, Fla, 2000, 2007, & 2008; solo exhibs, Gov Jeb Bush, Capital Bldg, Tallahassee, Fla, 2002, Cummer Mus, Jacksonville, Fla, 2005 & Thomas Ctr, Gainesville, Fla, 2006, Jimmy Z's Barbecue Bistro, 2010; St Petersburg Mus Fine Art, Fla, 2007; Thomasville Center, Gainesville, 2008; William Penn, Philadelphia, Pa, 2009-2011; Art at Night, Tampa Mus Art, Fla, 2010; The Arc of Dallas, Tex, 2009-2011. *Pos:* teaching artist, VSA Fla, 96-2012; Ky Festival, North Port, Ala, 96-2013; Bryn Mawr Rehab Hosp, 2000-2012; Mennalb Mus, Orlando, Fla, 2003-2013; Eckard Coll, Lewis House, St Petersburg, Fla, 2012; Ladies Book Club, Vero Beach, Fla, 2013. *Teaching:* instr, Art Students Unltd Regional Schs, Hillsborough & Tampa, Fla & Pasco County, Fla. *Awards:* Emerging Artist Grant, Hillsborough Co, 95; Purchase Award, Vero Beach Ctr Arts, 95; Very Special Arts Fla Outstanding Contributions, 98-2000; First Place, Princeton Med Ctr, 2003-2006, Best of Show, 2005-2006; Best of Show, Moss Rehab, Elkin Park, Pa, 2011. *Bibliog:* Erika Duckworth (auth), One for folk art, St Petersburg Times, 95; Leslie L Neumann, Folk Art Finder, Florence Laffal Publ, 95; Untrained Folk Artists, St Petersburg Times, 99; Life, Tuscaloosa News, 99; Folk Art, Tampa Tribune, 2000; Pasco News, 2000; Kristin G Congdon & Tina Bucuvalas (coauths), Just Above the Water, Univ Press Miss, 2006; Gary Monroe (auth), Extraordinary Interpretations, 2006; Gary Monroe (auth), St. Joseph's River, 2009; Marsha Saxton (auth), Sticks and Stones, 2009. *Mem:* Folk Art Soc Am; Very Special Art Nat. *Media:* Acrylic on Board. *Specialty:* Charlotte Terry, Vero Beach, Fla. *Interests:* His dog. *Collection:* Tom and Donna Brumfield, Ann Oppenhimer, Marian Winters, Glenda Hood, Jeb Bush, Erin Friedburg, Kristin Congdon, Gary Monroe, Dr Kear, Dr Cardona, Bob Hart, Mr Creed, Charlotte Terry, Carol Webb. *Publ:* Contribr, Fla Living Mag, 98; Very Special Arts 25th Anniversary Bk, 99; St. Petersburg Times, 1997-2008; Tampa Tribune, 1997-2008. *Dealer:* Lisa Stone 965 Beach Comber Ln Vero Beach Fl 32963; Charlotte Terry 3507 Ocean Dr Vero Beach FL 32963

BHABHA, HUMA
SCULPTOR
b Karachi, Pakistan, 1962. *Study:* RI Sch Design, BFA, 1985; Columbia Univ, MFA, 1989. *Work:* Whitney Mus Am Art, New York; Saatchi Gallery. *Exhib:* Feature, New York, 1991; Solo exhibs, Kim Light Gallery, Los Angeles, 1993, Cokkie Snoei, Rotterdam, Netherlands, 1997, AN Gallery, Karachi, 1998, ATM Gallery, New York, 2004, 2006-07, Mario Diacono Gallery, Boston, 2006, Greener Pastures Contemp Art, Toronto, 2007, Salon 94, New York, 2007, Aldritch Contemp Art Mus, Ridgefield, Conn, 2008; Stand-Ins, PS1 Mus, Inst Contemp Art, Long Island City, NY, 1992 & Greater New York, 2005; Four Walls Benefit, David Zwirner, New York, 1993; Who Killed Mr Moonlight, Exit Art, New York & Mus Contemp Art, Los Angeles, 1994; Not a Lear, Gracie Mansion, New York, 2001; Momenta Art, Brooklyn, 2002, Arena Mex Art Contemp, Guadalajara, Mex (with Jason Fox), 2004, Peter Blum Gallery (with Matthew Day Jackson), 2007; The Empire Strikes Back, ATM Gallery, New York, 2002; USA Today: New Am Art from the Saatchi Gallery, Royal Acad Arts, London, 2006; Every Revolution is a Roll of the Dice, Ballroom Marfa, Tex, 2007; Clay Today, Hudson Valley Ctr Contemp Art, Peekskill, NY, 2008; Whitney Biennial, Whitney Mus Am Art, 2010. *Awards:* Emerging Artist Award, Aldritch Contemp Art Mus, 2008. *Dealer:* Salon 94 12 E 94th St New York NY 10128; ATM Gallery 619 B W 27th St New York NY 10001

BIALOBRODA, ANNA
PAINTER
b Lodz, Poland, 1946. *Study:* Otis Art Inst, BFA, 71, MFA, 73; Whitney Mus Am Art Independent Study Prog, 73. *Work:* Albright-Knox Art Gallery, Buffalo, NY; Chemical Bank, DeBevoise & Plimpton, Capitol Holding Group, Neuberger Berman & Atlantic Bell, NY; Europ Fine Art Found, Geneva; Israel Mus, Jerusalem; Arthur Andersen & Co, Chicago, Ill; Nat Mus Warsaw, Poland; and others. *Comn:* GTE Corp, Dallas, Tex, 94. *Exhib:* Patricia Shea Gallery, Santa Monica, Calif, 92; 45th Acad Purchase Exhib, Am Acad Arts & Lett, NY, 93; Jason McCoy Inc, NY, 93; Ars Erotica, Nat Mus Warsaw, Poland, 94; Burnt Whole, traveling, Inst Contemp Art, Boston, Mass & Wash Proj for Arts, Washington, 94; Murder, Asher/Faure Gallery, Santa Monica, Calif, 94; and others. *Awards:* Nat Endowment Arts Grant, 74; NY Found Arts Grant, 91; Rockefeller Found Fel, Bellagio, Italy, 95. *Bibliog:* Eileen Myles (auth), Anna Bialobroda at Jason McCoy, Art in Am, 12/91; David Page (auth), The Hunter Hunted, Los Angeles Times, 12/31/92; Terry Myers (auth), Anna Bialobroda, Flash Art, summer 93. *Media:* Acrylic, Oil. *Publ:* Richard Hertz (auth), Theories of Contemporary Art, Prentice-Hall, Englewood Cliffs, NJ, 85; Barbara Rose, Twentieth Century American Painting, Skira-Rizzoli, Rizzoli Int Publ, New York, 86; Barbara Rose, Autocritique, Essays on Art and Anti-Art 1963-1987, Weidenfeld & Nicholson, New York, 88; Marek Bartelik, Anna Bialobroda-Exits, Galeria Krytykow Pokaz, Warsaw, Poland, 91; John Yau, Anna Bialobroda, Jason McCoy Gallery, New York, 91. *Dealer:* Patricia Shea Gallery 2042 Broadway Santa Monica CA 90404. *Mailing Add:* PO Box 20237 New York NY 10009

BIBLOS, MAHIA
SCULPTOR, DESIGNER
b Buenos Aires, Arg. *Study:* Nat Sch Fine Art, with Prilicliano Pueyrredon, BA; Sch Design, Inst Nat Fine Arts, Mex; Nat Sch Fine Art, Univ Nat Art Mod, Mex, MA. *Work:* Mus Art Contemp José Luis Cuevas, Mex City; Mus Art Contemp, Morelia, Michoacan, Mex; Casa Cult Morelia, Michoacan, Mex. *Exhib:* 4th & 5th Int Triennales of Tapestry, Cent Mus, Lödz, Poland, 81 & 85; Textil Mexicano Contemporaneo, Ft Mason, San Francisco, 90; Mexico-Polonia-Textil Contemporaneo, Rufino Tamayo, Mex, 91; Coleccion Latino Americana, José Luis Cuevas, Mex, 92. *Pos:* Dept head, textile design & color, Sch Design, Nat Inst Fine Arts, Mex, 76-. *Awards:* Creadores Intelectuales, 91 & Proj Promote Cult, 93, Nat Found Cult Arts. *Bibliog:* Juan Acha (auth), Piel Andina (exhib catalog), Galeria Juan Martin, Mex, 86; Alicia Azuela (auth), La Magia del Tapiz, Banco, BCH, Mex, 88. *Mem:* Agrupación Mex Art Textil (vpres). *Dealer:* Galeria Juan Martin Dickens 33 letra B Colonia Polanco Mexico DF 11560. *Mailing Add:* Pueblo 126-2 Piso Colonia Roma Mexico DF 06700 Mexico

BICKLEY, GARY STEVEN
EDUCATOR, SCULPTOR
b Lebanon, Va, Apr 25, 1953. *Study:* E Carolina Univ, BFA, 76; Univ Ga, MFA, 78. *Work:* Southeastern Ctr Contemp Art, Winston-Salem, NC; Portsmouth Community Arts Ctr, Va; City of Rockville, Md; First Nat Bank, Roanoke, Va. *Exhib:* Painting and Sculpture Today, Indianapolis Mus Art, 78; solo exhibs, Southeastern Ctr Contemp Art, Winston-Salem, NC, 78, 80 & 82; Am Drawing III, Portsmouth Fac & Smithsonian Inst, traveling, 80; Rutgers Nat Works on Paper, Stedman Art Gallery, Camden, NJ, 81; Virginia Painting and Sculpture, Va Mus Fine Arts, Richmond, 81; Clayworks, NY; Exhib 280, Huntington Galleries, WVa; 20 Sculptors Outdoor Exhib, Va Mus Fine Arts. *Teaching:* Asst prof, Va Polytech Inst & State Univ, Blacksburg, 78-; vis prof, Univ Ga, Cortona, Italy, 81. *Awards:* Ford Found Scholar, Univ Ga, 77-78; Summer Stipend, Nat Endowment Humanities, Va Polytech Inst & State Univ, 81; Work Stipend for Clayworks Workshop, Nat Endowment Arts. *Media:* Welded & Cast Metals. *Mailing Add:* Va Tech Dept Art & Art Hist 201 Draper Rd Blacksburg VA 24061-0103

BIDLO, MIKE
CONCEPTUAL ARTIST
b Chicago, Ill, Oct 20, 1953. *Study:* Univ Ill, Chicago, BA, 73; Southern Ill Univ, MFA, 75; Teachers Col, Columbia Univ, MA, 78. *Work:* Chase Manhattan Bank & New York Stock Exchange, NY; Sezon Mus, Tokyo; Omaha Nat Bank, Nebr; Mod Mus Stockholm; Fashion Inst Technol, Univ Colo, Boulder; Phila Mus Art. *Exhib:* Grey Art Gallery, NY Univ, 89; Daniel Templon, Paris, 90; Sezon Mus, Japan, 91; Saatchi Collection, London, 91; Bruno Bischofberger and Tony Schafrazi, NY, 98, Gallery, Fountain Drawings; Picasso's Women, Leo Castelli Gallery, 88; Astrup Fearnley Mus, Oslo, 02; Nat Gallery Art, Iceland, 03; Erased DeKooning Drawings, Francis Naumann Gallery, NY, 2005; and others. *Teaching:* Guest lectr, Art Ctr, Pasadena, 88, Pratt Inst, NY, 84, Univ Colo, Boulder, 85, Univ Calif, Los Angeles, 88, Otis Art Inst, Los Angeles, 88, Bard Col, 89 & State Univ Calif, Fullerton, 91, The Tate Mus, 99, Pollock Krasner Study Ctr, 99, Univ of Iceland, 03, State Univ of NY, 04, Pollack Krasner Study Ctr, 2012. *Awards:* Fel, Nat Endowment Arts. *Bibliog:* Robert Rosenblum (auth), Masterpieces, Bruno Bischifberger Gallery, 89; Olivier Zahm & Joseph Masheck (auths), Not Dechirico (catalog essays), Daniel Templon Gallery, 90; Joseph Masheck, Thomas McEvilley & Francis Naumann (auths), Not Leger (catalogue), Bischofberger Gallery, 92; Francis Naumann, Arthur Danto & Mike Bidlo in Conversation; Robert Rosenblum (auth, Erased DeKooning Drawings (catalog essays), 2005. *Mem:* Am Art Therapy Asn (cert mem). *Media:* All Media. *Dealer:* Bruno Bischofberger, Zurich. *Mailing Add:* 432 W 38th St New York NY 10018-2816

BIDSTRUP, WENDY
ADMINISTRATOR
b Pittsburgh, Pa, Feb 15, 1940. *Study:* Wells Col, BA, 1962. *Work:* Marion Art Ctr, Marion, Mass. *Collection Arranged:* Cecil Clark Davis: A Woman Ahead of Her Time, New Bedford Art Mus, 2002. *Pos:* exec dir, Marion Art Ctr, 84-; cur, New Bedford Art Mus, New Bedford, Mass, summer 2002. *Teaching:* art history lectr, Tabor Acad, Marion, Mass, 74-86. *Bibliog:* David B Boyce (auth) Cecil Clark Davis, The Standard Times, summer, 2002; Paul Kandarian (auth), Cecil Clark Davis, The Boston Globe, 8/2002; John Robeson, Cecil Clark Davis (documentary, video). *Mem:* Nat Mus Women in the Arts; Sippican Hist & Preserv Soc. *Mailing Add:* Marion Art Center 80 Pleasant St Box 602 Marion MA 02738

BIEDERMAN, JAMES MARK
PAINTER, SCULPTOR
b New York, NY, Nov 8, 1947. *Study:* Whitney Mus Independent Study prog; Yale Univ, MFA, 73. *Work:* Kroller-Muller Riks Mus, Otterlo, Netherlands; Pompidou Ctr, Paris; Mus Mod Art & Metrop Mus Art, NY; Mus Contemp Art, Chicago; Hirshhorn Mus, Washington, DC. *Comn:* Wall sculpture, Home Box Off, NY, 85. *Exhib:* Sculpture, Clocktower Gallery, NY, 81; 2nd Int Jugend, Kunsthalle, Nuremberg, WGer, 82; Choix Pour Aujourd'hui, Ctr Pompidou, Paris, 82; Documenta 7, Kassel, WGer, 82; Kunstmuseum Aalborg & Rander, Denmark, 83; Mus Mod Art, NY; Triennale, Musee Cantonal des Beaux Arts, Lausanne, Switz; Geometric Abstraction, Bronx Mus, NY, 85. *Teaching:* Vis artist sculpture, Boston Mus Sch, 83 & Yale Univ, formerly; painting, NY Univ, 84-86; Hofstra Univ, 98-. *Awards:* Nat Endowment Arts Drawing Award, 79 & Sculpture Award, 82; Painting Award, New York Found Arts, 86; Adolph and Esther Gottlieb Found Grant, 2005; John Simon Guggenheim Memorial Foundation Fine Arts Fel, 2011. *Bibliog:* Ronnie Cohn (auth), rev, Art Forum, 4/83; Himmel Freeman (auth), New Art, Harry Abrams, 84; Curt Barnes (ed), Art J, spring 91; and others. *Media:* Oil on Linen, Oil on Wood. *Dealer:* John Weber Gallery 142 Greene St New York 10012; Galerie Winkelman Neubruckstabe 12 Dusseldorf Fed Repub Ger

BIEL, JOE
PAINTER, DRAFTSMAN
b Boulder, Colo. *Study:* Drake Univ, Des Moines, BFA (painting & art hist, summa cum laude), 1988; Univ Mich, ANn Arbor, MFA (painting), 1990. *Exhib:* Oregon Biennial, Portland Art Mus, 1997; solo exhibs, Bemis Ctr for Contemp Art, Omaha, 2001, Kucera Gallery, Seattle, 2002, 2005, Kuckei/Kuckei, Berlin, Ger, 2003, 2006, 2009, Acuna-Hansen Gallery, Los Angeles, 2004-05, Nettie Horn Gallery, London, 2009; Art on Paper, Weatherspoon Art Mus, NC, 2002; What a Painting Can Do, Hayworth Gallery, Los Angeles, 2003; Drawn Fictions, Marylhurst Univ, Ore, 2004; Contemporary Erotic Drawing, Aldrich Contemp Art Mus, Conn, 2005; The O-Scene: Contemporary Art and Culture in OC, Laguna Art Mus, Calif, 2006; The Diane and Sandy Besser Collection, De Young Mus, Calif, 2007; Looky-See, Ben Maltz Gallery, Otis Coll Art Design, Calif, 2008. *Pos:* Artist-in-residence, Ballinglen Found, Ireland, 2004 & 18th St Arts Complex, Santa Monica, Calif, 2004-07. *Awards:* Pollock-Krasner Found Grant, 2003 & 2008; Ludwig Vogelstein Found Award, 2008. *Bibliog:* Holly Myers (auth), Delicate and Inquisitive, Los Angeles Times, 12/7/2001; DK Row (auth); Dark Star of Humor, The Oregonian, 9/12/2003; Sue Taylor (auth), Joseph Biel at Mark Woolley, Art in Am, 2/2004; Tom Morris (auth), Bedtime Fairy Tales These Are Not, Artreview, 7/2006. *Mailing Add:* 936 Chung King Rd Los Angeles CA 90012

BIELER, TED ANDRE
EDUCATOR, SCULPTOR
b Kingston, Ont, July 23, 1938. *Study:* Sculpture with Ossip Zadkine, Paris, 53; tapestry with Jean Lurcat, St Cere, France, 54; Slade Sch Art, London, 54; Cranbrook Acad Art, BFA, 61. *Work:* Montreal Mus Fine Arts; Can Coun, Ottawa; Univ Toronto; Agnes Etherington Art Centre, Queen's Univ, Kingston; McMaster Univ; York Univ; Nat Capital Comn, Ottawa, Ont; Univ Windsor, Ont; McMullen Mus, Boston Col, Chestnut Hill, Mass; Georgetown Univ, Lauinger Libr, Washington, DC; New England Coll Gallery, Henniker, NH; Sir Wilfred Grenfell Coll Art Gallery, Corner Brook, Nfld. *Comn:* Star-Cross'd (sculpture ballet set), comn by Brian MacDonald, Ottawa, 73; stainless steel sculpture, Forensic Sci Bldg, Govt Ont, 75; aluminum tetrahedras sculpture, Portsmouth Harbour, Kingston, Govt Can, 75; sculpture for Govt of Can Bldg, comn by Macy Dubois & Shore Tilbe Henschel Irwin, Architects, Toronto, 77; cast aluminum relief sculpture for Wilson Sta, comn by Spadina Subway Line, Toronto, 78; Boat Bridge (laminated birch relief wall), Govt Ont Bldg, Kingston, 84; Wave Breaking (cast bronze sculpture), Can Chancery, Dept External Affairs, 91; Tower Song (cast aluminum sculpture), Windsor Sculpture Garden, Ont, 98; and others. *Exhib:* Signs & Symbols, Art Gallery Ont Traveling Show, 71; Rehearsal, Harbourfront Art Gallery, Toronto, 77; solo exhibs, York Univ, 77, Univ Rochester, 77, Geraldine Davis Gallery, Toronto, 86, Lindsay Gallery, Ont, 89, Vessels: bronze sculptures, Geraldine Davis Gallery, Toronto, 89, Drawings from the Lake, Faculty Club, York Univ, 89; Columns, Valuts, Bridges and Other Sculptures, Glendon Gallery, Toronto, 91; Performance, Harbourfront Art Gallery, Toronto, Ont, 78; Monumental Sculpture, Toronto Dominion Ctr, 78; Artists with their Children, Art Gallery at Harbourfront, Toronto, Ont, 83; York Work, York Univ, Downsview, Ont, 86; The Building of Architectural Vision, City Gallery, NY, 87; Firing the Imagination: Artists & Architects Use Clay, Urban Ctr Gallery, NY & Bennington Col, Vt; Shadows Grow Longer, Ofrenda, Days of the Dead Installation, Harbourfront, Toronto, 94. *Pos:* dir, Graduate Studio Program Visual Arts, York Univ, Toronto, 80-83 & 86-90, chmn, Dept Visual Arts, 87-90; coordr, Odette Ctr for Sculpture, York Univ, 90-91. *Teaching:* Prof fine arts, York Univ, Toronto, 69-. *Awards:* Allied Arts Medal, Royal Archit Asn Can, 69; Can Silver Jubilee Medal. *Bibliog:* L Sabbath (auth), Sculpture in Canada, 62 & H McPherson (auth), Scope of Sculpture, 64, Can Art; William Withrow (auth), Canadian Sculpture, Graph, Montreal, 67; R Burnett & M Schiff (coauths), Contemporary Canadian Art, Hurtig Publ, 83. *Mem:* Royal Can Acad Arts (mem coun, 75-77); Int Sculpture Ctr, Lawrence, Kans; The Sculpture Garden, Toronto (bd dir, 84-). *Mailing Add:* Visual Arts Dept Room 232 CFA York Univ 4700 Keele St North York ON M3J 1P3 Canada

BIELTVEDT, ARNOR G
PAINTER, INSTRUCTOR
b Akureyri, Iceland, May 25, 1963. *Study:* Univ Ger, Vordiploma, 87; Johnson & Wales Univ, BS, MS, 89; RI Sch of Design, BFA, 92; Wash Univ, MFA, 94. *Work:* Reykjavik Art Mus, Reykjavik, Iceland; N Shore Community House, Winnetka, Ill; N Shore Art League, Winnetka, Ill; Embassy of Iceland, Tokyo; Embassy of Iceland, London; Akureyri Art Mus, Iceland; Embassy of Iceland, Copenhagen. *Comn:* Homescapes, Anne Loucks Gallery; Portraits of Home & Portraits of People, Glencoe, Ill, 2002-. *Exhib:* 175th Anniversary, Galeri Commeter, Hamburg, Ger, 96; Viking Celebration, Icelandic Embassy, Wash, DC, 2000; Biennial Int Juried Exhib, Brad Cooper Gallery, Tampa, Fla, 2004; Still Life Contemp Visions, Anne Loucks Gallery, Glencoe, Ill, 2004; Light & Carriers of Light, Icelandic Graphic Mus, Reykjavik, 2005; October Int Exhib, Marziart Int Gallery, Hamburg, Ger, 2006; 10 Yr Anniversary Exhib, Galerie Beeldkracht, Scheemda, The Neth, 2007; Open Art Fair, Galerie Beeldkracht, Utrecht, The Neth, 2008. *Teaching:* Instr art dept head, Logos Sch, St Louis, Mo, 94-2001; instr art dept head & gallery dir, N Shore Country Day Sch Winnetka, Ill, 2001-2006; instr art dept head, Polytechnic Sch, Pasadena, Calif, 2007-. *Bibliog:* Leslie Korengold (auth) Creating Life from Stillness, N Shore Home, 2003; Vala Bergsveinsdotter (auth) Still a Youngster In Art, Morning Paper (Iceland), 2005; Ragna Siguroardottir (auth) Play with Live & Color, Morning Paper (Iceland), 2005. *Mem:* Gardens Art Guild, Huntington Libr & Gardens, Pasadena, Calif. *Media:* Mixed Media. *Dealer:* Anne Loucks Gallery Glencoe IL; Galerie Beeldkracht Scheemda The Neth; Crest Mount Fine Art Salt Lake City UT; Art Iceland Gallery Reykjavik Iceland. *Mailing Add:* 1436 N Chester Ave Pasadena CA 91104

BIERBAUM, GRETCHEN ANN
COLLAGE ARTIST, EDUCATOR
b Cheyenne, Wyo, Mar 25, 1942. *Study:* Kent State Univ, BA, 64, MA, 68; Pahlavi Univ, Iran, 71-72. *Work:* N Coast Galleries, Hudson, Ohio. *Comn:* Commemorative painting, Hudson Libr & Hist Soc, Ohio, 85; univ campus collage, Kent State Univ, Ohio, 92; biographical collage of the founder of the Akron Conv & Visitors Bur, Ohio, 94; corp collage, Michelin Tire Co, Akron, Ohio, 94; and others. *Exhib:* 42nd Ann Show, Butler Inst Am Art, Youngstown, Ohio, 80; 5th Ann Midwest Watercolor Soc Show, Burpee Mus, Rockford, Ill, 81; Barker Gallery, Palm Beach, Fla, 82; 52nd Ann Exhib, Butler Inst Am Art, Youngstown, Ohio, 90; and others. *Pos:* Docent, Kent State Univ Art Gallery, Ohio, 78-79; auth & ed, North Coast Collage Soc Newslett Quart, 84-90. *Teaching:* Instr watercolor, Univ Akron, Ohio, 79-81; painting at international workshops in Panama & the British West Indies, 93-94. *Awards:* Ruppel Award, Ohio Watercolor Soc Ann, Ruppel's Co, 79; First Place, Solon Show, Anixter-Cleveland Inc, 81; Purchase Award, Westerville Art Festival, Otterbein Col, Marketing Serv Inc, 84. *Bibliog:* Helen Cullinan (auth), North coast: Collage mecca, The Plain Dealer, 89; Don Breedlove (auth), Artists of Ohio the Fine Arts Catalogue, Mountain Productions Inc, 93; Virginia Williams (auth), Creative Collage Techniques, North Light Books, 94. *Mem:* N Coast Collage Soc Inc (founder/pres, 84-); Hudson Soc Artists (pres, 80-81). *Media:* Watercolor. *Mailing Add:* 254 W Streetsboro St Akron OH 44236

BIERMAN, IRENE A
EDUCATOR
b Bogota, NJ. *Study:* Harvard Univ, MA, 66; Univ Chicago, PhD, 80. *Collection Arranged:* The Warp & Weft of Islam (auth catalog), Seattle, Portland & Tocoma, Reno, 79; The Common Cord, Seattle Art Mus, 86; Permanent Near East Collection, Seattle Art Mus. *Teaching:* Vis lectr Islamic art hist, Univ Wash, Seattle, 76-80; prof Islamic art hist, Univ Calif, Los Angeles, 82-. *Awards:* Fel, Ctr for Advanced Study in the Visual Arts, 81-83; Fel, Am Res Ctr Egypt, 80-81; Fulbright-Hays Fel to Egypt & Turkey, 81-82. *Mem:* Coll Art Asn; Middle East Studies Asn; Am Oriental Soc; Am Res Ctr Egypt; NAm Hist Islamic Art. *Res:* Public arts in the Islamic world with emphasis on the Mediterranean areas. *Publ:* Coauth, The Warp & Weft of Islam, Univ Washington, 78; auth, The Message of Urban Space: The Case of Crete, Espace et Société; Oriental Carpets, In: Decorative Arts & Household Furnishings Used in Am, Winterthur Mus, 86; co-auth, Symbols of Islam, Univ Wash Int Studies, 86; auth, The fatimid public text, In: Actes, Congress International de l'Histoire de l'arte XXVI, 86; co-ed, Urban Structure and Social Order: The Ottoman City and its Parts, Caratzas Bros, New York, 91. *Mailing Add:* UCLA Art Histr Box 951417 100 Dood Los Angeles CA 90095-1417

BIESENBACH, KLAUS
CURATOR, MUSEUM DIRECTOR
Collection Arranged: Douglas Gordon, Timeline, 2006, Doug Aitken, Sleepwalkers, 2007, Projects 87, Sgalit Landau, 2008, Take your time, Olafur Eliasson, 2008, Pipilotti Rist, Pour Your Body Out, 2008, Performance 4, Roman Ondak, 2009 & Performance 1, Tehching Hsieh, 2009 . *Pos:* Founding dir & chmn emer, Kunst-Werke Inst Contemp Art, Berlin, 1990-; founder, Berlin Biennale, 1996; cur, PS1 Contemp Art Ctr, 1996-2004, chief curatorial adv, 2004-2009, dir, 2009-; cur dept film & media, Mus Mod Art, 2004, chief cur dept media & performance art, 2006-2009. *Mailing Add:* Museum Modern Art 11 W 53 St New York NY 10019

BIFERIE, DAN (DANIEL) ANTHONY, JR
PHOTOGRAPHER, EDUCATOR
b Miami, Fla, Dec 17, 1950. *Study:* Daytona State Col, AS (with honors), 71; Ohio Univ, BFA (summa cum laude), 72, MFA, 74. *Work:* High Mus; New Orleans Mus Art; Baltimore Mus Art; Santa Barbara Mus Art; Bibliotheque Nationale, Paris; Nat Mus Am Art; Southeast Mus Photog (permanent collection). *Comn:* Art in Public Places Commission New Smyrna; Beach Regional Libr, 99. *Exhib:* Solo exhibs, Albany Mus Art, 86, Lakeland's Unique Architectural Heritage, Polk Mus Art, Fla, 87, Southeast Mus Photog, 94; Four Photographers, Mass Inst Technol, Boston, 76; Fla Light Invitational, Orlando Mus Art, Fla, 79; Four Southeastern Photographers, Contemp Arts Ctr, New Orleans, La, 81; Contemp Photog as Phantasy (with catalog), Santa Barbara Mus Art, 82-83; Fact & Fiction: The State of Fla Photog (traveling exhib), Norton Gallery Art, West Palm Beach, Fla, 90; Digital Am, Orlando Mus of Art, 98; Dan Biferie, Digital/Photogr Traveling Exhib, 99-2001; Fla Individual Artists Fellowship Program, 25th Ann Traveling Exhib, Cummer Mus of Art, Jacksonville, Fla, 2002-2004; Southeast Invitational show, Crealde School Art, 2009; Dan Biferie-40 Years in Photography, Southeast Mus Photography, Daytona Beach, Fla. *Pos:* Found, Southeast Mus Photog, Daytona State Col, Fla, 1978-1990, chmn visual arts dept, 1985-1988; pres, Arts Coun Volusia Co, 1991-1995; chair, School of Photog, 2005-. *Teaching:* Sr prof, Daytona State Col, Fla, 1975-. *Awards:* Our Children to the South Photo-documentary project Grant, Fla, Int Alliance, 1985; Lakelands Architectural Heritage, Photo-documentary Grant, Polk Mus Art; Fla Endowment for the Humanities; Individual Artists Fel, Fla Div of Cult Affairs, 1996-1997 & 2008; Honored Educator, Society for Photographic Edn, Southeast Region, 2012. *Bibliog:* Lakeland's Unique Architectural Heritage (exhib catalog) Polk Mus Art, 87; The New Movement, Focal Point Press, 87; Churchscapes in Black & White (studio photog), 88; Digital Photogr, Greece, 98; Digital Fine Artists Mag, 2000; The Digital Da-Kloom US Art Gallery Mag, 10/2001. *Mem:* Soc Photog Educ (pres 77-84); Daytona Beach Community Coll Photog Soc (founder & pres 79-81); Am Asn Mus. *Media:* Giclee Print. *Res:* History and criticism of photography, photographic aesthetics. *Interests:* Photogr, Art Education, Film, Antiques, Religious Artifacts. *Collection:* National Mus of Am Art, Smithsonian Inst Washington, DC; Bibliothegue Nationale, Paris, France; New Orleans Mus of Art La; High Mus of Art, Atlanta, Ga. *Publ:* Contribr, Photographic Annual, Middle Tenn State Univ, 75; Florida Light, Loch Haven Art Ctr, 79; Photographers Forum, Darkroom Section, 81; Photography in Florida, Catskill Ctr for Photog Quart Mag, 85; Churchscapes, Studio Photog, 88; Dreaming in B & W Photo's Electronic Imaging Mag, 96. *Dealer:* Holden Luntz Gallery West Palm Beach FL. *Mailing Add:* Daytona State Coll 1200 W International Speedway Blvd Daytona Beach FL 32114

BIGELOW, ANITA (ANNE) (EDWIGE LOURIE)
GRAPHIC ARTIST, PRINTMAKER
b Los Angeles, Calif, Mar 3, 1946. *Study:* Reed Col, with Lloyd Reynolds & Willard Midgette, BA, 67; San Francisco Art Inst, with Jack Stauffacher & Gerry Gooch: Portland State Univ, MA, 75; Portland Community Col, AA, 85. *Work:* Lloyd Reynolds Collection, Portland Mus Art, Ore. *Comn:* Bookplates (set of 4), comn by Mary Barnard, Vancouver, Wash, 79-81; bookplates (set of 10), Reed Coll Libr, Portland, Ore, 81; bookplates (set of 2), Boston Atheneum, Mass, 82. *Exhib:* Contemp Ex-Libris 1980-1982, XIX Int Ex-Libris Cong, Oxford, Eng, 82; The World of Ex Libris, Belgrade, 95. *Mem:* Portland Boat Club; US Rowing. *Media:* Woodcut, Linoleum Cut; Pastel, Pencil. *Publ:* Illusr, Mississippi Mud and various articles-items, Joel Weinstein, 82-86; Time and the White Tigress, B Breitenbush Books, 86

BIGGERS, SANFORD
SCULPTOR
b Los Angeles, California, 1970. *Study:* Syracuse Univ (Dept Int Progs Abroad), Florence, Italy, 1991; Morehouse Coll, Atlanta, BA, 1992; Md Inst Coll Art, Baltimore, 1997; Skowhegan Sch Painting & Sculpture, Maine, 1998; Sch Art Inst Chicago, MFA, 1999. *Comn:* Somethin' Suite, Performa 07, New York, 2007; Cosmic Conundrum, The Kitchen, New York, 2008. *Exhib:* Solo exhibs include Matrix Gallery, Berkeley Art Mus, Calif, 2002, Trafo Gallery, Budapest, 2002, Contemp Arts Mus, Houston, 2002 Mary Goldman Gallery, Los Angeles, 2004, 2006, Triple Candie, New York, 2005, Ctr Contemp Art Ujazdowski Castle, Warsaw, 2005, Kenny Schachter Rove, London, 2006, Grand Arts, Kansas City, Mo, 2007, D'Amelio Terras Gallery, New York, 2008; group exhibs include Full Service, Kenny Schachter, New York, 2000; Altoid's Curiously Strong Collection, New Mus Contemp Art, New York, 2001; Whitney Biennial, Whitney Mus Am Art, New York, 2002; Shuffling the Deck, Princeton Mus Art, NJ, 2003; Art Rock, Rockefeller Ctr, New York, 2006; Black Moving Cube, Tate Britain, London, 2006; Pretty Baby, Mod Art Mus Fort Worth, 2007; Black Light/White Noise, Contemp Art Mus, Houston, 2007; Illuminations, Tate Modern, 2007; Shuffle, Schloss Solitude, Stuttgart, Germany, 2008; Neo Hoodoo: Art for a Forgotten Faith, Menil Collection, Houston, 2008. *Teaching:* Asst Prof Sculpture & Expanded Media, Va Commonwealth Univ, Present. *Awards:* Art Matters Grant, 2007; Creative Capital Found Grant, 2008. *Mailing Add:* Mary Goldman Gallery PO Box 94 New Suffolk NY 11956-0094

BILDER, DOROTHEA A
PRINTMAKER, PAINTER
b Dayton, Ohio, Oct 4, 1940. *Study:* Ill Wesleyan Univ, BFA, 62; Southern Ill Univ, Carbondale, MFA, 64. *Work:* Portland Art Inst, Ore; Columbia Col/Mo Arts Coun, Columbia, Mo; Art Inst Chicago, Ill; Fine Arts Mus Long Island, Hempstead, NY; Cincinnati Art Mus, Ohio. *Comn:* Ymagos Atelier di Arte, Ltda, Sao Paulo, Brazil. *Exhib:* Solo shows, Monotypes & Lithographs, Lee Scarfone Gallery, Univ Tampa, Fla, 90, Prints & Works on Paper, Marbeck Ctr Gallery, Bluffton Col, Ohio, 90, Fragments/Painting on Canvas, Gallery 1792, Winter Park, Fla, 93, Hellenic Mus & Cult Ctr, Chicago, 93, Recent Print Work, Expressions Graphics, Oak Park, Ill, 98; 12th Ann Paper in Particular, Nat Exhib Works on/off Paper, Columbia Coll & Mo Arts Coun, Columbia, Mo, 91; Look at the World Through Women's Eyes, NGO Forum on Women, United Nat 4th World Conf on Women & Nat Mus Women Arts, Washington, DC, 96; 9th Nat Drawing & Print Competitive Exhib, Coll Notre Dame of Md, Gormely Gallery, Baltimore, 97; 10th Ann Nat Exhib Fine Art by Women, Old Courthouse Arts Ctr, NW Area Arts Coun, Woodstock Sq, Ill, 97; Nat Print Exhib Celebrating 200 Yrs of Lithography, Xavier Univ, Dept Art, Cincinnati, Ohio, 98; 15th Nat Biennial Exhib, Los Angels Printmaking Soc, Laband Art Gallery, Loyola Marymount Univ, Los Angeles, 99; over 96 Int & Nat Exhibs. *Pos:* Artist-in-Residence, Red Deer Coll, Alta, Can, 89 & 94. *Teaching:* Prof drawing & printmaking, Northern Ill Univ, De Kalb, 68-; instr printmaking, Penland Sch Crafts, NC, summers 70-80. *Awards:* Merit Award, Emerging Woman Artist Nat, Ind Univ, 87. *Mem:* Coll Art Asn; Southern Graphics Coun; Art Inst Alumni Asn; Print Consortium; Chicago Women's Caucas Art. *Media:* Serigraphy, Lithography; Oil, Pastel. *Publ:* Auth & illusr, Silk Screening Printing, In: Art, Fuller & Dees/Times Mirror Co, 74. *Dealer:* Glatt, Sao Paulo & Rio de Janiero Brazil. *Mailing Add:* 2707 Greenwood Acres Dr Dekalb IL 60115

BILLIAN, CATHEY R
ENVIRONMENTAL ARTIST, EDUCATOR
b Chicago, Ill, 1946. *Study:* Art Inst Chicago, Univ Ariz, BFA (fine arts); Pratt Inst, fel, MFA (summa cum laude), 78. *Work:* Philadelphia Mus Art; NY Pub Libr Print Collection; Morris Mus; Norton Simon Inc & Chem Bank, NY; Brooklyn Mus; Nat Park Serv; City of Phoenix, Ariz; US Forest Serv; Libr Congress; Smithsonian Inst; Poet's House, NY; pvt collection, former vpres Al Gore; plus others. *Comn:* Sculpture, Creative Time, Battery Park, NY, 81; light, sculpture & dance environment, Whitney Mus, 84; sculpture, Prospect Park, NY, 85; archit sculpture, US Forest Serv: Southwest Region, 90-91 & City of Phoenix, 92. *Exhib:* Recent Trends in Light, Morris Mus, 83 & Hofstra Univ (with catalog), 83; Stopped Time, Four Projected Environments, Sculpture Ctr, NY & Rockland Ctr Arts (with catalog), 84; Recent Acquisitions/Louis Comfort Tiffany Found Purchase, Brooklyn Mus, NY; Cathey Billian, Michael Graves, Charles Simonds at Liberty State Park, Jersey City Mus, (with catalog); NY Experimental Glass, Soc Art Craft, Pittsburgh, Pa (with catalog); Luminous Visions, FIT Gallery, NY (with catalog); Four Sculptors from the NY Experimental Glassworks, Nina Owen Ltd, Chicago, Ill; solo exhibs, Cross-Cut Piedra Lumbre, Pratt Inst Gallery, NY, Frozen Moments, Gallery of NY Experimental Glassworks, Future Antiquities, Whitney Mus Sculpture Court, NY, Art Omi Int Arts Ctr, Fields Sculpture Park, Columbia Co, NY & Mary Boone Gallery, NY. *Collection Arranged:* Knowing Limits, Travelling Exhib of Poetry & Art, 2000-01. *Pos:* Consult, Artpark, NY; NY & NJ State Coun Arts, 82-; artist-in-residence, NY Experimental Glassworks, Bob Blackburn's Printmaking Workshop, NY, Nat Park Serv, Utah, Del Water Gap, NJ, Yellowstone Nat Park & Dept Interior, NMex & AIR Banff Ctr for Arts; adv bd & corresp, Pub Art Rev; dir, Wild America; interdisciplinary environ arts initiatives & design res, Nat Parks and Arts Colls, incl Univ Arts & Cooper Union, 97-. *Teaching:* Lectr interdisciplinary environ design, NY State Coun Humanities; instr, Parsons Sch, 80-81, Pratt Inst Grad Dept, 80, Rutgers Univ, 80-82, Cooper Union, 95; fac, Pratt Inst, 84-, prof, 2005-. *Awards:* Sculpture Fel, Nat Endowment Arts, 84; 6 Proj Grants, NY State Coun Arts, Whitney Mus, 85. *Bibliog:* Lucy Lippard (auth), Overlay: Contemporary Art and the Art of Prehistory, 83; Cathey Billian/Frozen Moments, Craft Int, 6/88; Lynn Miller (auth), Lives and Works - 14 Women Artists, 92, plus others. *Mem:* Public Art Review (nat advisory bd); Coll Art Asn; fel Hirsch Farm Proj Environ Art; Maine Coast Artists. *Media:* Photographic Works, Environmental Structures & Drawing. *Res:* The intersection of environmental interpretation & public art. *Interests:* Music, Architecture, Nature as they intersect with Visual Art. *Publ:* Guest ed Public Art Review, Nature Trails jour, Fall 2000. *Mailing Add:* 456 Broome St New York NY 10013

BILLS, LINDA
SCULPTOR
b New York, NY, July 22, 1943. *Study:* Beaver Col, BFA, 65. *Work:* Am Craft Mus, NY; Nat Mus Am Art; Wustum Mus Fine Arts, Racine, Wis; Del Art Mus, Wilmington; Ark Art Ctr, Little Rock. *Exhib:* Solo exhib, Sybaris Gallery, Royal Oak, Mich, 93 & 96, Villa Julie Coll, Stevenson, Md, 2000; Touch, The Handworkshop, Va

Ctr Craft Arts, Richmond, Va, 93; Art Sites 6-, Natural Meaning, Rockville Art Pl, Rockville, Md, 94; Gomez Gallery, Baltimore, Md, 95; In Wood: Material Variations, Md Art Place, Baltimore, 95; Venerable Gardens/Artistes '96, Tudor Pl, Washington, 96; Biennial '96, Del Art Mus, Wilmington, 96; Celebrating Am Craft 1975-1995 (with catalog), Danish Mus Decorative Art, Copenhagen, Denmark, 97; Poetic Objects: Technique and Vision, Del Art Mus, Wilmington, 97; Biennial 96: Mus Acquisitions, Del Art Mus, Wilmington, 98; Subject To Change, Part I and Part II, Linda Bills, Jann Rosen-Queralt, Jason Swift (with catalog), Md Inst Coll Art, Baltimore, 99; Drawing The Line, Philadelphia Art Alliance, Pa, 99; Blurring Boundaries: Objects in Craft Media from the Collection, Del Art Mus, Wilmington, 99; Grandstand Sculpture, Contemp Mus, Baltimore, Md, 99; Nature Re-Bound, Palo Alto Art Ctr, Calif, 2000; Nine Artists/Five Decades: Works by Beaver Coll Alumni Beaver Coll, Glenside, Pa, 2000; Biennial 2000, Del Art Mus, Wilmington, 2000. *Awards:* Swan Prize, Philadelphia Craft Show, Swan Gallery, 87; Visual Artist Fel Grant, Nat Endowment Arts, 88, 90 & 92; Grant-In-Aid, Md State Arts Coun, 87 & Visual Art Fel Grant, 88 & 97; Vt Studio Ctr fel, 99. *Bibliog:* Jack Lenor Larsen cur, The Tactile Vessel, Erie Art Mus, 89; Margo Shermeta (auth), Linda Bills: a balance between strength & delicacy, 9-10/91 & Patricia Malarche (auth), The vessel form, summer 92, Fiber Arts Mag. *Media:* Miscellaneous

BILLS, MITCHELL
DESIGNER, VIDEO ARTIST
b Auburn, NY, Dec 23, 1950. *Study:* Tyler Sch Art Temple Univ with Joe Scorsone & Peter D'Agostino, MFA, 84. *Work:* Tyler Sch Art Libr, Elkins Park, Pa; Intermedia Arts Minn; Pa State Univ Libr, University Park; Experimental Television Ctr, Owego, NY, 91; UCLA Film & Television Arch, Los Angeles, 92. *Exhib:* Univ & the Arts, Wayne State Univ, Detroit, Mich, 89; 48th Ann Juried Show, Sioux City Fine Arts Ctr, Iowa, 89; Siggraph 92: 19th Int Conf on Computer Graphics & Interactive Techniques, Chicago, 92; About Face, Real Art Ways, Hartford, Conn, 94. *Pos:* Design assoc, Home Viewer Publ, Philadelphia, 85-88. *Teaching:* Asst prof graphic design, SDak State Univ, Brookings, 88-90 & Southern Conn State Univ, 90-. *Awards:* Second Place Award, Prof/Experimental Video, Video 12 regional juried competition, 92. *Mem:* Arts Coun of Greater New Haven/Media Arts Ctr; Coll Art Asn; Asn Comput Mach/Siggraph, NY. *Media:* Computer, Video. *Publ:* Auth & illusr, Zero Through One; Poems & Drawings, Moonlight Express, 84; auth, Dog star man, Home Viewer, 88. *Mailing Add:* 53 Hamilton Dr Bethany CT 05624-3414

BILODEAU, DANIEL ALAIN
PAINTER, DRAFTSMAN
b Montreal, Que, Can, US Citizen. *Study:* Ringling Sch Art & Design, BFA, 96-2000; Studio Art Centers Int; NY Art Acad, MFA, 2013. *Work:* The Citadel Mus, Canadian, Tex; Univ Tampa Medical Sch, Tampa, Fla; Sarasota Film Festival, Sarasota, Fla; New York Law Sch, New York; Ringling Coll Art & Design. *Comn:* Mural, Sarasota Film Festival, Sarasota, Fla, 99; large scale painting/installation, Semilla Estrella, Puerto Jimenez, Costa Rica, 2005. *Exhib:* Solo exhib, Body English, Dabbert Gallery, Saratoga, Fla, 2008; Beaux & Eros II, Peninsula Mus Art, Belmont, Calif, 2007; Factory Fresh, Pajama Factory, Williamsport, Pa, 2010, Going Pastel, Inst Contemp Arts, London, 2010, Art Hamptons, Bridgehampton, New York, 2010; Take Home a Nude, Sothebys, NY, 2012; Single Far 3, RH Gallery, NY, 2013; Works from the Terra Found, NYAA, 2013. *Awards:* George Sugarman Found Grant, George Sugarman Found, 2004; Leslie T and Francis Posey grant, 2011; Summer Fellowship, Terra Found for Am Art Europe, Giverny, Fr, 2012. *Bibliog:* Marty Fugate (auth), Bilodeau's Art is Divine but Down to Earth, The Observer, 3/16/2006; Int Artist Mg, Dec 2009/Jan 2010; Art Renewal Ctr Int Salong Catalogue, 2010. *Media:* Oil on Linen, Canvas, Graphite, Mixed Media. *Dealer:* Robin Rile Fine Art Miami FL. *Mailing Add:* 988 Blvd of the Arts #609 Sarasota FL 34236

BINGHAM, GEORGANNE C
EXECUTIVE DIRECTOR
Pos: Dept dir, NC Mus Art, Raleigh, formerly; dep dir, develop & membership, NC Mus Art Found; exec dir, Art Mus Western Va, Roanoke, 2003-. *Mailing Add:* Art Museum of Western Virginia 1 Market Square 2nd Floor Roanoke VA 24011

BINKS, RONALD C
PHOTOGRAPHER, PAINTER
b Oak Park, Ill, Oct 20, 1934. *Study:* George Eastman House, with Minor White, 54; RI Sch Design, BFA, 56; Berlin Art Acad, cert, 58; Yale Univ, MFA, 60, Am Acad in Rome, 62. *Work:* Southwest Art Mus, Lubbock, Tex; San Antonio Mus Art, Tex; Ammon Carter Mus, Ft Worth, Tex; Del Mar Col, Corpus Christi, Tex; Springfield Art Mus, Mo; and others. *Comn:* Nature Conservancy Tex. *Exhib:* Fulbright Artists, Whitney Mus Am Art, NY, 58; 20th Century Photog, George Eastman House, Rochester, 60; Abilene Mus Fine Arts, 83; Berlin Fotos, Univ Tex, San Antonio, 98; Sequences, Blue Star Art Ctr, 2005; Binks, 50 Years Photog, Univ Tex San Antonio Gallery, 2006. *Pos:* Ed adv, Photographer's Forum, 79-. *Teaching:* Assoc prof art, RI Sch Design, 62-76, chmn film dept, 68-72; prof, Div Dept Art & Art History, Univ Tex, San Antonio, 76-. *Awards:* Fulbright Fel, 56-8; Prix de Rome, 60-62. *Bibliog:* Beaumont Newhall (auth), Young photographers, Art in Am, 60. *Publ:* Aperture, spring 61; Voices of Art, 2004; Articles, 2006; Artists at Your Doorstep, Trinity Univ Press, 2008. *Dealer:* REM Gallery San Antonio TX. *Mailing Add:* Dept Art Univ Tex San Antonio One University Cir San Antonio TX 78249

BIN MOHAMMAD BIN ALI AL-THANI, SHEIKH SAUD
COLLECTOR
b Qatar, 1964. *Pos:* Pres, Qatar Nat Coun for Cult, Arts, Heritage, 1997-2005; founder, Al Wabra Wildlife Preservation (AWWP); founder, Al-Thani awards, 2000. *Awards:* Named one of Top 200 Collectors, ARTnews mag, 2009-13. *Collection:* Antiquities; Old Masters; rare books; photography; Islamic art; contemporary art

BIOLCHINI, GREGORY PHILLIP
PAINTER
b Peoria, Ill, Mar 24, 1948. *Study:* Famous Artist Course, Westport, Conn, 70; Edison Community Col, Ft Myers, Fla, printmaking, 80 & 88; Ringling Art Inst, Sarasota, Fla, figure sculpture, ceramics, workshops in watercolor, pastel & oil, 90. *Work:* State Fla, Capitol Bldg, Tallahassee; Ft Myers Hist Mus, Barbara B Mann Performing Arts Hall, Univ SFla Campus, Harborside Conv Ctr, Edison Mus, Ft Myers, Fla; Embry Riddle Aeronautical Univ, Daytona, Fla. *Comn:* Oil portrait, Mayor Zee Butler, comn by Brent Scheneman, LaBelle Gallery, Sanibel, Fla, 81; oil portraits, J Paul Riddle, 86, T H Embry, 87, Embry-Riddle Univ, Daytona, Fla; oil portrait, Barbara B Mann, comn by Sen Frank Mann, Ft Myers, Fla, 88; bronze portrait, Chief Billy Bowlegs, comn by D J Wilkins, Ft Myers, Fla, 90; Mrs Thomas Alva Edison (oil portrait), The Edison Found, Ft Myers, Fla, 98. *Exhib:* Pastels Only, Nat Arts Club Gallery, NY, 81-2003; solo exhib, Fla Cowboy, Ft Myers Hist Mus, 84; Societee des Pastellistes de France, Paris, 87; Degas Pastel Soc Second Biennial, Nat Exhib, New Orleans, La, 88, 2002; Three Notable Pastelists, Fla Southern Univ, Lakeland, 90; Nat Pastel Soc Master Pastelists, Harmon-Meek Gallery, Naples, Fla, 92; Butler Inst, Youngstown, Ohio, 2003; Fla State Capital Building; and others. *Pos:* Co-founder & vpres, Co-operative Gallery, Bell Tower, Ft Myers, Fla, 83-86. *Awards:* Award for Nude, Pastels Only, Nat Arts Club, Vincent Giffuni, 83; Award for Nude, Pastels Only, Nat Arts Club, Hon & Mrs DiGiovanna, 88; Best of Show, Fla State Wildlife Comn, 2001; Grumbacher Gold Medallion, 2002. *Bibliog:* The Art of Pastel Portraiture (featured artist), Watson-Guptil Publ, 96; The Best of Pastel, Pure Color, Northlight Pub, 2006. *Mem:* Pastel Soc Am (master pastelist status, 88); Degas Pastel Soc; Fla Artists Group; Int Pastel Soc. *Media:* Pastel. *Dealer:* Harmon-Meek Gallery 386 Broad Ave S Naples FL 33940. *Mailing Add:* Studio 412 81 W North Shore Ave Fort Myers FL 33903-4403

BIONDI, FLORENCE GLORIA
PAINTER, PASTEL
b Sept 25, 1924. *Study:* Brooklyn Mus Art Sch, studied with Isaac Soyer, 1968-1975; Art Student League, studied with John H Sanden & Daniel Greene, 1 yr scholar, 1976-1979. *Work:* Princeton Univ, NJ; Harvard Univ, Cambridge, Mass. *Comn:* Portrait John F Kennedy, Italian Execs of Am, NY, 1967; Prehistoric elephant for book, Dr V Maglio, Cambridge, Mass, 1971; Prehistoric man (drawing), Dr V Maglio, Princeton, NJ, 1972. *Exhib:* Salmagundi Club Ann (juried), NYC, 2004; Pastel Soc Am Ann (juried), NYC; Am Artists Prof League Ann (juried), NYC, 2005; Pen & Brush Club Invitational (juried), NYC, 2005; Audubon Artists Ann (juried), NYC, 2005. *Awards:* Pastel Award, CLW Art Club, 2001; Pastel Soc Am Gold Medal, Salmagundi Club, 2004; Audubon Artists Gold Medal, Art Spirit Found, Diane B Bernhard, 2005; Gold Medal Hon, Frank C Wright, 2010. *Mem:* Am Artists Prof League; Pastel Soc Am; Catharine Lorillard Wolfe Art Club; Audubon Soc; Art Students League NY. *Media:* Oil. *Publ:* Art, book on prehistoric elephants, Harvard Univ, 1971; art, Contemporary Women Artists Date Book (calendar), Panz Corp, Calif. *Mailing Add:* 426 McDonald Ave Brooklyn NY 11218

BIRBIL, PAUL GREGORY
PAINTER, PRINTMAKER
b Chicago, Ill, 1965. *Study:* Univ NMex; Calif Coll Arts & Crafts, BFA (hon), 85; Spec course in Salzburg, Bildendkunst with Sandro Chia, cert, 93. *Work:* Museo de Santo Domingo, Mexico City, Mex. *Comn:* Oil painting, Alazraki y Assoc, Mex, 93; painting, Producciones por Marca, Mex, 94; wall painting, New Art Digital, Mex, 94; oil painting, Artes Graficas Panorama, Mex, 96. *Exhib:* Jovenes Nacidos en los 60's (traveling), Mex, 93; solo shows, Mus Contemp Art, Morelia/Michoacan, Mex, 94 & Museo del Chopo, Mex, 96; Contemp Painters from Mexico, Museo de Arte Contemporaneo, Bogata, Colombia, 95. *Awards:* Louis Siegrist Painting Award, 85. *Media:* Oil Paint. *Dealer:* Andres Siegel 40 Veracruz Mexico City Mexico. *Mailing Add:* Madrid 209-Coyoacan 04100 Mexico DF Mexico

BIRCHLER, ALEXANDER
FILMMAKER
b Baden, Switz, 1962. *Study:* attended, Schule fur Gestaltung, Basel, 83-87; attended, Univ Art & Design, Helsinki, 85; Nova Scotia Coll Art & Design, Halifax, MFA, 92. *Work:* Columbus Mus Art, OH; Neues Mus, Nuremberg, Ger; Ulrich Mus Art, Wichita, Kans; Yokohama Mus Art, Japan; and numerous others. *Exhib:* solo shows, Slow Place, Mus fur Gegenwartskunst, Basel, 97; Stripping, Kunstlerhaus Bethanien, Berlin, 89; Gregor's Room, Gallery Bob van Orsouw, Zurich, 99; Motion Pictures, Gallery Barbara Thumm, Berlin, 99; Arsenal, Bonakdar Jancou Gallery, NY, 2000; Tanya Bonakdar Gallery, NY, 2002; ArtPace Found Contemp Art, San Antonio, Tex, 2002; County Line Road, 2003; Single Wide, Whitney Mus Am Art, NY, 2004; Editing the Dark, Kemper Mus Contemp Art, Kansas City, 2005; House with Pool, Miami Art Mus, 2006; Galerie Barbara Thumm, Berlin, 2006; group shows, Nonchalance Revisited, Akademie der Kunste, Berlin, 98; Solitude in Budapest, Kunsthalle, Budapest, 99; Every Time, La Biennale de Montreal, 2000; New Work, Tanya Bonakdar Gallery, NY, 2001; Out of Place: Contemp Art & the Architectural Uncanny, Mus Contemp Art, Chicago, 2002; Adolescence, Reina Sofia Mus, Madrid, 2003; Eight, Centre Culturel Suisse, Paris, 2004; Swiss Experimental Film, Image Forum, Tokyo, 2005; Roaming Memories, Ludwig Forum, Aachen, 2005; Melancholy, Nationalgalerie, Berlin, 2006; Picture Ballot, Kunsthaus, Zurich, 2006; Raised by Wolves, Art Gallery Western Australia, Perth, 2006. *Pos:* lectr at various univs & insts, 92-, including Univ Zurich, 93-94. *Teaching:* core fac mem, Milton Avery Grad Sch, Bard Col, NY, 2005-. *Bibliog:* Dora Imhof (auth), Teresa Hubbard & Alexander Birchler, House with Pool, Kunstforum, Vol 161, 3-4/2004, 504-505; Amoreen Armetta (auth), Teresa Hubbard/Alexander Birchler, Flash Art, 1/2005, 69; Rene Morales, Teresa Hubbard & Alezander Birchler, MAM Portrait: Miami Art Mus, Miami, 7-9/2006, 6; and many others. *Mailing Add:* c/o Tanya Bonakdar Gallery 521 W 21st St New York NY 10011

BIRDSALL, BYRON
PAINTER
b Buckeye, Ariz, Dec 18, 1937. *Study:* Seattle Pacific Col, BA; Stanford Univ, MA. *Work:* Anchorage Hist & Fine Arts Mus; Jean Haydon Territorial Mus, Pago Pago, Am Samoa. *Comn:* Painting, Alaska Bank of Com, Anchorage, 76; Alaska Pipeline Co, Anchorage, 77; RCA, Anchorage, 77; stone lithos, Anchorage Opera Soc, 85; painting, Anchorage Olympic Organizing Comt, 85; King Co Libr System, 86; and others. *Exhib:* All Alaska Watercolor Exhib, Alaska Watercolor Soc, 75-77; Anchorage Hist & Fine Arts Mus, 76 & All Alaska Exhib, 78; and many solo exhibs. *Teaching:* Instr, Makerere Univ, Kampala, Uganda, 66-70; feature prog, art dir, KVZK Television, Pago Pago, Am Samoa, 72-73 & Graphix West Advertising Agency, Anchorage, Alaska, 75-76. *Awards:* Alaska Arts & Crafts League First Prize in Watercolor; Alaska Watercolor Soc First Prize, 76 & Second Prize, 77, Alaska Watercolor Show; Third Prize, All Alaska Art Exhib, 82. *Bibliog:* Lana Johnson (auth), Watercolorist forsakes his palm trees, Anchorage Times, 11/77; Barbara Whipple (auth), Byron Birdsall paints Alaska, Am Artist, 4/81; Janet O'Hara (auth), Byron Birdsall, artist of the world, Wien Air Alaska Flight Time, 9/83. *Mem:* Alaska Watercolor Soc (pres, 76); Alaska Artists Guild. *Media:* Watercolor, Stone. *Publ:* Auth, Letters from Africa, Anchorage Times, 6/81. *Dealer:* Kirsten Gallery 5320 Roosevelt Way NE Seattle WA 98105. *Mailing Add:* c/o Artique Ltd 314 G St Anchorage AK 99501

BIRDSALL, STEPHANIE
ARTIST
b Atlanta, Ga, 1952. *Study:* Univ Ga, 70-71; Rhodes Col, 71-72; City & Guilds London Art Sch, London, Eng, 72-76. *Work:* Fla State Art Collection, Fla State Capitol, Tallahassee, Fla; Fla Mus Art & Cult, Avon Park, Fla; Mus of the Everglades, Everglades Nat Monument, Fla. *Exhib:* Seaweed Gallery, Sanibel Island, Fla, 2001; 4th Ann Int Asn Pastel Socs Competition, Chablis Gallery, Placerville, Ga, Gallery on Fifth, Naples, Fla, 2002; Renaissance in Pastel, Nat Exhib W Hartford Art League, W Hartford, Conn, Nat Pastel Exhib, Lone Star Pastel Soc, Amarillo, Tex, 12th Ann Nat Pastel Painting Exhib, Pastel Soc NMex, Albuquerque, NMex, 2003; Eastern Regional Juried Exhib Traditional Oils, Oil Painters Am, Kewaunee, Wis, Southeastern Pastel Soc Int Show, Marietta-Cobb Mus Art, Ga, 2004; 109th Ann Exhib, Catherine Lorillard Wolfe Art Club, NY, 74th Ann Exhib, Hudson Valley Art Asn, Hastings on Hudson, NY, Int Asn Pastel Socs, Art Source Gallery, Raleigh, NC, Putney Painters, Village Arts Gallery, Putney, Vt, 2005; Tucson Plein Air Painters, Northern Trust Bank, Tucson, Ariz, Two Women, Rising Stars, Putney Painters & Friends, Susan Powell Fine Art Gallery, Madison, Conn, 2006; solo exhib, Fla Mus Art & Cult, Avon, Fla, Rocky Mountain Plein Air Painters, 5th Ann Show, Elkhorn Gallery, Winter Park, Colo, 2006; Richard Schmid Fine Art Auction, Bellevue, Colo, 2006; and others. *Awards:* Daniel Smith Award, Pastel Soc Northern Fla, 2002; 2nd Place, Nat Pastel Exhib, Lone Star Pastel Soc, 2003; First Place Award of Excellence, Degas Pastel Soc, 2004; 14th Ann Pastel Exhib, Artisan/Santa Fe Award, Pastel Soc NMex, 2005; Exceptional Merit Award, Degas Pastel Soc, 2005; Finalist Artist Art prize Challenge, Int Artist Mag, 2005; and numerous others. *Bibliog:* Lonni Pierson Dunbier (auth), Artist's Blue Book, Am Artists, Mountain Press Publ, 2004; Sara Shlussel & Ron James (coauths), Parks Portrayed in Pen and Paint, 2005; Sylvie Fauvel Cabal (auth), L'Art du Pastel en France, 2006. *Mem:* Pastel Soc Conn (signature mem); Plein Air Soc Fla (signature mem); Pastel Soc Am (signature mem); Nat Asn Women Artists (juried mem); Pastel Soc NMex (signature mem); Catharine Lorillard Wolfe Art Club; and others. *Mailing Add:* 3131 N Deer Track Rd Tucson AZ 85749

BIRENBAUM, CYNTHIA See Barber, Cynthia

BIRK, SANDOW
PAINTER, SCULPTOR
b Detroit, Mich, 1962. *Study:* Parsons Sch Design, Otis Art Inst, BFA, 81-88; Am Coll Paris, 84; Bath Acad Art, Eng, 85. *Work:* San Francisco Mus Mod Art; Laguna Art Mus, Laguna Beach, Calif; Mus da Republica, Rio de Janeiro, Brazil; Renee di Rosa Mus, Napa, Calif; Sonoma Valley Mus Art, Calif; Metropolitan Mus Art, NY; Los Angeles Co Mus Art; San Diego Mus Contemp Art; De Young Mus, San Francisco. *Comn:* lobby, Lincoln Properties Bldg, Philadelphia, Pa; City Place Shopping Ctr, City of Long Beach, Calif; Hollenbeck LAPD Station, Los Angles, Calif; Tarzana MTA Station, Tarzana, Calif; lobby, Jazz Theatre, San Francisco; Avalon Lifeguard Station, Avalon, Calif. *Exhib:* Carioca, Laguna Art Mus, Laguna Beach, Calif, 97, San Jose Mus Art, Calif, 99; When Borders Migrate, Mus Art & Hist, Santa Cruz, Calif, 99; Made in Calif, Los Angeles Co Mus Art, 00; In Smog and Thunder, Laguna Art Mus, Calif, 00; Incarceration, Santa Barbara Contemp Arts Forum, Calif, 01; Sandow Birk's Divine Comedy, San Jose Mus Art, 05; Leading Causes of Death in Am, San Diego Mus Art, 05. *Awards:* the Basil H Alkazzi Award, 98; J Paul Getty Fel for the Visual Arts, 99; Individual Artist Fel, City of Los Angeles, Calif, 01; Guggenheim fel, 95; Int Exchange fel to Mex, NEA, 95; Fulbright fel to Brazil, 97. *Bibliog:* JSM Wittette (auth), Sandow Birk and the killing of Los Angeles, Visions Art Qrtly, 93; Greil Marques (auth), Flotsam and jetsom of California state of mind, NY Times, 98; Claudine Ise (auth), Sly scenes of California Civil War, Los Angeles Times, 98. *Media:* Oil on Canvas. *Interests:* surfing. *Publ:* Gallery - Barry McGee (Twist), Surfers J, 96; Graffiti, 96 & Views of the Getty Museum, 98, Juxtapoz Mag; In Smog and Thunder: The Great War of the Californias, Last Gasp Publ, 2000; Incarcerated: Visions of California in the 21st Century, Last Gasp Publishing, 2001; Dante's Inferno, Chronical Books, 04, Dante's Purgatorio, 05, Dante's Paradiso, 05. *Dealer:* Koplin Del Rio Gallery 6031 Washington Blvd Culver City Ca 90232; Catharine Clark Gallery 150 Minna St San Francisco Ca 94105; PPow Gallery 511 W 25th St #301 New York NY 10001. *Mailing Add:* 835 Locust Ave #316 Long Beach CA 90813

BIRMELIN, ROBERT
PAINTER, DRAFTSMAN
b Newark, NJ, Nov 7, 1933. *Study:* Cooper Union Art Sch; Yale Univ, BFA, 56, MFA, 60; RI Coll Hon Dr Fine Arts, 96. *Exhib:* Solo exhibs include Claude Bernard Gallery, NY, 88 & 90, Jersey City Mus, NJ, 97-98, Eugene Olson Gallery, Bethel Col, St Paul, Minn, 98, Lore Degenstein Gallery, Susquehanna Univ, Selinsgrove, Pa, 98, Peter Findlay Gallery, NY, 97 & 2000, Luise Ross Gallery, NY, 99 & Jaff-Friete Gallery, Dartmouth Col, Hanover, NH, 99, Luise Ross Gallery, 2006; group exhibs include Galeria Mara, Buenos Aires, Argentina, 89; Am Imagist and Abstract Painting, Moscow, USSR, 89; Contemp Realist Gallery, San Francisco, 94 & 95; Radix Gallery, NY, 96; Recent Paintings, Bannister Gallery, RI Col, Providence, 96; Powerful Expressions: Drawing Today, Am Acad Design, NY, 96; Sex/Industry, Stefan Stux Gallery, NY, 97; Summer Group Show, Radix Gallery, NY, 97; Re-presenting representation III, Arnot Art Mus, Elmira, NY, 97; 10th Ann Exhib, Hackett-Freedman Gallery, San Francisco, Calif, 97, 2001. *Teaching:* Prof art, Queens Col, NY, 64-, retired. *Awards:* Am Acad Fel, Rome, 61-64; Nat Endowment Arts, 82 & 90; NJ Coun Arts, 88; Nat Endowment of Arts, 1976, 1982, 1989. *Bibliog:* Laurie Hurwitz (auth), Contemporary Masters: Robert Birmelin, Am Artist, 4/90; Robert Berlind (auth), From the corner of the minds eye: the paintings of Robert Birmelin, Art in America, 3/91; Fred Stern (auth), To make the unreal real: the art of Robert Birmelin, Art Leisure, 8/98. *Mem:* Nat Acad Design (assoc, 86, acad, 94). *Media:* Acrylic, Oil. *Dealer:* Hackett-Freedman Gallery 250 Sutter St San Francisco CA 94108; Peter Findlay Gallery 41 E 57th St New York NY 10022

BIRNBAUM, DARA
VIDEO ARTIST
b New York, NY, Oct 29, 1946. *Study:* Carnegie Mellon Univ, Pittsburgh, Pa, BA (archit), 69; San Francisco Art Inst, BA, 72; New Sch Social Res, New York, 76. *Work:* Mus Mod Art, NY; Ctr Georges Pompidou, Paris; Mus Contemp Art, Chicago; San Francisco Mus Mod Art; Castello Di Rivoli, Turin, Italy. *Comn:* RIO Videowall, RIO Shopping/Entertainment Complex, Atlanta, Ga; MTV ArtBreak, MTV Network; Fourt Gates, St Polten Kunst & Raum Project, St Polten, Austria. *Exhib:* Whitney Biennial Exhib, Whitney Mus Am Art, NY, 85; Solo exhibs, Portikus, Frankfurt, Ger, 94, CAPC Mus Art Contemp Entrepot, Bordeaux, France, 94, X Works at l'Esec, Paris, France, 94, Rena Bransten Gallery, San Francisco, Calif, 94, Paula Cooper Gallery, NY, 94, Norrtalje Konsthall, Swed, 95 & Kunsthalle Wien, Vienna, Austria, 95; L'Effetcinéma, Mus Art Contemp, Montréal, Can, 95; Polyphonix 28, Mus Art Africaine Océanien, Paris, France, 96; Surfing Systems, Mus Fridericianum, Kassel, Ger, 96; 13th Kasseler Dokumetarfilm & Videofest, Filmladen, Kassel, Ger, 96; Women's Work, Greene-Naftali Gallery, NY, 96; and others. *Teaching:* Instr video & post-studio, Calif Inst Arts, Valencia, 82; experimental video instr, Sch Visual Arts, New York, 83-86; Perkins jr fel, Prog Vis Arts, Princeton Univ, 87-88 & vis jr fel Coun Humanities, 87-88; video & media arts, Hunter Col Grad Sch, New York, 90-91; Heinz & Gisela Friedrich-Stiftung guest prof, Stadel-Hochschule for Bildende Kunst & Inst New Media, Frankfurt, Ger, 92. *Awards:* Maya Deren Award for Indep Film & Video Artists, Am Film Inst, 87; Cert, Harvard Univ, 88; Special Jury Prize, Deutcher Videokunstpries Sudwestfunk, 92. *Bibliog:* Dara Birnbaum (monogr), Succes de bedac No 10, Le Coin du Miroir, Dijon, France, 86; Benjamin Buchloh (ed), Rough Edits: Popular Image Video (monogr), Press of Nova Scotia Coll Art & Design, 87; Dara Birnbaum (monogr), IVAM, Ctr del Carve, Valencia, Spain, 91. *Mem:* Found Independent Video & Film, NY (bd dir, 83-85); Creative Time (bd dir, 88-96). *Media:* Video, Media Installation. *Publ:* Auth, Playground (The damnation of Faust), Zone, No 1/2, 85; Out of the Blue, in Discourses: Conversations In: Postmodern Art & Culture, Mass Inst Technol Press, 90; The RIO Experience: Video's New Architecture Meets Corporate Sponsorship, In: Illuminating Video: An Essential Guide to Video Art, Aperture Found, New York, 90; Overlapping Signs, In: War after War, City Lights Press, San Francisco, 92; Every TV Needs a Revolution, IMSCHOOT, Uitgevers, Ghent, 92. *Mailing Add:* 140 Thomson St Apt 3A New York NY 10012

BISGYER, BARBARA G (COHN)
SCULPTOR, DESIGNER
b New York, NY, June 7, 1933. *Study:* Sarah Lawrence Coll; Sculptors & Ceramic Workshop, New York; also indust design with R R Kostellow. *Work:* US Consular Small Sculpture Collection, Smithsonian Inst; Larry Aldrich Mus Contemp Art; Savin Bus Machines Corp. *Comn:* Sculpture, pvt residence, Delray, Fla, 84. *Exhib:* Union Carbide; Aldrich Mus; Avery Fisher Hall, Lincoln Ctr; Hudson River Mus; Pratt Sch Design; Sarah Lawrence Coll; London, 92; Can, 99; Switz, 99; Frankfurt, 2001; San Francisco, 2002; South West Waterfront Exhib, Portland, Ore, 2012, 2013, 2014. *Pos:* serving on numerous committees; juried numerous exhibits. *Awards:* Merit Award for Outstanding Design & Craftsmanship in Sculpture, Artists Craftsmen, New York; President's Award, Mamaroneck Artists Guild, Westchester Art Soc; Audubon Beaux Arts Award; many others. *Bibliog:* Articles in Art News, Today's Art & La Revue moderne des et de la vie. *Mem:* Artists Craftsmen, New York; Mamaroneck Artists Guild; Artists Equity Asn, New York; Am Soc Contemp Artists; Abraxas. *Media:* Cast Bronze, Welded Steel, Precious Metal. *Dealer:* Braswell Galleries. *Mailing Add:* 3550 Bond Ave Apt 1008 Portland OR 97239

BISHOP, BUDD HARRIS
PAINTER, MUSEUM DIRECTOR
b Canton, Ga, Nov 1, 1936. *Study:* Shorter Coll, Ga, AB, 58; Univ Ga, MFA, 60, with Lamar Dodd & Howard Thomas; Arts Admin Inst, Harvard Univ, 70. *Work:* Sequatchie Sundown, Bridgestone Collection, Tenn State Mus, 2000; 4 paintings, Phillips Performing Arts Ctr, Univ Fla; Grand Valley, Bellmont Univ, Nashville, Tenn. *Comn:* 4 large paintings Fla Landscapes, The Greens Develop, Gainesville. *Exhib:* Solo exhibs, Cumberland Univ, Lebanon, Tenn, 2002, Arnold Gallery, Shorter Coll, Rome, Ga, Moon Gallery, Berry Coll, Mt Berry, Ga, Parthenon Mus, Nashville, Deland Mus Art, Fla, 2003. *Collection Arranged:* Tenn State Collection of Sculpture; The First Am Collections of Hunter Mus of Art; Sculpture Collection, Columbus, Mus; Ogilvy Collection Chinese & Japanese Art; Asian Art Collections, Harn Mus

Art; Sirak Collection of European Art, Ohio; E Tenn Currents ii, Knoxville Mus Art, 99; Exhib of Shey Private Collection, Harm Mus, 2000. *Pos:* Dir creative serv, Transit Advert Asn, NY, 64-66; dir, Hunter Mus Art, 66-76 & Columbus Mus Art, Ohio, 76-87; dir, Harn Mus Art, Gainesville, Fla, 87-98 & dir emer, 99-; dir, Fla Art Mus Asn, 91-98 & officer at large, 91-93; bd dir, Fla Asn Mus Found Inc, 94-98; indep cur & mus consult, 99-; bd dir, Upper Cumberland Arts Coun, Tenn & Friends of Cordell Hull Mus, Tenn. *Teaching:* Lectr art hist, Vanderbilt Univ, 61-62; art dir children's prog, Ensworth Sch, Nashville, Tenn, 61-64; lectr art, Univ Chattanooga, 67-68. *Awards:* Tenn Arts Comt Award, 71; Shorter Coll Alumni Award, 79; Lifetime Achievement Mus Service Award, Fla Asn Mus, 97; James R Short Award, SE Mus Conf, 98; Harn Mus Study Ctr renamed Bishop Study Ctr, 98. *Mem:* Am Asn Mus; Tenn Asn Mus (pres, 70-71); Asn Art Mus Dirs; Fla Art Mus Dir Asn; Tenn Arts Comn. *Media:* Landscapes in acrylic, pastel, pencil. *Res:* Early Tennessee artists; early Southern American painting; George Bellows; American and European sculpture. *Publ:* Contribr, Italian Old Master Drawings & Insights and Conclusions: American Master Drawings, Ark Arts Ctr; America's Mirror: Painting in the United States 1850-1950; Inner Eye: Contemporary Art from the Marc and Livia Straus Collection; auth, Linda Howard: Star Flower, 94, Lachaise's Head of a Woman, Harn Mus Art, 96; Shared Treasures: Vero Collects II, Vero Beach Mus Art. *Dealer:* The Arts Co Nashville TN. *Mailing Add:* PO Box 258 Livingston TN 38570

BISHOP, JACQUELINE K
PAINTER
b Long Beach, Calif, Oct 1, 1955. *Study:* Univ Kansas, Lawrence, 73-75; Univ New Orleans, BA, 76-78; Tulane Univ, MFA, 80-82. *Work:* New Orleans Mus Art, La; Huntsville Mus Art, Ala; City New Orleans - Arts Coun, New Orleans, La; Albrecht-Kemper Mus Art, St Joseph, Mo; Tulane Univ, New Orleans, La. *Exhib:* Bird Space, Hudson River Mus, NY; Terra, Brazil, 96, Albrecht Kemper Mus, 2002; The Texture of Memory, Arthur Roger Gallery, New Orleans, La, 2002; Trespass, Arthur Roger Gallery, New Orleans, La, 2005. *Teaching:* Instr drawing & painting, Newcomb Col, Tulane Univ, New Orleans, 82-84, instr drawing, 93-94; asst prof advan painting, Loyola Univ, New Orleans, La, 90; Loyola Univ, Art & Environment, 2003-2005. *Awards:* La Div Arts Grant. *Bibliog:* D Eric Bookhardt (auth), Color, Time & Space, Gambit Weekly. *Media:* Oil, Mixed Media. *Dealer:* Arthur Roger Gallery 432 Julia St New Orleans LA. *Mailing Add:* 1217 Philip St New Orleans LA 70130

BISHOP, JEFFREY BRITTON
PAINTER, EDUCATOR
b Berkeley, Calif, Feb 18, 1949. *Study:* Boston Mus Sch, Dipl (with honors), 73; Tufts Univ, BFA, 74; Univ Wash, MFA, 77. *Work:* Seattle Art Mus, Wash. *Comn:* Large wall installation, City Seattle, Wash, 80. *Exhib:* New Ideas, Seattle Art Mus, Wash, 78; Wash Open, Seattle Art Mus, Wash, 79; Solo exhibs, Linda Farris Gallery, Seattle, Wash, 80, 82, 88 & 93, Mirage Gallery, Los Angeles, Calif, 81 & Seattle Art Mus, 83, San Diego State Univ Gallery, Calif, 94 & Meyerson & Nowinski Art Assocs, Seattle, Wash, 97; Eight Seattle Artists: Installations, Los Angeles Inst Contemp Art, 80; Wash Yr, Henry Gallery, Univ Wash, Seattle, 81; Collage & Assemblage, Miss Mus Art, Jackson & traveling, 81-83; Bellevue Art Mus, Wash, 83; Betty Bowen Tenth Anniversary Exhib, Seattle, Wash, 88; 20th Anniversary Show, Linda Farris Gallery, Seattle, Wash, 90; Watercolor, Bellevue Art Mus, Wash, 91; Betty Bowen Legacy, Security Pacific Gallery, Seattle, 92; Elizabeth Leach Gallery, Portland, Ore, 94; Vox Populi, NY, 95. *Teaching:* Lectr mod art, Univ Wash, Seattle, 78; program dir, Henry Gallery Lecture Series, Seattle, Wash, 78-82; lectr & instr mod art, drawing & painting, Cornish Inst, Seattle, Wash, 79-82. *Awards:* 66th James William Paige Traveling Fel, Boston Mus Fine Arts, 74; Betty Bowen Award, Seattle Art Mus, 82. *Bibliog:* Mathew Kangas (auth), Seattle, Artforum, 5/79 & Art in Am, 81; Barbara Taylor (auth), Eight Seattle Artists, Los Angeles Inst Contemp Art, 80. *Mem:* Allied Arts of Seattle; founding mem Ctr Contemp Art. *Media:* Water Media, Charcoal. *Publ:* Auth, interview with Susan Sontag, Insight, 82. *Mailing Add:* 240 Carlton Ave Brooklyn NY 11205-4002

BISHOP, JEROLD
EDUCATOR, PAINTER
b Salt Lake City, Utah, Apr 14, 1936. *Study:* Southern Utah State Col, Cedar City, AB, 56; Utah State Univ, Logan, BS, 60, MFA, 66. *Work:* Valley Nat Bank, Phoenix; Glendale Community Col, Ariz; Starr Commonwealth Boys, Albion, Mich; Court House Collection, Douglas, Ariz. *Comn:* Ariz Hwy Mag, Phoenix, Ariz, 84-86; Collector Plate Series, Fine Arts Mktg, 85. *Exhib:* Mormon Festival Arts, Brigham Young Univ Art Ctr, Provo, Utah, 77-79; Watercolor USA, Springfield Art Mus, Mo, 77 & 80; Univ Ariz Fac Shows, Mus Art, Tucson, 77-85; Watercolor Biennial, Scottsdale Ctr Arts, Ariz, 80; and others. *Pos:* Art dir, Thiokol Chemical Corp, Brigham City, Utah, 63-64 & 66-67; production artist & art dir, Utah State Univ, Logan, 64-66. *Teaching:* Asst prof art, Univ Ariz, Tucson, 67-72, assoc prof, 72-. *Awards:* Masters Meed Medallion, Tubac Festival Arts, Santa Cruz Valley Art Asn, 76; Special Award, 4th Ann Western Fedn Watercolor Socs Exhib, 79; Silver Medal, 57th Ann Nat, Springville Mus Art, Utah, 81; Merit Award, Ariz Watercolor Asn, Scottsdale, 84; Phippen Family Award, Prescott, Ariz, 85. *Mem:* Western Fedn Watercolor Socs; Southern Ariz Watercolor Guild; Ariz Watercolor Asn. *Media:* Watercolor, Mixed. *Mailing Add:* 9133 E Speedway Blvd Tucson AZ 85710-1818

BISSELL, PHIL
CARTOONIST, ILLUSTRATOR
b Worcester, Mass, Feb 1, 1926. *Study:* Sch Practical Art, Boston; Art Instr Inc, Minneapolis, grad. *Hon Degrees:* Lesley Univ, BFA, 2007. *Work:* Baseball Hall Fame, Cooperstown, NY; Basketball Hall Fame, Springfield, Mass; Football Hall Fame, Canton, Ohio; Hockey Hall Fame, Toronto; Swimming Hall of Fame, Ft Lauderdale; Eisenhower Mus, Abilene, Kans; NE Patriots Hist Mus, 2008; Agganis Arena, Boston Univ; Hamilton Wenham Hall of Fame; Gerald Ford Mus, Ann Arbor, Mich; William J Flynn, Boston Coll Recreation Complex, Chestnut Hill, Mass; Rev Francis J Hart SJ, The Hart Recreation Ctr, Holy Cross Coll, Worcester, Mass. *Comn:* New Eng Patriots (Nat Football League) insignia; Rourke Bridge Plaques, Lowell, Mass. *Exhib:* Southern Calif Expo, 64; Nat Cartoonists Soc, NY, 71 & Washington, DC, 72-79; Man & His World, Ninth Int Salon Cartoons, Montreal. *Awards:* Best Ed Cartoons, 74-88; Mass Bay Chiefs Award, 81. *Mem:* Hon mem Baseball Writers Asn. *Media:* Ink, Tempera. *Publ:* The World Encyclopedia of Cartoons, Horn, Chelsea House, 80; Sport Spot, Tall Tales from Tall Ships. *Mailing Add:* 19 Landmark Ln Rockport MA 01966

BJORKLUND, LEE
PAINTER, EDUCATOR
b Wadena, Minn, June 20, 1940. *Study:* Univ Minn, Minneapolis, BA, 69 & MFA, 73. *Work:* Walker Art Ctr, Minneapolis Inst Art, Fed Reserve Bank, Norwest Nat Bank & First Nat Bank, Minneapolis; Amerada Hess Corp, NY. *Comn:* Norwest Bank, Minneapolis, Minn, 78; RAUTI, Rochester, Minn, 87; Mayo Clinic, Scottsdale, Ariz, 87. *Exhib:* Walker Art Ctr, 66, 72 & 75; Univ Gallery, 67, 71 & 81; Minn Inst Arts, 75, 81, 86 & 90; Peter M David Gallery, 80-82 & 85; Kuopio Mus, Kuopio, Finland, 81. *Pos:* Visual art coordr, Minn State Arts Bd, Minneapolis, 74-75, co-founder, Minn Artists Exhib Prog, 75, chmn, Visual Studies Div, 75-78, acad adv, 82 & acting dean students, 85-86. *Teaching:* Instr, Univ Minn, 70-72, Art Ctr Minn, 71-72, Minn Mus Art Sch, St Paul, 72-73, Winona State Univ, 72, Minneapolis Col Art & Design, 73-90, assoc prof. *Awards:* Minn State Arts Bd Grant, 72 & 79; Ford Found Grant, 77; Mellon Found Grant, 82-84; and others. *Bibliog:* Mike Steele (auth), Practitioners explore the modern art mystique, Minneapolis Tribune, 5/18/75; Eleanor Heartney (auth), article, New Art Examiner, summer 81; William Hegeman (auth), article, Art News, 11/81; Margot Kriel Galt (auth), The artists who came in from the cold, Minn Monthly, 1/86. *Mem:* Minneapolis Soc Fine Arts. *Media:* Mixed. *Dealer:* Peter M David Gallery 400 First Ave N Minneapolis, Minn. *Mailing Add:* 326 W Elmwood Pl Minneapolis MN 55419

BLACK, DAVID EVANS
SCULPTOR
b Gloucester, Mass, May 29, 1928. *Study:* Skowhegan Sch, Maine, summer 49; Wesleyan Univ, AB, 50; Ind Univ, Bloomington, MFA, 54. *Work:* Neue Nat Galerie, West Berlin, Ger; Dayton Art Inst; Utsukushi-Ga-Hara Mus, Japan; Kalamazoo Col, Mich; Ft Wayne Mus Art, Ind; Cent Mich Univ Mt Pleasant, Clarkson Univ, Potsdam, NY; Univ Alaska, Fairbanks; Zanesville Art Ctr, Ohio. *Comn:* Island Park, Belmont, Calif, 90; Main Libr Plaza, Tucson, Ariz, 91; Ottawa Park, City of Toledo, Ohio, 94; Univ Circle, Cleveland, Ohio, 95; Flyover (auth, catalog), Wright Brothers Mem, City Dayton, Ohio, 96; City of DC, 2009; City of Ft Myers, Fla, 2010. *Exhib:* Solo exhib, Amerika-Haus, W Berlin, 71; Neue Nat Gallerie, Berlin, Ger, 77; Lehmbruck Mus, Duisberg, Ger, 77; Taft Mus (with catalog), Cincinnati, Ohio, 85; Indianapolis Mus Art, 85; Kalamazoo Art Inst (with catalog), Mich, 87. *Pos:* Mem, DAAD Artists Prog, Berlin & WGer Govt, 70-72. *Teaching:* Prof sculpture, Ohio State Univ, 54-84. *Awards:* Fulbright Grant, Italy, 62-63; Nat Endowment Arts Individual Artist Grant, 65; Int Sculpture Prize, Hakone Mus, Japan, 85; Special Award, Nat Coun Engineers Asn, 1999; German Gov grant, Berlin, 71-73. *Bibliog:* Charlotte Lowe (auth), Sonora, Tucson Citizen, 7/4/91; article, Sculpture Mag, 5/92; article, Competitions Mag, 1/95; Flyover, Dayton Daily News, 1994-96; Black on White (film), Umbrella Films Berlin, 2002. *Media:* Metals, Environments. *Interests:* Reading, classical music, museums, travel. *Publ:* Auth, Flyover (booklet), City of Dayton, Ohio, 97; David Black, Urban Sculpture as Proto Architecture. *Dealer:* David Black Sculpture 1066 Lincoln Rd Columbus OH 43212. *Mailing Add:* 1066 Lincoln Rd Columbus OH 43212

BLACK, DEBRA & LEON DAVID
COLLECTOR
Study: Dartmouth Coll, AB, 1973; Harvard Univ, MBA, 1975. *Pos:* With Drexel Burnham Lambert Inc, New York, 77-90, financial dept assoc, 77, head mergers and acquisitions, 85-90, co-head corp financial dept, formerly; co-founder, The Apollo Orgn (incl Apollo Mgt LP, Apollo Advisors LP, Apollo Real Estate Advisors LP), 90-; bd dirs, Vail Resorts Inc, Sequa Corp, United Rentals Inc, Allied Waste Industries Inc, 2000-, AMC Entertainment Inc, 2001-, Sirius Satellite Radio Inc, 2001- & Wyndham Int Inc; trustee, Mus Modern Art, New York, Mt Sinai Hosp, Lincoln Ctr for Performing Arts, Metrop Mus Art, Prep for Prep, The Jewish Mus, Cardozo Sch Law, The Asia Soc, Spence Sch & Vail Valley Found; bd trustees, Dartmouth Coll, 2002-2011. *Awards:* Named one of Top 200 Collectors, ARTnews mag, 2004-13. *Collection:* Old Masters, Impressionist, Modern and Contemporary Art, and Chinese Sculpture

BLACK, JAPPIE KING
SCULPTOR, TEXTILE ARTIST
Study: RI Sch Design, BFA; Syracuse Univ, MFA. *Exhib:* Solo exhibs, Adams Gallery, RI Coll, 1975, Interlochen Arts Acad, 1980, 1987, East End Arts Coun Gallery, NY, 1990, ComArt Gallery, Syracuse Univ, 1992, Tower Fine Arts Gallery, SUNY Brockport, 1996, Mohawk Valley Ctr Arts, NY, 2001; Fiber Sculpture National, Nazareth Coll Art Ctr, NY, 1982; Fiber at the End of the Century, Corvallis Arts Ctr, Ore, 1994; Materials: Hard & Soft, Ctr for Visual Arts, Tex, 1994; Grateful Threads, Delaplaine Visual Arts Ctr, Frederick, Md, 1999; Elements 2000, Snug Harbor Cult Ctr, Staten Island, 2000. *Teaching:* Asst prof, Syracuse Univ, NY, 1996-98, Kean Univ, NJ, 2001-; adj prof, Rochester Inst Technol, NY, 2000. *Awards:* Empire State Craft Alliance Grant, 1995; Cmty Arts Grant, 1999 & Individual Artist Grant, 2001, Arts & Cult Coun, Rochester, NY; NY Found Arts Fel, 2009

BLACK, LISA
PAINTER, PHOTOGRAPHER
b Lansing, Mich, June 19, 1934. *Study:* Univ Paris, Sorbonne, dipl, 55; Univ Mich, BA, 56. *Work:* Conn Bank & Trust; Stamford Hosp, Conn; Darien Physical Therapies, Darien, Conn; Internal Med of Darien, Darien, Conn. *Comn:* Mural, Easter Seal Rehabilitation Ctr, 89; Painting, Travel Store, Darien, Conn, 93. *Exhib:* New Haven Paint & Clay Club Art Exhib, Conn, 71-72 & 83; Springfield Art League 53rd Nat

Exhib, Mass, 72; 32nd Ann Art Exhib, Cedar City, Utah, 72; 15th Nat Exhib Am Art, Chautauqua, NY, 72; Milford Fine Arts Art Exhib, 83; Stamford Mus Conn Art, 89-90, 92 & 94; Juried Exhib, Rowayton Art Ctr, 94, 97-99; Milford Arts Coun, 99; Greenwich Art Soc, 2003-2005; Juried Show, The Blues, Art Soc Old Greenwich, 2006; Far Away Places (juried), Stamford Art Asn, 2006; Juried Photography, New Canaan soc Arts, 2007; Monotype Guild New Eng (juried), 2007; Hot Hot Hot (juried) Greenwich Art Soc, 2007; Nano Int Art Festival, Kotka, Finland, 2007; Rowayton Arts Ctr, 2008; ArtUp Gallery (juried), Westport, Conn, 2009; Banner Exhib, Fairfield Arts Coun, 2009, 2011; participant, Nano Int Arts Festival, Stuttg art, 2011. *Pos:* Historian, Greenwich Art Soc, 92-93; bd mem, Rowayton Art Ctr, 2000; founder, Fairfield Public Sch Private Art Coll, 2011. *Teaching:* Children's art lessons, pvt studio, 78-79; Art hist 5th grade (volunteer), 97-98; Arts in Action, Fairfield Middle Sch. *Awards:* First Prize, Rowayton Arts Ctr, 89, 91, 93, 96 & 98; Fred Kraus Mem Award, Stamford Mus Conn Art, 92; Best in Show, Rowayton Arts, Ctr, 97; 1st Prize, Art Soc Old Greenwich, 2005, 2007; Juried Show Award, Greenwich Art Soc, 2007; Judge's Merit Award, Rowayton Arts Ctr, 2008; 2nd Prize (Prints), Rowayton Arts Ctr, 2009; 2nd Prize Rowayton, Cater Community Awards, Show, 2010; 1st prize, Mavis Fenner Juried Show, 2009; 1st prize, Carraytan Arts Ctr, 2010; 2nd prize, RAC multimedia, 2011; 3rd prize, Rowayton Arts Ctr, 2011. *Mem:* Rowayton Arts Ctr; New Haven Paint & Clay Club; Greenwich Art Soc; Art Soc Old Greenwich; Greenwich Art Coun; Center for Contemp Printmakers; Ridgefield Guild of Artists; Fairfield Arts Ctr; Monotype Guild of New England. *Media:* All Media. *Interests:* Family, art hist, museums & poetry. *Dealer:* Wilton Gallery Wilton CT; Ninth Life Fine Art Gallery St Thomas VI; Barbel Gallery New Canaan CT; Art Up Gallery 42 Main St Westport CT 06880-3401. *Mailing Add:* 368 Brookhaven Ct Sebastopol CA 95472

BLACK, MARY MCCUNE
CURATOR, PAINTER

b Broadwell, Ohio, Feb 14, 1915. *Study:* Ohio Univ, BS (educ), 37, MFA, 58; Amagansett Sch Art, Sarasota, Fla; workshop study with Charles Burchfield, William Thon, Aaron Bohrod, Paul Sample, Eliot O'Hara & Hilton Leech. *Work:* McJunkin Corp; Kanawha Co Pub Libr; WVa State Col, Permanent Collection; Lutheran Church, Parkersburg, WVa; First Christian Church, Charleston, WVa; Venice (Fla) Art Ctr. *Exhib:* Smithsonian Inst, 63; Nat Exhib, Sacramento, 78; WVa Juried Exhib, 79 & 83; Allied Artists WVa, 82; Duo exhib, WVa State Col, 86; solo invitational, Venice Art Ctr, Fla, 94, 2000. *Collection Arranged:* Permanent collection exhibition; Fiber & Fabrics; Collectors Exhib of Kanawha Valley. *Pos:* Dir, Charleston Art Gallery Sunrise, 63-75, cur fine arts Sunrise, 75-77; art juror, Fine Arts Exhib Art & Craft Fair, Cedar Lakes, WVa, 79-88; retired; mem adv bd, Fine Arts Dept, West State Col. *Teaching:* Instr art, Sandusky Jr High Sch, 37-39; instr painting, adult prog, Kanawha Co Bd Educ, 58-64; instr art, Valley Day Sch, 60-63; instr painting, YMCA & Charleston Art Gallery, 63-68. *Awards:* Pat Buster Award, Venice Area Art League, 90 & 96; Purchase Award, Tri-State Asn, Huntington, WVa, 90; Merit Award, WVa Watercolor Soc Juried Exhib, 92 & 96; Best of Show WVa Watercolor Soc Regl Exhib, 99; Winners Circle Award, Venice Art Ctr, 2000; plus others. *Mem:* Allied Artists WVa; Nat League Am Pen Women; Southern Watercolor Soc (signature mem); Venice Area Art League, Fla; charter mem WVa Watercolor Soc. *Media:* Watercolor, Acrylic. *Specialty:* Painting, juried crafts. *Interests:* painting/all media. *Dealer:* Gallery Eleven 1033 Quarrier St Charleston WV 25301

BLACKBURN, DAVID
PAINTER

b Huddersfield, UK, June 22, 1939. *Study:* Huddersfield Sch Art, NDD, 59; Royal Coll Art, London DesRCA, 62. *Hon Degrees:* Univ Huddersfield, DLit (hon). *Work:* Fogg Mus, Harvard, Cambridge, Mass; Mus Mod Art, NY; Phillips Collection, Washington; Albertina, Vienna; Nat Gallery Victoria, Melbourne; British Mus, London. *Exhib:* Yale Ctr Brit Art, New Haven, 88; retrospective, Dulwich Picture Gallery, London, 89 & Schloss Cappenberg, Frankfurt, 94; Peter Bartlow Gallery, Chicago, 92; Gallery Bentley, Phoenix, 96; Hart Gallery, London, 94, 96, 98, 00, 02, 04. *Teaching:* Vis prof fine art, Univ Calif, Davis, 79 & Georgetown Univ, Washington, 81; vis artist, Humanities Res Centre, Australian Nat Univ, Canberra, 95. *Bibliog:* R S Phillips (auth), Light & Landscapes, Hart, 92; Peter Fuller (auth), Modern Painters, Methuen, 93; Sasha Grishin (auth), David Blackburn & the Visionary Landscape Tradition, Hart, 95; C Mullins (auth), David Blackburn: The Sublime Landscape, 2002. *Media:* Pastel. *Dealer:* Peter Bartlow Gallery 44 E Superior St Chicago IL. *Mailing Add:* 113 Upper St Islington/London United Kingdom N11QN

BLACKBURN, ED M
PAINTER

b Amarillo, Tex, June 15, 1940. *Study:* Univ Tex, BFA, 62; Brooklyn Mus, Beckman Scholar, 63; Univ Calif, Berkeley, MA, 65. *Work:* Ft Worth Art Mus; Dallas Mus Fine Art. *Comn:* Mural on canvas, USAA, San Antonio, 75; Larger Canvas II (billboard), Houston Nat Bank, 78. *Exhib:* Off the Wall, San Antonio Mus Art, 81; solo exhib, Ft Worth Art Mus, 82; Am Still Life 1945-1983, Contemp Arts Mus, Houston, 83; Texas Images and Vision, Univ Tex Huntington Gallery, Austin & Amarillo Art Ctr, 83; 38th Corcoran Biennial & Second Western States, 83-84. *Awards:* Painting Grant, Nat Endowment Arts, 77 & 89-90. *Bibliog:* Ken Harrison (dir), Ed Blackburn (film), PBS, 75. *Media:* Acrylic, Oil. *Dealer:* Moody Gallery 2815 Colquit Houston TX 77098

BLACKBURN, LOREN HAYNER
PAINTER, ILLUSTRATOR

b South Glens Falls, NY, Mar 5, 1929. *Study:* Self-taught. *Work:* Coopers Cave Collection Lake George; Summer Youth Theater Group, Lake George, NY; US Air Force Permanent Collection; US Navy Collection; William J Clinton Presidential Lib. *Comn:* First Nat Bank, Glen Falls; NAm Med Instrument Corp; Champlain Stone Ltd; Garwood Boat Manufacturing; Albany Int. *Exhib:* Solo exhibs, Crandall Libr Mus, Glens Falls, NY, 79, Saratoga Golf & Polo Club, NY, 81, Appleland Gallery, Burnt Hills, NY, 83, Aqueduct Race Track, Jamaica, NY, 83, Smith Opera House, Geneva, NY, 84, Saratoga City Ctr, NY, 84 & 85 & Gallery of Arts Guild, Old Forge, NY, 85, Legends of Lake George, Recent Watercolors, Lake Shore, Gallery Bolton Landing; Fine Arts Pavilion, Worlds Fair, Knoxville, Tenn, 82; Nat Am Watercolor Exhib, Old Forge, NY, 84 & 85; Sarasota Racing Series Paintings, 87 & 88; Saratoga Series, Chapman Hist Mus, 89. *Awards:* Blue Ribbon, 32nd Ann Glens Falls Regional Art Exhib, 79; Second Place & Artists Choice, 12th Ann Old Saratoga Hist Asn Exhib, 80; Best of Watercolors, Lower Adirondack Regional Art Coun Outdoor Show, 80; Todah Moshe Award, Nat Am Exhib, Old Forge, NY, 84. *Bibliog:* Introductions, US Art, 32, 8/97; O Christmas Tree, US Art, 12/97; article, US Art, 9/98. *Mem:* Lower Adirondack Regional Art Coun (mem exec bd, 80-85, pres, 81-82). *Media:* Watercolor, Pastels; Oil. *Specialty:* Lithography & Giclee of org watercolors. *Publ:* Auth, Watercolor page, Am Artist Mag, 3/83. *Dealer:* Blackburn Gallery 261 Bay Rd Glens Falls NY 12801; Primrose Press New Hope PA; Blackburn Gallery 286 Bay Rd Queensbury NY. *Mailing Add:* 46 Lyon Ct Queensbury NY 12804-1750

BLACKEMORE, AMY
PHOTOGRAPHER

b Tulsa, Okla, 1958. *Study:* MFA, 1985. *Exhib:* Jill in Woods, 2005; Group show, Inman Gallery, Houston, Tex. *Pos:* Prof photog, 1986-. *Awards:* Whitney Biennial, Whitney Mus Art, NYC, 2006. *Mailing Add:* 3901 Main St Houston TX 77002

BLACKEY, MARY MADLYN
PAINTER, PRINTMAKER

b Glen Cove, NY. *Study:* Albright Art Sch, NY, cert; State Univ NY, Buffalo, BS (art educ); Art Students League; Ruth Leaf Etching Studio; Donn Steward Etching Workshop, Fleisher Art Memorial Etching Workshop, Philadelphia, PA. *Work:* Columbia Broadcasting Studio, New York; Hofstra Univ; Int Bus Machines; Conoco Oil; Nassau Community Coll; James Mitchner Mus; Hyatt Regency Hotel Corp, Tex; Champlain Petroleum Corp, Colo; NY Bankers & Bond Buyers, New York; Art Tech Aircraft Serv Ctr, New York; Gary Lucidon, Manchester, Vt. *Exhib:* Project Diomede, Inst Contemp Art, The Clocktower, 89; Positive Actions: Visual Aids, billboard design, Inst Contemp Art, New York, 90; Urban Paradise-Gardens in the City, public art design, Proj Pub Art Fund, New York, 93; solo exhibs, Ariz Aqueous, Tubac, Ariz, 1994, 1999, 2004, 2008, Spatial Ventures, Germantown Acad Art Ctr, Pa, 96, St Joseph's Coll, Philadelphia, Pa, 97, Planetfest, The Pasadena Ctr, Los Angeles, 97, Gloucester Co Coll, NJ, 98, Magical Encounters - Sky and Earth, Pennswood Art Gallery, Pa, 2000; Three Artist Exhib-Thomas Moser, Philadelphia, Pa, 95; Night of 1000 Drawings, Artists Space, New York, 95; Spiritual Matters, Trenton City Mus, NJ, 95; Works on Paper, Am Coll, Pa, 98; Watercolor USA, Springfield Art Mus, Mo, 99-2008; A Wintry Mix, Gallery 125, Trenton, NJ, 2005; Spring Exhib, Gallery 125, Trenton, NJ, 2006; Am Color Print Soc Exhib, Philadelphia Sketch Club, Pa, 2006; The Art of Printmaking-Spring, Bull Gallery, Newport, RI, 2006; Am Color Print Soc 63rd Exhib, Cheltenham Art Ctr, Pa, 2007; Dangerous Women-Homage to Female Artists of Mid-Atlantic Area, Mercer Gallery at Community Coll, Trenton, NJ, 2007; Artsbridge Ann Exhib, NJ, 2007; Homage to Areas Women in Art Post Interpretation, Mercer Co Community Coll, E Windsor, NJ, 2007; Watercolors, Germantown Gallery, Germantown, Pa, 2008; Ellarslie Open, Trenton City Mus, Trenton, NJ, 2008; Phillips Mus, Franklin & Marshall Coll, Lancaster, Pa, 2008; Chestnut Hill Gallery Print Exhib, Philadelphia, Pa, 2008; Color Print Exhib, Villanova Univ, Philadelphia, Pa, 2009; Hicks Art Gallery, Bucks County Comm Coll, Newtown, Pa, 2009; Watercolor Exhib, Montgomery County Comm Coll, Pa, 2009; Artsbridge Ann, New Hope Center for the Arts, Pa, 2011; Positively Transparent, Artworks, Trenton, NJ, 2012; Am Color Print Soc, Phila, Pa, 2013; Founders Exhib, Bucks County Community Coll, Pa, 2013. *Teaching:* Instr watercolor, Jackson Heights Art Club, 71-72, Five Towns Music & Art Found, 77-79, Great Neck Adult Prog, 81-83 & Islip Art Mus, 86. *Awards:* Fourth Prize, Arches Nat Watercolor Competition, 91; Patron Purchase Award, Watercolor, USA, Springfield Art Mus, Mo, 92 & 2000; Award Excellence, Aqueous 94, Tubac, Ariz, 94; Crest Award, Philadelphia Watercolor Soc, 2000; Purchase award, Mitchner Mus, Doylestown, Pa, 2001; Jeanne Clair Mem Award-Etching, Am Color Print Soc, Philadelphia, Pa, 2005; Jurors Award, Works on Paper, Artsbridge, Lambertville, NJ, 2006; Frank Nofer Award, Phila Watercolor Soc, 2007; Dorothy & Hugh Hutton Intaglio Award, Color Print Exhib, Philadelphia, Pa, 2008; 2nd prize watercolor, Prallville Mill Exhib, NJ, 2009; 1st prize watercolor, Artsbridge Ann Exhib, Lambertville, NJ, 2010; Phyllis Reif Memorial Award, Philadelphia Watercolor Soc, Reading, Pa, 2010; Graphics award, Goggle Art Ctr, Reading, Pa, 2010; Phillis H Reif Memorial award, Phil WC Soc, 2010; 2nd Prize Watercolor, Artsbridge Annual, Stockton, NJ, 2011; 2nd Prize, Phil W.C. Soc Montgomery Coll, Pottstown, Pa, 2012. *Bibliog:* Malcolm Preston (auth), Vision in Space and Form, Newsday, 90; Peter A Juley & Son Collection-Nat Mus Am Art, Smithsonian Inst; The Best of Watercolor, Rockport Publ, 95; Doris Brandes (auth), Artists of the River Towns: Their Works & Their Stories, River Arts Press, 2002; Doris Brandes (auth), Artists of the River Towns: Their Works and Their Stories, River Arts Press. *Mem:* Am Watercolor Soc; Nat Soc Painters Casein & Acrylic (bd dir, 82-84); Pa Watercolor Club; Found for Archit, 90-; Philadelphia Watercolor Club, 90-; Am Color Print Soc, 2004-; Goggle Works Ctr Arts Exhib, Reading, Pa, 2010. *Media:* Watercolor, Acrylic; Etching. *Specialty:* paintings, prints. *Interests:* Walking, travel, architecture, local history. *Publ:* The American Medium (watercolor), Am Watercolorists Visual Travel Prog; Watercolor - The Creative Experience, N Light Publ; The Best of Watercolor, Vol 3, vol 5, Rockport Publ, 95 & 99. *Dealer:* Riverbank Art Gallery, Rosemont, NJ. *Mailing Add:* 1032 Radcliffe St C-15 Bristol PA 19007

BLACKMAN, THOMAS PATRICK
DIRECTOR, PRINTMAKER

b Des Moines, Iowa, May 15, 1951. *Study:* Univ Iowa, Iowa City, BFA, 1976. *Collection Arranged:* Chicago Sculpture Int-Mile 1, 2, 3, 82-84. *Pos:* Sponger & shop asst, Landfall Press, Chicago, 1978-80; intaglio printer, Metropress, Chicago, 1980-81; dir, Chicago Int Art Exposition, 1980-93, Chicago Int Antique Show, 84-91, Art Chicago, 1993-2006; pres, Thomas Blackman Assoc Inc, Chicago, 1992-97; with Merchandise Mart Properties Inc, Chicago, 2006-. *Mailing Add:* Art Chicago Merchandise Mart Properties Inc Ste 470 The Merchandise Mart Chicago IL 60654

BLACKMON, JULIE
PAINTER
b Springfield, Mo, 1966. *Exhib:* Represented in permanent collections of Mus Contemp Photography, Midwest Photographers' Project, Chicago, Mus Fine Arts, Houston, Univ Ark, Little Rock; Solo exhibs, Drury Univ, 2005, Univ Ark at Little Rock, 2005, Arts Ctr Ozarks, Ariz, 2006, Good Girl Art Gallery, Springfield, Mo, 2006, Photoeye Gallery, Santa Fe, N Mex, 2006, Blue Sky Gallery, Portland, Oreg, 2006, Catherine Edelman Gallery, Chicago, 2006; Group exhibs, Selections from Photographers Showcase, Photoeye Gallery, Santa Fe, 2005; Group Portrait, Boston Univ, Photographic Resource Ctr, 2005; Family Pack, Soc Contemp Photography, Kansas City, 2006; Domestic Diaries, Rockford Mus Art, Ill, 2006; Constructed Illusions, Jenkins Johnson Gallery, San Francisco, 2006; Merit Award for body of work, Soc Contemp Photography, 2004; Merit Award, B&W Mag, 2005. *Mailing Add:* c/o Catherine Edelman Gallery 300 W Superior St Chicago IL 60610

BLACKMUN, BARBARA WINSTON
EDUCATOR, CURATOR
b Merced, Calif, June 29, 1928. *Study:* Univ Calif, Los Angeles, BA (fine arts; hons), 49 & PhD (art hist), 84; Ariz State Univ, MA (art hist), 71. *Collection Arranged:* Art Inst Chgo, 1994 & 2006-08; Art of Benin Kingdom, Field Mus, Chgo, 1990-93; Power and parody: European though African Eyes, Detroit Inst of Art, 2002-2010; Partners of the Soul, San Diego Mus of Art, 2003; Decoding design and Disguise, Mesa Coll, 2003; Understanding Women in African Art, Mesa Coll, 2004; Benin: Kings and Rituals, Mus fuer Voelkerkunde Vienna and Ethnologisches Mus Berlin, 2004-2006; African Arts of Disruption and Cohesion, Mesa Coll, 2005; Personal Pathways: Arts of Southeast Africa, 2010; Heads, Hats, & Hands in African Art, 2006; Touching the Mystery, 2007; Puppetry & Performance in Africa, 2008; Shapes, Colors, & Codes of Protection, 2009. *Pos:* Founding dir, Univ Arts Workshop, Malawi, Africa, 68-69; co-founder & chmn, Pub Arts Adv Coun, Co of San Diego, 76-78; consult, Kingdom of Benin Exhib, Field Mus Natural Hist, Chicago, 91-92, Cleveland Mus Art, 94 & Art Inst Chicago, 95-96; vis cur, San Diego Mus Art, 2003, 2010. *Teaching:* Lectr art hist & chmn art subject bd, Univ Malawi, Limbe, Malawi, Africa, 67-69; prof art hist, San Diego Mesa Col, Calif, 71-2000, prof emeritus, 2000-, chmn dept visual arts, 76-78 & 83-85; adj asst prof, Univ Calif, San Diego, 87, 2004, 2009; adj assoc prof, Univ Calif, Los Angeles, 88; vis prof art history, UCLA, Los Angeles, 2000. *Awards:* Fulbright Hays Doctoral Res Fel, 80; Grant for Advan Area Res on Africa, Am Coun Learned Soc & Social Sci Res Coun, 93; Nat Endowment for Humanities Collab Grant, Cleveland State Univ, 93-98. *Mem:* Coll Art Asn; Archaeol Inst Am; African Studies Asn; Art Historians Southern Calif. *Res:* The Nyau masks of the Maravi and their significance in African art; the bronze and terracotta sculpture of Ife, Nigeria, a classification through style analysis; the iconography of carved figural altar tusks from Benin Kingdom, Nigeria; African Ivories; art history of the Kingdom of Benin and its neighbors; Identification of Figures on Benin's Bronze Relief Plaques; Stylistic Authentication of Nigerian Antiquities. *Publ:* auth, Continuity and Change: The Ivories of Ovonranmwen and Eweka II, African Arts 30, 68-79, 94-96; auth, Icons and Emblems in Ivory, The Art Inst Chicago Mus Studies 23; auth, From Time Immemorial: Historicism in the Court Art of Benin, Nigeria, Symbols of Time in the History of Art, Belgium, 2002; auth, The hands of the Artist, Frank Willett, The Art of Ife, Glasgow, 04; Who are the Figures in Benin Art? Translations from Ivory to Bronze: In B Plankensteiner (ed), Benin: Kings and Rituals, Kunsthistoriche Mus with MVK, Vienna, pgs 161-169, 2007; Benin Art and Iwebo: The Place of the White Man, Power and Parody: The European Through African Eyes, Nii Quarcoopome (ed), Detroit Inst Arts, 2007; A Fashion History of Malawi, Berg Encyclopedia of World Dress and Fashion, London, 2007; Lake Twentieth Century Bronzes and Ivories in Benin City, Nigeria, in Ernst Pernicka, Silke von Berswordt-Wallrabe, and Hilke Wagners (ed), Original-Copy-Fake? Examining the Authenticity of Ancient Works of Art, Ruhr Univ, Bochum, Ger, von Zabern Press, pp 153-163, 2008; Contemporary Contradictions: Bronzecasting in the Edo Kingdom of Benin, M Visona and G Salami, A Companion Reader for Visona, Poynor & Cole, A History of Art in Africa, 2nd Ed, Prentice Hall, NJ, 2012. *Mailing Add:* 9850 Ogram Dr La Mesa CA 91941

BLACKSTOCK, VIRGINIA HARRIETT
PAINTER, JUROR
b St Louis, Mo. *Study:* Univ Mo, BS, 50; Univ Wis, MA, 52; studied with Frank Webb, Judi Betts, Cheng Khee Chee, Alex Powers, Steve Quiller, Don Andrews, Carla O'Connor, John Salminen, Paul Jackson. *Work:* St Mary's Hosp, Grand Junction, Colo; John Drazek DDS Periodontal Suite, Grand Junctions, Colo; Dr M Kleinsorge Offices, Delta, Colo; Matthew Drbohlav DDS offices, Hotchkiss, Colo; Craig Cayo DDS, Montrose, Colo; Palisade Public Libr, Colo. *Comn:* Outdoor Mural (40'x17'), City Delta, Colo, 95; paintings, Delta Co Mem Hospital, Colo, 2005-2006. *Exhib:* 59 solo exhibs; Rocky Mountain Nat Ann Watermedia Exhib, Foothills Art Ctr, Golden, Colo, 93-94, 2008-09; Allied Artists Am, 85th Ann Exhib, Nat Arts Club, NY, 93 & 98; Audubon Artists 56th & 58th Ann Exhib, Salmagundi Club, NY, 95, 98, 99 & 2000; Watercolor Soc Ala, 59th Ann Nat Exhib, Wiregrass Mus, Dothan, Ala, 2000; Colo Watercolor Soc, Ann Exhibs, Colo Hist Mus, Denver, Colo, 2003-07; RI Watercolor Soc, Nat Watercolor Exhib, Nat Register Hist Place, Pawtucket, RI, 2004, 2006; Transparent Watercolor Soc of Am, 30th Exhib, Elmhurst, Ill Art Mus, 2006; Kansas Watercolor Soc, Great 8 Exhib, Wichita Art Mus, Kans, 2006 & 08; Nat Ann Exhib, Missouri Watercolor Society (MoWS), 2007, 2010, 2012; 58th Annual Exhib and Traveling Exhib, Texas Watercolor Society (TWS), 2005, 07-08, 2012. *Pos:* Exhib chmn, Western Colo Watercolor Soc, 91- 93, 95, 98, 2011; Vice Pres, Western Colo Watercolor Soc, 2004-2013. *Teaching:* Instr, watercolor & drawing, Colo, Ala, Ariz, NMex & Utah, 95-2006. *Awards:* Honorable Mention, NMex Watercolor Soc, Nat Exhib Chen Khee Chee, 2000; Third place, Wyo Watercolor Soc XVII, Nat Exhib, 2002; First place, Black Canyon Exhib, 44th & 46th Ann, All Media, 2002 & 2004, Second Place, 47th & 48th Ann, 2005-2006, First Place, Still Life & Abstract, 50th Ann Exhib, 2009; Award of Excellence 4th Place, 25th Ann Int Exhib, San Diego Watercolor Soc, 2005; Jack Richeson Award, 58th Ann Exhib, Texas Watercolor Soc, 2007; Dorothy Garber Award, Western Colo Watercolor Soc, 2007, 2011, Framing Award, 2011; Award of Excellence, Mont Watercolor Soc 25th Ann Exhib, 2007; Holbein Award, Tex Watercolor Soc 59th Ann Exhib, 2007; Best of Show, Western Colo Watercolor Soc Mem, 2011. *Mem:* 13 signature mem; Rocky Mountain Nat Watermedia Soc (signature mem); Watercolor Soc, La, Mont, Kans, Pa, NMex, Tex, Mo, Colo & RI (Signature Mem); Western Colo Watercolor Soc (Signature Mem, chmn, 1991-93 & 98, vpres, 2004-2008, Statise-Master Painter 2011); San Diego Watercolor Soc (Signature Mem); Audubon Artists Inc (Signature Mem). *Media:* Watercolor, Acrylic, Oil. *Specialty:* original fine art. *Interests:* Photog, skiing, biking, hiking, swimming, gardening & traveling. *Publ:* Contribr, Creative Watercolor, A Step by Step Guide, Rockport Publ Inc, 95; contribr, The Artistic Touch I, Ideas & Techniques, Creative Art Press, 95; Abstracts in Watercolor, Rockport Publ Inc, 96; Exploring Color, North Light Bks, 98; Artistic Touch III, Works & Inspirations, Creative Art Press, 99; Best of American Artists, Kennedy Publ, 2007; Artistic Touch IV, Creative Art Press, 2010. *Dealer:* Home Gallery Hotchkiss CO 81419. *Mailing Add:* 31045 L Rd Hotchkiss CO 81419-9409

BLACKWELL, ELISE
WRITER, EDUCATOR
b Austin, Tex, July, 18, 1964. *Study:* Univ Calif, Irvine, MFA. *Teaching:* Asst prof & dir MFA prog, Univ SC. *Awards:* Michael J Mungo Undergraduate Teaching Award, 2009. *Publ:* Auth, Hunger, 2003, The Unnatural History of Cypress Parish, 2007, Grub, 2007, An Unfinished Score, 2010. *Mailing Add:* University of South Carolina Welsh Humanities Building 302 Columbia SC 29208

BLACKWELL, TOM (THOMAS) LEO
PAINTER
b Chicago, Ill, Mar 9, 1938. *Work:* Currier Gallery Art, Manchester, NH; Guggenheim Mus, Mus Mod Art, Metrop Mus Art, NY; Detroit Inst Fine Art, Mich; Herbert F Johnson Mus, Cornell Univ, Ithaca, NY; Phoenix Mus Art, Ariz; and many others. *Exhib:* Human Concern-Personal Torment, Whitney Mus Am Art, NY, 69; Whitney Mus Am Art Painting Ann, 72; Prospectus, Art in the Seventies, Aldrich Mus Contemp Art, Ridgefield, Conn, 79; Seven Photorealists from NY Collections, Solomon R Guggenheim Mus, NY, 81; Contemp Am Realism since 1960, Pa Acad Fine Art, Philadelphia, Pa, 81-82; solo exhibs, Selected works 1970-1980, Dartmouth Col, Hanover, NH, 80, Univ Ariz Mus Art, Tuscon, 81; Louis K Meisel Gallery, NY, 77, 80, 82 & 91, Currier Gallery Art, Manchester, NH, 85; Carlo Lamagna Gallery, NY, 86; Ten Super Realists, Ft Lauderdale Mus Art, 91-92; Really, Real, Realism, Jack Wright Gallery, Palm Beach, Fla, 93; Photo Realism, The Last Decade, Louis K Meisel Gallery, NY, 93; The Purloined Image, Flint Inst Arts, Mich, 93; Art After Art, Nassau Co Mus, Roslyn, NY, 94; and others. *Teaching:* Artist-in-residence, Dartmouth Col, Hanover, NH, 80; Univ Ariz, Tucson, 81; instr, Sch Visual Arts, New York, 85-89. *Awards:* Grant, New Hampshire Comn Arts, 85. *Bibliog:* John Russell (auth), Painters from Brussels, New York Times, 5/21/82; Terence Mullaly (auth), Icy reflections of life, London Daily Telegraph, 83; Vivien Raynor (auth), Tom Blackwell, New York Times, 5/2/86. *Media:* Oil. *Publ:* Auth, Photorealism, Harry N Abrams; Photorealism Since 1980, Harry N Abrams; American Watercolors, Abbeville Press; Contemporary American Realism Since 1960, New York Graphic Soc. *Mailing Add:* 14 Sunset Rd Rhinebeck NY 12572

BLACKWOOD, DAVID (LLOYD)
PAINTER, PRINTMAKER
b Wesleyville, Nfld, Can, Nov 7, 1941. *Study:* Ont Coll Art, Toronto, 59-64. *Work:* Nat Gallery Can; Nat Gallery Australia; Art Gallery Ont; Montreal Mus Fine Arts; NB Mus. *Exhib:* Int Graphics, Montreal Mus Fine Arts, 71; 1st Norweg Biennial, Frederickstad, 72; Biennial Int de l'Estampe, Paris, France, 73. *Pos:* Artist-in-residence, Univ Toronto, 69-75. *Teaching:* Art master, Trinity Col Sch, Port Hope, Ont, 63-75. *Awards:* Ingres Medal, Govt France, 63; Purchase Award Can Biennial, Nat Gallery Can, 64; Hornansky Award Int Graphics, Montreal Mus Fine Arts, 71. *Bibliog:* Rex Bromfield (auth), David Blackwood (film), CBC, 72; Farley Mowat (auth), Survivor, Wake of the Great Sealers, McClelland & Little Brown, 73; Blackwood (film), NFB, 75. *Mem:* Royal Can Acad Art (vpres, 79). *Dealer:* Gallery Quan 112 Scollard St Toronto ON M5R 1G2 Can. *Mailing Add:* 22 King St Port Hope ON L1A 2R5 Canada

BLAGDEN, ALLEN
PAINTER, PRINTMAKER
b New York, NY, Feb 21, 1938. *Study:* Hotchkiss Sch; Yale Univ Summer Art Sch; Cornell Univ, BFA. *Work:* Berkshire Mus, Pittsfield, Mass; Garvan Collection, Peabody Mus, New Haven, Conn; New Britain Mus Am Art, Conn; Adirondack Mus, Blue Mountain Lake, NY; Leigh Yawkey Woodson Mus, Wausau, Wis; and others. *Comn:* Many pvt portrait commissions. *Exhib:* Father and Son Show, Mongerson Wunderlich Gallery, Chicago, 89; one-man shows, Rehn Gallery & Kennedy Galleries, NY, Indian Images, Mongerson Wunderlich Gallery, Chicago, 90; Birds in Art, Leigh Yawkey Woodson Art Mus, Wausau, Wis, 90; Artists of Am, Denver, Colo, 90; Howard Godel Fine Arts, NY; and others. *Pos:* Illusr dept ornithology, Smithsonian Inst, Washington, DC, 62-63. *Teaching:* Instr painting, Hotchkiss Sch, 68-69; artist-in-residence, Cornell Univ, 82. *Awards:* Allied Artist Award, 63; Century Club Art Prize, 71; Marine Award, Arts for the Parks, 2000. *Mem:* Century Asn, NY; Artists' Fel, NY. *Media:* Watercolor, Oil; Etching, Lithography. *Publ:* Wildlife Painters at Work, Watson-Gupthill. *Dealer:* Mongerson-Wunderlich 704 N Wells St Chicago IL 60610; Howard Godel 39A E 72 New York NY 10021. *Mailing Add:* Box 625 Salisbury CT 06068

BLAGDEN, THOMAS P
PAINTER
b Chester, Pa, Mar 29, 1911. *Study:* Yale Univ, BA, 33; Pa Acad Fine Arts, 33-35; spec study with Henry Hensche & George Demetrios. *Work:* Addison Gallery Am Art, Andover, Mass; Wadsworth Atheneum, Hartford, Conn; Berkshire Mus, Pittsfield, Mass; New Britain Mus Am Art, New Britain, Conn; Neuberger Mus, Purchase, NY;

Currier Gallery, Manchester, NH. *Exhib:* Pa Acad Fine Arts, Philadelphia, 38; Corcoran Gallery Art, Washington, DC, 41; Metrop Mus Art, NY, 50; Am Acad Arts & Lett, NY, 61; Loeb Drama Ctr, Harvard Univ, Cambridge, Mass, 71; solo exhibs, Keene State Col, NH, 79 & 21 other one-man exhibs, incl nine in NY (Milch Galleries & others), St Gaudens Mus, New Britain Mus, American Art. *Teaching:* Instr art, Hotchkiss Sch, Lakeville, Conn, 35-56. *Awards:* Purchase Prize, Wadsworth Atheneum & Berkshire Mus. *Mem:* Century Club, NY; Conn Watercolor Soc. *Media:* Oil, Watercolor

BLAGG, DANIEL
PAINTER
b 1951. *Work:* Mus S Tex, Corpus Christi; Tyler Art Mus, Tex; Deloitte & Touche, Washington, DC; Bank One, Ft Worth, Tex; Tex Instruments, Plano; Southwestern Bell, Dallas; GTE, Irving, Tex; Shell Oil, Houston; Exxon, Dallas; Grand Bank, Dallas; Arthur Young Co, Dallas; First City, Dallas; Belo Broadcasting, Dallas; FRK Properties, San Antonio; Fluor Corp, Houston. *Exhib:* Urbanscapes, Tarrant Co Jr Coll, S Campus, Ft Worth, Tex, 1993; Artspace111, Ft Worth, Tex, 1996; Abilene Art Mus, Tex, 1997; Dallas Visual Art Ctr, Dallas, 1998; Tyler Mus Art, Tex, 1999; Urban Realities, Galveston Art Ctr, Tex, 2000; Kidder Smith Gallery, Boston, 2002 & 2004-2005. *Bibliog:* Amy Sorter (auth), Art & Soul, Woodstock Times, 8/2000; Gaile Robinson (auth), Public Art, Ft Worth Star-Telegram, 6/2005. *Mailing Add:* DFN Gallery 46 W 85th St #A New York NY 10024

BLAINE, FREDERICK MATTHEW
SCULPTOR, EDUCATOR
b Baltimore, Md, May 24, 1947. *Study:* Univ Miss, BA, 70. *Work:* Blithe Spirit, Frogpond & Japan Phyle, Int Soc Copier Artists; The Tate Gallery, London; Metrop Mus Art, NY; Mus Mod Art, NY; The Smithsonian; Australia Nat Gallery; Pompidou Ctr Gallery, Paris; Laurel Historical Soc; Del Mus Natural History; Freshwater Mussel Soc; Am Malacologist. *Exhib:* 24th, 25th & 26th Ann Nat Show, Acad Arts, Easton, Md, 88; 47th Ann Nat Competition, Lakeworth, Fla, 88; Artist's Equity 3rd & 4th Ann Awards Exhib, Washington, DC, 88; Solo exhib, DCCA Gallery, Wilmington, Del, 89; Biannual Show Del Art Mus, 89. *Pos:* Bd trustees, Rehoboth Art League, 88-94; chmn art dept, Seaford Sch Dist; curatorial assoc, Del Mus Nat History, 2013. *Teaching:* Instr art-sec, Seaford Sch Dist, 70-02; asst prof ceramics & sculpture, Salisbury State Univ, 83-, lectr art, 84-89. *Mem:* Am Malacological Soc; Conchologists Am; Lepidoptera Soc; S Lepidopterrist Soc; Eutomological Soc Wash. *Media:* All. *Interests:* Malacology, conchology, entomology. *Publ:* Contribr, Sculpture: Technique, Form, Content, Davis Publ, 88; auth, Brithespirit, Frogpond, Int Soc Copier Artists. *Dealer:* Art South Philadelphia PA. *Mailing Add:* 908 W St Laurel DE 19956

BLAIR, DIKE
PAINTER, SCULPTOR
b New Castle, Pa, Aug 2, 1952. *Study:* Univ Colo, 71-75; Skowhegan Sch Painting & Sculpture, 74; Whitney Mus Independent Study Prog, 76; Sch Art Inst Chicago, MFA, 77. *Comn:* Construction (7ft x 30ft), Hosp Corp Am, Nashville, 82; photo glass mural (7 ft x 1/2 ft), Murray Hill Cinema, NY, 90. *Exhib:* Painting & Sculpture Today, Ind Mus Art, 86; Landscape in the Age of Anxiety, Lehman Coll Art Gallery, 86; The New Romantic Landscape, Whitney Mus, Fairfield Co, 87; Image World, Whitney Mus Am Art, NY, 89; Bellevue, Mus Mod Art, Vienna, Austria, 89; The Winter of Love, Mus Mod Art, Paris, France; Let's Entertain, The Walker Art Ctr, Minneapolis, Minn, 2000; Elysian Fields Ctr, Georges Pompidou, Paris, France, 2000. *Pos:* editor, Purple Mag. *Teaching:* adj painting instr, RISD. *Awards:* Fel, Mid-Atlantic Regional, Nat Endowment Arts, 88-89; Louis Comfort Tiffany Found Award, 95. *Bibliog:* Mary Ellen Haus (auth), The Unnatural Landscape, Art News, 1/88; Robert Mahoney (auth), Reviews, Arts Mag, 1/92; Jeff Rian (auth), Ouverture, Flash Art, 97; Tim Griffin (auth) The Intangible Economy, Art & Text, 2000. *Media:* Paint & Photo on Glass. *Publ:* Auth, GFWFQ recalled, Issue No 6, summer 86

BLAIR, PHILIPPA MARY
PAINTER, EDUCATOR
b Christchurch, NZ, Nov 18, 1945; US citizen. *Study:* Univ Canterbury, NZ, Diploma Fine Arts, 67; Massey Univ, NZ, BA English, 68; Auckland Univ, NZ, BA Art Hist, 73-74; Auckland Secondary Teachers Col, Diploma of Art Teaching, 76. *Work:* Long Beach Mus, Calif; Mus of New Zealand (Te Papa), Wellington, NZ; Conn Graphic Arts Ctr, Norwalk; Citicorp/Citibank, NY; Atlantic Richfield Corp, Los Angeles; Pfizer Corp, Conn; General Electric Co, NY; Hong Kong & Shanghai Bank; Nat Gallery, Canberra, Australia; Christchurch Gallery, NZ; Auckland City Art Gallery, NZ; Bank of NZ; Chan Liu Mus, Taiwan; Chartwell Collection, Hamilton, NZ; Centre of Contemp Art, Christ Church, NZ; Lincoln Univ, NZ; Univ Wellington, NZ; Univ Auckland, NZ; Auckland City Art Gallery, NZ; ANZ Nat Bank, NZ; Griffis Art Ctr, New London, Conn; BNZ art collection, NZ; Govett-Brewster Art Gallery, NZ; Bishop Suter Gallery, Nelson, NZ; Conn Graphic Arts Ctr, Conn; Hocken Libr, Dunedin, NZ; Manawatu Art Gallery, NZ; Nat Womens Hosp, Auckland, NZ; Rangi Ruru Sch, Christ Church, NZ; Saatchi & Saatchi, Wellington, NZ; Univ Auckland, NZ; Waikato Mus Art Hist, Hamilton, NZ; Dunedin Art Gallery, NZ; British Mus, London; Riverside Art Mus, Calif. *Comn:* Mural, Univ Auckland, NZ, 83; stained glass, Cook Island Church, Auckland, NZ, 83; mural, Auckland City, NZ, 89; After Crazy Horse, Origins Dance Theatre, Auckland, NZ, 90; lithographs, Sky City Hotel & Casino, Auckland, NZ, 95; Interactive educ poster, Celebrate Art NZ, 2006. *Exhib:* Gestural Maps, Post Gallery, Los Angeles, 2000; TransMotion, DoubleVision Gallery, Los Angeles, 2001; Maximal Abstraction, Judith Anderson Gallery, 2001; Trajectories, J Land Gallery, Wellington, NZ, 2001; New Paintings, Pacific Art Gallery, Zug, Switz, 2002; TransMotion, J Land Gallery, Wellington, New Zealand, 2002; Between Heaven and Earth, W Wickiser Gallery, 2003; New Work, Pfizer Global Research Ctr, New London, Conn, 2003; Maps, Fyr Arte Contemporanea, Florence, Italy, 2003; Cutting Loose, D Vision Gallery, LA and Janne Land Gallery, NZ, 2004; Double Vision, Cypress Col, Calif, 2005; Point and Line to Plane, COCA, 2005; Llano Quemado, Fyr Arte Contemporanea, Florence, Ital, 2005; Recent Paintings, Warwick Henderson Gallery, Auckland, NZ, 2005; Flow Show, Riverside Art Mus, Calif, 2005; NZ Artists Chan Liu Museum, Taipei, Taiwan, 2006; Alternate Routes: mapping in the studio, Sam Francis Gallery, Crossroads Sch, Santa Monica, Calif, 2006; Spring-Break, Janne Land Gallery, Wellington, NZ, 2007; Attivare, Lawrence Asher Gallery, Los Angeles, Calif, 2007; Themes & Variations: New Abstraction in LA, Torrance Art Mus, Calif, 2007; New Paintings: Works on Paper, Catchment Gallery, Nelson, NZ, 2008; Paintings, Ming Jen Gallery, Kaoshiung City, Taiwan, 2008; Works on Paper, Warwick Henderson Gallery, Auckland, NZ, 2009; Tracks, Lawrence Asher Gallery, Los Angeles, 2009; Inbetween, Jancar McCorkle Projects, Los Angeles, 2009; Out of Line, Warwick Henderson Gallery, Auckland, NZ, 2010; Densities, Beacon Arts Bldg, Calif, 2010; OU Boum, Long Beach City Coll, Calif, 2010; Opening Show, Gallery Reis, Singapore, 2010; Global Visions, Griffis Art Center, New London, Conn, 2010; Camouflage, Warwick Henderson Gallery, Auckland, New Zealand, 2011; Solid Stripes, Launch Los Angeles, Merry Karnowsky Gallery, Calif, 2011; 5 on Paper, Warschaw Gallery, San Pedro, Calif; Focus on Abstraction, Eva Breuer Gallery, Sydney, Australia, 2012; Under Glass: Warwick Henderson Gallery, Auckland, NZ, 2012; PSST: Warschaw Gallery, San Pedro, Calif, 2012; 25 Years in Parnell, Warwick Henderson Gallery, Auckland, NZ; Women Artists of the Permanent Collection, Riverside Art Mus, 2013; Warschaw Gallery, San Pedro, Calif, 2013. *Teaching:* Artist-in-residence, Canberra Sch Art, Australia, 84, Griffis Art Ctr, New London, Conn, 2002 and Rangi Ruru School, Christchurch, NZ, 2005; lectr painting, Univ Canterbury, NZ, 84, Univ Auckland, 87-94 & Otis Col Art & Design, 2001-2004; vis artist, Art Ctr Col Design, Pasadena, Calif, 95-2001; painting instr, Otis Col Art & Design; painting tutor, Santa Reparata Sch of Art, Florence, Italy, 2002, 2005, 2007, 2009; painting tutor (emeritus), Santa Monica Col, Calif; private painting tutor, 2002-2009, mentor for MFA student from Mass Coll Art, 2010-2011; painting tutor, Quarry Art Ctr, Whangarei, NZ. *Awards:* Travel Award, Air NZ / QEII Arts Coun, 87. *Bibliog:* Michael Dunn (auth), Concise History of NZ Painting, 91; Beate Starck (auth), Philippa Blair, Univ of Auckland, 91; W Brown (auth), 100 NZ Paintings, 94; Michael Dunn (auth), Contemp NZ Painting, Craftsman's Press, Australia, 96; Michael Dunn (auth), NZ Painting: A Concise History, 2003; Greg O'Brien (auth), We Set Out One Morning, BNZ Art Collection, BNZ, NZ, 2006; Tessa Laird (auth), LenLyes Color: A Carnival of Soul, Govett-Brewster Gallery, New Zealand, 2009. *Media:* Oil, Acrylic, Lithography. *Specialty:* Abstract contemp art. *Interests:* Walking, piano, contemp dance, travel & languages. *Publ:* auth, Acts of Inclusion, Spirit of P Blairs Recent Painting, Art NZ, 82, Metamorphosis in P Blairs Recent Painting, 86 & Paint for your Life, 94; Micro-Organisms: Pacific Circuits, private publ, 96; A Hutchison (auth), Maximal Abstraction, 2001; C Fusco, Transmotion: Drawings & Painting by P Blair, 2002; C Fusco (auth), P Blair at DoubleVision Gallery, Asian Art News, 2002; A Hutchison (auth), Cutting Loose, 2004; A Hutchison (auth), Eye Blast, 2005; P Frank, Flow, Riverside Art Mus, 2005; auth, Out of Line, A. Kirker and W. Henderson Gallery, 2010; P Frank, Densities, Beacon Arts, Inglewood, Calif, 2010; auth, Camouflage, A Kirker and W. Henderson Gallery, 2011, 2012; PSST: Art in San Pedro, 2000-2012. *Dealer:* Paper Graphica 192 Bealey Ave Christchurch NZ; Warwick Henderson Gallery 32 Bath St Parnell Auckland NZ; Brooke-Gifford Gallery 112 Manchester St Christchurch NZ; Eva Breuer 83 Moncur St Woollahra Sydney Australia; Ming Jen Gallery Taiwan No 143-1 Guang Zhou Kaohshiung City Taiwan ROC; Gallery Reis, Palais Renaissance 390 Orchard Rd #03-01/02 Singapore 238872; Launch LA 170 S LaBrea Ave Los Angeles Calif 90036

BLAKE, JANE SALLEY
PUBLISHER, EDITOR
b Tallahassee, Fla, Sept 3, 1937. *Study:* Fla State Univ, Tallahassee, BA (fine arts & journalism), 58. *Pos:* Founder, pres & chmn bd, Arts Forum Inc, Louisville, Ky, 78-84; publ, exec ed, Beaux Arts mag, 80-84; pres, Blake Publ Inc, Louisville, Ky, 83-86; pres, principal, J S Blake Commun Group, Louisville, Ky, 86-; pres, principal, Ctr Mag, Inc, 86. *Awards:* 13 Louie Awards, Advert Club, Louisville, Ky, 81-84; 4 Landmarks Excellence Awards, PRSA & IABC, Louisville, Ky; Gov's Arts Award for Media Excellence, 89; Above & Beyond the Call of Duty Award, 90. *Mem:* Sigma Delta Chi Prof Journalism Soc; Pub Relations Soc Am; Women in Commun. *Publ:* Ctr Mag Ky Ctr Arts, 83; Publ, Practical Pub Relations for Non-professionals, 85; Kentucky Marquee, 86. *Dealer:* The Center Magazine Inc PO Box 22312 Louisville KY 40252. *Mailing Add:* PO Box 22312 Louisville KY 40252-0312

BLAKE, WENDON See Holden, Donald

BLAKELY, COLIN
PHOTOGRAPHER, ADMINISTRATOR
Study: Syracuse Univ Division of Internat Programs Abroad, Florence, Italy, 1994; BA with honors in Studio Art), Williams Col, Mass, 1995; Univ New Mexico, MFA (in Photography), 2001. *Exhib:* Solo, 2 and 3 person exhibitions Colo Ctr for Photographic Arts, 2000, Robert Steele Gallery, NY, 2003, 2005, Adrian Col Art Gallery, 2004, Salon E, Tex, 2004; Group exhibitions Jacob Javits Convention Ctr, NY, 2000, Ann Arbor Art Ctr, 2004, Jen Beckman Gallery, NY, 2007, Griffin Mus of Photography, Mass 2007 and others. *Pos:* Web designer, Design Sources Southwest, Albuquerque, New Mexico, 2000. *Teaching:* Middle Sch Math/Science/Photography teacher, The Annunciation Orthodox Sch, Houston, Tex, 1995-98; assoc prof Eastern Michigan Univ, 2001-, chair, currently. *Publ:* Photo District News, 2000, Fotofest 2002 and 2004, Photo Review, 2004, Flak Photo, 2007 and others. *Mailing Add:* 510 Keech Ave Ann Arbor MI 48103

BLASCO, ISIDRO M
SCULPTOR, ARCHITECT
b Madrid, Spain, Mar 12, 1962. *Study:* Sch of Fine Arts of Madrid, BFA, 89, Sch of Arch of Madrid, MArch, 93. *Work:* Mus Modern Art, NY; Mus Modern Art, San Francisco; New Mus, NY. *Comn:* Sculpture, City of ELX, Spain, 92; Public Art, Sculpture Space, Utica, NY, 2000. *Exhib:* Solo exhibs, Macula Gallery, Alicante, Spain, 1990, Diario Levante, Valencia, Spain, 1994, Queens Mus Art, Bulova Ctr, NY,

1999, Stefan Stux Gallery, Project Room, NY, 1999, PS 1, NY, 1999, Museo de Arte y Diseno Contemporaneo, San Jose, Costa Rico, 2000, Roger Smith Gallery, NY, 2001, Fucares Gallery, NY, 2002, 2006, Museo Patio Herreriano, Valladolid, Spain, 2003, Museo National Centro de Arte Reina Sofia, Madrid, Spain, 2004, DCKT Contemp, NY, 2004, 2005, 2007, CAB, Burgos, Spain, Savannah Coll Art and Design, ACA Gallery, Ga, 2006, College of Saint Rose, Ctr Art and Design, Albany, 2007, Hilger Gallery, Vienna, Austria, Contrasts Gallery, Shanghai, China, 2007; Group exhibs, Roma '91, Spanish Acad in Rome, Italy, 1991; Amerika in Immigrant Hands, Jamaica Ctr for Arts and Learning, NY, 1999; Insights: Interior Spaces in Contemp Art, Whitney Mus Am Art, Champion Beach, Conn, 2000; Eccentric Photography, Islip Art Mus, NY, 2001; Metaphors for Architecture, Five Artists Revisit Utica, NY, 2002; Magische Expeditionen, Mus Folkwang, Essen, Germany, 2002; S-Files, El Museo del Barrio, NY City, 2002; Slingshot Project Gallery, NY, 2003; El Estudio del Artista, Domestico, Madrid, 2003; Parklife, Public Art Fund, Metro Teck, Brooklyn, NY, 2003; Not To Scale, Dorsky Gallery, NY, 2003; Temporary Spaces, Charlotteenborg Exhib Hall, Denmark, 2003; Emerging Artists Fel, Socrates Sculpture Park, NY, 2004; Untethered Architecture, Numark, Gallery, Washington, DC, 2004; Queens International, Queens Mus, NY, 2004; In Practice, Sculpture Ctr, NY, 2004; Under Construction, Morcel Gallery, NY, 2005; Odd Lots, White Columns, NY, 2005; Welcome 2 the Jungle, DCKT Contemp, NY, 2005; Off the Wall, Hunter Coll Art Galleries, NY, 2005; That Which is Built, Patricia Sweetow Gallery, San Francisco, 2005; Identidades Criticas, Univ de Cordoba, Spain, 2006; Substance and Light, Munson-Williams-Proctors Inst NY, 2006; Expansiones Implosivas, Centro Cultural de la Villa, Madrid, 2007; Thirtyseven Degrees, Contemp Fine Art Gallery, Sydney, Australia, 2007; PHOTO+, Blue Star Art Space, Tex, 2007. *Awards:* Rome Prize, Spanish Acad Rome, 90-91; Pollock-Krainer Award, Pollock Krainer Found, 97-98; Guggenheim Fel, Guggenheim Found, 2000-01. *Media:* All Media. *Dealer:* Stefan Stux, 329 W 20th, 9th Fl, New York NY 10011

BLAUGRUND, ANNETTE
MUSEUM DIRECTOR, ART HISTORIAN
Study: Columbia Univ, PhD (art history). *Pos:* Dir, Nat Acad Mus, 1997-. *Teaching:* Tchr, Columbia Univ, formerly. *Awards:* Am Art J Award (AAMD, AAM, CAA), 1984; Chevalier in the Order of Arts & Letters, France, 1992; Victorian Soc Award, 1997. *Interests:* Theatre, literature, golf & tennis. *Publ:* Auth, Paris 1889 American Artists at the Universal Expos, 1989; auth, The Watercolors for the Birds of America, 1998; auth, The Essential Audubon, 1999; auth, The Tenth Street Studio Building: Artist Entrepreneurs from the Hudson River Sch to the Am Impressionists (and chapters in other bks), 1997. *Mailing Add:* Nat Acad Design Mus 1083 5th Ave New York NY 10128

BLAYTON, BETTY BLAYTON-TAYLOR
PAINTER, ADMINISTRATOR
b Williamsburg, Va, July 10, 1937. *Study:* Syracuse Univ, BFA, 59; Art Students League, 61; studied with Arnold Prince, 61-62 & Munoru Niizuma, 64-67. *Work:* Studio Mus Harlem; Metrop Mus Art, NY; Fisk Univ; Philip Morris Corp; Chase Manhattan Bank; Spellman Coll, Atlanta, Ga; Norfolk State Univ, Norfolk VA; The Robert Blackburn Printmaking Workshop; Beatrice Corp; Virginia State Coll; Tugaloo Coll; The Blanchette Rockefeller; The Reginald Lewis; The Bryon Lewis; The Bettina Hunter & The Evelyn Cunningham; and others. *Comn:* Uniworld Group, NY, 98. *Exhib:* Thirty Contemp Black Artists, Minneapolis & traveling, 68; Prof Artist for Young Artists, Metrop Mus Art, NY; Black Am Contemp Artist, Zamoia, Africa, 75; Solo exhibs, Caravan House Gallery, NY, 75, Fisk Univ, 80, Syracuse Univ, NY, 83, Bedford Stuyvesant Gallery, Brooklyn, NY, 89, Isabel Neal Gallery, Chicago, 90 & Lubin House Gallery, NY, 91; Three Women, Howard Univ Gallery, 76, Brown Univ Gallery, Washington, 87; San Francisco Mus Art; Boston Mus Art; High Mus Art; Minneapolis Inst Art; Everson Mus Art; Milwaukee Art Ctr; Pace Univ Gallery, NY, 94; Cinque Gallery, NY, 97; NCA Int Conference Exhib at the Nat Mus, Accra Ghana, 2001; UFA Gallery, NY, 2001-2003; Parsons Aronson Galleries--African-Am Women Artists, 2004; Smithsonian-The Bob Blackburn Printmaking Workshop Travel Show, 2004; Something to Look Forward To Phillip Mus Franklin & Marshall Coll (auth, catalog), Lancaster, 2004. *Pos:* Supv artist graphics & plastics, Harlem Youth Unlimited, 64-67; pres & artistic dir, Children's Art Carnival, New York, 68-98; New York State Comn Educ Curriculum & Assessment Comt Arts & Humanities, 94-95. *Teaching:* Consult, New York City Bd Educ, 72-; prof art educ, City Col New York, 78-. *Awards:* Award Empire State Woman of Yr, 84; Black Women in Arts Award, 88; CBS TV's Martin Luther King, Jr Fulfilling the Dream Award, 95; Woman's Caucus for the Arts Life Time Achievement Award, 2005. *Bibliog:* Five (film), Silvermine Films, 72; Forever Free, Univ Ill Press, 81; Muriel Silverstein (auth), Doing Art Together, 81; African Am Art, The Long Stuggle, Crystal Britton, 96; Collecting African AM Art, Halima Taha, 98. *Mem:* Arts & Bus Coun (bd mem, 75-96); Printmaking workshop, NY, (bd mem, 79-); founding mem Harlem Textile Works; Advisor, The Bob Blackburn Printmaking workshop, 99. *Media:* Multi Media, Monoprints, Painting. *Res:* Arts in Educ, ages 4 - 21 years, Arts in Hist. *Interests:* Metaphysical Studies, Theatre, Mythology, Anthrop & Health. *Publ:* Auth, People who make things happen, Art Gallery Guide, 69; Making Thoughts Become, 78. *Dealer:* Jan Harrison 509 W 110th St New York NY 10025; Picture That Gallery LLC 84 Courtland Ave Stanford CT, 06902; Synchronicity Fine Arts 106 W 13th St New York NY 10011. *Mailing Add:* 2001 Creston Ave Bronx NY 10453

BLAZEJE, ZBIGNIEW (ZIGGY) BLAZESE
SCULPTOR, PAINTER
b Barnaul, USSR, June 2, 1942; Can citizen. *Study:* Royal Conserv Music, Toronto; Ont Coll Art. *Work:* Art Gallery Ont, Toronto; Norman McKenzie Art Gallery, Regina, Sask; Confedn Art Gallery, Charlottetown, PEI; Hart House, Univ Toronto; Sir George William Univ, Montreal, PQ. *Comn:* Structural sculpture, Libr-Ross Bldg, York Univ, 72; and others. *Exhib:* Canadian Art, Art Gallery Can Pavilion Expo 67, Montreal; Sculpture 67, City Hall Toronto; Electric Art, Univ Calif, Los Angeles Art Gallery & Phoenix, Ariz, 69; Sensory Perceptions Traveling Exhib, Art Gallery Ont, 70-71; Electronic Paintings, Cybernetic Environment, Hart House Art Gallery, Univ Toronto, 81; and others. *Pos:* Pres & dir, Arts Sake Inc, Inst Visual Art, 79-. *Teaching:* Instr environ, Ont Col Art, 70-81; instr environ, New Sch Art, Toronto, 71-72. *Awards:* Can Coun Jr Grants, 66, 67 & 69; Ont Art Coun Grants, 79 & 81. *Bibliog:* H Malcomson (auth), Sculpture in Canada, Artforum, 10/67; G M Dault (auth), In the galleries Toronto, Artscanada, 6/71; Electric Gallery plus 3, McCurdy-Bursell Films, Toronto, 4/72. *Mem:* Royal Can Acad Arts. *Mailing Add:* 1254 Dundas St W Toronto ON M6J 1X5 Canada

BLEACH, BRUCE R
PRINTMAKER, PAINTER, SCULPTOR
b Monticello, NY, Mar 23, 1950. *Study:* Orange County Community Col, AA, 70; Hartford Art Sch, Univ Hartford, BFA, 72; State Univ NY, New Paltz, MFA, 74. *Work:* Lucent Tech, Orlando Magic, British Airways, Pfizer, Intel, DuPont, Lockheed Martin, AOL, Jackson Nat Life, Motorola, Hyatt, IBM, Merrill Lynch Pierce Fenner Smith Inc & Nat Westminster Bank, NY; Provincial Mus, Taiwan; Southeast Banking Corp, Fla; plus others. *Comn:* XEROX, Novartis, Montefiore Children's Hosp, NY, Triptych, RCA Americom, Princeton, NJ, 80; embossed aluminum, Shulte Inc, NY, 84; monoprint series on hand-made paper, Gallery Sho, Tokyo, Japan, 85; cast paper with multi-media, Fred Dorfman Inc, NY, 86; metal tryptech, comn by Skoke-Koo Gallery for ADP Corp, Calif; Murals for the Pres's Off, 2001; Int Asn of Machinists and Aerospace Workers, 2001; Booz, Allen, and Hamilton, Va, 2000; Johnson & Johnson, Washington, DC, 2000. *Exhib:* Contemp Prints, Nat Prov Mus, Taiwan, 77; Works on Paper, Hudson River Mus, Yonkers, NY, 78; Artists Who Make Prints, Fordham Univ at Lincoln Ctr, NY, 81; Invitational, Cayman Gallery, NY, 83; Solo exhibs, Contemp Ltd Eds, Fla, 85, Hersh Gallery, Long Island, 86, Fred Dorfman Inc, NY, 87, Syd Entel Gallery, Tampa, Fla, 88, Art Forms Gallery, Redbank, NJ, 89, Inner Visions of Georgetown, Washington, DC, 89; Faculty Exhib, Parsons Sch Design, Lake Placid, NY, 84-85; Five Printmakers, Castle Gallery, Coll New Rochelle, NY, 85; Zola Fine Art, Los Angeles, 86; Alumni Art, State Univ NY, New Paltz, 87; Los Angeles Expo, 88; NY Expo, 88-90; Save Our Shores, Art Forms Gallery, 88; John Szoke Gallery, NY, Reele Gallery, NY; CS Schulte Gallery, NY, 89. *Pos:* Lead Guitarist, Vocalist in, Boystown. *Teaching:* art prof, Orange Co Community Col, NY (10 yrs). *Awards:* Best of Show, Sullivan Co Art Asn, 73; Directors Award Graphics, Knickerbocker Artists, 75; Drawing Award, Paperworks Exhib, Hastings Gallery, 80; Cover Art for the Guild 8 Designers Source Book. *Bibliog:* Robert Smallman (dir), Printmaking (film), 78. *Media:* Etchings, Monoprints; Mixed Media on Wood & Aluminum, Etched Bronze Wall Sculpture, Collage, Acrylic on Canvas and Wood. *Publ:* Printworld Mag, The Guild Source Book, Art Bus News, NY Gallery Guide, Art in Am, Interior Design Mas, The Village Voice, NY Times. *Dealer:* Innervisions Inc 12211 Folkstone Dr Oak Hill VA 20171. *Mailing Add:* 146 Coleman Rd Goshen NY 10924

BLECKNER, ROSS
PAINTER
b New York, NY, 1949. *Study:* NY Univ, BA, 71; Calif Inst Arts, MFA, 73. *Work:* Joslyn Art Mus; J B Speed Art Mus. *Exhib:* Group exhibs, 10 Plus 10: Contemp Soviet and Am Painters, Milwaukee Art Mus, Wis, The Corcoran Gallery Art, Washington, Artists' Union Hall of the Tretyakov Embankment, Moscow, USSR & Tsentralnyi Zal Khudozhnikov, Tbilisi, USSR, 90; The Last Decade: Am Artists of the 80's, Tony Shafrazi Gallery, NY, 90; Weitersehen, Mus Haus Esters & Mus Haus Lange, Krefeld, Ger, 90; Solo exhibs, Art Gallery, Ontario, Toronto, Can, 90, Galeria Soledad Lorenzo, Madrid, Spain, 90, Heland Wetterling Gallery, Stockholm, Sweden, 90, Kunsthalle, Zurich, Switz, 90, Kolnscher Kunstverein, Koln, WGer, 91, Moderna Museet, Stockholm, Sweden, 91, Galerie Daniel Templon, Parish, France, 97, Galerie Ghislaine Hussenot, Paris, France, 97, Galeria Aglutinador, Havana, Cuba, 98, Glenn Horowitz Bookseller, East Hampton, NY, 98, Lehmann Maupin Gallery, NY, 98, Mary Boone Gallery, NY, 98, 01, Baldwin Gallery, Aspen, Colo, 98, Julie M Gallery, Tel Aviv, Israel, 98, Betsy Senior Gallery, NY, 99, Wetterling Gallery, Stockholm, Sweden, 99, Emilio Mazzoli Galleria d'Arte Contemporanea, Modena, Italy, 99, Martin Browne Fine Art, Sydney, Australia, 99, Mario Diacono Gallery, Boston, 2000, Fay Gold Gallery, Atlanta, 2000, Zaknin Schwartz Gallery, Atlanta, 2000, Rebecca Camhi Gallery, Athens, Greece, 2000, Galerie Ernst Beyeler, Basel, Switz, 2000, Inarco Gallery, Italy, 2001, Thomas Ammann Fine Art, Zurich, 2007; Pintura de los Ochenta en las Americas, Museo de arte contemporaneo de Monterrey, Mex, 91; Carnegie Inst, Mus Art, Pittsburgh, Pa, 88; The Binational/Die Binationale, Kunsthalle Dusseldorf, W Ger, 88; The Image Of Abstraction, Mus Contemp Art, Los Angeles, Calif, 88; Stephen Wirtz Gallery, San Francisco, 98; Cleveland Mus Art, 98; Inst Contemp Art, Boston, 99; Katonah Mus Art, NY, 99; Whitney Mus Am Art, NY, 99; Galerie Daniel Templon, Paris, 99; Solomon R Guggenheim Mus, NY, 2000; Victoria Miro Gallery, London, 2000; Chicago Cult Ctr, 2000; Steffany Martz Gallery, NY, 2000; Barbara Gladstone Gallery, NY, 2000; Mus Contemp Art, North Miami, Fla, 2001; Los Angeles Co Mus Art, 2001; and many others. *Bibliog:* Roberta Smith (auth), article, Art in Am, 1/81; Peter Halley (auth), article, 5/82 & Robert Pincus-Witten (auth), Defenestrations, 11/82, Arts Mag; Elizabeth Hess (auth), Celestial Navigations, Village Voice, 88; Kay Larson (auth), article, New York Mag, 11/88; Michael Brenson (auth), article, New York Times, 10/88; Ross Bleckner's Capri Sketchbook, Travel & Leisure, Mar 98; Annabelle Kerins (auth), An Intimate Exhibition: Bleckner in Miniature, Long Island Newsday, 8/21/98; Rand Gener (auth), Ross Bleckner: A Study in Contrasts, HX Magazine, 11/13/98; Steven Vincent (auth), Bleckner at Mary Boone and Lehmann Maupin, Art and Auction, 11/16/98; Kim Levin (auth), Voice Choices: Ross Bleckner, The Village Voice, 12/1/98; Joyce Korotkin (auth), Ross Bleckner, Cover, Feb 99; Barry Schwabsky (auth), Ross Bleckner, Artforum, Mar 99; Carol Diehl (auth), Ross Bleckner, Art News, Mar 99; Lucy Fremont (auth), Ross Bleckner, Animal Fair, Oct 99; Demetrio Paparoni (auth), Ross Bleckner, Tema Celeste, Jan 2000; Pilar Viladas (auth), Posh Spice, The NY

Times, 10/29/2000; Martin Herbert (auth), Ross Bleckner, Tema Celeste, Jan 2001; Elisa Turner (auth), Mythic Proportions, Art News, May 2001. *Media:* Oil on Canvas. *Dealer:* Mary Boone Gallery 745 Fifth Ave New York NY; Lehmann Maupin 39 Greene St New York NY. *Mailing Add:* c/o Mary Boone Gallery 745 5th Ave New York NY 10151

BLESER, KATHERINE ALICE
PAINTER
b Los Angeles, Calif, Apr 3, 1942. *Study:* Northwestern Univ, Evanston, Ill, BA, 73; Ga State Univ, Atlanta, MA, 75. *Work:* Ga Inst Technol & Fed Reserve Bank, Atlanta; Chattahoochee Valley Art Mus, LaGrange, Ga; State of Ga, Atlanta; Springfield Art Mus, Mo; Telfair Mus Art, Savannah, Ga. *Comn:* Six oil paintings, S Trust Bank, Birmingham, Ala, 87; two oil paintings, Anheuser-Busch, Cartersville, Ga, 93; two oil paintings, Kaiser Permanente, Atlanta, Ga, 95; oil painting, Med Ctr, Columbus, Ga, 96; eight oil paintings, Oshner Found Hosp, New Orleans, La, 97. *Exhib:* Am Artists Mag Nat Art Competition, Grand Cent Gallery, NY, 85; Allied Artists Am, Nat Arts Club, NY, 87, 91 & 97; Knickerbocker Artists, Salmagundi Club, NY, 87 & 95, Fine Arts Inst Ann Exhib, San Bernardino Co Mus, Redlands, Calif, 87, 92 & 93; Springfield Art League Ann Exhib, George Walter Vincent Smith Mus, Mass, 88, 90, 94 & 96; Nat Asn Women Artists Exhib to India, Sanskar Kendra Mus, Ahmedebad, India, 89-90; Arts for the Parks Ann Competition, Lakeview Mus Arts & Sci, Peoria, Ill & Cincinnati Mus Nat Hist, Ohio, 89-90 & 94-95; South Bend (Ind) Regional Mus Art, 94; Asn Visual Arts Ann Exhibit, Hunter Mus Am Art, Chattanooga, Tenn, 96, 97 & 2000. *Awards:* Hon Mention, Artists Mag Landscape Painting Competition, 87; Catharine Lorillard Wolfe Art Club Medal of Honor, Oil, 90; Merit Award, Springfield Art League Ann Exhib, 88. *Bibliog:* Valerie Rivers (auth), Entering art competition, Am Artists, 9/86; Bebe Raupe (auth), the 1987 landscape painting competition winners, 12/87; Greg Schaber (auth), Entering national competitions, Artist's Mag, 6/96. *Mem:* Catharine Lorillard Wolfe Art Club; Nat Asn Women Artists; Am Artists Prof League; Academic Artists; Audubon Artists. *Media:* Oil. *Publ:* Getting Into - And Staying With - Galleries, Art Calendar, 2/96; Creating a Garden of Hues, Artists Mag, 5/96. *Dealer:* The Little Gallery 6 Bridgewater Plaza Moneta VA 24121; Off the Wall Gallery, 123 E Broughton St, Savannah GA. *Mailing Add:* PO Box 219 Decatur GA 30031-0219

BLESSING, JENNIFER
CURATOR
Study: Brown Univ, AB (with honors); New York Univ, MA (art history), PhD candidate. *Collection Arranged:* Cur, A Rose is a Rose is a Rose: Gender Performance in Photog, 97; cur, Seven Easy Pieces, 2005; cur, Speaking with Hands: Photography from The Buhl Collection, 2006; cur, Family Pictures: Contemporary Photographs and Videos from the Collection of the Guggenheim Museum, 2006. *Pos:* Project asst cur, Solomon R Guggenheim Mus, 89, cur photog, 2006-. *Publ:* Contribr, Art/Fashion, Skira, 97; contribr, Modernism, Gender and Culture, Garland, 97; contribr, Veronica's Revenge: Current Perspectives in Contemporary Photography/The Lambert Photography Collection, Scalo, 98; contribr, Robert Mapplethorpe and the Classical Tradition, Guggenheim Mus, 2004; contribr, Allegorie II: Vedio, NRW-Forum Kultur und Wirtschaft, 2005. *Mailing Add:* Curator of Photography Solomon R Guggenheim Museum 1071 Fifth Ave New York NY 10128-0173

BLEVINS, JAMES RICHARD
ART ADMINISTRATOR, EDUCATOR
b Feb 1, 1934; US citizen. *Study:* David Lipscomb Col, BA, 56; George Peabody Col, MA, 60, PhD, 70; Univ Calif, Los Angeles, 75. *Pos:* Dean, Sch Liberal Arts, Univ Southern Ind, 69-; mem bd dir, Evansville Mus, 70-, chmn, Fine Arts Comt, 76-; chmn, Ohio River Arts Festival, 72; prod, New Harmony Theatre, 88-; prod, Young Abe Lincoln, 89-. *Awards:* Mayors Arts Award, Evansville, 94. *Mem:* Evansville Arts & Educ Coun (vpres, 73); Int Comt Humanities, 80-86 (chmn, 83-84); Nat Fedn State Humanities Couns, 83-85. *Mailing Add:* Univ Southern Ind 8600 University Blvd Evansville IN 47712

BLISS, HARRY JAMES
PAINTER, ILLUMINATOR
b May 21, 1923; US citizen. *Study:* Studied at Dickinson Jr Col, 47 & Edinboro State Teachers Col, 48; Pratt Inst, cert, 51. *Work:* Lincoln Trust Collection, Rochester, NY; Hartford Insurance Collection, Conn; General Motors Collection; Am Motors Asn Collection, Rochester, NY; Merrill Lynch Pierce Fenner & Smith, Rochester, NY. *Exhib:* Chautauqua Exhib Nat Art, Chautauqua Gallery Art, NY, 90; Finger Lakes Exhib, Memorial Art Gallery, Rochester, NY, 95; Adirondacks Nat Exhib Am Watercolors, Old Forge Gallery, NY, 95; Arts for the Parks, Jackson Hole, Wyo, 95; Cooperstown National, Cooperstown Mus, NY, 96. *Pos:* Art dir & designer, Mel Richmond Studio, Philadelphia, 52-53; designer/illusr, Kilborn Studios, Rochester, NY, 59-61; illusr, Studio 5, Rochester, NY, 63-73; owner, Harry Bliss Gallery, Pittsford, NY, 74-. *Teaching:* Instr watercolor, Rochester Inst Technol, 75-77, instr illus & design, 77-83; instr illus & design, Graphic Careers, 80-87. *Awards:* Robley McCarthy Award, Chautauqua, Exhib National Art, 70; Dale Myers Cooper Medal, Adirondacks Nat Exhib Am Watercolors, 92; Elizabeth Ling Reamer Mem Award, Rochester Finger Lakes Show, 93. *Bibliog:* Pat Hooley (auth), Harry Bliss as fine artist, Pittsford Brighton Post, 82; Teresa Sharp (auth), Artist Harry Bliss creates masterpieces, Pittsford Brighton Post, 84; Judith Reynolds (auth), Heaven's back porch, City Newspaper, 87. *Mem:* Rochester Art Club (v pres). *Media:* Acrylic, Watercolor; Graphite. *Mailing Add:* 581 Marsh Rd Pittsford NY 14534-3331

BLITZ, NELSON, JR
COLLECTOR
Pos: President Nelson Air Device Corp, Maspeth, NY, Nelson Acquisition Corp, Rye. *Awards:* Named one of Top 200 Collectors, ARTnews Magazine, 2004-2006, 2011, 2012, 2013. *Collection:* Germen expressionism, modern & contemporary art, Wiener Werkstatte metalwork and furniture. *Mailing Add:* Nelson Air Device Corp 46-28 54th Ave Maspeth NY 11378

BLIZZARD, ALAN
PAINTER, EDUCATOR
b Boston, Mass, Mar 25, 199. *Study:* Mass Sch Art, Boston, with Lawrence Kupferman; Univ Ariz, with Andreas Andersen; Univ Iowa, with Stuart Edie, James Lechay & Byron Burford. *Hon Degrees:* Mass Coll of Art, BFA. *Work:* Brooklyn Mus, NY; Metrop Mus Art, NY; Art Inst Chicago; Denver Art Mus, Colo; La Jolla Mus Art, Calif; Crocker Mus Art, Sacramento, Calif; Ashland Univ; Columbia Univ; and over 250 other pub & pvt collections. *Exhib:* Many exhibs in leading Mus, Coll & Univs, incl Oxford Univ, Eng. *Teaching:* Chmn & prof painting, Scripps Col & Claremont Grad Sch, currently; chmn art dept, Scripps Col. *Mailing Add:* Scripps College 1030 Columbia Ave Claremont CA 91711

BLOCH, BABETTE
ARTIST, SCULPTOR
b New York City, 1956. *Study:* Univ Wis, 1973-1975; Univ Calif Davis, BS 1975-1977; San Francisco Art Inst, summer 1976; Sch of Visual Arts, 1980; Residency Fel, Chateau Rochefort En Terre, Brittany, France, 1996. *Work:* Int Hillel, Washington DC; Temple Soc Concord, Syracuse, NY; Md Inst Art, Baltimore, Md; Brookgreen Gardens & Sculpture Mus, Murrells Inlet, SC; Enterprise Corporate Park, Shelton, Conn. *Comn:* Lowcountry Sculptures, Brookgreen Gardens, Murrells Inlet, SC; The Pioneers, Hudson Manufacturing, Chicago, Ill for Hudson Heritage Farm, Fennville, Mich; In the Garden, Dolph & Naomi Shayes, Syracuse, NY; Steeloglyph, Boca Rio Golf Club, Boca Raton, Fla; Ark Doors, Eternal Light & Candelabras, Morse Sr Campus, Tradition's Sanctuary, W Palm Beach, Fla; Vitruvian Man, R.D. Sinto for Enterprise Cor Park, Shelton, Conn, 2012. *Exhib:* solo exhibs, Nat Arts Club, NY, 1999, Harmon Meek Gallery, Naples, Fla, 2001, Soho Arts S, Palm Beach Fla, 2003, Steel Garden: Fort Wayne Mus Art, Fort Wayne, Ind, 2015, Portraits Inc, New York, 2015, Housatonic Mus Art, Bridgeport, Conn, Magna Magnolias, 2015, Mattatuck Mus Art, Waterbury, Conn, 2014: Steel Garden ; Elaine Benson Gallery, Bridgehampton, NY, 2000-2001; Cavalier Galleries, Greenwich, Conn & Nantucket, Mass, 2001-; Chairs, Coins & Candlesticks, Sculpture in Everyday Life, Brookgreen Gardens, Rainey Sculpture Pavilion, Murrells Inlet, SC, 2003; Elaine Baker Gallery, Boca Raton, Fla, 2003-2013; Paul Mellon Arts Ctr- Choate Rosemary Hall, 09/2006-11/2006; Rarity Gallery, summer 2008-2015; Nat Arts Club-Member's Show, New York, 92-2015; Salmagundi Club, 2008-. *Pos:* Pres, Ex-Officio, Artists' Fellowship, Inc; cochair, Nat Arts Club Roundtable. *Awards:* Dr Max Ellenburg Award, Nat Asn of Women Artists, 1986; Salzman Award for Achievement in Sculpture, Nat Arts Club, 1992; President's Medal of Honor, Nat Arts Club, 1994; Philip Isenberg Mem Award, 125th Ann Mem Exhib, Salmagundi Club, 2008, 2012 & 2015; Highest Sculpture award, Nat Arts Club, 2011, 2012. *Bibliog:* Peggy Kinstler (auth), Inform Art, Spring 2002; Fairfield Conn Home Home, 3/2006-4/2006; Redding Pilot, 8/2006; American Artist Studios, 2011; ARTnews, 2012; American Artist Workshop, 2012; Internat Artist, 2012. *Mem:* Artist's Fel Inc (pres ex officio); Nat Arts Club, Exhibiting Artist Member, (co-chair Roundtable Comt); Salmagundi Club (mem); Century Asn. *Media:* Stainless Steel. *Specialty:* Fine Art Sculpture & Painting. *Publ:* The Grand Rapids Press, 5/25/1996; Fairfield County Home Mag, Mar/April 2006; Hartford Courant, 4/3/2006; The Redding Pilot, 1/1/96, 10/3/96, 6/21/2001, 8/10/2006, 6/12/2008, 1/26/2014, 6/4/2015; Fine Art Connoisseur, 8/2015. *Dealer:* Elaine Baker Gallery Boca Raton FL; Harmon/Meek Galleries Naples FL; Portraits Inc New York NY; Wit Gallery Lenox MA. *Mailing Add:* 61 Pheasant Ridge Rd Redding CT 06896

BLOCH, HENRY WOLLMAN
COLLECTOR
b Kansas City, Mo, Jul 30, 1922. *Study:* Univ Mich, BS, 44. *Pos:* Trustee, Nelson-Atkins Mus Art. *Collection:* Impressionist and post-impressionist art. *Mailing Add:* 1 H and R Block Way Kansas City MO 64105-1905

BLOCK, HOLLY
MUSEUM DIRECTOR
b 1959. *Study:* Bennington Coll, Vt, BA (photog & sculpture). *Pos:* Mem, Washington Project for Arts, DC, 3 years; cur satellite galleries, Bronx Mus Arts, NY, 85-88, exec dir, 2006-; dir Art in General, New York, 88-2006, established residency program for open studio on-site artists, 96; co-comnr Cairo Biennial, US Dept State, 2003. *Mem:* Nat Asn Artists Orgn (co-vpres bd dirs, 90-95, pres bd dirs, 94-96, adv, 96-). *Publ:* Auth, Art Cuba: The New Generation, Harry N Abrams, 2001. *Mailing Add:* Bronx Museum of Arts 1040 Grand Concourse Bronx NY 10456-3999

BLOCK, VIRGINIA SCHAFFER
PAINTER, ASSEMBLAGE ARTIST
b Newark, NJ, Apr 24, 1946. *Study:* William Paterson Coll, Wayne, NJ, BA, 68, MA (visual arts), 69; Rutgers State Univ (serigraphy, advan printmaking), 89, studies with Tom Vincent, 74-78, Jeanne Jaffe, 94. *Work:* Hoesct Celanese, NJ; Mead Data Cent, Cincinnati, Ohio; Nabisco Brands USA, Hanover, NJ; Berlex Laboratories, Wayne, NJ; Warner Lambert, NJ; The Quantum Group, NJ; Thacher, Proffitt & Wood, New York; Charles & Lynn Kramer Family Found, NJ; Mutual Benefit Life, NJ; Merrill Lynch, NJ; St. Thomas Univ, Miami, Fla. *Comn:* Canvas, Kimmelman, Wolff & Samson, Roseland, NJ, 86; canvas, Mandelbaum, Salsburg, Gold, West Orange, NJ, 87; canvas/acrylic, Sandoz Pharmaceuticals, Hanover, NJ, 90. *Exhib:* Juried Nat Exhib: Ann Metro Show of Small Works, City Without Walls, Newark, 97 & 2000; solo exhibs, Berlex Lab Corp Gallery, Montville, NJ, Patterns and Placement, 99, Fredrick Clement Gallery, Montclair, NJ, Wavelengths, 2001 & Beneath the Layers, Pierro Gallery, South Orange, NJ, 2007; The NJ Arts Ann, The Noyes Mus Art, Oceanville, NJ, 2001; Under the Chuppah, Kansas City Jewish Mus, Kans, 2002; Group invitation, City Without Walls at Seton Hall Univ Sch Law, Newark, Color and Concept, 2003; Int Juried Show, NJ Ctr Visual Arts, Summit, NJ, 2004; 68th & 69th Nat Midyear, Butler Inst Am Art, Youngstown, Ohio, 2004-2007; Connection, St Thomas Univ, Sardiñas Gallery, Miami, Fla, 2005; Invitational Exhibs, Genesis and Evolution, SMI Gallery, Acad Sq, 2010, Considering Collage, SMI Gallery, Acad Sq,

2011, Holy Lives, Therese A Maloney Art Gallery, Coll St Elizabeth, Morristown, NJ, 2012. *Pos:* Advert artist, 69; freelance artist, 74-80; co-founder, pres, Studio Montclair Inc, 96-2002, dir, Virginia S Block Gallery, 2010-; adv bd, George Segal Gallery, Montclair State Univ, NJ, 2007-, recording secretary, 2012, 2013. *Teaching:* Grad asst fine arts, William Paterson Coll, Wayne, NJ, 68-69; art teacher, Hanover Twp Pub Sch System, 70-73. *Awards:* Harry & Ruth Kaltish Award for Best Design, NJ Watercolor Soc Open Exhib, 95; Mitsuki Kovac Award, NJ Watercolor Soc Open Exhib, 96; Silver Medal of Honor, Audubon Artists Inc, 2003; Cert of Speical Congressional Recognition for Comm Serv, Bill Pascrell, 2009, 2010, 2011 & 2012. *Bibliog:* Intzides, Angelik (auth), Works of the N.A.W.A., Athens, 96; Tu, Hsiao-Ning (auth), Crossing Boundaries (exhib catalog), Noyes Mus Art, 10/2001; Shevchenko, Olya (auth), Connections (exhib catalog), Montclair-Graz Int Cult Exchange, 2003. *Mem:* Allied Artists Am; Audubon Artists Inc; Nat Asn Women Artists Inc (chmn, traveling painting exhib, 83-85 & exhibs, 84-85, exec bd, 83-89, newsletter ed, 86-89); NJ Watercolor Soc; Studio Montclair Inc (co-founder, 97, pres, 97-2002). *Media:* All. *Dealer:* Fredrick Clement Gallery 310 E 46th St Ste 3P NY NY 10017; Patricia G Selden Selden Assocs Inc Montclair NJ 07042. *Mailing Add:* 300 Highland Ave Upper Montclair NJ 07043

BLODGETT, ANNE WASHINGTON B.
PAINTER
b New York, NY, Apr 17, 1940. *Study:* Smith Col, BA, 61; Boston Mus Sch Fine Arts, 61-62; with George Demetrios, Boston, 64; Sch of Fine Arts, Cambridge, Eng, 63. *Work:* Berkshire Mus, Pittsfield, Mass; Fitzwilliam Coll Collection, Cambridge, Eng; Corp collections: Wilson Learning Co, Minneapolis; Quixote Co, Chicago; InnerAsia Co, San Francisco; Heublein Co, Hartford, Conn; Meml Hosp, New York City; Davis, Polk & Wardwell, Inc, New York City. *Comn:* Davis, Polk & Wardwell Co, NY, 81; landscape, Roberto Mendoza, 2001. *Exhib:* Solo exhibs, Berkshire Mus, 71, Caravan House Gallery, NY, 71 & 74, Medici Gallery, London, 73, Northeast Harbor Libr, Me, 73, 75; Carspecken-Scott Gallery, Wilmington, Del, 78; Bodley Gallery, NY, 80 & 83; Marbella Gallery, NY, 85, 88, 95, 98; Millbrook Gallery, NY, 88; Chapin Sch, 95; Mass Gen Downtown Hosp, Boston, 95; Ann Norton Gallery, Palm Beach, Fla, 97; Group exhibs, New Grafton Gallery, London, 72, Red Barn, Fishers Island, NY, 76, Buck Hill Falls Art Asn, Pa, 76, Pioneer Gallery, Cooperstown, NY, 78, Ferguson Gallery, Hartford, Conn, 80, Erikson Gallery, 81, Tomlyn Gallery, Jupiter, Fla, 82, Maplebrook Art Show, Amenia, NY, 87, Saxon Gallery, Southampton, NY, 89, First Nat Bank, Peterborough, NH, 90, Tremaine Gallery, Hotchkiss Sch, Lakeville, Conn, 98, Spring Island Trust Vis Artists Program, SC, 2001, Smith-Killian Fine Art Gallery, Charleston, SC, 2003, Art Placement, Scapes: Sea and Land, 717 Fifth Ave Lobby, NY, 2003, Century Asn, NY, 94, 2001, 2010, Smith Coll, 2011. *Bibliog:* Les Krantz (auth), The New York Art Review, 88. *Mem:* Century Asn, 92. *Media:* Oil, Acrylic. *Collection:* Robert Murray, Mr & Mrs Robert Burch, Mr & Mrs Michael Ainslie, Richard Spizziri, Mr & Mrs Ward Woods. *Publ:* Auth, article in Artspeak, 85; Pictures on Exhibit, 89; Miss Porters Sch, Art Issue, 85; Berkshire Eagle, Pittsfield, Mass, 71; Union Leader, 81. *Mailing Add:* 829 Park Ave New York NY 10021-2468

BLOODGOOD-ABRAMS, JANE MARIE
PAINTER
b Queens, NY, Jan 7, 1963. *Study:* Coll St Rose, Albany, NY, BS (studio art), 85; State Univ NY, New Paltz, MFA (painting), 87. *Work:* AIG Insurance, NY; Federal Express, NY; Barclays Financial Group, NY; First Albany Corp, NY; McGraw-Hill, NY; Mt St Mary Coll, Newburgh, NY; Samuel Dorsky Mus, New Paltz, NY; City of Edinburgh, Scotland. *Comn:* Omni Corp, Albany, NY. *Exhib:* The Art of Nature, N Mus, Lancaster, Pa, 93; Images 94, Pa State Univ Mus, 94; NY State Biennial Invitational, NY State Mus, Albany, 98; Envisioned in a Pastoral Setting, Shelburne Mus, Vt, 98; Solo exhib, Allen Sheppard Gallery, Piermont, NY, 98; Landscapes, Carrie Haddard Gallery, Hudson, NY, 2000; Sacred Visions, Austelling, Austria, 2000; Pastel Soc of Am, Nat Arts Club, NY, 2000; Catharine Lorillard Wolfe Art Club, NY, 2000; Degas Pastel Soc, New Orleans, La, 2000; United Pastelists of Am, Nyack, NY, 2001; Florence Int Biennial, Italy; Gallery Abtei Braweiller, Koln, Ger, 2003; Mohawk Hudson Regional, Albany, NY, 2003; Living Room Gallery, Kingston, NY, 2003; Albert Shahinian Gallery, Poughkeepsie, NY, 2004; River Gallery, Chattanooga, Tenn, 2005; DFN Gallery, NY, 2006 & 2008; Menden Hal Sobieski Gallery, Los Angeles, Calif, 2006; Meyer East Gallery, Santa Fe, NMex, 2007; Harrison Gallery, Williamstown, Mass, 2007. *Awards:* Best of Show, Clermont State Hist Site, 93; Special Opportunity Stipend Award, NY State Coun Arts, 98; Mem of Yr Award, Ulster Co Arts Coun; Pastel Soc Am, 2000; Ludwig Vogelstein Found Grant, 2004. *Bibliog:* Luminist paintings in Hudson, Northeast Art and Antiques, 12/99; The luminous landscapes of Jane Bloodgood-Abrams, The Country Mag, 11/2000; Luminist pleasure: a marriage of meteorology and physics, Art Ideas, Vol 5, No 3; Back to (the Hudson river) school, Hudson Valley Mag, 4/2002; Fine Art Connoisseur, 4/2005; Am Art Collector, 2/2006, 6/2007 & 9/2008. *Mem:* Pastel Soc Am (signature mem); Woodstock Art Asn; Nat Asn Women Artists; Catharine Lorillard Wolfe Art Club. *Media:* Oil, Pastel. *Interests:* The Art of George Inness and the Hudson River Sch. *Dealer:* Carrie Haddad Gallery Hudson NY; River Gallery Chattanooga TN; DFN Gallery New York NY; Meyer East Gallery Santa Fe NM. *Mailing Add:* 30 Staples St Kingston NY 12401

BLOOM, ALAN DAVID
PAINTER, STONE SCULPTOR
b Tucson, Ariz, June 29, 1945. *Study:* Univ Ariz, BS, 67; master apprenticeship/gemstone carving with R Lenius, 78; independent study at Rifkind Ctr Ger Expressionist Studies, Los Angeles Co Mus Art, 94; Int Center for Creative Photog, 2008; Studies at Studio I, Westport, Conn, 72, Mus de Nat, Mexico City, 77, Vatican, Rome, 89; Study by Invitation of Hans Namuth Film and Photo Archives of Jackson Pollack in Studio, Springs, Long Island, NY, 2008. *Work:* Europ Am League Art, Geneva, Switz & San Francisco, Calif; Thomas M Golden Found, Freestone, Calif. *Comn:* Spirit of Youth in America Mural (20th anniversary repainting with Charles Lobdell), City San Francisco, 76-96. *Exhib:* Face to Face, Art for life Invitational, Santa Rosa, Calif, 1989-; Calif Mus Art, Santa Rosa, 94; Plein Air Mountainscapes, Rogue Gallery, Rogue Valley Art Ctr, Medford, Ore, 94; The Spirit of Table Rock Mountain, Wiseman at Rogue Coll, Grants Pass, Ore, 95; Whispers Gallery, 97, Gallery on the Rim, San Francisco, 97; Am Passionist Exhib, Humbolt Arts Comn (31st ann), Eureka, Calif, 98; Homage and Inspiration, Sebastopol Ctr Art, Sebastopol, Calif, 98; The Passion Seven, Ore Mus Modern Art, Grants Pass, Ore, 99; Jega Art Ctr, Ashland, Ore, 2000; Quicksilver Mine co, Front Street Gallery, 2001; The Passion Seven Expressionst Painters, Morris Graves Mus, Eureka Graves, Calif, 2001; US Dept State, Am Embassy Show File, 2001; Vacant Oasis, Works on Paper at Spring & Wooster, Manhattan, New York, 2001; Linda Penzur Gallery, San Anselmo, Calif, 2002; Catherine Finn Gallery, Tiburon, Calif, 2002; Snyder-Highland Found Art Mus, Passion 7, Weaverville, Calif, 2003; Bodega Now, New York in Oil, Bodega, Calif, 2005; UNICEF Int Invitational, Paramount Bldg, San Francisco, Calif, 2005; Zebulon, Petaluma, Calif, 2006; Hammerfriar Gallery, Healdsburg, Calif, 2006; Ricardo Zulmira Gallery, Tucson, Ariz, 2008; Cry of the Land, Moise Paternina Gallery, Columbia, S Am, 2009; The Silent Ones, Linda Penzur Gallery, San Anselmo, Calif, 2009; Lewellan Gallery, Forrestville, Calif, 2011; Art Takes, Times Square, NY, 2012; Bodega Now, Bodega, Calif, Alain Bloom, New Work in Oil, 2012; Refined by Fire, Point Richmond Calif, 2012. *Pos:* dir, Work Work Work Inc, 79-81; dir, Love Harmony Inc, 87-; founder, Studio Bodega, 2002-. *Awards:* Int Vis Artist of the Yr, 2004; Gold Medal of Excellence, Intl Biographical Soc, Cambridge, Eng; NS Law, Dir Gen. *Bibliog:* Alan Bloom, Pleinnaire Landscapes Abstracted (doc), Ore Pub Television, 1994; Kathleen Ayres (auth), Alan Bloom, Moody mountains equals rock solid art, Ore Courier, 95; Edith Decker (auth), Museum trove of treasures Bloom, teases with tenderness, Grants Pass Courier Entertainment, 99; Si & Ann Frazier (for corresp), Gem Artists, Lapidary J, 25, 99; Biographical Encyclopedia of Am Painters, Sculptors, and Engravers of the United States, Colonial thru Current Yr; Oregon Fine Art Gallery Guide (front cover image and review of painting pages 34-35), 2007-2008; The Paintings of Alain Bloom, Southern Oregon Arts Mag; Alain Bloom: California Expressionist (guide review, pgs. 28-34), Oregon Fine Art Gallery Guide, 2012. *Mem:* sig mem Passion Seven Expressionist Painters; Europe Am League Art. *Media:* Oil, Mixed Media; Gemstone Carving. *Dealer:* Studio Bodega Now Bodega CA. *Mailing Add:* 14201 Bodega Hwy Bodega CA 94922

BLOOM, DONALD S
PAINTER, ILLUSTRATOR
b Roxbury, Mass, Sept 3, 1932. *Study:* Mass Coll Art, BFA, 53; Art Students League, 53-55, with Barnet, Levi & Trafton; Inst Allende, San Miguel Allende, Mex, MFA, 57. *Work:* East Brunswick Pub Libr, NJ; South River Pub Libr, NJ; Fairleigh Dickinson Univ, Madison, NJ; Montclair State Coll, NJ; Rutgers Univ; Bloomfield Coll, NJ; Upsala Coll, East Orange, NJ. *Comn:* Mural, Judge Raymond Del Tufo, Newark, NJ, 63. *Exhib:* Boston Arts Festival, 1955; Butler Inst Ann Youngstown, Ohio, 58; four solo exhibs at NY City Galleries, 59-64; Whitney Ann Am Painting, Whitney Mus Am Art, NY, 60; Silvermine Guild Ann, New Canaan, Conn, 63; Audubon Artists Ann, Nat Acad Galleries, NY, 63; NJ Pavilion, NY World's Fair, 65; Springfield Watercolor Asn Traveling Show, Mo, 65; NJ State Mus Ann, 66 & 73; Charles Press Gallery, Colts Neck, NJ, 70; Art Barn, Monmouth, NJ 73; oil paintings, Acad Music on Main St, 2008; The Cachets of Don Bloom, Americover exhib, Oak Brook, Ill, 2010; Triumph Brewing Company, Princeton, 2011. *Collection Arranged:* Butler Inst Ann Youngstown, Ohio, 58; Charles Press Gallery, Colts Neck, NJ, 70; Art Barn, Monmouth, NJ 73. *Pos:* Staff cartoonist, Sentinel (newspapers), 78-90. *Teaching:* Art instr, Piscataway Schs, 58-92; instr painting & collage, Morris Co Art Asn, NJ, 60-68; instr painting, Bloomfield Coll, 65-66; dist chmn art dept, Piscataway Schs, NJ, 66-84; instr watercolor, Summit Art Ctr, 74; instr art, Trenton State Coll, 83. *Awards:* Guggenheim Fel Creative Painting, 61; Huntington Hartford Found Fel, 64; Second Place Cachets Award, Am First Day Cover Soc Nat Conv, 98; full scholar to Inst Allende, 56-57; 1st Prize, Prof Oils, NJ State Senior Exhibit, 2007. *Bibliog:* E Genauer (auth), rev in NY Herald Tribune, 9/61; J Beck (auth), rev in Art News, 10/61; V Raynor (auth), rev in Arts, 10/61. *Mem:* Nat Cartoonists Soc. *Media:* Oil; Watercolor; Pastel; Ink. *Publ:* Auth, We learned about color & design, Sch Arts Mag, 58; illusr, Seventeen Mag, 61; Country & Western Issue, Billboard Mag, 63; auth, Batik in the Classroom & Woodcuts by Children, 72 & Two for One, 75; illusr, Shards, Michael Kesler, 2008; illusr, Letters and Laughs from A to Z, Maureen Feit, 2009; illusr, Vestiges of Memory, Sid Winter, 2010. *Mailing Add:* 31 Dexter Rd East Brunswick NJ 08816

BLOOM, MARTHA
COLLAGE ARTIST, PHOTOGRAPHER, EDUCATOR
b Paterson, NJ, Aug 5, 1951. *Study:* Green Mountain Coll (art maj), 69-70; Art Inst Boston, 70-71, Art Students League, 71-80. *Work:* Assoc Am Artists, NY; Sylvan Cole Gallery, NY; Art Students League; Columbia Mus, Columbia, SC; McNay Mus, San Antonio, Tex; Permanent installation, Art student league children's class etchings, D'Arcy-Massive-Benton-Bowles, NY, 90; Metrop Mus, NY; Libr of Cong; Nat Acad; Delaware Mus; and many pvt collections; Libr Congress. *Comn:* Union Settlement Asn, NY, 92. *Exhib:* Solo exhibs include MacDowell Sch, Art Students League, NY, 77; group exhibs include Audubon Soc, Nat Acad Gallery, NY, 74; theme shows, Asn Am Artists, 80-85; McNay Ann Collector's Show, McNay Mus, San Antonio, Tex, 84-87; Midtown-Payson Gallery, NY, 89; Book Arts Gallery, NY, 91; Graphics Arts Ctr, Conn, 95 & 97; Salander O'Reilly Gallery, 2002, 2003 & 2004; Westport Arts Center, Conn, 2009; and others. *Teaching:* Lectr, printmaking, Cooper-Hewitt Mus, NY, 80-81; Nat Acad Sch, 2000-; art instr childrens half day, Art Students League, 85-2012, art instr adults, 2012-; Inner City Outreach Prog, NY & Conn, 91-; Silvermine Sch Art, Ct, 92-; Westport Arts Ctr, Ct, 92-; Carriage Barn Ctr, Conn, 97; Whitney Mus Am Art, Champion, Conn; Nat Acad Sch of Fine Arts, NY, 99-; Nat Acad Mus, 2006-; Aldridge Mus, Ridgefield, Conn, 2007; ASC, NYT Campus, 2008; Westport Arts Ctr, Conn, 2009. *Awards:* MacDowell Traveling Scholarship, Art Student League, 74-77. *Bibliog:* B Bloom (auth), Magical Thinkin, Art Students

League Linea Fall 2009. *Mem:* Artists Equity Asn; life mem Art Students League (bd control, 3 yrs); Artists Fel Inc; Artists Union Asn; Silvermine Guild; Artist Fellowship Asn. *Media:* All Media. *Interests:* Video; Music; Dance; Singing; Yoga. *Publ:* Photographs pub in mags and newspapers; NY Mag, Linea ASC, 2009. *Mailing Add:* 111 Compo Rd S Westport CT 06880

BLOOM, SUZANNE See Manual, Ed Hill & Suzanne Bloom

BLOOMFIELD, LISA DIANE
PHOTOGRAPHER, CONCEPTUAL ARTIST
b Los Angeles, Calif, Aug 9, 1951. *Study:* Univ Calif, Berkeley, BA, 73; Calif Inst Arts, MFA (art & design; scholar), 80. *Work:* J Paul Getty Mus, Malibu, Calif. *Exhib:* Phantasy, Santa Barbara Mus Art, 82; solo show, Arco Ctr Visual Art, 83, Visual Studies Workshop, Rochester, NY, 89; Franklin Furnace, NY; two-person show, Lightwork, Syracuse, NY, 88; Biennial I, Calif Mus Photo, Riverside, 90; Systems, Los Angeles Munic Art Gallery, 90. *Collection Arranged:* Photographs: Griffith Observatory: 1935-1978, Los Angeles, 78; The Theater of Gesture, Los Angeles Ctr Photog Studies, 83. *Teaching:* Instr Otis Art Inst, 81-; lectr, Univ Washington; lectr, Univ Calif Los Angeles, 89; lectr, Univ Calif Riverside & Santa Barbara, 90. *Awards:* Purchase Award, Six State Exhib, Univ NMex, Albuquerque, 82; Calif Arts Coun Grant, 83; Visual Arts Fel, Nat Endowment Arts, 86; Fac Develop Fund, New Sch Soc Res, NY, 89. *Bibliog:* J Hugunin (auth), Mocking objects, Afterimage, 12/80; D Berland (auth), On photography, Los Angeles Times, 5/15/83; J Brumfield (auth), Loaded implications, Art Week, 5/28/83. *Mem:* Friends Photog; Los Angeles Ctr Photog Studies; Soc Photog Educ. *Publ:* Contribr, Impulse Mag, vol 10 #1, 82; Top stories #28, 89; CAA J, 90. *Mailing Add:* 1525 S Stanley Ave Los Angeles CA 90019-3849

BLOOMFIELD, SARA J
MUSEUM DIRECTOR
Study: Northwestern Univ, BA (Eng lit), MA (educ). *Hon Degrees:* several hon doctorates. *Pos:* vpres, Cleveland Financial Group; deputy dir opers, US Holocaust Mem Mus Coun, Washington, 1986-88, exec dir, 1988-94; assoc dir mus programs, US Holocaust Mem Mus, Washington, 1994-98, acting dir, 1998-99, dir, 1999-. *Awards:* Young Leadership Award, Am Jewish Com, 1986; Jan Karski Award, Anti-Defamation League, Washington chap, Officers Cross of the Order of Merit of the Jewish Com. *Mem:* Women's Political Caucus (bd mem); Cleveland City Club (bd mem); Am Jewish Com (bd mem). *Mailing Add:* US Holocaust Memorial Museum 100 Raoul Wallenberg Pl SW Washington DC 20024-2126

BLOOMFIELD, SUZANNE
PAINTER, PRINTMAKER
b Cleveland, Ohio, June 23, 1934. *Study:* Ohio Univ, BS, 55; Univ Ariz, MEd, 75. *Work:* Pima Coun Aging, Tucson, Ariz; Univ Ariz, Tucson; Albany Print Club, NY; Ariz State Sen Ruth Solomon pvt collection; Nat Asn Women Artists, New York. *Comn:* Univ Ariz Dept Judaic Studies. *Exhib:* UN World Conf Women, Nairobi, Kenya, 86; Nat Asn Women Artists Centennial Yr, Foreign Exhib Tour India, 89-90; Am Album Res Arch, Nat Mus Women Arts, Washington, DC, 90; Global Focus - UN Fourth World Conf Women, Beijing, China & Moscow, Russ, 95; Galeria Berta Armas, Ensenada, Mex, 97; Mus Contemp Art, Los Angeles, 97; Univ Ariz, Tucson, 98; Traveling Printmaking Exhib USA, 98-2000; Millennium Collection, United Nations, New York, 2001; Univ Alaska, Anchorage, 2003; Univ Tex, 2004; Tucson Mus Art, 2005-2009; Unity Canvas, World Trade Ctr Mem Foun, 2006; 25-27th Miniprint Int tour, 2005-2008; NY Hall Science, 2008; Tucson Int Airport, 2008; Purdue Univ, 2008; Western Nat Paints Assoc, 2008; Herberger Theater Ctr Gallery, Phoenix, Ariz, 2009; Nat Assn Women Artists, NY, 2010, 2011; Johnson & Johnson World Headquarters Gallery, New Brunswick, NJ, 2012. *Collection Arranged:* Univ Ariz; Albany Print Club, NY. *Awards:* Irwin Zlowe Memorial Award, 2002. *Bibliog:* Calif Art Rev, 89; Ariz Illus, KUAT Tv, Tucson, Ariz, 90; Women - Your Voice (doc), Albright Productions, San Antonio, Tex, 92; Into the New Century (exhib catalog), Univ Ariz, 98. *Mem:* Nat Asn Women Artists. *Media:* Encaustics, Oil, Printmaking. *Mailing Add:* 4270 E Holmes Tucson AZ 87111

BLOVITS, LARRY JOHN
PAINTER, EDUCATOR
b Detroit, Mich, Oct 19, 1936. *Study:* Wayne State Univ, Detroit, BFA, 64, MFA, 66; study with Daniel Greene, summers 83-86. *Work:* Muskegon Mus Art, Mich; Battle Creek Art Ctr, Mich; Beta Rho Delta Zeta Nat Sorority Mus, Oxford, Ohio; Mich Supreme Court Chambers, Lansing; Grand Rapids Art Mus, Mich. *Comn:* Pres Martin Essenberg, Covenant Col, Lookout Mountain, Tenn, 88; Pres John Bernhard, Western Mich Univ, Kalamazoo, 90; GW Haworth, Chmn, Haworth Corp, Holland, Mich, 91; Sen Eva M Hamilton, Lansing, Mich, 94; Sen Paul Henry, Allendale, Mich, 95. *Exhib:* Soc Des Pastellistes de France Int, Palais Rameau, Lille, France, 87; OPA 5th Int, Ky Highlands Mus, Ashland, 88; Salmagundi Members Exhib, NY, 88; solo exhib, Muskegon Mus Art, Mich, 88; 20th Ann Pastel Soc Ann Nat, Nat Arts Club, NY, 92; and others. *Pos:* Visual arts adv, Mich Coun Arts, Detroit, 76-81; apprentice master teacher, Nat Endowment Arts, Washington, DC, 83; vis artist, Mich Tech Univ, Houghton, 89. *Teaching:* adj instr drawing, Wayne State Univ, Detroit, 66-67; instr drawing & painting, Northern Mich Univ, Marquette, 67; prof art, drawing & painting, Aquinas Col, Grand Rapids, Mich 67-93. *Awards:* Member's Award, 9th Ann Nat, Pastel Soc Am, 81; 9th Ann Salmagundi nat, Metrop Portrait Soc, 86; Outstanding Achievement Portraiture, Nat Portrait Seminar, 91. *Bibliog:* Who's Who Midwest, Marquis, 23rd ed, 91; Madlyn Woolwich (auth), The Art of Pastel Portraiture, Watson-Guptill Books, 96. *Mem:* Am Soc Portrait Artists; Pastel Soc Am; Am Portrait Soc; Midwest Pastel Soc; Salmagundi Club, NY. *Media:* Oil, Pastel. *Publ:* Contribr, Photographing your art, Profile Mag, 84 & Directory of American Portrait Artists, 85, Am Portrait Soc; contribr & coauth, Artist in residence, Larry Blovits multipurpose studio, Am Artists Mag, 90; auth, Pastel Landscape, Technique & Procedure, video, pvt publ, 91; Pastel for the Serious Beginner, Watson-Guptill Books, 96. *Dealer:* Arnold Klein Gallery 4520 N Woodward Royal Oak MI 48072. *Mailing Add:* 0-1835 Luce SW Grand Rapids MI 49504-9503

BLUE, CHINA
DIRECTOR
Berkeley, Calif. *Study:* Calif Coll Arts, Oakland, Calif, BFA, 92; Hunter Coll, NY, MFA, 94. *Work:* Newport Art Mus, Newport, Rhode Island; Aine Mus, Tornio, Finland; Internet Archives, San Francisco, Calif; Galerie Barnoud, Dijon, France; Roger Williams Mus, Providence, Rhode Island. *Comn:* Research: Sounds of the Eiffel Tower, Eiffel Tower, Paris, France, 2007; Research: Sounds of the Vertical Gun, NASA/RI Space Grant, Providence, Rhode Island, 2009; Movie: Listening with More Than Ears, NASA/Rhode Island Space Grant, Providence, Rhode Island, 2010; Firefly Festival, City of Pawtucket, Pawtucket, Rhode Island, 2011. *Exhib:* Solo exhibs, Architectural Therapy, Lance Fung Gallery, NY, 2003, Fluid Paths, Interface and l'Atheneum, Dijon, France, 2004, Newport Art Mus, Newport, Rhode Island, 2011; Group exhibs, Limo Juried Show, Armory Show, NY, 2007, Flatland Limo, Armory Show, NY, 2008, Aqua Alta, Venice Architecture Biennale, Venice, Italy, 2008. *Pos:* founder & exec dir, Engine Inst, Providence, Rhode Island, 2010-. *Awards:* Research & Residency grant, Eiffel Tower, 2007; NASA/Rhode Island Space grant, Research Recording Vertical Gun, 2009, Listening with More Than Ears, 2010; Arts grant, Firefly Festival, City of Pawtucket, Rhode Island, 2011; RISCA Fel, New Genres, Firefly Projects, Rhode Island State Coun Arts, 2012. *Bibliog:* Ken Johnson (auth), Weekend in Review, NY Times, 2003; Sarah Valdez (auth), China Blue at Lance Fung, Art in Am, 2003; Lori Waxman (auth), Mikey vs. Fabio, Art Forum, 2006; Jill Connor (auth), China Blue and Carol Salmanson, Brooklyn Rail, 2007; Ed Rubin (auth), China Blue: Newport Art Mus, Sculpture Mag, 2012. *Mem:* Coll Arts Asn (94-); Godzilla Asian Am Art Network (mem bd dirs, 95-97); Engine Inst (exec dir, 2010-); Art Project: Birch Forest (mem bd dirs, 2010-). *Media:* Mixed Media. *Publ:* contbr, Demonstrations of Simple and Complex Auditory Psychophysic Multiple Platforms and Environments, Acoustics Today, 2005, What is the Sound of Eiffel Tower, 2009; auth, 7th Kingdom, Univ Rhode Island, 2010; contbr, To Be an Artist: Musicians, Visual Artists, Writers and Dancers Speak, EL Kurdyla Pub, 2011; auth, Firefly Projects, Newport Art Mus, 2011. *Dealer:* Galerie Barnoud 12 Rue Burlier Dijon France 21000. *Mailing Add:* 256 Maple St Warwick RI 02888

BLUE, PATT
PHOTOGRAPHER, WRITER
b Paducah, Ky, Apr 27, 1943. *Study:* State Univ NY, Stony Brook, BA (studio art & art hist), 74; Art Inst Chicago, MFA, 87. *Work:* Brooklyn Mus, NY; John F Kennedy Libr, Boston; City Mus New York; Light Work, Syracuse Univ, NY; also pvt collections of David C Ruttenberg & Francis Kohler; NY Pub Libr. *Exhib:* Light Work Retrospective, Everson Mus, Syracuse, NY, 85; solo exhibs, Heart of Man, Sch Art Inst Chicago, 87; Photo Active, Feldman Fine Arts, NY, 88; Myself, My Mother, My Grandmother, (Flesh & Blood), Kilkady Mus, Fotofeis, Scotland, 93, Ansel Adams Ctr Photog, San Francisco, 94; Living on a Dream: Words & Images, Los Angeles Ctr Photog Studies, 94; Life I: Within a Foot, James Howe Gallery, Kean Univ, NJ, 94; Mother's Who Think, 99; Facetime Series: Re-viewing Photog, Univ Arts, Philadelphia, Pa, 2002; and others. *Pos:* Arts & educ adminr, Int Ctr Photog, NY, 75-81; ed photogr, Life Mag, People, Der Stern, Paris Match, and others, 80-86; cur, New Spirit of Photography, Fashion Inst Technol, NY, 85; coordr, Contemp Europ Photog Lect Series, SAIC, Chicago, 87; ed, Findings, Interdisciplinary J Creative Works, 91-92. *Teaching:* Lectr, numerous mus & insts, 82-2003; fac, Int Ctr Photog, 75-81 & NY Univ, 83-84; vis artist, RI Sch Design, Providence, 84; adj fac, Moore Col Art, Philadelphia, 84-85; asst prof photog & resident fac, Kean Univ, Union, NJ, 87-97; grad thesis adv, Sch Visual Arts, NY, 95. *Awards:* Leica Medal of Excellence, 82; W Eugene Smith Found Humanities Photography, 84; Nat Endowment Arts, 88-89; NY Found Arts Fel, 89-90 & 93-94; and others. *Bibliog:* A D Coleman (auth), Documentary solution or problem?, New York Observer, 12/26/88-1/2/89; Review, Sunday Star Ledger, 11/3/91; Ann Marie Rousseau (auth), The larger questions of life: An interview, Photo Rev, Vol 19, No 3, summer 96. *Publ:* Photogr, Babies having babies, Life Mag, 83; John Loengard, Classic Photog, 88; ed, D Friend, The Meaning of Life, Little Brown & Co, 91; Flesh and Blood, George/Heyman/Hoffman, The Picture Project, 92; auth, Living on a Dream: A Marriage Tale, a photog/lit memoir, Univ Press, Miss, 98

BLUE MAN GROUP See Goldman, Matt

BLUE MAN GROUP See Wink, Chris

BLUHM, NEIL GARY
PATRON, COLLECTOR
b 1938. *Study:* Univ Ill, BBA; Northwestern Univ, JD. *Pos:* Partner, Mayer, Brown & Platt, Chicago, 1962-70; co-founder, JMB Realty Corp, 1969, pres, 1970-1972, pres trustee, JMB Realty Trust, 1972-; bd dirs, Chicago Cares Inc, Urban Shopping Ctrs Inc, 1993-2000; mng principal, Walton Street Capitol, currently; trustee, Art Inst Chicago, Northwestern Univ; pres bd trustees, Whitney Mus Am Art. *Awards:* Named one of Top 200 Collectors, ARTnews Mag, 2007-13. *Mem:* Bar State Ill; Real Estate Roundtable; Standard Club; Chicago Club; Alzheimer's Disease & Related Disorders Asn (bd mem). *Collection:* Contemporary art. *Mailing Add:* Walton Street Capital, LLC 900 N Michigan Ave, Suite 1900 Chicago IL 60611

BLUM, ANDREA
SCULPTOR
b New York, NY, Apr 6, 1950. *Study:* Univ Denver; Boston Mus Sch Fine Arts, BFA, 73; Sch Art Inst Chicago, MFA, 76. *Work:* Art Inst Chicago; AT&T, Chicago; Marina Bank, Chicago; Univ Iowa Mus Art, Iowa City; Nat Collection Fine Arts, Washington, DC. *Exhib:* Boston Mus Sch, 73; Fel Exhib, Art Inst Chicago, 76, Drawings of '70's, 77 & Works on Paper, 78; 3 Sculptors, Northern Iowa Univ Gallery Art, Cedar Falls, 79; Art from Chicago, Koffler Found Collection, Nat Collection Fine Arts, Washington, DC; Solo exhibs, Marianne Deson Gallery, Chicago, 78 & 80; Beyond Object, Aspen Ctr for Visual Arts, Colo, 80; Creative Time, NY, 81; Installation, Hudson River Mus, NY, 81; DeCordova Mus, Mass, 81; and others. *Teaching:* Vis

artist & lectr, Univ Iowa, Iowa City, 77, Kalamazoo Inst Art, Mich, 77, Univ Ill, Chicago Circle, 77, Univ Hartford, Conn, 78, Univ Northern Iowa, Cedar Falls, 79 & Univ Chicago, 79; vis artist, Art Inst Chicago, 81. *Awards:* Nat Endowment for Arts individual grants, 76 & 78. *Bibliog:* Franz Schulze (auth), Nothing but abstract, summer 76 & Kay Larson (auth), Rooms with a point of view, 10/77, Art News; C L Morrison (auth), rev in Artforum, 10/76. *Mem:* Coll Art Asn Am. *Mailing Add:* 428 Broome St New York NY 10013-3252

BLUM, ERIC
PAINTER
b Fresno, California. *Study:* Univ Calif, Los Angeles, 1976-78; Cent Saint Martin's Coll Art & Design, London, 1984-85. *Exhib:* Solo exhibs: M-13 Gallery, New York, 1989, 1990; Rule Mod, Denver, 1998; Littlejohn Contemp, New York, 1999, 2000, 2003; Marcia Wood Gallery, Atlanta, 2002, 2003, 2004; Lemmons Contemp, New York, 2005, 2007; group exhibs include Michael Kohn Gallery, Los Angeles, 1986; Arte Contemp, Madrid, Spain, 1995; Hot Wax, Cummings Art Ctr, New London, Conn, 2002; Blue, Baxter Chang Patri Fine Art, San Francisco, 2005; Rule Gallery, Denver, 2007; Lemmons Contemp, New York, 2007; Waxing Eloquent, The Rooms, St Johns, Newfoundland, Canada, 2007; Marcia Wood Gallery, Atlanta, 2008; Boltax Gallery, Shelter Island, NY, 2009; David Weinberg Gallery, Chicago, 2009. *Awards:* Pollock-Krasner Found, 1998, 2001; NY Found Arts Grant, 2008. *Dealer:* Marcia Wood Gallery 263 Walker St Atlanta Georgia 30313; Julie Baker Fine Art 246 Commercial St Nevada City CA 95959; Littlejohn Contemp 245 E 72nd Street 6E New York NY 10021; Boltax Gallery 21 North Ferry Rd Shelter Island NY 11964; Opus Art 2-4 Hoxton Square London NI 6 NU

BLUM, HELAINE DOROTHY
SCULPTOR, PAINTER
b Cleveland, Ohio. *Study:* Cleveland Art Inst; Western Reserve Univ; Art Students League; Columbia Univ. *Work:* Detroit Inst Art; Israel Mus Art, Jerusalem; Skirball Mus, Los Angeles. *Comn:* Portrait Samuel Golter, City Hope Med Ctr, Duarte, Calif, 72; portrait Marcel Marceau, Friends Marcel Marceau, Paris, 76. *Exhib:* May Show, Cleveland Mus Art, 45-60s; Am Sculpture, Metrop Mus Art, NY, 51; Max Weber Exhib, Jewish Mus, NY, 56; Jewish Art, Smithsonian Inst, 60s; Sculpture, Corcoran Mus, 65; Acad Med, NY, 68; Am Art, Calif Palace Legion Hon, 68; Sculpture, O'Hara Gallery, London, 69. *Awards:* L'Esprit, Silvermine Guild Artists, 59 & 65; Nat Coun Jewish Women Award, 67-82; Nat Asn Women Artists Award, 68. *Bibliog:* Articles, New Yorker, 60, New York Times, 66 & Art News, 71. *Mem:* Artists Equity Asn; Nat Asn Women Artists; Silvermine Guild. *Media:* Bronze. *Mailing Add:* 535 Ocean Ave Unit 7B Santa Monica CA 90402-2646

BLUM, JUNE
PAINTER, SCULPTOR
b Maspeth, NY, Dec 10, 29. *Study:* Brooklyn Coll, MA, 59; Brooklyn Mus Art Sch, with Reuben Tam & Tom Doyle, 59-67; New Sch, New York, with Laurie Goulet, 65. *Work:* Brooklyn Col, New York; Okla Art Ctr Mus; Cocoa Beach Libr, Fla; Long Island Univ, Brooklyn Campus Art Dept; Rowan Univ Art Dept, Glassboro, NJ. *Comn:* Light Environments (Time-Space), Suffolk Mus, Stony Brook, NY, 70, Okla Art Ctr Mus, Oklahoma City, 72, Hudson River Mus, Yonkers, NY, 73 & Nassau Co Mus Fine Arts, Roslyn, NY, 80. *Exhib:* Works on Paper/Women Artists (with catalog), Brooklyn Mus, 75; Sons & Others, Queens Mus, Flushing, NY, 76; solo exhibs, Paintings, Bronx Mus, NY, 76, Brevard Community Coll, Cocoa, Melbourne, Fla, 84, Soho 20 Gallery (with catalog), Chelsea, New York, 98-2005 & Brevard Mus Art & Sci, Melbourne, Fla, 98, Long Island Univ (with catalog), Brooklyn Campus, 2011; Group exhibs, The Sister Chapel, PS#1, Queens, NY, 78 & Stony Brook Univ, Stony Brook, NY, 78; The Opposite Sex, A Realistic Viewpoint (with catalog), Univ Mo, Kansas City, 79; Three Contemp Am Realists, June Blum, Audrey Flack, Alice Neel, Miami Dade Community Coll, S Campus (with catalog), 78; A Woman's Space, Nassau Co Mus Fine Arts, Roslyn, NY, 80; Art to Wear, Barbara Gillman Gallery, Miami, Fla, 81; Women's Art, Miles Apart (with catalog), Valencia Coll, Orlando, Fla & Aaron Berman Gallery (with catalog), New York, 82; Brevard Performing Arts Ctr, Melbourne, Fla, 88; Brevard Mus, Cocoa, Fla, 95; Mus Stonybrook, NY, 96; National Art Club, New York, 2003. *Collection Arranged:* The Artists Use of Paper, Watercolors, Contemp Outdoor Sculpture, 74, Suffolk Mus; Contemp Figure/New Realism, Suffolk Mus, 71; Unmanly Art (catalog), Suffolk Mus, 72; Figures of 5 (catalog), Miami Dade Community Coll, 79; Form & Figure, Western Asn Mus, 80. *Pos:* Cur contemp art, Suffolk Mus, Stony Brook, NY, 71-76; dir, Women for Art, 76-. *Awards:* Anne Eisner Putnam Mem Prize, Nat Acad, Nat Asn Women Artists, 68; Hon Mention, White Mountain Festival Arts, Jefferson, NH, 77; Medal of Honor Award, National Arts Club, New York, From Veteran Feminists in the arts, 2003. *Bibliog:* Pam Harbaugh (auth), Artists work reflects how 70's women struggled, Fla Today, 7/98; Ann Samuels (auth), Blum in bloom, Spacecoast Press, 8/98; Lyn Dowling (auth), Artist displays work on women's subject, Cocoa Beach Current, 9/98; Benita Budd (auth) June Blum, environmental images, Women Artists News, Spring 85; Womens Art Pioneer, Brooklyn Daily Eagle, 2011; Emily Bachman (auth), June Blum Pioneer in Womens Art Movement, Fort Green Clinton Hill Patch, 2011; Feminist of the Month, June Blum, Veteran Feminists Am, 2011; plus others. *Mem:* Women's Caucus for Art (nat chap); Coll Art Asn Am; Brevard Art Mus; Brevard Cult Alliance; Friends Cocoa Beach Libr (art chair); Nat Mus Women in the Arts. *Media:* Oil, Fabric. *Publ:* Auth, Metamorphosis of June Blum, 76, Betty Friedan ser, 76, Female connection, 78, A woman's space, 80, Women for Art, June Blum's Line Black & White Paintings, 2005; Women's Art, Miles Apart (catalog intro), Valencia Community Coll, Fla, 82; June Blum, Fiberarts, 3/86; June Blum Black and White Paintings, 2011; Blue Note Books, Andrew D. Hottle, 2011. *Dealer:* NN Gallery Seattle WA. *Mailing Add:* 120 Boca Ciega Rd Cocoa Beach FL 32931

BLUMBERG, RON
PAINTER
b Reading, Pa. *Study:* Nat Acad Design; Art Students League, New York; Acad Grande Chaumiere, Paris, France. *Work:* Joseph Hirshorn Mus, Washington; Los Angeles Co Mus Art, Calif; Exec Mansion, State of Calif, Sacramento; Bonita Granville; Mrs Mel Blanc. *Exhib:* Dallas Mus Fine Arts, Tex, 35-36; Los Angeles Co Mus Art, Calif, 55-58; MH DeYoung Mem Mus, San Francisco, 67; Art LA 88 & 89, Feingarten Galleries, Los Angeles, 88 & 89; Art Show, New York, 89 & 90; New York Modernism, New York, 2000, 2008, 2009; LAAS, Los Angeles, 2005, 23006, 2009, 2010. *Teaching:* Westwood Studio, 50-78. *Mem:* Calif Confederation Arts (bd dir, 80-81); Artist Economic Action (chmn). *Media:* Oil. *Dealer:* Trigg Ison Fine Art West Hollywood CA; Feingarten Gallery Los Angeles CA

BLUME, PETER F
MUSEUM DIRECTOR
b Syracuse, NY, Jun 5, 1946. *Study:* Syracuse Univ, BFA, 1967, 1973; Attingham Summer Sch, Eng, 1976; Univ Berkeley, Calif, 1986. *Collection Arranged:* Gustav Grunewald 1805-1878, Allentown Art Mus, Pa, 92; Joan Snyder: Works with Paper, Allentown Art Mus, Pa, 93; Charles Sheeler in Doylestown: Am Modernism and the Pennsylvania Tradition, Allentown Art Mus, Pa, 97; All That Jazz: Printed Fashion Silks of the 20's and 30's, Allentown Art Mus, Pa, 99; John Clem Clarke: Comforts, Near Disasters, and Pentimenti, Allentown Art Mus, Pa, 99; Honoring Tradition: Perspectives of Three Asian-Am Artists, Indira Freitas Johnson, Naoko Matsubara, Komelia Hongia Okim, Ball State Univ Mus Art, Muncie, Ind, 2004. *Pos:* Cur, Allentown (Pa) Art Mus, 1974-84, dir, 1984-2002; Ball State Univ Mus Art, Ind, 2003-. *Awards:* Rockefeller Found fel Metrop Mus Art, New York City, 1973-74. *Mem:* Mus panel Pa Coun on Arts, Harrisburg (mem, 1983-87); Rotary. *Publ:* Auth exhib catalogs; Auth, George Bellows Dawn Of Peace, Am Art Rev, fall 93. *Mailing Add:* Ball State Univ Mus Art 2000 W University Ave Muncie IN 47306

BLUMENTHAL, ARTHUR R
MUSEUM DIRECTOR EMERITUS, CONSULTANT
b Cleveland, Ohio, May 25, 1942. *Study:* Kent State Univ, BS (art educ), 64; Inst Fine Arts, NY Univ, MA (art hist), 66, PhD (fine arts), 84; Mus Training Cert, Metrop Mus, 68; Travel grant, Am Coun Learned Socs, 79; Mus Mgt Prog, Univ Colo, Boulder, 94; Rollins Coll, Prog for Effective Leadership, 2000. *Exhib:* Cubist Prints, Collection Dr Abraham Melamed (auth, catalog), Elvehjem Art Ctr, Univ Wis 72; Portraits at Dartmouth, Dartmouth Coll, 78; Theater Art of the Medici (auth, catalog), Dartmouth Coll, 80; Treasures of Cornell Fine Arts Mus (auth, catalog), 93; Italian Renaissance & Baroque Paintings in Fla Mus (auth, catalog), Cornell Fine Arts Mus, 91; Degas to Delaunay: Masterworks from Robert & Maurine Rothschild Family Collection (auth, catalog), Cornell Fine Arts Mus, 99; Cosimo Rosselli: Painter of the Sistine Chapel (auth, catalog), Cornell Fine Arts Mus, 2001; Honoré Daumier! Paintings, Sculpture, & Prints from the UCLA Hammer Mus, 2003; Director's Choice: European Art 1345-1901, Cornell Fine Arts Mus, 2006; The Art of Francesco de Mura: In the Light of Naples (auth, catalog), Cornell Fine Arts Mus, 2015. *Pos:* Cur, Elvehjem Mus Art, Univ Madison, Wis, 68-74; cur art, Hood Mus, Dartmouth Coll, 76-82; dir, The Art Gallery, Univ Md, 82-84 & Cornell Fine Arts Mus (dir, 88-2007, emeritus, 2007-); Rollins Coll; art mus consult, Loving Art Partnerships, Winter Park, Fla, 2006-; guest curator, Cornell Fine Arts Mus, Rollins Coll, 2013. *Teaching:* Assoc prof mus studies, Rollins Coll, Winter Park, Fla, 91-94; instr, How to Look at Art, Vero Beach Mus, Vero Beach, Fla, 2009-. *Awards:* Ford Found Fel, 65-67; Spec Proj Grant, Eng Speaking Union-Cent Fla br, 91; Best Art Mus Dir in Cent Fla, The Orlando Weekly, 99, 2002 & 2006; Fla Art Mus Directors Asn Lifetime Achievement Award, 2006-2007; Petters Int Initiative Award, Rollins Coll, 2006. *Mem:* Coll Art Asn; Am Asn Mus; Fla Art Mus Dir Asn; Fla Asn Mus; Int Coun Mus. *Specialty:* Italian Renaissance & Baroque theater; contemporary American art; Francesco de Mura. *Interests:* Collecting; Reading; Travel; Acting. *Publ:* Auth, Italian Renaissance Festival Designs, Univ Wis Press, 73; Theater Art of the Medici, Univ Press of New England, 80; Theater Designs in the Collection of Cooper-Hewitt Mus, Smithsonian Press, Washington, DC, 86; Giulio Parigi's Stage Designs: Florence and The Early Baroque Spectacle, Garland, NY, 86; articles In: The Dictionary of Art, London, 96; Cosimo Rosselli: Painter of the Sistine Chapel, Cornell Fine Arts Mus, Rollins Coll, Winter Park, Fla, 2001. *Mailing Add:* Loving Art Partnerships 1740 Bryan Ave Winter Park FL 32789-3957

BLUMRICH, STEPHEN
DESIGNER
b Gotha, Ger, June 9, 1941; US citizen. *Study:* Kunstgewerbeschule Dept Fabric Design, BFA, 58. *Work:* Nat Collection Fine Arts; Opryland Hotel, Nashville, Tenn; White House Christmas Ornament Collection, 2001. *Comn:* S Cent Bell, Nashville, Tenn. *Exhib:* Ann Southern Tier Art Show, Corning Mus Glass, NY, 70-74; Lake Superior Int Craft Exhib, Tweed Art Mus, Duluth, Minn, 74; The New Fabric Surface, Renwick Gallery, 78; Surface Design Invitational, Purdue Univ, West Lafayette, Ind, 78; Games & Crafts, Philadelphia Art Alliance, 79; Show Biz, Fashion Inst Technol, NY, 80; Opening Exhib, Greenwood Gallery, 80. *Pos:* Ed, Surface Design J, 76-88; designer, Pea Ridge Purties, 84-2002. *Awards:* Craft/Art S, Thomson, Ga, 81; Golden Isles Art Festival, St Simons Island, Ga, 81. *Bibliog:* Dona Z Meilach (auth), The Great Batik Revival, Sphere Mag, 73; Mike O'Brien (auth), A special craftsman, Regist Guard, Eugene, Ore, 75. *Mem:* Surface Design Asn. *Media:* Fabrics, Quilts

BLUNK, JOYCE ELAINE
ASSEMBLAGE ARTIST, PAINTER
b Moorland, Iowa, May 13, 1939. *Study:* Univ Iowa, with Stuart Eddy, Hans Breeder & Byron Burford, BA, 63, MA, 70, MFA, 71. *Work:* Kebbel Villa, Oberpfalzer Kunstlerhaus, Schwandorf, Ger; Harvey Littleton Printmaking Studios, Spruce Pine, NC; Allan Stone pvt collection, NY; Univ Iowa Sch Art & Art Hist; W Carolina Univ Fine Art Mus, Cullowhee, NC; Blanden Mus Art, Fort Dodge, Iowa. *Exhib:* Group Exhibs: Two Artist Invitational, Oberpfalzer Kunstlerhaus, Schwandorf, Ger, 90,

Southeastern Juried Triennial, Fine Art Mus S, Mobile, Ala, 93, Exhib 280: Works Off Walls, Huntington Mus Art, WVa, 93, Artists in Residence, Chateau de la Napoule Found, France, 94, Nat Juried Exhib, Muse Gallery, Found Visual Arts, Philadelphia, Pa, 96, Nat Indoor & Outdoor Sculpture Show, Hoyt Inst Fine Arts, New Castle, Pa, 98, William King Regional Art Ctr, Abingdon, Va, 99, Border Biennial, Mus York Co, Rock Hill, SC, 2000, Herndon Gallery, Antioch Coll, Yellow Springs, Ohio, 2001, Tryon Ctr for Visual Art, Spirit Sq Galleries, Charlotte, NC, 2002, The Hunter Mus Am Art, Chattanooga, Tenn, 2002, Fayetteville Mus Art, NC, 2004, 88 Greenwich St Gallery, Nat Asn Women Artists, Ann Exhib, New York, 2004, Inaugural Exhib, Fine & Performing Arts Center, Western Carolina Univ, Cullowhee, NC, 2005, Goggle Works Center for the Arts, Reading, Pa, 2006 & Black Mt Ctr Arts, Black Mt, NC, 2007; Kunst and Gewerbeverein, Regensburg, Ger, 2008; Foundry Arts Ctr, St Charles, Mo, 2009, 30th Mini Print Int Cadaques, traveling to Cadaques, Spain, England, France, 2010-2011, Univ North Carolina, Asheville, 2010, Breverd Coll, NC, 2011; Solo Exhibs: Mint Mus Art, Charlotte, NC, 91, Kimura Gallery, Univ Alaska, Anchorage, 99, Black Mountain Ctr for the Arts, NC, 2002 & 2009, The Cecilia Coker Bell Gallery, Coker Coll, Hartsville, SC, 2002, Lipscomb Gallery, SC Gov's Sch for Arts & Humanities, Greenville, 2004, Artspace Gallery One, Raleigh, NC, 2004, Santa Fe Gallery, Santa Fe Coll, Gainesville, Fla, 2005 & Rockford Coll Art Gallery, Rockford, Ill, 2007, M.E. Blowers Gallery, Univ NC, Asheville, NC, 2008, Blanden Mus Art, Fort Dodge, Iowa, 2011-2012, Raleigh Fine Arts Soc, NC Artists Exhib, Raleigh, NC, 2013. *Teaching:* Artist-in-residence, W Carolina Univ, Cullowhee, NC, 97; artist-teacher visual art, Vt Coll, Norwich Univ, Montpelier, Vt, 97-2000; artist, teacher, Vt Coll Fine Art, Montpelier Univ, 2011-2012. *Awards:* Pollock-Krasner Found Grant, 91-92; NC Arts Coun & Nat Endowment Arts Residence Fel, La Napoule, France, 94; NC Arts Coun Visual Artist Fel, 96-97; Fel Residency, Va Ctr Creative Arts, Stadt Salzburg, Austria, 99; Fel Residency, Cill Rialaig Int Artists' Retreat, Ballinskelligs, Ireland, 2003, 2008, 2014; Fel Residency, Nota Bene Loft Studio, Cadaqués, Spain, 2005; Fel Residency, No Boundaries Int Artist Colony, Bald Head Island, NC, 2006; Fel Residency, Va Ctr Creative Arts, Stadt Salzburg, Austria, 2012; Gottlieb Found Individual Support Grant, 2015. *Bibliog:* Tom Klobe (auth), The Third Int Shoebox Sculpture Exhib (catalog), Coun Cult Planning & Develop, 88; Mark Richard Leach (auth), Art Currents Six Material Redemptions (exhib catalog), Mint Mus Art, 91; Anne Forcinito & Jeff Petus (auths), NC Arts Coun Visual Artist Fel Traveling Exhib (catalog), Mint Mus Art, 97; Margaret A. Skove (auth), Joyce Blunk Painting and Assemblage (exhib catalog), Blandeau Mus Art, Fort Dodge, Iowa, 2011. *Mem:* Int Sculpture Ctr; Nat Asn Women Artists. *Media:* Mixed Media; Acrylic & Oil. *Mailing Add:* 31 Samayoa Pl Asheville NC 28806

BOARDMAN, DEBORAH
PAINTER, CONCEPTUAL ARTIST
b Salem, Mass, 1958. *Study:* Mt Holyoke Col, BA, 80; studied with Atelier Lucio Loubet, Paris, 81; Mass Coll Art, BFA, 84; Tufts Univ, Sch Mus Fine Arts, MFA, 87. *Work:* Artist Book Collection, Mus Mod Art Libr, NY; Artist Book Collection, Mus Contemp Art, Chicago; Ryerson & Burnham Libr, Art Inst Chicago; Joan Flasch Artists' Book Collection, SAIC; Wing Collection, Newberry Libr, Chicago; Houghton Libr, Harvard Univ, Cambridge, Mass; Rare Books Collection, Waldo Libr, W Mich Univ; Rare Books Collection, Boston Public Libr; Chicago Cultural Ctr. *Exhib:* Solo exhibs, Good Luck (Lame Horse), Armstrong Gallery, Cornell Coll, Mt Vernon, Iowa, Stations of Mary, Gallery Eleven, Tufts Univ, Medford, Mass, 87, Mobius Performance Space, Boston, 88, Crane Gallery, Chicago, 89, Memento Mori, McAuley Gallery, Mt Mercy Col, Cedar Rapids, Iowa, 92 & Mutual Borders, Community United Methodist Church, Chicago, 94; NAME, The Enunciation (Or What the Oxen Said), Set Design, Waldorf Auditorium Theater, Chicago, 95; The Initiation, Set Design, Chicago, 95; Paper in Particular, Columbia Col, Mo, 96; Mary Mary, Quite Contrary, Women Made Gallery, Chicago, 96; Installation, Prairie Ave Gallery, Chicago, 97; Illumination, Ornamentation, Collaboration Decoration with Jeff Hillard, Prairie Ave Gallery, Chicago, 97; Domestic Taboo, Suburban Fine Arts Ctr, Highland Park, Ill, 98; Death, Dreams & Heraldry, Chicago Cult Ctr, 99; Fla Women Artists: The New Millennium, Taipei Fine Arts Mus, 1999; Out of Line: Drawings by Ill Artists, Chicago Cult Ctr; Picturing Death Project, McLean Co Arts Ctr, Bloomington, Ill, 2001; Deborah Boardman, Jan Cicero Gallery Project Space, Chicago, 2002; Remembrance, Evanston Art Ctr, Ill, 2003; Figures of Invention, The Work Space, NY, 2003; Deborah Boardman, Richard Rezac, Amy Vogel, Track House, Oak Park, Ill, 2004; New Work in Gilles, Werewolves & Other Dilemmas, Gescheidle Gallery, Chicago, 2005; 2nd Int Biennial for the Artist's Book, Bibliotheca Alexandrina, Egypt, 2006. *Pos:* Educ comt, NAME Gallery, Chicago, Ill, 91-93. *Teaching:* Vis painting, Univ Iowa, 88-89, asst prof 89-95; vis artist, Moorhead State Univ, Minn, 91; instr, School Art Inst Chicago, 97-; vis artist, Univ Southern Ind, 99. *Awards:* Ill Arts Coun Access Prog; Chicago Artists Int Prog Grant, City Chicago Dept Cult Affairs, 94; Regional Arts Projs Grant, 93; Visual Artists Fel, Ill Arts Coun, 2001. *Bibliog:* Eliot Nusbau (auth), Des Moines Register, 1/28/90; Elisabeth Condon (auth), The Mussell Secretes the Shell Which Shapes It, New Art Examiner, 9/90; Elisabeth Condon (auth), Communion, New Art Examiner, 3/94. *Media:* Painting, Artist Books, Installation. *Publ:* Memory & Influence (limited ed booklet); Mutual Borders (limited ed booklet), 94; Picturing Death (limited ed), 2000. *Mailing Add:* 1436 W Highland Ave Chicago IL 60660

BOARDMAN, SEYMOUR
PAINTER
b Brooklyn, NY, Dec 29, 1921. *Study:* City Coll New York, BSS, 42; Art Students League; Ecole Beaux Arts, Paris, France; Acad Grande Chaumiere, Paris; Atelier Fernand Leger, Paris, 46-52. *Work:* Whitney Mus Am Art, Guggenheim Mus & NY Univ; Walker Art Ctr, Minneapolis, Minn; Santa Barbara Mus Art; plus others. *Exhib:* Solo exhibs, Galerie Mai, Paris, 51, Martha Jackson Gallery, NY, 55 & 56 & Stephen Radich Gallery, NY, 60-61: & Dorsky Gallery, NY, 72; Whitney Mus Am Art, 55, 61 & 67; Kunsthalle, Basel, Switz, 64; Albright-Knox Gallery, Buffalo, NY, 67; Andrew Dickson White Mus of Art, Cornell Univ, 71; Anita Shapolsky Gallery, NY, 86; Anderson Gallery, Buffalo, NY, 94; and others. *Collection Arranged:* Whitney Mus, Guggenheim Mus, Santa Barbara Mus Art, Calif, Walker Art Ctr, Minn. *Teaching:* Instr painting & drawing, Wagner Col, Staten Island, NY, 57-58. *Awards:* Longview Found Award, 63; Guggenheim Fel, 72; Gottlieb Found Award, 79 & 83; Krasner-Pollock Found Award, 85, 91 & 98, 2001, 2003. *Bibliog:* Arts Digest, 4/55; Art News, 3/68; Arts, 1/80 & 3/92. *Media:* Acrylic, Oil. *Specialty:* Abstract Art. *Dealer:* Anita Shapolsky Gallery NY

BOB, DADDY-O See Wade, Robert Schrope

BOB & BOB
PERFORMANCE ARTISTS
b Santa Monica, Calif, May 8, 53 (F Shishim); b Detroit, Mich, Feb 8, 52 (P Velick). *Study:* (P Velick), Art Ctr Coll, Antioch Coll, BFA, 75; (F Shishim), Art Ctr Coll, BFA, 75; (Bob & Bob), studies with Tom Wudl, Llyn Foulkes & Lorser Feitelson. *Work:* Ace Gallery, Toronto, Can. *Exhib:* Sex is Stupid, Los Angeles Inst Contemp Art, 79; Nature Is Perfect, Animals Are Perfect, What Are Humans?, Washington Hall Performance Gallery, Seattle, 80; Bob to Bob, Marianne Deson Gallery, Chicago, 82; We're All Lucky, Mus Contemp Art, Los Angeles, Calif, 85; retrospective (with catalog), Otis/Parson, 86; Philadelphia Mus Art, Pa, 98; Los Angeles 1955-1985: Birth of an Art Capitol, Pompidou Ctr, Paris, France, 2006. *Teaching:* Otis/Parson, Art Ctr Coll Design. *Awards:* Golden Turkey Award, Young Turks, DTLA Admin. *Bibliog:* Alyson Pov (auth), Across America, Art Papers, 1/81 & Retrospective rev, Los Angeles Times, 86; California Stories, KCET PBS-TV, Los Angeles. *Mem:* The Young Turks, Los Angeles. *Publ:* Contribr, High Performance/Public Spirit, Astro Arts, 79; Performance Anthology, Carl Loeffler, 80; Across America (record), MITB Records, Beverly Hills, 81; The Least I Can Do (record), MITB Records, Beverly Hills, 82; We Know You're Alone (record), Polydor Records, 83; Linda Montano (ed), Performance Artists Talking, Univ Calif Press, Berkeley, 2001; and many other forms of technological reproduction. *Mailing Add:* PO Box 6461 Beverly Hills CA 90212

BOBICK, J BRUCE
EDUCATOR, PAINTER
b Clymer, Pa, Oct 25, 1941. *Study:* Indiana Univ Pa, BS, 63, MS, 67; Univ Notre Dame, MFA, 68. *Work:* Mt Mercy Col, Cedar Rapids, Iowa; Western Ill Univ, Macomb; Springfield Art Mus, Mo; Ill State Mus, Springfield; Krannert Art Mus, Univ Ill, Champaign-Urbana. *Comn:* Stainless-steel kinetic sculptures, Carrollton Parks, Recreation & Cult Arts Dept, 88, Pinnacle Insurance Co, Carrollton, Ga, 89; wall-hung quilt, Omni Int Hotel, St Louis, Mo; two paintings for use as bedspread designs, All Star Sports & All Star Music; Disney World, Orlando, Fla, 92; oil painting, Ga Sports Hall Fame, Macon, Ga, 99. *Exhib:* Watercolor, USA Springfield Art Mus, Mo, 68-70,73, 75, 77, 89-90 & 93; Nat Watercolor Soc, Oakland Art Mus, Calif, 70, Otis Arts Inst, Los Angeles, Calif, 73, Palm Springs Art Mus, 73, Calif State Univ, Northridge, Calif, 77, Laguna Beach Mus Art, Calif, 69, 71-72, 79, Muckenthaler Cult Ctr, Fullerton, Calif, 2004, Brand Art Galleries, 2004; Nat Exhib Watercolor Soc of Ala, Birmingham Mus Art, 69-82; 164th Ann Am Watercolors, Prints & Drawings, Pa Acad Fine Arts, Philadelphia, 69; Nat Acad Design Galleries, NY, 70, 71; 17th Hunter Ann Exhib Paintings & Drawings, Hunter Mus Art, Chattanooga, Tenn, 78; Ga Mus Art, 89, Mus Art, Columbus, 91; Watercolor Now Fourth Biennial, Salt Lake City Art Ctr, Utah, 93-94; Albany Mus Art, 94; Watercolor Now Fifth Biennial, Knoxville Mus Art, Tenn, 95; From the Avant-Garde to the Present Day, Artists Union Exhib Gallery, St Petersburg, Russ, 96; Southern Quilts: A New View, Mus Am Quilters Soc, Paducah, KY, Huntsville Mus Art, Huntsville, AL, 90, 92. *Pos:* artist-in-residence High Mus of Art, Atlanta, Ga, 2000; Univ Pittsburgh, Semester-at-Sea, 2003; Natl Watercolor Society, Los Angeles, CA, 72, 73. *Teaching:* Assoc prof art, Western Ill Univ, 68-76; from assoc prof to prof & chmn dept art, WGa Col, 76-; vis prof painting, Univ Ga Studies Abroad, Cortona, Italy, 80; vis prof painting, Arrowmont Sch Arts & Crafts, Gatlinburg, Tenn, 84, 85, 86, 87, 88, 95 & 98, Guangxi Teachers Univ, Guilin, Peoples Repub China, 93; prof, chmn dept art State Univ of W Ga. *Awards:* Purchase Award, Ill State Mus, 71, Watercolor USA, 71 & 75; Ga Watercolor Soc Award, 82, 86, 91 & 93. *Bibliog:* Dorothy M Joiner (auth), Bruce Bobick: Images upon the subconscious, Art Papers, 1/85; Laura Stewart Dishman (auth), A patchwork of memory, imagination, Orlando Sentinel, 2/20/86; Carlotta M Eike (auth), Artifacts from imaginary culture explore archeological implications, Mus News, 11/88. *Mem:* Nat Watercolor Soc, Watercolor USA Honor Soc; Pittsburgh Watercolor Soc; Ga Watercolor Soc; Ala Watercolor Soc. *Media:* Watercolor. *Res:* Communication between artist and viewer. *Publ:* Auth, Images upon the subconscious, The Flying Needle, 5/86; Markings: Aerial Views of Sacred Landscapes (book review), Vol V, Visual Resources, 89; auth, Professional Practices Committee Re-examines MFA Standards, CAA News, vol 27, No 6, 11/2/2002. *Dealer:* Dorothy Moye & Associates, 866 E Ponce de Leon Ave Decatur GA 30030. *Mailing Add:* State Univ of W Georgia Dept of Art Carrollton GA 30118

BOBINS, NORMAN R
PATRON
Study: Univ Wis, BS, 64; Univ Chgo, MBA, 67. *Pos:* Sr vpres Am Nat Bank and Trust Co, 67-81; sr exec vpres, chief lending officer, Exchange Nat Bank Chicago, 81-90; chmn, pres & ceo, LaSalle Nat Bank, Chicago, 90-; pres & ceo, LaSalle Bank Corp; sr exec vpres, ABN AMRO Bank, NV, Neth; vchmn, Standard Federal Bank, NA, bd dirs; bd trustees, Chicago Community Trust, Field Mus, Art Inst Chicago, Univ Chicago Hospitals; bd dirs, Terra Found Art; exec bd, Auditorium Theatre Coun, Chicago; treas, bd dirs, Financial Services Roundtable, Washington; chmn bd, Chicagoland CofC, formerly; mem, Bd Educ Chicago, 94-. *Awards:* Human Rights Medallion, Am Jewish Comt, 92; Kreshet Rainbow Award, 97; Reach for Excellence Award, Midtown Educational Found, 98; Business Leadership Award, DePaul Univ, 99; Jane Addams Hull House Medal, 2000; Chairman's Award, Boys & Girls Club, 2002; Lifetime Achievement Award, Asn Corp Growth, 2003; Richard J Daley Medal, 2005

BOBROWICZ, YVONNE PACANOVSKY
INSTRUCTOR, WEAVER
b Maplewood, NJ, Feb 17, 1928. *Study:* Cranbrook Acad Art; study with Anni Albers; with Paolo Soleri at Haystack Mountain. *Work:* Philadelphia Mus Art, 90; Chicago Art Inst 20th Century Collection, 92; Racine Mus Art Textile Collection, 2012. *Comn:* Woven wall, comn by Louis I Kahn, Kimball Mus, Ft Worth Tex, 72; woven wall hanging, Savings & Loan Bank, Pittsburgh, Pa, 77; Dupont Corp, Wilmington, Del, 85; Woodcock & Washburn, CIRA Bldg Phila, Pa, 2007; Berwind Corp, Phila, Pa, 2010. *Exhib:* Walker Art Ctr, Minneapolis, Minn, 53; Mus Contemp Crafts, NY, 60; Philadelphia Mus Art, 63 & 300 yrs of Philadelphia Art, 76; Civic Ctr Mus Philadelphia, 67-73; Univ Pa Mus, Philadelphia, 75; Lousanne 14th Biennial of Tapestry, 89; group show, Tilburg Textile Mus, The Neth, 89; and others. *Teaching:* Lectr textiles & weaving, Drexel Univ, Philadelphia, 66-97; instr weaving, Peters Valley, Leyton NY, summers 72, 76, 79, & 2003. *Awards:* First Prize, Los Angeles Co Fair, 51; Grant for Excellence in Fiber Art, Leeway Found, 97. *Mem:* Am Craft Coun; World Craft Coun; Philadelphia Guild Handweavers. *Media:* Thread, fiber or metal. *Publ:* Contribr, Rugmaking, Golden Bks, 72; contribr, Hooked and Rya Rugs, Van Nostrand Reinhold, 74; contribr, Am Rugs and Carpets, William Morrow, 78. *Dealer:* Helen Drutt 1625 Spruce St Philadelphia PA 19103; Snyderman-Works Galleries 303 Cherry St Philadelphia Pa 19106. *Mailing Add:* 2312 Spruce St Philadelphia PA 19103

BOCCHINO, SERENA MARIA
PAINTER, EDUCATOR
b Englewood, NJ, Mar 22, 1965. *Study:* Wroxton Coll, Oxfordshire, England, Humanities, 80; Fairleigh Dickinson Univ, Hon Coll, BA, Teaneck, NJ, 82; New York Univ, MA, 85; Fairleigh Dickinson Univ, Post Grad Art, Sabbatical, Russia, 82. *Work:* Springfield Art Mus, Ohio; Morris Mus, NJ; Zimmerli Art Mus, NJ; Montclair Art Mus, NJ; Trenton State Mus, NJ. *Comn:* mural, Jersey City Medical Ctr, NJ, 2002; installation, Somerset Co Cult & Heritage Commission, 2010. *Exhib:* Solo exhibs, Bergen Mus Art & Sci, Paramus, NJ, 75, Dela Ctr Contemp Art, Dela, 2003, Morris Mus, NJ, 2003; group exhibs, Drawing Exhib, Lyman Allen Mus, Conn, 92; Zoo Extracts, islip Art Mus, NY, 98; Brodsky Ctr Prints, Jersey City Mus, NJ, 2002. *Pos:* Studio assist drawing, Raritan Valley Coll, NJ, 2005-; prof develop provider painter, NJ Dept Educ, Trenton, NJ, 2005-2008; expert art & aging, Rutgers Univ, NJ, 2010. *Awards:* PS1 Studio Residency, PS1 Int Studio Prog, Pvt & State of NY, 87; Artists Grant, Artist support grant for exhib, Artists Space, New York, 89; Artist Fel, NJ State Coun Arts, 90, 2002; Pollock-Krasner Grant, Pollock-Krasner Found, 91; Residency, Brodsky Ctr, Pvt & Rutgers Univ, 2002. *Bibliog:* Yvette Pineyro (auth), Observer Highway, Wildchild, 94; Yvette Pineyro (auth), Rhythms, Wildchild, 96; Monica Sharf (auth), Observer Highway Revisited, Inversion Films, 2000; Greg Smith (auth), Blue, Down the Line Produc, 2007; Greg Smith (auth), Pop, Down the Line Prod, 2009. *Mem:* CUE Art Found; Marie Walsh Sharpe Art Found; Mus Mod Art; Coll Art Asn; Lucia Bocchino Fund for Promising Young Artists (exec dir, 2007-). *Media:* Oil, Enamel Paint. *Publ:* Art, M/E/A/N/I/N/G, Bee & Schorr, 94, 95; auth & illustr, What Am I? The Story of an Abstract Painting, His Perfect Time, 2005. *Dealer:* Tria Gallery 531 West 25th St Ground Floor #5 New York NY 10001; James Bacchi Arthaus 411 Brannon St San Francisco CA 94107; Simon Gallery 48 Bank St Morristown NJ 07960

BOCCIA, EDWARD EUGENE
PAINTER, WRITER
b Newark, NJ, June 22, 1921. *Study:* Pratt Inst Art Sch, New York; Art Students League; Columbia Univ, BS & MA. *Work:* Univ Mass; St Louis Univ; State Hist Soc Mo; Mus Art, Ft Lauderdale, Fla; Nat Picture Gallery, Athens, Greece; Steinberg Gallery Art, Washington Univ, St Louis. *Comn:* Stained glass, Clayton Inn, Mo; four wall paintings, First Nat Bank, St Louis; mural, Stations of the Cross & stained glass windows, Newman Chapel, Washington Univ, St Louis; religious drawings & 14 mural paintings, Temple Brith Sholom Kneseth Israel, St Louis; and others. *Exhib:* Gallery of the Masters, 90 & 92, St Louis, Mo; Am Gallery, 92; Pompeii Gallery, 95; Parkland Coll Art Gallery, Champaign, Ill; Retrospective exhib, St Louis Univ, 96; Fontbonne Coll, 98; Fac Exhib, Steinberg Gallery, Wash Univ, St Louis, 98; Borders Books, Philadelphia, 99; Atelier A-E Gallery, New York, 99; St Louis Gallery, Mocra, 99; solo exhibs, Sheldon Concert Hall, Bellweather Gallery, St Louis, 99, St Bonaventure Univ, New York, 2000, Monday Club, St Louis, 2003 & Creative Art Gallery, St Louis, 2007; Concordia Lutheran Church Art Exhib, 2003; McCaughen & Burr Gallery, St Louis, Mo, 2005-2006; AJ Brewington Gallery, St Louis, 2011; and others. *Teaching:* Dean, Columbus Art Sch, Ohio, 48-51; guest instr, Univ Sask, summer 60, Webster Groves Coll, summer 65 & Univ Minn, 86; prof emer fine arts, Washington Univ, St Louis, Mo, 51-86; var lectures, St Louis, 2007. *Awards:* Bronze Medal, Temple Israel, St Louis, 62; Knighted to Cavaliere, Pres Ital Repub, 79; Order of the Crown of King St Louis IX of France, St Louis Univ, 90. *Bibliog:* An Artist Who's Gone His Own Way, St Louis Post Dispatch, 85; Who's Who: Artist Edward Boccia, Dan's Papers Inc, Bridgehampton, NY, 92; Renaissance Man Edward Boccia, St Louis Post Dispatch, 96; Interview with the Artist, Webster-Kirkwod Times, 9/2005; Color theory, St Louis Mag at Home, 5-6/2007. *Mem:* Nat Soc Arts & Letters, St Louis Poetry Ctr; St Louis Poetry Center; St Louis Writers Guild. *Media:* Painter - Oil. *Publ:* Contribr, Writers Challenge Voyages, 99; Missouri State Poetry Anthology, 99; Memories and Memoirs, Anthology of Missouri Poets, 2000; Flash Point, 2001; The Magic Fish, Pudding House Press, 2002; auth, Answering Neruda (poetry), Pudding House Press, 2006; The Light of City and Sea (anthology), Suffolk Co Press, NY, 2006; Long Island Sounds (anthology), N Sea Poetry Scene Press, NY, 2006; Gems from the Past, Mo State Poetry Soc, 2006; Poetry J, Margie Mag, 2007. *Dealer:* McCaughen & Burr St Louis MO; A J Brewington St Louis Mo. *Mailing Add:* 600 Harper Ave Webster Groves MO 63119

BOCK, WILLIAM SAUTS-NETAMUX'WE
ILLUSTRATOR, PAINTER
b Sellersville, Pa, Sept 18, 1939. *Study:* Philadelphia Coll of Art, BFA (illus), spec study with Robert Riggs; Lutheran Sem, Philadelphia, MA. *Work:* US State Dept. *Comn:* Watercolor series of Am cities, comn by Marriott Corp for reproduction in many cities, 3-dimensional art (Indian Mex) & murals, Marriott Camelback Inn, Phoenix, Ariz, 69-70; watercolor for Christmas card, Book of the Month Club, NY, 71 & 74; Olympic designs for Plexiglas etching, McDonalds, Willow Grove, Pa, 75. *Awards:* Honored by Exhib for Illustrations for Crusader King, Am Inst of Graphic Arts, New York, 74; Monthly Choice Award for Illustrations for Malcolm Yucca Seed, Philadelphia Children's Reading Round Table, 78. *Bibliog:* Mr & Mrs Philip Berman (interview), Berman Collection, Pub TV, Allentown, Pa, 69; B A Bergman (auth), The First Aristocrats, Sunday Bulletin, Philadelphia, 2/75; Gerry Wallerstein (auth), William Sauts-Netamux'we Bock, Wolf-Clan Chief of the Lenape, Bucks Co Panorama Mag, 1/76. *Mem:* Philadelphia Children's Reading Round Table. *Media:* Pen & Ink; Watercolor, Acrylic. *Publ:* Illusr, Wolf Hunt, Little Brown, 70; illusr & auth, Coloring Book of the First Americans, Lenape Indian Drawings, Middle Atlantic Press, 74; illusr, Tom Sawyer, Field Enterprises, World Bk, 75; Of Whales & Wolves, Lothrop, Lee, 78; White Fang (film strip), Spoken Arts, 78. *Mailing Add:* 252 E Summit St Souderton PA 18964-1341

BODEM, DENNIS RICHARD
CONSULTANT
b Milwaukee, Wis, July 27, 1937. *Study:* Wabash Col, BA, 59; Grad Sch, Univ Wis-Madison, 59-61. *Pos:* Asst archivist, State Hist Soc Wis, 61-64; chief resources div, Buffalo & Erie Co Hist Soc, NY, 64-66; state archivist, Div Mich Hist, Dept State, 66-72, cur, State Mus, 72-74; cur, Mann House, Concord, Mich, 74; dir, Jesse Besser Mus, 74-98; State Bd Very Spec Arts, Mich, 92-93; with Points North Rsch. *Mem:* Thunder Bay Arts Coun; Mich Coun Arts; Mich Mus Asn; Mich Asn Community Arts Agency; Am Records Mgt Asn; Soc Am Archivists. *Interests:* Representative works of outstanding US, Midwest and Michigan artists of the late 19th and 20th centuries for museum collection. *Publ:* Nine articles, three signed reviews and one booknote in professional journals; numerous articles and notes in newspaper. *Mailing Add:* 121 E White Alpena MI 49707

BODENMANN, HANS U
COLLECTOR
Pos: inventor and investor. *Awards:* Named one of Top 200 Collectors, ARTnews mag, 2009-13. *Collection:* Contemporary art

BODIN, KATE
EDUCATOR
Study: Boston Univ, BFA; Arts & learning, Endicott Col, Med. *Pos:* Dean of fac, Montserrat Col of Art, Beverly, Mass, 92-; Chairperson Gloucester Committee for Arts (mayoral appointment). *Mailing Add:* Montserrat College of Art 23 Essex St Beverly MA 01915

BODINE, WILLIAM B, JR
MUSEUM DIRECTOR
b New Brunswick, NJ, Sept 30, 1948. *Study:* Univ Va, BA, 1970. *Pos:* Prog Adminstr, Nat Endowment for Arts, Washington, 1974-1980; develop office mgr, Mus Fine Arts, Boston, 1980-83; Asst dir, Corcoran Gallery of Art, Washington, 1983-1992; assoc dir, High Mus Art, Atlanta, 1992-94; chief cur, Columbia Mus Art, SC, 1994-2002; dir, Frick Art & Hist Ctr, Pittsburgh, 2002-. *Mem:* Am Asn Mus, Asn Art Mus Dir. *Mailing Add:* Frick Art and Historical Center 7227 Reynolds St Pittsburgh PA 15208

BODNAR, PETER
PAINTER, EDUCATOR
b Andrejova, Czech, Nov 27, 1928; US citizen. *Study:* Flint Inst Arts, Mich, 41-44; Western Mich Univ, BS, 51; Mich State Univ, MA, 56. *Work:* Dallas Mus; Isaac Delgado Mus, New Orleans; Ft Worth Art Mus; Lakeview Ctr Arts, Peoria, Ill; State of Ill Ctr, Chicago. *Exhib:* Solo retrospectives, Isaac Delgado Mus, 66, Ill Art Coun Galleries, Chicago, 71, Newport Harbor Art Mus, Newport Beach, Calif, 74, Ill State Mus, Springfield, 77, Danforth Mus, Framingham, Mass, 93 & Aaron Galleries, Chicago, 96; Spirit of the Comics, Inst Contemp Art, Univ Pa, 69; Solo exhibs, Lakeview Ctr Arts, Peoria, 72 & Univ Ill, 82. *Pos:* Vis artist, Bradley Univ, spring 70, Univ Southern Calif, 74 & Univ NMex, 83; vis artist, Southern Methodist Univ, Dallas, 72 & 81, artist-in-residence, summer workshop, Taos, NMex, 72. *Teaching:* Asst prof art, State Univ NY, Col Plattsburgh, 56-58 & Univ Fla, 60-62; prof painting, Univ Ill, Urbana-Champaign, 62-92. *Awards:* Tamarind Lithography Workshop Inc Grant, 64; Univ Ill Fel, Ctr Advan Study, 67-68; Nat Endowment Arts Fel, 75-. *Bibliog:* Hiram Williams (auth), Notes for a Young Painter, Prentice-Hall, 65; Franz Schulze (auth), article, Art Int, summer 67; Peter Frank (auth), Peter Bodnar, Mauretania Inc, 92. *Media:* Oil, Acrylic. *Publ:* Contribr, Strung Out with Elgar on a Hill, 70; Portrait: Converse, 75. *Dealer:* Aaron Gallery Chicago. *Mailing Add:* 2504 E Perkins Rd Urbana IL 61801

BODYCOMB, ROSALYN
PAINTER
b Honolulu, Hawaii, 1958. *Study:* Tex Christian Univ, Ft Worth, BFA (printmaking), 1984, MFA (painting), 1989. *Work:* Dallas Mus Art; var pvt collections. *Exhib:* 500X Gallery, Dallas, 1994-95; Arts Coun Exhib, Ft Worth, 1996; Juried Exhib, Alternative Mus, New York, 1997; Introduction 2000, Mulcahy Mod, Dallas, 1999; Upstate Art, Phoenicia, NY, 2000; Habeas Corpus, Univ Dallas, Irving, 2001; Meanwhile, Arlington Mus Art, Tex, 2003; Texas Biennial, Gallery Lombardi, Austin, 2005; Peopled People, Nohra Haime Gallery, New York, 2008. *Awards:* Joan Mitchell Found Grant, 2005; Guggenheim Found Fel, 2007; Pollock-Krasner Found Grant, 2008. *Bibliog:* Andrew Marton (auth), Three from Texas: Introduction 2000 at Mulcahy

Modern, Ft Worth Star-Telegram, 12/17/1999; Kim Smith (auth), Mabye Perspective is like another theory of relativity, Ft Worth Mag, 8/2001; Mike Daniel (auth), Rosalyn Bodycomb at Mulcahy Modern, Dallas Morning News, 10/24/2003; Charles Dee Mitchell (auth), Nocturnes, Art in Am, 10/2005. *Media:* Oil

BOEPPLE, WILLARD
SCULPTOR, EDUCATOR
b Oct 18, 1945. *Study:* CCUNY, BFA, 68. *Work:* Met Mus Art, NY; Boston Mus Fine Arts; Storm King Art Ctr, Mountainville, NY; Nat Gallery of Kenya, Nairobi; Edmonton Art Gallery, Alberta, Can; Nat Gallery of Botswana, Gaborone. *Comn:* Vermont State Coun on the Arts Goldstone Mem. *Exhib:* Mead Art Mus, Amherst Col, Mass, 88; Andre Emmerich Gallery, NY, 1991, 93; Francis Graham-Dixon Gallery, London, 94; Galerie du Tableau, Marseille, France, 95; Tricia Collins Grand Salon, NY, 97, 99; NY Studio Sch Gallery, NY, 99; Broadbent Gallery, London, 2001, 2003, 2005, 2008; Andrew Mummery Gallery, London, 2002; Salander O'Reilly, NY, 2004; several group exhibitions 1971-2007. *Pos:* Chmn, Triangle Artists Workshop, 93-2001. *Teaching:* prof sculpture, Boston Mus Sch, 77-87; asst. faculty Bennington Coll Vermont, 69-73. *Bibliog:* Stephen Sandy (auth), The Sculpture of Willard Boepple, Acquavella Contemporary Art; Judith Barter (auth), Willard Boepple: Sculpture, Mead Art Mus, Amherst Col; Andrew Hudson (autho), Breaking Loose from Conventions, Willard Boepple: Sculpture 70-90. *Mem:* Century Asn; Nat Acad. *Media:* Metal, Wood, Resin. *Dealer:* Salander O'Reilly Gallery 20 E 79 New York NY 10021; Broadbent Gallery 25 Chepstow Corner London England W2 4XE. *Mailing Add:* 75 Grand St North Bennington VT 05257

BOGART, MICHELE HELENE
HISTORIAN, CURATOR
b New York, NY, Oct 5, 1952. *Study:* Art Students League; Smith Col, BA, 79; Univ Chicago, MA, 75, PhD, 79. *Exhib:* The Seelye Yrs, Smith Coll Mus Art, Northampton, Mass, 74; Am Art Quest for Unity, Detroit Inst Art, Mich, 82-83; Fauns and Fountains, Parrish Art Mus, Southampton, NY, 85. *Pos:* Guest cur, Parrish Art Mus, 82-84; guest cur sculpture, Detroit Inst Art, Mich, 80-83; mem Art Commission, City of NY, 1998-2003 (renamed Public Design Commission), vpres, formerly, conservation advisory group mem, currently; bd dirs, Fine Arts Federation of NY, currently; pres, Associates of the Art Commission of the City of NY. *Teaching:* Instr art, Am Sch, Chicago, Ill, 76-77; asst prof art hist, Univ Ga, Athens, 79-82; assoc prof to prof, State Univ NY, Stony Brook, 1982-, graduate program dir, currently. *Awards:* Fel, Smithsonian Inst, 77-78; Joint Award, Res Found State Univ NY, 83; Winterthur Res Fel, Fel for Coll Teachers & Independent Scholars, Nat Endowment Humanities, 94-95; Provost Fac Travel Grant, 85 & 87; Am Coun Learned Socs Grant-in-Aid, 87; Benno M Forman Fel, Winterthur Mus, 88; Nuala McGann Drescher Leave Fund Award, 88; Smithsonian Sr Postdoctoral Fel, 90. *Mem:* Coll Art Asn; Am Studies Asn; Asn Am Art Historians (co-chair). *Res:* Nineteenth & twentieth century sculpture; archit sculpture; reproductions & copies; illus, photog, posters & com art. *Publ:* Auth, Photosculpture, Art Hist, winter 80; auth, On women and art, Ga Review, winter 80; auth, Development of a popular market for sculpture, J Am Cult, spring 81; auth, Four sculpture sketches for the New York Public Library, Bulletin Ga Mus, winter, 82; The Importance of Believing in Purity, Archives Am Art J, 84; Barking Architecture: the Sculpture of Coney Island, Smithsonian Studies Am Art, winter 88; Public Sculpture and the Civic Ideal in New York City 1890-1930, Univ Chicago Press, 89; Artistic Ideals and Commercial Practices: The Problem of Status for the American Illustrator, Prospects 15, 90; auth, Artists, Advertising, and the Borders of Art, Univ Chicago Press, 95. *Mailing Add:* Department of Art Room 4215 2224 Staller Center for the Arts State University of New York at Stony Br Stony Brook NY 11794-5400

BOGART, RICHARD JEROME
PAINTER
b Highland Park, Mich, Oct 30, 1929. *Study:* Art Inst Chicago, dipl, 52; Univ Ill, 54; Black Mountain Col, NC, 56. *Work:* Brooklyn Mus; Yellowstone Art Ctr, Billings, Mont; Achenback Found, San Francisco; Mint Mus Art; Detroit Inst Art. *Exhib:* Solo exhibs, Poindexter Gallery, NY, 68-83, Meredith Long & Co, Houston, Tex, 77 & J P Natkin Gallery, 85-88; Conn Painting, Drawing & Sculpture Exhib, 78; Artist Showcase, Conn Comn on the Arts, 84; State of the Artists, Aldrich Mus, Ridgefield, Conn, 87; Douglas Drake Gallery, NY, 90-92; Gallerie 454, Birmingham, Mich, 93; The Artist As Native: Reinventing Regionalism, Babcock Galleries, NY, 93-94; Experiment in Art, Black Mountain Col, 2002-03; Museo Nacional Centro de Arte Reina Sofia, Madrid, Spain, 2002. *Awards:* Artist of yr, Art/Pl Gallery, Fairfield, Conn, 2000; Dir Choice, Copley Soc of Art, Boston, Mass, Jan, 2007. *Bibliog:* Alan Gussow (auth), A sense of place, the artist & the American land, Sat Rev Press; Alan Gussow (auth), The Artist as Native: Reinventing Regionalism, Pomegranate Art Books, Calif; Robert Natkin (auth), Subject Matter and Abstraction, In Exile, Claridge Press St Albans; Artist & their spaces, Conn Mag, 10/87; other reviews in Art News, Arts, Art in Am, Time Mag & NY Times. *Media:* Oil, Pastel. *Publ:* Auth, Richard Bogart: The Reflected Landscape (exhib catalog), 87; Richard Bogart: Latitudes (catalog), 93; No Other Shore (catalog), 99; Still Ponds (catalogue), 2001; Black Mountain College: Experiment in Art; ed, Vincent Katz. *Dealer:* Gallerie 454 15105 Kercheval Grosse Pointe MI 48230. *Mailing Add:* 378 Judd Rd Easton CT 06612

BOGER, CHRISTYL
CERAMIST, EDUCATOR
Study: Miami Univ, Oxford, Ohio, BFA; Mich State Univ, East Lansing; Ohio Univ, Athens, MFA, 2000. *Exhib:* Solo exhib, Longstreth-Goldberg Gallery, Naples, Fla, 2006; two-person show, Swanson-Reid Gallery, Louisville, 2007; group exhibs include The Common Denominator, Sculpture Ctr, Cleveland, 1998; Couplets: Duality in Clay, Clay Studio, Philadelphia, 2000, Chymical Object, 2001, Looking Back: 10 Yrs of the Evelyn Shapiro Fel, 2002; Pygmalion's Gaze Reconsidered, Nat Coun Educ Ceramic Arts, Baltimore, 2005; A Tale to Tell: Contemp Narratives in Clay, John Michael Kohler Arts Ctr, Sheboygan, Mich, 2005. *Teaching:* Teaching asst, Ceramics Dept, Ohio Univ, Athens, 1997, teaching assoc instr, 1999, 2000; summer resident & instr, Archie Bray Found, Helena, Mont, 2000; teaching assoc, Clay Studio Sch, Philadelphia, 2001; vis asst prof, Indiana Univ, Bloomington, 2001-05, asst prof, 2005-; emerging artist, Nat Coun Educ Ceramic Arts, 2003; vis artist, Sch Art Inst Chicago, 2005, instr, 2006. *Awards:* Evelyn Shapiro Found Fel, Clay Studio, Philadelphia, 2001. *Mailing Add:* 2684 McCartney Ln Bloomington IN 47401

BOGGS, MAYO MAC
SCULPTOR, EDUCATOR
b Ashland, Ky, Mar 22, 1942. *Study:* Univ Ky, with Mike Hall, BA (art); Univ NC, Chapel Hill, with Robert Howard, MFA (sculpture). *Work:* Gerald R Ford Libr; NC Govs Mansion; SC Govs Mansion; Huntington Galleries, WVa; NC Nat Bank, Charlotte; Jimmy Carter Libr. *Comn:* sculpture, comn by Ms Barbara Plott, Tryon, NC, 89; sculpture, comn by Mr & Mrs Marshall Chapman, Spartanburg, SC, 90; large scale computer graphics (3' x 6'), office of Rick Harris Law Firm, Spartanburg, SC, 92; sculpture, comn by Lillian Jackson Braun, Tryon, NC, 94; sculpture, comn by Mr & Mrs Jack Kenan Four Sabot Farm, Landrum, NC, 94. *Exhib:* Spartanburg Co traveling exhib of twelve paintings, 91; Invitational Sculpture Exhib, Stone Hedge, Tryon, NC, 91; Invitational Group Exhib, Carolina Editions Gallery, Artista Vista, Columbia, SC, 91; Invitational exhib Art of the Upstate Gallery, Spartanburg/Greenville Airport, 91; Fourth Ann NCNB Art Exhib, Spartanburg, SC, 92; and others. *Teaching:* Tech asst, Univ Kentucky, 1968; fellowship, tchr basic and beginning sculpture, Univ NC, 1969-70; instr, Penland Sch Crafts, NC, 1973-75, vis scholar, 1976, summer faculty, 1977; asst dean, counselor, Ghost Ranch, Abiquiu, NMex, 1992; instr in art, Converse Col, Spartanburg, SC, 70-73, asst prof art, 1974-77, assoc prof, 1978-94, prof, 1994-, dept chair, 1997-. *Awards:* John W Oswald Res & Creativity Award, Univ Ky, 69; Kathryne Amelia Brown Fac Award, Converse Col, 72; Named Hon Artist of Spartanburg by proclamation of the Mayor of Spartanburg, 91; Best in Show Award, Fourth Ann NCNB Art Exhib, Spartanburg, SC, 92. *Mem:* Spartanburg Artists Guild; Am Asn Univ Profs; Tri-State Sculptors. *Media:* Steel Construction, Bronze Casts; Computer Graphics. *Mailing Add:* Converse College Art Dept 580 E Main St Spartanburg SC 29301

BOGHOSIAN, VARUJAN
SCULPTOR, EDUCATOR
b New Britain, Conn, June 26, 1926. *Study:* Cent Conn Teacher's Coll, New Britain, 46-48; Vesper George Sch Art, Boston, 48-50; Yale Univ Sch Art & Archit, BFA, 57, MFA, 59; Brown Univ, MA (hon), 65; Dartmouth Coll, MA (hon), 69. *Hon Degrees:* Brown Univ, MA(hon), 59. *Work:* Mus Mod Art & Whitney Mus Am Art, NY; Albright-Knox Art Gallery, Buffalo, NY; Brooklyn Mus, NY; Boston Mus Fine Arts; Addison Gallery Am Art, Andover, Mass. *Exhib:* Solo exhibs, Stable Gallery, 63-66, Cordier & Ekstrom, NY, 69-88, Am Acad Rome, 86, Aldrich Mus Contemp Art, Ridgefield, Conn, 88, Claude Bernard Gallery, NY, 91, David Winton Bell Gallery, Brown Univ, 92 & Berry Hill Galleries, 97-99; Boîtes, Mus d'Art Moderne de la Ville de Paris & Maison de la Cult de Rennes, France, 76-77; Artists-in-Residence at Dartmouth, Hopkins Ctr, Dartmouth Coll, Hanover, NH, 88; Berry Hill, NY, 96; Alpha, Boston, 97; Irving Gallery, Palm Beach, 97; many others. *Pos:* Sculptor-in-residence, Am Acad Rome, 66-67, 75; artist-in-residence, Dartmouth Coll, Hanover, NH, 68; bd trustees, MacDowell Colony, Peterborough, NH, 82-, co-chmn bd trustees, 84-. *Teaching:* Instr drawing & painting, Univ Fla, Gainesville, 58-59; asst prof advanced drawing, Cooper Union, NY, 59-64; instr, Pratt Inst, NY, 61; instr drawing, Yale Univ, 62-64; assoc prof art hist, Brown Univ, Providence, RI, 64-68; prof sculpture, Dartmouth Coll, 68-96, George Frederick Jewett art prof, 82-96, prof emer, 96-. *Awards:* Fulbright Grant for Painting, Italy, 53; Nat Inst Arts & Lett Award, 72; Guggenheim Fel, 85; others. *Bibliog:* Dore Ashton (auth), article, Studio Int, 4/65; article, Time Mag, 2/9/70; article, Art Int, 3/81. *Mem:* Am Acad & Inst Arts & Lett; Nat Acad Design (assoc, 90, acad, 93). *Media:* Constructions, Collage. *Dealer:* Cordier & Ekstrom Inc 417 E 75th St New York NY 10021; Lori Booksteen Fine Art New York NY. *Mailing Add:* One Read Rd Hanover NH 03755

BOHAN, RUTH L
EDUCATOR, HISTORIAN
b Galesburg, Ill, Dec 27, 1946. *Study:* Univ Ill, BA, 69; Univ Md, MA, 72, PhD, 80. *Pos:* Res assoc, Yale Univ Art Gallery, 79-80. *Teaching:* Prof art hist, Univ Mo, St Louis, 81-, chair, Dept Art & Art Hist, 95-03 & 09-10, interim assoc dean, Coll Fine Arts & Commun, 2010-2013. *Awards:* Smithsonian Fel-Nat Collection Fine Arts, 75-76; Mellon Fel, Washington Univ, 80-81; J Paul Getty Fel, 85-86. *Mem:* Am Studies Asn; Coll Art Asn; Mid-America Am Studies Asn; Mod Language Asn. *Res:* Early twentieth-century American modernism; Walt Whitman and the visual arts; material culture. *Publ:* Auth, The Societe Anonyme's Brooklyn Exhibition: Katherine Dreier and Modernism in America, UMI Res Press, 82; contrib ed, The Societe Anonyme and the Dreier Bequest at Yale University: A Catalogue Raisonne, Yale Univ Press, 84; American drawings and watercolors, 1900-1945, The St Louis Art Mus Bull, summer 89; Looking into Walt Whitman: American Art 1850-1920, Penn State Press, 2006. *Mailing Add:* Dept Art & Art History Univ Missouri 1 University Blvd Saint Louis MO 63121

BOHEN, BARBARA E
HISTORIAN, MUSEOLOGIST
b Bradford, Wiltshire, Eng, Apr 24, 1941; US citizen. *Study:* Queens Coll, City Univ NY, BA, 69; NY Univ Inst Fine Arts, MA (fine arts), 73, PhD (classical art), 79, Mus Mgt Inst, 82. *Work:* Kerameikos Mus, Athens, Greece; World Heritage Mus, Urbana, Ill. *Collection Arranged:* In Search of the Ancient Egyptians, 88, Kings Crusaders & Craftsmen, 89, Beyond the Himalayas, 90; and others. *Pos:* lectr, NYU, Washington Sq, 72-73; asst dir, Kerameikos Mus, Athens, Greece, 76-78; Dir, World Heritage Mus, Urbana, Ill, 81-98; coauth & ed, Heritage (biann), Newsletter of the World, Heritage Mus, 81-98. *Teaching:* Lectr art hist, Queens Coll, City Univ NY, spring & summer, 73, Univ Ill, Urbana, fall 82; mus studies, Univ Ill, Urbana, 94-97, asst prof, 2012-. *Awards:* Fulbright Fel, Greek Archaeology (vases), 73; Danforth Fel, Greek vase painting studies, 74-76; Deutscheforschunggemeinschaft Fel, 79-81; Arnold O

Beckman Research Award, Univ Illinois, 94; Chancellor's Academic Professional Excellence Award, 95. *Res:* Greek vase classification, Apulian vase studies, Egyptian mummies. *Interests:* Early Iron Age archaeology. *Publ:* Auth, Origins of Greek Civilization, 75 & Greece, the Foundations of Greatness (audio visual progs), Reading Lab Inc, 87; Geometrischen Pyxiden, Walter de Gruyter, Berlin, 88; The Boeotian origin of an unusual geometric vase, J Paul Getty J, Vol 20, 92; Collaborative Investigation of the UI Egyptian Mummy, ACTA Cong Int Mummy Studies, 95; New Light on a Dark Age, Univ Mo, fall 96; Early Attic Krater

BOHLEN, NINA (CELESTINE EUSTIS BOHLEN)
PAINTER, DRAFTSMAN, PRINTS
b Boston, Mass, Mar 5, 1931. *Study:* Radcliffe Col, BA, 53; studied drawing & painting, Hyman Bloom, 52-56. *Work:* Fogg Mus Art; Boston Pub Libr; Brockton Mus; Fuller Mus; Tides Inst & Mus Art, Eastport, Maine, 2009; Danforth Mus, Framingham, Mass. *Exhib:* Solo exhib, Siembab Gallery, Boston, 62, Shore Gallery, 68, Tragos Gallery, 71, 74, Libr Boston Athenaeum, 77, Far Gallery, New York, 78, Mus Comparative Zoology, Harvard Univ, 82, Tichenor Libr, Harvard Univ, 83, Boston Pub Libr, 88, 92, Pine Manor Coll, Chestnut Hill, Mass, 88, 91, St Botolph Club, Boston, 89, Martin Sumers Graphics, New York, 91, Univ Maine, Machias, 92, Ann Weber Gallery, Georgetown, Maine, 93, June Fitzpatrick Gallery, Portland, Maine, 94, Middlesex CC, 2007, Danforth Mus Art, Framingham, Mass, 2012, Tides Inst Mus Art, Eastport, Me, 2012; Two person exhib, Van Buren Gallery, Cambridge, Mass, 85; Group exhibs, Swetzoff Gallery, Boston, 59; Boston Mus Sch, 63; Boston Arts Festival, 63; Fuller Mus, Brockton, Mass, 69; Far Gallery, 73; Westmoreland Mus, Pa, 73; Am Acad Arts & Letters Recipients for Awards Exhib, 77; Hassam Fund Exhib, Am Acad Arts & Letters, 78, 81; Impressions Gallery, 78, Boston, 79; Boston Athenaeum, 79; Silo Gallery, Conn, 85; De Cordova Mus, Lincoln, Mass; Bumpus Gallery, Duxbury, Mass, 87; Boston Pub Libr, 87, 90, 91, 93, 94, 99, 2003; Little Rock Art Asn, 92; McGowan Fine Arts, Concord, NJ, 94; Martin Sumers Graphics, 91-97; Middlesex CC, Bedford, Mass; Wendell Gilley Mus, Southwest Harbour, Maine, 97; Kelley Gallery, Charlestown, Mass, 99-2002; St Botolph Club, Boston, 2000, 2007-2008; Tides Inst & Mus Art, East Port, Main, 2004; Ctr for Maine Contemp Art, Rockport, 2005; Maine Print Proj, Bath, 2005-2006; LC Bates Mus Hunckley, Maine, 2007-2014; Maine drawing proj, 2011; Boston Print Biannual, Danforth Mus, Framinpham, Mass; St Botolph Club, Boston group exhib, Danforth Mus. *Pos:* vice pres, Tideo Inst & Mus Art, Eastport, Me. *Teaching:* Pvt instr drawing & painting, 73-77, Newton Arts Ctr, 84-89, Pine Manor Coll, 85-94; Tide's Inst & Mus of Art, 2003-2004; instr monotype workshop, Maine Coll Art, 93. *Awards:* Am Acad Arts & Lett Award in Art, 77; Camargo Found, Cassis, France. *Bibliog:* Drawing from Boston, 87; Something about the Author, 90; Expose Mag, Harvard Univ, 2000; Drawing to See Goldstein & Fishman, 2004. *Media:* All. *Interests:* gardening. *Publ:* Illusr, Baboon Orphan, EP Dutton, 81. *Mailing Add:* 56 Fuller St Waltham MA 02154-5053

BOHLER, JOSEPH STEPHEN
PAINTER
b Great Falls, Mont, June 12, 1938. *Study:* With Robert Lougheed, Wilson Hurley, John Pike, Robert Wood, Bill Reese & others; Art Instruction Sch, Minneapolis, Minn, 60. *Work:* Coca Cola Bottling Co, Kansas City, Mo; Johnson Co Bank, Kansas City, Kans; Phoenix Bank & Trust, Ariz; Smithsonian Inst, Washington, DC. *Comn:* Portrait of Tex Ritter, Cowboy & Western Heritage Mus, Okla City. *Exhib:* Solo exhib, C M Russell Mus, Great Falls, Mont, 72; Pastel Soc Am, NY, 80; Am Watercolor Soc, NY, 81; Allied Artists Am, Nat Arts Club, NY, 81-82; two-man exhib, CM Russell Mus, Great Falls, Mont, 94; Gilcrease Mus, Tulsa, 2000. *Pos:* Bd dir, Stuart Anderson Black Angus Enterprises, 80-81; pres, NW Rendevous Group. *Teaching:* Jade Fon Watercolor Workshops, Pacific Grove, Calif, 84-86 & Venice, Italy, 95. *Awards:* Arjomari/Arches/Rives Award, Am Watercolor Soc, 90; Gold Medals, Drawing, Silver and Bronze, Watercolor, Nat Acad Western Art Exhibit, Nat Cowboy & Western Heritage Mus. *Mem:* Rocky Mountain Nat Watermedia Soc; Allied Artists Am; Am Watercolor Soc; Nat Acad Western Art; Midwest Watercolor Soc. *Media:* Watercolor, Pastel. *Interests:* Boogie, blues & ragtime piano player. *Publ:* Peggy & Harold Samuels, Contemp Western Artists, 82; The Artistic Touch, 94. *Dealer:* Grapevine Gallery Box 132 Oklahoma City OK 73101; Wilcox Gallery Jackson WY. *Mailing Add:* Box 387 Monument CO 80132-8161

BOHNEN, BLYTHE
CONCEPTUAL ARTIST, PHOTOGRAPHER
b Evanston, Ill, July 26, 1940. *Study:* Smith Col, BA (art), 62; Boston Univ, BFA, 67; Hunter Col, MA (painting), 72. *Work:* Dallas Mus Fine Arts, Tex; McCrory Corp, Whitney Mus Am Art, Mus Mod Art, Metrop Mus Art, Brooklyn Mus Art, NY; Fogg Art Mus, Harvard Univ, Cambridge, Mass; Art Inst Chicago; Albright-Knox Art Gallery, Buffalo, NY; Guggenheim Mus, NY; Int Ctr Photog, NY. *Comn:* Ceramic tile relief, wall mural (15' x 30'), Libr Blind, Record Storage Ctr, Trenton, NJ, 80-82. *Exhib:* Annual Survey of Am Painting (with catalog), Whitney Mus Am Art, 71-72; Penthouse, Mus Mod Art, NY, 72, 91; Reflections 1971-72, Aldrich Mus Contemp Art, Conn, 71-72; Wadsworth Atheneum, Hartford, Conn, 75; Extraordinary Women, Mus Mod Art, NY, 77; Drawings of the 70's, Chicago Art Inst, 77; Permanent Collection of 20th Century Drawings, Metrop Mus Art; solo exhibs, Int Cult Ctr (with catalog), Antwerp, Belg, 78, Galerie Camomille, Brussels, Belg, 78, Artline Gallery (with catalog), Hague, The Neth, 79, Contemp Art Ctr (with catalog), New Orleans, La, 80, PS 1, NY, 81, Light Gallery, NY, 84 & Galerie Mukai, Tokyo, Japan, 84; Self Portraits (with catalog), Gallery Plaza, Security Pac Nat Bank, Los Angeles, 85; Artists' Self-Portraits, Acad Arts, Honolulu, Hawaii, 85; New Portraiture, Light Gallery, NY, 86; First Person Singular, Self-Portrait Photog, 1840-1987 (with catalog), High Mus, Atlanta, Ga, 88; group exhib, San Jose Mus Art, San Jose, Calif, 98, Visions from America, Whitney Mus Art, New York City, 2002. *Collection Arranged:* Addison Gallery of Am Art, Phillips Academy, Andover, Mass; Aldrich Mus of Contemp Art, Ridgefield, Conn; Allen Art Mus, Oberlin Col, Oberlin, Ohio; Akron Art Mus, Akron, Ohio; Mus Art, Univ Mich, Ann Arbor; Art Mus, Princeton Univ; Ashville Art Mus, Ashville, NC; Baltimore Mus Art; Brooklyn Mus Art; Mus Fine Art, Boston; Art Mus, Univ Calif-Berkeley; Carnegie Mus Art, Pittsburgh; Ctr for Creative Photography, Univ Ariz, Tucson; Chase Manhattan Bank; Chrysler Mus, Norfolk, Va; Art Institute Chicago; Cincinnati Art Mus; Cleveland Mus Art; Dallas Mus Fine Art. *Teaching:* Lectr, Metrop Mus Art, 67-72; guest lectr mod mathematics & mod art, Metrop Mus Art, 78; FID; instr, Parsons Sch Design, 79-88. *Awards:* Artist-in-Residence Grant, 76 & Fel, 78, Nat Endowment Arts. *Bibliog:* Edward Lucie-Smith (auth), Art of the Seventies, 1980; Tom E Hinson (ed), Catalogue of Photography: The Cleveland Museum of Art, 1999; Willy Rotzler (auth), Constructive Concepts: The History of Constructive Art from Cubism to the Present, 1977; Ellen Handy (ed), Reflections in a Glass Eye, 1999; Victoria Thorson & Wendy Shore (eds), Great Drawings of all Times, 1981; Metrop Mus Art Bulletin, Old Masters-New Apprentices, 12/68; Sylvia Wolf (auth), Visions from America, 2002. *Media:* Acrylic, Graphite, Silver, Gelatin Print. *Mailing Add:* 13 Orchard Hill Rd Norwalk CT 06851

BOHNERT, THOM (THOMAS) ROBERT
CERAMIST, EDUCATOR
b St Louis, Mo, Jan 3, 1948. *Study:* Southern Ill Univ, Edwardsville, BA, 69; Cranbrook Acad Art, Bloomfield Hills, Mich, MFA, 71. *Work:* Flint Inst Art, Mich; Minneapolis Art Inst, Minn; Univ Iowa Mus, Iowa City; Cranbrook Acad Art, Bloomfield Hills, Mich; Boyman Mus, Rotterdam, Holland. *Exhib:* Young Americans/Clay Glass, Tucson Mus Art, Ariz, 78; Century Ceramics in the US 1878-1978, Everson Mus, Syracuse, NY, Renwick Gallery, Smithsonian Inst, Washington, DC & Cooper-Hewitt, NY, 79; one-person show, Exhibit A Gallery, Chicago, Ill, 79 & 81; A Response to Wedgewood, 2 Yr Traveling Exhib, Mus Philadelphia Civic Ctr, Pa, 80; Basket-Works, John M Kohler Arts Ctr, Sheboygan, Wis, 81; Painting and Sculpture Today: 1982, Indianapolis Mus Art, 82; Am Clay Artists: Philadelphia 83, Marian Locks Gallery East, 83; plus many others. *Teaching:* Instr ceramic & drawing, Southern Ill Univ, 71; instr ceramics & drawing, C S Mott Community Col, 71-; vis artist ceramics, Univ Mich, 77-78; prof art. *Awards:* Award, Detroit Inst Art, 76; Nat Endowment Arts Craftsmen Fel, 78-79; Creative Artists Grant, Mich Coun Arts, 83-84; John Simon Guggenheim Fel, 86-87. *Bibliog:* Helen Williams Drutt (auth), Contemporary Ceramics: A Response to Wedgewood, 81; Christopher Young (auth), Six Experiments in Sculpture: Thom Bohnert, Flint Inst Arts, 86; Gottfried Borrmann (auth), Ceramics of the world, Kunst & Handwerk, Dusseldorf, WGer, 84; Alice Westphal (auth), Putting Pottery in Perspective, Rockford Col, 90. *Media:* Ceramic, Metal. *Dealer:* Braunstein/Quay Gallery San Francisco; Loveed Fine Arts New York. *Mailing Add:* 6337 Flushing Rd Flushing MI 48433-2548

BOIGON, BRIAN JOSEPH
CONCEPTUAL ARTIST, WRITER
b Toronto, Ont, Aug 14, 1955; Can citizen. *Study:* Ont Coll Art, 73-76; Univ Toronto Sch Archit, BA, 76-80. *Work:* Art Gallery Ont, Toronto; Can Coun Art Bank, Ottawa, Ont. *Exhib:* Rauman und Installation, Wurttembergischer Kunstverein, Stuggart, WGer, 84; Mapping the Surface, Mendell Art Gallery, Saskatoon, Sask, 86; Logic Display, PS1, NY, 88; Speed Neutralization and the Spectacle of Sleep, 49th Parallel (with catalog), NY, 88. *Pos:* Ed, Impulse Mag, Toronto, 84-90. *Teaching:* Asst prof, Univ Toronto, Dept Fine Art & Archit, 86-90. *Bibliog:* Gordon Lebredt (auth), Staging Mondrian, C Mag, 84; Rick Rhodes (auth), Review, Art Forum, 88. *Media:* Mixed Media, Photography. *Publ:* Auth, Downtown, Impulse, 87; Kiss sugar good bye, Impulse Mag, 88; Victorian spacing and the international style, New Observations, 88; Inboard/Outboard, Fifth Column, 89; auth, Speed Reading Tokyo, P3 Mus, Tokyo, 90. *Dealer:* S L Simpson Gallery 515 Queen St W Toronto ON Canada M5V 2B4. *Mailing Add:* 299 Rushton Rd Toronto ON M6C 2X8 Canada

BOL, MARSHA C
MUSEUM DIRECTOR, HISTORIAN
b Shelbyville, Ind. *Study:* Univ NMex, MA (art hist) 1980, PhD (art hist) 1989. *Exhib:* Behind the Mask in Mexico, Mus of Int Folk Art, 1988; Alcoa Found Hall of Native Ams, Carnegie Mus, 1998; Mexican Modern: Masters of the 20th Century, NMex Mus Art. *Pos:* Cur of educ, Maxwell Mus, Univ NMex, 1982-84; cur Latin Am Folk Art, Mus Int Folk art, 1984-90; cur anthropology, Carnegie Mus Nat Hist, 1990-98; dir, NMex Mus Fine arts, 2001-. *Teaching:* Assoc prof mus studies, Univ Tex, San Antonio, 1999-2001. *Res:* Native American Art History, specifically Plains Indian Womens' Arts. *Publ:* Auth, Painting & Sculpture, The Spanish Borderlands, 1993; Collecting Symbolism Among the Arapaho, 1996; North, South, East West: Am Indians & the National World, 1998; Defining Lakota Tourist Art, 1880-1915, 1999; Identity Recovered: Portrait of a Northern Arapaho Quillworker, 2001; Early Euro-Am Ethnographers and the Hopi Tihu, 2001; Maria Martinez: For all the People, 2004. *Mailing Add:* NMex Mus Art PO Box 2087 Santa Fe NM 87504

BOLAS, GERALD DOUGLAS
MUSEUM DIRECTOR, CONSULTANT
b Los Angeles, Calif, Nov 1, 1949. *Study:* Univ Calif, Santa Barbara, BA, 72, MA (art hist), 75; City Univ NY, PhD, 98. *Collection Arranged:* Gyorgy Kepes, 78, Richard Hunt: Three Places, 79, Old and Modern Master Drawings, 80, Greek Vases and Roman Glass, 80 & Arthur Osver: The University Years, 81, Washington Univ Gallery Art; Paris in Japan: The Japanese Encounter with European Painting, 87; Ketav: Flesh and Word in Israeli Art (auth, catalog), 96; and others. *Pos:* Asst to dir, Yale Univ Art Gallery, 75-77; dir, Washington Univ Gallery Art, 77-88, Portland Art Mus, Ore, 88-92, Ackland Art Mus, Univ NC, Chapel Hill, 94-2006; pub art & mus consult, 2006-2011; exec dir, Raleigh Arts Commission, 2011-. *Teaching:* Asst, Univ Calif, Santa Barbara, 73-74; adj asst prof, Washington Univ, 77-88; adj prof, Univ NC, Chapel Hill, 94-2006. *Awards:* NEH Mus Training Internship, Yale Univ Art Gallery, 75; Fel, Winterthur Mus & Nat Mus Am Art, Smithsonian Inst, 93. *Mem:* Asn Art Mus Dir Emeritus. *Res:* Nineteenth century Am art; hist of art auctions, museums

patronage and connoisseurship, pub art, electric & digital art. *Publ:* Auth, Illustrated Checklist of the Washington University Collection, 81; American Responses to Western-Style Japanese Painting, In Paris in Japan: The Japanese Encounter with European Painting, Tokyo & St Louis, 87; numerous other articles and catalog forewords

BOLDING, GARY WILSON
PAINTER, CURATOR
b El Dorado, Ark, Nov 30, 1952. *Study:* Hendrix Col, BA, 75; Brooklyn Col, with Philip Pearlstein, MFA, 89. *Work:* Chattahoochee Valley Art Mus, Lamar Dodd Art Ctr, La Grange, Ga; Duncan Gallery Art, De Land, Fla; Cornell Mus Art, Rollins Col, Winter Park, Fla; Polk Mus Art, Lakeland, Fla. *Exhib:* solo exhibs, Gallerie Michael Rasche, Freiburg, Ger, 99; Lorraine Ogilvie Gallery, Marlburg, Ger, 2002; Tatistcheff Gallery, NY, 2002; Bernice Steinbaum Gallery, Miami, Fla, 2003; Cornell Mus, Rollins Col, Fla, 2003; Polk Mus, Lakeland, Fla, 2006. *Collection Arranged:* Robert Fichter, Duncan Gallery Art, 91; The Ethical Object, Duncan Gallery Art, 91; Oscar Bluemmer: Watercolors & Gouaches, Duncan Gallery Art, 94; Worlds on Paper, Duncan Gallery Art, 94; Surrealist Sculpture with a Southern Gothic Twist, Duncan Gallery Art, 94. *Teaching:* Prof painting, Stetson Univ, De Land, Fla, 89-. *Awards:* Bank of Boston Award, 52nd Nat Soc 4 Arts, 90; Purchase Award, LaGrange Nat XVII, Chattahoochee Valley Art Mus, 92; Fla Individual Artist Fel, Fla Arts Coun, 94 & 2003. *Bibliog:* Joan Altabe (auth), Boldings work irreverent, well done, Sarasota Herald Tribune, 9/2/94; Cris Hassold (auth), Gary Bolding; Terror in the suburbs, Art Papers, 3-4/94; Roberta Favis (auth), Artists/Educators: Five in Florida, De Land Mus, 1/94. *Mem:* Coll Art Asn. *Media:* Oil, Acrylic. *Dealer:* Arts on Douglas 123 Douglas St New Smyrna Beach FL 32168; Bernice Steinbaum Gallery Miami Fla. *Mailing Add:* 1105 S Beresford Rd Deland FL 32720-3521

BOLEN, JOHN E
ART DEALER, COLLECTOR
b Ft Gordon, Ga, Aug 27, 1953. *Study:* Univ Calif, Los Angeles, AB, 75. *Collection Arranged:* Painting into Bronze: The Polychromed Bronze of Harry Jackson, Southwest Mus, Highland Park, Calif, 79; The Cowboy, San Diego Mus Art, 81. *Pos:* Co-dir, Bolen Gallery, Inc, Santa Monica & Los Angeles, Calif, 78-84, Bolen Publ, Playa del Rey, Calif, 79-84; co-owner, John & Lynne Bolen Fine Arts, Huntington Beach, Calif, 84-, John & Lynne Bolen Fine Arts, Irvine, Calif, 99-. *Teaching:* Lectr art collecting, privately, 76-78; pvt art marketing consult, 76-78. *Mem:* Art Dealers Asn Calif (bd dir, 80-83, vpres, 82-83). *Specialty:* Nineteenth and twentieth century American paintings, sculptures and original prints. *Publ:* Ed, Arthur Secunda, Monograph, 80, co-ed, Six Decades of American Prints, 1900-1960, 82, Grant Wood: Paintings, Drawings & Lithographs, 83 & The American Landscape: Current Visions, 83, Bolen Gallery, Inc. *Mailing Add:* PO Box 53394 Irvine CA 92619-3394

BOLEN, LYNNE N
ART DEALER, COLLECTOR
Study: Univ Calif, Los Angeles, BS, Calif State Univ, Dominguez Hills, MBA, Calif State Univ, Long Beach, MSHCA. *Pos:* Co-dir, Bolen Gallery, Inc, Santa Monica & Los Angeles, Calif, Bolen Publ, Playa del Rey, Calif; co-owner, John & Lynne Bolen Fine Arts, Huntington Beach, Calif. *Teaching:* Univ Phoenix. *Bibliog:* Critical reviews in Santa Monica Evening Outlook; var issues, Art Voices. *Mem:* Art Dealers Asn Calif (secy & mem bd dir, 82-83). *Specialty:* Nineteenth and twentieth century American paintings, sculptures and original prints. *Publ:* Co-ed, Six Decades of American Prints 1900-1960, Grant Wood: Paintings, Drawings & Lithographs, The American Landscape: Current Visions, Bolen Gallery, Inc. *Mailing Add:* PO Box 53394 Irvine CA 92619-3394

BOLER, JOHN ALFRED
ART DEALER, COLLECTOR
b Minneapolis, Minn, Aug 26, 1942. *Study:* Univ Minn, BA, 65; Univ Iowa, MA, 70. *Collection Arranged:* Guest cur, Minnesota Voices, Minn Mus Am Art, 92-93. *Pos:* Dir & owner, Avanyu Gallery, Minneapolis, Minn, 82-87; pres & founder, Art Dealers Asn Twin Cities (Minneapolis & St Paul), 83-86; pvt dealer, John A Boler Indian and Western Art, Minneapolis, Minn, 87-; judge, Twin Cities Indian Market, 5/91; panelist, Dakota Arts Cong, 92; co-cur exhib, Minn Mus Am Art, 92-93; dir & owner, John A Boler Fine Art, Minneapolis, Minn, 87-2007, Las Cruces, NM 2007-09. *Teaching:* Arts Law Conf, Walker Art Ctr, 85. *Awards:* Minn Gov's Award for Volunteerism in the Arts, 91. *Mem:* Indian Arts Am (adv bd); Minn Am Indian Ctr Gallery; Minn Sate Arts Board (adv panelist); docent, Las Cruces Mus Art, NM. *Res:* Survey of Am Indian art of the Upper Midwest from prehistory to present. *Specialty:* Classic and contemp Am Indian and southwestern art. *Interests:* Contemp Am Indian and Southwestern art, 19th and 20th century French art, int folk art. *Publ:* Understanding American Indian Art, Parts I & II, 7 & 8/87, Anatomy of an Art Dealers' Association, 9/87 & Indian Artists Are on Warpath, 9/88, Art Business News. *Mailing Add:* 4372 Camino Dos Vidas Las Cruces NM 88012

BOLGE, GEORGE S
MUSEUM DIRECTOR
b Trenton, NJ, 1942. *Study:* State Univ NJ, Rutgers, BA & BS; Inst Fine Arts, NY Univ, MA; 1987. *Hon Degrees:* Nova Univ, Ft Lauderdale, Fla, Honorary Dr of Humane Letts. *Collection Arranged:* The Dr & Mrs Meyer B Marks Cobra Art Collection; The Maurice Lipschult Collection of Constructed Reliefs; The Jean & David Colker Collection of Pre-Columbian Art; Eng Victorian Doulton Lambeth Stoneware from the Bernard J & Florence F Starkoff Bequest; Isadore & Kelly Friedmen Collection. *Pos:* Grad res asst & asst cur, Ancient Art Dept, Brooklyn Mus Art, NY; Fel, Nat Trust Hist Preserv; exec dir, Mus Art, Ft Lauderdale, Fla, 1970-88; Fine Arts Consult, 1989-91; curatorial consult, Broward Co, Fla, 1991-; exec dir, NJ Ctr Vis Arts, Summit, NJ, 1991-94; dir, Boca Raton Mus Art, Fla, 1995-. *Bibliog:* Graphic Work of Renoir, Catalogue Raisonne compiled by Dr. Joseph Stella, Lund Humphries, Bedford & London, Eng, 1975. *Mem:* Am Asn Mus; Fla Asn Mus; Fla Art Mus Dirs Asn; Appraisers Asn Am; Pub Art & Design Committee; Broward Cult Coun. *Mailing Add:* c/o Boca Raton Mus Art Mizner Park 501 Plaza Real Boca Raton FL 33432

BOLGER, DOREEN
RETIRED MUSEUM DIRECTOR, CURATOR
b Far Rockaway, NY, Jan 10, 1949. *Study:* Bucknell Univ, BA, 71; Univ Del, Newark, MA, 73; Grad Ctr, City Univ NY, PHD, 83. *Collection Arranged:* J Alden Weir: An Am Impressionist (auth, catalog), Metrop Mus Art, 83; William M Harnett, Metrop Mus Art, 92-93; Am Impressionism and Realism, The Painting of Modern Life: 1885-1915 (coauth, catalog), Metrop Mus Art, 94-95. *Pos:* Field rep, Mus Early Southern Decorative Arts, Winston-Salem, NC, 73; rsch assoc, then asst cur dept Am paintings and sculpture, Metrop Mus Art, 76-82, Assoc cur Am paintings and sculpture, 82-88; cur, Metrop Mus Art, 89 & Amon Carter Mus, Ft Worth, Tex, 89-94; mem educ and fel com, The John Nicholas Brown Ctr for the Study of Am Civilization, Brown Univ, formerly; ann fund worker, Gordon Sch, East Providence, formerly; trustee, Williamstown Art Conservation Lab, Mass, formerly; reviewer gen operating support, Inst Mus and Libr Svcs, 96-97; dir, Mus Art, RI Sch Design, 94-98 & Baltimore Mus Art, 98-2015. *Teaching:* Adj prof, Brown Univ, 97. *Awards:* Unidel Fel, Univ Del, 72-73; City Univ New York Grad Ctr Fel, 73-74; Chester Dale Fel, Metrop Mus Art, 74-76; Metrop Mus Art Travel Grants, 78, 84 & 88; Ailsa Mellon Bruce Vis Sr Fel, Nat Gallery Art, 90; Nat Endowment for Humanities Travel to Collections Grant, 92. *Mem:* Asn Art Mus Dirs; Phi Beta Kappa; Md Hist Soc (vis com, 96-); Providence Art Club. *Res:* Late 19th century American art. *Publ:* Auth, American Paintings in the Metropolitan Museum of Art: Volume III (a catalog of works by artists born between 1846 and 1864), Princeton Univ Press & Metrop Mus Art, 80; J Alden Weir: An American Impressionist, Univ Del Press, 83; co-auth (H Barbara Weinberg and David Park Curry), American Impressionism and Realism: The Painting of Modern Life, 1885-1915, Metro Mus of Art, 94; co-ed, Thomas Eakins and the Swimming Picture, Amon Carter Mus, Ft Worth, Tex, 96; auth, articles in jours including Antiques Mag & Am Art Jour

BOLLERER, FRED L
MUSEUM DIRECTOR
Study: Ohio Univ, BBA; Thunderbird Sch Global Mgmt, Phoenix, MBA. *Pos:* Exec vpres, First City Nat Bancorporation, Houston, Tex, formerly; chmn & CEO, First Am Metro Corp, 1988-1993, bd chmn & CEO, First Am Bank Va; pres & CEO, Riggs Bank NA, 1993-1997; mgmt adv, Morino Inst, Washington, DC, 1998-, pres & CEO Potomac KnowledgeWay Project, 1997-2000; partner, Venture Philanthropy Partners, 2000-2007, Real Change Strategies, LLC, McLean, Va, 2007-2009; bd dirs, Southern Nat Bancorp Va, Inc, 2007-; chief operating officer, Corcoran Gallery Art, 2009-2010, dir, pres, 2010-. *Mailing Add:* Corcoran Gallery Art 500 17th St NW Washington DC 20006

BOLLIGER, THERESE
EDUCATOR, SCULPTOR
b Walde, Switz, Apr 28, 1944; Swiss & Can citizen. *Study:* Sch Visual Arts, Berne, Switz, 60-61; Sch Visual Arts, Basel, Switz, 65-69. *Work:* Govt Ont, Hart House-Univ Toronto, Toronto Dom Bank, Can; Univ Western Ont, London, Ont; Mohawk Coll, Hamilton, Ont; Govt Ont; Hart House, Univ Toronto; Oakville Galleries, Oakville, Ont; Univ Lethbridge, Lethbridge, Alberta; St Michael's Coll, Univ Toronto. *Exhib:* Transference, Mercer Union, Toronto, 86; Word Perfect, Art Gallery Hamilton, Ont, 90; Nickle Mus, Calgary, Alta, 91-92; Kevin Vergleich (with catalog), Southern Alta Art Gallery, Can, 91-92; Edmonton Art Gallery, Alta, 92; Stutter, Cold City Gallery, Toronto, 93; Solo exhibs, Dressing Hair and Wounds (with catalog), Kamloops Art Gallery, BC & Burnaby Art Gallery, BC, 93-94, Correspondences, Cold City Gallery, Toronto, 96, Blutbild/Wortbild, Moersbergerstrasse, Basel, Switz, 97 & Volatile Body/Volatile Language, Cold City Gallery, Toronto, 98; Snappy Title, YYZ, Toronto, 97; Cold City Artists, Cold City Gallery, Toronto, Cutting Edge (with catalog), ARCO, Madrid, Spain, 97 & 98 & Exquisite Corpse in Lotusland, Presentation House Gallery, Vancouver, 97; Coming to One's Senses, Longdale Gallery, Toronto, 97; Common Ground, Harbourfront Gallery, Toronto, 98; The Word in Contemp Canadian Art, Mus Contemp Canadian Art, Toronto; Ellipsis, Koffler Gallery, Toronto, Hartnett Gallery, Univ Rochester, NY; Mask and Metamorphosis, Art Gallery Hamilton, Ont; Contemp Canadian Drawing Series, Gallery Stratford, Ont; The Cold City Years, The Power Plant, Toronto; Fray, Mus Textiles & The Koffler Gallery, Toronto; Alphabeb, Stewart Hall, Montreal; Four Echoes, Oakville Galleries; Identity and Place, Kamloops Art Gallery. *Pos:* Acquisition Comt, Oakville Galleries, Ont, 91-93; Toronto Art Coun Interdisciplinary Jury, 96; Sabbatical, Basel, Switz, 97-98. *Teaching:* Instr drawing, Ont Coll Art, Toronto, 82-89 & Univ Guelph, 82-84; prof sculpture, Erindale Coll, Univ Toronto, 83-. *Awards:* Can Coun B, 86, 88. *Bibliog:* Dianne Bos, Ian Gray & Jane Perdue (auths), Artists Gardens at Harbourfront Centre 1990-1995, Harbourfront Centre, 96; Kym Preusse (auth), Volatile Body/Bolatile Language, Cold City Gallery, Toronto, 10/8-31/98; Carolyn Bell Farrell (auth), ellipsis, The Koffler Gallery, 1/7-2/21, 99; Shirley Madill (auth), Mark and Metamorphosis, Art Gallery Hamilton, Ont; Shannon Anderson (auth), Four Echoes, Mercer Union, Toronto. *Mem:* Sculpture Garden, Toronto (bd dir, 89-92). *Publ:* Auth, Cutting Edge, ARCO, Cold City Gallery, Madrid, Spain, 2/97. *Dealer:* Cold City Gallery 686 Richmond St W Toronto M61 3C3. *Mailing Add:* 404 Markham St Toronto ON M6G 2K9 Canada

BOLOMEY, ROGER HENRY
SCULPTOR
b Torrington, Conn, Oct 19, 1918; US & Swiss citizen. *Study:* Acad Bella Arte, Florence, Italy, 47; Univ Lausanne, 47-48; Calif Coll Arts & Crafts, Oakland, 48-50. *Work:* Mus Mod Art, Whitney Mus Am Art, NY; Univ Calif Mus Art, Berkeley; San Francisco Mus Mod Art, Calif; Stadtische Kunst, Mannheim, Ger. *Comn:* Aluminum sculpture, Southridge Mall, Milwaukee, Wis, 70; two reliefs, Mutual of NY, Syracuse,

71; two bronze sculptures, S Mall Proj, Albany, 71; stainless steel sculpture, NY State Off Bldg, Hauppauge, 73. *Exhib:* Carnegie Inst Int, Pittsburgh, 64; Whitney Mus Am Art Sculpture Ann, 64; Quatriene Exposition Suisse Sculpture, Bienne, Switz, 66; Contemp Am Paintings & Sculpture, Univ Ill, Urbana, 67; American Sculpture, Univ Nebr, Lincoln, 70. *Collection Arranged:* Forgotten Dimension: A Survey of Small Sculpture in California Now Traveling Exhib, 82-84. *Teaching:* Assoc prof art, Herbert H Lehman Col, 68-75; prof & chmn dept art, Calif State Univ, Fresno, 75-83. *Awards:* First Prize & Purchase Award, Bundy Art Mus Sculpture Int, Waitsfield, Vt, 63; Sculpture Prize, San Francisco Art Inst 84th Ann, 65; Res Found Award, City Univ NY, 70. *Mem:* San Francisco Art Inst; Am Fedn Arts; hon fel Acad Fine Arts, The Hague, Netherlands. *Media:* Steel, Aluminum

BOLT, RON
ENVIRONMENTAL ARTIST, PAINTER
b Toronto, Ont, 1938. *Study:* Northern Tech Sch (Gold Medalist), 55; Ryerson Polytech Sch, 57; Ont Art Col, 58. *Work:* Can Coun Art Bank; Gov Ont-Nat Libr Can; Metrop Toronto Reference Libr; Nat Art Libr, Victoria & Albert Mus; McGill Univ, Rare Bks Libr; Queen's Univ, Kingston - York Univ, Toronto; Concordia Univ, Montreal, Que; McMaster Mus Art; MacKenzie Art Gallery, Regina, Saskatchewan; Kitchener/Waterloo Art Gallery; Canadian Broadcasting Corp. *Comn:* Stamp design, Can Post, 79; Newmarket Courthouse (mural), Govt Ont, 80; tapestry designs, Indo-Asian Tapestries Ltd, Toronto, 82; waterworks, Sheraton Hotels Int, Halifax, NS, 85; Govt Can, Can House, Sydney, Australia, 92. *Exhib:* Over 65 Can solo exhibs, 65-; Int Union Tourist & Cult Asn, Istanbul, 79; Canadian Printmakers (traveling, US & Mex), Bronx Mus, NY, 82; Int Biennial Print Exhib, Taipei, Repub China, 85 & 87; 39th NAm Print Exhib, Boston, 87; 3rd Biennial Exhib Prints, Wakayama, Japan, 89; Mexico (traveling, 6 pub galleries), Ont, 95-97; Le Mur Vivant Fine Art, London, Eng, 98; Pollock House, Glasgow, 98; Tate West, St Ives, Cornwall, Eng, 2000; Art Inst Shen Zhen, China 2000; Contemp Art Mus, Guang Zho, China; Liu Hai Su Art Mus, Shanghai, China, 2000; Albemarle Gallery, West End London, Eng, 2006; Three Rivers (Yukon) Traveling Across Can, 2004-; Le Mur Vivant, Fine Art London, 98; Pollock House, Glasgow, 98; Tate West, St Ives, Cornwall, Eng, 2000; Art Mus Shen Zhen, China, 2000; Contemp Art Mus, Guang Zho, China, 2000; Liu Hai Su Art Mus, Shanghai, China, 2000. *Collection Arranged:* Queens Univ, 75; McMichael Canadian Collection, 76; Art Gallery Windsor, 77; Art Gallery Algoma, 84; Art Gallery Northumberland, 1990, 2007; Art Gallery Peterborough, 1995,2006; McLaughlin Gallery, 2006. *Pos:* Assoc, Royal Conservatory Music, Toronto; mem, Toronto City Hall Arts Adv Bd, 1970; co-found, Art Mag; Trustee, Nat Portrait Gallery, Royal Ontario Mus, 2001. *Teaching:* Instr art, Northern Tech Sch, 71-74, Learning Resources Ctr, Toronto, 72-73 & Hibbs Cove Art & Music Ctr, Nfld, 72-73; guest speaker, juror & lectr, 80-. *Awards:* Purchase Award, Univ Guelph, Ont, 79; 125 medal, Govt Can, 92; Second Prize, Kochi Int Triennial Exhib, Japan, 90; Yukon 3 Rivers Journey, 2003; Queen's Jubilee Medal, 2003; Medallion, Royal Canadian Acad Arts, 2005. *Bibliog:* High North, Beaver Mag, 79; St Ives, Portrait of an Art Colony, Tate Gallery, Eng, 94; Ron Bolt on Mexico, Mag Art, 96; Arts Atlantic, 2003; LA Times Supplement, 2003; Albemarle Gallery (catalogue), London, Eng, 2004-2008; Paintings of Nova Scotia, 2004; Loch Gallery (catalogue), Can, 2006; and 12 pages more. *Mem:* Visual Arts Ont (dir, 75-81); Soc Can Artists (hon life mem); Arts & Letts Club, Toronto (prof mem); Royal Can Acad Art (elected mem, exec coun, 86-92). *Media:* Oil, Acrylic; Printmaking. *Interests:* Travel, painting & music. *Publ:* Contribr, Art Mag, 68-70; auth, Acrylics, Govt Ont Dept Cult & Recreation, 76; The Inner Ocean, Merritt Publ, 80; The Beat and the Still, North Eds Ltd, 90; Rendezvous/Boreal Forest, 2004; Three Rivers: Yukon/Great Boreal, 2005. *Dealer:* Loch Gallery 16 Hazelton Ave Toronto Ont M5R 2E2; Christina Parker Gallery 7 Plank Rd St John's Nfld A1E 1H3; Albemarle Gallery 49 Albemarle St London Eng W1X 3FE. *Mailing Add:* 856 Lees Ave Cobourg ON K9A 0B Canada

BOLTON, ROBIN JEAN
PAINTER, GRAPHIC ARTIST
b Americus, Ga, Sept 13, 1943. *Study:* Univ Ga, BFA (graphic design), 65. *Work:* Liverpool NY Pub Libr; Cobb Co Bd Educ, Marietta, Ga; Liverpool United Methodist Church, NY; Bridgeport United Methodist Church, NY; Dewit Community Church, NY; Federation Hall, Talluhah Falls Sch, Ga; Georgia Com on Women, Labor Dept. *Comn:* 12 paintings, IBM Collection, Binghamton, NY, 81-85; 3' x 6' paintings, Cannon Corp, Rochester, NY, 84; two 4' x 5' paintings, CitiBank, Nat Landmark Bldg, Albany, NY, 84-85; Mobil Oil Corp, Rochester, NY, 84-85; 4' x 5' painting, comn by Lee Iacocca, New York, 87-88; painting, Ga Dept of Ed, 2001; designed label, Persimmon Creek Vineyard, Clayton, Ga; two 48" x 60" paintings, bd rm & CEO office, Farash Corp, Rochester, NY; 25th anniversary painting of the Carter Ctr Pres Libr, Atlanta, 2007, Javy Lopez Collection. *Exhib:* 100 Yrs-100 Works, Kirkpatrick Art Ctr, Oklahoma City, Conguien Mus Art, Longview, Tex, Chatanooga Regional Hist Mus, Tenn, Fine Arts Mus South, Mobile, Ala, Islip Art Mus, NY, 89; Spring Showhouse, Lionsgate Mansion, Atlanta, Ga. *Pos:* Printer & painter. *Teaching:* Com Art Supply, Syracuse, NY. *Awards:* First Prize, Cooperstown Nat Juried, Cooperstown NY Art Asn, 76; First Prize, Arena Nat, Binghamton, NY, 76; Henry Mallory Mem Award, Cooperstown Art Asn, 78. *Bibliog:* TV documentary, WCNY Public Television, Liverpool, New York, Syracuse, 87; Gail Mountain (auth), Gloucester Daily Times, 92; Sharon Carson (auth), Boston Sunday Globe; Bev Leesman (auth), Syracuse New Times, 94. *Mem:* Nat Asn Women Artists, NY; Liverpool Arts & Crafts Guild, NY (lifetime hon mem); Alpharetta Art Guild. *Media:* Acrylic; Canvas. *Specialty:* fine arts and crafts. *Interests:* Reading, Cooking. *Dealer:* Nan Miller Gallery 3450 Winton Pl Rochester NY 14623; Lagerquist Gallery 3235 Paces Ferry Place NW Atlanta GA 30305

BOLTON-SMITH, ROBIN LEE
CURATOR, HISTORIAN
b Washington, DC, Oct 30, 1941. *Study:* Smith Col, Northampton, Mass, BA, 63; Inst Fine Arts, NY Univ, MA, 75. *Collection Arranged:* Lilly Martin Spencer: The Joys of Sentiment (co-auth, catalog), Smithsonian Inst, 73; Portrait Miniatures in Private Collections, Smithsonian Inst, 76; Miniature Collection (auth, catalog), Cincinnati Mus, 85; Tokens of Affection: The Miniature in Am, Met Mus, 90 & 91, Nat Mus Am Art, Smithsonian Inst, 91 & Art Inst Chicago, 91. *Pos:* Cur res asst, Nat Collection Fine Arts, Smithsonian Inst, 63-67, asst cur, 71-76, assoc cur, formerly; cur res asst, Metrop Mus Art, New York, 67-69; consult, 93-. *Res:* History of the American portrait miniature. *Publ:* Auth, Portrait Miniatures in Private Collections, Smithsonian Inst, 76; Five miniature collections, Coll Art J, summer 79; Fraser's place in the evolution of miniature portrait, In: Charles Fraser of Charleston (exhib catalog), Gibbes Art Gallery, Charleston, SC, 83; Intro to Anson Dickinson, The Celebrated Miniature Painter 1779-1852 (exhib catalog), Conn Hist Soc, 83; The Miniature in America, Vol CXXXVIII, No 5, Antiques Mag, 11/90. *Mailing Add:* 108 Warren Hill Rd Cornwall Bridge CT 06754-1303

BOMFORD, DAVID
CONSERVATOR, MUSEUM DIRECTOR
Collection Arranged: Art in the Making, Nat Gallery, London, 1998-2004. *Pos:* Asst restorer paintings, Nat Gallery, London, 1968-1974, sr restorer paintings, 1974-2005, head registrar & art handling depts, formerly; vis scholar, J Paul Getty Mus, 2005 & assoc dir collections, 2007-; ed, Studies in Conservation. *Teaching:* Slade prof fine art, Univ Oxford; vis prof, Churubusco Nat Inst Conserv, Mexico City & Vitae Found Art Mus, Sao Paolo. *Awards:* Heritage Preservation award for Distinction in Scholarship & Conservation, Coll Art Asn, 2010. *Mem:* Int Inst Conserv (sec gen). *Publ:* Auth, Conservation of Paintings, Nat Gallery Publ, 1997. *Mailing Add:* 1200 Getty Center Dr Los Angeles CA 90049-1679

BONANSINGA, KATE
CRITIC, CURATOR
b Lafayette, Ind, Aug 2, 1962. *Study:* Univ Mich, Ann Arbor, BA, 83; Ind Univ E Asian Language Inst, 90; Univ Ill, Urbana-Champaign, MA, 91. *Collection Arranged:* Arts and Crafts Furnishings from Portland Collections, 95. *Pos:* Cur & dir, Hoffman Gallery, Ore Sch Arts & Crafts, 91-95; co-owner, BonaKeane Gallery, 95-98; visual arts critic, Willamette Week. *Teaching:* Asst prof art hist, Ore Col Art & Craft, 91-; instr fine arts, Univ Portland, 93-94, Nike Corp, 95-. *Mem:* Coll Art Asn; Am Craft Asn; Soc Nam Goldsmiths. *Res:* Crafts; interiors; Contemporary ceramics. *Publ:* Auth of numerous reviews in Artweek, Reflex, Am Craft, Am Ceramics & Ceramics Monthly. *Mailing Add:* c/o Oregon Sch Arts & Crafts Hoffman Gallery 8245 SW Barnes Rd Portland OR 97225

BONINO, FERNANDA
ART DEALER
b Torino, Italy, Jan 5, 27. *Pos:* Pres & dir, Galeria Bonino, Ltd, New York, 63-86, Buenos Aires, 74-81. *Mem:* Art Dealer Asn Am. *Specialty:* Contemporary paintings and sculptures; American; European; South American. *Mailing Add:* 48 Great Jones St New York NY 10012

BONNER, JONATHAN G
SCULPTOR
b Princeton, NJ, 1947. *Study:* Philadelphia Coll Art, BFA, 71; RI Sch Design, MFA, 73. *Work:* Am Craft Mus, NY; Ariz State Univ Art Mus, Tempe; Marshall Fields, Chicago; RI Sch Design Mus Art; Mus Fine Arts, Boston, Mass; and many pvt collections. *Comn:* Triple Inversion, Fidelity Investments, London, 95; At Rest, Harcourt Gen Corp Headquarters, Chestnut Hill, Mass, 95; Facing AS220 Bldg, Providence, RI, 99; Twin, Fidelity Mgmt, Smithfield, RI, 99; Metamorphosis, RI Col, Providence, 2000; Nashu Street Park, Boston, 99; many others. *Exhib:* Solo exhibs, Virginia Lynch Gallery, Tiverton, RI, 91, Hokin Kaufman Gallery, Chicago, Ill, 91, Peter Joseph Gallery, NY, 92 & 93, Newport Art Mus, RI, 93, Kavesh Gallery, Ketchum, Idaho, 94, Gallery Camino Real, Boca Raton, Fla, 94 & Peter Joseph Gallery, NY, 95, MA Ginsberg Gallery, Iowa City, 95 & 99, Wheeler Gallery, Providence, 98 & many others; Am Works in Metal, Pritam & Eames, East Hampton, NY, 90-92; Joseph Gallery, NY, 91, 94 & 96; Masterworks, 91 & Masterworks Two (coauth, catalog), Peter Joseph Gallery, NY, 94; Formed by Fire, Carnegie Mus Art, Pittsburgh, Pa, 93; Inaugural Exhib, Donald Becker Gallery, Miami Beach, Fla, 94. *Awards:* Nat Endowment Arts, 76 & 88; RI State Coun Arts Fel, 87 & 90; LEF Found Project Grant, 98; City of Providence Art Project Grant, 98. *Bibliog:* Bill Van Siclin (auth), Providence J, 5/28/93; Casa Vogue, 2/94; Jamie Epstein (auth), Metalsmith Mag, winter 94; Karen Chambers (auth), Metalsmith Mag, winter 96

BONTECOU, LEE
ARTIST, SCULPTOR
b Providence, RI, Jan 15, 1931. *Study:* Art Students League, New York, 1952-55. *Exhib:* Solo exhibs, Leo Castelli Gallery, 1960, 1962, 1966, 1971, 1999, Galerie Ileana Sonnabend, Paris, 1965, Mus Boymans-van Beuningen, Rotterdam, 1968, Mus Contemp Art, Chicago, 1972, 2003, Davison Art Ctr, Wesleyan Univ, 1975, Halper Gallery, Palm Beach, Fla, 1976, Hathorn Gallery, Skidmore Coll, 1977, Mus Contemp Art, Los Angeles, 1993, Bonnefanten Mus Maastricht, Holland, 1995, Daniel Weinberg Gallery, 1995, 2001, Knoedler & Co, New York, 2004, 2005; Group exhibs, Schneider Gallery, Rome, 1957-58; Spoleto, Italy: Festival of Two Worlds, 1958; Leo Castelli Gallery, New York, 1960-1962, 1966, 1967, 1972, 1974, 1980, 1994, 1999, 2002; Whitney Mus Am Art, New York, 1960, 1961, 1963, 1964, 1966, 1968, 1982, 1984, 1999; Mus Mod Art, 1960, 1961, 1963, 1964; World House Galleries, New York, 1960; Seattle World's Fair, 1962; Corcoran Gallery Art, Wash, DC, 1963; Tate Gallery, London, 1964; Denver Art Mus, 1969; Met Mus Art, New York, 1976; Kunsthaus Zurich, 1980; Aldrich Mus Contemp Art, 1981; Contemp Art Mus, Austin, 1982; Ronald Feldman Gallery, New York, 1984; Mus Contemp Art, Los Angeles, 1993; Mus Fine Arts, Houston, 1996; Michael Rosenfeld Gallery, New York, 1996; Daniel Weinberg Gallery, Los Angeles, 2000, 2001; Cleveland Art Mus, 2003; Carnegie Mus Art, 2004; Elizabeth Leach Gallery, Portland, Ore, 2005; Frances Young Tang Teaching Mus & Art Gallery, Skidmore Coll, 2006; Bowdoin Coll Mus Art, 2007-08. *Teaching:* Art dept, Brooklyn Coll, City Univ NY, 1970-91. *Awards:*

Mademoiselle Woman of Yr, 1960; Second Prize, 28th Biennial Am Art, Corcoran Gallery Art, Wash, DC, 1963; First Prize, Nat Inst Arts and Letters, 1966; Francis J Greenburger Award, 2003; Skowhgan Medal for Sculpture, 2004; Int Asn Art Critics Award, 2005. *Mem:* Nat Acad; Am Acad Arts and Letters; Am Acad Arts and Scis. *Media:* Miscellaneous Media. *Dealer:* Valerie Carberry Gallery 875 N Michigan Ave Chicago IL 60611; David Floria Gallery 525 E Cooper Ave Aspen CO 81611; Larissa Goldston Gallery 530 W 25th St New York NY 10001; David Klein Gallery 163 Townsend St Birmingham MI 48009; Knoedler & Co 19 E 70th St New York NY 10021; Barbara Mathes Gallery 22 East 80th St New York NY 10021; Michael Rosenfeld Gallery 24 W 57th St New York NY 10019; Senior & Shopmaker Gallery 21 E 26th St New York NY 10010; Amy Simon Fine Art 275 Post Rd E Westport CT 06880. *Mailing Add:* c/o Leo Castelli Gallery 18 E 77th St New York NY 10075

BOOKER, CHAKAIA
SCULPTOR, PAINTER

b Newark, NJ. *Study:* Rutgers Univ, E Brunswick, NJ, BA, 76; City Coll New York, MFA, 93; studied clay crafts with Deena Kolbert, New York, 79-81 & clay biz with Kent Kraus, 81-82. *Work:* Studio Mus Harlem, NY; Queens Mus Art, Flushing, NY; US Embassy, Dakar, Senegal; also pvt collections of Vera G List & Richard Bellamy; Snite Mus Art; Neuberger Mus Art. *Comn:* 3D tire sculpture, Neuberger Mus Art, Purchase, NY, 97; sculpture relief, Nat Aeronautics & Space Admin, dedicated Nat Mus Women, Washington, DC, 98; outdoor sculpture, Pub Art Fund, Metro Tech Ctr, Brooklyn, NY, 98; outdoor sculpture, Neuberger Mus Art, 98. *Exhib:* Solo shows incl Jamaica Arts Ctr, NY, 94, Queens Mus Art Bulova Corp Ctr, NY, 96, Neuberger Mus of Art, Purchase Coll, 97, June Kelly Gallery, New York, 98, Laumeier Mus, St Louis, 99, Akron Art Mus, 2000, Galerie Simonne Stern, New Orleans, 2001; group shows incl Int '94, Socrates Sculpture Park (exhib catalog), Long Island City, NY, 94-95; Outdoor Sculpture Party '95 DeCordova Mus & Sculpture Park, Lincoln, Mass, 95; The Listening Sky: An Inaugural Exhib of the Studio Mus in Harlem Sculpture Garden (with catalog), Studio Mus Harlem, NY, 95; Heat Up, Fukuyama Mus, Hiroshima, Japan, 96; 20th Century Am Sculpture at the White House, Washington, 96; Postcards from Black Am: Contemp African Am Art, DeBeyerd Centre for Contemp Art, Breda, The Neth, 98, Frans Hals Mus, The Neth, 98; RUBBER, Robert Miller Gallery, NY, 98; New Mus Contemp Art, New York, 99; Whitney Biennial, 2000; N'Namdi Art Gallery, Chicago, 2000, 2001; Seton Hall Univ, Walsh Libr Gallery, South Orange, NJ, 2002. *Pos:* Artist-in-residence, Studio Mus Harlem, 95-96; Designed/Produced Pottery for plays, Extenuating Circumstances, Division Street & Mass Appeal, 81. *Awards:* Connor Award, 90-92; Joan Mitchell Found Grant, 95; Gregory Miller Fel, NY Found for Arts, 99; Anonymous Was A Woman Grant, 2000. *Bibliog:* Michael Kimmelman (auth), Turning an alley into a showcase for sculpture, NY Times, 9/22/95; Holland Cotter (auth), Art in review, NY Times, 7/26/96; Sarah Schmerler (auth), Standing on ceremony, Time Out, Vol 49, 96. *Mem:* Am Acad Arts and Letters. *Media:* Tires, Bones; Installationist, Mixed Media. *Publ:* A Guide of Sculpture Parks & Gardens, Publishing Ltd, 96. *Dealer:* Max Protetch Gallery 511 W 22nd New York NY 10011-1109; Anthony Archibald J 602 Tenth Ave New York NY 10036. *Mailing Add:* 608 E Ninth St No 2 New York NY 10009

BOOTH, DOT
PAINTER, PRINTMAKER

b Chicago, Ill. *Study:* Univ Ala, Birmingham, 63-64; Univ South Fla, Tampa, 68-70. *Work:* Miss Mus Art, Jackson; Macon Mus Arts & Sci, Ga; City Miami, Fla; Columbus Mus, Ga; Pensacola Art Ctr, Fla. *Comn:* Orlando Exec Airport, Fla. *Exhib:* 40th & 43rd Ann Contemp Am Paintings, Soc Four Arts, Palm Beach, Fla, 69, 78, 81 & 87; Best of Fla, Pensacola Art Ctr, 70; Invitational, Mus Arts & Sci, Daytona Beach, Fla, 72; Selections from Permanent Collection, Miss Mus Art, Jackson, 78; Artists in Ga, High Mus Art, Atlanta, 78-79; Loch Haven Art Ctr Show, Orlando, Fla, 83. *Pos:* Scenic artist, EPCOT, 82. *Teaching:* Vis instr, Ringling Sch Art, 89. *Awards:* Philip Hulitar Award, 49th Ann Soc Four Arts, Palm Beach, Fla, 87; Purchase Award, Frontal Images, Jackson, Miss, 70; Best of Show, Gasparilla, Tampa, Fla, 78. *Bibliog:* Dot Booth--Hard Edge Realism, Orange Co Public TV, Fla, 73. *Media:* Oil, Acrylic; Serigraphy. *Mailing Add:* Booth Davis Studios 1939 Taylor Ave Winter Park FL 32792-3130

BOOTH, LAURENCE OGDEN
SCULPTOR, ARCHITECT

b Chicago, Ill, July 5, 1936. *Study:* Stanford Univ, BA, 58; Mass Inst Technol, BArch, 60. *Work:* Art Inst Chicago. *Exhib:* Richard Gray Gallery, 76; Chicago 7 Architects, Walter Kelly Gallery & Richard Gray Gallery, 77; Frumkin Struve Gallery, Chicago, 80-81; New Chicago Architecture, Verone, Italy, 81; Harvard Grad Sch Design, 81; and many other solo & group exhibs. *Pos:* Vis critic, Harvard Univ, 81-82; bd dir, Mus Contemp Art, Chicago. *Teaching:* Instr archit, Univ Ill, Chicago Circle, 69-71; vis prof, Univ Ill, 82. *Bibliog:* Amy Goldin (auth), Vitality vs greasy kid stuff, Art Gallery Mag, 72; article, Chicago Archit J, 81; article, New Chicago Archit, 81; and others. *Media:* Multimedia. *Publ:* Auth, Spiritual content of order, Arc Mag, 68; auth, Review of Stanley Tigerman sculpture, Art Scene Mag, 69

BOOTH, MARK
PAINTER

b Camden, NJ, 1964. *Study:* RI Sch Design, BFA (Printmaking), 1987; Sch Art Inst Chicago, MFA, 1995, continuing studies, 1999-2000. *Exhib:* Solo exhibs include Gov Drummer Acad, Byfield, Mass, 1992, St Lawrence Univ, Canton, NY, 1993, RX Gallery, Chicago, 1996, 1997, Bodybuilder & Sportsman Gallery, Chicago, 2005, Inst Contemp Art, Chicago, 2008; group exhibs include New Talent I, Contemp Arts Workshop, Chicago, 1995; Baubien, Booth, Carmichael, Lineage Gallery, Chicago, 1996; Out of the Shadow of Ivan Albright: 12 Contemp Chicago Artists, Ill Art Gallery, Chicago, 1997; Evanston Art Ctr Biennial, 2000; Print + Mass, Gallery 2, Sch Art Inst Chicago, 2000; Contextual: Art & Text in Chicago, Chicago Cult Ctr, 2001; Painting: Nine Chicago Painters, Univ Wis, Green Bay, 2002; Bodybuilder & Sportsman Gallery, Chicago, 2003 & 2005

BOOTH, MICHAEL GAYLE
PAINTER, SCULPTOR

b Soda Springs, Idaho, June 13, 1951. *Study:* Boise State Univ, 74; Utah State Univ, BA, 78, MFA, 79. *Work:* Blue Mountain Community Coll Grounds, Pendleton, Ore; State Capital Bldg Governors Chambers, Boise, Idaho; Large Monumental Sculpture, Freeway Junction, Pendleton, Ore; Quarterhorse Hall of Fame, Amarillo, Tex; Large Monumental Sculpture, CofC Visitors Ctr, Pendleton, Ore. *Comn:* Painting of Historic Boise, J R Simplot, Idaho, 88; Monumental Mural, Gold Beach Athletic Asn, Ore, 88; Series of Large Paintings, Park Ctr Sports Club, Boise, 89; Monumental Sculpture, Pendleton City, Ore, 93; Series/Collection of Sports Cars, US Sen Gordon Smith, Pendleton, Ore, 95; Hermiston Pub Libr, Ore, 98; Hermiston Ore Convention Ctr, 98; mural. *Exhib:* Ore Watercolor Soc, Ore Capital Bldg, Salem, 85; Watercolor USA, Mo, 86; Audubon Artists of Am, NY, 87; Nat Soc of Painters in Casein & Acrylic, NY, 88; The Cayuse Indians, Ore Trail Interpretive Ctr, Ore, 92. *Collection Arranged:* Regional Sculpture Masks, Alliance Varied Arts, 75; Nat Works on Paper, Coop Show with Utah State Univ, 76; Painting 78, Alliance Varied Arts, 78; Happy Canyon Western Art Invitational, 90-96. *Pos:* Dir, Alliance Varied Arts, 77-79; own, Artist Gallery & Frames, 83-88. *Teaching:* Art prof basic design & drawing, Utah State Univ, 79-80, drawing, design, appreciation, painting & sculpture, Blue Mountain Col, 88-, Eastern Ore Univ, 98-. *Awards:* First Place, Watercolor Div, Rock Springs Nat Art Exhib, 79; First Place, Artists Showcase, Utah State Univ, 80; Best of Show, Watercolor Soc Ore, 81. *Bibliog:* Mindy Carrel (auth), Gallery, Western Horseman, 5/92; Vicki Stavig (auth), One on one, Art of the West, 11-12/93; Diane Nodurft (auth), Balancing act equine images, 2-3/96. *Mem:* Audubon Artists Am; Watercolor Soc Ore; Nat Watercolor Soc; Nat Soc Painters in Casein & Acrylic. *Media:* Acrylic, Oil; Bronze, Concrete. *Publ:* Auth, Creating Dynamic Contrast Through the Properties of Color, Artwise Publs, 79; A Sketch of Pendleton, Artwise Publs, 93; Cayuse Indians, The Art of Michael Booth, Artwise Publs, 94; Watercolor Strategy, Artwise Publs, 95; The Paintings of Michael G Booth, The Reservation, Artwise Publs, 96. *Mailing Add:* 1335 Tutuilla Rd Pendleton OR 97801

BOOTH, ROBERT ALAN
SCULPTOR

b Mt Kisco, NY, 1952. *Study:* Art Inst Boston, 71-73; Mass Coll Art, BFA, 76; Syracuse Univ, MFA, 78. *Work:* Equitable Life Assurance Soc, Syracuse Univ; Burchfield-Penney Art Ctr, Wright State Univ. *Comn:* Site sculpture, comn by Ted Stetler, Syracuse, NY, 77; sculpture, TRW Bearings Corp, Jamestown, NY, 81; site sculpture, Artpark, Lewiston, NY, 83; pub fountain restoration, Fredonia, NY, 91. *Exhib:* 43 Western NY Exhibs, Albright-Knox Art Gallery, Buffalo, NY, 90; X Sightings, Anderson Gallery, Buffalo, NY; Working With Tradition: The Academic Artists, Birchfield Art Ctr, Buffalo, NY & NY State Mus, Albany, 93; 45 Western NY Exhib, Albright-Knox Art Gallery, Buffalo, NY, 94; Solo exhib, Burchfield Penny Art Ctr, Buffalo, 95, St Georges Sch, newport, RI, 2010, traveling exhib, Wounded in Action, Am Acad Orthopedic Surgeons, 2010-2011; New Work, Henri Gallery, Washington, DC, 96; Chautauqua Ctr Visual Arts, NY, 97; Mass Coll Art, Boston, 98; Wright State Univ, 99; Rosewood Art Gallery, 2003; Gallery 15, Rochester, NY, 2003; Buffalo Art Studio, NY, 2003; Univ Mass, Dartmouth, 2006; Moscone Ctr, San Francisco, 2008; Emotion Pictures: Orthopedics in Art, Chicago Cult Ctr, 2008; ArtPark 1974-1984, Univ Buffalo, NY, 2010; Hunter Gallery, St Georges Sch, Newport, RI, 2010; Figuration, Buffalo Arts Studio, NY, 2011. *Pos:* Pres, Coun Art Dept Chairs, State Univ NY, 93-96; bd mem, Mid-Am Coll Art Asn, 97-2003. *Teaching:* Distinguished Teaching Prof sculpture, State Univ NY Coll, Fredonia, 78-2005, chmn, dept art, 88-96, distinguished teaching prof, 2005-, dept chair, 2009-. *Awards:* State Univ NY Fac Res Fel, 82-83; Artist Fel Grant, Chautauqua Funds for the Arts, NY, 95. *Mem:* Int Sculpture Ctr; Hallwalls Contemporary Art Ctr. *Media:* Mixed. *Mailing Add:* 3197 Rte 83 Fredonia NY 14063

BOOTHE, POWER
PAINTER, ADMINISTRATOR

b Mar 12, 1945; US citizen. *Study:* Colo Col, BA, 67; Whitney Mus, Independent Study Prog, 67-68; Colo Coll. *Hon Degrees:* Hon Doctor of Arts, 1989. *Work:* Guggenheim Mus; Whitney Mus Am Art; NJ State Mus; Stanford Univ Art Mus; and others; Mus Mod Art; British Mus; New Britain Mus Am Art. *Exhib:* Theodoron Award Show, 71, Art of this Decade, 74 & Recent Acquisitions, 75, Guggenheim Mus, NY; one-person exhibs, Power Booth, Paintings, 71-88, A M Sachs Gallery, 73, 74, 76, 77, 81, 82 & 85, Pvt Images, Los Angeles Co Mus Art, Calif, 77, Painting Show, PS1 Gallery, Brooklyn, NY, 77, Art & Dance, Inst Contemp Art, Boston, 82 & Hurlbutt Gallery, Greenwich, Conn, 88, Souyun Yi Gallery, 87 & 89, Harrison Gallery, 90, Time-Life Bldg, NY 90, Trenkmann Gallery, 91 & Robert Morrison Gallery, 92; Book-Objects by Contemp Artists, Albright-Knox Art Gallery, Buffalo, NY, 77; Between the Sexes, Md Art Place, NY, 94; The Persistence of Abstraction, Noyes Mus, Ocean Park, NJ, 94; Scratching the Surface, Stephen Haller Gallery, 94; New Paintings, Power Boothe, 95; Pioneers of Abstraction, Sidney Mishkin Gallery, 96. *Pos:* Co-dir, Mt Royal Grad Sch, Md Inst, Col Art, 95-98; ed, Am Abstract Artist J, 96-98; dir, Sch Art, Ohio Univ, 98-. *Teaching:* Instr painting, Sch Visual Arts, NY, 79-88; Princeton Univ, 89-95; Mt Royal Grad Sch, Md Inst, Col Art, 93-98; Sch Art, Ohio Univ, 1998-2001; Dean, Hartford Art Sch, Univ Hartford, 2001-. *Awards:* Int Arts Grant, Nat Endowment Arts, 86 & 88; Guggenheim Fel Grant, 89; NY State Grant, 87 & 89; Pollock Krasner Found Grant, 89; NY State Arts Grant, 91; and many others. *Bibliog:* Gerard Haggerty (auth), Boothe at Haller, Art News, 94; Roberta Smith (auth), Power Boothe, NY Times, 95; Robert Edelman (auth), Power Boothe at Stephen Haller Gallery, 96. *Mem:* Am Abstract Artists; Coll Art Asn; Nat Asn Sch of Art & Design. *Media:* Oil, Acrylic; Film, Performance. *Publ:* When the Fourth Soldier Falls, A Study of Pielo Della Francesca's Resurrection, issue, Reflex Horizons, 86; Abstraction and Meaning, Am Abstract Artists J, 98. *Mailing Add:* Hartford Art Sch Univ Hartford 200 Bloomfield Ave Hartford CT 06117-1599

BOOTZ, ANTOINE H
PHOTOGRAPHER
b Paris, France, Feb 27, 1956. *Study:* Sciences-Politiques, Paris, 74-75; Sorbonne, Paris, 76-77; Univ St Charles, Marseille, France, 77-78. *Work:* Fonds Nat d'Art Contemporain, Paris; Galerie Baudoin Lebon, Paris. *Exhib:* Des Photographies dans le Paysage, Galerie de France, Paris, 81; Une Autre Photographie, Mus Andre Malraux, Creteil, France, 82; Saus Titre, Galerie Baudoin Lebon, Paris, 83-85; Saus Titre, Contemp Photog & Video from France, traveling US, 85-87. *Pos:* Freelance photogr for mags, 89-. *Awards:* Fel, Nat Endowment Arts, 86-87

BORA (BORAEV), VADIM MAKHARBEKOVICH
SCULPTOR, PAINTER
b Beslan, No Ossetia-Alania, Russia, Apr 9, 1954. *Study:* Vladikavkaz Pedagogical Tech Col, Design & Drawing degree, 1969-73; Leningrad State Pedagogical Inst, Auditing, 1973-74; Leningrad Acad of Art, Auditing, 1973-74. *Work:* Spartanburg Co Mus of Art, Spartanburg, SC; Ministry of Culture Collection, Moscow, Russia; No Ossetia Mus of Art, Vladikavkaz, Russia; Anderson Arts Ctr, SC. *Comn:* Meditation - Terra Cotta, Bishop Chapel Retirement Ctr, St Louis, MO, 1996; Cat Walk, City of Asheville, NC, 1999; Animal Alley, Bronze, Buckhead Condominiums, Atlanta, Ga, 2000; Crucifix, synth Marble, St Mary's Episcopal Parish, Asheville, NC, 2000; The Wings of Freedom, Va Medical Ctr of WNC, NC, 2001; sculpture, On the Mend, Mission Hospitals, Asheville, NC, 2006; Sheriff, Bronze, Haywood County, Waynesville, NC, 2008; Cornelia & Cedric Bittmore estate, Bronze, Asheville, NC, 2010; synthetic stone, Nine Grotesque, Modesto, Asheville, NC, 2010. *Exhib:* Solo Exhibs incl: New & Different, The Artists Gallery, Wilmington, NC, 2004, Am Retrospective, Spartanburg Mus of Art, SC, 2005, Armida Gallery, Moscow, Russia, 2006, In the Russian Tradition, Anderson Arts Ctr, 2006; group exhibs incl: The Artists, The Asheville Arts Coun, Asheville, NC, 2000, Sculpture Invitational, The Burke Country Arts Coun, Morganton, NC, 2001, 16 Patton, Asheville, NC, 2002, Int Florence, Biennale of Contemp Art, Florence, Italy, 2005; Twisted Tree Gallery, Hickory, NC, 2005; Ctr for Craft, Creativity & Design, Hendersonville, NC, 2006; 16 Patton Gallery, Asheville, NC, 2010; Fine Arts League of the Carolinas, Asheville, NC, 2010; Conn-Artist Gallery, Hendersonville, NC, 2010. *Teaching:* Art instr, Vladikavkaz Lycee of Art, Russia, 1988-90; instr, Singleton Arts Ctr, Flat Rock, NC, 1994-95; Principal, instr, Vadim Bora Studio-Gallery, Asheville, NC, 1998, Battery Park Sculpture Club, Asheville, NC, 2003, Spartanburg Mus Art, SC, 2004-05. *Mem:* Nat Sculpture Soc; Portrait Soc of Am; Mountain Sculptors; Tri-State Sculptors; Prof Artists Union of Russia; Prof Artists Union of N Ossetia-Alania. *Media:* Bronze, Terra Cotta, Oil, Canvas, Silver, Copper. *Specialty:* Portraiture, figurative, landscape, narrative. *Publ:* Arnold Wengrow, Artist Faces up to his works, Asheville Citizens, Times Gannet, 2004; Staff Publisher, Never at Rest, The Laurel of Asheville, Laurel Publ, 2004; Constance E Richards, Artists Retreat - Nuances of the Land, Pinnacle Living, Leisure Publ, 2005; Linda Conley, Vadim Bora, Spartanburg Herald Journal, 2005; Ali Marshall, Words for his Art Language, Mountain Xpress, 2011. *Mailing Add:* 171 Peterson Dr Asheville NC 28801

BORAX, EDITH See Morrison, Edith Borax

BORDEAUX, JEAN-LUC
ART HISTORIAN, CURATOR, ART EXPERT
b Laval, France, Feb 13, 1937. *Study:* Univ Paris, Fac Sci, PCB, 1959; Mus Nat d'Art Mod, Paris, study of museology with Jean Cassou, 1958-60; Iowa State Univ, BS (journalism), 1964; Ariz State Univ, MA (art hist), 1966; Univ Calif, Los Angeles, PhD (art hist), 1970. *Collection Arranged:* Baroque Paintings from the Getty Mus; Roman Portraits from the Getty Mus; Rodin from the Maryhill Collection, J Paul Getty Mus; The Rococo Age: French Masterpieces of the Eighteenth Century, High Mus, Atlanta; The First Painters of the King, NY, New Orleans & Columbus, Ohio; Unstretched Surfaces, Pompidou Ctr, Paris and LAICA, Los Angeles; Abstraction in Los Angeles, 1950-1980, Gribin Collection, CSUN and Univ Calif Irvine; The Fundamental Aspects of Modernism, Los Angeles & Albuquerque, NMex. *Pos:* Art critic & writer, Connaissance des Arts & Art Int, 1973-86; asst cur paintings, J Paul Getty Mus, Malibu, Calif, 1969-72; dir, Fine Arts Gallery, Calif State Univ, Northridge, 1972-2005; guest cur, Calif Palace of the Legion of Honor, San Francisco, 1975; chargé de mission, Mus du Louvre, France, 1979-80; organized and cur numerous exhibs since 1972; dir & head expert, Christie's France & Monaco Old Master Paintings & Drawings, 1989-93. *Teaching:* Instr art hist, Univ Calif, Los Angeles, 1969-72; dir fine arts gallery, Calif State Univ, Northridge, Calif, 1972-81; prof art hist, Calif State Univ, Northridge, 1969-, dir Mus Studies, 1994-. *Awards:* Kress Fel, 1970-71; Calif Arts Coun Exhib Grants, 1974-75; J Paul Getty Trust Publ Award, 1984; Found Paribas Publ Award, 1984; Officier des Palmes Academiques, France, 1986. *Mem:* Fr Soc Hist Art; Coll Art Asn; Les Amis du Louvre; Los Angeles Coun Mus Art; Mus Contemp Art Los Angeles. *Res:* French painting from 17th to early 19th centuries; Twentieth Century Art & Criticism; Italian Baroque art; Mus Studies; Twentieth Century: The Age of the Collage. *Interests:* Contemp art in New York & Los Angeles. *Publ:* Auth, articles, Burlington Mag, Am Art Rev, Art Int, Art in Am, Jour J Paul Getty Mus, Artibus et Historiae Gaz des Beaux Arts, Connaissance des Arts, and others; François Le Moyne and His Generation 1688-1737, (catalog raisonné), Arthena, 1984-85. *Mailing Add:* Calif State Univ Northridge 18111 Nordhoff St Northridge CA 91330

BORDES, ADRIENNE
PAINTER, INSTRUCTOR
b New York, NY, 1935. *Study:* NY Univ, with Philip Guston, BA, 57; Hunter Col, New York, with Tony Smith & Vincent Longo. *Exhib:* One-person shows, Capricorn Gallery, NY, 67 & 68 & Wilkes Col, Pa, 78; Six Artists, NY Univ, 68; Some New Beginnings, Brooklyn Mus, 68; Women in the Arts, Univ Wis, 72; Transitions, Wallace Gallery, State Univ NY, 79; Four Artists & A Writer, Fed Hall, NY, 82. *Teaching:* Adj instr painting, Hunter Col, New York, 78-80 & Adelphi Univ, 79-80; tenured asst prof hist archit & interior design, Fashion Inst Technol, 80-. *Awards:* Painting Grant, Millay Colony Arts, Austerlitz, NY, 75. *Bibliog:* Julia Ballerini (auth), Four Artists and a Writer, catalog, Fed Hall, NY, 82. *Mem:* Interior Design Educators Coun. *Media:* Acrylic. *Mailing Add:* 369 Seventh Ave New York NY 10001

BORDO, ROBERT
PAINTER
b Montreal. *Study:* McGill Univ, 1967-70; NY Studio Sch, 1972-75. *Exhib:* Solo exhibs, Concordia Art Gallery, Montreal, 1984, Brook Alexander, New York, 1987, 1989, 1991-92, Tibor de Nagy Gallery, New York, 1996, Alexander and Bonin, New York, 1999, 2002, 2005, 2008, Galerie Rene Blouin, Montreal, 2000, Rubicon Gallery, Dublin, 2007 & Mummer + Schnelle, London, 2009; Aerial Perspectives, DC Moore Gallery, New York, 1997; The Continuous Mark: 40 Years of the New York Studio School, NY Studio Sch, 2005; The Good, Bad, and the Ugly, New Langton Arts, San Francisco, 2007; Am Acad Arts & Letts Invitational, 2007 & 2010; Slough, David Nolan Gallery, New York, 2009. *Teaching:* Visiting faculty, Calif Inst Arts, 1995 & Parsons Sch Design, New York, 1995; assoc prof, Cooper Union Sch Art, New York, 1995-. *Awards:* MacDowell Fel, 1994; Artist Fel Award, Tesuque Found, 1998. *Bibliog:* Valerie Gladstone (auth), Reviews: New York: Robert Bordo, Artnewsm 11/2005; Ken Johnson (auth), Air, NY Times, 7/2006; David Cohen (auth), The Heady Hedonist, NY Sun, 9/2008. *Media:* Oil. *Mailing Add:* c/o Alexander and Bonin 132 Tenth Ave New York NY 10011

BORETZ, NAOMI
PAINTER, EDUCATOR
b New York, NY. *Study:* Art Students League; Boston Mus Sch; Rutgers Univ, MA (art hist); City Univ New York, MA (fine arts). *Work:* Joslyn Art Mus, Omaha, Nebr; Solomon R Guggenheim Mus, Metrop Mus Art Prints Coll, Mus Mod Art, Whitney Mus Am Art, Queens Coll Art Collection, New York; Brit Mus London, Eng; Glasgow Mus, Scotland; Walker Art Ctr, Minneapolis, Minn; Mus Fine Arts, Boston; Fogg Art Mus, Harvard Univ, Mass; Coos Art Mus,Ore; DeLand Art Mus, Fla; Yale Univ Art Gallery; Mus Southwest, Midland, Tex; Asheville Art Mus, NC; San Jose Art Mus, Calif; Miami Univ Art Mus, Oxford, Ohio; Missoula Art Mus, Mont; Crawford Munic Art Gallery, Ireland; and others; Hove Mus Art. *Exhib:* Westminster Arts Council Arts Centre, London, England, 71; Awards Exhib, Brooklyn Mus Art, 72; Middlesex Co Mus, NJ, 81; Condeso Lawler Gallery, New York, 87; Carnegie-Mellon Art Gallery, Pittsburgh, 89; Ulrich Mus Wichita State Univ, Kans, 92; Noyes Mus, NJ, 94; Nelson-Atkins Art Mus, Mo, 94; Westbeth Gallery, 96; Mishkin Gallery, Baruch Coll, 97; Muhlenburg Coll Art Gallery, 2002; and others. *Awards:* Va Ctr Creative Arts Fel, 86; Ossabaw Arts Found Fel, 75; Artist Fel, NJ State Coun Arts, 85-86; Tyrone Guthrie Art Ctr Fel, Ireland, 87; Writers-Artists Guild, Can, 88. *Bibliog:* Ian Woodcock (auth), article, Arts Mag, 7/72; interview, Brit Broadcasting co Radio, 72-73; article, NY Times, 3/81; and others. *Mem:* Am Abstract Artists. *Media:* All Media. *Publ:* Auth, The reality underlying abstraction, In: Perception and Pictorial Representation, Praeger, 79; Watercolors with acetate, Leonardo, 78; and others

BORG, JOSEPH
PRINTMAKER, COLLAGE ARTIST
b New York, NY, Jan 26, 1942. *Study:* Studied intaglio with Ruth Leaf; studied lithography with Dan Weldon; Nassau Community Col, AA, 80. *Work:* Mus Modern Art, Barcelona, Spain; Queensboro Col, NY; Tama Art Univ, Tokyo; World Bank, Washington, DC; Off of Lieutenant Gov, State Capital, Honolulu. *Exhib:* Int Print Show, Nat Libr Paris, France, 86; Int Prints, Mus de La Estaupa, Mex, 88; Print Int, Found de Collioure, France, 88; Mini Print Int, Mus Fine Arts, Boston, 89; solo exhib, Saigado Gallery, Akita City, Japan, 90; Mozart Exhib, Gallery Lincoln Ctr, NY, 91; Art Embassies Prog, US Dept State. *Pos:* Vpres, Rockville Ctr Arts Coun, 84-88; demonstr/lectr, various sch-art groups; master printer/tech adv, Ruth Leaf Print Studio, 88-. *Mem:* Southern Graphics Coun. *Media:* Intaglio, Etching. *Publ:* Auth, New York Moments, Book of Collages. *Mailing Add:* 159 Gordon Rd Valley Stream NY 11581

BORGATTA, ISABEL CASE
SCULPTOR, EDUCATOR
b Madison, Wis, Nov 21, 22. *Study:* Smith Coll, 39-40; Yale Univ Sch Fine Arts, BFA, 44; Studio of Jose de Creeft, 44-45; Art Students League, 46. *Work:* Benton Mus, Univ Conn; Hudson River Mus; Coll New Rochelle Mus; 4 pieces NYNEX Hqs, NY & Grand Hyatt Hotel, NY; Smith Coll Mus; Okla Art Ctr; Chrysler Mus; Brooklyn Mus; Kranert Mus, Univ Ill; Yeshiva Univ; City Univ Graduate Ctr; Wadsworth Atheneum, Hartford, Conn; Donald Trump Buildings; Norfolk Mus; Coll New Rochelle; Hudson River Mus. *Comn:* Mem sculpture, New Rochelle, NY, 72; Grand Hyatt Hotel, NY; Zofital Spa, Rome; NYNEX, NY; Transnational Develop, NY; and others; Harry Belafonte, Jennings Lang, Senator William Benton, Morris Ernst, Mrs Rudoff Wunderlich, Alfred Kazin Dan Talbot, Donald Trump, etc. *Exhib:* Metrop Mus, 47; Pa Acad Fine Arts Ann, Philadelphia, 49-55; Whitney Mus, New York, 51-52; Village Art Ctr, 51; Am Sculpture, Metrop Mus Art, 51; solo exhibs, Galerie St Etienne, 54 & 56 & Frank Rehn Gallery, 68, 71, 74 & 77, Hudson River Mus, 61, Hastings on Hudson Mus, 61, Roko Gallery, New York, 72, Briarcliff Coll Mus, 70, Cathedral Mus, St John the Divine, New York, 78, Westbeth Gallery, 88; Hartford Atheneum, Nat Acad Ann Sculptors Guild, 71-88; Elaine Benson Gallery, 82 & 85; Sid Deutsch Gallery, 84 & 87; Ceres Gallery, 85; Sweet Briar Coll Mus, 86; Galerie Coach, Paris, 86; Oklahoma Art Ctr, 87; Camp Gallery, 87; NY Carlsbad Glyptotek Copenhagen, Denmark, 80; Closson Gallery 87; Women Sculptors of the Nineties, Newhouse Mus, 92; Kyoto City Mus, Japan, 93; Newhouse Mus, 95; Retrospective Exhib, The Century Asn, NY, 2011. *Pos:* Deleg, Fedn Fine Arts; exec bd, Sculptors Guild, currently. *Teaching:* Lectr sculpture, City Coll New York, 60-71; assoc prof, Col New Rochelle, 73-78, prof, 78-80. *Awards:* MacDowell Colony Fel, 68, 73, 74; Yaddo Fel, 71, 72 & 73; Va Ctr Creative Arts Fel, 85-92; Sculpture residency, Govt Greece, Delphi, 92-93, Crete, 94-96; Ettl Grant, Nat Sculpture Soc, 95. *Bibliog:* Mark van Doren (auth), The sculptures of Isabel Case Borgatta, Galerie St Etienne, 54; William D Allen (auth), Borgatta's marbles, Arts Mag, 68; James R Mellow (auth),

article in NY Times, 74; Virginia Watson-Jones (auth), American Women Sculptors, Oryx Press, 86; Isabel Case Borgatta: The Persistence of the Figure, Cincinnati Univ, 87; Shaping Space, Zelanski & Fisher, Hancourt Brace, 95, 2nd ed, 2006; Smith Voices, Smith College Press, 99; Mary Pat Fisher (auth), Women & Religion, Laurence King Publ, London, 2006; Roxanne Guerrero (auth), A Maternal Art Life mag, Dec 69; Anthony Padovano (auth), The Process of Sculpture, Doubleday, 81; Marion Roller (auth), Meeting the Challenge of Space, Nat Sculpture Soc, 82; Profile of Isabel Case Borgatta, Nat Sculpture Soc, 2005; Jane Fallo (auth), The Shape of Things, Smith Coll Alumnae Quarterly, 2012. *Mem:* Women's Caucus Art; Artists Equity; Sculptors Guild (exec bd); Nat Sculpture Soc; The Century Asn. *Media:* Stone, Wood. *Res:* Continued research for publications, including Health Hazards for Artists. *Interests:* Environment, liberal politics. *Publ:* Auth, A Sculptor Changes, Women Artists Newsletter, 77; Casting landscapes in paper, Artists Mag, 86; The Persistence of the Figure, College Art Assoc, 87; The Figure Today, Women's Caucus for Art, 88; Profile of Isabel Case Borgatta, Nat Sculpture Soc, 2005; Series of Articles on Health Hazards for Artists, Pub Sculptors Guild Bulletins. *Dealer:* Westbeth Gallery NY. *Mailing Add:* 463 West St Apt 1105 New York NY 10014-2010

BORN, JAMES E
SCULPTOR
b Toledo, Ohio, Nov 16, 1934. *Study:* Toledo Mus Sch, cert; Univ Toledo, BA, 59; Univ Iowa, Iowa City, MFA, 62. *Work:* Univ Iowa, Iowa City; Art Ctr Mus, Pine Bluff, Ark; Trans World Airlines, Los Angeles, Calif; Chartoff Productions, Santa Monica, Calif. *Exhib:* Solo exhibs, Cent Mich Univ, 69, 77 & 84, Muskegon Community Coll, 79, Ferris State Univ, 85, Gallery Abbott Kiney, Venice, Calif, 92, Mich Fine Arts Competition, Bloomfield Art Ctr, Birmingham, 92, Commun Trans World Airlines, Los Angeles Airport, Calif, San Diego Mus Art, 95, Mt Clemens Art Mus, Mich, 93-95 & Saginaw Art Mus, 93-95; Sculpture & Ceramics, Butler Inst Am Art, Youngstown, Ohio, 68, 74, 75 & 77; Mich Fine Arts Competition, Bloomfield Art Ctr, Birmingham, 92; Saginaw Mus, Mich, 93-95; Mt Clemens Art Ctr, Mich, 93-95; juried exhib, San Diego Mus Art, Calif, 95. *Teaching:* Asst prof sculpture, painting, design & drawing, Univ Calif, Humboldt, Arcata, 62-64 & Calif Western Univ, San Diego, 64-65; asst prof sculpture, design & painting, Univ Calif, Stanislaus, Turlock, 65-68; assoc prof sculpture, Cent Mich Univ, Mt Pleasant, 68-76, acting chmn, 72-74, prof sculpture, 76-. *Awards:* Sculpture Award, 92 & Laatsch Award-Sculpture, 93, Mich Competition, Saginaw Art Mus; Trustee Award, Mich Competition, Mt Clemens Art Ctr, 94. *Mem:* Coll Art Asn; Mid-Am Art Asn. *Media:* Bronze

BORNSTEIN, ELI
PAINTER, SCULPTOR
b Milwaukee, Wis, Dec 28, 1922; US & Can citizen. *Study:* Univ Wis, BS, 45 & MS, 54; Art Inst Chicago; Univ Chicago, 43; Acad Montmartre of Fernand Leger, Paris, 51; Acad Julian, Paris, 52, Univ Saskatchewan, D Litt, 90. *Work:* Walker Art Ctr, Minneapolis, Minn; Nat Gallery Can, Ottawa; Univ Calgary, Alta; Univ Sask & Mendel Art Gallery, Saskatoon; Ft Lauderdale Mus Art, Fla; Milwaukee Art Mus; Florsheim Collection, Chicago; Canadian Ctr Archit, Montreal; Beaverbrook Art Gallery; Frederickton; and others. *Comn:* Aluminum construction, Sask Teacher's Fedn, Saskatoon, 56; structurist relief, Univ Sask, Saskatoon, 58; structurist relief, Int Air Terminal, Winnipeg, 62; structurist construction, Wascana Ctr Authority, Regina, 83; hexaplane structurist relief, Synchrotron, Can Light Source Bldg, Univ Sask, 2003; Int Univ Bremen, Germany, 2006; Univ Manitoba, Winnipeg, 2008; Univ Wisc Milwaukee Found, 2012. *Exhib:* Retrospectives, Mendel Art Gallery, Saskatoon, 64, 82, 96, & 2003; Nat Gallery Can Biennial, Ottawa, 67; 2nd Int Biennial, Medellin, Colombia, 70; Can Cult Centre, Paris, France, 76; Glenbow-Alta Inst, Calgary, 76; York Univ Art Gallery, Toronto, 83; Fine Arts Gallery, Univ Wis, Milwaukee; Forum Art Gallery, NY, 2005-12; and others. *Pos:* Founder, Ed, The Structurist, 60-2010. *Teaching:* Instr drawing, painting & sculpture, Milwaukee Art Inst, 43-47; instr design, Univ Wis, 49; prof art, Univ Sask, 50-, head dept art, 63-71, prof emer, 90. *Awards:* Allied Arts Medal, Royal Archit Inst Can, 68; Hon mention, 2nd Int Biennial Exhib, Medellin, Colombia, 70; Gov Gen's Queen Elizabeth Silver Jubilee Medal, 77; Saskatchewan, Order of Merit, 2008. *Bibliog:* Eli Bornstein: Selected Works/Oeuvres Choisies, 1957-1982, Kazimir Karpuszko, Mendel Art Gallery, 82; Eli Bornstein: Art Toward Nature, Jonneke Fritz-Jobse, Mendel Art Gallery, 96; Eli Bornstein, Gerald Nordland, Forum Gallery, New York, 2007; An Art at the Mercy of Light, Recent Works by Eli Bornstein, curated by Oliver Botot with essays by him and Rodney La Tourelle, Mendel Art Gallery, 2013; Univ Manitoba Sch Art Gallery, 2014. *Mem:* Canadian Artists Representation. *Media:* Structurist Relief, Structurist Construction. *Publ:* Auth of numerous articles and essays in The Structurist since 60-; In Directions in Art, Theory and Aesthetics, Faber & Faber, London, 68; Canadian Art Today, 69; Time as a Human Resource, Univ Calgary Press, 91; A Celebration of Canada's Arts 1930-1970, Scholar's Press, Toronto, 96; Perspectives of Saskatchewan, Univ Manitoba Press, 2009. *Dealer:* Forum Art Gallery New York NY. *Mailing Add:* Box 378 RPO Univ Sask Saskatoon SK S7N 4J8 Canada

BORNSTEIN, JENNIFER
PRINTMAKER
Study: Univ Calif, Berkeley, BA, 1992; Univ Calif, Los Angeles, MFA, 1996. *Work:* Hammer Mus, Los Angeles; Centre Georges Pompidou, Paris; Mus Contemp Art, Los Angeles; Mus Contemp Art, Chicago; Orange County Mus Art, Newport Beach. *Exhib:* Solo exhibs, Studio Guenzani, Milan, 1997, Jay Gorney Mod Art, New York, 1998, Blum & Poe, Santa Monica, 1999, 2002, Mus Contemp Art, Los Angeles, 2005, Hammer Mus, Los Angeles, 2008, Fargfabriken Ctr for Contemp Art, Stockholm, 2009; Sightings: New Photographic Art, Inst Contemp Art, London, 1998; Greater New York, PS1, Long Island City, NY, 2000; A Passion for Art: The Disaronno Originale Photography COllection, Mus Contemp Art, Chicago, 2001; Faking Real, Columbia Univ, New York, 2003; General Ideas: Rethinking Conceptual Art 1987-2005, CCA Wattis Inst for Contemp Art, Calif, 2005; Uncertain States of America, Ctr for Curatorial Studies, Bard Coll, 2006; Mobile Museum, Latvian Ctr for Contemp Art, Riga, 2007; Index: Conceptualism in California from the Permanent Collection, Mus Contemp Art, Los Angeles, 2008. *Awards:* Rema Hort Mann Found Award, 1997; Elizabeth Found Studio Grant, 2000; Pollock-Krasner Found Grant, 2008. *Bibliog:* Holland Cotter (auth), The Name of the Place, NY Times, 1/31/1997; Bruce Hainley (auth), Legend of the Fall, Artforum, 56-63, 3/1999; Christopher Knight (auth), Art in LA, Los Angeles Times, 5/18/2001; Jerry Saltz (auth), A Two-Headed Butterfly Flaps its Wings, Village Voice, 7/6/2006; Kenneth Baker (auth), A Bunch of Amateurs, San Francisco Chronicle, 5/25/2008

BOROFSKY, JONATHAN
SCULPTOR, PAINTER
b Boston, Mass, 1942. *Study:* Carnegie-Mellon Univ, Pittsburgh, Pa, BFA, 1964; Yale Sch Art and Archit, New Haven, Conn, MFA, 1966. *Work:* Kunstmuseum Basel; Dallas Mus Art; Tate Gallery; Los Angeles Mus Contemp Art; Milwaukee Art Mus; Walker Art Ctr; Mus Mod Art; Whitney Mus Art; Nat Mus Osaka, Japan; Philadelphia Mus Art; Carnegie Inst Mus Art. *Comn:* Seattle Art Mus; US Fed Bldg Los Angeles; Tokyo Opera City; Messeturm Frankfurt; Swiss Bank Corp Basel; General Mills Corp Minneapolis; Nasher Corp Collection, Dallas; City of Kassel, Ger; Ice Palace Arena, Tampa, Fla; Atlantic City Convention Ctr, Atlantic City, NJ; Nat Mus Korea; Boston Mus Fine Arts; City of Baltimore. *Exhib:* Solo exhibs, Philadelphia Mus Art, Walker Art Ctr, Whitney Mus Am Art, NY City, Tokyo Met Mus Art, Israel Mus Jerusalem, Moderna Museet Stockholm, Mus Mod Art, Museum van Hedendaagse Kunst Ghent, Mus Contemp Art, Los Angeles, Kunstmuseum Basel, Corcoran Gallery Art, Wash, DC, Boston Mus Fine Arts; Group exhibs, Artists of the Heath Gallery 1965-1998, Mus Contemp Art Ga, 2002. *Teaching:* instr, Sch Visual Arts, NY, 1969-77, Calif Inst Arts, Los Angeles, 1977-80. *Dealer:* Paula Cooper Gallery 465 W 21st St New York NY 10011; Anton Meier Gallery 2 rue de l'Athenee 1205 Geneva Switzerland; Adam Baumgold Gallery 74 E 79th St New York NY 10021; Russell Bowman Art Advisory 311 W Superior Chicago IL 60610; Rudolf Budja Galerie Palais Kinsky Freyung 4 1010 Vienna Austria; CAIS Gallery 99-5 Chungdam-Dong 135-100 Seoul Korea ; Concept Art Gallery 1031 South Braddock Ave Pittsburgh PA 15218; Cynthia Drennon Fine Arts Inc 223 North Guadalupe Santa Fe NM 87501; Gemini GEL 8365 Melrose Ave Los Angeles CA 90069; Gemini GEL at Joni Moisant Weyl 980 Madison Ave New York NY 10019; Bobbie Greenfield Gallery 2525 Michigan Ave Santa Monica CA 90404; Barbara Krakow Gallery 10 Newbury St Boston MA 02116; Galerie Susanna Kulli Dienerstrasse 21 8004 Zurich Switzerland; Mixografia 1419 East Adams Blvd Los Angeles CA 90011; Jack Rutberg Fine Arts 357 N La Brea Ave Los Angeles CA 90036; Carrie Secrist Gallery 835 West Washington Blvd Chicago IL 60607; Amy Wolf Fine Art 47 Vestry St New York NY 10013; Yorkshire Sculpture Park W Bretton W Yorkshire Wakefield WF4 4LG United Kingdom

BOROS, CHRISTIAN
COLLECTOR
b Poland, 1949. *Study:* With Bazon Brock (communications), Wuppertal, Ger, 1984-88. *Pos:* Founder & owner, Boros Group, Wuppertal & Berlin, 1990-; founder, Boros Collection (Sammlung Boros), Berlin, 2008-; bd mem, Zeppelin Univ, Friedrichshafen. *Awards:* Named one of Top 200 Collectors, ARTnews mag, 2006-13. *Collection:* 700 works of contemporary art, especially German & British. *Mailing Add:* Sammlung Boros Hofaue 63 Wuppertal 42103 Germany

BORSHCH, DMITRY GENNADIEVICH
PRINTMAKER, DRAFTSMAN
b Dnepropetrovsk, USSR, Mar 21, 1973. *Study:* V.I. Surikov Inst Art, 88; Studied with Eli Mikhailovich, 89; Studied with Boris Petrovich, 90. *Work:* State Tretyakov Gallery, Moscow; State Russian Mus, Saint Petersburg; Moscow Mus Art; Russian Acad Art; Pushkin State Mus Art, Moscow. *Exhib:* Nat Arts Club, New York; Brecht Forum, New York; Exit Art, New York; City of NY Grad Ctr, New York; Salmagundi Club, New York; ISE Cult Found, New York; Frieze Art Fair, London. *Awards:* award for graphics, Nat Arts Club, New York, 2008; visual artist, ISE Cult Found, New York, 2010. *Bibliog:* L. Lawrence (auth), Backstory: Adoption for Art Lovers, Christian Science Monitor, 2007; A.L.B. Berman, Masterpieces on a Dime, Express Night Out, Washington Post, 2008; A. Simon, Fine Art Adoption Network, Art in General, 2009; S. Nikolopoulos, 7 Minutes in Heaven with Dmitry Borshch, Asphalt Eden, 2009; M. Alexenberg, The Future of Art in a Postdigital Age: From Hellenistic to Hebraic Conciousness, Univ Chicago Press, 2010. *Publ:* Illusr, Rio Grande Review, Univ Texas, El Paso, 2010; illusr, Salt Hill, Syracuse Univ, 2010; illusr, Tulane Review, Tulane Literary Soc, 2010. *Dealer:* Russian American Cultural Center 520 East 76th St Suite 7E New York NY 10021

BORSTEIN, ELENA
PAINTER, EDUCATOR
b Hartford, Conn, Feb 5, 1946. *Study:* Skidmore Col, BS; Univ Pa, BFA & MFA. *Work:* Mus Mod Art; Mass Inst Technol; Everson Mus; Newark Mus; Phoenix Mus; and others. *Comn:* Ottawa Silica Corp, Ill; Whitco Chemical Co, NY. *Exhib:* Contemp Reflections, Aldrich Mus Art, Ridgefield, Conn, 74; 14 Am Artists, Corcoran Gallery/Aarhus Kunstmuseum Traveling Exhib, 77; Gifts of Drawing, Mus Mod Art, NY, 79; Everson Mus, 81; Skidmore Col, Saratoga Springs, NY, 82; Kathryn Markel Gallery, NY, 83; Andre Zarre Gallery, 90, 92, 93, 97 & 2000; JJ Brookings, San Francisco; and others. *Pos:* Art consult, Aarhus Kunstmuseum, Denmark, 74-75; vis artist, St Mary's Coll, Ind, Md Art Inst & Sch Visual Arts, 81. *Teaching:* Prof painting & photog, York Coll, City Univ NY, 70-. *Awards:* Nat Endowment Arts Grant, 80; Creative Artists Pub Serv Prog Grant, 80; City Univ New York Res Award, 89, 91 & 93. *Bibliog:* David Shirey (auth), article, Arts Mag, 9/78; articles, Art Int, 1/80, NY Times, 3/16/80 & Art in Am, 12/2000. *Mem:* Coll Art Asn (mem, Women's Caucus). *Mailing Add:* Fine Arts Dept York Col 9420 Guy Brewer Blvd Jamaica NY 11451

BOSMAN, RICHARD
PAINTER, PRINTMAKER
b Madras, India, 1944. *Study:* Byam Shaw Sch Painting & Drawing, London, 64-69; NY Studio Sch, NY, 69-71; Skowhegan Sch Painting & Sculpture, Maine, 70. *Work:* Albright-Knox Art Gallery, Buffalo, NY; Australian Nat Gallery, Canberra; Brooklyn Mus, NY; Fogg Art Mus, Harvard Univ, Cambridge; Nat Mus Am Art, Washington,

DC; Weatherspoon Art Gallery, Greensboro. *Exhib:* Solo exhibs, Galerie La Maquina Espanola, Madrid, 90, Galerie Biedermann, Munich, 91, Brooke Alexander, 91, 93 & 94, Galleria Toselli, Milan, 92, Fairfield Univ Gallery, Conn, 93, RI Sch Design Print Gallery, 93, Timmesh Gallery, Minneapolis, 93; Works on Paper, Curt Marrus Gallery, NY, 88; Sounding the Depths: 150 Yrs of Am Seascape, Am Fedn Arts, NY, 89; First Impressions, Walker Art Ctr, Traveling from Minneapolis to Baltimore, 89; Monoprints/Monotypes-Images by Twenty Contemp Artists, Univ Maine Mus Art, Orono, 89; Group exhib, Galeria La Maquina Espanola, Madrid, 89; Images of Death in Contemp Art, Patrick & Beatrice Haggerty Mus Art, Milwaukee, 90; Selected Paintings, Drawings and Sculpture, John Berggruen Gallery, San Francisco, 90 718. *Teaching:* Instr, NY Studio Sch, 72, Skowhegan Sch Painting & Sculpture, Maine, 82 & Sch Visual Arts, NY, 82-84; Teacher Skowhegan Sch Painting and Sculpture, Maine, 1982, Sch Visual Arts, New York City, 1983-1985, Univ Pa, Philadelphia, 1986, Temple Univ, Philadelphia, 1987, Columbia Univ, New York City, 1988-1990, Temple Univ, Philadelphia, 1991, RI Sch Design, Providence, 1992, State Univ of NY, Purchase, 1993, Fairfield Univ, 1993, Yale Univ, Norfolk, Conn, 1994-1998, Vassar Col, Poughkeepsie, NY, 1995-. *Awards:* Guggenheim fel, 1994. *Bibliog:* Jole de Sanna (auth), Milan: Richard Bosman, Toselli Gallery, Artforum, 12/86; Chavarri Ardujar (auth), La Pintura con sangre entra, Las Provincias, 7/87; Joy Hakanson Colby (auth), Richard Bosman, The Detroit News, 11/1/88. *Mem:* Nat Acad (assoc, 94, acad, 94). *Publ:* Coauth, Exit the Face, Mus Mod Art, NY, 82; illusr, Grasping at Emptiness, Kulchur Found, 85; The Captivity Narrative of Hannah Duston, Arion Press, San Francisco, 87; Nat Mus Am Art & Library of Congress, Washington, DC; Dannhoiser Found, Metrop Mus Art, Mus Mod Art, Whitney Mus Mod Arts Pub Libr, NY. *Mailing Add:* c/o Mark Moore Gallery 5790 Washington Blvd Culver City CA 90232

BOSTICK, WILLIAM ALLISON
PAINTER, CALLIGRAPHER, DESIGNER, ILLUSTRATOR, PRINTMAKER
b Marengo, Ill, Feb 21, 1913. *Study:* Carnegie Inst Technol, BS; Cranbrook Acad Art, with Zoltan Sepeshy & Maija Grotel; Detroit Soc Arts & Crafts, with John Foster; Wayne State Univ, MA (art hist). *Work:* Detroit Inst Arts, Cranbrook Acad Art Mus, Detroit Pub Libr, Wayne State Univ & Detroit Hist Mus; Evansville Mus Arts & Sci, Ind. *Comn:* 32 calligraphic panels on wood, 11 calligraphic lecterns & 1 large calligraphic quotation (with Christopher Bostick), Cath Cemeteries of Chicago for Resurrection Mausoleum, Justice, Ill, 71; 6 large acrylic paintings on architectural roots of Mich Nat Corp Hq Bldg, 90. *Exhib:* Exhib Mich Artists, Detroit Inst Arts, 36-63; Pepsi-Cola Exhib, 45; Scarab Club Gold Medal Exhib, 47-94; Mich Watercolor Soc, 48-94; Solo exhibs, Arwin Galleries, 67 & 75 & Preston Burke Gallery, 96. *Pos:* Typographer, Detroit Typesetting Co, 35-36; graphic designer, Evans-Winter-Hebb, Detroit, 36-37; exec secy, Founders Soc, Detroit Inst Arts, 46-60, adminr & secy, 46-76; ed, Midwest Mus Quart, 59-60. *Teaching:* Instr drawing, Wayne State Univ, 46-47; instr calligraphy, Detroit Soc Arts & Crafts Art Sch, 61-63; instr hist of the book, Wayne State Univ Grad Sch, 62-67; instr calligraphy & art hist, Grosse Pointe War Mem & Edison Inst, 73-86 & Ctr Creative Studies, Detroit, 86-94; instr, Italic Handwriting in suburban Detroit, over 40 years, formerly. *Awards:* Scarab Gold Medal, Scarab Club Detroit, 62, 68 & 79; Knight, Order of Italy Solidarity; Chevalier, French Order of Arts & Lett. *Mem:* Scarab Club Detroit; Mich Watercolor Soc (cofounder); Soc Scribes, NY; Mich Asn Calligraphers; Soc Italic Handwriting. *Media:* Watercolor, Acrylic, Lithography. *Publ:* Illusr, Many a Watchful Night, 45; auth & illusr, England Under GI's Reign, 46; illusr, The Mysteries of Blair House, 48; auth, A Guide to the Guarding of Cultural Property, UNESCO, 77; auth & publ, A Manual on the Acquiring of a Beautiful and Legible Handwriting, 77, rev ed, 80 & Calligraphy for Kids, 91, La Stampa Calligrafica; Back to the Second Basic R-Ritin, 98. *Dealer:* Preston Burke Gallery 30448 Woodward Royal Oak MI 48073

BOSWORTH, BARBARA
PHOTOGRAPHER, EDUCATOR
b 1953. *Study:* Bowling Green State Univ, BFA; Rochester Inst Technol, MFA. *Exhib:* Solo exhibs include Phoenix Mus Art, 2008, Smithsonian Am Art Mus, 2008. *Teaching:* Prof photog, Mass Coll Art & Design. *Awards:* Buhl Found Grant; John Simon Guggenheim Mem Found Fel; New England Found Arts Fel; Bernheim Found Fel; Ruttenberg Fel, Friends of Photog. *Mailing Add:* Mass Coll Art & Design 621 Huntington Ave Boston MA 02115

BOTERO, FERNANDO
SCULPTOR
b Medellin, Colombia, 1932. *Study:* Acad San Fernando, Spain, 53; Prado Mus, Madrid, 54; Univ Florence, Italy, art hist with Roberto Longhi. *Work:* Mus d'Arte Mod del Vaticano, Rome; Birmingham Mus Art, Ala; Mus de Arte Mod, Bogota, Colombia; Mus Mod Art, Metrop Mus Art, Solomon R Guggenheim Mus, NY; Baltimore Mus Art, Md; Smithsonian Inst, Washington, DC; Ateneumin Taidemuseo, Helsinki, Finland; Museo de Bellas Artes, Caracas; Milwaukee Art Mus, Wis. *Exhib:* Solo exhibs, Dider Imbert Fine Art, Paris, 92, Traveling exhib, Avignon, 92-93, Marlborough Gallery, NY 93, Galeria Marlborough, Madrid, 94, Nac de Bellas Artes, Buenos Aires, 94, Fernando Botero, Museo d'Arte Moderna, Lugano, Switz, 97, Botero em Sao Paulo, 98, Museu de Arte de Sao Paulo, Brazil, 98 & Museo Nacional de Artes Visuales, Montevideo, Uruguay, 98, Abu Ghraib, Marlborough Gallery, NY, 2006, Tasende Gallery, 2010; Group exhibs, Gulf Caribbean Art Exhib, Mus Fine Arts, Houston, 56; Solomon R Guggenheim Mus, 58; Paintings from the Gres Gallery, Baltimore Mus Art, 59; Recent Acquisitions: Painting & Sculpture, Mus Mod Art, NY, 61; An Invitation to See: 125 Paintings from the Mus of Modern Art, Mus Mod Art, NY, 73; Retrospectives, Traveling, Ger, 70, Mus Boymans-van Beuningen, Rotterdam, The Neth, 75, Traveling, Hirshhorn Mus & Sculpture Garden, 79, Traveling, Tokyo Art Gallery, Japan, 86, Helsinki City Art Mus, 94; Fall 1977: Contemp Collectors, Aldrich Mus Contemp Art, 77; Recent Develop in Latin Am Drawing, Art Inst Chicago, 87; The Ellen & Jerome Westeimer Collection, Okla Art Ctr, 87; Figures of Contemp Sculpture (1970-1990): Images of Man Traveling Exhib, Isetan Mus Art, Tokyo, Japan, 92; Latin Am Artists of the 20th Century, Traveling Exhib, Estacion Plaza de Armas, Seville, Spain, 92-93; Lateinamerikanische Kunst Im 20 Jahrhundert, Mus Ludwig, Cologne, Ger, 92-93; Biennale de Sculpture Monte Carlo, Marisa del Re Gallery, NY, 93; Art Mus Americas, 96; Marlborough Gallery, 96; O'Hara Gallery, 97; Forma eta Figunazion: Blake-Parnell Bildumako Maisa-Lanak, Guggenheim Bilbao Mus, 98; Botero a Dinard, Palais des Arts de Dinard, 2002; Botero a Venezia: Sculpture e dipinti, 2003; Palazzo Duccale, Venezia, Ital, 2003; Les Artistes des Animaux, Festival Int de Sculpture de Monet-Carlo, Monaco, 2002. *Bibliog:* Pierre Daix, Charles Virmaitre & Jean Cau (auths), Botero aux Champs-Elysees, fall 92; Edward J Sullivan (auth), Fernando Botero: Drawings & Watercolors, Rizzoli, New York, 93; Miguel Canbajal (auth), Una Charla con Fernando Botero en nueva York, El Pais de los domingos, 11/15/98; and many others. *Publ:* Auth, Esta Noche Con Usted, Interview by Maria Elvira Salazar, Telemundo TV, USA, 7/27/88 & 9/24/88; Anna Marie Escallon, Botero New Works on Canvas, New York, Rizzoli, 97. *Mailing Add:* c/o Marlborough Gallery 40 W 57th St New York NY 10019

BOTT, H(ARVEY) J(OHN)
SCULPTOR, PAINTER
b Greeley, Colo, Dec 28, 1933. *Study:* Art Ctr Sch Los Angeles; Inst Fine Arts, NY Univ; Art Students League; Kunstakademie-Dusseldorf & Bamberg, Ger, MBK, 55. *Work:* Rice Univ; New Orleans Mus Art; San Antonio Art Mus; Denver Art Mus; Bakersfield Art Mus, Calif; and many others. *Exhib:* Solo exhibs, San Jose, Calif, 77, Contemp Arts Ctr, New Orleans, La, 85, Ga Southern Univ, Statesboro, 89, Crocker Art Mus, Sacramento, Calif, 86, San Antonio Col, Tex, 95 & Sculpture Court, Houston Art League, Tex, 96; Contemp Arts Mus, Houston, Tex, 85; Texas Art Celebration, Houston, 89, Condeso-Lawler Gallery, NY, 90 & Galerie Muhlenbusch-Winklemann, Dusseldorf, Ger, 90-92; El Palomar, Houston, Tex, 94; Infinite Airport, Lamar Univ, Beaumont, Tex, 94; and many others. *Pos:* Artist-in-residence, Loft-on-Strand, Galveston, Tex, 69-78. *Teaching:* Glassell Sch Art, Mus Fine Arts, Houston, Tex, 92-. *Awards:* Plastik Reisestipeduim, Museen der Stadt Koln, Ger, 56; Premier Les Plus Sculpture, Prix de Paris, France, 65; and many others. *Bibliog:* Wendy Paris (auth), HJ Bott: Recent Systemic Structures, Sally Reynolds Fine Arts, Houston Chronicle, 8/27/94; Catherine Anspon (auth), Minimalist, Geometric, Idiosyncratic, Pure: Harvey Bott, Public News, 12/97; Shaila Dewan (auth), DoV-ine Inspiration, Houston Press, 12/97. *Media:* All. *Publ:* Auth, ROBOTT Opera: A Time-warp Newscast, Univ St Thomas, Houston, 83. *Dealer:* Thom Andriola New Gallery 2639 Colquitt Houston TX 77098

BOTT, JOHN
PAINTER, CRITIC
b Gassaway, WVa, Sept 12, 1936. *Study:* Troy State Univ, BS, 61; Univ NC, Chapel Hill, MFA, 69. *Work:* Witherspoon Gallery, Univ NC, Greensboro; NH Comn Arts, Concord; New Harmony Gallery Contemp Art, Ind; Bank NH, Concord; Chrysler Mus, Norfolk, Va; Swope Gallery, Terre Haut, Ind; Springmills Inc, Lancaster, SC; Burlington Industs; Colby Sawyer Col; Bank of New Hampshire. *Comn:* Mural, Thoren Mus, Petersburg, Ind, 76-77; paintings, Highwood Building, Tewksbury, Mass. *Exhib:* Solo exhibs, Davidson Col, NC, 70 & Vanderbilt Univ, Nashville, 74; New Eng Contemp Artist, Ctr Arts, Nashua, NH, 87-88; New Harmony Gallery Contemp Art, Ind, 88; McGowan Fine Art, Concord, NH, 91; Kimball-Jenkins Mansion, Concord, NH, 97; Milbrook Gallery, Concord, NH, 99; Kimball Union Academy, Plainfield, NH; and others. *Pos:* NH revs ed, Art New England, Boston, 84-86. *Teaching:* Prof painting, Greensboro Col, NC, 69-72 & Univ Evansville, Ind, 72-76; prof, Colby-Sawyer Col, New London, NH, 77-. *Awards:* Burlington Industs Award, Guilford Co Exhib, 71; Excellence Award, 30th Wabash Valley, 74 & Hoffman Award, 33rd Wabash Valley, 77, Sheldon Swope Gallery. *Bibliog:* Margo Clark (auth), New England contemporary art, Art New Eng, 12-1/88. *Media:* Watercolor, Acrylic. *Publ:* Paul Pollaro (exhib catalog), Phillips Exeter Sch & Lamont Gallery, 88. *Dealer:* New Harmony Gallery Contemp Art New Harmony IN; Gallery Mack Seattle Wash. *Mailing Add:* Colby-Sawyer Col Dept Art New London NH 03257

BOTT, MARGARET DEATS See Deats, (Margaret)

BOTTINI, DAVID WILLIAM
PAINTER, EDUCATOR
b Harrisburg, Pa, 1961. *Study:* Mt St Mary's Univ, BA, 83; Savannah Coll Art & Design, MFA, 91. *Work:* Mt St Mary's Univ, Emmitsburg, Md; Fat Hat Films, Philadelphia, Pa; The Madeira Sch, McLean, Va; Farmers & Mechanics Bank, Waynesboro, Pa; The House on Cherry St, Bed & Breakfast Inn, Jacksonville, Fla; Orris House Inn, Mechanicsburg, PA; Harrisburg Area Com Col, Midtown-Campus, Harrisburg, Pa. *Comn:* 3 panel paintings, Alexander Baer Asid, Bact, Md, 88; 2 paintings, lithograph prints, The Potomac Sch, McLean, Va, 96; 2 large paintings, The Madeira Sch, McLean, Va, 2004; large painting, John P Hunt, Philadelphia, Pa, 2004. *Exhib:* Wash Co Regional Exhib, Wash Co Mus, Hagerstown, Md, 82 & 84; Ann Nat Juried Exhib, Verizon Gallery, N Va Community College, Fairfax, Va, 2001; Ann Juried Nat Exhib, Arts Ctr, Shippensburg Univ, Shippensburg, Pa, 2003; group exhib, Artist Tree Exhib, Gallery Neptune, Bethesda, Mo, 2005; invitational, Int Salon of Small Works, New Arts Prog, Kutztown, Pa, 2006; invitational one-person, Featured Artist, Mary Condon Hodgson Gallery, Frederick Community College, Frederick, Md, 2006; Images 2008, Regional Juried Art Exhibit, Robeson Gallery, Penn State Univ, Pa, 6-7/2008; Small Works Juried, York Art Asn, 7/2008; Adams Co Art Council, Ann Juried Show, 6/2008; solo exhib, Lancaster Arts Hotel, Lancaster, Pa, 2009; Ann Juried Art Exhibit, Adams Country Art, Gettysburg, 2009; Summer Artist Showcase, Foxhall Gallery, 2009. *Pos:* Chair, Visual Art Dept, The Madiera Sch, McLean Va, 98-2003. *Teaching:* Instr, Art Studio, Episcopal High Sch, Jacksonville, Fla, 87-90, The Potomac Sch, McLean, Va, 92-97 & Susquehanna Univ, Selinsgrove, Pa, 2006-; interim instr, Studio, Sidwell Friend's Sch, Washington DC, 2005-2006; Frederick Community Col, 2005-. *Awards:* Master Teacher, Madiera Sch, 2001. *Bibliog:* Southern Accents Mag, 6/88; Madiera Today Mag, McLean, Va, Fall 2002; Hagerstown Herald Mail, 8/2006; Pa Arts Mag (cover and feature), May 2008; feature

article, Showcase Now Arts Mag, 6/2009. *Mem:* Kids-in-Design, Prof Volunteer Orgn, 92-99; Nat Gallery Art Teacher Adv bd, 95-98; Wash Proj for the Arts, 2001-2002. *Media:* Acrylic. *Dealer:* Foxhall Gallery Wash DC; Gallery 30 Gettysburg Pa; Gallerie 13 Mechanicsburg Pa. *Mailing Add:* 2315 Edgewood Rd Harrisburg PA 17104

BOTWINICK, MICHAEL
MUSEUM DIRECTOR
b New York, NY, Nov 14, 1943. *Study:* Rutgers Coll, BA, 1964; Columbia Univ, MA, 1967. *Collection Arranged:* Coordr exhib, The Year 1200, Metrop Art Mus, NY, 1969-70 & Masterpieces of 50 Centuries, 1971. *Pos:* Asst cur, Medieval Art & the Cloisters, Metrop Mus Art, NY, 1969, assoc cur, 1970, asst cur in chief, 1970-71; asst dir art, Philadelphia Mus Art, 1971-74; dir, Brooklyn Mus, 1974-83, Corcoran Gallery Art, Wash, 1983-87, Newport Harbor Art Mus, 1990-97, Univ Calif, Irvine, Calif, 1997-98, Staten Island Inst Arts & Science, NY, 1998; sr vpres, Knoedler-Monarco, 1986-88; pres, Fine Art Group, 1988-90; dir, Hudson River Mus, currently. *Teaching:* Instr, Columbia Univ, NY, 1968-69 & City Univ NY, 1969. *Awards:* Order of Leopold II, Belgian Govt, 1980; Royal Order of Polar Star, Swedish Govt, 1983. *Mem:* Am Asn Mus; Int Coun Mus; Coll Art Asn; Asn Art Mus Dirs. *Mailing Add:* c/o Hudson River Museum 511 Warburton Ave Yonkers NY 10701

BOUCHARD, PAUL E
PAINTER
b Providence, RI, Sept 26, 1946. *Study:* Calif State Univ, Long Beach, BFA, 78. *Work:* Munic Collection, Beverly Hills, Calif; Art Mus, Calif State Univ, Long Beach; Coos Art Mus, Coos Bay, Ore; Combined Forces Vet Mus Art, Dural, NSW, Australia; US State Dept, Washington, DC; Nat Vietnam Vet Art Mus, Chicago; SUNY Oneonta. *Comn:* Paul Kasnits; C Lewis; San Diego Fallbrook Field Station, Calif State Univ; SPCA LA, Long Beach, Calif. *Exhib:* Solo exhibs, Dreams of Ancient Answers, Franklin Furnace, NY, 89, Univ SDak, Vermillion, 91, Calif Brand Munic Gallery, Glendale, 92, Chabot Coll, Hayward, Calif, Human Condition, Eastern Wash Univ, Cheney, 92, Vietnam Vets, Carriage House Art Ctr, Sydney, Australia, 92; group exhibs, Artists You Should Know, Los Angeles Art Asn, Calif, 87; Healing the Wounds, Chapman Coll, Orange, Calif, 88; Mixing It Up, Coos Art Mus, Ore, 88. *Awards:* Contribs to the Arts, Torrance, Calif, 85. *Bibliog:* Laurel Darrow (auth), Oh Say Can You See, Grants Pass Daily Courier 4/3/87; Russ Leadbrand (auth), Art Matters, Cambrian, 10/21/87; Keith Dilis (auth), Art, San Luis Obispo Telegram Tribune, 10/31/87. *Media:* Mixed Media, Watercolor, Sculpture. *Dealer:* Los Angeles Co Mus Art Rental Gallery; Laguna Beach Mus Art Rental Gallery; Albany Mus Hist & Art. *Mailing Add:* 166 Denton Rd Saratoga Springs NY 12866-9196

BOUCHET, MARK
SCULPTOR, VIDEO ARTIST
b Castro Valley, Calif, 1970. *Study:* UCLA Sch Fine Arts, Los Angeles, 1994. *Work:* LVMH Collection, Paris; Jumex Collection, Mex; Deutsche Bank; DekaBank; Centre Georges Pompidou, Paris; Astrup Fearnley Mus Mod Art, Oslo. *Exhib:* Solo exhibs, AB Gallery, Los Angeles, 1993, Boss Exhibs, Los Angeles, 1999, Maccarone Inc, New York, 2003, Calerie Michael Neff, Frankfurt, 2004, Kunstraum Innsbruck, 2005, Galerie Vallois, Paris, 2007, Mus Contemp Art, Los Angeles, 2007, Circus Gallery, Los Angeles, 2007, Galerie Parisa Kind, Frankfurt, 2008 & Central De Art Contemporaneo, Guadalajara, 2008; Slum Loard, Main St Gallery, Napa, Calif, 1993; Common Denomination Language Expo, FAR, Los Angeles, 1994; Special K Projects, Los Angeles, 1996; Life After The Squirrel, Location One, New York, 2000; Casino, SMAK, Gent, 2001; Out of True, Santa Barbara Univ Art Mus, Calif, 2002; Dedicated to a Proposition, Extra City, Ctr for Contemp Art, Antwerp, 2004; Situational Prosthetics, New Langston Art Ctr, San Franciso, 2005; Uncetain State of America, Bard Curatorial Ctr, New York, Serpentine Gallery, London & Reykjavik Art Mus, Iceland, 2006; New Economy, Artists Space, New York, 2007; Meet Me Around the Corner, Astrup Fearnley Mus Mod Art, Oslo, 2008; 53rd Int Art Exhib Biennale, Venice, 2009. *Mailing Add:* 6086 Comey Ave Los Angeles CA 90034

BOUGHTON, DOUG
ADMINISTRATOR, EDUCATOR
Study: Univ Alberta-Edmonton, PhD. *Pos:* World Pres, InSEA (International Society for Education through Art); chief examiner Visual Arts for the International Baccalaureate Organization; foundation dir, Nat Art Educ Research Council of the Australian Inst of Art Educ; consulting prof art educ, Inst of Educ, Hong Kong. *Teaching:* Art teaching at elementary, secondary, college and univ levels in Australia, Canada, and the US; art dept chair and head of the sch of art and design educ, Salisbury Col of Advanced Educ and the Univ of South Australia; prof Assessment, Curriculum, International Issues in Art Edu, dir Sch of Art, Northern Illinois Univ, currently. *Awards:* Studies in Art Educ Invited Lecture award, 1997; USSEA Edwinf Ziegfeld award, 2006. *Mem:* Coun for Policy Studies in Art Educ; Nat Art Educ Asn (fellow); Australian Inst of Art Educ (now Art Educ Australia) (honorary life mem); South Australian Visual Arts Educ Asn (honorary life mem). *Publ:* Published over 80 articles and book chapters. *Mailing Add:* Northern Illinois University Room 215A Art Building 300 Gilbert Way Dekalb IL 60115

BOURDEAU, ROBERT CHARLES
PHOTOGRAPHER
b Kingston, Ont, Nov 14, 1931. *Study:* Univ Toronto; Queens Univ, Kingston, Ont. *Work:* Nat Gallery Can; Nat Film Board Can, Pub Arch Can, Ottawa; Smithsonian Inst; Mus d'art Contemp, Montreal. *Comn:* A photography study of bank archit, Parnassus Found, NY, 87. *Exhib:* Light 7, Hayden Gallery, 68; two-man exhib, New Eng Sch Photog, Cambridge, Mass, 75; Nat Gallery Can, 75; Solo exhibs, Int Ctr Photog, NY, 80, Vancouver Art Gallery, 80, Art Gallery Ont, 81 & Aferimage Gallery, Dallas, 83. *Bibliog:* P Cousineau (auth), The Banff Purchase, John Wiley Publ, 79; monograph, Mintmark Press, 80. *Mem:* Royal Can Acad Arts. *Dealer:* Jane Corkin Gallery 179 John St Toronto M5T 1X4 Ont; Edwynn Houk Gallery 745 Fifth Ave NY 10151. *Mailing Add:* 1462 Chomley Crescent Ottawa ON K1G 0V1 Canada

BOURGEOIS, DOUGLAS
PAINTER
b Gonzales, La, Aug 31, 1951. *Study:* La State Univ, Baton Rouge, BFA, 74. *Work:* Southeastern Ctr for Contemp Art, Winston-Salem, NC; Nat Mus Am Art, Washington, DC; Virlane Found, New Orleans, La; Life Equitable, NY; Morris Mus Art, Augusta, Ga. *Exhib:* Solo exhibs, Arthur Roger Gallery, New Orleans, La, 92, 94, 96, 99, 2003 & 2006, Contemp Arts Ctr, New Orleans, 2002-03; group exhibs, A New Quarter: Contemp New Orleans Artists, Lauren Rogers Libr & Mus Art, Laurel, Miss, 83; Gallery Review: New Orleans, Pensacola Mus Art, Pensacola, Fla, 86; Fine Arts Mus of the South, Mobile, Ala, 84; Boxes, Southeastern Ctr Contemp Art, Winston-Salem, NC, 85, Elvis, 87, SECCA 7 Eleven, 88; 1986 New Orleans Triennial, New Orleans Mus Art, La, 86; Visionary Imagists, Contemp Arts Ctr, New Orleans, La, 90; Grand Tradition: Permanent Collection in Context, Miss Mus Art, Jackson, Miss, 96; Body and Soul: Contemp Southern Figures, Columbus Mus Art, Ga, 97; The Ghost of Cornell, Contemp Art Ctr, New Orleans, La, 98; Spirit and Flesh, Art Mus WVa, Roanoke, 99; Visual Arts Fel Invitational, Baton Rouge, 99; True Colors: Meditations on the Am Spirit (traveling exhib), 2002-05; Story of the South: Art & Cult, 1890-2003, Ogden Mus Southern Art, New Orleans, 2003; Context/Content, Baum Gallery Art, Univ Cent Ark, 2005; Made in New Orleans, Space 301, Mobile, Ala, 2006; New Orleans Rebirth-Significant Artists Return, Opelousas Mus Art, La, 2006; Katrina: Catastrophe & Catharsis, Colo Springs Fine Arts Ctr, 2007; Unsung, Nicole Klagsbrun Gallery, New York, 2007. *Awards:* Visual Arts Fel; SECCA/RJR Indiv Arts Fel, Southeast 7, 87; La Div Arts Fel, 92; Joan Mitchell Found Grant, 2007. *Bibliog:* Roger Green (auth), Ten for the 90's, Art News, 90. *Media:* Oil. *Dealer:* Arthur Roger Gallery 136 Prince St New York NY 10012. *Mailing Add:* c/o Arthur Roger Gallery 432 Julia St New Orleans LA 70130-3671

BOURQUE, LOUISE
FILMMAKER
Study: Univ de Moncton, BA (comm), 1986; Concordia Univ, BFA (film produc), 1990; Sch Art Inst, Chicago, MFA (filmmaking), 1992. *Exhib:* Dir Films: The People in the House; 1994, Going Back Home, 2000; Self Portrait Post Mortem, 2002; The Bleeding Heart of It, 2005. *Teaching:* Film instr, Sch Mus Fine Arts, Boston. *Awards:* Whitney Biennial, Whitney Mus Art, NYC 2006. *Mailing Add:* 230 The Fenway Boston MA 02115

BOURSIER-MOUGENOT, CÉLESTE
INSTALLATION SCULPTOR
b Nice, France, 1961. *Work:* Centre Pompidou, Paris France; Israel Mus, Jerusalem, Israel; Mus of Contemp Art San Diego, La Jolla, Calif; MONA FOMA, Tasmania, Australia; CAPC Musée De la Ville de Bordeaux, Bordeaux, France; Henry Art Gallery, Univ Wash, Seattle, Wash. *Exhib:* Solo Exhibs, Untitled- A Sound Installation, Rice Univ Art Gallery, Houston, Tex, 2001, capcMusée de Bordeaux, France, 97, Herzliya, Herzliya Museum of Art, Herzliya, Israel, 2001, Le Maillon, Théâtre de Strasbourg, Strasbourg, France, 2004, Céleste Boursier-Mougenot, Les Halles Place du Bouffay, Nantes, France, Univ Wash, 2009; Group exhibs, 1999 Nat & Int Studio Prog, PS 1 Inst for Contemp Art, NY, 99; Soundwaves: the art of sampling, Mus Contemp Art, San Diego, 2007 ; Ensemble, Inst of Contemp Art, Philadelphia, Pa, 2007; Glow 2010, Santa Monica, Calif. *Awards:* AFAA Artists' Studio Prog, 98; FIACRE grant, 97, 2004; Golden David, 2009; Marcel Duchamp Award Nominee, 2010. *Bibliog:* Céleste Boursier-Mougenot, Le Journal des arts, May 9-22, 2008; Céleste Boursier-Mougenot Wins 2009 Golden David Award, Artforum, 2009; French Connection, Black Jack Editions, 2008; États Seconds, French Ministry of Cult & Communication, 2008; Celeste Bocrsier, Mougenut, the Curve, Barbican Art Gallery, Art Forum, 2010. *Dealer:* Paula Cooper Gallery 534 W 21st St New York NY 10011. *Mailing Add:* Paula Cooper Gallery Céleste Boursier-Mougenot 534 W 21st St New York NY 10011

BOUSSARD, DANA
PAINTER, STAINED GLASS ARTIST
b Salem, Ore, 1944. *Study:* Univ Chicago; St Mary's Coll; Art Inst Chicago; Univ Mont, BFA, MFA. *Work:* Fed Reserve Bank, Minneapolis, Minn, 98; Casey Found, Seattle, Wash, 2000; Alaska Pub Health Lab, Anchorage, Alaska, 2001; Big Bend Coll, Moses Lake, Wash, 2004; Holy Spirit Catholic Parish, 2008. *Exhib:* Minneapolis Art Inst, 71; Portland Art Mus, Ore, 72; Am Craft Coun Invitational, New York, 72, 73; Mus Contemp Crafts, New York, 74; JPL Art Gallery, London, 75; Contemp Paper Works, Los Angeles, 77; Univ Houston Art Gallery, 77; Boise Gallery Art, 79; Mod Masters Tapestries, New York, 83; Foster/White Gallery, Seattle, 84, 93, 94; Zhenjing Acad Art, Hanzhow, China, 84; Carson Sapiro Gallery, Denver, 86; Munson Gallery, Santa Fe, 87; Oaxaca Mus Contemp Art, Mex, 89; Boulder Art Ctr, Colo, 91; Sutton West Gallery, Missoula, Mont, 96; Hockaday Art Ctr, Noice Gallery, Kalispell, Mont, 97; Nat Mus Women in Arts, Wash, DC, 99; Groveland Gallery, Minneapolis, 2001; Denise Roberge Gallery, Palm Desert, Calif, 2003; Tacoma Art Mus, Wash, 2004; Heidi Cho Gallery, New York, 2006; Moridian Found Nat Mus of China, 2007; Holter, Mus Art, 2008. *Awards:* Fel, Western States Art Fed, 75; Fel, Nat Endowment for Arts, 80; Visual Art Award, Mont Gov's Award, 87; Design Award, Holter Mus, 99; Fine Arts Outstanding Alumni Award, Univ Mont, 2003, Career Achievement Award, 2005; Cult Achievement Award for Art, Missoula Cult Coun, 2005. *Bibliog:* Feature article, Nat Mus Women in the Arts Mag, 99; feature article, Murdoch Family Trust, Messages from Idaho, 2007; feature article, Glass Art Mag, 2009; feature article, Mont Quarterly, 2009. *Media:* Stained Glass, Painted Fiber, All Media. *Publ:* cover art, Mont Mag, 97; cover art, How Can I Be Trusted by Nancy Nyquist, 2009; article, Ministry & Liturgy Mag, 2009. *Mailing Add:* 24425 Doney Ln Arlee MT 59821

BOUTIS, TOM
PAINTER, PRINTMAKER
b New York, NY, Aug 25, 1922. *Study:* Cooper Union, New York, BFA, 48; Skowhegan Sch Painting & Sculpture, summer 51; Cooper Union, hon BS. *Work:* Art Inst Chicago: CIBA-Geigy Collection, Ardsley, NY; Canton Art Inst, Ohio; Colby Col; Everson Mus, Syracuse, NY; Russell Sage Col, Albany NY; St Michaels Hosp,

Newark, NJ; Atlanta Univ, New Orleans, La; Billard Univ, New Orleans, La. *Comn:* Drawings, NY Hilton Collection Am Art, 62. *Exhib:* Solo exhibs, Landmark Gallery, NY, 73, 75 & 77 Am Acad Arts & Letters, 88 & 89, Nat Acad, 91 & Greek Consulate, 94; Drawings Exhib, Uffizzi Mus, Florence, Italy, 57; Selected Painters of Soho, Lehigh Univ Mus, 74; CIBA-Geigy Collection, Summit Art Mus, NJ, 74; Gathering of the Avant-Garde, Kenkeleba, NY, 88; and others. *Teaching:* Artist in residence painting, Summer Art Prog, Cooper Union, 69. *Awards:* Mark Rothko Found, 76; Nat Endowment for the Arts, 76; Adolphe Esther Gotleib Found Grant, 83; Am Acad Art Inst, 88-90; Rockefeller Found, Bellagio, Italy, 89; Two fulbright grants, 55-57. *Bibliog:* Sidney Delavante, (auth), Arts, 75; Peter Frank (auth), Art News, 77. *Mem:* Nat Acad. *Media:* Monoprints, Oils; Collage. *Mailing Add:* 162 E 82nd St New York NY 10028

BOVE, CAROL
INSTALLATION SCULPTOR
b Geneva, Switz, 1971. *Study:* NY Univ, BS, 2000. *Exhib:* Solo exhibs include Bronwyn Keenan Gallery, New York, 2000, Team Gallery, Art 33, Basel, 2002, Team Gallery, New York, 2003, Cubitt Gallery, London, 2003, Inst Contemp Art, Boston, 2004, Kunsthalle Zurich, 2004 Hotel, London, 2004, Galerie Dennis Kimmerich, Dusseldorf, Ger, 2006, Blanton Mus Art, Austin, 2006, Maccarone Inc, New York, 2007; group exhibs include Draw, Barry Whistler Gallery, Dallas, 2000; Perfunctory, Team Gallery, New York, 2001, Burst, 2002; XEROS, Le Magasin, Centre Nat Art Contemp Grenoble, France, 2002; Reproduction II, Galerie Georg Kargl, Vienna, 2003; When I Think About You I Touch Myself, New York Acad Art, 2004; Hysterical, Galerie Dennis Kimmerich, Ger, 2004; Model Modernisms, Artists Space, New York, 2005; I Love My Scene: Scene 1, Mary Boone Gallery, New York, 2006, Hiding in the Light, 2006; An Ongoing Low-Grade Mystery, Paula Cooper Gallery, New York, 2007; Strange Events Permit Themselves the Luxury of Occurring, Camden Arts Center, London, 2007; Whitney Biennial, Whitney Mus Am Art, New York, 2008; 54th Int Art Exhib Biennale, Venice, 2011. *Media:* Miscellaneous Media. *Dealer:* Galerie Dennis Kimmerich Heinrich-Heine-Allee 19 D-40213 Dusseldorf Germany; Hotel 53 Old Bethnal Green Rd London E2 6QA England. *Mailing Add:* 135 Plymouth St Apt 405 Brooklyn NY 11205

BOVE, RICHARD
PAINTER, EDUCATOR
b Brooklyn, NY, Oct 21, 1920. *Study:* Pratt Inst, BFA; Art Students League; Brera Acad, Milan, Italy. *Exhib:* Am Acad Design, New York; Philadelphia Mus Art; Corcoran Gallery Art, Washington, DC; Whitney Mus Art & Metrop Mus Art, New York; Brooklyn Mus. *Teaching:* Instr painting, Art Students League, 55-65; chmn dept painting, Pratt Inst, 70-74, prof painting, Grad Sch, 73-. *Awards:* Nat Acad Design Award; Louis Comfort Tiffany Found Award; Fulbright Fel, Italy. *Mem:* Life mem Art Students League. *Media:* Concrete, Plastics. *Mailing Add:* 501 Atwood Ct Newtown PA 18940

BOWEN, PAUL
SCULPTOR
b Wales, Britain, July 12, 1951. *Study:* Chester Sch Art, 68-69; Newport Coll Art, Wales, diploma, 69-72; Md Inst Coll Art, Baltimore, MFA, 72-74. *Work:* Solomon R Guggenheim Mus, NY; Mus Fine Art, Boston; Welsh Arts Coun, Cardiff, Wales; Provincetown Art Asn & Mus, Mass; Walker Art Ctr; Fogg Art Mus, Cambridge, Mass. *Comn:* Shapeshifting, Uchidayoukou Corp, Tokyo. *Exhib:* one man shows, Mus Contemp Art, Ghent, Belgium, 89, Saidye Bronfman Ctr, Montreal, Can, 90, Cherry Stone Gallery, Wellfleet, Mass, 91, 93 & 98, Howard Yezerski Gallery, Boston, 93, 97-98, Provincetown Art Asn Mus, Mass, 96 & New Eng Sch Art, Boston, 98; Jaffe-Fried Gallery, Dartmouth Coll, Hanover, NH, 74-04; Cape Mus of Fine Art, Dennis, Mass, 74-04. *Collection Arranged:* Innovations in Contemp Sculpture, Aldrich Mus, Ridgefield, Conn, 88. *Pos:* Artist in residence, Dartmouth Coll, Hanover, NH, 05. *Teaching:* Truro Ctr Arts, Mass; Fine Arts Work Ctr, Provincetown, Mass. *Awards:* Welsh Arts Coun Award to Artists, 78; Fel, Mass Artists Found, 81 & New Eng Found Arts, Boston; Pollock-Krasner Found Grant, 87. *Bibliog:* Ann Wilson Lloyd (auth), Artifacts Reborn, Contemporanea, 10/89; BH Friedman (auth), Sculpture as Autobiography, Paul Bowen (exhib catalog), Provincetown Art Asn & Mus, 95; Sara London (auth), Paul Bowen: Beyond the Mythological 1986-1996 (exhib catalog), Provincetown Art Asn & Mus, 96; Jennifer Liese (auth), Paul Bowen: Sculptures 1974-2004 (catalog essay), Jaffee-Fried Gallery, Dartmouth Coll,. *Media:* Mixed. *Mailing Add:* 130 Dover Rd Williamsville VT 05362-9721

BOWEN-FORBES, JORGE C
PAINTER
b Georgetown, Guyana, May 16, 1937. *Study:* Chelsea Sch Design, MFA, Eng, 72. *Work:* Nat Collection, Georgetown, Guyana; El Paso Mus Art, Tex; Kindercare Corp & Sellers Investment Corp, Montgomery, Ala; McCreary Cummings Fine Art Collection, Washington, Iowa; Leon Loards Gallery; Bomani Gallery, San Francisco. *Exhib:* Nat Sun Carnival, El Paso Mus, Tex, 74; Am Watercolor Soc, 74, 75, 77 & 84; Allied Artists of Am, Nat Acad, 75; African/Am Art of 80's, Mus African Arts, Buffalo, NY, 82; Nat Acad Design, NY; Frye Mus, El Paso, Tex; Wichita Centennial, Kans; Newark Mus; 10 solo exhibs worldwide. *Pos:* Art dir, Corbin Advt Agency, Bridgetown, Barbados; tech advisor, Ministry of Information & Cult, Georgetown, Guyana; com artist, Guyana Lithographic, Georgetown; nat juror Nat Arts Club, New York, 85, Nat Soc Painters in Casein and Acrylic. *Teaching:* Burrowes Sch Art, Guyana. *Awards:* Gold Medal of Honor, Allied Artists of Am, 75; High Winds Medal, Am Watercolor Soc; Gold Medal of Honor, Knickerbocker Artists, 78; Silver Medal of Honor, Allied Artists of NY, 78. *Mem:* Nat Watercolor Soc; Am Watercolor Soc (signature mem); Nat Soc Painters in Casein & Acrylics; Audubon Artists Am; Knickerbocker Artists. *Media:* Watercolor. *Publ:* Am Artist Mag, 85; Splash 2, Am Contemp Watercolors, 92; Creative Watercolors, Rockport, 96; Best of Watercolors, Rockport, 96; Best of Oil Painting, Rockport, 96; Best in Acrylic Painting; Am Poetry Ann. *Dealer:* Leon Loard Gallery 2781 Zelda Rd Montgomery Al 36106

BOWER, JOHN ARNOLD, JR
ARCHITECT, EDUCATOR
b Philadelphia, Pa, Apr 22, 1930. *Study:* Student, Pa State Col, 49; Student, OH State Univ, 51; Univ Pa, BArch with hons, 53. *Comn:* Principle works incl Vance Hall, Wharton Grad Ctr (gold medal Am Inst of Architects Philadelphia chapter 1973, design citation 1968), Int House (gold medal Am Inst of Architects Philadelphia chapter 1967), Milles Sculpture Group (silver medal Am Inst of Archits Philadelphia chapter 1972), Gallery at Market E (cert excellence - urban design 1978), Soc Hill Townhouses (1st hon award Pa Soc Archits 1966), Princeton Forrestal Village (Merit award Pa Soc Archits 1987), Market St E Transp Mall Ctr, One Reading Ctr Off Tower, Baltimore Mus Art (restoration, additions), 1234 Market St Off Bldg, 1500 Walnut St Off Bldg, Marriott Philadelphia Conv Ctr Hotel. *Pos:* Draftsman John A. Bower, Sr Archit, Philadelphia, 50-51; designer Philadelphia Planning Comn, 53-54; sr designer, Vincent G Kling Archits, Philadelphia, 54-61; partner, Bower & Fradley Archits, 61-78, Bower Lewis Thrower Archits, Philadelphia, 78-; mem design adv panel, Dept Housing & Community Develop, Baltimore, 64-. *Teaching:* Prof archit, Univ Pa. *Awards:* Albert F Schenk traveling fel Univ Pa 54; fel, Fontainebleau Sch Fine Arts-Music, Paris, 54. *Mem:* Fel Am Inst of Archits (nat urban planning and design comt 74-75, nat comt on design 76-78); Nat Acad of Design (assoc, 75, acad, 94), Carpenter's Co, Hexagon Hon Soc, Tau Sigma Delta Clubs: Germantown Cricket. *Mailing Add:* Bower Lewis Thrower Archits 1216 Arch St Ste 9 Philadelphia PA 19107-2835

BOWER, MARILYN KAY
PAINTER, INSTRUCTOR
b Concordia, Kans, June 24, 1941. *Study:* Kans State Univ (grad with honors, Magna Cum Laude) BS, 1963; Studied with Skip Whitcomb, Jim Wilcox & Hal Holoun, 1990-1998. *Work:* Great Plains Art Mus (Moseman Collection), Lincoln, Nebr; Mus Nebr Art, Kearney, Nebr; Peru State Col, Peru, Nebr; Bone Creek Mus Agrarian Art, David City, Nebr. *Comn:* Painting, City of Seward, Nebr (gift to Seward, Alaska), 1983. *Exhib:* Solo exhib, Midwest Landscapes, Plainsman Mus, Aurora, Nebr, 1989, The Lay of the Land, Bone Creek Mus of Agrarian Art, David City, Nebr, 2008; Impact-the Art of Nebraska Women (juried traveling show), Kearney, Nebr, 1988; TJ Majors Competitive, Peru State Col, 1989; 19th Joslyn Biennial, Joslyn Art Mus, Omaha, Nebr, 1986; Art in the Woods, Overland Parks Arts Comn, Overland Park, Kans, 1993, 1989, 2000; Arts for the Parks Top 100 (juried nat competition), Jackson, Wyo, 1997; Paint the Parks (juried nat competition), Topeka, Kans, 2007. *Teaching:* Instr, adult educ (oil, watermedia painting), Southwest Community Col, 1978-1990. *Awards:* Purchase Award, Reflections 1986, Norfolk Arts Ctr, 1986; Nebr Women Artists (top 36), Impact-the Art of Nebr Women, Sheldon Art Mus, 1988; Purchase Award, TJ Majors Competition, Peru State Col, 1989; Purchase Award, Art in the Woods, regional competition, Overland Park Arts Comn, 1989. *Bibliog:* Dora Hagge (ed), Impact-The Art of Nebraska Women, 1988; Elizabeth Torak (auth), Preserving Our Natural Resources, Am Artist Mag, 1990; Slusser & Margaret (coauths), Watercolor Impressions (bk), 1995; Arts for the Parks, Arts for the Parks Org, 1997; Leslie Busler (auth), Wyoming Through artists Eyes, Southwest Art Mag, 1998 . *Mem:* Rocky Mountain Plein Air Painters (RMPAP), formerly; Am Plains Painters Asn (APA), formerly; Peninsula Art League; Oil Painters Am; Plein Air Wash Artists. *Media:* Oil on linen. *Dealer:* Anderson O'Brien Fine Art 8724 Pacific St Omaha NE 68114; Bluewater Artworks Paulsbo Wa. *Mailing Add:* 9800 Harland Lane Port Orchard WA 98367

BOWERS, ANDREA
VIDEO AND INSTALLATION ARTIST
b Wilmington, OH. *Study:* Bowling Green State Univ, BFA, 1987; Calif Inst Arts, MFA, 1992. *Work:* Armand Hammer Mus Art & Cult Ctr, Mus Contemp Art, Los Angeles; Hirshhorn Mus; Ingvild Goetz Collection, Munich, Ger; Mus Mod Art, Whitney Mus Am Art, NY; Mus Fine Arts, Houston; Mus Contemp Art, San Diego; Mus Abteiberg, Moenchengladbach, Ger. *Exhib:* One-woman shows, Damaged Goods, Bliss, Pasadena, Calif, 1994, Spanish Box, Santa Monica, Calif, 1996, Spectacular Appearances, Santa Monica Mus Art, Calif, 1998, Moving Equilibrium, Sara Meltzer Gallery, NY, 1999, Intimate Strangers, 2000, Box with Dance of Its Own Making, Chouakri Brahms, Berlin, 2002, From Mouth to Ear, Goldman Tevis, Los Angeles, 2002, Virtual Arena, Sara Meltzer Gallery, NY, 2002, Magical Politics, Chouakri Brahms, Berlin, 2003, Nonviolent Civil Disobedience Training, Sara Meltzer Gallery, NY, 2004, Magazine 4 Voralberger Kunstverein, Austria, 2004, Mary Goldman Gallery, Los Angeles, 2004, Culture of Choice, Van Horn, Dusseldorf, 2005, Letters to an Army of Three, Core Prog, Glassell Sch Art Mus Fine Arts, Houston, 2006, The Weight of Relevance, Power Plant, Toronto, 2007, Sanctuary, Van Horn, Dusseldorf, 2008; Dave's Not Here, Three Day Weekend, Los Angeles, 1994; Unfinished Hist, Walker Art Ctr, Minneapolis, 1998-99; Me Mine, Luckman Fine Arts Gallery, Calif, 1999; Moving Pictures, Galerie Tommy Lund, Copenhagen, Denmark, 2000; Subject Plural, Contemp Arts Mus, Houston, 2001; Everybody Now, Bertha & Karl Leubsdorf Gallery, NY, 2001; Time-Share, Sara Meltzer Gallery, NY, 2002; Munic Art Gallery, Barnsdale Art PK, Los Angeles, 2003; COLA 2003, Rendered, Sara Meltzer Gallery, NY, 2003; 100 Artist See God, Laguna Art Mus, San Francisco, 2003-04; Whitney Biennial Am Art, Whitney Mus Am Art, 2004; Touch of Evil, Gallery Estacion Tijuana, Mex, 2005; The Last Christmas, Mehdi Chouakri, Riverside Wall, Berlin, 2005; This is Not a Love Song, Susanne Vielmetter Gallery, Los Angeles, 2006; Particulate Matter, Mills Coll Art Mus, Oakland, 2006; Radical Hospitality, The Suburban, Chicago, 2007; The Way That We Rhyme, Yerba Buena Ctr Arts, San Francisco, 2008; Memory is your Image of Perfection, Mus Contemp Art, San Diego, 2008. *Awards:* Regional Fel Visual Arts Sculpture, Western States Arts Fedn/Nat Endowment Arts, 1995-96 & 1998; Fel, Visual Arts, City LA, 2003; US Artists Fel, 2008; Louis Comfort Tiffany Found Grant, 2009. *Bibliog:* David Pagel (auth), Window on LA, Los Angeles Art Fair Catalog, 1991; Eleanor Heartney (auth), The Imp of the Perverse, ARTnews, 9/1993; Leanne Alexis Davidson (auth), Three Day Weekend, Real Life Mag, 35-36, No 23, 1994; Kenneth Baker (auth), Taking Art into Their Own Hands, San Francisco Chronicle, C1 & C5, 6/2/1995; Michael Darling

(auth), Box Tops, Santa Barbara News-Press, 2/1996; David A Greene (auth), Hot Coffee, Frieze, 76, Issue 43, 5/1997; Franceso Bonami (auth), Unfinished History, exhib catalog, Walker Art Ctr, Minneapolis, 1998; Hildegund Amanshauser (auth), A Living Theatre, exhib catalog, Salzburger Kunstverein, 1999; Doug Harvey (auth), It's Chinatown, LA Weekly, 49, 5/5-11/2000; Kelly Klassmeyer (auth), Group Mentality, Houston Press, 4/12-28/2001; Sara Gavlak (auth), Andrea Bowers, Intimate Strangers, Time Out, 1/11-18/2002; Renna Jana (auth), California Dreamin, Tema Celeste, 20-21, 2003; Pamela M Lee (auth), Crystal Life, Artforum, 174, 5/2004; Katy Siegel (auth), All Together Now, Artforum, 169, 1/2005; Mar Herbst (auth), Marc Herbst on Andrea Bowers, InterReview, 36, 2006; Sharon Mizota (auth), Filling the Gap, Art Ltd, 7/2007; Julia Bryan-Wilson (auth), The Way That We Rhyme: Women, Art & Politics, Artforum, 1/2008

BOWERS, CHERYL See Olsen Bergman, Ciel (Cheryl) Bowers

BOWES, FRANCES
COLLECTOR
b San Francisco, Calif. *Pos:* Founder & pres, Kransco (sold to Mattel, 94); owner, Yakima Products Inc (sold to Watermark), Arcata, Calif, 1994-2001, Camelback outdoor products (sold to Bear Stearns Merchant Banking), 1995-2003. *Awards:* Named one of Top 200 Collectors, ARTnews Magazine, 2004-12. *Mem:* UCSF (bd dirs); DIA Art Found; Trustees Am Patrons of Tate Haward Collectors Comt. *Collection:* Modern and contemporary art. *Mailing Add:* 800 Francisco St San Francisco CA 94109

BOWLER, JOSEPH, JR
PAINTER, ILLUSTRATOR
b Forest Hills, NY, Sept 4, 1928. *Study:* Charles E Cooper Studios, New York; Art Students League. *Work:* Ann Exhib of Published Work for 1977, Soc Illusr 78. *Comn:* Portraits, Rose Kennedy, Rose Kennedy Wing, Albert Einstein Hosp, 71; Geri DeGaulle, Time cover; Julie & David Eisenhower, Saturday Evening Post cover; Family of Dr & Mrs Ellis Jones, GA, 90 - 05; Daughters of Mr & Mrs Hank Cram, SC 98 - 04. *Exhib:* Ann Exhib of Published Work for 1977, Soc Illusr, 78. *Pos:* judge, Portrait Soc of Am, self-portrait contest, 2006. *Teaching:* Instr painting, Parsons Sch Design, New York, 68-72; instr, MFA Independent Study Degree Prog, Syracuse Univ, 80-86. *Awards:* Artist of Yr, Artists' Guild New York, 67; Elected to the Illustr Hall of Fame, 92. *Bibliog:* Cory SerVaas (auth), Artist in the White House, Saturday Evening Post, summer 72; Joe Bowler--Artist Illustrator (film), & Arts the Thing Joe Bowler--Portraits (film), SCE-TV; Artist Joe Bowler, Southern Accents, winter 82. *Mem:* Soc Illusr. *Media:* Oil. *Specialty:* Joe Bowler Collection; The Red Piano Gallery, Hilton Head Island, SC. *Publ:* Portraits, The Artists Mag, 9/88; At My Easel, Thoughts of a Master Portraitist, Int Artist, 12/2000. *Dealer:* Marilyn C Bowler Artist's Representation 9 Baynard Cove Rd Hilton Head Island SC 29928. *Mailing Add:* Nine Baynard Cove Rd Hilton Head Island SC 29928

BOWLES, MARIANNE VON RECKLINGHAUSEN See von Recklinghausen, Marianne Bowles

BOWLING, GARY ROBERT
PAINTER
b Lamar, Mo, Feb 1, 1948. *Study:* Mo Southern State Col, BS (art educ), 70, Univ Ark, Fayetteville, MFA, 74. *Work:* Sheldon Mem Art Gallery, Lincoln, Nebr; Mitchell Art Mus, Mt Vernon, Ill; Sioux City Art Ctr, Iowa; Johnson Co Community Col, Kans; Univ Mo, Columbia; Univ Iowa, Iowa City; Brunnier Art Mus, Iowa State Univ; Kemper Mus Contemporary Art, Kansas City, Mo; Jule Collins Smith Mus Fine Art, Auburn Univ, Ala; Daum Art Mus, Sedalia, Mo. *Comn:* Paintings, Northwestern Life Insurance, Minneapolis, Minn, Iowa State Gateway Ctr, Ames, Norwest Bank, Hopkins, Minn, Fairview-Southdale Hosp, Minneapolis; McDonald's Hamb Univ, Chicago; N Lake Shore Hyatt, Chicago; Farm Bureau Hdq, Des Moines, Iowa. *Exhib:* Prairie Vistas, Joslyn Art Mus, Omaha, Nebr, 86; Contemp Landscape, Inst Creative Arts, Fairfield, Iowa, 87; Brunnier Art Mus, Ames, Iowa, 88; Mid Am Landscape, SW Minn, St Univ, Marshall, 89; New Masters, Huntington Mus Art, WVA, 92; Land of the Fragile Giants, Brunnier Art Mus, Ames, Iowa, 94; Midwestern Romanticism (with catalog), Ill Arts Coun, Lakeview Mus Art, Peoria & Beach Mus Art, Manhattan, Kans, 96-97; Obsessed with Weather, Brunnier Art Mus, Ames, Ia, 2007; Not Just Landscapes, Highland Park Art Ctr, Highland Park, Ill, 2008; Silver Lining, The Citadelle Art Found, Canada, Tex, 2010. *Teaching:* Instr painting & drawing, Univ Ark, Fayetteville, 74; chmn art dept, Westmar Col, Le Mars, Iowa, 74-83. *Bibliog:* John Couper (auth), A sense of place, Joplin Mag, 86; C Butler et al (auths), Of Vapor & Denser Surfaces, (exhib catalog), Mitchell Mus, 87; Mark Stegmaier, Gary Bowling, Am Artist Mag, 88. *Mem:* Yaddo Fel. *Media:* Oil, Mixed Media. *Publ:* Auth, Land of the Fragile Giants, Univ Iowa Press; Lela Gilbert, Lit by the Sun, Carpe Diem Books, 2001. *Dealer:* Groveland Gallery 25 Groveland Terr Minneapolis MN 55403; Olson-Larson Gallery 203 5th St W Des Moines IA 50265; M A Doran Gallery 3509 S Peoria Tulsa OK 74105; Sherry Leedy Gallery 2004 Baltimore; Anderson Obrien Gallery 1108 Jackson St Omaha Ne 68102; Meyer Gallery East 225 Canyon Rd Santa Fe NM 87501; Leopold Gallery 324 W 63rd St Kansas City MO 64113; Hyde Gallery 221 E Walnut St Springfield MO 65806. *Mailing Add:* PO Box 207 Lamar MO 64759

BOWLING, KATHERINE
PAINTER
b Washington, DC, 1955. *Study:* Va Commonwealth Univ, BFA, 78. *Work:* Metrop Mus Art, NY; Orlando Mus Contemp Art, Fla; Phoenix Art Mus, Ariz; Brooklyn Mus Art, NY; Fisher Landau Center, Long Island City, NY. *Exhib:* Va Arts Biennial, Va Mus Fine Arts, 79; New Painting, Va Mus Fine Arts, 83; solo exhibs, Albright-Knox Mem Gallery, Buffalo, NY, 88, Blum Helman, Los Angeles, 90 & NY, 90, 92 & 94 & Orlando Mus Art, Fla, 94, Joseph Helman Gallery, NY, 96, 98, 01; Nocturnal Landscape, Whitney Mus Am Art, 89; group exhib, The Modern Landscape, Queens Libr Gallery, Queensborough, NY, 96; Landscapes, David Floria Gallery, Woody Creek, Colo, 97; The Secret Garden, The Art Mus at Fla Int Univ, Miami, 97; Joseph Helman Gallery, NY, 98, 2000; Exurbia, Gallery Luisotti, Santa Monica, Calif, 2000; and others. *Awards:* Mid Atlantic Arts Found Fel, 88; NY State Found for the Arts Fel, 89; Grant, Nat Endowment Arts, 91. *Bibliog:* Grace Glueck (auth), Katherine Bowling, The New York Times, 4/98; Robert M Murdock (auth), Katherine Bowling, Review, 4/98; Mary Hrbacek (auth), Land to See (exhib catalog), Joseph Helman Gallery, 01

BOWLT, JOHN
ART HISTORIAN, EDUCATOR
b London, Eng, Dec 6, 1943. *Study:* Univ Birmingham, Eng, BA, 65 & MA, 66; Moscow Univ, USSR, 66-68; Univ St Andrews, Scotland, PhD, 71. *Pos:* Dir, Inst of Modern Russian Cult. *Teaching:* Lectr Russian, Univ St Andrews, Scotland, 68-69; asst prof Russian, Univ Kans, Lawrence, 70-71; prof Russian art & lang, Univ Tex, Austin, 71-88; prof Russian art & lang, Univ Southern Calif, Los Angeles, Calif, 88-. *Awards:* Woodrow Wilson Nat Fel, 71; Fel Nat Humanities Inst, Yale Univ, 77-78; Fulbright-Hays Award to France, 81; Int Res & Exchanges Bd, 86, 88, 90, 96; Borehard Found to France, 95; Raubenheimer Outstanding Senior Faculty Award, Univ Southern Calif, 97. *Mem:* Am Asn Advan Slavic Studies. *Res:* Russian art and architecture of 18th, 19th and 20th centuries. *Interests:* Antique books. *Collection:* Russian books. *Publ:* Auth, Kalman & the Labyrinth of Decadence, 2008; auth, Russia - St Petersburg: The Russian Silver Age, 2008; and numerous other bks & articles

BOWMAN, BRUCE
PAINTER, ART WRITER
b Dayton, Ohio, Nov 23, 1938. *Study:* San Diego City Coll, Calif, AA; Calif State Univ, Los Angeles, BA & MA; Univ Calif, Los Angeles. *Exhib:* Cypress Coll, Calif, 77; Designs Recycled Gallery, Fullerton, Calif, 77; Pierce Coll, Los Angeles, 78; Pepperdine Univ, Malibu, 78; Leopold-Gold Gallery, Santa Monica, 80-81. *Teaching:* Instr art, West Los Angeles Coll, Culver City, 69-83, chmn art dept, 75-76, 83; instr art, Cypress Coll, 76-77. *Media:* Oil. *Res:* Contemp art forms and techniques. *Interests:* Karate (black belt). *Publ:* Auth, articles in Arts & Activities Mag, Design Mag & Sch Arts Mag; Shaped Canvas, 76 & Toothpick Sculpture & Ice Cream Stick Art, 76, Sterling; Ideas: How to Get Them, R & E Publ, 85. *Dealer:* The Options Gallery 2665 Shell Beach Rd Shell Beach CA 93449. *Mailing Add:* 1711 Ramona Dr Camarillo CA 93010

BOWMAN, GEORGE LEO
PAINTER
b Newburyport, Mass, Dec 25, 1935. *Study:* Boston Sch Mus Fine Arts, 60; Tufts Univ, Medford, Mass, BS, 60. *Work:* Harvard Univ, Brookline, Mass; Va Mortgage Co, Norfolk; Honeywell Corp, Minn. *Exhib:* Adelson Gallery, 70-72, Copley Soc, 70-73, Boston, Mass; Grand Cent Gallery, NY, 73-76; Rockport Art Asn, Mass, 74-82; Joseph Kilbridge Gallery, Groton, Mass, 89. *Pos:* Asst art dir, DC Heath Publ Co, Boston, Mass, 63-67; illusr & designer, ASEC, Burlington, Mass, 78-92. *Teaching:* Instr design & drawing, Boston Sch Mus Fine Arts, 63-70. *Awards:* Nat Casein Show Painting Award, NY; Aldro Hibbard Painting Award, Rockport Art Asn, Mass; Copley Soc Painting Award, Boston, Mass. *Media:* Oil. *Publ:* New York Life Calendar, 80-81. *Mailing Add:* 749 Main St Unit C Osterville MA 02655-1944

BOWMAN, JERRY W
PAINTER, DESIGNER
b Columbia City, Ind, Aug 3, 1952. *Study:* Kalamazoo Col, BA, 74; Univ Mich, Ann Arbor; Kalamazoo Inst Arts. *Work:* Upjohn Co Corp Collection; Pharmacia Inc, Corp Collection; Springfield Art Mus, Mo; Pfizer Inc, Corp Collection; Bronson Mem Hosp Collection. *Comn:* Painting, George Handley, Denver, Colo, 98; painting, Aaron Maule, Belfast, Ireland, 2000; Jerry Colca, Kalamazoo, Mich, 2010; Casa Bolero, Kalamazo, Mich, 2012. *Exhib:* Watercolor West, Art & Cult Ctr, Brea, Calif, 92, 94, 96 & 97, 99; San Diego Watercolor Soc Int Exhib, Poway Ctr Performing Arts, Calif, 93; Watercolor USA, Springfield Art Mus, Mo, 93-94, 97, 2000-2001, 2003 & 2011; Rocky Mountain Nat, 93-94, 96, 98, 2000, 2003 & 2006; Northwest Watercolor Soc, Howard/Mandville Gallery, Kirkland, Wash, 94; Philadelphia Watercolor Club 95th Exhib, Pa, 95; Watercolor Now: Best of WC, Springfield Art Mus, 2003; Red River Watercolor Soc Ann, 2005; Adirondack OFAG Ann, 2006; Solo Exhib: Pfizer (Kalamazoo), Corporate Invitational, 2007; Juried Mich Show, Kalamazoo Inst Arts, 2008, 2012, 2013; Ariz Aqueons, Tubac Center for the Arts, 2009; Three Rivers, Carnegie Ctr, Mich, 2009-2014; Park Club, Kalamazoo, Mich, 2010; 21st Salon Internat d'Aquarelle, Uckange, France, 2011, 2012; Mich Watercolor Soc Ann, 2011-2014; Univ Mich, Dearborn, 2011, 2012; Mich Arts, Arts Council, Holland, Mich, 2012; Art Prize, Grand Rapids, Mich, 2012, 2013, 2014; Signature Am Watercolor Exhib, 2013-2014; Ella Sharp Mus, 2013; Greater Mich Art Exhib, Midland Art Mus, 2013; Midtown Gallery, Kalamazoo, Mich, 2013; NHS Small Works Ehib, 2014; Transparent Watercolor Soc Exhib, 2014; Winter Art Exhib, View Arts Ctr, Old Forge, NY, 2014; ArtPrize, Devos Place Convention Ctr, Grand Rapids, Mich, 2015; Rocky Mountain Nat Watermedia Ann Exhib, Foothills Art Ctr, Golden, Colo, 2015; Int Soc of Experimental Artists Ann Exhib, Dennos Mus, Traverse City, Mich, 2015; Lakeland Hosp, one-person exhib, St Joseph, Mich, 2015. *Pos:* Pres, Bowman Art LLC, 2010. *Teaching:* guest lectr, Southwestern Mich Watercolor Soc, 2009; guest lectr, Paw Paw Mich Art Asn, 2009; pvt studio instr, 2010-; Head watercolor Instr, Beth Charles Art, Holland, Mich, 2011, 2012. *Awards:* 1st Prize, Kalamazoo Inst Arts, 99; Golden Palette Award, Rocky Mountain Nat, 2000; Major Cash Award, Watercolor USA, 2000 & 2003; Cohen award, Adirandack Ann, 2006; Rosenfield Award, MWES, 2011; Prix Credit Mutual prize, 2012; Billboad Competition Winner, KIA, Kalamazoo, Mich, 2012; 1st Pl, Carnegie Ctr, All Mich Show, 2013; MWCS award, Mich WC Soc, 2013; DIA award, Mich Watercolor Soc 98th Ann Juried Competition and traveling exhib, Bloomfield Hills, Mich, 2015; 2nd Pl, Carnegie Ctr Ann Open Competition, Three Rivers, Mich, 2015. *Mem:* Kalamazoo Inst Art; Sig mem, Watercolor W & Rocky Mountain Nat Watermedia Soc; Watercolor

USA; Paw Paw Art Asn; Southwestern Mich Watercolor Soc; Mich Watercolor Soc; Asn Mem NWS; Transparent Watercolor Soc. *Media:* Watercolor. *Specialty:* watercolor. *Publ:* Splash 5: Best of Watercolor, NLight, Cincinnati, OH, 98; Watercolor Mag, 2012. *Dealer:* Urban Cottage Kalamazoo MI; Davanna G and Su Casa South Haven MI; Kalamazoo Inst of Art Kalamazoo MI. *Mailing Add:* 83626 Waldron Lawton MI 49065

BOWMAN, JOHN
PAINTER
b Sayre, Pa, 1953. *Study:* Rutgers Univ, BFA, 76. *Exhib:* Solo exhibs, Nine Gallery, NY, 83, White Columns & Virtual Garrison Gallery, New York, 84, Holly Solomon Gallery, NY, 85, 86, 87 & 89 & Jon Oulman Gallery, Minneapolis, Minn, 88; Petits Tableaux, Galerie Charles Cartwright, Paris, France, 86; Interiors, Proctor Art Ctr, Bard Col, Annandale-on-Hudson, 88; The Silent Baroque (with catalog), Galerie Thaddaeus Ropac, Salzburg, Austria, 89; Romance & Irony (traveling exhib), Mus Western Australia, Perth, Sydney, Australia, Auckland, NZ & Tampa, Fla, 90; Fernando Alcolea, Barcelona, Spain, 90. *Bibliog:* Richard Martin (auth), Fictions, Arts, 2/88; Eleanor Heartney (auth), Review: Fictions, Artnews, 2/88; Kim Levin (auth), Choices: Dwelling, Village Voice, 1/3/89. *Mailing Add:* Tibor Denagy Gallery 724 Fifth Ave New York NY 10019

BOWMAN, LESLIE GREENE
MUSEUM DIRECTOR
b Springfield, Ohio, Nov 9, 1956. *Study:* Miami Univ, Ohio, BPhil, 1978; Univ Del, MA (Early Am Cult), 1981. *Pos:* Curatorial asst, Los Angeles County Mus Art, 1980-81, asst cur decorative arts & European sculpture, 1981-84, assoc cur decorative arts, 1984-88, cur decorative arts & asst dir exhib programs, 1989-97; consult cur, Oakland Mus, Calif, 1986, Santa Barbara Mus Art, 1986-90; curatorial bd dirs, Decorative Arts Study Ctr, San Juan Capistrano, Calif, 1990; mem, Comt for the Preservation of the White House, 1993-; bd trustees, Nat Trust Hist Preservation; with Nat Mus Wildlife Art, Jackson Hole, Wyo, 1997-99; dir & CEO, Winterthur Mus & Country Estate, Winterthur, Del, 1999-. *Teaching:* Adj prof, Univ Southern Calif, 1988; instr, Univ Calif Los Angeles, 1988. *Awards:* Winterthur Mus Fel, 1978-80; Crowninshield Fel, 1986-87 & 1987-88; Florence J Gould Found Scholar, 1989; Charles F Montgomery Award, Decorative Arts Soc of Soc Archit Historians, 1990; Univ Del Presidential Citation, 2001. *Mem:* Am Ceramic Arts Soc; Am Ceramic Circle; English Ceramic Circle; Furniture Hist Soc; French Porcelain Soc; Glass Circle; Nat Early Am Glass Club; AAM (accreditation comn); Asn Art Mus Dirs (bd dirs); Charles Rennie MacIntosh Soc (Scotland); Soc Winterthur Grads; Soc Silver Collectors. *Publ:* Auth, Am Arts & Crafts: Virtue in Design, 1980; co-auth, Am Rococo, 1750-1775: Elegance in Ornament, 1992, Silver in the Golden State, 1986, The Gilbert Collection of Gold & Silver, 1988. *Mailing Add:* Winterthur Mus Garden & Libr Rte 52 Kennett Pike Winterthur DE 19735

BOYD, BLAKE
PAINTER, INSTALLATION SCULPTOR
b Slidell, La, 1970. *Study:* Memphis Coll Art. *Work:* Arts Coun New Orleans; Gershwin Hotel, New York. *Exhib:* Solo exhibs include Contemp Arts Ctr, New Orleans, 1997, Barrister's Gallery, New Orleans, 2000, Galerie Simonne Stern, New Orleans, 2001, Cheekwood Botanical Gardens & Mus Art, Nashville, 2003, Arthur Roger Gallery, New Orleans, 2003, 2005 & 2007; group exhibs include Artists on War: An Open Forum, Contemp Arts Ctr, New Orleans, 1991, Discovering Columbus, 1992, Under Your Skin, 1995, The Body Photographic, 1995, The 1st New Orleans Banana Festival, 1996, Homage to the 20th Century, 2000 & La Biennial, 2003; Hall-Barnett Gallery, 1991-94; Comic Release: Negotiating Identity for a New Generation, Carnegie-Mellon Univ, Pittsburgh, 2003; Motion Stills, Savannah Coll Art & Design, Ga, 2004; Young, Willing & Hungry, Jen Bekman Gallery, New York, 2005. *Awards:* Percent for Art Purchase Prize, Arts Coun New Orleans; Pollock-Krasner Found Grant, 2007. *Dealer:* Arthur Rogers Gallery 432 Julia St New Orleans LA 70130. *Mailing Add:* PO Box 1677 Slidell LA 70459

BOYD, KAREN WHITE
EDUCATOR, FIBER ARTIST
b Akron, Ohio, Sept 8, 1936. *Study:* Kent State Univ, BA (art educ), 58 & MA (studio art), 64; Tyler Sch Art, Temple Univ, MFA (weaving), 75. *Exhib:* Regional Craft Biennial, J B Speed Mus, Louisville, Ky, 70; Mid-States Craft Exhib, Evansville Mus, Ind, 73; Nat Fiber Design Show, Calif Polytech State Univ, San Luis Obispo, 75; 3rd Int Exhib Miniature Textiles, Brit Crafts Centre, London, 78. *Teaching:* Assoc prof weaving & textiles, Murray State Univ, 67-81, prof, 81-. *Awards:* Juror's Award, Ted Hallman, Nat Fiber Design Show, 75; Honorable Mention, Southeast 80 Craft Exhib, Tallahassee, Fla. *Mem:* Ky Guild Artists & Craftsmen; Handweaver's Guild Am; Asn British Craftsmen. *Dealer:* Am Art Inc Atlanta GA

BOYD, LAKIN
EDUCATOR, PRINTMAKER
b Athens, Ala, Aug 27, 1946. *Study:* Univ Ala, BFA, 68 & MA, 70; Pratt Graphic Ctr, 70-71, intaglio with Michael Ponce de Leon. *Work:* Oscar Wells Mem Mus, Birmingham, Ala; Univ Ala, Tuscaloosa; Ala Arts Comn; Univ South; Pratt Graphic Ctr Print Collection, NY. *Exhib:* Nat Student Printmakers Travel Exhib, 68; 13th Dixie Ann, 72; Solo exhibs, Univ Ala & Judson Col, 73; 14th Ann Reece Regional, 74. *Teaching:* Asst prof graphics & art hist, Ala A&M Univ, Huntsville, 71-82. *Awards:* Purchase Award, Birmingham Art Asn, 67; Fulbright Grant to Belg & Neth, 75. *Mem:* Southeastern Coll Art Conf; Am Asn Univ Prof; Nat Art Educ Asn; Am Crafts Coun; Ala Art Educ Asn. *Media:* Intaglio, Lithography. *Mailing Add:* 426 Eustis Ave SE Huntsville AL 35801-4110

BOYD, (DAVID) MICHAEL
PAINTER, GRAPHIC ARTIST
b Waterloo, Iowa, Nov 27, 1936. *Study:* With Philip Evergood, 57; Univ Northern Iowa, BA, 59. *Work:* Baltimore Mus Art; Albright-Knox Art Gallery, Buffalo, NY; Chrysler Mus Art, Norfolk, Va; Mint Mus Art, Charlotte, NC; Knoxville Mus Art, Knoxville, Tenn; Waterloo Mus Art, Iowa; Univ Ky Art Mus, Lexington; Robert Wood Johnson Univ Hosp, New Brunswick, NJ. *Comn:* Mural, EF MacDonald co, Dayton, 82. *Exhib:* Recent Acquisitions, Albright-Knox Art Gallery, 81 & Baltimore Mus Art, 82; Ana Sklar Gallery, Miami, Fla, 84; Geometric Abstraction: Selections from a Decade, 1975-1985, Bronx Mus Art, New York, 85; JJ Brookings Gallery, San Jose, Calif, 87; solo exhibs, Davenport Mus Art, Iowa, Charles H MacNider Mus, Mason City, Iowa, Waterloo Munic Galleries, Iowa, 89-90, Andre Zarre Gallery, New York, 90 & 94, Herbert F Johnson Mus Art, Ithaca, NY, Clinton, NY & Univ Ky Art Mus, Lexington, 91-92; retrospective, Upstairs Gallery, Ithaca, NY, 95 & Pardo Lattuada Gallery, NY, 2000; Galleria Le Bateleur, Rome, Italy, 2003; Coastline: Recent paintings, Artefact Pardo Gallery, Milan, Italy, 2003; Coastlines/Kustenlinie: Recent paintings, Artefact Pardo Gallery, Zurich, Switz, 2005. *Teaching:* Prof design, Cornell Univ, 68-96, prof emer, 96. *Awards:* Purchase Award, Everson Mus Art, 71; Yaddo Fel, 74; New York Found Arts, 88. *Bibliog:* Pat Sloan (auth), article, Arts Mag, 79; Lawrence Campbell (auth), Michael Boyd, Art in Am, 84. *Mem:* Am Asn Mus. *Media:* Acrylic on Canvas and Paper. *Mailing Add:* 78 Greene St New York NY 10012

BOYD, ROBERT
SCULPTOR, VIDEO ARTIST
b 1969. *Study:* Southwest Mo State Univ, Springfield, 1987-89; Tyler Sch Art, Temple Univ, Pa, 1989-90; Cooper Union Sch Art, New York, 1990-91. *Exhib:* Solo exhibs, Islip Art Mus, NY, 1999, Zilkha Gallery, Wesleyan Univ, Conn, 2007, Indianapolis Mus Contemp Art, 2007, Pinchuk Art Centre, Kiev, Ukraine, 2008, PS1 Contemp Art Ctr, New York, 2008, Feldman Gallery, Pacific Northwest Coll Art, 2009; Anthology of Art, Akademie der KUnste, Berlin, Ger, 2004; In the Absence of Recombination, Jawaharlal Nehru Univ, India, 2005; Darkness Ascends, Mus Contemp Canadian Art, Toronto, 2006; Float, Socrates Sculpture Park, New York, 2007; Wedded Bliss, The Marriage of Art and Ceremony, Peabody Essex Mus, Salem, Mass, 2008. *Pos:* Guest lectr, New Sch for Social Res, New York, 1999, Pratt Inst, New York, 1999, New York Univ, 2003, CUNY, New York, 2005, Parsons New Sch Design, 2007, Coll NJ, Hamilton, 2008, Pacific Northwest Coll, Portland, 2009; vis artist, New Coll Univ S Fla, 2000, Ringling Sch Art & Design. *Teaching:* Instr sculpture, Cooper Union Sch Art, 2006-. *Awards:* New York Found Arts Fel, 2004 & 2009; Rema Hort Mann Found Grant, 2006; Civitella Ranieri Found Fel, 2009. *Bibliog:* Holland Cotter (auth), Pop Politics Power, NY Times, 9/30/2005; Murray Whyte (auth), Things That Go Bump in the Night, Toronto Star, 6/20/2006; Valerie Gladstone (auth), Float Drifts into Socrates Sculpture Park, New York Sun, 8/24/2007; Jacob Stringer (auth), Politically Curate, Salt Lake City Weekly, 1/17/2008; Lyra Kilston (auth), Time-Based Art Festival: 09, Freize Mag, 9/28/2009

BOYER, NATHAN P
VIDEO ARTIST, EDUCATOR
Study: Tufts Univ, BFA, 1998; Yale Univ Sch Art, MFA, 2002. *Teaching:* Asst prof, Coll Arts & Sciences, Univ Mo, Columbia. *Awards:* Fulbright Grant, 2010. *Mailing Add:* University of Missouri A102 Fine Arts Bldg Columbia MO 65211

BOYLAN, JOHN LEWIS
PAINTER, PRINTMAKER
b Cleveland, Ohio, Oct 8, 1921. *Study:* Oberlin Col, 39-42; Cleveland Inst Art, 42; Univ NMex, BFA, 47; Art Students League, 47-50; study with Vaclav Vytlacil, Morris Kantor, Harry Sternberg, Will Barnet & Peter Piening. *Work:* Metrop Mus Art, NY; NY Pub Libr; Roswell Mus, NMex; Univ Pa Art Mus. *Exhib:* Soc Am Graphic Artists, 50 & 71; Royal Soc Painter-Etchers & Engravers, London, 54 & 56; solo exhib, Roswell Mus, 59 & 66; Japan Print Soc, Tokyo, 67. *Teaching:* Dir painting & design, Roswell Mus Art Sch, 50-51; instr painting & design, Inst Am Indian Art, Santa Fe, NMex, 66-, actg head fine arts, 74-75. *Awards:* Award of Merit, Am Asn State & Local Hist, 60. *Media:* Oil, Acrylic; Woodcut, Metal Plate Lithograph

BOYLE, RICHARD J
ART HISTORIAN, WRITER
b New York, NY, June 3, 1932. *Study:* Adelphi Univ, BA; Oxford Univ, with Edgar Wind & John Pope-Hennessy; Art Student League, with Will Barnet. *Collection Arranged:* John Twachtman Retrospective, 66, Laser Light: A New Visual Art, 69, The Early Work of Paul Gauguin, 71 & Robert S Duncanson: A Centennial Exhibition, 72, Cincinnati Art Mus; Am Paintings from Newport, Wichita Art Mus, 69; Young Am Painters from PA Acad Fine Arts, 75; Milk & Eggs: The Am Revival of Tempera Painting, Brandywine River Mus, PA, 30, 50, 2002; Double Lives, Am Painters as Illustr 1850-1950, New Britain Mus Am Art, 2008. *Pos:* Cur, Int Art Found, Newport, RI, summer 62; dir, Middletown Fine Arts Ctr, Ohio, 63-65; cur painting, Cincinnati Art Mus, 65-73; dir, Pa Acad Fine Arts, 73-83; art comn chmn, Redevelop Authority, Philadelphia, 75-83; consult, continuing educ prog, Philadelphia Col Art, 85-86; mem low illustration comt, New Britain Mus Am Art, 1999-. *Teaching:* Vis scholar, Moore Col Art, Philadelphia, 83-84; instr, Philadelphia Univ Arts, 84-87; adj prof art hist, Temple Univ, Philadelphia & Japan, 87-2005. *Awards:* Benjamin Franklin Fel, Royal Soc of Art, London, Eng; Literary Award for book (John H Twachtman), Athenaeum of Philadelphia, 76. *Mem:* Am Asn of Mus; Asn Historians Am Art. *Res:* Late nineteenth & twentieth century American art & culture, history of painting technique and technology, Hist Am Illustration. *Interests:* Research, travel, jogging, reading, movies. *Publ:* Contribr, French impressionists influence Am impressionists, Lowe Art Mus, Fla, 71; Auth, John Twachtman's Gloucester Years, Twachtman in Glouster: His Last Years, 1900-1902 (exhib catalog), IRA Spanierman Art, 87; auth, Lewis Henry Meakin: An American Landscape Painter Rediscovered, Cincinnati Art Galleries, 87; coauth, Sunlight & Shadow: Life & Art of Willard Metcalf, 88; auth, Technique, Technology and Gentility: The Style of American Impressionism, World Impressionism and Pleinairism, Chunichi Shimbun/Matsuzakaya Art Mus, Nagoya, Japan, 91; Connection with a Place: The Collection of the Brandywine River Museum (catalog), Chadds Ford, Pa, 91; Dow: American Sensei, Arthur Wesley Dows: His Art and His Influence, Ira Spanierman, Inc, 99; Max Kuehne: Artist & Craftsman, Hollis Taggart Galleries, 2001; Milk & Eggs: The American Revival of Tempera Painting, Brandywine River Mus and Univ Washington Press, 2002; Bob Kane: People &

Places, Rizzoli Int Inc, 2002; From Hawthorne to Hofmann: Provincetown Vignettes, 1899-1945, Hollis Taggart Galleries, 2002; auth, Robert Kipniss: Paintings 1950-2005, Hudson Hills Press, 2007; The Comic Book Art of Artur Pinajidu; Arthur Panajian: Discovering a Master of Abstraction, Woodstock Art Mus, 2009; Remington's Infantryman, Exploring Illustration/Remington's Infantryman, Rockwell Ctr American Visual Studies, Norman Rockwell Mus, 2013. *Mailing Add:* Box 177 Salisbury CT 06068

BRADBURY-REID, ELLEN A
ADMINISTRATOR, EDUCATOR
b Louisville, Ky, Feb 26, 1940. *Study:* Yale Univ; Univ Vienna, Austria, 60; Univ NMex, BA & MA, 66. *Collection Arranged:* African Oceanic Art, Am Indians, North and South; Am 20th Century, Regis Collection; Artifacts from Manhattan Project, Los Alamos. *Pos:* Res asst, Minneapolis Inst Art, 69-70, asst registr, 70-72, registr, 72-75 & cur primitive art, 75-79; dir, Mus Fine Arts, Mus NMex, 79, Santa Fe Festival Arts, 82; founder, Recursos Santa Fe, 84- & Royal Road Art Tours, 98. *Teaching:* Inst, Univ NMex, 67, Col Santa Fe, 96. *Mem:* Int Women's Forum; NMex Quincentennial Comn; Albuquerque Mus Arts (adv bd); Founding Mem NMex Coalition for Hist Preservation. *Res:* American Indian Ghost Dance. *Publ:* Four-State Survey, the State of Regional Arts, ARTSPACE, Fall, 83; auth, Art Reviews, Albuquerque J, 85-86; co-ed, From the Faraway Nearby, A Biography of Georgia O'Keeffe, Addison-Wesley, 92; Auth, Native Arts and Crafts, (Southwest Indian Arts and Crafts Series), Salamander, 95; K. Villea & L Wagner (coauth), Contemporary Mexican Architecture and Design, Gibbs Smith, 2002. *Mailing Add:* 510 Alto St Santa Fe NM 87501-2517

BRADFORD, MARK
COLLAGE ARTIST
b Los Angeles, Calif, 1961. *Study:* Calif Inst Arts, BFA, 1995, MFA, 1997. *Exhib:* Solo & two-person shows: Distribution, Deep River, LA, Calif, 1998, Floss, Walter McLean Gallery, San Francisco, 1998, European Wavy, Two Rivers Gallery, Pittsburgh, 1999, Color Theory, Luggage Store, San Francisco, 2000, I Don't Think You're Ready For This Jelly, Lombard-Freid Arts, NY, 2001, That Wasn't My Car You Saw, Finesilver Gallery, San Antonio, 2002, Patricia Faure Gallery, Santa Monica, Calif, 2002, Caught Up, Suzanne Vielmetter, LA Projects, 2002, Very Powerful Lords, Whitney Mus Am Art, NY, 2003 & Neither New Nor Correct, 2007, Bounce, REDCAT, LA, Calif, 2004, Grace & Measure, Sikkema Jenkins & Co, NY, 2005, Niagara, LAXART, 2006, Artspace, San Antonio, 2008; Biennale Internazionale, Palazzo delgi Affari, Florence, Italy, 1999; Contemp Art By African American Artists, Art Mus Princeton, NJ, 2000; Freestyle, Studio Mus in Harlem, NY, 2001, Black Belt, 2003; Ghetto Fabulous, Watts Tower Art Ctr, LA, 2002; Mixed Feelings, USC Fisher Gallery, LA, 2002; ARCO, Madrid, Spain, 2003; California Biennial, Orange County Mus Art, Newport Beach, 2004; inSite: Art Practices in the Public Domain, San Diego and Tijuana, 2005; Cut, Susanne Vielmetter LA Projects, 2005; Whitney Biennial: Day for Night, Whitney Mus Am Art, New York, 2006; USA Today, Royal Acad Arts, London, 2006; Art on Paper, 2006, Weatherspoon Art Mus, Univ NC, Greensboro, 2006-07; Brave New Worlds, Walker Art Ctr, Minneapolis, 2007; Eden's Edge, Hammer Mus, UCLA, 2007; Life on Mars, Carnegie Int, Carnegie Mus Art, Pittsburgh, 2008. *Awards:* Nancy Graves Found Grant, 2002; Joan Mitchell Found Grant, 2002; Louis Comfort Tiffany Found Grant, 2003; Bucksbaum Award, 2006; USA Fellowship, US Artists, 2007; MacArthur Fel Grant, 2009. *Media:* All Media. *Mailing Add:* c/o Sikkema Jenkins & Co 530 W 22nd St New York NY 10011

BRADLEY, BETSY
MUSEUM DIRECTOR
Study: Millsaps Col, BA; Vanderbilt Univ, MA in Eng. *Pos:* Deputy dir, and community arts dir, Miss Arts Commission, exec dir, 1995-2001, Miss Mus Art, Jackson, 2001-; bd mem, Nat Assembly of State Arts Agencies; panelist, Nat Endowment for Arts; adv panel mem, Miss Sch Arts. *Awards:* Named one of Top 50 Bus Women, Miss Business J. *Mailing Add:* Mississippi Museum of Art 380 South Lamar Street Jackson MS 39201

BRADLEY, JOE
PAINTER
b Old Orchard Beach, Maine, 1975. *Study:* RI Sch Design, BFA (Painting), 1999. *Exhib:* Solo exhibs include Allston Skirt Gallery, Boston, 2002, Contemp, New York, 2003, PS1 Contemp Art, Long Island City, NY, 2006, CANADA, New York, 2006, Dicksmith, London, 2007, Peres Projects, Berlin, LA, 2007, Greener Pastures Contemp Art, Toronto, 2007; group exhibs include Here Comes Rhodey, Allston Skirt Gallery, Boston, 2000, Gone Fishing, 2003; Friends & Family, Lombard-Freid Fine Arts, New York, 2002; What's Growing In Your Garden, ATM Gallery, New York, 2003, Joy to the Max, 2003, Goose Steppin;, 2005; No Platform, Just a Trampoline, Marcus Ritter Gallery, New York, 2003; Under the Sun, Greener Pastures Gallery, Toronto, 2004; New York's Finest, CANADA, New York, 2005; Under Pressure, Art Concept, Paris, 2006; Mangoes, Peres Projects, LA, 2006; Silicone Valley, PS1 Contemp Art, Long Island City, NY, 2007; Beneath the Underdog, Gagosian Gallery, New York, 2007; Whitney Biennial, Whitney Mus Am Art, New York, 2008

BRADLEY, SLATER
PHOTOGRAPHER
b San Francisco, Ca, 1975. *Study:* UCLA, BA, 1998. *Work:* Annandale-on-Hudson, NY, Ctr Curatorial Studies Mus, Bard Col, NY, 2003, Armory Photog Show, 2002, Here are the Young Men, Team Gallery, 2002, Universitatsstadt Kaiserslautern, Ger, 2002, Art + Pub, Geneva Switzerland, 2002, Arndt & Partner, Berlin, Ger, 2002, Video Cube, FIAS, Paris, 2001, Trompe Le Monde, Galerie Yvon Lambert, 2001, Home Town Hero, Refusalon, San Francisco, 2001, Spec Projects Series, PS1, NY, 2000, Charlatan, Team Gallery, New York City, 2000, Fried Liver Attack, 1999. *Exhib:* Solo exhibs incl, Taka Ishii Gallery, Tokyo, 2005, Matrix 216: Year of the Doppelganger, Univ Calif Berkeley Art Mus & Pacific Film Archive, 2005, Blum & Poe, Los Angeles, 2004, Stoned & Dethroned, Team Gallery, New York City, 2004, Annandale-on-Hudson, NY, Ctr Curatorial Studies Mus, Bard Col, NY, 2003, Armory Photog Show, 2002, Here are the Young Men, Team Gallery, 2002, Universitatsstadt Kaiserslautern, Ger, 2002, Art + Pub, Geneva Switz, 2002, Arndt & Partner, Berlin, Ger, 2002, Video Cube, FIAS, Paris, 2001, Trompe Le Monde, Galerie Yvon Lambert, 2001, Home Town Hero, Refusalon, San Francisco, 2001, Special Projects Series, PS1, NY, 2000, Charlatan, Team Gallery, New York City, 2000, Fried Liver Attack, 1999. *Dealer:* Galeria Helga de Alvear Doctor Fourquet 12 28012 Madrid Spain; Max Wigram Gallery 99 New Bond St London W1S 1SW United Kingdom; Meridian Gallery/Rita Krauss Fine Art 41 East 57th St 8th Fl NY City NY 10022; Rago Arts and Auction Ctr 333 North Main St Lambertville NJ 08530; Taka Ishii Gallery 1-3-2 5F Kiyosumi Koto-ku Tokyo #135-0024 Japan; Serge Ziegler Galerie PO Box 27 CH-8024 Zurich Switzerland

BRADLEY, WILLIAM STEVEN
MUSEUM DIRECTOR, EDUCATOR
b Salina, Kans, Aug 20, 1949. *Study:* Univ Colo, BA, 71; Friedrich-Alexander Univ, 72; Northwestern Univ, MA, 74, PhD, 81. *Collection Arranged:* Gene Kloss: Six Decades of Printmaking, 84; Frank Reaugh: Scenes from the Texas Range, 84; Honky Tonk Visions, 86; Nine Texas Printmakers, 86; The Blue Star Exhibition: Contemporary Art in San Antonio, 86; Lin Emery/Emery Clark, 89; Kazuo Kadonaga, 90; Richard Johnson/John Scott, 91; Contemporary Art from the K & B Corp Collection, 91; Elemore Morgan Photographs, 92; Edouard Duval Carrie: Migration of the Spirit, 2002. *Pos:* Cur art, Tex Tech Univ Mus, 83-85; chief cur, San Antonio Mus Art, 85-86; dir, Alexandria Mus Art, 87-92 & Davenport Mus Art, 92-2001; Resident fel, Cody Inst Western Am Studies, 2009; Fulbright-Leipzig Chair for Am Studies, Univ Leipzig, Germany, 2010. *Teaching:* Instr mod art, Wells Coll, 79-81; lectr mod art, Cornell Univ, 80-81, Univ Tex, 86-87; instr, Northwestern State Univ, La, 88-92; prof, Colorado Mesa Univ, Colo, 2003-. *Mem:* Coll Art Asn; Am Asn Mus; Tex Art 150 (secy, 84-87); La Asn Mus (vpres, 88-89); Asn Art Mus Dirs; Am Studies Assn; Am Assn Univ Professors. *Res:* Modern European art; contemporary American art. *Publ:* Auth, Gene Kloss: Six Decades of Prints, Tex Tech Univ, 84; Emil Nolde and German Expressionism, UMI Res Press, 86; Contemp Art in San Antonio, CASA, 86; contribr, Lynda Benglis/Keith Sonnier: A Decade of Sculpture, Alex Mus Art, 87; Elemore Morgan, Jr, Where Land Meets Sky, U Southwest La, 99; Roger McCoy: Encounters, 2006; contbr, A Seamless Web: Emro-American Art in the 19th Century, Cambridge Scholars, 2013

BRADSHAW, DOVE
PAINTER, SCULPTOR
b New York, NY, Sept 24, 1949. *Study:* Boston Mus Sch Fine Arts, BFA, 74. *Work:* Metrop Mus Art, Mus Mod Art & Whitney Mus Am Art, NY; Brooklyn Mus, NY; Philadelphia Mus Art; Ark Art Mus, Little Rock; Art Inst Chicago; Nat Gallery, Washington, DC; Mattress Factory Mus, 98; Mus Contemp Art, Los Angeles, Calif; Carnegie Mus Art, Pittsburgh, PA; Mattress Factory Mus, Pittsburgh, PA; Le Pompidou Ctr, Paris; The Getty Ctr, Los Angeles; Fogg Art Mus, Cambridge; Rubin Mus Art, NY; Kunst Mus, Dusseldorf; Ingreja do Convento de Santo Antonio, Trancoso, Portugal; Mus Contemp Art, Roskilde, Denmark; Pier Ctr, Orkney, Scotland; Sirius Art Ctr, Cobh, Ireland; The Marble Palace, State Russian Mus, St Petersburg; Centre Pompidou, Paris; Mus Mod Art, New York; The British Mus, London; Esbjerg Mus Mod Art, Esbjerg, Denmark; San Franisco Mus Art; Walker Arts Ctr, Minneapolis; NY Pub Lib Performing Arts; Honolulu Mus Contemp Art; Birmingham Mus; Bowdoin Coll Mus Art, Brunswick, Me; Antonio Dale Nogare Collection, Blazano, Italy. *Comn:* Radio Rocks, comn by Baronessa Lucrezia Durini, Bolognano, Italy. *Exhib:* Break to Activate (wall piece), PS1, Inst Art & Urban Resources, NY, 77.; Merce Cunningham Dance Co: Phrases & video: Deli Commedia, Costumes, 84, Native Green, Arcade, 85, Points in Space, costumes & lighting, 86, Brit Broadcasting Co, 86, Carousel, costumes & Lighting, 87, Fabrications, decor & lighting, 87, Cargo X, decor & lighting, 89, The Paris Opera Ballet, 90, Trackers, 91, Philadelphia Ballet, Arcade.; Dazzle Camouflage Set Design, Time and Space Theatre, NY, 83.; Plain Air: Sandra Gering Gallery, 89, The Mattress Factory, Pittsburgh, Pa, 90 & P S 1 Mus, Long Island Ctr, NY, 91.; Indeterminacy, 16 mm film,; Drawings of the 80's (from the permanent collection), Mus Mod Art, 90; The Drawing Ctr, NY; Carnegie Int, Pittsburgh, Pa; Drawings of the '90's, Katonah Mus, NY; Rolywholover a Circus, Mus Contemp Art, Los Angeles, 93 & 98; Work from the Permanent Collection, Art Inst Chicago, 94; Guggenheim Mus, NY, 94; Menil Collection, Houston, Tex, 94; Mito Tower, Japan, 94; Philadelphia Mus, Pa, 95, 96, 99, 2000; Del Mus of Contemp Art, 2000; Rooseum Mus, Malmö, Sweden, 2000; Anastasi Bradshaw Cage, Mus Contemp Art, Roskelde, Denmark, 2001, Univ Va Art Mus & Univ Art Gallery, UCSD, San Diego, 2005; Form Formlessness: Dove Bradshaw, 1969-2003, Mishkin Gallery, NY, 2003; The Invisible Thread: Buddhist Spirit in Am Art, Sag Harbor, NY, 2003; Diferenca Gallery, Lisbon, 2003; Volume Gallery, NY, 2004; Edge Level Ground, Shering Gallery, Berlin, 2005; Reality, Stalke Gallery, Copenhagen; The Missing Peace, Artists and the Dalai Lama, traveled to US, Eur, Asia, 2006; Spirit of Discovery I & II, Trancoso, Portugal, 2006-2007; 360 Tokyo, 2006; Dedicated to Sol Lewitt, Bjorn Ressel Gallery, NY, 2007; Senza Titolo, Rome, 2007; One More, Esbjerg Mus Mod Art, Denmark, 2008. *Pos:* Artistic adv, Merce Cunningham Dance Co, 84-; Sandra Gering Gallery, NY, 89, 90, 93, 95 & 98; Barbara Krakow Gallery, Boston, 97; Linda Kirkland Gallery, NY, 98; Stalke Gallerie, Copenhagen, 96, 98, 2001, 2004; Lary Becker Contemp Art, 2000, 2005, 2008, & 2012; Stark Gallery, NY, 2001; Volume Gallery, NY, 2004; Solway Jones Gallery, Los Angeles, 2005; Time & Material, Trancoso, Portugal, 2006-2007; 6th Biennial, Gwangju, S Korea; Gallery 360 Degrees, Tokyo, 2006; Senzatitolo, Rome, 2007; Pierre Menard Gallery, Cambridge, Mass, 2008. *Teaching:* Sculpture, Sch Visual Arts, NY, 75-81; Sch Contemp Art, Pont-Aven, Brittany, France, 2007; lectr, Univ Pa Art Dept, Philadelphia & Sothebys, 2008, Mus Mod Art, New York, 2009; Sorbonne, 2012. *Awards:* Sculpture, Nat Endowment Arts, 75; Pollock-Krasner Painting Award, 85; NY State Coun Arts, Design & Lighting Merce Cunningham Dance co, 87; Furthermore Grant for Monogr, 2003; Nat Sci Found, 2006. *Bibliog:* Gene Moore (auth), Windows at Tiffany's: The Art of Gene Moore, Harry N Abrams, 80; Judith

Collishan Van Wagner (auth), Lines of Vision, Hudson Hills Press, New York, 89; Thomas McEvilley (auth), New York reviews, Art Forum, 1/90; The Odyssey of a Collector, Carnegie Mus Art, 96; New Art on Paper, Phila Mus Art, Hunt Mfg Coll, 96; Thomas McEvilley (auth), Sculpture in the Age of Doubt, Allworth Press, New York, 2000; Dede Young (auth), Ethereal and Material (intro by Douglas Maxwell), Del Ctr Contemp Arts, 2000; Anastasi Bradshaw Cage, Mus Contemp Art, Roskilde, Denmark, 2001; Thomas McEvilley (auth), Dove Bradshaw, Nature Change and Indeterminacy, Batty Publ, West NY, NJ, 2003; Charles Stuckey (auth), Time & Material, Senzatitolo, Rome, 2007; Charles Stuckey (auth), Time Matters, Pierre Menard Gallery, 2008; The Third Mind, Am Artists Contemplate Asia, 1860-1989, Guggenheim Mus, New York, 2009; 560 Broadway, A New York Drawing Collection at Work 1991-2006, Yale Univ Press, Conn, 2008; Richard Koslelanitz (auth), Conversing with Cage 2nd ed, Routledge, New York & London, 2004; The Invisible Thread: Buddhist Spirit in Contemporary Art, Snug Harbor Cultural Ctr, New York, 2004; James Putnam (auth), Art and Artifact: The Mus as Medium, Thames and Hudson, London, 2003; Richard Kostelanitz (auth), Conversing with Cage, 2nd ed, Routledge, NY & London, 2001. *Mem:* Pataphysical Soc, Laval, France. *Media:* All. *Specialty:* Fine Art. *Interests:* Reading philosophy & lit, running, yoga, meditation, landscape, gardening. *Publ:* Fire Hose Postcard 1976-1992, Metrop Mus Art, NY; Indeterminacy Contingency, Removal, Riverstone, Equivalents, Full, self produced, NY, 90-94; Plain Air, silver prints in portfolio, ed of 5, Art Inst Chicago, 91; Indeterminacy (film), 95 & Indeterminacy Stones (film), 95-98; Negative Ions I & II, Watersones, 96; Spent Bullets photogravure, Nils Borch Jensen, Copenhagen, 99; Notations (outdoor sculpture), 99-; Radio Rocks, 98-2008; Self Interest, 99-2003; Angles 12 Rotations, 2000-2005; Material/Immaterial Stones, 2000-2005; One of the boys, And so & All, Daguerreotype, 2003; Six Continents, 2003-; Herself in her element, They were & went, 2004; Body Music, 2006; Quick Constructions, 2006-2010; Partial Portrait, 2010; Artists Books, 2008-2011; Libido (copperwork), 2011; Spacetime (film), 2011; Performance (film), 2012. *Dealer:* Danese Gallery NY; Stalke Gallery Kirke-Sonnerup Denmark; Larry Becker Contemporary Art Philadelphia PA; Gallery 360, Tokyo; Thomas Rebbein Galerie Cologne 360

BRADSHAW, ELLEN
PAINTER
b Rochester, NY, 1961. *Study:* Pratt Inst, Brooklyn, NY, BFA, 84. *Exhib:* Solo Exhibs: Bridge Cafe, NY, 95, Pace Univ, Schimmel Ctr for Arts, NY, 99, Pleiades Gallery, NY, 2000, 04, 06-08, Citibank Financial Ctr, NY, 2002, A Taste of Art, NY, 2003; Group Exhibs: Lever House, NY, 98, Pleiades Gallery, NY, 99, Tribeca Fine Arts, NY, 2000, Butler Inst of Am Art, Youngstown, Ohio, 2001, Nat Arts Club, NY, 2002, Caesarea Gallery, Boca Raton, Fla, 2003, Pen & Brush, NY, 2003. *Pos:* Pres, Pleiades Gallery 2000-. *Awards:* William & Theresa Meyerowitz Mem Award, Audubon Artists Am 86th Annual, 2000; Sophia & Emmanuel Zimmer Award, Pen & Brush Reg non-mem Juried Show, 2001; Jane Peterson Mem Award, Salmagundi Club, Annual Combined Exhib, 2003; Arthur T Hill Memorial Award, Salmagundi Club, 2004 & 2005. *Bibliog:* Bonnie Barney (auth), Perspectives, Yates Co Arts Coun, Vol 28, no 1, 2002; Thomas Lawrence (auth), Manhattan Arts International, 3-4/2000; Peggy Platonos (auth), Waterside Weekly, 8/98; Kathleen Willcox (auth), The New York Sun, Vol 121, no 242, 4/4/2006; Chad Smith (auth), Downtown Express, Vol 18, no 48, 4/14-20/2006; The Tribeca Trib, Vol X, no 5, 1/2004; The Villager, Vol 74, no 24, 10/13-19/2004; Kathleen Willcox (auth), The New York Sun, Vol 121, No 242, 4/4/2006 ; Amanda Folts (auth), Finger Lake Times, 10/26/2008; Anya Harris (auth), Life in the Finger Lakes Mag, Vol 8, No 4, winter 2008. *Mem:* Allied Artists Am Inc; Am Artists Prof League; Pleiades Gallery Contemp Art, NY (pres, 2000-); Pen and Brush Inc; Audubon Artists Inc; Salmagundi Club. *Media:* Miscellaneous Media, Oil. *Mailing Add:* 100 Beekman St Apt 25N New York NY 10038

BRADSHAW, LAURENCE JAMES JOSEPH
EDUCATOR, PAINTER
b St Paul, Kans, Sept 21, 1945. *Study:* Pittsburg State Univ, Kans, BFA, with Reed Schmickle, Bert Keeney, Alex Barde, Robert Blunk, Robert Russell, MA; Ohio Univ, MFA, with William Kortlander, Dana Loomis, Gary Pettigrew. *Hon Degrees:* Academia Italia. *Work:* Mercantile Libr, NY; Sioux City Art Ctr, Iowa; Joslyn Art Mus, Omaha; Sheldon Art Mus, Univ Nebr, Lincoln; Harmony House, Omaha; Alumni Center Univ Nebr, Omaha; Pittsburg State Univ, Omaha; plus many others. *Comn:* Metrop Arts Coun, Omaha, 76; Omaha Symphony Assoc, 86; Reviewer of Manuscript, Collegiate Press Publ, Alta Loma, Ca, 96; Map Drawing, Univ Nebr Alumni Asn, Omaha, 97; Medal Design, Univ Nebr, Omaha, 98. *Exhib:* 38th Mother Load Nat, El Dorado Hills, Calif; 7th Celebration of the Arts, Montpelier Cult Ctr, Laurel, Baltimore MD, 2004; 22nd Ann Nat, Alvin Community Coll, Houston, Tex; Looking for Am, Nat Washington Gallery of Photog, Bethesda, MD, 2004; Int Invitational, United Arab Emirates, 2005; Acad Invitational Mus Neb Art, Kearney, Neb, 2009-2010. *Collection Arranged:* 16th Ann All Media Int, 2014; 16th Ann Faces Int, 2014; 16th Ann Contemp Art Int, 2014; 14th Ann Collage & Mixed Media Int, 2012; and over 150 others. *Pos:* Dir, Univ Art Gallery, 74-76; Dir, Upstream People Gallery, Selected Works Gallery, Omaha, Nebr, 98-2014. *Teaching:* Instr life-drawing, painting & silkscreen, Akron Art Inst, Ohio, summer 73; prof drawing, design & painting, color & visual literature, Univ Nebr, Omaha, 73-2011. *Awards:* Abby Award, Nebr Asn Advertisers, 2001; Hon Mention, 2nd National Exhib, Georgetown, Tex, 2004; 100 Top Educators, Eng, 2005; plus over 60 nat & int art & teaching awards. *Mem:* Visual Artists & Galleries NYC; Joslyn Art Mus. *Media:* Mixed. *Res:* The consequences of combining the right then left brain hemispheres in drawing. *Specialty:* Hosting Int Juried Exhib in all Media. *Interests:* Gardening, reading & travel. *Collection:* Prints & paintings by Thomas Majeski, Gary Day, Bart Vargas & others. *Publ:* Illusr, Painting with Acrylics, Van Nostrand-Reinhold, 74; August Fires, Glover Davies, Abattoir Press, 78; Folk & Progressive Art, Ancient & New Values in Contemp Art, Acad Italia, 84; New York Art Rev Am References Publ, Chicago, 88. *Dealer:* Upstream People Gallery; Anderson O'Brien Fine Art Gallery. *Mailing Add:* Univ Nebr at Omaha Dept Art Omaha NE 68182-0011

BRADY, CHARLES
PAINTER, SCULPTOR
b New York, NY, July 27, 1926. *Study:* Art Student League, 48-51, with John Groth & Morris Kantor; with Marjorie Fitzgibbon, Ireland. *Work:* Seven works in Irish Arts Coun Collection, Dublin; Northern Ireland Arts Coun; NW Trust; Northern Bank Finance Corp; Bank of Ireland Collection; Art Students League. *Exhib:* Pa Acad Fine Arts, Philadelphia, 67; Solo exhib, Keys Gallery, Derry, Northern Ireland, 77; John Taylor Gallery, Dublin, 79, 81, 86, 88, 89 & 90; Delighted Eye, London, 80; Keys Gallery, Derry, Northern Ireland, 80; and others. *Teaching:* Artist-instr graphics, dept archit, Col Technol, Dublin, 70-71; lectr, Nat Col Art, Dublin, 75-83. *Awards:* P J Carroll Award, Living Art Exhib, Trinity Col, Dublin, 78; Appointment to the Institution of Honor for Creative Artists, Irish Arts Coun, Aosdána, 81; Landscape Prize, Oireachtas Exhib, 9/89. *Mem:* Life mem Art Student League; United Arts Club (hon chmn artist group, 71), Dublin; Figurative Image Group, Dublin (chmn, 85); L&P Financial Trustees of Ireland Ltd. *Media:* Oil; Lost-Wax into Bronze. *Dealer:* John Taylor 34 Kildare St Dublin 2 Ireland; Charles Cambell Gallery 647 Chestnut St San Francisco CA 94133

BRADY, LUTHER W
COLLECTOR, EDUCATOR, PATRON
b Rocky Mount, NC, 1925. *Study:* George Wash Univ, Wash, AA, 44, AB, 1946, MD, 1948. *Hon Degrees:* DFA, Colgate Univ, 1988; DSc, Lehigh Univ, 1990; MD, Toyama Univ, 1996; Dr Honoris Causa, Heidelberg Univ, 1997; DFA, George Wash Univ, 2004; DFA, PA Acad Fine Arts, 2006. *Work:* Picker Gallery, Colgate Univ; Villanova Univ Gallery; Pa Acad Fine Arts; George Wash Univ; Philadelphia Mus Art; Ackland Mus. *Comn:* Joyce, comn by Sam Martin for George Wash Univ; Untitled, comn by Joe Mooney for George Wash Univ. *Pos:* Chmn, Friends Philadelphia Mus Art, 67-70; bd dir, Settlement Music Sch, Philadelphia, 75-; bd trustees, Philadelphia Mus Art, 75-; bd dir, Art Alliance Philadelphia, 78-80; bd dir, Santa Fe Opera, 79-; trustee, Curtis Inst Music, 90-; bd, Fleisher Art Mem, 1998-. *Teaching:* Prof & chmn, Hahnemann Univ, 59-; prof, Distinguished Univ, Sch Med Drexel Univ, 1998-. *Awards:* Distinguished Hon Medal, Curtis Inst Music, 93; George Wash Univ Soc Medal, 95; James B Colgate Soc Medal, 95; Luther W Brady Curatorship of Japanese Art, Philadelphia Mus Art, 96. *Mem:* Int Arts-Med Asn; Asn of Artists Equity of Philadelphia; PAA (bd dir, 77-79); Found for Archit (bd dir, 82-87). *Media:* Collector paintings, sculptures. *Interests:* Abstract expressionists. *Collection:* American contemp art; Asian and Far Eastern porcelains and stone carvings; English sculpture; Works by John Walker, Jules Olitski, Sam Gillian, Oscar Bluemner, Fritz Scholder and others. *Publ:* Coauth, Principles and Practice of Radiation Oncology, Lippincott. *Mailing Add:* 230 N Broad St Philadelphia PA 19102-1121

BRADY, ROBERT D
SCULPTOR
b Reno, Nev, 1946. *Study:* Calif Coll Arts & Crafts, BFA, 1969; Univ Calif, Davis, MFA, 1975. *Work:* San Francisco Mus Mod Art; Oakland Mus; Crocker Mus, Sacramento, Calif; Stedelijik Mus, Amsterdam, Holland; Am Telegraph & Telephone, NY. *Exhib:* Solo shows include Braunstein/Quay Gallery, San Francisco, 1991, 1993, 1995, 1996, 1998, 1999, 2001-03, NDak Mus Art, Grand Forks, 1993, Horwitch, Lew Allen Gallery, Santa Fe, NMex, 1994, 1996, 1998 & 2000, Calif State Univ, Sacramento, 1994, Craft & Folk Art Mus, San Francisco, 1995, Natalie & James Thompson Gallery, San Jose State Univ, Calif, 1996 & John Elder Gallery, NY, 1998 & 1999, Lew Allen Contemp, 2006; group shows include Calif Ceramics & Glass, Oakland Mus, 1974; Modern Masks, Whitney Mus Am Art, 1984; Best Picks, Oakland Mus, 1986; Ten Yr Retrospective Traveling Exhib, Crocker Mus Art, Sacramento, 1989; de-Persona, Oakland Mus, 1991; In Reverence of Wood, Univ Art Gallery, Calif State Univ, Haywood, 1993; Human Nature/Human Form, Laguna Gloria Art Mus, Austin, Tex, 1993; Made of Wood Traveling Show, Hewlett Packard, Palo Alto, Calif, 1993-94; A Labor of Love, New Mus, NY, 1996; Ceramic Sculpture from the East Bay, Calif State Univ, Hayward, 1996; Prints from Wash Square Editions, San Jose State Univ Art Galleries, Calif, 1997; Soc Arts Crafts, Boston, 1997; Earth and Air, San Francisco Craft & Folk Art Mus, Calif, 1997; The Mus of Arts and Sciences, Macon, GA, 1999; Made in Calif: Art, Image and Identity, 1900-2000, Los Angeles Co Mus of Art, 2000; Lew Allen Contemp, NMex, 2003, 2006. *Pos:* Prof art, Sacramento State Univ. *Bibliog:* Mary Webster (auth), The initiation, Artweek, 4/8/1993; Lis Bensley (auth), City Focus, Santa Fe Hip and Hopping, Art News, 6/1996; Michael Rush (auth), Robert Brady and Steven Whittlesey, Am Craft, 6-7/1998. *Mem:* ENSECA. *Media:* Ceramic, Wood. *Publ:* Auth, Ceramic Sculpture (catalog). *Dealer:* Braunstein-Quay Gallery 430 Clementia San Francisco CA 94103. *Mailing Add:* c/o Lew Allen Contemp 129 W Palace Ave Santa Fe NM 87501

BRAFF, PHYLLIS
CRITIC, CURATOR
b Boston, Mass. *Study:* Simmons Col, BS, BA; Columbia Univ, MA (art hist), MPhil, PhM; Harvard Univ exten program. *Collection Arranged:* Images of George Washington, 76; Artists & East Hampton: A 100 Year Perspective (auth, catalog), Guild Hall Mus, 76; Falaise - historical collection house, 81; Thomas Moran: A Search for the Scenic(auth catalog), Guild Hall Mus, 80-81; The Surrealists & their Friends on Eastern LI at Mid Century (auth catalog), Guild Hall Mus, 96-97; Women Artists on Eastern LI, 98. *Pos:* Mus admin/dir, chief art cur & dir of mus collection, NY State (Nassau Co) Mus Services, 68-91; art critic, East Hampton Star, 69-85; art critic, New York Times (Long Island Section), 81-; coed, Thomas Moran Catalogue Raisonne proj, 81-. *Teaching:* Queens Coll, Sch Visual Arts, LI Univ (CW Post grad div). *Awards:* NYSCA Grant, Artists and East Hampton: A Hundred Year Perspective, 76; NY Coun for the Humanities, The Castle Theme in Am Archit, 84; NEA Grant, The Surrealists and their Friends on Eastern LI at Mid Century, 96; Distinguished Criticism Award, LI Press Asn. *Mem:* Am Soc for Hispanic Art Hist Studies (pres,

86-88); Int Asn Art Critics (pres, USA section, 92-94, 2007-2010, vpres, Int, 95-98). *Res:* Thomas Moran Catalogue Raisonne. *Publ:* auth, Bibliography of 20th Century Art & Architecture, Worldwide Art Books, 68; auth, Bibliography of American Art & Architecture, Worldwide Art Books, 68. *Mailing Add:* 333 E 55th St New York NY 10022

BRAGAR, PHILIP FRANK
PAINTER, SCULPTOR
b New York, NY, May 10, 1925. *Study:* Esmeralda Sch Painting & Sculpture, Mex City, with Raul Anguiano, Carlos Orozco Romero, Alfonso Ayala & Ignacio Aguirre, 54-59. *Work:* NY Pub Libr; Pasadena Art Mus, Calif; NJ State Mus, Trenton; Los Angeles Co Mus Art; Libr Cong, Wash, DC; Mus Mod Art, Mexico City; Jose Luis Cuevas Mus, Univ Mus Contemp Art, Mexico City; National Print Mus, Mexico City. *Exhib:* Solo Exhibs, Galeria Antonio Souza, Mexico City, 68; Galeria Pecanins, 69 & 73; Lynn Kottler Gallery, NY, 81; Palace Fine Arts, Mexico City, 92; Mus Jose Luis Cuevas, Mexico City, 95; Mus Univ Contemp Arte, Univ Nacional Autónoma de México, 97; Chopo Univ Mus, 2005; Galeria Pecanins, Mexico, DF, 2006; Nineteen Yrs of Woodcut Prints, 78, & Kafka by Bragar, 85, Galeria Pecanins, Mexico City; Biennial of Graphics, Mus Fine Arts, Mexico City, 79; Mus Mod Art, Mexico City, 87; Nat Print Mus, Mexico City, 90; Pre-hispanic Man/Contemp Man, Deleg Venustiano Carranza, Mexico City, 94; Paintings and Sculptures, Galeria Pecanins, Mexico City, 98; Metropolitan Univ, Mexico City, 2000. *Teaching:* Instr drawing, painting, design & printmaking & dir art dept, US Int Univ, Mexico City, 70-75. *Awards:* 1 yr grant paintings, Pre-hispanic Man/Contemp Man, Nat Fund for Cult & Art, 90; Grant, Nat System Creators Art, Mexico City, 93-96, 97-2000; Nat Fund Cult Art Us, The Human Beings, 2000-2001. *Bibliog:* Antonio Espinoza (auth), The Savage Expressionism of Philip F Bragar, El Nacional-Mexico City, 4/92; Lorna Scott Fox (reporter), Inseparable Man-Philip F Bragar, Polyester and Cotton-Mexico City, no 2, summer 92; Alfredo Rodriguez Ramirez (auth), Philip F Bragar, the alien, Novedades, Imágenes, Mexico City, 10/14/94, The City of Mexico Reflected in the painting of Philip F. Bragar (auth), Eduardo Alexandro Hernandez, Uel Universal, 01/14/2000. *Media:* Oil, Wood. *Publ:* Illusr poem, In: Armando Zarate's El Corazon Cae Fuera del Camino, 63; illusr, Dr Oswaldo Schon's Americans Under Mexican Law, 71. *Mailing Add:* Iztaccihuatl No 21 Col Hippodrome Condesa Mexico DF 06100 Mexico

BRAGG, E ANN
PAINTER
b Liberty, NY, Mar 8, 1935. *Study:* State Univ Col, Buffalo, NY, BS, 58; study with Edgar A Whitney, 75-80 & Paul Wood, 80-85. *Work:* American Bond Inc. *Exhib:* Am Standard Gallery, NY, 85; Firehouse Gallery, Nassau Community Col, 86; Women's Art Show, Purdue Univ, Ind, 86; Autotech Show, Long Island Coliseum, Nassau Co, 86; Nat Asn Women Artists, Tweed Mus Art, Univ Minn, 87; Nassau Mus Fine Arts, Roslyn, NY, 89; and others. *Pos:* Guest inst, Valley Stream High Sch & Celebration of Drawing, Workshop, Nassau Community Col; Judge & Demonstrator for Art Leagues, New York & Long Island. *Teaching:* Pvt lessons for problem children in elementary sch, 76-81; instr, abstract experiment watercolor, 5 Towns Mus & Art Found, 81-92; guest instr, drawing, Nassau Community Col, 86. *Awards:* Mario Cooper Award, Am Watercolor Soc, 81; Elizabeth Morse Genius Found Award, Nat Asn Women Artists, 88; Heckshire Mus Award, 90. *Bibliog:* Malcolm Preston (auth), Showing a bit of abstraction, News Day, 4/20/85; Helen A Harrison (auth), Heart of the matter figures as motif, 1/22/89 & From exuberant abstraction to detailed realism, 6/10/90, NY Times. *Mem:* Nat Asn Women Artists; Nat Art League. *Media:* All. *Mailing Add:* 2921 Cleveland Ave Oceanside NY 11572-1114

BRAIG, BETTY LOU
PAINTER, EDUCATOR
b Naylor, Mo, Apr 21, 1931. *Study:* Phoenix Col, AA, 64; Ariz State Univ, BA, 70, MA, 73; int, nat & state seminars. *Work:* Tretyakov Gallery Art Sch, Moscow; Prague Acad Fine Art, Prague; Dean of Charles Univ, Prague; Frostburg State Univ, Frostburg, MA; Glendale Community Col, Ariz; Gold Canyon Golf Resort, Gold Canyon, Ariz; Maryvale High Sch, Phoenix, Ariz; Glendale Community Coll, Glendale, Ariz. *Comn:* Free Hanging Cross, Am Evangelical Lutheran Church, Phoenix, 72; Keith Herring, Mural, City of Phoenix, 83; Heavenly Valley Resort, Lake Tahoe, Calif, 83; Gold Canyon Golf Resort, Ariz; 20 ft high cross, Mountain View Lutheran Church, 2003; 18' x 10' mural, North Valley Medical Plaza, Paradise Valley, Ariz, 2002. *Exhib:* Solo Exhib, City of Chandler Ctr for Arts, Ariz, Visual Conversations, Chandler Ctr Arts, 2001; Nat Soc Painters Casein & Acrylic, NY, 80; San Diego Int Watercolor Exhib, San Diego Art Mus, 82; Nat Energy Art Exhib, Denver, 82; Ariz Biennial, Tucson Mus Art, 82; Western Fedn Watercolor, Rocky Mountain Nat; Atrium Gallery, Ft Worth Mus Sci & Hist, Tex; Am Watercolor Soc Traveling Exhib, 80, 82, 83, & 2008; Glendale Community Coll, 2013. *Pos:* Phoenix Col, Ariz, Corrizo Sch Art, Ruiodoso, NMex; gallery dir, Phoenix Union High Sch Dist; Ambassador to Eastern Europe for Humanities (Delegation), 92; Int Fine Art examiner, Int Baccalaureate, UK, IBA. *Teaching:* Instr art, Phoenix Union High Sch Dist, 70-92, Ariz Artists Sch Art Teacher, Int Baccalaureate Examine, UK, elected art seminars, 98-; instr fine art, experimental painting & misc medias; art coordr, Superstition Mountain Mus, Ariz. *Awards:* Grumbacher Art Award, Ariz Watercolor Asn, 81; David Gayle Found Award, Western Fedn Watercolor, 82; Best of Show, Int Soc Experimental Artists, 94 & 2007; Cutting Edge Award, 2006; Award of Excellence, Ariz Watercolor Asn; Nautilus Award, I SEA, 2007; Third Place Award, Ga Nat Watercolor, 2009. *Bibliog:* Sue St John (auth), A Walk Through Abstraction, 2010. *Mem:* Assoc mem Am Watercolor Soc; Ariz Watercolor Asn; Ariz Artist Guild; 22-30 Watercolorist Ariz; Int Soc Experimental Artists (signature); Western Fedn Watercolor Soc (signature); Mo Watercolor Asn; Ga Watercolor Asn. *Media:* Watercolor, Acrylic; Mixed. *Res:* Southwest wild flowers with medicinal properties. *Specialty:* Experimental water medias, mix of art disciplines; Res & Create mural for mountain view Luthern Church, Narthex, Ariz, Abstract Spiritual Art. *Interests:* Global trends in art; visual lang. *Publ:* Ariz Arts & Travel, Scottsdale Mag, 85; Southwest Art, Southwest Profile, 85; Creative Watercolor, 95, Best of Watercolor II, 97 & Best of Composition, Rockport Publ, 98; Watercolor Expressions, 2000; Watercolor Magic Mag, 2001-03; A Walk Through Abstraction, North Light Pub, 2008. *Dealer:* Braig Studio 5271 S Desert Willow Gold Canyon AZ 85219. *Mailing Add:* 5271 S Desert Willow Dr Gold Canyon AZ 85218

BRAINARD, BARBARA
PRINTMAKER, PAINTER
b Mar 21, 1952. *Study:* Tulane Univ, BFA (printmaking/painting; magna cum laude, 85, Tulane Grad Fel), 1988. *Work:* New Orleans Mus Art; Rutgers Univ; Bloomsberg Univ; Springfield Mus. *Exhib:* Solo exhibs include Still-Zinsel Gallery, New Orleans, 1994, 1996, 1998, 2000, Cole Pratt Gallery, New Orleans, 2002, 2003, 2005, 2009, 2011, Spring Hill Coll, Mobile, Ala, 2008, Valencia Coll, Orlando, Fla, 2012; Group exhibs, Prospect I, New Orleans, 2008-2009; Vestiges/Trinitas, Coastal Carolina Univ, NC; ArtNow, Contemporary Arts Ctr, New Orleans, 2012. *Collection Arranged:* Arts in Educ, New Orleans Mus Art, 2010; Cold Drink, DuMois Gallery, 2010. *Teaching:* Loyola Univ, New Orleans, 1989-. *Awards:* Pollock/Krasner Found Grant, 2005, 2007. *Media:* Monotype, Mixed Media. *Specialty:* Contemporary Southern Art. *Publ:* New Orleans Review, 2011. *Dealer:* Cole Pratt Gallery

BRAITSTEIN, MARCEL
SCULPTOR, EDUCATOR
b Charleroi, Belg, July 11, 1935; Can citizen. *Study:* École Beaux-Arts Montreal, dipl; Inst Allende, San Miguel Allende, Mex. *Work:* Montreal Mus Fine Arts, PQ; Art Gallery Ont, Toronto; Winnipeg Art Gallery, Man; Confederation Ctr, PEI; Can Coun Art Bank, Ottawa; Musée de Québec, Can. *Comn:* Monument, Right Hon A Meighen, Dept Pub Works, Can Govt, 69; wall sculpture & fireplace, Ministry of Social Affairs, Québec, 85; relief mural, Alcan House, Montreal, 89. *Exhib:* Spring Show, Montreal Mus Fine Arts, 61; Vermont USA, Bundy Art Gallery, 66; Panorama of Québec Sculpture, Mus Rodin, Paris, France, 70; First Int Biennial Small Sculpture, Budapest, Hungary, 71; Musée du Québec, 92. *Pos:* Dir, Dept Fine Arts, Univ Québec, Montreal, 86-91, retired. *Teaching:* Prof sculpture, Ecole Beaux-Arts Montreal, 65-69 & Univ Quebec, Montreal, 69-73 & 75-97; prof, Mt Allison Univ, 73-75. *Awards:* Sculpture Prizes, Quebec Govt, 59 & Montreal Mus Fine Arts, 61; Sculpture Prize, Montreal Mus Fine Arts, 61. *Bibliog:* E H Turner (auth), Sculpture in Canada, Can Art, 62; Jean Simard (auth), Marcel Braitstein, Sculpteur (monogr), Québec Sculptors Asn, 69; Yves Racicot (dir), Traces (video), Univ Que, Montreal, 91. *Mem:* Quebec Sculptors Asn (vpres, 69-71); Royal Can Acad Arts. *Media:* Welded Steel, Miscellaneous Media. *Publ:* Auth, Le temps, l'artiste et ses traces (essay) In: Ecrits et temoignages de 21 sculpteurs, Montreal, edition Fini-infini, 23-31, 93; Enfant traque, enfant cache (biography), Montreal, editions XYZ, 95; Les Mysteres de lile de Saber (novel), Granby, Que, Editions de la Paix, 10/98. *Mailing Add:* 3045 Montée Alstonvale Vaudreuil-Dorion PQ J7V0G4 Canada

BRAMAN, IRMA
COLLECTOR
Pos: founder, Norman and Irma Braman Chair in Holocaust Studies, Univ Fla, 2008. *Awards:* Named one of Top 200 Collectors, ARTnews mag, 2009-13. *Collection:* Modern and contemporary art, especially American. *Mailing Add:* 1 Indian Creek Dr Miami FL 33154

BRAMAN, NORMAN
COLLECTOR
b West Chester, Pa, Aug 22, 1932. *Study:* Temple Univ, BA, 1955. *Pos:* With marketing and sales dept, Seagrams Distributors, New York, 1955-57; founder, Keystone Stores, Philadelphia, 1957-72; pres, Braman Enterprises, Miami, Fla, 1972-; owner, Philadelphia Eagles, 1985-94; chmn, ARCONA, Miami, 1985-87; bd dirs, US Holocaust Memorial Coun & Am Israel Public Affairs Comt, Miami; campaign chmn, United Jewish Appeal, Miami; bd govs, Univ Miami Med Sch & Tel Aviv Univ; founder & trustee, Mount Sinai Med Ctr, Miami; trustee, United Israel Appeal; founder, Norman and Irma Braman Chair in Holocaust Studies, Univ Fla, 2008. *Awards:* Named one of Top 200 Collectors, ARTnews Mag, 2004-13. *Mem:* Greater Miami CofC; Dade County Planning and Adv Bd. *Collection:* Modern and contemporary art, especially American. *Mailing Add:* Braman Enterprises 2060 Biscayne Blvd Fl 2 Miami FL 33137-5024

BRAMHALL, KIB
PAINTER
b Morristown, NJ, June 12, 1933. *Study:* Princeton Univ, AB (art & archeol), 55. *Work:* First Nat Bank of Boston, John Hancock Mutual Life Insurance Co & New England Life, Boston; Russell Reynolds Assoc, NY; Smart Fabrics, Ltd, Montreal. *Comn:* Painting for Cox Cancer Ctr, comn by Henry Guild, Boston, 75. *Exhib:* Seventeen solo exhibs, NY, Boston, Santa Fe, Cincinnati, Palm Beach, New Haven, Martha's Vineyard, Cape Cod and Nantucket, 60-86; 24 New Eng Realists, Munson Gallery, Santa Fe, 78; 300 Yrs of Northeast Art, Copley Soc, Boston, 80; Am Realists, Coe Kerr Gallery, NY, 82, 83, 86 & 89; Craven Gallery, 97, 99. *Media:* Oil. *Dealer:* Bramhall & Dunn Vineyard Haven MA 02568; Luce House Gallery Tisbury MA; Craven Gallery W Tisbury MA 02575. *Mailing Add:* RFD 900 Seven Gates Farm Vineyard Haven MA 02568

BRAMLETT, BETTY JANE
ADMINISTRATOR, PAINTER, COLLAGE ARTIST
b Augusta, Ga. *Study:* Converse Col, Spartanburg, SC, BA; Univ NC, Chapel Hill; Columbia Univ, MA; Univ SC, Columbia, EdD, 83. *Work:* SC State Collections, Columbia; Spartanburg Arts Ctr Gallery, SC; Springs Mills Res & Develop Bldg, SC; C S Nat Bank Collection, Columbia, SC; Greenville City Hall Collection, SC. *Exhib:* 38th Ann Guild SC Artists, Juried Art Exhib, 88; 52nd Ann Exhib, Greenville Artists Guild, SC, 88; Joyce Dickinson Dowis Mem Art Exhib, Florence Mus Art, SC, 88; Invitational Women's Exhib, Roe Art Gallery, Furman Univ, Greenville, SC, 88; 16th

Ann Shelby Art League Nat Show, Works on Paper, Rutgers Nat, 94; 30 Juried Shows, 95-2000; many exhibs up to 2005. *Pos:* Fine arts coordr, Spartanburg Co Sch Dist 7, 59-99, retired; arts comnr, SC Arts Comn, 77-80. *Teaching:* Instr art hist & art educ, Univ SC, Columbia, 69-73. *Awards:* SC Art Educator of the Yr, 88, Southeastern Supervisor of the Yr, 89; SC O'Neill Verner Award Art Educ, 89; Award of Merit, SC Watercolor Soc, 95-96. *Bibliog:* Jack Bass (auth), Porgy Comes Home, World Publ, 70; Seth Vining (ed), article, Tryon Daily Bulletin, NC, 70; Bramlett's Art Goes on Display, Spartanburg Herald-J, 70. *Mem:* Greenville Artists Guild; SC Watercolor Soc; SC Artists Guild (pres 77); So Watercolor Soc. *Media:* Watercolor, Acrylic, Collage. *Res:* A Comparison study of two methods for teaching art appreciation. *Interests:* Piano; beading. *Collection:* Many private collections. *Publ:* Auth, Glass on Glass, Sch Arts, 4/63; auth, Spartanburg's Adventure in Art, 4/67 & A Federal Program Can Be Successful, spring 73, SC State Dept; auth, Elementary Art Media, 73 & co-auth, Fine Arts Curricula, Spartanburg Co Sch Dist, 96. *Dealer:* Carolina Gallery Spartanburg SC; City Art Columbia SC. *Mailing Add:* c/o Carolina Gallery 523 W Main St Spartanburg SC 29306

BRAMSON, PHYLLIS HALPERIN
PAINTER, EDUCATOR
b Madison, Wis, Feb 20, 1941. *Study:* Yale Summer Art Sch, Norfolk, Conn, 62; Univ Ill, Urbana, BFA, 63; Univ Wis, Madison, MA (Vilas Fel, full hon), 64; Art Inst Chicago, MFA, 74. *Work:* Hirshhorn Mus; Mus Contemp Art, Chicago; Art Inst Chicago; Mus de Toulon, France; Corcoran Mus of Art; Libr Congress; Smart Mus; New Mus Contemporary Art; Orlando Mus Contemporary Art. *Exhib:* Chicago & Vicinity Show, Art Inst Chicago, 74; Smithsonian Inst, Wash, DC, 76; Works on Paper, Art Inst Chicago, 78; Solo Exhibs: Dart Gallery, Chicago, 80, 83, 85, 88 & 92, Brody's Gallery, Wash, 87 & 93, Douglass Libr Gallery, Douglass Col, Rutgers Univ, New Brunswick, NJ, 91, G W Einstein Gallery, NY, 91, Printworks Gallery, Chicago, 92 & 97 & Phyllis Kind Gallery, Chicago, 94 & 96; Fort Wayne Mus, Ind, 2001; Carl Hammer Gallery, Chicago, 2002; Boulder Art Mus, Boulder Colo, 2004; Claire Oliver Gallery, NY, 2006; Grover/Thurston Gallery, Seattle, Wash, 2007, 2008; Chicago Cult Center, 2005; S Eastern Center Arts, Winston-Salem, NC, 2006; Cynthia Broan Gallery, New York, NY, 2007; Group Exhibs: Seattle Art Mus, 85; 43rd Biennial Exhib Contemp Am Painting; Corcoran Art Gallery, 93; 25 Yrs Printing at Landfall Press, Art Inst Chicago, 96; Constructivists, Ctr Gallery, Creative Studios, Detroit, 96; First Center Arts, Nashville, Tenn, 2003; Nat Acad Mus, NY, 2004; S Eastern Center Arts, Winston-Salem, NC, 2006; Laura Mesaros Galleries, W Va Univ, 2009; Carrie Secrist Gallery, Chicago, 2010; Natalie & James Thompson Art Gallery, San Jose State Univ, 2010. *Pos:* Prof studio arts, Univ Ill, Chicago, 1985-2007, prof emeritus, 2007; vis artist, painting & frawing MFA prog, Sch of the Art Inst, Chicago Ill, 2007-. *Teaching:* Instr drawing & painting, Columbia Col, Chicago, 72-82; vis artist, Univ Ill, 75, Univ Iowa, 79, Univ Chicago, 80, Art Inst Chicago, 81, Ind State Univ, 81, Univ Wis, 83 & Northwestern Univ, 83; assoc prof, Univ Ill, Chicago, 85-; vis artist & lectr, Univ Colo & Univ Nebr, 86 & Univ NMex, 90. *Awards:* Louis Comfort Tiffany Grant, 1980; Nat Endowment Arts Fel Grant, 76, 83 & 93; Sr Fulbright Scholar, Australia, 88; Guggenheim Fel, 93; Rockefeller Found Residency Grant, 1997; Fund Art & Dialog, Jury Award, 2004; Anonymous Was a Woman Award, 2009; Distinguished Alumni Award, Sch Art & Design, Univ Ill, 2010. *Bibliog:* John Russell (auth), article, New York Times, 3/12; Lisa Peters (auth), article, Arts Mag, 3/82; Cody Westerbeck (auth), Phyllis Bramson, Artforum, summer 86; Robert Berlind (auth), Art in Am, 6/2000; Jenni Sorkin (auth), Friez, 11/12/2000; Philip Berger (auth), Phyllis Bramson at Carl Hammer Gallery, Time Out Chicago, 2006. *Mem:* Coll Art Asn (bd dir, 89-92). *Media:* Oil, Mixed Media, Drawing. *Dealer:* Printworks/Chicago 311 W Superior Suite 105 Chicago IL 60610; Claire Oliver Gallery 513 W 26 St New York NY 10001; Philip Slein Gallery 1319 Washington Ave St Louis MO 63103; Carrie Secirst Gallery 835 W Washington Blvd Chicago IL 60607. *Mailing Add:* 411 S Sangamon 4C Chicago IL 60607

BRAND, MICHAEL
MUSEUM DIRECTOR
b Canberra, 1958. *Study:* Australian Nat Univ, Grad, 1979; Harvard Univ, MA, 1982, PhD, 1987. *Pos:* Founding head, Asian art Nat Gallery of Australia, 1988-96; asst dir, Queensland Art Gallery, Australia, 1996-2000; dir, Va Mus Fine Arts, Richmond, 2000-2005 & J Paul Getty Mus, LA, Calif, 2006-2009. *Mailing Add:* J Paul Getty Mus 1200 Getty Ctr Dr Los Angeles CA 90049-1679

BRANDENBERG, ALIKI LIACOURAS See Aliki, Liacouras Brandenberg

BRANDHORST, UDO
COLLECTOR
Pos: Founder, Brandhorst Art Mus, Munich, 2009-; chmn, Udo and Anette Brandhorst Found, Cologne, Ger. *Awards:* Named One of Top 200 Collectors, ARTnews mag, 2004-13. *Collection:* Contemporary art. *Mailing Add:* Brandhorst Mus Tuerkenstrasse 19 Munich 80333 Germany

BRANDT, KATHLEEN WEIL-GARRIS
EDUCATOR, ART HISTORIAN
b Cheam, Surrey, Eng. *Study:* Vassar Col, AB, 56; Univ Bonn, 57; Harvard Univ, AM, 58, PhD, 65. *Hon Degrees:* MA Oxford Univ. *Pos:* Ed-in-chief, Art Bull, 77-81; art historian-in-residence, Am Acad Rome, 75 & 81; consult Renaissance art, Vatican Mus, 87-. *Teaching:* Prof Renaissance art, NY Univ, 65-, Inst Fine Arts, 66-; Harvard Univ, 80-81. *Awards:* Lindback Found Award for Distinguished Teaching, 67; Research Prize, Alexander von Humboldt Found, 85; Officer, Order of Merit of The Italian Repub, 93. *Mem:* Coll Art Asn; Renaissance Soc Am; Soc Archit Hist; NY Acad Sci. *Res:* painting, sculpture & architecture of the 15th and 16th centuries in Italy. *Publ:* Auth, The Santa Casa di Loreto, Garland Press, 77; coauth (with J D'Amico), The Renaissance Cardinal's Ideal Palace, Elefante Press, Rome, 82; auth, On Pedestals, Roemisches Jahrbuch fuer Kunstgeschicte, 84; Twenty-Five Questions About Michelangelo's Sistine Ceiling, Apollo, 87; Michelangelo's Pieta, Studies for Andre Chastel, 87; A marble in Manhattan: Ike Case for Michelangelo, Burlington Mag, 96. *Mailing Add:* 37 Washington Sq W No 16C New York NY 10011

BRANFMAN, STEVEN
CERAMIST, INSTRUCTOR
b Los Angeles, Calif, Mar 5, 53. *Study:* Cortland State Univ, BA, 74, RI Sch Design, MAT, 75, studied with Gerald DiGusto, Norm Shulman, Jun Kaneko, John Jessiman. *Work:* Schein-Joseph Inst-Mus Ceramic Art, Alfred, NY; Canadian Clay and Glass Asn, Toronto; Concordia Coll Art Mus, Ann Arbor, Mich; Fuller Mus of Art, Brockton, Mass; Weisman Art Mus, Minneapolis, Minn. *Comn:* Numerous pvt comns. *Exhib:* Artful Crafts, Fitchburg Art Mus, 89; Great Am Crafts, Starr Gallery, Mass, 90; Nat Invitational Exhib, Fisher Gallery, Farmington Valley, Conn, 92; Nat Invitational Raku Exhib, Kreft Ctr Arts, Ann Arbor, Mich, 92, 94 & 95; Art by Choice, Art Complex Mus, Duxbury, Mass, 95; Solo exhib, Thayer Gallery, Braintree, Mass, 94 & 95; Steven Branfman & Students, 96; Six int recognized Raku Artists, Vt Clay Studio, Montpelier, 96; Dowd Fine Arts Ctr, State Univ NY, Cortland, 97; Escuela de Artesania, Mexico City, 98; NY in Raku, Currier Art Gallery, Manchester, NH, 98; Weisman Art Mus, Minneapolis, Minn, 2000; Guilford Handcrafts Ctr, Ct, 2003, 2005; NIT Inst Art, Natl Ceramics, Biennial, 2004; Lexington Arts & Crafts Soc, MA, 2004. *Pos:* Pres-dir, Potters Shop, Needham, Mass, 77-; mem, RI Sch Design Alumni Coun, 86; vpres & bd trustees, Studio Potter Organization, 90-. *Teaching:* Instr ceramics, Thayer Acad, Braintree, Mass, 78-; artist-in-residence ceramics, Lasell Jr Col, Newton, Mass, 85-88, Potters Sch, Needham, Mass; lectr, Osgood Lectr Series, Thayer Acad, 3/93 & Asn NE Prep Sch, 4/94. *Awards:* RI Sch Design Alumni Serv Award, 85; First-Prize Crafts, Concord Art Asn, 86. *Bibliog:* Potter Adds New Twists Using An Old Technique, Boston Sunday Globe, 9/10/95; Steven Branfman Leads Raku Weekend, Clay Times Mag, Jan/Feb 97; Raku At Amatlan, Ceramics Monthly, 1/2000. *Mem:* Am Crafts Coun; Mass Asn Crafts; Nat Coun Educ Ceramic Arts. *Media:* Clay-Raku Technique. *Publ:* Auth, Raku Basics, Pottery Making Illustrated, Supplement to Ceramics Mo, 1/94; contrib, Make it in Clay, Mayfield Publ, 97; ed & contrib, Clay Times Mag; auth, Raku: a Practical Approach, Second Ed, Krause Publ, 2001; auth, Ireland Glass Technique, Ceramics Monthly, May 2002; auth, Potters Professional Handbook, Am Ceramic Soc, 2003. *Dealer:* Signature Galleries Boston MA; Baak Gallery Cambridge MA. *Mailing Add:* The Potters Shop 31 Thorpe Rd Needham MA 02494

BRANGOCCIO, MICHAEL DAVID
PAINTER, COLLAGE ARTIST
b Denver, Colo, July 18, 1954. *Study:* Univ Northern Colo, BA, 77, MA, 80. *Work:* Arvada Ctr Art, Arvada, Colo; Nautilus Found, Tallahassee, Fla; IBM, Chicago, Ill; Southern Methodist Univ, Dallas, Tex; Hilton Hotel, Tokyo, Japan. *Comn:* Suite of collage on paper, Hilton Hotel, Shanghai, China, 88; acrylic on canvas, Infinity World Headquarters, Los Angeles, Calif, 89; 2 canvas murals, GKBI Towers, Indonesia, 95. *Exhib:* solo exhibs include Nautilus Found, Tallahassee, Fla 92, 1/1 One Over One Gallery, Denver, 95, Olson-Larsen Gallery, Des Moines, 97, 99, 2001, 2002, 2004, William Havu Gallery, Denver, 99, 2001, Ruth Bachofner Gallery, Santa Monica, 99, 2004, Finer Things Gallery, Nashville, Tenn, 2001, Clarke Galleries, Stowe, Vt, 2004, Sardella Fine Arts, Aspen, 2005; Underwraps, Irvine Fine Arts Ctr, Calif, 88; Invitational, Claremont Grad Sch, Calif, 89; Iowa Artists, Des Moines Art Ctr, 94; National Artists Work on Paper, Riverside Art Mus, Calif, 96; Olson-Larsen Gallery, Des Moines, 96; Susan Street Gallery, Solana Beach, Calif, 97; The Des Moines Club, 98; Ruth Bachofner Gallery, 98, 2001, 2002, 2004; Antelope Valley Col, Lancaster, Calif, 98; Fine Things Gallery, 2002; Birds in Painting, Clarke Galleries, 2004. *Teaching:* Guest lectr, Octagon Ctr Arts, Ames, Iowa, 96, Legion Arts, Cedar Rapids, Iowa, 96, William Penn Univ, Oskaloosa, Iowa, 2005. *Bibliog:* Rick Deragon (auth), A Synthesis of Influences, Artweek, 7/89; Orville O Clark (auth), Michael Brangoccio, Chicago Tribune, 1/18; Mark Hinson (auth), Gallery brings back abstract expressionist, Tallahassee Democrat, 2/7/92. *Media:* Mixed Media on Canvas; Paper Collage. *Dealer:* William Havu Gallery 1040 Cherokee Denver Co 80204

BRANNON, MATTHEW
PRINTMAKER
b Saint Maries, Idaho, 1971. *Study:* Univ Calif, LA, BA, 95; Columbia Univ, MFA, 99. *Exhib:* Solo exhibs include Soft Rock, Kunstlerhaus Bethanien, Berlin, 2000, Tatum O'Neals Birthday Party, Kevin Bruk Gallery, Miami, 2003, Exhausted Blood & Imitation Salt, John Connelly Presents, New York, 2004, Penetration, Jan Winkelmann, Berlin, 2005 & Hyena, 2006, Meat Eating Plants, David Kordansky Gallery, LA, 2005, Shoegazers & Graverobbers, Art 37 Statements, David Kordansky Gallery, Basel, 2006, Come Together, Friedrich Petzel Gallery, New York, 2006, Try & Be Grateful, Art Gallery York Univ, Toronto, 2007, Where Were We, Whitney Mus Art Altria, NY, 2007; group exhibs include Made Especially for You, Artists Space, New York, 99; Luggage, Galerie Max Hetzler, Berlin, 2000; Dedalic Convention, MAK, Vienna, 2001; Inaugural Exhib, Golinko Kordansky Gallery, LA, 2003, Tapestry from an Asteroid, 2004; Snowblind, John Connelly Presents, New York, 2003, Cave Canem, 2004; Collection: How I Spent a Year, PS1 Contemp Art Center/Mus Mod Art, New York, 2004, Curious Crystals of Unusual Purity, 2004, Greater New York, 2005; Post No Bills, White Columns, New York, 2005; Temporary Import, Art Forum Berlin, 2005; Uncertain States of America: Am Art in the 3rd Millennium, Astrup Fearnley Mus Mod Art, Oslo, 2005, Center Cur Studies, Bard Coll, Reykjavik Art Mus & Serpentine Gallery, London, 2006, Mus Serignan, Herning Art Mus, Copenhagen & Center Contemp Art, Zanek Ujazdowski, Warsaw, 2007; Slow Burn, Galerie Edward Mitterand, Geneva, 2006; On the Marriage Broker Joke, Office Baroque Gallery, Antwerp, 2007; Whitney Biennial, Whitney Mus Am Art, 2008. *Media:* Serigraphy, Silkscreen, Miscellaneous Media. *Mailing Add:* c/o Petzel Gallery 456 W 18th St New York NY 10011

BRANSBY, ERIC JAMES
MURALIST, EDUCATOR
b Auburn, NY, Oct 25, 1916. *Study:* Kansas City Art Inst, Mo, with Thomas Hart Benton & Fletcher Martin, cert (painting & printmaking); Colorado Springs Fine Arts Ctr & Colo Coll, with Boardman Robinson & Jean Charlot, BA & MA (mural painting); Yale Univ, with Josef Albers & Carol Meeks, MFA (painting). *Hon*

Degrees: Park Coll, Kansas City, Mo, DFA, 95; Univ Colo, LHD, 97; Commendation, US Cong. *Work:* Colorado Springs Fine Arts Ctr; Mo State Hist Soc Collection, Columbia; Brigham Young Univ Mus Art; Nelson Atkins Mus Art, Kansas City; Princeton Univ; Print Research Found, New York; Ga Mus Art, Athens; Kirkland Mus Art, Denver; Denver Art Mus; El Pomar Found, Colo Springs, Colo; Denver Public Libr, Denver, Colo. *Comn:* Fresco mural, Univ Ill, Urbana, 52; mixed media mural, Brigham Young Univ, Provo, Utah, 58; mixed media mural, Univ Mo, Kansas City, 75; mixed media mural, St Paul Sch, Skokie, Ill; panel mural, Colo Springs Fine Arts Ctr, 85, 2012; 12 panel mural, Kans State Univ, Manhattan, 86; 8 panel mural, Loveland Mus, Colo, 88; fresco mural, Park Coll Libr, Mo, 91; 36 panel mural, Pioneer Mus, Colorado Springs, 94; 8 panel mural, US Air Force Accad, 95. *Exhib:* Housing & Urban Develop Nat Community Art Competition; Joslyn Mus Biennial, Omaha, 72 & 78; Nat Ctr Fine Arts, Washington, DC, 73-75; Solo exhibs, Univ Mo, 78, Colorado Springs Fine Arts Ctr, 2002 & Ga Mus Art, Univ Ga, 2004; Smithsonian-Traveling Print, 79-80; West Surrey Coll, Eng, 80; Albrecht Kemper Mus, 93; Nat Soc Mural Painters Centennial, NY Art Students League, 95; Ind State Univ, 97. *Teaching:* Asst instr, Yale Univ, 49-50; instr beginning drawing & design, Univ Ill, Urbana, 50-52; prof freehand drawing & design, Univ Mo, Kansas City, 65-84; prof emer advan figure drawing, painting & printmaking Univ Mo, Kansas City. *Awards:* Edwin Austen Abbey Found, Fel (mural painting), 52; Kansas City Asn Trusts & Founds, 70; Veatch Award, Distinguished Res, Univ of Mo, 77; Weldon Springs Grant, Univ Mo, 80; Lifetime Achievement Award, Pres Benezet, Colo Coll, 99; Pollock-Krasner Award, 2001-2002 & 2006-2007; Lifetime Achievement Award, Pikes Peak Coun Arts. *Bibliog:* Nat Community Art Prog, US Govt Printing Off (HUD), 73; Under the Influence, Students of Thomas Hart Benton (catalogue), Albrecht Kemper Mus, 93; From Roots to Soaring Visions (catalogue), Colorado Springs Fine Arts Ctr, 2001; Eric J Bransby (auth), Figurative Connections, selected works (catalogue), Ga State Mus Art, 2003. *Mem:* Nat Soc Mural Painters; and others. *Media:* Multimedia, Buon Fresco. *Res:* Design analysis of Piero della Francesca's mural cycle in the Church of San Francesco at Arezzo, Italy; develop of lightweight portable fresco panels; design analysis of a Byzantine mosaic mural cycle in the Kariye d'Jami church in Istanbul, Turkey. *Interests:* Renaissance & Mex mural fresco techniques. *Publ:* The Buon Fresco Process (video), Univ Mo Video Network; Art-Do It, (A handbook for artists), Kendall/Hunt Publ; auth, Figurative Connections (catalogue), Univ Ga Press; auth, From Roots to Soaring Visions (catalogue), Colo Springs Fine Arts Ctr; Under the Influence (the students of Thomas Hart Benton, Catalogue), Albrecht-Kemper Mus; The Muralists of Colorado. *Dealer:* Bransby Fine Arts 9080 Hwy 115 Colorado Springs CO 80926. *Mailing Add:* 9080 Hwy 115 Colorado Springs CO 80926

BRANT, PETER M
PATRON
Exhib: Remembering Henry's Show: 1978-2008, 2009-2010; Urs Fischer: Oscar the Grouch, The Brant Found Art Study Ctr, Greenwich, Conn, 2010-2011, Josh Smith: The American Dream, 2011, David Altmejd, 2011-2012, Karen Kilimnik, 2012, Nate Lowman: I wanted to be an artist but all I got was this lousy career, 2012-2013, Andy Warhol, 2013, Julian Schnabel, 2013; Dan Colen: Help, 2014. *Pos:* Chmn & chief exec officer, Brant Industries, Inc; owner, Brant Publ (Interview, Art in Am Mag, The Mag Antiques, Modern Magazines); co-founder, Greenwich Polo Club, 1995-; bd trustees, Mus Contemp Art, Los Angeles. *Awards:* Named one of Top 200 Collectors, ARTnews, 2008-13. *Collection:* Contemporary art, design & furniture. *Publ:* Exec producer (films), Basquiat, 1996, Pollock, 2000 & Warhol, 2006; producer, The Homesman, 2014. *Mailing Add:* The Brant Foundation Inc 80 Field Point Rd Greenwich CT 06830

BRANTLEY, JAMES SHERMAN
PAINTER
b Philadelphia, Pa, Feb 1, 1945. *Study:* Pa Acad Fine Arts; Philadelphia Coll Art; Univ Pa. *Work:* Afro-Am Hist & Cult Mus; Am Mus at PAFA Chamber of Commerce of Del; Hampton Univ Mus; Fed Res Bank, Philadelphia, Pa. *Exhib:* Contemp Black Artists (with catalog), Whitney Mus Art, NY, 73; one-man shows, Sande Webster Gallery; Visions, Atmosphere Gallery, NY, 2000; New Acquisitions, Hampton Univ Mus, Va; From the Collection, Am Mus @ PAFA; Absence of Color, Philadelphia Mus of Art. *Awards:* Hallgarten Prize, Nat Acad Design; Louis Fine Purchase Award, Pa Acad & Francis Bergman Portrait Award. *Bibliog:* Int Rev of African-Am Art, Vol 17, 2000; Wall St Jour, Mar 2000; Wilson Quarterly, Summer 2000; Painter's Progress, Gerard Brown (auth), Phila Weekly, 99. *Media:* Acrylic. *Publ:* Int Rev of African-Am Art, Vol 15, 99; Ed Sozanski, Philadelphia Inquirer, 2/28/99; Brantley Exhib, Philadelphia Tribune, 1/6/99; African-Am Wishing Book, Running Press, 96. *Mailing Add:* 6915 Greenhill Rd Philadelphia PA 19151-2320

BRASELMAN, LIN EMERY See Emery, Lin

BRASETH, JOHN E
ART DEALER, CONSULTANT
b Seattle, Wash, May 23, 1959. *Study:* Studied Northwest Art from 1930's to present. *Pos:* Dir & owner, Gordon Woodside-John Braseth Galleries. *Specialty:* Northwest masters: Morris Graves, William Ivey, Mark Tobey, Paul Horiuchi, Guy Anderson, Joseph Goldberg, Kenneth Callahan, Jacob Lawrence; plus others. *Mailing Add:* 2101 Ninth Ave Seattle WA 98121

BRATCHER, COLLEN DALE
PAINTER
b Rockport, Ky, Jan 10, 1932. *Study:* Univ Louisville, BCE, 1955, MCE, 1972. *Work:* Citizens Bank, Evansville, Ind; Evansville Mus Arts & Sci, Ind; Morehead State Univ, Ky; Coca Cola Co, Elizabethtown, Ky; Household Int Corp, Prospect Heights, Ill; Lucille Parker Markey Cancer Ctr, Lexington, KY; Lilly Enterprise Coatings, Indianapolis; Doncaster Mus Art, Eng; Hillard & Lyons Ctr, Louisville, Ky; numerous pvt collections. *Comn:* Paintings, Lewisport Sch & Lewisport City Hall, Ky, 77; Pate House, Hancock Co, Ky, 77; 3 paintings, Hancock Co, Ky; painting, Liberty Nat Bank & Trust, Louisville, Ky; Summer on the River, Liberty Nat Bank & Trust Louisville, Ky, 1981; Chinn's Farm, Danville, Ky, 1991. *Exhib:* Watercolor USA, Springfield, Mo, 74, 83 & 88; 8 State Ann Paintings-Graphics, JB Speed Art Mus, Louisville, Ky, 1975-77, 81; 39th Watercolor Soc Ala Ann Nat Competitition Exhib, Birmingham Mus Art, 79; Midwest Watercolor Soc Ann, 78-79 & 83; Rocky Mountain Nat Watermedia, Golden, Colo, 80-82; Nat Arts Club Open Watercolor Exhib, NY, 81-82; Solo exhibs, Grand Canyon Nat Park, Ariz, 81 & 83, Morehead State Univ, Ky, 83 & Doncaster Mus, South Yorkshire, Eng, 86 & 90; 3rd Ann Georgia Watercolor Soc Exhib, Mus Arts & Scis, Macon, 82; El Paso's NatSun Carnival Art Exhib, El Paso Mus Art, 82-85; Aqueous Ky Watercolor Soc Ann Nat Exhib, Owensboro Mus Fine Art, 83-91; Realism Today Ann Exhib, Evansville Mus Art, 83-85, 89-92; Headley-Whitley Mus Art, Lexington, Ky, 87; Evansville Mus Arts & Sci, Indiana, 91; Liberty Gallery, Louisville, Ky, 92. *Collection Arranged:* Evansville Mus Art, Ind; Owensboro Mus Art, Ky; Hilliard and Lyons Corp Headquarters, Ky; Morehead State Univ, Ky; Doncaster Art Mus, Eng. *Pos:* Artist. *Awards:* Purchase awards, An Exhib for Corp Collecting for Citizens Fidelity Bank I and II, JB Speed Art Mus, Louisville, 71 and 77; First Prize Representational Painting, Ky State Fair-Crafts & Fine Arts Section, 75; Bellinger award, 18th Nat Jury Show, Chautauqua Exhib Am Art, 75; First Place-Grand award, Art Works Show Ann Exhib, Paul Sawyler Art Club, Frankfort, KY, 81; Best of Show, Woman's Club Louisville, Ky, 82; Siegfried Weng Purchase award, 35th Ann Mid-States Art Exhib, Evansville Mus Arts & Scis, 82; Purchase Award, Reflections '83, Covington, Ky, 83; Travelling Exhib, 39th Waterworks Mich Water Color Soc Ann Exhib, Nat Competition, 85-86. *Bibliog:* Lansdell, Sarah (auth), Floyd County Show spotlights sophistication of area artists, Courier-Journal Newspaper, 07/12/81; Booth, Bill R (auth), Dale Bratcher and the Grand Canyon, North Light Mag, 3/83; Williams, Jane (auth) Dale Bratcher-Manifestation of the Mythic Chasm, Southwest Art Mag, 9/84; Articles, Am Artist, 3/85; Kay, Joan (auth), Trip to England opens new vistas for painter of the Grand Canyon, Courier-Journal Newspaper, 9/9/86; Booth, Bill R (auth), Through the Eyes of the Artist: Dale Bratcher, Four Colour Print Group (book), 8/2015. *Mem:* Watercolor Soc Ala; Ky Watercolor Soc; Southern Watercolor Soc; Midwest Watercolor Soc; Ga Watercolor Soc. *Media:* Watercolor, Egg Tempera. *Publ:* Sketching While Travelling, Am Artist Mag, 3/85; Booth, Bill R (ed), A Life in the 20th Century, Four Colour Print Group, 5/2015. *Dealer:* Owensboro Mus Fine Art 901 Frederica St Owensboro KY 42301; Indianapolis Mus Art 1200 W 38th St Indianapolis IN 46208. *Mailing Add:* 1529 Crosstimbers Dr Louisville KY 40245

BRATSCH, KERSTIN
PAINTER, INSTALLATION SCULPTOR
b Hamburg, Germany, 1979. *Study:* Columbia Univ, MFA, 2007. *Exhib:* Group exhibs, Max Hans Daniel Present, Autcenter, Berlin, 2009, No Bees, No Blueberries, Harries Liberman, NY, 2009, The Pursuer, Greene Naftali Gallery, NY, 2010, Behind the Curtain, Gio Marconi Gallery, Milan, 2010, Kaya, 179 Canal, NY, 2010, Held Up By Columns, Renwick Gallery, NY, 2010, Greater NY, PS1, Mus Modern Art, NY, 2010, Deste Found, Athens, 2011, 54th Int Art Exhib Biennale, Venice, 2011; solo exhibs, THUS!, NJ, 2010, Centre d'art contemporain, Parc Saint Leger, 2010, Deste Found, Athens, 2011, Kunsthalle Zurich, 2011. *Awards:* Agnes Martin Fellowship Award, 2006; Gamblin Award, 2007. *Media:* Acrylic, Oil. *Mailing Add:* c/o Gavin Brown's Enterprise 620 Greenwich St New York NY 10014

BRATT, BYRON H
PRINTMAKER
b Everett, Wash, Dec 12, 1952. *Study:* Western Wash Univ, BA (fine arts), 75. *Work:* Libr Cong, Wash, DC; Brooklyn Mus; Am Mus, Bath, England; New York Pub Libr; Addison Gallery Am Art, Phillips Acad, Andover, Mass. *Exhib:* Am Prints Today & 22nd Ann Print Exhib, Brooklyn Mus, NY; Am Color Print Soc, Philadelphia; 24th Nat Print Exhib, Smithsonian Inst, Wash, DC; RI Sch Design, Providence; Carnegie Inst, Pittsburgh; Int Print Co, Tokyo, Japan & Philadelphia. *Bibliog:* Andrew Stasik (auth), Am Prints & Print Marlow, 56-81, Print Rev, 82; Van Deventer (auth), Six Masters of Mezzotint, 87; Carol Wax (auth), The Mezzotint, Abrams, 90. *Media:* Mezzotint

BRATTON, CHRISTOPHER ALAN
ADMINISTRATOR, VIDEO ARTIST
b Akron, Ohio, July 3, 1959. *Study:* Atlanta Coll Art, BFA, 82; Whitney Mus Independent Study Prog, 84-86; Univ Wis, MFA, 94. *Hon Degrees:* Atlanta Coll Art, DHC, 2004. *Exhib:* Abu-Jamal Interview excerpts, NBCS, CBS, ABC, CNN, 1993-1995; Entreta pueblo y mi pueblo hay puntos y rayas, Unconventional Film and Video Festival curated by Countermedia at Near NE Arts Ctr, 1996; Nat Poetry Video Festival at Mus of Contemporary Art, Chgo, Ill, 1998; Video Machete screenings on commercial TV, PBS website, Taos Talking Picture Festival, 2000-present. *Pos:* dean undergraduate studies, Sch Art Inst Chgo, 2001-2003; pres and CEO, San Francisco Art Inst, 2004-2010; pres, dep dir, Mus Fine Arts, Boston, 2010-. *Teaching:* Guest lectr, Sch of Visual Arts, New York City, 1990; guest lectr, Sch of the Art Inst, Chicago, 1990, fac mem, 1992-2004, chmn Video Dept, 1993-95, chmn, Dept Film, Video, and New Media, 2000-2001, dean undergraduate studies, 2002-04; pres, San Francisco Art Inst, 2004-10; pres, Sch of Mus of Fine Arts (SMFA), Boston, 2010-. *Awards:* Nat Endowment Arts, 82, 88, & 90; The MacArthur Found grant, 2000-2003; Fund for Leadership Advancement award, James Irvine Found, Calif, 2005. *Mem:* Boston Art Acad (bd mem); Professional Arts Consortium (bd mem); Innovation Lab, Harvard Univ (founding mem); Nat Council on Youth, Education, and Media (founding mem). *Publ:* Mucho Coco, quarterly writings and art review, editorial mem, 97-98; The Global Studio, in Conditions and Strategies: Cont Art Edn and Comm, China Acad of Art Press, Hanzhou, China, 2008; Art, Censorship, Violence, Invited editorial for the Art Newspaper, 2008. *Mailing Add:* School of Musuem of Fine Arts, Boston 230 The Fenway Boston MA 02115

BRAUDY, DOROTHY
PAINTER, PHOTOGRAPHER
b Los Angeles, Calif. *Study:* Univ, Ky, BA; NY Univ, MA (art educ); pvt study with Richard Pousette-Dart; Art Students' League, with Stamos, Kantor & Glasier; Columbia Univ Teachers Coll. *Work:* Fed Reserve Bank, Richmond, Va; Mason Co Mus, Maysville, Ky; Rutgers Univ Mus, New Brunswick, NJ; Ellen Kim Murphy Gallery, 2000; Univ S Calif, 2006. *Comn:* Portrait, comn by Richard Poirier, New York, 75; George Davis family, Calistoga, Calif, 79; John Irwin family, Baltimore, Md, 80; William Chamness family, Aberdeen, Ohio; Ira Brind family, Philadelphia, 85; Dorothy Lyman-Vincent Malle, Los Angeles, 86. *Exhib:* Viridian Gallery, NY, 77-78; Solo exhibs, B R Kornblatt Gallery, Baltimore, 79, Washington, DC, 81, Goucher Coll, 82, UPB Gallery, Berkeley, Calif, 84, Orlando Gallery, Los Angeles, 86 & 88, 871 Fine Arts, 93, USC Fisher Gallery, 94, Ellen Kim Murphy Gallery, 2000 & Hamilton Galleries, 2006, 2009, 2011, Gallery 360, Northeastern Univ, Boston, 2010. *Teaching:* Prof art educ, Pratt Inst, New York, 71-77; prof art hist & drawing, Towson State Univ, Md, 78-79; prof visual arts, Goucher Coll, Towson, Md, 79-83. *Awards:* BAU Inst Fellowship, 2006, 2008; Toledo Artmaker Fellowship, 2010-2012. *Bibliog:* Articles, New Art Examiner, 10/81, Baltimore Sun, 9/81 & 9/83 & Santa Monica Mirror, 10/2000; revs, Los Angeles Times, 86, 88 & 94, ArtScene 12/88, Dreamworks, 88 & Art Week, 1/95; Women's Studies, 2003; Los Angeles Review (books website), 2012. *Mem:* Los Angeles Inst Humanities (fellow); Nat Mus Women in the Arts. *Media:* Oils, Watercolor, Photography. *Publ:* Auth, Finishing the Hat, 2000; Marking Time, 2006. *Dealer:* Hamilton Galleries; Frank Pictures. *Mailing Add:* 2008 N Oxford Ave Los Angeles CA 90027

BRAUN, EMILY
EDUCATOR, CURATOR, WRITER
Study: Victoria Col, Univ Toronto, BA, 1979; NY Univ, MA. *Pos:* Fine arts consult, Lila Acheson Wallace Found, 1982-84; curator, Leonard and Evelyn Lauder Collection, currently, Alex Hillman Family Found Collection, 2000-; active curator and has contributed to numerous mus exhibition catalogues in Great Britain, Europe, Canada, Mexico, and the United States. *Teaching:* Asst prof, Hunter Col and Graduate Ctr, 1992, distinguished prof, 2007-, dir of the Art History Program, currently, dep chair, Dept Art and Art History, currently. *Awards:* Sr Rsch Grant, Getty Found, 1993; Fellowship, NY Pub Libr, Dorothy and Lewis B. Cullman Ctr for Scholars and Writers, 2002-03; Henry Allen Moe Prize, NY State Hist Asn. *Publ:* contrib auth, Northern Light: Realism and Symbolism in Scandinavian Painting, 1982; co-auth, Gardens and Ghettos: The Art of Jewish Life in Italy, 1990; auth, Mario Sironi and Italian Modernism: Art and Politics Under Fascism, 2000; co-curator, co-auth, The Power of Conversation: Jewish Women and their Salons (recipient Nat Jewish Book award, 2005); essays and reviews have been featured in the Times Literary Supplement, Modernism/Modernity, Journal of Contemporary History, Art in America, Art Journal, Arts Magazine and the Short Oxford History of Italy. *Mailing Add:* Hunter Art Department 695 Park Ave 11th Floor North Building New York NY 10065

BRAUNSTEIN, MARK MATHEW
CURATOR, PHOTOGRAPHER
b New York, NY, Aug 6, 1951. *Study:* Carnegie-Mellon Univ, 72; Pratt Inst, 73, MS, 78; State Univ NY, Binghamton, BA, 74. *Exhib:* Images 1990, Images 1994, Images 2002, Images 2008 & Images 2015, Guilford Art Center, Conn; solo show, Conn Col, 91 & Mystic Nature Ctr, 92; Danforth Mus Art, Framingham, Ma, 2001; Hygienic Art Gallery, New London, Conn, 2002; Conn Coll Arboretum, 2001-2007; Emerging Artists Exhib, Windham Arts Center, Willimantic, Conn, 2007; group photo shows, Photo Show 36, Mystic Arts Ctr, Conn, 2014, The F-Stops Here, Hygienic Art Gallery, New London, Conn, 2014. *Collection Arranged:* Wetmore Print Collection, Conn Coll Website; Conn Coll Asian Art Collection, ARTstor Website. *Pos:* Ed & researcher, Rosenthal Art Slides, Chicago, 78-80; asst ed, Art Index, 80-83; head, Slide & Photog Collection, RI Sch Design, Providence, 83-87; visual resources cur, Art Hist Dept & cur campus artworks, Conn Col, New London, 87-. *Teaching:* Photoshop workshops, Conn Col, 99-; Visual Resources Asn (VRA), ann conferences, 2002, 2005, 2009, 2013; Windham Arts Center, Willimantic, Conn, 2007; Stonington (high Sch), 2007-2009, continuing educ, 2007-2009. *Awards:* Fac Develop Grants, RI Sch Design, 84-86; Art Libr Soc Travel Award, 95; Visual Resources Asn Travel Award, 2009. *Bibliog:* Contemporary Authors, Vol 113, new revisions series, vol 50 & 105; I Witness Video (9 minutes), NBC, 3/94; From There to Here, No Limits Commun, 2004. *Mem:* Visual Resources Asn. *Publ:* Auth, Vegetarianism in art (cover story), Vegetarian Times, 80; Rembrandt's Cologne Self-Portrait, Iris: Notes in the Hist of Art, 83; full-page photo, Flora, Graphis, 129, 2002; My Wildest Dreams (photo essay on nature), Healing Our World, 1-2/2012; As it Is on Earth: A Novel (cover photo), 2012; Microgreen Garden (all 60 photos), 2013. *Mailing Add:* PO Box 456 Quaker Hill CT 06375-0456

BRAUNSTEIN, RUTH
ART DEALER
b Minneapolis, Minn. *Collection Arranged:* California Era, Update, Huntsville Art Mus, Ala; Richard Shaw: Illusionism in Clay (auth, catalog), 71-85. *Pos:* Dir, Braunstein/Quay Gallery, San Francisco, 61-. *Awards:* Woman of the Year, Art Table Inc, 96. *Bibliog:* David Jones (auth), 1971 early work (catalog), 71; Peter Voulkos (auth), Anagama works (catalog), 91; Robert Brady (auth), Sculpture, 96. *Mem:* San Francisco Art Dealers Asn (pres, 75-77, 95 & 96); Hadassah; Art Table Inc. *Specialty:* Contemporary art: sculpture, painting and drawing; ceramic sculpture, mostly American artists. *Publ:* Richard Shaw, New York, 2007; catalog essay, Richard Whittaker. *Mailing Add:* Braunstein/Quay Gallery 580 14th St San Francisco CA 94103

BRAUNSTEIN, TERRY (MALIKIN)
PAINTER
b Washington, DC, Sept 18, 1942. *Study:* l'Ecole des Beaux Arts, Aix-en-Provence, France, 62; Univ Mich, Ann Arbor, BFA, 64; Md Inst Art, Baltimore, MFA, 68. *Work:* Mus Mod Art, NY; Victoria & Albert Mus, London, Eng; Long Beach Mus Art, Calif; Bibliotheque Nat, Paris; Corcoran Gallery Art & Nat Mus Am Art, Washington; Getty Ctr, Los Angeles, Calif; Contemp Art Ctr, Moscow, Russia; Libr Cong, Washington, DC; Los Angeles Co Mus Art; Yale Univ, Conn; Nat Mus Women Arts, Washington, DC; Univ Art Mus, Calif State Univ, Long Beach. *Comn:* book and ser photographs Imagina Project, Universal Exposition, Seville, Spain, 92; Open Channels Video, Long Beach Mus Art, 92; pub art, Metro Blue Line Sta, Long Beach, 94; book Nat Mus Women in the Arts, 94; pub art, Dirty Windows (metro proj), Berlin, Ger, 96; serigraph, Moscow Studio, Russ, 96; Windows on Wilshire, Los Angeles Co Mus Art, 97; bronze and steel Navy Mem, City Long Beach, Calif, 2003; Porcelain enamel work Elevator Cabinet Improvement Project, City Hall, Long Beach, 2001; Bluff Erosion & Enhancement Project (with Craig Cree Stone), City of Long Beach, 2002; Navysphere, stainless, brass & bronze sculpture & Porcelain enamel panels, Long Beach Hanvy Mem, Queensway Bay, Long Beach, 2004; Illuminations, Cerritos 50th Anniversary Mem, Cerritos, Calif, 2006; Sun Salutation, Byzantine glass & ceramic tile murals, Sun Valley Healthcare Facility, 2007. *Exhib:* Photomontage/Photocollage: The Changing Picture 1920-1989, Jan Turner Gallery, Los Angeles, 89; Solo exhibs, Almediterranea (catalog), Almeria, Spain, 90, Long Beach Mus Art, Calif, 91, Turner/Krull, Los Angeles, 92, Craig Krull, Los Angeles, 94, 95, 97, & 09, Troyer Fitzpatrick Lassman, Washington, 94, Universidad de Salamanca, Spain, 96, Feria Int de Arte (ARCO 97), Madrid, Spain, 97, Centro de Exposiciones de Radaquilar, Almeria, Spain, 98 & Centro Andaluz de la Fotografia, Almeria, 2002, Piazza delle Erbe, Montecassiano, Italy, 2005, Museo Civico Villa Colloredo Mels, Recanati, Italy, 2005-2006, Seeing with Other Eyes, Cerritos, Libr, 2006-2007, Univ San Francisco, Thacher Gallery, 2007, Station Identification: Terry Braunstein Works from 1982-Present, Torrance, Calif, 2009; Amb els Media, Contra els Media with (catalog), Sala Arcs Gallery, Barcelona, Spain, 90; Biennial I (with catalog), Calif Mus Photog, Riverside, 90; Primavera Fotografica (with catalog), Sala Arcs Gallery, Barcelona, Spain, 90; Virgin Territories, Long Beach Mus Art, 92; Imagina, Salas de Arenal, Universal Expos, Seville, Spain & traveling exhib (with catalog), 92-; Photog Los Angeles Now, Los Angeles Co Mus Art, 95, LA Current: A Female Perspective, Armand Hammer Mus Art, Los Angeles, 95, Palazzo del Consoli, Gubbio, Italy, Viaggiatori, 98; Fractured Identity: Cut and Paste, Julie Saul Gallery, New York City, 94; Magic Realism: Violating Expectations, Univ Art Mus, Calif State Univ, Long Beach, 94; Redefining the Book: Eight Invited Artists, Braunstein/Quay Gallery, San Francisco, 94; Oltre la Grande Soglia (catalog), Centro Esposito della Rocca Paolina, Perugia and Milan, Italy, 94; Still Life, Still Here, Hunsaker/Schlesinger Gallery, Los Angeles, 96; LA Current: A Female Perspective, Armand Hammer Mus Art, Los Angeles, 96; Imagine (traveling exhib), Salas de Arenal, Universal Exposition, Seville Spain, 97; Via Ggiatori-Travelers, Palazzo dei Consoli, Gubbio, Italy & Los Angeles, 98; Imagina, Centro Andalus de la Fotografia, Almeria, 2000; Rooms With a View-Enter Laughing, Long Beach Mus Art, Calif, 2000-01; Insomnia, Nat Mus Women Arts, Washington, DC, 2003; California Landscape, Long Beach Mus Art, Calif, 2005. *Pos:* Vis artist, Smithsonian Inst, 78; guest cur Bookworks, Wash Project Arts, Washington, 80, artist bd mem, 80-84, bd dirs, 80-; guest juror & cur, 82-91; vpres, fac asn, Corcoran Sch Art, Washington, DC, 83-; artist mem, Advisory Comt Pub Art, Long Beach Percent-for- Art-Program, 90-94; design team, Street Facade Improvement Proj, Long Beach, 98. *Teaching:* Instr, Prince Georges Community Coll, Largo, Md, 70-74; Northern Va Community Col, Annandale, 76-78; instr printmaking, Corcoran Sch Art, Washington, 78-79, assoc prof & coordr 3rd yr Fine Arts Prog, 79-86; guest artist, Chicago Art Inst, 84, Long Beach Mus Art, 88, Univ Mich, 89, Otis Art Inst, 91, Mills Col, 92 & San Francisco Art Inst, 93, Contemp Art Ctr, Moscow, 96; prof emer, Corcoran Sch Art, 86; prof painting & mixed media, advanced students, Calif State Univ, 89; guest lectr, Pomona Coll, Claremont, Calif, 89, Hampshire Coll, Northampton, Mass, 90, Art Ctr Coll Design, Pasadena, Calif, 91, Univ Complutense, Roqueta del Mar, Spain, 91, Art Inst, Los Angeles, 95 & Orange Coast Coll, 98, Cerritos Libr, 2006, Long Beach Mus Art, 2007. *Awards:* Visual Artist fel, Nat Endowment for Arts, 85; Open Channels Video Grant, Long Beach Mus Art, 92; Distinguished Arts Award, Visual Artist, Long Beach, 92; Nat Book Award, Nat Mus Women Arts, Washington, 94; Yaddo Artists Residency, Saratoga Springs, NY, 97, 99, 2005; Artists fel, Long Beach, Calif, 99; Durfee Grant, 2009. *Bibliog:* Lewis (auth), Braunstein's fantasy montages, Wash Post, 10/18/86; Hunt (auth), Windows in Art, Los Angeles Times, 11/97; Gottleib (auth), Windows Turning Heads on Wilshire, Press Telegram, 10/97; Joselow (auth), Terry Braunstein, Envisioning Art for the People, 98; Barbara Crane (auth), Three Women of Influence in Long Beach tell different stories, Long Beach Bus J, 1/2004; Joe Segura (auth), The Sphere is Here, Long Beach Press Telegram, 5/20/2004; Shirle Gottleib (auth), Book Mark, Long Beach Press Telegram, 12/15/2006; Tom Hennessey (auth), Cerritos Artist Has it Covered, Long Beach Press Telegram, 2/18/2007. *Mem:* Long Beach Arts Coun (bd dirs). *Media:* Photomontage Artist, Public Artist. *Publ:* Auth, Windows, Vis Studies Workshop Press, 82; Theater or Life? (exhib catalog), Charlotte Salomon exhib, Judaic Mus, Washington, 83; Station identification, Kalliope Mag, 85; A Tale from the Fire, Nat Mus Women Arts, 95; Creating a Particular Horizon, Writing & the Artists Bk, Abracadabra, 96. *Dealer:* Craig Krull Gallery Bergamot Sta 2525 Michigan Ave Bldg B3 Santa Monica CA 90404. *Mailing Add:* 262 Belmont Ave Long Beach CA 90803

BRAUNTUCH, TROY
PAINTER
b Jersey City, NJ, 1954. *Study:* Calif Inst Arts, Valencia, BFA, 75. *Work:* Lannan Found, Los Angeles, Calif; Metrop Mus Art, Mus Mod Art, NY. *Exhib:* Solo exhibs, The Kitchen, NY, 79, Mary Boone Gallery, NY, 82, 83 & 85, Akira Ueda Gallery, Tokyo, Japan, 84, Kent Fine Art, NY, 88 & 90, The Living Room, Amsterdam, 89, Liliane & Michel Durand-Dessert, Paris, 90 & Gallerie Mai 36, Zurich, Switz, 97, Galerie Capitain Petzel, Berlin, 2010, Mildred Lane Kemper Art Mus, St Louis, 2011;

New Talent/NY, Gallery Contemp Art, Cleveland, Ohio, 80; US Art Now, Konsthallen, Goteborg, Sweden, 81; Venice Biennale, Venice, Italy, 82; Nat Mus Art, Osaka, Japan, 83; Mus Mod Art, 84; Mus & Sculpture Garden, Washington, 84; Whitney Mus Am Art, NY, 89-90, Whitney Biennial, 2006. *Awards:* Guggenheim Found Fel, 2010. *Media:* Conté, C-Prints

BRAVMANN, RENE A
ART HISTORIAN, EDUCATOR
b Marseilles, France, Dec 10, 1939; US citizen. *Study:* Cleveland Mus Art, 57-61; Western Reserve Univ, BA, 61; Univ Wis, 61-63; Ind Univ, MA (fine arts), 65, PhD, 71. *Teaching:* Asst prof art hist, Univ Wash, Seattle, 68-72, assoc prof, 72-76, prof, 77-, chmn African studies, 69-75. *Awards:* Ford Found Fel, Am Coun Learned Socs, 66-68; Post-doctoral Res Grant, Soc Sci Res Coun, 72-73; Am Philos Soc Grant, 74. *Publ:* Auth, West African Sculpture, 70 & auth, Open Frontiers: The Dynamics of Art in Black Africa, 73, Univ Wash; auth, The diffusion of Ashanti political art, In: African Art & Leadership, 72; auth, Islam & Tribal Art in West Africa, Cambridge Univ, 74; auth, An urban way of death, African Arts, Vol 8, No 3. *Mailing Add:* Univ Wash Dept Art Hist Seattle WA 98195

BRAZDA, BONIZAR
INSTALLATION SCULPTOR, CONCEPTUAL ARTIST
b Cambridge, Can, 1972. *Exhib:* Solo exhibs include Hegel's Angels, Maccarone, Inc, New York, 2003, Legendary Yangtze Punks, Swiss Inst Contemp Art, New York, 2004, The Journalist, Haswellediger & Co Gallery, New York, 2004 & Cafécore, 2006, EyeShadow, The Moore Space Miami, 2005, Bread, The Kitchen, New York, 2006, Beat Meat Table Eat, Bortolami, New York, 2007; group exhibs include Majority Rules, Free Gallery, Glasgow, 2003; Sense of Place, Boulder Mus Contemp Art, Colo, 2004; Greater New York, PS1/Mus Mod Art, New York, 2005; In Practice Series, Sculpture Center, LIC, New York, 2006; Just Kick It 'Till It Breaks, The Kitchen, New York, 2007; Substance & Surface, Bortolami, New York, 2007; Whitney Biennial, Whitney Mus Am Art, New York, 2008

BREAREY, SUSAN WINFIELD
PAINTER, EDUCATOR, GALLERY DIRECTOR
b Biddeford, ME, Sept 9, 1964. *Study:* Ecole des Beaux Arts, Paris, France, Certificate de lithographie, 87; Evergreen State Coll, BA, 88; RI Sch of Design, MFA, 94. *Work:* Cheekwood Mus of Art (permanent collection), Nashville, TN; Meditech Corp (permanent collection), Westwood, MA; Bank of Boston (permanent collection), Boston, MA; Putney Sch (permanent collection), Putney, VT. *Comn:* Paintings, Works on Paper, Three Creek Ranch, Jackson, WY, 2007; paintings, works on paper, Ryan Garrett Fine Art consulting; several pvt collector comns: Santa Fe, NYC, & Jackson, WY. *Exhib:* Cheekwood National Painting Exhibition, Cheekwood Mus Art, Nashville, TN, 93; The Centennial Open, Parrish Art Mus, Southampton, NY, 98; Post Pastoral, New Images of the New England Landscape, Hood Mus, Dartmouth Coll, Hanover, NH, 99; Out West, the Great American Landscape, Nat Art Mus of China, Beijing, China, 2007-2008; Solo exhibs, Susan Brearey, New Work, Gerald Peters Gallery, Santa Fe, NM, 2005 & 2007, Muse Gallery, Jackson, Wyo, Aug-Sept, 2007, 2009, Forest Silhovettes, 2009-2010; Taylor Piggott Gallery, Jackson, Wy. *Pos:* Gallery coordr, Putney Sch, Michael S Currier Ctr, 2004-; painting prof, RISD, Providence, 2014. *Teaching:* Visual arts faculty, painting/drawing, Putney Sch, Putney, VT, 91-; instr, drawing, Keene Col, Keene, NH, 95-96; vis prof, painting/drawing/sculpture, Pont-Aven Sch Contemp Art, France; Prof, Port Aveu Sch Contemp Art, France, 2009. *Awards:* Art Materials Award, Liquitex Corp, 88; Barnes Fund Award, Putney School, VT; Grad Artist-in-Residence, Univ Leeds, Bretton Hall Coll, 2000. *Bibliog:* Vivian Raynor (auth), The Smoothest of Lineups, Hopper House, NY Times, 95; Megan Smith (auth), Susan Brearey, NY Art New Eng, 98; Gail Kelley (auth), Painter of Wildlife, Boston Globe, 98; Out West, The Great American Landscape, Nat Art Mus China, Beijing; var catalogs & revs, Meridian Int Ctr, Washington, DC. *Mem:* Coll Art Asn (ann mem); World Wildlife Fund; NRDC (Natural Resources Defense Council); Folk New England NE Folk Music Archives (bd mem). *Media:* All Media. *Specialty:* Putney School faculty, alumni, student & visiting artist exhibitions. *Interests:* Gardening, Skiing. *Dealer:* Gerald Peters Gallery 1011 Paseo de Peralta, Santa Fe NM 87501

BRECKENRIDGE, BRUCE M
CERAMIST, EDUCATOR
b Chicago, Ill, Oct 29, 1929. *Study:* Wis State Col-Milwaukee, BS, 52; Cranbrook Acad Art, Bloomfield Hills, Mich, MFA, 53; Acad Grande Chaumier, Paris, 56. *Work:* Elvehjem Art Ctr, Univ Wis-Madison; Wustum Mus, Racine, Wis. *Comn:* Two Ceramic Mural tiles, Apache Corp, Houston, Tex, 94. *Exhib:* Objects as Objects, Mus Contemp Crafts, NY, 68 & Coffee Tea and Other Cups, 71; Nat Ceramics Invitational Exhib, Nelson Gallery Atkins Mus, Kansas City, 69; Nat Ceramics Invitational, Scripps Col, 71; The Plastic Earth, John Michael Kohler Arts Ctr, Sheboygan, Wis, 73. *Collection Arranged:* Richmond Art Ctr, Calif, 59-61; Mus Contemp Crafts, NY, 65-66. *Pos:* Asst dir, Richmond Art Ctr, Calif, 59-61; installation asst, Mus Mod Art, New York, 64-65; asst dir, Mus Contemp Crafts, New York, 65-66. *Teaching:* Instr ceramics, Brooklyn Mus Art Sch, 65-68; prof art-ceramics, Univ Wis-Madison, 68-. *Awards:* Residency, Vcross Found, Wyo. *Mem:* Nat Coun Educ Ceramic Arts. *Media:* Ceramics. *Publ:* Auth, New ceramic forms, 65, Wisconsin designer-craftsman, 69, Don Reitz exhibition, 70 & National invitational exhibition II, glass, 71, Craft Horizons. *Mailing Add:* 1715 Regent St Madison WI 53705-4117

BRECKENRIDGE, ETHAN
SCULPTOR
b Madison, Wis, 1977. *Study:* Sch Visual Arts, New York, BFA, 2002; Columbia Univ, New York, MFA, 2005. *Exhib:* On the Beach, Printed Matter, New York, 2005; Six Laws of Motion, Max Protetch Gallery, New York, 2005; Peace Tower, Whitney Biennial, Whitney Mus Am Art, New York, 2006; EAF Exhib, Socrates Sculpture Park, New York, 2006; Am Acad Arts & Letts Invitational, 2010

BREDER, HANS DIETER
SCULPTOR, VIDEO ARTIST
b Herford, Ger, Oct 20, 1935; US citizen. *Study:* Hochschule fuer Bildende Kunste, Hamburg, Ger, with Willem Grimm, asst to sculptor, George Rickey. *Work:* Cleveland Mus, Ohio; Joseph H Hirshhorn Collection, Washington, DC; Whitney Mus of Am Art, NY; Mus of Art, State Univ NY Col, Purchase; Mus of Art, Iowa City; Am Asn Advan Sci, Washington, DC; Prudential Ins Co NAm, Newark, NJ; Mus Mod Art, NY. *Comn:* Three outdoor sculptures, City of Hanover, Ger, 71. *Exhib:* Mus Contemp Art, Chicago, Ill, 68; Jewish Mus, 69, Exhibit Recent Acquisitions, Mus Mod Art, 84, Whitney Mus Am Art, NY, 87, 89 & 91; one-artist exhibs, Richard Feigen Gallery, Chicago, 67, 70, 72, NY, 67, 70, The Kitchen, Ctr Video & Music, NY, 75, Wolfgang Foerster Galerie, Munster, Ger, 79, 81, 82, 88 & 91, Schreiber/Cutler Inc, NY, 87, 88 & 89, Ruth Siegel Gallery, NY, 90; 2nd Videonale, Bonn, Ger, 86; 3rd Fukui Int Video Biennale, Japan, 89; Painting Beyond the Death of Painting, Kuznetzky Most Exhib Hall, Moscow, 89. *Pos:* Co-dir, Corroboree: Gallery of New Concepts, Univ Iowa, Iowa City, 77-. *Teaching:* Prof multimedia, Univ Iowa, Iowa City, 77-. *Bibliog:* Stephen Foster, Estera Milman (auths), The Media as Medium: Hans Breder's Berlin Work, Kans Quart, Vol 17, No 3, 85; Herman Rapaport (auth), Hans Breder and the Auras of Video, Art Criticism, Vol 4, No 1, 88; Donald Kuspit (auth), New York Reviews, Artforum, 5/89. *Publ:* Coauth, Speculum, Ctr for New Performing Arts, 73; coauth, Participatory Art and Body Sculpture with Mirrors, Leonardo: Art, Sci & Technol, 74. *Mailing Add:* 623 E College St Iowa City IA 52240-5122

BREED, CHARLES AYARS
SCULPTOR, DESIGNER
b Paw Paw, Mich, Jan 31, 1927. *Study:* Western Mich Univ, BS; Univ Wis, MA. *Work:* Midland Ctr Arts, Mich; Dow Chemical, Mich. *Comn:* Eternal Flame (Plexiglas), Temple Beth El, Spring Valley, NY, 66; Icon Screen (polyester), Hellenic Orthodox Church, Bloomfield Hills, Mich, 68; sculpture, Alden D Dow Ctr Arts, Midland, 82; sculpture, steelcase, Grand Rapids, Mich, 92; sculpture, Nat Endowment Arts, Washington, DC, 93; and others. *Exhib:* Craftsman USA 66, Mus Contemp Crafts, NY, 66, Plastic as Plastic Nat Invitational, 68; Made of Plastic Nat Invitational, Flint Inst Art, Mich, 68; Exhib 70, Columbus Art Gallery, Ohio, 70; First Biennial Int Small Sculpture Exhib, Budapest, Hungary, 71. *Pos:* Bd dir, Awareness Inc, Lansing, Mich, 62-64; bd dir, Midland Ctr Arts, 67-72. *Teaching:* Dir art, Nat Music Acad, 58-62; prof art & chmn dept, Delta Col, 62-83. *Awards:* Nat Merit Award, Mus Contemp Crafts, NY, 66; Outstanding Teacher Year, Bergstein Found, 67; Mich Coun Arts Artist Grant, 81; Delta Scholarly Achievement Award, 90; Beautification Award, City Midland, Mich, 92 & 93. *Bibliog:* Jack Brickhouse (auth), Everything is Double in Paw Paw, Paramount Films, 48; Curtis Bessinger (auth), Where does the design of a house begin, House Beautiful, 1/62; Rite of Spring--Detroit (videotape), PM Mag, 81-83. *Media:* Plastic. *Publ:* Auth, Plastic as a new art form, House Beautiful, 2/62; co-auth, Plastic-the visual arts in crafts, Crafts & Craftsmen, 67; auth, Unite equal opposites, Symposium, 80; Conceptual Art, Art in Am, 2/84. *Dealer:* Northwood Galleries 144 E Main Midland MI 48640. *Mailing Add:* Equiline Design 1320 W Main Midland MI 48640-2648

BREEN, HARRY FREDERICK, JR
PAINTER, SCULPTOR
b Chicago, Ill, Mar 4, 1930. *Study:* Art Inst Chicago, with John Rogers Cox & Paul Wiegarht, BA, 53; Univ Ill, Urbana-Champaign, MA, 59. *Work:* Ill State Mus, Springfield; Butler Mus Am Art, Youngstown, Ohio; Krannert Art Mus, Champaign, Ill; Union League Club, Chicago; Lakeview Ctr Arts & Sci, Peoria, Ill. *Comn:* Paintings & sculpture, Bishop's Chapel, St Mary's Cathedral Rectory, Peoria, Ill, 91; stained glass windows & sculpture, St Philomena's Church, Monticello, Ill, 92 & 94; mural, St Joseph's Cathedral, Mo, 95; mural, St Matthew Cath Church, Champaign, Ill, 97; sculpture & painting, High Sch St Thomas More, Champaign, Ill, 2000. *Exhib:* Mid-Yr Ann, Butler Mus Am Art, Youngstown, Ohio, 62-63 & 65; Pa Acad Fine Art (traveling), 63, Europe, 64; Realism Revisited, Flint Art Inst, Mich, 66; 5th Biennial Relig Art, Cranbrook Acad, Detroit, 66; Ill Arts Coun Traveling Exhib, 67; Retrospective, Lakeview Ctr Arts & Sci, Peoria, Ill, 77; Univ Ill Painting Fac, Univ Tokyo & Nat Hist Mus Taipei, 81; Blossoms, The Art of Flowers, Houston Mus Natural Sci, 2007; and others. *Teaching:* Instr art, Pub Schs, Gary, Ind, 54-57 & Univ High Sch, Univ Ill, 57-59; prof art, Sch Art & Design, Univ Ill, Champaign, 59-85; vis prof art, Univ Wis, Madison, 68-69. *Awards:* Second Purchase Prize, Fourth Union League Exhib, Chicago, 61; Fourth Purchase Prize Oils, Mid-Yr Ann, Butler Mus Am Art, 63; Second Prize Sculpture, Ann Exhib, Hoosier Salon, Indianapolis, 63. *Mem:* Nat Soc Arts & Lett (hon mem). *Media:* All; Clay. *Dealer:* Green Street Studio 24 E Green St Champaign IL 61820. *Mailing Add:* 1107 W Church St Champaign IL 61820

BREEN, SUSAN
PAINTER
Study: Boston Coll, BA, 1991; Sch Vis Arts, New York, MFA, 1996. *Exhib:* Solo exhibs include Gallery at Classic Stage Corp, New York, 1999, Woodward Gallery, New York, 2002, 2004; group exhibs include Boston Coll, Chestnut Hill, Mass, 1991; Reggio Gallery, New York, 1996; Paper Invitational III, Woodward Gallery, New York, 2000, Paper Invitational VI, 2003, Winter Paper 7, 2005; 6th Ann Postcards from the Edge, Galerie Lelong, New York, 2003; Huntsville Mus Art, Ala, 2003; Trash Art Event, Black Rock Art Ctr, Bridgeport, Conn, 2003, Four from the Rock, 2004; Community Word Proj Benefit Exhib/Auction, Nat Arts Club, New York, 2004. *Awards:* Marianne Martin Award, 1991; AGNI Phillip Guston Prize, 1999. *Mailing Add:* Woodward Gallery 133 Eldridge St New York NY 10002

BREIGER, ELAINE
PRINTMAKER, PAINTER
b Springfield, Mass. *Study:* Art Students League; Cooper Union. *Work:* Brooklyn Mus, NY; Libr Cong, Washington, DC; Honolulu Acad Art, Hawaii; Chase Manhattan Bank, NY; Mus Prints & Printmaking, Albany, NY. *Comn:* Print, Container Corp Am, 70. *Exhib:* Glaser Gallery, La Jolla, Calif; Contemp Gallery, Dallas; Martha Jackson

Gallery, NY, 74; Pace Gallery, NY, 76; Source Gallery, San Francisco, Calif, 77; Silicon Gallery, Philadelphia, Pa, 99. *Pos:* Mgr, Printmaking Workshop, 68-70; chmn dept art, 92nd St YMCA, 72-76. *Teaching:* Instr techniques etching & intaglio printing, 92nd St YMHA, NY, 71-76; color etching, photogr image, Sch Visual Arts, NY, 77-. *Awards:* Nat Endowment Arts Grant, 75. *Bibliog:* Una Johnson (auth), American Prints & Printmakers, Doubleday, 80. *Mem:* Soc Am Graphic Artists; Boston Printmakers; LAPS. *Media:* Etching; Acrylic, Oil

BREITENBACH, WILLIAM JOHN
SCULPTOR, EDUCATOR
b Milwaukee, Wis, Jan 21, 1936. *Study:* Univ Wis, Milwaukee, BS, 62 & MS, 65; Stephen F Austin State Univ, MFA, 71. *Work:* Brentwood Col, NY; Del Mar Col, Corpus Christi, Tex; Stephen F Austin State Univ, Tex; Houston Baptist Univ, Tex; Sam Houston State Univ, Tex. *Comn:* Sculptural fountain, William Robert Murfin, Houston, 72; plywood wall sculpture, Performing Arts Ctr, Sam Houston State Univ, Huntsville, Tex, 76; Cent Tex Col, Killeen, 83. *Exhib:* Creative Collab, Rice Univ, Houston, 72; 9th Monroe Ann, Masur Mus Art, Monroe, La, 72; Southwest Graphics Invitational, Mex-Am Cult Exchange Inst, San Antonio, Tex, 72; Inst Visual Arts, Puebla, Mex, 81; Cult Activities Ctr, Temple, Tex, 84; and others. *Pos:* Chmn, Houston Area Art Curric Develop Comt, 82-86. *Teaching:* Supvr elem art, South Door Co Sch Dist 1, Brussels, Wis, 62-65; full prof art educ, design & drawing, Sam Houston State Univ, 65-. *Awards:* First Prize in sculpture, 5th Ann Exhib, Del Mar Col, 71; Merit Award for creative collab, Rice Univ, 71; Third Place Award, Assistance League Houston, 73. *Mem:* Tex Art Educ Asn; Nat Art Educ Asn. *Media:* Paper Mache, Fabricated Plywood; Ark. *Publ:* Auth, Art education and the modern age, Tex Trends in Art Educ, 68. *Dealer:* Umbrella Arts 2615 Old Houston Rd Huntsville TX 77340. *Mailing Add:* Sam Houston State University Art Dept PO Box 2089 Huntsville TX 77341

BREJCHA, VERNON LEE
GLASS BLOWER, PHOTOGRAPHER
b Ellsworth, Kans, Jan 30, 1942. *Study:* Ft Hays State Univ, BA & MS; Univ Wis-Madison, MFA with Harvey K Littleton. *Hon Degrees:* prof emeritus. *Work:* Corning Mus of Glass, NY; Mus of Contemp Crafts, NY; Kunstmuseum, Dusseldorf, Ger; Los Angeles Co Mus Art; Smithsonian Inst, Washington, DC. *Comn:* Chandelier Overland Park, Convention Ctr, Overland Park, Kans, Picken Hall, FHKSU Hays, Kans; Field Flow Wall Projects, KU Medical Ctr; Prairie Bounty De Bruce Grain Co, Kansas City, Mo; Sculpture, H & R Block World Center, Kansas City, Mo. *Exhib:* Great Am Gallery, Atlanta, Ga, 86; Two-person exhib, Glass Gallery, Bethesda, Md, 87; Solo exhibs, Marx Gallery, Chicago, Ill, 90, Hall Fame, Bonner Springs, Kans, 91, Vetro Marmo Arte, Columbus, Ohio, 95, Michael Kelly Gallery, San Antonio, 96, Wichita Ctr Arts, Kans, 97 & Soc Fine Arts, Chicago, 98, KL Fine Arts, Chicago, 99; Vessel Transformed, Pensacola Mus Art, Fla, 93; Graceland Col, Lamoni, Iowa, 93; Goblet Show, Porta Gallery, Chicago, 96; Glass Now 2002, Nat'l Liberty Mus, Philadelphia; Solo exhib, Leopold Gallery, Kansas City, MO, 2004; Retrospective, Ft Hays State Univ, 2009; Ruben Saunders Gallery, Wichita, Kans, 2012; One Man Birger Sandzen Mem Gallery, Lindsborg, Kans, 2013; Brejcha-Six Decade Retrospective Phoenix Gallery, Lawrence Creates, and Art Emergency, Lawrence, Kans, 2014. *Pos:* Prof Emer, 2003. *Teaching:* Asst prof glass, ceramics & sculpture, Tusculum Col, Greenville, Tenn, 72-76; asst prof design glass, Univ Kans, 77-81, assoc prof, 81-2002. *Awards:* First Place Purchase, Ceramics Northwest, CM Russell Mus, Great Falls, Mont, 70; Purchase Award, Tenn Bicentennial Art Exhib, State of Tenn, 76; Artist Fel, Nat Endowment Arts, 84; Kans Governor's Artist, 85. *Bibliog:* Polly Rothenberg (auth), The Complete Book of Creative Glass Art, Crown, 74; Elizabeth Campbell (auth), Kansas-Theme of glass artist Vernon Brejcha, Neues Glas, Dusseldorf, 82; Phyllis George (auth), Craft in America, Summit Group, 93; Dale & Diane Barta, Czech Glass & Collectables Book II, Collector Books, 97; Paul Dorrell (auth) Living the Artists Life, Hilstead Pub, 2004, 2012. *Mem:* Am Crafts Coun; Nat Coun on Educ for the Ceramic Arts (glass panel chmn, 77); Glass Art Soc; Kans Artist-Craftsmen Asn. *Media:* blown glass. *Interests:* Photography, Figure Studies, Life Drawing; Nature photography. *Publ:* Auth, Throw the Lid First, Ceramics Monthly, 70; contribr, The Complete Book of Creative Glass Art, Crown, 74; Crafts & Craftsmen of the Tennessee Mountains, Summit Press; auth, British hot glass, Glass Studio, 82; Craft in America, Summit Group, 93. *Dealer:* The Bender Gallery 57 Haywood St Asheville NC 28801; Saunders Gallery 230 W Superior St Chicago Il 60610; ArtWorks 7724 E Central Wichita KS 67206. *Mailing Add:* 1111 E 1500 Rd Lawrence KS 66046

BREMER, MARLENE
PAINTER, SCULPTOR
b Coburg, Ger; US Citizen. *Study:* Fairleigh Dickinson Univ, NJ, BA, 79; William Paterson Univ, NJ, MA, 81; New York Univ, NY, cert (fine art appraisal), 89. *Work:* Pvt collections USA & Europe; Spritzwerke Herman Koch, Creidlitz, Ger; Treppen Zentrum Schaarschmidt GMBH, Hamburg, Ger; Bimar Int Asn, Allendale, NJ; Lotz Medizin Technik GMBH, Munich, Ger; Namtar House of Carpets, Paramus, NJ; Union Camp Headquarters, NJ; Dr RH Aveson, Wayne, NJ; Lotz Medizintechnik, Munich, Ger; Karl Brandt KG, Coburg, Ger. *Exhib:* Munic Gallery, Athens, Greece, 96; Catharine Lorillard Wolfe Art Club 106th Ann, New York, 2002 & 2008; The Art of Collecting, Morris Mus, Morristown, NJ, 2002 & 2003; Haworth Munic Libr, NJ, 2004; Cynon Valley Mus, Aberdare, Wales, UK, 2004; Bergen Pac, Englewood, NJ, 2005; Maurice M Pine Pub Libr, Fairlawn, NJ, 2005; Gallery Merz, Sag Harbor, NY, 2005; Synagogue for the Arts, NY, 2006; Goggle Work Ctr Arts, Reading, Pa, 2006; Karpeles Libr Mus, Newburgh, NY, 2006; Port of Calls, Warwick, NY, 2006; Belski Mus, Closter, NJ, 2007; Adelphi Univ, Garden City, NY, 2007; Blue Hill Art & Cult Ctr, Pearl River, NY, 2007; NAWA: 119th Annual Exhibition, GoggleWorks, Reading, PA, 2008; Int Soc Experimental Artists Watercolor Art Society, Houston, Tex, 2008; Penn State Univ, Pa, 2009; 121st Ann Exhib, Nat Arts Club, NAWA, New York, 2010; Sylvia Wald And Po Kim Art Gallery, NY, 2011-2013; Midday Gallery Englewood, NJ, 2012; Northshore Arts Asn, Gloucester, Mass, 2012; BergenPac, Englewood, NJ, 2012; Art 9 Connection, George Segal Gallery, Montclair State Univ, 2013; The Gallery of the High Mountain Presbyterian Church, Franklin Lakes, NJ, 2013. *Pos:* Appraiser fine art, currently. *Teaching:* Instr sculpture, Ridgewood Community Sch, NJ, 84-85; adj prof art hist, Bergen Community Coll, NJ, 85-88. *Awards:* Salute Award, Jacob Javits Bldg, NY, 88; Award Excellence, Old Church Cult Ctr, Demarest, NJ, 93; Beatrice G Epstein Mem, Nat Asn Women Artists, NY, 96; Award Excellence, Manhattan Arts Int, NY, 2000; Hazel Witte Mem Award, NAWA 111th Ann Exhib, NY, 2000; Award, NY/Paris Competition, Inst Visual, Paris, France; Celebration of Women in the Arts, Women's Rights Information Center, NJ, 2002; Elizabeth Howard Memorial Award, NAWA, NY, 2009; S Magnet Knapp Memorial award, NAWA, NY, 2011. *Bibliog:* Justin Lim (auth), Korean-Am Times, NJ, 93; Eileen Watkins (auth), Star Ledger, NJ, 95; Renee Phillips (auth), Manhattan Arts Int, NY, 96; 111th Exhib Catalog, NAWA: Atelier 14, New York, 2000; plus others. *Mem:* Nat Asn Women Artists, (asst hist, New York Chap, bd mem jury, exhibs comt); Artists Equity Asn; Salute to Women in the Arts, NJ; Painting Affiliate Art Ctr, NJ; City Without Walls, Newark, NJ; JSEA, Int Soc Experimental Artists, Chicago. *Media:* Mixed Media, Acrylic, Painting, Assemblages. *Interests:* Music, Theater, Nature. *Mailing Add:* 440 Egan Pl Englewood NJ 07631

BREN, DONALD L
COLLECTOR
b 1932. *Study:* Univ Wash, BA & MBA. *Collection:* Contemporary American art. *Mailing Add:* The Irvine Co 550 Newport Center Dr Newport Beach CA 92660

BRENDEL, BETTINA
PAINTER, LECTURER
b Luneburg, Ger; US citizen. *Study:* Hamburg, Ger, BA, 40; Kunstschule Schmilinsky, Hamburg, 41-42; Landes Hochschule Bildende Kuenste, Hamburg, 45-47, with Erich Hartmann; Univ Southern Calif, 55-58; New Sch Social Res, 68-69. *Work:* San Francisco Mus Art; Long Beach Mus Art; Mus fuer Konkrete Kunst, Ingolstadt, Ger; Max-Planck-Inst, Munich, Ger; Grunwald Graphic Art Collection; Los Angeles Co Mus Art; Hammer Mus, Los Angeles, Calif; pvt collection, Travis Spitzer; and others. *Comn:* Painting, Auditorium Werner-Heisenberg Inst, Munich, Ger. *Exhib:* Los Angeles Co Mus Ann, 55, 57, 59 & 61; Ester Robles Gallery, 56-63; 58th Ann, San Francisco Mus Art, 66; On Mass and Energy, Santa Barbara Mus Art, 66; Women Artists, Santa Monica Coll Art Gallery, Calif, 77; Los Angeles Artcore Gallery, 84; A Digital View, Art Store Gallery, Pasadena, 90; Digitals & Modules, Glendale, Calif, 90; Crossroads Sch, Santa Monica, Calif; solo exhibs, Gallery 16-34, Santa Monica, Calif, 91, Particles & Waves, Bettina Brendel 1957-97, Long Beach Mus Art, 98 & Symmetry & Sequences, David Lawrence Gallery, Beverly Hills, Calif, 2000; retrospective (with catalog), Long Beach Mus Art, 98; Downey Mus Art, Calif; computer art exhib, Gallery Wosimsky, Giessen, Ger, 2003, 2005. *Pos:* Computer artist, Calif Mus Sci & Indust, Los Angeles, 88-92. *Teaching:* Instr, The Emergence of Mod Painting, Univ Calif, Los Angeles, 58-61, lectr art, Exten, spring 76; lectr, Thematic Option Prog, Univ Southern Calif, 80; lectr, symp Arte c Technologia, Gulbenkian Found, Paris, 85, Lisbon, Portugal, 87, Max Planck Inst Physics, Munich, Ger, 91, Loughborough Univ Technol, Eng, 96. *Awards:* Long Beach Mus Art, 60, 61; First Purchase Award, San Francisco Mus Art, 66; 2nd Prize, Palm Springs Art Mus, Calif, 99. *Bibliog:* Dr John Marburger (auth), Bettina Brendel, Paintings 70-82, 84; Peter Frank (auth), Bettina Brendel, 1907; Bethany Price (auth), article, Long Beach Bus J, 3/98; William Wilson (auth), article, Los Angeles Times, 4/98; and others. *Mem:* Friends Graphic Arts, Univ Calif, Los Angeles; Univ Calif Los Angeles Art Coun; Am Physical Soc; Archives Am Art; Los Angeles Printmaking Soc; YLEM, Artists using Science & Technology, San Francisco. *Media:* Acrylic, Collage; Computer Art. *Res:* Theoretical physics and its relation to the arts. *Interests:* Classical music, modern dance, poetry. *Publ:* Auth, The painter and the new physics, Art J, fall 71; The influence of atomic physics, Leonardo Mag, 73; Whenever in the World (poems), Stockton Press, 77; Atomic Patterns, YLEM Newsletter, Oakland Calif, 97, Symmetry. Art as Metaphor, 2000; Springer (auth), Experiments in Art and Technology, 2002. *Dealer:* David Lawrence Gallery 9507 Santa Monica Blvd Beverly Hills CA 90210; Gallery Wosimsky Germany

BRENNER, BIRGIT
INSTALLATION SCULPTOR
b Ulm, Württemberg, Germany, 1964. *Study:* Studies Graphic Design, Darmstadt, Germany, 1985-90; Hochschule der Künste (at Rebecca Horn), Berlin, 1990-95, Master of Arts, 1996. *Exhib:* Solo exhibs include Art-Acker, Berlin, 1991; Galerie EIGEN + ART, Berlin, 1996, 1999, 2001, 2003, 2007, Verein für Junge Kunst, Wolfsburg, Germany, 2006, Galerie EIGEN + ART, London, 2007, About Change Collection, Berlin, 2008; group exhibs include 37 Räume, Kunstwerke eV, Berlin, 1992; Kunstverein an der Finkenstrasse, München, Germany, 1997; Now more than ever, Citylights, Melbourne, Australia, 2002; Red Riviera Revisited, Red House Ctr Cult & Debate, Sofia, Bulgaria; Into Me Out of Me, PS1 Contemp Art Ctr, New York, 2007; True Romance, Kunsthalle Wien, Austria, 2007; Sommer bei EIGEN + ART, Galerie EIGEN + ART, Berlin, 2008. *Teaching:* Prof Photog/Drawing/New Media, Staatliche Akad Bildenden Künste, Stuttgart, Germany, 2007. *Mailing Add:* Galerie EIGEN + ART Auguststrasse 26 Berlin 10117 Germany

BRESCHI, KAREN LEE
SCULPTOR
b Oakland, Calif, Oct 29, 1941. *Study:* Calif Coll Arts & Crafts, BFA, 63; Sacramento State Univ, 60-61; San Francisco State Univ, MA, 65; San Francisco Art Inst, 68-71; Calif Inst Integral Studies, San Francisco, PhD, 87. *Work:* Oakland Mus, Calif; Crocker Art Gallery, Sacramento; San Francisco Mus Art; Univ Art Mus (Berkeley); St Mary's Coll Art Gallery (Moraga); Univ Ariz Art Mus. *Exhib:* Fac Show Sculpture, 73 & Ceramic Sculpture, 74, San Francisco Art Inst; Solo exhibs, Braunstein/Quay Gallery, 73, 75, 78, 81 & 84; Clay, Whitney Mus, NY, 74; Exchange DFW/SFO, San Francisco Mus Art, 76; Illusionistic-Realism Defined in Contemp Ceramic Sculpture, Laguna Beach Mus, Calif, 77; The Great Am Foot, Mus Contemp Crafts, NY, 78;

West Coast Sculptors, 78 & A Century of Clay, 79, Everson Mus; Clayworks, Univ Santa Barbara Mus, 79; A Century of Ceramics in the US 1878-1978, Renwick Gallery, Smithsonian Inst, 79-80; solo show, Braunstein/Quay Gallery, 81; and many others. *Teaching:* Instr sculpture, San Francisco Art Inst, 71-77; instr sculpture, San Francisco State Univ, 74-79; instr, Univ Calif, Davis, 80-81. *Awards:* First Place for Painted Flower, Oakland Art Mus, 62; Women's Archit League Award, Crocker Art Mus, 63; Award, Calif State Fair, 63. *Mem:* West/East Bag. *Media:* Clay, Mixed. *Mailing Add:* 4042 22nd St San Francisco CA 94114

BRESLAW, CATHY L
PAINTER, EDUCATOR
b Coral Gables, Fla, Nov 7, 1957. *Study:* George Washington Univ, BA, 79; Howard Univ, Washington, DC, MSW, 81; Claremont Grad Univ Fel, 04; Sue Arlene Walker Mem Fel, 05; Claremont Grad Univ, MFA, 06. *Work:* Maxwell Technologies, San Diego, Calif; Frontier Analytics, La Jolla, Calif; Che Bella, Phoenix Ariz; Ariz Fast Foods, Phoenix, Ariz; Saigon & Assocs, Los Altos, Calif; American Graphics, Inc, Amerigraph LLC, San Diego, Calif; GEA Power Cooling Systems, San Diego, Calif; ADC Telecommunications, Minneapolis; Residential Wholesale Mortgage Inc, San Diego, Calif. *Comn:* Series of 8 paintings, comn by Randall Moore, San Diego, 98. *Exhib:* Nat Watercolor Soc Travel Tour, Wichita Falls Mus & Art Ctr, Tex & Bade Mus, Berkeley, Calif, 97; Ann Nat Exhib (with catalog), Brea Civic & Cult Ctr Gallery, Los Angeles, 97; Nat Watercolor Soc, Downey Mus Art, Calif, 97; Soc Layerists Multimedia, Bradford Col, Haverhill, Mass, 98; Nat Oil & Acrylic Soc, Columbia Col, Osage Beach, Mo, 98; Art in Flux, San Diego, Calif, 2000; Abstractions, Balboa Park, San Diego, Calif, 2000; Riverside Art Mus, Huntington Beach Art Ctr, Ruth Bachofner Gallery, Coleman Gallery Contemporary Art, Grand Central Art Ctr; Solo exhibs, West Valley Art Mus, Chico Art Ctr, Charleston Heights Art Ctr, Earleville Art Ctr, Southern Ore Univ, Fitton Ctr for Arts, Univ St Mary, Riverviews Art Space, Waterworks Art Ctr. *Teaching:* Instr painting & drawing, N Co Jr Community Col, 92-97; mixed media, Quail Gardens, Encinitas, 96-97; workshops in creativity, San Diego Watercolor Soc, 98-. *Awards:* Gold Medallion, Calif Watercolor Soc 29th Int Ann Open Exhib, Grumbacher, 97; Soc Experimental Artists Int Exhib Merit Award, Sarasota Art Ctr, 97. *Bibliog:* New American Paintings, 03 & 15th Anniv ed, 09. *Mem:* Sig mem Nat Watercolor Soc; Int Soc Multimedia Layerists; Int Soc Experimental Painters. *Media:* Acrylic, Mixed Media. *Interests:* Travel, Skiing, Golf, Reading

BRESLIN, NANCY
PHOTOGRAPHER
b Orange, NJ, Aug 18, 1957. *Study:* Rutgers Univ, BA, 79; Univ Pittsburgh, MD, 83; Univ De, MFA, 00. *Exhib:* Int show, NJ Ctr for Visual Arts, Summit, 2001-02 & 2004-05; Mem Exhib, De Ctr for Contemp Arts, Wilmington, 2001-02, 2004, 2010, & 2014; Life and Death in Paris, Mezzanine Gallery, Wilmington, 2002; Biggs Mus Am Art, Dover, Del, 2003, 2009, 2011; A Pinhole Diary of Eating Out, Arlington Arts Ctr, Va, 2005; A Pinhole Diary of Eating Out, Saint Joseph's Univ, Philadelphia, 2006; Old Media: New Visions, Delaware Center Contemp Arts, Wilmington, 2006; Del Women's Conf Fine Art Exhib, Del Art Mus, 2007, 2009; Wonder and Fear: Pinhole Photographs, Mezzanine Gallery, Wilmington, 2008; Intervals, Visual Arts Ctr, San Antonio Coll, 2008; Pinhole Diary, Colourworks, Wilmington, 2010; Photo Month 2011, Packard Reath Gallery, Lewes, Del, 2011; Fragile Boundaries, Del Ctr Contemporary Arts, Wilmington, Del, 2012; Viridian Artists, NY, 2012; Nancy Breslin: Pinhole Projects, Delapaine Visual Arts Edn Ctr, Frederick Md, 2013; NWAA and Winterthur: A Collaboration, Chris White Gallery, Wilmington, De, 2013; Biggs Picture, Biggs Mus Am Art, Dover, Del, 2014. *Collection Arranged:* Arresting Images, Luther Brady Art Gallery, Washington, DC, 2003; (with Peter Caws) Del Women's Conf Fine Arts Exhib, Newark, 2005. *Pos:* vis artist, Winterthur Mus, Del, 2012. *Teaching:* Adj instr photog, Univ Del, Newark, 2001-2013; adj instr photog, Corocoran Coll Art & Design, 2014. *Awards:* Artist Fel, De Div of Arts, 2003 & 2008. *Bibliog:* Atlas Janel (auth), Nancy Breslin: Life Through a Pinhole, Delmarva Quart, summer 2007; Artist Profile, Tusculum Rev, Vol 5, p 103-106, 2009; Steve Hoffman (auth), Pinholic Photographer Finds a Way to Savor the Moments, Newark Life Mag, 2009. *Mem:* Soc for Photog Educ, sec mid-Atlantic board, 2002-2006; De Ctr for Contemp Arts; Newark Arts Alliance (gallery comt, bd dirs, 2007). *Media:* Pinhole Photography, Video. *Publ:* Auth, Deborah Turbeville, The Encyclopedia of Twentieth Century Photography, Lynne Warren (ed), Routledge, 2006; Light Leaks, Issue 15, p. 46-49, 2009; Square Mag Pinhole Issue (p 76-87), 2011. *Mailing Add:* 2475 Virginia Ave NW Apt 230 Washington DC 20037

BRESLIN, WYNN (WINIFRED)
PAINTER, SCULPTOR
b Hackensack, NJ, 1932. *Study:* Syracuse Univ, 50; Ohio Wesleyan Univ, BFA, 54; Univ Del, MFA, 60. *Work:* 3 oil paintings, Del Division of Libr; Univ DE; Syracuse Univ; Wesleyan Univ. *Comn:* Sculpture, Immanuel Episcopal Church, Wilmington, Del, 62; painting, First Federal Bank, Newark, Del, 79. *Exhib:* Del Art Mus Regional Shows, 56-75; Benedictine Art Awards, Am Fedn Arts, 67; Woodmere Art Gallery, Philadelphia, 73-75; Philadelphia Art Alliance, 74; Catharine Lorillard Wolfe Art Club, Nat Arts Club, 74; Four State Regional show, Univ Del, 88; Chester Co Art Asn, 2002-2003; Boothbay Region Art Found, 2011-2012; Newark Arts Alliance, 2011, 2013. *Pos:* Owner studio, Del & Maine, Wynn Breslin Studio Gallery, 1976-2013. *Teaching:* Art instr, Del Pub Schs, 54-63, Del Art Mus, 56-76 & Tatnall Sch, 64; instr adult pvt classes, 63-90; artist-in-educ series, 81-94. *Awards:* First Prize Watercolor, Nat Orgn Women Art Exhib, Wilmington, 73; Ethel M Schnader Art Prize, Woodmere Art Gallery, Philadelphia, 74; 1st Prize Watercolor, 77, 1st Prize Oil, Chester Co Art Asn, 85; First Prize Acrylic Painting, Univ Del, 88. *Bibliog:* From an artistic viewpoint, Univ News, Univ Del, 67; News-Journal, Wilmington, Del, 2013; Crossroads (cover & 2 page spread), 6/2013. *Mem:* Nat League Am Pen Women (treas, Diamond State Br, 72-74); Wilmington Soc Fine Arts; Del Ctr Contemp Art; Chester Co Art Asn; The Boothbay Region Art Found; Newark Arts Alliance, 2008-2013. *Media:* Oil, Watercolor. *Specialty:* painting, watercolors, oils, acrylics, sculpture. *Interests:* On-site travel painting, seacapes, florals, landscapes. *Publ:* Delaware Women Remembered. *Mailing Add:* 470 Terrapin Lane Newark DE 19711-2118

BRESS, BRIAN
COLLAGE ARTIST
b Norfolk, Va, 1975. *Study:* RI Sch Design, BFA, (Film/Animation/Video), 1998; Univ Calif Los Angeles, MFA (Painting & Drawing), MFA, 2006; Skowhegan Sch Painting & Drawing, Maine, 2007. *Exhib:* Solo exhibs include Open-End Gallery, Chicago, 2003, RC Art Gallery, Univ Mich, 2006, Angstrom Gallery, Los Angeles, 2007, Zach Feuer Gallery, New York, 2007; Group exhibs include Fel Invitational, Hudson D Walker Gallery, Fine Arts Work Ctr, Provincetown, Mass, 2001; Anti-Spacesuit: The Dirty Future, G1 Gallery, Chicago, 2003; Exhibition #9 - Some Romantic Landscape, Champion Fine Arts, Los Angeles, 2005; Character Traits, New Collaborative Works, I-5 Gallery, Los Angeles, 2005; The Latest Fiction, Cirrus Gallery, Los Angeles, 2006, Naïve Set Theory, 2006; Rough Trade, Michael Kohn Gallery, Los Angeles, 2006; Just My Funny Way of Laughing, S La Brea Gallery, Los Angeles, 2006; Supersonic 2006, LA Municipal Art Gallery, Los Angeles, 2006; Chain Letter, High Energy Constructs, Los Angeles, 2006; Beyond Image, Armory Ctr Arts, Pasadena, Calif, 2007; Big Secret Cache, Angstrom Gallery, Los Angeles, 2007; Machine Imaginaire, Lisa Boyle Gallery, Chicago, 2007; Against The Grain, Los Angeles Contemp Exhibs, Los Angeles, 2008. *Dealer:* Kantor/Feuer Gallery 7025 Melrose Ave Los Angeles CA 90038

BREST VAN KEMPEN, CATEL PIETER
PAINTER
b Murray, UT, May 2, 1958. *Work:* Leigh Yawkey Woodson Art Mus, Wausau, Wis; Bennington Ctr for the Arts, Bennington, Va; Springville Mus Art, Springville, Utah; World Ctr for Birds of Prey, Boise, Ind; Arizona-Sonora Desert Mus, Tucson, Ariz. *Exhib:* Christie's Wildlife Art Auction, Brit Mus, London, UK, 1995, 1998; Birds in Art, Leigh Yawkey Woodson Art Mus, Wausau, Wis, 1996, 2001, 2002, 2005; Art of the Living World, Bonham's, Singapore, 1997; Taipei Eco Art Exhib, Nat Mus Hist, Taipei, Taiwan, 1999; solo exhibs, Wildlife Experience Mus, Denver, Colo, 2003; Rose Wagner Art Ctr, Salt Lake City, Utah, 2005; Wilding Art Mus, Los Olivos, Calif, 2006; Western Visions, Nat Mus Wildlife Art, Jackson, Wyo, 2004-2006. *Awards:* Wildlife Medallion, Arts for the Parks, Nat Park Acad Arts, 1992; Award of Excellence, Art & the Animal, Soc Animal Artists, 1994, 1996, 1997, 2004; Most Honored Artist, 150 Yrs of Utah Art, Springfield Mus Art, 2002. *Bibliog:* Scott Bestul (auth), Natures Diversity, Inform Art, fall 1997; Janet Rae Brooks (auth), A Natural Obsession, Wildlife J, spring 2001; Darryl Whey (auth), Science, Art & Science Art, Birding, 2004. *Mem:* Soc Animal Artists. *Media:* Acrylic, Oil, Watercolor. *Publ:* Contribr, Natural Habitat, Spanierman Gallery, 1998; Illusr, Dinosaurs of Utah, Univ Utah, 1998; Contribr, Wildlife Art: 60 Comtemp Masters, Portfolio Press, 2001; Illusr, Biology of the Gila Monsters & Beaded Lizards, Univ Calif Press, 2005; Auth, Rigor Vitae: Life Unyielding, Eagle Mountain Publ, 2006. *Dealer:* Mill Pond Press 310 Center Ct Venice, FL. *Mailing Add:* PO Box 17647 Salt Lake City UT 84117-0647

BRETT, NANCY
ARTIST
b Jackson, Mich. *Study:* Univ Michigan, Independent Study, 1967-68; Wayne State Univ, BFA, 1969; Cranbrook Acad Art, MFA, 1972. *Work:* Cranbrook Acad Art Mus, Bloomfield Hills, Mich; Herbert Johnson Mus Art, Cornell Univ, Ithaca, NY; Kidder Peabody, NY; Prudential, IBM, JP Morgan, Chemical Bank, NY; Library of Congress, Washington, DC. *Exhib:* Solo exhibs, Painting Ctr, NY, 1997, (auth, catalog) Cranbrook Acad Art Mus, Bloomfield Hills, Mich, 1998, (auth, catalog) Hyde Collection Art Mus, Glens Falls, NY, 1999, Lesley Heller Gallery, NY, 2006 & 2008; group exhibs, Kindred Spirits, Hillwood Art Mus, CW Post, Long Island Univ, NY, 1986; Distant Vision: Contemp Landscape, Janice Charach Epstein Mus, West Bloomfield, Mich, 1992; K&E Gallery, NY, 1994; OIA Show, Police Bldg, 1994; Pleasant Pebble, Workspace, NY, 1995; Gas Works Gallery, London, Eng, 1997; Cornerhouse Gallery, Manchester, Eng, 1997; Weatherspoon Art Gallery, Univ NC, Greensboro, 1997; HAIR DO, Work Space, New York, NY, 1997; Drawing in Present Tense, (auth, catalog) Parsons Sch Design, NY, 1999; Williamsburg Art & Historical Ctr, Brooklyn, NY, 2000; Exit Art, Air Gallery, NY, 2002; Courthouse Gallery, Lk George Arts Project, 2002; IT Space, New York, NY, Art During Wartime, 2003; Ind State Univ, Terre Haute, Contemp Women Artists, 2005; Sweet Tragedy, Planaria Gallery, NY, 2005; The Winter Salon, Lesley Heller Gallery, NY, 2006; Hot House, Cranbrook Acad Art Mus, Mich, 2007; Ann Invitational Exhib Contemp Art, Nat Acad Mus, NY, 2008. *Teaching:* Vis artist, Sarah Lawrence Col, Bronxville, NY, 1989, 1993 & 2000-01, Skidmore Col, Saratoga Springs, NY, 1993 & 1997, Bennington Col, Vt, 1993, State Univ NY, Purchase, 1995, Yale Univ, 1995, State Univ, NY, Albany, 1999 & Columbia Coll, Chicago, 2001; guest lectr, RI Sch Design, Providence, 1993 & Sch Visual Arts, New York, 1994 & 1997; adj Prof, BFA Prog, Parsons Sch Design, NY, 1995-2002, MFA Prog, 1998-2002; pvt study, master classes & individual tutoring, 2002-. *Awards:* Yaddo Art Fel & Residency, 1983-88; Nat Endowment Arts, Visual Arts Fel, 1991-92; Pollock-Krasner Found Grant 2003-04; Edwin Palmer Mem Prize, Nat Acad Design, 2008. *Bibliog:* Judy Collischan (auth), Something Other, catalog, 1982; Helen Harrison (auth), Something beyond seeing, NY Times, 3/6/83; Judy Collischan (auth), Kindred Spirits, catalog essay, 1986; Judy Collischan (auth), Nancy Brett, ARTS Mag, 1991; Joy Hakanson Colby (auth), Artist paints a harsh view of the precarious world of childhood, Detroit News, 7/30/98; Keri Guten Cohen (auth), Painter casts an edgy eye on childhood, Detroit Free Press, 7/21/98; Debra Bricker Balkan (auth), Drawing in the Present Tense, 1999. *Mem:* Artists Space; Coll Art Asn. *Media:* Oil. *Publ:* Kathleen Monaghan (auth), A Loaded Brush, Hope Coll, Mus Art, Glens Falls, NY. *Mailing Add:* 457 Broome St New York NY 10013

BRETTELL, RICHARD ROBSON
EDUCATOR, CONSULTANT
b Rochester, NY, Jan 17, 1949. *Study:* Yale Univ, BA, MA, PhD, 76. *Collection Arranged:* Four Directions in Modern Photography (auth, catalog), Yale Art Gallery, 73; The Drawings of Camille Pissarro (coauth, catalog), Ashmolean Mus, Oxford, England, 79; Camille Pissarro, Mus Fine Arts, Boston, 80-81; Paper and Light: The Calotype in France & Great Britain (coauth, catalog), Mus Fine Arts, Houston, 82-83; The Golden Age of Naples: Art & Civilization Under the Bourbons, 82, Mauristshuis: Dutch Painting of the Golden Age, 83-84, Degas in the Art Institute of Chicago (with Suzanne Folds, McCullagh, coauth catalog) 84 & The Art of the Edge: European Frames 1300-1900(coauth catalog), 86, Art Inst Chicago; Permanent Galleries, European Painting & Sculpture 1300-1900 (installation designer), Art Inst Chicago, 87-; The Art of Paul Gauguin, Nat Gallery Art, Washington, DC, Art Inst Chicago & Mus d'Orsay, Paris, 88-89; The Impressionist & the City, 91-92; Impression: Painting Quickly in France 1860-1890, Nat Gallery Art, London, Van Gogh Mus, Amsterdam, The Netherlands, Clark Inst, Williamstown, 2000-01; Pissarros's People, Clark Art Inst, San Fran Mus Art, 2011-2012. *Pos:* Cur, European Painting & Sculpture, Art Inst Chicago, 80-88; dir, Dallas Mus Art, Tex, 88-92; independent art historian & consult, 92-. *Teaching:* Asst prof hist art, Univ Tex, Austin, 75-80; vis prof, Yale Univ, 93 Harvard Univ, 95; prof, aesthetic studies Univ Tex Dallas, 98-. *Awards:* Chevalier, Commander, Order of Arts & Letters, France. *Mem:* Coll Art Asn; Soc Archit Hist. *Res:* French drawing, printmaking & painting, 1800-1914; American architecture of the 19th century; landscape painting; history of photography 1839-1900. *Publ:* Coauth, The Drawings of Camille Pissarro in the Ashmolean Mus (with Christopher Lloyd), Oxford Univ Press, 80; Painters & Peasants, Skira, 83; auth, An Impressionist Legacy: The Collection of Sara Lee Corporation, Abbeville Press, 86; French Paintings of the 19th Century: The Art Institute of Chicago, 3 vols, Abrams, New York/Art Inst Chicago, Ill, 87; and many other books, catalogs and articles. *Mailing Add:* 5522 Montrose Dr Dallas TX 75209-5610

BREUER, BRADFORD R
PATRON, MUSEUM DIRECTOR
Study: Austin Col. *Pos:* Dir, The Alamo, San Antonio, formerly; pres, San Antonio Mus Asn, formerly; mem adv bd, Ctr for Southwestern & Mexican Studies Austin Col; bd trustees, Amon Carter Mus, Ft Worth

BREUNING, OLAF
PHOTOGRAPHER, SCULPTOR
b Schaffhausen, Switzerland, 1970. *Study:* Zurich, Switzerland, prof photog educ, 1993, post grad photog studies. *Work:* Whitney Mus Am Art, New York; Saatchi Gallery. *Exhib:* Solo exhibs include Metro Pictures gallery, New York, 2001, 2004, 2005, 2006, Air de Paris, Paris, France, 2000, 2001, 2005, Galerie Meyer & Kainer, Vienna, Austria, 2001, 2005, Nils Staerk Contemp Art, Copenhagen, Denmark, 2004, 2006, Kodama Gallery, Osaka, Japan, 2004, 2005, 2007, Nicola von Senger Gallery, Zurich, Switzerland, 2005, 2006, 2007, Sketch, Home, London, UK, 2006, Migros Mus, Zurich, Switzerland, 2007; Group exhibs include Au-delà du spectacle, Ctr Georges Pompidou, Paris, France, 2000, bdv (Video), 2001; Swiss Mix, Mus Ctr de Arte Reina Sofia, Madrid, Spain, 2003; Playback, Mus d'Art Mod, Paris, France, 2007; Le Spectrarium (les fantÓmes de la machine), Fondation Suisse, Sité Univ, Paris, France, 2008 ; After Effects, the art of production & post production, Mus de Arte Contemp, Santiago, Chile, 2008. *Dealer:* Air De Paris 32 rue Louise Weiss Paris France 75013; Art & Public 37 rue des Bains Geneva Switzerland 1205; Greider Contemporary Lärchentobelstrasse 25 Küsnacht Bei Zürich Switzerland 8700; Meridian Gallery/Rita Krauss Fine Art 41 E 57th St 8th Floor New York NY 10022; Metro Pictures 519 W 24th Street New York NY 10011; Carolina Nitsch Project Room 534 W 22nd St New York NY 10011; Parkett Editions 145 Avenue of the Americas New York NY 10013; Galerie Nicola von Senger Limmatstr 275 Zurich Switzerland 8005

BREVERMAN, HARVEY
PAINTER, PRINTMAKER
b Pittsburgh, Pa, Jan 7, 1934. *Study:* Carnegie-Mellon Univ, BFA; Ohio Univ, MFA. *Work:* Whitney Mus Am Art, New York; Albright-Knox Art Gallery, Buffalo; Baltimore Mus, Md; Jewish Mus, New York; Mus Mod Art, New York; Nat Portrait Gallery, Washington, DC; British Mus, London, Eng. *Comn:* Print ed, Asn Am Artists, 67; bronze ed, NY State Soc Pathologists, 73; print ed, Rochester Print Club, 80; print ed, Boston Pub Libr, 81; mural, Niagara Frontier Transportation Authority, Buffalo, 84. *Exhib:* Solo Exhibs: Grand Rapids (Mich) Art Mus, 77; FAR Gallery, New York, 74; 79; Gadatsy Gallery, Toronto, 76; 78; 81; 84; 87; Nardin Galleries, New York, 80; Art Gallery Hamilton, Can, 1981; Canton Art Mus, Ohio, 87; Babcock Galleries, New York, 90, 91; Kalamazoo (Mich) Inst Arts, 97; Butler Inst Am Art, 97; Yeshiva Univ Mus, New York, 97; 2002; Gertrude Herbert Inst Art, Augusta, Ga; 2000 Ind Univ Art Gallery, 2001; Univ at Buffalo Art Gallery & David Anderson Gallery, Buffalo, NY, 2004; Dowd Fine Arts Gallery, SUNY Cortland, NY, 2005; Woodbury Art Mus, Orem, Utah, 2008, Kennedy Mus Art, Ohio, Univ, Athens, Ohio, 2010; 35 Yrs in Retrospect, Butler Inst Am Art, Youngstown, Ohio, 71; Works on Paper: Recent Acquisitions, Albright-Knox Art Gallery, Buffalo, 79; Minn Mus Art, 82 & 86; Mus Fine Arts, Houston, 88; Florian Mus, Carbonari, Romania, 99; Mus Civico Di Grafica, Brunico, Italy, 99; 12 Deutsche Int Print Biennale, Frechen, 99; De Mini Gravura, Vitoria, Brazil, 2000; Quingdao Int Print Biennial, China, 2000; Bankside Gallery, London, 2000; 4th Int Print Triennial, Lahti Art Mus, Finland, 2001; Zeichen Der Gegenwart, Vienna Art Ctr Gallery, Austria, 2002; 4th Egyptian Int Print Triennale, Cairo, 2003; 1er Concours Int d'Ex-libirs, Ankara, Turkey, 2003; Int Print Triennial, Krakow, Poland, 2003; Silpakorn Univ Art & Culture Ctr, Bangkok, Thailand, 2003, 2004; Gracefield Arts Ctr, Dumfries, Scotland, 2004; Lefkas, Greece, 2005; Mona Bismark Found, Paris, 2005; Inst Zacatecano Cultura, Guadalupe, Mex, 2005; US Embassy-Hollar Soc Gallery, Prague, Czech Republic, 2006; Tipoteca Italiana Foundazione, Treviso, Italy, 2006; Nat Inst Mus, Bitola, Republic of Macedonia, 2006; Museo Civico, Cremona, Italy, 2007; Bienal Int de Gravura, Municipal de Alijo, Alijo, Portugal, 2007; 1st Int Print Exhib, Univ Insubria Varese, Italy, 2008; 4th Int Print Exhib, Bodio Lomnago, Italy, 2008; Biennial Int des Arts Graphique, Mus Graphic Arts, Istanbul, Turkey, 2008; Bridge: East Coast USA Meets East Coast Australia, Fyre Gallery, Braidwood, Australia, 2010; Pyramida Ctr for Contemp Arts, Haifa, Israel, 2010; 8th Int Print Biennale, Guangzhou, China, 2010; Print Internacional de Cadaques and Fondacio Tharrats d'Art Grafic, Barcelona, 2010; Second Kulisiewicz International Graphic Arts Triennial, IMPRINT, 2011; Royal Castle, Warsaw, Poland, 2011. *Teaching:* Prof art, Univ Buffalo, 61-, SUNY Disting prof, 99-; artist-in-residence, State Acad Fine Arts, Amsterdam, Neth, 65-66; vis artist, Oxford Univ Ruskin Sch Fine Arts, Eng, summer 74 & 77; Pont Aven Sch Art, France, 95; Jagiellonian Univ, Poland, 97. *Awards:* Tiffany Found Grant, 62; Creative Artists Pub Serv Grant, 72; Nat Endowment Arts Fels, 74-75 & 80-81; award, Am Acad Arts & Lett, 80-81; Va Ctr Creative Arts Fel, 93; Distinguished Teaching of Art award, Coll Art Asn, 2002-2003. *Bibliog:* Madeline Burnside (auth), New York Reviews: Harvey Breverman at the FAR Gallery, Art News, summer, 79; Martin Heavisides (auth), Harvey Breverman at Gadatsy Gallery, Artsmagazine, Toronto, 3/79; Gerrit Henry (auth), New York Review: Harvey Breverman at Nardin Galleries, Art News, 12/80. *Mem:* Nat Acad Design (assoc, 92, acad, 94); Soc Am Graphic Artists; Audubon Artists Inc. *Media:* Oil; Etching, Lithography. *Dealer:* Babcock Galleries 724 Fifth Ave New York NY; Wenniger Graphics Gallery 174 Newbury St Boston MA 02116. *Mailing Add:* 76 Smallwood Dr Buffalo NY 14226-4027

BREWER, PAUL
PAINTER, ILLUSTRATOR
b Jan 24, 1934. *Study:* La Co, BA, 56; Famous Artists Sch, degree in advert design, 59; Studied at Syracuse Univ & Am Art Acad, Chicago. *Hon Degrees:* La Col, 2008. *Work:* Portraits of: Jack Benny, Danny Kaye, Red Buttons, Danny Thomas, Don Murray, Phil Silvers, EG Marshall, Pablo Picasso, David Susskind, Leonard Bernstein, Merv Griffin, Edward P Morgan, Carole Kuhrt, Rev Adolph Bohn, Dorsey Connors, Rev Dr J McClure, Jack Paar & Christopher Plummer, Ed and Susan Halle, John and Nicole Walsh, Elvis Presley, Michael Jackson; Krantzen Studio, Chgo; Ford Motor Co, Detroit; Union League Club, Chgo; Ill Bell Telephone, Chgo; Standard Rate & Data, Chgo. *Comn:* Am Bankers Assn, Chgo; Ford Motor Co, Detroit, Mich; Follet Publishing, Chgo; KALB TV, Alexanoria, La; New Orleans Public Svc, La; Chgo Sun Times. *Exhib:* Solo exhibs, La Coll, 63, Chicago Sun-Times, North Shore Art League, Famous Artists Sch, Chicago Pub Libr & Chicago Press Club; and others. *Collection Arranged:* Union League Club, Chicago, Ill; Bell Telephone Co; Standard Rate & Data; Krantzen Studio; Commonwealth Edison; Ford Motor Co; Hartford Insurance Co; and others. *Pos:* Designer, art dir, portrait painter, art teacher. *Teaching:* Instr painting, Art Ctr, Highland Park, Ill; Instr, Deerpath Art League, Lake Forest, Ill. *Awards:* Recipient award, Am Newspaper Guild, Artists Guild Chicago, Famous Artists Sch & Graphic Arts Coun; Nat Award, Louisville Rotogravure Asn; Awards of excellence in painting for In View exhib, 2004-; Graphic Arts Coun; Union League Club; Chicago 3; Hartford Illus Award; Award in caesin and acryllics, Nat Soc Painters, 2008; and over 100 others. *Bibliog:* Famous Artist Mag; Newsweek; Am Business Mag. *Mem:* La Alumni Asn, North Shore Art League; Chicago Soc Typographic Arts; Chicago Soc Commun Arts (bd dirs); Deerpath Art League; Am Soc Portrait Artists; Famous Artists Sch Alumni Asn; Am Watercolor Soc (assoc); The Art Ctr; Artist Guild Chicago. *Media:* Portrait. *Res:* Early Americans. *Specialty:* Fine Art; Portraits. *Interests:* Touring Art Galleries; photog; painting on location. *Publ:* Illusr, New in the City, Follett; Who Am I, McKnight; Count a Lonely Cadence, Follett. *Dealer:* Carole Lynn Kuhrt. *Mailing Add:* 1160 S Green Bay Rd Lake Forest IL 60045

BREWSTER, MICHAEL
INSTALLATION SCULPTOR, EDUCATOR
b Eugene, Ore, Aug 15, 1946. *Study:* Pomona Col, Claremont, Calif, studied with John Mason, David Gray, BA, 68; Claremont Grad Sch, with David Gray & Mowry Baden, MFA, 70. *Work:* La Jolla Mus Contemp Art, Calif; Guggenheim Mus, NY; Fine Art Gallery, Univ Mass, Amherst; Mus RI Sch Design; Mus Contemp Art, Los Angeles; Panza Collection, Varese, Italy; and others. *Comn:* Sonic installations for pvt parties in NY, 77, San Francisco, 78, Los Angeles, 80 & Hollywood, 84; Villa Panza, Varese, Italy, 2002. *Exhib:* Newport Harbor Art Mus, 72 & 75; Artists Space, NY, 77 & 84; Ft Worth Mus Art, 77; Baxter Art Gallery, Calif, 77; Joslyn Mus Art, Nebr, 79; Galleria del Cavallino, Venice, Italy, 79; Whitney Mus Am Art, NY, 81; Los Angeles Co Mus Art, Calif, 81; Commune di Rimini, Italy, 82; MOCA, Los Angeles, 85; Santa Monica Mus Art, 1988; Ace Contemp Exhibs, 1988; Musee Art Moderne, Ville de Paris, 1990; Art Gallery New South Wales, 1991; Bennett Roberts Fine Art, 1995; LA Municipal Art Gallery, 1996; Orange Co Mus Art, 1999; Los Angeles Contemp Exhibs, Hollywood, 2002; Times Square Gallery, NYC, 2004; Getty Res Inst, 2007. *Teaching:* Instr sculpture, drawing & painting, Pomona Col, 71-73; prof art, Claremont Grad Univ, 1973-. *Awards:* Nat Endowment Arts Fel, 76, 78, 84 & 90; Fel, Guggenheim Found, 88. *Bibliog:* Richard Armstrong (auth), review, Artforum, 11/79; Kay Larson (auth), reviews, New York Mag, 3/2/81 & 6/25/84; Suzanne Muchnic (auth), review, 8/25/81 & Robert Pincus (auth), review, 1/31/85, Los Angeles Times; Barry Schwabsky (introd), Peter Clothier (essay), Brandon LaBelle (interview), See Hear Now (catalog LACE Exhib), Feb 2002; Christopher Miles (auth), Critics Picks, Artforum web site, Mar, 2002; Giuseppe Panza di Biumo (introd), The Panza Collection, Villa Menafoglio Litta Panza, Skira, Brewster in Varese, Pages, 27, 33, 150, Sept 2002; Peter Grueneisen (ed), Soundspace (archit for sound & vision), Birkhauser, page, 26 Sept 2003; Holland Cotter (auth, review), Moved, NY Times, page e37, Apr 9, 2004; Giuseppe Panza (auth), Memories of a Collector, Abbeville Press, 2007; Brandon La Belle (auth), Background Noise, Continuum Press, 2008. *Mem:* Int Sculpture Ctr; Los Angeles Contemp Exhib; Am Asn Univ Prof; LACMA; MOCA, LA; Am Bamboo Soc; Orchid Soc. *Media:* Sound, Light. *Publ:* Auth, Inside, Outside, Down & Soliloquies, Baxter Art Gallery, 77; Michael Brewster, Galleria de Cavallino, Italy, 79; Happen-Stance, Herron Sch Art, 79; Touch and Go, Fine Arts Gallery, Calif State Univ, 85; Gone to Touch, Words & Spaces, Smith & Delio, Univ

Press Am, 89; auth (essay), Where, There or Here? Site of Sound-of architecture and the ear, LaBelle & Roden (eds.) June 1999; See Hear Now, Catalog, B Schwabsky (introd), Peter Clothier (essay), Brandon LaBelle (interview) Fellows of Contemporary Art, Los Angeles, Feb 2002. *Mailing Add:* 1165 Palms Blvd Venice CA 90291-3524

BRIANSKY, RITA PREZAMENT
PAINTER, INSTRUCTOR
b Grajewa, Poland, July 25, 1925; Can citizen. *Study:* Montreal Mus Fine Arts, with Jacques de Tonnancour; also with Alexandre Bercovitch & Anne Savage, Montreal; Ecole Beaux-Arts Montreal; Art Students League, NY. *Work:* Mus Que; Nat Art Gallery, Ottawa, Ont; Montreal Mus Fine Arts, Que; Can Dept External Affairs, Ottawa, Ont; Dofasco, Hamilton, Ont; and others. *Exhib:* Second Int Biennial Exhib of Prints, Tokyo & Osaka, Japan, 60-61; Salon Int Femme Vichy, France, 60-61; UNICEF Int, UN, NY, 65; La Soc des Artistes Prof du Que, Edinburgh, Scotland & London, Eng; Solo exhibs: Accents Gallery, Ottawa, 88-89,92; Galerie L'Art Francais, Montreal, 89-90; Galerie de Bellefeuille, Montreal, 91; Emma Ciotti Gallery, Iroquois Falls, Ont, 92; Galerie Jean-Pierre Valentin, Montreal, 95, 97; Cole St Luc Libr, Cote St Luc, Quebec, 97; Montreal Holocaust Mem Centre, 97; Temple Emanuel, Montreal, 98; McGill Univ, Birks Bldg, Montreal, 1999-2001; Gemst Gallery, Montreal, 2002, 2007; Group exhibs, Canadian Artists Jerusalem 3000, Jerusalem, 96, Au Feminin, Chorxd'ouvres de la Collection du musee du Quebec, 97 & 98, Eradication de la pauvrete, Le Musee Marc-Auvele Fortin, Montreal, 97, Centre Cult Marie Fitzback, St George de Bauce, 98 & Pavilion des arts du palais Montcalm, Quebec, 98, Gems & Gallery, Montreal, 2002. *Teaching:* Instr, Ctr for Creative Lifestyles, Montreal. *Awards:* Third Prize, 1st & 2nd Nat Exhib Prints, Burnaby, BC, 60 & 63; Purchase Award, Dawson Col, Montreal, 82; Purchase Award, Thomas More Inst, Montreal, 85. *Bibliog:* E Kilbourn (auth), 18 print-makers, Can Art, 61; Henriette Giordan (auth), Rita Briansky-Du vetement comme portrait, Printemps, 95; Corinne Bolla-Paquet (auth), Rita Briansky-Fragments de Pologne-du desastre, Vie Arts, autumn 96. *Media:* Oil, Pastel. *Publ:* Illusr, Rubaboo Reader, 68; Grandmother Came From Dworitz, Tundra Bks, Montreal, 69; Ten Etchings from Wm Shakespeare's Sonnets, 72; On Stage Please, McClelland & Stewart, Toronto, 77 & Holt, Rinehart & Winston, New York, 79; Le Nu dans l'art au Quebec, Marcel-Broquet Publ, 82; Le Paysage dans la Peinture au Quebec, Marcel Broquet, Publ, 84; Agenda D'Art 1997, Musée Du Quebec, 97; Can Collection of Nat Art Gallery of Can Ottawa, CD-Rom, 98; Se Me Souviens, Coffret Commemoratif De La Chanson Québecoise, 98; The View from Here, Winnipeg Art Gallery, 2000; Holocaust Literature and Education, University Guelph, Ont, 2000. *Dealer:* Galeria Brigitte Des Roches 2110 Crescent St Montreal PQ H3G 2B8. *Mailing Add:* 4545 Girouard Ave Apt 203 Montreal PQ H4A0A1 Canada

BRICKNER, ALICE
PAINTER, PRINTMAKER
b New York, NY, 1931. *Study:* Sarah Lawrence Col, with Kurt Roesch, Ezio Martinelli, Lux Feininger & Theodore Roszak, BA, 52; Pratt Graphic Art Ctr, with Seong Moy, Arnold Singer, Erich Monch & Ansei Uchima, 57. *Work:* Johnson & Johnson, Surgikos Collection; Pratt Graphic Art Ctr; Stuttgart Univ, Ger; plus pvt collections. *Exhib:* Solo exhibs, Donnell Libr Ctr, New York City, 1999, Howell Ctr, Beacon, NY, 1998; Chrysalis Gallery, Southampton, NY, 1998-2001; Sch House Gallery, Croton Falls, NY, 1997, 1999, 2000; Galye Wilson Gallery, Southampton, 1997; Scarborough Gallery, Chappaqua, NY, 1993, 1994, 1997. *Collection Arranged:* Works at PaintingsDirect.com, 2000-. *Mem:* New York Artists Equity Asn; Artist's Space. *Media:* Watercolor, Acrylics; Collage on Canvas

BRIDENSTINE, JAMES A
MUSEUM DIRECTOR, COLLECTOR
b Detroit, Mich, Nov 29, 1945. *Study:* Coll Holy Cross, AB, 1967; George Washington Univ, MA, 1975; Harvard Univ, Cert Mus Studies, 1978. *Pos:* Assoc Cur, Detroit Inst Arts, 1976-86; dir, Edsel & Eleanor Ford House, 1986-90; exec dir, Kalamazoo Inst Arts, Mich, 1990-2015. *Teaching:* Adj prof art hist, Western Mich Univ, 1992-96. *Mem:* Am Asn Mus; Coll Art Asn; Midwest Mus Asn; Mich Mus Asn; Asn Art Mus Dirs. *Res:* American art history - 19th century- contemporary art

BRIDGES, MARILYN
PHOTOGRAPHER
Study: Rochester Inst Technol, BFA, 79, MFA, 81. *Exhib:* Solo exhibs, Mus at Hartwick Col, Oneonta, NY, 97, Peabody Mus Natural History, Yale Univ, 97, Etherton Gallery, Tucson, Ariz, 98, Devena's Gallery, Tulsa, Okla, 98, Lehigh Univ, Bethlehem, Pa, 99, Soho Triad Fine Arts, NY, 99, Apex Gallery, Los Angeles, 200, Carleton Col, Northfield, Minn, 2000, Beacon Gallery, Bellport, NY, 2001, Joseph Bellows Gallery, La Jolla, Calif, 2001, Mus Nat, Lithuania, 2002, Rose Lehrman Arts Ctr, Pa, 2002, Nat Ctr Am Art, Tex, 2003, Throckmorton Gallery, NY, 2003, 2007; group exhibs, San Francisco Mus Art, 97; Rico Gallery, Los Angeles, 98; Yancey Richardson Gallery, NY, 99; Art Inst Boson, 2000; Woodstock Ctr Photography, NY, 2000; Brooke Alexander Gallery, NY, 2001; Gallery Fine Art, Univ RI, 2001; Burden Gallery, NY, 2003; AXA Gallery, 2003. *Awards:* Guggenheim Fellowship, 82; CAPS Grant, 83; NEA Grant, 84; Fulbright Grant, 88-89; Makedonas Kostas Award (Greece), 89; Medal of Arles, Recontres Internationals de la Photographie, France, 91; Wings Trust Award, 2003. *Mem:* Fel, The Explorers Club, 88. *Mailing Add:* PO Box 269 Warwick NY 10990

BRIGGS, ALICE LEORA
DRAFTSMAN, INSTALLATION SCULPTOR
b Borger, Tex, Nov 17, 1953. *Study:* Utah State Univ, BFA, 77; Univ Iowa, MA 80, MFA, 81. *Work:* Fine Art Mus San Francisco; El Paso Mus Art, Tex; Scottsdale Mus Contemp Art, Ariz; Phoenix Art Mus, Ariz; Denver Art Mus, Colo; Ark Art Ctr, Little Rock, Ark; Univ Oxford, Bodleaian Lib; Lib Congress, Rare Books Special Collections; Crystal Bridges Mus Am Art, Bentonville, Ark; Univ NMex Art Mus, Albuquerque, NMex; Univ Ark, Little Rock, Ark; Univ Chgo Libr Special Collections, Rare Books; Rochester Inst Technology Libr, Cary Coll; Ross Art Mus, Ohio; Wesleyan Univ, Del, Oh. *Comn:* 7th Ave Streetscape, Phoenix Office Art & Cult, Ariz, 2005. *Exhib:* Solo exhibs, Neviem Viem Neviem: Alice Leora Briggs, Galerie mesta Bratislavy, Bratislava, Slovak Rep, 2002; Contemp Forum Award, Phoenix Art Mus, 2004; Graft, Int Mus Surgical Sci, Chicago, 2005; Diane & Sandy Besser Collection, deYoung Mus, San Francisco, 2007; New Prints, Int Print Ctr, New York, 2009; Ni una mas, Drexel Univ, Pa, 2010; Dreamland: The Way Out of Juarez, El Paso Mus Art, Tex, 2010; Re-Imagining the West, Scottsdale Mus Contemp Art, Ariz, 2010; Near Impunity, Eide/Dalrymple Gallery, Augustana Col, Sioux Falls, SD, 2012; Abecedario de Juarez, Nau-Haus Art, Houston, Tex, 2012; La Linea: Alice Leora Briggs, Southwest Sch Art, San Antonio, Tex, 2013; Bipolar, Mesa Contemporary Arts Mus, Mesa, Ariz, 2013; In the Wake of Juarez, Univ NMex, Albuquerque, NMex, 2013; Surface Tension, Etherton Gallery, Tucson, Ariz, 2013; Alice Leora Briggs, The Gallery at UTA, Univ Tex Arlington, Tex, 2014. *Teaching:* asst prof, Utah State Univ, 86-91; vis artist, Univ Ariz Sch Art, 2004-2005. *Awards:* Materials grant, Contemp Forum, Phoenix Art Mus, 2004; Proj Grant, Ariz Comm Arts, 2005; Dozier Travel Award, Dallas Mus Art, 2008; Border Art Residency, El Paso Community Found, 2008-2009; Artist in Residence, Anderson Ranch & Art Ctr, 2010; Fulbight, Slovak Rep, 2011; Distinguished Lecture Series, Univ NMex Albuquerque, NMex, 2013. *Bibliog:* Charles Bowden (auth), Deadly Sins/Measured Virtues, catalog/Nora Eccles Harrison Mus Art, 2006; Julie Sasse (auth), Translations, catalog/ Etherton Gallery, 2009; Harmony Hammond (auth), Suffering & Sanctuary, Albuquerque Journ, Santa Fe North, 2009; Mike Melia (auth), An Unflinching Look at Violence in Juarez, PBS Newshour, 2009; Alix McKenna (auth), Alice Leora Briggs: Art from Juarez, Calif Literary Rev, 2010; Susan Wider (auth), In the Wake of Juarez, The Magazine, 2013; Margaret Regan (auth), Heaven and Hell, 2013; Heather Wodrich (auth), Alice Leora Briggs Draws a Light in the Dark, Ariz Public Media, 2013. *Mem:* Southern Graphics Council Internat. *Media:* Drawing, Printmaking, Installation. *Publ:* illustr, The Eighth Letter, Limited ed letterpress book, self publ, 86; illustr, The Essence of Beeing, Sherwin Beach Press, Chicago, 92; illustr, Kililng is Fun, Ken Sanders Rare Books, 2009; illustr, Collapse of the Home: Tejas, Railsmith, Austin, 2010; coauth, illustr, Dreamland: The Way Out of Juarez, Univ Tex Press, 2010. *Dealer:* Davidson Galleries 313 Occidental Ave S Seattle WA 98104; Etherton Gallery 135 S 6th Ave Tucson AZ 85701; Evoke Contemporary 130 Lincoln Ave Ste F Santa Fe NMex 87501

BRIGGS, PETER S
CURATOR, HISTORIAN
b Oak Park, Ill. *Study:* Northern Ill Univ, BA, 72; Univ Ky, MA, 75; Univ NMex, PhD, 86. *Collection Arranged:* Landscape Art, Univ NMex Art Mus, 83; 100 Years of French Prints, Chronicles: Historical References in Contemp Clay & From 2 to 3 Dimensions: Richard Santiago's Sculpture & Drawings, 85; New Western Directions: Mark Klett & Rick Dingus, 86; 4x4: Sixteen Printmakers from the Four Corner States & The Brian Ransom Ceramic Ensemble, 87; Life & Land: The FSA Photographers in Utah, 1936-1941, Harrison Mus Art, 88; Human Components, Univ Ariz Mus Art, 92; Max Cole, 93; Day by Day: Am Daily Life, 94; La Cadena que No Se Corta, Traditional Arts Tucson's Mex Am Community, 96; Eminent Delights, Images of Time, Space and Matter, 96; Tucson Artists: 1970-1997, 97; Reasoned Excess, 17th Century European Prints, 98; The Order of Pictures, 2000; Rudolf Baranik, 2000; Lewis Alquist, 2000; Groundwork: Drawings by Jim Waid (auth, catalog), 2001; Robert Stackhouse, 2001 & 2008; Ernest DeSoto, 2001-02; Bruce McGrew: A Retrospective (auth, catalog), 2002; Burning Images: Cage, Bennet, Chejnowski, 2002; Kolomon Sokol: The Human Spirit, 2003; Olivier Mosset; Recent Work, 2003; Natural Pursintis, 2003; Mario Morreno Zazueta, 2003; A Physical Art; The Intaglio Prints of Andrew Rush, 2003; Bahe Billy, 2004; James G Davis (auth, catalog), 2004; Jasper Johns, 2004 & 06; Labor and Leisure, 2005; Terry Winters, 2007; A Family Collects, 2008; Color Print USA, 40 Ann, 2010; Art and Style, 2011; War Babies, 2012; Just Not Yet, 2012; Fresco y Dicho: Frederico Vigil, 2013; Gain, 2013; Arizona, New Mexico, Texas: 20th and 21st Century Art, 2013; Line Up, 2014; Ansel Adams, 2015; Changing Places, 2016. *Pos:* Asst cur of collections, Maxwell Mus Anthrop, 76-78; registr, Univ NMex Art Mus, 79-82, cur collections, 82-84; dir & chief cur, Nora Eccles Harrison Mus Art, 84-89; chief cur, Tucson Mus Art, 89-90; cur collections, Univ Ariz Mus Art, 90-99, chief cur, 99-2004; Helen Jones Cur of Art, Tex Tech Univ Mus, 2004-. *Teaching:* Instr, Univ Ky, 73-74, Univ NMex, 76-77 & 81; asst prof, Utah State Univ, 85-89; grad fac, Tex Tech Univ, 2005-. *Awards:* Res Fel, Orgn Am States, 79; Tinker Found Res Grant, 80; Bainbridge Bunting Fel, 80-81; Nat Endowment Art research grant, 83-84; Nat Endowment Art Prof Fel, 83 & 92; Fac Res Grant, Utah State Univ, 88 & Univ Ariz, 94; Fulbright Scholar, 2009, 2016. *Mem:* Coll Art Asn; Am Asn Mus; ICOM. *Res:* Pre-columbian art hist especially lower Cent Am; 20th Cent Am & Latin Am Art Hist; Social Art Hist; Village planning & archit, 20th and 21st Century American Art. *Publ:* Auth, La diversidad social de Panama Central: Los Restos Mortuorios del sitio de el Indio, Los Santos, Patrimonio Historico, Panama, 92; A Portion of Space, Larry Elsner Found, 92; Fatal Attractions: Central American Mortuary Arts and Social Organization in The Central Americans and Their Neighbors, Univ Colo, 93; Emigres: Ceramics in Cross-Cultural Perspective, NCECA, 94; The Order of Pictures, 2000; Groundwork; Drawings by Jim Waid, 2001; Bruce McGraw, A Retrospective, 2002; Concrete Art, 2003; Reasonable Probabilities; Collected Notes on Paintings of James G. Davis, 2004; ArtLies, 2005-2010; NMex Artists: Paintings & Drawings, 2007; Voices of Art, 2009; Afterimage, 2009-2014; Color Print: 40th Ann, 2010; Just Not Yet, 2012; Line Up, 2014; Graphic Impressions, 2012-2015; Changing Places (ed), 2016. *Mailing Add:* 3410 40th ST Lubbock TX 79413

BRIGHAM, DAVID R
MUSEUM DIRECTOR, ADMINISTRATOR
Study: Univ Conn, BA (Eng & accounting); Univ Pa, MA (mus studies & Am civilization), PhD (Am civilization), 1992. *Pos:* Dir, Worcester Art Mus, Mass, 1996-2002 & Allentown Art Mus, Pa, 2002-07; pres & chief exec officer, Pa Acad Fine Arts, 2007-. *Teaching:* Instr, Univ S Calif, George Mason Univ, Fairfax, Va & Lebanon Valley Coll, Annville, Pa. *Mailing Add:* Pa Acad Fine Arts 118-128 N Broad St Philadelphia PA 19102

BRIGHT, SHEILA PREE
PHOTOGRAPHER
Study: Univ Mo, BA, 1998; Ga State Univ, MFA (Photography), 2003. *Work:* High Mus Art, Ga; Libr of Congress, Washington; Diggs Gallery, Winston-Salem State Univ; King & Spalding Art Collection, Ga; Hammond House Mus, Ga. *Exhib:* Solo exhibs include Hammonds House, Atlanta, 2001, Wertz Contemp, Atlanta, 2003, Mus Contemp Art, Cleveland, 2008, Wadsworth Atheneum Mus Art, Hartford, Conn, 2008, High Mus Art, Atlanta, 2008; Group exhibs include Locating the Spirit: Religion & Spirituality in African Am Art, Smithsonian Anacostia Mus & Ctr for African Am History & Culture, Washington, 1999; New Works Proj, Lehman Art Gallery, Bronx, 2000; Spiritual Transformations, Our Dream Gallery, Portland, Ore, 2001; Face Time, Atlanta Contemp Art Ctr, Atlanta, 2002; Saturday Night, Sunday Morning, Leica Gallery, New York, 2003; The Georgia 7, Mus Contemp Art of Georgia, Atlanta, 2004; Mothers & Daughters, Clark Atlanta Univ Art Galleries, Atlanta, 2005; If It Ain't Broke, 138 Gallery, New York, 2007; Double Exposure: African Ams Before & Behind the Camera, Mus African Diaspora, San Francisco, 2008. *Awards:* New Works Photography Award, En Foco, Inc, Bronx, 1999; Nat Bronica Award, Tamron USA, New York, 2001; Santa Fe Prize, Santa Fe Ctr for Photography, Santa Fe, 2006

BRILLIANT, RICHARD
EDUCATOR, WRITER
b Boston, Mass, Nov 20, 1929. *Study:* Yale Univ, BA, 51, MA, 56, PhD, 60; Harvard Univ, LLB, 54. *Comn:* The Fayum Portraits, Prog for Art on Film, NY, 88. *Exhib:* Jewish Portraits in Colonial & Federal Am, NY, 97; Likeness & Beyond, Portraits from Africa & Beyond, NY, 90; Group Dynamics, NY Hist Soc, 2006. *Pos:* Ed-designate, Art Bull, 90-91, ed-in-chief, 91-94; dir, Ital Acad, Columbia Univ, 96-2000; consultant to pres & CEO, New York Historical Soc, 2004 & 2005; prof emer, Anna S. Garbedian prof humanities, Columbia Univ. *Teaching:* From asst prof to prof art hist, Univ Penn, 62-70; vis Mellon Prof fine arts, Univ Pittsburgh, 71; vis prof, Scuola Normale Superiore, Pisa, 74, 80 & 88, Princeton, 86; prof, Columbia Univ, 70-2004. *Awards:* Fulbright Grant, 57-59; Am Acad Rome, 60-62; Guggenheim Found Fel, 67-68; Nat Endowment Humanities Sr Fel, 72-73; Distinguished Senior Scholar, College Art Asn, Feb 2005; Elected mem Am Acad Art & Scis, 2005. *Mem:* Coll Art Asn; Ger Archaeol Inst; Am Acad Arts & Sciences. *Res:* Greek and Roman art and archaeology; theory and method in art history; portraiture. *Interests:* Portraiture, Narrative, Historiography of Art History. *Publ:* Gesture and Rank in Roman Art, 63; The Arch of Septimius Severus in the Roman Forum, 67; Arts of the Ancient Greeks, 73; Roman Art from the Republic to Constantine, 74; Pompeii, AD 79: the Treasure of Rediscovery, Volair, 79; Visual Narratives, 84; Portraiture, Reaktion & Harvard, 91; Commentaries on Roman Art, Pindar Press, 94; Facing the New World, Prestel, 97; Un Americano a Roma, 2000; My Laocoon, California, 2000; Group Dynamics, NY Hist Soc, 2006; Reuse Value, Ashgate, London, 2011

BRITE, JANE FASSETT
CURATOR, DIRECTOR
b Chicago, Ill. *Study:* Marjorie Webster Col, BS, 57; Univ Wis, Milwaukee. *Work:* Fiber Revolution - Textile Mus, Washington, DC, 87; Exploration & Innovation, Textile Mus, Washington, DC, 90. *Exhib:* Exhibs juried, Wis Art Bd, Percent for Art Prog, 2003-, 2006, 2009, Sharon Lynn WIlson Ctr, 2008, Oconomowoc Plein Air Art Fair, 2009, Cedarburg Art Ctr (2 shows), 2008, 2009, Anderson Art Ctr, Racine, Wis, 2008, Charles Allis Art Mus, Wis Painter-Sculptors, 2007, West Bend Day of the Dead exhib, 2008-2009. *Collection Arranged:* Wisconsin Directions Three (auth, catalog), 84 & Wisconsin Directions Four (auth, catalog), 85; Emerging Imagist (auth, catalog), 85; Fiber R/Evolution, History of Fiber 50's-80's (auth, catalog), 86-87; The Force, Brian Richie & Dennis Nechtavel (performance/site installation cur), 87; Triangulation, Women of Substance, Walker's Point Ctr, 88-90; Diverse Works, Maryland Art Place (bd trustees), 88-89; Walkers Point Ctr Arts, 89-2006. *Pos:* Bd mem, Wis Arts, Madison, 82-85 & Art Reach, Milwaukee, 82-86; rev, Inst Mus Serv, Washington, DC, 83-84; ed bd, Acad Sci, Arts & Letts, 85-86; Art Reach, 82-85 & 88. *Teaching:* Safe & Sound, YMCA, Milwaukee, Wis, 99-2003; dir, Walker's Point, 89-2006; develop & implemented classes for homeless women; Art After School progs with accompanying guide book; Developed prog veterans & housing proj/teen girls, Charles Allis Art Mus, Villa Terrace, 2010. *Mem:* bd trustees, Dance Circus bd, 86-2007; Woodland Pattern bd, 2007-2009; cult bd, St John's, 2007-2009; AWE bd 99-2009; Milwaukee Metrop Singers bd, 2008-2009; W Bend Art Mus bd, 2006-2008; TEMPO- Prof women; Wis Painters & Sculptors; Wis Designer-Craftsmen; Tal-N-Art Consortium Inc Adv, 86. *Media:* Fiber, Crafts. *Res:* Development of fiber arts of the last thirty years; history of Wisconsin art of the 30's & 40's; Develop Fiber Arts of last 60 years; Hist of Wis art of last century. *Interests:* cur & Jurying national & regional exhibs & art fairs. *Publ:* Fiber/R Evolutioin, Milwaukee Art Mus, 86-87; Ed Rossbach: Exploration & Innovation, Textile Mus, DC, 90; Contemp Crafts: The Saxe Collection, Toledo Mus, 93; co auth, The New Direction-Old Pleasures in Ceramic Art, 85; The Evolution of Art in Milwaukee, 86; Wis Acad Rev, Wis Acad Sci, Arts, & Letters; auth, The Milwaukee Joun Gallery of Wis Art (exhib catalog); co auth, Art After School, 99; plus more than 50 catalogues. *Mailing Add:* 1610 N Prospect Ave No 1001 Milwaukee WI 53202-6702

BRITO, MARIA
SCULPTOR, PAINTER
b Havana, Cuba, Oct 10, 1947; US citizen. *Study:* Fla Int Univ, Miami, BFA, 77, MS, 76; Univ Miami, Coral Gables, Fla, MFA, 79. *Work:* Olympic Sculpture Park, Seoul, Korea; Archer M Huntington Mus, Austin, Tex; Univ Fla, Tallahassee; Art in Public Places, Metro-Dade Ctr, Miami; Lowe Art Mus, Coral Gables, Fla. *Comn:* Sculpture, Seoul Olympic Organizing Comt, Seoul, Korea, 88. *Exhib:* The Decade Show, Studio Mus Harlem, New Mus Contemp Art & Mocha, Mus Contemp Hispanic Art, NY 90; Southern Exposures, High Mus Art, Atlanta, 91; Cuban Artists of the Twentieth Century, Mus Art, Ft Lauderdale, Fla, 93; Revelations/Revelaciones: Evanescene and Latino Art, Johnson Mus Art, Cornell Univ, Ithaca, NY, 93; Transcending the Borders of Memory, Norton Gallery Art, West Palm Beach, Fla, 94; and others. *Teaching:* adj prof, Barry Univ, Miami Shores, Fla. *Awards:* Visual Artists Fel, Nat Endowment Arts, 84 & 88; Pollock-Krasner Found Grant, 90; Virginia A Groot Found Grant, 94. *Bibliog:* Ricardo Pau-LLosa (auth), The Dreamt Objectivities of Maria Brito-Avellana, Dreamworks, Human Sci Press Inc, 86; Charlotte S Rubenstein (auth), American Women Sculptors, G K Hall & Co, 90; Lynette M F Bosch (auth), Maria Brito: Metonymy and metaphor, Latin Am Art Mag, 93; and others. *Mem:* Coll Art Asn; Ctr Fine Arts; Ctr Contemp Art. *Media:* Mixed. *Mailing Add:* 8995 SW 75th St Miami FL 33173

BRITT, SAM GLENN
EDUCATOR, PAINTER
b Ruleville, Miss, Sept 26, 1940. *Study:* Memphis Acad Art, BFA; Univ Miss, MFA; Cape Cod Sch Painting, Provincetown, Mass, with Henry Hensche; Frudakais Acad Sculpture, Philadelphia, with Angelous Frudakais. *Work:* Union Bldg, Delta State Univ, Munic Art Gallery, Jackson, Miss; First Nat Bank, Cleveland, Miss. *Comn:* Drawing depicting the lifestyle of ancient Indians, Winterville Mounds Mus, Miss, 67; painting, Union Planters Nat Bank, Memphis, Tenn; painting, Mrs Pat Kerr, Memphis, Tenn. *Exhib:* Solo exhib, Gov's Mansion, Jackson, Miss; Bryant Galleries, Jackson, Miss & New Orleans, La, 83; Nat Bank Com, Memphis, Tenn, 83; Symphony Ball, Peabody Hotel, Memphis, Tenn, 83; 7 Am Impressionists, Gallery 3, Roanoke, Va, 85; and others. *Teaching:* Instr drawing & painting, Delta State Univ, 66-73, asst prof, 73-78, assoc prof art, 78-; pvt instr, Clarksdale, Miss, 73-; instr, Painting City Park, New Orleans, summer 85, Painting Workshops Unlimited, Jackson, Miss, 85 & 86 & Drawing Studio One, Gray, La, 85 & 86. *Awards:* Second Prize, Nat Painting Exhib, 64; Most Outstanding Work, Nat Small Painting Exhib, Hadley, 74; Best in Show, Crosstie Festival, 79. *Bibliog:* Ed Phillips (auth), Finding God's beauty in a simple world, Delta Scene Mag, 75; Featured on Miss Educ TV as a Miss Artist, spring 80. *Media:* Oil, Pastel. *Mailing Add:* 1105 University St Cleveland MS 38732-3665

BRITTON, DANIEL ROBERT
PRINTMAKER, EDUCATOR
b Colorado Springs, Colo, Apr 1, 1949. *Study:* Univ Colo, BFA, 74, MFA, 76. *Work:* Corcoran Mus, Washington, DC; Portland Art Mus, Ore; Haggin Art Mus, Calif; Scottsdale Mus Contemp Art, Ariz; Tamarind Inst, NMex; Nelson Art Mus, Ariz; Bibliotheque Nat, Paris; Utah Mus Fine Arts, Salt Lake City; Lauren Rodgers Art Mus, Laurel, Miss; Huntsville Mus Fine Arts, Ala. *Comn:* McDonalds Corp, Chicago & Denver, 88. *Exhib:* Tenth Nat Print Competition, Univ Art Gallery, Minot, NDak, 81; DeKalb 81 Nat Print Competition, Swen Parsons Gallery, Ill, 81; Moravian Print Nat, Church Street Gallery, Bethlehem, Pa, 81; Am Drawing IV, Portsmouth Mus, 83; Haggin Art Mus, Stockton, Calif, 88; Albrecht Art Mus, St Joseph, Mo, 91; Bradley Univ Nat Print Exhib, Peoria, Ill, 91; NDak Nat Print & Drawing Competition, 92; 5th Int Biennial Graphic Arts, Novomesto, Slovenia, 98; 8th Int Print & Drawing Biennial, Taipei Art Mus, Repub China, 98; Monotypes, Fine Arts Gallery, Brigham Young Univ, Utah, 98; Am Printmaking, Moderna Galleria, Croatia, 99. *Teaching:* Vis prof lithography, Univ Utah, Salt Lake City, 91; prof art, printmaking, Ariz State Univ, 76-. *Awards:* Award of Merit, DeKalb Print Nat, 81; Stockton Nat Print Competition, Haggin Art Mus, Stockton, Calif, 88; Nat Honor Soc, Ariz State Univ, 91; Heitland Found Grant, Ger, 91; Artist fel Ariz Comn of the Arts, 98. *Bibliog:* Roberta Loach (auth), Printmakers, Visual Dialogue Mag, 79; Art in the Sun Belt, Art News, 80; Carol Kotrozo (auth), Drawing and Printmaking, Art Week, 81; Yingxue/Malone/Wampler, Contemp Am Painting, Jilin Fine Arts Pub, 99. *Mem:* Los Angeles Printmaking Soc; Southern Graphics Coun. *Media:* Lithography, Monotypes, Oil. *Publ:* Tamarind Technical Papers, 79 & 80. *Dealer:* G-Z Gallery Scottsdale AZ. *Mailing Add:* Sch Art Ariz State Univ Tempe AZ 85287

BROAD, EDYTHE & ELI
COLLECTOR, PATRON
b New York, NY, June 6, 1933. *Study:* Mich State Univ, BA (cum laude), 1954. *Hon Degrees:* Southwestern Univ, LLD, 2000. *Pos:* Co-founder, chmn, pres, chief exec officer, SunAmerica Inc (formerly Kaufman & Broad, Inc) Los Angeles, 1957-2001; founding chmn & bd trustees, Mus Contemp Art, Los Angeles, Calif, 1980-; nat trustee, Baltimore Mus Art, Md, 1985-91; bd trustees, Arch of Am Art, Smithsonian Inst, Washington, DC, 1985-; painting & sculpture comt, Whitney Mus Am Art, New York, 1987-89; chmn adv bd, Art/89, Los Angeles, Calif, 1989; founder & chmn, Kaufman and Broad Home Corp, Los Angeles, Calif, 1993-; trustee, Mus Modern Art, New York, currently. *Teaching:* Asst prof, Detroit Inst Tech, 1956. *Awards:* Founders Award, Occidental Coll, 2000; Trustees Award, Calif Inst Arts, 2000; Chairman's Award, Asia Soc Southern Calif, 2000; Named one of Top 200 Collectors, ARTnews Mag, 2004-13. *Mem:* Hillcrest Country Club; The Regency Country Club, Los Angeles. *Collection:* Museum quality works from approximately 1913 to present with a concentration on American art of the 70's, 80's & 90's; Contemporary art. *Publ:* auth, The Art of Being Unreasonable: Lessons in Unconventional Thinking, 2012 (Eli). *Mailing Add:* Broad Foundation Ste 1200 10900 Wilshire Blvd Los Angeles CA 90024

BROCK, ROBERT W
SCULPTOR, EDUCATOR
b Tacoma, Ohio, June 27, 1936. *Study:* Sch Dayton Art Inst, 54-60, dipl, with Robert C Koepnick; Univ Dayton, BFA, 60; Ohio Univ, MFA, 62, with David Hostetler. *Work:* Dayton Art Inst; State Univ NY Col, Fredonia. *Comn:* Sculpture, Fillmore Suburban Hosp, 96. *Exhib:* Artists of Southern Ohio, Dayton Art Inst, 60 & 61; Ohio Sculpture & Ceramic Show, Butler Inst Am Art, Youngstown, 62; Western NY Show, Albright-Knox Art Gallery, Buffalo, 65-67, 69 & 75 & Outdoor Sculpture Exhib, 68; Unordinary Realities, Xerox Ctr, Rochester, 75. *Pos:* Mem adv comt, Burchfield Ctr, 70-84; chmn fine arts dept, State Univ Col, Buffalo, 70-73 & 81-85; pres, Patteran Artists Inc, Buffalo, 77-78; mem adv comt, Art in Subway, Buffalo, 81-85. *Teaching:* Prof sculpture, State Univ NY Col, Buffalo, 62-. *Mem:* Int Sculpture Ctr. *Media:* All Media. *Mailing Add:* 104 Fordham Dr Buffalo NY 14216

BROD, STANFORD
DESIGNER, EDUCATOR
b Cincinnati, Ohio, Sept 29, 1932. *Study:* Coll Design, Archit, Art & Planning, Univ Cincinnati, BS (design), 55; Art Acad Cincinnati, DFA. *Hon Degrees:* (Hon) DFA, Art Acad Cincinnati, 2013. *Work:* Nat Collection Fine Arts, Washington, DC; Mus Mod Art, New York; Hebrew Union Coll, Jewish Inst Relig Mus, Los Angeles; Contemp Art Ctr & Cincinnati Art Mus, Ohio. *Comn:* Urban Walls: Cincinnati (ten story bldg wall mural), Solway Gallery for Cincinnati Community, 72; Six Urban Banners, Contemp Art Ctr, 75, 520 Paolo, Brazil, US Pavilion; Archit Graphic Design for Interior of Wise Temple, Cincinnati, Ohio, 2005. *Exhib:* Greetings, Mus Mod Art, NY, 66; Int Calligraphy Today; Urban Banner Designs Cincinnati Downtown Commercial Districts, 81; Tel Aviv Mus, 82; Int Art Exhib DRUPA, Dusseldorf, Ger, 82; traveling show, Calligraphia USA/USSR, Russia & USA, 90-92; and others. *Pos:* Designer, Rhoades Studio, Cincinnati, 55-62; designer, Lipson, Alport & Glass Inc, Cincinnati, 62-94, wood/brod design, 94-. *Teaching:* Exp typography, Art Acad Cincinnati, 60, 75, 91 illus, 91, 92, packaging design, 91, 92, 94, 96, 98, 2000, 2004-2010 & corp design, 92, 93, 95, 97, 99, 2001, 2003, 2005-2010; adj prof graphic design, Coll Design, Archit, Art & Planning, Univ Cincinnati, 62-2012. *Awards:* Communication Arts Award, Community Arts J, 59, 64, 66 & 70; Typomundus 20/2 Int Award, 70; Int Typographic Composition Award, 70-72 & 75. *Media:* Brush, Pen & Ink, Computer. *Res:* Development of computer art and design. *Publ:* Auth, Trademarks & Symbols of the World, 87; Letterheads 2; A Collection of Letterheads from Around the World, 89; Greeting Cards: A Collection from Around the World, 89; Expressive Typography, The Word As Image, 90; Fresh Ideas in Promotion 2, Graphic Brochures 2, 96; Designers Stationary, 2001; Big Type, 2002; Design Rules for Letterheads, 2004; auth, iFishie, Toddler Tweets, i Go to the Zoo, 2010-2011; auth, Numbirds (childrens book); auth, Mastering Hebrew Calligraphy, 2012. *Mailing Add:* 3662 Grandin Rd Cincinnati OH 45226

BRODERICK, HERBERT REGINALD, III
EDUCATOR
b Bethesda, Md, July 16, 1945. *Study:* Columbia Coll, AB, 67; Columbia Univ, MA, 68, MPhil, 75, PhD, 78. *Teaching:* Instr art hist, Columbia Univ, 74-77, asst prof, 78; asst prof, Herbert H Lehman Coll, City Univ NY, 78-84, assoc prof, 85-2010. *Awards:* Mrs Giles Whiting Found Fel, 74-75; Nat Endowment Humanities Fel, 81-82; PSC/City Univ NY Fac Res Awards, 81-82 & 88-89, 2004-05. *Mem:* Int Ctr Medieval Art; Int Soc Anglo Saxonists; Soc Antiquaries of London. *Res:* Iconography of the Old Testament in medieval art; Anglo-Saxon manuscript illumination. *Publ:* Auth, Some attitudes toward the frame in Anglo-Saxon manuscripts of the 10th and 11th centuries, Artibus & Historiae, Vol V, 82; Observations on the method of illustration in manuscript Junius II, Scriptorium, Vol XXXVII, 83; Observations on the creation cycle of the Sarajevo Haggadah, Zeitschrift, für Kunstgechichte, XLVII, 84; A Note on the Garments of Paradise, Byzantion, LV, 250-254, 85; Early Medieval Aspects of the American Renaissance, Medievalism in Am Culture, Vol I, Binghamton, NY, pg 89-114, 87; and others; Metatexuality, Sexuality & Intervisuality, in Ms Junius II, Word & Image, 2009

BRODERICK, JAMES ALLEN
GRAPHIC ARTIST, CONSULTANT
b Chicago, Ill, 1939. *Study:* St Ambrose Coll, BA, 62; Univ Iowa, MA, 66. *Exhib:* SAMA-Open, 86, San Antonio Mus Art, 86; Recent Photog, Blue Collar Gallery, San Antonio, 86; Heat & Light, Univ Tex, San Antonio, 87; Close-Up, San Antonio Mus Art, 87; solo exhibs, Martin Rathburn Gallery, San Antonio, 93 & Inst Cult Pernano Norte Americano, Lima, Peru, 94; and others. *Pos:* Dir, UTSA Pub Art Commn, 93-2003; bd dir, Nat Coun Art Adminstrs, 95-97; pres, Nat Asn Sch Art & Deisgn, 99-2002. *Teaching:* Asst Prof, Northwest Mo State Univ, Maryville, 66-76, dir art gallery, 67-76, chmn, Dept Art, 70-76; prof & chairperson, Dept Art, Tex Tech Univ, Lubbock, 76-83; prof, art, Univ Tex, San Antonio, 83-currently, dir, Div Visual Arts, 83-2002, chmn, Dept Art & Art Hist; prof emer, 2003. *Mem:* Tex Asn Schs Art (bd dir); Nat Coun Art Adminr (bd dir); Nat Asn Schs Art & Design, fel & life member (pres, 99-2002, bd dir, 85-,); Coll Art Asn. *Media:* Miscellaneous Media, Photography. *Mailing Add:* 1643 Ranch Rd 473 Boerne TX 78006

BRODIE, REGIS CONRAD
CERAMIST, PAINTER
b Pittsburgh, Pa, Nov 19, 1942. *Study:* Ind Univ Pa, BSc (art educ) & MEd; Temple Univ, MFA. *Work:* World Ceramic Exposition Found, Icheon, Korea (outdoor installation); Escuela de Arte Francisco Alcatara (Nat Sch of Ceramics), Madrid, Spain; Museo de Ceramica, (Nat Ceramics Mus of Spain), Barcelona, Spain; Musee Nat de la Ceramique, (Nat Ceramics Mus of France), Sevres, France; Embassy of the United States of Am, Cairo, Egypt; Permanent Collections Nat Ariz State Univ, Tempe, Ariz; Everson Mus of Art, Syracuse, NY: Delaware Art Mus, Wilmington, Delaware, Tang Teaching Mus and Gallery, Skidmore Col, Saratoga Springs, NY; Southern Conn State Univ, New Haven, Conn, The Hyde Collection, Glens Falls NY, Long Beach Mus of Art, Long Beach, Calif. *Exhib:* Invitational Porcelain Exhib, Am Craft Mus, NY, 2000; The Int Exposition of Sculpture Objects & Functional Art (SOFA), Chicago, 2000, NY, 2001 & 2002; Am Masters, Santa Fe, NMex, 94-99; Inter-D2, Int Craft Exhib, McAllen, Tex; Interconnections, Univ Wales Inst, Cardiff, Wales, Eng. *Teaching:* Prof studio art, Skidmore Col, 69-, dir, Six summer art prog & AP summer art prog for high sch students, 72-. *Awards:* The Edwin M Moseley Fac Research Lectr, Skidmore Col, 88; The Ella Vandyke Tuthill Endowed Chair in Studio Art, Skidmore College (First Recipient 93-99); Vis Fel, Univ of Wales Inst, Ctr for Art and Design Ed, Cardiff, UK, May, 2001; 2004-2005 Residency Prog, Int Symposium on & construction of Outdoor Ceramic Sculpture, World Ceramic Exposition Found, Yeoju, Korea (One of Ten Ceramic Artists Invited). *Bibliog:* Charlotte F. Speight & John Toki (auth), Make it in Clay: A Beginner's Guide to Ceramics, 2nd ed, Mayfield Publishing Company, 2001; Susan Peterson (auth), Working with Clay, 2nd ed, Prentice Hall, Laurence King Publ, London, Eng, 2002; Roberta Griffith (auth), Regis Brodie-A Vision Defined, Revista Ceramica, Nat Ceramics Mag of Spain, Madrid, Issue No 86, 2003. *Media:* Clay, Mixed Media. *Publ:* Auth, The Energy-Efficient Potter, Watson-Guptill Publ, 5/1982; auth, The Studio Potter, 6/97, Re-firing a Second Chance (article), Vol 25, #2 Ceramics Monthly, 5/94, The Creative Process (article), 5 & 31-33; contribr auth (with Richard Zakin), Ceramics, Mastering the Craft (a section on multi-firing with step-by-step photos and text), 238-241, Chitton Book Company, Radnor, Pa, 1990. *Dealer:* Loveed Fine Arts 575 Madison Ave Ste 1006 New York 10022

BRODKIN, ED
PAINTER, CONCEPTUAL ARTIST
b New York, NY, Aug 21, 1925. *Study:* Brooklyn Mus Art Sch, 51; Cooper Union, BFA, 75. *Work:* Stull & Benoit Assoc, Jersey City, NJ; Moore, Berson, Lifflander & Mcwhinney, NYC; De Steno Assoc, Ridgewood, NJ. *Exhib:* Solo exhibs, Pleiades Gallery, New York, 89, 91-92, 94, 96-97, 99, 2000-2003, 2005, & 2011; group exhibs, New Yorkers in Barcelona, Cartoon Gallery, Spain, 91, NJ Ctr Visual Arts Int Juried Show, Summit, NJ, 97 & City Without Walls Gallery, Newark, NJ, 97, 98 & 2001, Gwangju Biennial Int, Art Ctr, Gwangju, S Korea, 2003, Int Juried Show, NJ Ctr Visual Arts, Summit, NJ, 2005, 58th Ann Art of the Northeast, Silvermine Art Guild, New Canaan, Conn; 48th Ann NE USA, Silvermine Gallery, New Canaan, Conn, 97, 2001 & 2004; Galerie Roessler, Munich, Ger, 99-2000; Jersey City Mus Invitational, 2002; Gwanguu - Biennal, Int Art Ctr, Gwangju, S Korea, 2003; Art from Detritus, Williamsburg Art and Historical Ctr, 2011. *Pos:* Mem, Art & Design Adv Comn, Mercer Co Community Col, Trenton, NJ, 70-73; chmn, Pleiades Gallery, NY, 94-96, comt chmn, NY, 97-2007. *Teaching:* Instr fine & appl art, Mechanics Inst, NY, 61-62. *Awards:* Painting Award, Bergen Mus Art & Sci, 84; Award of Distinction, Rockport Publ, 97; Artist Showcase Award Winner, Manhattan Arts Int, 98, 99; Selected Artist of the Week, Manhattan Arts, 2007. *Bibliog:* Alexandra Shaw (critic), Manhattan Arts, 10/97; Sean Simon (critic), Artspeak, 10/97; Creative Inspirations, Rockport Publ, 12/97; and many others; Cornelia Seckel (critic), Art Times, 6/99; Gallery & Studio, 11/2003, 3/2005. *Mem:* NY Artists Equity Asn. *Media:* Various Paints, Varnishes, and non-rectangular grounds. *Res:* Worldwide art history, (Lascaux to today with many visits to US, Canada, Mexico, Europe, & Asia). *Specialty:* Quality art in a variety of genres. *Interests:* Chamber Music, Cosmology, Philosophy, Art History. *Collection:* Chagall, Kollwitz, Hiroshiqe, Utamaro. *Publ:* The Best of Acrylic Painting, 96 & Creative Inspirations, 97, Rockport Publ; Ed McCormack (auth), Gallery and Studio, 4/2002, 3/2005. *Dealer:* Pleiades Gallery 530 W 25th St New York NY 10001-5516. *Mailing Add:* 167 Garden Ave Paramus NJ 07652-1918

BRODSKY, ALEXANDER ILYA UTKIN
ARCHITECT, SCULPTOR
b Moscow, Russia 1955. *Study:* Moscow Archit Inst, 78. *Work:* Mus Mod Art, NY; Hirshhorn Mus & Sculpture Garden, Washington, DC; Inst Contemp Art, Boston, Mass; Portland Art Mus, Ore; Bayly Art Mus, Univ Va. *Comn:* Interior, Atrium Restaurant, Moscow, Russia 88; Pedestrian Bridge, Tacoma, Wash, 90; Monumental Sculpture in Courtyard, Euroean Ceramics Work Ctr, Hertogenbosch, Neth, 91; lighting project 93-96, Yamagiwa Art Found, Tokyo, Japan, 92; Palazzo Nero, Wellington City Art Gallery, NZ, 92. *Exhib:* Paper Architecture: New Projects from the Soviet Union, List Visual Arts Ctr, Mass Inst Technol, Cambridge, Mass, 90; solo exhibs, Mus Art, Univ Ariz, Tucson, 92, Bayly Art Mus, Univ Va, Charlottesville, 93, Portland Ctr Visual Arts, Ore, 93 & Gallery 210, Univ Mo, St Louis, 94; group exhibs, SKVC Gallery, Ljubljana, Yugoslavia, 86, La Grande Halle de La Villette, Paris, France, 88, Deutsches Architektur mus, Frankfurt, Ger, 89, Found pour l'Archit, Brussels, Belgium, 90, Irving Galleries, Sydney, Australia, 91, Ewing Gallery, Univ Tenn, Knoxville, 92, The Rye Arts Ctr, NY, 93, de Saisset Mus, Santa Clara, Calif, 94, Wessel & Lieberman Books, Seattle, Wash, 95, Milwaukee Art Mus, Wis, 96, Govett-Brewster Art Gallery, New Plymouth, New Zealand, 2000. *Awards:* Second Prize, Theater for Future Generations, OISTT Competition, Paris, 78; First Prize, Crystal Palace, Cent Glass Competition, Tokyo, 82; First Prize Archit, East Meets West in Design Competition, Jacob K Javits Conv Ctr, New York, 88. *Bibliog:* Lois Nesbitt (ed), Brodsky & Utkin, Princeton Archit Press, 91; Gregory Burke (ed), Palazzo Nero & Other Projects, Wellington City Art Gallery, NZ, 92; Constantin Boym (auth), New Russian Design, Rizzoli, 92. *Media:* Installation. *Mailing Add:* c/o Ronald Feldman Fine Arts 31 Mercer St New York NY 10013

BRODSKY, BEVERLY
PAINTER, ILLUSTRATOR
b Aug 16, 1941. *Study:* Brooklyn Col, BA, 1965; Painting with Ad Reinhardt; Color Theory with Burgoyne Diller. *Work:* The Mazza Collection; Raich Ende & Malter; Leonard Braunschweigger & Co; Mazza Mus Internat Art, Ohio; Mus Internat Art, Univ Findlay, Ohio; Paintings on loan, The American Embassies, Freetown, Sierra Leone, West Africa, 2014-2017; Bandar Seri Begawan Brunei, 2015-2018. *Comn:* Phoenix Dance Theater (poster), Cubiculo Theater, New York, 1977; poster, Nat Endowment for the Arts, New York, 1980; poster, Long Wharf Theater, CT, 1980; New York City Opera (poster), Lincoln Center, New York, 1981; Jewish Book Month (poster), Jewish Welfare Comn, New York, 1982. *Exhib:* Yeshiva Univ Museum,

NYC, 1983; The Jewish Mus, 88, Danger, Deliverance, and Art, Lorhl Gallery, 90, Gallery 18 New York, Galerie Bernhardt Steinmetz, Bonn, Germany, 1993; The Painting Center, New York, 1996; Broom Street Gallery, NY Artist's Equity, New York, 1997-1998; The Am Century Part II 1950-2000, The Whitney Mus, New York, 2000; Guild Hall, NY, 2000; Buying Time, Sotheby's, New York, 2001; Three Voices, Flinn Gallery, Greenwich, Conn, 2005, Art Fair Verona, Italy, 2005, Barbara Paci Gallery, Pietra Santa, Italy, 2005; M-13 Gallery, 1992; Etra Fine Art, Miami, Fla, 2007; Westbeth Gallery, New York, 98, 2010; Cheryl Pelavin Gallery, 2011; Solo exhib: Telcom, NY, 2001, Studio Gallery, NY, 2004, Art Basel, Miami, 2005,Pearson Art Gallery, NY, 2009, Vermont Studio Ctr, 2010, Kunstraum No 10, Germany, 2010, Painted Through, Westbeth Gallery, 2010, First St Gallery, NY, 2013, 0-68 Gallery, The Netherlands, 2013, B.E.L. Gallery, Westport, Carter Burden Gallery, 2016; Invitations: Westbeth Gallery Opening, Figuring Abstraction, NYC, 2015, Hebrew Union Col Mus Opening, The Intent of Evil, Soho, NY, 2015, Carter Burden Galley Opening, NYC, 2016, Chazou Gallery Opening, Kamloops, BC, Canada, 2016; Paintings on Loan-The American Embassies-Freetown, Sierra Leone, West Africa, 2014-2017, Bandar Seri Begawan Brunei 2015-2018; Figuring Abstraction, Westbeth Gallery, NYC, 2015; The Intent of Evil, Hebrew Union Col Mus, Soho, NY, 2015; Chazou Gallery, Canada, 2016. *Collection Arranged:* The Power of Drawing, Westbeth Gallery, 1997-1998. *Teaching:* field adv drawing, Vermont Grad Sch (Norwich Univ), 1987-1988; part time prof painting & color theory, Parsons Sch Design, New York, 1979-; Adj prof drawing, Adelphi Univ, Long Island, NY 1980-1985; prof painting, color theory, New School, Parsons Univ, New York. *Awards:* Caldecott Medal, 1977; Conn Comn Arts, 79; Nat Fine Arts Com Medal, 80; NY Found for Art Fel, 2000; Henry Bergh Award, 2004; Fel, Vt Studio Ctr, 2010; Book Awards, 77, 84; Outstanding merit, Bank St Coll Book Award, 2000; Fel, NCSS-CBC Social Studies Trade Book; Ind Support Program Finalist, Gottlieb Found, 2004; Triangle Artist's Workshop Fellowship; Adolf & Esther Gottlieb Found grant, 2012. *Bibliog:* A Change of Art, NY Mag, 90; Eighteen From New York, Juni Magazin fur Kuitur & Politik, 91; William Stover (auth), Sotheby's Catalog (NYFA), 2001; Concept Mag, 2005; Greenwich Time, 2005; PMNL Magazine, 74; The New York Times, 76, 77; The Washington Post, 86; Kirkus Mag, 2003; The Villager Art Rev, 2007; Kunstraumo 10, Ger, 2012. *Mem:* Hon mem, Poets House; Author's Guild; Mus of the Am Indian; The Jewish Museum, NYC; First Street Gallery. *Media:* Oil, Egg Tempera, Watercolor, Pastel. *Res:* Native Am hist & cult. *Specialty:* Abstract Painting, Sculpture. *Interests:* Music, nature, hiking, poetry, ballet, opera, travel. *Collection:* Int private collections, geology, mythology; Mazza Mus; Leonard Braunschwiegger & Co, Charles Reich, Ende & Malter Mazza, Mus Int Art, Univ Findlay, Isaac Giudi, Century 21. *Publ:* auth, The Crystal Apple, Viking, NYC, 1974; auth, Sedna, Viking, NYC, 1975; auth, The Golem, 76, Jonah, 77, Secret Places, 79, JB Lippincott; auth, The Story of Job, George Braziller, 86; auth, Buffalo, Marshall Cavandish, 2003; Reprinted, Fitzhenry & Whiteside, Can, 2005; Gihon Series: Montotypes, 2011; A Passion for Color, Paintings (catalog). *Dealer:* Etra Fine Art 50 NE 40th St Miami FL 33137; First St Gallery 526 W 26th St NY. *Mailing Add:* 55 Bethune St New York NY 10014

BRODSKY, EUGENE V
PAINTER
b New York, NY, 1946. *Study:* George Washington Univ, 63-64. *Work:* Metrop Mus Art, New York; Picker Art Gallery, Colgate Univ, Hamilton, NY; Detroit Inst Art; Nat Gallery of Art, Washington, DC; Baltimore Mus Art, Md; Yale Univ Art Gallery, New Haven, Conn; Mus Contemp Art, San Diego, Calif. *Exhib:* Imago Galleries, Palm Desert, Calif, 2004; Butler's Fine Art, East Hampton, NY, 2005; Gallery Camino Real, Boca Raton, Fla, 2005; Sears Peyton, New York, 2006, 2009, 2011. *Teaching:* Mixed media teacher, Art Students League, 98-2001. *Awards:* Grant, Creative Artists Pub Svc, 75; Painting, Nat Endowment Arts, 1976; John Simon Guggenheim Fel, 79 & 87; Nat Endowment Arts, 85; Drawing fel, NY Found Arts, 89; Louis Comfort Tiffany Fellowship, 77. *Bibliog:* Alan G Artner (auth), Brodsky paintings save exhibition, Chicago Tribune, 82; Dore Ashton (auth), An art of process, Arts Mag, 85, 96; Phyllis Braff (auth), NY Times, 2000. *Media:* Mixed Media. *Dealer:* Sears-Peyton 210 Eleventh Ave New York NY 10001; Imago Galleries 45-450 Highway 74 Palm Desert CA 92260. *Mailing Add:* 121 Prince St Apt 4W New York NY 10012

BRODSKY, JUDITH KAPSTEIN
PRINTMAKER, EDUCATOR
b Providence, RI, July 14, 1933. *Study:* Radcliffe Col, BA (art hist); Tyler Sch Art, Temple Univ, MFA. *Work:* Libr Cong, Washington, DC; Fogg Art Mus, Cambridge; NJ State Mus, Trenton; Princeton Univ, NJ; Newark Mus. *Comn:* The Magic Muse, traveling art environ (with Ilse Johnson, M K Johnson & Jane Teller), Asn Arts NJ State Mus, 72; Bicentennial Portfolio, Princeton, NJ, 75. *Exhib:* one-person shows, Brown Univ, 73, NY State Mus, 75, Douglas Col, 78 & Assoc Artists, Philadelphia, 79; many group shows, US & abroad. *Pos:* Assoc dir, Princeton Graphic Workshop, Inc, 66-68; owner, Castle Howard Press; nat pres, Women's Caucus Art, 76-78; assoc dean, Rutgers Univ, 81-82, assoc provost, 82-. *Teaching:* Lectr art hist, Tyler Sch Art, 66-71; asst prof printmaking, Beaver Col, 72-77, assoc prof, 77, actg chmn art dept, 77; assoc prof & chmn art dept, Rutgers Univ, 78-81. *Awards:* Purchase Prizes, NJ State Mus, 70 & 71 & Boston Printmakers, 71; Stella C Drabkin Mem Award, Am Color Print Soc, 77; and others. *Bibliog:* Miller & Swenson (auth), Lives and Works: Talks with Women Artists, Scarecrow Press, 81. *Mem:* Coll Art Asn Am; Philadelphia Print Club; Calif Soc Printmakers; Boston Printmakers; Soc Am Graphic Artists; founding mem Coalition Women's Art Orgn. *Media:* Intaglio, Lithography. *Publ:* Auth, Some notes on women printmakers, Art J, summer 76; designed & publ, B J O Nordfeldt, Etchings, 77, Friends and Foes from A to Z, by Dorothea Greenbaum, 78 & Woman, A Portfolio, 78; auth, Rediscovering Women Printmakers: 1500-1850, Counterproof, spring 79; The Status of Women in Art, Feminist Collage, Columbia Teachers Coll Press, 79. *Dealer:* Assoc Am Artists 20 W 57th St New York NY. *Mailing Add:* Visual Arts Mason Gross Sch Arts 33 Livingston Ave New Brunswick NJ 08901-1959

BRODSKY, STAN
PAINTER, EDUCATOR
b Brooklyn, NY, Mar 23, 1925. *Study:* Univ Mo, BJour; Univ Iowa, with Jim Lechay & Byron Burford, MFA; Columbia Univ, EdD. *Work:* Baltimore Mus Art; Heckscher Mus, Huntington, NY; Dayton Art Inst, OH; Wm A Farnsworth Mus, Rockland, Maine; Parrish Mus, Southampton, NY; Telfair Mus Art, Savannah, Ga; Hyde Collection, Glen Falls, NY; Neuberger Mus, Purchase, NY; Hofstra Univ Mus Art, Hempstead, NY; Del Univ, Newark; Univ Mus, Richmond, Va; New Britain Mus Art, Conn; Mus Art, Bero Beach. Fla; Pensacola Mus Art, Fla; Parrish Mus Art, East Hampton, NY; Newsday Lowe Art Mus, Univ Miami, Coral Gables; pvt collection, Dr James Watson, Cold St Harbor, NY; and others; Maier Art Mus, Randolph Coll, Wa; Smith Coll Mus Art; Northampton Mus Art. *Comn:* Abstract Symbols (lobby mural), PRD Electronics, Syosset, NY, 70. *Exhib:* Solo exhibs, 89, 91, 94, 99, 2003 & 2006, Gesture of Art, Port Washington, NY, 2009, The Figure 1951-2006, Hofstra Univ Mus Art, 2008; two-person exhibs, June Kelly Gallery & Gallery Merz, Sag Harbor, NY, 2006; Centennial Open, Parrish Mus, Southampton, NY, 98; 173rd Ann, Nat Acad Mus, NY, 98; Retrospective 70's-90's (with catalog), Univ Bridgeport, Conn, 99; Labscapes, Coldspring Harbor Lab, NY, 2000; Long Island: Morning Noon and Night, Long Island Mus Art, Stonybrook, NY, 2001; Westport Art Ctr, About Paint, 2005, Gallery N, Abstraction Forty, Setauket, NY, 2005, June Kelly Gallery, NY, 2008, Long Island Morderns (with catalogue), Heckscher Mus Art, NY; three person exhib, Gallery North, Setauket, NY, 2006, 2010; Children's Pleasures, Hofstra Univ Mus Art; The Impact of Color, June Kelly Gallery, NY, 2011; Absorbing Art, Heckscher Mus Art, Huntington, NY; Retrospective, Hechscher Mus Art, Huntington, NY, 2013; 50 Yrs of Celebration, Hofstra Univ, Hempstead, NY, 2013; Abstract Expressionism Reconsidered, Nassau Co Mus Art, NY, 2012. *Teaching:* Prof art, C W Post Ctr, Long Island Univ, 60-, prof emer, 91-. *Awards:* MacDowell Colony, Petersboro, NH, 71; Va Ctr Creative Arts, 85, 86 & 89; Yaddo Fel, Saratoga Springs, NY, 87, 96 & 2004; Trustees Award Scholarly, Creative Achievement, C W Post, Long Island, NY, Univ Brookville, Long Island, 91; and others. *Bibliog:* Ron Pisano (auth), Long Island Landscape Painting in the 20th Century, Little Brown & Co, 90; NY Review of Art, 4th ed, Krantz Pub Co, Chicago, 90; Dr J Collischan (auth), Transformations Into Color (catalog), Mus Retrospective, 91; Amei Wallach (auth), Seeing Through Seeing Beyond, Univ Bridgeport, 99; Marek Bartelik (auth), Synthesis: Redefining the Landscape; June Kelly Gallery, rev, Art News, 168, summer, 2008; Being Stan Brodsky, The Figure 1951-2006, Ameiwallach; Alicia Longwell (auth), Gesture of Art (essay), Port Washington, NY. *Media:* Oil, Acrylic, Gouache, Paint Stick, Watercolor. *Specialty:* Contemporary painting, sculpture, photography and wall hangings. *Interests:* Travel, music, literature, film. *Publ:* Illusr for poster, Enclosure VI, 2000 edition, Graphique de France, Boston, Mass, 88; Ionian Green IV, 500 Ed Color Q, Dayton, Ohio; Riding at Anchor, Waterline Bks, 94; The Uncertainty of Experience, An Artists Journey (memoir), Mid-March Press, NY, 2010. *Dealer:* June Kelly Gallery 166 Mercer St New York NY 10012. *Mailing Add:* 22 Sammis St Huntington NY 11743

BRODY, ARTHUR WILLIAM
PRINTMAKER, PAINTER
b New York, NY, Mar 2, 1943. *Study:* Harvey Mudd Col, BS, 65; Claremont Grad Sch & Univ Ctr, MFA, 67. *Work:* Southern Ill Univ, Carbondale; St Lawrence Univ Mus, Canton, NY; Ariz State Univ, Tempe; Hist & Fine Arts Mus, Anchorage, Alaska; Portland Mus, Ore; Kenai Borough Sch Dist; Mus of the North, Fairbanks, Alaska; Alaska State Mus, Juneau, Alaska. *Comn:* Oil on carved copper (28'x4'), Rabinowitz Courthouse, Fairbanks, Alaska, 2001; 2 panels (13.5x4x2.5), oil on carved bronze, Hutchison Technology Center, Fairbanks, Alaska; Acrylic on carved bronze (10'x4'), Su Valley High School, Talkeetna, Alaska, 2009; Alaska Percent, Art Rabinowitz Courthouse, 2001; Alaska Percent, Art Hutchison, Technol Center, 2005; Alaska Percent, Art State Virology Lab, 2008; Alaska Percent, Art, Su-Valley High Sch, 2009; Alaska Percent, Art State Criminology Lab, 2012. *Exhib:* Print Club, 91; Harper Nat, 92; Print Club Albany, 92; Cimmeron Works on Paper, 93; Prints & the Paper, 95; Los Angeles Printmakers, 2003; and others. *Collection Arranged:* Gilkey Collection, Portland Art Mus, Portland, Oregon. *Pos:* visualization res spec Arctic Region Supercomputing Ctr, Fairbanks, Alaska, retired. *Teaching:* Instr printmaking, design, drawing, painting & art hist, beginning & advan; instr, Univ Alaska, 67-69; asst prof, Ripon Col, Wis, 70-75; from asst prof to assoc prof, 77-84, prof, 84-; printmaking & computer art, Univ Alaska; prof emeritus, Univ Alaska, Fairbanks, 2000-. *Awards:* Second Prize Printmaking, Harrisburg Nat, 92; Purchase Award, Cimmeron Works on Paper, 93; Prints & the Paper Award, 95; Los Angeles Printmakers, 2003. *Mem:* Los Angeles Printmakers; Pacific Arts Northwest; Boston Printmakers; Explorers Club. *Media:* Woodcut, Intaglio, Watercolor, Oil, Plein Air Painting. *Res:* Virtual Reality user Interface; Landscape in virtual reality Panoramic photography. *Specialty:* Alaskan Art. *Interests:* Wilderness travel, hiking, canoeing, cycling, reading. *Publ:* Auth, Communications & Intent, Communications--Tyrant or Liberator?, Ripon Col, 74; Painting the Landscape, Proceedings of Artic Sci Conf, 95. *Dealer:* The Alaska House Gallery 1003 Cushman St Fairbanks AK 99708; Stephan Fine Arts 5th Ave Anchorage AK 99501; Gallery 14 Vero Beach Fl. *Mailing Add:* 11365 SW Mountain Ash Cir Port Saint Lucie FL 34987

BRODY, BLANCHE
PAINTER, PRINTMAKER
b Brooklyn, NY, April 17, 1925. *Study:* Hunter Coll, 41-44; Boston Univ, BS, 49, MEd, 51; San Francisco Art Inst, with Richard Diebenkorn, 57-59. *Work:* Itel, San Francisco, Calif; El Dorado Press, Berkeley, Calif; Rene di Rosa, Bay Area Figuratives Mus; Alan Stone. *Comn:* Logo, Anti-Defamation League Biennale Brit, 88. *Exhib:* San Francisco Women Artists, San Francisco Mus Art, Calif, 57-58, 60, 62-63 & 66-67; Calif Painters Ann, Oakland Mus, 58 & 62-64; Painted Flower Invitational, Oakland Mus, Calif, 59 & 64; Jack London Square, Oakland Mus, Calif, 59-67; Mid Yr Ann, Butler Inst Am Art, Youngstown, Ohio; West Coast Oil Painting Ann, Frye Art Mus, Seattle, Wash, 62-63 & 65-66; Natural & Supernatural, 64-66 & The Contemp Landscape, 68-69, San Francisco Art Inst, Calif; The Artist Looks at

Peace, St Marys Coll; Nat Mus Women in the Arts (2014-). *Collection Arranged:* curator, The Artist Looks at Peace, St Mary's Coll. *Awards:* Second Prize, Oakland Mus, Jack London Square, 61; Ed Hill, El Paso, Tex; First Hon Mention, Biennale Int de Vichy, 64; First Prize, San Francisco Women Artists, 66-67; Hon Mention, Biennale Int del Deporter en las Bellas Artes, Barcelona, Spain, 67. *Bibliog:* James Normile (auth), The subject is children, Archit Dig, 11-12/73; NY Art Yearbook, 75-76; Louis Chapin (auth), Looking west--to exuberance, Christian Sci Monitor, 10/25/78; Thomas Albright (auth), Art in the San Francisco Bay Area, 1945-1980. *Mem:* Artists Equity (mem bd, 60-63); Valley Art Ctr. *Media:* All Media. *Interests:* Psychology, reading, cooking, travel. *Collection:* Renee de Rosa, Tufts Med Sch, Alan Stone, St Marys; Dan & Margie Horan. *Mailing Add:* 19 Vista Del Orinda Orinda CA 94563

BRODY, CAROL Z
PAINTER, COLLAGE ARTIST
b Brooklyn, NY, July 5, 1941. *Study:* Brooklyn Coll, BA (cum laude), 62; Parsons Sch Design, 82-84. *Work:* Staten Island Borough Hall, NY; Snug Harbor Cult Ctr, Staten Island, NY; St Vincent's Med Ctr, Staten Island, NY; Kidder-Peabody Offices, NY, Carmel, Calif & Mich; Metrop Savings Bank, Brooklyn, NY; Kent State Univ Sch Art. *Comn:* Cover design (portrait), Women in History Month, Staten Island Borough Hall, 84; collage & watercolor painting, Smith Kline Beecham Pharmaceuticals Co, Parsippany, NJ, 91; cover design (invitation), Staten Island Inst Arts & Scis, 92. *Exhib:* Ann Nat Exhib, Knickerbocker Artists, Salmagundi Club, NY, 83 & 92; Layerists: Level to Level, Johnson-Humrickhouse Mus, Coshocton, Ohio, 90; solo exhibs, Recent Watercolors, AT&T Corp Educ Ctr, Hopewell, NJ, 90, Pen & Brush Club, NY, 92, 95, 2001, Jeanette Hare Gallery, Northwood Univ, 2006; Ga Watercolor Nat Exhib, Columbus Mus, 91; 167th Ann Exhib, Nat Acad Design, NY, 92; Soc Four Arts, Palm Beach, Fla, 97; Allied Artists of Am at Butler Inst of Am Art, Ohio, 2001; Ann Nat Exhib, Nat Watercolor Soc, Brea, Calif, 2001. *Teaching:* Instr watercolor, Art Lab, Snug Harbor, Staten Island, NY, 86-95 & Armory Art Ctr, West Palm Beach, Fla, 97-98; adj instr art educ, Coll Staten Island City Univ, NY. *Awards:* Adriana Zahn Award, 90; First Place Solo Award, Pen & Brush Ann Mem, 90; Emil Carlson SCNY Award, Salmagundi Club, 96; Third Place, Louisiana Watercolor Soc, 2011. *Bibliog:* Sue St John (auth), A Walk into Abstracts, How Did They Do That?. *Mem:* Nat Watercolor Soc; Catharine Lorillard Wolfe Art Club (vpres painting, 95); Salmagundi Club (jury awards, 89, admiss comt, 90-92); Soc Layerists Multi-Media; Pen & Brush (chmn watercolors, selection comt 90-96); Allied Artists; Audubon Artists; Nat Asn of Women Artists. *Media:* Watercolor, Acrylics. *Publ:* Illusr, Watercolor Mag, Am Artist Publ, 90; Layering, An Art of Time and Space, Soc Layerists Multi-Media, 91; The Best of Acrylic Painting, Rockport Publ, 96; Watercolor Mag (article), 2004; Splash 11, Northlight Books, 2010; Don Unwin (auth), The Artistic Touch 4, 2010; Creativity Workshop, Watercolor Artist Mag, 2012; Journeys to Abstraction by Sue St. John, Northlight Pub, 2012; Best of Am, Watercolor, Kennedy Pub, 2012. *Mailing Add:* 801 Caraway Ct Wellington FL 33414

BRODY, DAVID
PAINTER, EDUCATOR
b New York, NY, Feb 16, 1958. *Study:* Columbia Univ, 1975-79; Bennington Col, BA, 1979-81; Yale Univ, MFA, 1983. *Exhib:* Gun as Image, Mus of Fine Arts, Florida State Univ, Tallahassee, 1997; The Perception of Appearance, Frye Art Mus, Seattle, WA, 2002; Sex, Death, and Geometry, A Thirty Year Retrospective, Central Wash Univ, Ellensburg, Wash, 2013. *Collection Arranged:* Springfield Mus, Springfield, Ohio. *Teaching:* Carnegie Melon Univ, 1990-91; SACI, Florence, Italy, 1992-96; Asst prof, Univ of Wash, Seattle, WA, 1996-2000, assoc prof painting & drawing, 2000-2008, chair, 2000-2007, prof 2008-. *Awards:* Guggenheim, 1991; Fulbright, 1992; Elizabeth Found, 1994; Basil Alkazzi Award, 1998. *Bibliog:* Francine Koslow-Miller (auth), David Brody: Selected Paintings 1985-1994; Elisabeth Sussman (auth), David Brody: Selected Paintings 2001-2002. *Mem:* CAA. *Media:* Oil. *Dealer:* Prographica Fine Works on Paper, Seattle, WA. *Mailing Add:* University of Washington School of Art Box 353440 Seattle WA 98195

BRODY, J(ACOB) J (EROME)
HISTORIAN, MUSEOLOGIST
b Brooklyn, NY, Apr 24, 1929. *Study:* Brooklyn Mus Art Sch, with Gross & Ferren, 46-50; Art Students League, with Groth, 47; Cooper Union, cert, 50; Brooklyn Coll, 50-52; Univ NMex, BA, 56, MA, 64 & PhD, 71. *Collection Arranged:* Early Masters of Modern Art, Isaac Delgado Mus Art, New Orleans, La, 59; Indigo, Mus Int Folk Art, Santa Fe, NMex, 61; Between Traditions (auth, catalog), Univ Iowa Mus, 76; Myth, Metaphor & Mimbreno Art, Maxwell Mus Anthrop, Univ NMex, Albuquerque, 77; The Chaco Phenomenon (auth, catalog), Maxwell Mus Anthrop 83-85; Mimbres Painted Pottery (auth, catalog), Am Fedn Arts 83-85; Mimbres Pottery, Roswell Mus Fine Arts, 83; Beauty From the Earth; Anasazi & Pueblo Indian Pottery (auth, catalog), from Collection of Univ Pa Mus, 90-93; A Bridge Across Cultures: Pueblo Painters in Santa Fe 1910-1932 (auth, catalog), Wheelwright Mus, 92; To Touch the Past: The Painted Pottery of the Mimbres People (auth, catalog), from collection of Weisman Mus Art, Univ Minn, 96; Better than the Picture of the Camera: Early Twentieth Century Pueblo Indian Painting, Univ Art Mus, NMex, 98. *Pos:* Cur art, Everhart Mus, 57-58; cur collection, Isaac Delgado Mus Art, 58-60 & Mus Int Folk Art, 61-62; dir & cur, Maxwell Mus Anthrop, NMex, 62-84; res cur, Sch Am Res 87-; res cur, Maxwell Mus Anthrop, NMex 88-; res assoc Lab Anthrop, Mus Indian Art & Cult, 90-. *Teaching:* Prof museology, Univ NMex, 63-, prof Am Indian art, 65- & emer status. *Awards:* Non-Fiction Award, Border-Regional Libr Asn, 71; Award of Honor, NMex Cult Properties Rev Comt, 78; Archaeol Soc NMex (honoree, 92); Conservation Award, Am Rock Art Res Asn, 98; Honoree, Native Am Art Studies Asn, 98; Disting Alumni Award, Coll Fine Arts, 2000; Lifetime Contribution to the Humanities Award, NMex Endowment for the Humanities, 2001. *Bibliog:* Joyce Szabo (auth), J J Brody, Archaeology, Art and Anthropology, Papers in Honor of J J Brody, Archaeol Soc NMex, 92. *Mem:* Soc Am Archaeol; Native Am Art Studies Asn; Am Rock Art Res Asn. *Res:* Native American art; Southwest Pueblo Indian prehistoric & historic arts, ethnic and modern art. *Publ:* Indian Paintings & White Patrons, UNM Press, 70; Between Traditions, Univ Iowa Mus, 76; Mimbres Painted Pottery, UNM Press, 77; co-auth, Mimbres Pottery: Ancient Art of the American Southwest, Hudson Hills Press, 83; Co-dir, Painted Earth, Program for Art on Film (film), Metrop Mus Art & Getty Found, 89; The Anasazi, Jaca Books, Milan and Rozzoli, 90; Auth, Anasazi and Pueblo Painting, UNM Press & Sch Am Res, 91; Co-auth, To Touch the Past: The Painted Pottery of the Mimbres People, Hudson Hills Press, 96; auth, Pueblo Indian Painting: Tradition & Modernism in New Mexico 1900-1930, Sch Am Res Press, 97; A Day in the Life of a Mimbres Indian, Jaca Books, Milan, 98; Mimbres Painted Pottery, Revised Edition, Sch Am Res Press, 2004. *Mailing Add:* 15 Blue Crow Lane Sandia Park NM 87047

BRODY, MYRON ROY
SCULPTOR, PHOTOGRAPHER
b New York, NY, 1940. *Study:* Nat Inst Fine Arts, Mexico City; Philadelphia Coll Art, BFA, 65; Grad Sch Fine Art, Univ Pa, MFA, 68; Ateneum, Helsinki, Finland, 68-69; Univ Va, 70-71; Harvard Univ, 75. *Work:* Univ of Arts; Princeton Univ Art Mus, NJ; Univ Va Art Mus, Charlottesville; Mus Nac Bellas Artes, Rio de Janeiro; US Dept of State; and others. *Comn:* Polished bronze, N Patrol Sta, Kansas City Police Dept, Mo, 77; polished bronze, Prudential Insurance Co Am, Plymouth, Minn; polished bronze, Technical Audit Ltd, Surrey, Eng. *Exhib:* Nelson Gallery-Atkins Mus, Kansas City, Mo; Allan Stone Gallery, NY; Wichita Art Mus, Kans; Kansas City Art Inst; Minneapolis Inst Arts; Dusseldorf Kunstakademie, Ger; Ark Art Ctr; and other group & one-person exhibs. *Pos:* EXPO 92, Seville, Spain; consultant US Information Agency. *Teaching:* Asst prof sculpture & design, Va Western Community Col, 69-76, chmn dept art, 69-72; adj prof ceramics, art educ & sculpture, Univ Va Sch Continuing Educ, 70-76; lectr sculpture, Hollins Col, Va, 75-76; chmn art dept & prof, Avila Col, Kansas City, Mo, 76-85; chmn art dept, Univ Ark, Fayetteville, 85-91, prof, 85-. *Awards:* Cert for Distinguished Serv, Mus Nacional de Belas Artes, Rio de Janeiro, 83; Fulbright-Hays Fels, Finland, 68, Eng, 73 & Ger, 91; Artists' Work Programmer, Irish Mus Mod Art, Dublin; and others. *Media:* Multimedia. *Publ:* Contribr, New Designs in Ceramics, 70; Decorative Art in Modern Interiors, 73-74; Visual Art & The End User: Who Uses Whom, Int Forum Design, Ulm, Ger, 90. *Mailing Add:* Univ Ark Main Campus Dept Art FNAR 116 Fayetteville AR 72701

BRODY-LEDERMAN, STEPHANIE
PAINTER, DRAWINGS
b New York, NY, 1939. *Study:* Univ Mich Sch Archit & Design, Ann Arbor, 59; Finch Col, BS (design), 61; C W Post Ctr, Long Island Univ, MA (studio art), 75. *Work:* Chase Manhattan Bank, Mus Mod Art, New York, NY; Newark Mus, NJ,; Prudential Insurance Co, NJ; Edward Albee Found, Montauk, NY; Insurance of NAm, NY; Am Womens Economic Develop Corp, NY; Amherst Col, Amherst, Mass; Cooper Hewitt Mus, NY; Harvard Business Sch, Boston, Mass; Montclair Art Mus, Montclair, NJ; Mus Mod Art, New York; and others. *Comn:* Edition of 100 small artworks, Franklin Furnace, New York, NY, 83; poster, funded by Nat Endowment Arts Alternative Mus, NY. *Exhib:* Penthouse Aviary, Mus Mod Art, NY, 80; Butler Libr, Metrop Mus Art, NY, 85; NY Artists Bookworks, Mus Modern Art Libr, NY, 90; Solo Exhibs: Hebrew Home Aged, Riverdale, NY, 95; La State Univ, Shreveport, 95; Galerie Caroline Corre, Paris, 95; Marc Miller Gallery, East Hampton, NY, 96; Williamsburg, Brooklyn, NY, 96; Heroes To Go, Arlene Bujese Gallery, East Hampton, NY, 97; Recent Work, 123 Watts Gallery, NY, 98; Edison Col, Fort Meyers, Fla, 2001; Iconic Imagery, Arlene Bujese Gallery, E Hampton, NY, Appetites, Cleary, Gottlieb, Steen & Hamilton Artists Prog, NYC, 2003; Role Call, Guild Hall Mus, E Hampton, NY, 2004; Pilot Light, OK Harris Fine Art, NYC, 2004; Out Gallivanting, OK Harris Gallery, NY, 2006; Begin, Again, Islip Art Mus, East Islip, NY, 2008, Stories that AddUp, OK Harris Fine Art, New York, 2009, Stories That Add Up, Hudson Opera House, Hudson, NY, 2010, Warm Uncertainty, The Forge Gallery, 2012, One Wall, Big Room, OK Harris Fine Art, NY, 2012; A Woman's Place, Mus Stonybrook, NY, 96; The L Word, 473 Broadway Gallery, NY, 96; Box, Fotouhi Cramer Gallery, NY, 96; Fields & Bulls, 123 Watts Gallery, NY, 96; Current under current: Working in Brooklyn, Brooklyn Mus, NY, 97; NY Drawers, Gasworks, London, Manchester, UK, 97; Art on Paper, Weatherspoon Gallery, Univ NC, Greensboro, NC, 97; The Next World: Text and/as Image/and/as Design and/as Meaning, Johanna Drucker (cur), Newberger Mus, Purchase, NY, 98; The Centennial Open, Parrish Art Mus, Southampton, NY, 98; Group Shows: Material Cult, Univ Bridgeport, Conn, 2000; Text: Word and Image, Nassau Community Col, Garden City, NY, 2000; Here, There & Everywhere, Jean Deux Gallery, Brooklyn, 2000; Bookworks, Brooklyn Mus, 2000; City Arts Benefit, Matthew Marks Gallery, Brooklyn, 2000; Pierogi 2000/The Flat Files, Univ Arts, Philadelphia, Pa, 99; Animal, Limn Gallery, San Francisco, Ca, 99; Waxing Poetic, Montclair Art Mus, NJ, 99; ARTeur: Visual Codex, 450 Gallery, NYC, 2002; Insomnia: Landscapes of the Night, Nat Mus Woman Arts, DC, 2003; 30 Years of Innovation, Ctr Book Arts, NYC, 2004; Diversity, Pratt Inst, Brooklyn, NY, 2005; Making Your Mark, Brooklyn Arts Coun, Brooklyn, NY, 2006; Brooklyn/Nature, Saint Joseph's Col, Brooklyn, NY, 2007; Punchbowl, Metaphor Gallery, Brooklyn, NY, 2008; Books, Broadsides et alia, art6 Gallery, Richmond, Va, 2008; Galerie Beatrix Soulie, Paris, France, 2008; Kentler Gallery, Brooklyn, NY, 2009; NY Grad Sch for Psychoanalysis, New York, 2009; OK Harris Gallery, New York, 2009; Univ de Rouen, Mont-Saint-Aignan, France, 2009; Islip Art Mus, Islip, NY, 2009; Heidi Cho Gallery, New York, 2010; OK Harris, New York, 2010; Central Booking, Brooklyn, 2010; Text=Art=Text: Art from the Kramarsky Collection, Univ Va Mus, Richmond, 2011; Vaoyage of the Oenanauts, Projective City, Paris, 2011; ABC/123, Eric Firestone Gallery, East Hampton, NY, 2011; Butlers Fine Art, East Hampton, NY, 2011; Brodsky, Brody-Lederman, Perlman, Butler Fine Art, East Hampton, NY, 2012; Arcadia, OK Harris, NY, 2012; Visual Vernacular, Southampton Cultural Ctr, NY, 2012. *Collection Arranged:* Edward Albee Foundation, Montauk, NY, Am Women's Econ Develop Corp, NYC, Archive of Concrete & Visual Poetry, Miami Beach, FL, Art Mus of Peale, Brampton, Ontario, Canada, ASCAP, NY, Barnes Hospital, St Louis, Brooklyn Mus Art, NYC, Center for the Arts, Vero Beach, FL, Fine Arts Mus Long Island, Hempstead, NY; Cumberland Health Facility, Brooklyn, NY; Doubleday

Books, Garden City, NY; Erasmus Haus, Basel, Switz; Grafikhuset Futura, Stockholm, Sweden; Librairie Arcade, Osaka, Japan. *Awards:* LINE Grant, NYS Coun on the Arts & NEA, 1984; Hassam & Speicher Purchase Award, Am Acad & Int Arts & Letters, NYC, 1988; Artists Grant, Artists Space, NYC, 1989; E D Foundation Project Grant, 1991; Arthur C Danto Award, Guild Hall Mus Ann, East Hampton, NY, 97; Selected artist, On the Verge, Neuberger Mus, Purchase, NY, 98; Guild Hall Mus Exhib Award, Carolyn Lancher, 2003; Art for "The Poet's Eye", Issues Mag, 2009. *Bibliog:* Janis Edwards (auth), Extensions of the Book, Art Week, 8/10/85; Peter Stack (auth), Airport Shoe: One Show Fits All, San Francisco Chronicle, 12/87; Karin Lipson (auth), article, Newsday, 7/22/88. *Media:* Oil. *Publ:* Auth & illusr, Chocolate Cake, 79 & He Doesn't Walk Funny-He Wore Corrective Shoes, 79, pvt publ; Romantic couplet (the hustle) (portfolio), Paris Rev, 79, cover, winter 2003; Spring Chicken, Artifacts at End of Decade, 81; The adventuress tries fantasy, Whitewalls, 83; Domestic Screams, 85. *Dealer:* OK Harris 383 W Broadway New York NY 10012. *Mailing Add:* 822 Madison Ave-Ste 4 New York NY 10021

BROEKE, JAN TEN See Ten,

BROER, ROGER L
PRINTMAKER, PAINTER
b Omaha, Nebr, Nov 9, 1945. *Study:* Eastern Mont Col, BA, 74; Cent Wash Univ, 74-75. *Work:* Mus Native Am Cult, Spokane, Wash; US Dept Interior, Browning, Mont; MSU, Billings; Univ SD; Evergreen Col; Heritage Ctr, Red Cloud Indian Sch, Pine Ridge, SD. *Comn:* Murals: Denver Int Airport; City Kent Wash; Tahoma Sch Dist, Maple Valley, Wash. *Exhib:* Seventy group and thirty-five solo exhibs incl at Dept Interior, Washington, DC and Espace de Pierre Cardin, Paris. *Collection Arranged:* Univ SDak, Vermillion, SDak. *Teaching:* Iowa State Arts Comn Workshop, 81; artist in schs, Arts Alaska Inc, 83-87; artist-in-residence, Wash State Arts Comn; workshop (Oscar Howe), Univ SDak; mentorship (Lloyd New), Buffalo Bill Cody Mus. *Bibliog:* Jill Rowley (auth), Indian Country Today, 10/2000. *Mem:* Indian Arts & Crafts Asn; Artists of the Black Hills. *Media:* Monotype; Mixed Media, Oil, Sculpture. *Publ:* Articles in various publications, including Contemp Western Artists and The Nebraskaland Mag; Art of the Hills Mag. *Mailing Add:* PO Box 324 Hill City SD 57745-0324

BROKER, KARIN
DRAFTSMAN, PRINTMAKER
b Pa, July 27, 1950. *Study:* Univ Iowa, Iowa City, BFA, 72; Atelier 17, Paris, with Stanley Hayter, 73; Univ Wis, Madison, MFA, 80. *Work:* Cabo Frio Biennial Collection, Brazil; US Info Serv, Middle East; Brooklyn Mus Art, NY; Boston Mus Fine Arts, Mass; Smithsonian Instn; Nat Mus Am Art; plus others. *Comn:* Trophy (3-D drawing), InterFirst Bank & Houston Symphony, 83; RSVP, Bechtler Gallery, Charlotte, NC, 92. *Exhib:* Solo exhibs, McClain Gallery, 03, Univ Denver, Colo, 95, Dakota Galleries, Houston, Tex, 95, Los Angeles on paper, Santa Monica, Calif, 95, Tex Myths and Realities, The Mus of Fine Arts, Houston, 95, Three Tex Artists of Yr in Russia (traveling) 96, London Original Print Fair, Royal Acad Art, London, 99, Gerhard Wurzer Gallery, Houston, 2000, and many others. *Pos:* Pres, Southern Graphics Coun, 84-86; studio coordr, CAA Conf, Houston, Tex, 88. *Teaching:* Prof, Rice Univ, Houston, Tex, currently. *Awards:* Nat Endowment Arts Visual Artist Fel, 85 & 87; Dewar's Texas Do-ers, Tex, 89; Tex Art of Yr, Art League of Houston, 94. *Bibliog:* Carey Rote (auth), essay, Corpus Christi State Univ, 88; David Brauer (auth), essay, Rice Univ, 92; Susanna Sheffield (auth) BBK, Koln, Germany, 91; New Orleans Mus Art, La, 86; Alison de Lima Green (auth) Texas: 150 Works from the Museum of Fine Arts, 2000; Robin Montana Turner (auth) State of the Art Program Portfolios, Barrett Kendall pub, 99; plus many others. *Mem:* So Graphics Coun. *Media:* Drawing, Intaglio. *Publ:* Auth, Mad Artist-Printmaker (catalog), Tex Tech Univ, 83. *Dealer:* McClain Gallery, Houston. *Mailing Add:* 4916 Gibson St Houston TX 77007-5329

BROMMER, GERALD F
PAINTER, WRITER
b Berkeley, Calif, Jan 8, 1927. *Study:* Concordia Teachers Col, BSc (educ), 48; Univ Nebr, MA, 55; Chouinard Art Inst; Otis Art Inst, Univ Southern Calif; Univ Calif, Los Angeles. *Hon Degrees:* Concordia Univ, Irvine, Calif, DLitt, 85. *Work:* Hughes Labs, Malibu; Pac Telesis, San Francisco; State of Calif Collection, Sacramento; Utah State Univ; Owensboro Mus Fine Art, Ky; TRW, Sunnyvale, Calif; Firestone Collection; Laguna Beach Mus Art; Univ Utah; Birmingham (Ala) Mus Art; Springfield Art Mus, Mo; Hickory Mus Art, NC; Howard Ahmanson Collection, Los Angeles; Sam Maloof, Claremont, Calif; Ed & Gail Roski, Toluca Lake, Calif; Joseph Miller, Boone, NC; Janice Donelson, Vienna, Va; Peter Uberoth, Los Angeles. *Comn:* Series watercolors, Hilton Hotels, Las Vegas, Reno, Anaheim & San Francisco; Intercontinental Hotel, Los Angeles; Epcot Ctr, Orlando; James Earl Jones, New York. *Exhib:* Am Watercolor Soc, NY, 69, 72 & 73; Nat Acad Design, NY, 71; Watercolor USA, Springfield, Mo, 73, 75 & 76; Nat Watercolor Soc, Los Angeles, 74, 75 & 77-; Royal Watercolor Soc, London, 75; Calif Art Club 2004-2014; plus over 180 solo exhibs. *Pos:* Chief designer, Daystar Designs, Inc, 63-73; Artist-in-residence, Jonathan Club, Los Angeles, 98-2014. *Teaching:* Chmn dept art, Lutheran High Sch, Los Angeles, 55-74; instr, workshops, US & abroad, 75-2014. *Awards:* Landmark Purchase Award, Watercolor USA, 69; Crescent Cardboard Co Purchase Award, Nat Watercolor Soc, 72; Utah State Purchase Award, Watercolor West Invitational, 73. *Bibliog:* Splash 2, 10/93, Splash 3, 10/94, Creative Collage Techniques, 10/94, Splash 6, 10/98, North Light; The Best of Acrylic Painting, 96 & The Best of Watercolor Painting, 95, 96, 97, Quarry Bks, Rockport Publ; Landscape Inspirations, Rockport Publ, 97; Northlight: Watercolors in a Weekend, A David Charles Book, London, UK, 2000; Watercolor Expressions, Rockport Publ, 2001; Splash 7, The Power and Beauty of Light, 2002; Work Small/Learn Big, Int Artist, Australia, 2005; Splash 9, Strokes of Genius, 2007, 2012; Strokes 4: Exploring Line, 2012. *Mem:* Nat Watercolor Soc (treas, 63, vpres, 65-66, 80-81, pres, 67-68, 81-82); Nat Art Educ Asn; Watercolor USA Hon Soc; Nat Art Club, NY; Calif Art Club, Los Angeles; Int Soc Painters in Acrylic (hon pres). *Media:* Transparent Watercolor, Collage. *Interests:* art history. *Collection:* contemporary American Art, primarily watercolors. *Publ:* Auth, Exploring Transparent Watercolor, 93, The Art of Collage, 78, Discovering Art History, 81, 3rd ed, 93, 4th ed, 97 & Exploring Drawing, 87, Davis; Watercolor and Collage Workshop, 86, Collage Techniques, 94, Watson-Guptill; Careers in Art, Davis, 99; Emotional Content: How to Create Paintings that Communicate, Int Artist, Random House, 2003; and many others. *Dealer:* New Masters Gallery PO Box 7009 Carmel CA 93921; Schroeder Studio Gallery Orange CA 92866; Galleria Beretich 1034 Harvard Claremont Ca 91711. *Mailing Add:* 11252 Valley Spring Lane Studio City CA 91602

BRONNER, FELIX
PAINTER, COLLAGE ARTIST, EDITOR
b Vienna, Austria, Nov 7, 1921; US Citizen. *Study:* Univ Calif, BS, 1941; Mass Inst Technol, PhD, 1952. *Hon Degrees:* Ecole Pratique des Hautes Etudes, Paris, 1996. *Work:* Univ Conn Libr, Storrs, Conn; Univ Conn Health Ctr, Farmington, Conn; Univ Conn at Avery Point, Groton, Conn; Mandell Jewish Community Ctr, West Hartford, Conn; Am Physiological Society, Bethesda, Md. *Exhib:* Silver Mine Show, Conn, 1985; Choices (invitational show), Guilford, Conn, 1996; New Britain Art League, New Britain, Conn, 1999; Discovery Mus, Barnum Festival, Bridgeport, Conn, 2001; Pump House Gallery, Hartford, Conn, 2004; JCC W Hartford, 2008; New Haven Libr, 2009; 50th anniv show, Ctr Artists Gallery. *Pos:* Vpres, W Hartford Art League, W Hartford, Conn, 2002-2004; treas, Artworks Inc, Hartford, Conn, 2004-2007. *Teaching:* Prof emeritus, Univ Conn Health Ctr, Farmington, Conn; Univ Conn, Storrs, Conn. *Awards:* Painting Award, W Hartford Art League, 1984; 1st prize painting, Green Art Gallery, Guilford, Conn, 1986; 2nd prize painting, Choices, Shoreline, Alliance for the Arts, Guilford, Conn, 1986; Prize for painting, Wintonbury Art League, Bloomfield, Conn, 1989; Gallery on the Green, Canton, Conn, 1993; Prize for drawing, Gallery on the Green, 1996. *Bibliog:* Jennifer Ball (auth), Felix Bronner Artworks, Artviews (page 167), summer 2003. *Mem:* W Hartford Art League (vpres, 2002-2004); Artworks Gallery (treas, 2004-2007); Canton Artists League. *Media:* Acrylic, Oil, All Media. *Res:* Bone physiology. *Interests:* Abstract Art; Abstract Expressionism. *Publ:* sr ed, Topics in Bone Biology, 2009; five books in abstract art. *Mailing Add:* 160 Simsbury Rd West Hartford CT 06117-1469

BRONSON, A A (MICHAEL WAYNE TIMS)
POST-CONCEPTUAL ARTIST, WRITER
b Vancouver, BC, June 16, 1946. *Work:* Art Gallery Ont, Toronto; San Francisco Mus Mod Art; Musee d'Art Contemporain, Montreal; Vancouver Art Gallery, Vancouver; Mus Mod Art, NY. *Comn:* Ursa Major and Taurus: Pavilion Fragments from the Starry Vault, Relief Mural, Toronto Stock Exchange, 83; Exterior Relief Sculpture, Ottawa Courthouse, 86. *Exhib:* Solo exhibs, Art Gallery Ont, 85, Albright-Knox Art Gallery, 86, Wexner Ctr Visual Arts, Columbus, 93, San Francisco Mus Mod Art, Columbus, 93, San Francisco Mus Mod Art, 93, Stedelijk Mus, Amsterdam, 94, Nat Gallery Can, 95 & Mus Mod Art, NY, 96, Last Visual Arts Ctr, MIT, 2002; Group exhibs, Paris Biennale, Paris, 77; Venice Biennale, Can Pavilion, 80; Documenta 7 & 8, Kassel, Ger, 82 & 87; Int Survey Painting & Sculpture, Mus Mod Art, NY, 84; Artistic Collaboration in the Twentieth Century, Hirshhorn Mus, Washington, 84; Galerie Frédéric Giroux, Paris. *Pos:* Ed, File Mag, Toronto, 72-89; dir, Printed Matter, New York, 2003-. *Teaching:* dept art, UCLA, Los Angeles, 91-92; visiting artist in res, U Toronto, 2007; visiting sr critic, Yale Univ Sch Art, 2006, 2008; grad critic, Workplants Typographie, Netherlands, 2009. *Awards:* Toronto Arts Award, 89; Banff Ctr Arts Nat Award, 93; Jean A Chalmers Award Visual Arts, 94; Bell Canada Award in Visual Art, 2001; Media Award, Gov Gen Visual Art, Canada, 2002; Skowhegan Award, New York, 2006; Office of the Order of Canada, 2008 ; Knight of Arts and Letters, France, 2011. *Bibliog:* General Idea 1968-1984, Kunsthalle Basel, 84; Fin de Siecle, Wurttembergischer Kunstveren, Stuttgart, 92; Jean-Christophe Ammann (auth), Pharmacopia, Centre d'Art Santa Monica, Barcelona, 92. *Media:* Multi-media. *Publ:* Auth, Menage A Trois, Gen Idea, 78; co-ed, Performance by artists, Art Metropole, 79; auth, Getting Into the Spirits Cocktail Book, Gen Idea, 80; co-ed, Museums by artists, Art Metropole, 83. *Mailing Add:* Printed Matter 195 10th Ave New York NY 10011

BRONSON, CLARK EVERICE
SCULPTOR
b Kamas, Utah, Mar 10, 1939. *Study:* Art Instr Inst, 56-57; Univ Utah, 59. *Comn:* Hartford Stag (bronze), Hartford, Conn, 80; Chadwick Ram (bronze), Boone Crockett Buffalo Bill Hist Ctr, Cody, Wyo, 82. *Exhib:* Nat Acad Western Art, Nat Cowboy Hall Fame, 73, 74 & 75; Mzuri Safari Found Conf, Reno, Nev, 73 & 74; Mont Hist Soc, Helena, 78; C M Russell Art Show & Auction, Great Falls, Mont, 79-81; Nat Sculpture Soc, NY, 81. *Pos:* State of Utah Fish & Game Staff Artist, 60-63. *Awards:* First Prize, Nat Art Competition, Art Instr Inst, 57; Silver Medal (bronze sculpture), Nat Acad Western Art, 74, 75 & 77; Silver Medal (bronze sculpture), Nat Sculpture Soc, 81. *Bibliog:* Don Jardine (auth), The continuing success of Clark Bronson, Illustrator, 71; Scott Dial (auth), Symbols of freedom, Southwest Art, 1/80; Richard P Christenson (auth), Bronson's love of life is forever frozen in bronze, Desert News, 9/81. *Mem:* Nat Acad Western Art; Nat Sculpture Soc; Soc Animal Artists; Wildlife Artists Int; Northwest Rendezvous Group. *Media:* Bronze sculpture and painting. *Publ:* Illusr, Nat Wildlife Mag, 63 & High Uintahs--Hi, 64, Album of North American Animals, 66, Album of North American Birds, 67 & Biography of a Grizzly, 69. *Mailing Add:* 1125 E Aspen Ridge Ln Provo UT 84604-6322

BROOKE, DAVID STOPFORD
MUSEUM DIRECTOR
b Walton-on-Thames, Eng, Sept 18, 1931. *Study:* Harvard Univ, AB, 58, AM, 63. *Pos:* Asst cur, Fogg Art Mus, Cambridge, Mass, 60-61; asst to dir, Smith Col Mus, Northampton, 63-65; chief cur, Art Gallery Ont, Toronto, 65-68; dir, Currier Gallery Art, Manchester, NH, 68-77; dir, Clark Art Inst, 77-94. *Mem:* Asn Am Art Mus Dirs. *Res:* British painting of the eighteenth and nineteenth centuries. *Publ:* Coauth, James

Tissot (catalog), Art Gallery Ont, 68; auth, Mortimer at Eastbourne and Kenwood, Burlington Mag, 68; James Tissot's amateur circus, Boston Mus Bulletin, 69; coauth, The Dunlaps of New Hampshire, Antiques, 70; auth, Raeburn's portrait of John Clerk of Eldin, Currier Gallery Bulletin, 71. *Mailing Add:* 414 Blanketflower Ln West Windsor NJ 08550

BROOKE, PEGAN
PAINTER
b Orange, Calif, July 19, 1950. *Study:* Univ Calif, San Diego, BA (literature), 72; Drake Univ, BFA (painting), 76; Univ Iowa, Iowa City, MA (painting), 77; Stanford Univ, MFA (painting), 80. *Work:* Guggenheim Mus; Univ Nebr Art Mus, Omaha; Iowa State Capitol Bldg, Des Moines; Bank Am Int Hq, San Francisco; San Francisco Mus Mod Art; and others. *Exhib:* Solo exhibs, Scottsdale Ctr Arts, Ariz, 83, Saxon-Lee Gallery, Los Angeles, 89, Images Transformed, Oakland Mus, 92, Univ Calif Davis, 92, Joan Roebuck Gallery, Lafayette, Calif, 94 & 96, R B Stevenson Gallery, La Jolla, Calif, 96, 97, 99 & Winfield Gallery, Carmel, Calif, 98, Percival Galleries, Des Moines, 2000, Friesen Gallery, Sun Valley, Idaho, 2002, RB Steverson Gallery, San Diego, 2002, Anne Loucks Gallery, Glencoe, Ill, 2004, RB Stevenson Gallery, La Jolla, Calif, 2005; New Perspectives in Am Art, 83, Emerging Artists 1978-86, 88, Guggenheim Mus; CA Directions in Painting, Alaska State Mus, 86; Survey of Calif Women Artists, Fresno Art Mus, 87; Landscape as Presence, San Jose Inst Contemp Art, 89; Joan Washburn Gallery, NY, 95. *Teaching:* Lectr, Univ Calif, Berkeley, 82, Davis, 83, Calif Col Art & Crafts, 83, Sonoma State Univ, 83 & prof art, San Francisco Art Inst, 84-; grad dir & full prof, San Francisco Art Inst. *Awards:* Marin Arts Coun Painting Grant, 92 & 98; Millary Colony Artist Residency, Austerlitz, NY, 2003; Artist Residency, Pont Aven Sch Contemp Art, Pont Aven, France, 2005. *Bibliog:* Christine Tamblyn (auth), Pegan Brooke at Fuller Goldeen, Art News, 87; Mark Levy (auth), Pegan Brooke at Fuller Goldeen, Art in Am, 88; Suvan Geer (auth), Pegan Brooke, LA Times, 89; David Bonetti (auth), San Francisco Examiner, 92; Leah Ollman (auth), Art in America, 97; Robert Pincus (auth), San Diego Union-Tribune, 97, 99. *Mem:* Coll Art Asn. *Media:* Oil. *Dealer:* R B Stevenson Gallery La Jolla CA; Winfield Gallery Carmel CA; Hemphill Fine Arts Washington, DC; Friesen Gallery Seattle WA. *Mailing Add:* PO Box 857 Bolinas CA 94924

BROOKNER, JACKIE
ENVIRONMENTAL ARTIST, SCULPTOR
b Providence, RI. *Study:* Wellesley Col, BA, 67; Harvard Univ, MA, 70; New York Studio Sch, 76-77. *Comn:* Grossenhain, Ger; Cincinnati, Ohio; Salway Park; Dreher Park, West Palm Beach, Fla; Roosevelt Community Center, San Jose, Calif; Salo, Finland; The Fargo Project. *Exhib:* Varieties of Sculptural Ideas, Max Hutchinson Gallery, NY, 84; traveling exhib, NY/Beijing, Shanghai Art Mus, Beijing Art Inst & Hong Kong Arts Festival, 87-88; Pamela Auchincloss Gallery, NY, 91; Exit Art, NY, 2006; solo exhibs, Diggs Gallery, Winston-Salem State Univ, NC, Hunter Mus Art, Chattanooga, Tenn, 95, Columbus Mus, Ga, 95, Univ N Tex Art Gallery, Denton, Nat Civil Rts Mus, Memphis, Tenn, 96, Crossing Borders, Krakow Poland, 94- & Native Tongues, Fundacio Joan Miro, Centre d'Estudio d'Art Contemporano, Barcelona, Spain, 97; and others. *Collection Arranged:* Dow Jones Collection; Becton Dickinson. *Pos:* Guest ed, Art J, Art & Ecology, summer 92. *Teaching:* Undergrad & grad, Parson Sch Design, NY, 77-; instr, Grad Sculpture Fac, Bard Col, 87; dean & instr, NY Studio Sch, 87; grad sculpture fac, Univ Pa, 94-2000; Harvard Univ, 2002. *Awards:* Trust for Mutual Understanding, Gaia Inst, 97; Nat Endowment Arts Grant, 2002-03; NY Found Arts Fel, 2009; Fargo Project, Nat Endowment for the Arts, 2011. *Bibliog:* Lauren de Boer (auth), Making Sense of Matter, Earthlight, fall 2000; Mara Scrupe (auth), Environment, Audience and Public Art in the New World (Order), Sculpture, 3/2000; Micke Bal (auth), Quoting Caravaggio, Univ Chicago Press, 99; A Boetzkes (auth), The Ethics of Earth Art, Univ Mn, 2010. *Media:* Ecological Art. *Publ:* Is Feminism An Issue for Students of the 80's and 90's?, Art J, Vol 50, No 2, summer 91; guest ed, On Art and Ecology, Art J, Vol 51, No 2, summer 92; M/E/A/N/I/N/G, Forum: On Creativity and Community, No 15, 5/94; Natural Reality/Artistic Positions Between Nature and Culture, Ludwig Forum fur Int Kunst, Aachen, Germany, 99; poetry, NY, winter, spring, 85-89, 99; The Gift of Water, Cultures & Settlements, Malcolm Miles & Nicola Kirkham (eds), Intellect Books, Bristol, Eng, 2003; Urban Rain/Stormwater as Resource, ORO editions, 2009. *Mailing Add:* 131 Spring St New York NY 10012

BROOKS, BRUCE W
PAINTER, SCULPTOR
b New York, NY, July 10, 1948. *Study:* Pratt Inst, BFA, 70, MFA, 75. *Work:* Queens Mus; SUNY, New Paltz; Best Products; Prudential. *Exhib:* Miss Mus Art, 81; Solo exhibs, OK Harris, NY, 81, 83 & 92; Brodway Windows, 95-96; Toby Fine Arts, 2001. *Teaching:* Dir com photog prog, City Univ NY; prof & coordr visual arts, LaGuardia Community Col, CUNY. *Awards:* PSC, City Univ NY, 83, 85, 94 & 2002-03. *Mem:* USHA; Am Civil War Soc; Coll Art Asn; ISHA; Friends of Bonsai. *Media:* Oil, Alkyd. *Mailing Add:* 108 Wyckoff St Brooklyn NY 11201-6307

BROOKS, DREX M
PHOTOGRAPHER, EDUCATOR
b Seattle, Wash, Dec 14, 1952. *Study:* Ore State Univ, Corvallis, BFA (photog), 76; RI Sch Design, Providence, MFA (photog), 80. *Work:* Nat Mus Am Art, Smithsonian Inst; The Art Mus, Princeton Univ; RI Sch Design Mus Art; Bibliotheque Nationale, Paris; San Francisco Mus Modern Art; Amon Carter Mus; Mus of Fine Arts Utah. *Exhib:* Regional Photographers, Denver Art Mus, 87; Mountain West Biennial, Nora Eddes Harrison Mus, Logan, Utah, 89, 91; Sweet Medicine, Utah Mus Fine Arts, Salt Lake City, 92; Between Heaven & Home (with catalog), Nat Mus Am Art, Washington, DC, 92; Solo shows, Sweet Medicine, Utah Mus Fine Arts, Salt Lake City, 92, Reservations, Arvada Ctr Arts & Humanities, Colo, 2000, Am Perspectives: Photographs From the Polaroid Collection, Tokyo Metrop Mus Photog, 2000 & Drwx Brooks 25 Yrs, Salt Lake Art Ctr, 2001; Between Heaven and Home, Contemp Am Landscape Photographs, Nat Mus Am art, Smithsonian Inst, Washington, DC 1992. *Teaching:* Instr photog, Univ Colo, Denver, 83-88; prof photog & art, Weber State Univ, Ogden, Utah, 88-. *Awards:* Visual Artist Fel, Nat Endowments Arts, 88 & 92; Visual Artist Grant, Utah Arts Coun, 97; Hemingway Found Grant, 2000; Fr Ministry of Cult and Nat Endowment for the Arts, Residency Fel at LaNapoule Found, France, 93. *Bibliog:* Lucy R Lipparad (auth), The Lure of the Local: Senses of Place, 182-183, 97 & On the Beaten Track: Tourism, Art and Place, 126-127, 99, The New Press; Rebecca Solnit (auth), The Struggle of Dawning Intelligence: On Monuments and Native Americans, Harvard Design Mag, 54-56, fall 99. *Mem:* Soc Photog Educ. *Media:* Photography. *Publ:* contribr, Colorado: Visions of an American Landscape, Roberts Rhinehart Publ, 106, 91; Between Heaven and Home: Contemporary American Landscape Photographs, 13 & 42, 92; Sweet Medicine: Photographs of Indian Massacre Sites, Battlefields and Treaty Sites, Univ NMex Press, 95; RISD Views, Meridian Printing, 44, 96; Black and White Photography: An International Collection, Rockport Publ, 23 & 135, 2000. *Dealer:* Robischon Gallery 1740 Wazee Denver CO 80202. *Mailing Add:* 1210 SW 3rd Ave Ontario OR 97914

BROOKS, ELLEN
PHOTOGRAPHER
Study: Univ Wis, Madison; Univ Calif, Los Angeles, BA, 68, MA, 70, MFA, 71. *Work:* Mus Mod Art, NY; Nat Mus Am Art, Washington, DC; Nat Gallery Can, Ottawa; Musee d'Art Contemporain Montreal, Can; Albright-Knox Mus, Buffalo, NY. *Exhib:* Solo exhibs, Polaroid Project: Ellen Brooks, Vikky Alexander, Dorothy Goldeen Gallery, Santa Monica, Calif, 91, Wooster Gardens, NY, Vikky Alexander/Ellen Brooks, Ansel Adams Ctr, Friends Photog, San Francisco & Urbie et Orbie, Paris France, 92, Cleveland Ctr Contemp Art (traveling), Ezra & Cecile Zilkha Gallery-Wesleyan Univ, Middletown, Conn & Stux Gallery, NY, 93-94; Departures Photog 1923-1990 (traveling), Independent Curators Inc, 92; Between Home and Heaven, Nat Mus Am Art, Washington, DC, 92; Bennington Col, Vt, 92; Concept/Construct: Photog in Los Angeles Art 1960-1990, Laguna Art Mus, Calif, 93; Thomas Segal Gallery, Boston, Mass, 93. *Teaching:* Instr, San Francisco Art Inst, Calif, 73-82, Sch Visual Arts, New York, 85, Tisch Sch Arts, New York Univ, 84-92. *Awards:* Individual Fel, Nat Endowment Arts, 79 & 91; Phelan Award, Oakland, Calif, 72. *Bibliog:* Mary Ellen Haus (auth), Beyond Nature, Ellen Brooks, Tema Celeste, 1-2/89; Leslie Tonkonow (auth), Ellen Brooks, J Contemp Art, fall/winter 91; Carol Squires (auth), review, Artforum, 11/91. *Mailing Add:* 28 Hubert St New York NY 10013-2041

BROOKS, JAN
SCULPTOR, LECTURER
b Quanah, Tex, Jan 28, 1950. *Study:* Columbia Col, Mo, AA, 70; Southern Ill Univ, Carbondale, BA, 72, MFA, 74. *Work:* Ark Art Ctr, Little Rock; Mint Mus Art, Charlotte; Nat Ornamental Metal Mus, Memphis; Southern Ill Univ Mus, Carbondale; Wustum Art Mus, Racine, Wis. *Comn:* Bronze & steel cross, St Barnabas Episcopal Church, Denton, Tex, 75; eight bronze panels, NC Dept Com-NC Arts Coun, Charlotte, 82; mixed metal interior relief, Aeronca Corp, Charlotte, 85. *Exhib:* The Goldsmith, Renwick Gallery, Smithsonian Inst, Washington, DC, 74; The Metalsmith, Phoenix Art Mus, 77; solo exhib, Southeastern Ctr Contemp Art, Winston-Salem, 80; Young Americans: Metal, Mus Contemp Crafts NY, 80; Toward a New Iron Age, Victoria & Albert Mus, London, Eng, 82; Am Metal Work, Kyoto Mus Traditional Indust, Japan, 83; USA-Portrait of the South, Palazzo Venezia, Rome, Italy, 84; Nine From NC, Nat Metal Mus, Memphis, Tenn. *Teaching:* Instr metal, Southern Ill Univ, Carbondale, 74-77; asst prof, Univ NC, Charlotte, 77-83. *Awards:* Designer-Craftsmen Award, NC Artists Exhib, NC Mus Art, 79; Merit Awards, 12th Competitive Exhib, Fayetteville Mus, 84 & Metal Sculpture Exhib, Millersville Univ, 84. *Bibliog:* Julie Hall (auth), Tradition and Change: The New American Craftsmen, E P Dutton, 76; Thelma R Newman (auth), The Container, Crown Publ, 76; Jane Kessler (auth), Jan Brooks-Loyd, Art Papers, 80. *Mem:* Am Craft Coun (vpres, bd trustees, 86); Soc NAm Goldsmiths; Nat Campaign Freedom of Expression; Am Studies Asn. *Media:* Metal. *Publ:* Auth, Strategies for Interpretation (catalog), Cincinnati Arts Ctr. *Mailing Add:* 2120 Conejo Santa Fe NM 87505

BROOKS, KELLY GAVIN
PAINTER
b Baltimore, Md, Sept 29, 1960. *Study:* Lynn Univ, Boca Raton, Fla, 80-81; Coll Notre Dame, Baltimore, Md, 85-86; Schuler Sch Fine Art, Baltimore, Md, 99-2003; Studied with Scott Christensen, Jackson, Wyo. *Work:* Acad Art Mus, Easton, Md. *Exhib:* Oil Painters of Am, Regional Juried Exhib, Richmond, Va, 2001, Nat Juried Exhib, Taos, NMex, 2002; Plein Air Easton, Acad Mus Art, Easton, Md, 2005, 2006, 2008, 2009, 2010; 12th Ann Invitational, Laguna Art Mus, Calif, 2010. *Teaching:* instr landscape oil, Easton STudio & Sch, 2006-2010; instr landscape oil, Stratford Seminar, 2009-2010; lectr landscape, Bellamy Mansion/Walls Gallery lecture, 2009. *Bibliog:* Jennifer Ling (auth), Gavin Brooks, Plein Art Mag, 2006; Michelle Morton (auth), Gavin Brooks, Am Artist, 2009; Bruce Doherty (auth), Gavin Brooks, Workshop Mag, 2009; Mitch Abala (auth), Landscape Painting Essentials, Watson-Guptil, 2010. *Mem:* Plein Air Painters of the Southeast. *Media:* Oil. *Dealer:* David Leadman-Walls Fine Art Wrightsville Beach Rd Wilmington NC; South St Fine Art 5 South St Easton MD 21502; Gallery Antonia Chatham MA

BROOKS, WENDELL T
PRINTMAKER, EDUCATOR
b Aliceville, Ala, Sept 10, 1939. *Study:* Ind Univ, BS (art educ), 62, MFA (printmaking; Martin Luther King Jr Fel, scholar, Southern Fel), 71; Woodstock Artist's Asn, scholar, summer 61; Pratt Graphic Art Asn, scholar, 62; Univ Md, 65-66; Howard Payne Col, 66-67. *Work:* Libr of Cong, Washington, DC; Nasson Col; Mount Union Col; Carleton Col; Bethel Col; plus others including pvt collections. *Exhib:* A Return to Humanism, Burpee Art Mus, Rockford, Ill, 71; Social Comment in Recent Art, Concordia Teachers Col, Seward, Nebr, 71; The Black Experience in Prints, Pratt Graphic Ctr, NY, 72; Black Artists of Am, NJ State Mus, Trenton, 72; Jew Jersey,

1972, 7th Ann Exhib, Trenton, 72; A Very Spec Invitational Show, McCarter Theatre, Princeton, NJ, 79; Black Artists/South, 79; and many other solo & group exhibs. *Teaching:* Instr printmaking, Ala A & M Univ, 67-68; asst prof printmaking & artist-in-residence, Nassan Col, 70; asst prof printmaking, Trenton State Col, 71-; lectr art at var art groups, cols & univs, 69-72. *Bibliog:* Article in Negro Heritage, 10/68; article in Chalkboard, 11/68; article in Christian Sci Monitor, 6/22/70; plus many other newspapers. *Mem:* Philadelphia Print Club. *Mailing Add:* 63 Florance Ave Apt 6 Ewing NJ 08618

BROOME, RICK (RICHARD) RAYMOND
PAINTER
b Pueblo, Colo, Oct 13, 1946. *Study:* Northrop Univ, 67-71; Northrop Inst Tech, 68. *Work:* USAF Acad, Colorado Springs, Colo; Naval Air Mus, Pensacola, Fla; Air Force Mus, Dayton, Ohio; San Diego Art & Space Mus, Calif; Northrop Univ, Inglewood, Calif. *Comn:* T-33/Colo Rocky Mountains, 74, F-105/Vietnam, 75, B-1/USAF Acad, 79, F-15/USAF Acad, 81 & T-Birds/USAF Acad, 82, USAF Acad Cadets, Colorado Springs. *Exhib:* JOC Aviation Art Show, Craig Air Force Base, Selma, Ala, 76 & Scott Air Force Base, Ill, 77. *Awards:* Best Cover/Year, Rocky Mountain Collegiate Asn, 75. *Bibliog:* Will Robinson (dir), From Time to Time (film), KRDO TV, 80 & 81; Gary Olson (auth), Airplanes in art: Broome a master, Weekend, Colo Springs Sun, 3/7/80. *Media:* Acrylic. *Res:* Created 1450 plus historically accurate aviation originals involving complete detailed research. *Publ:* Illusr, 12 covers of Frontier Mag, Inflight Publ, 74-82; 3 covers of Talon Mag, USAF Acad, 75-82; 2 covers of Check Points Mag, USAF Acad, 80; 3 covers of Aerospace Historian, Univ Kans, 79-82. *Dealer:* Kemper Galleries 1624 N Academy Blvd Colorado Springs CO 80915. *Mailing Add:* 2809 Old Broadmoor Rd Colorado Springs CO 80906-3643

BROSIUS, KAREN
MUSEUM DIRECTOR
Study: Butler Univ; Ecoles d'arts Americaine; Juilliard Sch Music; Hunter Col, City Univ of NY, MA summa cum laude,. *Pos:* Researcher, Res Found of City of NY, formerly; pub affairs officer, Pierpont Morgan Libr, formerly; sr philanthropic, arts, and commun exec Altria Group, Inc, New York City, formerly; dir Columbia Mus Art, SC, 2004-; bd dir, Arts & Bus Coun, ArtTable, currently. *Mem:* Am Asn Mus; Nat Endowment Arts. *Mailing Add:* Columbia Mus Art PO Box 2068 Columbia SC 29202

BROSK, JEFFREY
SCULPTOR
b New York, NY, Feb 15, 1947. *Study:* Univ Pa, BA & BS, 70; Mass Inst Technol, MA (archit), 76. *Work:* Bank Am, San Francisco. *Comn:* IBM, Dallas, Tex. *Exhib:* Aldrich Mus Contemp Art; Hudson River Mus, Yonkers, NY, 78; solo exhibs, Max Hutchinson Gallery, NY, 83, Roanoke Mus Fine Arts, Va, 85, Fine Arts Ctr, Univ Mass, Amherst, 87, Stephen Rosenberg Gallery, NY, 88 & 90, Joan Robey Gallery, Denver, 91, Clark Univ, Worcester, Mass, 92 & Stephen Rosenberg Gallery, NY, 92; Construct Gallery, Chicago, 81; Galerie Alain Oudin, Paris, 81; Anne Reed Gallery, Ketchum Idaho, 90; Current Minimalists, Art Festival, Atlanta, Ga, 91; and many others. *Awards:* Grant, Pollock-Krasner Found, Inc. *Bibliog:* Hal Foster (auth), article, Artforum, 12/79; Michael Brenson (auth), Rev/Art, NY Times, 12/2/88; Stephen Westfall (auth), rev, Art Am, 4/89; Eleanor Heartney (auth), Rev, ARTnews, New York, 90; Mizue, Tokyo, Japan, 91. *Media:* All Media. *Dealer:* Stephen Rosenberg Gallery 115 Wooster St New York NY 10012. *Mailing Add:* 135 Spring St New York NY 10012-3858

BROTHERS, BARRY A
PAINTER, MURALIST
b Brooklyn, NY, Jan 18, 1955. *Study:* Brooklyn Coll, City Univ NY, BS (photog & art), 77, MFA (painting), 80. *Work:* Herbert F Johnson Mus Art, Cornell Univ, NY; Brooklyn Coll Collection, New York; Am Broadcasting co Inc; Capital Cities/ABC Inc, New York. *Comn:* 7 paintings, 6 photographs for portfolio, US oil refineries & Fortune Mag, New York, 81; six murals (two triptychs), Am Broadcasting co Inc, Broadcast Opers Complex, New York, 85-86; mural, Capital Cities/ABC Inc, Corp Hq, New York, 89. *Exhib:* New Realists, Adelphi Univ, Garden City, NY, 82; Brooklyn 1983 & 1985, Brooklyn Mus, 83 & 85; The Brooklyn Landscape, Ammo Artists Space, Brooklyn, 84; 12 Yr Retrospective, Brooklyn Mus, 84; 11th Ann Invitational, Henry Hicks Gallery, Brooklyn, 86; Printmaking at British Columbia, Mus Borough Brooklyn, New York, 87; In Search of the Am Experience, Mus Nat Arts Found, 89. *Pos:* Independent graphic & advert artist, illusr & photogr, 74-; room screen, furniture design, computer software develop, 89-. *Awards:* DESI 9, Graphic Design, USA, 86; Landscape Painting Competition, Artists Mag, 87; In Search of the American Experience, Mus Nat Arts Found, 89. *Bibliog:* American Artists - Survey of Leading Cont Am, essay, 85 & The New York Art Rev, essay, 89, Krantz co; Art Product News Mag, article, Grady Publ co, 3/87 & 4/87; Contemporary Graphic Artists, essay, Gale Research co Publ, Vol 2, 87. *Media:* Oil, Acrylic. *Publ:* Contribr, Print Mag XXXVIII:2, article, 3-4/84; Gran Bazaar Maf, essay, Milan, Italy, 85; Graphic Design: USA, Kaye Publ Corp, 8/86. *Mailing Add:* 1920 E 17th St Brooklyn NY 11229

BROTHERS, CAMMY R
EDUCATOR
Study: Harvard Univ, BA (summa cum laude, Fulbright Fel, 1991-92), 1991 & PhD (Rome Prize Fel, 1996-97), 1999; Courtauld Inst Art, Univ London, MA, 1992. *Pos:* Cur intern, Univ Iowa Mus Art, 1989; cur asst, Fogg Mus Art, 1990-91. *Teaching:* Asst prof dept archit, Univ Va, 1999-2006, assoc prof Italian Renaissance Archit, 2006-. *Awards:* Villa I Tatti Fel, Harvard Univ Ctr for Renaissance Studies, 2001-2002; Canadian Ctr for Archit Fel, 2006; Garden & Landscape Fel, Dumbarton Oaks, 2006-2007; Vis Sr Fel, Ctr for Advanced Study of Visual Arts, 2007; Charles Rufus Morey Bk award, Coll Art Asn, 2010. *Publ:* Auth, Michelangelo, Drawing, and the Invention of Architecture, Yale Univ Press, 2008. *Mailing Add:* Univ Virginia 412 Campbell Hall PO Box 400122 Charlottesville VA 22904-4122

BROUDE, NORMA FREEDMAN
HISTORIAN, EDUCATOR
b New York, NY, May 1, 1941. *Study:* Hunter Col, AB, 62; Columbia Univ, MA (Woodrow Wilson Found Fel), 64, PhD (Woodrow Wilson Dissertation Fel), 67. *Collection Arranged:* co-cur with Mary D Garrard, Claiming Space: Some Am Feminist Originators, Am Univ Art Mus, 2007. *Pos:* Mem of the Art Bulletin Editorial Advisory Comm, Col Art Asn of Am, 96-98. *Teaching:* Instr art hist, Conn Col, New London, 66-67; vis asst prof, Oberlin Col, Ohio, 69-70; asst prof art hist, Columbia Univ, NY, 72-73; vis asst prof, Vassar Col, Poughkeepsie, NY, 73-74; asst prof art hist, Am Univ, Washington, DC, 75-77, assoc prof art hist, 77-86, prof art hist, 86-2011, prof emer art history, 2011-. *Awards:* Nat Endowment Humanities Fel, 81-82; Mina Shaughnessy Scholar, 82; Bellagio Study & Conf Ctr Fel, Rockefeller Found, 91; Art Hist Recog Award, Women's Comm, Coll Art Asn of Am, 2000. *Mem:* Coll Art Asn Am; Women's Caucus Art. *Res:* Late 19th and early 20th century European painting. *Publ:* Auth, Degas and French Feminism Circa 1880, Art Bull, 88; auth & ed, World Impressionism: International Movement, 1860-1920, Harry N Abrams Inc, 90; auth, Impressionism, A Feminist Reading, 91, Georges Seurat, 92 & gen ed, The Rizzoli Art Series, 92 Rizzoli; co-ed (with Mary D Garrard), The Expanding Discourse; Feminism and Art History, Harper Collins, 92; The Power of Feminist Art: The American Movement of the 1970's, History and Impact, Abrams, 94; Gustave Caillalootte and the Fashioning of Identity in Impressionist Paris, Rutgers Univ Press, 2002; co-ed (with Mary D Garrard), Reclaiming Female Agency: Feminist Art History after Postmodernism, Univ of CA Press, 2005; GB Tiepolo at Valmarana, Art Bull, 6/2009. *Mailing Add:* Dept Art American Univ 4400 Massachusetts Ave NW Washington DC 20016-8004

BROUDO, JOSEPH DAVID
EDUCATOR, PAINTER
b Baltimore, Md, Sept 11, 1920. *Study:* Alfred Univ, BFA, 46; Boston Univ, MEd, 50. *Work:* Int Mus Ceramics, Faenza, Italy, Alfred Univ, NY; Prieto Collection, Mills Coll, Calif; Joan Mannheimer Collection; Mus Ceramic Art, Alfred Univ. *Comn:* mosaics, temples, Goversville, NY, Amsterdam, NY, Beverly, Mass. *Exhib:* Int Exhib, Ostend, Belg, 60; Ten Boston Area Craftsmen, NY World's Fair, 64-65. *Teaching:* Dept head & prof art, Endicott Coll, 46-94, distinguished emer prof, 94-. *Awards:* Grand Prize, Int Exhib, Ostend, Belg, 60; Top Honors, Eastern States Expos & De Cordova Craftsmen Exhib; and others. *Mem:* Mass Asn Craftsmen (chmn, 55-56, dir, 72); Am Crafts Coun (exec coun, 71-72); Boston Soc Arts & Crafts (dir, 62-78); Cult Connection (dir, 87-90). *Media:* Acrylic, Oil; Watercolor; Ceramics. *Res:* red reduction glazes in oxidation fire. *Interests:* painting, politics. *Mailing Add:* Endicott College Dept Art 5 Gary Ave Beverly MA 01915

BROUGHER, KERRY
MUSEUM DIRECTOR, CURATOR
Study: Univ Calif, Irvine, BA (Art History), 1974; Univ Calif, Los Angeles, MA (History of Film & Television), 1978. *Pos:* Various cur positions, Mus Contemp Art, Los Angeles, 1982-1997; dir, Mus Mod Art, Oxford, England, 1997-2000; chief cur, Hirshhorn Mus & Sculpture Garden, Washington, 2000-, dir, Art & Progs, 2002-2006, deputy dir, 2007-. *Awards:* Co-recipient Int Asn, Art Critics Award, 2005. *Mailing Add:* Smithsonian Institution Hirshhorn Museum and Sculpture Garden PO Box 37012 Washington DC 20013

BROUN, ELIZABETH GIBSON
MUSEUM DIRECTOR, HISTORIAN
b Kansas City, Mo, Dec 15, 1946. *Study:* Univ Bordeaux, cert advanced study, 1967; Univ Kans, BA, 1968, MA, 1969, PhD 1976; Woodrow Wilson Fel, 1968-69; Ford Found Fel, 1970-72. *Collection Arranged:* Spencer Mus Art, Lawrence, Kans; Albert Pinkham Ryder, Nat Mus Am Art, Washington, DC, 1989. *Pos:* Cur prints & drawings, Spencer Mus Art, Univ Kans, Lawrence, 1977-83, actg dir, 1982-83; asst dir, chief cur, Nat Mus Am Art, Smithsonian Inst, Washington, DC, 1983-88, actg dir 1988-89, Margaret & Terry Stent dir, Smithsonian Am Art Mus (formerly Nat Mus Am Art) & Renwick Gallery, 1989-. *Teaching:* Asst prof, Univ Kans, 1978-83. *Mem:* Phi Beta Kappa. *Res:* History of American art and graphic arts; Contemporary art, 19th-century art, prints and drawings. *Publ:* Coauth, Benton's Bentons, 1980 & Engravings of Marcantonio Raimondi, 1981; auth, Contents of Whistler's Art, Arts Mag, 1987; The Art of Lithography, Univ Houston, 1987; Benton, A Politician in Art, Smithsonian Studies in Am Art, spring 1987; Albert Pinkham Ryder, Smithsonian Press, 1989. *Mailing Add:* Smithsonian Am Art Mus MRC 970 PO Box 37012 Washington DC 20013-7012

BROWER, STEVEN
GRAPHIC DESIGNER, EDUCATOR
b New York, NY. *Study:* Calif State Univ, BA. *Pos:* Principal, Steven Brower Design; former creative dir, Print Mag. *Teaching:* Instr graphic design, Sch Visual Arts, New York. *Publ:* Auth, Woody Guthrie Artworks, Rizzoli, 2005; coauth, 2D: Visual Basics for Designers, Cengage Learning, 2006; auth, Satchmo: The Wonderful World and Art of Louis Armstrong, Abrams, 2009. *Mailing Add:* School of Visual Arts 209 E 23 St New York NY 10010-3994

BROWN, AARON MORGAN
PAINTER
b Wichita, Kans, April 4, 1964. *Study:* Wichita State Univ, Painting; Univ Kans, BFA (Painting); Syracuse Univ, MFA (Painting). *Exhib:* Solo exhibs include Strecker-Nelson Gallery, Manhattan, Kans, 2002, 2003, 2004, Wichita Ctr Arts, Wichita, Kans, 2005, Brian Marki Fine Art, Portland, Ore, 2007, Limbo Fine Arts, San Diego, 2007; Group exhibs include 68th Ann Regional Exhib, Arnot Art Mus, Elmira, NY, 2002; Stillness In The Din, Erman B White Gallery, Butler C Coll, El Dorado, Kans, 2004; Red Ball Auction, Sushi Visual Art, San Diego, 2004; Second Nature, Proj Creo, St Petersburg, Fla, 2004; Arts Coun Ann Juried Exhib, CityArts, Wichita,

Kans, 2005; Klaudia Marr Gallery, Santa Fe, 2005; Empirical/Experimental, Manifest Creative Research Gallery, Cincinnati, 2005; Bestiary, Froelick Gallery, Portland, Ore, 2006; Languages of Silence, Greater Reston Arts Ctr, Reston, Va, 2006; A Sense of Place, Trish Higgins, Wichita, Kans, 2007; Real & Imagined, Elder Art Gallery, Charlotte, NC, 2007; Apparitions, Curious Matter, Jersey City, 2007. *Awards:* Pollock-Krasner Grant, 2005 ; Best in Show, Nat Competition, Masur Mus Art, Monroe, LA; 1st Place Prize, Experimental Category, Artist's Magazine Nat Competition, 2006; George Sugarman Found Grant, 2007. *Dealer:* Blue Gallery 118 SW Blvd Kansas City MO 64108

BROWN, ALAN M, JR
DEALER, CONSULTANT
b New Rochelle, NY. *Study:* Syracuse Univ, BS, 69. *Collection Arranged:* Textiles of the Andes. *Pos:* Owner, Alan Brown Gallery, Naples, FL. *Awards:* Arts Award, Westchester Arts Coun, 94. *Mem:* Coun Arts Westchester (trustee, formerly); Westchester Pub Art (bd dir, formerly); Pelham Art Ctr (art adv bd). *Res:* Contemporary artists. *Specialty:* American Pop Art & American Art 1950-1990. *Interests:* Curating Public & Private Art Collections. *Collection:* Contemporary American art; folk art; Ancient Peruvian Textiles. *Dealer:* Alan Brown Gallery 901 7th St South Naples FL 34102. *Mailing Add:* 901 7th St S Naples FL 34102

BROWN, ALICE DALTON
PAINTER
b Danville, Pa, Apr 17, 1939. *Study:* Acad Julian, Paris, 57; Cornell Univ, 58-60; Oberlin Coll, Ohio, BA, 62. *Work:* Maier Mus Art, Lynchburg, Va; Springfield Mus Art, Mo; Tampa Mus Art, Fla; Met Mus Art, NY; Ashville Mus Art, NC. *Comn:* Painting, General Electric Co, 90; Am Home Products Corp, 94. *Exhib:* Collectors Choice, McNay Art Inst, San Antonio, Tex, 81, 89 & 90; solo exhibs, AM Sachs Gallery, NY, 82-84, Katharina Rich Perlow Gallery, NY, 85; Fischbach Gallery, NY, 87, 89, 91, 93, 95, 98, 2000, 2002, 2004, 2006, 2008, 2010, 2012; William Sawyer Gallery, San Francisco, 88; Springfield Art Mus, Mo, 99; Fischbach Gallery, 2010, 2012; Herbert Johnson Mus Art, 2013; Cornell Univ, Ithaca, NY, 2013. *Awards:* Purchase Award, West Collection: Art & Law, 85. *Bibliog:* April Kingsley (auth), The Paintings of Alice Dalton Brown, Hudson Hills Press, 2002; poster reproductions pub by McGraw Publ; Gerrit Henry (auth), Alice Dalton Brown at Fischbach, Art in America, 2003; Margie Goldsmith and Richard Matthews (auths), Making Miracles of Light and Shadow: An Interview with Alice Dalton Brown, Tampa Review, ed. 40, Univ Tampa Press, 2010; Valerie Gladstone (auth), Review: New Yorks Alice Dalton Brown, Art News, 2010; Stephanie Wiles (auth), A Conversation with Alice Dalton Brown, Herbert F Johnson Mus, Cornell Univ, 2013. *Media:* Oil, Pastel. *Specialty:* Am Realist Art. *Dealer:* Fischbach Gallery 210 Eleventh Ave New York NY 10001. *Mailing Add:* 817 Central Ave #2 Peekskill NY 10566-2039

BROWN, ANITA
PAINTER
b Rosario, Argentina, Aug 8, 1916; US citizen. *Study:* Nat Acad Design, 34; Hunter Col, BA, 38. *Work:* Louise E Thorne Mem Art Gallery, Keene State Univ, NY; Roberson Ctr Arts & Sci, Binghamton, NY; Griffiths Art Ctr Gallery, St Lawrence Univ, Canton, NY; Butler Inst Am Art, Youngstown, Ohio. *Exhib:* New Talent, Country Art Gallery, Westbury, NY, 60; group exhibs, Ligoa Duncan Gallery, NY, 64, Gallery 1199, NY, 78, Nat Acad Design, NY; Still Life Exhib, Japan Europe & Am, Storm King Art Ctr, Mountainville, NY, 67; Visions Past, Visions Present, Roberson Ctr Arts & Sci, Binghamton, NY, 80. *Awards:* Honorable Mention, Long Island Artists 13th Ann, Hofstra Coll, 62; Molly Morpeth Canaday Mem Award, Nat Asn Women Artists, 75. *Mem:* Nat Asn Women Artists. *Media:* Oil, Woodcut, Etching

BROWN, BETTY ANN
EDUCATOR, CRITIC
b Oklahoma City, Okla, June 6, 1949. *Study:* Southern Methodist Univ, BFA, 71; Univ Tex, Austin, MA, 73; Univ NMex, Albuquerque, PhD, 77. *Collection Arranged:* Faces of Fiesta, San Diego State Univ, 82; Susan Kleinberg, Univ Southern Calif, Davidson Conf Ctr, 82; Sensuous Surfaces, Univ Southern Calif, 82; Generations, Conejo Valley Art Mus, 83; Caretas Mexicanas, Mexican mask exhib, Southwest Mus, 83; Space (Artists Spaces), Occidental Col, 86; Roland Reiss Retrospective, 91. *Pos:* Dir visual arts prog, Col Continuing Educ, Univ Southern Calif, Los Angeles, 81-; art critic for weekly newspaper, Reader, 81-83; auth, monthly series of previews on Los Angeles art exhibs, Artscene, 82-; auth, monthly column, Arts Mag, 82-; ed, Visions Mag, 86-87. *Teaching:* Asst prof art hist, Ill State Univ, 77-79; asst prof, Calif State Univ, Northridge, 79-81 & 86-; adj prof, Univ Southern Calif, 81-85; assoc prof art, Calif State Northridge, 88-. *Mem:* Art Table; Women's Caucus Art; Asn Latin Am Art (secy, 81-83); Inst Hispanic Media & Cult (bd dir, 82-83). *Res:* Contemporary Art, Ancient and contemporary arts of Latin America. *Publ:* Auth, numerous articles on Pre-Columbian art history and contemporary folk arts of Latin America; Exposures: Women and Their Art, 89; auth, numerous articles on contemp criticism. *Mailing Add:* Art Dept Cal St Univ Northridge 18111 Nordhoff St Northridge CA 91330-0001

BROWN, BRUCE ROBERT
PAINTER, SCULPTOR
b Philadelphia, Pa, July 25, 1938. *Study:* Tyler Sch Art, Temple Univ, BFA (painting), 62, MFA (sculpture), 64. *Work:* Telfair Acad Arts & Sci, Savannah, Ga; Festival Arts Collection, Erie, Pa; WVa Arts & Humanities Coun; Damon Ctr, Monroe Community Coll (sculpture on permanent loan), Rochester, NY. *Comn:* Five Coins for Medal Arts Co, 71; Heroes of God, Rochester, NY, 72; Inauguration medallion for pres of Monroe Community Col, Rochester, NY, 72; Bronze relief, Dr Stabins Monroe Community Coll bd trustees, 75; Acad achievement medallion for Monroe Community Col, 76; Bronze relief, pastor of church congregation in Rochester, NY, 77; Portrait of Canonized St, Davao City, Philippines, 2002. *Exhib:* Nat Show, Pa Acad Fine Arts, Philadelphia, 62; Nat Show, Butler Inst Am Art, Youngstown, Ohio, 62-63; 21st Ann Int Exhib, Beaumont, Tex, 72; Bertrand Russell Peace Found Show, London, Eng, 72; Sunbird Gallery, Los Altos, Calif, 87; Tyler Alumni Gallery, Temple Univ, Philadelphia, 87; Beaumont Nat Art Show, Beaumont Mus, Beaumont, Tex, 72; solo exhib La State Univ, Baton Rouge, La, 73; Gallery G, 2003; Big and Little Gallery, 2004; plus others. *Pos:* sculptor-in-residence St Gauden's Natural Hist Site, NH 69. *Teaching:* instr, adult painting prog, Dept Recreation, Philadelphia, 61-64; instr ceramics & art, Philadelphia Pub Sch, 65-66; instr art, West Liberty State Col, 67-68, head of sculpture dept; assoc prof art, Monroe Community Col, NY, 68-99, chmn, Art Dept, 79; instr, Rochester Inst Technol, 79-80; instr, Ford Acad of Fine Arts, Davao City, 2001-03; instr, Philippine Women's Coll, 2004-06. *Awards:* Purchase Award, Arts & Humanities Coun WVa, 67; Purchase Award, Am Acad Arts & Lett, 68; Purchase Award, Erie Summer Festival Arts; Huntington 180 Exhib Award in Sculpture, Charleston, WVa, 68; Painting Award Appalachian Corridors, 68. *Bibliog:* Folio Mag Tyler Sch of Fine Art, Temple Univ, Philadelphia, Pa; Cabbages & Kings Mag, Monroe Community Col, Rochester, NY; Mindanao Times, Davao City, Philippines. *Mem:* Coll Art Asn Am; Southern Sculptors Asn; Rochester Print Club; Artist's Equity Asn, NY. *Media:* Oil & Acrylic. *Res:* Inter-disciplinary art/math course, drawing the human figure. *Publ:* Auth, Robert Henkes, Sport in Art (guide for beginning illus); Artists USA; Printmaking USA

BROWN, CAROL K
PAINTER, SCULPTOR
b Memphis, Tenn. *Study:* Univ Miami, BFA, 78; Univ Colo, MFA, 81. *Work:* Denver Art Mus; Jacksonville Art Mus, Fla; Art Mus, Fla Int Univ, Miami; Miami Art Mus, Fla; Tampa Mus Art, Fla; Memphis Brooks Mus Art, Tenn; Polk Mus, Fla; Mus Contemp Art, San Diego, Calif; and others. *Comn:* Sculpture, Fla Int Univ, Miami, Dade Co Art Pub Places, Miami, Fla, 87, Univ Fla, Gainesville, 88; Southeast Banking Corp, 89; Progressive Insurance Co, 2006; and others. *Exhib:* Denver Art Mus Invitational, 81; Art of Miami, Southeastern Ctr Contemp Art, Winston-Salem, NC, 85; Nat Endowment Arts-Fel Artists, Fla State Univ, Tallahassee, 85 & 86; The Hortt Exhib, Mus Art, Ft Lauderdale, Fla, 85, 86 & 87; Solo Exhibs: Bacardi Sculpture Plaze & Gallery, Miami, Fla, 88; Ctr Fine Arts, Sculpture Plaza, 87; Gloria Luria Gallery, Bay Harbor Island, Fla, 91; Nohra Haime Gallery, NY, 92, 94, 96, 2000, 01, 03, 06, & 08; Jacksonville Art Mus, 93; Jeff Baker Blau Gallery, Boca Raton, Fla, 93; Frederic Snitzer Gallery, 95; Lehman Col, Bronx, NY, 96; Ambrosine Gallery, Fla, 2000 & 2004; Whitney Mus, 97; Whitney Mus Am Art, 97; Nat Mus of Women in the Arts, Washington, DC, 2004, 2005; Beijing Biennial, 2005; and others. *Teaching:* Instr, Miami-Dade Community Col, 86-87; fac, New World Sch Arts, 91-. *Awards:* State Fla Fine Arts Fel, 83 & 92; Nat Endowment Arts Fels, 84 & 86; Southeastern Ctr Contemp Art Fel, 84. *Bibliog:* Janet Koplos, rev, Art in Am, 5/2001; Douglas F Maxwell (auth), rev, Carol K Brown at Nohra Haime Gallery, NY Arts, 2/2001; Michael Arog (auth), Art in America, 5/2004. *Media:* All Media; Acrylic. *Dealer:* Nohra Haime Gallery 41 E 57th St New York NY; Scott White Contemporary Art 2400 Kettner Blvd Loft #238 San Diego CA 92101; Blueleaf Gallery 10 Marino Mart Fairview Dublin 3 Ireland

BROWN, CECILY
ARTIST
b London, 1970. *Study:* B-Epsom Sch Art, Surrey, England, B-TEC Diploma in Art & Design, 1987; Morley Col, London, Attended Drawing & Printmaking classes, 1987-89; NY Studio Sch, 1992; Slade Sch Art, London, BA in Fine Arts, First Class Hon, 1993. *Work:* At Century's End: John P Morrissey Collection 90's Art, Mus Contemp Art, Fla, 1999; Directions, Hirshhorn Mus & Sculpture Garden, Washington, DC, 2002, Off, Murray Guy, NY; Off, Murray Guy, NY, 2003; Art, Whitney Mus Am Art, 2004. *Exhib:* Exhib incl Fete Worse Than Death, Laurent Delaye, London, 1994, Eagle Gallery, London, 1995, Taking Stock, NY, 1996, Deitch Projects, NY, 1997, Janice Guy Gallery, NY, 1997, Vertical Painting, PS 1 Contemp Art Ctr, NY, 1999, Pleasure Dome, Jessica Fredericks Gallery, NY, 1999, Facts & Fictions, Galleria in Arco Turin, Italy, 1999, Deitch Projects, NY, 2000, The Skin Game, Gagosian Gallery, Beverly Hills, Calif, 2000, Serenade, Victoria Miro Gallery, London, 2000, Gagosian Gallery, NY, 2000, Emotional Rescue: Contemp Art Project Collection, Ctr Contemp Art, Seattle, 2000, Days of Heaven, Contemp Fine Arts, Berlin, 2001. *Mailing Add:* c/o Gagosian Gallery 555 W 24th St New York NY 10011

BROWN, CHARLOTTE VESTAL
MUSEUM DIRECTOR, HISTORIAN
b Siler City, NC, June 3, 1942. *Study:* Univ NC, Greensboro, BA (with honors), 64; Univ NC, Chapel Hill, PhD, 75. *Collection Arranged:* The New Narrative: Contemporary Fiber Art, 92; The Art of Building in North Carolina, 92; This is Not Tramp Art, 93; Bob Trotman: A Retrospective of Furniture and Sculpture, 94; A Multitude of Memories: The Work of Annie Hooper, 95; Textiles: Tradition and Innovation, Bedovin, Israeli, Palestinian, 96; Mark Hewitt Potter, 97; The Neugents: Close to Home, the Photographs of David Spear, 98; The Little Black Dress: From Sorrow to Seduction, 98. *Pos:* City of Raleigh, Hist Preservation, 81-82. *Teaching:* Asst prof, Duke Univ, 71-79; asst prof mod archit, NC State Univ, 89-90. *Mem:* Royal Oak Found; Am Asn Mus; NC Preservation/Hist Preservation Found; Vernacular Archit Forum. *Res:* Architectural history and theory, 19th and 20th century; American and English. *Publ:* Coauth, The Humanities, D C Heath, 89, 93 & 96; Architects and Builders in NC, Univ NC Press, 90. *Mailing Add:* NC State Univ Gallery Art & Design Box 7306 Univ Student Ctr Raleigh NC 27695-7306

BROWN, CHRISTOPHER
PAINTER
b Camp Lejeune, NC, 1951. *Study:* Univ Ill, Champaign-Urbana, BA, 73; Univ Calif, Davis, MFA, 76. *Work:* San Francisco Mus Mod Art, Univ Art Mus, Fine Arts Mus San Francisco & Security Pac Nat Bank, Calif; Chase Manhattan Bank, Metrop Mus, New York Pub Libr, Grey Art Gallery & New York Univ, NY; Gen Mills, Walker Art Ctr, Minneapolis, Minn; Sheldon Mem Art Gallery, Lincoln, Nebr; Mod Art Mus, Ft Worth, Tex. *Comn:* Painting, Fed Aviation Comn, Kansas City, Mo, 96. *Exhib:* Solo exhibs, Mod Art Mus, Ft Worth, Tex (traveling), 95-96, Campbell Thiebaud Gallery,

San Francisco, 96 & 98, Pasadena City Coll Art Gallery, Calif, 97 & Edward Thorp Gallery, New York, 98, Friesen Gallery, Seattle, 2000, Byron Cohen Gallery, Kansas City, Missouri, 2001, John Berggruen Gallery, San Francisco, 2002, 2006 & 2008; The Painted Room (traveling), Madison Art Ctr, Wis, 85-86; Chicago Int Art Exposition, Ill, 86 & 88; traveled to San Francisco Art Inst, Calif, 86; Newport Harbor Art Mus, Calif, 86 & 87; Contemp Arts Ctr, Cincinnati, Ohio, 87; Am Acad & Inst Arts & Letts, NY, 88; The Water Paintings, 1976-1987 (traveling), Univ Tex, Arlington, 88; Blum Helman, Los Angeles, Calif, 89; 10 Plus 10: Contemp Soviet & Am Painters, Mod Art Mus, Ft Worth, Tex, traveled to San Francisco Mus Mod Art, Milwaukee Art Ctr, Corcoran Gallery Art & Soviet Union, 90; Edward Thorp Gallery, NY, 92 & 95; Lyricism & Light, Palo Alto Cult Ctr, Calif, 94; Toward the Millennium: Contemp Paintings from Northern Calif, Monterey Mus Art, La Mirada, 97; Shasta Coll Gallery, Redding, 99. *Teaching:* Prof art, Univ Calif Berkeley, 81-92. *Awards:* Fel, Nat Endowment Arts, 87; Award, Am Acad & Inst Art & Letts, 88. *Bibliog:* John Yau (auth), Christopher Brown - New Paintings 1990 (exhib catalog), Gallery Paule Anglim, 90; Jeff Kelley (auth), Christopher Brown - New Paintings 1994 (exhib catalog), Campbell-Thiebaud Gallery, 94; Michael Brenson (auth), History and Memory: Paintings by Christopher Brown, Mod Art Mus, Ft Worth, 95; John Yau (auth), Christopher Brown - Buildings, Birds and Box Cars (exhib catalog), Johg Berggram Gallery, 2006. *Dealer:* John Berggrmen Gallery San Francisco CA; Edward Thorp Gallery New York NY. *Mailing Add:* c/o John Berggruen Gallery 228 Grant Ave San Francisco CA 94108

BROWN, CONSTANCE GEORGE
GALLERY DIRECTOR, ART DEALER
Study: Perry Normal Sch, Boston, Dipl, 54, Northeastern Univ, 73-76. *Collection Arranged:* F Ladd, 76, F Brown, 77, Ingersoll & Bloch, 77, Dr A Noonan, 79 & G White & A Brown, 85, Seventeen Wendell Street. *Pos:* Chair & mem adv bd, Nat Ctr Afro-Am Art Mus, 80-; mem, Local Site Comt, Mass Art & Humanities, 85 & Art Planning Coun, Lena Park Develop Corp, Boston, Mass, 86; comt mem & chair, Archives of Am Art. *Mem:* Archives of Am Art. *Res:* Contemporary Black-American artists

BROWN, DANIEL
CRITIC, CURATOR
b Cincinnati, Ohio, Nov 4, 1946. *Study:* Middlebury Coll, AB, 68; Univ Mich, MA, 70; post-grad, Princeton Univ, 72-3. *Comn:* catalogs, Todd Reynolds, John Stewart, Tom Bacher, Burang Kim, David Bumbeck, Robert Kempshild, Beverly Erschell, Jymi Bolden. *Collection Arranged:* Constance McClure: A Retrospective & Rita Zimmerman: New Monoprints (guest cur), 86; New Art from Academe: An Overview, The Cent Exchange (guest cur), Kansas City, Mo, 88; Cincinnati Past & Present: The Golden Ages in the Visual Arts, Tangeman Fine Arts Gallery (guest co-cur), Univ Cincinnati, 88; Contemporary Landscape, KenCabCo (guest cur), 88; Figure It Out, Katz & Dawgs Gallery Inaugural Exhib (guest cur), Columbus, Ohio, 88; Lyrical Abstractions (guest cur), 89 & the Artist at Mid- Career: A Dialogue Between Cincinnati & Columbus (guest cur), 89-90,Katz & Dawgs Gallery, Columbus, Ohio; Arts Consortium, Cincinnati, Ohio; Interpretations of the Everyday Object, 91; Frescoes of Working People, 91; Landscape East and West, 91-92; Union Terminal, Cincinnati Multiculturalism: the Evolution and the Celebration Group Show, African-Am Mus, 91-92; Black Not White, in black and white, 92; Maple Knoll Retirement Community, 2001-; The Univ Club Cincinnati, paintings by Frank Satogata, photos by John Chewning & Ann Asbury, paintings by Greg Storer, photos by Tuck Krielbuhl & Lisa Britton, paintings by Cole Carothers, and a group show, Beauty is Back, 2005-2006; group show, The Healing Power of Beauty, The Kidney Found of Cincinnati, 2006; group fundraiser, Beauty Matters, The United Way of Greater Cincinnati, 2006; Calligraphic Expresionism, Xavier Univ Art Gallery, 2008; Sandra Small Gallery, Covington, Ky, 2008-2009; Daniel Brown at the Ascent, United Way Greater Cincinnati, 2009; Wrator & Fuess lecturer, Cinn Bell Collector of Art, Am Artist, Art Consoritum, Cinn, 92; guest cur, Sandra Small Gallery, Covington, Ky, 2008-10; cur, Gardens & Earthly Delights, Cinn Art Galleries, 2010, cur, for fundraiser, Living Arrangements for the developmentally disaled, 2010; guest cur, The Weston Gallery at the Aronoff Ctr, 2011. *Pos:* Art critic, Cincinnati Mag, 79-82, Dialogue Art J, Columbus, 83-, WCPO-TV, Cincinnati, 86- & Provincetown Arts, 88-, Cincinnati Herald, 92-, Everybody's News, 93-94, Artist's Mag, 2006-, Diere Gallery, Cincinnati, 2007; artist's model, Constance McClure, 84-, David Bumbeck, 84-85, Dan Boldman, 85-, Jerome Mussman, 85-, David DeVaul, 86 & Cole Carothers, 87-; art commentator, WKRC-TV, Cincinnati, 85; pres, Daniel Brown Inc, Independent Art Consultants; cur, KZF Gallery, Cincinnati, 87-94, 2004, Kidney Found Cincinnati, 2006-, Sandra Small Gallery, Covington, Ky, 2008-; regular guest columnist art issues, Cincinnati Post, 91-; founding art ed & essayist, City Beat, 94-95; ed-in-chief, Antenna Arts Mag, 96-98; ed, www.Blvc Chip Review.com (politics/arts), 2004; juror, 1st Ann Juried Show, Xavier Univ, 2007; contrib writer, The Artist's Mag, 2008-. *Teaching:* Guest lectr, Contemp Arts Ctr, Cincinnati, 84-86, Cincinnati Art Mus, 86, Univ Cincinnati, 86 & 93-95, Contemporary Art, Fifth St Gallery, 2007 & Sandra Small Gallery, 2008-; part-time lect printmaking, drawing & painting, Art Acad Cincinnati, currently; Mercantile Libr, Univ Cincinnati, Fiction 2004-; asst prof writing & criticism, The Baker-Hunt Found for the Arts, Covington, Ky, 2009-. *Awards:* Winner, the Critics Purse, Dialogue Mag, 85. *Mem:* Contemp Arts Ctr, Cincinnati (trustee, 84-88); Enjoy the Arts, Cincinnati (trustee, 85-88, vpres, 86-88); Int Soc Art Critics, NY & Paris; Mercantile Libr, Cincinnati (trustee, 84-90); Art Acad Cincinnati (trustee, 86-92 & 93-97); Visiting nurses of Cincinnati (art ad), 2004; Artists Without Boundaries (trustee, 2008-). *Res:* Psychoanalytic and political implications of contemporary art. *Collection:* Contemporary prints, drawings and paintings of both national and regional artists. *Publ:* Auth, The Zen of Seeing (exhib catalog), Southern Ohio Mus & Cult Ctr, Portsmouth, 94; The Art of David Bumbeck (exhib catalog), Dartmouth Coll, 95; Bukang Kim: A Retrospective (exhib catalog), Springfield Arts Ctr, Ohio, 96; Robert Knipschild (exhib catalog), Springfield Arts Ctr; Beverly Erschell (exhib catalog), Washington DC Gallery and Weston Gallery, Cincinnati; Contemp Neo-Pub, KZF, 2005; The Little Black Dress, Tuck Krekbiel; Bill Paris, Photographs (exhib catalog), 2008; Bill Davis, The Palimpsest Series Photographs (exhib catalog), Krazl Mus, Mich, 2008. *Mailing Add:* 2365 Madison Rd Apt 205 Cincinnati OH 45208

BROWN, DAVID ALAN
HISTORIAN, CURATOR
b Bellevue, Ohio, July 25, 1942. *Study:* Harvard Col, BA (magna cum laude), 64; Cambridge Univ, Fulbright fel, 64-65; Yale Univ, MA, 67, PhD, 73. *Collection Arranged:* Berenson and the Connoisseurship of Italian Painting, 79, From Leonardo to Titian: Italian Renaissance Paintings from the Hermitage, 79, Raphael and Am, 83 & Leonardo's Last Supper: Before and After, 84, Nat Gallery Art, Washington, DC. *Pos:* Cur Italian Renaissance painting, Nat Gallery Art, Washington, DC, currently. *Teaching:* Lectr art hist, Yale Univ, New Haven, Conn, 73-74 & Smithsonian Assoc Prog, Washington, DC, 75-. *Awards:* Finley Fel, Nat Gallery Art, 68-71; Fel Villa I Tatti, Harvard Ctr for Renaissance Studies, Florence, 69-70; Excellency Award, Found for Italian Art & Culture, 2007. *Mem:* Renaissance Soc Am; Coll Art Asn. *Res:* Italian Renaissance painting; Leonardo Da Vinci; Correggio. *Publ:* Auth, articles on Leonardo Da Vinci and on Correggio, Mitteilungen des Kunst Historischen Inst, Florence, 71, Mus Studies, 72, Master Drawings, 74 & 75. *Mailing Add:* Nat Gallery Art Sixth & Constitution Sts Washington DC 20565

BROWN, DAVID LEE
SCULPTOR
b 1939. *Study:* Cass Tech, 57; NC Sch Design, 60; Cranbrook Acad Art, 62. *Work:* John Hopkins Univ, Baltimore, Md; De Cordova Mus, Lincoln, Mass; Hirshhorn Mus & Sculpture Garden, Washington, DC; Milwaukee Art Ctr, Wis; Chase Manhattan Bank, New York. *Comn:* Sculptures, Reynolds Aluminum Corp, Richmond, Va, 76, Xerox Corp (monumental), Stamford, Conn, 78, Warner Lambert Co, Morris Plains, NJ, 81, Fla Nat Bank, Jacksonville, 86 & Fort Lauderdale Airport. *Exhib:* Hammer Gallery, New York. *Teaching:* Instr sculpture, Cranbrook Acad Art, 60-61; prof design, Pratt Inst, New York, 72-. *Media:* Stainless Steel, All Media. *Interests:* racing a "DN" ice boat. *Dealer:* Richard Lynch Hammer Galleries 33 W 57th St New York NY 10019. *Mailing Add:* 10 John St Southampton NY 11968

BROWN, EDITH RAE
SCULPTOR, MEDALIST, PAINTER
b Flushing, NY, Nov 9, 1942. *Study:* Art Students League; Pietra Santa, Italy, studios and workshops of prof sculptors & painters. *Work:* Smithsonian Inst, Washington; Am Numismatic World Mus, Colorado Springs, Colo; Newark Mus, Newark, NJ; Nat Arts Club, NY; Nat Art Mus Sport, Ind. *Comn:* Comn by pvt collectors. *Exhib:* Chesterwood Mass, 1989; Nat Arts Club, NY, 1989-2003, Roundtable Exhib, 2010, 2011; Hecksher Mus, NY, 1990; Fedn Int de'la Medille, Helsinki Art Mus, Finland, 1990; Newark Mus, NJ, 1991; Hungarian Nat Gallery, Budapest, 1994; Patac Sztuki, Krakow, Poland, 1995; Gallery Emanual, NY, 1995; Gallerie Art Viva, Paris, 1995-2003; Parsons Sch Design, Paris, 1995; Venezuela Consulate, NYC Lehman Col, UN 50th Ann, 1996; L'Assemblee Nationale, Paris, 1997; Festival Des Arts, Vayolles, France, 1997; Salon D'Automne, Paris, 1996-2008; Am Numismatic Soc Mus, Colorado Springs, 1998; Beelden aan Zee Mus, The Hague, 1998, Nat Asn Women Artists,1998; Nassau Mus Fine Arts, NY, 1998; Biennale Int Citta di Firenza, 2000 & 2001; Westwood Gallery, NYC, 2006; Roundtable Exhib, Nat Arts Club, 1997-2008; Wisser Gal, NY Inst Tech, Brookville, NY, pub TV WLIW Chan 21, 2005; Port of Call Gallery, Warwick, NY, 2006; Karpeles Libr Mus, Newburg, NY, 2006; Ann Masters Show, Huntington Arts Coun, 2005-2007; Bennington Ctr Arts, Vt, 2007; Nat Art Mus of Sport, Indianapolis, Ind, 2008; Art Students League, 2008; Hudson Pointe Art Show, N Bergen, NJ, 2008; Long Island Prof Artosts Showcase, CW Post Univ, Brookville, NY, 2008; Red River Valley Mus, Int Exhib, Vernon, Tex, 2008; Art Guild of Pt Washington, Elderfields, Port Washington, NY, 2009, 2010; Nat Asn Women Artist, 2011, 2012. *Pos:* Chmn sculpture exhibs; juror sculpture exhibs; lectr, demonstrate carving stone sculpture. *Teaching:* Stone carving. *Awards:* Salzman Award, Nat Arts Club, 95 & 96; Lelia Garin Sawyer Mem Award, Am Artists Prof League, 93, 95 & 96; Pietro Montana Mem Award, Hudson Valley Art Asn, 96; Tooker Foundry Award, 2007. *Mem:* Allied Artists of America, 2006-; Artists Equity, NY; Coun Am Artists Soc Inc (pres); Am Medallic Sculpture Asn; Fed Int de la Medaille, Nat Asn Women Artists; Nat Arts Club (Exhib artist mem & com chair); Pen & Brush, 1994-2001; Nat Sculp Soc (assoc mem); Artists Fel (bd mem); Town of N Hempstead Art Advisory Coun; Salon D'Automme; Huntington Arts Coun, NY; Hudson Valley Art Asn, NY. *Media:* Sculpture, Painting. *Specialty:* Contemp Art. *Publ:* Auth, Artist expresses her need to create, Intermountain Jewish News, 6/11/85; Contemporary Sculpture, Chesterwood, 89. *Dealer:* Gallery Studio 55 Glen Cove Rd Greenvale NY 11548; Art Viva, Levallois-Perret, France. *Mailing Add:* PO Box 504 Glen Head NY 11534

BROWN, ERIC L
GALLERY DIRECTOR
b New York, Sept 5, 1967. *Study:* Vassar Coll, 90. *Pos:* Archivist, asst to Nell Blaine, New York & Gloucester, Mass, 86-91; co-owner, co-dir, Tibor de Nagy Gallery, New York, 93-; mem bd, Frances Lehman Loeb Art Ctr, Vassar Coll, Poughkeepsie, NY, 94-; fel, Morgan Libr, New York, 94-. *Mailing Add:* Tibor de Nagy Gallery 724 5th Ave New York NY 10019

BROWN, GARY HUGH
PAINTER, EDUCATOR
b Evansville, Ind, Dec 19, 1941. *Study:* DePauw Univ, Greencastle, Ind, BA, 63; Acad Belli de Arti, Rome & Florence, Italy, 63-64; Univ Wis-Madison, MFA, 66. *Work:* Elvehjem Art Ctr, Madison, Wis; Yale Univ, New Haven, Conn; Glenbow Art Mus, Alta, Can; Utah Mus Fine Arts, Salt Lake City; Tyler Mus Art, Tex; and others; 20th Century Fox; Int Mus Photography, George Eastman House; Mus Modern Art, Univ

Art Mus; plus many others. *Comn:* Ltd ed paper suite, Source Gallery, San Francisco, publ by Twinrocker, Ind, 76; mural, Osaka Univ, 85; tile courtyard & fountain, Sarah House, Santa Barbara, Calif, 94; Inst Cult Inquiry: 1997 AIDS Chronicle. *Exhib:* One-man shows, Fleischer-Anhalt Gallery, Los Angeles, Calif, 68, de Saisset Art Gallery, Univ Santa Clara & Santa Barbara Mus Art, 71-72, Comsky Gallery, Beverly Hills, Calif, 75, United Arts Club, Dublin, Ireland, 75, Source Gallery, San Francisco, 76 & 78, Art/Life Gallery, Santa Barbara, 82 & Ventura Col, 94, LifeLine, Villa Lila, Nijmegen, The Neth, 2000, plus others; Art-Space, Osaka-Tokyo, Japan, 85; Tokyo Munic Mus Art, 86; The Drawing 2000 Int Period Gallery, Omaha, Nebr; The Blake House Collection, Blake House, Kensington, Calif, 2000; Signs of His Times, Univ Art Mus, Univ Calif Santa Barbara, 2009; View From Here: Santa Barbara Artists, SBMA, 2011. *Pos:* Artist-in-residence, Int Inst for Experimental Papermaking, Calif, 74, New Harmony, Ind, 76, Ateliershaus Worpswede, WGer, 82, Artist Union, Nishinomiaya, Univ Japan, 85 & Fez, Morocco, 93. *Teaching:* Prof painting & drawing, Univ Calif, Santa Barbara, 66-2008 (Emeritus). *Awards:* Greenshields Found Grant for European Travel/Study, 63. *Mem:* Coll Art Asn. *Media:* Drawing, Oil. *Interests:* Drawing, Painting, Papermaking, Art Jour. *Publ:* Illusr, Peter Whigham's The Blue Winged Bee, Anvil, 69; John Logan (auth), Poem in Progress, Dryad, 75; The Santa Cruz Mountain Poems, Morton Marcus (auth), Capra, 75, 2nd ed, 92; The Music of the Troubadors, Ross-Erikson, 79; Electroworks, George Eastman House & Chanticleer Press, 80; Male Nude Now, Universe, 2001; Art of the Jounal, Princeton Archit Press, 2005; The Vietnam War in American Memory, Univ Mass Press, 2009; Patrick Hagopian (auth), The Vietnam War in Am Memory, Univ Mass Press, Amherst, 2009; The Address Book, Pacific Standard Time: Art in LA, 1945-1980, 2011. *Mailing Add:* Art Dept Univ Calif Santa Barbara CA 93106

BROWN, GILLIAN
CONCEPTUAL ARTIST, PHOTOGRAPHER
Study: Brown Univ, Providence, RI, BA, 73; RI Sch Design, Providence, MAE, 77; Univ Calif, Los Angeles, MFA (photog), 80. *Work:* Addison Gallery Am Art, Andover, Mass; Art Mus, Princeton Univ; Bibliot Nat, Paris; Calif Mus Photog, Univ Calif, Riverside; Calif Inst Arts, Valencia. *Comn:* Permanent site works, Washington Proj Arts, 90. *Exhib:* Solo exhibs, Andover Gallery, Mass, 86, Gatehouse Gallery, Mt Vernon Col, 87, Constructions, Kathleen Ewing Gallery, Washington, 87, Notre Dame Col, Baltimore, Md, 90, Jones, Troyer, Fitzpatrick Gallery, Washington, 92 & Troyer, Fitzpatrick, Lassman Gallery, Washington, 96; Doubletake, Hans & Walter Bechtler Gallery, Charlotte, NC, 94; A View from Baltimore to Washington, Fine Arts Gallery, Univ Md, 94; Off the Mall, Corcoran Gallery Art, Washington, 94; Boston Now, Inst Contemp Art, Boston, 94; The Drawing Show, Bernard Toale Gallery, Boston, 95; Anxious Libraries, Photog Resource Ctr, Boston, 96; Constructed Photog, Addison Gallery Am Art, 97. *Awards:* Nat Endowment Art Fel, 90; Md State Arts Coun Grant, 92; Iowa State Arts Coun Grant, 93. *Bibliog:* Lenore D Miller (auth), Manipulated environments: photomontage into sculpture, Camerawork, spring/summer 94; Eric Renner (auth), Pinhole Photography, Focal Press, Boston, 95; Ferdinand Protzman (auth), It's the thought that counts, Wash Post, 3/2/96

BROWN, HILTON
PAINTER, EDUCATOR
b Momence, Ill, Sept 22, 1938. *Study:* Goodman Theatre & Sch Drama, Art Inst Chicago, 56-58; Univ Chicago, 59; Skowhegan Sch Painting & Sculpture, Maine, summers 60 & 61; Sch of Art Inst Chicago, dipl fine arts (George T & Isabelle Brown foreign travel fel), 62, BFA, 63, MFA, 64; Univ Ill, Chicago, 62-63. *Work:* Baltimore Mus Art; Ball State Univ Art Collection; Macomb Community Col, Detroit; Univ Md, College Park; Nat Gallery of Art, DC. *Comn:* Exterior wall paintings, City of Baltimore, 73-75; mural, T Johnson Sch, Baltimore, 79-80. *Exhib:* Chicago & Vicinity Show, Art Inst Chicago, 60; Nat Print Exhib, Brooklyn Mus, 64; Twelve Chicago Painters, Walker Art Ctr, Minneapolis, 65; 20th Mo Show, City Art Mus, St Louis, 66; Md Regional Exhib, Baltimore Mus Art, 75; Kornblatt Gallery, Baltimore, Md, 79; Leslie Lohman Gallery, NY, 80; Baltimore Mus Art, 86; Susan Isaacs Gallery, Wilmington, Del, 90; Akron Art Mus, Ohio; Spencer Mus Art, Univ Kans, Lawrence, 2002. *Collection Arranged:* The Art and Archives of Ralph Mayer, Art Technologist, 94, Univ Del Gallery, Newark; Milk and Eggs - Am Tempera Paintings 1930-50, Brandywine River Mus, Chadds Ford, PA, 2002. *Pos:* Mem contemp art accessions comt, Baltimore Mus Art, 68-78; contrib ed, Am Artist Mag, 81-86. *Teaching:* Instr color, drawing, design & painting, Sch of Art Inst Chicago, 62-65; asst prof drawing & compos, Sch Fine Arts, Washington Univ, 65-68; prof drawing, painting & printmaking, Goucher Col, 68-78, chmn art dept, 76-78; vis prof art hist, Winterthur Prog Conserv Art, Univ Del, 74-78, assoc dir, 78-80, prof art, art history and conservation, 78-84, coordr, Ralph Mayer Ctr Artists Techniques, 84-88, Ralph & Bena Mayer prof, 84-88, Harriet T Baily prof art, art conserv, art hist, mus studies & women's studies, 92-2011; consult & lect, Ed Dept, Nat Gallery of Art, Wash, DC, 1990-2011. *Awards:* Renfrow Art Award, City Art Mus, St Louis, 65; Berney Award Painting, Baltimore Mus Art, 70. *Bibliog:* Franz Schultz (auth), Chicago Art Inst, 3/67; John Brod Peters (auth), Art views: Hilton Brown: New directions, St Louis Globe Democrat, 8/12/67; Lincoln F Johnson (auth), Retrospective shows Brown growth, The Sun, Baltimore, 2/24/77; Hilton Brown, the artist comes out, The Gay Paper, Baltimore, 9/80. *Mem:* Coll Art Asn; Am Asn Univ Prof. *Media:* Acrylic, Pastel, Oil, Printmaking, Watercolor, Drawing, All Media. *Res:* History of the technology of Western European and Am art from 500 to the Present; history of gay and lesbian art, queer art. *Interests:* Gay, lesbian & queer art & artists; Anglo-Catholicism; gardening; health, cooking, food. *Publ:* Auth, Looking at paintings: Joseph Stella and John Storrs silverpoint drawings, 5/81, Looking at paintings: Paul Cadmus' playground, 1/82, History of watercolor, 3/83 & History of landscape painting, 2/84, Am Artist Mag; Auth, Art and Archives of Ralph Mayer, exhib catalog, 94; Co-auth, exhibition catalog, Milk and Eggs, American Tempera Painting, 1930-50, 3/02. *Dealer:* Gary Snyder/ Project Space Contemp Am Art NYC. *Mailing Add:* 826 N Jefferson St Wilmington DE 19801

BROWN, IONA ROZEAL
PAINTER
b Washington, 1966. *Study:* Univ Maryland, BS (Kinesiological Sciences), 1991; Pratt Inst, Brooklyn, NY, 1996; San Francisco Art Inst, BFA (Painting), 1999; Skowhegan Sch Painting & Sculpture, ME, 1999; Yale Univ Sch Art, MFA (Painting), 2002. *Work:* Collections of Eileen Harris Norton and Peter Norton, Santa Monica, Calif; Hirshhorn Mus & Sculpture Garden, Smithsonian Inst, Wash DC; Milwaukee Art Mus, Wisc; New Mus Contemporary Art, NY; Wadsworth Atheneum Mus Art, Hartford, Conn. *Exhib:* Solo exhibs include Gallery Upstairs, MD, 1995, Sandroni Rey, Los Angeles, 2002, 2004, 2007, Caren Golden Fine Art, New York, 2002, 2004, G Fine Art, Washington, 2004, 2006, Wadsworth Atheneum Mus Art, Conn, 2004, VOLTA4: Voltany, Basel, Switz, 2008, Mythologies and Mash-ups, Saltworks Gallery, Atlanta, Ga, 2010; Group exhibs include Int Paper, Hammer Mus, Los Angeles, 2003; New Wave, Kravets/Wehby Gallery, New York, 2003, Japan, INC, 2007; Skin Deep, Numark Gallery, Washington, 2003; Pop Rocks, Caren Golden Fine Art, New York, 2003; Altoids Curiously Strong Collection, New Mus Contemp Art, New York, 2004; When The East Is In The House, Saltworks Gallery, Atlanta, 2006; Sweet Sweetback's Baadasssss Song, Von Lintel Gallery, NY, 2007; New Acquisitions, Milwaukee Art Mus, Wisc, 2009, Pattern ID, Akron Art Mus, OH, 2010; The Global Africa Project, Mus Arts & Design, NY, 2010; Battle of Yestermorrow, Performa via Salon 94, NY, 2011; 30 Americans, Corcoran Gallery Art, Wash DC, 2012. *Awards:* Camille Hanks Brosby Fel, Skowhegan Sch Painting & Sculpture, 1999; Schickle-Collinwgwood Prize, Yale Univ, 2001; Blair Dickinson Award, Yale Univ, 2002; Matrix Artist, Wadsworth Atheneum Mus Art, 2004; US Japan Creative Artists Fel Prog, 2005; Joan Mitchell Found Grant, 2007; Louis Comfort Tiffany Found Grant 2008

BROWN, JAMES
PAINTER, GRAPHIC ARTIST
b Brooklyn, NY. *Study:* Long Island Univ, BA, 54; Brooklyn Col, MS, 55; NY Univ & Yeshiva Univ. *Work:* Corpus Christi Mus, Tex; New York City Tech Col; York Coll City Univ NY; Medgar Evers Col, Brooklyn, NY; Voluntariado del Museo de las Casa Reales, Casa de Bastidas, Santo Domingo, Dom Repub; House of Humour & Satire, Gabrova, Bulgaria. *Comn:* Portraits, New York City Pub Schs, 79; illus, Nat Asn Advan Colored People, NY, 80; illus, Revlon, USV Lab, 80; Black Winners (illus), comn by Melvin Douglas, 84; York Col, NY, 85; and others. *Exhib:* Minn Mus Art, Saint Paul, 79; Albrecht Art Mus, Saint Joseph, Mo, 80; Mus Philadelphia Civic Ctr, Pa, 80; Univ Mo, 80; Tulane Univ, La, 80; Queens Mus, NY, 84; Schenectady Mus, NY, 85; poster Shop Galerie, Martinique (WI), 86; Le Centre d'Arte, Haiti (WI), 88; Festival Arts, Port-au-Prince, Haiti, 89; US Pavilion, World's Fair, Seville, Spain, 92; Voluntariado del Museo de las Casas Reales, Santo Domingo, Dom Repub, 94; Sotheby's NY, 97. *Pos:* Supervisor art, New York Bd Educ, 74-83. *Teaching:* Critic, New Jersey State Col, 75; instr drawing, painting & printmaking, Intermediate Sch, New York, 76-78; guest artist, Corpus Christi Mus, 78; lectr bus of art, Col New Rochelle, NY, 79; panelist, Artists as Agents of Social Change: Five Views, Heckscher Mus, Huntington, NY, 86. *Awards:* Purchase Award & First Prize, C of C, Union, NJ, 79; Award, Greater Patterson Arts Coun NJ, 80; Best in Show, Festival on the Green, NJ, 81; and others. *Bibliog:* Georges Paul Hector (auth), Atelier de Reflexion: Conjonction ou itineraire a deux, Valcin II et James Brown, Le Nouvelliste, Port-au-Prince, Haiti, 11/11/89; Abril Peralta (auth), James Brown, Ventana: List in Diario, Santo Domingo, Dom Repub, 4/6/94; Rafael Median (auth), James Brown: Una Extraordinaria Exposition Individual en la Casa de Bastidas, Listin USA Mag Revista de Variodados, 3/2/94; and others. *Mem:* Coalition Black Artists (dir, 78-); Long Island Black Artists Asn (pres, 83-85). *Media:* Oil, Pastel; Carbon Pencil. *Publ:* Contribr, Interracial Books for Children, Coun on Interracial Bks for Children, New York, 79; illusr, Ten Little Niggers, St Albans Printing, New York, 81; Black Winners, Nat Asn Advan Colored People, 84. *Dealer:* Dorsey's Art Gallery 553 Rogers Ave Brooklyn NY 11225; Festival Arts Distributors Petionville Haiti. *Mailing Add:* 117-54 219th St Cambria Heights NY 11411

BROWN, JONATHAN
HISTORIAN
b Springfield, Mass, July 15, 1939. *Study:* Dartmouth Col, AB, 60; Princeton Univ, PhD, 64, Guggenheim Mem Fel, 81-82. *Pos:* Dir, Inst Fine Arts, New York Univ, 73-78; vis mem, Inst Advan Study, 78-79. *Teaching:* Asst prof art hist, Princeton Univ, 65-71, assoc prof, 71-73; from assoc prof to prof, Inst Fine Arts, NY Univ, 73-84, Carroll & Milton Petrie prof, 84-; Slade prof fine art, Oxford Univ, 81-82; Andrew W Mellon lectr fine arts, Nat Gallery Art, 94. *Awards:* Order of Isabel la Católica Award, 86; Medalla de Oro de Bellas Artes, Govt Spain, 86; Gran Cruz de Al Fonso X el Sabio, Gout, Spain, 96. *Mem:* Spanish Inst (bd dir, 87-96); Am Philos Soc; Real Acad de Bellas Artes de San Fernando (corresp mem); Am Acad Arts & Sci. *Res:* Spanish art 16th-19th centuries. *Publ:* Velázquez, Painter and Courtier, 86; The Golden Age of Painting in Spain, 91; Kings and Connoisseurs, 95; Picasso and the Spanish Tradition, 96; La Pintura de los Reinos, 2011. *Mailing Add:* 1 E 78th St New York NY 10021

BROWN, JULIA
ADMINISTRATOR
b Washington, DC, Mar 9, 1951. *Study:* Sarah Lawrence Coll, BA, 72. *Pos:* Docent, Nat Gallery Art, Washington, 73-74; art historian, Gen Servs Admin, Washington, 74-75, project mgr, 75-80; cur, Hudson River Mus, Yonkers, NY, 80-81; cur, Mus Contemp Art, Los Angeles, 81-83, sr cur, 83-86; dir, Des Moines Art Ctr, 86-91 & Skystone Found, 91-95; cur spec exhibs, Guggenheim Mus, NY, 95-2000; dir, Am Fedn Arts, NY, 2000-. *Awards:* Alfred Bar Award, distinguished publ, Coll Art Asn, 92. *Mailing Add:* Am Fedn Arts 10th Fl 305 E 47th St New York NY 10017

BROWN, JUNE GOTTLIEB
PAINTER, INSTRUCTOR
b Dunn, NC, June 21, 1932. *Study:* With Leon Stacks, 64-70, Frederick Taubes, 73 & 75 & Robert F Calrow, 77 & 81. *Work:* DuPont & Co, Leland, NC; Dalton Collection, Charlotte, NC; Springs Mills, NY; United Carolina Bank, Southport, NC; Brunswick Co, Bolivia, NC; Fed Reserve Bank, Richmond, Va; J Arthur Dosher Memorial

Hospital, Southport, NC; Fairley Jess & Isenberg, Southport, NC; Allegacy Fed Credit Union, Winston Salem, NC; pvt collection of Mr & Mrs Dennis Hatchell, Winston Salem, NC. *Exhib:* North Carolina Realism, Mint Mus, 74; Hoyt Nat Painting Show, Hoyt Inst Fine Arts, New Castle, Pa, 82; Allied Artists Am Ann Exhib, NY, 82, 86 & 2005; Nat Mid-Year Exhib, Butler Inst Am Art, 82 & 83; Salmagundi Club Open Competition, NY, 83; Henley Southeastern Spectrum, Galleries 214, Winston-Salem, NC, 83; Mariner's Museum, Mystic, Conn, 89; Int Soc Marine Painters, 97-99; Dimensions, Winston Salem, NC, 2000; 20th Spring Fine Art Show, Wilmington, NC, 2002; Am Artists Professional League, NY, 2004-2005. *Pos:* Co-founder, Franklin Square Gallery, Southport, NC. *Teaching:* Instr art, Brunswick Community Col, 78-99. *Awards:* Emily Morse Mem Award, Salmagundi Club, 83; Traveling Show Award, Henley's Southeastern Spectrum, 83; Dorothy Watkeys Barberis Award, Catharine Lorillard Wolfe Show, 86; First Place Moore Co Arts Coun, NC, 2000, second place acrylic, 2003 & 2004; Grumbacher Gold Medallion, 20th Spring Fine Art Show, Wilmington, NC, 2002; John Collins Mem Award, Am Artists Prof League, 2005. *Mem:* Am Artists Prof League & Am Soc of Marine Artists; Catherine Louillard & Wolfe Art Club; Assoc Artist Winston Salem, NC; Assoc Artists, Southport, NC (co-founder). *Media:* Acrylic, Oil. *Dealer:* City Art Works Gallery New Bern NC; Sunset River Gallery Calabash NC; Ricky Evans Gallery, Southport, NC. *Mailing Add:* 230 River Dr Southport NC 28461

BROWN, LARRY
PAINTER
b New Brunswick, NJ, June 1, 1942. *Study:* Wash State Univ, Pullman, BA, 67; Univ Ariz, MFA, 70. *Work:* Walker Art Ctr, Minneapolis; Indianapolis Mus Art; Minn Mus Am Art; Norton Mus Art, W Palm Beach, Fla; Newark Mus Art, NJ; Daum Mus Art, Sedalia, Mo; Portland Mus Art, Oreg. *Exhib:* Walker Art Ctr, Minneapolis, 74; Milwaukee Art Mus, 75; Indianapolis Mus Art, 78; Carnegie Mus Art, Pittsburgh, 88; and many others. *Teaching:* Vis artist painting, Mont State Univ, Bozeman, 78, Iowa State Univ, Ames, 82, Ohio State Univ, Columbus, 83 & 86, NTex State Univ, 85, Rutgers Univ, 87, State Univ NY, Stonybrook, 87 & 91, NMex State Univ, 88, Ariz State Univ 88, Syracuse Univ, 88 & Sarah Lawrence Coll, 97-2006; adj prof, The Cooper Union, 91-. *Awards:* Nat Endowment Arts Fel, 79-80. *Bibliog:* Leslie Luebbers (auth), Mind & Matter/New American Abstraction (exhib catalog), 87; John Caldwell (auth), Ten Americans (exhib catalogue), Carnegie Mus Art, 88; Curt Barnes (auth), Constructed painting, Art J, 91; and others. *Mem:* Coll Art Asn. *Media:* Oil. *Dealer:* Sears Peyton Gallery 210 11th Ave Ste 802 New York NY 10001 ; John Davis Gallery 362 1/2 Warren St Hudson, NY 12534 ; Butters Gallery 520 NW Davis St Portland OR 97209. *Mailing Add:* 54 Franklin St Apt 4R New York NY 10013

BROWN, LAWRIE
PHOTOGRAPHER, EDUCATOR
b San Jose, Calif, 1949. *Study:* San Jose State Univ, Calif, BA, 72; San Francisco State Univ, MA, 75. *Work:* Oakland Mus, Calif; San Francisco Mus Mod Art, Calif; Bibliotheque Nationale, Cabinet Des Estampes, Paris, France; Ctr Creative Photography, Tucson; Stanford Univ Mus Art, Calif; Metropolitan Mus Art, New York, NY; Univ Louisville, KY; Univ Tex, Austin; Mus Fine Arts Houston; and others. *Comn:* Stephen F Austin State Univ, Tex, 2007; Wayne Art Ctr, Pa, 2007; Rawls Art Mus, Va, 2007; Crave Mag, Featured Photographer, Hong Kong. *Exhib:* Everson Mus Art, Syracuse, NY, 77; San Francisco Mus Mod Art, Calif, 78; Arco Ctr Visual Art, Los Angeles, 79; Il Diaframma-Canon, Milan, 82; Oakland Mus, Calif, 83; Boise Gallery Art, Idaho, 83; Hudson River Mus, Yonkers, NY, 84; Alternative Mus, NY, 84; Canon Photogallery, Amsterdam, 85; Friends Photog, Carmel, Calif, 85; Int Ctr for Photog, NY, 87; Houston Ctr for Photog, 87; Bank of Am, San Francisco; Univ Washington, Seattle, 2004; Barrett Art Ctr, NY, 2004; Mus Fine Arts, Fla State Univ, Tallahassee, 2004; Monterey Mus Art, Calif, 2005; Univ Toledo Ctr Visual Arts, Ohio, 2005; Visual Arts Ctr NJ, Summit, 2006; Spiva Arts Ctr, Joplin, Mo, 2006; Southeastern La Univ, 2008; Nicolet Col, 2008; E Tenn State Univ, 2008; Andrews Art Mus, NC, 2009; Amarillo Mus Art, Tex, 2010; Mus Art & Hist, Santa Cruz, Calif, 2010-2011; Scott Nichols Gallery, San Francisco Calif, 2012; 20th Anniv Exhib, Scott Nichols Gallery, 2013. *Collection Arranged:* Sheldon Mem Art Gallery, Lincoln, Nebr, 2005; Who Is Imitating Whom? Photography & Photo-Realism in Art. *Teaching:* dir, Photog Dept, Cabrillo Col, Calif, 79-. *Awards:* Nat Endowment Photogrs Fel, 79; Polaroid Grants, 85, 86, 87 & 2005. *Bibliog:* Peter Hunt Thompson (auth), Untitled 6, Quarterly Friends Photog, 73; Hal Fischer (auth), Don Worth, Barbara Thompson, Lawrie Brown, Casey Williams, Art Week, 9/25/76; Leland Rice (auth), Contemporary California Photography, Camerawork Gallery, 78; ZOOM Int Mag, Milan, Italy, 2006. *Mem:* Soc Photog Educ; Friends Photog; San Francisco Mus Modern Art, Ctr for Photographic Arts, Carmel, Calif; SF Camera Work Gallery, Calif; Mus Art & History, Santa Cruz, Calif. *Media:* Photography. *Specialty:* Photography. *Collection:* Laundry Series, 24x36″ archival digital black & white photos; Trash series 2007; Colored Food Series; Painted Plant Series; Landscape Series. *Publ:* Auth, Legacy of Light, Knopf, 87; Darkroom Photog, San Francisco, 9-10/83 & 86; Exploring Color Photography, William Brown Pub, 89; 7x7 Mag, San Francisco; Focus Mag, Milan, Italy; Colored Food Series went viral on 64 websites including ABC.com, Huffington Post.com and National Public Radio websites. *Dealer:* Scott Nichols San Francisco; Saret Gallery Sonoma Calif. *Mailing Add:* 2623 Willowbrook Ln No 114 Aptos CA 95003

BROWN, MARY RACHEL See Marais

BROWN, PEGGY ANN
PAINTER, INSTRUCTOR
b Ft Wayne, Ind, Mar 15, 1934. *Study:* Marquette Univ, BS (jour); Ft Wayne Art Inst. *Work:* Ind Univ, Bloomington; Columbus Art Ctr, Ohio; Ricks Coll, Rexburg, Idaho; Cooperstown NY Art Asn; Mus Art, Ft Wayne, Ind. *Comn:* Painting, Amoco Corp Int Hq, Chicago, Ill; painting, Marshall Town Bank, Ames, Iowa; painting, Office Controller of Currency, Chicago, Ill; painting, Standard Chartered Bank, Hong Kong; painting, Miami Herald, Fla. *Exhib:* Allied Artists Am, NY, 70-93; Nat Watercolor Soc, Los Angeles, 72-76, 79-85 & 93-94; Am Watercolor Soc, NY, 74, 76, 79 & 82; Nat Acad Design, 79 & 82; Watercolor USA, Springfield, Mo; Rocky Mountain Watermedia Nat, Golden, Colo; and others. *Pos:* Sem panelist & instr, currently. *Teaching:* Instr creative watercolor, Ind Univ, Ft Wayne, 74-82; instr workshops. *Awards:* Best of Show NWS Purchase, Nat Watercolor Soc, 93; Cash Award & Purchase Award, Watercolor USA, 94; Merit Award, Rocky Mountain Watermedia Nat, 94 & 2001; Int Quilt Asn, 2008, 2009; Am Quilting Soc, 2010 & 2011. *Bibliog:* Gerald Brommer (auth), Collage Techniques; Nita Leland & Virginia Williams (coauths), Creative Collage Techniques, 94; The Best of Watercolor, 96, The Best of Watercolor II, 98, Rockport Publ. *Mem:* Nat Watercolor Soc; Allied Artists Am; Watercolor USA Honor Soc; Am Watercolor Soc (bd dir, 92); Rocky Mountain Watermedia Soc. *Media:* Transparent Watercolor, Drawings & Fiber Art. *Specialty:* Fine art. *Interests:* Golf, camping and travel. *Collection:* Nat Academy of Design, Indiana University, Fort Wayne Museum of Art. *Publ:* SAQA Jour, 2010; Quilting Arts Mag, 2010. *Dealer:* Editions Limited Indianapolis IN; Polonaise Art Gallery Woodstock VT; Brown County Art Guild Gallery Nashville IN. *Mailing Add:* 1541 N Claylick Rd Nashville IN 47448

BROWN, PETER C
SCULPTOR, PAINTER
b Port Chester, NY, Oct 10, 1940. *Study:* Ohio Wesleyan Univ, BFA, 63; Cranbrook Acad of Art, MFA, 65. *Work:* Dannheisser Found, NY, The Prudential, NY, Brooklyn Union Gas Co, Brooklyn, NY; First Nat Bank Chicago, Ill; Sydney & Frances Lewis Found, Richmond, Va; Miami Univ Art Mus, Oxford, Ohio. *Exhib:* solo exhibs, 55 Mercer Gallery, NY, 80 & 82, Harm Bouckaert Gallery, NY, 82 & 84, Queens Mus, Flushing, NY, 82, M-13 Gallery, NY, 87 & 88, Winston Gallery, Wash, DC, 87; Approaches to Abstractions, Shanghai Exhib Ctr, Shanghai, China, 86; Dwellings, Althea Viatora Gallery, NY, 87; Vital Forces, Nature in Contemp Abstraction, Hecksher Mus, Huntington, NY, 91; Ten From Queens Mus, Paine Webber Gallery, NY, 92; Howard Scott Gallery, NY, 94 & 97; Grossman Gallery, Lafayette Col, Easton, Pa, 2003. *Teaching:* Asst prof fine art, Western Col, Oxford, Ohio, 65-70; instr painting, Philadelphia Art Mus, 71-72; prof fine art, LaGuardia Col, City Univ NY, 73-02. *Awards:* Creative Artists Pub Serv Prog Fel, NY State Coun Arts, 83-84; Fel, New York Found Arts, 85; Research Award, City Univ New York, 85, 88. *Bibliog:* Corinne Robins, rev, Sculpture, 3/89; Karin Lipson (auth), Nature in the abstract, around us and within, Newsday, 7/26/91; Helen Harrison (auth), The natural world and its mysteries, NY Times, 8/11/91; Karen S Chambers (auth), Pete Brown New Sculpture, Review, p 16, 4/15/97. *Media:* Wood, Acrylics

BROWN, PETEY
PAINTER
b W Orange, NJ. *Study:* Boston Univ Sch Fine and Applied Arts, BFA (painting), 75; Boston Univ Grad Sch Painting, 76. *Comn:* Hyatt Regency Hotel, Tampa, Fla, Four Seasons Hotel, Maui, Hawaii, Meridien at Coronado, San Diego, Hyatt Regency Hotel, Waikiki, Hawaii, Embassy Suites Hotel, Parsippany, NJ, Floridian Hotel, Vero Beach, Fla, Conrad Hotel, Uruguay. *Exhib:* Solo exhibs at Newton Arts Ctr, Massachusetts, 81, 84, Helen Shlein Gallery, Boston, 83, Patricia Heesy Gallery, NY City, 85, 86, David Brown Gallery, Provincetown, Massachusetts, David Brown Gallery, 87, Hunsaker/Schlesinger Gallery, Los Angeles, 89; group exhibs at Salem State Col, NH, 77, Cambridge Art Asn, Mass, 78, Fed Reserve Bank, Boston, 79, Danforth Mus, Framingham, Mass, 81, Helen Shlien Gallery, Boston, 82, Boston Visual Artists Union, 83, Provincetown Group Gallery Invitational, 84, Patricia Heesy Gallery, NY City, 85, 86, 87, Baltimore Mus Art, 86, Van Straaten Gallery, Chicago, 88, Hunsaker/Schlesinger Gallery, Los Angeles, 89, Gallery 99, Miami, 89, OIA Gallery, NY City, 90, Artists Space, 92, Gallery 148, NY City, 95, 96, New Art Ctr, 97, AIR Gallery, 2000, 2001, I-20 Gallery, 2003, Nat Acad Design Invitational, 2006

BROWN, ROBERT K
DEALER
b Springfield, Mass, May 22, 1942. *Study:* Boston Univ, BS; Annenberg Sch Commun, Univ Pa, MCommun Arts. *Pos:* Dir & co-owner, Reinhold-Brown Gallery, New York, currently. *Mem:* Antiquarian Booksellers Asn Am; Int League Booksellers. *Specialty:* Rare posters relating to the early avant-garde including constructivism, functionalism, art nouveau-deco, Vienna secession; rare books on 20th century art and architecture. *Publ:* Contribr, Art Deco Minneapolis Inst, 70; ed, Art in Design in Vienna, 72; auth, Art Deco Internationale, Quick Fox, 77. *Mailing Add:* 120 E 86th St No 6B New York NY 10028-1062

BROWN, SARAH M
PAINTER, INSTRUCTOR
b Longview, Tex, Jan 30, 1935. *Study:* Univ Chicago & Art Inst Chicago, BFA (with honors in figure drawing & figure painting), 1957; student, Tulane Univ, 1960, Odyssey Studio, Atlanta, 1978 & Watercolor Seminar, 1980. *Work:* former Pres Jimmy Carter; Sen Geraldine Ferraro; Reynolds Plantation; Great Waters, Eatonton, Ga; St Ives Country Club; Yoshima Ibashi, Asahi Inc, Tokyo; Portrait of Michael Feinstein, Calif State Univ, Los Angeles; poster, Ducks Unlimited, Ga; mural, Road to War, AH Stephens Mem; portrait, Franklin D Roosevelt, Warm Springs Lodge; portrait, Archbishop Wilton Gregory, Ga, 2013. *Exhib:* Solo exhibs, Longview (Tex) Art Asn, Pensacola Art Asn & Douglasville Cult Arts Ctr, 1995; Festival of the Masters, Lake Buena Vista, Fla; Knickerbocker Artists 31st Ann, NY; Catherine Lorillard Wolfe Art Club Exhibit; Nat Western Small Painting Exhib, Bosque Farms, NMex; Palm Beach Galleries, New Orleans; ABC Art and Frame Show, Atlanta, 1995; Safari Int Exhib, Galleria Mall, Atlanta, 1995; Callawolde Cult Arts Ctr, 2001; Delgado Mus No, La; Southeastern Wildlife Exposition, Charleston, SC; Christmas in Savannah, 2014. *Pos:* dir art dept, Pensacola Adult Vocat Sch, 58-59; owner, Sarah Brown Studio-Gallery, New Orleans, 59-63, Atlanta, 63-89 & Roswell, Ga, 86-89; owner, Sarah Brown Studio-Gallery, Atlanta, 89-; founder, Sarah Brown Tours, 73-; The Little Brown Press, 76-. *Teaching:* ceramics, drawing & painting, Pensacola (Fla) Jr Col, 58; condr, seminars in field. *Awards:* Best of Show, 1st Place Nat Western

Small Painting Exhib, 1982; 3rd Place show, 1st Place western category, Palm Beach Galleries; 1st place oils, NLAPW Ga State Competition. *Bibliog:* Articles in Veranda Mag, Ga. Wildlife Fedn Mag & Southeastern Wildlife Expo Dir. *Mem:* Nat League Am Pen Women; Nat Mus Women in the Arts (charter); Portrait Soc Am Inc; Atlanta Botanical Gardens; Ga Wildlife Fedn; Atlanta Artists Club. *Media:* oil, watercolor. *Specialty:* Portraits, landscapes, florals & wildlife. *Interests:* Piano & golf. *Dealer:* Keep It Art Sea Lincoln City OR; The Willard Washington DC; Christmas in Savannah

BROWN, STEPHEN PAT
PAINTER, SCULPTOR
b Greeley, Colo, Aug 26, 1950. *Study:* Colo State Univ, BFA, 72; Skowhegan Sch Painting & Sculpture, with Paul Georges, 72; Art Students League, with Gabriel Laderman; Brooklyn Col, with Philip Pearlstein, Allan D'Arcangelo, Lennart Anderson & Lois Dodd, MFA, 78. *Work:* Colo State Univ Gallery, Ft Collins; collections appear at Hosta Mus, New Britain Mus of Am Art, The Speed Mus, The Albany Mus, Mattatuck Mus. *Exhib:* New Realism, Terrain Gallery, NY, 80; solo exhib, Rosenberg Gallery, NY, 82; Hobart & William Smith Col, Geneva, NY, 82; Cortland Univ Gallery, NY, 82; Bodies and Souls, Artists Choice Mus, NY, 83; Contemp Am Still Life, One Penn Plaza, NY, 85; First Eight Years, Artists Choice Mus, 85; Life That Is Still, Sherry French Gallery, NY, 86; 161st Ann, Nat Acad Design, 86; Allan Stone Gallery, New York City, 87; Prince St Gallery, Rockefeller Gallery, State Univ of NY at Fredonia, 88; group exhib, Allan Stone Gallery, 89. *Pos:* Studio asst, Alice Neel, NY, 74-75. *Teaching:* Guest artist studio art, La State Univ, 79; instr printmaking, Sch Art League, Brooklyn, NY, 79-80; guest lectr painting, Cortland Univ, NY, 82; artist-in-residence, Parsons Sch Design, 83, vis artist, 85, guest lectr, 86; Asst prof, Hartford Univ, 1988-. *Awards:* Charles Shaw Painting Scholar, Brooklyn Col, 78; Yaddo Residency, NY State Coun Arts, 79; Millay Residency, Edna St Vincent Millay, 80; recipient, Acad Award in Art, Am Acad of Arts and Letters, 94. *Bibliog:* Harold Lujar (auth), Stephen Brown, Arts Mag, 11/78; John Perrault (auth), New talent in NY, Soho Weekly News, 79; Michael Brenson (auth), Contemporary American still life, New York Times, 7/5/85; Judd Tully (auth), Still life feast, Art World, 85. *Mem:* Nat Acad. *Media:* Oil

BROWNAWELL, CHRISTOPHER J
MUSEUM DIRECTOR
Study: Wilkes Col, BA (art); George Washington Univ, MA (museum edn). *Pos:* With, Commonwealth Conservation Ctr, Pa Hist Mus Commission and Smithsonian American Art Mus, formerly; curator, Acad Art Mus, 1988-93 dir, 1993-2010; dir, Farnsworth Art Mus, 2010-. *Mailing Add:* Farnsworth Art Museum 16 Museum St Rockland ME 04841

BROWNING, DIXIE BURRUS
PAINTER, WRITER
b Elizabeth City, NC, Sept 9, 1930. *Study:* Mary Washington Col; Richmond Prof Inst; and with Barclay Sheaks, Ray Prohaska & Ric Chin. *Work:* US Coast Guard Mus, New London, Conn; Statesville Mus Arts & Sci, NC; Duke Hosp Collection, Durham, NC; Wachovia Bank & Trust, Z Smith Reynolds Found, Winston-Salem. *Exhib:* Marine Exhib, James River Juried, Mariners Mus, Newport News, Va; Irene Leache Mem Biennial, Norfolk Mus Art, Va, 68; Regional Gallery Art, Boone, NC, 71 & 74; Manufacturers Hanover Trust Gallery, NY, 71; Southeastern Ctr for Contemp Art, Winston-Salem, 76. *Pos:* Founder & co-dir, Art Gallery Originals, Winston-Salem, 68-73; co-dir, Art V Gallery, Clemmons, NC, 74-75; pres, co-owner, Browning Artworks, Ltd, Frisco (Cape Hatteras) NC, 84-. *Teaching:* Teacher watercolor & acrylics, Arts & Crafts Asn Inc, Winston-Salem, 67-73; watercolor lectr & demonstr in schs & art orgns, NC, currently. *Awards:* Three First Prizes & one Second Prize, Southport Art Festival, 67, 68 & 71; Best in Show, Asn Artists NC, 71; Third Prize, Watercolor Soc NC, 76. *Bibliog:* Ola Mae Foushee (auth), North Carolina Artists, Univ NC; Anthony Swider (auth), Going to the Gallery, Winston-Salem & Forsyth Co Sch Syst, 69; Ward Nicholls (auth), Artists & Craftsmen in North Carolina, Wilks Art Guild, 74. *Mem:* Int Soc Artists; Assoc Artists Winston-Salem (vpres, 68-69); Watercolor Soc NC (co-organizer & pres, 72-73); Winston-Salem Arts Coun; Arts & Crafts Asn, Inc. *Media:* Watercolor, Chinese Ink. *Publ:* Illusr, North Carolina Parade, Univ NC, 66; contribr, Drawing & Painting the Natural Environment, Davis, 74; auth introd, Artists/USA 79-80, Found Advan Artists; auth film, Acrylics, The Contemporary Colors, Hunt Mfg Co. *Mailing Add:* Browning Studios of Hatteras Island PO Box 275 Frisco NC 27936

BROWNING, MARK DANIEL
PAINTER, SCULPTOR
b Miles City, Mont, Dec 26, 1946. *Study:* Self taught. *Work:* Plains Art Mus, Fargo, ND; USDA/Human Nutrition Res Ctr & Univ NDak, Grand Forks, NDak; Custer Co Art Ctr, Miles City, Mont; Pillsbury Co/Corp Offs, Minneapolis. *Exhib:* Solo exhibs, Yellowstone Art Ctr, Billings, Mont, 81, Talley Gallery, Bemidji State Univ, Minn, 83, Plains Art Mus, Moorehead, Minn, 84 & Bismark Art Gallery, NDak, 92; 113th Am Watercolor Soc, Salmagundi Club, NY, 80; Watercolor USA, Springfield Art Mus, Mo, 82, 83 & 90; 10th Midwest Watercolor Soc, Neville Mus, Green Bay, Wis, 86; Collection of Mid-Am Artists, Art Ctr Minn, Wayzata, 87; and many others. *Pos:* Dir & bd dir, Custer Co Art Ctr, 76-79, exec dir; pres, Mont Inst Arts, 76-78, bd dir, 76-81; studio artist & gallery owner, 79-; pres, Greater Grand Forks Arts & Humanities Asn, 86-88; exec dir, Custer Co Art Ctr, 95-; adv panel mem, Mont Cult & Aesthetic Trust, 96-; pres bd dir, Mont Art Gallery Dirs Asn. *Awards:* Purchase Selection, Am Art, Pillsbury Co, 80; Honorable Mention, Midwest Watercolor Soc, Manitowoc, Wis, 80; Purchase Award, Midwestern Invitational, Plains Art Mus, 85. *Bibliog:* Sebby Wilson Jacobson (auth), Zaner gallery review, Times-Union, Rochester, NY, 85; Ron Netsky (auth), Art Agenda, Democrat & Chronicle, Rochester, NY, 85. *Mem:* Mont Arts Coun; signature mem Midwest Watercolor Soc; NDak Coun Arts; signature mem Nat Watercolor Soc. *Media:* Watercolor; Smooth Surface, Non-Traditional. *Publ:* Creative Watercolor, Rockport Publ

BRUBAKER, JACK
SCULPTOR, BLACKSMITH, DESIGNER, PAINTER
b Chicago, Ill, Aug 30, 1944. *Study:* studied painting & drawing with Mary Brubaker, also at Art Inst Chicago, 64, Syracuse Univ, BFA, 66, Ind Univ, MFA, 68. *Work:* Joseph Hirshhorn Collection, Naples, Fla; Ind Univ Mus, Bloomington; and many others; Larry Hagman Collection; Douglas Cramer Collection; Ali McGraw Collection. *Comn:* Architectural works for pvt residences, pub bldgs, and churches. *Exhib:* Let There Be Light, Nat Ornamental Metal Mus, Memphis, Tenn, 84; Contemp Iron 87, traveling show, 87-89; solo exhib, Indianapolis Mus Art, Ind, 87, Jack Brubaker Sculpture, Judi Rotenburg Gallery, Boston, 89, Jack Brubaker Hand Forged Metals, Indianapolis Mus Art, 87; Sculpture, Bell Ross Gallery, 88; Toys, Metal Mus, 2000; Windvanes and Whirlygigs, Metal Mus, 2000; and many others. *Pos:* owner Jack Brubaker Designs. *Teaching:* teacher, advanced blacksmithing and design workshops for profls. *Awards:* Gold Trouser Button, Ctr for Metal Design, Aachen, WGer, 86. *Bibliog:* D Meilach (auth), Decorative and Sculptural Ironwork, Schiffer Pub, 2000; D Meilach (auth), The Contemporary Blacksmith, Schiffer Pub, 2000; D Meilach (auth), Direct Metal Sculpture, Schiffer Pub, 2000. *Mem:* Artist Blacksmith Asn Am (pres, 83-84); Brit Artist Blacksmith Asn. *Media:* Hot forged iron, bronze, copper, aluminum, paint. *Specialty:* Design history, sailing, boatbuilding. *Publ:* Dir, Forging Stone Cutting Tools (video), Artist Blacksmith Am, 81; and many others. *Mailing Add:* 5035 Earl Young Rd Bloomington IN 47408

BRUCH, CHRIS
SCULPTOR
Study: Univ Kans, Lawrence, BFA (ceramics/sculpture); Univ Wis, Madison, MA (video), MFA (sculpture). *Exhib:* Solo retrospective, Lawrimore Project, Seattle, 2007; solo exhibs include Salt Lake Art Ctr, 2001, Univ Colo, Colorado Springs, 2004, Kittredge Gallery, Univ Puget Sound, Tacoma, Wash, 2006; group exhibs include Northwest Biennial Exhib, Tacoma Art Mus, Wash, 2007. *Awards:* Betty Bowen Mem Award; Artist Trust GAP Grant; Neddy Artist Fel; Pollock-Krasner Found Grant, 2006-07; Artist Trust Fel, 2006. *Dealer:* Elizabeth Leach Gallery 417 NW 9th Ave Portland OR 97209; Lawrimore Project 831 Airport Way S Seattle WA 98134. *Mailing Add:* 3737 NE 135th St Seattle WA 98125-3831

BRUDER, HAROLD JACOB
PAINTER, EDUCATOR
b Bronx, NY, Aug 31, 1930. *Study:* Cooper Union, cert, 51; New Sch Social Res; Pratt Graphic Art Ctr. *Work:* NJ State Mus, Trenton; Sheldon Mem Gallery, Lincoln, Nebr; Hirshhorn Mus, Washington, DC; Univ NMex Mus. *Exhib:* Corcoran Gallery Biennale, Washington, DC, 63; Modern Realism & Surrealism, Am Fedn Arts Traveling Show, 64, The Realist Revival, 72-73; 22 Realists, Whitney Mus Am Art, NY, 70; Aspects of the Figure, Cleveland Mus Art, 74; Am Family Portraits, Philadelphia Mus Art, 76; solo exhibs, Armstrong Gallery, NY, 84 & 86 & Contemp Realist Gallery, San Francisco, 88; and others. *Pos:* Artist-in-residence, Aspen Sch Contemp Art, summer 67. *Teaching:* Assoc prof art, Kansas City Art Inst, 63-65; vis lectr, Pratt Inst, 65-66; prof emer art, Queens Col, 65-95, chmn art dept, 82-85. *Awards:* Purchase Prize, Am Acad Arts Letters, 78; PSC-BHE Fac Res Award, 76, 79, 84 & 88; Nat Endowment Arts Grant, 85-86. *Bibliog:* Ralph Pomeroy (auth), Harold Bruder and immediate family, Art & Artists, 10/68; Alan Gussow (interviewer), A sense of place, Saturday Rev Press, 72; Ralph Pomeroy (auth), Harold Bruder's Metaphors, Arts, 10/82. *Media:* Oil. *Publ:* Auth, Notes from the Prado, Art J, fall 72; Monumental Miniatures: The Drawings of Pierre Bonnard & Edward Vuillard, Drawing, 3-4/92; Breaking the ice: Emma Eames in search of the ideal, Opera Quart, winter 92; Romanized and romanticized: Mantegna's great Judith, Drawing, 9-10/92; Using linear rhythms for composition, Am Artist, 1/97. *Mailing Add:* 211 W 56st #24C New York NY 10019

BRUGUERA, TANIA
KINETIC ARTIST, VIDEO ARTIST
b Havana, Cuba, 1968. *Study:* Sch Art Inst Chicago, MFA, 2001. *Work:* New Mus for Latin Am Art, UK; Museo Nacional de Bellas Artes, Havana; Bronx Mus, New York; Mus Mod Art; JP Morgan Chase. *Exhib:* Solo exhibs, Academia de San Alejandro, Havana, 1986, Centro de Desarrollo de las Artes Visuales, Havana, 1992, Sch Art Inst Chicago, 1997, Vera van Laer Gallery, Antwerp, Belgium, 1999, San Francisco Art Inst, calif, 2002, Museo Nacional de Bellas Artes, Havana, 2003, Rhona Hoffman Gallery, Chicago, 2004; Proteo, Academia de Artes Plasticas, San Alejandro, 1986; I Festival de la Creacion y la investigacion, Instituto Superior de Arte, Havana, 1987; 2nd Int Poster Biennial, Museo Jose Luis Cuevas, Mex City, 1992; XI Int Drawing Biennial, Middlesbrough Fine Arts Mus, England, 1993; New Art from Cuba, Tullie House Mus and Art Gallery, England, 1995; 23rd Sao Paolo Int Biennial, Parque do Ibirapuera, Sao Paolo, Brazil, 1996; Videodrome, New Mus Contemp Art, 1999; The Stone and water, Helsinki Art Mus, Helsinki, Finland, 2002; The living museum, Mus fur Modern Kunst, Frankfurt, 2003; Island Nations, RI Sch Design Mus, 2004; Gwangju Biennale, Gwangju, Korea, 2008. *Teaching:* Coord dir, Escuela Victor Marante, Tomas Sanchez Found, Havana, 1992-93; prof, Instituto Superior de Arte, Havana, 1992-96; instr, Comunidad Las Terrazas, Pinar del Rio, Cuba, 1994; lectr, Sch Mus Fine Arts, Boston, 1998, Royal Coll, London, 2001, RI Sch Design, 2002; fac, San Francisco Art Inst, Calif, 2002, Skowhegan Sch Painting & Sculpture, Maine, 2002, Sch Art Inst Chicago, 2004, Columbia Coll, 2004; founder & dir, Catedra Arte de Conducta, Havana, 2002-. *Awards:* Guggenheim Meml Found Fel, 1998; Prince Claus Prize, Rotterdam, Neth, 2000; Louis Comfort Tiffany Found Grant, 2009; Meadows Prize, Meadows Sch Arts, Southern Methodist Univ, Dallas, 2013

BRULC, LILLIAN G
PAINTER, SCULPTOR
b Joliet, Ill. *Study:* Art Inst Chicago, MFA (George D Brown Foreign Travel Fel), 64; Univ Chicago, MFA, 64; also with Franz Gorse, Austria. *Work:* Major works in permanent archit environ, smaller works in pvt collections; pvt collections, Charles Craig, Santa Barbara, Calif, Dorothy & Allen Solom, Oxnard, Calif, Andrew Koval,

Washington, DC. *Comn:* Life-size bronze, mural, environ design, SVD Theologate, Chicago, 79-80; bronze relief, 83 & mural & mosaic, 86, Iron Range Interpretative Ctr, Chisholm, Minn; Holocaust Mem bronze & ceramic, Joliet Jewish Congregation Temple, Joliet, Ill, 89; bronze bas relief, Capitol Develop Bd, State of Ill, 92; series of 6 large murals, St Elizabeth Seton Church, Naperville, Ill, 2000; restoration ceiling murals, Daprato-Rigali Co, Chicago, 2004; and others. *Exhib:* Prints, Drawings & Watercolors 2nd Biennial by Ill Artists, Art Inst Chicago, 64; Solo exhib, Drawings & Lithographs, Casa de Escultura, Panama City, 69; Murals for People (slide of Chicago works), Mus Contemp Art, Chicago, 71; 3rd Ann Celebration Women's Day, Erector Sq Gallery, New Haven, Conn, 88; Gallery Genesis, Chicago, 88, 89, 90, 91, 92 & 93; Univ Wis, Milwaukee, 94; Art Colony, Most Na Soci, Slovenia, 96; Paintings, prints and drawings, Courtyard Gallery, CTU, Chicago, 2004. *Pos:* Artist-in-residence, Chicago Archdiocese Panama Mission, San Miguelito, 65-70, art adv & part-time resident, 73-79; artist-in-residence, Archdiocesan Latin Am Comt, Chicago, 71-72 & SVD Theologate, Chicago, 79-80; consult, Gallery Genesis, Chicago, 88; adv bd, Ill State Mus, Lockport, 95-97. *Teaching:* Asst instr lithography, Art Inst Chicago, 61-64; lectr theol & art, Divine Word Sem, Techny, Ill, 66-68; instr design, mat, portrait & drawing, Chicago Acad Fine Arts, 72-78. *Awards:* Merit Award, Slovenian Arts Coun, Univ Wis, Milwaukee, 94; Grant, Slovenian Arts Coun, Univ Wis, Milwaukee, 94; Resident, Artists' Colony, Slovenia, 96. *Bibliog:* Charlando (TV presentation), Univ Chicago WGN-9, 68; Edward Gobetz (auth), Lillian Brulc, Painter, Sculptor, Printmaker, Success Stories, SRCA; Darja Groznik (auth), interview, JANA, Ljubljana, Yugoslavia, 88; Mario Lewis Morgan (auth), Lillian Brulc Y Los Murales De San Miguelito, Panama City, Panama, 97. *Mem:* Environ & Art Comt, Archdiocese of Chicago; Chicago Women's Caucus for Art; Chicago Artists' Coalition. *Media:* Acrylic; Bronze. *Publ:* Illusr, Thirsting For the Lord, Alba House, 76; auth, Visit with Franz Gorse in Carinthia, Austria, SRCA Publ, 78; illusr, Dream Visions, SRCA Publ; Old Testament Message (23 vols), Michael Glazier Inc; illusr, State Historical Soc. Murals, 94. *Dealer:* Studio L' Atelier. *Mailing Add:* L' Atelier 909 Summit Joliet IL 60435

BRUMER, MIRIAM
PAINTER
b New York, NY, Oct 7, 1939. *Study:* Univ Miami, BA (art & Eng); Boston Univ, MFA (painting). *Work:* Chase Manhattan Bank, Citibank, NY; Boston Univ, Mass; Bell Labs, NJ; Payne Gallery Art, Moravian Coll, Pa; and many pvt collections. *Comn:* Painting for office, NY Bank Savings, 73. *Exhib:* A Woman's Place: The Central Hall Gallery in the 1970's, Mus Stonybrook, NY, 96; A Woman's Place: Central Hall Gallery Artists in the 90's, Gallery North, Setauket, NY, 96; Found and funky, Hunterdon Art Ctr, Clinton, NJ, 97-98; solo exhibs, The World Imagined, Payne Gallery Moravian Coll, Bethlehem, Pa, 2001, Conant Hall, Princeton, 2002, Wooster Arts Space, NY, 2005, Visitors: The World of Miriam Brumer, Rockland Ctr Arts, Nyack, NY, 9/2007, Miriam Brumer: Works on Paper, Wooster Arts Space, NY, 9/2007; City Without Walls, NJ, 2000, 2002; Obsession/Fixation, Invitational, Ceres Gallery, NY, 2002; Nat Arts Club, NY, 2003; Skoto Gallery, NY, 2005; Love's Secret Domain, 3rd Ward Gallery, NY, 6/2007; Group exhibs Bravin Lee Programs, 5-7/2009, NY, McKenzie Fine Arts, 6/2009, NY, Elisa Tucci Contemporary Art, NY, 2008-9; Two person exhib, Alpan Gallery, Huntinton, NY, 3/2009; Berkeley Coll Gallery, NY, 2012; 69th Regiment Armory, Fountain Art Fair, 2013, 2014. *Pos:* Writer & ed, Feminist Art J, NY, 72-74; educator, Queens Mus, 87-2005. *Teaching:* Asst prof studio art & art hist, NY Inst Technol, Old Westbury, 69-75; instr, Hunter Coll, 76-81 & New York Univ, 83-; lectr studio art & art hist, Marymount Manhattan Coll, New York, 83-; lectr art, The Looking Series, Queens Mus Art, 89-2009. *Awards:* Ludwig Vogelstein Found Grant, 76-77; Comt Visual Arts Grants, 79 & 80; Artist-in-Residence, NY Found Arts, 85; Artspeak, Will Grant, 87, 90. *Bibliog:* Kay Kenny (auth), Views by Women Artists, 82; Diana Morris (auth), Eight, Women Artist News, 83; Michelle Kidwell (auth), Miriam Brumer, Arts Mag; Hedy O'Beil (auth), More than meets the eyes, Arts, 5/84; The Mojo of Masks, Dan Bischoff (auth), The Star Ledger, 8/2000; Sheila McKenna (auth), Miriam Brumer, Newsday, 9/5/2000; Myra Yellin Outwater (auth), Small Intimate Pieces Reveal Artist's Enormous Range, The Morning Call, 3/2001; Dan Bischoff (auth), Newark Show Uncovers 'Hidden Things', The Newark Star Ledger, 2/2002; Tony Sienzant (auth), Imagining Worlds Unseen, The Easton Times, 3/2001. *Media:* Acrylic on wood, Assemblage, Works on Paper. *Mailing Add:* 250 W 94th St New York NY 10025

BRUMFIELD, WILLIAM CRAFT
PHOTOGRAPHER, WRITER
b Charlotte, NC, Jun 28, 1944. *Study:* Tulane Univ, BA, 66; Univ Calif, Berkeley, MA, 68, PhD, 73. *Work:* New Orleans Mus of Art, La; Nat Gallery of Art, Photographic Archives, Washington, DC; Libr of Congress, Prints and Photogs, Washington, DC; Arkhangelsk Mus of Art, Arkhangelsk, Russ; Nat Mus of Archit, Moscow, Russ. *Exhib:* Lost Russia: Duke Univ Mus of Art, Durham, NC, New Orleans Mus of Art, La, 96-97, Univ of Mich Mus of Art, Ann Arbor, 97-98; The Romanov Legacy, Memphis Brooks Mus of Art, Tenn, 97-98; Orthodox Shrines of the North, Arkhangelsk Mus of Art, Arkhangelsk, Russia, 99-2000; The Russian North, Nat Mus of Archit, Moscow, Russia, 2001. *Pos:* Cur, William C Brumfield Collection Univ Wash, Seattle, 2003-. *Teaching:* Asst prof, Harvard Univ, Cambridge, Mass, 74-79; prof, Tulane Univ, New Orleans, La, 81-; assoc prof, Univ Va, 85-86. *Awards:* Notable book of the year award, NY Times Book Rev, 93; AAUP award, Illustration book category, 96; Fel, Guggenheim Found, 2000. *Bibliog:* Suzanne Massie (auth), Pleasures of Domes, NY Times Bk Rev, 93; Chris Waddington (auth), Brumfield Captures Essence, New Orleans Times-Picayune, 97; Maya Chaplygina (auth), William Brumfield on Assignment, Ogonyok, Russia, 4/2001. *Mem:* Russian Acad of Archit; Inst of Modern Russian Cult; Soc of Archit Historians; Soc of Historians of East European & Russian Art; Russian Acad of the Arts (hon mem 2006). *Media:* Black/White Photography. *Res:* The history and photographic documentation of Russian architecture. *Collection:* William C Brumfield Russian architecture collection. *Publ:* Auth, photogr, Gold in Azure, David Godine, 83; auth, Origins of Modernism Russian Archit, Univ of Calif, 91; auth, photogr, Hist of Russian Archit, Cambridge Univ Press, 93; Lost Russia, Duke Univ Press, 95; Landmarks of Russian Archit, Gordan & Breach, 97; Vologda Album, Tri Quadrata, 2005; Totma: Archit Heritage in Photographs, Tri Quadrata, 2005; Irkutsk: Archit Heritage in Photographs, Tri Quadrata, 2006; Velikii Ustiug Tri Quadrata, 2007; Tobolks, 2006, Solikamsk, 2007, Cherdyn, 2007, Kargopol, 2007, Chita, Archit Heritage in Photographs, TriQuadrata, 2008, Buriatiia, 2008, Solovki, 2008, Kirillov, Ferapontovo, 2009, Kolomna, 2009, Suzdal, 2009; Ustiuzhna, 2010; Torzhok: Archit Heritage in Photographs, 2010; Belozersk, 2011; Vologda, 2012; Usol'e: Archit Heritage in Photographs, 2012; Usol'e: Zemilia Stroganovykh na Kame, 2013. *Mailing Add:* Tulane University 305 Newcomb Hall New Orleans LA 70118

BRUMMEL, MARILYN REEDER
COLLAGE ARTIST, PRINTMAKER
b Syracuse, NY, Dec 29, 1926. *Study:* Syracuse Univ, BFA, 48; also studied with Roberto De La Monica, 72 & Krishna Reddy, 78. *Work:* Newark Mus, NJ; Passaic Co Hist Soc, NJ; Govt Off Bldg (NJ State Coun Arts), Atlantic City; Nat Elec Rural Co-op Asn, Washington, DC; Pub Serv Elec & Gas Co, Bergen Co, NJ. *Comn:* Odyssey (30 prints), Art Ctr NJ, Tenafly, 76; Cryogenic Landscape (print), Arde Inc, Norwood, NJ, 83. *Exhib:* Women's Show Invitational, Everson Mus, Syracuse, NY, 74; Nat Arts Club Show, NY, 74; Silvermine Guild Artists, New Canaan, 75; 1st Biennial NJ Artists, Newark Mus, 77; Print Club Ann, Philadelphia, Pa, 78; Audubon Artists Ann, Acad Design, NY, 81; solo exhibs, Transformed Visions, Printmaking Coun NJ, 97 & Time and Space, Interchurch Ctr, NY, 98. *Awards:* Gold Medal Award, Catharine Lorillard Wolfe Ann, 78; Director's Award, Bergen Community Mus, 89; Best Contemp Award, Kerygama Gallery, 90. *Bibliog:* David Speiegler (auth), Art Review, Bergen Record, 71 & 78; John Zeamon (auth), Art Review, Bergen Record, 89. *Mem:* Nat Asn Women Artist (chmn, mem extn), 92-93; Printmaking Coun NJ; Art Ctr Painting Affiliates (co-chmn); Computer Art Prints Asn. *Media:* Miscellaneous. *Dealer:* Prints Etcetera 1517 163rd St Whitestone NY 11357

BRUNET-WEINMANN, MONIQUE
CRITIC, CURATOR
b Toulon, France, Apr 30, 1943; Can citizen. *Study:* Univ Paris X, with Pierre Francastel, Ecole des Hautes Etudes, Diplome d'Etudes Superieures en Lettres, 67; Univ Montreal, MA (hist art), 90. *Hon Degrees:* Directrice honoraire du Cetnre Copie-Art, Montreal, 91. *Exhib:* Group Exhib, Juried Int, Copigraphy, Montage (cur), Rochester, NY, 1993. *Collection Arranged:* Louise Gadbois Retrospective, 1932-1982 (with catalog), 83, James Guitet, Propositions, X Positions (with catalog), 88 & Pastel Quebecois Comtemporain, 92, Univ UQAM Gallery, Montreal; Copigraphy: What Happened to the Women Pioneers?, ISEA, Galerie Arts Technologiques, Montreal, 95; Christian Tisari, 1977-1997, Désordre et des astres, Maison des arts de Laval & Des ordres et dèsastre, Maison de la Culture Côte-des-Neiges, 98; D'où Venons-nous? Que sommes-nous? Où allons-nous?, Maison de la cult Frontenac, Maison des arts de Laval, 2000; Photos Géniques, Maison des arts de Laval, 2000; Mutations de Riopelle, MAC des laurendides, 03-04. *Pos:* Art critic, freelance, Vie des Arts, Montreal, Que, 74- & Contemporanea, Provincetown Arts, Parcours, 90-; cur, freelance, Univ Gallery, UQAM Montreal, 83- & Maison des arts de Laval, 95-; pres, CRITIQ, Complexe de Realisations Independant Transculturel et Interartiel du Que, 89-; Musee d'art contemp des laurentides, 2003-. *Teaching:* Lectr Fr Lit, McGill Univ, 71-73. *Awards:* Grand Prix Lit Conseil de la culture des Laurentides, 93-. *Bibliog:* Louise Gadbois er Mary Bouchard, review by Rene Viau, Vie die Arts, 2009; Entrevue avec Monique Brunet, La Parole météque, no 33, 10/99; review by Jeanne Maranda, Canadian Women Studies, 2010. *Mem:* Int Art Critic Asn. *Res:* Life & work of Jean Paul Riopelle, Louise Gadbois, Simone Mary Bouchard, James Guitet, Father Marie Alain Couturier. *Collection:* Contemp Quebec art: Benoit, Cantieni, Jaque, L Gadbois, Betty Goodwin, James Guitet. *Publ:* Contribr, Medium Photocopy, Transatlantic Press, 87; Fluid Exchanges: Artists & Critics in the Aids Crisis, Univ Toronto Press, 92; La Copigraphie et ses Connexions, Hull, Montcalm CRITIQ, 93; Esthetique des Arts Mediatiques I, Presses de l'Universite du Quebec, 95; Jean-Paul Riopelle, des Visions d'Amerique, Ed de l'Homme, Montreal, 97; Catalogue Raisonné Jean Paul Riopelle, vol I 1939-53, Hibou éd, 99; CDRom, Copigraphy: Elements for a Global History, Loplop ed, Montreal, 2000; Raisonné, vol II 1954-59, Acatos 'ed, Paris, 2004; Jean Paul Riopelle, Catalogue Raisonne des estampes Hibou Editeurs, Montreal, 2005; Marie Alain Couturier, Un combat pour l'art sacre, 2005; Jean Paul Riopelle, Catalogue Raisonnè vol III 1960-1965, Hibou Edieen, Montreal, 2009; auth, Louis Jaque Genèse d'une signature, Montreal, 89; Marcel Broquet ed, Simone Mary Bouchard et Louise Gadbois, l'art nail dans la modernite Harscel Broquet, Montreal, 2009. *Mailing Add:* 229 Des Bois Rd Rosemere PQ J7A 1S4 Canada

BRUNI, STEPHEN THOMAS
MUSEUM DIRECTOR
b Philadelphia, Feb 3, 1949. *Study:* George Wash Univ, BA, 1971. *Pos:* Curatorial asst, Del Art Mus, Wilmington, 1972-74, prog asst, 1974-77, admin asst, 1977-79, mgr support servs, 1979-82, asst dir admin, 1982-84, deputy dir admin, 1984-85, acting dir admim, 1985-86, exec dir, 1986-; Mem arts selection comt, Del State Arts Coun, 1985-86, State Division Librs., 1984-86; mem Gov's Arts Adv Comt, 1983-85; mem adv bd, Siena Hall and Seton Villa, Creative Artists Network; bd dir, Studio Group, Inc. *Mem:* Am Asn Mus, Asn Art Mus Dir, Bd Greater Wilmington Conv and Visitors Bur. *Mailing Add:* Delaware Art Mus 2301 Kentmere Pkwy Wilmington DE 19806

BRUNI, UMBERTO
PAINTER, GRAPHIC ARTIST
b Montreal, Que, Nov 24, 1914. *Study:* With Guido Nincheri, Montreal, 30-37; Ecole Beaux-Arts, Montreal, grad prof, 37. *Comn:* Bust of Brother Andre, St Joseph Shrine, Montreal, 39; religious scene at church (fresco), Montreal, 58; historical scene (oil), Rougier et Freres, Montreal, 59; Da Giovanni (mosaic mural), Montreal, 60; religious mosaic mural, Ste Elizabeth Church, Ville Emard, Que, 61; portrait of ex-Prime Minister Sauve, Quebec Parliament. *Exhib:* Solo exhibs, Figuratif a L'Abstrait, Mus Beaux-Arts, Montreal, 61 & Giotto Art Gallery, Rome, Italy, 62; Can Artist in Paris,

Maison Que, France, 62; Art Coun Can, O'Keefe Ctr, Toronto, 62; Univ Quebec, 77-86; and many others. *Pos:* Cur, Univ Que, Montreal, 70-80, founder & dir, Gallery, 74-80. *Teaching:* Prof, Ecole Beaux-Arts, Montreal, 47-69; prof, Univ Que, Montreal, 70-80; Retired. *Awards:* Fel to Rome & Paris, Art Coun Can, 61-62; Research Fel to Rome & Paris, Que Govt, 72. *Mem:* Royal Can Acad Arts; Acad Gentium Pro Pace, Rome; Int Inst Conserv Hist & Artistic Works. *Media:* All. *Interests:* Didactical presentation of exhibitions. *Publ:* Auth, Signatures, Marcel Broquet Ed, 81. *Mailing Add:* 1325 Blvd D'Auteuil Laval PQ H7E 3J4 Canada

BRUNO, PHILLIP A
DIRECTOR
b Paris, France. *Study:* Columbia Col, BA (hist fine arts & archit); Inst Fine Arts, New York Univ. *Comn:* Restored 17th century house on Martha's Vineyard, Mass, 64. *Collection Arranged:* Ralph Rosenborg Retrospective, Washington, DC, 52; Jose Luis Cuevas, Paris, 55; Elmer Livingston Macrae, Nashville, 63; Tschang-yeul Kim, 79 & Enrico Donati, 80, FIAC, Grand Palais, Paris; Tschang-yeul Kim/Wolfgang Kubach & Anna Marie Wilmsen, 81; Dale Chihuly, Red Grooms, Claudio Bravo, Magdelina Abakanowicz, Bill Jackin, Manolo Valdes, Chakaia Booker, Fernando Botero. *Pos:* Weyhe Gallery, New York, 50-51; co-founder & assoc dir, Grace Borgenicht Gallery, 51-55; dir, World House Gallery, New York, 56-60; dir, Am Exhibs for La Napoule Found, New York & France; dir, Staempfli Gallery, New York, 60-89, co-dir, 81; adv bd mem, Ossabaw Island Found, Savannah, Ga, 78-; art consult, First Am Nat Bank, Nashville, 80-81; assoc dir, Marlborough Gallery, New York, 89-2007. *Teaching:* Guest lectr, Foreign Ministry Finland, Helsinki, 78 & Cornell Univ, 92. *Mem:* Hon life mem St Paul Art Ctr; hon mem Tenn Fine Arts Ctr Cheekwood, Nashville; Dukes Co Hist Soc, Edgartown, Mass; Munic Art Soc; Nat Trust Hist Preservation. *Specialty:* Contemporary. *Collection:* Mainly mid-twentieth century American watercolors and drawings, ranging from Marin to Kline, including Lachaise, Demuth, Tobey, Bravo, Lopez-Garcia, Wunderlich; Selections of the collection have been exhibited at the Palmer Art Mus, Penn State Univ, Hunverian Art Gallery, Glasgow, Scotland, Krannert Art Museum, Tennessee Fine Arts Center, Finch College Museum Art, Minn Mus, Vassar Art Coll Gallery, Quqanheim Mus & The Phillips Collection. *Mailing Add:* 342 E 67th St No 11A New York NY 10065-6238

BRUNO, SANTO M
PAINTER
b June 29, 1947. *Study:* Tyler Sch Art, Temple Univ, Philadelphia, Pa, BFA, 69, MFA, 71; studies with David Pease, Romas Viesulas & Steven Green. *Hon Degrees:* Atlanta Coll Art, 80. *Work:* High Mus Art, Atlanta; Kilpatrick, Cody & Regenstein Collection; Stampe Nacional de Italia; Univ Osaka, Japan; Creiger Assocs, Boston. *Comn:* Five major painting-constructions, New Atlanta Hartsfield Int Airport, Ga, 80. *Exhib:* Solo shows, First Impressions of Atlanta, Image South Gallery, Atlanta, Ga, 72, Illusions of a Greek Spring, Gallerie Illien, 73, Crow Carter Presents Santo Bruno: A Five-year Select of Work, Crow-Carter & Assocs, 76, Recent Work, Javo Gallery, 77, A Selection of Work: 78-80, Atlanta Art Workers Coalition Gallery, 80; Mark Miller Gallery, EHampton, NY, 96, State Street Real Estate Gallery, Charleston, SC, 2012; Flight Patterns, Forest Ave Consortium, Atlanta, 80; Artists and the Cyclorama Project, Colony Square, 82; Abstraction/Attraction, Newhouse Gallery, Staten Island, NY, 86; Bruce Lurie Gallery, NY, 87 & 88; Gotham Fine Arts, Ltd, 87; Dome Gallery, 88. *Pos:* Conserv contractor, Santo Bruno Fine Art, 83-; owner, Santo Bruno Fine Art, 91-. *Teaching:* Instr painting, Tyler Sch Art, Temple Univ, Rome, Italy, 70-71; instr painting & drawing, Atlanta Col Art, 71-78, head dept painting, 77-78; instr drawing, Western Conn St Univ, 2010. *Awards:* Nathan Margolis Mem Award, Temple Univ, 78; Exhib grant, NY State Council Arts, 91. *Bibliog:* Preview essay, Art Voices S, 1/78; Sherry Baker (auth), Interview with Santo Bruno, Off-Peachtree Mag, 2/78; Michael Fressola (auth), What's new at Newhouse, Staten Island Advan, 2/86. *Media:* Acrylic. *Interests:* Owns & maintains a personal collection of art work from the 16th century to modern art. *Dealer:* Marc Miller Gallery 3 Railroad Ave East Hampton NY 11937; Hermus Fine Art 20 Woodrow Rd Staten Island NY

BRUNO, VINCENT J
HISTORIAN, ADMINISTRATOR
b New York, NY, Feb 8, 1926. *Study:* Bard Col, 46-48; Academie Julian, Paris, cert painting, 49; Kenyon Col, BA (philos art), 51; Columbia Univ, MA, 62, PhD, 69; Kenyon Col, DFA, 84. *Hon Degrees:* D, Kenyon Col, 84. *Teaching:* Instr art hist, Wellesley Col, 64-65; assoc prof, C W Post Col, Long Island Univ, 65-66; assoc prof, State Univ NY, Binghamton, 66-76, chairperson, 72-76; chmn dept art, Univ Tex, Arlington, 76-84, Ashbel Smith Chair prof, 84-93, dept art & art hist, prof emer, 94-. *Awards:* John Simon Guggenheim Mem Fel, 78-; Am Coun Learned Soc Grant-in-Aid, 80; Am Philos Soc Grant-in-Aid, 82; Nat Endowment Humanities, Fel, 86-87; Getty Found Grant, 89. *Bibliog:* Martin Robertson (auth), The classical palette: Review of Form and Color in Greek Printing, Times Lit Suppl, London 8/5/77; S R Roberts (auth), Review of form and color in Greek painting, Art Bulletin LXII, 80; A O Koloski Ostrow (auth), Review of Hellenistic painting techniques, Am J Archeol 91, 87. *Mem:* Coll Art Asn Am; Archeol Inst Am; Am Inst Nautical Archeol; Am Sch Classical Studies, Athens; hon fel Am Acad Rome (mem, adv comt). *Res:* Conducted excavations at Cosa under auspices of American Academy in Rome and State Univ of New York at Binghamton, 68-72; ancient painting techniques. *Publ:* Contribr, Princeton Encyclopedia of Classical Sites, Int J Nautical Archaeol, In Memoriam Otto J Brendel; Hellenistic painting techniques: The evidence of the Delos fragments, Columbia Studies in the Classical Tradition, Vol XI, Leiden (monogr), 85; coauth, Cosa IV: The Houses; Memoirs of the American Academy in Rome, Vol XXXVIII, University Park, Pa, 93; Classical and post classical studies in memory of Frank Edward Brown (1908-1988), Studies Hist Art, Vol 43, 93; Functional and spatial analysis of wall painting: proceedings of the Fifth International Congress on ancient wall painting, Amsterdam Bulletin, 93

BRUNSVOLD, CHICA
PAINTER, INSTRUCTOR
b Ypsilanti, Mich, 1940. *Study:* Univ Mich, Sch Art, BS (design), 61, Sch Educ, cert, 62, MA (art), 62; studied with watermedia specialists Glen Bradshaw, Katherine Liu, Carole Barnes, Carlton Plummer, Cheng Khee Chee, George James, Virginia Cobb, MarilynHugheyPhillis, John Salminen, Ralph Smith, Betsy Dillard Stroud, Mary Todd Beam & others. *Work:* Birdlam; Waiting II; Bonding with Noah; Zooillogicals; Possums at Play; Gulf Stream; Bird in Haud; The Mediator; Trunk Show; The Secret Garden; Jurassic. *Exhib:* Solo exhibs, Art League Torpedo Factory Arts Ctr, Alexandria, Va, 96, Lombardi Cancer Ctr, Georgetown Univ Hosp, Washington, DC, 97, Children's Nat Med Ctr, 97, Burroughs-Chapin Art Mus, 97, Strathmore Hall Arts Center, Bethesda, Md, 97, Touchstone Gallery, Washington, DC, 98 & Ellen Noel Art Mus, 98, MSC Forsyth Gallery, Tex A&M Univ, 99, The Artists Mus, Washington, 99, Children's Art Mus, San Angelo, Tex & Northwood Univ, Cedar Hill, Tex, 2000; Paine Art Ctr, Oshkosh, Wis, 2001; Art Station, Stone Mountain, Ga, 2001; Atrium Gallery, Fairfax Inova Hospital, Fairfax, Va, 2002; Longwood Univ, Farmville, Va, 2003; Goodyear Cottage, Jekyll Island, Ga, 2003; This Century Gallery, Williamsburg, Va, 2003; Black Rock Arts Center, Germantown, Md, 2005; Visual Arts Center, NW Fla, Panama City, Fla, 2006; group exhib, Nat Watermedia, 95- & over 160 others; Goodwin House, Alexandria, Va, 2007; Crossroads Art Center, Richmond, Va, 2007; Strathmore Hall Arts Center, Bethesda, Md, 2007; Green Springs Gardens Horticultural Ctr, Alexandria, Va, 2009; Fairfax Co Arts, Pinnacle Buldg, McLean, Va, 2010; Glenview Manision, Civic Ctr, Rockville, 2011; First Stage Theater, McLean, Va, 2011; Green Spring Gardens Park, Alexandria, Va, 2011, 2013, 2015. *Collection Arranged:* Arts in Embassies Program, Burma; The Art Station, Stone Mountain, Ga; Resurrection Med Ctr, Pediatric Wing, Chicago; Burroughs-Chapin Art Mus, Myrtle Beach, SC; Ellen Noel Art Mus, Odessa, Tex; Finnegan & Henderson, Atlanta; Longwood Univ, Farmville, Va; Paine Art Ctr, Oshkosh, Wis; Fairfax Inova Hosp, Va. *Pos:* Illusr gen, Cent Intelligence Agency, 62-67 & Ind Col Armed Forces, 67-68; First vpres, Potomac Valley Watercolorists, 91-93, pres, 93-95. *Teaching:* Instr water media painting at art clubs & organizations for past 30 years; instr workshop Stretching the Boundaries for Creative People, Ohio Watercolor Soc, 1997, 1999, 2002; sole juror, judge, Va Women in the Arts, Elkins, WVa, 2010, DE Watercolor Soc Regional Exhib, 2012; workshop instr, Peninsula Fine Arts Ctr, Norfolk, Va, 2013. *Awards:* Holbein Award, Tex Watercolor Soc, 97; Daler-Rowney Award, Taos Nat Exhib Am Watercolor IV, 98; Harrison Cady Award, Am Watercolor Soc, 99; Virginia Watercolor Soc, 2005; M. Graham & Company Award, Southern Watercolor Soc, 2006; Va Watercolor Soc, 2009; Potonac Valley Watercolor, 2010, 2013; Nat Watercolor Soc, 2011; Gallery Underground, 2015. *Bibliog:* Josef Woodard (auth), Notable works surface in watercolor exhibit (rev), Los Angeles Times, 5/2/96; Phaedra Greenwood (auth), Awards presented in national watercolor show (rev), Taos News, NMex, 10/9/97; Maureen Bloomfield (auth), Ones to Watch, Watercolor Magic (mag) Yearbook, 2001; It Ain't Over Till it's Over, Watercolor Magic mag., Creativity, 2001; Mary Beam (auth), Celebrating your Creative Self, Northlight Bks, 2001; Betsy Dillard Stroud (auth), Painting the Now, Watercolor Magic, 2006, Watercolor Artist, June, 2014; Betsy Dillard Stroud (auth), The Artist's Muse, Northlight Bks, 2006; Splash 10, Northlight Books, 2008; Mary Todd (auth), The Creative Edge, Northligh Books Publ, 2009; Creativity Workshop, The Watercolor Artist, 2/2009; Competition Spotlight, The Artist's Mag, 3/2009; The Artistic Touch (3, 4, 5 and 6), Creative Art Press. *Mem:* Nat Watercolor Soc (signature mem); NW Watercolor Soc (signature mem); Va Watercolor Soc (signature mem); Am Watercolor Soc (sig mem, 2011). *Media:* Watercolor, Acrylic, Watermedia. *Interests:* Choir, tennis, bridge, salmon fishing. *Collection:* Zooillogicals-bright whimsical paintings, florals and abstracts of birds and animals. *Publ:* Illusr, Birdlam, York Graphic Servs, 96; Illusr Waiting II, York Graphic Svcs, 99; The Doll & the Secret Garden II, The Finer Image, 2003; illusr, Confetti Mag, summer 2004; Night Blooms II, Exuberance, Who? & Eclipse, Old Town Editions, 2006; The Journey, The Cathedral, Bird Bath, Cat Bird Seat, Under Cover, Yellow & Purple, December, Old Town Eds, 2009; Parrotdise II, Unstill Life, Creation I and II, Catty Corner, Eclipse, Old Town Editions, 2011; Faces in the Crowd, Gossip, Old Town Editions, 2013; Hen Party, Coon Caper, The Reunion, Mother Goose, The Bayou, Basket of Posies, Checkered Past, Checks & Balances, Just Ducky II, Let's Fly, Misty Mountains, Night Blooms III, Pink Sky, Rainy Day Bouquet, Sanctuary, Swirl, Totem Pole and Woodland Dance, Old Town Editions, 2015. *Dealer:* Gallery Underground 2100 Crystal Dr Arlington Va 22202. *Mailing Add:* 3510 Wentworth Dr Falls Church VA 22044

BRUNSWICK, CECILE R
PAINTER
b Antwerp, Belg, Jul 26, 1930; US citizen. *Study:* Queens Col, BA, 52; Columbia Univ, MIA, 54; Art Students League, with Frank O'Cain, 92. *Work:* World Children's Art Mus of Okazaki, Japan; Canadian Mus of Civilization, Quebec; Pfizer Inc, NY; Sumitomo Marine & Fire Insurance Co, NY; Nat Westminster Bank, NY; Assilah Forum Found Mus, Morocco; Wills Eye Hosp, Pa; IBM, NY; Arthur Andersen, Va; Nestle's, Calif. *Comn:* Erica Stone Collection. *Exhib:* Paris-Washington Echange Artistique, Arts Etoiles, Paris, 93; Visual Perceptions, Nour Found, NY, 93; Relationships, Kavehaz Gallery, NY, 96; SomArts Gallery; A Celebration of Possibilities, San Francisco, 99; Provence Paintings, Broome St Gallery, NY, 98 & Hidden Assets, 2000; Artsforum Gallery, NY, 2000; World Festival of Art, Slovenia, 01, Matthew Travis Gallery, Houston, Tex, 03; Paul Mellon Art Ctr, Choate, Wallingford, Conn, 2004; Artspace 129, Montclair, NJ, 2005; Mercedes-Benz, Manhattan Gallery, NY, 2005; Franklin 54 Gallery, NY, 2006; The Landmark Lobby Gallery, Tarrytown, NY, 2006; Karin Sanders Gallery, Sag Harbor, 2006; City Without Walls, Newark, NJ, 2006; Affordable Art Fair, Franklin 54 Gallery, NY, 2007; Pool Art Fair, Basel/Miami Art Fair, Miami, 2007; Fashion Ctr Space for Pub Arts, NY, 2008; Art Source Int, NY, 2009; Gallery 8, Fashion Ctr Arts Festival & Open Studio, New York, 2009; The Artists Proj, Toronto, 2010; No Rules, Dorian Grey Gallery, NY, 2011; Architectural Home Design Show, NY, 2011, 2012, 2013; McKenzie Tribe Gallery, Southampton, NY, 2011; Quick Ctr Mus, St Bonaventure Univ Mus, NY, 2011, 2012; Navillus Gallery, Toronto, 2011, 2012, 2013; Grace Inst, NY, 2011;

Fashion Ctr Arts Festival, 2011, 2012, 2013; Quick Ctr Mus Exhib of Morocan Paintings, 2011-2012; Affordable Art Fair, 2012; Art Southampton, Dorian Gray Gallery, 2012; Exhale Unlimited Gallery, LA, 2013. *Awards:* Mus Prize, Hudson River Mus, 80; Third Prize, City of NY - Parks Dept, 90; Assilah Forum Found Residency, Morocco, 2002; Valparaiso Residency, Spain, 2006. *Bibliog:* Valerie Kellogg (auth), VOICE Art, 1/8/98; ABC Television, Business Now, BA-TV - Kathy Ryan, 6/4/2000; Antiques & the Arts Weekly, 11/19/04; Cecile Brunswick, Interior Design, 4/06; Eric Ernst (auth), Southampton Press, 8/2006; Apartment Therapy (web review), 2011; Michele Keith (auth), Trove, Array Mag, 2012. *Mem:* NY Artists Equity; Japan Soc; NY Artists Cir. *Media:* Oil, Watercolor, Pastels, Collage. *Interests:* Travel, choral singing. *Collection:* colorful abstract oil paintings on linen canvas. *Publ:* Auth, New York Windows Calendar, Pomegranate Artbks, 88; illus, Bologna Children's Book, Itabashi Mus, 94; Sites Unseen: Paintings, Cecile Brunswick, 2010, 2012. *Dealer:* Dorian Grey Gallery 437 E 9th St New York NY. *Mailing Add:* 127 W 96th St 15D New York NY 10025-6482

BRUSH, LEIF
SOUND SCULPTOR, INSTRUCTOR
b Bridgeport, Ill, Mar 28, 1932. *Study:* Art Inst Chicago, dipl (fel), 70, MFA (fel), 72. *Work:* Mills Coll Libr; Inst Recherche Coordr Acoustique & Musique Libr; Audio Arts Libr, London; Electroacoustique de Bourges, France, 2002; and others. *Comn:* Minn Dept Trans/State Arts Bd, Milaca, 86. *Exhib:* Minneapolis Inst Arts, 77, 79, 86 & 89; Walker Art Ctr, Minneapolis, 79 & 80; Neuberger Mus, Purchase, NY, 81; Suono/Ambiente/Musica, Milan, Italy, 82; Minneapolis Coll Art & Design, 82; Hudson River Mus, NY, 82; Mail Music, Monza, Italy, 83; Tweed Mus Art, 84; New Music Am, 80, 87; Yellow Springs Inst, Chester Sps, Pa, 87; The Aerial (cassette/CD), Nonsequitur, Issue 4, 92; Jukebox-in-the-sky (over deconstructed voting booth installation), Tweed Mus Art, Duluth, 94; Red Eye Theater, Minneapolis, 94; The Sound Symposium Lend Me Your Ears: Sound City Spaces, St John's, Nfld, Can, 94; Ear to the Ground (interactive, on-the-floor, sound installation), Nash Gallery, Minneapolis, 97; CD Zero, FACT, UK, 2000. *Pos:* Vis artist, Univ Victoria, 73, Univ Colo, 75, State Univ NY, Alfred, 76, Univ Md, Baltimore Co, 77, Wright State Univ, 78, Art Res Ctr, Kansas City, Univ NDak & ZBS Found, Fort Edward, NY, 79; res artist, Visual Studies Workshop, 84. *Teaching:* Instr audible constructs, Art Inst Chicago, 70-72; asst prof, Univ Iowa, Iowa City, 72-76; asst prof sculpture, Univ Minn, Duluth, 76-79, assoc prof, 79-87, prof art in tech, 87-2002; Terrain Instruments presentation & lect, Banff Centre Arts & Univ Calgary, 93. *Awards:* Fels, Jerome Found, 82 & Nat Endowment Arts, 73 & 83; Bush Found, 80; Minn Percent for the Arts, 86. *Bibliog:* David Moss (prod) Art You Can Hear, NPR, 86; New Music America, Am Pub Radio Network, 88; Soundviews: Sources, Nonsequitur, Santa Fe, 90; Sztuka Fabryka Radio, Belgium, 93 & 94; and others. *Media:* Multimedia. *Publ:* Contribr, Fifth Assembling, New York, 75; Soundings, Neuberger Mus, 81; Ear Mag, Vol IX, No 5, New York, 85; New Music America, Hartford, 84; Leonardo, Pergamon, Vol 17, 84 & Vol 23, Issue 20, 90; Musicworks, Toronto, 85; Experimental Musica Instruments, Vol VII, No 5, 92. *Mailing Add:* 2909 Jefferson Ct Duluth MN 55812

BRUSKIN, GRISHA
PAINTER, SCULPTOR
b Moscow, Russia, Oct 21, 1945. *Study:* Art Inst Moscow, Russia, BA, 68. *Work:* Mus Mod Art, NY; Ludwig Mus, Cologne, Ger; Israel Mus, Jerusalem; State Pushkin Mus Fine Arts, Moscow; Art Inst Chicago. *Exhib:* Von der Revolution zur Perestroika, Kunst Mus Luzern, Switz, 83; Ich lebe Ichsehe, Kunst Mus Bern, 88; 100 Yrs of Russian Art 1889-1989, Barbican Art Gallery, London, 89; Chagall to Kitaj: The Jewish Experience in 20th Century Art, Barbican Art Gallery, London, 90; Ost-Kunst West-Kunst,Ludwig Forum Int Art, Aachen, 91; Von Malewitschbis Kabakov, Ludwig Mus, Cologne, Ger, 93; one-man show, State Pushkin Mus Fine Arts, Moscow, 93; Europa Europa, Kunst & Ausstellungshalle der Bundesrepublix, Bonn, Ger, 94. *Bibliog:* Suzanne Muchnie (auth), The unknown Soviet artist who won the West, Los Angeles Times Calendar, 7/31/88; Peter Selz (auth), Grisha Bruskin-The Unique Work, Cimaise No 220, 9-10/92; Jana Markova (dir), Grisha Bruskin in New York (film), 93. *Media:* Oil, Linen, Bronze, Steel. *Dealer:* Marlborough Gallery 40 W 57th St New York NY 10013. *Mailing Add:* 236 W 26th St No 705 New York NY 10001

BRUSO, ARTHUR
CURATOR, SCULPTOR
b Albany, NY, Aug 12. *Study:* State Univ New York, New Paltz, BS; Univ Pa, MFA, Philadelphia, Pa. *Exhib:* Aether, Curious Matter, 2008, Hocus Pocus, 2008, Poison, 2009, A Lesser Doxology, 2009, Psychopomp, 2010; Falling City, Curious Matter, 2011; Naming the Animals, Curious Matter, 2011; The Fools Journey, Curious Matter, 2012; Dangerous Toys, Curious Matter, 2012; A Time in Arcadia, Curious Matter, 2013; Theres a Moon in the Sky, Its Called the Moon, Curious Matter, 2013. *Pos:* exhib dir, ArtGroup, New York, 93-99; co-found, Studio Galleries, Jesey City, NJ, 2000-2006; co-found, Curious Matter, Jersey City, NJ, 2007-2009. *Bibliog:* Brendan Carroll (auth), Curious Matter, Features Photos of Falling City, Arthur Broso, Jersey Jour, 7/29/11; Summer Hortillosa, Curious Matter and JC Public Library, Team Up for A Time in Arcadia, Art Exhib, Jersey City Independent, 2013. *Mem:* AAM. *Media:* Found objects, Photography, Painting, Drawing. *Res:* Bomarzo, Chartre, cabinets of curiosity, Greek/Roman Mythology, Astronomy. *Specialty:* Contemporary art. *Interests:* tarot, symbolism, garden hist. *Publ:* auth & artist, Photography Book, Into the Magic Space, 2008; Structure of the Church, Jersey City, 2010; Mingst (coauth), Curious Matter, Jersey City, NJ, 2007; Mingst (coauth), Hocus Pocus, Jersey City, NJ, 2007; Mingst (coauth), Between Worlds, Jersey City, NJ, 2008; Mingst (coauth), Poison, Jersey City, NJ; Mingst (coauth), Curious Matter, 2009; The Line Holds, The Space Beckons, Jersey City, 2009; Mingst (coauth), The Ecstatic, Jersey City, NJ, 2010; auth, A Narrow World, 2012; Mingst (coauth), Fool's Journey (catalog), 2012; Minst (co-auth), A Time in Arcadia (catalog), 2013. *Mailing Add:* Curious Matter Arthur Bruso 272 Fifth St Jersey City NJ 07302

BRUST, ROBERT GUSTAVE
PAINTER, WRITER
b Pittsburgh, Pa, Aug 14, 1945. *Study:* Carnegie Mellon Univ, BA, 68; Conn Col, MA, 75; Pittsburgh Ctr Arts, 76-91. *Work:* Highmark Blue Cross Blue Shield, Pittsburgh, Pa; Monroeville Pub Libr, Pa; Hoyt Inst Fine Arts, New Castle, Pa; Washington & Jefferson Col, Washington, Pa. *Exhib:* Westmoreland Art Nat, Twin Lakes Park, Greensburg, Pa & Westmoreland Co Community Col, Youngwood, Pa, 90-91 & 93-95; Assoc Artists of Pittsburgh Ann, Carnegie Mus Art, 92; Three Regional Artists, Hoyt Inst Fine Arts, New Castle, Pa, 93; W&J Nat Painting Show, Olin Fine Arts Gallery, Washington & Jefferson Col, Pa, 92-97; Triennial, Southern Alleghenies Mus Art, Loretto, Pa, 96-97; Gallery Space, Monroeville Pub Libr, Pa, 84, 89, 93 & 97; Undercroft Gallery, Pittsburgh, Pa, 96; Pittsburgh Soc of Artists, Butler Inst Am Art, Salem, Ohio, 99; Southwestern Pa Regional, Southern Alleghenies Mus Art, Ligonier, Pa, 2000-2001. *Pos:* writer and ed, self employed, 67-01, Penn Art Asn, 78-01. *Teaching:* Instr painting, Penn Art Asn, Penn Hills, Pa, 82-83 & 87-90 & demonstr painting, 83-98; demonstr, E Suburban Artists League, Murrysville, Pa, 92 & 95. *Awards:* Best of Show, Penn Art Asn, 84, 85, 87, 89, 90, 93 & 95; Jurors Award, Pittsburgh Soc Artists, 90 & 97; Purchase Award, W&J Nat Painting Show, 94. *Bibliog:* Niles Campbell (auth), Photography influences perception of art, Pittsburgh Business Times, 7/88; Jane Crawford (auth), Painter brings nature's brilliance to light, Pittsburgh Post-Gazette, 8/88; Donald Miller (auth), Today at the arts festival, Pittsburgh Post-Gazette, 6/90. *Mem:* Penn Hills Arts Coun (bd mem, 88-2001 & vpres, 94-2001); Penn Art Asn (bd mem, 76-2001, pres 78-80); ESuburban Artists League (bd mem, 86-90); Pittsburgh Soc Artists (bd mem, 83-87); Assoc Artists Pittsburgh. *Media:* Acrylic. *Publ:* Coauth, Picture perception: An alternative view of reversible figures, Arts Educ Int J, 73; E&A, Penn Art Asn Newsletter, 78-2001; Interaction effects of picture & caption on humor ratings of cartoons, J of Social Psychology, 79; Humor & interpersonal attraction, J of Personality Assessment, 85; ed, Pittsburgh Soc Artists Newsletter, 87. *Dealer:* Pittsburgh Ctr for the Arts 6300 Fifth Ave Pittsburgh PA 15232; Studio Z Gallery 1415 E Carson St Pittsburgh PA 15203

BRUTVAN, CHERYL
CURATOR
Study: SUNY BUffalo, BA (art hist); Williams Coll, MA (art hist). *Pos:* Asst cur, Contemp Arts Mus, Houston; cur, Albright Knox Art Gallery, Buffalo, 1985-1998; Beal cur & head dept contemp art, Mus Fine Arts, Boston, 1998-2008; cur contemp art, Norton Mus Art, 2009-. *Mailing Add:* 1451 S Olive Ave West Palm Beach FL 33401-7162

BRUZELIUS, CAROLINE ASTRID
HISTORIAN
b Stockholm, Apr 18, 1949. *Study:* Wellesley Coll, BA, 71; Yale Univ, MA, 73, MPhil, 74, PhD, 77. *Exhib:* Paesaggi Perduti Granet a Roma 1802-1822, Am Acad, Rome, 96. *Pos:* Dir, Am Acad Rome, Italy, 94-98. *Teaching:* Asst prof, Duke Univ, Durham, NC, 92, assoc prof, 86-89, chmn art dept, 89- & prof, 91-2008. *Awards:* Fulbright Award, 85-88 & 93; Rome Prize, Am Acad Rome, 85-86; Guggenheim Found Fel, 97. *Mem:* Coll Art Asn; Redieval Acad; Soc Archit Historians; Soc andcade d'archeologie, Avista; Int Ctr Redieval Art. *Res:* Medieval architecture and sculpture, Italy & France. *Publ:* Auth, Longpont and the Architecture of the Cistercian Order in the Thirteenth Century, Analecta Cisterciensia, 79; The Thirteenth Century Church of St Denis, Yale Press, 85; The Stones of Naples: Church Building on the Angevin Kingdom, 1266-1343, Yale Univ Press, 2005. *Mailing Add:* Dept Art & Art History Campus Box 90764 Duke Univ Durham NC 27708-0764

BRYAN, JACK L
PAINTER, SCULPTOR
b Lawton, Okla, Aug 30, 1942. *Study:* Univ Okla, BFA, 65, post-grad work, 73-74; Tulsa Univ, MA (art hist, hons), 67. *Work:* Comanche Mem Hosp. *Comn:* Sculpture, YMCA, 88. *Exhib:* Arts Festival 1985, Carrier Found, Belle Mead, NJ; Songs of the Wichita Mountains, Kirkpatrick Gallery Okla Artists, 89; Wichita Landscapes (solo exhib), Wichita Falls Mus Art, Tex, 90; group exhib, Leslie Powell Gallery, Lawton, Okla, 91; Leslie Powell Landscape Show, 93; and others. *Pos:* Chmn, visual arts panel, Okla Arts Inst. *Teaching:* Chmn dept art, Cameron Univ, Lawton, Okla, 67-. *Awards:* Teacher of the Year, Lawton Arts & Humanities Coun, 84; Lawton Artist of the Year, 90. *Mem:* Nat Asn Sch Art & Design; Okla Summer Arts Inst; Leslie Powell Found. *Media:* Oil, Acrylic. *Publ:* Illusr, Meadowlark, 81, Cross Stitch, 82 & Southwest Pass, 83, Valentine Series, Hosanna Press, Chicago. *Mailing Add:* 10 NW 35th St Lawton OK 73505-6115

BRYAN, SUKEY
PAINTER
b Summit, NJ, Apr 4, 1961. *Study:* Yale Univ, BA (fine arts), 83; Md Inst Coll Art, MFA, 90. *Work:* Cathedral of the Incarnation, The Baltimore Mus Art, Baltimore; Piper & Marbury, Baltimore. *Exhib:* Next Generation, Addison Gallery Am Art, Andover, Mass, 93; solo exhibs, Galerie Francoise et ses freres, Baltimore, Md, 94 & 2000 & C Grimaldis Gallery, Baltimore, Md, 95, 97 & 2000; Metamorphosis, Corcoran Gallery Art, Washington, 96; Juried Exhib, Lancaster Mus Art, Pa, 97; Elemental Forces, Univ Pac, Stockton, Calif, 98; Susan Cummins Gallery, Mill Valley, Calif, 98; Colo State Univ, Ft Collins, 99; Indianapolis Art Ctr, 99; Burroughs and Chapin Art Mus, SC, 2000; Wanatchee Valley Coll, Washington, 2000. *Pos:* Vis critic & lectr, Md Inst, Col Art, 95-97, Univ Md, Baltimore Co, 96 & Carroll Community Col, Md, 96, The Bently Sch, Berkeley, Calif, 2000. *Awards:* Individual Artist Award, Md Stat Arts Coun, 91; Nat Endowment Arts Visual Artists Fel, 93-94. *Bibliog:* Tony Merino (auth), Growth and atrophy: The empathetic landscape, Art Papers, Atlanta, 5/6/94; Mike Giuliano (auth), Land ho, Baltimore City Paper, 9/13/95; John Dorsey (auth), A refocused Sukey Bryan pours on talent, Baltimore Sun, 9/14/95; Mike Givliano (auth), Blow Up, Baltimore City Paper, 2/12/97; John Dorsey (auth), Dispassionate Paintings Show nature acting up, Baltimore Sun, 1/28/97. *Media:* Oil. *Publ:* Auth & illusr, Tidal Grass, pvt publ, 93. *Dealer:* C Grimaldis Gallery 523 N Charles St Baltimore MD 21201. *Mailing Add:* 921 Cottrell Way Stanford CA 94305

BRYANS, JOHN ARMOND
INSTRUCTOR, PAINTER
b Marion, Ohio, 1925. *Study:* Ringling Sch Art, Sarasota, Fla, 47-49; Burnsville Painting Classes, NC, 48-50; Jerry Farnsworth Studio, Sarasota, 50. *Work:* Columbus Mus, Ga; Abilene Mus & McMurray Coll, Abilene, Tex; Muskingum Coll, New Concord, Ohio; Appalachian State Univ, Boone, NC; Ohio State Univ, Marion, Ohio; Goodwin House, Baileys Crossoads, Falls Church, Va. *Comn:* Murals, Foundry Methodist Church, Washington, DC, 72 & 78; mural, Coral Gables Methodist Church, Fla, 83; mural, US Embassy, Madrid, Spain, 94; mural, St Michael's Episcopal Church, Arlington, Va, 94; mural, Strathmore Hall Arts Ctr, Bethesda, Md, 00. *Exhib:* Ga Watercolor Nat, 85 & 92; Irene Leach Mem, Chrysler Mus, Norfolk, 88, 96 & 98; Watercolor USA, Springfield Mus, 89, 95, 96, 98 & 99; Aqueous Nat, Louisville, KY, 92 & 2000; Adirondacks Nat, Old Forge, NY, 92; Butler Inst Am Art, Youngstown, Ohio, 2000; Nat Watercolor Soc, Calif, 2000. *Pos:* Retired. *Teaching:* Instr drawing & painting, Hill's Art Sch, Arlington, Va, 52-77; head dept art, McLean Arts Ctr, Va, 65-73 & 78-99; co-dir, Painting in the Mountains, Burnsville, NC, 65-83; instr watercolor, Md Col Art & Design, Silver Spring, 80-81. *Awards:* Awards, Va Watercolor Soc, 91-93, 95, 96, 98 & 2000; Second Award, Baltimore Watercolor Soc, Mid Atlantic Regional, 92; Award, Nat Watercolor Soc, Calif, 2000. *Bibliog:* Best of Watercolor 1 and 2, Rockport Press, Mass. *Mem:* Southern Watercolor Soc; Va Watercolor Soc; Ky Watercolor Soc; Baltimore Watercolor Soc; The Art League, Alexandria, Va. *Media:* Watercolor, Acrylic. *Dealer:* Art Scene, Inc, Bethesda, Md

BRYANT, DONALD L, JR
COLLECTOR
b Mount Vernon, Ill, June 30, 1942. *Study:* Denison Univ, Granville, Ohio, BA, 1964; Washington Univ, St Louis, JD, 1967; Chartered Life Underwriter, Chartered Fin Consultant. *Pos:* Chmn & chief exec officer, Donald L Bryant Assoc, St Louis, 1968-75, Bryant Group, Inc, St. Louis, 1975-2010, chmn emeritus, 2010-. *Awards:* Named Outstanding Alumni, Sch of Law Washington Univ, 1990; named one of Top 200 Collectors, ARTnews mag, 2004-13. *Mem:* Million Dollar Round Table (life mem); The Int Forum; Asn Advanced Life Underwriters; St Louis Asn Life Underwriters; Estate Planning Coun St Louis; Mo Bar Asn; Am Bar Asn; Bellerive Co Club;, Vintage Club, Indian Wells, Calif;, Winged Foot, Mamaroneck, NY;, Castle Pines, Castlerock, Calif; Meadowood, Napa Valley, Calif; Golf Club of Okla, Broken Arrow; Herbert Hoover Boys Club, St Louis (pres, 1987-); Arts and Educ Coun Greater St Louis; Dance St Louis; Opera Theatre St Louis; Boy Scouts Am; St. Louis Art Mus. *Collection:* Abstract Expressionism, especially de Kooning; contemporary art. *Mailing Add:* Bryant Group Inc Ste 1200 701 Market St Saint Louis MO 63101-1884

BRYANT, LAURA MILITZER
WEAVER
b Detroit, Mich, Mar 3, 1955. *Study:* Univ Mich Sch Art, BFA (summa cum laude), 78. *Work:* Xerox Corp, Rochester, NY; Seton Hall Univ Law School, NJ; Valparaiso Univ, Ind; City of St Petersburg; Mobil Oil Corp. *Comn:* Eli Lilly; Buffalo Lights, Foit-Albert Assoc; Sky Song, comn by Mr & Mrs D Bomberger, Indianapolis, Ind. *Exhib:* Albright-Knox Art Gallery, Buffalo, NY, 92; solo exhibs, Mod Art Gallery, Sarasota, Fla, 93, 94 & 95; Fiberart Int, 93, Pittsburgh Ctr Arts, Pa, 93; Crafts Nat, Pa State Univ, 93 & 95; Chataugua Fiber Int, Adams Art Gallery, Dunkirk, NY, 94; solo exhibs, Mod Art Gallery, Sarasota, Fla, 94 & 95 & Casements Cult Ctr, Ormond Beach, Fla, 96; Crafts Nat 30, Zoller Gallery, Penn State Univ, Pa, 96; Under Currents: Over View, Area Survey, Tampa Mus Art, Fla, 97; SE Fine Crafts Biennial II, Fla Gulf Coast Art Ctr, Bellair, 97; Spotlight 98, Arrowmont Sch Arts & Crafts, Gatlinburg, Tenn & Venice Art Ctr, Fla, 98; 45th Fla Craftsman Exhib, Art & Cult Ctr, Hollywood, 98; and many others. *Pos:* Own, Prism, currently. *Teaching:* Lectr fabric design & color, State Univ Col Buffalo, 87-89. *Awards:* Vern Stein Fine Art Award, Albright-Knox Art Gallery, 92; Fla Individual Artist Fel, 94-95; HGA Award of Distinction Spotlight 95, ACCSE, 95; Award of Merit, 45th Fla Craftsman Exhib, 98. *Mem:* Am Craft Coun; Fla Craftsman. *Media:* Fiber. *Dealer:* Modern Art Gallery 1665 10th St Sarasota FL 34236; Art Resources Gallery 494 Jackson St St Paul MN 55101

BRYANT, LINDA GOODE
ART DEALER, GALLERY DIRECTOR
b Columbus, Ohio, July 21, 1949. *Study:* Spelman Col, BA, 72; City Univ New York, MA candidate. *Pos:* Dir, Just Above Midtown Gallery, NY, 74-86; dir educ, Studio Mus in Harlem, 74-75; panelist, NY State Coun on the Arts & DCA, 77-86; freelance artist. *Awards:* Grad Intern, Metrop Mus, 73, Rockefeller Fel, 73-74. *Bibliog:* Satterwhite (auth), Black Dealer/57th St, New York Post, 11/74; USA's Linda Bryant, African Woman, 76; Essence Woman, Essence Mag, 7/77. *Res:* American abstract art; theory on stylistic development in the 1970s termed contextures. *Specialty:* New and emerging artists working in contexturalist vein; utilizing materials not heretofore used as primary in art object (smoke, hair, clothes, nylon mesh). *Publ:* Co-auth, Contextures (American Abstract Art 1945-1978), Just Above Midtown, 78. *Mailing Add:* 215 W 90th St New York NY 10024-1221

BRYANT, OLEN L
SCULPTOR, EDUCATOR
b Cookeville, Tenn, May 4, 1927. *Study:* Murray State Col, BS; Cranbrook Acad Art, MFA; Inst Allende, San Miguel, Mex; Cleveland Inst Art; Art Students League. *Work:* Tenn Fine Arts Ctr Collection, Nashville; Hunter Gallery, Chattanooga, Tenn; Carroll Reece Mus, Johnson City, Tenn. *Comn:* Aura, St Phillips Episcopal Church, Franklin, Tenn, 87; The Actors, Tenn Performing Arts Ctr, Nashville, Tenn, 85; Sentinel, Austin Peay State Univ, Austin, 80 & Seeds, Libr, 87; Humanitarian Awards, Country Music Found, 86-89. *Exhib:* Solo exhibs, Tenn Fine Arts Ctr, 68 & 82, Hunter Gallery, 69, Evansville Mus, Ind, 70, Haas Gallery Bloomsburg, Pa, 71, Morehead Univ, 71 & Vanderbilt Gallery, Nashville, 83. *Teaching:* Instr art, Shaker Heights Schs, Ohio, 58-61; instr art, Union Univ, 62-65; prof art, Austin Peay Univ, 66-91. *Mem:* Am Crafts Coun. *Media:* Wood, Clay. *Mailing Add:* 816 New Deal Potts Rd Cottontown TN 37048-4821

BRYANT, TAMARA THOMPSON
PAINTER, SCULPTOR
b Anderson, Ind, Apr 8, 1935. *Study:* Univ Ky, BA (art); Ind Univ, MFA; study with Leon Golub & Creighton Gilbert. *Work:* Ind Univ, Bloomington; Colgate Univ; Univ Ky; Syracuse Univ. *Comn:* Mural, Children & Sports, Albuquerque Pub Schs, 85. *Exhib:* 17 Conn Artists, Wadsworth Atheneum, Hartford, 60; Arts of Cent NY 36th & 38th Ann, Munson-Williams-Proctor Inst, Utica, 73 & 75; Solo exhibs, Picker Art Gallery, Colgate Univ, 78, Photogenesis, Albuquerque, 81 & Hoshour Gallery, Albuquerque, 83; Electroworks, Int Mus of Photog, George Eastman House, Rochester, 79-80; Multiples 80, Contemp Arts Ctr, New Orleans; Spring Arts Festival, Taos, 85; On the Wall-Off the Wall, Ctr for Contemp Arts, Santa Fe, 85; Statements 88 Invitational, Albuquerque, 88; Magnifico, Albuquerque, 91. *Pos:* Dir art classes, Wadsworth Atheneum, 59-61; vis artist-in-residence, Univ Ky, 65, Everson Mus, Syracuse, 79 & Int Mus Photog, George Eastman House, Rochester, 80. *Teaching:* Instr art, Univ Ky, 65-66; instr fine arts, Colgate Univ, 72-80, asst prof, 80; art specialist, The Montessori Sch, Albuquerque, 86-95; Art Specialist & Teacher, Mountain Shadows Montessori School, Boulder, CO, 95-2004, Lexington Montessori Sch, Spring, 2011; teacher, demonstrator, Lexington Montessori Sch, Versailles, Ky, 2013. *Awards:* First Prize, Hartford Soc Women Painters, 60 & 61; Colgate Univ Fac Develop Fund Grant, 77-78, Res Coun Grant, 79-81. *Bibliog:* Catherine Lord (auth), Women and photography, Afterimage, 1/80 & Modern photography, 9/80; Ellen Land-Weber (auth), Processes: Copying Machines, Afterimage. *Mem:* Coll Art Asn Am; Albuquerque United Artists; Light Work. *Media:* Multi. *Res:* Use of standing movable screens (as in Japan); Hanging banners in large-scale installations. *Interests:* Photos, prints, paintings on wood, canvas, watercolor. *Collection:* Italian baroque drawings; African sculpture; Folk Art; Contemporary paintings, prints, sculpture. *Publ:* Contribr, Drawings of the Italian Renaissance, Ind Univ Press, 58

BRYCE, EILEEN ANN
PAINTER
b Tulsa, Okla, June 8, 1953. *Study:* Inst European Studies, Vienna, Austria, 73; Southern Methodist Univ, BFA, 75; Univ Tulsa, MA, 78. *Work:* Chautauqua Art Mus, NY. *Exhib:* Chautauqua Nat Exhib of Am Art, Chautauqua Art Mus, NY, 81; Art Ann Two, Okla Art Ctr, Oklahoma City, 81; Tex Fine Arts Asn Nat Exhib, Laguna Gloria Mus, Austin, 82; Alexandria Mus Visual Arts, La, 82; First Ann, Provincetown Art Mus, Mass, 83; Nat Print & Drawing Exhib, Lee Hall Gallery, Clemson Univ, 83. *Awards:* Purchase Prize, Chautauqua Nat Exhib Am Art, New York, 80; Plaque of Distinction, Marietta Nat Exhib Am Art, 81; Painting Award, Alexandria Mus Vis Arts Invitational, 82. *Bibliog:* Articles, Art Voices, 9-10/81 & Tulsa Mag, 6/82; Arts Chronicle, Okla Educ TV Authority, 82. *Media:* Oils, Acrylic. *Dealer:* Leslie Levy Gallery 7141 Main St Scottsdale AZ 85251. *Mailing Add:* 1732 S College Tulsa OK 74104-6122

BRYCE, MARK ADAMS
PAINTER, PRINTMAKER
b San Francisco, Calif, July 4, 1953. *Study:* Philadelphia Coll Art, 69-71; Pa Acad Fine Arts, with Hobson Pitman, Morris Blockburn, Mayo Bryce & Arthur DeCosta, 70-74. *Exhib:* Nat Mid-Year Show, Butler Inst Am Art, 82; Allan Stone Gallery, NY, 88-89; Contemp Philadelphia Art, Philadelphia Mus Art, Pa, 90; Allan Stone Gallery, NY, 91; James Corcoran Gallery, Santa Monica, Calif, 92; John Berggruen Gallery, San Francisco, 93; Contemp Landscapes & Recent Acquisitions of Sculpture, Larry Evans Gallery, San Francisco, 94; Mid-winter Exhib, Brian Grass Fine Art, San Francisco, 95; Brian Gross Fine Art, San Francisco, 95. *Teaching:* Instr drawing, Philadelphia Col Art, 80-82; lectr painting, Wilmington Soc Fine Arts, 83-84. *Awards:* Charles Smith Endowment Prize, Woodmere Open, 76; Award Merit, Reading Art Mus, 83; Outstanding Landscape Award & Award of Merit, Calif State Fair. *Bibliog:* David Fathergill Quinlan (auth), Raissonne (catalog), NJ, 85; John Driscoll & Arnold Skolnick (co-auth), The Artist and the American Landscape; Randall Barton (auth), Sacred Journey. *Media:* Oil, Pencil, Lithography. *Publ:* Am Artist, 90; color reproduction (oil), Guardian, 143, 95. *Dealer:* John Cacciola Gallery, 501 W 23rd St, NYC. *Mailing Add:* 1569 Robyn Rd Escondido CA 92025

BRYCELEA, CLIFFORD
PAINTER, ILLUSTRATOR
b Shiprock, NMex, Sept 26, 1953. *Study:* Ft Lewis Col, Durango, Colo, study with Mick Reber & Stan Englehart, BA (art), 75. *Work:* Los Angeles Athletic Club, Calif; Transcoe Co, Houston, Tex; Norwest Bank & Jackson David Bottling Co, Durango, Colo; Albuquerque Federal Savings And Loan Asn, NMex; Burns Nat Bank & Tamarron Resort, Durango, Colo; and others. *Comn:* Mural, The Indian Ctr, Ft Lewis Col, Durango, Colo, 73; mural, Ft Lewis Admin, Durango, Colo, 74; mural, The Indian Ctr, Durango, Colo, 74; Dulce High Sch Gym, 83. *Exhib:* Gallup Ceremonial, Red Rock Park, NMex, 76-81; Am Inst Contemp Art Ann, San Dimas Exhib Hall, Calif, 80-82; Navajo Show, Mus Northern Ariz, Flagstaff, 80-82; Death Valley 49'ers Show, Mus Death Valley, Calif, 81; Indian Shows, Navajo Tribal Mus, Window Rock, Ariz, 82; Indian Market, Santa Fe, NMex, 80-96; IACA Markets, Denver & Mesa, Ariz, 87-96. *Awards:* Purchase Awards, NMex Watercolor Soc II, 76 & NMex State Fair, 77; Gold Medal Winner, Am Indian & Cowboy Asn Show, 81; 1st Place & Mem Award, Gallup Ceremonial, NMex. *Bibliog:* Carey Vicanti (auth), Clifford Brycelea, Jicarilla Chirtain Newspaper, 6/81; Julie Pearson (auth), Southwest Art Mag, 6/92. *Mem:* Indian Arts & Crafts Asn. *Media:* Acrylic, Watercolor; Stonelitho, Photoprint. *Publ:* Contribr, Art Fever, Gallery West Inc, 81; illusr, Pieces of White Shell, 84; illusr-cover, Haunted Mesa, Bantam Books, 85; Southwest Art Mag, 92; Moon & Otter & Frog, Hyperion Books, 95. *Dealer:* Tohatin Gallery 145 W Ninth St Durango CO 81301; Tekakinitha Gallery Helen GA. *Mailing Add:* 1721 Montano St Santa Fe NM 87501-3389

BRYSON, LOUISE HENRY
PATRON
Study: Pomona Col, 93. *Pos:* Sr vpres, FX Networks, formerly; dir & chmn, KCET TV, LA, formerly; dir, SCalif Pub Radio, formerly; dir, Investment Co of Am, formerly; trustee, J Paul Getty Trust, 1998-, vchmn, chmn, 2006-; exec vpres distribution & bus develop, Lifetime Television, 1999-2005, pres distribution & bus develop, 2005-; exec vpres, gen mgr Lifetime Movie Network, 2005-; bd, councilors Annenberg Sch for Communications, Univ SCalif, currently

BRZOZOWSKI, RICHARD JOSEPH
ARTIST, PAINTER
b New Britain, Conn, Sept 9, 1932. *Study:* Paier Art Sch, New Haven, Conn. *Work:* Grumbacher Collection, NY; Phoenix Mutual Inst, Hartford, Conn; Springfield Mus Art, Mass; CBT Bank, Hartford, Conn; Otis Elevator, Farmington, Conn. *Exhib:* Nat Acad Design, 92-96; Am Watercolor Soc, 94-96 & 2005, 2012, 2014; Copley Soc, Boston, Mass, 2000-2001; Watercolor USA, 2001-2002 & 2007, 2012; Adirondacks Nat Exhib Am Watercolors, 2004, 2007, 2008, 2009, 2010; Allied Artists, 2007, 2008, 2009, 2011; and others. *Awards:* Medal of Hon, Knickerbocker Artists, 86; Paul Remmey Mem Award, Am Watercolor Soc, 95; Adolph & Clara Obrig Award, Nat Academy, 96; John Singleton Copley Award, Copley Soc Boston, 97; Silver Medal, Allied Artists,, NY, 99; Sagendorph Memorial Award, Copley Soc, 2003; David Jeck-Key Award, 2003; John Young-Hunter Award, 2009; John-Young-Hunter Mem Award, Allied Artists, 2005; Old Forge Award, Adirondack; The Arthur Baker Mem, 2009; Adirondack Lewis Nemeth Mem Award, Casein Soc, 2010; High Winds Medal Am Watercolor Soc, 2014. *Mem:* Am Watercolor Soc (bd dir, 87-88, corresp secy, 2nd vpres); Conn Watercolor Soc (bd dir, 69-70); Nat Soc Painters Casein & Acrylics; Allied Artists Am. *Media:* Watercolor, Acrylic. *Interests:* Antiques. *Publ:* Watercolor magic (article); Reproduction of painting included in Watercolor Expressions, The Best of Acrylic Paintings; Landscape Inspirations. *Mailing Add:* 13 Fox Rd Plainville CT 06062

BUBRISKI, KEVIN E
PHOTOGRAPHER
b North Adams, Mass, Nov 29, 1954. *Study:* Bowdoin Col, BA, 75; Bennington Col, MFA, 97. *Work:* Ctr Creative Photog, Tucson, Ariz; Bibliot Nat, Paris; Mus Photographic Arts, San Diego; Boston Mus Fine Arts; Houston Mus Fine Arts; Mus Modern Art, NY; Metropolitan Mus Art, NY; Smithsonian Am Art Mus. *Exhib:* Mus Photog Art, San Diego, Calif, 90; In Tibet, traveling exhib, 91; Introductions, Robert Koch Gallery, 91; Contemp Photo Journalism, ICP Uptown Gallery, NY, 91; Nat Arts Club, NY, 95; Freeman Ctr, Wesleyan Univ, Conn, 99; NY Hist Soc, New York City, 2002; Decordova Mus, Lincoln, Ma, 2002; Hallmark Mus, Turners Falls, Mass, 2006; Nepal in Black and White, Rubin Mus Art, NYC, 2008. *Pos:* Fine Art Photog. *Teaching:* Instr photog, Harvard Univ, summer 92, Bennington Col, 95-96, Williams Col, 99-2003; adj prof, Williams Col, 1999-2009; Union Coll, 2009-10; Green Mountain Coll, 2010-. *Awards:* Nat Endowment Arts, 88; Fulbright Award, 89-90; Guggenheim Fel, 94-95; Asian Cult Coun Fel, 94-95; Hasselblad Masters Award, 2004; Robert Gardner Visiting Artist Fel, Peabody Mus, Harvard Univ, 2010-2012. *Bibliog:* Double Take, 12/2001; Vince Aletti (auth), Village Voice, 8/15/2002; Ad Coleman (auth), Photography in NY, 1-2/2003; David Friend (auth), Watching the World Change-The Stories Behind the Images of 9/11. *Mem:* Explorers Club of NY. *Media:* Photography. *Specialty:* Photog. *Collection:* Documentary Photog. *Publ:* Auth, A Fine Art Book: Portrait of Nepal, Chronicle Books, fall 93; Power Places of Katmandu, Inner Traditions, 95; Pilgrimage: Looking at Ground Zero, 2002; auth, Pilgrimage, Power House, 2002; Michael Rockefeller Photographs, New Guinea 1961, Harvard Univ Press, 2006; Maobadi, Himal Books, 2011. *Dealer:* Gallery Kayafas 450 Harrison Ave Boston MA 02118. *Mailing Add:* PO Box 559 Shaftsbury VT 05201

BUCHANAN, BEVERLY
SCULPTOR, PAINTER
b Fuquay, NC, Oct 8, 1940. *Study:* Bennett Coll, Greensboro, NC, BS, 62; Columbia Univ, MS, 68, MPH, 69. *Work:* High Mus Art; Metrop Mus Art, NY; Tampa Mus Art, Fla; Chrysler Mus; Whitney Mus; Columbia Mus; Mead Art Mus; also many pvt collections. *Exhib:* Silvermine Guild Arts Ctr, 73; High Mus Art (two exhibs), 88; Albright Knox Gallery, 89; solo exhibs, Schering-Plough Hq Gallery, Madison, NJ, 92, Steinbaum Krauss Gallery, NY, 93 & 96, Gallery Contemp Art, Sacred Heart Univ, Fairfield, Conn, 96, Tubman African Am Mus, Macon, Ga, 96, Spirit Sq Ctr Arts Educ, Charlotte, NC, 96 & Beverly Buchanan, Art Mus Missoula, Mont, 97; retrospective (traveling), Montclair Mus Art, NJ, 94-96; Mus Mod Art, NY, 94; African-Am Women Artists, Sweet Briar Col, Va, 96; Bearing Witness (with catalog), Spelman Coll Mus Fine Art, 96-99; Woman's Work, Columbus Mus, Ga, 96; Resonant Forms: Contemp African-Am Woman Sculptors, Smithsonian Inst, Anacostia Mus & Ctr African-Am Hist & Cult, Washington, DC, 98; House and Home: Private Spaces, Bernice Steinbaum Gallery, Miami, Fla, 2001; Common Ground, Corcoran Mus Art, 2004. *Teaching:* Lectr & vis artist, var institutions, 90-96. *Awards:* Guggenheim Fel, 80; Nat Endowment Arts Sculpture Fel, 80, 94; Pollock-Krasner Found Award, 94; Distinguished Art Career, Coll Art Asn, 2005; Lifetime Achievement Award, Women's Caucus for Art, 2010. *Bibliog:* Robert Morton (ed), American Images, The SBC Collection of Twentieth Century American Art, Harry N Abrams Inc, New York, 96; Henry Sayre (interviewer), Beverly Buchanan: Works in progress, In: A World of Art, Ore Pub Broadcasting, Annenberg/CPB Proj, 96; William Zimmer (auth), Sculptural installation of large intention, NY Times, 11/3/96; Richard J Powell (auth), Black Art and Culture, 97; Henry Sayre (auth), A World of Art, 2nd ed, 97. *Media:* Acrylic, Oil; Wood. *Mailing Add:* c/o Bernice Steinbaum Gallery 3550 N Miami Ave Miami FL 33127

BUCHANAN, NANCY
VIDEO ARTIST, CONCEPTUAL ARTIST
b Boston, Mass, Aug 30, 1946. *Study:* Univ of Calif, Irvine, BA, 69, MFA, 71. *Work:* Mus Mod Art, NY; Mus Contemp Art, La Jolla, Calif; Mus Art, Long Beach, Calif; Allen Mem Art Mus, Oberlin, Ohio. *Exhib:* API Nat Video Fest, Am Film Inst, Los Angeles, 84 & 91; New Television, WNET, KCET, KGBH, NY, Los Angeles & Boston, 89 & 90; The 90's various PBS stations, NY, Calif & Chicago, 91; Committed Visions, Mus Mod Art, NY, 92; Zones of Disturbance, Steirischer Herbst, Graz, Austria, 97; City of Los Angeles, UCLA Hammer Mus, Westwood, Calif, 2000; Art/Women/California 1950-2000: Parallels and Intersections, San Jose Mus Art, Calif, 2002; Calif video, Getty Research Inst, 2008; Los Angeles 1955-1985, Centre Pompidou, Paris, France. *Teaching:* Asst Prof non-static art, Univ Wis, Madison, 82-84; fac, Sch of Film, Video, Calif Inst Arts, Valencia, 88-2005. *Awards:* Individual Artist's Fel (video), Nat Endowment Arts, 83 & 89; Rockefeller fel, multimedia, 96; City of Los Angeles Indiv Artist's grant, 99. *Bibliog:* Nancy Grub (ed), Making Their Mark: Women Artists Move into the Mainstream, Abbeville Press, 89; Christine Tamblyn (dir) & Doug Hall & Sally Jo Fifer (eds), Significant Others, Illuminating Video, Aperture, 91; Linda Burnham & Steven Durland (eds), The Citizen Artist: 20 Years of Art in the Public Arena, The Critical Press, 98; Laura Cottingham, Not for Sale: Feminism and Art in the USA during the 1970s (videotape), Hawkeye Productions, 98. *Media:* Video; installation. *Mailing Add:* c/o Calif Inst Sch of Film Dept 24700 McBean Pkwy Valencia CA 91355

BUCHANAN, SIDNEY ARNOLD
SCULPTOR, COLLAGE ARTIST
b Superior, Wis, Sept 12, 1932. *Study:* Univ Minn, Duluth, BA, 62; NMex Highlands Univ, Las Vegas, MA, 63. *Work:* Joslyn Art Mus, Omaha, Nebr; Springfield Art Mus, Mo; Jacksonville Art Mus, Fla; City Art Gallery, Manchester, Eng; Neuberger Mus, Purchase, NY; Civic Art Center, Sioux Falls, SD; Sheldon Art Gallery, Lincoln, NE; Tweed Gallery, Univ Minnesota, Duluth, MN; Bemidji State Coll, MN; Asheville. *Comn:* Sculpture (26'), Omaha Int Airport, 86; sculpture new bldg Omaha, Enron Corp Am, 91; sculpture (46' high & 10 ton), Kutak Found Univ Nebr, Omaha, 92; 62' high sculpture, Pace Setter Corp, Omaha, Nebr, 94; 60' high sculpture, Wilkensin Mfg Co, 95. *Exhib:* Midwest Biennial, 64-70 & Nebr, 75, Joslyn Art Mus, Omaha, Nebr; Mid-Am Exhib, William Rockhill Nelson Gallery of Art, Atkins Mus Fine Arts, Kansas City, Mo, 65-66; Colo/Nebr Exchange Exhib, Omaha & Denver, 67; Report on the Sixties, Denver Art Mus, 69; Northwestern Biennial, SDak Mem Art Ctr, 72; solo exhibs, Turner Park, Nebr, 80, Sheldon Mem Gallery, Univ Nebr, Lincoln, 86, Coll St Mary, Omaha, 89-90 & Jackson Art Works, Omaha, 2000; Invitational Sculpture, SIll Univ, 96; Invitational Sculpture, SW Mo State Univ, 98; Sculpture of the 20th Century, Neuberger Mus, Purchase, NY, 2002; Wind & Water Sculpture Exhib, 2002; Nebr AIDS Project, Fluxion Gallery, 2003. *Pos:* Vis sculptor, Manchester Coll of Art & Design, Eng, 69-70; artist-in-residence, Southern Ill Univ, Edwardsville, 72, Bemidji State Col, Minn, 75 & Plattsburg State Univ, 78. *Teaching:* Prof sculpture, Univ Nebr, Omaha, 64-95. *Awards:* Purchase Awards, Midwest Biennial, Joslyn Art Mus, Omaha, Nebr, 64-66 & Western Wash State Coll, 67; Nat Endowment for the Arts Grant, 75. *Bibliog:* Dr Judith Van Wagner (auth), Metal Paintings, Leonardo Mag, Spring 77 & Award Winning Sculpture, Margaret Harold Publ, 67; Dr Judith Collichan (auth), Welder sculpture of the 20th century, Neuberger Mus; Judy Van Wagner (auth), Leonardo May, Tornado Sculpture, 79. *Media:* Steel, Welded, Metal. *Specialty:* Sculpture. *Interests:* Classical Music. *Publ:* Award Winning Sculpture, Margaret Harold Publ, 67; Leonardo Magazine, Pub NY, London, Paris, Dr. Judy Van Wagner; Who's Who Nebraska Art, Merit Pub Co.; Sculpture Techniques, Form, Content, Arthur Williams Davis Pub, Worcester, MA, 90. *Dealer:* Gallery 72 Omaha. *Mailing Add:* 1202 S 62nd St Omaha NE 68106

BUCHER, KAREN
PHOTOGRAPHER
b Lebanon, Pa, Jan 24, 1949. *Study:* Cornell Univ, BS, 70; NM State Univ, MFA, 94; Visual Studies Workshop with Carrie Mae Weems, Rochester, NY, 93. *Work:* Corcoran Gallery of Art, DC; Denver Art Mus, Denver, Colo; Portland Art Mus, Ore; Gibson Gallery, SUNY Potsdam, NY; Ctr for Documentary Studies, Duke Univ, NC. *Exhib:* El Paso Observed, El Paso Mus Art, Tex, 94; Gun as Image, Mus Fine Arts, Fla State Univ, Tallahassee, Fla, 97; Game Face, Smithsonian Inst, DC, 2001; Am Photography, Rockefeller Arts Ctr, Fredonia, NY, 2002; Both Sides of the Street, Corcoran Art Gallery, DC, 2003; Rendering Gender, Truman State Univ Art Gallery, Kirksville, Mo, 2004; Southwest Biennial, Albuquerque Mus, Albuquerque, NM, 2006, 2008; Nosotras, Museo Alameda, San Antonio, Tex, 2008. *Awards:* 1st Place (Fine Art), Golden Light Competition, Maine Photo Workshop, 96; Purchase Award, Denver Dark Room Show, Denver Art Mus, 98; Hon Mention, Int Photo Award, 2003; Juror's Hon, Terrain, Las Cruces Mus Art, 2004; Grant, Puffin Found, 2004. *Bibliog:* Double Take, Duke Univ, summer 99. *Mem:* Soc for Photographic Educ. *Publ:* Sunnydell Farm, Visual Studies Workshop, Rochester, NY, 2004

BUCHLOH, BENJAMIN
HISTORIAN, CRITIC
b East Ger. *Study:* Freie Universitat Berlin, MPhil, 1969; City Univ NY, PhD (art history), 1994. *Pos:* Co-editor, October mag; dir critical & cur studies, Whitney Independent Study Prog, NYC, 1991-93. *Teaching:* Assoc prof, MIT, 1989-94; prof art history, Barnard Coll/Columbia Univ, NYC, 1994-2005, dept chair, 1997-2000, Virginia B Wright prof 20th-century & contemp art, 2004-05; Franklin D & Florence Rosenblatt prof mod art, Harvard Univ, 2005-. *Awards:* Golden Lion Award, Venice Biennale, 2007. *Mem:* Fel Am Acad Arts & Sci. *Publ:* Auth, Formalism and Historicity: Essays on American and European Art Since 1945, 1999; Photography and Painting in the Art of Gerhard Richter: Four Essays on Atlas, 2000; Neo-Avantgarde and Culture Industry: Essays on European and American Art from 1955 to 1975, 2001; coauth, Experiments in the Everyday: Allan Kaprow and Robert Watts, 2002; Art Since 1900: Modernism, Antimodernism, Postmodernism, 2005. *Mailing Add:* Harvard Univ Dept Art Sackler Mus 485 Broadway Cambridge MA 02138

BUCHMAN, ARLES (ARLETTE) BUCHMAN
PAINTER, ASSEMBLAGE ARTIST
b Liverpool, England; US citizen. *Study:* Lycee Jules Ferry, Paris, France; Herne Bay Collegiate Sch, Eng; Silvermine Art Sch, Conn. *Work:* Randolph-Macon Col, NC; Guild Hall, Easthampton, NY. *Comn:* Mem portrait, Ardsley Sch, NY. *Exhib:* Parrish Art Mus, Southampton, NY; Monmouth Mus, NJ; Inst Mod Art, NY. *Pos:* Pres, Victor D'Amico Inst Art, 85-91. *Teaching:* Instr art, Mus Mod Art, 61-71; Victor D'Amico Inst Art, 63-96; Metrop Mus Art, 61-71. *Awards:* First Prize, Westchester Art Soc, 70; Best Abstract, Nat Asn Woman Art, 89. *Bibliog:* Brian O Doherty (auth), Art, wide variety display, NY Times, 62; Robert Blaisdell (auth), An Artist-Teacher, Video VDIA, 90. *Mem:* Nat Asn Women Artists; NY State Teachers Asn; Mamaroneck Artists Guild; Jimmy Ernst Alliance. *Media:* Multi-media. *Publ:* Coauth, Assemblage, Mus Mod Art, 70; contribr, Palate to Palate, Times Book, 78; Jardin des Modes, France, 82; You're Never Too Thin or Too Rich, Southampton, 88. *Dealer:* Media-Loft 50 Webster Ave New Rochelle NY 10801. *Mailing Add:* Eight Wildwood Cir Larchmont NY 10538-3427

BUCHMAN, JAMES WALLACE
SCULPTOR, EDUCATOR
b Memphis, Tenn, Dec 3, 1948. *Study:* Dartmouth Col, BA; Skowhegan Sch Painting & Sculpture. *Work:* Mus Fine Arts, Springfield, Mass. *Comn:* 1980 Olympic Games, Lake Placid, NY; Gen Serv Admin, Pittsfield, Mass. *Exhib:* Solo exhibs, 75, Max Hutchinson Gallery, 79 & 83 & Haenah-Kent, NY, 91; Sculpture Invitational, Zabriskie Gallery, NY, 82; Rochester Polytechnic Inst, 87; Haenah-Kent, NY, 91, 92 & 94. *Teaching:* Marlboro Col, 80-82; asst prof, State Univ NY, Albany, 83-. *Awards:* Guggenheim Fel, 77; Nat Endowment Arts, 80. *Bibliog:* Ingeborg Hoesteret (auth), Buchman (Sculpture Now), Art Int, 6/15/75; Donald B Kuspit (auth), James Buchman at Sculpture Now, Art Am, 7-8/75; Alan Singer (auth), article, Arts Mag, 4/85

BUCHMAN, LORNE M
ADMINISTRATOR
Study: Univ Toronto, BA; Stanford Univ, PhD. *Pos:* prin, founder, Buchman Associates, 2000-; Provost, Calif Col of Arts and Crafts, formerly, pres, formerly; pres, Saybrook Grad Sch and Rsch Ctr, 2006-09; pres, chief exec officer, Art Ctr Col of Design, Pasadena, Calif, 2009-. *Mailing Add:* Art Center College of Design Office of President 1700 Lida St Pasadena CA 91103

BUCKINGHAM, MATTHEW
VIDEO ARTIST
b Nevada, Iowa, 1963. *Study:* Univ Iowa, BA, 1988; Bard Coll, MFA, 1996. *Exhib:* New Histories, Inst Contemp Art, Boston, 1996; The American Century, Whitney Mus Am Art, New York, 1999; Greater New York, PS1 Contemp Art, NY, 2000; solo exhibs, Statens Mus for Kunst, Copenhagen, 2001, PS1 Contemp Art, New York, 2002, Mus Mod Kunst Stiftung Ludwig, Vienna, 2003, Kunstverein und Kunstmuseum, St Gallen, Switz, 2005, Camden Arts Centre, London, 2007, Museo Nacional Centro de Arte Reina Sofai, Madrid, 2009; No Reservations: Native American History and Culture in Contemporary Art, Aldrich Contemp Art Mus, Conn, 2006; The Cinema Effect: Illusion, Reality, and the Moving, Part II: Realisms, Hirshhorn Mus and Sculpture Garden, Washington, DC, 2008. *Awards:* Louis Comfort Tiffany Found Grant, 2009. *Bibliog:* Gregory Williams (auth), Matthew Buckingham: Murray Guy, New York, Frieze, 5/1999; Orla Ryan (auth), In Between Lost and Found: The Films of Matthew Buckingham, Afterimage, 3-4/2001; Tacita Dean (auth), Historical Fiction: The Art of Matthew Buckingham, Artforum, 3/2004; Marck Godfrey (auth), The Artist as Historian, 10/2007. *Mailing Add:* c/o Murray Guy 453 W 17th St New York NY 10011

BUCKNALL, MALCOLM RODERICK
PAINTER
b Twickenham, Eng; US citizen. *Study:* Univ Viswa-Bharati, West Bengal, India, 54-55; Chelsea Art Sch, London, Intermediate Nat Dipl Design, 58; Univ Tex, Austin, BFA, 61; Univ Wash, Seattle, MFA, 63. *Work:* Butler Inst Am Art, Youngstown, Ohio; Okla City Art Mus; Univ Va Art Mus, Charlottesville; Crescent Collection, Crescent Marketing Ctr & State Art Work Environment, Dallas, Tex; Austin Mus Art, Tex. *Comn:* Portrait of Dean Sharlot (oil), Law Sch Univ Tex, comn by Law Sch Found; portrait of Willie Nelson, W Hotel, Austin, Tex, 2011. *Exhib:* Southwest Biennial, NMex Mus Art, Santa Fe, 74, 76, 78 & 2003; Graham Gallery, Houston, Tex, 85, 87 & 91; Third Coast Review, Aspen Art Mus, Colo, 87; Texas Dialogues: Blue Star Art Space, San Antonio, Tex, 91; Martin-Rathburn Gallery, San Antonio, 93-95 & 98; Familiar Faces, Okla City Art Mus, 93; Realism: With a Twist, Arlington Mus, Tex, 96; D Berman Gallery, Austin, Tex, 2000, 02, 04, 06, 08, 10. *Pos:* Art critic, Amherst J Record, Mass, 63-65; gallery artist, Greenwich Village Art Ctr, New York, 63-65, Graham Gallery, Houston, Tex, 82-92, Martin Rathburn Gallery, San Antonio, Tex, 92-99 & D Berman Gallery, Austin, Tex, 2000-. *Teaching:* Instr drawing & design, Univ Wash, Seattle, 61-63. *Awards:* Medal, Mid Yr Show, Butler Inst Am Art, 72 & 76; Artist Fel, Nat Endowment Arts, 85-86; Nat Drawing Show, Del Mar Coll, Corpus Christi, Tex, 95. *Bibliog:* Melissa Hirsch (auth), Malcolm Bucknall: Apprehension of Mystery, Dart Mag, spring 83; Greg Kot (auth), It's the Jesus and Nirvana Chain, Rolling Stone, 4/1/93; Wim Niehaus (auth), De Jesus - Liz Art, Oor, Amsterdam, Holland, 9/94. *Media:* Oil, Ink Drawing. *Dealer:* Wally Workman Gallery, Austin, Tex. *Mailing Add:* 4205 Shoal Creek Blvd Austin TX 78756-3518

BUCKNER, PAUL EUGENE
SCULPTOR, EDUCATOR
b Seattle, Wash, June 16, 1933. *Study:* Univ Wash Sch Art, BA (sculpture), 59; Claremont Grad Sch, MFA (sculpture), 61, study with Albert Stewart; Fulbright grant, Slade Sch, Univ Col, London, 61-62. *Work:* Olympic Col, Bremerton, Wash; Salem Civic Ctr, Ore; Ore Mus Art, Eugene; Multnomah Athletic Club, Portland, Ore; West Seattle High School, Seattle, Wash. *Comn:* wood carvings, carved doors, Sacred Heart Gen Hospital, Eugene, Ore, 82-83; Entry Court Sculpture, Eastern Ore Correctional Inst, Pendleton, Ore, 88; wood carvings, Mount Angel Abbey, St Benedict, Ore, 85-86; two carved wood figure groups, Timberline Lodge, Ore, 90; copper/gold leaf wind vane & ceramic tile totem, South Seattle CC Duwamish Ctr, 2003-06; copper/gold leaf sculpture, Washington High Sch, Tacoma; and others. *Exhib:* Northwest Artists, Seattle Art Mus, Wash, 64; solo exhib, Ore Mus Art, Eugene, 64, Jadite Galleries, NY, 88 & Frye Art Mus, Seattle, Wash, 93, The Well-tempered Clavicle, Hult Performing Arts Center, Jacobs Gallery, 1999; Sculpture 67, Seattle Art Mus, Wash, 67; Mountain High III, Timberline Lodge, Ore, 81; Sculpture on the Green, Univ Portland, 82; retrospective, The Figure-Twenty-Five Yrs, Ore Mus Art, Eugene, 86; Contributing Artist: 1939-1989, Ore Hist Soc, Portland, Ore, 89; A Garden for Sculpture, Seattle Ctr, 92; Thirty-three Yrs of Sculpture with Paul Buckner, Chetwynd Stapylton, Gallery, Portland, 96; Drawings by the Buckners, Chung Chi Col, Chinese Univ Hong Kong, 2009. *Teaching:* Prof emer sculpture, Univ Ore, Eugene, 62-. *Awards:* Nat Sculpture Rev Prize, Nat Sculpture Soc, 77; Award of Distinction, Mainstreams 77, Marietta Col, Ohio, 77; Thomas F Herman Fac Achievement Award for Distinguished Teaching, Univ Ore, 95; West Seattle High Sch Hall of Fame, 2007. *Bibliog:* Lorraine Widman (auth), Sculpture: A Studio Guide, Concepts, Methods, and Materials, Prentice Hall, Englewood Cliffs, NJ, 89; Mary Balcomb (auth), Paul Buckner: Sculptor, Am Artist, 6/80; Charlotte Graydon (auth), Nationally known sculptor takes crisp view of wood, The Oregonian, 9/10/84; Lane Tompkins (auth), Paul Buckner: The Man, The Teacher, Sculpture Northwest, 09-10/2008 & Paul Buckner: Part Two - The Art, Sculpture Northwest, 11-12/2008; Hon-Ching Lee (auth), Drawings by the Buckners, 2009. *Media:* Wood Carving, Bronze Casting. *Mailing Add:* 2332 Rockwood Ave Eugene OR 97405

BUDD, LISA C
PAINTER
b NJ, 1962. *Study:* Fashion Inst of Technol, AA (applied sci), Jan, 83. *Exhib:* Audubon Artists Inc, Salmagundi Club, New York, 2007-2012; Salmagundi Club Non Member, Salmagundi Club, New York, 2007-2012; Philadelphia WC Soc, Berman Art Mus, Collegeville, Pa, 2006, 2009-2011, 2013; Allied Artists of Am, Nat Arts Club, New York, 2008, 2010, 2011; Noyes Mus of Art, Assoc Exhib, Oceanville, NJ, 2008-2011; Am Water Color Soc, Salmagundi Club, New York, 2009, 2011. *Awards:* Contessa Bonardi Award, NJ Watercolor Soc, 2007; Catherine Lorillard Wolfe Award, Salmagundi Non-mem, 2007; Dale Meyers Medal Award, Salmagundi Non-mem, 2008; Henry Grasser Memorial Award, Allied Artists of Am, 2008; Dagmar Tribble Award, Garden State Watercolor Soc, 2009; Paul Schwartz Mem, Am Watercolor Soc, 2009; Hon Mention, Salmagundi Club Ann Mem Show, 2010; Paul B Remmey Memorial Award, Am Watercolor Soc, 2011; Ogden Pleisner Mem award, Salmagundi Club, 2012; Pat Dews award, NJ Watercolor Soc, 2012; Utrecht Supply award, Garden State Watercolor Soc, 2012. *Bibliog:* Pat Johnson (auth), Lisa Budd Creates Fluid Fish Art, The Sandpaper, 1/2009; Bobbi Seidel (auth), Jersey Shore Now, Asbury Park Press, 5/2007. *Mem:* Philadelphia Water Color Soc (elected mem); NJ Watercolor Soc (elected mem); Garden State Watercolor Soc (elected mem); Audubon Artists Inc (elected mem); Allied Artists of Am (elected mem); Am Watercolor Soc. *Media:* Watercolor. *Publ:* Visions in Watercolor, Courier Post Trenton, 5/2009; contribr, Long Beach Island Rhapsody, Jersey Shore Publ, 2006. *Mailing Add:* 189 John St West Creek NJ 08092

BUDICIN, JOHN
PAINTER
b 1944, Rovigno, D'Istria, Italy, 1944. *Study:* Riverside Community Coll, Calif, 1963-65. *Work:* Mission San Juan Capistrano; Caribbean Princess Line; pvt collections of Joan Irvine Smith, Jean Stern, Roy Rose, Ray Redfern; Fisher-Haas Infinity; Birtcher Enterprises; Fechin Workshop. *Exhib:* Group exhibs, Esther Wells Collection, Laguna Beach, Calif, 90-96; Plein-air Painters of Am, Avalon, Catalina Island, Calif & Lake Tahoe, Calif, 94-2005; Gold Medal Juried Exhibition, Calif Art Club, Pasadena Mus Calif Art, 96-2011; solo exhibs, Echoing Nature, Galerie Gabrie, Los Angeles, 98 & A Year in Retrospect, 99, Galerie Gabrie, Pasadena, Calif, 2000, Debra Huse Gallery, Balboa Island, Calif, 2005, Michael Hollis Fine Art Exhib, 2009; 85 Yrs of Art, Calif Art Club, Carnegie Art Mus, 98; Treasures of the Sierra Nevada, Muckenthaller Mus & Natural Hist Mus, Los Angeles, 98; Southwest Painters, Mus Western Art, Prescott, Ariz, 98; Inland Exhib, San Bernardino County Mus, Calif, 98; On Location in Malibu, Frederick F Weisman Mus Art, Pepperdine Univ, Malibu 99-2000, 2003, 2006 & 2009; Laguna Plein Air Painting Competition, Laguna Beach Art Mus, Calif, 99-2000; Desertscapes, Calif Art Club Gallery at the Old Mill, San Marino, 2003; Glories of the Sonoran Desert, Desert Caballeros Western Mus, Wickenburg, Ariz, 2003; The Allure of Light, The Depot, Steamboat Springs, Colo, 2003; Plein Air Color & Lifht, Lyme Art Asn, Old Lyme, Conn, 2004; Sea to Shining Sea: A Reflection of America, Haggin Mus, Stockton, Calif, 2004-2005 ; Maynard Dixon Country Invitational, 2004-2013; Painting the North Coast, Trailside Galleries, Scottsdale, Ariz, 2005; Six Masters on Cumberland Island, Fraser Fox Fine Art, Charleston, SC, 2005; Bakersfield Mus Art, Bakersfield, Calif, 2007; From the Heart, Plein Air Painters of Am, Haggin Mus, Stockton, Calif, 2007; On location with Plein Air Painters Am, The Haggin Mus, Stockton, Calif, 2009; Masters of the American West, Autry Nat Ctr, Los Angeles, Calif. *Teaching:* Teacher, Plein-Air Painters of Am Workshops, 97-2003, Scottsdale Artists' Sch, Ariz, 98-2008, Calif Art Club, 99, Tuscany & Umbria, Italy, 99, Fechin Inst, Taos, NMex, 2000-01, Art in the Aspens, Aurora, Colo, 2000-01, Fredericksburg Artist Sch, Tex, 2000-2007, Tuscany Artist Tours group, 2002, Calif Art Club, 2002, Sedona Arts Ctr, Tuscany Italy, 2006 & Sedona Arts Ctr, Ariz, 2007. *Awards:* Grumbacher Gold Medal, San Bernardino County Mus, 89 & 97; Bud Rickerts Art Ctr Award, Fine Arts Inst, 94; Award of Excellence, Oil Painters Am, 96; First Place, Multimedia Mini Show, Redlands Art Mus, 96 & 97; Second Place, Sights of Santa Ana, 98; Award of Excellence, Oil Painters of Am, 2002; Artists Choice Award, Calif Art Club, Mission San Juan Capistrano, 2003; Palm Springs Life Award, La Quinta Arts Found Plein Air Event, 2004. *Bibliog:* Norman Koplas (auth), Global Perspective, SW Art, 10/2004; James Lightner (auth), Land of Sunlight, Contemporary Paintings of San Diego Co, 2007; Disappearing Beauty, Am Art Collector, 2/2007; From the Site to the Studio, Am

Artist Mag, 10/2007; Vicky Stavig (auth), Chasing the Light, Art of the West, 07/2011, 08/2011; Jean Stern & Moly Siple (auths), California Light: A Century of Landscapes, Rizzoli Publ, 2011; Lois Griffel (auth), Painting Impressionistic Colon, 2010. *Mem:* Plein-Air Painters of Am (pres); Calif Art Club; Oil Painters of Am; Laguna Plein Air Painters Asn. *Media:* Oil. *Specialty:* landscape. *Interests:* gilding. *Publ:* From Sea to Shining Sea, Painting the American Landscape, Haggin Mus, 2004; cover art, Stephen Doherty (auth), The Secret of Success - Never Settle, Am Artist Mag, 2005; cover art, Bob Bahr (auth), Making mountains subtle, Am Artist Workshop Mag, spring, 2006; Disappearing Beauty, Am Art Collector, 2/2007; From the Site to the Studio, Am Artist Mag, 10/2007. *Dealer:* American Legacy Gallery 5911 Main St Kansas MO 64113; Debra Huse Studio Gallery 229 Marine Avenue Ste E Balboa Island CA 92662; Michael Hollis Fine Art S Pasadena CA. *Mailing Add:* 638 W 34th St San Bernardino CA 92405

BUDNY, VIRGINIA
SCULPTOR, WRITER

b Maui, Hawaii, 1944. *Study:* Vassar Coll, with Concetta Scaravaglione, AB, 65; Columbia Univ, with Peter Agostini, 65-66; Univ NC, Greensboro, with Peter Agostini, MFA, 70; Inst Fine Arts, NY Univ, MA, 88; Inst Fine Arts, NY Univ and Metrop Mus Art, New York, curatorial studies certificate, 92. *Work:* Smithsonian Inst; Vassar Coll Art Gallery; Weatherspoon Art Gallery. *Exhib:* North Carolina Sculpture 79, Weatherspoon Art Gallery, Univ NC, Greensboro, 79; Am Porcelain Traveling Exhib, Renwick Gallery, 80-83; Illusion, Southeast Ctr Contemp Art, Winston-Salem, NC, 83; Contemp Trompe l'Oeil Painting and Sculpture, Boise Gallery Art & traveling, 83-85; Equitable Gallery, NY, 84; Alternative Mus, NY, 85; Brenda Kroos Gallery, Columbus, Ohio, 85; Desires, A Personal Gallery, Greensboro, 88; Sculptors Draw the Nude, Luise Ross Gallery, NY, 90; Left Bank New York, La Maison Française of New York Univ, NY, 2006; NY's Left Bank Snug Harbor Cult Ctr, Staten Island, NY, 2007. *Pos:* Res asst to Everett Fahy (chmn, Dept Europ paintings) Metrop Mus Art, NY, 93-2009; consult, The Lachaise Found, 2003-. *Teaching:* Asst prof sculpture, Univ NC, Greensboro, 73-80; instr art hist, Continuing Educ, Cooper Union, NY Univ, 87-88; lectr art hist, Parsons Sch Design, 91-92, instr, 92; adj instr art dept, City Coll NY, 97 & 2000; lectr, Parsons Sch Design & New Sch, 2004; lectr, IRP, New Sch, 2006. *Awards:* Yaddo Found Fel, 81; Am Philos Soc Grant, 84; June & Morgan Whitney Fel, Metrop Mus Art, 92-94; and others. *Bibliog:* William Zimmer (auth), rev, Arts Mag, 1/77; Jane D Scholl (auth), article, Smithsonian Mag, 2/81; Vivien Raynor (auth), rev, NY Times, 1/11/85; Gary Shapiro (auth), rev, New York Sun, 10/27/06; Peter Trippi (auth), Fine Art Connoisseur, 11/12/2007. *Mem:* ArtTable: Catalogue Raisonne Scholars Association (CRSA); Metrop Chap Victorian Soc Am; Nat Sculptor Soc. *Media:* Clay. *Res:* Benedetto da Maiano & Gaston Lachaise. *Publ:* Auth, The poses of the child in the composition sketches by Leonardo da Vinci for The Madonna and Child With a Cat, Weatherspoon Gallery Asn Bull, 80; The sequence of Leonardo's sketches for The Virgin and Child with Saint Anne and Saint John the Baptist, Art Bull, 83; coauth (with Frank Dabell), Hard at work 'di notte chome di dì': A close reading of Cosimo Rosselli's career with some new documents, in: Cosimo Rosselli: Painter of the Sistine Chapel, Cornell Fine Arts Mus, 2001; Benedetto da Maiano, and Benedetto da Maiano: Pulpit, Church of Santa Croce, in:Encyclopedia of Sculpture, 2004; Gaston Lachaise's American Venus:The genesis and evolution of Elevation, The American Art J, 2003-2004; New York's Left Bank: Art and Artists Off Washington Square North, 1900-1950, NY, 2006; Gaston Lachaise: The applied arts, Sculpture Review, spring 2008; Musical themes in sculpture: A forceful appeal to the "imaginative intellect", Sculpture Rev, winter 2008; A "new Eve": Gaston Lachaise's portrait of Christiana Morgan, Archon, the Gov's Acad, Byfield, Mass, fall, 2009; The female form in twentieth century sculpture, Sculpture Rev, winter, 2009; coauth (with Julia Day, Jens Stenger, Katherine Eremin, & Narayan Khandekar), Gaston Lachaise's bronze sculptures in the Fogg Museum, JAIC, spring-summer, 2010; catalogue entries, in Maine Moderns: Art in Seguinland, 1900-1940, New Haven: Yale Univ Press, Portland Maine: Portland Mus Art, 2011; A Beautiful Goddess with Heavy Breasts: Gaston Lachaise's Muse, in: Gaston Lachaise: A Modern Epic Vision, NY, Gerald Peters Gallery, 2012; coauth, (with Julia Day, Jens Stenger, Katherine Eremin, & Narayan Khandekar), Gaston Lachaise: Characteristics of His Bronze Sculpture, Cambridge, Mass, 2012; New York's Left Bank: Art and Artists Off Washington Square North, 1900-1950; A Roster, New York, 2013; Provocative extremes: Gaston Lachaise's women, Sculpture Rev, summer, 2014. *Mailing Add:* 324 E 81st Apt 6RW New York NY 10028

BUECKER, ROBERT
GALLERY DIRECTOR, PAINTER

b Pittsburgh, Pa, 1935. *Study:* Pa State; Carnegie Tech. *Exhib:* Solo exhibs, Richard Feigen Gallery, NY, 63, 66 & 69 & Zolla/Lieberman Gallery, Chicago, 77; Other Ideas, Detroit Inst Arts, Mich, 69; Six Greek Crosses, 77 & Religious Work Retrospective, 79, Cathedral St John the Divine Mus Religious Art; and others. *Pos:* Owner, Buecker & Harpsichords, NY, 70-. *Bibliog:* Suzy Gablic (auth), article, Art News, 1/64; Michael Andre (auth), article, Village Voice, 8/11/75; Tom Johnson (auth), article, Village Voice, 3/25/81. *Res:* Contemporary New York art history. *Specialty:* Contemporary American art. *Mailing Add:* 465 W Broadway New York NY 10012-3147

BUERGEL, ROGER M
CURATOR, HISTORIAN

b Berlin, 1962. *Study:* Acad Fine Arts, Vienna; Univ Vienna. *Collection Arranged:* Painting Between Vulgarity and the Sublime, 1999; Things We Don't Understand, 2000; Governmentality, 2003. *Pos:* Co-founder, Springerin-Hefte für Gegenwartskunst; artistic dir, Documenta 12, Kassel, Germany, 2007; chief cur & dep dir programs, Miami Art Mus, 2008-. *Teaching:* Lectr, Luneburg Univ, Germany, 2001-05; vis prof art hist, Acad Fine Arts, Karlsruhe, Germany, 2007. *Awards:* Walter Hopps Award for Curatorial Achievement, Menil Collection, 2002. *Mailing Add:* Miami Art Mus 101 W Flagler St Miami FL 33130

BUFFINGTON, SEAN T
ADMINISTRATOR, EDUCATOR

Study: Harvard Univ, BA (English and Am lit and Afro-Am studies), 1991; Univ Mich, MA (Am culture), 1994. *Pos:* Adminr, Alumni and Univ Develop Office, Harvard Univ, 1994-99, asst provost interfaculty programs, 1999-2002, dep cheif staff to pres and provost, 2002-05, assoc provost, 2005-07; pres, Univ of the Arts, 2007-; bd mem, Philadelphia Art Comn, Greater Philadelphia Chamber of Commerce's Col and Univ Pres's Coun, Greater Philadelphia Cultural Alliance and Kimmel Ctr for Performing Arts, currently. *Mailing Add:* University of the Arts Philadelphia Office of President 320 Broad St Philadelphia PA 19102

BUGBEE-JACKSON, JOAN (MRS JOHN M JACKSON)
SCULPTOR, EDUCATOR, PAINTER

b Oakland, Calif, Dec 17, 1941. *Study:* Univ Mont; Univ Calif, San Jose, BA & MA; Art Students League, with R B Hale; Sch Fine Arts, Nat Acad Design; also with M Wildenhain, EvAngelos Frudakis, Joseph Kiselewski, Granville Carter & Adolph Block. *Work:* Cordova Pub Libr, Alaska; Harbor Art Gallery, Cordova, Alaska. *Comn:* Alaska's Wildlife (bronze medal), 80 & 93; two sculpture murals, Alaska State Capitol Bldg, Juneau, Alaska, 81; Gruening & Bartlett busts, Alaska State Capitol Bldg, Juneau, 82; plaque, Armin F Koernig, 85; two portraits, comn by Mr & Mrs Robert B Atwood, 85; Cordova Fisherman's Mem Statue, 85; bronze relief, Alaska's Five Govs, Loussac Libr, Anchorage, 86; Charles E Bunnell Bronze Statue, Univ Alaska, Fairbanks, 88; bronze, Sitka, Alexander Baranof Monument, Alaska, 89; bronze plaque, Wally Noerenberg, Prince William Sound, Alaska, 89; Russian-Alaskan friendship plaques, Kayak, Is & Cordova, Alaska, Vladivostok & Petropavlovsk-Kamchatskiyi, Russia, 91; Alaska Veteran's Monument, Anchorage, 2001; Pioneer Aviators Statue, Anchorage, 2005. *Exhib:* Solo exhib, Springvale, Maine, 70; Nat Sculpture Soc Ann, New York, 70-73; Allied Artists Am Ann, New York, 70-72; Nat Acad Design Ann, New York, 71 & 74; retrospective, New York, 72; Cordova Woman Art Show, 86-88; Fish Follies Nat Exhib, 2013. *Teaching:* Instr design, De Anza Coll, Cupertino, Calif, 67-68; instr pottery & glaze chem, Greenwich House Pottery, New York, 69-71; instr pottery, Prince William Sound Community Coll, Cordova, 72-88. *Awards:* Helen Foster Barnet Prize, Nat Acad Design, 71; Allied Artist Am Award, 72; Citation, Alaska State Legislature, 81; Alaska Gov's Art Award, 2001. *Bibliog:* Jim Seay (auth), A move for inspiration, Anchorage Daily News, 8/13/72; New Issues, Alaskan Medal Series, The Numismatist, 1/81; Ron Dalby (auth), Cordova's contemporary realist, Alaska Mag, 86; Rebecca Hom (auth), Cordova's Sculptor, Rualite Mag, 9/88. *Mem:* Fel Nat Sculpture Soc. *Media:* Fired Stoneware Clay, Cast Bronze, Oil & Watercolor. *Specialty:* Harbor Art,. *Interests:* Hunting, fishing, hiking. *Publ:* Contribr, Nat Sculpture Rev, winter 70-71, spring 71 & winter 81-82. *Dealer:* Harbor Art Gallery Cordova AK. *Mailing Add:* PO Box 374 Cordova AK 99574

BUHLER, KEN
PAINTER, PRINTMAKER

Study: Univ Iowa, BFA; Ind Univ, MFA. *Work:* Prudential Corp; McCrory Corp; IBM; de Saisset Mus, Santa Clara Univ; Boston Co. *Exhib:* Solo exhibs, Rosefsky Art Gallery, SUNY Binghamton, 2001, Beach Mus, Manhattan, Kans, 2001, Randolph Macon Coll, Va, 2002, Sioux City Art Ctr, Iowa, 2002; Milestones for Peace, Int Artists Mus, Tel Aviv, 2001; All Drawing, Gallery 817, Univ Arts, Philadelphia, 2002; Thinking In Line: A Survey of Contemporary Drawing, Univ Fla, 2003; Obsessions, Int Ctr for Contemp Art, Pont-Aven, France, 2005; Thirteenth Anniversary Show, Painting Ctr, New York, 2006. *Teaching:* Instr & asst prof, Pratt Inst, 1995-2000, artist-in-residence, 2000-. *Awards:* MacDowell Colony Fel, 1983, 2003; Nat Endowment for the Arts Fel, 1987; Pollock-Krasner Found Grant, 1987; NY Found Arts Fel, 1994, 2009; Yaddo Colony Fel, 2003. *Bibliog:* Nick Baldwin (auth), Iowa's Best, Des Moines Sunday Register, 5/21/1978; Laura Tuchman (auth), Less and More Vie for Attention, San Jose Merchant News, 9/19/1993; William Zimmer (auth), Abstract Expressionism Is Alive and Well, NY Times, 11/27/1994. *Mailing Add:* Bard College PO Box 5000 Red Hook NY 12504

BUIST, KATHY
PAINTER

b Allendale, MI, Nov 12, 1959. *Study:* Kendall Sch Design, BFA, 81; Vt Studio Ctr, 93-97; NY Acad Art (cum laude), MFA, 96. *Exhib:* Group exhibs, Long Island Mus, 97; Nabi Gallery, 99-2006; Parrish Art Mus, Southampton, NY, 99; Holiday Show, Nabi Gallery, NY, 1999; Parrish Art Mus, Southampton, NY, 1999; Seasons, Elsa Mott Ives Gallery, NY, 2000; Landscapes Real & Imagined, Rye Arts Gallery, NY, 2001; Inaugural Show, Boston Art, Mass, 2002; Rye Arts Ctr, NY, 2002-2007; Barret Arts Ctr, Rhinebeck, NY, 2002-2007; Scott Freidrick Gallery, Allenhurst, NJ, 2003-2004; Frederick Gallery, 2003-2007; Edgewood Orchard Galleries, Wisc, 2006; Diana Ferrone, Laguna Beach, Calif, 2006-2007; Water Street Gallery, Douglas, Mich, 2006-2007; Sage Moon Gallery, Charlottesville, Va, 2006-2007. *Pos:* Vis artist, Caldwell Community Coll, 98; Vis artist, Jersey Shore Arts Ctr, 2005. *Awards:* Fel, Va Ctr for the Creative Arts, 98 & 2002; Artist Grant, Vt Studio Ctr, 2000. *Bibliog:* Phyllis Braff (auth), NY Times, 97 & 98; L Mag, 2005; Expression of Nature, TriCity News, 2006. *Mem:* Jersey Shore Plein Art Painters; Nat Plein Air Painters; The Guild Shrewsbury; Audubon Artists Art Soc, NY; The Salmagundi Art Club, NY. *Media:* Oil, Pastels. *Dealer:* Water St Gallery; Diana Ferrone Gallery. *Mailing Add:* 201 E 21st St Apt # 16E New York NY 10010

BUITRON, ROBERT C
PHOTOGRAPHER, VIDEO ARTIST

b E Chicago, Ind, Sept 21, 1953. *Study:* Ariz State Univ, BFA, 80; Univ Ill, Chicago, MFA, 96. *Work:* Mexican Mus, San Francisco; New Orleans Mus Art; Bibliotheque Nationale, Paris, France; Ctr Creative Photog, Tucson; Consejo Mexicano de Fotografia, Mex. *Exhib:* Hecho En Latinoamerica II, Museo del Palacio de Bellas Artes, Mex, 81; Ten Photographers: Olympic Images, Mus Contemp Art, Los Angeles,

84; Chicago Art: Resistance & Affirmation, Wight Art Gallery, Univ Calif, Los Angeles, 90; Arizona Photographers, Ctr Creative Photog, Tucson, 90; Syncretism, The Art of the XXI Century, Alternative Mus, NY, 91; Turning The Map, Part two, Camerawork, London, Gt Brit, 92; From the West: Chicano Narrative Photog, Mex Mus, San Francisco, 95; Image and Identity, pARTs Photog Arts, Minneapolis, Minn, 2000; Cowboys, Indians, and The Big Picture, McMullen Mus Art, Boston, 2002; Only Skin Deep: Changing Visions of the Am Self, Int Ctr Photog, NY, 2003; 1984 Olympics Los Angeles to Present Work, Louis Carlos Bernal Gallery, Pima Coll, Tucson, Ariz; Post-Ironic Lull, Galaxy Gallery, Univ Mo, St Louis, 2005; Photography Midwest, Wis Union Galleries, Univ Wis, Madison, 2006. *Collection Arranged:* Chicanolandia, MARS Artspace (traveling exhib), 93; Am Voices: Latino Photographers in the US, Foto Fest, Smithsonian Inst, 94; Picarte: Photography Beyond Representation, Heard Mus, 2003. *Pos:* Exec dir, MARS Artspace, Phoenix, 82-84; independent cur & writer, 89-. *Teaching:* Asst prof photography, Univ Minn, 98-2000; instr, Sch Art Inst Chicago, 2000-2002; instr, Col DuPage, 2000-. *Awards:* Visual Artist Fel, Nat Endowment Arts, 82; Artist Fel, Art Matters Found, 95; Photog Fel, Ill Arts Coun, 98. *Bibliog:* Richard Nilsen (auth), Calendar Captures Cultural Ironies, Arizona Republic, 1991; Holland Cotter, Loyal to Two Cultures: From Chicano Roots to a New Ambiguity, NY Times, 01. *Media:* Photography. *Publ:* Lucy Lippard (auth), Mixed Blessing, 1990; Gary D Keller, Contemporary Chicana & Chicano Art: Artist, Works, Culture & Education, Vol 1, 2002; Heather Fryer (auth), Cowboys, Indians, and The Big Picture, McMullen Mus Art, Boston, 2002; Coco Fusco & Brian Wallis (auth), Only Skin Deep, Int Ctr Photography, NYC, 2003; Catriona Rueda Esquibel, Aztec Princess Still at Large, 04. *Mailing Add:* 124 Division St Geneva IL 60134

BUJESE, ARLENE
CURATOR, ART DEALER

b Hillsdale, NJ. *Study:* Corcoran Sch Art, 64-70; Hood Col, Md, AB, 75, MA, 78. *Work:* Parrish Art Mus, Southampton, NY. *Exhib:* Four Graphic Artists, Parrish Art Mus, 70; Nat Exhib Prints & Drawings, Okla Art Ctr, 72; 11 Contemp Printmakers, Int Monetary Fund, Washington, 74; Printmakers of the Region, Guild Hall Mus, NY, 75; Artist of the Springs, 78-2012; solo exib, Arts Club Washington, 84; NJ National Print Exhib, Hunterdon Art Ctr. *Pos:* Dir & vpres, Phoenix II Gallery, Washington, 81-83; dir, Benton Gallery, Southampton, NY, 86-94; owner & dir, Arlene Bujese Gallery, East Hampton, NY, 94-2006; cur, Ossorio Foundation, Southampton, NY, 2006-2007; Spanierman Gallery, East Hampton, 2007-2010; resident cur, Southampton Cult Ctr, Southampton, NY, 2010-; bd dirs, East End Hospice, RI, NY. *Teaching:* Instr design, Hood Col, Md, 81-84. *Awards:* Best in Any Media, Guild Hall Ann, 80; Exhib Comt Prize, Arts Club Washington, 82. *Media:* Etching. *Specialty:* Major contemporary American artists and the new generation of artists of Eastern Long Island. *Interests:* East End Hospice, gardening. *Publ:* Ed, 25 Artists: Hans Namuth and 24 Artists, Univ Publ Am, 82. *Mailing Add:* 40 Whooping Hollow Rd East Hampton NY 11937

BUJNOWSKI, JOEL A
PRINTMAKER, PAINTER

b Chicago, Ill, Dec 16, 1949. *Study:* Western Ill Univ, BA, 72, MA, 74; Northern Ill Univ, MFA, 78. *Work:* State Ill Ctr Collection, Chicago, Ill; Lamar Dodd Art Ctr Collection, La Grange Col, Ill; Univ NDak Collection, Grand Forks; Univ Dallas Collection, Irving, Tex; Clemson Univ Collection, SC. *Exhib:* 11th Monroe Nat Art Exhib, Masur Mus Art, Monroe, La, 79; Wesleyan Int Exhib Prints & Drawings, traveling exhib, 80-81; 7th Univ Dallas Print Invitational, Tex & Gt Brit, 81-83; 79th & 80th Chicago & Vicinity Exhib, Art Inst Chicago, Ill, 81 & 84; New Am Graphics III, Mus in Europe, Africa & Asia, 83; 20th Ann All Media Exhib, Brea Civic Cult Ctr Gallery, Calif, 86; Int Biennial Print Exhib, Taipei Fine Arts Mus, Repub China, 87; solo exhib, Univ Ariz Mus Art, Tucson, 89; Third Biennial Exhib of Prints, Mus Mod Art, Wakayama, Japan, 89; 16th, 22nd, 23rd, 25th Bradley Nat Print & Drawing Exhib, Peoria, Ill, 77, 89, 91 & 95. *Teaching:* Asst prof printmaking & drawing, Univ Hawaii, Manoa, Honolulu, 86-87; dir, Harper Col Nat Print & Drawing; adj fac, currently; asst prof drawing & printmaking, Eastern Ill Univ, Charleston, Ill, currently. *Awards:* Award Excellence, Memphis State Univ, 85; Best of Show, Bradley Univ, 89; Arts Midwest & Nat Endowment Asn Regional, 90. *Bibliog:* Marcia Morse (auth), Fresh faces, new visions, Honolulu Sunday Star Bull, 9/14/86; Karl Moehl (auth), review, New Art Examiner, 90; Jerry Klein (auth), Peoria J Star, 90. *Dealer:* Chicago Ctr for Print 1509 Fullerton Chicago IL. *Mailing Add:* 11284 Lorenson Rd Montague MI 49437

BULKA, DOUGLAS
PAINTER, EDUCATOR

b 1954. *Study:* Univ Mich, Ann Arbor, 73-75; Wayne State Univ, Detroit, Mich, BFA, 77, MFA, 86. *Work:* Detroit Inst Arts, Mich; Detroit Receiving Hosp, Mich; Northern Mich Univ Art Mus, Marquette; Wayne State Univ, Detroit, Mich. *Exhib:* Mich Artists 80/81, Univ Mich Mus Art, Ann Arbor, 81; Reactions to Mich, Muskegon Mus Art, 86; Isolate, Lemberg Gallery, Birmingham, Mich, 92, Curb Marks, 95; Mich Artists from the Permanent Collection, Detroit Inst Arts, 97; Drawn From Nature: Landscape Drawings & Watercolors from the Permanent Collection, Detroit Inst Arts, 97; Artists of the Midwest, Northern Mich Univ Mus, Marquette, 98. *Collection Arranged:* Ambient Luminosity, Detroit Artists Market, 97; The Print, Ann Arbor Art Ctr, 98. *Pos:* conservation program coordr, Commn Art Pub Places, State of Mich, 90; bd dir & exhib com chair, Detroit Focus Gallery, Mich, 91-95; bd dir & exhib com chmn, Detroit Artists Market, Mich, 95-. *Teaching:* adj fac painting & drawing, Lawrence Tech Univ, Southfield, Mich, 81-82; adj fac painting & drawing, Wayne State Univ, Detroit, Mich, 84-87, 99-2000. *Awards:* Creative Artists Grant, Arts Found Mich and Mich Coun Arts & Cult Affairs, 92; Arts Midwest/NEA Regional Visual Artists Painting Fel, 96; Purchase Award Artworks Fund, 97; NEA & Arts Midwest, 97. *Mem:* Detroit Artists Market (exhib com 95-, bd dir exec com 99-2002, bldg com 99-2001); Detroit Inst of Arts (founder soc 2001). *Media:* Oil, Watercolor, Pastel. *Publ:* Joy Hakanson Colby (auth) There's Beauty in Freeways if You Ride with this Painter, The Detroit News, 9/7/95; Glen Mannisto (auth), Illuminating Visions, The Metro Times, 9/20/95; Marsha Miro (auth), Beauty in Unusual Places, The Detroit Free Press, 11/25/92. *Dealer:* Lemberg Gallery 23241 Woodward Ave Ferndale MI 48220-1361. *Mailing Add:* 1438 Iroquois St Detroit MI 48214

BULKA, MICHAEL
CRITIC

Study: Va Commonwealth Univ, BFA in Sculpture, minor in Painting; Univ Ill, Chicago Circle, MFA in Studio Arts. *Exhib:* Critic contrib to P-Form, dialogue, C, Art in Am, World Art, New Art Examiner, New City ArtNet. *Mem:* Chicago Art Critics An. *Publ:* Critic contrib to P-Form, dialogue, C, Art in Am, World Art, New Art Examiner, New City ArtNet

BULKIN SIEGEL, WILMA
PAINTER

b Philadelphia, Pa, Dec 2, 1936. *Study:* MD, Women's Med Coll Pa, 62; New Sch, with Bruno Lucchesi, 74-84; Nat Acad Design, NY, 89-93; Art Inst Fort Lauderdale, with Barbara Dix, 91; studied with Rowena Smith, 91-94. *Hon Degrees:* Drexel Univ Sch of Nursing & Pub Health, Philadelphia, Pa, LHD, 2006. *Work:* NY Presby Hosp, New York; Hollywood Mem Regional Hosp, Fla; Sylvester Center Univ Miami, Fla; numerous pvt collections. *Comn:* Daniel D Cantor Ctr, Ft Lauderdale, Fla; painting, St Paul's Episcopal Church, Paterson, NJ, 98; painting, Gold Found, New York City, 99-2000. *Exhib:* The Golden Yrs, Morani Gallery, Philadelphia, 96; Fla Int Univ, Miami, 97; Faces of AIDS Quilt, Mus Art, Ft Lauderdale, 97, Geneva, Switz, 98; Carnell Mus, Fla, 98; Shelter of the Home Within, Villanova Univ Art Gallery, Pa, 99; Marcella Geltman Gallery, Northern NJ, 95; Bigger Than Life, Coral Springs Mus, Fla, 99, Young at Art Mus, Ft Lauderdale, Fla, 2001; solo exhibs Coral Springs (Fla) Mus, 99, Survivors of AIDS (rotating exhib), 99, State of Fla Pharmacy Conv, Naples, 99, Hollywood (Fla) Memorial Regional Hosp, 99, Art Explosion 2000, Jr League Ft Lauderdale, 2000, Ft Lauderdale Mus Art, 2005-2006, Holocaust Survivors, Whitespace Collection, West Palm Beach Fla, 2008, Women Collared for Work, Coral Springs Mus Art, Coral Springs, Fla, 2009, Delaplaine Art Ctr, Frederick, Md, 2009, Del Art Mus, Wilmington, Del, 2010, Villanova Univ Bull Gallery, Pa, 2011, West Chester Univ, West Chester, Pa, 2012, Returning Veterans from Iraq and Afghanistan, Holy Cross Hospital Women's Hospital Gallery Opening, 2013. *Pos:* Rotating internship, Mt Sinai Hosp, NY, 63, med resident, Temple Univ Hosp, 64-65, hematology fel Mt Sinai Hosp, 66, chemotherapy fel Mem Sloan-Kettering Hosp, 67, asst prof medicine, emer oncology, Montefiore Med Ctr & Albert Einstein Col Medicine, Bronx, 67-; med dir hospice Beth Abraham Hosp, Bronx, 83-89; ret practice of medicine, 90; speaker, Soc Art in Healthcare, Gainesville, Fla, 2002; keynote speaker, First Nat Conf Grandmakers for the Arts in America, 2012; adj clinical asst prof dept medical educ, Nova Southern Univ, 2012-. *Teaching:* instr art in medicine, Univ Miami, 2000-. *Awards:* Dick Blick Award, Gold Coast Watercolor Soc, Fort Lauderdale, Fla, 94; First Prize, Am Physicians Art Asn Art Exhib, New Orleans, La, 98, Orlando, 2000, Washington, 2002; Janice Palmer Award, Soc for Arts in Healthcare, Buffalo, NY, 2009; Cecil Schapiro Mem Award, Nat Asn Women Artists Exhib, New York City, NY, 2000; NAWA merit award for photog, Ann Norton Sculpture Gardens, West Palm Beach, 2001; Medal Honor for works on paper, Ann NAWA Show, Salmagundi Club, New York City, NY, 2009; Honorable Mention, Northern Trust Bank, North Palm Beach, Fla, 2010; First Prize, Northwood Univ Annual, 2012. *Bibliog:* The Golden Years, Channel 66, Philadelphia; The Faces of Aids, Milwaukee News, 97; The Fire of Life, Aids Resource Ctr Wis Benefit, 97; Art in Medicine, Am Asn Medical Coll; Enhancing Professionalism through Arts in Medicine, Assn Am Medical Coll, 11/2000; Reflexions, Benny and Lenny, 2010. *Mem:* Gold Coast Watercolor Soc (vpres 97-98, chmn community outreach 98-99); 2+3 Artist Group Inc (pres 2000-2001); Nat Asn Women Artists Inc (pres Fla chap, 2002-); Fla Artist Group Inc; Ga Watercolor Soc; Catharine Lorillard Wolfe Asn (assoc); Int Arts-Medicine Asn; Am Physicians Art Asn; Soc Arts in Healing; Boca Raton Mus Art Artists Guild (juried exhibiting mem). *Media:* Watercolor. *Collection:* many pvt collections. *Publ:* featured CNN-TV interview, 98, other TV interviews; The Art of Wholeness in Medical Education, Speaker Soc Art in Healthcare, Gainesville, Fla, 2002; Hope Center, Art of Nursing, American Jour of Nursing, 2003; Healing Art Publication of Detroit Receiving Hospital, 2007. *Mailing Add:* 2504 Laguna Terrace Fort Lauderdale FL 33316

BULL, FRAN
PAINTER, PRINTMAKER

b Orange, NJ, Sept 22, 1938. *Study:* Bennington Coll, Vt, BA, 60; Fashion Inst Technol, textile design, 62-63, New York Univ, MA, 80; pvt study/apprenticeship, Malcolm Morley, New York. *Work:* Baltimore Mus Art; Brooklyn Mus Art, New York; Indianapolis Mus Art; NJ State Mus Art, Trenton; Speed Art Mus, Louisville, Ky; Mus Mod Art, New York; Nat Mus Women Arts, Washington, DC; John McEnroe Libr Collection; New York Studio Sch; Yale Univ, New Haven, Conn; John Hopkins Univ, Baltimore; Amherst Coll, Mass; Johnson & Johnson, New Brunswick, NJ; pvt collection, Bo Alveryd, Malmo, Sweden; Guilin Mus, China. *Exhib:* The Am Photo Realist--an Anthology, Fisher Fine Art Gallery, London, 86; Pulp Art: Investigations into Slurry, Katherine E Nash Gallery, Minneapolis, 98; City Without Walls, Newark, NJ, 2000; Brava Diva!, Karpeles Manuscript Mus, Charleston, SC, 2002; Here Comes the Bride, Woman Made Gallery, Chicago, 2006; Four Points of View, Galeria Nac Del Centro-Costarricense de Ciencia y Cult, Costa Rica, 2006; Gallery Gora, Montreal, Can, 2007; Paintings and Prints, The Christine Price Gallery, Castleton State Coll, Vt, 2007; Dark Matter, Gallery in the Field, Brandon, VT, 2007. *Teaching:* Adj fac painting, New York Univ, New York, 80-86; vis artist, Towson State, Md, 86-87 & Univ W Bohemia, Plzen, Czech Republic, 2002-2003; vis instr painting, Univ Wis, 88; guest lect, The Carving Studio, Rutland, Vt, 2007-2008. *Awards:* AIGA Award; Cert of Merit, 7th Ann Feed the Baby, Feed the Soul, Competition, Hamilton, Ohio, 2000; Featured Artist, NJ State Coun Arts, Artist Gallery, 2002; Best in Show, Food Chain, Printmaking Coun NJ, 2002. *Bibliog:* Louis K Meisel (auth), Photo Realism, Harry Abrams Inc, 80; David Bourdon (auth), Art: A painters aviary, Archit

Digest, 81; Eileen Watkins (auth), Women paint women, Newark Star Ledger, 89; Douglas Anderson (auth), Barn dance, Vt Magazine, 10/2002; Gwen Donovan (auth), Local artists have broad scope, Star-Ledger, 9/22/2002; Marc Awodey (auth), There's something about Mary, Seven Days, 10/1/2003; Harriet Brainard (auth), Studio reflects world-renowned artist, Addison Independent, 5/22/2006; Richard L Brown (auth), Sculpture and beyond in West Rutland, Rutland Herald, 5/20/2007; Marc Awodey (auth), Coming Together, Seven Days, 11/2007. *Mem:* Nat Asn Women Artists; Nat Mus Women Arts; Orgn Independent Artists; Contemp Art Network; Woman Made Gallery. *Media:* Acrylic, Mixed Media. *Publ:* Mordant Rhymes for Modern Times, Middletown Press, 90; Balm of My Dreams, 2003. *Dealer:* Walker Fine Art 300 W 11th Ave #A Denver CO 80204. *Mailing Add:* PO Box 401 Brandon VT 05733

BULL, HANK
CONCEPTUAL ARTIST, VIDEO ARTIST
Can citizen. *Study:* New Sch Art, Toronto, Can, 69. *Comn:* Mural, McMaster Univ, Hamilton, Ont, 72. *Exhib:* HP Show, A Space, Toronto, 76; Dokumenta 8, Kassel, 87. *Pos:* Pres & dir, Western Front, 73-88. *Awards:* B Award, Canada Coun, 80 & 87. *Publ:* HP in a Pickle, 74. *Mailing Add:* c/o Western Front 303 E 8th Ave Vancouver BC V5T 1S1 Canada

BULLARD, EDGAR JOHN, III
MUSEUM DIRECTOR
b Los Angeles, Calif, Sept 15, 1942. *Study:* Univ Calif, Los Angeles, BA, 1965, MA, 1968; Nat Gallery Art, Samuel H Kress Found Fel, 1967-68; Harvard Univ Inst Arts Admin, 1971. *Hon Degrees:* Loyola U, New Orleans, LHD, 1987. *Collection Arranged:* German Expressionist Watercolors in Am Collections, 1969, Mary Cassatt 1844-1926, 1970 & John Sloan 1871-1951 (auth, catalog), 1971, Nat Gallery Art, Washington, DC; Richard Clague 1821-1873, 1974 & Zenga & Nanga: Paintings by Japanese Monks & Scholars, 1976, New Orleans Mus Art; The Contemp South: Photog, US Info Agency, 1977; The Wild West: Paintings and Sculpture by Frederic Remington and Charles M Russell, 1979, Robert Gordy: Paintings and Sculpture 1960-80, 1981 & Edward Weston and Clarence John Laughlin: An Introduction to the Third World of Photography (auth, catalog), 1982, New Orleans Mus Art; Odd Nerdrum: The Drawings, New Orleans Mus Art, 1994; Henry Casselli: Master of the Am Watercolor, New Orleans Mus Art, 2000; Great Collectos/Great Donors, The Making of the New Orleans Mus Art, 2010. *Pos:* Asst cur, J Paul Getty Mus, Calif, 1967; cur, Nat Gallery Art, Washington, 1968-70, asst to dir, 1970-71, cur spec projs, 1971-73; dir, New Orleans Mus Art, 1973-2010, dir emer, 2010-; trustee, Ga Mus Art, Univ Ga, 1975-80, Knessel Hall Music Sch, Blue Hill, Maine, 1986-2002, La SPCA, 1986-90, New Orleans Opera Asn, 1999-2006, Tulane Univ Col, 1999-2002, Amistad Rsch Ctr, Tulane Univ, 2001-, Haystack Mountain Sch Crafts, Deer Isle, Maine, 2003-2012; Xavier Univ, New Orleans, 2010-; La State Univ Mus Art, Baton Rouge, 2011-; Nat Hospice Found, Wash DC, 2011-. *Awards:* Order of the Republic of Egypt, 1978; Louis Brandeis Humanitarian Award, 1985; commander, Order of Arts & Letts, Republic of France, 2009. *Mem:* Am Asn Mus (trustee, 1996-98); Asn Art Mus Dir; Am Contract Bridge League; Knights Order of St John of Jerusalem. *Res:* Late 19th & 20th century American and European art. *Publ:* Auth, Mary Cassatt: Oils and Pastels, Watson-Guptill, 1972; A Panorama of American Painting (exhib catalog), 1975; Two visions of the wild west: Frederic Remington & Charles M Russell, Southwest Art, 12/79; The Kinetic Sculpture of Lin Emery (exhib catalog), 1982; auth, In Celebration of Light: Photographs from the Cheryl and James S Pierce Collection (exhib catalog), 2003; Robert Kipniss: Paintings 1950-2005, 2007; George Rodrigue Prints: A Catalogue Raisonne 1970-2007, 2008; Leah Chase: Paintings by Gustave Blache III, 2012. *Mailing Add:* 1805 Milan St New Orleans LA 70115

BUMBECK, DAVID
PRINTMAKER, EDUCATOR
b Framingham, Mass, May 15, 1940. *Study:* RI Sch Design, BFA, 62; Syracuse Univ, with Robert Marx, MFA, 66. *Work:* NY Pub Libr; Metrop Mus Art, NY; Brooklyn Mus, NY; Wiggin Collection, Boston Pub Libr; Libr Congress, Washington, DC. *Exhib:* Boston Printmakers Nat Exhib, 67-86; Living Am Artists & the Figure, Mus Art, Pa State Univ, 74; 31st Nat Print Exhib, Brooklyn Mus, 78; Nat Print Exhib, Philadelphia Print Club, 79; Nat Exhib, Soc Am Graphic Artists, 79. *Pos:* Dir, Christian A Johnson Gallery, 73-85. *Teaching:* Instr painting & printmaking, Mass Col Art, Boston, 66-68; prof, Middlebury Col, 68-2002, prof emeritus, 2002-. *Awards:* David Berger Mem Award, Boston Printmakers Nat Exhib, 68; Purchase Award, Soc Am Graphic Artists Nat Exhib, NY, 79. *Mem:* Boston Printmakers (mem exec bd, 68-); Soc Am Graphic Artists; Nat Acad Design (assoc, 88, acad, 92). *Media:* Intaglio, Sculpture, Painting. *Mailing Add:* 63 Drew Ln Middlebury VT 05753

BUNNELL, PETER CURTIS
EDUCATOR, CURATOR
b Poughkeepsie, NY, Oct 25, 1937. *Study:* Rochester Inst Technol, BFA, 59; Ohio Univ, MFA, 61; Yale Univ, MA, 65. *Comn:* Masters of American Photography, US Postal Svc, 2002. *Collection Arranged:* Photography as Printmaking, 68, Photography into Sculpture, 70, Clarence H White, 71, Mus Mod Art, NY; Princeton Univ Art Mus: Robert O Dougan Collection, 83 (auth catalogue); Minor White: The Eye That Shapes, 89 (auth catalogue); The Art of Pictorial Photography, 92; The Florence Gould Found Collection, 94; Ruth Bernhard: Photographs, 96; Photography at Princeton (ed, catalog), 98; Nineteenth-Century British Art, 99; M Jay Goodkind Collection of Photographs, 99; Edward Ranney Photographs, 2003; auth, Two Views: Eugéne Atget and Lee Friedlander, 2012. *Pos:* Cur photog, Mus Mod Art, NY, 66-72; cur photog, Art Mus, Princeton Univ, 72-2002, prof emer, 2002, dir, 73-78; actg dir, The Art Mus, 98-2000. *Teaching:* Vis lectr hist photog, Dartmouth Col, 68 & Inst Film/TV, NY Univ, 68-70; vis lectr hist photog, Yale Univ, 73; McAlpin prof hist, photo & modern art, Princeton Univ, 72-02, prof emer, 02. *Awards:* Guggenheim Mem Fel, 79; George Wittenborn Award, Art Libr Soc, 89; Hon Fel, Royal Photog Soc Gt Brit, 93. *Mem:* Soc Photog Educ (nat chmn, 73-77); Coll Art Asn Am (bd dir, 75-79); Friends of Photog (bd trustees, 74-86, pres, 78-87, chmn, 87-92); Aperture Found (bd advisors, 2013). *Media:* Photography. *Res:* History of photography with primary emphasis on the 20th century. *Publ:* Auth, Degrees of Guidance, 93; ed, The Florence Gould Foundation Collection of Nineteenth-Century French Photographs, 94; auth, Michael Kenna: A Twenty-Year Retrospective, 94; Thomas Joshua Cooper, 95; Ruth Bernhard: Photographs, 96; Siskind: The Bond and the Free, 97; Michiko Kon: Introduction, 97; ed, Photography at Princeton, 98; Jerry N Uelsmann: Museum Studies, 99; Walter Chappell: Time Lived, 2000; Remembering Limelight, 2001; A Photographic Vision: Pictorial Photography, 1889-1923, 2003; La Photographie Pictorialiste, 2004; Inside the Photograph, 2006, 2nd ed, 2009; Eye Mind Spirit: The Enduring Legacy of Minor White, 2008; ed, Aperture Magazine Anthology: The Minor White Years 1952-1976, 2012. *Mailing Add:* 40 McCosh Circle Princeton NJ 08540

BUNNEN, LUCINDA WEIL
PHOTOGRAPHER, COLLECTOR
b Katonah, NY, Jan 14, 1930. *Study:* Atlanta Coll Art, 70-71; also study with Michael Lesy, Minor White, Linda Connor, Duane Michaels & George Tice. *Work:* Mus Mod Art & Whitney Mus Am Art, NY; Pushkin Mus, Moscow; High Mus Art, Atlanta; R J Reynolds Industs, Winston-Salem, NC; Mus Fine Arts, Boston. *Comn:* 40 photographs, O'Hare Hyatt House, Chicago, 72; 40' mural & 5-screen slide show, High Mus Art, Atlanta, 74; film from slides, US Comn Civil Rights, Montgomery, 78; prints, Northside Hosp, Atlanta, 86; videos, High Mus Art, 88. *Exhib:* Portrait of Am, Smithsonian traveling exhib, 75-79; Movers and Shakers in Georgia, High Mus Art, Atlanta, 78; Atlantic Artists in Buenos Aires, Buenos Aires, Arg, 89; New Southern Photog: Between Myth and Reality, Aperture Found, NY, 91; The Rocker, Bernice Steinbaum Gallery, NY, 92; Out of Bounds, City Gallery East, Atlanta, Ga, 94; Exceptions; Artists' books and art books (touring), US Info Agency, Washington Project Arts, 94. *Collection Arranged:* Subjective Vision: The Lucinda Bunnen Collection of Photographs (with catalog), High Mus Art, Atlanta, 84. *Pos:* Bd dir, High Mus Art, 78-, Image Film & Video, 82-, Art Papers, 82-; Chair Hambidge Art Ctr, 98-02. *Awards:* Outstanding Leadership Award, Am Asn Univ Women, 75; Governor's Award Arts, Ga, 86; First Place, 2nd Ann Photog Contest, Atlanta Women's News, 90. *Bibliog:* profile, Lear's Mag, 5/90; Sarah Ferrell (auth), The Last Word, NY Times Bk Rev, 7/28/91; Picks & Pans, People Mag, 3/25/91. *Mem:* Friends of Photog; Int Ctr Photog; Eastman House; Visual Studies Workshop; and others. *Media:* Photography, Video. *Collection:* Contemporary photography, Outsider art, Coca Cola bottles, cows, heart rocks, knives, live dogs from New Mexico. *Publ:* Auth, Movers and Shakers in Georgia, Simon & Schuster, New York, 78; contribr, Family of Women, Ridge Press, 79; coauth, Scoring in Heaven: Gravestones and Cemetery Art of the American Sunbelt States, Aperture, 91; Alaska: Trail Tales and Eccentric Detours, Icehouse Press, 92; The Rocker, Rizzoli, New York, 92. *Dealer:* Richard Eagan Fine Art, PO Box 190449, Miami Beach, Fl, 33119. *Mailing Add:* 3910 Randall Mill Rd NW Atlanta GA 30327-3102

BUNTS, FRANK
PAINTER, EDUCATOR
b Cleveland, Ohio, Mar 2, 1932. *Study:* Yale Univ; Cleveland Inst Art; Case Western Reserve Univ, BA & MA. *Work:* Philadelphia Mus Art, Pa; Fine Arts Gallery, San Diego, Calif; Libr Cong, Washington; Corcoran Gallery Art, Washington; Cleveland Mus Art, Ohio; Boise Art Mus, Idaho; and others. *Comn:* Exhib catalog design: Univ Md; Duncan phillips, Retrospective for a Critic; Hommage A Baudelaire; The Drawings of Arshile Gorky; Jasper F Cropsey 1823-1900, A Retrospective View of America's Painter of Autumn. *Exhib:* Cleveland Mus Art, Ohio; San Francisco Mus Art, Calif; Corcoran Gallery Art, Washington, DC; Indianapolis Mus Art, Ind; Mus Mod Art, Rijeka, Yugoslavia; San Diego Fine Arts Gallery, Calif; Nat Acad Sci, Washington, DC; Black & Herron Gallery, NY; Christie's, NY; Marion Deson Gallery, Chicago, Ill; Franz Bader Gallery, Washington, DC; Comara Gallery, Los Angeles, Calif; Solo exhibs, Comara Gallery, Los Angeles, 1967, 68, St John's Coll, Annapolis, Md, 1972, Gallery 118, Mpls, 1974, Cath Univ Am, Washington, DC, 1978, Plum Gallery, Washington, DC, 1979, Flatiron Studio, New York City, 1987, Maryanne McCarthy Fine Art, New York City, 1988-89, Roberta Wood Gallery, Syracuse, NY, 1993, Effect/Cause Mail Project, 1993-95; Yale Univ Sterling Libr, New Haven, CT, 2005; Boise Art Mus, Idaho, 2010, 2011; and others. *Collection Arranged:* Cleve Mus Art; Fine Arts Gallery, San Diego; Libr Congress; Corcoran Gallery Art, Washington, DC; Cooperstown Art Asn, NY; Chinese Artists Asn, Beijing. *Pos:* prof emeritus, Dir Grad Studio Prog, Univ Md. *Teaching:* Cleveland Inst Art, Ohio, 63-64; Ark State Univ, Jonesboro, Ark, 65-67; Univ Md, College Park, 67-77, dir, Grad Art Studio Prog, 71-77. *Awards:* Purchase Prize, Cleveland Mus Art, Ohio; and others. *Bibliog:* ICC Artist Database, CD Rom, Nippon Tel & Tel, Tokyo, Japan; The Catalog of American Drawings, Watercolors, Pastels and Collages, Corcoran Gallery Art Washington, DC; numerous articles in many newspapers; artwork in videos, The Man from UNCLE, 1966, Callanetics, MCA, 1986, Portrait of an Artist by Konrad Gylfson, 1986; music video, Always and Forever, Whistle, C C Productions, 1990; documentary video, San Francisco Center for Visual Studios, 1990; film and edit, Breaking Some Eggs-A Wisconsin Breakfast, 2003. *Media:* Oil and Organic Resin on Canvas. *Dealer:* VIA Art Foundation. *Mailing Add:* 15 W 24th St New York NY 10010

BUONAGURIO, EDGAR R
PAINTER, MURALIST
b Yonkers, NY, July 4, 1946. *Study:* City Coll New York, BA, 69; Teachers Col, Columbia Univ, MA, 72. *Work:* Joseph Hirshhorn Mus & Sculpture Garden, Washington, DC; Mint Mus Art, Charlotte, NC; Bronx Mus Arts, NY; Herbert F Johnson Mus Art, Cornell Univ; Everson Mus Art, Syracuse, NY. *Comn:* Fantail (mural), The Continental Group, Stamford, Conn, 80-81; Byzantine Dream, Continental Nat Bank, Ft Worth, 82; Labyrinth (mural), City Nat Bank, Baton Rouge, 83; Olympia & York, Inc, NY, 85; Develop Specialists, Inc, Chicago, Ill, 86. *Exhib:* Mint Mus Art, Charlotte, NC; Everson Mus Art, Syracuse, 83; Zolla-Lieberman Gallery, Chicago, Ill, 84; Gloria Luria Gallery, Bay Harbor Islands, Fla, 85; Jerald

Melberg Gallery, Charlotte, NC, 85; Hadler/Rodriquez, Houston, Tex, 86; Oscarsson-Siegeltuch, NY, 87; and others. *Pos:* Critic, Arts Mag, New York, 77-80. *Teaching:* Instr painting, Hudson River Mus, Yonkers, NY, 69-74; instr art & art hist, Riverdale Country Sch, Bronx, NY, 69-79; adj prof painting, Westchester Community Col, 72, Col New Rochelle, 74. *Awards:* Creative Artists Pub Serv Prog Fel Painting, 81-82. *Bibliog:* Ellen Lubell (auth), Edgar Buonagurio at Andre Zarre, Art in Am, 83; Phillip Verre (auth), Recent painting by Edgar Buonagurio, Arts Mag, 84; Grace Glueck (auth), Edgar Buonagurio, NY Times, 84. *Media:* Acrylic, Canvas. *Dealer:* Oscarsson-Siegeltuch Gallery 568 Broadway New York NY 10012; Zolla-Lieberman Gallery 356 W Huron Chicago IL 60610. *Mailing Add:* 1723 Holland Ave Bronx NY 10462

BUONAGURIO, TOBY LEE
SCULPTOR
b Bronx, NY, June 28, 1947. *Study:* City Coll New York, BA (fine arts), 69, MA (art educ), 71. *Work:* Heckscher Mus, Huntington, NY; Everson Mus Art, Syracuse, NY; Mint Mus Art, Charlotte, NC; Alternative Mus, NY. *Exhib:* Solo exhibs, Gallery Yues Arman, NY, 82, Everson Mus Art, Syracuse, NY, 82, Bronx Mus Arts, NY, 83, Contemp Arts Ctr, New Orleans, 83, Jerald Melberg Gallery, Charlotte, NC, 85 & Fine Arts Gallery, State Univ NY, Stony Brook, 86; Contemp self-portraits, Allan Frumkin Gallery, NY, 83; and others. *Teaching:* Prof and dir undergrad study, art dept, State Univ NY, Stony Brook, 76-. *Awards:* Creative Artists Pub Serv Fel for drawing, 80-81. *Bibliog:* April Kingsley (auth), Toby Buonagurio, Arts Mag, 80; Robert Lubar (auth), Toby Buonagurio, Arts Mag, 82; Thomas Piche (auth), Toby Buonagurio, Am Ceramics, 82; Ellen Lee Klein (auth), Toby Buonagurio: More optical bounce to the ounce, Arts Mag, 86; Ceramics Today: Toby Buonagurio USA (monogr), Editions Olizare, Geneva, Switz, 84; and others. *Mem:* Coll Art Asn. *Media:* Ceramic, Mixed Media. *Publ:* Coauth, Ceramic directions: A contemporary overview, 83. *Mailing Add:* 1723 Holland Ave Bronx NY 10462-3926

BURCH, G. DAVID
PHOTOGRAPHER, SCULPTOR
b Charlottesville, VA, Oct 31, 1925. *Study:* Clines Sch Photog, G.J. Bill, Chattanooga, Tenn, 46; Univ of the Arts, Philadelphia, 61-65 & 88; Towson Univ, Towson MD, 89-2006; PGCC, Largo, MD, 89-2006. *Hon Degrees:* AA, Accademia Intern, Greci-Marino, Italy, 2001; Acadenical Knight, Accademia Intern, Greci-Marino, Italy, 2004. *Work:* Penn State Delaware Campus Lib, Media, PA; Am Center for Physics-Out Bldg Entry, College Park, MD; Cecil County Arts Council, Elkton, MD. *Exhib:* The Creature Within, Arnold & Porter, Wash CD, 92; Inaugural Installation of Art, Am Center for Physics, College Park, MD, 94-5; Exploration in Form: Sculpture, Acad of the Arts, Easton, MD, 98 ; Grounds for Sculpture, Hamilton, NJ, 2000; Sculpture in Bronze & Granite, Maryland Fed Art, City Gallery, Baltimore, 2001; Maryland Hall for the Creative Arts, Annapolis, 2003; Maryland Fed of Art, Annapolis, 2007. *Pos:* mgr art & photog dept, Elkton Division of Thiokol Corp, Elkton, MD, 56-88. *Teaching:* instr photog, Cecil Community Coll, North East, MD, 74-84. *Awards:* 1st Pl Sculpture Award, Artfelt 94, Epilepsy Soc, New York City, 94; 1st Pl Sculpture Award, Perry House Galleries, Alexandra, VA, 96; Per Meriti Artistici, Premio Alba 2003, Casa Editrice Alba, Ferrara, Italy, 2004; Best in Show, Mattawoman Creek Art Ctr, Marbury, MD, 2005. *Bibliog:* Susi Haj Livy, Adel El Siwi, Moutashar, G. David Burch (auths), Department of Culture and Information, Sharjah, United Arab Emirates; Wendy Gilbert (auth), A Monster This Way Comes, Cecil Whig, Elkton, MD, 92; Mike Purvis (auth), Artist Marries Bronze, Granite to Recreate His Archetypes, The Capital, Annapolis, 95; Moutussi Acharyya (auth), Sharjah's Visual Oasis, Khaleej Times, 97; Ahmed Moualla (auth), Visual Experiments, Int Arts Biennial, 97; Phil Greenfield (auth), Sculpture by G. David Burch Featured at Maryland Hall for Creative Arts, The Sun, Baltimore, MD, 2003; Arthur Williams (auth), The Sculpture Reference, Sculpture Book Publishing, Gulfport, MS, 2004; Casa Editrice (auth), Dictionary of Contemporary Art, Ferrara, Italy, 2000-6. *Mem:* Wash Sculptors Soc. *Media:* Cast Bronze & Granite

BURCHETT, DEBRA
ADMINISTRATOR, CURATOR
b Bremerhaven, Ger, Sept 26, 1955; US citizen. *Study:* Univ Ky, Lexington, 74-75; Univ Calif, Irvine, with Craig Kauffman, Alexis Smith & Tony DeLap, BFA, 77, independent res under Melinda Wortz, BA, 78. *Collection Arranged:* Clothing Constructions, 79, Michelangelo Pistoletto, 79, Barry Le Va, New York Artist, Nat Endowment Arts Exhib, 80, Architectural Sculpture, Nat Endowment Arts Mus Prog, 80, Il Modo Italiano, Nat Endowment Arts Mus Prog, 83-84 & others, Los Angeles Inst Contemp Art. *Pos:* Gallery asst, Univ Calif, Irvine & Newport Harbor Art Mus, Newport Beach, Calif, 76-77; ed, Jour: Contemp Art Mag, 77-80; cur, Main & Entrance Galleries, Los Angeles Inst Contemp Art, 79-84; develop asst, Fine Arts Gallery, Mount St Mary's Col, 81 & Calif State Univ, Los Angeles, 83; dir, sales & admin, Gemini-G E L (graphics ed ltd), Los Angeles, 84-92 & The Litho Shop Inc/Sam Francis, Santa Monica, Calif, 92-; advert rep, Art Forum Mag. *Awards:* Nat Endowment Visual Arts Mus Prog Grant, 79; Critics Residency Grant, 79 & Artist Residency Grant, 80, Nat Endowment Arts; and others. *Bibliog:* Jennifer Seder (auth), Closet art, Los Angeles Times, 6/8/79; Germano Celant (auth), Culture, L'Europeo, Rome, Italy, 8/79; Melinda Wortz (auth), Clothing constructions, Art News, 9/79. *Mem:* Nat Asn Artists' Orgn (founding bd dir, 82-83); Graphics Arts Coun. *Publ:* Ed, Art and music, 70, issues 17-25, 77-80 & Another look at conceptualism, 79, J Southern Calif Art Mag; contribr, Visits: Kisch, Lere, Vogel & Scoops: Nordman, Irwin, Wheeler, 78 & ed spec issue, Art in Latin America (bilingual ed), 79, J Los Angeles Inst Contemp Art. *Mailing Add:* 1146 N Central Ave Apt 181 Glendale CA 91202

BURCHETT, KENNETH EUGENE
EDUCATOR, CONSULTANT
b Stockton, Mo April 26, 1942. *Study:* Mo State Univ, BS, 66; Univ Tulsa, MA, 70; Univ N Tex, PhD, 80. *Exhib:* 47th Ann Ten State, Moody Art Ctr, Shreveport, La, 70; 39th Ann Ten State, Springfield Art Mus, Mo, 70; 30th Okla Ann, Philbrook Mus, Tulsa, 70; Drawing Mid-USA 1, Spiva Art Ctr, Joplin, Mo, 76; Fine Arts Ann, Dallas Mus Fine Art, Tex, 78; Nat Painting, Pensacola Coll, Fla, 80; Mid-Four Regional, Nelson-Atkins, Kansas City, Mo, 84; Group Invitational, Ark Arts Ctr, Little Rock, 87. *Pos:* bd mem, AIC Jour. *Teaching:* Prof & chmn art, Coll Ozarks, Branson, Mo, 72-85 & Univ Cent Ark, Conway, 85-2000, prof 2000-. *Awards:* Alumni of the Year, Univ N Tex. *Mem:* Inter-Soc Color Coun; Coll Art Asn Am; Nat Art Educ Asn; Am Asn Univ Prof. *Res:* Color Theory: Attributes of Color Harmony, Color Design and Color Applications. *Publ:* Auth, Art Vocabulary, Mental Measurements Yearbook, Gryphon, 78; Twelve Books on Color, 89, Color Harmony Attributes, 91 & Color Harmony, 2002, Color Research & Application, Wiley & Sons; Faber Birren, Leonardo JISAST, Pergamon, 90; Color Education, Inter-Soc Color Coun News, 91; Artist and Audience and Living with Art, Studies in Art Education, J Issues & Res Art Educ, NAEA, 93; Bibliographical History of the study & use of color from Aristotle to Kandinslay, Mellen, 2005; The Battle of Carthage: A History of the First Civil War Battle of the Trans-Mississippi, McFarland, 2012. *Mailing Add:* Univ Cent Ark Dept Art McAlister Hall No 101 Conway AR 72032

BURCKHARDT, TOM
PAINTER
b New York, 1964. *Study:* State Univ NY, BFA, 1986; Skowhegan Sch Painting and Sculpture, Maine, 1986. *Exhib:* Solo exhibs include PMW Gallery, Stamford, Conn, 1991, Frankel Nathanson Gallery, Maplewood, NJ, 1993, Frick Gallery, Belfast, Maine, 1993, Urban Tantra, Esso Gallery, New York, 1996, 1998, Bernard Toale Gallery, Boston, Mass, 1997, 1998, 2000, Works on Paper, Bridgewater, Lustberg & Bloomfield, New York, 2000, Caren Golden Fine Art, New York, 2000, 2002, 2003, 2005, Geoffrey Young Gallery, Great Barrington, Mass, 2001, Byron Cohen Gallery, Kansas City, Mo, 2002, Totem, Tibor de Nagy Gallery, New York, 2002, 2004, 2006, Hunterdon Mus Art, Clinton, NJ, 2005, Aldrich Contemp Art Mus, Conn, 2006; group exhibs include Salon, Art in General, New York, 1992; Point Now, Black and Greenberg Gallery, New York, 1995; Maine Coasts Artists, Rockport Maine, 1997; Summer Slam, Anna Kustera Gallery, New York, 1999; Self-Made Men, DC Moore Gallery, New York, 2001; Artists to Artists: A Decade of The Space Program, Marie Walsh Sharpe Found, 2002; New York, New Work, Now! Currier Gallery Art, Manchester, NH, 2002; In the Land of Nod, McDonough Mus Art, Youngstown, Ohio, 2004; Design for Living, Islip Art Mus, NY, 2005; Work in Progress, DUMBO Arts Ctr Gallery, Brooklyn, 2006. *Awards:* Studio Grant, Marie Walsh Sharpe Art Found, 1992-93; NY Found Arts Fel, 1996 & 2009; Pollock-Krasner Found Grant, 1997 & 2005; George Hitchcock Award, Nat Acad Arts, 2002; Richard & Hinda Rosenthal Found Award, Am Acad Arts and Letters, 2002; Best Emerging Artist Award, Int Asn Art Critics, 2003. *Dealer:* Blumenfeld/Lustberg Fine Art 23 Fiske Pl Brooklyn NY 11215; Byron C Cohen Gallery for Contemp Art 2020 Baltimore Ave Kansas City MO 64108; Tibor De Nagy Gallery 724 Fifth Ave New York NY 10019

BURCKHARDT, YVONNE HELENE See Jacquette, Yvonne Helene

BURDA, FRIEDER
COLLECTOR
b Gengenbach, Germany, 1936. *Pos:* Dir finances, participatory interests & admin, Burda GmbH, 1975-86; founder, Darmstadt, Ger, Found Frieder Burda, Baden-Baden, Ger, 1998- & Mus Frieder Burda, Baden-Baden, 2004-; mem acquisition panel, Ctr Georges Pompidou, Paris, currently. *Awards:* Named one of Top 200 Collectors, ARTnews mag, 2005-13. *Collection:* Modern and contemporary art, German Expressionism. *Mailing Add:* Museum Frieder Burda Lichtentaler Allee 8b Baden-Baden D-76530 Germany

BURDIN, ANTHONY
INSTALLATION SCULPTOR
b Encino, Calif, 1971. *Exhib:* Solo exhibs include CCA Wattis Inst Contemp Arts, San Francisco, 2008, Maccarone Gallery, New York; Group exhibs include Tri-Annuale Part 1, Los Angeles Contemp Exhib, Los Angeles, 1999; Selections from the Collection of Heather Hubbs, Shane Campbell Gallery, Chicago, 2004; Whitney Biennial, Day for Night, Whitney Mus Am Art, New York, 2006; Uncertain States of Am, Am Art in the 3rd Millennium, Ctr Curatorial Studies at Bard College, NY, 2006; Quotidian, BUIA Gallery, New York, 2007; Fit To Print: Printed Media In Collage, Gagosian Gallery, New York, 2007; Unmonumental: Object In The 21st Century, New Mus Contemp Art, New York, 2007, Sound of Things: Unmonumental Audio, 2008 . *Mailing Add:* Maccarone Gallery 630 Greenwich St New York NY 10014

BURDOCK, HARRIET
HISTORIAN, PRINTMAKER
b Buffalo, NY. *Study:* Univ NMex, with Garo Antresian, BFA, 66; Kean Col, MA, 69; Pratt Graphics Ctr, New Sch Social Res, with Clare Romano & Federico Castellon. *Pos:* Lectr, NJ State Mus, Trenton, 67-68; asst, Art, Prints & Photog Div, NY Pub Libr, 80-. *Teaching:* Instr art hist, Bergen Co Col, Paramus, NJ, 78-79. *Mem:* Coll Art Asn Am; Am Asn Mus; Int Coun Mus; Asn Hist Am Art; Print Club New York (founding comt, 92-). *Publ:* Auth, Notes from Russia, Graphic Arts Coun NY Newsletter, 77; auth, Woodcuts in China, Print Collector's Newsletter, 81. *Mailing Add:* c/o Art Prints & Photog Div NY Public Libr New York NY 10018

BURFORD, JAMES E
PAINTER, EDUCATOR
b Vancouver, Wash, July 25, 1945. *Study:* Univ Oreg, BS, 71; Carnegie Mellon Univ, MFA, 78. *Work:* Portland Art Mus, Ore; Coos Art Mus, Coos Bay, Ore; Univ Art and Design, Helsinki, Finland; Superior Ct Pa Judges Chambers, Pittsburgh, Pa; Westinghouse Corp Collection, Pittsburgh, Pa. *Comn:* Murals, Sheraton-Washington Hotel, DC, 84-85; dry ice pieces, Univ Ore, Eugene, 70; Corcoran Gallery Art, Mentorship Program, Washington, DC, 2004-2005. *Exhib:* Grand Galleries Nat, Cascade Gallery, Seattle Ctr, Seattle, Wash, 72; 58th Ann NW Artists, Seattle Art Mus, Seattle, Wash, 72; Artists of Ore, Portland Art Mus, Portland, Ore, 72, Works on Paper, 74; solo exhib, Coos Art Mus, Coos Bay, Ore, 74; Seattle Arts Festival, Seattle

Ctr, Seattle Art Mus, Seattle, Wash, 75; LaGrange Nat, Columbus Mus Art, Columbus, Ga, 78; Assoc Artists Pittsburgh, Carnegie Mus, 92 & 97; Carnegie Mus, Pittsburgh, 72, 88, 89 & 92; Fac & group exhib, Corcoran Gallery Art, Washington, DC, 2004-2005 & 2007. *Pos:* Dir, Gatehouse Gallery, Mt Vernon Coll, Washington, DC, 78-99. *Teaching:* Instr painting, Carnegie Mellon Univ, Pittsburgh, Pa, 76-78; assoc prof, Mt Vernon Coll, Washington, DC, 78-99; lectr color, Hirshhorn Mus, Washington, DC, 89-90 & 92; adj instr, Univ Md, College Park, 99-2001, Marymount Univ, Arlington, Va, 99-, Art League Sch, Alexandria, 99- & Corcoran Coll Art & Design, Washington, DC, 2001-. *Awards:* Purchase Award, Coos Art Mus, Coos Bay, Ore, 1975; Jury Award, 68th Ann Carnegie Mus, US Steel, 78; Jury Award, Three Rivers Arts Festival Pittsburgh, Pa, 78; Arts and Humanities Grant, Mt Vernon Coll, Washington, DC, 81-83, 89; Fac Develop Grant, Mt Vernon Coll, Washington, DC, 86 & 96-97; Puchase award, Ore Art Mus, Portland, Ore. *Mem:* Assoc Artists of Pittsburgh, Pa. *Media:* Oil, Acrylic, Alkyd, Video, Color Pencil. *Publ:* John Wall (auth), Blair Art Museum Show, Portland Art Mus, 72; George Johanson (auth), Portland Art Mus Ann, The Oregonian, 1972; Nancy Unger (auth), The Teachers Show, Entertainment Gazette, 98. *Mailing Add:* 3222 1st Rd N Arlington VA 22201

BURG, PATRICIA JEAN
PAINTER, PRINTMAKER
b Windsor, Ont, Can, Jan 9, 1934; US citizen. *Study:* Otis Art Inst, Los Angeles, MFA (cum laude), 66. *Work:* IBM Co, Los Angeles; Art in Embassies, White House Loan Collection; Standard Oil Co, NY. *Comn:* Oil paintings, Latham & Watkins, Los Angeles, 75 & 79, Allison Corp, Los Angeles, 75, Roberts Scott & Co, San Diego, 76 & Carson City Hall, Calif, 77. *Exhib:* Northwest Printmakers, Seattle Art Mus, Wash, 69; New Work-New Talent, Los Angeles Co Mus Art, Los Angeles, 74; Miriam Perlman Gallery, Chicago, 1990; Int Triennial, Krakow, Poland, 1994; Laguna Art Mus, 2001; Contemp Prints, Nat Arts Club, NY, 2004; Belfast Print Workshop Gallery, Ireland, 2006; and others. *Pos:* Co-founder & dir, Triad Graphic Workshop, Los Angeles, 66-; co-owner, Art Source Gallery, Los Angeles, 75-. *Teaching:* Instr drawing, Otis Art Inst-Parsons, Los Angeles; instr drawing, Occidental Col, Eagle Rock, Calif; faculty, Woodbury Univ, Burbank, Calif. *Awards:* Purchase Awards, Mus Fine Arts, Boston, 68, Otis Art Inst, Los Angeles, 69, 10th Nat Calif Poly, Pomona, 1988; Merit Award, Western Books, 1986. *Bibliog:* Bentley Schaad (auth), The Realm of Contemporary Still Life, Reinhold Press, 65; Thelma R Newman (auth), Innovative Printmaking, Crown, 75; Constructions, Art Scene Mag, 3/90. *Mem:* Los Angeles Inst Contemp Art; Los Angeles Printmaking Soc (bd dir, 76-); Artists Econ Action. *Media:* Etching, Painting. *Specialty:* Modern art with emphasis on graphics and paintings. *Publ:* Contemporaries, LA Times, 5/98; 22 Printmakers, Sierra Vista Herald, summer 2003. *Dealer:* Tang Gallery 32 Main St Bisbee AR 85603. *Mailing Add:* 3666 Longridge Ave Sherman Oaks CA 91423-4918

BURGER, GARY C
MUSEUM DIRECTOR
b Greenville, SC, Nov 6, 1943. *Study:* Williams Col, BA, 65; Williams Col, Clark Art Inst, MA, 76. *Pos:* Assoc dir, Mass Coun Arts & Humanities, 76-78; consult, New Eng Found Arts, 78-79; dir, The Berkshire Mus, 79-89, Williamstown Art Conserv Lab, 89-. *Mem:* New England Mus Asn (past pres); Nat Inst Conserv (trustee); Mass Arts Advocacy Comt; Asn Regional Conserv Ctrs (pres); Williams Coll Mus AA vis comt. *Publ:* Auth, 100 American Drawings from the J D Hatch Collection, Heim Galleries, 76. *Mailing Add:* 324 Oblong Rd Williamstown MA 01267-3043

BURGER, W CARL
EDUCATOR, PAINTER
b Baden, Ger, Dec 27, 1925; US citizen. *Study:* NY Univ, BS, MA; Studies at Columbia Univ; Rutgers Univ; Parsons Sch Design, Art Students League, New Sch, NY. *Work:* Kean Univ, NJ; Bergen Mus; Chubb Asn; Newark Mus & State Mus, NJ; Exxon, NJ; Morris Mus; AT&T; Johnson & Johnson; Bristol Meyers; Schering Plough; Rutgers Univ Law Sch, Newark; British Airways, Newark Liberty Int Airport; Butler Inst Am Art; The Frame Gallery, Lambertville, NJ; Rider Univ; Noyes Mus; Rabat Gallery, E Brunswick, NJ; Jersey Art Gallery, Lambertville, NJ; British Airways; and numerous int private collections. *Comn:* Space Mural, Lockheed Electronics, Woodbridge, NJ, 60. *Exhib:* solo exhibs, Newark Acad, NJ, 2006, The Butler Inst Am Art, Youngstown, Ohio, 2007, Rider Univ, Lawrenceville, NY, 2007, Noyes Mus, NY, 2008, NJ State Mus, Morris Mus, Noyes Mus, Somerset Art Ctr, NJ Ctr Visual Arts, Kean Univ, Rider Univ; Watercolor Show, Holyoke Mus, Mass, 78; Newark Mus Triennial, 82; Am Drawing, Morris Mus, 85; Retrospective, NJ State Mus, 87; Co Coll Morris, NJ, 2004; Somerset Coll, Tri-State Show, Somerville, NJ, 78; Noyes Mus, Butler Inst Am Art, 2011; NJ State Mus, 2011; Drumthwacket, Governor's Mansion, Princeton, NJ. *Pos:* Set designer, Cape May Playhouse, 54-55 & Hillson's Theatre Stars, Binghamton, NY, 56. *Teaching:* Prof design & drawing, Kean Univ, Union, NJ, 60-93, prof emer, 93-; prof, NJ Center Visual Arts, Summit, NJ, Morris Co Coll, NJ, Ctr Contemp Art, Far Hills, NJ, & Fairleigh Dickinson Univ, Newark Mus, Contemporary Arts, Bedminster, NJ. *Awards:* NJ State Coun Arts Grant, 81; Winsor Newton Award Excellence; Allied Artists Award, Nat Arts Club, NY, 2004; NY Central Award, Audubon Artists, 2005; Arts Bridge Award, Drawing, 2006; Patrons Award, Phillips Mill Ann, Bucks Co, Pa; Marquis Who's Who in Am Art References Award for aquamedia, Audubon Artists, New York, 2009, 2012; and over 70 group show awards; Art Gallery on Kean Univ, NJ, Campus Named in Honor of Karl & Helen Burger. *Bibliog:* Article in Art News, 9/83; featured numerous times on NJ Artists Series, NJ Pub TV, 86-; Morris Mus (catalog), 2001; Butler Inst Am Art (catalog), 2007. *Mem:* NJ Watercolor Soc (trustee, 69-72); Audubon Artists (hon mem); Assoc Artists NJ (past pres, 80-83); Phi Delta Kappa; Am Legion; NJWE. *Media:* Watercolor, Ink Drawings, Acrylic incorporated with Sand, Watercolors with Organic Plant Stains, Collage. *Res:* Thesis, animal forms in Mayan art. *Specialty:* Contemporary Art. *Interests:* Weight training, swimming & concerts. *Publ:* Revs, Art News, 85 & NY Times, 2002-2011; Star Ledger, 2011. *Dealer:* Pedersen Gallery Lambertville NJ; Jersey Art Gallery Lambertville; Studio 7 Bernardsville NJ; NJ Art Lambertville NJ; Skidmore Assn Princeton NJ; Rabat Gallery New Brunswick NJ. *Mailing Add:* 85 Tumble Falls Rd Stockton NJ 08559

BURGER-CALDERON, MONIQUE & MAX
COLLECTOR
b Switz, Sept 29, 1954. *Study:* Cantonal Coll, Aarau, Switz, 1974; Univ St Gallen, Switz, Licentiatus Oeconomiae, 1978; Harvard Univ, MBA, 1981. *Pos:* Trainee, syndication div, Dresdner Bank AG, Singapore, 1978-79; assoc, Boston Consult Group, Munich, Ger, 1980; mng dir, Burger Söhne GmbH, Emmendingen, Ger, 1981-85; mem group bd mgt, Burgher Söhne AG, Burg, Switz, 1985-87; mng partner, Apax Partners & co AG, Zollikon, Switz, 1987-2009, chmn 2009-. *Awards:* Named one of Top 200 Collectors, ARTnews mag, 2005-13. *Collection:* Post-1980s art

BURGESS, DAVID LOWRY
ARTIST
b Philadelphia, Pa, Apr 27, 1940. *Study:* Pa Acad Fine Arts, Philadelphia; Univ Pa; Inst Allende, San Miguel, Mex. *Work:* Lamont Libr & Houghton Libr, Harvard Univ, Cambridge, Mass; Mus Fine Arts, Boston; Smithsonian Collection, Washington; Archives, Boston Pub Libr; Pa Acad Fine Arts Mus, Philadelphia; Herning Mus, Herning, Denmark; De Cordova Mus, Lincoln, Mass; Archives of Lincoln Ctr, NY; MIT Archives, Cambridge, Mass; Carnegie Mus Art, Pittsburgh, Pa; Fogg Mus, Harvard Univ; Boston Mus Fine Art; Carnegie Mus Art. *Comn:* Common Light, City of Cambridge, Mass, 2000. *Exhib:* 25 Yr Retrospective, Mass Inst Technol List Visual Art Ctr; Earth, Air, Fire, Water, The Elements, Mus Fine Arts, Boston, 71; Master Drawings of the 19th & 20th Centuries, Mus Fine Arts, Boston, 72; Sky Arts Conference (co-ed catalog), Mass Inst Technol List Visual Art Ctr, 81, Linz, Austria, 82 & Munich, WGer, 83; De Cordova Mus, 85; Monocle, Hamburger Kunsthalle, 85; Pa Acad Fine Arts; Art Transition, Mass Inst Technol, Cambridge, 92; DLight, Univ Mass Gallery, Boston, 93; Pittsburgh Biennial, Pa, 94 & 95; Joseloff Mus, Hartford, Conn, 2000; Space Soon, Roundhouse, London, 2007; Deep Space Signatory Group, NASA, Ames, Calif, 2008; Carnegie Mus Art, 2007-2008; Art Outsiders, Paris, France, 2007; CNES, The French Space Agency, Paris, France, 2008; Mus Photography, Paris, 2011, 2012; Riverside Mus, Calif, 2013; and others. *Pos:* Fel & sr consult, Ctr Advan Visual Studies, Mass Inst Technol, 71-; distinguished artist, ECHO, Univ Que, Montreal, 89; distinguished fel, Studio for Creative Figuring, Carnegie Mellon. *Teaching:* Prof, Mass Coll Art, Boston, 69-; dean, Coll Fine Arts, Carnegie Mellon Univ, Pittsburgh, prof fine arts; Koopman Distinguished Chair Visual Arts, Hartford Sch Art, 2001-2002. *Awards:* Am Acad Arts & Letters, 73; Nat Inst Art, 73; Guggenheim Found, 74; Rockefeller Found Grant, 84; Mass Coun Arts Proj Grant, 85; Nat Endowment Arts Individual Artist Grant, 86; Kellogg Found, 2001-2002; Berkman Grant, 2003 & 2005. *Bibliog:* articles, Boston Mag, 11/85 & Art in Am, 2/86; T Frick (auth), article, Sacred Theories of the Earth, 2/86; and var articles in mag & publ. *Mem:* Arts Educ Am (adv bd, 78-); Nat Humanities Fac. *Media:* All Media. *Res:* Deep Space Signaling Group, Moon Arts Group, Studio for Creative Inquiry. *Specialty:* experimental arts. *Interests:* Cosmology-space art. *Publ:* Auth, Fragments, 69, Looking and Listening, 72 & Memory, Environment & Utopia, 75; Burgess, The Quiet Axis, 2008; Living in Space, 2009; Outrage, 2012. *Mailing Add:* 1375 Cordova Rd Pittsburgh PA 15206

BURGESS, JOSEPH JAMES, JR
PAINTER, EDUCATOR
b Albany, NY, July 13, 1924. *Study:* Hamilton Coll, BA, 47; Yale Univ, MA, 48; Pratt Inst, 52-54; Cranbrook Acad Art, MFA, 54. *Exhib:* Two-person exhib, Flint Inst Art, 56-65 DeWaters Art Ctr, Flint, Mich 64; Recent Drawings USA, Mus Mod Art, NY, 56; Solo exhib, Albany Inst Hist, Art, NY, 58 Ball State Teachers Col, 58, Historic Costume of the Orient, Santa Fe, NMex, 83; Drawing Nat, Calif Palace Legion Hon, San Francisco, 59; Calif Design Ten Show, Pasadena Art Mus, 68; First Ann City of Angels Int Exhib Photog, 74; Santa Fe Festival of Arts, 79. *Pos:* Designer & co-owner, Origins, retail & K/B Designs, wholesale, Carmel, Calif, 66-75 & The Gold Persimmon, retail & K/B Designs, wholesale, Santa Fe, NMex, currently; dir, Blair Galleries, Ltd, Santa Fe, NMex, 76-79. *Teaching:* Asst prof fine arts & head dept, St Lawrence Univ, Canton, NY, 54-55; art instr, chmn dept & dir, DeWaters Art Ctr, Flint Community Jr Col, 56-65; asst prof design, Ariz State Univ, Tempe, 65-66; asst prof art, NMex Highlands Univ, 82-83; instr drawing & design, Santa Fe Community Col, NMex, 86-90; workshops at Valdes Inc, Santa Fe NMex, 87-2000; lectr, Renesan Lectr Series: Art in Age of Transition, Col Santa Fe, 1-2/2000. *Media:* Mixed. *Specialty:* Painting, sculpture and graphics. *Publ:* Auth, Three Chinese Poems, Translations from Tang Dynasty poets, winter 61-62, Four Chinese poems, translations from Tang poetry, fall 61 & Some thoughts on non-communication in the arts, spring 63, Mich Voices; auth, A random poem, translation from the Tang Dynasty poet Wang Wei, 10/12/73, A shining legend, 9/10/74, Asia's first iron-clad warship, 5/19/75, Christian Sci Monitor; and many others. *Mailing Add:* 16 Caliente Rd Santa Fe NM 87505

BURGESS, LOWRY
PAINTER, EDUCATOR
Study: Inst Allende, San Miguel, Mex, 1959-63; Pa Acad Fine Arts, Univ Pa, Grad Degree, 1961. *Exhib:* Solo exhib, Carnegie Mus Art, Pittsburgh, 2008. *Pos:* Sr consultant, Ctr Advanced Visual Studies, Mass Inst Technol, 1989-; fel, Studio Creative Inquiry, Carnegie Mellon Univ, Pittsburgh, 1989-, dir, SIMLAB, 1995. *Teaching:* Prof art, Mass Coll Art, 1969-89, prof emeritus, 1989-; prof art, Carnegie Mellon Univ, Pittsburgh, 1989-, dean, Coll Fine Arts, 1989-92. *Awards:* AAAL Grant, 1972; Guggenheim Found Fel, 1973; Penn Found Fel, 1976; Rockefeller Found Fel, 1980 & 1984; Mass Arts Coun Fel, 1982; Imperishable Gold Award, Ledevoir, Montreal, 1989. *Mailing Add:* Carnegie Mellon Sch Art DH C312 5000 Forbes Ave Pittsburgh PA 15213-3890

BURGGRAF, RAY LOWELL
PAINTER, EDUCATOR
b Mt Gilead, Ohio, July 26, 1938. *Study:* Ashland Col, BS, 61; Cleveland Inst Art, BFA, 68; Univ Calif, Berkeley, MA, 69, MFA, 70. *Work:* Mint Mus Art; Western Ill Univ; Montgomery Mus Fine Arts; Greenville Co Mus; Dekalb Col. *Comn:* Royal Caribbean Cruise Lines Inc, 85. *Exhib:* Artists of the Southeast & Texas, Isaac

Delgado Mus Art, New Orleans, 71; The Great Buffalo Show, Cameron Univ Art Gallery, Lawton, Okla, 86; Ann Juried Exhib, Orlando Mus Art, Fla, 87; Four From Fla, Kennesaw State Col, Marietta, Ga, 90; Works on Paper, Nat Acad Sciences, Washington, DC, 90. *Teaching:* Asst prof painting & drawing, Fla State Univ, 70-. *Awards:* First Nat Bank Award, Mobile Art Patrons League, Ala, 71. *Mem:* Coll Art Asn Am. *Media:* Acrylic. *Mailing Add:* 1507 Marion Ave Tallahassee FL 32303-5830

BURGOS, JOSEPH AGNER, JR
PAINTER, WRITER
b Hato Rey, San Juan, Puerto Rico. *Study:* New York City Community Coll, Liberal Arts & Sci, Brooklyn, 75; Pratt Inst Found Arts, Brooklyn, 89. *Work:* PR Collection Olga Nolia, Univ Metrop, San Juan, PR; Libr Collection, Univ PR, Humacao, PR; Libr Collection, Univ PR, Rio Piedras, PR; UPR Collection, Inst Hostos Studies, San Juan, PR. *Exhib:* Solo exhibs, Temple of Writers & Poets, New York, 84, Brooklyn Heights Libr, Brooklyn, 86, Oller/Compeche Gallery, New York, 87, Boricua Coll, Brooklyn, 88, Cafe-Teatro Julia de Burgos, Super Concert Gloria Mirabal, New York, 89, La Casa de la Herencia Cult Puertoriquena, Conference Eugenio Maria de hostos, New York, 89, Comite de Afirmacion Puertoriqueha, Homage to Julia de Burgos, New York, 93, Lat American Awareness Month, Eastern Conn State Univ, Willimantic, Conn, 2008, Princeton Univ, Carl A Fields Ctr, NJ, 2009; Group exhibs, An Evening of Music & Poetry, Mus City of New York, 85; PR Art Recognition Day, Rotunda Gallery, City Hall, New York, 88; In Celebration of PR Heritage Month, State Univ NY, Old Westbury, 99; Boricua en la luna, Clemente Soto Velez Cult Ctr, New York, 2008; Boricuas at Broricua, Boricua Coll, NY, 2011. *Pos:* cur, Boricuas at Boricua, Boricua Coll, 2011. *Teaching:* Eastern Conn State Univ, Hispanic Heritage Month, speech & paintings, 2008; Hispanic Heritage Month, A Tribute to Julia de Burgos, Princeton Univ, 2009; instr, Essays about Creativity, Boricuas at Boricua, Boricua Coll, 2011. *Awards:* Cert Merit, PR Art Recognition Day, Counc Andrew Stein, City Hall, 88; Corresp Acad, In Hon Pablo Picasso, Acad del Verbano, Italy, 2001; Fac Awards, Committee of Haaren High Sch, Major H award, 64; Cert Contribution to Latino Heritage Month, A Tribute to Julia de Burgos, Princeton Univ, NJ. *Bibliog:* Peter Bloch, ARTS CLOSE-UP CANALES, Revista Canales Publ, 84; Maurice Horn, Ed Painting & Biography, Contemp Graphic Artist 3, 88; Roberto Puviani, Painting-Tribute to Picasso, Int Encyclopaedic Dictionary of Mod & Contemp Art, Italy, 2000, 2001; Karunesh Agrawal, Hostos & Julia de Burgos, Taj Mahal Joun, India, 2008. *Mem:* Bd Educ City New York; Bureau of Audio-Visual Instruction; Aerial Phenomena Res Org, Tucson, Ariz, 73; Rosicrucian Order, Calif, 76-2009. *Media:* all media. *Res:* Mercury, Gemini, Apollo, Space Shuttle, Mission to Mars Program. *Interests:* Working on 9 ft robots since 1990, writing a biography, video recordings of cultural programs in NY poetry, music, art, and awards. *Collection:* Large Vincent Van Goegh painting. *Publ:* Art Exhibition por Myrna Llush, El Vocero de PR, 87; Julia de Burgos painting of Burgos Jr, El Vocero de PR, 97; Painting of Eugenio Maria de Hostos, El Vocero de PR, 99; Tribute to Pablo Picasso of Burgos Jr, El Vocero de PR, 2000; Eugenio Maria de Hostos and Julia de Burgos, Taj Mahal Review, Allahabad, India, 2008; Picture of 9ft high, 3ft wide Robot with Literary Paragraph, Taj Mahal Review, Vol. 9, No. 2, 12/2010

BURK, A DARLENE
DEALER, COLLECTOR
b Wheatland, Wyo, Dec 24, 1929. *Study:* Calvin Goodman Sem, 76-80. *Pos:* Owner, Burk Gallery, currently. *Mem:* Rotary; Boulder City Arts Coun; Boulder City Chamber Commerce. *Specialty:* Western art, Indian culture, landscape and wildlife. *Collection:* Painting, Jeff Craven, Carol Harding; Clyde Ross Morgan

BURKE, DANIEL
MUSEUM DIRECTOR, EDUCATOR
Study: La Salle Univ, PhD. *Pos:* Vpres, acad affairs La Salle Univ, Philadelphia, pres, 69—77; founding dir, La Salle Univ Art Mus, 76—. *Teaching:* Teacher, Eng West Philadelphia Cath High Sch. *Mailing Add:* La Salle Univ Art Mus 1900 W Olney Ave Philadelphia PA 19141

BURKE, DANIEL V
PAINTER, EDUCATOR
b Erie, Pa, Apr 21, 1942. *Study:* Columbus Coll Art & Design, 60-62; Mercyhurst Col, BA (art), 69; Edinboro State Col, MEd (art), 72; MacDowell Colony, Peterborough, NH, 70 & 73. *Work:* Del Mar Coll Art Gallery, Corpus Christi; Laguna Gloria Art Mus, Austin, Tex; Southern Utah State Col; IBM Corp, Austin; NC Nat Bank, Boone; and others. *Comn:* Arrival (10'x20' wall display), Bayfront Convention Ctr, Erie, Pa, 2007. *Exhib:* Solo exhibs, Williams Coll Mus Art, Mass, 81, Rike Ctr Gallery, Univ Dayton, Ohio, 83, Gallery 937, Assoc Artists Pittsburgh, Pa, 96 & Arlington Arts Ctr, Va, 2006; Drawings USA, Minn Mus Art, St Paul, 75; Megahan & Penelec Galleries, Allegheny Col, Pa, 84; Second Street Gallery, Charlottesville, VA, 92; 35th Nat Chautauqua Art Asn Show, NY, 92; Rosewood Arts Ctr Gallery, Kettering, Ohio, 93; Erie Art Mus, Pa, 93. *Teaching:* Prof art, Mercyhurst Col, 69-, dir dept art, 79-. *Awards:* Visual Arts Fel, Pa Coun Arts, 86, 92 & 2003; Director's Award, 35th Nat Show, 92; Joseph M Katz Mem Award, 84th Ann, Carnegie Mus Art, 94. *Mem:* Northwestern Pa Artists Asn (co-exec chmn, 75-); Assoc Artists Pittsburgh. *Media:* Acrylic

BURKE, JAMES DONALD
MUSEUM DIRECTOR, ADMINISTRATOR
b Salem, Ore, Feb 22, 1939. *Study:* Brown Univ, AB, 62; Univ Pa, AM, 66; Fulbright-Hayes Fel, Holland, 68-69; Harvard Univ, PhD, 72. *Hon Degrees:* LHD, Maryville Univ, 97; DHL, Univ Mo, 98. *Collection Arranged:* Charles Meryon (auth, catalog), 74-75. *Pos:* Cur, Allen Art Mus, Oberlin Col, 71-72; cur drawings & prints, Art Gallery, Yale Univ, 72-78; asst dir, St Louis Art Mus, 78-80, dir, 80-99, dir emeritus, 99-. *Teaching:* Instr, Yale Univ, 72-78; scholar in residence, Univ Mo, 99-; E Desmond Lee scholar in residence, sr lectr art history & archaeology, Washington Univ, 2001. *Awards:* Nat Endowment Arts Mus Fel, 73. *Mem:* Am Asn Mus; Coll Art Asn; Print Coun Am. *Res:* Sixteenth and seventeenth century Dutch and Flemish art; contemporary and modern art; American art; photography. *Publ:* Auth, Jan Both: Paintings, Drawings & Prints, 75. *Mailing Add:* PO Box 759 Neskowin OR 97149

BURKE, JONATHAN
ADMINISTRATOR
Study: Kansas City Art Inst, BFA (painting); Boston Univ, MFA (painting). *Pos:* Dean fine arts, gallery dir, Laguna Col of Art & Design, Calif, 1985-2011, dean visual commun, 2000-02, pres, 2011-. *Mailing Add:* Laguna College of Art & Design Office of President 2222 Laguna Canyon Rd Laguna Beach CA 92651

BURKE-FANNING, MADELEINE
PAINTER, EDUCATOR
b New Orleans, La, Feb 12, 1941. *Study:* Davids Sch Art, New Orleans, 76-78; Pensacola State Coll, 82-88; workshops with Gerald Brommer & Don Andrews, 99. *Work:* Wise Choice Mus & Gallery, Sandestin, Fla; Kate Holms-Branton Gallery, Pensacola, Fla; Corner Copia, Orange Beach, Ala; Expressions Gallery, Pensacola, Fla; Artist Three, Perdido Key, Ala; Woodcock Gallery and Interiors, Pensacola, Fla; Stockamp Gallery, Pensacola, Fla; Michelle Ray Gallery, Pensacola, Fla; On Site Plants & Serv, Pensacola, Fla; Pel-Tex Oil Co, Houston, Tex. *Comn:* portrait, comn by Susan M Galens, United Way, Chattanooga, Tenn, 96; watercolor, St Johns Hospital, Harahan, La, 2000; portrait, comn by Earl P Burke Jr, Pel-Tex Oil co, Houston, Tex, 2000; portrait, comn Daniel Gough, Pace, Fla, 2000; portrait, comn by Cathy and Peter Butler, MD, 2004; portrait, comn by Dr and Mrs Noel Pacheco, 2004-2005; portrait, comn by Mr and Mrs Sims, Kurt and Tommi Stockamp MD, Pensacola, Fla; portrait, comn by Mr and Mrs Michael Heller, Pensacola, Fla; portrait, comn by Melba Harrell, Milton, Fla; portrait, comn by Vernon and Angele Hargis, New Orleans, La; portrait, comn by Lauren E Glenn, Baton Rouge, La; portrait, comn by Peter and Cathy Butler, Pensacola, Fla; portrait, comn by, Jeanne Nicole Glenn, New Orleans, La; portrait, comn by Mr and Mrs Michael Burtt; On Site Plants & Serv, comn by Terry O'Brien, 2009; portrait, Andrea Arnof, Carmel, Calif, 2011. *Exhib:* Eclectic, World Trade Ctr, New Orleans, La, 96 & Pensacola Mus Art, Fla, 97-98; Stages: Then and Now, Art and Design Mus, Ft Walton, Fla, 2000; solo exhibs, Ducks Unlimited, Pensacola, Fla, 98 & 2000, Sam Houston Racetrack, Jockey Club, Houston, Tex, 2001 & Portraiture in Watercolor, Stockamp Gallery, Northwest Fla, 2005; Go Figure 96! 97! & 98!, Cultural Ctr Pensacola, Fla, 96-98; Art with an Edge, Artel Gallery, Pensacola, Fla, 99-2000; 26th Ann Transparent Watercolor Exhib, Visual Arts Ctr, Panama City, Fla, 2001; Algiers Point Heritage show, New Orleans, La, 2007-2009; Simply Southern, Milton, Fla, 2011. *Pos:* Presenter, Watercolor Workshops, Destin, Fla, 2008, Georgetown, Maine, New Orleans, La, Pensacola, Fla & Houston, Tex, 96-2000 & 2004-2005; Bay St Louis, Miss, 2005. *Teaching:* Instr watercolor, Pensacola State Coll & City Pensacola, Fla, 97-2010, 2011. *Awards:* Best in Show, Int Trade Mart, 96; Distinction, Best of Collected Watercolor, Rockport Press, 97 & 2002. *Bibliog:* Art and Healing, Univ W Fla (TV), 97 & Go Figure 96!, 97! & 98!, 97; Donna Freckman (auth), Central Lights, Pensacola Today Mag, 98. *Mem:* Nat Mus Women Arts; Am Soc Portrait Artists; Fla Watercolor Soc; Woodbine Figure Painters (secy, treas, 95-98); Bay Cliff Watercolor Soc (founder & pres, 96-2001 & 2006-2007); New Orleans Mus Art; La Watercolor Soc; Pensacola Mus Art; Northwest Fla Arts Coun; Eastern Shore Art Ctr & Mus. *Media:* Watercolor. *Interests:* Travel, photography, gardening, reading, horse back riding. *Publ:* contribr, Best of Watercolor, Painting Texture, Rockport Press, 97; Pensacola Today: Coastal Lights Art and Healing, Buschnell Publ, 98; The Insider, Sanpiper Publ, 2000; The Weekender, Pensacola News J, 2000; Collected Best of Watercolor, Rockport Press, Northlight Bks, 2002; Coming of Age Mag, Pensacola, Fla, 2009/2010; WSRE, Coming of Age (TV interview), Art & Ceremony, 2010. *Mailing Add:* Palm Cottage Studio 4160 Rommitch Ln Pensacola FL 32504

BURKHARDT, RONALD ROBERT
PAINTER, CONCEPTUAL ARTIST, COLLAGE ARTIST
b Jackson, MI, Jul 25. *Study:* Western Mich Univ, BA, 71; Art Students League of New York, 2003-04; Nat Acad Fine Art, New York, 2005-2006. *Work:* Muhammad Ali Ctr & Mus, Louisville, Ky; Gallery Asto, Los Angeles; Western Mich Univ, Kalamazoo; Mus Coral Springs, Fla; George Bush Presidential Libr, Dallas, Tex; Ella Sharp Mus, Jackson, Mich; Shacknow Mus, Boca Raton, Fla; Eisenhower Medical Ctr, Palm Springs, Calif; Stonybrook Hosp, NY. *Comn:* Solar Hieroglyphs (acrylic on canvas 10' x 6') Robert Hernreich, NY & Vail, 2005; Vector (collage, acrylics, assemblage, 48'x71') & Arena V (oil & metal on canvas, 36x24), Greenfield Partners, Fairfield, Conn; Dogs Name.com, SoNo, Conn; Confetti, Luke Scott, Westport, Conn; Painted Violin, Ft Worth Symphony, Tex, 2007; Lakers Hist Notism, Shaquille O'Neal, Los Angeles, 2010; Wave Over Tampa, Nicole Johnson, Miss America 99, Tampa, Fla, 2011. *Exhib:* Solo exhibs, STAR-t Gallery, New York, 2001, Rockefeller's Business Comt For The Arts, Forbes Gallery, New York, 2002, Grand Havana Gallery, New York, 2003, Think Art Gallery, New York, 2003, One Fine Art Gallery, Chicago, 2005, Sublime Gallery, Tribeca, NY, 2006, Peter Marcelle Contemp Gallery, NY & Southampton, 2008, Paul Fisher Gallery, W Palm Beach, Fla, 2008, Marion Meyer Gallery, Laguna Beach, Calif, 2008, LuminArte Gallery, Dallas, 2013, Vertu Fine Art Gallery, Boca Raton, Florida, 2015; Group exhibs, 7 Degrees Gallery, Laguna Beach, Calif, 2006, The McKinney Ave Contemp, Dallas, Tex, 2007, Phillps de Pury Gallery, New York, 2008, Forster Gallery, Miami Beach, Fla, 2010, Ron Burkhardt Retrospective, Ella Sharp Mus, Jackson, Mich, 2011; Art Release Gallery / Trump Tower, New York, 2003, Watermill Mus, Long Island, NY, 2008; Banking on Art, Wells Fargo Bank, Laguna Beach, CA, 2003-2004; Watermill Mus, Watermill, NY, 2004; BJ Spoke Gallery, Huntington, NY, 2005; Muhammad Ali "Quotations", Muhammad Ali Mus, Louisville, KY, 2005; Biennale Int Dell'Arte Contemporanea, Fortezza Da Basso, Florence, Italy, 2005; Magidson Fine Art, Sao Paolo, Brazil, 2005; Int Biennale Contemp Art, Klagenfurt, Austria, 2006; Casa Decor, Art Basel, Miami, Fla, 2006; Phillippe Guionnet Gallery, Palos Verdes, Calif, 2006; Hampton Road Gallery, Southampton, NY, 2008; Long Beach Arts Gallery, Long Beach, Calif, 2007,

2010; Los Angeles Co Mus Art Biennial, Calif, 2007; Sotheby's New York, 2009; US Biennale Artists, Broadway Gallery, New York, 2010; LuminArte Gallery, Dallas, Tex, 2011; Art Prize, Top 25, Grand Rapids, Mich, 2011; Galerie Daliko, Krems, Austria, 2012; Guild Hall Mus, East Hampton, NY, 2012, 2013; Melissa Morgan Fine Art, Palm Desert, Calif, 2013; Featured Spotlight Artist at Art Hamptons/Bridgehampton, NY, 2015; Art on Exhibit, Art Southampton, NY, 2015; Three Man Show, Leonard Tourne Gallery, NY, 2015. *Pos:* contemporary artist, founder of notism and earth art. *Teaching:* Guest prof, Western Mich Univ, 2006; lectr, Earth Art Workshop, Ella Sharp Mus, Jackson, Mich, 2011. *Awards:* Paperworks, B.J. Spoke Gallery, NY, Faye Hirsch, Juror, Sr Ed Art in Am Mag, 2005; Medici Medal for Mixed Media at Florence Biennale Contemp Art, 2005; Long Beach Arts, Calif, 2007, 2009, 2010; Am Art Awards, Calif, 2010, 2011. *Bibliog:* John Capos (auth), Who's Here, Dan's Papers, Southampton, NY, 2004; Roberta Carasso (auth), Burkhardt Discovers There's Art in Taking Notes, Laguna News Post, 2005; Debbie Sklar (auth), The Art of Notetaking, Orange Co Register, LNN, 2005; Burkhardt Selected for Florence Biennale, Southampton Press, NY, 2005; Art Hamptons, interview, WVVH-TV, 7/2008; Ron Burkhardt returns to the Hamptons, CBS, The Insider, 7/2008; Artists to Watch in 2009, Art & Living Mag, 2009; Notism of Ron Burkhardt interview, WNBC-TV 12/2008; Art and Living Mag, Devoss' Art Prize, 2011; Devoss Attracts International Artist Ron Burkhardt, Art Prize, 2011; Burkhardt TV Interview, Art Southhampton, Cognacs Corner, 2012; Beach Lane, 2012; Worth Mag, 2013. *Mem:* Whitney Mus Am Art, New York; MOMA, New York; One Club, New York; Laguna Art Mus, Laguna Beach, Calif; Guggenheim Mus, New York; Parish Art Mus, Watermill, NY. *Media:* Acrylics, Oil, Collage, Mixed Media. *Interests:* Traveling, writing, karate, motorcycling, tennis, films. *Publ:* Auth, Is Creativity a Product of its Environment?, Adweek Magazine, NY, 80; Return of the Creative Mind, Ad Age Mag, 80; Keeping the Pasture Green, Adweek Magazine, NY, 84; Between the Lines, One A Magazine, NY, 2004. *Dealer:* Melissa Morgan Fine Art 73040 El Paseo Palm Desert Ca 92260; Peter Marcelle Hampton Rd Gallery Bridgehampton NY; Paul Fisher Gallery 433 Flamingo Dr W Palm Beach FL 33401; Lee Scott, Charlton Rose Gallery New York; Jeff Forster Forster Gallery 400 Alton Rd Miami Beach FL 33139; Matt Anzak Lumin Arte Gallery 1727 E Levee St Dallas TX 75207. *Mailing Add:* PO Box 1070 Quogue NY 11959

BURKHART, KATHE K
CONCEPTUAL ARTIST, WRITER
b Martinsburg, WVa, June 18, 1958. *Study:* Calif Inst Arts, BFA, 82, MFA, 84. *Work:* Flash Art Mus; Smak Mus, Ghent, Belg Collections; also pvt collections of Rogier & Hilde Matthys, Ghent, Belg, Ellen & Richard Sandor, NY, Andre Wilcox, Bruges, Belg, Carlo Pappruco, Turin, Italy & Robert Shiffler, Greenville, Ohio; Participant, INC 2003; Mitchell Algus Gallery, NY, 2003-2004; Galerie Lumen Travo, Amsterdam, Neth; PS 1, Mus Mod Art, 2007-2008; Seavest Coll, NY. *Comn:* Banner, Los Angeles Contemp Exhib, 85; Fuoi Uso, Italy, 95; Mus Fine Art, Bruges, Belg, 97; John Waters, San Francisco, Calif. *Exhib:* Selected Works from the Liz Taylor Series, Shoshana Wayne Gallery, Santa Monica, 92; Reframing Cartoons, Wexner Ctr, Columbus, Ohio, 92; From Media to Metaphor: About AIDS, Mus d'Art Contemp, Montreal, Que, 93; Rijksakad, Amsterdam, 94-96; Bad Girls, UCLA Wight Mus, 94; Real Fake, Neuberger Mus, Purchase, NY, 95; Printemps/Etc, Groningen Mus, The Neth, 96; solo exhibs, Serge Sorokko Gallery, NY, 97, Galerie DeLege Ruimte, Gent, Belg, 97, Mus V Schone Kunsten, Bruges, Belg, 97, 99, Shores Gallery, Amsterdam, 2000; NYU 80 WSE, 2012; Nudes, Osmos Gallery, NY. *Pos:* Bookstore mgr, Los Angeles Contemp Exhibs, 82-85; freelance graphic designer for var clients, 85-; prof, New York Univ, 2000-. *Teaching:* Vis artist painting, Mason Gross Sch Art, Rutgers Univ, New Brunswick, NJ, 91-92 & San Francisco Art Inst, 98; teacher Ohio State Univ, 94; teacher RISD, 99, New York Univ, 2000-; Sch of Visual Arts, 2012; Rietveld Acad, Amsterdam. *Awards:* Arts Int Award, 93; Art Matters, 94; Funds for Fine Arts, Amsterdam, 98-2001; Haven Found, 2011; Mondriaan Found, 2012. *Bibliog:* Helena Kontova (auth), Bad girl made good, Flashart, 10-11/90; Gianni Romano (ed), Velvet Revolution (exhib catalog), Galleria Arco, Turin, Italy, 93; Women and Performance, Osmos Mag, 2002; Barbara Pollack, Art In America, 10/2004; Bad Girl Work 1983 - 2000, Hanus Press, 2005; Schambelan, Elizabeth Art Forum, 3/2005; Martha Schwendener (auth), The Liz Taylor Series: Selections from 1983-2007, NY Times, 2007; Esopus, 2011. *Mem:* Coll Art Asn. *Media:* Interdisciplinary. *Specialty:* Contemporary Art. *Interests:* Feminism, Literature, Politics, Psychology. *Publ:* Auth, From Under the 8 Ball, LINE, 85; The Torture Paintings, Culturcentrum, Bruges, Belgium, 97; The Double Standard Participant Press, 2005; The Liz Taylor Series the First 25 Years (auth), Regency Arts Press, 2007. *Dealer:* Galerie Lumen Travo Amsterdam Participant Inc New York; Annie Gentils, Antwerp, Belg. *Mailing Add:* 47 S Fifth St Brooklyn NY 11211

BURKO, DIANE
PAINTER, PHOTOGRAPHER
b Brooklyn, NY, Sept 24, 1945. *Study:* Skidmore Coll, BS, 66; Univ Pa Grad Sch Fine Arts, MFA, 69. *Work:* Philadelphia Mus Art; DeCordova Mus, Lincoln, Mass; Reading Pub Mus; AT&T; Wells Fargo Bank; Pa Acad Fine Arts; IBM, Tucson, Ariz; CIGNA Corp; Art Inst, Chicago, IL; Frederick Weisman Art Mus, Minneapolis, MN; Hood Mus Art; Dartmouth Coll; Chgo Mus; Mich Mus Art. *Comn:* One percent RDA, Philadelphia Marriott, 95-96. *Exhib:* Whitney Mus Am Art, 81; Art Inst Chicago, 83; Tampa Mus Art, 86; Md Art Inst, 86; solo exhibs, Hollins Coll, 87, Marian Locks Gallery, 88, 90, 92 & 94, Nat Acad Sci, Washington, 91 & Moravian Coll, 95-96; Perspectives - PA, Carnegie Mellon Univ, Pittsburgh, Pa, 88; Landscape: Work by Women Artists, Bryn Mawr Col, Pa, 94; Artist Made Objects, Locks Gallery, Philadelphia, 95; The River, Philadelphia Art Alliance, Pa, 98; A Sense of Place: Paintings by Diane Burko, Parthenon Mus, Nashville Tenn, 99; Volcano series, Locks Gallery, 2001; Earth, Water, Fire, Locks Gallery, Pa, 2004; Paint/Pixel, Rider Univ Art Gallery, NJ, 2005; Flow, Aidekman Art Center, Tufts Univ, Mass, 2006; The Michener Mus, Pa, 2006; Diane Burko: Photographs, Locks Gallery, Pa, 2006, 2010; Politics of Snow, Locks Gallery, 2010; Politics of Snow II, Woodrow WIlson Sch, Princeton Univ, 2011; Photographs: Diane Burko, Locks Gallery, 2011; Water Matters, Lewallen Galleries, 2012. *Pos:* Pres & founder, Philadelphia Focuses on Women in Visual Arts, 73-75; Mayors Cult Adv Coun, 88-90; Art Comn Philadelphia, 92-96. *Teaching:* Prof drawing, painting & design, Philadelphia Community Coll, 69-95, prof art, 73-, head art dept, 80-85; vis prof, Princeton Univ, 85. *Awards:* Pa Coun Arts Individual Artists Grant, 81 & 89; Nat Endowment Arts Visual Arts Fel, 85-86, 91-92; Bessie Berman Painting Grant, Leeway Found, 2000; Distinguished Feminist Award, 2008; Lifetime Achievement Award, Women's Caucus for Art, 2010. *Bibliog:* Alexandria Anderson (auth), Burko-Locks, Art News, 91; Robert Rosenblum (auth), Luci ed Ombra di Bellagio - The Light & Shadow of Bellagio (exhib catalog), Locks Gallery, 94; David Bourdon (auth), Diane Borko, Land Survey: 1970-95 (exhib catalog), Moravian Coll, 95; Diane Burko: Politics of Snow, Locks Gallery, 2011. *Mem:* Coll Art Asn Am (bd mem, 94-98-); Women's Caucus Art (treas adv bd, 77-78 & 82-85); Philadelphia Volunteer Lawyers for Arts, (bd mem 86-89); Philadelphia Art Comn; Fleisher Art Mem (bd mem 2006-); Philaguatika (bd mem 2007-). *Media:* Oil, Acrylic, Digital Camera. *Collection:* Colgate Univ, Picker Art Gallery, Hamilton, NY; De Cordova Mus, Lincoln, Mass; Hahnemann Hosp, Pa. *Dealer:* Lew Allen Galleries 1613 Paseo de Peratta Santa Fe NMex 87501. *Mailing Add:* 310 S Juniper St Philadelphia PA 19107

BURLEIGH, KIMBERLY
PRINTMAKER, EDUCATOR
b Meadville, Pa, Apr 1, 1955. *Study:* Ohio Univ, Athens, BFA, 77; Ind Univ, Bloomington, MFA, 80. *Comn:* Progressive Corp, Cleveland, Ohio; One person shows, Carnegie Mellon Univ, 2001, Fine Arts Work Ctr, Provincetown, Mass, 99. *Exhib:* One-person shows, Pittsburgh Plan for Art, Pa, 85 & Feature Gallery, Chicago, 86 & 87; John Michael Kohler Arts Ctr, Sheboygan, Wis, 92; Galerie 1900-2000, Paris, France, 94; Print Club, Philadelphia, Pa, 94; Galerie Toner in Sens en Bourgogne, France, 97 & 98; NY Digital Salon, Visual Arts Mus, NY, 98; Gallery N-Space at Siggraph, 2001; CEPA Gallery, Buffalo, 99. *Collection Arranged:* Progressive Corp, Cleveland, Ohio; Joan Flasch Artists Bk Collection, Art Inst Chicago; Bibliotheque Nat de France; Robert J Shiffler Collection & Archive; Galerie Toner in Sens en Bourgogne, France. *Pos:* Vis artist, Murray State Univ, Ky, 83. *Teaching:* Vis asst prof painting, Univ Utah, Salt Lake City, 81-82 & Ohio Univ, Athens, 86-89; asst prof, State Univ Tex, Nacogdoches, 82-83; assoc prof/grad prog dir fine art, Univ Cincinnati, 90-; prof, grad program dir fine art, Univ Cincinnati, 99-. *Awards:* Visual Artists Fel, Nat Endowment Arts, 87; Ohio Arts Coun Grant, 89 & 99; Artist Proj Grant, Ohio Arts Coun, 95, 97 & 99. *Bibliog:* David McCracken (auth), Words help tell the message in painting, Chicago Tribune, 9/25/87; Barbara Gallati (auth), New work, Arts Mag, 11/81. *Publ:* Cincinnati Portfolio II (lithograph), Mark Patsfall Graphics Inc, Cincinnati, Ohio, 93; Counterfeits I, self publ, Cincinnati, Ohio, 97; Device & Devices, self publ, Cincinnati, Ohio, 98; Reversions, self publ, Cincinnati, 2000. *Mailing Add:* c/o Univ Cincinnati Sch Art PO Box 210016 Cincinnati OH 45221

BURLESON, CHARLES TRENTMAN
PAINTER, EDUCATOR
b Charlotte, NC, June 15, 1952. *Study:* Philadelphia Coll Art, BFA, 74; RI Sch of Design, MFA, 76. *Work:* NC Arts Soc, Raleigh; Surry Col, Dobson, NC; Providence Jour Collection, RI; Mint Mus, Charlotte, NC; Queens Univ, Ont, Can. *Comn:* Outdoor mural, RI State Coun Arts, Providence, 77; A Case for Boxes (house box), RI Sch of Design Mus, 80, 2001. *Exhib:* Solo exhibs, Central Falls, NY, 80, Gallery Z, NY, 86 & Virginia Lynch Gallery, Tiverton, RI, 88; Group exhibs, Alan Stone Gallery, NY, 80 & RI Sch of Design Mus Art, 90; Helander Gallery, NY, 90. *Collection Arranged:* Burelson Painting Prize Competition Exhib, 2003-04. *Pos:* Chief critic, EHP Prog, Rome, Italy, 85. *Teaching:* Prof illustr dept, RI Sch Design, 76-2005. *Awards:* Second Place Award, NC Arts Soc, 69; Purchase Award, Mint Mus Art, Charlotte, 74; Purchase Award, NC Mus Art, 75. *Bibliog:* Edward Sozanski (auth), Burleson's landscapes are striking, Providence J, 82; Edward Booth-Clibborn (auth), American Illustration, Abrams, 84; Drawings-Gallery Z, East Village Rev, 3-4/87; Chronos Mag, winter 2003. *Media:* Oil. *Specialty:* Am Art. *Publ:* Painting (cover piece), Where I'm Calling From Raymond Carver, Atlantic Monthly Press, 88. *Dealer:* Grand Central Gallery, Boston, MA; Erlich Gallery, Marblehead MA; Virginia Lynch, Tiverton, RI. *Mailing Add:* 7 Hayward Pl Rumford RI 02916

BURNET, PEGGY & RALPH W
COLLECTOR
b 1945. *Study:* St Lawrence Univ; Univ Minn. *Pos:* With Bermel-Smaby, Minneapolis, 1969-73, branch mgr, 1971-73; founder, Burnet Realty, Minneapolis, 1973, pres Eastern region, 1983-88, chief exec officer, 1990-95; chief exec officer, Prudential Burnet Realty, Minneapolis, 1995-1998; chmn, Coldwell Banker Burnet, Minneapolis, 1998-; sr vpres, Midwest region, Title Resource Group, 1998-; pres bd dirs, Walker Art Ctr, Minneapolis, formerly. *Awards:* Named one of Top 200 Collectors, ARTnews, 2007-10. *Collection:* Contemporary British art, especially young British artists. *Mailing Add:* Coldwell Banker Burnet Ste 3 7550 France Ave S Minneapolis MN 55435

BURNETT, AMY LOUISE
GALLERY OWNER, WRITER
b Bremerton, Wash, Nov 3, 1944. *Study:* Central Univ, Ellensburg, MA, 66. *Pos:* cur, Pyrex Mus, Bremerton, 2008-. *Teaching:* instr, Olympic Coll, 1978-; instr, Amy Burnett Gallery, 1978-. *Awards:* Woman of the Year, YWCA Kistsap County; Hall of Fame, Olympic Coll; Arts in Embassy, US State Dept. *Specialty:* landscape, Victorian women, horses and salmon. *Interests:* interior design; bridge. *Publ:* Contribr, Kisap Newspaper Group, Patriot, 99-05; filmmaker, Self for Bremerton Kitsap Access Television, 2000; contribr, Westsound Home and Garden, 2005. *Mailing Add:* 402 Pacific Ave Bremerton WA 98337

BURNS, IAN
SCULPTOR, KINETIC ARTIST
b Newcastle, Australia, 1964. *Study:* Swinburne Univ, Melbourne, BS (eng), 1989; Univ Newcastle, BFA, 2000; CUNY Hunter Coll, MFA, 2003; Griffith Univ, Brisbane, PhD, 2008. *Exhib:* In-Practice Series, The Sculpture Ctr, New York, 2004; Greater New York, PS1 Mus Contemp Art, New York, 2005; solo exhibs, The Soap Factory, Minn, 2005, Spencer Brownstone Gallery, New York, 2005 & 2007, Art Basel Miami, Fla, 2005, Hilger Contemp, Vienna, Austria, 2006, Big Orbit, Buffalo, NY, 2006, Galeria Espacio Minimo, Madrid, 2007, Queensland Coll Art, Brisbane, 2008, Mothers Tankstation, Dublin, 2008, St Louis Mus Contemp Art, Mo, 2008, Indpls Mus Contemp Art, 2009; Now Voyager, Islip Art Mus, NY, 2006; StereoVision, Univ South Fla Contemp Art Mus, 2007; New Acquisitions, Mus Contemp Art, Sydney, 2008; Fax, The Drawing Ctr, New York, 2009. *Awards:* Fel, New York Found for Arts, 2008; Emerging Artist New Work Grant, Australia Coun, 2009. *Bibliog:* Elisabeth Kley (auth), Greater New York 2005, ART News, Vol 104, No 5, 139, 5/2005; Barbara A MacAdam (auth), Object Overruled, ART News, 124-127, 12/2007; Julia Morrisroe (auth), Art Basel - Miami, Sculpture Mag, 79, 4/2008. *Mailing Add:* c/o Spencer Brownstone Gallery 39 Wooster St New York NY 10013

BURNS, JOSEPHINE
PAINTER
b Llandudno, North Wales, July 2, 1917. *Study:* Cooper Union Art Sch, grad, 39, BFA, 76; Art Students League, 49 & 50. *Work:* C W Post Coll Mus, Long Island Univ; Okla Mus Art, Oklahoma City; Bristol City Art Gallery, Whitworth Art Gallery, Manchester Univ, England. *Exhib:* Brooklyn & Long Island Artists, Brooklyn Mus, 58; Solo exhibs, Alonzo Gallery, NY, 66 & Auld Alliance Gallery, Nashville, Tenn, 94; Community Gallery, Brooklyn Mus, 76, 77 & 80; Bergen Co Community Mus, 82; Mostyn Art Gallery, NWales, UK, 82 & 85-92; Salena Gallery, Long Island Univ, 84; Broekman Gallery, Chester, UK; Gallery Ynys Mon, Anglesey, North Wales, UK, 98; and others. *Pos:* Co-dir, Hicks Street Gallery, Brooklyn, 58-63; assoc dir, Brownstone Gallery, Brooklyn, 69-76. *Awards:* Resident Fel, MacDowell Colony, 60, 62, 64, 65 & 68; Resident Fel, Yaddo, Saratoga Springs, NY, 61. *Mem:* Artists Equity Asn, NY. *Media:* Oil, Pastel. *Publ:* Paintings 1982-1997, A Window on Two Worlds (catalog), 98. *Dealer:* Christine Holt Auld Alliance Gallery Westgate Ctr 6019 Highway 100 Nashville TN 37205

BURNS, MARK A
CERAMIST
b Springfield, Ohio, Oct 5, 1950. *Study:* Sch Dayton Art Inst, BFA, 72; Univ Wash, Seattle, MFA, 74. *Exhib:* Everson Mus Art, Syracuse, NY & Renwick Gallery, Smithsonian Inst, Washington, DC, 79; solo exhibs, Helen Drutt Gallery, Philadelphia, Pa, 75, 76, 82, 84 & 89, Happy Birthday Frank Furnets, Pa Acad Fine Arts, Philadelphia, Pa, 84, A Decade in Pennsylvania: 1975-1985, Soc Art & Craft, Verona, Pa, 86 & As Seen on TV, Univ Gallery, Calif State Univ, Chico, 86; Mus Philadelphia Civic Ctr, traveling, 80; Contemp Artists: An Expanding View (with catalogue), Wellesley Coll Mus, Mass, Monmouth Mus Art, Lincroft, NJ & Squibb Gallery, Princeton, NJ, 86; Am Ceramics Now: 27th Ceramic Nat Exhibit, Everson Mus Art, 87; Perch Int Crafts, Triennial Twenty Americans: Am Figurative Ceramics, Art Gallery Western Australia, 89; Metamorphosis, Contemp Mus Ceramic Art, Shigaraki, Japan, 92. *Pos:* Asst prof, Philadelphia Col Art, Pa, 75-83, Tyler Sch Art, Temple Univ, Philadelphia, Pa, 81-82, Moore Col Art & Design, Philadelphia, Pa, 85 & Univ Nev Las Vegas, 91-92; vis prof, Univ Ariz, Tucson, 82-83 & RI Sch Design, Providence, 89-91; prof & head ceramics, Univ Nev, 92-. *Awards:* Nat Endowment Arts, 76 & 88. *Publ:* Coauth (with Louis DiBonis), Fifties Homestyle: Popular Ornament of the USA, Harper & Row, 88. *Dealer:* Helen Drutt Gallery 1721 Walnut St Philadelphia PA 19103

BURNS, MARSHA
PHOTOGRAPHER
b Seattle, Wash, Jan 11, 1945. *Study:* Univ Wash, 63-65; Univ Mass, Amherst, 67-69. *Work:* Mus Mod Art, Metrop Mus Art, NY; Nat Mus Am Art, Smithsonian Inst, Libr Cong, Washington, DC; Ctr Creative Photog, Tucson, Ariz; Seattle Art Mus, City of Seattle Collection, Wash; Stedelijk Mus, Amsterdam; Dallas Mus Fine Art, Tex; San Francisco Mus Contemp Art, Fed Reserve Bank of San Francisco, Calif; Libr of Congress, Washington; and others. *Exhib:* Charles Cowles Gallery, NY, 92, 2001 & Portraits from Am, Susan Spiritus Gallery, Costa Mesa, Calif, 92; China 1989, One Path Three Vision, Ital, Seattle, Wash, 90; Western Women Photographers, Maveety Gallery, Portland, Ore, 90; Anniversary Show, Linda Farris Gallery, Seattle, Wash, 90; 1991 Nat Governors Asn Art Exhib, Wash State Convention & Trade Ctr, Seattle; People & Places, Northern Ill Univ Art Mus Gallery, Chicago, 91; SoHo at Duke, Five Artists from Charles Cowles Gallery, Duke Univ Mus Art, Durham, NC; To Collect the Art of Women: The Jane Reese Williams Collection of Photog, Mus NMex, Santa Fe, 92; Photographs: Jock Sturges, Plauto, Marsha Burns, Charles Cowles Gallery, NY, 92; group exhibs, Horse, The Male as Sexual Entity, Ron Judish Fine Arts, Denver, Colo, 2000, Am Perspectives: Photographs from the Polaroid Collection, Tokyo Metrop Mus of Photog, 2000-01. *Awards:* Photogr Fel, Nat Endowment Arts, 78; Awards in Visual Arts, Nat Mus Am Art, Southeastern Ctr Contemp Art, 81; photography fel, Nat Endowment for the Arts, 87-88. *Bibliog:* Gerard Malanga (ed), Scopophilia: The Love of Looking, Alfred Van de Mark Ed & Harper & Row, 85; Chris Bruce (auth, catalog) Cities, Henry Gallery Mus, Univ Wash, 87; articles, Korper, Polaroid Corp, 88; and others. *Dealer:* Charles Cowles Gallery 420 W Broadway New York NY 10012

BURNS, SHEILA
PAINTER, LECTURER
b Scotland; US citizen. *Study:* Detroit Soc Arts & Crafts; Wayne State Univ, BA. *Work:* Grand Rapids Mus, Mich; Wayne State Univ; Founders Soc Gallery Loan Collection, Detroit Inst Art; Hillberry Theatre, Wayne State Univ, Detroit. *Comn:* Grosse Prep Acad, Am Spoon Foods; Children's Hosp Mich. *Exhib:* Mich Biennial Exhib Painters & Printmakers, Grand Rapids Mus; Mich Acad Sci, Art & Lett & Mich Regional Exhib, Univ Mich; Blue Water Int Exhib, US & Can, 74 & 75; Eastern Mich Int, 75; plus many others. *Teaching:* Instr, secondary schs. *Awards:* Purchase Award, Mich Biennial Painters & Printmakers, Grand Rapids Mus; Watercolor Awards, Scarab Club Detroit. *Mem:* Am Asn Prof Artists. *Media:* Watercolor, Oil. *Publ:* Illusr, Detroit Free Press; illusr, Are Nursery Rhymes for Children? by Dr Edward Southern; Centennial Poster (ltd-ed), and other ltd-ed posters. *Dealer:* Galerie de Boicourt Birmingham MI 48011

BURNS, STAN
PAINTER, SCULPTOR
b Sutersville, Pa. *Study:* Wayne State Univ, BA & MA; Detroit Soc Arts & Crafts, with Reginald Bennett, Sarkis; Pewabic Pottery with Mary Chase Stratton. *Work:* Wayne State Univ; Ford Motor Co; Founders Gallery Loan Collection, Detroit Art Inst. *Comn:* Numerous pvt comns & portrait comns. *Exhib:* Mich Acad Sci, Art & Lett & Mich Regional Exhib, Univ Mich; Mich Artists Exhib, Detroit Inst Art; Mich Watercolor Soc; Blue Water Int Exhib, 73 & 74; Eastern Mich Int, 75; solo-invitational, Bacardi Gallery, Miami; plus many solo exhibs incl galleries in Dallas, Miami, Washington, DC, Detroit, Chicago & Kalamazoo. *Awards:* Board of Directors' Award, Scarab Gold Medal Show, Detroit; Blue Water Int Exhib, Port Huron Mus, Mich; Eastern Mich Int Exhib Award; Best of Show, Scarab Art Club; Gold Plaque, Detroit/Windsor Int Freedom Festival. *Mem:* Nat Asn Prof Artists; Scarab Club

BURNSIDE, CHRIS
PAINTER
b Sept 23, 1973. *Study:* Univ Wash, Seattle, BFA, 1996; Univ Pa, MFA, 2001. *Exhib:* Solo exhibs: Nexus Found for Today's Art, Philadelphia, 2002; Open Air, NY, 2004; Washington Art Asn, Washington, Conn, 2006; Alpan Gallery, Huntington, NY, 2007; two-person exhib, Fox Gallery, Philadelphia, 2001; Group exhibs: The Object: Color & Carrier, Ramapo Coll, NJ, 2003; Vital Signs: Drawing as Inquiry (juror Robert Reed), Creative Arts Workshop, New Haven, Conn, 2000; Tastes Like Chicken, Art Space, Brooklyn, NY, 2007; Abstraction Obstruction: Working the Meridians, Soil Gallery, Seattle, 2005; Night of 1000 Drawings, Artists Space, New York 2006; 183rd Ann: Invitational Exhib Contemp Am Art, Nat Acad Mus, New York, 2008; Inquiry, Gross McCleaf Gallery, Philadelphia, 2008. *Pos:* Archivist, Cheim & Read Gallery, NY. *Awards:* Juror's Prize, Nat Spring Open Juried Exhib, Barbara Grossman, 2000; Stuart Egnal Scholar, 2000; SJ Wallace Truman Fund Prize, Nat Acad, 2008. *Bibliog:* William Zimmer (auth), Among a Show of Drawings, Looking for Ones With Bite, NY Times, 5/14/2000; RB Strauss (auth) Nexus Abides, Around Philly.com, 2/2002; Orlando Lima (auth), Profile: Chris Burnside; The Artist's Vision Soars in Greenpoint, NY Sun, 3/3/05. *Media:* Mixed Media, Acrylic. *Publ:* Mark Brosseau, Inquiry: 5 Painting Practices, Gross McCleaf Gallery, Philadelphia, 2008; Nancy Malloy, 183rd Annual: An International Exhibition of Contemporary American Art, Nat Accad Mus, NY, 2008

BURNSIDE, MADELEINE HILDING
CRITIC, MUSEUM DIRECTOR
b London, Eng, Oct 18, 1948; US citizen. *Study:* Warwick Univ, Eng, BA, 70; Univ Calif, Santa Cruz, PhD (history of consciousness), 76. *Collection Arranged:* Universal Limited Art Editions: The First 10 Years (auth, catalog), Islip Art Mus, 83 & Guild Hall Mus, 84; Preparation & Proposition (auth, catalog), 84, The Living Carousel, 84, The Writing on the Wall (auth, catalog), 85 & Myths & Rituals for the 21st Century (auth, catalog), 86, Islip Art Mus. *Pos:* Ed assoc, Art News Mag, 73-79 & Arts Mag, 79-80; dir, Islip Art Mus, 80; exec dir, Mel Fisher Maritime Heritage Soc and Mus, Key West, Fla, 91-. *Teaching:* Asst art hist, Univ Calif, 72-73; adj prof art hist, Dowling Col, 83-. *Awards:* Fels, Harkness, 70, Ford Found, 73 & Helena Rubinstein, 75; Nat Endowment Arts, 80. *Res:* Contemporary art. *Publ:* Auth, Hard Line, Drawing as a Primary Medium, 84 & Luis Camnitzer, the Torture Series, 85, Islip Art Mus; coauth, Houston Conwill's St Matthew Passion, Alternative Mus, 86; coauth with Rosemarie Robotham, Spirits of the Passage, Simon & Schuster, 97. *Mailing Add:* Mel Fisher Maritime Heritage Soc and Mus 200 Greene St Key West FL 33040

BURPEE, JAMES STANLEY
PAINTER, INSTRUCTOR
b Oakland, Calif, Feb 12, 1938. *Study:* San Jose State Col, BA, 58; Calif Coll Arts & Crafts, with James Weeks, MFA, 60. *Comn:* Painting, 13 x 4 ft, Dain Bosworth, Minneapolis, 92. *Exhib:* A Sense of Place: Artists & the Am Land, Sheldon Mem Art Gallery, Lincoln, Nebr, 73-74; Solo exhibs, Coll St Catherine, St Paul, Minn, 78, Nash Gallery, Univ Minn, 82 & 85, Artbanque Gallery, Minneapolis, 84, Katherine Nash Gallery, Univ Minn, 82 & 85, Flanders Contemp Art, Minneapolis, Minn, 93; Am Art; The Challenge of the Land, Pillsbury Co Sponsor, 81; two person exhibs, Meetings & Archetypes: Minn Artists exhib prog, Minneapolis Inst Arts, 87 & Forum Gallery, Minneapolis, Minn, 90; Environmental Show, MC Gallery, Minneapolis, 91; 22nd Anniversary Show, Flanders Contemp Art, Minneapolis, 94; and others. *Teaching:* From instr to asst prof & chmn, Art Dept, Midwestern Univ, Wichita Falls, Tex, 60-67; from asst prof to prof painting & drawing, Minneapolis Col of Art & Design, 67-; vis artist painting, Kansas City Art Inst, 74 & Calif Col of Arts & Crafts, 74 & 75; guest lectr, Calif Col Arts & Crafts, 79-80; lectr, Wash Univ, St Louis, 84; lectr, Tour for Milton Avery Show, Walker Art Ctr, Minn, 83. *Awards:* Fel Residency Found Karolyi, Venice, France, 89; Nat Endowment Arts Artist-in-residence, Volcanoes Nat Park, Hawaii, 73-74; Fel, MacDowell Colony, 76. *Media:* Acrylic. *Publ:* Illusr, Visual Studies by Frank Young, Prentice-Hall, 84. *Dealer:* Flanders Contemp Art 400 N First Ave, First Flr, Minneapolis, MN 55401; Bridge Square Gallery 16 Bridge Sq PO Box 341 Northfield MN 55057. *Mailing Add:* 3208 Aldrich Ave S Minneapolis MN 55408-3602

BURR, RUTH BASLER
PAINTER
b Chicago, Ill, Feb 12, 1932. *Study:* Glendale Col; Pierce Col; UCLA; Laguna Beach Sch Art, Calif. *Work:* Calif Inst Technol, Pasadena; Univ Calif, Los Angeles Med Ctr, Westwood, Calif; Glendale Fed, Glendale, Calif; Transamerica Corp, Los Angeles. *Comn:* Over 100 murals, 53-70, over 100 portraits, 68-72, People in Los Angeles Co, Calif; 3 large oils of ships, Robinson Develop Co, Newport, Calif, 79; 75 paintings, Trans Am Corp, Los Angeles, Calif, 80-84. *Exhib:* Brand II, Brand, Glendale, Calif, 70; solo exhibs, Descanso Gardens, Hospitality Mus, La Canada, Calif, 70-92; Art Expo Cal Ann, Conf Ctr, Los Angeles, 87-92; featured artist, Los Angeles Co Fair, 92; Artist of Yr, Buena Park, Calif, 92; Phillips Gallery, Carmel, Calif. *Pos:* Co-chmn with Johnny Ray, Hear Found, Pasadena, Calif, 70-71; co-chmn, Art Under Oaks, Descanso Gardens Guild, 85-88. *Teaching:* Instr art, Los Angeles City Sch, 72-80; instr, Pasadena City Col, 75-80; instr, Brand Art Ctr, 80-86. *Awards:* Best of Year, 3 categories, Ebell Club, 82; First Place, Under Oaks, Descanso Gardens, 90. *Media:* Watercolor. *Mailing Add:* 27071 Glenar FF Ln San Juan Capistrano CA 92675

BURR, TOM
ARTIST
b New Haven, 1963. *Work:* Update 92, 92-93, Tom Burr, 95-96, Stainless, 96-97, Parasite, 97-98, Slung Low, Kunstverein Braunschweig, 2000, Deliberate Living, Greene Naftali Gallery, NY, 2001, Deep Purple, Whitney Mus Am Art, 2002-03, Whitney Biennial Am. Art, 2004, It's All An Illusion, A Sculpture Project, Migros Mus fur Gegenwartskunst, Zurich, 2004, The Future Has a Silver Lining-Genealogies of Glamour, 2004

BURR, TRICIA
PAINTER
b Plainfield, NJ, Sept 15, 1943. *Study:* Marshall Arisman Sch Visual Arts, 95; studied with Gerardo Ruiz, painting & engraving, 2004-05; studied with Anne Seelbach, Victor D'Amico Inst, NY & Keith Keller La Escuela, Mex; Collegio de Belles Artes, San Miguel de Allende, Mex; Mus Temporary Art, Tubingen Ger; Int Mus Coll Mex. *Work:* Kulturhaus, Bremen, Ger; Mus of Contemp Art, Santiago, Chile; Contemp Art Ctr, New Orleans, LA; Yoshkar Ola Mus Fine Arts, Russia; Int Mus Collage, Mex; Popov Mus, St Petersburg, Russia. *Comn:* Two works, Popov Mus, Russia. *Exhib:* Bakers Dozen Int Coll Exhib, Mex; Human Artifacts Exhib, Bremen, Ger; I Miss You Exhib, Acorn Gallery, Los Angeles, Calif; Human Pixel Project, Harvard Univ; Three Columns Gallery, Cambridge, Mass; Cult Festival of the Arts, Wellington, NZ, 2007-2008; Russian Soul - Am Soul, St Petersburg, Russia & US, 2008. *Pos:* Vpres, Savannah Coll Art & Design, 86-92. *Teaching:* Pvt sessions in studio, currently. *Awards:* 1st prize, Painting Environ Scapes, 99, Univ Ga & Painting Watercolor Underwater, 2000. *Mem:* Int Lomographic Soc; Int Orgn United Mail Artists (IOUMA), (pres at large); Int Breakfast Club (charter, bd dirs), 86-. *Media:* Oils, Watercolors, Mixed Media & Acrylic. *Res:* Survivors of the blockade & seige of Leningrad during WWII. *Dealer:* Beacon Gallery 1606 Butler Ave Tybee Island GA 31328; Win Gallery St Petersburg Russia. *Mailing Add:* Pelican House 142 Pelican Dr Tybee Island GA 31328

BURSON, NANCY
PHOTOGRAPHER, CONCEPTUAL ARTIST
b St Louis, Mo, Feb 24, 1948. *Study:* Colo Women's Coll, 66-68. *Work:* San Francisco Mus Mod Art; Libr Cong, Washington, 84-86; Whitney Mus; Victoria & Albert Mus, London; Metrop Mus Art; Creative Time: Visualize This, 1991; Creative Time: Theres No Gene for Race (billboard), NY, 2000; Creative Time with Lower Manhattan Cultural Council (posters), 2002; Deutch Bank, 2005. *Comn:* Big Brother, CBS News Special, NY, 83; updates of missing children, FBI, Washington, DC, 84-86; Mick & Keith, Rolling Stone Mag, NY, 86; Aged Marilyn Monroe, Good Morning Am, NY, 86; Beauty in the Future, NY Times Mag, 96; Clinton/Obama Image, The New Republic (cover), 2008. *Exhib:* Solo exhibs incl Int Ctr Photog, NY, 85; Jayne Baum Gallery, NY, 90; Clamp Art Gallery, New York, 2006; The Hand of God, Clamp Art Gallery, NYC, 2006; group exhibs incl Identity, Palais de Tokyo, Paris, 85; Stills: Cinema & Video Transformed, Seattle Art Mus, 86; Photog of Invention: Am Pictures of the 80's, Nat Mus Am Art, Washington, Whitney Mus Am Art, 90, Photog after Photog, 95-96 & Identity & Alternity, Venice Biennale, Italy, 95, After Photoshop, Metropolitan Mus Art, NY, 2012; solo retrospectives, Contemp Arts Mus, Houston, 92 & Recoutres Int Photographie, Arles, France, 96; Traveling Retrospectives: Seeing & Believing: The Art of Nancy Burson, Grey Art Gallery, NYC, Blaffer Gallery, Houston, Tex, Weatherspoon Mus, NC, Photo Espana, Madrid, 2002; Metropolitan Mus, NY; After Photoshop: Photography in the Digital Age, 2012-13; I, You, We, Whitney Mus, NY, 2013. *Teaching:* Vis artist photog, Kansas City Art Inst, Mo, 85; photog course, Tisch Sch Arts, NY Univ, 90-94; Vis artist, Harvard Univ, 98; Vision & Style, NY Film Acad, 2013. *Awards:* Art Matters, 96; Nomination best mus show in NYC, Int Asn Art Critics, 2002; Anonymous was a Woman Grant, 2002. *Bibliog:* Elizabeth Hoyt-Atleins (auth), Art News Review, 5/90; Vince Aletti (auth), About Face: Redefining Normality with Nancy Burson, The Village Voice, 94, 4/21/92; A Defining Reality: The Photographs of Nancy Burson, Rebecca Busselle Aperture, 94. *Media:* Computer Generated Photography, Real Photography, Video, Public Art Installations, Drawing. *Specialty:* Contemp photog. *Interests:* Design for Public Art Installations, Drawing, Interactive Childrens ibooks. *Publ:* Photogr, Am Photogr, 85, Newsweek, 85, New York Post (cover), 85, Manipulator Mag, 85-86 & Smithsonian Mag; Composites, William Morrow, 86; Faces: Nancy Burson, publ by CAM, Houston, essay by Lynn Herbert, 92; FACES, Nancy Burson, Twin Palm Publ, 93; auth, Seeing & Believing: The Art of Nancy Burson, Twin Palm Publ, 2002; auth, Focus: How Your Energy Case Changes the World, 2004; You Can Draw the Way You Feel (interactive children's ibook). *Dealer:* ClampArt 521-531 W 25th St New York NY 10001

BURT, DAVID SILL
SCULPTOR
b Evanston, Ill, Feb 20, 1917. *Study:* Harvard Univ, BA, 40. *Work:* Fine Art Ctr, Univ Wis, Milwaukee; US Art in Embassies Prog, Stamford Mus. *Comn:* Excelsior Hotel, Tulsa, 81; Bradley Int Airport, Hartford, Conn, 86; Philips Electronic Corp, Mahwah, NJ, 88; Chartwell Reinsurance Inc, Stamford, Conn, 90; Reliance Nat, NY, 96. *Exhib:* Pa Acad Fine Arts Exhib, 64; Northeast USA Exhib, 65, 67, 69, 70, 77, 80 & 81; 18 solo exhibs, NY, Conn, RI, Colo, Tex & Ireland. *Pos:* Promotion writer, Archit Forum, Indust Design & Interiors. *Mem:* Sculptors League; Silvermine Guild Artists. *Media:* Hammered & Braised Sheet Metal. *Publ:* Auth, Detour to sculpture, Am Artist Mag

BURTON, JUDITH ANN
PAINTER
b Salt Lake City, Utah. *Study:* Pacific Lutheran Univ, BA (art and lit); Sonoma State Univ, MA (counseling). *Exhib:* Solo exhibs incl Merced Coll, Calif, 2000, Wired Cafe, Merced, 2001, Playhouse Merced, 2002-03, Univ Calif, Merced, 2003, Hourian Gallery, San Francisco, 2004. *Awards:* Best of Show, Soc Western Artists, Fall Show, 1994, First Place, Spring Show, 1997, Ann Show, 1998, Regional Show, 1998; Best of Show, Chowchilla, Calif, 2002. *Mem:* Soc Western Artists; Asn Calif Artist; Nat Watercolor Soc; Colored Pencil Soc Am; Am Watercolor Soc. *Media:* Oil. *Dealer:* Mariposa Arts Coun 5022 Hwy 140 Mariposa CA 95338; Hourian Gallery 1843 Union St San Francisco CA 94123. *Mailing Add:* c/o Arbor Gallery 645 W Main St Merced CA 95340

BURTON, RICHMOND
PAINTER
b Talladega, Ala, 1960. *Study:* Rice Univ, BA (archit), 1984. *Exhib:* Solo exhibs include Postmasters Gallery, NY, 1987, 1988, Mario Diacono Gallery, Boston, 1989, 1990, 1991, 1994, Daniel Weinberg Gallery, Los Angeles, 1990, 1991, Simon Watson, NY, 1990, Matthew Marks Gallery, NY, 1991, 1994, 1996, A/D Gallery, NY, 1992, Laura Carpenter Fine Art, Santa Fe, 1992, Galleria In Arco, Turin, Italy, 1993, Rhona Hoffman Gallery, Chicago, 1993, Turner and Byrne Gallery, Dallas, 1993, Turner Byrne and Runyon Gallery, Dallas, 1995, Velge & Noirhomme, Brussels, 1996, 1997, Anthony Meier Fine Arts, San Francisco, 1996, Cheim & Read Gallery, NY, 1997, 1999, 2001, 2004, Lawing Gallery, Houston, 1999, Hamilton's Gallery, London, 2001, Goss Gallery, Dallas, 2005, The Drawing Room, NY, 2005; group exhibs include Drawing in the Present Tense, Parsons Sch Design, NY, 1999; Vanishing Point, Cynthia Broan Gallery, NY, 1999; Opulent, Cheim & Read Gallery, NY, 2000, Simple Marks, 2003; Reconstructions: The Imprint of Nature/The Impact of Science, Sidney Mishkin Gallery, Baruch Col, NY, 2000; Butler Inst Am Art, Youngstown, Ohio, 2002; Fresh Paint, Hampton Road Gallery, NY, 2004; Affinities, The Drawing Room, NY, 2005; Big Band, Galerie Les Filles due Calvaire, Paris, 2005; The Food Show, The Hungry Eye, Chelsea Art Mus, NY, 2006; Long Island Abstraction - 1950s to the Present, Spanierman Modern, NY, 2006; Still Missing: Beauty Absent Social Life, Visual Arts Museum, Sch Visual Arts, NY, 2006; Hampton Design Showhouse, McNeill Art Group, NY, 2006; Intersections, Emily Davis Gallery, Univ Akron, Ohio, 2006. *Mailing Add:* Cheim & Read Gallery 547 W 25th St New York NY 10001

BURTT, LARICE ANNADEL ROSEMAN
PAINTER, SCULPTOR
b Philadelphia, PA, June 22, 1928. *Study:* BS, Bucknell Univ, Penn. *Work:* Grand Canyon Nat Park Mus, North, Ark; Bucknell Univ, Penn; Cent Bucks CC; Yale Univ Sch Nursing; Childrens Cult Ctr. *Comn:* Joan Krats, Noah, Lancaster, Pa, 88; Mr John Marcinek, Peaceable Kingdom, Calif, 90; Dr Bertram Brown, Give me your Tired, 95. *Exhib:* Stone Painting, Abington Art Ctr, Abington, PA, 76; Upstairs Gallery, 80-90; Newton & Nova, 86; Arnot Art Mus, Elmira, NY, 87; Congressional Bldg, Washington, DC, 90-2000; Yale Univ, New Haven, Conn, 95; Phillips Mill juried show, New Hope; Accents Images, Peddlers Village, Lahaska, Pa; Gaileria Veroneze, Rue de Royal, New Orleans; Bushkill Falls Gallery, Bucks County, Penn; Coryell Gallery, Lambertville, NJ; and numerous others from 72-2002. *Pos:* Demonstrator, workshops, Bucks Co Sch, 77-2002; art league, speaker, Doylestown AAW, Pa Craft Guild, 80-2000. *Teaching:* Demonstrations, CR Sch System, Neshaminy, Central Buck, PA. *Awards:* Hon mention, Woodmere Art Mus, 78; New Sculptor, Phillips Mill, 79; hon mention, Doylestown Art League, 85. *Mem:* Artsbridge; Jane Michener Art Mus; Doylestown Art League (juried mem); Cult Arts Center, Bucks, Co; Pa Guilds of Craftsmen (juried mem). *Media:* Acrylics, GA Marble. *Interests:* Music, shows, tennis. *Publ:* Buck Co Courier Times, Art Sec, 77-90; Intelligencer, Art, 80-2000; Philadelphia Inquirer (bull), 90; New Hope Gazette, Art, 2002; Town & Country. *Dealer:* Philadelphia Art Mus Gallery of Sales; Jane Anthony Gallery 15 S State St Newtown PA 18940. *Mailing Add:* 310 E Winchester Ave Langhorne PA 19047

BUSARD, ROBERTA ANN
PAINTER, SCULPTOR
b Muskegon, Mich, Apr 20, 1952. *Study:* Study under Victor A S Robinson, 69; San Francisco Art Inst, 70-73; Silvermine Coll Art, 71; Art Inst Boston, 71; Experimental Etching Studio Boston, 71 & 77; Laguna Beach Coll Art & Design, 72; Eastern Mich Univ, 72; Arica Inst, Boston, 74-75 & New York, 75; Mass Coll Art, BFA, 77; Wayne State Univ, MFA, 98; Tamalpa Inst, 2005. *Work:* US West Telecommunications, Denver; Diekmann & Assoc Ltd, Chicago; Sales, Goodloe & Golden, Atlanta; Anchorage Mus Hist & Art; Thomas M Morrisey/KATZ Television, Chicago. *Exhib:* 50th Nat Ann Midyear Painting Exhib, Butler Inst Am Art, 86; A World of Maps, Anchorage Mus Hist & Art, 94-95; Art in Embassies Prog, Am Embassy, Kuwait, 95-98; Selections NGO Forum, Elite Gallery, Moscow, 95; NGO Forum, Nat Mus Woman in the Arts, 96; and many others. *Pos:* Founding mem, exhib & bus comts, Vt Artists Collective, Burlington, 89-90; cur, The Black & White Project, Vt Women's Caucus for Art, 89-91; founding dir, The Kids Art Studio, S Burlington, 90-91; leader, No Limits for Women in the Arts, Ann Arbor, Mich, 91-92; exhib comt mem, Detroit Focus Gallery, 94-95; founder, Mich Woman's Caucus for Art, 94, pres, 94-95,

co-pres, 96; dir found, Wild Heart Designs LLC, Ann Arbor, Mich, 98-; creative dir, Body Waves, Ferndale, Mich, 2006-. *Teaching:* Int Sch Genoa, Italy, 76; Single Mothers' Project, Burlington, 90; The Kid's Art Studio, South Burlington, 90-91; guest lectr, Univ Mich, 92; Go Like the Wind Sch, Ann Arbor, 93-94; The Women's Art Project, Ann Arbor, 92-94; artist-in-residence, Summer Sch Sch Art Inst Chicago Ox-Bow, Saugatuck, Mich, 95. *Awards:* Jurors' Choice, Mary Mellor Mem Fund Award for Painting Mixed Media & Drawing, San Francisco Women Artists Gallery, 94; Jurors' Choice Award, Paper Stars Nat Women's Exhib, San Francisco Women Artists, 94; Thomas C Rumble Graduate Fels, Wayne State Univ, 96-98. *Bibliog:* Marika Christenson (auth), Busard-Thompson Show at Margolis Gallery, Arts & Entertainment, Co, 84; Nancy Booth Stringer (auth), Roberta Ann Busard: The art of poetic form, Art Light, J Mich, 12/92; John Carlos Cantu (auth), Busard's Paintings, Sculptures Worth Seeing at Arts Council Loft, Ann Arbor News, 3/95. *Mem:* Coll Art Asn; Nat Women's Caucus Art; Chicago Artists Coalition; Nat Mus Women Arts; Int Sculpture Inst. *Media:* Miscellaneous Media. *Publ:* Contribr, New letters, Vol 59, No 4 (Etching Series, 71 & 77), Univ Mo Press, Kansas City, 93; contribr, Danahy Ed, Tampa Review (cover & interior art), Univ Tampa Pres, 2008. *Mailing Add:* P O Box 130051 Ann Arbor MI 48113

BUSCH, RITA MARY
PAINTER, SCULPTOR
b Middletown, RI, July 14, 1926. *Study:* Watercolor workshops: Robert Wood, 72, Charles Reid, 75 & Doug Walton, 85, Jane Burnham, 93 & Margaret M Martin, 94. *Work:* Fidelity Nat Bank, Oklahoma City; Presby Hosp Found, Oklahoma City; Consolidated Insurance Co, Tulsa, Okla; Country Club Publ, Oklahoma City; Weyerhauser Corp Hq. *Comn:* Watercolor paintings, Dorothea Land, Oklahoma City, 86; watercolor painting, Preston Nichols, Moore, Okla, 86; pastel portrait, Mrs Jack J Wells, Oklahoma City, 86; watercolor painting, (World Neighbors, Commemorative Piece), Mr & Mrs Douglas Ormseth, NY, 87; Watercolor painting, House of Hunan, Norman, Okla. *Exhib:* Okla Art Guild, North Park Mall, Oklahoma City, 84; Newport Art Festival, RI, 84, 86 & 94; Nat League Am Pen Women, Pirates Alley, Oklahoma City, 86; Okla Watercolor Traveling Exhib, 86; Narragansett Art Festival, RI, 94. *Pos:* Jr art coordr, State Fair Okla, 76-90. *Teaching:* Teacher, watercolor, St Lukes Sch Continuing Ed, Oklahoma City, 86, Geatches Art Sch, Oklahoma City, 86 & Arts Annex, Oklahoma City, 88-89; artist-in-residence, Skyview Elem Sch, Yukon, Okla, 90. *Awards:* Equal Merit Award, Okla Art Guild Juried Show, 84; First Place Watercolor & Oils, McAlester Art Fest, McAlester Art Guild, 81; First Place Pastel, Pen Women's Show, Nat League Am Penwomen, 86. *Mem:* Okla Art Guild (3rd vpres, 76-77, 2nd vpres Shows, 77-79, pres, 79-80); Okla Watercolor Asn; Nat League Am Pen Women, (pres, 90-92). *Media:* Watercolor, Pastels, Metal, Cast. *Dealer:* Margo K Shorney Shorney Gallery Fine Art 6616 N Olie Oklahoma City OK 73116. *Mailing Add:* 1220 N Glade Oklahoma City OK 73127-4158

BUSH, CHARLES ROBERT See Robb, Charles

BUSH, JILL LOBDILL
PAINTER
b Grand Island, Nebr, May 11, 1942. *Study:* Tex Tech Univ, BA (adv art & design), 64. *Work:* Collection five paintings, First Fed Savings & Loan, Ft Smith, Ark; Holt Crock Clinic, Ft Smith, Ark, 80; Peace oil painting, Harris Methodist HEB Hosp, Ctr Women's Health, Bedford, Tex, 91. *Comn:* Dr OJ Wallenman Jr mem portrait, St Joseph Hosp Drs, Ft Worth, 79; Marion Day Mullins DAR portrait, Ft Worth Woman's Club, 80; Brig Gen Victor Carey, portrait, Darby's Rangers Mus, Ft Smith, Ark, 80; Coach Indian Jim Malone, portrait, Southern La State Univ, Hammond, 80; Dr Paul Parham mem portrait, TCU Libr Asn, Ft Worth, 87. *Exhib:* Knickerbocker 29th Ann, Nat Arts Club, NY, 79; Pastel Soc Am Exhib, Copley Mus, Boston, 79; 1st Ann Main St Tex Invitational, Ft Worth, 86; Pastel Soc Am Invitational, 3rd Salon Des Pastellists, Lille, France, 87; PSA Invitational Exhib, Ashland Area Gallery, Ky, 89; and others. *Teaching:* Instr figure drawing & oil painting, Ft Worth Art Mus Sch, 65-70; instr figure drawing & oil painting, Ft Worth Woman's Club, 73-76, instr oil, pastel & drawing, 74-79. *Awards:* Pastel Soc Am Award, San Marcus Nat, 79; Schwann Weber Award, Pastel Soc Am Eighth Ann, 80; First Place, Pastel Soc SW Ann, 85. *Bibliog:* Madlyn-Ann Woolwich (auth), Pastel Interpretations, Northlight Bks, 92; Madlyn-Ann Woolwich (auth), Profiting from children's portraits, Artists Mag, 10/95; Madlyn-Ann Woolwich (auth), The Art of Pastel Portraiture, Watson Guptill, 96. *Mem:* Pastel Soc Am; Pastel Soc SW. *Media:* Pastel, Oil. *Specialty:* Children's portraits. *Publ:* Contribr, Pastel Interpretations, Northlight Bks, 92-93; Still Life Techniques, Northlight Bks, 94; Art of Pastel Portraiture, Watson Guptill, 96. *Mailing Add:* 6440 Curzon Fort Worth TX 76116

BUSH, MARTIN H
MUSEUM DIRECTOR, HISTORIAN
b Amsterdam, NY, Jan 24, 1930. *Study:* State Univ NY Albany, BA & MA, 58; Syracuse Univ, PhD, 66. *Collection Arranged:* Photo Realism: Rip-Off or Reality, 75; George Grosz, 75; Wayne Thiebaud, 75; Robert Goodnough, 75; Richard Pousette-Dart, 75; Duane Hanson, 76; W Eugene Smith, 77; Milton Avery, 78; Joan Miro, 78; Louise Nevelson, 78; Theodoros Stamos, 79; Kenneth Noland, 80; Figures of Contemporary Sculpture 1970-1990, 92; Kunst Haus Wien, Vienna, Austria, 94; and many others. *Pos:* Dir, E A Ulrich Mus Art, Wichita State Univ, 71-89, vpres acad resource develop, 74-89; pres, ACA Galleries, 89-93, Martin Bush Fine Arts Inc, 93-. *Teaching:* Instr, Syracuse Univ, 63-65, asst dean, 65-70. *Awards:* Wichitan of the Year, Wichita Sun, 76; Outstanding Educator, Kans Art Educ Asn, 79; Outdoor Sculpture collection named after Martin H Bush, Wichita State Univ, 92. *Mem:* Am Asn Art Mus; Coll Art Asn; Art Dealers Asn Am. *Res:* 20th century American art. *Publ:* Auth, Ben Shahn, Syracuse Univ, 68, & Dorris Cesar, 70; Duane Hanson, 76; Ernest Trova, 77; Robert Goodnough, Abbeville, 82; The Photographs of Gordon Parks, Ulrich Mus Art, 83; Philip Reisman: People are His Passion, Ulrich Mus Art, 86; and many articles, brochures and catalogs. *Mailing Add:* 117 77th St 7C New York NY 10021-1824

BUSHNELL, KENNETH WAYNE
PAINTER, EDUCATOR
b Los Angeles, Calif, Oct 16, 1933. *Study:* Univ Calif, Los Angeles, BA (art), 56; Univ Hawaii, MFA (painting), 60. *Work:* Honolulu Acad Art, Hawaii State Found Cult & Arts; Bibliot Nat, Paris; S Guggenheim Mus, NYC; Whitney Mus Am Art; MOMA, NY. *Comn:* Nieman Marcus (mural), 2001; steel sculpture Pearl Ridge Ctr, Hawaii, 84; two 23 ft wall reliefs, Kaiser Clinic Honolulu, 86; Kalakaua Ctr Proj, five wall reliefs 20 ft x 9 ft, Honolulu, 89; Painting on glass, 9 ft x 16 ft, Japan Travel Bureau, Honolulu, 89; Four Panels 6 ft x 17 ft mural project, First Hawaiian Bank, Main Branch, Honolulu; mural, Honolulu Airport, Inter Island Terminal, 2001. *Exhib:* Painting USA: The Figure, NY Mus Mod Art, 62; Baltimore Mus Art, 62; Drawings USA, St Paul Art Ctr, Minn, 63; 158th Ann Exhib, Pa Acad Fine Arts, Philadelphia, 63; NW Printmakers Ann, Seattle Mus & Portland Mus, 64; New Talent in the West, Salt Lake City Art Ctr, 68; Calif-Hawaii Exhib, San Diego Mus, 70; Int Print Biennial, Krakow, Poland, 74; Int Print Biennial, Honolulu Acad Art, 78-82; solo exhibs, Contemp Arts Ctr, Honolulu, Hawaii, 65 & 86, 92, Honolulu Acad Art, 68 & 73, 2000, Sande Webster Gallery, Philadelphia, 81, 85, 88 & 92, Meissner Editions, Hamburg, 84, Maghi Betini Gallery, Amsterdam, 84 & Karen Fesel Gallery, Dusseldorf, WGer, 90, Contemp Art Ctr. *Pos:* Prof Emer Univ of Hawaii; Prof Art Emer, Univ of Hawaii at Manoa. *Teaching:* Prof art painting, Univ Hawaii, 1961-1999; prof art painting, C W Post Ctr, Long Island Univ, 78-79 & 83; chmn, Dept Art Univ Art Manoa, 91-. *Awards:* Purchase Awards, Honolulu Acad Art, 1968, 1986, 2001; First Award Painting, Calif-Hawaii Exhib, San Diego Mus, 74; Hawaii State Found Purchase Awards, 75, 81, 84, 86, 87, 2000, 06; Honolulu Acad Arts Biennial, The Mescaline Award for Painting. *Mem:* Honolulu Printmaker's & Soc Am Graphic Artists; Am Abstract Artists. *Media:* Oil, Acrylic Polymer . *Collection:* Whitney Mus of Am Art, Monk, NY; S Guggenheim Mus; Fogg Mus, Harvard Univ; Honolulu Academy of Arts, Hawaii State Foundation on Culture and the Arts; IBM Collection, New York City. *Dealer:* Fine Art Associates Ward Ctr Honolulu HI 96814; Karen Fezel Gallerie Dusseldorf Ger. *Mailing Add:* 2081 Keeaumoku St Honolulu HI 96822

BUSHNELL, KENNETH WAYNE
PAINTER
b Los Angeles, Calif, Oct 16, 1933. *Study:* Univ Ill, BA, 1970; The Barnes Found, 1976-1978; Mass Coll of Art, studied under Patricia Tobacco Forrester, 2001. *Work:* Widener Univ Mus of Art, Chester, Pa; Colgate Palmolive Corp, NYC; Pfizer Inc, Morris Plains, NJ; Sankyo Pharma Inc, Parsippany, NJ; Senior Care & Activities Center, Montclair, NJ; Becton Dickinson, Mountain Lakes, NJ. *Comn:* CBS Inc, NY, 1983. *Exhib:* Flora, Univ City Arts League, Philadelphia, Pa, 1980; Montclair Art Colony, Past & Present, Montclair Art Mus, Montclair, NJ, 1997; Allied Artists Mems Exhib, Butler Inst Am Art, Youngstown, Ohio, 2001; Connections, Kunstlerbund, Graz, Austria, 2004; Butler 69th Midyear, Butler Inst Am Art, Youngstown, Ohio; Allied Artists Am 93rd Ann Exhib, Nat Arts Club, New York, 2006; Visions in Watercolor, Dupre Gallery, Montclair, NJ, 2006; Allied Artists Am Invitational Exhib, Bennington Ctr Arts, Vt, 2007. *Collection Arranged:* Watercolor in Tuscany, 2014. *Pos:* Pres, PS Art Tours, Montclair, NJ, 2005-; watercolor workshops, Les Pradailles, France & Gold Coast Watercolor Soc, Fort Lauderdale, Fla, 2006; Watercolor Jour in Tuscany, 2011; Artist in Res, Strickley Mus, 2012. *Teaching:* Instr, watercolor, Adult Sch of Montclair, NJ, 1995-2005; instr, Montclair Art Mus, 1999-; watercolor instr, Visual Arts Ctr, Summit, NJ, 2007-; Cent Jersey Art Studios, Cranford, NJ, 2007-; Canyon Ranch, 2010, 2011; NY Open Ctr, 2011. *Awards:* 1st Prize Watercolor, The Art Show, Town of Montclair, 1988; 1st Prize Watercolor, Art in the Park, Montclair Co-Op Sch, 1990; Best in Show, 5th Ann Juried Show, Louisa Melrose Gallery, 2004. *Bibliog:* Sheryl Weinstein (auth), Watercolorist Showcases Blooming Creations, Star Ledger, 1997; William Zimmer (auth), Three Rare Invitations to Inner Sanctum, NY Times, 1997; Teri Murphy (auth), Louisa Melrose Gallery Presents Art Blooms, Nouveau, 2005. *Mem:* Women Artists of Montclair (publicity), 1992-2003; Studio Montclair Inc (publicity), 1995-2005; Artists Fel, 1997-; Allied Artists of Am (dir watercolor), 97-. *Media:* Watercolor, Acrylics. *Interests:* reading, travel, gardening. *Dealer:* Dupre Gallery 127 Valley Rd Montclair NJ 07042; Essex Fine Arts 13 S Fullerton Montclair NJ 07042. *Mailing Add:* 184 Christopher St Montclair NJ 07042

BUSINO, ORLANDO FRANCIS
CARTOONIST
b Binghamton, NY, Oct 10, 1926. *Study:* State Univ Iowa, BA, 52. *Pos:* Cartoonist, Sat Eve Post, McCall's, Ladies Home J, Sat Rev, Look, True, Argosy, Boys' Life, Family Circle & other US & foreign mags. *Awards:* Best Mag Cartoonist of Year, Nat Cartoonists Soc, 65, 67 & 68. *Mem:* Nat Cartoonists Soc; Mag Cartoonists Guild. *Mailing Add:* 12 Shadblow Hill Rd Ridgefield CT 06877-5221

BUSSCHE, WOLF VON DEM
PHOTOGRAPHER, PAINTER
b Ger; US citizen. *Study:* Columbia Col, studied art hist, 56-62; Columbia Univ Sch Painting & Sculpture, 59-62; Art Students League, 61-62; self-taught in photog. *Work:* San Francisco Mus Mod Art; Mus Mod Art, Int Ctr Photog, Metrop Mus, NY; George Eastman House, Rochester, NY; NY Pub Libr; Bancroft; and others. *Exhib:* Vision & Expression, George Eastman House, Rochester, NY, 69; Soc Encouragement Contemp Art Award Exhib, San Francisco Mus Mod Art, 80; Int Triennial Exhib Photog, Musee d'art et d'hist, Fribourg, Switz, 81; Metrop Mus, NY, 82; Pleasures & Terrors of Domestic Comfort, MoMA, NY, 91; MNS of Photographic Arts, San Diego, Calif, 2000; Mus de L'elysee, Lausanne, Switz, 2002; numerous one-person exhibs. *Awards:* Who's Who in the West, 91. *Bibliog:* Carole Kismaric (auth), article, Camera, No 10, 71; Jerome Tarshis (auth), article, Art in Am, 1/81; Thomas Albright (auth), article, Art News, 4/82. *Media:* All. *Mailing Add:* 841 Contra Costa Ave Berkeley CA 94707

BUSTO, ANA MARIE
PHOTOGRAPHER, SCULPTOR
b Bilbao, Spain, Jan 15, 1952. *Study:* Barcelona, Spain, BA (journalism). *Exhib:* Counter-Representations, Brooklyn Mus, 85, Dream Machinations in Am, Minor Injury, Brooklyn, NY, 90; Race and Cult, City Coll NY, 91; one-person shows, Entre Naturalezas, Forun, Tarragona, Spain, 92, Love Song, Rekalde, Bilbao, Spain, 94 &

2000, Working Shoes, Spais, Gerona, Spain & El Museo Del Barrio, NY, 96, Transportar, Museo de Arte Carrillo Gil, Mexico City, Mex, 97 & Night Flights, Metronom, Fundacio Privada d'Art Contemporani, Barcelona, Spain; Am Discover Spain 1, Spanish Inst, NY, 92; Fragments, Koldo Mitxelena, San Sebastian & Macba, Museu d'Art Contemporani, Barcelona, Spain, 96; Pierogi Files, Brooklyn Mus, NY, 98; Tal Como Nos Vemos, Circulo de Bellas Artes, Madrid, Spain, 99; The Eyes Have It, Porter Troupe Gallery, San Diego, 2000; Women at Work, Southwester Col, Calif, 2001; Playa Giron, Valencia Biennale, Spain, 2001; and many others. *Awards:* NY Found Arts, 90; Nat Endowments Arts, 90; Spain Ministerio de Cultura, 97. *Publ:* Village Voice, New Observations, 85; NY Times, La Vanguardia, Spain, 89, El Pais, Spain, 90. *Mailing Add:* 107 Roebling Brooklyn NY 11211

BUSZKO, IRENE J
PAINTER
b Brooklyn, NY, Sept 22, 1947. *Study:* Pratt Inst, BFA, 69; Queens Col, MFA, 72. *Work:* Lehman Brothers Collection; Lloyd's Bank Int, NY; Chemical Bank & Citibank, Citicorp Ctr, NY; Mitsubishi Int, NY; Exxon, Tex. *Exhib:* Group Exhibs: 157th Ann Exhib, Nat Acad Design, NY, 82; Suburban Landscape (with Rosemary Hamilton), Suffolk Community Col, 2007; one-person exhib, Tatistcheff & Co, NY, 82, 85, 89, 94, 96 & 2001, Plandome Gallery, NY, 92, Queens Coun Arts, Woodhaven, NY, 94; Three Painters from NY, Bloomsbury Theater, London, Eng, 85; The Richmond Hill Series, Queens Mus, Flushing, NY, 86. *Pos:* Artist-in-residencies, Bear Mt Palisades Interstate Park, 77, Altos de Chavon, Dominican Republic, 83, Alfred Univ, NY, 83, Yosemite Nat Park, Calif, 93; Artist art colonies, Ossabaw Island Project, 79, Virginia Ctr for Arts, 83, Yaddo, 86-91, Blue Mountain Ctr, 2000, Millay Colony, 2003. *Teaching:* Instr painting, Nat Acad Design, 87-88. *Awards:* Creative Artist Pub Serv Grant, NY State Coun Arts, 76. *Media:* Oil on Canvas. *Publ:* Article, Am Artist Mag, 4/94. *Mailing Add:* 652 Broadway New York NY 10012

BUTCHKES, SYDNEY
PAINTER, SCULPTOR
b Covington, Ky, Oct 13, 1922. *Study:* Cincinnati Art Acad, Ohio; Art Students League; New Sch Social Res, NY. *Work:* Metrop Mus; Brooklyn Mus, NY; Cincinnati Art Mus; Wadsworth Atheneum, Hartford, Conn; Nat Collection Fine Arts, Smithsonian Inst, Washington, DC; and others. *Comn:* Sculpture for lobby of Financial Progs Bldg, Denver, 69; hanging sculpture for bar of Ritz Carlton Hotel, Boston, 69; painting for lobby of Skidmore, Owings, Merrill, Chicago, 70; paintings, World Trade Ctr, NY & Continental Tel Co, Washington, DC. *Exhib:* Art for the Collector, San Francisco Mus Art, 65; Painting Without a Brush, Inst Contemp Art, Boston, 65; Painting Out from the Wall, Des Moines Art Ctr, Iowa, 67; Plastic as Plastic, Mus Contemp Crafts, NY, 69; Mus Acquisitions, Colorado Springs Art Ctr, 69; Art, Design and the Modern Corp, Nat Mus Am Art, Washington, DC, 85. *Awards:* Am Crafts Coun Hon Fel. *Mem:* Abstr Am Artists. *Media:* Acrylic Paint; Wood. *Mailing Add:* PO Box 351 Sagaponack NY 11962-0351

BUTERA, VIRGINIA FABBRI
CURATOR, HISTORIAN
b Norristown, Pa, Nov 15, 1951. *Study:* Trinity Col, Conn, BA, 73; Johns Hopkins Univ, MA (art hist), 75; City Univ NY, MPhil, 91, PhD program, ongoing. *Collection Arranged:* The Graphic Side of the Second Empire, Philadelphia Mus Art, 78; The Great Am Fan Show (auth, catalog), Lerner-Heller Gallery, NY, 81; The Folding Image: Screens by Western Artists of the 19th and 20th Centuries (coauth, catalog), Nat Gallery Art, Washington, DC & Yale Univ Art Gallery, 84-85; Contemporary Screens (auth, catalog), Contemp Arts Ctr, Cincinnati, Lowe Art Mus, Toledo Art Mus & City Gallery Contemp Art, Raleigh, 86-88. *Pos:* Fel, Nat Mus Am Art, Washington, DC, 76-77; asst, Dept Prints, Drawings & Photographs, Philadelphia Mus Art, 78-79, asst to dir, 79-81; co-chair & bd trustees, AIR Gallery, New York, 84-85; curatorial consult, Everything for Industry, Jersey City Mus, 88-89; bd trustees, NJ Ctr Visual Arts, 93-95. *Teaching:* Lectr art hist, Col St Elizabeth, Madison, NJ, 98-99. *Awards:* Smithsonian Mus Fel, 76-77; Nat Endowment Arts Grant, 78-79; First Prize, 50th Annual Frick Symposium, 90. *Mem:* Coll Art Asn; Asn Am Mus. *Res:* European and American painting and sculpture, 1860 to the present. *Publ:* Auth, The fan as form and image in contemporary art, 81 & Investigating Jim Jacobs' sculpture and painting, 86, Arts Mag; Contemporary screens, Art Mus Asn Am, 86; Jim Jacobs: Screens, Mus of Art, Ft Lauderdale; co-auth, The Folding Image: Screens By Western Artists of the Nineteenth and Twentieth Centuries, New Haven: Yale Univ Art Gallery, 84. *Mailing Add:* 18 Fay Pl Summit NJ 07901

BUTLER, CHARLES THOMAS
MUSEUM DIRECTOR, CURATOR
b Pearisburg, Va, 1951. *Study:* Univ Del, with William Inness Homer, BA (cum laude), 1976; Univ NMex, with Beaumont Newhall & Tom Barrow, grad studies, 1976-78. *Collection Arranged:* Recent Graphics from Am Print Shops (auth, catalog), 1986; Michael Eastman: Color Photographs (auth, catalog), 1988; Gardens of Paradise: Oriental Prayer Rugs (textiles), 1989; Enduring Impressions: Prints, 1960-1990 (graphics), 1990; Dick Arentz: Outside the Mainstream (photographs; auth catalog), 1991; Close to the Surface: The Expressionist Prints of Edvard Munch & Richard Bosman (graphics; auth catalog), 1996; Body and Soul: Contemporary Southern Figures (painting & sculpture; auth, catalog), 1997. *Pos:* Asst dir, Sioux City Art Ctr, Ind, 1979-85; exec dir, Mitchell Mus, Mt Vernon, Ill, 1985-88; dir, Huntington Mus Art, WVa, 1988-94, exec dir, currently, Columbus Mus, GA, 1994-. *Awards:* Prof Year Award, Ga Asn Mus & Galleries, 1998. *Mem:* Midwest Mus Conf; Am Asn Mus; Southeastern Mus Conf (exec comt, 1989-, vpres, 1994-96, pres, 1996-98); WVa Asn Mus (exec comt, 90-93); Mus Trustee Asn Adv Counc (chair, 1998-2003); Asn Art Mus Dirs. *Media:* Photography, Graphics, Contemporary Painting, Drawing. *Publ:* auth, New Talent, New York, Sioux City Art Ctr, 1984; coauth, Edward McCullough: The Elegy Series, Mitchell Mus, 1987; auth, Close to the Surface: Prints by Edvard Munch and Richard Rosman, Columbus Mus, 1996; gen text ed, Heartland: Paintings by Bo Bartlett, 1978-2002, 2002; gen, Am Art in the Columbus Mus: Painting, Sculpture and Decorative Arts, 2003; gen text ed, Lines of Discovery, 250 Years Am Drawing in Columbus Mus, 2006. *Mailing Add:* 1251 Wynnton Rd Columbus GA 31906

BUTLER, CONNIE
CURATOR
Study: Scripps Coll, Claremont, BA (art hist); Univ Calif, Berkeley, MA (art hist). *Collection Arranged:* The Power of Suggestion, Narrative and Notation in Contemporary Drawing, 1996-97; Afterimage, Drawing Through Process, 1999; Willem de Kooning, Tracing the Figure, 2002; Robert Smithson, 2004; WACK! Art of the Feminist Revolution, 2007. *Pos:* Cur, Artists Space & Mus Contemp Art, Los Angeles, formerly; chief cur drawings, Mus Mod Art, New York

BUTLER, DAVID
MUSEUM DIRECTOR
Study: Fla State Univ, BA (Art History), 1976, MA (Art History), 1980; Wash State Univ, PhD, 1991. *Pos:* Cur asst, John & Mable Ringling Mus Art, 1978-1979; educ coordr, registrar Mus Art & Archeology, Univ Mo, 1980-1984, asst dir, 1984-1986; asst proj coordr, St Louis Arts in Transit, Metrolink Light Rail, 1987-1988; dir, Emerson Gallery, Hamilton Coll, 1992-1995; dir, Swope Art Mus, Terre Haute, Ind, 1995-2000; dir, Ulrich Mus Art, Wichita State Univ, 2000-2006; exec dir, Knoxville Mus Art, 2006-. *Teaching:* Instr art history, Univ Mo, 1988-1991, Wash Univ, St Louis, 1987-1992. *Mem:* secy, Friends of Hist, Allen Chapel, 1997-2000; design coun, City of Wichita, 2003-2006; bd dirs, Trees, Inc, 1996-2000; vpres, Arts Illiana, 1995-2000; Asn Coll & Univ Mus & Galleries, bd secy, 2000-2005; Am Asn Mus. *Mailing Add:* Knoxville Museum of Art 1050 Worlds Fair Pk Dr Knoxville TN 37916

BUTLER, GEORGE TYSSEN
PHOTOGRAPHER, FILMMAKER
b Chester, England, 1943. *Study:* Univ NC, BA (English), 1966; Hollins Col, Va, MA (English), 1967. *Exhib:* Films: Pumping Iron, 1977; Pumping Iron II: The Women, 1983; In the Blood, 1989; The Endurance: Shackleton's Legendary Antarctic Expedition, 2000; Shackleton's Antarctic Adventure, 2001; Going Upriver: The Long War of John Kerry, 2004; Roving Mars, 2006; Group exhib, Whitney Biennial, Whitney Mus Art, 2006; The Lord God Bird, 2008; Tiger, Tiger, 2014. *Pos:* Writer, reporter, Newsweek Mag, NYC, 1969; freelance writer, photog, NH, 1970-75; pres, White Mt Films, NH & NY, 1975-. *Awards:* Nat Academies Communication award, 2008; Nat Bd Review award, Best Documentary Film for Endurance Film, 2001. *Mem:* Fellow Royal Geographic Soc, London; Century Assn, NYC. *Interests:* Collecting antique photographs; farming; hunting; fishing; mountain climbing. *Publ:* Photog contribr (with Charles Gaines) Pumping Iron, 1974; auth, photog, Schwarzenegger-A Portrait, 1990; ed (with John F. Kerry), The New Soldier, 1971; auth, photog, John Kerry: A Portrait, 2004. *Mailing Add:* White Mountain Films PO Box 61 Holderness NH 03245-0061

BUTLER, JAMES D
PRINTMAKER, PAINTER
b Ft Dodge, Iowa, Aug 30, 1945. *Study:* Omaha Univ, Nebr, BS, 1967; Univ Nebr, Lincoln, MFA, 1970. *Work:* Brooklyn Mus, New York; Brit Mus, London, Eng; Metrop Mus Art, New York; Chicago Art Inst; Whitney Mus Am Art, New York; Northwestern Hosp Collection, Chicago, 2006. *Comn:* First Ill Print Comn, Ill Arts Coun, 1973; Ill State Libr, Springfield, 1991; Gen Services Admin/US Post Office/Courthouse, Oklahoma City, 1993; Fed Reserve Bank Chicago, 2002; MD Anderson Cancer Res Hosp, Houson, 2004. *Exhib:* Corp Collections Show, Minn Mus of Art, St Paul, 1972; Prints: Midwest Invitational, Walker Art Ctr, Minneapolis, 1973; 19th Nat Print Exhib, Brooklyn Mus, 1974; Mod Printmaking Exhib of Contemp Prints, Bevier Gallery, Rochester Inst of Technol, NY, 1974; New Am Colorists, World Print Coun, San Francisco, 1981; 30 Am Printmakers, Columbus, Ohio, 1982; Rapture/Rupture: Life Along the Mississippi River, Anna Lamar Switzer Visual Arts Ctr, Fla, 2007, Lakeview Mus Arts & Sci, Peoria, Ill, Forum Gallery, New York & Dubuque Mus Art, Iowa. *Teaching:* Asst prof, Southern Ill Univ, Edwardsville, 1970-76; assoc prof, Ill State Univ, Normal, 1976-81, prof, 1981-2000, disting prof, 2000-. *Awards:* Robert Cooke Endowment Award, 1971 Mid-States Art Exhib, Evansville Mus of Arts & Sci, Ind, 1971; First Place, Fine Art of Printmaking, Lexington, Ky, Nat Soc of Arts & Lett, 1971; Nat Endowment Arts, 1975-76 & 1979-80; Ill Arts Coun Fel, 1985 & 1989; Anna Lamar Switzer Disting Artist, Anna Lamar Switzer Ctr Visual Arts, Pensacola, Fla, 2007. *Bibliog:* Clinton Adams & Susan Ellis (auths), Drawing Color Separations on Surfaced Mylar, Tamarind Tech Papers, 1974; Experiments in affordable custom lithography, Print News, Vol 3, 2-3/81; Dr Linda S Ferber, Kristin H McKinsey (auths), Views Along the Mississippi River: James D Butler, Lakeview Mus Arts & Sci, Peoria, Ill, 1998; Grace Glueck (auth), James D Butler-Views Along the Mississippi River, NY Times, 7/10/98. *Mem:* Mid-Am Coll Art Asn; Coll Art Asn; Mid-Am Print Coun; Southern Graphics Coun; Boston Printmakers. *Media:* Lithography; Drawing; Oil. *Publ:* Andrea Guthmann, Arts Along the Mississippi River, WTTV, Chicago, 1/03. *Dealer:* Forum Gallery 745 5th Ave New York NY 10151; Tory Folliard Gallery 233 N Milwaukee St Milwaukee WI 53202

BUTLER, JOSEPH THOMAS
CURATOR, WRITER
b Winchester, Va, Jan 25, 1932. *Study:* Univ Md, BS, 54; Univ Ohio, MA, 55; Univ Del, MA (Winterthur Fel), 57. *Exhib:* Am Furniture from Westchester Collections: 1650-1880, Katonah Gallery, Katonah, NY, 86; The Am Eagle: An Enduring Symbol, Katonah Gallery, Katonah, NY, 89; Am Painted Furniture, Scarsdale Historical Soc, 90; Visions of Washington Irving, 91. *Collection Arranged:* Divided Loyalties, Philipsburg Manor, North Tarrytown, NY, 76-79 & Four Centuries of History, A

Decade of Restoration. *Pos:* Cur & dir Collections, Hist Hudson Valley, Tarrytown, NY, 57-, emer, 93-; Am ed, The Connoisseur, 68-78; ed bd, Art & Antiques, 78-83; adj prof mus studies, Fashion Inst Tech, NY, 86-97; adj prof, Columbia Univ, Grad Sch Archit, 1976-1986. *Teaching:* Adj assoc prof archit, Columbia Univ, 71-81. *Mem:* Furniture Hist Soc; Victorian Soc in Am; Am Ceramic Circle; The Century Asn; SAH. *Res:* Am decorative arts archit. *Publ:* Auth, American Antiques, 1800-1900, 65; Candleholders in America, 1650-1900, 67; coauth, The Arts in America, the 19th Century, 70; auth, Washington Irving's Sunnyside, 75; Van Cortlandt Manor, 78; Sleepy Hollow Restorations: A Cross Section of the Collection, 83; Field Guide to American Antique Furniture, 85; American Painted Furniture, 90. *Mailing Add:* 222 Martling Ave Tarrytown NY 10591-4756

BUTT, HARLAN W
SILVERSMITH, ENAMELIST

b Princeton, NJ, Mar 30, 1950. *Study:* Tyler Sch Art, with Stanley Lechtzin, BFA, 72; Southern Ill Univ, with Brent Kington, MFA, 74. *Work:* Southern Ill Univ, Carbondale. *Comn:* University mace & jazz band commemorative, NTex State Univ, Denton; University mace, Southwest Adventist Col, Keene, Tex. *Exhib:* Solo exhibs, Wichita Art Assoc, Wichita, Kans, 88, Seika-do Gallery, Kyoto, Japan, 82 & 85, Nat Ornamental Metal Mus, Memphis, 83 & Contemp Crafts Gallery, Portland, Ore, 86; Int Exhibition Enameling Art, Ueno Royal Mus, Tokyo, 85; Enamels Int, Long Beach Mus Art, Calif, 85; Biennale, La Maison des Arts, Laval, Can, 86. *Collection Arranged:* Kyoto Metal: An Exhib of Contemp Japanese Metalwork (auth, catalog), 83-84. *Teaching:* Lectr metalworking, San Diego State Univ, Calif, 75-76; prof metalworking, Univ NTex, Denton, 76-. *Awards:* Merit Award, Int Exhib Enameling Art Comt, 85. *Mem:* Soc NAm Goldsmiths; Am Crafts Coun; NTex Enamel Guild; Enamel Guild West. *Media:* Metal. *Mailing Add:* 2375 Wood Hollow Rd Denton TX 76208

BUTTER, TOM
SCULPTOR, INSTRUCTOR

b Amityville, NY, Oct 19, 1952. *Study:* Philadelphia Coll Art, BFA, 75; Wash Univ, St Louis, Mo, MFA, 77. *Work:* Acad Fine Arts, Philadelphia; Metrop Mus Art, NY; Chase Manhattan Bank; Walker Art Ctr, Minneapolis; Indianapolis Mus Art, Ind; Albright-Knox Art Gallery, Buffalo, NY. *Exhib:* Transformation of the Minimal Style, Sculpture Ctr, NY, 84; Solo exhibs, Curt Marcus Gallery, 86, 88, 91, 93 & 97, Nina Freundenheim Gallery, Buffalo, NY, 87 & 92, John Berggruen Gallery, San Francisco, 87-, Pence Gallery, Los Angeles, 88; Perspectives from Pennsylvania, Carnegie Mellon Univ Art Gallery, Pittsburgh, 87; Sculpture Inside Outside, Mus Fine Arts, Houston, 88-89; The 1980's A New Generation, Metrop Mus Art, NY, 88; Aronson Gallery, Parsons Sch of Design 99; and others. *Teaching:* Adj, Parsons Sch Design; assoc prof sculpture, RI Coll Design. 96-97; corp fac, Sculpture Prog, Parsons, Sch Design, 98-; coordr, Parsons Mus Fine Arts, currently. *Awards:* Nat Endowment Arts Grant, 80 & 82; NY Found Arts Grant, 87, 97; Silver Star Alumni Award, Univ Arts, Philadelphia; Print Project, Univ Arts, Philadelphia, 95, Washington Univ, St Louis, 96. *Bibliog:* Wade Saunders (auth), Interview with ten sculptors, Art Am, 11/85; Michael Brenson (auth), rev, NY Times, 3/91; Nancy Princenthall (auth), rev, Art Am, 12/93; George Melrod (auth), rev, Sculpture Mag, 1-2/94. *Interests:* Bookkeeping

BUTTERFIELD, DEBORAH KAY
SCULPTOR

b San Diego, Calif, May 7, 1949. *Study:* San Diego State Coll, Calif; Univ Calif, San Diego; Univ Calif, Davis, BA (with honors), 71, MFA, 73; Rocky Mountain Coll, DFA (hon), Billings, Mont, 97; Montana State Univ, DFA (hon), 98. *Hon Degrees:* Rocky Mountain Coll, Billings, Mont, Hon DFA, 97; Mont State Univ, Bozeman, Hon DFA, 98; Whitman Coll, Walla Walla, Wa, DFA, 2004. *Work:* Whitney Mus Am Art, Metrop Mus Art, NY; San Francisco Mus Contemp Art; Israel Mus, Jerusalem; Walker Art Ctr, Minneapolis; Denver Art Mus; Smithsonian Am Art Mus, Washington, DC; US Embassy, Ottawa, Can. *Comn:* Copley Square, Boston; Portland Airport, Ore; Univ Calif Los Angeles, Franklin Murphy Sculpture Garden; Denver Art Mus; Kans City (Mo) Zoo; White House, Washington, DC, 2000; Monte Carlo, Monaco, 2000; Smithsonian Inst, Washington; San Francisco Int Airport. *Exhib:* Solo exhibs, Seattle Art Mus, 81, Walker Art Ctr, Minneapolis, 81, Dallas Mus Fine Arts, 82, Oakland Mus, Calif, 83, (auth, catalog), San Diego Mus Art, 96, Bellevue Art Mus, Wash, 2001, Holter Mus Art, Helena, Mont, 2002, Abby M Taylor Sculpture, 2010; Group exhibs, 2 Sculptors, Univ Mus Berkeley, Calif, 74; Whitney Biennial & The Decade in Review, Whitney Mus Am Art, NY, 79; 8 Sculptors, Albright-Knox Gallery, Buffalo, 79; Israel Mus, Jerusalem, 80; Arco Ctr Visual Art, 81; Walker Art Ctr, Minneapolis, 82; Dallas Mus Fine Arts, 82; Oakland, 83; Mile of Sculpture, Chicago, 85; Contemp Art Ctr, Honolulu, 86; 20th Century Am Sculpture at the White House, Exhib VIII, 2000; Zwirner and Writh, NY City, 2006. *Teaching:* Asst prof, Mont State Univ, Bozeman, 79-83, adj prof, cons, 84-87; asst prof sculpture, Univ Wis, Madison, 75-76. *Awards:* John Simon Guggenheim Mem Fel, 80; Individual Artist Fel, Nat Ednownment Arts, 80; Golden Plate Award, Am Acad Achievement, 93. *Bibliog:* Kenneth Baker (auth), Galleries: Butterfield horses, San Francisco Chronicle, 5/28/94; Robert Gordon (auth), Deborah Butterfield, Harry N Abrams. *Mem:* Nat Acad. *Media:* Natural Materials, Steel. *Publ:* Auth, Horses: The Art of Deborah Butterfield, Chronicle Bks, 92. *Dealer:* Edward Thorp Gallery 210 Eleventh Ave New York NY 10001; Zolla Lieberman Gallery 325 W Huron Chicago IL 60610. *Mailing Add:* 11229 Cottonwood Rd Bozeman MT 59718

BUTTERLY, KATHY
SCULPTOR

b Amityville, NY, 1963. *Study:* Moore Coll Art, Philadelphia, BFA, 1986; Univ Calif, Davis, MFA, 1990. *Exhib:* Solo exhibs, Moore Coll Art, Philadelphia, 1992, Clay Studio, 1993, Franklin Parrasch Gallery, New York, 1994-1999, Bernard Toale Gallery, Boston, 2000, Tibor de Nagy Gallery, New York, 2002, 2004, 2007, 2011, Shoshana Wayne Gallery, Santa Monica, Calif, 2003; Group exhibs, Fourth Concorso Nazionale della Ceramica d'Arte: Savona-Fortezza Primiar, Savona, Italy, 1990; Contemp Ceramics, Bennington Coll Gallery, Vt, 1992; Talentborse Handwerk, Munich, 1994; Forms and Transformations of Clay, Queens Borough Pub Libr Gallery, Jamaica, NY, 1997; Byron Cohen Gallery Contemp Art, Kansas City, Mo, 2000, 2002; 15th Anniversary Exhib, Franklin Parrasch Gallery, New York, 2001; Kanazawa World Craft Forum, Japan, 2003; Very Familiar: Celebrating 50 Years of Collecting Decorative Arts, Carnegie Mus Art, Pittsburgh, 2004-2005; Pretty is as Pretty Does, SITE Santa Fe, 2009; Dirt on Delight Impulses that Form Clay, Inst Contemporary Art, Phila, Pa, 2009; Figuring Color, Inst Contemporary Art Boston, 2012. *Awards:* Anonymous Was a Woman Grant, 2002; Evelyn Shapiro Found Grant, 1993; Empire State Crafts Alliance Grant, 1995; NY Found Arts Fel, 1999 & 2009; Joan Mitchell Found Grant, 2009; Pollock-Krasner Found Grant, 2011; Contemporary Artist award, Smithsonian Am Art Mus, 2012. *Media:* Clay. *Dealer:* Lemberg Gallery 23241 Woodward Ave Ferndale MI 48220; Shoshana Wayne Gallery 2525 Michigan Ave B1 Santa Monica CA 90404. *Mailing Add:* c/o Tibor de Nagy Gallery 724 Fifth Ave New York NY 10019

BUTTI, LINDA
PAINTER, EDUCATOR

b Brooklyn, NY, Jan 15, 1951. *Study:* Brooklyn Col, New York, with Philip Pearlstein & William T Williams, BA, 72, MFA (painting), 75. *Work:* Art Network, Staten Island, NY; Iona Coll Permanent Collection of Art, New Rochelle, NY; Bell Atlantic, Atlanta, Ga; NBC Studios, NY; Staten Island Univ Hosp. *Comn:* Watercolor (mural, 4' x 5'), Catholic Telecommunication, NY, 88; wall mural, Network America; murals (two, 42" x 30"), Swanston Fine Arts Inc, Atlanta, Ga, 88. *Exhib:* Brooklyn '77 & Brooklyn '78, Brooklyn Mus, NY; solo exhibs, Newhouse Ctr Contemp Art, Snug Harbor Cult Ctr, NY, 85, New Visions, Princeton Univ, NJ, 89, St John's Univ, 93, SI Community Television Studios, 94 & Elaine Benson Gallery, 2000; Mem Exhib, Staten Island Mus, NY, 88; Contemp Spiritual Art Nat, Paul VI Inst Arts, Washington, 88; 51st Ann Artists Exhib, Guild Hall, Mus, Easthampton, NY, 89; Brenau Coll Nat Exhib; Elaine Benson Gallery, 2000; New World Gallery, 2004; Mohawk Valley Art Ctr, 2006. *Collection Arranged:* Women in Art, Art Lab, Staten Island, NY, 2000. *Pos:* Assoc prof art, City Univ NY, 2001-. *Teaching:* Assoc prof, St Johns Univ, 81-, Iona-Seton Col, 84-88 & LaGuardia Community Col, 88-90, Molloy Col, 94-; lectr, Bronx Community Col, 83-85, Cult Pluralism, LaGuardia Community Col, 89 & Seurat & European Art, Staten Island Mus, Staten Island Inst Art, 91-98 & Molloy Col, 94; art prof, Art Lab Sch, Snug Harbor Cult Ctr, Staten Island, NY. *Awards:* NY State Coun Arts Grant, 91-98; NY Dept Cult Affairs Grant, 93. *Bibliog:* M Fressola (auth), Best of Both Worlds, SI Advance, 92; Marion Weesberg (auth), Dan's Papers, Honoring the Artist, 12/99; Diane Cable (auth), Columns, Profile of Artist Linda Butti, 10/99. *Mem:* Women in Arts Inc (pres, 2005-); Cath Artists Am (vpres, 94-); Coll Art Asn. *Media:* Oil on Canvas, Mixed Media, digital art. *Specialty:* Digital artwork, New World Gallery, NY. *Interests:* Horticulture, Botan. *Collection:* Brenau Univ, NBC Studies, Mitsubishi Corp, St Vincent's Hosp. *Publ:* Auth, A few stars shine, NJ Star, 95. *Dealer:* Nancy Stein Gallery 340 W 57th St New York NY. *Mailing Add:* 65 Beverlyn Ave Staten Island NY 10301

BUTTS, H DANIEL, III
GALLERY DIRECTOR

b Pittsburgh, Pa, July 15, 1939. *Study:* Yale Univ, BA, 60, BFA, 61; Pa State Univ, MA, 62. *Pos:* Dir, Arts & Crafts Ctr Pittsburgh, 65-68; dir, Mansfield Art Ctr, 68-. *Teaching:* Instr hist art, painting & drawing, Shady Side Acad, Pittsburgh, 62-65. *Mailing Add:* 699 Sloane Ave Mansfield OH 44903-1836

BYARS, DONNA
SCULPTOR, COLLAGE ARTIST

b Rock Island, Ill. *Study:* Stephens Col, Columbia, Mo; Iowa State Univ, BA; Parsons Sch Design, NY. *Work:* Va Mus Fine Arts, Richmond; Bellevue Hosp Collection, NY; Pub Art Prog, Long Island Univ-C W Post; Santa Fe Mus; Chicago Art Inst. *Comn:* Site sculpture, Bard-Hudson Valley Studies, 78; site sculpture, New Wilderness Found, 78; site sculpture, Wave Hill, Bronx, NY, 79; Women & Wood, Katonah Mus, NY, 93. *Exhib:* Solo exhibs, 55 Mercer, 75, AIR Gallery, 77, 79, 84 & 87 & Hudson River Mus, 89; Aldrich Mus Contemp Art, Ridgefield, Conn, 75-76; Lunds Konsthall, Lunds, 81, & Kulturhurst, Stockholm, 82, Sweden; Schweinfurth Mus, Auburn, NY, 82; Va Mus Fine Art, 88; Hudson River Mus, 89; Max Hutchinson's Sculpture Fields, 88-96; In Three Dimensions: Women Sculptors of the 90s, Snug Harbor Cult Ctr, Staten Island, NY, 96. *Pos:* Dir, Parsons Gallery, Parsons Sch Design, New York, 84-86. *Teaching:* Instr drawing, Parsons Sch Design, 76-92; instr collage, New Sch for Social Res, New York, 77-. *Awards:* Artist-in-Residence Grant, Palisades Interstate Park, Am the Beautiful Fund, Washington, 76; Creative Artists Pub Serv Program Fel, 82. *Bibliog:* Gloria Orenstein (auth), The Reflowering of the Goddess, Pergamon Press; James J Kelly (auth), The Sculptural Idea, Arts Rev; Lucy Lippard (auth), Overlay: Ancient Images & Contemporary Art, Pantheon Bks. *Mem:* Women's Caucus Art, NY; Coll Art Asn

BYERS, FLEUR
PAINTER

b Washington, DC. *Study:* Pomona Col, Claremont, Calif; BA, Univ Penn, Corcoran Gallery Art, Washington, DC, 51; Pa Acad Fine Arts, 59; studies with Elliot O'Hara. *Work:* Salomon Brothers, NY; Polyclinic Hosp, Harrisburg, Pa; Bank America, Boston, Mass; McNees, Wallace & Nurick, Harrisburg, Pa; Shumaker & Williams Ins Co, Camp Hill, Pa; and many pvt collections. *Exhib:* 11th Biennial Northeast Regional Exhib, Susquehanna Art Soc, Selinsgrove, Pa, 96, 12th Biennial, 98, 13th Biennial, 2001, 14th Biennial, 2004; 26th Ann Juried Exhib, York Art Asn, Pa, 96; Greater Lafayette Mus Art, Ind, 96; Sheldon Swope Mus Art, Terre Haute, Ind, 96; juried traveling exhib, Nat Asn Women Artists, 96-99 & 2002-2003; Lancaster Mus Art, Pa, 95 & 2002-2006; Saginaw Art Mus, Mich, 98; Purdue Univ Gallery, West Lafayette, Ind, 99; Midwest Mus Am Art, Elkart, Ind, 99; Laney Col, Oakland, Calif, 99; 8th Ann Nat Akron Soc of Artists Grand Exhib, Ohio, 98; Juried Exhib Doshi Gallery, Harrisburg, Pa, 98-99 & 2006-2010; Ann Juried Exhib York Art Asn, Pa, 98-2000,

2002-2003 & 2005; Ann Exhib Nat Asn Women Artists, NY, 99, 2002-2003 & 2005-2007, & 2012; 9th Ann Juried Art Exhib, Elizabethtown Col, Pa, 99; Ann Juried Exhib, State Ms of Pa, Harrisburg, 99, 2003, 2005; Juried Exhib, Whitaker Ctr for Sci and the Arts, Harrisburg, 99-2000, 2004, 2006; Ann Juried Exhib United Pastelists of Am, Clifton Arts Ctr, NJ, 2000; Juried Exhib United Pastelists of Am, Edward Hopper House, Nyack, NY, 2001; solo exhibs incl Gallery at Walnut Pl, Harrisburg, 99, 2001, 2004, 2006, Pen and Brush Galleries, NY, 2000; Wyomissing Inst Fine Arts, Pa, 2001; York Art Asn, Pa, 2002; Pine Street Presbyterian Church, Harrisburg, Pa, 2003; Ann Exhib of Catharine Lorillard Wolfe Art Club, Nat Arts Club, Nat Arts Club, NY, 10/2003, 2005, 2007, 2009, 2010; Doshi Gallery's Juried Exhib at Morrison Gallery, Penn State Univ, 2003-2004; Juried Exhib at Wayne Art Center, Wayne PA, 2003-2007; Juried War Exhib, National Assoc of Women Artists Gallery NY, Feb 2004; Pen and Brush Galleries, NYC, 2005-2007, 2009, York Art Assoc, PA, 2006-2007, Studio Gallery 234, York, 2005-2012; 35th Ann Juried Art Exhib, Lebanon Valley Coll, Annville, Pa, 4/2006. *Collection Arranged:* Arts for Peace & Justice Exhib, Strawberry Sq, Harrisburg, Pa, 90-2009; Adventures in Creativity, Strawberry Sq, Harrisburg, Pa, 2000; Salomon Bros, NY; Charles Dear, Interior Design, NY; Polyclinic Hosp, Harrisburg; Dauphin Deposit Bank, Harrisburg. *Pos:* Cur, Arts for Peace & Justice Exhibs Harrisburg, 90-2009; critic, York Art Asn, Nat Asn Women Artists, Bald Eagle Art League, Mechanicsburg Art Center, PA, 2009. *Teaching:* Instr oil painting, Mechanicsburg Art Ctr, Pa, 90; instr all mediums, Home Studio, New Cumberland, Pa, 93-2010; instr drawing & pastels, Lower Paxton Twp, Harrisburg, Pa, 94-98, Boscov's Campus of Courses, Camp Hill, Pa, 94; Bald Eagle Art League, Williamsport, Pa, 12/94 & 6/98; York Art Asn, York, Pa, 1999-2005; instr painting & drawing various art ctrs. *Awards:* Hon Mention, Ann Pastel Exhib, Pen & Brush, NY, 2/97; Catharine Lorillard Wolfe Art Club Cash Award, 101st Ann Exhib, Nat Arts Club, NY, 10/97; William Meyerowitz Meml Award, 109th Ann Exhibition Nat Asn Women Artists, NY, 98; Solo Show Award, Pen and Brush, NY, 99; HK Holbein Award, Oil Pastel Asn, Nyack, NY, 99; Mister Art.com Award, Oil Pastel Asn, Edward Hopper Art Ctr, Nyack, NY, 2000; 1st Prize Graphics Winter Exhibit, York Art Asn, 2000; Art Times Award, 105th Ann Exhib, CL Wolfe Art Club, NY, 2001, Charlotte Dunwiddle Memorial Award, 106th Ann Exhib, 2002; Merit Award United Pastelists Am, Nyack, NY, 2001; First Prize/Pastels, 32nd Ann Juried Exhib, York Art Asn, Pa, 2002; 1st Prize, Pastels, Mechanicsburg Art Ctr, PA, April, 2003; Atlantic Papers Award, 62nd Ann Juried Exhib, Audubon Artists, NY, Oct 2004; Award of Excellence, Regional Juried Exhib, 2005; 1st Award, Pen and Brush Galleries, NYC, 2006; Rottler Award Excellence, York Art Asn, 6/2007; Most Extreme Award, Art Ctr Mechanicsburg, Pa, 6/2007; 3rd Prize, Pastels, Arts Asn Harrisburg, Penn, 2006, 2nd Prize, 2007; 3rd Prize, 35th Ann Exhib Arnold Art Gallery, Annville, Penn, 2006; Rottler Award, York Art Asn, York, Pa, 2007; Myra Biggerstaff Memorial Award, Nat Asn Women Artists Ann Members Exhib, NY, 2011. *Bibliog:* Pastel Drawings, Patriot-News, Harrisburg, Pa, 12/19/97, Local Artist is part of exhibit in NY, 9/26/97; Traveling Art, Daily Rocket-Miner, Rock Springs Wyoming, 6/30/98; The Best of Drawing & Sketching, Rockport Publ, 98; Patricia Seligman (auth), How to Paint Trees, Flowers & Foliage; Linda Barr (auth), Artist Brings Skills to Mechanicsburg, 99; Zachary Lewis (auth) Arts for Peace, Patriot-News, 00; Ruth Summer (auth), Fleur Byers, Oil Pastel Artist, The Pastel Jour, 3-4/2002; USA Showcase, Fleur Byers, Pastel Artist Int, 9-10/2002; March Meeting, Franklin County Art Alliance, Chambersburg Pa, March, 2000; Fleur Byers & Maureen Buckholz to Exhib, Berks Arts, Reading, Pa, April-May, 2001; Three Artists Show at YAA, The York Dispatch, York Pa, 1/31/2002; Exhib features Area Artists, Community Courier, York Pa, 2/13/2002; Endless Options, Intelligencer Journal, Lancaster PA, 6/14/2003; Best of Pennsylvania Artists, 2006; Catching Up With the CLWAC Members' Exhib 2007 at the Broome St Gallery, Gallery & Studio, New York, 4-5/2007. *Mem:* Nat Asn of Women Artists; Catharine Lorillard Wolfe Art Club; Nat League of Am Pen Women; Oil Pastel Asn Int; Susquehanna Art Mus; Lancaster Art Mus; Art Asn of Harrisburg; York Art Asn; Art Ctr of Mechanicsburg; Pen & Brush Inc. *Media:* Oil Pastel, Charcoal, Graphite, Colored Pencil, Etching. *Res:* Study combinations of various mediums; Study effects of light and weather. *Specialty:* Fine Art; Impressionist city and country scenes. *Interests:* Soc Concerns, poetry, literature, music, hiking, swimming. *Publ:* Coauth, Committee Sponsors Harrisburg Exhib,West Shore Shopper, Camp Hill, Pa, 7/29/98; Arts for Peace, Justice Exhib to Open with Reception Today, Patriot-News, Harrisburg, Pa, 7/31/98; Art, Poetry, & Prose Featured at Exhib, Harrisburg Times, Harrisburg, Pa, 8/7/98; Art for Peace and Justice, Sentinel, Carlisle, Pa; Exhib of Fleur Byers, Art Work, Harrisburg City Calendar, Harrisburg, PA, April, 99; Inst of the Art-Multmedia Works, Patriot-News, Harrisburg PA, 4/20/2001; Pine Street Church-Painting by Fleur Byers, Patriot, News, Harrisburg, PA, 3/21/2003. *Dealer:* Gallery at Walnut Place 413 Walnut St Harrisburg PA 17101; Studio Gallery 234 300 S Pershing Ave York PA 17403; Second Floor Gallery 105 S Market St Mechanicsburg PA 17055; Middletown Area Arts Collective 35 Union St Middletown PA 17057

BYNUM, E (ESTHER PEARL) ANDERSON
CURATOR, PRINTMAKER
b Henderson, Tex, Dec 19, 1922. *Study:* Dallas Mus Fine Arts, 52; NTex State Univ, BA, 65; Univ Md, MA, 72, advan grad specialist cert, 73; also lithography with Tadeusz Lapinski. *Work:* US Civil Serv Bldg, Washington, DC; Montgomery Co Contemp Print Collection & Montgomery Co Pub Schs, Md. *Exhib:* NY Int Art Show, 70; Baltimore Mus, 73-74; Jersey City Mus, NJ, 74; 26th Ann Exhib, McNay Art Inst, San Antonio, 75 & 32nd Ann, 81, Tex Watercolor Soc; Lowe Art Mus, Univ Miami, Fla, 75. *Pos:* Cur, Four Oaks Gallery, Henderson, Tex, 80-. *Teaching:* Instr art, Montgomery Co Pub Schs, Rockville, Md, 65-75, elem art coordr, 75-79; artist in educ, Longview Pub Sch, Tex Art Coun, 84-86. *Bibliog:* Articles in Henderson Daily News & Longview, Tex Arts Coun. *Mem:* Tex Watercolor Soc; Am Craft Coun; Graphics Soc. *Media:* Watercolor, Lithographs. *Publ:* Contribr, monthly visual arts article, Henderson Daily Newspaper. *Dealer:* Four Oaks Gallery 709 Hwy 43 Henderson TX 75652. *Mailing Add:* 711 Highway 43 Henderson TX 75652

BYRD, JERRY
PAINTER
b Fullerton, Calif, Mar 6, 1947. *Study:* Univ Calif, Irvine, BFA, 70, MFA, 72. *Work:* Mus Contemp Art, Melbourne, Australia; Crocker Art Mus, Sacramento, Calif; Newport Harbor Art Mus, Newport Beach, Calif; Laguna Beach Mus Art, Calif. *Comn:* Paintings on canvas, AT&T, San Francisco, 77, IBM, San Jose, 82, Carol Beadel, Santa Barbara, 84 & Peabody Hotel, Orlando, Fla, 86. *Exhib:* The First Decade, Fine Arts Gallery, Univ Calif, Irvine, 75; Painting and Sculpture Today, Indianapolis Mus Art, 76; Current Concerns, 76 & New Directions in Southern California Art, 78, Los Angeles Inst Contemp Art; Geometric Abstraction, Inst Art, Boston, 81; Calif Contemp Artists, Laguna Beach Mus Art, Calif, 84. *Awards:* Fine Arts Patrons Award, Univ Calif, Irvine, 69; Nat Endowment Arts Fel, 74. *Bibliog:* Robert Hutchinson (auth), Scale and modern comfort, Archit Digest, 79; Clark Poling (auth), Geometric Abstraction: A New Generation, Boston Inst Contemp Art, 81; Suvan Geer (auth), Emphasis on formalism, Art Week, 84. *Media:* Oil, Acrylic. *Publ:* Illusr, College Algebra (auth, Louis Leithold), Macmillon Publ Co, Inc, New York, NY, 80. *Dealer:* Ivory-Kimpton 55 Grant Ave San Francisco CA 94108. *Mailing Add:* 1137 Palms Blvd Venice CA 90291-3524

BYRNE, CHARLES JOSEPH
DESIGNER
b Louisville, Ky, Oct 15, 1943. *Study:* Univ Louisville, BS; Wayne State Univ. *Comn:* Various Exhib Designs, Detroit Inst of Arts, 73-80; Contemp Arts Ctr, Cincinnati, 81-84; Univ Calif, Berkeley. *Exhib:* Buckminster Fuller Portfolio, Gettler Paul Gallery, 81, NY Art Dir Club Ann Exhib, 82, 83 & 84; Archit Photog Exhib, CAGE Gallery, 82, Local Color Photog Exhib, Tangeman Fine Arts Gallery, Univ Cincinnati, 82, Advert Club Cincinnati Ann Exhib, 81-84, Cincinnati Art Dir Club Ann Exhib, 79-84, Poster, Brodie Gallery, Univ Cincinnati, 82 & 83, Color and Contract, Photog Exhib, Carl Solway Gallery, Cincinnati, 84; Cult Posters Exhib, Univ Louisville, 82, Posters, Portland Mus, Louisville, Ky, 84. *Pos:* Cur, Dept of Fine Arts, Univ Louisville, Ky, 63-66, asst univ designer, 66-70; chief designer graphics & signage, Smith, Hinchman & Grylls Assoc, Inc, Detroit, 70-76; owner, Colophon Design Studio, Cincinnati & Colophon, San Francisco, 78-84, Chuck Byrne Design, Oakland, Calif, 85-; contrib ed, Print Mag, 88-. *Teaching:* Instr, Interior Designers Guild, San Diego, 77-78; instr, Cincinnati Acad Art, 80, Acad Art Col, San Francisco, 92-93; adj fac, Univ Cincinnati, 81-84; assoc prof design, Calif Col Arts & Crafts, 88-91; fac, San Jose State Univ. *Awards:* Commun Arts Mag Award, 74, 81 & 85; Commun Graphics Award, Am Inst of Graphic Arts, 74, 75 & 82-85; Awards, Art Dirs Club Cincinnati, 79-83. *Bibliog:* Print Magazine Casebook 8, Environ Graphics, 90; Carol Stevens (auth), Chuck Byrne, Print Mag, Sept/Oct, 90; Gatta, Lange, Lyons (auths), Foundations of Graphic Design, Davis Publ Inc, Worcester, Mass, 90. *Mem:* Am Inst Graphic Arts. *Media:* Print Graphics. *Publ:* Coauth, Computer Graphics, Mich Soc Archit Bull, 4/75; Downtown vs Suburban Shopping Centers: a Clear Case of Identity, Detroit Free Press Mag, 2/76; numerous articles for Print Magazine, 86-. *Mailing Add:* 5528 Lawton Ave Oakland CA 94601

BYRNES, JAMES BERNARD
ART HISTORIAN, MUSEUM DIRECTOR
b New York, NY, Feb 19, 1917. *Study:* Nat Acad Design, New York, 36-38; Am Artists Sch, New York, 38-40; Art Students League, 41-42; Univ Perugia; Istituto Meschini, Rome, 51-52. *Exhib:* Man Ray, Paris & Los Angeles (catalog); Track 16, Robert Berman Galleries; Degas and New Orleans (catalog essay), New Orleans Mus Art, 1999. *Collection Arranged:* Edgar Degas, His Family & Friends in New Orleans (auth, catalog), 65; Odyssey of an Art Collector--The Collection of Mr & Mrs Frederick S Stafford, Paris (auth, catalog), 66; Arts of Ancient & Modern Latin Am (auth, catalog), 68; Rothko (auth, catalog), 74; Artist as Collector--Ethnic Art (auth, catalog), 75. *Pos:* Cur mod & contemp art, Los Angeles Co Mus, 46-54; dir, Colorado Springs Fine Arts Ctr, 54-56; assoc dir, NC Mus Art, 56-58, dir, 58-60; dir, New Orleans Mus Art, 61-72; dir, Newport Harbor Art Mus, Newport Beach, Calif, 72-75; consult fine arts, 1978-; symposium, Modern Art in Los Angeles in the Late Forties, Getty Res Inst, 2003. *Teaching:* Vis prof hist 20th century art, Univ Southern Calif, 50, Univ Fla, Gainesville, 60-61. *Awards:* Knight in the Order of Leopold II, Belg Govt, 72; Hon Title, Dir emer, New Orleans Mus Art, 89; Man of Yr for Art, Isaac Delgado Fellows Award, New Orleans Mus Art, 1999. *Mem:* Appraisers Soc Am (sr mem); Appraisers Asn Am; Am Asn Mus; Int Coun Mus; Am Inst Designers (hon life mem); and others. *Res:* Nineteenth and twentieth century art; Edgar Degas; pre-Columbian and African art. *Mailing Add:* James B Byrnes & Assoc 7820 Mulholland Dr Los Angeles CA 90046

BYRON, MICHAEL
PAINTER
b Providence, RI, 1954. *Study:* Kansas City Art Inst, BFA, 76; NS Coll Art & Design, MFA, 81. *Exhib:* Mus Mod Art, NY, 83; Boymans-Van Beuningen, Rotterdam, The Neth, 86; Solo exhibs, Aldrich Mus Contemp Art, 87, Mus Boymans-Van Bueningen, Rotterdam, 91, Galerie Barbara Farber, Amsterdam, 91, Elga Wimmer Gallery, Broadway, NY, 93, Galerie Philippe Gravier, Paris, France, 93 & Anders Tornberg Gallery, Lund, Swed, 94; Whitney Biennial, Whitney Mus Am Art, NY, 89; Maryland Inst Art, Baltimore, 91; Selections from the Permanent Collection, Phoenix Art Mus, Ariz, 92; Recent Donations & Acquisitions, Whitney Mus, NY, 92. *Teaching:* Vis artist, RI Sch Design, 85, NS Col Art & Design, Halifax, 85 & 92 & Hochsch voor Kunsten (grad level), Arnhem, Neth, 91-92; guest lectr, Sch Visual Arts, New York, 88 & Hochsch Hertenbosch voor Kunst, Den Bosch, Neth, 91; asst prof, Washington Univ, St Louis, Mo, 94-. *Bibliog:* Anna Tilroe (auth), Volkskrant, Een Kolossale Bruine Mandarijn, 11/1/91; Wouter Welling (auth), Het Poetische Theater van Michael Byron, Kunstbeeld, 91; Jurriaan Benchop (auth), Interview with Michael Byron, Metropolis M, 91. *Dealer:* Baron-Boisante 50 W 57th St New York NY 10019. *Mailing Add:* 329 Belt Ave #301B Saint Louis MO 63112-4512

BYRUM, DONALD ROY
PRINTMAKER, PRINT DEALER
b Hertford, NC, June 19, 1942. *Study:* RI Sch Design, BFA, 67; Univ Mich, MFA, 69; spec studies in lithography with John Maggio, 79. *Work:* Minn Mus Am Art, St Paul; Chrysler Mus Art, Norfolk, Va; BYK Gulden Lomberg Chemische Fabrik GMBH, Konstanz, WGer; Am Embassy, Madrid, Spain; Yale Univ Art Gallery; Bank of America; Lehrman Inst; Galerie Chatitre, France. *Comn:* Etching & aquatints, comn by Dryden Gallery, NY. *Exhib:* Contemp Master Prints, Winthrop Univ Gallery, 76; US Print Exhib, Spirit Sq Art Ctr, NC, 79-81; Southeastern Ctr Contemp Art, NC, 80; Don Byrum/Rick Crown, Mint Mus Art, 81; New Am Graphics US State Dept Tour, Spain & Moracco, 82-83; Southern Printmakers, Southern Graphics Coun, 84, 88 & 90; Md Inst Coll Art, 93; New Art Media, Marlboro Art Gallery, Md, 93; Mid America Prints 97, Art & Design Gallery, Univ Kans; Don Byrum/Digital Printmaking, Stringer Fine Arts Ctr, Kans, 2000; Colorprint USA International, Landmark Gallery, Tex Tech Univ, 2002; Don Byrum/Works on Paper, Steckline Art Gallery, Newman Univ, Kans, 2004; 11th, 12th, 13th, 14th, & 15th Faculty Biennial Art Exhib, Ulrich Mus Art, Wichita, Kans; State of the Art, Art of the State, Cameron Art Mus, 2011; Contemporary South, Visual Art Exchange Gallery; Donald Byrum Printmaking, Hagersmith Design Gallery, 2014; Scope: The Southern Landscape, Visual Art Exchange Gallery, 2014. *Pos:* chmn dept arts & art history, Univ NC, Charlotte, 82-93; dir sch art & design, Wichita State Univ, 93-2008. *Teaching:* Asst prof printmaking, Minnesota State Univ Mankato, 69-74; asst/assoc prof, Univ NC, Charlotte, 74-93, prof printmaking, 93-2008, sch art & design, Wichita State Univ, retired, 2008. *Awards:* Purchase Awards, Minn Printmakers, Minn Arts Coun, 70 & NC Artists, Asheville Mus, 77; Fayetteville Mus Art Award, 79; Purchase Award, Eastern US Print Exhib, Fac Res Grant Computer Graphics, 89 & 92 & Res Leave, Computer Graphics, fall 92; Outstanding Computer Curric Award, 89; Seven Artist Project Grants; North Carolina Arts Council Regional Artist Grant, 2012. *Mem:* Nat Coun Art Adminrs; State Bd; Southeastern Coll Art Asn (conf comm); Conf Comt, Southeastern Coll Art Conf; Coll Art Asn Am; NC Art Ed Asn (State bd); SGC Int (former pres); Brunswick Arts Council (bd); Wilmington Art Assn Brand. *Media:* Etching & Lithography. *Specialty:* original prints. *Interests:* owner, Donald Byram Prints. *Dealer:* Visual Art Exchange 309 W Martin St Raleigh NC 27601; Wilmington Art Asn Hannah Block Arts Ctr Gallery 120 S Second St Wilmington NC 28401. *Mailing Add:* 3906 Meeting Pl Ln Southport NC 28461

C

CABLE, MAXINE ROTH
SCULPTOR
b Philadelphia, Pa. *Study:* Tyler Sch Fine Art, Temple Univ, AA; Corcoran Sch Art, George Washington Univ, AB; Am Univ, with Hans Hofmann. *Work:* Allied Chem Corp Gallery, NY; Nat Acad Sci, Washington, DC; George Washington Univ. *Comn:* Environ sculpture, Allied Chem Corp, 69-70; sculpture, Wolf Trap Farm Performing Arts, Va, 73. *Exhib:* Area Exhibs, Corcoran Gallery Art, 55-67; Artists Equity Traveling Exhib, Columbia Mus, SC, 73-74; Solo exhibs, Adams Morgan Gallery, Washington, DC, 64, Hodson Gallery, Hood Coll, Frederick, Md, 69, Gallery Ten, Washington, DC, 75-76, 79 & 83 & Art Dept, Cath Univ Am, 83. *Pos:* Dir, Glen Echo Graphics Workshop, Md, 75. *Teaching:* Consult art, Montgomery Co, Md, 57-65 & Head Start Prog, Washington, DC, 70. *Awards:* Sculpture Award, David Smith, Corcoran Gallery Art, 55; First Prize in Painting, Smithsonian Inst, 67. *Bibliog:* Washington Artists Today, Artists Equity Asn, 67; Art for Public Places, Dept Housing & Urban Develop, 73. *Media:* Mixed, Natural and Man-Made. *Mailing Add:* 7000 Buxton Terr Bethesda MD 20817-4404

CABOT, HUGH
PAINTER
b Boston, Mass, Mar 22, 1930. *Study:* Vesper George Sch Fine Arts; Boston Mus Fine Arts Sch; Coll Americas, Mexico City; Asmolean, Oxford Univ, Cambridge, Eng. *Work:* Univ Ariz, Tucson; Harwood Found Art, Taos, NMex; Tucson Med Ctr; Washburn Univ, Topeka, Kans; Starmont Vail Med Ctr, Topeka, Kans; Chandler Ctr Arts, Chandler, Ariz; Booth Mus Western Art, Cartersville, Ga. *Comn:* Great American Rodeo Cowboy (lifesize figure), Las Vegas Hilton Hotel, 85. *Exhib:* Korea, Mitsubishii Gallery, Tokyo, Japan, 58 & Tokyo Press Club; La Marine Americaine, Mus de la Marine, Paris, 63; Oper Palette, every maj city in free world incl Nat Gallery Art. *Pos:* Off combat artist, Korean War. *Awards:* First, Second & Third Awards, Tex Tri State, 69; Artist of Year, Scottsdale, Ariz, 78. *Bibliog:* Jim Newton (auth), Those Cabots, Phoenix Gazette, 74; Meet Hugh Cabot, Ariz Living, 75; Danny Medina (auth), Hugh Cabot, Ariz Art Talk, 82; David M Brown (auth), Tubac Artist---Hugh Cabot, Greyhawk Mag, 85; Allen Scott (auth), Cabots cowboy, Tucson Lifestyle, 86; Hugh Cabot, Kathy Engle editor Green valley News, 2003. *Mem:* Salmagundi Club. *Media:* Oil, Watercolor, Charcoal, Pastel. *Specialty:* Works by Hugh Cabot. *Publ:* Auth-illusr, Korea one, Globe Publ, 54. *Dealer:* Olivia Cabot, Hugh Cabot Gallery, # 10 Calle Iglesia, Tubac, Ariz, 85646. *Mailing Add:* PO Box 1478 Tubac AZ 85646

CABOT, MARY A. BOOTH
PAINTER, PRINTMAKER
b Winston-Salem, NC, Sept 28, 1942. *Study:* Univ Tenn, 66-67; Ga State Univ, 68-70. *Work:* Arthur Anderson & co, Coca-Cola Inc, Kilpatrick & Cody Attorneys, Delta Airlines, Atlanta, Ga; Simon & Schuster Doubleday Publ, NY; Shamrock Hilton, Houston, Tex; Johnson & Johnson Inc, Mass; and others. *Comn:* Four art deco murals, Noelles Restaurant, Atlanta, Ga,; Delta Air Lines Crown Room (4 watercolors), Hartsfield Int Airport, Atlanta, Ga; Park Seed co, Greenwood, SC; Atlanta Flower Show. *Exhib:* Southern Watercolor Soc 4th Exhib (with catalog), Columbia Mus Arts & Sci, SC, 80; Southern Watercolor Soc 5th Exhib (with catalog), La Polytechnic Inst, Ruston, 81; 5th Int Exhib Botanical Art & Illus (with catalog), 83; Arnold Arboretum, Harvard Univ, Boston, Mass, 84; Southern Watercolor Soc 9th Exhib (with catalog), Miss Mus Art, Jackson, 85; Marie Selby Botanical Gardens, Sarasota, Fla, 85 & 94; State Botanical Garden, Athens, Ga, 88; Nat Flower Shows (Spring Exhibs), Philadelphia, Boston, Atlanta, Ann Arbor, Washington, DC, Syracuse, Mobile, Ala, & St Louis, Mo, 91-2014; and others. *Teaching:* watercolor classes, workshops. *Bibliog:* Inside Cobb Mag, spring 84; Les Krantz (auth), American Artists: an illustrated survey of leading contemporary Americans, 85; article, Southern Homes Mag, 84, 86 & 88; Female Artists in the United States 1900-1985: a Research and Resource Guide, Rutgers Univ Press, 86; Artists of Georgia, Vol I, 89 & Artists of the South II, 92, Mountain Productions Inc, Albuquerque; Cincinnati Post Newspaper, 2001; Power of Color & Light, InformArt Mag, 2005; Mary Booth Cabot Finds Her Joy Through Art, InformArt Mag, 2005; color feature article, Rosewell Neighbor Newspaper, 2007. *Mem:* Southern Watercolor Soc; Ga Watercolor Soc; Ky Watercolor Soc. *Media:* Watercolor. *Specialty:* watercolor, paintings. *Interests:* Florals; books; landscapes; nature; birds. *Dealer:* Swan Coach House Atlanta Ga; Gibbs Botanical Gardens Ball Ground Ga. *Mailing Add:* c/o Wren Hill Gallery 3961 Loch Highland Pass Roswell GA 30075

CABRERA, MARGARITA
SCULPTOR
b Mexico, 1973. *Study:* Maryland Inst Art, 1997; Hunter Coll City Univ New York, BFA (Sculpture), 1997, MFA (Combined Media), 2001. *Exhib:* Solo exhibs include Sara Melzer Gallery, New York, 2003, 2004, 2006, 2008, Adair Margo Gallery, El Paso, Tex, 2005, Walter Maciel Gallery, Los Angeles, 2007; Group exhibs include Staff Show, Metrop Mus Art, New York, 1999; Weight as Real, House Gallery, Long Island City, New York, 2000; Critical Consumption, Rotunda Gallery, Brooklyn, 2003; Domicile, Ctr Contemp Art, Seattle, 2004; Rearranged/Redefined: Domestic Objects Reconsidered, Mainline Art Ctr, Pa, 2005; As Good As Your Next Gig, Walter Maciel Gallery, Los Angeles, 2006; Gimme Shelter, Shelter Island Heights, New York, 2006; Frontera 450+, The Station Mus, Houston, 2006; Phantom Sightings: Art After the Chicano Movement, Los Angeles County Mus Art, 2008. *Awards:* Joan Mitchell Found Grant, 2007. *Mailing Add:* c/o Sara Meltzer Gallery 73 Worth St Apt 5B New York NY 10013

CADDELL, FOSTER
PAINTER, WRITER
b Pawtucket, RI, Aug 2, 1921. *Study:* RI Sch Design; pvt study with Peter Helck, Robert Brackman & Guy Wiggins. *Work:* Lyman Allyn Mus, New London, Conn; Senate Gallery Washington, DC; Brown Univ Military Libr, Providence, RI. *Comn:* Official portraits of Sen Thomas J Dodd, Washington & Judge LP Moore, US Circuit Ct Appeals, Second Dist, NY, Sen Christopher J Dodd, Washington, (only Artist to paint Official Portraits of Father and Son US Senators, Both Hanging in Washington); portrait of Dr George S Avery, Brooklyn Botanical Gardens, NY; portrait of Carl Cuttler, Mystic Seaport Mus, Conn; relig paintings for many denominations incl Church of Eng; portraits of many bus & civic leaders. *Exhib:* Solo exhibs, Providence Art Club, 48 & 63, Slater Mem Mus, Norwich Free Acad, 76 & Heritage Plantations, Sandwich, Mass, 85; Am Artists Prof League Grand Nat Exhib, 70-92; Am Watercolor Soc Ann, Nat Acad Galleries, 71; Slater Mus, Norwich Acad, 71-80; Nat Arts Club, NY, 73-80; Pastel Soc of Am, 85-2004; Conn Pastel Soc, 85-2005; Soc Rep Pastellistes De France & Inst Exhib, Lille, France, 87; Acad Fine Arts, Beijing, China, 97. *Pos:* Lithograph artist, Providence Lithograph Co, 39-51; artist with Far East Air Force, 43-46. *Teaching:* Instr, Foster Caddell's Art Sch, 55-2005. *Awards:* Best Show, Conn Pastel Soc, 89 and awards 90, 94, 98, 99, & 2001-2006; Grumbacher Award, Pastel Soc Am, 91 & 2005, Master Panelist, 97 & elected to Hall of Fame, 98; Allied Artist Award, Pastel Soc Am, 94; Conn Soc of Portrait Artist Lifetime Achievement Award, 2005; and many others. *Bibliog:* David Lewis (ed), Landscape Painting Techniques, Watson-Guptill, 84; Madlyn Woolwich (ed), Pastel Interpretations, Northlight, 93; Madelyn Woolwich (ed), The Art of Pastel Portraiture, Watson-Guptill, 96; Richeson (auth), My Friends, Todays Great Masters, 2007. *Mem:* Am Portrait Soc; Am Artists Prof League; Acad Artists Am; New Eng Plein Air Painters (hon mem); Pastel Soc Am; Lyme Art Asn (Elected Life Member); and others. *Media:* Oil, Pastel. *Interests:* Collecting Antique Arms. *Publ:* Illusr, series sports bks, Little, Brown & co; auth & illusr, Keys to Successful Landscape Painting, 76, Keys to Successful Color & Keys to Painting Better Portraits, 82, Pitman & Sons, London & Watson-Guptill; Foster Caddell's Keys to Successful Landscape Painting, Northlight, 93; The Best of Pastels II, 98; The Best of Sketching & Drawing, Rockport Publ, 98; contrib to work on websites; Pastel Jour, 2000; Pastel Artist Int, 2002. *Dealer:* Court Yard Gallery 12 Water St Mystic CT 06355. *Mailing Add:* Northlight 47 Pendleton Hill Rd Voluntown CT 06384

CADE, WALTER, III
PAINTER, COLLAGE ARTIST
b New York, NY, Jan 17, 1936. *Study:* Inst Mod Art, New York. *Work:* City of Miami Beach, Fla; Va Beach Art Mus; Rockefeller Found; Bruce Mus; Fine Arts Mus S; Nat Mus Am Art, Smithsonian Inst. *Exhib:* Art Ann, 69-70 & Contemp Black Artists in Am, 71, Whitney Mus Am Art, New York; Corcoran Gallery, Washington, DC, 72; Solo exhibs, Ocean Co Coll, 77, Jackson State Univ, 80 & Olin Mus Art, Bates Coll, Maine, 93; Miss Mus Art, Jackson, 81; Tampa Mus, Fla, 82; Tucson Mus Art, Ariz, 83; Two-person exhib, Lewiston-Auburn Coll, Maine, 93; Group exhibs, New Eng Fine Arts Inst, Mass, 93 & Lewiston-Auburn Coll, Maine, 94. *Awards:* First Prize, Fine Arts Mus South, Mobile, Ala, 82; Best in Show, Bruce Mus, Greenwich, Conn, 84 & 94. *Bibliog:* The Florida Arts Gazette, article, 5/80; The Christian Sci Monitor, article, 7/93; Maine Sunday Telegram, article, 9/93. *Media:* Acrylic, Collage. *Dealer:* Sande Webster Gallery 2018 Locust St Philadelphia PA 19103. *Mailing Add:* 172-03 119th Ave Jamaica NY 11434

CADIEUX, MICHAEL EUGENE
EDUCATOR, PAINTER
b Missoula, Mont, June 15, 1940. *Study:* Univ Mont, BA & MA. *Work:* Univ Mont Fine Arts Collection, Missoula; Yuma Fine Arts Asn, Ariz. *Exhib:* Spokane-Pac NW Ann, Cheney Cowles Mus, 66; SW Yuma Fine Arts, 66-68; Ariz Ann, Phoenix Art Mus, 67; Tucson Art Mus Ann, Ariz, 68; Mid-Am, Nelson-Atkins Mus, Kansas City, Mo, 72, 30 Miles, 75; Mid-Am, St Louis Art Mus, 72; Davidson Nat Drawing, Davidson Coll Galleries, 75. *Collection Arranged:* Univ Wis Ctr Syst, 67; Univ Md, 67; Western Asn Art Mus Traveling Exhib, 69; fac shows, Spiva Art Ctr, Memphis Acad, 75-78; Mo Art Coun-Mid Am Arts Alliance Shows. *Pos:* Reviewer art publ, SE Asia in Rev, 76-. *Teaching:* Instr painting & drawing, Ariz Western Col, Yuma, 66-69; assoc prof art hist, Kansas City Art Inst, Mo, 69-. *Awards:* Third Place, 2nd Southwestern, Yuma Fine Arts, 67; Grant Study in India, US Off Educ, 71. *Bibliog:* Donald Hoffman (auth), Here's Art all in a row, Kansas City Star, 72 & Michael Cadieux, Kansas City Star, 77. *Media:* Painting Collage. *Res:* Cross-cultural art history. *Publ:* Auth, The mural tradition in Indian painting, SE Asia in Rev, 77. *Mailing Add:* Dept Art Hist Kansas City Art Institute 4415 Warwick Kansas City MO 64111

CADILLAC, LOUISE ROMAN
PAINTER, INSTRUCTOR
b Central City, Pa. *Study:* Univ Northern Colo, BA, 54, MA, 64; with Sylvia Glass, Calif, Gene Matthews, Colo & Chen Chi, NY. *Work:* Denver Pub Libr Western Hist Div; Jefferson Sch Credit Union, Lakewood, Colo; Jewish Community Ctr, Denver; Leroy Springs & Co, Myrtle Beach, SC. *Exhib:* Metrop Exhib, Denver Art Mus, 60; Rocky Mountain Nat Watermedia, Foothills Art Ctr, Golden, Colo, 74-91; Nat Watercolor Soc, Palm Springs Mus Fine Art, Calif, 82-93; solo exhib, Univ Northern Colo, 84; Nat Acad Design, NY, 86 & 88; Am Watercolor Soc, NY, 92-94. *Pos:* Juror, Painting Competitions, Critic & Group Sessions. *Teaching:* Instr sec & elem art, Jefferson Co Pub Sch, Lakewood, Colo, 57-67, adaptive art specialist, 74-83; instr, Watermedia Workshops; Dillman's Sand Lake, Wis; Acapulco with Flying Colors Workshops; Leech Studio, Sarasota, Fla; Ed Day Gallery Workshops, Ont, Can; Italy and Greece with Flying Colors Workshop. *Awards:* Rocky Mountain Nat Watermedia Top Award, Foothills Art Ctr, 91; Gold Medal Hon, Am Watercolor Soc, 92; Leila Gardin Sawyer Award, Nat Acad Design, New York, 86 & 88. *Bibliog:* Watercolors for Grades 4, 5 & 6 (film), KRMA TV, Denver Pub Sch, 75. *Mem:* Nat Watercolor Soc; Rocky Mountain Nat Watermedia Soc; Am Watercolor Soc; Soc Experimental Artists. *Media:* Watermedia, Mixed Media. *Publ:* Artists Mag, 92; Splash I & II & IV, 92, 93 & 95; Judging Watermedia Competitions and Your Workshop Dollars, Watercolor, spring 96 & Loosen Up, fall 96; Art Clinic, Professional art instructors evaluate your work, Artist's Mag, 3/99. *Dealer:* Edward Day Gallery Kingston Ont K7L 2Z4 Canada. *Mailing Add:* 880 S Dudley St Lakewood CO 80226

CADY, DENNIS VERN
CONSERVATOR, PAINTER
b Portland, Ore, Nov 10, 1944. *Study:* Portland State Univ; Brooklyn Mus Art Sch, (Max Beckman Mem Grant), Painting & drawing with Rubin Tam, 69-71; Pratt Inst Graphic Ctr; Empire State Col, BS, plus independent study of tech aspects of paper restoration; Margo Fieden Galleries, New York, apprenticeship in restoration and preserv of works on paper, 74-77. *Work:* Franklin Furnace, NY; NY Publ Libr, South Street Seaport Mus; South Street Seaport Mus, NY; Univ Toronto, Can. *Comn:* Poster, 72, costumes for dance (with Frank Garcia), 74, costumes, 77, Phillis Lamhut Dance Co; poster, Emery Hermans Dance Theatre, 75; sets & props, Murray Louis Dance Co, 76. *Exhib:* Solo exhibs, Brownstone Gallery, Brooklyn, NY, 91, Mapletree Gallery, Pauling, NY, 94, Gallery at Hunter Mountain, NY, 94; Regional Art Ann, Schenectady Mus Art, 92; Kelmscott Gallery, Cold Springs, NY, 93; Catskill Watercolors, Gallery at Hunter Mountain, NY, 93; Millbrook Gallery, NY, 94; Greene Co Arts Coun Landscape Show, Chatham, NY, 94. *Pos:* Freelance restorer, New York, 77-. *Awards:* Nat Scholastics Award, New York, 62; America the Beautiful Fund Grant, 91. *Bibliog:* The Print Collector's News Letter, XV, 4, 9/84 & 10/84; Dennis Cady (auth), Amy Winter, Nature Imitates Art, Brownstone Gallery, Brooklyn, NY, 91. *Media:* Oil, Watercolor. *Publ:* Auth, Block Prints by Dennis Cady, Hillside Ctr, Portland, Ore, 71; Wall Street Blue Prints by Dennis Cady, Baun Printshop, New York, 84. *Dealer:* Art Adv Serv Inc New York NY; Art Planning Consult New York NY. *Mailing Add:* 57 Courtney Ave Newburgh NY 12550-6303

CADY, SAMUEL LINCOLN
PAINTER, INSTRUCTOR
b Boothbay Harbor, Maine, July 21, 1943. *Study:* Univ NH, Durham, BA, 65; Ind Univ, Bloomington, MFA, 67. *Work:* Addison Gallery Am Art, Andover, Mass; Prudential Insurance Co, Newark, NJ; Pac Securities Int Bank, Los Angeles, Calif; Gen Elec, Fairfield, Conn; Peabody Essex Mus, Salem, Mass; Butler Inst, Youngstown, Ohio; Orlando Mus of Art, Fla; Farnsworth Art Mus, Rockland, Maine; Portland Art Mus, Portland, Maine; United Cent Bank Denver; Maryland Mus Art, Md; Univ NH, Durham; Univ Maine Mus Art, Bangor. *Comn:* NH State Percent for Art Prog, Laconia Vocational Tech; Maine State Percent for Art Prog, Knox Co Courthouse, Rockland, Me. *Exhib:* Whitney Biennial (with catalog), Whitney Mus Am Art, New York, 75; solo exhibs, Holly Solomon Gallery, New York, 76, 78-80 & 83-84, Hampshire Coll, Amherst, Mass, 78, Capricorn Gallery, Bethesda, Md, 79, Castelli-Goodman-Solomon Gallery, E Hampton, NY, 82, Fujii Gallery (with catalog), Tokyo, 84 & 88, Howard Yeserski Gallery, Boston, 90, 94 & 96, Round Top Ctr Arts, Damariscotta, Maine, 94, Mary Ryan Gallery, New York, 94, 98, 2004 & 2009, Barbara Gillman Gallery, Miami Beach, Fla, 95, Portland Mus of Art, Maine, Mapping Maine, Portland Mus of Art, Biennial, 98, 2003 & 2005, Yezerski Gallery, 2000, 2002 & 2007, Caldbeck Gallery, 2001, 2003, 2005, 2007, 2009, & 2012, & Univ Maine Mus Art, Bangor, 2006; retrospective 1966-1986, Addison Gallery Am Art (with catalog), 87; Gwenda Jay Gallery, Chicago, 89; Mainstream Am: The Collection of Philip Desind, Ohio, 87 & Masters of The Masters, Sch Vis Arts Fac, Butler Inst, Youngstown, Ohio, 98; On the edge: 40 yrs of Maine Painting, Maine Coast Artists Gallery, Rockport, 92; Islands, Caldbeck Gallery, Rockland, Maine, 97 & 99; Work of the 90's; Resurfaced, Boston Univ Art Gallery, Mass, 2005; Portland Show III, Greenhut Gallery, Portland, Maine, 2006 & Anniversary Show, 2008, 2010; 181st Ann Exhib, Nat Acad Design, New York, 2006; drawings, Art House Gallery, Portland, Maine, 2010. *Teaching:* Instr drawing, painting & printmaking, Univ NH, Durham, 68-69; instr grad workshop & MFA prog, Sch Visual Arts, New York, 84-2008. *Bibliog:* Ken Greenleaf (auth), Cady, A native son, forges images into icons, Maine Sunday Telegram, 8/94; Cate McQuade (auth), Angels come down to earth, Boston Globe, 9/26/96, revs, 9/14/2000, 9/20/2002 & 4/19/2007; Carl Little (auth), Art of Maine Islands, 97, Paintings of Maine, 2006 & Shaped Art of Sam Cady, Maine Boats, Homes & Harbors Mag, 8/2009; Ken Johnson (auth), rev, NY Times, 5/8/98; Edgar Allen Beem (auth), Back home in friendship, Down East Mag, 9/2002; Grace Glueck (auth), NY Times, 11/12/2004; Harpers Mag, reproductive edition, 1/2005; Edward Gomez (auth), Art & Antiques, 2/2005; Cynthia Nadelman (auth), Art News, 3/2005; Ken Greenleaf (auth), The Real Deal, MidCoast Me, Portland, Me, Phoenix, 2012. *Media:* Oil on Canvas, Silkscreen, Lithography, Graphite Pen & Ink, Woodblock Prins. *Interests:* Boating, hiking, tennis & reading. *Publ:* Contrib, Inner/Urban, First St Forum, St Louis, Mo, 81; Time Out: Sport and Leisure in America Today, Tampa Mus, Fla, 83; Fujii Gallery (with catalog), Tokyo, Japan, 84 & 88; Addison Gallery Am Art Retrospective (with catalog) Andover, Mass, 87; Paintings and snapshots (exhib catalog), Caldbeck Gallery, 2005; Reality and Reverie (exhib catalog), Univ Maine Mus Art, 2006. *Dealer:* Howard Yezerski Gallery 460 Harrison Ave Boston MA 02118; Mary Ryan Gallery 527 W 26th St New York NY 10001; Caldbeck Gallery Rockland 12 Elm St ME 04841. *Mailing Add:* Box 208 Friendship ME 04547

CAESAR, JEDEDIAH
SCULPTOR
b Oakland, Calif, 1973. *Study:* Sch Mus Fine Arts, BFA, 98; Univ Calif, Los Angeles, MFA, 2001. *Exhib:* Solo exhibs, Black Dragon Soc, Los Angeles, 2002, 2004, D'Amelio Terras Gallery, New York, 2007, Blanton Mus Art, Austin, 2007, Susanne Vielmetter LA Projects, 2007, Galerie Nathalie Obadia, 2008; Group exhibs, Welsh-Beck Gallery, Los Angeles, 2000; The Panoptic Mind, Eyedrum Gallery, Atlanta, 2001; Frozen Wisdom, Raymond Lawrence Gallery, Atlanta, 2001; Face Off, The Smell, Los Angeles, 2001; Black Dragon Soc, Vienna, Austria, 2002, Los Angeles, 2002, New York, 2004; Beautiful Artists, Yamaguchi Inst Art, Japan, 2002; Jack Tilton/Anna Kustera Gallery, NY, 2002; Andrew Kreps Gallery, NY, 2003; Hiromi Yoshii Gallery, Tokyo, Japan, 2003; Run for the Hills, Locust Projects, Miami, 2004, Rule the Wasteland, 2004; Surface Tension, Lombard-Fried Fine Arts, NY, 2004; Thing, Armand Hammer Mus & Cult Center, LA, 2005; Sculpture New Spirit, Galerie Nathalie Obadia, 2005, 2006; Ask the Dust, d'Amelio Terras Gallery, New York, 2005, Circumventing the City, 2007; Trace, Whitney Mus Am Art, New York, 2006, Whitney Biennial, 2008; Sculptors' Drawings, Angles Gallery, Santa Monica, Calif, 2007; Paper Bombs, Jack Hanley Gallery, LA, 2007; Calif Biennial, Orange County Mus Art, Newport Beach, Calif, 2008

CAFFERY, DEBBIE FLEMING
PHOTOGRAPHER
b Mar 6, 1948. *Study:* San Francisco Art Inst, BFA, 75. *Work:* Mus Mod Art, NY; Metrop Mus Art, NY; Mus Photog Arts, San Diego, Calif; George Eastman House, Rochester, NY; Smithsonian Inst. *Exhib:* Mus Photog Arts, San Diego, 89; Carry Me Home, Nat Mus Am Hist, Smithsonian Inst, 90; O'Coracao Da Cienca, Centros Estudo Photographie, Coimbra, Port, 91; Visages, Paysages et Autves Rivages, Centre Art Contemporain, Brussels, Belg, 92; Photo Essays from the South, Ctr Creative Photog, Tucson, Ariz, 92; The South by its Photographers, Burmingham Mus Art, 96. *Pos:* Freelance photogr & teacher. *Awards:* Governor's Art Award, La, 89; Lou Stouman Prize Photog, San Diego Mus Photog Arts, 96-97. *Bibliog:* Debbie Fleming Caffery, Carry Me Home, Smithsonian Press, 90. *Publ:* Double take, Ctr Photog, Duke Univ, 96. *Dealer:* Howard Greenberg Gallery 120 Wooster New York NY. *Mailing Add:* 115 Florida Ct Lafayette LA 70503-2005

CAHANA, ALICE LOK
PAINTER
b Budapest, Hungary, Feb 7, 1929; US citizen. *Study:* Talpiot Teachers Coll, Tel Aviv, 49-51; independent studies, Boras, Sweden, 51-56; Univ Houston, Tex, 61-66; Rice Univ, with prof Joe Tate, Dadi Virz, Bob Camblin & Basilous Poulos, 69-77. *Work:* US Holocaust Mem Mus, Washington, DC; Sarvar-Auschwitz (diptych), Yad Vashem, Jerusalem, 95; Pope Benedict XVI, Vatican Collection. *Comn:* The Wollstein Family, 2005. *Exhib:* From Ashes to the Rainbow--A Tribute to Raoul Wallenberg, Skirball, Los Angeles, 87; Rotunda US Cong, 87; Pa Acad Fine Art, 88; Sacred Text, B'nai Brith Klutznic Nat Jewish Mus, Washington, DC, 95; Remembering not to forget, Holocaust Mus, Houston, 96. *Awards:* To Everything there is a Season (mono print), presented to Pres Carter, Pres Sadat & Prime Minister Begin, to hon Israel-Egypt peace treaty, 79; recognized by Pres Clinton, nat gathering Holocaust survivors, 95. *Bibliog:* Triumph of the Spirit (video), EDAR, PBS, Baltimore, 95; Pres Clinton tribute & art presentation, CBS, Yad Vashem, Jerusalem, 95; James Moll (dir), The Last Days (film), 98-99. *Media:* Acrylic, Mixed Media

CAIN, DAVID PAUL
PAINTER, PHOTOGRAPHER
b Indianapolis, Ind, Oct 14, 1928. *Study:* Univ NMex, Albuquerque, 48-49; Earlham Coll, Richmond, Ind, BA, 50; Madison Art Sch, Conn, 79. *Work:* Old Jailhouse Found, Austin, Tex; Int Ctr Photog, NY; many pvt collections in US, Mex & Puerto Rico. *Exhib:* US Army Art Show, European Command, Munich, Ger, 52; solo exhibs, Earlham Coll, Ind, Aiden House, Mass, Yale Univ, Conn, and others. *Pos:* Freelance, 78-. *Teaching:* Teacher art & photog, Grove Sch, Madison, Conn, 70-74; teacher art, Lincoln High Sch, San Jose, Costa Rica, 75; photog. teacher, Guilford Art Sch, Conn,

76-77; instr oil painting, Meridian Art Gallery, Conn, 78- & Hamden Arts Comn, Conn, 78-. *Mem:* Brownstone Group, Meriden, Conn; Guilford Art League, Conn; Madison Art Soc, Conn (pres, 81-); Mt Carmel Art Asn; Conn Pastel Soc, Meriden, Conn; Arts & Crafts Asn, Meriden, Conn. *Media:* All. *Dealer:* Fischer Gallery Boston St Guilford CT 06437

CAIN, SARAH
COLLAGE ARTIST
b Albany, NY, 1979. *Study:* San Francisco Art Inst, BFA (Bernard Osher Scholar), 2001; Univ Calif, Berkeley, MFA, 2006; Skowhegan Sch Painting & Sculpture, 2006. *Exhib:* Solo exhibs include LAB Annex, San Francisco, 2001, Lucky Tackle Gallery, Oakland, Calif, 2003, San Francisco Art Comn, 2004, Queens Nails Annex, San Francisco, 2005, Anthony Meier Fine Arts, San Francisco, 2006; Group exhibs include Reference Check Number One, San Francisco Pub Libr, 2001; Space is the Place, Berkeley Art Ctr, Calif, 2005; Murphy & Cadogan Fel Award Show, San Francisco Art Comn, 2005; The Flaming Sword of Truth, Berkeley Art Mus, Calif, 2006; A Century of Collage, 25th Anniversary Show, Elizabeth Leach Gallery, Portland, Ore, 2006; SECA Art Award Exhib, San Francisco Mus Mod Art, 2007; Like color in pictures, Aspen Art Mus, Colo, 2007; Calif Biennial, Orange County Mus Art, Newport Beach, Calif, 2008. *Awards:* Schmidt Family Fel, 2000; Inst Int Educ Travel Fel, 2000; John Anson Kittredge Fel, 2002; Demonstration Grant, Univ Calif Inst Res Arts, 2005; Murphy & Cadogan Fel, 2005; SECA Art Award, San Francisco Mus Mod Art, 2006; Pollock-Krasner Found Grant, 2007. *Dealer:* Anthony Meier Fine Arts 1969 California St San Francisco CA 94109

CAIVANO, ERNESTO
ARTIST
b Madrid, Spain, 1972. *Study:* The Cooper Union, BFA, 99; Columbia Univ, MFA, 2001. *Exhib:* Group exhibs, Intercontinental Gallery, Montreal, Can, 1999, Part 01, Wallach Gallery, New York City, 2000, Thesis Exhib, Columbia Univ, New York City, 2001, Medium, Roy Neiman Gallery, New York City, 2001, Miami Ambassador, Fredric Snitzer Gallery, Miami, 2002, Shallow Interiors, Rivington Arms Gallery, New York City, 2002, Amenities, Gershwin Hotel, New York City, 2002, My Sources Say Yes, Guild & Greyshkul, New York City, 2003, Terrarium, Bronx River Art Ctr, NY, 2003, Druid Wood as a Superconductor, Space 101, Brooklyn, 2003, Game Over, Grimm/Rosenfeld, Munich, 2003, New Topography, Geoffrey Young Gallery, Great Barrington, Mass, 2003; Grant/Selwyn Fine Art, Los Angeles, 2003, St Valentine's Day Massacre, 85 Chambers, New York City, 2003, Placemaker Gallery, Miami, 2004, PS1 Contemp Art Ctr, Long Island, 2004, Whitney Biennial, Whitney Mus Am Art, 2004 Summer Drawing Exhib, David Zwirner Gallery, New York City, 2004; Solo exhibs, Arboreal, 31 Grand Inc, Brooklyn, 2003, Mating Grounds, Richard Heller Gallery, Los Angeles, 2004. *Awards:* Recipient Joan Sovern award, 2000, 2001; Hayward prize, Am Austrian Found, 2001 & 2002; Salzburg Kunstakademie Fel, 2002. *Mailing Add:* 48 Eldridge St #6E New York NY 10002

CAJERO, MICHAEL RAY
ENVIRONMENTAL ARTIST, SCULPTOR
b Tucson, Ariz, May 26, 1947. *Study:* Univ Ariz, BFA (studio art), 69; Kent State, MFA (drawing, painting & art hist), 76. *Exhib:* Alumni exhib, Mus Art, Univ Ariz, Tucson, 85; solo exhib, Shemer Art Ctr, Scottsdale, Ariz, 89; The Death Cart, Roswell Mus Art, NMex & Central Arts Collective, Tucson, Ariz, 90; Human Components - Light Altars, Mus Art, Univ Ariz, Tucson, 92; The Painted Bride, A Triangular Rotation, Philadelphia, 93. *Teaching:* Part-time instr drawing & design, Community Servs Campus, Pima Community Col, Tucson, Ariz, 77-94; instr drawing & sculpting, Tucson Mus Art Sch, Ariz, 84-; adj prof drawing & design, Pima Community Col, 99-. *Awards:* Nat Endowment Arts Visual Arts Fel, 93-94; Artist in Residence Fel, Tucson Partnership Inc, 93; Pima Arts Coun Visual Arts Fel, Tucson, 94; New Genre fel, Tucson. *Bibliog:* Wesley A Rusnell (auth), Invitational Exhib, Roswell Mus Art, 90. *Media:* Installation, Environments. *Mailing Add:* 2740 E 6th St Tucson AZ 85716-4408

CALABRESE, KAREN ANN
PAINTER, INSTRUCTOR
b New York City, May 27, 1952. *Study:* Ridgewood Sch Art, Cert, 73. *Exhib:* Lake Mohawk Country Club, Sparta, NJ, 95; Skylands Asn, Ringwood, NJ, 97; The Public Gallery, Newton, NJ, 2001; Ringwood Manor Asn Arts, Ringwood, NJ, 2004; 21st Ann Skylands Exhib, Newton, NJ, 2008. *Pos:* Designer (paste-up artist), Ridge Type Serv, Ridgewood, NJ, 73-77; artist (production mgr), Eastern Art, Garfield, NJ, 77-81. *Teaching:* Pvt instr (drawing), Pvt Studio, Highland Lakes, NJ, 95-2002; instr (perspective drawing & painting), Phoenix Sch Art, Vernon, NJ, 98-2005. *Awards:* 1st Place (painting), Highland Lakes Country Club, 94; 1st Place (drawing), Ringwood Manor Asn Arts, 2004; 1st Place (pastel), 2nd Place (drawing), St Catherine of Bologna 8th Ann Photo & Art Exhib, 2007; 1st Place (painting), 3rd Place (pastel), St Catherine of Bologna 9th Ann Photo & Art Exhib, 2008; 1st Place (drawing), St. Catherine of Bologna, 10th Ann Photo and Art Exhib, 2009; 1st Place (greeting card design), Decorative Artists Wrkbk Mag, 98. *Mem:* Warwick Art League; Middletown Art Group; Sussex Co Arts & Heritage Coun. *Media:* All Media, Watercolor & Gouache, Pencil. *Dealer:* Sussex Co Arts & Heritage Council Gallery 137 Spring St Newton NJ 07860; Flying Pig Gallery 15 Main St Sussex NJ 07461

CALABRO, JOANNA SONDRA
PAINTER, SCULPTOR
b Waterbury, Conn. *Study:* Paier Coll Art, 65-66; Rice Univ, 77; studied with Bruno Lucchesi, Italy, 82. *Work:* US Embassies, Bratisbva, Slovakia; Ambassador Theodore E Russell pvt collection. *Comn:* Sculpture, comn by Graham Doorland, Airborne Express, Seattle, Wash, 84. *Exhib:* Juried exhib, Champions Art Show, Houston, 74 & Art League Houston, 74, 76 & 77; Solo exhibs, Wilmington Coll, Ohio, 83 & Rockport Art Asn, Mass, 89-92; Salmagundi Art Club Nat Show, NY, 84; N Am Sculpture Exhib, Golden, Colo, 85. *Pos:* Juror, numerous art shows in Conn, Tex, Ohio & Mass, 70-98; bd selectman, Rockport Art Coun, 94. *Teaching:* Instr sculpture & painting, Five Star Gallery, Houston, 74-76. *Awards:* First Place Award, Am Pen & Brush Women, 75; Martha Moore Award, Rockport Art Asn, 89 & Excellence in Any Medium, 98. *Bibliog:* Kit Van Cleave (auth), Winning a Struggle, SW Art, 78. *Mem:* Am Artist Prof League; Rockport Art Asn; Am Metallic Sculpture Asn; Copley Soc; Guild Boston Artists. *Media:* Oil; Clay, Metal. *Publ:* Contrib, Goddesses for Every Season, Element Books, 95; Best of Oil Painting, Rockport Publ, 96; Portrait Inspirations, Quarry Books, 97; Arts Pleiades N, Pleiades Publ, 97; A Gallery of Marine Art, Rockport Publ, 98. *Dealer:* Fine Arts Rockport Gallery 49-B Main St Rockport MA 01966

CALABRO, RICHARD PAUL
SCULPTOR, PAINTER
b Yonkers, NY, June 27, 1937. *Study:* Univ Ga, BLA, 62; Sch Visual Arts, New York, 66; Pa State Univ, MFA, 68. *Work:* Pa State Univ Mus, State College, Pa; Univ Mass, Amherst; Mus Mod Art, NY; Venice Video Libr, Italy. *Exhib:* Information, Mus Mod Art, NY, 70; solo exhibs, Henri Gallery, Washington, DC, 70, Max Hutchinson Gallery, NY, NY, 72 & Shippee Gallery, NY, 85 & 86; Categorizing (solo exhib), Moore Coll Art, Philadelphia, Pa, 75; Lenore Gray Gallery, Providence, RI, 88. *Teaching:* Prof sculpture, Univ RI, 68-. *Awards:* Fulbright Fel, 68; Nat Endowment Arts Grant, 77; RI State Arts Coun Grant, 79 & 88. *Dealer:* Shippee Gallery 41 E 57th St New York NY

CALAMAR, GLORIA
PAINTER
b New York, NY, Sept 7, 1921. *Study:* Otis Art Inst, Los Angeles, 39-43; Art Students League, scholar, 43-45, State Univ NY, New Paltz, BA (art hist), 69-70. *Work:* Nat Mus Am Art, Washington, DC; Santa Barbara Mus, Calif; Mt St Mary Coll; Art Students League. *Exhib:* Solo exhibs, Mus d' Art Moderne dela Ville de Paris, France, 67, Univ Calif, Berkeley, 69, Georgetown Univ, 74, Alkamal Gallery, Jerusalem, Israel, 81 & Beaux Arts Ctr, Tunis, Tunisia, 81; Los Angeles Mus Art, 54; Bertrand Russel Centenary Invitational, London, 72-73; Drawings & Watercolors of India, Swastika Gallery, Jaisalmer India, 84; Victorian Houses, Humboldts Finest Gallery, Eureka, Calif, 88; Lighthouses, Starr King Gallery, Unitarian Church, San Francisco, Calif, 88; Santa Barbara Faulkner Gallery, 92-94. *Teaching:* Instr studio courses & art hist, Orange Co Community Coll, 63-68 & Santa Barbara City Coll, 75-79; art hist, Mt St Mary Coll, New York, 68-69; instr drawing, Univ Calif, Santa Barbara, 79. *Awards:* Nat Endowment Arts Grant, 80-81; Residency Grant, Dorland Mountain Art Colony, Temecular, Calif, 83; Award, Santa Barbara Visual Artists League, 92-96. *Bibliog:* A gift is indicated, Trumpeteer Mag, 49; Gloria Calamar has affinity for her subject, Am Artist Mag, 4/69. *Mem:* Life mem, Woodstock Art Asn; life mem, Art Students League, New York; charter mem, Artists' Equity Asn, New York. *Media:* Watercolor, Oil. *Publ:* Auth, The Adventuress a Remarkable Travel Experience, Independent News Alliance, 69; Palette Talk, Grumbacker, Publ, #28; Kalavita: A Little Town Where a Clock Never Moves; Tar Pits Park Landmark Proposal, Santa Barbara Co Hist Landmark Adv Comn. *Mailing Add:* Studio 12 PO Box 2517 Santa Barbara CA 93120-2517

CALATRAVA, SANTIAGO
ARCHITECT
b Valencia, Spain, 1951. *Study:* Escuela Tecnica Superior de Arquitectura de Valencia, Spain, 1974; ETH Zurich, PhD, 1981. *Exhib:* Solo exhibs, Retrosepctive, traveling exhib, 1992, La Lonja, Spain, 1993, Dynamics of Equilibrium, Ma Gallery, Tokyo, 1994, Mus de Navarra, Pamplona, Spain, 1995, Milwaukee Art Mus, Wis, 1996,Meadows Mus, Southern Methodist Univ, Dallas, 2001; group exhibs, Mus Mod Art, New York, 1993, 2004, 2005; Mus Applied & Folk Arts, Moscow, Russia, 1994; Nat. Mus Sci, Tech & Space, Haifa, Israel, 1997; Kunsthistorisches Mus Wien, Vienna, Austria, 2003. *Teaching:* lectr, Archit dept, ETH Zurich, 98, Mass Inst Tech, 98. *Awards:* City of Zurich Award for Good Building, Switzerland, 1991; Brunel Award, Stadelhofen Railway Station, Zurich, 1992, Madrid, Spain, 1998; City of Toronto Urban Design Award, Canada, 1993; Canton of Lucerne Award for Good Building Lucerne, Switzerland, 1995; Algur H Meadows Award for Excellence in the Arts, Meadows Sch Arts, Dallas, Tex, 2010; Award for Excellence in Design, Am Mus Natural Hist, New York, 2001; Best of 2001, Time Mag, New York, 2001; Illuminating Design Award of Merit, Illuminating Engring Soc North Am, New York, 2003; Golden Plate Award, Acad Achievement, Chicago, 2004; Time 100, Time Mag, New York, 2005; AIA Gold Medal, Am Inst Arhchit, DC, 2005; Sidney L Stauss Award, NY Soc Archit, New York, 2006; Urban Visionaries Award for Archit, Cooper union for the Advancement Sci & Art, New York, 2007; Golden Belgian Building Award, Brussels, Belgium, 2009. *Mailing Add:* Santiago Calatrava Inc 713 Park Ave New York NY 10021

CALDWELL, ELEANOR
JEWELER, EDUCATOR
b Kansas City, Mo, May 1, 1927. *Study:* Southwest Mo State Univ, Springfield, BS in Educ, 48; Columbia Univ, MA, 53, EdD, 59. *Work:* Colo Women's Coll, Denver; Ft Hays Kans State Coll, Hays; Denver Pub Schs; Northern Ill Univ, DeKalb; Sheldon Mem Art Gallery, Lincoln, Nebr. *Comn:* Presidential medallion, Northern Ill Univ, 70; 3 graphic images, pvt collection, 2002. *Exhib:* Am Jewelry, Smithsonian Inst Traveling Exhib, 55-57; Handweaving II, Smithsonian Inst Traveling Exhib, Denver Art Mus, 58-59; Own Your Own Exhib, Denver Art Mus, Colo, 61-63 & 65-67; Jewelry & Precious Metalsmiths, Wichita Art Asn, 72; Toys Designed by Artists, Ark Art Ctr, Little Rock, 75 & 78; Am Metalwork 1976, Sheldon Mem Art Gallery, Lincoln, 76; The Metalsmith Int Exhib, Phoenix Art Mus, Ariz, 77; Metalsmith Int, Univ Kans, Lawrence, 81; Soc N Am Goldsmiths' Int, Cranbrook Acad Art, 87; Wichita Nat Decorative Arts, Wichita, 88; Contemp Jewelry Invitational, NY, 89; D'Art, Mus Art, Tucson, Ariz, 98, 2002 & 2004; and others. *Pos:* Bd trustee, Tucson Mus Art, 96-; Fine Arts Bd, Univ Ariz, Tucson, 99-. *Teaching:* Assoc prof jewelry & graphics, Ft Hays Kans State Univ, 54-57 & 64-67 & Edinboro State Coll, Pa, 60-62;

prof jewelry & metals, Northern Ill Univ, 67-83, prof emer, 83- & Arrowmont Sch Crafts, Univ Tenn, Gatlinburg, 74-77 & 82-88. *Awards:* Jewelry Award, 12th Nat Decorative Arts, Cent States Craftsmen's Guild, 57; Purchase Award, 5th Ann Own Your Own Exhib, Denver Pub Schs, 61; Res Grant, Northern Ill Univ Grad Sch, 68-82. *Bibliog:* Meg Torbert (ed), American Jewelry, Design Quart, Walker Art Ctr, 59 & 61; Lois E Franke (auth), Handwrought Jewelry, McKnight & McKnight, 62; Jon Nelson (auth), American Metalwork 1976 (slide set), Sheldon Mem Art Gallery, Lincoln, 76; Slide Bank, Phoenix Arts Comm, Ariz, 90. *Mem:* Soc of N Am Goldsmiths; Am Crafts Coun; Mus Art Tucson; Nat Mus Women Arts (charter mem). *Media:* Jewelry and related objects in gold and silver; graphic and collage images. *Interests:* Contemporary glass, paintings & prints by American Indian artists. *Dealer:* Sanders Galleries 6420 N Campbell Tucson AZ 85718. *Mailing Add:* 4949 E Placita Alisa Tucson AZ 85718

CALDWELL, GRAHAM
ARTIST
b Philadelphia, 1973. *Study:* Eugene Lang Col; Parsons Sch Design, New Sch for Social Res, NY City, 1992-95; RI Sch Design, BFA (glass), 1998. *Exhib:* Solo exhibs include Systems, Millennium Arts Ctr, Washington, DC, 2001, Elizabeth's Tears, Broadway Windows, NY City, 2002, New Sculpture, Addison/Ripley Fine Art, Washington, DC, 2003, Slowly Growing Things, 2005; group exhibs include Love Show, The Arcade, Providence, RI, 1996; Woods Gerry Gallery, Providence, RI, 1997; Mus Contemp Art, Washington, DC, 1998; Craft House, Penland, NC, 2000; Through the Looking Glass, The Octagon, Mus Am Archit Found, Washington, DC, 2001; Emerging Artists, Bergdorf Goodman, NY City, 2002; US Embassy, Prague, 2003; Meat and You, Strand on Volta, Washington, DC, 2003; Census 03, New Art From DC, Corcoran Gallery of Art, Washington, DC, 2003; Art From the Past to the Present, A Selection, Osuna Art, Bethesda, MD, 2004; US Consulate, Istanbul, 2004; Installations/Drawings, G Fine Art, Washington, DC, 2005. *Bibliog:* A Tale of Two Houses, 2/9/2001, Seeing the Light at Millennium, 6/22/2001, Splendor in the Glass, 12/19/2002, Caldwell's Biomorphic Glass Action, 12/20/2002, & Graham Caldwell: New Language in Glass, 12/30/2004, The Washington Post; Glenn Dixon (auth), Graham Caldwell: New Sculpture, Glass, spring/2003. *Media:* glass. *Dealer:* G Fine Art 1514 14th St NW DC 20005. *Mailing Add:* 4660 Broad Branch Rd NW Washington DC 20008

CALIBEY, GREGORY
PAINTER
b Conn, 1959. *Study:* Wesleyan Coll; Univ NC. *Exhib:* Solo exhibs, Eleanor Ettinger, NY, 2000, 2003, 2005, 2007; Group exhibs, New Masters of Realism, Eleanor Ettinger, NY, 1998, Figure in Am Art, 1999-2007, Int Summer Salon, 1999-2000, 2003-2004, 2006, Int Autumn Salon, 2005; Am Figurative Painting, Albemarle Gallery, London, 1999; It's All About the Figure, Bob Rauschenberg Gallery, Edison Coll, Ft Myers, Fla, 2007. *Mailing Add:* c/o Eleanor Ettinger Gallery 24 W 57th St Ste 509 New York NY 10019

CALIFF, MARILYN ISKIWITZ
PAINTER, COLLAGE ARTIST
b Memphis, Tenn, Apr 27, 1932. *Study:* Memphis Coll Art, BFA, 70; Univ Memphis, MFA, 88. *Work:* Memphis Brooks Mus Art, Overton Park; Leo Bearman, Sr Collection, Memphis, Tenn; Boyle Investments, Memphis, Tenn; Nathan Walberg Collection, Miami, Fla; The Pie Lady Corp Collection, Memphis, Tenn; Tenn State Art Mus, Nashville, Tenn. *Comn:* Glass mosaic murals (with Barbara Shankman), Memphis Hebrew Acad, 62, Baron Hirsch Synagogue, 64 & Memphis Jewish Community Ctr, 68. *Exhib:* Solo exhibs, Earth Art Gallery, West Palm Beach, Fla, 89, Univ Northern Ala, Florence, 91 & Oak Ridge Cult Arts Ctr, Tenn, 91, Stamp Francisco, Rubber Stamp Art Gallery, San Francisco, Calif, 95 & Salem Col, Winston-Salem, NC, 97; First Int Fe-Mail Artistamps Exhib, Rubber Stamp Art Gallery, San Francisco, Calif, 97; Nat League Am Penwomen Biennale, Univ Tampa, Lee Scarfone Gallery, Fla, 98; Morocca Cafe, 99; Germantown Pub Libr, 2000; Wimbledon Sportsplex, 2001; Germantown Performing Arts Ctr, 2001; Tenn Art Mus, Nashville; Lilly Oncology on Canvas Exhib, Royal Coll Art, London Eng, 2007; Memphis in May Sanctioned Turkish Delights, Artists on Central, 2008; Dixon Gallery and Gardens, Memphis, Tenn, 2009; Mid South Community Coll, 2010; WKNO TV, 2011; Caritas Village, 2011; Wings Gallery, Memphis, Tenn, 2011; Dixon Gallery & Gardens, 2012; Goldsmith's Botanic Garden, 2012. *Teaching:* adj prof (art appreciation), SW Tenn Com Col, Memphis, 2002-08. *Awards:* Three Purchase Prizes, First Tenn Artists & Craftsman Show, 72; First Place Acrylics, Tenn State Art Competition, Nat League Am Penwomen, 89, First Place Mixed Media, 91, First Place Photog, 95; Purchase Prize, All Tenn Artist, Tenn State Mus, 01; Arts in Park Photography Prize, Memphis, Tenn; 1st prize in oils, Mid South Exhib, 73. *Bibliog:* Fine Arts Trader, 6/94; USA Weekend, 8/25-27/95; Memphis Mag, Vol XXI, No 11, 2/97. *Mem:* Nat Mus Women Arts; Nature Conservancy; Hadassah; Artists' Link (pres 2004-2005); Nat Womens' History Mus. *Media:* Mixed Media, Collage, Photography. *Interests:* Travel & snorkeling. *Publ:* Auth, Your First Quilt, 72; The Pillow Book, 73; Travelin' with Marilyn, Newsletter, pvt publ, 96. *Dealer:* Paul Edelstein Gallery, Memphis. *Mailing Add:* 5305 Denwood Ave Memphis TN 38120

CALKINS, ROBERT G
HISTORIAN, EDUCATOR
b Oakland, Calif, Dec 29, 32. *Study:* Princeton Univ, BA, 55; Harvard Univ, MA, 62, PhD, 67. *Teaching:* Prof hist art, Cornell Univ, 66-; prof emer, 2002; seminar dir, 83,85, 87, 89, 90, 92, 93, 94, 95, 96, 97, 99, 2001. *Awards:* Grant, Am Coun Learned Soc, 73 & APS, 80. *Mem:* Int Ctr Medieval Art (mem bd adv, 71-, dir & vpres, 80-81, pres, 81-82); Coll Art Asn; Medieval Acad Am. *Res:* Medieval art & archit. *Publ:* Auth, Distribution of labor: The illuminators of the hours of Catherine of Cleves, Transactions Am Philos Soc, 79; Monuments of Medieval Art, Dutton, 79; Illuminated Books of the Middle Ages, Cornell Univ Press, 83 & 85; Programs of Medieval Illumination, Helen Foresman Spencer Mus Art, 84; Medieval Architecture in Western Europe from AD 300 to 1500, Oxford Univ Press, 98. *Mailing Add:* 4 Indigo Run Dr Apt 2720 Hilton Head Island SC 29926

CALLAHAN, AILEEN LOUGHLIN
PAINTER, MURALIST
b Dayton, Ohio. *Study:* Boston Univ, BFA, 68, MFA, 70; Skowhegan Sch Painting & Sculpture, Summer Grants, 68 & 69; Escuela Nac de Pintura y Escultura, Mex City, Fel study with David Alfaro Siquieros & Juan O'Gorman, 70-72. *Work:* Hotel Camino Real, Mexico City; Boston Univ; Clinic Collection, City of Boston; McMullen Mus Art, Boston Coll; New Bedford Whaling Mus. *Comn:* Interior wall, Skowhegan Sch Painting & Sculpture, Maine, 69; interior mural (2 walls), Inst Contemp Art, Boston, 75; exterior wall, San Felipe Church, Albuquerque, NMex, 79. *Exhib:* Nat Competition Exhib, Pindar Gallery, New York, 89; Nat Affiliate Members Exhib, Soho 20 Gallery, New York, 90; Small Works Nat Exhib, Amos Eno Gallery & New York, 90-91; Invitational Exhib, Pratt Manhattan Gallery, 91; Invitational Exhib, Am Acad Arts & Letts, New York, 94; Drietzer Gallery, Brandeis Univ, 97; McMullen Mus, Boston Coll, 99; Hofstra Univ, New York, 2001; New Bedford Art Mus, Mass, 2005; Lied Gallery, Creighton Univ, NE, 2007; Kauffman Gallery, Shippensburg Univ, Pa, 2009; Grad Theological Union Libr, Berkeley, Calif, 2010; Imagining Moby, New Bedford Whaling Mus, 2011; A Community of Artists, Danforth Mus, 2012; Cruel Sea: Law of the Fishes, Danforth Mus, Framingham, Mass, 2012; A Community of Artists, Danforth Art, Framingham, Mass, 2013, 2014; Off the Wall, Danforth Art, Framingham, Mass, 2015. *Teaching:* Lectr fine arts, Boston Coll, 79-, Regis Coll, Weston, Mass, 79-98 & Lesley Coll, Cambridge, Mass, 88-91, Univ Mass, Boston, 91-. *Awards:* Blanche E Coleman Award, Coleman Trust, 84; Jurors Award, Small Works, Amos Eno Gallery, 90. *Bibliog:* P Fernandez Marquez (auth), Aileen Loughlin Callahan, El Nac, 7/23/72; Theresa Gawlas (auth), Regis Professor collaborates with poet on book, Wayland-Weston Town Crier, 10/1/87; Joyce Cohen (auth), Corporal places: paintings by Aileen Callahan, Art New Eng, 6/94. *Media:* Oil, Fresco. *Publ:* Auth, A painter's language: the color of wind, Regis Today Mag, 87; The Face of Art Once Removed, Regis Today Mag, 92; Dante's Heads: The Plume & The Pallette, 2001; Eye to Eye: Leviathan, 2003; The Drawings, Conversations In An Icon (auth Francis Patrick Sullivan), 2008. *Mailing Add:* 69 Harvey St No 12 Cambridge MA 02140

CALLARI, EMILY DOLORES
PAINTER, RESTORER
b New York, NY. *Study:* Sch Indust Arts, New York, 37; Art Students League, 45-69; Bryant Youth & Adult Ctr, Queens, 50; Wash Irving Evening Trade, 53; Wall St Art Asn, 64-68; studied with Brackman, Olinsky, Green. *Work:* Portrait, Venice Art Ctr, Fla; two religious paintings, pvt collection of Bishop Nevins, Diocese of Venice, Fla. *Comn:* Life-size Madonna, comn by J Chorbajian, Church Bd, Holy Martyrs Armenian Church, Bayside, NY, 58; portraits of family, owners of Duke Garden Ctr, Venice, Fla, 75-99; portrait of late dist Judge James Gordon, comn by Mrs J Gordon, Louisville, Ky, 90; portrait of Chloe Embree, Jacaranda, Venice, Fla, 96; various portraits mems of Blumenstaad family, Chicago, 98. *Exhib:* Knickerbocker Artists, Nat Acad Exhibs, New York, 59; Wall St Art Asn, New York, 64-68; Travel Award Exhib, Wall St Art Asn, London, Amsterdam, Paris & Bourse, 68-69; retrospective, Caldwell Trust, Venice, Fla, 96; Italian Heritage Fest, Venice Art Ctr, Fla, 98; Women's Support & Enrichment Ctr, Venice, Fla, 98. *Pos:* Art adv, Hollywood Jewelry Co, New York, 47-60; secy, Salmagundi Art Club, New York, 70-73, Artists Fel, New York, 70-73. *Teaching:* Portraiture, Venice Recreation, Sarasota Co, 74-80, Venice Art Ctr, 74-96. *Awards:* First Prize, Nat NY State Pavilion, 68; First Prize, Wall St Art, New York, 68; First Prize, Venice Art Ctr, Fla, 90; First awards and travel awards for portrait paints, London, Paris & Amsterdam. *Bibliog:* Various articles, Venice Gondolier, 73-96; The Weekly, 96. *Mem:* Life mem, Art Students League; Catharine Lorillard Wolfe Art Club; fac mem, Venice Art Ctr; Sarasota Co Coun Arts; Nat Mus Women Arts. *Media:* Oil, Pastel, Portraits. *Specialty:* Portraits. *Interests:* Travel. *Collection:* First prize winners of black models. *Publ:* Illus, ad copy, Women's Wear, 50. *Dealer:* Final Touch Frame Gallery Venice FL

CALLE, PAUL
PAINTER, WRITER
b New York, NY, Mar 3, 1928. *Study:* Pratt Inst. *Work:* Thomas Gilcrease Inst Am Hist & Art, Tulsa, Okla; Nat Cowboy Hall Fame & Western Heritage Ctr, Oklahoma City; Nat Air & Space Mus, Washington, DC; NASA Fine Art Collection; US Dept Interior; Booth Mus, Cartersville, Ga; and others. *Comn:* NASA, Cape Kennedy, Jet Propulsion Lab, Star City, Moscow, USSR, 68-75; Basic History of Iron & Steel, Basic Indust, 68-70; Nat Park Serv, Mesa Verde, Yosemite, Cape Hatterus, 70-74; Classics in Surgery, Schering co, 71-73; and others. *Exhib:* 1st & 2nd Convocation Western Art, Dallas, Tex; NASA Eyewitness to Space, Nat Gallery Art, Washington, DC, 70; NASA Apollo-Soyuz, Moscow, 75; 25 Yr Retrospective, Thomas Gilcrease Mus, 92; Prix de West Invitational, 92-2007; and others. *Awards:* Mill Pond Press Award, Northwest Rendezvous, 79-80; Silver Medal Drawing, Nat Acad Western Art, 92; Nona Jean Hulsey Award, Prix de West Invitational, 95; and others. *Mem:* Soc Illusr; Northwest Rendezvous Group. *Media:* Oil, Pencil. *Publ:* Auth & illusr, The Pencil, Watson & Guptill, 75; Paul Calle An Artist's Journey, Mill Pond Press. *Mailing Add:* 316 Old Sib Rd Ridgefield CT 06877-2317

CALLE, SOPHIE
PHOTOGRAPHER
b Paris, France, 1953. *Work:* Mus Mod Art, New York; Solomon R Guggenheim Mus, New York; Ctr Georges Pompidor, Paris, France; Los Angeles Co Mus Art. *Exhib:* Solo exhibs include Fred Hoffman Gallery, Los Angeles, 1989, Pat Hearn Gallery, New York, 1991, Leo Castelli Gallery, New York, 1993,Contemp Arts Mus, Houston, 1994, High Mus Art, Atlanta, 1995, Paula Cooper Gallery, New York, 2001, 2005, 2009, Venice Biennale, 2007, Take Care of Yourself, Paris France, Montreal, Can, 2008, Brazil, 2009, White Chapel Gallery, London, 2009, De Pont Found, The Netherlands, 2009, La Mus Mod Art, Humlebaek, Denmark, 2010; Group exhibs include Whitney Biennial, Whitney Mus Art, New York, 1993; Taking Pictures, Int Ctr Photography, New York, 1994; Premises, Solomon R Guggenheim Mus, New York, 1998; Urban Mythologies, Bronx Mus Arts, New York, 1999; Mus as Muse, Mus Mod

Art, New York, 1999; Vanitas Parsonae, Robert Miller Gallery, New York, 2000; The Photographic Impulse, Henry Art Gallery, Seattle, Wash, 2002; Realm of the Senses, James Cohan Gallery, New York, 2004; Beauty Matters, Tina Kim Fine Art, New York, 2004; Seeing Things, Dorsky Gallery, Long Island City, NY, 2007; The New Normal, Artist Space, New York, 2008; Swift Inst, New York, 2009; Paula Cooper, 2009; Guggenheim Mus, Bilbao, Spain, 2009; Haunted: Contemp Photography/Video/Performance, Soloman R Guggenheim Mus, New York, 2010; Exposed, Voyeurism, Surveillance & the Camera, Tate Modern, London, 2010. *Awards:* Spectrum-Int Preis fur Fotografie der Stifung Niedersachsen, 2002; Int Award in Photog, Hasselblad Found, 2010; Named one of 10 Most Important Artists of Today, Newsweek mag, 2011. *Bibliog:* Sophie Calle, Take Care of Yourself, Actes, Sud, Press, 2007; Sophie Calle, Appointment with Sigmund Freud, Thomas Hudson, New York, 2005; Sophie Calle, Exquisite Pain, Thomas Hudson, 2005. *Dealer:* Paula Cooper Gallery 534 W 21st St New York NY. *Mailing Add:* Paula Cooper Gallery 534 W 21st St New York NY 10011

CALLIS, JO ANN
PHOTOGRAPHER
b Cincinnati, Ohio. *Study:* Univ Calif, Los Angeles, BA (art), 74; MFA (photog), 77. *Work:* Biblio Nat, Paris, France; Carnegie Inst, Pittsburgh, Pa; Corcoran Gallery Art, Washington; Mus Mod Art, NY; San Francisco Mus Mod Art; Getty Mus, Los Angeles, Calif; Nat Mus of Modern Art, Tokyo. *Exhib:* Oakland Mus, 77, 83 & 91; Milwaukee Art Ctr, 79; Fogg Art Mus, 80; Whitney Mus Am Art, 81 & 86; Contemp Arts Mus, Houston, 81; Los Angeles Co Mus Art, 82 & 87 (with catalog); San Francisco Mus Mod Art, 83 & 84; Mus Contemp Art, Los Angeles, 84; Solo exhibs, Mus Contemp Art, Los Angeles (with catalog), 85, Dorothy Goldeen Gallery, Santa Monica, 92, G Gibson Gallery, Seattle, 93, Laurence Miller Gallery, NY, 93, Cleveland Mus Art, Ohio, 94 & Craig Krull Gallery, Santa Monica, 94-95, 99 & 2001; Cranbrook Acad Art Mus (with catalog), 88; High Mus Art (traveling, with catalog), 89; Mus Mod Art, NY, 89 & 91; Denver Art Mus, 91; (Basically) Black & White, Riverside Art Mus, Calif, 92; Patterns of Influence, Ctr Creative Photog, Univ Ariz, Tucson, 92; Clay Out of Context, Univ Art Gallery, San Diego State Univ, 93; Am Made-The New Still Life (with catalog), Isetan Mus Art, Tokyo, 93; Group exhibs, Armory Ctr for the Arts, Calif, 2000, Ctr for Creative Photog, Univ Ariz, 2000, USC Fisher Gallery, Los Angeles, 2000. *Pos:* Workshop, San Francisco Art Inst, 78, Friends Photog & Ansel Adams Ctr Photog, San Francisco, 80, 86 & 90; juror, Friends Photog, Ferguson Grant & Ansel Adams Ctr Photog, San Francisco, 87; panelist, Bush Artist Fel Preliminary, St Paul, Minn, 90. *Teaching:* Instr photog, Calif State Univ, Fullerton, 77-78, Univ Calif, Los Angeles, 77-, Calif Inst Arts, Valencia, 76-. *Awards:* Awards in the Visual Arts, 89; Guggenheim Fel, 90; Photogr Fel, Nat Endowment Arts, 91; City of Los Angeles Cult Affairs Grant, 2001. *Bibliog:* Susan Kandel (auth), Enigmatic fabrications, Los Angeles Times, 6/11/92; Lita Barrie, On the scene: Los Angeles, Artspace, 9-10/92; JoAnn Callis: A fascination with transformation, Cal Arts Current, Vol 5, No 3, 5/93. *Mailing Add:* c/o Craig Krull Gallery Bergamot Sta 2525 Michigan Ave Bldg B3 Santa Monica CA 90404

CALLISTER, JANE
PAINTER
b Isle of Man, United Kingdom. *Exhib:* Solo exhibs, Bergamot Station, Santa Monica, 1999, Tiffany Szilage Gallery, St Petersburg, Fla, 2000, Southfirst art, Brooklyn, 2001, Peter Miller Gallery, Chicago, 2003, Susanne Veilmetter: Los Angeles Projects, 2004, 2006 & Contemporary Arts Forum Santa Barbara, 2007; California Girls, Purple Orchid Gallery, Dallas, 2000; Fresh, The Altoids Curiously Strong & Original Art Collection, The New Mus, NY, 2001; Las Vegas, James Kelley Contemp, Santa Fe, 2002; Wheeling: Krad-Kuit-Tour, J ette Rudolf Gallerie, Berlin, Germany, 2002; Paintings as Paradox, Artists Space, NY, 2002; 2003 Prague Biennial, Veletrzni Palace Mus Contemp Art; Possible worlds, Sch Visual Arts Gallery, Ind Univ, 2004; Bonkers ((Loco paisajes)!, WunderKammerII, Nina Menocal Gallery, Mexico City, 2005; California Biennial, Orange County Mus Art, 2006; Las Vegas Diaspora, Las Vegas Art Mus, 2007 & Laguna Art Mus, Calif, 2008; Prescient, Michael Berger Gallery, Pittsburgh, 2008. *Teaching:* Instr, Painting, Dept Art, Univ Calif, Santa Barbara. *Awards:* Art Matters Found Grant, 2009. *Media:* Acrylic. *Publ:* Colin Gardner (auth), Jane Callister's Artificial Elegance: Beyone the Pleasure Principal, UTSA Satellite Space, 9/1999; Vicky Perry (auth), Abstract Painting: Techniques & Concepts, Watson & Gutlipp, 9/2005; Jan Tumlir (auth), LA Artland, Blackdog Press, 11/2005. *Mailing Add:* UCSB Dept Art Bldg 434 Rm 123 Santa Barbara CA 93106-7120

CALLUORI HOLCOMBE, ANNA
CERAMIST
b Newark, NJ, Sept 15, 1952. *Study:* Montclair State Univ, NJ, BA, 70; La State Univ, MFA, 74. *Exhib:* Solo exhib, Wash Univ, St Louis, 81 & Mem Art Gallery, Rochester, NY, 91 & Archie Bray Found Gallery, Helena, Mont, 91; 51st Int Ceramic Art Competition, Int Mus Ceramics, Faenza, Italy, 98; The Still Life Transfigured, Clay Place, Pittsburgh, Pa, 2000; Albert Kemper Mus, St Joseph, MO, 2002; Mulvane Art Mus, Topeka, Kans, 2002; Birger Sandzea Gallery, Lindsburg, Kans, 2002; Solo, ATR Vallauris Gallery, France, 2003; Int Acad of Caramils mems Exhib; World Ceramils Exposition, Icheon & Korea, 2004; First Int Triennial of Silicats Arts, Kecskenet, Hungary, 2005. *Collection Arranged:* Ceramics Invitational, 80, Functional Ceramics with a Decorative Approach, 81 & Retrospective: Fred Brian, 84, Ill Wesleyan Univ, Bloomington; Nat Coun Educ Ceramic Arts Show (auth, catalog), traveling, 83-86 & 91; New Approaches to Figurative Art & Retrospective: Jack Wolsky, 86, Tower Fine Arts Gallery, Brockport, NY; Off the Pedestal, On the Walls, Village Gate Art Ctr, Rochester, NY; Int Mus Ceramics, Faenza, Italy; Jingdezen Ceramic Inst, China; Keramikmuseum, Westerwald, Germany. *Pos:* Dir, Tower Fine Arts Gallery, State Univ NY, Brockport, 84-94; head, art dept, Kansas State Univ, Manhattan, 94-2000; juror, Am Ceramic Soc Centennial Nat Juried Exhib, 96 & Int Cone Box Exhib, Orton, Found, 98. *Teaching:* Asst prof art, Ill Wesleyan Univ, Bloomington, 79-84; assoc prof art & gallery dir, State Univ NY, Brockport, 84-94; assoc prof art, Kans State Univ, 94-, prof, 98-. *Awards:* Int Ceramics Award, Sidney Meyer Found, Australia; Gold Medal, 46th Int Exhib Ceramics, Italy, 89; Sidney Meyer Found Int Ceramics Award, Shepperton Art Gallery, Australia, 97. *Bibliog:* Richard Zakin (auth), Ceramics, Mastering the Craft, Chilton Bk Co, 90; Richard Zakin (auth), Electric Kiln Ceramics (3rd ed), Chilton, 94; Craft & Art of Clay, Susan Peterson (4th ed), Richard Zakin (auth), Hand-Formed Ceramics: Creating From and Surface, Chilton Bk Co, 96; Best of Pottery, Rockport Publ, 96. *Mem:* Nat Coun Educ Ceramics Arts (pres-elect 92-94, dir exhibs, 83-86 & 89-91, pres, 92-94, past pres, 96-98, fel, currently); Empire State Crafts Alliance, NY; Am Crafts Coun; Coll Art Asn (prof practice comt, 2000-03); Nat Coun Art Admin (bd mem, 98-); Elected Mem of Int Acad of Art, (2002); Coll Art Asoc, Int Committee, (2005); Prof Practices Comn (2001-2005). *Media:* Ceramics. *Res:* Ceramic Sculpture. *Publ:* Auth, Master of fine Arts and careers, Nat Coun Art Adminrs Ceramics Art J, 80; Still life vignettes, 11/93 & Faenza: group study at the National Institute, 5/97, Ceramics Monthly; About My Work, Chinese Potters Newsletter, 2000; Building a Better Box, Pottery Making Illust, Vol 2, 99. A residency in Vallauris, Ceramics Tech, (No.18), 2004. Give and Take: using Slip Tech, Pottery making Illust, 2004. *Dealer:* Strecker-Nelson Gallery Manhattan KS; Oxford Gallery Rochester NY. *Mailing Add:* Univ Florida Sch of Arts and History 101B Fine Arts Bldg C PO Box 115801 Gainesville FL 32611

CALMAN, W(ENDY) L
PRINTMAKER, PHOTOGRAPHER
b New York, NY, Feb 23, 1947. *Study:* Univ Pittsburgh, BA (art hist), 69; Tyler Sch Art, Temple Univ, MEd, 70, MFA (printmaking), 72. *Work:* Honolulu Acad Arts; Ark Art Ctr, Little Rock; Del Mar Col; Int Ctr Photog, George Eastman House, NY; House of Humor and Satire, Gabravo, Bulgaria. *Exhib:* Photog Unlimited, Fogg Art Mus, Harvard Univ, 74; Uniquely Photog, Honolulu Acad Arts, 79; 16th Joslyn Biennial, Joslyn Art Mus, 80; Photofusion, Pratt Manhattan Ctr Gallery, NY, 81; Sights Unseen, AIR Gallery, NY, 82; Works on Paper, Am Haus, Hamburg, Ger, 87; Group Invitational, Aula Acad Fine Arts, Warsaw, Poland, 92; 2nd Bharat Bhavan Int Biennial Prints, Bhopal, India, 95. *Teaching:* Instr drawing & printmaking, Univ Tenn, Knoxville, 72-76; assoc prof printmaking, Ind Univ, Bloomington, 76-. *Awards:* Best Graphic Award, 16th Joslyn Biennial, Joslyn Mus Art, 80; Master Arts Fel, Ind Arts Coun, 85. *Bibliog:* K Wise (auth), Photographer's Choice, Addison House Found, 75; Thelma Newman (auth), Innovative Printmaking, Crown Publ, 77; Virginia Watson-Jones (auth), Contemporary American Sculptors, Oryx Press, 86. *Mem:* Coll Art Asn; World Print Coun; Philadelphia Print Club. *Media:* All. *Mailing Add:* 500 S Hawthorne Dr Bloomington IN 47401

CAMARATA, MARTIN L
ARTIST, EDUCATOR
b Rochester, NY, June 10, 1934. *Study:* NY State Univ, Buffalo, BA, 56; NY Univ, MA, 57. *Work:* Mus Belles Artes, Caracas, Venezuela; Univ of the Pac; Mus Palace of Legion Fine Arts, San Francisco. *Exhib:* Twenty-Second Painting Ann, Butler Inst Am Art, 57; Boston Printmakers Ann, 62-66; Philadelphia Print Club Ann, 65 & 66; Print-Drawing Ann, Pa Acad Fine Arts, 65, 66 & 68; Potsdam Ann Print-Drawing, NY, 74; Solo exhibs, McKissick Mus, Univ SC & Ore State Mus Fine Arts, Eugene, Ore. *Teaching:* Prof drawing & printmaking, Calif State Univ, Stanislaus, 64-. *Awards:* First Prize Print, William J Keller Award, 56; Best of Show, Calif State Fair Art Exhib, 65; Fulbright Fel, Rome, Italy, 58-59. *Bibliog:* T Albright (auth), rev in San Francisco Chronicle, 72 & 75. *Publ:* Auth, Lithography at Collectors Press, Artists Proof Mag, 72. *Mailing Add:* Art Dept Calif State Univ 801 W Monte Vista Ave Turlock CA 95382

CAMERON, BROOKE BULOVSKY
EDUCATOR, PRINTMAKER
b Madison, Wis. *Study:* Univ Wis, Madison, BS (art educ; honors); Univ Minn summer art hist tour of Europe with Prof Lorenz Eitner; Univ Iowa, with Mauricio Lasansky, MA (printmaking); NY Univ, viscosity printing workshop with Krishna Reddy, 82-83; Pratt Manhattan Graphics Ctr, litho & photo litho with James Martin & Ryo Watanabe; studied with Vito Giacalone, China & Japan, 84. *Work:* Emory Univ, Atlanta, Ga; Univ Ga Mus Art; Springfield Art Mus, Mo; Ringling Mus, Sarasota, Fla; Rockford Coll Dept Art Collection; Univ Wis, Madison, Wis; Stephens Col, Columbia, Mo; Indianapolis Mus Art, Ind; Ga Mus Art & Univ Ga, Athens; Portland Art Mus, Ore; United Telephone, Kansas City; Tri-con Indust(s), Matto City Japan. *Comn:* Miss Willie, ed prints, Lakeside Studios, Mich, 77. *Exhib:* "Americas 2000: Works on Paper", Minot, NDak, 94; 16th Ann Quad State Juried Exhib, Quincy Art Ctr, Ill, 96; For the Visual Arts 4th Anniversary 5 State Regional Show, Juanita Hammons Hall Performing Arts, Springfield, Mo, 96; Two-person exhib, Western Ill State Univ, Macomb, 96; Int Print Exhib, Portland Mus Art, Ore, 97; 49th Ann Nat Juried Print Exhib, Hunterdon Mus Art, Clinton, NJ, 2005; 30th Bradley Int Print & Drawing Exhib, Peoria, Ill, 2005; Ann Boston Printmaker's Exhib, Boston Univ, 2005. *Collection Arranged:* Heart of Am Nat Printmaking Exhib, Univ Mo. *Teaching:* Instr art & art hist, Tex Christian Univ, Ft Worth, 66-67; from instr to prof fine arts, Univ Mo, 67-, chmn dept art, 79-82. *Awards:* Printmaking Award, Crown Ctr Exhib Halls, Kansas City, Mo, 74; Univ Mo Res Coun Grant for Contemp Chinese Painting, 94; Purchase Award, Lynward Mem Purchase Prize, 44th Nat Hunterdon Mus Art, Hunterdon, NJ. *Bibliog:* many reviews in newspapers. *Mem:* Coll Art Asn; Women's Caucus Art; Kansas City Print Coalition; Southern Graphics Coun. *Media:* Intaglio, Photo-intaglio. *Specialty:* prints. *Interests:* travel. *Publ:* Contribr, Managing the Academic Department 17-18, Am Coun Educ & Macmillian Publ Co, 83; Greater Midwest Int, (catalogue), Central Mo State Univ, Warrensburg, 2005; Boston Printmakers, N Am Print Biennial (catalogue), Boston Univ, 2005; 30th Bradley Int Print & Drawing Exhib (catalogue), Peoria, Ill, 2005. *Dealer:* Lakeside Studios 150 S Lakeshore Rd Lakeside MI 49116; Paint Box Gallery Sister Bay WI. *Mailing Add:* 923 College Park Columbia MO 65203

CAMERON, DAN
CURATOR
b NY. *Study:* Syracuse Univ; Bennington Coll, Vt, BA (philos), 1979. *Collection Arranged:* New Orleans Triennial, New Orleans Mus Art, 1995; Living Inside the Grid, New Mus Contemp Art, New York, 2003, East Village USA, 2004; Poetic Justice, Int Istanbul Biennial, 2003; Dirty Yoga, Taipei Biennial, 2006; NY Interrupted, PKM Gallery, Beijing, 2006-07. *Pos:* Sr cur, New Mus Contemp Art, New York, 1995-2006; dir visual arts, Contemp Arts Ctr, New Orleans, 2007-; founding dir & chief cur, Prospect.1 New Orleans P.1 biennial int art, 2008-. *Awards:* Named one of Eight to Watch, Times-Picayune, 2008. *Mailing Add:* Contemp Arts Ctr 900 Camp St New Orleans LA 70130

CAMERON, ELSA S
CURATOR, ART CONSULTANT
b San Francisco, Calif, Nov 19. *Study:* San Francisco State Univ, BA, MA. *Comn:* pub collections, Richard Serra, Sol Lewitt, Jonathan Borofosky, Katerina Grosse, Jaume Plensa, Ned Kahn, Anthony Gormley, James Carpenter, Zang Wang, Zheng Chong Bin. *Exhib:* San Fran Airport Mus Exhib, 81-99; Fine Art Mus of San Francisco, 76-99. *Collection Arranged:* Native Am Ceramics: Contemporary Pueblo Works, 73, Works of Benemeno Serrano, The Beat Poets, Food Show, 76, Foot Show, 76 & 86, Downtown Ctr & Downtown Dog Show, 78, M H de Young Mem Mus, San Francisco, Calif; The Right Foot 80, Midcentury Modern Design, Lights, Chairs, Tools, S Fairport; French Marionettes; Treasures of the Yellow River: Xian China, Guam Int Airport; Architecturally Integrated Public Art for GTAA/Toronto Pearson Int Airport, 99-2006; Mexican Folk Art, 99; Magic Lanterns, 2000; Historic Aviation Collection, Malton Gallery, History of EyeWas, 2001-2006; History of Canadian Aviation, 2005; History of Toronto, 2006; Contemp Installation & Sculpture, Almaty Financial Dist; Xian Warrrior Figures of the Yellow River; MBS Pub Art, Singapore; Nansam State Tower, Seoul, Korea. *Pos:* Pres, Community Arts Int, 76-; cur in charge, Fine Arts Mus San Francisco; dir, Fine Arts Mus Sch & Mobile Outreach Prog, 76-82; founding dir & chief cur, San Francisco Int Airport Mus, 83-99; art mgr & consulting cur, Greater Toronto Airports Authority, Toronto, Can, 99-2006; art consultant, Design Ave: Chen Du City Project, China, 2005-2006; art consultant, archit projects, M Safdie, Boston, 2006-2008; art consultant, MBS Singapore, 2007; art proj mgr, Almaty New Financial Dist, 2007-2008; art adv, Nansam Tower, Seoul, Korea, 2010-2011; Street Mus, 2012; art adv, New Stanford Hospital Art Commission, 2014-. *Teaching:* Prof mus studies, Univ Art Mus, Berkeley, Calif, 81-82; asst prof art, Univ Southern Calif, 82-83, prof public art & mus studies, 95-96. *Awards:* Nat Endowment for the Arts Grant to Mus Prof & Res Grant; LIFF Found Exhib Grant; Ford Found Grant Special Mus Proj; Distinguished Art Award, 96; San Francisco Art Comn, Pub Art Award, Embassy Suites, 98; Distinguished Alumni, San Francisco State Univ, 2000; San Francisco CofC Bus & Arts Award, 2008. *Bibliog:* Museum as Educator, Univ Cailf Press, 89. *Mem:* Am Asn Mus; Int Coun Mus; Profl Art Consultants; ICOM. *Res:* Mus educ & community arts. *Specialty:* Pueblo ceramics & Native Am art forms; contemp Am art; Int public sculpture. *Interests:* Environmental studies; Urban art. *Publ:* Contribr, Museum as educator, Univ Calif, Berkeley, 78; assorted mus publs & pub art documents. *Mailing Add:* Community Arts International 15 Douglass St San Francisco CA 94114

CAMERON, ERIC
PAINTER, EDUCATOR
b Leicester, Eng, Apr 18, 1935. *Study:* Kings Col, Univ Durham, Newcastle, Eng, BA, 57, study with Lawrence Gowing, Victor Pasmore & Richard Hamilton; Courtauld Inst, Univ London, Acad Dipl (hist art), 59. *Work:* Art Gallery Ont, Toronto; Nat Gallery Can, Ottawa, Ont; Mus Art Contemp Montréal; Glenbow Mus Calgary; Vancouver Art Gallery, BC; Montreal Mus Fine Arts. *Exhib:* Woods II, Nat Gallery Can, 71 & Woods I, Art Gallery Ont, 71; Videoscape, Art Gallery Ont, 74; Int Video Exhib, Aarhus, Denmark, 76; Paintings in Mixed Exhib, Art Gallery NS, Halifax, 77; Newspaper Paintings & Lawn, Anna Leonowens Gallery, Halifax, NS, 77; Keeping Marlene Out of the Picture--and Lawn, Vancouver Art Gallery, BC, 78; Divine Comedy, Nat Gallery Can, 90; Exposer/Cacher, Mus Art Contemp Montreal, 93; Eng Roots, Tate St Ives, Leeds City Art Gallery, 98; Voici, Palais des Beaux-Arts de Bruxelles, 2000; L'Oeuvre Programme, Musee d'Art Contemporain, Bordeaux, 2005. *Pos:* Dir grad prog, NS Col Art & Design, Halifax, 76-87; dept art, Univ Calgary, head, 87-97. *Teaching:* Lectr art & art hist, Univ Leeds, Eng, 59-69; assoc prof painting & video, Univ Guelph, Ont, 69-76. *Awards:* Governor generals Award in Visual and Media Arts, 2004; Gershon Iskowitz Prize, 94. *Mem:* Univs Art Asn Can (Ont rep, 72-73, secy-treas, 73-76 & 76, vpres, 76-79); fel Royal Soc Arts; Royal Can Acad. *Media:* Oil, Acrylic. *Publ:* Auth, Mac Adams: The Mysteries, 76, Dan Graham: Appearing in Public, 76, Art as Art and the Oxford Dictionary, Vanguard, 77 & Bill Beckley's Lies, 77, Artforum; Bent Ayis Approach, Nickle Arts Mus, Calgary, 84; Divine Comedy, Nat Gallery Can, 90. *Mailing Add:* Dept Art 2500 Univ Dr NW Calgary AB T2N 1N4 Canada

CAMFIELD, WILLIAM ARNETT
HISTORIAN
b San Angelo, Tex, Oct 29, 1934. *Study:* Princeton Univ, AB, 57; Yale Univ, MA, 61, PhD, 64. *Teaching:* From asst prof to assoc prof mod Am & mod Europ art, Univ St Thomas, Houston, Tex, 64-69; from assoc prof to prof, Rice Univ, Houston, Tex, from 69 & Joseph & Joanna Nazro Mullen prof, 80, prof emeritus, currently. *Awards:* Am Philos Soc Grant, 65; Am Coun Learned Socs Grant-in-Aid, 68, Fel, 73-74; Nat Endowment Humanities Fel, 81; Guggenheim Fel, 88; Mellon Found Emer Fel, 2005-06 & 2007-08; Sr Fellowship, Dedalus Found, 2007 & 09. *Bibliog:* F Will-Levaillant (auth), Picabia et la machine: symbole et abstraction, Rev l'Art, Paris, No 4, 69; Douglas David (auth), Big Dada, Newsweek, 9/70; Christopher Green (auth), Francis Picabia, his art, life and times, Burlington Mag, 11/81; David Hopkins (auth), Max Ernst: Dada and the dawn of surrealism, Burlington Mag, 7/93. *Mem:* Coll Art Asn; founding mem Asn l'Etude Dada Surrealisme; co-founder Tex Conf Art Historians. *Res:* Emphasis on Dada in Paris and art in France from about 1910 to 1925. *Publ:* Francis Picabia, Guggenheim Mus, 70; Francis Picabia, Princeton Press, 79; Tabu Duda, Kunsthalle Bern, 83; Marcel Duchamp Fountain, Menil Collection, 89; Max Ernst, Prestel Verlag, 93; The Paintings of Frank Freed, Mus Fine Arts, Houston, 93; and others. *Mailing Add:* Rice University Dept Art & Art History 6100 Main St Houston TX 77005

CAMNER, ANNA INGRID
PAINTER
b Stockholm, Sweden, Dec 5, 1977. *Study:* Royal univ Coll Fine Arts, MA, 2003. *Work:* Magasin 3, Sweden; Nat Pub Art Coun, Sweden. *Exhib:* Night & Daydream, Natalia Goldin Gallery, Stockholm, 2008; The Triumph of Time, Stellan Holm Gallery, New York, 2010; Thrice upon a time, Magasin 3, Stockholm, 2010. *Awards:* Bernadotte Art Award, Sigvard Bernadotte, 2007; AIT, Tokyo, 2008. *Bibliog:* Dreams of Death on Glass, Scanorama, 02/2008; Peter Cornell (auth), Spindeln I Natet, Expressen, 03/2008; Clemens Poellinger, Forganglighet med tunna penseldr, Svenska Dagbladet, 12/2008; Milou Allerholm, Fantasivarld parad med teknisk, Dagens Nyheter, 04/2006; Lars-Erik Selin (auth), Forbluffande sakert och vackert om doden, Svenska Dagbladet, 04/2006. *Dealer:* Stellan Holm Gallery New York; Natalia Goldin Gallery Stockholm Sweden

CAMP, DONALD EUGENE
PHOTOGRAPHER
b Meadville, Pa, July 28, 1940. *Study:* Tyler Sch Art, BFA, 87, MFA, 89. *Work:* Mus Am Art, Philadelphia; Philadelphia Mus Art; Pa Convention Ctr, Philadelphia; Arco Corp, Philadelphia; Blue Cross Blue Shield, Philadelphia. *Comn:* Smithsonian Inst; Bklyn Mus. *Exhib:* Philadelphia Selection, Alternative Mus, NY, 91; Art Now, Philadelphia Mus Art, 91; Dust Shared Hearts, Noyes Mus, Brigantine, NJ, 92 & Swarthmore Col, Pa, 95; Mich State Univ Mus Art. *Pos:* Staff photogr, Philadelphia Evening & Sunday Bull, 72-81; professor emeritus, Ursinus Coll. *Teaching:* Asst prof photog, Tyler Sch Art, 89-91; sr lectr pub image, Univ of the Arts, 95; vis asst art, Ursinus Coll, 00-01, prof emer 2011-. *Awards:* Guggenheim Fel, John Simon Guggenheim, 95; Nat Endowment Arts Fel, 95; Pew Fel, 95. *Mem:* Soc Photog Educators (nat bd dir, 90-94); The Print Ctr. *Media:* Photography, Works on Paper. *Mailing Add:* 4511 Spruce St Philadelphia PA 19139

CAMPBELL, BETH
PAINTER, INSTALLATION SCULPTOR
b Dwight, Ill, 1971. *Study:* Truman State Univ, Kirksville, Mo, BFA, 1993; Ohio Univ, Athens, MFA, 1997; Skowhegan Sch Painting & Sculpture, 1997. *Work:* Mus Mod Art; New School Univ; New Mus Contemp Art; Whitney Mus Am Art; Altoids Curiously Strong Collection. *Exhib:* Outer Boroughs, White Columns, New York, 1999; solo exhibs, Roebling Hall, Brooklyn, 2000, 2002, Sandronio Rey Gallery, Los Angeles, 2003, Art Acad Cincinnati, 2004, Nicole Klagsbrun Gallery, New York, 2004, 2005, 2008, Art Basel Miami Beach, 2004, Sala Diaz, San Antonio, 2005, Whitney Mus Am Art, New York, 2007, Feldman Gallery & Project Space, Pacific Northwest Coll Art, Portland, Ore, 2007; Greater New York, PS1 Contemp Art Ctr, New York, 2000; Altoids Curiously Strong Collection, New Mus Contemp Art, New York, 2001; Hello, My Name Is, Carnegie Mus Art, Pittsburgh, 2002; High & Inside, Marlborough Chelsea, New York, 2003; Open House: Working in Brooklyn, Brooklyn Mus Art, 2004; Looking at Words, Andrea Rosen Gallery, New York, 2005; On Being an Exhibition, Artists Space, New York, 2007; Open House: Cincinnati Collects, Contemp Arts Ctr Cincinnati, 2007; Skipping the Page, Ctr Book Arts, New York, 2008. *Awards:* Emerging Artist Fel, Socrates Sculpture Park, 2000; Rema Hort Mann Found Art Grant, 2000; Art OMI Grant, 2001; Artist's Pension Trust Selection, 2005; Pollock-Krasner Found Grant, 2006; Louis Comfort Tiffany Found Grant, 2009. *Bibliog:* David Humphrey (auth), New York E-Mail, Art Issues, 3-4/2001; Jerry Saltz (auth), Repeat Performances, Village Voice, 10/9/2002; Randy Kennedy (auth), What's on Sale There? Confusion, But It's Cheap, NY Times, 5/15/2007

CAMPBELL, COLIN G
DIRECTOR
b New York City, Nov 3, 1935. *Study:* Cornell Univ, AB, 1957 ; Columbia Univ, JD, 1960; Amherst Coll, LLD, 1972; Williams Coll, LLD, 1973; Dickinson Coll, LLD, 1982; Univ Hartford, LLD, 1983; Wesleyan Univ, LLD, 1989; Conn Coll, LLD, 1990; Fairfield Univ, LLD, 1999; Trinity Coll, DHL, 1981; Georgetown Univ, DHL, 1984; Cedar Crest Coll, PhD (Pub Sci), 1997. *Pos:* Atty, Cummings & Lockwood, Stamford, Conn, 1960-1962; asst to pres, Am Stock Exchange, New York, 1962-1963, secy, 1963-1964, vpres, 1964-1967; adminr vpres, Wesleyan Univ, Middletown, Conn, 1967-1969, exec vpres, 1969-1970, pres, 1970-1988, pres emeritus, 1988-; pres, Rockefeller Bros Fund, 1988-2000; pres, chief exec officer, Colonial Williamsburg Found, Va, 2000-; trustee, Coll's Mason Sch of Business Educ. *Awards:* Prentis Award, Coll William & Mary, 2008; DeWitt Clinton Medal, NY Hist Soc. *Mem:* mem, Colonial Williamsburg Found, Bd Trustees, 1989, chmn, 1988-2008. *Mailing Add:* Colonial Williamsburg Foundation PO Box 1776 Williamsburg VA 23185

CAMPBELL, CRYSTAL Z
SCULPTOR
b Prince Georges County, MD. *Study:* Univ Okla, BFA, 2004; Skowhegan Sch Painting & Sculpture, 2003; State Univ New York, Albany, MFA(Africana Studies), 2007; Univ Calif San Diego, MFA, 2007-10. *Exhib:* Exhibs include Univ Kans, Lawrence, Kans, 2003; Momentum, Okla City, Okla, 2003; Free Play, Islip Art Mus, East Islip, NY, 2007. *Awards:* Presidential Int Travel Fel, Univ Okla, 2003; Skowhegan Partial Fel, 2003; Mary Clarke Miley Scholar, Univ Okla, 2004; Prof Develop Travel Grant, 2006; Chair's Distinguished Service Award, State Univ NY, Albany, 2007, Initiatives for Women Grant, 2007; Vermont Studio Ctr Artist's Grant, 2007; George Sugarman Found Grant, 2007; Russell Found Grant, 2008

CAMPBELL, DAVID PAUL
PAINTER, INSTRUCTOR
b Takoma Park, Md, 1936. *Study:* Art Students League, 57-58 & 61. *Work:* Mus Fine Arts, Boston; Metrop Mus Art, NY; Art Inst Chicago; Boston Pub Libr; Pierce Atwood (corp collection) Portland, Maine; Maine Maritime Mus, Bath, Me; San Francisco Mus Art; Portland Public Libr, Portland, Me. *Comn:* Painting, Gillette Co, Boston, 80. *Exhib:* A Sense of Place, Univ Nebr & Joslyn Mus, 73; Brockton Art Mus Triennial, Mass, 80; Perspectives on Contemp Am Realism, Pa Acad Fine Arts, 82 & Art Inst Chicago, 83; San Francisco Mus Mod Art, 85; Contemp Drawings from Boston Collections, Mus Fine Arts, Boston, 86-87; Boston Ann Drawing Show, 87-88 & 91; The Pursuit of Excellence, Hubbard Mus, Ruidoso Downs, NMex, 91; Nat Acad Ann Show, Nat Acad NY, 94, 96, 2006, & 2012; Bergen Mus, Paramus, NJ, 95; Biennial, Portland Mus of Art, Maine, 98 & 2005; Maine Maritime Mus, Bath, Maine, 2010. *Teaching:* Instr life drawings, Montserrat Coll, Beverly, Mass, 89; instr watercolor, NE Sch Art, Boston, 90, Jewish Community Ctr, Newton, Mass, 90-; instr watercolor & drawing, Mus Fine Arts, Boston, 92-2001, Maine Coll Art, Portland, 2001-2014. *Awards:* Appreciation Award, City Somerville, Mass, 93; Grant, Gottlieb Found, 87; Grant, Pollock-Krasner Found, 89, 97. *Bibliog:* Frank H Goodyear Jr (auth), Perspectives on Contemporary American Realism, Pa Acad Fine Arts, 82; Peter Merchant, John Pennington & Wendy Mason (dirs), David Campbell, Words and Watercolors (videotape), Somerville Educ TV, 84; Alvin Martin (auth), American Realism, San Francisco Mus Mod Art & Henry N Abrams, 85; Carl Little (auth), The Art of Maine in Winter, Down East Bks, 2002. *Media:* Oil, Drawing. *Publ:* Looking at trees, The Sun Mag, 11/92; poem, Beloit Poetry J, fall 95; Windows of the Soul (anthology), 95; 5 poems, Struggle Mag, 2003; 4 poems, Sensations Mag, fall, 2003, 2005, 2006, 2010; poem, Goose River Anthology, 2006, 2009, 2010. *Dealer:* Thomas Segal Gallery 4 W University Pkwy Baltimore MD 21218; Greenhut Gallery 146 Middle St Portland Me 04101; Frost Gully Gallery PO Box 202 Freeport ME 04032. *Mailing Add:* 1 Fitchburg St C 416 Somerville MA 02143

CAMPBELL, GRAHAM B
PAINTER
b Kent, Eng, 1946. *Study:* Chesterfield Art Coll, Eng, 61-65; Birmingham Art Coll, studied with John Walker, 66-69; Yale Sch Art, MFA, 78. *Work:* Walker Art Gallery, Liverpool Art Mus, Eng; Touchstone Gallery, NY; Ikon Gallery, Birmingham, Eng; Midland Art Ctr, Eng; NY Studio Sch Gallery. *Exhib:* Art of the State, Rose Art Mus, 82; Four, Rose Art Mus, 82; CDS Gallery, NY, 84-87, 89, 91-92 & 94-95; Recent Acquisitions, Rose Art Mus, 85; Emerging Artists, EF Hutton Collection, NY, 87. *Teaching:* Instr, Brandeis Univ, currently. *Awards:* Mazer Grant, Brandeis Univ, Mass, 82 & 85; Louis Comfort Tiffany Found Award in Painting, Tiffany Found, 86; Grant, John Simon Guggenheim Mem Found, 96. *Bibliog:* Grace Glueck (auth), Graham Campbell, New York Times, 9/20/85; M Poirier (auth), Graham Campbell, New York reviews, ArtNews, 11/85; Theodore F Wolff (auth), Further exposure, Christian Science Monitor, 7/7/86. *Mailing Add:* Art Dept Brandeis Univ PO Box 9110 Waltham MA 02454-9110

CAMPBELL, NANCY B
PRINTMAKER
b Syracuse, NY, May 28, 1952. *Study:* Syracuse Univ, BFA, 74; Univ Mich, MFA, 76. *Work:* Philadelphia Mus Art, Pa; Libr Cong, Washington, DC; Worcester Art Mus, Mass; Mt Holyoke Coll Art Mus, S Hadley, Mass; Syracuse Univ Art Collection, NY; Ill State Univ, Normal; Lamar Univ, Beaumont, Tex; Haggin Mus, Stockton, Calif; Amoco Products, Denver; Mich Bell Tel; NS Coll Art & Design, Halifax; Tenn Technol Univ; Univ Conn, Storrs; Univ Dallas, Irving, Tex; Univ Hartford, W Hartford; Univ Mass, Amherst; Univ Mass, Boston; Univ NH, Durham; Univ RI, Kingston; Univ Vt, Burlington; and others. *Exhib:* Collaboration in Print, Stewart & Stewart Prints: 1980-90, Detroit Inst Arts, Mich, 91 & Kalamazoo Inst Arts, Mich, 91; Southern Graphics Coun Traveling Exhib, Ohio Univ, Athens, Univ Ga, Athens & Adams State Coll, Alamos, Colo, 98-99; Janet Turner Nat Print, Calif State Univ, Chico, 99; Nat Printmaking 2000, Coll NJ, Ewing; Pacific States Nat Exhib, Univ Hawaii, 2000; Bangain US, Flusso Gallery, New York, 2004; NAZU Int Biennale, NAZU, Japan, 2004; American Impressions (grand prize winner), Ben Shahn Galleries, William Paterson Univ, Wayne, NJ, 2007; New Prints, Int Print Ctr, New York, 2010. *Pos:* Chmn art dept, Mt Holyoke Coll, S Hadley, Mass, 92, 95, 2003 & 2005, chmn studio art prog, 2008-. *Teaching:* Asst prof studio art, Oberlin Coll, Ohio, 79-80 & Univ Hartford, Conn, 80-81; prof art, Mount Holyoke Coll, S Hadley, Mass, 81-, dir printmaking workshop, 98-. *Awards:* Patron Award, Ralph E Cades Family Found, 63rd Int Exhib Print Club, Philadelphia, 87; Juror's Commendation, Boston Printmakers 43rd Am Print Exhib, 91; Award, Springfield Art League 72nd Ann Exhib, 91. *Bibliog:* Richard Field & Ruth Fine (auth), A Graphic Muse: Prints by Contemporary American Women, Hudson Hills Press, 87; Ellen Sharp, Collaboration in Print: Stewart & Stewart Prints: 1980-1990, Mich Coun Arts, 91; Gloria Russell (auth), Mediums come together at art exhibition, Sunday Republican, Springfield, Mass, 92. *Media:* Screenprinting, Lithography. *Collection:* Univ of VT, Burlington, Vt. *Dealer:* Alice Simsar Fine Art 1103 Baldwin Ave Ann Arbor MI 48107. *Mailing Add:* 369 Middle St Amherst MA 01002

CAMPBELL, NAOMI
INTERDISCIPLINARY VISUAL ARTIST, PUBLIC ARTIST
Study: Art Students League, NY; Graduate College de Champlain, Quebec, Can. *Work:* Arts for Transit (div MTA), New York; NY Pub Libr, New York; Art Students League, New York; ASPCA, New York & Fla; SWIFT Pan-Americas Corp, New York; Amity Art Fund; Trenton City Mus, NJ; NY State Mus. *Comn:* City of NY: MTA Arts for Transit Permanent Subway Art, Faceted Glass, 2005; London Int Advertising, Eng, 2005, 2006; Mosaic Mural, City of Irving Permanent Art, East Branch Libr & College Entrance (Mosaic Mural), Tex, 2006; Painted Wall Scroll, Maimonides Hosp, Entrance Cancer Treatment Ctr, New York, 2006; Granite Sculpture, City of Geochang, Korea, 2007. *Exhib:* Butler Mus Am Art, 2001, 2002; Exhib of Int Art of the Fan (traveling, Seoul, Korea), Tokyo Metrop Mus Art, Japan, 2003; Heidi Cho Gallery, New York, 2003; Umeda Sky Gallery, Osaka, Japan, Okayama Sculpture Exhib, Okayama, Japan, Harold B Lemmerman Gallery, NJ, 2004; Along the Way, (MTA Arts for Transit 20 yr Retrospective), Paine Webber UBS Gallery, New York, 2005; The League Then & Now, Gallery Salute to the 130th Anniversary of the Art Students League NY, 2005; Lehman Coll MTA Arts for Transit Exhib, New York, 2006; Susan K Black Found Nat (traveling), 2007-2009; Trenton City Mus Exhib, NJ, 2007; New York City Invitational Exhib, Allied Artists Am, Bennington Ctr Arts, Vt, 2007; Scope, Miami Basel, Fla, 2008; Asian Contemp Art Fair, New York, 2008; Alte Poste, Berlin, Germany, 2008; Paramida Ctr Contemp Art, Haifa, Israel, 2009; Whitebox, Theatre of More/21, NY, 2009; White Box Proj, New York, 2010; George Billis Gallery, NY; Boscobel Gallery, NY; Governors Island Art Fair, NY, 2011; Arte et Amicitae, Amsterdam, Netherlands and NY, 2011-2012; Third Int Pastel Artists Exhib, Taipei, Taiwan; Seeing Ourselves, Mus Photog and the Moving Image, NY, 2012. *Pos:* Selection Comt, Arts for Transit, NY; judge & guest lectr, various art orgns & colls in New York, including Salmagundi Ctr Am Art & Lehman Collection Art Div & NY Transit Mus. *Teaching:* prof fine arts, Art Students League NY. *Awards:* Top Placing, Am Soc Portrait Artists, New York, 2002; Top Placing, Portrait Div, Artist Mag Competition, 2002; Gold Medal Hon (4): Salmagundi Ctr for Am Art; Catharine Lorillard Wolfe Art Club; Audubon Artists of Am, NY, 2004, 2009; Pastel Journal Award, Pastel Soc Am Ann Exhib, 2006; and others. *Bibliog:* Vera Haller (auth), 100 Years of the Subway, Newsday NY.com (video interview with artist), NY, 2004, Finding Beauty in the Subway, LA Times, Chicago Tribune, 2004; Celia McGee (auth), Sunday Now, Carving Out a Niche, Daily News NYC, 2005; Janet Purcell (auth), Times Trenton, Detour to Fame, 2007; Am Artist Mag; and others including, The NY Times, Daily News, Wash Post, NY Post, Int Artist, The Artists Mag & Voice of Am. *Mem:* Allied Artists of Am; Pastel Soc Am (honors signature mem); Nat Watercolor Soc (honors signature mem); Am Soc Portrait Artists (honors signature mem); Audubon Artists Am; Catharine Lorillard Wolfe Art Club; Transparent Watercolor Soc Am (honors signature mem); Salmagundi Club (art adv bd). *Media:* Visual, Installation, Sculpture. *Publ:* 15 Books including, Looking Beyond, A Constant Process, Int Artists Publ, 2004; auth, The Source of Life, Watercolor Magic Mag, 8/2005; The Portraits of Life, Pastel J Mag, 12/2006; Pure Color: The Best of Pastel, North Light, 2006; Along the Way, MTA Arts for Transit, Monacelli Press, 2006; 100 MidAtlantic Artists, Schiffer Pub, 2010, The Complete Painters Handbook, 2012; contribr, Linea Art Jour, winter, 2003 & summer, 2004; interviews in Newsday, 2004, Daily News, 2005, WatercolorMagic Mag, 2005 & The Pastel Jour Mag, 2006; Strokes of Genius II, North Light, 2009; contribr, Artscape Mag, 2009; Am Artist Mag, 2011. *Dealer:* Russo Karbin Fine Art

CAMPBELL, REBECCA
ARTIST, INSTRUCTOR
b Salt Lake City, Utah, 1971. *Study:* Pacific Northwest Coll Art, Portland, Ore, FRA, 1994; Vt Studio Ctr, resident, 1998; Univ Calif, Los Angeles, MFA, 2001. *Exhib:* Solo exhibs include Dreaming in Vertigo, Gallery 8, Portland, Ore, 1992, Domestics, Crossroad, Portland, 1993, Consent, Blue Boutique, Salt Lake City, 1997, Pink, Cordell Taylor Gallery, Salt Lake City, 1998, sky garden, Art Barn, Salt Lake City Arts Council, 1999, Boy Crazy, Atrium Gallery, Salt Lake City Library, 1999, Thin Skin, LA Louver, 2002, 2005, Xanadu, Ameringer Yohe Fine Art, NY, 2006; group exhibs include Sex and Death, Boyde Gallery, Portland, 1992, Regeneration, 1993; Scarcity and Excess, Portland Art Mus North, 1993; Out of the Closet, Salt Lake Art Ctr, 1999; Women's Work, Union Gallery, Univ Utah, 1999; LA Louver, 2003, 2004, 2005; Am Acad Arts & Letts Invitational, New York, 2010. *Pos:* Input colorist, Dark Horse Comics, Mikwaukie, Ore, 1994; chair adv bd, Zoos, Arts and Parks Fun, Tier II Cultural/Botanical Orgns, 1997; cur educ, Salt Lake Art Ctr, Utah, 1997-99; project coordr, Youth Educ, Dept Cultural Affairs, Los Angeles, 1997. *Teaching:* High sch art instr, Int Learning Program, Ore, 1995-96; art specialist, Salt Lake City Sch Dist; teaching asst/Artsbridge fellow, Univ Calif Los Angeles, Artsbridge emer scholar mentor, 2001; visual arts specialist/curriculum author, The Accelerated Sch, Los Angeles, 2000; vis prof, Calif State Univ, Fullerton, 2002. *Awards:* Werner Hirsch Drawing Award; Feitelson Arts Found Award. *Bibliog:* Peter Clothier (auth), Art Walk: L.A., The Huffington Post, 3/2009; Leah Ollman (auth), Memories of a searching spirit, LA Times, 3/2009; Erin Clark (auth), Rebecca Campbell, Artworks Mag, 2007. *Mailing Add:* c/o LA Louver 45 N Venice Blvd Venice CA 90291

CAMPBELL, RICHARD HORTON
PAINTER, PRINTMAKER
b Marinette, Wis, Jan 11, 1921. *Study:* Cleveland Sch Art; Art Ctr Sch, Los Angeles; Univ Calif, Los Angeles. *Work:* Theater Guild Am, NY; Hilton Hotel, Denver. *Exhib:* Los Angeles Co Mus, Calif; Denver Mus; Frye Mus, Seattle, Wash; Oakland Art Mus, Calif; De Young Mus, San Francisco. *Pos:* Dir, Los Angeles Art Asn. *Awards:* Second Prize, Los Angeles All-City Exhib, 51; First Prize, Cleveland May Show, 54; First Prize, 7th Festival of Arts, Los Angeles, 58. *Mem:* Nat Watercolor Soc; Los Angeles Art Asn; fel Int Inst Arts & Lett. *Media:* Oil, Acrylic

CAMPBELL, THOMAS P
MUSEUM DIRECTOR
b Cambridge, Eng, 1962. *Study:* Oxford Univ, BA (Eng lang & lit), 84; Christie's, London, diploma (fine & decorative arts), 85; Courtland Inst Art, London, MA, 87, PhD, 99. *Collection Arranged:* Tapestry in the Renaissance: Art and Magnificence, Metrop Mus Art, New York, 2002 & Tapestry in the Baroque: Threads of Splendor, 2007. *Pos:* Founder, Frances Tapestry Archive, London, 87-94; asst cur Dept European Sculpture & Decorative Arts, Metrop Mus Art, New York, 95-97, assoc cur, 97-2003, cur, 2003-08, dir & chief exec officer, 2009-, supervising cur, Antonio Ratti Textile Ctr, currently. *Awards:* Exhib of Yr, Apollo Mag, 2002; Alfred H Barr, Jr Award, Coll Art Asn, 2003; Iris Found Award, Bard Grad Ctr, 2003. *Publ:* Auth, Henry VIII & the Art of Majesty: Tapestries at the Tudor Court, 2007. *Mailing Add:* Metrop Mus Art 1000 Fifth Ave New York NY 10028-0198

CAMPELLO, FLORENCIO LENNOX
CRITIC, PAINTER
b Guantanamo, Us Naval Base, Cuba, Sept 6, 1956. *Study:* Univ Wash Sch Art, BS (art), 81; Naval Postgrad Sch, Monterey, Calif, MS, 87. *Work:* McManus Mus, Scotland, Brusque Mus, Brazil, San Bernardino Co Art Mus, Calif, Musee des Duncan, France, Frick Mus, Ohio, Meadows Mus Art, Shreveport, La, Hunter Mus, Tenn. *Exhib:* Solo exhibs, The Hub Gallery, 79, Arts Northwest Gallery, Wash, 81, Galeria Sevillana, Spain, 84, Warehouse Gallery, Scotland, 92, Chevrier's Presidio Gallery, Calif, 93-94, Fraser Gallery, Wash, DC, 96-99, 2001, 49 West, Md, 97, Eklektikos Gallery, Wash, DC, 2000, represented by, Fraser Gallery; exhib incl, Sacramento Fine Arts Ctr, Calif, Rock Springs Art Ctr, Wyo. *Pos:* Art critic, Dimensions Mag, Norfolk, Va, 94-99, Greater Reston Arts Center, Reston, Va, 97, Gallery West, Alexandria, Va, 97, Pitch Mag, City Beat, Manassas J; Adv, DC Arts & Humanities Commission, Wash, 99-2001; guest cur, Athenaeum, Alexandria, Va, 2001; assoc dealer Sothebys.com; cur From Here and From There: A Survey of Contemp Cuban Art Frazer Gallery, Bethesda, Md, 2003; info warfare adv, KSI, Arlington, Va, 97-, Visions Mag for the Visual Arts, Va Beach, 95-2000, Crier Media, Alexandria, 99-. *Awards:* Decorated Meritorious Service medal US Navy, Navy Commendation Medal (4), Navy Achievement Medal (2); recipient second prize, Bellgrade Art Festival, 97 & 98. *Mem:* Art Dealers Asn of Greater Wash. *Media:* Watercolor. *Mailing Add:* c/o Crier Media Group Inc 112 S Patrick St Alexandria VA 22314-3027

CAMPER, FRED
EDUCATOR
b Chicago, Il, 1947. *Study:* Mass Inst of Tech, BS in Physics, 71; NYU, Dept Cinema Studies. *Pos:* Lab technician, for a co specializing in environ measurements of radioactivity. *Teaching:* teacher, film-making, and film history Sch Art Inst Chicago, 76-82; teacher asst, NYU, 72, instr, 73; teacher, Am Melodrama, 2000; Lectr on art, photog, and film for coll and univ in NY, NJ and Ill; lecturer in the field; teacher, reading course in art issues Univ Ill at Urbana-Champaign; co-founder, member a film by, 2003-. *Awards:* Recipient Lisagor award, 99, Film Preservation Honor, Anthology Film Archives, 2001, Best DVD award, Cinemarati, Exceptional Achievement in Criticism award, 2004. *Mem:* Nat Writers Union, Int Asn of Arts Critics, Chicago Art Critics Asn (co-found, mem). *Publ:* Freelance writer, publisher (film articles for a variety of periodicals, catalogues and books), 1968-, writer on film Chicago Reader, 1976, 1986-, writer on art, 1989-, writer (of reviews of art and photog exhib and interviews with artists), 1993-

CAMPUZANO, ANTHONY
COLLAGE ARTIST
b 1975. *Study:* Tyler Sch Art, Temple Univ, BFA (Hecht Meml Award in Sculpture & Corso Scholar Prize), 2000. *Work:* Pa Acad Fine Arts. *Exhib:* 15 Different Recipes, Temple Univ Gallery, Pa, 1996; Ideal, Tyler Sch Art Gallery, Elkins Park, Pa, 1997; The Willow House, Ukrainian Inst Mod Art, Chicago, 2001; The New Acropolis, Fleisher-Ollman Gallery, Pa, 2003; Fabulous Histories: Indigenous Anomalies in American Art, Harvard Univ, 2004; Looking at Words, Andrea Rosen Gallery, New York, 2005; solo exhibs, White Columns, New York, 2005, Moore Coll Art & Design, 2005, Fleisher/Ollman Gallery, Pa, 2006-07, Inst Contemp Art, Pa, 2009; Everything Else, Franklin Parrasch Gallery, New York, 2008. *Awards:* Pew Ctr for Arts Fel, 2009. *Bibliog:* Miriam Seidel (auth), Curators Mount a New Acropolis, Philadelphia Inquirer, 1/9/2004; William Pym (auth), Mr. Anthony Goes to School, Moore Coll Art & Design, 11/2005; Steven Stern (auth), Liberal Arts, NY Times Style mag, 2006. *Dealer:* Franklin Parrasch Gallery 20 W 57th St New York NY 10019

CANDAU, EUGENIE
LIBRARIAN
b San Francisco, Calif, Jan 26, 1938. *Study:* Fat City Sch Finds Art, MFA, 73; San Francisco State Univ, BA, 74; Univ Calif, Berkeley, MLS, 78. *Collection Arranged:* Kaethe Kollwitz, San Francisco Mus Art, 70; Hand Bookbinding Today, An International Art (traveling exhib), San Francisco Mus Mod Art, 78. *Pos:* Librn, Fine Arts Libr, San Francisco Mus Mod Art, 68-91. *Mem:* Coll Art Asn; Art Libr Soc NAm (exec bd, 90-91); Pac Ctr Bk Arts (exec bd, 83-86); Berkeley Civic Arts Comn, 83-90; Berkeley Art Ctr (exec bd, 90- & pres, 95-97). *Interests:* Arts of the book; modern & contemporary art. *Publ:* Bibliographies for San Francisco Mus Mod Art publ: Edward Ruscha, Philip Guston, Sigmar Polke, and others, 70-; auth, articles and reviews in Fine Print and Art Week, 76-; Hand Bookbinding Today, An International Art (exhib catalog), 78; contribr, P Selz, In: Art in Our Times, Abrams, 81; and others. *Mailing Add:* 2108 Derby St Berkeley CA 94705

CANDIOTI, BEATRIZ A
PAINTER
b 1935. *Study:* Coll Nac, with Ramos Mejia, AA, 50; Univ Louisville, BA, 80, Univ KY, 86-90. *Work:* Nat Mus Am Art, Smithsonian Inst, Washington, DC; Floyd Co Art Mus, New Albany, Ind; Galerie Triangle, Washington, DC. *Exhib:* Solo exhib, Galerie Triangle, Washington, DC, 83; James Hunt Baker Galleries, NY, 83; Kentucky Tradition in Am Landscape Painting 1800 to the Present, Owensboro Mus Fine Art, Ky, 83; Capital Art from Kentucky, Lazenby Assoc, Washington, DC, 85; Kentucky Art Exhib, J B Speed Art Mus, Louisville, 86. *Awards:* First prize, Art Asn Harrisburg, Pa, 84; Catharine Lorillard Wolfe Award, 85; Kentucky Artist Award, Ky Gen Assembly, 90. *Mem:* Nat Asn Women Artists

CANIER, CAREN
PAINTER, EDUCATOR
b New York City, NY, Mar 25, 1953. *Study:* Cornell Univ, BFA, 74; Boston Univ, MFA, 76. *Work:* Herbert F Johnson Mus Art, Ithaca, NY; Art Mus, SUNY, Albany; Am Acad, Rome, Italy; corp collections, Chemical Bank, New York, Am Hess, New York & AT&T, Chicago. *Exhib:* Solo exhibs, Robert Schoelkopf Gallery, 85 & 91, Bowery Gallery, New York, 2001 & Boston Univ Sherman Art Gallery (traveling), Mass, 2002, Civitella Ranieri Gallery, Umbertide, Italy, 2009, Dorothy Young Ctr for Arts, Drew Univ, Madison, NJ, 2009, The Painting Center, NY, 2010; Les Fables de LaFontaine (traveling), Cent pour l'Art et la Cult, Inst Am Univ, 2002-2003; Allegories Imagined Landscapes, Concord Art Asn, Concord Mass, 2003; Between Perception & Invention, Sharon Arts Ctr, Petersburgh, NH, 2005. *Teaching:* Prof art, Rensselaer Polytechnic Inst, 78-, department head, currently. *Awards:* Rome Prize, Am Acad, Rome, 77-78; Artist Fel, NY Found Arts, 85 & 90; Ingram Merrill Found Grant, 86; Pollock Krasner Found Grant, 90. *Bibliog:* Ken Johnson (auth), Caren Canier, Arts Mag, 85; Katherine French (auth), Caren Canier, Boston Univ, 2002; Jeanne Duval (auth), Between Perception & Invention, Sharon Arts Ctr, 2005; Koren Christofides (auth), Fables of LaFontaine, Univ Wash Press, 2006. *Mem:* Coll Arts Asn Am; Soc Fels, Am Acad Rome. *Media:* 2D Mixed Media, Oil, Matte Acrylic

CANNIFF, BRYAN GREGORY
DESIGNER, DIRECTOR
b Minneapolis, Minn, Dec 26, 1948. *Study:* Minneapolis Coll Art & Design, BFA, 71. *Collection Arranged:* Designer, The Life of Florence Ziegfeld (and 40 other maj shows), NY City Mus, 75 & Bicentennial Exhib, South St Seaport Mus, 76. *Pos:* Art dir, New York City Mus, 72-75; designer, South St Seaport Mus, NY, 75-76 & Mus Mod Art, NY, 76-79; art dir, Saturday Rev Mag Corp, NY, 79-80, Panorama Mag, 81 & Boating Mag, 81-83; creative dir, Popular Mechanics Mag, 83-2004, Canvas Mag, 2006-present. *Awards:* NY Art Dirs Club Awards, 80, 84 & 87; Creativity Awards, 82-98; Design Awards, 82-98. *Mem:* Visual Club; Soc Illusr; Am Inst Graphic Arts; Soc Pub Designers; NY Art Dir Club

CANNING, SUSAN M
HISTORIAN, CRITIC
Study: Calif State Univ, BA, 70; Pa State Univ, MA (art hist, Fulbright Fel), 73; PhD (art hist), 80. *Collection Arranged:* Henry Van de Velde (auth, catalog), Konniklijk Mus & Kroller Muller, 88; The Order of Things (auth, catalog), Trinity Col, Hartford, 93; Myself: Your/other (auth, catalog), Castle Gallery, 93, Mediums the Message (auth, catalog), 95 & Alternative Measurer (auth, catalog), 98. *Teaching:* Asst prof art hist, Univ NC, 79-86; assoc prof art hist, Oberlin Col, Ohio, 88 & Col New Rochelle, NY, 89-. *Awards:* Fulbright Res Fel, Belgium, 86; Scholar in Residence, NY Univ, 95. *Mem:* Coll Art Asn; Asn Historians 19th Century Art; NY Univ Assoc; Nat Asn Arts Admin; Visual Resource Asn. *Res:* 19th century Belgian art, especially James Ensor, Henry Van de Velde and Les Vingt. *Publ:* Auth, Henry Van de Velde, Painhryst Drawings, Royal Mus Antwerp, 88; Le Cercle des XX, Tzwern-Aisinber, 89; The Order of Anarchy, Coll Art Asn, 94; Le foule et le boulevard: James Ensor the sheer politics of everyday life, Peter Lang Publ, 97; Visionary politics: the social subject of James Ensor, Barbican, London, 97. *Mailing Add:* Art Dept SAS Col New Rochelle 29 Castle Place New Rochelle NY 10805

CANNULI, RICHARD GERALD
PAINTER, GALLERY DIRECTOR
b Philadelphia, Pa, Feb 2, 1947. *Study:* Villanova Univ, BFA, 73; Art Students League, 75; Pratt Inst, MFA, 79. *Comn:* Paintings, St Nicholas Tolentine Church, Bronx, 77-79, Assumption-St Paul Parish, Mechanicville, NY, 78 & St Augustine Prep Chapel, Richland, NJ, 80-81; Dedication Cross, Connelly Ctr, Villanova Univ, 80; Design the Chapel, Biscayne Col, Fla, 81. *Exhib:* Expressions, Earth Art, Mus Philadelphia Civic Ctr, 79; Creative Dimensions, Carrier Found, Bellmead, NJ, 79; Liturgical Art, Pavilion Gallery, Mt Holly, NJ, 81; Watercolors of Europe, Palace of Arts Gallery, Minsk & Byelorussia House Artist Creations Gallery, Riga, Latvia, 91-92; New Watercolors, E China Normal Univ Art Gallery, Shanghai, China, 92 & 95; A Survey of Work 1968-1995: Paintings, Fabric and Sculpture, Villanova Univ Art Gallery, Pa, 95; Art and Religion, Balch Inst Ethnic Studies, Philadelphia, Pa, 97; Connections: Religion and Art (traveling exhib), Asn Uniting Religion & Art, 98; A Brushed with God: Contemp Religious Icons, Lawrence Gallery, Rosemont Col, Pa, 98; Behold the Wood of the Cross: The Crucifix in Art and Worship, Galleria Inter-Cult Ctr, Georgetown Univ, Washington, DC, 99. *Teaching:* Instr studio art & hist, Msgr Bonner High Sch, Drexel Hill, Pa, 73-78; asst prof studio art, Villanova Univ, 7996, dir, Art Gallery, 79-, chmn, Dept Art & Art Hist, 90-, assoc prof, 96-. *Media:* Oil, Fabric. *Mailing Add:* Studio Art/Theater Dept Villanova Univ 800 Lancaster Ave Villanova PA 19085

CANO, MARGARITA
PAINTER
b Havana, Cuba, Feb 27, 1932. *Study:* Univ Havana, PhD, 56, MLibSc, 62; studies in art hist & mus conserv with Helmut Ruheman from Nat Gallery, London, Eng. *Work:* Univ Miami Lib; Miami Dade Public Lib System. *Exhib:* South Fla Arts Ctr, Miami Beach, 94; Cult Res Ctr, Miami, 98; Dade Co Cult Resource Ctr, Miami, 2003; Coral Gables Libr, Fla, 2003; Books and Books Art Gallery, Coral Gables, Fla, 2005, The Still Life, 2012; Onate Art Gallery, Miami, Fla, 2006; Cremata Art Gallery, Miami, 2006, 2008; Viota Art Gallery, San Juan, 2008. *Collection Arranged:* Cintas Fellows, Paintings by Cuban Artists (auth, catalog), Miami-Dade Pub Libr, Fla, 77; The Romance of an Era, Colonial Art in Cuba, Main Libr, 80; The Miami Generation, Cuban Mus, Miami, 83; Art of the Bound Book, 85 & Some of Our Favorite Things, 86, Main Libr; Cintas Fellows Revisited, Main Libr, 88. *Pos:* Registr, Julio Lobo Found, Napoleonic Art Mus, 57-58; art librn, Miami-Dade Pub Libr, 63-93; bd dir, Cuban Mus, Miami & Cintas Found, NY, Miami Book Fair Int & Bass Mus, Miami Beach, 97; panelist, National Endowment for the Arts, Washington, DC, 97. *Teaching:* Instr contemp Latin Am art, South Campus, Miami-Dade Community Col, 77, instr hist Latin Am art, 82. *Awards:* Cintas Found Fel, 75-76; Lifetime Achievement award, Cintas Found, 2009; Lifetime Achievement award, The Three Graces, Miami-Dade Public Lib, 2011. *Mem:* Art Libr Soc NAm; Am Libr Asn. *Media:* Encaustic, Mixed-Media, Prints. *Res:* Contemporary Latin American art. *Publ:* Auth, How to

Bridge the Art Gap, Art Libr Soc NAm, 76; Dictionary of Latin American Artists (bibliog), Cintas Found, 76; Cuba Paradise Lost, 2004; Memories and Metaphors (DVD), 2006; Words of Wisdom, 2009; auth, illusr, Isabel y su Cama Nueva, Isabel y su Gato Coco (two books for pre-schoolers), 2010-2012. *Mailing Add:* 501 SW 24th Ave Miami FL 33135

CANO, PABLO D
SCULPTOR, EDUCATOR
b Havana, Cuba, Mar 11, 1961; US citizen. *Study:* Miami-Dade Community Col, Wolfson Scholar, AA, 80; Md Art Inst, BFA, 82; Queens Col, MA (Cintas fel), 86. *Work:* Miami-Dade Pub Libr & Miami-Dade Community Col, Miami; Cintas Found, NY. *Exhib:* Carnival of Critters, Main Libr Gallery, Miami, 81; The Miami Generation (with catalog), Cuban Mus Arts & Cult, Miami 83 & traveling nationally, 83-85; Celebration The Holiday Tradition, Mus Art, Ft Lauderdale, Fl, 88; and many others in the US, Colombia & France. *Teaching:* Instr advan drawing, New World Sch Arts, 88; prof humanities, Miami Dade Community Col, Med Ctr Campus, 92. *Bibliog:* Helen Kohen (auth), Bright days for art in South Florida, Art News, 12/80; Giulio V Blanc (auth), Pablo Cano, Noticias de Arte, 9/81; and others in Miami Herald, Miami News, El Herald & Diario Las Americas, 80-81. *Media:* Miscellaneous. *Publ:* Illusr, The Thorns are Green My Friend, Ediciones Universal, 88; El Niño de Guano, Poemario Angel Gaztelu. *Dealer:* Pablo Cano Portrait Art Studio; Gomez Gallery Baltimore MD. *Mailing Add:* 501 SW 24th Ave Miami FL 33135-2933

CANRIGHT, SARAH ANNE
PAINTER
b Chicago, Ill, Aug 20, 1941. *Study:* Art Inst Chicago, BFA. *Work:* Kresge Found, NY; Art Inst Chicago; Nat Collection Fine Art, Washington, DC; Chase Manhattan Bank, London; AT&T Corp, Richmond, Va; and others. *Exhib:* Whitney Biennial, NY, 74; Phyllis Kind Gallery, Chicago, 74-79; Franklin Furnace, NY, 79-81; Pam Adler Gallery, NY, 79-81 & 83-84; Walker Art Ctr, Minneapolis, 81; Artemesia Gallery, Chicago, 86; Marvin Seline Gallery, Austin, Tex, 87; and others. *Teaching:* Instr, Princeton Univ, 78-; instr, Skowhegan Sch Painting & Sculpture, 80; sr lectr, Univ Tex, Austin, 82-. *Awards:* Armstrong Award, Art Inst Chicago, 71; Nat Endowment Arts Fel Grant, 75 & 78-85; Creative Artists Pub Serv Prog Grant, 77. *Bibliog:* Robert Storr (auth), article, Arts Mag 9/81 & Art in Am, 2/85; Douglas Cameron, (auth), article, Art News, 5/85; Mel McCombie (auth), article, Art News, 5/87. *Mem:* Am Abstract Artists. *Media:* Oil. *Dealer:* Pam Adler Gallery 37 W 57th St New York NY 10019

CANTINE, DAVID
PAINTER
b Jackson, Mich, June 7, 1939. *Study:* Univ Iowa, BA, 62, MA, 64. *Work:* Mazur Mus, Monroe, La; Alta Art Found; Edmonton Art Gallery. *Exhib:* Solo exhibs, Univ Saskatchewan, Univ Alberta & Northern State Univ, 66-67 & 69, Mazur Mus, 72, Kraushaar Galleries, New York, 77, 82, 88, 2002 & 2004, Vanderleelie Gallery, Edmonton, 94, 97, 2000, 2002, 2004 & 2006, Cristopher Cuits Gallery, Toronto, 2000 & 2004, Art Gallery Alberta, 2007 & Latitude 53, 2007. *Pos:* Prof artist, currently. *Teaching:* Prof art, Univ AB, 65-96. *Bibliog:* Roald Nasgaard (auth), Abstract Painting In Canada, 2007; Patricia Ainslie & Beth Lavioltte (auths), Alberta Art and Artists, 2007. *Media:* Acrylic Polymer. *Res:* Color as structure. *Specialty:* Contemporary. *Dealer:* Kraushaar Galleries 724 Fifth Ave New York NY; Vanderleelie Gallery Edmonton AB Canada; Christopher Cutts Gallery 21 Morrow Ave Toronto Ont Can; Aaron Galleries Chicago. *Mailing Add:* 99 St Georges Crescent Edmonton AB T5N 3M7 Canada

CANTINI, VIRGIL D
EDUCATOR, ENAMELIST, SCULPTOR
b Italy, Feb 28, 1920. *Study:* Carnegie Inst Technol, BFA, 46; Univ Pittsburgh, MA, 48; Duquesne Univ, Hon DFA, 81. *Work:* Wichita Mus Art, Kans; Carnegie Mus Art, Pittsburgh, Pa; Westmoreland Co Mus Art, Greensburg, Pa; Hillman Libr, Univ Pittsburgh; Point Park Col. *Comn:* Three sculptures & two tapestries, Hillman Libr, 69 & Nat Sci Bldg, 74, Univ Pittsburgh; Joy of Life (fountain sculpture), Urban Redevelop Authority, Pittsburgh, 69; Skyscape (enamel mural), Oliver Tyrone Co, Pittsburgh, 71; enamel murals, Univ Pittsburgh, 75 & 77. *Exhib:* Assoc Artists Pittsburgh, 45-70; Pittsburgh Int, Carnegie Mus Art, 61, 64 & 67; Solo exhibs, Westmoreland Co Mus Art, 62 & Pittsburgh Plan Arts, 62, 67, 72, 75 & 78; Enamels 50-80, Brookfield Craft Ctr Gallery, Conn, 81. *Pos:* Vpres, Pittsburgh Coun for Arts, 68-70; Pres, Asn Artists Pittsburgh. *Teaching:* Prof art & chmn dept studio arts, Univ Pittsburgh, 52-99. *Awards:* Guggenheim Fel, 58; Pope Paul VI Bishop's Medal, 64; Davinci Medal-Ital Sons & Daughters Am, Cult Heritage Found, 68. *Bibliog:* Dorothy Sterling (auth), article, Am Artist, 52; Helen Knox (auth), article, Pitt Mag, 64; Lloyd Davis (auth), article, Appalachian, 67. *Mem:* Assoc Artists Pittsburgh (pres, 62-64); Arts & Crafts Ctr (vpres, 55-57); Pittsburgh Plan Arts; Coll Art Asn Am; Am Crafts Coun. *Media:* Enamel. *Mailing Add:* 354 S Highland Ave Pittsburgh PA 15206-4232

CANTONE, VIC
CARTOONIST, LECTURER
b New York, NY, Aug 7, 1933. *Study:* Sch Art & Design, New York, grad, 52; Art Inst Schs, Inc, Minneapolis, grad, 78; Nassau Col, Garden City, NY, AA (cum laude), 78; Hofstra Univ, with Prof John Wildeman, Hempstead, NY, BA, 79; post-grad, 85-; Fulbright Scholar, Japan, 87. *Work:* Mus Cartoon Art, Ohio State Univ; US Presidential Librs (Johnson, Ford & Reagan); Geo-Graphics: Political Cartoons and the Environment, Hofstra Univ Mus, 90; Smithsonian Inst. *Exhib:* Int Pavillion Humor, Montreal, Can; Smithsonian Inst. *Collection Arranged:* Political Cartoons/Caricatures, Int Salon Cartoons, Montreal, 76-89; Best Editorial Cartoons of the Year, 75-2004; Reins of Power, Mus Cartoon Art, Boca Raton, Fla, 79; Geo-Graphics: Political Cartoonists on the Environment, 90 & The Reagan Presidency, 93, Hofstra Mus; No Laughing Matter: Political Cartoonists on the Environment, Smithsonian Inst, 91-96. *Pos:* Newsroom, cartoonist, Newsday, Melville, NY, 54-59; political cartoonist, caricaturist, NY Daily News, 59-91; ed art, Newsweek, 74-82; political cartoonist & caricaturist, King Features/North Am Syndicate, 91-; Wall Street Journal Report (nat tv), 82-83; cur & dir, Geo Graphics, Political Cartoons & The Environment, Hofstra Mus, 90; courtroom artist, Cablevision News 12, 91-2001; No Laughing Matter: Political Cartoonists on the Environment, Smithsonian Inst, 92-96; ed & pub mag, 74-79, editl cartoons Travel Weekly Mag, 73-91, others; editorial cartoonist, The Brooklyn Papers, 95-2002. *Teaching:* Lectr, Nassau Col, 77, Hofstra Univ, 79 & 86, NY Press Club, 80, 86 & 98, Asn Am Ed Cartoonists, 83, 84 & 86 & John Jay Col Criminal Justice, 85 & 98, Queens Col, 96, 97, & 98. *Awards:* George Washington Honor Medal, Freedoms Found, 78; Golden Press Award, 79; Hon Legion Award, NY, Police Dept, 94 & 96; The Reuben Award, Deadline Club, NY, 2003; Nat Cartoonist Soc. *Bibliog:* Cover story, Vic Cantone, Editorial Cartoonist, Illusr Mag, 79; Reach Out, Cable & Satellite, 5/83; Faces & Places, NY Daily News, 85. *Mem:* Soc Prof Journalists; Asn Am Ed Cartoonists. *Media:* Print, Video. *Res:* Acquired Knowledge of Nonverbal Communication Theory. *Publ:* Auth & illusr, Topo the Mouse, T S Denison & Co, 69; The Sea Circus, Chicago Tribune, 70; newspaper articles; first amendment themes, Ed & Publ Mag, 74-79. *Dealer:* Rothco Cartoons Syndicate 1463 44 St Brooklyn NY 11219; King Features/North Am Syndicate 235 E 45 St New York NY 10017

CANTOR, FREDRICH
PAINTER, PHOTOGRAPHER
b New York, NY, July 8, 1944. *Study:* Pratt Inst, 62-64, 66 & 67; San Francisco Art Inst, 66; Cooper Union, 69; studied with Philip Pearlstein. *Work:* Pa State Mus; New Orleans Mus Art; Sheldon Mem Art Gallery, Univ Nebr, Lincoln; Univ Mass Mus Art, Amherst; Bibliotheque Nat & Mus Carnavalet, Paris; Musee Nicéphore Niépce, Chalon S/Saone, France. *Exhib:* Solo exhibs, Robert Schoelkopf Gallery, NY, 76, Sheldon Mem Art Gallery, Univ Nebr, Lincoln, 79, Galeria Diaframma, Milan, Italy, 80, Galerie Delpire, Paris, France, 80 & 82, La Galerie Le Trepied, Geneva, Switz, 81, Marcuse Pfeifer Gallery, NY, 81 & Musee Nicephore Niepce, Chalon, S/Saone, France, 85; Galerie Philippe Fregnac, Paris, 83; Am Ctr, Paris, 84; Spazi Contemp Art, Housatonic, Mass, 94; Nicholas Davies & Co, NY, 95; and others. *Teaching:* Special instr photographic printing, St Martin's Sch Art, London, Eng, 71; adj lectr photog, Brooklyn Col, NY, 74-76; instr photog & drawing, Sch Visual Arts, NY, 75-76, Parsons Sch Design, New York, 77-78. *Awards:* Fel, Yaddo, 78; Fel, Va Ctr Creative Arts, 79, 80 & 84; Fel, McDowell Colony, 80; Fel Grant, NY State Found Arts, photog, 87. *Bibliog:* Hilton Kramer (auth), Fredrich Cantor, New York Times, 3/27/76 & 5/17/81; Janet Malcolm (auth), Fredrich Cantor, The New Yorker, 5/29/76; Carole Naggar (auth), Fredrich Cantor-Dictionnaire des Photographes, Editions Seuil, Paris, 83. *Media:* Silver Gelatin & Kodalith Prints; All. *Publ:* Auth, Rome: Vol 1, 77 & Paris: 1982, 82, pvt publ; illusr, Soul Survivors, Ticknor & Fields, 83

CANTOR, MIRA
PAINTER, DRAFTSMAN
b New York, NY, May 16, 1944. *Study:* State Univ NY, Buffalo, BFA, 66; Univ Ill, Champaign-Urbana, MFA, 69. *Work:* Mus Fine Arts, Boston; Boston Pub Libr; Honolulu Acad Arts, Hawaii; State Found, Honolulu; Rose Art Mus; Brandeis Univ, Waltham, Mass. *Comn:* Portraits comn by Negroponte Family, Brookline, Mass, 78; portraits comn by Baumann Family, Dusseldorf, Ger, 79; portrait comn by Renate Bohmer, Essen, Ger, 79; portrait comn by Dieter Schroder, Dusseldorf, Ger, 79. *Exhib:* One-person show, Galerie Lohrl, Ger, 78, De Cordova Mus, 86, Tokyo Am Ctr, Japan, 87 & Northeastern Univ, 88, 90; Boston Invitational '78, Brockton Art Ctr, Mass, 78; Three Dimensional Possibilities, Rose Art Mus, Waltham, Mass, 79; Centerbeach, Ctr Advan Visual Studies, Mass Inst Technol, 79 & 80; Fitchburg Art Mus, 92; Am Ctr, Egypt, 95, Genovese Sullivan Gallery, Boston, 99, 2002, 2005. *Collection Arranged:* Rose Art Mus, Brandeis Univ. *Pos:* Consult, Massport, 81-82; coordr visual arts, Northeastern Univ, 85-87; consult, Urban Arts, Boston, 89-90. *Teaching:* Instr painting & drawing, Univ Hawaii, Honolulu, 70-71; instr drawing, Mass Inst Technol, 78-80; instr, Northeastern Univ, Boston, 83-87, asst prof, 88-91, assoc prof, 91-2004, prof, 2004-. *Awards:* Artist-in-residence Award, Univ Hawaii, 82; Res & Develop Fund, Northeastern Univ, 89; Fac Exchange, Univ Alexandria, 91; Fulbright Scholar, 94. *Bibliog:* Robert Taylor (auth), Show Yields Fresh Perspectives, 4/84, Christine Temin (auth), Mira Cantor: Drawings that Dance, 5/88, Running Freeze 4/90, Boston Globe; Nancy Stapen (auth), New England Portraitists in 80's Keep Faces Fresh, 1/89, Artist Wasteland Embodies Life-and-Death Questions, 5/90, Boston Herald; Mira Cantor (article), Arts and Sciences Chronicle, Northeastern Univ Coll of Arts and Sciences, 3/90. *Mem:* Coll Art Asn. *Media:* Multi-Media, Drawing, Painting. *Dealer:* Genovese Sullivan Gallery Boston. *Mailing Add:* 99 Dunster Rd Apt 2 Jamaica Plain MA 02130-2733

CANTWELL, WILLIAM RICHARD
PAINTER, PRINTMAKER
b Philadelphia, Pa, July 24, 1947. *Study:* Trinity Col, Conn, BA, 69; Sch Visual Arts, studied drawing & illustration with Jack Potter, 77-84; Pratt Inst & Manhattan Graphics Ctr, studied etching with David Finkbeiner, 85-86. *Comn:* Public Relations Booklet, Consolidated Edison, NY, 77; Citibank Bldg & New York Skyline (drawings), Citibank, NY, 78; portrait series, Fairbanks Rehabilitation Asn, Alaska, 85. *Exhib:* Key West Art Festival, Fla, 86, 87, 88; Westport Art Festival, Conn, 86, 87, 88; Mystic Art Festival, Conn, 86, 87, 88; Gracie Sq Art Festival, NY, 86-88; Miami Beach Festival Arts, 87, 88; Maitland, Fla Art Fest, 87-88; Gasparilla Art Festival, Tampa, 89; Beaux Arts Festival, Coral Gables, 88-89; Wickford Art Festival, RI, 89-90; Coconut Grove Arts Festival, Fla, 92, 93 & 94; Cherry Creek Arts Festival, Denver, Colo, 92, 93 & 94; Festival of the Masters, Disney World, Fla, 92, 93 & 94; Winter Park Arts Festival, Fla, 95; and others. *Teaching:* Art therapist & painting instr, The Grove Sch, Madison, Conn, 69-70; instr graphics & photog, The Reece Sch, NY, 70-77. *Awards:* First Place, graphics, Washington Square Outdoor Exhib, New York, 79 & 85 & Key West Old Island Days Art Festival, 86; Philip Isenberg Award, Salmagundi Club, New York, 81; Rowland A Dufton Award for best of Watercolor

show, 88; Second-Third Place, watercolor, Washington Square Art Exhib, 88. *Media:* Watercolor, Etching, Serigraphy. *Publ:* Illusr, Around the system: We don't just work here, Consolidated Edison, New York, 77; Celebrity choice, Playbill Mag, New York, 83; Circling Manhattan, Dramalogue, Hollywood Co, New York, 83; Portraits, Fairbanks Rehabilitation Asn, Alaska, 85

CAO, GILDA
PHOTOGRAPHER, PAINTER
b Cienfuegos, Cuba, Dec 17, 1956; US Citizen. *Study:* Abroad Studies Eng, Univ of London, BFA, 86; NY Univ, Tisch Sch Arts, 88; Parsons Sch of Design, currently attending. *Work:* Gerald W Moore, Banker, Miami, Fla; Gunther Weiss, Art Collector; Paul Steiner; Douglas Oliver, Philanthropist, NY. *Exhib:* Tribeca Art Loft, New York City, 98; Fleet Bank, Empire State Bldg, NY, 99; Salon Di Pierro Martin, Ger, 2000. *Pos:* Cur, Zepol, Cuban Fine Art, 92; art posing, Pratt Sch of Design, 97-2004; poet, auth, Free lance assignments, currently. *Teaching:* instr, yoga, self mastery, pvt sessions, currently. *Bibliog:* Jewish Voice, NYC, 2006. *Media:* Photography, Poet. *Collection:* Silver gelatin modern heroine, a multifaced mobile image with alternate point of view

CAPES, RICHARD EDWARD
GRAPHIC ARTIST, INSTRUCTOR
b Atlanta, Ga, Nov 6, 1942. *Study:* Univ Ga, Athens, BS, 65, MA, 69; Univ Ga, Cortona, Italy, 70. *Work:* Barnwell Mem Garden Art Ctr, Shreveport, La. *Comn:* 200 Years (painting), Collectors Wall Gallery, Sarasota, Fla, 76; illus, Southside Sch, Sarasota, Fla, 83; graphic symbol of Venice, Fla, Chamber Commerce, 92; painting, City Sarasota, Fla, 94; Arthur Andersen LLP, Sarasota, Fla, 2000. *Exhib:* Two Southern Draughtsmen, Addison Gallery Am Art, 72; Brooks Mem Art Gallery, 72; 32nd Ann Exhib, Jacksonville Art Mus, Fla, 81; 36th Ann Exhib, Lee Scarfone Gallery, Univ Tampa, Fla, 86; two person show, Creative Edge, Bradenton, Fla, 92; 43rd Ann Fla Artists Group Inc Show, Sarasota, Fla, 92. *Teaching:* Asst prof art educ, Univ Southern Miss, 71-73; asst prof art, Morehead State Univ, 73-74. *Awards:* Southeast Bank Award, 80 & Hamel Mem Award, 81, Fla Artist Group Inc; First Prize, Arvida State Fla, 83; First Place Art, United First Fed Savings & Loan, Fla, 86. *Bibliog:* Wayne Mayhail II (auth), Gulfcoast People, Gulf Coast Publ, 89; Ralph Montgomery (ed-auth), article, Bus Mag, 89. *Mem:* Manatee Art League; Sarasota Visual Arts Ctr; Fla Artist Group Inc; Anna Maria Island Art League; Fla Watercolor Soc; and others. *Media:* Ink, Watercolor. *Publ:* Illusr, Sarasota Scene - Historical, 4/90; illusr, cover, Bus Magazine Yearbook, 90; cover, SARASOTA: A Sentimental Journey, Libr Cong, 91; auth & illusr, Richard Capes Drawings Capture Siesta Key, Libr Cong, 92. *Dealer:* Art for the World Gallery Sarasota FL; Island Gallery West Holmes Beach FL. *Mailing Add:* 2116 Florinda St Sarasota FL 33581

CAPLAN CIARROCCHI, SANDRA
PAINTER, EDUCATOR
b Winnipeg, Man, 1936. *Study:* Univ Man, BFA, 57; Boston Univ, MFA, 60; Yale Univ, 60-61; studied with David Aronson, Bernard Chaet, John Schuler, N Carone, Wm Bailey. *Work:* Winnipeg Art Gallery; J A MacAulay Collection, Winnipeg, Can; Boston Mutual Life Insurance; Bellevue Hosp, NY; Connor Clark Inc, Toronto; Dewey, Ballantine, New York; Town Sch, New York. *Comn:* and many pvt collections. *Exhib:* Solo exhibs, Winnipeg Art Gallery, 74, Atlantic Gallery, New York, 86, First St Gallery, New York, 89, Cast Iron Gallery, NY, 94 & Brooklyn Botanic Garden, 97, Cooperstown Art Assn, 98, Paintingsdirect.com, 2005, Civitella Del Tronto, Italy, 2005, World Financial Ctr, New York, 2008, Westbeth Gallery New York, 2003, 2008; Group exhibs, Maine Coast Artists Exhibs, 74-77; Watercolor, Contemp View, Fairleigh Dickinson Univ, 81; Views by Women Artists, Fordham Univ, 82, Gallery 53, Cooperstown, NY, Still Life-Landscape; Artists Equity Show, 97, 98; Westbeth Gallery, NY, 2003; Moveable Feast- Zeuxis, Westbeth Gallery, New York, 2003-2010; Two-person exhib, San Benedetto Del Tronto, Palazzina Azzura, Italy, 2009; All About Drawing, WestBeth Gallery, NY, 2012; Cooperstown Art Asn, NY, 99; Winter Light, First St Gallery, NY, 2012; First St Gallery, 2013; New Gallery, Colonella, Italy, 2013. *Teaching:* Instr art, Mus Mod Art, NY, 65-71, Village Community Sch, NY, 71-79, Lenox Sch, NY, 79-89, & Nat Acad Design 99-2003, Town Sch, NY, 89-2001, private students, 2005-2013. *Awards:* Can Coun Award, 61-62; Woodstock Art Asn Award Watercolor, 83; 3rd Prize Painting, Cooperstown Art Asn Nat Competition. *Bibliog:* David Daniel (auth), In the Galleries Art & Antiques, 4/89; Simona Clementoni: Monograph, 2009; Susan Hartenstein, Monograph, 2/22/2008. *Mem:* Artists Equity Asn; Nat Asn Women Artists; First Street Gallery NY. *Media:* Oil, Pastel, Watercolor, Charcoal. *Interests:* still life with landscape & archit views. *Publ:* Winnipeg Art Gallery, Sandra Caplan, Pastel Drawings, 74; Giovani Artisti Stranieri Galleria San Luca, Rome, 61; Views by Women Artists, Fordham Univ, NY, 82; Illusr, Fair Game--Hunter's Cookbook (Great American Cooking Schools), Irena Chalmers Cookbooks Inc, 83; Sentieri (Paths), Sandra Caplan, Ray Ciarrocchi, 2009; Freeman's Jour, Cooperstown, NY, 4/1996

CAPONI, ANTHONY
SCULPTOR, EDUCATOR
b Pretare, Italy, May 7, 1921. *Study:* Univ Flore, Italy; Cleveland Sch Art; Walker Art Ctr, Minn; Univ Minn, BS & MEd. *Work:* Minneapolis Inst Art; St Cloud State Col; Minn Mus Am Art, Caponi Art Park and Learning Ctr. *Comn:* Wax models for all bronze motifs, Eisenhower Libr, Abilene, Tex, 60; The Granite Trio, (32 tons carved granite sculpture), St Cloud Mall, Minn, 73; Copper Christ, (24 ft hammered copper sculpture), Edina, Minn, 78; Boulders on Boulders, (3 ton carved limestone sculpture), Minneapolis, Minn, 82; Pompeii, (17 panel bronze sculpture, 150 ft length), Caponi Art Park, Eagan, Minn, 88. *Exhib:* Walker Art Ctr, Minneapolis, 47-58; St Paul Gallery Art, 47-58; Iowa State Teachers Col, 58; Minneapolis Art Inst Ann; solo-show, Minnesota Mus Art, Rochester Art Ctr & Tweed Gallery, Duluth, Minn, 72; Minnesota Artists Look Back 1948-1988, Minn Mus Art & Salone del Palazzo Communale, Modena, Italy, 88-89; retrospective, Macalester Col, St Paul, Minn, 91. *Pos:* founder and artistic dir Caponi Art Park and Learning Ctr. *Teaching:* Prof art & chmn dept, Macalester Col, 1949-1991. *Awards:* Two Purchase Prizes, Minn Inst Art, 47-48; Ford Found Grant, 64; Italian Heritage Award, City of St Paul, 91; 2011 Eleven Who Care, KARE TV11. *Bibliog:* Moira Harris (auth), Monumental Minnesota: A Guide to Outdoor Sculpture; Public Art in Minnesota, Forecast Pub Artworks; various articles in St Paul Pioneer Press, ThisWeek Newspaper, Minneapolis Star Tribune & Eagan Sun Current. *Media:* Stone. *Publ:* Auth, Boulders & Pebbles of Poetry & Prose, Independence Press, 72; Auth, Voice from the Mountains, Ruminator Press, 2002; auth, Voice from the Mountains: A Memoir, Reprinted Nodin Press, 2010; auth, Meaning Beyond Reason, Nodin Press, 2011. *Mailing Add:* 1215 Diffley Rd Eagan MN 55123-1415

CAPONIGRO, PAUL
PHOTOGRAPHER
b Boston, Mass, Dec 7, 1932. *Study:* With Benjamin Chin & Minor White. *Work:* Comfort Gallery, Haverford Col, Pa; Int Ctr Photog, NY; Portable Works Collection, Phoenix, Ariz; Mus voor Fotografie, Antwerpen, Belig. *Exhib:* Solo exhibs, Mus Mod Art, NY, 68 & 69, San Francisco Mus Art, 70, Art Inst Chicago, 72, Albright-Knox Art Gallery, Buffalo, 76, High Mus Art, Atlanta, 79, Simon Lewinsky Gallery, San Francisco, 80, Univ Wis-Lacrosse Fine Arts Gallery, 80, Images, Cincinnati, 81, Marlborough Gallery, NY, 81, Photog Gallery, Philadelphia, 81 & Worcester Art Mus, Mass, 81; Looking at Photographs, Mus Mod Art, NY, 73; Am Masters, Smithsonian Inst, 74; Photog in Am, Whitney Mus Am Art, 74; 14 Am Photographers, Baltimore Mus Art & traveling, 75; The Land: Twentieth Century Landscape Photogs, Victoria & Albert Mus, London, Eng, 76; 100 Master Photographers, Mus Mod Art, NY, 76; Mirrors and Windows: Am Photog Since 1960, Mus Mod Art, NY & traveling, 78-80; Am Photog of the '70's, Art Inst Chicago, 79; Discovering Am 1959-70, Art Inst Chicago, 79; American Landscape, Mus Mod Art, 81; A Century of Am Landscape Photog, High Mus Art, Atlanta, 81; Seattle Art Mus, 83; Nat Mus Am Art, Smithsonian Inst, Washington, 84; Mus Mod Art, NY, 85; Photog and Light, Los Angeles Co Mus Art traveling exhib, 87; Decade by Decade-20th Century American Photog, Ctr Creative Photog, Tucson, Ariz, 89; Photographs from the Permanent Collection: A Sesquicentennial Celebration (with catalog), Haverford Comfort Gallery, Haverford Col, Pa, 90; The Beauty of Essence retrospective, Vision Gallery, Calif, 90; Megaliths, Cymbeline, NY Shakespeare Festival, 90; Photo Lore, Hartnell Col, Salinas, Calif, 90; Inlaid Silver: Polaroid Images from the 1960's, Ctr Photog Art, Carmel, Calif, 96; Meditations in Light, Farmsworth Art Mus, Rockland, Maine, 96 & Mus NW Art, La Conner, Wash, 99; Ancient Sentinels, Schmidt-Bingham Gallery, NY, 98; Megaliths, Markosian Libr Gallery, Salt Lake Community Col, 98; Photographs from the Permanent Collection: People and Places, DeCordova Mus & Sculpture Park, Lincoln, Mass, 98; Measure of Nature: Landscape Photographs from the Permanent Collection, Art Inst Chicago, 98; Courtesy of the Artist, Princeton Univ Art Mus, 98. *Pos:* Consult photo res dept, Polaroid Corp, Cambridge, 60-70; workshops at numerous places, 70-74; in residence, Maine Photog Workshop, 79-81. *Teaching:* Instr creative photography, NY Univ, 67-71; instr photography, Yale Univ, 71-86; lectr at numerous universities & art schs throughout the US. *Awards:* Guggenheim Fel, 66 & 75; Nat Endowment Arts Photog Fel, 71 & 74 & Grants, 75 & 82; Art Dirs Club NY Award, 74. *Bibliog:* Hal Fischer (auth), Sensual luminosity and misplaced beauty, Artweek, Vol II, No 24, 13, 7/5/80; Owen Edwards (auth), The gravity of Stone, Am Photogr, Vol 7, No 2, 13-14, 8/81; Margaret Lake (auth), Paul Caponigo (article), ARTnews, 9/98. *Mem:* Founder Am Heliographers Asn. *Publ:* Megaliths, Little Brown & Co, 86; Graphis No 252, Tribute to Polaroid, 11-12/87; Seasons, Little Brown & Co, 88; Photography: Art & Technique, Focal Press, 89; Writing with Light (photo essay), Parabola Mag, fall 91. *Dealer:* Andrew Smith Gallery 76 E San Francisco Santa Fe NM 87501. *Mailing Add:* 20 Prior Ln Cushing ME 04563-3111

CAPORAEL, SUZANNE
PAINTER
b New York, NY, Aug 5, 1949. *Study:* Otis Art Inst, Los Angeles Co, BFA, 77, MFA, 79. *Work:* Los Angeles Co Mus Art; Los Angeles; San Francisco Mus Mod Art; Art Inst Chicago, Ill; High Mus Art, Atlanta; JB Speed Art Mus, Louisville; Carnegie Inst, Pittsburgh; Nat Mus of Women in Arts, Washington; Los Angeles Ms of Contemp Art, Los Angeles Co Mus of Art; plus others. *Exhib:* Suzanne Caporael, Newport Harbor Art Mus, Newport, 1984 & Santa Barbara Mus Art, Calif, 1986; Summer 1985, Mus Contemp Art, Los Angeles, 1985; Avant Garde In The Eighties, Los Angeles Co Art Mus, Los Angeles, 1987; Presswork, Nat Mus Women in the Arts, Washington, DC, 1991; Individual Realities, Sezon Mus Art, Amagasaki, Japan, 1991; solo exhibs incl The Elements of Pigment, Kohn Turner Gallery, Los Angeles, 1998, Richard Gray Gallery, Chicago, 1998, The Lemberg Gallery, Birmingham, Mich, 1998, Suzanne Caporael, Karen McCready Gallery, NY, 2000, Melt New Paintings, Kohn Turner Gallery, Los Angeles, 2000, plus others; Cleveland Collects: Contemporary Art, Cleveland Mus Art, 1998; Linger, Artemis, Greenberg Van Doren Gallery, New York, 2002; Less is More, 511 Gallery, New York, 2007; New Prints: Spring 2008, Int Print Ctr, New York, 2008; Am Acan Arts & Letts Invitational, New York, 2010; The Memory Store, New York, 2010. *Teaching:* Univ Calif, Santa Barbara & San Francisco Art Inst. *Awards:* Nat Endowment Arts, 86. *Bibliog:* Kenneth Baker (auth) Abstracts with a hint of nature, San Francisco Chronicle, 4/16/94 Suzanne Caporael at the Wirtz gallery, 5/26/92, Galleries, 5/27/87; Monroe Hodder (auth) Inner natures, Visions, summer 95; Kim Levin (auth), Suzanne Caporael, Village Voice, 5/97; Nancy Doll (auth), Suzanne Caporael (catalog) Kohn Turner Gallery, Los Angeles, Richard Gray Gallery, Chicago, 96; Howard Fox (auth) Avant-garde in the eighties, (catalog) Los Angeles Co Mus of Art, 87, California viewpoints - Suzanne Caporael, Santa Barbara Mus of Art, 86; plus others. *Media:* Oil on Canvas. *Specialty:* Modern & Contemporary Masters. *Mailing Add:* c/o Richard Gray Gallery Suite 2503 875 N Michigan Chicago IL 60611

CAPORALE-GREENE, WENDE
PAINTER, INSTRUCTOR
b Bronx, NY, Dec 13, 1956. *Study:* Paier Coll of Art / Albertus Magnus Col, BFA, 83; Art Students League; Nat Acad of Design; NY Acad, with Ken Davies & Rudolph Zallinger; Private workshops with Daniel Greene, Nelson Shanks, Burton Silverman, Richard Whitney, Thomas Fogarty, Mary Beth Mackenzie & Frank Mason. *Work:* Phillips Med Systems, Inc, Shelton Conn. *Comn:* illus assignments, Readers Digest, Macmillan Publ, Harper & Row, Xerox & Tennis Mag; portraits, John & Caroline Walker, NY, 98, Diana & Will Fiske, Conn, 99, Cornelia Guest, 2004, Laurie & Eric Widing, 2005, Virginia & Jim Collins, Va, 2006. *Exhib:* Pastel Soc of Am Exhibs, NYC, 1983-2005; Allied Artists Am Nat Exhib, NYC; Hammond Mus, N Salem, NY; Hermitage Mus, Norfolk, Va; The One Show, Children's Bk Illus, Master Eagle Gallery, NYC; Soc Illusr Mus Ilus, NY; Monmouth Co Mus, Monmouth, NJ; Nat Art Competition / Am Artist Mag at Grand Central Gallery, NY; Contemp Master Pastelists, Galerie Luminous, Taichung, Taiwan. *Pos:* lectr/demonstr, for Nat Orgn including the Portrait Soc Am, Pastel Soc Am. *Teaching:* instr, pastel painting, Northern Westchester Ctr for the Arts, NY, 1993-2005; instr painting, Katonah Art Ctr, NY, 2005-; pvt workshops, Kimberly, Wis, Hilton Head, SC, Scottsdale, Ariz, Santa Fe, NMex & Asheville, NC, 2004-. *Awards:* Honor Award, Conn Pastel Soc, 1993; Howard Chandler Christy Award for portrait or figure, Pastel Soc Am, NY, 95; Am Artist Prof League for Realistic Pastel, Pastel Soc of Am, 2000; Canson, Inc Award, Pastel Soc Am, NY, 2004; MH Hurlimann Armstrong Award, Pastel Soc of Am, 2005. *Bibliog:* Madlyn Ann Woolwich, The Art of Pastel Portraiture, Watson-Guptill, 95; Feature Article, Pastel Artist Int, 9/99; Madlyn Ann Woolwich (auth), Pastel Interpretations, N Light Publs, 2003; Featured Artist, Pastel J, 11/03-12/03; Ginia Bellafante (auth), Formal Portraits Dress Down, NY Times, 2005; Maureen Bloomfield (auth), Pure Color, The Best of Pastel, N Light Publs, 2005. *Mem:* Pastel Soc of Am (master pastelist); NY Portrait Soc of Am. *Media:* Oil, Pastel. *Publ:* auth, The pastel page, Am Artist Mag, 4/99; auth, Painting Children's Portraits in Pastel, Int Artist Mag, 2001; auth, Words from the wise; the art of the portrait, Int Artist Mag, 4/2006-5/2006. *Dealer:* Portraits Inc New York NY; Portraits S Raleigh NC; ThePortraitSource Flat Rock NC. *Mailing Add:* 742 Titicus Rd PO Box 438 North Salem NY 10560

CAPPELLETTI, SHEILA
PAINTER
b New York City, NY, July 19, 1936. *Study:* Sch Visual Arts, New York, NY, 1968-1970; Parsons Sch Design, NY, 1980; Art Student's League, NY, 1980-2007; Studied with Francis Criss, Mario Cooper & Dale Meyers. *Hon Degrees:* Watercolor USA, Springfield, Mo. *Work:* Springfield Art Mus, Springfield, Mo; Zimmerli Art Mus, New Brunswick, NJ. *Exhib:* Pa Watercolor Soc, Lancaster, Pa, 2002; Salmagundi Art Club, New York, NY, 2002-2007; Watercolor, USA, Springfield Art Mus, Springfield, Mo, 2004; Audubon Artists Inc, NY, 2004-2007; Butler Inst, Youngstown, Ohio, 2005 & 2008; Roberson Mus & Sci Center, Binghamton, NY, 2007; Hall of Science, Queens, NY; RI Watercolor Soc, 2009; Pittsburgh Watercolor Soc, Pa, 2009; Nat Asn Women Arts, Nat Arts Club, New York, 2010. *Pos:* Juror of Selection, Salmagundi Club, NY. *Teaching:* art classes pvtly. *Awards:* Gold Medal for Watercolor, Springfield Art Mus, 2004; Purchase Award, Springfield Art Mus & City of Springfield, Mo, 2004; Allied Artists Award, Pen & Brush, NYC, 2005; Lucille Davis Grimm Mem Award, Springfield, Mo, 2005; Rita Davis Mem Award, Salmagundi Art Club, NYC, 2006; Best in Show Christmas Award, Salmagundi Art Club, 2006; Appelby Mem Award, 2007; Mary K Karasick Mem Award, Nat Assoc Women Artists, NY, 2008; Rita Fruis Mem Award, Salmagundi Art Club, New York, 2009; Jack Richardson and Co Art Supplies Award, Audubon Artists, NY, 2010; Salmagundi Holiday Award, NY; MO Award & Patron Purchase, Springfield Art Mus. *Mem:* Honorary mem, Watercolor USA, Mo, 2004; Salmagundi Art Club, NY, 2002-2007; Nat Asn Women Artists, NYC, 2004-2007; Audubon Artists Inc, NYC, 2007; North East Watercolor Soc, Kent, Conn, 2007; Baltimore Watercolor Soc, Baltimore, Md, 2007; Louisiana Watercolor Soc; Pittsburgh Watercolor Soc, 2009. *Media:* Mixed media. *Mailing Add:* 41-34 42nd St Long Island City NY 11104

CAPPS, KENNETH P
SCULPTOR
b Kansas City, Mo, April 10, 1939. *Study:* Univ Calif, San Diego, BA, 73, MFA, 75. *Work:* Storm King Art Ctr, Mountainville, NY; Sculpture Park Alfred Schmela, Düsseldorf, Ger; Oakland Mus, Calif; San Diego Mus Contemp Art, Calif; Fed Res Bank, Los Angeles, Calif; Mus of Modern Art, NY; The Irvine Co, San Diego, Calif; The Port of San Diego, Bayside Park, Chula Vista, Calif. *Comn:* Konoids, outdoor sculpture, San Diego Unified Port Dist, Calif, 85; sculpture, Garden Grove, Calif, 87. *Exhib:* Sculpture in the Fields, Storm King Art Ctr, Mountainville, NY, 73; Pub Sculpture Urban Environ, Oakland Mus, Calif, 74; The Minimal Tradition, Aldrich Mus, Ridgefield, Conn, 79; Sculpture in Calif 1975-80, San Diego Mus, Calif, 80; Constructed Metal, Univ Calif Santa Barbara, 84; solo exhibs, Kenneth Capps Sound Sculpture, 84-92, Calif Ctr for Art Mus, Escondido, Calif, 97, Quint Contemp Art, La Jolla, Calif Sculpture and Drawings, 98; A San Diego Exhib, San Diego Mus Contemp Art, La Jolla, Calif, 85 & Sculpture Arenas, Mandeville Gallery, Univ Calif, La Jolla, 87; Metered Atmosphere, Brandstater Gallery, Loma Linda Univ, Calif, 87; Metaphor of Function, San Diego State Univ, Calif, 90; Send and Receive Comm Sound Work, Hyde Gallery, Grossmont Coll, El Cajon, Calif, 99; Sharjah Arts Mus, Sharjah United Arab Emirates, 2000; New Additions Outdoors, Grounds for Sculpture, Hamilton, NJ, 2003; Rodin to Now: Modern Sculpture Springs Art Mus, Palm Desert, Calif, 2012; Pub Projects, Calif Ctr for the Arts, Escondido, Calif, 2001-2002; ArtExchange, San Francisco, Calif, 2003; "Backyard" Carlsbad Sculpture, Garden 2004-2005; The Elapses Invitational, Palm Desert, Calif, 2006-2008; Metered, Cannon Gallery, Carlsbad, Calif, 2008; Drawings, Cardwell Jimmerson Contemp Art, Los Angeles, 2009; Honing In: 50 San Diego Artists, Quint Contemp Art, La Jolla, Calif, 2009; Quint: Three Decades of Contemporary Art, Calif Ctr for Arts, Escondido, Calif, 2009; Kenneth Capps Early Sculpture 1969-1975, Royale Projects, Palm Desert, Calif, 2012; The Very Large Array, Mus Contemporary Art, San Diego, Calif, 2013. *Collection Arranged:* Public Sculpture Urban Environment, Oakland Mus, Calif, 74; The Minimal Tradition, The Aldrich Mus of Contemporary Art, Ridgefield, Conn, 79; Sculpture in Calif 1975-1980, San Diego Mus Art, Calif, 80; Sculpture at Storm King, Storm King Art Ctr, Mountainville, NY, 80; Forty Two Emerging Artists, Mus Caontemporary Art, San Diego, Calif, 85; San Diego Artist, Arta Publishing Inc, 88; Public Sculpture in Duesseldorf, Ger, by Wolfgang Funken, 2012. *Awards:* Fel, drawing, 83, sculpture, 87, Nat Endowment Arts, 86; Pollock-Krasner Found, 86; Engelhard Found, Boston, Mass, 88. *Bibliog:* Tara Collins (auth), Kenneth Capps, Arts Mag, 9/76; Francis Colpitt (auth), Art in Am, 5/87; Robert Pincus (auth), On the cutting edge with steel, San Diego Union, 87; Dona Z Meilach (auth) The Contemporary Blacksmith, Schiffer Pub, Ltd, 2000; Dona Z Meilach (auth), Direct Metal Sculpture, Schiffer Pub, Ltd, 2001; Robert Pincus (auth), In Plain Sight, SDak Union, 2008; Patricia Buckley (auth), Sculptor finds motion in the inanimate, NC Times, 2008; Dona Z Meilach (auth), Iron Work Today Inside & Out, Schiffer Publ Ltd, 2006; Adam levine & Rob Cardillo (auths), Great Gardens of the Philadelphia Region, Temple Univ Press, 2007; Kenneth Capps Metered Exhib catalogue, Cannon Art Gallery, Calif, 2008; Kenneth Capps early Sculpture 1969-1975, Exhib Catalogue, Royale Projects, Palm Desert, Calif. *Media:* Steel/Mixed. *Specialty:* Contemporary Art. *Dealer:* Quint Contemporary Art La Jolla CA; Royale Projects Indian Wells CA. *Mailing Add:* 1175 Hoover St Carlsbad CA 92008

CARBONE, DAVID
PAINTER, CRITIC
b New York, NY, Nov 29, 1950. *Study:* Skowhegan Sch Painting & Sculpture, with Laderman, Noland, Diao, Marden, Blaustein, Morley, Beal, 70; Sch Mus Fine Arts, Tufts Univ, with Feininger, Cox, Schwartz & Rubenstein, BFA, 71; Brooklyn Col (fel), with Holty, Holtzman, Bontecou, Stone, Ernst, Pearlstein, Russell & Groell, MFA, 74. *Comn:* Babette Whipple, Belmont, Mass. *Exhib:* Solo exhibs, Zoe Gallery, Boston, David Brown Gallery, Provincetown, 86, Mass, Contemp Realist Gallery, San Francisco, 93 & Art Mus, Univ Wis, Milwaukee, 95; Landscape Painting, 1960-1990, Spoleto Festival, Gibbes Mus & Bayly Mus, 90; New Am Figure Painting, Contemp Realist Gallery & Clemson Univ, 92; Shooting Gallery, 2001; B Rubstein & His Legacy, SMFA, Boston, 2002; Courtland Jessup Gallery, 2003; Drawing Conclusions, Paintings, NY Art Gallery, 2004; The Body & its Dangers, The Painting Ctr NY, 2005; Between Perception and Invention, Sharon Arts Ctr, Peterborough, NH, 2005; Three Paintings: Selected Works, The Painting Ctr, 2008. *Teaching:* Instr painting, Brooklyn Coll, 74-75; lectr art hist, Boston Mus Sch, 75- & instr grad sem, 76-81; vis artist painting & art hist, Knox Coll, 83; vis artist painting, Montserrat Art Sch, 85; vis assoc prof, Pratt Inst, 87, Stanford Univ, 90 & Parsons Sch Design, 91; assoc prof & dir, Grad Studies in Studio Art, State Univ New York, Albany, 93-. *Awards:* Ingram-Merrill Award, 85; Charlene Engelhard Award, 86. *Bibliog:* John Hollander (auth), The Italian Tradition in American Art in Landscape Painting 1960-1990, 90; Thomas Bolt (auth), New American Figure Painting (catalog), 92; The Nude in Contemporary Art, Aldrich Mus Contemp Art, 99; Perception and Invention: Four painters talk about figurative art, Catalog Essay, 2005; and others. *Mem:* Coll Art Asn; Inst Asn Art Critics. *Media:* Oil. *Publ:* The Field Beyond Chassy, Antaeus, 80; Francis Bacon, 9/90, Carlo Maria Mariani, 1/91, Susana Jacobson, 3/91, Eugene Leroy, 4/91 & Jim Nutt, 12/91, Art Antiques; Alfred Russell, Modern Painters, fall 91 & Art Antiques, 92; The Subject Matter in View, Mod Painters, autumn 97; The Return of the Mad Mahatma, Mod Painters, winter, 2001; Edwin Dickinson: A Transcendental Vision, Mod Painters, Autumn, 2003; On Nadelman's standing male nude, No 1, 2007 & Tracing Giovanni's Shadow, No 2, 2008, The Sienese Shredder #3, John Graham's Apostasy, 2009; Gabriel Laderman: An Unconventional Realist, Univ New Hampshire, 2008; A Delicate Poignancy: Langdon Quin's Paintings, 1990-2010, Univ New Hampshire, 2010. *Dealer:* Hackett-Freedman Gallery 250 Sutters 4th Fl San Francisco CA 94108

CARBONI, STEFANO
CURATOR
Work: Auth: Glass From Islamic Lands: The al-Sabah Collection, 2001; co-auth (with David Whitehouse): Glass of the Sultans: Twelve Centuries of Islamic Masterworks, 2001; Co-cur (with Linda Komaroff) (exhibs) The Legacy of Genghis Khan: Courtly Art and Culture in Western Asia, 1256-1353 (Alfred H Barr Junior Award for exhib catalogue, Coll Art Assoc, 2004). *Pos:* Assoc cur, dept Islamic Art Metrop Mus Art, New York City

CARDILLO, RIMER ANGEL
PRINTMAKER, SCULPTOR
b Montevideo, Uruguay, Aug 17, 1944. *Study:* Nat Sch Fine Arts, Uruguay, MFA, 68; Weissenssee Sch Art & Archit, Berlin, Ger, 70; Leipzig Sch Graphic Art, Leipzig, Ger, 71. *Work:* Prints Cabinet of Berlin, EGer; Chicago Art Inst, Ill; Mus Mod Art, NY; Cabinet Des Estampes, Bibliotheque Nationale, de Paris, France; Allen Mem Art Mus, Oberlin Col, Ohio. *Comn:* Charruas y Montes Criollos, Installation, Museo Fernando Garcia, Montevideo, Uruguay, 91; Camera Sixtine, street light boxes, First Biennial of Mercosur, Porto Alegre, Brazil, 97; Nandu, Installation Islip Art Mus, Long Island, 98; Suite of prints, Galeria Sur, Montevideo, Uruguay, 98; Suite of bronze sculptures, Ulla & Greger Olsson Art Collection, Belgium, 99. *Exhib:* Int Biennial Graphic Art, Sakaide, Japan, 88; Europe and the Third World, Messepalast, Vienna, Austria, 88; Ceremony of Memory, Ctr Contemp Art, Santa Fe, NMex, 89; Arte dell Uruguay nel Novecento, Inst Italo-Latin Am, Roma, Italy, 89; La Tierra: Visiones de Am Latina, Mus Contemp Hispanic Arts, NY, Mus de Bellas Artes, Caracas, Venezuela, 90; Echoes of the Spirit, Atlanta Coll Art Gallery, 90; solo exhibs, Rimer Cardillo: Works on Paper (with catalog), Galeria Sur, Uruguay, 92, Espinillo, Nat Mus Anthrop, Montevideo, 94, Pachamazon, Calvin Morris Gallery, NY, 96, Rimer Cardillo: Recent Work, Calvin Morris Gallery, NY, 98 & Araucaria (with catalog), Bronx Mus Art, 98; Rejoining the Spiritual: The Land in Contemp Latin Am Art, Md Inst Coll Art, Baltimore, 94; Twenty-fifth Anniv Exhib, Artists Talk Back: Reaffirming Spirituality, Part III, El Museo del Barrio, NY; In the Making: The First Ten Yrs of the Permanent Collection, Islip Art Mus, NY, 96; Landscapes: An Exhib of Sculpture, The Wash

Sculptors Group & Art Mus Am, Org Am States, Washington, DC, 97; First Mercusol Biennial, Porto Alegre, Brazil, 97; Araucaria, Rimer Cardillo, Ten Yrs Journey, Bronx Mus Arts, NY, 98; Biennial Venice Italy, 2001, Uruguayan Pavillion, Int Biennial Graphic Arts, Ljubljana, Yugoslavia, 2005. *Pos:* Artist-in-residence, Southern Ill Univ, 79-81; Bd dir, NY Found Arts, 93-96; panel mem, N State Coun Arts, 94-95; bd adv, Intar Gallery, N, 91-96 & Gallery Montevideo, 98-. *Teaching:* Prof painting, Nat Circle Fine Arts, 72-74; prof graphics, State Univ NY, Purchase, 88-90; instr graphics, Printmaking Workshop, NY, 88-; part time prof, State Univ NY, Col Purchase, 88-94; prof, State Univ NY, Col New Paltz, 94-. *Awards:* Fel, Adolf and Esther Gottleib Found, 88; Spec Proj Fel, NY State Coun Arts, 89; Fel, Pollock-Krasner Found, 90; Guggenheim Fel, 97. *Bibliog:* Victor Zamudio-Taylor (auth), Ceremony of Memory (contemp commentary), Santa Fe Ctr Contemp Arts, 88; Susana Torruella Leval (auth), Identity and Change, The Latin American Challenge, Hispanic Art Tour III, 88-89; Sullivan Edward (ed), Latin Am Art in the Twentieth Century, Phaidon Press, 96; Grady T Turner (auth), Rimer Cardillo at Cavin-Morris, Art in Am, 10/96; Joe Vojko, Rimer Cardillo at Calvin-Morris, Rev 1, No 1, 4/96; Lucy R Lippard (auth), Travel & Hierarchy in the Work of Rimer Cardillo, Bienal Venice, Italy, 2001. *Mem:* Fodo Del Sol Gallery, Washington, DC. *Media:* All Media. *Dealer:* Chace-Randall Gallery 49 Main St Andes NY 13731; Rimer Cardillo 72 Tillson Lake Rd Wallkill NY 12589. *Mailing Add:* 208 W 105th St Apt 1 New York NY 10025-3983

CARDINAL, MARCELIN
PAINTER, COLLAGE ARTIST
b Gravelbourg, Sask, Can, 1920. *Study:* Self-taught. *Work:* Quebec Mus, Que; Mus Fine Arts of New Mex, Santa Fe; Hirshhorn Mus, Wash; Mus d'Art Mod, Dunkerque, France; Mus d'Art Contemporain, Montreal; Smithsonian Inst. *Comn:* Mural, Metro St Michel, Montreal, CTCUM, 86; L'Art Dans la Rue/paintings on billboards, Benson & Hedges, Montreal, 77; paintings on billboards, Montreal Olympics, 76. *Exhib:* Artisans Gallery, New York, 53; Guggenheim Mus, NY, 54 & 58; Biennial Int, Menton, France, 55; Matthiesen Gallery, London, Eng, 58; Albright-Knox Art Gallery, Buffalo, NY, 60; Feingarten Galleries, Chicago & NYC, 60-61; Galerie Denyse Delrue, Montreal, 62; Galerie Gilles Corbeil, Montreal, 73, 74 & 75; Int Art Fair, Basel, Switz, 74; Mus du Quebec, 76; Mus d'Art Mod, Dunkerque, France, 77; Mus d'Art Contemporain, Montreal, 77 & 78; Don Stewart Gallery, Toronto, 82; Galerie Daniel Beauschene, Montreal, 85; Galerie Frederic Palardy, Montreal, 90; plus others. *Awards:* Creation et Recherche, Minister Cult Affairs, Quebec, 72, 73, 75 & 78. *Bibliog:* Christian Allegre (auth), article, Vie des Arts, 72; Profile: Marcelin Cardinal, Art Mag, 3/79; Germain Lefebvre (auth), Marcelin Cardinal, Temps, Espace Et Continuite--Vie Des Arts, 82. *Mem:* Soc Prof Artists Quebec (vpres, 72-73); hon mem Conseil de la Peinture Du Quebec. *Media:* Acrylic, Collage Artist, Canvas on Canvas. *Mailing Add:* 4897 Queen Mary Rd Apt 15 Montreal PQ H3W 1X1 Canada

CARDOSO, ANTHONY
PAINTER, SCULPTOR
b Tampa, Fla, Sept 13, 1930. *Study:* Univ Tampa, BS (Art); Art Inst Minn, BFA; Univ S Fla, MA (Art Educ), MA (Fine Art); Elysion Coll, PhD. *Work:* Minn Mus Art, St Paul; Suncoast Credit Union Bldg, Tampa, Fla; Ringling Mus Archives Sarasota, Fla; and others. *Comn:* Sports Authority, Tampa Stadium Off, 71; sports theme paintings, Leto High Sch & Pierce High Sch, Tampa, 71; two murals, Sun Coast Credit Union Bldg, Tampa, Fla, 75; Immigrant Statue, Tampa, Fla, 93. *Exhib:* Drawings USA, Minn Mus Art, St Paul, 71; Rotunda Gallery, London, Eng, 72; Brussels Int, Belg, 73; Ringling Mus Archives, Sarasota, Fla, 78; Acad Ital Exhib, Terma, Italy, 80-85; Centro Studi E Ricerche Della Nazioni, Italy, 86; and many others. *Collection Arranged:* Sculpture, Remingtons (6), J. E. Fraser (1); etchings, Rembrandt, Monet, Whistler, Picasso, Goya, Dali, others; prints, Norman Rockwell, Lasey Rivers, others. *Pos:* Supvr art, Hillsborough City Schs, 85-89, art supvr, 85-91, studio dir, 89-94, gallery dir, 91-94, 2003, pvt instr, 2010. *Teaching:* Instr Jefferson High, A P Leto High; teaching supvr, art & humanities, Hillsborough Co, Tampa. *Awards:* Gold Medal Award & Victory Statue; Palma D'Oro D'Europa, Accademia D'Europa, 89; Merit Award, Hillsborough Co, Fla State Fair, 94-96; Int Photogrs Asn Award; Prix de Paris, France; Smithsonian XXI Biennial Art Award; President Award, St Paul Mus. *Bibliog:* Bertrand Sorlot (auth), article in La Rev Mod, 71; articles, Tampa Tribune, 75-92 & Acad Italia, 80-86; Fla Mus Photographic Arts, Tampa Tribune, 2010. *Mem:* Fla Arts Coun; Ringling Art Mus Archives; Fla League Arts; Acad Italia, Italy; Tampa Art Coun; Univ Fla, 2010. *Media:* Oil, Acrylic. *Res:* Art education - the tactile-visual concept. *Specialty:* Fine arts. *Interests:* Sculpture collection & etchings. *Collection:* Western art paintings & sculpture, prints & etchings. *Publ:* Contribr, La Rev Mod, 71 & 72; Acad Italia, 80-86; Tampa Tribune, 83-92; St Petersburg Times, 92; Gazeta Newspaper, Tampa, 2003; auth (book), The Philosophical Foundations of Art Education, 2010. *Dealer:* Art Studio I & Gallery 3208 Nassau St Tampa FL 33607; El Prado Art Gallery 4318 El Prado Blvd Tampa FL 33629

CARDUCCI, JUDITH
PAINTER
b Norwood, Mass, Feb 25, 1935. *Study:* Quinnipiac Coll, Conn, Hist Art, with CA Brodeur, 60; Myers Sch Art, Univ of Akron, Ohio. *Work:* Univ Maine, Mus Art, Bangor, Maine; Hosp Special Surgery, NY; City Hall Coun Chamber, Hudson, Ohio; Cleveland State Univ, Ohio; State Teachers Retirement Syst & Educ Asn Bldgs, Columbus, Ohio; Kent State Univ, Ohio; Children's Hosp, Akron, Ohio; Case Barlow Hist Farm, Hudson, Ohio; Butler Inst Am Art, Ohio; Univ Hosp, Cleveland, Ohio; Walpole High Sch, Mass. *Comn:* Many portrait comn's. *Exhib:* Pastels Only, Ann Nat Shows, Nat Arts Club, NY, 96, 97, 99, 2000-2006; Cincinnati Art Club, Ann Nat Shows, View Point, Ohio, 96, 98, 2001-; Am Artists Prof League, Salmagundi Club, NY, 97; La Fond Galleries, Ann Nat Show, La Fond Gallery, Pittsburgh, Pa, 98 & 99; Degas Pastel Soc, Biennial Shows, Int Trade Ctr, New Orleans, La, 98 & 2000; Catharine Lorilard Wolfe Ann Nat Show, Nat Arts Club, NY, 98 & 2000; Lexington Art Club, Ann Show, The Nude, Lexington, Ky, 2001; Portraits Exhib (invited), Butler Inst Am Art, Youngstown, Ohio; Plein Air Show, Summit Art Space, Akron Area Arts Alliance, 2009. *Pos:* Bd & fac, Portrait Soc Am, 2006-; chmn, Cecilia Beaux Forum, Portrait Soc Am. *Teaching:* Instr, Cuyahoga Valley Art Ctr, Ohio, 98-; fac mem, Portrait Soc Am, 99-; Workshops, en plein air & portraiture, Southern France, 2006 & 2009; Siena, Italy, 2007; Richeson Sch Art, Kimberly, Wis, 2008; Andreeva Portrait Acad, Santa Fe, NM, 2008; Southern Atelier, Fla, 2009; workshops in pastel & portraiture by invitation; Master Class, Int Asn Pastel Soc biennial Conv, 2007. *Awards:* Best of Show, Portrait Soc Am, Wash, DC, 98; Best of Show, La Fond Galleries Nat Annual Show, Pittsburg, Pa, 98; Best of Show, The Nude, Lexington Art Club, 2001; Artist of the Year Award & Solo Show, Akron Life & Leisure Mag, 2007; Outstanding Visual Artist Award, Akron Area Arts Alliance, 2007; People's Choice, Portrait Soc Am Conv, DC, 2009; 1st Pl, Hudson Soc Artists, 2009, Best of Show, 2007, 2008; Portrait Painting in Pastel, 2 disk video & booklet, Signilar Art Videos. *Bibliog:* Betsy Hosegood (auth), Paint! Portrait & Figure, Roto Vision (Watson-Guptill), 2000; DC Selor (auth), Judith B Carducci, The Pastel J, 8/04; M Stephen Doherty (auth), Drawing on Life, Am Artists Mag, 02; articles: Int Artist; The Pastel J; The Pastelagram, 2006-2007. *Mem:* Portrait Soc Am (founding mem, 99-); Pastel Soc Am (chmn, Critique Comt, 2004-); Degas Pastel Soc (juried mem, currently); Am Artists Prof League; Salmagundi Club (juried mem, currently); Cincinnati Art Club (juried mem); Akron Soc Artists (signature mem). *Media:* Pastel, Charcoal, Conte Crayon, Ink, Graphite. *Interests:* Portraiture, still life, interiors, plein air, nude figure. *Collection:* Many private collections in USA, Canada, Europe, Israel. *Publ:* auth, Dare to See Fleshtones, Artists Mag, 98; auth, Drawing, The Foundation for Portraiture, Portrait Soc Am, 2001; contribr, Best of Portrait Painting, North Light Books, 98; contribr, How Did you Paint That? 100 Ways to Paint People & Figures, Int Artists, 2004. *Mailing Add:* 197 Sunset Dr Hudson OH 44236

CARDUCCI, VINCE
ADMINISTRATOR, CRITIC
b Detroit, Mich, June 30, 1953. *Study:* Mich State Univ, BFA, 75; New Sch for Social Rsch, MA, 2002. *Work:* Blue Cross/Blue Shield, Mich; Bank of Am, Mich; Franklin Furnace Arch Inc, NY; Gilbert & Lila Silverman Found, Mich. *Exhib:* Urbanology: Artists View Urban Experience, Ctr for Creative Studies, Detroit, 89; Text/Image, Detroit Artists Market, 92; The Detroit Show, Ctr Galleries, 94. *Pos:* Regional ed (Mich), New Art Examiner, Chicago, Ill, 84-96; contribr, Art Forum, New York, 89-92; ed, Detroit Focus Quart, 93-98; contrib ed, New Art Examiner, Chicago, 96-2002; contrib writer, Metro Times, Detroit, 2002-2009; coordr, Critical Studies/Humanities, Cranbrook Acad Art, 2007-2008; dean, undergraduate studies, Coll Creative Studies, Detroit, 2012-. *Teaching:* Instr lib arts, Coll for Creative Studies, Detroit, 2006-; lectr art hist, Wayne State Univ, Detroit, 2009-2010. *Awards:* Kresge Artist Fel, Art Crtiticism, 2010. *Bibliog:* Gerhard H Magnus (auth), Vincent A Carducci at Creative Arts Gallery, New Art Examiner, 86; Joy Hakanson Colby (auth), The Art of the Real, Detroit News, 92; Dennis Alan Nawrocki (auth), Art in Detroit Public Places, Wayne State Univ Press, 99. *Mem:* Coll Art Asn. *Res:* Esthetic and social issues in contemp art & cult. *Publ:* Lynne Avadenka: The Work of Art in the Wake of Sept 11, Metrotimes, 2002; Chromatic Interactions: Alison McMaugh, Art & Australia, 2002; Tom Otterness: Public Sculpture and the Civic Ideal for the Post Modern Age, Sculpture, 2005; Artists of the Great Lakes: 1910-1960, Am Art Rev, 2007; Lois Teicher: Private Voice, Pub Benefit, Sculpture, 2009. *Mailing Add:* 1305 E Fifth St Royal Oak MI 48067

CAREY, ELLEN
PHOTOGRAPHER
b New York, NY, June 18, 1952. *Study:* Art Students League, NY, 70; Kansas City Art Inst, BFA, 76; State Univ NY, Buffalo, MFA, 78. *Work:* Albright-Knox Art Gallery; Fogg Mus; Mus Fine Art, Houston; Patrick Lannan Found, Palm Beach, Fla; Chase Manhattan Bank, NY; Lightworks, Syracuse, NY; Dannheiser Found, NY; Picker Art Gallery, Colgate Univ, Hamilton, NY; Brooklyn Mus, NY; Whitney Mus Am Art, NY; and others. *Comn:* 7 Light Boxes, Madison Sq Garden, Exec Hq, NY, 90-93; Highland Hosp, Rochester, NY; Wadsworth Atheneum; Saint Francis Hosp, Hartford, Conn. *Exhib:* In Western NY (with catalog), Albright-Knox Gallery, 77; Contemp Photog, Fogg Art Mus, Harvard Univ, 80; The Markers (with catalog), San Francisco Mus Mod Art, 81; Some Contemp Portraits, Contemp Arts Mus, Houston, 82; Painting, Pattern, Photograph, Addison Gallery Am Art, Phillips Acad, Andover, Mass, 82; Figures: Forms and Expressions (with catalog), Albright-Knox Gallery, 82; Contemp Self-Portraiture in Photog, Hayden Art Gallery, Mass Inst Technol, 83; Hallwalls Ten Yrs (with catalog), Albright-Knox Gallery, 84; Self-Portrait/Photog 1840-1985 (with catalog), Nat Portrait Gallery, London, Eng, 86; Recent Acquisitions, Brooklyn Mus Art, 86; one-person exhibs, Art City, NY, 86, Simon Cerigo, NY, 87, Int Ctr Photog, NY, 87, John Good Gallery, NY, 89, Schneider-Bluhm-Loeb Gallery, Chicago, 90, Nat Acad Sci, Wash, DC, 92 & Gallery 954, Chicago, 94, Cleveland Ctr for Contemp Art, 97, Lougheborough Univ Sch Art & Design, Leicestershire, Eng, 99; First Person Singular: Self-Portrait in Photog, 1840-1988 (with catalog), High Mus, Atlanta, 88; Appropriation and Syntax: Uses of Photog in Contemp Art, Brooklyn Mus, 88; The Photog of Invention: Am Pictures of the 1980's, Nat Mus Am Art, Smithsonian Inst, Washington, DC, Mus Contemp Art, Chicago & Walker Art Ctr, Minneapolis, 89; David C Ruttenberg Collection (with catalog), Art Inst, Chicago, 91; Colt 4 (with catalog), Wadsworth Atheneum, 92; Life Lessons, Art Inst Chicago, 94; The Instant Image, Park Ave Atrium, NY, 94; The Abstract Urge, Ansel Adams Ctr Photog, San Francisco, 94; The Camera I, Self Portraits from the Audrey & Sydney Irmas Collection (with catalog), Los Angeles Co Mus Art, 94; Beyond the Camera, Large-Scale Manipulated Photographs, Artspace, New Haven, Conn, 94; Making Pictures, Caldwell Col, NJ, 94; Issues and Identities: Recent Acquisitions in Contemp Photog, Art Inst Chicago, 94; Abstract Photographs, Baltimore Mus Art, 95; Eye of the Beholder: The Avon Collection, Int Center for Photog, NY, 97; Photog's Multiple Roles, The Mus of Contemp Photog, Chicago, 99; and others. *Pos:* Cur, Vrej Baghoomian, Gallery, NY. *Teaching:* Asst, State Univ NY Buffalo, 76-78, instr, 77, 78; vis artist, instr, Int Ctr Photog, NY, 81-83; vis artist, RI Sch Design, Providence, 83; vis artist, Columbia Col, Chicago, Ill, 90; asst prof photog, Hartford Art Sch, Univ Hartford, Conn, 85-. *Awards:* Coffin Grant, Univ Hartford, Conn, 81, 90 & 91; Nat Endowment Arts Grant, 84; Polaroid 20 x 24, Polaroid Corp, Boston, Mass & NY,

84-98; Conn Comn on the Arts Grant, 98; Te Found Grant, 99. *Bibliog:* Vince Aletti (auth), Voice Choice, Village Voice, 11/26/96; William Zimmer (auth), A family album with no pictures, The NY Times, 12/10/2000; Barbara Pollack (auth), National reviews, Artnews, 1/01; Lyle Rexer (auth), Ellen Carey at Real Art Ways, Art in Am, 6/01. *Mailing Add:* c/o Jayne H Baum Gallery 26 Grove St Apt 4C New York NY 10014

CARIOLA, ROBERT J
PAINTER, SCULPTOR
b Brooklyn, NY, Mar 24, 1927. *Study:* Pratt Inst Art Sch; Pratt Graphic Ctr. *Work:* Fordham Univ; De Pauw Univ; La Salle Coll; Hofstra Coll; Topeka Pub Libr, Kans; N Merrick Pub Libr & Long Beach Mus, Islip Libr, NY; St Brendans Church, NY; Albright Knox Mus, Buffalo, NY; St Raymond's Mausoleum, Bronx, NY. *Comn:* four chapel murals, paintings, St John's Mausoleum, Queens, NY, 73-74; Murals, Walker Mem Baptist Church, Bronx, NY, 75; two chapel murals, Mt St Mary Cemetery, Queens, NY, 77; mural painting, St Johns Lutheran Church, Merrick, NY, 92; Indian monument sculpture, Merrick, NY, 93; metal murals, etched glass windows & doors, 2 Large Mosaics, St Raymonds, Bronx, NY; four foot bronze statue, Mother Teresa, Outdoor Grotto, Our Lady of Lourdes Church, 2004 & Massapequa Pk, NY, 2004; life size horses, Painted Design, Americana Plz Mall, Manhasset, NY. *Exhib:* Boston Mus Printmakers Exhib, 62; Corcoran Gallery Art, Washington, DC, 63; Pa Acad Fine Arts, Philadelphia, 63; Vatican Pavilion, NY World's Fair, 64; Nat Acad Design, NY, 70; Solo exhib, Long Beach Mus, Long Beach, NY, 85; Huntington Libr Art Gallery, 2005; Merrick Libr, 2013. *Collection Arranged:* Vatican Pavilion, 64; Temple Emanuel, 97; Our Lady of Lourdes Church, 2004-2006. *Pos:* Art consult, Cath Youth Orgn, Rockville Centre, NY, 67-; art coordr, St John's Cloister, Queens, NY, 72-74. *Teaching:* Instr art, La Salle Acad, Oakdale, NY, 63-65, Catholic Youth Orgn Summer Wkshop & Huntington Twp Art League, 71 & Nat Art League, Douglaston, NY, 94-. *Awards:* Grantee, Tiffany Found, 64 & 66; Grumbacher Cash Award, Silvermine Guild Artists, New Canaan, Conn, 76; Grantee, NY State Coun Arts, 92; and others. *Bibliog:* A V LesMez (auth), Cariola, Long Island Rev Mag, 64; Balt Carlson (auth), Vatican Pavilion gets Long Island exhibit, New York Times, 8/27/64; Jeanne Paris (auth), Cariola's works on exhibit at Merrick Gallery, Long Island Press, 5/28/67. *Mem:* Prof Artists Guild (pres, 69-70); hon mem Cath Fine Arts Soc. *Media:* Acrylic, Metal, Mosaics, Stained Glass. *Res:* Ancient art & old masters tech. *Specialty:* Mixed techniques & theme shows. *Interests:* Classical Music, opera, photog. *Collection:* High Schs Murals; Jacqueline Kennedy Onnasis, Dina Merrill (actress), Coll of Wooster, Hofstra Coll, Fordham Univ; three painted life size horses at Americana Plz in Mahasset; and many other private collections. *Publ:* Illusr, Writers's Ann, 58; Sign Mag, 71; contribr, Liturgical Arts Mag, 71-72; Equine Images, fall 91; Shroud-Art Images, 2008; Esperanza, Ava Maria and More, 2009. *Dealer:* Landing Gallery Woodbury NY; Soundview Gallery Port Jefferson NY. *Mailing Add:* 1844 Gormley Ave Merrick NY 11566

CARL, JOAN
SCULPTOR, PAINTER
b Cleveland, Ohio, Mar 20, 1926. *Study:* Cleveland Sch Art; Chicago Art Inst; Mills Coll; with Dong Kingman; Bordman Robinson; Carl Morris; apprenticeship, Albert Wein; New Sch Art, with Arnold Mesches & Ted Gilien. *Work:* NC Mus Art, Raleigh; Int Cult Ctr for Youth, Jerusalem, Israel; The Temple Mus, Cleveland, Ohio; Thomas Bros Maps, Irvine Calif; Judah Magnes Mus, Berkeley; NE Ohio Mus, Cleveland, Ohio; also pvt collections. *Comn:* Bronze Family Group, CPC, Brea, CA; aluminum pillars, Zinkal Ltd, Tel Aviv, Israel; GFRC Relief, Mountain View, Brea, Calif; Bronze Relief, CHP, Sacramento, Calif; Marble Wall Relief, Temple Bat Yahm, Newport Beach, Calif; Bronze portrait bust: Dr B Schifrin; bronze portrait bust, Mrs N Weissman; Bronze, Family Fugue, Dr Bruce Gillis; Garvey Court, El Monte, Calif; Mr & Mrs Norman Lynn, Lake Worth, Fla; Temple Beth El, Bloomfield, Mich; bronze, From Generation to Generation, Garvey Senior Affordable Partners, El Monte, Calif; Natures Melody, Terracotta, CJ, Brady, Fla; portrait bust, AE Wright; AE Wright Sch, Agoura, Calif; Generation to Generation, bronze, Mt Sinai Memorial Park, Hollywood, Calif. *Exhib:* Chai (graphics), Nat & Int Traveling Show, 74-75; Brand Libr Gallery, Glendale, Calif, 83; Feldhyme Libr Gallery, San Bernardino, Calif, 87; Milkin Gallery, Los Angeles, Calif, 88; Burbank Art Ctr, Calif, 90; Courtwright Gallery, Los Angeles, Calif, 94; Decker Studio Gallery, North Hollywood, Calif, 96; North Hollywood Gallery, 97; Gallery 825, North Hollywood, 98. *Pos:* Fac, Valley Ctr of Arts, Los Angeles, 59-64 & Univ Judaism, 90-94; lectr Title III Prog, San Bernardino, Inyo & Mono Co, Calif, 67-69. *Teaching:* Instr, Univ Judaism, 84-88, 94-95. *Awards:* Honorable Mention, Nat Orange Show, San Bernardino, 58 & Calif State Fair, Sacramento, 70 & 72; Design Award, Ceramic Tile Inst, 75. *Bibliog:* Will H Tagress (auth), Valley sculptor believes in reflecting world around her, The News, 74; Joel Pashby (dir), Living in 3d, film; M Landis (dir), Creative Legacy, film; Veronica Aberham (dir), Documentary video, studio-online.com; Video Interview: Art in LA, interviewer John Armillas, UTUBE. *Mem:* Founding mem Calif Confederation Arts; Artist Equity Asn, Inc (past pres); Los Angeles Art Asn (pres, 94-97). *Media:* Sculpture. *Interests:* Family, humanity & global warming. *Collection:* Works in all sizes and materials: Bronze, marble, welded steel, hardwood, watercolors, drawings, and oils. *Publ:* illusr, A World of Questions and Things (cover design), 50; illusr, Discovery Unlimited, A Guide to Raising a Creative Child, 81; illusr, The Canrelvalis of Eusebius Asch (cover design), 99. *Mailing Add:* 4808 Mary Ellen Ave Sherman Oaks CA 91423

CARLBERG, NORMAN KENNETH
GRAPHIC ARTIST, PHOTOGRAPHER
b Roseau, Minn, Nov 6, 1928. *Study:* Brainerd Jr Col, Minn, 47-49; Minneapolis Sch Art, 50; Yale Univ, BFA, 58, MFA, 61. *Hon Degrees:* Md Inst Coll Art, Baltimore, PhD. *Work:* Addison Gallery Am Art, Phillips Acad, Andover, Mass; Whitney Mus Am Art, NY; Schenectady Mus, NY; Pa Acad Fine Arts, Philadelphia; Hirshhorn Mus, Washington, DC; Guggenheim Mus, NY. *Comn:* Modular screen, Baltimore City Hosp, 65; four modular sculptures, Baltimore City Schs, Northern Parkway Jr High, 70-73 & for PS 39, 73-75; modular column, Harry Seidler, Trade Group Complex, Canberra, Australia, 73-75 & Black Widow (steel modular), 75-; Winter Wind, Painted Steel 26' x 26', Riverside Ctr, Brisbane, Australia; Uno Y Dos, Steel 12' x 12' x 10', Milford Mills, Baltimore, Md. *Exhib:* Recent Sculpture USA, Mus Mod Art, NY, 59; Structured Sculpture, Galerie Chalette, NY, 60; Solo exhibs, Cath Univ, Santiago, Chile, 60 & Baltimore Mus Art, 68; Whitney Ann, Whitney Mus Am Art, 62. *Teaching:* Instr sculpture, Cath Univ, Santiago, 60-61; sculptor in residence, Rinehart Sch Sculpture, Md Inst Col Art, Baltimore, 61-97. *Awards:* Fulbright Teaching Grant, Santiago, Chile, 60; Purchase Award, Ford Found, 62; Mus Prize, Baltimore Mus Art, 66. *Bibliog:* Josef Albers (auth), The Yale School-Structured Sculpture, Art in Am, 61; George Rickey (auth), Constructivism, George Braziller, 67; Peter Blake (auth), Architecture for the New World, the work of Harry Seidler, Wittenborn & Co, 73. *Media:* All Media. *Mailing Add:* 4450 Roland Springs Dr Baltimore MD 21210

CARLHIAN, JEAN PAUL
ARCHITECT
b Paris, Nov 7, 1919; arrived in US 1948; naturalized 1954. *Study:* Univ Paris, Bachelier es Lettres, 36; Harvard Univ, M (city planning), 47; Ecole des Beaux Arts, architecte diplome par le goubernement, 48. *Comn:* Principal works include Christian A Johnson Memorial Bldg, Middlebury Col, Mather House, Quincy House, Leverett House, Harvard, Baker Hall and McCollum Ctr of Harvard Bus Sch, Coll Ctr, Vassar Coll, The Quadrangle, Brown Univ, Mus Nat Heritage, Univ Vt Billings Ctr, Nat Mus African Art, Sackler Mus, S. Dillon Ripley Ctr, GE Co, Management Develop Inst, Cornell Univ, The Andover Cos, Smith Col, Ctr for African, Near Eastern, and Asian Cultures at Smithsonian Inst. *Pos:* Designer Harrison and Abramowitz, NY City, 49, Coolidge, Shepley, Bulfinch & Abbott, Boston, 50-57; assoc Shepley, Bulfinch, Richardson and Abbott, 58-62, partner, 63-72, vpres, dir, 72-89, consulting principal, 89-; mem, Royal Comn on Teaching Archit, 63-64, Back Bay Archit Comn, Boston, 66-79, Landmarks Comn, Boston, 69-76; bd dirs Boston Architectural Ctr, 78-80, Western European Architectural Found, 90-92, adv 93-. *Teaching:* Instr, asst prof Grad Sch Design, Harvard Univ, 48-55; vis critic Yale Univ, 58-61, 63-64, RI Sch Design, 62-63, 77 Rice Univ, 65, Harvard Univ, 78, 81; artist-in-residence Am Acad Rome, 75. *Awards:* Nat Endowment Arts Design fellow, 76-77, 78-79; Wheelwright fellow, Harvard Univ, 47; named Chevalier de l'Ordre des artes et des lettres. *Mem:* Fel, AIA (chmn comt aesthetics, 68, chmn comt on design 69, AIA Firm Award, 73, Edward C Kemper Award, 89); Royal Soc Arts; mem, Nat Acad Design (assoc, 81, acad, 94); Acad d'Architecture; Boston Soc Architects; Soc Architectural History; Smithsonian Inst. *Publ:* Contribr, Encyclopaedia Britannica, Dictionary Am Biography & articles to prof jour. *Mailing Add:* Shepley Bulfinch Richardson & Abbott 2 Seaport Ln Boston MA 02210

CARLILE, JANET (HILDEBRAND)
PAINTER, EDUCATOR
b Denver, Colo, 1942. *Study:* Cooper-Union, BFA, 66; Pratt Inst, MFA, 72. *Work:* Brooklyn Mus, NY; Brooklyn Coll Print Collection, NY; Printmaking Workshop Print Collection, NY; Libr Cong Collection; Neuberger Mus, Purchase, NY; Hirshhorn Collection, Smithsonian, Washington, DC; Metrop Mus Print Collection; Dutchess Co Community Coll; Mus at Purchase Women's Mus. *Comn:* Sneffel's Range (drawing), NY Health & Hosp Corp, 84; ed of prints, Woodstock Sch Art, NY, 84; poster, Ouray Alpine Holiday, Ouray, Colo, 93. *Exhib:* Soc Am Graphic Artists Show; Assoc Am Artists Gallery, NY, 71-84; 50 Yrs Am Printmaking, 74 & Am Landscape Paintings, 76, Brooklyn Mus, NY; solo exhib, Blue Mountain Gallery, NY, 80; Alpine Artists Show, Ouray Colo Arts Asn, 84; Woodstock Artists, Woodstock Artists Asn, NY, 82; solo exhib, Red Mt Gallery, Ouray, Colo, 2003-2014. *Pos:* Adv, Printmaking Workshop, 68-86 & Woodstock Sch Art, 80-86; asst dir, Brooklyn Mus Art Sch, 73; pres, Ouray Arts Asn, 92 & 93. *Teaching:* Instr printmaking, Sch Visual Arts, 70-72 & Brooklyn Mus Art Sch, 71-80; prof & dir printmaking, Brooklyn Coll, NY, 71-2004, head BFA prog, 94 & 2008-14, dir drawing & 2D design, 2003-14, dir MFA prog, 2006-08. *Awards:* Hirshhorn Purchase Award, Soc Am Graphic Artists, 72; Creative Artists Pub Serv Drawing & Printmaking Award, 80; Creative Incentive Grant, City Univ New York, 93 & 98-2000; Pollack/Knasner Grant, 2002-03; Nominated Am Acad Arts & Letters, 2005 & 09. *Bibliog:* Kaplan (auth), American landscape painting, Am Artist Mag, 84. *Media:* Watercolor; Oil; Prints (etching). *Res:* 2-D Media. *Interests:* Gardening, Traveling. *Dealer:* Carlile Fine Arts; Red Mountain Gallery. *Mailing Add:* PO Box 1004 Ouray CO 81427

CARLSON, CYNTHIA J
PAINTER, EDUCATOR
b Chicago, Ill, Apr 15, 1942. *Study:* Chicago Art Inst, BFA; Pratt Inst, MFA. *Work:* Va Mus Fine Art, Richmond; Guggenheim Mus, NY; Philadelphia Mus of Art; Metrop Mus Art, NY; Allen Mem Art Mus, Oberlin, Ohio; Neuberger Mus Art, Purchase, NY; Denver Mus Art, Denver, Colo; Brooklyn Mus Art, Brooklyn, NY; Princeton Mus Art, Princeton, NJ. *Comn:* Mendik Co Inc, Eleven Penn Plaza, NY, 84; mural, Md State Arts Coun, Baltimore-Washington Int Airport, 85; Los Angeles Metro Rail System, 92; Percent for Art Comn, Criminal Justice Ctr, Philadelphia, Pa, 95. *Exhib:* Artpark, 77; Solo exhibs, Allen Mem Art Mus, Oberlin, Ohio, 80; Lowe Art Mus, Coral Gables, Fla, 82; Milwaukee Art Mus, Wis, 82; Albright-Knox Art Gallery, Buffalo, NY, 85; Queens Mus, Flushing Meadow, NY, 90; Hudson Opera House, Hudson, NY. *Teaching:* Assoc prof art, Philadelphia Col Art, 67-81, prof, 81-86; prof, Queens Col, City Univ NY, 86-. *Awards:* Nat Endowment Arts Grant, 75, 78, 80, 87; PSC-CUNY Res Award, 88, 90. *Bibliog:* Patricia Stewart (auth), High decoration in low relief, Art in Am, 2/80; April Kingsley (auth), Cynthia Carlson: The subversive intent of the decorative impulse, Arts Mag, 3/80; Regan Upshaw (auth), Cynthia Carlson: Memento Mori, Art in Am, 7/86. *Mem:* Coll Art Asn (bd dir). *Media:* Acrylic, Oil. *Mailing Add:* 139 W 19th St New York NY 10011

CARLSON, GEORGE ARTHUR
SCULPTOR, PAINTER
b Elmhurst, Ill, July 3, 1940. *Study:* Am Acad Art; Chicago Art Inst; Univ Ariz. *Hon Degrees:* Doctorate Fine Arts, Univ Idaho, Moscow. *Work:* Amon Carter Exhib Hall, Ft Worth, Tex; Indianapolis Mus Fine Arts, Eiteljorg Mus Am Indian & Western Art; Outdoor Mus Art, Englewood, Colo; Genesee Mus, Rochester, NY; also pvt collections of Harrison Eiteljorg, Senator Barry Goldwater, Mr & Mrs John Marion, Edward Bass, Art Nicholas, Lois Rice, Fritz Scholder, Arnold Schwarzenegger, Bill Cosby, Robert Mehi, Dr Bane Travis; Western & Wildlife Mus, Jackson Hole, Wyo; Bank Am, Los Vegas; Mobile Oil, Houston, Tex; Washington Park, Denver, Colo; Colo Sch Mines, Golden, Colo; Gonzaga Univ, Spokane, Wash; Autry Nat Mus, Los Angeles; NMex Mus Fine Art, Santa Fe; Denver Art Mus. *Comn:* Monument of Early Day Miner, Washington Park, Denver, 77; portrait bust, comn by Bill Cosby, 79 & Bill Harrah, 81; Navajo John (bronze sculpture), Foreign Diplomat Coun, Washington, 81; Paul Robeson, comn by Bill Cosby; St. Ignatius, Gonzaga Univ, Spokane, Wash. *Exhib:* Nat Acad Western Art, Okla, 74-80; retrospective, Indianapolis Mus Fine Arts, Ind, 79-80; one man shows, Smithsonian Inst, Nat Hist Mus, Washington, 82, The Tarahumara, Indianapolis Mus Art, Stremmel Galleries, Reno, Nev, 82 O'Grady Galleries, Chicago, Ill, 83 & Gerald Peters Gallery, Santa Fe, NMex, 77, 85 & 88; Artist Am Show, Denver, 81-98; Nat Sculpture Soc, NY, 81-; Artists of Am show, Denver, Colo, 81-98; Kyoto World Expos Hist Cities, Traveling Show, 87; Ky Derby Mus, Lexington, 88; Spirit of the West, West One Bank tour of Utah, Idaho & Washington, 91; Hakone Open-Air Mus, Tokyo, 91; High Plains Heritage Mus, Spearfish, SDAk, 91-92; Denver Seven, Nat Cowboy Hall Fame, Okla City, 92; Western Rendezvous Show, Park city, Utah, 95; Prix de West, Nat Cowboy Hall Fame, Okla City, 95-98; Leading the West, Munson Gallery, Santa Fe, NMex, 98; Western Invitational, Autry Western Heritage Mus, Los Angeles, 98; Coors Invitational, Denver, Colo, 98; The Governor's Invitational, Denver, Colo, 98; Major Retrospective, Denver Art Mus, Colo, 2007-; The Art Spirit Gallery, Coeur d'Alene, Idaho, 2008. *Awards:* Gold Medals, 74, 78, 80 & 85, Prix de West, Best of Show, 75, Silver Medals, 76 & 81, Nat Acad Western Art; Artists of America, AOA Master, 1992; Idaho Gov's Award for Excellence in the Arts, 1996. *Bibliog:* Gene Autry (auth), George Carlson, Dignity in Art, Western Heritage Mus, 93; Donald Martin Reynolds (auth), Masters of Americas Sculpture, Abbeville Press, Gilcrease Mus Rendezvous, Tulsa, Okla, 94; Donald J Hagerty (auth), Leading the West: One Hundred Contemporary Painters and Sculptors, Northland Publ, 97; Sherrie McGraw (auth), The Language of Drawing, Bright Light Publ, 2005. *Mem:* Nat Acad Western Art; Nat Sculpture Soc (dir, 1989); Lionel Hampton Nat Jazz Festival (Nat Board Dirs, 2001); Calif Art Club, 2003. *Media:* Bronze; Mixed. *Publ:* Auth, The Tarahumara, pvt publ, 77; auth, The Strength of the Spirit, Gerald Peters Gallery, Santa Fe, NMex, 1992; auth, Dignity in Art, Autry Western Heritage Mus, 1993; auth, Year of the Horse, Nicholas Gallery, Billings, Mont, 2002. *Mailing Add:* PO Box 28 Harrison ID 83833

CARLSON, JANE C
PAINTER
b Boston, Mass, Sept 1, 1928. *Study:* Art Students League; Mass Coll Art; study with Charles Kinghan & Robert Davis. *Exhib:* Allied Artists Am, 69-83; Am Artists Prof League, 70-83; Am Watercolor Soc, Nat Acad Design, NY, 71-83; Audubon Artists, 73-83; Art for the Parks, Nat Exhib, 87; Nat Acad of Design, NY; Nat Arts Club, NY; NY World Trade Ctr; Knickerbocker Artists Nat Exhib; Grand Central Galleries, NY; Lever House, NY; Frye Mus, Seattle; Muckenthaler Cult Ctr, Calif; Ctrl Wyoming Mus of Fine Arts. *Teaching:* Watercolor demonstrations; watercolor & oil workshops. *Awards:* Robert Simmons Award, 71, Maynard Landa Memorial Award, 77, Windsor Newton Award, 81, Muriel Alvord Award, 82, Hudson Valley Art Asn; Twin Brooks Award, 77, William McKillap Prize, 79, Gold Medal, 82 & 97, Best in Show (Gold Medal), 85, Award for Excellence (Gold Medal), 87, Members Award with Solo Show, 91, Gold for Oil, 93, Award for Watercolor, 95, Kent Art Asn; High Winds Medal, 83 & 85, American Watercolor Society; James Holton Award, 72, Knickerbocker Artists; Robert Simmons Award, 78, Catherine Lorellard Wolf; Open Show Award, 80, Salmagundi Club; Jules Bauer Award, 81, New Rochelle Art Asn; Guilia Palermo Award, 82, Audubon Artists of Am; Dassler Award, 85, Adirondacks National; Award for Excellence, 87, Arts for the Parks National Show (100 paintings for Nat Tour). *Mem:* Am Watercolor Soc (bd dir, 77); Am Artists Prof League; Audubon Artists; Allied Artists Am; Hudson Valley Art Asn; Knickerbocker Artists. *Media:* Oil, Watercolor. *Specialty:* Contemporary Realism. *Publ:* Am Artists Mag Watercolor Pg. *Dealer:* The Hughes Gallery Boca Grande FL. *Mailing Add:* Candlewood Isle PO Box 364 New Fairfield CT 06812

CARLSON, MARY
SCULPTOR
b Stevens Point, Wis, Mar 21, 1951. *Study:* Sch Visual Arts, BFA, 73. *Work:* Chase Manhattan Bank, NY. *Exhib:* Solo exhibs, Curt Marcus Gallery, NY, 86, Michael Klein Inc, NY, 87, Max Protetch Gallery, NY, 92, Holly Solomon Gallery, NY, 94 & Bill Maynes Gallery, NY, 96, 97 & 99; Identia E Alterita, Venice Biennale, Italy, 95; Shirts & Skins, Contemp Mus, Honolulu, 96; Body Language, Fla State Univ, 96; and others. *Awards:* Guggenheim Found, 93. *Bibliog:* William Zimmer (auth), Everyday Expectations With a Twist, NY Times, 12/23/90; Gretchen Faust (auth), New York in Review, Arts Mag, 2/91; Holland Cotter (auth), Art in Review, NY Times, 4/10/92

CARLSON, ROBERT MICHAEL
GLASS BLOWER, PAINTER
b Brooklyn, NY, Nov 19, 1952. *Study:* City Coll NY, 70-73; Pilchuck Sch, 81-82. *Work:* Corning Mus Glass, NY; Glasmuseum, Frauenau, Ger; Glasmuseum, Ebeltoft, Denmark; Los Angeles Co Mus Art; Toledo Mus Art; Indianapolis Mus Art; Tampa Mus Art. *Exhib:* Design Visions-Int Directions, Art Gallery West Australia, Perth, 92; Clearly Art/Pilchuck Connection, Whatcom Co Mus, Bellingham, Wash, 92; Interglas Symposium Exhib, Crystalex, Novy Bor, Czech, 91; The Frozen Moment, Bellevue Art Mus, Wash, 91; Glass Inventions/Silica Dreams, Mus Craft & Folk Art, San Francisco, 89; Masters of Contemp Glass: Selections from the Glick Collection, Indianapolis Mus Art, 97; Telling Compelling Tales: Narration in Contemp Glass, Holter Mus, Helena, Mont, 98; Clearly Inspired, Contemp Glass and Its Origins, Tampa Mus Art, 99; Contemp Craft from the Saxe Collection, Fine Arts Mus San Francisco, 04; Int Glass Invitational, Habatat Galleries, Boca Raton, Fla, 2004. *Teaching:* Vis artist, glass art, Calif Col Arts & Crafts, Oakland, 89; fac, glass art, Pilchuck Sch, Stanwood, Wash, 89-90 & 92; fac, Penland Sch Crafts, NC, 94 & Bild-Werk Art Acad, Frauenau, Ger, 96. *Awards:* Award of Merit, Ariz Biennial, Tucson Mus Art, 86; Jurois Award, 5th Ann Capitol Invitational, The Glass Gallery, 86; Nat Endowment Arts, Fel, 90; John Hauberg fel, Pilchuck Sch, Stanwood, Wash, 2000; Hon Lifetime Membership award, Glass Art Soc, 2004; John Hanberg Fel, 2012; Artist in Res, Mus Glass, Tacoma, Wash, 2012. *Bibliog:* Dick Weiss (auth), Robert Carlson, Class Work Mag, 90; Bonnie Miller (auth), Chronical Books, 91; Ron Glowen (auth), The Symbolism of Alchemy, Am Craft, 94. *Mem:* Glass Art Soc (bd dir 92-, vpres, 93); Glass Art Society (pres, 94-96); Am Crafts Coun. *Media:* Multimedia. *Mailing Add:* PO Box 11590 Bainbridge Island WA 98110

CARLSTROM, LUCINDA
PAINTER, PRINTMAKER
b Jamestown, NY, Sept 8, 1950. *Study:* Ringling Sch Art, Sarasota, Fla, 68-70; Atlanta Coll Art, Ga, BFA, 74; Inst Allende, San Miguel, Mex, 73. *Work:* Contemp Hotel, Walt Disney World, Lake Buena Vista, Fla; DeKalb Jr Col, McClatchey, Cody Rodgers & Regenstein, Atlanta, Ga; Barnett Banks, Barnett Holding Co, Jacksonville, Fla; El Dorado Hosp, Tucson. *Exhib:* Walt Disney World, Lake Buena Vista, Fla, 74-79; New Orleans Mus Art, 75; US Info Agency Traveling Exhib, 76-78; High Mus Art Gallery, Atlanta, Ga, 79-. *Awards:* Best Graphics, Space Coast Arts Festival, Cocoa Beach, Fla, 75; Best Watercolor, Southeastern Arts & Crafts Festival, Macon, Ga, 76; Second Award, Art Festival Atlanta, 79. *Mem:* Artists Equity Asn; Univ Mich Artists Guild; Ga Watercolor Soc. *Media:* Watercolor; Etching. *Mailing Add:* 1075 Standard Dr NE Atlanta GA 30319-3357

CARMEAN, E A, JR
HISTORIAN, CURATOR
b Springfield, Ill, Jan 25, 1945. *Study:* MacMurray Col, BA (hist art), hon PhD, 81; Univ Ill, with Allen Weller. *Collection Arranged:* The Collages of Robert Motherwell (with catalog); Friedel Dzubas (with catalog); Modernist Art 1960-1970 (with catalog); Morris Louis: Major Themes & Variations (with catalog); The Subjects of the Artist (with catalog); Mondrian: The Diamond Compositions (with catalog); Morton G Neumann Collection (with catalog); Picasso: The Saltimbanques (with catalog); Kadinsky: The Improvisations. *Pos:* Cur 20th century art, Mus Fine Arts, Houston, 71-74; cur 20th century art, Nat Gallery Art, 74-84; dir, Ft Worth Art Mus, Tex, 84-91, Memphis Brooks Mus Art, 92-. *Teaching:* Lectr art hist, Univ Ill, Urbana, 67-69; vis prof 20th century art, Rice Univ, 73-74; vis prof 20th century art, George Washington Univ, 75-76. *Awards:* Guggenheim Found Fel, 78-79. *Mem:* Coll Art Asn; Am Asn Mus. *Res:* Picasso & cubism; abstract expressionism; modern sculpture. *Publ:* Auth, Braque the papier colles, 82; David Smith, 82; Je suis le cahier: The sketchbooks of Picasso, 87; Nancy Graves, 87; Helen Frankenthaler - A painting retrospective, 89. *Mailing Add:* 954 Harbor View Dr Memphis TN 38103-8838

CARMICHAEL, DONALD RAY
PAINTER
b Elnora, Ind, Dec 26, 1922. *Study:* Herron Art Inst, BFA, 51; Univ Tenn, Knoxville, MFA, 75; also with John Taylor & David Freidenthal, New York & Edwin Fulwider, Ford Times & Garo Antreasian, NMex. *Work:* Tenn State Mus, Nashville; Jackson-Madison Co Pub Libr, Tenn; Casey Jones Railroad Mus, Jackson, Tenn; Tarble Arts Ctr, Charleston, Ill; Bristol Art Ctr, Tenn; and others. *Comn:* Life size statue, Carl Smith Agency, Jackson, 67; official seal (engraving), Jackson State Community Col, 67; five panel mural, History of Jackson, McDonalds, Inc, 68. *Exhib:* Three-man show, Lynn Kottler Galleries, NY, 71; 23rd Grand Prix Int, Deauville, France & Palace Fine Arts, Rome, Italy, 72; Watercolor USA, Springfield Art Mus, 74-75; Southeastern Collection of Contemp Art, Mich Artrain Tour, 74; and others. *Collection Arranged:* Lawrence Calcagno Retrospective, 82-83; Walter Sorge Retrospective, 83-84; Watercolor III, Fourth and Fifth Biennial, 83-85; Med Illustr, CIBA Collection, Frank Netter, Md, 84. *Pos:* Pres, Jackson Art Asn, 65-67; pres, Jackson Arts Coun, 68-70; chmn visual arts adv panel, Tenn Arts Comn, 72-75, field rep, 75-78; dir, Tarble Arts Ctr, Eastern Ill Univ, Charleston, 78-85, emer dir, 85-; bd mem, Cent Ill Arts Consortium, 78-84; mem rev comt, Art in Archit, Capital Develop Bd, Ill, 79-82; dir exhib, Venice Art Ctr, FL, 87-, pres 93-94. *Teaching:* Instr painting, Shelbyville Art League, Ind, 51-55; instr art appreciation, Union Univ, Tenn, 64-66, instr drawing, painting & composition, 66-74; grad asst, Univ Tenn, Knoxville, 74-75; instr evening classes, Dyersburg State Community Col, Tenn, 76-77; instr art theory, Eastern Ill Univ, Charleston, 80-84; instr watercolor, Venice Art Ctr, Fla, 87. *Awards:* Purchase Award, Enjay Chem Nat, 66; Tennessee Painting Today Purchase Award, Tenn Arts Comn, 67; Tennessee Watercolor Soc Purchase Award, 75. *Bibliog:* William T Alderson (auth), Tennessee lives, Historical Rec Asn, 71; article, La Rev Mod, 72; Mary Ann Beckwith (auth), Creative Watercolor & Techniques, 96. *Mem:* Fla Suncoast Watercolor Soc; Tenn Watercolorist (dir & mem chmn, 71-73); Southern Watercolor Soc; Tenn Watercolor Soc (co-founder, pres, 74); Fla Artist Group Inc (dir, 97, vpres, 99, pres, 2001-03). *Media:* Watercolor, Oil. *Publ:* Contribr, Edward Betts, auth, Creative Seascape Painting, 81; Jerry McLish (auth), Marine Art - A Collection of Fine Art, 98. *Dealer:* Venice Art Ctr Venice FL 34285. *Mailing Add:* 25 Max Lane Dr Apt 214 Jackson TN 38305

CARNWATH, SQUEAK
PAINTER
b Abington, Pa, May 24, 1947. *Study:* Goddard Col, 69-70; Calif Coll Arts & Crafts, MFA, 77. *Work:* Oakland Mus; San Francisco Mus Mod Art. *Exhib:* group exhibs, Professor's Choice, Pomona Col, Claremont, Calif, 92, Contemp Uses of Wax & Encaustic, Palo Alto Cult Ctr, Calif, 92, New Additions 1991-1992, Alice Simsar

Gallery, Ann Arbor, Mich, 92, Fine Arts Presses, City Hall, Civic Ctr, San Francisco, Calif, 92, Art Contact, Central Exhib Hall, St Petersburg, Russia, 92, Am Art Today: Heads Only, Art Mus Fla, Int Univ, Miami, 94, Here & Now: Bay Area Masterworks from the di Rosa Collections, Oakland Mus, Calif, 94; solo exhibs, Ledis Flam Gallery, NY 93 & 94, OK Harris/David Klein Gallery, Birmingham, Mich, 94, Chrysler Mus, Norfolk, Va, traveling, 94, David Beitzel Gallery, NY, 96 & 98, Cohen Berkowitz Gallery, Kansas City, Mo, 97, Squeak Carnwath, Seeing in the Dark, Calif Mus Art, Luther Burbank Ctr Arts, Santa Rosa, Calif, 98 & Undraped Human Being, John Berggruen Gallery, San Francisco, Calif, 98, Nielsen Gallery, Boston, Mass, 2006, Univ Berkeley, Townsend Ctr, Berkeley, Calif, 2007, Anderson Ranch at the Aspen Art Mus, Colo, 2008, Squek Carnwath: Painting is no Ordinary Object, Oakland Mus Calif, 2008, American Printmaking Now, Nat Art Mus China, Beijing, Guan Shanyue Art Mus, Shenzen, China, 2010, The Missing Peace: Artists Consider the Dalai Lama, Nobel Mus, Stockholm, Sweden, 2010-2011, Triton Mus Art, Santa Clara, Calif, 2011, Fifty Years of Bay Area Art-the SECA awards, SFMOMA, Calif, 2011-2012, Choose Paint! Mus African Diaspora, San Francisco, Calif, 2012, The Female Gaze: Women Artists Making their World, Pennsylvania Academy of the Fine Arts, Phila, Pa, 2012-2013, Here is, James Harris Gallery, Seattle, Wash, 2013, When Collecting Becomes a Collection-Sharing the Gifts of Wilfred Davis Fletcher with the Community, Long Beach Mus Art, Long Beach, Calif, 2013-2014, Peter Mendenhall Gallery, Los Angeles, Calif 2014. *Teaching:* Teaching asst ceramics, Calif Col Arts & Crafts, Oakland, 71, 76, guest artist, 77-78, 79, 82, shopmaster ceramics, 80-82; instr, Ohlone Col, Fremont, Calif, Calif Col Arts & Crafts, Oakland, 78; vis artist, Univ Calif, Berkeley, 82-83; prof art, Univ Calif, Davis, 83-, grad adv, 85-88, 90-92; vis prof & assoc dean, Sch Fine Arts, Calif Col Arts & Crafts, 93-94; prof in residence, Dept Art Practice, Univ Calif, Berkeley, 98. *Awards:* Guggenheim Fel, 94; Artist-in-Residence, Alma B C Shapiro Residency for a Woman Painter, Yaddo, Sarasota Springs, NY, 96; Hometown Heroes, Oakland Artists Who Have Made a Difference, Office of the Mayor, Oakland, Calif, 96. *Bibliog:* S Winn (auth), Ramps & ghosts, Artnews, 11/80; S Boettger (auth), From the sunnyside, Art in Am, 1/83 & Impolite figure, Artforum, 10/83. *Media:* Oil. *Dealer:* Gail Severn Gallery Ketchum ID; Clark Gallery Lincoln MA; James Harris Gallery Seattle WA; Peter Mendenhall Gallery Los Angeles CA; Melissa Morgan Fine Art Palm Desert CA; Tayloe Piggott Gallery Jackson WY; Turner Carroll Gallery Santa Fe NM. *Mailing Add:* 248 3rd St #737 Oakland CA 94607

CAROOMPAS, CAROLE J
PAINTER, INSTRUCTOR
b Oregon City, Ore. *Study:* Calif State Univ, Fullerton, BA, 68; Univ Southern Calif, MFA, 71. *Work:* Los Angeles Co Mus Art; New Mus, NY; Nora Eccles Harrison Mus of Art, Utah State Univ, Logan; Berkeley Mus; Orange Co Mus; Santa Barbara Mus; and others. *Exhib:* Los Angeles - New Work, Mus Mod Art, NY, 76 & Maps, 77; Art about Art, Whitney Mus Art, NY, 78; Michael & Dorothy Blankfort Collection, Los Angeles Co Mus Art, 82; Corcoran Biennial, Corcoran Gallery Art, Washington, DC, 93; Around the Dinner Party, Armand Hammer Mus, Calif, 95-96; Some Grids, Los Angeles Co Mus Art, 96; Patterns of Excess, Beaver Col, Pa, 96; Cirrus Gallery, Los Angeles, 96; solo exhibs, Mark Moore Gallery, Santa Monica, Calif, 97, 99-2000 & Western Project, 2003-2007 & 2009, 2011; Otis Gallery, Otis Coll Art & Design, Los Angeles, 97; San Jose Mus Art, 2002-; Riverside Mus, 2007; LA Munic Art Gallery, 2007; Track 16 Gallery, Santa Monica, 2007-2008; Under the Big Black Suns Calif Art 1974-1981, MOCA, 2011; Lace, LA Spirit, Resurrection (web based archive), 2011; 1940-1980 Abject Figurative Expressionism, Calif Mus Art, Pasadena, 2012; Bacon, Western Project, LA, 2012; Sanctified: Spirituality in Contemporary Art, Vincent Price Art Mus, Monterey Park, Calif, 2013. *Teaching:* Prof Fac mem painting, Otis Coll Art Design, 81-, Fine arts of grad studies, Otis Coll Art Design, Los Angeles. *Awards:* NEA Grants, 1987, 1993; Adolph Y Esther Gottlieb Grant, 93; Guggenheim Mem Fel, 1995; Grant, City of Los Angeles, 2000; Grant, Calif Community, 2005; Grant, Peter S. Reed Found, 2006. *Bibliog:* Terry Myers (auth), Reviews, New Art Examiner, 10/94; Amelia Jones (auth), Reviews, Art Forum, 11/94; Michael Duncan (auth), LA rising, Art in Am, 12/94 & Essay, 11/98; Christopher Knight (auth), LA Times, 97-2000 & 2007; David Pagel (auth), Art Issues, 98; Michael Duncan (auth), article, Art in Am, 98 & 2007; and others. *Media:* Acrylic. *Specialty:* Contemporary Art. *Publ:* Auth, Dreams of the lady of the castle perilous & portfolio: the songs she sang to herself, Paris Review, 81; The Weavers Dream - A Lullaby, Whitewalls, 81; La Lucha (the Struggle) Record Album with Chas Smith & Tim Biskup, self-publ, 89; Intro - & Another Fairy Tale, Lace, 89; Before & After Frankenstein: The Woman who knew too much, Sue Spaid Gallery, 92; Dancing with Mistfits: Eye Dazzler, Western Product, 2007. *Dealer:* Western Project La Cienaga Culver City CA. *Mailing Add:* 1250 Long Beach Ave #118 Los Angeles CA 90021-2339

CARP, RICHARD M
ADMINISTRATOR, EDUCATOR
b Madison, Wis, June 10, 1949. *Study:* Stanford Univ, BA, 71; Pacific Sch Relig, MA, 77; Grad Theological Union, PhD, 81. *Pos:* Dir grad prog, Calif Col Arts & Crafts, 86-87; vpres acad affairs, Kansas City Art Inst, 89-91; chair, Northern Ill Univ, DeKalb, 91-. *Teaching:* Assoc prof interdisciplinary, Calif Col Arts & Crafts, 82-88; prof, Art Inst Southern Calif, 88-89; spec proj image bank teaching world religions, Nat Endowment Humanities, 88-92; prof & sr grad fac interdisciplinary, Northern Ill Univ, DeKalb, 91-; spec proj co-dir, Nat Endowment Humanities, Univ Hawaii, 93. *Mem:* Am Acad Relig; Asn Integrative Studies; Coll Art Asn; Soc Values Higher Educ; Am Asn Univ Women. *Res:* Art; material culture; religion and the construction of perception. *Publ:* Contribr, Tracing Common Themes: Comparative Courses in the Study of Religion, Scholars Press, 93; contribr & ed, Saber es Poder/Interventions: Urban Revisions: Current Projects for the Public Realm-Museum of Cont Art LA, ADOBE-LA, 94; auth, Lost in the desert: Mark C Taylor, disfiguring art, architecture, religion, Art J, spring 94; auth, Perception & Material Culture: Historical & Cross-Cultural Perspectives, Historical Reflections/Reflexions Historiques, fall, 97; contribr, Beyond Schultz: Absence Face to Face, Wish I Were: Felt Pathways of the Self, Magna Publ, 98. *Mailing Add:* Northern Ill Univ Sch Art Dekalb IL 60115

CARPENTER, DENNIS (BONES) WILKINSON
PHOTOGRAPHER, EDUCATOR
b Meridian, Miss, June 7, 1947. *Study:* Univ Ky, BArch, 72; Univ Fla, MFA, 79. *Work:* Jacksonville Art Mus, Fla; Polaroid Corp, Clarence Kennedy Gallery, Cambridge, Mass; Polaroid Int, Amsterdam, Neth; St Petersburg Mus Fine Art, Fla; Univ Fla, Gainesville. *Exhib:* Graphics Invitational, Mint Mus, 80; solo exhib, Univ Denver, 82, Light Factory, Charlotte, NC, 83, Webster Univ, St Louis, 83 & Photogenesis Gallery, Albuquerque, 83; Photographers Choose Photographers, Name Gallery, Chicago, 83. *Pos:* 606-257-9000, Home: 606-254-5146. *Teaching:* Assoc prof photog, Univ Ky, Lexington, 73-; grad teaching asst, Univ Fla, Gainesville, 77-79; dir photog, Penland Sch Crafts, NC, 83. *Awards:* Best of Show, The Landscape, Crealde Sch Art, 81 & Each Image Unique, Catskill Ctr Photog, 81; Nat Endowment Arts Fel, 83. *Mem:* Soc Photog Educ; Coll Art Asn; Friends Photog. *Media:* Mixed. *Mailing Add:* Univ Ky Col Fine Arts/Art Dept 207 Fine Arts Bldg Lexington KY 40506-0022

CARPENTER, EARL L
PAINTER
b Long Beach, Calif, Nov 13, 1931. *Study:* Chouinard Art Sch, 1 yr; Art Ctr Coll Design, 4 yrs. *Work:* Mus Northern Ariz, Flagstaff; also in pvt collections of Olaf Weighorst, Sen Barry Goldwater, John Colton, James Russell, Barbara Wilhelm, Will Auther, Tim Forsythe. *Comn:* 8 paintings, Mus Northern Ariz. *Exhib:* Retrospective, Wyo State Arch & Hist Dept, 74; Grand Canyon Art, Northern Ariz Univ, Flagstaff, 78; Artist of the Rockies 10th Anniversary Exhib, Pueblo, Colo, 83; Nat Park Acad Art, Wyo, 87; Gov's Invitational, Cheyenne, Wyo; Northern Ariz Univ, Flagstaff, 98; Grand Canyon Asn Art, Kolb Studio, 2000; Grand Canyon Painters, Mus of N Ariz, 2006-2007; Historic Home Tour, Phoenix, AZ, 2010; Leanin Tree Mus, Boulder, Colo. *Pos:* Tech illusr, Advert Art (Agency), 60-65; fine artist, 1965-. *Teaching:* pvt instr. *Awards:* Stacey Scholar, 67 & 69. *Bibliog:* My Technique, American Artist. *Mem:* Grand Canyon Art Asn. *Media:* Oil, Watercolor. *Res:* On location Grand Canyon, other. *Specialty:* Traditional. *Interests:* Photography, archery. *Publ:* Illusr, paintings in Ariz Highways Mag, Phoenix, 73, 74 & 87; article, Southwest Art Mag, 1/81 & US Mag, 9/88; Art of the West, 4-5/90, 11-12/92 & 11-12/97; The Majesty of the Grand Canyon, First Glance Bks, 98; Art Talk 98, Scottsdale, Ariz, 98; askart.com; Ed Trumble (auth), Lean'n Tree, Western Art (bk), 2007. *Dealer:* Blue Coyote Gallery Cave Creek Ariz. *Mailing Add:* PO Box 5325 Lake Montezuma AZ 86342

CARPENTER, JOSEPH ALLAN
GRAPHIC ARTIST, CARTOONIST
b Providence, RI, Feb 8, 1921. *Study:* RI Sch Design, BFA, 47. *Work:* Rehoboth Antiquarian Soc Mus, Mass. *Comn:* Portraits of retirees, Allied Signal Co, E Providence, RI, 65-78. *Exhib:* Solo exhibs, Attleboro Mus, Mass, 79 & Providence Art Club; Bard Co Showcase, NY. *Pos:* Ad mgr, Mason Can Co, 56-60; art dir, Fram Co Bendix, 60; creative dir, Automotive Div, Allied Signal, 84. *Media:* Watercolor. *Publ:* Auth & illusr, Only Golfers Know The Feeling, Mobray Co, 83 & 84, Bob Adams Inc, 91. *Mailing Add:* 72 Elm St Rehoboth MA 02769

CARR, CAROLYN K
CURATOR, HISTORIAN
b Providence, RI. *Study:* Smith Col, BA; Oberlin Col, MA; Case-Western Reserve Univ, PhD. *Collection Arranged:* Ohio: A Photographic Portrait (auth, catalog), 1980, The Image in Am Painting and Sculpture 1950-1980 (auth, catalog), 1982, Akron Art Mus, Ohio; Gaston Lachaise: Portrait Sculpture (auth, catalog), Nat Portrait Gallery, Wash, DC, 1985; Then and Now: Am Portraits of the Past Century (auth, catalog), Nat Portrait Gallery, 1988; Am Art at the 1893 World's Columbian Exhib (auth, catalog), Nat Portrait Gallery, 1993; Rebels: Painters & Poets of the 1950s, 1999; Hans Namuth: Portrait, 1999; A Brush with History: Paintings from the Nat Portrait Gallery, 2001; Retratos: 2000 Years of Latin Am Portraits, 2004; Legacy: Spain & the United States, Age of Independecne 1263-1848, 2007. *Pos:* Art critic, Akron Beacon Journal, Ohio, 1968-74; chief cur, Akron Art Mus, Ohio, 1978-83; deputy dir & chief curator emer, Nat Portrait Gallery, Washington, DC, 1984-. *Teaching:* Instr art hist, Kent State Univ, 1963-65. *Awards:* La Encomienda de la Orden de Isabel la Católica, 2008. *Mem:* Coll Art Asn; Am Asn Mus. *Res:* Post 1945 American art; late 19th century American Art; photography. *Specialty:* 18th, 19th, & 20th Century Portraiture. *Publ:* Legacy: Spain and the US in the Age of Independence, 1763-1848, 2007. *Mailing Add:* 4943 Hillbrook Lane NW Washington DC 20016

CARR, SIMON
PAINTER
Study: Goddard Coll, BFA (painting); Parsons Sch Design, MFA (painting), 1981. *Comn:* Eight Stations of the Cross, Church of St Luke in the Fields, New York. *Exhib:* Solo exhibs include Cantor Fitzgerald Gallery, Haverford Coll, Pa, 2005, Salena Gallery, Long Island Univ, Brooklyn, 2007; group exhibs include 183rd Annual: Invitational Exhib Contemp Am Art, Nat Acad Mus, New York, 2008. *Teaching:* Asst prof art, Borough of Manhattan Community Coll, City Univ New York. *Awards:* Nat Endowment Arts Fel; Gottlieb Found Grant; Pollock-Krasner Found Grant, 1999-2000; Joseph S Isidor Mem Award & Medal, Nat Acad, 2008. *Mailing Add:* 463 West St Apt 635B New York NY 10014

CARRERO, JAIME
PAINTER, EDUCATOR
b Mayaguez, PR, June 16, 1931. *Study:* Polytechnic Inst, Columbia Univ, BA (art hist); Pratt Inst, MS. *Work:* Ponce Mus, PR; Mus Inst PR Art & Univ PR, San Juan; Inter-Am Univ Collection, San German. *Comn:* Illus for bk, Cuentos Puertorriquenos, 73. *Exhib:* Univ PR, San Juan, 60 & 65; Inst Cult PR, San Juan, 62; Acad Fine Arts, Calcutta, India, 65; Ateneo Puertorriqueno, San Juan, 66; Ponce Mus, 86; Springfield Mus, Mass, 90. *Teaching:* Prof painting, drawing & art hist, Inter-Am Univ, 57-; prof art hist, Rum, Mayaguez, PR, 74-75. *Bibliog:* Josemilio Gonzalez (auth), Jaime Carrero, Pintor, El Mundo, 60; Drawings by Jaime Carrero, El Corno Emplumado, Mex, Nos 26, 28 & 30, 64-66; Drawings: The San Juan Star. *Media:* Acrylic, Watercolor. *Mailing Add:* c/o Galeria Petrus Calle Hoare #726 Santurce PR 00907

CARRICO, ANITA
LIBRARIAN
b Bronx, New York, June 30, 1938. *Study:* State Univ NY, Buffalo, BA (art history), 74, MLS, 79. *Pos:* Asst Librn, Albright-Knox Art Gallery, Buffalo, NY 79-81; librn, Baltimore Mus Art, Md, 81-89; head librn, Philadelphia Mus Art, Pa, 89-94 & Univ Archit Libr, Md, 94-. *Mem:* Art Libr Soc NAM (secy 89-91); Asn Archit Sch Libr; Wash Art Libr Resources Comt (co-chmn, 96-). *Mailing Add:* c/o Univ Md Archit Libr College Park MD 20742

CARROLL, JAMES F L
PAINTER, SCULPTOR
b Postville, Iowa, Sept 4, 1934. *Study:* Colo State Coll, BA, 56, MA, 62; Univ Colo, Boulder, MFA, 66; also studied with Richard Ellinger, Sir Robin Phillipson, Joan Brown, Roland Reiss. *Work:* Kutztown Univ, Kutztown, Pa; St Mary's Coll Md; Muhlenberg Coll, Allentown, Pa; Pa State Univ, Berks Campus, Reading, Pa; Reading Pub Mus, Pa; Butler Inst Am Art, Youngstown, Ohio; and others. *Exhib:* Solo exhibs: 112 Greene St Workshop/Gallery, NY, 77, Lehman Coll Gallery, City Univ NY, 77, Martin Art Gallery (with catalog), Muhlenberg Coll, Allentown, Pa, 97, Rosefsky Gallery, Binghamton Univ, NY, 2004, Tompkins Gallery, Cedar Crest Coll, Allentown, Pa, 2005, 2010, Clay on Main Gallery, Oley Pa; Group exhibs: Invitational, Summer Gallery Outdoor Sculpture Show, Pa State Univ Berks Campus, Reading, Pa, 88-91; Masterpieces, Martin Art Gallery Exhib, Muhlenberg Coll, Allentown, Pa, 98; Maria Feliz Gallery, Jim Thorpe, Pa, 2000; MCS Gallery, Easton, Pa, 2000; Cedar Crest Coll, Art Gallery, Paper Forms, Allentown, Pa, 2000; Reading Area Community Coll, Works on Paper, Reading, 2002. *Pos:* Founder, New Arts Prog, Kutztown, Pa, 74- (dir & pres, currently); nominator, Award in Visual Arts, AVA, 90-91 & Nat Found for Advancement in Arts, NFAA, 92-97; panel mem, Pa Coun on the Arts, 90-92; juror, Gallery 33, Hershey, Pa, 91; juror, NEPA Regional Art, AFA Gallery, Keystone Coll, Marywood Univ, Univ Scranton, Pa, 2010. *Teaching:* Prof fine arts, Kutztown Univ, Kutztown, Pa, 66-99; lectr, Yale Univ, 82, Pratt, Bklyn, 86, Lehigh Univ, Bethlehem, Pa, 88, Slade Sch Art, London, 92, WITF-FM PBS Radio, Harrisburg, Pa, Phoenix Gallery, NYC, 2002, SUNY, 2004, Cedar Crest Coll, Allentown, Pa, 2005; adj fac, Muhlenberg Coll, Allentown, PA, 91 & Cedar Crest Coll, Allentown, 99-2001; instr, Alvernia Coll, Reading, 2003 & La Guardia Community Coll, NY, 2004, 2005, 2007. *Awards:* Exceptional Acad Serv Cert, Commonwealth of Pa, 78; Nat Sculpture Show, Touring Exhib, Statesboro, Ga, 79; Visual Arts Grant, Nat Endowment Arts, 80; Visual Arts Award, Kutztown Univ, 82, 85, & 88; Pollock-Krasner Found Grant, 2004 & 2008; Excellence in Art Educ Pagoda Award, Berks Art Coun, Reading, Pa, 2006. *Bibliog:* Tim Higgins (auth), Carroll's NAP brings mtns, 8/5/86, Geoff Gehman (auth), Nature plays host to 43, Morning Call Newspaper, 8/26/90; Marilyn J Fox (auth), A solo new arts exhib, Eagle/Times Newspaper, 8/2/92; Tim Higgins (auth), James Carroll drawing convey his cerebral concepts of space, 8/30/97; Myra Yellin Outwater (auth), Article, Morning Call Newspaper, 12/4/2000. *Mem:* Am Asn Mus; Int Sculpture Ctr; Lehigh Valley Arts Coun (bd mem, 89-92); Coll Art Asn. *Media:* Paint. *Publ:* Auth, 71 Small Works on Paper, 65-81, & In and Out of Kutztown, 82, James Carroll; Contribr, 11th, 10th, Critical & 8th Assembling, Assembling Press, 78-81; In and Out of New York, Hunter Yoder, 80; Essay, Paul Harryn (catalogue), Ideas from Individual Impressions and Marks: Prints of Non-Printmakers, Lehigh Univ, 91; Foreword essay, Julius Tobias (catalogue), 92; Dance On Paper (with catalog), Lehigh Univ Art Galleries, Bethlehem, Pa, 2001; 80 Individual artists booklets, 97-. *Mailing Add:* 173 W Main St Kutztown PA 19530

CARSON, G B
CONSULTANT, ART DEALER
b Helena, Mont, Feb, 28, 1950. *Study:* Univ Calif, Berkeley, BA (art hist), 77. *Collection Arranged:* Le Desert de Retz: An 18th Century French Folly Garden, Calif Palace Legion Hon, San Francisco, 91; Nathan Oliveira Figure Studies, Schneider Mus Art, So Oregon Univ, Ashland, 2002. *Mem:* Graphic Arts Coun, Fine Arts Mus, San Francisco; Asn Study of Dada & Surrealism. *Specialty:* California art of the 1960's. *Mailing Add:* PO Box 8502 Berkeley CA 94707

CARSON, SOL KENT
PAINTER, PRINTMAKER, EDUCATOR
b Philadelphia, Pa, Jun 7, 1917. *Study:* Temple Univ, Tyler Sch Fine Arts, BFA (with hon), 44, Teachers Coll, BSc Ed (with hon), 45 & MEd (fine arts), 46; Minerva Univ Grad Sch, Bari, Italy, PhD, 58-60; Phi Delta Kappa. *Work:* Philadelphia Mus Art, Archives-prints, Pa; Philadelphia Libr, Pa; Millersville Univ, Pa; Temple Univ, Medical Sch, Philadelphia, Pa; Mus Mod Art; Dublin Galleries; Federal Arts Galleries, Okla Art Ctr; Acad Fine Arts; Cheltenham Art Asn; Woodmere Art Galleries; Temple Univ, Tyler Galleries. *Comn:* Stone mask, Mother Katherine Drexel, Convent, Cornwells Heights, Pa; bronze bust, Dean Ladd Thomas, Temple Univ Sch Theology, Philadelphia, Pa; Paul Bunyon Mural Panel, Am Lumber Corp, Philadelphia, Pa; bronze bust, Morris Harvey Coll, WVa; restoration, 3 Thomas Eakins canvases. *Exhib:* New York World's Fair, 39; Pa Acad Fine Arts, 64-66; Art Alliance, 66; solo exhib, Wis State Univ, Wis, 67; Int League Peace & Freedom, Philadelphia, 67; Int Exhib, Civic Ctr Convention Mus, Philadelphia, Pa, 68; Carson, Paintings & Prints, Los Gatos Chambers, Calif, 94; Calif CofC, Los Gatos. *Pos:* Dir, dept visual educ, Temple Univ Dental Sch, Philadelphia, Pa, 44-47, Eckels Coll, 46-55; consult mus, Univ Pa Mus, 45-46; consult art, Bristol Township Sch Dist, Pa, 56-66. *Teaching:* Asst to prof, graphic arts dept, Temple Univ, 40-45; instr, drawing & painting, Philadelphia Bd Educ, Adult Div, 47-58; summer fac, drawing & painting, Wis State Univ, 65-67; assoc prof, art dept, Millersville Univ, Pa, 66-79, assoc prof, drawing, painting & printmaking. *Awards:* Barnes Found Scholar, 39; Fel, Established printmaking dept, Tyler Sch, Temple Univ, Philadelphia, 40-46; 100 distinguished painters award, Philadelphia Fidelity, Pa, 67. *Bibliog:* WPA Artist, From pic and should to professor. *Mem:* Nat Educ Asn; Am Asn Univ Prof; Pa State Educ Asn; Artist Equity; Asn Higher Educ; Phi Delta Kappa. *Media:* Acrylic, Oil. *Res:* Carburundum etching, carbograph from WPA times. *Interests:* Drawing, painting, printmaking, poetry & music. *Publ:* Auth, To my son, my wife, to myself, Nat Libr Poetry, Harbinger House, 95; med illusr, Temple Univ Schs. *Mailing Add:* 447 Alberto Way C128 Los Gatos CA 95032

CARSWELL, JOHN
MUSEUM DIRECTOR, PAINTER
b London, Eng, Nov 16, 1931. *Study:* Wimbledon Sch Art, Surrey Eng, 46-48; Royal Coll Art, London, ARCA, 48-51. *Work:* Arts Coun Gt Brit. *Exhib:* Solo exhibs, Hanover Gallery, London, 56 & Fischbach Gallery, NY, 66. *Collection Arranged:* Islamic Binding & Bookmaking (auth, catalog), 81-82; Blue & White: Chinese Porcelain & Its Impact on the Western World, (auth, catalog), 85; The Mosaics of Jordan (with catalog), 92. *Pos:* Cur, Oriental Inst Mus, Univ Chicago, 78-85, dir, David & Alfred Smart Gallery, 85-87; dir, Sotheby's Asian Islamic Dept 88-. *Teaching:* Prof fine art, Am Univ Beirut, Lebanon, 56-76. *Bibliog:* G Hovrari (auth), Arab Seafaring (new ed), Princeton Univ Press, 95. *Mem:* Oriental Ceramic Soc (coun mem); Royal Soc Asian Affairs (vpres). *Media:* Oil, Paper. *Res:* Islamic art and architecture; Far eastern ceramics; cross-cultural contacts in Asian Art. *Publ:* Auth, Coptic Tattoo Designs, Am Univ Beirut, 58; New Julfa: Armenian Churches & Other Buildings, Oxford Univ Press, 68; coauth, Kutahya Tiles and Pottery in Armenian Cathedral of St James, Jerusalem, Oxford Univ Press, 72; Chinese Ceramics in Sadbeok Hanim Museum, Istanbul, 95. *Mailing Add:* Islamic Dept 34-35 New Bond St London United Kingdom W1A 2AA

CARTER, (CHARLES) BRUCE
PRINTMAKER, EDUCATOR
b North Adams, Mass, May 15, 1930. *Study:* Albright Art Sch, Buffalo, NY, dipl, 51; State Univ NY Buffalo, BS, 52; Pa State Univ, Univ Park, MEd & DEd, 58. *Work:* Nat Hist Mus, Univ Oslo, Norway; Philadelphia Mus Art; State Art Mus, Raleigh, NC; Amarillo Art Ctr, Tex. *Comn:* Painted mural, Narvik City Coun, Norway, 62 & mosaic mural, 63; mosaic mural, Kiruna, Sweden, 62; painted mural, Nat Mus, Gettysburg, Pa; mosaic mural, Nordsland Banken, Leknes, Norway, 68. *Exhib:* Soc Am Graphic Artists, NY, 71; 2nd Triennial Int Exhib Contemp Xylography, Nat Mus Xylography, Carpi, Italy, 72; Hokkaido Print Asn Int Exhib, Sapporo, Japan, 72; 3rd Int Print Biennial Exhib, Art Mus, Epinal, France, 75; Return to the Crucible, The Pentagon, DC, 76; Wounded Knee: An Am Tragedy, Amarillo Art Ctr, Tex, 76; 6th Nat Print Exhib, Los Angeles, 78; Nat Hist Mus, Univ Oslo, Norway, 80; The Warsaw Woodcuts, Ghetto Fighters Mus, Israel, 81. *Pos:* Art consult, Poetry on the Buses, Pittsburgh, 76-. *Teaching:* Prof printmaking-drawing, Carnegie Mellon Univ, Pittsburgh, 63-93; retired. *Awards:* Purchase Prizes, Nat Mus Xylography, Carpi, Italy, 72 & Univ Wis-Madison, 75. *Mem:* Coll Art Asn; Philadelphia Print Club; Artists' Equity Asn. *Media:* Woodcut, Lithography. *Publ:* Coauth, Wounded Knee: An American Tragedy (film), WQED-TV, 72. *Mailing Add:* 343 Sperryville Rd Glenfield NY 13343

CARTER, CAROL
PAINTER
b Sumter, SC, 1955. *Study:* Principia Col, Elsah, Ill, BA, 77; Washington Univ, St Louis, Mo, MFA, 84. *Work:* Arjomari, Arches, Rives Paper, Inc; Blue Cross/Blue Shield, St Louis, Mo; Citicorp, Maui, Hawaii; Renaissance Ctr Club, Detroit, Mich; Suwa Art Mus, Japan; and others. *Comn:* Edison Brothers, St Louis, Mo; Renaissance Ctr, Detroit, Mich. *Exhib:* Solo exhibs, Elliot Smith Gallery, St Louis, Mo, 90, Diane Nelson Gallery, Laguna, Calif, 90, Ethical Soc, St Louis, Mo, 92, Galleria Blagas, Detroit, Mich, 93, R Duane Reed Gallery, St Louis, Mo, 94 & 96 & Stein-Bartlow Gallery, Chicago, Ill, 94; Artists and The Am Yard, Wustum Art Mus, Racine, Wis, 91; Watercolor USA, Springfield Art Mus, Mo, 93; Watercolor, Strecker Gallery, Manhattan, Kans, 93; Boats, Elliot Smith Gallery, St Louis, Mo, 93; H2O Color Invitational, Univ Wis, Whitewater, Wis, 93; St Louis Art, Cedar Rapids Art Mus, Iowa, 98; Belgade, Ctr Contemp Art, St Louis, Mo; Fla Skies, Maryville Univ, 2000; and many others. *Pos:* Gallery owner & operator, Rockport, Mass & St Louis, Mo, 76-79; asst, B Z Wagman Gallery, St Louis, 85-86. *Teaching:* Teaching assistantship, Wash Univ, St Louis, 83-84; watercolor instr, Fine Arts Inst, Wash Univ, 85-, drawing instr, Sch Archit, 89-91, Principia Col, 91; vis artist, Metrop Honors Art, St Louis, 88 & 90, Univ of Denver, 89. *Awards:* Award, Five State Watercolor, Wichita Art Mus, Kans, 89; Purchase Award, Watercolor USA, Springfield Art Mus, Mo, 91; M-AAA/Nat Endowment Arts Fel Award in Painting & Works on Paper, 94; Art Award, Nat Asn Women Bus Owners, 98. *Bibliog:* J P Wolf (auth), Introspective Reflections, Am Artist Mag, 10/89; Paul Harris (auth), Ideas are the Work of These Six Area Artists, St Louis Post-Dispatch, 6/91; Carol Shepley (auth), Appropriate Art: Group Show is all about Boats, St Louis Post Dispatch, 8/93; Carol Shepley (auth), Work by Gallery Artists, St Louis Post Dispatch, 5/94. *Mem:* Art St Louis. *Media:* Acrylic, Watercolor. *Dealer:* Peter Bartlow 44 E Superior Chicago IL 60611

CARTER, CURTIS LLOYD
MUSEUM DIRECTOR, EDUCATOR
b Moulton, Iowa, Oct 10, 1935. *Study:* Taylor Univ, Upland, Ind, 60; Spec student, Harvard Univ, 61 & Brandeis Univ, 66; Boston Univ, PhD, 71. *Collection Arranged:* Jan Fabre: Passage, 98; A Passion for Porcelain: Three Centuries of Meissen Floral Painting, 98; Joseph Friebert at Ninety, 98; In the Lion's Den: The Bible Images of Marc Chagall, 98; Feng Mengbo: Video Games, 98. *Pos:* Chmn, Comt Fine Arts, Marquette Univ, 76-84; dir, Haggerty Mus Art, Marquette Univ, 84-; pres, Dance Perspectives Found Inc, 87-98. *Teaching:* Asst prof aesthet & philos, Marquette Univ, 7684, prof, 84-; instr, Les Aspin Ctr Govt, Wash, DC, 96-. *Awards:* Wis Dance Coun Award, 92. *Mem:* Wis Alliance Arts Educ (co-chmn, 74-79); ARTREACH Milwaukee Inc (founding pres & bd mem 75-81, mem, currently); Nat Endowment Arts & Humanities (panelist & referee, 84-); Dance Perspectives Found (vpres 78-87, pres 87-). *Res:* Cultural identity of works of art; curatorial frameworks for understanding art in culturally diverse societies; improvisation in the arts; arts and technology; dance

aesthetics; contemporary visual arts. *Publ:* Ed & contribr, Franta (exhib catalog), 92; Contemporary Folk Art (exhib catalog), 93; The Art of Design 2 (exhib catalog), 93; Wisconsin Artists: A Celebration of Jewish Presence (catalog), 94. *Mailing Add:* Marquette Univ Haggerty Mus Art 13th Clybourn Milwaukee WI 53233

CARTER, DAVID GILES
MUSEUM DIRECTOR, CURATOR
b Nashua, NH, Nov 2, 1921. *Study:* Princeton Univ, with CR Morey & AM Friend, AB, 44; Harvard Univ Grad Sch Arts & Sci, with P Sachs, CR Post, C Kuhn & others, MA, 49; Inst Fine Arts, New York Univ, 51, with W Cook, E Panofsky & G Schoenberger. *Collection Arranged:* San Diego Art Mus, 56; Turner in Am (with Wilbur D Peat), 56; The Young Rembrandt and His Times, 58; The GHA Clowes Collection, 59; Dynamic Symmetry, 61; El Greco to Goya (with Curtis Coley), 63; The Weldon Collection, 64; Masterpieces from Montreal, 66; The Painter and the New World, 67; Rembrandt and His Pupils, Art Gallery of Toronto, 69; Jan Menses, 76. *Pos:* Curatorial asst, Metrop Mus Art, New York, 50-54; cur paintings & prints, John Herron Art Mus, 55-59; dir, Mus Art, RI Sch Design, 59-64 & Montreal Mus Fine Arts, 64-76; self employed consult; mem adv comt, Mt Holyoke Col Art Mus Art, 76-; trustee, Eli Whitney Mus and Related Landmarks of the Nat Monument, Hamden, Conn, 78- & New Haven Colony Hist Soc, 90-97; trustee, New Haven Colony Hist Soc, 90-97, pres, 97-2000, bd mem, 2000-. *Teaching:* Lectr, Ind Univ, Bloomington, 58-59. *Awards:* Gold Medal of Ital Cult, Ital Ministry Foreign Affairs, 63; Eli Whitney Medal, 11 and naming of Gallery, David Giles and Carter Studio. *Mem:* ICOM; Mediaeval Acad; Grolier Club; Royal Soc Arts; plus others; Arms and Armor Club Am; AAM; CAA. *Res:* Northern Renaissance; secondary interest in Mannerist and Northern Baroque painting. *Collection:* iconography, medieval art and architecture. *Publ:* Auth, Rencontre avec Valentin, l'Oeil, 70; The Winnipeg flagellation and the master of the View of St Gudule, Miscellanea in Memoriam Paul Coremans (1908-1965), Bull de l'Institut royal du Patrimoine artistique, xv, 75; Spanish itinerary, 5/76 & Northern Baroque and the Italian connexion, 5/76, Apollo; Montreal mus des beaux-arts, Art Gallery, 4-5/76; and others. *Mailing Add:* 100 Edgehill Rd New Haven CT 06511-1320

CARTER, GARY
PAINTER, SCULPTOR
b Hutchinson, Kans, Mar 12, 1939. *Study:* Art Ctr Coll Design, BFA, 71. *Work:* Nat Cowboy Hall Fame, Oklahoma City; C M Russell Mus, Great Falls, Mont; Mont Hist Soc, Helena; Gould Inc, Chicago; Cowboy Artists Am Mus, Kerrville, Tex; Wrigley Collection, Chicago, Ill. *Comn:* Mont Centennial Painting Comn (1889-1989), Pepsi-Cola Corp; mural, 1st Security Bank of West Yellowstone; mural, Big Sky Ski Resort; Phillip Anshutz Corp; Cutthroat Communs. *Exhib:* Cowboy Artists of Am Ann, Phoenix Art Mus, 82-2003; Western Heritage, Shamrock Hilton, Houston, 84; Buffalo Bill Art Show, Cody, Wyo, 86; Cowboy Artists of Am miniature show Ann, Kerrville, Tex, 90-96 & retrospective, 96; Wildlife of the Am West Art Mus, Jackson, Wyo, 88, 89 & 90; Booth Western Art Mus, Cartersville, Ga; Int Mus Horse, Lexington, Ky, 92; Eiteljorg Mus Am Indian & Western Art, Indianapolis, 95; Southwest Mag Traveling Show, 96. *Teaching:* Taught Art Seminar, C Mus, Kerrville, Tex, 86; head group workshop, Cowboy Artists Am Mus, 82, 83, 85, 88, 91, 93, 95. *Awards:* Artist of the West 1990, San Dimos Festival of Western Arts; Gold Medal Award, Cowboy Artist Am Exhib, Phoenix Art Mus, 90 & 97; Award Excellence, Western Heritage Invitational Art Show, 96. *Bibliog:* Dale Burk (auth), A Brush with the West; Chase Reynolds, Old Masters of the West. *Mem:* Cowboy Artists Am (pres, 85-86). *Media:* Oil. *Publ:* Auth, Western Horseman, 9/88; auth & illusr, Horse & Rider, 7/87; auth, Art of the West Mag, 4-5/88, feature article & cover, 11-12/93; Southwest Art Mag, 3/89; Big Sky J, winter 94-95. *Dealer:* GCWAPC Inc 12075 Marina Loop West Yellowstone MT 59758; Carter Western Art PO Box 338 West Yellowstone MT 59758. *Mailing Add:* PO Box 338 West Yellowstone MT 59758

CARTER, HARRIET (ESTELLE) MANORE
PAINTER
b Grand Bend, Ont, Mar 22, 1929. *Study:* Dundas Valley Sch Fine Arts, Ont. *Work:* Sarnia Pub Libr & Art Mus, Ont; Art Gallery Brant, Brantford, Ont; Can Coun Art Bank; Hart House, Univ Toronto; Can Soc Painters Watercolour Diamond Jubilee Collection presented to her Majesty Queen Elizabeth II for the Royal Collection of Drawings and Watercolours at Windsor Castle; and many other pvt collections both in Can & US. *Comn:* Cloud Flowers (show), comn by Univ BC. *Exhib:* Traveling Exhib, 70-83 & Fifty Yrs, 75, Can Soc Painters Watercolour; On View Traveling Exhib, Ont, 76-77; Can Watercolour Soc Japan & Can Exhib, 76-77; Ont Soc Artists Ann Exhib, Oakville Centennial Gallery, 77; Cloud Flowers Traveling Exhib, 81-82; solo exhib, Nancy Poole's Studio, Toronto, 72-83. *Pos:* Commercial designer, Dominion Glass Co, Wallaceburg, Ont, 49-52. *Teaching:* art classes, secondary adult night sch. *Awards:* Hon Award, Can Soc Painters Watercolour, 69; Ont Soc Artists 100th Ann Exhib Awards, 72; Purchase Award, London Pub Art Gallery & Mus, 72; Royal Can Merit Award, Energy Mint Coin Design, 81. *Bibliog:* Tom Thompson Memorial Gallery Museum of Fine Art Show, Art Mag, 71; Kay Kritzwiser (auth), Four exhibits mind stretching style, Toronto Globe & Mail, 72; Lenore Crawford (auth), Manore Carter art gets message across, London Free Press, 73. *Mem:* Can Soc Painters Watercolour; Ont Soc Artists; Royal Can Acad Arts. *Media:* Watercolor. *Interests:* Antiques, collecting. *Collection:* The Royal Collection of Drawings and Watercolours, Windsor Castle; Can Coun Art Bank; London Reg Art Gallery. *Publ:* Illus, Art View Mag, Toronto; Cloud Flowers, The Botanical Gardens, Univ British Columbia; Canadian Artists in Exhibition 1972-1973. *Mailing Add:* 78 MacLennan Ave Hamilton ON L8V 1X6 Canada

CARTER, JERRY WILLIAMS
SCULPTOR, ARCHITECT, VIDEO ARTIST, MOSAIC ARTIST
b Wichita, Kans, Apr 19, 1941. *Study:* Univ Md, BA,1968; Chicago Art Inst, 1969; Atheneum Nat Acad Fine Arts Helsinki, Finland, 1970; Centro Int Studi L'Insegnamento Mosaico, cert, Ravena, Italy, 1970; L'Ecole Nat Superieur Beaux Arts Paris, with Gustave Singier, Paris, 1971; Acad Belli Arti Ravenna, with Pomadoro, 1972; Paleo Christian Art Hist, Univ Studi Bologna, cert, with Prof Bovini, 1971; Nat Inst Design, Helsinki, Finland, 1973; Antioch Univ, Columbia Visual Arts Ctr, MFA, 1981; Ctr Creative Imaging, Camden, Maine, 1993, Beta Test Site: Day Star Digital, Harvard Graphics Sys, 1992-1994. *Work:* The Phillips Collection, Washington; Pinacoteca Comunale Ravenna, Italy; Kunstgewerbemuseum der Stadt Köln, Cologne, Ger; Nat Mus Am Art, Washington, DC. *Comn:* Descent of the Holy Spirit (venetian glass mosaic), Church Holy Spirit, Forrestville, Md, 78; Cascade (ceramic & venetian glass mosaic sculpture), Vista Int Hotel, Washington, DC, 83; mosaic monument, UNESCO, Ravenna, Italy, 83; Second Genesis, American Peace/Ecology Monument (cast concrete relief & glass mosaic monument), UNESCO competition comn by High Patronage of the Pres of Italy & European Parliament, Ravenna, Italy, 1984-1988; Flight of Fantasy (plastic & glass relief-mosaics), Montgomery Co Sch, Bethesda, Md, 1986; Human Rights/Andrei Sakaharov Monument (cast concrete monolith & glass mosaic) & Ctr for Democratic Principles Action Prog, comn by City of Moscow, Russia, 92; Immortal Diamond design, Lauinger Libr, Georgetown Univ, comn by Fr Timothy Healey, Univ Pres, 1988; Pyramid of Souls, World Trade Ctr Int Monument & Mus, 2001-05; Pyramid of Peace and Reconciliation, Astana, Kazakhstan, 2005-06. *Exhib:* Solo exhibs, Layering in Stone & Glass, Am Asn Advan Sci, Washington, DC, 87, Galleria MARC, Moscow Artist's Gallery, Moscow, 90, Spaso House, Am Ambassador's Gallery, Moscow, 90, Scottish Rite Ctr, Washington, DC, 2000, Objects of the Mysterion, Arcetri Observatory, Florence, Italy, 2004, Amhurst Gallery, Silver Springs, Md, 2004, Washington Summit on Climate Change, 2006; M'ysuri, Georgian Cult Ctr, Moscow, USSR, 90; Galeria Esplanade (Metsovaara), Helsinki, Finland, 90; Amerika Hauser (USIS), Cologne, Munich, Ger, 90; retrospective, Natcher Ctr, Bethesda, Md, 96; Florence Int Biennale Contemp Art, Florence, Italy, 2003; and many others. *Pos:* Art dir, ABC-TV, Washington, DC, 66-68; artist-in-residence, Iittala Nuutijärvi Glass Factory, Finland, 89-; forensic art consult, tech expert witness & investigator specializing in virtual property theft, 84-. *Awards:* Fulbright, Italy, 84; Medallion of Ravenna, Italy, 84; 100 Most Significant, Corning Glass Int Rev, 86; invited participant, Global Forum for Spiritual and Political leaders on the Salvation of Humanity, Supreme Soviet & Soviet & Acad Sci, Moscow, USSR, 90; invited participant, Solidarnosc 10th Anniversary, Gdansk, Poland, 90; Mac Users Group Digital Art Competition, New York, 96; Lorenzo Il Magnifico Award, Florence Int Biennale Contemp Art, Florence, Italy, 2003. *Bibliog:* L Krantz (auth), American Artists, 85; Jennifer Gibson, PhD (auth), Reflections in Stone and Glass, an American Reinterprets the Art of Mosaics, The World and I, 10/87; Igor Ignatiev (auth), The creative process and creations of Jerry Carter, Echo of the Planet, Tass, Moscow, USSR, 10/88; C Frazier Smith (auth), Monumental Mosaic, Baltimore Sun Mag, 11/88; J C Topping Jr (auth), PROCEEDINGS, Second North American Conference on Preparing for Climate Change Institute, Wash, DC, 88; I Wiman, PhD (auth), Expecting the unexpected: Some ancient roots to current perceptions of nature, Ambio, Royal Swedish Acad Sci Publ, Stockholm, Sweden, XIX, No 24, 90; TA Yasui (auth), Jerry Carter and the international mural mission, Wash Post, 4/16/90; E Egoreva (auth), Artist Jerry Carter, Decorative Arts USSR, Moscow, USSR, 7/90; G Nicola (auth), Jerry W Carter-Glass Mosaic, Neues Glass, Freschen, Ger, 2/91; ML Trechovich (auth), Artist in the City, Moscow, 88; G. Bovini (auth), Ravenna Art and History, 91; Prof I Fiorentin (ed), Mosaico Ravenna incontra San Pietroburgo, Longo Ed Ravenna, Italy, 94; E M Goodwin (ed), Encyclopedia of Mosaic, 2003; John T Spike & Daniel Y Gezari (auths), Il Mysterion Del Cosmo: Jerry Carter all'Osserfvatoriao di Arcetri, Florence, Italy, 2004. *Mem:* Int Asn Contemp Mosaicists, Ravenna, Italy (founding mem); MARS Gallery Asn, Moscow, Russ. *Media:* All Media. *Publ:* Auth, Presso il centro stampa del comune di Ravenna, Italy, 80, Parco Della Pace Ravenna, Longo Ed, 90 & Mosaic: Medium for the Times, 90. *Dealer:* JW Carter & Assoc 10502 Bucknell Dr Silver Spring MD 20902. *Mailing Add:* 10602 Bucknell Dr Silver Spring MD 20902-4254

CARTER, MARY
PAINTER, PRINTMAKER
b Hartsdale, NY. *Study:* Art Students League, with Reginald Marsh, Robert Beverly Hale & E Dickenson, 51-55; Hunter Coll, 67, Sch Visual Arts, 68; Parsons Sch, 81. *Exhib:* Audubon Artists Ann, 54 & Nat Acad Design, NY, 56, 57 & 72; Hartford Atheneum Show, Conn, 56; Pa Acad Fine Arts, 57; Philadelphia Sketch Club, 58; Ball State Art Gallery, 58 & 63; Nat Competition, Springfield Art Mus, Mo, 66; Ann Drawings & Sculpture Show, Del Mar Coll, Corpus Christi, Tex, 67; Hudson Guild Invitational, NY, 75- & solo exhib, 85-; visual dialogues show, office of C Virginia Fields, Borough Pres Manhattan, 2005; Art Tango, Lafayette Grill, 2006; Inner Bridges to Outer Scenes, Venezuelan Ctr, 2007; Now and Then, Eurlan Gallery, 2008. *Mem:* Art Students League; Women Arts Found. *Media:* Oil, Tempera, Casein. *Mailing Add:* 253 W 16th St New York NY 10011

CARTER, NANETTE CAROLYN
PAINTER, PRINTMAKER
b Columbus, Ohio, Jan 30, 1954. *Study:* L'Acad di Belle Arti, Italy, 75; Oberlin Coll, Ohio, BA, 76; Pratt Inst Art, New York, MFA, 78. *Work:* Newark Mus, NJ; Herbert Johnson Mus Art, Cornell Univ, Ithaca, NY; Studio Mus, Harlem, New York; Libr Cong, Washington, DC; and many others; and numerous other pub, pvt & corp collections. *Comn:* Mural, Dwight Englewood Sch, NJ, 80; color poster for concert, Jazzmobile, Avery Fisher Hall, New York, 85; color poster exhib, Black Women in the Arts 1990, Montclair State Coll, NJ; poster, Snug Harbor Hills ASSN, 2005. *Exhib:* Solo exhibs, GRN 'Namdi Gallery, New York, 2006; Group exhibs, Biennial Print Exhib, Brooklyn Mus, New York, 81; Bennington Col, Vt, 91; Hillwood Art Mus, Brookville, NY, 92; Nat Mus Women Arts, Washington, DC, 92; Univ Mass Amherst, 93; Del Art Mus, 93; RI Sch Design Mus; Parrish Art Mus, Southampton; Yale Gallery Art, Conn; Philadelphia Mus Art; and others. *Pos:* Artist-in-residence, New York State Coun Arts, 84. *Teaching:* Instr printmaking & drawing, Dwight Englewood Sch, Englewood, NJ, 78-87; prof, City Coll New York, 92; Prof Pratt Inst Art, Brooklyn, New York, 2001. *Awards:* Fels, Bob Blackburns' Printmaking Workshop, New York, 89, Lower East Side Printshop Inc, New York, 97 & Brandywine Workshop,

Philadelphia, Pa, 99; New York Found Arts, 90; Pollock-Krasner Found Inc Grant, 94; Wheeler Found Grant, 96. *Bibliog:* Phyllis Braff (auth), rev, NY Times, 12/1/91; Richard Leslie (auth), The New Art Examiner, Chicago; Ann Gibson (auth), A Century of African American Art: The Paul R Jones Collection, 2004. *Media:* Oils, Monoprints. *Publ:* Illusr (cover), Midnight Birds, Mary Helen Washington (auth), Japan, 82; Bearing Witness, Rizzoli Int Publ Inc, New York; auth, The Chemistry of Color (catalog), Pa Acad Fine Arts, 2005. *Dealer:* GR N'Namdi Gallery Detroit MI NY IL; Sandi Webster Gallery Philadelphia PA. *Mailing Add:* 788 Riverside Dr New York NY 10032

CARTER, PATRICIA
PRINTMAKER, EDUCATOR, ADMINISTRATOR
Study: Rutgers Univ, Douglass Col for Women, New Brunswick, NJ, BA (Studio Arts and Journalism), 1987; Rutgers Univ, Mason Gross Sch of the Arts, New Brunswick, NJ, MFA (Printmaking), 1989; Georgia Southern Univ, Statesboro, Ga, MED (Art Edn), 1993. *Teaching:* Department chair, prof foundation studies and printmaking/paper/book arts, Betty Foy Sanders Department of Art, Ga Southern Univ, currently. *Publ:* Instructional Materials, Instructor's Guide, Student Study Guide; World of Art; Art Forms; Art Connections, p, grade age 5 Art Education Classroom Text, K-1; Georgia Artists Collection at Georgia Southern Univ. *Mailing Add:* Georgia Southern Univ PO Box 8032 233 Pittman Dr Center for Art & Theatre 2005 Statesboro GA 30460

CARTER, SAM JOHN
PAINTER, SCULPTOR
b Des Moines, Iowa, Mar 20, 1943; Can citizen. *Study:* Calif State Univ, Long Beach, BA, 65, MA, 82; Univ Toronto, BL Arch, 70; Ikenobo, Ikebana, Kyoto, Japan, 82. *Work:* Ont Sci Ctr & Ont Place, Toronto; Nat Gallery, Ottawa; Expo 86 & Artists Gallery, Vancouver. *Comn:* Flower Totoms, Govt Can, Vancouver, BC, 80; Vancouver Sea Flowers, Jonathan's Seafood, BC, 81; China Lion, Wons, Vancouver, BC, 82; Vancouver-Papal Visit, Pageant & Chair of Catholic Church, BC, 84; Parade, Theme Pageant, Expo 86, Vancouver, 86. *Exhib:* Summer Numbers, A Space, Toronto, 70; Ont Coll Art Gallery, Toronto, 71; Spoleto Festival, Italy, 71; World Wildlife Event, United Nations Conf, Stockholm, Sweden, 71; Art-Subterranean, Mus Mod Art, Mexico City, 80; Kado-Flower Way, Contemp Fine Arts Gallery, Tokyo, Japan, 85. *Pos:* Sr designer, Ont Sci Ctr, 65-71; Chmn, found div, Emily Carr Col Art & Design, 73-86. *Teaching:* Instr cult probe, Ont Col Art, 70-71. *Bibliog:* Yamashita (auth), Gardens of the world project, Ikenodo J, Kyoto, 83-84; Rule (auth), Art in season, Western Living, Vancouver, 85; De Vecchi (auth), Fantasy as partner, Vogue Decoration, Paris, 4/86. *Mem:* Ikenobo Ikebana Soc; Craftsman's Asn BC; Vancouver Community Arts Coun; Circle Craft Cooperative. *Publ:* Auth, Celebration of Paper, Arts Coun, 80; Some Roads to Here, Can Soc For Educ through Art, 80; Art and the City, Peregrine, 80; Kado-World Garden, Ikenobo J, 83. *Dealer:* Dianne Farris Gallery BC Canada. *Mailing Add:* Emily Carr Col Art & Design 1399 Johnston St Vancouver BC V6H 3R9 Canada

CARTER, WARRICK LIVINGSTON
EDUCATOR, COMPOSER
Study: Tenn State Univ, BS, 1964; Mich State Univ, MusM, 1966, PhD, 1970. *Comn:* created commissioned work for the Nat Endowment for the Arts, Chgo Symphony Orchestra Asn, Chgo Chamber Orchestra. *Pos:* dir entertainment arts Walt Disney Entertainment, 1996-2000; guest lecturer, Northwestern Univ, Calif State Univ, Univ of Santa Catarina, Brazil; music composer, 1971-; Bd dirs Arts in Public Places, Chgo, 1976-82, Partners of Americas, 1975-84, Internat House of Blues Found, 1993-, New Orleans Ctr Creative Arts, 1996-, Ill Chamber of Commerce, Federation of Independent Col; past bd mem Nat Asn of Jazz Educators, Mass Arts and Humanities Council, Found for the Advancement of Music; corp council Interlochen Ctr for Arts, 1999-; bd adv Jikei Group, Osaka, Japan, 2001-; chmn Jazz panel, Nat Endowment of the Arts. *Teaching:* Asst prof, dir bands, Univ Md, 1966-71, assoc prof Northwestern Univ, Evanston, Ill, 1978-84, prof music, chmn fine and performing arts Governors State Univ, University Park, Ill, 1971-84, dean of faculty, provost, vice-president acad affairs Berklee Col Music, Boston, 1984-96, pres Columbia Coll Chgo, 2000-2013. *Awards:* Recipient Outstanding Service award Nat Black Music Caucus, 1980, Composition grant, NEA, 1977, 82, 87, Lawrence Berk Leadership award, Internat Asn Jazz Educators; named Outstanding Music Educator, School Musician Magazine, 1983, Best Drummer, Notre Dame, 1970; named to Internat Jazz Educators Hall of Fame. *Mem:* NEA (chmn music 1982-85), Internat Asn Jazz Educators (pres 1982-84), Music Educators Nat Conf, Nat Black Music Caucus (sec 1974-78, exec dir), Nat Asn of Recording Arts and Sciences, American Soc of Composers, Authors and Publishers. *Publ:* articles have been published in professional journals

CARTER, YVONNE PICKERING
PAINTER, EDUCATOR
b Washington, DC, Feb 6, 1939. *Study:* Traphagen Sch, cert, 59; Howard Univ, AB, 62, MFA, 68. *Work:* NC Mus, Raleigh; Federal Reserve Bank, Richmond, Va; Gibbes Gallery, Charleston, SC; Miami-Dade Co Libr, Fla; Montgomery Co Print Collection, Md; Artery Orgn, Md. *Exhib:* Gathered Visions: Selected Works by African-Am Women Artists; Performance Art: Maverick Street Litany, Dock St Theatre, Charleston, SC, 92; Book As Art VI, Nat Mus Women in the Arts, Washington, 94; Beyond Africa: Cult Influences in Am Art, Greensboro Cult Ctr, NC, 94; Gathering Medicine: Coast to Coast: Nat Women Artists of Color, Art in General, NY, 94; Fondo Del Sol Visual Art Ctr, Washington, 95; Nathan Cummings Found, NY, 96; My Magic Pours Secret Libations, Fla State Univ Mus Fine Arts, Tallahassee, 96; and others. *Pos:* Dept chair, Mass Media, Visual & Performing Arts Dept. *Teaching:* Prof design & painting, Univ District of Columbia, Washington, 71-. *Awards:* DC Comn Arts & Humanities Visual Arts Award, 81, 82 & 94; Fac Res Grant, 84. *Bibliog:* Curtia James (auth), Review of Gathered Visions, Art Papers, 91; Beth Joselow (auth), The Book As Art VI, Washington Rev, 4-5/94; Gumbo Ya Ya: Anthology of Contemporary African-American Women Artists, Mid March Press, 95. *Mem:* Washington Women's Art Ctr; Women's Caucus Art; Coll Art Asn. *Media:* Watercolor, Constructions. *Mailing Add:* 6620 Bears Bluff Rd Wadmalaw Island SC 29487

CARTIN, MICKEY
COLLECTOR
Collection Arranged: Joe Coleman retrospective, Jack Tilton Gallery, NY, 2006, Palais de Tokyo, Paris. *Pos:* Pres, Rexel CLS, Hartford, Conn, 1984, bd chmn, 2000-; owner, Cartin Collection, New York; trustee, Wadsworth Atheneum, Hartford, Conn. *Awards:* Named one of Top 200 Collectors, ARTnews mag, 2007-13. *Collection:* Early Netherlandish painting, 20th-century painting, emerging artists, illuminated manuscripts. *Mailing Add:* Rexel CLS 270 Locust St Hartford CT 06114

CARTWRIGHT, DERRICK R
MUSEUM DIRECTOR
b San Francisco, Calif, 1962. *Study:* Univ Calif, Berkeley, BA; UCLA, MA, 88; Univ Mich, PhD (art hist), 94. *Collection Arranged:* Jose Clemente Orozco in the US, 1927-1934; Ambassadors of Progress: American Women Photographers in Paris, 1900-1901; Luis Gispert: Loud Image; Coming of Age in Ancient Greece: Images of Childhood From the Classical Past; Lateral Thinking: Art of the 1990s. *Pos:* Dir, Founders Gallery, Univ San Diego, 93-98; dir, Musée d'Art Américain, Giverny, France, 98-2000, Hood Mus Art, Dartmouth Coll, 2000-04; Maruja Baldwin exec dir, San Diego Mus Art, 2004-09; Illsley Ball Nordstrom dir, Seattle Art Mus, 2009-2011, consultant, 2011-. *Teaching:* Prof art hist, Univ San Diego, 93-98. *Mem:* Asn Art Mus Dirs; Baleda Park Cult Partnership (vpres). *Mailing Add:* Seattle Art Mus 1300 First Ave Seattle WA 98101-2003

CARTWRIGHT, ROY R
CERAMIST
Study: Mt San Antonio Col, Walnut, Calif, 55-56, 57-58; Univ Southern Calif, Los Angeles, 56-57; Calif Coll Arts & Crafts, Oakland, BFA (ceramics), 61; Rochester Inst Technol, NY, MFA (ceramics), 63. *Work:* Cincinnati Bell System; Univ Fla, Miami; Cleveland Mus Art; Johnson Collection Am Crafts; Everson Mus, Syracuse, NY. *Exhib:* Solo shows, Art Asn Harrisburg, Pa, 89, Contemp Art Ctr, Cincinnati, Ohio, 89, Swindler Gallery, Royal Oak, Mich, 91 & Carnegie Art Ctr, Covington, Ky, 92, Miami Univ Mus Art, Ohio, 97-98 & Ohio Univ, 98; Carnegie Art Ctr, Covington, Ky, 90; Dawson Gallery, Rochester, NY, 90; Northeast Mo State Univ, Kirksville, Miss, 91; Design Smith Gallery, Cincinnati, Ohio, 98. *Teaching:* Cleveland Art Inst, 63-64; Univ Ill, 64-65; Univ Cincinnati, 65-; lects, talks & panel discussions, var cols & univs, 76-91. *Awards:* Research Equip Award, Univ Res Coun, 90; Visual Artist Fel, Nat Endowment Arts, 90; Individual Artist Grant, Ohio Arts Coun, 91 & 94. *Bibliog:* Rev, Panorama, 10/89; rev, City Beat, Cincinnati, 2/12-18/98; rev, Dialogue, 11-12/89 & 5-6/98; and others. *Mem:* Delta Phi Delta. *Mailing Add:* 8164 Kemperidge Ct Cincinnati OH 45249

CARULLA, RAMON
PAINTER, PRINTMAKER
b Havana, Cuba, Dec 7, 36; US citizen. *Study:* Self taught. *Work:* Detroit Inst Art, Mich; Mus Tamayo, Mex; Mus Fine Art, Montreal, Can; Mus Latin Am Art, Washington, DC; Bass Mus, Miami Beach, Fla; CBS Int Corp Collection, New York; Cincinnati Art Mus; Contemp Mus Art, Panama City, Panama; New Sch Social Res, New York; Japan Print Asn Collection, Tokyo; Boca Raton Art Mus, Fla; Cuban Mus Art & Cult, Miami, Fla; Taiwan Mus Art; Florean Mus, Maramures, Romania; Patricia & Phillip Frost Art Mus, FIU Miami, Fla; Tampa Mus Art, Tampa, Fla; and numerous others. *Comn:* Eastern Nat Bank, Coral Gables, Fla. *Exhib:* Paper as a Medium, Fla Int Univ & Smithsonian Inst, 79-80; solo exhibs, VI Graphic Biennial, San Juan, PR & Malcolm Brown Gallery, 85, Le Grand le Jeunne Auhordi-Grand Palais, Paris, France, 88, Cuban Collection Fine Art, The Dreamer Series, Miami, 98, Breaking Barriers, Mus Art, Ft Lauderdale, Fla, 98 & People and Places, Corbino Galleries, Longboat Key, Fla, 2000; 20 Yrs After, Bacardi Gallery, Miami, 87; Carbunar '99', The Int Small Engraving Salon, Florean Mus, Rumania, 99 & Carbunar '2000', 2000; Contemp Art Auction, Durban Segnini Gallery, Coral Gables, Fla, 2000; I Bienal Argentina de Grafica Latinoamericana, Museo Nacional del Grabado, Buenos Aires, 2001; Latin-Am Masters of Today & Tomorrow, Artspace, Virginia Miller Gallery, Coral Gables, Fla, 2001; and others. *Collection Arranged:* Cincinnati Mus Art, Contemp Mus de Valez Malaga, Malaga, Spain, Jersey City Mus, Joan Miro Found, Lowe Art Mus, Lehigh Univ Art Mus, Museo Rufino Tamayo, Museo José Luis Cuevas Mus Art, Ft Lauderdale, and more. *Teaching:* Guest lectr, Cranbrook Acad Art, Bloomfield Hills, Mich, Wayne State Univ, Detroit, 83 & Cleveland State Univ, Ohio, 85; private art instr. *Awards:* Fel, Cintas Found, Inst Int Educ, 73-74 & 79-80; Silvia Daro Dawidowicz Award, Metrop Mus & Arts Ctr, Coral Gables, Fla, 82; First Prize, Sixth Biennial Latin Am Graphic Art, San Juan, PR, 83; Hon Men, IX Biennial Ibero-Am Art, Palacio de Bellas Artes, Mex, 94; Cintas Fel Ann, 1973-1974, 1979-1980. *Bibliog:* R Pau Llosa (auth), The origins of Cuban art, Miami Herald, 10/81; Ramon Carulla and the Latin American Expression, Vanidades Mag, 10/82; Armando Alverez Bravo (auth), El mundo alucinante de Ramon Carulla, El Nuevo Herald, 10/91; Carol Damian (auth, art critic), Carmilla Catalogue-Life is a Masquerade; Carol Damian (art critic), Ramon Carilla, Black & White, Coral Gables Publ Lib, Fla; Ivy Olga Connor (art critic), Arts Latino Americano Mag. *Mem:* Miami Art Mus, Miami, Fla; Frost Art Mus, Fla Int Univ. *Media:* Oil on Canvas & Paper, Mixed Media, Printmaking. *Res:* Prado Mus investigation of Goya the black paintings, 2002-2003. *Specialty:* Latin Am Artist Galleries. *Interests:* Art, sports, traveling, football, basketball. *Publ:* Auth, Schweyer-Galdo Eds, 85; The Forgotten, A Series 32 works, oil/paper. *Dealer:* Gora Gallery, Montreal, Canada; P Jorn Hamburg Germ; Commenoz Gallery 328 Crandon Blvd Key Biscayne Fl 33149. *Mailing Add:* 4735 NW 184th Terr Miami FL 33055-2936

CARVALHO, JOSELY
PRINTMAKER, PAINTER
b Sao Paulo, Brazil, Sept 21, 1942. *Study:* Printmaking with Marcelo Grassman & Darel, 61-63, Woodcut with Shiko Munakata, 65, Sch Archit, Washington Univ, St Louis, Mo, BA, 67. *Work:* Casa de las Americas, Havana, Cuba; Mus Mod Art, NY; Bronx Mus Art, NY; Mus de Bellas Artes, Caracas, Venezuela; Brooklyn Mus, NY. *Comn:* Spectacolor Board-Times Square, Pub Art Fund, NY, 88. *Exhib:* Committed to Print, Mus Mod Art, NY, 88; Diary of Images: It's Still Time to Mourn, Hillwood Mus, Brookville, NY, 91; Diario De Imagens: Dia Mater, Museu De Arte De Sao Paulo (MASP), Sao Paulo, Brazil, 92; Mus Contemp Art, San Paolo, Brazil, 94; Olin Gallery, Kenyon Col, Ohio, 95; North Gallery, Miami-Dade Community Col, Fla, 96. *Teaching:* vis prof, Sch Archit, Nat Univ Mex, 71-73; vis prof silkscreen, State Univ NY, Purchase, 88; artist-in-residence, Franklin & Marshall Col, Lancaster, Pa, 88; vis artist painting, State Univ NY, Purchase, 92. *Awards:* Nat Endowment Arts Fel, 75-76 & 95-96; NY State Coun Arts, 78-82; NY Found Arts Fel, 84, 85. *Bibliog:* Arlene Raven (auth), Rape, Ohio State Univ, 85; Lucy Lippard (auth), Following the Dots, Connecting Project/Conexus, 87; Deborah Wye (auth), Committed to Print, Mus Mod Art, 88. *Mem:* Heresies Collective; Women Caucus Art. *Media:* Multi Media. *Publ:* Mothers, Mags & Movie Stars, Heresies Collective, 85 & Story of Elza; auth, The Meal, 86; coauth, with Conexus, Connection Project, 87; illusr, We Hold Our Ground, Ikon, 88; illusr (cover), Abortion and Woman's Choice, Northeastern Univ Press, 90. *Dealer:* Terne Gallery 38 E 57th St 6th Floor New York NY 10022. *Mailing Add:* 216 E 18th St New York NY 10003

CASADEI, GIOVANNI
PAINTER
b Rome, Italy, Mar 13, 1956; US citizen. *Study:* Scuola-Libera-Del-Nudo, Rome, Italy, 78-83; Pa Acad Fine Arts, Philadelphia, cert, 88-92. *Exhib:* Recent Paintings, Philadelphia Mus Art, 94; Still Life and Landscape, Mulligan-Shanoski Gallery, San Francisco, 96; Paintings of Landscapes & Interiors, Design Art Gallery, Drexell Univ, Pa, 96; Italian Journey, Hahn Gallery, Philadelphia, 97; recent paintings, Carspecken-Scott Gallery, Wilmington, Del, 97; The Unbroken Line, Philadelphia, 97. *Teaching:* Instr landscape painting, Manayunk Art Ctr, Philadelphia, 97- & Main Line Art Ctr, Haverford, Pa, 97-. *Awards:* Henry Scheidt Travel Scholarship, Ann Student Show Pa Acad Fine Arts, 91 & Philadelphia Mayor's Award, 92; Elizabeth-Greenshields Found Grant, Montreal, Can, 98. *Bibliog:* Judith West (auth), Portfolio-Giovanni Casadei, Seven Arts Mag, Vol 4, No 4, 4/96. *Media:* Oil. *Dealer:* Hahn Gallery 8439 Germantown Ave Philadelphia PA 19118. *Mailing Add:* 1326 Moore St Philadelphia PA 19148-1500

CASAS, FERNANDO R
PAINTER, DRAFTSMAN
b Cochabamba, Bolivia, Mar 25, 1946. *Study:* Colo Col, BA; Rice Univ, MA, PhD; pvt training with Raul Prada. *Work:* Nat Mus Art, La Paz, Bolivia; Pinacoteca Nac, Cochabamba, Bolivia; Art of the Americas Collection (B Duncan), NY; Mus Fine Arts, Houston. *Comn:* Five paintings about Society, Baker World Trade, Houston, 80; mural, Hermman Hosp, Houston, 90. *Exhib:* Solo exhibs, Harriet Griffin Gallery, NY, 76 & Mus Nacional De Arte, La Paz, Bolivia, 88; Toni Jones Gallery, Houston, 79 & 80; Heritage Gallery, Los Angeles, 79; Duveen Gallery, Houston, 79; Galeria Emusa, Bolivia, 86; Blue Mt Gallery, NY, 89. *Awards:* First Nat Award Painting & First Nat Award Drawing, Concurso Nac de Artes Plasticas, Bolivia, 72 & 73. *Bibliog:* Itsuo Sakane (auth), The Asahi Shimbun, Japan, 8/83, 5/84 & others; Flocon (auth), Curvilinear Perspective, Univ Calif Press, 87; Pintura Boliviana del siglo XX, BHN Bolivia, 89. *Media:* Oil; Mixed. *Publ:* Auth, Flat sphere perspective, Vol 16, No 1, 83 & Polar perspective: A graphical system for creating two dimensional images representing a world of four dimensions, Vol 17, No 3, 84, Leonardo; and others. *Dealer:* Beowulf Fine Arts Ltd 12620 I-45 N Suite 218 Houston TX 77060 Tel: 713-872-1342. *Mailing Add:* 22214 Meadowsweet Dr Magnolia TX 77355-3572

CASAS, MELESIO (MEL)
PAINTER, EDUCATOR
b El Paso, Tex, Nov 24, 1929. *Study:* Univ Tex, El Paso, BA, 56; Univ of the Americas, Mex, MFA, 58. *Work:* Nat Mus Am Art, Smithsonian Inst; pvt collections incl Jim & Ann Harithas, NY, Robert Wilson, Houston, Tex, Joe Nicholson, San Antonio, Tex & Todd Spites, Santa Fe, NMex, June A Nickles, Austin; Smithsonian Nat Mus Am Art; Janet & Jim Dicke, New Bremen, Ohio. *Exhib:* Artists of the Southeast & Tex, Biennial Painting & Sculpture, 71; Tex Painting & Sculptures: 20th Century, 72; Mex-Am Art Symp, Trinity Univ, 73; 12 Tex Artists, Contemp Art Mus, Houston, 74; 1975 Biennial Contemp Am Art, Whitney Mus Art, 75; Dale Gas--Chicano Art of Tex, Contemp Arts Mus, Houston, 77; Showdown, Alternative Mus, NY, 83; Chicano Expression, INTAR, NY, 86; Ft Worth Art Festival, Tex, 86; Solo exhib, Laguna Gloria Mus, Austin, Tex. *Pos:* Book reviewer, Choice Mag, Am Libr Asn, 54-; panels, San Antonio Art Coun & Nat Endowment Arts, 86. *Teaching:* Prof art, design & painting, San Antonio Col, Tex, 61-90; retired. *Awards:* Purchase Prize, 59 & Cash Award, 64, El Paso Art Mus; Cash Award, San Antonio Art League, 66 & Ft Worth Art Festival, 86. *Bibliog:* Jacinto Quiarte (auth), The Art of Mexican Americans, Univ Tex, 73; article, Art News, 12/77; Mimi Crossley (auth), Dale Gas at the Contemporary Art Museum, Art in Am, 1-2/78. *Mem:* Founding mem Con Safo Painters; Fine Arts Comn, San Antonio, Tex. *Media:* Acrylic. *Mailing Add:* 40 Silverhorn Dr San Antonio TX 78216

CASEBERE, JAMES E
PHOTOGRAPHER, SCULPTOR
b Lansing, Mich, Sept 17, 1953. *Study:* Mich State Univ, 71-72; Minneapolis Coll Art & Design, BFA, 76; Whitney Mus Independent Study Program, 77; Calif Inst Arts, MFA, 79. *Work:* Neuberger Mus, Purchase, NY; Walker Art Ctr, Minneapolis, Minn; Victoria Albert Mus, London; Tampa Mus, Fla; Mus Mod Art, NY; Mus Fine Art, Boston. *Comn:* Minn Hist Ctr, St Paul, 91. *Exhib:* Solo exhibs include Addison Gallery of Am Art, Phillips Acad, Andover, Mass, 2000, Lisson Gallery, London, 2000, Bernier Eliades, Athens, Greece, 2001, Goldman Fine Art, Boston, 2001, Gallerie Tanit, Munich, 2001, Inst of Contemp Arts, Phila, 2001 & Sean Kelly Gallery, New York City, 2001, Sean Kelly, New York City, 2007, Sean Kelly Gallery, 2010; group exhibs include Fabricated to be Photographed, San Francisco Mus Mod Art, Albright-Knox Gallery, Buffalo, NY, Newport Harbor Art Mus, Newport Beach, Calif & Univ NMex, Albuquerque, 79-80; Sculpture on the Wall, Aldrich Mus Am Art, 86; Photog Fictions, Whitney Mus Am Art, 86; Arrangements for the Camera: A View of Contemp Photog, Baltimore Mus Art, Md, 87; Suburban Life: Plotting the Am Dream, Whitney Mus Am Art, 89; Pleasures and Terrors of Domestic Comfort, Mus Mod Art, NY, 91; More Than One Photog, Mus Mod Art, NY, 92; Photog & Art: Interactions Since 1946, Los Angeles Co Mus Art; Architecture as Metaphor, Mus of Modern Art, New York City, 97; Selections from the Permanent Collection, Whitney Mus of Am Art, 97; Within These Walls, Kettle's Yard, Cambridge, Eng, 97; Elsewhere, Carnegie Mus of Art, Pitts, 97; The Luminous Image, Alternative Mus, New York City, 97; PhotoImage: Printmaking 60s to 90s, Mus of Fine Arts, Boston, 98; Where: Allegories of Site in Contemp Art, Whitney Mus of Am Art, Stamford, Conn, 98; Insties: Interior Space in Contemp Art, Whitney Mus of Am Art, Stamford, Conn, 2000; Supermodel, Mass Mus of Contemp Art, North Adams, 2000; Inside Out: Reality of Fiction?, Sean Delly Gallery, New York City, 2000; Making Pictures: Contemp Am Photog, Asheville Art Mus, NC, 2000; Staged and Manipulated: Photog Fictions from St Louis Collections, St Louis Art Mus, Mo, 2000; Open Ends: Architecture Hot and Cold, Sets and Situations, Mus of Modern Art, New York City, 2000; Flash Back, Barbara Farber/La Serre, Trets, France, 2000; Art on Paper 2000, Weatherspoon Art Gallery, 2000; Photo-Synthesis: Recent Develop in Contemp Photog, Dela Ctr for Contemp Arts, 2001; Whitney Biennial, Whitney Mus Am Art, 2010. *Teaching:* Asst prof photog, Rockland Community Col, 85-88; vis artist, Calif Inst Arts, 84, Boston Mus Sch, 89, RI Design, 91, Cooper Union, 94, Sch Visual Arts, 94-95, Harvard Univ, 96 & Yale Univ, 97. *Awards:* Visual Artist Fels, 82, 86 & 90, Nat Endowment Arts; Visual Artist Sponsored Proj Grant, NY State Coun Arts, 82; Fel, New York Found Arts, 85, 89 & 94; Guggenheim Fel, 95. *Bibliog:* Art: James Casebere, W, 5/2001; William L Hamilton (auth), An Artist's Novel Take on History: he lets the walls talk, NY Times, 5//28/2001; Deborah Everett (auth), James Casebere, NYArts, 6/6/2001. *Publ:* Auth, In the 2nd Half of the 20th Century, CEPA Gallery, Buffalo, 82

CASELLAS, JOACHIM
PAINTER, DIRECTOR
b Gerona Prov, Spain, Aug 1, 1927; US citizen. *Study:* Coll Sacred Heart, Gerona, Spain, BA, 48; Inst Escolar. *Work:* Mus Provincial & Tossa de Mar Mus, Gerona, Spain; The White House, Washington, DC; The Golden Bourgh, Austin, Tex; MD'A Mus D'Ar, Gerona, Spain; Fort Walton Beach Art Mus, Fort Walton Beach, Fla. *Exhib:* Salon de Octobre, Galleria Leytana, Barcelona, Spain, 50; Brazil Biennial, Brazil, 51; Paris Group, Paris, France, 52; Art Who? Ocean Springs, Miss, 88-90; Casell Gallery, New Orleans, La, 88; Artist Showroom, New Orleans, La, 88. *Pos:* Pres Casell Gallery. *Teaching:* lectr art, pastel technique. *Awards:* Merit Award, Ocean Springs Art Asn, 88; First Place, Fall Festival, Biloxi Art, 88; First Place, Biloxi Art Asn, 89 & 90; First Place, New Orleans 12, La, 94 & 2001; Blue Ribbon, Wyes Art Collection Twelve, 1993, 2001, & 2004; and others. *Bibliog:* Sota La Boira, Diputacio de Gerona, Mus D'Art; Biographical Encyclopedia of American Painters, Sculptors, and Engravers of the USA, Colonial to 2002. *Mem:* Ocean Springs Art Asn. *Media:* Pastel, Miscellaneous Media. *Specialty:* Southern art. *Interests:* Ancient history, plants, travel. *Collection:* African art. *Dealer:* Casell Gallery 818 Royal St New Orleans LA 70116. *Mailing Add:* Casell Gallery 818 Royal St New Orleans LA 70116

CASEY, JOHN THAYER
PAINTER, SCULPTOR
b New London, Conn, June 27, 1931. *Study:* Univ Ore, BA (Ina McClung Scholar, 57-58); Calif Coll of Arts & Crafts, MFA with Nathan Oliveira & Harry Krell. *Work:* Univ Ore, Eugene; State of Ore, Salem, Monmouth & Pendleton; Coos Art Mus, Ore. *Exhib:* 68th Western Ann, Denver Art Mus, 62; 22nd Spokane Ann, Cheney Cowles Mus, Wash, 70, 72, 74 & 76; 32nd Ann NW Watercolor Exhib, Seattle Art Mus Pavilion, Wash, 71; Watercolor West, Brea, Calif, 96 & Riverside, 97; All-Ore Art Ann, Salem, 98, 2001 & 2002; Expressions West, Coos Art Mus, 2000 & 2002; Expressions West, 2005; Watercolor West, Brea, Calif, 2006. *Teaching:* Assoc prof drawing, painting & design, Western Ore Univ, Monmouth, 65-88, emer prof. *Awards:* Grad Teaching Scholar, Calif Coll Arts & Crafts, 61-62. *Bibliog:* Lorraine B Widman (auth), Sculpture: A Studio Guide to Concepts, Methods & Materials, Prentice-Hall, 90-; A Duca & L Loscutoff (coauths), The Best Acrylic Painting, Rockport Publ, 96 & Creative Inspiration, 97. *Media:* Acrylic, Watercolor; All Media

CASEY, KIM L
PAINTER, EDUCATOR
b Dexster, Maine, Apr 18, 1964. *Study:* Plymouth State Col, BS (art educ), 82; Brooklyn Col, MFA, 97. *Work:* So Ho Soda Corp, NY. *Exhib:* Graduate Show, Brooklyn Col, NY, 97; Currier Mus, Manchester, 97; Weber Nat, Weber State Univ, Ogden, Utah, 2000; 20th Century Fairwell, Central Mich Univ, 2000; Plymouth State Univ, NH, 2000; Invitational, Shelburne Farms Mus, Vt, 2000; Franco Am Ctr, 2003; Franklin Pierce Col, 2003. *Collection Arranged:* Soho Soda, Brooklyn Coll. *Teaching:* prof studio art, Plymouth State, NH, 97-2000, Notre Dame Col, NH, 98-99 & Univ NH, 99-2000. *Awards:* NH State Coun on Arts Fel; prof artists grant, state of NH. *Mem:* Cause Women in Arts; NH Art Asn; Coll Art Asn. *Media:* Oil. *Publ:* contribr, Artists, The Daily Chautaugua, 97, New York Gallery Guide, 98, Landscape Artists, Boston Globe, 99 & 2000, art sect, Manchester Union Leader, 2003. *Dealer:* NH Art Asn State St Portsmouth NH 03801; The Barn Gallery Ogunquit ME; New Hampshire Art Asn Portsmouth NH. *Mailing Add:* 244 Locust St Dover NH 03820

CASEY, TIM (TIMOTHY) WILLIAM
PAINTER, EDUCATOR
b Lawton, Okla, July 19, 1947. *Study:* Art Acad Cincinnati, 65-68; RI Sch Design, BFA, 70, MFA, 72. *Work:* Chase Manhattan Bank, New York; Jewish Mus, New York; Nat Gallery Art, Washington, DC; Weatherspoon Art Gallery, Univ NC; and pvt collections of Wynn Kramarsky, Vera List Estate, Martin Margulies & Tom Solomon.

Comn: Painting, Vera List for Jewish Mus, New York, 86. *Exhib:* Solo exhibs, Gabrielle Bryers, New York, 85-86, Tomoko Liguori, New York, 88 & 90 & John Davis Gallery, Hudson, NY, 2006-2007; A Radical Plurality, William Paterson Coll, Wayne, NJ 86; Artists Space, New York, 90-91; Ten, Eye Grind Gallery, Los Olivos, Calif, 93; Margulies-Taplin Gallery, Miami, Fla, 99; Momenta Art Benefit, Momenta Art, Williamsburg, Brooklyn, NY, 2002; Incredible Lightness of Being, Black & White Gallery, Williamsburg, Brooklyn, NY, 2003; John Davis Gallery, Hudson, NY, 2005; Lesley Heller Gallery, New York, 2006. *Teaching:* Instr drawing, RI Sch Design, 70-75; adj instr drawing & painting, State Univ NY at Purchase, Exten Sch, 86-89; artist-in-residence, Studio in a Sch, PS 11, 89-; adj instr painting, NY Univ, 2000-2002; vis artist, Middlebury Coll, Vt, 2002 & Bard Coll, Hudson, NY, 2004. *Awards:* Studio Artist, Nat Studio Prog, Inst Art Urban Resources, The Clocktower, New York, 86. *Bibliog:* John Russell (auth), rev, NY Times, 10/85; Grace Glueck (auth), rev, NY Times, 2/85; Stephen Westfall (auth), rev, Art in Am, 88; Joan Crowder (auth), Santa Barbara News-Press, 1/15/93 & 8/19/93; Holland Cotter, NY Times, 2/14/2003; Andrew Amelinckx, Register Sun, Hudson, NY, 3/3/2006. *Media:* Oil, Watercolor. *Mailing Add:* 2 Broadway Ter Apt 36 New York NY 10040-2774

CASH, SARAH
MUSEUM DIRECTOR, CURATOR
b New Haven, Conn, Oct 26, 1958. *Study:* Smith Col, BA, 80; Williams Col (art hist), MA, 86; Mus Mgt Inst, Berkeley, cert, 96. *Collection Arranged:* Ominous Hush: The Thunderstorm Paintings of M J Heade (auth, catalog), Amon Carter Mus, 94; Thomas Cole's Paintings of Eden, Amon Carter Mus, 95; Thomas Eakins and the Swimming Picture (auth, catalog), Amon Carter Mus, 96-97; The Gilded Cage: Views of Am Women 1872-1921, Corcoran Gallery of Art, 2002. *Pos:* Sr res assoc Am paintings, Nat Gallery Art, 86-89; asst cur, Amon Carter Mus, Fort Worth, Tex, 90-95; dir, Maier Mus Art, Randolph-Macon Woman's Col, 95-98; Bechhoefer cur am art, Corcoran Gallery Art, Washington, DC, 98-. *Teaching:* Adj fac mus studies, Randolph-Macon Woman's Col, Va, 96-98. *Mem:* Am Asn Mus, Washington; Coll Art Asn Am, NY. *Publ:* Coauth, American Naive Paintings in the National Gallery of Art (catalog), 91; auth, Martin Johnson Heade's paintings of Manchester, Mass, Am Art J/Kennedy Galleries, 96. *Mailing Add:* 412 S Taylor St Arlington VA 22204

CASIDA, KATI
PRINTMAKER, SCULPTOR
b Viroqua, Wis, Mar 28, 1931. *Study:* Univ Wis-Madison, BS (art educ), 53; New Sch Social Res, with Antonio Frasconi, New York, 55. *Work:* Genentech, San Francisco, City Percent Art Prog, Brea, Calif; Ore Art Comn, Salem; Int Paper Co, NY; Hastings Coll Law; 3 sculptures, Bank of Am Art Collection, NC, Santa Clara, City Plaza. *Comn:* Sculpture (steel), Spectrum Ctr, Criswell Co, Dallas, 83; sculpture (wood & trees) & bldg sculptures, Viroqua City Park & Medical Office, Wis, 87; sculpture (aluminum), Oakland City Ctr, Calif; sculpture, Marina, Berkeley, Calif. *Exhib:* Oakland Mus, 94; Contract Design Ctr, San Francisco, 94; '94 Sculpture, Syntex Corp, Palo Alto, Calif, 94; '94 handmade papers sculptures, Magnolia Edits, Oakland, Calif, 94; sculpture, San Francisco, Calif, 2000; Oakland Mus, Calif, 2002; solo exhib, Gallery 555, Solvorn, Norway, 2004; Steel Gallery, 2005; New Nordic Designs, Nordic 5 Arts, San Francisco, 2006; 3 Sculptors, Atrim Gallery, San Francisco, Calif; Cyprus Chair-Memorial for Missing Persons-1974, Oakland, Calif, 2008; Sculpturesite Gallery, San Francisco, 2010. *Pos:* Sculptor, currently. *Teaching:* Instr art & art hist, Upsala Coll, East Orange, NJ, 55-56. *Awards:* Am Asn Univ Women, La Crosse, Wis, 50; Open Proposals, City of Oakland, 91. *Bibliog:* Radio, Jonsok sculpture, Nat Norweg Broadcasting co, 6/85; Andrea Workman (auth), Casida-modern sculptor, Viking Mag, Minneapolis, Minn, 12/85; Margret Schaefer (auth), Steel Magnolia: interview with Kati Casida, Claremont Grad Univ, Women's Studies J, Vol 36, No 8, 12/2007. *Mem:* Int Sculpture Ctr; Calif Soc Printmakers; Nat Women's Art Caucus; The Nat Mus of Women in the Arts, Washington, DC; Pacific Rim Sculptures Group; Am Scandinavian Found, Sons of Norway & Am Indian Mus; Greek Cypriot Asn, San Francisco. *Media:* Woodcut, Metal, Aluminum, Copper & Handmade papers. *Res:* Rome, Italy. *Specialty:* outdoor sculptures. *Interests:* dance; traveling. *Collection:* Mindocino, Calif, Ketchum, Id, Berkeley, Calif, and others. *Publ:* Coauth, Jonsok sculpture, Viking Mag, Minneapolis, Minn, 12/85; Sculpture for Missing Persons, Hellenic J, San Francisco, 3/92. *Dealer:* Sculpturesite Gallery Sonoma Ca. *Mailing Add:* c/o Studio 1570 La Vereda Rd Berkeley CA 94708

CASPE, LYNDA
PAINTER, SCULPTOR
b New York, NY. *Study:* BA, Univ Chicago, 61; MFA, Univ Iowa, 1964; Atelier 17, Paris, 1964-1965; New York Studio Sch, 1966-1968. *Work:* Nat Gallery of Australia; Inst Women & Arts, NJ; Schering-Plough Art Collection, Madison, NJ; Greater Middletown Art Coun, NY; Derfner Judaica Mus. *Exhib:* Artist Postcard Show, Cooper Hewett Mus, New York, 1978; Artist Postcard Show, Inst Contemp Art, Oslo, Norway, 1979; Artist Postcard Show, Inst Contemp Art, England, 1980; Dura Europos Proj, Philadelphia mus Jewish Art, 2010; Solo exhib, City Paintings, Inside & Out, 2011-2012, Sovereign/Santander, Landscapes for Every Season, 2012-2013; Biblical Bronze Reliefs, Derfner Judaica Mus, 2013-2014; Cityscapes, Elma and Milton A Gilbert Pavillions Gallery, 2013-2014; Hebrew Union Col Mus Show, 2015; Mus of Biblical Art, Dallas, Tex, 2015; Lynda Caspe, Sculpture, Sculptural Reliefs and Preparatory Drawings, Gallery of the Office of the Manhattan Borough President, Gale A Brewer, 2015; Bowery Gallery, Founding Members 1969, Westbeth Gallery, NY, 2014. *Collection Arranged:* cur, Scenes from the Bible, Synagogue for the Arts, 2007; Yeshiva University Mus. *Teaching:* adj assoc prof, Borough of Manhattan CC, 1978-2013; instr, Parsons Sch Design, 1977-1989; instr, Univ Chicago. *Awards:* Yaddo Fel, Yaddo Found, 1973; Creative Art Pub Serv Grant, NY State, 1974; Prof Staff Congress, Prof Achievement Award, City Univ, NY, 2008, 2009, 2010; grant, Memorial Found for Jewish Culture, 2011-12. *Bibliog:* Charles Berger (auth), Rev of Lynda Caspe Bowery Gallery Exhib, 2010; Richard McBee (auth), Bible Scenes, The Jewish Press, 2007; Jane Necol (auth), Rev of Shows at Art Students League Online, 2001; City Arts, Digital Ed Review of Linda Caspe's Sovereign/Santander Exhib, City Paintings, Inside and Out, 2011-2012; Dianne Resulli (auth), Ars Gratis Argentaria, Broadsheet Daily, 2012; John Goodrich (auth), Review of Lynda Caspe's Sovereign/Santander Exhib, City Paintings, Inside and Out (catalogue with critical essay), 2011-2012; Gerald Haggerty (auth), Review of Lynda Caspe's Sovereign/Santander Exhib, Landscapes for Every Season (catalogue, essay), 2012-2013; McBee (auth) Biblical Reliefs and Citiscapes, The Jewish Press, 2013; Gloria Kestenbaum (auth) Treasures in the Bronx, The Jewish Week, 2013; Gabrielle Alfiero (auth), The Bible Cast in Bronze, Our Town Downtown, City Arts, 2015; Dusica Sue Malesevic (auth) Bowery Gallery's Radical Notions Persist, The Village, 2014. *Mem:* Artist Equity, 1991, 1998, 2000; Fed Mod Painters & Sculptors 2001-(co-pres, 2005-2006). *Publ:* auth, Art & Poetry, 2013. *Mailing Add:* 150 Franklin St New York NY 10013

CASSARA, FRANK
PAINTER, PRINTMAKER
b Partinico, Sicily; US citizen. *Study:* Colorado Springs Sch Fine Arts, Colo; Univ Mich, MS (design); also spec study, Atelier 17, Paris, France. *Work:* Libr Cong, Washington, DC; Bibliot Nat, Paris, France; Stedelijk Mus, Amsterdam, Neth; Detroit Inst Arts; Free Libr Philadelphia; Nat Mus Am Art, Smithsonian, Washington, DC; Owen Ill, Toledo, Ohio; and others. *Comn:* Mural, US Post Off, East Detroit, 39; mural, Donald Thompson Sch, Highland Park, Mich, 39; mural, US Post Off, Sandusky, Mich, 40; mural, Water Conditioning Plant, Lansing, Mich, 41; mural, Palio, Ann Arbor, Mich, 96. *Exhib:* Seventh Int Exhib Lithography & Wood Engr, Art Inst Chicago, 39; 1st Exhib Am Printmakers, Gallerie Nees Morphes, Athens, Greece, 65; 22nd Nat Exhib Prints, Libr Cong, 71; Atelier 17: A Retrospective, Elvehjem Art Ctr, Madison, Wis, 77; Toledo Mus Art, Ohio, 82; Mus Art, Univ Mich, Ann Arbor, Mich, 86; DeWaters Art Ctr, Flint, Mich, 90; Birmingham Bloomfield Art Center (BBAC), Birmingham, Mich, 2006; and others. *Teaching:* Instr drawing, Detroit Soc Arts & Crafts, 46-47; prof printmaking, Univ Mich, 47-83, emer prof art, currently. *Awards:* Over 50 awards in nat & regional exhibs; Rackham Res Grants, Univ Mich, 61, 68, 74 & 75. *Bibliog:* Kresge Art Mus Bulletin, Vol VII, 92, Mich State Univ. *Mem:* Nat Acad Art. *Media:* Oil; All. *Publ:* Contribr, Artists' Proof, A Collectors Edition, 71. *Mailing Add:* 1122 Pomona Rd Ann Arbor MI 48103

CASSELL, BEVERLY
PAINTER
b Montgomery, Ala, 1936. *Study:* Univ Ga, Athens, MFA (art & philos), 60, study with Lamar Dodd & Howard Thomas; NY Univ, NY, 63. *Work:* Disney Studios, Burbank, Calif; Ga Mus, Athens; Taiwan Mus Art, Taichung; US Embassy, Manila, Philippines; Univ House, Univ Calif, Santa Cruz. *Exhib:* Taiwan Mus, Taichung, Taiwan, 89; Los Angeles Co Mus Art, 92; Nagasaki Mus Art, Japan, 92, 93 & 94-96; Judson Gallery, New York City, 99; Modern Art Gallery, Los Angeles, Calif, 99; NOHO Art Gallery, North Hollywood, Calif, 2000. *Pos:* Founder & dir, Artist Conf Network, Int, 83-; regional arts coun, City of Los Angeles, Calif, 98, adv coun, 99. *Teaching:* Univ Colo, Denver, 67-69; Univ Calif Santa Cruz, 72-80; UCLA Exten, 86-89; Getty Mus Art Educ Ser, Los Angeles, 92. *Awards:* Los Angeles Cult Affairs Coun Grant for Los Angeles Inner City Youth Water Sculpture Proj. *Bibliog:* Article, Calif Art Review, 89; 4th International Contemp Art Fair Catalog, Art Los Angeles, 89. *Mem:* Artist Conf Network Int (dir). *Media:* Oil, Gouache. *Publ:* Leaven, NY, 80; Design Int, 89; Calif Art Rev, 89; Quarry West, rev ed 94

CASSELL, ROBERT E, JR
PHOTOGRAPHER, ADMINISTRATOR
b Jackson, Tenn. *Study:* Vanderbilt Univ, BE, 64; Univ Tenn, MS, 66; Univ Mass, Arts Mgt, 2006; Va Intermont Coll, BFA, Photography & Art History, 2010. *Exhib:* Members Gallery, Arts Depot, Abingdon, Va, 2005-; Selected Work, Va Int Coll, Bristol, Va, 2006; Juried Photog Show, Va Highlands Festival, Abingdon, Va, 2006, 2008; Appalachian State Pushpin Exhib, 2007; Appalachian Photog Salon, 2008. *Pos:* Arts admin, Depot Artists Asn, Abingdon, Va, 2001-2012; grants reviewer, Va Arts Commission, 2004-2006, 2009-2011; grants reviewer, Tenn Arts Commission, 2012-. *Mem:* Pro Art Asn, Wise, Va (pres, vpres, secy, 93-); Va Highlands Fest (bd dir & fine art chmn, 2003-09); Va for the Arts (2004-); Southwest Va Artisans Ctr (steering comt, 2005-2007); Art Asn Abingdon (2009-2012); Abingdon Tourism Adv Comt, 2011; Abingdon Arts Incubator (bd 2011-2012); Depot Artist Asn (life mem); Tennesseans for the Arts (2012-). *Media:* Silver Gelatin, Color Print, Digital. *Dealer:* Arts Depot 314 Depot Sq Abingdon VA 24210. *Mailing Add:* 2100 Louita Ave Kingsport TN 37660

CASSELL, STEPHEN
ARCHITECT
Study: Priceton Univ, BA (archit), 1986; Harvard Univ, M (archit), 1992. *Exhib:* Recent Work, Harvard Univ Grad Sch Design, 1997; Architecture Research Office: Work, Princeton Univ Sch Archit, 2000; Forever Modern: 50 Years of Record Houses, Archit Record and Pratt Inst, 2005; Post, Syracuse Univ Sch Archit, 2008; From the Ground Up, Van Alen Inst, 2009. *Pos:* Architect, Mathieu et Virnot Architects, Paris, 1983-84, Steven Holl Architects, New York, 1986-89, 1993-94, Edwin Schlossberg, Inc, New York, 1993-94; founding partner, Archit Res Office LLC, 1993-. *Teaching:* vis prof, RI Sch Design, 1993 & 1994, Harvard Univ Grad Sch Design, 1996, 1998, 2004 & 2006 & Syracuse Univ Sch Archit, 2008; Harry S Shure prof, Univ Va, 2001 & Porter distinguished vis chair, 2007; instr, Calif Col Arts Summer Design Intensive, 2005; lectr, Princeton Univ Sch Archit, 2002 & 2009; Friedman assoc prof, Univ Calif Berkeley, 2009. *Awards:* Young Architects Forum award, AIA New York Chap, 1996, Archit Award, 2000, Honor Award for Interior Archit, 2008, Honor Award, Bldg Type Awards, Educ Facility category, 2008; Award for Design Excellence, Art Comn City of NY, 1999; Independent Projects Award, NY State Coun on Arts, 1998; Emerging Voices Award, Archit League, New York, 2001; Design Innovators Award, House Beautiful and Chrysler, 2005; Design Award, RI Monthly, 2007; Design Award, Contract Mag, 2008; Honor Award for Interior Archit, Boston Soc Architects, 2008; Archit Award, Am Acad Arts & Letts, 2010. *Mailing Add:* Archit Res Office 170 Varick St 7th Fl New York NY 10013

CASSELLI, HENRY CALVIN, JR
PAINTER
b New Orleans, La, Oct 25, 1946. *Study:* Student, John McCrady School Fine and Applied Arts, 1967. *Work:* Libr Congress; New Orleans Mus; Hunter Mus, Tenn; Greenville Mus, SC; Albany Mus, Ga; Am Tel & Tel, NY; The White House, Nat Portrait Gallery, Washington, DC. *Comn:* La State Univ, Baton Rouge, 78; WC Bradley, Columbus, Ga; portrait of Pres R Reagan, Nat Portrait Gallery, Smithsonian Inst & The White House. *Exhib:* Solo exhibs, Lauren Rogers Mus, 72 & Greenville Co Mus, SC, 80; Smithsonian Traveling Drawing Exhib, 72-75; Hunter Mus, Tenn, 81; Am Watercolor Soc, NY, 71-86; and others. *Awards:* High Winds Medals, 76, 77, 79 & 88, Silver Medal, 86 & Gold Medal, 87, Am Watercolor Soc. *Bibliog:* Doreen Mangan (auth), Henry Casselli, Am Arts; Susan Meyer (auth), 20 Figure Painters, Watson-Guptill, 79; article, Southern Accent Mag, 81; Betty Harvey (auth), Henry Casselli, Art West Digest, 85; John Kemp (auth), Henry Casselli, Am Artist. *Mem:* High Winds medal 1976, 77, 79, 88, Silver medal 1986, Gold medal 1987; Am Watercolor Soc (vpres, 79-80); nat juror 1979; Nat Acad Design, NY (assoc, 88, acad, 94). *Media:* Watercolor, Pastels. *Publ:* Contribr, The Natural Way to Paint, Davis, 78; Using Color, Dobie, Watson-Guptill, 86. *Dealer:* Tex Art Gallery Dallas TX; Mongerson-Wunderlich Chicago IL. *Mailing Add:* 4015 N Labarre Rd Metairie LA 70002-1820

CASSULLO, JOANNE LEONHARDT
PATRON
b Glen Cove, NY, Dec 2, 1955. *Study:* Roanoke Col, Salem, Va, BA (eng, elementary educ & fine arts) 78; So Methodist Univ, MFA, 82. *Pos:* Dir, counseling & educ, PCI Inc, Ft Worth, Tex, 78-80; vpres, bd dir, Phoenix House Found, Inc, New York City, 82-; gallery asst, Washburn Gallery Inc, New York City, 83-86; trustee, Whitney Mus Am Art, New York City, 85-, secy; pres, Dorothea L Leonhardt Found, New York City, 88-. *Teaching:* Cert teacher, elementary educ, Va, formerly. *Awards:* Helen Rubinstein Fel in Mus Studies. *Mem:* RxArt, Children's Advocacy Ctr of Manhattan; Housing Enterprises for Less Privileged (HELP USA). *Publ:* Contribr, articles and jour's

CASTAGNO, JOHN EDWARD
ART DEALER, PAINTER
b Philadelphia, Pa, July 19, 1930. *Study:* Univ Arts, Philadelphia, 50; Pa Acad Fine Arts, 60-61; Fleisher Art Mem, Philadelphia, 62; Barnes Found, Pa, 63-64. *Work:* Butler Inst Am Art, Ohio; Tweed Mus, Duluth, Minn; Los Angeles Co Mus, Calif; Lakeview Mus Arts & Sci, Peoria, Ill; Birmingham Mus Art, Ala; Villanova Univ, Pa; St Josephs Univ, Pa; La Salle Coll, Pa; Widener Univ, Pa; Haifa Mus, Israel; Munic Dublin, Ireland. *Comn:* Philadelphia Poster, United Van Lines/Quaker Storage, Pa, 76. *Exhib:* Makler Gallery, Philadelphia, 70; Philadelphia Sketch Club, 70; solo exhibs, Pa Acad Fine Arts, Philadelphia, 71, Lakeview Mus Arts & Sci, Peoria, Ill, 72, Cedar Rapids Mus Art, Iowa, 72 & Tweed Mus, Duluth, Minn, 72; Mus NMex, 73; Civic Ctr Philadelphia, 71 & 74; Mus Art, Univ Ore, 76. *Collection Arranged:* Europahaus, Vienna, Austria, 72; Mus NMex, 73; Art Alliance, Philadelphia, 76; Tweed Mus, Duluth, Minn, 76; Newman Galleries, Philadelphia, 76. *Pos:* Artists' Signatures Identification expert. *Teaching:* Artist-in-residence, Villanova Univ, Pa, 73; lectr, Rennasaince Cruise Lines, formerly. *Awards:* 1st Prize Painting, Del Co Arts Festival, 69; 1st Prize Sculpture, Upper Merion Cult Ctr, Pa, 72. *Bibliog:* Victoria Donohoe (auth), article, Philadelphia Inquirer, 3/7/71; Cedar Rapids Gazette, 4/23/72; The Flag in the Art of Our Country, Am Heritage Bk, 76. *Mem:* Pa Acad Fine Arts Alumni; Villanova Univ Pres Forum. *Media:* Mixed Media. *Res:* Abstract Artists of the World. *Specialty:* 19th & 20th century Am/European paintings. *Publ:* Auth, Artists As Illustrators, 89, American Artists Signatures & Monograms 1800-1989 & European Artists Signatures & Monograms 1800-1990, 90, Artists' Monograms and Indiscernible Signatures 1800-1991, 91, Old Masters' Signatures & Monograms 1400-born 1800, 96 & Latin American Artists Signatures & Monograms, Colonial Era - 1996, 97, Scarecrow Press; Old Glory (illus), US Postal Svc, 2004. *Mailing Add:* 1142 Synder Ave Philadelphia PA 19148-5522

CASTELLANOS, LAURA
PAINTER, GRAPHIC ARTIST
b New York, 1963. *Study:* Fla Int Univ, BFA. *Comn:* Poster, Bumbershoot Festival, Seattle, 1993. *Exhib:* Solo exhibs include Catherine Person Gallery, Seattle, 2005, CoCA, Seattle, 2007. *Awards:* Pollock-Krasner Found Fel, 2007

CASTILE, RAND
MUSEUM DIRECTOR
b NC, July 15, 1938. *Study:* Drew Univ, BA; Urasenke Tea Ceremony Hq, Kyoto, Japan; also study with Grand Master Sen Soshitsu, XV, diploma, Drew Univ, LHD, 94. *Hon Degrees:* Drew Univ, LHD, Madison, NJ. *Collection Arranged:* Four exhibs per yr, Japan House Gallery, 71-86. *Pos:* Lectr, Japanese art & tea ceremony, US & Japanese Univs & mus; dir, Japan House Gallery, Japan Soc Inc, NY, 70-85; consult-panelist, Nat Endowment Arts, 75; consult, Nat Endowment Humanities, 75-; bd adv, Japan Study Ctr, Columbia Univ; dir emer, The Avery Brundage Collection, Asian Art Mus San Francisco, 85-94; mem, Maine Arts Comn, 97. *Awards:* Fulbright Scholar, 66-67; Mayor's Award of Honor for Arts & Culture, New York, 82. *Mem:* Asn Art Mus Dir Emer; Metrop Mus Art (vis comt); Am Asn Mus; US-Japan Educ & Cult Conf; US Can Cult Coun; Century Asn. *Publ:* Auth, numerous articles in Art News, Geijutsu Shincho, Bijutsu Techo, Orientations, J of Nat Tokyo Nat Mus & Print Collector's Newslett, 63-; The Way of Tea, 72; Ikeda & Ida: Two Japanese Printmakers, 74; Japanese Art Now: Tadaaki Kuwayama & Rikuro Okamoto. *Mailing Add:* 120 SW Peacock Blvd # 203 Port Saint Lucie FL 34986

CASTILLO, MARIO ENRIQUE
PAINTER, MURALIST, EDUCATOR
b Rio Bravo, Coah, Mex, Sept 19, 1945. *Study:* Ill Inst Design, cert, 64; Sch Art Inst Chicago, BFA, 69; Sch Fine Arts, Univ Southern Calif Los Angeles, post grad studies, 69-70; Calif Inst Arts, Valencia, MFA, 72, post grad studies, 73-74; Pasadena City Col, 77; Calif State Univ Los Angeles, 80; East Los Angeles City Coll, 81 & 82 & Univ Calif Dominguez Hills, 87 & 88; Nat Univ, Inglewood, Calif, 89. *Work:* Nat Mus Am Art, Washington, DC; San Francisco Mus Art; Denver Art Mus; Albuquerque Mus, NMex; Portland Art Mus, Ore; Art Inst Chicago; San Diego Art Mus; San Diego Mus Contemp Art; Tucson Mus Art; Denver Mus; Mex Mus, San Francisco; San Antonio Mus; Nat Hispanic Cult Ctr, Mus Albuquerque, NMex; Notre Dame Univ; City Hall, City of Chicago; Western Ill Univ; Univ Guadalajara, La Cierega Campus; Evergreen State Coll, Olympia, Wash. *Comn:* Metafisica (mural), 68 & Wall of Brotherhood (mural), 69, City of Chicago, Ill; four paintings, Latino Inst, Chicago, 91; two murals, Mex Am Fine Arts, Chicago, 92; mayahuel mural, Nat Mus Mex Art, 96. *Exhib:* Sacred Images-New Visions, Riverside Art Mus, Calif, 89; solo exhibs, Inst Hispanic Cult Studies, Santa Monica, Calif, Orlando Gallery, Sherman, Okla, 89, Sangre De Cristo Arts Ctr, Pueblo, Colo, 91 & Prospectus Art Gallery, Chicago, 91-92; Day of the Dead, Mex Fine Arts Mus, Chicago, Ill, 90; Cara (traveling show), Fresno Art Mus, 91, Tucson Mus Art, 91 & Smithsonian Inst Nat Mus Am Art, 92. *Pos:* Artist/designer, Lukas & Assocs, 65-66; artist, City of Chicago, Bd of Educ, 67-68; artist/designer, El Mercado Co, Los Angeles, 81-83. *Teaching:* Art instr design, Santa Monica City Coll, summer 73; asst prof fine arts, Univ Ill, Champaign-Urbana, 73-76; art instr design, Immaculate Heart Coll, Los Angeles, 79-80; painting instr fine arts, Exceptional Children's Found, Los Angeles, 85-86; art instr fine arts, Plaza de La Raza, Los Angeles, summer 89; full time fac mem, Dept Art & Design, Columbia Coll, Chicago, 90-. *Awards:* First Place Painting, 74, First Place Drawing, 75 & First Place Photog, 75, Hispanic Art Exhib, Mus Sci & Indust, Chicago. *Bibliog:* Sebastian Rotella (auth), Ancient art inspires a modern man, LA Times, 12/8/89; Lyman Pitman (auth), Hands, feet, eyes, lead viewers to artist's mind, Chieftain, Pueblo, Colo, 4/28/91; Olga Herrera (auth), Castillo exhibit opens innovative local gallery, Lawndale News, Chicago, 10/24/91. *Media:* Acrylic, Mixed Media. *Res:* Mesoamerican art; Mexican murals. *Interests:* Archeology and music. *Collection:* Collector of prints & works on paper. *Publ:* Towards's A People's Art-The Contemporary Mural Movement, Dutton & Co, 77; Canto Al Pueblo Anthology, Penca Bks, San Antonio, 78; Community Murals: The People's Art, Assoc University Presses, Cranbury, NJ, 82; The Course of Mexican History (front cover art), Oxford Univ Press, 2011. *Dealer:* Prospectos Gallery Chicago Ill; LA LLorona Gallery Chicago Ill. *Mailing Add:* 10101 S Ave M Chicago IL 60617

CASTLE, WENDELL KEITH
SCULPTOR
b Emporia, Kans, Nov 6, 1932. *Study:* Univ Kans, BFA & MFA; various hon degrees. *Hon Degrees:* MD Inst of Art, DFA, 79; St John Fisher Col, LHD, 87; State Univ NY, DFA, 97. *Work:* Mus Fine Arts, Boston; Nordenfieldske Kunstindustrimus, Norway; Philadelphia Mus Art; Metrop Mus Art, Am Craft Mus, NY; Renwick Gallery, Smithsonian Inst; and others. *Comn:* Clock sculpture, Pillar Bryton Partners, Orlando, Fla; commemorative piano, Steinway & Sons, Long Island, NY; outdoor clock sculpture, Hammerson Can, Inc, Toronto; art furniture, Cincinnati Art Mus; clock sculpture, Maccabees Mutual Life Insurance Co, Southfield, Mich. *Exhib:* Art & Relig, Vatican, Rome, 78; Masterpieces of Time, Taft Mus, Cincinnati, Ohio, 85 & Renwick Gallery, Nat Mus Am Art, Smithsonian Inst, Washington, 85-86; Mus Fine Arts, Boston, 88; Furniture of Wendell Castle, Detroit Inst Arts, 89, Delaware Art Mus, 90, Va Mus Fine Arts, 90; Solo exhibs, Morgan Gallery, Kansas City, Mo, 94 & 97, Peter Joseph Gallery, NY, 94-96, Anne Reed Gallery, 95 & 96, Savannah Coll Art & Design, 96, Leo Kaplan Modern, NY, 97 & 99, Indigo Galleries, Fla, 98 & R Duane Reed Gallery, St Louis, 98, Riley Hawk Galleries, Seattle, 2000 & 2001 & Habatat Gallery, Boca Raton, Fla, 2001; The White House Collection of Am Crafts, George Walter Vincent Smith Art Mus, Mass, 96; The White House Collection of Am Crafts, Mint Mus, Charlotte, NC, 99 & Decorative Arts Mus, Little Rock, Ark, 99; SOFA, Seventh Regiment Armory, NY, 98-2001; Recent Acquisitions, Metrop Mus of Art, New York City, 99 & Recent Acquisitions: Selected Additions to the Modern Design Collection, 99. *Pos:* hon trustee, Renwick Art Gallery, Smithsonian Inst, 90; bd mgrs, Mem Art Gallery, Rochester, 86-92; Bd dir, Nat Mus Am Art & Rochester Mem Art Gallery, NY, 92. *Teaching:* Instr drawing, Univ Kans, 60-61; assoc prof furniture design, Rochester Inst Technol, 62-70; prof sculpture, Wendell Castle Workshop, 80-88; artist-in-residence, Rochester Inst Technol, 84-. *Awards:* Nat Endowment Arts Grants, 73, 75, 76 & 88; Gold Medal Award, Am Craft Coun, 97; Lifetime Achievement Award, Arts & Cultural Coun for Greater Rochester, 98; Masters of Medium Award, James Renwick Alliance, 99; Award of Distinction, Furniture Soc, 2001; and many others. *Bibliog:* Tod Riggio (auth), Carpenter, Castle, Frid, Krenov and Maloof Honored, Woodshop News, 6/2001; Designer's Whimsical Works Blur Line Between Furniture and Sculpture, The Plains Dealer, 6/2001; Gregory Kuharic (auth), Gregory Kuharic to speak about twentieth century crafts, Antiques & The Arts Weekly, 5/29/2001. *Mem:* Am Craftsman Coun; NY State Coun Arts; Am Craft Coun (trustee, 86-); Nat Mus Am Art Comn (comn alumni group, 2000); Arts & Cult Coun for Greater Rochester (arts award comt, 97); Am Craft Mus (hon mem dir's forum, 91). *Media:* Wood. *Publ:* coauth, The Wendell Castle Book of Wood Lamination, Van Nostrand Reinhold, 80; The Fine Art of the Furniture Maker, Mem Art Gallery, 81; Furniture by Wendell Castle, Giovannini/Taragin/Cooke, Hudson Hills Press, 89. *Dealer:* Gerald Peters Gallery 1011 Paseo de peralta Santa Fe Nm 87501; Habata Gallery 608 Banyan Trail Boca Raton FL 33431; Leo Kaplan Modern Fuller Building 41 E 57th St NY 10022; Morgan Gallery 114 SW Blvd St Louis MO 64108. *Mailing Add:* 80 Oakwood Ln Scottsville NY 14546

CASTRILLO, REBECCA
PRINTMAKER, PAINTER
b Santurce, PR, Feb. 26, 1954. *Study:* Art Students League, 71-73; Univ PR, Rio Piedras, BFA (1 year interchange prog Univ Piso, Italy, 73), 75; Pratt Inst, Brooklyn, MFA, with Clare Romano, Walter Ragalsky, George Mackneil & Claudio Júarez, 78; studied printmaking with Robert Blackburn, 79. *Work:* Asoc Artes Graficas Panamericanas, Venezuela; Museo Del Barrio-Bronx, NY; Lincoln Hosp, Printmaking Workshop Collections, NY; Saloon de la Sociedad de Bellas Artes, Rueil De Mal Maison, France, Pratt Inst, NY. *Comn:* El Rostro De La Bailarina, Carton De Venezuela, 86. *Exhib:* Printmaking Workshop Traveling Exhib, USA, 85; Biennial of

Latin Am Graphics, Mocha Mus Contemp Arts, NY, 86; Saloon Vardol en el Centro Cult de Orval, Saloon Mus, Orval, France, 90; Biennial of Latin Am Graphics, Mus Arsenal De La Marina, Inst PR Arts, San Juan, PR, 94; IX Biennial Ibeoamericana of Graphics, Pàlacio De Bellas Artes, Mexico City, 94. *Teaching:* Prof fine arts, Art Student League, San Juan, PR, 80-94, Univ Interamericana PR, 86-94 & Eckerd Col, St Petersburg, Fla, 88. *Awards:* First Prize in Painting, Certamen Ateneo Puertorriqueño, San Juan, PR, 75; First Prize, Mobil Oil Corp, 84; Merit of Professional Growth Award, Inst Cult PR, 94; and others. *Mem:* Nat Asn Women Artists, NY; Assoc Mujeres Artistas De PR (vpres, 83-94); Women Caucus for Arts, NY. *Media:* All Media. *Mailing Add:* 1012 Calle Puerto Principe URB Las Americas Rio Piedras PR 00921

CASTRUCCI, ANDREW
PAINTER, SCULPTOR
b West Hoboken, NJ, Sept 14, 1961. *Study:* Sch Visual Arts, BFA, 83. *Work:* Mus Modern Art, NY; Whitney Mus Am Art, NY; Stedelijk Mus Modern Art, Amsterdam, Holland; Mus Zu Berlin, Ger; Centre Georges Pompidou, Paris, France. *Comn:* mural, 99 Park Ave Office Bldg, Sammy Ofer, NY, 96; mural, World Trade Ctr, Allesandra Grassi, Milan, Italy, 97; mural, Water Surface, Galerie Christian Schneeberger, St Galen, Switzerland, 98; mural, Fish Hook Falls Asleep, Andrea Stillacci, Milan, Italy, 99; mural, Skyline, Bullet Space, NY, 2000. *Exhib:* If You Lived Here, Dia Art Found, NY, 89; In Transit, New Mus, NY, 93; The Realm of the Coin, Queens Mus, NY, 93; Fever, Traveling Exhib, Wexner Ctr, Columbus, Ohio, 94; In Memory of..., Mus Modern Art, NY, 94; Urban Encounters, New Mus, NY, 98; The End, Ind Vision Contemp Art, NY, 2000; Le Case D'arte de Pasquale Leccese, New York City (a) Self-Portrait, Milan, Italy; Life of the City, Mus Modern Art, NY, 02; The River Speaks, Generous Miracles (catalog), 99; Tower I, II, Sch of Visual Arts, 02-03; Blood, Rubber, Fixative, Tribes Gallery (with catalog), 03. *Collection Arranged:* Ave D - DADA, Bullet Space, 90; Your House is Mine, Bullet Space (catalog), 91; A Continuation of Something Else, Bullet Space (catalog), 97; Confusion, Sch visual Arts, 99; Zeor Infinite/Finite, Sch Visual Arts, 2000. *Pos:* co-dir, A&P Gallery, NY, 84-86; dir, Bullet Space Printshop, NY, 88-98; mem, cur, Bullet: An Urban Artists collaborative, NY, 85-2003. *Teaching:* teacher fine arts dept, drawing, Sch Visual Arts, 85-86; teacher hosp audiences, drawing, painting, sculpture, Hosp Audience, 98-2003; teacher graphic design, artists books, Sch Visual Arts, 98-2003; teacher painting & drawing, CW Post Col, Long Island Univ, 01-03; teacher, Experimental TV, Conn, 2000; teacher, Art Matters, 88-89; teacher, North Star Found, 84. *Awards:* Award, Andy Warhol Found, 92; Grant, Artists Colony, Macdowell/Yadoo, 94-95. *Bibliog:* Art in America, 2/2000; Art Forum, 10/91; The River Speaks (catalog), 99; Your House is Mine, 88-92. *Mem:* Bullet Space: An Urban Artists Collaborative. *Media:* Acrylic, Oil; Metal, Wood, Printmaking. *Res:* Painting, sculpture, prints, artists books, drawings. *Publ:* Newsweek, 1/25/93; Time Out NY, 8/28/97; NY Times, 8/14/98. *Dealer:* Bullet Space Alexandra Rojas 292 E 3rd St New York NY 10009-8963; Generous Miracles Gallery 524 W 20th St New York NY 10011. *Mailing Add:* 292 E 3rd St New York NY 10009-8963

CASWELL, HELEN RAYBURN
PAINTER, WRITER
b Long Beach, Calif, Mar 16, 1923. *Study:* Univ Ore Sch Fine Arts. *Comn:* mural, Villa Sienna, Redwood City, Calif, 99; mural, St Ignatius Ch, San Francisco, 2000; stain glass window, Meth Ch, Sebastopol, Calif, 98; mural, St Elizabeth Sch, Palo Alto, Calif. *Exhib:* De Young Mus Show, Soc Western Artists, 61; Solo exhibs, Northwest Mo State Coll, 66 & Rosicrucian Mus, San Jose, 70; Montalvo Cult Ctr, Saratoga, 68; Church of the Incarnation (Episcopal), Santa Rosa, Calif, 2007. *Awards:* James D Phelan Award for Narrative Poetry, 58; San Francisco Browning Soc Award, 66; Roberts Writings Award, 90. *Media:* Oil, Printmaking. *Publ:* Auth, Growing in Faith Library, Abingdon, 89; Jesus for Little People, Broadman-Holman, 94; A Little Book of Friendship, Thomas Nelson, 95; A Little Book of Prayers, Thomas Nelson, 95; The Parables of Jusus, Abingdon, 98; illusr St Francis Celebrate Christmas, Loyola Press, 99. *Mailing Add:* 13207 Dupont Rd Sebastopol CA 95472-9787

CASWELL, JIM (JAMES) DANIEL CASWELL-DAVIS
SCULPTOR, CERAMIST
b St Boniface, Man, Nov 9, 1948. *Study:* Calif State Univ, Northridge, with Peter Plagens, Walt Gabrielson, Karen Carson & Howard Tollefson, 66-71. *Comn:* Vases, Manufacture Nat de Sevres, Sevres, France, 86. *Exhib:* Scripps Ann, Lang Art Gallery, Claremont, Calif, 82; Pacific Currents, San Jose Mus Art, 82; Art and/or Craft, Kanazawa, Japan, 82; Clay for Walls, Renwick Gallery, 83; On and Off the Wall, Oakland Mus, 83; Triennale de la Porcelaine, Nyon, Switz, 86; 27th Ceramic Nat Exhib, Everson Mus, Syracuse, NY, 87; Am Ceramics Now, Am Craft Mus, NY, 87; East-West Contemp Ceramics, Olympic Invitational, Seoul, Korea, 88. *Awards:* Nat Endowment Arts Fel, 83; Fel, Centre Nat des Arts Plastiques, 85 & 86. *Media:* Ceramic. *Dealer:* Jane Corkin Gallery 179 John St Suite 302 Toronto ON Canada. *Mailing Add:* 2208 Cloverfield Blvd Santa Monica CA 90405

CASWELL, SALLY (CASWELL-LINHARES)
PAINTER, PRINTMAKER
b Brockton, Mass, Nov 1, 1941. *Study:* Studied with George Lockwood, 61-62; Mass Coll Art, Boston, BFA, 65; RI Coll, Providence, MAT, 77; Univ Mass, Dartmouth, MFA (Distinguished Thesis), 90. *Work:* US Naval War Coll Mus, Newport; Slide Libr, RI Sch Design, Providence; Slide Libr, Copley Soc Boston; Antique Automobiles: Reflections, Sweet-T, Sleek 31 (Watercolor Triptych), Autozone Corp, off Chief Exec Officer & Pres, Memphis, Tenn, 2002. *Comn:* Portrait & landscape paintings, comn by many pvt collectors, 62-; New Eng Watercolors, NEICO Microwave co, Hopkinton, Mass, 81; The Four Seasons (watercolor paintings), Blue Cross Boston, Framingham, Mass, 85; Spinakers Sailing Past Prudence Island (watercolor diptych), Citizens Bank, Pawtuxet, Providence, RI, 85; and others. *Exhib:* S Wharf Gallery, Nantucket, Mass, 80-90; Market Barn Gallery, Falmouth, Mass, 81-86; Pittsburgh Nat Aqua Media, Pittsburgh Ctr Arts, 83; Int Energy Art Show, Foothills Art Ctr, Golden, Colo, 83; Riggs Gallery, San Diego, Calif, 84-85; Japan-Am Exchange, Japan Watercolor Soc, Tokyo, 86; Bristol Art Mus; Faculty Exhib, Woods-Gerry Gallery, RI Sch Design, Providence, 87-94; Art Northeast USA, Silvermine Galleries, New Canaan, Conn, 88; All New Eng Exhib, Duxbury Art Complex Mus, Mass, 89 & 97; Emerging Artists, Univ Mass, Dartmouth, 90; Cornwall Gallery Invitational, Jamaica Plains, Mass, 92; Hera Gallery Invitational, 92; Then & Now, Mass Coll Art Tower Gallery, Boston, 93; Copley Soc Art, Boston, 1993, 94, 95, 97, 98; solo exhibs, Providence Art Club, Dodge House gallery, 97, 2000, 2002 & 2005; Embracing Diversity, Attleboro Mus, Mass, 98; Reveal and Conceal, 19 on Paper, Newport Art Mus, RI, 2002-2003; Ann Nat Exhib, Chautauqua Ctr Visual Arts, Chautauqua, NY, 2006; Ann Nat Exhib, RI Watercolor Soc, Pawtucket, RI, 2006-2007 & 2009; Invitational, with 19 on Paper, Gallery 297, Bristol, RI, 2007; Breslin Gallery, E Greenwich, RI, 2007; three-person exhib, RI Watercolor Soc, Pawtucket, RI, 2007; Beyond the Surface, with 19 on paper, Spring Bull Gallery, Newport, RI, 2009; Multiplicity, with 19 on paper, Cotuit Ctr Arts, 2009; with 19 on Paper, Judith Klein Art Gallery, New Bedford, Mass, 2010; Invitational Guest Artist, Spring Bull Gallery, Newport, RI, 2010; Nat Exhib, Cape Cod Art Asn, 2010, 2011; Contemporary Still Life, Copley Soc art, Nat WGBH Art Auction, Boston, 2012; Art Essex Gallery, Essex, Conn, 2012, 2013; Fresh Paint Auction, Copley Society, 2013; gallerie ellipsis, Newport, RI, 2013; 19 on Paper, Silver Anniv Exhib, Newport Art Mus, Newport, RI, 2013. *Collection Arranged:* Community Col RI Gallery, Knight Campus, Warwick, En Plein Air: Six RI Masters, 1998; Flanagan Campus, Lincoln, Contemp Printmakers, 2003; Marjorie Dalenius, Whimsical Sculptures & Assemblages (wit, wisdom, icons & fantasy) 2006. *Pos:* Bd mem, Pawtucket Arts Coun, 86-88 & Nat Mus Women Arts, RI, 97-98; dir art gallery, Community Coll RI, Warwick, 95-99; Flanagan Campus, Lincoln, 2003-2006. *Teaching:* Instr watercolor & design, RI Sch Design, 86-94; adj asst prof drawing, life drawing, 2-D design, color, watercolor, acrylic painting, Community Coll, RI, 87-2010; grad teaching asst, 2-D Design & Color, Univ Mass, Dartmouth, 88-89, grad asst to curator, 89,90; instr spec studies, watercolor painting, Chautaugua Inst, NY, 96-; pvt instr watercolor painting & art hist tour of Florence, Siena, and Tuscany, 2000; pvt workshops, watercolor landscape & drawing, 2007-. *Awards:* First Prize, RI Watercolor Soc, 89; Minna Walker - Smith Award, New Haven Paint & Clay Club, New Eng & New York, 80; Joseph Boland Watercolor Award, Bristol Art Mus, 83; Finalist, Art for Preserving Our Nat Resources, Am Artist Mag, 90; Providence Art Club Award, 96; First Prize & Best of Show, Fall River Art Asn Ann Regional Exhib, 96; First Prize, Cape Cod Art Asn Open Jurried Exhib, 97; Hon Mention, All New England Exhib, Duxbury Art Complex Mus, 89; 3rd prize painting, Wickford Art Asn, Art of the Ocean State, RI, 97. *Bibliog:* Arturo Vivante (auth), rev, Boston Rev Arts, 6/72; Bill Van Siclen (auth), Sensing emotion in city & sea, Providence J, 3/88; Robert C Fisher (auth), A little greatness, Am Artist Mag, 8/90. *Mem:* Wickford Art Asn; Copley Artist, Copley Soc Boston; Providence Art Club; signature mem, RI Watercolor Soc; 19 on Paper. *Media:* Watercolor, Oil, Acrylic; All Media, Lithography. *Publ:* Illusr, The Watchman, Identity Press, Cambridge, 71; The Trident: Centennial Edition, Yearbook of US Naval War Coll, 84; An Anniversary Collection 1984-1988; Winning Poems from the Pawtucket Arts Council Annual Poetry Competition, RI State Coun Arts, 88; Spiritual energy, Innerview Mag, summer 89; and others. *Dealer:* Sally Caswell Studio www.sallycaswell.com; Farmstead Mercantile Warren RI; Arnold Art Gallery Newport RI; Copley Soc Boston MA; Art Essex Gallery Essex CT; gallerie ellipsis Newport RI. *Mailing Add:* 611 Warren Ave Swansea MA 02777

CATANIA, PHILIP
PAINTER, SCULPTOR
b Brooklyn, NY, Nov 2, 1946. *Study:* Pratt Inst BFA (graphic arts), New York, 68; Coll New Rochelle, MA (art educ, therapeutic), 84; Studied with Ben Clements, Max Ginsberg, Alvin Hollingsworth, Richard Bove, Martha Earlbacker, Roger Rogalski, Claire Romano, William Folger. *Work:* High Sch Art & Design Gallery, New York. *Comn:* Peterskill Landscape, Kingston, NY, 73; Mixed Media Mobile, Kingston, NY, 73; Landscape, Wassaic, NY, 78. *Exhib:* Konstmasson, Sollentuna, Stockholm, Sweden, 2008; Art Nocturne Knokke, Scharpoord, Meelaan 32, Belgium, 2008; Art Monaco, Diaghilev Exhib, Grimaldi Forum, Monaco, 2010; Marb Art IV Feria, Margella, Picasso Mus, Spain, 2008; Open Art Fair, Van Gogh Mus, Netherlands, 2008; Le Salon Des Artistes Europeens, Mus Urbanisme de Beijing, China, 2008; Salon de la Culture et de l'Art Sino, Europeens Carrousel du Louvre, Paris, France, 2010; Who's Who Art Club Int, Salon of Artist Members, SAM, 2012; Giverny, France, SAM 2013, Paris, France; Mus Americas, Doral, Fla, 2014. *Pos:* Art monitor, Pratt Inst, 67-68. *Teaching:* Poughkeepsie Community Ctr, NY, 76-77, Davenport Central Sch, NY, 87-88, McLaren Sch, NY, 70-71; Wassaic Developmental Ctr, NY, 74-80; instr, Green Haven Correctional Facility, Stormville, NY, 80-86. *Awards:* Excellence in painting, Graduation Portfolio, Robert Simmons, 64; Best in show, Pratt Summer show, Pratt Inst, 67; Blue Ribbon, Ulster Co Fair, 72; Hon mention, Herkimer Co Art Show, 2008. *Bibliog:* Catherine Bourlet (auth), Philip Catania, Monograph, 2009; Hans Janstad (auth), Mojligheternas Land, Monograph, 2010; Art Acquisitor, Vol 6, 9-11, Amsterdam Whitney Gallery, 2008, 2011-14; A World of Artists, Michael Joseph publ, 2010; Artists Haven Gallery Artist Members Spring Ed, Michael Joseph Publ, 2012; Energia Creativa, Art Jour, Italy, pp 71, 2013. *Mem:* Windsor Whip Works Art Ctr; Who's Who Art Club Int; Community Arts Network of Oneonta. *Media:* Acrylic, Oil. *Dealer:* Svenska Konstgalleriet Mickaella Himmelstrom Friisgatan 9C Malmo S-21421 Sweden; Amsterdam Whitney Int Fine Arts Inc Ruthie Tucker 511 W 25th St Chelsea New York NY 10001; Trevisan Int Art Paola Trevisan Via Gurzone 31E-16 45030 Occhiobello Italy; Galerie Thuillier Denis Cornet 13 rue Thorighy 75003 Paris France. *Mailing Add:* PO Box 337 Edmeston NY 13335

CATCHI
PAINTER, PRINTMAKER
b Philadelphia, Pa, Aug 27, 1920. *Study:* Briarcliff Jr Col, 37; Commercial Illus Studios, 38-39; also with Leon Kroll, Harry Sternberg & Hans Hofman & with Angelo Savelli, Positano, Italy. *Hon Degrees:* Acad Int Medicea Bella Arte Firenze, Italy, hon degree, 83. *Work:* Rosenberg Found; Hofstra Univ, Hempstead, NY; Jane Voorhees

Zimmerli Art Mus Rutgers, State Univ NJ. *Exhib:* Solo exhibs, Co Art Gallery, Locust Valley, NY, 91, Kiya Galerie, Konoha, Tokyo, Japan, 95, She He Rock Gallery, Manhasset, NY, 95, Heckshер Mus Art, Huntington, NY, 2001 & Graphic Eye Gallery, Port Washington, NY, 2005; retrospectives, 60 Yr Retrospective, Manhasset, NY, 94, Diatel Gallery, Emma Willard Sch, Troy, NY, 2001 & Nat Asn Women Artists, New York, 2005; Manhasset Pub Libr, NY, 2008; Graphic Eye Gallery, Port Washington, NY, 2009. *Pos:* Artist-in-residence, Friends Acad, Locust Valley, NY, 84, Vt Studio Ctr, Johnson, Vt, 2002-2009. *Awards:* First Prize, Riverside Mus, NY; Dr Maury Leibouvitz Art Award, 86; Emily Lowe Award, 89; Beatrice Jackson Award, 2000; Helen Jennings Founder Award, 2002; Community Leadership Award, Port Washington Pub Libr, 2009. *Bibliog:* Nan Ickeringill (auth), Art & at home with Catchi, New York Times, 68; Doris Herzig (auth), She has painted since she was 12, Newsday, 68; Molly Sinclair (auth), Oil brush & canvas, Atlanta Constitution, 69. *Mem:* Audubon Artists; Int Platform Asn; New York Soc of Women Artists (pres, 84-87); Artists Equity, New York (bd, 86-90); Art Adv Coun, Port Washington Pub Libr (past pres); Nat Coun Prominent Am (exec adv coun); Nat Asn Women Artists (past pres). *Media:* Oil, Watercolor, Stone, Cast Metals. *Publ:* Illusr (cover), La Revue Art Moderne Mag, France, 7/75 & 6/78; doc book, Int Sculpture Symp, Tex, 76

CATE, PHILLIP DENNIS
HISTORIAN, DIRECTOR
b Washington, DC, Oct 19, 1944. *Study:* Rutgers Univ, BA (art hist), 67; Ariz State Univ, MA (art hist), 70. *Collection Arranged:* Meryon's Paris/Piranesi's Rome (with catalog), 71; The Ruckus World of Red Grooms (with catalog), 73; Japonisme: Japanese Influence on French Art, 1854-1910 (with catalog), 75; The Color Revolution, color lithography in France 1890-1900 (with catalog), 78; Circa 1800: The Beginning of Modern Printmaking, 1775-1835 (catalog), 80; Theophile Alexander Steinlen, 1859-1923 (auth, catalog), 82; The Circle of Toulouse-Lautrec (auth, catalog), 85; Matsukata Collection of Ukiyo-e Prints from Tokyo National Mus (auth, catalog), 88; Eiffel Tower: A Tour de Force (auth, catalog), 89; Pissarro to Picasso Color Etching in France, 92; The Spirit of Monmartec Cabarets Humor and the Advant-garde 1875-1905 (auth catalog), 96. *Pos:* Asst to dir, Pa Acad Fine Art, 67-68; dir, Jane Voorhees Zimmerli Art Mus, Rutgers Univ, 70-; Supervision of Curatorial and Acad Activities, 2003-present. *Mem:* Print Coun Am; Asn Art Mus Dirs; Coll Art Asn; Grolier Club. *Res:* 19th century French Art & Soc. *Publ:* Ed & essayist, The Graphic Arts & French Soc, 1871-1914, Rutgers Press, NB, 88; essayist, L'Estampe Originale: Artistic Printmaking in France 1893-1895, Van Gogh Mus, Amsterdam, 91; From Pissarro to Picasso; Color Etching in France, Bibliotheque Nationale, Paris, 92; The Spirit of Martwartu Cabarets, Humor and the Avant-garde 1875-1905, 96; Breaking the Mold; Sculpture in Paris from Dauimer to Rodin, 2005

CATEURA, PATTY
PAINTER
b New York, New York. *Study:* Md Inst Coll Art, Baltimore, MFA, 1993; Skowhegan Sch Painting & Sculpture, Skowhegan, Maine, 1994. *Exhib:* Solo exhibs include Gregory Lind Gallery, San Francisco, 2003, Carol Shen Gallery, Packer, Brooklyn, NY, 2004, Cooler Gallery, White River Junction, Vt, 2006; group exhibs include Artworks Artworkers, Basilico Fine Arts, NY, 1996; Scapes, Ernst Rubenstein Gallery, New York, 2000; Life of the City, Mus Mod Art, New York, 2002; Musical Modes, Clifford Chance, New York, 2005; Mother Lode, Cheryl McGinnis Gallery, New York, 2006; Groundswell Benefit, Exit Art, New York, 2007; Finish This, Cooler Gallery, White River Junction, Vt, 2007; Works on Paper, Cuchifritos Gallery, New York, 2008. *Awards:* MacDowell Fel, Peterborough, NH, 2000; NY Found Arts Grant, 2008. *Mailing Add:* Elizabeth Foundation for the Arts 323 W 39th St #614 New York NY 10018

CATON, DAVID
PAINTER
b Pasadena, Calif, Sept 13, 1955. *Study:* Univ Houston, BFA, 79; Yale Univ, MFA, 81. *Work:* Tex Commerce, Houston, Tex; Tex A&M Univ, Houston. *Exhib:* Wilhelm Gallery, Scottsdale, Ariz, 87 & 88; Bill Ross Gallery, Memphis, Tenn, 88; Bienville Gallery, New Orleans, 88; Harris Gallery, Houston, 90 & 95; Harris Gallery, Houston, 98, 99, 00, 01, 02; A Sense of Place, Williams Tower, Houston, 2001. *Awards:* Visual Arts Fel Painting, Nat Endowment Arts, 85 & 87. *Dealer:* Harris Gallery 1100 Bissonnet Houston TX 77005

CATTAN, EMILIA
PAINTER, PRINTMAKER
b Mexico City. *Study:* Escuela Nal Bellas Artes 80; Draw-Paint E Elizondo, 95; Art Claustro De Sar Juana, Art 88; Univ Ibero Americana, Lit, 90. *Work:* Galeria Centro Deportivo Isdaelita, Mexico, DF; Mus Techologico Chapultepec, Mexico, DE; Banco Mercantil, Mexico, DF; Alianza Francesa, Mexico, DF; Inst Mex Northamericano De Relacidnes Exteridres, Mexico, DF. *Comn:* Cruz-Roja Mex Sieche Mex DF, 86; Les Artistes DUXX, Paris, 93; Pro Mo-Arte, 95; Directorio Re Las Artes Plasticas, Mexico, DF, 94. *Publ:* Les Artistes Del XX Siècle, Arts Est Images De Monde, Paris; Directorid De Las Artes Plasticas, Mexico, DF. *Mailing Add:* Reforma 2233 Mexico DF 11020 Mexico

CATTANEO, (JACQUELYN A) KAMMERER
PAINTER, INSTRUCTOR
b Gallup, NMex, June 1, 1944. *Study:* Tex Women's Univ, Denton, 62-64; studied with Frederick Taubes, 72-73, Sergei Bongart, 78, Bettina Steinke, 85, Ben Konis, 76-77, Daniel Greene, 84, Everett Raymond Kinstler, 85, Albert Handell, 96-98 & 2006-2007. *Work:* Gallup Pub Libr Permanent Collection, NMex; NMex State Capitol, Gov & Mrs Bruce King Collection & Lt Gov & Mrs Casey Luna; Blessed Katharine Drexel (portrait), Sacred Heart Cathedral; Rehoboth McKinley Christian Hosp; Univ NMex, Gallup Branch, NMex; Rico Motor Co. *Comn:* Portrait of Calvin C Hall, Univ NMex; portraits, Sunwest Bank, First State Bank, City of Gallup & El Rancho Hist Hotel, Gallup, NMex; Sisters Blessed Sacrement, Bensalem, Pa; Blessed Mother Teresa of Calcutta, Sacred Heart Cathedral, 2004; portrait of Joseph A Caretto comn by Rollie Mortuary, Gallup, NMex, 2006-2007 ; portrait, Enrico Menapace comn by Rico Motor co, Gallup, NMex; Gurley Family Portrait, Gurley Hall, Univ NMex; portrait, St Katharine Drexel. *Exhib:* Catharine Lorillard Wolfe Art Club, NY, 84-2007; Best & the Brightest Invitational, O'Briens Art Emporium, Scottsdale, 86; Ann Exhib, Pastel Soc W Coast, Sacramento, Calif, 89-2007; Asn pour Du Prom Du Patrimone Artistique Francois, Paris, France, 91; Ann Exhib, Pastel Soc West Coast, Sacramento, Calif, 89-94; Int Nexus, 92 Fine Art Exhib, Trammell Crow Pavilian, Dallas, Tex; Women Reflect, Carlsbad Mus Fine Arts, Carlsbad, NMex, 92; solo exhib, Carol's Art & Antiques, Liverpool, NY, 97; Pastel Soc NMex Visions Show, Geary Gallery, Santa Fe, 2007; Schaknoa Mus Plantation, Fla, 2011-; Legacy Fine Art, Hot Springs, Ark, 2011; Amsterdam Whitney Fine Art, NY, 2011; Artists Haven Gallery, Ft Lauderdale, Fla, 2011. *Pos:* Vchmn, Gallup Area Arts Coun & Coop Gallery, 70-88; judge fine arts, Inter-tribal Ceremonial Gallup, NMex, 80, 84, 92, 2000, & 2012; comt mem, Gallup NMex Multi-Cultural Ctr, 87-88; mem, Soviet Union Deleg to Leningrad, Moscow, Russ & Kiev, Ukraine, 90; mem, US Women Artists Middle East Deleg Exchange Prog, Jerusalem, Ibillin, Tel Aviv, Israel, Cairo & Egypt & Italy, 92; mem, US Women Artists Deleg to Rio de Janeiro, Igaccu Falls, Manaus & Amazon Village, Brazil, 94; US Women Artist Deleg Spain, Greece, Turkey, 96; US Women Artist Deleg, The Maritimes, ThunderBay, Konoca, Ont, 2000; Nova Scotia, Prince Edward Island; bd mem, New Deal Art Preserv, NMex. *Teaching:* Instr art for children, Studio Corner, Gallup, NMex, 65-78 & pvt instr, 97-; instr portraiture, Carizo Lodge, Ruidoso, NMex, 78, San Juan Col, Farmington & Univ NMex, Gallup, 85-86. *Awards:* Pastel Soc Am, 2004; Second Place Pastel, Catherine Larillar Wolfe Art Club, New York, 2005; Merit Award, Pastel Soc, West Coast's Signature Mem, 2006; selected for Best 100 Paintings in Am, 2006-10, 2011. *Bibliog:* Herbert Lieberman (auth), A Guide to Contemporary Art, 81; Artists Dictionary, 2011. *Mem:* Oil Painters Am; Allied Artists Am; Salmagundi Club, NY; Pastel Soc of the West Coast (signature mem); Am Portrait Soc (signature mem); Pastel Society Am (signature mem); Landscape Artist Int (cert signature mem); Pastel Soc NMex; Catharine Lorillard Wolfe Art Club (signature mem, 84-); NMex New Deal Art Reservation (bd mem). *Media:* Oil, Pastel. *Interests:* reading, walking, travel, gardening. *Publ:* Contribr, Southwest Art, Pastel Society of West Coast Profile, 11/87; Artists of New Mexico Vol III, Mountain Productions, Albuquerque, NMex, 90; Northlight, Northlight Book Club, Vol 23, No 162, 10/91; NMex Art Buyers Guide (cover & insert), 98; Momentum NCEA Mag (cover & ed); Int Artist Mag, 2005; New Mexico Traveler & Gallup Life; and others. *Mailing Add:* c/o Studio Corner 210 E Green Gallup NM 87301

CATTELAN, MAURIZIO
ARTIST
b Padua, Italy, 1960. *Work:* Projects 65, Mus Modern Art, NY, 98; Centre Pompidou, Musée National d'Art Moderne, Paris, 2000; Over the Edges, Stedelijk Mus voor Acutuele Kunst, 2000; Felix, Mus Contemp Art, Chicago, 2002; Dreams & Conflicts: Dictatorship of the Viewer, La Biennale di Venezia, Venice, 2003; Whitney Biennial Exhib, Whitney Mus Am Art, 2004. *Exhib:* 49th Int Art Exhib Biennale, Venice, 2001; Irony, Fundación Joan Miró, Barcelona, 2001; HOLLYWOOD IS A VERB, Gagosian Gallery, London, 2002; Dreams & Conflicts: Dictatorship of the Viewer, La Biennale di Venezia, Venice, 2003; Bodily Space: New Obsessions in Figurative Sculpture, Albright-Knox Art Gallery, Buffalo, NY, 2004; The Big Nothing, Inst Contemp Art, Philadelphia, 2004; None of the above, Swiss Inst, NY, 2004; 54th Int Art Exhib Biennale, Venice, 2011. *Mailing Add:* c/o Marian Goodman Gallery 24 W 57th St New York NY 10019

CATTERALL, JOHN EDWARD
PAINTER, EDUCATOR
b Sheridan, Wyo, Jan 12, 1940. *Study:* Univ Wyo, BA, 66; Wash State Univ, MFA, 68. *Work:* Brooklyn Mus, NY; Detroit Inst Arts, Mich; Cranbrook Acad Art; Univ Colo, Boulder; Tex Tech Univ. *Comn:* Triptych, Barnett Winston Co, Jacksonville, Fla, 78; diptych, R J Reynolds Corp, Winston-Salem, NC, 80; IBM Corp, Boca Raton, Fla, 86; Apache Corp, 95. *Exhib:* New Am Graphics, Elvehjem Art Ctr, Madison, Wis, 75; Int Print Biennial, Ministry Cult & Art, Krakow, Poland, 76; Int Print Exhib, Cranbrook Acad Art, 80; solo exhib, Yellowstone Art Ctr, Billings, Mont, 80; Recent Acquisitions, Brooklyn Mus, 81; Western Skies--Western Eyes, Colo Inst Arts, Denver, 82; Int Print Invitational, Korean Print Soc, Seoul, 83. *Pos:* Bd dir, Artspace Mag, 86; adv bd, Ucross Found, 93-. *Teaching:* Asst prof painting & printmaking, Univ SFla, 71-75; prof & dir, Mont State Univ, 75-82; prof & dept head, NMex State Univ, 82-88; chmn & prof, Art Dept, Univ Fla, 88-. *Awards:* Purchase Awards, Boston Printmakers Exhib, 70 & Potsdam Prints, State Univ NY, 75; Best of Show, Printmaking Exhib, Univ Colo, 75. *Bibliog:* Coke Van Deren (auth), The Painter & The Photographer, 72. *Mem:* Northwest Print Coun, Portland, Ore (bd mem, 80-82); World Print Coun; Coll Art Asn; Nat Coun Arts Admin. *Media:* Acrylic, Oil. *Dealer:* Art Sources Jacksonville Fla; Adair Margo Gallery El Paso TX

CAUDILL, DAVE
SCULPTOR
Study: Univ Ky, Lexington, BA, 1970; Louisville Sch Art, MA, 1973. *Work:* Univ Louisville Sch Music; Louisville Zoo; Lexington Arboretum, Ky; Singletary Ctr for the Arts, Univ Ky; Rauch Planetarium, Louisville; and var corp & pvt collections. *Exhib:* Solo exhibs, Deemer Gallery, 1992, Jefferson Cmty Coll, 1995, Louisville Free Pub Libr, 1999, Cathedral of the Assumption, Louisville, 2000; Rendezvous, Kennedy Gallery, Nassau, Bahamas, 1997; Gallery on the Square, Danville, Ky, 2000-2001; Capitol Arts Alliance, Bowling Green, 2001; Ky Art & Craft Found, 2002; Common Wealth, Bernheim Forest Arboretum, Clermont, 2002; Mid-States Art Exhib, Evansville Mus Art, Hist & Sci, Ind, 2002. *Awards:* Ky Arts Coun award, 1998 & 2000; Pollock-Krasner Found Grant, 2008. *Mem:* Ky Mus Arts & Design (bd mem); Ky Guild Artists & Craftsmen; Louisville Artisans Guild. *Media:* Steel. *Dealer:* Cerlan Gallery 522 W Short St Lexington KY 40507. *Mailing Add:* c/o Promenade Gallery 204 Center St Berea KY 40403

CAUDURO, RAFAEL
PAINTER, MURALIST
b Mexico City, Mex, Apr 18, 1950. *Study:* Univ Iberoamericana, indust design, 68-72. *Work:* Mus Mod Art, Cuevas Mus, Alfa Cult Ctr, Mex; Contemp Art Mus (MARCO), Monterrey, Mex. *Comn:* Postage stamp, Dept Communs, Mexico City, 85; Communications (mural), Dept Communs, Mex, Vancouver, Brit Columbia, Can, 86; London Underground (mural), Paris Metro (mural), City Coun, Mexico City, 89; History Travels in the Caboose (mural), Ministry Commun & Transport, Mexico City, 93. *Exhib:* Images for the Children, Children's Mus Manhattan, 90; The Blessing of Spring, Casa de la Cultura Mex-Japan, Mexico City, 91; one-man shows, Colegio Bachilleres, Mex, 92, Flint Inst Art, Mich, 93, La Poética Tiempo, Kennesaw State Coll Gallery Art, Atlanta, Ga, 93, Inst Cult Mex, NY, 94, Inst Tecnológico y Estudios Superiores Monterrey, Mex, 95, Gráficas y Dibujo, Mus Nac Estampa, Mex, 95 & De Angeles Calvarios y Calaveras, Mus Palacio Bellas Artes, Sala Nac, Mex, 95; Drawings and Prints, Museo Nacional Estampa, Mexico City, 95; De Angeles, Calvarios y Calaveras, Palace Fine Arts, Nat Hall, Mexico City, 95; and many others. *Bibliog:* Jorge A Manrique (auth), Cauduro: cual realismo, La Jornada, 4/91; Donald Kuspit, Rafael Cauduro (exhib catalogue), Mex Cult Inst, NY, 94; Alfonso Ruiz Soto, Ilusionismo critico (catalogue), Palace Fine Arts Show, 95. *Media:* Oil, Acrylic. *Publ:* Coauth, Rafael Cauduro, MoArt Mus, Mex, 91; Elena Poniatowska, Cauduro, Leon's City Mus, 92; Donald Kuspit, Rafael Cauduro, Mex Cult Inst New York, 94. *Dealer:* Louis Newman Galleries 322 N Beverly Dr Beverly Hills CA 90210. *Mailing Add:* c/o Saturno 12 Jardines de Cuernavaca Cuernavaca 62360 Mexico

CAVALIERE, BARBARA
CRITIC, HISTORIAN
b New York, NY. *Study:* State Univ NY Stony Brook, BA, 75; Queens Col, City Univ New York. *Pos:* Contrib ed, Arts Mag, New York, formerly; contribr, Acad Am Encycl, 21 vols, Arete Publ Co Inc, Princeton, NJ, 78-80, Contemp Artists, St Martin's Press; prod ed, Metrop Mus, currently. *Awards:* Helena Rubenstein Fel, Whitney Mus Am Art, 75; Art Critic's Fel, Nat Endowment Arts, 80. *Mem:* Int Asn Art Critics (chmn, mem comt, 81-84, treas 84-90); Found Community Artists, NY; Nat Writer's Union. *Res:* 19th & 20th century art, especially abstract expressionism & contemp art of 1940's to present. *Publ:* Auth, Theodoros Stamos in perspective, 12/77, The making of ometa, 10/80, Vir heroicus sublimis: Building the idea complex, 1/81 & Possibilities II, 9/81, Arts Mag; Notes on Mark Rothko & Early abstract expressionism: The 1940's, Flash Art, 1-2/79. *Mailing Add:* Metropolitan Mus Art Editorial Dept 1000 Fifth Ave New York NY 10028

CAVAT, IRMA
PAINTER, EDUCATOR
b New York, NY. *Study:* New Sch Social Res; Archipenko Art Sch; Acad Grande Chaumiere, Paris; also with Ozenfant, Paris & Hans Hofmann; William de Kooning Studio. *Work:* Mus Modern Art; Flint Mus; Art Inst Detroit; Delgado Mus; SB Mus. *Comn:* wall of portraits, Fac Club, Univ Calif, Santa Barbara, 68; mural, pvt hotel, Athens, Greece, 70; wall piece, Los Angeles, Calif, 70; Santa Barbara Mall & Ventura Mall, Calif, 76. *Exhib:* Festival of Two Worlds, Spoleto, Italy, 58-59; Ten Americans, Palazzo Venezia, Rome, 60; solo exhibs, Santa Barbara Mus, Calif & Phoenix Mus, Ariz, 66-67; Kennedy Galleries, 82 & 84; Feingarten Gallery, Los Angeles, 86; Preston Burke, Detroit, 87; Arts and Letters, Santa Barbara, 2000. *Teaching:* Prof painting & drawing, Univ Calif, Santa Barbara, retired. *Awards:* Yaddo Fel, Trask Found, 50; Fulbright Fels, 56-58; Creative Arts Inst Award, Univ Calif, 70; Humanities Award, Univ Calif, 88. *Media:* Oil, Mixed Media, Clay, Wood. *Res:* Italian and German Museums. *Specialty:* California painters. *Interests:* painting, drawing, sculpture. *Mailing Add:* 802 Carosam Rd Santa Barbara CA 93109

CAVENER STICHTER, BETH
CERAMIST
b Pasadena, Calif, 1972. *Study:* Cecil Acad Arts, Florence, Italy, 94; Haverford Col, BA (sculpture), 95; Ohio State Univ, MFA (ceramics), 2002. *Exhib:* Solo exhibs include Acme Art Co, Columbus, Ohio, 2000, tremble, shiver, 500 W Nationwide Blvd, Columbus, 2002, River Gallery and Mus, Chattanooga, Tenn, 2004, Contemp Crafts Gallery, Portland, 2004, The Wildness Within, G-Spot Gallery, Baltimore, 2005, Garth Clark Gallery, NY, 2006; group exhibs include Expressing the Human Form, Baltimore Clayworks, 2001, Ravens, 2002; Animal Body, Human Space, Archie Bray Found Warehouse Gallery, Helena, Mont, 2003; The Art Spirit Gallery, Coeur d'Alene, Idaho, 2003; The Art of Imitating Life, Herron Gallery, Indianapolis, 2004; American Masters, Santa Fe Clay, 2005; Animated Earth, Craft Alliance, St Louis, Mo, 2005; Made at the Clay Studio, The Clay Studio, Philadelphia, 2005; A Tale to Tell: Contemp Narratives in Clay, John Michael Kohler Arts Ctr, Sheboygan, Wis, 2005; Dominion: Man in Nature, Gallery Materia, Scottsdale, Ariz, 2005. *Teaching:* Artist-in-residence, lectr, instr, Archie Bray Found, 2002; summer guest artist-in-residence, The Clay Studio, 2004. *Awards:* Edith Fergus Gilmore Grant, 2001 & 2002; Emerging Artist Grant, Am Crafts Council, 2003; Individual Artists Fellowship, Ohio Arts Council, 2005; Virginia A Groot Found Grant, 2005. *Mailing Add:* PO Box 977 Helena MT 59624

CAWLEY, JOAN MAE
ART DEALER, PUBLISHER
b McKeesport, Pa. *Study:* Okla State Univ, BA, 48; Univ Okla, teaching cert, 52; Univ Mich, MA, 57. *Pos:* Docent prog chmn, Wichita Art Mus, 63-68; pres, Wichita Art Mus, 68-69. *Mem:* Scottsdale Gallery Asn. *Specialty:* Art of the southwestern United States; posterprints; Publ of posters and prints, 1 location in Scottsdale, Ariz, 1 location in Tempe, Ariz. *Mailing Add:* Joan Cawley Gallery Ltd 7135 E Main St Scottsdale AZ 85251

CAWOOD, GARY KENNETH
PHOTOGRAPHER
b Chattanooga, Tenn, Jan 17, 1947. *Study:* Auburn Univ, BArchit, 70; E Tenn State Univ, MFA, 76. *Work:* Baltimore Mus Art, Md; Nat Mus Am Art; Libr Cong; New Orleans Mus Art; Corcoran Gallery Art, Washington, DC. *Exhib:* Solo exhibs, Hass Gallery, Bloomsburg Univ, Pa, 2000, Stevenson Union Gallery, S Ore Univ, Ashland, 2000, Gallery A4, Southern Ill Univ, 2001, Historic Ark Mus, Little Rock, 2002, A4 Gallery, Boston Coll Art, Mass, 2002, New Harmony Gallery Contemp Art, Ind, 2002, Aquinas Coll, 2004, Gallery 1401, Univ of Arts, Philadelphia, 2005, Hannah Davis Gallery, Memphis, Tenn, 2009, Multicultural Arts Ctr, Merced, Calif, 2010, Artspace Gallery, Richmond, Va, 2010, Morris Graves Mus Art, Bureke, Calif, 2013, Viewpoint Gallery, Sacramento, Calif, 2013, Charro Gallery, Kans City, Mo, 2014; two-person exhibs, Ascherman Gallery, Cleveland, Ohio, 82 & Project Art Ctr, Cambridge, Mass, 82, New Harmony Gallery, Indiana, 2002, Vestiges (with Rene West), Austin Coll, Sherman, Tex, 2009; Current Works, Soc Contemp Photog, Kansas City, 87-89; Obstacles (auth, catalog), traveling exhib; Photog in the Minimalist Era, Iowa State Univ, Ames; Three Photographs, Munson-Williams Proctor Inst, Utica, NY, 98; Recent Acquisitions, Corcoran Gallery Art, Washington, DC; invitational exhib Art and Science, York Arts, York, Pa, 2000, Brooks Perspective, Memphis Brooks Mus, 2001, Cazenovia College, Cazenovia, NY, 2006; Soho Photo Nat Juried Exhib, New York, 2007; Masterworks of Am Portraiture, Amon Carter Mus, Fort Worth; Material Afterlife, Urban Inst for Contemp Art, Grand Rapid, Mich, 2009; Photowork, Barrett Art Ctr, Poughkeepsie, NY, 2010; Small, Cordon-Potts Gallery, San Francisco, Calif, 2010. *Pos:* prof emeritus, Univ Ark, Little Rock. *Teaching:* Adj prof photog, Univ Del, 75-76; assoc prof, La Tech Univ, 76-85; assoc prof, Univ Ark, Little Rock, 85-96, prof, 96-2012; fac, Sch Photog Studies, Prague, Czech Repub, 95-98. *Awards:* Magic Silver Juror's Award, Murray State Univ, 2008. *Bibliog:* Mark Power (auth), The Spiritual Landscape, Photo Rev, winter, 89; John Cunnally (auth), Take Only Pictures, Leave Only Footprints, No 12, 9/90; John Dorsey (auth), Photos Show Us What We Miss If We Can't See - Or Don't, Maryland Life, Baltimore Sun; Michal Janta (auth), U(S) Porny Realisimns Garyho Cawooda, Cesky Tydenik, 8/5/96; Roy Proctor (auth), Cawoods' still pictures will put your mind in motion, Richmond Times Dispatch, Va, 11/11/99; Pam Dillon (auth), The everyday and odd shown in new light, Dayton Dailey News, Ohio, 1/16/2000; Edawrd J Sozanski (auth), Life After Dark, Philadelphia Inquirer, 2/8/2005. *Media:* Digital Pigment Prints. *Interests:* creative writing. *Publ:* Contribr, Southern Eye, Southern Mind: A Photographic Inquiry, Memphis Acad Arts, 81; American Infra Red Survey, Photo Survey Press, 82; Century of Vision, SW Louisiana Univ Mus Art; Scenes Unseen, White Rose Press; The Watchmans Room (monogr), Whatelseitis, 2002. *Dealer:* Gallery 26 Little Rock Ark. *Mailing Add:* 1703 Raiv Park Little Rock AR 72204

CAZORT, MIMI
CURATOR, HISTORIAN
b Little Rock, Ark. *Study:* Washington Univ, St Louis, Mo, BFA, 53; Univ Mich, Ann Arbor, MA, 61, PhD, 70. *Pos:* Cur prints & drawings, Nat Gallery Can, Ottawa, 67-97; mem, Int Adv Comt, Keepers Pub Graphic Collections. *Teaching:* Adj prof art hist, Carleton Univ, Ottawa, 77-. *Awards:* Osler Fel, Hist Med, 88. *Mem:* Print Coun Am. *Res:* European drawings, concentration in North Italian, late eighteenth century; anatomical illustration, 1400-1900. *Publ:* Coauth (with Catherine Johnston), Bolognese Drawings in North American Collections, Ottawa, 80; auth, Bella Pittura: The Art of the Gandolfi, Ottawa, 94; The Ingenious Machine of Nature: Four Centuries of Art and Anatomy, Ottawa, 96. *Mailing Add:* 91 Concord N Ottawa ON K1S 0Y7 Canada

CECIL, CHARLES HARKLESS
PAINTER, EDUCATOR
b Kansas City, Mo, May 12, 1945. *Study:* Haverford Coll, Pa, BA (with honors), 67; Yale Univ Grad Sch, 67-69; with RH Ives Gammell, Boston, Mass, 69-71 & Richard F Lack, Minneapolis, Minn, 72-73. *Work:* Haverford Coll Libr, Pa; West Bend Gallery Fine Arts, Wis; House, Children's Hosp, Philadelphia, Pa; Am Philos Soc, Philadelphia, Pa; Thomas Jefferson Univ, Philadelphia, Pa. *Comn:* Portrait, Dr Gilbert White, past pres, Haverford Coll, 72; portraits comn by Count & Countess Carl Klingspor, (Sweden), 88; portrait, Henry S Cecil MD, President Emer, Children's Seashore House, Children's Hosp, Philadelphia, Pa, 90; portrait, Jonathan Evans Rhoads, MD, past pres, Am Philos Soc, Philadelphia, Pa, 92; portrait, Francis E Rosato, MD, Samuel D Gross prof surgery & chmn Dept Surgery, Thomas Jefferson Univ, Philadelphia, Pa. *Exhib:* Twin City Art Exhib, Minneapolis, Minn, 75; 154th & 155th Ann, Nat Acad Design, New York, 79-80; solo exhib, Univ Club Chicago, Ill, 80; Boston Painters of the Light, Dallas, Tex, 84; Am Realism Abroad, Colby Coll, Waterville, Maine, Butler Inst Am Art, Youngstown, Ohio & Wichita Art Mus, Kans, 90; 10th Anniversary Exhib, Charles H Cecil Studios, London, 2001; Florence and Beyond, Cohasset, Mass, 2003. *Teaching:* Dir, Charles H Cecil Studios, Borgo San Frediano, Florence, Italy, currently; instr, Brit Inst, Florence, Italy, currently; co-dir, Studio Cecil-Graves, Florence, Italy, formerly; instr, Villa Schifanoia Grad Sch Fine Arts, Florence, Italy, formerly. *Awards:* Julius T Hallgarten First Prize for Oil Painting, 79 & Benjamin Altman Second Prize Landscape, 80, Nat Acad Design; Grant for Painting, John F & Ann Lee Stacey Found, 80; Three ann grants, Elizabeth Greenshields Found, Montreal; RHI Gammell Found Grant, 86-2001; Excellence of Art Educ Award, Portrait Society of Am, 2008. *Media:* Oil. *Publ:* Coauth, Realism in Revolution, The Art of the Boston Sch, 86. *Dealer:* Ann Long Fine Art 54 Broad St Charleston SC 29401. *Mailing Add:* Borgo San Frediano 68 Florence 50124 Italy

CECIL-WISHING, DEVIN
PAINTER, ILLUSTRATOR
b 1981. *Study:* Calif Coll Arts, 2005. *Exhib:* Audubon Artists Online Ann Exhib, 2012. *Pos:* illusr, Bay Nature Mag, San Francisco Chronicle. *Teaching:* instr cast drawing, Grand Central Acad Art, NY, currently. *Awards:* Alfred Ross Prize for Excellence in Cast Drawing; Marquis Who's Who in Am Art References award in Graphics, Audubon Artists, New York, 2012. *Bibliog:* Am Artist mag. *Mem:* Audubon Artists. *Mailing Add:* 53 W 21st St Fl 3 New York NY 10010

CELENTANO, FRANCIS MICHAEL
PAINTER, EDUCATOR
b New York, NY, May 25, 1928. *Study:* NY Univ Inst Fine Arts, MA, 57; Acad Fine Arts, Rome, Italy, Fulbright Fel, 57-58. *Work:* Mus Mod Art, New York; Albright-Knox Art Gallery, Buffalo; Fed Reserve Bank, San Francisco; Seattle Art Mus, Wash; Rose Art Gallery, Brandeis Univ, Waltham, Mass; The Whitney Mus Am Art, New York; Hallie Ford Mus Art; Willamette Univ Salam, Ore; Halie Ford Mus, Salem, Ore. *Comn:* Painting, Hwy Bldg, Wash State Hwy Dept, 70; mural, Port of Seattle, Seattle-Tacoma Airport, 71; mural, Seattle City Light, 74; mural, Lincoln Mutual Savings Bank, Seattle, 79. *Exhib:* The Responsive Eye, Mus Mod Art, New York, 65; Kinetic & Optical Art Today, 65 & Plus by Minus: Today's Half Century, 68, Albright-Knox Art Gallery; Whitney Ann, Whitney Mus Am Art, 67; Pacific Cities, Auckland City Art Gallery, NZ, 71; 1st Western States Biennial Exhib, Nat Gallery Fine Arts, Washington, DC, 79; retrospective, Portland Ctr Visual Arts, Ore, 86; Optic Nerve, Perceptual Art of the 60's, Columbus Mus Art, Ohio; Extreme Abstraction, Albright Knox Mus, Buffalo, NY. *Teaching:* Prof art, Univ Wash, 66-97, prof emer, 97-. *Awards:* Int Artist's Sem Award, Fairleigh Dickinson Univ, 65; Nat Endow Arts Fel, 90; Western States Arts Fedn. *Bibliog:* Kingsbury (auth), Art, Francis Celentano, 1/70, Seattle Mag, 1/70; Kangas (auth), Francis Celentano, transcendence & negation, exhib catalog, 81; catalog, Francis Celentano, Selected Paintings, 1954-995, Safeco Exhib Catalogue, Seattle, 3/2-4/20, 95. *Media:* Acrylic on Plastic, Acrylic on Canvas. *Dealer:* Laura Russo Gallery Portland OR; Loretta Howard Gallery NY. *Mailing Add:* 1399 NE 106th St Seattle WA 98125-7538

CELLI, PAUL
PAINTER, EDUCATOR
b Boston, Mass, May 8, 1935. *Study:* Mass Coll Art, BFA, 60; RI Sch Design, MFA, 62. *Work:* Bank of Boston. *Exhib:* Providence Art Festival, RI, 61-69; New Eng Contemp Artists Asn, Boston, 63; Berkshire Mus, Pittsfield, Mass, 66; Solo exhibs, Bennett Coll, Millbrook, NY, 67, Carpenter Ctr, Harvard Univ, 76, Mass Coll Art, 2001. *Teaching:* Prof 4D theory, Mass Coll Art, 70-. *Bibliog:* Horn (auth), Contemporary Graphic Artists, Vol 1, 85. *Media:* Oil, Acrylic. *Publ:* Auth, Ink Comics, Number 3: An Art Comic Book, Nat Distribution

CELMINS, VIJA
PAINTER
b Riga, Latvia, Oct 25, 1939; arrived in Indianapolis, 1949. *Study:* John Herron Inst, Indianapolis, BFA, 1962; Univ Calif, Los Angeles, MFA, 1965. *Work:* Art Inst of Chicago; Baltimore Mus of Art; Carnegie Inst Mus of Art, Pittsburgh; Met Mus Art, NY; Whitney Mus Am Art, NY; San Francisco Mus of Modern Art; Nat Gallery of Art, Washington; and many others. *Exhib:* Retrospectives, Whitney Mus Am Art, NY, 1993, Metrop Mus Art, NY, 2002, Ctr Pompidou, Paris, 2006-07, traveled to Hammer Mus, UCLA; solo exhibs, David Stuart Galleries, La, 1966, Riko Mizuno Gallery, La, 1969, 1973, Felicity Samuel Gallery, London, 1975, Pence Gallery, Santa Monica, Calif, 1990, McKee Gallery, NY, 1996 & 2001, Inst Contemp Art, London, 1996-97, Reina Sofia, Madrid, 1996-97, Kunstmuseum Winterthur, Switz, 1996-97, Mus fur Moderne Kunst, Frankfurt, Ger, 1996-97, Anthony d'Offay Gallery, London, 1999, Cirrus Gallery, Los Angeles, 2000-2001, Mus Contemp Art, Basel, Switz, 2001, Metrop Mus Art, NY, 2002, Mus Fine Arts, Houston, 2002-03, Herron Sch Art, Indianapolis, 2003, Susan Sheehan Gallery, NY, 2003, Douglas Hyde Gallery, Trinity Coll, Dublin, 2003; group shows, Phila Mus Art, 1966; Tampa Bay Art Ctr, Fla, 1968; Contemp Am Drawings, Ft Worth Mus, Tex, 1969; Am Drawings, Whitney Mus Am Art, NY, 1973, Biennial Exhib, 1977, 1997, 2002, The Decade in Rev, 1979, The Am Century, 1999; Paperworks, Mus Modern Art, NY, 1970, Calif Prints, 1972, For 25 Years: Gemini GEL, 1991, Tempo, 2002, Contemp Voices, 2005, Against the Grain, 2006; Am Exhib, Art Inst Chicago, 1974; Nancy Hoffman Gallery, NY, 1974; Contemp Graphics Ctr, Santa Monica Mus Art, 1975; 30 Yrs of Am Printmaking, Brooklyn Mus, 1977, The Am as Printmaker, Nat Print Exhib, 1983, Public & Private: Am Prints Today, 1986; Margo Leavin Gallery, LA, 1978; Contemp Am Realism, Pa Acad Fine Arts, Philadelphia, 1981; Hassam & Speicher Fund Purchase Exhib, Am Acad & Inst Arts & Letters, NY, 1983-84; Pasadena Collects, Pasadena Art Mus, 1986; Individuals, Mus Contemp Art, LA, 1986; Of Another Nature, Loughelton Gallery, NY, 1988; Making Their Mark, Cincinnati Art Mus, 1989; The Persistence of Vision, Tibor de Nagy Gallery, NY, 1990; The Times, The Chronicle & The Observer, Kent Fine Art, NY, 1991; Pamela Auchincloss Gallery, NY, 1993; Barbara Mathes Gallery, NY, 1993; Daniel Weinberg Gallery, San Francisco, 1996; La Mus Modern Art, 1997; Fondation Cartier pour l'art contemporain, Paris, 1997-98; Mus Fine Arts, Boston, 1998; Whitechapel Art Gallery, London, 1998 & 2001; Aspen Art Mus, Colo, 1999; Exhib Ctr Centro Cult de Belem, Portugal, 1998; Found Joan Miro, Barcelona, 1998; Montreal Mus Fine Arts, 1999-2000; Hirshhorn Mus & Sculpture Garden, Washington, 1999-2000; James Cohan Gallery, NY, 2000; San Francisco Mus Mod Art, 2000-01; Pori Art Mus, Finland, 2001; Painting: From Rauschenberg to Murakami, Venice Biennale, 2002; The Undiscovered Country, Hammer Mus, LA, 2004; Craig F Starr Assoc, NY, 2006; Nat Gallery Art, Washington, 2006; Life on Mars, Carnegie Int, 2008. *Teaching:* Univ Calif, Irvine; Calif Inst of the Arts, Valencia, 1976-77; Resident artist Skowhegan Sch Painting and Sculpture, Maine, 1981; Cooper Union, New York, 1984; Yale Grad Sch, 1987. *Awards:* Cassandra Found Award, 1968; Artist Fel, NEA, 1971, 1976; Guggenheim Fel, 1980; AAAL Art Award, 1996; Medal for Painting, Skowhegan Sch Painting & Sculpture, 1997; MacArthur Found Fel, 1997; Coutts Contemp Art Found Award, 2000-2001; Athena Award for Excellence in Painting, 2006; Carnegie Prize, 2008; Roswitha Haftmann Prize, 2009; US Artists Broad Fel, 2009. *Bibliog:* Dennis Cooper (auth), rev, Artforum, 2/89; Gerard Haggery (auth), article, Art Am Mag, 3/89; Rev, Art Am Mag, 1993; Dave Hickey (auth), Vija Celmins, Artforum, Dec 1999; Keith Patrick (auth), Formal Dress, Contemp Visual Arts, issue 26, 2000; Karl Erickson & Andrew Falkowski (auth), Style Representation, New Art Examiner, Mar 2000; Vija Celmins, Art on Paper, Nov-Dec 2000; Toba Khedoori/Vija Celmins, Mus fur Gegenwartkunst, Apr 3, 2001. *Mem:* Nat Acad Design (academician elect 2004). *Publ:* Contemporary Women Artists, Laurie Collier Hillstrom and Kevin Hillstrom (ed), St. James Press, 99; Examining Pictures: Exhibiting Paintings, Cornerhouse Pubs, Manchester, UK, 1999; Art at Work: 40 Years of the Chase Manhattan Collection, New York, 2000; Painting as a Language: Material, Technique, Form and Content, Jean Robertson and Craig McDaniel, Harcourt Coll Pub, New York, 2000; Treasure from the Art Institute of Chicago, Hudson Hills Press, New York, 2000; Celebrating Modern Art: Highlights of the Anderson Collection, San Francisco Mus of Modern Art, Mondadori Printing, Italy, 2000. *Mailing Add:* McKee Gallery 745 Fifth Ave New York NY 10151

CEMBALEST, ROBIN
EDITOR
Study: Yale Univ, BA art history and English, 1982. *Pos:* Ed Asst, Art Forum, 1982-86; staff, Forward Newspaper, 1994-98; sr ed, ARTnews Mag, NYC, 88-94, exec ed 98-; contrib writer, New York Times, Wall Street Journal. *Awards:* Recipient, National Headliner Award, Siluruians Award for Arts/Cultural Reporting. *Mailing Add:* ARTnews Magazine 48 W 38th St New York NY 10018-0042

CEMIN, SAINT CLAIR
SCULPTOR
b Cruz Alta, Brazil, 1951; arrived in US, 1978. *Study:* Ecole Nat Superiore Beaux-Arts, Paris, 1974. *Work:* Whitney Mus Am Art, New York; Mus Contemp Art, Los Angeles; Mus de Arte Contemporaneo, Monterrey, Mex; Eli Broad Family Found, Los Angeles; Emily Fisher Landau Collection, Long Island City, NY. *Exhib:* Solo exhibs include Galeria Projecta, Sao Paulo, Brazil, 1979, 1981, 1982, Red Bar, Daniel Newburg Gallery, New York, 1985, 1986, Massimo Audiello Gallery, New York, 1987, 1989, 1990, Daniel Weinberg Gallery, Los Angeles, 1988, 1989, Santa Monica, 1991, Hirshhorn Mus & Sculpture Garden, Smithsonian Inst, Washington, 1991, Witte de With, Rotterdam, 1991, Robert Miller Gallery, New York, 1994, 1995, 1997, Cheim & Read, New York, 1999, 2002, Arts Club Chicago, 1999, Brent Sikkema, New York, 2004, Sikkema Jenkins & Co, New York, 2008; group exhibs include Pratt Graphic Ctr, New York, 1979; Binational Am Art of the Late 80's, Inst Contemp Art, Boston, 1988; Whitney Biennial, Whitney Mus Am Art, New York, 1989, Altered & Irrational, 1995; Doubletake, Collective Memory & Current Art, Hayward Gallery, London, 1992; 15th Anniversary Exhib, Rhona Hoffman Gallery, Chicago, 1992; 20 Yrs Daniel Weinberg Gallery: A Series of Anniversary Exhibs, Daniel Weinberg Gallery, Santa Monica, Calif, 1993; Venice Biennale, 1995; The Mediated Object, Fogg Art Mus, Harvard Univ, 1996; Decorative Strategies, Ctr Curatorial Studies, Bard Coll, NY, 1998; 78th Exhib Artist Mems, Arts Club Chicago, 1999; Rough Edge: Selections from the Broad Art Found, Crocker Art Mus, Sacramento, 2000; Secret Victorians/Contemp Artists & a 19th Century Vision, Fabric Workshop & Mus, Philadelphia, 2001; Cool & Collected, Weatherspoon Art Mus, Greensboro, NC, 2004; Here Comes the Bogey-Man, Chelsea Art Mus, New York, 2005; 183rd Ann: Invitational Exhib Contemp Am Art, Nat Acad, New York, 2008. *Mailing Add:* c/o Sikkema Jenkins & Co 530 W 22nd St New York NY 10011

CENCI, SILVANA
SCULPTOR
b Florence, Italy, Aug 4, 1926. *Study:* Manzoni Inst, Italy; Acad Fine Art, Italy, 49; Acad Grand Chaumiere, Paris, 49-50. *Work:* Uffizi Gallery Mod Art & Numero Gallery, Florence, Italy; Bundy Art Mus, Waitsfield, Vt; Metrop Boston Transit Authority; Merchants Bank, Manchester, NH; and others. *Comn:* Monumental sculpture, Pavilion Archit, New Haven, Conn, 61; two lions explosively formed, Graham Jr Col, Boston, 63; baptistry doors, Carter & Woodruff Archit, Keene, NH, 65; fountains, Western Front Restaurant, Cambridge, Mass, 67 & Sasha Montagu, Brookline, 69. *Exhib:* New Eng Art Today, Northeastern Univ, 62; Bristol Art Mus, RI, 67; New Eng Sculptors Asn, Boston City Hall, 69 & Contemp Art-Italian Heritage, 75; ten-year retrospective, Bristol Art Mus, 77; and others. *Pos:* Artist-in-residence, City of Boston, 71-73. *Teaching:* Instr art, Brookline Art Ctr, 66-69. *Awards:* Gold Hammer Award, Medea, Italy, 58; First Honorable Mention, Design in Transit, Inst Contemp Art, 71; Blanche Coleman Award, 74; World Culture Prize, Salsomaggiore Terme, Italy. *Bibliog:* Al Kaliman (auth), Odyssey Implosion/Explosion, WBZ-TV, 64; John A Hughes (auth), Explosion in Northwood, NH Profiles, 64; Richard Hadley (auth), The state we are in, Channel 11 TV, NJ, 75. *Mem:* NH Art Asn; Artists Equity Asn

CENSOR, THERESE
SCULPTOR
b Antwerp, Belgium; US citizen. *Study:* Mus Mod Art, New York; New Sch Social Studies; Art Life Studio, New York. *Work:* Smithsonian Inst, Washington, DC; Mus Art, La Jolla, Calif; Bergman Collection, Israel Mus, Jerusalem; Butler Inst, Youngstown, Ohio. *Exhib:* Small Sculpture from USA, Int Arts Prog; US Comt Int Asn of Art, Helsinki, Finland; Princeton Univ, NJ; New Eng Shows, Silvermine Guild of Artists, New Canaan, Conn. *Mem:* Audubon Artists; Nat Asn Women Artists; NY Soc Women Artists; Artists Equity of NY; Hudson River Contemp Artists. *Media:* Welded Metal, Stone. *Mailing Add:* 525 E 86 St New York NY 10028-7512

CERVENKA, BARBARA
EDUCATOR, PAINTER
b Cleveland, Sept 28, 1939. *Study:* Siena Heights Col, Studio Angelico, Adrian, Mich, 57-64, BA, 64; Wayne State Univ, Detroit, 67-69; Univ Mich, Ann Arbor, 69-71, MFA, 71. *Work:* Alumni Mem Mus & Univ Mich, Ann Arbor; Eastern Mich Univ, Ypsilanti; Jesse Besser Mus, Alpina, Mich; Clarke Col, Dubuque, Iowa; Dennos Mus, Traverse City, Mich; and others. *Exhib:* Watercolor USA, Springfield, Mo, 69, 73 & 75; Mid-Mich Show, Midland, 71; Am Watercolor Soc Show, NY, 73; Mich Watercolor Soc Show, 89-91 & 97; Toledo Area Artists Show, Ohio; Entradas Da Bahia, Salvador, Brazil, 2001, Univ of Mich, 2002; Through a Distant Mirror, Macomb Community Coll, 2006, Fermilab, Batana, Ill, 2007; Bandits and Heroes, Poets and Saints in Popular Art from the Northeast of Brazil, 2007. *Collection Arranged:* Cuadros of Pamplovia Atta: Textile Pictures by Women of Peru - traveling exhib, 89-96; O Pelourinho Popular Art from the Historic Heart of Brazil - traveling

exhib; Ayacucho - Tradition and Crisis in Peruvian Popular Art - traveling exhib, 98-. *Teaching:* Instr drawing & watercolor, Siena Heights Col, 71-78; adminr, Adrian Dominican Sisters, Mich, 78-82; asst dean, Univ Mich Sch Art, 84-94; assoc prof art dept, Siena Heights Univ, Adrian, Mich, chair, 97-2000. *Awards:* First Prize, Toledo Area Artists Show, 73; First Award, Detroit Inst Arts, Mich Watercolor Soc, 97; Award, Mich Watercolor Exhib, 2000. *Mem:* Mich Watercolor Soc; Coll Art Asn; Watercolor USA Hon Soc. *Media:* Watercolor. *Res:* Popular Art of Central and South America, especially of Peru and Brazil; Co-director of Con/Vida, Popular Arts of the Americas. *Mailing Add:* 307 Maple Ridge Ann Arbor MI 48103

CESARCO, ALEJANDRO
INSTALLATION ARTIST, PAINTER
B Montevideo, Uruguay. *Study:* UCUDAL, BA, Montevideo, Uruguay, 1998; NY Univ, MA (studio art), New York, 2000. *Work:* Mus Contemp Art, Denver; Colby Coll Mus Art; Microsoft Art Collection; Deutsche Bank Art Collection; Princeton Univ Mus Art. *Exhib:* Solo exhibs, Rosenberg Gallery, New York, 1999, Colección Engelman-Ost, Montevideo, Uruguay, 2001, Art Resources Transfer, New York, 2001, Centro Municipal de Exposiciones, Montevideo, 2002, Fluent-Collaborative, Austin, Tex, 2004, Miroslav Kraljevic Gallery, Zagreb, Croatia, 2004, Galerie ARTkITECT, Universidad de Los Andes, Mérida, Venezuela, 2005, Art in General, New York, 2006, Murray Guy, New York, 2006-07, 2009, New Langton Arts, San Francisco, 2008, Turtle Point Press, New York, 2009, Charles H Scott Gallery, Emily Carr Univ, Vancouver, 2009, Tanya Leighton Gallery, Berlin, Germany, 2009, Fundación PROA, Buenos Aires, 2010, & ArtPace, San Antonio, 2010; Invisible, Centro Cultural de España, Montevideo, 1999-2000; Artists in the Marketplace, Bronx Mus of Arts, 2000; Ellipsis (...), Leslie Tonkonow Artworks+Projects, New York, 2001; EAF02, Socrates Sculpture Park, Long Island City, NY, 2002; Now Playing, D'amelio-Terras, New York, 2003; No lo llames Performance, Museo del Barrio, New York & DA2, Salamanca, Spain, 2004; Rub Out the Word, Dumbo Arts Ctr, Brooklyn, 2005; 2nd Biennial of Young Artists, Bucharest, Romania, 2006; Textual Insight, Gallery W52, New York, 2007; Deep in the Heart of Southie, Lamontagne, Boston, 2008; Before and After, Eugene Binder Gallery, Marfa, Tex, 2009; Nine Screens, Mus Mod Art, New York, 2010. *Awards:* Emerging Artist Fel, Socrates Sculpture Park, Long Island City, 2003; Rolex Mentor and Protégé Arts Initiative Award, 2006; Art Matters Found Grant, 2009. *Bibliog:* Alicia Haber (auth), Sobre Lo Invisible, Diario del Pais, 1999; Alfredo Torres (auth), Invisible, Semanario Brecha, 5/2000; Franklin Sormans (auth), (...) Ellipsis, Time Out NY, 8/2001; Gabriela Forcadell (auth), Masterbox 5, Buenos Aires, 2002; Dedications, ART Press, 2003; Break even, New York Times, 10/20/2006; Lara Bullock (auth), Open and Shut, Time Out Chicago, 2/2007; Tim Giffin (auth), Notes on Jokes, Artforum, 1/2008; John Quin (auth), Alejandro Cesarco - Tanya Leighton, MAP, Winter/2009. *Media:* Film, Miscellaneous Media. *Mailing Add:* c/o Murray Guy 453 West 17 St New York NY 10011

CETÍN, ANTON
PAINTER, PRINTMAKER
b Bojana, Croatia; Sept 18, 1936; Can citizen. *Study:* Sch Applied Arts, dipl, 59; Acad Fine Arts, Masters dipl, 64. *Work:* Ontario Collection, Toronto, Can; Univ Mich, Dearborn; Princeton Univ; Salon XX, Bogota, Colombia; Oberhausmuseum, Passau, Herman Hesse Mus, Calw, Germany; Nat Librs, Paris, France, Zagreb, Croatia & Ottawa, Can; Palais de Glace, Buenos Aires, Arg; Museo del Chopo, Mexico City; Vatican, Rome; Mus Arts & Crafts, Gallery Klovicevi dvori, Modern Gallery, Zagreb, Croatia; Art Gallery Hamilton, Can; and others; Mus Moslavina, Kutina, City Mus, Split, Croatia. *Exhib:* Solo exhibs, Atelier E Noel, Paris, France, 1968, Isetan Gallery, Tokyo, Japan, 74, Galerie Le Creuset, Brussels, Belgium, 74, Art Gallery Hamilton, Can, 78, Heritage Gallery, Los Angeles, 79, Galeria Juan Martin, Mex, 79, Salon XX, Bogota, Columbia, 81, Mannheimer Abendakademie, Ger, 81 & Gilman Galleries, Chicago, 83; Mus del Chopo, Mex, 93; Salas Nac de Cultura, Palais de Glace, Buenos Aires, 94; Mus Mcpl de Arte J C Castagnino, Mar del Plata, Argetina, 95; Mus & Gallery Ctr (with catalog), Zagreb, Croatia, 96; Mus Bjelovar, Croatia, 97; City Mus, Varazdin, Croatia, 98; Art Gallery, Split, Croatia, 98; Gallery Fine Arts & Waldinger Gallery, Osijek, Croatia, 2000, Hermann Hesse Mus, Calw, Ger, 2000, Mercedes Zentrum, Stuttgart, Ger, 2000-2001, Gallery Anton Cetín, Cazma, Croatia, 2001, State Archives in Rijeka & Gallery Kortil, Rijeka, Croatia, 2002, Multicultural Art Gallery, Halifax, Can, 2003, Mus Mimara (with monograph), Zagreb, Croatia, 2004 & 05, CsI, Vienna, Austria, 2004-05 & Mus Vukovar, Croatia, 2005; Kamern Theatre, Sarajevo, 2005; Mus Mimara, Zagreb, Croatia, 2005; Gallery Anton Cetin, Cazma, Croatia, 2006; City Museums, including, Kutina, Koprivnica, Krizevci, Bjelovar, Cazma, Vinkovci, Nasice, Slatina, Virovitica, Zagreb, Split, Croatia, 2006-2008; Gallery Murska Sobota, Slovenia, 2007; The Print Studio, Hamilton, Canada, 2007; City Mus, including Cazma, Zagreb, Split, Bjelovar, Vinkovci, Croatia, 2009; Gallery Moos, Toronto, Canada, 2009; Gallery Anton Celín, City Mus, Bjelovar, Kutina, Croatia, 2011; Mus Franciscan Gallery, Siroki Brijeg, Bosnia Hercegovina, Gallery Emanuel, Vidovic, Split, Croatia, 2012; Modern Gallery, Zagreb, 2013; Gallery Krsto Hegedusic, Petrinja, Croatia, 2013. *Awards:* Artist of the Year, Toronto, Can, 86; The Order of Croatian Danica (Morning Star), highest honor in the field of Cult in Croatia, 95; The Order of Croatian Interlace, highest honor in the field of development and high repute of Croatia, 95; Mare nostrum Croaticum, for outstanding contribution to culture and historic values, 2001. *Bibliog:* Stuart Reid, Rudolf Wesner, Josip Depolo (auths), shows at City Mus (catalog), Varazdin & Art Galllery (catalog), Split, Croatia, 98; Art Gallery and Waldinger Gallery (catalog), Osijek, Croatia, 2000; Cetíns Life and Work, MIL Media, Zagreb, Croatia, 2002-05; Branka Hlevnjak (auth), Cetín, Life and Work, Zagreb, Croatia, 2004; and others; David Burnett (auth), Cetin, Life & Work, Toronto, Canada, 86. *Media:* Oil, Acrylic; Etching, Aquatint, Lithography; Pastel. *Mailing Add:* 916-5 Greystone Walk Dr Toronto ON M1K 5J5 Canada

CHABOT, AURORE (MARTHA)
SCULPTOR
b Nashua, NH, July 30, 1949. *Study:* Pratt Inst, BFA, 71; Univ Colo, Boulder, MFA, 81. *Work:* Taipei Fine Arts Mus; Tucson Mus Art; Pushkin Mus, Moscow; Mus Decorative Arts, Riga, Latvia; Mint Mus. *Comn:* Tile mural, Univ Ariz Marley Bldg, 97; tile mural, Skyharbor Airport, Phoenix, 2001; Tile Mural, Vortex of Time & Space, Sky Harbor Internat'l Airport, Phoenix, AZ, 2002. *Exhib:* Solo exhibs, Mary H Dana Women Artist Series, Mabel Douglass Libr, Douglass Col/Rutgers Univ, 90, Univ of Ariz Art Mus, 90, Univ Nebr, Lincoln Gallery Art, Dept Art & Art Hist, 94, Manchester Craftsmen Guild, Pittsburgh, Pa, 94; Featured Artist Sandy Carson Gal, Sofa, Chicago, 97; Substance: Materials, Process and Vision in Clay, Tex Woman's Univ, Denton, 98; San Angelo Mus Fine Arts, Tex, 99; Paper Pots II & III, John Elder Gallery, New York City, 99 & 2001; The World Community of Ceramists, The Herndon Gallery, Antioch Col, 99; Freewheeling, Five Ceramic Masters from the Univ Colo, Dairy Ctr for Arts, Boulder, 2000; Clay Out West, Laramic Community Col, Cheyenne, Wy, 2000; Clay Odyssey Civic Ctr, Helena, MT; Ceramics Cult Connections, State Mus, Suny, Plattsburgh; Clay on the Wall, Gallery 128, New York City, 2001; Clay West, 2003, Inter Mountain Invitational, Nora Eccles Harrison Mus of Art UT State Univ, Logan UT; Clay, Making Connections Ceramic Triennial Roswell Mus & Art Ctr, Roswell, NMex, 2003; Glaze Storm Artists, Univ of Indianapolis, IN, Tile; Matter and Motif, Baltimore Clayworks, Baltimore, MD, 2004. *Awards:* Artist-in-Residence Award, Va Ctr Creative Arts, 94; Individual Artist Fel Grant, Western Arts Fedn, 95 & Tucson Pima Arts Coun, 97; Small Res Grant, Univ Ariz, Tucson, 96; Univ of Ariz, Coll of Fine Arts Incentive Grant, 2001; Sabbatical Leave Award, Univ AZ, 2002; Fel of the Council Award, Nat Council on Educ for the Ceramic Arts, 2005. *Bibliog:* Joyce Tognini (auth), A Soviet Reunion, 6-7, 2-3/92; Richard Zakin (auth), Electric Kiln Ceramics (cover Jacket), 93; Charlotte Speight (auth), Hands in Clay, Photog Portfolio, 4th edit, 99; The Craft and Art of Clay, by Susan Peterson, 99; Ceramics Ways of Creation by Richard Zakin, 99; Making Ceramic Sculpture by Raul Acero, 2000; Contemporary Ceramics by Susan Peterson, 2000; Ceramic Mastering the Craft by Richard Zakin, 2001; Allan Chasanoff Ceramic Collection Catalogue, Mint Mus, 2000; Di Morgenthal & SJE Tourtilloh, Ceramics Art and Perception Cellular Synchronicity, Issue 48, 2002; 21st Century Ceramics (catalog), The Penland Book of Ceramic; Master Classes in ceramic techniques, 2003; 21st C. Ceramics in the US & Canada...Review by Robert Silberman pp45-85; Electric Kiln Ceramic, 3rd ed, 2004, Richard Zakin (auth), American Craft, Mag, April/May, 2004; The Sculpture Reference by Arthur Williams, Tile Making & Installing, by Angelica Pozo, 2005. *Mem:* Coll Art Asn; Am Craft Coun; Nat Coun Educ Ceramic Arts (dir at large, bd dir, 99-2001, juror emerging artists, 2000-01); Nat Council of Educ for the Ceramic Arts (pub dir, Nat bd dir, 2001-04). *Media:* Ceramics, Mixed. *Publ:* Auth, articles, Nat Coun Educ Ceramic Arts J, 84, 85, 87, 89, 91-92, 92-93 & 95; Editor, NCECA Journals, 2001, & 2003. *Dealer:* Sandi Carson Gallery. *Mailing Add:* 823 S Second Ave Tucson AZ 85701

CHADWICK, WHITNEY
CRITIC, HISTORIAN
b Niagara Falls, NY, 1943. *Study:* Middlebury Col, BA, 65; Pa State Univ, MA, 68, PhD, 75. *Hon Degrees:* Dr Honoris Causa, Univ Gothenburg, Sweden, 2003. *Teaching:* Assoc prof art hist, Mass Inst Technol, Cambridge, Mass, 72-78; prof art hist, San Francisco State Univ, 78-; vis prof, Art Hist, Williams Col, 2003. *Awards:* Fel, Mary Ingraham Bunting Inst, 92; Vis Res Scholar, Univ Ulster, Belfast, 2002; Clark Fel, Sterling and Francis Clark Art Inst, 2002; Radcliffe fellow, Radcliffe Inst, 2011; Lifetime Achievement award, Women's Caucus for Art's, 2012. *Mem:* Coll Art Asn. *Res:* Surrealism; contemporary art; feminism. *Publ:* Woman, Art and Soc, Thames and Hudson, 90; coed (with Isabella de Courtivron), Significant Others: Creativity & Intimate Partnership, Thames & Hudson, 93; auth, Leonora Carrington: La Realidad de la imaginacion, Ediciones ERA, Mexico City, 94; Mirror Images: Women, Surrealism and Self Representation, MIT, 98; The Art of Romaine Brooks, Univ Calif, 2000; coed (with Tirza Latimer), The Modern Woman Revisited: Paris Between the Wars, Rutgers Univ Press, 2003; co auths, Eija-Lissa Ahtila, Jesper Just, Annika Larsson, Annica karlsson Rixon, Bent: Gender & Sexuality in Contemp Scandinavian Art, San Francisco State Univ Fine Arts Gallery & Univ Wash Press, 2006; Women Artists & the Surrealist Movement, London: Thames & Hudson, Boston: new york Graphic Soc Books, ParisL Editions du Chene, 86, Tokyo: Parko Editions, 89; Myth in Surrealist Painting, 1929-1939: Dali, Ernst, Masson, Ann Arbor: UMI Res Press, reissued, 88. *Mailing Add:* 871 DeHaro St San Francisco CA 94107-2705

CHAFETZ, SIDNEY
PRINTMAKER, EDUCATOR
b Providence, RI, Mar 27, 1922. *Study:* RI Sch Design, BFA, 47; Acad Julian, Paris, 47-48; L'Ecole Am Beaux Arts, Fontainebleau, 47; with Fernand Leger, Paris, 48 & SW Hayter, Atelier 17, 50-51. *Work:* Libr Cong, Washington; Morgan Libr, NY; Dahlem-Staalische Mus; Philadelphia Mus Art; British Mus; Mus Art, NY. *Comn:* Dedication etching, Ohio State Univ Coll Law, 64; Hawthorne Keepsake, Ohio State Univ, 64; Robert Lowell Poster, Int Poetry Forum, Pittsburgh, Pa, 67; F Scott Fitzgerald Keepsake, Fitzgerald Newsletter, Ohio State Univ, 68; Poor Richards Almanacks Original Woodblock Portrait, Imprint Soc, Barre, Mass, 70; Ozick Epodes, Logan Elm Press, Ohio State Univ. *Exhib:* Ten Yrs of Am Prints, 1947-57, Brooklyn Mus, NY, 57; Young Am Printmakers, Mus Mod Art, NY, 58-59; 1st Biennial Int Gravure Sur Bois, Banska Bystrica, Czech, 70; 2nd Triennial Int Graphica Contemp, Capri, Italy, 72; 30-Yr Retrospective, Antioch Coll & throughout Ohio, 78-79; Satire & Homage, Chafetz Graphics, 88; Perpetrators, exhib of original prints circulating in US & Europe, 92-. *Teaching:* Emer prof art, Ohio State Univ, 48-82, prof emer, 82-; vis prof art, Univ Ariz, spring 65, Univ Wis-Madison, summer 67 & Univ Denver, summer 71 & 79; Fulbright Sr lectr, Univ Belgrade, Yugoslavia, 80. *Awards:* Fulbright Fel, 50-51; Governors Award, Ohio, 91; Outstanding Printmaker, Mid Am Print Coun,

98. *Mem:* Soc Am Graphic Artists; Am Color Print Soc; Am Asn Univ Prof; Nat Acad Design (assoc, 81, acad, 91). *Media:* Woodcut, Intaglio. *Publ:* Auth, Chafetz Graphics: Satire and Homage, The Ohio State Univ Pres, 88. *Dealer:* Susan Teller Gallery 568 Broadway New York NY 10012. *Mailing Add:* Ohio State Univ Dept Art Columbus OH 43210

CHAIKLIN, AMY
PAINTER
b Newark, NJ, Oct 4, 1955. *Study:* New York Studio Sch, Paris, France, studied with Elaine de Kooning, 76; Wash Univ, Sch Fine Arts, BFA, 77. *Work:* Mus Mod Art, Libr, NY; Franklin Furnace Arch, NY; Visual Studies Workshop Arch, Rochester, NY; Art Circolo, E V, Munich, Ger; Sergei Diaghilev Art Ctr, Marble Palace, St Petersburg, Russ. *Comn:* Eyes on You (mural), Fashion Moda, Bronx, NY, 83; Media Girls (mural), Eyes and Ears Found, San Francisco, Calif, 84; Girl with Pet Rat (mural), Limbo Gallery, NY, 84; Berlin Beauties (mural), comn by Maria Makkaroni, Berlin, Ger, 84. *Exhib:* Purgatory & Paradise, Metrop Mus Art Libr, NY, 86; solo exhibs, New Paintings, Galerie Schrill, Berlin, Ger, 90, Sergei Diaghilev Art Ctr, Marble Palace, St Petersburg, Russia, 92, Hamburg Messe, Hamburg, 93 & Galerie im Saalbau (with catalog) Berlin, Ger, 95; Fine Arts Mus Long Island, Hempstead, NY, 91; Erotische Kunst, Galerie Schwarz, Griefswald, 93 & 10 Jahre Druckhof Schwarz, 94; Nature Morte, NY Studio Sch Gallery, 93; Art Multiple, Dusseldorf, 94; Erotik Mit Dem Weiblichen Auge, Galerie Art of Fee, Hamburg, Ger, 95; Am Art, Galierie Mainz, Berlin, Ger, 96; Sex Sells, Galerie Boudoir, Berlin, Ger, 96; Gallery Onetwentyeight Invitational, NY, 98. *Awards:* Artist-in-Residence, Cite Int des Arts, Wash Univ, 88; Artist-in-Residence, Stiftung Starke, Berlin, Ger, 92-94; Artist Fel, Women Studio Workshop, Rosendale, NY, 98. *Bibliog:* Tina Fleisher (auth), Radio SFBIII, Red Zeitpunkle, Berlin, 9/8/95; Katrin Betting Muller (auth), TIP, Kunst Notizen, 104, 9/21/95; Aber aha Klein (auth), MT Lokal Anzeiger Kreuzberg, Galerie Mainz, Berlin, 2/7/96. *Media:* Oil, Watercolor. *Mailing Add:* 380 Malcolm X Blvd Apt 10A New York NY 10027-2384

CHALIF, RONNIE
SCULPTOR
b New York, NY. *Study:* Parsons Sch Design (with hon), 53; NY Univ, BS (art ed), 54; studies at Art Students League, New York. *Work:* Guild Hall Mus, East Hampton, NY; Zimmerli Art Mus, New Brunswick, NJ; World Trade Ctr, NY; Continental Tel Co, Washington; Gen Elec Int Hq, Fairfield, Conn; McGraw Hill, Inc, New York; Grey Advertising, New York; US Home Corp Nat Hq, Houston. *Comn:* Cadillac Fairview (lobby sculpture), comn by Barbara Tamerin, Dallas, Tex, 80. *Exhib:* Solo exhibs, Guild Hall Mus, East Hampton, NY, 68, Fed Courthouse, NY, 84-85, Jacob J Javits Federal Bldg, NY, 86-87, Marymount Manhattan, Col, NY, 86, Benton Gallery, Southampton, 87-89 & Arlene Bujese Gallery, E Hampton, 96-2005, Gayle Wilson Gallery, 2000, 2003-2004; New Directions in Sculpture, Heckscher Mus, Huntington, NY, 77; On the Leading Edge, GE Inaugural Exhib, Fairfield Conn, 83; NY Soc Women Artists, 85-94; Nat Asn Women Artists, 87, 89-92; Benson Gallery, Sculpture Garden, Bridgehampton, NY, 2000-2002; Gus and Judith Lieber Mus, Sculpture Garden, Springs, NY; Southampton Cultural Ctr, Southampton, NY, 2012, 2013; and many others. *Pos:* Pres, Neuropathy Asn, 2005-2009, Hon Pres, 2009-. *Teaching:* Sculpture, 74-89. *Awards:* Award in Sculpture & Painting, Guild Hall Mus, 68 & 83; B G Epstein Award, Nat Asn Women Artists, 91, Freelander Mem Award, 92. *Bibliog:* Rose C S Slivka (auth), From the studio, East Hampton Star, 3/11/93, 7/25/96 & 7/30/98, 4/8/99; Aspects of Abstraction, July 27, 1997; Sheridan Sansegundo (auth), At the Galleries, 7/30/98 & 9/8/99; Rose Sliuka (auth), From the Studio, 9/23/99; Robert Long (auth) One Foot Over the Line, 10/07/2004; Ronnie Chalif at Gayle Wilson Marion (auth) Marion Wolberg Weiss. *Mem:* NY Soc Women Artists; Nat Asn Women Artists; Artist Craftsmen NY (bd mem, formerly); Women in the Arts Found; Women Caucus for Art; Co-Founder and Hon Pres, Neuropathy Asn. *Media:* Stone. *Specialty:* Contemporary Long Island Artists of East End. *Interests:* Opera, Medical Research. *Publ:* auth, Exercising with Neuropathy. *Dealer:* Arlene Bujese Gallery Newton Lane East Hampton NY 11937. *Mailing Add:* 815 Park Ave New York NY 10021

CHALLIS, RICHARD BRACEBRIDGE
DEALER, LECTURER
b London, Eng, Aug 12, 1920; US Citizen. *Study:* King's Coll Sch, London, 34-37; Chelsea Col, 38-39. *Collection Arranged:* Roger Kuntz Retrospective, Laguna Beach Mus Art, Calif, 77; Moderator, The Ruth Stoever Fleming Collection, Newport Beach, 85; Publ, Newport-Mesa Unified Sch Dist. *Pos:* Founder & dir, Challis Galleries, 50-82; art dir, Los Angeles Home Show, 65-67; consult, Esther Wells Collection, 1983-; pres, Adele Bednarl Galleries, Los Angeles, 1976-77. *Teaching:* Lectr, Marketing of Fine Art, Orange Co Dept Educ & Univ Calif Irvine. *Bibliog:* Chronicled in archives of Am Art Smithsonian Inst (as Challis Galleries). *Mem:* Laguna Beach Festival Arts; Art Inst S Calif; life mem Laguna Art Mus, Orange Co Mus Art. *Media:* Contemporary Paintings & Sculpture. *Specialty:* 20th century paintings and sculpture. *Mailing Add:* 1390 S Coast Hwy Laguna Beach CA 92651

CHALMERS, KIM
EDUCATOR, STUDIO ARTIST
b New York, NY, 1945. *Study:* Univ Southwestern La, BFA, 71; Fla State Univ, MFA, 73. *Comn:* Clock and Compass, centennial mosaic, Western Ky Univ. *Exhib:* Solo exhibs, Nothing Up My Sleeve, Univ North Fla, Jacksonville, 74, Endless Maze and Sarcophagal Robes, Francis Marion Col, SC, 78, Simple Explanations, Florence Mus, SC, 86, My Blue Haven, Univ Western Carolina, Cullowhee, NC, 88, 2000, Museo Int de Electrografia, Cuenca, Spain, 92, Guild of Instruction, Daito Bunka Univ, Higashimatsuyama, Japan, 95, Sailors Garden, Downtown Glass Gallery, Hartsville, SC, 97, Labyrinth, Ivan Wilson Fine Arts Center, Bowling Green, Ky, 2000, They Seemed as Giants, Centennial Art Ctr, Tenn, 2002, Quagmire, Lindsey Wilson Collection, Ky, 2003, Hazmat Janice Mason Art Mus, Cadiz, Ky, 2004, Selection, Tenn Tech, 2004, Anne Wright Wilson Gallery, Georgetown, Ky, 2009; Faculty Art Exhibition, Western Ky Univ, Bowling Green, 2000; Ownesboro Art Guild 35th Juried Competition, Ky, 2000; Firstar Juried Competition, Bowling Green, Ky, 2000; New Works, Houchens Gallery, Bowling Green, 2002; Kinderkite, Franklin, Ky, 2002; They Seem as Giants, Centennial Art Ctr, Nashville, Tenn, 2002; Ky Nat Juried Competition, Murray, 2003; Owls, Youngsan Univ, Musan, Korea, 2005; Tattoo, Berea Col, Ulmann Galleries, Berea, Ky, 2006; Paper Memorial, KY Visions at the Capital, KAC, US Senate Annex, Wash DC, 2008. *Pos:* founder & dir, Art Dept Gallery, 73-80, New Gallery, 80-83, Bell Art Gallery, 83-91 & Downtown Glass Gallery, 96-98. *Teaching:* prof, Coker Col, 73-99, dept chmn, 85-99; prof, head dept art, Western Ky Univ, 99-2007. *Awards:* Fulbright Fel, 80; Coker Prof Devel Grant, London, Eng, & Paris, 88; Southeast Arts Fedn Regional Fel, Nat Endowment Arts, 94; Fac Devel Grant, Studio Sabbatical, 95; Al Smith Individual Fel, Ky Arts Coun, 2006. *Mem:* CAA; SECAC. *Media:* Painting, all media

CHAMBERLAIN, BEAU
PAINTER
b Portland, Ore, 1976. *Study:* Pratt Inst, BFA, 2003. *Exhib:* Solo exhibs include Jessica Murray Projects, New York, 2005, Mogadishni Gallery, Copenhagen, 2007, Project 4 Gallery, Washington, 2007, CTRL Gallery, Houston, 2007; group exhibs include Arlene Schnitzer Performing Arts Ctr, Portland, Ore, 2003; Night of 1000 Drawings, Artist Space, New York, 2003; Network Baraka, Nicole Klagsbrun, New York, 2004; All Sentient Beings, Dumbo Arts Ctr, Brooklyn, 2006; Visual Aids, Sikkema Jenkins Gallery, New York, 2006; Year_07 Art Projects London, CTRL Gallery, Houston, 2007; 183rd Ann: Invitational Exhib Contemp Am Art, Nat Acad Mus, New York, 2008. *Awards:* Julius Hallgarten Prize, Nat Acad, 2008. *Dealer:* CTRL Gallery 3907 Main St Houston TX 77002. *Mailing Add:* c/o Jessica Murray Projects 150 Eleventh Ave Btwn 21sr & 22nd St New York NY 10011

CHAMBERLAIN, CHARLES
CERAMIST, EDUCATOR
b Brockton, Mass, 1942. *Study:* Mass Coll Art, BFA; Coll Ceramics, Alfred Univ, MFA. *Work:* Smithsonian Inst, Washington, DC; Mass Coll Art, Boston; Coll Ceramics, Alfred Univ, NY. *Comn:* 14 Stations of the Cross, St Paul's Episcopal Ch, Greenville, NC. *Exhib:* Artist, Craftsmen, Inst Art, Jacksonville, Fla, 73; Solo retrospective, NC Mus Art, Raleigh, 73; 27th Ceramics Nat, Everson Mus, Syracuse, NY, 74; Craft Multiples, Smithsonian Inst, Washington, DC, 75; NC Clay, Raleigh, 92. *Teaching:* Instr ceramics, Worcester Art Ctr, Mass, 65 & Univ NH, 66-67; prof ceramics, East Carolina Univ, Greenville, NC, 67-2003, chmn design dept, 82-85, prof art; retired. *Awards:* Best in Show, Mass Asn Craftsmen, 65; Merit Award, Emerging Craftsmen of New Eng, 65; Hon Mention, Piedmont Craftsmen Ann, 71. *Mem:* Piedmont Craftsmen; Am Crafts Coun; Nat Coun Educ Ceramic Art. *Media:* Clay, Mixed Media. *Mailing Add:* 2307 E Third St Greenville NC 27858-1606

CHAMBERLAIN, DAVID (ALLEN)
SCULPTOR, PAINTER
b Canton, Ohio, Aug 11, 1949. *Study:* Princeton Univ, with Joe Brown & James Seawright, BA (archit design), 71, Teaching Art Inst; Colo Col, 72; Univ Pa, with Robert Engman & Neil Welliver, MFA (sculpture), 77. *Work:* Nat Mus Am Art, Washington; Delaware Mus Art, Wilmington; Detroit Inst Art, Mich; British Art Mus, London, Eng; Asian Art Mus, San Francisco; and many others. *Comn:* Cantata, Horne Libr, Babson Col, Wellesley, Mass, 81; TORUS, Stratus Computer Inc, Marlboro, Mass, 86; A Une Passante, M C Wallace Libr, Wheaton Col, Norton, Mass, 91; Ballette, Southworth Libr, Canton Col, NY, 91; Eroica, Morgridge Auditorium, Univ Wis, Madison, 92. *Exhib:* Pucker/Safrai Gallery, Boston, Mass, 79-97; solo exhibs, Everson Mus Art, Syracuse, NY, 83, 85, Lyme Acad Fine Arts, Old Lyme, Conn, 85 & 86, Gibson Gallery, SUNY at Potsdam, NY, 87, Pucker/Safrai Gallery, Boston, Mass, 81, 84 & 88 & MacLaren/Markowitz Gallery, Boulder, Colo, 91; solo retrospectives, The Art Complex Mus, Duxbury, Mass, 88, McKissick Mus Art, Columbia, SC, 90 & Muskegon Mus Art, Mich, 96; Renjeau Gallery, Concord, Mass, 89-98; Aspen Grove Galleries, Aspen, Colo; Muse A Muse Gallery, Tokyo; and many others. *Pos:* Fel/panelist, Conf World Affairs, Boulder, Colo, 89-98; vis artist collabr, US Indochina Arts Proj, Repub Vietnam, 95; vis artist, Johannesberg, South Africa, 97. *Teaching:* Co-dir & artist-in-residence, Arts Col House Prog, Univ Pa, 75-77; assoc prof, Univ SC, Columbia, 90-91; adj prof, Rivier Col, Nashua, Ntl, 91-94. *Awards:* Red Ribbon Award, Am Film Festival, 82; SC Arts Comn Individual Artist Grant, 91; KBK Found Grant, 91. *Bibliog:* Search for Perfection (film), FIS/Pucker Safrai, 82; Melodic Form: The Sculpture of David Chamberlain, David Godine, 90; David Chamberlain: Artistry in Motion (film), SC-ETV/PBS, 92. *Mem:* New Eng Sculptors Asn; Coll Art Asn. *Media:* Bronze, Oil Monotypes. *Publ:* Haven't We Met (album), 91, Released (album), Cahoots Quartet, 93. *Mailing Add:* c/o Pucker-Safrai Gallery 171 Newbury St Boston MA 02116

CHAMBERS, PARK A, JR
EDUCATOR, PHOTOGRAPHER
b Wheeling, WVa, Oct 29, 1942. *Study:* Kent State Univ, BFA, 68, MFA, 70. *Work:* The Chicago-Tokyo Bank & Shatkin Trading Company, Chicago, Ill; Johnson & Johnson, Elmhurst, Ill; Kent State Univ, Ohio. *Comn:* Wrist Sculpture, comn by Fred Gordon, Skokie, Ill, 73; Installation/Performance, Focus on the Arts, Highland Park, Ill, 75; Body Sculpture, Friedman Leather Fashions, NY, 79-80; Body Sculpture, SSF Inc, Chicago, Ill, 75-88. *Exhib:* 51st Ann, Cleveland Mus Art, Ohio, 69; 22nd Ann, Butler Inst Am Art, Youngstown, Ohio, 70; Form in Fiber, Deson-Zaks Gallery, Chicago, Ill, 72; Sculpture in New Media, Ill State Mus, Springfield, 73; Fiber Forms, Cincinnati Art Mus, Ohio, 78; Fiber as Art, Metrop Mus, Manila, Philippines, 80; Art for AIDS, Vopol Gallery, San Francisco, Calif, 86; Figure & Place, Artemisia Gallery, Chicago, Ill, 88; Private/Pub, Betty Rymer Gallery, 92. *Collection Arranged:* Extensions & Spirit & Image: Art of Voodoo, SAIC Gallery, 86 & 87; SAIC, Idaho State Univ, Pocatello, 87. *Pos:* Juror, Univ Chicago, Ill, 72; lectr, Mus Contemp Art, 72; artist-in-residence, Highland Park High Sch, Ill, 74-75; vis artist, Ctr Creative Studies, Detroit, Mich & Univ Ariz, Tucson, Ariz, 88. *Teaching:* Instr metal & fiber,

Kent State Univ, Ohio, 68-69; instr fiber, Akron Art Inst, Ohio, 69-70; prof emer, Art Inst, Chicago, Ill, 70-. *Awards:* Experiment Materials, Brunswick Corporation, Chicago, Ill, 69; Individual Grant, Nat Endowment Arts, 76; Ill Arts Coun, Independent Artist Grant, 98. *Bibliog:* Robert Glauber (auth), Skyline, Chicago, 72; E Chung & A Sandoval (coauth), The New Plastics, Vis Arts Ctr Alaska, 82; D Consentino (auth), Spirit & Image, Vol 21, No 1, African Arts, 87. *Media:* Photo Images, Embellishment. *Publ:* Contribr, Decorative Art in Modern Interiors, Studio Vista Limited, London, 71; Techniques of Rya Knotting, Van Nostrand Reinhold Co, 71; Soft Sculpture, Crown Publishers, 74; How to Create Your Own Designs, Doubleday & Co, 75; Hardcore Crafts, Ballantine Books, 76. *Mailing Add:* 2764 Valencia Dr Sarasota FL 34239

CHAMBERS, WILLIAM MCWILLIE
PAINTER, ART DEALER
b Baton Rouge, La, Aug 6, 1951. *Study:* La Tech Univ, Ruston, 69-71; Kansas City Art Inst, Mo, BFA, 73; New York Studio Sch, with Leland Bell, 73-74. *Work:* NY Pub Libr; Weatherspoon Art Mus, Greensboro, NC; Leslie Lohman, Gay Art Mus, NY. *Exhib:* Solo Exhibs: Bowery Gallery, NY, 93; Peter Madero Gallery, NY, 94 & Tricia Collins-Grand Salon, NY, 95 & 97, Barbara Levy Gallery, Fire Island, NY, 98, Fischbach Gallery, NY, 2002; John Davis Gallery, Hudson, NY, 2007 & 2008; Figureworks, Brooklyn, 2008; George Billis Gallery, NY, 2013. *Pos:* VPres, Grace Borgenicht Gallery, NY, 74-95 & co-cur, Fifty Years of Canadian Landscape Painting, 86; dir, DC Moore Gallery, NY, 95-96; pvt dealer 96-. *Bibliog:* Articles in Art in Am, 3/95 & NY Times, 3/97. *Media:* Oil, Watercolor, Woodcut. *Specialty:* 20th century American, & European Art/Milton Avery, Max Beckmann, Jean Arp, Wolf Kahn, Doris Lee. *Publ:* Ed of numerous exhib catalogues, 74-; Jose de Rivera-Constructions, Taller Ediciones, Madrid, 80. *Dealer:* Studio visits by appointment; John Davis Gallery Hudson NY; Figureworks Brooklyn NY; New Hope Sidetracks Gallery New Hope PA. *Mailing Add:* 319 E 50th St New York NY 10022

CHAMBERS, WILLIAM THOMAS
PAINTER
b Chicago, Ill, Feb 12, 1940. *Study:* Am Acad Art, dipl, 62; Northeastern Ill Univ, BA, 73. *Work:* Northwestern Univ, Evanston, Ill; Ill State Capitol, Springfield; Kennedy Ctr & Comsa Corp, Washington; Carol Jones Contemp Art Collection, Chicago; Wheaton Coll, Ill; Transylvania Univ, Ky; Trinity Int Univ, Ill; Fla State Univ; Duke Univ; Lawrence Univ, NY; Univ Ala; Supreme Court, Montgomery, Ala. *Comn:* Painting, comn by Arnold Weber, Northwestern Univ, Evanston, Ill, 90; painting, comn by Gov James R Thompson, Springfield, Ill, 92; painting, Carol Jones Gallery, Chicago, 93; painting, comn by Melvin Laird, Comstat Corp, Washington, 95; painting, comn by Martin Feinstein, Washington Opera Co, 96. *Awards:* Award, Portrait Inst Ann Competition, 83; Best Show, Oil Painters Am Ann Midwest Show, 95; Award, Oil Painters Am Ann Nat Competition, 96; Grand prize, Portrait Soc Am, 99; People's Choice Award, Portrait Soc Am, 99; Top Ten Award, Portrait Soc Am, 2008. *Mem:* Oil Painters Am (master signature mem); Portrait Soc Am. *Media:* Oil, Pastel. *Mailing Add:* 1607 S Harvard Ave Arlington Heights IL 60005

CHAMPLIN, ANDREA
PAINTER
Study: Wayne State Univ, BFA (painting), 1989; Yale Univ, MFA (painting/printmaking), 1996. *Exhib:* Solo shows include Clifford-Smith Gallery, Boston, 1999, 2003, Cummings Art Center, Connecticut College, 2000, Michael Steinberg Fine Art, New York, 2004; group exhibs include Imaginary Anatomy, Pasinger Fabrik, Munich, 1998; Escape, DNA Gallery, Provincetown, Mass, 1999; Cool Abstraction, Cummings Art Ctr, Conn Coll, New London, 2000; Future Maybe, Oni Gallery, Boston, 2000; Buzz, Clifford-Smith Gallery, Boston, 2001; Anywhere But Here, Gallery 414, Hunter Coll, New York, 2002; Clean, It Only Looks Dirty, GV/AS Gallery, Brooklyn, NY, 2003; 183rd Ann: Invitational Exhib Contemp Am Art, Nat Acad Mus, New York, 2008. *Teaching:* Vis prof painting, Sch Mus Fine Art, Boston. *Dealer:* Michael Steinberg Fine Art 526 W 26th St Ste 215 New York NY 10001. *Mailing Add:* 223 W 21st St Apt 4K New York NY 10011-3138

CHAN, ERIC
PAINTER
b 1968. *Study:* Univ Calif, Berkeley, Grad, 90; Columbia Univ, MFA, 98. *Exhib:* Exhibs with Heather Schatz (as ChanSchatz) include Columbia Univ, New York, 98, Deep Thought, Basilico Fine Arts, New York, 98, XXIV Bienal de Sao Paulo, Brazil, 98, Open House, Shiffler Found, Greenville, Ohio, 98, The Production of Production, Apex Art, New York, 99, Too Wide Enough, Swiss Inst, New York, 99, Basilico Fine Arts, New York, 99, Real Art Ways, Hartford, Conn, 2000, Representing, Parrish Art Mus, Southampton, NY, 2000, Grand Arts, Kansas City, Mo, 2001, Lemon Sky, Los Angeles, 2002, Before & After Science, Marella Contemp Art, Milan, 2003, Life By Design, Beall Ctr, Univ Calif, Irvine, 2003, Lukas & Sternberg, Inc, New York, 2003, Portrait Masterworks, New York, 2003, Augmentation, Massimo Audiello, New York, 2003, Here & There, 2006 & Remix, 2006, Starring, Armory Art Fair, New York, 2004, One in a Million, Austrian Cult Forum, New York, 2004, Ctr Curatorial Studies, Bard Coll, NY, 2004, INterVENTIONS, Bowling Green State Univ Art Gallery, Ohio, 2004, FloorPlay, Brooklyn Coll Art Gallery, NY, 2004, Multiple Studies, Contemp Art Ctr, Cincinnati, Ohio, 2004, Crib Sheets, Univ Calif, Los Angeles & Monacelli Press, 2005, Extreme Abstraction, Albright-Knox Art Gallery, Buffalo, NY, 2005 & Ideas First, 2006, Mutiny, The Happy Lion, Los Angeles, 2006, Meeting in the Drawing Project, Univ NC, Greensboro, 2007, In Situ, Galerie Michael Janssen, Berlin, 2007, Cress Gallery, Univ Tenn, Chattanooga, 2007, Hunter Mus Am Art, Chattanooga, Tenn, 2007. *Teaching:* Adj asst prof visual arts, Columbia Univ, New York. *Media:* Serigraphy, Silkscreen. *Mailing Add:* ChanSchatz 423 W 14th St 2R New York NY 10014

CHAN, GAYE
EDUCATOR, ADMINISTRATOR, CONCEPTUAL ARTIST
Study: San Francisco Art Inst, MFA; Univ Hawaii-Manoa, BFA. *Work:* Collaborative works include being part of Eating in Public and Downwind Productions. *Teaching:* Prof, dept chair, Univ Hawaii-Manoa, currently. *Res:* Art in General-NYC, Articule-Montreal, Artspeak-Vancouver, Asia Soc-NYC, Gallery 4A-Sydney, Honolulu Mus Art, SF Camerawork-San Francisco, Southern Exposure-San Francisco, Queens Mus and YYZ Artist Outlet-Toronto. *Mailing Add:* Department of Art & Art History University of Hawaii Manoa 2535 McCarthy Mall Honolulu HI 96822

CHAN, PAUL
VIDEO ARTIST
b Hong Kong, 1973. *Study:* Art Inst Chicago, BFA (video/digital arts), 1996; Bard Coll, MFA (film/video/new media), 2002. *Exhib:* Contemp Artist & Popular Culture, Contemp Ctr at Folk Art Mus, New York, 1999; All Power to the people, The Kitchen, New York City, 1999; Black Panther Omega 2000, Walker Art Center, Minneapolis, 1999; Visual Codex, 450 Gallery, New York, 2002; MOOV, White Box Gallery, New York, 2002; Baghdad Home Movies, Ocularis, Brooklyn, 2003; Lean, ISE Found Gallery, New York, 2003; solo exhibs, MOMA Film, Gramercy Theater, New York, 2003, Greene Naftali Gallery, New York, 2004, 2008, Hallwalls, Buffalo, 2005, Franklin Art Works, Minneapolis, 2005, Inst Contemp Art, Boston, 2005, Hammer Mus, Los Angeles, 2005, Galleria Massimo De Carlo, Milan, 2006, Blanton Mus Art, Austin, Tex, 2006; History Makes a Comeback Prog, NY Video Festival at Lincoln Ctr, New York, 2003; Election Show, Am Fine Arts, New York, 2004; Carnegie Int, Carnegie Mus Art, Pittsburgh, 2004; Greater New York, PS1 Contemp Art Ctr, Long Island City, NY, 2005; New Work/ New Acquisitions, Mus Mod Art, New York, 2005; Whitney Biennial, Whitney Mus Am Art, New York, 2006; Belief & Doubt, Aspen Art Mus, Colo, 2006; Paper Trail: A Decade in Acquisitions, Walker Art Ctr, Minneapolis, 2007; 53rd Int Art Exhib Biennale, Venice, 2009. *Awards:* Jerome Found New York Media Arts Grant, 2001; Andy Warhol Found/ Lower E Side Printshop Van Lier Fel, 2001; Rockefeller Found New Media Arts Fel, 2003; US Artists Fel, 2007. *Mailing Add:* Greene Naftli Gallery 508 W 26th St 8th Floor New York NY 10001

CHANDLER, ANGELYN SANDERS
MUSEUM DIRECTOR
b Atlanta, Ga. *Study:* Emery Univ, BA, 57. *Pos:* Exec dir, Atlanta Int Mus Art Design, formerly. *Mailing Add:* c/o Atlanta Int Mus Art & Design 1315 Peachtree St NE Atlanta GA 30309

CHANDRA, FREDDY
INSTALLATION SCULPTOR
b Jakarta, Indonesia, 1979. *Study:* Univ Calif, Berkeley, BA (archit), 2002; Mills Coll, Oakland, MFA (studio art), 2004. *Work:* TSG Corp, New York; Capital Group, Los Angeles; Neiman Marcus, Los Angeles; Orrick Herrington & Sutcliffe LLP, Menlo Park; Holland Group, San Francisco; McKenna Long & Aldridge LLP, Washington DC. *Exhib:* Solo exhibs, Worth Ryder Gallery, Univ Calif, 2001, Kala Art Inst, Berkeley, 2007, Headlands Ctr for Arts, San Francisco, 2007, Brian Gross Fine Art, San Francisco, 2009, Walter Maciel Gallery, Los Angeles, 2010; Emerge, 8th Ann GenArt Exhib, San Franciso, 2005; Close Calls, Headlands Ctr for the Arts, San Francisco, 2007; WorkADay, Blankspace Gallery, Oakland, 2007; The Space Between, San Jose Inst Contemp Art, 2008; Pattern ReDefined, Walter Maciel Gallery, Los Angeles, 2008. *Pos:* Lectr, Univ Calif, Berkeley, 2004-05; vis artist instr, Mills Coll, Oakland, 2004-; artist-in-residence, Headlands Ctr for the Arts, Sausalito, Calif, 2007 & Dejerassi Resident Artists Program, Woodside, Calif, 2009. *Awards:* Kala Art Inst Fel, Berkeley, 2006; Joan Mitchell Found Grant, 2009. *Bibliog:* Tim White (auth), Urban Images, Sacramento News & Rev, 7/22/2004; Kenneth Baker (auth), Nice surprises at this year's Emerge show of new talents, San Francisco Chronicle, 11/15/2005; Peter Selz (auth), Compositions of Space and Light, Berkeley Daily Planet, 7/22/2007; Frank Cebulski (auth), The Space Between, Artweek, Vol 39, No 5, 6/2008

CHANG, JASON
PAINTER
b Taiwan, 1940; US Citizen. *Study:* Coll New Rochelle, MA (arts). *Work:* Asia Bank, NY; Pastel Mus, Suzhow, China; N Am Pastel Artists Gallery; Golden Eagle Inst; Taipei Cult Ctr. *Comn:* Portrait, Pres Windstar Construction Co, 2003; portraits, pvt comn by Dr Cheng, 2004. *Exhib:* Solo exhib, Master Pastelist Jason Chang, 99 Art Ctr, Taipei, Taiwan; Allied Artists Am, Butler Inst Am Art. *Collection Arranged:* Contemp Master Pastelists Exhib, Pastel Soc Am, Taiwan, 94 & 2006. *Pos:* Pres, N Am Pastel Artists Asn, 97-; vpres, Golden Eagle Inst; organizer & juror, Int Pastel Artists Exhib, Taiwan & New York, 2005-2007. *Teaching:* instr, Nat Taiwan Acad Fine Art, formerly; instr, Coll New Rochelle, formerly; instr, Pastel Soc Am, Sch Past & Nat Arts Club, currently. *Awards:* Am Artists Prof League Award, 2000 & 2001; Pastel Soc Am, Ann Exhib Award & Master Pastelist; Award, 72nd Am Artists Prof League, 2000; First Place, Am Artists Prof League, 2004; Silver Medal, Audubon Artists, 2005. *Mem:* Allied Artists Am; Pastel Soc Am (master pastelist); N Am Pastel Artists Asn; Audubon Artists Inc. *Media:* Pastels, Oil. *Publ:* Contribr, Int Pastel Mag, Pastel Soc of Am, Butler Inst of Am Art, il Pastello Conteporaneo in Europe (Europastello), The Pastel Jour, L'Art du Pastel, The World Jour and many others; auth, Pastel World of Jason Chang, 99. *Mailing Add:* 151-56 21st Ave Flushing NY 11357

CHANG, LISHAN
INSTALLATION SCULPTOR, PHOTOGRAPHER
b Taiwan. *Exhib:* Solo exhibs, Amerasia Gallery, Flushing, NY, 2004-05, Crystal Art Gallery, NY, 2005, Gallery Korea, NY, 2007, Art Ctr William Patterson Univ, NJ, 2007, Brooklyn Pub Libr, 2008, Washington Pavilion Arts & Sci, Sioux Falls, 2008, Earlville Opera House, NY, 2008; Nexus-Taiwan in Queens, Queens Mus Art, NY,

2004; Diverse Version, Walsh Libr Gallery, NJ, 2007; Float, Socrates Sculpture Park, NY, 2007; Dare to Art, Kuandu Mus Fine Arts, Taipei, 2007; Taipei Fine Arts Mus, Taiwan, 2008; How Chinese, Gallery 456, Chinese Am Arts Coun, New York, 2009. *Awards:* Artist Grant, Nat Culture & Arts Found, Taiwan, 2004; Jerome Fel, Franconia Sculpture Park, Minn, 2007; Artist Fel, Coun Cult Affairs, Taiwan, 2007; Freeman Fel, Vt Studio Ctr, 2008; NY Found Arts Fel, 2008; Pollock-Krasner Found Grant, 2008

CHANG-IL, KIM
COLLECTOR, GALLERY OWNER
Pos: Owner, Arario Gallery, 1989-. *Awards:* Named one of 100 Most Influential People in the Int Art World, Monopole mag; named one of Most Influential People in Korean Contemporary Art, Art Price mag; named one of Top 200 Collectors, ARTnews mag, 2009-13. *Collection:* Contemporary art

CHANNING, SUSAN ROSE
ADMINISTRATOR, PHOTOGRAPHER
b Englewood, NJ, Aug 16, 1943. *Study:* Pa State Univ, BA (fine arts) & BA (gen arts & sci), 65; George Washington Univ, MFA, 67. *Work:* Polaroid Corp. *Exhib:* Cleveland Mus Art; Eighteenth Ann Corcoran Gallery of Art Area Show, Washington, 67; Camera Movements, Moore Coll Art Gallery, Philadelphia, 83. *Collection Arranged:* Design in Transit, State Subway Station Competition, Inst Contemp Art, Boston, 71; Points of View, Recent Work by Area Photographers (auth, catalog), Inst Contemp Art, Boston, 72; Art of the State, Recipients & Finalists in Painting, Printmaking & Drawing, Rose Art Mus, Brandeis Univ, Waltham, Mass, 77 & 79; Photography Fellowship Recipients, Mass Inst of Technol Creative Photog Gallery, Cambridge, Mass, 78; Uncensored: An Exhibition of Previously Censored Work from the Midwest, 87; In Their Own Space, 88; Interaction: New Video Installations, 89; Urban Evidence, Contemporary Artists Reveal Cleveland, Cleveland Ctr Contemp Art & Cleveland Mus Art, 96. *Pos:* Performing arts prog coordr & art instr, Wadsworth Atheneum, Hartford, Conn, 68-70; dir urban action prog & spec proj, Inst Contemp Art, Boston, 70-72; asst dir, Mass Coun Arts & Humanities, Boston, 72-73; dir artists fel prog, Artists Found Inc, Boston, 73-82; consult, WGBH New TV Workshop, Boston, 78-79, and others, 86-96; dir, Prints in Progress, Philadelphia, 83-85; dir, Spaces Gallery, Cleveland, Ohio, 86-; panelist, Nat Endowment Arts & Photog Fel; on-site evaluator, Visual Artists Orgn advan prog. *Teaching:* Instr photog & serigraphy, Wadsworth Atheneum, Hartford, Conn, 68-70. *Mem:* Ohio Arts Coun; Visual Arts & Crafts (adv panel); Percent for Art (core comt mem). *Publ:* Ed, Cleveland: New Possibilities, Civic Re-Vision, Buster Simpson-West Sixth Streetscape (exhib catalog), Spaces, 88; Creating in Crisis: Making Art in the Age of AIDS (exhib catalog), Spaces, 94; Radical Ink (exhib catalog), Spaces, 95. *Mailing Add:* 3069 Scarborough Rd Cleveland OH 44118-4064

CHAO, BRUCE
SCULPTOR
b Boston, Mass, Nov 17, 1948. *Study:* Wayne State Univ, Detroit, Mich; RI Sch Design, Providence, BFA, 73, MFA, 75; Univ Wis, Madison. *Work:* Corning Mus Glass, NY. *Exhib:* Solo exhibs, An Invisible Barrier, 77, Angels, 78 & 89, O K Harris Gallery, NY, Suspended, PS1 Auditorium, NY, 79, Joslyn Art Mus, Omaha, Nebr, 81 & RI Col, Providence, 93; Washington Proj Arts, 80; Glas 86, Leerdam, The Neth; Glass: Another View, Univ Hawaii, 87; Glassworks, Renwick Gallery, Smithsonian Inst, Washington, 90; Glass Installations, Am Craft Mus, NY, 93. *Teaching:* Asst prof, RI Sch Design, Providence, 82-88, assoc prof, 88-92, prof art, glass dept head, 94-. *Awards:* Finalist Award, sculpture, Mass Artists Fel Prog, 91; RI Sch Design Res Grant, 94; US/Japan Creative Artist Fel, Nat Endowment Arts, 96; NEA Artist Fel Grant, 76, 81, 90. *Bibliog:* Carol Doran-Khewhok (auth), Glass: Another View, New Work, summer 87; Helmut Ricke (auth), Again - Glass and the Fine Arts, Neus Glas, 10-12/86; Donald Kuspit (auth), Bruce Chao's Arc From Purity to the Uncanny, Glass Mag, 93; and others. *Mem:* Glass Art Soc. *Mailing Add:* Rhode Island Sch Design 2 College St Providence RI 02903

CHAPELLIN, HELENA See Wilson, Helena Chapellin Wilson

CHAPIN, DEBORAH JANE
PAINTER, INSTRUCTOR
b Fort Collins, Colo, 1954. *Study:* Univ Va, BS, 76; USDA, cert, 90-93; Nat Acad Design, with Raymond Kinstler, 99, with Sam Adoquei, 2002. *Work:* Fed Reserve Bank, Richmond, Va; John Nuveen Co, NY; Pardoe Properties, Washington, DC; Schultz Inc, St Louis, Mo. *Comn:* Wetlands and Wildlife 2007 calendar, DNR restoration projects & Chesapeake Bay Wetlands (fundraising prog). *Exhib:* Artist of Am Exhib, Colo Hist Mus, Denver, 88, 90; ASMA Marine Exhib, Md Hist Mus, Baltimore, 89; ASMA Marine Exhib, RJ Schaffer Mus, Mystic, Conn, 92; solo Exhibs, Meridian Int Ctr, Washington, DC, 92, 97, Nat Arts Club, New York, 98 & 2003; Salon des Independants, Grand Palais, Paris, France, 93, 94; Salon Societe Nationale des Beaux Arts, Louvre, Paris, France, 99-2001; Ketterer 17-20th Century Marine Art Exhib, Hamburg, Ger, 2000; Arts for the Parks Top 100, Jackson Hole, Wyo, 2004-2005; SEWE, Charleston, SC, 2005-2008; Natural World Observed, Nat Arts Club, NYC, 2005; Paint Am Touring Exhib, 10/2006-10/2008; NWO Tex Art Gallery, Dallas, Tex, 2007; CM Russell Art Auction, CM Russell Mus, Great Falls, Mont, 2007; Mystic Int, Mystic, Conn, 2007; NWO, Adam Whitney Gallery, Nebr, 2008 & Tweed Mus Art, Minn, 2009. *Collection Arranged:* Nat Acad Prof Art Plein Air Painters, Tweed Mus Exhib, 2009; Cultivating the Mind (film doc on contemp realistic art), 2009-11. *Teaching:* Instr painting, NAPPAP, 97-2007; Pub Arts Prog, Smithsonian Am Art Mus, 2007-. *Awards:* President's Award, Chesapeake Bay Found, 90; Paint Am Grand Prize Winner, Paint Am, 2007. *Bibliog:* Edward Archibald (auth), Dictionary of Sea Painters, London, 89; Gerlinde de Beer (auth), Allgemeines Kunstlerlexikon, 97; The Artists Blue Book, 2000-2009. *Mem:* Nat Arts Club; Artists Fel; Calif Arts Club; Nat Acad Prof Plein Air Painters (founder, 99); Societe Nat des Beaux Arts. *Media:* Oil on Linen. *Specialty:* Plein air painting, marine, wildlife and nature art. *Interests:* Conservation Programs, wildlife & nature walks & safaris. *Collection:* Casa Genota, Historic Home of Eugene O'Neill, Sea Island, Ga. *Publ:* Contribr, Chesapeake Bay Mag, 5/83, 5/90; Marine Art, Am Art Mag, 6/88; US Art, Adams Pub, 12/90; auth, Recording the Sea & Surf, Am Artist Mag, 10/95; Capturing Life & Movement en Plein Air, New Horizon Studios, 11/2000; Gerlinde de Beer (auth), Ludolf Backhysen, 2001; Smithsonian Butterflies et al, Vol 1, NHS Press, 10/2008; Natural World Observed, Adam Whitney Catalog & Tweed Mus Catalog, NHS Press, 8/2008; Capturing Life and Movement en plein air (marine), NHS Press, 2009; The Professional Artist (plein air), NHS Press, 2009; auth, Dust on My Shoes, Sun at My Back (200pgs color, 50 plates) NHS Press, 2010. *Dealer:* Mystic Maritime Gallery 47 Greenmanville Ave Mystic CT 06355. *Mailing Add:* 7034 Woodstream Terrace Lanham Seabrook MD 20706

CHAPLIN, GEORGE EDWIN
PAINTER, EDUCATOR
b Kew Gardens, NY, Aug 30, 1931. *Study:* Yale Univ Sch Art, with Josef Albers, BFA & MFA. *Work:* Yale Univ Gallery; Trinity Col, Conn; World Bank, Washington, DC; Mattatuck Mus, Conn; Bayer Corp, Tarrytown, NY; New Britain Mus Am Art, Conn. *Exhib:* Carpenter Ctr, Harvard Univ, 74; Dept of State, Washington, DC, 76-80; New Britain Mus, Conn, 77; Conn 78 Invitational, Carlson Art Gallery, Univ Bridgeport; Mattatuck Mus, Waterbury, Conn, 78; Slater Mem Mus, Norwich, Conn, 81; Munson Gallery, New Haven, Conn, 91; Corbino Gallery, Longboat Key, Fla, 98; Swanson Reed Contemp, Louisville Ky ; Longboat Key Ctr for the Arts, Fla; Ringling Col Art & Design, Longboat Key Ctr Arts, Fla, 2010. *Pos:* prof emeritus, Fine Arts, Trinity Coll, Hartford, Conn. *Teaching:* Head dept painting, Silvermine Coll Art, 65-71; dir studio prog, Trinity Coll, Hartford, Conn, 72-91, prof fine arts, 88, Charles S Nutt prof fine arts (emer). *Awards:* David G Lyon Award, 31st New England Ann, Conn, 81; 1st Prize, 1st Faber Birren Color Award Exhib, Stamford Art Asn, Conn, 81. *Bibliog:* Bernard Chaet (auth), The Art of Drawing (1st ed), Hold Rinehart and Winston, Inc; Paul Zelanski (auth), Color, Fourth & Fifth Ed, The Art of Seeing, Third Ed, Prentice Hall, Inc,; Nature's Transcendent Painter: George Chaplin (dvd), Dore Hammond Films. *Media:* Oil, Pastel. *Interests:* Music. *Dealer:* Erdreich White Fine Arts Boston Ma; Art and Interiors Westport CT; Fox Gallery Hartford CT. *Mailing Add:* 162 Spring Place Way Annapolis MD 21401

CHAPLINE, CLAUDIA BEECHUM
PAINTER, WRITER, CURATOR, ASSEMBLAGE ARTIST
b Oak Park, Ill, May 23, 1930. *Study:* Corcoran Sch Art, 48-53; George Wash Univ, Wash, AB, 53; Conn Coll Sch Dance, 54 & 56; Wash Univ, St Louis, Mo, MA, 56; Univ Mo, 56-57; Phi Beta Kappa. *Work:* Univ Calif, Los Angeles; Downey Mus Art, Calif; Fine Arts Mus, San Francisco; Norcal, San Francisco; Morris Graves Mus, Eureka, Calif; Crocker Mus Art; New York Public Lib; Calif State Lib; Haiku Coll; Poets House Coll, NY; San Fran Peninsula Art Mus, Belmont, Calif. *Comn:* Performance proj, City Santa Monica, Calif, 81; Subway, Nuremburg, Ger, 94; sculpture, Hotel Radisson, Antigua, Guatemala. *Exhib:* Galerie Christa Riedel, Frankenthal, Ger, 2000; Marin Civic Ctr, San Rafael, Calif, 2000; War Meml Mus, Seoul, Korea, 2001; Olema Valley Ranches Today, Claudia Chapline Gallery, 2002; Exchange Exhib, Somarts, Axis Mundi, San Francisco & Paris, 2002; Calif State Univ Dominquez Hills, 2005; Rosicrucian Egyptian Mus, San Jose, Calif, 2007; Peninsula Mus Art, Belmont, Calif, 2009; Artist in Res, Arts Benicia, Benicia, Calif, 2011. *Collection Arranged:* Performance Series 74-80, Inst Dance & Experimental Art, Introductions, 85-86; San Francisco Civic Arts Festival, 88 & 89; Calif Arts Coun, Artists-in-residence, 82 & Art in Pub Bldg, 84-90; Art at the Cheese Factory, 2010-13; Art Contemporary Marin, 2013-14. *Pos:* Founder dir, Inst Design & Experimental Art, Calif, 74-87; coordr, Artists in Social Inst, Calif Arts Coun, Sacramento, 82-84; mgr, Art in Pub Bldgs, Calif Arts Coun, 84-90; owner, Claudia Chapline Gallery, Stinson Beach, Calif, 87-2014; dev dir, Bolinas Mus, 90; pub art consult, City Berkeley, Calif, 2002-010; pres, Art at the Cheese Factory, 2008-14. *Teaching:* Instr dance, Wash Univ, 53-56; instr, Univ Mo, 56-67; asst prof, Univ Calif, Los Angeles, 60-67 & Calif State Univ, Northridge, 61-64; vis artist & mentor, Univ San Francisco, 2007; instr poetry workshops, Stinson Beach Lib, 2011-13. *Awards:* Artist Res, Norcal, San Francisco, 99, Stinson Beach, Bolinas Community Fund, 2000 & DeYoung Mus Arts, San Francisco, 2000; Marin Arts Coun Community Arts Grant, 2001; Zellerbach Family Fund, 2002; Lifetime Achievement Award, NCWCA, 2007; Artist Res, Arts Benicia, Benicia, Calif, 2011. *Bibliog:* Pacific Sun, 10/28/98; San Francisco Chronicle, Evening News Mag, 99; Niche Mag, winter 2003; Craft of No Calif, 2003; J Rigler (auth, video), Conversations with Interesting Characters, 99; Passages (video), 2007; Ebb and Flow (catalog), Peninsula Art Mus; Marin Poetry Live 5, 2013. *Mem:* San Francisco Art Dealers Asn; Art Table; Pub Art Works Marin; Coll Art Asn; Women's Caucus Art. *Media:* Acrylic, Assemblage, Installation. *Res:* Dance Therapy in the United States. *Specialty:* Contemporary art of Northern California. *Interests:* Environment, recycling & reuse, movies, poetry. *Collection:* Fred Blackman, Italo Scanga, Harold Schwarm. *Publ:* Auth, Tension-Line, High Performance, 78; ed, numerous articles in Artists News, 81; Egret, 96; Calle Aldama, 96; Artists Dialogue, 97-98; auth, Collage: Pop Poetry & Sound Bytes; Selected Works Catalog, 2002; Art & Healing, Calif Biofeedback Soc, 2007; Artswell, West Marin Citizen (column), 2008-12; ed, Women Artists in Marin: Five Decades, 2010; Sea Glass: Stinson Beach Poems, 2010; Falling up the Stairs, a Memoir, 2013. *Dealer:* Claudia Chapline Gallery. *Mailing Add:* PO Box 1117 Stinson Beach CA 94970

CHAPMAN, GARY HOWARD
PAINTER
b Xenia, Ohio, July 25, 1961. *Study:* Berea Col, Ky, BA (art), BS (indust art), 84; Cranbook Acad Art, Mich, MFA (painting), 86. *Work:* Birmingham Mus Art; Huntsville Mus Art, Ala; Montgomery Mus Art & Ala State Coun Arts, Montgomery, Ala; Mobile Mus Art, Ala; the Ogden Mus Art, New Orleans, La; The Meridian Mus Art, Miss. *Comn:* oil painting, Hoar Construction Co, Birmingham, Ala. *Pos:* CAA mentor, 2003. *Teaching:* Prof painting & drawing, Univ Ala, Birmingham, 1990-; instr painting, Arrowmont Sch Arts & Crafts, Gatlinburg, 1998, 2000, 2002. *Awards:* Painting Fel, Ala State Coun Arts, 1994, 2002 & Nat Endowment Arts/Southern Arts

Fedn, 1996; Red Clay Survey Purchase Award, Huntsville Mus Art, Ala, 1998; Purchase Award, Meridian Mus, 2000. *Mem:* Southeastern Cols Art Conf; CAA Coll Art Asn. *Media:* Oils. *Publ:* Contribr, New American Paintings, book 3, 16 & 52, Open Studio Press. *Mailing Add:* 2008 3rd Ave N Apt 14C Birmingham AL 35203-3362

CHAPPELL, BERKLEY WARNER
PAINTER, PRINTMAKER
b Pueblo, Colo, Mar 21, 1934. *Study:* Univ Colo, BFA, 56, MFA, 58; studied with Mark Rothko, Jimmy Ernst, Cari Morris. *Work:* San Francisco Mus Art; Henry Gallery, Univ Wash, Seattle; Tacoma Mus Art, Wash; Univ BC, Vancouver; Salishan Lodge, Gleneden Beach, Ore; Univ Colo, Boulder; Univ Puget Sound, Tacoma, Wash; Salish Inn, Stevenson, Wash; Portland Art Mus, Ore; Portland Pub Sch System; corp collections, Colt Firearms, Conn & I Magnin; and many more; pvt collections, Larry Kirkland, John & Betty Gray, Carolyn Kizer, Carl & Hilda Morris, Cheryl Glenn & Jon Olson. *Exhib:* Young West Coast Artists, Pasadena, Calif, 59; Abstract Expressionism Today, San Francisco, 60 & Landscape Painting Today, 61; Am Printmaking Today, Ger, Greece, France, 69; Grand Gallerie, Seattle, 75; Hunterdon Mus NJ; Pasadena Mus Art; Multiples, Western Mich Univ, Kalamazoo, 79; Fish: An Exhib, Hockaday At Ctr, Kalispell, Mont; Northwest Print Coun, Portland Art Mus, Ore, 82; Sun River Exhib, Bend, Ore, 83; Art & Agriculture, Guistina Gallery, Ore & State Univ, Corvallis, Ore, 84, 86, 90 & 92; Printmakers, Blackfish Gallery, Portland, Ore, 89; Am Engravers on Copper, Portland State Univ, Ore, 92; Into the Woods, Woodcuts, and Wood Sculpture, Eugene Arts Asn, Mahlon Sweet Airport, Ore, 95; Ore Painters, Mirror Pond Gallery, Bend, Ore, 2005. *Collection Arranged:* Portland Mus Art, Portland, OR. *Teaching:* Asst painting, Univ Colo, 56-58; instr to asst prof painting, Univ Puget Sound, Tacoma, 58-63; asst prof to prof painting & printmaking, Ore State Univ, Corvallis, 63-97; prof emer, Ore State Univ, Corvallis, Ore, 97. *Awards:* Purchase Awards, San Francisco Art Inst, 61 & Henry Gallery, Univ Wash, 64 & 69; Oregon State Univ Found; Grayco Found, Portland, Ore; Grants, finish the unprinted editions of the late Wendell H. Black, printmaker and mentor, Univ Colo. *Media:* Oil; Engraving. *Mailing Add:* 2230 NW 29th St Corvallis OR 97330-1244

CHAPPELL, KATE CHENEY
PRINTMAKER, PAINTER
b Hartford, Conn. *Study:* Univ Southern Maine, AB (summa cum laude), 1983; Sarah Lawrence Coll; Sorbonne & l'Atelier Goetz, Paris, 1965-66; Haystack Sch Arts & Crafts, Deer Isle, Maine, 1993, 1995, 1998 & 2006; Maine Coll Art, 1997-2000; Vt Studio Ctr, Printmaking Residency, 2001, 2002, 2004, 2007, 2009. *Hon Degrees:* Chatham Coll, 1997; Colby Coll, 2009. *Work:* Bates Coll Mus, Maine; Colby Coll Mus, Maine; New Britain Mus Am Art, Conn; Portland Mus Art, Maine; Univ New England; NY Pub Libr; Bowdoin Coll Mus; Farmsworth Mus. *Comn:* Ramblers Way Farm. *Exhib:* Solo exhibs include Baker's Table, Portland, Maine, 1984, Harvard Divinity Sch, 1987-91, South Congregational Church, Kennebunkport, 1990-94, Round Top Ctr Arts, 2003, True North Conf, 2004, New Britain Mus Am Art, Conn, 2008; group exhibs include Maine Printmakers, Ctr Maine Contemp Art, Rockport, 1980-2006; Univ Southern Maine, 1981-84; River Clubs Ann Juried Show, Kennebunkport, Maine, 1985-2007; Women Artists of Monhegan Island, Lupine Gallery, 1996-99, 2002, 2003 & 2005; Invitational Print Show, River Tree Ctr Arts, 1999, Splendid Splashes, 2000, Island Visions/Island Voices, 2000, Visions/Voices II, 2001, Monhegan, 2003; Peregrine Press Juried Group Show, Aucocisco Gallery, 2002, 2003, 2004; 10x10 Group Show, June Fitzpatrick Gallery, Portland, 2004-07; On Island, Univ New England Art Gallery, Portland, 2007; Saco Mus, Main, 2008; Portland Mus Art, Collage Show, 2009; Peregrine Show & UNE Works from the collection, 2009. *Collection Arranged:* co-cur, On Island works of Monhegan Artists at Univ New Eng, 2007; cur, Island Visions/Island Voice's, Collaboration of Monhegan Island Artists & Poets, 2000-2009. *Pos:* Co-founder & vpres, Tom's of Maine, Kennebunkport, 1968-. *Teaching:* Monotype workshop (with Alice Spencer), Kaystack, Maine. *Awards:* Best of Show, Watercolor, River Club Ann Juried Show, Kennebunkport, 1986, Hon mention, 95, 98, 2000, 2005, 2008; Scholastic Art Award, Gold Key, Wadsworth Athenaeum, Hartford, Conn. *Mem:* Women Artists of Monhegan Island; Pa Watercolor Soc; Peregrine Press; 10x10. *Interests:* Poetry, French culture & literature, yoga, hiking, tennis, family. *Publ:* Carl Little (auth), Spotlight Review for Maine, Art New Eng, 2004; Lost at Sea & Standing Stones, Words & Images, 2000 & 2001; Inner Terrain article, Farmington Life, 2008; Emma Bouthilletee (auth), Center for Book Arts article, Kennebunk Post, 2008; Chana Bloch (auth), Blood Honey, Cover Image for Autumn House Press, 2008. *Dealer:* Mast Cove Gallery PO Box 2718 Kennebunkport ME 04046; Lupine Gallery 48 Main St Monhegan ME 04852. *Mailing Add:* PO Box 301 Monhegan ME 04852

CHAPPELL, MILES LINWOOD
HISTORIAN, EDUCATOR
b Norfolk, Va, June 6, 1939. *Study:* Coll William & Mary, BS, 60; Univ NC, Chapel Hill, with Philipp Fehl, Frances Huemer & Joseph Sloane, PhD (art hist), 71. *Collection Arranged:* Rubens in Prints (auth, catalog), Coll William & Mary, 77; Arthur Strauss and the German Expressionists (auth, catalog), Coll William & Mary, 78; Disegni dei Toscani a Roma 1580-1620 (coauth, catalog), Uffizi Gallery, Florence, 79; Drawings from the Herman Collection (auth, catalog), Muscarelle Mus Art, Coll William & Mary, 83; Cristofano Allori (auth, catalog), Pitti Gallery, Florence, 84; Age of Caravaggio (catalog), NY, 84; Il Seicento Fiorentino (contribr, catalog), Florence, 86; Disegni di Lodovico Cigoli (auth, catalog), Uffizi Gallery, 92; Cigoli tra manierismo e barocco (intro, catalog), Pitti Gallery, 92; Fine Art of Drawing, Muscarelle Mus Art, Coll William & Mary, Va, 93 & Drawn on the Spot: Landscape Drawings, 16C-20C, 95; Tuscan Drawings, NY, 2000; Figline, Cigoli, e i suoi amici, 2008; Galileo and the Arts, Pisa, 2009. *Pos:* Assoc ed, Studies in Iconography, 76-81, ed, 81-82; art adv bd, Interlochen Ctr Arts, 90-; art historian and critic. *Teaching:* Assoc fel, Harvard Univ Ctr Italian Renaissance, Florence, 90; prof art hist, Col William & Mary, 71-, chancellor prof, 86-2005. *Awards:* Nat Endowment Humanities Fel, 83; Res Grants, Nat Endowment Humanities, Samuel Kress Found & Am Philosophical Soc. *Mem:* Coll Art Asn Am; Southeastern Coll Art Conf (mem bd dir, 78-84); Renaissance Soc Am; Kunsthistorisches Inst, Florence. *Media:* Drawing. *Res:* Renaissance and Baroque art; old master drawings; British and Colonial American painting. *Interests:* Drawing. *Publ:* Auth, Cristofano Allori's depictions of St Francis, Burlington Mag, 71; Cigoli, Galileo and Invidia, 75 & John Smibert's Italian sojourn, 82, Art Bulletin; Missing paintings by Cigoli, Paragone, 82; Identification of S Coccapani drawing collection mark, Master Drawings, 83; Fuseli: Antique and Nightmare, Burlington Mag, 86; Drawings by Cigoli, Master Drawings, 89; auth, Artistic Education of Marie de Medicis (Le siecle de Marie de Medicis), 2003; On Cigoli's Prospettiva Pratica, Paragone, 2006; Cigoli and Galileo (catalog), Galileo, Pisa, 2009. *Mailing Add:* Dept of Art & Art Hist Col William & Mary Williamsburg VA 23185

CHAPPELLE, JERRY LEON
CERAMIST, SCULPTOR
b Fredericktown, Mo, Nov 14, 1939. *Study:* Murray State Univ, BS; Univ Minn, MFA. *Work:* High Mus Art, Atlanta, Ga; Greenville Co Mus Art, SC; Ga Coun Arts; Mobile Mus Art, La; Pres Carter Ctr, Atlanta, Ga. *Comn:* Ceramic mural, Sally Julius Mem, Miller Libr, La Plume, Pa, 80 & Kelly Airforce Base, San Antonio, Tex, 85; ceramic & stucco mural, St Gregory's Episcopal Church, Athens, Ga, 81; mural, Mohasco Entrance, High Point, NC, 86; ceramic mural, Mus Arts & Sci, Macon, Ga, 90; ceramic mural, Veterans Admin Hospital, Dallas, Tex, 98. *Exhib:* Fun and Fantasy, Xerox Corp Gallery, Rochester, NY, 73; Regional Invitational, Gallery Contemp Art, Winston-Salem, NC, 75; Hopkins Gallery Art, Ohio State Univ, Columbus, 80; Greenville Co Mus Art, SC, 81; Carrol Reece Mus, Johnson City, Tenn, 88; Ceramic Mural Cohen's of Atlanta, 2005; Contemporary Ceramics, North Ga State Univ, 2009; Lyndon House Art Ctr, Athens, Ga, 2011. *Pos:* Dir, Scorpio Rising Workshops, 70-77; co-owner, Happy Valley Pottery Inc, 70-; vis artist, Ohio State Univ, 80; co-owner, Chappelle Gallery, 99-. *Teaching:* Instr ceramics, Univ Minn, 69-70; asst prof ceramics, Univ Ga, 70-76. *Awards:* Two First Prizes, Atlanta Arts Comt, 75; Second Prize, Covington Arts Exhib, Covington Art Ctr, 74; Artist Initiated Grant, Ga Endowment Arts, 89. *Bibliog:* Larry Smith (auth), Ceramic Art (film), Univ Ga, 74; Evolution of the Artist Craftsman in Georgia, Highlight of Contemporary Ceramics (film), Ga NEA-TV, 74; HGTV, The Good Life, 2001. *Mem:* Am Crafts Coun; Piedmont Craftsmen Inc. *Media:* Clay, Glass. *Dealer:* Sandler Hudson Gallery 1009 A Marietta St NW Atlanta GA 30318

CHARKOW-HOLLANDER, NATALIE
SCULPTOR
b Philadelphia. *Study:* Taylor Sch Fine Arts. *Work:* Nice Caves & Their Inhabitants, 97; Birth of the Milky Way, 2002. *Exhib:* Solo exhib Reliefs in Stone, Lohin Geduld Gallery, 2004. *Teaching:* Founder, prof, sculpture dept, Philadelphia Col Art (now Univ Arts); prof Yale Univ, Boston Univ, Queens Col, City Univ NY, Univ Pa. *Mem:* Nat Acad (acad, 2003)

CHARLES, DURANT See Rizzie, Dan

CHARLES, LARRY
PAINTER, LECTURER
b South Bend, Ind, Mar 17, 1951. *Study:* Ind Univ; Ariz State Univ; Scottsdale Artists' Sch. *Exhib:* The Art of Illusion, Woodson Art Mus, Wausau, Wis, 2003; Trompe L'Oeil Style, Phoenix Art Mus, Phoenix, Ariz, 2003. *Teaching:* instr liberal arts, Univ So Calif, Los Angeles, 86-87. *Mem:* Trompe L'Oeil Soc Artists (co-founder 2001-). *Media:* Acrylic, Oil. *Publ:* Auth, International Artist, 2002. *Dealer:* Eleanor Ettinger Gallery 119 Spring St New York NY 10012. *Mailing Add:* 14926 N 86th Ln Peoria AZ 85381

CHARLOT, MARTIN DAY
PAINTER, MURALIST
b Athens, Ga, Mar 6, 1944. *Study:* Apprenticeship with Jean Charlot & Ansel Adams. *Work:* Bishop Mus, Honolulu; State Found Cult & Arts, Honolulu; The Queen Emma Found, 91; Metrop Mus Art, NY; City of Honolulu. *Comn:* King Kamehameha IV and Queen Emma (6' x 7' mural), Queen Emma Found, 91; Hawaii at Peace, Fruits of our Labor (6' x 27' mural), New Honolulu Police Hq, 93; Beyond Words (4' x 14' mural), Children's Dental Ctr, Inglewood, Calif, 96; Science, Nature & Technology (7' x 15' mural), Ventura Co Discovery Ctr, Thousand Oaks, Calif, 98; (mural) The Children's Dental Center, 99; Legal Offices Steve Thomas, Wilshire Blvd, Santa Monica, 2001; and many others. *Exhib:* One-man shows, De Mena Gallery, NY, 67, Hawaii State Libr, Honolulu, 72, Volcano Art Ctr, 76, Contemp Arts Ctr, Hawaii, 79, Fed Bldg, 80, Kauai Libr, 80, Ala Moana Center, Honolulu, 83 & Hawaii Loa Col, 84; East West Ctr, 86; State Found Cult & Arts Retrospective, 87; An Am Palette, a Dance Celebration of Am Art & Mus, Principia Col, Ill, 89; Brockman Gallery, Los Angeles, 89; Louis Stern Fine Arts, Los Angeles. *Pos:* Illusr, Collins Assoc, NY, 69; art dir, Bravura Films, Mountain View, Calif, 70; contribr, Ha'ilono Mele, 79-80; illusr, Honolulu Advertiser Progress Edition, 82. *Teaching:* Lectr art & film, Univ Hawaii, 62-; lectr filmmaking, St John's Univ, Minn, 69; teacher cinema, Honolulu Acad Arts, 70; artist-in-schs, Doe Sch Syst, Hawaii, 75; lectr, Fresno Calif Univ, 83 & Honolulu Acad Arts. *Awards:* Fel in Perpetuity, Metrop Mus Art, NY, 79; Akamai Business Award, Kaneohe Bus Group, 83. *Bibliog:* On paper gallery, Commun for Peace, Aqua Planet Inc, Japan, 89; Les Krantz (auth), Calif Art Rev, 89; Made in Paradise (film), 95; Harry N Abrams Inc (auth), Art of the State Hawaii, 99; and others. *Mem:* Hawaii Film Bd (perpetual mem); Pac Film Inst; mem Screen Actors Guild; Film Makers Coop, NY; Hawaii Orgn Arts (founder, 92); NAACP (hon chmn); Waiahole-Waikane Community Asn (founding steering com mem, art dir); First Hawaii Int Film Festival (founding bd dir, art dir). *Media:* Oil, Acrylic. *Publ:* Illusr, How to Make Your Own Hawaiian Musical Instrument, Bess Press, Inc, 88; cover, White Bread, Hawaii Rev, Univ Hawaii, 89; J Am Planning Asn, Hunter Col, NY, 90; contribr, Kalapana Will Be Forever, film, 90; illusr, Design Stock Certificate, Blue Rider Entertainment Inc, 97;

auth & illusr, Surfaces, WW Norton & Co, New York, 96; Art of the State Hawaii, Harry N. Abrams, Inc, 99; Contemporary Chicana and Chicano Art, Bilingual Press, 2002, Arizona State Univ,; The Crucifixion in American Art, McFarland & Co, Inc, North Carolina and London, 2003. *Mailing Add:* 123 C N Maple St Burbank CA 91505

CHASE, DORIS (TOTTEN)
VIDEO ARTIST, SCULPTOR
b Seattle, Wash, Apr 29, 1923. *Study:* Univ Wash; also with Mark Tobey. *Work:* Mus Mod Art, Kobe, Japan; Art Inst Chicago; Nat Collection Fine Arts & Smithsonian Inst, Washington, DC; Mus Fine Arts, Boston; Mus Mod Art & NY Univ, New York; and others. *Comn:* Steel & Bronze, Wash State Arts Comn, 70; Wash State Conv Ctr; Kerry Park, Seattle; Nat Endowment Arts; Seattle Ctr Found, 99. *Exhib:* Solo exhibs, Western Mus Asn Circulating Exhib, 70-72 & Henry Gallery, Univ Wash, Seattle, 71, 78 & 98; Metrop Mus Art, New York, 74; Calif Palace Legion Hon, 78; Mus Mod Art, New York, 78, 81 & 93; Georges Pompidou Ctr, Paris, 82-85; AIR Gallery, New York, 83; 911-Media Arts Ctr, 89, 92 & 94; DC/TV 90, New York; Woodside/Braseth Gallery, Seattle, Wash, 90 & 93; Seattle Art Mus, 92 & 94; Mus NW Art, La Conner, Wash, 94; Am Inst Architects, 95; New Acquisitions, Mus Northwest Art, La Corner, Friesen Fine Arts, Seattle, Wash, 2003. *Awards:* Nat Endowment Arts Fel, 76; NY State Coun Arts Grant, 80; Govs Art Award, State Wash, 92; Retirement Res Found Grant, 93; Seattle Arts Comn Grant, 95; Coll Art Asn Tribute, Seattle Art Mus, 2004. *Bibliog:* Articles in Newsweek, 7/3/78, NY Times, 3/18/81 & Videography, 9/81, Sightlines, spring, 86 & Seattle Times; Robin Schanzenbach (dir), Doris Chase: Portrait of the Artist (documentary film), Pub Broadcasting Serv, 85; Dr Patricia Failing (auth), Doris Chase: Artist in Motion (book & video), Univ Wash Press, 92; Cynthia Goodman (auth), Digital visions, Sculpture Mag, 97 & 99; KCTS, Doris Chase - Circle at the Center (video), 99. *Mem:* Women/Artist/Filmmakers (pres, 78); Asn Independent Video & Filmmakers; NY Film Coun (bd mem); 911-Media Arts (bd mem). *Publ:* dir, Doris Chase Dance Series, 70-79, Concept Series, 80-85, Sophi, 89, By Herself, 90-95 & The Chelsea, 93; auth, "By Herself" series discussion guide, 95. *Dealer:* Terra Nova Films, Whitney Mus New York NY, MoMA

CHASE, JACK S(PAULDING)
SCULPTOR
b Burlington, Vt, Mar 4, 1941. *Study:* US Military Acad, BS, 63; Univ Vt, Burlington, MS, 72. *Work:* Cathedral Church St Paul, Burlington, Vt; Champlain Valley Union High Sch, Hinesburg, Vt; Smithsonian Mus (Nat Zoological Park) & Am Cancer Soc, Washington, DC. *Comn:* Bronze tree, Heckler & Koch, Arlington, Va, 81; steel mobile, Nat Zoological Park, 90; bronze mem trophy, Lake Champlain Yacht Club, Shelburne, Vt, 83; bronze tree, comn by Bishop Harvey Butterfield, South Burlington, Vt, 83; welded mem Sculpture, US Army For Sci & Technol Ctr, Charlottesville, Va. *Exhib:* Nat Vietnam Mem Design Winners, Am Inst Archit, Washington, DC, 81; Nat Defense Univ, Washington, DC, 86; US Army Intelligence Agency, Washington, DC, 88; US Army War Coll, Carlisle, Pa, 90; Fisher Galleries, Washington, DC, 96 & 98. *Pos:* Owner, Birch Pond Sculpture, Jericho, Vt, 82-. *Awards:* Most Popular Sculpture Award, Exhib Vt Artists, Norwich Univ, 80 & 82; Phillippe Citation Distinguished Pub Serv Art, Gen Elect Found, 82; and others; Best of Show, WestFest, Westfield, Mass, 99. *Bibliog:* Donna Carpenter (auth), Yankee Artist, Monogram, Gen Elect Co, 83; Anne Brown (auth), Witness Trees, High Roads Folio, 85; Catherine Orr (auth), A man for all seasons: Jack Chase, Lookout Mag, 86. *Mem:* Vt Crafts Coun. *Media:* Welded Metal, Computer Design in Stainless Steel. *Mailing Add:* 42 Snipe Island Rd Jericho VT 05465

CHASE, JEANNE NORMAN
PAINTER, PRINTMAKER
b Spokane, Wash, Feb 15, 1929. *Study:* Calif State Univ, BFA, 59. *Work:* LaGrange Col, Ga; Chattahoochie Mus Art, Ga; Kyoto Internat Wood Soc, Japan; Portland Mus of Art, Ore; Spencer Mus Art, Univ of Kans; Centre for Japan, Johannsburg, South Africa. *Exhib:* Manhattan Graphic Soc, NY, 99; Print exhib, Veliko Art Gallery, Bulgaria, 2000; Women Contemp Artists Exhib, Selby Gallery, 2001; Exh Van Horn Art Ctr, Tex, 2003; Venice Art Ctr, Fla, 2003; Fine Arts Collectors Exhib, Sarasota, Fl, 2004; Nat Pen Women Exhib, Tampa Univ, Fla; Depalo Center, Abruzzi, Italy, 2007; Pratt Gallery, Seattle, Wash, 2008; Mini Print Exhib, Roovebaeksholm, Denmark, 2008. *Collection Arranged:* Spencer Mus Art, Kans; Muban Found, Chonqing, China; Pres Jimmy and Rosalyn Carter, Plains, Ga. *Pos:* Lectr, Women in the Arts. *Teaching:* Instr, figure drawing & painting & chmn fine arts, Ringling Sch Art, Fla, 79-93 & workshops, Wild Acres, NC, 84-87. *Awards:* First Prize, Southeastern Art Exhib, 76; Merit Awards, Longboat Art Ctr Nat & Daytona Mus Art, 79; Peoples Choice Award, Venice, Fla, 2008; Peoples Choice Award, Sarasota Art Ctr, 2009; People's award, Venice, Fla, 2013; Animals in Art, Manatee, Fla, 2013; Best of Show, Venice Art Ctr, 2013. *Bibliog:* Alicia Caldwell (auth), Activist artist prepares series, Bradenton-Herald, Fla, 12/29/85; Joan Altabe (auth), A Creative Force, Sarasota Herald-Tribune, 96; Thirza Jacocks (auth), Hello Sincerity, 96 & Studio Work of Jean Norman Chase, 98, Pelican Press; Lisa Sidmundson (auth), Artistic License, Undiscovered Fla Mag, 2010. *Mem:* Artists Equity; Women's Caucus Arts; Fla Artists Group; Nat League Pen Women; Women's Contemporary Artists; Baren Woodblock Inc, Wood Engravers Net Work. *Media:* Pencil, Oil, Printmaking. *Interests:* Music. *Publ:* Auth, Drawing in another dimension, Design Mag, 76; Artists and Their Cats, Midmarch Press, 90; New American Paintings, Open Studios Press, 96; Claymaniacs Are cookin, Cover Art, 2007; Undiscovered Florida, Artistic License, 2008; Cities of the World, 2013. *Dealer:* Mickelson Gallery 707 G St NW Washington DC 20001; Esposito Gallery Alpine TX. *Mailing Add:* 1817 Ingram Ave Sarasota FL 34232

CHASE, LOUISA L
PAINTER
b Panama City, Panama, Mar 18, 1951; US citizen. *Study:* Syracuse Univ, BFA, 73; Yale Univ Sch Art, MFA, 75. *Work:* New York Pub Libr, Mus Mod Art, Metrop Mus Art & Whitney Mus Am Art, NY; Morton Neumann Family Collection, Chicago, Ill; Newsweek, NY; Corcoran Gallery Art, Libr Cong, Washington, DC; Albright-Knox Art Gallery, Buffalo, NY. *Comn:* Silkscreen print, Lincoln Ctr, New York, 81. *Exhib:* Solo shows incl Robert Miller Gallery, NY, 81, 82, 84 & 86, Harcus-Krakow Gallery, Boston & Galerie Inge Baker, Cologne, 83, Mira Goddard Gallery, Toronto, 84 & 89, Paul Cava Gallery, Philadelphia, 84, Margo Levin Gallery, Los Angeles, 85, Texas Gallery, Houston, 87 & Brooke Alexander, NY, 89; group shows incl Whitney Biennial, Whitney Mus Am Art, NY, 81; Am Landscape, Whitney Mus, Fairfield Co, Conn, 81; New Visions, Aldrich Mus, Ridgefield, Conn, 81; Block Prints, Whitney Mus Am Art, 82; Am Artist as Printmaker: 23rd National Print Exhib, Brooklyn Mus, 83; Prints from Blocks: Gauguin to Now, Mus Mod Art, NY, 83; Currents, Inst Contemp Art, Boston, 84; An Int Survey of Recent Painting & Sculpture, Mus Mod Art, NY, 84; Drawing Acquisitions: 1981-1985, Whitney Mus Am Art, 85; Selections from the Frederick R Weisman Collection (traveling), 87; The New Generation, The 80's, Am Painters & Sculptors, Metrop Mus Art, NY, 88; Making Their Mark, Women Artists Move into the Mainstream, 1979-85 (traveling), 89; Landscapes, Brooke Alexander, 89; Tokyo Art Ctr Hall, 91; Kyoto Art Ctr Hall, 91; Brooke Alexander New York, 91. *Teaching:* Instr painting, RI Sch Design, Providence, 75-79, Sch Visual Arts, New York, 80-82. *Awards:* Nat Endowment Arts, 78-79 & 82-83; Creative Artists Pub Serv Prog, 79-80. *Bibliog:* Margaret Moorman (auth), Louisa Chase, Brooke Alexander, Artnews, summer 89; Richard Kalina (auth), Louisa Chase, Arts Mag, 5/89; Michael Brenson (auth), Works from nature, Louisa Chase, NY Times, 2/17/89. *Media:* Oil. *Dealer:* Brooke Alexander 59 Wooster St New York NY 10012; Viviane Bregman Fine Art 1010 Fifth Ave New York NY 10028; ClampArt 521-531 W 25th St New York NY 10001; Gallery Karl Oskar 3008 W 71 Prairie Village KS 66208; Goya Contemporary/Goya-Girl Press Inc 3000 Chestnut Ave Baltimore MD 21211; Hartje Gallery 4 Brington Rd Brookline MA 02445; RoGallery.com 47-15 36th St Long Island City NY 11101; Spanierman Gallery 45 E 58th St New York NY 10022; Tandem Press 201 S Dickinson St Madison WI 53703; Diane Villani Editions 285 Lafayette Street #3-d New York NY 10012. *Mailing Add:* 52 Spring Close Hwy East Hampton NY 11937-2654

CHASE, W(ILLIAM) THOMAS
CONSERVATOR
b Boston, Mass, May 31, 1940. *Study:* Oberlin Col, Ohio, BA, 62; NY Univ, MA, 67, conserv cert, 67; Brit Coun Course on conserv of antiquities, 69. *Pos:* Wadsworth Atheneum, Hartford, Conn, 62 & 63; conservator to Nemrud Dagh Excavations, Adiyaman Villayet, Turkey, 64; Chester Dale Fel in Conserv Dept, Metrop Mus Art, New York, 66; asst conservator, Freer Tech Lab, 66-68, head conserv, 68-97; adv to John D Rockefeller 3rd Fund for Thai Bronze Treatment Proj, 73-75; head, Chase Art Serv, 97-. *Mem:* Fel Int Inst Conserv Hist & Artistic Works; hon fel Am Inst Conserv (pres, 2003-2005); Washington Conserv Guild (vchmn, 68-69, pres, 70). *Res:* Technical studies of Oriental art, particularly ancient Chinese bronzes and belt-hooks, mirrors and other objects; corrosion study and analysis. *Publ:* Coauth (with Gettens & Clarke), Two early Chinese weapons with meteoritic iron blades, Freer Occasional Papers, 71; auth, Bronze Disease and Its Treatment, Dept Fine Arts, Thailand, 75; co-ed, Corrosion and Metal Artifacts, Nat Bur Stand, 77; co-auth (with U Franklin), Early Chinese Black Mirrors and Pattern-Etched Weapons Ars Orientalis XI; coauth, Islamic metalwork, Freer Gallery, 85

CHASE-BIEN, GAIL
PAINTER
b Lowell, Mass, May 16, 1946. *Study:* Calif Coll of Art, BFA (with High Distinction), 1978; Calif Coll of Art, MFA (with High Distinction), 1980. *Work:* di Rosa Mus, Sonoma, Calif; Sonoma Art Mus, Sonoma, Calif; Hughes Corp, Los Angeles, Calif; Shearson Lehman Corp, NY; Mustard's Restaurant, Napa Valley, Yountville, Calif. *Comn:* Art Work Int, Sultan of Brunei, Beverly Hills Hotel, Los Angeles, Calif; Carneros Alambic, Remy Martin Winery, Napa, Calif. *Exhib:* Ann 111th Exhib, San Francisco, Art Inst, San Francisco, Calif, 1992; California Landscape, Hewlett Packard Corp, San Mateo, Calif, 1994; California Grandeur and Genre Exhib, Bedford Gallery, Walnut Creek, Calif, 1996; Calif Coll of Arts & Crafts, Alumni Exhib, CCAC Gallery, San Francisco, Calif, 1999; Gail Chase-Bien, I Wolk Gallery, St Helena, Calif, 2003, 2006; Parallel Convergence, Napa Valley Mus, Yountville, Calif, 2004. *Pos:* Foun River Sch, Middle Sch for the Arts, Napa, Calif, 1995; Dir Fine Arts, River Sch, Napa, Calif, 2004; Bd, Napa Col Performing Arts Center, Napa, Calif, 2006; Bd Mem, Napa Arts Coun, Napa, Calif, 2006. *Teaching:* Instr painting, Col of the Redwoods, Fort Brag, Calif, 1983-1986; Visual artist, Napa Arts Coun, Napa, Calif, 2003-2004. *Awards:* Curator's Choice, Terra Infirma, Napa Valley Mus, 2004. *Bibliog:* Robert Taylor (auth), Brockton Mus Exhib, Boston Globe, 1989; Terri Cohen (auth), Gail Chase-Bien, Artweek Mag, 1992; Leonard Shlain (auth), The Paintings of Gail Chase-Bien, Parallel Convergence Catalog, 2004. *Mem:* Napa Arts Coun (bd mem, 2006); Napa Coll Performing Arts (bd mem, 2006). *Media:* Pastel, Oil. *Publ:* Coauth, Gail Chase-Bien, Napa Valley Mus, 2004. *Mailing Add:* 1086 La Londe Ln Napa CA 94558

CHASE-RIBOUD, BARBARA
SCULPTOR, WRITER
b US, June 26, 1939. *Study:* Temple Univ, BFA, PhD; Yale Univ, MFA; Mulhouse Col, PhD; Univ Conn, PhD. *Work:* Mus Mod Art, NY; Newark Mus, NJ; Beaubourg Mus, Paris; NY State Off Bldg; Metrop Mus Art, NY; Nat Collections, France; Foley Sq Off Bldg, NY; and others. *Comn:* Fountain, Kiron Arts & Communications, Paris, 92; multi-colored bronze sculpture, Lannan Found, Los Angeles; bronze & silk sculpture, Metrop Mus, NY; Gen Serv, Washington. *Exhib:* Solo exhibs, Mass Inst Technol, Boston, 70, Berkeley Univ Mus, 73, Detroit Art Inst, 73, Indianapolis Art Mus, 73, Mus Mod Art, Paris, 74, Kunstmuseum, Dusseldorf, 74, Kunstmuseum, Baden-Baden, 79, Mussee Reatu, Artes, 80, Bronx Mus, NY, 81 & Passadena Coll Mus, Los Angeles, 90; Kiron Arts & Communications, Paris, 94; Equitable Life Gallery, 96; Mus NC, 97; Mus Mod Art, Ft Worth, 97; Smithsonian Inst, 98. *Pos:* Lectr, US State Dept, Tunisia, Senegal, Mali, Ghana, Ivory Coast, and others. *Awards:* John Hay Whitney Fel; Carl Sandberg Prize, Best Am Poet, 88; Knighthood in Arts & letters, French Govt, 96. *Bibliog:* American Women Sculptors, Rubinstien, 91;

Abrahms Jenson (auth), The Sculpture of Barbara Chase-Riboual, Munro Women Artists, 97. *Mem:* Century Asn, NY; PEN; Am Ctr NY. *Media:* Multicolored Bronze, Silk. *Publ:* Auth, Sally Hemings--A Novel, (French, Ger, Ital, Spanish & Swed transl), Viking, 79; Valide--A Novel(French, Ger, Ital transl), William Morrow, New York, 86; Portrait of a Nude Woman as Cleopatra, 88 & Echo of Lions, 89, William Morrow; The President's Daughter, Crown, NY, 94; Egypt's Nights, Felin, Paris, 94. *Mailing Add:* c/o Pegalston Fine Arts 407 Central Park W Suite 6C New York NY 10025

CHATMAS, JOHN T
PAINTER, SCULPTOR
b Marlin, Tex, Nov 1, 1945. *Study:* Univ Tex, Austin, BFA, 68; Pratt Inst, MFA, 70. *Work:* Univ Tex, Austin; Baylor Univ, Waco, Tex; Bank Paribas, Dallas; Waterloo Capital Management, Austin, Tex. *Exhib:* solo exhibs, Tex Christian Univ, Fort Worth, 78, Max Hutchinson Gallery, Houston, 79, Graham Gallery, Houston, 82, Cult Activities Ctr, Temple, Tex, 83, E Tex State Univ, Commerce, 85, Baylor Univ, Waco, 72, 92, Art Forum of Waco, 2012; Group exhibs, Artists Biennial, New Orleans Mus Art, La, 73; 112 Green St Gallery, New York, 75; Southwest Tarrant Co Ann, Ft Worth Art Mus, Tex, 77; Southwest Fine Arts Binnial, Santa Fe, NMex, 78; Ann Delta Art Exhib, Ark Art Ctr, Little Rock, Ark, 77; Natl Small Sculpture & Drawing Exhib, San Diego State Univ, Calif, 72; Made in Tex, Univ Tex, Austin, 79; N Tex Invitational, N Tex State Univ, 79; Small Works, 80 Wash Sq E Galleries, NY Univ, 80; New Am Talent, Laguna Gloria Art Mus, Austin, Tex, 86; New Am Talent, Austin Mus Art, Tex, 95; City Images, Divaldo Archa, Prague, Czech Repub, 96; McLennan Community Coll, Waco, 70, 97, 2005, 2011, 2013; Visions Int Competition, Art Ctr Waco, 2002. *Teaching:* prof art & art hist, McLennan Community Coll, 70-. *Awards:* First Place Award, Art Ctr Waco, Tex, 77; Fac Develop Leave Grant, McLennan Community Coll, 85; Visual Artists Fel, Art Matters Inc, New York, 90; Merit Award, Contemp Art Ctr Ft Worth, Tex, 97. *Bibliog:* Charlotte Moser (auth), Abstract Expressionists Inspire Newer Painters, Houston Chronicle, 7/79; Paul Rogers Harris (auth), John Chatmas: Paintings, The Art Center, Waco, Tex, 2/79; Susie Kalil (auth), Texas Ranges: Houston From Boogeymen to the End Result of Constructivist Theory, Art News, 12/82; Gordon McConnell (auth), The paintings of John Chatmas, Cult Activities Ctr, Temple, Tex, 10/83; Janet Kutner (auth), Mystery Cloaks Intriguing Show, Dallas Morning News, 10/14/91; Joseph Kagle (auth), City Images, Divaldo Archa, Prague, Czech Repub, 96. *Media:* Acrylic, Oil, Miscellaneous Media. *Mailing Add:* 1315 N 34th St Waco TX 76710

CHATTERJEE, JAY (JAYANTA)
ADMINISTRATOR, EDUCATOR
b Calcutta, India, Mar 19, 1936; US citizen. *Study:* Indian Inst Technol, BArch (hons), 58; Univ NC, MRP, 62; Harvard Univ, MArch, 65. *Pos:* Dean Emeritus, Col Design, Archit, Art & Planning, Univ Cincinnati, 82-2001. *Awards:* Thomas Jefferson Award, AIA; Disting Svc Award, ACSP; Post-Corbett Award Lifetime Achievements in the Arts; Visionary Award, Contemp Arts Ctr, Cincinnati, Ohio; Martin Mayerson Award for Leadership in Higher Educ. *Mem:* Am Planning Asn; Asn Collegiate Schs of Planning (pres, 83-85); ICFAD; Contemp Arts Ctr (emer); AIA (assoc). *Media:* photography. *Publ:* Contribr, Managing University Team in Partnership Planning, Sage, 82; Schools and the Private Sector in Partnership, Rutgers, 84. *Mailing Add:* 20 Rawson Woods Cir Cincinnati OH 45220-1331

CHATTERLEY, MARK D
SCULPTOR
b Highland Park, Mich, Aug 22, 1957. *Study:* Mich State Univ, BFA, 79, MFA, 81. *Work:* Holocaust Mus, St Petersburg, Fla; NC State Univ Visual Art, Raleigh; Jinro, Seoul, Korea; James Wallace Art Trust, Auckland, NZ; Kresge Art Mus, Mich State Univ, East Lansing. *Comn:* Three sculptures, Wharton Ctr Performing Arts, East Lansing; installation, Governor's Mansion, Lansing, Mich. *Exhib:* Lansing Art Gallery, Mich, 88 & 98; Kendall Coll Art & Design, Grand Rapids, 88; Clay USA, Radford Univ, Va, 89; Univ Cincinnati, Ohio, 90; Kresge Art Mus, Mich State Univ, East Lansing, 91; Sculpture Exhib, Pa State Univ, 91; Egner Fine Arts Ctr Gallery, Univ Findlay, Ohio, 92; Adrian Coll Art Gallery, Mich, 93; Raynor: Master and His Circle, Muskegon Mus Art, 94; Sixteenth Mich Artist's Competition, Art Ctr Battle Creek, Mich, 94; Life Imitating Art of Art Imitating Life?, Mackerel Sky Gallery, East Lansing, Mich, 95; Cincinnati Art Mus Spec Exhib, 96; Ester Prangley Rice Gallery, Western Md Col, 97; The Spirit of Clay, Art Works Gallery, Norfolk, Va, 97; The Artfull Home, Ann Arbor Art Ctr, Mich, 97; Mythic Fire, Edenside Gallery, Louisville, Ky, 97; Sculpture Michigan, Frederick Meijer Gardens, Grand Rapids, Mich, 98. *Awards:* Festival of the Masters First Place for Sculpture, Walt Disney World, Fla, 93; Mich Potter's Asn First Place Ceramics '95, Habatat-Shaw Gallery, Pontiac, Mich, 95; Fletcher Challenge Ceramics Award of Merit, Auckland, NZ, 98. *Mailing Add:* 231 Turner Rd Williamston MI 48895

CHAVEZ, JOSEPH ARNOLD
SCULPTOR, INSTRUCTOR
b Belen, NMex, Dec 25, 1939. *Study:* Univ Albuquerque, BS (art educ), 63; Univ NMex, MA (art educ), 67, MA (art), 71; Univ Cincinnati, 74. *Work:* Slide Libr Collection, Univ Southern Ala; plus numerous works in pvt collections across the nation. *Exhib:* Solo exhibs, Jonson Gallery, Univ NMex, 71 & 76; NMex Arts & Crafts Fair Ann, Albuquerque; Southwest Arts & Crafts Fair Ann; Southwest Crafts Biennial, Santa Fe Folk Art Mus, 74; State Fair Dallas, Tex, 75; Gallery A, Taos, NMex; Aldridge Gallery, Albuquerque; Hispanic Market, San Francisco Nat Mus, 90; Denver Art Show, 90. *Teaching:* Art, Lincoln Jr High, Albuquerque, 63-70; supvr student teachers art educ, Univ NMex, 70-71; teacher art, Sandia High Sch, Albuquerque, 71-; instr art, Univ Albuquerque, summer 70; supvr student teachers art educ, Univ Cincinnati, 74; artist-in-residence, Pueblo, Colo, 90. *Awards:* Sculpture, Festival in the Pines, Flagstaff, Ariz, 90; Second Place, Pottery & Sculpture Expos, Rio Grande Art & Crafts Fair, 74; Spec Merit, State Fair Tex, 75; Fourth Place, NMex State Fair Sculpture Exhib, 83. *Bibliog:* Dr Jacinto Quirarte (auth), Mexican-American Artists, Univ Tex, 73; The Man Who Fell to Earth, London Film Co, 75; Joseph Chavez (auth, videotape), The Art of Carving Stone. *Mem:* Designers & Craftsmen NMex (pres, 73); Art Advocacy. *Media:* Stone, Wood. *Publ:* Auth, Critique on art, Coll St Joseph News, 64; auth, Space filled & fulfilled, Southwest Art, 4/82. *Dealer:* Gallery A Taos NM; Aldridge Gallery Albuquerque NM. *Mailing Add:* 4618 Sorrel Ln SW Albuquerque NM 87105-6388

CHAVEZ, JUAN ANGEL
EDUCATOR
b La Junta, Chihuahua, Mex, Sept 25, 1971; arrived in US, 1985. *Study:* Sch Art Inst Chicago Early Coll Prog. *Pos:* Intern, Educ & Performing Arts Dept, Mex Fine Arts Ctr Mus, Chicago; arts rep, City of Chicago Pub Art Comt. *Teaching:* Sculpture dept, Sch Art Inst Chicago. *Awards:* Richard H Driehaus Individual Artist Award; Louis Comfort Tiffany Found Grant, 2008. *Mailing Add:* Chicago Pub Art Group 1259 S Wabash Chicago IL 60605

CHAVOOSHIAN, MARGE
PAINTER, EDUCATOR
b New York, NY, Jan 8, 1925. *Study:* Art Students League, New York, 41-45; study with Reginald Marsh, 41 & Mario Cooper, 77. *Work:* NJ State Mus, Trenton; Morris Mus, Morristown; Rutgers Univ, New Brunswick, NJ; Mercer Co Cult & Heritage Comn; Johnson & Johnson, New Brunswick, NJ; Mus at San Lazarre, Venice, Italy; Zimmerli Mus, Rutgers Univ, New Brunswick, NJ; and others. *Comn:* Holiday design (reproduction), Multiple Sclerosis Soc, Trenton Chap, 73 & Nat Dist, 74; historic bldg series (30 paintings), NJ State Coun Arts, 80; holiday poster, Port Authority NY & NJ, 81; painting (reproduction), Armenian Sisters Acad, Philadelphia, Pa, 81; 2 full sheet watercolors, Capital Health Systems, Mercer Hospital, Trenton, NJ, 2008. *Exhib:* Solo exhibs, Rider Univ, 74, 2000, NJ State Mus, 81 & Trenton City Mus, 84 & 88, Arts Club of Washington, DC, 91, Louise Melrose Gallery, Frenchtown, NJ, 2002, Coryell Gallery, Lambertville, NJ, 2006; Group shows, Frye Mus, Seattle, Wash, 83; Owensboro Mus Fine Art, Ky, 83; Allied Artists Am Nat Exhib, Salmagundi Club, NY, 83; 200 Yrs of Am Drawings, Morris Mus, NJ, 84; Catharine Lorillard Wolfe Nat Exhib, Nat Arts Club, NY, 85; Nat Asn Women Artists, Jacob Javitz Fed Bldg, NY, 86; Philadelphia Watercolor Club 70th Ann Exhibit, Port Hist Mus, 88, Ursinus Col, 94 & 96; Nat Watercolor Soc, 98; Lancaster Art Mus, PA, Newark Mus, NJ, Noyes Mus, NJ, Phillip-Muriel Berman Mus, PA, Woodmere Mus, PA; Philadelphia Watercolor Soc, Noyes Mus Art, Oceanville, NJ, 2002; Butler Inst Am Art, Youngstown, Ohio, 2007; Two Person Exhib: Nora (daughter) and Marge C (watercolor and sculpture), Chapin School, Princeton, NJ, 2007, Related Artists, Medford Arts Ctr, Medford, NJ, 2010; Adirondacks Nat Exhib Am Watercolors, Old Forge, NY, 2007, 2009; Salmagundi Club, New York, 2009; Nat Arts Club, New York, 2009; and others. *Pos:* illustrator, John David Mens Store, NY, 43-44; artist, Fawcett Publs, 45-46; artist on campus, Pa State Univ, 46-48; Consult art, Title 1 Prog, teacher-student workshop, Trenton Pub Sch, NJ, 66-73; artist-at-large, NJ Chap Nat Orgn, Alliance Art Educ, 79-81; corresp secy, Trenton Artist Workshop Asn, 86-. *Teaching:* Studio instr painting & drawing, Princeton Art Asn, NJ, 77-79; asst prof watercolor, Mercer Co Col, West Windsor, NJ, 85-91; Watercolor Workshops, Chalfonte Hotel, Cape May, NJ, 88-2008, workshops, 2009. 2010, Hilton Leech Studios Workshops, 98-99, Art Ctr, Sarsota, Fla, 2001-2003, and others. *Awards:* Silver Medallion, Garden State Watercolor Soc, Grumbacher, 81; Bermel Award Traditional Watercolor, Monmouth Mus, NJ Watercolor Soc, 84; Gold Medallion, Am Artists Prof League, 90, Title of Fel, 91 & Best in Show, 91; Bronze Medal, Catharine L Wolfe Art Club, NY, 2000, 2004, 2007, 2009 (medal of hon); Ken McCann Mem Award, Garden State Watercolor Soc 35th Ann Open, 2005; Thomas Moran Award for Watercolor, Salmagundi Nat Show, NY, 2006-2007; Silver Medal of Honor, NJ Watercolor Society, 2007; Hist Soc Purchase Award, Lambertville, NJ, 2008; Distinguished Merit Award, Am Artists Prof League, Middlesex Co Coll, Edison, NJ, 2008; Winsor & Newton Award, Ridgewood Art Inst, Barn Galleries, NJ, 2008, David Davis Award, 2010; Katlan Seascape Award, Salmagundi Nonmembers Show, New York, 2009. *Bibliog:* William D Gorman (auth), Marge Chavooshian paints the cities, Artform Mag, NJ, 11/81; Nancy Alderman (auth), Woman of the month, Woman's Newspaper, Princeton, 9/84; Pat Van Gelder (auth), The Watercolor page, Am Artist, 10/88. *Mem:* Catharine Lorillard Wolfe Art Club; Philadelphia Watercolor Soc; Nat Asn Women Artists; Allied Artists Am; Nat Watercolor Soc (signature mem); Am Artists Prof League (nat and NJ chpts); NJ Watercolor Soc, Garden State Watercolor Soc; Am Watercolor Soc (signature mem). *Media:* Watercolor, Pen & Ink. *Specialty:* Paintings, sculpture, and prints. *Interests:* Piano, gardening, travel, plein air painting. *Collection:* Public: Zimmerli Mus, Rutgers Univ, NJ, NJ State Mus, Trenton Rider Univ, NJ, Art Mus, Venice, Italy; PSE&G, Johnson & Johnson, Schering Plough Corp, Arts Club of Wash, Mercer County Culture & Heritage Comm, Bristol Myers Squibb, Capital Health System, Mercer Hospital, Trenton, NJ, 2008. *Publ:* Auth, Travel tips from the pros, 3/85, Quick tips, 7/85 & The watercolor page, 10/88, Am Artist Mag; Best in Watercolor, 95, Places in Watercolor, 96 & Landscape Inspirations, 97, Rockport Publ; The Best of Sketching and Drawing, Rockport Pubs, 99; The Artistic Touch 3, Creative Art Press, 99; Trenton Artist Workshop Asn, 25 Years, 2004; Phillips Mill 75th Anniversary Retrospective Exhibit, Phillip Mill Community Asn, 2005; Bennington Ctr for the Arts, Vt Invitational for Allied Artists of Am (catalog), 2007; The Invisible Watercolorist, In Your Prime, Pa & NJ Publ, 2009. *Dealer:* Coryell Gallery Lambertville NJ; Lawrence Gallery Lawrenceville NJ; Farnsworth Gallery Bordentown NJ; Ellarslie The Trenton City Mus, NJ. *Mailing Add:* 537 Riverdale Ave Apt 1114 Yonkers NY 10705

CHAVOOSHIAN, NORA
SCULPTOR, DESIGNER
b Trenton, NJ, Oct 25, 1953. *Study:* Pa Acad Fine Art, 1970-1973; San Francisco Art Inst, BFA, 1975. *Comn:* Bronze (sculpture), Brookdale Playground Community, Brookdale Park, Essex Co, NJ, 1997; Sculpture (featured on wine label), Angelbeck's Fine Wines, Montclair, NJ, 2001; Pub Art (bas relief murals), Community in Schs, Orange High Sch, Orange, NJ, 2007. *Exhib:* 1997 Int Show, NJ Center Visual Arts, Summit, NJ, 1997; Bronze Sculpture of Nora Chavooshian, Winfisky Gallery, Salem

State Coll, Salem, Mass, 1998; Recent Works of Nora Chavooshian, Pierre DePont Arts Center, Wilmington, Del, 1999; 2000 Winter Goodwill Games, Goodwill Galleries, Lake Placid, NY, 2000; Project Vision, Montclair State Univ, Montclair, NJ, 2000; Look Back - Recent Work of Nora Chavooshian, Denise Bibro Fine Art, NY, 1999, 2006; Connections, Ben Shahn Gallery, William Peterson Univ, 2006; The Gallery at Chapin, Princeton, NJ, 2007; Armenian Women's Art, The Village Quill, NY, 2007. *Awards:* Rose Goldstein Mem Award for Sculpture, 54th Ann Audubon Artists Exhib, NY, 1996; Salmagundi Club Award, 22nd Ann Open Jury Show, Ridgewood Art Inst, 2002. *Bibliog:* William Zimmer (auth) review, NY Times, 1992, 1993; Eileen Watkins (auth), review, Star Ledger, 1993; Edward J Sozanski (auth), review, Philadelphia, Inquire, 1993; Joyce Korotkin (auth), Look Back NY Arts (review), 2000; Janet Purcell (auth), Princeton Show, The Two of Us (review), Trenton Times, 2007. *Media:* Cast Sculpture, Clay, Installation Sculpture, Metal Cast. *Dealer:* Denise Bibro Fine Art 529 W 20th New York, NY. *Mailing Add:* 53 Gordonhurst Ave Montclair NJ 07043

CHEE, CHENG-KHEE (JINYI XU)
PAINTER, EDUCATOR
b Fujian, China, Jan 14, 1934; US citizen. *Study:* Nanyang Univ, Singapore, BA, 60; Univ Minn, Minneapolis, MA, 64; studied watercolor painting with Dong Kingman & Edgar Whitney. *Work:* Univ Minn & 3-M Co, St Paul; Tweed Mus Art, Duluth, Minn; Purdue Univ, Calumet, Ind; China Acad Fine Arts, Hangzhou, China; Fujian Prov Art Mus, China. *Comn:* Lakeshore Surf (painting) 88, Winter Lake View (painting), 95, Lake Superior Paper Industs, Duluth, Minn. *Exhib:* Minn Mus Art, St Paul, 76; Am Watercolor Soc Ann, 75, 78-79, 81, 91, 94, 95 & 98, 2001, 2003; Rocky Mountain Nat Watermedia Exhib, Foothills Art Ctr, Golden, Colo, 76, 78, 80, 84 & 90-93; Allied Artists Am Ann, Nat Art Club, NY, 80, 82 & 91-97, 99-2001, 2003; Nat Watercolor Soc Ann, 83-85 & 92, 2002-2003; Adirondacks Nat Exhib Am Watercolors, 82-83, 86, 89, 91-92 & 95, 97-98, 2000, 2002-2004; Singapore Nat Art Mus, 97; Bloomington Art Ctr, 2003. *Pos:* Sr librn, Univ Minn, Duluth, 65-78. *Teaching:* Instr, Univ Minn, Duluth, 78-80, asst prof, 81-88, assoc prof, 88-. *Awards:* Gold Medal, Allied Artists Am 67th Ann, 80; Gold Medal, Knickerbocker Artists Ann, 90 & 93; Silver Medal, Am Watercolor Soc Ann, 91; and others. *Bibliog:* Marcia Brown (auth), The Eastern Mountain Walks on Water, Cheng-Khee Chee China Exhib (catalog), 87; Hugh E Bishop (auth), Chee Pursuing Excellence, Lake Superior Mag, 5/95; Lok Tok (auth), Master Watercolorist Cheng-Khee Chee, Cheng-Khee Chee Southeast Asia Exhib (catalog), 97. *Mem:* Am Watercolor Soc; Transparent Watercolor Soc Am; Nat Watercolor Soc; Allied Artists Am; Watercolor USA Honor Soc. *Media:* Watercolor, Chinese Brush Painting. *Publ:* Contribr, Learn Watercolor the Edgar Whitney Way, 94; Splash 3: Ideas and Inspirations, 94; The Best of Watercolor, Rockport Pub, 95; Splash 4: The Splendor of Light, 96; Splash 5: The Glory of Color; The Watercolor World of Cheng-Khee Chee; Old Turtle Illustrations, 91; Noel Illustrations, 2005. *Dealer:* Chee Studio 1508 Vermilion Rd Duluth MN 55812. *Mailing Add:* 1508 Vermilion Rd Duluth MN 55812-1526

CHEEK, RONALD EDWARD
PAINTER, INSTRUCTOR
b Greenville, SC, Dec 6, 1942. *Study:* Ringling Coll Art & Design, BFA, 71; Art Students League, with Frank Mason, Theodoros Stamos & Charles Alston; New Sch Social Res, with Joseph Floch. *Work:* Columbia Mus Art & SC State Mus, Columbia; Augusta Mus, Ga; The Citadel Mus, Charleston, SC; Albany Mus Art, Ga; Jasper Rand Art Mus, Westfield, Mass; Lakeland Mus Art, Fla; Sioux Indian Mus, US Dept Interior, Rapid City, SDak. *Comn:* Plant Remedies: Medicine of the American Indians, Blair-Murrah Exhibs, 91; Anniston Mus Art, Ala, 96; Cox Arboretum, Dayton, Ohio, 96; Bartlesville Art Mus, Okla, 97; Clark Co Heritage Mus, Las Vegas, Nev, 97; Charlotte Mus History, NC, 2002; Charlotte County Historical Ctr, Port Charlotte, Fla, 2010. *Exhib:* Solo exhibs, Jasper Rand Art Mus, Westfield, Mass, 79, Old Hyde Park Art Ctr, Tampa, Fla, 81, Cayuga Mus Hist Art, Auburn, NY, 81, Citadel Mus, Charleston, SC, 81, Sioux Indian Mus, Rapid City, SDak, 82, Manatee Community Coll, Bradenton, Fla, 83 & Univ S Fla, Sarasota, 85, Albany Mus Art, Ga, 78, Lakeland Mus Art, Fla, 76, Columbia Mus Art, SC, 78, Florence Mus Art, SC, 78; Venice Art Ctr, Fla, 90; Anderson Co Art Ctr, SC, 91; Longwood Gardens, Kenneth Sq, Pa, 92; Cartwright Ctr, Univ Wis, Lacrosse, 93; Nat Hist Ore Trail Interpretive Ctr, US Bur Land Mgt, Baker City, Ore; Jefferson Patterson Park & Mus, Prince Frederick, Md, 98; Lewis & Clark Interpretive Ctr, Great Falls, Mont, 99. *Teaching:* Instr figure & drawing, Manatee Art League, Bradenton, Fla, 78-80; instr all media & drawing, Manatee Area Vocational-Technical Ctr, 78-, Manatee Community Coll, 96-, Pickens Co Mus Art & Hist, 96- & Manatee Art League, 96-; instr portrait & drawing, Sarasota Co Vocational-Technical Ctr, 78-90; instr pastel painting & drawing, Sarasota Visual Ctr Art, 91-. *Awards:* Golden Jubilee Award, Sarasota Art Asn, 76; First Place, Paul Dorfmuller Mem Pastel Competition, 82; First Place, Pickens Co Mus Art Invitational, 88. *Bibliog:* Drawings by Ronald Cheek, Sioux Indian Mus & US Dept Interior, 82; Forty works at forty, Sarasota Herald Tribune, 83; South Carolina Art Collection, Columbia Mus Art, 86; Biographical Encyl American Painters, Sculptors, and Engravers of the US - Colonial to 2002. *Mem:* Old Hyde Park Art Ctr, Tampa, Fla; Art Ctr, St Petersburg, Fla; Venice Art Ctr, Fla. *Media:* Pastel. *Mailing Add:* 617 E Main St Easley SC 29640

CHEIM, JOHN
GALLERY DIRECTOR
b San Jose, Calif, April 4, 1953. *Study:* RI Sch Design, BFA. *Pos:* Dir, Robert Miller Gallery, 1977; co-founder, prin/head exhibutions, Cheim & Read, 1997-. *Mailing Add:* Cheim & Read 547 W 25th St New York NY 10001

CHEMECHE, GEORGE
PAINTER, SCULPTOR
b Baghdad, Iraq, May 11, 1934; US citizen. *Study:* Avni Sch Fine Arts, Tel Aviv, 56-59; Ecole des Beaux Arts, Paris, 60-63. *Work:* Guggenheim Mus, NY; Denver Art Mus; Fogg Mus, Boston; San Francisco Mus Mod Art; Herbert F Johnson Mus Art, Cornell Univ, Ithaca, NY; and others. *Awards:* Am-Israel Cult Found Award, 60. *Bibliog:* Jean Pierre Vandigaum (auth), Interview with the artist, Art Press, Paris, 77; John Perreault (auth), article, in: Soho News, 77; Ruth Bass (auth), article, in: Art News, 81. *Media:* Oil, Pastel, Metal. *Mailing Add:* 222 W 23rd St No 422 New York NY 10011-2311

CHEN, ANNA CHAIHUE
PAINTER
b Taiwan. *Study:* Art Inst Philadelphia, AS, 1973. *Work:* Daytona Beach Mus of Arts & Sci, Daytona Beach, Fla; Polk Mus of Arts, Lakeland, Fla; Walt Disney World, Co, Orlando, Fla; Orlando Int Airport, Orlando, Fla; Kissimmee Ct House, Kissimmee, Fla. *Comn:* (watercolor), comn by Patrick Knipe, 1996; (watercolor), comn by Noreen Schumann, Naples, Fla, 2001; (watercolor), comn by Chalotte Houser, Merritt Island, Fla, 2002; (watercolor), comn by Ether Van Kessel, DeBary, 2002; (watercolor), comn by Marrianne Dowling, DeBary, Fla, 2002. *Exhib:* Fla Watercolor Soc Am Exhib, Mus of Fine Arts, St Petersburg, Fla, 1991-1996; Collectors Exhib, Daytona Beach Mus of Arts, Daytona Beach, Fla, 1993; FWS Ann Exhib, Deland Mus of Art, Deland, Fla, 1994; The Artis Mag Competition, Cincinnati Art Club, Cincinnati, Ohio, 1997; AWS Ann Int Exhib, Galleries of the Salmagundi Club, NY, 2004-2006. *Awards:* Best of Show, Mt Dora Art Festival, Mt Dora Art Ctr, 1993-1995; Arts Mag Competition, Arts Mag, 1997; Best of Show, Sausalito Art Festival, Sausalito Art Festival LLc, 2005; Edgar Whitney Mem Award, Am Watercolor Soc Exhib, Salmagundi Art Club, NYC, 2006. *Bibliog:* Marilyn Watman-Feldman (auth), Winter Spring Watercolor Painter, Winter Park Outlook, 1990; Dianne Copelon (auth), Heritage Flavors Chens Work, Orlando Sentinel, 1995; Jennifer Modenessi (auth), Spotlight, Contra Costa Sunday Times, 2005. *Mem:* Am Watercolor Soc (signature mem); Nat Watercolor Soc (signature mem); Fla Watercolor Soc (signature mem); Int Artist Soc (signature mem). *Media:* Watercolor. *Publ:* Contribr, Tropical Joy Artists of Taiwan, Artists Mag Point Fine Arts Inc, 1994; contribr, Best of Watercolor Painting Texture, Rockport Publs Inc, 1997; Best of Watercolor Painting Composition, Rockport Publs Inc, 1997. *Mailing Add:* 9604 Velevetleaf Cir San Ramon CA 94582

CHEN, HILO
PAINTER
b Taiwan, Repub of China, Oct 15, 1942; US citizen. *Study:* Chong Yen Col, BS (archit). *Work:* Guggenheim Mus; Byer Mus, Evanston, Ill. *Exhib:* Wadsworth Atheneum, Hartford, Conn, 74; Indianapolis Mus of Art, 74; Pa State Mus of Art, 74; Baltimore Mus of Art, 75; Lafayette Natural Hist Mus & Planetarium, La, 75; Edwin Ulrich Mus, Wichita State Univ, Kans, 76. *Collection Arranged:* New-Photo Realism, Wadsworth Atheneum, 74. *Bibliog:* Robert Hughes (auth), An omniverous & literal dependence, Arts, 6/74; Andrea Mikotajuk (auth), American realists at LKM, Arts, 1/75; Dorothy Belden (auth), Realism exaggerated in Ulrich Art Exhibition, Wichita Eagle, 3/76. *Media:* Oil on Canvas, Watercolor on Paper. *Dealer:* Louis K Meisel 141 Prince St New York NY 10012

CHEN, HSIN-HSI
GRAPHIC ARTIST
b Sept 1969. *Study:* Tunghai Univ, Taiwan, BFA, 1992; Univ Md, MFA, 1996. *Exhib:* Solo exhibs include Troyer Fitzpatrick Lassman Gallery, Washington, 1996, C Grimaldis Gallery, Baltimore, 1998, Korean Embassy, Washington, 2000, Montpelier Cult Arts Ctr, Laurel, Md, 2001, Harmony Hall Regional Ctr Arts, Ft Washington, Md, 2004, Glenview Mansion Art Gallery, Rockville, Md, 2005, NIH, Bethesda, Md, 2006, McLean Proj Arts, Va, 2006, Monroe Gallery, Arts Club Washington, 2008; group exhibs include Government House, Annapolis, Md, 1997; C Grimaldis Gallery, Baltimore, 1999, 2007; Global Women Project, traveling exhib, 2000-05; Leaded: The Materiality & Metamorphosis of Graphite, Univ Richmond Mus, Va, 2007. *Awards:* Solo Show Competition Award, Montpelier Cult Arts Ctr, 2000; Pollock-Krasner Found Grant, 2007. *Mailing Add:* 304 Deep Trail Ln Rockville MD 20850-7770

CHEN, PIERRE TM
COLLECTOR
Pos: Founder, chmn, chief exec, Yageo Corp, 1977-. *Awards:* Named one of top 200 art collectors, ARTnews mag, 2011, 2012, 2013. *Collection:* Western and Chinese modern and contemporary art; Chinese imperial porcelain and art. *Mailing Add:* Yageo Corporation Xindian Dist 3F, 233-1, Baoqiao Rd Taipei Taiwan 23145

CHENEY, LIANA DE GIROLAMI
ART HISTORIAN, CURATOR
b Milan, Italy, 1942; US citizen. *Study:* Univ Miami, BA, 68, MA (art hist), 70; Worcester Art Ctr, Mass, studied ceramics, 70; Wellesley Col, Mass, 71, post-grad study, Renaissance art; Boston Univ, PhD (Renaissance, Mannerism & Baroque art), 78. *Collection Arranged:* Karl May, 80, Thomas Nast, Illustrator, 84 & J Beuys, 84, Univ Lowell; Whistler, 84, Lawrence Kupferman, 85, Samuel P Howes, 86 & Photographs of Cambodia, 87, Whistler House Mus, Lowell; and many other exhibitions at Univ Mass Lowell and Whistler House Mus Art, Lowell. *Pos:* Consult, Nat Endowment Humanities Art Hist Grants, 80-; cur, Whistler House Mus, Lowell, 84-; president, ATSAH. *Teaching:* prof art history, Instr art hist, Boston Col, 73-74; from instr to prof art hist, Univ Mass-Lowell, 74, chairperson art dept, 83-97; chair, Cult Studies Dept, 2000-2013; Univ Coruna, Spain, 2013; Univ Bari, 2014. *Awards:* Samuel H Kress Found Grants, 73, 73 & 74; Nat Endowment Humanities Grants, 77-78, 79-82, 89 & 92; Mass Coun Arts & Humanities Grant, 85-86; Teaching Award, Univ Mass, Lowell, 2002, 2005, 2009. *Mem:* Coll Art Asn Am; Renaissance Soc Am; Emblematic Soc; Save Venice Inc; PreRaphaelite Soc; SECAC; SRC; ATSAH Soc;

Symbolist Soc. *Res:* Italian art history; Pre-Raphaelite painters; Women's Art. *Interests:* Classical music, astrology, walking, knitting & theater; reading, collecting stamps, cinema. *Publ:* Coauth (with P Marks), The Whistler Papers, 86 & The Whistler Notes, Lowell, 88; ed, Vanitas and Vanities: Symbols in the Arts, Edwin Mellen Press, 92; Pre-Raphaelitism, Edwin Mellen Press, 92; Botticelli's Neoplatonic Images, Scripta Humanitatis, 93; Self-Portraits of Women Artists, Ashgate Press, 97; Essays on Women Artists, 2 vols, Edwin Mellen Press, 2002; Vasari's Homes, Lang Press, 2006; Vasari's Teachers, Lang Press, 2006; Italian Mannerism, Lang Press, 2007; Vasari's Prefaces, Edwin Mellen Press, 2007; Arcimboldo, Parkstone Press, 2008, 2013; Vasari's Prefaces: Art and Theory, Lang Press, 2011; New Academia, 2011; Vasari's Emblematic and Artistic Manifestations, New Academia, 2011; Self portraits, Women Painters, New Academia, 2009; Edward Burne-Jones (Mythical) Paintings, Lang Press, 2013; Bronzino, 2014; Vasari Elements: Symbolism, Lang, 2013; Giorgio Vasari in Context, Eric, 2013. *Mailing Add:* 112 Charles St Boston MA 02114

CHENG, CARL F K
SCULPTOR
b San Francisco, Calif, Feb 8, 1942. *Study:* Univ Hawaii, 63; Univ Calif Los Angeles, Dickson Art Ctr, BA, 63, MA, 67; Folkwang Art Sch, Essen, Ger, 64-65. *Work:* Fred Weisman Collection, Pepperdine Coll, Malibu, Calif; Exploratorium, San Francisco; George Eastman House, Eastman Kodak, Rochester, NY; David Bermant Collection, Santa Barbara; many other pvt collections. *Comn:* Marine Station, Metro Rail, Metrop Transit Authority, Los Angeles, 95; Tilted Landscape, Tempe Arts Comn, Ariz, 95; Community Island Pond, Pier 11, Percent for Arts Proj, New York, 97-98; Everglades Trespass, Libr Proj, Broward Co, Fla, 2000; Santa Monica Art Tool, Calif, 88; Santa Monica Libr, Calif, 2005; Aerial Plaza, Long Beach, Calif, 2009; Ghost Fish, La Port, 2012. *Exhib:* Water Projects, ASG Gallery, Nagoya, Japan, 88; Impression of an Invisible Sculp, List Visual Arts, Mass Inst Technol, Cambridge, 88; 66 Percent Water, Capp St Projs, AUT, San Francisco, 89; 40 Yrs of Assemblage, Wight Gallery, Univ Calif Los Angeles, 89; solo exhibs, Survey, 25 years of John Doe Co, Contemp Art Forum, Santa Barbara, Calif, 91, Quality of Light, Int Exhib, Cornwall Eng, Newlyn Art Gallery, Penzance, 97 & Installation, Santa Monica Art Mus, Bergamont Ctr, Calif, 98; Artec Bianale, Nagoya, Japan, 93; 5th Bienal of Havana, Cuba, 94; Investigations, Munic Art Gallery, Los Angeles, 96; Turbulent Landscapes Exploratorium (3 yr traveling exhib), San Francisco, Calif, 96; COLA: Individual Artist Grant Exhib, Munic Art Gallery, Barnsdall Park, Los Angeles, 97; Organic Lab Mus, Santa Monica Mus Art, Calif, 98; Nature Observed, installation, Sculpture Ctr, New York, 2000; Photo into Sculpture, Cherry Martin Gallery, 2011; Pacific Standard Time, MOCA, Los Angeles, 2012. *Teaching:* Instr, Otis Art Inst, Claremont Grad Sch art dept & Dickson Art Ctr, Univ Calif, Los Angeles. *Awards:* Visual Arts Grant, Nat Endowment Arts, 82 & 86; Getty Visual Arts Grant, Getty Mus, 90; Los Angeles Cult Arts Grant, 90 & 96-97; Flintridge Found Grant, 2004. *Bibliog:* JS Willette (auth), Profile of artist vision, Art Quart, fall 93; Peter Frank (auth), Art pick of the week, rev, LA Weekly, 6/96; W Wilson (auth), Investigations Show rev, LA Times Calendar, 6/4/96; Mark Johnston (auth), Contemporary Art in Southern California, Craftsman House, 99; Shifting Perceptions, Pacific Asia Mus, Pasadena, Calif, 2000; R Whitaker (ed), Carl Cheng, Works Mag No. *Mem:* Mus Contemp Art, Los Angeles; Sculpture Inc. *Media:* Installations, Public Art. *Dealer:* John Doe Co Santa Monica CA. *Mailing Add:* 1518 17th St Santa Monica CA 90404

CHENG, EMILY
PAINTER
b New York, NY, July 28, 1953. *Study:* Rhode Island Sch Design, BFA, 75, New York Studio Sch of Painting, Drawing & Sculpture. *Hon Degrees:* fellow, Nat Endowment, 82-83, Yaddo, 95, NY Found, 96. *Exhib:* Solo exhibs, Hanart TZ Gallery, 96, Bravin Post Lee, New York City, 97, Metrop Mus Manila, Philippines, 97, Schmidt/Dean Gallery, Phila, 98, Byron Cohen Gallery, Kansas City, Mo, 2001, Plum Blossoms, NY, 2004, Ayala Mus, Makati, Manila, Philippines, 2006; Group exhibs, Hanart 20th Anniversary Exhib, Hong Kong Art Ctr, HK The Ann, Nat Acad Arts, NY, 2004, Microcosm Brewery Projects Space, Los Angeles, Calif, Magical Gardens, Kidspace at MASS MoCA, North Adams, Mass, 2005. *Teaching:* instr, Sch Visual Arts, RI Sch Design, currently. *Awards:* Nat Endow Arts Fel, 82-83. *Bibliog:* Yeon-Shim Chung (auth), Emily Cheng Unity of East and West, The Art Mag Wolgan Missol, 7/2000; Abstracting the Meaning, The NY Times, 9/24/2000; Jonathan Goodman (auth), Ornament as Knowledge, Ornament as Desire, Yishu, winter, 2003; Impy Pilapil (auth), Rekindling Wonder, Philippine Star, 7/3/2004; Chris Moylan (auth), Emily Cheng and Lois Conner, Arts Asia Pacific, fall, 2004. *Mem:* Coll Art Asn. *Media:* Oil. *Dealer:* Winston Wachter Fine Art NY; Plum Blossom Gallery NY; Schmidt Dean Gallery Philadelphia PA. *Mailing Add:* 439 Lafayette St New York NY 10003-7007

CHENG, FU-DING
FILMMAKER, PAINTER
b Palo Alto, Calif, Feb 5, 1943. *Study:* Sch Archit, Univ Southern Calif; Alliance Francaise, Paris; Univ Calif, Berkeley, BArch. *Exhib:* New Am Filmmakers, Whitney Mus Am Art, NY, 70; Yale Film Festival, 72; Belg Int Film Festival, 73; Asian-Am Film Festival, NY, 86 & 92; Tokyo Int Film Festival, 87; Houston Int Film Festival, 90; Art retrospective Magic Realism and Beyond, Available Light Gallery, Los Angeles, 98; film retrospective Zen-Tales for the Urban Explorer, UCLA/Armand Hammer Mus, Los Angeles, 2000. *Teaching:* Instr art, Univ Calif, Los Angeles, 76-82, Shamk Apprentice Gallery, 97-. *Awards:* Independent grant, Film Proj, Am Film Inst, 77; First Place, Foothill Nat Film Festival, Foothill Col; Gold Prize, Houston Int Festival, 90. *Bibliog:* Zen-tales for the Urban Explorer (video), LA Weekly, 2000; Urban Mystic (videolage), Brave New Artists of Video, LA Times. *Mem:* Independent Feature Project, West. *Media:* Film video; Watercolor, Acrylic. *Publ:* Auth, Los Angeles Times Calendar, Brave New Artists Video, 87; auth, Video Lace, Urban Mystic, 87; illusr (children's book), Dream-House, Hampton Rds Publ, 2000. *Dealer:* Cinergy Entertainment Santa Monica CA. *Mailing Add:* 209 Seventh Ave Venice CA 90291

CHEPP, MARK
MUSEUM DIRECTOR, ADMINISTRATOR
b Milwaukee, Wis. *Study:* Univ Wis, Milwaukee. *Collection Arranged:* Howard Schroedter Retrospective Exhib, 87; Robert Von Neumann: Works On Paper, 1930-1970, (auth, catalog) 89; African Art From the Richard Hunt collection, 89; The Quentin and Emmy Lou Schenk Collection of Ehtiopiana, 90; Ethel Cook: The Young'n With A Wild Brush, 91; Imaging Faith: Greek And Russian Icons, 1500-1900, 91; The Columbian Encounter, 92; An Unexpected Orthodoxy: The Paintings of Lorenzo Scott (auth, catalog), 93; Conversations: The Paintings of Frances Hynes (auth, catalog), 93. *Pos:* Cur, Univ Wis, Milwaukee Art Mus, 74-91; dir, Springfield Mus Art, 91-. *Mem:* Am Asn Mus; Ohio Mus Asn; Asn Midwest Mus. *Publ:* Auth, Remains To Be Seen (exhib catalogue) John Michael Kohler Arts Ctr, Sheboygan, 83; Howard Schroedter (exhib catalogue) Univ Wis, Milwaukee, 87. *Mailing Add:* 107 Cliff Park Rd Springfield OH 45501

CHERMAYEFF, IVAN
DESIGNER, GRAPHIC ARTIST
b London, Eng, June 6, 1932; US citizen. *Study:* Harvard Univ, 50-52; Inst Design, Ill Inst Technol, four Moholy-Nagy scholar, 52-54; Yale Univ Sch Design, BFA (Mohawk Paper Co Fel), 55. *Hon Degrees:* Portland Sch Art LLD, 81; Corcoran Sch Art, D Fine Arts, 91; Univ Arts, Philadelphia, D fine Arts, 91; Corcoran Mus Art Sch, Hon DFA, Wash DC, 96; Coll Creative Studies, Hon DFA, Detroit, 2012. *Work:* Addison Gallery; Mus Modern Art, NY. *Comn:* 9' sculpture, 9W57, NY, 91; Gene Segment (sculpture), Mt Sinai; Med Ctr, NY, 95. *Exhib:* Industry Sculpture Show, Butler Inst Am Art, Youngstown, Ohio, 71; Venice Biennale, 72; Va Mus Art, Richmond, 74; Jacksonville Art Mus, 75; Addison Gallery, Andover, Mass; Corcoran Mus Art, Washington, 95; Visual Arts Mus, NY, 95; Brno, 2001; Pera Mus, Istanbul, 2004. *Collection Arranged:* Mobile Corp Worldwide, London, Wash, 80, 81, Tokyo, 82; Mobile Worldwide Hq, Arlington, Va, 80-85. *Pos:* Trustee & comt mem painting & sculpture, film, design, Mus Mod Art, NY, 65-85; vpres, Yale Arts Asn, 68-76; mem comt arts & archit, Yale Univ Coun, 71-; mem comt Visual & Environmental Studies, Harvard Univ Bd Overseers, 72-80; vpres, Am Inst Graphic Art, pres, 65-68; bd trustees, New Sch Social Res, 1986-2002; bd overseers, Parsons Sch Design, 1986-2002. *Teaching:* Instr design, Brooklyn Col, 56-57 & Sch Visual Arts, 59-65; Andrew Carnegie prof design, Cooper Union; Joyce C Hall distinguished prof, Kansas City Art Inst; vis prof, Univ Calif, Los Angeles, 98; instr, Sch vis Arts, NY, 2011-2012. *Awards:* Yale Arts Medal, 85; Hon Doctorate Fine Arts, Corcoran Mus Art, Washington & Univ Arts, Philadelphia, 91; RDI Hon, Roy Soc Arts, Conn, 92; Soc of Illustrators, gold medal, 2002; Brno, 2005. *Bibliog:* Douglas Davis (auth), article, Newsweek Mag, 71 & 200 American leaders, Time Mag, 74; article, NY Times, 98. *Mem:* Am Inst Graphic Arts (vpres, pres & bd dir, 60-64); Int Design Conf Aspen (vpres & co-chmn bd dir, 67 & 90); Indust Designers Soc Am; Alliance Graphique Int; Benjamin Franklin fel Royal Soc Arts. *Media:* Collage. *Specialty:* David Findlay Jr; Contemporary Art. *Interests:* architecture, art; design. *Collection:* Antique toys. *Publ:* Auth, Observations on American Architecture, Viking, 72; First Shapes, Firstwords, Abrams, 92; TM, Princeton, 93; Designing, Graphics, 94; Identify Print, 2011. *Dealer:* Ricco/Maresca Gallery New York NY; David Findlay Junior Gallery. *Mailing Add:* 140 E 81st St New York NY 10028

CHERNICK, MYREL
VIDEO ARTIST
b Minneapolis, Minn, 1952. *Study:* RI Sch Design, 70-72; Rutgers Univ, BA, 74; Art Inst Chicago, MFA, 76. *Exhib:* Washington Sq Windows, Grey Art Gallery, NY, 90; Collage: New Applications, Lehman Coll Art Gallery, Bronx, NY, 91; Dirt and Domesticity: The Construction of the Feminine, (with catalog) Whitney Mus Am Art, NY, 92; Under Contract, Randolph St Gallery, Chicago, Ill, 93; Living with Cobwebs, Video Pool Studio, Winnipeg, Can, 95; Projects, (with catalog), Islip Art Mus, NY, 96; Giftland VI, Printed Matter, NY, 97; Generations, AIR Gallery, NY, 97; Big Art in Small Places, Judson Mem Church, NY, 97 & El Bohio Cult Ctr (video), NY, 98; Relics and Remembrance, The Bristol Art Mus, Bristol, RI, 98; Mothers Mother Other Lover, Hanes Art Ctr, Univ NC, Chapel Hill, 98; Motherlode, Mills Pond House Gallery, St James, NY, 99; Now We're Thirteen, Synagogue for the Arts, NY, 99; Generations II, AIR Gallery, NY, 2000; Review/New, Synagogue for the Arts, NY, 2000; The Judson House Project, NY, 2000; Jewish Women's Film Festival, 2002; Doublebind, 2003; Maternal Metaphors, 2004; Beggars Opera, 2008; Reel Mothers, 2009. *Collection Arranged:* New Work, New York/Outside New York, (catalog), New Mus, 84; In Three Dimensions: Women Sculptors of the 90's, (catalog), Snug Harbor Cult Ctr, 95. *Teaching:* instr 4-D design, Pratt Inst Found, 2001. *Awards:* Creative Artists Pub Serv Prog Fel, 80; Nat Endowment Arts Visual Artist Fel, 89-90 & 95; US/Can Creative Artist Residency, Nat Endowment Arts, 95. *Bibliog:* David McKracken (auth), Under Contract, The Chicago Tribune, 2/12/93; Cliff Eyland (auth), Transition and Trajectory: The Art of Myrel Chernick, 97; Myrel Chernick (auth), Curating Winnipeg/NY, Poolside, Video Pool Mag, 98; Michelle Grabner (auth), Test Family: Children in Contemporary Art, New Art Examiner, Oct 99; Mother Reader, Moyra Davey (ed), Spring 2001 (text by the artist). *Mem:* Coll Art Asn. *Media:* Video Photography. *Publ:* In Three Dimenstions: Women Sculptors of the '90s, Catalogue of Women Sculptors, The Snug Harbor Cult Ctr, 95; Cathy Valenza (auth) essay, Projects, Islip Art Mus, 96; Cliff Eyland (auth), essay, Living with Cobwebs, 99; The M Word: Real Mothers in Contemporary Art, Demeter Press. *Mailing Add:* 7 Mercer St Apt 4R New York NY 10013

CHERNOW, ANN
PAINTER, PRINTMAKER
b New York, NY, Feb 1, 1936. *Study:* Syracuse Univ, 53-55; NY Univ, BS, 57, MA, 69; with Irving Sandler, Jules Olitski, Hale Woodruff & Howard Conant. *Work:* Yale Univ Art Gallery; Zimmerli Mus Rutgers Univ; Portland Mus, Ore; Nat Mus Women Arts, Washington, DC; Reading Pub Mus, Pa; Davison Art Ctr, Wesleyan Univ, Conn; Metrop Mus Art, NY; Brooklyn Mus, Mus of the City of New York; Legion of Honor, San Francisco; Toledo Mus; Libr Cong; Nat Gallery of Art, Vogel Coll; Oakland Mus

Art, Calif; Sacred Heart Univ, Conn; Metropolitan Mus Art, NY; Nat Acad, NY; NY Public Lib Print Collection. *Comn:* Artist of the year, United Way, Tri-towns, Conn, 85; Friends of Music 91, Year of Mozart Celebration; Soc Am Graphic Artists; The Art of Persuasion (poster), Nat Arts Club, NY Soc of Etchers, 2006; Artist of the Year, Print Club of Albany, 2012. *Exhib:* Solo exhibs, Munic Mus, St Paul, France, 96, Westchester Comm Coll, NY, 97, Janer Gallery, NY, 98, Stamford Mus & Nature Ctr, Conn, 98, Kincannon Fine Arts, Tex, 99, Siena Coll, Mich, 99, Queens Coll, NY, 99 & Uptown Gallery, NY, 99, Dorothy Rogers, Santa Fe, 9/2011, PMW Gallery, Stamford, Conn; Stonemetal Press, Tex, 96; Broadway Gallery, Troy, NY, 97; Assoc Artists Southport, NC, 97; Institut Franco-Americain, Rennes, France, 97; Harwick Mus, Oneonta, NY, 97; World Fine Art Gallery, NY, 98; Boston Ctr Arts, 98; Gallery 551, San Francisco, Calif, 98; Housatonic Mus Art, Conn, 98; Stamford Mus & Nature Ctr, Conn, 98; Graphicarts Ctr, Conn, 98; Uptown Gallery, NY, 98 & 2006; Silvermine Guild, 2005; Dorothy Rogers Fine Art, 2007; Rockwell Gallery, 2008; Albert Merola Gallery, 2008. *Pos:* Qualified appraiser, AAA; pres, Conn Fine Arts. *Teaching:* Instr studio work, Mus Mod Art, NY, 66-70; instr painting & drawing, Silvermine Coll & Silvermine Guild, 68-80; instr art hist, Univ Conn, 69; prof emer, Norwalk Community-Tech Coll, 82-; printmaking, Univ Ind, 99; Nat Acad, NY, 2000; mentor, Univ Mass, 2011. *Awards:* Audubon Artists Award for Etching, 97; Eisner Found Award, NY, 98; Lifetime Honors, Silvermine Guild, Conn, 2005; Lifetime Achievement, Soc Am Graphic Artists, 2011. *Bibliog:* Herbert Lust (auth catalog), 9/92; Ann Chernow's Work at Yale, Conn Post, 2/98; feature article & cover mag, Fairfield Co Times, 3/98; Gifted Choices of a Guest Curator in Stamford, NY Times, 4/19/98; Article in NY Times, 99 & Westport Mag, 2/2000; Catalog Raisonee of Prints, 1968-2005, Amity Art Foundation, CT; Catalog of the Picasso Project, 2008; Fairfield County Mag, 2011. *Mem:* Silvermine Guild Art; Print Club Philadelphia; Soc Am Graphic Artists, NY; Nat Drawing Asn; Am Print Alliance; Albany Print Club; Calif Soc Printmakers; Los Angeles Printmakers; Nat Acad; New York Etchers Soc. *Media:* All Media. *Res:* Catalogue Raisonne of Graphic Work, Amity Art Found, Woodbridge, Conn. *Interests:* writing poetry and short stories. *Publ:* Auth, Reuben Nakian, sculptor, 69, Palette Mag, Conn Art Asn; art ed & contribr, Communitas, New Eng, 79; contribr, The NY quart, Greens Mag & Art Life, 94; writer, researcher & interviewer of documentary, A Gathering of Glory, 2004; writer, researcher & interviewer of documentary, Years in the Making, 2009; Carrier Pigeon Mag, 2012; Cream of Tomato. *Dealer:* Dorothy Rogers Fine Art Santa Fe NM; Albert Merola Gallery Provincetown MA; Miguel Herrara 220 W 16th St NY; Patsy Whitman 530 Roxbury Rd Stamford Conn; Vida Florian Art Gallery Ct; The White Gallery. *Mailing Add:* 2 Gorham Ave Westport CT 06880

CHERUBINI, NICOLE
SCULPTOR
b Boston, Mass, 1970. *Study:* Rhode Island Sch Design, BFA (Ceramics), 1993; New York Univ, MFA (Visual Arts), 1998. *Exhib:* Solo exhibs include Ruby, Brooklyn, 2000, Jersey City Mus, New Jersey, 2004, ADA Gallery, Richmond, VA, 2005, Samson Projs, Boston, 2005, Jane Harstook Gallery, New York, 2006, Smith-Stewart, New York, 2008; Group exhibs include Innovation & Tradition, Henry St Settlement, New York, 2002; Scope: New York, Samson Projs, Boston, 2005; Material Abuse, Caren Golden Fine Art, New York, 2006; Beauty's Gold is Clay, Alexandre Gallery, New York, 2006; The Bong Show, Leslie Tokonow, New York, 2006; Mutiny, Happy Lion, Los Angeles, 2006; Lucky Draw, Sculpture Ctr, New York; Newman Popiashvili Gallery, New York, 2007; Circumventing the City, D'Amelio Terras Gallery, New York, 2007; Irrational Profusion, PS 1/MOMA, Queens, NY, 2007. *Awards:* Louis Comfort Tiffany Found Grants, 2008. *Mailing Add:* 112 Saint James Pl Brooklyn NY 11238

CHESHIRE, CRAIG GIFFORD
PAINTER, EDUCATOR
b Portland, Ore, Dec 31, 1936. *Study:* Univ Ore, BA, 58, with David McCosh, MFA, 61; also with Francis Chapin. *Work:* Mus Art, Eugene, Ore; Univ Ore; Eastern Ore Col. *Exhib:* Northwest Artists Ann, Seattle; Artists of Ore Ann, 58-75; Northwest Painters, Smithsonian Inst Traveling Exhib, 59; Mus Art, Eugene, 61-74; Gallery West, Portland, 72; Visions & Perceptions Gallery, Eugene, 80; Littman Gallery, Portland State Univ, 87 & 94. *Teaching:* Assoc prof drawing & painting, Portland State Univ, 63-81, prof, 78-92, emer prof, 92-. *Awards:* Ina McClung Award in Painting, 61 & Ore Develop Fel, 62, Univ Ore; Purchase Award, Mus Art, Eugene & Ore Arts Comn, 74. *Mem:* Portland Art Mus; Am Asn Univ Prof. *Media:* Oil, Watercolor. *Publ:* Ed, David McCosh (monogr), Mus Art, Univ Ore, 85; Sketchbooks of David McCosh, Mus Art, Univ Ore, 94. *Mailing Add:* 3540 SW 108th Ave Beaverton OR 97005

CHESLEY, JACQUELINE
PAINTER, MOSAIC ARTIST
b New York City, Jan 4, 1936. *Study:* Workshop with Wolf Kahn, 1975; Vt Studio Sch (scholar), 1995. *Work:* Newark Mus, Newark, NJ; Morristown Mus, NN; D I Dupont Nemours, Del; Horsham Hospital, Ambler, Pa; Monmouth Col, Long Branch, NJ. *Comn:* Ballentine Mansion, Newark, Mus, Newark, NJ, 1990. *Teaching:* pastel workshops, Pastel Soc, Somerset Art Asn, Princeton Art Asn. *Mem:* Pastel Soc of Am. *Media:* All Media, Pastel. *Publ:* coauth, American Artist, 1983 & 1989; contrib, Oil Pastel, Watson Guptil, 1990; contrib, New Jersey, Harry Abrams, 1999; contrib, Creative Composition & Design, N Light Books, 2003. *Dealer:* Walker Kornbluth Gallery 7-21 Fairlawn Ave Fairlawn NJ. *Mailing Add:* 95 Clark Ave Ocean Grove NJ 07756

CHESLEY, PAUL ALEXANDER
PHOTOGRAPHER
b Red Wing, Minn, Sept 10, 1956. *Study:* Ariz State Univ; Univ Minn; Colo Mountain Col. *Work:* Bell Mus of Natural Hist, Minn; Honolulu Acad, Hawaii. *Exhib:* Solo exhibs, Ecuador, Colorado Springs Fine Arts Ctr, 74 & Gargoyle Gallery, Colo, 75; Nature, Nishi Ginza Galleries, Tokyo, Japan, 75; Indians of the Andes, Birmingham Mus Art, Ala & Sci Mus Minn, 75; retrospective, James Ford Bell Mus Natural Hist, Minn, 75; Nature, Honolulu Acad Art, Hawaii, 76. *Awards:* Photo Design Stock Award. *Bibliog:* Julia Scully (auth), Four photographers, Mod Photog, 7/77; Constance Brown (auth), It's always hot springs time in the Rockies, Smithsonian, 11/77 & Woman Alive, Quest, 11/77; and others. *Media:* Color Photography. *Publ:* Along the Continental Divide, Nat Geographic Bk; Compass Guide to Colorado; Compass Guide to Hawaii; Thirteen Day in the Life, Book Projs; Compass Guide to Minnesota, Bangkok Thailand Book, Passage to Vietnam Book Proj

CHESNEY, LEE R, JR
PAINTER, PRINTMAKER
b Washington, DC, June 1, 1920. *Study:* Univ Colo, BFA, 46; Univ Iowa, MFA, 48; Univ Michoacan, Morelia, Mex; also with James Boyle, James Lechay & Mauricio Lasansky. *Work:* Rosenwald Collection, Nat Gallery, Art, Washington, DC; Mus Mod Art, New York; Tate Gallery Art, London; Bibliot Nat, Paris; Nat Gallery Art, Stockholm, Sweden; Portland Mus Print Arch, Ore; Indianapolis Mus & Krannert, Mus, Ill; Harn Mus, Gainsville, Fla. *Comn:* Honolulu Print Soc, 75 & 83; Honolulu Acad Art, 77; Univ Hawaii Centennial Comn, 82; Wycross Press Comn, 84. *Exhib:* Six Artists in Paris, Am Cult Ctr, Paris, 64; Epinal Print Biennial, France, 70-71; Cite Int des Arts, Paris, France, 79; Contemp Arts Ctr, Honolulu, 80; 10 yr retrospective, Fisher Gallery, Univ Southern Calif, 68; BMIC Galerie, Paris, 81; Salon de Mai, Paris, 82; Honolulu Acad Art, 85; Portland State Univ Gallery, 88; Univ Fla Gallery, 89; Amon Carter Mus, Ft Worth Tex, 90; Worcester Art Mus, Mass, 91; Mona Bismark Fedn, Paris, France, 91; Spectrum of Innovation, Nelson-Atkins Mus, Kansas City, Mo, 90; Williams/Lamb Gallery, Long Beach, 90-92; Solo exhibs: Parsons Sch Art & Design, Paris, France, 98; Davis Dominquez Gallery, Tucson Ar, 99; Abstract Expressionism: Then and Now, Hofstra Mus, New York, 2001; Inauqural Exhib, Hawaii State Mus Art, 2002; Cleveland Mus Art, 2003; Hawaii State Mus Art, 2005; Domingus Gallery, Tucson, Ariz, 2005-2007; three-person exhib, Univ Hawaii, Hilo, 2007; Image & Abstraction, Good Design Gallery, New York; Pacific Standard Time, Norton Simon Mus, 2011. *Pos:* Adv bd, Los Angeles Printmaking Soc, 67-. *Teaching:* Univ Ill, 50-67; assoc dean fine arts, Univ Southern Calif, 67-72; fac mem, Univ Hawaii, 72-84; Louis D Beaumont vis distinguished prof, Wash Univ, 79; Lacoste Sch France, 89; UCLA, 89-90. *Awards:* Sr Fulbright Res Award, Am Acad Rome, 64; Vera List Purchase Award, Soc Am Graphic Artists, 65; Univ Hawaii/Ford Found Fac Enrichment Award, Paris, 78-80; Fond Gardilanne-Moffat Studio Award, Cite Intern des Arts, Paris, 78-83. *Bibliog:* Wayne Miyamoto (auth), Lee Chesney--25 years of printmaking. *Mem:* Soc Am Graphic Artists; Coll Art Asn Am; Los Angeles Printmaking Soc (adv bd, 67-); Hawaii Artists League; Honolulu Printmaking Soc; NW Prints Coun; Southern Graphics Conf. *Media:* Oil; Acrylic, Etching, Engraving. *Publ:* Contribr, Printmaking today, Coll Art J, Vol XIX, No 2; A brief glance at Ukiyo-e and Hanga, Japan Print Quart, winter 67; Teaching in art grad progs, J Educ Perspectives, fall 77. *Dealer:* Davis Dominquez Gallery 154 East 6th Tucson AZ 85705; Tobey C Moss Gallery 7321 Beverly Blvd Los Angeles CA 90036; Annex Gallery 604 College Ave Santa Rose CA 95404. *Mailing Add:* 14601 Whitfield Ave Pacific Palisades CA 90272-2645

CHESNEY, LEE ROY, III
PRINTMAKER, EDUCATOR
b San Antonio, Tex, July 5, 1945. *Study:* Univ Ill, with Dennis Rowan, Eugene Telez, BFA; Univ Calif, Los Angeles, with Ray Brown; Ind Univ, with Rudy Pozzatti, Marvin Lowe, MFA. *Work:* Honolulu Acad Arts; San Diego State Univ Mus; State Univ NY Potsdam; Dickinson State Coll Mus, NDak; Graphic Chem & Ink Co Collection, Chicago. *Exhib:* Libr Cong, Nat Collection Fine Arts, Smithsonian, Washington, DC, 69 & 73; 1st Int Pratt Graphics, Bath, Eng, 73-74; Int Print Biennials, Epinal, France, 75 & 77; Boston Printmakers, 82; Prints USA, 82; Pratt Graphics, NY, 82; and others. *Pos:* Prog dir art dept, Univ Tex, 78-81, grad adv, 81-88. *Teaching:* Assoc instr printmaking, Ind Univ, Bloomington, 69-72; instr design & prints, Univ Tex, Austin, 72-75, asst prof printmaking, 75-78, assoc prof art, 78-, assoc chair Dept Art & Art History, interim chair, formerly. *Awards:* Graphic Chem & Ink Purchase Award, Soc Am Graphic Artists, 73; Honolulu Acad Arts Purchase Award, 73; Prints from Am Univs Purchase Award, US Info Agency, 74. *Mem:* Coll Art Asn Am; The Southern Graphics Coun; Soc Am Graphic Artists, NY. *Media:* Intaglio, Mixed Media. *Mailing Add:* Univ Tex at Austin Fine Arts 1 University Station D1400 Austin TX 78712-0340

CHEVINS, CHRISTOPHER M
PAINTER, DRAFTSMAN
b New York, NY, May 31, 1951. *Study:* Yale Univ, BA, 73; Rutgers Univ, with Leon Golub, MFA, 81 (Teaching Fel). *Work:* Jane Voorhees Zimmerli Mus, Rutgers Univ, New Brunswick, NJ; Continental Insurance Co, Piscataway, NJ. *Exhib:* New Galleries of Lower East Side, Artists Space, NY, 84; Fusion, Paulo Salvador, NY, 84 & 85; Smart Art, Harvard Univ, Sert Gallery, Cambridge, Mass, 85; New Art NY, Lidewij Edelkoort, Paris, France, 85; Urban Mythologies, Fine Arts Ctr, Univ RI, Kingston, 86; 12 Emerging Artists, Hudson River Mus, 87-88. *Teaching:* Instr painting, Mason Gross Sch of Arts, 81-82. *Bibliog:* Joseph Masheck (auth), Smart Art, Willis, Locker & Owens, 84. *Mem:* Found Community Artists. *Media:* Oil on Canvas. *Mailing Add:* 10 Beach St Third Flr New York NY 10013-2425

CHI, KE-HSIN (JENNY)
PAINTER
b Taiwan. *Study:* Tainan Junior Coll Art, Taiwan, Assoc Deg; Lewis Univ, Romeoville, Ill, BA; Sch Figurative Art, New York Acad Art, MFA, 1998; Florence Acad Art, Italy, 2001, 2002. *Exhib:* Exhibs include Fairfax Gallery, Jacksonville, Fla, Verde Gallery, Champaign, Ill, Palakta, Fla. *Teaching:* Asst Prof, Eastern Ill Univ, 2002-Present. *Awards:* White House Blue Ribbon Christmas Proj; Cultural Council Fel, Jacksonville, Fla; Carl Steinsieck Memorial Award; George Sugarman Found Grant, 2007. *Dealer:* Hawthorn Gallery 2017 3rd Ave N Birmingham AL 35203 .

CHIANESE, CAROL BURNARD
PAINTER
b Susquehanna, PA, Feb 01, 1942. *Study:* Bloomsburg Univ, BS Bus, 1963; Meredith Col, Credit Hours, 1977-1978; Art Study, Giverny, France, Cert, 2005. *Work:* IBM Corp, Poughkeepsie, NY; SAS Inst, Cary, NC; Morehead Planetarium, Chapel Hill, NC; Carolina Power & Light, Raleigh, NC; Wachovia Bank & Trust, Raleigh, NC. *Comn:* Branch Bank & Trust Co, Raleigh, NC, 1997; Carolina Power & Light, Raleigh, NC, 1998; Elon Col, Elon, NC, 2000; SAS Inst, Cary, NC, 2001; Raleigh Red Wolf Sculpture, City of Raleigh Arts Comn, Raleigh, NC, 2001. *Exhib:* A Colorist Vision, Kinston Coun of Arts, Kinston, NC, 1986; Twelve Women Artists, Fayetteville Mus Art, Fayetteville, NC, 1991; Landscape Impressions, Wilkes Art Gallery, N Wilkesboro, NC, 1994; Shades of Pastel, Lauren Mus Art, Laurel, Miss, 2000; Celebrating 25 Years, Fayetteville Mus Art, Fayetteville, NC, 2004; For Pastels Only, Pastel Soc of Am 33rd Ann, NYC, 2005; Three in Giverny, Artspace Upfront Gallery, Raleigh, NC, 2006. *Awards:* Allied Artists Award, Pastel Soc Am, Allied Artists of Am 28th ann, 2000; Jim Lynch Award, Pastel Soc of Am 29th ann, Jim Lynch Co, 2001; Strathmore Award, Pastel Soc of Am 30th ann, Strathmore Artist Papers Co, 2002. *Bibliog:* Valerie Rivers (auth), Small Art Groups, Am Artist Mag, 1988; Raleigh Red Wolf Ramble, City of Raleigh Arts Comn, 2002; Blue Greenberg (auth), 3 Impressionist Artists, Durham Herald Sun, 2006. *Mem:* Pastel Soc Am (Master pastelist); Pastel Soc West Coast (Signature mem); Pastel Soc Southeast; Artspace Artists Asn (Juried mem); Capital Art League (Charter mem). *Media:* Oils, Pastels. *Publ:* Contribr, Small Art Groups, Am Artist Mag, 1988; contribr, Artists of the Carolinas, Mountain Productions, 1990; contribr, Raleigh Red Wolf Ramble, City of Raleigh Arts Comn, 2002; contribr, 3 Impressionist Artists, Durham Herald Sun, 2006. *Dealer:* Artspace Inc 201 E Davie St Raleigh NC 27601. *Mailing Add:* 4900 N Hills Dr Raleigh NC 27612-4006

CHIARENZA, CARL
PHOTOGRAPHER, ART HISTORIAN
b Rochester, NY, Sept 5, 1935. *Study:* Rochester Inst Technol, AAS, 55, BFA, 57; Boston Univ, MS, 59, AM, 64; Danforth Found Teacher Grant, 66-68; Harvard Univ, PhD, 73. *Work:* Los Angeles Co Mus Art; Nat Mus Am Art, Washington, DC; Philadelphia Mus Art; Mus Mod Art & Int Ctr Photog, NY; Art Inst Chicago, Contemp Photog & Exchange Nat Bank, Chicago; Minneapolis Inst Arts; Mus Fine Arts, Boston & Houston; Int Mus Photog, George Eastman House, Rochester; Ctr Creative Photog, Tucson; Fogg Art Mus, Cambridge; Cleveland Mus; San Francisco Mus Mod Art; Getty Mus, Los Angeles; Amon Carter Mus, Ft Worth, Tex; Santa Barbara Mus; Tampa Mus; Worcester Mus; RISD Mus Art; Princeton Mus; Yale Art Gallery; Int Ctr of Photography, New York; Mead Mus Art, Amherst, Mass; Shadai Gallery, Tokyo, Japan; The Joy of Giving Something Inc, New York; and many others. *Exhib:* Solo exhibs, SE Mus Photog, 95-96, Rochester Int Technol, 96, Witkin Gallery, NY, 96, Castellani Art Mus, 97, Hobart & William Smith Col, 97, High Mus Art, Atlanta, 97 & Univ Iowa Mus Art, 97-98, Stephen Cohen Gallery, Los Angeles, Calif, 99, Robert Klein Gallery, Boston, Mass, 99, Spectrum Gallery, Rochester, NY, 99, Troyer Gallery, Washington, DC, 99, Alan Klotz/Photocollect, New York City, 2000 & Spectrum Gallery, 2002, Spectrum Gallery, 2002, Hartnett Gallery, Rochester, NY, 2003, Photog Gallery, Univ RI, 2003,-2004, Carl Solway Gallery, Cincinnati, Ohio, 2004-2005, Center for Photog Arts, Carmel, Calif, 2005, Selected Works, Studio Hart Buffalo, NY, 2007, Peace Warriors and Solitudes, Univ Richmond Art Mus, Va, 2008 & Through This Lens Gallery, Durham, NC, 2009, Daura Galley, Lynchberg, Va, 2010, Pictures Come from Pictures, Mark Arts Ctr, Coll of the Desert, Calif, 2011, Anderson Galleries, Univ Buffalo, 2012-2013; Group exhibs, Garden of Civilization, Ansel Adams Gallery, 96; Everson Biennial, Everson Mus Art, Syracuse, NY, 96; La Photographie au present: L'annee 1996 dans les collections de la Bibliotheque Nationale de France, 97; Bibliotheque Nationale, Paris, Faculty Show, Hartnett Gallery, 97; The Jude Peterson Collection, Fitchburg Art Mus, 98; Heliography: The Retrospective, Hugo de Pagano Gallery, NY, 98; Years Ending in Nine, Photographs from 1889-1989, Mus Fine Arts, Houston, Tex, 98; The Hotchkiss Sch, Lakeville, Conn, 98; Works on Paper: Digital Printmaking at Singer Editions, Robert Klein Gallery, Boston, 98; On the Nature of Landscape, Mt Holyoke Coll Art Mus, 98; Sun Valley Ctr Arts, 98; Princeton Univ Art Mus, 98-99; Ctr Creative Photog, Tucson, 99, 2001; Yale Univ Art Gallery, 99; The Fitchburg Art Mus, 2000; Harvard Univ Art Mus, 2000; Visual Arts Gallery, Adirondack Community Coll, Queensbury, NY, 2000, 2001; Mill Art Ctr & Gallery, Honeoye Falls, NY, 2000; Nazareth Coll Arts Ctr, 2000; DeCordova Mus and Sculpture Park, Lincoln, Ma, 2000-01; Boise Art Mus, 2001; Fitchburg Art Mus, 2001; Davison Art Ctr, Wesleyan Univ, 2001; Kiyosato Mus Photog Arts, Japan, 2001; Spectrum Gallery, Rochester, 2001; Amon Carter Mus, Ft Worth, 2002; The Rosenwald-Wolf Gallery, Univ Arts, Philadelphia, 2002; Dunedin Fine Art Ctr, Fla, 2002; Visual Studies Workshop Gallery, 2002; The Troyer Gallery, Washington, DC, 2002; Nazareth Coll Arts Center, Foyer Gallery, Rochester, NY, 2004 & 2006; Fitchburg Art Mus, Mass, 2004-2005; Ryerson Univ Gallery, Toronto, 2006; Studio Hart, Buffalo, NY, 2007; Ackland Art Mus, Chapel Hill, NC, 2006; Light Factory, Charlotte, NC, 2006-2007; HP Garcia Gallery, NY, 2007; The Art Of Looking: Selections from the Collection of Charles Millard, Ackland Art Mus, Chapel Hill, NC, 9-12/2007; The Digital Print: Work from Singer Eds, Edwards Art Gallery, Holderness Sch, Plymouth, NH, 1-2/2008; Amon Carter Mus, Ft Worth, Tex, 2008; Minor Impact, Howard Greenberg Gallery, New York, 2008; Four Masters, Image City Gallery, Rochester, NY, 2009; Jude Peterson Photography Collection, Fitchburg Art Mus, 2011; Portland Art Mus, 2012; and many others dating back to 1955. *Pos:* Ed, Contemp Photogr, Boston, 66-69; co-founder, Imageworks Ctr & Sch, Cambridge, Mass, 71-73; chmn, Dept Art Hist, Boston Univ, 76-81; vis comt, Harvard Univ Art Mus, 95, chair, Photogr Collections Comt, 95-; bd trustees, Visual Studies Workshop, 80-2000. *Teaching:* Prof art hist, Boston Univ, 63-86; vis prof photog hist & theory, Visual Studies Workshop, Rochester, NY, 73-74; Harnish vis artist, Smith Coll, 83-84; Fanny Knapp Allen prof art hist, Univ Rochester, 86-98 & artist-in-residence, 98-; vis prof, Cornell Univ, 91-92. *Awards:* Mass Arts & Humanities Foun Fel, 75-76; Nat Endowment Arts Fel, 77-78 & 90-91; Arts Coun Artist Award, Greater Rochester, 96; Special Opportunity Stipend Award, NY Found for Arts, 97; Lillian Fairchild Artist Award, 99; Best in Show, 5th & 6th Biennial Exhib of Italian-Am Artists, Nazareth Coll Arts Ctr, 2000, 2002; Best in Photography, 7th & 8th Biennials Exhib of Italian-Am Artists, Nazareth Coll Arts Ctr, 2004, 2006; Lifetime Achievement Award, Photographic Resource Ctr, Boston Univ, 2010. *Bibliog:* AD Coleman (auth), Carl Chiarenza: Pushing the Envelope (exhib catalog), High Mus, 11/97; Stephen Prokopoff (auth, exhib catalog), Landscapes of the Imagination, Univ Ia Mus Art, 1/98; AD Coleman (auth), Tears and Pressures, Photo Review, 15-19, winter 98; Brooks Jensen (auth), interview, LensWork, No 79, 66-93, 11-12/2008; Robert Hirsch (auth), Internal Landscapes, The Photo Rev, Vol 28, No 4, 2-6, 2009; Stuart Low (auth), Re-Created Visions, The Democrat & Chronicle, Rochester, NY, Apr 14, 2002; Jean Dykstra (auth), Photo Book Beat, Art on Paper, Dec 2002; Robert Hirsch (auth), Transmutations: Photographic Works by Carl Chiarenza, Univ Buffalo Art Gallery, 2012. *Mem:* Soc Photog Educ (bd dir, 63-); Photog Resource Ctr (bd trustees, '77-); Friends of Photog (adv trustee, 79-83); Visual Studies Workshop (86-99); and others. *Media:* Collage & Black and White Photography. *Res:* Twentieth century American photography. *Interests:* Classical Music, jazz, reading, making art. *Publ:* Coauth, Heinecken, Friends Photog, 80; Aaron Siskind: Pleasures and Terrors, Little Brown, Boston, 81; auth, Eye & Mind: The seriousness of wit, Kenneth Josephson, Mus Contemp Art, Chicago, 83; Chiarenza: Landscapes of the Mind, David R Godine, Boston, 88; Gary Winogrand (essay), Image, vol 34, no 3-4, 91 & vol 35, no 1-2, 92; Evocations, Nazraeli Press, Tucson, 2002; The Peace Warriors of 2003, Nazraeli Press, Tucson, Ariz, 2005; auth, Solitudes, Lodima Press, Ottsville, Pa, 2005; Interaction: Verbal/Visual, Nazraeli Press, 2007; Carl Chiarenza: Pictures Come From Pictures, Selected Photographs 1955-2007, David R Godine Pub, Boston, 2008; author of many other essays. *Dealer:* Stephen Cohen Gallery 7358 Beverly Blvd Los Angeles CA 90036; Robert Klein Gallery 38 Newbury St Boston Ma 02116; Alan Klotz Gallery 511 W 25th St Ste 701 New York NY 10001. *Mailing Add:* 5 Edgemere Dr Rochester NY 14618

CHIARLONE, ROSEMARIE
CONCEPTUAL ARTIST
b Philadelphia, Pa, June 12, 1951. *Study:* Pa Acad Fine Arts, 1969-1971; Fla Int Univ, BFA, 1972-1974; Fla Int Univ, MA, 1977-1979; Visual Arts Fel, Fla Dept State, Fla, 1982, 2000; Pollock Krasner Found Grant, NY, Found, NY, 1985; Fla Enhancement Grant, Miami-Dade Dept Cult Affairs, 2004. *Work:* Nat Mus Women in the Arts, Washington, DC; Art in Public Places, Miami; Art in Public Places, Tampa, Fla; Arthur & Matta Jaffe Collection of Bks & Aesthetic Objects, Boca Raton, Fla; Fla Int Univ, Miami. *Comn:* Carolina Monaco (2 paintings), Royal Carribbean Cruise Lines, Miami, 1985; Assemblage for Princess, Miami City Ballet, Miami Beach, 1987. *Exhib:* 10th Anniversary Exhib, Ctr Book & Paper Arts, Chicago, Ill, 2004; Matter & Spirit, Wells Book Ctr Wells Col, Aurora, NY, 2004; For Everyone & No One, Mus of Contemp Art, N Miami, Fla, 2005; Lifestyle, Space Lab, Spaces Gallery, Cleveland, Ohio, 2005; Journey, Noyes Mus Art, Oceanville, NJ, 2006; Book as Art, Nat Mus Women in Art, Washington, DC, 2006. *Bibliog:* Fred B Adelson (auth), Narrative Images Alluring World, NY Times, 2000; Christopher Healy (auth), Book It Art Gallery or Libr, Cleveland Scene, 2003; Helen Frederick (auth), Collaboration as a Medium, Pyramid Atlantic, 2005. *Mem:* Nat Mus of Women Arts; Pa Acad Arts; Mus Contemp Art; Noyes Mus Art; Fontaneda Soc. *Publ:* Auth, Rosemarie Chiarlone, Boxes & Books, Art Papers, 1994; auth, In Three Shows: Mus Looks Beyond Region, NY Times, 2002; auth, Book It Art Gallery or Library, Cleveland Scene, 2003; auth, Dissent: Political Voices, 2005. *Mailing Add:* 200 E San Marino Dr Miami Beach FL 33139

CHICAGO, JUDY
PAINTER, SCULPTOR
b Chicago, Ill, July 20, 1939. *Study:* Univ Calif, Los Angeles, BA, 62, MA, 64. *Hon Degrees:* Russell Sage Coll, DFA, 1992; Smith Coll, Northampton, Mass, DFA, 2000; Lehigh Univ, Bethlehem, Pa, LHD, 2000; Duke Univ, Durham, NC, DFA, 2002. *Work:* Brooklyn Mus; San Francisco Mus Mod Art; Oakland Mus Art; Butler Inst Am Art, Youngstown, Ohio; Pa Acad Fine Arts, Philadelphia; Los Angeles Co Mus Art; New Orleans Mus Art; Nat Mus Women in the Arts; Mus Art, Santa Fe, NMex; Albuquerque Mus Art, NMex; Brooklyn Mus Art; and numerous others. *Exhib:* Solo exhibs, ACA Galleries, NY, 84-86, Marilyn Butler Fine Art, Santa Fe, NMex, & Scottsdale, Ariz, 85, Lyons Matrix Gallery, Austin Tex, 94, Flanders Gallery, Minneapolis, 96, Cline Lew Allen Gallery, Santa Fe, 96 & Galerie Simonne Stern, New Orleans, 96, Chicago in Glass, Lew Allen Contemp, 2006, Setting the Table: Preparatory Work for The Dinner Party, ACA Galleries, NY, 2007, ACA Galleries, New York, 2010; Group exhibs, The Dinner Party, San Francisco Mus Mod Art, 79, Traveling throughout US, Can, Scotland, Eng, Ger & Australia; Holocaust Project: From Darkness Into Light (traveling, auth catalog), Spertus Mus, Judaica & 6 venues in US, 93; Sources and Collaborations (traveling), Austin Mus Art, Tex & three other locations, 94; In a Different Light, Univ Art Mus, Univ Calif, Berkeley, 95; Division of Labor: Women's Work in Contemp Art, Mus Contemp Art, Los Angeles, 95; Sniper's Nest: Art That Has Lived with Lucy R Lippard (traveling), Ctr Curatorial Studies Mus, Bard Coll, 95; Sexual Politics: Judy Chicago's Dinner Party & Feminist Art History, Armand Hammer Mus, Univ Calif, Los Angeles, 96; Hanart TZ Gallery, Taiper, Taiwan, 97; Trials and Tributes, New Orleans Mus Art, La, 2001; Voices from the Song of Songs, Fitzwilliam Mus, Cambridge, Eng, 2001; Resolutions: A Stitch in Time, Am Craft Mus, NY, 2000 & Skirball Cult Ctr, Los Angeles, Calif, 2001. *Pos:* Co-founder, Feminist Art Prog, Calif Inst Arts, Valencia, 71-73. *Teaching:* Asst prof, Calif State Univ, 69-71; founder, instr, Feminist Studio Workshop, 73-74; artist-in-residence, Coll of St Catherine, St Paul, Minn, 75; vis prof, Ind Univ Bloomington, 97, artist-in-residence, 99; vis prof, artist-in-residence, Duke Univ, Durham, NC, 2000, Univ NC, Chapel Hill, 2000; prof-in-residence, Western Ky Univ, Bowling Green, 2001; Chancellor's Artist in Residence, Vanderbilt Univ, Tex, 2006. *Awards:* Nat Endowment Arts, 77; Streisand Found Grant, 92; Serv to Field Award, Spertus Mus Judaica, 94; proclamation, City of Albuquerque, 96; Getty Grant Prog, 97. *Bibliog:* Guy Cross (auth), An Interview with Judy Chicago, The Mag, Santa Fe, 9/96; Susan Fernandez (auth), Judy Chicago: artist and woman, St Petersburg Times,

10/6/96; Paula Harper (auth), The Chicago Resolutions, Art in Am, 6/2000; and others; Gail Levin (auth), Becoming Judy Chicago, 2007. *Mem:* Women's Caucus Art. *Media:* Mixed Media. *Publ:* Auth, Birth Project, Doubleday/Anchor, 79; Judy Chicago: The Dinner Party, Athenaum, Ger, 87; The Dinner Party, Viking/Penguin, 1996 Beyond the Flower: The Autobiography of a Feminist, 96; Through the Flower: My Struggle as a Woman Artist, Yuan-Liou Publ Co Ltd, Taiwan, 97; coauth, Women and Art, 99; Fragments from the Delta of Venues, Power House, 2004; Kitty City: A Feline Book of Hours, Harper Design Int, New York, 2005; The Dinner Party, Merrell Publ, 2007. *Dealer:* Lew Allen Contemporary 129 W Palace Ave Santa Fe NM 87501; ACA Galleries 529 W 20th St New York NY 10011. *Mailing Add:* PO Box 1327 Belen NM 87002

CHICHURA, DIANE B
ADMINISTRATOR, ART DEALER
b Queens, NY. *Study:* Pratt Inst, BS, 54; Columbia Univ, MA, 57; Fordham Univ, PhD, 80. *Pos:* Dist dir, Related Arts, W Hempstead Pub Schs, 68-98; co-owner, Isis Gallery Ltd, Searingtown, NY, 82-; consult, NY State Educ Dept, 99-2006. *Teaching:* Fordham Univ Grad Sch, 77-79. *Mem:* Int Soc Educ Art; US Soc Educ Art; Nat Art Educ Asn; NY State Art Teachers Asn (prog chmn, 70, 74 & 82); Long Island Art Teachers Asn. *Publ:* Coauth, Super Sculpture: Using Science, Technology and Natural Phenomena in Sculpture, Van Nostrand Reinhold, 74; contribr, Cognition and the Visual Art Experience, In: Tapestry: The Interrelationships of the Arts in Reading & Language Development, Collegium Book Publ, Elmsford, 79; coauth, Cognitive Model for Visual Arts Experience & Interactive Development of a Cognitive Curriculum for Visual Arts Experience-Based on the Dynamic Process of Equilibrium, Fordham Univ, 80. *Mailing Add:* 47 Dogwood Rd Searingtown NY 11507

CHIHULY, DALE PATRICK
SCULPTOR, GLASS ARTIST
b Tacoma, Wash, Sept 20, 1941. *Study:* Univ Wash, Seattle, BA, 65; Univ Wis, Madison, MS, 67; RI Sch Design, Providence, MFA, 68. *Hon Degrees:* RI Sch Design, Hon Dr Art, 86; Univ Puget Sound, Tacoma, Wash, Hon Dr Art, 86; Calif Coll Arts & Crafts, Oakland, Hon Dr Art, 88; Pratt Inst, Hon D, 95; Gonzaga U, Spokane, Wash, Hon D, 96; Brandeis U, DHL, 2000; Univ Hartford, Conn, Hon DFA, 2001. *Work:* Am Craft Mus, Cooper-Hewitt Mus, Metrop Mus Art, Mus Mod Art & Whitney Mus Am Art, NY; Contemp Arts Ctr Hawaii & Honolulu Acad Arts, Hawaii; Seattle Art Mus; Wadsworth Atheneum, Hartford, Conn; San Francisco Mus Mod Art, Calif; Los Angeles Co Mus Art, Calif; Nat Mus Am Hist & Renwick Gallery, Nat Mus Am Art, Smithsonian Inst, Washington, DC; numerous others. *Comn:* Victoria and Albert Mus, London, Eng; Atlantis, Paradise Island, Bahamas; Bellagio, Las Vegas, Nev; Naples Mus Art, Fla; Benaroya Hall, Wash. *Exhib:* Solo exhibs, Oklahoma City Mus Art, Okla, 2002, Phoenix Art Mus, Ariz, 2002, Ft Wayne Mus Art, Ind, 2002, Monterey Mus Art, Calif, 2002, Wash State Hist Mus, Tacoma, 2002, Tyler Mus Art, Tex, 2002, Mus Centre Vapriikki, Tampere, Finland, 2002, Frederick R Weisman Mus Art, Pepperdine Univ, Malibu, Calif, 2004, Fairchild Tropical Botanic Garden, Coral Gables, Fla, 2004, Colorado Springs Fine Arts Ctr, 2005, Royal Botanic Gardens, Kew, Surrey, UK, 2006, Marlborough Gallery, NY, 2006, Franklin Park Conservatory, Columbus, Ohio, 2006, R Duane Reed Gallery, St Louis, Mo, 2006; Group exhibs, Habitat Gallery, Detroit, 80-83; Charles Cowles Gallery, NY, 81-83; Betsy Rosenfield Gallery, Chicago, 81-83; World Glass Now, Hokkaido Mus Mod Art, Sapporo, Japan, 82; The Wisconsin Movement-Glass in Form, Priebe Art Gallery, Univ Wis, Oshkosh, 82; The Descendents, NDak Mus Art, Grand Forks, 83; 11th Ann Nat Invitational Contemp Am Glass, Columbus Coll Art & Design, Ohio, 83; Mus Arts & Crafts, Hamburg, 92; Alaska Baskets, Skagway City Mus, Alaska, 98; Montana Macchia, Holter Mus Art, Helena, Mont, 98, Paris Gibson Sq Mus Art, Great Falls, Mont, 98, Hockaday Ctr Arts, Kalispell, Mont, 98 & Custer Co Art Ctr, Miles City, Mont, 98; Mus Tower David, Jerusalem, Israel, 99; Chihuly: Glass Master, Hsinchu Municipal Cult Ctr, Taiwan, 99; Installations, Hiroshima Mus Contemp Art, Contemp Art Ctr Va, Va Beach & Mint Mus Craft & Design, Charlotte, NC, 99; Masterworks in Glass, Nat Gallery Australia, Canberra, 99; Installations, Knoxville Mus Art & Ark Arts Ctr, Little Rock, 2000; A Transparent Legacy, Seattle Art Mus, 2006; Niijima Float Installation, Tacoma Art Mus, Wash, 2006; Material Matters, LA County Art Mus, Calif, 2006; New Work, Marlborough Gallery, New York, 2006. *Teaching:* instr ceramics, RI Sch Design, 69-75, head dept sculpture and prog glass, 76-80; educ coordr & co-founder, Pilchuck Glass Ctr, Stanwood, Wash, 71-; affil prof, Univ Wash, 94-95. *Awards:* Distinguished Artists Gold Medal Award, Univ Arts, Philadelphia, 2000; Lifetime Achievement Arts Award, Corp Coun Arts/Artsfund, 2001; Gold Medal Award, Nat Arts Club, NY, 2002. *Bibliog:* Liz Seymour (auth), Man of glass, Attaché, 11/1998; Sarah Greenburg (auth), Glass act: Dale Chihuly in Seattle, London and Jerusalem, Art Newspaper, 5/1999; John Russell Taylor (auth), Sculpting with light, London Times, 06/27/2001. *Mem:* Seattle Int Film Festival (bd adv, 93); Seattle Art Fair (adv comt, 93); Pilchuck Artistic Adv Comt, 93-94; Northwest Aids Found (assoc bd mem, 94). *Media:* Blown Glass. *Publ:* Auth, Dale Chihuly: Chihuly in the light of Jerusalem 2000, Ariel, Israel Rev Arts and Letters, 55-57, 99; Chihuly Jerusalem 2000, 2000, Chihuly Projects, 2002 & Chihuly Gardens & Glass, 2002, Portland Press. *Mailing Add:* Chihuly Studio 1111 NW 50th St Seattle WA 98107-5120

CHILDERS, MALCOLM GRAEME
PHOTOGRAPHER, PRINTMAKER
b Riverside, Calif, Feb 19, 1945. *Study:* Humboldt State Univ, Arcata, Calif, BA, 69; Fullerton State Univ, Calif, MA, 72. *Work:* Springfield Art Mus, Mo; Tenn State Mus, Nashville; Meadows Mus Art, Shreveport, La; Brooks Mem Art Gallery, Memphis, Tenn; Standard Oil Co-Ind; McGraw Hill; Merck Corp. *Exhib:* Appalachian Corridors Biennial Art Exhib 4, Charleston, SC 75; Bradley Print Show, Peoria, Ill, 75-76; La Grange Nat Competition II, Ga, 75-76 & 86; Tenn Bicentennial Exhib, Nashville, Tenn, 76; Solo exhib, Western Colo Ctr Arts, 2009; and others. *Pos:* Fine art photographer, Mesa Co & Conservancy. *Teaching:* Instr printmaking, Loma Linda Univ, Calif, 72-74; asst prof drawing, painting & printmaking, Southern Col, Collegedale, Tenn, 74-86; Instr Cleveland State Col, Tenn, 84; Instr Printmaking Univ of Tenn, Chattanooga, 85; Mesa State Col, Grand Junction, Colo, 2006. *Awards:* Purchase Awards, La Grange Nat II, La Grange Art Mus, 75, Mid-South Biennial, Brooks Mem Art Gallery, 75 & Tenn Bicentennial, State of Tenn, 76. *Media:* All Media, Printmaking, Photography, Video, Poetry. *Publ:* Roadsongs: A Journey Into The life and Mindscapes of An American Artist, The Real Earth, Wind River Press, 2001. *Dealer:* Real Earth Art Productions

CHILDS, CATHERINE O See Catchi

CHILDS, ELIZABETH CATHARINE
ART HISTORIAN, EDUCATOR
b Denver, Colo, July 5, 1954. *Study:* Wake Forest Univ, BA, 76; Columbia Univ, MA, 80, PhD, 89. *Collection Arranged:* Co-cur, Femmes d'Espirit: Women in Daumier's Caricature, 90; co-cur, The Political Eye: French Caricature and Mass Media. *Pos:* Lectr & prog asst Educ Dept, Metrop Mus Art, NY, 76-81; mus lectr, Mus Mod Art, NY, 79; res assoc, Solomon R Guggenheim Mus, 87-91. *Teaching:* Lectr & asst prof mod art hist, State Univ NY, Purchase, 87-92; asst prof, Washington Univ, 92-98, assoc prof, 98-2011, dept chair, 2007-, prof, 2012-; prof art hist, dept chair, Etta & Mark Steinberg prof art history, 2012. *Awards:* Gould Fel, Princeton Univ, 92-93; Univ Fel, NEH, 96-97; CASVA Sr fel, Nat Gallery Art, 97; Disting Fac Award, Washington Univ, 2008; Millard Meiss award, College Art Asn, 2011. *Mem:* Coll Art Asn; Midwest Art Hist Soc; Asn Historians Nineteenth Century Art; Soc French Hist Studies; Asn Women Fac. *Res:* Mod art in Europe & Am, The European avant-garde, exoticism & primitivism, gender & art, art & colonialism, censorship, caricature, photography, art, travel, art of exploration, global modernisms. *Publ:* ed, Suspended License: Censorship & the Visual Arts, Univ Washington Press, 97; contribr auth, Degas to Picasso: the Artist and the Camera, Dallas Mus Art with Yale, 99; contribr auth, Vincent Van Gogh and the Painters of the Petit Boulevard, Rizzoli, 2000; contribr auth, Gauguin: Tahiti, Boston Mus of Fine Arts, Musee d'Orsay, 2003; auth, Daumier and Exoticism Satirizing the French & the Foreign, Peter Lang, 2004; contrubr, auth, John Lafarge's Second Paradise, Yale Univ Press, 2010; contribr auth, Ganjun: Polynesia, 2012; auth, Vanishing Paradise: Art and Exoticism in Colonial Taliti, Univ Calif Press, 2013; Gauguin Metamorphoses, Mus Modern Art, NY, 2014. *Mailing Add:* Washington Univ Dept Art History & Arch Campus Box 1189 1 Brookings Dr, CB 1189 Saint Louis MO 63130-4899

CHILTON, FRED
PAINTER
b Las Cruces, NMex, June 14, 1944. *Study:* Ctr for Creative Studies, Detroit, Mich, 63-66. *Work:* One-man shows Branigan Cult Ctr, 83, Adobe Patio Gallery, 87, Studio W Gallery, 92, Glenn Cutter Gallery, 99, 2000; juried shows NM W/C Soc, 99, 2000. *Comn:* Mural, Lady of Guadalupe Cath Church, Tortugas, NMex, 85; vicariate banners, comm by Cath Diocese of Las Cruces, NMex, 85; book cover, illustrated history of Las Cruces, Linda Harris (auth); poster, NMex Wine & Vine Soc, 96; commemorative poster, 5th Ann Las Cruces Mariachi Conf, 98; commemorative poster, Internat Mariachi Conf, 98, 99, 2000. *Exhib:* 50th Ann Mid-Year, Butler Inst Am Art, Youngstown, Ohio, 86; Watermedia 86, Mont Watercolor Soc; Close to the Border, NMex State Univ, Las Cruces, 86; Rio Bravo Watercolor Exhib, El Paso Mus Art, 87; 121st Ann Exhib Am Watercolor Soc, 88; El Paso Art Asn Ann Exhib, Sierra Med Ctr, 92; Am Watercolor Soc, 94; and others. *Teaching:* Carrizo Lodge, Riudoso, NMex, Rio Grande Artes Workshops. *Awards:* Bronze Medal Color Photog, Scarab Club of Detroit, 78; Grumbacher Gold Medal, Salmagundi Club, 82; Huthsteiner Purchase Award, 88; Silver Medal, El Paso Mus Art, 88; Best of Show, NMex Watercolor Soc, 92, 93, 94; Best of Show, Sierra-Providence Annual Exhib, El Paso Internat Mus, 2000; 2d Pl Figure, 3d Pl Figure, 4th Pl Figure, Hon Mention, Watercolor Mag Ann Competition, 2006. *Mem:* El Paso Art Asn; NMex Watercolor Soc; signature mem Am Watercolor Soc. *Media:* Watercolor, Oil. *Publ:* Contemp Western Artists, Southwest Art Publ, 82; NMex Mag, 5/93; Watercolor magic, Artists Mag, 4/95; The Artist's Mag, 2001-04; La Ventana Mag, 2005; Watercolor Magic Mag, 2006. *Dealer:* Patio Gallery Las Cruces NMex; William Bonney Gallery Mesilla NMex. *Mailing Add:* PO Box 8436 Las Cruces NM 88006

CHIN, MEL
SCULPTOR
b Houston, Tex, 1951. *Study:* Peabody Col, Nashville, Tenn, BA, 75. *Work:* Birmingham Mus Art, Ala; Harold Wash Libr, Chicago, Ill; Menil Found, Houston, Tex; Mus Fine Arts, Houston, Tex; Prudential Service Corp, Newark, NJ. *Comn:* Ecliptic Fence, Houston, Tex, 86; Conditions for Memory, Central Park, NY, 89. *Exhib:* Solo exhibs, Frumkin/Adams Gallery, 1988, Hirshhorn Mus & Sculpture Garden, Washington, 1989 Walker Art Ctr, 1990, Menil Collection, Houston, 1991, Storefront for Art & Archit, NY, 1991, Fabric Workshop, Philadelphia, 1992, Swarthmore Coll, Pa, 1992, Colo State Univ, Ft Collins, 1995, Frederieke Taylor Gallery, New York, 2001, 2003 & 2007, Contemp Arts Ctr, Cincinnati, 2002, Station Mus, Houston, 2006; group exhibs, The Manila Palm, Contemp Art Mus, Houston, 1978, Fire, 1979, Out of This World, 1994; Landscape As Metaphor (with catalog), Denver Art Mus, Colo & Columbus Mus, Ohio, 1994; Equal Rights & Justice (with catalog), High Mus, Atlanta, 1994; Refuse/Refuse, Honolulu Acad Arts, 1994; Old Glory: The Am Flag in Contemp Art, Cleveland Ctr Contemp Art, 1994; Robert McClain & Co, Houston, 1994; Sculpting with the Environment/A Natural Dialogue, Pratt Inst, New York, 1994; Black Male (with catalog), Whitney Mus Am Art, New York, 1994, Art at the End of the 20th Century (traveling), 1996; Murder, Bergamot Sta Arts Ctr, Santa Monica, Calif, 1995; Grounded, ART/OMI, 1995; Texas Myths & Realities, Mus Fine Arts, Houston, 1995; Thinking Print, Mus Mod Art, New York, 1996; Money-Making, The Fine Art of Curreney, Fed Reserve, Washington, 2000; One Planet Under a Groove, Bronx Mus Art, NY, 2002; Signatures of the Invisible, PS1 Contemp Art Ctr, New York, 2003; Down the Garden Path, Queens Mus Art, Long Island City, NY, 2005; Invitational Exhib Visual Arts, Am Acad Arts & Letters, New York, 2008. *Pos:* Vis artist & lectr at numerous mus & univs, 89-94; Lamar

Dodd hon chair fine arts, Univ Ga, Athens, 94-97; consult prof, Stanford Univ, Calif, 98; sculpture prof, Cooper Union, NY City, 99. *Awards:* Nat Endowment Arts Grant, 88, 90 & 91; Penny McCall Found Award, 91; Cal Arts Alpert Award Visual Arts, 95; Joan Mitchell Found award, 97; Creative Capital Grant, 2001; Nancy Graves Found award, 2004. *Bibliog:* William Zimmer (auth), Everything I say is art is art, she said, NY Times, 5/1/94; Mary Voelz Chandler (auth), Off the wall art, Rocky Mountain News, 5/15/94; Tracey C Hummer (auth), dialogue, Rev, 11-12/94. *Mailing Add:* c/o Frederieke Taylor Gallery 145 E 29th St Apt 1A New York NY 10016

CHIN, RIC
LECTURER, PAINTER, CALLIGRAPHER
b Hong Kong, July 16, 1935; US & UK citizen. *Study:* State Univ NY, BA; Art Students League; Sch Chinese Brushwork, New York; also with Barse Miller, Cheng Dai-Chien & Wang Chi-Yuan; Normal Univ Taiwan, MFA. *Work:* Nat Palace Mus, Taiwan; Penang Mus, Malaysia; Manhattan Savings Bank, Eastchester, NY; Houston's Ethan Allen Gallery, Greensboro, NC; Wantagh Sch Syst, NY; and pvt collections. *Exhib:* Am Artists Prof League Grand Nat, Lever House, NY, 71-75; Nat Palace Mus Ann, Taiwan, 74; Solo exhibs, Winston-Salem Hyatt House, NC, 74 & Ctr Asian Studies, St John's Univ, NY, 75; United Va Bank; and others. *Pos:* Dir, Bertrick Assoc Artists Inc, Seaford, NY, 65-74. *Teaching:* Lectr Chinese cult & art, Long Island Univ, 70-71; instr Chinese brushwork, var workshops, Southeastern US & Nat Art League, Douglaston, NY; nat painting & cooking lectr tour in 78 cities & on 34 TV shows, 77-78. *Mem:* Salmagundi Club (mem bd dir, 74 & 75); Am Artists Prof League; Sumi-e Soc Am; Nat Art League; Art League Nassau Co; Va Beach Arts Ctr; Chinese Calligraphy Asn, NY. *Media:* Watercolor, Water-Ink. *Res:* Rice paper with controlled texture. *Mailing Add:* PO Box 444 Pleasant Garden NC 27313

CHIROUSSOT-CHAMBEAUX, JANE
CURATOR, CRITIC
b France, July 7, 1943. *Study:* Ecole de Beaux Arts, Alger, Master, 64 & conservateur, Paris, 84; Mus de Beaux Arts, Directeur, 90. *Hon Degrees:* Master Beaux Arts Conservateur. *Comn:* Queen of England; King of Spain; Vatican, Elysee Palace; Sappor Beer, CNN, Luxembourg Mus. *Exhib:* Grand Prix & Bienials, France, USA, Japan. *Collection Arranged:* Les 3 Ameriqus, Mus du Luxembourg, 89; L' Aura de Createous, Chapeue de la Sorbonne, 90 & 91; Grand Prix de Paris, Found Napoleon, 92; Biennale d' Aquitaine, Mus de Beaux Arts, 93; Salon d' Automne, Mus de Beaux Arts, 95 & 96; Biennale Grand Prix, Japan, 95-99; Biennial Grand Prix, USA, 1995-2000. *Pos:* Pres, IAP, IAC, Inst IC & AM, 87-96; cur, Mus de Beaux Arts, 90-96, Mus de Sapporo, Japan, 97-. *Teaching:* teacher Inst d'Art Contemp Paris. *Awards:* Meda1, Mayor Miami, 92; Grand Cordon, Encouragement Pub, 95 & Inst Art Cult, 96; various medals in art field; City of Paris Silver Medal, 02; Governor Gold Medal, 02. *Media:* Sand, metallic oxyds. *Interests:* Organ, piano, guitar, painting, sculpture. *Dealer:* Music des Beaux Arts d'Unet

CHIU, MELISSA
MUSEUM DIRECTOR
b Australia. *Study:* Univ Western Sydney, BA, PhD; Univ S Wales, Coll Fine Arts, MA. *Collection Arranged:* Paradise Now? Contemp Art from the Pacific, Cai Guo-Qiang, An Explosion Event: Light Cycle Over Cent Park, China Refigured: The Art of Ah Xian, Asia Soc. *Pos:* Dir Asia-Australia Arts Ctr, Sydney, 1996-2001; cur contemp Asian & Asian Am art, Asia Soc, New York, 2001-2004, mus dir, 2004-2013, vpres global arts programming, 2008-2013; dir Hirshhorn Mus & Sculpture Garden, Wash DC, 2013-. *Teaching:* Fac, RI Sch Design (Asian contemp art & design), formerly; vis prof, City Univ New York Grad Sch, currently. *Awards:* Getty Res Fel, 2003-04. *Mem:* founding member, Asian Contemp Art Consortium; Asn Art Mus Dirs. *Publ:* Auth, Chinese Contemporary Art: 7 Things You Should Know, 2008. *Mailing Add:* Hirshhorn Museum & Sculpture Garden 700 Independence Ave SW Washington DC 20560

CHO, MIKA MIKYUNG
EDUCATOR, ADMINISTRATOR, CONSULTANT, VISUAL ARTIST
Study: Sook Myung Women's Univ, Seoul, Korea, MFA, BFA (Studio and Industrial Arts); Illinois State Univ, Normal, Doctor of Education, MA (Art Education & Educational Administration). *Exhib:* Solo shows include: Abstract Paintings, Robert Art Gallery, Santa Monica, Calif, 1998, Multiple Personality, Multiple Intelligence, and Multiple Whatever, Storage Gallery, Santa Monica, 2001, Untitled Paintings, Da Vinci Gallery, Los Angeles, 2003, University Gallery Kunst Universitat, Austria, 2005, Bronco Gallert, Pomona, 2007, Uni-Tech, Technology Univ, Auckland, New Zealand, 2011; Group Shows include: Now, CSULA Fine Arts Gallery, 1993, View, 1994, Diverse Vision, 1997, Montage, Village Square Gallery, Montrose, Calif, 1997, Groove-A-Ganza, DiRT Gallery, Hollywood, 2001, Route 66, Eagle Rock Arts Organization, 2004-2006, Angel's Ink Gallery, San Pedro, 2007, Biannual Faculty Show, Fine Arts Gallery, Calif State Univ, Los Angeles, 2000, 2003, 2007, 2008, 2010, Group Exhibition, Altanadena City Gallery, Calif, 2012 and others; Curatorial work includes: Process Painting, AlteWelt Gallery, Autria, 2004, Conceptual Painting, Moviemento Gallery, Austria, 2005, Conceptual Drawing, Bruder Baum Gallery, Austria, 2006, Morphoam, Bronco Gallery, 2007, Art and Social Justice, Univ Art Gallery, Austria, 2011 and others. *Pos:* Project consultant, Korean-American Teacher Project, Los Angeles, 1993-1994; consultant, juror, Beverly Hills Community Ctr, Annual Arts Fair, 1993, 1994, 1998; consultant, Korean Educational Development Inst, Seoul, Korea, 1999, 2001, 2005, Liaison for the Exchange Program for Global Teacher Education, Pusan Nat Univ, Korea, 2011, 2012; mem review board, Calif Commission on Teacher Credentialing, Calif Single Subject testing Credential Subject Matter Competency Standards and State Exam, 2003, Journal of Art and Design Education, England, 2007-, International Journal of Education Through Art, England, 2009 and others; Juror in the field; editor, Journal of Art Education, Seoul, Korea, 2004-2005; presenter in the field; univ representative, Nat Asn of Schools of Art and Design, 2013; board mem Eagle Art Ctr, Los Angeles, 2008. *Teaching:* Prof, Art Dept, Calif State Univ, Los Angeles, 1991-, dept chair, 2013-; vis prof, artist, Art Dept, Univ Arts and Communication, Kunst Universitat, Linz, Austria, 2003-2009, 2011; guest teaching at San Pedro Alternative School, Los Angeles, Univ Calif Irvine, Pusan Nat Univ, Korea, Nat Hsinchu Teachers Col, Taiwan. *Awards:* Recipient Outstanding Higher Education Art Educator, State Council of Calif Art Education Asn, Sacramento, 1996, Disting Women award, Calif State Univ, Los Angeles, 2000, and Nat Art Education Asn Painter award, 2002, 2011. *Mem:* Col Art Asn (education comt mem 2003-2006); Korean Art Education Asn (board mem 2004-2005); Calif Faculty Asn; International Soc for Education Through Art; Nat Art Education Asn; US Soc for Education Through Art. *Publ:* several publications, papers, reviews and catalogs. *Mailing Add:* California State University FA 329 5151 State University Drive Los Angeles CA 90032

CHO, Y(EOU) J(UI)
PAINTER
b Taiwan, China, Nov 3, 1950; US citizen. *Study:* Nat Taiwan Normal Univ, BFA, 73; State Univ NY, Albany, MA, 77. *Work:* Hong Kong Fine Art Mus; pvt collections of Martin Margulies, Coconut Grove, Fla & Max Palevesky, Los Angeles; Taipei Fine Art Mus; Taiwan Mus Art, Taichung; Miss Mus Art, Jackson. *Exhib:* Solo exhibs, OK Harris Works Art, NY, 86, 88, 90, 93, 97 & 2002, Hong Kong Inst Prom Chinese Cult, 88, Frank Bernarducci Gallery, 89, Kiong Gallery, Atlanta, 94, Asia Art Ctr (auth, catalog), Taipei, Taiwan, 95, Gallery 456, New York City, 99, Brushstrokes Gallery, Hong Kong, 2007, Invasion Gallery, Taipei, Taiwan, 2010, Moon Gallery, Taichung, Taiwan, 2012, 2015, The A Lift Gallery, Platform, Shenzhen, China, 2013; NY Observed, Frank Bernarducci Gallery, NY, 89; Chinese Am Arts Coun, NY, 89; Contemp Drawing Exhib, Cheng Piin Gallery, Taipei, Taiwan, 90; Dual Cultures, Nassau Co Mus Art, Roslyn, NY; Norton Ctr for Arts, Centre Col, Danville, Ky, 95; The World Bank, Washington, DC, 95; Cherng Pun Gallery, Taipei, Taiwan, 95; Alternative Mus, NYC, 95-96; Asia Art Ctr, Taipei, Taiwan, 96 & 2002; New World Art Ctr, New York City, 96; Heritage Arts Int Auction, Taipei, 97; Kao Hsiung Mus Fine Arts, Taiwan, 97; Raritan Valley Community Coll Gallery, Somerville, NJ, 97; Taiwan Int Art Fair, Taipei, 98 & 2000; Nat History Mus, Taipei, 2000; 15th Asian Int Art Exhib, Taipei, 2000; OK Harris Works of Art, New York City, 2000; Dimensions Art Ctr, Taipei, 2001; Hammond Mus, North Salem, NY, 2001; New Realist Painting in Taiwan Since 1970s, Asia Art Ctr, Taipei, Taiwan, 2002; Below the Canal after 9/11, Asia Art Ctr, NY, 2003; Everything OK at OK Harris, Brevard Mus Art & Sciences, Melbourne, Fla, 2003-2004; Mountain Jade Show, Natural History Mus, Taipei, Taiwan, 2004; Asian Fusion Gallery, Asian Cult Ctr, NY, 2005; The Odyssey of Art in Taiwan, 1950-2000, Nat Art Mus China, Beijing, 2006; NY to New Hampshire: Artists of the OK Harris Gallery, New England Col Gallery, Henniker, NH, 2007; Shanghai Art Fair, Shanghai MART, China, 2008; Impression of the Repulse Bay, HS modernart Gallery, Hong Kong, 2009; Asia Top Gallery Hotel Art Fair, Grand Hyatt Hotel, Hong Kong, 2010; Art Taipei 2011, Taipei World Trade Center Exhib Hall, Taiwan, 2011; Tenderness Hong Kong Oil Paintings Joint Exhib Wan Fung Art Gallery, 2012; Memory and Imagination Ping Tung Art Mus, Taiwan, 2013; Women--Home: in the name of Asian Female Artists, Kaohsiung Mus Fine Arts, Taiwan, 2014; Gaze of Sins (Painting On and On 6), Koo Ming Kown Exhib Gallery, Communication and Visual Arts Bldg, Hong Kong Baptist Univ, 2015. *Pos:* Vis artist and teacher, Nat Changhua Univ, Taiwan, 95, Chinese Univ, Hong Kong, 96 & Taitung Teachers Col, Taiwan, 2000; teaching, Hong Kong Baptist Univ, 2005-11, vis artist, 2011-12. *Awards:* First Prize, Prov Mus Taiwan, 73; Nat Endowment Cult & Art, Changhua Univ, Taiwan, 95; Gottlieb Found, 2004; Pollack-Krasner Found, 2005; Hong Kong Oil Painting Competition, Merit award, 2012. *Bibliog:* Mun-Lee Lin (auth), Mind and Spirit: Women's Art in Taiwan, Taipei Fine Art Mus, Taiwan, 98; Huang K-Nan (auth), Wall, Nat History Mus, Taiwan, 2000; The 15th Asian Int Art Exhib, China Times, Tainan, Taiwan, 2000. *Media:* Acrylic, Oil; Watercolor. *Publ:* Auth, Family Ties, Krasdale Foods Gallery, White Plains, NY, 93; Visions in Between, Taipei Gallery, New York, 93; Between East & West: Transformations of Chinese Art in the Late 20th Century, Discovery Mus, Bridgeport, 94; A Woman's Views: Equality, Development & Peace, World Bank Staff Art Soc, Washington, 95; Artist-Taiwan Art, Tsai-C Ni, Artist Mag, Taiwan, 95; and others. *Dealer:* O K Harris Gallery 383 W Broadway New York NY 10012

CHODKOWSKI, HENRY, JR
PAINTER, EDUCATOR
b Hartford, Conn, Mar 30, 1937. *Study:* Univ Hartford, BFA, 61; Yale Univ, MFA, 63. *Work:* Nat Gallery Greece, Athens; Phillips Collection, Nat Collection Fine Arts, Washington, DC; Philadelphia Mus; DeCordova Mus, Mass. *Exhib:* Solo exhibs, JB Speed Art Mus, 68, 72 & 78, Duke Univ Mus, 72, Middendorf Gallery, Washington, DC, 75, Allan Stone Gallery, NY, 79 & The Hellenic-Am Union, Athens, 85 & 91, Miami Univ Art Mus, Oxford, Ohio, 1999, Univ Ky Art Mus, Lexington, 1999-2000, Dishman Art Gallery, Lamar Univ, Beaumont, Tex, 2000; Gallery Contemp Art, Winston-Salem, NC, 74; Hassam & Speicher Exhib, Am Acad & Inst Arts & Letters, NY, 82; Twenty-one Am Artists on Paper, Warsaw Acad Fine Arts, Warsaw, Poland, 88. *Teaching:* Prof advan & grad painting, Univ Louisville, 73-. *Awards:* Polaroid Corp Grant, 68; Award for Excellence in Teaching & Scholarship, Univ Louisville, 78; Al Smith Fel, Ky Arts Coun, 89-90; Richard Florsheim Art Fund grant, 1988. *Bibliog:* Jay Kloner (auth), The precisionist paintings of Henry Chodkowski, 10/75 & Henry Chodkowski, 3/79, Arts Mag; Mary Machas (auth), Taoism and the Minoan Labyrinth, The Athenian, 5/85. *Media:* Acrylic, Miscellaneous Media. *Dealer:* Heike Pickett Gallery 110 Morgan St Versailles KY 40383; B Deemer Gallery 2650 Frankfort Ave Louisville KY 40206. *Mailing Add:* 2015 Baringer Ave Louisville KY 40204-1401

CHONG, ALBERT VALENTINE
PHOTOGRAPHER, EDUCATOR
b Kingston, Jamaica, Nov 20, 1958. *Study:* Sch Visual Arts, NY, BFA, 81; Univ Calif, San Diego, MFA, 91. *Work:* Baltimore Mus Art; Tampa Mus Art; Schomberg Ctr Res Black Cult, NY; Mus Nat Ctr African Am Artist, Boston; Bronx Mus Arts. *Comn:* Absolut Chong for Abolut Expressions (campaign mission), Absolut Spirits Company.

Exhib: Constructed Images, Studio Mus Harlem, NY, 89; Am Pictures of 1980's, Nat Mus Am Art, Washington, 89; Convergence, Photo Resource Ctr, Boston, 90; Decade Show, New Mus Art, NY, 90; Interrogating Identity, Grey Art Gallery, NY, 91; Pleasures & Terrors Domestic, Mus Modern Art, NY, 91; Ancestral Dialogues, Ansel Adams Ctr Photog, San Francisco, 94; 5th Havana Biennial, Wifredo Lam Ctr, Cuba, 94; solo exhibs, Projections, Throckmorton Fine Arts, New York City, 2001, Family Love: Photographs by Albert Chong, Zora Neale Hurston Nat Mus of Fine Arts, Eatonville, Fla, 2002, Nurturing Spirits: Photographs by Albert Chong, African Am Mus, Philadelphia, 2003, others; group exhibs, Mundos Creados: Ijans Amerikanse Fotografie, 2002 Photo Festival at Fries Mus, Leeuwarden The Neth, 2002, Un/familiar Territory, San Jose Mus of Art, 2003, others; Venice Biennial, Venice, Italy, 2001; Ritter Art Gallery, Fla, 2001; Committed to the Image, Black Photographers Contemp Brooklyn Mus of Art, 2001. *Teaching:* Instr photog, Sch Visual Arts, 85-88; vis scholar art/photog, Mira Costa Col, 89-91; asst prof art/photog, Univ Colo, 91-; assoc prof, RI Sch Design, 96. *Awards:* Regional (WESTAF), Los Angeles Conv Ctr, Nat Endowment Arts, 91; Nat Endowment Arts Fel, 92; CoVisions Award, Colo Coun Arts, 93; Guggenheim Fel, 98; Pollock/Krasner Grant, Pollock Krasner Found, 98; WESTAF Award, 2001. *Mem:* Soc Photog Educators. *Media:* Mixed. *Dealer:* Chelsea Galleria Miami FL; Skoto Gallery NY. *Mailing Add:* 140 Cherokee Way Boulder CO 80303-4202

CHONG, PING
DIRECTOR, VIDEO ARTIST, CHOREOGRAPHER, VISUAL ARTIST
b Oct 2, 1946. *Study:* Pratt Inst, 64-66, Sch Visual Arts, 67-69. *Hon Degrees:* Cornish Col, DFA, 98; Kent State Univ, DHL, 2004. *Work:* Site-specific installations, Mass Inst Technol, Albert & Vera List Visual Arts Ctr, Cambridge, 85 & Three Rivers Arts Festival, Pittsburgh, 88. *Comn:* In the Absence of Memory (light installation), New England Found Arts, 89; Tempus Fugit, Haggerty Mus Art, Marquette Univ, Milwaukee, Wis, 90; A Facility for the Containment and Channeling of Undesirable Elements, Artists Space, NY, 92. *Exhib:* Haggerty Mus Art, Milwaukee, Wis; Lafayette Coll Gallery, Easton, Pa; Austin Ctr Arts, Hartford, Conn; Artists Space, NY; Testimonial, Transculture, Venice Biennala, Italy, 95; Testimonial II, Lafayette Coll, Pa, 2006. *Pos:* Founder & dir, Ping Chong & Co. *Awards:* Five Nat Endowment Arts Fel, USA; Bronze Star Award, Sacramento Int Film & Video Festival, Calif, 89; Silver Award, Dance on Camera Festival, 93; sustained achievement, Obie Award, 77 & 2000; Bessie Award, 92 & 99; Prudential fellow, USA Artists, 2006; Falstaff award for Best Director, Best Adaptation for Throne of Blood, 2010; Doris Duke award, 2013. *Media:* Theatre. *Publ:* Dir, Education of the Girl Child (video), 73; co-dir, Paris, KCTA-TV, 82 & Turtle Dreams, WGBH-TV, (videos), 87; dir, A M/A M--The Articulated Man (film), 82; Plage Concrete (video) WGBH TV Ser, 88; script auth, Kindness, 88; script author, Nuit Blanchz, 88; script auth, Snow Captain, 89; I Will Not be Sad in this World, WNYE TV, 93; script auth, Gaijin, 95; script auth, Truth & Beauty, 2001; script auth, The East-West Quartet, 2005; Undesirable Elements: Real People, Real Lives, Real Theater, 2012. *Mailing Add:* 47 Great Jones St New York NY 10012

CHOO, CHUNGHI
SILVERSMITH, FIBER ARTIST, EDUCATOR
b Inchon, Korea, May 23, 1938; US citizen. *Study:* Cranbrook Acad Art, Bloomfield Hills, Mich, MFA, 65. *Work:* Metrop Mus Art, Mus Mod Art, Am Craft Mus, Cooper Hewitt Mus, NY; Musee des Arts Decoratifs, Paris, France; Art Inst Chicago; Victoria & Albert Mus, London, Eng; Mus fur Kunsthandwerk, Frankfurt, Ger; Detroit Inst Art, Detroit, Mich; Mus Fine Arts, Houston, Tex; Long House Res, East Hampton, NY; plus others. *Exhib:* Young Americans 1969, Mus Contemp Crafts, NY; solo exhib, Jack Lenor Larsen Show Rm, NY, 71; Fabric Vibrations, Eastern & Western Europe, Near & Far East & Pac Islands sponsored by Smithsonian Inst, 72-75; N Am Goldsmith, Renwick Gallery, Washington, DC & traveling, 74-77; Forms in Metal: 275 yrs of Metalsmithing in Am, Mus Contemp Crafts, NY & traveling, 75-76; Dyers Art, Mus Contemp Crafts, NY, 76; Int Fiberworks, Cleveland Mus Art, Ohio, 77; For the Table Top, Am Craft Mus, NY and traveling, 80-82; Craft Today: Poetry of Physical, Am Craft Mus, NY and traveling, 86-88; Craft Today USA, Europ traveling exhib, Am Craft Mus & US Information Agency, 89-92; Seoul Int Metal Artists Exhib, Seoul Arts Ctr, Korea, 99; Defining Craft, Am Craft Mus, NY, 2000; Women Designers in the USA 1900-2000; Diversity and Difference, Bard Grad Ctr, NY, 2000; plus others. *Teaching:* Prof jewelry & metalsmithing, Sch of Art & Art Hist, Univ Iowa, 68-, F Wendell Miller Disting Prof art, head of jewelry and metal arts program. *Awards:* Nat Endowment Art Grant, 81; AMOCO Excellence in Teaching Award, 87; Regents Award for Faculty Excellence, 93; plus others. *Bibliog:* Jack Lenor Larsen (auth), Dyer's Art, Reinhold; Katherine Pearson (auth), American Crafts; Robert Rorex (auth), Chunghi Choo, works in Metal & Silk, 10/82; Robert Rorex (auth) Metalsmith, Winter/91, American Craft, Univ Iowa metal artists, Oct/Nov 94. *Mem:* Soc Am Silversmiths. *Publ:* Photog, American Crafts, Stewart Tabori and Chang, Art in the World, 3rd dit., Holt Rinehart; Modern Design in the Metropolitan Museum of Art 1890-1990, Harry N Abrams; Art in Context, 4th edit., Harcourt Brace Jovanovich. *Mailing Add:* 2 Glenview Knolls NE Iowa City IA 52240

CHOPRA, NIKHIL
PHOTOGRAPHER
b Kolkata, India, 1974. *Study:* Md Inst Coll Art, Balitmore, BFA, 2001; Ohio State Univ, Columbus, MFA, 2003. *Exhib:* Solo exhibs, Kinnear Warehouse, Columbus, Ohio, 2003, 4th Fl, Kitab Mahal, Mumbai, 2005 & Chatterjeee & Lal, Mumbai, 2007; Central Asia Biennale, Bishkek, Kyrgzstan, 2004; The Taste of Others, Apexart, New York, 2005; Asian Contemp Art Week, Brooklyn Mus, New York, 2006; Beings and Doings, British Coun, New Delhi, India, 2007; House of Mirrors, Grosvenor Gallery, London, 2007; Khoj Int Artist's Asn, New Delhi, 2008; Mori Art Mus, Tokyo, Japan, 2008; Astrup Fearnley Mus, Oslo, Norway, 2009; 53rd Int Art Exhib Biennale, Venice, 2009. *Teaching:* Fac, MS Univ, Baroda, India, 1997-1999; artist-in-residence, Khoj International Artists Asn, New Delhi, 2007. *Mailing Add:* Chatterjee & Lal Arthur Bunder Rd Colaba 01/18 Kamal Mansion Fl 1 Mumbai India 400 005

CHRISMAS, DOUGLAS JAMES
GALLERY DIRECTOR
b Vancouver, Canada, April 9, 1944. *Pos:* Dir, Douglas Gallery, Vancouver, 1961-65, ACE Gallery, LA, 1966-; founder, ACE Mus, 1986. *Mailing Add:* ACE Gallery Wilshire Tower 5514 Wilshire Blvd Los Angeles CA 90036

CHRIST-JANER, ARLAND F
PAINTER, PRINTMAKER
b Garland, Nebr, Jan 27, 1922. *Study:* Carleton Col, BA, 43, LLD, 67; Yale, BD, 49; Univ Chicago, JD, 52; Coe Col, hon LLD, 61; Monmouth Col, hon LHD, 67; Carleton Col, LLD, 67; Colo Col, hon LLD, 71. *Hon Degrees:* Curry Col, hon LHD, 72; Cornell Col, hon LHD, 99. *Work:* Am Repub Ins Co, Des Moines, Iowa; Bankers Trust Co, NY; Hershey Foods Corp, Pa; Montclair Art Mus, NJ; Motion Picture Asn Am, NY; Indianhead Mills, NY; and others. *Exhib:* Nat Print Competition, Auburn Univ, Ala; Nat Print & Drawing Exhib, NMex Univ; Columbia Art League, Mo, 76; Solo exhibs, Carleton Coll, 80, Columbia Coll, 81; and others. *Pos:* Pres, Cornell Col, Boston Univ, New Col & Stephens Col, formerly; pres, Ringling Sch Art & Design, Sarasota, Fla, 84-96, emer pres, 96-; dir, Independent Col Univ Fla, Fla Independent Col Fund; trustee, New Col Found, Marie Selby Botanical Gardens; assoc, Independent Col Art & Design; vpres, Nat Asn Sch Art & Design, 93-96; adv bd, Sun Bank/Gulf Coast; interim dir, Ringling Mus Art & Ringling Mus Art, Sarasota, Fla, 2000. *Mem:* Am Acad Arts & Scis; Nat Asn Sch Art & Design (future's comt, 2 yrs). *Media:* Graphic. *Mailing Add:* Ringling Sch Art & Design 2700 N Tamiami Tr Sarasota FL 34234

CHRISTENBERRY, WILLIAM
PAINTER, SCULPTOR, PHOTOGRAPHER
b Tuscaloosa, Ala, Nov 5, 1936. *Study:* Univ Ala, Tuscaloosa, BFA, 58, MA (painting), 59; Kansas City Art Inst, Hon DFA, 83. *Work:* Corcoran Gallery Art, Libr Cong & Nat Mus Am Art, Washington; Mus Mod Art, Whitney Mus Am Art, NY; San Francisco Mus Mod Art; Baltimore Mus Art, Md; Philadelphia Mus Art, Pa; Pace McGill Exhibit, New York City, 2001, Creager Mus, 2001, Univ Cincinnati Galleries, 2001. *Comn:* Southern Wall, US Gen Serv Admin, Washington, DC, 78; Cola Wall, Arnold and Porter, Washington, DC, 83; Of Time & Place: Walker Evans & William Christenberry, Amon Carter Mus, Ft Worth, Tex & Friends of Photography; Potomac Wall, Phillip Morris Corp, 89. *Exhib:* Washington: 20 Yrs, Baltimore Mus Art, 70; New Sculpture: Baltimore-Washington-Richmond, Corcoran Gallery Art, 70; Eastern Cent Regional Drawing Exhib, Philadelphia Mus Art, 70; Wilderness, Corcoran Gallery Art, Washington, DC, 71; Artists at Work, Baltimore Mus Art, 72; Solo exhibs, Corcoran Gallery Art, 73, Baltimore Mus Art, 73, Corcoran Gallery Art (with catalog), 77, Philadelphia Mus Art, 91, Southside Gallery, Oxford, 94, Nancy Drysdale Gallery, Washington, 94, Pace McGill Gallery, NY, 95, Smithsonian Am Art Mus, 2006-07; Fourteen Am Photogrs, Baltimore Mus Art, 75; The Presence of Walker Evans (with catalog), Inst Contemp Art, Boston, 78; Washington Art on Paper: 1962-1978 (drawing), Corcoran Gallery Art, 79; Am Photog of the '70s, Art Inst Chicago, 79; Southern Fictions, Contemp Arts Mus, Houston, 83; A Second Talent: Painters & Sculptors Who Are Also Photographers, Aldrich Mus Contemp Art, 85; Recent Acquisitions, Mus Mod Art, NY, 88; Looking South: A Different Dixie, Birmingham Mus Art, 89; Morgan Gallery, Kansas City, Mo, 93; Debut, Kemper Mus Contemp Art & Design, Kansas City, Mo, 94; Worlds in a Box, White Chapel Art Gallery, London & Sheffield, Eng, Edinburgh, Scotland & Norwich, 94; Duchamps Leg, Walker Art Ctr, 94; Am Studies, Art Forum Praterinsel, Munich, Ger, 94; In Response to Place: Photographs from the Nature Conservancy's Last Great Places, Corcoran Gallery Art, Washington, DC, 2001; Am Acad Arts & Letts Invitational, New York, 2010. *Pos:* Vis artist painting, Yale Univ Summer Sch Art & Music, 91 & 93; self-employed artist, currently. *Teaching:* Instr art, Univ Ala, Tuscaloosa, 59-61; from asst prof to assoc prof art, Memphis State Univ, 62-68; assoc prof art, Corcoran Sch Art, Washington, DC, 68-74, prof, 74-; vis artist painting, Yale Univ Summer Sch Art & Music, 91 & 93. *Awards:* Individual Artists Fel, Nat Endowment Arts, 76; John Simon Guggenheim Mem Fel, 84; Art Matters Grant, New York, 94; Jimmy Ernst Award in Art, Am Acad Arts & Letts, 2010. *Publ:* William Christenberry Southern Photographs, Aperture Inc, 83. *Dealer:* Hemphill 1515 14th St NW 3rd Fl Washington DC 20005. *Mailing Add:* 2739 Macomb St NW Washington DC 20008

CHRISTENSEN, BETTY (ELIZABETH)
ILLUSTRATOR, PAINTER
b Collingdale, Pa. *Study:* Philadelphia Coll Art, cert; Art Students League; Nat Acad, with Jack Pellew, Am Watercolor Soc. *Work:* Mattatuck Mus, Waterbury, Conn; Hoffman Fuel, Danbury, Conn. *Exhib:* Am Watercolor Soc Ann, Nat Acad, NY, 57-59, 61-63, 66, 69 & 78; 200 Yrs: Watercolor Painting in Am, Metrop Mus Art, NY, 66; Invitational, 81 & Conn Classic Arts, 82, Mus Art, Sci & Indust, Bridgeport, Conn; Putman Arts Coun, Mahopac, NY, 81 & 85; Allied Artists Ann, Nat Arts Club, NY, 85; Conn Watercolor Soc Ann, New Haven, 85; Sheffield Art League Spring Show, Mass, 85 & 86; Catherine Lorillard Wolfe Art Club, NY; Art on the Mountain, Wilmington, Vt; Solo shows, Brooks libr, Brattleboro, Vt. *Awards:* Best-in-Show, Bethel Art League, 91; Ridgewood Award, Kent Art Asn, 95; Grumbacker Gold Medal, Richter Art Asn, 95. *Mem:* Am Watercolor Soc; Allied Artists Am; Conn Watercolor Soc; Kent Art Asn; Conn Classic Arts. *Media:* Watercolor, Oil. *Publ:* Illusr, A Few Thoughts on Trout, Simon & Schuster, 86. *Mailing Add:* 25 W St Newtown CT 06470

CHRISTENSEN, LARRY R
PAINTER, INSTRUCTOR
b Manti, Utah, Jan 18, 1936. *Study:* Utah Tech Col, cert, 2 yrs. *Work:* Salt Lake Co Fine Arts Collection; Utah Arts Coun, Salt Lake City; Salt Lake City Chamber Com, Vet Admin & Am Express, Salt Lake City; First Interstate Bank, Salt Lake City; Fairview Mus of Art, Fairview, Utah, 2000; Sanpete Co Comn, Mantl, Utah, 2001. *Comn:* Idaho Telephone Dir Cover, 61, portrait of pres, 62, Mountain Bell; Eccles Art Ctr, 2003. *Exhib:* Springville Mus Art Nat, Utah, 69-93; Univ Utah Mus Fine Art, 76-79; Watercolor West Transparent Watercolor, Calif, 80-84; Western Fedn

Southwestern Watercolor Socs, NMex, 84, Tex, 93; Southam Gallery, 88-95; Dixie Coll Invitational, St George, Utah, 91-95; and others. *Pos:* Art dir, Mountain Bell, 71-79; instr, Christensen Watercolor Workshop, Salt Lake City, 75, 76, 79, 80 & 93; Div Continuing Educ, Univ Utah, 75, Photo Blue Workshop, 77-. *Teaching:* Kimball Art Ctr, Park City, Utah, 92. *Awards:* Silver 2nd Award, Utah State Expos, 70; First Place, Cody Country Art 70 & 81; Cash Award, Salt Lakes Art Coun, 81. *Mem:* Assoc mem Am Watercolor Soc; Utah Watercolor Soc; assoc mem Watercolor Soc Calif. *Media:* Watercolor, Pencil. *Publ:* Contribr, Art West, 72. *Dealer:* Southam Gallery 50 E Broadway Salt Lake City UT 84111. *Mailing Add:* 3534 Dover Hill Dr Salt Lake City UT 84121-5527

CHRISTENSEN, NEIL C
PAINTER
b Imperial, Nebr, Oct 28, 1947. *Study:* Univ Nebr, Lincoln, BFA, 78, MFA, 84. *Work:* Peru State Col, Nebr; Mus Nebr Art, Kearney; Sioux City Art Ctr, Iowa. *Exhib:* 18th Joslyn Biennial, Joslyn Art Mus, Omaha, Nebr, 84; People on Paper, Sheldon Mem Art Gallery, Lincoln, Nebr, 86; 37th Spiva Art Ctr, Joplin, Mo, 87; Ceremonial Gardens, Haydon Gallery, Lincoln, Nebr, 90; Rall Gallery, Doane Col, Crete, Nebr; Celebrations & Ceremonies, Haydon Gallery, 91; Solo exhib, Sioux City Art Ctr, Iowa, Mus Nebr Art, Kearney. *Awards:* Vreeland Award, Univ Nebr, 84; Cash Award, 18th Joslyn Biennial, Joslyn Art Mus, 84; Purchase Award, 1987 Biennial, Sioux City Art Ctr, 87; Purchase Award, T J Majors Exhib, Peru State Col, Nebr. *Bibliog:* Am Szabat (auth), Christensen still lifes reveal reverence, Lincoln J, 1/18/90; Kyle MacMillian (auth), Minimalism an influence on painter's still life work, Omaha World Herald, 7/31/91; Kathryn Cates Moore, Artist keeping strict hours now, Lincoln J-Star, 9/15/91. *Media:* Oil on Panel. *Dealer:* Haydon Gallery Hardy Bldg Suite A 335 N 8th St Lincoln, NE 68508

CHRISTENSEN, SHARLENE
PAINTER, INSTRUCTOR
b Fountain Green, Utah, Aug 24, 1939. *Work:* Equitable Life & Casualty Utah Collection; Salt Lake Visitor Ctr, Salt Lake City; Salt Lake Co Fine Arts Collection, 87; Salt Lake CofC; W C Swanson Family Foun, Ogden, Utah, 2000; Fairview Mus of Art, Fairview, Utah, 2000. *Comn:* Salt Lake Visitor & Convention Center, Salt Lake City, Utah. *Exhib:* Springville Mus Art, Utah, 69-93; Eccles Art Ctr, Ogden, Utah, 75, 79, 88 & 2003; Audubon Artists 38th Ann, NY, 80; Utah Watercolor Soc, 75-95; Watercolor West, Riverside, Calif, 80; San Diego Int Watercolor Exhib, 81; Kimball Art Ctr, Park City, Utah, 84, 89 & 92; Southam Gallery, 88-99; Am Watercolor Soc, NY; and many others. *Pos:* Artists-in-schs prog, Nat Found Arts & Utah Inst Fine Arts, 73-74. *Teaching:* Instr watercolor, Salt Lake Art Ctr, 72-84; Christensen Workshops, 75-, Summer Arts Inst, Kimball Art Ctr, Park City, Utah, 92; instr watercolor, subjects in nature, Kimball Art Ctr, 88; A Way of Seeing through Watercolor, 92. *Awards:* Award of Excellence, Utah Watercolor Soc, 78; Equitable Life & Casualty Utah Collection Purchase Award, 85; Jurors Choice Award, Loge Gallery, 85. *Bibliog:* Ann Poore (auth), article in Salt Lake Tribune, 3/88; George Dibble (auth), Art Scene, Salt Lake Tribune, 5/88. *Mem:* Am & Utah Watercolor Soc; assoc mem Am Watercolor Soc. *Media:* Transparent Watercolor. *Publ:* Contribr, Art West, 72; Dict Utah Artists; Robert Olpin, 80; Women Artists of Utah, Springville Mus of Art, 80. *Dealer:* Southam Gallery 50 E Broadway Salt Lake City Utah 84111. *Mailing Add:* 3534 Dover Hill Dr Salt Lake City UT 84121

CHRISTENSEN, VAL ALAN
PRINTMAKER, GALLERY DIRECTOR
b Valentine, Nebr, Jan 26, 1946. *Study:* Univ Nebr-Lincoln, with Thomas P Coleman, BFA, 68; Wichita State Univ, MFA, 70; Cambridge Univ, Eng. *Work:* Sioux City Art Ctr, Iowa; Sheldon Mem Art Gallery, Lincoln, Nebr; Kearney State Col, Nebr; Hastings Col, Nebr; Springfield Art Mus, MO. *Exhib:* Thirty-fifth Nat Graphic Arts & Drawing Exhib, Wichita Art Asn, Kans, 71; 29th Nat Print Exhib, Silvermine Guild of Artists, New Canaan, Conn, 72; 3rd Ann Nat Print Exhib, Ga State Univ, Atlanta, 72; 43rd Ann Art Exhib, Springfield Art Mus, Mo, 73; Nebraska 75, Joslyn Art Mus, Omaha, 75; one-person show, Sheldon Mem Art Gallery, Lincoln, 76. *Collection Arranged:* John and Pam Finley Collection of African Art; Marianne Keown Collection; Vivian Olson Collection. *Pos:* Artist-in-sch, Grand Island Cent Cath, 75-79; panel mem, Community Arts Prog, Nebr Arts Coun, Omaha, 77-79; dir, Spiva Atr Ctr, 79-93; assoc prof of art, Mo Southern State Univ, Joplin, 79-. *Teaching:* Asst prof printmaking, Univ Nebr-Lincoln, 71-72; instr printmaking/drawing, Hastings Col, Nebr, 72-75; asst prof art, Mo Southern St Univ, 79-2002; assoc prof, 2002-. *Awards:* Vreeland Award, Univ Nebr-Lincoln Found, 67; Purchase Awards, 40th Ann Art Exhib, Springfield Art Mus, Mo, 70 & 33rd Ann Fall Show, Sioux City Art Ctr, 71. *Mem:* Mid-Am Coll Art Asn; Coll Art Asn. *Media:* Intaglio prints. *Interests:* African Art. *Mailing Add:* 426 N Pearl Ave Joplin MO 64801-2463

CHRISTIANSEN, DIANE
PAINTER, CARTOONIST
b Grinnel, Iowa, Oct 27, 1958. *Study:* Grinnel Col, Iowa, BA (antrhop), 81; Loyola Univ, Chicago, MSW, 90; Art Inst Chicago, MFA (painting), 90. *Work:* South Bend Art Ctr, Ind. *Exhib:* Solo exhibs, Artemisia Gallery, Chicago, 85 & 91, Race St Gallery, Grand Rapids, 86, Ill Cent Gallery, Peoria, 88, World Tattoo Gallery, Chicago, 90, Chicago Cult Ctr, 92, Lorenzo Rodriguez Gallery, Chicago, Ill, 93 & Second St Gallery, Charlottesville, Va; Gigantic Women, Miniature Work, Gallery II, Chicago, 90; Itinerary, MWMWM Gallery, Chicago, 91; group show, Lannon Cole Gallery, Chicago, 91, Narratives of Loss, Univ Wis, Milwaukee, 93 & Three Paintings, Edinboro Univ, Pa, 94. *Awards:* Purchase Prize, Michiana Regional Show, South Bend, Ind, 86; Full Merit Scholarship, Art Inst Chicago, 88; Visual Arts Fel Award, Arts Midwest, Nat Endowment Arts Regional, 92. *Bibliog:* Susan Alexis Collins, Diane Christiansen, Walter Andersons, New Art Examiner, 12/91. *Media:* Oil on plaster. *Publ:* Chicago Tribune, 4/93 & 4/94. *Mailing Add:* 2022 W Crystal St Chicago IL 60622-3129

CHRISTISON, MURIEL B
EDUCATOR, MUSEUM DIRECTOR, ART HISTORIAN
b Minneapolis, Minn. *Study:* Univ Minn, BA & MA; Univ Paris Inst Art & Archaeol, dipl (grad study art hist); Univ Brussels, dipl (grad study art hist). *Exhib:* The Impressionist & Post-Impressionists, 51, Goya, 53, Masterpieces of Chinese Art, 55, Les Fetes Galantes, 55, Masterpieces of Am Silver, 60 & Sport & the Horse, 60, Va Mus Fine Arts, Richmond; Am Painting & Sculpture, for your home, New Environment, 63-82, Art of India & Southeast Asia, 63. Krannert Art Mus, Univ Ill, Urbana/Champaign. *Collection Arranged:* Va Mus Fine Arts; Krannert Art Mus; Muscarelle Mus. *Pos:* Cur researcher, Minneapolis Inst Arts, 36-42, head educ dept, 44-47; assoc dir, Va Mus Fine Arts, Richmond, 48-61; consult, Ark Art Ctr, 61; assoc dir & oper dir, Krannert Art Mus, Univ Ill, Champaign-Urbana, 62-71, dir, 71 & 75-82, dir emer, 82-; bd mem, Am Asn Mus, 72-82, sr examiner, 82-; interim dir, Muscarelle Mus, Col William & Mary, Williamsburg, Va, 84-85 & 93-94; evaluator, Univ Tex, Austin, 78, Wash Univ, St Louis, 80, Ohio Arts Coun, 84 & SC Arts Comn, 86. *Teaching:* Instr art in civilization & Am art, Univ Minn, Minneapolis, Minn Mpls Inst Arts, 45-47; dir grad prog art mus studies, Univ Ill, 72-82; adj prof art, Col William & Mary, 83-98. *Awards:* Carnegie Scholar, Inst Int Educ, 36; CRB Fel, Belg-Am Educ Found, 38; Distinguished Serv, Midwest Mus Conf, 82. *Mem:* Asn Art Mus Dirs; Am Asn Mus; Soc Preserv Va Antiquities; Soc Archit Hist (Va chap). *Publ:* The artmobile, an experiment in education, Art J, 55; Le Museobus de Virginia Museum of Fine Arts, Mus, Unesco, 55; 25th anniversary in Virginia, 60 & The design game, Art Journal, 71; Professional Practices in University Art Museums (mus news), 80; plus many exhib catalogues & other mus publ, auth of about 75 mus titles

CHRISTMAN, REID AUGUST
PAINTER
b Brooklyn, NY, Oct 28, 1948. *Study:* Nat Acad Fine Art, NYC, scholarship with Daniel Green, 1971; Art Students League, New York, 1972; Scholarship studies with Robert Brackman & Everett R Kintsler. *Work:* Elliott Mus, Stuart, Fla. *Comn:* many pvt comn. *Exhib:* ASMA Contemp Am Marine Art, Vero Beach Mus Art, Fla, 2004; Save the Bay, Invitational Exhib, Gallery on Merchants Square, Williamsburg, Va, 2004-2005. *Awards:* Leonard Kestenbaum, Ann, Allied Artist Am, 1993; Leon Stacks Mem, 81st Ann, Allied Artist Am, 1994; M Grumbacher Gold Medallion, Grand Nat, Am Artists Prof League, 1994. *Bibliog:* Contrib, Vero Beach Magazine, Moulton Publ, 2005. *Mem:* Allied Artists of Am; Am Artists Prof League; Am Soc Marine Artists. *Media:* Acrylic, Oil, Pastel. *Interests:* Marine art, landscapes & still life. *Publ:* Contrib, Best of Oil Painting, Rockport Publ, 1996. *Dealer:* Admiralty Gallery 3315 Ocean Dr Vero Beach FL 32963-1959. *Mailing Add:* 165 23rd Ave Vero Beach FL 32962

CHRISTO AND JEANNE-CLAUDE
ARTISTS
Christo: b Gabrovo, Bulgaria, June 13, 1935; Jeanne-Claude: b France, June 13, 1935, died Nov 18, 2009 (died Nov 18, 2009); immigrated to New York, NY, 1964. *Study:* Christo: Fine Arts Acad, Sofia & Vienna, 53-56, Fine Arts Acad Vienna, 56, Jeanne-Claude: Univ Tunis, BA, 52. *Hon Degrees:* 12 times Doctors Honoris Causa. *Work:* Centre National d'Art et de Culture Georges Pompidou & Musee d'Art Moderne de la Ville, Paris; Corcoran Gallery Art, Washington DC; Found Beyeler, Basel-Riehen, Switz; Fogg Mus, Cambridge, Mass; Henie-Onstad Kunstsenter, Hovikodden, Norway; La Mus Mod Art, Calif; Mus Boijmans Van Beuningen, Rotterdam, Neth; Mus Ludwig, Cologne, Germ; Mus Contemp Art, San Diego, La Jolla, Calif; Mus Wurth, Kunselsau, Germ; Philadelphia Mus Art, Pa; Rijksmuseum Kroller-Muller, Otterlo, Neth; Smithsonian Inst, Hirshhorn Mus & Sculpture Garden, Wash DC; Smithsonian Am Art Mus, Washington, DC; Stedelijk Mus, Amsterdam, Neth; Nat Gallery, DC; Mus Modern Art, NY; Whitney Mus Am Art; Guggenheim Mus Art; and many others. *Exhib:* Iron Curtain-Wall of Oil Barrels, blocking the Rue Visconti, Paris, 62; Wrapped Fountain & Wrapped Medieval Tower, Spoleto, 68; Wrapped Kunsthalle, Berne, Switz, 68; 5,6000 Cubic Meter Package, Documenta 4, Kassel, Air Package 280 ft high, 68; Wrapped Mus Contemp Art, Chicago, 69; Wrapped Coast, Little Bay, One Million Sq Ft, Sydney, Australia, 69; Wrapped Vittorio Emanuele, Piaza Duomo & Wrapped Leonardo de Vinci Monument, Piazza Scala, Milan, 70; Valley Curtain, Grand Hogback, rifle Colo, 1970-72; The Wall, Wrapped Roman Wall & Wrapped Ocean Front, Newport, RI, 74; Running Fence, Sonoma and Marin Counties, Calif, 70-72; Wrapped Walk Ways, Loose park, Kansas City, MO, 77-78; Surrounded Islands, Biscayne Bay, Greater Miami, Fla, 80-83; The Pont Neuf Wrapped, Paris, 75-85; The Umbrellas, Japan, USA, 84-91; Wrapped Reichstag, Berlin, 71-95; Wrapped Trees, Foundation Beyeler and Berower Park, Riehen-Basel, Switz, 97-98; The Wall, 13,000 Oil Barrels, Gasometer, Oberhausen, Ger, 99; The Gates, Central Park, New York City, 2005. *Awards:* Award of Excellence(Christo), Cheltenham Art Ctr, 80; Kaiser Ring Award for Art Achievement, Ger, 80; Crystal Award, Switzerland, 95; Praemium Imperiale, Tokyo, Japan, 95; Award for Distinction in Sculpture for lifetime achievements, Sculpture Ctr, New York, 96; Inspiration Award, New York Found Arts, 2004; Artist of the Yr, NY State Art Teachers Asn, 2004; Urban Visionaries Award, Cooper Union, New York, 2004; President's Award, NY Chap Am Soc Landscape Archit, New York, 2005; Life Trustee Award, NY Archit League, New York, 2006. *Bibliog:* Guy and Linda Pieters (auths), Christo and Jeanne-Claude, Over the River, Project for the Arkansas River, State of Colorado, 2007, Christo and Jeanne-Claude, The Mastaba, Project for the United Arab Emirates, 2007; Christo and Jeanne-Claude: Early Works 1958-64, 2009; Masa Yanagi (auth), Christo and Jeanne-Claude: Life=Works=Projects, 2009; Christo and Jeanne-Claude, 2010. *Media:* Fabric, Aluminum, Steel

CHRISTOPHERSON, HOWARD MARTIN
PHOTOGRAPHER, ART DEALER
b Duluth, Minn, Sept 26, 1955. *Study:* Self taught. *Work:* Arthur Andersen Company, St Paul, Minn; AT&T Minneapolis, Minn; Minn Hist Soc; Univ Minn Art Mus; First Bank, Minneapolis, Minn; Dahl and Assoc, St Paul, Minn; Heritage Insurance Company, Sheboygan, Wis; Schneido USA, Plymouth, Minn; Lessors Inc, Egan,

Minn; Medtronic Inc. *Exhib:* Minnesota Collects, Minn History Center, St Paul, 94; Art on the Plains, Plains Art Mus, Fargo, NDak, 98; The Nest, Minn State Fair, 98; Return to the Satiric Dancer, Fed Reserve Bank Gallery, Boston, Mass, 99; Figural Works in all Media, Watkins Gallery, Winona State Univ, 2000; solo exhibs, Icebox Gallery, 90, 91, 92, 97, 99. *Pos:* dir & owner, Icebox Gallery, Minneapolis, Minn, 88-. *Awards:* grant, Forecast Pub Artspace Productions, 82; Que Award for Art-A-Whirl, Mayor of Minn; grant, Union Depot Place, St Paul; Second Place for photog, Minnesota State Fair, St Paul, 95

CHRISTY, BONNIE BETH
PAINTER, DIRECTOR, EDITOR
b Chicago, Ill, Jan 9, 1955. *Study:* Ind State Univ, Terre Haute, 62-63; Miami Univ, Oxford, Ohio, 64-65; Joseph Sulkowski, NY Students League, NY, 2003. *Work:* Garst Mus, Greenville, Ohio; Art Instruction Collection, Minneapolis; Robert Shefler Collection, Dayton, Ohio; Richmond Art Mus, Richmond, Ind; Cleveland Mus Natural Hist; Greenacres Arts Ctr, Cincinnati Art Galleries. *Exhib:* Ann Juried Exhib, Richmond Art Mus, Richmond, Ind, 70-2012; Am Painters in Paris, Palais des Congres, Paris, 75; Hoosier Salon, Ind State Mus, Indianapolis, 2002, 2012; Journey to the Edge of the Appalachia Preserve, Cincinnati Mus of Natural Hist, 2004; Oil Painters of Am, Hilligoss Galleries, Chicago, 2005; Ann Regional Exhib, Garst Mus, Greenville, Ohio, 2006; Endangered Species-The Wilds, Cincinnati Art Galleries, 2006; Indianapolis Zoo Invitational; Darke Co, Agricultural Soc. *Pos:* Workshop instr, North Shore Art Asn, 96; Western Ohio Watercolor Soc, 2000; Hoosier Salon-New Harmony, Ind, 2003-2006; Springfield, Ohio, Springfield Art Mus, Western Art Acad, Schreiner Univ, Kerrville, Tex, 2003-2014, Susan K Black Found, Dubois, 2014. *Teaching:* Instr, painting, Greenville Art Guild, Greenville, Ohio, 70-90; Artist in res, painter, Hayes Found, Richmond, Ind, 86; instr, Studio Gallery, Greenville, Ohio, 90-; Instr, Richmond Art Mus, Richmond, Ind, currently. *Awards:* Jurors Choice Award, Oil Painters Am, 92; Best of Show, SKB Found, Jim Parkman, 2005; Grand Award, Headwaters Art Ctr, Headwaters Bd, 2005. *Mem:* Master Works for Nature (web designer); Tri-Arts (pres); SKB Found (ed legacy news); Darke Co Center for the Arts DCCA (bd mem); Oil Painters Am; Hoosier Salon, Indianapolis, Ind; Ind Plein Air Painters Asn. *Media:* Oil; Watercolor. *Specialty:* Greenacres Arts Ctr, Cincinnati, Ohio. *Publ:* Auth, Tradition: The Art and Artists of the Hoosier Salon, Hoosier Salon Patrons Asn Inc; Painting Indiana III-Heritage of Place Book. *Dealer:* North Shore Art Asn 11 Pirates Ln Gloucester MA 01930. *Mailing Add:* 6441 Daly Rd Greenville OH 45331

CHRISTY, BONNIE BETH
PAINTER
b Chicago, Ill, Jan 9, 1955. *Study:* Kansas City Art Inst, BFA (painting), 82, studied with Wilbur Niewald; Research Rockhurst, Kansas City, Mo, BS (nursing), 86. *Work:* Salmagundi Club, New York; Sierra Point Marina Harbor, Calif. *Comn:* Morning Light, comn by Judith Moran, 2004; Wisteria in Spring, comn by Dave Dawney, 2004, Back of House of Flowers, 2006; Realistic rep of the Sierra Point Marinain Brisbane Calif, comn by Ted Warburton Harbor Master & the dir of marina serv, Brisbane Calif, 2008; San Francisco Sailor, comn by Zachary Reed, 2009; Portugal Princess, comn by Michael Bell, 2010. *Exhib:* Amarillo Art Ctr, Amarillo, Tex, 81; Abilene Fine Arts Mus, Abilene, Tex, 81; Fall Salon, Limner Gallery, 2003; Newington Cropsey Found Gallery, 2004; JMS Gallery, Phila, Pa, 2006; Art and the American Experience, Santa Cruz Art League, 2008; The Am Artists Prof League, Salmagundi Club, New York, 2009; 67th Annual Exhib, Audubon Soc, 2009, online exhib, 2011; 81st Grand Exhib, Am Artists Prof League, 2009; Impact Artists, 2010; 69th Annual Exhib, Salmagundi Club, 2011; California Dream, Chgo Art Ctr, 2012, Only in San Francisco, 2012; 70th Audubon Soc annual exhib online, 2012; 84th Grand Nat Am Artist Profl League, Online, 2012, Syncronisity, 2012; 85th Grand Nationals Am Artist Professional League, 2013, 86th Grand Nat Exhib, 2014; Audubon Soc Annual Exhib, 2013. *Awards:* Back Cover award, House of Flowers, New Art Internat Vol X, 2005-2006; Marquis Who's Who in Am Art Reference Award in oils, Audubon Artists, 2009; Certificate of Merit for Traditional Realism and Gold Plaque for Painting, 70th Annual Audubon Soc Exhib, Online, 2012, online 71st,, 72nd, Salmagundi Club, 2014. *Bibliog:* Jeremy Sedley (auth), New Art Int, Book Art Press, 2005-2009. *Mem:* Am Artists Prof League (elected mem, fellow mem 2014); Am Soc Marine Artists; Audubon Soc (active mem 2013); Portrait Soc Am; Cecilia Beaux Forum. *Media:* Oil

CHU, ANNE
SCULPTOR
b NY City, 1959. *Study:* Philadelphia Coll Art, BFA, 1982; Columbia Univ, MFA, 1985. *Exhib:* Solo exhibs include Bess Cutler Gallery, NY, 1991, Neuberger Mus at SUNY, Purchase, 1993, TZ'Art & Co, NY, 1995, AC Project Room, NY, 1996, 1999, Dallas Mus of Art, Tex, 1998, Marc Foxx, Los Angeles, Calif, 1998, Monica de Cardenas, Milan, Italy, 1999, Donald Young Gallery, Chicago, 1999, 2002, Berkeley Art Mus, Calif, 2000, Indianapolis Mus Art, 2000, Galerie Karlheinz Meyer, Karlsruhe, Germany, 2001, Victoria Miro Gallery, London, 2001, 2005, Marlborough Graphics, NY, 2001, Christine Burgin, NY, 2002, 303 Gallery, NY, 2003, Weatherspoon Art Mus, Greensboro, NC, 2005, Miami Mus Contemp Art, Fla, 2005; group exhibs include Annual Small Works Show, Sculpture Ctr, NY, 1988; Bess Cutler Gallery, NY, 1989, The New Eccentricity: Sculpture, 1990; New Generations: New York, Carnegie Mellon Art Gallery, Pittsburgh, Pa, 1991; 55 Ferris Street, Brooklyn, NY, 1992; NaturalUnnatural, TZ'Art & Co, NY, 1993; Summer Survey, Alternative Mus, NY, 1994; Happy Valley, AC Project Room, NY, 1995, Drawings from the Mad Library, 1996, New Digs, 1998; In Three Dimensions: Women Sculpors of the '90s, Snug Harbor Cultural Ctr, NY, 1995; Prop Fiction, White Columns, NY, 1997; Surrogate: The Figure in Contemporary Sculpture and Photography, Henry Art Gallery, Seattle, Washington, 1998; Girlschool, Brenau Univ Galleries, Gainsville, Ga, 1999; Making the Making, Apex Art, NY, 2001; Paper 1, Galerie Friedrich, Basel, Switzerland, 2002; Extended Painting, Victoria Miro Gallery, London, 2003; Annual Carnegie Int Exhib, Carnegie Mus, Pittsburgh, 2004; deja vu, Frederieke Taylor Gallery, NY, 2005; Collections, Mus Contemp Art, Chicago, 2006; Figures in the Field: Figurative Sculpture and Abstract Painting from Chicago Collections, Mus Contemp Art, Chicago, 2006; New Now Next: The Contemp Blanton, Blanton Mus Art, Austin, Tex, 2006; Am Acad Arts & Letts Invitational, New York, 2010. *Pos:* Co-dir, AC Project Room, 1996-2002. *Awards:* Joan Mitchell Found Grant, NY, 1999; Penny McCall Award, Anonymous Was a Woman Found, NY, 2001; Guggenheim Found Fel, 2010. *Bibliog:* Gregory Volf (auth), Ane Chu at A/C Project Room, Art in America 85, 2/1997; Martha Schwendener (auth), Anne Chu, Art on Paper 2, 1997. *Dealer:* Donald Young Gallery 224 S Michigan Ave Ste 266 Chicago IL 60604. *Mailing Add:* 303 Gallery 525 W 22nd St New York NY 10011

CHU, JULIA NEE
PAINTER
b Shanghai, China, Dec 10, 1940; US citizen. *Study:* Univ Calif Los Angeles, BA, 78, MFA, 81. *Work:* MCA Music Corp, Nashville, Tenn; Hong Kong Mus, Sumitomo Co, Osaka, Japan; Landmark Tower, Yokohama, Japan; Calif Mart, Los Angeles; Four Seasons Hotel, Hong Kong; and others. *Comn:* Central Plaza, Hong Kong; paintings (14' x 16'), GKBI Tower, Jakarta, Indonesia, 95; painting (9' x 12'), New Island Printing Ltd, Hong Kong, 96; paintings (12' x 10'), Grand Hyatt, Hong Kong; MGM Studios, Calif. *Exhib:* Solo exhibs, Taipei Fine Arts Mus, Taiwan, 89, Tokyu Bunkamura Art Ctr (catalog), Tokyo, 95 & Hong Kong Univ Sci & Technol Art Gallery (catalog), 96; Sydney Univ, Australia, 92; Macau Mus Invitation Show, 92; Composite Expression (catalog), Chinese Cult Found, San Francisco, 95; Now a Dream of East, New Asian Invitational (catalog), Kirin Plaza, Osaka & Japan Forum, Tokyo, 95; In Search of Identity, Invitational Calif Chinese Artists, Chinese Cult & Info Ctr, Taipei Gallery, NY, 96; and others. *Teaching:* Grad, Teaching fel, Univ Calif, Los Angeles, 80-81. *Awards:* Ford Found Grant, 80. *Bibliog:* Amano Taro (auth), A Challenge to Modernism: Julia Nee Chu (exhib catalog), Yokohama Mus Art, 95; Belinda Chang (auth), In search of identity, World J, World Daily, Monterey Park, Calif, 8/18/96; Holland Cotter (auth), 7 artists on the trails of cultural identity, NY Times, 8/23/96. *Mem:* Asian Am Art Ctr, NY; Art Action, Hong Kong. *Media:* Acrylic, Oil. *Dealer:* Annex Gallery 453 6th Ave San Diego CA 92101; EDL Assocs 3221-B Cains Hills Pl Atlanta GA 30305; Sin Sin Fine Art G/F No1 Prince's Terr Mid-Levels Hong King; Fresh Paint Arts 9355 Culver Blvd Ste B Culver City CA; Jim Robischon Gallery 1740 Wazee St Denver CO; Daniel Fine Arts 3337 Laguna Canyon Rd Ste D LaGuna Beach, CA. *Mailing Add:* 1520 17th St Santa Monica CA 90404

CHUPIK, KEVIN KING
PAINTER
b Ft Worth, Tex, 1967. *Study:* Tex Christian Univ, BFA, 1992; Univ Colo, Boulder, MFA, 1995. *Exhib:* Solo exhibs, Joe B Rushing Ctr Gallery, Ft Worth, Tex, 1990, Tex Christian Univ, Ft Worth, 1992, Tarratn County Coll, Ft Worth, 1992, Univ Colo, 1995, Nev State Legis, Carson City, 1999, Winchester Gallery, Las Vegas, 2002, Las Vegas Art Mus, 2002, Coll Southern Nev, 2007; Grace Cult Ctr, Abilene, Tex, 1994; La Creme, Contemp Arts Collective, Las Vegas, 1998; Austin Mod Gallery, Tex, 2002; CSN Fac Show, Las Vegas, 2004-2006 & 2009; Contemp Arts Collective Juried Exhib, Las Vegas, 2004; Jack the Pelican Presents, Brooklyn, New York, 2007; Bridge Gallery at City Hall, Las Vegas, 2008. *Teaching:* Instr painting, drawing & design, Coll Southern Nev, 2003. *Bibliog:* Spotlight, Las Vegas Rev J, 9/13/2002; Whipping Boys, Mercury Mag, 10/10-16/2002; Artful Pursuits, Luxury Las Vegas, 128, 2/2007; Atomic Ranch, Polished Mag, 37-42, 4/2008; Mad for Mid Mod, H&D Mag, 42-53, 1-2/2009. *Mailing Add:* c/o Brett Wesley Gallery 1112 Casino Ctr Blvd Las Vegas NV 89104

CHURCH, MAUDE
PAINTER, ILLUSTRATOR
b Berkeley, Calif, June 15, 1949. *Study:* Calif Coll Arts & Crafts, Oakland, BFA, 72; Byam Shaw Coll Art, London, Eng, MA, 73. *Comn:* Red & Yellow (mural), Calif Sch Prof Psychology, San Francisco, Calif, 74; Curved Space (mural), comn by J V Ferrero Jr, Palos Verdes, Calif, 76; Oasis (triptych), comn by Pamela & Joe Bonino, Palm Springs, Calif, 84. *Exhib:* Retrospective, Riverside Art Mus, Calif; Starburst: Maude Church, Bank Am World Hq, San Francisco; Exchange Exhib: San Francisco-Berlin, Amerikahaus Gallery, Berlin, Ger; California Artists, 81, Oakland Mus, Calif; 3rd Ann Women's Nat, Triangle Gallery, Washington, DC; Marine Art, Coos Art Mus, Coos Bay, Oregon. *Pos:* Pres, North Calif Artists Equity Asn, 78-79; adv bd dir, Bay Area Lawyers Arts, 78-79; nat bd dir, Women's Caucus for Art, 89-92; art dir, Mindscape, Novato, Calif, 94-96; sr artist, Sega-Soft, Redwood City, Calif, 96; creative dir, Classroom Connect, Burlingame, Calif. *Teaching:* Adj fac, Calif Sch Prof Psychology, Alameda, 74-93; assoc prof art, Lone Mountain Col, San Francisco, Calif, 75-76. *Awards:* Fine Art Merit Award, San Francisco Arts Festival, 77; Outstanding Young Woman of the Year, 79; Sculpture Award, small sculpture exhib, Medocino Art Ctr, Calif, 90. *Bibliog:* Arthur Bloomfield (auth), City's Art in the Right Place, San Francisco Examiner, 9/28/78; Sylvie Roder (auth), Tight formats, Artweek, 10/15/83; Kim Anno (auth), A propensity for animals, Bay Area Reporter, 9/12/85. *Mem:* Women's Caucus Art; Artists Equity Asn (pres, 78-79); Pro Arts, Oakland, Calif. *Media:* Acrylic paint, Prismacolor Pencil, Pen & Ink, Assemblage, Computer Graphics. *Publ:* Album cover, Holly Near, Watch Out, 84; Two posters, The Nature Co, 87; art dir, The Adventures of Peter Rabbit (CD-Rom), Mindscape, 95; illusr (album cover & illus), Jeff Rosedale, Scenes from an Observation Car, 2008

CHURCHILL, DIANE
PAINTER
b Bronxville, NY, Jan 8, 1941. *Study:* Wellesley Col, BA(art hist); Brooklyn Mus Art Sch; Hunter Col, MA (painting). *Work:* Chase Manhattan Bank Collection, NY; Reliance Group Inc, Mass; Jay Hambridge Art Found, Rabun Gap, Ga; Weehawken Twp; Grolier Publ; Wellesley Coll Collections; Robert Yaeger Health Ctr, Pomona, NY. *Comn:* Lori Adler, NY. *Exhib:* Soho 20 Gallery, 76, 78 & 80; solo exhib, Gallery 107, Brooklyn Hopper House, Nyack, Cal Tech, San Luis Obispo, Calif; William Carlos Williams Ctr, Rutherford, NJ; St Peter's Artcorp Ctr, NY; Gallery 93, Nyack,

NY, 98; Rockland Ctr for the Arts, 2000; Tweed Gallery, NJ, 87; Soho 20 Gallery, NY. *Pos:* Artist catalyst, Brigade-In-Action, NY, 68-73; publ & ed, Fourth St, 71-73; field rep, Visual Arts Dept, NY State Coun Arts, NY, 76-77. *Teaching:* Teacher art, Hudson Sch, Hoboken, NJ, 79-88 & Fieldston Lower Sch, 87-. *Awards:* Yaddo, 68; NJ State Coun Arts Fel, 79-80 & 85-86; Karoly Found, Vence, France, 88; Fondaçion Valparaiso, Spain, summer 2001. *Bibliog:* Carlotta Swardon (auth), Artist makes masks to reveal, not conceal, NY Times, 2/17/91; Beth Kissinger (auth), Unmasked, Jersey J, 5/22/91; Nancy Capiocco (auth), Windows to the Soul, Rockland J News, 10/30/92. *Mem:* NY Wellesley Artists Group. *Media:* Acrylics. *Interests:* Imagery connected to women, color. *Mailing Add:* 88 Clinton Ave South Nyack NY 10960-4617

CHUSID, EVETTE
PAINTER
b Newark, NJ. *Study:* Newark Sch Fine & Indust Art; Traphagen Sch Fashion, studied with Virginia Cobb, Nicholas Reale, Catherine Chiang Liu & Fran Larsen, 80-90's. *Exhib:* Solo exhib, NJCVA Mus, Summit, NJ, 87, Lever House, NY, 91; Bergen Mus, Bergen Co, NJ, 89; Mennen Corp, NJ, 90; Bellmead Corp, NJ, 90-94; Monmouth Mus, NJ, 94. *Awards:* Best Show, Essex Watercolor Club, 96. *Mem:* Audubon Artists, NY; Nat Asn Women Artists (bd, 92-94); NJ Ctr Visual Arts; Essex Watercolor Club, NJ. *Media:* Watercolor, Acrylic. *Publ:* Articles, Newark Star-Ledger, 80, 90 & 93

CHUTJIAN, SETA LEONIE See Injeyan, Seta L

CIANFONI, EMILIO F
CONSERVATOR, PAINTER
b Rome, Italy, Oct 9, 1946; US citizen. *Study:* Drawing, painting & restoration with Giustino Caporali, 58-63, Manieri Art Inst, 60-63, Acad di Belle Arti, 64-66; conserv of paintings at Inst Centrale del Restauro, 66-67, Rome; studies under Edwig Dickinson, Art Students League, New York, 70-72; Baldwin Sch (glazes chemistry), New York, 73. *Comn:* Paintings, Lowenbrau Co, Munich, Bavaria, Ger, 67; painting & sculpture, comn by Pacifici Family, Rome, Italy, 67; mural, Church Hosp Comples, Vilalba, Italy, 69; Bicentennial Coins Competition, Metrop Mus Art, NY, 74. *Exhib:* Galleria Borgognona, Rome, Italy, 7-8; Galeria Modigliani, 63, 20th Century Competition, City Bldg, 64 & Mus Mod Art, 65, Rome; New Talent (2 shows), Betty Parsons Gallery, NY, 74; Primitive & Contemp Art, Tucson, Ariz, Betty Parsons Gallery, 75; UN Group Am Exhib, NY, Truman Gallery, 77. *Pos:* asst to Ben Shahn, NY, 68; Design painter-conservator, Gucci Shops, Rome & NY, 68-70; sr craftsman, Alva Reproductions, NY, 70-72; restorer, Metrop Mus of Art, NY, 72-74; chief conservator, Vizcaya Mus & Gardens, 75-2011; asst to Boris Vasilov, Acva Mus LePlica; pres, Cianfoni Art Restoration Inc, 2001-. *Awards:* First Prize, 20th Anniversary of Italian Partisans Competition, Rome, 64; Second Prize, Ciac Poetry & Arts Competition, Rome, 66. *Mem:* Am Inst Conserv Hist & Artistic Work; Int Inst Conserv Hist & Artistic Work; Asn Preserv Technol. *Media:* Mixed. *Dealer:* Truman Gallery 38 E 57th St New York NY 10022. *Mailing Add:* 270 NN 36 St Miami FL 33127

CIARDIELLO, JOSEPH G
ILLUSTRATOR
b Staten Island, NY, July 22, 1953. *Study:* Parsons Sch Design, with Maurice Sendak & Jim Spanfeller, BFA, 75. *Work:* Soc of Illusrs, NY, (permanent collection). *Exhib:* Soc Illusrs Ann Exhib, NY, 1974-; Soc Publ Designers, NY, 79 & 86; Art Dirs Ann, Art Dirs Club, NY, 80 & 87; Graphic Art & Illustration, Quebec City, Can, 85; The Illustrator & The Environment, Soc of Illusrs, NY, 90; Sci/Fi & Fantasy, Soc Illusrs, 92; Eye on Am: Editorial Illustration in the 90s, Norman Rockwell Mus, 99; One Man Show, Soc Illustrators, 99; Illustrating the Sea, Mystic Seaport, 2004; Lines of Attack, Conflicts in Caricature, Nasher Mus Art, Duke Univ, 2010; Earth: Fragile Planet Soc Illustrators, 2010; PCNJ Collaborative Editions Project, Four by Four, 2012. *Teaching:* Guest lectr illus, Fashion Inst Technol, Parsons Sch Design & Montclair State Col, 80- & Moore Col Art; adj prof illus, Montclair State Col, Upper Montclair, 81; co-instr illus, Parsons Sch Design, 87; Syracuse Univ MFA Prog, summer 2000; Jack Davis distinguished visiting artist lectr, Univ Ga, 2012. *Awards:* Silver Medal, Soc of Illusrs, 92, 99, 2006, 2012; Steven Dohanos Award, 2006. *Bibliog:* Tom Goss (auth), Mini-portfolio Joe Ciardiello, Print Mag, 84; Marion Muller (auth), Drawing pens & drumsticks, Upper & Lower Case, 84; Scott Gutterman (auth), article, How Mag, 1-2/87; article, Idea Mag, Japan, No 208, 88 & No 219, 90; Warren Burger (auth), Communication Art, 94. *Mem:* Soc Illustrators. *Media:* Pen & Ink, Watercolor. *Interests:* Jazz/blues music (plays drums). *Publ:* Illusr, Around the World in 80 Days, 88; Moby Dick, 89, 20,000 Leagues Under the Sea, 90, Dr Jekyll & Mr Hyde, 91, Reader's Digest; Art for Survival, Graphis Press, 92; The Savage Mirror: Contemporary Caricature, Watson Guftill, 92; Like Jazz, Spanfeller Press, 92; The Illustrated Portraits, Rolling Stone Press, 2000; The Illustrator in America, publ 2000; The Blues, Harper Collins, 2003; Illus Now, Taschen, 2005; Black, White, & Blues, Strike Three Press, 2011. *Mailing Add:* 35 Little York Mt Pleasant Milford NJ 08848

CIARROCCHI, RAY
PAINTER, EDUCATOR
b Chicago, Ill Aug 23, 1933. *Study:* Chicago Acad Fine Arts; Wash Univ, BFA, with Fred Conway & Stephen Pace; Boston Univ, MFA, with David Aronson. *Work:* Citibank, NY; Owens-Corning Glass Found; Brooklyn Mus; The Hosp Corp of Am; The World Bank; Greenwich Public Lib, Conn; Univ Mass, Amherst; C Hoate Mem Hosp, Boston; Archives of Am Art; Smithsonian Inst; Lincoln Ctr Libr; NYC Public Libr; Joel and Lila Harnett; Mus Art, Univ Richmond. *Exhib:* Solo exhibs, Tibor De Nagy Gallery, 71, 72, 74, 76, 78, 80, 83 & 85, Fischbach Gallery, 86 & 89, landscapes 78-91, Marsh Gallery, Modlin Fine Arts Ctr, Univ Richmond, Va, Katharina Rich Perlow Gallery, 93 & 96; Ray Ciarrocchi-Latitudes of Light, A Traveling Exhib in Italy, Aug-Sept, 2004; Am Watercolors, 1800 to the Present, Brooklyn Mus, NY, 76; Works on Paper from the Ciba-Geigy Collection, Neuberger Mus, Purchase, NY, 77; The Face of the Land, Southern Alleghenies Mus Art, Loretto, Pa, 88; Painterly Realism, traveling exhib, Houston, Tex; Sentieri, Palazzina Azzurra, Italy, 2009. *Collection Arranged:* All About Drawing, Works by R. Ciarrocchi, S. Caplan, S. Gechtoff, R. Granne, Westbeth Gallery, NY, 2012. *Teaching:* Instr painting & drawing, Parsons Sch Design, New York, 66-71; adj prof, Sch Arts, Columbia Univ, 69-71 & 76- & Baruch Coll, City Univ New York, 76-94; vis artist, Md Inst Coll Art, 71-72; instr, Brooklyn Coll, 72-76. *Awards:* Fulbright Grant to Italy, 63-64; Tiffany Grant, 67; Ingraham Merrill Found Grant, 77 & 82-83; Pollock-Krasner Found Grant, 2009-2010. *Bibliog:* Richard Waller (auth), Ray Ciarrochi - Landscapes 1978-91; Julia Ayres (auth), Monotype: Painterly Printmaking, 91; Nina Mallory (auth), Ray Ciarocchi: Italian Landscapes, 99; Simona Clementoni (auth), Ray Ciarrocchi: Silent Landscapes, 2009; Francesco Tentarelli (auth), Latitudes of Light, 2004. *Media:* Oil, Mixed Media, Monotypes. *Mailing Add:* 55 Bethune St Apt D 1004 New York NY 10014-2010

CICANSKY, VICTOR
SCULPTOR
b Regina, Sask, Feb 12, 1935. *Study:* Univ Sask, Saskatoon, BEd, 64; Univ Sask, Regina, BA, 67; Univ Calif, Davis, MFA, 70, with Bob Arneson & Roy DeForrest; studies at Haystack Mountain Sch Art, Deer Isle, ME. *Hon Degrees:* DFA, Univ Regina. *Work:* Sask Govt Arts Bd; Can Coun Art Bank; Sacramento State Col; Mus of Mod Art, Tokyo, Japan; Mus of Mod Art, Montreal; Mus Fine Arts, Montreal; The Glenbow Mus, Calgary; Nat Gallery Can; and many others. *Comn:* The Grain Bin (group sculpture), Sask Olympics Art Comt, Montreal, 76; The Old Working Class (sculpture), Saskatoon, 77 & The New Working Class (sculpture), 81, Sask Govt; Regina-My World (sculpture), Co-op Life Insurance Co Bldg, Regina, Sask, 79; The Garden Fence (mural), Can Broadcasting Corp, 83-84; Founders Awards (sculpture), Sask Writer's Guild, 84; Heritage Seeds (sculpture), Sask Govt, 85. *Exhib:* Contemp Ceramics, Mus of Fine Arts, Kyoto, Japan, 71; Int Ceramics, Victoria & Albert Mus, London, Eng, 72; Trajectories 73, Musee de Art Moderne de Ville de Paris, France, 73; Espace 5, Montreal, Que, 74; Fired Clay Show, Greater Victoria Art Gallery, Victoria, BC, 75; NY Clay, Monique Knowlton Gallery, NY, 75; Solo exhib, MacKenzie Gallery, Regina, Glenbow Mus, Waterloo Art Gallery & Mendel Art Gallery, 83, Susan Whitney Gallery, 84, Woltjen/Udell Gallery, Edmonton, 85 & Grunwald Gallery, Toronto, 85; and many others. *Teaching:* From assoc prof art to prof, Univ Regina, Sask, 70-92; Banff Sch Fine Arts, Nova Scotia Coll Art, Univ Calif, Davis, formerly. *Awards:* Can Coun grants/travel & work, 68-69, 71, 74 & 83; Kingsley Ann Award/Sculpture, Sacramento, 69; Royal Albert Award, Ceramic Sculpture, Toronto, 71; Sask Order of Merit; Sask Centennial Medal. *Bibliog:* Personal bests, Can Art, fall 85; Christopher Hume (auth), Voluptuous clay veggies set off titters at the Grunwald's, Toronto Star, 10/11/85; Karen Wilken (auth), Sculpture, Can Encyl, 85; Don Kerr (auth), The Garden of Art: Vic Cicansky, Sculptor, Univ Calgary Press, 2004. *Mem:* CARFAC. *Media:* Clay, Bronze, Wood. *Publ:* Contribr to Arts Mag, Fall 70, Mus of Mod Art J, Amsterdam, 4/71, Arts Can, 5/73; Art & Artists, 8/73, Time, 4/73 & ArtsCan, 230/231; Hand & Eye, Glorious Mud (television series), CBC Television, 2/16/84. *Dealer:* Mira Godarad Gallery Toronto Can; Galerie de Bellefeuille Montreal Can; Douglas Udell Gallery Edmonton & Vancouver Can; and others

CICCONE, AMY NAVRATIL
LIBRARIAN
b Mich, Sept 19, 1950. *Study:* Wayne State Univ, 72, BA (art hist); Univ Mich, 73, AMLS, specializing in art librarianship. *Collection Arranged:* Hidden treasures, The Chrysler Mus, 85-86; Samuel Johnson (auth), Univ Southern Calif, 88. *Pos:* Librn, Norton Simon Mus, Pasadena, Calif, 74-81; ed, Art Librs Soc of NAm Directory of Members, 75-77; chief librn, Chrysler Mus, Jean Outland Chrysler Libr, Norfolk, Va, 81-88; Archit & Fine Arts Libr, Univ Southern Calif; head librn, Archit & Fine Arts Libr, Univ Southern Calif, Los Angeles, 88-97; bibliographer art & archit, Univ Southern Calif, Los Angeles, 97-; Actg asst univ librn pub serv, Univ Southern Calif, Los Angeles, 93-95; Assoc Coord. collection develop, 2004-2008, dir collection develop, 2008-. *Mem:* Art Libr Soc NAm (mem chmn, 75-77, mem coordr, 79, facilities standards comt, 86); Dec Arts Roundtable (coord, 91-93); Strategic Planning Task Force (chmn, 94-96, conference co-chair, 2001). *Res:* Art Mystery fiction. *Interests:* Decorative Arts, Medieval Art/Architecture. *Publ:* Contribr, Art Libr Soc NAm Newsletter, 75-77; Art Documentation, 83-88; contrib ed, Art Reference Serv Quart, 90-98; mysteries for Art libraries, column, Arlis/na update, 1999-2005. *Mailing Add:* 12718 Westminster Ave Los Angeles CA 90066

CICERO, CARMEN LOUIS
PAINTER, EDUCATOR
b Newark, NJ, 1926. *Study:* Newark State Col, NJ, BS, 51; Hunter Col, NY, 53; Montclair State Univ, MFA, 91. *Work:* Guggenheim Mus, NY; Mus Mod Art, NY; Whitney Mus, NY; Metropolitan Mus Art, NY; Nat Mus Am Art, Washington, many others; Fogg Art Mus, Harvard; Hirshhorn Mus, Washington, DC; Mint Mus, NC; Montclair Art Mus; works in collections of 35 mus; and others. *Exhib:* 6 Whitney Mus Anns, 55-66; (26) solo exhibs, incl Peridot Gallery; Premiere Bienale de Paris, France; Graham Gallery, NY; June Kelly Gallery, NY; Karen Johnson Gallery, San Francisco. *Teaching:* Mem fac, Sarah Lawrence Col, 59-68; retired prof, Montclair State Col, 60-02. *Awards:* Guggenheim Fel, 57, 65; Purchase Prize, Ford Found, 65; Purchase prize, Am Acad Arts & Letts, 97; Lifetime Achievement Award, Pollock-Krasner Found, 2007; Pollock-Krasner Found Grant, 2008. *Bibliog:* Charles Le Clair (auth), The Art of Watercolor, Prentis-Hall & Color in Contemporary Painting, Watson-Guptil; William Gerdts (auth), Painting & Sculpture in NJ, Nostrand Co; Deborah Forman (auth), Perspectives on the Provincetown Art Colony. *Mem:* Nat Acad (assoc, 91, acad, 93). *Media:* Oil, Acrylic, Watercolor. *Interests:* Music. *Publ:* The Art of Carmen Cicero, Schiffer Pub Ltd. *Dealer:* June Kelly Gallery 166 Mercer St New York NY 10012. *Mailing Add:* PO Box 460 Truro MA 02666-0460

CIEZADLO, JANINA A
CRITIC, EDUCATOR
Study: Ind Univ, Bloomington, MFA in Printmaking; Ind Univ, Bloomington, MA in Comparative Lit. *Teaching:* adj prof, dept liberal educ Columbia Col; adj asst prof, dept art and design Univ Ill at Chicago. *Mem:* Chicago Art Critics Asn. *Publ:* Published (reviews, scholarly monographs, articles, poetry, exhib work), art critic Chicago Reader, Afterimage, Journal of Media Arts and Cultural Criticism

CIFOLELLI, ALBERTA
PAINTER, PRINTMAKER
b Erie, Pa, Aug 19, 1931. *Study:* Cleveland Inst Art, dipl(painting), 53; Kent State Univ, BS(art educ), 55; Fairfield Univ, MA, 75 (commun). *Comn:* Mitsubishi Capital, Rockefeller Ctr. *Exhib:* Solo exhibs, Noho Gallery, 82; Kaber Gallery, NY, 83; Sacred Heart Univ, 98; Reece Galleries, NY & Housatonic Mus Art, Bridgeport, Conn, 2000, Listed Archives of American Art, 2005, Softening the Edge, Silvermine Guild, 2010; A State of Artists, Invitational, Aldrich Mus Contemp Art, Ridgefield, Conn; The Natural Image Invitational, Stamford Mus, Conn, 88; Harmon-Meek Gallery, Naples, Fla, 89; 400 Yrs of Women Artists Touring Exhib, Nat Mus Women Arts, Washington, DC; The Conn Biennial, Bruce Mus; 50 Yr Retrospective, Stamford Mus, 99; Distinguished Alumni Exhib, Cleveland Inst Art, 2007; House Project, Westport Arts Center, Conn, 2009; Women: Diverse Interludes, Andre Zarre, NY, 2009; Cummings Gallery, Merlyhurst Col, Erie, PA, 2009; and others. *Collection Arranged:* Nat Mus Women Arts; Reagan Libr, Semi Valley, Calif; Housatonic Mus Art, Bridgeport, Conn; Francis Lehman Loeb Art Ctr, Vassar Coll; United Nations, NY. *Pos:* Chairwoman, Art Dept Laurel Sch, Shakerhts, 65-69; vpres, Westport Weston Arts Coun, Conn, 78-79; artists-in-residence, Djerassi Found, 86; chairwoman, Inst Visual Artists, 88-89; juror undergrad achievement, State Univ NY, Stony Brook, 2000; cur, Special Exhib About Paint, Westport Arts Ctr, 2005. *Teaching:* Instr painting & life drawing, Cleveland Inst Art, 67-70; prof life drawing & design, Sacred Heart Univ, 79-; prof, Grad Sch Painting, Col New Rochelle; invited guest instr, Fairfield Schs. *Awards:* Doris Kreindler Mem Award, Nat Soc Painters in Casein & Acrylic, 74; four grants, Conn Comn Arts; Residency to live and work at Djerassi Found, Woodside, Calif, Summer 86; 100 Outstanding Women in Conn, UN Woman's Conf, 2000; Artist of Yr Award, Art Place, Southport, Conn, 2000 & 2001; Alberta Cifolelli: Housatonic Mus Art, 2002; Dir's Choice, Silvermine Galleries, New Canaan, Conn, 2003. *Bibliog:* Deborah Frizzell (auth), Alberta Cifolelli, 98; Donald Kuspit (auth), Biophiliac Paintings, Nature All the Way, 98; William Zimmer (auth), Flowers and More, NY Times, 99; Jaquiline Moss (auth), Alberta Cifolelli, Arts Mag, 4/82; Mark Daniel Cohen (auth), Brightening of the Spirit - Art of Alberta Cifolelli, 2002. *Mem:* Visual Artist & Gallery Asn; Westport Arts Ctr (vis arts chmn, 76-); trustee Silvermine Guild Artists (bd dir, 78-83); Women's Caucus for Art, NY Chap; Artists Fel, NY; Artists Fel Inc; NY Artists Equity Archives Am Art. *Media:* Oil, Pastel, Printmaking. *Specialty:* White Gallery, Lakeville, Conn, 2004-2006. *Interests:* Politics (democratic). *Dealer:* PMW Stamford Conn; Silvermine Galleries New Canaan Conn; White Gallery Lakeville Conn; Elaine Wechsler New York; Larry Sarolli New York; Alexis Chasman New York; Art Services International Westport Conn. *Mailing Add:* 8 Plover Lane Westport CT 06880

CIKOVSKY, NICOLAI, JR
CURATOR, HISTORIAN
b New York, NY, Feb 11, 1933. *Study:* Harvard Coll, AB; Harvard Univ, AM & PhD. *Collection Arranged:* Sanford Robinson Gifford, Univ Tex Art Mus, 70-71; The White Marmorean Flock; Nineteenth Century Am Women Neoclassical Sculptors, Vassar Coll Art Gallery, 72; William Merritt Chase: Summers at Shinecock (catalog), 87; Raphaelle Peale Still Lifes (catalog), 88; Paintings, Manoogian Collection, 89, Whistler, 95, Winslow Homer (auth, catalog), 95. *Pos:* Dir, Vassar Coll Art Gallery, 71-74; sr cur, Am & Brit Painting Nat Gallery Art, Washington, DC, 83. *Teaching:* Assoc prof art, Vassar Coll, 71-74; prof art, Univ NMex, 74-83. *Awards:* Guggenheim Fel, 78-79; Kress Sr Fel, Ctr Advan Study in Visual Arts, Nat Gallery Art, 82-83. *Res:* Nineteenth & twentieth century American painting and sculpture. *Publ:* Ed, Samuel FB Morse's Lectures on the Affinity of Painting with the Other Fine Arts, 83; coauth, George Inness, 85; Winslow Homer, 90; Winslow Homer Watercolors, 91; George Inness, 93. *Mailing Add:* Nat Gallery Art 4th St & Constitution Ave Washington DC 20565

CIMBALO, ROBERT W
PAINTER, PRINTMAKER
b Utica, NY. *Study:* Pratt Inst, Brooklyn; Syracuse Univ; Socita Di Dante Alighari, Belle Arte & Univ Studi Roma, Rome. *Work:* Kirkland Art Ctr, Clinton, NY; Munson-Williams-Proctor Inst, Utica, NY; Syracuse Univ; State Univ NY Coll Cortland; Pratt Inst. *Comn:* Portrait of Past Pres, Utica Col, NY. *Exhib:* Dante's Inferno Traveling Exhib to various cols and univs; many works incl in public & pvt exhibs. *Teaching:* Assoc prof art hist & studio art, Utica Col, Syracuse Univ, 78-2000. *Awards:* Targo D'oro Premio D'italia, 86. *Media:* Oil. *Publ:* Illusr, East Utica, Munson Williams Proctor Inst, fall 71; Frank, Catherine and Vito, Black Locust Press, 79; September 11, 2001 Victory Poster; The Graphic Art of Robert Cimbalo, The Ethnic Heritage Studies Ctr, Utica Coll, Utica, NY, 2010; Italian American Themed Illustrations, Fra Noi Mag, Chgo, Ill, 1998-. *Mailing Add:* 1602 Harrison Ave Utica NY 13501

CINGILLIOGLU, HALIT
COLLECTOR
b 1954. *Hon Degrees:* Erciyes Univ, Hon Dr Finance. *Pos:* principle shareholder, Demir-Halk Bank, The Netherlands; exec council mem, Istanbul Stock Exchange; advisory bd mem, Sotheby's. *Awards:* Merit of State Eminent Svcs, Turkish Parliament, 2009; named one of Top 200 collectors, ARTnews mag, 2011, 2012, 2013. *Collection:* Impressionism; postwar, modern, and contemporary art

CINTRON, JOSEPH M
PAINTER, EDUCATOR
b Ponce, PR, Aug 4, 1921. *Study:* Univ Dayton, BA, 43; Ohio State Univ, 51; Cleveland Inst Art, dipl, 54; with Robert Brackman, Madison, Conn, 62; Art Students League, with Sidney Dickinson, David Leffel, Howard Sanden, Gustav Rehberger & Harvey Dinnerstein. *Work:* Univ Hospitals Cleveland; La Fortaleza, San Juan, Puerto Rico; Case Western Reserve Univ, Cleveland; The Cleveland Clinic, Ohio; Cleveland Play House; and others. *Comn:* Portrait, Eric Fromm, Case Western Reserve Univ, Cleveland, Ohio, 69; Portrait, Gov Luis a Ferre, La Fortaleza, San Juan, PR, 74; Portrait Dr Dudley Allen, Univ Hospitals, Cleveland, 80; Portrait Bishop Gregory Rozman, Klagenfurt, Austria, 85; Portrait Jack Anderson, Washington, DC, 96; and others. *Exhib:* Canton Art Inst Regional, 65-69; Cleveland Mus Art Regional, 69; Nat, Butler Inst Am Art, 70; Sch of Fine Arts, Willoughby, Ohio, 72; Int Platform Asn, Washington, DC, 81-98; Northern Ohio Invitational, 83; Kuban Galleries, Cleveland, 84; and others. *Teaching:* Prof painting & drawing, Cleveland Inst Art, 56-, Cooper Sch Art, 63-82, Sch Fine Arts, Willoughby, Ohio, 82-96. *Awards:* Painting Award, Cuyahoga Valley Art Ctr, 67 & 68; First Place, 81 & 94, Popular Award, 83, Second Place, 84, Merit Award, 86, 94 & 97, Int Platform Asn; and others. *Bibliog:* Marie Kirkwood (auth), Cintron Trademark is Realism, Sun Press, Cleveland, 8/5/71; Gloria Borras (auth), Pintar Rostros es Captar Almas, Puerto Rico Ilustrado, San Juan, 3/30/75. *Mem:* Int Platform Asn; Art Students League, NY. *Media:* Oil, Pastels. *Dealer:* The Bonfoey Galleries Cleveland Ohio. *Mailing Add:* c/o The Bonfoey Gallery 1710 Euclid Ave Cleveland OH 44115

CIPOLLA, VIN
ADMINISTRATOR
Pos: Exec vpres, Nat Trust for Historic Preservation, formerly; pres & CEO, Nat Park Found, 2005-2009; pres, Munic Art Soc, 2009-; bd dirs, Nat Parks New York Harbor Conservancy & Ballet Hispanico

CIPRIANO, MICHAEL R
PAINTER, EDUCATOR
b Waterbury, Conn, 1942. *Study:* Cent Conn State Coll, BS, 67, MS, 69; Univ Conn, 70; Columbia Univ, MA, 75, EdD, 77. *Work:* Coll New Rochelle, NY; Richard Judd Collection, Cent Conn State Univ, New Britain; Howell Cheney Vocational Inst, Manchester, Conn; Manchester Community Coll, Manchester, Conn; Wheaton Coll, Norton, Mass; Mus Am Art, New Britain, Conn; William Benton Mus, Univ Conn, Storrs; Housatonic Mus, Bridgeport, Conn; Arguments for Abstraction, Eastern Conn State Univ (with catalog), 94 & Atelier Lizio, Naples, Fla, 2003. *Comn:* Large painting canvas, 84 & installation six large mural paintings, Conn Comn on the Arts, Manchester, 84; six large murals (restoration), comn by Conn Comt Cult & Tourism, Howell Cheney Tech Sch, Manchester, Conn, 84 & 2006. *Exhib:* Wadsworth Atheneum, Hartford, Conn, 82; Works on Paper, Cartwright Hall Gallery, Bradford, Eng, 84; Hewlett-Woodmere Gallery, NY, 85; Atria Gallery, Hartford, 86; Watson Gallery, Norton, Mass, 89; Bushnell Gallery, Conn Artists Showcase & Conn Coun Arts, Hartford, 89; solo exhibs, Artworks Gallery, Hartford, Conn, 95, Farmington Art Guild, Conn, 93 & Akus Gallery Eastern Conn State Univ, 94, Coll New Rochelle, NY, 96; Chen Gallery, Central Conn State Univ, 98 & 2004; SUNY Westchester, 99; Maxwell Fine Arts, 2002-2005. *Pos:* Univ Arts Coun, New York, 82; Fine Arts, Cent Conn State Univ, 88; Conn Acad Fine Arts, 95-; consult acquisitions comt, New Brit Mus Am Art, 96-, acquisition and loan comt, 2001-; Art Space, Ctr Visual & Performing Arts, 96-; Media & the Arts, Conn Bus & Indust Asn; consult, Pia-Sgolin Gallery, Cantor, Conn. *Teaching:* Prof fine arts, Cent Conn State Univ, 73-86, chmn dept art, 86-96; Charter Oak State Coll, 95-; vis artist, Farming Sch Dist, 95; prof emer, Coll New Rochelle, 96-; Prof, CSU, 66, chair, prof emeritus, 2000. *Awards:* Purchase Award, Conn Comn on the Arts, 84. *Bibliog:* Bernard Hanson (auth), Museum of American Art, New Britain, Saltbox Gallery & West Hartford-Michael Cipriano, Art in New England, 81; William Zimmer (auth), Diverse show opens gallery, 11/25/84 & Charlotte Libov (auth), Public art thrives with State support, 4/27/86, NY Times; New abstracts display strength, Emotion in Manchester Exhib, Hartford Courant, 10/89. *Mem:* Artists Equity Asn; Arts Space, Visual & Performing Arts; Conn Art Asn; Conn Watercolor Soc. *Media:* Acrylic, Mixed Media. *Specialty:* Contemp Art. *Publ:* Auth, Artist, an unused resource, Sch Arts, 72; Arts: Frills or fundamentals, CAEA, 77. *Dealer:* Maxwell Fine Arts, Peekskill, NY. *Mailing Add:* 76 Pendleton New Britain CT 06053

CIRICLIO, S(USAN) E (FAY)
PHOTOGRAPHER, EDUCATOR
b New York, NY, Nov 27, 1946. *Study:* Phoenix Col, Ariz, AA, 69; Calif Coll Arts & Crafts, BFA, 72; Mills Col, Oakland, Calif, MFA, 74. *Work:* San Francisco Mus Mod Art; Oakland Mus, Calif; Barnsdall Collection, Los Angeles; Siebu Mus, Tokoyo; Kiyosato Mus Photog Art, Yamanashi, Japan; Mills Coll. *Comn:* Eyes & Ears Found, 79. *Exhib:* New Photog, MH deYoung, San Francisco, 74; SF/LA/NY, San Francisco Art Inst, 77; Billboard Show, San Francisco Mus Mod Art, 79; Calif Women in Photog, Axiom Ctr Arts, Cheltenham, Eng, 87; Young Californians, Siebu Mus, Tokoyo, 89; Forecast, Mus NMex, Santa Fe, 94; An Artist and His Circle, Kiyosato Mus, Yamanashi Japan, 98. *Pos:* Acad vpres, Calif Coll Arts & Crafts, 86-87, 89-92, dept chair photog, 88-93, 99-2008 . *Teaching:* Instr photog, Chabot Coll, Hayward, Calif & San Francisco Art Inst, 73-86; prof photog, Calif Coll Arts & Crafts, 77-. *Awards:* Photog Fel, National Endowment, 79. *Bibliog:* Thomas Garver (auth), New Photography, MH deYoung Mus, 74; Robert Heinecken (auth), West Coast Revision, SF Camerawork Quart, 85; Van Deren Coke (auth) Forecast, Mus of NMex, 94. *Mem:* Coll Art Asoc; Society for Photog Educ; San Francisco Mus of Mod Art; SF Cameraworks (bd mem, 83-86); Oakland Mus; UC Berkeley Mus. *Media:* Photography. *Interests:* History, gardening. *Mailing Add:* 2095 Arrowhead Drive Oakland CA 94611

CISCLE, GEORGE
CURATOR, EDUCATOR
b Baltimore, Md, Sept 15, 1947. *Study:* Loyola Coll, BA, 69; Univ NC, MEd, 72; studied under Isamu Noguchi. *Collection Arranged:* Keith Martin Retrospective, 87; Kindred Spirits, 88; Outcry: Artists Answer AIDS (ed, catalog), 90; Photo Manifesto, 91; Catfish Dreamin', 92; Ignisfat, 96; 15 Year Survey of Baltimore Art, 96; Joyce J Scott Kickin it with the Old Masters, Baltimore Mus Art, 2000; Everlasting by Ann Fessler, 2003. *Pos:* Dir, George Ciscle Gallery, 85-89; dir & founder, The Contemp, Baltimore, Md, 89-96; cur-in-residence, Md Inst Art, 97. *Teaching:* Instr fine arts, Cardinal Gibbons High Sch, Baltimore, 69-72, State Coll Pub Sch, 74-76; teacher-coordr, Baltimore Co Pub Sch, 76-85. *Mem:* Am Asn Mus. *Publ:* Contribr, Mining the Museum, The New Press, 94; Eyewinkers, Tumbleturds and Candle Bugs: The Art of Elizabeth Talford Scott, Md Inst, 98; At Freedrom's Door, MICA, 2007. *Mailing Add:* 4000 N Charles St Unit 1509 Baltimore MD 21218

CISNEROS, ELLA FONTANALS
COLLECTOR, DIRECTOR
b Cuba. *Pos:* Founder, Together Found, 1990; pres bd dirs & founder, Cisneros Fontanals Art Found, 2002- & Miami Art Ctrl, 2003-; trustee, Miami Art Mus, 2003-. *Awards:* Spectrum Philanthropy Award, Am Red Cross, 2003; Visionary Award, Mus Arts & Design, 2007; Women Together Award, United Nations, 2008; named one of Top 200 Collectors, ARTnews mag, 2009-13. *Mem:* Am Patrons of the Tate (bd trustees); Cintas Found; US Artist; Int Womens Forum. *Collection:* Contemporary art; geometric abstraction from Latin America. *Mailing Add:* 5960 SW 57 Ave Miami FL 33143

CISNEROS, PATRICIA & GUSTAVO ALFREDO
COLLECTOR
b Caracas, Venezuela, Jun 1, 1945. *Study:* Babson Coll, Wellesley, Mass, BBA, 68. *Pos:* Pres & chief exec officer, Organización Diego Cisneros, Venezuela, 68-, Galerías Preciados, Spain, Spalding-Evenflo; chmn bd, All Am Bottling co, Coral Gables, Fla; int adv comt, Chase Manhattan Bank, 81-; int adv coun, Pan-Am World Airways, 83-; founding mem & worldwide adv bd, Beatrice Foods Corp, 84-; former shareholder, mem bd dirs Univision. *Awards:* Decorated Order of El Libertador, Order Andrés Bello, Order Francisco de Miranda, Order Cruz de las Fuerzas Armadas de Cooperación, Order Mérito al Trabajo (Venezuela), Order of Isabel La Católica (Spain); named one of 200 Top Collectors, ARTnews mag, 2004-13; World's Richest People, Forbes mag., 1999-current. *Bibliog:* Pablo Bachelet (auth), Gustavo Cisneros: The Pioneer, Planeta Publ, 2004. *Mem:* Knights of Malta. *Collection:* Modern and contemporary Latin American, European, and North American art; Amazonian ethnographic objects; colonial and Federalist furniture; Ibero-American decorative art. *Mailing Add:* Apartado 60039 Chacao Caracas Venezuela

CITRON, HARVEY LEWIS
SCULPTOR
b New York, NY, June 26, 1942. *Study:* Pratt Inst, Brooklyn, BFA, 65, Academia di Belli Arti, Rome, Italy, 68. *Comn:* St John Baptist, Archdiocese of Philadelphia, Pa, 76. *Exhib:* Contemp Am Realism Since 1960, traveling exhib in US & Europe, 81-83; Neo-objective Sculpture, Dart Gallery, Chicago, 82; Artists Choice: First 8 Yrs, Artists Choice Gallery, NY, 85; Works on Paper, Tianjin Acad Fine Arts, Tianjin, China, 85; Group Sculpture/Painting, Union Club, NY, 89; Works on Paper, Drawing Univ Arts, Phildelphia, 89; group exhib, Artists Notebook Preliminary Study, Univ Arts, Phildelphia, 91, Painting Sculpture Grad Sch Figurative Art, NY Acad Art, 92, 18 Sculptors, Philadelphia Art Alliance, Philadelphia, 92. *Teaching:* Adj assoc prof sculpture, Univ Arts, 81-89; assoc prof sculpture, NY Acad Art, 87-89. *Bibliog:* Hilton Kramer (auth), Five gallery realist show, New York Times, 80; F H Goodyear Jr (auth), Contemporary American Realism Since 1960, New York Graphic Soc, 81; A G Artner (auth), Dart displays contemporary view of human form, Chicago Tribune, 82. *Media:* Bronze, Clay. *Mailing Add:* 57 Warren St No 7 New York NY 10007-1018

CIVALE, BIAGIO A
PRINTMAKER, PAINTER
b Rome, Italy, Aug 11, 1935. *Study:* Acad Grande Chaumiere, Paris, 53-55; Fine Arts Acad, Rome, dipl (art educ), 58; NY Univ, 83-90; State Univ NY, Purchase, 84. *Work:* Gabinetto Naz Stampe, Rome; Mod Sacred Art Gallery, Montecatini Mus, Florence, Italy; Argenton-Sur-Creuse Mus, France; Mus Espanol Arte Contemp Madrid, Spain; Mod Mus, Stockholm; Sforza Castel Pub Collection of Prints, Milan, Italy; World Bank, Wash, DC; Westchester Co Bldg, White Plains, NY; and others. *Comn:* Large Panels for Ital Air Force Club, Cagliari, Italy, 58; Large Panels for NATO Ctr, Chateauroux, France, 62; Crucifixion for Sacrestia, Scarperia Church, Florence, Italy, 74; New Testament & Christmas Panels, Dicomano Church, Florence, Italy, 75. *Exhib:* Over 60 solo exhibs & over 200 group exhibs in 4 continents; 40 yr retrospective, Palazzo Ranghiasci, Gubbio, 90; 42 yr retrospective, Yonkers Educ & Cult Ctr, NY, 92; San Ban Kan Ginza Gallery, Tokyo, Japan, 92; Zhejang Acad Fine Arts, Hangzhou, Peoples Republic of China, 92; Silpakorn Univ, Bangkok, Thailand, 93; Nat Taiwan Art Inst, 95; Karmer Mus, Kulturforum, Kempen, Ger, 97; Sarah Lawrence Col, Bronxville, NY, 98; Upper View, Peekskill, NY, 2002; The Coffey Gallery, Kingston, NY, 2002; Molloy Coll Art Gallery, Rockville Centre, NY, 2004; GR Art Gallery, Mamaroneck, NY, 2004 & 2005; Irvington Public Libr, 2008; Claude Gallery, Eastchester, 2008 & 2009; Blue Door Gallery, Yonkers, 2009. *Pos:* Art critic, 50-90, cur, 74-2014. *Teaching:* Instr art educ, Roosevelt High Sch, Yonkers, NY, 79 & 80. *Awards:* Various, France, Italy & USA. *Bibliog:* Luigi Servolini (auth), Incisori D'Italia, EIA, Milano, 74; Biagio Civale, Woodcuts and Linocuts, 1950-1990, Edition Heliodor, Westbury, NY, 90; New American Paintings, Open Studios Press, 94; various titles & books with Bookstand Publishing, 2010 & 2011. *Mem:* Blue Door Artists Asn; Yonkers Arts Council. *Media:* Oils, Etchings, Woodcuts, Tempera, Serigraphs. *Dealer:* Castillon Fine Arts 159 Madison Ave New York NY 10016; Noel Fine Art Bronxville NY; Artemisia Gallery Udine Italy. *Mailing Add:* 311 Lee Ave Yonkers NY 10705

CIVITELLO, JOHN PATRICK
PAINTER
b Paterson, NJ, Aug 17, 1939. *Study:* William Paterson Coll, BA, 61; New York Univ, MA, 62. *Work:* Nat Mus Am Art, Smithsonian Inst, Washington; Monterey Peninsula Mus Art, Calif; 3M co, St Paul, Minn; NBC-TV, NY; Lloyd's Bank, Calif; Comput Sci Corp, Los Angeles. *Comn:* 3 paintings, Silk City Series, Broadway Bank & Trust Co, Paterson, NJ, 72-3. *Exhib:* 30th Biennial Am Art, Corcoran Gallery Art, Washington, 67; What's Happening in Soho, Univ Md Art Gallery, 71; solo exhib, Art Club Chicago, 74; Am Acad Arts & Lett Ann, 76; Drawing Today in NY, Sewall Art Gallery, Houston, Tex & Dayton Art Inst, Ohio; and others. *Pos:* Art project dir, Great Falls Historic District, Paterson, NJ, 78. *Teaching:* Fairleigh Dickinson Univ, Madison, NJ; Montclair State Coll; Staten Island Coll; New Sch Social Res, NY; Union Coll, Union, NY. *Awards:* Prix-de-Rome, Italy, 68-70; Creative Artists Pub Serv Grant, Cult Coun Found, 72; Childe Hassam Purchase Award, Am Acad Arts & Lett, 76. *Bibliog:* E Bilardello (auth), Pittori Americani a Roma, Margutta-Periodico d'Arte Contemporanea, Rome, 70; article, Arts Mag, 7/75. *Mem:* Am Acad Rome Alumni Asn; Found for Community Artists, NY. *Media:* Acrylic, Wood, Photography. *Res:* Electrostatic Transducers. *Interests:* photography, national park. *Publ:* Lenswork Quart, 5/95. *Dealer:* AM Sachs Gallery, NY; Dubins Gallery, Los Angeles, Calif. *Mailing Add:* 3239 N Arrowhead Ave San Bernardino CA 92405

CIVITICO, BRUNO
PAINTER, EDUCATOR
b Dignano D'Istria, Italy, Sept, 1, 1942; US citizen. *Study:* Rutgers Univ, 60; Pratt Inst, BFA, 66; Ind Univ, MFA, 68. *Work:* Bayly Mus, Univ Va, Charlottesville; Boston Pub Libr; Chemical Bank & Claude Bernard Galleries, New York. *Comn:* Silkscreen poster, NH Comn Arts, Theater by the Sea, Portsmouth, NH, 80; mural, Clemson U. SC, 2000. *Exhib:* Brooklyn Coll Faculty Past & Present, Davis & Long & Schoelkopf Gallery, NY, 77; Realism and Metaphor, USF Art Galleries, Tampa, Fla, 80; Narrative Painting, Alan Frumkin, NY, 81; Cleveland Mus Ann, Ohio, 83; solo exhibs, Robert Schoelkopf Gallery, NY, 72, 74, 77, 80 & 84, Manchester Inst Art & Sci, NH, 87 & Contemp Realist Gallery, San Francisco, 90 & 92; and others. *Pos:* Cur, Landscape Pty, 60-90, Gibbes & Bayly Mus, 92, Univ SC, 2000. *Teaching:* Instr, Pratt Inst, 69; lectr, Brooklyn Coll, 71, Princeton Univ, 72, Boston Univ, 79, Sch Art, Yale Univ, 82, Wash Univ, St Louis, 85 & NY Acad Art, 91; asst prof, Univ NH, 73-79; vis artist, Tyler Sch Art, Philadelphia, 80-81 & Cleveland Inst Art, 82-83; adj asst prof painting, Queens Coll, NY, 83-85; vis prof, Parsons, New York, 91. *Awards:* Fel, Guggenheim Found, 79; Nat Endowment Arts Fel, 81; Fel, Ingram Merill Found, 89; and others. *Bibliog:* Edward Lucie-Smith (auth), American Art Now, William & Morrow, 85; Charles Jencks (auth), Post Modernism, Rizzoli, 87; John L Ward (auth), American Realist Painting 1945-1980, UMI Res Press, 89. *Media:* Oil. *Publ:* Auth, An analysis of recent landscape and narrative paintings by Gabriel Laderman, Am Artist, 86. *Dealer:* Horchetl/Friedman Gallery San Francisco. *Mailing Add:* 2 Wragg Sq Charleston SC 29403-6209

CLARK, CAROL
ART HISTORIAN, CURATOR
b New York, NY, July 21, 1947. *Study:* Univ Mich, AB (with distinction), 69, MA, 71; Cleveland Mus Art, Kress Found Fel, 72-75; Case Western Reserve Univ, PhD, 81; Amherst Col, AM (hon), 92. *Pos:* Cur paintings, Amon Carter Mus Western Art, Ft Worth, Tex, 77-84; exec fel, Prendergast Proj, Williams Col Mus Art, 84-87. *Teaching:* Instr art hist & mus studies, Tex Christian Univ, Ft Worth, 75-77; lectr art hist, Williams Col, 85-87; assoc prof fine arts & Am studies, Amherst Col, 87-92, prof, 92-. *Awards:* William R Kenan, Jr Professorship, 2000-2004; William McCall Vickery 1957, Prof 2008-. *Mem:* Coll Art Asn; Am Studies Asn; Western Hist Asn. *Res:* American 19th & early 20th century painting. *Publ:* Auth, Thomas Moran's Watercolors of the American West, Univ Tex Press, 80; A Romantic Painter in the American West, Alfred Jacob Miller: Artist on the Oregon Trail, 82; Charles Deas, Am Frontier Life, 86; coauth, Maurice Brazil Prendergast & Charles Prendergast, Catalogue Raisonne, 90; The Robert Lehman Collection, Vol VIII: American Drawings and Watercolors, Metrop Mus Art, 92; Charles Deas & 1840s Am, Univ Okla Press, 2009. *Mailing Add:* Amherst Col Dept Art & Hist Art Amherst MA 01002

CLARK, EDWARD
PAINTER
b New Orleans, La, May 6, 1926. *Study:* Art Inst Chicago, 46-51; Acad de la Grande Chaumiere, Paris, France, 52. *Work:* Aldrich Mus Contemp Art, Ridgefield, Conn; Centio des Arts Mod, Guadalajara, Mex; Mus Solidarity, Titograd, Yugoslavia; La State Univ, Baton Rouge. *Exhib:* Salon D'Automme, 52 & Salon des Realites Nouvelles, 55 & 85, Mus d'Art Mod, Paris; Prix d'Othn Friese, Mus des Arts Decoratifs, Paris, 55; The Brata Groupe, Mus Mod Tokyo, Japan, 60; Biennial, Whitney Mus, NY, 73; Bicentennial Banners, Hirshhorn Mus, Washington, DC, 76; Icarus Odyssey, Centro de Arte Moderno, Guadalajara, Mex, 79; retrospective, Studio Mus of Harlem, NY, 80; Realities Nouvelles, 1984, Grand Palais, Paris, 84. *Awards:* Creative Artists Pub Serv Award, New York, 59; Nat Endowment Arts Grant Painting, 72 & 81. *Bibliog:* Article, Edward Clark, pushbroom in action, Art Int, 70; Corrine Robbins (auth), Pluralist Era in American Art, Harper & Row, 83; article, Edward Clark, statement, Issue Mag, 85. *Mem:* Asn des Anciens de la Cite Internationale des Arts, Paris. *Media:* All. *Dealer:* Larry Randall 82-30 138th St Kew Gardens NY 11435; Julia Hotton 202 E 76th St New York NY 10021. *Mailing Add:* 4 W 22nd St New York NY 10010-5802

CLARK, EMERY ANN
PAINTER, ENVIRONMENTAL ARTIST
b New Orleans, La, Sept 12, 1950. *Study:* Newcomb Col, BFA, 72; Sch Fine Arts, Boston Univ, 69; Skowhegan Sch Painting & Sculpture, 71; Tulane Univ, MFA, 81. *Work:* New Orleans Mus Art & Virlane Found, New Orleans, La; IBM, Washington, DC; Chase Manhattan Bank, Miami, Fla; Hunter Mus Art, Chatanooga, Tenn. *Comn:* NOMA Nile (29' 6″ 45 mile color environ installation), New Orleans Mus Art, La, 77;

Art by the Yard (1000' x 5' painted canvas), Art Coun New Orleans, La, 82 & Barbara Gillman Gallery, Miami, Fla, 83; Sea Wall (environ installation 40 x 41), Touro Med Off Bldg, New Orleans, La, 83; New Orleans Intl Airport & Arts Council with NO Art Installation, 89-92; Ochsner Clinic Fdtn, Healing Arts Prog, 2003-2005. *Exhib:* Artists' Biennial, New Orleans Mus Art, La, 75 & 77; La Major Works, La World Expos, New Orleans, 84; The Art of New Orleans, Southeastern Ctr Contemp Art, Winston-Salem, NC, 84; Landscape, Cityscape, Seascape, Contemp Arts Ctr, New Orleans, La & NY Acad Art, NY, 86; Barbara Frederick Gallery, Washington, DC, 86; Fishbach Gallery, NY, 86; Tampa Triennial, Tampa Mus Art, Fla, 88; 50th Ann Nat Exhib Contemp Am Paintings, Soc Four Arts, Palm Beach, Fla, 88; one-person show, Lowery Sims (with catalog), Alexandria Mus Art, Univ Art Mus, Univ La in Lafayette, Southern La, Univ La, State Univ, 98-99. *Teaching:* Vis artist, New Orleans Ctr Creative Arts, 74-76; instr, Tulane Univ, 79-81. *Awards:* Thomas J Watson Traveling Fel, 72; 1st Prize, 50th Ann Nat Exhib Contemp Am Painting; Spec Guest, Aspen Inst Humanistic Studies, Aspen Co, 74. *Bibliog:* John Kemp (auth), An Artist's Sense of Place, Am Artist, Vol 52, 62-65, 6/88; Lowery Sims (auth), catalog, Alexandria Mus, 89. *Mem:* Contemp Arts Ctr New Orleans (bd mem, 76-89, co-chmn Arts Comt, 77, Arts Comt, 78-81 & 86-88, chmn Arts Comt, 80-81, vpres, 78 & 82-84); Women's Caucus Arts; Coll Art Asn; Nat Asn Artists Orgn; New Orleans Ctr Creative Arts Community (Liaison bd, 80-89, pres, 84-85). *Media:* Painting, Environmental Art. *Publ:* Univ Art Mus Catalog, Bomb Mag, New York, No XXII, 46-47, fall 90. *Mailing Add:* 2407 Lakeshore Dr Mandeville LA 70448-5737

CLARK, GARTH REGINALD
DEALER, HISTORIAN
b Pretoria, Republic SAfrica, May 15, 1947. *Study:* Royal Coll Art, London with Lord Queensberry & Edwardo Paolozzi, MA, 76. *Exhib:* Hans Coper: A Retrospective, Gardiner Mus, Toronto, Can, 85. *Collection Arranged:* A Century of Ceramics in the US Traveling Exhib (auth, catalog), 79; The Contemporary Am Potter Traveling Exhib (auth, catalog), Smithsonian Inst, 80; Michael Carden: A Portrait, NCECA Conference, 81; Ceramic Echoes: Historical References in Contemporary Ceramic Art (auth, catalog), Nelson Atkins Mus, 83. *Pos:* Dir, Inst Ceramic History, Los Angeles, 79-81. *Teaching:* Art historian ceramics, Univ Calif, Los Angeles, 78. *Awards:* Morton Professor, Ohio Univ, 81; Eleventh Wittenborn Mem Award for Art Book of the Year, 89; Fel, Royal Coll Art, 96. *Mem:* Decorative Art Soc; Inst Ceramic History; Art Libr Soc NAm. *Publ:* Auth, Ceramic echoes, Contemp Art Soc, 83; co-auth, American Potters Today, Victoria & Albert Mus, London, 86; auth, American Ceramics: 1876 to the Present, 87, The Eccentric Teapot, 89, The Mad Potter of Biloxi: The Life and Art of George E Ohr, 89 & The Book of Cups, 90, Abbeville Press; co-auth, American Ceramics in The Everson Museum, Rizzoli, 88; The Potters Art: A Complete History of British Pottery, Phaidon, 95. *Mailing Add:* c/o Garth Clark Gallery 223 N Guadalupe St Santa Fe NM 87501-1868

CLARK, JON FREDERIC
EDUCATOR, GLASS BLOWER
b Waterloo, Wis, Aug 13, 1947. *Study:* Univ Wis, BSc; Royal Coll Art, London, MFA. *Work:* Royal Coll Art, London, Eng; Archie Bray Found, Helena, Mont; Portnoy Ltd, NY; Hadler Galleries, NY; Lannan Found, Palm Beach, Fla. *Exhib:* New Am Glass, Focus WVa, Huntington, 76; Contemp Art Glass, Lever House, NY, 76; Art of Craft, The Am View, Ill State Univ, Normal, 76; Nat Glass III, Univ Wis, Madison, 76; Nat Craft Exhib, Del Mus Art, Wilmington, 76; Philadelphia Craft Show, Philadelphia Mus Art, 77. *Collection Arranged:* Cup Show, Fritz Driesbach, 76 & Eisch Retrospective, Littleton Collection, 77, Tyler Sch Art, Temple Univ, Philadelphia. *Teaching:* Glass technician, Calif Col Arts & Crafts, Oakland, 73; assoc prof, Tyler Sch Art, 73-82. *Bibliog:* Judith Stein (auth), Exhibition Review, Vol 3 (1) & Richard Avidon (auth), Exhibition Review, Vol 4 (1), Glass Art Mag. *Mem:* Am Crafts Coun; Glass Art Soc; Nat Coun on Educ for Ceramic Arts. *Media:* Glass, Polyester. *Mailing Add:* 7703 Union Ave Elkins Park PA 19027-2621

CLARK, LYNDA K
MUSEUM DIRECTOR, PAINTER
b Miami, Fla. *Study:* Fla Atlantic Univ, BFA, 69; Calif State Univ, Long Beach, MA, 86. *Exhib:* Maurice Le Grand Le Seuer Sullins (catalog), 87-88, Robert Lostutter, 89, New Work, John Balsley, 90, Native Am Workers of Clay: 2500 BC-1500 AD, 92; Point of Contact: Western Artists/Japanese Artisans (colored woodblock prints), (catalog), 93; The Ness Collection: Northern Plains Tribal Art, 94; To Make a Proud Appearance, Native Am Dance & Ceremonial Clothing, 94; Signe Stuart: Retrospective (catalog), 95, Native Sons: Harvey Dunn & Oscar Howe, 97; Robert J Aldern: Retrospective, 99; Corporals, Cooks & Cowboys: African Americans in the Black Hills, 2000; Sacred Duty: Warriors and Weapons of the Northern Plains (catalog), 2000; Pursuit of Art: Grace French Pioneer Artist and Teacher. *Pos:* Asst cur, Long Beach Mus Art, Calif, 83-86; cur, Ill State Mus, Springfield, 86-88; dir, Niu Art Mus, Dekalb, Ill, 89-93, SDak Art Mus, Brookings, 93-98; exec dir, Journey Mus, Rapid City, SDak, 98-; ind curator, 2000-; gov appointee, SDak Arts Coun, 2003-; SDak for the Arts, 2005-; owner, Herons Flight Studio, SDak, 2010-. *Teaching:* Art hist & studio art, Spokane Falls Community Col, 80-83; Art Hist (contemp Am Art, 50-present), Sangamon State Univ, Springfield, Ill, 88; Mus studies, Northern Ill Univ, 90-93. *Awards:* Fel Nat Endowment Arts, 86; Fel Kellogg Found, 86. *Mem:* Am Asn Mus; Soc Am Mosaic Artists; Surface Design Asn; Rotary Int; AAUN. *Media:* Acrylic on canvas, mosaic, fiber. *Res:* Contemporary American artists; 20th century folk and outsider art; traditional and contemp Native Am art. *Specialty:* Mosaics, fiber, paint & mixed mediums, 2-D & 3-D by contemporary Western and Native American artists. *Collection:* Native American art (Northern Plains), outsider art, contemporary Western. *Publ:* Maurice LeGrand Leseuer Sullins: Paintings, Ill State Mus, 87; Outside USA: Out of This World, Maurice Sullins, Kunstforum Int, Cologne, Ger, 3-4/91; Native Sons: Harvey Dunn & Oscar Howe, 97; Sacred Duty: Warriors and Weapons of the Northern Plains, 2000. *Mailing Add:* Heron's Flight Studio 211 Founders Park Dr Rapid City SD 57701

CLARK, MICHAEL
MUSEUM DIRECTOR
Study: Corcoran Sch Art, BA. *Work:* Clark in Context: Day of the Revolutionary, Mus Contemp Art, 2003; rep in permanent collections, Nat Gallery Art, DC. *Exhib:* exhib incl, Clark & Hogan: Paintings & Collab, Barry Gallery, 2002-03. *Pos:* Founder & co-dir Mus Contemp Art, Wash, 91-. *Mailing Add:* Museum of Contemporary Art 1054 31st St Washington DC 20007

CLARK, MICHAEL VINSON
PAINTER, PRINTMAKER
b Tex, Nov 20, 1946. *Work:* Corcoran Gallery Art, Nat Collection Fine Art, Nat Gallery Art & Phillips Collection, Washington, DC; Everson Mus, Syracuse, NY. *Exhib:* Solo exhibs, Mus STex, Corpus Christi, 78 & Harry Lunn Gallery, DC, 79; The Art of Organic Form, Smithsonian Inst, Washington, DC, 68; New Painting: Structure, Corcoran Gallery, 68; Nat Drawing Soc Show, Philadelphia Mus Art, Pa, 70; Ten Washington Artists 1950-1970, Edmonton Art Gallery, Can, 70; Washington Art: Twenty Yrs, Baltimore Mus of Art, 70; 75th Anniversary, Cooper-Hewitt Mus, NY, 77; Critics Choice 1977, Lowe Mus, Syracuse Univ, Syracuse, NY, 77; Dimock Gallery, George Washington Univ, DC, 79; Images of the 70's, Nine Washington Artists, Corcoran Gallery Art, DC, 80. *Awards:* Purchase Award, Nat Drawing Soc, Philadelphia Mus, 70; Purchase Award, 35th Corcoran Biennial Contemp Painting, 77. *Bibliog:* James Harithas (auth), Michael Clark, Everson Mus Art, 73. *Publ:* Illusr, The Art of Organic Form, Smithsonian Inst, 68. *Mailing Add:* 220 E 60th St Suite 6H New York NY 10022-1406

CLARK, ROBERT CHARLES
PAINTER, LECTURER
b Minneapolis, Minn, Aug 31, 1920. *Study:* Minneapolis Sch Art; Walker Gallery Art Sch, Minneapolis. *Work:* Los Angeles Co Mus Hist, Sci & Art, Los Angeles; Norton B Simon Inc, Hunt's Foods & Industs Found, Los Angeles; Glendale Fed Collection of Calif Art. *Comn:* The Resurrection (mural), Forest Lawn Mem Park, Glendale, 65. *Exhib:* Artists of Los Angeles & Vicinity, Los Angeles Co Mus Art, 55-58; Illusion & Reality, Santa Barbara Mus Art, Calif, 56; Solo exhibs, Calif Palace of Legion of Honor, San Francisco, 56 & Rosicrucian Egyptian Mus, San Jose, 73; Charles & Emma Frye Mus, Seattle, Wash, 57-58. *Pos:* Background artist, Natural Hist Dept, Los Angeles Co Mus, 54-62. *Awards:* Artists of Los Angeles & Vicinity Award, Los Angeles Co Mus Art, 55; Purchase Award, Palos Verdes Estates Art Gallery, 56. *Bibliog:* Janice Lovoos (auth), The tempera paintings of Robert Clark, Am Artist, 12/69; William F Taylor (auth & producer), Robert Clark: An American Realist (film), 74; Elizabeth Rigby (auth), Robert Clark: A perfectionist's medium, Southwest Art, 1/79. *Media:* Tempera, Watercolor. *Mailing Add:* c/o Zantman Art Galleries PO Box 5818 Carmel CA 93921

CLARK, ROBERTA CARTER
PAINTER, ILLUSTRATOR
b St Louis, Mo, May 2, 1924. *Study:* Purdue Univ; Ctr Creative Studies, Detroit, 48-51; Art Ctr Sch, Los Angeles, 53-54; Art Students League, with Hirsch, 59; also studied with John Terelak, Don Stone & Charles Reid. *Work:* Brookdale Coll, Lincroft, NJ; Rutgers Univ, New Brunswick, NJ; Monmouth Med Ctr, Long Branch, NJ; Wash & Lee Univ, Lexington, Va; Seton Hall Univ, South Orange, NJ; Monmouth Co Courthouse; and others. *Comn:* Numerous portraits. *Exhib:* Soc Western Artists, De Young Mus, San Francisco, 54; Transparent Watercolor Soc, 83-92, 2001, 2005; Am Watercolor Soc, 85, 87, 89 & 92; Nat Acad Exhib, NY, 90; Adirondacks Nat Exhib Am Watercolors, 90-92; Garden State Watercolor Soc, 2000-2008; Philadelphia Watercolor Club, 2005; Pa Watercolor Soc, 2005; NJ Watercolor Soc, 75-2009. *Teaching:* Instr workshops, Calif, St Louis, Hilton Head, Rockport, Mass, Vt, Pocono Pines, Pa, Ohio, Tex & NJ. *Awards:* Silver Medals, NJ Watercolor Soc Ann, 78, 81 & 85 & Grumbacher Inc, 82, 85, 87-88 & 2007; Adirondacks Nat Exhib Am Watercolors, 90, Harold Coopersmith Award, 91 & Paul Mowrey Mem Award, 92; Garden State Watercolor Soc Award, 91 & 2008; Transparent Watercolor Soc, Master Painter, 2005; and others. *Mem:* NJ Watercolor Soc (secy, 76-78, pres, 79-82); Rockport Art Asn; Master Transparent Watercolor Soc Am; Am Watercolor Soc; Garden State Watercolor Soc; Guild of Creative Art; Ocean Co Artists Guild; Pine Shores Art Asn; Somerset Art Asn. *Media:* Watercolor, Pastel, Oils. *Publ:* Illusr, The Littles, thirteen bk ser, Scholastic Inc, 70-2004; auth & illusr, How to Paint Living Portraits, North Light, 90; Painting Vibrant Children's Portraits, North Light, 93; 12 images, A Successful Career in Portraiture, Am Artist Mag, 5/2008. *Dealer:* Anchor & Palette Gallery Bay Head NJ. *Mailing Add:* 47B Cheshire Sq Little Silver NJ 07739-1433

CLARK, TIMOTHY JOHN
PAINTER, EDUCATOR
b Santa Ana, Calif, June 30, 1951. *Study:* Art Ctr Coll Design, with Paul Marciel Souza & Harry Carmean, 69-70; Chouinard Art Inst, with Donald W Graham & Harold M Kramer, Emerson Woelffer, CFA, 72; Calif Inst Arts, BFA, 74; Calif State Univ, Fullerton, with Victor Joachim Smith, 75; Calif State Univ, Long Beach, with Joyce Wahl Treiman, MA, 78. *Work:* Nat Portrait Gallery/Smithsonian; Sherman Found; Millard Sheets Collection; El Paso Mus Fine Art; Mus Mission San Juan Capistrano; Farnsworth Art Mus, Rockland, Maine; Butler Inst Am Art, Youngstown, Ohio; Mus City of NY; Springfield Art Mus, Mo; Whistler House Mus, Lowell, Mass; Libr Cong Works on Paper, Washington, DC; Buck Collection, Laguna Beach, Calif; E Gene Crain Collection, Newport Beach, Calif; Golisano Mus Art, Naples, Fla; Loyola Univ Mus Art, Chicago, Ill; Laguna Art Mus, Laguna Beach, Calif. *Comn:* Various portrait comns; Sir Eldon Griffith. *Exhib:* Ann Exhib, Nat Acad Design, NY, 80, 98 & 2000; Group exhibs: Grand Cent Art Galleries, NY, 93; Worcester Art Mus, Mass, 98; Artists of Am, Colo History Mus, Denver, 2000, Hammer Galleries, 2004-2009, Vose Galleries, Realism Now, 2004, Ctr for Maine Contemp Art, 2005, Topkapi Mus, Istanbul, 2002, Von Liebig Art Center, Naples Fla, 2007-8, Bennington Arts Center, Vt, 2007-8, Morris Mus Art, Augusta, Ga, 2012, Harmon-Meek Gallery,

Naples, Fla, 2011-14, Burrough-Chapin Art Mus, SC, 2013; Solo exhibs: Mus Mission San Juan Capistrano, 96-97; Bowers Art Mus, Santa Ana, Calif, 2000; Parker Ranch Art Mus, Kamuela, Hawaii, 2000; Butler Inst Am Art, Youngstown, Ohio, 2008; Pasadena Mus Calif Art, 2008; Whistler House Mus Art, Lowell, Mass, 2008; Hammer Galleries, NY, 2009, Nev Mus Art, Reno, 2010-11, Laguna Art Mus, Laguna Beach, Calif, 2012-13; Lois Wagner Fine Arts, NY, 2014. *Teaching:* Prof drawing & painting, Orange Coast Col, Costa Mesa, Calif, 74-79 & Coastline Col, Fountain Valley, Calif, 76-2006; instr watercolor, Univ Hawaii, 82, Worcester Art Mus, Mass, 94-98, Art Students League, New York, 95-; National Academy School, 2004-2006; lectr, Yale Archit Grad Classical Educ Prog, Rome, Italy, 2005-. *Awards:* First Place, San Diego Int Watercolor Exhib, 77; Nominated for Emmy, Focus on Watercolor, PBS-TV, 89; Excellence in Educ NISOD Award, Univ Tex, Austin, 97; William A Paton Award, The Nat Acad, NY, 2000; The President's Award, Nat Arts Club, Exhibiting Members Show, 2003, 2012; The Salzman Award, Nat Arts Club Exhibiting Members Show, 2004; Allied Artists Watercolor Award, 2005; best in show, Political Animals, Von Liebig Art Center, Naples, Fla, 2008. *Bibliog:* Brad Bonhall (auth), His Art and Soul, Los Angeles Times, 3/27/2000; Daniel Chang (auth), The Art of Being Prepared, Orange Co Register, Calif, 3/18/2000; Virginia Wright (auth), Painting by Painting Room by Room, The Times Record, Brunswick, Maine, 5/11/2000; Richard Chang (auth), In the Eye of the Artist, Orange Co Register, 9/10/2002; Holland Cotter (auth), Luminaries at the League, Now All Over Town, NY Times, 9/9/2005; Kelly Compton (auth), Timothy J Clark: Master of Color, Light, & Shadow, Fine Art Connoisseur, NY, July/Aug 2008; Jean Stern & Lisa Farrington (coauths), Timothy J Clark, Pomegranate Communs, Petaluma, Calif, 2008; Avery Hunt (auth), The Vision of Timothy J. Clark, Coastal Journal, Bath, ME, 10/2/08; Raymond Steiner (auth), Timothy J. Clark at Hammer Galleries, Art Times, Mt. Marion, NY, 3/2009; Twenty Great Masters, Am Artist, NY, 5/2011; Cathy Thomas (auth), An Artist's Palate, Orange Co Register, Calif, 4/2011; Janet Blake (auth), Timothy J Clark, Laguna Art Mus (brochure), 2012-2013. *Mem:* Nat Arts Club, NY; Artist's Fel, NY; Century Assn, NY. *Media:* Watercolor, Oil. *Publ:* Contribr, Learning from the Pros, Watson-Guptill, 85; Tips on analyzing your subject, Am Artist Mag, 87; Focus on Watercolor, Watson-Guptill 87; Learning from the Best, Watercolor Mag, fall 96; Winslow Homer's Watercolor Techniques, Watercolor Mag, fall 98; Art Review, The Art Times, Aug. 2004-2010; auth, Noteworthy: Expressive Luminescence, Watercolors, Watercolor Mag, NY, 2010; Out and About, Fine Art Comn, New York, NY, 3/2011; Twenty Great Masters, Am Artist, 2011. *Dealer:* Lois Wagner Fine Art 15 E 71st St New York NY 10021; Harmon-Meek Gallery 599 Tamiami Trail Naples Fl 34102. *Mailing Add:* PO Box 2728 Capistrano Beach CA 92624

CLARK, VICKY A
CURATOR, HISTORIAN

b Atlanta, Ga. *Study:* Univ Calif, Los Angeles, BA, 72; Univ Calif, Davis, MA, 74; Univ Mich (teaching fel, 75-77), PhD, 79. *Collection Arranged:* Lothar Baumgarten, Jeff Wall, Meg Webster, Barbara Bloom, Carnegie Mus Art. *Pos:* Cur educ, Carnegie Mus Art, Pittsburgh, 81-89, assoc cur contemp art, 89-94; cur, Pittsburgh Ctr Arts, 96-. *Teaching:* Instr, Univ Toledo & Toledo Mus Art, 79; asst prof, Univ RI, 80 & Skidmore Col, Saratoga Springs, NY, 80-81; adj prof, Chatham Col, 87-, Univ Pittsburgh, 91-, Carnegie-Mellon Univ, 96-. *Mem:* Coll Art Asn. *Res:* Contemporary art. *Publ:* Richard Serra in Pittsburgh, Carnegie Mag, Vol LVIII, No 4 8/86; On the Meaning of Art at the End of the Century in Carnegie International, Carnegie Mus Art, 88; Auth & Ed, International Encounter: The Carnegie International & Contemporary Art, 1896-1996, Carnegie Mus Art, 96; auth, Recycling Art History (exhib, catalog), Pittsburgh Ctr Arts, 98; auth, Women in Mus, The New Art Examiner, 95. *Mailing Add:* Pittsburgh Ctr Arts 6300 5th Ave Pittsburgh PA 15232

CLARK, VICKY JO
PAINTER

b Lamesa, Tex, Sept 14, 1937. *Study:* Abilene Christian Univ Tex, 56-59, studied with Ben Konis, Albert Handell, Daniel Greene. *Work:* Abilene Christian Univ, Tex; Seminole High Sch, Tex; First Int Bank, Houston, Tex; Plaines Nat Bank, Lubbock, Tex; Post Nat Bank, Tex. *Comn:* Mural, Primary Cafeteria, Seminole Pub Sch, Tex, 91; Ten paintings of children, Southwest Meml Hosp, Houston. *Exhib:* Salmagundi Club, NY, 88-92; Catharine Lorillard Wolfe, Nat Arts Club, NY, 88-90; Maryland Pastel Soc, Johns Hopkins Sch Med, Baltimore, 89 & 91; Pastel Soc SW, Dallas, Tex, 90; Pastel Soc NMex, 96. *Teaching:* Workshops pastel, Tex & NMex. *Awards:* First Place, Southeastern Pastel Soc, 89; Purchase Award, A&A Guffuni, Pastel Soc Am, 89; Pastel Soc Am Plaque, Salmagundi, 89; Merit Awards in Chicago, 89, Dallas, 90 & Seattle, 91. *Mem:* Pastel Soc Am; Catharine Lorillard Wolfe; Pastel Soc Southwest. *Media:* Pastel. *Interests:* painting children & western landscapes. *Publ:* Auth, The best of Pastel & Floral Inspirations, Rockport Publ, Inc; The Best of Pastel 2, Rockport Pub, Inc, Cover Story, The Pastel Jour, Oct/Nov 99; articles and paintings The Pastel Jour, Oct/Nov 2000; cover and article, Pastel Artist Int, 1-2/2001; cover, Feist Phonebook, High Plains, 2003-2004; High Panhandle, 2003-2004; cover, Daniel Smith Catalogue, 2005-2006. *Mailing Add:* 607 SW Avenue 1 Seminole TX 79360

CLARK, WILLIAM W
HISTORIAN

b Tampa, Fla, Jan 17, 1940. *Study:* Pa State Univ, BA (with hons); Columbia Univ, MA & PhD. *Pos:* Ed, Gesta, 88-91; prof art, Queens Col, City Univ New York, 67-. *Teaching:* Prof medieval archit, Queens Col & Grad Ctr, City Univ NY, Flushing, 67-. *Awards:* Grants, Nat Endowment Arts, Am Coun Learned Soc & J Paul Getty Trust. *Mem:* Coll Art Asn; Societe Francaise d'Archeologie; Int Ctr for Medieval Art; Centre des Recherches d'Archeologie Medievale; Medieval Acad Am. *Res:* Twelfth-century early Gothic architecture and sculpture in France and England. *Publ:* Auth, Spatial innovations in the chevet of Saint-Germain-des-Pres, J Soc Archit Historians, no 38, 79; Laon Cathedral: Architecture, Harvey Miller Publ, London, vol 1, 83 & vol 2, 87; The first flying buttresses: A new reconstruction of the nave of Notre-Dame de Paris, Art Bull, no 66, 84; Suger's church at Saint-Denis: The state of research, In: Abbot Suger and Saint-Denis, 86; Medieval Architecture, Medieval Learning, Yale Univ Press, New Haven, 92. *Mailing Add:* Dept Art Queens Col Flushing NY 11367

CLARK-LANGAGER, SARAH ANN
GALLERY DIRECTOR, CURATOR

b Lynchburg, Va, May 14, 1943. *Study:* Randolph-Macon Woman's Col, Lynchburg, Va, BA (art hist), 65; Univ Wash, Seattle, MA (art hist), 70; City Univ New York, Grad Ctr, PhD (art hist), 88. *Collection Arranged:* Northwest Traditions (auth, catalog), Seattle Art Mus, 78; Sighted/Sited at Western: Drawings for Sculpture, Western Gallery, Western Wash Univ, 90; Northwest Native Am & First Peoples Art, Western Gallery, 93; Chairs: Embodied Objects (catalog), Western Gallery, 93; Stars & Stripes: 20th Century Prints & Drawings, Western Gallery, 94; Photographs from Am, 96; Focus on WWU Collections: The Last Five Decades (catalog), Western Gallery, 99; Northwest Artists' Books (coauth), Western Gallery; Decades of Giving: Virginia Wright and Sculpure at Western (auth), Western Gallery, 99; Western Tableaux: 100 Years (coauth), Western Gallery, 99; Surface Tension, Western Gallery, 2003; A Sofa and..., Northwestern Artists & 20th Century Designer Furniture, 2003; Noguchi & Dance, Western Gallery, WWV, 2005; The Al & Vera Leese Collection, Gift of Marian Boylan, Western Gallery, 2006; Critical Messages: Contemp Northwest Artists on the Environment, Western Gallery, WWU, 2010. *Pos:* Assoc cur, modern art, Seattle Art Mus, 75-79; cur, 20th century art, Munson-Williams Proctor Inst, Utica, NY, 81-86; gallery dir, Univ NTex, Denton, 86-88; gallery dir & cur of Outdoor Sculpture Collection, Western Gallery, Western Wash Univ, Bellingham, 88-. *Teaching:* Assoc, Educ Dept, Yale Univ Art Gallery, 65-67; assoc, Educ Dept, art history, Albright-Knox Art Gallery, Buffalo, 67-68; assoc, Educ Dept, art hist, Seattle Art Mus, Wash, 71-75; asst prof, art hist, Univ N Tex, Denton, 86-88; adj prof, Western Wash Univ, 88-. *Awards:* Outstanding Achievement Award (fund raising), Western Foundation, Western Washington Univ, 99; Faculty Recognition Award, Board of Trustee, Western Washington Univ, 2003; and many others. *Mem:* Wash Art Consortium (mem, bd dirs); Am Asn Mus. *Publ:* Perspective on Excellence: A Century of Teaching and Learning at Western Washington Univ, 2000; Sculpture in Place: A Campus as Site, Marquand Books/Western Wash Univ, 2002; Susan Bennerstrom, Univ Wash Press, 2000; Isamu Noguchi; Beyond Red Square In Isamu Noguchi and Skyviewing Sculpture. Japan Week 2004; essay, 22nd Rosen Outdoor Sculpture Competition and Exhib, Appalachian State Univ, 2008; Messengers in the Northwest, Critical Messges: Contemp Northwest Artists on the Environment, Bellingham, WWU,2010

CLARK-MENDES, CYBELE
PHOTOGRAPHER

b Los Angeles, California, 1975. *Study:* RI Sch Design, MFA; Cornell Univ, BFA. *Exhib:* group exhibs include Palm Beach Inst Contemp Art, Lake Worth, Fla, 2001; Urban Inst Contemp Arts, Grand Rapids, MI, 2002; Exit Art, New York, 2002; Ctr Cult Pablo de Torriente Brau, Havana, Cuba, 2002; Mus Contemp Art, Atlanta, 2002; Art in General, New York, 2003; Woman Made Gallery, Chicago, 2004; Print Ctr, Philadelphia, 2004; FLATFILE Galleries, Chicago, 2004; Gallery 825, Los Angeles, 2005. *Awards:* Pamela Joseph Fel, Anderson Ranch Arts Ctr, 2005; New York Found Arts Fel, 2008

CLARKE, ANN
PAINTER, EDUCATOR

b Norwich, Eng, Aug 27, 1944; Can citizen. *Study:* Slade Sch Fine Art, Univ Col, London, dipl fine art & design. *Work:* Can Coun Art Bank; Westburne Collection, Montreal; Hill Trust Fund Collection, Calgary, Alta; Prov Courthouse Collection, Edmonton, Can; Queensland Art Gallery, Brisbane, Australia. *Exhib:* Abstraction West: Emma Lake and After, Nat Gallery, Ottawa, Ont & Mendel Art Gallery, Saskatoon, Sask, 76; Mus d'Art Contemp, Montreal, Que, 76; one-person shows, Edmonton Art Gallery, 77, Southern Alta Art Gallery, 79 & Gallery One, Toronto, 86, Gallery One, Toronto, Ont, 99 & 2000, 30 Yr Survey, The Thunder Bay Art Gallery, Ont, 2000; Seven Prairie Artists, Art Gallery of Ont, 79; Threshold of Colour, Edmonton Art Gallery, 82; Ultima Thule, Definitely Superior Gallery, Thunder Bay, Ont, 95; Inner Landscapes-16xOne, Gallery One, Toronto, Ont, 96; The Tweed Contemp Artists' Series, the Tweed Gallery, Duluth, Minn, 98; Faculty Show, Thunderbay Art Gallery, Ont, 2004; solo, Paths of Desire, Prairie Art Gallery, Grandeprairie, Alta, 2004, Triptych, Verb Gallery, Kingston, Ont, 2006, Random Courses, Swamp Ward Project, Kingston, Ont, 2006. *Pos:* Art coordr, Royal Ont Mus, Toronto, 85-86; artistic dir, Kingston Artists Asn Int, 88-90. *Teaching:* Asst prof art, NS Col Art & Design, Halifax, 75-76; lectr art, Univ Alta, Edmonton, 76-84 & Red Deer Col, 79-80, Grant McEwan Col, 80-84; lect art, Univ Guelph, Ont, 85-91; lectr art, Queen's Univ, Kingston, Ont, 88-91; prof, Visual Arts, Lakehead Univ, Thunder Bay, Ont, 92-. *Awards:* Can Coun Art Bank Award, 73 & 76; Govt Alta Cult Award, 74; Can Coun Art Award, 78-79; Can Council Senior Award, 1999; Ont Arts Council Senior Award, 2003. *Bibliog:* Article, Ken Carpenter (auth), Ann Clarke, Art Mag, 6/81; David Burnett & Marilyn Schiff (auths), Contemporary Canadian Art, 83; Karen Wilkin (auth), Ann Clarke, Vie des Arts, 86. *Media:* All Media. *Dealer:* Gallery One Toronto Ont; Roomz Thunderbay Ont. *Mailing Add:* 294 Pearl St Thunderbay ON P7B 1E6 Canada

CLARKE, ANN
EDUCATOR

Study: Univ of Mich, BFA (painting and printmaking), 1981; RI Sch of Design, MFA (textiles), 1994. *Exhib:* Wearables Exhibition, Peters Valley Craft Center Gallery, Layton, NJ, 2004, Under One Roof, SOHO20, NY, 2004, Missing Pieces, Rochester Contemporary, Rochester, NY, 2005, Beckstrand Gallery, Calif, 2006, Under One Roof Reprise, Everson Mus of Art, NY, 2007, Seams: Contemporary Art to Wear, Noyes Mus of Art, Oceanville, NJ, 2008. *Pos:* Asst prof, Dept Art, Women's Studies, Appalachian Studies, East Tenn State Univ, 1994-98; prog coord fiber arts and materials studies, Dept Art, Syracuse Univ, 1998-2005, chair Dept of Art, 2005-07, assoc dean, Col of Visual and Performing Arts, 2007-08, dean, 2008-. *Teaching:* bd trustees, Syracuse State, 2009-, Everson Mus of Art, 2010-. *Mailing Add:* Syracuse University College of Visual and Performing Arts 200 Crouse College Syracuse NY 13244-1010

CLARKE, BUD (WARREN) F
DESIGNER, PAINTER
b Windsor, Vt, Jan 10, 1941. *Study:* Art Students League, 59-63; Sch Visual Arts, with Milton Glazer. *Pos:* Art dir, McCalls Corp, 68-70; art dir, McGraw Hill Inc, NY, 70-81; founder, Bud Clarke & Assocs, 81-84; pres, Clarke/Thompson Design, 84-. *Teaching:* Instr mag design, 77-, instr media commun, 78-, Sch Visual Arts, NY. *Awards:* Cert of Merit, Art Dir Mag; Soc Publ Designers; Jesse H Neal Award, Am Bus Press, 80 & 82. *Bibliog:* Roy Paul Nelson (auth), Publication Design, William C Brown, 78. *Mem:* Soc Publ Designers; McGraw Hill Art Dirs Club (pres, 74-78). *Media:* Magazines, Printed Material, Watercolor, Mixed Medium. *Mailing Add:* 65 Pokonoie Rd Ulster Park NY 12487-5080

CLARKE, JOHN CLEM
PAINTER
b Bend, Ore, June 6, 1937. *Study:* Ore State Univ; Mexico City Col; Univ Ore, BFA, 60. *Work:* Whitney Mus Am Art, NY; Dallas Mus Art, Tex; Va Mus Fine Arts; Metrop Mus Art & Mus Mod Art, NY; Baltimore Mus Fine Arts, Md. *Exhib:* Bi-Ann, Whitney Mus, 67-73; Realism in Am, touring USA; Mus Mod Art, NY; Aspects of Realism, touring Can, 76-78; Illusion and Reality, touring Australia, 77-78; Art About Art, Whitney Mus, NY, 78; Contemp Am Realism Since 1960, Pa Acad Fine Arts, Philadelphia, 81; The Ponderosa Collection, Butler Inst Am Art, Youngstown, Ohio, 83. *Media:* Oil on Canvas. *Mailing Add:* c/o Louis K Meisel Gallery 141 Prince St New York NY 10012

CLARKE, JOHN R
HISTORIAN, CRITIC
b Pittsburgh, Pa, Jan 25, 1945. *Study:* Georgetown Univ, AB, 67; Yale Univ, MA, 69, PhD, 73. *Teaching:* Asst prof hist art, Yale Univ, 75-80; asst prof, Univ Tex, Austin, 80-82, assoc prof, 82-87, prof, 88. *Awards:* NEH grants, 95, 99 & 2008; Guggenheim grant, 2002. *Mem:* Coll Art Asn Am (vpres, 96-98, pres 98-2000); Archeol Inst Am; Int Asn Study Ancient Mosaics; Am Coun Learned Soc (bd dir, 2000-2010). *Res:* Publ of the Roman Villa at Oplontis. *Publ:* Auth, Roman Black & White Fiigural Mosaics, NY Univ Press, 79; The Houses of Roman Italy, 100 BC-AD 250: Ritual, Space and Decoration, Univ Calif Press, 91; Looking at Lovemaking: Constructions of Sexuality in Roman Art, 100 BC-AD 250, Univ Calif Press, 98; Roman Sex, 100 BC-AD 250, Abrams, 2003; Art in Lives of Ordinary Romans: Visual Representation & Non-elite Viewers in Italy, 100 BC-AD 315, Univ Calif Press, 2003; Roman Life, 100 BC-AD 200, Abrams, 2007; Looking at Laughter: Humor, Power & Transgression in Roman Visual Culture, 100 BC-AD 250, Univ Calif Press, 2007. *Mailing Add:* Univ Tex Dept Art & Art Hist Austin TX 78712

CLARKE, KEVIN
PHOTOGRAPHER, CONCEPTUAL ARTIST
b New York, NY, Mar 20, 1953. *Study:* Cooper Union, BFA, 76; studied sculpture under Chris Wilmarth, Hans Haacke, Dore Ashton & Reuben Kadish. *Work:* Brooklyn Mus, NY; San Antonio Mus Art, Tex; Mus Wiesbadan & Fluxeum, Wiesbaden, Ger; Nat Gallerie, Berlin; Int Ctr Photog, NY; Smithsonian Inst; Cold Spring Harbor Lab. *Comn:* 7 murals for atrium, B-W Bank, Stuttgart, Ger; Portrait James D Watson, Cold Spring Harbor Lab, NY; Portrait Jacques Lowe, NY Acad Sci. *Exhib:* The Red Couch, Int Ctr Photog, NY, 84, Summer Rencontres, Ampitheater Arles, France, 84 & Tampa Mus Art, Fla, 90; Kaufhauswelt (Dept Store World), Frankfurter Kunstverein, Ger, 80; Blood, Schirn Kunsthalle, Frankfurt, Ger, 2003; Photo Espagne, 2002; Hecksher Mus Art, NY, 2003. *Bibliog:* Encounters with the Portrait, catalog Ralf Christofori, 2002; The End of the Art World. Vernal Passage, by Robert C. Morgan, Allworth Press, NY, 1999. *Interests:* genetics. *Collection:* William N Copley, Ann and James Harithas, DG Bank, others. *Publ:* Coauth, Kunstund Medien, Materialien Zur Documenta 6, Documenta, 1977; auth, Kaufhauswelt, Schirmer & Mosel, Muarch, 1980; The Red Couch, a Portrait of America, Harper & Row, 1984; Kevin Clarke Portraits, NY Kunsthalle; coauth, Gene Worlds, Bundeskunsthalle, Bonn, 1998; Kevin Clarke, by Alan Jones, Tema Celeste, 1999; Blood, Prestel Publs, 2001; Dust to DNA, Ars Genetica, Inc, 2002. *Dealer:* Galerie Michael Sturm, Stuttgart, Ger; Galleria de Arte Pilar Parra, Madrid, Spain

CLAYBERGER, SAMUEL ROBERT
PAINTER, EDUCATOR
b Kulpmont, Pa, Mar 26, 1926. *Study:* Chouinard Art Inst, Los Angeles; Jepson Art Inst; study with Don Graham, Rico Lebrun & Richard Haines. *Work:* Pasadena Art Mus, Calif. *Exhib:* Solo exhibs, Pasadena Art Mus, 60, Laguna Beach Mus Art, Calif, 67, Era Marguerite Gallery, San Marino, 91, Prufrock Gallery, Pasadena, 2000, Heritage Gallery, La, 93 & 98, Art Acad, La, 2001, Chouinard Found Sch Art, South Pasadena, 2003-2005, Unitarian Universalist Church, St Monica 99 & 2005; group exhibs, Calif, Longbeach Mus Art, 65-66, La Jolla Mus Art 69-70, Oceanside Mus Art, 2001 Calif Watercolor Soc. *Pos:* Designer-colorist, UPA Pictures Inc, Burbank, 53-58 & Jay Ward Prod Inc, Los Angeles, 59-64. *Teaching:* Instr design, Chouinard Art Inst, 60; instr design & painting, Otis Art Inst of Los Angeles Co, 63-69, asst prof drawing & painting, 69-79; instr drawing, Otis Parsons, 79-91; instr figure painting, landscape, Chouinard Found Art Sch, South Pasadena, 2003-2006. *Awards:* Nat Watercolor Soc, 56, 58, 60 & 69; Los Angeles All-City Exhib, Home Savings & Loan, 62. *Bibliog:* Joseph Mugnaini & Janice Loroos (auths), Drawing: A Search for Form, Reinhold, 65; George De Groat (auth), Sam Clayberger eyes the human condition, Star News, Pasadena, 70; Paul J Karlstrom (interviewer), taped interview archives, Am Art, Smithsonian Inst, 81; Joseph Mugnaini, Expressive Drawing, Davis Publ, 88; Gerald W Brommer (auth), The Art of Sketching, Clinker Press, ltd ed portfolio, 2000. *Media:* Acrylic, Watercolor. *Publ:* The Erotic Drawings of Sam Clayberger, Clinker Press, ltd ed portfolio, 2000. *Mailing Add:* 486 Mavis Dr Los Angeles CA 90065-5054

CLAYSON, S HOLLIS
ART HISTORIAN
b Itasca, Ill. *Study:* Wellesley Col, BA, 68; Univ Calif, Los Angeles, MA, 75, with T J Clark, PhD, 84. *Teaching:* Asst prof art hist, Wichita State Univ, 78-82; Asst prof Northwestern Univ, Evanston, Ill, 82-90, assoc prof & chair, 91-2001, Charles Deering McCormick prof teaching excellence, 93-96, prof art hist, 2001-, dir, Alice Kaplan Inst Humanities, currently; Koldyke outstanding teaching prof, 2004-2006. *Awards:* Coll Art Asn Teaching Award, 90; Am Coun Learned Soc Fel, 90-91; Sr Fel, Northwestern Univ Humanities Ctr, 94-95; Clark fel, 2003; Scholar, Getty Res Inst, 2004; Chercheur invité, INHA, Paris, 2009; Vis fel, Res Sch Humanities, Australian Nat Univ, 2010; Fel, Columbia Univ Inst Scholars, Reid Hal, Paris, 2010. *Bibliog:* Jill Foulston (ed), Regrettable Meals, Virago Book of Food, The Joy of Eating, London, 2006; Janet McLean (ed & cur), Threshold space: Parisian modernism betwixt & between 18969-1891, Impressionist Interiors, Nat Gallery Ireland, Dublin, 2008; Paul Smith (ed), The Grande Jatte and its Absences, Re-viewing Seurat,Penn State Univ Press, 2010. *Mem:* Coll Art Asn; Midwest Victorian Studies Asn; Midwest Art Hist Soc; Asn Art Historians, Eng. *Res:* Social iconography of later 19th century French art. *Publ:* Auth, catalog for The Second Exhibition, 1876, A Failed Attempt, The New Painting, Impressionism 1874-1886, The Fine Arts Mus, San Francisco & The Nat Art Gallery Art, Washington, DC, pp 145-159, 86, Painted Love: Prostitution in French Art of the Impressionist Era, Yale Univ Press, 91, (co-edited) Understanding Paintings: Themes in Art Explored and Explained, 2000, Paris in Despair: Art and Everday Life Under Siege, 1870-71, Paris in Despair: Art and Everyday Life under Siege 1870-71, Univ Chicago Pressm 2002, paperback, 2005; essay: The Sexual Politics of Impressionist Illegibility, Dealing with Iegas: Representations of Women and the Politics of Vision, Richard Kendall & Griselda Pollock (eds), London, 92, *Mailing Add:* Northwestern Univ 2439 Ridgeway Ave Evanston IL 60201

CLAYTON, CHRISTIAN
PAINTER
b Denver, Colo, 1967. *Study:* Art Ctr Coll of Design, BFA, 1989-91. *Exhib:* Clayton Brothers solo shows: Green Pastures, La Luz de Jesus Gallery, Calif, 2001, Candy Lackey, Roq La Rue Gallery, Seattle, 2002, Six Foot Eleven, La Luz de Jesus Gallery, 2003, Art Statements, Art Basel, Miami, Fla, 2004, I Come From Here, Mackey Gallery, Houston, Tex, 2004, Wishy Washy, Bellwether Gallery, NY, 2006, The Armory Show, 2006, Madison Mus Contemp Art, Wis, 2006, Alyce de Roulet Williamson Gallery, Calif, 2006; Clayton Brothers group shows: Tribute to La Luz de Jesus Gallery, Track 16 Gallery, Santa Monica, 1998, Collaborations, New Image Art Gallery, Calif, 2000, School Girls, Fish Tank Gallery, Brooklyn, 2001, Decipher, Eighth Floor Gallery, NY, 2002, Burning Brush, Six Space Gallery, Calif, 2002, The Burbs, DFN Gallery, NY, 2003, Assembly, Front Room Gallery, Brooklyn, 2003, Qee Show, OX-OP Gallery/Toy 2R Company, Tokyo, 2004, Tree Trimmings, Track 16 Gallery, 2004, Stranger Town, Dinte Fine Art, NY, 2005, Move 13, Clementine Gallery, NY, 2005, Visual Language, Mackey Gallery, Houston, Tex, 2005, Drawn to Expression, Alyce de Roulet Williamson Gallery, Calif, 2006; solo shows: 17 Souls, La Luz de Jesus Gallery, Calif, 1995, Out of Order, 14996, Loved to Give, 1998, I am Little, 2000; group shows: The Narrative Image, Ozone Art Gallery, SoHo, NY, 1996, The Young and the Restless, Bucheon Gallery, San Francisco Gallery, Calif, 1998, Move 2, New Image Art Gallery, 1998, California Artists, Ann Nathan Gallery, Chicago, 1998, The Portrait Show, New Image Art Gallery, 2001. *Pos:* Mem, The Clayton Brothers. *Teaching:* Tchr experimental media, Art Ctr Col of Design, Pasadena, Calif, 1995-. *Media:* Miscellaneous Media

CLAYTON, ROBERT
PAINTER
b Dayton, Ohio, 1963. *Study:* Colo Inst Art, 1981-83; Art Ctr Coll of Design, BFA, 1986-89. *Exhib:* Clayton Brothers solo shows: Green Pastures, La Luz de Jesus Gallery, Calif, 2001, Candy Lackey, Roq La Rue Gallery, Seattle, 2002, Six Foot Eleven, La Luz de Jesus Gallery, 2003, Art Statements, Art Basel, Miami, Fla, 2004, I Come From Here, Mackey Gallery, Houston, Tex, 2004, Wishy Washy, Bellwether Gallery, NY, 2006, The Armory Show, 2006, Madison Mus Contemp Art, Wis, 2006Alyce de Roulet Williamson Gallery, Pasadena, Calif, 2006; Clayton Brothers group shows: Tribute to La Luz de Jesus Gallery, Track 16, Santa Monica, 1998, Collaborations, New Image Art Gallery, Calif, 2000, School Girls, Fish Tank Gallery, Brooklyn, 2001, Decipher, Eighth Floor Gallery, NY, 2002, Burning Brush, Six Space Gallery, Calif, 2002, the Burbs, DFN Gallery, NY, 2003, Assembly, Front Room Gallery, Brooklyn, 2003, Qee Show, OX-OP Gallery/Toy2R Company, Tokyo, 2004, Tree Trimmings, Track 16 Gallery, 2004, Stranger Town, Dinter Fine Art, NY, 2005; solo shows: 75 Pints, La Luz de Jesus Gallery, 1994, Lucky 13, 1995, No Rhyme or Reason, 1997, 14 Gold Teeth, 1999; group shows: Antagonist, Pacific Design Ctr, Calif, 1995, California Artists, Ann Nathan Gallery, Chicago, 1998, Move 2, New Image Art Gallery, 1998, The Portrait Show, 2001. *Pos:* Mem, The Clayton Brothers. *Teaching:* Tchr experimental media, Art Ctr Col of Design, Pasadena, Calif, 1996-. *Media:* Miscellaneous Media

CLEARY, BARBARA B
PAINTER, INSTRUCTOR
b Durant, Okla, Aug, 10, 1935. *Study:* Univ Okla, BS, 58; Univ Central Okla, MA, 63; also studied with John Pike, Edgar Whitney & M Douglas Walton. *Work:* Muchnic Gallery, Atchinson, Kans; Winfield Art Ctr, Kans; City of Salina, Kans; City of Newton, Kans; Main Hurdman, Kans. *Exhib:* Kansas Watercolor Soc 5-State, Wichita Art Mus, 85, 86, & 88; Art Ann V,Cult Arts Ctr, Tulsa, Okla, 86; Southern Watercolor, Okla Art Ctr, Okla City, 87-88; National Watercolor Oklahoma, Okla Art Ctr, Oklahoma City, 88-89; 115th Am Watercolor Soc, Nat Gallery, NY. *Teaching:* Ft Scott Community Col. *Awards:* Past Pres Award, Fall Nat, Bakersfield, Calif, 85; Patron Award, Kans Watercolor Soc 4-State, 85; Patron Arts Award, Southern Watercolor Soc, 87. *Mem:* Kans Watercolor Soc (bd dir, 78-79, 84-85 & 86-87); Images II, Fine Arts (chmn, 88-90). *Media:* Watercolor; oil. *Publ:* Contribr, The Best of Kansas Arts and Crafts, State of Kans, 88. *Dealer:* Richard Hamilton 17201 E 40 Hwy Independence MO 64055

CLEARY, SHIRLEY CLEARY COOPER
PAINTER, WRITER
b St Louis, Mo, Nov 14, 1942. *Study:* Washington Univ, St Louis, BFA, 64; Tyler Sch Art, Temple Univ, MFA, 68; The Corcoran Mus Sch, 69-71. *Work:* Fedn Flyfishers Int Mus, W Yellowstone, Mont; Washington State Art Pub Places Collections; Herning Hojskole, Denmark; Nat Parks Found, Jackson, Wyo; Hokonui Heritage Ctr & Mus, Gore, NZ. *Comn:* Portrait of Gov Swinden, Sen Melcher, Sen Baucus, Cong Williams (medallion), comn by Mont Democratic Party, Helena, 85-90; Limited prints, Mont ambassadors, comn by State of Mont, Helena, 86; Poster, Mont Water Quality Month, comn by State of Mont, 91; Poster, 100 Years Fish Technology Ctr (USTD), 92; Patron Paintings, Mont State Trout Unlimited. *Exhib:* C M Russell Mus, Great Falls, Mont, 83 & 86-2013; Western Wildlife Gallery, San Francisco, Calif, 88; Arts for the Parks (US Tour), 89, 94, 97-98 & 2002; Women Artists of the West, Calif, 90 & 92; Maryland Waterfowl Festival, 93-96; Women Artists & the West, Tucson Mus Art, 94-95; Am Mus Fly Fishing, Manchester, Vt, 97; Casper Artist Guild Int Miniature Exhib, 2004; Grand Prize, Rocky Mountain Art Show, 2005; Holter Mus Art, Helena, Mont, 2009-2012; Paint the Parks, 2010. *Pos:* Bd mem, Mont Arts Coun, 73-82; guest artist, Herning Hojskole, Denmark, fall 81; artist-in-residence, Rivermeadow, Jackson Hole, 89-94 & 97. *Awards:* Best of Show, 3rd Ann Miniature Exhib, El Dorado Gallery, Colo, 84; First Place Acrylic & Gouache Painting, Bosque Art Gallery, NMex, 84 & 85; First Place, Ore Trout Stamp, 90; First Place, Asn NW Steelheaders Stamp, 92; Nat Trout Unltd Conservation Comms Award, 99; Artist of the Year, Nat Trout Unltd, 2001; First Place, Casper Artist Guild Int Miniature Exhib, 2004; finalist, Int Artist Mag Floral Competition, 2007. *Bibliog:* Ann Geracimos (auth), Shirley Cleary-artist of the West, Am Artist Mag, 4/81; Vivian A Paladin (auth), Shirley Cleary-eclectic artist in the West, Art W, 7/81; Judy Hughes (auth), Feeling the Splash of the Water, The Angling Art of Shirley Cleary, Wild Life Art News, 9/92; The Fine Art of Flyfishing, US Art, 7/94. *Media:* Gouache, Oil. *Publ:* Illusr, covers, Mont Outdoors, 81-86, 92 & Flyfisher's Mag Int Fedn Flyfishermen, 86; La Forza Opaca della Tempera, Disegnare & Dipingere, 11/87; illusr, Fly Fishing Quart; Fly Fisherman Mag; Diane Inman (auth), The Fine Art of Angling: Ten Modern Masters, Atlantic Salmon J, 10/2008. *Dealer:* Horizon Fine Art 165 N Center St Jackson WY 83001; Wild Wings Inc S Hwy 61 Lake City MN 55041-0451; Ponderosa 944 Springhill Hamilton MT 59840; Spirits in the Wind 1211 Washington Ave Golden CO 80401. *Mailing Add:* 1804 Beltview Dr Helena MT 59601

CLEAVE, MARCIE VAN
MUSEUM DIRECTOR
Pos: Exec Dir, Folk Art Ctr, 1988-. *Mailing Add:* Folk Arts Center 10 Franklin St Stoneham MA 02180

CLEAVER, RICHARD BRUCE
SCULPTOR
b Camden, NJ, 1952. *Study:* Md Inst Coll Art, BFA (magna cum laude), 77; Univ, Wis, MA, 80. *Work:* Erie Art Mus, Pa; Sallie May Loan Corp, Washington; St Paul Companies, Minn; Del Art Mus, Wilmington; De Young Mus. *Exhib:* Art Sites, Corcoran Gallery Art, Washington, DC, 96; Contemp Am Ceramics, Loveland Mus, Colo, 97; All the World's a Stage: Mixed Media Dioramas by Tom Duncan & Richard Cleaver, Noyes Mus, Oceanville, NJ, 98; Del Art Mus Biennial, Wilmington, 98; Family Ties, Peabody Essex Mus, Salem, Mass, 2003; Kentucky Mus Art & Craft; Fuller Craft Mus; Baltimore Mus Art; Ariz State Mus; John Michael Kohler Art Center. *Collection Arranged:* Diane and Sandy Besser Collection. *Awards:* Ind Artist Grant, Md State Arts Coun, 92, 95, 99, 2003; Crafts Fel, NEA, 94; Trawick Prize, 2007. *Bibliog:* Joe Vajtko (auth), Icons for Iconoclasts: Recent works by Richard Cleaver, Joel H Springer & Christian Vergane (rev), 21-26, 12/15/96; Barry Schwabsky (auth), Schwabsky: Critic, 14-15, Washington Rev, Critics' Residency Prog, 4/5-97; Hidden Stories in the Work of Richard Cleaver, Sch Arts, 1/98. *Dealer:* Sandy Besser Santa Fe Clay Santa Fe. *Mailing Add:* 4000 N Charles St Apt 1509 Baltimore MD 21218-1767

CLEMENT, KATHLEEN
PAINTER, GRAPHIC ARTIST
b Ord, Nebr, May 28, 1928. *Study:* Univ Nebr, BA, 50; with Frank Gonzalez, 67-69; Univ Am, with Toby Joysmith, 77-79; Mus Studies, Paris, 80. *Work:* Mus Mod Art, Isidro Fabela Cult Ctr & Inst N Am Cult Relations, Mexico; House of Humour & Satire, Gabravo, Bulgaria, 88. *Comn:* Paintings comn by, Co Minera Autlan, Univ Zacatecas, Rudolf Mosny & Embotelladora De Sinaloa. *Exhib:* Solo exhib, Rossi Gallery, Morristown, NJ, 83, Mus Puebla, Mex, 91, Mus Fine Arts, Toluca, Mex, 92 & San Miguel De Allende, GTO, British Am Mus, Mexico, 2008; Latin Am Art, Ger & Austria, 88; Biennal-Humour & Satire, Gabravo, Bulgaria, 89; Rafael Matos Gallery, Mex, 90; 2n Bienal, Mus de Monterrey; Museo de Historia Natural, Mex, DF, 2000 & Grupo de Los 100, Mex, DF; Mus City, Leon, Queretaro, Mex, 99; Pablo Goebel Fine Arts, Mex, DF, 2003; and others. *Pos:* Bd Dir, British Am Mus, Mexico. *Awards:* Prize in Graphics, Nebr Reg Competition, 48; Delta Phi Delta; Purchase Prize, Bienal, Gabrovo, Bulgaria, 88. *Bibliog:* Jorge J Crespo de la Serna (auth), article, Novedades, 3/30/76; Berta Taracena (auth), article, Tiempo, 5/24/82; John Maxim (auth), www.herald.com, Int Ed, The Miami Herald, 9/7/2003 & www.mexiconews.com.mx; Ricardo Pacheco Colin (auth), article, Cronica, 3/13/2004; Vicky Cowel (auth), article, The Herald, Mex, 1/31/2006; Dauido Marlow (auth), photo, Archit Digest, 135, 8/2006; Sylvia Navarrete, Revistai, Octubre, 2000. *Mem:* SOMART; Foro de Arte Contemporanio. *Media:* Acrylic, Pen & Ink. *Interests:* Reading, building houses, travel & family. *Dealer:* Sibley 75 St Mark Pl #3 New York NY 10003; Pablo Goebel Fine Arts Mexico DF. *Mailing Add:* Tulipan 359 Col El Toro Contreras Mexico 10610 DF Mexico

CLEMENT, SHIRLEY
PAINTER
b New York, NY July 7, 1922. *Study:* Ringling Sch Art, two yrs; Amagansett Art Sch, Sarasota, Fla, two yrs. *Work:* Univ Fla, Gainesville; Davenport Munic Gallery, Iowa; Henry Ward Ranger Fund, NY. *Exhib:* Am Watercolor Soc, Nat Acad, NY, 50-; Watercolor Show, Phoenix Mus, 68; Winterpark Sidewalk Art Festival, Fla, 71; Disneys Festival of the Masters, Lake Buena Vista, Fla, 74; Nat Acad Show, NY & High Mus, 74; Allied Artists, Nat Arts Club, NY, 74. *Awards:* Salmagundi Award, Am Watercolor Soc, 69; William A Paton Award, Nat Acad Design, 74; Verda Karen McCracken Young Award, Am Watercolor Soc, 77. *Mem:* Am Watercolor Soc; Fla Artist Group; Fla Watercolor Soc; Sarasota Art Asn; Manatee Art League. *Media:* Watercolor, Acrylic. *Publ:* Auth, article on The watercolor page, Am Artist, 4/48. *Mailing Add:* PO Box 5771 Sarasota FL 34277-5771

CLEMENTE, JOANN P
PAINTER, CONSULTANT
Study: Univ Tampa, Arts Mgmt & Painting Concentration, Fla; NY Sch Interior Design, 83; Barbizon Sch, Forest Hills, NY, 84; Internship, Plant Hall Mus. *Work:* Restoration of Religious Statues, St Columbkille Church, Ft Myers, Fla. *Comn:* Painting, World Reknown Scuba Diver, Bruno Cherubini, Rome, Italy, 97; painting, rep to President Clinton, Washington, DC, 98. *Pos:* Interior decorator, sales, Nebr Furniture & Belmont Furniture, Tampa, Fla; Designer of jewelry & motifs, Ft Myers, Fla, currently; Art consult to prestigious galleries. *Mem:* Am Soc Portrait Painters. *Media:* Acrylic, Oil, Watercolor, Designer. *Mailing Add:* 11110 Caravel Cir #206 Fort Myers FL 33908-3980

CLEMENTS, DAWN
PRINTMAKER
b Woburn, Mass, 1958. *Study:* Brown Univ, BA, 1986; SUNY Albany, MFA, 1989. *Work:* Mus Mod Art; Whitney Mus Am Art; Deutche Bank; Tang Mus; Princeton Univ; Saatchi Collection, London. *Exhib:* Solo exhibs, Rensselaer Polytechnic Inst, NY, 2002, Herter Art Gallery, Univ Mass, 2006, Middlebury Coll Mus Art, Vt, 2006, Allcott Gallery, Univ NC, Chapel Hill, 2007, Potter Gallery, Taft Sch, Watertown, Ct, 2009, Hales Gallery, London, 2010, Acme Los Angeles, Calif, 2010, The Boiler, Pierogi, Brooklyn, NY, 2010, 2011, Sint-Trudoabdij, Male, Belgium, 2011; True North, Miami Int Airport, Fla, 2005; Twice Drawing, Wachenheim Gallery, Tang Mus, Skidmore Coll, 2006; Nieuwe Collectie, Wuyts van Campen Mus, Lier, Belgium, 2007; Contemporary Large-Scale Drawings from the West Collection, Pollock Gallery, Southern Methodist Univ, Dallas, 2009; Whitney Biennial, Whitney Mus Am Art, New York, 2010; Ark Art Ctr, 2012. *Pos:* artist in res, Middlebury Coll, 2000, Farpath Res, Dijon, France, 2004, Taft School, Watertown, Conn, 2009, Sint-Trudoabdij, Male, Belgium, 2011; guest printmaker, Princeton Univ, 2006; critic, RI School Design, Providence, RI, currently. *Teaching:* Lectr, Lewis Ctr for the Arts, Princeton, NJ; visiting faculty, Calif Inst Arts, Valencia, Calif, currently. *Awards:* Art Matters Grant, 1993; Arts Int Grant, Rockefeller Found, 1993; NY Found Arts Fel, 2005; Guggenheim Fel, John Simon Guggenheim Mem Found, 2012. *Bibliog:* Leah Ollman (auth), Fine art, to be seen every day, Los Angeles TImes, 8/13/2004; Jillian Steinhauer (auth), Artist Dawn Clements Draws Big at Williamsburg's Pierogi Gallery, Village Voice, 10/30/2007; Miriam Bale (auth), Melodramatic Interiors: Talking About the Movies with Dawn Clements, L Mag, 5/21/2010. *Dealer:* Pierogi Gallery Brooklyn NY. *Mailing Add:* c/o Pierogi Gallery 177 N 9th St Brooklyn NY 11211-2009

CLEMENTS, ROBERT DONALD
SCULPTOR, EDUCATOR
b Pittsburgh, Pa, Dec 24, 1937. *Study:* Carnegie-Mellon Univ, BFA (painting), 59; Pa State Univ, MA (art), 62, PhD (art educ), 64. *Work:* Nat Mus Am Arts, Smithsonian Inst, Washington; Jacksonville Mus Arts; Chase Manhattan Bank; Coca Cola USA; Georgia Mus Art. *Comn:* Indian Creek MARTA Sta, Atlanta; sculpture, SE Atlanta Park & Recreation Ctr; folk art plazas, Corp Olympic Development, Atlanta; sculpture, Musical Gambol, Los Altos, Calif; sculpture, Isabel Gates Webster Park, Atlanta, 2008. *Exhib:* Solo exhibs, Totems to Southerners & the South, Hunter Mus Art, Montgomery Mus & Asheville Mus; Nat Sculpture, 80; South Exhib, Palazzo Venezia, Rome, 84; Atlanta in France, Sorbonne, Paris & Toulouse, 85. *Pos:* Art consult, Arts & Humanities Prog, US Off Educ, 68-69. *Teaching:* Asst prof art, Ball State Univ, 64-68; assoc prof art, Univ Ga, 69-81, prof art, 81-94, emer prof, 94-. *Awards:* Energy Art Award, 82; Univ Affil Fel, Ga VAP, 86-; Ga Endowment Arts, Artist Grant, 87; Meigs Teaching Award, 93; Atlanta Urban Design Commission, 1997. *Bibliog:* Cynthia Bickley Green (auth), Robert Clements, Art Papers, Vol 10, No 5, 86; Joy Lee (auth), Wood sculpture, Arts/Crafts, spring 80; Charlotte von Glasersfeld (auth), article, Art Papers, 11/83; Barbara Mackenzie (auth), Old & new blend in Clements' sculpture, Atlanta Constitution, 7/22/86. *Mem:* Nat Art Educ Asn; Ga Art Educ Asn; Southern Asn Sculptors; Int Sculpture Ctr. *Media:* Metal. *Res:* art learning, humanities, education. *Interests:* bas-relief sculpture, public art. *Publ:* Auth, The inductive method of teaching visual art criticism, J Aesthetic Educ, 7/79; Modern architecture's debt to creative education, Gifted Child Quart, summer 81; Metaphor in Art Education, Art Educ, 9/82; The inductive method of teaching visual art criticism, J Aesthetic Educ, 7/79; coauth (with Claire Clements), Art and Mainstreaming, Art Instruction for Exceptional Children in Regular Classrooms, Charles C Thomas, 84; Emphasis Art: A Qualitative Art Program for Elementary & Middle School, Pearson Education/Allyn & Bacon,, 1992, 1996, 2001, 2005 & 2009. *Mailing Add:* 155 Bar H Ct Athens GA 30605

CLEVELAND, R. EARL
ADMINISTRATOR, ART RESTORER
b Union, Miss, June 8, 1936. *Study:* Miss Coll, BA; Univ Miss, MFA; Univ Tenn, EdD. *Work:* Univ Miss Fine Arts Ctr, University, Miss; Miss College, Clinton, Miss; Carson-Newman Coll, Jefferson City, Tenn; Univ Miss Alumni Center Coll; E. TN Riverboat Mus; Jefferson Co Hist Soc; Ft Sanders Medical Center; Blair E Batson Children's Hosp; TN First Peoples Bank Coll; Citizens Bank of TN Coll. *Comn:* Redwood sculpture, Carson-Newman Coll, 76; redwood sculpture, First Nat Bank, 85; wood & fibre glass resin sculpture, First People's Bank, 85; Emporium Center, Nat Comp, 2010. *Exhib:* Second Nat Print & Drawing Exhib, Dulin Gallery Art, Knoxville, Tenn, 67; Tenn Watercolor Exhib, Cheekwood Mus, Nashville, 75; Quinlan Ann Art Exhib, Gainesville, Ga, 76; Carroll Reece Mus, Johnson City, Tenn, 77;

Owensboro Mus Fine Arts, Ky, 79; Somerhill Gallery, Durham, NC, 80; Goldsboro Ann Art Exhib, NC, 85; Sacred Arts Seven Exhib, Wheaton, Ill, 85; Whiting Gallery, Fairhope, Ala, 86; Oak Ridge Art Ctr & Mus, Oak Ridge, Tenn, 86; Carson-Newman Coll, 92 & 2007. *Pos:* Artist-illusr, Ling-Temco-Vought Inc, Dallas, Tex, 61-62; retired, 95; art restorer, administrator, educator, currently. *Teaching:* Instr art, Univ Miss, Oxford, 63-64; prof art & chmn dept, Carson-Newman Coll, Jefferson City, 64-95. *Awards:* First Prize Painting, Morristown Art Competition, Tenn, 66 & Macon Ann Arts Exhib, Macon Arts Coun, 73; First Prize Drawing, Oak Ridge Relig Art Exhib, Oak Ridge Art Ctr, Tenn, 76; Second Prize, Centennial Photography Exhib, Knoxville, Tenn, 85; Best in Show, Sacred Arts Seven Exhib, Wheaton, Ill, 85. *Bibliog:* Introduction to Art, B and W Photography, Desktop Publishing; 200 Years in Pictures, TN Valley Pub; Religious Faith in an Artistic Journey, Mossy Creek Pub; A Personal Search for God. *Mem:* Nat Asn Schs Art; Nat Coun Art Adminrs; Southeastern Coll Art Conf; Tenn Watercolor Soc. *Media:* Watercolor, Drawing, Oil, Acrylic. *Res:* Arts administration in higher education, art and law issues. *Interests:* reading, trout fishing, travel. *Publ:* Auth, Art and the Law, 77 & The Art Department Chairperson: An Ambiguous Role, 78, Nat Coun Art Adminrs; The law: Public aid and the private sector, 78 & Art administration in pursuit of efficacy, 83, Fac Studies; Structured Models for Managing Conflict, Fac Studies, Secac Rev 85, An Overview of Professional Opportunities in Art, 87 & Evaluating Student Art: More Than Just Grading, 88; Reflections of Faith in an Artistic Journey, Mossy Creek Publ, 2004. *Mailing Add:* 143 E Old Andrew Johnson Hwy Jefferson City TN 37760

CLIFF, DENIS ANTONY
PAINTER, INSTUCTOR

b Victoria, BC, Aug 8, 1942. *Study:* Univ Victoria, BEd, 65; New Sch Art, 66-67. *Work:* Nat Gallery Can, Art Bank Gallery, Ottawa; Charlottetown Confederation Ctr Arts, PEI; Univ Sask, Saskatoon; Art Gallery Northumberland, Cobourg, Ont. *Comn:* Murals, Ostler Sch Nursing, Toronto, 70, Simcoe Bd Educ, Ont, 71, Eaton Ctr, Toronto, 78 & Fisher-Price, Toronto, 79; Parkdale Focus Mural, Toronto, 92. *Exhib:* New Blood, Rodman Hall Art Ctr, St Catherines, Ont, 73; Can Invitational, Can Consulate, Chicago, 77; Artists Coop Toronto at Nexus, Philadelphia, 78; Explorations, Thames Art Ctr, Chatham, Ont, 80; Toronto Exchange, Mem Univ, St Johns, Nfld, 81; retrospective, Contor Gallery, Toronto, Can, 2000; Sir Sandford Fleming Coll, 2007. *Pos:* Dir, Artist's Co-op, Toronto, 77-82; pres, Arts Sake Inc, 78-80; vpres, Workscene Co-op Gallery, 88-89; prog coordr, Sir Sanford Fleming Coll, 99-. *Teaching:* Artist-in-residence, Canador Coll, North Bay, Ont, 72-74 & Arts Sake, Toronto, 77-79; vis prof, York Univ, Toronto, 79-82; asst prof, Univ Victoria, 82-84; instr, Toronto Sch Art, 85-, steering comt mem, 91-; Sir Sandford Fleming Coll Diploma Prog, 2000-, Visual & Creative Arts Diploma Prog, 2007-. *Awards:* Best Painting, 70 & Best in Show, 71, City Toronto Ann; Can Coun Grant, 79; Ontario Arts Coun Award, 88. *Bibliog:* Sandra Shaul (auth), Altered egos: An exhibition of drawings by Denis Cliff, 77; Diane Pugen (auth), article, 78, Art Mag; Margie Kelk (auth), Denis Cliff: Drawings, 92; Martha Perkins (auth), Cliff changes the way people view paintings, 2006. *Mem:* Royal Can Acad Art. *Media:* Acrylic on Canvas, Drawing on Paper Collage. *Interests:* Film; Food; Reading; Travel. *Dealer:* Contor Galleries 51 Yonge St Toronto Ont Can. *Mailing Add:* 207A Cowan Ave Toronto ON M6K 2N7 Canada

CLIFT, WILLIAM BROOKS
PHOTOGRAPHER

b Boston, Mass, Jan 5, 1944. *Study:* Workshop Paul Caponigro, 59. *Work:* Metrop Mus Art, Mus Mod Art, NY; Art Inst Chicago; Mus Fine Arts, Boston; Nat Gallery, Canberra, Australia; Fogg Art Mus, Yale Univ; Mus Fine Arts, Santa Fe; Libr Congress, Washington, DC; Nat Mus Am Art. *Comn:* Photographs, Old City Hall, Boston, Mass Coun Arts, 70, American Co Courthouses, Joseph Seagrams & Sons, NY, 75-76, American Images, Am Tel & Tel, NY, 78 & Hudson River, Readers Digest Asn, 85-88. *Exhib:* Solo exhibs, Old City Hall, Boston, Worcester Art Mus, Mass, 71, Landscapes, Mus Fine Art, Santa Fe, 79, Phoenix Art Mus, 81, Boston Atheneum, Mass Eclipse Gallery, Boulder, Colo, 83, Bank Santa Fe, NMex & Susan Harder Gallery, NY, 84, Chicago Art Inst, 87 & Amon Carter Mus, Ft Worth, Tex, 87, Gerald Peters Gallery, 2010; Court House, 77, Mirrors and Windows, 78 & Am Landscapes, 81, Mus Mod Art, NY; Counterparts, Metrop Mus Art, NY, 82; Landmarks Reviewed, Pensacola Mus Art, Fla, 83; Western Spaces, Burden Gallery, NY, 85; retrospective, Equitable Gallery, NY, 93. *Awards:* Fels, Nat Endowment Arts, 72 & 79 & Guggenheim Found, 74 & 80. *Bibliog:* Erla Zwingle (auth), Romancing the stones, Am Photogr, 6/87. *Mem:* Charter mem Asn Heliographers; NMex Coun Photog. *Publ:* Coauth, American Images, McGraw-Hill, 79; contribr, American Photographers in the National Parks, Viking, 81; Counterparts-Form and Emotions in Photographs, Metrop Mus Art, 82; Landmarks Reviewed, Pensacola Mus Art, 83; Photographic Viewpoints, Boston Mus Fine Arts, 85; auth, Certain Places, William Clift Eds, 87; A Hudson Landscape, William Clift Eds, 93. *Mailing Add:* PO Box 6035 Santa Fe NM 87502

CLIFTON, MICHELLE GAMM
SCULPTOR, FILMMAKER

b Los Angeles, Calif, July 11, 1944. *Study:* Yale Univ, summer scholar, 65; Univ Ill, Urbana, with Lee Chesney, BFA, 66; Pa State Univ, with Carol Summers, MFA, 68. *Work:* Mus City New York; Los Angeles Co Mus Art; Meany Ctr for Labor Studies, Silver Spring, Md; State Univ NY Col, Potsdam; US Info Agency, Washington, DC. *Comn:* Soft NY Times, comn by Carey Peck, A O Sulzberger at NY Times, 76; Bathroom Faucet (3-D billboard), Pasco Hernando Community Col, Brookville, Fla, 79. *Exhib:* Libr Cong, Washington, DC, 69; Fun & Fantasy, Xerox Ctr, Rochester, NY, 73; Renwick Gallery, Smithsonian Inst, Washington, DC, 74-75; Dayton Art Inst, Ohio, 77; two-person show, Cordy Gallery, NY, 77; Whimsy, Taft Mus & Cincinnati Inst of Fine Arts, 78; one-person shows, Great Am Foot Show, Mus Contemp Crafts, NY, 78 & US Military Acad, West Point, 81; Mus Art, Carnegie Inst, Pittsburgh, 79; and others. *Pos:* Art dir, Hardtimes Movie Co, Garrison, 72-; art dir & vpres, Hudson River Film Co, Garrison, 77-; art dir & production mgr, Henry Hudson's River: A Biography (film), 79. *Teaching:* Asst drawing & printmaking, Pa State Univ, 66-68. *Awards:* Hon Mention as Art Dir, Emmy Winner Christina's World, 77; Cine Golden Eagle Award, 79; Grand Award, Houston Int Film Festival, 79. *Bibliog:* Steven Lindstedt (auth), Soft Sculpture, Family Creative Workshop, 76; Erica Brown (auth), Bunking in a barnyard, New York Times, 12/25/77; Carol Sama (auth), Michelle Gamm Clifton lives in a material world, Houston Home & Garden, 5/77. *Mem:* Am Crafts Coun; Nat Acad TV Arts & Sci. *Media:* Fabric, Stuffing. *Publ:* Illusr series, Gerald Ford's America, San Francisco Pub TV, 75; auth & illusr cover, New York City couch, Art Now Gallery Guide, summer 77

CLIMO, LINDEE
PAINTER, ILLUSTRATOR

b Mass, 1948. *Study:* Univ Ariz, Chico State Coll, Chapman Coll World Campus Afloat. *Work:* Confederation Ctr Art Gallery, Nova Scotia, Robert McLaughlin Gallery, Acadia Univ, Art Gallery Newfoundland & Labrador, Dept External Affairs, Ohawa. *Comn:* Painting for Gov Gen of Canada, commissioned by Province of Prince Edward Island. *Exhib:* Solo exhibs, Confederation Ctr Art Gallery, Prince Edward Island, 78, 80, 82, Nat Gallery Women Arts, 96, Meadows Mus, Dallas, Texas, 97; Group exhibs, Nat Gallery Canada, Ottwa, 76; Woman as Viewer, Winnipeg Art Gallery; Mirror Images, Mit List Gallery, Miami Art Mus; Mus Mod Art, San Francisco, Calif. *Awards:* Amelia Frances Howard-Gibbon Illustrator's Award, 83. *Bibliog:* documentary film, Lindee Climo, CBC, 81; The Art of Lindee Climo, Women inthe Arts, Nat Mus Women Arts Mag, holiday ed, 96; Christopher Mills (auth), art rev Mirrors, Boston Phoenix, 6/11/98. *Media:* Oil. *Interests:* animal husbandry, ox teaming. *Publ:* Auth, Chester's Barn, 83 & Clyde 86, Tundra Books. *Dealer:* Mira Godard Gallery 22 Hazelton Ave Toronto ON Canda M5R 2E2

CLINE, CLINTON C
PRINTMAKER, EDUCATOR

b Granite City, Ill, Oct 21, 1934. *Study:* E Los Angeles Col, AA, 62; Calif State Univ, Long Beach, BA, 65, MA, 68. *Work:* Univ Tex, Irving; Univ SDak; Downey Art Mus, Calif; Palm Springs Mus, Calif; Drake Univ, Des Moines, Iowa. *Exhib:* 15th Joslyn Biennial, Joslyn Art Mus, Omaha, Nebr, 78; 21st Nat Exhib, Okla Art Ctr, Oklahoma City, 79; Univ Tex Nat, Irving, 79; traveling group, Collagraph Problem Solving, 88-90; 16th Harper Coll Nat, 92; 36th Ann, Unterdon Art Ctr, 92. *Collection Arranged:* 1975 Governor's Awards for the Arts and Humanities, 75; In Their Own Image, Southern Conn State Col, 76. *Teaching:* Lithography, Univ Colo, Boulder, 69-, full prof, currently. *Awards:* Purchase Awards, Los Angeles Printmaking Soc, 79 & Vermillion Nat Print & Drawing, 79. *Bibliog:* Leonard Edmundson (auth), Etching, Van Nostrand Reinhold, 73; Eldon L Cunningham (auth), biog, A Primary Form of Expression. *Media:* Lithography, Intaglio. *Publ:* Publisher, First National Colorado Print and Drawing, 74; Border to Border print publ, Univ SDak, Univ Colo, Univ Neb, Univ Minn; Int Juried, Univ SDak; First Nat Printmaking Slides & Video Exchange, E C Cunningham. *Dealer:* One Over One Denver CO. *Mailing Add:* 10909 Patterson Ct Denver CO 80234-3945

CLINTON, PAUL ARTHUR
PRINTMAKER, INSTRUCTOR

b Salem, Ore, 1942. *Study:* Ore State Univ, BA, 68; Tamarind Lithography Workshop, master printer, 70; Univ SFla, MFA, 77. *Work:* Mus Mod Art, NY; Brooklyn Mus; Pasadena Art Mus, Calif; Tex Technol Univ, Lubbock; Gruenwald Graphics Art Found, Univ Calif, Los Angeles. *Comn:* Sculpture, City of Tacoma, 84. *Exhib:* Univ Wis, Madison, 75; Univ Dallas, Irving, 75; State Capitol Mus, Olympia, Wash, 78; Brooklyn Mus, 79; Okla Art Ctr, Oklahoma City, 81; Wash Painting & Sculpture, 83; and others. *Collection Arranged:* Collaboration, Prints by Major Am Artists, Tacoma Art Mus, 81. *Pos:* Master printer, Tamarind Lithography Workshop, Los Angeles, 69-70; master printer, Gemini, Los Angeles, 70; master printer, Cirrus Ed, Los Angeles, 70-71; master printer, Graphicstudio, Univ SFla, Tampa, 71-76; proprietor, Arch Press. *Teaching:* Asst prof, Univ SFla, Tampa, 71-76; instr, Pierce Col, Tacoma, Washington, 77-. *Awards:* Printers Fel & Ford Found, 69. *Mem:* NW Print Coun; World Print Coun. *Media:* Lithography, Intaglio. *Publ:* Contribr, Printmaking: History and Process, Holt, Rinehart, Winston, 78; contribr, Graphic Studio, National Gallery of Art, Prestel

CLOSE, FRANK
STAINED GLASS ARTIST, SCULPTOR

b Dec 28, 1947. *Study:* Univ Ky, BA, 71; stained glass with Casey Lewis & Peter Mollica, Berkeley, Calif, 75; glass design with Kenneth van Roenn, Univ Ky, 76 & Ludwig Schaffrath, Berkeley, Calif, 77; glass painting with Albinas Elskus, Washington, DC, 78; hot glass with Fred Mercer, Louisville Sch Art, Ky. *Comn:* entry piece, Oliver Wendell Holmes Libr, Phillips Acad, Andover, Mass, 89; lead & glass piece (5' x 5'), Costain Group, Lexington, Ky, 90; two works, (73″ x 94″ each), Office Ctr, Short Hills, NJ, 90; Totem MCMXCI, IBM Data Ctr, Rochester, NY, 91; Suspended Construction, Minn Percent Arts, Alexandria, 92. *Exhib:* Wood & Glass, 86 & Crafts Invitational, 87, Southeastern Ctr for Contemp Art, Winston-Salem, NC; Glass Invitational, Ind Univ Southeast, New Albany, 86; Glasswork, Ky Art & Craft Gallery, Louisville, 87; group shows, Triangle Gallery, Lexington, Ky, 88 & John Davis Gallery, NY, 88; 2e Salon Int du Vitrail 1989, Chartres, France. *Pos:* Cur, Waller Gallery exhibs, Lexington, Ky, 79-82; Henry Faulkner, Opera House Gallery, Lexington, Ky, 82; lectr, many univ & mus. *Teaching:* Instr, Univ Ky, Lexington, 70-83. *Bibliog:* Contemporary glass (catalog), Louisville Art Gallery, 86; New Work in New York, New Work, winter-spring 86; Glasswork (catalog), Ky Art & Craft Found Gallery, 87. *Mailing Add:* 444 W 6th St Lexington KY 40508

CLOSE, MARY
PAINTER

b Morristown, NJ, Nov 30 1951. *Study:* Coll of New Rochelle, BFA, 1973; Parson's Sch of Design, 1979; Int Ctr of Photog (Pat Blue), 1999. *Collection Arranged:* Wit, Whimpsy & Humor, Castle Gallery, New Rochelle, 1997. *Pos:* Illusr, Kukasiewicz Design & Freelance, 1976-1986. *Awards:* Adriana Brina Award, Pastel Soc of Am,

1991; Beatrice Vare Award, Pastel Soc of Am, 1995; Pastel J Award, Pastel Soc of Am, 2000. *Bibliog:* Tom Nicholas & John Terelak (auths), Best of Oil Painting, Rockport Publs, 1996; Karen Frankel (auth), Mary Close's Significant Still Lifes, Am Artist Mag, 1997; Best of Drawing & Sketching, Rockport Publs, 1998. *Mem:* Pastel Soc of Am. *Media:* Acrylic, Oil, Pastel. *Publ:* Illusr, A Book of Cut Flowers, William Morrow & Co, 1983. *Dealer:* New Arts Gallery (Tony Carretta) 513 Maple St Litchfield CT 06759. *Mailing Add:* PO Box 1496 Lakeville CT 06039

CLOSE, (JOHN) TIMOTHY
MUSEUM DIRECTOR
Study: Ariz State Univ, BFA; Calif Inst Arts, MFA; Mus Mgt Inst, J Paul Getty Trust, Cert. *Work:* Houston Art Mus; Mus Mod Art, New York. *Pos:* Exec dir, Arlington Arts Ctr, Va, formerly, Albany Mus Art, Ga, 1994-2000, Boise Art Mus, Idaho, 2000-06; dir, Mus Glass, Tacoma, Wash, 2006-. *Mem:* AAM; AAM Accreditation Comt (peer reviewer); Inst Mus & Libr Services (panel reviewer); Asn Art Mus Dirs. *Mailing Add:* Mus Glass 1801 Dock St Tacoma WA 98402-3217

CLOTHIER, PETER DEAN
WRITER, CRITIC
b Newcastle-on-Tyne, Eng, Aug 1, 1936; US citizen. *Study:* Cambridge Univ, Eng, BA & MA; Univ Iowa, PhD. *Work:* Los Angeles Co Mus Art; Univ Southern Calif. *Pos:* Dean Col, Otis Art Inst, 76-79, actg dir, 77-79; dean, Col Fine & Commun Arts, Loyola-Marymount Univ, 81-85. *Teaching:* Asst prof comparative lit, Univ Southern Calif, Los Angeles, 68-76. *Awards:* Dart Award for Acad Innovation, Univ Southern Calif, 72; Art Critics Fel Grant, Nat Endowment for Arts, 76-77; Rockefeller Found Humanities Fel, 80. *Bibliog:* Joseph E Young (auth), Re-evaluating the tradition of the book, Art News, 75; Peter Plagens (auth), Chiaroscuro by Peter Clothier, Art in Am, 86; Rebecca Solnit (auth), Dirty-Down by Peter Clothier, Artweek, 87. *Publ:* Auth, Otto Natzler, Am Ceramics, 91; Christos Umbrella Fantasy, Art News, 92; Richard Koshalek, MOCA's Maverick, Art News, 92; David Hockney, Abbeville Modern Masters, Abbeville Press, 94; While I am not Afraid, High Mountain Press, 97

CLOUDMAN, RUTH HOWARD
CURATOR
b Oklahoma City, Okla, June 11, 1948. *Study:* Washington Univ, St Louis, BA, 70; Bryn Mawr Col, Pa, MA, 73. *Pos:* Asst cur, Joslyn Art Mus, Omaha, Nebr, 73-75, chief cur, 75-78; guest cur, Sheldon Gallery, Univ Nebr, Lincoln, 78-79; assoc, Newhouse Galleries, New York, 80-84; sr cur, Portland Art Mus, 84-90; chief cur, Mary & Barry Bingham, sr cur Europ & Am Art, J B Speed Art Mus, Louisville, 90-. *Mem:* Coll Art Asn; Am Asn Mus. *Res:* Early 20th century modernism; contemporary art. *Publ:* Preston Dickinson, 1889-1930 (exhib catalog), Sheldon Mem Art Gallery, Univ Nebr, 79-80; Perspectives 4: Cindy Sherman (exhib catalog), Portland Art Mus, 86; Frederick Bridgman, The Funeral of a Mummy, Am Art Rev, summer 92; In Pursuit of Excellence: The Wendell and Dorothy Cherry Collection (exhib catalog), J B Speed Art Mus, 94; The Speed Art Museum: Highlights of the Collection (bk), 2007. *Mailing Add:* J B Speed Art Mus 2035 S Third St Louisville KY 40208

CLOUGH, CHARLES SIDNEY
PAINTER
b Buffalo, NY, Feb 2, 1951. *Study:* Pratt Inst, Brooklyn, NY, 69-70; Ontario Coll Art, Can, 71-72. *Work:* Albright-Knox Art Gallery, Buffalo, NY; Everson Mus, Syracuse, NY; Brooklyn Mus, NY; Dayton Art Inst, Ohio; Indianapolis Mus Art; Newport Art Mus, 2003; Blanton Mus Art, Austin, Tex; Nat Gallery Art, Wash, DC; Smithsonian Am Art Mus, Wash DC; Mus Contemp Art, Los Angeles; Delaware Art Mus, Wilmington, Del; Eastman House, Rochester, NY; High Mus Art, Atlanta, Ga; Hood Mus Art, Hanover, NH; Fogg Art Mus, Boston, Mass; Joslyn Art Mus, Omaha, Nebr; Metrop Mus Art, New York; Miami Mus Art, Miami, Fla; Milwaukee Mus Art, Milwaukee; Yale Univ Art Gallery, New Haven, Conn; and others. *Comn:* Mural, Niagra Frontier Transportation Authority, 84; video, Music Television Network, 85; Sony Corp, 92. *Exhib:* Solo Exhibs: Brooklyn Mus, NY, 85 & 94; aleria Peccolo, Livorno, Italy, 86; m Fine Arts Co, New York, 87; Nina Freudenheim Gallery, Buffalo, NY, 88; Scott Hanson Gallery, New York, 90; Burchfield Ctr, State Coll NY, 91; Barbara Gillman Gallery, Miami, 91; State Univ NY at Potsdam, 91; Castellani Art Mus, Niagara Falls, NY, 92; Grand Salon, New York, 93-94 & 99; Galerie Liesbeth Lips, The Neth, 94 & 2000; Newport Art Mus, Newport, RI, 2003; Revival House Western, RI, 2006; Geisai Pulse Fair, Miami, Fla, 2007; Norwich Art Council, Norwich, Conn, 2007, The Way to Cluffalo, Univ Buffalo Art Gallery, 2012, David Findlay Jr Gallery, 2013; The Pictures Generation, Metrop Mus of Art, NY. *Pos:* Co-founder, Hallwalls Inc, Buffalo, NY, 74, pres bd dir, 77-79. *Teaching:* teacher, Columbia Univ, NY, 2001; RI Sch Design, Prov, RI, 2008. *Awards:* Painting Fel, Nat Endowment Arts, 82 & 89; Graphic Artists Fel, Creative Artists Pub Serv Prog, 83; Pollock-Krasner Found Grant, 2008; Gottlieb Found Grant, 2013. *Bibliog:* Carter Ratcliff (auth), Playful redemption, paintings by Charles Clough (catalog essay), State Univ NY, Potsdam, 91; Elizabeth Licata (auth), Charles Clough's dreampix, Art in Am, 7/92; Charles A Riley II (auth), Uncanny likeness-recent paintings by Charles Clough (catalog essay), Grand Salon, 94; Nancy Whipple Grinnell (auth), Newport Folio, Newport Art Mus, 2003; Sandra Q Firmin (auth), The Way to Cluffalo, 2012. *Media:* Mixed. *Publ:* Charles Clough (auth), Pepfog Clufff, 2007. *Dealer:* David Findlay Jr Gallery NY. *Mailing Add:* 124 Thompson St #7 New York NY 10012

CLUTZ, WILLIAM
PAINTER
b Gettysburg, Pa, Mar 19, 1933. *Study:* Mercersburg Acad, 47-51; Univ Iowa, 51-55; Art Student's League, NY, 57. *Work:* Mus Mod Art & Chase Manhattan Bank, NY; Joseph H Hirshhorn Collection, Washington, DC; Fogg Art Mus, Cambridge, Mass; Metrop Mus Art, NY; plus many others. *Comn:* Salomon Bros, NY; 3rd Nat Bank, Dayton, Ohio; Minn Mutual Life Insurance, St Paul; Mobil Corp; and others. *Exhib:* Solo exhibs, Condon Riley Gallery, NY, 59, David Herbert Gallery, NY, 62, Bertha Schaefer Gallery, 63-64, 66 & 69, Triangle Gallery, San Francisco, Calif, 67, Graham Gallery, 72, Brooke Alexander Gallery, NY, 73, NY Stock Exchange, 2002; Pa Acad Fine Arts Ann, Philadelphia, 64-66; Alonzo Gallery, 77- 79; Tatistchaff & Co, NY, 81-82 & 84; John C Stoller Co, Minneapolis, 83; Nicholas Davis Gallery, NY, 97; Katharina Rich Perlow Gallery, NY, 99-2002 & 2005-2006, 2008-2010. *Teaching:* Instr, Parsons Sch Design, New York, 69-95. *Awards:* Distinguished Univ Teaching Award, Parsons Univ Sch Design, NY, 89. *Bibliog:* Of Time and Place: American Figurative Art from the Corcoran Gallery, Smithsonian, Inst, 81; Janice C. Oresman (auth), William Clutz, ARTS Mag, 11/84; Gerrit Henry (auth), Art in America, 2/98. *Mem:* Nat Acad Art (mem). *Media:* Oil, Canvas, Pastel. *Publ:* auth, Five Decades of NY Streets, 2002; auth, Pictorial Overview, 2004. *Dealer:* Katharina Rich Perlow Gallery. *Mailing Add:* Katharina Rich Perlow Fine Arts 40 East 84 St New York NY 10028

CLYMER, ALBERT ANDERSON
PAINTER
b Memphis, Tenn, Feb 16, 1942. *Study:* Tex A&M Univ, with Joseph Donaldson, Napa Coll with Frank Altamura. *Work:* White House, Washington; Newport Mus Mod Art, Calif; Oakland Mus Mod Art, Calif; Berkeley Mus Mod Art, Calif; San Francisco Mus Mod Art, Calif; Levi Straus, San Francisco, Nut Tree, Calif. *Comn:* Ten paintings for Army Recruiting, US Army Reserve, Mountain View, Calif, 77; 30 paintings for Episcopal Homes Found, Santa Rosa, Calif, 77; 20 Abstract Indian Forms, Shorebirds, Tiburor, Calif, 87. *Exhib:* Dallas Mus Fine Arts, Tex, 65; Depot Gallery, Yountville, Calif, 90; Shore Birds, Tiburon, Calif, 90; Mesa Gallery, San Francisco, 90; Blue Heron Gallery, Yountville, Calif, 94; Mondavi Winery, Oakville, Calif, 94; plus 224 solo exhibs. *Pos:* Bd dir, Depot Gallery, Yountville, Calif, Blue Heron Gallery, Yountville, Calif, 93. *Teaching:* Instr, Experimental acrylic tech on paper & masonite, Blue Heron Gallery, 94. *Awards:* First Prize in Mod Oil, Vintage 76 Int, 68 & Santa Rosa Statewide Ann, 71 & 72. *Bibliog:* Stephens (auth), Albert Anderson Clymer, La Rev Mod, Paris, 66 & 74; Paul Gillette (auth), The Single Man's Indispensable Guide Handbook, Playboy Press, 73; Artist of Northern California, Mountain Publ, 89. *Mem:* Berkeley Arts Crafts Coop. *Media:* Acrylic on Masonite, Paper. *Publ:* Illusr, Oakland Redevelopment Agency's Annual Report, Abby Press, 66; Bodega Bay, Nut Tree, 75; (catalog), Works by Albert Anderson Clymer, Arlene Lind Gallery, 78. *Dealer:* Naked Horse Gallery 4151 N Marshall Way Suite B Scottsdale AZ 85251; Shore Birds On The Boardwalk Tiburon CA 94920

COATES, ANN S
CURATOR, PHOTOGRAPHER
b Louisville, Ky. *Study:* Univ Louisville, BA, 63, MA, 69; New York Sch Interior Design, Cert, 65; Arrowmont Sch Arts Crafts, Tenn. *Work:* Brown-Forman Distillers Corp; James G Brown Regional Cancer Ctr; Actors' Theatre Louisville; Kentucky Fried Chicken, Brown & Williamson. *Exhib:* China Triptych, Speed Mus, Louisville, Ky; Paper 90, Headley-Whitney Mus, Lexington, Ky; Southeast 81 Craft Competition, Lemoyne Art Found, Tallahassee; Thread and Fiber, Alexandria Mus, La; Handmade Paper Nat Invitational, Liberty Gallery, Louisville; Paradigms of Perserverence, Louisville Visual Art Asn; and others. *Collection Arranged:* Edward Weston 1958-1968, 68; Kentucky Threads, Louisville Art Gallery. *Pos:* Cur slides, Univ Louisville, 69-. *Teaching:* Instr mod art, Univ Louisville, 69-; lectr, Univ Ky, Lexington & Louisville Craftsmen's Guild. *Awards:* Bronze Medal, Great Quilts of America, Good Housekeeping, 78; Ky Found for Women Grant. *Bibliog:* Sarah Lansdell (auth), Paper works show uncovers artist's passion for the medium, The Courier, 7/20/80; Karen Hisle (auth), Ann Coates mixes work with pleasure, Scripps-Howard Press, 7/9/80; Fiber Arts Design Book, Hasting House, 80. *Mem:* Coll Art Asn; Art Libr Soc NAm; Soc Archit Historians. *Media:* Fiber. *Res:* Paper Conservation; preservation; women artists. *Publ:* The Female Image in the Nineteenth Century (film), Univ Louisville, Women's Studies Ctr, 78. *Mailing Add:* 1819 Woodbourne Ave Louisville KY 40205-2147

COATES, ROSS ALEXANDER
HISTORIAN, PAINTER
b Hamilton, Ont, Nov 1, 1932. *Study:* Univ Mich; Art Inst Chicago, BFA; NY Univ, MA & PhD. *Work:* Finch Col; Univ Calif, Berkeley; Univ Alta; State Univ NY, Stonybrook; NY Univ; and others. *Exhib:* Whatcom Mus, Bellingham, 83; Space Gallery, Los Angeles, 84; Northwestern Artists Workshop, Portland Ore, 85; Art Gallery Hamilton, Ont, Can, 88; Some Assembly Required, Bumbershoot, Seattle, Wash, 89; Solo exhibs, Thirteen Whirlwinds (installation), Gallery II, Wash State Univ, Pullman, WA, 90, Northview Gallery, Portland Community Coll, Ore, 90, Fisher Gallery, Cornish Sch Art, Seattle, 91, & UOP Gallery, McCaffrey Ctr, Univ Pacific, Stockton, Calif, 92, Getting From One Place, Fine Arts Ctr, Port Angeles, Wash, 91, Dreamtime, Pritchard Gallery, Univ Idaho, Moscow, 92; Sun Valley Ctr Arts, Idaho, 91; Storie Naturali, Artists' Books, Genoa, Italy, 91; Come to Your Senses, collaborative pieces with Marilyn Lysohir, Bellevue Art Mus, Wash, 91; Dreams and Shields, Salt Lake Art Ctr, Utah, 92; Inter, Kunsthalle, Holstebro, Denmark, 92; Installation with Marilyn Lysohir: Secrets of an Ancient Heart, SPF Rodovre, Denmark, 94; Installation: Hunting, Salt Lake Art Ctr, 94. *Teaching:* Art tutor, Canon Lawrence Col, Uganda, EAfrica, 68-70; prof dept fine arts, Wash State Univ, 77-. *Awards:* Idaho Arts Comn Artists Grant, 90 & 94. *Media:* Oil. *Res:* Non-Western art, particularly Africa; occult and how it relates to contemp art. *Publ:* Ed, Some Thoughts on the Problems of Artists in Contemporary Africa, J African Studies, Univ Calif, LosAngeles, 78; Gard Okello in Six Artists, African Arts, Univ Calif, Los Angeles, 79; Gods Among Us: American Indian Masks, State Univ San Diego, 90. *Mailing Add:* Wash State Univ Dept Fine Arts Pullman WA 99164-7450

COBB, VIRGINIA HORTON
PAINTER, LECTURER
b Oklahoma City, Okla, Nov 23, 1933. *Study:* William Schimmel, Ariz, 1966; Community Col, Denver, 1967; Edgar Whitney, NY City, 1966; Univ Colo, 1967; Chen Chi, NY City, 1974. *Work:* Foothills Art Ctr, Golden, Colo; Nat Acad of Design, NY; NMex Watercolor Soc, Albuquerque; St Lawrence Univ, Canton, NY; NM Mus

Art, Albuquerque, NM; Mus Fine Arts, Santa Fe, NM. *Exhib:* Am Watercolor Soc, Nat Acad Galleries, NY, 73-85; Butler Inst Am Art, Youngstown, Ohio, 75; Nat Acad Design, NY, 78-85; San Bernadino Co Mus, 78; Nat Watercolor Invitational, 81; one-person exhib, Stuhr Mus, Grand Island, Nebr, 82; and others; Jung Ctr Invitational, Houston, Tex, 2009. *Teaching:* Lectr & demonstr, Emphasis-KRDO Channel 13, Colorado Springs, Colo, 77; instr, Crafton Hills Col Master Seminars, Yucaipa, Calif, 77, 78 & 81; instr, Univ Alaska, Anchorage, 81; lectr & demonstr, Pub Broadcasting Serv, KAKM, Anchorage, 81; Master Class/Santa Fe Painting Workshops/Friedman Cobb Studios, 1989-; guest lectr, Watermedia 2000; Houston; lectr, Station KRDO-TV, 1977, Francis Marion Col, Florence, 1981, Station KAKM, Anchorage, 1981. *Awards:* Walter Biggs Mem Award, Nat Acad Design, 78 & 81; High Winds Medal, 81; Silver Medal Honor, Am Watercolor Soc, 83; Adolph & Clara Obrig Prize, 85; Am Artist Achievement award, 1994. *Bibliog:* Southwest Art Mag, 11/79; Todays Art Mag, 3/79; Houston Home & Garden, 2/80. *Mem:* Nat Acad Design (assoc, 78, acad, 94); Dolphin fel Am Watercolor Soc; Watercolor USA Honor Soc; Rocky Mountain Watermedia Asn. *Media:* Mixed Watermedia; Graphics. *Publ:* Contribr, Am Artist Mag, 1/79

COBURN, BETTE LEE
PAINTER
b Chicago, Ill, July 31, 1922. *Study:* Grinwell Col, Iowa; Chicago Art Inst; Univ NC. *Work:* Fed Reserve Bank, Charlotte, NC; SC Arts Comn, State Art Col, Columbia; Greenville Co Mus Arts, SC; Univ SC, Columbia; Univ Ga, Athens. *Comn:* Painting, comn by Pres, Ivey's, Greenville, SC, 62; city seal, Greenville City Bd, SC, 65; painting, First Fed Bank, Henderson, NC, 68; State Governor's Comt, Columbia, SC 69; Astro Theatre's I & II, Greenville, SC, 73. *Exhib:* Atlanta High Mus Art, Ga, 69; Nat USA Travelling Exhib Oils, London Pub Art Mus, Ontario, 70; 23rd Grand Prix Int, Deuville Expo Mus, France, 72; retrospective, SC State Mus, Columbia, 88; Greenville Co Art Mus, SC, 88; Florence Mus Art, SC, 89; Invitational Exhib, State Mus Art, Columbia, SC, 89; Art's Symposium 2nd Exhib, Greenville Co Mus, SC, 89. *Teaching:* Instr painting, Greenville Co Art Mus Sch, 65-83. *Awards:* Selected for Artworks, McCormick Arts Coun, 92; Selected 10,000 Plus Exhib, Sch Art Inst Chicago, 94; Selected Invitational Exhib, SC Governor's Sch Arts, 94. *Bibliog:* Rene Borel (auth), Le Semaines International de La Femme, 69; Jack A Morris (auth), 39 Contemporary Artists of SC, 70; Elizabeth Montgomery (auth), Poet without words, Greenville Woman Mag, 5/87. *Mem:* Greenville Mus Art Sch (chmn, educ comt, 61-62); Greenville Artists Guild (pres, 65); Nat Asn Women Artists (mem comt, 70); SC State Arts Comn (selection comt, 74 & 75); SC State Artists Guild (pres, 81). *Media:* Oils & Acrylics; Mixed Media. *Dealer:* Hampton III Gallery 10 Gallery Ctr Taylors SC 29687. *Mailing Add:* 31 Harvest Ln Greenville SC 29601

COBURN, RALPH (M H)
PAINTER
b Minneapolis, Minn, Aug 10, 1923. *Study:* Mirski Art Sch, with Esther Geller, Carl Nelson, Barbara Swan & John Wilson, 46-49; Mass Inst Technol, 47; Acad Julian, 50. *Work:* Stedlijk Mus, Amsterdam; Mus Mod Art, Caracas, Venezuela; Brockton Art Mus, Mass; Chase Manhattan Bank, NY; Smithsonian Inst. *Exhib:* Mass Inst Technol, 54 & 76; Mirsks Gallery, 55; Alpha Gallery, 69 & 80; West End Gallery, Gloucester, Mass, 96; Alpha Gallery, 96. *Media:* Oil, Acrylic; Pen and Ink, Watercolor. *Dealer:* Alpha Gallery 14 Newbury St Boston MA 02116

COCCHIARELLI-BERGER, MARIA GIOVANNA
PAINTER, MURALIST
b Brooklyn, NY, Apr 10, 1956. *Study:* Syracuse Univ, NY, BA (art hist), 1978; Queens Col, CUNY, MS (art ed), 1985, MFA, 2004. *Hon Degrees:* Queens Col, BFA, 85. *Work:* Sprint Contemp Art Col, Overland Park, Kan; Hallmark Contemp Art Col, Kansas City, Mo; Manelst Mus, Oslo, Norway; Wyo State Mus, Cheyenne; Omaha Children's Mus, Nebr; Mus Friends, Walsenburg, Colo; mural, Rainbow Pet Hospital, Kansas City, Kansas, 2001; Asian Am Arts Ctr, New York. *Comn:* Interior Tile Installation, Sites for the students publ art, Bronx, NY, 1991-92; 6 interior banners, World, NYC School Construc Auth, Bronx, NY, 1992-93; mural, Struggle, Socrates Sculpture Park, Long Island City, NY, 1993; art garden, Art of Envi, Wyo Alliance Arts Ed, Laramie, 1996; art garden, Art of Envi, Gem Theater Jazz Mus, Kansas City Mo, 1999. *Exhib:* Metamorphosis of a Butterfly, Penn State Zolar Gal & Travel, Pa, 1991; Visual Aids: Positive Action, Clock Tower Mus, New York City, 1991; Self-Images of Wyo Artists, Wyo Arts Council, (traveled thru stat), 1994; Woman The Artist's View, Bennington Ctr for Arts, Vt, 1995; Reinventing the Emblem, Yale, Univ Art Gal, New Haven, Conn, 1995; Wyo Artists, Nicolaysen Art Mus, Casper, 1996; H2O Works on Paper, Manêlyst Mus, Oslo, Norway, 1999; Leedy Volkos Invitational, Kansas City, Mo,1999; State of the Art Gallery, Kansas City, Mo, 2000; Digital Sandbox Gallery, NY, 2004-2005; Permanent Collection exhib, Mus of Friends, 2007, Mus of Friends, Eddie Dominquez, Tierra Culture, 2009, Mus of Friends, Cocchiarelli-Berger, Berger-Cocchiarelli, 2009, Mus of Friends, Walsenburg, Colo, 2009; Brendt Berger Monumental Paintings/Linda Fleming Wood Sculptures form 1988-1992, Peggy Zehring in process, Mus Friends, Walsenburg, Colo, 2010. *Collection Arranged:* Freeing The Angel From The Stone (sculpture) (auth, catalog), Attilio Piccirilli, 2005; Sicilian Journey (photographs) (auth, catalog), Janine Coyne, 2006; Identity Theft (auth, catalog), Antonio Petracca, 2006; Painting Up the Town (auth, catalog), Ital Am Mus, 2006; Not Paved with Gold (auth, catalog), Vincenzo Pietropaolo, 2007; Diorbhail Cameron Cetic Reflections, 2008. *Pos:* ed cur, Unv Wyo Art Mus, 1993-96; prog dir, Grand Arts, Kansas City, Mo, 1997-98; cur collec, Italian Am Mus, New York City, 2004-; co-founder, Mus of Friends, Walsenburg, Colo, 2007-. *Teaching:* instr, watercolor & art hist, Kansas City Art Inst, 1998-2000 (summer); muralist mural painting, Mo Arts Coun Statewide, 1999-2000; adj prof art visual, Kean Univ, Union, NJ, 2004-05; painting instr, summer children prog, Space Gallery, Laveta, Colo, 2009. *Awards:* Emerging Artist Award, Ollantay Gal, Asn Queens Artists, 1984; Fellowship Award, Vt Studio Colony Artists, 1988; Best in Show, Culture Without Borders, Affil Group, 1998. *Bibliog:* Tom FinKelpearl, Michele Cohen (auth), Art for Learning, Municipal Art Soc, 1994; Liliane Francuz (auth), Self Images of Wyo Artists, Wyo Arts Coun, 1995; Lesley K. Baier (ed), Reinventing the Emblem, Yale Univ Press, 1995. *Mem:* Am Asn Mus. *Media:* Oil, Acrylic, Watercolor, All Print Media. *Res:* Contemp Ital Am Artists in the market place. *Interests:* Developing a new mus in Southern Colo called: Mus of Friends, Walsenburg, Colo. *Publ:* Not Paved with Gold (auth, catalog), Vincenzo Pietropaolo's Photographs, 2007; Painting Up the Town (auth, catalog), 2006; Identity-Theft, Antonio Petracca (auth, catalog), 2006, Janine Coyne (auth, catalog), Photographs; Freeing the Angel from the Stone (auth, catalog), The Work of the Piccirilli Brothers, 2005. *Dealer:* Jane St. Lifer 140 Riverside Blvd New York NY 10069. *Mailing Add:* PO Box 301 Gardner CO 81040

COCHRAN, DOROTHY PARCELLS
PRINTMAKER, CURATOR
b Teaneck, NJ, Aug 4, 1944. *Study:* Montclair Univ, BA, 66, MA, 70; Sch Arts, Columbia Univ, MFA, 84; studied with Bob Blackburn, Anthony Harrison, Roberto DeLamonica, John Ross, Claire Romano, kathy Caraccio, Michael Mazur & Jane Wilson. *Work:* Zimmerli Mus, Rutgers Univ; Ga Mus Fine Arts; Mus Mod Art Libr, NY; New York Pub Libr; Bristol-Myers-Squibb, Princeton, NJ; Free Libr Philadelphia; Prudential Life Insurance; Coopers & Lybrand Siemans Corp; Public Service Electric & Gas Co; Delta Dental Plan; Educational Testing Services; Valley Hospital, NJ; Newark Public Lib; Columbia Univ. *Comn:* Design Harmony, principal, Gail Lindsey, Wake Forest, NC. *Exhib:* 37th Boston Printmakers Nat, Rose Art Mus, Brandeis Univ, 85; Selections, Artists Space, NY, 86; NJ Arts Ann: Printmaking & Photog, NJ State Mus, Trenton, 89; Editions: The 1st 5 years-An Artist Book Collaboration, Newark Mus, 94; The Guardians, The Ctr Gallery, Demarest, NJ, 94; A View of One's Own, Jane Voohees, Zimmerli Mus, New Brunswick, NJ, 94; UMA Gallery, NYC; Nicholas Harrison Gallery, Mass; Truro Center Arts, Castle Hill, Mass; Franklin 54, NY, 2008; UMA Gallery, NY 2008; Provincetown Art Mus, Mass, 2009; The Art Mus State Univ Minn, 2010; Ctr Contemporary Printmaking, Norwalk, Conn, 2011; Printmaking Ctr, Branchburg, NJ, 2011; Po Kim Gallery, NY, 2011, 2012; Art Connection, George Segal Gallery, Montclair State Univ, 2011, Pressing Matters, Montclair Art Mus, Yard Sch Art, 2012; 40 Yrs of Women Artists, Douglass Lib, Inst of Women and Art, New Brunswick, NJ, 2012; Belskie Mus, Closter, NJ, 2012; NAWA, 310 Art Gallery, Ashville, NC, 2013; 10077 Bau Gallery, Beacon, NY, 2013; The Way in, Left Bank, Gallery, Wellfleet, Mass, 2013; Red, A Gallery, Provincetown, Mass, 2013; 4 Great Printmakers, Castle Hill Gallery, Truro, Mass, 2013. *Collection Arranged:* Toshiko Takaezu installation, Moon Series, 2009; Print Matrix, revealing the layers, Montclair Pub Libr, Montclair, NJ, 2010; The Interchurch Center, NYC. *Pos:* Dir & cur, The Galleries at the Interchurch Ctr, NY, 86-2009. *Teaching:* Asst prof printmaking, Columbia Univ, NY, 83-84 & City Univ NY, 85-86; printmaking chr, Old Church Cult Ctr, School of Art, NJ, 88-; vis artist, Southwest Crafts Ctr, San Antonio, Tex, 94; Castle Hill Center for the Arts, Truro, Mass, 94-; Fac, Montclair Art Mus, Yard Sch Art, 2010-; presenter, 5th, 7th Int Encaustic Conf, Provincetown, Mass, 2011; workshops in art venues around the country; Silvermine Ctr Arts, 2013; Manhattan Graphics Ctr, NYC. *Awards:* Fel, NJ State Coun Arts in Printmaking & Mixed Media, 82 & 85; Jane Turner Mem Award, Nat Asn Women Artists Ann, 92 & Esther Gayner Mem Award, 94; Shikler Prize, Nat Acad Design. *Bibliog:* Kay Larson (auth), Selections from the artist file, Artist Space, 9/85; William Zimmer (auth), High spirits in Montclair, New York Times, 1/19/86; Dan Cameron (auth), The old back & forth, Arts Mag, 2/86; Byron Coleman (auth), Gallery and Studio, June, July, Aug, 2006. *Mem:* Coll Art Asn; Nat Asn Women Artists (bd mem, 2010-); Studio Montclair (bd mem). *Media:* Printmaking, Drawing, Painting, Mixed Media, Collage, All Media, Encaustic. *Specialty:* contemporary art. *Mailing Add:* 13 Galena Rd Little Falls NJ 07424

COCKER, BARBARA JOAN
PAINTER, GALLERY DIRECTOR
b Uxbridge, Mass, Oct 16, 1923. *Study:* Becker Col, 43; Mt St Mary Col, 45; NY Sch Interior Design, 68. *Work:* Central Jersey Bank & Trust, Rumson, NJ; Midlantic Bank, Edison, NJ; President's House, Monmouth Col, West Long Branch, NJ; Riverview Hospital, Red Bank, NJ; First Union Bank, NJ; Frist Union Bank, Rumson, NJ. *Comn:* Ocean paintings, comn by Judge William Kirkpatrick, Rumson, NJ, 69; ship painting, comn by William Crawford, Singer Island, Fla, 70; ocean paintings, comn by Dr J Putnam Brodsky, Rumson, NJ, 70; sea marsh painting, comn by Daniel Riley, Greenwich, Conn, 92; mural sea painting, comn by Nancie B Taylor, Montecito, Calif. *Exhib:* Catharine L Wolfe Club, Nat Acad, NY, 70; Solo exhibs, Guild Creative Artists, NJ, 76, 94 & 95, Nantucket Art Asn, 88, 91 & 95, Monmouth Co Libr, NJ, 91, 95 & 99, Art Alliance, Red Bank, NJ, 92, Captiva Island Civic Ctr, Fla, 94, 97, Pen & Brush Club, NY 96, Sun Trust Bank, Fla, 97, PNC Bank, NJ, 97; Monmouth Beach Cult Ctr, NJ, 2000, 01 & 03. *Pos:* Pres, owner & dir, Paintings of the Sea Gallery, Nantucket, Mass, 75-98. *Teaching:* Pvt instr sea painting. *Awards:* Woman of the Year, Zonta Int, 83; Spec Award, Pen & Brush Club, NY, 84; Blue Ribbon, Monmouth Arts Gallery, NJ, 92 & 94; Best in Show, Mammouth, Arts, NJ, 95, 01 & 03. *Bibliog:* Capturing the surf, Art & Antiques, 89; Nino Marini (ed), Profile of the sea, Captiva Chronicle, 92; Stella Farwell (auth), Sea creativity, Captiva Current, 94. *Mem:* Coast Guard Arts Program. *Media:* Acrylic on Canvas. *Res:* sea poetry. *Specialty:* painting of the sea. *Interests:* sea. *Publ:* Prayer for Nantucket, 96; The Sea Around Me (feature article), Becker Coll Alumnis Magazine, Warcester, Ma, 71 & 05. *Mailing Add:* PO Box 1376 Nantucket MA 02554-1376

COCKRILL, SHERNA
PAINTER, INSTRUCTOR
b Chicago, Ill. *Study:* Univ Ark, BA & MA; Malden Bridge Sch Art, 67 & 68; also study with R V Goetz, 65-69; with Albert Handell, 80-81. *Work:* Smithsonian Inst Archives Am Art, Washington, DC; Ozark Art Ctr, Springdale; Nat Mus Women Arts, Washington, DC; Mid-Am Mus, Hot Springs, Ark. *Comn:* Many portrait comn. *Exhib:* Greater New Orleans Nat Exhib, 73; Tex Fine Arts Asn Ann, Austin, 73-74; Governor's Distinguished Artists Exhib, 76; Five State, Univ Ark, 79-83; Art Expo '83, Dallas; Laguna Gloria Mus Austin, Tex Fiesta Exhib, 84, 86; Sequoya Exhib

(Univ Ark), 80-86; Easton Rooms, Rye, E Sussex, Eng, 87; Romney Bay Gallery, Kent, Eng, 87; Gov Collection, Ark, 95; Ark Artists Registry Invitational, 96; Faberge Competitive Exhib, 96; Solo exhibs: Arts Ctr Ozarks, Ark, 97; Walton Arts Ctr, Ark, 98; Sager Creek Arts Ctr, Siloan Springs, Ark, 2000; Eighteenth & Nineteenth Nat Womens juried exhib, League Am Penwomen at the Walton Art Ctr, 2001-2002; WRMC Found Permanent collection (2 paintings), 8/2002; Cent Ark Libr System, Arts Ctr Ozarks, 7/2002; 12 th Annual Fall Regional exhib, 2005, Salon Int,San Antonio, Tex, 5/2006; and others. *Teaching:* Instr oil painting, Ozarks Arts Ctr, 72-75; also pvt classes. *Awards:* Grand Prize, Arkansas State Festival Art, 73; First Prize in Art, Little Rock Ten State Arts Fair, State of Ark, 73; Top Award Ark Festival Art, 73 & 74 & Top Award Ark Festival & Art Invitational, 75; 5 State Competitive Award for Sequoia, Univ Ark, 86; 2d Prize, Greater New Orleans Nat. *Mem:* Ozark Artists & Craftsmen (bd dir, 75-). *Media:* Oil, Acrylic. *Specialty:* The New Realism; Rivermarket and Boswell. *Publ:* Auth, Women artists in mid-USA, Feminist Art J, Brooklyn, 74-75. *Dealer:* Boswell Gallery 5606 R St Little Rock AR 72701; Selby Pictures Ltd, London; Rivermarket Art Space, Little Rock, AR; Rocky Creek Gallery Fayetteville AR; Greg Thompson, Fine Arts, Little Rock, AR. *Mailing Add:* 1295 Wood Creek Apt 8 Fayetteville AR 72701

CODDING, MITCHELL ALLAN
MUSEUM DIRECTOR, ADMINISTRATOR

b Bartlesville, Okla, Sept 20, 1954. *Study:* Univ Okla, BA in Spanish, 1954; Univ Ky, PhD in Spanish, 2000. *Teaching:* visiting asst prof, Univ Calif, Riverside, 1983-83. *Awards:* Edward Larocque Tinker Fel, The Hispanic Soc Am, 1982; John Carter Brown Libr Fel, Brown Univ, 1982. *Publ:* Co-Ed: The Hispanic Society of America: Tesors, The Hispanic Society of America, 2000; Archer Milton Huntington, the Champion of Spain in America, Spain and the United States: the Origins of American Hispanism, Univ of Illinois Press, 2002; A Legacy of Spanish Art for America: Archer M. Hungtington and The Hispanic Society of America, Manet/Velázquez: the French Taste for Spanish Painting, The Metropolitan Museum of Art, 2003; Coauth: Cinco siglos de exploración:Fondos cartográficos de la Hispanic Society, CaixaGalicia, 2005; The Decorative Arts in Latin America, 1492-1820, The Arts in Latin America, 1492-1820, Philedelphia Museum of Art, 2006. *Mailing Add:* Hispanic Soc Am 613 W 155th St New York NY 10032-7501

CODE, AUDREY
PAINTER

b Pittsburgh, Pa, Oct 6, 1937. *Study:* Carnegie Mellon Univ, with Balcomb Greene, BFA, 59, MFA, 61; Provincetown Workshop, Mass, 61. *Work:* Aldrich Mus Contemp Art, Ridgefield, Conn; Chautauqua Art Mus, NY; Fulton Co Arts Coun, Gloversville, NY. *Comn:* Murals, St John's Church, 62 & Sr Citizens Ctr, 75, Pittsburgh, Pa; mural, Cyclerama, Los Angeles, 70. *Exhib:* Contemp Reflections, Aldrich Mus, Ridgefield, Conn, 78; Arte Fiera, Bologna, Italy, 78; PS1, NY, 78; solo show, Frank Marino Gallery, NY, 79, PSI, NY, 86; West End Gallery, Portland, Maine, 88, Los Angeles Nicola Gallery, Los Angeles, Calif, 88, Celebrity Ctr, NY, 88; Herbert F Johnson Mus, Ithaca, NY, 81; Alchemy, Hankook Gallery, NY, 83; More Than Meets the Eye, NY, 85; PSI Mus, 86; Group Shows, Andre Zarre, NY, 86, 88, 90 & 93 Rabbett Gallery, New Brunswick, NJ, 89; Blondie's Gallery, NY, 93-94; Dactyl Fed, 97; Robert Steele Gallery, 98, 2000-2005; Atlantic Gallery, 2006; Miller Gallery, Carnegie Mellon Univ, 2009; Andrew zatte Gallery, 2009; Broome St Gallery, 2009. *Teaching:* Vis artist, San Francisco Art Inst, 79; lectr, Stuyvesant Group, New York, 80-94; Westchester Community Col, 88. *Awards:* Creative Artists Pub Serv Fel, NY State Coun Arts, 81. *Bibliog:* Corinne Robbins (auth), Audrey Code's Paintings Arts, 79; Diana Morris (auth), Eight, Women Artists News, 83; Alchemy, Artspeak, 83; Sherry Miller (auth), West End Gallery, Oct 88. *Mem:* Women Arts; Women's Caucus Art. *Media:* Acrylic, Graphite. *Publ:* Illusr, Life Forms of the 70's, Independent Press, 75; auth & illusr, Eggplants and Other Murders, Chrome Press, 82; auth, Alchemy, Chrome Press, 83. *Mailing Add:* 70 Grand St New York NY 10013-2264

CODELL, JULIE FRANCIA
HISTORIAN, ADMINISTRATOR

b Chicago, Ill, Sept 19, 1945. *Study:* Vassar Col, AB (English), 67; Univ Mich, MA (English), 68; Ind Univ, MA (art hist), 75, cert (renaissance studies), 77, PhD (comparative lit & arts), 78. *Collection Arranged:* Montana Women Artists and the Environment (auth, catalog), Missoula Mus Arts, 82; Photographs of Edward S Curtis, Custer City Art Ctr, Miles City, Mont, 88; Scene/Seen out the window, retrospective exhib of Gennie DeWeese, Missoula Mus Art, 96. *Pos:* Chair, Art Dept, Univ Mont, 88-90; dir, Sch Art, Ariz State Univ, Tempe, 91-2001, prof art history, affliate fac religious studies, gender & women's studies, film & media studies, English, interim chair, film & media, 2011-12; ed, J pre-Raphaelite Studies, 91-94, book rev ed, 95-99. *Teaching:* Instr, Western Ill Univ, 68-71; asst prof art hist & criticism, Univ Mont, Missoula, 79-83, head slide libr, Dept Art, 79-90, assoc prof, 83-89, prof, 89-90; prof, Ariz State Univ, 91-. *Awards:* AIIS Fel, 2002; Ransom Humanities, 2002; NEH Fel, 1993, 2003; Huntington Fel, 2004; Getty Fel, 2006; Scholar award, Yale Ctr British Art, 2011; Fel, Inst Humanities Rsch, Ariz State Univ, 2012-13; Kress Digital Workshop Fellowship, 2014; Getty Digital Workshop Fellowship, 2014; Project Grant, Ariz State Univ Herberger Inst, 2014-2015; Inst for Humanities Research, Ariz State Univ, Seed Grant, 2015-2016. *Bibliog:* D McNamer (auth), Julie Codell, art historian, Missoulian, 80; Carol Woodruff (auth), From Renaissance to Robocop, Visions, 88; Trudy Thompson Rice (auth), Women in the Arts, Ariz State, 94. *Mem:* Coll Art Asn; Research Soc Victorian Periodicals; Victorian Interdisciplinary Studies Western US (Pres); N Am Victorian St Asn; Midwest Victorian Studies Asn (pres); Historians of British Art. *Res:* Film, India under the Raj, colonial Photog, Victorian cult. *Publ:* From Rebels to Representatives, Writing the Pre-Raphaelites, 2009; The Ideological Adventure of The Man Who Would Be King, John Huston, McFarland Publ, 2010; The Sacred Celebrity Body, Celebrity Colonialism, CSP, 2010; Ponzanesi & Waller (eds) Blackface Faciality & Colony Nostalgia in 1930s Empire Film, PostColonial Cinema Studies, Routledge, 2011; Brown & Vidal (eds), Gender, Genius, & Abjection in Artists Biopics, The Biopic in Contemporary Culture, Routledge, 2014; Transculturation in British Art, 1770-1930, 2012; Power & Resistance, The Delhi Coronation Durbars, 2012; Eds Glazer & Merrill, Aestheticisms Bric a Brac, Palaces of Art, Smithsonian, 2013; Int Exhibs, Companion of British Art, 1600 to the Present, Arnold and Peters Corbett, Wiley Blackwell, 2013; Victorian Portraits: Re-Tailoring Identities, 19th C Contexts, 2012; Artistic, Blackwell Companion to Victorian Literature and Culture ed Tucker, 2014; Exotic, Fetish, Virtual, The Uses of Excess, ed Skelly, 2014; Nationalizing Abject American Artists, ed Epstein, 2014; Robbins & Tokayer (eds), Collection and Museum of Baroda, Jews and the Indian National Art Project, 2014; Easley, et al, Art Periodicals, Research Companion to 19th Century Periodicals, 2015; From English School to British School: Nineteenth-Century Art Worldwide, 2015. *Mailing Add:* c/o Sch Art Ariz State Univ Tempe AZ 85827-1505

COE, ANNE ELIZABETH
PAINTER

b Henderson, Nev. *Study:* Ariz State Univ, BA, 70, MFA, 80; Univ PR, 78. *Work:* Centro Arte Mod Guadalajara, Mex; NDak Mus Art, Grand Forks; Scottsdale Ctr Arts, Ariz; Smithsonian Inst; Eiteljorg Mus, Indianapolis; Columbus Mus Art, Ga; Mus Contemp Art, Glasgow, Scotland; Tucson Mus Art, Ariz; Whitney Mus Western Art, Cody, Wyo; Midwest Mus Am Art, Elkhart, Ind; Scottsdale Mus Contemp Art, Ariz; Figge Mus, Davenpor, Iowa; Northern Ariz Univ Art Mus, Flagstaff; Autry Mus, Los Angeles. *Comn:* McDonald's Corp, Ill; mural & set design, Warner Brothers, Tempe, Ariz, 76. *Exhib:* Tucson Mus Art Biennial, 82; Whatever Happened to the Avant Garde, Ctr Contemp Art, Santa Ana, Calif, 83; Segal Gallery, New York, 85; Am Art Now, Columbus, Ga, 85; Women of the American West, Bruce Mus, Greenwich, Conn, 85; Art From the Drivers Seat traveling exhib, 93-96; 4th Ann New Art of the West, Eiteljorg Mus, Indianapolis, 94; Art & the Law traveling exhib, 94. *Pos:* Arts producer, KAET-TV, Phoenix, Ariz, 77-80; artist-in-residence, Ariz Comn Arts, 81-83. *Teaching:* Drawing & life drawing, Ariz State Univ, 76-78; painting, Scottsdale Artists Sch, Ariz, 96; prof art, Cent Ariz Coll, 2002-. *Bibliog:* Robert Ewing (auth), Esthetic badness, Artweek, 82; Jesse Mullins (auth), Razing Ariz, Art Today, 9/88; Kiana Dicker (auth), Anne Coe, Southwest Art, 6/92; Hannah Brown (auth), Where to read all about it, New York Post, 4/1/97; Donald J Hagerty (auth), Leading the West, One Hundred Contemporary Painters and Sculptor, Northland Publ, 97; Sarah E Boehme (auth), Whitney Gallery Western Art, 98; J Gray Sweeney (auth), Anne Coe: Life examined, 98; Carolyn C Robbins (auth), A Century of Arizona women artists, Am Art Rev, 2/2001; Michael L Walsh (auth), The New Frontier, US Art, 6-7/2001; Nicholas Roukes (auth), Arftful jesters, Ten Speed Press, 2003; Todd Wilkinson (auth), cover article, Southwest art, 6/2005. *Media:* Acrylic on Canvas. *Interests:* Land conservation and restoration. *Publ:* Nicholas Roukes (auth), Humor in Art, Davis Publ, 97; Albert W Porter, Joseph A Gatto & Jack Selleck (auths), Exploring Visual Design, Davis Publ, 2000; Rutgers Univ Press, Sci, cover, spring; Peter Hassrick (auth), Drawn to Yellowstone, Artists in America's first national park, Autry Mus, Univ Wash Press, 2002. *Dealer:* Larsen Gallery Scottsdale AZ; Austin Gallery Austin TX; Visions W Denver CO; Jackson Street Gallery Jackson WY; Ogilvie/Pertl Gallery Chicago IL. *Mailing Add:* 5776 E Forest St Apache Junction AZ 85219-9506

COE, HENRY
PAINTER

b Baltimore, Md, Oct 23, 1946. *Study:* Roanoke Col, Salem, Va, BA, 69; Md Inst Coll Art, MFA, 72. *Work:* Kanagawa Mus Mod Art, Japan; Acad Arts, Easton, Md; L'Association des Amis de La Grande Vigne, Dinan, France. *Comn:* Mural, Baltimore City Sch System, Md, 78; M D Anderson Cancer Ctr, Houston, Tex, 93. *Exhib:* Maryland Art Place, Baltimore, Md, 88; Horizons, Maryland Landscapes, Md State Arts Coun & Md Hist Soc; An Outside View, Univ Md, Univ Col, College Park; Musee du Chateau de Bochefort-En-Terre, Brittainy, France, 94; Hoffberger Gallery, Balt Hebrew Congregation, Md, 98. *Pos:* artist-in-residence, Rochffort-Enterre, France, 94. *Teaching:* art instr, Chesapeake Col, Md, 73-74. *Awards:* Edward Maxwell Award, Md Biennial Exhib, Baltimore Mus Art, 80; Md State Arts Coun Grant, 92; Artist Residency, Les Amis de La Grande Vigne, Dinan, France, 98. *Bibliog:* Joanne Dudziak, (auth), Heart Works, Baltimore Mag, 12/88; Sarah Tanguy (auth), A Brush with Maryland, Mid-Atlantic Country, 3/94; Sally Faulkner (auth), The Disappearing Landscape, Am Artist, 9/94. *Media:* Oil. *Dealer:* C Grimaldis Gallery 523 N Charles St Baltimore MD 21201; Marybell Galleries 740 N Franklin St Chicago IL 60610; Harris Gallery 1100 Bissonnet Houston TX 27005

COE, SUE
PAINTER

b Tamworth, Staffordshire, Eng, 1951. *Study:* Royal Coll Art, London, Eng, 70-73. *Work:* Metrop Mus Art, Mus Mod Art & NY Pub Libr, NY; Nat Mus Am Art, Smithsonian Inst, Washington; Whitney Mus Am Art, NY; Brooklyn Mus Art, NY; Nat Mus Women in the Arts, Washington; Libr Congress, Washington; San Francisco Mus Mod Art; plus others. *Exhib:* Solo exhibs, Brody's Gallery, Wash, 94, Jonson Gallery, Univ NMex, 94, Sue Coe: Recent Works, Visual Arts Gallery, Univ Ala, 95, Mesa Coll Gallery, San Diego, 95, Sweatshops 1995: Works by Sue Coe, Bread and Roses, NY, 95, Sue Coe's Ship of Fools, Galerie St Etienne, NY, 96, Sue Coe: We All Fall Down, Salt Lake Art Ctr, Utah, 96, Heel of the Boot: Prints by Sue Coe, Ariz State Univ Art Mus, Tempe, Univ Ill, others, 97-99, Sue Coe: The Pit, Galerie St. Etienne, NY, 99, The Tragedy of War, Galerie St Etienne, NY, 2000, Selections from Sleep of Fools, Emmanuel Gallery, Denver, Colo, 2006, Graphic Witness, Pacific Northwest Col Art, Portland, Ore, 2007, Cycles, Smokebrush Gallery & Found for Arts, Colo Springs, Colo, 2007, Elephants We Must Never Forget: Paintings Drawings, and Prints by Sue Coe, Galerie St Etienne, NY, 2008, Mad as Hell! New Work and Some Classics by Sue Coe, Galerie St Etienne, NY, 2012; Group exhibs, Biennale, San Francisco Mus Mod Art, 84, Am Drawings, Nordiyllands Kunst Mus & Ranger Kunst Mus, Denmark, 1984, The Downtown Show: The New York Art Scene 1974-1984, Grey Art Gallery, NY, Andy Warhol Mus, Pa, Austin Mus Art, Tx, 2006, Lit Graphic: The Art of the Graphic Novel, Norman Rockwell Mus, Mass, 2007, Make Art/Stop Aids, Fowler Mus UCLA, Calif, 2008, Blab!, Marianna Lester Beach Mus Art, Kans, 2008; Art Inst Chicago, 86; The New Avant-Garde, Los Angeles Co

Mus Art, 87; Committed to Print, Mus Mod Art, NY, 88; Advocacy in Art, Aldrich Mus Contemp Art, 91; Concept in Form, Artists' Sketchbooks & Maquettes, Palo Alto Cult Ctr, Calif, 95; Art & the Law (traveling), West Publ, 95; In the Light of Goya, Univ Art Mus, Berkeley, 95; Working in the 90s, Coll Mainland Art Gallery, Texas City, Tex, 96; A Critical Reality: Sue Coe and Paul Marcus, ACA Galleries, NY, 97; Art on the Edge: The Werner and Elaine Danheiser Collection, Mus Mod Art, NY, 97; Taboo: Repression and Revolt in Modern Art, Galerie St Etienne, NY, 98; Open Ends, The Mus of Modern Art, NY, 2000. *Pos:* Illusr, Time Mag, New York Times. *Teaching:* instr Reportage/Social Political Art, Parsons New Sch, 2001-2004. *Awards:* Outstanding Nat Activist Award, The Culture and Animals Found; Nat Academician, 94; book of the yr, Sheep of Fools: A Blab! PETA, 2005; prize, 175th Open Ann Exhib, Nat Acad Design, NY, 2008. *Bibliog:* Susan Gill (auth), Sue Coe's inferno, Artnews, 10/87; Peter Schjeldahl (auth), My Coe Dependency, Village Voice, 5/8/96. *Mem:* Nat Acad (assoc, 93, acad, 94). *Media:* Graphite, Gouache, Watercolor, Printmaking, Oil. *Specialty:* German and Austrian Expressionism, Am & European Self-taught Art, Grandma Moses. *Publ:* How to Commit Suicide in South Africa, 83; auth, Paintings and Drawings, 85; Auth, X (The Life & Times of Malcolm X), 86; Police State (exhib catalog), 87; Liverpool's Children, New Yorker, 12/13/93; Scenes from an AIDS ward, Village Voice, 2/22/94; The Sweatshop, 1994, 11/7/94, Keeping Vigil, 1/9/95, New Yorker; Dead Meat, (auth) Four Walls Eight Windows, 96 (Genesis Award 91); AIDS Prevention Mural computer work (auth), RedHot Orgn, 98; Pit's Letter (auth), Four Walls Eight Windows, 2000; Political Illustration of the Late Twentieth Century, 2001; Bully: Master of the Global Merry-Go-Round, 2004; Sheep of Fools...a song cycle for 5 voices, 2005; Ghost Sheep, Blab Mag No 13, autumn 2002; Weapons of Mass Destruction, Blab Mag No 14, autumn 2003; Faul Plague, Blab Mag No 15, autumn 2004; Run, Blab Mag No 16, autumn 2005; Hurrican, Blab Mag No 17, autumn 2006; Cruel, O/R Books, 2012. *Dealer:* Galerie St Etienne NY. *Mailing Add:* Galerie St Etienne 24 W 57th St New York NY 10019

COFFEY, JOHN WILLIAM, II
CURATOR, ADMINISTRATOR
b Raleigh, NC, Mar 12, 1954. *Study:* Univ NC, Chapel Hill, BA, 76; Williams Coll, MA (hist art), 78. *Collection Arranged:* Four artists: Biederman, Maddrell, Ross, Saganic (auth, catalog), 81, Maine Artists Invitationals, 82-84, Alex Katz: Small Works, 85 & Yvonne Jacquette: Tokyo Nightviews (auth, catalog), 86, Bowdoin Coll Mus Art; Twilight of Arcadia: Am Landscape Painters in Rome, 1830-1880 (auth, catalog), 87, Lucy Sallick: In the Vicinity of the Self (auth, catalog), 87 & New England Now: Contemp Art from Six States (coauth, catalog), 87, Bowdoin Coll Mus Art; Referees: Dotty Attie, Christopher Hewat, John O'Reilly (auth, catalog), 90 & Making Faces: Self-Portraits by Alex Katz (auth catalog), 90, NC Mus Art; Finding the Forgotten: Landscape Paintings by John Beerman (auth, catalog), 91 & Moshe Kupferman: Between Oblivion and Remembrance (auth, catalog), 91, Louis Remy Mignot: A Southern Painter Abroad (coauth, catalog), 96. Sign and Gesture: Contemporary Abstract Art from the Haskell Collection, NC Mus Art (auth, catalog), 99, Color, Myth & Music: Stanton Macdonald-Wright and Synchromism (contribr, catalog), 2001. *Pos:* Asst to dir, Williams Coll Mus Art, 78-79, actg dir, 79-80; cur, Bowdoin Coll Mus Art, 80-88; mem adv comt, Maine State Comn Arts & Humanities, 82-85, Maine Coast Artists Gallery, 86 & Baxter Gallery, Portland Sch Art, 86-88; cur, American & Modern Art, 88-; visual arts panel, NC Arts Coun, 90-91; dir, visual arts, Israel-NC Cult Exchange, 94-97; bd mem, NC Global Ctr, 98-2000; chief cur, 94-2005, NC Mus Art, dept dir art, 2001-. *Teaching:* Instr art hist, Williams Coll, 79-80; adj assoc prof, Univ NC, Chapel Hill, 2004-. *Mem:* Maine Festival Arts (vpres, 82-83, pres, 83-84); Assn Art Mus Curators. *Res:* Am & Mod Art. *Publ:* Christine Woelfle (sculptor), Baxter Gallery, Portland Sch Arts, 87; auth, Vantage on High essay, in: Yvonne Jacquette (exhib catalog), DC Moore Gallery, 96; Louis Remy Mignot, Antiques, 11/96; contribr, North Carolina Museum of Art Handbook of the Collections, 98; Moshe Kupferman: Work Diary (exhib catalog), Tel Aviv Mus Art, 98; contribr, In Pursuit of Refinement: Charlestonians Abroad, 1740-1860 (catalog), Gibbes Mus Art, 99; contribr, NC Mus Art, Handbook, 2010; Arms for Art and Other Shenanigans, Southern Cultures, Winter, 2013. *Mailing Add:* NC Mus Arts 4630 Mail Svc Ctr Raleigh NC 27699-4630

COFFEY, SUSANNA JEAN
PAINTER
b New London, Conn. *Study:* Univ Conn, Storrs, BFA, 1977; Yale Sch Art, MFA, 1982. *Hon Degrees:* Penn Coll Arts, 96. *Work:* Art Inst Chicago, Catherine T & John D MacArthur Found, Vanderberg Foods, Chicago, Ill; Mariam Coffin Canaday Libr, Bryn Mawr Coll; Minneapolis Mus Art; Northwestern Univ. *Exhib:* Solo exhibs incl Sazama Gallery, Chicago, 1991 & 1992, Gallery Three Zero, New York, 1994, Lyons Wier & Ginsberg Gallery, Chicago, 1996, Tibor de Nagy, New York, 1997, 1999, 2001, 2003, Galeria Alejandro Sales, 1998, Dartmouth Coll, Hanover, NH, 1998, Marguerite Oestreicher Fine Art, New Orleans, La, 2000, Alpha Gallery, Boston, Mass, 1995, 2000, 2004, Weatherspoon Art Gallery, Univ NC, 2001, Kendall Art Gallery, 2002, Isabel Ignacio Gallery, Seville, Spain, 2006, Pi 37 Gallery Pireus, Greece, 2006; group exhibs incl Statewide Survey, Rockford Art Mus, Ill, 1995; Inside Out (with catalog), Aldrich Mus Contemp Art, 1995; Image & Eye, NY Studio Sch, 1995; 47th Ann Am Acad Purchase Exhib, 1995; Evanston Art Ctr, Ill, 1996; Artists to Artists, the Marie Walsh Sharpe Art Found Exhib, Ace Gallery, New York, 2002; Painting: a Passionate Response, the Painting Ctr, New York, 2002; NY Acad Sci, 2003; Nat Acad Design, New York, 2003; Ill State Mus, Chicago, 2004; Nat Acad Mus, New York, 2005; 55 Mercer Gallery, New York, 2006; Smithsonian, Nat Portrait Gallery, 2006; Nat Mus Contemp Arts, Greece, 2006; Invitational Exhib Visual Arts, Am Acad Arts & Letters, New York, 2008. *Pos:* Vis critic, Royal Col Art, London, 1995, Vt Studio Ctr, 1994; panel mem, Harvard Ctr for Religious Studies, 2001. *Teaching:* Teaching asst, Yale Univ, 1982; prof, painting Sch of the Art Inst of Chicago, 1982-, Oxbow, Mich, 1985-; vis artist, var schs, 1983-; adj assoc prof, Univ Ill, 1983; artist in resident, Dartmouth Coll, 1998; resident fac, Skowhegan, Maine, 2007. *Awards:* Louis Comfort Tiffany Found Award, 1993; Acad Award, Am Acad Arts & Letters, 1994, 1995 & Purchase Award, 2008; Guggenheim Fel, 1996; named to Nat Acad, 2001. *Bibliog:* Eileen Myles (auth), Rev, Art in Am, 7/1994; Vivien Raynor (auth), Rev, NY Times, 6/11/1995; Charles Hagan (auth), Rev, NY Times, 7/14/1995. *Mem:* Nat Acad (coun). *Dealer:* Maya Polsky Gallery 215 W Superior St Chicago IL 60610; Alpha Gallery 14 Newbury St Boston MA 02116; Galeria Alejandro Sales Julian Romea 16 08006 Barcelona Spain; Marguerite Ostreicher Fine Arts 720 Julia St New Orleans LA 70130; Sala Pelaires C Can Veri 3 E-07001 Palma de Mallorca

COFFIN, ANNE GAGNEBIN
ARTS ADMINISTRATOR
Study: Smith Col, BA. *Pos:* feature writer Look Mag, New York City, 66-71; Cur, exhib organizer, Am Art: The Last 4 Decades, London, 77; NY rep, newsletter ed, Villa I Tatti, Harvard Univ Ctr for Italian Renaissance Studies, Florence, 84-92; dir, Int Print Ctr, New York City, 2000-. *Mem:* Century Asn, NY; NY Landmarks Conservancy, Chamber Music Soc Lincoln Center (trustee); Cosmopolitan Club, New York. *Mailing Add:* 20 E 9th St 3AB New York NY 10003

COFFIN, J DOUGLAS
SCULPTOR, PAINTER
b Lawrence, Kans, Aug 6, 1946. *Study:* Kans Univ, BFA, 71; Cranbrook Acad Art, MFA, 75. *Work:* Nat Mus Am Indian, Smithsonian Inst, NY; Inst Am Indian Arts Mus, Mus Indian Arts Cult, Wheelwright Mus Am Indian, Santa Fe; US Embassy, Malawi, Africa. *Comn:* Sun Shield, Inn Anasazi, Santa Fe, 92; African Spirit Totem, Madhvani Group, Nairobi, Kenya, 93; Medicine Wheel Totem, Haskell Indian Nations Univ, Lawrence, Kans, 94; Kansas Totem #1, City of Lawrence, Kans, 95; Mountain Spirit Totem, Markham Winery, Napa, Calif, 95. *Exhib:* Celebrations (inaugural exhib), Nat Mus Am Indians, Smithsonian Inst, NY, 94-95; Ceremony: From the Inside Out, Inst Am Indian Arts Mus, Santa Fe, NMex, 96; 20th Century Am Sculpture at the White House, Washington, DC, 97-98; Many Moons (with video catalog), Wheelwright Mus, Santa Fe. *Bibliog:* Michelle Wolford (auth), Southwest Artists, Am Net TV, 94; Linda Barskey (auth), Art of Doug Coffin, E Net TV, 98. *Media:* Steel. *Mailing Add:* c/o Waxlander Gallery 622 Canyon Rd Santa Fe NM 87501

COGAN, JOHN D(ENNIS)
PAINTER
b Wichita Falls, Tex, Feb 24, 1953. *Study:* Tex A&M Univ, BS, 75; Rice Univ, MA, 78, PhD, 81. *Work:* San Juan Coll & Citizens Bank, Farmington, NMex. *Comn:* Acrylic painting, Afternoon at Echo Amphitheater, San Juan Coll, 97; triptych acrylic, The gentle Light of Evening, Bernalillo Co Courthouse, 2000; ongoing, Sultan of Oman. *Exhib:* Arts for the Parks Top 100, Nat Park Acad Arts, Jackson, Wyo, 92, 94, 95, 96, Grand Canyon Modern Masters & Plein Air on the Rim, 2009; solo invitational, Henderson Fine Arts Bldg, San Juan Col, Farmington, NMex, 94. *Awards:* Landscape Merit Award, Arts for Parks, Nat Park Acad Arts, 94; Arts for Parks Collectors Award, Nat Park Acad Arts, 95. *Bibliog:* Netta Pfeifer (auth), John Cogan, Southwest Art Mag, 10/89; Vicki Stavig (auth), Isn't it grand, Art West Mag, 3/90; Shirley Behrens (auth), A Spiritual Peace, Art West Mag, 9/95. *Media:* Acrylic. *Specialty:* fine art. *Interests:* landscape, animal, plein air. *Publ:* Auth & illusr, Landscape painting pitfalls, Artists Mag, 9/93; Capitalize on the versatility of acrylic, Art Materials Today Mag, 9/94; The varied faces of acrylics, Artists Mag, 7/95. *Dealer:* Chris and Joyice Gere El Prado Galleries Tlaquepaque Village PO Box 1849 Sedona AZ 86339; Bill & Debbie Bunch Galleries W 260 N Cache Jackson WY 83001. *Mailing Add:* 5102 Lee Ln Farmington NM 87402

COGGER, CASSIA ZAMECKI
PAINTER
Study: Univ Colo, Boulder, degree in art hist and studio arts; Art Students' League, NY. *Exhib:* Solo exhibs at Nemick and Thompson Gallery, 2002; group exhibs include Nat Acad Mus, NY, 2006. *Pos:* Vpres Art Students' League, NY, 2006

COGSWELL, MARGARET PRICE
INSTRUCTOR
b Evanston, Ill, Sept 15, 1925. *Study:* Wellesley Col, BA, 47; Pratt Inst; Art Inst Chicago; Columbia Univ; Art Students League, Georgetown Univ, MA, 89. *Collection Arranged:* Communication Through Art, 64; The Am Poster (ed, catalog), 68; Am Exhib, 34th & 35th Venice Biennales, 68 & 70; Explorations, 70; The Audio-Visual Mag, 72; George Catlin's Am Indians, 74; Images of an Era: The Am Poster (with catalog), 75. *Pos:* Head dept publ & assoc foreign exhib, Am Fedn Arts, 55-66; ed, The Am Artists Series, 59-63; chmn, 50 Bks of the Yr, Am Inst Graphic Arts, 64; dep chief, Off Prog Support, 66-80, Nat Collection Fine Arts, Smithsonian Inst, 66-, mem, Women's Coun, 77-81, vchmn, 79, deputy cur of educ, 81-84, coord spec academic progs, 84-. *Teaching:* Smithsonian Inst, 70. *Awards:* Gold Medal for Printmaking, Am Artist Mag, 53. *Mem:* Am Asn Mus; Coll Art Asn. *Publ:* Ed, The Ideal Theater: Eight Concepts, 63; co-ed, The Cultural Resources of Boston, 64; ed, Sao Paulo 9, 67; Images of an Era: The American Poster 1945-75, 76; National Survey of Assembility in Museums, 89. *Mailing Add:* 2929 Connecticut Ave NW Washington DC 20008-1435

COHAN, JAMES
GALLERY DIRECTOR
b 1960. *Study:* Wash Univ, St Louis, BA; New Mus, New York City, Intern. *Pos:* With John Weber Gallery; dir, Paula Cooper Gallery; sr dir, Anthony d'Offay Gallery, 91-99; owner, dir, James Cohan Gallery, New York City, 2000-. *Mailing Add:* James Cohan Gallery 533 W 26th St New York NY 10001

COHELEACH, GUY JOSEPH
PAINTER, SCULPTOR
b New York, NY. *Study:* Cooper Union, with Don Eckelberry, grad. *Hon Degrees:* Coll of William & Mary, Hon Dr Arts, 75. *Work:* Nat Wildlife Gallery, Washington, DC; Nat Audubon Soc; Am Mus Natural Hist; Beware, presented to Pres of US. *Comn:* American Eagle, US Govt, presented to VPres Agnew, 71; Elephant, African

Safari Club, Washington, DC, for Pres of US, 72; Leopard & Elephant, World Wildlife Fund, 72; and others. *Exhib:* Houston Mus Natural Hist, Tex, 94; Cleveland Mus Natural Hist, Ohio, 94-95; Blauvelt Mus, Oradell, NJ, 95; Newark Mus, 96; Carnegie-Mellon, Pittsburgh, 96-97; Newark Mus, NJ, 96; John J Audubon Mus, Ky, 97; Rory Tory Peterson Inst, NJ, 97, 2002; Haly Libr Mus, Tex, 97-98; Fort Worth Zoo, Tennison Gallery, Tex, 98; Blauvelt Mus, NJ, 98; Neville Pub Mus, Wis, 99; Michelson Mus, Tex, 99; Burpee Mus, Ill, 99-2000; West Valley Art Mus, Ariz, 2000-01; Courthouse Cult Arts Ctr, Fla, 2002; The Wildlife Experience Mus, Colo, 2003; R W Norton Art Gallery, La, 2003; Vero Beach Mus Art, Vero Beach, Fla, 2004-2005; Ward Mus of Wildfowl Art, Salisbury, Md, 2005; Hiram Blaurelt Mus, Oradell, NJ, 2005; Oshkosh Pub Mus, Oshkosh, Wis, 2006-2007; Schiele Mus, Gastonia, NC, 2007; Roger Tory Peterson Inst, Jamestown, NY, 3-6/2008; Anniston Mus, Anniston, Ala, 6/1/2008-9/30/2008. *Pos:* freelance. *Awards:* Prints Mag, 79 & Mich Outdoors, 79; Master Artist, Leigh Yawkee Art Mus, Wis, 83; 8 Awards of Excellance, from SAA; First occidental artist to exhibit in post-WWII Peking; Award of Excellence, Artists for Conservation, 2010; Soc Animal Artists. *Bibliog:* Roger Caras (auth), Quest: An Artist & His Prey; Terry Weiland (auth), Coheleach, Briarpatch Press, 88; Terry Weiland (auth), Guy Coheleachs Animal Art, DDR Publ, 94. *Mem:* Soc Animal Artists; Explorer's Club; African Safari Club; Adventurer's Club. *Media:* Oil, watercolor. *Specialty:* Animals in Art. *Interests:* Fishing, Shooting. *Publ:* Illusr, Nat Wildlife Mag, 67-; Readers Digest, 67-; Int Wildlife Mag, 71-; auth, The Big Cats-The Paintings of Guy Coheleach, Harry Abrams, 82; Wildlife Art News, 84 & 93; auth/illustr, The African Lion as Man-Eater, Panther Press, 2003. *Dealer:* K & K Wildlife Art; Trailside Gallery. *Mailing Add:* c/o Coheleach Art Box 527 Hobe Sound FL 33475

COHEN, ALAN BARRY
PHOTOGRAPHER, EDUCATOR
b Harrisburg, Pa, Aug 28, 1943. *Study:* NC State Univ, BS, 66; Ill Inst Technol/Inst Design, MS (photog), 72. *Work:* Art Inst Chicago, Ill; High Mus Art, Atlanta, Ga; Baltimore Mus Art, Md; Nat Mus Am Art, Washington, DC; Metrop Mus Art, NY. *Exhib:* The Picture in the Picture, Galerie Neumann, Dusseldorf, Ger, 93; Visions of a Nation: Photographs by Mex & Am Photog, Smart Mus Art, Chicago, 94; Now (death camps), Friedrich-Ebert-Stiftung: Landesburo Thuringen, Erfurt, Ger, 95; 50 Yrs-Liberation from Auschwitz-Birkenau, Literaturhaus, Frankfurt, Ger, 95; Indelible Traces, Chic Cult Ctr, 96; The Holocaust: Voices, Portraits, Places, Gallery 312, Chic, 97; All Chic: An Electronic Exhib: U-Turn E-Zine Issue #2, 98; Works from the Gallery, Carol Ehlers Gallery, Chic, 98; Opening the Shutter: 150 Yrs of Photog, Kresge Art Mus, Mich State Univ, E Lansing, Mich, 98; Narrative & Abstraction in 20th Century Photog: Works by W Eugene Smith & Alan Cohen, Block Mus, 98; Not on any Map, Betty Rymar Gallery, Sch Art Inst Chic, 99; Block Mus Art, Northwestern Univ, Evanston, Ill, 2001. *Pos:* Bd dir, New Art Examiner, 90-92; reviewer, Nat Endowment Humanities, 80-85. *Teaching:* Instr photog, Ill Inst Tech, Chicago, 72-74; vis artist photo hist/photog, Columbia Col, Chicago, Ill, 76-86; adj assoc prof, Art Inst, Chicago, Ill, 86; vis artist photog & photo hist, DePaul Univ, Chicago, Ill, 92. *Awards:* Grant & Fel Nat Endowment Arts & Nat Endowment Humanities, 78. *Bibliog:* Alan Artner (auth), Photographic Memory, Chic Tribune (vol #7, p13), 5/18/97 & Cohen's Death Camp Photographs (vol #5, p7), 3/28/96; Michael Weinstein (auth), The Holocaust: Voices, Portraits, Places, New Art Exam (reproduction, p98), 12/97; W E Smith & Alan Cohen (photog), 20th Century Photography of Print World (reproduction, pp39), 98; Mark Towner (auth), Three Decades of Midwestern Photography: 1960-1990, Davenport Mus Art, 92; Sander Gilman (lect & pub), Contemporary Photography Sees History: The Work of Alan Cohen, 2001. *Publ:* Coauth, From Pictorialism to Precisionism, A B Bookman, 84; JNO Cook: Radically recycled cameras, Mass Inst Tech, 90; interview (text) with Cook; The Black Trans-Atlantic Experience: The Photographs of Stephen Marc (interview), Univ Ill Press, 92; Midwestern Photography: 1960-1990 (includes statement), Davenport Mus Art, 92; An as Yet Untitled Mono, Univ Chicago; On European Ground, 2001. *Dealer:* Eleanor Barefoot Gallery New York

COHEN, CHARLES E
HISTORIAN, EDUCATOR
b New York, NY, July 11, 1942. *Study:* Columbia Univ, AB, 63; Princeton Univ, MFA, 65; Harvard Univ, PhD, 71. *Pos:* cur drawings, Pordenone 500th Anniversary, 84. *Teaching:* Tutor Harvard Univ, Cambridge, Mass, 67-68; head teaching fel, 69-70; asst prof art Univ Chicago, 70-75; assoc prof, 75-80; chmn art dept, 85-89; Resident Master Pierce Hall, prof art, Mary L Block, 80-; chmn comt visual arts. *Awards:* Delmas Found Fel, 80; Guggenheim Found Fel, 83-84; Nat Endowment Humanities Univ Fel, 89-90. *Mem:* Coll Art Asn Am; Midwest Art Hist Soc; Renaissance Soc Am. *Res:* Venetian & North Italian painting and drawing in the Renaissance. *Publ:* Auth, I disegni di Pomponio Amalteo, GEAP, 75; Pordenone's Cremona Passion Scenes & German Art, Arte Lomberda, 76; The Drawings of Giovanni Antonio da Pordenone, La Nuova Italia, 80; Pordenone not Giorgione, Burlington Mag, 80; The Art of Giovanni de Pordenone, Cambridge, 96. *Mailing Add:* Univ Chicago Art History Dept 5540 S Greenwood Ave Chicago IL 60637

COHEN, CHERRYL & FRANK
COLLECTOR
b Cheshire, Eng, 1944. *Pos:* Founder, Glyn Webb Home Improvement Stores; mem judging panel, Turner Prize, Tate Mus, Britain, 2003. *Awards:* Named one of 200 Top Collectors, ARTnews mag, 2004-13. *Collection:* Modern British & contemporary art. *Mailing Add:* The Frank Cohen Collection 3 Grafton Pl London 1 United Kingdom 5

COHEN, CORA
PAINTER
b New York, NY, Oct 19, 1943. *Study:* Bennington Coll, with Paul Feeley, David Smith & Tony Caro, BA, 64, MA, 72; studied with Richard Haas. *Work:* Chase Manhattan Bank, NY; RCM Capital Management, San Francisco, Calif; NY Pub Libr, NY; Swed State Art Coun, Stockholm, Yale Univ, New Haven, Conn. *Exhib:* Solo exhibs, Everson Mus, Syracuse, NY, 74, Max Hutchinson Gallery, NY 79, 80, 84, Wolff Gallery, 88, Holly Solomon Gallery (with cataloque),88, 90, New Arts Program, Kutztown PA, 93, Jason McCoy Gallery, 93, David Beitzel Gallery, NY, 94, Joslyn Art Mus, Omaha, Nebr, 96, Paintings & Altered X-Rays (with catalog), Gallerie Mariann Ahnlund, Umea, Sweden, 99, Sarah Moody Gallery Art, 96, Hering Raum Bonn, Ger, 97-99, Rena Bransten Gallery, San Francisco, Calif, 97, Michael Steinberg Fine Art, 2008, Painting, N3 Project Space, New York, 2003, Benefit Photog Auction, CEPA Gallery, NY, 98, Belvedere Strabe 149a, Koln, 99; Bentley Gallery, Scottsdale, Ariz, 99, 2002, 2005, MCoy, Chelsea, NY, 2001, Emory & Henry Col, Emory, Va, 2003, Abaton Garage, Jersey City, NJ, 2005 & 2007, Markus Winter Gallery, Berlin, 2007, Oblique Forms: Spray Paint Paintings, Photographs, The Hybrid Indexical Adventure Series, Abaton Garage, Jersey City, NJ, 2007, Come in a Little Closer, Recent Paintings, Michael Steinberg Fine Art, NY, 2008, Field Inst Hombroich, Mus Insel Hombroich, Neuss, Dinter Fine Art, 2011, D.M. Allison Art, Houston, Tex, 2012, Heather Gaudio Fine Art, New Canaan, Conn, 2012, The Responsibility of Forms, Guided by Invoices, NY, 2013, Cora Cohen-on paper, Galerie Hafemann, Wisebaden, 2013; Group exhib, Sandra Gering Gallery, NY, 92; Painting Self-Evident: Evolutions in Abstraction, Piccolo Spoleto Festival, Charleston, SC, 92; An Esemplastic Shift, 92 & The Fetish of Knowledge, 92, A/C Proj Room, NY; Contemp Surfaces, Pamela Auchincloss Gallery, NY, 92; Libidinal Painting, White Columns, NY, 93; 30th Anniversary Exhib, Leo Castelli Gallery, NY, 93; Inaugural Show, The Painting Ctr, NY, 93; Heterogeneity, Abstraction & Virtual Space, Out of the Blue Gallery, Edinburgh, Scotland, 94; Mirage, Penine Hart Gallery, NY, 94; Stalke Out of Space, Copenhagen, 98; Art on Paper, Weatherspoon Art Gallery, Greensboro, 98; Coalition for the Homeless Benefit & Auction, NY, 98; Barbara Davis Gallery, Houston, Tex, 98; Galerie Mariann Ahnlund, Stockholm Art Fair, 98; A Sustaining Passion, The Tsagaris/Hilberry Collection, Cedar Rapids Mus Art, Iowa, 98 & Dubuque Mus Art, Iowa, 98; Benefit Photog Auction, CEPA Gallery, NY, 98; Immediaces of the Hand: Recent Abstract Painting in New York, Hunter Coll, Times Sq Gallery, NY, 99; Positionen 33 Painting, Hering Raum Stahlwerk Willich, Ger, 99; The Five & Dime Series, The Record, The Death, The Surprise, Jan van der Donk, New York, 2001; Back to the Future, Cynthia Broan Gallery, New York, 2002; im + provisus: Compositions in Jazz, Sheldon Art Galleries, St Louis, 2003; No Words & Words on Paper, Stalke Kirke Sonnerup, Denmark, 2007; Dutch Barn Fall Show, Clinton Corners, NY, 2007; Painters of Calif & NY, Elder Gallery, Charlotte, NC, 2007; Shape Shifters: NY Painters Univ NC at Pembroke, Pembroke, NC Sideshow Gallery, Brooklyn, NY 2008; It's a Wonderful Life, Sideshow Gallery, Brooklyn, New York, 2009; Back to the Drawing Board, Michale Steinberg Fine Art, New York, 2008; Strokes, Univ Tex, Dallas, 2009; Willaim Shearburn Gallery, Santa Fe, 2009; The World, Other World, Firehouse Gallery, Burlington, Vt, 2010; Carl Plansky and Friends, Sam and Adele Golden Gallery, New Berlin, NY, 2010; 70 Yrs Abstract Painting-Excerpts, Jason McCoy Gallery, NY, 2011, Its All Good, Apocalypse Now! Sideshow Gallery, Brooklyn, NY, 2011, Scripted, Gross McCleaf Gallery, Phila, Pa, 2011, Polis, Art Blog, 2011, Drawn out Death, Houston, Tex, 2011, American Women, Elder Gallery, Charlotte, NC, 2011, Auf Papier, Galerie Hafemann, Wiesbaden, 2011; Mic: check, Sideshow Gallery, Brooklyn, NY, 2012, Hex, Janet Kurnatowski Gallery, Brooklyn, NY, 2012, I Surrender, devening projects and editions, Chicago, Ill, 2012, Am Acad Arts and Letters, NY, 2012; Paper Bend, Jason McCoy Inc, NY, 2012; Assembly, 2012; Edward Thorp Gallery, NY, 2012; Sideshow Nation, Sideshow Gallery, NY, 2013; Paparazzi 2, Janet Kurnatowski Gallery, NY, 2013; Signature Works, Guided by Invoices, NY; Signs and Systems, Gross Mcleaf Gallery, Philadelphia, Pa, 2013; Season Review, Edward Thorp Gallery, NY. *Collection Arranged:* cur, Snippits Samplings Statis, Educ Alliances, Ernests Rubenstein Gallery, New York, 2009. *Teaching:* Vis artist painting, Art Inst Chicago, 83, 85, 91, 92, 97, & 2012, Univ Chicago, 84, Boston Mus Sch Fine Arts, 85, 94; lectr, NY Studio Sch, 89 & Tyler Sch Art, 90; adj fac, NY Univ, 90-97; vis prof, Sch Art Inst Chicago, 93; vis artist, New Arts Prog, Kutztown, Pa, 93, Vt Studio Ctr, 97, 98, 99, 2006-2011; assoc prof art, Univ NC, Greensboro, 98-2003; vis artist, Corcoran Mus & Sch Art, 2000, Emory & Henry Coll, Emory, Va, 2003, Wash Univ, St Louis, 2003, The New Sch, New York, 2004 & New York Univ, 2005; adj fac, State Univ NJ, Newark, 2004 & Md Inst Coll Art, Baltimore, 2006; vis critic, Vt Studio Ctr, Johnson, Vt, 2006-2011; Educ Alliance, New York, NY, 2007-2011; NY Studio Sch, NY, 2012; Medicine Hat Coll, Canada, 2012. *Awards:* NY Found Arts, 89; Pollock/Krasner Award, 98; The National Endowment for the Arts, 87; Adolph & Esther Gottlieb Found Award, 2006; Marie Walsh Sharpe Art Found Space Prog, Brooklyn, NY, 2008; Edward F. Albee Found Residency Award, Montauk, New York, 2009; Purchase award, Am Acad Arts & Letts, NY, 2012; John Simon Guggenheim Meml Found, Fellowship, 2013. *Bibliog:* Anders Bjorkman (auth), Vasterbottens-Kuriren, The Earth Reddens and Bursts, Umea, Sweden, 96; Holland Cotter (auth), NY Times, 4/99; Stephen Maine (auth), Art in Am, 2/2005; Barbara MacAdam (auth), The New Abstraction, Art News, Vol 106, No 4, 4/2007; Laurie Fendrich (auth), The Interface of Art & Humanity, Chronicle of Higher Educ, Chronicle Review, Brainstorm, 2/2008; Cathy Nan (auth), Shape Shifters: NY Painters, 5/2008; Gillian Sneed (auth), Trends in Contemporary Painting, NY Arts Mag, July/Aug 2008; Joan Waltemath (auth), The Brooklyn Rail, 11/2008; Jennifer Riley (auth), Cora Cohen: Come in a Little Closer at Michael Steinberg, 2008; Edith Newhall (auth), Going Off Script with a Show Called Scripted, The Philadelphia Inquirer, 2011; Mitchell Mettelstadt (ed), Cora Cohen's Writerly Art, F Newsmagazine, 2011; Anne M Wagner (auth), Art Forum, 2012; David Rhodes (auth), Dirty/Clean Painting: Cora Cohen at Guided by Invoices, 2013; William Eckhardt Kohler (auth), The Huffington Post, Cora Cohen-Divine Madness, 2013; Nora Griffin (auth), The Brooklyn Rail, Cora Cohen, The Responsibility of Forms, 2013. *Mem:* CAA. *Media:* Oil, Acrylic. *Interests:* Visual art. *Dealer:* Michael Steinberg Fine Art PO Box 2065 New York NY 10011; Guided by Invoices 558 W 21st St New York NY 10011

COHEN, DAVID
CRITIC, CURATOR
b London, Eng, Apr 20, 1963, UK & US citizen. *Study:* Univ Sussex, Eng, BA, 1985; Courtauld Inst Art, London, MA, 1987. *Collection Arranged:* Academie Matisse: Henri Matisse & his Nordic & American Pupils, New York Studio Sch Drawing, Painting & Sculpture, 2001; Thomas Nozkowski: Drawing, New York Studio Sch Drawing, Painting & Sculpture, 2003; Alex Katz Collages, Colby Coll Mus Art, Maine, 2005; Merlin James: Painting to Painting, New York Studio Sch Drawing, Painting & Sculpture, 2007; Francoise Gilot, New York Studio Sch Drawing, Painting & Sculpture, 2007. *Pos:* gallery dir, NY Studio Sch Drawing, Painting and Sculpture, 2001-2010; critic, art, & contrib ed, The New York Sun, 2003-2008; ed, publ, artentical.com, currently; Moderator, Rev Panel, Nat Acad Mus & Sch Fine Arts, New York, 2004. *Teaching:* Vis prof, Western Carolina Univ, NC, 2004-2005; adj prof, State Univ New York, Albany, 2000-2001; vis prof, Western Carolina Univ, Cullowhee, NC, 2004-2005; instr, New York Studio Sch, New York, 2009-; critic in residence, Triangle Int Workshop, World Trade Ctr, New York, 98. *Mem:* Internat Asn Art Critics. *Res:* The Life & Work of RB Kitaj and Alex Katz. *Publ:* Auth, Henry Moore in the Bagatelle Gardens, Paris, Lund Humphries, 93; coauth, Un siécle de sculpture anglaise, Galerie nationale Jeu de Paume, 96; coauth, Lucian Freud: Etchings in the Collection of Paine Webber, Yale Ctr British Art, 99; ed, Artcritical.com, 2000-; auth, Jock McFadyen: A book about a painter, Lund Humphries, 2001; coauth, Henry Moore: Sculpting the 20th Century, Yale, 2001; auth, Alex Katz Collages (exhib catalog), Colby College Mus Art, 2005

COHEN, GEORGE MICHAEL
EDUCATOR
b Brookline, Mass, Sept 24, 1931. *Study:* Harvard Univ, AB, 55, AM, 58; Boston Univ, PhD, 62. *Teaching:* Prof, Hofstra Univ, 70-. *Bibliog:* A History of American Art; Essential American Art. *Mem:* Appraisers Asn Am. *Publ:* Auth, The bird symbolism of Morris Graves, Coll Art J, 58; The paintings of Charles Sheeler, 59 & The lithographs of Thomas Hart Benton, 62, Am Artist; The sculpture of John B Flannagan, Artvoices, 65; The art of George Catlin, Art & Antiques, 81; The Early Art of Thomas Cole, Fineart Connoisseur, 2006. *Mailing Add:* 80 Wintercress Ln East Northport NY 11731

COHEN, HAROLD
ARTIST, THEORIST, EDUCATOR
b London, Eng, May 1, 1928. *Study:* Univ London, Diploma (fine arts), 51. *Work:* Tate Gallery, London; Stedelijk Mus, Amsterdam, Holland; Victoria & Albert Mus, London; Los Angeles Co Mus Art, Calif; Walker Art Ctr, Minneapolis, Minn. *Comn:* Wall hanging, Milan Triennale, 63; tapestry, Brit Petroleum Co, 65. *Exhib:* Documenta, Kassel, WGer, 64 & 77; 33rd Venice Biennale, 66; Solo exhibs, Mus d'Art Contemporain, Montreal, Que, 67, Victoria & Albert Mus, 68 & Stedelijk Mus, 77; Three Behaviors for the Partitioning of Space, Los Angeles Co Mus Art, 72; Retrospective, Scottish Arts Coun Gallery, Edinburgh, 76; Harold Cohen: Drawing, San Francisco Mus Mod Art, 79; Computers & the Visual Arts: The Research & Drawings of Harold Cohen, Sierra Nevada Mus Art, 79; and others. *Pos:* Vis scholar, Artificial Intelligence Lab, Stanford Univ, 73-75. *Teaching:* Instr art, Univ Col London, 61-65; prof art, Univ Calif, San Diego, 68-, chmn visual arts dept, 68-69, dir, Ctr Art/Sci Study, 74-, emer prof, currently. *Awards:* Harkness Fel of Commonwealth Fund, 59-61; Purchase Award, Gulbenkian Found, 61; Nat Endowment Arts Workshop Grant, 76. *Publ:* Auth, The making of a tapestry, 67, Apropos work in progress, 68 & On purpose, 74, Studio Int; The material of symbols, First Ann Symposium on Symbols & Symbol Processing, Univ Nev, 76; What is an Image?, Int Joint Conf Artificial Intelligence, Tokyo, Japan, 79. *Mailing Add:* Univ Calif San Diego 9500 Gillman Dr Circa-0037 La Jolla CA 92093-0327

COHEN, HAROLD LARRY
DESIGNER, EDUCATOR
b Brooklyn, NY, May 24, 1925. *Study:* Pratt Inst Art Sch, Brooklyn; Northwestern Univ; Inst Design, BA. *Pos:* Dir, Inst Behav Res, Silver Spring, Md, formerly; dean sch archit & environ design, State Univ NY, Buffalo, formerly, prof, currently. *Teaching:* Prof design, chmn dept & dir design res & develop, Southern Ill Univ, Carbondale, formerly. *Awards:* Five Good Design Awards, with Davis Pratt; Mus Mod Art Awards, 49-53. *Mailing Add:* 600 Main St Buffalo NY 14202-3030

COHEN, JEAN
PAINTER
b New York, NY, Aug 1, 1927. *Study:* Pratt Inst, Brooklyn, 44-45; Cooper Union Art Sch, New York, 46-49; Skowhegan Sch Painting & Sculpture, Maine, summer 50. *Work:* Ciba-Geigy Corp, Ardsley, NY; Hampton Inst Mus, Va; Bocour Color Collection, Garnersville, NY; Colby Coll Mus, Waterville, Maine; Wright State Univ Mus. *Exhib:* Contemp Artists, Riverside Mus, NY, 63; Pa Acad Regional, Philadelphia, 64; Visual R&D, Univ Tex Art Mus, Austin, 73; Contemp Am Painting, Randolph-Macon Col, 74; West Bronx Art League, Bronx Mus, 75. *Pos:* Consult, West Bronx Art League, 69-75; founder, Landmark Gallery, NY; cur, Magic Circle Exhib, Bronx Mus Arts, 77. *Teaching:* Instr painting & design, Cooper Union, spring & summers, 51-63; lectr painting, Philadelphia Col Art, 62-69; lectr painting, Queens Col Art Dept, 72-75; Jersey City State Col, Philadelphia Col Art, 81-86 & La State Univ, spring 90. *Awards:* Landscape Painting Prize, Skowhegan Sch Painting, 50; Creative Artists Pub Serv Grant, 80; Adolph Gottlieb Grant, 84. *Mem:* Artists Equity; Am Abstract Artists. *Media:* Oil, Compressed Charcoal. *Dealer:* Cape Split Place Addison ME 04606. *Mailing Add:* 60 Westminster Dr Shirley NY 11967

COHEN, JEAN R
CERAMIST, COLLECTOR
b Colorado Springs, Colo, Apr 13, 1935. *Study:* Penland Sch Crafts; Maples Mills Sch Crafts; Arrowmont Sch Crafts; Visual Arts Ctr; also, study with Richard La Fean, Jane Peiser, Elsa Rady, Ralph Baccera, David Leach, Don Pilcher, Rudi Staffel, Catherine Hiersoux & Sally Silberberg. *Work:* Towson State Univ Gallery, Baltimore; Vessels Aesthetic, Taft Col, Calif. *Exhib:* Md Craft Coun Biennial Exhib, Maryland, 81 & 83; Contemp Crafts Exhib, Del Art Mus, Del, 82; Lloyd Herman Selects, Arlington Arts Ctr, Va, 82; Am Hand Inc, Washington, DC & NY, 83 & 84; Everson Mus Art, NY, 84; Crafts Nat, Buffalo State Col, NY, 85; Am Ceramic Nat, Calif, 86. *Teaching:* Teacher, Potters Guild Baltimore, Md, 77-82; workshop instr, Washington Kiln Club, 84 & Santa Barbara State Col, 86. *Awards:* Purchase Award, Vessels Aesthetic, 83. *Mem:* Clayworks of Baltimore, Md; Potters Guild of Baltimore, Md; Am Craft Coun. *Publ:* Ceramics Monthly, 4/86. *Mailing Add:* 6104 Eastcliff Dr Baltimore MD 21209-3514

COHEN, JOAN LEBOLD
ART HISTORIAN, PHOTOGRAPHER
b Highland Park, Ill, Aug 19, 1932. *Study:* Smith Coll, BA, 54. *Work:* Smith Coll Mus Art; Harvard Law Sch; Atlantic Richfield Corp Collection; NYNEX; Paul, Weiss, Rifkind, Wharton & Garrison, New York, Hong Kong, Beijing; US Embassy, Phnom Phen, Cambodia; US Asia Law Inst; Law Sch NY Univ; and numerous pvt collections. *Exhib:* Shadows of Mt Huang, Univ Art Gallery, Berkeley, Calif, Austin, Tex & Princeton, NJ, 81; Alisan Fine Arts, Hong Kong, 87 & 89; Smith Coll Alumnae House, 90, 94, 98 & 2004; Kendall Gallery, Wellfleet, Mass, 91; Soho Photo Gallery, New York, 94-2012; Castle Hill Gallery, Truro, Mass, 2001-2011; Photo New York, 2004. *Collection Arranged:* Painting the Chinese Dream, 82 & The New Generation of Chinese Art, 90, Northhampton, Mass; New York, The City and It's People, Bejing, 85; Artists from China, Bronxville, NY, 87; Between East & West, Bridgeport, Conn, 94-95; CCIC, Hong Kong, 86. *Pos:* Guest cur, Smith Coll Mus Art, 82, 90, & 2009, Brooklyn Mus, New York, 83, Worker's Cult Palace, Beijing, 85, Sarah Lawrence Coll Art Gallery, 87, Discovery Mus, Bridgeport, Conn, 94, Univ Pa, 2011; Registrar, Corcoran Gallery Art, Washington, DC, 1955-56. *Teaching:* Lectr, Dept Pub Educ, Mus Fine Arts, Boston, 65-71; lectr Asian art & film, China, Japan & India, Sch Mus Fine Arts, Tufts Univ, Boston, 68-90. *Awards:* Two awards for bk, China Today & Her Ancient Treasures, 74 & 75; Smith Coll Medal, 90. *Bibliog:* Ralph Croizier (auth), Review of the New Chinese Painting, Journal of Asian Studies, 1988; Landscapes of Asia photo exhib, Art News, 6/1997; Lotus Eyes photo exhib, Art News, 2004. *Mem:* Fairbank Ctr E Asian Studies, Harvard Univ; Mod China Seminar Columbia Univ. *Media:* Photography. *Res:* Art & politics in contemp Chinese art. *Specialty:* Contemp photog. *Interests:* Contemp Chines art. *Publ:* Buddha, Seymour Lawrence Delacorte, New York, 69; co-auth, China Today and her Ancient Treasures, Abrams, New York, 74, 2nd ed, 80 & 3rd ed, 86; Anchor, Monuments of the God Kings, Abrams, New York, 75; The New Chinese Painting, 1949-1986, Abrams, New York, 87; Yunnan School, A Rennaissance in Chinese Painting, Fingerhut Group Publ, Minneapolis, MN. *Dealer:* Photo Researchers 60 E 56th New York NY 10522. *Mailing Add:* 1095 Park Ave New York NY 10128-1154

COHEN, LYNNE G
PHOTOGRAPHER, EDUCATOR
b Racine, Wis, July 3, 1944. *Study:* Slade Sch Art, London, 64-65; Univ Wis, Madison, BS (art), 67; Univ Mich, 68, Eastern Mich Univ, MA (art), 69. *Work:* Int Mus Photog, George Eastman House, Rochester, NY; Mus Mod Ville Paris; Nat Gallery Can, Ottawa; Victoria & Albert Mus, London; Metrop Mus Art, NY. *Comn:* Centre d'Art Contemporain de Guerigny, France, 91; Wexner Ctr Arts, Columbus, Ohio, 96; Univ Valencia, 98. *Exhib:* Solo Exhibs, Int Ctr Photog, NY, 78, Mus Gestaltung Zurich, Switz, 89, FRAC Limousin, 92, PPOW, NY, 92 & 96, Robert Klein Gallery, Boston, 95, Karsten Schubert Gallery, London, 96, Galerie des Archives, Paris, 96, PPOW, NY, 96, Kirkland Fine Arts Ctr, Millikin Univ, Ill, 98 & Mus voor Fotografie, Antwerp, 98; Victoria & Albert Mus, London, 89; Double Mixte, Galerie Nat Jeu Paume, Paris, 95; Passions Privees, Mus d'Art Mod Paris, 96; Wexner Ctr Arts, Columbus, Ohio, 97; and others. *Collection Arranged:* Art Inst Chicago, Ill; Kinsthaus, Zurich, Switzerland; Met Mus Art, MYC; Musee d'Art Moderne de la Ville Paris, France; Nat Gallery Can. *Teaching:* Lectr photog art, Eastern Mich Univ, Ypsilanti, 68-73; from lectr to prof visual art, dept visual arts, Univ Ottawa, 74-; vis artist & prof, Sch Art Inst Chicago, 84 & 92; Ecole des Beaux-Arts de Bordeaux, 94 & 96; Nova Scotia Col Art & Design, 96. *Awards:* Logan Award, Art Inst Chicago, 67; Sr Arts Grant, Ont Arts Coun, 85; Sr Arts Grant, Can Coun, 86, 89 & 95. *Bibliog:* Marc Freidus (auth), Typologies, Nine Contemporary Photographers, Newport Harbor Art Mus (exhib catalog & bk); Jean-Pierre Criqui (auth), Double Mixte, Galerie Nat du Jeu de Paume (exhib catalog & bk), Paris, 95; Mark Robbins and Sarah Rogers (auths), Evidence: Photography and Site (group exhib catalog & bk), 96. *Media:* Art, Photography. *Publ:* Contribr, Creative Cameria, 4/78; Occupied Territory, Aperture, NY, 88; Contact Sheet, 89 & 96; Lost and Found, FRAC-Limousin, 92. *Dealer:* PPOW 476 Broome St New York NY 10013; Galerie Rodolphe Janssen 35 rue de Livourne 1050 Bruxelles

COHEN, MICHAEL S
CERAMIST, PHOTOGRAPHER
b Boston, Mass, Mar 7, 1936. *Study:* Mass Coll of Art, BFA, 57; Cranbrook Acad of Art, Bloomfield Hills, Mich, 61; Haystack Mountain Sch Crafts, Deer Isle, Maine, 61. *Work:* Mus of Mod Art, NY; Mus Contemp Crafts, NY; Johnson Collection Contemp Crafts, Wis; Everson Mus, Syracuse, NY; Addison Gallery, Andover, Mass. *Exhib:* Syracuse Int, Everson Mus, 62, 64 & 66; Am Studio Pottery, Victoria & Albert Mus, London, Eng, 63; 10th Int Exhib Ceramic Art, Smithsonian Inst, Washington, DC, 65; Objects USA, Mus Contemp Crafts, NY, 70; Crafts 1970, Boston City Hall, Mass; solo exhibs, Soc Arts & Crafts, Lexington, Mass, 74 & Gallimaufry, Croton-on-Hudson, NY, 76; Potter's Wheel, DeCordova Mus, Lincoln, Mass, 76; and others. *Pos:* Owner Michael Cohen Tiles. *Teaching:* Haystadt, Mass Art, Phoenix Potter, Notre Dame, Holl Potter, Berkeley Potters Guild, NH League of Crafts. *Awards:* Nat Endowment Arts grant, 74; Master Craftsman grant, Nat Endowment Arts, 75; 2nd Int Symposium, Tenn, 75. *Bibliog:* Peter Sabin (auth), Studio Production, Studio Potter, 76. *Mem:* Am Crafts Coun; Mass Asn of Craftsmen; Asparagus Valley Potters Guild (pres, 75-). *Media:* Stoneware. *Interests:* Tile production. *Publ:* Smithsonian Archives of American Art, 8/2001. *Mailing Add:* 107 Amherst Rd Pelham MA 01002

COHEN, MILDRED THALER
ART DEALER, GALLERY DIRECTOR
b New York, NY, 1921. *Study:* Hunter Coll, New York, BA, 42; Pratt Inst Libr Sch, Brooklyn, NY, BLS, 43. *Collection Arranged:* Women Students of William Merritt Chase, 73; Ethel Paxson, 76; Nell Choate Jones, 79; Frederic Taubes, 81; Three Generations of Wiggins: Carleton, Guy C, Guy A, 81; Robert Hallowell, 83; Anne Blodgett, 85, 88, 92 & 95; Eliot Clark, 88; Samuel Rothbort, 89; Rachel Hartley, 91; Frank Kleinholz, 92; Anthony Springer, 96; Joseph Margulies, 97; Allen Blagden, 98; Hildegarde Hamilton, 99; Samuel Brecher, 99, 2003; James Bowman Consor, 2000-04; Tsar, Valery Tsarikovsky, 2007; Aleen Aked, 2008. *Pos:* Librn, Mus French Art, French Inst, New York, 43-45; dir, The Marbella Gallery Inc, New York, 71-. *Mem:* Appraisers Asn Am Inc. *Specialty:* Nineteenth and early twentieth century American Paintings. *Publ:* Auth, Tonalism, an American Interpretation of the Landscape, 93; Robert Hallowell, an artist Rediscovered, 83 & Eliot Clark, artist, scholar, world traveler, 90. *Mailing Add:* 28 E 72nd St New York NY 10021

COHEN, NICOLE
VIDEO ARTIST
b Falmouth, Mass, 1970. *Study:* Hampshire Col, Amherst, Mass, BA, 1992; Univ Southern Calif, Los Angeles, MFA, 1999. *Comn:* Forever, Forever, Univ Southen Calif, Los Angeles, 2005. *Exhib:* Solo exhibs include Guards, Harold Johnson Gallery, Amherst, Mass, 1992, Video Drawings, Helen Lindhurst Fine Arts Gallery, Univ Southern Calif, Los Angeles, 1998, Fantasy Space & Crystal Ball: Dreamhouse, Shoshana Wayne Gallery, Santa Monica, Calif, 2000, 40-Love, 2003, New Work, 2007, Van Fantasies, Sara Meltzer Gallery, NY City, 2001, My Vie en Rose, Media Field, Williams Coll Mus Art, Williamstown, Mass, 2003, How to Make Your Windows Beautiful, LUXE Gallery, NY City, 2005; group exhibs include Miller Durazo, Los Angeles, 1999, 2000; Art for Art Sake, Threadwaxing Space, NY City, 1999; Live Fictions, Sch Cinema and Television, Univ Southern Calif, Los Angeles, 1999; Trajectories, Shoshana Wayne Gallery, Santa Monica, Calif, 1999, Summer 2001; Art In Motion, Interactive & Multimedia Event, Helen Lindhurst Gallery, Los Angeles, 2000; It's About Time, Riverside Art Mus, Calif, 2000; Video Blowout, Crazy Space, 18th Street Complex, Santa Monica, Calif, 2000; Seizure!, Artplace, Los Angeles, 2000; Travelogue, Orange County Mus Contemp Art, Santa Ana, Calif, 2001; I See You 2, Fredericks Freiser Gallery, NY City, 2001; Seeing, Los Angeles County Mus Art, 2002; Still Life-Still Here, Armory Ctr for Arts, Pasadena, Calif, 2003; Light and Spaced-out, Loevenbruck, Paris, 2003; Surface Tension, The Fabric Workshop, Philadelphia, 2003; Stop & Stor, LUXE Gallery, NY City, Simply Drawn, 2004, It's Not About Sex, 2005, What A Great Space You Have..., 2006; Domicile: A Sense of Place, CoCa, Seattle, 2004; Loop, Interactive Gallery, New Media Caucus, Boston, 2005. *Awards:* Artist Space Independent Grant, 2000. *Dealer:* LUXE Gallery 24W 57th St NY 10019. *Mailing Add:* c/o Shoshana Wayne Gallery Bergamot Station 2525 Michigan Ave B1 Santa Monica CA 90404

COHEN, PETER GRAY
PAINTER, DESIGNER
b New York, NY, Nov 12, 1925. *Study:* Univ Chicago, 42-43; Art Inst Chicago, 43; Art Students League, NY, 47-48; Sch Painting & Sculpture, Mex City, 50-51. *Comn:* pvt comn by GD Birla, Culcutta, India, 52; Carib Theater, Clearwater, Fla, 53; They Served for Freedom, Little Italy, New York, NY, 58. *Exhib:* Eggleston Galleries, NY, 48; Archit League, NY, 56; Crown Galleries, NY, 57; Vietnam, 1st Reformed Church, Somerville, NJ, 65; New Paintings, Everhart Mus, Scranton, Pa, 66; Fred Waring Gallery, Stroudsburg, Pa, 87; Am Assoc for Advancement of Science, Wash, DC, 89; Open Space Gallery, Allentown, Pa, 90; Lycoming Coll, Williamsport, Pa, 92; South Bend Mus, In, 2010. *Teaching:* dir, Art School Poconos, Pa, 70-75. *Awards:* Emily Lowe Purchase Award, 49; Nat Community Arts Competition, HUD, 73; Interdisciplinary Grant, Pa Coun on Arts, 90. *Bibliog:* interview, Portraits, PBS-WVIA, 88; and others. *Mem:* Nat Soc Mural Painters, 51-57. *Media:* Alkyd, Enamels, Oil, Fresco. *Res:* developed colored concrete and plaster as mural materials. *Publ:* The Viable Culture, Pa Coun Arts, 90; Environmental Conservation, 90; Magic of Conception series, based on electron micrographs, reproduced extensively worldwide. Covers include Science, report of Lawrence Berkeley Labs, paintings & article, Newton, Japan. *Mailing Add:* 1116 N Milpas St Santa Barbara CA 93103

COHEN, REINA JOYCE
GRAPHIC ARTIST, PRINTMAKER
b New York, NY, Mar 28, 1931. *Study:* Cooper Union, NY, 51; The New School, 66. *Work:* Nassau Co Med Ctr, Hempstead, NY; Vitelco, St Thomas, US VI; St Laurence Univ, Canton, NY. *Comn:* Monoprints, Winrock Inn, Albuquerque, NMex, 90; Ltd Ed Collector Plates, Braford Exchange, Eng, 99. *Exhib:* Firehouse Gallery, Nassau Comm Col, Hempstead, NY, 81; Space Group Korea, Seoul, 82 & 84. *Awards:* First Prize, Freeport Arts Coun, 79; Award of Excellence, Independent Art Soc, 84 & 90; Grant, Mid Atlantic Arts Found, Baltimore, Md, 91. *Mem:* Nat Asn Women Artists; Independent Art Soc. *Media:* Miscellaneous Media, Etching. *Publ:* Floral Prints, Manor Art Ent Ltd, 93-94. *Dealer:* Art Rep Inc 279 Woodmere St Islip Terrace NY 11752; Printworks 251-27 Gaskell Rd Little Neck NY 11363. *Mailing Add:* 306 Roosevelt Blvd Fl 1 Long Beach NY 11561

COHEN, SOREL
CONCEPTUAL ARTIST, PHOTOGRAPHER
b Montreal, Que. *Study:* Concordia Univ, Montreal, BFA, 74, MFA, 79. *Work:* Nat Gallery Can, Ottawa, Ont; Bibliot Nat, Paris; Mus d'Art Contemporain, Montreal Mus Fine Arts; Winnipeg Art Gallery, Manitoba. *Exhib:* An Extended and Continuous Metaphor, PS 1, NY, 83; Productions and the Axis of Sexuality, Walter Philips Gallery, Banff, 84; Visual Facts, Third Eye Ctr, Glasgow, 85; Doppleganger/Cover, Galerie Aorta, Amsterdam, 85; et les ateliers de femmes, Mus d'Art Contemporain, Montreal, 86; Songs of Experience, Nat Gallery of Can, 86; Figures, Cambridge Darkroom, 87. *Pos:* Bd mem, Galerie Optica, 80-88. *Awards:* Bourse du Quebec, Ministere des Affairs Culture, 83; Arts Grant B, Can Coun, 85; Duke & Duchess Award in Photogr, Can Coun, 88. *Bibliog:* R Graham & G Godmer (auths), monogr essays, Mus d'Art Contemporain, 86; Therese St Gelais, rev, Parachute, 86-87; Bob Wilkie (auth), Telling pictures, revealing histories, Afterimage, Vol 17, No 9, 4/90. *Dealer:* Wynick Tuck Gallery 80 Spadina Ave Toronto Ont M5V 2J3 Canada; Samuel LaLourre Gallery Montreal Can. *Mailing Add:* 631 Lansdowne Ave Montreal PQ H3Y 2V7 Canada

COHEN, STEVEN A
COLLECTOR
b 1956. *Study:* Univ Pa Wharton Sch, BS (econ). *Pos:* Trader, Gruntal & co, 1978-92; chmn & founder, Strategic Air Command Capital Adv, 1992-. *Awards:* Named one of Top 200 Collectors, ARTnews mag, 2004-13; Forbes 400: Richest Americans, 2003-; The World's Richest People, Forbes mag, 2004-; The World's Most Influential People, TIME mag, 2007; 50 Most Influential People in Global Fin, Bloomberg Markets, 2011. *Mem:* Michael J Fox Found (bd mem, currently); Steven & Alexandra Cohen Found (co-founder, currently); Mus Modern Art (painting & sculpture comt). *Collection:* Impressionism; modern & contemporary art. *Mailing Add:* SAC Capital Adv 72 Cummings Pt Rd Stamford CT 06902

COHN, BARBARA G See Bisgyer, Barbara G (Cohn)

COHN, FREDERICK DONALD
DEALER, APPRAISER
b Monroe, Mich, May 3, 1931. *Study:* Univ Wis, BA, 54; Detroit Coll Law, LLB, 57. *Pos:* Art dealer, Images Gallery, Toledo, Ohio, currently. *Mem:* Toledo Mus Art, Pres Coun. *Specialty:* Nineteenth to twenty-first century American painting, print and sculpture. *Mailing Add:* 4343 W Bancroft St Apt 4F Toledo OH 43615-3958

COHN, MARJORIE B
CURATOR, HISTORIAN
b New York, NY, Jan 10, 1939. *Study:* Mt Holyoke Col, BA, 60; Radcliffe Col, AM, 61. *Hon Degrees:* Mt Holyoke Col, DFA, 96. *Collection Arranged:* Albrecht Durer, 1471-1528 (auth, catalogue), Mt Holyoke Col, 71; Wash & Gouache, Watercolor at Harvard, Fogg Art Mus, Harvard Univ, 77; Ingres Collection (auth, handbook), 81 & Gray Collection of Engravings (auth, handbook), 86, Fogg Art Mus; A Noble Collection: the Spencer Albums of Old Master Prints (auth, handbook), Fogg Art Mus, 92; Touchstone: 200 Years of Artists' Lithographs, Fogg Art Mus, 98. *Pos:* Conservator works of art on paper, Fogg Art Mus, Harvard Univ, 62-89, curator prints, 89-, actg dir, 90-91; mem bd examr (paper), Am Inst for Conserv, 76-78, mem nominating comt, 77 & ed jour. *Teaching:* Guest lectr print hist, Boston Univ, 73; vis lectr print hist, Wellesley Col, 73; vis asst prof print hist, Brown Univ, 75; sr lectr fine arts, Harvard Univ, 77-. *Mem:* Fel Int Inst for Conserv; fel Am Inst for Conserv; fel Am Acad Arts Sci. *Res:* History, materials & techniques of traditional graphic arts. *Publ:* Contribr, A Note on Media and Methods, Tiepolo, A Bicentenary Exhibition, Fogg Art Mus, 70; Wash & Gouache: A Study of the Development of the Materials of Watercolor, Fogg Art Mus, 81; contribr, Pursuit of Perfection: Works by J A D Ingres, J B Speed Mus, 83; Francis Gallery Gray and Art Collecting for America, Harvard Univ Art Mus, 86; A Noble Collection: The Spencer Albums of Old Master Prints, Harvard Univ Art Mus, 91. *Mailing Add:* Harvard Univ Art Mus Print Dept-Mongan Ctr 32 Quincy St Cambridge MA 02138

COHN, RICHARD A
DEALER
b New York, NY, Feb 20, 1924. *Study:* Univ Wis. *Pos:* Pres, Richard A Cohn Ltd, New York, 65-; partner, Kimmel/Cohn Photography Arts, New York, 74-. *Specialty:* Twentieth century German Expressionism. *Mailing Add:* Richard A Cohn Ltd One W 64th St New York NY 10023

COIT, M B
PAINTER, SCULPTOR
b New London, Conn. *Study:* Univ Conn, BFA, 68. *Comn:* Triptych, Mitsui Manufacturers Bank, Los Angeles, Calif, 83. *Exhib:* Images, Bowers Mus, Santa Ana, Calif, 87; LA Art, Gallery Q, Tokyo, Japan, 87; Designations, Los Angeles Co Mus Art, Calif, 87; solo exhib, Branslater Gallery, Riverside, Calif, 89; Artist's Book, Anchorage Mus, Alaska, 90; traveling exhib, Southern Calif Decade 1980-89; Contemp Artists, Univ Calif, Los Angeles, 90. *Bibliog:* Suzanne Muchnic (auth), Galleries downtown, LA Times, 11/2/84; Melinda Wortz (auth), article, Loma Linda Univ, 89; Roger Churches (auth), M B Coit: lucid lights, Loma Linda Univ, 89. *Media:* Acrylic, Oil; Plastic

COKENDOLPHER, EUNICE LORAINE
PAINTER, INSTRUCTOR
b Sonora, Tex, April 17, 1931. *Study:* Tex Womans Univ, 48-50; studied with Don Stone, Edgar Whitney, Zoltan Szabo, George Cherepov, Bud Biggs, Naomi Brotherton & Howard Wexler, 75-89. *Work:* Southern Guild Artists & Craftsmen, Bowling Green, Ky; Baptist Med Ctr Found, Oklahoma City. *Comn:* Noah and the Ark, First United Methodist Church, Burkburnett, Tex, 81. *Exhib:* Tex Fine Arts Citation Exhib, Laguna Gloria Mus, Austin, Tex, 80; Aqueous 79', Ky Watercolor Soc, 79; The Best of Southwest Watercolor Soc, Brookhaven Col, Dallas, 81 & 84; Southern Watercolor Soc Seventh Ann, Asheville Art Mus, NC, 83; Ga Watercolor Soc Fifth Nat Exhib, Valdosta State Coll Fine Arts Bldg, 84. *Teaching:* former instr watercolor, Wishing Well Studio, Burkburnett, Tex, 84. *Awards:* Award Merit, Aqueous 79, Ky Watercolor Soc Nat Exhib, 79; Mary Jo Weale Award, Southern Watercolor Soc Nat Exhib, 83; Second Place, Best of Southwest Watercolor Soc, 84. *Mem:* Southwestern Watercolor Soc; Tex Watercolor Soc. *Media:* Watercolor, Oil

COKER, CARL DAVID
PAINTER, EDUCATOR, SCULPTOR
b Greensboro, NC, Feb 8, 1928. *Study:* Art Students League with Robert Beverly Hale; Univ NC; Univ NMex with Randall Davey, Raymond Jonson, Richard Diebenkorn & Enriique Montenegro, BFA & MA; Ill State Univ, DTA. *Work:* Philbrook Mus, Tulsa; Univ Okla Mus, Norman; Jonson Gallery, Univ NMex,

Albuquerque; Mus of NMex, Santa Fe; El Paso Mus Art, Tex; Internat Mus Art, El Paso Tex; US Embassy, Lima, Peru; JS Nunnely, Fort Worth, Tex; MA Blue, San Antonio, Tex. *Comn:* Welded steel altarpiece, Holloman Air Force Hosp Chapel, USAF, 67; painting, Farmers & Merchants Bank, Tulsa, 75; fiberglass painting, 76 & welded steel sculpture, 77, Hicks Park, City of Tulsa; stainless steel sculpture (36' high) Gerald Hines Int, Redman Plaza, Tulsa OK, 83. *Exhib:* Tex Ann, Dallas Mus of Fine Arts, 60; Ill Print & Drawing Show, Art Inst Chicago, 63; Nat Drawing Show, Bucknell Univ, 65; Five NMex Artists, Pronaf Mus, Juarez, Mex, 65; NMex Sculptors, 66 & NMex Painters, 67, Mus of NMex, Santa Fe; Instituto Cult Peruano Norte Americano, 79; Galeria Forum, Lima, Peru, 80; Arte Sin Limetes, 4 cities in Mex & US; Amaro Gallery, Las Cruces, NMex, 2011; Preston Contemporary Art Mus, Mesilla, NMex, 2012; El Patio Gallery, Mesilla, NMex, 2013. *Teaching:* Instr painting, ETex State Univ, Commerce, 56-61; asst prof painting-sculpture, NMex State Univ, Las Cruces, 64-68; prof painting, Univ Tulsa, 68-87, retired, 89; guest artist, Escuela Nacional de Bellas Artes, Lima, Peru, 79-80, Claremont Col, Calif, 84. *Awards:* Fulbright Teaching/Res Grant, Lima, Peru, 79-80; Gold Medal, Painting, El Paso Mus, 88; Best of Show, El Paso Ann, 92; Best of Show, Internat Mus Art, El Paso, Tex, 2000. *Mem:* Taos Art Assoc; Asociacion Peruana de Artistas Plasticas; Coll Art Asn; Fullbright Asn. *Media:* Acrylic, Wood Sculpture. *Mailing Add:* 2250 Rosedale Las Cruces NM 88005

COLANGELO, CARMON
ADMINISTRATOR, PRINTMAKER
b Toronto, Can, Oct 29, 1957. *Study:* Univ Windsor, BFA, 81; La State Univ, MFA, 83. *Work:* Fogg Art Mus, Harvard Univ; Butler Mus Am Art, Steubonville, Ohio; Nelson-Atkins Mus Art, Kansas City, Mo; Univ Minn, Minneapolis; Clemson Univ, SC; Natl Mus Am Art, Washington, DC; Whitney Mus Art, NY; Exhib prints in shows US-Korea Int, 89; Boston Printmakers 42nd, 90; silvermine Int, 92, New World Contemp Prints, Balt, 93. *Exhib:* Colorprint USA, Lubbock Fine Arts Ctr, Tex, 94; solo exhib, Philadelphia Print Club, 95; Minn Nat Print Biennial, Katherine E Nash Gallery, 96; A Thought Intercepted, Calif Mus Art, Santa Rosa, 97; Litografia Contemporanea, Museo Nacional, Buenos Aires, 97; Drawn To Stone, Kennedy Mus Art, Athens, Ohio, 98; Slovenia Print Biennial, Slovenia Graphic Art, Novomesto, 98; Allographies, Univ Mus, Indiana, Pa, 98; Blasted Impulses and Beautiful Impossibilities, Univ Delaware, Newark, Del, 2000; Re-Tracings, Univ Chapel Hill, NC, 2001; Fountains of Age, Sandler-Hudson Personal Gallery, Atlanta, Ga, 2002; Da, Da, Da, Hope St Gallery, Liverpool Contemp Biennial, Eng, 2002; Phantasmogoria, Scuola Int di Grafica, Venice, Italy, 2003; Laura Mesaros Gallery, WVa Univ, WVa, 2004; Phantasmogoria, Museo de Pueblos, Guanajuato, Mex, 2004. *Pos:* Chmn div art, WVa Univ, 93-97; dir, Sch Art, Univ Ga, Athens, 97-; Instr Louisiana State Univ, Baton Rouge; 84; asst prof art W VA Univ, Morgantown, 84-88; assoc prof, 88; dir grad studies in art, 89; assoc chair div art, 93; dir & distinguished res prof Lamar Dodd Sch Art, Athens, GA, art prof. *Teaching:* Prof printmaking, WVa Univ, 84-97 & Univ Ga, 97-. *Awards:* Judith Lieber Award, Soc Am Graphic Arts, 93; Governors Award, WVa Juried Exhib, Arts & Humanities, 95; Applebaum/Charbonnel, Minn Nat, Charbonnel Inks, 96; Senior Research Grant Fine Arts, Univ GA, 98; Distinguished Research Prof, Univ GA, 2003; Deem Distinguished Lectr, WVa, Univ, WV, 2004. *Bibliog:* E C Cunningham (auth), Printmaking: A Primary Form of Expression, Colo Press, 92; Paul Krainak (auth), Appalachian high, Art Examiner, 97; Lynn Allen & Phyllis McGibbon, Best of Printmaking, Rockport Pupl, 97; Cong Zhiyuan, The Window Overseas, Chinese Printmaking, Vol 12, 98; Joel Ginson (AUTH), Carmon Chameleon, Georgia Magazine, June 2003; Michael Slaven (auth), Phantasmogoria, Art Papers, 2004. *Mem:* Coll Art Asn; Southern Graphics Coun (bd mem, 95-96); Contemp Art Ctr, Atlanta, GA; Ga Mus Art; Natl Coll Art Administrators; Southern Graphics Council (bd mem, 95-97). *Publ:* Contribr, Remote Simulations, Contemp Impressions, 95. *Dealer:* Sandler-Hudson Gallery, Atlanta, GA. *Mailing Add:* Univ of GA Lamar Dodd Sch Art 100 B Visual Arts Athens GA 30602

COLAO, RUDOLPH
PAINTER
b Peekskill, NY, Dec 26, 1927. *Study:* Art Students League, with Frank V Dumond, Edwin Dickinson & Frank Mason, 49-52. *Work:* Springville Mus, Utah. *Exhib:* Ann Exhib, Hudson Valley Art Asn, White Plains, NY, 83; Allied Artists Am, NY, 84; Nat Acad Design, NY, 84; Western Heritage Fair, Houston, Tex, 84-85; Summer Exhib, Rockport Art Asn, Mass, 88. *Teaching:* Instr drawing & painting, Art Students League, NY, 84-87; instr oil painting, Scottsdale Artists Sch, 87-88. *Awards:* Silver Medal, 81 & Gold Medal, 85, Rockport Art Asn; John Young Hunter Award, Allied Artists Am, 84. *Bibliog:* Herbert E Abrams (auth), The Teaching of Frank Dumond, Am Artist, 74; Jill Warren (auth), Rudolph Colao, Southwest Art, 82; Charles Movalli (auth), A Conversation with Rudy Colao, Am Artist, 84. *Mem:* Allied Artists NY; Knickerbocker Artists; Rockport Art Asn; Hudson Valley Art Asn. *Media:* Oil, Watercolor. *Mailing Add:* 2 S St Rockport MA 01966

COLARUSSO, CORRINE CAMILLE
PAINTER, INSTRUCTOR
b Boston, Mass, Mar 22, 1952. *Study:* Yale Summer Sch Art & Music, 72; Univ Mass, BFA, 73; Tyler Sch Art, Temple Univ, Philadelphia, MFA, 75. *Exhib:* Corcoran Gallery Art, Washington, DC, 75; Inst Contemp Art, Recife, Brazil, 76; O'Kane Gallery, Univ Houston, Tex, 77; 30 Women Artists, Peachtree Ctr, Atlanta, Ga, 78; one-person show, Oglethorpe Univ, Atlanta, 78; Personal Statements: Drawing, Southeastern Ctr Contemp Art, Winston-Salem, NC, 79; Atlanta Women's Invitational, Agnes Scott Col, 79. *Teaching:* Asst drawing, Univ Mass, Amherst, 72-73; grad teaching asst, Tyler Sch Art, 74-75; fac mem found design & drawing, Atlanta Col Art, 75-, dept head found studio, currently. *Awards:* MacDowell Colony Fel, 77 & 79; Fulbright-Hayes Res Grant, India /Nepal, 78

COLBY, BILL
PRINTMAKER, PAINTER
b Beloit, Kans, Jan 8, 1927. *Study:* Univ Denver, BA, 50; Univ Ill, Champaign, MA, 54. *Work:* Libr Cong, Pennell Print Collection, Washington, DC; Seattle Art Mus; Wichita Art Mus, Kans; Portland Art Mus, Ore; Tacoma Art Mus, Wash; Nat Art Acad, Hangzhou, China. *Comn:* Painting, Kilworth Chapel, Univ Puget Sound, Tacoma, Wash, 67; prints, Weyerhauser Corp, Tacoma, 82; prints, NW Print Coun, Portland, Ore, 93 & 97; prints, Everett Event Ctr, Wash, 2005. *Exhib:* State Capitol Mus, Olympia, Wash, 74, 76, 78, 80 & 91; solo exhib, Kittredge Gallery, Tacoma, 79, 87, 89, 95, 2002, 2008; Art Alliance Gallery, Philadelphia, 79; Bellevue Art Mus, Wash, 79, 83 & 85; retrospective, Tacoma Art Mus, 86; Univ Hawaii, Hilo, 93; Sandpiper Gallery, Tacoma, 93, 95, 98, 2000, 2003, 2004, 2006 & 2008; and others. *Teaching:* Prof printmaking, Univ Puget Sound, Tacoma, Wash, 56-89, dir Kittredge Gallery, Univ Puget Sound, 58-65 & 83-89. *Awards:* Arts award, Pierce Co, Wash, 2002. *Mem:* Am Color Print Soc, Philadelphia; Puget Sound Sumi; Tacoma Arts & Crafts Asn; NW Printmakers. *Media:* Woodcut, Etching; Acrylic, Watercolor. *Publ:* Portrait of an Artist, Pierce Co Mag, 2/82; Jet Dreams: Art of NW 50's, Univ Wash Press, Seattle, 95; Best of Northwest Art, Tacoma Art Mus, Wash, 2012

COLBY, JOY HAKANSON
CRITIC
b Detroit, Mich. *Study:* Detroit Soc Arts & Crafts; Wayne State Univ, BFA; Hon Dr. Fine Arts, Ctr Creative Studies, 98. *Pos:* Art critic, Detroit News, 50-. *Awards:* Art Achievement Award, 83, Wayne State Univ; Detroit Press Club Award Arts Writing, 84; Award for Achievment, Ctr for Creative Studies, 89. *Mem:* Mich Coun Arts (adv, 72-79); Detroit Coun Arts; New Detroit Inc Arts Comt; Bloomfield Hills Arts Coun. *Publ:* Auth, Art & A City, 56; Arts and Crafts in Detroit, Detroit Inst Arts, 76. *Mailing Add:* Detroit News 615 W Lafayette Detroit MI 48231

COLBY, VICTOR E
SCULPTOR, EDUCATOR
b Frankfort, Ind, Jan 5, 1917. *Study:* Corcoran Sch Art; Ind Univ, AB, 48; Cornell Univ, MFA, 50. *Work:* Ithaca Coll Mus; Munson-Williams-Proctor Inst, Utica, NY; St Lawrence Univ, Canton, NY; State Univ NY Coll Cortland; Roberson Mus, Binghamton, NY. *Comn:* Wall sculpture, Wilson Nuclear Physics Lab, Cornell Univ, 68. *Exhib:* Solo exhibs, Hewitt Gallery, 58, The Contemporaries, 66 & Hartley Gallery, 74. *Teaching:* Prof sculpture, Cornell Univ, 50-82; retired. *Media:* Wood. *Mailing Add:* 642 Peru S Lansing Rd Groton NY 13073-9733

COLE, DONALD
PAINTER
b New York, NY, Oct 31, 1930. *Study:* Bucknell Univ, BS (civil eng); Univ Iowa, MFA. *Work:* Worcester Art Mus, Mass; Portland Art Mus, Oreg; ARCO Ctr Visual Arts, Los Angeles; Tacoma Art Mus, Wash. *Exhib:* One-man exhibs, Frank Marino Gallery, 81 & 82, State Univ NY, Plattsburgh, 86, Kidi Gallery, Japan, 92, Toyama Ginko, Japan, 92, Ishikawa Denki, Japan, 92 & Gallery 17, Kanazawa, 93, Nancy Hoffman Gallery, New York City, 73, 75, 78; Foster/White Gallery, Seattle, Wash, 2001; Jeffrey Moose Gallery, 2001; Gallery 070 Vashon, Wash, 2004 & 2006; ARTXCHANGE Gallery (with catalog), Seattle, Wash, 2007, 2010, 2012. *Teaching:* Parsons Sch Design, NY, 77-94 & Fashion Inst Technol, 83-94. *Awards:* Creative Artists Pub Serv Grant/Painting, NY State Coun Arts, 75; Nat Endowment Arts Artists Fel Grant, 78. *Bibliog:* Ellen Lubell (auth), article in Arts Mag, 73, 75 & 78; Sheila Farr (auth), The Seattle Times, 2001; Regina Hackett (auth), The Seattle p. 1, 2007; Alex Clayton (auth), Unexpected Arrivals, Art Access, 12/2007-1/2008; John Levy (auth), Unpredictable Arrivals, Artxchange Gallery, 2007; Elaine Hanowell (auth), Donald Cole, Mountain Visions, Artxchange Gallery, 2010. *Media:* Acrylic on Canva. *Specialty:* Contemporary Art by International Artists. *Dealer:* ArtXchange Gallery 512 First Ave S Seattle WA 98104. *Mailing Add:* 25718 Wax Orchard Rd SW Vashon WA 98070

COLE, GRACE V
PAINTER, INSTRUCTOR
b Chicago, Ill, Jan 23, 43. *Study:* École Albert du Fois with Ted Seth Jacobs, Vihiers, France; Lill St Studio, Chicago; Prairie State Coll, Chicago Heights, Ill; Art Inst Chicago; Univ Chicago; pvt apprenticeships in painting, drawing & sculpture. *Work:* Bristol Meyers Gallery, Evansville, Ind; Ill Coll & Trinity Episcopal Church, Jacksonville, Ill; Sigma Alpha Epsilon, Univ Tenn, Knoxville; Coe Coll, Cedar Rapids, Iowa; The MacArthur Found, Chicago, Ill; Northern Trust Corp Ctr, Ill; Rosalind Franklin Univ, Ill; Stephen F Austin State Univ, Nacogdoches, Tex. *Comn:* 4 portraits, Scharfman Orgn, New York, 87; 1 portrait, Rockford Coll, Ill, 88; 2 portraits, Episcopal Diocese Chicago, Ill, 88; 10 portraits, Medinah Country Club, Ill, 88-90; 3 portraits, Bank Louisville, Ind, 89-90; The MacArthur Found, Chicago, Ill, 2003. *Exhib:* Arts Club of Chicago, Ill, 98-2005; Fine Art Bldg Gallery, Ill, 99-2006; Chicago Athenaeum Mus, Ill, 2000-03; Arts Club of Wash, DC, 2000; Univ W Fla, 2000; Univ of Ill, Chicago, 2000; Cahoon Mus of Am Art, 2001-06; Coll Lake Co, Ill, 2001; Anne Loucke Gallery, 2001-05. *Teaching:* Instr drawing & painting, Cole Studio, Chicago, 80-; instr painting, Prarie State Coll, Chicago Heights, 84-95; instr painting & portraits, Suburban Fine Art Ctr, Highland Park, Ill, 90-93; instr drawing & painting, Old Town Triangle Asn, Chicago, 91-; pvt instr. *Awards:* Golden Apple Award, Prairie State Coll, Chicago Heights, Ill, 94. *Bibliog:* Karl Moehl (auth), Illinois artist, New Art Examiner, 9/86; Chicago Tribune, 8/16/91 & 3/20/92; Star Publ, Chicago Heights, 3/19/92. *Mem:* Ill Arts Alliance, Chicago; Ill Comt for the Nat Mus Women Arts, Washington, DC, (pres, 2002-03); The Arts Club, Chicago. *Media:* Oil; Drawing Materials. *Dealer:* Portraits Inc 985 Park Ave New York NY 10028; Anne Louchs Gallery Glencoe Ill; Fine Arts Bldg Gallery; Ellen Posture Highland Park Ill Agt; Jean Leigh Gallery Chicago Ill

COLE, HAROLD DAVID
HISTORIAN, EDUCATOR
b Tulsa, Okla, Feb 28, 1940. *Study:* Univ Tulsa, BA, MA (art criticism), with Alexander Hogue & Harry A Broadd; Ohio State Univ, MA (art hist), PhD, with Franklin Ludden. *Work:* Art Gallery, Univ Tulsa, Okla; Art Gallery, Baldwin-Wallace Col, Berea, Ohio; Art Gallery, Cumberland Col, Williamsburg, Ky; Art Gallery, Nicholls State Univ, Thibodaux, La. *Exhib:* 32nd Ann Springfield Ann Ten-State Exhib, Springfield Art Mus, Mo, 62; 12th Ann Own Your Own Exhib, Denver Art Mus, Colo, 68; 51st Ann May Show, Cleveland Mus Art, Ohio, 69; Solo exhibs, Cumberland Coll, 70 & 72 & Nicholls State Univ, 71; H Cole Retrospective, 92-2012. *Collection Arranged:* Kenneth R Weedman Exhib (auth, catalog), 73. *Pos:* Mem visual art panel, Ohio Arts Coun, 77-79. *Teaching:* Prof art hist, Baldwin-Wallace Col, 66-, Malicky chair humanities, 94-2006. *Awards:* Special Jury Mention, Cleveland Mus Art May Show, 69; Strosacker Award for Excellence in Teaching, 77; Bechberger Award for Excellence in Counselling, 95. *Mem:* Coll Art Asn; Midwest Art Hist Asn; Int Ctr Medieval Art; Monument Historique. *Res:* Thirteenth century French sculpture & archit; 19th century French painting. *Publ:* Auth, Kenneth R Weedman Sculpture Exhibition, Crafts Horizons, 72; coauth, Grant Reynard: His Life & Work, Baldwin-Wallace Col, 75. *Mailing Add:* Baldwin Wallace Univ Dept Art Berea OH 44017

COLE, HERBERT MILTON
HISTORIAN, PHOTOGRAPHER
b Newton, Mass, Apr 15, 1935. *Study:* Williams Col, BA, 57; Columbia Univ, MA, 64, Columbia Univ, PhD, 68. *Collection Arranged:* African Arts of Transformation (auth, catalog), Univ Calif, Santa Barbara, 70; The Arts of Ghana (auth, catalog), Mus Cult Hist, Univ Calif, Los Angeles, 75-77; Igbo Arts: Community & Cosmos (coauth, catalog), Los Angeles, 84; Icons: Ideals & Power in the Arts of Africa (auth), Natural Mus African Art, Smithsonian Inst; Deceptive Realities: Authenticity & Quality in African Art, Univ Art Mus, Univ Calif, Santa Barbara; I Am Not Myself: The Art of African Masquerade, UCLA, 85. *Pos:* Consult ed, African Arts, Univ Calif, Los Angeles, 70-. *Teaching:* Prof African art hist, Univ Calif, Santa Barbara, 68-. *Awards:* Ford Found Foreign Area Fel, 66-67; Nat Endowment Humanities Younger Humanist Fel, 72-73; Rockefeller Sr Fel, Smithsonian Inst, 87-88; Leadership Award, Arts Counc African Studies Asn. *Mem:* Coll Art Asn; Arts Coun African Studies Asn. *Media:* Photography. *Res:* Arts of tropical Africa. *Publ:* Ed, African Art and Leadership, Univ Wis-Madison, 73; auth, The Arts of Ghana, Univ Calif, Los Angeles, 77; Mbari: Art and Life Among the Owerri Igbo, Ind Univ Press, 80; Igbo Arts: Community & Cosmos; A History of Art in Africa. *Mailing Add:* 2020 ElCamin de la Luz Santa Barbara CA 93109

COLE, JEAN (DAHL)
PAINTER, WATERCOLOR
b Greeley, Colo, Jan 30, 1947. *Study:* Univ Calif, Berkeley, BA (design), 68; studied with Charles Reid, Irving Shapiro, Frederic Wong, Zolton Szabo & Steve Quiller. *Work:* Leanin' Tree Mus Western Art, Boulder, Colo; Sisters Charity Health Care Systems; Storage Technology, Inc, Invesco; pvt collections of Clayton G Mammel, Thomas Cousins, Donald & Susan Sturm & Philip Anchutz; Jackson Nat Life Insurance. *Exhib:* Six on Paper, Metro State Coll, Denver, 94; Watercolor West, Brea Cult Ctr, Colo, 94; Rocky Mountain Nat, Watermedia Exhib, Foothills Art Ctr, Golden, Colo, 94, 96, 98, 99, 2002 & 2005; Solo exhib, Arvada Ctr for the Arts & Humanities, 2000, Republic Plaza Botanica Spectaculum, Univ Northern Colo, 2000; Colo Watercolor Soc State Watermedia Exhib, Colo Hist Mus, Denver, 94-96, 98-99; Am Watercolor Soc, 94, 97, 99, & 2010; Watermedia VIII, Univ Colo, Colorado Springs, 96; Contemp Watermedia Invitational, Univ Southern Colo, 97; Watermedia IX, Colorado Springs Fine Art Ctr, 98; Colo Wyo Biennial, OneWest Art Ctr, Ft Collins, 98; NW Watercolor Soc Ann Open Exhib, Wash State Conv & Trade Ctr, Seattle, 98. *Teaching:* Demonstrations & workshops for var art groups. *Awards:* Award for Excellence, Colo Watercolor Soc State Exhib, 97 & Pres Award, 98, 99; Merchandise Award, NW Watercolor Soc Ann Open, 98; Reed Memorial Award, Calif Watercolor Asn Watercolor Competition, 98; Best of Show, Rocky Mountain Nat, 98. *Bibliog:* Flowers that Grow on You, The Artists Mag, 11/92; The Secret Life of Flowers, Rocky Mt News, 4/10/2000; Am Artists Watercolor, Know Your Paints, 2008. *Mem:* Signature mem Nat Watercolor Soc; signature mem Colo Watercolor Soc (treas, 90-91, pres, 92); signature mem Am Watercolor Soc,; signature mem Rocky Mt Nat Watermedia Soc; Signature mem Transparent Watercolor Soc Am; Int Guild of Realism. *Media:* Transparent Watercolor. *Publ:* Spotlight, Rocky Mountain News, 12/93, 11/94 & 4/2000; Light and Shadow, 97 & Best of Watercolor 2, 97, Basic Flower Painting, Northlight, Watercolor Magic, 95-98, Rockport Publ; The Scene, Denver Post, 8/29/98; Collected Best of Watercolor, 2002; The Secret to Fabulous Flowers, Watercolor Basics, 2004. *Dealer:* Tom O'Neil Fine Arts Denver CO. *Mailing Add:* 3800 E 4th St Denver CO 80206-4558

COLE, JULIE KRAMER
PAINTER
b Springfield, Ohio, June 9, 1942. *Study:* Colo State Univ, Ft Collins, 60-62; Colo Inst Art, Denver, grad, 63. *Work:* San Dimas City Hall, Calif; Home St Bank, Loveland, Colo. *Exhib:* Am Royal Western Art Show, Kansas City, 84 & 85; Governor's Western Art Show, North Platte, Nebr, 84-88; Am Indian and Cowboy Asn Show, San Dimas, Calif, 88-91; Minneapolis Western & Wildlife Show, Minn, 89, 90 & 92; Classic Am Western Art Show, Beverly Hills, Calif, 90 & 91. *Pos:* Freelance fashion illusr, 63-80; illusr, Leanin' Tree Publ Co, 84-, Antrock, 90, Johnson Creative Arts, 90 & Bradford Exchange, 92; prof western artist, Cole Fine Art Inc, 86-. *Awards:* Festival Choice, 88; Silver Medal, 89; Gold Medal, Am Indian & Cowboy Asn Show, 90; Hall of Fame, Colo Inst Art, 92. *Media:* Pastel, Gouache. *Publ:* Auth, Western Horseman, 4/89; US Art, 4/91, 3/93, 7/93, 8/93, & 3/94; Bradford Exchange, 7/93 & 11/94; Collectors Mart Mag, 7/93. *Dealer:* Cole Fine Art Inc PO Box 7268 Loveland CO 80537. *Mailing Add:* c/o Thunderbird Art Gallery 1309 E 16th St Greeley CO 80631

COLE, MAX
PAINTER
b Hodgeman Co, Kans, Feb 14, 1937. *Study:* Univ Ariz, Tucson, MFA, 64. *Work:* La Jolla Mus Contemp Art; Dallas Mus; Utah Mus; Los Angeles Co Mus; Tel Aviv Mus; Metrop Mus; and others. *Exhib:* Whitney Mus Am Art Biannual, 75; New Abstract Painting, Los Angeles Co Mus, 76; 35th Biannual, Corcoran Gallery Art, 77; Solo exhibs, Sidney Janis Gallery, NY, 77 & 79, Los Angeles Louver Gallery, 79, 80 & 83, Miami-Dade Col, 82, Cologne Art Fair, Ger, 90, Kiyo Higashi Gallery, Los Angeles, 91, 93-95, Kunstraum, Kassel, Ger, 91 & Mus Folkwang, Essen, Ger, 92; Zabriskie Gallery, NY, 87; Galerie Helene Grubair, Miami, 88; Haines Gallery, San Francisco, 88, 91 & 96; Stark Gallery, NY, 96; Galerie Schlegl, Zurich, 96; and others. *Teaching:* Asst prof painting, Pasadena City Col, Calif, 67-79; adj assoc prof, Columbia Univ, New York, 85-91. *Awards:* Nat Endowment Arts Fel, 83; Pollock-Krasner Fel, 86; Res Fel, Indo-US Subcommission, 88; and others. *Mailing Add:* 195 E 3rd St New York NY 10009

COLEMAN, A(LLAN) D(OUGLASS)
CRITIC, CURATOR
b New York, NY, Dec 19, 1943. *Study:* Hunter Col, Bronx, NY, BA, 64; San Francisco State Col, MA, 67; New York Univ. *Collection Arranged:* Silver Sensibilities, Snug Harbor Cultural Ctr, Staten Island, NY, 80 & Catskill Ctr Photog, 82; The Erotic in Photography: Contemporary Trends, Cameravision, Los Angeles, 82; Testimonies: Photography and Social Issues, Houston Fotofest, 90; Saga: The Journey of Arno Rafael Minkinnen, DeCordova Mus, Lincoln, Mass, 2005; Saga, Lianzhou Int Photo Festival, 2006; Saga Nat Mus Contemp Art, Bucharest, 2006, Saga Palace of Art, Bratislava, 2006; Saga, Salon Tai de Museo, Salo, Finland, 2007; China: Insights, Fred Jones Jr Mus Art, Norman, Okla, 2008; Saga, See, Beijing, 2008; Jerry Uelsmann & Maggie Taylor, See, Beijing, 2008; China: Insights, The Light Factory, Charlotte, NC, 2008; Saga, Palazzo del Principi, Reggio Emilia, Italy, 2008; Saga, Winnipeg Art Gallery, 2008; Light Quartet, See, Beijing, 2009; Wynn Bullock & Harold Feinstein, See, Beijing, 2010; Insights, May Gallery, Webster Univ, St. Louis, 2010; Insights, Cedar Rapids Mus Art, 2010; Ralph Gibson and Arthur Tress, Beijing, 2011; Insights, Pomona Coll Mus Art, 2011; Mary Ellen Mark, Beijing, 2011; Insights, Nash Gallery, Univ Minnesota, 2011; George Tice, Beijing, 2011; Insights, Lowe Art Mus, Univ Miami, 2011; Silent Strength of Liu Xia, City Univ Hong Kong, 2012, Silent Strength, Centro Cultural Galileo, Madrid, 2012. *Pos:* Photog columnist, Latent Image, Village Voice, 68-73; photog critic, New York Times, 70-74; contrib ed, Camera 35, 75-82, Lens' on Campus, 83-87; vpres, Photog Media Inst, Inc, 77-; founder/organizer, Conf on Photog Criticism, 77-; bd dir, Photog Resource Ctr, 78-82; critic-in-residence, Int Ctr Photog, NY, 79; founding ed, Views: A New Eng J Photog, 79-81; mem bd advisors, Ctr Photog Woodstock, 82-93 & Los Angeles Ctr Photog Studies, 82-; photog critic, New York Observer, 88-97; columnist, Camera & Darkroom, 89-95, European Photog, WGer, Photo Metro, 89- & Photography in New York, Juliet Art Mag, Italy, 93-98; exec dir, The Photography Criticism Cyber Archive, 2003-. *Teaching:* Mem fac photog criticism, New Sch Social Res, New York, 70-71, 79-81; vis lectr, Col Art, Md Inst, 71-73; Instr photog, Dept Film/TV, New York Univ, 78-82, asst prof, Dept Photog, 83-93, faculty mem, VASA Project, 2010-. *Awards:* Hasselblad Found Grant, Sweden, 91; Fulbright Scholar, Sweden, 94; Writing on Photography Infinity Award, Int Ctr Photog, 95; Kulturpreis, Deutsche Gesellschaft fur Fotografie, 2001; Lifetime Achievement in Writing on Photography, Royal Photographic Soc, 2010. *Bibliog:* Video interview, Video Databank, Sch Art Inst Chicago, 77; Craig Morey & Ted Hedgpeth (auths), interview, San Francisco Camerawork Newslett, 10/82; Video interview, Md Inst Coll Art, 83. *Mem:* Int Asn Art Critics (exec vpres & chmn, mem comt, 87-93); Authors Guild; PEN Am Ctr; Int Soc Gen Semantics; Nat Writers Union; Am Soc Journalists & Authors. *Res:* Hist of photography, examining the impact of the invention of the lens on Western culture between 1500 to present. *Interests:* Contemp Poetry & short fiction, jazz & world music, experimental music. *Publ:* The Grotesque in Photography, Ridge Press/Summit, 77; Light Readings: A Photography Critics Writings, 1968-1978, Oxford Univ Press, 79; Coauth, The Photography A-V Program Directory, PMI Inc, 80; Looking at Photographs: Animals Chronicle, 95; Tarnished Silver: After the Photo Boom, Midmarch, 96; auth, Dept of Field: Essays on Photography, Mass Media and Lens Culture, Univ NMex Press, 98; The Digital Evolution, Nazrael Press, 98; Critical Focus, Photography in the Int Image Community, Nazraeli Press, 95. *Mailing Add:* 465 Van Duzer St Staten Island NY 10304

COLEMAN, CONSTANCE DEPLER
PAINTER, DESIGNER
b Macomb, Ill, Sept 9, 1926. *Study:* Dominican Col, San Raphael, Calif, 45-47; Calif Sch Fine Arts, San Francisco, with Mark Rothko & David Parks, 47-49; Cincinnati Art Acad, Ohio, with Paul Chitlaw, 63-65. *Work:* City Hall, City of Carmel by the Sea, Calif. *Comn:* animal and people portraits by private clients. *Exhib:* James Hunt Barker Gallery, Palm Beach, 79; Wondrous Wildlife, Int Wildlife Juried Show, Cincinnati, Ohio, 83; A B Crosson Jr Gallery, Cincinnati, Ohio, 84; Portraits for Commission, McIntosh-Drysdale Gallery (with Gifford Myers & Bruce Sharp), Washington, DC, 86; Albion Gallery, Santa Barbara, Calif, 87; Durenberger Friends, San Juan Capistrano, 92; Waterhouse Gallery, Santa Barbara, Calif, 98-; Portraits by Artists, Beverly Hills, 98; Sarah Davenport Gallery, London, 98; Zantman Galleries, Carmel, Palm Desert, 98; William Secord Gallery, NY, 98; Carmel Art Asn, 98; Dog and Horse Art Gallery, Charleston, SC, 2001-; Eisele Gallery of Fine Art, Cincinnati, Ohio, 2010-. *Collection Arranged:* American Kennel Club Mus of the Dog St Louis. *Pos:* Designer & illusr, paper products, greeting cards & wall paper, portraying animals in human situations, 49-70; "Original Depler" gift products, dept, 56, Nostalgic art work and products. *Teaching:* Dir, teacher & founder, Primary Art Dept, Cincinnati Country Day Sch, Ohio, 62-68. *Bibliog:* Marcia Smith (auth), They pant for arf art, Dallas Times Herald, 5/14/84; article, Pet Portraits, Epcot Mag, Disney Cable-TV, Matt & Mutley, TV Program 84; feature articles in numerous mag & newspapers incl USA Today, Los Angeles Times, Prints Mag, Best Mag, & Venue Mag, Cincinnati, Ohio. *Mem:* mem, Carmel Art Assn, Carmel, Calif. *Media:* Oil, Silverpoint, Pen & Ink

Pastel. *Res:* Domestic Animals of Tibet; dogs. *Collection:* Oprah Winfrey, Lily Pulitzer, Oscar de la Renta, Jenny Iovine, Michael McDonald, and others. *Publ:* Illusr, Joy in a Wooly Coat, H J Kramer, Inc, 89. *Dealer:* Eisele Gallery Cincinnati; Dog & Horse Art, Charleston, SC; William Secord Gallery, NY; Carmel Art Asn Carmel CA. *Mailing Add:* 2121 Alpine Pl Cincinnati OH 45206

COLEMAN, DONNA LESLIE
PAINTER, EDUCATOR
b Philadelphia, Pa, Nov 16, 1954. *Study:* RI Sch Design, BFA (honors), 77; Brooklyn Coll, MFA, 82; Univ DC, educ courses, 96; Univ Zurich, English lit courses, 72-73, Switzerland; Mercy Coll, educ courses, Dobbs Ferry, NY, 87-89. *Exhib:* Solo exhib, Arlington Arts Ctr, Va, 92, Gallery K, Washington, DC, 96 & 2000 & New Horizons Gallery, Children's Hosp, Washington, DC, 96; Options 93, Washington Proj for Arts, 93; Fashion Happening, Gallery K, Washington, DC, 98; Mather Gallery, Case Western Reserve Univ, 2002; Meditated Nature, HereHere Gallery, Cleveland, Ohio, 2003; Featured Artist, Dead Horse Gallery, Cleveland, Ohio, 2003; Go Figure, Sandusky, Ohio, 2004; Vanishing Borders: Contemp Environmental Art, Herndon Gallery, Antioch Coll, Yellow Springs, Ohio, 2006; Riffe Gallery, Columbus, Ohio, 2009; Unapologetic, Touchstone Gallery, Washington, DC, 2009; Intown Club, Cleveland, Ohio, 2010; River Gallery, Cleveland, Ohio, 2011. *Pos:* Dir, Dreamcatcher Summer Arts Camp, Washington, DC, 97-2000. *Teaching:* Art teacher, Rye Country Day Sch, NY, 86-89, Browne Acad, Alexandria, Va, 89-98, Fillmore Arts Ctr, Washington, DC, 91-, Sidwell Friends Sch, 97- & Firelands Asn Vis Arts, 2001-; vis ast prof art, Oberlin Coll, 2002-; visiting prof, Lorain Co Community College, 2010-. *Awards:* Grants-in-Aid, DC Comn Arts, Washington, DC, 92, 95 & 98; Fel Award, Art Matters, New York, 92 & 95; Ohio Arts Coun, Indiv Artist Fel Award, 2002 & 2007. *Media:* Oil on Canvas. *Res:* Narrative paintings. *Mailing Add:* 22 King St Oberlin OH 44074

COLEMAN, FLOYD WILLIS
EDUCATOR, PAINTER
b Sawyerville, Ala, Jan 13, 1939. *Study:* Ala State Univ, with Hayward L Oubre, BA, 60; Univ Wis, with Robert Burkert, MS, 62; Univ Ga, with Edmund B Feldman, PhD, 75. *Work:* Oakland Mus, Calif; High Mus Art, Emory Univ, Spelman Col, Atlanta Univ, Atlanta, Ga. *Exhib:* Am Drawing Ann, Norfolk Mus Arts & Sci, Va, 62; 18th Southeastern Ann, High Mus Art, Atlanta, Ga, 63; 30 Contemp Black Artists, Minneapolis Inst Arts, Minn, 68; Spiral: Afro-Am Art of the Seventies, Mus Nat Ctr Afro-Am Artists, Boston, 80; Recent Works on Paper, Last Stop Gallery, Richmond, Va, 88. *Teaching:* Asst prof, Clark Col, Atlanta, Ga, 65-71; assoc prof, Southern Ill Univ, Edwardsville, 76-80, prof, 81-83; prof & chair, Jackson State Univ, 83-87; prof & chair, Howard Univ, 87-. *Awards:* Fels, Ford Found, 68-70, Esso Found, 71 & Nat Endowment Humanities, 76-77. *Mem:* Coll Art Asn Am; Nat Conf Artists (co-chmn, 70-71). *Media:* Mixed-Media on Paper. *Res:* African continuities in Afro-Am art; Mex influences on Mayan archit; the art of Felrath Hines & the Spiral group; Black artists of the South. *Publ:* Auth, African influences on Black American art, 76 & Toward an aesthetic toughness in Afro-American art, 78, Black Art Quart; Popular images in Afro-American art, J Soc Ethnic & Special Studies, 80; coauth, Black Design: Systems, Elements, Applications, 84, Prentice-Hall. *Mailing Add:* 13014 Daley St Silver Spring MD 20906-5104

COLEMAN, GAYLE
LECTURER, CONSERVATOR
b Allentown, Pa, Mar 15, 1954. *Study:* Lehigh Univ, Bethlehem, Pa, BA; Art Restoration Tech Inst, cert & apprenticeship; Nova Law Sch. *Pos:* Art conservator, Lehigh Univ, Bethlehem, Pa, 76-; freelance art restorer, Pa; partner, Coleman Art Gallery, Allentown, 76-; lectr var cols & univ. *Mem:* Am Inst for Conserv of Hist & Artistic Work; Asn for Preservation Technol; Am Bar Asn. *Res:* Microchemical analysis of art work; moral rights & art conservation. *Mailing Add:* 17216 Hampton Blvd Boca Raton FL 33496

COLEMAN, LORING W
ARTIST
b Boston, Mass, Apr 1918. *Study:* Middlesex Sch, Grad; Scott Carbee Sch of Art, Grad, Boston. *Work:* exhib in group shows, High Art Mus, Milton Col, Mus of Fine Arts, Rep in permanent collections, Mus of Fine Arts, Parrisch Art Mus. *Exhib:* Exhibs incl Retrospective, Concord Art Assoc, Francesca Anderson Fine Art, St Botolph Club, Central Place Galleries, Shore Galleries, exhib in group shows, Am Watercolor Soc, Knickerbocker Artists, Munson Gallery, Milton Col, Addison Gallery of Am Art, Represented in permanent collections, Salmagundi Club, Butler Inst of Am Art, Canton Art Inst, Concord Pub Libr. *Pos:* rep, Francesca Anderson Find Art, Lexington, Mass. *Teaching:* Prof, painting, sculpture Middlesex Sch. *Awards:* Salmagundi Club, Lifetime Achievement Award; recipient Strathmore Paper Co Award; Elizabeth K Ellis Artists Fel Award. *Mem:* Nat Acad (assoc, 91, acad, 94). *Mailing Add:* Francesca Anderson Fine Art 3720 SW Bond Ave Unit 910 Portland OR 97239

COLEMAN, M L (MICHAEL LEE)
PAINTER, INSTRUCTOR
b Livingston, Mont, May 11, 1941. *Study:* Univ Wyo, BS, 63; studies with James Disney, Loveland, Colo, 69 & 75, Hall Diteman, Billings, Mont, 77 & Wilson Hurley, Albuquerque, NMex, 85. *Work:* Northern Natural Gas, Omaha, Nebr; Iowa Beef Producers; Home Nat Banks, Arkansas City, Kansas City & Scottsdale, Ariz; JW Holmes & Assoc, Scottsdale, Ariz; Webtrend Graphics, Vista, Calif. *Exhib:* Mus Native Am Cult Art Show & Auction, Spokane, Wash, 80-81; Sun Valley Western Art Auction & Exhib, Idaho, 80-81; Stockmen's Found Art Show & Auction, Calgary & Edmonton, Alta, 81; Art of the West, Ger Mus, Munich, 81. *Teaching:* Instr workshops, Sedona, Ariz. *Awards:* Best of Show, Stockmen's Found Art Show and Auction, Calgary, Alta, 81. *Bibliog:* Kathe McGehee (auth), M L Coleman's dramatic landscapes, Art West Mag, Vol III, No 6; Dale Burk (auth), A Brush with the West, Mountain Press, 80; Peggy & Harold Samuels (auths), Contemporary Western Artists, SW Art Publ, 82. *Mem:* Ariz Plein Air Painters; Sedona Guild of Artists (master signature artist); Sedona Visual Artists Coalition. *Media:* Oil. *Dealer:* Sheri D Coleman 200 Sunset Pass Rd Sedona AZ 86351. *Mailing Add:* Sunset Pass Studios 200 Sunset Pass Rd Sedona AZ 86351-9519

COLEMAN, MICHAEL B
PAINTER
b Provo, Utah, June 25, 1946. *Study:* Brigham Young Univ. *Work:* Buffalo Bill Hist Mus, Cody, Wyo; J N Bartfield Galleries, NY; Legacy Galleries, Jackson, Wyo. *Comn:* Boone & Crockett Club; Alaska Prof Hunters Asn. *Exhib:* Springville Mus Nat; Nat Acad Western Art, Nat Cowboy Hall of Fame, Oklahoma City; Buffalo Bill Hist Ctr; Charlie Russell Mus; Kennedy Galleries; Wunderlich Gallery; Gerold Peters Gallery, Santa Fe, NMex; Artists Am, Denver; J N Bartfield Gallery, NY. *Awards:* Hubbard award, Prix de West. *Bibliog:* Diane Cochrane (auth), Romantic Western landscapes, Am Artist, 1/75; Susan Myers (auth), Twenty American Landscape Painters; Romantic Western painter, SW Art Mag, 2/77; Peter Hassrick (auth), Under Eagles Wings: The Art of Michael Coleman; and others. *Media:* Oil. *Dealer:* J N Bartfield Galleries 30 W 57th St New York NY 10019. *Mailing Add:* 2822 Rolling Knolls Dr Provo UT 84604-4832

COLEN, DAN
ARTIST
b Leonia, NJ, 1979. *Study:* RI Sch Design, BFA (painting), 2001. *Work:* Secrets & Cymbals, Smoke & Scissors (My Friend Dash's Wall in the Future), 2004-2006; Untitled (going, going, go...), 2005; Holy War, 2006; The Awesome Power of Nature, 2006; Rama Lama Ding Dong, 2006; Untitled (Vete al Diablo), 2006. *Exhib:* solo exhibs, Seven Days Always Seemed Like A Bit of An Exaggeration, Rivington Arms, NY, 2003; Potty Mouth, Potty War, Pot Roast, Pot is a Reality Kick, Gagosian Gallery, NY, 2006; Secrets & Cymbals, Smoke & Scissors (My Friend Dash's Wall in the Future), Peres Projects, Los Angeles, 2006; group exhibs, First Show, Rivington Arms, NY, 2002; Art Works for Hard Money, Gavin Brown's Enterprise, 2003; Galerie du Jour, Paris; The Armory Show with Peres Projects, NY, 2005; Bridge Freezes Before Road, Barbara Gladstone Gallery, 2005; Interstate, Nicole Klagsbrun Gallery, NY, 2005; Whitney Biennial, Day for Night, Whitney Mus Am Art, NY, 2006; Infinate Painting with Villa Manin-Centre for Contemp Art, Passariano, Codroipo, Ital, 2006; Axis of Praxis, Midway Contemp Art, Minneapolis, Minn, 2006; USA Today, Royal Acad Arts, London, 2006; Fantastic Politics, Nat Mus Art, Architecture & Design, Oslo, Norway, 2006. *Media:* Mixed Media

COLESCOTT, WARRINGTON W
PRINTMAKER, PAINTER
b Oakland, Calif, Mar 7, 1921. *Study:* Univ Calif, Berkeley, BA & MA; Acad Grande Chaumiere, Paris; Slade Sch Art, Univ Col, London. *Work:* Metrop Mus Art, Mus Mod Art, NY; Brooklyn Mus, NY; Art Inst Chicago; Nat Collection Art, Smithsonian Inst, Washington; Milwaukee Art Mus, Wis; Whitney Mus Am Art; Chasen Mus Art, Madison, Wis; Fogg Mus, Harvard Univ, Mass; Racine Art Mus, Wisc; New Orleans Mus Art; Corcoran Gallery, Wash DC; Kathe Kollwitz Mus, Berlin; Purer Studio and Mus, Nurenberg; Mus Contemp Art, Madison, Wisc. *Comn:* Milwaukee Art Mus Print Forum, 96, 2001; Albany NY Print Club, 96; Color print USA, 98; NY Print Club, 2002; Corcoran Gallery, Wash, DC, 2006. *Exhib:* Biennial Int, Ljubljana, Yugoslavia, 81, 83, 85 & 87; Solo exhibs, Tampa Mus Art, 87, Perimeter Gallery, Chicago, 88, 91, 93, 95, 98, 2002 & 40 Yrs of Printmaking, Elvehjem Mus, Univ Wis, 88; Warrington Colescott Retrospective, Univ SDak Galleries, 92; Art Galleries, State Univ NY, Albany, 95; Milwaukee Art Mus, 96, 2001, 2006, 2008; Int Print Triennial Crakow, Poland, 97; Integrafia 200, Poland; Macau Int Prints, 2000; 10th Int Print Biennial, Varna, Bulgaria, 99; Millenium Grafica, Yokohama & Taipei, 2000; Grolier Glub, NY, 2012. *Collection Arranged:* Warrington Colescott archive, Miluwaukee Art Mus, 2008; Warrington Colescott, Dillinger Prints, Racine Art Mus, Racine, Wisc, 1963-1966. *Pos:* Co-dir, Mantegna Press, Hollandale, Wis. *Teaching:* Prof art, Univ Wis, Madison, 49-86, Leo Steppart chair emer, dept art, 86-; Richard Koopman Distinguished chair visual arts, Hartford Art Sch, Conn, 94-95. *Awards:* Guggenheim Fel, 65; Nat Endowment Arts Artists Fel, 76, 79, 83-84 & 93-94; Fulbright Fel, 57-58; Printmaker Emeritus, Southern Graphics Coun, 1991; Major award, Int Print Triennial Krakow, 1997; Lifetime Achievement Award, Mus of Wis Art, West Bend, Wis; Lifetime Achievement in Printmaking, Southern Graphics Coun, 2005. *Bibliog:* EC Cunningham (auth), Printmaking, Univ Colo Press, 91; Tim Porges (auth), New Art Examiner, 5/95; Pat Gilmour (auth), Warrington Colescott, Milwaukee Art Mus, 96; Mary Weaver Chapin (auth), The Prints of Warrington Colescott, 1948-2008. *Mem:* Fel Wis Acad Sci, Arts & Lett; Mid Am Print Counc; Am Print Alliance; Nat Acad Design (assoc, 91, acad, 92); Southern Graphics Conf. *Media:* Etching; Painting on Paper. *Res:* Color intaglio. *Specialty:* Prints, Printmakers, Wisc Artists. *Collection:* Dr. Robert Dickens, Manitonic, Wisc, Karen Johnson Boyd, Racine, Wisc, J.C. Lessring, Santa Rosa, Calif, Milwaukee Art Mus, Wisc, Dr Robert Leff, Duluth, Mn. *Publ:* Illusr, Death in Venice, Aquarius Press, 71; The Mariposa Ste No 1-VI Pems by Carl Thayer, Etchings by Warrington Colescott, Tetrand Press, London, 71; Prime Time Histories, Warrington Colescott, Eleven Etchings, 73; illusr (covers), 30 Years of Printmaking, Brooklyn Mus, 76 & Art News Mag, 3/77; illusr, Since Man Began to Eat Himself, Perishable Press, Mt Horeb, Wis, 85; Improvisations, Dieu Donne Press, NY, 92; interview & comnd print, Contemp Impressions, vol 10 no 1, Spring 2002; co-auth (with Arthur Hove), Progressive Printmakers: Wisconsin Prints and the Print Renaissance, Univ Wis Press, 1999; auth, Mary Weaver Chopin, The Prints of Warrington Colescott, a catalogue raisonne 1948-2008, Milwaukee Art Mus, Univ Wis Press; Wisconsin Sesquicentenial Portfolio, Andrew Balkin Ed, Madison, Wisc, 2001; Univ Wisconsin Art Dept Faculty Exhib (exhib catalog), Chasen Mus Art, 2008. *Dealer:* Peltz Gallery 1119 E Knapp St Milwaukee WI 53202; Perimeter Gallery 210 W Superior St Chicago IL 60610; Grace Chosy Gallery 1825 Monroe St Madison Wis. *Mailing Add:* 8788 County Rd A Hollandale WI 53544-9423

COLINA, ARMANDO G
GALLERY DIRECTOR, EDITOR
b Veracruz, Mex, Mar 30, 1935. *Study:* Univ Mex, BA. *Exhib:* Zoologia Fantastica Homenaje A Jorge Luis Borges, Inst Artes Graficas De Oaxaca, Mex, 12/3/99-3/9/2000, Casa De Am, Madrid, Spain, 5/5-6/4/2000, Centro Cult Circulo De Arte, Barcelona, Spain, 7/26-9/11/2000; La Vitalidad De Un Artista, Kunstforeningen, Copenhague, Denmark, 11/27/99-2/27/2000, Helsinki City Art Mus, Finland, 3/31-5/28/2000; Homenaje Al Lapiz, Mus Jose Luis Cuevas, Mex, 12/9/99-3/9/2000; Sol Y Vida Mexican Modern Art: 1900-1950, Nat Gallery of Can, 2/24-5/17/2000; Francisco Toledo, Whitechapel Art Gallery, Londres, 4/14-6/7/2000, Mus Nat De Arte Reina Sofia, Madrid, Spain, 6/20-6/28/2000. *Collection Arranged:* Francisco Zuniga: Ten Years of Graphic Work, Montreal, NY & Wash, 84; Itinerant exhib 17 mus throughout world, 85-94; Carlos Merida: An Hommage, Museo de Arte Moderno, Guatemala; Imagen de Mex: Frankfurt Kunsthalle, Vienna & Dallas, Tex, 87; Art in Latin Am: London, Stockholm & Madrid, 87-88; Remedios Varo, Madrid & Monterrey, Mex, 88-89; Francisco Toledo, Homage to Jorge Luis Borges, Fantastic Zoology; Frida Kahlo, Japan & Australia, 89-90; Un panorama del Arte Mex, Inst Cult Mex, Washington, 90; Mex Masters, CDS Gallery, NY, 90; V Triennale Klein-plastik, Fellbach, Ger & Wilhelm Lehmbruck Mus, Duisburg, Ger, 92; Nat Homage to Carlos Merida, Fine Arts Palace Mus, Mus de Monterrey, Mex, 92-93; Voces de Ultramar, Las Palmas de Gran Canaria & Madrid, 92; The World of Frida Kahlo, Schirn Kunsthalle, Frankfurt, Ger, Mus Fine Arts, Houston, Tex, Hague, Holland, 93; V Trienale of Small Scale Sculpture, Fellbach, Ger & Wilhelm Lembruck Mus, Duisburg, Ger, 93; Bilder un Visionen, Mexikanische Kunst zwichen Avantgarde und Aktualltat, Mus Wurth, Kunzelsau, Santiago de Compostela, Spain & Dusseldorf, Kunsthalle, Ger, 95-96; Siqueiros/Pollack Pollack/Siqueiros, Dusseldorf, Kunsthalle, Ger, 95. *Pos:* Art consult, currently; owner, Arvil Art Gallery, currently; trustee, Mus Monterrey, NL, Mex; Museo Arte Contemporaneo, Oaxaca, Mex; art advisor & appraiser to Secretaria de Hacienda y Credito Pub, Mex; greeting card oper consult, Unicef, 92-93; mem, Visual Arts Comt, INBA, Mex. *Awards:* Europalia Mexico, 93. *Mem:* Asn Mex Comerciantes Arte & Anticuarios (pres, 96). *Specialty:* Contemporary Latin American & Mexican art. *Publ:* Arte Precolombino de Mex, 88; The World of Frida Kahlo, 93; Homenaje Nacional a Carlos Merida, 93; Siqueiros, El lugar de la utopia, 94; Imagenes y Visiones, arte mexicano entre la vanguardia y la actualidad, 96. *Mailing Add:* c/o Galeria Arvil SA Cerrada de Hamburgo No 9 Mexico 6 DF Mexico

COLKER, EDWARD
PAINTER, GRAPHIC ARTIST
b Philadelphia, Pa, Jan 5, 1927. *Study:* Philadelphia Coll Art, grad; NY Univ, BS & MA; spec study with E&J Desjobert, Paris. *Work:* Mus Art, Philadelphia; Univ Ariz, Tucson; NY Pub Libr Print Collection; Mus Mod Art, NY; NY Univ; Worcester Art Mus; Michener Art Mus; Brooklyn Mus; Whitney Mus. *Comn:* Lithography ed, Print Club, Philadelphia, 66, Int Graphic Art Soc, NY, 66 & 69 & Ill Arts Coun, 73; Ed for Print Club of NY, 2004. *Exhib:* Philadelphia Mus Art, 67; Am Art Today, Pa Acad Fine Arts, 68; solo exhibs, Kenyon Gallery, Chicago, 75, Neuberger Mus, Purchase, NY, 85-86 & Univ Ill, Chicago, 86; Nat Collection Fine Arts, Washington, DC, 77; Works on Paper, Yugoslavia, 82; Univ of Arts, 86; State Univ NY, Albany, 90; Cooper Union, 93; Univ Ariz, 98-99; Bates Coll Mus Art, Lewiston, Maine, 98-99; Neuberger Mus Art, State Univ NY, Purchase, 98-99; Poets House, NY, 2003 & 2010. *Collection Arranged:* FMC Collection, 20th Century Art, 74-75. *Pos:* Consult, Works on Paper, US Int Commun Agency, 82; Natl Endowment for the Arts, 80, 88; consult, Israel Coun Higher Educ, 2007. *Teaching:* Assoc prof fine arts, Univ Pa Grad Sch Fine Arts, 68-70; prof & dir, Sch Art & Design, Univ Ill, Chicago Circle, 72-78, res prof art, 77-80; dean, visual arts, State Univ NY, Purchase, 80-85; chmn dept art, Cornell Univ, 85-86; provost, Univ Arts, 86-91, Cooper Union, 91-95 & Pratt Inst, 95-98, 2003. *Awards:* Guggenheim Fel, 61; Univ Ill Res Bd, 77; Graham Found, 77; R Florsheim Art Fund, 97; residency, Rochefort-En-Terre, France, 2007. *Bibliog:* Zigrosser (auth), The Appeal of Prints (appreciation), 70; introd essay In: New York Landscape, 81; Five Decades in Print, 98; The Stamp of Impulse, 2003; Caxtonian, 2008. *Mem:* Coll Art Asn Am; Caxton Club; Ctr for Bk Arts; Grolier Club. *Media:* Lithography, Book Arts, Watercolor. *Publ:* Contribr, The Fall (lithos), 77; From South Dakota (lithos), 78; Aesthetique du Rale (lithos), 78; Selections, Essay on Nature, Emerson, Sky at Ashland, Anania (lithos), 85; All Souls (lithos), Norris, 93; Sutzkever, Beneath the Trees, 2004; Elephants by Night, 2005; Open the Gates (with Dave Brubeck), Haybarn Press, 2006; The Summons of Becoming, 2009; Desertstones, 2008-2009; Gathering, 2010; Voices to Share, 2011; Opposed to Indifference, 2012; Poems from Africa II, 2013. *Mailing Add:* 512 Millwood Rd New York NY 10549

COLLADO, LISA
COLLAGE ARTIST, ASSEMBLAGE ARTIST, PAINTER
b Washington, DC, June 24, 1944. *Study:* Radcliffe Coll, 62-63; Art Students League, with Edward Giobbi, Leo Manso & Xavier Gonzales 78-80; Empire State Coll, State Univ NY, BA, 85; NY Univ, MA, 93. *Work:* Adirondack Community Coll, Queensbury, NY; Everson Mus Art, Syracuse, NY; Wash Co Mus Fine Arts, Hagerstown, Mass; New Eng Community of Contemp Artists, Brooklyn, Conn; Casa Argentina en Tierra Santa, Jerusalem; Phillips Acad, Addison Gallery of Am Art; pvt collections of Thomas M Messer, Nasser Ovissi, Dr Donald Rubel & Mary Daly; Nat Collage Soc Teaching Collection, Kent State Univ, Oh. *Comn:* Hist placque, Egyptian Tourist Off, NY, 86; biog in collage, F Aley Allen, NY, 86; glass sculpture, comn by Nasser Al Nassir, NY, 89; Ode to Black Hist Month, 99; Art Gallery, Nat Asn of Women Artists Millennium Collection. *Exhib:* Diana Fever, The Emerging Collector, NY, 90; Women Artists Series, Rutgers Univ, NJ, 96; World Youth Summit-Peace Agenda, St Ulrich bei Steyr, Austria, 96; Galerie pro arte Kasper, Morges, Switz, 96 & 2004; Global Art Project, Tucson, Ariz, 98, 2002 & 2006; Alchemy, Nabisco Brands Gallery, East Hanover, NJ, 2000; Blue, City Without Walls Gallery, Newark, NJ, 2001; Cathedral Center for the Arts, Phoenix, Ariz, 2005; Karpeles Manuscript Mus, 2006; Art Gallery, Saratoga Springs, NY, 2007; Ariz State Univ, Phoenix, Ariz, 2007; Celebrate Faith Ringgold, Rutgers Institute for Women & Art, 2009; 40th Anniv Exhib, Mary H Dana Womens Art Series, Rutgers Univ; Mesa Arts Ctr, Ariz, 2012, 2013. *Pos:* Lectr, Nat Asn Women Artists traveling Painting Exhib; organizer, Nat Asn Women Artists; cur, Collage Insights, NY, 2003. *Awards:* Florence B Anderson Mem Award, 96, 2003, & 2009; Pollick-Krasner Found Grant, 97; Hontense Fern Mem Award, 2000; Adolph and Esther Gottlieb Found Grant, 2002; Prix due Pub, section Art Brut, Singulier et Insolite, 2004. *Bibliog:* Cynthia Maris Dantzic (auth), Design Dimensions: An Introduction to the Visual Surface, Prentice-Hall, 89; Cynthia Maris Dantzic (auth), 100 NY Painters, Schiffer, 2006. *Mem:* Am Soc Contemp Artists; Nat Collage Soc; Lower Adriondack Regional Art Coun (LARAC). *Media:* Acrylic, Mixed Media, Collage. *Interests:* Classical music, reading, helping women artists in their careers, gardening, cats. *Publ:* Coauth, article on Nasser Ovissi, Editorial La Gran Enciclopedia Vasca, 88

COLLENS, DAVID R
DIRECTOR, CURATOR
Study: Franklin Pierce Univ, BA (Am lit), 69; studies in print making, New York, 71-72; studies in art hist, New Sch Social Res, New York, 72-73. *Collection Arranged:* David Smith, 76; Alexander Liberman, 77; Anthony Caro, 81; Mark di Suvero, 25 Years of Sculpture and Drawings, 85; The Reemergent Figure - Seven Sculptors, Storm King Art Ctr, 87; William Tucker: The Am Decade 78-88, 88; Alexander Calder: Five Grand Stabiles, 88; Wandering Into Memory: Sculpture by Anne and Patrick Poirier, 89; Complex Visions: Sculpture and Drawings by Alice Aycock, 90; Enclosures and Encounters: Architectural Aspects of Recent Sculpture, 91; Ursula von Rydingsvard: Sculpture, 92; Siah Armajani: Recent Work, 93; Mia Westerlund Roosen: Sculpture and Drawings, 94; Mark di Suvero, 95-96; The Fields of David Smith, 97-99 (auth, catalog, 96); Andy Goldsworthy, Storm King Art Ctr, 2000; Grand Institutions: Calder's Monumental Sculptures, 2001-2003, (auth, catalog, 03); Chakaia Booker, Storm King Art Ctr, 2004; Richard Bellamy & Mark di Suvero, 2005-2006, (auth, catalog, 06); Louis Bourgeois, 2007; Deborah Masters, Travellers and Big Head, 2007; Sol Lewitt, 2008; Mark di Suvero, Lithographs, Drawings and Indoor Sculptures, 2008; Maya Lin, Bodies of Water, 2009; The View from here, Storm King at Fifty, 5t5: New Perspectives, Storm King at Fifty, 2010-2011; Mark di Suvero at Governors Island: Presented by Storm King Art Center, 2011. *Pos:* dir, chief cur Storm King Art Ctr, Mountainville, NY, 74-, bd trustees, 74-; adjudicator, Winston-Salem Univ Sculpture Garden Contest, NC, 83; mem arts adv comt, Metrop Transportation Authority, New York, 85-94. *Bibliog:* Louise Bourgeois, 2007; Deborah Masters, Travellers & Big Head, 2007; Sol LeWitt, 2008; Mark di Suvero, Lothographs, Drawings & Indoor Sculptures, 2008; Maya Lin, Bodies of Water, 2009; The View from Here, Storm King at Fifty, 2010. *Mem:* AAM. *Publ:* contribr, Sculpture at Storm King, 80, A Landscape for Modern Sculpture: Storm King Art Ctr, 85; co-auth, Mark di Suvero at Storm King Art Ctr, Abrams, 96; contribr, The Fields of David Smith, 99, Earth, Sky and Sculpture, 2000, Calder, 2003 & Richard Bellamy & Mark di Suervo, Storm King Art Ctr, 2006. *Mailing Add:* Storm King Art Ctr Old Pleasant Hill Rd PO Box 280 Mountainville NY 10953-0280

COLLERY, PAULA
PAINTER
b Glen Cove, NY, Dec 15, 1954. *Study:* Tyler Sch Art, Temple Univ, Philadelphia, BFA (painting & photog), 79. *Exhib:* Solo exhibs, Gracie Mansion Gallery, 83 & Germans Van Eck Gallery, 85, NY, Gallery Six to Six, 87; Hats Off, New Mus, NY, 83; Totem Show, NY, 84; Chill Out, Kenkeleba Gallery, NY, 84; Bernice Steinbaum Gallery, NY, 84; Harm Bouchaert Gallery, NY, 85; Edinburgh Festival, Scotland, 85; Group nude show, Gallery Six to Six, NY, 90; Starving Artist Cookbook, Dooley Le Cappellaine Gallery, NY, 92; group exhibs, Maxfish, NY, 95, Hayday, E Village artist from the 80's, Life Cafe, NY, 98, Starving Artist Cookbook, video series, Anthology Film Archives, NY, 2001, Reaction, EXITART, NY, 2002. *Awards:* Art Fel Residency Va Ctr Arts, 88, Cummington, 85; MacDowell Colony Residency, 84, 85; Konstepedemin Residency, Gothenberg, Sweden, 2000. *Bibliog:* David Herhkovits (auth), Art in Alphabetland, Art News, 9/83; Ted Castle (auth), article, Art Monthly, London, 83; Vivien Raynor (auth), article, New York Times, 2/84; George Dellea (auth), Starving Artists, New York Times, Style Sect, 5/1992. *Mem:* AAM. *Media:* Oil. *Mailing Add:* 100 St Mark's Pl No 3 New York NY 10009

COLLIER, ANNA
PHOTOGRAPHER
b Los Angeles, Calif, 1970. *Study:* Calif Inst Arts, Valencia, Calif, BFA, 93; Univ Calif, LA, MFA, 2001. *Exhib:* Solo exhibs include One to One, Three Day Weekend, Los Angeles, 95, Inst Visual Arts, Univ Wis, 98, MARCH FOXX, West Gallery, Los Angeles, 2001, 2002, Jack Hanley Gallery, San Francisco, 2004; group exhibs include LACE video screening of LA video artists, 93; Summer Group Show, Three Day Weekend, LA, 94, Thanks! 94, Dave's Not Here, 95; Art Dogs, George's, Calif, 2000; Summer Group Show,Goldman Tevis, 2000; I Want More, Temple Bar Gallery, Dublin, Ireland, 2001; New Wight Art Gallery, UCLA, 2001; MARC FOXX, 2001, 2002, 2003; A Show That Will Show That a Show Is Not Only a Show, The Project, 2002; Bay Area Now III, Yerba Buena Ctr Arts, San Francisco, Calif, 2002; Portraiture, Karyn Lovegrove Gallery, Calif, 2003; Makeshift World, Stephen Wirtz Gallery, San Francisco, Calif, 2003; 17 Reasons, Jack Henley Gallery, 2003; Nicole Klagsbrun Gallery, NY, 2004; Whitney Biennial: Day for Night, Whitney Mus Am Art, 2006; represented in collections of San Francisco Mus Modern Art, Mus Contemp Art San Diego, La Jolla, Calif, LA County Mus Art. *Teaching:* Vis faculty Art Ctr, Pasadena, Calif, 2002-2003, Calif Col Arts, San Francisco, 2002-, new genres dept San Francisco Art Inst, Calif, 2003. *Mailing Add:* c/o MARC FOXX Gallery 6150 Wilshire Blvd Los Angeles CA 90048

COLLINGS, BETTY
SCULPTOR, WRITER
b Wanganui, NZ, Jan 15, 1934. *Study:* Ohio State Univ, BFA, cum laude, 71, MFA, 74. *Work:* Israel Mus; Carnegie Art Ctr, Covington, Tex; Wallace Arts Trust, New Zealand. *Exhib:* Solo shows, Urdang Gallery, New York, 79, 80, 83, 89 & 90, Antioch Univ, 82, Grad Ctr, City Univ NY, 83 & Ukraine Union Artists, Kiev, 92, Castleton

Col, 94, 97, Retrospective Cultural Arts, Carnegie Gallery, Ky, 2004, Upper Arlington Arts Comn, Ohio, 2009; Groups exhibs, TAO III, Ohio Wesleyan Univ, 89; The Figure's Edge, Akron Univ, 92; Art League Invitational, Ft Hayes, 92; Celebrating Our Own, Arlington, 93; TAO VI, 97; Seeing Abstractly, Va Cult Arts Comn, 97; Action Replay: Post Object Art, Artspace & Govett Brewster Gallery, NZ, 98; Convergence VI, Providence, RI, 98; Carnegie Art Center, 2003-06; Contemp Art & The Mathematical Instinct, Tweed Mus 2004; Five Women Sculptors, Upper Arlington, 2007. *Collection Arranged:* Contemp Collection of Ohio State Univ, 75-80. *Pos:* Dir, Ohio State Univ, Gallery Fine Arts, 74-80, ed acquisitions, 76-78; consult, Oberlin Col, 81-82; invited cur, Wright State Univ, 81, Va Commonwealth Univ, 82, Bard Col, 82 & Cleveland Ctr Contemp Art 85; Int exhib consult, Ohio Arts Coun, China, 88; cur, Ohio-Shaaanxi Exchange, 90-91, Kiev-US exchange, 92-93; cur & prog dir, Artists Org, 97; cur, Democracy Steps for Cedar Falls, Ohio, 1997; dir, Artists On Art, 2002-; Democracy Steps to Lonely Bay, Coromandel, New Zealand, 2003. *Awards:* Distinguished Service Award, Art League, 80; Sculpture Fel, 81-82 & Critism Fel, 83-84, Ohio Arts Coun; Eleven Misc Awards for Sculpture, 76-90; Distinguished Serv Award, Ohio Dept Nat Resources, 98. *Bibliog:* Robert Pincus Witten (auth), Drawing on Sculpture, 1979; Roberta Smith (auth), article, NY Times, 12/22/89; V Watson Jones (auth), American Women Sculptors, Oryx Press, 90; N & J Heller (auths), An Ency of 20th Century American Women Artists, Garland, 93. *Mem:* Int Asn Art Critics; Artists' Orgn (pres, 85-87, dir prog, 87-). *Media:* Plastic, Clay, Bronze. *Interests:* science, gardening, geology. *Publ:* Auth, Sculptural Views on Perceptual Ambiguity: Thomas Macaulay 1968-1986 (catalog), Dayton Art Inst, 86; 10 From the File, Dialogue, 80-83; Judy Pfaff, 80, George Woodman, 81, John Davies, 81, Judy Rifka, Arts Mag, 83, Mel Bochner, 84, Richard Killeen 85,; Shaanxi-Ohio (posterlogue), The Artists Orgn, 90; Akio Hizume's Democracy Steps for Cedar Falls, TAO posterlogue, 97. *Mailing Add:* 1991 Hillside Dr Upper Arlington OH 43221

COLLINS, BRADFORD R
EDUCATOR, ADMINISTRATOR, PAINTER
Study: Amherst Col, BA (American Studies), 1964; Yale Univ, PhD (art history), 1980. *Teaching:* Assoc prof art history, department chair, Univ South Carolina, currently. *Publ:* edited and contributed one of the essays to 13 Views of Manet's Bar, 1996. *Mailing Add:* University of South Carolina College of Arts and Sciences McMaster 228 Columbia SC 29208

COLLINS, DAN (DANIEL) MCCLELLAN
PAINTER
b Los Angeles, Calif, Aug 20, 1954. *Study:* Ark State Univ, 76; Santa Monica Col, AA, 79; Art Center Coll Design, Los Angeles, BFA, 83. *Comn:* Franklin & Argyle, Hollywood C of C, 86. *Exhib:* Mus Sci & Indust, Ontario, Calif, 83; Hollywood-Inside & Out, Los Angeles Munic Art Gallery, 86; Small Works, Jose Drudis-Biada Gallery, Los Angeles, 87; group exhib, Mus Neon Art, Los Angeles, 88. *Pos:* Dir-cur, Goski Gallery, Los Angeles, 84-86. *Media:* Wood, Oil. *Mailing Add:* c/o Lisa Sette Gallery 4142 N Marshall Way Scottsdale AZ 85251

COLLINS, DAVID
PAINTER, PRINTMAKER
Study: RI Sch Design, BFA, 1988. *Exhib:* Solo exhibs include Nightingale Gallery, Water Mill, NY, 1999, Kenise Barnes Fine Art, Larchmont, NY, 2000, 2001, 2003, 2005, 2007, Jeffery Coploff Fine Art, New York, 2000, 2002, Marcia Wood Gallery, Atlanta, 2001, Vernacular Press, New York, 2004, Mount Mercy Coll, Cedar Rapids, Iowa, 2007; group exhibs include Introductions, Gallery Paule Anglim, San Francisco, 1992; Painting Ct, New York, 1999; Anita Friedman Fine Art, New York, 2001; Neobotanica, Jacksonville Mus Mod Art, Fla, 2001; Prints From Within, Conn Graphic Arts Ctr, Norwalk, 2002; Beautiful Male Objects, Nightingale Gallery, Water Mill, NY, 2004; Brave New Worlds, Dorsky Curatorial Programs, New York, 2005; Sanbao Int Printmaking Exhib, Jingdezhen Sanbao Ceramic Art Inst, China, 2007; 183rd Ann: Invitational Exhib Contemp Am Art, New York, 2008. *Awards:* Yaddo Fel, 2003 & 2005. *Mailing Add:* c/o Kenise Barnes Fine Art 1955 Palmer Ave Larchmont NY 10538

COLLINS, HARVEY ARNOLD
MURALIST, EDUCATOR, PAINTER
b High Springs, Fla, Aug 22, 1927. *Study:* Univ Fla, with Fletcher Martin, BFA, 51; MFA, 52; LHD, 82; Doc of Letters, Olivet Nazarene Coll, 82. *Hon Degrees:* (hon) DFL, Olivet Nazarene Univ, Bourbonnais, Ill, 60901. *Comn:* All Faiths Mural, St; 75 Year History of Olivet Coll (mural), Bourbonnais, Ill, 82; mural, Nazarene Publ House, Kansas City, Mo, 83; Weakley Mem Mural, Bradley Pub Libr, Ill. *Pos:* Chmn dept art, Olivet Nazarene Univ, Bourbonnais, Ill, 71-91, retired, 91. *Teaching:* Instr painting, drawing & ceramics, Largo Jr High Sch, Fla, 58-71; prof painting & art hist, Olivet Univ, Bourbonnais, Ill, 71-91; art instr, Santa Fe Community Col, Gainesville, Fla, formerly. *Bibliog:* 75th Anniversary Mural (exhib catalog), Nazarene Publ House, Kansas City, Mo, 1/84. *Media:* Acrylics, Oils. *Interests:* painting, reading, collecting plants. *Mailing Add:* 7220 8th Ave Loop West Bradenton FL 34209

COLLINS, HOWARD F
HISTORIAN
b Buffalo, NY, Oct 28, 1922. *Study:* Albright Art Sch, Buffalo, with Charles Burchfield, Ralston Crawford & Isaac Soyer, dipl, 43; State Univ NY Col, Buffalo, BS, 47; Columbia Univ, MA, 54; Univ Pittsburgh, with William S Heckscher & Charles Seymour Jr, PhD, 70. *Teaching:* Assoc prof art hist, Kutztown State Col, 60-65; from assoc prof to prof, WVa Univ, 65-72, chmn div art, 69-71; prof, Univ Nebr, Lincoln, 72-. *Mem:* Coll Art Asn Am; Mid-Am Coll Art Asn; Renaissance Soc Am; assoc Int Inst Conservation; Asn Historians Am Art. *Res:* Fifteenth century Venetian painting. *Publ:* Major narrative paintings by Jacopo Bellini, Art Bull, 9/82; The Cyclopean Vision of Jacopo Bellini, Pantheon, 82; Time, space and Gentile Bellini's Miracle of the Cross at Ponte S Lorenzo, Gazette Beaux Arts, 12/82; Pictorial space in Donatello's relief panels on the high altar of the santo in Padua, Arte Veneta, XLII, 87; The Decagonal Temples of Jacopo Bellini, Paragone, 9/90. *Mailing Add:* 1930 C St Lincoln NE 68502-1649

COLLINS, JIM
SCULPTOR, COLLAGE ARTIST
b Huntington, WVa, Sept 12, 1934. *Study:* Marshall Univ, AB, 57; Univ Mich, Ann Arbor, MPH, 61; Ohio Univ, MFA, 66. *Work:* Tenn Aquarium, Chattanooga; Milwaukee Art Ctr; Tenn State Mus, Tenn; Vols (Stainless Steel Fountain), Bicentennial Libr, Chattanooga, Ten; The Community (stainless steel), Sheriff's Bldg, Rockland Co, NY; City of Suwanee, Ga. *Comn:* Limerick Herd (32 silhouettes of life-sized animals, powder-coat aluminum), four sites along dual carriageways in Co Limerick, Ireland, 2004; Mile Markers on the River Walk (9 sculptures), Chattanooga, Tenn, 2007; Pub Art, #1 Fire Station, Plano, Tex, 2008; Three Individual Sculptures for Three Villages, Carlingford, Collon, & Heynestown County, Louth, Ireland, 2009; Three Shades of Green (Sculpture), Univ Tenn, 2012; St George's Nat Sch, Balbriggan, Ireland, 2012. *Exhib:* Solo Exhibs: Encounters Huntsville Mus Art, Huntsville, Ala, 2007; Sculpture Walk, Best of Show, Columbus, Ga, 2007-2008, 2008-2009, Art in Public Places, Knoxville, Tenn, 2009, 2010, 2012-13, 2013-14, Irish Encounters (solo touring exhib of 20 mixed media collages), throughout Ireland, 2010-2011, 5th Annual Downtown Sculpture Exhib, Asheboro, NC, 2010, Discover What's Outside Sculpture Show, Salisbury, NC, 2010, 2011, Sculpture Walk V, Kingsport, Tenn, 2011-12, Public Art League Sculpture Exhib, Champaign-Urbana, Ill, 2012-13, Midwest Sculpture Initiative, Mich, Big Wheel Watcher, Ohio, 2011, Canton, Mich, 2012-13, Fenton, Tecumseh and Kochville, Mich, 2013-14, Canton, Fenton, and Hastings, Mich, 2014-2015, Art on the Streets, Colorado Springs, Colo, 2012, 27th Rosen Exhib, Appalachian State Univ, Boone, NC, 2013-14, Salisbury Sculpture Show, NC, 2013-14, Public Art on Hilton Head Island, SC, 2013-14, Sculpture Walk VII, Kingsport, Tenn, 2013-14, Sculpture Biennial, Gadsden, Ala, 2014-15, Sculpture Walk, Johnson City, Tenn, 2014-15, Suwanee Sculptour, Ga, 2012-13, 2013-15, 2015-17, Outdoor Sculpture Show, Gulfport, Miss, 2015 and several others. *Teaching:* Prof art, Univ Tenn, Chattanooga, 66-83. *Awards:* The Best of Tenn, Tenn State Mus, 2001; Distinguished artist award, presented by Mayor Bob Corker, Chatanooga, TN, 2004; Jackson, Tenn/Union Univ Sculpture Tour, Purchase Award, 2007; Sculpture Walk, Columbus Ga, Best of Show, 2007-2008; Merit Award, Art in Public Places, Knoxville, Tenn, 2011, People's Choice award. *Bibliog:* Jim Collins Art: 1963-2003, Two Hands Art Publishing, NC, 2003; Art of Tenn, Frist Center for the Visual Arts, Nashville, Tenn, 2003; Jim Collins Addendum, 2004-2009. *Mem:* Southern Asn Sculptors (pres, 70-71); Int Sculpture Ctr; Mid-South Sculpture Alliance, Visual Artists, Ireland. *Media:* Metals, Mixed Media, Collage. *Publ:* Auth introd, A Handbook to British Landscape Painters, 70; auth, Women Artists in America, 18th Century to the Present, 75 & Women Artists in America II, 76; Addendum, 2004-2009. *Dealer:* Chivaree Southern Art & Design Cashiers NC 28717

COLLINS, LARRY RICHARD
PAINTER, PHOTOGRAPHER
b Spokane, Wash, July 15, 1945. *Study:* Univ Okla, BFA, 67, studied with Emilio Amero; Ind Univ, studied with James McGarrell; Mass Coll Art, MFA, 80, studied with George Nick; La Napoule Art Found, studied with Jack Beal. *Work:* Mus Fine Arts Boston, Mass; Sheldon Mus Art, Lincoln, Nebr; Wadsworth Atheneum, Hartford, Conn; Worcester Art Mus, Worcester, MA; Berg Collection, NY Pub Libr, NY; Wallach Photog Div; NY Public Libr; Mabee-Gerrer Mus Art, Shawnee, Okla; Int Ctr Photography, NY; Provincetown Art Asn, Mass; Leslie-Lohman Mus, NY. *Comn:* serigraph, Okla City Symphony Soc, 64; Paintings, Tiffany & Co, NY, 96. *Exhib:* Solo exhibs, Mabee-Gerrer Mus Art, Shawnee, Okla, 84; NY Pub Libr, 87; Newbury Coll, Brookline, Mass, 2000; Hampshire Coll, Amherst, Mass, 2004, Larry R Collins: Finding Light, Provincetown Art Asn & Mus, Mass, 2010, Larry R. Collins: The Night Laundromat, Loveland, Provincetown, 2012, Larry R. Collins: My Life, Loveland, Provincetown, Mass; Group exhibs, Ann Exhib, Nat Acad Design, NY, 82, 86; Realistic Directions, Zoller Gallery, Pa State Univ, 83; Recent Acquisitions, Sheldon Mem Art Gallery, Lincoln, Nebr, 83; Ann Eight State Exhib of Southwest Am Art, Okla Art Ctr, Okla, 62-66; Am Artist Mag: 50th Anniversary Exhib (traveling) 87; Emerging Artists, Provincetown Art Asn & Mus, Mass, 96; Horrors of War, Worcester Art Mus, Worcester, Mass, 2006; Suffering & Smiles, Univ RI, 2007; The Night Laundromat: Larry R Collin, Loveland, Provincetown, MA; Ken Fulk's Peep Show, San Francisco, Calif, 2012; Woodman Shimko Gallery, Palm Springs, 2013; Stadler-Kahn, Phila, Pa, 2013; A-Gallery, Provincetown, Mass, 2015; TB Projects, Provincetown, Mass, 2015; Celebrating Veterans, Univ RI, 2015. *Collection Arranged:* David Davis Collection, Kennedy to Kent State: Images of a Generation, Worcester Art Mus, Mass; Michael Sodomick Coll, NY. *Pos:* Gallery Dir, Schoolhouse Ctr for Art & Design, Provincetown, Mass, 98-2003; dir, Larry Collins Fine Art, Provincetown, MA, 2004-2013. *Teaching:* Prof anat, Mass Col Art, Boston, 79-82 & 85-95; instr drawing, Univ NH, Durham, 86-88; prof, Montserrat Col Art, Beverly, Mass, 94-95; instr figure drawing, Provincetown Art Asn & Mus, Provincetown, Mass, 2007-09. *Awards:* Bronze Star, combat art, US Army, Republic Vietnam, 1968; Travel Fel, Creative Arts Studies Found, 84; Individual Arts Fel, NH State Coun Arts, 88; Artists Opportunity Grant, NH State Coun Arts, 90. *Bibliog:* Norman A Geske (auth), The American Painting Collection of the Sheldon Memorial Art Gallery, Univ of Nebr, 88; Liz McLean (auth), Larry Collins in his Studio (film), 2009; Larry Collins: Finding Light, Provincetown Art Asn and Mus (monograph), Provincetown, Mass, 2010; Norman Lloyd (auth), The MIA's of Tiger Mountain (film), 2011. *Mem:* Provincetown Art Asn. *Media:* Oil on cancas, charcoal drawings, vintage Vietnam war photog. *Res:* Vintage War Photog. *Specialty:* Vintage photos; Antiques. *Publ:* Illusr, Old Love Story (with Allen Ginsberg), Lospecchio Press, NY, 1986; Illusr, The Hopper House at Truro (with Lawrence Ferlinghetti), Lospecchio Press, NY, 1996; Auth, Painting in Boston: 1950-2000, Provincetown Arts, 2003-2004; Illusr, TOW (with Eileen Myles), Lospecchio Press, NY, 2005; Auth, Artists Heart, Provincetown Arts, 2005-2006; Auth, I Couldn't Bear to Look, in Kennedy to Kent State: Images of a Generation, Worcester Art Mus, 2013; Auth, Barmaid, in John Arsenault: Barmaid, Daylight Books, 2015. *Dealer:* Larry Collins Fine Art 145 Commercial St Provincetown MA 02657. *Mailing Add:* PO Box 2 Provincetown MA 02657

COLLINS, PAUL
PAINTER
b Muskegon, Mich, Dec 11, 1937. *Study:* Self-taught. *Work:* Gerald R Ford Mus, Grand Rapids, Mich; off pres, Jerusalem; Amway Japan Ltd, Tokyo; Puskin Mus, Moscow, USSR; Palace de la Presidence du Senegal, Dakar, Senegal, Africa. *Comn:* Special Olympics (series of 14 portraits), Joseph P Kennedy Found, 79; Martin Luther King Non-Violent Peace Prize Medal (sculpture), comn by Corretta Scott King, 80; Challenger VII Logo (sculpture & logo), & First US Women Astronaut (commemorative plaque), NASA, 82; America at Work (series of 24 portraits), Amway Corp, 83; American Portrait of Japan (15 painting series), Amway Japan Ltd, Tokyo, 95. *Exhib:* Ill State Mus, Springfield; Mus Sci & Indust, Chicago & Los Angeles; Sioux Indian Mus, SDak; Studio Mus, Harlem, NY; Smithsonian Mus, Washington, DC; Am Cult Ctr, Paris, London, Nairobi, Kenya, Lagos, Nigeria, Dakar, Senegal & Madrid, Spain; White House, Washington, DC; Palais Des Congress, Paris; Collegium Artisticum, Sarajevo; Meguro Gajoen Mus, Tokyo; Mus Performing Arts, NY. *Awards:* Mead Book Award, New York, 72; Am Artists Top Twenty Figure Painters in US, 80; Golden Centaur, Accademia Italia, del Artie delle Lavoro, Italy, 82. *Bibliog:* Save the Children, Paramount Pictures; Paul Collins in Israel, Israeli Films Inc; Paul Collins Voices of Israel, CBS Sunday Morning Show. *Media:* Dry Oil, Own Media. *Publ:* Black Portrait of an African Journey, Eerdmans Publ, 71; Other Voices-A Native American Tableau, NAEC Publ, 74; Gerald R Ford-A Man in Perspective, Eerdmans Publ, 76; Great Beautiful Black Women, Johnson Publ, 78; 20 Figure Painters & How They Work, Watson-Guptill Publ, 79. *Dealer:* Collins Fine Art Amway Grand Plaza Hotel 220 Lyon NW Grand Rapids MI 49503. *Mailing Add:* 615 Kent Hills Dr Grand Rapids MI 49505

COLLINS, THOM
MUSEUM DIRECTOR
Study: Swarthmore Coll, Pa, BA, 1988; Northwestern Univ, MA (art hist). *Pos:* Exhib coordr, Mus Mod Art, 1994-96, cur, 1996-99; assoc cur, Henry Art Gallery, Univ Wash, Seattle, formerly; chief cur, Contemp Arts Ctr, Cincinnati, 2000-03; exec dir, Contemp Mus, Baltimore, 2003-05; dir, Neuberger Mus, Purchase Coll, Purchase, NY, 2005-2010, Miami Art Mus, 2010-. *Awards:* Newhall Curatorial Fel, Mus Mod Art, New York, 1994. *Mem:* Asn Art Mus Dirs; Asn Art Mus Curs; Coll Art Asn. *Mailing Add:* Miami Art Museum 101 W Flagler St Miami FL 33130-1504

COLLINSON, JANICE
PAINTER, GALLERY DIRECTOR
b Newark, NJ, June 27, 1948. *Study:* Westminster Col, 66-68; Georgian Court Col, BA, 70; studied painting with James Leslie, Jr, Art Alliance, 98-99. *Work:* Hist Allaire Village, Allaire State Park, Wall, NJ; Med Ctr Ocean Found, Brielle, NJ; Spring Lake Community Theatre, NJ; White Lilac Inn, Spring Lake, NJ. *Comn:* archtl renderings of homes, Diane Turton Realtors, NJ, 80-; design commemorative postmarks, Hist Allaire Village, Wall, NJ, 82-2000; archtl rendering of Kidsbridge, Chetkin Gallery, Red Bank, NJ, 99; bldg renderings Law Offices of Norman Hobbie, Toms River, NJ, 2000. *Exhib:* Ann Miniature Show, Paper Mill Playhouse, Millburn, NJ, 95; invitational exhibs Sr Christina Geis Gallery, Lakewood, NJ, 90, Gallery at Medford Leas, NJ, 99, Peck Sch Gallery, Morristown, NJ, 2000. *Pos:* arranger exhbns Evergreen Gallery, Spring Lake, NJ, 87-. *Teaching:* art tchr K-12, Borough of Point Pleasant, NJ Schs, 70-74; watercolor tchr, Sea Girt Lighthouse, Sea Girt, NJ, 90-. *Bibliog:* Three Artists, Garden State Home & Garden, 92; Spring Show: Favored Season, The Coast Star, 94. *Mem:* Manasquan River Group of Artists (co-pres, 84-86, prog chair 91-2000). *Media:* Watercolor, Ink. *Publ:* illus Cooks and Artists of the Jersey Shore, Hoffman Press, 80; illus Cuisine and Art, Hoffman Press, 89. *Dealer:* Evergreen Gallery 308 Morris Ave Spring Lake NJ, 07762. *Mailing Add:* 2421 Beech St Manasquan NJ 08736

COLLISCHAN, JUDY K
CRITIC, CURATOR, ARTIST
b Red Wing, Minn, Oct 19, 1940. *Study:* Hamline Univ, BA, 62; Nat Univ Mex, 63; Ohio Univ, MFA, 64; Univ Iowa, PhD, 72. *Exhib:* Small Works, NY Univ Galleries, NYC, 2002; Drawing Conclusions: Work by Artist-Critics, NYArts Gallery, NYC, 2003; Funky Fine/Fall Line, Berliner Kunstprojekt Gallery, Berlin, Ger, 2003; The Valentine Sail & The New Scream, Jacklight Gallery, NYC, 2004; Over the Top-Under the Rug, Shore Inst Contemp Arts, Long Branch, NJ, 2005; Eviction Blues, Asian Am Arts Center, NYC, 2005; That's Not Funny, Jacklight Gallery, NYC, 2005; Carnival, Wilder Gallery, Catskill, NY, 2006; Alternate Westchester Libr, NY, 2013. *Collection Arranged:* Monumental Drawings by Sculptors: Serra, Westerlund, Nonas, Jensen, Fishman, Nozkowski and others, 82, Paintings from the Mind's Eye, 83, Seymour Lipton, 84-85, Michelle Stuart, 85 & Walter Murch, 86; Lines of Vision: Drawings by Contemporary Women, 89; End Papers (19th & 20th century drawings), Paper Spaces, 97, Biennial for Public Art, 97, 99 & 2001, Glass Houses, 98, Clay Bodies, 99, Comtemp Classicism, 2000. *Pos:* Admin Dir, The Printmaking Workshop, 95-96, Dir, Hillwood Art Mus, Long Island Univ, C W Post Campus, Greenvale, NY, 82-94; critic, Arts Mag, 84-; co-chmn, New York State Coun Arts, Visual Art Panel, 87-90; assoc dir curatorial affairs, Neuberger Mus Art, SUNY, Purchase, 96-2000; mentoring dir & lectr, Art Sch; mentoring dir & lectr, Oogie Art Sch, 2010-. *Teaching:* Instr, Kansa Sate Univ, 64-66; instr, Univ No Iowa, 70-71; asst prof, Univ Omaha Nebr, 72-75; assoc prof contemp art, State Univ NY, Plattsburgh, 75-83; adj prof contemp art, Long Island Univ, C W Post Campus, Greenvale, NY, 82-. *Awards:* Kress Found Res Grant, 70; Award, State Univ NY, 81. *Bibliog:* Charles Giuliano (auth), A Servant of Two Masters: Drawing Conclusions, NYArts, Sept/Oct 2003. *Mem:* AICA. *Media:* Mixed Media. *Res:* Contemporary art, particular art by women and minorities. *Interests:* fine arts. *Publ:* Auth, Women Shaping Art, Praeger, 84; Lines of Vision: Drawings by Contemporary Women, Hudson Hills, 89; Welded Sculpture of the Twentieth Century, Hudson Hills Press, Inc, New York, 2000; Made in the USA, i Universe, 2010; Barnes and Noble Nook. *Mailing Add:* 248 E 7th St Apt 11-12 New York NY 10009

COLLYER, ROBIN
SCULPTOR, PHOTOGRAPHER
b London, Eng, Mar 7, 1949; Can citizen. *Study:* Ont Coll Art, Toronto, 67-68. *Work:* Nat Gallery Can & Can Coun Art Bank, Ottawa; Art Gallery Ont, Toronto; Mus d'Art Contemporain, Montreal; Can Cult Ctr, Paris, France. *Exhib:* Carmen Lamanna Gallery, Toronto, Ont, 71, 72, 74, 76, 78, 79, 81 & 83, Mt Allison Univ, 76 & Etherington Art Ctr, 82; Nat Gallery Can, Ottawa, 73; Kunsthalle, Basel, Switz, 78; Seven Toronto Artists, Artists' Space, NY, 80; Frankfurter Kunstverin, Frankfurt; Akademie der Kunste, Berlin; traveling retrospective, Can & US, 82 & 84; Ctr Int d'Art Contemporain, Montreal, 85. *Pos:* Bd dir, Trinity Square Video, 79-82. *Teaching:* Instr, Ont Col Art, Toronto, 75; NS Col Art, Halifax, 77. *Awards:* Can Coun Grants, 69-71, 73, 74 & 76-69; Can Coun Sr Arts Grant, 80. *Bibliog:* David Burett & Marilyn Schiff (auths), Contemporary Candian Art, Hurtig Publ, Edmonton, 83. *Mem:* Can Coun Adv Art Panel; Trinity Square Video. *Media:* Mixed Media; Photography, Video. *Publ:* Contribr, Impulse, summer 80; co-prod & co-dir, The Girl Can't Fly It (film), A Space & Broadcast Serv, Toronto, 80; Darn These Hands (film), A Space & Rogers Cable TV, Toronto, 80; co-prod, Sculpture of Here and Now (film), Toronto. *Dealer:* Susan Hobbs Toronto ON. *Mailing Add:* 57 Pemberton Ave Willowdale ON M2M 1Y2 Canada

COLMER, ROY DAVID
VISUAL ARTIST
b London, Eng; US citizen. *Study:* Hochschule für Bildender Künste, Hamburg, Ger, 60-65; New Sch/Parsons with George Tice, 78 & Lisette Model, 82. *Work:* Mus Mod Art, Mus City New York & Chase Manhattan Bank, New York, NY; Brooklyn Mus, NY; Mus d'Ixelles, Brussels, Belg; NY Pub Libr; Jack S Blanton Mus Art; Univ Tex, Austin; and others. *Exhib:* Recent Acquisitions, Mus Mod Art, NY, 87; Selected Photographs, Brooklyn Mus, NY, 89; Mean Streets: Photographs From the Collection, 1940's-1980's, Mus Mod Art, NY, 91; Open Mind: The LeWitt Collection, Wadsworth Atheneum, Hartford, Conn, 91; Queens Mus Art, Bulova Corp Ctr, NY, 93; solo exhib, OK Harris Works Art, NY, 2000; Red, Mitchell Algus Gallery, NY, 1999; Für Hanne, Galerie Ascan Crone, Hamburg, Ger, 2001; Life of the City, Mus Modern Art, NY, 2002; Mitchell Algus Gallery, NY, 04; Jack S Blanton Mus Art, Univ Tex, Austin, 04; Recent Aquisitions: New York Street Photography From the 1960's and 1970's, NY Pub Libr, 2006; America/Americas, Jack S Blanton Mus of Art, Univ Tex, Austin, 2006; High Times/Hard Times (traveling exhib), 2006; solo exhib, Mitchell Algus Gallery, New York, 2007; High Times, Hard Times, New York Painting 1967-1975, Nat Acad Mus, New York & Tamayo Mus, Mex City, 2007; Short Distance to Now, Paintings from New York, 1967-1975, Gallery Kienzle & Gmeiner, Berlin, 2007; Making the Scene: The Midtown Y Photography Gallery 1972-1996, NY Pub Libr, New York, 2007; Short Distance to Now, Part 2, Paintings from NY, 1967-1975, Gallery Thomas Flor, Dusseldorf, Ger, 2008; High Times/Hard Times (traveling exhib), NY Paintings, 1967-1975, ZKM Ctr Art & Media, Karlsruhe, Ger, 2008; New American Abstraction, 1960-1975, Gary Snyder/Project Space, New York, 2008; Mixed Use, Manhattan: Photography & Other Practices, 1970s to the Present, Reina Sofia Mus, Madrid, Spain, 2010; Colorscope: Abstract Painting 1960-1979, Santa Barbara Mus Art, Calif, 2010; Overture: New Ways of Seeing the Blanton Coll, Blanton Mus Art, Austin, Tex, 2011; Vision is Elastic, Thought is Elastic, Murray Guy, NY, 2011. *Teaching:* Asst prof painting, Univ Iowa, 70-71; vis lectr, Univ Cincinnati, Ohio, 71; instr photog, New Sch/Parsons, NY, 87-95. *Awards:* Guggenheim Fel, 88; Found Contemp Performance Arts Inc, 90. *Bibliog:* David Reed (auth), Blanton Museum of Art: American Art since 1900, Univ Tex, Austin, 2006; Raphael Rubinstein (auth), High Times, Hard Times (review), Art in America/Annals of Painting, 9/2007; Roberta Smith (auth), Space Redefined in Chelsea, Art Review, New York Times, 2007; Lynna Cooke and Douglas Crimp with Kristen Poor (eds), Mixed Use, Museo Nacionaal Centro de Arte Reina Sofia, Madrid, MIT Press, Cambridge, Mass, 2010; Moyra Davey and Zoe Leonardd (guest ed), Blind Spot 43, Bard Coll, Annandale on Hudson, NY, 2010. *Publ:* auth, Roy Colmer/Photographs, pvt publ, 87; Doors NYC, 2001; Trucks NYC, 2001; Movie Houses, 2003; Headlines, 2003. *Dealer:* Algus Greenspon 71 Morton St New York NY 10014. *Mailing Add:* 1425 Silver Lake Blvd #2 Los Angeles CA 90026

COLNURN, MARTHA
FILMMAKER, ANIMATOR
Study: Md Inst Coll Art, Baltimore, BA, 94; Royal Acad Art, Holland, MA, 2002. *Comn:* Spiders In Love: An Arachnogasmic Musical, 2000, Skelehellavision, 2001, Cats Amore, 2002, Groscher Lansangriff: Big Bug Attack, 2002, Secrets of Mexuality, 2003, A Little Dutch Thrill, 2004, Cosmetic Emergency, 2005 and many others. *Exhib:* solo exhibs, INSE(X)CTS Major Art Fair, Amsterdam, Neth, 2002, Frankfurter Kunstverein, Young & Upcoming, Frankfurt, Ger, 2003, WINDOW gallery, Walter Van Beirendonk Fashion shop, Antwerp, Belg, 2003; group exhibs, Courthouse Gallery, Anthology Film Archive, NY, 2000, Las Palmas, Transmision: Emerging Artists living around the North Sea, Rotterdam, Neth, 2001, Outline Gallery, Haunted House of Art, Amsterdam, Neth, 2002, Diana Stigter Gallery, Amsterdam, 2003, Site Specific, Deiska, Amsterdam, 2003, Luggage Nanjing Art Inst Gallery, Nanjing, China, 2004, Vixens, Diana Stigter Gallery, Amsterdam, 2004, Liste Art Fair, Diana Stigter Gallery, Basel, Switz, 2004, Sideshow Gallery, Williamsburg, NY, Whitney Biennial: Day for Night, Whitney Mus Am Art, NY, 2006 and others; film screenings, LA Film Festival, Egyptian Theatre, Calif, 2004, Utah Arts Festival, 2004, Super 8 Special 2004, Basel, Switz, 2004, Rotterdam Int Film Festival, Neth, 2005, DUTCH OPEN, Amsterdam, 2005, Brampton Indie Arts Festival, Calif, 2005 and many others. *Pos:* vis artist, Norway, 2003, MIT, Mass, 2005 & Sch Mus Fine Arts, Boston, 2005. *Teaching:* vis prof animation, San Francisco Art Inst, 2001; Basics of Subversive & Traditional Animation, Rotterdam, Neth, 2002; vis tutor, Dutch Art Inst, Enschede, Neth, 2003; lectr, animation workshop, Nanjing Art Inst, China, 2004; vis artist & prof, Calif Inst Arts, 2004. *Awards:* Best Animated Film, NY Underground Film Festival, 99 & 2003; Sarah Lawrence Coll Film Award, 2002; and many others. *Mailing Add:* c/o Stux Gallery 530 W 25th St New York NY 10001

COLOMBINI, SUSAN MURPHY See Murphy, Susan Avis

COLOMBO, CHARLES
PAINTER
b Wilmington, Del, Nov 3, 1927. *Study:* Pa Acad Fine Arts, Philadelphia; Art Students League with Charles DeFeo; privately with Frank E Schoonover. *Work:* Pvt collections throughout US & abroad including The Vatican, Rome, Italy, Prince Ranier, Monaco, former Vpres & Mrs Walter Mondale & Senator Joseph R Biden, Jr. *Comn:* Hagley Powder Mills, comn by State of Del for Pres J F Kennedy, 62. *Exhib:* Am Watercolor Soc, 66-81; Nat Arts Club, NY, 66-75; Charles & Emma Frye Mus, Seattle, 75; Colonnade Des Artes Gallery; Lake Buena Vista, Disneyworld, Fla. *Awards:* Watercolor Award, Pa Acad Fine Arts, 49; Scholar Award, Pa Acad Fine Arts; Watercolor Award, Del Art Mus, Wilmington, 56. *Bibliog:* Frederick Kramer (auth), Brandywine Tradition Artists, Great Am Ed, New York, 71; Nancy Mohr (auth), Charles Colombo, A part of the Brandywine tradition, Delaware Today, Wilmington, 71; article, Art News, 5/83. *Mem:* Am Watercolor Soc; Rehoboth Art League. *Dealer:* Gallery At Greenville Wilmington DE; Maxwell Gallery San Francisco CA. *Mailing Add:* 402 Surrey Ct Sellersville PA 18960

COLOSI, DAVID
INSTALLATION SCULPTOR
b Rochester, NY, 1967. *Study:* State Univ New York, Plattsburgh, BA, 1989; Calif Inst Arts, MFA, 1991; New York Univ, MA, 2006. *Work:* Sherman Art Lib, Dartmouth Coll. *Exhib:* In Between, Floating Gallery, Tokyo, 1993; Science Friction, Dorsch Gallery, Miami, 2002; There's Got to Be a Morning After, Jeff Bailey Gallery, New York, 2003; Art Positions, Art Basel, Miami Beach, 2004; solo exhibs, Art Basel Switz, 2005, Galerie Catherine Bastide, Brussels, 2007, Lower Manhattan Cult Coun, New York, 2008, Cueto Project, New York, 2009; NADA Art Fair, Miami, 2005. *Awards:* Louis Comfort Tiffany Found Grant, 2009. *Bibliog:* Jessica Misener (auth), Hallucinogenic Ogres and Anatomical Machinery, Miami Hurricane, 10/31/2002; Don Miller (auth), Bizarre Bazaar, Naples Daily News, 12/3/2004; Robert Shuster (auth), David Colosi's Imaginary Numbers, Village Voice, 11/17/2009. *Publ:* Auth, Laughing Blood: Selected Poems 1987-2003, Left Hand Bks, 2004

COLP, NORMAN B
PHOTOGRAPHER, CURATOR
b Bronx, NY, Sept 3, 1944. *Study:* Queens Col, Flushing, NY, BA (art), 67; Pratt Inst, Brooklyn, NY, 67; Parsons Sch Design, NY, 71. *Work:* Corcoran Gallery Art, Smithsonian Archive Am Art & Smithsonian Inst, Washington; Univ Calif, Berkeley Art Mus; Victoria & Albert Mus, Nat Art Libr, London, Eng; Wadsworth Atheneum, Hartford, Conn; Whitney Mus Am Art; and others. *Comn:* Porcelain enamel signs, Creative Sta/MTA, NY, 91; zoetrope-B/W photo images with John Billingham, Nat Shopping Ctrs, Hamden, Conn, 91. *Exhib:* After the Fact: Select from LeWitt Collect, Wadsworth Atheneum, Hartford, 96; Small Wonders, CEPA, Buffalo, 97; Role Model, Hugo de Pagano, NY, 98; The Tiny Cinema, Red Mills, Claverack, NY, 2001; FotoFest, Houston, 2002 & 06; Art in Embassies Program, US Dept State, Havana, Cuba & Lima, Peru, 2003; Fine Print Auction, Foto Fest Int, Houston, 2004; Collage, Univ Calif, Berkeley Art Mus, 2004; Daumenhimp The Flipbook Show, Kunstalle, Dusseldorf, Ger, 2005, Foto Mus, Antwerp, Belg, 2006. *Collection Arranged:* Stories Your Mother Never Told You, White Plains Publ Libr, 82; Less is More, Pratt Graphics Ctr, 82; One Cubic Foot, Metrop Mus Art, 83; From the Beginning, Pratt Graphics Ctr, 84; The Impractical-Practical, White Plains Pub Libr, 84. *Pos:* Assoc cur, Alternative Mus, NY, 79-80; cur exhibs, Ctr Book Arts, NY, 80-83 & exhib coord, 83. *Teaching:* Instr, book art, Sch of Visual Arts, NY, 82-86 & Pratt Graphics Ctr, NY, 83-84. *Awards:* Workshop in Residence, Mus Holography, 85, Fieldcrest Cannon Inc, 91; Creative Stations, MTA, 91; The Merchant and Ivory Found, 2002; Foto Fest Award, 2002. *Bibliog:* Don Williams (reporter), News 4 New York, WNBC-TV, 6/3/92; Cathy Courtney (auth), Private Views & Other Containers, estamp/London, 6/92; Melissa Bank (auth), The Girls' Guide to Hunting and Fishing, 99, 2000. *Media:* Sequential Images, Framed & Accordion Books. *Specialty:* Contemp photography & Painting. *Publ:* Auth, The Thrice Told Tale, 77, pvt publ; An Old Saw, 82, A Primer on Art Criticism, 83, Crazy Hair, 83 & Freud's Recipe, 83, Hand & Mind Books. *Dealer:* Marsha Ralls The Ralls Collection 1516 31st St NW Washington DC 20007

COLPITT, FRANCES
HISTORIAN, CRITIC
b Tulsa, Okla, Dec 19, 1952. *Study:* Univ Tulsa, BFA, 74, MA, 77; Univ Southern Calif, PhD, 82. *Collection Arranged:* Finish Fetish: LA's Cool School, Univ Southern Calif, 91; Knowledge: Aspects of Conceptual Art, Univ Calif, Santa Barbara, 92; In Plain Sight (abstract painting in Los Angeles), Blue Star Art Space, San Antonio, 94; Chromaform: Color in Sculpture, Univ Tex, San Antonio, 98; wall painting, Univ Tex, San Antonio, 2005; Material Culture, Tex Christian Univ, 2008. *Pos:* Corresp ed, Art Am, currently; Deedie Rose Chair Art Hist, Tex Christian Univ, 2005. *Teaching:* Vis asst prof art hist, Univ Calif, Santa Barbara, 82-88; vis asst prof, Cornell Univ, 85-86 & Univ Southern Calif, 88-90; asst prof, Univ Tex, San Antonio, 90-94, assoc prof, 94-; dept chair art & art history, Univ Tex, 2002-2005. *Mem:* Int Asn Art Critics; Coll Art Asn; Art Table. *Res:* Contemporary abstract painting and sculpture; theories of 20th century criticism; minimal and conceptual art. *Publ:* The Shape of Painting in the 1960s, Coll Art J, 91; Minimal Art: The Critical Perspective, Univ Wash Press, 93; Between Two Worlds, Art Am, 98; Space City Takes Off, Art Am, 2000; ed, Abstract Art in the Late Twentieth Century, Cambridge Univ Press, 2002; Hard-Edged Cool, Birth of the Cool, Orange County Mus Art/Prestel, 2007. *Mailing Add:* TCU PO Box 298000 Fort Worth TX 76129

COLQUHOUN, PETER LLOYD
PAINTER, INSTRUCTOR
b New York, NY, Dec 1, 1955. *Study:* Pratt Inst, BFA, 89; Brooklyn Mus Art Sch, with Francis Cunningham; Art Students League, with Robert B Hale. *Work:* Bank of NY; Southeast Mo State Univ Mus; Fine Arts Mus Long Island. *Comn:* portrait, Giussepe Manzari, Rome, Italy, 85; portrait, Henry Barnett, NY, 97, 98; Lower Manhattan (cityscape), Zweig/Glaser Advs, NY, 98. *Exhib:* Roerich Mus, NY, 87; Audubon Artists, NY, 93-2000; Fine Arts Mus Long Island, Hempstead, NY, 93; Nat Acad Design, 97, 2000. *Pos:* artist-in-residence, Helene Wurlitzer Found, Taos, NMex, 2001, Rochefort en terre, Md Inst Col Art, 2002. *Teaching:* teacher painting, NY Acad, 80-83, Ctr del Arte Verrochio, Siena, Italy, 84-85. *Awards:* Internship, Peggy Guggenheim Mus, Venice, 84; Grant, Adolf & Esther Gottlieb Found, 93 & 2001; Pollack-Krasner Found Grant, 2002. *Bibliog:* Shyka Cohen (auth), catalog entry, Ice Gallery, 96; Tracy O'Shaughnessy (auth), Exhibit Is the Art of Evocative, Waterbury Republican Am, 99; Familiar Views of Downtown, Tribeca Tribune, 99. *Mem:* NY Artist Equity Asn (bd dir, 98-, columnist Artist's Proof 98-); Audubon Artists; Fedn Mod Painters & Sculptors; Orgn Independent Artists. *Media:* Oil. *Specialty:* American and German artists (2Dd & 3D). *Dealer:* Galorie Von Stechow Frankfurt Am Main. *Mailing Add:* 105 Duane St Studio Apt 4C New York NY 10007

COLSON, GREG J
SCULPTURE, CONCEPTUAL ARTIST
b Seattle, Wash, 1956. *Study:* Calif State Univ, Bakersfield, BFA, 78; Claremont Grad Sch, Calif, MFA, 80. *Work:* Mus Mod Art, NY; Hirshhorn Mus, Washington, DC; Panza Collection, Lugano, Switz; Tsaritsino Mus Contemp Art, Moscow, Russ; Mus Contemp Art, Los Angeles; Getty Research Inst, Los Angeles; Metrop Mus Art, New York; Moderna Museet, Stockholm, Sweden; New York Pub Libr; Samlung Rosenkranz, Berlin, Ger; UBS Collection, Zurich, Switz; Whitney Mus Art, NY; Hammer Mus, Los Angeles, Calif. *Exhib:* Solo exhibs, Lannan Mus, Lake Worth, Fla, 88, Sperone Westwater, NY, 90-91, 94, 2001, Konrad Fischer Gallery, Dusseldorf, Ger, 91, Kunsthalle Lophem, Brugges, Belg, 94, Krannert Art Mus, Champaign, Ill, 96, 1000 Eventi, Milan, Italy, 98, Galleria Cardi, Milan, Italy, 2001, 2003, Griffin Contemp, Venice, Calif, 98-2001, 2004-2005 & 2007, Gian Enzo Sperone, Rome, 92, 99, Baldwin Gallery, Aspen, Colo, 2002, 2006; Laboratory, Russian Mus, Leningrad, 90; Colson, Pardo, Murakami, Tower, Mars Gallery, Tokyo, 92; Mapping, Mus Mod Art, NY, 94; 100 Yrs of Calif Art, Orange Co Mus Art, Newport Beach, Calif, 97; Panza Collection, Mus Contemp Art, Los Angeles, Calif, 2000; da Warhol al 2000, Palazzo Cavour, Regione Piemonte, Turin, Italy, 2000; Arte Americana: Ultimo Decennio, Museo d'Arte della Ravenna, Italy, 2000; Amerika-Europa: Sammlung Rosenkranz, Von der Heydt Mus, Wuppertal, Ger, 2002; Outside the Box, Hammer Mus, Los Angeles, Calif, 2010; Astrazione Figurazione, Galleria Cardi, Pietrasanta, Italy, 2012; Untitled (Giotto's O), Sperone Westwater, Lugano, Switz, 2012; Patrick Painter Inc, Santa Monica, Calif, 2012, 2013; Baldwin Gallery, Aspen, Colo, 2012. *Bibliog:* Pontus Hulten and Peter Wegner (auth's), Greg Colson, Wale and Star Press, 1999; Robert Evren (auth), Greg Colson, Galleria Cardi, Milan, 2001; Genevieve Devitt (auth), Greg Colson: The Architecture of Distraction, Griffin, Santa Monica, Calif, 2006. *Media:* Wood, Metal, Paint. *Dealer:* Sperone Westwater 415 W 13th St New York NY 10014; Galleria Cardi Piazza S Erasmo 3 Milan Italy I-20121; Baldwin Gallery 209 S Galena St Aspen CO 81611; Griffin Contemporary 55 N Venice Blvd Venice CA 90291; Gian Enzo Sperone Via di Pallacorda 15 Rome Italy 00186; Patrick Painter Inc 2525 Michigan Ave Unit B2 Santa Monica CA 90404. *Mailing Add:* 751 Palms Blvd Venice CA 90291

COLVILLE, PAT
PAINTER
b New Orleans. *Study:* Univ Houston, BS; Univ Okla, MFA. *Exhib:* Solo exhibs include Condeso/Lawler Gallery, New York, 1996 & 1998, Moody Gallery, Houston, 2004 & 2005, Galveston Arts Ctr, Tex, 2008; group exhibs include 183rd Ann: Invitational Exhib Contemp Am Art, Nat Acad Mus, New York, 2008. *Awards:* Benjamin Altman Prize, Nat Acad, 2008. *Mailing Add:* c/o Moody Gallery 2815 Colquitt Houston TX 77098

COLWAY, JAMES R
PAINTER
b Oneida, NY, Nov 12, 1920. *Study:* Syracuse Univ Sch Art, 45-48, Univ Col, 46-48. *Work:* US Embassy Prog (17 paintings shown), Washington; Butler Inst Am Art, Youngstown, Ohio; Lyman Allyn Mus, Univ Conn, New London; Munson-Williams Proctor Inst, Utica, NY; Slater Mem Mus, Norwich, Conn; and others. *Comn:* 41 painting reproductions, comn by Aaron Ashley & Hedgerow House. *Exhib:* Grumbacher Show, Grand Cent Art Gallery, NY, 64; Solo exhibs, Chase Gallery, NY, 69, St Lawrence Univ, 70, Grand Haven Art Ctr, Mich, 70 & 75 & Arvest Galleries, Boston, 76; Munson-Williams-Proctor Inst, Utica, NY; Schweinfurth Mus, Auburn, NY. *Pos:* Sr vpres & dir, Oneida Ltd, retired; pres, Colway Assocs, retired. *Bibliog:* Show rev, Art News, 5/69; Grumbacher's Palette Talk, 78. *Mem:* Am Artists Prof League; Cent NY Watercolor Soc; Artists Equity Asn. *Media:* Water Media, Oil. *Mailing Add:* 101 The Vineyard Oneida NY 13421

COMINI, ALESSANDRA
HISTORIAN, WRITER, EDUCATOR
b Winona, Minn, Nov 24, 1934. *Study:* Barnard Coll, with Julius Held, BA, 56; Univ Calif, Berkeley, with Herschel Chipp, MA, 62; Columbia Univ, PhD with distinction, 69. *Teaching:* Asst prof art hist, Columbia Univ, 69-74; vis prof, Yale Univ, 73; prof, Southern Methodist Univ, 74-83, univ distinguished prof, 83-2005; prof emer, 2006-. *Awards:* Grand Medal Hon for serv to Austrian Repub, 90; Lifetime Achievement Award, Womens Caucus Art, 95; United Methodist Scholar Teacher Award, 96; Tex Women's Hall Fame (nominee), 2002; Vet Feminists of Am Award, 2010; Distinguished Alumna Award, Barnard Coll, 2011. *Mem:* Am Soc Composers, Auth & Publ; Tex Inst Letters; Coll Art Asn. *Res:* Foreign artists in Rome 1750-1914; Gothic revival and German romanticism, Austrian art nouveau & Expressionism; the visual Brahms, the visual Schoenberg, Berg, Webern, Mozart, R Strauss, Bruckner & Mahler; Alma Mahler and her Vienna; women artists; Scandinavian artists. *Interests:* Chamber music, flute. *Publ:* Gustav Klimt, George Braziller publ, NY, 75-2002, 2009; Egon Schiele, George Braziller publ, NY, 76-2002, 2009; The Changing Image of Beethoven: A Study in Myth-Making, Rizzoli Int Publ, 87, 2008; Käthe Kollwitz, Yale

Univ Press, 92; Egon Schiele, Abrams, 94; Violetta & Her Sisters, Faber & Faber, 94; auth, In Passionate Pursuit: A Memoir, George Braziller Publ, NY, 2004; and others; Schiele in Prison, NY Graphic Soc, 73; Egon Schiele's Portraits, Univ Calif Press, 74, 90 (nominated for Nat Book Award). *Mailing Add:* 2900 McFarlin Dallas TX 75205

CONANT, JAN ROYCE
PAINTER, ILLUSTRATOR
b Boston, Mass, Sept 14, 1930. *Study:* Boston Mus Sch Fine Arts, 48-51; Cincinnati Art Acad, 51-53. *Work:* Wyndham Rose Hall Hotel, Montego Bay, Jamaica, West Indies; Smith-Worthington Saddlery Co, Hartford, Conn; Chukka-Cove Farm, Ltd, St Ann, Jamaica, West Indies. *Comn:* 4 Paintings, Contract Art, Centerbrook, Conn; painting & logo, Source Inc, Branford, Conn; more than 360 commissioned paintings in pvt collections. *Exhib:* Solo exhibs, Conn Bank & Trust Co, Hartford, 71, Jamaica by Jan, Runaway Bay Hotel, West Indies, 80, Chester Art Gallery, 87 & Lyman Allyn Mus, New London, Conn, 89, Jamaica Mutual Life, Kingston, 97, Lyme Acad Fine Arts, 98-2003, Pet Connection, Lyme Art Asn, 99-2008; Catherine Lorillard Wolfe Art Club, NY, 86 & 89; Am Soc Equine Art, Lexington, Ky, 87, 90 & 95; W Graham Arader Gallery, NY, 93. *Bibliog:* Paul Smith (prod), Meet Jan Royce Conant, CPTV Your Public Media, 7/15/2010. *Mem:* Am Soc Equine Art; Lyme Acad Coll Fine Arts; Conn Comn Arts; Lyme Art Asn (dir, currently). *Media:* Oil, Watercolor. *Specialty:* Equestrian sports; Animal Portraits; Nature. *Interests:* Animal behavior; Equestrian arts. *Publ:* Children of Light, Ithaca Pres, 2005; Dowsing for Animals Well-being, 2005-2013. *Dealer:* Stonefield Farm Studio LLC. *Mailing Add:* Stonefield Farm Three Bridges Rd East Haddam CT 06423

CONAWAY, GERALD
SCULPTOR, PAINTER
b Manson, Wash, Feb 15, 1933. *Study:* Everett Jr Col, Wash, ABA; Univ Wash, Seattle, with George Tsutakawa & Everett Dupen, BA (art educ), MFA (sculpture). *Work:* Anchorage Fine Arts Mus, Alaska; Alaska Methodist Univ, Anchorage; Nat Gallery Art. *Comn:* William H Seward (marble monument), Mutual Ins Co, NY & Anchorage Centennial, Anchorage, 67; concrete wall sculptures, Raymond Lawson, AIA, 73; aluminum sculptures, Gen Serv Admin Fed Bldg, Fairbanks, Alaska, 79 & Pub Safety Bldg, Fairbanks, Alaska, 81; Benny Benson Mem (aluminum), Anchorage, 83. *Exhib:* All Alaska, Anchorage, 65-70; Western Regional Craft Show, Portland, 67; Sculpture Northwest, Seattle, 68. *Pos:* Sign writer & artist, Univ Wash, 54-65; graphic artist, Boeing Airplane Co, 57. *Teaching:* Instr art, Northshore Sch Dist, Wash, 57-65; from assoc prof to prof art, Alaska Methodist Univ, 65-76. *Awards:* Sculpture Award, All Alaska, 65-70; Jewelry Award, Western Regional Craft Show, 67. *Mem:* Nat Art Educ Asn. *Media:* Wood, Stone. *Mailing Add:* 2457 Cottonwood St Anchorage AK 99508-3931

CONAWAY, JAMES D
PAINTER, EDUCATOR
b Granite City, Ill, Oct 9, 1932. *Study:* Southern Ill Univ, Carbondale, Ill, BA; Univ Iowa, Iowa City, MA, MFA. *Work:* Am Embassy Collection; Waterloo Munic Art Gallery, Iowa; Davenport Munic Art Gallery, Iowa; Sloan Kettering Cancer Inst, New York; Frederick Weisman Mus, Minneapolis, Minn; New England Journ Medicine Boston; Fed Res Bank, Minneapolis; Univ Iowa; Augustana Coll, Rock Island, Ill; Central Coll, Pella, Iowa; & many pvt collections. *Comn:* Painting, Texaco Oil co, Houston, 81; CoBank, Minneapolis, 2006; Hazelden Found, St Paul, Minn; Target Corp, Minneapolis; Cargill Corp, Minneapolis; Tai Tam Bldg, Hong Kong; 3M Corp, St Paul, Minn. *Exhib:* Art for the Embassies, Smithsonian Inst, Washington, DC, 67; Midwestern Ann Competition, Joslyn Art Mus, Omaha, 73; Mid Yr Biennial, Butler Inst Am Art, Youngstown, Ohio, 74; Manisphere, Winnepeg Art Ctr, 74; Marietta Int Painting Exhib, Ohio, 76; Wisemann Art Mus, Minneapolis; New Am Painting Number II, Exhib in Print, Open Studio Press; Minn Marine Art Mus, 2011; Am Embassy, Ankara, Turkey, 2009; Minnetonka Ctr Arts, 2012. *Teaching:* Asst prof, Univ Wis, Stevens Point, 67-68; prof painting & drawing, Anoka Ramsey Coll, Minneapolis, 68-77; prof painting, Hamline Univ, St Paul, 77-96. *Awards:* Purchase Award, Davenport Munic Art Gallery, 63, Waterloo Munic Art Galleries, 65; Donors Prize, Walker Art Ctr Biennial, 66. *Bibliog:* By the time he got to Phoenix, Arizona Arts & Lifestyle, Spring; Worn wood helps to define the landscape, Minneapolis Star Tribune, 4/97. *Mem:* Mid-Am Coll Art Asn (treas, 77-78); Artist Equity; Traffic Zone Co-Operative, 95-. *Media:* Acrylic, Oil. *Interests:* International travel. *Publ:* New Am Paintings, 97; James Conaway (auth), Minneapolis-Santa Fe connection, Southwest Profiles, 5/83. *Dealer:* Groveland Gallery 25 Groveland Terr Minneapolis MN 55403; Artsource LA 11901 Santa Monica Blvd #555 Los Angeles 90025. *Mailing Add:* 250 3rd Ave N #204 Minneapolis MN 55401

CONCANNON, GEORGE ROBERT
PAINTER
b Berkeley, Calif. *Study:* Stanford Univ, BA; Harvard Univ, MA; Can Col. *Exhib:* Gulbenkian Nat Mus, Lisbon, Port. *Teaching:* Univ Calif, Berkeley. *Mem:* World Affairs Coun; Urban Land Inst; Am Indust Coun. *Media:* Oil on Canvas, Expressionistic Realism. *Dealer:* Woollahra Gallery Sydney Australia; Wind-Borne Gallery Darien CT. *Mailing Add:* 2995 Woodside Rd Woodside CA 94062

CONDESO, ORLANDO
PRINTMAKER
b Lima, Peru, Dec 31, 1947. *Study:* Visual Arts, Lima; Pratt Graphics Ctr, NY. *Work:* Nat Mus Hist, Repub China; Harlem Art Collection, NY; Orgn Am States, Washington, DC; Braniff Int, Lima; Cult Peruvian NAm Inst, Lima. *Exhib:* Second Biennial of Latin Am Prints, San Juan, PR, 72; 2nd Int Print Exhib, Mus Mod Art, Sao Paulo, Brazil, 72; 18th Nat Print Exhib, Brooklyn Mus, NY, 72; Young Artists 1973, Int Play Group Inc, NY, 73; Calif Palace Legion Hon, San Francisco, 73; Nat Mus Hist, Repub China, 73; 2nd Miami Graphics Biennial, Fla, 75; Solo exhibs, Pensacola Art Ctr, Fla, 77, Ivone Briceno Gallery, Lima, Peru, 78, Usdan Gallery, Bennington, Vt, 79, Nobe Gallery, NY, 79, Forum Gallery, Lima, Peru, 81 & 85, Wilson Arts Ctr, Rochester, NY, 82 & Pancho Fierro Gallery, Lima, Peru, 91; NJCVA Fac Exhib, Schering-Plough Corp, Madison, NJ, 89; Printers of The Vinalhaven Press, Fogg Gallery, Vinalhaven, Maine, 89; Earth Works JJCVA, Summit, NJ, 91. *Pos:* Co-owner, Condeso-Lawler Gallery, currently. *Teaching:* Photog tech printmaking, Lower East Side Printshop, NY, 82-84; etching instr, Cooper Union, NY, 83; etching instr, NJ Ctr Visual Arts, Summit, 89-90. *Awards:* First Prize, 5th Nat Print Competition, USA Embassy, Lima, 70; Award, 5th Ann Exhib, Pratt Graphics Ctr, 72; Purchase Award, 2nd Miami Graphics Biennial, 75. *Media:* Acrylic, Silkscreen. *Publ:* Art News, 3/71; Printshop Calendar, New York, 75; Escandalar Mag No 7, New York, 79; Art Gallery Scene, Jan Issue, 83. *Mailing Add:* 217 E 22nd New York NY 10010

CONDO, GEORGE
PAINTER, SCULPTOR
b Concord, NH, 1957. *Study:* Univ Mass, Lowell. *Work:* Corcoran Gallery, Wash DC; Mus Fine Arts, Houston; Mus Modern Art, NY; Solomon R Guggenheim Mus, NY; Whitney Mus Am Art, NY. *Comn:* book cover, Jack Kerouac's Book of Sketches, 2006; designed album covers for numerous musicians; series of paintings with Kanye West for his album, My Beautiful Dark Twisted Fantasy, 2010. *Exhib:* Perspectives @ 25: A Quarter Century of New Art in Houston, Contemp Art Mus, Houston, 2004; Traveling exhib, One Hundred Women, Mus Modern Art, Salzburg, Austria, Kunsthalle Bielefeld, Ger, 2005; 48th Corcoran Biennial: Closer to Home, cur by Stacey Schmidt, Corcoran Gallery of Art, Wash, 2005; East Village, New Mus Contemp Art, NY, 2005; Dreams and Nightmares of the Queen, Wrong Gallery, Tate Modern, London, 2006; Infinite Painting: Contemporary Painting and Global Realism, cur by Francesco Bonami, Villa Canarutto, Manin Centro d'Arte Contemporanea, Codroipo, Italy, 2006; Comic Abstraction: Image-Breaking, Image-Making, Mus Modern Art, NY, 2007; La Civilisation Perdue, Musee Maillol, Paris, France, 2009; Whitney Biennial, Whitney Mus Am Art, NY, 2010; Traveling exhib, George Condo: Mental States, New Mus, NY, Mus Boijmans van Beuningen, Rotterdam, The Netherlands, Hayward Gallery, London, UK, 2011, Schirn Kunsthalle, Frankfurt, Ger, 2012; 55th Int Art Exhib Biennale, Venice, 2013. *Pos:* founding mem, Hi Sheriffs of Blue, 1980. *Teaching:* visiting lectr, Visual and Environmental Studies, Harvard Univ, Boston, Mass, 2004. *Awards:* Acad Award in Art, Am Acad Arts and Letts, 99; Francis J Greenberger Award, 2005; Anderson Ranch Nat Artist Award, 2008; Ann Artists' Award, Arts Connection, NY, 2008. *Bibliog:* Mark Sanders (auth), George Condo: The Condo Effect, Another Mag, pp 410-423, Autumn/Winter, 2004; Jennifer Higgie (auth), Time's Fool,' Frieze, pp 110-117, 5/2007; Calvin Tomkins (auth), Portraits of Imaginary People: How George Condo Reclaimed Old Master Painting, The New Yorker, pp 56-65, 1/17/2011. *Specialty:* Modern and Contemporary art. *Publ:* George Condo: One Hundred Women, Ostfildern-Ruit, Hatje Cantz Verlag, 2005; George Condo: Existential Portraits, Luhring Augustine, NY, Holzwarth Pub, Berlin, 2006; George Condo: Mental States, Hayward Pub, London, 2011. *Dealer:* Simon Lee Gallery. *Mailing Add:* Simon Lee Gallery 12 Berkeley St London W1J 8DT United Kingdom

CONDREN, STEPHEN F
PAINTER
b Chicago, Ill, Sept 4, 1951. *Study:* Sch Art Inst Chicago, BFA, 1980; Northern Ill Univ, MSA, 1996. *Work:* Chicago Hist Soc, Ill; Cuneo Mus & Gardens, Libertyville, Ill; Harris Bank, Libertyville, Ill; Village of Libertyville, David Adler Mus, Ill; David Adler Cult Ctr, Ill. *Comn:* Pen & Ink Wash, John F Cuneo, Grayslake, Ill, 1985; oil painting, Kenneth Eichelburger, Libertyville, Ill, 1985; watercolor painting, Mr Webber, Grayslake, Ill, 1986; oil painting, Alier Jorgenson, Libertyville, Ill, 2004; oil painting, Rotary Club Chicago, Ill, 2004. *Exhib:* Landscapes, David Adler Cult Ctr, Libertyville, Ill, 1994; Lake Forest Art Show, Lake Forest Gallery, Ill, 1995; Open Show, Studio, Libertyville, Ill, 1995; Lake Co Vistas, Galerie Brang & heinrich, Stuttgart, Ger, 2000; Current Works, Union League Club, Chicago, Ill, 2004. *Teaching:* instr, Chicago Sch Art & Design, 1973-75; instr, Col Lake Co, 1985-; instr, Chicago Pub Sch, 2003-. *Awards:* First Place, USS Midway Frequent Winds, NY, 1976. *Mem:* Arts Club Chicago; Univ Club Chicago; Union League Club Chicago; Int Vis Ctr (bd mem, currently); Rotary One, Chicago (bd mem, currently). *Media:* Acrylic, Oil, Watercolor, Educator, Illustrator, Instructor. *Dealer:* Marty Lazer 329 W 18th St Suite 306 Chicago Il 60616

CONE, MICHELE C
HISTORIAN, LECTURER, CURATOR
b Paris, France, May 21, 1932; US citizen. *Study:* Studied at Inst d'Art et d'Archeol, Sorbonne, 67-68; Bryn Mawr Col, BA; NY Univ, PhD, 88. *Pos:* contribr, Art in Am. *Teaching:* fac, Sch Visual Arts, NY, 80-2011. *Awards:* Chevalier daus l'ordre des Arts en Lettres, 79. *Mem:* Art Table; Coll Art Asn; AICA; Pen; NY Inst Humanities Fellow. *Res:* Art and Visual Propaganda in the 20th Century. *Interests:* Contemp art; music; 1940's art and design; asian art. *Publ:* auth, The Roots and Routes of Art in the 20 Century, Horizon Press, 1975; auth, Artists under Vichy: A Case of Prejudice and Persecution, Princeton Univ Press, 92; contribr, The Art of the Everyday, NY Univ Press, 97; The Jew in the Text, Thames & Hudson, 96; Fascist Visions in France and Italy 1890-1945, Princeton, 97; auth, French Modernisms: Perspectives on Art Before, During and After Vichy, Cambridge, 2001. *Mailing Add:* 260 W Broadway 8F New York NY 10013

CONELLI, MARIA ANN
ADMINISTRATOR, EDUCATOR, HISTORIAN
b Brooklyn, NY, Nov 1, 1957. *Study:* Brooklyn Col, BA, 1980; NY Univ, MA, 1983; Columbia Univ, MPhil; Columbia Univ, PhD, 1992. *Pos:* Chair, Parsons/Smithsonian Inst, New York City and Washington, 1992-2001; dean, Fashion Inst Tech, New York City, 2001-2005; dir, Am Folk Art Mus, 2005-. *Teaching:* Educator, Metrop Mus of Art, New York City, 1981-84; instr, Parsons Sch of Design, 1983-2001. *Awards:* J Paul Getty Postdoctoral fel, 1997; Pub Works Challenge grantee, Nat Endowment for the Arts, Wash, 2002-03. *Mem:* Fel: Am Acad in Rome (fel 1987-88); Coll Art Assoc. *Publ:* Contr articles to prof jour; co-edit: Newsletter Decorative Art Soc, 1995—; books

CONFORTE, RENEE See McKee, Renee Conforte

CONFORTI, MICHAEL PETER
MUSEUM DIRECTOR, HISTORIAN
b Bradford, Mass, Apr 3, 1945. *Study:* Trinity Col, Conn, BA, 1968; Harvard Univ, MA, 1973, PhD, 1977. *Collection Arranged:* Cur, Sweden: A Royal Treasury, 1988; cur, The Am Craftsman & the European Tradition, 1620-1820, 1989; cur, Art & Life on the Upper Mississippi, 1890-1915, 1994; cur, A Grand Design, The Hist of London's Victoria & Albert Mus, 1997; Uncanny Spectacle: The Public Career of John Singer Sargent, 1997; Impression: Painting Quickly in France, 1820-1890, 2001; Gustav Klimt: Landscapes, 2002; Turner: The Late Seascapes, 2003; Jacques-Louis David: Empire to Exile, 2005; The Clark Brothers Collect: Impressionist & Early Modern Paintings, 2006; Claude Lorrain: The Painter as Draftsman, Drawing from the British Mus, 2007; The Unknown Monet: Pastels & Drawings, 2007; Like Breath on Glass: Whistler Inness & the Art of Painting Softly, 2008; Dove/O'Keeffe: Circles of Influence, 2009; Picasso Looks at Degas, 2010; Pissaro's People, 2011; Unearthed: Recent Archaological Discoveries from Northern China, 2012; Winslow Homer: Making Art, Making History, 2013. *Pos:* Cataloguer, Sotheby & Co, London & NY, 1968-71; cur sculpture & decorative arts, Fine Arts Mus, San Francisco, 1977-80; chief cur & Bell Mem cir, Minneapolis Inst Arts, 1980-94; dir, Sterling & Francine Clark Art Inst, Williamstown, Mass, 1994-. *Teaching:* Adj prof art hist, Univ Minn, 1986-94 & Williams Coll, 1995-. *Mem:* Trustee, Am Acad Rome, 1999-, mem exec comt, trustee Amon Carter Mus, 2006-2011, mem exec comt 2011-, Comite Int d'histoire de l'art, (CIHA), 2003-2009, Int Coun Mus, Am Asn Mus, 2005-; chair Art Mus Image Consortium, 2003-2005; Asn Art Mus Dirs, (trustee 2001-, pres 2008-2010, chair nominating and governance comt 2011-); Mass MoCA, (trustee, 2007-); State Hermitage Mus (2010-); Int Advisory Bd. *Res:* Sculpture and decorative arts, 17th to 20th centuries; museum history and history of collecting. *Publ:* Auth, Deaccessioning in American Museums: Some Thoughts for England, Apollo, 8/89; Expanding the Canon of Art Collecting in Museums, Mus News, 9-10/89; History, Value and the 1900s Art Museum, J Mus Mgmt & Curatorship, 9/93; Museums Past and Museums Present: Some Thoughts on Institutional Survival, J Mus Mgmt & Curatorship, 12/95; The Idealist Enterprise and the Applied Arts, in A Grand Design (exhib catalog), Baltimore et al, 1997; La tradition éducative et la concept des musees des beaux-arts aux États-Uris, Musée de Louvre; and others. *Mailing Add:* c/o Sterling & Francine Clark Art Mus PO Box 8 225 South St Williamstown MA 01267

CONGER, WILLIAM
PAINTER, EDUCATOR
b Dixon, Ill, May 29, 1937. *Study:* Art Inst Chicago, 56-57; Univ NMex, with Elaine deKooning, BFA, 61; Univ Chicago, MFA, 66. *Work:* Mus Contemp Art, Chicago; Art Inst Chicago; Ill State Mus, Springfield; Jonson Mus, Albuquerque; Portland Mus, Wash; Rockford Art Mus, Univ Club Chicago; Davis Mus, Wellesley College, Union League, Chicago; Smart Mus, Chicago; Wichita Art Mus, Kans; West Virginia Mus of Art; Eli & Edythe Broad Mus of Art, Lansing, Michigan; Loyola Univ Mus of Art, Chgo; DePaul Univ Art Mus, Chgo; Mus of Contemporary Art, Madison, Wis. *Comn:* Painting for IBM Corp, 86; City of Chicago Painting & Glass Windows, 2002; McCormick Place, Chicago, 2006; Chgo Public Library, Edgewater Branch. *Exhib:* Chicago & Vicinity, Art Inst Chicago, 63, 71, 73, 78, 80-81 & 84-85; Solo exhibs: Krannert Ctr Performing Arts, Urbana, Ill, 76, Zaks Gallery, Chicago, 78, 80 & 83, Boyd Gallery, Chicago, 85, 87, 90, 92, 94, 97-2002, 2004, 2007, 2009, 2010; Janus Gallery, Santa Fe, 92 & Jonson Mus, Albuquerque, NMex, 98; Walters Gallery, Tulsa OK, 2001; Tadu Contemp, Santa Fe, NMex, 2003, 2005. Happy, Los Angeles, 2010, Zolla Luberman Gallery, Chicago, 2013, Printworks Gallery, Chicago, 2013, Vendome Gallery, NY, 2014, Tarble Art Mus, Charleston, Ill, 2014, and Zolla Lieberman Gallery, Chgo, 2016; Visions-Painting & Sculpture of Distinguished Alumni 1945 to present, Art Inst Chicago Sch Gallery, 76; Chicago Abstractionists, Grae Gallery, St Louis, Mo, 87; Printmaking in Chicago 1935-95, Block Gallery, Northwestern Univ, 96, 2005; Art in Chicago 1945-1995, Mus Contemp Art, Chicago, 96-97; Albuquerque '50s, Univ Mus, Albuquerque, 90; Ill State Mus, 2005; Metcap, Chicago, 2006; Retrospective 1958-2008, Chicago Cult Ctr, 2009; Group exhibs: Chgo Cultural Ctr, 2014, Fred Jones Mus of Art, Univ of Oklahoma, Norman, 2014, Bruno Favid Gallery, St Louis, Missouri, 2015, Ed Paschke Art Ctr, Chgo, 2015, and Loyola Univ Art Mus, Chgo, 2015. *Pos:* Mem bd dir, Oxbow, Saugatuk, Mich, 83-86; adv bd, Renaissance Soc, 88-2002; Adv Bd, DePaul Univ Art Mus, 2005. *Teaching:* Prof art, DePaul Univ, Chicago, 71-85, chmn dept, 71-77 & 80-85; vis artist, Univ Southern Ill, 84, Sch of Art Inst Chicago, 85, Univ Iowa, 96; prof & chmn dept art theory & practice, NWestern Univ, Evanston, Ill, 84-98; Northwestern Univ, 98-2006, prof emer, 2006. *Awards:* Bartels Prize, 71 & Cluseman Prize, 73, Art Inst Chicago; Ill Acad Fine Arts Award Nominee, Chicago, 92; Pollock-Krasner Found Grant, 2008. *Bibliog:* Art in Am, 11/85; M Gedo (auth), The meaning of artistic form & the promise of the psychoanalytic method, Vol 2, No 3, Art Criticism, 86; Carol Volk (auth), Art & Antiques, 4/92; S Taylor, auth, Art in Am, 7/97; G Holg (auth), William Conger, Art News, 1/95; Art News, 5/2007, 12/2000; Art in Am, Dec 2007; Donald Kuspit (auth), catalog essay; Julia Karabenick (auth), www.geoform.net; D Golden (auth) ArtCritical, Oct 2014 (online); S Ostrow (auth), Catalog Essay, Vendome Gallery, NYC, 2014. *Mem:* Arts Club Chicago; Union League Club Chicago. *Media:* Oil, Gouache, acrylic. *Res:* Manet & Perspective, other art hist & practice topics; Career records in Archives of Am Art, Smithsonian Inst, Northwestern Univ Archives. *Specialty:* Contemp Art. *Interests:* US Hist, Science, Philosophy. *Collection:* Mod & Contemp Art, mainly Chicago; Native Am; Rare books & Hist Doc. *Publ:* Looking & dreaming in New York & Chicago, No 1, Chicago/Art/Write, 85 & Abstract painting: Fact, fiction, paradox, No 2, & Art Limits, No 4, 87; Drawing, No 13, WhiteWalls, 86; The Journal of Eugene Delacroix, Psychoanalytic Studies of Biog, Int Univs Press Inc, 87; contribr, Gedo, Looking at Fine Art from The Inside Out, 94; The MFA Filling the Gap between Seeing & Saying, Alumni Exhib Catalog, Northwestern Univ, 2001; auth, Toward a New Revolutionary Art, Again, Prompt, Vol I, No 1, 10/2008; Contributor: Gedo, Monet and His Muse (Chapter 5), Univ of Chgo Press, 2010; Abstract Painting & Integrationist Linguistics, Language Sciences, Vol 33, 2011; An Assessment in What Do Artists Know, edited by James Elkins, Univ Penn, 2013; What is Painting?, Neoteric, 9/14 and The New Art Examiner, 9/14. *Dealer:* Printworks Gallery Chicago Il; Zolla Lieberman Gallery 325 W Huron Chicago Il; Bruno David Gallery St Louis Mo. *Mailing Add:* 3500 N Lake Shore Dr Apt 15A Chicago IL 60657

CONKLIN, ERIC
ARTIST
b Baltimore, Md, Apr 20, 1950. *Work:* Historic Ark Mus, Little Rock; The Sherlock Holmes Mus, London; Leigh Yawkey Woodson Art Mus, Wausau, WI. *Exhib:* Works by Contemp Md Artists, The Govt House, Annapolis, Md, 2000; Phoenix Art Mus, 2003; Leigh Yawkey Woodson Art Mus, Wausau, Wis, 2003; The Art of Illusion, Teopel Oeil Soc of Artists, Philabrook Mus of Art, Tulsa, Okla, 2004; Smith Kramer Mus Toor, 2004-2007. *Pos:* research historian, Trompe l'Oeil Soc Artists, 2001-. *Teaching:* Mus Lectures & Demonstr, Phoenix Art Mus, Phoenix, Ariz; Philbrook Art Mus, Tulsa, Okla; Woodson Art Mus, Wausau, Wis. *Awards:* Exhib III, Works by Contemp Md Artists, 1st Lady Glendening, 2000; Best of Show, York Art Asn, 2001; Annie Award, 2003; Cult Arts Found of Awwe Arundel Co, Visual Arts, Md. *Mem:* Trompe l'Oeil Soc Artists (founding mem, rsch historian, 2001-); Md Hall Sch Arts; Delaplaine Visual Arts Ctr; York (Pa) Art Asn; Md Fedn Art; Allied Artists Am. *Media:* Hand mixed Oil on Panel. *Res:* Dutch perspective boxes, Am & European trompe l'oeil painting; Anamorphic Cylindees & Conical mirror Images. *Specialty:* Trompe l'Oeil. *Publ:* Ed, Best of the West: New Mexico, Southwest Art, 2002; Birds in Art, Woodson Art Mus; Edgaetown Art Gallery original paintings, 2004. *Dealer:* Cynthia McBride McBride Gallery 215 Main St Annapolis MD 21401; Eleanor Ettinger Gallery New York NY; Edgartown Art Gallery Edgartown MA. *Mailing Add:* c/o Eleanor Ettinger Gallery 24 W 57th St Ste 609 New York NY 10019

CONKLIN, JO-ANN
MUSEUM DIRECTOR, CURATOR
b Great Barrington, Mass, Dec 22, 1952. *Study:* Md Inst Coll of Art, BA, 79; Univ Iowa, MA (art hist), 88. *Collection Arranged:* Landscape: James Casebere, Univ Iowa Mus Art, 91, Pajama: An Artist's Coterie at Play, 94, Inscape: Odd Nerdrum, 95 & Rudolf Koppitz: Viennese Master of the Camera (auth, catalog), 96; Map of Temper, Map of Tenderness: Annette Messager (auth, catalog), Brown Univ, 97 & False Witness: Joan Fontaebera and Kahuf Selesnick, 2000. *Pos:* registr, Univ Iowa Mus Art, 86-96 & cur of graphic arts, 86-96; dir, David Winton Bell Gallery, Brown Univ, 96-. *Publ:* auth & ed, Art by Women: The Louis Noun Collection, Univ Iowa Mus Art, 90 & Photographs from the Collection of Carlton Willer, 93; ed, Crafting the Media: Patrons & Certisums in Theme, Brown Univ, 99. *Mailing Add:* 69 Hillside Ave Providence RI 02906

CONLEY, ZEB BRISTOL, JR
COLLECTOR, GALLERY DIRECTOR
b Andrews, NC, Feb 12, 1936. *Study:* Mars Hill Col, 55-57; Coll William & Mary, 57-61; NMex Highlands Univ, 63. *Collection Arranged:* Alfred Murang Retrospective, Mus of the Southwest, Midland, Tex, 85. *Pos:* Dir, Jamison Galleries, Santa Fe, 73-98, bd mem, 74-98, pres, 81-98; guest cur, Mus of the Southwest, Midland, Tex, 85. *Specialty:* Traditional Southwestern art, specializing in Taos and Santa Fe masters. *Mailing Add:* 1 Taos Trail S Corrales NM 87048-9661

CONLON, JAMES EDWARD
SCULPTOR, HISTORIAN
b Cincinnati, Ohio, Dec 9, 1935. *Study:* Ohio State Univ, BS (art educ), 59, MA (fine arts), 62. *Work:* Fine Arts Mus South Mobile; Fine Arts Mus York, Ala; Symbiotic Series, Mobile Arts Coun; Moses, Springhill Ave Temple, Mobile, Ala. *Comn:* sculptural relief, Mobile, Ala Airport; Three Angels (wall relief), Seventh Day Adventist Church, St Elmo, Ala, 82; Gateway, Cathedral Sq, Mobile Arts Coun & Mainstreet Mobile, Ala, 93; At Play (life-size tableau) Univ S Ala Women's & Children's Hosp, 96. *Exhib:* Southern Asn Sculptors Traveling Exhib, Smithsonian Inst; Competition 75, Mobile, Ala, 75; two-person show, Fine Arts Mus South-Mobile, 77; Montgomery Mus Art, 78-79; Ala Sculptors Invitational, 80. *Teaching:* Instr, Ind Univ, Bloomington, 62-65; from asst prof to assoc prof, Univ S Ala, Mobile, 65-73, prof, 74-97, prof emer art & art hist, 98-. *Awards:* Award to Develop the Ethnic Am Art Slide Libr, Samuel H Kress Found, 72-75; Award to Produce a Reference Index of Afro-Am Art, Am Revolution Bicentennial Comn, 73; Univ Res Grant, 76-77. *Mem:* Ala Alliance Arts Educ; Mobile Watercolor and Graphic Arts Soc (pres, 2003). *Media:* Woods, Limestone, Cast & Laminated Plastics. *Res:* An investigation of stylistic development in Afro-American, Mexican American and Native American art from 1800 to the present; adaptation of the industrial process of cultured marble to the production of hollow-cast figurative forms 1983-1986. *Interests:* figurative & organic forms in sculpture. *Publ:* Coauth, An Afro-American slide project, Coll Art Asn J, winter 70. *Dealer:* Gallery 54 54 Upham St Mobile AL 36607. *Mailing Add:* 1613 Sugar Creek Dr W Mobile AL 36695-2938

CONN, DAVID EDWARD
PRINTMAKER
b Jersey City, NJ, Apr 10, 1941. *Study:* Newark Sch Fine Arts, NJ; Md Inst Coll Art, Baltimore, BFA, with Peter Milton, 67; Univ Okla, Norman, MFA, 70. *Work:* Ark Art Ctr, Little Rock; Ft Worth Art Mus, Tex; Modern Mus Art, Campinas Sao Paulo, Brazil. *Exhib:* 20th Exhib Southwestern Prints & Drawings, Dallas Mus Art, 75; Joslyn Art Mus, 78; 1984 int Art Competition, Los Angeles; Texas Visons, Mus Art Am Southwest, Houston, 86; 4th Int Exhib, Lodz, Poland; Int Prints II, John Szoke Graphics Gallery, NY, 88. *Pos:* Chmn dept art & art hist, Tex Christian Univ, 90-94. *Teaching:* Prof art-printmaking, Tex Christian Univ, 69-. *Awards:* Ford Fel, Painting, 66-67; Purchase Award, Ark Print, Drawing & Crafts, Ark Art Ctr, 71; Individual Fel Printmaking, Drawing & Artists Bks, Nat Endowment Arts, 84. *Bibliog:* American Printmakers 74--Graphics Group, Arcadia, Calif, 74. *Media:* Intaglio, Waterless Lithography. *Mailing Add:* 1024 Shaw Fort Worth TX 76110

CONNEEN, JANE W
PRINTMAKER, BOOK ARTIST
b Montclair, NJ, April 19, 1921. *Study:* With George Parker, Emily Hatch, Sally Kugelmeyer & David Sander; Lehigh Univ. *Work:* Hunt Inst Botanical Doc, Pittsburgh, Pa; Mus City New York; Skillman Libr, Lafayette Col, Easton, Pa. *Comn:* Drawings, Allentown Art Mus, Pa, 75 & Pa Chamber Commerce, Harrisburg, 76. *Exhib:* Solo exhib, Lehigh Univ & Kemerer Mus, Bethlehem, Pa, 85 & Skillman Libr, Lafayette Col, Easton, Pa, 95; Philadelphia Print Club, 82; Royal Soc Miniature Painters, London, 83; 20-yr Retrospective Exhib, Lehigh Univ, 90; Book Arts 93, Can Bookbinders & Book Artists' Guild. *Pos:* miniature book pub. *Awards:* Best in Show & First in Graphics, Am Nat Miniature Show, Laramie, Wyo, 80; First in Graphics, Miniature Painters, Sculptors & Gravers Washington, DC, 83, Miniature Art Soc Fla, 84 & Miniature Art Soc NJ, 85; Distinguished Book award from The Miniature Book Soc, 90; Norman Forgue Award, Miniature Book Soc, 2001. *Bibliog:* Louis Bondy (auth), Miniature Books, Sheppard Press, London, 81; Lillian Wachtel (auth), Miniature Herb Books, The Herb Quarterly; David P Richards (auth), How to Discover Your Own Painting Style, North Light Books; Christina Feliciano (auth), Making Books by Hand, Quarry books, Rockport Publishers, Inc. *Mem:* Miniature Painters, Sculptors & Gravers Soc, Washington, DC; fel Int Guild Miniature Artisans; Printmaking Coun NJ; Miniature Book Soc. *Media:* Hand-Colored Etchings; Limited Edition Miniature Books, Gouache Landscapes, Wood Engraving. *Publ:* Auth & illusr, The Winding Roads of Ireland, 90; The Language of Herbs I, II, & III (miniature bks), 91; Staithes; The Story of a Yorkshire Fishing Village (miniature bk); Covered Bridges of Bucks County, Pennsylvania, 96; Wildflowers of Wickham Park, Florida, 96; Violets, 93; Dixie Cups, 95; Strawberries, Their History & Uses, 95; Santas, 97; Angels, 98; The Star Spangled Banner, 2000; Assisi, 2000; Ireland: A Gallery of Small Gouache Paintings, 2002; Achill Island, 2003. *Dealer:* The Snow Goose Gallery, Main St, Bethlehem, PA, 18018

CONNEEN, MARI M
PAINTER
b Allentown, Pa, Dec 21, 1946. *Study:* Self taught. *Work:* Lowe Art Mus, Miami, Fla; Pensacola Visual Arts Mus, Fla; Loch Haven Art Ctr, Orlando, Fla; Walt Disney World, Orlando, Fla; Hunt Botanical Inst, Pittsburgh, Pa; Brevard Mus Art & Sci, Melbourne, Fla; Orlando Mus Art, Fla; IBM Corp, NC; Southern Progress, Birmingham, Ala. *Comn:* Two large watercolors of sea life, Song of Norway Cruise Line, Miami, Fla, 87. *Exhib:* Allied Artists of Am 85th Watercolor Exhib, Nat Arts Club, New York, 84; Adirondacks Nat Exhib, Old Forge Art Ctr, 84-99; Miss Watercolor Exhib, Mus Art Jackson, 87 & 93; Okla Watercolor Exhib, Okla Art Ctr, 87-88 & 92-93; Boca Raton Mus, 90; Nat Watercolor Soc, 93-94. *Awards:* Best of Show, Winter Park Art Festival & Coconut Grove Art Festival, 83; Experts Choice, Artist Soc Int, 84; Nat Watercolor Soc, 93. *Bibliog:* Article on Camelias, Southern Accents Mag, 12/91; Orlando Mag, 3/94; Fla Today Newspaper; Watercolor Magic, 2003; Space Coast Living, 2003. *Mem:* Nat Mus Women in Arts; Am Artist Prof League; Guild Natural Sci Illusr; Southern Watercolor Soc; Nat Watercolor Soc; Fla Watercolor Soc; Watercolor USA Honor Soc. *Media:* Watercolor; Lithography. *Interests:* Environmental issues. *Publ:* Auth, Watercolor '86, Am Artists, 86; Best of Flower Paintings, 96; Painting Texture, Rockport Press, 97; Best of Watercolor, 97; Best of Flower Painting II, 99. *Dealer:* J Lawrence Gallery 535 W Eau Gallie Blvd Melbourne Fla; Grand Cent Art Galleries Inc 24 W 57th Ave New York NY 10019. *Mailing Add:* 457 Crystal Tree Dr Waynesville NC 28785

CONNELLY, CHUCK
PAINTER
b Pittsburgh, Pa, 1955. *Study:* Tyler Sch Art, Philadelphia, Pa, BFA, 77. *Work:* Metrop Mus Art, NY; Brooklyn Mus Art, NY; Portland Art Mus, Ore; J B Speed Mus, Louisville, KY; Tucson Mus Art, Ariz. *Exhib:* New Narrative Painting, Museo Tamayo, Mexico City, Mex, 84; solo exhib, Northern Ill Univ Art Gallery, Chicago, 84-85; Aldrich Mus Contemp Art, Ridgefield, Conn, 84 & 86; Painting & Sculpture Today, Indianapolis Mus Art, Ind, 86; Nassau Co Mus Art, Roslyn, NY, 91; Big Ideas, Tucson Mus Art, Tucson, Ariz, 92; Transport, Maier Mus Art, Lynchberg, Va, 94; The Figure: Another Side of Modernism, Snug Harbor Cult Ctr, Staten Island, NT, 2000; A Gift of Vision, Tucson Mus Art, Ariz, 95; East Oak Lane, DFN Gallery, NY, 2007. *Awards:* Gottlieb Found Grant, 99. *Bibliog:* Eleanor Heartney (auth), Chuck Connelly at Lennon, Weinberg, Art in America, 5/92; Ronny Cohen (auth), Chuck Connelly, Artforum, 2/93; Judith Page (auth), Chuck Connelly, ArtPapers, 3/95. *Media:* Oil. *Dealer:* Lennon Weinberg Inc 560 Broadway Suite 308 New York NY 10012-3945

CONNER, ANN
PRINTMAKER
b Wilmington, NC, Aug 11, 1948. *Study:* Salem Coll, NC, BFA, 70; Salem-Hofstra Summer Prog, Asolo, Italy, 70; Univ NC, Chapel Hill, MACT, 72, MFA, 75. *Work:* Fogg Art Mus, Harvard Univ, Cambridge, Mass; Mus Fine Arts, Boston; Libr Cong, Washington, DC; New York Pub Libr; List Visual Arts Ctr, Mass Inst Technol; and others; Ritz Carlton Hotels; Federal Reserve Bank, Richmond; Bank of America; Federal Reserve, Fidelity Investments. *Comn:* Cinnamon, Philip Morris USA, Charlotte, NC; NC Gov Business Art Print Ed, 91-. *Exhib:* Independant Exhib of Prints, Kanagawa Prefectural Gallery, Yokohama, Japan, 84-95; 69th Int Competition Prints, Print Club, Philadelphia, 94; Releif Prints, Winthrop Univ Galleries, Rock Hill, SC, 94; After Appalachia, WVa Univ, Morgantown, 95; In Relief, Contemp Am Relief Prints, Lincoln, Nebr, 98; Solo Exhibs: Gray Gallery, Greenville, NC, 98; Flatbed Press, Austin, Tex, 98, 2010, 2013; Printed in Beauty: Ann Conner Recent Work, Cameron Art Mus, Wilmington, NC, 2007; Ann Conner, Recent Woodcuts, Flatbed Press Gallery, Austin, Tex, 2007; Int Print Ctr, New York, 2002-2006; Holocaust, Cameron Art Mus, 2008; Colorprint USA 40th Anniversary, Mus Tex Tech, Tex, 2010; Selections from Flatbed Press, Austin, Tex, 2010; Boston Printmakers, 2011; Print Biennial, Ann Conner, Hodges Taylor Gallery, Charlotte, NC, 2011; New Prints, 2012; IPCNY, NY; Two Visions, New Elements Gallery, Wilmington, NC, 2012; Manler Fine Art, Raleigh, NC, 2012; Democratic Convention Exhib, Charlotte, NC, 2013; Flatbed Press Gallery, Austin, Tex, 2013; Prints: CA, LA and Beyond Part II, Gray Loft Gallery, Oakland, CA, 2015, New Editions and Monotypes, Flatbed Press Gallery, Austin, Tex, 2014-2015, Palate to Plate, Newport Art Mus, RI, 2014-2015. *Collection Arranged:* State Dept Art in Embassies. *Awards:* Ture Ben Prize, Boston Printmakers, 2003. *Bibliog:* Susan Tallman (auth), Utopia/Dystopia, Print Club, Philadelphia, 92; David Acton (auth), 60 years of North Am Prints, 1947-2007, Boston, 2009; Ann Conner (auth), Park Art on Paper, 2002. *Mem:* Print Club, Pa; Boston Printmakers; Drawing Ctr, New York; Mus Mod Art, New York; Renaissance Soc, Univ Chicago. *Media:* Woodcut. *Publ:* Les Krantz (auth), New York Art Rev, 88; Modern Graphics, Art of the 80's, Libr Cong, 89; Printworld Directory of Contemporary Prints, 85-86, 88-89 & 93; Print News, Prints from Blocks, 85; The Complete Manual of Relief Printmaking, Kindersley, 88. *Dealer:* Flatbed Press 2832 E Martin Luther King Blvd Austin Tx 78702; Hodges Taylor Art Consultancy 118 Kingston Ave Ste 25 Charlotte NC 28203; The Mahler Fine Art 228 Fayetteville St Raleigh NC 27601

CONNER, LOIS
PHOTOGRAPHER
b Long Island, NY, Feb 12, 1951. *Study:* Pratt Inst, BFA, 75; Yale Univ, MFA, 81. *Work:* Mus Mod Art & Metrop Mus Art, NY; Smithsonian Inst, Nat Mus Art, Washington, DC; Victoria & Albert Mus, London, Eng; Nat Gallery Victoria, Melbourne, Australia. *Comn:* Wave Hill, Botanical Gardens, NY, 90; The Cuyahoga River, Gund Found, Cleveland, Ohio, 91. *Exhib:* Photographs from the Collection, Victoria & Albert Mus, London, Eng, 87; Photographs of China, Canton Art Mus, China, 88; China, Cleveland Mus Art, Ohio, 88; Landscapes, Bombay Ctr Photog, Bombay, India, 90; In the Shadow of the Wall (auth, catalog), Taiwan Mus Art, Taichung, Rep China, 92; Between Heaven & Home, Smithsonian Inst, Washington, DC, 92; Mus Mod Art, NY, 92. *Teaching:* Adj prof photog, Fordham Univ, New York, & Cooper Union, New York, 91; asst prof photog, Yale Univ, New Haven, Conn, 91-. *Awards:* Fel, Nat Endowment Arts, 83; Guggenheim Fel, 84; Fel, NY State Coun Arts, 79. *Bibliog:* Dang Ho Liu (auth), In the Shadow of the Wall, Taiwan Mus Art, 92. *Dealer:* Laurence Miller Gallery 138 Spring St New York NY 10012. *Mailing Add:* 36 Gramercy Park E No 4-E New York NY 10003

CONNIFF, GREGORY
PHOTOGRAPHER, WRITER
b Jersey City, NJ, May 3, 1944. *Study:* Columbia Univ, BA, 66; Univ Va Law Sch, LLB, 69; with William Weege (printmaker), 71-72. *Work:* Mus Mod Art, NY; Ctr Creative Photogr, Tucson, Ariz; Mus Fine Arts, Boston, Mass; San Francisco Mus Mod Art; Corcoran Gallery Art, Washington; Art Inst Chgo. *Comn:* Nat Rd Proj, John Hopkins Univ Press; Urban Gardens, George Gund Found. *Exhib:* Solo exhibs include Corcoran Gallery Art, 79, Toledo Mus Art, 83, Akron Art Mus, Ohio, 86, Mus Contemp Photogr, Chicago, 86, Cleveland Mus Art, 2002, Ludwig Mus, Budapest, 2002; group exhibs include Fogg Art Mus, 80; A Century of Landscape, High Mus Art (catalog), 81; The Lens in the Garden, Hudson River Mus, Yonkers, NY, 84; Two Days in Louisiana, Milwaukee Art Mus, Wis, 89; Between Home and Heaven, Nat Mus Am Art, Washington, 92; Crossing the Frontier (catalog), San Francisco Mus Mod Art, 96, 2001; Camera and Ink; Judy Pfaff and Gregory Conniff; Milwaukee Mus of Art, 2004; Candace Dwan Gallery, NY City, 2006. *Pos:* Consult ed (landscape), Johns Hopkins Univ Press. *Awards:* Nat Endowment Arts Photog Fel, 80-81, 92-93; Wis Arts Bd Visual Arts Fel, 78, 84 & 90; John Simon Guggenheim Mem Fel, 89-90. *Bibliog:* Jane Livingston (auth), Gregory Conniff, Corcoran Gallery Art, 79; David Tannous (auth), Gregory Conniff, Art Am, summer 80; Kent Williams (auth), In His Own Image, Isthmus, 11/24/89. *Media:* Photography. *Specialty:* photography. *Interests:* Gardening. *Publ:* Auth & illusr, Common Ground: Vol 1 of an American Field Guide, Yale Univ Press, 85; Between Home & Heaven: Contemporary American Landscape Photography, Univ NMex Press, 92; Crossing the Frontier, SFMOMA, Chronicle Books, 96; Twenty Years in the Field, Sordoni Gallery, 99; Wild Edges, Chazen Mus Art, 2006. *Dealer:* Joseph Bellows Gallery 7661 Girard Ave La Jolla Ca 92037. *Mailing Add:* 1426 Rutledge St Madison WI 53703-3835

CONNOLLY, JEROME PATRICK
PAINTER, MURALIST
b Minneapolis, Minn, Jan 14, 1931. *Study:* Univ Minn, BS (art educ); also with Francis Lee Jaques. *Work:* Diorama backgrounds & murals in 36 mus, incl Carnegie Mus, Pittsburgh, James Ford Bell Mus, Minneapolis, George C Page Mus, Los Angeles, Smithsonian Mus Nat Hist, Taipei Zoo Educ Bldg, Taiwan, Transp Mus & many others. *Exhib:* Sportsman's Gallery of Art & Bks, NY; Crossroads of Sport, NY; Abercrombie & Fitch, NY & San Francisco; Petersen Gallery, Los Angeles; Solo exhib, Abercrombie & Fitch, NY, 72; and others. *Pos:* Staff artist, Ill State Mus, Springfield, 58-60, Natural Sci Youth Found, Westport, Conn, 60-65; free lance artist, 65-. *Awards:* First place, Wildlife Art Show, East Stroudsberg Univ, 93. *Mem:* Susquehanna Valley Art Soc. *Media:* Oil, Acrylic. *Interests:* fishing & ballooning. *Publ:* Illusr, Adelbert the Penguin, 69; The Deer Family, 69; Aise-ce-bon: a Raccoon, 71; Saga of a Whitetail, 81; 15 children's books & contribr, Audubon Mag, Nat Wildlife, Hartford Life Insurance Co calendar & Pa Game News. *Mailing Add:* 804 Sunbury Rd Shamokin Dam PA 17876

CONNOR, MAUREEN
SCULPTOR, EDUCATOR
b Baltimore, Md. *Study:* Pratt Inst, NY, MFA, 73. *Work:* Irish Mus Mod Art; The Avon Corp, NY; Zentrum Fur Kunst Und Medientechnologie, Karlsruhe, Ger. *Exhib:* Aldrich Mus Contemp Art, Ridgefield, Conn, 93 & 94; Nat Mus Art, Seoul, Korea, 93; Whitney Mus Am Art Biennial, 93; solo exhibs, Alternative Mus, NY, 94-95, Baxter Gallery, Maine Coll Art, Portland, 95, PPOW, NY, 95, William F Brush Gallery, St Lawrence Univ, Canton, NY, 96, Galerie Sima, Nuremburg, Ger, 96, Mus of Modern Art, NY, 96, Kunstraum Munich, Ger, 97 & Inst Contemp Art, Philadelphia, 97, Curt Marcus Gallery, 98, Museo de Arte Modern, Buenos Aires,Argentina, Queens Mus of Art, Corona Park, NY, 2000, Curatorial Studies, Riverdale, NY, 2006; The Telematic

Room, Neue Gesellschaft fur Bildende Kunst, Berlin, Ger, 96; The Visible & the Invisible, Inst Int Visual Arts, Univ Col, London, 96; Feed and Greed, Mus Angewande Kunst, Vienna, Austria, 96; Dress for Millenium Eve, Fabric Workshop, Philadelphia, 96; Mus Mod Art, Screening Video Viewpoints, 96; City Canibal, 98; Memorable Histories & Historic Memories, Bowdoin Col, Mus Art, 98; Queens Artists: Highlights of the 20th Century, Queens Mus Art, NY, 98; Xmas, Kent Gallery, NY, 99; A room with a view, Sixth@Prince, Fine Art, 99; Salome, Castle Gallery, New Rochelle, NY, 99; Size Matters, Gate Gates et al, Brooklyn, NY, 99; The End, Exit Art/The Third World, NY, 2000; Representing: A Show of Identities, The Parish Art Mus, Southampton, NY, 2000; Likeness of Being: Contemp Self Portraits, DC Moore Gallery, 2000; All You Need is Love, Laznia Ctr for Contemp Art, Gdansk, Poland, 2000; Do You Have Time?, Liebman Magnan Gallery, NY, 2001; Mirror, Mirror, Mass MoCa, North Adams, Mass, 2002; New Hotels for Global Nomads, Cooper Hewitt Mus, NY, 2002; Individuals, Mendel Art Gallery, Saskatoon, Saskatchewan, Can, 2002; Food, Katonah Mus, NY, 2003; Health & Safety, Whyspa Inst Art, Gdansk, Poland, 2004; Inside Out Loud, Kemper Art Mus, St Louis Mo, 2005; When Artists Say WE, Artists Space, NYC, 2006; Everyone Dance Now, EFA Gallery, NYC, 2006; Feeding Desire, Cooper Hewitt Mus, NYC, 2006. *Teaching:* numerous lectures at art schs & universities, 76-2001; guest prof, Akad Bildenden Kunst, Munchen, Ger, 95-96; prof sculpture & installation, Queens Col, City Univ NY, 90-. *Awards:* Guggenheim Fel, 95; Nat Endowment Arts Fel, 95; NYFA Individual Artists Fel, 99; NYSCA Finishing Funds Award for "Growing Older" at QMA, 2000; NYSCA Media Project Grant, Queens Mus of Art, 2000; Harvestworks Digital Media Arts Artist-in-Residence, 2000. *Bibliog:* Martha Schwendener (auth), Maureen Connor, Love at First Site, Time Out, 2/5-12/98; Mira Schwirtz (auth), Maureen Connor, Curt Marcus Gallery, Flash Art, 5/98-6/98; Laura Frost & Tim Griffin (auth), She saw/He saw, Two Views of Maureen Connor, 6/98-7/98; Amelia Jones (auth), Performing Bodies, Calif Univ Press, 98; Ken Johnson (auth), Review: Seductions and Games: Recent Video Installations by Maureen Connor, The NY Times, 1/19/2001; Sarah Valdez (auth), Rules of the Game: Maureen Connor Makes Socially Conscious Art with a Twist, Time Out NY, 1/18-25, 2001; Jean Robertson & Craig McDaniel (coauths), Themes of Contemporary Art: Visual Art After 1980, NY/Oxford, Oxford Univ Press, 2005. *Publ:* Contribr, Testing Resources, 2007; Making Art History: Changing Discipline & its Institutions, Elizabeth C Mansfield (ed), 2007. *Mailing Add:* 10 Leonard St New York NY 10013-2929

CONRAD, NANCY R
PAINTER
b Houston, Tex, Jan 29, 1940. *Study:* Randolph Coll, BA; Glassell Sch Art, Mus Fine Arts, Houston. *Work:* El Paso Mus Fine Arts, Tex; Continental Oil Co Collection & Dresser Indust Collection, Houston; Aviation Am Bldg, Love Field, Dallas; Chase Banks, Corpus Christi, Midland, New Braunfels, Arlington, Tex; Toyota Corp; Chevron Corp; Merril Lynch, Denver & Baker; Hughes, ACL Resources; MD Anderson Med Ctr; Randolph Coll; Burlington Northern Santa Fe Collection, Methodist Hospitals; Exxon, Houston; Herman Hospitals; Conoco, Houston. *Comn:* Allied Bank Systems, First City Banks, 84-85; Stauffer Hotel, Trammel Crow Properties, Austin, Tex, 86; Astrodome Sheraton, 89; Methodist Hospitals; Memorial, Herman Hospitals; BNSF; Northwestern Mutual Life, Chicago. *Exhib:* Group exhibs, Sun Carnival Exhib, El Paso Mus Fine Arts, 73-75; Tex Painting & Sculpture, Dallas Mus Fine Arts; 52nd Ann Nat Exhib, Shreveport, La, 74; Nat Women's Yr Exhib, 79; Women & Their Work, touring show, 80-81; Staged & Stages, Blaffer Gallery, Univ Houston, 85; Tex Visions, 86; Summer Group Show, Gallery 3, 2002, Art Crawl, 2002; Artists of Tex, Harris Gallery, 2004; Hockaday Mus Mems Kalispell, 2004-2005; Solo exhib, Harris Gallery, 2005; Mayor Houston Art Exhib, 2007; 2 person exhib, Harris Gallery, 2010. *Collection Arranged:* BNSF (cur Sally King), Fort Worth, Tex, 2008. *Teaching:* Pvt instr. *Awards:* Foley Award, Foley's of Houston, 70; Purchase Award, El Paso Mus Art, 73. *Bibliog:* Articles In: Southwest Art Mag, Art Mag, Art Voices S, Artweek Newspaper, San Francisco, Texas Artist, Vol II; Paintings of the Silent Land, monograph, 2011. *Mem:* Mus Fine Arts Houston. *Media:* Oil, Drawing. *Specialty:* Oil painting, photography, realism. *Interests:* Mont & Tex landscapes in oil, pastel & archival photog. *Collection:* Burlington, Northern, Fort Worth, Tex; Memorial, Herman Hospitals; Methodist Hospitals, MD Anderson Cancer Ctr. *Publ:* Illusr, Little Flower, Child Welfare League, 2000; The Paintings of Nancy Conrad, 2013. *Dealer:* Harris Gallery 1100 Bissonet Houston TX 77005; harrisgalleryhouston.com

CONSEY, KEVIN E
MUSEUM DIRECTOR, PROFESSOR
b New York, NY, Jan 15, 1952. *Study:* Hofstra Univ, BA, 74; Univ Va, Charlottesville, 75; Univ Mich, Ann Arbor, MA (mus practice art hist), 77; Kellogg Sch of Mich, Northwestern Univ, MBA, 99. *Collection Arranged:* African Art (auth, catalog), Art Mus, Univ Mich, 76 & 77; Real, Really Real, Super Real, 81. *Pos:* Dir, San Antonio Mus Art, 80-83 & Newport Harbor Art Mus, 83-89, dir & Chief Exec Officer, Mus Contemp Art, Chicago, 89-98; dir, Univ Calif Berkeley Art Mus, 99-05, SFAI prof, 2011-. *Teaching:* Instr art hist, Univ Toledo, 75-76; asst prof & dir, Emily Lowe Gallery, Hofstra Univ, 77-80; vis prof, Univ Tex, San Antonio, 81-83. *Mem:* Asn Art Mus Dirs; Coll Art Asn; Visual Arts Panel, Tex Comn Arts; Int Coun Mus. *Res:* Twentieth century European & Am art. *Publ:* Coauth, Pompeii as Style, In: Pompeii as Source and Inspiration, Univ Mich, 77; ed, Art for the People--New Deal Murals on Long Island, Hofstra Univ, 78; Off the Wall--Environments and Installations, San Antonio Mus Art, 81. *Mailing Add:* 78 San Mateo Rd Berkeley CA 94707-2016

CONSTANTINE, GREG JOHN
PAINTER, EDUCATOR
b Windsor, Ont, Can, Feb 14, 1938. *Study:* Andrews Univ, Mich, BA; Mich State Univ with Angelo Ippolito, MFA; Univ Calif, Los Angeles. *Work:* Grand Rapids Art Mus, Mich. *Exhib:* Ark Nat, 69; Chicago & Vicinity, Chicago Art Inst, 71; Mich Artists, Detroit, 71; Philbrook Art Ctr, Tulsa, Okla, 75; LaGrange Nat, Ga, 75. *Teaching:* Chmn dept painting & art hist & prof art, Andrews Univ, 63-. *Awards:* W & B Clusman Prize, Chicago Vicinity Show, Chicago Art Inst, 71. *Bibliog:* J Heriksen (auth), Artist, Insight Mag, 70; O Young (auth), Editor, Focus Mag, 75. *Mem:* Mus Contemp Art, Chicago; Coll Art Asn; Mid-Am Art Asn. *Media:* Acrylic; Photography. *Publ:* Auth, article, Spectrum Mag, 75. *Mailing Add:* 9648 Painter School Road Berrien Center MI 49102

CONTINI, ANITA
ADMINISTRATOR, CURATOR
b Cleveland, Ohio, Jan 16, 1944. *Study:* Cleveland Music Settlement, scholar, 60; Elizabeth Seton Col, Yonkers, NY, AAS, 64; Hofstra Univ, Long Island, NY, BA, 66. *Collection Arranged:* Ruckus Manhattan by Red Grooms (auth, catalog), 75-76, Ruckus Manhattan, 81 & Art on the Beach (auth, catalog), 82, Creative Time Inc. *Pos:* Exec dir & pres, Creative Time Inc, New York, 73-86; pres & bd mem, Athena Found Inc, New York, 78-; vpres & dir, World Finan Ctr Arts & Events Prog, 86-. *Awards:* Certs Merit, Ruckus Manhattan, 76 & Masstransiscope, 81, Munic Art Soc. *Bibliog:* Grace Glueck (auth), New home, new look for Ruckus Manhattan, New York Times, 12/18/81; Carrie Rickey (auth), Taking care of artists' business, Village Voice, 1/5/82; Damon Wright (auth), Art and commerce, New York Times, 4/17/94. *Mem:* Arts & Bus Coun New York. *Mailing Add:* 4630 Center Blvd Apt 512 Long Island City NY 11109

CONTINOS, ANNA
PAINTER, DESIGNER
b New York, NY. *Study:* Hunter Col, BA. *Work:* Gov Christine T Whitman; Am Fuji Seal Inc, NJ; IE DuPont De Nemours & Co, Wilmington, Del; Bell Labs - Holmdel, Piscataway, NJ; Ctr for Health Affairs, Princeton, NJ; also many pvt collections in the US, Can, Taiwan, S Africa, Spain, Eng, Ireland, PR & Japan. *Exhib:* Solo shows, Art Spirit Gallery, Clinton, NJ, 82, Zeta Gallery, Shrewsbury, NJ, 85 & New Brunswick Cult Ctr, NJ, 85 & Short Hills Art Gallery, NJ, 88; Trenton City Mus Invitational, NJ, 84; NJ Watercolor Soc Montclair Mus & Monmouth Mus, 84-92; Nat Asn Women Artists Traveling Painting Exhib (7 locations), 91-92; 73rd Ann Philadelphia Watercolor Club, Noyes Mus, Oceanville, NJ, 92. *Awards:* Award for Excellence, Somerset Art Asn Ann, 80; Best Show, Princeton Art Asn Ann, Princeton Microfilm Corp, 83; Forbes Award, NJ Watercolor Soc Ann, Forbes Mag, 90. *Mem:* NJ Watercolor Soc; Catharine Lorillard Wolfe Art Club; Nat Asn Women Artists. *Media:* Watercolor. *Dealer:* Short Hills Art Gallery, NJ

CONVERSE, ELIZABETH
PAINTER, WRITER
b Springfield, Ill, Jan 17, 1946. *Study:* Lake Forest Col, BA, 67; Performance Group/Drama, 70-72; Sarah Lawrence Writing Ctr, 90-92; Pasadena City Col, 96; Pacific Oaks Col, teaching degree, MA (human develop/creativity), 99. *Work:* Provincetown Art Mus, Provincetown, Mass; Pasadena Hist Mus; Sierra Madre Art Comn; Pasadena Cent Libr; Salon Zero, Armory. *Comn:* Harvest Ball, pvt comn, Darien, Conn, 88; murals & paintings, Susan Chen, Zonshine Develop, Los Angeles, 92; Calif Living Histories, City of Los Angeles; Mayor Riordan; Lightbringer Gallery; Hope Thru Housing, 2007-2008. *Exhib:* Provincetown Art Mus, Conn; Sound/Shore Gallery, Port Chester, NY, 86-88; Gallarie Bonheur, Greenwich, Conn, 87; Lozano Restaurant, 94; Pasadena Armory, 95; PAS Histo Mus, Salon Zero; Sierra Madre, City Hall, Los Angeles, City Hall. *Pos:* Writer, dir & actor, Alexyz Partnership, 78-83; vpres & creative dir, Productions Syst, Inc, 82-89; exec dir/found, Livinghistories.us, 99-; Elizabeth Converse Inc, Pasadena Rotary, Pasadena Found, Verron Communication, 2010-. *Teaching:* S Bay Contemp Art Mus, 92, Monrovia Unified Sch Dist, La Canada Unified Sch Dist, Pasadena Unified Sch Dist, Pacific Oaks Col; Hope Through Housing. *Awards:* Nat Endowment Arts Grant, 77; Stewart Found Calif Coun for Humanities, City of Sierra Madre. *Publ:* Articles in Pasadena Weekly, Visions Mag, The Muses, Art Week & LA Reader; Pasadena Star News, Mountain Views, Sierra Madre. *Mailing Add:* 851 Woodland Dr Sierra Madre CA 91024

COOGAN, JAY
ADMINISTRATOR
Study: Brown Univ, BA (visual arts), 1980; Hunter Col, City Univ of NY, MFA (sculpture), 1982. *Comn:* Fidelity Investments; Hasbro Inc; Zambarano Hosp, RI. *Pos:* Fac mem, RI Sch of Design (RISD), 1982-2009, provost, 2005-08; pres, Minneapolis Col of Art and Design (MCAD), 2009-, trustee, currently. *Mailing Add:* Minneapolis College of Art and Design Office of President 2501 Stevens Ave Minneapolis MN 55404

COOK, JOSEPH STEWART
PAINTER
b Glendale, Calif, Aug 5, 1935. *Study:* Art Ctr Sch Design (scholar), Los Angeles, 53; Otis Art Inst (scholar), Los Angeles, 53-54; Chouinard Art Inst, Los Angeles, 55-58. *Work:* Springfield Mus, Mo; Home Savings & Loan, Los Angeles; Joslyn Art Mus. *Exhib:* Solo exhibs, RJ Dibbs Gallery, Pacific Palisades, Calif, 55, Marian Gallery, Mt St Mary's Col, Los Angeles, 61, WAA Wilshire Gallery, Los Angeles, 62, Paideia Gallery, Los Angeles, 64; Oakland Art Mus, 65; Calif Palace Legion Hon, 66; San Francisco Mus Mod Art, 66; Joslyn Art Mus, 67; Va Mus Fine Arts; Palm Springs Desert Mus, Calif, 79, 82 & 94; Chateau Tours Mus, France, 86; Brand Libr Gallery, Glendale, Calif, 87; Northern Ariz Univ Gallery, Flagstaff, 89. *Pos:* Asst art coordr, City Los Angeles, 59-61. *Awards:* James Phelan Biannual Award, Calif Palace Legion, Hon, 65; Watercolor USA Purchase Award, 73; Second Place, Watercolor W Ann, 77. *Mem:* Watercolor USA; Pacific Palisades Art Asn (pres, 60); Westwood Art Asn (pres, 61-62); Nat Watercolor Soc (pres, 76). *Media:* Watercolor, Oils. *Mailing Add:* 25195 Stewart Pl Carmel CA 93923

COOK, KATHLEEN L
PAINTER
b Amarillo, Tex, Mar 19, 1949. *Study:* Amarillo Col, AA (sci), 69; Tex Tech Univ, BFA, 73; studied with Daniel Greene, 79; studied with Albert Handell, 82. *Work:* San Antonio Art League; San Marcos Telephone Co, Tex. *Comn:* 300 portrait comns in various cities, Tex, 82-2010. *Exhib:* Images, McAllen Int Mus, Tex, 86; solo exhibs,

About Light, Mus SW, Midland, Tex, 87, Green House Gallery, San Antonio, Tex, 92 & Ellen Noel Art Mus, Odessa, Tex, 95; Plains Hist Mus, Canyon, Tex, 89-91; Animals In Art, La State Univ Sch Vet Med, 98; Degas Pastel Soc Biennial Exhib, New Orleans, La, 2000; Pastel Soc Southwest, Dallas, 2009; Pastel Soc Am, New York, 2010. *Pos:* Illusr, art dir, Hemphill-Wells, Lubbock, Tex, 70-80; bd dir, Hill Country Arts Found, Ingram, Tex, 83-85. *Teaching:* Instr pastel-figure/still-life, Hill Country Arts Found, Ingram, Tex, 82-2010; invitational one-week workshops pastel, Dallas, Houston, McAllen, Midland, Amarillo & Lubbock, Tex. *Awards:* Best of Show, Pastel Soc W Coast, 89 & Pastel Soc NMex, 97, Grand Prize, Pastel Artist Int Mag Competition, 2000; Best of Show, Pastel Soc of SW, 2000. *Bibliog:* Survey of contemporary art of the figure, Am Artist Mag, 2/85; Susan Embry (auth), Kathleen Cook, SW Art Mag, 8/89. *Mem:* Pastel Soc Am; Knickerbocker Artists. *Media:* Pastel, Oil. *Collection:* Portrait/Figure, Landscape, Still-life, animals, Contemp Realism. *Publ:* Coauth, Looking around the color wheel, Am Artist Mag, 92; Auth, Exploring the How and Why of Painting Pastel, Artist Internat Mag, 2002. *Dealer:* Marta Stafford Fine Art Marble Falls TX. *Mailing Add:* 218 Old Ingram Loop Ingram TX 78025

COOK, LIA
TAPESTRY ARTIST, EDUCATOR

b Ventura, Calif, 1942. *Study:* Univ Calif, Berkeley, BA, 65, MA, 73. *Work:* Am Craft Mus, NY; Galerie de la Tapisserie et d'Art Textile, Beauvais, France; Mus Mod Art, Metrop Mus Art, NY. *Comn:* Embarcadero Ctr, San Francisco, 74; City Hall, Fairfield, Calif, 76; Art in Archit Prog, US Gen Serv Admn, Richmond, Calif, 76; Rensselaer Polytechnic Inst, 79; Mercantile Bank, Tex, 86. *Exhib:* Solo exhibs, Renwick Gallery, Nat Mus Am Art, 80, San Jose Mus Art, Calif, 80, Nat Mus Am Art, Smithsonian inst, 96, R Duane Reed Gallery, St Louis, 98, Perimeter Gallery, Chicago, 99, Miami Univ Art Mus, 00, Nancy Margolis Gallery, 01, Arlene LewAllen Gallery, Santa Fe, NMex, 02, Mills Coll Art Mus, Oakland, Calif, 2004, Nancy Margolis Gallery, New York, NY, 2006; group exhibs, The Art Fabric: Mainstream, San Francisco Mus Mod Art, traveling, 81-84; Celebration 25, 81 & The Pattern Show, 82, Am Craft Mus, NY; Jacquard Textiles, Cooper-Hewitt Mus, NY, 82; Fiber Directions, Brunnier Gallery and Mus, Iowa State Univ, 82; retrospective, Galerie Nat de la Tapisserie et d'Art Textile, Beauvais, France, 83; Mus Fine Arts, Boston, 02; Dean Lesher Regional Ctr for the Arts, Walnut Creek, Calif, 02; Am Textile History Mus, Lowell, Mass, 03; Boulder Mus Contemp Art, Colo, 2004; Temple Gallery, Tyler Sch Art, Pa, 2004; Kala Art Inst, Berkeley, Calif, 2004; Dhal Art Ctr, Rapid City, SDak, 2004; Ormeau Baths Gallery, Belfast, Northern Ireland, 2005; Art Works Downtown, San Rafael, Calif, 2005; Mus of Design, Atlanta, Ga, 2005; GalleryOne, Washtenaw Community Coll, Ann Arbor, 2005; Smithsonian Mus Am Art, Renwick Gallery, Washington, DC, 2005; City Art Gallery, City Coll San Francsico, 2005; Nat Gallery Australia, Canberra, 2005; Cheongju City, Republic of Korea, 2005; Salt Lake City Ctr, 2007. *Collection Arranged:* Racine Art Mus, Wis; Cleveland Mus Art; Mus Bellerive, Zurich; Am Craft Mus; Metrop Mus Art; Milwukee Art Mus; Mus Art, RI Sch Design; Nat Mus Am Art, Smithsonian Inst; Mus Mod Art; Oakland Mus, Calif. *Pos:* artist-in-residence, Fondazione Arte della Seta Lisio, Florence, Italy, 90, Jacquard Project, Muller-Zell, Ger, 91, Philadelphia Col Textiles & Scis, 95. *Teaching:* Prof art, Calif Col Arts & Crafts, Oakland, 76-. *Awards:* Fels, Nat Endowment Arts, 74-75, 77-78, 86, 92-93, 94; Special Proj Grant, Nat Endowment Arts, 81; Calif Arts Coun Artist Fel Grant, 90; fel, Am Craft Coun, 97; Flintridge Found Fel, 00. *Bibliog:* Barbaralee Diamonstein (auth), Handmade in America: Conversation with Fourteen Craftsmasters, Harry M Abrams, New York, 84; Maureen Conner (auth), The tapestries of Lia Cook, Arts Mag, 2/85; Nancy A Corwin (auth), Lia Cook, Monograph from Nat Acad Sci Exhib, 90; Jon Carver (auth), Lia Cook, THE Mag, 10/2002. *Media:* Rayon. *Publ:* Auth, Ed Rossbach as Educator: A Personal View, Ed Rossbach: 40 Years of Exploration and Innovation in Fiber Art, Textile Mus, Lark Bks, Washington, DC, 90. *Dealer:* Perimeter Gallery Chicago IL; Arlene LewAllen Gallery Santa Fe NM. *Mailing Add:* 2127 Bonar St Berkeley CA 94702

COOK, MICHAEL DAVID
PAINTER, VIDEO ARTIST

b Ramey, PR, July 16, 1953. *Study:* Fla State Univ, BFA, 75; Univ Dallas, MA, 76; Univ Okla, MFA, 78. *Work:* Mus Contemp Art, San Diego; Sandra Conn & Assoc, Chicago; World Book Corp, Chicago; Polaroid Corp, NY; New Mus Contemp Art, New York; Univ NMex Art Mus, Albuquerque, NMex; Univ Nebr, Omaha, Nebr; Ind State Univ, Evansville, Ind. *Exhib:* 77th Ann Exhib by Artists of Chicago & Vicinity, Art Inst Chicago, 78; New Dimensions--Time, Mus Contemp Art, Chicago, 80; Working Drawings, Hunter Gallery, NY, 81; War Games, Kitchen, NY, 82; solo exhibs, NAME Gallery, Chicago, 82, Grayson Gallery, Chicago, 83, Wenger Gallery, La Jolla, Calif, 84, Janet Steinberg Gallery, San Francisco, Calif, 86, Recent & Past Work, Art Mus, Univ NMex, Albuquerque, 89, Animal-Vegetable or Mineral?, Mus Fine Arts, Santa Fe, 90 & Charity, Shidoni Contemp,Tesuque, NMex, 90; The End of the World, New Mus Contemp Art, NY, 83-84; System and Structure, Allen Priebe Art Gallery (traveling), 83-84; Myth & Magic, Wenger Gallery, Los Angeles, 87; Social Space, Janet Steinberg Gallery, San Francisco, 88; 20 X 40, Jayne Baum Gallery, NY, 89; Playing with Fire (with catalog), Ctr Contemp Arts, Santa Fe, 90-91; Worlds at Risk: Dangerous Environments and Vanishing Traditions, Cambridge Multi-Cult Arts Ctr, Cambridge, Mass, 93; Re-Inventing the Emblem: Contemporary Artists Recreate a Renaissance Idea (with catalog), Yale Univ Art Gallery, New Haven, Conn, 95; Instructions: Paintings 1991-1996 (with catalog), Ctr for Contemp Arts, Santa Fe, NMex, 96-97; Our Good Earth, Hemphill Fine Arts, DC, 99; Michael Cook: Painting and Video, Canfield Gallery, 2004; Modern and Contemporarym Canfield Gallery, 2004; Museum Window, Univ NMex Art Mus, Albuquerque, NMex, 2008. *Teaching:* Vis artist painting & drawing, Video Univ Ill, Champaign-Urbana, 78-80; asst prof, Univ Ill, Chicago, 80-83; vis lectr, Univ Calif, Berkeley, 83-85, Univ Calif, Davis, 85; Spec vis fac, San Francisco Art Inst, 85; prof painting & drawing, Univ NMex, Albuquerque, currently. *Awards:* Ford Found Fac Res Grants, 78 & 79; Ill Arts Coun Fel, 82; Nat Endowment Individual Artists Fel, 84-85; Teacher of Year Award, Univ NMex, 89-90. *Bibliog:* Janet Kutner (auth), Graf-feet-i, glitter and crab claws, Artnews, 79; Pat Tomson (auth), article, New Art Examiner, 82; Lynn Gumpert (auth), The End of the World (catalogue), New Museum, New York, 83; Kenneth Baker (auth), Filtering Apocalypse through illusions, San Francisco Chronicle, 5/13/86; Ina Russell (auth), Signs of the global village, Artweek, 2/6/88; Hillel Swartz (auth), The End of the Century, The End of the Centuries 990 to the Present, Doubleday, 90; Richard Tobin (auth), Michael Cook, Instructions, THE Mag, 1/97; Ellen Berkovitch (auth), Mythical American Landscape Laid Bare, Jour N, 12/5/97; Jan E Adlmann (auth). Michael Cook, Dirge, THE Mag, 01/2009. *Publ:* Auth, Radiation Remains the Same, Phono Record, Grayson Gallery, 83

COOK, R SCOTT & SOUSSAN A E
ART DEALER, CRITIC

Study: NY Univ, MA, 75. *Specialty:* 20th Century European paintings, sculpture & drawings; Latin American art. *Publ:* Auth, Space Shots, Art Am, 82; Bruce Conner, Artforum, 82; Andre Masson, Arnold Herstand, 84; The Brothers Duchamp, Arnold Herstand, 86; Rene Magritte, Arnold Herstand, 86

COOK, RICHARD L
ADMINISTRATOR, SCULPTOR

b Big Spring, Tex, Oct 30, 1934. *Study:* Univ NMex, BA (art), 67, MA (sculpture), 68; studied with Charles Mattox, Van Derem Coke & John Pearson. *Work:* Mus Fine Arts, Univ NMex, Albuquerque; New Orleans Mus Art, La; Masur Mus Art, Monroe, La; Fine Arts Gallery, Nicholls State Univ, Thibodaux, La; La Bi-Centennial Arts Ctr Collection, Baton Rouge, La. *Exhib:* Southern Asn Sculpture Nat Traveling Exhib, Southern States & DC, 69-70; Masur Ann, Masur Mus Art, Monroe, La, 69, 70 & 72; 8-State Exhib, Okla Art Ctr, 70; Mobile Nat, Mobile Art Ctr, Ala, 72; New Orleans Biannual, New Orleans Mus, La, 73; Sculpture-NMex, Mus Fine Arts, Santa Fe, 75. *Collection Arranged:* New Mexico Collects the 20th Century (auth, catalog), 85; Selections '90-Minority Artists of New Mexico (auth, catalog), 90. *Pos:* Pres, Southern Asn Sculptors, 71-72; deputy dir, NMex Arts, 80 & 81; pres, Nat Coun Art Admin, 89 & 90. *Teaching:* Assoc prof sculpture, Nicholls State Univ, 68-74; prof, Col Santa Fe, NMex, 84-; vis scholar art, Eastern Washington Univ, 93. *Awards:* First Award, 7th Monroe Ann, Mazur Mus, 70; Second Award, Southern Asn Sculptors, Ga Southern Col, 70; Purchase Award, La Bicentennial Exhib, La Art Comn, 73. *Mem:* Nat Mus Neon Art; Coll Art Asn Am; Nat Coun Art Adminr (bd dir, 88, pres, 89-90). *Media:* Mixed Media. *Publ:* Auth, On kinetic art with electric light, 72 & Kinetic art-the luminetic system with no sound, 75, Leonardo Peraiagon Press; ed, The Sculpture Quarterly, Southern Asn Sculptures, 72-74; auth, Art in the schools, Albuquerque J, 85; coauth, Selections-90 minority artists of New Mexico, Arts Advocate, Vol 4, No 6, 90. *Mailing Add:* Dept Art Col Santa Fe 1600 St Michael's Dr Santa Fe NM 87505-7634

COOK, ROBERT HOWARD
SCULPTOR, MEDALIST

b Boston, Mass, Apr 8, 1921. *Study:* Demetrios Sch, 38-42; Beaux Arts, Paris, under Marcel Gaumont, 45. *Work:* Whitney Mus Am Art, NY; Pa Acad Fine Arts, Philadelphia; Va Mus Fine Arts, Richmond; Hirshhorn Collection, Washington, DC; State Univ NY, Oneida; Mobile Mus Art, Ala; British Mus, London. *Comn:* Lifeline, Sun co, Radnor, Pa, 78; Off the Water, Sun-co, 79; Emerging, Saudi Arabia, 81; Camel, Saudi Arabia, 82; Stretch, Saudi Arabia, 82; Giant, Woodlands, Tex; Flight-Canale Monterano, Italy, 2003. *Exhib:* Solo exhibs, Inst Contemp Art, Boston, 51, Birmingham Mus Fine Arts, Ala, 67, Mint Mus Art, Charlotte, NC, 68, Va Mus Fine Art, Richmond, 68 & Schenectady Mus Art, NY, 77; Pa Acad Fine Arts; Whitney Ann; Nat Acad Design; Boston Art Festival; Univ Ill; Biennale Venezia, Italy, 51; Antwerp Belgium, 2010; Wayne, PA, 2011; Canale Martino, Italy, 2011. *Awards:* Second Prize, Prix de Rome, Am Acad Rome, 42; Cash Award & Best-of-Show, Nat Acad Arts & Lett, 48; Tiffany Award, Tiffany Found, 48. *Bibliog:* Tracy O'Kates & Arnold Eagle (auth), World of Robert Cook (27-minute doc), Beechtree Productions, 77; work of Robert Cook (10 min film), CBS Sunday Morning with Charles Kuralt, 6/30/91. *Mem:* Sculptors Guild; Nat Sculpture Soc; British Art Medal Soc. *Media:* Bronze, Wood, Silver, Gold. *Collection:* 104 Pieces in Bronze. *Publ:* Auth, Family Album in Bronze (photographs by Franco Romagnoli), 76, Twelve commissions, 78, In motion, 80, Circles & Cycles, 97, Jasillo. *Dealer:* Henry Cook 79 St Rose St Jamaica Plain Boston MA 02130. *Mailing Add:* V1A Quarto Grande Canale Monterano Rome 00060 Italy

COOK, SILAS BALDWIN
DIRECTOR

b Exeter, NH, Oct 10, 1961. *Study:* Wesleyan Univ, BFA, 87. *Exhib:* Curator, Performing Judaism, Douglas F Cooley Mem Art Gallery, 2002; Curator, A Selection of Print from the Collection of William and Nell Givler, Douglas F Cooley Mem Gallery, 2001; Curator, Raymond Saunders: Paintings and Drawings, Douglas F Cooley Mem Art Gallery, 2001; Curator, Differences Preserved: Reconstructed Tombs from the Liao and Song Dynasties, Douglas F Cooley Mem Art Gallery, 2000; Curator, William Kentridge Films and Prints, 1989-99, Douglas F Cooley Mem Art Gallery, 1999. *Pos:* Art Dir/Cur, DF Conley Mem Art Gallery, Reed Col, Portland, Ore, 89-. *Mailing Add:* Reed College Douglas F Cooley Art Gallery 3202 SE Woodstock Blvd Portland OR 97202-8199

COOK, STEPHEN D
PRINTMAKER, DRAFTSMAN

b Jackson, Miss, Sept 10, 1951. *Study:* Miss Coll, BA, 73; Univ Miss, MFA, 75; Royal Coll Art, London, cert, 76. *Work:* Victoria & Albert Mus, London; Southern Graphics Coun Print Arch, Oxford, Miss; Miss Sch Supply Co, Jackson; Meridian Mus Art; Mississippi Mus Art. *Exhib:* Mid-South Biennial, Brooks Mem, Memphis, 74; Solo exhibs, Miss Art Asn Gallery, Jackson 77, Meridian Mus Art, 79, Janet Redmont Gallery, Millsaps Coll, 87, Samuel Marshall Gore Gallery, Miss Coll, 99; Comparisons & Contrasts, Soviet Union Tour, 79-81; Southeast Mo State Univ Nat Print Invitational Exhib, 81; Southern Graphics Coun Member Touring Exhib, 86-88;

Art Around Miss, Meridian Mus Art, 2006; Inaugural Exhib, Irby Center, Belhaven Coll, 2005; The Mississippi Story, Mississippi Mus Art, 2007. *Pos:* Guest lectr, Ioan Andrescu Visual Arts Acad, Cluj, Romania, 95. *Teaching:* Chmn dept printmaking, Miss Mus Art Sch, 77-78; instr printmaking & drawing, Univ Miss, Oxford, 78; instr, Hinds Junior Coll, Raymond, 80, Miss Coll, Clinton, 83-90, asst prof, 90-2003, assoc prof, 2003-2008, prof, 2009-; adj instr, Jackson Pub Schs, 82. *Awards:* Bellamann Mem Found Ann Award, 75; ITT Corp Int Fel, London, 75-76; Award of Merit, Miss Artists Competitive, 78. *Mem:* Southern Graphics Coun (vpres, 86-88, pres, 88-90). *Media:* Etching, Wood Engraving; Charcoal, Pastel. *Interests:* Folk music. *Publ:* Contribr, J Royal Coll Art, 76; Interchange, ITT Fel Publ, 87; Perspective, Miss Mus Art, 92; Faithworks Mag, 2000. *Mailing Add:* 3924 Oakridge Dr Jackson MS 39216

COOKE, JUDY
PAINTER
b Bay City, Mich, July 8, 1940. *Study:* Boston Mus Sch Fine Arts, Hons dipl, 63; Tufts Univ, Medford, Mass, BFA, 65; Reed Col, Portland, Ore, MAT, 70. *Work:* Boston Mus Sch of Fine Arts; Portland Art Mus, Ore; Ranier Bank & Pac Northwest Bell, Seattle; Itell Corp, San Francisco; Bank Am, San Francisco; Hewlett Packard Co, Portland, Ore. *Comn:* Hewlett Packard Co, Portland, Ore; Spieker Properties, Lake Oswego, Ore, 2000. *Exhib:* Prospect: Northwest 72, Seattle Art Mus Pavilion, 72; Northwest Ann, Seattle Art Mus, 73 & 74; Aesthetics of Graffiti, San Francisco Mus Mod Art, 78; Blackfish Gallery 6th Anniversary Exhib, Portland, Ore; Expo 86, Vancouver, BC; Elizabeth Leach Gallery, Portland, Ore, 87, 91, 93, 95, 97 & 2001; Esther Saks Gallery, Chicago, Ill, 90; solo show, Fassbender Gallery, Chicago, Ill, 96. *Pos:* Founding mem, Blackfish Gallery, 79-84. *Teaching:* Assoc prof, Pac NW Col Art, Portland, Ore, 86-. *Awards:* Purchase Award, Portland Art Mus, 73; Painting Award, Seattle Art Mus Pavilion, 73; Boston Mus traveling fel, 65 & 74; Visual Artist Fel Painting, Nat Endowment Arts, 89; Bonnie Bronson Fel, Portland, Ore, 93; Edvard Munch Residency, Oslo, Norway, 96. *Bibliog:* Bruce Guenther (auth), Fifty Northwest Artists, Chronicle Bks; Lucy Lippard (auth), Northwest passage, Art in Am, 7-8/76; Lois Allen (auth), Contemporary Art in the Northwest Craftsman House, Gordon & Beach Publ Int, 95. *Media:* Oil Paint, Mixed Media

COOKE, LYNNE
CURATOR
b Geelong, Australia; arrived in US, 89. *Study:* Univ Melbourne, Australia, BA (with honors), 74; Univ London, MA, 79, PhD, 87. *Collection Arranged:* Co-cur: Venice Biennial, 86; Carnegie Int, 91. *Pos:* Co-cur, Carnegie Mus Art, Pittsburgh, 91; cur, Dia Ctr Arts, New York, 91-2008, cur-at-large, 2008-; artistic dir, Sydney Biennial, Australia, 95-96; mus/exhib panelist, Nat Endowment Arts, Washington, 96; chief cur & dep dir, Ctr Reina Sofía, Madrid, 2008-. *Teaching:* Lectr, Dept Art Hist, London Univ, 79-80. *Mailing Add:* Dia Art Found 535 W 22nd St New York NY 10011

COOKE, SAMUEL TUCKER
PAINTER, EDUCATOR
b Gainesville, Fla, Dec 4, 1941. *Study:* Stetson Univ, with Fred Messersmith, BA; Univ Ga, with Lamar Dodd & Howard Thomas, MFA. *Work:* Asheville Art Mus, NC; Mint Mus Art, Charlotte, NC; Univ Ga Collection; Hunter Gallery Art, Chattanooga, Tenn; Davidson Col, NC. *Exhib:* Nat Drawing & Small Sculpture Exhib, Ball State Univ, 72-74; Davidson Coll Nat Print & Drawing Exhib, 74-75; Gallery Contemp Art Realist, Winston-Salem, NC, 74-75; Southeastern Drawing Invitational, Mint Mus, Charlotte, 79; Solo exhibs, New Morning Gallery, Asheville, 78, Somerhill Gallery, Durham, 79 & 81 & Asheville Art Mus, 80. *Teaching:* Chmn dept art, Univ NC, Asheville, 68-79. *Awards:* 3rd Davidson Nat Drawing & Print Award, Knight Publ Co, 74; 39th Southeastern Painting & Drawing Award, Wachovia Bank NC, 74; Mint Mus Award for Realism in North Carolina, NC Arts Coun, 74. *Dealer:* New Morning Gallery 3 1/2 Kitchen Pl Asheville NC 28803; Somerhill Gallery 5504 Chapel Hill Blvd Durham NC 27707. *Mailing Add:* 65 Kenilworth Rd Asheville NC 28803-2542

COOLIDGE, MATTHEW
DIRECTOR, EDUCATOR
Study: Boston Univ, BA (environmental studies & contemp art), 91. *Pos:* Dir & founder, Ctr for Land Use Interpretation, 94-. *Teaching:* Instr curatorial practice program, Calif Coll Arts, San Francisco. *Awards:* Mem Fel, John Simon Guggenheim Found, 2004; Grant for Emerging Fields, Creative Capital Found, 2009. *Publ:* Auth, The Nevada Test Site: A Guide to America's Nuclear Proving Ground, 96 & Back to the Bay: An Examination of the Shoreline of the San Francisco Bay Region, 2001, CLUI. *Mailing Add:* 9331 Venice Blvd Culver City CA 90232

COOPER, DIANA
SCULPTOR
b 1964. *Study:* Harvard Coll, BA, 1986; NY Studio Sch, New York, Cert Fine Arts, 1990; Hunter Coll, New York, MFA, 1997. *Exhib:* The Love Show, Ah! space Gallery, New York, 1996; solo exhibs, Ah! space Gallery, New York, 1997, Postmasters Gallery, New York, 1998-99, 2002, 2005, 2007-08, Mus Contemp Art, Cleveland, Ohio, 2007; Benefit Show, New Mus Contemp Art, New York, 1998; Bricolage, Rudolph Projs, Houston, 2002; Kerlin Gallery, Dublin, Ireland, 2003; Lines Signs & Codes, Galerie Anne de Villepoix, Paris, 2003; Burgeoning Geometries, Whitney Mus Am Art, New York, 2006; Process & Promise, 92nd Street Y Art Ctr, New York, 2006; Holiday Reading, Number 35, New York, 2007; Capricious & Mercurial Systems, A&D Gallery, Columbia Coll, Chicago, 2008. *Awards:* Artist Fel, NY Found Arts, 2000; Gugenheim Fel, 2000; Rome Prize, Am Acad Rome, 2003; Pollock-Krasner Found Grant, 2008. *Bibliog:* Kim Levin (auth), The Short List: Voice Choice, Village Voice, 3/1998; David Bonetti (auth), Driven to Dynamic Abstraction, San Francisco Examiner, 1/28/2000; Holland Cotter (auth), Second Sight, NY Times, 3/22/2002; David Cohen (auth), Open House: Working in Brooklyn, New York Sun, 2004; Lilly Wei (auth), Line Analysis, Art in Am, 2008. *Dealer:* Numark Gallery 625-27 E Street Washington DC 20004; Carl Berg Gallery 6018 Wilshire Blvd Los Angeles CA 90036; Rotwand Sabina Kohler & Bettina Meier-Bickel Rotwandstrasse 53 ch-8004 Zurich Switzerland; Hales Gallery Tea Building 7 Bethnal Green London E1 6LA; Postmasters 459 W 19th St New York NY 10011. *Mailing Add:* 310 Dodge Hall Mail Code: 1806 3022 Broadway New York NY 10027

COOPER, ELIZABETH
PAINTER
b Queens, NY, 1972. *Study:* Cooper Union, BFA, 1994; Columbia Univ, MFA, 1998. *Exhib:* Solo exhibs include Roger Smith Gallery, New YOrk, 1996, 1998, 2000, Galerie Rolf Ricke, Cologne, 2002, Galerie Scmidt Maczollek, Cologne, 2005, 2008, Thrust Projects, New York, 2006, 2008; group exhibs include Abstraction in Process 2, Artists Space, New York, 1998; Wish You Luck, PS1 Contemp Art Ctr, New York, 1998; Reconciliations, DC Moore Gallery, New York, 1999; The Stroke, Exit Art, New York, 1999, Collector's Choice, 2000; Some Are Painting, Artist Alliance, New York, 2003; Cloudless clearcuts, Castle Raab, Switzerland, 2006; Freeze Frame, Thrust Projects, New York, 2008; 183rd Ann: Invitational Exhib Contemp Am Art, Nat Acad Mus, New York, 2008. *Awards:* George Hitchcock Prize, Nat Acad, 2008. *Mailing Add:* c/o Thrust Projects 114 Bowery #301 at Grand St New York NY 10013

COOPER, MARK F
SCULPTOR, COLLAGE ARTIST
b Evensville, Ind, Oct 5, 1950. *Study:* Ind Univ, BS, 72; Tufts Univ, MFA, 80. *Work:* Corcoran Mus, Washington DC; Fogg Art Mus, Cambridge Mass; Duxbury Art Mus Complex, Duxbury, Mass; Fuller Mus, Brockton, Mass; Children's Mus for the Arts, New York; Capital Children's Mus, Washington, DC; W Licht Mus, Vienna, Austria. *Comn:* Collage sculpture, Cambridge Hosp, Mass, Praecis Pharmaceutical, Walthem, Mass & Bates Sch, Salem, Mass, 2000; bronze sculpture, Driscoll Sch, Brookline, Mass, 2000; Anderson Consult, Boston; sculpture, comn by Roger Williams Col, Univ Middle East, 2008; Berlin Wall Proj, Boston Coll, 2009. *Exhib:* 50 Yrs of Collecting, City Mus Paris, France, 98; Artists as Teachers, Mc Mullen Mus, Chestnut Hill, Mass, 99; solo exhibs, Duxbury Art Mus, Duxbury, Mass, 99, Nao Project Gallery, Boston, 2002 & 511 Gallery, New York, 2003, 2005 & 2007; Collaborative, Boston Mus Fine Arts, 99 & 2002-2003; Getting Along, Peabody Essex Mus, Salem, Mass, Whitney Mus Am Art, Philip Morris, New York & Newhouse Ctr Contemp Art, Snug Harbor Cult Ctr, Staten Island, 2000; Open Circle, Davis Mus, Wellesley, Mass, 2000, From Polaroid to Impossible, Westlicht Mus, 2011; More is More, Samson Projects, 2011; New Blue and White, Boston Mus Fine Arts, 2013; Foster Prize Exhib, Boston Inst Contemporary Art, 2013. *Teaching:* Prof, Boston Coll, 78-; fac, Sch of Boston Mus Fine Arts, 78-. *Awards:* Grant, Mass Cult Coun, 99 & 2011; Commun Fel, Open Soc, 99-2000. *Bibliog:* Molly Hochkeppel (auth), Gardens Become Galleries, The Patriot Ledger, 5/23/2000; Work of Art, The Evening Star, Salem, Mass, 6/22/2000; Judith Montminy (auth), Art Museum Dusts Off Its Treasures, Boston Globe, 10/3/99; Diane C Lore, Getting Along at Snug Harbor, Staten Island, 12/7/99. *Media:* Mixed Media. *Res:* Visual Language-how meaning begins with context. *Publ:* auth, Making Art Together, Beacon Press, 2007. *Dealer:* 511 Gallery New York NY. *Mailing Add:* 52 St James Ave Somerville MA 02144

COOPER, PAULA
DEALER
b Mass, Mar 14, 1938. *Study:* Pierce Col, Athens, Greece; Sorbonne, Paris; Goucher Col, Baltimore, Md; Inst Fine Arts, NY Univ, Art Students League, 59-60. *Hon Degrees:* RI Sch Design, DFA (hon), 95. *Pos:* Asst, World House Galleries, NY, 59-61; pvt dealer, NY, 62-63; Paula Johnson Gallery, NY, 64-65; dir, Park Place Gallery, 65-67; owner/dir Paula Cooper Gallery, 68-. *Awards:* ArtTable Award for Distinguished Svc to the Visual Arts, 2001; hon, NY Studio Sch, 2001; Archives of American Art Medal, Smithsonian Inst, 2006. *Mem:* Art Dealers Asn Am (bd dir, 82-86, 88-90, vpres, 97-2000). *Specialty:* Contemp art. *Mailing Add:* 534 W 21st St New York NY 10011

COOPER, RHONDA H
GALLERY DIRECTOR, CURATOR
b New York, NY, Nov 5, 1950. *Study:* Hunter Col, BA, 71; Univ Hawaii, Honolulu, MA, 72; Cornell Univ, 74-75. *Collection Arranged:* The Asian Collection (auth, catalog), Dayton Art Inst, 79; World of Japanese Theater (auth, catalog), Queens Mus, 83; Carl Andre Sculpture (ed, catalog), 84, Toby Buonagurio Selected Works (auth, catalog), 86, Eight Urban Painters, 86 & Permutation and Evolution: Edgar Buonagurio 1974-1988 (auth, catalog), 88, State Univ NY, Stony Brook; Robert Kushner: Silent Operas (auth, catalog), 89; Kit-Yin Snyder: Enrico IV (auth, catalog), 90; City Views (ed, catalog), 92; Wood (ed, catalog), 93; Paper Works (ed, catalog), 94; Maura Sheehan: Dora: Big Girls Don't Cry (coauth, catalog), 94; Eighteen Suffolk Artists (ed, catalog), 95; Pat Hammerman (auth, catalog), 95; Long Island Artists: Focus on Materials (ed, catalog), 98; Loren Madsen: Six Million Monkeys (ed catalog), 1999; 15 Asian Am Artists (co-cur, ed catalog), 2001; Susan Shatter: Tracking the Terrain, 2003; Lucio Pozzi: Photoworks (ed, catalog), 1975-2004; Younhee Park: Ascending River (auth, catalog), 2005; Philip Pearlstein: Paintings and Watercolors (co-cur, ed catalog), 2007; Elizabeth Murray, 2008; Mel Pekarsky: Things in the Desert, 2009; Re-Natured: Cui Fei & Roy Nicholson (auth catalog), 2011. *Pos:* Cur Asian art, Dayton Art Inst, 1976-1979; cur exhibs, Queens Mus, NY, 1982-1983; dir, Univ Art Gallery, State Univ NY, Stony Brook, 1983-2013. *Teaching:* Instr Asian art, Univ Bridgeport, Conn, 1974-76 & Art Inst Boston, 1980-1981; adj lectr Asian art & arts mgt, State Univ NY, Stony Brook, 1984-2013. *Mem:* Am Asn Mus. *Publ:* Auth, Orthodoxy & Eccentricity in 17th Century China, Dayton Art Inst, 78; Zeng Shanqing, Hsiung Shih Art Monthly, 9/91; co-auth, Masterpieces of Chinese Art, Todtri, 97; The paintings of Yang Yanping, catalog essay, Goedhuis Contemp, 1999. *Mailing Add:* University Art Gallery SUNY Stony Brook NY 11794-5425

COOPER, SUSAN
SCULPTOR, PAINTER
b Los Angeles, Calif, Apr 25, 1947. *Study:* Univ Calif, Berkeley, BA, 68, MA, 70; Calif State Univ, Northridge. *Work:* Denver Art Mus, Colo; Kaiser Permanente, Colo; Westin Hotel, Cancuun, Mex; City & Co Denver; Denver Pub Libr; Denver Parks & Recreation Dept. *Comn:* Sculpture, Denver Parks & Recreation, 91; painting, Kaiser Permanente, 92; sculpture, Denver Pub Libr, 93; relief murals, City & Co Buildings, 93; Kaiser Permanente, Lafayette, Colo, 2004. *Exhib:* Centennial Exhib, San Francisco Mus Mod Art, Calif, 71; Four Corners Biennial, Phoenix Mus Art, Ariz, 73; solo exhib, Roswell Mus, NMex, 73, Inkfish Gallery, Denver, Colo, 83, 85, 88 & 90; Colo Ann, 76 & 80 Recent Acquisitions, 83 & Mayor's Awards, 88, Denver Art Mus, Colo; retrospective, Jonson Gallery, Univ NMex, Albuquerque, 80; Nat Mus Women in Arts, Significant Colo Women Artists of 20th Century, 88; Henri Gallery, 89; Galeria Expositum, Mexico City, 92. *Pos:* Dir, Rocky Mountain Women's Inst, Denver, Colo, 77-80, pres, 83-84. *Teaching:* Instr drawing, Community Col of Denver, Red Rocks, Colo, 77; instr, painting & drawing, Metrop State Col, 87-; instr, Univ Colo, Denver, 89-90. *Awards:* Guest Residency, Yaddo, Saratoga Springs, NY, 73; First Prize, Poster Competition, Colo Lawyers for the Arts, 86; Colo Visions Proj Grant, Colo Coun Arts, 94 & 95. *Bibliog:* Lindy Lyman Moore (auth), Susan Cooper, winter 78-79 & Katharine Smith-Warren (auth), Susan Cooper, fall 84, Artspace Mag; Irene Clurman (auth), Pastels at Inkfish, Rocky Mountain News, 1/18/83; Howard Rissoti (auth), Susan Cooper at Henri, Art Forum, 2/90; Jennifer Heath (auth), The Art is at Home, Rocky Mountain News, 1/8/88; Mary Chandler (auth) Rocky Mt News, 10/05. *Mem:* Ctr for Idea Art, Denver (bd mem); Pirate, Contemp Art Oasis; Mizel Cult Arts Ctr. *Media:* Wood, Steel. *Dealer:* Inkfish Gallery 1810 Market St Denver CO 80202; Henri Gallery 1500 21st St NW Washington DC 20036. *Mailing Add:* 1 Winwood Dr Englewood CO 80110-6023

COOPER, THEODORE A
DEALER, ART APPRAISER
b Cleveland, Ohio, Feb 20, 1943. *Study:* Muskingum Col, BA, 65; Ind Univ, 67. *Pos:* Asst dir, IFA Galleries, 68-70; dir, Studio Gallery, 70-71; pres & dir, Adams Davidson Galleries, Inc, 71-; mem art adv panel, Internal Revenue Serv. *Teaching:* Teaching asst introd art, Ind Univ, 65-67; instr, George Washington Univ, 95-. *Mem:* Sr mem Am Soc Appraisers; Wash Art Dealers Asn (pres, 81-87, 91-93); Art Dealers Asn Am. *Specialty:* 19th and early 20th Century American Masters; European Masters 16th-19th Century. *Publ:* Marble and Bronze: 100 Years of American Sculpture 1840-1940, Garamond Pridemark Press, 84; The Artist as Explorer: Luminist Visions of 19th Century America, Mus Press, Washington, DC, 86; Intimate and Visionary: 200 Years of American Master Drawings, 1790-1990, Weadon Publ, 90. *Mailing Add:* 2727 29th St NW Washington DC 20008

COOPER, WAYNE
PAINTER, SCULPTOR
b Depew, Okla, May 7, 1942. *Study:* Valparaiso Univ; Famous Artist Sch; Gary Artist League, Cowboy Artists Am, Kerrville, Tex; American Atelier, NY. *Work:* Paint Horse Gallery, Breckenridge, Colo; Joe Wade Gallery, Santa Fe; Concetta D Gallery, Albuquerque; Heritage Gallery, Scottsdale, Ariz; Tribes Gallery, Norman, Okla; Black Hawk Gallery, Saratoga, Wyo; Gilcrease Mus Inst Am Hist & Art, Tulsa, Okla; Gilcrease Mus; Woolaroc Mus; Okla State Capital; Forks Lodge Wyo; Oneok Bldg, Tulsa, Okla. *Comn:* Twelve ft bronzes, Perkins Okla; Painting of Christ, Church of God, Depew, Okla, 74; lithograph ed, Am Express Co, NY; four large paintings (oil), Will Rogers Mus, Claremone, Okla; fourteen hist paintings, Okla State Capitol; Life Size bronzes, Bristow, Okla. *Exhib:* Country Beautiful, Minn, 68; Nat Show, Tyler, Tex, 69; Ft Wayne Mus, 75; Valparaiso Univ, 75; Gilcrease Mus, Tulsa; Will Rogers Mus, Claremont, Okla, Ky Univ & Circle Galleries; Rennes, France, NMex Univ; Ind Capitol, Ind Mansion. *Awards:* Best of Show, Twas Bay Show, Gilcrease Mus, Tulsa, 76 & America Beautiful Miniature, Nat Small Painting Show, Albuquerque, 91; First Place for Oils, Southern Shores, Gary, Ind, 70; First Place for Watercolor, Ft Wayne Mus, 75. *Mem:* Ind Artists & Craftsmen; Cowboy Hall of Fame; Cowboy Artists of Am. *Media:* Oil, Bronze. *Interests:* Western, Indian and Landscapes

COOPERSMITH, GEORGIA A
MUSEUM DIRECTOR
b Phillipsburg, NJ, May 19, 1950. *Study:* Syracuse Univ, 68-70, MFA, 77, PhD, 92; Rochester Univ Technol, BFA, 73. *Collection Arranged:* Expressionist Impulses in Recent Am Art, 84; Variations on a Theme-Figurative Art, 85; The North Country Landscape, 86; Howardena Pindell Paintings & Drawings, 92-95; Shattering the Southern Stereotype: Jack Berl, Nell Blaine, Dorothy Gillespie, Sally Urnn, Cy Twumbly, 98. *Pos:* Asst cur, Mem Art Gallery, Rochester, 79-81; dir, Roland Gibson Gallery, Potsdam, NY, 81-91,; Ctr Visual Arts, Farmville, Va, currently. *Teaching:* Instr mus studies & gallery practices, State Univ & Col Arts & Science, Potsdam, 81-91, Longwood Col, 95. *Mem:* Am Asn Mus; Northeast Mus Conf; Coll Art Asn; Piedmont Coun for the Humanities. *Publ:* Auth, Paintings & Photographs, Moholy-Nagy, Mem Art Gallery, 78; Drawings & Watercolor, Mem Art Gallery, 79; Sculpture from the Johnson Atelier, Brainerd Art Gallery, 82; The Twentieth Anniversary Exhibition of the Vogel Collection, 82. *Mailing Add:* Longwood Ctr Visual Arts Longwood Col 129 N Main St Farmville VA 23901

COOVER, DORIS GWENDOLYN
PAINTER, PRINTMAKER
b Beaverdam, Wis, Aug 8, 1917. *Study:* Woodbury Univ, 37; studied with Fred Mitchum, Dallas Mus Arts. *Work:* Int Sci Technol Mag, NY; Scoville Manufacturing Co, Danbury, Conn. *Exhib:* 34th Ann Autumn Exhib, Delgado Mus, New Orleans, 58; Dallas Mus Art, 59; Mus Fine Arts Houston, 59; Showcase Plus & 60, Neuberger Mus, Purchase, NY, 60; solo exhibs, Briarcliff Col, NY, 69, Silvermine Guild Artists, Conn, 70, Katonah Gallery, NY, 71, Am Can Corp, Greenwich, Conn, 71, Village Gallery, Croton, NY, 74, Kirby Ctr, Cameron Park, Calif, 85-89 & Va Barrett Gallery, Chappaqua, NY, 92-95; Whitney Mus & Guggenheim Mus, NY; Carnegie Inst, Pittsburgh, Pa; Art Inst Chicago; Boston Mus Art; Parsons Sch Design; and 46 other int & regional exhibs. *Teaching:* Painting for Enjoyment, Chappaqua Sch System, NY, 67-74. *Awards:* Best of Show, Friday House, 85; Best of Show, 85, First & Second Prize, 90 & Hon Mentions, 94-95, Motherlode Art Show, Placerville, Calif; W Colo Watercolor Show Hobbin Award, 98. *Bibliog:* Marian Kisch (auth), Silk screens, Patent Trader Newspaper, NY, 68; Les Krantz (auth), 1990 Calif Art Review, Am References Inc, 90; Betsy Peses (auth), Designs for nature with dash of emotion, Mountain Democrat Newspaper, Calif, 92. *Mem:* Westchester Art Soc. *Media:* Oil, Watercolor; Silk Screen. *Publ:* Illusr, cover design, Int Sci Technol Mag; Best of Watercolor-Painting Color & Best of Drawing and Sketching, Rockport Publ. *Dealer:* Virginia Barrett Gallery 11 Memorial Dr Chappaqua NY 10514. *Mailing Add:* 3008 Twin Oaks Rd Cameron Park CA 95682

COPE, LOUISE TODD
COLLAGE ARTIST
b Ventnor, NJ, June 17, 1930. *Study:* Syracuse Univ, BA (fine arts), MLA & MA; Independent Textile Res, Guatemala, Scandinavia, Nepal, Bhutan & Thailand. *Work:* Australian Crafts Coun; NC Mus Art, Raleigh; Del Art Mus, Wilmington; Kutztown State Coll Collection, Pa; Helen Drutt Collection; Pfannebecker Collection; 3000 Gifts of service to the world prayer shawls, Parliament of the World religions, S Africa. *Comn:* quilt for Stella Kramish, comn by Helen Pratt, Philadelphia Mus Art, 2001. *Exhib:* Invisible Artist, Philadelphia Mus Art, 73-74; Women's Work, Am Art, Civic Ctr Mus, Philadelphia Nat Exhib, 74; 2nd & 3rd Int Miniature Exhib; Thread Poem Traveling Show, Australia, 78; NC Mus Hist, 83; collab with Marcia Plevin Dance Co, Two Survivors, NC Mus Art, 83; Silkworks, Gayle Willson Gallery, Southampton, NY, 84; Arvada Ctr Arts, Colo, 85-86; Wearable Art: A National Experience, Springfield, Ill, 85; Columbia Mus Art, 88-89. *Teaching:* Instr fibers, Haystack Sch Crafts, 69-89; chmn dept textiles, Moore Col Art, 70-74; teacher textiles, Penland Sch Crafts, NC, summers 70-72 & 81-86; tutor textiles, Wincester Sch Art, Eng, summer 73; teacher fibers, var workshops in US, Eng & Can; asst fac, Starking Sch Ministry, Berkeley, 96-, Sophia Ctr, Oakland, 96-. *Awards:* NC Mus Art Purchase Award, 71; Del Art Mus Purchase Award, 70; NC Mus Art Award, 83. *Mem:* World Crafts Coun; Am Crafts Coun. *Media:* Fiber. *Publ:* Auth, Thread Poems, 76 & Sleeves, A treasury of ideas, techniques & patterns, 88, Coat of Arms Press. *Mailing Add:* 1683 Scenic Ave Berkeley CA 94709

COPENHAVER-FELLOWS, DEBORAH LYNNE FELLOWS
SCULPTOR, PAINTER
b Spokane, Wash, Jan 2, 1948. *Study:* Holy Names Col, Fort Wright, BA (fine art), 70. *Work:* Bronze Stage Coach, Pro Rodeo Hall Fame, Colorado Springs, 81; Monumental Statue, Hecla Mining Co, Coeurdalena, Idaho, 91; Life Size Bronze Scout, Boy Scouts Am, Diamond Lake, Wash, 92; Frank Irwin Mem, Univ Tex, Austin, 86; BUSI Bronze Sculpture, Remington Park, Oklahoma City, 90. *Comn:* Vietman War Mem, Mont State, Missoula; Inland Pacific Vietnam War Mem, Spokane, Wash; Bing Crosby Mem, Gonzaga Univ, Spokane, Wash; Benny Binion Mem, Las Vegas; Korean War Mem, Wash State, Olympia; Lady of the Sea, Anacortes, Wash. *Exhib:* Buffalo Bill Art Show, Whitney Mus, Cody, Wyo, 92. *Awards:* Best of Show Sculpture, Mus Native Am Cult, 85. *Bibliog:* Southwest Art Mag, 85. *Media:* Bronze; Oil. *Dealer:* BigHorn Gallery Copy WY; Alterman Morris Dallas TX. *Mailing Add:* PO BOX 805 Sonoita AZ 85637-0805

COPT, LOUIS J
PAINTER
b Emporia, Kans, Jan 29, 1949. *Study:* Emoria State Univ, BA, 71; Art Students League (New York), 85; Univ Kans - Landscape Class, 86. *Comn:* Grand Canyon (oil), Kans Geological Survey, Lawrence, Kans, 91; watercolor landscape, City of Lawrence, Kans, 91; Grand Canyon (oil), Mike Hayden (Asst Secy Interior), Washington, DC, 92. *Exhib:* Mid-4, Nelson-Atkins Mus, Kansas City, Mo, 87; Kans Watercolor Soc, Wichita Art Mus, 87-92; Kansas 9 - Kansas 8, Mulvane Art Mus, Topeka, 89-90. *Pos:* Pres, Lawrence Arts Comn, 85-86; bd mem, Asn Community Arts Kans, 91-; Kans Watercolor Soc, 85-93. *Awards:* Purchase Awards, Kans Watercolor Soc, 86, 89-90; Purchase Awards, Corporte Woods, 89-90; Am Artist Award, 5th Nat Midwest Pastel Soc, 90. *Bibliog:* Richard LeComte (auth), Artist scours landscape, Lawrence J World, 90; Jan Witkowski (auth), Craft art-survival, Topeka Capital J, 92; Louis Copt (auth), Winter watercolors, The Artist's Mag, 92. *Mem:* Kans Watercolor Soc; Assoc Arts Agencies of Kans; Lawrence Arts Comn (pres 85-86); Lawrence Art Guild (pres 84-85); Midwest Pastel Soc. *Media:* Oil, Watercolor. *Publ:* Auth, Finding color in the winter landscape, The Artists Mag, 92; illus, Battle for the prairie, Earthwatch, 92. *Dealer:* Kyle Garcia 2900 F Oakley Brookwood Ctr Topeka KS 66614. *Mailing Add:* 1935 E 850 Rd Lecompton KS 66050-4062

CORAOR, JOHN E
MUSEUM DIRECTOR, ADMINISTRATOR
b Woodbury, NJ, Nov 30, 1955. *Study:* Syracuse Univ, BFA, 77; Pa State Univ, MA, 81, PhD, 85. *Pos:* Managing ed, Museologist Quart, 80-83; exec dir, Tempe Arts Ctr, Ariz, 85-88; dir, Hecksher Mus Art, Huntington, NY, 88-. *Teaching:* Asst educ, HF Johnson Mus Art, Ithaca, NJ, 77-79; instr, Pa State Univ, State College, 81-85. *Awards:* Northeast Mus Conf Fel, 80; Mayoral Proclamation in Recognition of Outstanding Service, City of Tempe, 88. *Mem:* Am Asn Mus; Mid-Atlantic Asn Mus (actg ed, 82-83, chmn publs comt, 72-94); Mus Asn Ariz (rep to exec bd, 87-88); Suffolk Co Cult Affairs Adv Bd, 90-; NY State Asn Mus; and others. *Publ:* Auth, Documentation, Evaluation & Dissemination, Museologist, 82; The perforative viewer: some pedagogical reflections from a phenomenological perspective, Pa State, 84; Fifty years of the museologist, Museologist, 85. *Mailing Add:* 7 Newbury Pl Huntington NY 11743-3240

CORBIN, GEORGE ALLEN
HISTORIAN, WRITER
b Detroit, Mich, Oct 23, 1941. *Study:* Oakland Univ, Rochester, Mich, BA (art hist), 63; Bucknell Univ, Lewisburg, Pa, MA, 68; Columbia Univ, MA (art hist), 71, PhD (primitive & pre-Columbian art), 76. *Teaching:* From asst to assoc prof & chair art, Lehman Col, New York, 69-. *Mem:* Coll Art Asn. *Res:* Art of the South Pacific Islands, particularly Melanesia and Polynesia; African, North American Indian and pre-Columbian art. *Publ:* Auth, The art of the Baining: New Britain, Exploring the Visual Art of Oceania, Univ Press Hawaii, 79. *Mailing Add:* Dept Art City Univ NY Lehman Col 250 Bedford Park W Bronx NY 10468

CORBINO, MARCIA NORCROSS
CRITIC, WRITER
b Tulsa, Okla. *Study:* Duke Univ, BA, 49; Art Students League, 50. *Collection Arranged:* Multiple Visions: A History of Art in Sarasota, Selby Gallery, Ringling Sch Art and Design, 2000; Quintessential Contemp: Art from Pvt Collections on Longboat Key, Longboat Key Ctr for Arts, 2/04; The Circus, Art Ctr Sarasota, 1/2005. *Pos:* Writer & photogr, Sarasota Jour, 74-77; critic, Sarasota Herald Tribune, 77-82; consult, Corbino Galleries, 85-2003 & Speakers Bur Fla Humanities Coun, 96; critic, Longboat Observer, 96-2001. *Teaching:* instr, The Edn Ctr, Longboat Key, 96; instr Inst Creative Writing, Adult & Community Educ, 2003-07. *Bibliog:* Su Byron (auth), Artistic License: A Sarasota Wordsmith Lives Her Passion, Sarasota Downtown and Beyond, 4/2002. *Res:* Contemporary American and Latin American art. *Specialty:* Latin American Art. *Interests:* Reading. *Publ:* Helen Sawyer: Memories of a Morning Star, 95; Gail Symon Hicks: The Painted Garden, 96; contrib, Dorothy Gillespie, 98; Travels in the Labyrinth: Mexican Art in the Pollak Collection, Univ Pa Press, 2001; A History of Visual Art in Sarasota, Univ Press Fla, 3/2003; photograph of Evan Hunter, A Mystery Writers' Colony, Sarasota Mag, 2/05; Jon Corbino and The Pleasures of the Bathing Beach: A Slice of Life in America, 1939, Nassau County Hist Soc Journal, 04; Literary Lions, Sarasota Mag, 11/04; A Fine Madness: True Tales from the Days when Sarasota was an Artists' Colony, Sarasota Mag, 11/03; Lillian Burns, West Coast Woman, Sarasota, Fla, 2/01; Steir's waterfalls make a splendid exhibition, The Longboat Observer, Longboat Key, Fla, 2/10/00; catalog, Julio Antonio: Images and Commentaries, Panama Mus Art, 7/99. *Mailing Add:* 1111 N Gulfstream Ave No 6B Sarasota FL 34236

CORDOVA, WILLIAM
PAINTER, SCULPTOR
b Lima, Peru, 1972. *Study:* Art Inst of Chicago, BFA, 1996; Yale Univ Sch of Art, MFA, 2004. *Work:* Whitney Mus Am Art, New York. *Exhib:* Solo exhibs, Inst Contemp Art, Winnipeg, Can, 2002, Mus Contemp Art, Miami, 2003, Drylongso (Pichqa Suyo), PS.1 Contemp Art Ctr, Long Island, NY, 2005, 2006, Pálante, Arndt & Partner, Berlin, 2006, The Quickening, Marianne Boesky Gallery, New York, 2006, Arndt & Partner, Berlin, 2007, Sandroni Rey, Los Angeles, 2007, I Wish it Were True, Davidson Univ, NC, 2007; Altoids Curiously Strong Collection, New Mus, New York, 2003; ARCO, Caren Golden Fine Arts, Madrid, Spain, 2004; Thesis Exhib, Yale Univ, New Haven, CT, 2004; Scratch, The Studio Mus in Harlem, New York, 2005; two-person exhibs, I Wish it Were True, Proj Row House, Houston, (with Leslie Hewitt), 2005, I Wish it Were True, Jamaica Art Ctr, Queens, NY, (with Leslie Hewitt), 2006; Efface, Steve Turner Gallery, Los Angeles, 2006; Being There, Ingalls & Assocs, Miami, 2006; Youth of Today, Schirn Kunsthalle, Frankfurt, Germany, 2006; Street Level, Contemp Arts Ctr, New Orleans, 2007 ; Street Level Nasher Mus, Duke Univ, NC, 2007; Whitney Biannual, Whitney Mus, New York, 2008; Prague Triennial, 2008; San Juan Triennial, Instituto de Cultura Puertorriqueña, Puerto Rico, 2009. *Awards:* Travel Grant, Tigertail Productions, 1999; Art Matters Found Grant, 2009. *Bibliog:* John Lamb (auth), Maybe I'm Amazed, High Plains Reader, 11/2001; Robert Enright (auth), Peruvian Magic, The Glove and Mail, 9/2002; Roni Feinstein (auth), Expanding Horizons, Art in America, 12/2003; Jeff M Ward (auth), Round 23, Artlles, Winter/2006; Trevor Schoonmaker (auth), Street Level, 3/2007; Cate McQuaid, Street Wise, The Boston Globe, 2/2008. *Dealer:* Arndt & Partner Zimmerstrasse 90-91 Berlin Germany 10117. *Mailing Add:* c/o Sikkema Jenkins & Co 530 W 22nd St New York NY 10011

CORDY-COLLINS, ALANA (KATHLEEN)
CURATOR, EDUCATOR
b Los Angeles, Calif, June 5, 1944. *Study:* Univ Calif, Los Angeles, BA (art hist), 70, MA (archeol), 72, PhD (archeol), 76. *Pos:* Mem chmn, Archeol Inst Am, San Diego Chap, 77-78, pres, 79-81; cur, Latin Am Collections, San Diego Mus Man, 79-. *Teaching:* Instr archeol, Univ Calif, Los Angeles 72-74; instr art & archeol, Univ Calif, San Diego 74-79 & San Diego Mesa Col, Calif, 75-80; assoc prof anthrop, Univ San Diego, 80-. *Awards:* Altman Art Award, Univ Calif, Los Angeles, 72. *Res:* Iconographic study of Chavin & Peru art; shamanic art; function of art in culture. *Publ:* Ed, Pre-Columbian Art History, Selected Readings, Vol 2, 82; auth, The Cerro Sechin massacre: Did it happen?, Mus of Man Ethic Technotes, No 18, 83; Ancient Andean art as explained by Andean ethnohistory: An historical review, 83 & coauth (with D D McClelland), Upstreaming along the Peruvian north coast, 83, Brit Archeol Reports; Mega-Ninos, Spondylos Shells, and the Chimor-Calangone Connection, J New World Archaeol, Inst of Archeol, Univ Calif, Los Angeles (in press). *Mailing Add:* Mus of Man Balboa Park 1350 El Prado San Diego CA 92101

CORKERY, TIM (TIMOTHY) JAMES
PAINTER, EDUCATOR
b Washington, DC, Oct 30, 1931. *Study:* Univ Chicago Univ Col, 55-59; Art Inst Chicago, BFA, 60; Inst Allende Univ Guanajuato, Mex, MFA, 64. *Work:* Baltimore Mus Art; Idaho First Nat Bank, Boise; Alcoa Aluminum Co, Pittsburgh; Johnson & Johnson Inc, Newark, NJ. *Comn:* Mural for pub housing, Dept of Housing & Community Develop, Baltimore, 73; indoor mural for Univ Baltimore, Mayor's Adv Comt for Art & Cult, 79; indoor mural for Arts Tower, Baltimore, 80. *Exhib:* Eighteenth Area Exhib, Corcoran Gallery Art, Washington, DC, 67; Solo exhibs, Royal Marks Gallery, NY, 69 & 70, Jefferson Place Gallery, Wash, DC, 71 & Max Hutchinson Gallery, NY, 73 & 74; Univ Md, Baltimore Co, 75; Univ Ore Mus Art, 78. *Collection Arranged:* Seventeenth Area Exhib (cataloged), Corcoran Gallery Art, Washington, DC, 65; Washington 20 Years (cataloged), Baltimore Mus Art, 70; Mem Gallery, Albright-Knox Gallery, 70 & 75; New Washington Painting (cataloged), Hayden Gallery, Mass Inst Technol, 71; Washington Art, Richmond Mus Exten, 71; Artists Making Art, Baltimore Mus Art, 72; Synergy-Artists One Plus One Equals Three (cataloged), Thorpe Intermedia Gallery, Sparkill, NY, 82. *Pos:* Ed Art Depts: Washington Evening Star, 1950-1951; Chicago Sun Times, 1955-1958, 1963-1964; Chicago Daily News, 1958-1960; NY Daily News, 1964-1965; NY Post, 1980-1988. *Teaching:* Instr fine arts & painting, Corcoran Sch Art, Washington, DC, 65-67; instr painting, Md Inst Col Art, Baltimore, 67-77; vis artist painting, Univ Ore, Eugene, 77-78, Sch Art, Inst Chicago, 78 & RI Col, Providence, 89-95. *Awards:* Purchase Awards, Baltimore Mus 70 & Macht Found, 70; Munic Art Soc Award, 72. *Bibliog:* Sidra Stich (auth), Five Washington artists, Art Int Mag, 12/71; Carter Ratcliff (auth), article, Art Spectrum Mag, 2/75; Ellen Lubell (auth), article, Arts Mag, 2/75. *Mem:* Coll Art Asn Am. *Media:* Oil on Canvas. *Mailing Add:* 3 Theresa Ct Providence RI 02909

CORMACK, MALCOLM
CURATOR, HISTORIAN
b Birmingham, Eng, Dec 6, 1935. *Study:* Courtauld Inst Art Univ London, BA, 59; Cambridge Univ, Eng, MA, 65. *Pos:* Asst keeper, City Birmingham Mus & Art Gallery, Eng, 59-62; from asst keeper to keeper, Fitzwilliam Mus, Cambridge, 62-76; cur paintings, Yale Ctr Brit Art, 76-91; Paul Mellon cur, Va Mus Fine Arts, 91-. *Teaching:* Instr art hist, Cambridge Univ, 62-76; instr, Yale Univ, 76-. *Mem:* Walpole Soc. *Mailing Add:* 515 Wild Life Tr Richmond VA 23233-6427

CORMIER, CINDY
MUSEUM DIRECTOR
Study: Univ Conn, Sch of Bus. *Pos:* cur, Wistariahurst Museum, formerly; chairperson of editorial bd, Hog River Journal, formerly; dir educ & cur servs, Hill-Stead Mus, co-interim dir, 2007-. *Mailing Add:* Hill-Stead Museum 35 Mountain Road Farmington CT 06032

CORMIER, ROBERT JOHN
PAINTER, LECTURER
b Boston, Mass, May 26, 1932. *Study:* R H Ives Gammell Studios, cert. *Work:* Maryhill Mus, Goldborough, Wash; Superior Courthouse, Cambridge, Mass; Univ Sch, Shaker Heights, Ohio; Salem Courthouse, Mass; Suffolk Co Courthouse, Boston, Mass. *Comn:* Portraits for St Michael's Church, Charleston SC; John Hancock Mutual Life Insurance Co, 81; Mass Appellate Court, Boston, 83; Mass Supreme Judicial Court, Boston, 90; Boston Coll Law Sch, Newton MA, 90; 1st & 2nd Uninesralist, Unitarian Church, Boston, 92. *Exhib:* New Eng Artists Contemp Ann, 54-69; Guild of Boston Artists, 60-90; Boston Arts Festival, 62; Coun Am Artists Socs, NY, 66; Springfield Mus, Mass, 79. *Pos:* Mem, City Art Comn, Boston, 82-, Chmn, 90-95; bd mem, Brown Fund, Boston, 89-; designator, Henderson Found, 89-. *Teaching:* Instr drawing & painting, Vesper George Sch Art, 69-83; instr, studio & artasns. *Awards:* Gold Medal of Honor, Coun Am Artists Socs, 65; Greenshields Found Award, 70; Award Distinction, Guild Boston Artists, 93. *Mem:* Guild Boston Artists (secy, bd gov, 70-81 pres, 82-94); Copley Soc Boston (vpres, 70-77); Portraits, Inc. *Media:* Oil, Pastel

CORN, WANDA M
HISTORIAN, EDUCATOR
b New Haven, Conn, Nov 13, 1940. *Study:* Washington Square Col, New York Univ, BA, 63; Inst Fine Arts, New York Univ, MA, 65, PhD, 74. *Collection Arranged:* The Color of Mood: Am Tonalism, 1880-1910, (auth, catalog), 72; The Art of Andrew Wyeth (auth, catalog), 73; Am Art: An Exhibition from the Collection of Mr & Mrs John D Rockefeller 3rd, 76; Grant Wood: The Regionalist Vision (auth, catalog), 83-84; The Great American Thing, 2005-2006; Gertrude Stein: Five Stories, 2011-2012. *Pos:* Vis cur, Fine Arts Mus, San Francisco, 72, 73, 76 & 84 & Minneapolis Inst Arts, 82-84; comnr, Nat Mus Am Art, Smithsonian, 88-95; acting dir, Stanford Mus, 89-91; dir, Stanford Humanities Ctr, 92-95; Smithsonian coun, 2001; art adv com, Terra Found, 99-2008, bd dir, 2002; bd trustees, Wyeth Found for Am Art, 2002-. *Teaching:* Lectr Am art, Univ Calif, Berkeley, 70 & 76; from asst prof mod Europ & Am art to assoc prof, Mills Col, 70-80; assoc prof Am art hist, Stanford Univ, 81-88, prof, 89-, chmn, 89-91, 99-00 & assoc chair, 95-97; named Robert and Ruth Halperin prof in art history, 2000, retired, 2008. *Awards:* Smithsonian Fel, Nat Mus Am Art, 78-79; Fel, Woodrow Wilson Int Ctr Scholars, 79-80; Fel, Stanford Humanities Ctr, 82-83; Am Coun Learned Soc Awards, 82 & 86; Regents Fel, Smithsonian Inst, 87; Charles C Eldredge Prize for Distinguished Scholar in Am Art, 2000; Phi Beta Kappa Undergraduate Teaching Award, 2002; Radcliffe Inst Fel, Harvard Univ, 2003-2004; Clark Distinguished Vis Prof, Williams Coll, 2003; Samuel H Kress Prof, Ctr Advanced Study in Visual arts, Nat Gallery Art, 2006-2007; Distinguished Teaching of Art Hist Award, Coll Art Asn, 2007; Lawrence A Fleischman Award for Scholarly Excellence in Field of Am Art Hist, Archives of Am Art, 2006; Women's Caucus Art Life Time Achievement Award in Visual Arts, 2007; Fel, Clark Inst Art, 2010; fel, Georgia O'Keefe Rsch Ctr, 2013. *Mem:* Coll Art Asn (bd dir, 70-73 & 80-84); Women's Caucus Art (adv bd, 80-84); Am Studies Asn (nat coun, 86-89). *Res:* American art from the Civil War to 1945. *Publ:* Auth, Coming of Age: Historical Scholarship in American Art, Art Bul, LXX, pp 188-207, 6/88; auth, The Great American Thing: Modern Art and National Identity, 1915-1935, Univ of Calif Press, 99; auth, Women Building History: Public Art at teh 1893 Columbia Exposition, Univ. Calif Press, 2011; co-auth, Seeing Gertrude Stein: Five Stories, Univ Calif Press, 2011. *Mailing Add:* PO Box 1299 Sagamore Beach Sagamore Beach MA 02562

CORNELL, DAVID E
CERAMIST, SCULPTOR
b Kalispell, Mont, Feb 24, 1939. *Study:* Mont State Univ, BS (art); Archie Bray Found, with Kenneth Ferguson & David Shaner; Corcoran Sch Art, with Teuro Hara & Richard LaFean; Alfred Univ, MFA (ceramics), with Bob Turner, Val Cushing & Daniel Rhodes. *Work:* Greenville Art Mus, SC; Charles M Russell Gallery, Great Falls, Mont; Libby Dam, Treaty Tower, Vis Ctr, Libby, Mont; Archie Bray Found, Helena, Mont; Mont State Univ, Bozeman. *Comn:* Ceramic fountain fixtures, Mont State Univ Libr, 64; Treaty Panel (sculpture), US Army Corps 18 Engineers & Mont Hist Soc, 75. *Exhib:* Tenth Int Exhib Ceramic Art, Smithsonian Inst, Washington, DC, 66; Norfolk Mus Art, Va, 66; Harriman Gallery, Orange Co Community Col, Middletown, NY, 69; Handblown Glass Exhib, Corning Glass Ctr, NY, 69; Mint Mus Art, NC, 70; Appalachian Corridors: Exhib 2, Charleston, Wva, 70; NW Crafts Show, Henry Gallery, Seattle, Wash, 71; Cheney Cowles Mem Mus, Spokane, Wash, 73; Mont State Hist Soc Exhib, Poindexter Gallery, Helena, 75. *Pos:* Artist-in-residence, Penland Sch of Crafts, 69-70; dir, Archie Bray Found, 70-77; owner-mgr, Pear Blossom Pottery, Talent, Ore; pres, Clayfolk, Inc, 78-79. *Awards:* First Prize, Univ Exhib, Mont State Univ, 64; Jury Award, 11th Biennial NW Ceramics, Ore Ceramics Studio, 65; Best of Show, 11th Ann Own Your Own, Southern Colo State Col, 74. *Bibliog:* Mary Lou O'Neil (auth), Archie Bray Found, Mountain Lines, Mountain Bell Tel & Tel, 11/70; David Depew (auth), Archie Bray Found, Ceramics Mo, 5/72; Jerry Metcalf (auth), Today at the Bray, Mont Arts, Mont Inst Arts, 76. *Mem:* Helena Arts Coun (vpres, 73); Mont Art Gallery Dir Asn (secy, 75-76); Nat Coun Educ in Ceramic Arts; Am Crafts Coun; Glass Art Soc. *Media:* Ceramic. *Mailing Add:* 2316 S Pacific Hwy Talent OR 97540-9633

CORNELL, HENRY
PATRON
Study: Grinnell Col, BA, 76; NY Law Sch, JD, 81. *Pos:* Assoc, Davis Polk & Wardwell, New York City, 81-84, Goldman Sachs & Co, New York City, 84-94, partner, managing dir, 94-. *Mem:* Asian Art Mus, San Francisco (trustee, currently); Whitney Mus Am Art

CORONA, LIVIA
PHOTOGRAPHER
Study: Art Ctr Coll Design, Pasadena, BFA, 2001. *Exhib:* Inszenierte Kraft, Munich BMW Pavillon, Ger, 2000; Energy=, William Turner Gallery, Venice, Calif, 2001; The Drop, Los Angeles, 2001; Lisa Sette Gallery, Scottsdale, Ariz, 2004; Love Found Photog Exhib, New York, 2005; Take Home a Nude, New York Acad Art, 2006; Visa Pour L'Image, Perpignan, France, 2007; Parientes de Ocasion, Centro Fotografico Manuel Alvarez Bravo, Oaxaca, Mex, 2008; solo exhibs, 3A Gallery, San Francisco, 2008, Powerhouse Arena, Brooklyn, 2008, Galerija Herman Pacaric, Slovenia, 2009, Haus der Architektur, Graz, Austria, 2009; Occasional Relatives, Atheneum Arts Ctr, La Jolla, 2009. *Awards:* Named 30 under 30 Emerging Photogrs to Watch, Photo Dist News, 2002; Int Photog Award in Photojournalism, 2003-2004; Photog award, Mex Tourism Bd, 2005; Sony World Photog Award, Cannes, 2008; Guggenheim Found Fel, 2010. *Bibliog:* Andrew Blum (auth), The Original Tenant Was an Art Show, NY Times, 12/30/2004; Darren Ching (auth), Livia Corona and Los Enanitos Toreros, Magenta Mag, 11/2006. *Publ:* Auth, Ananitos Toreros, Powerhouse Bks, New York, 2008; Of People and Houses, Haus der Architektur, Graz, Austria, 2009

CORR, JAMES D
PAINTER, COLLEGE EDUCATOR
b Missoula, Mont, Feb 13, 1931. *Study:* Western Mont Col, BS (art); Univ Mont, ME (art); also with Peter Volkous & Walter Hook. *Work:* Western Gallery & Co High Sch, Dillon, Mont; Univ Collection, Missoula; Copper City Mus, Anaconda, Mont; Beaverhead Chamber Mus Dillon, Mont; Lewis & Clark Exped Center, Dillon, Mont. *Comn:* Pioneer Fed Bldg, Lewis & Clark Derama Beavrhead Co Mus. *Exhib:* Electra, Helena, Copper Camp Festival, Butte, Mont; Mondak, Sidney, Mont. *Collection Arranged:* Seidensticker Wildlife Collection. *Teaching:* Emer prof, Western Mont Col, 70-94; Prof Art Emeritus, Univ Mont Western. *Awards:* UM Western Distinguished Alumni. *Media:* Multimedia. *Publ:* Illustrated Poetry, Brushgold, Bannack Revisited. *Mailing Add:* 515 SDak Dillon MT 59725

CORRIEL, ERIC
VIDEO ARTIST, DESIGNER
Study: Cornell Univ, BA, 2001; Ecole Regionale Superieure d'Expression Plastique, France, MFA, 2007. *Comn:* Murals, CH Dron Maternity Ward, Tourcoing, France, 2005-06. *Exhib:* Al Andaluz, Musee des Beaux Arts, France, 2006; Surface, BAG Gallery, Brooklyn, 2009; Windows Brooklyn, Soula, Brooklyn, 2009; Artsummerweek, La Grange, France, 2009; Brooklyn Utopias, Brooklyn Hist Soc, 2009. *Pos:* Freelance web designer, 1998-; co-founder, Intellikit, Brooklyn, NY, 1999-2004; designer, Confetti, 2006; project mgr & designer, Dept Advertising & Graphic Design, Sch Visual Arts, New York, 2007-. *Awards:* New York Found Arts Fel, 2009

CORRIGAN, KARINA
CURATOR
b Boston, Sept 1, 1970. *Study:* Wellesley Coll, BA, 1993; Univ Pa, Philadelphia, MS (hist preservation), 1995; Univ Del, Newark, MA (early Am cult), 2001. *Pos:* Asst cur, Peabody Essex Mus, Salem, Mass, 1997-2001, H A Crosby Forbes cur of Asian export art, 2001-. *Mem:* Hamilton Hall Inc, Salem, (trustee, 2005-); Friends Nalamdana, Mt Vernon, (trustee, 2005-). *Mailing Add:* Peabody Essex E India Sq Salem MA 01970

CORRIN, LISA G
MUSEUM DIRECTOR
Study: Mary Wash Coll, Fredericksburg, Va, BA Art Hist; State Univ NY, Stony Brook; Johns Hopkins Univ. *Pos:* Co-Founder, Contemp Mus Baltimore, 1989-97; chief cur, Contemp Mus Baltimore, 1989-97, Serpentine Gallery, London, 1997-2001; contemp art cur, Seattle Art Mus, 2001-05; dir, Williams Coll Mus Art, Williamstown, Mass, 2005-2012; dir, Mary & Leigh Block Mus Art, Northwestern Univ, Evanston, Ill, 2012-. *Awards:* Rockefeller Fel Multicult Scholar, Coll Art Asn, 1993. *Mailing Add:* Northwestern University Mary and Leigh Block Mus Art 40 Arts Circle Dr Evanston IL 60208

CORRIS, MICHAEL
CONCEPTUAL ARTIST, WRITER
b Brooklyn, NY, Aug 14, 1948. *Study:* Brooklyn Col, BA, 70; Md Inst Coll Art, MFA, 72; Visual Artist fel, Nat Endowment Arts, 74; Artist Book Grant, NY State Coun Arts, 87; Univ Coll London, PhD (Hist of Art), 96. *Work:* Mus Mod Art, NY; Victoria & Albert Mus, London; Univ Maine Mus Art, Orono, Maine; Mus Contemp Art, Geneva, Switz; Tate Gallery, London. *Exhib:* Documenta V, Friedrichianum, Kassel, Ger, 72; Art Press, Victoria & Albert Mus, London, 76; Art and Language, Nat Gallery Art, Melbourne, Australia, 76; Drawing Now, Mus Mod Art, NY, 76; Committed to Print, Mus Mod Art, NY, 88; Souls Le Soleil, Villa Arson, Nice, France, 88; 1968, Le Consortium, Dijon, France, 92; The Magic of Numbers, Staatsgalerie, Stuttgart, Ger, 97; Philippe Meaille Collection, Art & Language, Mus Of Contemp Art, Barcelona, 2014. *Collection Arranged:* Public and private collections, including the Mus of Modern Art, NY, Le Consortium, Victoria and Albert Mus, London, Staatsgaleri, Progressive Art Collection, Cleveland and Tampa, Getty Research Inst, Los Angeles, Dallas Biennial, 2012 and several others. *Pos:* Corresp, Art Forum Int, NY, 91-95; adv, Arts Coun Eng, 93-95; ed adv, Art & Text, Sydney, NSW, formerly; participant in the collective Art & Language, NY, 1972-76; founding editor, The Fox; reviews editor, Art Journal, New York: Col Art Asn, 2013-2016; series editor, Art Since the 80s, Reaktion Books, London. *Teaching:* Sr lectr art theory, Oxford Brookes Univ, 90-96; vis lect art, Goldsmiths' Col, London, formerly, Slade Sch At, London, formerly; Reader, art theory & hist, Oxford Brookes Univ, formerly; prof, chair division of art, Southern Methodist Univ, Meadows Sch of the Arts, 2009-2013. *Awards:* Mary E Lopresti Award, ARLIS Southeast, 87; Gerald J Ford Fellowship, 2013-14; Fellow, Dedman Col Interdisciplinary Inst, 2012-2013, 2015-2016. *Bibliog:* Jan Avgikos (auth), Absence As Presence, New Works Univ Maine Mus Art, 88; Charles Harrison (auth), Essays on Art & Language, Basil Blackwell, 91; Thomas Dreher (auth), Konzeptuelle Kunst in Amerika und England Zwischen 63 & 76, Frankfurt: Lang, 92. *Mem:* AICA; Coll Art Asn. *Media:* Offset Lithography, Computer Aided Design; Digital Commun Networks. *Res:* Modernist art in the US 1930-1965; politics and theory in international art since 1965, contemporary video, film and artist organizations, information and exchange groups. *Publ:* Auth, As if the Pillars of Society, 87 & My Frankenstein, 91, Clarte Press; contribr, Art Has No History, Verso Press, 94; Art and Ideas: Postmodernism, Phaidon Press (in prep); Inside a New York Art Gang: Selected Documents of Art & Language in New York, in Artists Think: The Late Works of Ian Burn, Sydney: Power Publ, 96; We Have Submerged Victoriously, Art & Language, Barcelona Fondacion Tapies, 99; Conceptual Art: A Critical Anthology, 1999; Conceptual Art: Theory, Myth and Practice, 2004; Ad Reinhardt, 2008; Non-Relational Aesthetics, 2008; Art, Word & Image: 2,000 Years of Textual/Visual Interaction, 2010; Leaving Skull City: Selected Writings on Art, Les Presses du Reel, 2015; Dallasian Spring, Art in America, 2015. *Mailing Add:* Southern Methodist University Meadows School of the Art 6101 Bishop Blvd Room 2735 OAC Dallas TX 75275

CORSO, SAMUEL (JOSEPH)
STAINED GLASS ARTIST, PAINTER
b Monroe, La, Jan 11, 1953. *Study:* La State Univ, Baton Rouge, BFA (painting & drawing), 75, MFA (stained glass design), 77; studied mosaics, sumi-e & bronze sculpture with Paul A Dufour, 77, 78 & 79. *Work:* River Oaks Sq Arts & Crafts Ctr, Alexandria, La; Louisville Arts Club, Ky; Signal Corp, La Jolla, Calif; Duravent Corp, Redwood, Calif; Premier Bancorp, Baton Rouge, La. *Comn:* Mosaic & stained glass, St Francis Cabrini Hosp, Alexandria, La, 88; mosaic mural, Christus Health, Houston, Tex, 90; stained glass, Soc of Jesus Retirement Home, New Orleans, 90; bronze sculpture, Emmy Lou Biedenharn Found, Monroe, La, 90; stained glass, Jesus Good Shepherd Cath Church, Monroe, La, 94-97; stained glass, St Aloysius Cath Church, Baton Rouge, La, 1997; stained glass, La State Percent-for-Art project, Baton Rouge, La, 2003. *Exhib:* Mint Mus Art, Charlotte, NC, 78 & 80; Missoula Mus Art, Mont, 88; Materials, Hard & Soft, Denton, Tex, 88; La Festival Arts, Masur Mus Art, Monroe, 89; Tex & Neighbors Exhib, 90; Southeastern Juried Competition, Fine Arts Mus South, Mobile, Ala, 1990, 2004; and others. *Pos:* Pres, Dufour/Corso Studios, 2008-. *Teaching:* Instr, Arrowmont Sch Arts & Crafts, Gatlinburg, Tenn, 78, 83 & 88; asst prof drawing & design, La State Univ, Baton Rouge, 81, instr, 83-91, 2001-2006; Wanganui Polytechnic, Wanganui, NZ, 2000. *Awards:* Hon Mention, Am Crafts Coun Southeast, 86; 2nd Place, Terrebonne Hist & Cult Soc, 88; La Div Arts Fel, 82, 2001, 2002. *Bibliog:* Albert Lewis (auth), Stained glass goes to college, Glass Mag, Vol V, No 4, 78; Lisa Corbin (auth), A painter's viewpoint, Prof Stained Glass, 5/91; Robert Kehlmann (auth), Neus Glass. *Mem:* La State Arts Coun; Am Crafts Coun. *Media:* European & Domestic Glass; Watercolor, Oil Pastel. *Publ:* Contribr, Robert Jenson's & Patricia Conway's Ornamentalism, Clarkson N Potter, 81; auth, New glass review No 4, Corning Mus, 82; Spectrum, Glass Mag, 12/82; contribr, M Crespo (auth), Experiments in Water, Watson/Guptil Press, 88; contrib, CJ Peterson (auth), Glass House: The Art of Decorating with Light, Sterling Publ Co, NY, 2007. *Dealer:* Worldwide Art Resources & Design Inc 257 E Main St Harbor Springs MI; Creative Resources: Art & Imaging Gallery Inc 162 N Woodward Ave Birmingham MI. *Mailing Add:* 813 North St Baton Rouge LA 70802

CORTESE, DON F
PRINTMAKER, PAINTER
b Chicago, Ill, Dec 30, 1934. *Study:* Art Inst Chicago, BFA; Syracuse Univ, MFA. *Work:* Libr Cong, Washington; Art Inst Chicago; Boston Pub Libr; Houghton Libr, Harvard Univ; Uffizi Gallery, Florence, Italy. *Comn:* Intaglio Print, Impressions Workshop, Boston, Mass, 71; etching on experimental paper, Boise Cascade, 80; 60th Int Paper Conf, Ottawa, Can, 85; 25th Anniversary Syracuse Pulp & Paper Found, 85; 120th Anniversary King & King Architects, Handmade paper & print, Syracuse, NY, 88. *Exhib:* Int Print Competition, Seattle Art Mus, Wash, 71; Artists of Cent NY, Munson-Williams-Proctor Inst Mus, Utica, NY, 76; Breaking the Bindings-Am Book Art Now, Eivehjem Mus, Univ Wis, 83; Self-Portraits, Am Artists, Uffizi Gallery, Florence, Italy, 83; Int Exhib Hand Papermaking & Artists Books, AldenBiesen Castle, Belg, 94; paper/print/pulp, Frans Masereel Int Graphic Ctr, Belg, 95; Multiple Affinities: CEPA Gallery, Buffalo, NY, 96; 50th Anniversary Boston Printmakers, Bakalar Gallery, Boston, 97; Invitational Int Exhib, Digital Print Media, Florence, Italy, 2000. *Collection Arranged:* New England Land Grant Universities Workshop, 81; Exhib of Visiting Printmakers, Herter Gallery, Univ Mass, 82; Botany of Papermaking Invitational, Mo Botanical Garden Libr, St Louis, 81; Italian J/Solo, Schweinfurth Art Ctr, Auburn, NY, 92. *Pos:* chmn dept, experimental studios, Syracuse Univ, NY, 1973-5, chmn dept studio art 93-6; coordr studio arts, London, Eng 75-6; coordr studio arts, Florence IT program, Syracuse Univ, 2000-01; interim dir, Florence Italy Prog, Syracuse Univ, 2001-02; prof emeritus, Syracuse Univ, 2002. *Teaching:* Prof hand papermaking & book arts printmaking, Sch Art, Syracuse Univ, NY, 65-. *Awards:* US State Dept Grant, Fullbright Prog, 65; Ford Fount Grant, 76; NY State Artists Proj Grant, 94. *Bibliog:* E C Cunningham (auth), Printmaking-A Primary Form of Expression, Univ Press Colo, 92; The Best of Printmaking-An International Collection, Rockport Publ, 97. *Media:* Collage, Digital Media. *Mailing Add:* 8062 Cazenovia Rd Manlius NY 13104

COSTA, EDUARDO
CONCEPTUAL ARTIST, PAINTER
b Buenos Aires, Argentina. *Study:* Univ Buenos Aires, MA; studied Eng & Am Lit with Jorge L Borges. *Work:* Costume Inst, Metrop Mus Art, NY; New York Univ Libr; Columbia Univ Libr; Yale Univ Libr. *Exhib:* Fashion and Surrealism, Fashion Inst Tech, NY, 87 & Victoria & Albert Mus, London, Eng, 88; Latin-Am Spirit, Bronx Mus Arts, NY, 88-89; The Art Mall, New Mus, NY, 92; Talking Paintings, IBEU, Rio de Janeiro, Brazil, 94; Elga Wimmer Gallery, NY, 95. *Teaching:* Guest artist & lectr, Cooper Union, 84-88. *Bibliog:* Jeff Weinstein (auth), All fashion involves ideas, Village Voice, 10/5/82; Deborah Drier (auth), Obsession, Art in Am, 2/88; Berta Sichel (auth), chilinelron/Costa, Art Nexus, 10/92; Gilberto de Abreu (auth), Obra de Arte Tambem é Gente, O Globo, RJ, Brazil, 3/28/94. *Media:* Mixed Media; Acrylic Paint. *Publ:* Auth, The Shower Curtain, Even, Village Voice, 12/22/87; Tunga, Pellegrino, Art in Am, 7/94; Oiticica, Clark and Pape, Art News, 12/94; Tellez, Art in Am, 11/96. *Dealer:* Elga Wimmer Gallery 560 Broadway New York NY 10012

COSTAN, CHRIS
PAINTER, COLLAGE ARTIST
b Chicago, Ill, Sept 18, 1950. *Study:* Univ Ill, Chicago, BA, 73, Santa Reparata Print Workshop, Florence, Italy, 74, Univ Wis, Madison, MA/MFA, 75. *Work:* Mus Mod Art; Brooklyn Mus, NY; Nelson-Atkins Mus Art, Kansas City, Mo; Art Inst Chicago; Newark Mus, NJ. *Exhib:* New Work, NY (exhib catalog), Seattle Art Mus, & Spencer Mus Art, 88; Committed to Print, Mus Mod Art, NY, 88; Print Selections from the Permanent Collection, Brooklyn Mus, NY, 90; Return of the Cadavre Equis (exhib catalog), Corcoran Gallery Art, Drawing Ctr, 93-94; The Atmosphere, Art, Native Wisdom & Science, Univ Gallery, Albany, NY, 93; Xenographic Nomadic Wall, XLV Venice Biennale, 93; Drop Dead Painting, 103 Reade St, NY, 94; Internal External (auth, catalog), Goldstrum Gallery, 95; FAO Gallery, NY, 96; Solo Exhibs: Cheryl Pelavin Fine Art, 03; Body Suit, Smith Coll Mus Art, 2003; Body Suit, Cheryl Pelavin Fine Art, 2004. *Awards:* Nat Endowment Arts, 89-90; Gottlieb Found, 95; Nat Accad Arts and Letters, 1995; NY Found Arts, 99. *Bibliog:* Ronny Cohen (auth), New York reviews, Art Forum, 5/89; Kay Larson (auth), Art/Kay Larson, New York Mag, 3/9/92 Daniel Grant (auth), Art in brief, Berkshire Eagle, 7/21/94; Cover Mag, Joel Silverstein, 98; Tribeca Trib, Jennifer Dalton, 98; Joel Silverstein (auth), reviews, nyreview.com, 10/2000; Phoebe Mitchell (auth), Daily Hampshire Gazette (fine arts sect), 2004. *Media:* Acrylic, Collage/Montage. *Publ:* Auth, Art by Chance (exhib catalog), Nelson-Atkins Mus Art, 89; Intaglio Printmaking in the 1980's (exhib catalog), 90; Presswork: The Art of Women Printmakers (exhib catalog), 91; Int External, Richard Martin, 95. *Dealer:* Cheryl Pelavin Fine Art, 13 Jay St New York NY 10007. *Mailing Add:* 303 Park Ave S No 515 New York NY 10010

COSTANTINI, EDUARDO
COLLECTOR
b Argentina, 1947. *Study:* Universidad Catolica Argentina, grad, 1971. *Pos:* vice pres BBVA Banco Frances, 1991-1993; Founder & pres, Consult, Buenos Aires, currently; founder, Eduardo F Costantini Found, Buenos Aires, 1995-, MALBA (Museo de Arte Latinoamericano de Buenos Aires), Argentina, 2001-, Synergos Global Philanthropist Cir, NY. *Awards:* Named one of Top 200 Collectors, ARTnews mag, 2004-13. *Mem:* Mus Modern Art, NY (chmns coun). *Interests:* kite surfing. *Collection:* Modern and contemporary Latin American art. *Mailing Add:* Malba Collection Constantini Avda Figueroa Alcorta 3415 Buenos Aires C1425CLA Argentina

COSTANZA, JOHN JOSEPH
SCULPTOR, CERAMIST
b New York, NY, June 24, 1924. *Study:* Tyler Sch Fine Arts, Temple Univ, BFA, 49; Univ Pa, cert, 43. *Work:* Philadelphia Coll Performing Arts; Harcum Jr Col, Bryn Mawr, Pa. *Comn:* Ceramic murals, University City High Sch, Philadelphia Sch District, Pa; Paragon Industry, West Orange, NJ, Ampacet Corp, Mt Vernon, NY; Monsanto Corp, Montvale, NJ; Rauch, Duban & Venturi, Architects & Shubert Theatre, Philadelphia. *Exhib:* Nat Ceramic Competition, Everson Mus Art, Syracuse, NY, 58, 60, 62 & 64; NY World's Fair Invitational, 64-65; Smithsonian Drawing Nat, Washington, & traveling, 64-67; Painting, Drawing & Sculpture Invitational, Univ Del, Newark, 66-68; Philadelphia Regional Art Show, Philadelphia Mus Art, 67; Ceramics Invitational, Philadelphia Civic Ctr Mus, 67, 70 & 73; Ceramics Invitational, Mus Contemp Crafts, NY, 68, 75 & 77. *Pos:* Designer, Potters of Wall St, New York, 50-51. *Teaching:* Art, Devereux Sch, Devon, Pa, 51-53 & Sayre Jr High Sch, Philadelphia, 53-57; teacher ceramics, West Chester High Sch, Pa, 57-63; prof ceramics, Moore Col Art, Philadelphia, 63-73. *Awards:* Purchase Award, Univ Del Art Show, 65; Purchase Prize, Temple Univ Alumni Show, 68; First Prize, Sculpture, William Penn Mem Mus, Harrisburg, Pa, 71. *Bibliog:* Jack Bookbinder (dir), Black History, The Making of a Mural (film), Philadelphia Sch District, 75; Dr Burton Wasserman (auth), Exploring the Visual Art, Davis Publ, 76; Louis G Redstone (auth), Public Art-New Directions, McGraw Hill, 80. *Mem:* Artists Equity Asn; Am Craftsman Coun. *Media:* Clay. *Publ:* Ed, Gerry Williams's Nine Philadelphia Potters, Daniel Clark Found, 73. *Dealer:* Carol Schwartz Art Gallery Chestnut Hill & Bethlehem Pike Philadelphia PA 19118. *Mailing Add:* 737 Polo Rd Bryn Mawr PA 19010-3825

COSTIGAN, CONSTANCE FRANCES
PAINTER, EDUCATOR
b NJ, July 3, 1935. *Study:* Boston Mus Sch Fine Arts; Simmons Col, BA; Am Univ, MA; Univ Va; Univ Calif, Berkeley. *Work:* Phillips Collection, Washington; Hirshhorn Mus, Washington; Univ Iowa Mus; Dimock Gallery, George Wash Univ; also pvt collections in US, Eng, Can, Europe & India. *Exhib:* 19th Area Exhib, Corcoran Gallery Art, 74; solo show, Phillips Collection, Washington, 77; Barbara Fiedler Gallery, Washington, 79 & 82; 25 Washington Artists, Realism & Representation, Foundry Gallery, Washington, 80; Del Mus Art, Wilmington, 80; Surface/Structure: Fiber Innovations, Arlington Arts Ctr, Va, 82; 10 Yrs, A Retrospective, Northern Va Community Col, 83; Franz Bader Gallery, Washington, 85 & 90; Hampshire Coll Gallery, Amherst, Mass, 96; Soho 20 Gallery, NY, 97; Corkran Gallery, Rehoboth Art League, Del, 98; From The States, Nat Mus Women Arts, Washington, DC, 98; Visual Arts Gallery, Habitat Center, New Delhi, India, 2003; Lavinia Ctr, Milton, Del, 2003; Hodson Gallery, Hood Col, Frederick, Md, 2005; Del Center Contemp Art, Wilmington, Del, 2006; Biggs Mus, Dover, Del, 2007; Gallery 50, Rehoboth, Dela, 2009; Del by Hand Masters, Del Mus Art, Wilmington, Del, 2009-2010; Regional Juried Biennal, Rehoboth Art League, Del, 2010, 2012; Constance Costigan, The Presence of the Unseen, Venture Gallery, Del, 2011; Sacred Spaces, Gallery 50, 2012; Art is Healing, Rehoboth Art League, 2013; This Land, Salisbury Univ, MD, 2013; Landscapes of the Mind, Biggs Mus Am Art, Dover, Del, 2014. *Collection Arranged:* Elements of Art: Line (auth, catalog), Arlington Arts Ctr, Va, 80; Hirshhorn Mus & Sculpture Garden; Phillips Collection; Dimock Gallery, George Washington Univ, Washington, DC; Univ Iowa Mus, Iowa City; private Coll US, Can, Gt Brit, Europe, India. *Pos:* Exhib designer, Smithsonian Inst, 57-59, mus serv, 61-70. *Teaching:* Instr studio art & crafts, Arlington Co Pub Sch, 70-76; instr drawing, design & painting, Smithsonian Inst, Washington, 70-76; prof, George Wash Univ, 1976-2002, emerita prof fine arts, 2003-; distinguished vis prof, Am Univ in Cairo, Egypt, 80-81; vis prof, drawing, Haystack, Mt Sch Crafts, Deer Isle, Me, 90. *Awards:* GSAS Facilitating Fund, George Wash Univ, Washington, 90; and many others. *Bibliog:* Lenore Miller (auth), Constance Costigan, Phillips Collection, Washington, 77; Jean Lawlor Cohen (auth), Constance Costigan: Spirit Fields: Paintings and Pastels, Franz Bader Gallery, Washington, 90. *Mem:* Fel Royal Soc Arts; Fel MacDowell Colony; Fel Ossabow Island Project; Master, Del by Hand. *Media:* all medias. *Specialty:* fine arts. *Interests:* music, art history, cooking, gardening. *Publ:* Elements of Art: Line, Arlington Arts Ctr, Arlington, Va, 80. *Dealer:* Gallery 50 Rehoboth DE. *Mailing Add:* 210 NE Market St Lewes DE 19958

COTE, ALAN
PAINTER
b Windham, Conn, 1937. *Study:* Boston Sch Mus Fine Arts, MA, 60. *Work:* Solomon R Guggenheim Mus, Mus Mod Art, Whitney Mus Am Art, Paine Webber Group Inc, New York; J Patrick Lannan Found, Palm Beach, Fla; Suermondt Mus, Collection Ludwig, Aachen, Ger; Rutgers Mus Art, New Brunswick, NJ; Mus Fine Arts, Phoenix; Mus Contemp Art, Miami. *Exhib:* Biennial, Corcoran Gallery Art, Washington, DC, 75; American Drawing in Black and White, Brooklyn Mus, New York, 80; Three Am Painters, Axiom Gallery, Melbourne, Australia, 81; Recent Acquisitions: Paintings and Sculpture, Mus Mod Art, New York, 83; Big Abstract Drawings, Pratt Inst Gallery, New York, 86; Mark d'Montbello Fine Art Gallery, New York, 97; Recent Paintings, Marist Coll (illustr catalog), New York, 2002. *Teaching:* Prof emer, art-painting, Bard Coll, Hudson, NY, 70-2003; retired. *Awards:* Fel, Mus Fine Arts, Boston, 61-64; Guggenheim Award, 84; Painting Award, Nat Endowment Arts, 89. *Media:* Acrylic, Oil

COTHREN, MICHAEL WATT
EDUCATOR
b Nashville, Ark, Apr 9, 1951. *Study:* Vanderbilt Univ, BA, 73; Columbia Univ, MA, 74, PhD, 80. *Pos:* Consult cur medieval stained glass, Glencairn Mus, Bryn Athyn, Pa. *Teaching:* Prof art hist, Swarthmore Col, 78-. *Mem:* Int Ctr Medieval Art; Medieval Acad Am; Soc Francaise d'Archeologie; Corpus Vitrearum USA. *Res:* Gothic art and architecture, especially stained glass. *Publ:* Auth, The Iconography of Theophilus Windows in the First Half of the Thirteenth Century, Speculum 59, 84; The Choir Windows of Agnieres (Somme) and a Regional Style of Gothic Glass Painting, J Glass Studies 28, 86; The Twelfth-Century Crusading Window of the Abbey of Saint- Denis: Praeteritorum enim Recordatio Futurorum est Exhibitio, with Elizabeth A R Brown, Journal of the Warburg and Courtauld Institutes 49, 86; The Seven Sleepers and the Seven Kneelers: Prolegomena to a Study of the 'Belles Verrieres of Rouen Cathedral, Gesta 25, 86. *Mailing Add:* Swarthmore Col Dept Art Swarthmore PA 19081

COTNER, TERESA
EDUCATOR
Study: Calif State Univ, Sonoma, BA, 1986; Calif State Univ, Los Angeles, MA (art history), 1995; Stanford Univ, PhD (art educ), 2000. *Pos:* chair, prof, Dept Art and Art History, Calif State Univ, Chico, currently. *Teaching:* Tchr, Calif State Univ, San Bernardino, formerly. *Mailing Add:* California State University Department of Art and Art History Ayres Hall, Room 107 Chico CA 95929

COTTER, HOLLAND
CRITIC, HISTORIAN
b Conn, 1947. *Study:* Harvard Coll, AB, 70; CUNY, MA (Am Modernism); Columbia Univ, M Phil, 92. *Pos:* Ed, NY Arts J, 1976-1980; contrib ed, Art in Am; ed assoc, Art News; freelance writer, NY Times, 1992-1997, art critic, 1998-. *Awards:* Pulitzer Prize for Critisicm, 2009; Disting Lifetime Achievement award for Writing on Art, Coll Art Asn, 2010. *Mem:* Int Asn Art Critics (bd dirs). *Publ:* NY Times; Art in America; Art News; Arts Mag; Flash Art. *Mailing Add:* 750 Kappock St Apt 1005 Bronx NY 10463-4518

COTTER, JAMES EDWARD
SCULPTOR, DESIGNER
b Corning, Iowa, Mar 13, 1944. *Study:* Wayne State Col, BFA, 67; Univ Colo, 68; Univ Wyo, MA, 69. *Work:* Nat Broadcasting Corp, NY; Wayne State Col, Wayne, Nebr; Blount Found, Montgomery, Ala; McDonald's Corp, Oak Brook, Ill; Mr & Mrs Gerald Ford, Vail, Colo. *Exhib:* Midwest Biennial, Joslyn Art Mus, Omaha, Nebr, 64; Denver Art Mus, Denver, Colo, 69, 79 & 86; Artists Working in Metal, Sheldon Mus, Lincoln, Nebr, 76; Nat Ornamental Metal Mus, Memphis, Tenn, 79; Copper 2, Mus Art, Tucson, Ariz, 80; solo exhib, Nat Ornamental Metal Mus, Memphis, Tenn, 80; The Great Am Cowboy, traveling exhib, Libr Cong, 83-84. *Pos:* Mem, Design Rev Bd Comt, Town of Vail, Colo, 74; mem adv bd, Colo Mountain Col, Vail, Colo, 74-80; adminr, Summer Vail Workshops Symp, Vail, Colo, 75-76. *Teaching:* Instr metalsmithing, Colo Mountain Col, Vail, Colo, 71-76; instr jewelry, Pendland Sch, Pendland, NC, 78. *Bibliog:* Murray Bovin (auth), Jewelry Making, 67; Lee & Jay Newman, Electroplating & Electroforming, Crown Publ. *Mem:* Soc N Am Goldsmiths Conf. *Media:* Metal & Stone; Mixed Media. *Dealer:* J Cotter Gallery 234 Wall St Vail Co 81657. *Mailing Add:* PO Box 385 234 E Wall St Vail CO 81657

COTTINGHAM, LAURA JOSEPHINE
CRITIC, WRITER
b Alexandria, Ky, Feb 4, 1959. *Study:* Univ Chicago, BS, 81; Whitney Mus Independent Study Program. *Pos:* Managing ed, Art & Auction, 86-89; contrib ed, Contemporanea, Venice, Italy, currently; adv bd NY, Balcon, Madrid, Spain, currently. *Res:* Contemp art, Feminism. *Publ:* Auth, The Feminist De-Mystique, Flash Art, 89; Why Second Wave Feminism Failed, Silent Baroque, 89; Thoughts Are Things: What is a Woman?, Contemporanea, 90; The Prison House of Language, Contemporanea, 90; Critical Poetics, Contemporanea, 90. *Mailing Add:* 172 E Fourth St No 8H New York NY 10009-7312

COTTINGHAM, ROBERT
PAINTER, PRINTMAKER
b Brooklyn, NY, Sept 26, 1935. *Study:* Pratt Inst, New York, 1959-63, AA, 1962. *Work:* Guggenheim Mus Art; Whitney Mus Am Art; Metrop Mus Art; Mus Mod Art, NY; Art Inst Chicago; Philadelphia Mus Art; Baltimore Mus Art; Birmingham Mus Art, Ala; Butler Inst Am Art, Youngstown, Ohio; Fogg Art Mus, Harvard Univ, Cambridge, Mass; Honolulu Acad Arts; Hunter Mus Art, Chattanooga, Tenn; Libr Cong, Washington; Milwaukee Art Mus; St Louis Art Mus, Mo; Tate Gallery, London; Utah Mus Fine Arts, Univ Utah, Salt Lake City; Va Mus Fine Arts; Conn Artists Collection; Everson Mus Art, Syracuse, NY; Mus Fine Arts, Houston, Tex; Reagan nat Airport, Arlington Co, Va. *Comn:* Permanent Pub Installation of 12 enamel panels depicting Am Railroad Imagery, Union Station, Hartford, Conn. *Exhib:* Solo exhibs include Brenda Kroos Gallery, Cleveland, Ohio, 1992, Butler Inst Am Art, Youngstown, Ohio, 1992, Rahr-West Art Mus, Maritowoc, Wis, 1990, Lyman Allyn Art Mus, New London, Conn, 1991, Harcourts Contemp, San Francisco, Calif, 1991, Nat Mus Am Art, Smithsonian Inst, Washington, DC, 1998-99, Still Lifes, Forum Gallery, NY, 2000, New Still Lifes, 2004, Robert Cottingham: paintings, gouaches, drawings, prints Cline Fine Art, Santa Fe, NMex, 2000, Barbara Krakow Gallery, Boston, 2005, Galerie Patrice Trigano, Paris, 2005; group exhibs include Recent Acquisitions, Whitney Mus Am Art & Hirshhorn Mus & Sculpture Garden, 1977; Takada Gallery, San Francisco, 1994; Triton Mus, Santa Clara, Calif, 1994; Struve Gallery, Chicago, 1994; Robert Cottingham, An Am Alphabet, Montgomery Mus Fine Art, Ala, 1996; Realism Knows No Bounds, Van de Griff Gallery, Santa Fe, NMex, 1998; It's Still Life, Forum Gallery, NY, 98; Collector's Show, Art Art Ctr, Little Rock, 1998; Twentieth Century Am Drawings, Ark Art Cen, 1999; Nat Acad Design, NY, 1999; A Century Am Dream, The Chunichi Shimbun, Naka-ku Nagoya, Japan, 2000; Nat Acad Design: 176th Ann Exhib, New York City, 2001; Carol Craven Gallery, West Tisbury, Mass, 2002. *Collection Arranged:* Abilene Christian Univ, Tex; Ackland Art Mus, Univ NC, Chapel Hill; Amarillo Mus Art, Tex; Ark Arts Cen, Little Rock; Art Inst Chicago, Ill; Baltimore Mus Art, Md; Birmingham, Mus Art, Ala; Cleveland Mus Art, Ohio; Del Art Mus, Wilmington; Denver Art Mus, Colo; Long Beach Mus Art, Calif; Milwaukee Mus Art, Wis; Mus Am Art, Smithsonian Inst, Washington, DC; RI Sch Design, Providence; St Louis Art Mus, Mo; Tampa Mus Art, Fla; Univ Iowa Mus Art, Iowa City; Univ Ky Art Mus, Lexington; Univ Mich Mus Art, Ann Arbor; Utah Mus Fine Arts, Univ Utah, Salt Lake City; others; A Fine Line, Drwings by Nat Acad, Nat Acad Design, New York, 2003-2004; Here's The Thing: The Single Object Still Life, Katonah Mus Art, NY, 2008. *Pos:* Art dir, Young & Rubicam Advert, NY, 1959-64 & Los Angeles, 1964-68. *Teaching:* instr, Art Ctr Col Design, Los Angeles, 1969-70, Nat Acad Design, 1991; artist-in-residence, Wesleyan Univ, Middletown, Conn, 1987-92, Nat Acad Design, NY, 1991, Marie Walsh Sharpe Art Found, Colorado Spring, Colo, 1994. *Awards:* Nat Endowment Arts Grant, 74-75; Walter Gropius Fel, Huntington Mus Art, WVa, 1992; MacDowll Colony Residency, 1993-94; Chubb Life Am Fel, 1994. *Bibliog:* Roberta Smith (auth), Hudson Valley Conversations, NY Times, 7/18/97; JoAnn Lewis (auth), Man of letters: Robert Cottingham turned America's signs into symbols, Washington Post, 10/24/98; Ann Landi (auth), Who hails from Hopper, ARTnews, 4/98. *Mem:* Nat Acad (assoc, 1990, acad, 1994, coun). *Media:* Watercolor. *Dealer:* Forum Gallery 730 5th Ave New York NY 10151. *Mailing Add:* PO Box 604 Newtown CT 06470-0604

COTTON, WILL
PAINTER
b Melrose, Mass, 1965. *Study:* Cooper Union, NY City, BFA, 1987; NY Acad Art, NY City, 1988. *Exhib:* Solo exhibs, Silverstein Gallery, 1995-1996, 1998, Devil's Fudge Falls, I-20 Gallery, NY City, 1999, Mary Boone Gallery, NY City, 2000-2002, 2004, Jablonka Galerie, Koln, Germany, 2001, Mario Diacono Gallery, Boston, 2003, Galerie Daniel Tempion, 2003, Kunsthalle Bielefeld, Germany, 2004, Michael Kohn Gallery, Los Angeles, 2005; Group exhibs, A Room With A View, Sixth @ Prince Fine Art, NY, 1999; Tate, NY City, 1999; The Darker Side of Playland: Childhood Imagery from the Logan Collection, San Francisco Mus Art, 2000; Emotional Rescue: The Contemp Art Project Coalition, Ctr Contemp Art, Seattle, 2000; Contemp Art Project, Seattle Art Mus, 2002; Sweet Tooth, Copia, Am Ctr for Wine Food & The Arts, Napa, Calif, 2003; Giverny, Salon 94, NY City, 2003; La Grande Bouffe - The Big Eat in Art, Kunsthalle Bielefeld, Ger, 2004. *Media:* Oil, Linen. *Dealer:* Michael Kohn Gallery 8071 Beverley Blvd CA 90048; Michael Steinberg Fine Art 526 W 26th St NY 10001; Galerie Daniel Templon 30 rue Beaubourg France 75003. *Mailing Add:* c/o Mary Boone Gallery 745 Fifth Ave New York NY 10151

COTTONE-KOLTHOFF, CAROL
PAINTER, ILLUSTRATOR
b San Pedro, Calif, May 24, 1954. *Study:* Calif State Univ, Long Beach, BFA, 77, MFA, 80; Loyola Marymount Univ, Los Angeles, educ credential, 80. *Comn:* Tunnels (mural), Marymount Col, Palos Verdes, Calif, 80; Aviary-Hummingbirds, San Diego Zoo, 93. *Exhib:* Juried Exhib, Butler Inst Am Art, Youngstown, Ohio, 81; Nat Women's Caucus for the Arts, Nat World Exhib, New Orleans, 85; Twelve and Under Invitational, Golden West Col, Huntington Beach, Calif, 90; Wildlife 92, San Bernardino Mus, Calif, 92; 6th Ann Animals in Art, State Univ, Baton Rouge, 93; Calif State Expos, Del Mar, 93; and others. *Teaching:* Lectr art-draw/paint, Calif State Univ, Long Beach, 81-83; instr art-draw/paint, Monterey Pennisula Col, 87-89; instr art-design, Southwestern Col, Chula Vista, 91-. *Awards:* Award, Western Fedn Watercolors Soc Exhib, 90; First Place Show Award, City of Brea, Calif, 91; Del Mar Award, City of Del Mar, Calif, 93. *Bibliog:* Carol Katchen (auth), The natural beauty of birds, Artist's Mag, 10/94. *Publ:* Contribr, Splash III, North Light Publ, 94. *Mailing Add:* 5085 Argonne Ct San Diego CA 92117

COTTRELL, MARSHA
PRINTMAKER
b Philadelphia, 1964. *Study:* Tyler Sch Art, BFA, 1988; Univ NC, Chapel Hill, MFA, 1990. *Work:* Mus Mod Art, New York; San Francisco Mus Mod Art. *Exhib:* Solo exhibs include Derek Eller Gallery, New York, 1998, Revolution Gallery, Detroit, 2000, Henry Urbach Archit, 2002, G-Module, Paris, 2003; group exhibs include Multiples, Pierogi 2000, Brooklyn, NY, 1996; Summer Selections, Drawing Ctr, New York, 1996, 25th Anniversary Benefit Selections Exhib, 2002; Current Undercurrent: Working in Brooklyn, Brooklyn Mus Art, 1997, Digital Printmaking Now, 2001; Art on Paper 2000, Weatherspoon Gallery, Univ NC, Greensboro, 2000; Rendered, Sarah Meltzer Gallery, New York, 2003; The Drawn Page, Aldrich Mus Contemp Art, Conn, 2003; Architecture by Numbers, Whitney Mus Am Art at Altria, New York, 2004; Airborne, Henry Urbach Archit, New York, 2004; Happy Birthday to Me, G-Module, Paris, 2005, Double-Edged Abstraction, 2007; NextNext Visual Art, Brooklyn Acad Music, 2005. *Awards:* MacDowell Colony Grant, 1994, 1996, 1999 & 2002; Marie Walsh Sharpe Art Found Grant, 1999; NY Found Arts Grant, 1999 & 2003; John Simon Guggenheim Mem Found Fel, 2001; Lower East Side Printshop Special Eds Fel, 2003; Harvestworks Digital Media Educ Scholar, 2004; Pollock-Krasner Found Grant, 2007. *Mailing Add:* 295 Washington Ave Apt 6E Brooklyn NY 11205

COUCH, ROBERT
PAINTER, ARCHITECT
b Grenada, Mississippi, Oct 15, 1944. *Study:* Mass Inst Tech, MA Arch, 72; Univ Pa, Studio of Louis Kahn, MA Arch, 73; Pa Acad Fine Arts. *Exhib:* 61st Anniv Exhib, Philadelphia/Tri State Artists Equity, Philip and Muriel Berman Mus Fine Art, Ursinus Coll, Collegeville, Pa, 2009; Feast the Eyes, Wayne Art Center, Pa, 2010; Works in Black and White, Plastic Club, Philadelphia, Pa, 2010; 80th Ann, Hudson Valley Art Asn Inc, Lyme Art Asn Gallery, Old Lyme, Conn, 2011; 83rd Grand Nat, Am Artists Prof League, Salmagundi Club, NY, 2011; Cape Cod Art Asn, Barnstable, Mass, 2011; Outside-Inside, GoggleWorks Center for the Arts, Reading, Pa, 2011; Salmagundi Club, NY, 2011; Art of the State Pa 2011, State Mus Pa, Harrisburg, Pa, 2011. *Pos:* Am Inst Architects, Wash DC, 81-; Philadelphia Sketch Club, Pa, 2009-. *Teaching:* adj assoc prof architecture, Temple Univ, Philadelphia, Pa, 81-82; guest critic, Coll Architecture, Temple Univ, Philadelphia, Pa, 83-88; guest critic, Moore Coll Art and Design, Philadelphia, PA, 2009-2011. *Awards:* Alfred F. Lofgren Prize for Landscape Painting, Contemp Voices, Woodmere Art Mus, Philadelphia, Pa, 2010; Best Still Life Award, Philadelphia Sketch Club, Philadelphia, Pa, 2010; Purchase Award & Hon Mention, Berks Art Alliance, GoggleWorks Center for the Arts, Reading, Pa, 2010; Hon Design Judge, Easter Chapter, Am Soc Interior Designers, Ann Design Awards, 2010, 2011; Purchase Award, Berks Art Alliance, Reading Public Mus, Pa, 2011; Lucy Glick Award, Fel Pa Acad Fine Arts, Artists House Gallery, Philadelphia, Pa, 2011; Marquis Who's Who in American Art Reference Award in Oils/Acrylics, Audubon Artists, New York, 2011. *Mem:* Philadelphia Sketch Club; Am Inst Architects. *Media:* Oil, Charcoal, Graphite. *Mailing Add:* Studio 203 915 Spring Garden St Philadelphia PA 19123

COUGHLIN, JACK
PRINTMAKER, SCULPTOR
b Greenwich, Conn, Feb 19, 1932. *Study:* Art Students League; RI Sch Design, BFA, 54, MS, 61. *Work:* Metrop Mus Art & Mus Mod Art, NY; Norfolk Mus Arts & Sci, Va; Staedelsches Kunst Inst, Frankfort, Ger; Nat Collection Fine Arts, Washington; Mus Mod Art, NY; Worcester Art Mus, Mass; Univ Ulster, Northern Ireland; and several others. *Comn:* Ed original prints, Asn Am Artists, 62-79, Int Graphic Arts Soc, 66 & 68, Silvermine Guild Artists, New Canaan, Conn, 67, Graphic Studio, Dublin, Ireland, 71 & Franklin Mint, Pa, 77, Springfield Mus, 83; ongoing drawings for The New Republic. *Exhib:* Nat Inst Arts & Lett, 1970; Soc Am Graphic Arts, NY, 1971-92; Nat Acad Design Ann Exhib, 1974-2007; 4th Int Graphic Biennial, WGer, 1976; 3rd Norwegian Int Print Biennale, Norway, 1976; Fifth Int Print Exhib, Barcelona, Spain, 1985, 1988. *Pos:* Academican, Nat Acad Design, 72-2007. *Teaching:* Prof drawing & printmaking, Univ Mass, Amherst, 60-94, emer prof, 94-. *Awards:* Nat Exhib Award for etching, Soc Am Graphic Artists, 77 & 81; Nat Exhib Awards for drawing & printing, Nat Acad Design, 80, 82 & 83, 2005, 2007; NDak Am Drawing Biennial, 90. *Bibliog:* Robin Skelton (auth), Imagination of Jack Coughlin, 70, Jack Coughlin: Irish portraits, 72 & Jack Coughlin: A Perspective View, 80, Malahat Rev, Univ Victoria, BC; article, Am Artist Mag, 6/86. *Mem:* Nat Acad Design (assoc, 72, acad, 90); Soc Am Graphic Artists; Boston Printmakers. *Media:* Lithography, Woodcut, Metal, Cast, Etching. *Interests:* Playing blues harmonica. *Publ:* Illusr, Mnemosyne Lay in Dust, 66 & Synge-Petrarch, 71, Dolmen Press, Dublin, Ireland; Grotesques, 20 Etchings by Jack Coughlin, Aquarius Press, 70; 13 Irish Writers, Etchings, Godine Press, 73; Impressions of Bohemia, Pac Rim Galleries, 86; auth, A Brush with the Blues, 1997; Skyfish, 2G Drawings, 2011; With Dogs, HO Drawings, 2013. *Dealer:* Golden Cod Galleries E Commercial St Wellfleet MA 02667; Michaelson Gallery 132 Main St Northampton MA 01060. *Mailing Add:* N Leverett Rd Montague MA 01351

COULTER, LANE
SILVERSMITH, HISTORIAN
b Chelsea, Mass, Jan 16, 1944. *Study:* Univ Ill, BFA, 69; Univ Okla, MFA, 74. *Work:* Wustum Mus, Racine, Wis; Absolut Corp, New York City. *Comn:* MACE, Tex A&M Univ, College Station, 90; Absolut, Absolut Vodka, New York City, 90; Chalice, St Marks Church, Norman, Okla, 84. *Exhib:* Absolut Southwest, Mus Am Folk Art, New York City, 90; Double Vision 3, Wustum Mus, Racine, Wis, 95; Contemp Am Pewter, Nat Ornamental Metal Mus, Memphis, Tenn, 95; NMex Jewelers, Millicent Rogers Mus, Taos, NMex, 98; Souvenir NY, Aaron Faber Gallery, New York City, 92; Silver New Forms III, Fortunoff Corp, New York City, 92. *Collection Arranged:* Am Indian Jewelry, Nat Ornamental Metal Mus, 94; Hojalateria, Mus Internat Folk Art, 91. *Pos:* co-founder Summer Vail Metal Symposium, Colo, 75-85. *Teaching:* instr, Tex A&M, 69-72; assoc prof jewelry design, Univ Okla, Norman, 72-83; vis prof jewelry, Univ Tex, Austin, 86, Ariz State Univ, 87; prof metal work, Inst Am Indian Art, Santa Fe, NMex, 89-2001. *Awards:* Southwest Book award, Border-Regional Librs, 1990. *Mem:* Soc North Am Goldsmiths; Antique Tribal Art Dealers Asn. *Media:* Metal, Silver, Pewter. *Res:* Navajo Saddle Blankets; New Mexican Furniture, 19th Century; New Mexican tinwork. *Publ:* auth, Metalwork of Ann Orr, Ga Mus Art, 94; coauth, American Indian Jewelry, Dict World Art, 96; auth, American expressions, Am Craft, 97; auth, New Mexican Tinwork, Antiques Mag, 99; ed, Navajo Saddle Blankets, 2002. *Dealer:* Jett Gallery Old Santa Fe Mail Sante Fe NM 87501. *Mailing Add:* 2120 Conejo Santa Fe NM 87505

COUPE, JAMES
DIGITAL ARTIST
Study: Franklin & Marshall Coll, N Am Exchange Prog, Lancaster, Pa, 97; Univ Edinburgh, MA (fine art), 99; Univ Salford, Manchester, MA (creative technol), 2000; Univ Wash, Seattle, PhD (digital art & experimental media), 2009. *Comn:* Autonomous call ctr, Virtual Storey Project, Folly Gallery, Lancaster, 2004; telematic AI network, Mount Pleasant Media Workshop, Southampton, 2004, Artsway, Sway, 2004, Aspex, Portsmouth, 2004, Quay Arts, Isle of Wight, 2005, Salisbury Arts, Salisbury, 2005, Animation Station, Banbury, 2005, Living Archive, Milton Keynes, 2005, New Greeham Arts, Newbury, 2005 & Lighthouse, Poole, 2005. *Exhib:* Royal Scottish Acad, Edinburgh, Scotland, 99; Edinburgh Castle, 99; IDEA, Manchester, 2000; Northern Gallery Contemp Art, Sunderland 2001; Sunderland Mus, 2001; Camden Arts Ctr, London, 2001; Artsadmin, London, 2002; FACT, Liverpool, 2002; Custard Factory, Birmingham, 2003; Space Studios, London, 2003; Autonomous call ctr, Virtual Storey Project, Folly Gallery, Lancaster, 2004; telematic AI network, Mount Pleasant Media Workshop, Southampton, 2004, Artsway, Sway, 2004, Aspex, Portsmouth, 2004, Quay Arts, Isle of Wight, 2005, Salisbury Arts, Salisbury, 2005, Animation Station, Banbury, 2005, Living Archive, Milton Keynes, 2005, New Greeham Arts, Newbury, 2005 & Lighthouse, Poole, 2005; The Difference Engine, Lee Ctr for the Arts, Seattle, 2006; The Junction, Cambridge, 2007; 911 Media Ctr, Seattle, 2008. *Teaching:* Lectr digital art, London Coll Music & Media, Thames Valley Univ, London, 2000; sr lectr art & media & principal investigator, London South Bank Univ, London, 2003; lectr & rsch assoc, Ctr for Digital Arts & Experimental Media, Univ Wash, Seattle, 2004-2007, asst prof digital art & experimental media, 2007-. *Awards:* Res & Develop Grants, Thames Valley Univ, London, 2002-2003; Innovation Award, Arts & Humanities Res Bd, 2003; Fel in Cross-Disciplinary & Emerging Forms, Artist Trust, 2008; Grant for Emergin Fields, Creative Capital Found, 2009. *Bibliog:* Samson Spainer (auth), The Triumph of the Unexpected, Financial Times, 8/2005; Carrie Scott (auth), The Art of the Stars, The Stranger, 12/2005; Rachel Hazelwood (auth), Putting the Art in AlgoRiThm, Aesthetica, No 19, 10/2007; Francis DeVuono (auth), What are you F#&%ing Looking At?, ArtWeek, 12/2008. *Mailing Add:* DXARTS Univ Washington Box 353414 Seattle WA 98195-3414

COUPER, CHARLES ALEXANDER
PAINTER, INSTRUCTOR
b Portsmouth, NH, Feb 19, 1924. *Study:* Vesper George Sch Art, Boston, cert; Cape Sch Art, Provincetown, Mass, with Henry Hensche; Ernest Lee Major Studio, Boston. *Work:* Elizabeth T Greenshields Mus, Montreal; Attleboro Mus, Mass; Heritage Mus, Provincetown, Mass; Biblioteca Publica Collection San Migual de Allende, Mex; Smithsonian Inst; Cape Mus Fine Art, Mass; Beachcombers Cabinet Permanent Collection, Cape Mus Fine Art, Dennis, Mass. *Comn:* Pastel portrait, Judge Phillip, Wolaver QC, NS, Can, 80. *Exhib:* Solo exhibs, Cape Cod Art Asn, 73, Guild Boston Artists, 73, Soratoga Gallery-Bridgetown, NS, 92, STFX Univ Art Gallery, Antigonish, NS, 2004, Harris House Gallery, August 2009, Admiral Digby Mus, Nova Scotia, 2011; Allied Artists Am, NY, 74; Grande Prix Int, Cannes, France, 74; Deauville Int, France, 75. *Pos:* Mem, Provincetown Art Comn, Mass, 78-79. *Teaching:* Instr, life drawing & painting, Vesper George Sch Art, 55-; instr, Attleboro Mus, Mass; instr, Swain Sch Design, New Bedford, Mass, 65-68; instr, Aug Painting Workshops, Bear River, NS; instr, Bearcroft Studio, Mass. *Awards:* Award of Distinction, Pastel Soc Can, 92 & First Jury Award, 94, 2000; Gloria Layton Mem Award, Allied Artists Am, NY; Elizabeth T Greenshields Found Grant, Montreal; Medal of Distinction, 11th Grand Prix Int, Cannes, France; First Jury Awards, Cape Cod Art Asn, Hyannis, Mass; first jury award, Pastel Soc Canada, 2000. *Bibliog:* Critical rev in La Rev Mod, Paris, 69; The Best of Canadian Pastels, Art Instruction Assocs, Sarasota, Fla; Robin Metcalife (auth of text) Art and Craft of Nova Scotia. *Mem:* Pastel Soc Can; Artist de Peintre de La Cote d'Azur; Visual Arts NS; Provincetown Art Asn & Mus; Cape Cod Mus Art, Dennis, Mass. *Media:* Oil, Pastel. *Interests:* Archit, gardening, carpentry. *Publ:* Contribr to many Canadian art publications; An Artists Life Journey, 2013. *Dealer:* Flight of Fancy Gallery Bear River NS; Art Sales & Rental Gallery Halifax NS; Annapolis Art Gallery Ltd Wolfville NS; Egeli Gallery Provincetown Ma. *Mailing Add:* 735 Riverview Rd 7 Bear River NS B0S 1B0 Canada

COUPER, JAMES M
PAINTER, EDUCATOR
b Atlanta, Ga, Nov 21, 1937. *Study:* Atlanta Art Inst; Ga State Univ; Fla State Univ. *Work:* Ga Dept Natural Resources; John & Mable Ringling Mus, Sarasota, Fla; Miami Met Mus & Art Ctr, Coral Gables, Fla; Mus of Art, Ft Lauderdale, Fla; Art in Pub Bldgs, State of Fla; Art in Pub Places, Miami Dade Co, Fla; The Blount Collection, Montgomery, Ala; Frost Art Mus, Miami, Fla; Emory Univ, Atlanta, Georgia; Univ Fla; Miami Internat Airport. *Comn:* Mural, 20th Century Fox, 68; Two Large Oil Paintings, Miami Internat Airport, 2012. *Exhib:* Fla Int Univ, Miami, Fla, 93; Barbara Gillman Gallery, Miami, 93; Bellaire Art Ctr, Fla, 94; Ormond Beach Mem Mus, Fla, 96; Metro-Dade Cult Resource Ctr, 96; plus many others. *Collection Arranged:* Art of the Asian Mountains, 69; The Artist & The Sea, 69; Art of Italy, 69; Up & Out, 69-70. *Pos:* Asst to dir, Miami Art Ctr, 67-70; founding dir art mus, Patricia and Phillip Frost Mus, Fla Int Univ, 77-80. *Teaching:* Instr painting, Miami-Dade Jr Col, 64-68; instr painting, Miami Art Ctr, 65-72; from instr to prof painting, Fla Int Univ, 72-2005, chmn art dept, 77-78, MFA prog founder, dir, 98-2000. *Awards:* Fla Individual Artist Grant, 83 & 90; Yaddo Fel, 87; Hambidge Ctr Fel, 90, 91, 94 & 2001. *Bibliog:* Reviews, Art News, 87, Miami Herald, 86-2003 & St Petersburg Times, 96. *Media:* Oil. *Res:* Continuing use of landscape imagery in paintings concerned with ecological concerns, specifically the preservation of wilderness. *Interests:* Traveling. *Publ:* St Petersburg Times, Miami Herald, 1968-; Art News, 1980; Fla Times Union & Jacksonville J, 1982; Miami News, 1983; Am Artist, 1986; Diarrio de las Americas, 1992. *Dealer:* Micahel Murphy Gllery 2722 McDill Ave Tampa FL; Allyn Gallup Contemporary Art 1288 N Palm Ave. *Mailing Add:* 7845 SW 118th St Miami FL 33156

COURTNEY, SUZAN
PAINTER, PRINTMAKER
b Mobile, Ala, Sept 6, 1947. *Study:* Tulane Univ, 68-69; Kingston-Upon-Hull Coll Art, Hull, Eng, dipl art & design, 73; Whitney Mus Independent Study Prog, 74-75; Yale Univ Sch Art, MFA, 77. *Work:* Insurance Co N Am, Ericson Gallery & Davis, Markel and Edwards, NY; Gasperi Gallery, New Orleans; Fine Arts Mus of the South, Mobile, Ala. *Exhib:* Solo exhibs, Univ S Fla, 77, Fine Arts Mus, Mobile, Ala, 87, Gasperi Gallery, New Orleans, La, 89, 2009-2011, & Galerie Gordon Pym & Fils, Paris, 92; Two Decades of Abstraction, traveling nationally, 79; Five New York City Artists, Ericson Gallery, NY, 81; Invitational Exhib, Bristol Art Mus, Eng, 81; Perspectives South, 82 & Invitational, 84, Ericson Gallery, NY; Urban Spirit, City Without Walls, Newark, NJ, 85; New Urban Artists, Int Monetary Fund, Washington, DC, 85-86; Folk-Funk Show, Gasperi Gallery, New Orleans, La; Small Works, Parsons Sch Design, 89; Europa - Am, 360 E-Venti, NY - Rome, Pino Molica Gallery, 92; Miauhaus, NY, 92; Dieu Donne Papermill Inc Group Show; Ala Impact-Contemp Artists with Ala Ties, Mobile & Huntsville, Ala, 95; St Kolumba Exhib, Rapid Transit Gallery, Savannah Coll Art & Design, 98; Radiant Children: Art of the East Village-1980's, 99; Dog Days of Summer, Savage Gallery, Mobile, Ala, 2000-01; Miahaus Gallery, LA, 2001; 9/11 Exhib, Easter Shore Art Asn, 2003; Loft Pioneer Show VI, Pelican Gallery, 2008; From Afar: Documenting Traditions, Witnessing Transitions, Int Ctr Photog, 2008. *Pos:* Visiting artist, Princeton Univ, Rutgers Univ & Spring Hill Col, 84-86, Reading Univ & Slade Sch Art, London, Eng, 86, Parsons Sch Design, 95, Univ South Fla, 1996. *Teaching:* Instr painting & drawing, RI Sch Design, Providence, 79-83 & Univ South Fla, Tampa, currently; adj prof painting & drawing, Southampton Col, NY, 83-84; adj prof color theory, Rutgers Univ, NJ, 85-92; adj prof drawing, Parsons Sch Design, 87-92; adj prof, NY Univ Sch Educ, 2000, Marymount Coll, NJ, 2004. *Awards:* Skowhegan Sch Painting Fel; Susan Whedon Prize Painting, Yale Sch Art, 75; Edward Albee Studio Award, Montauk, NY, 80. *Media:* Oil on Canvas. *Publ:* New York Art Review, 88. *Dealer:* Gasperi Gallery New Orleans LA. *Mailing Add:* 530 Canal St No 3W New York NY 10013

COURTRIGHT, ROBERT
COLLAGE ARTIST, PAINTER
b Sumter, SC, Oct 20, 1926. *Study:* St John's Col, Annapolis, Md; New Sch Social Res, NY, 47-48; Art Students League, 48-52. *Work:* Musee de l'Art Moderne & de l'Art Contemporain, Nice, Franc; Collection de l'Etat, Paris; Metrop Mus Art, NY; Nichido Mus, Casama, Japan; San Francisco Mus Mod Art; Aldrich Mus Contemp Art, Ridgefield, Conn. *Exhib:* Smithsonian Inst, Washington, DC, 56; Mus Mod Art, NY, 57; Carnegie Int, Carnegie Inst, Pittsburgh, Pa, 59; Festival Int de la Peinture, Cagnes-sur-Mer, France, 76; Am & Europe, A Century Mod Masters from Thyssen-Bornemisza Collection, traveled in Australia & NZ, 79-81; C Grimaldis Gallery, Baltimore, 95, Kouros Gallery, NY, 95 & 97, Knocke, LeZout, 96, Galerie Bernard Cats, Brussels, 96 & 97, Galerie Jean Jacques Dutko, 96. *Bibliog:* Calvin Tompkins (auth), Robert Courtright, Andrew Crispo Gallery, NY, 79; Ralph Pomeroy (auth), Light and substance: The collages of Robert Courtright, Arts Mag, 12/79; Jeffrey Robinson (auth), Robert Courtright: Collage-Masks, Andrew Crispo Gallery, NY, 81. *Media:* Papier Mache, Acrylic. *Mailing Add:* 80 Varick St New York NY 10013

COUTURIER, MARION B
DEALER, COLLECTOR
Study: Univ Lausanne, Switz, cert de Francais et Langues; Univ Dijon; Columbia Univ. *Pos:* Owner, Couturier Galerie, 61- & consult, Los Angeles, 85-. *Teaching:* Instr, Broadies, art history extension courses. *Specialty:* Consultant, major pvt, muss & corp collections, impressionists, post impressionists & contemp art, pre-Columbian African tribal art sculpture & graphics. *Interests:* Work with major pvt and mus collections, selecting works from the mod to the contemp. *Collection:* Contemp artists in all media; Latin Am artists for merit & variety of their work; Cuban art all media & photog in Calif branch; Int exhibs incl, Victoria & Albert Mus, London

COUWENBERG, ALEXANDER
PAINTER
b Upland, Calif, 1967. *Study:* Art Ctr Coll Design, Pasadena, Calif, BFA, 1995; Claremont Grad Sch, Calif, MFA, 1997. *Comn:* Apax Partners, Menlo Park, Calif; Bellagio Hotel & Casino, Las Vegas; Hyatt, Capital Hill, Washington; Mandalay Bay Hotel & Casino, Las Vegas; Mandarin Hotel, New York; Metrop Hotel, New York; MGM Grand Hotel & Casino, Las Vegas; Mohegan Sun Casino, Uncasville, Conn; Wadsworth Publishing Company. *Exhib:* Solo exhibs include Ruth Bachofner Gallery, Los Angeles, 1999, 2001, 2002, Peter Blake Gallery, 2006, 2007, Katherine Markel Fine Arts, New York, 2008, William Turner Gallery, 2009; Group exhibs include Recent Paintings, Marcia Wood Gallery, Atlanta, 1997; Black & White, Ruth Bachofner Gallery, Los Angeles, 2003, 20th Anniversary Exhib, 2004; Continental Divide: LA/NYC, Planet Thailand, Brooklyn, 2004; Luster, Gensler, San Francisco, 2004; Inaugural Exhib, Sopa Fine Arts, British Columbia, Canada, 2005; Let There Be Light, Phantom Galleries, Los Angeles, 2007; Off the Grid, William Turner Gallery, 2007; Liquid Light, Mus Design Art & Architecture, Culver City, Calif, 2008. *Awards:* Joan Mitchell Found Grant, 2007

COVE, ROSEMARY
SCULPTOR, PAINTER
b New York, NY, Jan 11, 1936. *Study:* Parsons Sch Design; Master Class, studied with Knox Martin & Helen Beling. *Work:* Weatherspoon, NC; NY Times; Tallix Inc; CIBA Geigy, NY; Conti Commodities; Ingber Gallery. *Exhib:* Ingber Gallery, 73-90; Thompsen Gallery, 90; Lincoln Ctr, 92; Graham Modern, 92; Gremillion Gallery, 94-2000; Rivington Gallery, 98-2000; Gremillion Gallery, 2000-05; Rivington Gallery, 2000-05; Ann Norton Sculpture Garden, 2006; Artists' Museum of NY City, 2006; Art in the Garden, 2010; Beauties on the Beach, Milford Conn, 2011, Oakland Beach Park, Rye, NY, 2011, Central Park, 2012. *Awards:* Nat Endowment Residency Grant, 84; NY State Coun Arts Grant, 86; Ford Found Award. *Bibliog:* Allen Ellingswieg (auth), Rosemary Cove, 75 & Natalie Edgar (auth), Rosemary Cove, 78, Arts Mag; Dorothy Beskind (auth), Rosemary Cove (film), 77; Ed McCormack (auth), Art Speak. *Mem:* Women in Arts; Artists Equity; Am Medalists Soc. *Media:* Terra-Cotta, Corten Steel; Oil, Ink. *Collection:* Leon Kowalenko, Barbara Ingber, Dorthy Beskind, Norman Klein, Ciba Geigy. *Publ:* Art News, Arts Mag, NY Times, Art Speak, Westmore News. *Mailing Add:* 71 Waller Ave White Plains NY 10605

COVEY, ROSEMARY FEIT
PRINTMAKER, ILLUSTRATOR
b Johannesburg, S Africa, July 17, 1954. *Study:* Studied printmaking under Barry Moser, 68-72; Cornell Univ (archit), 74; Maryland Inst Coll Art (printmaking), 76. *Work:* Print Collection of Georgetown Univ, 27 prints, Washington; Cocoran Mus Art, Washington; Nat Mus Am Hist, Washington; NY Pub Libr, 16 prints; and many others. *Comn:* Seven cover illustrations, Wash Post/Book World, Washington, 80-90; 90th Anniversary Print, Int Fedn Metalworkers, Zurich, Switz, 83; seventeen illustrations, World & I Mag, Washington, 86-87; two wood-engravings prints, Gen Elec Astro-Space, Princeton, NJ, 91-92. *Exhib:* Solo exhibs, Jane Haslem Gallery, Washington, 92, Interlochen Ctr Arts, Mich, 92, Martin Sumers Graphics, 95, Georgia Southern Univ, Statesboro, Time Gallery, Chicago, 95, Saginaw Valley State Univ Art Gallery, Univ Ctr, Mich, 97, Butler Inst Am Art, Youngstown, Ohio, 97; Los Angeles 12th Nat Print Exhib, Frederick S Wright Gallery, Univ Calif, Los Angeles, 93; Women Printmakers: 18th Century to Present, Nat Mus Women Arts, Washington, 94; Am Self Portraits in Prints, Jane Haslem Gallery (traveling), 95; Calvin Coll Art Mus, Grand Rapids, Mich, 95; Indiana Art Mus, Bloomington, 95; Print Club Albany's 19th Nat Print Exhib, Schenectady Mus, NY, 95; William Floyd Gallery, NY, 2003; Grand Cent Art Ctr, Univ Calif, Fullerton, 2005. *Pos:* Permanent studio, Torpedo Fac Art Ctr, Alexandria, Va, 82-; artist in res, Grand Central Art Ctr, Santa Ana, CA, 2004. *Awards:* National Printmaking Grant, Alpha Delta Kappa Found, 92; Rockefeller Found Fel, Bellagio, Italy, 98. *Bibliog:* Marriott Michel (auth), Art reflects conflict, Wash Post, 85; Rosemary Covey's graphic response to emotions, Am Artists Mag, 86; Eric L Mackenzie (auth), Rosemary Feit Covey: The Prints 1970-1990, Eric L Mackenzie, 90. *Mem:* Torpedo Fac Artists Asn (pres Target Gallery, 93-94); Soc of Graphic Artists. *Media:* Wood Engraving. *Publ:* Shadows & Goatbones, Scop Publ, 92; Stark Naked on a Cold Irish Morning, Scop Publ, 92; Peking Street Peddlers, Bird & Bull Press, 94; Hearsay, Strange Tales from the Middle Kingdom, William Morrow Inc, New York, 98; Beauty and the Serpent: Thirteen Tales of Unnatural Animals, Simon and Schuster, 2001. *Mailing Add:* 118 N Patrick St Alexandria VA 22314

COVI, DARIO A
HISTORIAN
b Livingston, Ill, Dec 26, 1920. *Study:* Eastern Ill State Teachers Coll, BEd, 43; State Univ Iowa, MA, 48, with William S Heckscher; NY Univ, with Richard Offner, PhD, 58. *Hon Degrees:* Eastern Ill Univ, LHD, 2003. *Pos:* Mem exec comt, Ky Arts Comn, 65-70; part-time curator, Univ Art Coll, 96-. *Teaching:* From instr to prof art hist, Univ Louisville, 56-70; prof, Duke Univ, 70-75; Hite prof, Univ Louisville, 75-91, prof emer, 91-. *Awards:* Am Coun Learned Socs Fel, 64; Fulbright-Hays Fel, 68-69; Gladys Krieble Delmas Found Grant, 79. *Mem:* Coll Art Asn Am; Southeastern Coll Art Conf; Renaissance Soc Am; Midwest Art Hist Soc; Ital Art Soc; Leonardo Da Vinci Soc. *Res:* Italian Renaissance art. *Publ:* Auth, Prints from the Allen R Hite Art Institute Collection (exhib catalog), 63; contribr, McGraw-Hill Dict Art, Art Bull, Burlington Mag, Renaissance Quart & other nat art publ; auth, The Inscription in Fifteenth Century Florentine Painting; contribr, The Dictionary Art, Encyclopedia of Sculpture; Andrea del Verrocchio Life and Work, Leo S Olschki Editore, Florence, 2005. *Mailing Add:* Hite Art Inst Univ Louisville Louisville KY 40292

COVINGTON, HARRISON WALL
PAINTER, SCULPTOR
b Plant City, Fla, Apr 12, 1924. *Study:* Univ Fla, 42-43; Hiram Col, 43; Univ Fla, BFA (hons), 49, MFA, 53. *Work:* Herron Mus Art, Indianapolis, Ind; Everson Mus Art, Syracuse, NY; John & Mable Ringling Mus Art, Sarasota, Fla; Jacksonville Mus Art, Fla; Nat Gallery Art, Washington, DC. *Comn:* sculpture bas relief, Fla Fed Savings & Loan, 74; portraits of pres, 70, 76 & 84, sculpture bas relief, Univ South Fla, 75; sculptured figures, Int Shrine Hq, 80; bronze figure, Barnstormer, Tampa Int Airport, 2005; bronze figure, Firefighter Hillsborough Co, Fla, 2005; Hungarian Freedom Fighter (bronze), Cleveland, Ohio & Naples, Fla, 2006; bronze firefighter, Bartow, Fla, 2011. *Exhib:* Mus Dir's Choice, throughout Southeastern US, 56-59; Painting USA: The Figure, Mus Mod Art, New York, 62; New York World's Fair, 64; Fla 17, Pan-Am Union, Washington, DC, 68; Graphic Studio USF, Brooklyn Mus, 78; Tampa Mus Art, 87. *Teaching:* Instr art, Univ Fla, 49-61; prof art, Univ S Fla, 61-82, chmn visual arts prog, 61-67, dean, Div Fine Arts, 67-72, dean, Coll Fine Arts, 77-82, prof emer, 82- & dean emer, 82-. *Awards:* Sloan Found Grant, 47; Guggenheim Fel, 64; Artist of the Year, City of Tampa, 2007. *Bibliog:* Gene Baro (auth), Graphic Studio USF: An Experiment in Art and Education (exhib catalog), Brooklyn Mus, 78. *Media:* Acrylic, Plastic, Bronze. *Mailing Add:* 11809 Vera Ave Tampa FL 33618

COWAN, AILEEN HOOPER
SCULPTOR, PAINTER
b Windsor, Ont, June 11, 1926. *Study:* Univ Toronto, BA; Queen's Univ, Kingston, Ont; Univ Toronto. *Work:* Univ Western Ont; Robert McLaughlin Gallery, Oshawa, Can. *Comn:* J Gush, Toronto; Govt of Ont. *Exhib:* Agnes Etherington Gallery, Queen's Univ, Kingston, Ont, 74; Merton Gallery, Toronto, 79; McDowell Gallery, Toronto, 80; Sculptors Soc BC, Robson Sq Media Ctr, Vancouver, 80; J Aird Gallery, Toronto, 89-90; retrospective, Stock Exchange Tower, Toronto, 94; President's Exhib, SSC Gallery, 2003; Arch Exhib, St James Cathedral, Toronto, 2006-2007. *Collection Arranged:* Sculptor's Soc of Can, (traveling exhib), 81. *Pos:* Cur, permanent collection, Sculptor's Soc Can; pres, Sculptor's Soc of Can. *Teaching:* Univ Toronto, Ont, formerly. *Awards:* Augusts Kopmanis Mem Award, 80. *Bibliog:* Article, Athens News, Greece, 7/72; article, Art Mag, Toronto, Vol 5, No 15, 73. *Mem:* Sculptors Soc Can (life mem); Soc Painters Watercolors, formerly. *Media:* Bronze, Acrylic. *Res:* Polyesters. *Specialty:* Canadian art. *Interests:* Sculpture & painting. *Publ:* Earth and You, Vol XVI, 87. *Mailing Add:* 8 The Donway East Ste 467 Don Mills ON M3C 3R Canada

COWAN, RALPH WOLFE
PAINTER
b Pheobus, Va, Dec 16, 1931. *Study:* Art Students League, New York, 51. *Work:* Carter Presidential Ctr, Atlanta, Ga; Portsmouth Mus, Va; Royal Palace Monaco; Graceland, Memphis, Tenn. *Comn:* Palace Collection, comn by King Fahd, Saudi Arabia, 84; 3 portraits, comn by King Hassan II, Morocco, 84; 18 portraits, comn by HM Sultan Hassanal Bolkiah, Brunei, 85; 2 portraits, comn by Pres Augusto Pinochet, Chile; 4 portraits, comn by Pres Sheik Zayed, United Arab Emirates. *Exhib:* Solo retrospective, Portsmouth Mus, Va, 84; Ft Lauderdale Mus Art, Fla. *Awards:* Portsmouth Notable, Portsmouth Hall of Fame, Va, 87; Best in Show, Norton Mus Art, Norton Artist Guild, 88. *Bibliog:* Doug Stewart (auth), Making Faces is a Hard Days Fight, Smithsonian Mag 11-5-88; Linda Marx (auth), Painter Fights Back, People Mag, 9/4/89. *Mem:* Art Students League; Portrait Inst; Am Portrait Soc; Am Soc Artists. *Media:* Oil. *Publ:* Auth, A Personal Vision, self published, 88. *Mailing Add:* 243 29th St West Palm Beach FL 22407-5207

COWART, JACK
MUSEUM DIRECTOR, CURATOR
b Ft Riley, Kans, Feb 7, 1945. *Study:* Va Military Inst, BA, 67; Johns Hopkins Univ, PhD (art hist), 72. *Collection Arranged:* Henri Matisse: The Early Years in Nice, 1916-1930 (coauth, catalog), Nat Gallery Art, Washington, DC, 86-87; Georgia O'Keeffe, 1887-1986, Nat Gallery Art, Washington, DC, 87-88; Matisse in Morocco: The Paintings and Drawings, 1912-1913 (coauth, catalog), Nat Gallery Art, Washington, DC, 90-91; ROCI--Rauschenberg Overseas Culture Interchange, Nat Gallery Art, Washington, DC, 91; Ellsworth Kelly--The Years in France: 1948-1954 (coauth, catalog), Nat Gallery Art & Galerie Nal du Jeu de Paume, 92. *Pos:* Asst cur

paintings, Wadsworth Atheneum, Hartford, Conn, 72-74; cur 19th & 20th Century Art, St Louis Art Mus, St Louis, Mo, 74-83; head & cur, Dept Twentieth-Century Art, Nat Gallery Art, Washington, DC, 83-92; deputy dir & chief cur, Corcoran Gallery Art, Washington, DC, 92-. *Res:* Post-war American & European painting & sculpture. *Publ:* Coauth, Henri Matisse Paper Cut-Outs (exhib catalog), St Louis Art Mus & Detroit Inst Arts, 77; auth, Roy Lichtenstein, 1970-1980, Hudson Hills Press Inc, 81. *Mailing Add:* c/o Corcoran Gallery Art 500 17th St NW Washington DC 20006

COWIN, EILEEN
PHOTOGRAPHER, VIDEO ARTIST
b Brooklyn, NY, Aug 17, 1947. *Study:* State Univ NY, New Paltz, BS, 68; Ill Inst Technol, with Aaron Siskind & Arthur Siegel, MS, 70. *Work:* Mus Mod Art, New York; Los Angeles Co Mus Art; Fogg Mus; Brooklyn Mus; Nat Mus Am Art, Smithsonian Inst, Washington, DC; J Paul Getty Mus, Los Angeles, Calif; Hammer Mus Art, Los Angeles, Calif; Mus Contemp Photography, Chicago; Princeton Univ Art Mus, NJ; Mus Photographic Art, San Diego, Calif; Seattle Art Mus, Wash; Tokyo Metrop Mus Photography. *Comn:* How Many Billboards, Art in Stead, Mak Ctr Art & Architecture, 2010; Sundance Film Festival, 2002; Metro Rail Light Boxes, Calif, 2001. *Exhib:* Solo exhibs, Cooper Union, New York, 70, Witkin Gallery, New York, 71, Sch Dayton Art Inst, 72, 73, Portland Sch Art, Maine, 75, Light Gallery, New York, 76, OK Harris Gallery, New York, 77, Met State Coll, Denver, 78, The Light Factory, Charlotte, NC, 79, 84, Orange Coast Coll, Costa Mesa, Calif, 80, 83, Viviane Esders Gallery, Paris, 85, Min Gallery and Studio, Tokyo, 87, Cleveland Mus Art, 88, Jayne H Baum Gallery, New York, 88, 91, 93, 2000, Roy Boyd Gallery, Santa Monica, Calif, 89, 91, Mus Contemp Photog, Chicago, Ill, 91, Gallery 954, Chicago, 94, Contemp Arts Ctr, Cincinnati, 2000; Group exhibs, Calif Photog, Mus Art; The Diaristic Mode, Univ NMex Art Mus, Albuquerque, 83; The Image Scavengers, Inst Contemp Art, Philadelphia, 83; Mus Mod Art, Paris, 83; Whitney Biennial, Whitney Mus Art, 83; Los Angeles Co Mus Art, 85, 95-97, 2000; La Jolla Mus Contemp Art, 85; Viviane Esders Gallery, Paris, 85; The Photog of Invention, Nat Mus Am Art, 89; Jayne H Baum Gallery, New York, 90, 94; Pleasures and Terrors of Domestic Comfort (catalog), Mus Mod Art, NY, 91; de-Persona (catalog), Oakland Mus, Calif, 91; Erotic Desire (catalog), Perspektief, Rotterdam, Neth, 91; Tokyo Met Mus Photog, 92, 2000, 2005; Mus Fine Arts, Houston, 93; Mus Contemp Photog, Chicago, 98; Brewery Projects, Los Angeles, 2002; New Orleans Film Festival, 2004; Robert V Fullerton Mus, San Bernardino, Calif, 2006; Pasadena City Coll, Calif, 2009. *Teaching:* Prof emeritus art, Calif State Univ, Fullerton, 75-2008; vis artist photog, Art Inst Chicago, 80. *Awards:* Public Art Fund, Pa Sta Proj, 90; Best Experimental Film, USA Film Festival Dallas, 2003. *Bibliog:* Mark Johnstone (auth), Eileen Cowin, Min Gallery, Tokyo, 87; Max Kozloff (auth), The Privileged Eye, Univ NMex Press, Albuquerque, 87; Judi Freeman (auth), Eileen Cowin, Darryl Curran The Photographic: Two Points of View, Calif State Univ, Fullerton, 89; Sue Spaid, Still (And All) Eileen Cowin 1971-1998; Thomas McGouern, Witness Protection, 2006. *Mailing Add:* 2118 Wilshire Blvd #651 Santa Monica CA 90403

COWIN, JACK LEE
PRINTMAKER, PAINTER
b Indianapolis, Ind, July 29, 1947. *Study:* Herron Sch Art, Ind Univ, BFA, 69; Univ Ill, MFA, 71. *Work:* Chicago Art Inst, Ill; Okaido Mus, Japan; Ind Mus Art, Indianapolis,; Cleveland Mus Art, Ohio; Brooklyn Mus Art, NY. *Exhib:* Canadian Prints, Can Exhib Ctr, Tokyo, 85; Am Prints in Paris, Gallerie Chislaine Huosenot, France, 92; The Angling Art of Jack Cowin, Atlanta, Ga, 95; Landfall Press - 25 yrs Printmaking, Milwaukee Mus Art, Wis, 96; Basel Print Show, Switz, 97 & 98. *Teaching:* Prof printmaking, Univ Regina, Sask, Can, 71-. *Awards:* 20 American Printmakers, Soc Am Graphic Artists, 79; Purchase Award, Ind 500 Arts Festival, 79. *Bibliog:* Andy Oko (auth), Country Pleasures, Fifth House Press, 84. *Media:* Drawing, Etching. *Dealer:* The New Van Streaten Gallery 316 W Superior St Chicago IL. *Mailing Add:* 2029 Elphinstone St Regina SK S4T 3N5 Canada

COWLES, CHARLES
ART DEALER, COLLECTOR
b Santa Monica, Calif, Feb 7, 1941. *Study:* Stanford Univ, 63. *Pos:* Pres & publ, Artforum Mag, 65-79; cur mod art, Seattle Art Mus, 75-79; art dealer, Charles Cowles Gallery, 80-; bd trustee, New York Studio Sch, 85-2000; trustee, Wolfsonian, Fla Int Univ, Miami Beach, 95-; hon trustee, Laumeier Park, St Louis, 96-2000; trustee, Alliance for the Arts, NY, 2000; trustee, Alliance for the Arts, NY, 2000; trustee, Longhouse Reserve, East Hampton, NY, 2005; trustee, Moving Theater, NY, 2005. *Bibliog:* Laura de Coppett & Alan Jones (coauths), The Art Dealers, Potter. *Mem:* Art Dealers Asn Am. *Specialty:* Mod & contemp art. *Collection:* Contemp art, Japanese folk art & photog

COWLEY, EDWARD P
PAINTER, EDUCATOR
b Buffalo, NY, May 29, 1925. *Study:* Albright Art Sch; Buffalo State Col, BS, 48; Columbia Univ, MA, 49; Nat Coll Art, Dublin, Ireland, Ford Found Fel, 55. *Work:* Albany Inst Hist & Art, NY; Schenectady Mus, NY; Smith Col, Northhampton, Mass; Colgate Univ, Hamilton, NY; Berkshire Mus, Pittsfield, Mass. *Comn:* The Minerva Window (stained glass), The Sunya Alumni Asn, 94. *Teaching:* Prof art & chmn dept, State Univ NY, Albany, 56-75, prof art, 76-88. *Awards:* State Univ NY Res Grant, 66 & 74. *Media:* Pastels, Stained Glass. *Collection:* Altamont NY Stained Glass Panel Collection of Marijo Doucherty. *Mailing Add:* PO Box 198 Altamont NY 12009

COX, ERNEST LEE
SCULPTOR, EDUCATOR
b Wilmington, NC, June 1, 1937. *Study:* Coll William & Mary, BA (fine arts); Cranbrook Acad of Art, Bloomfield Hills, Mich, MFA (sculpture); Mich State Univ, Oakland. *Work:* St Petersburg Pub Libr, Fla; Acad Art Mus, Easton, Md, 2010; Univ S Fla, Tampa; 1st Nat Bank, Atlanta, Ga & Tampa, Fla. *Comn:* Steel sculptures, 64, Fed Deposit Ins Corp, Washington, DC, 65 & Gulf Life Ins Co, Jacksonville, 67. *Exhib:* The 17th Va Artists Exhib, Va Mus Fine Arts, Richmond, 58; 24th Ann NC Artists Exhib, NC Mus Fine Arts, Raleigh, 61; 20th-22nd Southeastern Ann Exhibs, High Mus Art, Atlanta, Ga, 65-67; Fla 17, Pan Am Union, Washington, DC, 68; 15 Fla Artists Sculpture Exhib, Gallery Contemp Art, Winston-Salem, NC, 70; solo exhibs, Jacksonville Mus Art, 73, Fla Art Fellows Art Exhib, Mus Fine Arts, St Pertersburg, Fla, 82 & Fla Art Fel Exhib, Norton Gallery Art, Palm Beach, 89. *Teaching:* From instr to prof sculpture, Univ S Fla, Tampa, 62-, chmn art dept, 71-73, prof emer, 94-. *Awards:* Second Prize, Fla Sculptors 7th Ann Exhib, 63; First Prize, Fla State Fair Fine Arts Exhib, 65; Purchase Prize, Southeastern Sculpture Exhib, Atlanta CofC, 69; Fla Art Fel, 82 & 89. *Media:* Welded, Forged Steel. *Mailing Add:* 7309 Bozman Neavitt Rd Bozman MD 21612

COX, RENÉE
PHOTOGRAPHER
b Colgate, Jamaica, Oct 16, 1960. *Study:* Syracuse Univ, Grad; Sch Visual Arts, MFA; Whitney Independent Study Prog. *Exhib:* Solo exhibs include Cristinerose Gallery, New York, 1996, Ambrosino Gallery, Coral Gables, Fla, 2000, Robert Miller Gallery, New York, 2001, 2005; group exhibs include Black Male: Representations of Masculinity in Contemp Art, Whitney Mus Am Art, New York, 1993; Bad Girls, New Mus Contemp Art, New York, 1993, Picturing the Mod Amazon, 1999; Sites of Being, Inst Contemp Art, Boston, 1995; No Doubt, Aldrich Mus Contemp Art, Ridgefield, Conn, 1996; Sexual Politics, Hammer Mus, Los Angeles, 1996; Gendered Visions, Johnson Mus Art, Cornell Univ, NY, 1997; Venice Biennale, 1999; Reflections in Black: A Hist of Black Photog, Smithsonian Mus & Ctr African Am Hist & Culture, Washington, 2000; Committed to the Image, Brooklyn Mus, 2001; Art & Outrage, Robert Miller Gallery, New York, 2002; Splat Boom Pow! The Influence of Comics in Contemp Art, Contemp Arts Mus, Houston, 2003-04; Who? Me?: Role-Play in Self-Portrait Photog, Zabriskie Gallery, New York, 2003; African Queen, Studio Mus Harlem, New York, 2005; The Forest: Politics, Poetics & Practice, Nasher Mus Art, Duke Univ, NC, 2005-06; Soul Food!, Wadsworth Atheneum, Hartford, Conn, 2006-08; She's So Articulate, Arlington Arts Ctr, Va, 2008. *Collection Arranged:* No Doubt, Aldrich Mus Contemp Art, Ridgefield, Conn, 1996. *Pos:* Asst fashion editor, Glamour, New York; fashion photog, Paris & New York, formerly

COX, RICHARD WILLIAM
HISTORIAN, WRITER
b Los Angeles, Calif, July 13, 1942. *Study:* Univ Calif, Los Angeles, BA (hist), 64, MA (hist), 66; Univ Wis, Madison, MA (art hist), 70, PhD (art hist), 73. *Teaching:* Instr Am art, Univ Wis, River Falls, 71-74; from asst prof to prof Am art & hist prints, La State Univ, 74-. *Awards:* Solon Buck Award for Best Article, Minn Hist, 75; Nat Endowment Humanities Fel, 75. *Bibliog:* Matthew Baigell (auth), The American Scene: American Painting of the 1930s, Praeger, 74; James Dennis (auth), Grant Wood, A Study in Art & Culture, Viking, 75. *Mem:* Coll Art Asn; Art Educ Asn; La Hist Soc. *Res:* Am painting & graphic arts in 1900-1945 period; contemp art. *Publ:* Art Young: Cartoonist from the middle border, Wis Mag Hist, 77; Caroline Durieux: The lithographs of the 1930's and 1940's La State Univ Press, 77; Adolf Dehn--jazz age satirist, Arch Am Art J, 78; Southern works on paper, 1900-1950, Southern Arts Fedn, 80; coauth (with Clinton Adams), Adolf Dehn, Catalogue Raisonne of the Lithographs, Minn Hist Soc Press, 87; (with Carlton Overland), Warrington Colescott, Forty Years of Printmaking, A Retrospective, Elvehjem Mus Art, Univ Wis, 89. *Mailing Add:* La State Univ Sch Art 123 Art Bldg Baton Rouge LA 70803

COYLE, TERENCE
PAINTER
b Williamstown, Mass, Sept 7, 1925. *Study:* Columbia Univ, 46-48; Hunter Col, 50; Art Students League, 64-70. *Work:* Mus City New York; Fordham Univ, Lincoln Ctr, New York; Billy Rose Collection, NY Libr Performing Arts; NY State Mus, Albany; Chubb & Son Inc, New York; Butler Mus Am Art. *Comn:* Anatomical Figures, Pain Erasure, 80; illustration, Discovering the Hudson, Ward Morehouse II, Watercolor, The Stage, 2007. *Exhib:* Am Artists Prof League, Lever Brothers Bldg, NY, 76; Nat Arts Club, Nat Arts Gallery, New York, 81; Last Days of the Helen Hayes Theatre, Sharon Creative Arts Found, Conn, 83; Places Please, Astor Gallery, Lincoln Ctr, New York, 84; Curtain Call at the Helen Hayes, Fordham Univ, Lincoln Ctr, New York, 86; Lincoln Ctr Gallery; Berkshire Mus, Pittsfield, Mass, 2005; Russian Embassy to UN, 2005; Retrospective at 80, Selected Works 1955-2005, Nat Arts Club, 2005; Butler Mus Am Art, 2006; Broadway in the 80's, Global Sandbox Gallery. *Teaching:* Instr oil painting, Art Students League, 74-; lectr artistic anatomy, Nat Acad Design, Sch Fine Arts, New York, 79-; instr figure portrait painting, Scottsdale Artists Sch, Ariz, ann workshop, 85; instr drawing workshop, Nat Arts Club. *Awards:* Award for graphic design, Communications Art Exhib, Am Inst Graphic Design, 79; Silver Medal, Nat Art League, 83. *Bibliog:* Artist chronicle's theatre demise, Lakeville J, Conn, 9/1/83; Richard Nielson (auth), The skin's game art/rev, Ariz Republic, 2/14/87; article, Hazelton Standard, 3/20/89. *Mem:* Life mem, Art Students League; Am Artists Prof League; Artist's Equity; Nat Art League; Nat Arts Club, NYC. *Media:* Oil, Watercolor. *Publ:* Coauth, Anatomy Lessons From the Great Masters, Watson-Guptill, 77; Albinus on Anatomy, Watson-Guptill/Dover, 79 & 88; auth, Master Class in Figure Drawing, Watson-Guptill, 85; (video) Terrence Coyle Landscape Watercolor, 96; Terence Coyle, Retrospective at 80, Jo An Pictures Ltd, 2005. *Dealer:* Jo An Fine Art PO Box 6020 New York NY 10150. *Mailing Add:* T Coyle c/o Jo An PO Box 6020 New York NY 10150

COYNE, JOHN MICHAEL
PAINTER, EDUCATOR
b St Stephen, NB, 1950. *Study:* Mt Allison Univ, BFA, 75; Univ Regina, MFA, 77. *Work:* Art Gallery NS, Halifax; Husky Oil, Calgary; Placer Dome, Inc, Toronto; Midland Doherty, Xerox Canada, Abitibi Price, Toronto; Air Canada, Toshiba Canada; Bank of NS, Toronto; Govt, Nfld & Labrador; Mt Allison Univ; Sir Wilfred Grenfell Col; and others. *Exhib:* Art Gallery NS, Halifax, 80; Acadia Univ Art Gallery, Wolfville, NS, 83; Edmonton Art Gallery, Alberta, 84; St Mary's Univ, Halifax, 84;

Mira Godard Gallery, Toronto, 86; Grenfell Col, Corner Brook, Nfld, 87 & 89; Gallery 78, Fredericton, NB, 88; Mem Univ Art Gallery, 90; Emma Butler Gallery, St John's, Nfld, 90; Arts & Cult Ctr, Corner Brook, Nfld, 97; Franklyn Gallery, Corner Brook, Nfld, 2003. *Teaching:* Asst prof, Acadia Univ, Wolfville, NS, 77-84, assoc prof & head art dept 83-86; founding head dept visual arts Mem Univ, Grenfell Col, Corner Brook, Nfld, 86-92, prof, 91-, head div arts, 99-2000. *Bibliog:* C MacLauglin (auth), Atlantic lines, Heritage Can Mag, 2/79; Dr Helen J Dow (auth), Michael Coyne: A Retrospective, Acadia Univ Art Gallery, 83; Arts Atlantic Winter 85, 87 & 91; Colleen O'Neill (auth), Michael Coyne, Sir Wilfred Grenfell Coll Art Gallery, 90. *Media:* Acrylic, Digital Imaging. *Mailing Add:* Dept Visual Art Mem Univ Sir Wilfred Grenfell Col Corner Brook NL A2H 6P9 Canada

COYNE, PETAH E
SCULPTOR, PHOTOGRAPHER
b Oklahoma City, Okla, Sept 30, 1953. *Study:* Art Academy Cincinnati, Grad, 77; Kent State Univ. *Hon Degrees:* Cincinnati Art Acad DArt (hon), 2001. *Work:* The Brooklyn Mus, Whitney Mus Am Art, Mus Mod Art, NY; San Diego Mus Contemp Art, La Jolla, Calif; The Speed Mus, Louisville, KY; Contemp Mus, Honolulu, Hawaii; Mus. Modern Art, NY; Phoenix Art Mus; Detroit Inst. of Art; and others. *Exhib:* Solo exhibs, Grand Lobby Installation, Brooklyn Mus, NY, 89, Petah Coyne Sculpture, Contemp Mus, Honolulu, Hawaii, Cleveland Ctr Contemp Art, Ohio, Ctr Contemp Art Santa Fe, NMex, 92-93, Corcoran Gallery Art, Wash, High Mus Art, Atlanta, Ga, Laurence Miller Gallery, NY, 96-97 & Fairy Tales, Galerie Lelong, NY, 98, 2001, Butler Gallery, Kilkenny Castle, Ireland, 99, Byron Cohen Gallery, Kansas City, Mo, 99, 2001, Julie Saul Gallery, NY, 2001, First Ctr for Contemp Art, Tenn, 2001, Des Moines Art Ctr, 2002, Cincinnati Art Mus, 2004; Group exhib, Art Contemporain Vision 90, Centre Int d'Art Contemporaine, Montreal, 90; Coyne-Hurtman Collaboration, Neuberger Mus, Purchase, NY, 92; Millennium Messages, Smithsonian Traveling Exhib, organized by Heckscher Mus Art, Huntington, Long Island, NY, 99, Contemp Mus, Baltimore, 2000, Mus of Modern Art (Glen Dimplex Artist's award), Dublin, 2000; Whitney Biennial, 2000; Detroit Inst of Arts, Mich, 2001, Galerie Lelong, NY, 2002, Memphis Coll of Art, Tenn, 2003. *Teaching:* Grad fac painting/sculpture, Sch Visual Arts, 90-94. *Awards:* Guggenheim Mem Foun, Guggenheim Found, 89; Nat Endowment Arts Fel Sculpture, 90; Sirus Proj, art-in-residence, Cobh, Co Cork, Ireland, 2000; Hon Doctorate, Cincinnati Art Acad, Ohio, 2001. *Bibliog:* Lasse Antonsen (auth), Installation by Petah Coyne, Massachusetts Contemp, 91; David Rubin (auth), Petah Coyne, Cleveland Ctr Contemp Art, 92; Tony Carlson (auth), Beauty and the Beast (film), 92. *Mem:* Skowhegan Sch Painting & Sculpture, NY (bd gov, 88-94); Orgn Independent Artist (bd dir, 88-92); Sculpture Ctr, NY (bd dir, 90-93). *Media:* All Media. *Dealer:* Galerie Le Long 526 W 26th St New York NY 10001; Byron C Cohen Gallery for Contemp Art 2020 Baltimore Ave Kansas City MO 64108; SOLO Impression Inc 601 W 26th St New York NY 10001. *Mailing Add:* 477 Broome St New York NY 10013

COZAD, RACHAEL BLACKBURN
MUSEUM DIRECTOR, ART APPRAISER
b Berkeley, Calif, 1964. *Study:* Texas Christian Univ, BA; Calif State Univ, Los Angeles, MA. *Pos:* Exhibs mgr & registrar, Calif Center for the Arts, San Diego, 93-94; cur exhibs, Iris and B Gerald Cantor Found, Los Angeles, Calif, 94-97, exec dir & chief cur, 98-2001; dir, Kemper Mus Contemp Art, Kansas City, Mo, 2001-2012. *Mem:* ArtTable; Mus Assessment Prog; Peer Rev Panel, US Gen Serv Admin, Art in Architecture Prog, 2002-; Appraisers Asn Am; Am Asn Mus; Aprraisers Asn Am (certified appraiser). *Specialty:* Mod & contemp art. *Publ:* El Dia de los Muertos: The Life of the Dead in Mexican Folk Art, 87; Rodin: A Magnificent Obsession, 2001; Frederick J. Brown: Jazz, Blues & Other Icons, 2002; Wayne Thiebaud: Fifty Years of Painting, 2003; The Kemper Mus of Contemp Art: The First Ten Years, 2004

CRABLE, JAMES HARBOUR
MULTI-MEDIA ARTIST, INSTRUCTOR
b Bronx, NY, Aug 30, 1939. *Study:* State Univ NY, Buffalo, BS, 62; Rochester Inst Technol, NY, MFA, 66; Chelsea Sch Art, London, Eng, HDA, 70. *Work:* Bell South Corp; AT&T Collection, Washington; Equitable Life Assurance Soc Am; State Univ NY Art Collection, Albany; IBM Collection; Chrysler Mus, Norfolk, Va; Everson Mus, Syracuse, NY; Duke Univ, Durham, NC; Stanford Univ, Palo Alto, Calif; Mem Art Gallery, Rochester, NY; Taubman Mus Art, Roanoke, Va. *Exhib:* Solo exhibs, Va Mus Fine Arts, Richmond, 76, Southeastern Ctr Contemp Art, Winston-Salem, 78, Gallery K, Washington, 79 & 82, Monterey Penninsula Mus Art, Monterey, Calif, 89, Interform Gallery, Osaka, Japan, 89, Fresno Metrop Mus Art, Calif, 90, Photo Forum, Pittsburgh, Pa, 91 & Camera Obscura, Denver, Colo, 93; Continuum VII, Dulin Gallery Art, Knoxville, 82; Over the Blue Ridge, Roanoke Fine Art Invitational, Va, 87; Collage: Four Directions, San Jose Mus Art, Calif, 88; Group exhibs, NY Art Expo, Jacob Javits Ctr, New York City, 92, Chrysler Mus, Norfolk, Va, 93; JJ Brookings Gallery, San Francisco, 95; Austin Mus, Tex, 97; Md Fedn Art, Annapolis, 97; Peninsula Fine Arts Ctr, Newport News, Va, 98; Mobile Mus Art, Ala, 99; Hite Art Inst, Univ Louisville, 2000; Touchstone Gallery, Washington, DC, 2003; Mus West, Palo Alto, Calif, 2004; AIPAD, The Photog Show, NY, 2005; Radius 250, Artspace Gallery, Richmond, Va, 2007; Colors of Life Int Exhib, Italian Embassy Cult Ctr, DC, 2008; Hoyt Mid Atlantic Juried Art Exhib, Hoyt Inst Fine Arts, New Castle, Pa, 2008; Tex Nat Photo Exhib, Dougherty Art Ctr, Austin, Tex, 2009; 23rd Int Juried Show, Visual Arts Ctr NJ, Summit, NJ, 2009; Motion, Int exhib, Ctr Fine Art Photography, Ft Collins, Colo, 2010; Gallery Internat Juried Photog, 12 12 Gallery, Richmond, Va, 2011; Fine Art Portfolio, Foto Week DC Interat awards, Wash DC, 2011; Northern Nat Art Competition, Nicolet Coll Art Gallery, Rhinelander, Wisc, 2012. *Teaching:* Assoc prof art survey, drawing & art educ, State Univ Col Brockport, NY, 66-69; lectr found studies, Croydon Col Art, Surrey, Eng, 70-71; prof drawing & art survey, James Madison Univ, Harrisonburg, Va, 73-. *Awards:* Fel, Nat Endowment Arts Fel, 79; Va prize invisual arts, presented by Gov Gerald Baliles, 87; Guild Award, Peninsula Fine Arts Ctr Exhib, Newport News, Va, 92; Shenandoah Valley Artist of Yr, Shenandoah Valley Ann Visual Arts Awards, 93; 1st Prize Photog, Peninsula Fine Arts Ctr, 2000; Award of Distinction, Southeastern Col Art Asn, 2000; Best in Show, Art Mus Western Va, 2001; Janet Shaffer Creativity Award, Acad Fine Arts, Lynchburg, Va, 2008; 1st Place award for Photog, Nat Will's Creek Survey, Cumberland, Md, 2011; Pro Camera award, 12th Ann Mid Atlantic Show, Lexington, Va, 2011; 1st Place award, Doorways and Passages, Profotio, Houston, Tex, 2012; Mayor Permanent Coll award, Va Artits Exhib, Charles H Taylor Ctr, Hampton, Va, 2012; Nat award of Excellence, Photograph of the Year, Westmoreland Art Nat, Pa, 2012; Best in Show, Nat Juried Photo Exhib, Acad Fine Arts, Lynchburg, Va, 2012. *Mem:* Coll Art Asn Am; Va Art Educ Asn. *Media:* Photo-collage. *Mailing Add:* 261 Green St Harrisonburg VA 22802-2046

CRAFT, DOUGLAS D
PAINTER, EDUCATOR
b Greene, NY, 1924. *Study:* Univ Iowa; Univ Chicago; Art Inst Chicago, BFA; Syracuse Univ; Univ NMex, MA in Painting. *Work:* Mus Mod Art & Whitney Mus Am Art, NY; Art Inst Chicago; Univ NMex, Albuquerque; Newark Mus, NJ; Smithsonian Inst, Washington, DC; Warner Lambert World Hq, Morris Plains, NJ; Butler Inst Am Art, Youngstown, Ohio; var pvt collections; many others. *Comn:* Paintings, comn by Mr & Mrs Daniel Weinstein for Edward Weinstein Ctr Performing Arts, Nat Coll Educ, Evanston, Ill, 72. *Exhib:* Solo exhibs, Royal Coll Art, London, 64, Traverse Festival Gallery, Edinburgh, 65, Mus Art, Carnegie Inst, Pittsburgh, Pa, 68 & Jersey City Mus, 78, 55 Mercer Gallery, NY, 80, Coll Ctr Art Gallery, New Rochelle, NY, 90, Bratton Gallery, Inc, NY, 90, Rosefsky Studio Art Gallery, State Univ NY, Binghamton, 93, Retrospective (with exhib & catalog), Butler Inst Am Art, Youngstown, Ohio, 93, Del Art Ctr Gallery, Narrowsburg, NY, 96, 2002, 2004; Butler Inst of Am Art, Youngstown, NY, 2005 and others; Rose Fried Gallery, NY, 68; Group exhib, Studio K, Long Island City, NY, 85; Montclair Art Mus, Montclair, NJ, 84; Contemp Syntax, Rutgers Univ, NJ, 87; Collage at NAME, NAME Gallery, Chicago, 88; Retrospective (exhib & catalog), Works on Paper (1974-1995), Makee Gallery, Mo, Gray Gallery, Ill & Keokuk Gallery, Ia, 97; Station Gallery, Katonah, NY, 93; Del Arts Ctr Gallery, Narrowsburg, NY, 95; Schick Art Gallery, Skidmore Coll, Saratoga, NY, 95; Paul McCarron Gallery, NY, 96; Pavel Zoubok Gallery, New York. *Collection Arranged:* Art Institute Chicago; Mus Modern Art, NYC; Whitney Mus Am Art, NYC; Newark Mus, NJ; Jersey City Mus, NJ; Butler Institute Am Art, Youngstown, Ohio; Smithsonian Inst, Washington, DC; Memorial Art Gallery, Univ Rochester, NY; Univ Ky, Lexington. *Pos:* Vis artist-in-residence, Univ Ky, 64; Am artist-in-residence, Royal Col Art, London, Eng, 64-65; vis artist-critic, Sunderland Col Art, Eng, 65 & Gloucestershire Col Art, Cheltenham, Eng, 65; cur, Fourteen Women Artists, Castle Gallery, New Rochelle, 82 & cur of Paper, Pigment & Glass, Castle Gallery, New Rochelle, 87. *Teaching:* Assoc prof painting, Art Inst Chicago, 55-66 & Carnegie Inst Technol, 66-69; vis artist, Cooper Union, 69-71 & Sch Visual Arts, New York, summer 88; prof painting, Col New Rochelle, 71-91; vis lectr, artist, Skidmore Col, Saratoga Springs, NY, 93. *Awards:* Harry Allison Logan Mem Award, Chautauqua Inst, NY, 63; Logan Bronze Medal & Prize, Art Inst Chicago, 66; Jury Award/Distinction in Painting, Mus Art, Carnegie Inst Int, 68. *Bibliog:* Max Wykes-Joyce (auth), Douglas Craft, Arts Rev, London, 64; Cordelia Oliver (auth), Exhibitions at Edinburgh, Guardian, 65; D L Shirey (auth), Douglas Craft Show in Jersey City, NY Times, 78; Vivien Raynor (auth), A magnetic group of 8 in Jersey City, NY Times, 80; Vivien Raynor (auth), Show of collages opens new exhibit hall in New Rochelle, New York Times, 88. *Media:* Acrylic, Oil. *Dealer:* Paul McCarron Fine Arts & Prints New York NY; River Gallery Narrowsburg NY; Paul Zoubok, Collages, NY, NY. *Mailing Add:* PO Box 245 Jeffersonville NY 12748

CRAFT, LIZ
ARTIST
b LA, 1970. *Study:* Otis Parsons, BA, 1994; UCLA, MFA, 1997. *Work:* It's All An Illusion, Migros Mus fur Gegenwartskunst, Zurich, 2004, Whitney Biennial, Whitney Mus Am Art, 2004, Seeing Other People, 2004. *Exhib:* Solo exhibs: Richard Telles Fine Art, Los Angeles, 1998; Centrum fur Gegenwartskunst Oberosterreich, Linz, Austria, 2001; Galerie Nathalie Obadia, Paris, 2001; Pub Art Fund, NY, 2002; A Real Mother For Ya, Sadie Coles HQ, London, 2002; Marianne Boesky Gallery, 2003; Group exhibs: Happy Trails, Coll Creative Studies, Univ Santa Barbara, 1999; Hot Spots, Weatherspoon Gallery, Univ NC, 1999; Good Luck for You, Transmission Gallery, Edinburgh, 2000; Calif Dreamin', Gallery Art, Carlsen Ctr, Johnson Co Community Col, Kansas City, 2000; Young & Dumb, ACME, Los Angeles, 2001; Play it as it Lays, The London Inst Gallery, 2002; Wheeling - Krad Kult Tour! Motorcycles in Art, Frankfurt Am Main, Ger, 2002; 3-D, Friedrich Petzel Gallery, 2003; The Thought That Counts, Sister, Los Angeles, 2003

CRAIG, GERRY
EDUCATOR, ADMINISTRATOR, WRITER
Study: Univ Kansas, BFA (History of Art), 1982, BFA (Textile Design), 1982; studied Philosophy and Art History at Univ Saint Andrews, Scotland, 1979-1980; Cranbrook Academy of Art, MFA, 1989. *Exhib:* solo exhibitions include: Journey Relics, Providence Athenaeum, RI, 1986, Second Skin, site specific installation, Mott Community Col, Flint, Michigan, 1995, Saints and Scrolls, Detroit Contemporary, 2001; group exhibitions include: The Fibre Art Exhibition, Mystic Art Assn, Conn, 1985, Fibers & Form Invitational, Seattle Ctr, 1987, Face to Face: Cranbrook to Mexico, Cranbrook Academy of Art Mus, 1988, The Stitch, Textile Arts Ctr, Chgo, 1991, Collision of Cool, Cranbrook Academy of Art Mus, 1999, 2000, Pin-Ups, Detroit Artists Market, 2002, Visual Inquiry, Kansas State Univ Art Faculty Exhibition Marianna Kistler Beach Mus of Art, 2013 and several others. *Collection Arranged:* Emprise Bank, Wichita, Kansas, Marianna Kistler Beach Mus of Art, American Craft Mus, NY and numerous private collections in RI, Washington, Michigan, Florida, and Kansas. *Pos:* Registrar's asst, Spencer Mus of Art, Lawrence, Kansas, 1981-1982; dir education/exhibitions, Slater Mill Historic Site, Pawtucket, RI, 1983-1986; assoc producer, Lyric Theater, Highline Community Col, Des Moines, Washington, 1987; registrar I, Detroit Inst of Arts, 1989-1990; exec dir, Detroit Artists Market, 1990-1995; curator of education, fine and performing arts, Wildlife Interpretive

Gallery, Detroit Zoological Inst, Royal Oak, Michigan, 1995-2001; regional artist, mentor, Vermont Col MFA program, 2005-; assoc fellow, International Quilt Study Ctr & Mus, Univ Nebraska, 2010; invited speaker in the field; managing editor, Cranbrook Academy of Art Viewbook, 2002, 2004, 2007, production editor, 2001-2006, Listen Up creative writing journal, 2005-2007; visiting artist, critic and juror for many organizations. *Teaching:* Instructor, Red Deer Col, Alberta, Canada, 1990, Fiber Dept, Col for Creative Studies, 1990-1993; asst dir for academic programs, Cranbrook Academy of Art, Bloomfield Hills, Michigan, 2001-2007; dept head, assoc prof art, dept of art, Coll of Arts & Sciences, Kansas State Univ, Manhattan, Kansas, 2007-; Dorothy Liesky Wampler Eminent Prof, James Madison Univ, Harrisonburg, Virginia, 2012-2013. *Awards:* James Renwick Senior Fellow in American Craft, Smithsonian Institution, 1994-1995. *Mem:* Textile Soc of America (board directors, juried exhibition co-chair, 2013-2014, membership com chair, 2012-2014, mem nominations com, awards com). *Publ:* Several publications in the field; published several book chapterss, catalog essays, articles and reviews (Art in America, Hmong Studies Journal, The Journal of Modern Craft, Suface Design Journal, Sculpture and others). *Mailing Add:* 2341 Grandview Terrace Manhattan KS 66502

CRAIG, JAMES HICKLIN
CONSULTANT
b Chester, SC, Jul 23, 1937. *Study:* Univ SC, 56; Cincinnati Coll Conservatory Music, 59; Juilliard Sch Music, 60; Paris, 60. *Pos:* Cur, decorative arts NC Dept Archives & Hist, Raleigh, 62-64; principal, James Craig Fine & Decorative Arts, 65-69; pres, Craig & Tarlton, Inc, Raleigh, 69-85; fine arts consult, Independence, Va, 85-; consult, to NC Gov's Mansion bd, acquisitions comt, currently. *Mem:* Sparta Mus Project, Raleigh Chamber Music Soc, New York City Chamber Opera Theater (bd dir, currently); Mint Mus Art, Charlotte, (trustee 2000-). *Interests:* Gardening. *Collection:* American Art & Antiques, violins & related meaterial. *Publ:* Auth, The Arts & Crafts in NC 1699-1840, 65 (listed by Montgomery as part of 100 best in field)

CRAIG, MORGAN
PAINTER
Study: Temple Univ, Tyler Sch Art, Philadelphia, BFA, 2000; Univ Arts, Philadelphia, MFA (Painting), 2003. *Exhib:* Solo exhibs include Redux Contemp Art Ctr, Charleston, SC, 2005, Penn State Univ, Altoona, Pa, 2005, Big Idea Gallery, Jim Thorpe, Pa, 2006, Artworks Gallery, Cincinnati, 2006, The Philadelphia Art Alliance, Philadelphia, 2006, City Arts Ctr, Okla City, Okla, 2007; Group exhibs include Works in Progress, Univ Arts, Philadelphia, 2001, 2002; New Blood 3, Invitational, Finer Things Gallery, Nashville, Tenn, 2004 ; Avalanche 2004, Juried Exhib, Avalanche Gallery, New York, 2004; 29th Juried Show, Allentown Art Mus, Allentown, Pa, 2005 ; Summer Invitational Exhib, OK Harris, New York, 2005; New Philadelphia Realism, Seraphin Gallery, Philadelphia, 2005; PLACE, Lawrence Asher Gallery, Los Angeles, 2006; South Bend Mus Art, S Bend, Ind, 2006; Delaware Ctr Contemp Arts, Painted Interior, Wilmington, Del, 2006; Bettcher Gallery, Miami, 2006. *Awards:* Univ Arts Merit Scholar, 2000-2003; O'Hern Family Memorial Award, 2004; George Sugarman Found Grant, 2008. *Mailing Add:* 2200 Arch St Unit 804 Philadelphia PA 19103

CRAIG, NANCY ELLEN
PAINTER
b Bronxville, NY. *Study:* Acad Julien, Paris, France; Art Students League, New York; Hans Hofmann Sch, Provincetown, Mass; Bennington Coll with Frederick Taubes. *Work:* Metrop Mus Art, New York; Baltimore Mus; New Britain Art Inst; John Ringling Mus, Sarasota, Fla; Provincetown Art Asn & Mus, Provincetown, Mass. *Comn:* Portraits comn by Assoc Justice Stanley Reed, Supreme Ct Bldg, Washington, DC, Gov & Mrs Herbert Lehman, New York, Mrs Franklin D Roosevelt, Jr, New York, Duke of Argyll, 69 & Princess Marie Luise of Prussia, 74, Paul Cadmus, Lady Jeanne Campbell, Edwin Dickinson, Princess Elizabeth of Yugoslavia, Christopher Forbes Family, Aileen Guinness Plunkett, Kieren Guiness, Hans Hoffman, Angelica Huston, Norman Mailer, John and Henry Ringley North, Frank Lloyd Wright, Lady Marcia Rose Leresson-Crower. *Exhib:* Nat Acad Design, New York; Audubon Artists, New York; Allied Artists Am, New York; Solo exhibs, Graham Gallery, New York & Galeria Betica, Madrid, Spain; Cape Cod Mus Art, Dennis, 2011; Groton Sch Mass, 2012. *Awards:* First Benjamin Altman Figure Prize, Nat Acad Design, 57; Gold Medal of Honor, Allied Artists Am; Patron's Prize, Audubon Artists; Pollock Krasner Found Grant, 2008. *Bibliog:* Nardi Campion (auth), Nancy Ellen Craig & her portraits, Am Artist. *Media:* Oil on Canvas. *Publ:* Auth, Portrait painting in oil, 60; Nassau Guardian, 71; New York Post, 73; New York Times, 78; Provincetown Banner, 2008; Boston Globe, 2008; Cape Cod Times, 2010; Provincetown Arts Mag, 2010. *Dealer:* Gail Browne Gallery Provincetown Ma; Triero Fine Arts Ma. *Mailing Add:* PO Box 57 Truro ME 02666

CRAIG, SUSAN V
LIBRARIAN
b Newton, Kans, Nov 11, 1948. *Study:* Univ Kans, BA, 70; Emporia State Univ, MLS, 71. *Pos:* Indexer, Art Index, H W Wilson Co, New York, 71-74; art hist & classics librn, Univ Calif, Berkeley, 75-81; art librn, Univ Kans, 81-. *Teaching:* Instr art bibliog, Univ Calif, Berkeley, 81. *Mem:* Art Libr Soc NAm (secy 75-77, chmn, 86). *Publ:* auth, Survey of Current Practices in Art & Architecture Libraries, Jour Libr Admin, Vol 39, No 1, 2003, 91-107; auth, Biographical Dictionary of Kansas Artists Active before 1945, web publ. *Mailing Add:* 1717 Indiana St Lawrence KS 66044-4049

CRAMER, DOUGLAS S
COLLECTOR, PATRON
b Louisville, Ky. *Study:* Northwestern Univ, 1949-50; Sorbonne, Paris, 1951; Univ Cincinnati, BA, 1953; Columbia Univ, MFA, 1954; Beta Theta Pi. *Pos:* Production asst, Radio City Music Hall, New York City, 1950-51; with script dept, Metro-Goldwyn-Mayer, 1952; managing dir, Cincinnati Playhouse, 1953-54; TV supv, Procter & Gamble, 1956-59; broadcast supv, Ogilvy, Benson & Mather, 1959-62; vpres, prog develop, ABC, 1962-66, 20th Century-Fox-TV, LA, 1966-68; exec vpres, in charge prod Paramount TV, 1968-71; ind prod, pres, Douglas S Cramer Co, 1971-; exec vpres, Aaron Spelling Prod, 1976-87, vchmn, 1988-90, bd trustess, 1983-96; pres, Mus Contemp Art, Los Angeles, 1990-93, 1st vchmn, 1993-96; trustee, Int Coun Mus Modern Art, New York City, 1993-; pres, bd trustees, Douglas S Cramer Found, 1993-; trustee, Mus Mod Art, New York, 1993-. *Teaching:* Instr, Carnegie Inst Tech, 1955-56. *Awards:* Named one of Top 200 Collectors, ARTnews Mag, 2004-08; Archives Am Art Medal, Smithsoanian Inst, 2009. *Bibliog:* Grace Glueck (auth), Artful LA, NY Times Mag, 11/23/86; Peter Clothier (auth), Douglas Cramer: Passionate Perfectionist, Art News, 2/87; Bob Colacello (auth), At Home on the Ranch, Vanity Fair, 4/88. *Mem:* Mus Contemp Art, Los Angeles; Ctr Theater Group (bd dir, 85-90); Int Coun Mus Mod Art (chmn painting & sculpture comt, 96); Am Ballet Theater (Nat bd dir, 88-93); Univ Club New York City. *Collection:* Approximately 600 works of contemporary American art from 1960 to the present; Contemporary art, especially '60s & '80s. *Publ:* Executive prodr.: Star Trek, 1968-69, Bridget Loves Bernie, CBS-TV, 1972-73, QB VII, 1973-74, Dawn: Portrait of a Teenage Runaway, NBC-TV, 1976, Danielle Steel's Fine Things, 1990, Kalediscope, 1990, Changes, 1991, Daddy, 1991, Palomino, 1990-91, Secrets, 1991, Heart Beat, 1992, Star, 1993, Message to Nam, 1993, Vanished, 1995, Family Album, 1994, Perfect Stranger, 1994, No Greater Love, 1995, Mixed Blessings, 1995, Zoya, 1995, Family of Cops I & II, CBS-TV, 1995-96, The Ring, 1996, Remembrance, 1996, Full Circle, NBC-TV, 1996, Family of Cops III, 1999; co-exec. prodr.: Love Boat, ABC, 1977-86, Vegas, ABC, 1978-81, Wonder Woman, ABC, 1975-77, CBS, 1977-78, Dynasty, 1981-89, Hotel, 1983-87, Trade Winds, 1993; prodr.: (feature film) Sleeping Together, 1995; author: (plays) Call of Duty, 1953, Love Is A Smoke, 1957, Whose Baby Are You, 1963, Last Great Dish, 1994, Lust For Murder, 1995

CRANDALL, DORRIS
INSTRUCTOR, PAINTER
b Brooklyn Heights, NY. *Study:* attended, Pratt Inst, New Sch, Art Students League, NYU; studied with, Reuban Tam & Edwin Dickinson, Brooklyn Mus Fine Art, Sheldon Kech, Mus Modern Art. *Work:* Zimon Found, NY; Alexander Liberman, NY; Frances McLaughlin Gill, NY; Lionel Kazan, Paris; Pablo Jacobi-Lugano. *Exhib:* Three Man show, Brooklyn Mus, NY; Two Man show, Bodley Gallery, NY; Group shows, Galleria 38, Wash DC, Michelson Gallery, Wash DC; The American Indian, Smithsonian Inst, Shrewsbury, NJ; Teacher/Student Exhib, Guild of Creative Art, Shrewsbury, NJ, 2011. *Pos:* art dir, Conde Nast, Vogue & Glamour mags, NY, 55-79; designer, Originala Designer Coats, NY, 79-80s; owner, Greeting Card Co, NY, 80s. *Teaching:* instr illustration & design, Parsons Sch Design, NY, 60-70; instr multi-media, New School, NY Inst Tech, Bennet Coll, NY, 60s-70s; instr drawing & multi-media, Guild of Creative Arts, Shrewsbury, NJ, 2000-2012. *Awards:* Graphics Ann, 50s; Grapics Int, 50s; AIGA, Revlon, 55; Cover Design award, Art Collector's Guide, 59; Certificate of Merit, The Commodore, Am Wool Coun, 63; Certificate of Merit, 15th Ann, Soc Illusrs, 65. *Bibliog:* Hilton Kramer (auth), Review of Dorris Crandall, 70s; Ink, Conde Nast. *Mem:* Guild of Creative Arts, Shrewsbury, NJ (exhibiting mem, 99-2012); Soc Illustration; Nat Arts Club; Graphic Artists Guild; Fashion Group (bd govs). *Media:* Fashion, Graphic Design, Illustration, Painting. *Publ:* contbr, Vogue, Glamour, House & Garden, Graphics Int, 50s-60s, Art Collectors Guild, 59. *Dealer:* Guild of Creative Arts 260 Broad St Shrewsbury NJ 07702

CRANDALL, JERRY C
PAINTER, HISTORIAN
b La Junta, Colo, Apr 1, 1935. *Study:* Woodbury Col, Los Angeles, Calif, 60. *Work:* Favell Mus, Klamath Falls, Ore; Koshare Indian Mus, La Junta, Colo; Bianchi Mus, Temecula, Calif. *Comn:* Robert Conrad as Pasquinelle in Centennial, comn by Robert Conrad, Malibu, Calif, 78; Wild Bill Hickok, Petersen Publ Co, Beverly Hills, Calif, 75; Custer's Last Stand, comn by Dr Larry Frost, Monroe, Mich; Luftwaffe aircraft for pvt Ariz collector; Aces of the Word Aircraft for pvt Tex collector. *Exhib:* Rotary Club Amarillo, 84-86; Tulsa Gilcrease Mus Art, 84-; Western Art in the Grand Traditon, 86-; Champlin Mus Art Show, 90 & 91; Air Aces Symp, 92 & 94; and others. *Pos:* Historical tech adv, Universal Studios film Centennial, 78, Columbia Pictures film The Mountain Men, 79 & Arts & Entertainment hist series The Real West; speaker, Professional Motivation in the Arts, Univ Calif, Riverside, 80-81, Forum Am Soc Aviation Artists, 90. *Awards:* Gold & Silver Medals, Western Artists Am Ann Exhib & Sale, 81. *Bibliog:* Phylllis Barton (auth), Creative credibility, Southwest Art, 10/80; Historical authenticity in art, Man at Arms, 11/83; Air Classics, 3/92, 12/92, 11/93 & 11/94. *Mem:* Little Big Horn Asn; Am Fighter Aces; Tailhook; Am Soc Aviation Artistsn; Los Angeles Soc Illusr. *Media:* Oil, Acrylic. *Publ:* Illusr, Marsielles, Star of Africa, 69 & Battle of Britain, 70, JWC Publ; Guns of the Gunfighters (cover), Petersen Publ Co, 75; General Custer and the Battle of the Little Big Horn, Garry Owen Press, 76; Aviation a History through Art, p-51, (cover); auth & illus, J626 pictorial (cover), Marseille (cover), Me109F,6,K (cover), J67 (cover), Eagles of the Luftwaffe, Fighter Aces of the Luftwaffe (cover); and others. *Dealer:* Eagle Editions Ltd PO Box 580 Hamilton MT 59840. *Mailing Add:* 752 Bobcat Ln Hamilton MT 59840-9355

CRANDALL, JORDAN
VIDEO ARTIST, ADMINISTRATOR, EDUCATOR
Comn: Video installations include Suspension, 1997, Drive, 1998-99, Trigger, 2002, Hotel, 2010. *Exhib:* Solo exhibitions include Mus of Contemporary Art Klasma, Helsinki, Neue Galerie am Landesmuseum Joanneum, Graz, ARTLAB, Tokyo, Museo de Arte Carillo Gil, Mexico City, Centre d'Art Contemporian de Basse-Normandie, Caen, Kunst-Werke, Berlin, Kitchen in NY, AGORA, Rio de Janeiro, Edith Russ Site fur Medienkunst, Oldenburg, and TENT Centrum Beeldende Kunst, Rotterdam; group exhibitions include the Whitney Mus, NY, Tate Mus and the San Francisco Mus of Modern Art; videos have been presented at many international film and media festivals. *Pos:* Honorary resident, Eyebeam Art and Technology Ctr, NY, currently; founding editor, VERSION; researcher in residence, Calif Inst for

Telecommunications and Information Technology (CALIT2), currently; writes and lectures regularly at various institutions across the US and Europe. *Teaching:* Chair, Visual Arts Department, Univ of Calif San Diego, currently. *Awards:* Vilem Flusser Theory award for Outstanding Theory and Research-Based Digital Arts Practice, Transmediale in Berlin, 2011. *Publ:* (auth) Suspension, 1997, Interaction: Artisitic Practice in the Network, 2001, Trigger Projekt, 2002, & Heatseeking, 2002. *Mailing Add:* The Visual Arts Department University California San Diego 9500 Gilman Dr VAF 413 La Jolla CA 92093-0327

CRANDALL, JUDITH ANN
GALLERY DIRECTOR, WRITER
b Milwaukee, Wis, Aug 20, 1948. *Study:* El Camino Jr Col, Univ Ariz. *Comn:* Cowgirls: Early Images & Collectibles, Schiffer Publ. *Collection Arranged:* Eleventh Ann Membership Show for Women Artists of the Am West, 83; Phoenix Forum Am Soc Aviation Artists, 88; coordr, Aviation Art Exhib, Champlin Mus, Mesa, Ariz, 90 & 91; Air Aces Symp, Mesa, Ariz & Atlanta, Ga, 92 & 93, Albuquerque, 95. *Pos:* Staff writer, Southwest Art Mag, Houston, 74-; dir, Saddleback Western Art Gallery, Calif, 78-80; owner, Eagle Ed, Hamilton, Mont, currently; ed, Aerobrush, Am Soc Aviation Artists, 99-90; guest ed, Great Am Aviation Artists, Challenge Publ, Calif. *Publ:* Auth, The Custer centennial, 76, Retrospective view of the year, 80 & Women artists of the American West, 82 & over 40 artists biography profiles, Southwest Art Mag; Little Chief, Air Classics Mag, 88; The artist's wife, AeroArt Mag, 88; auth, Cowgirls Early Images and Collectibles; contribr, various aviation art publ. *Mailing Add:* 752 Bobcat Ln Hamilton MT 59840-9355

CRANE, ARNOLD H
PHOTOGRAPHER
b Chicago, Ill, July 17, 1932. *Study:* Coll Law, DePaul Univ, Ill, JD, 55. *Work:* Metrop Mus Art & Mus Mod Art, NY; Art Inst Chicago, Ill; Kunsthaus, Zurich, Switz; Biblioteck Nat, Cabinet des Estampes, Paris, France. *Exhib:* Portraits of Photographers, Corcoran Gallery, Washington, DC, 74, Wellesley Col, Mass, 75, Kansas City Mus Art, 77, Univ Miami, Lowe Art Mus, Coral Gables, Fla, 79 & Univ Ill, Krannert Art Mus, 85; Selections Ruttenberg Collection, Art Inst Chicago, 92; Landscape of the Body, Mus Contemp Art, Chicago, 93. *Teaching:* adj prof, Univ Miami, 84. *Awards:* Photobuch Prize, Eastman Kodak Ger, 96; Int New Photo Award, White House News Photos, 2001. *Mem:* Am Soc Media Photogr; White House News Photog Asn. *Dealer:* Galerie AmDom Burkhart Arnold Cologne Germany; Arlene Lewallen Gallery Sante Fe NM. *Mailing Add:* 680 N Lake Shore Dr Apt 1202 Chicago IL 60611

CRANE, BARBARA BACHMANN
PHOTOGRAPHER, EDUCATOR
b Chicago, Ill, Mar 19, 1928. *Study:* Mills Col, with Alfred Neumeyer, 45-48; NY Univ, BA (art hist), 50; Inst of Design, Ill Inst Technol, with Aaron Siskind, MS (photog), 66. *Work:* Libr Cong, Washington, DC; High Mus Art, Atlanta; Art Inst Chicago; Mus Mod Art, New York; Bibliot Nat, Paris; Nat Mus Am Art, Smithsonian, Washington, DC; Mus Contemp Photog, Columbia Coll, Chicago; Ctr Creative Photog, Univ Ariz, Tucson; Mus Contemp Art, Chicago; Thessaloniki Mus Photog, Greece; Int Mus Photog, George Eastman House, Rochester, NY; John D & Catherine T MacArthur Found; The Nat Mus Mod Art, Kyoto, Japan; and others. *Comn:* 26 photomurals, Baxter Travenol Labs, Deerfield, Ill, 75; Chicago Epic (photomural), Chicago Bank Commerce, Standard Oil Bldg, Chicago. *Exhib:* Solo exhibs, Friends of Photog, Carmel, Calif, 69 & 75, Tweed Mus Art, Univ Minn, Duluth, 86, Spertus Mus Judaica, 92-93, Prague House Photog, Czech Repub, 93, Galerie Suzel Berna, Paris, 94, Gallery 954, Chicago, 94 & Mills Coll Art Gallery, Oakland, Calif, 97; San Francisco Mus Mod Art (with catalog), 85; Montreal Mus Fine Arts, Que (with catalog) & traveling, 94; When Aaron Met Harry, Mus Contemp Photog, Chicago, Ill, 96; Art in Chicago: 1945-1995, Mus Contemp Art, Chicago, 96-97; Midwest Photographers Project: Illinois Photography in the 1990's, Mus Contemp Photog, 96-97; Body in the Lens, Montreal Mus Fine Arts, Que, 97. *Pos:* Mem, educ adv bd, Polaroid Corp, 85; Visual arts panel, MacDowell Colony, 89-90. *Teaching:* Prof photog, Sch Art Inst Chicago, 67-93, emer prof, 93-; vis prof photog, Philadelphia Col of Art, 77, Sch Mus Fine Arts, Boston, 79 & Cornell Univ, Ithaca, NY, 83, Bezalet Acad Art & Design, Jerusalem, Israel, 87, Bezalel. *Awards:* Nat Endowment Arts Grant, 74 & 88; Guggenheim Found Fel in Photog, 79; Polaroid Corp Assistance Grant, 79-94; Ill Arts Coun Grant, 85 & 2001; Young Women's Christian Asn Outstanding Achievement Award, Art, 87; Artist of the Year, Union League Club of Chicago, 2006; Distinguished Artist, Brown Univ, 2006; Hon Educ & Artist, Midwest Region, Soc for Photog Educ. *Bibliog:* Mary Sherman (auth), rev, Chicago Sun Times, 3/25/88; Alice Thorson (auth), rev, Wash Times, 2/9/89; JoAnn Lewis (auth), rev, Wash Post, 2/11/89; Bernard Welt (auth), rev, New Art Examiner, 4/89. *Mem:* Soc Photog Educ (mem bd, 72-76); Friends of Photog (trustee, 75-81). *Media:* Gelatin Silver, Polaroid, Digital. *Publ:* Auth, Flora Photographica, Thames & Hudson, 92; contribr, A History of Women Photographers, Abbeville Press, New York, 94; Bystander: A History of Street Photography, Bulfinch Press, 94; The Body: Photographs of the Human Form, Chronicle Bks, 94; Exhibiting Photography: Twenty Years at the Center for Creative Photography, Univ Ariz, 96; Barbara Crane: 1948-1980; Barbara Crane: Urban Anomalies; Barbara Crane: Chicago Loop; Barbara Crane: The Evolution of a Vision; Barbara Crane: Still Lifes: Nature Mortes, 2002; and others. *Dealer:* Stephen Daiter Gallery Chicago; Flatfile Gallery Chicago; Francoise Paviot Gallery Paris. *Mailing Add:* 1017 W Jackson Blvd #1A Chicago IL 60607

CRANE, BONNIE LOYD
PRIVATE DEALER, APPRAISER
b Minneapolis, Minn, Aug 24, 1930. *Study:* Sweet Briar Coll Va, BA (cum laude), 50; Bryn Mawr Coll, Pa, MA, 72; studied with Hobson Pittman. *Collection Arranged:* Blanche Ames, Artist & Activist (auth, catalog), Brockton Art Mus, 82; Crane Collection: Special Exhibitions, Boston Sch, 85-86; Bruce Crane, Am Tonalist, 10-11/86; Tonalism, 10 & 11/87; Inspiration Cape Ann, summer 88; Gentle Art of Still Life, 89; Theresa Bernstein Centennial Exhib, 90; Interiors, 92; Russian Light I & II (auth, catalog), 95 & 96; Nikolai Timkov, 99; Three Boston Artists, 2003; Arthur Wesley Dow; Theresa Bernstein and Wm Meyerowitz, 2005; Play Ball, Art of Baseball, 2005; New England Sunlight, 2006; Theresa Bernstein, 2006; Little Picture Show: 87-2006; Don Stone & John Traynor, 2009. *Pos:* Cur & dir educ, Brockton Art Mus, Brockton, Mass, 81-82; cur, Clark Gallery, Lincoln Station, Mass, 81-85; owner, Crane Collection, Boston, Mass, 85-, Wellesley, 96-2005 & Cape Ann 2005-. *Teaching:* Lectr Am painting, Mus Fine Arts Sch, Houston, Tex, 75-76 & Rice Univ, 76; studio teacher drawing & painting, Cairo Am Coll, Egypt, 78-79. *Mem:* Arch Am Art; Nat Acad Design; Artcetera (bd mem); Handel & Haydn Soc (bd mem); Friends Art, Sweet Briar Coll (bd mem, 92); St Botolph Club (co-chair art com, 2002-03); Cape Ann CofC; N Shore Women Bus; Rockport Art Assoc; North Shore Art Assoc; Rockport Music; Vestry St John's Church, Beverly Farms. *Specialty:* Am painting of the 19th & early 20th centuries, especially Hudson River Sch, New Eng landscapes & the Boston Sch, also traditional contemp artists. *Interests:* Music, travel, volunteering. *Publ:* Auth, Artist & activist Blanche Ames, Brockton Art Mus & Smith Alumnae Quart, 82; The Gentle Art of Stilllife; Russian Light. *Mailing Add:* c/o Crane Collection 2 Old Salem Path Gloucester MA 01930

CRANE, DAVID FRANKLIN
CERAMIST, EDUCATOR
b Hamilton, Ohio, Aug 16, 1953. *Study:* Northern Ariz Univ, Flagstaff, BFA, 76, Ill State Univ, Normal, Ill, MFA, 78. *Work:* IBM Corp, Charlotte, NC; Souran Bank, Roanoke, Va; Fred Marer Collection, Los Angeles, Calif; Neville Pub Mus, Green Bay, Wis; Ill State Univ, Normal; Southern Progress Corp. *Exhib:* Marrietta Coll Crafts Nat, Grover Herman Fine Arts Ctr, Ohio, 78; Clay and Fiber: Fifteen View Points, Charles Wustain Mus, Racine, Wis, 78; Young Americans Clay/Glass, Mus Contemp Crafts, NY, 78; Biennial Exhib Crafts, Mint Mus Art, Charlotte, NC, 79; 36th Ann Nat Ceramics Invitational, Lang Art Gallery, Scripps Col, Claremont, Calif, 80; Earthenware USA, Hand & Spirit Gallery, Scottsdale, Ariz, 81; Southeast Seven 9, Southeastern Ctr Contemp Art, Winston-Salem, NC, 86; Clay Az Art, Crafts Mus, Helsinki, Finland, 87; Running Ridge Gallery, 89; Uncommon Vessels, Fla Gulf Coast Art Ctr, 90. *Pos:* Artist-in-Residence, Ford Found, Univ Ga, Athens, 78-79; dir, Armory Art Gallery, Va Tech, 89. *Teaching:* Visiting instr, art-ceramics, Univ Ga, Athens, 79-80; instr, ceramics, Callanwolde Fine Arts Ctr, Atlanta, Ga, 79-80; assoc prof art-ceramics, Va Tech, Blacksburg, Va, 80-. *Awards:* Award of Excellence, Radford Univ, 84; Secca-Seven Art Fel, RJ Reynolds Corp, 86; Va Mus Fel, 89. *Bibliog:* Mark Erikson (auth), Sophisticated Clay, Va Gazette, 84; Patricia Mattews (auth), David Crane, Am Ceramics, 5/88. *Mem:* Nat Coun Educ Ceramic Arts. *Publ:* Contrib, Low-Fire: Other ways to work in clay, Davis, 80; Images of Clay Sculpture, Harper & Row, 83. *Dealer:* Schneider Gallery 230 Superior St Chicago IL. *Mailing Add:* 1449 Lusters Gate Rd Blacksburg VA 24060

CRANE, JEAN
PAINTER
b Battle Creek, Mich, July 25, 1933. *Study:* Syracuse Univ, BFA, 55. *Work:* Wustum Art Mus, Racine, Wis; Madison Art Ctr, Wis; The Kemper Collection; Northwest Mutual Life Collection; Miller Brewery Collection. *Exhib:* Watercolor USA, Kohler Art Ctr; Wisconsin Biennale; Am Watercolor Soc, NY; Paine Art Ctr, Wis; Layering: An Art of Time and Space, Albuquerque Mus Art, 85; and others. *Teaching:* pvt teacher. *Awards:* First Place, Wustum Art Mus, 89; Emily Lowe Award, Am Watercolor Soc, New York, 81. *Bibliog:* Review, New Art Examiner, Chicago, 3/81. *Mem:* Wis Watercolor Soc; Wis Painters & Sculptors. *Media:* Watercolor. *Dealer:* Katie Gingrass Gallery 241 N Broadway Milwaukee WI 53202; Leslie Levy Gallery 7135 Main St Scottsdale AZ 85251

CRANE, JIM (JAMES) G
PAINTER, CARTOONIST
b Hartshorne, Okla, May 21, 1927. *Study:* Albion Col, BA; State Univ Iowa, MA; Mich State Univ, MFA. *Work:* Walker Art Ctr, Minn; Joslyn Mus, Omaha; Wis State Univ, River Falls; St Cloud State Col, Minn; Centro Colombo Amercano, Cali, Colombia; Armacast Libr, Eckord Coll. *Exhib:* 28th Biennial, Corcoran Gallery Art; 149th Ann, Pa Acad Fine Arts, Philadelphia; Mich Artists, Detroit Art Inst; Painting of the Yr, Smithsonian Inst; Ringling Mus, Sarasota; Centro Colombo Americano, Cali, Colombia; Walker Art Ctr, Minneapolis; Arts in Embassies Prog, Lima, Peru & Katmandu, Nepal; 50+ Retrospective, Eckerd Coll. *Teaching:* Chair & prof, Univ Wis, River Fall, 58-62; Prof art, Eckerd Col, 63-94, first chairman, Coll Creative Art, 72-75, artist-in-residence, 88-94, emer prof, 94-. *Awards:* Award Tampa Mus, Fla, 82; Robert A Straub Distinguished Teacher Award, Eckerd Col, 87; Friends Arts Art Educator Award, Pinellas, Art Coun, 95; Distinguished Alumni, Albion Coll, 72. *Media:* Acrylic Collage, Acrylic Painting. *Publ:* Auth, Great Teaching Machine, 66 & Parables, 71, John Knox; Inside Out, 67; illusr, A Funny Thing Happened on the Way to Heaven, 69; illusr, Kalabashee and His Sisters, 2002; ed, Aspects J, Acad Sr Professionals Eckerd Col, 96; plus others. *Mailing Add:* 11000 9th St E Saint Petersburg FL 33706-1112

CRANE, MICHAEL PATRICK
MUSEUM DIRECTOR, CURATOR
b St Louis, Mo, Dec 24, 1948. *Study:* Art Inst Chicago, MFA (design & commun), 76. *Work:* Jean Brown Arch, Tyringham Inst, Mass; Arch Sohm, Markgroningen, WGer; Mus Contemp Art, Univ Sao Paulo, Brazil; Mod Mus, Stockholm, Sweden. *Exhib:* 03-23-03, Nat Gallery Can, Ottawa, Ont, 77; Open Ring Gallery, Sacramento, 79; Berry Col, Mt Berry, Ga, 79 & 80; Union Gallery, San Jose, 80; La Mamelle, San Francisco, 81; and others. *Pos:* Original mem & co-dir, Name Gallery, Chicago, 73-74; ed, Running Dog Press, San Jose, 74-; adminr, All the Chicago Fog Performance Gallery, Chicago, 75-76; res fel, Inst Advan Studies in Contemp Art, San Diego, Calif, 77-78; gallery dir, Calif State Univ, Sacramento, 78-79; gallery dir, San Jose State Univ, 79-83; gallery & mus dir, Arvada Ctr Arts & Humanities, Colo,

83-86; gallery dir, Univ Colo, 86-94; sr cur, Bellevue Art Mus, 95-97; partner, SAY Terrazzo Designs, 97-. *Teaching:* Vis artist, Univ Chicago & Calif State Univ, Sacramento, 77; vis artist, San Diego State Univ, 78; lectr, Calif State Univ, Sacramento, 78-79 & San Jose State Univ, 79-83; vis artist, Sch Art Inst, Chicago, 79; vis artist, Ariz State Univ, 79; asst prof, Univ Colo, 86-94. *Publ:* Contribr, Anti-Object Art, Northwestern Univ Press, 74; auth, Fill in This Space, 75 & Landscapes I'd Love to Perform/Do, 76, Running Dog Press; ed, Correspondence Art, Contemp Arts Press, 83. *Mailing Add:* 7720 Missy Ct Saint Louis MO 63123

CRARY, JONATHAN KNIGHT
ART HISTORIAN
b New Haven, Conn. *Study:* San Francisco Art Inst, BFA, 73; Columbia Univ, BA, 75, MA, 78, PhD, 87. *Pos:* Found ed, Zone, 86-. *Teaching:* Vis lectr, Univ Calif, San Diego, 83 & 85; asst prof, Columbia Univ, 87, asst prof, Columbia Univ, 87; Meyer Shapiro, prof mod art & theory, 2005. *Awards:* J P Getty Fel Art Hist & Humanities, 90-91; Guggenheim Fel, 91; mem, Inst Adv Study, 93; Lionel Trilling Book Award, 2001. *Res:* Contemp art & culture. *Publ:* Auth, Passage from virgin to bride, 77 & Real estate opportunities, 78, Arts Mag; Delirious operations, 78, Artforum; Eclipse of the Spectacle, Art After Modernism, 84; Techniques of the Observer, MIT Press, 90. *Mailing Add:* 310 W 106th St New York NY 10025-3429

CRAVEN, DAVID JAMES
PAINTER, COLLAGE ARTIST
b London, Ont, Dec 18, 1946. *Study:* Univ Western Ont, BA, 69; Ont Coll Art, 71-73. *Work:* Nat Gallery Can, Ottawa, Ont; Art Gallery Ont, Toronto; Vancouver Art Gallery; Montreal Mus Fine Art; Winnipeg Art Gallery. *Exhib:* Solo exhibs, Musée d'Art Contemporain, Montreal, Que, 78 & Vancouver Art Gallery, BC, 78; Paris Biennale, Musée d'Art Moderne de la Ville de Paris, 80; Material Matters, Clocktower, NY & Norton Mus, Palm Beach, Fla, 80; Canada in Birmingham, Ikon Gallery, Birmingham, Eng, 81; Psychodrama, Philadelphia Art Alliance, Pa, 85. *Bibliog:* Peter White (auth), David Craven: Recent Work, Southern Alta Art Gallery, 78; Sandra Shavl (auth), David Graven: The Signification of Collage, Parachute Mag, 79; Stephen Westfall, David Craven, Art in Am, 84. *Media:* Acrylic on Board. *Dealer:* Sable-Castelli Gallery 33 Hazelton Ave Toronto ON M5R 2E3 Canada. *Mailing Add:* 329 W 21st St New York NY 10011-3025

CRAVEN, WAYNE
ART HISTORIAN, WRITER
b Pontiac, Ill, Dec 7, 1930. *Study:* John Herron Art Sch, Indianapolis, Ind; Ind Univ, BA, 55, MA, 57; Columbia Univ, PhD, 63. *Collection Arranged:* Co-cur, Exhib Celebrating the Creative Am (sculpture sect), White House, Washington, DC, 65; guest cur, 200 Years of Am Sculpture, Whitney Mus Am Art, NY, 76. *Pos:* Mem bd ed, The Am Art J, New York, 74-, Smithsonian Am Art Mus, Washington DC, Peale Family Papers, Yale Univ, New Haven; mem adv bd, Daniel Chester French Papers, Nat Trust, Washington, DC, 75-. *Teaching:* Instr art hist, Wheaton Col, Norton, Mass, 58-60; H F du Pont Winterthur prof art hist, Univ Del, Newark, 60-98, emeritus. *Mem:* Coll Art Asn; Victorian Soc in Am (mem adv comt, 72); NSS; AAS. *Res:* Eighteenth & nineteenth century Am painting & sculpture. *Publ:* Auth, Sculpture in America, Univ Delaware Press, 84 & Colonial American Portraiture, Cambridge Univ Press, 86; American Art: History and Culture, McGraw-Hill, 2002; plus many journal articles on Am art. *Mailing Add:* Art Hist Dept Univ Del 318 Old College Newark DE 19716

CRAWFORD, BILL (WILBUR) OGDEN
ILLUSTRATOR, ADMINISTRATOR
b Northfield, NJ, Oct 5, 1941. *Study:* Hussian Sch Art, AST, 65. *Hon Degrees:* Rocky Mt Coll Art Design, BFA. *Work:* Philadelphia Mus Art; Smithsonian Inst, Washington, DC; Am Bank. *Comn:* Paper sculpture and Poster for Exhib to Benefit the Philadelphia Aids Task Force, 90 & 92. *Exhib:* Bakers Art, Mus Contemp Crafts, NY; Christmas Exhib, Smithsonian Inst; Illustration, Philadelphia Art Alliance & Soc Illusr, NY; Design, Art Dir Show, NY; Int Design Exhib, Brussels, Belg, Japan & France; NY Art Dirs Ann. *Pos:* Pres, Artist Guild Del Valley; pres, Int Coun Design Schs, 93; art dir ann poster, Big Brothers Big Sisters, Phila chpt, 94-; adv bd, Upper Darby Sch System, 98-. *Teaching:* Instr advert design, Hussian Sch Art, 65-88, asst dir design, 74-88, vpres dir educ, 81-88 & asst dir bus art, 83-88; lectr & consult, graphic design & illus; lectr paper sculptures, Art Careers Portfolio Develop. *Awards:* Gold Award, Philadelphia Art Dirs Ann, 90; Gold & Silver Award, Int 3D Illus exhib, 90 & 92; Gold & Best of Show Award, Philadelphia Artists Guild, 91; Outstanding Career Achievement, Pa Asn Pvt Sch Admin Hall of Fame, 93. *Bibliog:* Raymond Ballinger (auth), Design with Paper, Van Nostrand Reinhold, 82. *Mem:* Philadelphia Watercolor Club; Artist Guild Del Valley (pres, 74-75, exec off, 76-90); Art Dir Club Philadelphia; Int Coun Design Sch. *Media:* Paper Sculpture, Calligraphy, Watercolor, Mixed Media. *Publ:* Contribr, Cookies and Breads--The Bakers Art, Van Nostrand Reinhold, 67; Illusr 20, Hastings House, 78; illusr, The Collector, 86; illusr, Vol I & Vol III, Rockport, 91-93. *Mailing Add:* 90 Bethel Rd Glen Mills PA 19342-1514

CRAWFORD, RACHEL See Imlah, Rachel Crawford

CRAWFORD, RAINIE
PAINTER
b East Lyme, Conn. *Study:* Studied with Robert Brackman, Nancy Reilly & William Schultz. *Work:* Bell Jar w/a Figurine, Butler Inst Am Art; Still Life w/a Pewter Teapot, New Britain Mus Am Art; Medicine Man, New Haven Paint and Clay Club. *Exhib:* Hudson Valley Art Asn; Pastel Soc Am; Salmagundi Club; Allied Artists Am; Academic Artists Asn; Catherine Lorillard Wolfe Art Club; Numerous Nat Exhibs; Conn Acad Fine Arts; Conn Pastel Soc; Butler Inst Am Art, Ohio; New Britain Mus Am Art, Conn; Slater Mem Mus, Conn; Mattatuck Mus, Conn; New HAven Paint & Clay Club, Conn. *Awards:* George Inness Jr, Mem Award; Joseph V Giffuni Mem Award; Mary Lou Fitzgerald Mem Award; Art Spirit Found Silver Medal, Pastel Jour Second Ann Pastel 100, 2000; Art Spirit Found Gold Medal, Audubon Artist in C, 2007; Hudson Valley Art Asn Gold Medal, 2007; Art Spirit Found Gold Medal, Hudson Valley Art Asn, 2008. *Bibliog:* featured artist, Pastel Jour, 3-4/2001, 3-4/2002, 4/2008; featured artist, Am Artist Mag, 11/2001; featured artist, The Country and Abroad, 07/2007; featured artist, L'Art du Pastel, Art du Paste en France Publ; featured artist, Pure Color: Best of Pastel, Northlight Books Publ; featured artist, 100 Ways to Paint Still Life and Florals, Int Artists Publ. *Mem:* Signature mem & Master Pastelist, Pastel Soc Am; Fel artist mem, Am Artists Prof League; Allied Artists Am; Acad Artists Asn; Conn Pastel Soc; Hudson Valley Art Asn; Conn Acad of Fine Art. *Media:* Pastels. *Publ:* Illustr, Best of Pastel II, Rockport Publ. *Mailing Add:* 21 Mountainview Ave New Milford CT 06776

CRAWFORD, THOM COONEY
PAINTER, SCULPTOR
b Boston, Mass, Sept 23, 1944. *Study:* Provincetown Workshop, 63 & 64; Spring Hill Col, Mobile, Ala, BS, 66-62; Syracuse Univ, MFA, 66-67; RI Sch Design, 69. *Work:* Univ Pa; Everson Mus; Prudential Insurance Co; Rockford Art Mus, Ill; Amoco Products. *Comn:* Interior & Exterior (painting & sculpture), Prickly Mt Architectural Project, Warren, Vt, 67; Exterior (painting & sculpture), Bundy Art Mus, Waitesfield, Vt, 69; Mem stone sculpture, Allassio, Italy, 90. *Exhib:* Solo exhibs, M-13 Howard Scott Gallery, NY, 91 & 96, Nama Gallery, Tel-Aviv Israel, 94, Albright Coll Ctr Arts, Reading, Pa, 94, Trinity Church & Art Initiatives, NY, 95, St Peter's Church, NY, 96 & Allentown Art Mus, 96; Post Modernism Metaphors, Alternative Mus, NY, 81; New Visions, Aldrich Mus Contemp Art, Ridgefield, Conn, 81; NY Visions, Janus Gallery, Los Angeles, 83; Queens Mus, 83; PS 1, Proj Rm, NY, 83; Monique Knowlton Gallery, NY, 84; M-13 Gallery, NY, 86; Basel Art Fair, Switz, 87; Sculpture Maquette, Hakone Open Air Mus, Japan, 94. *Teaching:* Asst prof sculpture, LaFayette Col, 90-95, Parsons Sch Design, New York, 95-. *Awards:* Creative Artists Pub Serv Prog Fel, 82-83; Nat Endowment Arts Fel, 85. *Bibliog:* Virginia Wiegand (auth), The Philadelphia Inquirer, 9/25/94; Barbara MacAdams (auth), Art News, 12/94; Holland Cotter (auth), NY Times, 8/95; and others. *Media:* Bronze, Mixed Media. *Publ:* Auth & illusr, Raising of the Heart, Limited Ed, Queen City Eds, 72; auth, Alpha Omega (print portfolio), Graphico Uno, 88. *Dealer:* M-13 Howard Scott Gallery 72 Greene St New York NY 10012

CREECY, HERBERT LEE
PAINTER, SCULPTOR
b Norfolk, Va, Aug 14, 1939. *Study:* Atlanta Coll Art, 64; Stanley W Hayter-Atelier 17, Paris, France, 64-65. *Work:* Whitney Mus Am Art, NY; High Mus Art, Atlanta, Ga; Akron Mus Art, Ohio; Indianapolis Mus Art, Ind; Norton Gallery Art, West Palm Beach, Fla; and others; pvt collections include AT&T, Chicago, McDonald Corp, Oak Brook, Ill, Fed Res Bank, Richmond, Va, IBM, Raleigh, NC, Chase Manhattan Bank, NY, Cannon chapel, Emory Univ, Atlanta, GA, Indianapolis Mus of Art, Ind, many others. *Exhib:* Herb Creecy: Recent Work, High Mus Art, Atlanta, Ga; 35th Biennial Exhib Am Painting, Corcoran Gallery Art, Washington, 77; Abstraction, Southeastern Ctr Contemp Art, 85; Painting & Things, Nexus Contemp Art Ctr, 88; Painting: 70's - 80's, Lamar Dodd Art Ctr, 88. *Teaching:* Lectr, Univ Ga; Studies Abroad Program, Cortona, Italy; vis lectr, Univ Tenn, Knoxville. *Awards:* Governor's Grant, Ga Coun Arts. *Media:* Acrylic, Oil; Miscellaneous. *Publ:* Artforum Int, summer 88; Southern Homes, 5-6/89; Southern Accent, 1-2/90; Veranda, summer 90; Pegasus, 9-10/99. *Mailing Add:* 55 25th St NW Atlanta GA 30309-2008

CREED, MARTIN
INSTALLATION SCULPTOR
b Wakefield, England, 1968. *Study:* Slade Sch Fine Art, London, 1986-90. *Exhib:* Solo exhibs include Camden Arts Ctr, London, 1995, 2000, Brit Sch Rome, 1997, 2003, Marc Foxx, Los Angeles, 1999, Gavin Brown's Enterprise, New York, 2000, 2005, Wrong Gallery, New York, Kunsthalle Bern, Switzerland, 2003, Hauser & Wirth, London, 2004, Hauser & Wirth, Zurich, 2006, Tate Modern, London, 2006, Ctr Curatorial Studies, Bard Coll, NY, 2007, Tate Britain, London, 2008; group exhibs include Ace! Arts Coun Collection, Hayward Gallery, London, 1996, How to Improve the World, 2006; Life/Live, Mus Art Mod, Paris, 1996; Nerve, Inst Contemp Art, London, 1999, Surprise, Surprise, 2006; 54x54x54, Mus Contemp Art, London, 1999; Turner Prize, Tate Britain, London, 2001, The Turner Prize: A Retrospective, 2007; Tempo, Mus Mod Art, New York, 2002, Out of Time: A Contemp View, 2006; Rock My World, Calif Coll Arts, San Francisco, 2002; Big Bang: Destruction & Creation in 20th Century Art, Ctr Pompidou, Paris, 2005; Draw a Straight Line & Follow It, Bard Coll, NY, 2006; Into Me/Out of Me, PS1 Contemp Art Ctr, Long Island City, NY, 2006; Words Fail Me, Mus Contemp Art Detroit, 2007; 54th Int Art Exhib Biennale, Venice, 2011. *Awards:* Turner Prize, 2001. *Dealer:* Hauser & Wirth London 196A Piccadilly London W1J 9DY England UK. *Mailing Add:* c/o Gavin Browns Enterprise 620 Greenwich St New York NY 10014

CREEVY, BILL
PAINTER, WRITER
b New Orleans, La, June 24, 1942. *Study:* La State Univ, New Orleans, BA(hist), 65, Baton Rouge, MFA, 68; Brooklyn Mus Art Sch, 69 (Max Beckmann Scholar). *Comn:* Paintings of New York, Munic Asst Corp, NY, 81. *Exhib:* 161st Ann Exhib, Nat Acad Art, NY, 85; Am Artist Mag Golden Anniversary Nat Art Competition, San Francisco, St Louis & NY, 87; Int Exhib, Pastels Only, Soc Pastellistes de France, Lille, France, 87; 38th Art of NE USA, Silvermine Guild Arts Ctr, New Canaan, Conn, 87; 16th Ann Open Exhib, Pastel Soc Am, NY, 88. *Pos:* Art dir, Brooklyn Pub Libr, New York, 69-; asst dir, First Street Gallery, New York, 76-; moderator, Pastel Annual of PSA, 2010. *Teaching:* Asst graphics & drawing, La State Univ, 66-68; instr painting, Brooklyn Mus Art Sch, 69; Pastel Painters of Maine, 2010-. *Awards:* J Klimberger Mem Award for Still Life, Pastel Soc Am, 87; Nat Arts Club Award for Excellence, 88; C R Gibson Award for Mixed Media, Silvermine Guild Arts Ctr, 87; Art Masters award, Am Artist Mag, 97; NY Cent Award, PSA, 99; Uschi Grueterich Mem Award, PSA, 2000; Shirley Epstein Award, PSA, 2002; Sennelier Award, PSA, 2003; HK Holbein Award, PSA, 2005. *Bibliog:* Golden Anniversary winners, Am Artist, 87; Eileen Myles (auth),

Bill Creevy at First Street, Art in Am, 88; Shirley Gonzales (auth), Pastels Expresses Range of Texture, Color, New Haven Register, 4/23/89; Barbara Fischman (auth), Bill Creevy: Art with a Punch, Pastelagram, fall/winter 98; Rita A Rogan (auth), Bill Creevy: The Key to the Creative Zone, Pastel J, May/June 2003. *Mem:* Pastel Soc Am; Degas Pastel Soc; Salmagundi Club, New York, 2008-2010; Pastel Soc Am, 2009-2010. *Media:* Pastel, All. *Publ:* Auth, What Counts is What's Underneath: Pastel techniques by Bill Creevy, Artist's Mag, 3/88, rev ed; The Pastel Book, Bill Creevy, 91 & The Oil Painting Book, 93, Watson Guptill; auth, Jane Lund: A Clear Vision, Am Artist, 3/99; Oddball Pastel Blenders, Pastelagram, spring/summer 99; Rigid Supports: the alternative to paper, Pastelagram, fall/winter 99; Sheldon Tapley: Where Past & Present Meet, Am Artist, 11/99; Alan Flattmann Deals with Katrina: A summer of too many storms, Pastelagram, winter 2006. *Dealer:* Cole Pratt Gallery 3800 Magazine St New Orleans LA. *Mailing Add:* 6 Greene St New York NY 10013

CRESPO, MICHAEL LOWE
WRITER, PAINTER
b New Orleans, La, Jan 3, 1947. *Study:* La State Univ, BA; Queens Col, MFA. *Work:* New Orleans Aquarium, Mclhenny Collection La State Univ, City Nat Bank Collection, Baton Rouge, La; Taco Bell Corp, San Diego, Calif; Entergy Corp, Little Rock, Ark. *Exhib:* Simms Fine Art, New Orleans, La; Mesur Mus, Monroe, La; McMurtrey Gallery, Houston, Tex; Transco Energy Tower Gallery, Houston, Tex; Kurts Bingham Gallery, Memphis, Tenn; Artists' Choice Mus, NY; Contemp Art Ctr, New Orleans, La. *Pos:* Dir, Sch Art, La State Univ. *Teaching:* Instr painting, Univ Southwestern La, 71; prof, La State Univ, 71-; vis artist painting, Purdue Univ, 74. *Awards:* La Div Arts Artist Fel; Southern Arts Fed Fel, Nat Endowment Arts. *Media:* Oil on Canvas, Watercolor. *Publ:* Auth, Watercolor Day by Day, Watson-Guptill, New York, 87; Experiments in Watercolor, Watson-Guptill, New York, 88; How to Make An Oil Painting, Watson-Guptill, New York, 90; Watercolor Class, Watson-Guptill, New York, 94. *Mailing Add:* 535 Cornell Ave Baton Rouge LA 70808-4613

CRESS, GEORGE AYERS
PAINTER, EDUCATOR
b Anniston, Ala, Apr 7, 1921. *Study:* Emory Univ; Univ Ga, BFA, MFA. *Work:* Tenn Fine Arts Ctr; High Mus, Atlanta, Ga; Ford Motor Co; Birmingham Mus, Ala; Mint Mus, Charlotte, NC; plus many others. *Exhib:* Pa Acad Fine Arts; Springfield Watercolor Ann; Solo exhibs, Grand Cent Moderns, NY, Addison Gallery Am Art 20 Yr & 50 Yr Retrospective, Hunter Gallery & var southeastern mus; Nat Mus Am Art, Washington, DC; Bampton Arts Centre, Oxon, Eng; and others. *Pos:* Pres SE Col Art Conf, 56, 66 & 83; chmn, Tenn Col Arts Coun, 66-68. *Teaching:* Instr art, Judson Col, Marion, Ala, 45-46, Mary Baldwin Col, Staunton, Va, 46-47, Univ Md, 47-48, Univ Ga, 49, 65 & 69, Univ Tenn, 49-51, Ont Dept Educ, 63 & Univ SC, 67; Guerry prof art, painter-in-residence, Univ Tenn, Chattanooga, 51-84, Guerry prof art emer, 84-. *Awards:* Southeastern Ann, Birmingham Mus Ann & Atlanta Arts Festival; Gov's Award in the Arts, Tenn, 90; Gov's Artist of Excellence Award, Ga, 90. *Mem:* Southeastern Coll Conf (pres, 56, 66 & 83). *Media:* Oil, Watercolor

CRETARA, DOMENIC ANTHONY
PAINTER, EDUCATOR
b Chelsea, Mass, Mar 29, 1946. *Study:* Boston Univ Sch Fine Arts, BFA (magna cum laude), 68, MFA, 70, Tanglewood Inst, summer 68. *Work:* Metrop Mus Art; Duxbury Art Complex, Mass; McBall Corp, Chicago, Ill; Triton Mus Art, Santa Clara; Univ Del; Riverside Art Mus, Calif; Wiggins Print and Drawing Coll, Boston Pub Libr; Collection of Cypress Coll. *Comn:* mural, comn by Joel Schumacher, 92; portrait, comn by Dr Sylvia Maxson, Long Beach, Calif, 2000; Schomburg Gall, Santa Monica, Calif, 2002. *Exhib:* Solo exhibs, Segal Gallery, New York, 84-85, Koplin Gallery, Los Angeles, 86, Victor McNeil Gallery, New York, 88, Koslow Gallery, Los Angeles, 90, John Thomas Gallery, Los Angeles, 91 & 93, Alon Gallery, Boston, 91 & 93, Brenda Taylor Gallery, New York, 95-96, Martin Zambito Gallery, Seattle, 98, Frye Art Mus, Seattle, 2001 & Schomburg Gallery, Santa Monica, 2002, Schomburg Gallery, Santa Monica, 2008, 2009, 2011, Todd Art Gallery, Middle Tenn State Univ, Murfreesboro, 2008, Calif State Univ Int Prog, Florence, Italy, 2008, Retrospective, Triton Mus Art, 2013; Group exhibs, West Art and the Law, Traveling, Kresge Art Mus, Mich, 95-96; retrospective, Las Vegas Art Mus, 98; Frye Art Mus, Seattle, 2001; Koplin Gallery, Los Angeles, 2000 & 2002; Carnegie Art Mus, Oxnard, Calif, 2003; Mid Tenn State Univ, Murfreesboro, 2004; Californians, CU Gallery, Daegu, Korea, 2012; Back View, Prographica Gallery, Seattle, 2012, Human Figure or Parts Thereof, 2012; The Figure in Contemporary Art, Cypress Coll Art Gallery, Calif, 2012; Art Inst Boston, 100th Anniv Exhib, Boston Public Libr, 2013; The Big Picture, Prographica Gallery, Seattle, 2013; Twenty Years of Drawing and Painting, Trition Mus Art, Santa Clara, Calif. *Pos:* Resident dir, Calif State Univ Int Prog, Florence, Italy, 2008-09. *Teaching:* Instr painting & design, DeCordova Mus Art, Lincoln, Mass, 71-74; chmn dept fine arts & prof painting & drawing, Art Inst Boston, 73-86; prof painting, Calif State Univ at Long Beach, 86-. *Awards:* Fulbright Hays Grant, Florence, Italy, 74; Camargo Found Grant Artist-in-Residence, Cassis, France, 78-79; Boston Padua Sister Cities Grant, 84; Distinguished Scholarly & Creative Achievement Award, CSULB, 94 & Distinguished Fac Teaching Award, 98; Outstanding Prof Yr, Calif State Univ, Long Beach, 2003. *Bibliog:* Articles, Arts Mag, 12/84, Artweek, Los Angeles, 4/87, 4/90 & 8/30/2002, Los Angeles Times, 4/87 & 4/90, Am Artists, 12/92, Oil Highlights: Figures, 1/96, Am Arts Quart, fall, 98 & 2000 & Art Scene, 4/2002; A Course in Figure Drawing, Artist's Mag, 6/90; Linda Krall & Amy Runyan (auths), Artists Clock Cured, 2012; Tina Datsko (auth), The Delirium of Simon Bolivar (Cover art), 2012; Frederick Turner (auth), Am Arts Quarterly (feature essay), 2013; Uploaded Mag, 10/22/2009; Geoff Tuck (auth), Notes on Looking, 9/20/2012; Christina Waters (auth), Smart Mouth, 3/24/2013; John Seed (auth), Huff Post Arts and Culture, 3/28/2013. *Mem:* Coll Art Asn; Seattle Acad Fine Arts (bd adv). *Media:* Oil, Charcoal. *Interests:* Writing, travel. *Publ:* Contribr, Figure Drawing, 76, The Art of Responsive Drawing, rev ed, 77 & Painting: Perceptual and Technical Fundamentals, 79, Prentice Hall; One Hundred American and European Drawings, Prentice Hall, 82; auth, A course in life drawing, Artist's Mag, 6/90; Planning a Well Structured Portrait, Am Artist, 96; contribr painting reproductions, In: Contemporary American Oil Painting, Jilin Fine Arts Publ House, 99 & Sex: Portraits of Passion, Watson Guptill, 99; contribr, Drawings to My Mother's Bolivian Kitchen: Recipes & Recollections, 2005; catalog essay, prints of Giorgio Morandi, Sixth Int Biennial Etching, Mus Contemp Art, Monsummano Terme, Italy; contrib/Foreword book, Portrait Painting Atelier, Watson Guptill, 2010; Artists Block Cured, Walter Foster, 2012; The Delirium of Simon Bolivar (cover art), Floricanto Press, 2014. *Dealer:* Schomburg Gallery Santa Monica CA. *Mailing Add:* Dept Art Calif State Univ 1250 Bellflower Blvd Long Beach CA 90840

CREWDSON, GREGORY
PHOTOGRAPHER
b Brooklyn, NY. *Study:* State Univ NY, Purchase, BA, 1985; Yale Univ, New Haven, Conn, MFA, 1988. *Work:* Brooklyn Mus Art, NY; Metrop Mus Art, Mus Mod Art & Whitney Mus Art, New York; Los Angeles Co Mus Art; Mus Fine Arts, Boston; John D & Catherine T MacArthur Found, Chicago; Solomon R Guggenheim Mus, NY; San Francisco Mus Mod Art; Nat Gallery of Victoria, Melbourne, Australia; Am Contemp Art, Tokyo. *Exhib:* Mus Mod Art, New York, 1991; solo exhibs, Houston Ctr Photog, 1992, Ruth Bloom Gallery, Los Angeles, 1992, 1995, Feigen Gallery, Chicago, 1993, 1994, Palm Beach Community Coll Mus Art, Fla, 1994, Luhring Augustine, NY, 1995, 1997, 2000, 2002, 2005, Jay Jopling/White Cube, London, 1995, Galleri Charlotte Lund, Stockholm, 1995, Galerie des Carmes, La Fleche, 1995, Ginza Artspace, Shiseido Co, Tokyo, 1996, 1999, Cleveland Ctr for Contemp Art, 1997, Marc Foxx Gallery, Los Angeles, 1998, Galleri Charlotte Lund, Stockholm, 1998, Emily Tsingou Gallery, London, 1999, Early Work 1987-88, Partobject Gallery, NC, 2000, SITE Santa Fe, 2001, Gagosian Gallery, Beverly Hills, Calif, 2002, John Berggruen Gallery, San Francisco, 2003, Fireflies, Skarstedt Fine Art, NY City, 2006, Williams Coll Mus Art, Williams, Mass, 2007; Shoshana Wayne Gallery, Los Angeles, 1992; Luhring Augustine, New York, 1993, 1994, 1996; Home Sweet Home and Other Fables, St Louis Art Mus, 1994; Recent Photograhpy Acquisitions: Selections for the Permanent Collection, Whitney Mus Am Art, New York, 1994; Perfect World, Univ Buffalo Art Gallery, NY, 1996; Show and Tell, Lauren Wittells Gallery, NY, 1996; Digital Gardens, Power Plant, Toronto, Ont, 1996; Nature/Cult and the Postmodern Sublime, Bard Ctr for Curatorial Studies, 1996; Prospect 96, Frankfurter Kunstverin, Frankfurt, Ger, 1996; Gothic, Inst Contemp Art, Boston, 1997; The Set Up, Barbara Farber Galerie, Amsterdam, 1997; Telling Tales, Art Gallery New S Wales, Sydney, Australia, 1998; Affinities with Archit, Belk Gallery, W Carolina Univ, Cullowhee, NC, Carroll Reece Mus, E Tenn State Univ, Johnson City & Anderson Gallery Sch Arts, Va Commonwealth Univ, Richmond, 1999; Under/Exposed, Varldens Storsta Fotoutstallning, Stockholm Tunnelbana, Sweden, 1999; Musee des Beaux Arts de Montreal, 2000; Art at MoMA since 1980, 2000; Mus Art, Atlanta, 2000; Eleni Koroneou Gallery, Athens, 2000; The City Gallery of Prague, 2001; Univ Auckland Art Gallery, New Zealand, 2001; Worcester Art Mus, Mass, 2002; Samsung Mus Modern Art, 2002; Paine Webber Art Gallery, New York City, 2002; Guggenheim Mus, NY City, 2002, 2003, 2005, 2007; Mus Contemp Art, Tokyo, 2003; Mass Mus Contemp Art, North Adams, 2003; Tina Kim Fine Art, NY City, 2004; Phoenix Art Mus, Ariz, 2004-05; Geoffrey Young Gallery, Great Barrington, Mass, 2006; The Arsenal Gallery in Cent Park, NY City, 2006; KW Inst Contemp Art, Berlin, 2006-07; Hudson River Mus, Yonkers, NY, 2007; World's Away: New Suburban Landscapes, Walker Art Ctr, 2008 & Carnegie Mus, 2008; Gagosian, New York, 2008; Bad-Habits, Alfred-Knox Art Gallery, Buffalo, NY, 2009; Am Acad Arts and Letts Invitational, New York, 2009. *Teaching:* Instr, State Univ NY, Purchase, 1988-93, Sarah Lawrence Col, Bronxville, NY, 1990, Cooper Union, NY, 1990-93, Sch Visual Arts, NY, 1993, Vassar Col, Poughkeepsie, NY, 1993 & Yale Univ, 1993-. *Awards:* Visual Arts Fel, Nat Endowment for the Arts, 1992; Skowhegan Medal for Photog, Skowhegan Sch Painting and Sculpture, 2004; Acad Award in Art, Am Acad in Arts and Letts, 2009. *Bibliog:* Hilarie M Sheets (auth), Gregory Crewdson: the burbs and the bees, Artnews, 10/1994; Alan Artner (auth), Photography exhibit exposes Plot against suburban sprawl, Chicago Tribune, 10/7/1994; Simon Grant (auth), Close encounters, Ikon Gallery, Art Monthly, 10/1994; Rick Moody (auth), Hover, Artspace Books, 1998; Gregory Crewdson Early Work (1986-88) (exhib catalog), Emilio Mazzoli Galleria D'art Contemporanea, 2002; Rick Moody (auth), Twilight: Photographs by Gregory Crewdson, Harry N Abrams Inc, 2003; Gregory Crewdson: Fireflies (exhib catalog), Skarstedt Fine Art and Luhring Augustine, 2006. *Dealer:* Luhring Augustine Gallery 531 W 24th St New York NY 10011. *Mailing Add:* 247 16th St Brooklyn NY 11215

CRIMMINS, JERRY (GERALD) GARFIELD
PAINTER, SCULPTOR
b Minneapolis, Minn, Feb 9, 1940. *Study:* Minneapolis Coll Art, BFA, 65; Pratt Inst, MFA, 67. *Work:* Pratt Inst, Brooklyn, NY; Southern Ill Univ, Carbondale; Philadelphia Mus Art; Minneapolis Inst Arts; Rotterdamse Kunstichting, Neth. *Exhib:* The Artists' Book, Univ Calif, San Diego at La Jolla, 77; Words & Images, Philadelphia Coll Art, 79; Southern Alleghenies Mus, Pa; Solo exhibs, Hansen Fuller Goldeen Gallery, San Francisco, Calif, 80, Touchstone Gallery, NY, 80, DC Armory, Washington, 81, Rodger LaPelle Galleries, Philadelphia, Pa, 82, Moore Coll Art & Design, 86; Imaginary Lands, Rotterdam Arts Found, The Neth, 83; Return of the Narrative, Palm Springs Desert Mus, Calif, 84; Group exhibs, Fleisher Mus, Palm Springs Desert Mus, Tyler Sch Art, Southern Alleghenies Mus; Snyderman Gallery, Philadelphia, Pa, 96; Alliance Francaise, NY, 2000; many others. *Collection Arranged:* Philadelphia Mus Art; Minneapolis Mus Art; Rotterdamse Mus Art; Southern Ill Univ; Pratt Inst; Philadelphia Free Libr; many pvt collections. *Teaching:* Instr, Tyler Sch Art, Philadelphia, 67-68; prof basic arts & sculpture, Moore Col Art & Design, Philadelphia, 68-2003. *Awards:* Purchase Award, So Ill Univ, 72 & Philadelphia Mus Art, 80; Men of Achievement Award, Cambridge, Eng, 81 & 82; Nat Endowment Arts Grant, 83; Pollock-Krasner Found Grant, Pa Coun Arts, 90. *Bibliog:* John Russel (auth), article, New York Times, 4/21/80; T Albright (auth), article, San Francisco Chronicle, 84; articles, Ariz Daily Star, 98, Miami Herald, 98, Kirkus Revs, 98 & Publ Weekly, 98. *Mem:* Marine Corps Asn; US Seagoing Marina Asn. *Media:* All Media. *Specialty:* fine art, paintings, sculpture, etc. *Publ:* Auth & illusr, Thicker than Blood,

Cold Chair Press, 76; The Song of the Fair Haired, pvt publ, 77; Visitors Guide to La Republique de Reves, Synapse Art Press, 80; The Secret History of La Republique de Reves, Reverian Govt, 83; The Republic of Dreams: Areverie, W W Norton & Co, New York, London, 98; French rights Editions du Seuil, German ed, Droemer-Knurde Die Republic der träume. *Dealer:* Jeffery Fuller Fine Arts Limted 730-32 Carpenter Philadelphia PA 19119

CRIMP, DOUGLAS
CRITIC, EDUCATOR
b Coeur d'Alene, Idaho, 1944. *Study:* Tulane Univ, BA (art hist), 68; City Univ New York, MPhil, 83, PhD, 94. *Pos:* Curatorial staff, Solomon R Guggenheim Mus, 68-71; ed assoc, Art News, 71-76; guest cur, Visual Arts Gallery, New York, 72 & Artists Space, New York, 77; managing ed, October, 77-83, exec ed, 83-86, ed, 86-90; series ed, October Bks, MIT Press, 88-90. *Teaching:* Instr art hist, Sch Visual Arts, New York, 70-76; vis instr, Dept Art Hist, NS Col Art & Design, Halifax, 82, Visual Arts Prog, Princeton Univ, 86, Mason Gross Sch Arts, Rutgers Univ, 88 & Cooper Union, New York, 88, Calif Inst Arts, Valencia, spring 89 & 90, Sarah Lawrence Col, 90-91; prof visual & cult studies, Univ Rochester, 92-. *Awards:* Art Critics Fel, Nat Endowment Arts, 73 & 84; Frank Jewett Mather Award, for distinction in art criticism, Coll Art Asn, 88; On the Museum's Ruins Grant, Getty Publ, 92. *Mem:* Int Asn Art Critics; Coll Art Asn. *Publ:* Auth, The Boys in my Bedroom, Art in Am, 2/90; Art acts up: A graphic response to AIDS, Out/look, summer 90; On the Museum's Ruins, Mass Inst Techol Press, 1993; Melancholia and Moralism, MIT Press, 2002. *Mailing Add:* 139 Fulton St New York NY 10038

CRISPO, DICK
PAINTER, PRINTMAKER
b Brooklyn, NY, Jan 13, 1945. *Study:* Ariz Sch Art; Carmel Art Inst; Monterey Peninsula Col; Hartnell Col; St Sophia Divinity Sch; also with Victor DiGesu, Sam Colburn, Jan Hannah, Alexander Napote, Kay Rodgers & others. *Work:* Libr Cong, Washington, DC; Bibliot Nat, Paris, France; Inst Nac de Bellas Artes, Mexico City, Mex; Mus Western Art, Tokyo, Japan; Nat Libr Ireland, Dublin; plus others. *Comn:* Ecology (mural), Monterey High Sch, Calif, 72; Ecology, Robert Louis Stevenson Sch, Pebble Beach, Calif, 72; Spirit of Youth, Carmel Youth Ctr, Calif, 73; History of the Migrant Worker (mural), Opportunity Indust Ctr, Salinas, Calif, 74; Twelve Master Teachers of the World (mural), Church of Antioch, Pacific Grove, Calif, 75. *Exhib:* Calif State Fair, Sacramento, 64; Small Painting Biennial, Purdue Univ, 68; Univ Calif, Berkeley, 72; Pan-Am Graphics, Mexico City, 72; Western Graphics, Tokyo, 73; and others. *Pos:* Chmn, Fine Arts Div, Monterey Co Fair, 72-74; co-founder, Mus on Wheels, Monterey, 74-; exhib dir, Pacific Grove Art Ctr, 74-; art counr, Monterey Co Probation Dept, 75-; Am cult specialist to Latin Am for USIS. *Teaching:* Instr arts & Crafts, York Sch, Monterey, 71-73; instr folk & ethnic arts, Monterey Peninsula Col, 74-75; instr folk & ethnic arts & art hist, St Sophia Divinity Sch, Pacific Grove, 75-; vis lectr, Univ Calif, Santa Cruz, Interdisciplinary Studies Dept, Porter, Col. *Awards:* All Calif Watercolor Competition Third Prize, Pacific Grove, 67; San Juan Bautista Invitational Second Prize, Calif, 68; Pan Am Graphics, 72; Am in Paris, Louve Mus, 76; Gold Medal, Acad Italy, 79; plus others. *Bibliog:* Pat Griffith (auth), An artist with a sense of humor, Carmel Valley Outlook, Carmel, Calif, 72; Robert Miskimon (auth), Social Consciousness of Art, Pine Cone, Carmel, 73; Dick Crispo, Artist of the Era. *Mem:* Artists Equity; Carmel Art Asn; Pacific Grove Art Ctr; Pac Art Asn (chmn); Art Workers United; Frick Mus. *Media:* All. *Res:* Eclectic study of world folk art. *Collection:* Folk and eccentric art from over 40 countries. *Publ:* Auth, Contemporary Print Making Renaissance in Japan, 69; dir, Dick Crispo Maker of Images, Frasconi-Selzer Films; History of the Carmel Art Association; Sea Scapes of Dick Crispo; Artworks mag (2 articles). *Dealer:* Bronstein & Sigg Gallery; Carmel Art Asn. *Mailing Add:* PO Box 1952 Carmel CA 93921

CRISS, CHERYL LYNN
PAINTER
b San Diego, CA, Dec 16, 1947. *Study:* The Design Inst, San Diego, 87-89; pvt studies. *Exhib:* Am Watercolor Soc Int, New York, 90-92, 97-98 & 2000; Mus Juried Exhib, San Diego Mus Art, Calif, 96 & 98. *Pos:* bd mem, San Diego Mus Art (Artists Guild), 92-96; vpres, San Diego Watercolor Soc, 92-94; pres, W Coast Watercolor Soc, 2006. *Awards:* Edgar Whitney, AWS Int, 98 & 2000; High Winds Medal, AWS Int, 2006. *Mem:* signature mem, Am Watercolor Soc; signature mem, Watercolor W; pres & signature mem, W Coast Watercolor Soc; past vpres, San Diego Watercolor Soc; US Coast Guard Artist. *Media:* Watercolor. *Publ:* Auth & illus, Getting the Size Right, The Artist's Mag, 94; Water Color Magic-Featured Artist, 98; The Quality of Light, N Light Bks, 2004; Textures of Life, The Artist's Mag, 2004; Dry Spell, The Artist's Mag, 2005. *Dealer:* Neora Matteucci Fine Art 555 Canyon Rd Santa Fe NMex. *Mailing Add:* 9574 Paseo Mountril San Diego CA 92129

CRIST, WILLIAM GARY
VISUAL ARTIST, EDUCATOR
b Pocatello, Idaho, Jan 17, 1937. *Study:* Univ Wash, Seattle, BA (art educ), 66; Cranbrook Acad Art, Detroit, MFA (sculpture), 71; study with Michael Hall, Julius Schmidt, Joseph Beuys, Nam June Paik & Klaus Rinke; Staatliche Kunstakademie, Dusseldorf, WGer, 81 & 83. *Work:* Cameron Univ, Lawton, Okla; Univ Mo, Kansas City; Gen Serv Admin, Washington. *Exhib:* Noho Gallery, NY, 79 & 80; Staatliche Kunstakademie, Dusseldorf, W Ger, 81; XVth Ann Int Electronic Music Festival, 85; Randolph Street Gallery, Chicago, 86; Oppression/Expression, Contemp Arts Ctr, New Orleans, 86; Pleiades Gallery, 10th Ann Juried, NY, 92. *Teaching:* Asst prof art, Wesleyan Col, Macon, Ga, 71-72; instr art, Cameron Univ, Lawton, Okla, 72-74; asst prof art, Univ Mo, Kansas City, 74-81, assoc prof art, 81-88, chair, dept art & art hist, 85-89, prof art, 88-; dir 2 and 3D computer graphics, Univ Mo Video Network, 89-. *Awards:* Interdisciplinary Arts Fel Prog, Rockefeller Found & Nat Endowment Arts, 86; Southwestern Bell Telephone Found, 92. *Media:* Mixed Media, Electronics. *Res:* Computer multimedia art; synthesis of various technologies into visual art; visual and audio relationships of space and time, art on the internet. *Publ:* Auth, article, High Performance Mag, Issue 32; Coherent light and Electronics as Creative Mediums, Okla State Arts Comn, 73; interview with Joseph Beuys, 82 & interview with Nam June Paik, Forum Mag, 5/86; auth, Underground Art in Poland, Coll Art Asn, Toronto. *Mailing Add:* Univ Mo Dept Art & Art Hist Kansas City MO 64110

CRISWELL, WARREN
PAINTER, SCULPTOR, ANIMATOR
b Sept 19, 1936. *Study:* Self-taught. *Work:* The Ark Arts Ctr, Little Rock; McKissich Mus, Univ SC, Columbia, SC; Univ Ark Little Rock; Hendrix Coll, Conway, Ark; Central Ark Lib Sys, Little Rock; Historic Ark Mus, Little Rock, Ark. *Exhib:* Solo exhibs, Ulysses at Circe's: Drawings of W Criswell, Capitol Arts Ctr, Taipei, Taiwan, 93, Works of Warren Criswell, Wichita Ctr Arts, Wichita, Kans, 2000, Warren Criswell: Perceptions & Conceptions, Historic Ark Mus, 2001 & Warren Criswell: Shadows, Ark Arts Ctr, Little Rock, 2003, Warren Criswell Moves, Hist Ark Mus, 2006; Body & Soul: Contemp Southern Figures, Columbus Mus, Columbus, Ga, 97, Mobile Mus Art, Mobile, Ala, 97, Miss Mus Art, Jackson, Miss, 98 & Cummer Mus Art, Jacksonville, Fla, 98; About Face (with catalog), Ark Arts Ctr, Little Rock, 2001; Little Rock Film Festival, 2008; Its About Time, Pulaski Tech Coll, Little Rock, Ark, 2012; Warren Criswell's Prints & Flicks, Austin Peah State Univ, Clarksville, Tenn, 2013; Disparate Acts: David Bailin, Warren Criswell, Sammy Peters, Ark State Univ, 2014; Delta Nat Small Prints Exhib, 2014. *Pos:* owner, Icarus Flicks; Warren Criswell Studio. *Awards:* Residency award, Mid-Am Arts Alliance, 94; Fel grant, Mid-Am Arts Alliance & NEA, 96; Individual Artist fellowship grant for painting, Ark Arts Coun, 2003. *Bibliog:* Gwen Diehn (auth), Simple Printmaking, Lark Books, New York, 2000; Werner Trieschemann (auth), A lighter Shade of Criswell, Ark Democrat Gazette, 7/15/2001; Peter Frank (auth), Warren Criswell: Shadows, 2003; Leslie Newell Peacock (auth), Criswell on the Move, Artists Six Moments, Ark Times, 5/2011; Ellis Widner (auth), Criswell Exhib, Still Crazy, Ark Democrat-Gazette, 2013. *Media:* Oil, Mixed Media. *Interests:* watercolor, printmaking, sculpture, animation. *Dealer:* Helen Scott Cantrell Gallery 8206 Cantrell Rd Little Rock AR 72227. *Mailing Add:* 7700 Rolling Manor Dr Benton AR 72015

CRITE, ALLAN ROHAN
PAINTER, ILLUSTRATOR
b Plainfield, NJ, Mar 20, 1910. *Study:* Boston Mus Sch Fine Arts, 29-36, Painter's Workshop, Fogg Art Mus, 40's, Harvard Univ, AB, 68, Suffolk Univ, Hon Doc Humanities, 78, Emmanuel Col, Hon Doc FA, 83, Mass Coll Art, Hon Doc FA, 88, Gen Theological Sem Episc Church, Hon Doc Div, 94. *Work:* Boston Pub Libr, Mass; Nat Ctr Afro-Am Artists, Mass; Mus Am Art, Washington, DC; Libr Boston Athenaeum, Mass; Mus Mod Art, NY; and many others. *Comn:* Insignia, USS Wilson, Navy; mural, Grace Church, Martha's Vineyard, Mass; Stations (Cross), Holy Cross Church, Morrisville, Vt; mural, St Augustine's Church, NY; banners & altar pieces, St Stephen's Episcopal Church, Mass. *Exhib:* Fogg Mus Art, Harvard Univ, 30 & 95; WPA exhib, Mus Mod Art, 36; Boston Mus Fine Arts, 78; Mus Nat Ctr Afro-Am Artists, 78, 85, 88 & 94; Afro-Am Hist & Cult Mus, Philadelphia, 79, 94; Allan Rohan Crite: A Retrospective, Mus Nat Ctr Afro-Am Art, 90; Against the Odds, Harlem Renaissance Artists, Newark Mus, NJ, 93; Alone in a Crowd, Black Printmakers - 30's & 40's, Equitable, NY, 93; Free Within Ourselves, Mus Am Art, Smithsonian, 94; Revelation, Nat Black Arts Festival, ITC, Atlanta, Ga, 94; and many others. *Pos:* Artist-historian, Semitic Mus, Harvard Univ; eng, draftsman/illustr Tech Equip, Naval Shipyard, Boston, 40-70; muralist, Rambusch Decorating Co, 49-50; libr, Grossman Libr, Harvard Univ, 74-89. *Teaching:* Lectr Christian art, Oberlin Col, 58; lectr drawing, Regis Col, 58; instr drawing, Roxbury Community Col, 77-78; lectr, Eye of the Beholder, Isabell Stewart Gardner Mus, 94; vis lectr art & liturgical art at many schs & cols nationally. *Awards:* 350th Ann Harvard Univ, Medal, Harvard Univ, Mass, 86; Men of Vision Award, Mus African-Am Hist, Mass, 92; Stain Glass Window, Christ Church, Bronxville, NY, 94; Cert Appreciation Life Contributions to Visual Art, St Bartholomew's Episcopal Church, 94; and many others. *Mem:* Community Fel, Mass Inst Technol, Mass. *Media:* Watercolor, Lithography. *Res:* Am Peoples of Color, Afro-Asian, Afro-Am; Cultural Heritage of US. *Publ:* Auth, Three Spirituals from Earth to Heaven, Harvard Univ Press, 48; Rediscovery of Cultural Heritage of US (paper), Libr Boston Athenaeum, 68; illusr, Book of Revelation, Limited Ed Book Club, NY, 94; The Lord's Prayer, an interpretation, The Seabury Press, Inc, 54; Blacks Who Died for Jesus, a history book by Mark Hyman, Winston-Derek Publ Inc, 83. *Dealer:* J Cox & Assocs PO Box 2414 Boston MA 02208

CRIVELLI, ELAINE
ENVIRONMENTAL ARTIST, SCULPTOR
b Philadelphia, Pa, Dec 4, 1950. *Study:* Westchester Univ, BFA, 78; Univ Del, with Joe Moss, MFA, 82. *Comn:* Sculpture installations, Univ NC, Chapel Hill, 82 & Gotham Design, Dobbs Ferry, NY, 88; Movement Int Theater, 87; Please Touch Mus, Philadelphia, Pa, 90. *Exhib:* Artists by Themselves, Sushi Gallery, San Diego, Calif, 87; Altered Sites, Fairmount Park, Philadelphia, 88; Playable Art, Moore Coll Art, Philadelphia, 89; Shadow Play, Please Touch Mus, Philadelphia, 90; Bergen Gallery, Savannah, Ga, 91; Common Wealth, Univ Mus, Ind Univ Pa, 95; Small Computers in the Arts, Silicon Gallery, Philadelphia, 96; Photog: Contemp Prospects, Hist Yellow Springs Inst, Chester Springs, Pa, 96. *Pos:* Gallery dir, Painted Bride Art Ctr, Philadelphia, 84-87; vis artist, Wimbledon Sch Art, Eng, Kingston Univ, Kingston-upon-Thames, Eng, Ruskin Sch Fine Arts, Oxford, Eng & Studies Abroad Prog, Univ Ga, Cartona, Italy, 93. *Teaching:* Lectr 3-D design, Philadelphia Col Art, 83-; prof design & drawing, Philadelphia Col Textiles & Sci, 87-; prof, Chestnut Hill Col, Pa, 87-89 Savannah, Ga, 89-93 & Am Sch London, 93-95. *Awards:* Fel, Univ Del, 80. *Bibliog:* Ronnie H Cohen (auth), Artpark, Artforum, 82; Deborah Curtis (auth), Introduction to Visual Literacy, Prentice Hall, 86; Edward J Sozanski (auth), On galleries, Philadelphia Inquirer, 2/26/87; Beth Wilcox (auth), Creating Art at Artpark, Sculpture Mag, 89. *Mem:* Sculptors Int; Coll Art Asn. *Media:* Mixed Media. *Mailing Add:* 413 E Front St Media PA 19063-3522

CRONIN, PATRICIA
SCULPTOR
b Beverly, Mass, 1963. *Study:* Rhode Island Coll, BFA, 1986; Brooklyn College, MFA, 1988; Skowhegan Sch Painting & Sculpture, Maine, 1991. *Exhib:* Solo exhibs include Brent Sikkema, New York, 1997, White Columns, New York, 1998, Deitch Projects, New York, 2002, UB Art Gallery, Univ at Buffalo, NY, 2004; Group exhibs include The Return of the Cadavre Exquis, The Drawing Ctr, New York, 1993; Stonewall 25: Imaginings of the Gay Past, Celebrating the Gay Present, White Columns, New York, 1994; Up the Establishment, Sonnabend, New York, 1994; The Name of the Place, Casey Kaplan Gallery, New York, 1997; Open House: Working in Brooklyn, Brooklyn Mus, New York, 2004; Its Not About Sex, Luxe Gallery, New York, 2005; The Title Of This Show Is Not GAY ART NOW, Paul Kasmin Gallery, New York, 2006; What F Word?, Cynthia Broan Gallery, New York, 2007; Neo-Integrity, Derek Eller Gallery, New York, 2007; Cincinnati Collects, Contemp Art Ctr, Cincinnati, 2007; Rest In Peace: Art & Objects for the Deadt, Bellweather, New York, 2008. *Awards:* Rome Prize, Am Acad in Rome, 2006; Louis Comfort Tiffany Found Grants, 2008

CRONIN, ROBERT (LAWRENCE)
PAINTER, DRAFTSMAN
b Lexington, Mass, Aug 10, 1936. *Study:* RI Sch Design, BFA, 59; Cornell Univ, MFA, 62. *Work:* Boston Mus Fine Arts; Brooklyn Mus; Nat Air & Space Mus, Washington, DC; Mus Art, Carnegie Inst, Pittsburgh, Pa; Nat Acad Mus, NY. *Comn:* On Speculation (sculpture), Lippincott Co, 82-; RS Reynolds Mem Award, 82. *Exhib:* Inst Contemp Art, Boston, 71; Gimpel Fils, London, 82; Gimpel & Weitzenhoffer Ltd, NY, 82, 84, 87 & 89; Gimpel-Hanover & Andre Emmerich Galerien, Zurich, 83; Klonaridis Gallery, Toronto, 84 & 86; Gallery Hiro, Tokyo, Japan, 89; Yoh Art Gallery, Osaka, Japan, 89; The Tin Yrs, A Survey of the 1980's, Fitchburg Art Mus, Mass, 90, Dillon Gallery, NY, 96 & 99; Kouros Gallery, NY, 2004; Zabriskie Gallery, NY, 2007; Galerie Gris, Hudson, NY, 2014. *Pos:* Self employed artist. *Teaching:* Instr painting, Bennington Coll, 66-68; instr art, Brown Univ, 68-71 & Sch Worcester Art Mus, 71-80. *Awards:* Mass Arts & Humanities Grant, 75; Mass Artists Found Grant, 79; Adolf & Esther Gottlieb Found Individual Support Grant, 91. *Bibliog:* Hilton Kramer (auth), New Talent, NY Times, 6/17/73; Hilton Kramer (auth), article, NY Times, 9/21/74; Max Wykes-Joyce (auth), Robert Cronin, Gimpel Fils, London Arts Rev, 4/9/82. *Mem:* Nat Acad Design. *Media:* Oil on canvas, Acrylic on paper, Ink on paper. *Interests:* Cycling. *Dealer:* Steven Isoz Galerie Gris 621 Warrent St Hudson NY 12534. *Mailing Add:* PO Box 74 Falls Village CT 06031

CROOKS, ROSELYN J
PAINTER, WRITER
b Lancaster, OH, Sept 15, 1924. *Study:* Studied with James R Hopkins, PhD (Oil Painting), 1945; Ohio State Univ, BFA, 1946. *Comn:* Numerous paintings local & US, 1989-2008. *Exhib:* Solo Exhibs: Skyline Country Club Gallery, Tucson, Ariz, 1980, 1982, 1983, 1986, 2001, 2005, 2011; Pima Co Art Competition for Painting, 2005; Group Exhibs: Tucson Mus Art Ariz, 1970, 1972; S Ariz Watercolor Guild, 1994, 1998; Skyline Country Club Gallery 1984, 1986, 1987, 1992, 1995, 1998, 2000, 2002, 2004, 2006, 2007, 2008, 2011; Artist of the month, Skyline Country Club Gallery, March 2011. *Pos:* Illus, Curtis-Wright Corp, Columbus, 1944; advert display mgr, Hickle's Dept Store, Lancaster, OH, 1947-1948; free lance artist, Tucson, Ariz, 1951; designer (notepapers) 1968 -1990; speaker in field. *Mem:* Southern AZ Watercolor Guild; Soc Southwestern Auths; Skyline Art Group (found 2004, chmn). *Media:* Oil, Watercolor. *Interests:* Crossword puzzles, reading, travel. *Publ:* auth (short story), Ariz Daily Star, 2007; Memoir, Ariz Daily Star, Feb 2011. *Mailing Add:* 5822 N Placita Bacanora Tucson AZ 85718

CROPPER, M ELIZABETH
HISTORIAN, LECTURER
b Dewsbury, Yorkshire, Eng, Aug 11, 1944. *Study:* Newnham Col, Univ Cambridge, BA (hon), 67; Bryn Mawr Col, PhD, 72. *Teaching:* prof art history, Temple Univ, 73-85; prof, Johns Hopkins Univ, 85-2000; AW Mellon prof, CASVA, Nat Gallery Art, 94-96. *Awards:* Jan Mitchell prize & Charles Rufus Morey prize (CAA) for Nicolas Poussin (with C Dempsey), 1997. *Mem:* Coll Art Asn; Renaissance Soc Am; vis mem Inst Advanced Study, Princeton; Fel Am Acad Arts & Scis; Am Phil Soc. *Res:* Italian Renaissance and Baroque art. *Publ:* co-auth (with Charles Dempsey), Nicholas Poussin: Friendship and the Love of Painting, Princeton Univ Press, 96; auth, Pontormo: Portrait of a Halberdier, Getty Mus, 97; auth, Life on the Edge: Artemesia Gentileschi, Famous Woman Painter, in Orazio and Artemisia Gentileschi (exhib catalog), Metropolitan Mus, 2001; auth, The Domenichino Affair, Yale Univ Pres, 2005; editor, Carlo Cesare Malvasia's Felsina Pittrice (1678): Lives of the Bolognese Painters, Vol 1, Early Bolognese Painting, Harvey MIller/ Brepols, 2012. *Mailing Add:* 1336 31st St NW Washington DC 20007

CROSBY, RANICE W
ILLUSTRATOR, EDUCATOR
b Regina, Sask, Can, Apr 26, 1915. *Study:* Conn Col, AB; Johns Hopkins Med Sch, under Max Broedel; also under Robert Brackman; Johns Hopkins Univ, MLA. *Pos:* Illusr for N J Eastman, Johns Hopkins Hosp, currently. *Teaching:* Assoc prof & dir emer, dept art as appl to med, Johns Hopkins Med Sch, 44-. *Awards:* Asn Med Illusr: Fel, Lifetime Achievement Award; William P Didusch Award, Am Urological Asn. *Mem:* Asn Med Illusr; Am Asn Univ Prof. *Publ:* Illustrator for medical textbooks and journals; Max Brôdel: The Man Who Put Art into Medicine, Springer/Verlag

CROSMAN, CHRISTOPHER BYRON
MUSEUM DIRECTOR, WRITER
b Chicago, Ill, June 25, 1946. *Study:* Washington & Lee Univ, BA, 68; Oberlin Col, 70-72. *Collection Arranged:* Painterly Panels: Jonathan Santlofer & Arlene Slavin; James Brooks: 25 Years of Work, 63-88; An Eye For Adornment; Shared Visions: Am Landscapes; Voyages of the Modern Imagination; By Land and Sea: Selected Works from the Collection of Andrew & Betsy Wyeth; and others. *Pos:* Cur educ, Albright-Knox Art Gallery, 80-84; peer rev panel, NY State Coun Arts, 82-84; dir, Heckscher Mus, 84-88 & Farnsworth Libr & Art Mus, 88-; field revs (reader), Inst Mus Servs, 85-86 & 92-93; chmn, Maine Arts Comn, 95-; reviewer, Am Asn Mus & Mapi, 96. *Teaching:* Instr art hist, Empire State Col, Buffalo, NY, 79-81. *Mem:* Am Asn Mus, Maine League Hist Soc and Mus, Rotary. *Publ:* Exhib catalogs & video interviews with artists; Co-auth, From Mus, Libraries & Galleries: Artists on Tape, 1984; contribr articles to prof jours; co-prod, video documentaries, 1974-84; cur exhib. *Mailing Add:* Farnsworth Art Mus 16 Mus St Rockland ME 04841-0466

CROSS, YVONNE
SCULPTOR, PAINTER
Study: Acad di Belli Arti, Florence, Italy, MFA, 1978; various additional studies throughout Italy, France & US, 1970-94. *Exhib:* Solo-exhibs, Gallery Juarez, Los Angeles, 82, Gallery Juarez, Palm Desert, 83, 44 Wilshire Gallery, Beverly Hills, 84-88, Pacific Design Ctr, Calif, 86 & Cross Art Gallery, Beverly Hills, 94-97, others; IV Bienal de Escultura, Portugal, 91; Touchables, Ga Tech Univ Gallery, Atlanta, 92; 1st Ann Art in Park Show, West Hollywood, Calif, 93; 20 Yrs Retrospect 1974-1994, Cross Art Gallery Exhib, Beverly Hills, Calif, 95; Les Oubliees d'Avignon, France, 1993. *Collection Arranged:* Embassy Collections, US Dept State, Washington, DC; Materials Res Collection, Pa State Univ, State College, Pa; Cedars-Sinai Med Ctr, LA, Calif; Nat Found for Prevention of Cancer, Denver, Colo; St James Episcopal Sch, LA, Calif. *Media:* Sculpture - All Media, Painting - Oil. *Interests:* Music composition and composing, antiques. *Mailing Add:* PO Box 5752 Beverly Hills CA 90209-5752

CROSSGROVE, ROGER LYNN
PRINTMAKER, EDUCATOR
b Farnam, Nebr, Nov 17, 1921. *Study:* Kearney State Coll; Univ Nebr, BFA; Univ Ill, MFA; Univ Michoacan, Mex. *Work:* Butler Inst Am Art, Youngstown, Ohio; Montclair Art Mus, NJ; William Benton Mus Art, Storrs, Conn; New Britain Mus Am Art; Inst Mex-Norteamericano Relaciones Cult, Mexico City. *Exhib:* Whitney Mus Am Art, NY, 56; Pa Acad Fine Arts, Philadelphia, 64; Audubon Artists, NY, 68; Conn Watercolor Soc, Wadsworth Atheneum, Hartford, Conn, 70; Monotypes, Pratt Graphics Ctr, NY, 72; New Am Monotypes, SITES, 78; William Benton Mus Art, Storrs, Conn, 91. *Pos:* Contribr & ed, Artists Proof, 67-68. *Teaching:* Prof art & assoc chmn dept graphic arts, Pratt Inst, 52-68; prof art, Univ Conn, 68-88, prof emer, 88. *Awards:* Emily Lowe Award, 51; Gold Medal, Nat Arts Club, 67; Am Watercolor Soc Award, 64 & 67. *Bibliog:* Henry N Rasmusen (auth), Printmaking with Monotype, Chilton, 60; Joann Moser (auth), Singular Impressions: The Monotype in America, Smithsonian Inst Press, Washington, 97; Phil Braham (auth), Exposed/Naked Men, Thunder's Mouth Press, 2000; David Leddick (auth), Male Nude Now, Universe, 2001; David Leddick (auth), The Nude Male: 21st Century Visions, Universe, 2008; Rutherford Witthus (editor), Live Oak, with Moss: A Restorative Edition, by Walt Whitman, Artists Edition Published by Rutherford Witthus, 2013. *Mem:* Conn Acad Fine Arts; Conn Watercolor Soc; Artworks Gallery, Hartford, Conn. *Media:* Monotype, Photography. *Collection:* Mex graphic art, Taller de Gráfica Popular, Alfredo Zalce and Jean Charlot. *Publ:* Contribr, Paperbound Books in Print, 63. *Mailing Add:* 362 Gurleyville Rd Storrs CT 06268

CROTTO, PAUL
PAINTER, SCULPTOR
b New York, NY, Oct 24, 1922. *Study:* Art Students League; Beaux-Arts, Florence, Italy; also with Fernand Leger, Paris. *Work:* Villeneuve-sur-Lot Mus, France; Mus Art Int, San Francisco; Galerie Grave, Munich, Ger. *Comn:* Portraits, LE Kaplan, NY & Robert Aries, Paris. *Exhib:* Mostra Artisti Am, Florence, 51; Mostra Int, Bordighera, Italy, 53; Am Painters in France, Galerie Craven, Paris, 53; Salon Automne, Paris, 56; Salon Comparaisons, Mus Mod Art, Paris, 68. *Awards:* Prix Int de Peinture, Villeneuve-sur-Lot, 63. *Bibliog:* T Ehrenmark (auth), American Artist in Sweden, Dagens Nyheter, 63; A Blasco Ibanez (auth), American Artist in Paris, Los Angeles Herald Examiner, 68; Betty Werther (auth), Art, Time-Life, Paris, 69. *Mem:* Soc Coop Entre Aide Artistes. *Media:* Oil; All. *Mailing Add:* 19 Rue Cauchois Paris F-75018 France

CROUCH, NED PHILBRICK
SCULPTOR, CURATOR
b Nashville, Tenn, Mar 14, 1948. *Study:* Austin Peay State Univ, Clarksville, Tenn, BS (art), 72; Cranbrook Acad Art, Bloomfield Hills, Mich, MFA (sculpture), 74. *Work:* Tenn Fine Arts Comn, Nashville; Cheekwood Fine Arts Ctr, Nashville; Ark Arts Ctr, Little Rock; Montgomery Bell Acad, Nashville; Austin Peay State Univ, Clarksville. *Exhib:* Mich II, Flint Inst Arts, Flint, Mich, 74; Mid-South Biennial, Brooks Mem Art Gallery, Memphis, Tenn, 75; Artists Biennial, New Orleans Mus Art, 75; Nat Sculpture USA, Huntsville Mus Art, Ala, 75; 18th Ann Delta Exhib, Ark Arts Ctr, Little Rock, 75; Tenn Bicentennial, Brooks Mem Art Gallery, Memphis, 76; Invitational, Southeastern Ctr Contemp Art, Winston-Salem, NC, 77. *Pos:* Guest cur, Am Folk-Exhib of 20th Century Quilts, Drawings & Sculpture, Vanderbilt Univ, Nashville, 76-; consult spec proj, Cheekwood Fine Arts Ctr, Nashville, 77-. *Teaching:* Instr sculpture, Austin Peay State Univ, Clarksville, 74-75. *Awards:* Hon Mention, Delta Exhib & Purchase Award, Toys by Artists, 75, Ark Arts Ctr, Little Rock; Purchase Award, Tenn Bicentennial, Tenn Fine Arts Comn, 76. *Mem:* Coll Art Asn Am; Midwest Regional Conservation Guild. *Media:* Welded Steel, Wood. *Mailing Add:* 114 E Glenwood Dr Clarksville TN 37040-3553

CROUSE, MICHAEL GLENN
EDUCATOR, PRINTMAKER
b Grand Rapids, Mich, June 20, 1949. *Study:* Kendall Sch Design, Grand Rapids, dipl, 70; Atlanta Coll Art, BFA, 77; Univ Mich, Ann Arbor, MFA, 79. *Work:* Ga Dept Educ, Atlanta; Huntsville Mus Art. *Exhib:* Serial Imagery, Huntsville Mus Art, Ala, 82; Southeastern Graphics Int, Mint Mus Art, 82; Wesleyan Second Int Exhib Prints &

Drawings, Macon Mus Arts & Sci, Ga, 82; Ninth Int Miniature Print Competition, Pratt Graphics Ctr, NY, 83; Second Int Miniature Print Exhib, Space Group Seoul, SKorea, 83; Red Clay V, Huntsville Mus Art, Ala, 83. *Teaching:* Instr art, Ill Col, 79-80; asst prof printmaking, Univ Ala, Huntsville, 80-. *Awards:* Charles Brand Machinery, Pratt Graphics Ctr Int Miniature Print Competition, 79; Purchase Award, LaGrange Nat VI, LaGrange Col, 81 & 24th NDak Print & Drawing Show, Univ NDak, 81. *Mem:* Coll Art Asn; Southeastern Coll Art Conf. *Media:* Mixed Media. *Dealer:* Absteins Gallery Art & Framing 1139 Spring St Atlanta GA 30309. *Mailing Add:* Bartow Tower SE 1530 Third Ave Birmingham AL 35294-0001

CROWLEY, CHARLES A
CRAFTSMAN
b Baltimore, Md, Oct 8, 1958. *Study:* Mass Coll Art, Boston, studied welding techniques, 83; Boston Univ, BFA (metalsmithing), 84. *Exhib:* Sculptural Objects, Wetsman Collection, Birmingham, Miss, 92; Celebration of Excellence, Soc Arts & Crafts, Boston, 93; Vessels Invitational, Iowa State Univ, 93; Metals Invitational 1994, Univ Akron, Ohio, 94; Don Brecker Gallery, Miami Beach, Fla, 94. *Teaching:* Instr metalsmithing, Brookline Ctr Adult Educ, 88-89; Lexington Ctr Arts & Crafts, 88-92; continuing educ instr metals, Mass Col Art, 89-92. *Awards:* Fel, Mass Coun Arts, 86; First Prize, Fortunoff Sterling Silver Design Competition, NY, 90; Fel, Nat Endowment Arts. *Media:* Metal. *Dealer:* Jan Wetsman Brimingham MI. *Mailing Add:* 6 Eveleth Rd Gloucester MA 01930

CROWLEY, TONY
ADMINISTRATOR
Study: Colo State Univ, BFA, 1975; Univ Nebr-Lincoln, MFA, 1980. *Exhib:* work featured in several exhibitions throughout the US, Japan and Canada. *Collection Arranged:* Permanent collections include Sheldon Memorial Art Gallery, Cedar Rapid Art Mus, New Orleans Art Mus, Harwell Art Mus, Kemper Group, Maytag Found and numerous colleges and universities. *Teaching:* tchr, Tarkio Col, Mo, formerly, Grinnell Col, Iowa, 1989-2002; chair dept art, Wayne State Univ, 2002-2007; Chair, dir, Col of Fine Arts, Ill State Univ, 2007-. *Mailing Add:* College of Fine Arts Illinois State Univ Campus Box 5600 CVA119 Normal IL 61790-5600

CROWN, ROBERTA LILA
PAINTER, CONCEPTUAL ARTIST
b New York, NY. *Study:* Queens Col, MA, 70. *Exhib:* Best Ann, Queens Mus, Flushing, NY, 89; solo exhib, Queens Coll Art Ctr, Flushing, NY, 89, Uniproperty Gallery, NY 98, Ezair Gallery, New York, 2009; A Salute to Women, Nat Mus Women Arts, Washington, DC, 91; Schering Plough Gallery, 95; Chubb Gallery, 97; Canajoharie Mus NY, 2000; Jamison-Carnegie Heritage Hall Mus, Ala, 2001; Cornell Medical Gallery, NY, 2002; Citicorp Gallery, NY, 2003; Pace Univ, NY, 2003; Queen Coll Art Ctr, Flushing, NY, 2005; Broome Street Gallery, NY, 2005; Maitland Art Center, Fla, 2005; Google Works, Reading, Pa, 2006; Karpeles Libr Mus, Newburgh, NY, 2006; Sage Coll - Opalka Gallery, Albany, NY, 2007; Monroe Art Center, Hoboken, NJ, 2007; Purdue Univ, Ind, 2008; Rutgers Univ, NJ, 2008; Ezair Gallery, New York, 2009. *Pos:* Exec coordr, Women Arts Found Inc, 80-2002. *Teaching:* Fine arts, Corlears JHS, 56 & 69-95. *Awards:* Mary K Karasick Mem Award, 91 & Leila Sawyer Mem Award, 92, Nat Asn Women Artists. *Mem:* Women in the Arts Found, Inc (exec coordr, 80-); Women's Caucus Art; Artists Equity; Nat Women's Asn Women Artists. *Media:* Oil on Canvas, Acrylic on Canvas. *Interests:* Travel. *Publ:* Contribr, Triangle Annual, Triangle, 87; IBM Nachrichton-Excellence, IBM, 89. *Dealer:* Maijana Bego. *Mailing Add:* 1175 York Ave New York NY 10021

CROWNER, SARAH
PAINTER
b Philadelphia, Pa, 1974. *Study:* Univ Calif, Santa Cruz, BA, 1996; Hunter Coll, CUNY, MFA, 2002. *Exhib:* Ceramics and Other THings, DAAD Galerie, Berlin, 2008; For the blind man in the dark room looking for the black cat that isn't there, Contemp Art Mus St Louis, Mo, 2009; Looking Back: The White Columns Annual, White Columns, New York, 2009; Whitney Biennial, Whitney Mus Am Art, 2010. *Bibliog:* Charles Darwent (auth), If the cat starts to talk, the future of art is in safe paws, The Independent, 12/20/2009; Holland Cotter (auth), At a Biennial on a Budget, Tweaking and Provoking, NY Times, 2/25/2010. *Mailing Add:* Nicelle Beauchene Gallery 383 Grand St Apt M904 New York NY 10002

CROZIER, RICHARD LEWIS
PAINTER, EDUCATOR
b Honolulu, Hawaii, Dec 28, 1944. *Study:* Univ Wash, Seattle, BFA (painting), 68; Univ Calif, Davis, with Wayne Thiebaud, MFA (painting) 74. *Work:* J B Speed Mus, Louisville, Ky; Am Embassy, Zaire; Greenville Art Mus, NC; Couric Cancer Ctr, Charlottesville, Va. *Comn:* Paintings Juvenile Court Bldg, Charlottesville-Albemarle Comt Arts, Va, 80-81; Cover, Am Libr Asn J, Chicago, 75; painting, Brown-Forman Corp, Louisville, 91; Art in Embassies Prog, US State Dept. *Exhib:* Maier Mus, Lynchberg, Va, Mt Holyoke Mus, South Hadley, Mass; Arts Club of Washington, DC, 2004; Pence Gallery, Davis, Calif, 2005; Roanoke Coll, Salem, Va, 2007; Chinese Univ of Hong Kong, 2008; Lychburg Acad Fine Arts, 2010. *Teaching:* Prof studio art, Univ Va, 74-2011, emer prof 2011-. *Awards:* Purchase Award, Southeastern Ctr Contemp Art, 77. *Bibliog:* John Arthur (auth), Spirit of Place, Bulfinch, 89; R Crozier & Thomas Bolt (coauths), Inventing the Landscape, Watson Guptill, 89; Green Woods and Crystal Waters, John Arthur (auth), Philbrook Mus of Art, Tulsa, Okla, 99; Kelly and Rasmussen (auths), The Virginia Landscape, Howell Press, 2000; Marianne Doezema (auth), Changing Prospects, Cornell Univ Press, 2002. *Media:* Oil. *Dealer:* Reynolds Gallery 1514 West Main St Richmond VA 23220. *Mailing Add:* 624 Preston Pl Charlottesville VA 22903

CRUM, DAVID
PAINTER
b Peoria, Ill, Dec 6, 1938. *Study:* Independently with John Chamberlain. *Work:* Long Beach Mus, Calif; Baruch Coll Gallery, NY; Mills Coll Art Mus, Calif. *Exhib:* Newport Beach Mus, Calif, 66; Paintings on Paper, Glassboro Coll Gallery, NJ, 72; Recent Acquisitions, Aldrich Mus, Ridgefield, Conn, 74; New Directions in Contemp Art, Santa Barbara, Calif, 82; Bank Am World Hq, San Francisco. *Teaching:* Vis assoc prof painting, La State Univ, 84. *Bibliog:* Peter Frank (auth), article, Soho Weekly News, 76; Sam Hunter (auth), New Directions in Contemporary Art, Princeton, NJ, 81; Judith Stern (producer), Fresh air, Nat Pub Radio, 81. *Mem:* Nat Arts Club. *Media:* Acrylic. *Dealer:* Frederich Spratt San Jose CA

CRUM, KATHERINE B
MUSEUM DIRECTOR, EDUCATOR
b Palo Alto, Calif, Dec 10, 1941. *Study:* Stanford Univ, BA, 62, MA, 64; Hunter Col, NY, MA (art hist), 74; Columbia Univ, PhD (art hist), 84. *Collection Arranged:* Richards Ruben & Michael Goldberg, 84, George Mayocole, Lynn Mayocole & Bill Taggart, 84, Color Abstraction in the 1980's, 85, Figurative Art of the NY School, 85, Women Artists of the Surrealist Movement, 86, Bradley Walker Tomlin, 89, Baruch Coll Gallery, City Univ NY & Clyde Connell, Mills Coll Art Gallery, 92; Ron Nagle: A Survey Exhibition, 93; Wally Hedrick on Love and Art, 93; Luis Cruz Pizaseta: Dislocations, 94; No Two Alike!, The Ceramic Art of George E Ohr, 2000; plus others. *Pos:* Dealer & owner, Nicholas Wilder Gallery, Los Angeles, 64-69; cur exhibs, Inst Res Hist, New York, 80-83; dir, Baruch Col Gallery, City Univ New York, 83-89 & Mills Col Art Mus, Oakland, Calif, 91-. *Teaching:* Adj asst prof art hist, Baruch Col, City Univ New York, 74-89. *Mem:* Coll Art Asn; Am Asn Mus. *Res:* 20th century art; 13th & 14th century Italian painting. *Publ:* Ed, Places of Origin, Inst Res Hist, 80; contribr, Western Civilization, Houghton Mifflin, 81; auth, The Cudner-Hyatt House, Scarsdale Hist Soc, 82; Figural Art of the New York School, Baruch Col, 85. *Mailing Add:* c/o Mills Col Art Gallery 5000 MacArthur Blvd Oakland CA 94613

CRUMB, ROBERT DENNIS
CARTOONIST, ILLUSTRATOR
b Philadelphia, Aug 30, 43. *Comn:* illusr (album cover), Cheap Thrills, Big Brother & The Holding Co, 68; illusr (book cover), The Monkey Wrench Gang, Edward Abbey, 85. *Exhib:* Solo exhibs include Modernism, San Francisco, 83 & 90, La Hune, Paris, 86, Gotham Book Mart, New York, 87, Alexander Gallery, New York, 93, Paul Morris Gallery, New York, 2000 & 2002, Dan Weinberg Gallery, Los Angeles, 2003, Ludwig Mus, Cologne, 2004, Whitechapel Art Gallery, London, 2005, Spruth Magers Proekte, Munich, 2006, Yerba Buena Center Arts, San Francisco, 2007; group exhibs include The Comics Art Show, Whitney Mus Am Art, New York, 83; Zap to Zippy: The Impact of Underground Comix, Cartoon Art Mus, San Francisco, 90; High & Low: Mod Art & Pop Cult, Mus Mod Art, New York, 90; 100 Drawings & Photographs, Matthew Marks Gallery, New York, 2001; New Mems & Award Recipients Exhib, Am Accad Arts & Letts, 2003; The Great Drawing Show, Michael Kohn Gallery, Los Angeles, 2003; Carnegie Int, Carnegie Mus Art, Pittsburgh, 2004; Beautiful Losers, Yerba Buena Center Arts, San Francisco, 2004, traveled to Contemp Arts Center Cincinnati, Orange County Mus Art, Calif, Contemp Mus, Baltimore, Univ South Fla, Milan Triennale, Le Tri Postal, France; Masters of Am Comics, Hammer Mus, UCLA, 2005, traveled to Mus Contemp Art, Los Angeles, Jewish Mus, New York, Milwaukee Art Mus; Summer Love: Art of the Psychedelic Era, Tate Liverpool, Eng, 2005, traveled to Kunsthalle Schirn Frankfurt, Kunsthalle Wien, Whitney Mus Am Art; Speak: Nine Cartoonists, Pratt Manhattan Gallery, New York, 2006; De Superman au Chat de Rabbin, Mus Art & Histoire Judaisme, Paris, 2007; 55th Int Art Exhib Biennale, Venice, 2013. *Pos:* Colorist, Am Greetings Corp, 63-67; cartoonist, Fantagraphics Books, Seattle, 67-; founder, publ & ed, Zap Comix, 68-, Weirdo Mag, 81-93; band mem, R Crumb & His Cheap Suit Serenaders, 72-. *Awards:* Harvey Special Award for Humor, 90; Grand Prix de la ville d'Angoulême, 99. *Bibliog:* Mary Dickinson (prodr), The Confessions of Robert Crumb, 87; Terry Zwigoff (dir), Crumb, 94; and others. *Collection:* 1920s & 1930s Jazz and Blues Records. *Publ:* Ed & publ, Zap Comix 0-14, 1968-2004; auth & illusr, Bijou Funnies 68-71; Head Comix, 68; Snatch Comics 68-69; R Crumb's Comics & Stories, 69; Motor City Comics, 69-70; Yellow Dog Comics Vol 2, #13, 69; R Crumb's Fritz the Cat, 69; Mr Natural, 70-71; San Francisco Comic Book #3, 70; Uneeda Comix, 70; Despair, 70; Hytone Comix, 71; Home Grown Funnies, 71; The People's Comics, 72; XYZ Comics, 72; Funny Aminals, 72; Black & White Comics, 73; El Perfecto Comics, 73; Artistic Comics, 73; Zam Zap, 74; Dirty Laundry Comics 74 & 78; Arcade Comics Revue, 75-76; Snarf #6, 76; American Splendor (with Harvey Pekar), 76-77, 79-80, 82-83; R Crumb's Carload o' Comics, 76; Best Buy Comics, 79; Snoid Comics, 79; ed & publ, Weirdo 1-28, 81-93; auth & illusr, Hup, 87, 89 & 92; co-auth (with Aline Kominski), My Troubles with Women, 91; auth & illusr, ID, 90-91; Weirdo Art of R Crumb, 92; The Life & Death of Fritz the Cat, 93; Complete Dirty Laundry Comics, 93; Introducing Kafka, 94; Self Loathing Comics 95 & 97; Art & Beauty, 96 & 2003; Mystic Funnies, 97, 99 & 2002; Your Vigor for Life Appalls Me, 98; Odds & Ends, 2000; Gotta Have'em: Portraits of Women, 2003; R Crumb's Kafka, 2004; The Sweeter Side of R Crumb, 2006; cover art for Eden and John's East River String Band, Some Cold Rainy Day, 2008, Drunken Barrel House Blues, 2009, Be Kind to a Man When He's Down, 2011; auth, The Book of Genesis (graphic novel), 2009; and many other album covers. *Dealer:* David Zwirner 525 W 19th St New York NY 10011. *Mailing Add:* 1150 Spaight St Madison WI 53703

CRUMP, JAMES
CURATOR, WRITER
Study: Ind Univ, BA & MA (art hist); Univ NMex, PhD (art hist). *Exhib:* Walker Evans: Decade by Decade, 2010; Doug and Mike Starn: Gravity of Light, 2012. *Pos:* Assoc cur photog, Kinsey Inst Sex Res, Ind Univ, Bloomington, formerly; founding dir, Arena Editions, formerly; chief cur & cur photog, Cincinnati Art Mus, 2008-. *Publ:* Auth, George Platt Lynes: Photographs from the Kinsey Inst, 1993; auth, F Holland Day: Suffering the Ideal, 1995; coauth, When We Were Three: The Travel

Albums of George Platt Lynes, Monroe Wheeler, & Glenway Wescott, 1998; coauth, Vik Muniz: Seeing is Believing, 1998; coauth, Garry Winogrand: 1964, 2002; coauth, Meridel Rubenstein: Belonging, 2004; auth, Albert Watson, 2007; writer, dir, prodr, (documentary) Black White + Gray: A Portrait of Sam Wagstaff & Robert Mapplethorpe, 2007; auth, Variety: Photographs by Nan Goldin, 2009; coauth, Starburst: Color Photography in Am 1970-1980, 2010; auth, Walker Evans: Decade by Decade, 2010; coauth, High Heels: Fashion Femininity and Seduction, 2011; coauth, Herb Ritts: LA Style, 2012; ed, Doug and Mike Starn: Gravity of Light, 2012; author, James Welling (monograph), 2013. *Mailing Add:* Cincinnati Art Mus 953 Eden Park Dr Cincinnati OH 45202

CRUMP, WALTER MOORE, JR
PRINTMAKER, PAINTER

b Winston-Salem, NC, Mar 18, 1941. *Study:* Gilford Col, NC, 61-64; Harvard Univ Exten, 64-66; Boston Univ, BFA, 70. *Work:* DeCordova Mus, Lincoln, Mass; Philadelphia Mus Art; Nat Mus Am Art, Smithsonian Inst; Libr Congress Print Collection; NC Mus Art, Raleigh; NY Pub Libr; Citicorp World HQ; RJ Reynolds World HQ. *Exhib:* Davidson Nat Drawing & Print Exhib, NC, 73; Color Print USA, Tex Tech Univ, Lubbock, 75; Artists Under 36, DeCordova Mus, 76; Int Miniature Print Exhib, Pratt Graphics Ctr, NY, 77; Boston Printmakers Nat Exhib, Mus Fine Arts, Boston, 75-88 & DeCordova Mus, 77 & 79; Korean Exchange Print Exhib, Seoul, 78; Silvermine Nat Print Exhib, New Canaan, Conn, 78, 80 & 83; Solo exhibs, Plum Gallery, Washington, DC, 80, 82 & 88; Tacer Gallery Tort, Spain, 85; Wauz Gallery, 86 & 87. *Teaching:* Chmn art dept & instr printmaking, Commonwealth Sch, Boston, 72-; lectr & slide presentations, DeCordova Mus, 78 & Nat Collection of Fine Arts, Washington, DC, 79. *Awards:* Purchase Prize & First Prize, Dulin Nat Print & Drawing Competition, Knoxville, Tenn, 78 & 79; A P Hanks Mem Purchase Prize, Print Club Int Biennial, Philadelphia, 79; Purchase Prize, Boston Printmakers Exhib, 76-79. *Mem:* Boston Visual Artists Union; Boston Printmakers. *Media:* Intaglio; Oil. *Mailing Add:* 516 E Second St Boston MA 02127-1463

CUBIÑÁ, SILVIA KARMAN
MUSEUM DIRECTOR, CURATOR

b Miami. *Study:* Boston Coll, BA (art hist), 1987. *Collection Arranged:* French Kissing in the USA, Moore Space, Miami, 2007. *Pos:* With Cuban Mus Art, Miami, formerly, Mex Mus, San Francisco, formerly; adj cur, inova Inst Visual Arts, Univ Wis, Milwaukee, formerly; Puerto Rico commissioner, Bienal de Sao Paolo, 1997; independent cur, 1997-2002; founding dir, Moore Space, Miami, 2002-08; juror, Hugo Boss Award, Guggenheim Mus, 2006; exec dir & chief cur, Bass Mus Art, Miami, 2008-. *Awards:* Fel Ctr Curatorial Leadership, 2007. *Mailing Add:* Bass Museum 2100 Collins Ave Miami FL 33139

CUCULLU, SANTIAGO
PAINTER

b Buenos Aires, Argentina, 1969. *Study:* Hartford Art Sch, BFA, 92; Minneapoplis Coll Art & Design, MFA, 99. *Work:* Mus Mod Art; Milwaukee Art Mus; Mus Fine Arts, Houston, Tex; Henry Art Gallery, Seattle; Walker Art Ctr, Minneapolis. *Comn:* MF Ziggurat, (mural), Milwaukee Art Mus, 2009. *Exhib:* Solo exhibs, Boom Gallery, Minneapolis, 99, Art Houston, Barbara Davis Gallery, Houston, 2002, Wiyya To Hell Owwa That, Julia Friedman Gallery, Chicago, 2003, Art Basel Miami: Art Statements, Barbara Davis Gallery, Houston, 2003, Arco: Madrid Project Room, Julia Friedman Gallery, Chicago, 2004, Works on Paper, Blum & Poe Gallery, Los Angeles, 2003, Delectable Reason of Sleeps, Perry Rubenstein Gallery, NY, 2005, The Dolphin Gallery, Kans City, 2007, On File (Mt Zigguarat), Milwaukee Art Mus, Milwaukee, 2008; Creaks & Shafts, Rochester Arts Ctr, 2007; group exhibs, Esacio de Pensamiento, Bueno Aires, Argentina, 95, Dumb & Evil, Calhoun Sq Gallery, Minneapolis, 98, Push, Pull Pop, 99, XL, Weinstein Gallery, Minneapolis, 2000, 13 From Minneapolis, Minneapolis, 2002, Fresh-The Altoids Collection, 2003, Fiction: Truth in Photography and Painting, Timothy Taylor Gallery, London, 2004, How Would You Light Heaven, Carlier I Gebauer, Berlin, 2004, How Latitudes Become Forms: Art in a Global Age, Contemp Art Mus, Houston, 2004, Whitney Biennial, 2004, Wanderlust, Julia Friedman Gallery, NY, 2005, Sticks and Stones, Perry Rubenstein Gallery, NY, 2005, Singapore Biennale, 2006, Archipeinture, Camden Arts Centre, London, 2006, New Perspectives in Latin Am Art, Mus Mod Art, New York, 2007; Carlier/Gebauer, Berlin, 2007; Calouste Gulbenkian Found, Lisbon, Portugal, 2007; Wisconsin Triennial, 2007; ARCO, Madrid, 2007. *Awards:* Jerome Emerging Artist Fel, Minneapolis Coll Art & Design, 2000; Art Matters Found Grant, 2009. *Mailing Add:* Green Gallery East 1500 N Farwell Ave Milwaukee WI 53202

CUEVAS, JOSE LUIS
DRAFTSMAN

b Mexico City, Mex, Feb 26, 1934. *Study:* Sch Painting & Sculpture (La Esmeralda, Inst Nac Bellas Artes), Mexico City. *Work:* Mus Mod Art & Solomon R Guggenheim Mus, NY; Brooklyn Mus, NY; Mus of Albi & Lyons, France; Metrop Mus Art, NY. *Exhib:* Biennial Venize, Italy, 72; Palais Beaux Arts, Brussels, Belg, 74; Warsaw Gallery, Poland, 75; Ludwig Mus, Cologne, Ger, 78; Mus Mod Art, Mexico City, 79; World Print Awards, San Francisco Mus Art, 83; Frederick S Wight Art Gallery of UCLA, 84; Mus Mod Art, Mexico City, 85; Musee d'Art Moderne de Liege, Belgium, 86; Alvar Alto Mus, Helsinki, Finland, 86; Pinacoteque Nationale Musee Alexandre Soutzos, Athens, Greece, 87; Orangerie Palais Auersperg, Vienna, Austria, 87. *Teaching:* Resident artist, Philadelphia Mus Sch Art, 57; lectr art, San Jose State Col, 70, Fullerton Col, 75 & Wash State Univ, 75. *Awards:* First Int Prize for Drawing, V Biennial of Sao Paulo, Brazil, 59; First Int Award, Mostra Bianco e Nero, 62; Award Excellence, 29th Ann Exhib, Art Dir Club, Philadelphia, 83. *Bibliog:* Carlos Fuentes (auth), Los mundos de Jose Luis Cuevas, Misrachi Gallery, Mexico City, 70; Daisy Ascher (auth), Revelando a Jose Luis Cuevas, Madero, Mex, 79; J B Ponce (auth), Jose Luis Cuevas: Genio O Farsante?, Ed Signos, 83; J M Tasende (auth), Tasende Gallery - 1982, La Jolla, Calif, 82. *Publ:* Illusr, Crime by Cuevas, Lublin Ed, 68; Homage to Quevedo, 69 & Cuevas Comedies, 71, Collectors Press; Roberto Sanesi, Jose Luis Cuevas, Centro Arte/Zarathustra, Milano, Italy, 78; J M Tasende, Jose Luis Cuevas Letters, 82, Peter Selz, Intolerance, 83 & J M Tasende, Twenty five years with Jose Luis Cuevas, La Jolla, Calif, 92, Tasende Gallery; Carlos Fuentes, The Buried Mirror, Houghton Mifflin, NY, 92. *Mailing Add:* c/o Tasende Gallery 820 Prospect St La Jolla CA 92037

CULBERTSON, JANET LYNN (MRS DOUGLAS KAFTEN)
PAINTER, ENVIRONMENTAL ARTIST

b Greensburg, Pa, Mar 15, 1932. *Study:* Carnegie Inst Technol, BFA, 53; Art Students League, 54; NY Univ, MA, 63; Pratt Graphic Arts Inst, 64-65. *Work:* Nat Mus Women Arts, Washington, DC; State Mus Harrisburg, Pa; St Petersburg Mus Art, Fla; Heckscher Mus, Huntington, NY; Stone Quarry Hill Art Park, Cazenovia, NY; Guild Hall, East Hampton, NY; Fogg Mus, Mass; Libr Cong; Islip Mus, NY; Hunterdon Mus, NY; Telfair Mus, Ga; Nat Acad Sci, Washington, DC. *Exhib:* Solo Exhibs: Lerner-Heller Gallery, New York, 71-73 & 75- 77; Benson Gallery, Bridgehampton, NY, 78, 81, 83, & 89; Nardin Gallery, New York, 81; Stone Quarry Hill Art Park, Cazenovia, NY, 96; Suffolk Coll, Riverhead, NY, 96; Atelier A/E, New York, 97; Univ Alaska, Anchorage, 97; Nat Acad Sci, Washington, DC, 98; Huntington Arts Coun Gallery, NY, 2002; Earth First, Univ of Nebr, Omaha, 2002; Cambridge Arts Ctr, Mass, 2003; Mythmaker, Nat Mus Women in the Arts, 2004-2005; Tomorrow's Landscape, Seton Hill Univ Greensburg, Pa, 2006; The Sacred Earth, Nat Museo de San Jose, Costa Rica, 2008; Eco-Feminism: Eve Defends her Garden, Floyd Memorial Libr, 2008; Adirondack Lakes Art Ctr, 2009, Vital Signs, South St Gallery, Greenport, NY, 2011, Possible Peril, Accola Griefen Gallery, NY, 2012; Group exhibs, Guild Hall Mus Invitational, E Hampton, NY, 89; Islip Mus, NY, 90 & 92; C W Post Hillwood Mus, Brookville, NY, 90 & 94; Acme Art Co, Columbus, Ohio, 91; Babcock Traveling Exhib, 93-94; Anita Shapkolsky Gallery, New York, 95; Listening to the Earth, Hamilton Univ, Clinton, NY, 95; Rediscovering the Landscape of the Americas (traveling exhib), Gerald Peters Gallery, NMex, 96-98; Women Realists, Ringling Sch Art & Design, Sarasota, Fla, 97; Univ Bridgeport, Conn, 99; What on Earth (8 works), Earth 2000, Univ of Miami, Fla, 2002 & 20 Industrial Park Works, Wave Hill, Bronx, New York, 98; Toxic Landscapes traveling exhib, Puffin Found, 2002; Cent Coll, Ohio, 2005; Antioch Coll, Ohio, 2005; Nat Drawing, Coll Ewing, NJ & Space 301, Environmental Concerns, Mobile, Ala, 2007; Accola Contemp, New York, 2008; Decordova Gallery, Greenport, NY, 2009; Future Tense, Islip Mus, 2010; Remembering 9/11, SUNY, Suffolk Coll, Riverhead, NY, 2011; Long Island Biennial, Heckscher Mus, NY, 2012; Petroleum Paradox, WCA, Ohio, 2013; Denise Bibro Gallery, All About Water, NY, 2013. *Teaching:* Instr art, Pace Coll, 64-68; adj prof, Pratt Art Inst, 73-74 & Southampton Coll, New York, 76, 11/9/80 & 5/20/90. *Awards:* Creative Artists Pub Serv Award, Graphics, New York, 89; First Prize & Mus Grant, Hillwood Art Mus, New York, 94; Purchase Award, Hoyt Mus, 95; Purchase Award, Nassau Co Mus, NY, 97; New York East End Arts Coun Grant, 2002-03; Ludwig Vogelstein Grant, 2003; Pollock Krasner Grant, 2007; Best in Show, East End Arts Council, Riverhead NY, 2008. *Bibliog:* Jenni Schlossman (auth), Political Landscapes, Women's Art J, 93; Rose Silvka, East Hampton Star, 5/26/94; Helen A Harrison (auth), NY Times, 3/96; Phyllis Braff (auth), NY Times, 89, 93, 95 & 2000; Joyce Beckenstein (auth), Janet Culbertson, The Toxic Wilderness, Women's Art Jour, 2011. *Mem:* Womens Caucus Art; Artists Equity; Greenpeace; Sierra Club; Earthwatch; Art Alliance of East Hampton. *Media:* Acrylic, Oil, Mixed media. *Specialty:* Contemporary art. *Interests:* Birds, Music. *Publ:* Auth, Articles in Feminism and Ecology, 81; Women Artists Newsletter, Article; Terra Nova, Article, 4/89; Gallerie, Article, Vol 8, 90. *Dealer:* Kristen Accola New York; Accola Griefen. *Mailing Add:* 46 Hilo Dr PO Box 455 Shelter Island Heights NY 11965

CULBRETH, CARL R
SCULPTOR

b Mineola, NY, Dec 2, 1952. *Study:* Nassau Community Col, AA (studio art), 73; Univ Vt, BS (art educ), 75; Univ Del, MFA (ceramic sculpture), 79. *Work:* Syracuse Univ; Roberson Ctr Arts & Sci, Binghamton, NY. *Exhib:* Ten Artists Under 30, Fine Arts Mus Long Island, Hempstead, NY, 81; Wards Island Sculpture Site, NY, 81; Brooklyn Mus, NY, 81; East Coast Clay, Sculpture Ctr, NY, 82; The Figure: New Form, New Function, Arrowmont Sch Gallery, Gatlinburg, Tenn, 83; Ancient Inspirations, Contemp Interpretations, NY State Mus, Albany, 83; Three Dimentions, Univ Tex, El Paso. *Pos:* Resident ceramist & gallery dir, Clayworks Studio Workshop, New York, 79-80; dept head, Terra Cotta, MJM Studios, Hoboken, NJ, 85-. *Teaching:* Adj assoc prof art, Long Island Univ, 80-85; coordr ceramics prog, Parsons Sch Design, 80-84. *Bibliog:* Donna Harkavay (auth), article, Am Ceramics, 8/82; Martin Ries (auth), article, Re-Dact, 11/83. *Mem:* Am Crafts Coun; Nat Coun Educ Ceramic Arts; Coll Art Asn. *Media:* Clay. *Mailing Add:* 189 Upper Mountain Ave Montclair NJ 07042-1905

CULLIGAN, JENINE ELIZABETH
CURATOR, ADMINISTRATOR

b Lexington, Ky, Dec 15, 1959. *Study:* Univ Kentucky, Lexington, KY, BA, 84; Case Western Reserve Univ, Cleveland, OH, MA, 87. *Collection Arranged:* Toulouse-Lautrec to Picasso-Master Prints from Watercolor, Switzerland, 95; Edward L Edwan Sr, From the Prism's Edge, 96; The Face of Justice: Portraits of John Marshall, 2001; A Grand Term: Over Here, Over There, Prints from Daywood Coll, 2002; Through Am Eyes: Two Hundred Yrs of Am Art, 2003; Winslow Anderson Coll Haitian Art, 2004; Never Done: Works By Women Artists from the Puzzudo Miller Collection, 2006. *Pos:* Asst Educ Coordr, Univ Kentucky Art Mus, Lexington, KY, 87-88; Assoc Cur, Delaware Art Mus, Wilmington, DE, 88-96; Sr Cur, Huntington Mus Art, Huntington, WV, 99-. *Awards:* Anne Worthington Callahan Award, Univ Ky, 84; Stone Fel, Case Western Reserve Univ, 85; AAM Cur Travel Stipend Award, AAM, 90. *Mem:* Am Asn Mus; Coll Art Asn; Asn Art Mus Cur. *Res:* Generalist; America Art late 19th Century-Contemporary. *Publ:* Ed, John O'Kulick: Transformations in Perspective, Deleware Art Mus, 91; ed, Robert Stackhouse,

Deleware Art Mus, 91; co-auth, Edward L Looper: From the Prism's Edge, Deleware Art Mus, 96; co-auth, Fifty years of Collecting Huntington Mus Art, 2001; co-auth, Through American Eyes, Huntington Mus Art, 2003. *Mailing Add:* Huntington Museum of Art 2033 McCoy Rd Huntington WV 25701-4999

CULLING, RICHARD EDWARD
PAINTER, COLLAGE ARTIST
b Detroit, Mich, Dec 5, 1951. *Study:* Wayne State Univ, BFA, 74, Univ Mich Sch Art, MFA, 88. *Work:* Univ Mich Permanent Collection, Ann Arbor. *Exhib:* 11th Mich Biennial, Kresge Art Mus, E Lansing, 88; Figuring It Out, Calvin Col, Grand Rapids, Mich, 88; What's New in Art, Galesburg Civic Ctr, Ill, 88; Animal Art, United Auto Workers, Gen Motors Resource Bldg, Auburn Hills, Mich, 88; Two Person, Univ Mich, Flint, 88; A Matter of Painting, Detroit Focus, Mich, 88. *Teaching:* Instr painting, Univ Mich, 86-88; instr painting, Paint Creek Ctr Arts, 88. *Awards:* Artist Grant, Mich Coun Arts, 84; Guggenheim Award, 85; Res Fel Award, Univ Mich, 87. *Bibliog:* Marsho Miro (auth), 2 Artists Find There's No Place Like Home, Detroit Free Press, 1/16/83. *Mem:* Coll Art Asn. *Media:* Oil. *Dealer:* Mary C Wright 568 N Woodward Birmingham MI 48154. *Mailing Add:* 38798 Kingsbury Livonia MI 48154

CULLUM, JERRY
EDITOR
Study: Eckered Coll, BA (lit); Univ Calif Santa Barbara, MA (religious studies); Emory Univ, Inst Liberal Arts, PhD. *Collection Arranged:* cur, Telfaire Mus Arts, Ga State Univ, Ga Perimeter Coll, Marietta-Cobb Mus Art, and more; co cur, Atlanta artists, Germany & England, 1996. *Pos:* assoc editor, Art Papers Mag, 1984-1997, sr editor, 1997-; art critic, Atlanta Journ & Contribution, 1988-; contribr, ARTnews, Art in America, 1998-; freelance critic, 1989-. *Teaching:* lectr, Atlanta Coll Art, Emeory Univ; visiting critic, New Castle, Tyne, United Kingdom, Shreveport & Alexandria, La. *Publ:* poems, Poetry, Chicago, Midwest Quarterly, and more mags. *Mailing Add:* Art Papers PO Box 5748 Atlanta GA 31107

CULVER, MARGARET VICTORIA
ADMINISTRATOR, ARTIST
b Liverpool, Eng, Aug 31, 1948. *Study:* Manchester Metrop Univ, BSc (graphic design), 69. *Work:* Real Tart Gallery, New Plymouth, New Zealand; Hill Country Arts Found, Ingram, Tex; Turchin Arts Ctr, Boone, NC; Public Gallery, Monmouth Medical Ctr, Long Branch, NJ; Monmouth Cty Clerks Offices, Freehold, NJ; Central Jersey Blood Ctr, Shrewsbury, NJ; Monmouth Mus; Kensington Court, Tinton Falls, NJ; Monmouth Co Libr. *Comn:* Taunton Sch, Gail Jordan, Prin, Howell, NJ, 1992. *Exhib:* Solo Exhibs: Art & Attic Gallery, Red Bank, NJ, 97; PNC Bank, Howell, NJ, 97; Little Silver Borough Hall, NJ, 98; Poricy Park Nature Ctr, Middletown, NJ, 98; Navesink Libr Theater, Middletown, NJ, 2003; Metuchen Libr, 2003, Nat Juried Art Exhib, Audubon Artists, Salamagundi Club, NY, 2011, 2012; Group Exhibs: New Comers Exhib, City Without Walls, Newark, NJ, 98, Black Box, 2008; Asbury Park, NJ, 2001; NJ Ctr for the Healing Arts, 99-2005; Botanical Awards, La Quinta Cult Ctr, Albuquerque, NMex, 2002; Guild Creative Art, Shrewsbury, NJ, 2002-2013; Art Alliance Monmouth Co, Red Bank, NJ, 2002; Focus on Sculpture, Grounds for Sculpture, Hamilton, NJ, 2005; 20th Ann Juried Show, Ocean County Artists Guild, Island Heights, NJ, 2006; 8th Int Collage Exchange, Real Tart Gallery, New Plymouth, New Zealand, 2006; Long Branch Arts Council, Art in the Park, 37th Ann Juried Exhib, Monmouth Festival Arts, 2009-2011; Music & Art Acad, Marlboro, NJ, 2003; Tratto'ria, Metuchen, Ger, 2004; Powys Gallery, 2004; Monmouth Beach Cult Ctr, 2005; West Long Branch Pub Libr, 2005; Small World Coffee, Princeton, NJ, 2006; Guild Creative Art Studio, Shrewsbury, NJ, 2006-2013; Georgian Court Univ, 2006; McKay Imaging Gallery, Red Bank, NJ, 2007; Noyes Mus Art, 2007-13; Women's Art Festival, Asbury Park, NJ, 2009; Terner Gallery, Ocean Twp, NJ, 2009; Shore Inst for Contemp Arts, Long Branch, NJ, 2009, Belmar Arts Council; Brookdale Community Col, Western Monmouth Campus; Oceanic Free Libr, Gallery 13, Asbury Park, NJ, 2008-2012; Dolphin Watch Gallery, Corolla, NC, Monmouth Mus, 2011, 2013, Salmagundi Club Non-Mem Photog & Graphics Exhib in Chelsea, NY, 2012, Aububon Artists' Ann Exhib, 2011, 2012, 2013. *Collection Arranged:* The Art of Healing, NJ Ctr for Healing Arts, 2000; The Flower Show, Cork Gallery, Lincoln Ctr, 2002; 43rd Anniversary Exhib, Guild at Monmouth Mus, 2003; Guild of Creative Art Exhib Mod, Agr Bldg, 2005-2013; 25th Cong Art Competition, 12th Dist High Sch Awards, 2006; Guild of Creative Art Bi-Monthly Exhib, Monmouth Cty Clerk's Offices, 2001-2013; Central Jersey Blood Center 2001-2013. *Pos:* Longman Publ, Harlow, Eng, 74-79; Can Govt, Dept Indust, Trade & Commerce, Ottawa, 74-79; Banfield Advert, Ottawa, Can, 81-84; Freelance graphic designer, Ottawa, Can, 84-87; Exec dir, Guild Creative Art, Shrewsbury, NJ, 2000-08, gallery exhib coordr, 2009-2013. *Teaching:* demonstrations: Old Bridge Libr, Raritan Camera Club, Freehold Art Soc, Pine Shores Art Asn, Sickles' Market Artists' Days, Monmouth County Libr, Howell Township Middle Sch, 2011. *Awards:* Botanical Awards, Gallery Print, Wis, 2002; Art Alliance, Jean Townsend 18th Ann Juried Show, Art Alliance of Monmouth Co, 2003 & 2006; Judge's Award, Members Juried Show, Art Soc Monmouth Cty, 2005-2013; First Place Photog, Art Soc Monmouth Co, Ruth Crown Mem Art Show, 2007-2013; hon mention, Audubon Artists, Salmagundi Club, NY, 2011, 2012; Presidents award for Innovation in the Collage & Mixed Media Category, Audubon Artists Juried Exhib, 2013; Marquis Who's Who in American Art References award in Collage & Mixed Media, Audubon Artists, 2014. *Bibliog:* Mitchell Seidel (auth), Some Assembly Required, Star Ledger, 4/1999; Anita Stratos (auth), Many Emotions Conveyed Through Art, Greater Media Newspapers, 6/2003; Shannon Mullen (auth), Releasing Memories, Asbury Park Press, 11/2005; Bobbi Seidel (auth), APP, 2006; Nicole Whitney Stevens (auth), Artistic Soul, State of the Art, 2006; Artist Wants Observers to Get the Big Picture, GM News, 2008; Bobbi Seidel (auth), Digital Doesn't Cut It; Around & About, Greater Media, 2011; and others. *Mem:* Guild of Creative Art (dir, 2000-11); Art Alliance of Monmouth Co (bd mem, 1996-2000); Freehold Art Soc; Art Soc of Monmouth Cty; Belmar Arts Coun, Shore Inst for the Contemp Arts; Monmouth Co Arts Coun; Monmouth Mus; Noyes Mus; Am Craft Coun. *Media:* Photo Collage, Mixed Media, Photography. *Specialty:* Contemporary. *Interests:* Travel; Cooking; Audio Books. *Publ:* Howell Reporter, APP, 2004; Monmouth Journal, 2005; APP (Entertainment Section), 2005; Jersey Alive, APP, 2006; Greater Media, 2008-2012; Discover JerseyArts (online). *Dealer:* The Guild of Creative Art Rt 35 Shrewsbury NJ; Dolphin Watch Gallery Corolla NC; Monmouth Mus NJ. *Mailing Add:* 39 Forrest Hill Dr Howell NJ 07731

CULVER, MICHAEL L
PAINTER, CURATOR
b Louisville, Ky, Sept 10, 1947. *Study:* Univ Louisville, BA (sculpture), 72, MA (painting), 77 & PhD (art hist), 86. *Work:* Ogunquit Mus Am Art, Maine; Owensboro Mus Fine Art, Ky; Univ Louisville, Brown & Williams Tobacco co & Humana Corp, Louisville, Ky; Kennebunk Savings Bank, Maine; RI Sch Design Mus Art. *Comn:* Poster & prog cover, Louisville Ballet, 83. *Exhib:* Nat Arts Club Gallery, NY, 87; solo-exhibs, Headley-Whitney Mus, Lexington, Ky & Owensboro Mus Fine Arts, Ky, 88; Nat Show, Viridian Gallery, NY, 88; US State Dept Art In Embassies Prog, Indonesia, 92-; Ctr for Maine Contemp Art, Rockport, 2002; Unity Coll Art Gallery, Maine, 2004. *Collection Arranged:* Painting & Drawing, 85-2005; Dozier Bell Exhib, 91; Walt Kuhn: Am Master, 92; The Art of Jack Levine, Ogunquit Mus Am Art, Maine, 92; Will Barnet: Works of six Decades (auth, catalog), 94; The Art of George Tooker, 96; Hughie Lee-Smith: A Retrospective, 97; Charles H Woodbury & His Students, 98; Painted Air: Am Impressionism, 2000; Landscapes by Wolf Kahn, 2002; The Art of Janet Fish, 2004; The Figure in Am, 2006; Paintings by Jamie Wyeth. *Pos:* Pres, Ky Art Educ Asn, 79; cur, Ogunquit Mus, Am Art, 83-, assoc dir, 95-2001, exec dir, cur, 2001-; chair, Maine Art Mus Trail Orgn, 2003. *Teaching:* Instr human Am studies, Univ Louisville, Ky, 81-82. *Awards:* Fulbright-Hayes Grant, 77; Grad Proj Award, Univ Louisville, 80, 82; Grad Dean's Fel, Univ Louisville, 81-83. *Media:* Acrylic. *Res:* Twentieth century American art. *Publ:* Auth, Examination of illustrations for pound's a draft of XVI Cantos, Paideuma J, Univ Maine, 83; Realistic art of Henry Strater (exhib catalog), Washington & Lee Univ, 86; Henry Strater an American original (exhib catalog), Owensboro Mus Fine Arts, 88; Charles H Woodbury and his Students, 98 & History of the Ogunquit Museum of American Art, 2000, Am Art Rev; exhib catalog, Landscapes by Wolf Kahn, 2002. *Dealer:* Mathias Fine Arts Trevett ME 04571; Swanson Reed Galleries 1377 Bardstown Rd Louisville KY 40204. *Mailing Add:* Shore Rd PO Box 815 Ogunquit ME 03907

CULVER, VICKY See Culver, Margaret Victoria

CUMMENS, LINDA TALABA See Talaba, L (Linda) Talaba Cummens

CUMMING, GLEN EDWARD
CONSULTANT
b Calgary, Alta, Can, July 2, 1936. *Study:* Alberta Coll Art, 4 yr dipl. *Exhib:* Chris Dikeakos: Sites and Place Names, 98; Monument: William Eakin, 98; The Word in Contemp Canadian Art, 98. *Collection Arranged:* Images; Photo Works from the Mocca Collection, 2000. *Pos:* Cur, Regina Pub Libr Art Gallery, Sask, 67-69; dir, Kitchener-Waterloo Art Gallery, Kitchener, Ont, 69-72, Robert McLaughlin Gallery, Oshawa, Ontario, 72-73, Art Gallery Hamilton, Ont, 73-89, 49th Parallel Gallery, Contemp Can Art, 89-92, Art Gallery North York, Ont, 93-95, Mus Contemp Canadian Art, Toronto Ontario, 95-2000 & Art Gallery Windsor, Ontario, 2001-2004. *Awards:* Queen Elizabeth Prize, 60; Alberta Visual Arts Bd Scholar, 60-62. *Mem:* Int Asn Art Critics; Int Coun Mus; Asn Art Mus Dirs (emer mem); McMurtry Law Garden Art Comt. *Specialty:* Can & Int art. *Publ:* Auth, Contemporary Art of Senegal, 79; Viewpoint: 29 by 9, 81; El Dorado, Gold from Ancient Colombia, 82; Living Imprssions, Contemp Can Graphics, 89; Walter Bachinski: Approaching Classicism, 91. *Mailing Add:* 207-70 Delisle Ave Toronto ON M4V1S7 Canada

CUMMING, ROBERT H
ARTIST, PHOTOGRAPHER
b Worcester, Mass, Oct 7, 1943. *Study:* Mass Coll Art, Boston, BA, 65; Univ Ill, Champaign, MFA, 67. *Work:* Mus Fine Arts, Houston; Mus Mod Art, NY. *Comn:* Outdoor sculpture, Walker Art Ctr, Minneapolis, Minn, 70; Nation's Capitol Documentation, Corcoran Gallery, Washington, DC. *Exhib:* Art by Telephone, Mus Contemp Art, Chicago, 69; 9 Artists-9 Spaces, Walker Art Ctr, Minneapolis, Minn, 70; 24 Young Los Angeles Artists, Los Angeles Co Mus, 71; Narrative Art, Palais des Beaux Arts, Brussels, Belg, 75; Whitney Biennial, NY, 77 & 81; Paris Biennale, Mus d'Art Mod, France, 77; Mirrors and Windows, Mus Mod Art, NY; and others. *Teaching:* Instr painting & drawing, Univ Wis, Milwaukee, 67-70; lectr photog,Univ Calif, Los Angeles, 74-. *Awards:* Frank Logan Prize, Chicago Art Inst, 69; Nat Endowment Arts Awards, 72, 74 & 83; Guggenheim Fel, 80. *Bibliog:* M Jochimsen (auth), Story Art, Mag Kunst, Mainz, Ger, 2/74; C Hagen (auth), Robert Cumming's Subject-Object, Artforum, summer 83. *Media:* Multimedia. *Publ:* Auth, Picture Fictions, Anaheim, Calif, 71; The Weight of Franchise Meat, Anaheim, Calif, 71; A Training in the Arts, Toronto, Can, 73; A Discourse on Domestic Disorder, Irvine, Calif, 75; Equilibrium and the Rotary Disc, Meriden, Conn, 80. *Dealer:* The Print Club Ctr Prints & Photographs 1614 Latimer St Philadelphia PA 19103. *Mailing Add:* 342 Haydenville Rd Whately MA 01093

CUMMINGS, DAVID WILLIAM
PAINTER
b Okmulgee, Okla, July 15, 1937. *Study:* Kansas City Art Inst, Mo, BFA, 63; Univ Nebr, Lincoln, MFA, 67. *Work:* Whitney Mus Am Art, NY; Los Angeles Co Mus Art, Calif; Phoenix Art Mus, Ariz; Mus Contemp Art, Antwerp, Belg; Aldrich Mus Contemp Art, Ridgefield, Conn; and others. *Exhib:* Lyrical Abstraction, Philadelphia Mus Art, Pa, 70 & Whitney Mus Am Art, 71; 20th Century Am Artists, Corcoran Gallery Art, Washington, DC, 71; Contemp Reflections, Aldrich Mus Contemp Art, 71-72; solo exhibs, Allan Stone Gallery, NY, 74-77 & 82, Gallery Alexandra Monett, Bruxelles, Belg, 75, 77, 79 & 82, Ericson Gallery, NY, 80, Shahin Requicha Gallery, Rochester, NY, 83, Gallery Jupiter, Little Silver, NJ, 87; AMB Galleries, Hoboken, 89; Cabrillo Coll, Aptos, Calif, 91; Rabbet Gallery, New Brunswick, NJ, 96; and others.

Pos: Vis artist, Ohio State Univ, Columbus, 74, Univ Iowa, Iowa City, 76, Univ NDak, Grand Forks, 81, SUNY, Purchase, 84, Cabrilllo Coll, Aptos, Calif, 91 & Ariz Western Univ, Yuma; coordr painting symposium, Colo Mountain Coll, Vail, 76-78; vis artist, RIT, Rochester, NY, 83. *Teaching:* Instr, State Univ NY, 67-71; assoc prof, City Univ NY, 71-89; prof, St Peters Coll, Jersey City, NJ, 85-2003; adj fac, Parsons Sch Design, NY. *Awards:* John Lehmann Award, St Louis Mus Art, Mo, 65; Woods Found Fel, Univ Nebr, 66-67; Painting Fels, NJ State Coun of the Arts, 85 & 91. *Bibliog:* Jacques Meuris (auth), David Cummings Plus Minus Zero, 11/79; Theodore F Wolff (auth), The Colorist's Art, The Christian Sci Monitor, 9/10/80; Susan Dodge Peters (auth), A master of color, Rochester City News, 4/28/83; Naomi Kenan (auth), Cummings' Work a Symphony of Color, Jersey Journal, 7/86; William Zimmer (auth), article, NY Times, 2/1/87. *Media:* Oil, Pastel, Watercolor. *Interests:* Prehistoric archaeological sites. *Dealer:* Rabbet Gallery 360 Georges Rd North Brunswick NJ 08902. *Mailing Add:* 106-108 Hopkins Ave Jersey City NJ 07306

CUMMINGS, MARY T
ADMINISTRATOR, CONSULTANT
b Minneapolis, Minn, May 22, 1951. *Study:* Univ Minn, BA (art hist), 73; Univ Mich, MA (art hist), 76; Ind Univ, MA (arts admin), 81. *Pos:* Lectr, Minneapolis Inst Arts, 77-78; asst to dir, Tweed Mus, Duluth, Minn, 78-79; dir, Missoula Mus Arts, Mont, 81-89; assoc dir, Minn Mus Art, St Paul, 89-. *Teaching:* Instr art hist, Macalester Col, St Paul, 77-78 & Univ Minn, Duluth, 78-79; vis prof art hist, Univ Mont, Missoula, 88-. *Mem:* Am Asn Mus; Women Mus Dir & Admin Caucus; Mont Art Gallery Dir Asn (pres, 83-86); Asn for Asian Studies. *Res:* Impact of museums on small communities; approaching art and visual images for the layman; nature of museums; Asian art (various topics). *Publ:* Auth, The Lives of the Buddha in the Art and Literature of Asia, Univ Mich, 85; Asian Di-Visions: A Contrast Between China and Japan (exhib catalog), 82 & The Primal Plastic Pool: Contemporary Art of the West (exhib catalog), 85, Missoula Mus; The artist and the museum: Some mutual expectations, The Crafts Report, 86; On learning to look and the function of museums, Mus Studies J, 88. *Mailing Add:* 137 E Curtice Saint Paul MN 55107-3271

CUMMINS, MAUREEN
PRINTMAKER, BOOK ARTIST
b 1963. *Study:* Cooper Union Sch Art, BFA, 1985. *Work:* Fogg Art Mus; Chicago Mus Contemp Art; Nat Gallery, Washington DC; New York Pub Libr; Minneapolis Inst Art. *Exhib:* Women in the Book Arts, Wellesly Coll, 1994; Scrolling the Page, Savannah Coll Art & Design, 1999; 2nd International Artists Book Triennial, Gallery Arka, Vilnius, Lithuania, 2000; Weir Farm Visiting Artist Exhib, Housatonic Mus Art, Conn, 2002; International Biennale for Hand Printed Artists Books, Bibliotheca Alexandria, Egypt, 2004. *Pos:* Founder, Inanna Press, 1991-. *Teaching:* Instr printmaking, Ctr for Book Arts, Women's Studio Workshop, Pyramid Atlantic, Conn Graphic Arts Ctr, 1993-; vis artist, West Baffin Eskimo Cooperative, 2001. *Awards:* Ctr for Book Arts Grant, 1994; Women's Studio Workshop Fel, 2000; Hearst Fel, Am Antiquarian Soc, 2000; Artist Grant, Puffin Found, 2003; Pollock-Krasner Found Grant, 2008. *Mailing Add:* 3 Church Ln High Falls NY 12440

CUNINGHAM, ELIZABETH BAYARD (MRS E W R TEMPLETON)
ART DEALER
b New York, NY. *Study:* Bronxville Sch, NY; Vassar Col, Poughkeepsie, NY; Finch Col, NY, BA; Hunter Col, New York, MA (art hist). *Pos:* Exec secy, Olana Preserv Inc, New York, 65-66; dir publicity, Comt to Rescue Italian Art, New York, 66-67; asst to pres, Nat Trust for Hist Preserv, 68-70; asst dir, Reese Palley Art Gallery, New York, 70-72; pres, Cuningham Ward Inc, 72-78; Betty Cuningham Gallery, 78-82; Hirsch & Adler Modern, New York, 82-. *Mem:* Drawing Soc Inc (exec comt, 70-80); Art Dealers Asn, 79-81. *Specialty:* Contemp painting. *Mailing Add:* 16 Studio Arcade Bronxville NY 10708

CUNNICK, GLORIA HELEN
PAINTER
b New York, NY. *Study:* Art Students League; New York Univ; Long Island Univ, CW Post, BFA, 87. *Work:* Fine Arts Mus Long Island, Hempsted, NY; Rutgers Univ, Zimmerli Art Mus; Pall Corp; Islip Mus, NY; Hillwood Art Mus. *Comn:* Touched by Light, Unitarian Church. *Exhib:* Tex Nat 95, Nacogdoches, Tex, 95; Islip Mus, NY, 96; BJ Spoke Gallery, Huntington, NY, 96; Nat Asn Women Artists, Athens Cult Ctr, Greece, 96; Omni Art Gallery, 2000; Hecksher Art Mus, 2001; Smithtown Township Art Mus, 2002; solo exhibs, Manhasset Libr, 2003, Graphic Eye Gallery, 2006 & Port Washington, Libr, 2007 & 08; Art League Long Island, 2004; Bryant Libr, 2007; James Beard Found, 2008; Great Neck Art Center, 2009; Painter and Poet Show, Man Hasset Lib, 2010. *Awards:* Winner, Fine Arts Mus, Long Island, NY, 93; Silver Award, Nassau Co Mus, 94; First Place Award, Nassau Co Arts Coun, 94; Best in Show Award, Great Neck Libr, 96 & First Prize, 2003; Award of Excellence, BJ Spoke Gallery, Nassau, 99; First Prize, Shelter Rock Art Gallery, 2001; Smithtown Township Arts Coun, 2002; First Prize, Great Neck Art Asn, 2005. *Bibliog:* Betty Ommerman (auth), Artist Math Equals Award, NewsDay, 1/26/92; Phyllis Braff (auth), Juried exhibition winners, NY Times, 94; Arlyne Boltson (auth), Membership plus three, Northport J, 96. *Mem:* Long Island Network Women Artists; Manhasset Art Asn Inc; Artist Network Great Neck; Art Asn Long Island; and others. *Media:* Acrylic, Encaustics. *Specialty:* abstraction, mixed. *Publ:* Biographical Encylclopedia American Painters, Sculptors & Engravers of US, Colonial, 2002. *Mailing Add:* Three Orchard Farm Rd Port Washington NY 11050

CUNNINGHAM, E C (ELDON) LLOYD
PRINTMAKER, EDUCATOR
b Colby, Kans, Mar 2, 1956. *Study:* Wichita State Univ, Kans, BFA, 79; Univ Colo, Boulder, MFA, 82. *Work:* Kaiser Med Found, US Univ Colo, Univ Dallas, Univ S Dakota; Quest Corp, Denver, Emprise Bank, Wichita. *Exhib:* Colorprint USA, Nat Invitational Exhib, Tex Tech Univ, Lubbock, 98; Midwest Select, South Bend Regional Mus Art, Ind, 94; Solo exhib, Clayton Staples Gallery, Wichita State Univ, Kans, 95; Twenty Twenty Vision, Arvada Ctr Arts & Humanities, Colo, 96; MAPC Bd Dir Print Exhib, Floyd Co Mus, New Albany, Ind, 96; Midlands Invitational 2000, Joslyn Art Mus, Omaha, NE; Invitational Print Exhib, State Univ NY, Brockport, 2000; The Sixteenth Nat Print Invitational, Univ Dallas, Irving, Tex, 99; Mapping Destinations Laredo, Tex, 2004; Walking on Water Int Invititional State Univ of NY, Brockport, 2004. *Pos:* Master printer, Master Eds Ltd, Englewood, Colo, 82-84. *Teaching:* Prof printmaking, Metrop State Col, Denver, 83-. *Awards:* Best Show, Works on Paper, Reuben Saunders Gallery, 80; Communs 1988 Best Show, 1999 Broadway Gallery, 88; Takach Corp Award, 3rd Biennial Print Exhib, Bus in the Arts Ctr Manitou Springs, Colo, 2000; Eagan Award for Excellence In Art, Wichita State Univ, 2001. *Bibliog:* Bloomsbury Rev, Vol 12, No 8, 12/92; Choice Current Revs Acad Librs, Vol 30, No 4, 12/92; Los Angeles Print Soc J, spring 93. *Mem:* Coll Art Asn; Nat Asn Schs Art Design; Southern Graphics Coun; Mid Am Print Coun (pres, 94-). *Media:* All Media. *Publ:* Auth, National Printmaking Slide/Video Exchange, Metrop State Col, 90; Printmaking A Primary Form of Expression, Univ Press Colo, 92; Higher Education Logic for Print Making, EC Cunningham Pub, 2000; Times They Are a Changin, article Graphic Impressions J, 2001; Book Introduction for Lynwood Kreneck, Printmaking, Texas Tech Univ Press, 2003. *Mailing Add:* Campus Box 59 PO Box 173362 Denver CO 80217-3362

CUNNINGHAM, FRANCIS
PAINTER, INSTRUCTOR
b New York, NY, Jan 18, 1931. *Study:* Art Students League, with Edwin Dickinson & Robert Beverly Hale; Harvard Coll, AB, 53. *Work:* Berkshire Mus, Pittsfield, Mass; Royal Theatre, Copenhagen; Security Pac Nat Bank, San Francisco; General Foods, Minneapolis; EP Dutton, NY; and other. *Exhib:* Solo exhibs, Hirschl & Adler Galleries, NY, 68, 70 & 75, Berkshire Mus, Pittsfield, Mass, 69, Distelheim Galleries, Chicago, 70 Mickelson Gallery, Washington, 71, Danish Consulate, NY, 87, Marsh Gallery, Univ Richmond, Va, 89, Gallerihusex, Copenhagen, Denmark, 95, Pro Persona Gallery, Stockholm, 98, Hudson River Gallery, Dobbs Ferry, NY, 2000 & Laurel Tracey Gallery, Red Bank, NJ, 2000-2008, 2010, 2012, St Francis Coll, Brooklyn, 2009, Century Master, 2013; two-man exhib, Forum Gallery, 79; Franciscan Provience, NY, 83; New Brooklyn Sch, NY, 82; Tel Aviv Mus, Isreal, 99; Laurel Tracey Gallery, 2000, 2002-2007, 2008-2010; Fedn of Modern Painters, New York City, 2001, 2007; Art Students League of NY, 2001, 2006; Galerie Susanne Ho/Jriis, Copenhagen, Denmark, 2002; exhib in group exhibs, Nat Acad Design, Butler Inst, & numerous others. *Pos:* Co-found & dir, NY Acad Sch Art, 83-86; co-found & dir, New Brooklyn Sch Life Drawing, Painting & Sculpture, Inc, 80-83. *Teaching:* Instr painting & drawing, Brooklyn Mus Art Sch, 62-80, Art Students League, NY, 80-83, 2003, New Brooklyn Sch, 80-85 & NY Acad Art, 83-85; Master classes, Art Student League, Nat Acad Design; Betzalel Jerusalem, Israel. *Awards:* Berkshire Art Asn Purchase Award, Berkshire Mus, 68; Louis Comfort Tiffany Found Grant, 73; Audubon Artists Awards, 73, 77, 80, 85, 93; Giula Palermo Award, 98; elected Nat Academician, Nat Acad of Design, 1994; fel, Bogliasco Found, 1997; Recipient of the Benjamin West Clinediust Medal for Exceptioal Artistic Merit, Artists Fel, 2004. *Mem:* Nat Acad Design (assoc, 92, acad, 94); Art Students League; Audubon Artists; Fel, Bogliasco Found, 97; Artists Fel. *Media:* Oil, Pencil, Charcoal. *Publ:* Coauth, Polykleitos' Diadoumenos: Measurement & Animation, Art Quart, summer 62; illusr, Fundamentals of Roentgenology, 64; articles in Linea, Art Students League, New York. *Dealer:* Laurel Tracey Gallery 10 White St Red Bank NJ 07701. *Mailing Add:* 789 W End Ave No 11D New York NY 10025-5469

CUNNINGHAM, J
SCULPTOR
b Greenwich, Conn, Sept 18, 1940. *Study:* Kenyon Col, BA, 62; Yale Sch Art & Archit, BFA, 63, MFA, 65. *Work:* Many pvt collections. *Exhib:* Many solo exhibs. *Teaching:* Prof art, Davidson chair, Skidmore Col, Saratoga Springs, 67-. *Awards:* Fel in Sculpture, Univ Pa, 66. *Publ:* Techniques of pyramid-building in Egypt, Nature, 3/3/88. *Mailing Add:* 35 Loughberry Rd Saratoga Springs NY 12866

CUNNINGHAM, SUE
PAINTER, ILLUSTRATOR
b Newton, Ill, Oct 19, 1932. *Study:* Southern Ill Univ, Carbondale; Millikin Univ, Decatur, Ill; study with Irving Shapiro, Zoltan Szabo & Maxine Masterfield. *Work:* Mead Johnson & Co; US Coast Guard; Quaker Oats Co, Danville, Ill; Bristol Myers Corp, Evansville, Ind; Hillside Acad, Hillside, Ill. *Comn:* Eight watercolor paintings, VA Kibler & Assoc, Architects, Newton, Ill, 81 & 85; eleven watercolor paintings, Comfort Inn, Vandalia, Ill, 85. *Exhib:* Mid-Am Biennial, Owensboro Mus Fine Art, Ky, 82 & 86; Nat Watercolor Soc Travel Show, 84; Ky Watercolor Soc Aqueous, 84; Adirondacks Nat Exhib Am Watercolors, 84 & 92; Am Watercolor Soc, 85; La Watercolor Soc, New Orleans, 85; Nat Arts Club Watercolor Open, NY, 86; Allied Artists Am, NY, 86; Nat Watercolor Okla, Okla Art Ctr, 86 & 87; Watercolor USA, Springfield, Mo Mus Art, 87; Gov Exec Mansion, Ill, 87. *Pos:* Regional Rep, Nat Watercolor Soc, 87-91; Official Coast Guard Artist. *Teaching:* Art marketing seminars; instr, watercolor workshops. *Awards:* First Place Watercolor, Ill State Fair Prof Art Exhib, 84; Award of Excellence, St Louis Art Affair, West Port Plaza & West Co Art Asn, 85; Juror's Award, Realism Today, Evansville Ind Mus Art, 89; St Louis Artists Guild, 86 & 87; Watercolor Ill Biennial, 85, 87 & 90. *Bibliog:* William Michael (auth), Self-portrait makes "watercolor page", Herald & Rev, Decatur, Ill, 9/18/86. *Mem:* Signature Mem, Nat Watercolor Soc; Assoc Am Watercolor Soc; Assoc Ky Watercolor Soc. *Media:* Watercolor. *Publ:* auth & illusr, Watercolor page, Am Artist Mag, 9/86. *Mailing Add:* 112 W Manchester Dr Decatur IL 62526

CUNO, JAMES
MUSEUM DIRECTOR
b St. Louis, Apr 6, 1951. *Study:* Willamette Univ, BA (hist), 73; Univ Ore, MA (art hist), 78; Harvard Univ, MFA, 80; Harvard Univ, PhD, 85. *Pos:* Asst cur, prints Fogg Art Mus, Harvard Univ, Cambridge, Mass, 80-83; asst prof, dept art Vassar Coll, Poughkeepsie, NY, 83-86; dir, Grunwald Ctr for Graphic Arts, UCLA, 86-89, Hood

Mus Art, Dartmouth Coll, Hanover, NH, 89-91, Univ Art Mus Harvard Univ, Cambridge, Mass, 91-2003 & Courtauld Inst Art, London, 2003-2004; mem pub grant adv comt, Getty Grant Prog, 91-96; pres & Eloise W Martin dir, Art Inst Chicago, 2004-2011; trustee, Wadsworth Atheneum; panelist, Nat Endowment of the Humanities, Nat Educ Assoc; mem vis comt, J Paul Getty Mus; pres, CEO, J Paul Getty Trust, 2011-. *Mem:* Asn Art Mus Dir (trustee, pres). *Publ:* Auth, ed exhib catalogues (with others) Foirades/Fizzles: Echo and Allusion in the Art of Jasper Johns, 87; Politics and Polemics: French Caricature and the Revolution, 1789-1799, 88; Scenes and Sequences: Recent Monotypes by Eric Fischl, 90; Jonathan Borofsky: Prints and Multiples, 1982-1991, 91; The Popularization of Images: Visual Culture Under the July Monarchy, 94; contribr articles to prof jour. *Mailing Add:* J Paul Getty Trust 1200 Getty Center Dr Los Angeles CA 90049-1679

CUOGHI, ROBERTO
VIDEO ARTIST, CONCEPTUAL ARTIST
b Modena, Italy, 1973. *Exhib:* Guarene Arte 99, Fondazione Sandretto Re Rebaudengo, Guarene d'Alba, Italy, 1999; Globale Positionen, Mus Progress, Vienna, 2000; Play, Openspace, Milan, 2000; The Gift, Palazzo delle Papesse, Siena, 2001; In Fumo, GAMC, Bergamo, 2001; Manifesta 4, Francoforte, 2002; Verso il Futuro, Museo del Corso, Rome, 2002; solo exhibs, Massimo De Carlo, Milan, 2002 & GAMC, Bergamo, 2003; Suillakku, Castello di Rivoli Contemp Art Mus, Turin, 2008; 53rd Int Art Exhib Biennale, Venice, 2009, 55th Int Art Exhib Biennale, 2013. *Awards:* Translating Words, Special Mention, Venice Biennale, 2009

CUPPAIDGE, VIRGINIA
PAINTER, EDUCATOR
b Brisbane, Queensland, Australia, Aug, 14, 1943; US & Australian citizen. *Study:* Orban Art Sch, Sydney, Australia, 62; Mary White Sch Fine Art, Sydney, Australia, MFA, 65. *Work:* Nat Jazz Mus, Harlem; New Castle Conservatory Mus; Neuberger Mus, State Univ NY, Purchase; Art Gallery NSW, Australia; Chase Manhattan Bank, New York; Whitney Commun, New York; Kingsborough Commun Col, Brooklyn, NY; Australian Nat Gallery; Queensland Univ, Brisbane, Australia; Australian Embassy, Washington D.C.; Citicorp, New York. *Comn:* Mural, Brisbane Grammar Sch, Queensland, Australia, 84; Australia Consulate, NY. *Exhib:* Solo exhib, Gallery A, Sydney, Australia, 74-82, Susan Caldwell Gallery, NY, 75, Penrith Regional Gallery, NSW, 83, Stephen Rosenberg, NY, 86-89, 93 & 95, Bloomfield Galleries, Sydney, Australia, 85-87; Robin Gibson Gallery, Sydney, 94, 96 & 2000; World Bank, Washington, 96; Can Heritage Touring Exhib, 98; The Nature of Painting, Blair Acad, Blairstown, NJ, 2000; Stella Downer Fine Art, Sydney, Australia, 2004-06 & 2010; plus many other solo exhibs; Group exhib, Seeing Jazz, Smithsonian Traveling Exhib, 97 & 99; Robin Gibson Gallery, Sydney, 2000 & 02; Bronx Community col, NY, 2001-06; Stella Downer Fine Art, Sydney, 2004 & 09; Gallery A, Newcastle Region Art Gallery; plus many other group exhibs. *Collection Arranged:* Juxtapositions Paintings & Constructions, Soho Art Space, NY, 94; The Liberating Spirit, St. Marks Church on the Bowery, NY, 96. *Teaching:* Vis artist painting, Univ Calif, Berkeley, 75 & Santa Barbara, 84; guest lectr, Pratt Inst, Brooklyn & Lehman Col, Bronx, 77-82; assoc prof, City Univ NY, 1992-08; assoc prof, Lehman Col Art, & Col Mt St Vincent, Bronx, 98-2001; Bronx Community Col, NY, 1995-2007; Borough of Manhattan Community Col, NY, 2002-present. *Awards:* CAPS Award, NY, 75; Macdowell Colony Fel Peterborough, NH, 75; Guggenheim Fel, 76. *Bibliog:* Art in Am, 90; Australian Weekend Mag, 92; The Australian, 94; Australian Embassy, 99; Virginia Prints & Paints, Textile Fibre Forum, Vol 86, 2007; Australian Artists Overseas, Art & Australia, 2007. *Mem:* Coll Art Asn; NY Found Arts; Women's Caucus Art NY; Art Table NY; Creative Coalition. *Media:* Oil, acrylic on canvas. *Specialty:* fine art. *Interests:* Art & jazz. *Dealer:* Stella Downer Fine Art Sydney. *Mailing Add:* 235 E 87th St #7G New York NY 10128-3225

CURMANO, BILLY X
CONCEPTUAL ARTIST, SCULPTOR
b 1949; US citizen. *Study:* Univ Wis, Milwaukee, BFA, 73, MS, 77; Art Students League, 82. *Work:* Franklin Furnace Arch, NY; Temple Univ, Philadelphia; Milwaukee Art Mus, Wis; Munic Mus, Ourense, Spain; Mus Mod Art, NY; and others. *Comn:* video, Franklin Furnace Archive, 99; mural, Ranch Community Svc, 99; sculpture & mural, Fosston Schs, 85; video, Canadian Pub Television, 80; sculpture, Winona Arts Center, 2007. *Exhib:* Wien Biennale, Vienna, Austria, 77; Orange Co 16th Ann, Brea Civic Cult Ctr, Calif, 82; 10th Small Works, NY Univ, 86; Oppresion/Expression, The Contemp, New Orleans, 86; The Drought, Minneapolis Inst Arts, 88; Fax & Sound Art, Artpool, Budapest, Hungary, 92; History of Disappearence, The Contemp, Gateshead, Eng, 2005; and others. *Pos:* dir, Witoka Contemporary. *Teaching:* Vis artist experimental art res, intermedia art, Univ NC, Chapel Hill, 95 & Ill State Univ, Normal, 96; drawing, Winona State Univ, Minn, 98. *Awards:* Mayor's proclamation: Billy X Curmano Day, St Louis, Mo, 92; Mayor's proclamation: Billy X Curmano Day, New Orleans, La, 97; McKnight Found Interdisciplinary Art Fel, 97. *Bibliog:* Tom Strini (auth), Doing The Mississippi, Stroke By Stroke, Milwaukee J Sentinel, 10/12/97; Mary Beth (auth), Adventures with Billy, LA WEEKLY, 2/12/99; Ann Rosenthal (auth), Bringing an Eco-Art Tributary into the Media Mainstream, Art J, spring, 2006. *Mem:* Coll Art Asn. *Media:* Mixed. *Publ:* Contribr, Libres D'Artista--Artists Books, Metronom, 81; Mail Art Book, Japan Artists Union, 82; High performance, Astro Artz, 81-83; Swimmin', Part II: The Drought, Minneapolis Inst Arts, 88; Art Journal, Coll Art Asn, New York, 92 & 2006; Billy X Curmano Futurisms Bastard Son, Mark Pezinger Verlag, Vienna, Austria, 2012. *Dealer:* Art Works USA Witoka MN 55987. *Mailing Add:* 27979 Country Rd 17 Winona MN 55987

CURRAN, DARRYL JOSEPH
PHOTOGRAPHER, PRINTMAKER
b Santa Barbara, Calif, Oct 19, 1935. *Study:* Ventura Coll, AA, 58; Univ Calif, Los Angeles, BA, 60 & MA, 64. *Work:* Mus Mod Art, NY; Nat Gallery Can, Ottawa; Int Mus Photog, George Eastman House, Rochester, NY; Royal Photog Soc, Bath, Eng; Norton Simon Mus; LA Co Mus Art; Nat Gallery Art, Wash DC; The Nelson Atkins Mus Art, Kans City, Mo; Mus Art, Rhode Island Sch Design; Cedar Rapids Mus Art, Iowa; J Paul Getty Mus, Los Angeles, Calif; Norton Mus Art, West Palm Beach, Fla; Harn Mus, Univ Fla, Gainesville, Fla; Daum Mus Contemporary Art, Sedalia, Mo; Boca Mus Art, Boca Raton, Fla; Boise Mus Art, Id; Crocker Art Mus, Sacramento, Calif; Ackland Mus Art, Univ NC, Chapel Hill, NC; David Winton Bell Gallery, Brown Univ, Providence, RI; Palm Springs Art Mus, Palm Springs, Fla; San Antonio Mus Art, Tex; Univ Md, Baltimore County; The Huntington Libr, San Marino, Calif; Mulvane Art Mus, Washburn Univ, Topeka, Kans; Spencer Mus Art, Univ Kans, Topeka, Kans; Fred Jones Jr Mus Art, Univ Okla, Norman, Okla; Colo Art Mus, Univ Colo, Boulder. *Exhib:* Vision & Expression, George Eastman House, 68; Photog into Sculpture, Mus Mod Art, NY, 70; Photog into Art, Brit Arts Comn, 73; solo exhibs, Focus Gallery, San Francisco, Calif, 74, Midway Studios, Univ Chicago, 75, Art Space, Los Angeles, 78 & Chaffey Col, 82; Traveling group exhib, Empowered Images, US Info Agency Collections, Los Angeles Co Mus Art. *Collection Arranged:* Graphic/Photographic (auth, catalogue), Art Gallery, Calif State Univ, Fullerton, 71; 24 From LA (auth, catalogue), San Francisco Mus Mod Art, 73; Photo Visionaries, Floating Wall Gallery, Santa Ana, Calif, 76; Los Angeles Perspectives, Secession Gallery, Victoria, BC, 76. *Pos:* Bd dir, Los Angeles Ctr for Photog Studies, 73-77, pres, 80-84, juror & chmn, Los Angeles Olympic Organizing Comt Photog Comn Proj for 84 Olympic Games. *Teaching:* Prof creative photog, Calif State Univ, Fullerton, 67-2001; vis artist photog, Sch of Art Inst Chicago, spring 75; retired, 2002-. *Awards:* First Place in Photog, 76 Calif Art Expo, Calif State Fair, 76; NEA Fel, 80; Calif Mus Photog Award, Career Achievement, 86; Hon Educator, Soc Photog Educ, 96. *Bibliog:* Robert Stuart (auth), Light & Substance, Univ NMex, Coke/Barrow, 74; Lewis/Alger (auth), Darryl Curran Photographs 1967-1981 (exhib catalog), Chaffey Col, 82; Judy Freeman (auth), The Photographic: Two Points of View (exhib, catalog), Calif State Univ, Fullerton. *Mem:* Soc Photog Educ (bd dir, 75-79); Coll Art Asn. *Media:* Photographic & Digital Media. *Res:* Extreme photography, Los Angeles in the 1960's-70's. *Specialty:* Photographs & variations of. *Interests:* Camerless imagery. *Publ:* Contribr, Revolution in a Box, Univ Calif, Riverside, contribr, Untitled 11, Emerging Los Angeles Photographers, Friends of Photog, Carmel, Calif; Object, Illusion, Reality, Calif State Univ, Fullerton, 79; LA Issue, Los Angeles Ctr Photog Studies, 79. *Dealer:* DNJ Gallery 2525 Michigan Ave Ste J1 Santa Monica Ca 90404. *Mailing Add:* 10537 Dunleer Dr Los Angeles CA 90064

CURRAN, DOUGLAS EDWARD
PHOTOGRAPHER, WRITER
b Seaforth, Ont, Aug 7, 1952. *Study:* Ryerson Polytech Inst, Toronto, BAA, 77; Banff Sch Fine Arts, Alta, scholar, 79. *Work:* Nat Film Bd Can, Ottawa; Alta Art Found, Edmonton; Walter Phillips Gallery, Banff Ctr, Alta; Olden Camera Gallery, NY; Edmonton Art Gallery; Winnipeg Art Gallery, Man. *Comn:* Alberta 1980, PhotoProject, Alta 57th Comn, Edmonton, 80; Metis Settlements of Alberta, Fedn Metis, Edmonton, 81; Structured Paradise: The National Park Experience, Banff Ctr, Parks Can & Whyte Mus, Alta, 85. *Exhib:* Recent Acquisitions, Nat Film Bd Can, Ottawa, 79; Seven, Walter Phillips Gallery, Banff, Alta, 81; Folk Concepts of Outer Space, Edmonton Art Gallery, 81 & traveling, 81-83; Primary Colour, Harbourfront, Toronto, 82; Document, Nat Film Bd Can, Ottawa, 83; Nat Touring Exhib, Edmonton Art Gallery, 85. *Teaching:* Sessional instr photog, Univ Alta, Edmonton, 83-84. *Awards:* Grants, Can Coun, 77 & 78; Alta Writers Guild Non Fiction Award, 85. *Bibliog:* Doug Clark & L Wedman (auth), Keepsake, Artswest Publ, 82; Metisism: A Cultural Identity, Fedn Metis Settlements, 82; Contemporary Photographs, Nat Film Bd Can, Hurtig Publ, 84. *Publ:* Auth & photogr, In Advance of the Landing: Folk Concepts of Outer Space, Abbeville Press, 86. *Mailing Add:* 2046 Curling Rd North Vancouver BC V7P 1X4 Canada

CURRERI-ERMATINGER, DYANA M
DIRECTOR, CURATOR
b New York, NY, May 26, 1952. *Study:* Calif State Univ, Sacramento, BA (fine art), 77, MA (fine art & technol), 79; Kellogg Found Fel arts educ, 84; Univ Calif, Berkeley, cert art admin, 86, J Paul Getty Found/Mus Mgmt Inst, 2000. *Collection Arranged:* Crocker Art Mus, Sacramento, Calif, 83-84; Hands to Work Hearts to God: Shaker Crafts from Western Collections, City of Palo Alto Cult Ctr, 87; Bay Area Sculpture: Metal, Stone & Wood, City of Palo Cult Ctr, 88; Accomodating Change: An Architectural Solution to Affordable Housing, Calif Coll Arts & Crafts Archit Sch, 90; From Plastic Form to Printers Plate: 16 Sculptor/Printmakers traveling exhib (auth, catalog), Calif Coll Arts & Crafts, 92; Hybridization: Contemporary California Crafts (1975-present), Nine Decades of Northern California Crafts (coauth, catalog), Calif Coll Arts & Crafts, 94; Silver Tears (an installation by Dennis Oppenheim), Calif Coll Arts & Crafts, 95; Judy Dater (a selected survey), Calif Coll Arts & Crafts, 96; Elwood Collection, WSA Mus of Art, 99-2000. *Pos:* Asst cur, Crocker Art Mus, Sacramento, 83-84; cur, City Palo Alto, 84-89; dir exhib & pub prog, Oliver Art Ctr, Calif Col Arts & Crafts, 89-; dir Washington State Univ Mus Art, 98-2000; exec dir, chief cur Fresno Art Mus, 2001-. *Teaching:* Lectr art practice, Consumnes River Col, Sacramento, 82; assoc prof art admin & mgt, Calif Col Arts & Crafts, 89-97; prof Honors Col, Washington State Univ, 99-2000. *Bibliog:* Sara Frankel (auth), Home is Where his Heart is, San Francisco Examiner, 9/12/90; Charles Talley (auth), Social Fiber, Art Week, 8/20/92; Mary Hull Webster (auth), Dater at CCAC, Artweek, Aug 96. *Mem:* ArtTable Northern Calif (chair, 94-96); Western Mus Asn; Am Asn Mus; Non-Profit Gallery Asn Bay Area (pres, 85-87); ArtTable Inc NY (bd mem/secy 96-98); Washington Art Consortium. *Res:* Northern Calif Art & Craft 1950; Northwest art 1930; Am Art 1900; Shaker Craft & Design. *Interests:* Mod & contemp Am Art, fine craft, design & archit. *Publ:* Coauth, Image/Object/Place: Photography and Installation, Calif Coll Arts & Crafts, 91; auth, Corollaries of Apprehension: West Coast Painting, Calif Coll Arts & Crafts, 92; Linda Fleming/Dennis Leon: Sculpture, Calif Coll Arts & Crafts, 93. *Mailing Add:* c/o Fresno Art Mus 2233 N First St Fresno CA 93703

CURRIE, BRUCE
PAINTER, PRINTMAKER
b Sac City, Iowa, Nov 27, 1911. *Study:* Art Students' League of New York, 31-32. *Work:* Nat Acad Design, NY; State Univ NY, Albany; Butler Inst Am Art, Youngstown, Ohio; Colorado Springs Fine Arts Ctr; Kalamazoo Inst Arts, Mich. *Exhib:* Whitney Mus Am Art, 57; Am Acad & Inst Arts & Letts, 60 & 77; Albany Inst Hist & Art, 65, 68, 70, 75 & 76; Munson, Williams Proctor Inst, Utica, NY, 68-69 & 72-73 & Nat Acad Design, 69-92; Colorado Springs Fine Arts Ctr, Colo, 71; Solo exhibs, Windham Fine Arts, Windham, NY, 2004; and many others. *Teaching:* Artist-in-residence, Syracuse Univ, 79. *Awards:* Am Watercolor Soc Awards, 58, 68, 75, 81, 85 & 97; Medal Hon, Audubon Artists, 62, 82, 98 & 2000, other awards, 63, 68, 70, 71, 76, 79, 82, 87, 89 & 90; Benjamin Altman Figure Prize, Nat Acad Design, 79. *Mem:* Nat Acad Design (assoc, 68, acad, 70); Am Watercolor Soc; Audubon Artists; Woodstock Artists Asn. *Media:* Oil, Acrylic, Woodcuts. *Dealer:* Fletcher Gallery 40 Mill Hill Rd Woodstock NY 12498. *Mailing Add:* 72 Boggs Hill Woodstock NY 12498

CURRIE, STEVE
SCULPTOR
b Flint, Mich, Sept 1, 1954. *Study:* Univ Mich, BFA, 77; Yale Univ, MFA, 84. *Work:* Metrop Mus Art, NY; Walker Art Ctr, Minneapolis, Minn; Albright-Knox Art Gallery, Buffalo; Des Moines Art Ctr, Iowa; Brooklyn Mus, NY; Weatherspoon Art Gallery, Univ of NC, Greensboro, NC; Modern Art Mus of Ft Worth, Tex; Orange Co Mus of Art Newport Beach, Calif; Flint Int Arts, Mich. *Exhib:* The 1980's: A New Generation of Am Painters & Sculptors, Metrop Mus Art, NY, 88; Innovations in Sculpture, Aldrich Mus Contemp Art, Ridgefield, Conn, 88; Height, Width, Length: Contemp Sculpture from the Weatherspoon Collection, Weatherspoon Art Gallery, Univ NC, Greensboro; Am Narrative Painting & Sculpture: The 1980's, Nassau Co Mus Art, Roslyn Harbour, NY, 91; Fabricated Nature, Boise Art Mus, Idaho, 94; solo exhibs, Weatherspoon Art Gallery, Greensboro, NC, 95, Miami-Dade Community Coll (with catalog), Miami, Fla, 95, Slusser Gallery, Univ Mich, Ann Arbor, Mich, 96 & Elizabeth Harris Gallery, NY, 2006-2007, 2010, 2012; Energy Inside- Bucksbaum Ctr for the Arts, Grinnell Univ Grinnell Iowa, 2001; Knockout Fairground 80 Wash Sq E Galleries NY Univ NY, 2002. *Awards:* Igor Found Grant, 86; Nat Endowment Arts Award for Sculpture, 88; NY Found Arts Award for Sculpture, 90 & 97. *Bibliog:* George Melrod (auth), Steve Currie, Art in Am, 5/94; Patricia C Phillips (auth), Steve Currie, Artforum, 4/94; Jonathan Goodman (auth), Sculpture, 6/2006, 73-74; Sol Ostrow (auth), Steve Currie at Elizabeth Harris Gallery, Art in Am, 153; Jonathan Goodman (auth), Steve Currie: Some Roads, Eliz Harris Gallery, New York, 2010; Faye Hirsch (auth), Art in America, 10/2012. *Media:* All Media. *Dealer:* Elizabeth Harris Gallery 529 W 20th St New York NY 10011. *Mailing Add:* 106 Franklin St Brooklyn NY 11222

CURRIN, JOHN
ARTIST
b Boulder, Colo, 1962. *Study:* Carnegie Mellon Univ, BFA, 84; Yale Univ, MFA, 86. *Exhib:* Solo exhibs, Andrea Rosen Gallery, 92, 94-95, 97, 2003, Regen Projects, LA, 96, 99, 2001-2002, 2004, Kerlin Gallery, Dublin, 2000, Mus Contemp Art, Chicago, 2000, 2003, Sadie Coles HG, London, 2000, 2003, Mus Contemp Art, San Diego, 2000, 2004, Victor Miro Gallery, London, 2001, Centre Pompidou Musée Nat d'Arte Moderne, Paris, 2002, Mus Fine Arts, Boston, 2003, Milwaukee Art Mus, 2003, Whitney Mus Am Art, 2003, 2004, Museo de Arte Moderne de la Ciudad de Buenos Aires, 2005, Inst Contemp Art, Boston, 2005, Fondos Regionales de Arte Comtemporaneo Ile-de-France y Poitou-Carentes, 2005, Gagosian Gallery, NY, 2007; Wide Walls, Stedelijk Mus, Amsterdam & Inst Contemp Art, London, 95; Narcissism: Artists Reflect Themselves, Calif Ctr for Arts, Escondido, 96; Projects 60, Mus Mod Art, NY, 97; Heart, Body, Mind, Soul: Am Art in the 1990s, Whitney Mus Am Art, 97; Tate Gallery Selects: Am Realities--Views From Abroad, 97; Pop Surrealism, Aldrich Mus Contemp Art, Conn, 98; Young Americans 2: New Am Art, Saatchi Gallery, London, 98; Carpenter Centre for Visual Arts, Harvard Univ, 99; Examining Pictures: exhibiting paintings, Whitechapel Art Gallery, London, 99. *Mailing Add:* c/o Regen Projects 6750 Santa Monica Blvd Los Angeles CA 90038

CURRY, AARON
SCULPTOR
b San Antonio, Tex, 1972. *Study:* Sch Art Inst Chicago, BFA, 2002; Art Ctr Coll Design, Pasadena, Calif, MFA, 2005. *Exhib:* Solo exhibs include David Kordansky Gallery, Los Angeles, 2006, Michael Warner Gallery, London, 2007, Galerie Daniel Buchholz, Germany, 2008, Hammer Mus, Los Angeles, 2008; Group exhibs include Anniversary Show, 1R Gallery, Chicago, 2002; Group Show, Worth Ryder Gallery, Univ Calif Berkeley, 2004; Autonomy, Fox Prod, New York, 2005; Southern Exposure, Wight Mus, Univ Calif Los Angeles, 2005; Flag Play Fox Dead, David Kordansky Gallery, Los Angeles, 2006; Untitled, Contemp Mus, Honolulu, Hawaii, 2006; Aspect, Forms & Figure, Bellwether Gallery, New York, 2007; Unmonumental: Object in the 21st Century, New Mus Contemp Art, New York, 2007; Friends & Family, Anton Kern Gallery, Los Angeles, 2008. *Mailing Add:* David Kordansky Gallery 3143 S La Cienega Blvd Unit A Los Angeles CA 90016-3110

CURRY, KEVIN LEE
CURATOR, DIRECTOR
b Louisville, Ky, Feb 2, 1957. *Study:* Centre Coll Ky, BA, 79; Univ N Tex, 86. *Work:* Univ NTex, Denton. *Comn:* installation, Cliff & Jody Cohen, Atlanta, Ga, 86; Installation, Murray Camp, Austin, Tex, 90. *Exhib:* 2nd Big Name Invitational, 500 Exposition Gallery, Dallas, 79; Accoutrements of Power, DW Gallery, Dallas, 86; Learning to Live with our Mistakes, Univ Tex-Dallas, Richardson, 86; Life in Airports, 2633 Commerce, Dallas, 87; Installed, 2633 Commerce, Dallas, 88; Kevin Curry, Jeff Elrod, Paul Meinel, 2633 Commerce, Dallas, 88; Critics Choice, D-Art Visual Art Ctr, Dallas, 88; Two of Everything, NRH Gallery, Ft Worth, Tex, 98. *Collection Arranged:* Distinctive Vision I-IV, 7-8/87, 8/88, 7/89, Distinctive Vision V, 9/89, Pivotal Signals, 7/90, Counter Signals, 8/90, Contemp Tex Art; Stars Over Texas, James Pace, Hills Snyder, Frank Tolbert, 3/90; Trance Medial: Mysticism and Technology in Contemporary Texas Art, 3/91; Substance and Subversion: New Political Art, 9/91; Joe Allen and Drew Deleo, 9/91; Small Works and Installations, 6/92; Individual Ideologies, 93; Ken Havis Retrospective, 93; Binary Ground: Contemporary Landscape & Environmental Art by Texas Artists, 94; The Figure Reconsidered, 95; New Texas Talent, 95. *Pos:* Gallery mgr, Foster Goldstrom, Dallas, Tex, 83-86; co-dir, Distinctive Vision Dallas & Austin, Tex, 87-91; dir, Univ NTex, Denton, 88-89; co-dir, Curry/Camp Exhibs, Dallas & San Antonio, 91-92; dir, Dallas Artists Res & Exhib, Tex, 91-92; Kevin Curry Exhibs, Arlington, Tex, 92-; co-dir NRH Gallery, Ft Worth, Tex, 97-99. *Teaching:* Grad fel, Drawing I & II, 86-88. *Bibliog:* Charles Dee Mitchell (auth), Staying Power, Dallas Observer, 7/90; Janet Kutner (auth), DARE selects Kevin Curry as first director, Dallas Morning News, 4/91; Shannon Dawson (auth), The Right Direction, Dallas Observer, 4/91. *Mem:* Kimbell Art Mus; Mus Fine Arts, Houston. *Media:* Installation. *Specialty:* Contemp Tex art. *Mailing Add:* 2514 White Oak Ln Arlington TX 76012-4849

CURTIS, DOLLY POWERS
SCULPTOR, WEAVER
b Bronx, NY, April 25, 1942. *Study:* Pa State Univ, BS, 60-63; NY Univ, MA, 63-65; Brookfield Craft Ctr, Conn, 73-86. *Work:* Southern Conn State Univ; Choate Sch Art Dept; Marymount Col; Gov Residence, State Conn; Smithsonian Inst Archives Am Art. *Comn:* Knotted sculpture, Landplan Partnership, Southport, Conn, 77; numerous comns for private residences, northeast US, 77-; woven wall, Richard Bergmann Architects, New Canaan, Conn, 80; weavings, Naperville Corp Ctr, Ill, 82; woven hanging, Coopers & Lebrand CPA, Hartford, Conn, 83; and others. *Exhib:* Solo exhibs, Woven Folds--Fabric Drawing in Space, Pindar Gallery, NY, 80, 81 & 82 & Woven Environmental Sculpture, Wesleyan Univ, Conn, 82; Art in Craft Media Traveling Exhib, 81-83; Pa State Univ Mus Art, 82; Fiber: The Artist's View, C W Post Ctr, Long Island Univ, 83; The Newport Art Mus, RI, 85; Mus Art, Sci & Industry, Conn, 85; and others. *Pos:* Owner, Archit Textiles, Easton, Conn, 73-; Independent TV producer, 86-. *Teaching:* Instr weaving, Brookfield Craft Ctr, Conn, 77, Haystack Mt Sch, Deer Isle, Maine, 77. *Awards:* State Conn Grant, 76; Outstanding Achievement Design, Women in Design Int, 83; Best in Fiber, Soc Conn Craftsmen, 85; Outstanding Service in Leadership Award, Pa State Coll Educ, 86. *Bibliog:* Patricia Hubbell (auth), Her weavings soar thru space & Kossia Orloff (auth), Reforming fabric, Women Artists News, fall 82; Martha B Scott (auth), article, Art Voices, 1-2/81; Donna Clemson (auth), Weaving Magician, The Penn Stater, 82; article on videotape, Dolly Curtis--Fiber artist, Crafts Report, 5/86. *Mem:* Artists Equity Asn; Am Crafts Coun; Women's Caucus Art; Surface Design Asn; Artist-Craftsmen New York. *Media:* Fiber, Textiles. *Publ:* Auth, State Grant: A two Way Street, Shuttle, Spindle, Dyepot, fall 77; contribr, Architectural Ornament, Van Nostrand Reinhold, 82; Designing for Weaving, Hastings House Publ, 82; Fiberarts Design II, Lark Publ, 83; Women Working Home, Rodale Press, 83. *Dealer:* Silvermine Galleries New Canaan Conn; Judy Birke Corp Consult New Haven CT. *Mailing Add:* 35 Flat Rock Rd Easton CT 06612-1703

CURTIS, ROBERT D
SCULPTOR
b Susanville, Calif, Mar 28, 1948. *Study:* Univ Ariz, BFA (sculpture), 70; Ariz State Univ, MFA (sculpture & design), 72. *Exhib:* Wis Directions 2, Milwaukee Art Mus, 78; Anita J Welch Mem Nat Competition & Sculpture Exhib, Scottsdale Ctr Arts, Ariz, 79; Wis Sculpture, Wustum Mus Fine Arts, Racine, 79; two-person exhib, Arts Club Chicago, Ill, 82; one-person exhib, Kit Basquin Gallery, Milwaukee, 82; Int Art Expo, Navy Pier, Chicago, 82 & 83. *Pos:* Consult restoration & installation of large scale sculpture, Bradley Family Found, Milwaukee, Wis, 78-; consult restoration & installation of large scale sculpture, Milwaukee Art Mus, 79. *Teaching:* Instr design & sculpture, Univ Wis, Milwaukee, 72-73; instr drawing, 3-D design, sculpture, Mt Mary Col, 75-. *Awards:* Shapes of 77 Stainless Steel Sculpture Competition, Vollrath Co, Wis, 77; Grant-in-Aid, Wis Arts Bd, 78; First in Sculpture Competition, City Madison, 83. *Bibliog:* Judith M Kaiser (auth), New Dimensions in Wisconsin Art: Robert Curtis, Exclusively Yours, The Patten Co, 80; Karen Thorsen-Collins (auth), Opening exhibition: Kit Basquin Gallery, New Art Examiner, 12/81. *Mem:* Int Sculpture Ctr; Coll Art Asn; Wis Painters & Sculpture Inc (pres, 76-78). *Media:* Steel, Stone. *Mailing Add:* 4109 Edgevale Ct Chevy Chase MD 20815-5909

CURTIS, VERNA P
CURATOR
Study: Univ Calif, Berkeley, BA, 67; Ariz State Univ, Tempe, 70-72; Univ Wis, Milwaukee, MA (art hist), 74. *Collection Arranged:* Walker Evans from the Collection of Arnold H Crane, 81, Lewis W Hine: Child Labor Photographs (auth, catalog), 82, Art in the Streets: 19th Century French Posters, 83, Atget's Paris, 84, Toulouse-Lautrec Prints from the Permanent Collection, 86 & La Tauromaquia: Goya, Picasso and the Bullfight, 86, Milwaukee Art Mus, Wis. *Pos:* Cur asst, Art Hist Galleries, Univ Wis-Milwaukee, 74; asst cur, Milwaukee Art Mus, 74-76, assoc cur, collections & exhibs, 77-80, assoc cur, prints, drawings & photographs, 81-85, cur, 86-. *Teaching:* Inst print connoisseurship, Univ Wis-Milwaukee, 79, instr photog hist, 84; instr print hist, Milwaukee Art Mus, 83. *Awards:* Nat Endowment Arts Grants, 82 & 84; Govt of Spain Grant, 86; Getty Trust Grant, 86. *Mem:* Print Coun Am. *Publ:* Auth, The Photograph and the Grid, 84 & Nic Nicosia's Realities, 85, Milwaukee Art Mus; Warrington Colescott, Perimeter Gallery, Chicago, 85. *Mailing Add:* 4109 Edgevale Ct Chevy Chase MD 20815-5909

CUSACK, MARGARET WEAVER
ILLUSTRATOR
b Chicago, Ill, Aug 1, 1945. *Study:* Pratt Inst, BFA (cum laude), 68. *Comn:* Hanging & poster, Am Express Co, NY, 84; hanging, Culinary Inst Am, Hyde Park, NY; hanging, Seagram's Bldg, NY; hanging, Yale New Haven Hosp, Conn; hanging, Bishop Mugavero Ctr Geriatric Care, Brooklyn, NY, 94. *Exhib:* 20th Century Images

of George Washington, Fraunces Tavern Mus, NY, 82; The Christmas Carol Sampler, Art Dir Club, NY, 83; NY Soc of Illustrators Exhib to Japan (traveling), Tokyo, 84; Looking at Earth, Smithsonian Nat Air & Space Mus, Washington, DC, 86; Fine Contemp Illustrators, E Tenn State Univ, 89; The Art Quilt, Atrium Gallery, NY, 91; Fiber Stars, Yeiser Art Ctr, Paducah, Ky, 91; Celebrating the Stitch, Newton Art Ctr, Mass, 92; Fiber Arts, Garrison Art Ctr, NY, 92. *Teaching:* Lectr dimensional illus, The Art Quilt & Fabric Col. *Awards:* Soc of Illusr Award, 74, 81, 82, 84 & 85; Art Ann Award, Communication Arts Mag, 76 & 81; Alumni Achievement Award, Pratt Inst, 88. *Bibliog:* Art Product News, 10/89; Step by Step Graphics Mag, 7/92; Needle Arts Mag, 9/94. *Mem:* Graphic Arts Guild; Am Crafts Coun; Children's Book Illusr Group; Brooklyn Commun Arts Prof; Art Quilt Network, NY. *Media:* Fabric Collage, Soft Sculpture. *Publ:* The Christmas Carol Sampler, Harcourt Brace Jovanovich, 83; Contemporary Pictorial Quilts, Gibbs Smith Pub, 93; Fabric Sculpture, Rockport Pub, 94; Fabric and Needlework Illustration, Graphic-Star, 94. *Mailing Add:* 124 Hoyt St Brooklyn NY 11217-2215

CUSICK, NANCY TAYLOR
COLLAGE ARTIST, ASSEMBLAGE ARTIST

b Washington, DC. *Study:* Am Univ, BA, 59, MA, 61, with Gates, Calfee, D'Artista and Summerford; Corcoran Art Sch, 68; Univ Calif, 71, with Lindgren, 71. *Work:* Mus Fine Arts, Pangborn Corp, Hagerstown, Md; Am Univ, Libr Cong, Nat Mus Women in Arts, Corcoran Gallery Art, Washington; US Embassy, Madagascar; Turkish-Am Assoc, Ankara & Izmir, Turkey; Helenic-Am Union, Athens, Greece; Mus de Arte Moderno, Buenos Aires, Arg. *Exhib:* Wash Artists Ann, Smithsonian Inst, 60-69; Area Exhib, Corcoran Gallery Art, 67; Southeastern Museums Tour, Corcoran Gallery Art, 73; solo exhibs, Antalya Mus Painting & Sculpture, Turkey, 90, Univ Calif, Los Angeles, 90, Gallery 10 Ltd, Washington, 90, Goldman Art Gallery, Rockville, Md, 91, Gallery 10 Ltd, 93, Cork Gallery, Lincoln Ctr, NY, 94, Nat Mus Women in Arts, Washington, 94; China World Trade Ctr, Beijing, China, 95; Elite Gallery, Moscow, Russia, 95; US Info Agency, Washington, 96; Nat Mus Women in Arts, Washington, 96; Gallery 10 Ltd, Washington, 96. *Pos:* Exec dir, Wash Women's Arts Ctr, DC, 79-80; contrib ed, Women Artists News, New York, 80-; Wash coordr, Int Festival Women Artists, UN Mid-Decade Conf Women, Copenhagen, Denmark, 80; proj dir, Focus Int-Am Women in Art, UN Decade Conf, Nairobi, Kenya, 85; pres, Gallery 10 Ltd, 91-92; arts caucus rep, Nat Women's Conf Comt, 91-92. *Teaching:* Instr painting & art hist, Dunbarton Col Holy Cross, 66-72; instr art, Prince George's Col, 72-77; lectr & workshop dir, Dokuz Eylul Univ, Izmir, Turkey, 89, Hacettepe Univ, Ankara, Turkey, 89, Bilkent Univ, Ankara, Turkey, 89. *Awards:* First Prize Painting, Soc Wash Artists, 66; Best Show, Hagerstown Mus, 67; Award of Excellence, Women's Caucus for Art, 96. *Bibliog:* David Barrows (auth), Nancy Cusick, The In Tower, 5/93; Mary D Garrard & Norma Broudee (auths), The Power of Feminist Art, 94; Diane Beal (auth), Artists in Beijing: Focus on Women, Koan, 11/95; Global Focus: Women in Art & Culture: Women in the arts, Nat Mus of Women in Arts, Winter/95; Cynthia Redecker (auth), Washington, Moscow artists stage a different kind of summit, Moscow Times, 9/95; Terry Parmelee (auth), Press patter, Washington Print Club, winter/96; Success on a Global Scale: Women artists Exhibit in China, Women in Arts, Nat Mus Women in the Arts, spring/96; Eleanor Kennelly (auth), Exhibit of Global Works of small art on view in museum's great hall, Wash Times, 5/12/96. *Mem:* Artists Equity Asn; Coll Art Asn; Coalition Women's Art Orgn; Women's Caucus Art; Soc Wash Artists. *Media:* Mixed Media, Oil. *Mailing Add:* Gallery 10 3005 Blueridge Ave Silver Spring MD 20902

CUSWORTH, CHRISTYL
PAINTER, CONSERVATOR

b Neptune, NJ, Mar 14, 1963. *Study:* Coll of NJ, BA, 1986; Univ of New Orleans, 1994; NY Univ, 2001. *Work:* ceramic tile mosaic, The Crusifix; ceramic tile mosaic, Columbus; oil on canvas, Star Night Over Lambertville; oil on canvas, Morning Tower; wood & steel, Nailed Cross. *Comn:* pvt, Murals (5), La Childrens Mus, La, 1994. *Exhib:* Art for Arts Sake, Contemp Arts Ctr, New Orleans, 1992; A Group of Women Artist, Ellarslie Mus, Trenton, NJ, 1996; 24th Ann Juried Art Exhib, Lambertville Hist Soc at Coryell Gallery, Lambertville, NJ, 2004. *Collection Arranged:* Julian Schnabel (Sculpture), Pace Gallery, NYC, 1990; Sartain Collection, Moore Col, 1997; The Philadelphia Ten, Moore Col, 1998; Ron Gorshov, 2005. *Pos:* Owner (conservator), Christyl Cusworth Paintings Conservator LLC, 1995-; Owner, Antietam (fine art bronze casting foundry), 1988-1991; Salah Hudson Conserv, 1991-1995. *Awards:* Joyce & Jermy Award, 24th Ann Coryell Gallery, 2004. *Bibliog:* Bibi Dietz (auth), Vanishing Paintings, Hunterdon Co Democrat, 2004. *Mem:* AIC (Prof assoc, 2002). *Media:* Oil, Mixed. *Specialty:* Painting. *Dealer:* Peoples Store, 28 N Union St Lambertville NJ 08530. *Mailing Add:* 54 S Main Lambertville NJ 08530

CUTLER, AMY
PAINTER, SCULPTOR

b Poughkeepsie, NY, 1974. *Study:* Staatliche Hochschule fur Bildende Kunste, Ger, 1994-95; Cooper Union Sch Art, NY, 1997; Skowhegan Sch Painting & Sculpture, 1999. *Work:* Art for Parks, Brooklyn Mus, 1999, Rural Crossing, 195 Bedford Av, NY, 1999, Artists in the Marketplace, Bronx Mus, 2000, Terrors and Wonders: Monsters in Contemp Art, De Cordova Mus & Sculpture Park, Lincoln, Mass, 2001, Stranger Than You, New Langton Arts, San Francisco, 2001, Works on Paper, The Weatherspoon Art Mus, Greensboro, NC, 2002; Open House: Working in Brooklyn, Brooklyn Mus Art, 2004, Whitney Biennial, Whitney Mus Am Art, 2004, The Drawn Page, Aldrich Mus Contemp Art, Ridgefield, Conn, 2004, About Painting, Tang Mus, Saratoga Springs, NY, 2004. *Exhib:* Solo exhibs include 80 Wash Sq East Galleries, NY, 1998, Summer Voices, Miller Block Gallery, Boston, 1999, Miller Block Gallery, Boston, 2000, Dialogues: Amy Cutler/David Rathman, Walker Art Ctr, Minneapolis, 2002, Inst Contemp Art, Philadelphia, 2002, Once Upon A Time, Kohler Art Ctr, Sheboygan, Wis, 2003, Kemper Mus of Contemp Art, Kansas City, Mo, 2004, David Winton Bell gallery, Providence, RI, 2006, Leslie Tonkonow Artworks + Projects, NY, 2007; group exhibs at Small Works, Rendered, Sara Meltzer Gallery, NY, 2003; Tina Kim Fine Art, NY, 2004; Rotunda Gallery, Brooklyn, 2004; Lucas Schoormans Gallery, NY, 2006; Mus Contemp Art KIASMA, Helsinki, Finland, 2006; Brooklyn Mus, 2007. *Awards:* Roma Hort Mann Found Grant, 1999. *Dealer:* Miller Block Gallery 14 Newbury St Boston MA 02116; Larissa Goldston Gallery 530 West 25th St NY City NY 10001; Blumenfeld/Lustberg Fine Art 23 Fiske Pl Brooklyn NY 11215. *Mailing Add:* c/o Leslie Tonkonow Artworks + Projects 535 W 22nd St New York NY 10011

CUTLER, BESS
ART DEALER

b Salem, Mass, Dec 13, 1949. *Study:* Brandeis Univ, BA, 71; Sch Mus Fine Arts, Tufts Univ, MFA, 76. *Pos:* Partner, Cutler-Stavandis Gallery, Boston, 78-82; owner & dir, Bess Cutler Gallery, New York, 83-. *Specialty:* Contemp artists. *Mailing Add:* 111 Manson Ave Kittery ME 03904-1221

CUTLER, JUDY A GOFFMAN
GALLERY DIRECTOR, MUSEUM DIRECTOR

b New Haven, Conn, Feb 7, 1942. *Study:* Univ Pa, BA, 63 & MA, 64. *Collection Arranged:* Rockwell, The Great American Story Teller (toured USA), 86; Norman Rockwell Illsr (toured Italy), 90; Norman Rockwell (toured Japan), 92; Great Am Illsr, (toured Japan & Asia), 93 & 95; Norman Rockwell & Sat Evening Post (toured France), 94; Maxfield Parrish Retrospective (toured Asia & USA), 95; Normal Rockwell: American Imagist, Naples Mus Art, Fla, 2009; Nassau Co Mus Art, 2009; Paine Art Ctr & Gardens, 2010; Norman Rockwell & His Mentor, JC Leyendecker, NMAI, 2010; Norman Rockwell's Am in England, Dulwich Picture Gallery, London, 2010-2011; Norman Rockwell's America, Birmingham Mus Art, 2012-2013. *Pos:* Gallery dir, Am Illustrators Gallery, New York, 85-; gallery dir & co-founder, Judy Goffman Fine Art, Pa & NY, 69-85; art dealer, Blue Bell, Pa, 65-69; museum dir, Nat Mus American Illustration, Newport, Rhode Island, 1998-2014. *Bibliog:* Ann Berman, An illustration Mus Debuts, Archit Digest, 99; Bill Van Siclen, Fine-Tuning The Picture, Providence Jour, 2000. *Mem:* Nat Arts Club; AAM; AFA; New England Mus Asn; Mus Store Asn; Soc Illustrators. *Specialty:* American illustration. *Interests:* Illustration Art. *Collection:* American Imagist Collection. *Publ:* Maxfield Parrish, 93; Maxfield Parrish: A Retrospective, 95; Parrish & Poetry: A Gift of Art and Words, Pomegranate Art Books, 95; Maxfield Parrish: A Treasury of Art, Thunder Bay Press, 2001; Maxfield Parrish and the American Imagists, 2004; JC Leyendecker, 2008, Abrams, Norman Rockwell & his Mentor, JC Leyendecker, NMAI, 2010, Norman Rockwell's Am in England, 2010, NMAI & Dulwich Picture Gallery; Normal Rockwell's America, Birmingham Mus Art, 2012. *Dealer:* American Illustrators Gallery 18 E 77th St New York NY. *Mailing Add:* Nat Mus Am Illus Vernon Ct 492 Bellevue Ave Newport RI 02840

CUTLER, JUDY GOFFMAN
ART DEALER, GALLERY OWNER

Study: Univ Penna, BA, 63, Grad Sch Educ, MS, 64. *Collection Arranged:* Norman Rockwell: An Am Tradition, Greenville Co Mus, Greenville, SC, 85-86; A Celebration of Am Illustration 1920-1950, C-TEC Corp, Wilkes-Barre, Pa, 87; Norman Rockwell: The Great Am Storyteller, Miss Mus Art, Jackson, 88-89; Am Illustrators 1880-1950, Parkersburg Art Ctr, Parkersburg WVa, 89; Norman Rockwell In Italy, Cortina d'Ampezzo & Rome, 90; Norman Rockwell in Japan, Tokyo, Osaka, Nagoya, 92; The Great Am Illustrators, Odakyu Mus, Tokyo, 93; Maxfield Parrish: A Retrospective, Norman Rockwell Mus at Stockbridge, 95. *Pos:* Guest cur for var travel exhibs of Am illstrs; guest lectr at Miss Mus Art, Lotos Club, Nat Arts Club & Norman Rockwell Mus; found, Nat Mus Am Illustration, Newport, RI; lectr, Nat Arts Club, NY; lectr, Carnegie Abbey Club, Portsmont, RI. *Mem:* Norman Rockwell Mus (Nat Steering Comt); Univ Pa Club of NY; Pa Soc. *Specialty:* Norman Rockwell, Maxfield Parrish, Paintings, drawings & watercolors by important American illustrators of the Golden Age (1890-1950); 19th Century American genre & landscape; early 20th century American Moderns, WPA, Ash-Can & American Impressionists. *Collection:* Golden Age of Great American illustrators, including Norman Rockwell, Maxfield Parrish, NC Wyeth, JC Leyendecker & Howard Chandler Christy. *Publ:* Contribr, Currier's Price Guide to American Artists, 1645-1945 at Auction, 87; auth, Artists as Illustrators: An International Directory with Signatures & Monograms, 1800 to the Present, 89; Maxfield Parrish, Brompton Bks, 93 & 99; Parrish & Poetry, Pomegranate Artbks, 95; Maxfield Parrish: A Retrospective, Pomegranate Artbks, 96; and others. *Mailing Add:* 18 E 77th St No 1A New York NY 10021

CUTLER, LAURENCE S
MUSEUM CHAIRMAN, ARCHITECT

b New Haven, Conn, Aug 27, 1940. *Study:* Univ Pa, BA, 62; Harvard, MArch, 66, MAUD, 67. *Work:* Chase Manhattan Bank Caribbean Hqrs; US Emb Staff Housing, Nigeria; Sugarloaf/USA Ski Area; Fire/Police Hqrs, Westford, Mass; pub housing project, Boston; Bally's Park Place Casino/Hotel; Reconstructed Biafra, Nigeria. *Collection Arranged:* cur, Norman Rockwell (auth, catalog), toured Japan, 92; cur, Great Am Illustrators, toured Japan, 93; cur, Maxfield Parrish: A Retrospective (coauth, catalog), toured Asia & US, 1995; cur, Norman Rockwell, American Imagist, Naples Mus Art, Fla, 2009; Dulwich Picture Gallery, London, 2010-2011; Norman Rockwell's America in England. *Pos:* co-founder, Ecodesign Int, Inc, 66, reacquired, 80; group dir, N Am, GGT/USA Adv, 88-91; founder, ARTShows and Products, 94; adv dir, Am Illustrators Gallery, NY, 84-; founder (with Judy Goffman Cutler), Nat Mus Am Illustration & Am Civilization Found, 98-. *Teaching:* teaching fel, Harvard, 65-71, asst prof, 65-71; asst prof, RISD, 64-69, MIT, 69-74. *Awards:* Fulbright-Hayes grant; Harvard Univ Milton Fund grants & scholarship; Three grants, NEA; design awards, AIA; Alpha Rho Chi bronze medal, Harvard Univ; honorific title Oniyasha Igwe of Okigwe, Igbo Tribe, Nigeria. *Bibliog:* Ann Berman (auth), Illustration museum debuts, Archtl Digest, 12/99; Lita Solis-Cohen (auth), National Mus of American Illustration, Maine Antiques Digest, 11/99; Bill Van Siclen (auth), Fine Tuning the Picture, Providence Jour, 9/21/2000; and many others. *Mem:* Nat Arts Club; Harvard Club; Am Asn Mus; AFA, New Eng Mus Asn; Royal Inst Brit Archs; Carnegie Abbey Club. *Res:* Collaborative efforts of Edith Wharton & Maxfield

Parrish. *Specialty:* Illus art from Golden Age Am Illus. *Interests:* Art, Archit, Urban Design, Poetry & Music. *Collection:* Am Imagist Collection; The Greatest Am Illust Collection in the Nation. *Publ:* Coauth, Industrialized Building Systems, MIT Press, 71; Recycling Cities for People, Van Nostrand Reinhold, 75; Housing Systems for Designers & Developers, 95; Maxfield Parrish: A Retrospective, 95; Maxfield Parrish and the American Imagists, 2004; J.C. Leyendecker: American Imagist, 2008; many books & catalogues, 18 all together. *Mailing Add:* Nat Mus Am Illus Vernon Ct 492 Bellevue Ave Newport RI 02840

CUTLER, RONNIE
PAINTER
b New York City, 1924. *Study:* Columbia Univ Art Sch, 57; Brooklyn Mus Art, Art Sch, 58; Art Students League, 59-60. *Work:* Art Students League Collections, NY; Commerce Bank, Memphis, Tenn; Nat Mus of Women in the Arts, Washington; Mus Southwest Minn, State Univ (25 Oil paintings), Marshall, Minn; plus pub and pvt collections. *Exhib:* Artists of Manhattan, Whitney Mus, NY, 54; 54th Ann Competition, Delgado Mus, New Orleans, La, 55; 5th Ann Competition, Berkshire Mus, Pittsfield, Mass, 56; Alumni Show, Brooklyn Mus, NY, 56 & 58; Casein Soc, Riverside Mus, NY, 57; Audubon Artists, Nat Acad Design, NY, 58 & 84; Solo exhibs, Bodley Gallery, NY, 79, Ronrich Gallery, NY, 89, 90 & 91, Art Mus Southwest Minn State Univ, 2005; Provincetown Art Mus, Mass, 93; Salmagundi Club exhib, Am Watercolor Soc, NY, 99, 2000; Monique Goldstorm Gallery, NY, 2002; International Works on Paper, Watercolor, 2003. *Awards:* Alumni Purchase Award, Art Students League, 60; Best of Show, Southern Berkshire Community Arts Coun, 79 & 80; Silvermine Guild Artists, New Canaan, Conn; First Prize in Oil, Painters & Sculptors Soc, NY; First Prize in Oil, Sheffield Art Asn, Mass, 86, 87 & 88; Frederix/Tara Award, Audubon Artists, 58th Ann Yr, 2000; First prize Oil Works on Canvas, Pen and Brush, NYC, 2003; First prize in Oil, Hal Frater Mem Award, Audubon Artists, 2009. *Bibliog:* An Illustrated Survey of the City's Mus, Galleries and Leading Artists, New York Art Rev. *Mem:* Art Students' League (life); Salmagundi Club, NY; Am Watercolor Soc; Pen & Brush. *Media:* Oil, Watercolor

CUTLER-SHAW, JOYCE
CONCEPTUAL ARTIST, SCULPTOR
b Detroit, Mich. *Study:* New York Univ, BA, 53; Columbia Univ, 53-54; Univ Calif, San Diego, MFA, 72. *Work:* Spec Collections Artists Bks, Mus Mod Art, NY; Teylers Mus Haarlem, Neth; Getty Ctr Libr, Artists Books, Los Angeles, Calif; Johnson Mus, Cornell Univ; Albertina Mus, Vienna, Austria; Welcome Inst, London, Eng. *Comn:* Namewall for Los Angeles Int Airport, Los Angeles Bd Airport Commissioners, Calif, 74; Charity Namewall for New Orleans Charity Hospital, New Orleans Downtown Development District, La, 80; Balboa Park Activity Ctr & Artist Mem Design Team, City of San Diego, 96-99; 2 metal street corner sculptures, Stone Crest Village Sculptures, Irvine Co, San Diego, Calif, 98-99; The Sycamore Leaf Canopy, The Railing of Wild River Grasses, The Sycamore Leaf Cascade, 3 works for Mission Valley Branch Library, San Diego, 99-2002; Into Flight, sculpture, White Sands of La Jolla, Calif, 2007-2008; Lightlines & the E Carnegie Libr, E Carnegie Libr, Pub Art Commission, San Jose, Calif, 2006-2009; Orbital Loops, Public Art Commission, Co Operations Center, San Diego, Calif, 2010-2011. *Exhib:* Three Directions, Newport Harbor Art Mus, Calif, 76; Am Narrative Art, Contemp Art Mus, Houston, Tex, 77; Un Espace Parle, Galerie Gaetan, Geneva, Switz, 78; Other Child Book, Palace of Cult and Sci, Warsaw, Poland, 79; Arteder 82, Balboa, Spain, 82; Nat Acad Sci, Washington, 86; Teylers Mus, Haarlem, The Neth, 90; Artist's Bks, Nat Mus Women in the Arts, Washington, 92; Calligraphia USA/USSR, Int Typeface Corp, Traveling Minsk, etc, USSR & USA, 90-93; Insite 94, Vet Admin Med Ctr, San Diego, 94; Hosp Gen, Tijuana, Mex, 94; Sci & Artists Book, Smithsonian Inst, Washington, 95-96; The New Anatomists, Wellcome Inst, 99; Festchrift für Konrad Oberhuber, Nordico Mus der Stadt, Linz, Austria, 2000; Libr Quartet, Four conCurrent exhibs; UC San Diego Coastal Libr, Athena, in Music & Art, Libr, two Pub Libr, 2003; The Biggest Draw, Millennium Galleries, Shefield, London, 2004; Chiayi Cult Ctr, Taiwan, 2005; Episodes of the City, Fales Libr Gallery, New York Univ, 2007; 1st Chinese Biennial, Beijing, China, 2008; Olympic Fine Arts Formal Exhib, Beijing, China, 2008; Your Documents Please Int Exhib, Mus Arts & Crafts, Itami-shi, Hyogo, Japan, 2008; Of Water & the River: Meditations on the Rio Grande, NMex State Univ, 2009; Body Narratives, NYU Medical Lib, 2011; Eco-Art, Pori Mus, Finland, 2011; Seeing Ourselves, MUSE Ctr Photography and the Moving Image, NYC, 2012; Splice, Blackwood Gallery, Univ Toronto Mississauga, Ontario, Can, 2012; What Comes to Mind, Athenaeum Music and Arts Libr, La Jolla, Calif, 2013; Word Processing, The LAB, Costa Mesa, Calif, 2013; Past Tense, Future Imperfect, ArtShare LA Gallery, LA, Calif, 2013; Public Art Matters, Woodbury Univ Sch Architecture, San Diego, Calif, 2013; SPLICE, Pratt Gallery, NY, 2013. *Collection Arranged:* Albertina Graphic Mus, Vienna; Getty Ctr Libr; Mus Mod Art, New York; Teyler's Mus, Haarlem, The Neth; Tate Gallery Libr, London; Univ Calif, San Diego (Joyce Cutler-Shaw Arch); Libr of Cong; Yale Univ Libr Special Collections; Univ Calif, Los Angeles, Libr Special Collections; Univ Wash, Seattle, Artists Books. *Pos:* Dir, Art & Artists: Video/Audio Arch, 74-80; chairwoman, Pub Art Adv Coun, San Diego, 78; TV interviewer/project dir, Art & Artists, KPBS-TV, San Diego, 79-80; adv coun, San Diego City Archit, 90-92; vis scholar (artist & residency), Sch Med, Univ Calif, San Diego, 92-; artist in res, Chiayi Co, Taiwan, 2005. *Teaching:* Vis arts fac contemp art, Palomar Coll, San Marcos, Calif, 74-78; vis fac contemp art, San Diego State Univ, Calif, 78-80 & Univ Calif, Irvine, 79-80; vis fac contemp art, Fine Art Drawing Sch of Medicine, Univ Calif, 97-; instr Master class, drawing, Theatre & Dance Dept, Univ Calif San Diego. *Awards:* Nat Endowment Arts Media Grant, Video Portrait, 81-82; Nat Endowment Arts Grant, 85-87; Purchase Prize, Alphabet of Bones Poster, Purchase Prize, State Univ NY, 91; Design Award, Am Inst Architects San Diego, Canopy, Mis Valley Libr, 2002; Distinguished Alumnus, 50th Anniv, Univ Calif, 2011. *Bibliog:* M Vogel (auth), Die Dame und der Vogel, Vaterland Luzern, Switz, 10/4/79; Moira Roth (auth), catalog essay, Johnson Mus, 86; catalogue essay, Johnson Mus, Cornell Univ, 86; Joyce Cutler Shaw (auth) Leonardo, MIT, Journal, 94; Bettyann Kevles (auth), Naked to the Bone, Rutgers Univ Press, NJ, 97; Library Quartet; Joyce Cutler Shaw (ex Catalogue) Athenaeum Music and Art Libr, 2003; Peter Selz (auth), Art of Engagement, Visual Politics in Calif & Beyond, Univ Calif Press, 2006; Suzanne JE Tourtillott (ed), 500 Handmade Books, Lark Books, 2008; Robin Price, Counting on Change, 25 Years of Artists' Books, Davison Art Ctr, Wesleyan Univ, Conn, 2010; Peter Selz (auth), Eco Art (catalog essay p 64-65, 124-127), Pori Art Mus Pub 108, 2011; Julie Dunn (editor), Athenaeum Music & Arts Library: Selections from the Permanent Collection, 1990-2010; Athenaeum Music & Arts Library, 2012. *Mem:* Coll Art Asn; Woman's Caucus Arts; Landmark Art Projects (founding mem, secy, 78-84 & pres, 85- 92); San Diego Coun Design Prof. *Media:* Multi-Media, Drawing; All Media. *Publ:* Alphabet of Bones, Kretschmer & Grossman, Frankfurt, W Ger 87; Three Cages, Ctr for Book Arts, New York, 92; The Anatomy Lesson: The Body, Technology and Empathy, In: Leonardo, Vol 27, No 1, 29-38, 94; Being Energy and Light, Semiotica Mouton de Bruyter, Berlin, NY, 95-115, 2001; The Anatomy Lesson; Univ The Fasciculus Medicine, Rubin Price Publ, Conn, 2004 (limited Ed of 50). *Mailing Add:* 7969 Engineer Rd Ste 211 San Diego CA 92111

CUTTLER, CHARLES DAVID
HISTORIAN, LECTURER
b Cleveland, Ohio, Apr 8, 1913. *Study:* Ohio State Univ, BFA & MA; Inst Art & Archeol, Paris, France; Univ Bruxelles; Inst Fine Arts, NY Univ, PhD. *Exhib:* Cleveland May Show, Ohio, 35-36; Philadelphia Watercolor Ann, Pa, 37. *Pos:* Guest lectr, Sem Europ Art & Civilization Belg, Ghent, summer, 69, Tokyo, 79, Brussels, 88. *Teaching:* Asst instr art hist, Ohio State Univ, 35-37; from instr to asst prof art hist, Mich State Univ, 47-57; from assoc prof to prof, Univ Iowa, 57-83, res prof, 65-75, emer, 83-. *Awards:* CRB Fel, Brussels, 53-54; Fulbright-Hays Sr Fel, Brussels, 65-66; Assoc mem, Royal Belgian Acad, 87. *Mem:* Coll Art Asn Am; founding pres Midwest Art Hist Soc; Renaissance Soc Am; Medieval Acad Am; Int Ctr Medieval Art; Hist Netherland Art (hon life). *Res:* Netherlandish and German art of the 14th to 16th centuries; art of Hieronymus Bosch. *Publ:* Lisbon Temptation of St Anthony by Jerome Bosch, 57; Northern painting, from Pucelle to Bruegel, XIVth, XVth & XVIth Centuries, 68, 73 & 91; Auth, Further Grunewald Sources, Zeitschrf Kstgesch, 87; Errata in Netherlandish art: Jan Mostaert's New World Landscape, Simiolus, 89; Exotics in Post-Medieval Art: Giraffes and Centaurs, Artibus et Historiae, 91. *Mailing Add:* PO Box 1700 Iowa City IA 52244-1700

CWIK, LARRY
PHOTOGRAPHER, FILMMAKER
Wheeling, WVa, 1959. *Work:* Portland Art Mus, Portland, Ore; Bibliotheque Nationale de France, Paris; Lewis and Clark Coll, Portland, Ore; Bank of Am, Seattle, Wash; Levi Strauss and Co, San Francisco, Calif; Regional Arts & Culture Coun, Portland, Ore. *Comn:* Bidwell & Co, Portland, Ore, 2001; Photoessay of Historic Bldg. *Exhib:* Oregon Biennial, Portland Art Mus, Ore, 87, Oregon's 20th Century in Photography, 2001, New on the Wall Recent Acquisitions in Photography, 2008; Blue Sky Gallery, Portland, Ore, 87; Oregon/Washington Biennial, Maryhill Mus Art, Goldendale, Wash, 87, 89; Introductions 1990, A New Decade, William Traver Gallery, Seattle, Wash, 90; Shelters and Structures, Rena Bransten Gallery, San Francisco, Calif, 90; Totems, Galeria 57, Madrid, 2001, Leslie Loman Gallery, NY, 2010, Rose Ctr Arts, Lower Columbia Coll, Longview, Wash, 2011; The Visitor: 20 Years Photographing Mexico, Galeria H2O, Barcelona, 2003; Asia 2011, Gallery 5, Milepost, Portland, Ore, 2012; Second Int Contemp Art Exhib, Gallery Systema, Osaka, Japan, 2012; Art Takes Time Square, NY, 2012; Art Connect Int Exhib, Oriel Bach Gallery, Mumbles, UK, 2012; Cwik/Stebvka, Gallery Homeland, Portland, Ore, 2012; Carnivals People Gallery, Portland, Ore, 2013; Second Annual Mountaineer Film Festival, Morgantown, W Va, 2011. *Pos:* mem bd dirs, Northwest Artists Workshop, Portland, Ore, 90; co-curator, Environmental Alarm, Blackfish Gallery, Portland, Ore, 92; vol photog, DaDa Ball, Portland Inst Contemp Art, Ore, 96, 97, 98; mem photog coun, Portland Art Mus, 2007-2008 & 2010-2011. *Teaching:* instr color printing, U-Develop Rental Darkrooms, Portland, Ore, 93-94; invited guest presenter photog short films, Int Student Ctr, Portland, Ore, 99. *Awards:* Purchase award, Lewis and Clark Coll, Portland, Ore, 85; Portland Photog Forum, Portland, Ore, 88; Hon Mention award, Northwest Biennial, Tacoma Art Mus, Tacoma, Wash, 99; Jurors award, 30th Ann Willamette Valley Juried Exhib, Corvallis Arts Ctr, Ore, 2000; Selected Artist, Portland Open Studios, 2002, 2003. *Bibliog:* Greg Smiley (auth), Cwik Brings Mexico to Portland, Vanguard, Portland State Univ, Ore, 91; Jae Carlsson (auth), Trapped Souls, G. Gibson Gallery and Italia, Reflex, Seattle, Wash, 92; Merce Planella (auth), Larry Cwik: El Autor, La Fotografia, Barcelona, 92; Journal de la Photographie, The Mexico of Larry Cwik, 2011; Richard Speer (auth), Asia 2011, Willamette Week, Portland, Ore, 2012; DK Row (auth), A Restless Mind's View of the World, in Threes, The Oregonian, Portland, Ore, 2012; Art Takes Time Sq, Chashama, NY, 2012; Yan Li (auth), Totems, Larry Cwik, Peoples Photography, Beijing, China, 2013; CAP Art Auction Catalog, Portland, Ore, 2013; Portland Alliance (illustrations), Ore, 2013. *Mem:* Portland Art Mus, Portland, Ore; Ore Ctr Photographic Arts; Portland Inst Contemp Art. *Media:* Photography, Drawing, Short Films. *Publ:* contbr, Photography, Impulse Mag, Honolulu, Hawaii, 81; auth, Artist Book, Self-Pub, 92; illusr, Cwik Study, WSU Today, Wash State Univ, Vancouver, Wash, 2005; contbr, Portland Project, Deck of Artist Cards, Portland Artists, Ore, 2010. *Mailing Add:* PO Box 5912 Portland OR 97228

CYPHERS, CHRISTOPHER J
ADMINISTRATOR
Study: Hampden-Sydney Col, BA (political sci); Wesleyan Univ, MA (liberal studies); Univ Albany-SUNY, PhD (history). *Pos:* Dir instl rsch and assessment, Sch Visual Arts, New York City, formerly, provost, 2000-08; pres, NY Sch Interior Design, 2008-2012; executive vice president, executive office, The Townhouse, LIM Col, 2012-. *Publ:* auth, The National Civic Federation and the Making of a New American Liberalism, 2002. *Mailing Add:* LIM College 12 E 53rd St New York NY 10022

CYPHERS, PEGGY K
PAINTER, PRINTMAKER
b Baltimore, MD, April 19, 1954. *Study:* Maryland Inst Coll Art; Towson Univ, BFA, 77; Pratt Inst, MFA, 79. *Work:* Saks Fifth Ave Hq, Cincinnati, Ohio; Libr Congress, Smithsonian Inst, Washington; Aldrich Mus, Conn; Nat Mus Women Arts, Washington; Weatherspoon Mus, Greensboro, NC; Johnson & Johnson, NJ; Anchorage Mus, Alaska. *Exhib:* Recent Acquisitions, Aldrich Mus, Conn, 86; solo exhibs, EM Donahue Gallery, NY, 88, 90, 91, 93, 96 & 98, Galerie Asback, Copenhagen, Denmark; Prints from Solo Impressions, Nat Mus Women Arts, Washington, 96; Cheryl Haines Gallery, San Francisco, 96; Proposition Gallery, 2003, 2005; Art Resources Transfer, 2003; Silent Space Gallery, NY. *Pos:* Auth, NY in Review (monthly article) Arts Mag, 88-90; Art Reviews, Tema Celeste, 2005, Mag, Milan, Italy. *Teaching:* Instr, painting & drawing, Parsons Sch Design, 88, Pratt Inst, 89-2007, New York Univ, 90-95 & Univ NC, Greensboro, 95; adj assoc prof of painting, Pratt Inst, 89-05, coord painting & drawing, 02-03, dir Pratt in Tuscany, 02, 03; vis artist-in-residence, Univ NC, fall 96. *Awards:* Yaddo Artist-in-residence, 94; Va Ctr Creative Arts, 95; Fac Develop Fund, Pratt Inst, 96; Award in Painting, Nat Endowment for the Arts; Elizabeth Found for the Arts Award, 98. *Bibliog:* Jed Perl (auth), Peggy Cyphers, Gallery Going: Four Seasons in the Art World, Harcourt Brace Jovanovich, 231-233, 91; Ellen Handy (auth), Peggy Cyphers, Art Mag, 2/92; Ronny Cohen (auth), Peggy Cyphers, Artforum, 7/96; Eleanor Heartney (auth), Peggy Cyphers, Art in Am, 1/99; Roberta Smith (auth), Peggy Cyphers, NY Times Mag, 2005; Sarah Valdez (auth), Peggy Cyphers, Art Am, 9/2005; Mario Navez (auth), Peggy Cyphers, NY Observer, 5/2005. *Mem:* Coll Art Asn. *Media:* Acrylic, Sand. *Specialty:* Contemporary painting and installation. *Interests:* Windsurfing, Flute, Astronomy. *Publ:* Ed, Progress (mag), New Observations, 58. *Dealer:* Donahue Sosinski Art New York

CYRUS, JAMAL D
ARTIST
b Houston, Tex, 1973. *Study:* Univ Houston, BFA (digital media & photog), 2004, Univ Pa Sch Design, 2006-. *Exhib:* Univ Mus, S Tex Univ; Station Mus Contemp Art, Houston; Lawndale Art Ctr, Houston; Arthouse, Austin, Tex; Whitney Biennale, 2006; When the Revolution Comes, Kathleen Cullen Fine Arts, NY, 2006; Alabama, Office Baroque Gallery, Antwerp, Belgium, 2007. *Pos:* Mem, Otabenga Jones & Assoc, Houston, 2002-. *Teaching:* Instr, art prog, Project Row Houses, Houston, Tex; instr, Shade Tree Project Fashion Club; mem staff, Workshop Houston. *Awards:* Artadia Houston Award, 2006. *Mailing Add:* Project Row Houses 2500 Holman PO box 1011 Houston TX 77251-1011

CYTTER, KEREN
VIDEO ARTIST, PHOTOGRAPHER
b Tel Aviv, Israel, 1977. *Study:* Avni Inst, Tel Aviv, 1997-1998; studied with Aram Gershuni & Jacob Mishori, 1999; De Ateliers Stichting 63, Amsterdam, 2002-2004. *Exhib:* Nice Plant, Gross Gallery, Tel Aviv, Israel, 1998; Shoes, Left Side, Tel Aviv, Israel, 2001; solo exhibs, Rozenfeld Gallery, Tel Aviv, 2002-2003, Stedelijk Mus Bureau, Amsterdam, 2004, Frankfurter Kunstverein, 2005, Kunsthalle Zurich, Switz, 2005, Galleria D'arte Moderna e Contemporanea di Bergamo, Italy, 2006, Elisabeth Kaufmann, Zurich, 2006, KW Inst for Cont Art, Berlin, 2006, Ellen de Bruijne Project, Amsterdam, 2006, Noga Gallery, Tel Aviv, 2006, Mus MOderner Kunst Stiftung Ludwig, Vienna, 2007, Collective Gallery, Edinburgh, 2007, Stuk Kunstcentrum, Leuven, Belgium 2007, Witt de With, Rottderam, 2008, Luttgenmeijer, Berlin, 2008 & Thierry Goldberg Projects, New York, 2009; Yanko Dada Mus, Ein Hod, Israel, 2002; Horse Hospital, London, 2003; Kav 16, Tel Aviv, 2004; Short Circuit, Motive Gallery, Amsterdam, 2005; The World State, Erik Steen Gallery, Oslo, 2006; The Floating Feather, Chantal Crousel Gallery, Paris, 2006; Zwischenbilanz II, Baloise Art Forum, Basel, Switz, 2007; Television Delivers People, The Whitney Mus Am Art, New York, 2008; Yokohama Triennale, Japan, 2008; 53rd Int Art Exhib Biennale, Venice, 2009; History in the Making, If I can't dance I don't want to be part of your revolution, Tate, 2009; Karen Kytter, Hammer Mus Proj Series, Los Angeles, 2010; Morality, Schau Ort, Elisabeth Kaufmann & Christiane Buntgen, Zurich, 2010; Repulsion, Kunsthaus Baselland, Muttenz, basel, 2010. *Awards:* Baloise Art Prize, Art27, Basel, Switz, 2006. *Bibliog:* Christoph Schutte (auth), article, Frankfurter Allgemeine, Mittwoch, 19, 1/2005; Barry Schwabsky (auth), On Keren Cytter, Artforum Int, New York, 10/2006; Melissa Gronlund (auth), True Romance, Frieze, 268-270, 10/2007; Karen Rosenberg (auth), What's on the Art Box? Spins, Satire and Camp, NY Times, 1/11/2008; Martin Coomer (auth), Timeout London, Domestics, Pilar Corrias, 4/2009; Daniel Birnbaum (auth), True Lies, Artforum Int, 2010. *Media:* Video. *Mailing Add:* Elisabeth Kaufmann Müllerstrasse 57 Zurich CH - 8004 Switzerland

CZACH, MARIE
HISTORIAN, CURATOR
b Chicago, Ill. *Study:* Sch Art Inst Chicago, BAE, 67; Columbia Univ, New York, MA, 68; Univ Ill at Urbana-Champaign, PhD, 85. *Pos:* Res assoc, George Eastman House, Rochester, NY, 68-70; asst cur photog, Art Inst Chicago, Ill, 70-72; dir, Mus Gallery, Western Ill Univ, Macomb, 74-78 & Sioux City Art Ctr, Iowa, 85; South Suburban Col, South Holland, Ill. *Teaching:* Dir studies, hist & criticism of photog & contemp art, Columbia Col, Chicago, 72-74. *Mem:* Coll Art Asn; Nat Coun Resource Develop; Nat Soc Fund Raising Exec; Develop Coun Chic. *Res:* Nineteenth-century art criticism; contemporary American art; history of photography; Semiotics. *Publ:* Auth, A Directory of Early Illinois Photographers, Western Ill Univ, 77; History of Photography Visual Resources (articles), Àfterimage. *Mailing Add:* 25862 Carey Plaza Wauconda IL 60084

CZARNIECKI, M J, III
MUSEUM DIRECTOR, CONSULTANT
b San Francisco, Calif, May 28, 1948. *Study:* Xaverius Col, Antwerp, Belg, dipl, 67; Wabash Col, Ind, BA, 71; Art Inst Chicago, 71-72; Columbia Col, Chicago, 73; Middlebury Col, Vt, 78; Salzburg Seminars, Austria, 89. *Work:* Magnolium, 82. *Collection Arranged:* Masters of Twentieth Century Photography (co-cur), Ringling Mus, 76; Before It's Too Late: The Photography of Edward S Curtis (cur, catalog), Miss Mus Art, 78; Southern Realism (dir), Miss Mus Art/Southern Arts Fedn, 78-81; Dance Image: A Tribute to Serge Diaghilev (dir), Miss Mus Art, 79; Russian Stage Designs: Scenic Innovation, 1900-1930 (dir), Miss Mus Art, 82; Paul Manship: Changing Taste in Am (dir, Catalog), Minn Mus Art, 85-88; A Lighter Shade of Pale: Photographic Influences in Other Media, Minn Mus Art, 89; Cuba-USA: The First Generation, Fondo del Sol Visual Arts Ctr with Minn Mus Art, 92; Shared Visions, Minn Mus Art, 93; A Bridge of Light (photog of John Varnier), Minn Mus Am Art, 93; Colo/Wyo Biennial 94, One W Art Ctr, 94; Diversity Art Works, 95; Shadow Catcher (ES Curtiss), 99-; Hennepin Govt Ctr, Visualizing the Blues, 1998-2000. *Pos:* Dir, Miss Mus Art, 76-83 & Minn Mus Art, 83-93; consult, Nat Endowment Arts & Inst Mus Services, 78-96; cur-in-residence, US Info Agency, Sofia, Bulgaria, 82; bd dir, Intermedia Arts, Minn, 85-91, Pub Art, St Paul, 88-, Concourse Arts, 89-94; visual arts chair, Minn/Cuba Proj, 85-; chair, Minn Archit Designer Selection Bd, 90-99; principal & chief exec officer, S/RI Cult Planners, Minn, 92-; pres, Inst Photog Studies, 93-98; bd trustees Coll Visual Arts, 97-, Franconia Sculpture Park, 96-, Am Mus Asmar Art, 2000-. *Teaching:* Instr photog, Wabash Col, Ind, 70-71; lectr hist photog, Art Inst Chicago, 72-74; dir educ, Ringling Mus Art, 74-76; lectr MBA arts prog, State Univ NY, Binghamton, 83-88, 90-94; lectr, Arts Admin, Metrop State Univ, Minn, 87. *Awards:* Am Field Serv Scholar, 66-67; Raymond Fund Grantee, 73; Hon Award Am Inst Archit, St Paul Chap, 87; McKnight Found Fel, 89; Fel, Salzburg Seminars, 89. *Mem:* Miss Inst Arts & Letts (founding dir, 79-83); Am Asn Mus (mem chair, 87-90); Int Coun Mus; Assoc Art Mus Dir (89-94); Nat Ctr Nonprofit Bds; Minn Coun Nonprofits. *Media:* Photography, Conceptual Art. *Publ:* Through the Sky in the Lake (photogs), Milkweed Editions, 90. *Mailing Add:* 472 Ohio St Saint Paul MN 55107-2101

CZARNOPYS, THOMAS J
SCULPTOR
b Grand Rapids, Mich, Dec 17, 1957. *Study:* Sch Art Inst, BFA (art educ), 82. *Work:* Mus Contemp Art, Chicago; Wexner Ctr Arts, Columbus, Ohio; Milwaukee Art Mus, Wis; Grand Rapids Art Mus, Mich. *Exhib:* Solo exhibs, Grand Rapids Mus, Mich, 87, Contemp Arts Ctr, Cincinnati, Ohio, 88, Mus Contemp Art, Chicago, 88 & 89, Va Mus Fine Arts, Richmond, 89, Zolla/Lieberman Gallery, Chicago, 95, Mark Moore Gallery, Santa Monica, Calif, 95-96 & Ill Art Gallery, 96-97; The Nature of Sculpture, Jacksonville Art Mus, Fla, 91; About Landscape, Wexner Ctr Arts, Columbus, Ohio, 91; Zolla/Lieberman Gallery, Inc, Chicago, 94, 95, 96 & 97; Wink Wink, Space Gallery, Chicago, 95; Szinhaz Galeria, Hungary, 95; Art in Chicago: 1945-1995, Mus Contemp Art, Chicago, Ill, 96; Paper Thin, Stephen Wirtz Gallery, San Francisco, Calif, 98; and others. *Teaching:* Vis artist, Sch Art Inst Chicago, 88 & Mich State Univ, East Lansing, 90. *Awards:* Nat Endowment Arts Fel Grant, 90; Ill Arts Coun Grant, 90. *Bibliog:* Lynne Warren (auth), Options 35: Tom Czarnopys, Mus Contemp Art, 88; Kathryn Hixson (auth), Latitudes: Focus on Chicago, Aspen Art Mus, 88; Sarah Rogers-Lafferty (auth), About Landscape, Wexner Ctr Arts, 91. *Media:* Mixed, Bronze. *Mailing Add:* c/o Zolla/Lieberman 325 W Huron Chicago IL 60610

CZESTOCHOWSKI, JOSEPH S
MUSEUM DIRECTOR
b Brooklyn, NY, Aug 8, 1950. *Study:* Univ Ill, Champaign-Urbana, BA, 71, MA, 73; Jagiellonian Univ, Cracow, Poland, dipl, 71. *Collection Arranged:* Memphis Brooks Mus, 74; Cedar Rapids Mus Art, 94; Dixon Gallery and Gardens, 97. *Pos:* Student asst, Krannert Art Mus, Univ Ill, 72; art ed, Perspectives Inc, Washington, DC, 72-75; cur collections, Brooks Mus Art, Memphis, 73; dir, Decker Gallery, Md Inst Coll Art, 75-78, dir, Cedar Rapids Mus Art, Iowa, 78-94, Parker Co, 93-, Dixon Gallery & Gardens, Memphis, 95-98 & Int Arts, Torch Press, 98-. *Awards:* Smithsonian Inst Foreign Currency Prog Res Award, 76-. *Bibliog:* Iowa's Young Successes, Des Moines Register, 8/7/83; Museum interview, Cedar Rapids Gazette, Iowa, 10/11/85; Building on a legacy, Horizon Mag, 3/86; Rev, Des Moines Regist, 12/3/89; Interview, The Iowan, fall 90. *Mem:* Polish Inst Arts & Sci Am Inc (trustee, 86-96); Am Asn Art Mus Dirs, Int Coun Mus & The Kosciuszko Found (mem, trustee 88-96); Ctr Study Presidency (trustee); Coll Lib Arts & Scis, Univ Ill Alumni Asn (trustee, 94-96); Coun Univ Ill Found, Urbana (mem & pres). *Res:* Nineteenth & early twentieth century American paintings, drawings and prints; contemporary American painters and printmakers; Polish art. *Publ:* Polish Poster, 1979; Grant Wood & John Stewart Curry, 1980; Am Landscape Tradition, 1982; Davies Catalog Raisonne, 1988; Marvin D Cone, Catalog Raisonne, 1990; Auth, Dixon Gallery & Gardens Permanent Collections Catalog, 96; Robert Rosenblum, Modern Masters, 2000; Anne Pingeot, Degas Sculptures, 2002; Apollo Degas, 6/2002; Georgia O'Keeffe: Visions of the Sublime, 2005; and numerous other exhib catalogs; Associated American Artists (catalog raisonne), 2010; Degas Sculptures, 2010; Photorealism Revisited, 2013; Eloquent Objects-Georgia O'Keeffe, 2014-15. *Mailing Add:* c/o International Arts 319 Goodwyn Memphis TN 38111

CZIMBALMOS, SZABO KALMAN
PAINTER, EDUCATOR
b Esztergom, Hungary, 1914. *Study:* Royal Hungarian Acad Fine Arts, Budapest, grad, 36; also with J Haranghy & E Domanowsky, Vienna, Prague, Munich, Paris, London & Rome. *Work:* Nat Gallery Budapest; City Mus Esztergom, Hungary; Staten Island Mus, NY; Staten Island Community Col. *Comn:* Murals 32 churches US; Hungarian Govt & pvt owners. *Exhib:* Pulitzer Art Gallery, NY; Int Inst, Detroit; Univ Del, 80; Staten Island Mus; Le Salon, Paris; solo & group exhibs in Hungary, Ger, France & Monaco. *Pos:* Owner, Czimbalmos Art Studio, Esztergom, 37-38, studio, Reichenbach, Ger, 45-49 & Staten Island, NY, 50-; art dir & partner, Hungarian Doll & Handcraft Factory, Reichenbach, formerly; art dir, Hungarian Relief, New York, 50; dir, Czimbalmos Pvt Art Sch, 55-. *Awards:* Hungarian Art Award, Budapest, 34; Staten Island Mus Prize, 62, 64, 67 & 71; St Stephan Gold Medal, Pannonia Exhib, 71; City Award, Ezstergom, Hungary, 85. *Mem:* Bavaryan Fine Art Soc; Staten Island Mus Art (vpres art sect, 61-62, pres, 63-64, exec bd, 63-75); Pannonia World Orgn Hungarian Artists (chmn bd dir, 67-). *Media:* All

CZUMA, STANISLAW J
HISTORIAN, CURATOR
b Warsaw, Poland, Oct 26, 1935; US citizen. *Study:* Jagiellonian Univ, BA & MA; Paderewski Found Scholar studies in India, 58-60; Nat Defense Foreign Lang Fel studies in India, 65-67; Banares Hindu Univ, with Vasudeva S Agrawala; Univ Calcutta, with S K Saraswati; Sorbonne, with Louis Renou; Univ Mich, with Walter Spink, PhD, 68. *Collection Arranged:* Cambodian Art, Asia Soc Gallery, NY (with catalog), 69; Permanent Indian Gallery, Brooklyn Mus; Indian Art from the George P Bickford Collection, Cleveland Mus (with catalog), 75; Kushan Sculpture, Cleveland Mus, Asia Soc Gallery, Seattle Mus (with catalog), 85-86; Asian Art and the Legacy of Sherman E Lee, Cleveland Mus, 2009. *Pos:* Ford Found curatorial trainee, Cleveland Mus, 68-69; cur Oriental art, Brooklyn Mus, 69-72; cur Indian & Southeast Asian Art, Cleveland Mus, 72-2005; emeritus. *Teaching:* Res asst Oriental art, Univ Mich, Ann Arbor, 62-64; adj prof, Case Western Reserve Univ, 72-2001. *Mem:* Asn Asian Studies. *Res:* Art of India and early southeast Asia, especially Kushan, Gupta & Early Medieval India, SE Asia with the focus on Cambodia, Himalayan Art. *Publ:* Auth, Gupta style bronze Buddha, 2/70, A masterpiece of early Cambodian sculpture, 4/74, Mathura sculpture in the Cleveland Mus Collection, 3/77 & Mon-Dvaravati Buddha, 9/80, The School of Kashmiri Ivories, 10/88, Bulletin Cleveland Mus; coauth, Masterworks of Asian Art, Cleveland Mus Art Catalog, 98; Ivory Sculpture, Art & Architecture of Ancient Kashmir, Marg Publ, Bombay, 89; The Kailasanatha Temple at Ellora, Makaranda, 90; Some Tibetan and Tibet Related Acquisitions of the Cleveland Mus of Art, Oriental Art, 92-93; Masterworks of Asian Art, The Cleveland Mus of Art, (Catalogue), Cleveland Mus Art, Cleveland, OH, 98; Great Acquisitions of Indian & Southeast Asian Art, Cleveland Mus of Art, Orientations, 01-02/2005; A Quest for the Best: The Enduring Legacy of Sherman E Lee, Orientations, 06/2009. *Mailing Add:* Cleveland Mus Art Asian Art Dept 11150 East Blvd Cleveland OH 44106

D

DABBERT, PATRICIA ANN
CERAMIST, SCULPTOR
b Albuquerque, NMex, Feb 22, 1943. *Study:* Univ Hawaii, 62; Univ NMex, Albuquerque, BFA, 65; Ind Univ, Bloomington, MA, 67. *Work:* Bowling Green State Univ, Ohio; Owens-Ill Corp, Toledo, Ohio; State Savings Bank, Columbus, Ohio; 1st of Am Bank, Michigan City, Ind; JG Blank Ctr Arts, Michigan City; Takeda Pharmaceuticals North Am Permanent Collection, Deerfield, Ill. *Comn:* Wall sculpture, Porter, Wright, Morris, Arthur, Miami, Fla, 88; wall sculpture, comn by Mr/Mrs L Hoodwin, Michigan City, 90; Holiday at the White House (Christmas ornament), comn by Hillary R Clinton, Washington DC, 93; wall sculpture, comn by Mr/Mrs G Abraham, Burr Ridge, Ill, 94; wall sculpture, comn by Mr/Mrs R Hull, Sarasota, Fla, 97. *Exhib:* Lakefront Festival Arts, Milwaukee Art Ctr, 93; Boca Raton Mus Art, Fla, 95; Las Olas Mus Arts Festival, Mus Art, Ft Lauderdale, Fla, 96; Beaux Arts Festival Art, Lowe Art Mus, Coral Gables, Fla, 96; Gasparilla Art Festival, Tampa Art Mus, Fla, 97; Flint Art Fair, Flint Inst Arts, Mich, 97; Members Ann Summer Exhib, Juror Art Ctr, Sarasota, 2007; Art Rageous, Juror Art Ctr, Manatee, 2007. *Pos:* Juror art show, Chesterton Arts & Crafts Fair, Ind, 88 & Prom Mgt Asn, Michigan City, 76. *Teaching:* instr art appreciation, Purdue North Cent, Westville, Ind, 68-73; instr advan art, Elston Sr High Sch, Michigan City, 73-84. *Bibliog:* Berk (auth), What to Do with 3 Tons of Clay, News Dispatch, 83; Grosswiller (auth), Area Artists Show New Paintings & Clay Works, Dunebeat, 83; Brewster (auth), Festival News, Crosby Gardens Art Festival Program, 87. *Mem:* Mich Guild Artists & Artisans; Artists & Craftsmen Porter Co; Sarasota Co Arts Coun; Fla Craftsmen. *Media:* Porcelain, Clay. *Specialty:* fine art. *Publ:* Contribr, Guild 3 Source Book of American Craft Artists, 87 & Guild 4 Source Book of American Craft Artists, 88, Guild Publ; contribr, Columbus Arts Festival Brochure & Poster, Greater Columbus Arts Coun, 91; auth, Sunshine Artist, Sunshine Artist Mag, 95; contribr (with S Peterson), The Craft & Art of Clay, 98. *Dealer:* Dabbert Gallery 76 S Palm Ave Sarasota Fl 34241. *Mailing Add:* 4819 Hoyer Dr Sarasota FL 34241

DABLOW, DEAN CLINT
PHOTOGRAPHER, EDUCATOR
b Superior, Wis, Aug 26, 1946. *Study:* Univ Wis, Stevens Point, BS (educ), 69; Univ Iowa, MA, 72, MFA, 74. *Work:* New Orleans Mus Art, La; Kansas City Art Inst, Mo; Mus Art, Univ Okla; Corcoran Gallery, Washington; Baltimore Mus Art. *Exhib:* Photog in Louisiana 1900-1980, New Orleans Mus Art, 80; Louisiana Major Works, La World's Fair, 84; traveling exhib, A Century of Vision: La Photog 1884-1984; LaGrange Nat XI, Ga, 86; Southeastern Juried exhib, Mobile Mus Art, Ala, 96; Red Clay Survey, Huntsville, Ala, 2005. *Collection Arranged:* The rain are fallin: Photographs from the Farm Security Admin in Louisiana 1935-1943 (traveling exhib), 95. *Teaching:* Prof art, La Tech Univ, Ruston, 76-, photo program coord, currently. *Awards:* Artist Fel Grant Color Photog, La Arts Coun, 82; Purchase Award, 16th Ann Prints, Drawings & Crafts, Ark Art Ctr, 83 & LaGrange Nat XI, Ga, 86; Southern Arts Fedn/Nat Endowment Arts, Regional Photog, Fel, 87. *Bibliog:* Natalie Canavor (auth), Popular Photography, 4/83; Turner Browne & Elaine Partnow (ed), Photographic Artists & Innovators, MacMillan, NY, 83. *Mem:* Soc Photographic Educ. *Media:* Archival Ink Jet Digital Photographs. *Publ:* Contribr, Creative Camera International Yearbook, Coo Press, London, 77; New Photographics/78 (cover), Cent Wash State Col, 78; Camera, CJ Bucher Ltd, Lucerne, Switz, 9/81; The rain are fallin: A Search for the People and Places Photographed by the Farm Security Administration in Louisiana, 1935-1943, Scrub Jay Press, Tollhouse, Calif, 2001. *Mailing Add:* La Tech Univ Ruston LA 71272

DACEY, PAUL
PAINTER, PRINTMAKER
b Toledo, Ohio, Jul 16, 1960. *Study:* Lacoste Summer Arts Prog, France, 82; Artists Environ Found, 82; Ellen Battell Stoeckel Fel, Yale Univ, 83; Cleveland Inst Art, BFA, 84. *Work:* Toledo Mus Art, Ohio; Progressive, Mayfield Village, Ohio; Dechert, New York and Philadelphia; Cleary, Gottlieb, Steen & Hamilton, New York; Novell, Provo, Utah; Taekwang Industrial Co, Seoul, South Korea; Warburg Pincus, NY; Airport Koltsovo, Yekaterinburg, Russia; McKenna, Long & Aldridge, Wash DC; White & Case, NY. *Comn:* Worlds without End (50 paintings) Nokia, Dallas, Tex, 99; Room of 18 Paintings, US Embassy, Ottawa, Can, 99; WWE (4 groups of 5 paintings), Credit Suisse First Boston, London, Eng, 99-2000; Grus (paintings), US Embassy, Kampala, Uganda, 2000; The Fall of Man (paintings), Mr & Mrs Banta, New York, 2002. *Exhib:* Winter Show, Cleveland Ctr Contemp Art, Cleveland, Ohio, 84; Small Works, NY Univ, New York, 96 & 98; The Form of the Formless, 2002, Ten Yrs, Kunstverein Grafschaft Bentheim, Neuenhaus, Ger, 2003; Toledo Area Artists, Toledo Mus Art, Ohio, 2004-2005; 39th Juried Exhib, Parrish Art Mus, Southampton, NY, 2005; Illuminators, Art Koltsovo, Yekaterinburg, Russ; Field of Vision, Beijing New Art Projs, Beijing; Mirrors of Continuous Change, Taekwang & Ilju Acad & Cult Found, Korea; Myths & Marks, Printmaking Coun NJ, Branchburg, NJ; The Abstract Universe, Maloney Art Gallery, CSE, Morristown, NJ; Big Queens Drawing Show, Jamaica Ctr Arts & Learning, Jamaica, NY. *Bibliog:* Rebekah Scott (auth), Art of the Disc, The Toledo Blade, 1/3/99; Heidi Mocklinghoff (auth), Stamp on the Wall, Munstersche Zeitung, 5/6/2002; Von Thomas Kern (auth), Of Cosmos, Game & Chaos, Graftchafter Nachreich Ten, 5/7/2002; Tahree Lane (auth), Museums Regional Exhib Shows Works of Whimsy, Charm, The Toledo Blade, 6/6/2004. *Media:* Acrylic on plastic discs. *Mailing Add:* 35-21 80th St Apt 23 Jackson Heights NY 11372

DADERKO, DEAN
CURATOR, CRITIC
Study: Tyler Sch Art, BFA (Sculpture), 1997. *Collection Arranged:* SIDE X SIDE, Visual AIDS, 50 Artists Photography The Future and Piece de Resistance. *Pos:* Curator, The Americas In Residence, Fonderie Darling, Montreal, Canada; dir, Parlour Projects, Williamsburg, Brooklyn, 2000-05; vis curator, Centro de Investigaciones Artisticas, Buenos Aires, Cooper Union Sch of Arts, New York, NY, MIT, Cambridge, Mass; curator, Contemporary Arts Mus Houston, 2011-; independent curator, currently. *Teaching:* Critic painting/printmaking, Yale Univ, 2010-. *Awards:* Curatorial Rsch Fellowship, French Am Cultural Exchange 2008-09. *Mailing Add:* Contemporary Arts Museum Houston 5216 Montrose Blvd Houston TX 77006-6547

DADI, IFTIKHAR
EDUCATOR, WRITER
Study: Cornell Univ, PhD (history of art). *Collection Arranged:* Curator (with Salah Hassan), Unpacking Europe, Mus Boijmans Van Beuningen, Rotterdam, 2001-2002; (with Leeza Ahmady and Reem Fadda) Tarjama/Translation, Queens Mus Art, 2009, Herbert F Johnson Mus Art, Cornell Univ, 2010; Anwar Jalala Shemza: Calligraphic Abstraction, Green Cardamom, London, 2009; Co-Curator (with Hammad Nasar, Ellen Avril & Nada Raza) Lines of Control: Partition as a Productive Space, Herbert F Johnson Mus Art, Cornell Univ, 2012, Nashar Mus, Duke Univ, 2013-2014. *Teaching:* Assoc prof, Dept of History of Art, Cornell Univ, chair Dept of Art, currently. *Publ:* Auth, Modernism and the Art of Muslim South Asia, 2010. *Mailing Add:* Cornell University Department of Art College Architecture, Art and Planning Goldwin Smith Hall G37 Ithaca NY 14853

D'AGOSTINO , CLAUDIO A
SCULPTOR, PAINTER
b Toronto, Canada, Apr 9, 1963. *Study:* Study under Laura Peterson, 91-95, Domenico Mazzone 95-98. *Work:* US Marine Corps Command Mus, San Diego; The White House, Washington, DC; Spreckels Organ, Balboa Park, San Diego, 2004; AFI, Los Angeles, Calif, 2007; pvt collections, Quincy Jones, Sophia Loren, Jack Valenti, Pres & Mrs Clinton, Liza Minnelli, Luciano Pavarotti, Oprah Winfrey & Pres Obama; Celine Dion, DisneyLand, Disney Family Mus. *Comn:* Pres and Mrs Clinton Flower Sculpture, Nat Italian American Found, Washington, DC, 94; Drill Instructor Sculpture, MCRD Mus Historical Soc, San Diego, 2002; Consul Gen Clin Robertson, Can, 2004; Congressman John R Lewis Ga, Washington, DC, 2006; Jack Valenti, AFI, Los Angeles, Calif, 2007. *Exhib:* San Diego Sculpture Guild, San Diego Sculpture Mus, 97; San Diego Mus Art, 96; Art Walk San Diego, 96; Sicilian Festa, San Diego, Calif, 2007; Los Angeles Feast of San Genaro, 2008; NaPua Gallery, Wailea, Maui, Hawaii, 2009. *Pos:* Instr, Claudio D'Agostino Studio, San Diego, 2005-, Maui, Hawaii, 2009-. *Teaching:* Sculpture, Portraiture, D'agostino Studio, 2004-. *Awards:* 1st Place, Ceramics Expo, City of San Diego, 95; Commanding Gen, Marines of MCRD, WRR, Medal and Award, 97; Tom LeBonge Award 4th Dist, Los Angeles, Calif, 2007. *Bibliog:* Nat Sculpture Soc NY issue newspaper, 5-6/2003; NIAF Wash DC news mag, 5/2003. *Mem:* Nat Sculpture Soc, NY; Cova San Diego; San Diego Sculpture Guild; San Diego Commn Arts & Culture; Nat Ital Am Found, DC. *Media:* Bronze, Miscellaneous Media. *Interests:* Human and life study, portraiture, bas-relief to monumental, bronze and others. *Publ:* Cpl Anthony D Pike, Sculpted in History, The Chevron MCRD, 2002; Nat Sculpture Soc, 2003; Nat Sculpture Soc, 2004-2005; and others including: Washington Post; NY Times; Los Angeles Times, 2007

DAHILL, THOMAS HENRY, JR
PAINTER, ILLUSTRATOR
b Cambridge, Mass, June 22, 1925. *Study:* Tufts Col, BS Chemistry, 49; Harvard Univ, summer 53; Sch Mus Fine Arts, Boston, dipl, 53, cert, 54; Skowhegan Sch Painting & Sculpture; Am Acad in Rome, Fel, 55-57; Max Beckmann Gesellschaft, Murnau, Ger, resident, 56; Emerson Col, AM, 67. *Hon Degrees:* Emerson Coll, Hon MA, 1966. *Work:* Fogg Mus, Lenin Libr, Moscow; Boston Pub Libr; Middlesex Canal Mus. *Comn:* Film strip, life of George Washington Carver, 61; portrait, Dr Richard D Pierce, 74; drawing series on Madagascar, 83 & Bali, 85; portrait, James & Susan

Jackson, Brookline, Mass, 95; portrait, Haig der Muderosian, Emerson Col, 95; Life Cycle (mural), First Church in Boston, 98; murals, Dock, 2005 & Village, 2006, Middlesex Canal Mus, Billerica, Mass. *Exhib:* Boston Art Festival, 55, 56 & 63; Archit League, NY, 58; Int Biennale Relig Art, Salzburg, Austria, 58-59; Emerson Col, 64 & 67; Drawings of NAfrica exhib through Mus Fine Arts Boston to galleries of New Eng prep schs, 67-69; St Botolph Club, 90; The Incredible Ditch (auth, catalog), Widener Libr, Harvard Univ, 98; Tufts Univ, 99; Middlesex Canal Mus, Billerica, 2005; Newton Free Libr: Paintings, Drawings, 2008. *Teaching:* Lectr gen art hist & contemp use of art in churches; instr hist art, Tufts Univ, 54-55 & 60-65; instr dept drawing, Sch Mus Fine Arts, Boston, 58-71; prof fine arts & chmn dept, Emerson Col, 67-95, summer sch abroad, Europe, Africa & Asia, 67-82, prof emer, 95-; guest, Minister of Cult, Moscow, USSR, summer, 74. *Awards:* Abbey Mem Fel to Am Acad in Rome, 55-57. *Bibliog:* Seaburg (auth), Botega a Roma, Anne Miniver Press, 2007. *Mem:* MacDowell Colonists; Boston Ctr Arts; Soc Fel Am Acad in Rome; Medici Soc. *Media:* Acrylic on Canvas; Pen & Watercolor. *Interests:* Swimming, Travel. *Publ:* Contribr, Seaburg, Dahill Publ, 97; illusr, Cambridge on the Charles, 01; Linda Yeaton Poetry, Magic House, illusr, 2004; Illustr, Lind Yeaton Poetry, White Nights, 2009. *Dealer:* Denise Powers. *Mailing Add:* 223 Broadway Arlington MA 02474

DAHL, SHERRI ANN
PAINTER, DIRECTOR

b Robbinsdale, Minn, June 26, 1984. *Study:* Minneapolis Coll Art & Design, BFA (Painting), 2006. *Exhib:* Solo exhibs include Dunn Brothers Coffee, Minneapolis, 2003, Accumulated Objects Gallery, Minneapolis, 2009; Group exhibs include Extremely Minn, Robin Gallery, Robbinsdale, Minn, 2004; Underg Showcase, Hopkins Ctr Arts, Hopkins, Minn, 2004; Minneapolis Coll Art & Design Art Show, Fallout Art Ctr, Minneapolis, 2006; Commencement Exhib, Minneapolis Coll Art & Design, 2006; Visual Arts Open Show, Perpich Ctr Arts, Golden Valley, Minn, 2007; Cultivate, Stevens Sq Ctr Arts, Minneapolis, 2007 ; Art A Whirl, Casket Company Arts Building, Minneapolis, 2007; Red Hot Art, Stevens Sq Park, Minneapolis, 2007; Bike Art II & III, Altered Esthetics, Minneapolis, 2007-08; 4th & 5th Ann Art Perchance, Minneapolis Inst Arts, 2007-08; Spotluck, SpotArt Gallery, Minneapolis, 2008; NEMMA Fall Fine Arts Show, Grainbelt Bottling House, Minneapolis, 2008; 98th Ann Minn State Fair Fine Art Competition, 2009. *Collection Arranged:* Found Mixed Media Collage by Aaron Hinkel, 2009; Spring Cleaning found object sclupture by Hugh Mann, 2009. *Awards:* Friends of Minneapolis Coll Art & Design Scholar, Minneapolis Coll Art & Design, 2002-06 ; Paul Olson Scholar, 2004-06; George Sugarman Found Grant, 2007; Peoples Choice Award, NEMAA, 2007, 08. *Bibliog:* Beth Peloff (producer), Access to Art episode 18, Minneapolis Television Network, 3-4/2009. *Mem:* N E Minneapolis Art Asn. *Media:* Oil. *Mailing Add:* 8117 Mount Curve Blvd Minneapolis MN 55445

DAHL, STEPHEN M
PHOTOGRAPHER

b Frederic, Wis, Sept 13, 1953. *Study:* Univ Wis, Eau Claire, BA, 71-75; Univ Wis, Madison, MA (social work), 78-79; Minneapolis Coll Art & Design, Minn, 84-85; Film in the Cities, St Paul, Minn, 84-87; Visual Studies Workshop, Rochester, NY, 85. *Work:* St Paul Co, Minn; Damark Int, Minneapolis, Minn; Minn Hist Soc, St Paul. *Exhib:* Heartland: Regionalist Vision of the Am Farm, Univ Art Mus, Univ Minn, 90; Black & White Photographs from My Goodhue Co Farm Family Documentary, 93; Farm Life, Opsis, NY, 93; solo show, Minn Governors Residence, St Paul, Minn, 93 & Univ Northern Iowa, Cedar Falls, 94; Katherine Nash Gallery, Univ Minn, 95; Face Value in Pursuit of the Person, Minn State Coll Art & Design, 98; Working: The Photogs of Stephen Dahl, Parts Photog Arts, Minn, 99; Minnesota 2000 Documentary Project Exhib, Minn Hist Soc, St Paul, 2000. *Pos:* Social worker, Waushara Co Dept Social Servs, Wautoma, Wis, 75-78 & Hopkins Sch Dist, Minn, 79-. *Teaching:* Artist-in-residence, Minn State Arts Bd, St Paul, Minn. *Awards:* Minn State Arts Bd Photog Fel, St Paul, Minn, 92 & 96; McKnight Fel, 93; Minn Hist Soc, 98; Jerome Found Travel & Study Grant, St Paul, 2000. *Publ:* working: Photographs of Working People by Stephen Dahl, Parts Photo Arts, 99; Minnesota in Our Time: A Photographic Portrait 12 Photographers Document the Turn of the Century, Minn Hist Soc Press, 2000

DAIGNEAULT, GILLES
CURATOR, CRITIC

b Montreal, Que, Apr 20, 1943. *Study:* Univ D'Aix-Marseille, Doctorate es lettres, 70. *Collection Arranged:* L'art au Quebec Depuis Pellan, Musee Quebec, 88; F Sullivan & D Moore, Musee de Rimooski, 89; Montreal 1942-1992, Galerie de L'ugam, 92; Art Actuel-Presences Quebecoises, Chateau Biron, France, 92. *Pos:* Art critic, Soc Radio-Can, 78-89 & LeDevoir, Montreal, 82-88. *Mem:* Asn Int des Critiques D'Art (depuis, 80). *Publ:* coauth, La Gravure au Quebec 1940-1980, Heritage, Montreal, 81; auth, L'Art au Quebec Depuis Pellan, Musee du Que, 88; coauth, Art Actuel-Presences Quebecoises, Paris, 92; coauth, Montreal 1942-1992, L'Anarchie Resplendissante de la Peinture, Univ du Que, 92. *Mailing Add:* 4596 Christophe Colomb Montreal PQ H2J 3G6 Canada

DAILEY, CHUCK (CHARLES) ANDREW
MUSEOLOGIST, PAINTER

b Golden, Colo, May 25, 1935. *Study:* Univ Colo, BA (art), 61; study in Western Europe, 62-63. *Work:* Mus NMex Permanent Collection, Santa Fe; Vincent Price Collection, Hollywood, Calif; US Dept Interior, BIA Collection, Washington, DC. *Exhib:* Fiesta Biennial, 64 & 65 & Southwest Biennial, 68, Mus NMex; NMex State Fair, Albuquerque, 68; Solo exhib, Gallery 5, Santa Fe, 64; J F Kennedy Performing Art Ctr, Washington, DC, 73. *Collection Arranged:* New Mexican Santero, 70-71 & World of Folk Costume, 71-72, Mus Int Folk Art, Spanish Endure (Spanish hist in Southwest), Palace of Governors, Mus NMex; Indian Arts & Crafts, J F Kennedy Ctr Performing Arts, Washington, DC, 73; One with the Earth traveling exhib, US & Can, 76-89; Mus Am Southwest, Canova, Italy, 94; 35th Anniversary Exhib, Inst Am Indian Arts Mus, 97. *Pos:* Mus preparator, Univ Colo Mus, Boulder, 59-61; exhibs tech, Mus Northern Ariz, Flagstaff, 62-63; cur-in-charge exhib div, Mus NMex, 64-71; mus workshop presentations, NMex, Alaska, Okla, Ariz & Wash & Smithsonian Inst. *Teaching:* Mus training dir, Inst Am Indian Arts, Santa Fe, 89. *Bibliog:* Catherine Wenzell (auth), Artists of Santa Fe, privately publ, 68. *Mem:* NMex Asn Mus; Am Indian Mus Asn; Am Asn Mus; Midwest Mus Asn; Far West Mus Asn; Nat Mus Am Indian. *Media:* Acrylic. *Publ:* Auth, Creating a Crowd, NMex Asn Mus, 72; Bringing a Unique Perspective to Museum Work, Mus News, 5-6/77; A Selection of contemporary art by Native Americans from the Museum of the Institute of American Indian Arts, Ohio Univ Press, 81; Major Influences in the Development of 20th Century Native American art, 82 & Many ways of seeing: The anniversary of the Institute of American Indian Arts, 83, Inst Am Indian Arts Press; Institute of American Indian Arts Mus Training, IAIA Printing, 2000. *Mailing Add:* 39 Apache Ridge Rd Santa Fe NM 87505-8906

DAILEY, DAN (DANIEL) OWEN
SCULPTOR, EDUCATOR

b Philadelphia, Pa, Feb 4, 1947. *Study:* Philadelphia Coll Art, BFA (glass), 69; RI Sch Design, MFA (glass), 72. *Work:* Corning Mus Glass, New York; Metrop Mus Art, New York; Smithsonian Mus, Washington, DC; Nat Gallery Victoria, Melbourne, Australia; High Mus Art, Atlanta, Ga; Philadelphia Mus Art; Los Angeles Co Mus Art; Boston Mus Fine Arts; Musee des Arts Decoratifs, Louvre, Paris; Mus Arts & Design, New York; and others. *Comn:* Orbit cast glass relief (mural), Rainbow Room Rockefeller Ctr, 87; cast glass relief (mural), Marietta Mem Hosp, Ohio, 88; Exuberance cast glass relief (mural), Vail Transportation Ctr, Colo; Sea Grass in Wind (12' x 16' cast glass mural), Northern Essex Co Courthouse, 91; cast glass mural, Los Angeles Co Mus, 93; Glass Mural, 92nd St Y, NY, 98; Vase, The Mayo Clinic, Rochester, MN, 2001; Chandelier, The Providence Performing Arts Ctr, RI, 2004; and numerous pvt collections. *Exhib:* Solo exhibs, Mass Inst Technol Gallery, 75, 77, Theo Portnoy Gallery, NY, 76-77, 79, 82, Habatat Galleries, Detroit, Mich, 81, 83, 90, Kurland/Summers Gallery, Los Angeles, 82, 85, 88, 90, Betsy Rosenfield Gallery, Chicago, Ill, 86, 88, 90, 94, Smithsonian Inst, Washington, DC, 87, Sanske Galerie, Zurich, Switz, 89-90, 92, 97, Habatat Galleries, Boca Raton, Fla, 89-2005, 2010, Leo Kaplan Modern, Scott Jacobson Gallery, NY, 90-2008, Imago Galleries, Palm Desert, Calif, 95, 99-2000, 2003, 2006 & Hawk Galleries, Columbus, Ohio, 2009; 1990 Economic Summit of Industrialized Nations, Rice Univ, Houston; Los Angeles Co Mus Art, 94; Kestner Mus, Ger, 94; Musee des Arts, Decoratifs Paris, 94; Toledo Mus Art, 94; Schantz Galleries, Mass, 2011 & 2012; Retrospective, Phila Coll Art, Renwick Gallery, Smithsonian Inst, Wash DC, 87; Fuller Craft Mus, Mass, 2012; and others. *Pos:* Guest designer, Fabrica Venini, Murano, Venice, Italy, 72-73; designer & freelance artist, Cristallerie Daum, Paris & Nancy, France, 76-, Steuben Glass, NY, 84-; Nat bd adv, Univ Arts, Philadelphia, Pa, 89-, Renwick Gallery, Smithsonian Inst, Washington, DC; owner, Dan Dailey Inc Studio, Kensington, NH, 77-; bd Governors, Mus of Art & Design, NY, 2000-11; adv coun, Urban Glass, Brooklyn, NY, 2002-; consult, The Artists Proj, Steuben Glass, Corning, NY, 2008-2009. *Teaching:* Teaching fel glass, RI Sch Design, Providence, 70-72; assoc prof glass, Mass Coll Art, Boston, 73-89, chmn three-dimensional fine arts dept, 74-79, dir glass prog, 73-89, glass prog prof, 89-2012, prof emer, 2012-; res fel sculpture & glass, Mass Inst Technol, Ctr for Adv Visual Studies, 75-80; fac mem, Pilchuck Glass Sch, Stanwood, Wash, 74-; Haystack Mountain Sch Crafts, Deer Isle, Maine, 76-, trustee, 83-92, prof emer, 2012-. *Awards:* Fulbright-Hays Grant as Designer, Fabrica Venini, Murano, Italy, 72-73; Nat Endowment for the Arts Fel, 79; Masters Fel, Creative Glass Ctr Am, 89; Masters of the Medium, James Renwick Alliance, 2001; The President's Distinguished Artist Award, The Univ of the Arts, Philadelphia, PA, 2001; Libensky Award, Pilchuck Glass Sch, Chateau Ste, Michelle Vinyards & Winery, Calif,. *Bibliog:* Jane Holtz Kay (auth), Architects expand use of glass art, NY Times, 7/90; Dan Dailey: Simple Complexities in Drawing & Glass 1972-1987 (catalog), Rosenwald Wolf Gallery & Renwick Gallery; Dan Dailey and Linda MacNeil: Art in Glass and Metal, Printed on the occasion of the Exhib at The Art Center at Hargate, St Paul's School, 99; Richard Wilfred Yelle (auth), International Glass Art, Schiffer Publ, 2003; Tina Oldknow, Milton Glaser & William Warmus (coauths), Dan Dailey, Abrams, New York, 2007; Dan Dailey & Allison MacNeil Dailey (auth), Glassgator, Toledo Mus Art, Ohio, 2007; Visions Realized: The Work of Dan Dailey, Fuller Craft Mus (catalog), 2012. *Mem:* Life Mem Glass Art Soc Am (bd dir, pres, chmn bd, 80-82); fel, Am Craft Coun; NY Experimental Glass Workshop (bd dir, 78-88). *Media:* Glass, Metal. *Res:* Began lecture series to define the Materialism art movement. Based on interviews & video recordings of artists in their studios. Describes development of contemp art since 1960 based on traditional artisans' processes & materials, including clay, wood, metal, glass. *Publ:* Coauth (with Allison MacNeil Dailey), Glassigator, Toledo Mus Art, Toledo, Ohio, 2007. *Dealer:* Imago Galleries Palm Desert CA; Schantz Galleries Stockbridge MA; Hawk Galleries Columbus OH; Habatat Galleries Palm Beach FL Royal Oaks MI; Wexler Gallery Phildelphia PA. *Mailing Add:* 2 North Rd Kensington NH 03833

DAILEY, JOHN REVELL
DIRECTOR

Quantico, Va. *Study:* UCLA, BS, 1956. *Pos:* Acting assoc dir, Nat Aeronautics and Space Admin, 1992-99; Dir, Nat Air and Space Mus, Washington, 2000-. *Awards:* Distinguished Serv Medal, Defense Superior Medal, Distinguished Flying Cross, Bronze Star. *Mailing Add:* Museum of the National Mall Independence Ave at 6th St Washington DC 20560

DAILEY, VICTORIA KEILUS
WRITER, ART DEALER

b Los Angeles, Calif, Jan 21, 1948. *Study:* Univ Calif, Los Angeles, BA, 70. *Collection Arranged:* Chemical Printing: The Invention of Lithography (auth, catalog), 80; The Poltroon Press: 10th Anniversary Retrospective (auth, catalog), 80; Joby Baker: Prints, Drawings Monotypes (auth, catalog), 80; Auguste Lepere Wood engravings (auth, catalog), 81; Terry De Lapp: Recent Still Life Paintings, 81. *Mem:*

Printing Historical Soc; Bibliographical Soc Am; Graphic Arts Coun; Antiquarian Booksellers Asn Am (bd govs, 80-); Groiler Club, NY. *Specialty:* 19th century prints and drawings, mainly French and English; art and illustrated books. *Publ:* Ed, Frijoles Canyon Pictographs, Pegacycle Press, 81; Henri Riviere, Peregrine Smith, 83

DAILY-BIRNBAUM, ELAINE
PAINTER
b Wichita, KS, Jan 02, 1943. *Study:* St Joseph's Col, BS, 1984; Special study with Glenn Bradshaw, 2000-2002. *Work:* Univ of Wis Hosp & Clinics, Madison, Wis; Wis Dept of Transportation, Green Bay, Wis; Powell & Goldstein LLP. *Exhib:* San Diego Watercolor Soc Int Exhib, 1998-1999, 2001-2003; Three-Women exhib, Women in Abstraction, Center for Visual Arts, Wausau, Wis, 2000; Am Watercolor Soc Int Exhib, 2002-2003, 2006; Nat Watercolor Soc Int Exhib, 2002, 2005; Rocky Mountain Nat Watermedia Exhib, 2005-2006. *Awards:* Gold Medal Award, Calif Watercolor Soc Nat Exhib, 2004; Best Show Award, Rocky Mountain Nat Watermedia Exhib, 2005; Silver Medal Award, Am Watercolor Soc Int Exhib, 2006. *Mem:* San Diego Watercolor Soc (signature mem 2001); Nat Watercolor Soc (signature mem 2002); Am Watercolor Soc (signature mem 2006). *Media:* Acrylic, Oil, Miscellaneous Media, Watercolor. *Mailing Add:* 5887 Woodsedge Rd Madison WI 53711

DALE, RON G
CERAMIST, SCULPTOR
b Spruce Pine, NC, Jan 26, 1949. *Study:* Penland Sch, 71, 74 & 78; Goddard Col, Plainfield, Vt, BA, 77; La State Univ, Baton Rouge, MFA, 79. *Work:* John Michael Kohler Arts Ctr, Sheboygan, Wis; Asher-Faure Gallery, Los Angeles; Lockerbie Manufacturing Inc, Los Angeles. *Exhib:* Westwood Clay Nat, Downey Mus, Calif, 81; Betty Asher's Cups, Triton Mus, Santa Clara, Calif, 82; Still Lifes, Asheville Art Mus, NC, 83; Solo exhib, Southeastern Ctr Contemp Art, Winston-Salem, NC, 83; Lagrange Nat, Lamar Dodd Art Ctr, Ga, 84; Nat Furniture Invitational, Am Crafts Coun, Tupelo Arts Ctr, Miss, 85. *Teaching:* Asst prof ceramics, Univ Miss, Oxford, 80-; vis instr ceramics, Penland Sch, NC, summer 85. *Bibliog:* Bova (auth), Ron Dale: Emerging talent, Nat Coun Educ Ceramic Arts J, 8/83; article, Ron Dale, Ceramics Monthly, 3/84; article, Paint on clay, Am Craft. *Mem:* Nat Coun Educ Ceramic Arts; Craftsmen's Guild Miss. *Media:* Clay, Wood. *Publ:* Auth, George E Ohr: Mad Biloxi Potter, Univ Miss, 83; George Ohr exhibition, Nat Coun Educ Ceramic Arts J, 83. *Dealer:* Martha Schneider Gallery 2055 Green Bay Rd Highland Pk IL 60035; Mario Villa Gallery 3988 Magazine St New Orleans LA 70115. *Mailing Add:* 42 County Rd 411 Oxford MS 38655

DALE, WILLIAM SCOTT ABELL
HISTORIAN, EDUCATOR
b Toronto, Ont, Sept 18, 1921. *Study:* Univ Toronto, BA & MA; Harvard Univ, PhD. *Comn:* full scale models for 4 stone heads, Trinity Coll, Univ Toronto, 44. *Collection Arranged:* Philip Aziz: Hidden Icons (exhib catalog), London Regional Art & Hist Mus, Ont, 96. *Pos:* Res cur, Nat Gallery Can, Ottawa, Ont, 51-57; cur, Art Gallery Toronto, 57-59; dir, Vancouver Art Gallery, BC, 59-61; asst dir, Nat Gallery Can, 61-66, dep dir, 66-67; chmn, visual arts dept, Univ Western Ont, 67-75, 85-87. *Teaching:* Prof art hist, Univ Western Ont, 67-87, Prof emer, 87-. *Bibliog:* Remaking the Shroud, film, Nat Geographic Channel, 2010. *Mem:* Coll Art Asn Am; Medieval Acad Am. *Res:* Romanesque ivories; sculpture of Chartres West; Exeter Cathedral; ancient & medieval perspective; Shroud of Turin. *Publ:* Contribr, Arts in Canada, 58; Oxford Companion to Art, 70; The British Museum Yearbook, 76; Latens Deitas: The Holy Sacrament Altarpiece of Dieric Bouts, Vol XI, No 1-2, Revue d'Art Canadienne/Can Art Rev, 84; Donatellos Chellini Madonna: Speculum Sine Macula, Vol CXLI, No 397, Apollo, 3/95. *Mailing Add:* 1517 Gloucester Rd London ON N6G 2S5 Canada

DALEY, CATHY
PAINTER
b Toronto, Ont. *Study:* Ont Coll Art, 73-75; Arts Sake Inc, 78-80. *Work:* Can Coun Art Bank, Ottawa, Ont; MacDonald Stewart Art Ctr, Guelph, Ont; Art Gallery Peterborough, Ont. *Exhib:* (K)ein Vergleich, Southern Alberta Art Gallery, Lethbridge, Alta, 91; Solo exhibs, Prince George Art Gallery, BC, 92, Art Gallery York Univ, North York, Ont, 94, Paul Petro Contemp Art, Toronto, 98 & Art Gallery of Kelowna, BC, 98; Identity, Main Access, Winnipeg, 92; Nat Drawing Show, Open Space, Victoria, BC, 94; Trames De Memoire (with catalog), Centre D'Expression, St Hyacinthe, Que, 96; Between Body & Soul, Leonard & Bina Ellen Gallery, Concordia Univ, Montreal, Que. *Teaching:* Instr Drawing, Univ Toronto, 88-89; instr drawing & painting, Ont Col Art, 88-. *Awards:* Arts Grant B, Can Coun, 93, 95 & 96; Sr Grant, Ont Arts Coun, 93 & 94. *Bibliog:* Roni Feinstein (auth), Art in Am, 2/96; Renee Baert (auth), Trames de Memoire (exhib catalog), 98; Nancy Tousley (auth), Calgary Herald, 3/99. *Mem:* Visual Arts Ont. *Publ:* Contribr, Borderlines, 89; Impulse, 90; Fireweed, 94; illusr, Kay Darling, Coach House Press, 94. *Dealer:* Paul Petro Contemp Art 265A Queen St W Toronto ON M5V 1Z4

DALEY, WILLIAM P
CERAMIST
b Hastings-on-Hudson, NY, Mar 7, 1925. *Study:* Mass Coll Art, BS; Columbia Univ Teachers Col, MA. *Hon Degrees:* The Univ of the Arts, DFA, 94; Maine Coll of Art, DFA, 93. *Work:* Philadelphia Mus Art; St Louis Mus, Mo; Everson Mus Art, Syracuse; Los Angeles Co Mus; Victoria & Albert Mus, London; and others; Met Mus of Art, NY; Newark Mus of Art, NJ; Mont Mus of Art, Charlotte, NC. *Comn:* Ceramic screen abacus, comn by Int Bus Machines Corp, Seattle World's Fair, 61; ceramic & copper modular wall, SAfrican Airlines, NY, 70; ceramic wall, Fairfield Maxwell Corp, NY, 72; ceramic screen (10ft x 20ft), Ritz Theatre, Philadelphia, 78; Baptismal font, St Pauls, Elkon Park, Pa, 89. *Exhib:* Philadelphia: Three Centuries of Am Art, Philadelphia Mus Art, 76; A Century of Ceramics in the United States, Everson Mus, Syracuse; Am Ceramics Now, Everson Mus, 88; Craft Today USA, Mus des Art Decoratifs, Paris, France, 89; Hartland Gallery, Philadelphia, Pa, 90. *Pos:* Mem adv bd clay studio, Philadelphia & Haystack Sch Crafts, 90. *Teaching:* Prof ceramics & design, Philadelphia Col Art, 57-, chmn crafts dept, 66-69, prof emer; guest prof ceramics, Univ NMex, 72; Disting prof emeritus, Univ of the Arts, Philadelphia, 90. *Awards:* Distinguished Achievement Arts Award, Mass Coll Art, 80; First Distinguished Univ Prof, Univ Arts, Philadelphia Coll Arts & Design, 89; Distinguished Teaching of Art Award, Coll Art Asn of Am, 91. *Bibliog:* Garth Clark (auth), American Potters - the work of twenty modern masters, Keramik der Welt, Gottfried Borman, 81; Peter Dormer, article in The New Ceramics, 86; article in Am Ceramics, 8/2/90. *Mem:* Hon life mem, Nat Coun Educ Ceramic Arts. *Media:* Clay. *Publ:* Auth, Notes on sources: A presentation, Nat Coun Educ Ceramic Arts J, Vol 1, No 1, 80; On drawing, Am Ceramics, Vol 1, No 1, 82; The geometry of residence, Nat Coun Educ Ceramic Arts J, Vol 4, 83. *Dealer:* Drutt Gallery 2220 Rittenhouse St Philadelphia, PA, 19103. *Mailing Add:* 307 Ashbourne Rd Elkins Park PA 19027

DALGLISH, JAMIE
PAINTER, VIDEO ARTIST
b Bryn Mawr, Pa, May 7, 1947. *Study:* Art Acad Cincinnati (scholar), 70; RI Sch Design, BFA, 74; Nat Ctr Experiments TV, San Francisco, Calif, 74. *Work:* Chase Manhattan Bank, NY; Sydney & Francis Lewis Wing, Va Mus, Richmond; Polaroid Corp, Cambridge; Armand Hammer pvt collection. *Comn:* Painting, comn by Mr & Mrs Stephen Abramson, NY, 82. *Exhib:* Eight from NY, State Univ Stony Brook, NY, 80; solo exhib, Port Washington Pub Libr, NY, 80, Braathen-Gallozzi Gallery, NY, 80, Barbara Braathen Gallery, NY, 81-82 & 85-89, Serra di Felice Gallery, NY, 83, Sarah Rentschler Gallery, NY, 85, OK Harris Works Art, NY, 91-93 & Hugo de Pagano Gallery, NY, 97; Signs, Semiotics, Behavior (video), Mus Art, RI Sch Design, Providence, 82; Video-USA, Centre d'Art Contemporain, Geneva, Switz, 84; King Lear's High Theatre of Sovereign Immunity-Come (T) Here (video), Limelight, NY, 86; Drawing Exhib, Long Island Univ, Brooklyn, NY, 86; Art Against AIDS (with catalog), NY, 87; Real Paint, Procter Art Ctr, Bard Col, NY, 88; Abstraction and Reality, Montogomery Ctr, NJ, 92; Young Guns: East Coast Artists, Nev Inst Contemp Art, Las Vegas, 94; Int Artists Established in New York City, Mus de la Ciudad, Madrid, Spain, 97; Hypertexture, Florence Lynch Gallery, NY, 2003; Vice Versa, MATCH Artspace, NY, 2005. *Awards:* Polaroid Corp Grant, 89; Pollock-Krasner Found Grant Award, 2006-07. *Bibliog:* Frederick Ted Castle (auth), Jamie Dalglish, Art Mag, 6/91; Lilly Wei (auth), Review of Exhibitions: Jamie Dalgish at OK Harris, Art Am, 5/94; Walter Robinson (auth), Review, Artnet Mag, 10/96; Jerome Davis (auth), Talking Heads, Vintage Mag Series, 86. *Mem:* ASCAP. *Media:* All. *Publ:* Contrib, photos, Mademoiselle, 9/92. *Dealer:* O K Harris Gallery 383 W Broadway New York NY 10012. *Mailing Add:* 325 N End Ave #8R New York NY 10282

DALGLISH, MEREDITH RENNELS
SCULPTOR, EDUCATOR
b Bryn Mawr, Pa, Apr 15, 1941. *Study:* Goddard Coll, Plainfield, Vt, BA, 65; Claremont Grad Sch, Claremont, Calif, MFA, 83. *Work:* Gallery Contemporanea, Jacksonville, Fla; Deland Mus Art, Fla; Albertson-Peterson Gallery, Orlando, Fla; Stetson Univ, Deland, Fla; Hilton Hotel, Atlanta, Ga; Orlando Fla Mus Art, IBM Corp, Miami, Fla, Ramada Inn, Beverly Hills, Calif, Sheraton, Scottsdale, Ariz, Omni Int, Miami, Fla, San Francisco Mus Art, and others. *Comn:* Mementoes in In-Laws (film), Los Angeles, Calif, 80; sculptures, Sheraton, Scottsdale, Ariz; sculptures, comn by Ralp Rudin, Los Angeles, Calif, 84, & Bill Bailey, Beverly Hills, Calif, 85; wall sculptures, Hilton Hotel, Atlanta, Ga, 96. *Exhib:* Westwood Ceramics Invitational, Downey Mus, Calif, 82; Ceramics Nat Invitational, Scripps Coll, Claremont, Calif, 84; Dimensions, Los Angeles Co Mus Art, 85; Sculpture Carved & Forged, Tampa Mus, Fla, 87; 100 Yr Nat Asn Women Artists Celebration, Jacob Javits Ctr, NY, 89; Spotlight '89, Univ Fla, Gainesville, 89; Solo exhibs, MIEL Ctr, Miami, 94, 1st Union Bank, Ft Lauderdale, Fla, 95; Earth Day Celebration, St Thomas Univ, Miami, 95-97; Take Back the Earth, Temporary Art Installation, Sao Paulo, Brazil, 97 & 2001; Int Ceramics Festival, Sãn Paulo, Brazil; Janovec Gallery, Portland, Oregon, 2007, 2008; Cult Sensitivities IV, Portland State Univ with Am & Korean Artists, Ore, 2009; two-person exhib, Water Resource Ctr, Vancouver, Wash, 2004; Solo exhibs, MIEL Ctr, Miami, 94, 1st Union Bank, Ft Lauderdale, Fla, 95; Door Show, Window & Door Designs/ Wilsonville, Ore, 2010; Door Show, Window & Door Designs/ Wilsonville, Ore, 2010; Beppu Waeppu Gallery, Portland, 2010; Albina Bank Juried Exhib, Portland, Ore, 2010; Swan Day Art Exhib, OWCA, Portland, Ore, 2010; Int Women's Day Art Exhib, Portland State Univ, Ore, 2010. *Collection Arranged:* Frances Lewis Collection, Richmond, Va; IBM Corp, Miami, Fl; Hilton Hotel, Atlanta, Ga; Ramada Inn, Beverly Hills, Ca; Sheraton-Scottsdale, Az; San Francisco Mus of Art; LA Co Mus, Los Angeles. *Pos:* Co-dir, Venice Ceramics Gallery, Calif, 77-78; dir, Ibis Fine Arts Gallery, Pasadena, Calif, 84-85; dir/cur, Ormond Mem Art Mus, Ormond Beach, Fla, 86-87; mem adv bd, Volusia Co Arts Comn, Daytona, 90-91; founder & dir, Women's Inst Creativity Inc, 92. *Teaching:* Assoc prof, ceramics, Rio Hondo Coll, Whittier, Calif, 84; prof, ceramics, Daytona Beach Community Coll, Fla, 87-88; art specialist, art appreciation, Volusia Co Schs, Deland, Fla, 89-90; prof, Miami-Dade Community Coll, Fla, 90-92, Fla Int Univ, Miami, 93-; artist-in-residence, Proj Leap, Palm Beach Co, 96- & Univ Miami, 96; arts-in-medicine, Univ Miami, 96 & 2001; artist-in-educ, State Fla, 97-2001; instr, workshops for artists, Sao Paulo, Brazil, 97 & 99; vis artist, guest artist & lectr in the field throughout the US and abroad; Mixed-Media Sculpt, Mountain View, Calif. *Awards:* Artistic Merit, Ruth Chenven, NY, 89; Artist-in-Education Award, State of Fla, 97-99; Project Leap Award, Palm Beach Co, Fla, 97-99; Lifetime Achievement Award & Catalog of Work, 1992-Present, Women's Inst Creativity Inc; Lifetime Achievement Award, Women's Inst for Creativity Inc. *Bibliog:* Judy Chicago (auth), The Dinner Party, Anchor Doubleday, 79, Dinner Party Project, 77; Mac McCloud (auth), Trends in clay, Artweek, 8/82; J Demetrakas (dir), Right Out of History: The Making of the Dinner Party (film). *Mem:* Nat Asn Women Artists, NY; Women's Caucus Arts; Nat Soc Multi-Layerists; Nat Coun Educ Ceramic Arts; Coll Art Asn; Nat Hon Soc. *Media:* Mixed-media. *Res:* Women and their creativity. *Interests:* Snorkel, boating, writing, dancing, healer music. *Publ:* Contribr, Old Market Craftsmen Cookbook, Ree Schonlau, 82; auth, Ron

Fondaw (catalog), Ormond Mus, 87; Art in America, Letters, 7/92; Mus of Arts & Sciences, Daytona, Fla; How to View Art Booklet for Middle & High School Age. *Dealer:* Albertson-Peterson Gallery 329 Park Ave S Winter Park FL 32789; Design Continuum Piedmont Ctr NE Atlanta GA 30305. *Mailing Add:* 12343 NE Holladay Pl Portland OR 97230

DALLAS, DOROTHY B
PAINTER, PRINTMAKER
b New York, NY. *Study:* Watercolor study with Ed Whitney, 78-80; Pratt Inst, Brooklyn, NY, BFA, 79, MFA, 81. *Work:* Bergen Co Freeholders, Courthouse, Hackensack, NJ. *Exhib:* Landscapes by Member Artists, Katonah Mus Art, NY, 88; 100 Yrs/100 Works Centennial Traveling Exhib, Islip Mus & others, 89; Hudson River Regional Watercolor Exhib, Woodstock Art Asn, NY, 89; NJ Watercolor Soc 50th Ann Exhib, Montclair Mus, NJ, 89; Am Watercolor Soc 129th Int Exhib, NY, 96; 175th Ann Exhib, Nat Acad Design, 2000. *Pos:* Guest cur, watercolor exhib, Art Ctr N NJ, New Milford, 76; judge, Teen Arts Prog, NJ State Dept Educ, Ramapo Col, 88-90. *Awards:* Grumbacher Medallion, Nat Asn Women Artists 99th Ann, Colo, 88; First Prize, Hudson River Regional Watercolor Exhib, Woodstock Art Asn/Ulster Co Art Asn, 89; Gold Medal for Watermedia, Catharine Lorillard Wolfe Art Club, 102nd Ann, 98. *Bibliog:* Best of Watercolor, 95, Best of Watercolor II, 97 & Abstracts in Watercolor, 96, Rockport Publ. *Mem:* Art Ctr Watercolor Affiliates (founder, 78, secy, 78-86, pres, 86-90); NJ Watercolor Soc (prospectus chmn, 81-, nominating chairperson, 96-); Catharine Lorillard Wolfe Art Club, Inc (bd dir, 82-88, pres, 89-92); Nat Asn Women Artists (bd dir, 85-89); Katonah Mus Artists Asn; Baltimore Watercolor Soc. *Media:* Watercolor, Collage. *Mailing Add:* 3381 Turner Mountain Rd The Plains VA 20198-1845

DALLMANN, DANIEL FORBES
PAINTER, PRINTMAKER
b St Paul, Minn, Mar 21, 1942. *Study:* St Cloud Univ, BS, 65; Univ Iowa, MA, 68, MFA, 69. *Work:* Nat Collection Fine Arts, DC; Art Inst Chicago; Yale Univ Art Mus, New Haven, Conn; Chemical Bank, NY; J B Speed Art Mus, Louisville, Ky; and others. *Exhib:* Contemp Self Portraits, Allan Frumkin Gallery, NY, 82; New Vistas: Contemp Am Landscape, Hudson River Mus, NY & Tucson Mus Art, Ariz, 84; Conjuring Reality: The Paintings and Drawings of Daniel Dallman and Paul Wiesenfeld, J B Speed Mus Art, Louisville, Ky, 84; Am Realism: Twentieth Century Drawings & Watercolors, San Francisco Mus Mod Art, 85; Realism Today, Nat Acad Design, NY, 88; The Landscape Observed, Md Inst, Baltimore, 90; Solo exhib, Etchings, Lithographs & Drawings, Davidson Gallery, 93, New Paintings,Tatistcheff & Co, NY, 93, Paintings, Davidson Gallery, Seattle, 94, Paintings & Drawings, Payne Gallery, Moravian Col, Bethleham, Pa, 97, Kendall Gallery, Miami-Dade Comm Col, Fla, 97, Little Sleepers and Other Small Works, Dartmouth Col, Hanover, NH, 98 & Dancers and Dreamers, Creighton Univ, Omaha, Nebr, 98; 20th century Figurative Paintings, Forum Gallery, NY, 94. *Teaching:* Prof drawing & printmaking, Tyler Sch Art, 69-. *Awards:* Visual Arts Fel, Pa Coun Arts, 87. *Media:* Oil; All Media. *Dealer:* Claire Oliver Fine Arts Philadelphia PA. *Mailing Add:* 144 Seville St Philadelphia PA 19127

D'ALMEIDA, GEORGE
PAINTER
b Paris, France, June 30, 1934; US citizen. *Work:* Joseph Hirshhorn Mus, Wash DC. *Exhib:* Rolly-Michaux Gallery, NY, 79, 81, 83 & 86 & Boston, 80, 82 & 86; Galleria Rotta, Genoa, 77, 80, 89 & 93; Solo exhib, Venice Biennial, 88; Galleria La Bussola, Turin, 89; and others. *Bibliog:* Venice Biennial, 1988 Catalogue. *Media:* Acrylic, Watercolor. *Mailing Add:* Casina di Selvole 53017 Radda in Chianti Siena Italy

DAL POGGETTO, SANDRA HOPE
PAINTER
b Sonoma, Calif, Nov 2, 1951. *Study:* Univ Calif, Davis, with Manuel Weri, Wayne Thiebaud, Robert Arneson, BA (hon), 75; San Francisco State Univ, with Robert Bechtle, MA (painting & drawing), 82. *Work:* South Bay Contemp Mus Art, Torrance, Calif. *Exhib:* Nature Morte (panelist), South Bay Contemp Mus Art, Torrance, Calif, 92; Gender/Geography: New Works by Montana Women Artists, Holter Mus Art, Helena, 95; Artists Who Teach (with catalog), Paris Gibson Mus Art, Great Falls, Mont, 95; SDP: An Exhib of Paintings, Augusta State Univ, Ga, 96; Mostra '96: Painting & Sculpture, Mus Italo Americano, San Francisco, 96. *Teaching:* Instr painting & drawing, Napa Valley Col, Calif, 85-86; instr life drawing, Archie Bray Found Ceramic Arts, Helena, Mont, 94-95; instr drawing, Mont State Univ, Bozeman, 95-96. *Awards:* Fel Painting, Helene Wurlitzer Found, NMex, 96; Artist-in-residence, Holter Mus Art, Helena Nat Forest, Mont, 96; Pouch Cove Found resident, Newfoundland, 2000. *Bibliog:* Will Torphy (auth), article, Artweek, 1/85; Kate Regan (auth), Shimmering Rays & A Troubled Lyricism, San Francisco Chronicle, 2/85; Jerome Tarshis (auth), Jerome's Unknowns, San Francisco Focus, 7/85. *Media:* Oil, Egg Tempera. *Publ:* Auth, Duccio in the eye of the hunt (essay), Gray's Sporting J, 10/96; In the eye of the elk (essay), The Structurist, 12/96. *Dealer:* Ed Russell Graystone Gallery 250 Sutter St San Francisco CA 94108. *Mailing Add:* 430 Monroe Ave Helena MT 59601

DALTON-MEYER, MARIE
MUSEUM DIRECTOR
Pos: exec dir, Farmington Valley Arts Ctr, formerly; Dir Develop & Communs, Hill-Stead Mus, currently; co-interim dir, Hill-Stead Mus, 2007-. *Mem:* Bd of Christian Serv. *Mailing Add:* Hill-Stead Museum 35 Mountain Rd Farmington CT 06032

DALY, STEPHEN JEFFREY
SCULPTOR, DRAFTSMAN
b Governors Island, NY, July 4, 1942. *Study:* San Jose State Univ, Calif, BA, 64; Cranbrook Acad Art, Mich, MFA (sculpture), 67. *Work:* Oakland Art Mus, Calif; Tex A&M Univ; Am Acad Rome, Italy; McNey Mus, San Antonio, Tex; Blanton Mus Art, Univ Tex, Austin; Polytechnic Univ, Valencia, Spain. *Comn:* Codema 2000, Commd Steel Sculpture, Havana, Cuba, 2000; Monumental wall work, Matthews & Branscom B Law Firm, San Antonio, Tex, 2000; Mentoring, Polytechnic Univ, Valencia, Spain, 2008. *Exhib:* 85th San Francisco Art Inst Ann, MH de Young Mem Mus, Calif, 65; Objects USA, Smithsonian Mus, Washington, 69; The Metal Experience, Oakland Art Mus, Calif, 71; Solo exhibs, Am Acad, Rome, 75, Triton Mus, Santa Clara, Calif, 77, William Campbell Contemp Art, Ft Worth, Tex, 87, 89-91, 93, 2002, 2004, 2008 and McNay Art Mus (catalog), San Antonio, Tex, 88; Group exhibs, Texas Currents, San Antonio Art Inst, 86 & New Sites-New Work, San Jose Inst Contemp Art, 86, The Blue Star Exhib, Blue Star Space, San Antonio, Tex, 86, Third Coast Review, Aspen Art Mus, Colo, 87, Another Reality (catalog), Hooks-Epstein Galleries Inc, Houston, Tex, 89 & A Century of Sculpture in Tex (catalog), Archer M Huntington Art Gallery, Univ Tex, Austin, 89; Hooks-Epstein Galleries, Houston, Tex, 91 & 93; The Figure, Grounds for Sculpture, Hamilton, NJ, 94-95; Pier Walk 97, Navy Pier, Chicago, 97; drawing, Ravel Fine Arts, Austin, Tex, 2000; Grounds for Sculpture, ISC Bd, Hamilton, NJ 2001; Mutamentum, Int Group Traveling Show, Italy, Ger & USA, 2001-2003; WM Havu Gallery, Denver, Colo, 2002, 2005 & 2007; Fusion of Art & Technol, Univ Gallery, Fresno State Univ, Calif, 2006; Peoples Gallery Exhib, Austin City Hall, Tex, 2009, 2010; Outdoor Sculpture Invitational, Kemp Ctr, Wichita Falls, Tex, 2009-2010; El Paseo Sculpture Invitational, Palm Desert, Calif, 2008-2009; Art in the Garden, San Antonio Botanical Garden, Tex, 2010-2011; G Gallery, TSG, Small Sculpture, Houston, Tex, 2011; Chicago Sculpture Exhib, Lincoln Park, 2012-2013; Drawing and Sculpture, EFA Gallery, Angelo State Univ, San Angelo, Tex, 2013; Gremillion Gallery, Dallas, 2014; Signals, William Campbell Contemp Art, Fort Worth, Tex, 2014; Drawings and Sculpture, Gremillion Co and Fine Art, Inc, Houston, Tex, 2015; GRIDMAN 3, Tex Sculpture Walk, Hall Art Ctr, Dallas, Tex, 2015. *Pos:* Art & archit Panel, Tex Comn Arts, Austin, 80-82; coordr, 4th Tex Sculpture Symp, 81-83; bd trustees, Int Sculpture Ctr, Hamilton, NJ, 97-2000; consult, Overland Partners, San Antonio, Tex, 2003-2005; pres, Tex Sculpture Group, 2009-2014, pres emeritus, 2014-. *Teaching:* Univ Minn, Minneapolis, 67-69, Humboldt State Univ, 69-79, Univ Tex, San Antonio, 79-81, Univ Tex, Austin, 81-2007, prof emer, 2007-. *Awards:* Prix de Rome, Am Acad Rome, Italy, 75; Louis Comfort Tiffany Award Sculpture, 77; Centennial Fel Fine Arts, Univ Tex, Austin, 83-84 & 88-91; Milam Centennial Fel, Univ Tex, 90-91; FRA Rsch Grant, Univ Tex, 95, 2001. *Bibliog:* Howard Smagula (auth), Texas Currents (catalog), San Antonio Art Inst, 85; Annette Carlozzi (auth), Third coast rev: a look at Tex art, Aspen Art Mus, Colo, 88; Susie Kalil (auth), Stephen Daly, McNey Mus (exhib catalog), 88; Marina Pastor (auth), The Art of Giant Fighting, Polytechnic Univ Press, Valencia, Spain, 2001; Michael Cochran(auth), Sculpture as Witness, Sculpture Mag, Oct 2006; Dave Hampton (auth), Pouring Metal in the South Bay, Art Investigation, Vol 2. *Mem:* Fel Am Acad Rome (FAAR), NY; Int Sculpture Ctr, Hamilton, NJ; Tex Sculpture Group; Drawing Ctr, NYC; Chgo Sculpture Int, Ill, 2014; Mid South Sculpture Alliance, Atlanta, Ga. *Media:* Metals, Cast, Drawing, Works on Paper. *Res:* Descrete object in cast metal; combination of drawing & sculpture; drawing with ink & watercolor. *Specialty:* Contemporary Art. *Publ:* Retrospective Catalogue, Polytechnic Univ, Valencia, Spain. *Dealer:* Wm Campbell Contemporary Art 49355 Byers Ft Worth TX 76107; Wm Havu Gallery 1040 Cherokee St Denver CO 80204; Gremillion & Co Fine Art 2501 Sunset Blvd Houston TX 77005. *Mailing Add:* 31350 Ranch Rd 12 Ste C Dripping Springs TX 78620

D'AMATO, JANET POTTER
ILLUSTRATOR, CRAFTSMAN
b Rochester, NY. *Study:* Pratt Inst; Harriet FeBland Workshop; Sarah Lawrence. *Comn:* Recreate church in miniature, 02. *Awards:* Merit Award, Dimensional Illusr Inc, 89; Art Dir Club, NY, 89. *Bibliog:* Anne Commire (auth), Something About the Author, Gale Publ, 75; Carmel Marchionni (auth), Lifestyles, Westchester Gannett Publ, 75 & 77; D Russo (auth), article, Westchester Spotlight; The Villa Voice, April 2004. *Media:* Acrylic, Collage, Wood Assemblage. *Res:* Primitive and folk art and crafts, American Indian and African. *Interests:* Miniatures, quillwork and various other crafts. *Publ:* Auth & illusr, Gifts to Make for Love or Money, Golden, 73; Colonial Crafts for You to Make, Messner, 75; Quillwork, Craft of Paper Filigree, 75 & Italian Crafts, 77, Evans; Native American Craft Inspirations (book), Evans, 92; How Do We Recycle Plastic (book), Greenwillow Press, 92; illusr, Ecology Basics, Prentice Hall, 86; and others. *Mailing Add:* 32 Bayberry St Bronxville NY 10708

D'AMICO, LARRY
PAINTER, PRINTMAKER
b Ossining, NY, 1951. *Study:* Sch Visual Arts, New York, 69-70; Silvermine Coll Art, Conn, 70-71; San Francisco Art Inst, 71-72; State Univ NY, Purchase, BA, 77. *Work:* US State Dept, Washington, DC; Kaiser Found, Chase Manhattan Bank, NY; Pace Univ, Brooklyn. *Exhib:* Plein-Air: A Tradition Honored, Castle Gallery, New Rochelle, NY, 88; solo exhib, Helio Gallery, NY, 89 & Scarborough Gallery, Chappaqua, NY, 89; Am Landscape, Broden Gallery, Madison, NY, 89; Hudson River Contemp, Hudson River Gallery, Ossining, NY, 89. *Bibliog:* Vivian Raynor (auth), Plein air tradition, New York Times, 6/88; Ina Pasch (auth), As landscapes vary, so do artists styles, Wis State J, 11/89. *Media:* Oil, Pastel; Print

DANCE, ROBERT BARTLETT
PAINTER, PRINTMAKER
b Tokyo, Japan, May 31, 1934; US citizen. *Study:* Philadelphia Coll Art, with Henry C Pitz & W Emerton Heitland. *Work:* NC Mus Fine Art, Raleigh; R J Reynolds Indust, Winston-Salem, NC; Hanes Dye & Finishing, Winston-Salem; Miss Mus Art, Jackson; Wachovia Bank & Trust, Winston-Salem. *Exhib:* Mystic Int, Conn, 86; Arts for the Parks, Smithsonian Inst, Washington, DC, 87; Artist's Sketchbooks, Southeastern Ctr Contemp Art, 88; Solo retrospective, Southeastern Ctr Contemp Art, 91; Mystic 100, Conn, 92. *Awards:* First Place, NC Watercolor Soc, 73, 74 & 77, Assoc Artists Winston-Salem, 72, 73 & 74; Smithsonian Inst, Washington, DC, 87. *Bibliog:* Susan E Meyer (auth), 40 Watercolorists and How They Work, Watson-Guptill, 76 & Sir Isaac Pitman & Sons Ltd, Great Brit, 76; Wendon Blake (auth), The Alkyd Painting Book, Watson-Guptill. *Mem:* NC Watercolor Soc; Assoc Artists Winston-Salem. *Media:*

Watercolor, Alkyd, Woodcut. *Publ:* Illusr, Things Invisible to See, Advocate Publ Group, 79; The Medium is the Message, Am Artist, 79; Yankee Mag, 9/80; Printing Atmospheric Effects, Am Artist, 85; Artist Mag, London, Eng, 1-2/88; plus others. *Dealer:* Southeastern Ctr for Contemp Art 750 Marguerite Dr Winston-Salem NC 27106; Mystic Seaport Gallery Mystic CT. *Mailing Add:* 1803 Cambridge Dr Kinston NC 28504-2005

D'ANDREA, JEANNE
EDITOR, DESIGNER
b Chicago, Ill, Dec 9, 1925. *Study:* Art Inst Chicago; Colo Col, with Rico Lebrun; Univ Chicago, with Joshua Taylor, Ulrich Middledorf & Carlos Castillo, PhB & MA. *Collection Arranged:* Gericault, Los Angeles Co Mus Art, 71; Women Artists: 1550-1950, 76; Treasures of Mexico, 78; and others. *Pos:* Designer sets, costumes, Turnau Opera Co, NY & Arlington Opera Theatre, Arlington, Va, 59-72; head dept educ, Ringling Mus Art, Sarasota, Fla, 60-62; coordr exhibs & publ, Los Angeles Co Mus Art, 69-81, ed & design consult, 81-. *Mem:* Coll Art Asn Am. *Mailing Add:* 751 Avenida Pequena Santa Barbara CA 93111

DANE, WILLIAM JERALD
LIBRARIAN
b Concord, NH, May 8, 1925. *Study:* Drexel Inst Technol, MLS; NY Univ Inst Fine Arts; Sorbonne, Paris, France; Attingham Park Summer Sch, Eng; Palladio Studies, Vicenza, Italy, 80; Victorian Soc Summer Sch, London, 81, Philadelphia, 83, Glasgow, 91, Budapest, 98, studied art & archit: Cent Ger, 96, Prague, 2000, Amsterdam, 2002, Slovenia, 2005, Iceland, 2007, Barcelona, 2007. *Collection Arranged:* Fine Print Collection, Newark Pub Libr; 150 Years of Graphic Art in NJ; Silkscreen, A Survey Show of Serigraphs & Screenprints for the NJ State Coun on Arts; Prints by Joseph Pennell; Posters & Prints from Puerto Rico, 195; Hidden Treasures: Japanese Art, 91; Glorious World Bk Illus, 92; Printmaking Workshop of Robert Blackburn, 94; Salute to SAGA, 94; Lorenzo Homar's Graphics, 94; Lasting Impressions: Greater Newark's Jewish Legacy, 95; Japanese Art in the 20th century, 96; A Potpourri of Pop Art: Prints, Posters & Pop-Ups, 97; Over There, 1917-1918: A Victory Salute to the USA in Posters, 98; 20th Century Am Illus, 98; Nostalgic & Unforgettable Travel Posters from the 20th Century, 99; Women Printmakers, 2000; New, Non-Objective & Abstract Prints, 2000; A Graphic Sanctuary for Animals, Birds and a Few Fish-A Zoo on Paper, 2000; Shopping Bags Go Worldwide-Fabulous Bag Designs as an Int Portable Art, 2000; The USA & World War II, 60 Years After; Sculptures As Printmakers, 2003; The Arts of Etching & Engraving to Hon Whistler, 2003; Hollywood Nostalgia: Great Stars in Movie Stills; Garbo, Hepburn & Brad Pitt, Too!, 2003; Celebration of the Vitality & Joys of Multiculturalism: A Century of Print Collecting, 2004; Archit Books, Posters & Prints from the Pre-Digital Era, 2004; The Essence of Illus Then & Now from Shaped Poetry to Peter Rabbit, 2004; Visual Recollections of The Music Scene: Clara Schumann to Ray Charles, 2005; 7th Gala Exhib, Shopping Bags! Infinite Design Solutions for an Everyday Product; A Salute to Two Great 20th Century Artists: Picasso & Lichtenstein in Prints, Posters & Notable Books, 2005; John Cotton Dana: Innovative Libr Mus Founder 50th Anniversary of His Birth in 1856, 2006; Gen George Washington's March through Newark, Nov 1776, An Anniversary Show, 2006; Robert Sabuda, Travels in Time, 2006; A Salute to the Grad Archit Assocs, 2007; A Poster Pageant (200 posters in an overview of the art of the poster), 2007; Old & New Just for You: Prints, Posters, Illustrated Books, Shopping Bags, Pop-Ups & Autographs for the 120th Ann of the Libr: 1889-2009; The History of Fine Printing: Notable Incunabula & Early Books plus Broadsides, 2009; Recent Maps Produced by Nat Geographics Maps for Nat Geographic Mag, 2009. *Pos:* Supvr art & music libr, Newark Pub Libr, 67-90; supvr spec collections, Newark Pub Libr, 91-. *Teaching:* moderator, Rutgers Univ, Newark, 95-2004. *Awards:* Distinguished Service Award, Art Libr Soc NAM, 98; Libr Service Award, NJ Libr Asn, 98; Lifetime Achievement Award, NY Chap, Victorian Soc in Am, 2002; Soc Am Graphic Artists Award, 2003; Personal Resolution from the Gen Assembly of the state of NJ, 2007; Center for the Book Arts, 2007; Aljira Center for Contemp Art, 2007, Newark, NJ, 2007. *Bibliog:* Ezra Shales (auth), The Artistic Librarian, Fine Arts Connoisseur, Vol 6 Issue 4, 2009. *Mem:* Victorian Soc Am (nat bd mem, 74-80, chmn NY chap, 72-74); Victorian Soc (co-chmn educ comm, 90); Grolier Club, NY; Art Libr Soc NAm (treas, 86-88); ARLIS; NJ State Coun Arts (Essex Co block grant juror, 88-93); Council for the Ctr Innovative Print, Rutgers Univ, 2003-; Adv Bd Mem Printmaking Council NJ, 2000-2006. *Publ:* Auth, Picture Collection Subject Headings, 69; contribr, Arts in America: A Bibliography, Smithsonian Inst Press, 79; auth, Networking and the Art Library, Drexel Libr Quart, fall 83; John Cotton Dana: A Contemporary Appraisal of his Contributions & Lasting Influence on the Library & Museum Worlds, 90; The History of Fine Printing in Newark, 88; The World in Prints: An International Survey of Graphic Arts, 2008; Over 50 Years of Major Art History: 1950-2000 in Posters, Pamphlets & Small Catalogs of 14 Major Artists of the Era, 2008; An International Survey of Graphic Arts: Contemporary and Historic, Robeson Gallery, Newark Campus, Rutgers Univ, 2007. *Mailing Add:* Five Washington St Newark NJ 07101

DANI
SCULPTOR, PAINTER
b Los Angeles, Calif, Mar 11, 1933. *Study:* Pasadena City Coll, 51; Laguna Beach Sch Art, 80; Orange Coast Coll, 90; Calif State, Long Beach, 90. *Work:* RW Norton Found; Favell Mus; Carnegie Arts Ctr Mus; and 36 original bronze sculptures & enumerable paintings, etchings, & serigraphs. *Comn:* Magic Doves, comn by Brenda Payne & Bob Brown, Sacramento, Calif, 80. *Exhib:* Solo exhibs, Simic New Renaissance Gallery, 2002-2003; Group exhibs, Traditional Artists' Exhib, San Bernardino Co Mus, Redlands, Calif, 77; Ann Invitational, Nat Acad Design, New York, 78; Hudson Valley Art Asn, Westchester Ctr, White Plains, NY, 78; Ann Exhib, Salmagundi Club, New York, 80; Fallbrook Invitational, 96; Art-A-Fair Festival, Calif, 98; Featured sculpture, Gallerie Gabrie, 2000, 2010; Calif Art Club 90th, 92nd & 94th Gold Medal exhib, Hist Mus, 2000 & 2002; Millard Sheets Gallery Sculpture Show, 2002; Am Artists Prof League, 76th Grand Nat Exhib, 2004, 84th Grand Nat Exhib, 2012; Catharine Lorillard Wolfe Art Club, 2004, 2007, 2013; Calif Art Club, 2000, 2002, 2005, 2011. *Pos:* Designer, catalogs and flyers, Aminco Int; co-chair Orange Co Artists Showcase, 2000. *Teaching:* Art instr, Costa Mesa Dept Recreation, 70-79; Newport Mesa Unified Sch Dist, Hard of Hearing Prog; Costa Mesa art league; instructional guide, Ramona High Sch & San Vicente Valley Club (pres, bd dirs). *Awards:* Mrs John Newington Award, Hudson Valley Art Asn, 81; First Place Sculpture Award, Catharine Lorillard Wolfe Mem Show, New York, 95; Art Fest Award for Sculpture, Am Artist Prof League, New York, 95, Leila Gardner Mem award, 2002; First Place Sculpture Award, Artist Eye Show, Calif, 2000; Inducted, Orange Coast Coll Hall of Fame; Featured Artist SVVC Ann Event, 2009; Upstream People award, 2009, 2011, 2012. *Bibliog:* Richard Buffum (auth), Dream woman exists, Los Angeles Times, 80; Noel Goldblatt (auth), People of the century, Presidential Villa, 82; Julia Carroll Myer (auth), Artists in the 1990's, Manhattan Arts, 91; Orange Co Illus, 77-78; South West Art Mag, 77; Ramona Sentinel, 2003; Union Tribune, 2004; San Vicente Valley News, 2004. *Mem:* Am Artists Prof League; Catharine Lorillard Wolfe Nat Arts Club; Hudson Valley Arts Asn; Acad Fine Arts Found (Rembrandt mem); CAC (sculptor mem). *Media:* Bronze. *Specialty:* Traditional fine art galleries. *Interests:* Golf, tennis, swimming & reading. *Publ:* Akim Exhib & Auction, Sotherbys, New York, 96. *Dealer:* Galerie Gabrie 597 Green St Pasadena CA 91101; Gail Roff Int Fine Art; Cosmopolitan Fine Arts 7932 Girard AVe La Jolla CA 92037. *Mailing Add:* 15619 Indian Head Ct Ramona CA 92065

DANIEL, KENDRA CLIVER KRIENKE
DEALER, PAINTER, COLLECTOR, CURATOR
b Plainfield, NJ. *Study:* Drew Univ, with Lee Hall & Peter Chapin, BA; Nat Acad Design, with Philip Isenberg, watercolor with Nicholas Reale. *Work:* Drew Univ Collection, Madison, NJ; Douglass Coll Collection, New Brunswick, NJ; US Steel. *Comn:* Portrait of retiring dean, Douglass Col, 70; portrait--US Steel, Coun Tennant, Summit, NJ, 70; Christmas card design, Spaulding for Children, Westfield, NJ, 72; drawing of AT&T Bldg, AT&T Int Hq, Basking Ridge, NJ, 78; and others. *Exhib:* Group show, AT&T Hq Gallery, Basking Ridge, 79; Flights into Fantasy, Brandywine River Mus, Eric Carle Mus, 2007, 2008. *Collection Arranged:* 19th Century American Paintings, 82; Am Paintings, Nabisco Gallery, 84; Fifty Years of 19th Century Am Painting, Schering-Plough, 86; Childhood Enchantments, Mus Cartoon Art, 89; Children's Illustrators, Johnson & Johnson Gallery, 90; Art for Children, Hotel Wales, NY; cur, Flights into Fantasy, Brandywine River Mus, 2007, Eric Carle Mus, 2008; Age of Enchantment, Dulwich Mus, 2007; Les Paruriers, Bijoux de la Haute Couture, 2006; Grand Hornu & Kay Nielsen, G1 Holtegaard, Denmark, 2007. *Pos:* Free lance portrait artist, 70-75; art dealer, framer & designer, Whistler's Daughter Gallery, 74-84; art dealer, Whistler Gallery, 84-90 & Kendra Krienke Fine Art, 90-2005; art dealer, Kendra & Allan Daniel, 2005-10. *Awards:* Purchase Award, Drew Univ, 68; Selection Award for Christmas Card, Spaulding for Children, 72. *Bibliog:* The seven hottest collectibles, Metrop Home Mag, 4/91; Works of Wonder, Country Living, 3/93; home collections featured, Mag Antiques, 1/2011 & 2/2011, Tendencias del Mercado del Arte, 6/2011. *Mem:* Soc Illusrs, 91-; ATCA. *Media:* Watercolor, Mixed Media. *Specialty:* Original Art By Illustrators For Children and Fantasy, 1880- 1950, incl Arthur Rackham, Kay Nielsen, Jessie Willcox Smith, Fanny Young Cory, Ludwig Bemelmans, and Edmund Dulac, among others. *Interests:* Am jazz, animal advocacy & rescue; reading, collecting art & antiques. *Collection:* Am folk art, original vintage illustration art for children, antique toys, Yves Saint Laurent vintage haute couture jewelry and clothes. *Publ:* Contribr, Art Lovers Cookbook, 75; American Illustrator Art, Random House, 91; Arpi Ermouyan, Famous American Illustrators, Soc Illusr, 98; Myth, Magic and Mystery, 96; ten full color exhib catalogs; Flights into Fantasy, The Kendra & Allan Daniel Collection children's illus; Auction Catalogs - American Folk Art from the Collection of Kendra and Allan Daniel, Christies, NY, 01/2001; Original Illus Art from the Collections of Kendra and Allan Daniel, Sotheby's, NY, 04/2011; contribr, Taschen edition, East of the Sun and West of the Moon; and many others. *Mailing Add:* 140 Ashley Pl Park Ridge NJ 07656

DANIELS, ASTAR CHARLOTTE LOUISE DANIELS
STAINED GLASS ARTIST, PAINTER
b Fostoria, Ohio, Nov 27, 1920. *Study:* Toledo Mus Sch of Design, 50-52; pvt study with colorist, Emerson Burkhart, Columbus, Ohio, 52-54; Thomas Moore Col, 71-73; Univ Cincinnati, Ohio, AA (summa cum laude), 77; Ohio Univ, Athens, 84-85. *Work:* Gallery of Findlay Col, Ohio; Gallery of Anne T Case Sch, Akron, Ohio; Gallery of Brown Univ, Providence, RI; Gallery of Defiance Col, Ohio; Ohio Youth Bldg, Columbus, Ohio; Gallery Gen Hos, Cincinnati, Ohio. *Comn:* Baptistry mural, comn by Mr & Mrs W J Poorman, Forest, Ohio, 53; choir loft mural, Buckland Congregational Christian Church, Ohio, 54; hereford mural, comn by Mr Jason Miller, Forest, Ohio, 57; outside mural, comn by Mr & Mrs Joseph Newhard, Carey, Ohio, 58. *Exhib:* Toledo Area Artists' Exhib, Toledo Art Mus, Ohio, 52-55; Columbus Art League Exhib, Columbus Art Mus, Ohio, 53; First Duo-Sister Show Gallery 8, Toledo Art Mus, Ohio, 55; Schaff Gallery, Cincinnati, Ohio, 96. *Pos:* Dir art, Ohio State Fair, Columbus, 55-57 & Sr Girl Scout Round-Up, Button Bay, Vt, 62. *Teaching:* Private lessons in Forest & Cincinnati, Ohio, 50-66; dir/instr art, Defiance Col, Ohio, 56-57; instr art/drama, Methodist summer camp, Sabina, Ohio, 60-64; instr art/drama, Fairview Arts Ctr, Cincinnati, 77-78; instr art, Acad Proj Succeed, Losantiville Sch, Cincinnati, 96. *Awards:* Scouters Award, 57; Cert of Achievement, Charlotte R Schmidlapp Found, 77. *Bibliog:* Emma Fundaburk & Thomas Davenport (coauths), Art in Public Places in the United States, Bowling Green Univ Popular Press, 75. *Mem:* Citizen Diplomat Soc for Positive Future (visit to USSR 1986); Soc for Universal Human (founding mem); Nat Mus of Women in the Arts (founding mem). *Media:* Leaded Stained Glass; Oil. *Interests:* World travel, mentoring young women, meta physical phenomena, healing arts. *Collection:* Works by Hal Lotterman, Raphael Gleitzman, Evelyn E Wentz, Emerson C Burkhart, Alan Melis, David Fisher, Irene Satala, Elisabeth Haley. *Publ:* Auth & illusr, Aiming in His Direction, Capozzolo, 71; illusr, Women's Spirit Bonding, Pilgrim Press, 83. *Mailing Add:* 8118 Wooster Pike Cincinnati OH 45227-4008

DANIELS, DAVID ROBERT
PAINTER, EDUCATOR
b Albion, Mich, Apr 26, 1948. *Study:* Cent Mich Univ, MA, 70; special study with Jack Beal & Sondra Freckelton, 92-94 & Janet Fish, 95. *Work:* Nat Inst Health, Bethesda, Md; Quadrangle Corp, Washington; Mich Educ Asn, East Lansing; East Jordan Hist Soc, Mich; Home Nat Bank, Arkansas City, Kans. *Comn:* Watercolor 28″ x 60″, Nat Inst Health, Bethesda, Md, 89; Quadrangle Watercolor, Quadrangle Corp, Washington, 90. *Exhib:* Montpelier/Invitational, Laurel, Md, 92; Rock Creek Gallery/Invitational, Washington, 93. *Pos:* Dir educ, A Salon, Washington, 92-96; instr, Coupeville Arts Ctr, 97. *Teaching:* Instr watercolor, Smithsonian Inst, 83-96, Northern Va Community Col, 84-96 & Haystack Mountain Workshops, 86-94. *Awards:* Best of Show, Capitol Hill Art League, 89; Best of Show, Washington Watercolor Asn, 89 & 96. *Bibliog:* Mood in watercolor, Am Artist Mag, 91; Al Avery (dir), Dave Daniels Watercolorist, Montgomery TV, 94; The color blue, Am Artist Mag, spring 95. *Mem:* Washington Watercolor Asn; Southern Watercolor Soc; Artist Equity; Capitol Hill Art League; Rockville Art Place. *Media:* Watercolor. *Publ:* Contribr, Mood in watercolor, Am Artist Mag, 91; Dave Daniels Watercolorist, Penn State Press, 94; illusr, Pathways/Cover Design, Lou DeSalba, 94; Contribr, The color blue, Am Artist Mag, 95; auth, Flowers in Watercolor, Rockport Publ. *Mailing Add:* 8012 Piney Branch Rd Silver Spring MD 20910-5244

DANIELS, MARTHA K
SCULPTOR, CERAMIST
b Brooklyn, NY, Sept 21, 1943. *Study:* Cooper Union, NY, 61-64; studied with John Hovannes, 62-64 & Dorothy Dehner, 62-64; Metrop State Col, Denver, Colo, BA (fine arts), 75. *Work:* Coll Contemp Art, Denver Art Mus; Kirkland Mus, Denver; Taco Bell Corp Art Collection, San Francisco; City & Co Denver; Playboy Art Collection, Chicago; Colo Dept of Transportation; Am Mus Ceramics, Pomona, Calif. *Comn:* Murals, Co Coun Arts, Trinidad, Colo, 89; Sculpture, Modern Archit, Denver, 90; Sculpture Installation, Kaiser Permanent, Aurora, Colo, 95; US Dept Interior, El Paso, Tex, 96; Tile Mural, Colo Dept Transp, Denver, 2004; Ceramic Screen, Chambers Family Found Bldg, Denver Colo, 2013. *Exhib:* Solo exhibs, Diana & Actaeon, Artyard, Denver, 94, Grotto, Denver Art Mus, 2000, Robert Nichols Contemp Clay, Santa Fe, NMex, 2004-2009; Wash Art 78, Annual Exhib, Int Art Dealers Asn, Washington, DC, 78; Mino Ceramics Exhib, Mino, Japan, 90; Egypt of the Mind, Denver Art Mus, 98; Kirkland Mus, Colo Art, Denver, 98; Website exhib, Int Mus Ceramics, Faenza, Italy, 2003-04; Colo Art, Denver Hist Mus, 2004; Scene, Denver Art Mus; Decade of Influence, Denver Mus Contemp Art, 2006; Am Crafts Council Exhib, San Francisco, 2010; Ceramic Ann Am, San Francisco, 2011; Earth & Fire, Denver Art Mus, 2012; Confluence, Emmanuel, Denver, Colo; Ventura Gallery, Palm Springs, Calif, 2012; World Interiors News, Annual Competition, London, 2013. *Teaching:* Tchr, Art Student's League, Denver; lectr, Logan Lectr Series, Denver Art Mus, 2012. *Awards:* Fel Award, Colo Coun on Arts, 89 & 01; Fel, Rocky Mountain Women's Inst, Denver, 95; Artists Grant, Denver Art Mus, 99. *Bibliog:* Dr Donald Kuspit (auth), The Myths in Depths (monograph), Denver Art Mus, 2000; Joshua Hassel (auth), Grotto, KBDI Channel 12 (video), Denver, 2001; Elizabeth Schlosser (auth), Colo Clay Artists, Lee Ballentine, 2005; Peyton, Paglia (auths), Decade of Influence, Denver Mus Contemp Arts, 2006; Chandler, Grant, & Paglia (auths), Colorado Abstract, Painting & Sculpture, Fresco Publ, Santa Fe, NM, 2009; Continental Divide, NCECA, Blurb publ, 2009; Carol Keller (auth), Confluence:35 Yrs of Art and Community, Blurb Pub, 2011; World Interiors Web News, 2013. *Mem:* Pirate Artist's Gallery (dir, 85-89); Spark Gallery (mem, 81); Fel Rocky Mountain Women's Inst; Art Student's League; Silica Studios, Palm Springs, Calif. *Media:* Clay, Bronze, Concrete. *Interests:* Historic preservation; Design and Ceramics, Collecting ceramics, mexicana, regional art; Modern and Contemporary Art. *Publ:* Ceramics Monthly Mag, 4/03; plus numerous articles. *Dealer:* Ventura Gallery 463 N Palm Canyon Dr Palm Springs Ca 92262. *Mailing Add:* PO Box 105 Desert Hot Springs CA 92240

DANIELSON, PHYLLIS I See Gillie, Phyllis I Danielson

DANK, LEONARD D
ILLUSTRATOR, CONSULTANT
b Birmingham, Ala, Dec 21, 1929. *Study:* Cornell Univ, BA, 52; Sch Med Illus, Mass Gen Hosp, Boston, cert, 55; Art Students League; Jules Laurents Studio, NY. *Work:* McGraw-Hill Publ co, NY; Stravon Educ Press Inc, NY; H S Stuttman co Inc, Conn; Proj-in-Health, NJ; Doubleday & co Inc, NY; PW Communications, NJ; Contemp Orthopedics, Calif. *Comn:* The Brain in Hypertension Parts I & II (animated films), Merck, Sharp & Dohme, 78; Drug Induced Movement Disorders (animated film), Dupont Pharmaceuticals, 83; health & fitness posters, Esquire Mag, 85-88. *Exhib:* Art of Medicine Exhib, Soc of Illustr, 86. *Pos:* Staff artist, Plastic Surgery Clin, Manhattan Eye & Ear Hosp, New York, 55-57 & Eye Bank for Sight Restoration, New York, 57-59; owner, Leonard Dank Studio, New York, 59-61 & Medical Illus Co, New York & Cutchogue, NY, 61-; consult med illusr, St Luke's-Roosevelt Hosp Ctr, New York, 61-83, Contemp Orthopaedics Publ, 81-83, Harper & Row, Publ, NY, 82-, PW Commun Inc, NJ, 82-86, Esquire Mag Health & Fitness Clinic, NY, 85-88 & Whittle-Time Commun Inc, 88-94. *Awards:* First Prize Motion Picture, Am Coll Surgery, 59 & 62; Better Teller Award, Asn Indust Advertisers, 73; Outstanding Children's Sci Book Award, Nat Sci Teachers Asn, 82; Cert Merit, Soc of Illus, 86. *Mem:* Asn Med Illusr; Guild Natural Sci Illusr. *Media:* Multi. *Publ:* Coauth, Clinical Obstetrics & Gynecology, 73-76, Gynecologic Operations, 78, Harper & Row; illusr, The Male His Body, His Sex, Anchor Press/Doubleday, 79; Dr Fishbein's Illustrated Medical Encyclopedia, 79 & Every Woman's Health 80, 82, & 85, Doubleday & co; Electromagnetic Spectrum 79, Jupiter 81 & Space Colony 82, Elsever-Nelson; Principles of Human Anatomy, 83, 86, 90, 92 & 95, 99, Principles of Anatomy & Physiology, 84, 87, 90, 92 & 96, 2000, Introduction to Human Body, 88, 90 & 92, 95, 97, Harper Collins. *Mailing Add:* Medical Illustrators Co PO Box 944 Cutchogue NY 11935

DANKO, LINDA AK
MUSEUM DIRECTOR
Pos: Group tour & prog sales mgr, Winterthur's Historic Houses of Odessa, Del, formerly; office mgr, Biggs Mus Am Art, Dover, Del, 2004-2005, interim dir, 2005-2006, exec dir, 2006-. *Mailing Add:* Biggs Museum of American Art PO Box 711 Dover DE 19903

DANLY, SUSAN
CURATOR, HISTORIAN
b Chicago, Ill, July 27, 1948. *Study:* Univ Wis, Madison, BA, 71; Brown Univ, MA, 77, PhD, 83. *Collection Arranged:* The Railroad in the Am Landscape (with catalog), 81; Shadow Catchers: Photographs of Native Am from the Huntington Collections (with catalog), 85; Prints & Drawings Am West, 85; The Modern Poster: Am Graphic Design in the 1890's, 85; Early Pasadena Artists, 86; Light, Air, and Color, 90; Telling Tales, 91; Language as Object: Emily Dickinson and Contemporary Art, 97. *Pos:* Asst cur Am art, The Huntington Libr, 84-86, assoc cur, 86; cur, Pa Acad Fine Arts, 88-93, Mead Art Mus, 93. *Teaching:* Vis fac am art, Univ Calif, Los Angeles, 85, Univ Pa, 90. *Awards:* Huntington Libr Fel, 90; Wintethur Fel, 93. *Mem:* Coll Art Asn; Am Studies Asn. *Res:* 19th Century American Art with specialty in history of photography. *Publ:* Auth, Edward Weston in Los Angeles, Huntington Libr, 86; The Railroad in American Art, Mass Inst Technol Press, 87; Facing the Past, Pa Acad Fine Arts, 92; Eakins and the Photograph, Smithsonian Inst Press, 94

DANOFF, I MICHAEL
PROFESSOR, ART ADVISOR
b Chicago, Ill, Oct 22, 1940. *Study:* Univ Mich, BA, 62; Univ NC, Chapel Hill, MA, 64; Syracuse Univ, PhD, 70. *Collection Arranged:* Art in Our Time, travelling exhib, 80; Image in Am Painting & Sculpture: 1950-1980 (co-auth, catalog), Akron Art Mus, 81; Cindy Sherman, Inc, 83; Robert Mangold, 84; Jeff Koons (auth, catalog), 88; Gerhard Richter: Painting (co-curator, catalog), Mus Contemp Art, Chicago, 88; Peter Halley: Paintings,89-92; Andy Warhol: Print Portfolios, 93; Contemplation: Five Installations, 96, Des Moines Art Ctr, Iowa; Cross Currents of Centurys End, 2004. *Pos:* Cur collections, Dickson Col, 70-73; cur, Michener Collection, Univ Tex, 73-74; cur collections & exhibs, Milwaukee Art Ctr, 74-80; assoc dir chief cur, Milwaukee Art Mus, 74-80; dir, Akron Art Mus, 80-84, Mus Contemp Art, Chicago, 84-88, San Jose Mus Art, 88-91 & Des Moines Art Ctr, 91-97; dir art prog, Neuberger & Berman, 1997-2011. *Teaching:* Asst prof 19th & 20th Century & contemp art, Dickson Col, 70-73, Univ Tex, Austin, 73; adj prof, Univ Wis, Milwaukee, 78, Univ Akron, Ohio, 84, Univ Ill, Chicago, 88; lectr, San Jose State Univ, Calif, 90; lectr, Mus Modern Art, 2011; adj assoc prof, NYU, 2012. *Awards:* Nat Endowment Arts Mus Prof Fel, 73. *Bibliog:* Rev, NY Times, 10/2/77; Helen Cullinan (auth), Italianate-Palazzo-Post Office, Art News, 9/81; Hilton Kramer (auth), An audacious inaugural, NY Times, 9/20/81; cover story, Arts & Books section, San Jose Mercury News, 11/20/88. *Mem:* Coll Art Asn Am, 67-; Am Asn Mus, 74-; Asn Art Mus Dir, 80-98; Ill Arts Alliance (trustee, 86-88); Creative Time (trustee 2000-2008); Vera List Ctr for Art & Politics (99-2009). *Res:* Contemporary art history & criticism. *Publ:* Auth, Gallery Guides to Collections, Milwaukee Art Ctr, 74-75; Mary Nohl: sophisticated naive, Midwest Art, 75; Europe in the Seventies, Art in Am, 1/78; Paintings That Make Your Retinas Dance, Art News, 11/81; Art and Commodities, Affinities and Intuitions: The Gerald S Elliott Collection of Contemporary Art, The Art Institute of Chicago/Thames & Hudson, Chicago/New York, 90; Cross Currents of Centuries End: Selections from the Neuberger Bermon Art Collection, Univ Wash Press, 2004. *Mailing Add:* 54 Riverside Dr 6d New York NY 10024

DANTZIC, CYNTHIA MARIS
EDUCATOR, ARTIST
b Brooklyn, NY, Jan 4, 1933. *Study:* Bard Col, 50-52; Yale Univ, with Josef Albers & Jose de Rivera, BFA, 55; Pratt Inst, MFA, 63. *Work:* Brooklyn Mus; Adirondack Mus, NY; Adelphi Univ Gallery; Bard Col; Rose Art Mus, Waltham, Mass; Univ Mass Gallery, Amherst; Edson Tool Bldg, Belleville, NJ; many private collections. *Comn:* Modular paintings, NY Soc Gen Semantics, 68 & Springbok Ed, Kansas City, Kans, 74; stained glass windows, Church Resurrection, Lakeland, Fla, 75; portrait Mary Susan Miller, Berkeley Inst, Brooklyn, 79; Above and Beyond (ed photog collages), Brooklyn Art & Cult Asn, 83; calligraphic parchment, Charles Ives, Berkshire Inst for Theology & Arts, 2004. *Exhib:* Solo Exhibs: East Hampton Gallery, NY, 66; Resnick Gallery, Long Island Univ, 83 & St John's Univ, NY, 95; Crosby Studio Gallery, New York City, 2005; Group Exhibs: Art Festival for NAACP Legal Defense (auth, catalog), Brooklyn Mus, 63, The Wit of It, Delgado Mus, New Orleans, 72; Affect-Effect, La Jolla Mus Art, 79; Interior-Exterior, 80 & 100 New Acquisitions, 81, Brooklyn Mus; Common Ground: NY Abstract, Galerie Arts Visuels, Que, 82; Donnell Libr, 95-; Blue Mountain Gallery, 95-2007; Jia-Xuan Zhang, Chinese calligraphy and photography, Long Island Univ, 98; China Inst, NY, 2007. *Pos:* Panelist, Regrant Panel NY Arts Funding, Brooklyn Arts & Cult Asn, 85-96; Consult/Analyst, NGDA, Online Database, Cooper Union, New York City, 99-2000. *Teaching:* Asst prof art, Brooklyn Ctr, Long Island Univ, 65-70, assoc prof, 70-75, prof, 75-, sen prof, 2009, dir dept, 77-79, chmn, 80-86; adj assoc prof, Cooper Union, 92-99, adj prof, 99-2002. *Awards:* Stipend Award Animation, Brooklyn Art & Cult Asn, 82; Newton Award for Excellence in Teaching, 88; Trustee Award for Scholarly Achievement, Long Island Univ, 90; Trustee Lifetime Award for Achievement in Art and Art Educ, 2000; 40 Yr Medal, Long Island Univ, 2007. *Bibliog:* Talk of the town, New Yorker, 5/28/66; Marie Avona (auth), Cynthia Dantzic, Multi-media Artist, Pratt Reports, 6/79; Herbert Keppler (auth), Expand Your View: Cynthia Dantzic's Photo collages, Mod Photog, 1/84; The Gang's All Here, photo-collage, Popular Photog, 2000; Venice, with an old Nikon, a 50 mm Lens and a Daily Diary, article & 7 photos, Popular Photography, 2001. *Mem:* Coll Art Asn; Am Asn Univ Prof; Founds Art & Teacher Educ; Soc Scribes (bd governors, vice pres, 2012); Park Slope Civic Coun (trustee); NY Soc General Semantics (bd gov), 2010; Nat Arts Club. *Media:* Pencil, Photography, calligraphy. *Interests:* Americana and Tribal Art, Piano, Non-Western Calligraphies. *Publ:* Auth, An invitation to the butterfly ball, NY Times Book Rev,

5/76; illusr, Biography, Confrontation, Long Island Univ, 79; auth & illusr, Design Dimensions: An Introduction to the Visual Surface, 90; auth & illusr, Prentice-Hall Drawing Dimensions: A Comprehensive Introduction, 99; auth & illusr, Antique Pocket Mirrors, Pictorial & Advertising Miniatures, Schiffer, 2002; auth, 100 New York Painters, Schiffer, 2006; Alphabet City, Signs of New York, Fotofolio, 2010; auth, 100 New York Photographers, Schiffer, 2009; 100 NY Calligraphers, Schiffer, 2015. *Mailing Add:* 910 President St Brooklyn NY 11215

DANZIGER, FRED FRANK
PAINTER
b Pittsburgh, Pa, Feb 24, 1946. *Study:* Pa Acad Fine Arts, cert, 70. *Hon Degrees:* Mary Butler Painting Prize, 00. *Work:* Philadelphia Mus Art; Pa Acad Fine Arts, Philadelphia; Ashville Mus Art, NC; Wichita Art Mus, Kans; Woodmere Art Mus, Philadelphia. *Comn:* Mural on medical history, Med Coll Pa, 95. *Exhib:* Art & the Law, Minn Mus Art, Minneapolis, 79; Recent Acquisitions, Noyes Mus, Oceanville, NJ, 86; Fel Ann, Pa Acad Fine Arts, Philadelphia, 88; Fel Ann, Michener Mus, Doylestown, Pa, 90; Recent Acquisitions, Woodmere Art Mus, Philadelphia, Pa, 92; Statewide Ann, State Mus Pa, Harrisburg, 92; Mainly Maine, Sherry French Gallery, New York, NY, 2006. *Teaching:* Instr painting & art hist, Art Inst Philadelphia, 73-; instr portrait painting, Pa Acad Fine Arts, 98-. *Awards:* Tiffany Grant, Nat Competition, Tiffany Found, 73; Alexander Prize, Painting Ann, Cheltenham Art Ctr, 89; Coyne Prize, Woodmere Painting Ann, Woodmere Mus, 92. *Bibliog:* Nicholas Roukes (auth), Acrylics Bold & New, Watson-Guptil, 87; Anna B Francis (auth), The Road to Recognition, Am Artist Mag, 91; Edward Sozanski (auth), On Art's Healing Edge, Philadelphia Inquirer, 91. *Mem:* Fel Pa Acad Fine Arts (treas, 80-84). *Media:* Acrylic, Oil. *Publ:* Auth, The Alone Ranger & Other Paintings, pvt publ, 79; What does big art have against nature, Philadelphia Inquirer, 91. *Dealer:* Rodger PaPelle Galleries 122 N Third St Philadelphia PA 19106; Sherry French Gallery 601 W 26th St New York NY 10001. *Mailing Add:* 22 Hunter Rd Coatesville PA 19320-4314

DANZIGER, JOAN
SCULPTOR
b New York, NY, June 17, 1934. *Study:* Cornell Univ, BFA, 54; Art Students League, 54-55; Acad Fine Arts, Rome, cert art, 56-58. *Work:* Nat Mus Am Art, Smithsonian Inst, Nat Mus Women's Art, Am Univ, Capitol Children's Mus, Discovery Channel, George Washington Univ, Washington, DC; Jacksonville Mus Arts & Sci, Fla; NJ State Mus, Trenton; New Orleans Mus Art, La; Susquehenna Art Mus, Pa; Artery Corp, Md, Discovery Channel, NY, Lab Sch, Washington, DC, Am Univ, George Washington Univ, Univ Md, Susquehenna Art Mus, Pa. *Comn:* Suspended sculpture, Md Fine Arts Comn & Frostburg State Col, Md, 75; two sculptures, AFL-CIO Labor Studies Ctr, Silver Springs, Md, 76; three sculptures, Convention Ctr, Washington, DC, 85; five sculptures, comn by George Taylor, Dist Ct, Md, 90; bronze sculpture, Grounds for Sculpture, Hamilton, NJ, 2000-2001; Discovery Channel, Md; Fish Out of Water, City of Baltimore; Party Animals, DC Commission of the Arts. *Exhib:* Solo exhibs, Jacksonville Mus Art & Sci, 79, Fendrick Gallery, Wash, 79, Terry Dintenfass Gallery, NY, 80, Joy Horwich Gallery, Chicago, 82, NJ State Mus, Trenton, 82, Benjamin Mangel Gallery, Philadelphia, 84, La World Expos, New Orleans, 84, Textile Mus, Wash, 85, Nat Mus Women Arts, 87, San Antonio Art Ctr, 87; Joy Horwich Gallery, Chicago, 82; La World Exposition, New Orleans, 84; Osuna Gallery, Wash, DC, 90; Stamford Mus, Ct, 96; Grounds for Sculpture, NJ, 99; Cork Gallery, London, Eng, 2002; Osuna Gallery, DC, 2009; Am Univ Mus, Katzen Art Ctr, 2012; Pittsburgh Children's Mus, Pittsburgh, Pa, 2013; Marywood Univ, Scranton, Pa, 2013. *Pos:* Visual arts panelist, DC Comn Arts & Humanities, 74-80; pres, Wash Sculptors Group, 94-99. *Teaching:* Visual arts panelist, DC Community Arts & Humanities, 74-79 & 84-85; artist-in-residence, AFL-CIO Labor Studies Ctr, 75; vis artist & lectr, Smithsonian Inst, 80-82; sculpture panelist, NJ State Coun Arts, 82. *Awards:* Nat Endowment Arts Grant, 75; Int des Arts, Paris, Grant, 86; Spokelos Found for Arts, Greece; Artist in Residence, Am Acad Rome, Italy, 2010. *Bibliog:* Constance Dodge (auth), Fantasy Sculpture, Albany News, NY, 78; Cynthia Nadelman (auth), article, Art News, 80; Maryse Pailla (auth), Profile, Art Voices, 81; Joanna Shaw Eagle (auth), American women in sculpture, Harpers Bazaar, 81; Michael Welzenbach (auth), The Magical Menagerie, Washington Post, 84; Virginia Watson-Jones (auth), Contemporary American Women Sculptors, 86; Richard Barrds (auth). Facing Sculpture, 2004; Michael O'Sullivan (auth), Wash Post, 2009; Elaine King (auth), Sculpture mag, July/Aug 2009; 100 Mid Atlantic Artists, 2011; Contemp Artists, Vol III, 2011; Sculpture Mag, July/August, 2013. *Mem:* Washington Sculptors Group; Int Sculpture Ctr; Soc Art Imagination; Sculpture Guild; Cosmos Club; Explorers Club. *Media:* Mixed-Media Sculpture, Woodcuts. *Publ:* Inside the Underworld: Beetle Magic (catalog), 2012; Mythic Landscape, 2008. *Mailing Add:* 2909 Brandywine St NW Washington DC 20008

DANZKER, JO-ANNE BIRNIE
DIRECTOR, WRITER
b Brisbane, Australia, 1945. *Study:* Univ Queensland, BA, 66, dip ed, 67, BEd, 71. *Pos:* Exhib programmer, Galleria Arte Bologna, Milan, 74-76; managing ed, Flash Art Mag, Milan, 74-76; cur, Vancouver Art Gallery, BC, 77-84, actg dir, 84, dir, 85-; dir, Mus Villa Stuck, Munich, Ger, formerly; dir, Frye Art Mus, Seattle, 2009-. *Teaching:* Asst Far Eastern art, York Univ, Toronto, 73-74. *Mem:* Coun Assoc Mus Dir; Can Mus Asn; Can Art Mus Dirs Orgn; Am Asn Mus Dir. *Publ:* Auth, William Hogarth: Nationalism, Mass Media and the Artist, 80, Mannerism: A Theory of Culture, 82, Vancouver: Art and Artists, 1931-1983, 83, Luxe, Calme et Volupte, 86 & Edvard Munch, 86 (exhib catalogs), Vancouver Art Mus, BC; Robert Flaherty: Photographer, Studies in Anthrop Visual Commun, Philadelphia, 80; Museum and Guerrilla Television, Video Art, Eine Dokumentation, Berlin, 81; Box of Daylight & Smokey Top, 84, Vanguard, Vancouver, BC. *Mailing Add:* Vancouver Art Gallery 750 Hornby St Vancouver BC V6Z 2H7 Canada

DAOU, ANNABEL
CONCEPTUAL ARTIST, DRAFTSMAN
b Beirut, Lebanon. *Study:* Barnard Col; Columbia Univ. *Exhib:* one man shows, Slipping, Conduit Gallery, Dallas, 2001, Striptease, Elizabeth Found for the Arts, NY, 2002, The Last Painting Show, Conduit Gallery Dallas, 2004, Ideas about the Thing & the Thing Itself, Gallery Joe, Philadelphia, 2005; New Space, Conduit Gallery, Dallas, Tex, 2002; A Three Week Show, Gallery Joe, Philadelphia, Pa, 2003; NADA, Josee Bienvenu Gallery, Miami, Fla, 2005; Series, Gallery Joe, Philadelphia, Pa, 2006; America, Josee Bienvenu Gallery, New York City, 2006. *Collection Arranged:* Sarah Ann & Werner H Kramarsky, NY; Howard Rachofsky, Dallas; US Trust, Dallas; Goldman Sachs, London; Museo Nacional de Bellas Artes, Havana. *Pos:* Cur, Aporia, Elizabeth Found Gallery, 2006. *Bibliog:* Roberta Fallon (auth) Artblog, 2006; David Markus (auth), Brooklyn Rail, 2006; Elizabeth Kley Time Out, NY, 2006. *Dealer:* Josee Bienvenu Gallery New York City NY; Gallery Joe Philadelphia PA

DARLING, SHARON SANDLING
HISTORIAN, MUSEUM DIRECTOR
b Mitchell, SDak, Feb 28, 1943. *Study:* NC State Univ, BA; Duke Univ, MAT; Winterthur Summer Inst, Am Dec Arts; Northwestern Univ, MBA. *Exhib:* Chicago Metalsmiths; Chicago Ceramics and Glass; Chicago Furniture; Haymarket! 1886; Motorola: A Journey Through Time & Technology. *Collection Arranged:* TC Industries. *Pos:* Cur dec arts, Chicago Hist Soc, 75-86; dir, Motorola Mus, 1986-2007. *Awards:* Charles F Montgomery Prize, Decorative Arts Soc, 85. *Res:* Decorative arts of Chicago and the Midwest; industrial arts; Architectural terra cotta. *Interests:* history, gardening. *Publ:* Coauth (with Gail Farr Casterline), Chicago Metalsmiths, 77; Chicago Ceramics and Glass, 80; Chicago Furniture, 84; TECO: Art Pottery of the Prairie School, 89; Coauth (with George A Berry III), Common Clay, 2003, Bars and Blades, 2007; Harry J Lucas, 2013. *Mailing Add:* 4N227 Burr Rd Saint Charles IL 60175

DARR, ALAN PHIPPS
CURATOR, HISTORIAN
b Kankakee, Ill, Sept 30, 1948. *Study:* Northwestern Univ, BA, 70, Inst Fine Arts, NY Univ, MA, 75, PhD (art hist), 80; Metrop Mus Art, cert mus training, 76; Univ Calif, Berkeley, mus mgt, 80; Harvard Univ, Ctr Italian Renaissance Studies, Villa I Tatti, Florence, postdoctoral fel, 88-89; Ctr Advan Study Visual Arts, Nat Gallery Art, Washington, DC, Paul Mellon Vis Sr Fel, 94. *Pos:* Grad intern, Metrop Mus Art, New York, 76; asst cur, Detroit Inst Arts, 78-80, assoc cur, 80-81, cur in charge European sculpture & decorative arts, 81-96, Walter B Ford II Family cur Europ sculpture & decorative arts, 97-; head of Dept European Painting, sculpture & decorative arts, 2009-2011, sr cur dept of European Art, 2011-, Walter B Ford II Family Cur European Sculpture and Decorative Arts, 2011-. *Teaching:* Instr, NY Univ, 76; adj prof, Wayne State Univ, Detroit, 82-. *Awards:* Bronze medal, Accademia del Discgno, Florence, 86; Fel, Nat Endowment Humanities & Rush H Kress Found, 88-89; Florence J Gould fel, 90; Paul Mellon Vis Sr fel, CASVA, Washington, DC, 94; award, Samuel Basil Trust Scholarship, Royal Collection Studies Prog, Eng, 2002; Cavaliere dell'Ordine della Stella della Solidarieta Italiana, Pres Italian Govt, 2007; Mentor of the Yr 2008, Provost & Vice Chancellor of Univ Mich Dearborn. *Mem:* Coll Art Asn; Renaissance Soc Am; ICOM; AAM; Am Ceramic Cir; Italian Art Soc; and others; AAMC. *Res:* Italian Renaissance and Baroque sculpture and decorative arts; Pietro Torrigiani and Italian Art in Renaissance England. *Publ:* Coauth, The Romantics to Rodin: Nineteenth Century French Sculpture from North American Collections (catalog), 80; The Influence of Paris: European and American Sculpture 1830-1930 (catalog), 81-82; auth, Italian Renaissance Sculpture in the Time of Donatello (catalog), 85; Donatello e i Suoi: Scultura fiorentina del primo Rinascimento (catalog), 86; coauth, Francesco da Sangallo, Burlington Mag, 12/87; co-ed & coauth, Donatello Studien (catalog), 89; Verrocchio and Late Quattrocento Italian Sculpture (catalog), 92; contribr, Kunst des Cinquecento in der Toskana, Kunsthistorisches Institut, Florence, 92; auth, The Figure Revisited (catalog), Int Ceramics Seminar, 94; coauth, Woven Splendor: Five Centuries of European Tapestry in the Detroit Institute of Arts (catalog), 96; organizer & coauth, The Dodge Collection: Eighteenth-Century French and English Art in the Detroit Institute of Arts (catalog), 96; org & co-auth, The Medici, Michelangelo and the Art of Late Renaissance Florence (catalog), Art Inst Chicago, Detroit Inst Arts, 2002; Italian Sculpture in the Detroit Inst Art (catalog), 2 Vols, 2002; auth, A Pair of Large Bronze Deities in Detroit, New Research, Attribution to Danese Cattaneo (catalog), Nat Gallery Art, Ctr Advan Study Visual Arts, Washington, DC, Yale Univ Press, 215-239, 2003; Francesco I de' Medici, Bernardo Buontalenti and a Medici Porcelain Ewer in Detroit, Arte Collezionismo Conservazione: Scritti in Onore di Marco Chiarini, Florence, Giunti & Ente, Ente Cassa di Risparmio di Firenze, 219-224, 2004; Two newly acquired sculptures by Rude and Rodin in the Detroit Institute of Arts, La sculpture en Occident: Etudes offertes a Jean- Rene Gaborit, Musee du Louvre, Paris, 273-283, 2007; organizer & coauth (with Brian Gallagher), Recent acquisitions of European Sculpture and Decorative Arts 2000-2006 at the Detroit Inst Arts, Burlington Mag, 449-456, 6/2007; auth, Virtuoso Carving: Three Eigheenth- Century British Portrait Sculptures by Le Marchand, Roubiliac & Chaffers, Bulletin of the Detroit Inst Arts, Vol 83, 2009; Discoveries, A Courtly Seventeenth Century Amber & Ivory Casket, Mag Antiques, 2009; The Return of the Prodigal Son by Antonio Montauti, Brillos en Bronce: Colecciones de Reyes (catalog), Madrid, 2009; 19th Century Royal Sevres Dejeuner Chinois Reticule: An Important New Acquisition at the Detroit Institute of Arts, French Porcelain Soc Jour, Vol IV, pp 121-160, 2011; Donatello, Desidero and Geri da Settignano, and Sculpture in Pietra Serena for a Boni Palace and Elsewhere in Florence: A Resassessment, pp 217-232, Desidero da Settignano, Venezia Marsilio, 2011; Pietro Torrigiani and His Sculpture in Henrician England: Sources and Influences, pp 49-80, The Anglo-Florentine Renaissance: Art for the Early Tudors, Yale Univ Press, 2012. *Mailing Add:* c/o Detroit Inst Arts 5200 Woodward Ave Detroit MI 48202

DARRIAU, JEAN-PAUL
EDUCATOR, SCULPTOR
b New York, NY, Nov 24, 1929. *Study:* Pratt Inst, 47-48; Brooklyn Col, BA, 51; Univ Minn, MFA, 54. *Work:* Hirshhorn Mus & Sculpture Garden; Ind Univ Fine Arts Mus; Colorado Springs Art Ctr; Minneapolis Inst Art; Albert List Collection; Interracial Movement/Entrance to City, City of Bloomington, Ind. *Comn:* Man and Woman (aluminum), Jersey City State Col, 69; Adam and Eve I (bronze), 68, Adam and Eve II (bronze), 73 & four portrait busts, 76, Ind Univ Campus; Red, Blond, Black and Olive (limestone), City Bloomington, Ind, 80. *Exhib:* Solo exhib, Grippi Gallery, NY, 62; Sculptors Guild, NY, 70-72; FAR Gallery, NY, 72-73; Privileges and Silences, Ind Univ, Bloomington, 82 & Univ Chicago, 83; Sch Fine Arts, Ind Univ, 84; Mussavi Arts Ctr, NY, 85. *Teaching:* Instr, State Col, Arkadelphia, Ark, 53, Oberlin Col, 54 & Colo Col, 57-61; instr, Ind Univ, Bloomington, 61-, head sculpture dept, 61-72. *Awards:* Fulbright Grant, 55-57 & 66-67; res grants, Colo Col, 59 & Ind Univ. *Mem:* Coll Art Asn; CAA Gay/Lesbian Caucus (bd mem). *Publ:* Contribr, Visions and Voice of the New Midwest, James A Rock & Co, 78; self-publ catalogs, 83 & 88. *Mailing Add:* 6 Greene St Apt 5B New York NY 10013-5817

DARROW, PAUL GARDNER
PAINTER, EDUCATOR
b Pasadena, Calif. *Study:* Colorado Springs Fine Art Ctr; Claremont Grad Sch & Univ Ctr. *Work:* Pasadena Art Mus, Calif; Times-Mirror Collection, Los Angeles; US Navy, Washington; Lytton Savings & Loan Collection, Los Angeles; Long Beach Mus Art, Calif. *Comn:* Murals, Air France, Los Angeles, 61, Balboa Yacht Club, 63 & Newport Bank, Calif, 71; Wells Fargo Bank, Costa Mesa, Calif, 78. *Exhib:* Corcoran Gallery, 54; Smithsonian Inst, 55; Oakland Art Mus, Calif, 64; solo exhibs, Newport Harbor, 72 & Gallerie Forma, El Salvador, 75; retrospective, Scripps Coll, 73 & (with catalog) Lang Gallery, 92; Southern California 100, Laguna Beach Mus Art, 77; California Photographers, Claremont Galleries, 78. *Teaching:* Prof emer art & chmn dept, Scripps Coll, 60-92, emer prof, 92-; prof emer art, Claremont Grad Sch, 70-92, emer prof, 92-; Cal Tech, 70-74. *Awards:* Purchase Award, Pasadena Art Mus, 58; Res Grant, Ford Found, 69; Nat Endowment Humanities Grant, 73. *Bibliog:* Bently Schaad (auth), The Realm of Contemporary Still Life Painting, 62 & Edmondson (auth), Printmaking, 72, Van Nostrand Reinhold. *Mem:* Calif Watercolor Soc; founding mem Los Angeles Printmaking Soc. *Media:* Collage, Mixed Media. *Specialty:* Contemp. *Publ:* Illusr, Aldous Huxley, Paris Rev, 62; Psychological Perspectives, C G Jung JG Jung Inst, 70; illusr, The Academic Bestiary, Wm Morrow, 74; auth, A Retrospective (catalog), Lake Gallery, Scripps Coll, 92; A Decade of Mixed Media & collage (catalog), Huntington Beach Art Ctr, 2001. *Mailing Add:* 690 Cuprien Way Laguna Beach CA 92651

DARTON, CHRISTOPHER
PAINTER
b New York, NY, Dec 9, 45. *Study:* New York Inst Technol, BFA, 69; Pratt Inst Grad Sch, MFA, 71. *Exhib:* Daniel Weinberg, San Francisco, Calif, 79; Mary Boone Gallery, 80. *Media:* Acrylic Paint. *Publ:* Auth, Matter as subject, Arts Mag, 11/77. *Mailing Add:* 9 E 16th St 4th Fl New York NY 10003-3189

DARTS, DAVID
DESIGNER, ADMINISTRATOR
Work: Pirate Box, featured in over 100 international online and print publications, including New Scientist, Ars Technical, and Wired Italia. *Pos:* Chair, department of art and art professions, NY Univ, Steinhardt Sch of Culture, Edu, and Human Development, currently, dir NY Univ Steinhardt MA in Studio Art program, Berlin, Germany, currently; curatorial dir, Conflux, 2009-. *Publ:* Research and writings about contemporary art, edu, emerging technologies and creative citizenship have been published in a number of top peer-reviewed journals and books. *Mailing Add:* NY University Steinhardt Department of Art & Art Professions 34 Stuyvesant St New York NY 10003

DAS, RATINDRA
PAINTER, INSTRUCTOR
b India, US citizen. *Study:* Univ of Calcutta, BA; Univ Toronto, MA; Am Acad Art (studied with Irving Shapiro); Workshops with Robert E Wood, Frank Webb, Serge Hollerbach. *Work:* Miller Art Mus, Sturgeon Bay, Wis; DuPage Co Courthouse, Winfield, Ill; Kane Co Courthouse, Geneva, Ill; Amoco Corp, Chicago, Ill. *Exhib:* Transparent Watercolor Soc, Elmhurst Art Mus, Elmhurst, Ill, 2004; Places & Faces, Gray Gallery Quincy, Univ, Quincy, Ill, 2005; Paintings from Around, Bloomingdale Art Mus, Bloomingdale, Ill, 2005; Transparent Watercolor, Kankakee Co Mus, Kankakee, Ill, 2005-2007; Am Watercolor Soc Ann, Salmagundi Club, NY, 2005-2007, 2010; Images of Mexico, Efren Gonzalez Gallery, Ajijic, Mex, 2006 & 2007; First Invitational Exhib Contemp Int Watermedia Masters, 2007; 2nd Invitational exhib, Contemp Int Watermedia Masters, 2010; 1st Shanghai Zhujia Jiao Int Watercolor Biennial Exhib, 2010. *Teaching:* Instr, Independent Teaching Workshops (throughout country & Mex). *Awards:* Louis Kaep Award, Am Watercolor Soc, 2004; Fred Albrecht Award, Am Watercolor Soc, 2005; Paul Schwartz Mem Award, Am Watercolor Soc, 2006; Mary and Maxwell Desser Memorial award, Am Watercolor Soc, 2011; Jan Gary & Wm Gorman Memorial award, Am Watercolor Soc, 2013. *Mem:* Am Watercolor Soc (signature mem, dolphin fellow); Nat Watercolor Soc, (signature mem); Watercolor West, (signature mem); Transparent Watercolor Soc Am, (master status, signature mem); Ariz Watercolor Asn (signature mem); Jiangsu Watercolor Research Inst, (hon mem), Nanjing, China; Rocky Mountain Nat Watermedia Asn. *Media:* Watercolor. *Specialty:* 2 and 3 dimensional artwork. *Interests:* travel. *Publ:* Contribr, Strengthen your Paintings by Dynamic Composition (B), Northlight Publ, 94; contribr, Best of Watercolor (B), Rockport Publ, 97; contribr, The Artistic Touch 3 (B), Creative Art Press, 99; auth, The Artists Mag (Art), 2001 & Watercolor Magic (Art), 2005, F E W Publ; Painting a Personal Reality (film), Creative Catalyst Video Production; article, Watercolor Mag, winter 2010; article, Watercolor Artist, April 2010; Watercolor Instructional Book, 2013; Watercolor Beyond Obvious Reality?. *Dealer:* Blue Dolphin Gallery Ephraim WI; Ajijic Mex; Diane Pearl Gallery; Mullaly's 128 Gallery Elk Rapids Mich; Li Fine Art Gallery Singapore. *Mailing Add:* 1938 Berkshire Wheaton IL 60189

DASENBROCK, DORIS (NANCY) VOSS
DESIGNER, PAINTER
b Horicon, Wis, Nov 6, 1939. *Study:* Wis State Univ, Oshkosh, BS, 62; Fla State Univ, Tallahassee, MFA, 67; Univ Md, College Park, BS, 89. *Work:* Fla State Univ Fine Arts Collection, Tallahassee; Mus Art, Ft Wayne, Ind; US House Rep, Washington, DC. *Comn:* Contemp design, St Matthew's Episcopal Church, St Petersburg, 69; altar, Bowie, Md, 70, stained glass designs, 79, All Saints Lutheran Church, Bowie, Md. *Exhib:* Am Acad Arts & Lett, NY, 69 & 70; West Bend Gallery Fine Art, Wis, 76; St Paul Mus Art, Minn, 77; Tweed Mus Art, Duluth, Minn, 77; South Alleghenies Mus, Loretto, Pa, 78; Mus Tex Tech Univ, Lubbock, 78; Fed Bldg, Washington, DC, 79. *Collection Arranged:* Artists Today Traveling Exhib, Prince George's Col, Marlboro Gallery, 79; Photography 79, Capital Ctr Gallery, 79. *Pos:* Exhib specialist, Capital Park Planning Comn, Riverdale, Md, 78-79; designer & illusr, Sterling Inst, Washington, DC, 79; media designer & coordr, Am Genetics Corp, Bethesda, Md, 79-; dir advert, GTCO Corp, Rockville, Md, 85-87, advert & mktg consult, 87-. *Teaching:* Instr, Montgomery Col, Takoma Park, Md, 69-70; instr, Bowie State Col, Md, 75-76, George Mason Univ, Fairfac, Va, 78-79. *Awards:* Childe Hassom Purchase Award, Am Acad Arts & Lett, 69; Art Purchase Award, Benedictine Corp, 76; Award Excellence, Simpson Paper Co, 80. *Bibliog:* Brian Abbott (auth), Artist profile, Bowie Blade, Md, 6/3/76. *Mem:* Washington Women's Art Ctr; Women's Caucus Art; Artists Equity Asn; Md Fedn Art; Southern Watercolor Soc. *Media:* Watercolor, Oil; Pen & Ink. *Publ:* Illusr, Probing the physical world: Excursions, Fla State Univ, Tallahassee, 67; Air Conditioning - Refrigeration and Heating, Nat Radio Inst, Washington, DC, 73; Householder's Appliance Repair Course, McGraw-Hill, 74; Job Assessment and Career Development Guide, Sterling Inst, 79; Photography, McGraw-Hill, CEC, 88. *Dealer:* Jansson Art Gallery Rte 6A Barnstable MA 02637. *Mailing Add:* 1407 Pennington Ln Bowie MD 20716-1829

DASH, ROBERT
PAINTER
b New York, NY, June 8, 1934. *Work:* Brooklyn Mus, NY; Hirshhorn Mus, Washington; Pittsburgh Mus Art; Joslyn Art Mus, Omaha, Nebr; Philadelphia Mus Art; Parrish Mus, Southhampton, NY; Heckscher Mus, Huntington, NY; Guggenheim Mus; Boston Mus Fine Arts; Guildham (Easthampton) Yale Univ; MIT; The Nelson Gallery, Kansas City, KS; US Delegation to the United Nations. *Comn:* Centennial, Cheseborough-Pond's Inc. *Exhib:* Landscapes by Five Americans, Festival of Two Worlds, Mus Mod Art Traveling exhib, 66; The New Realism, Hirschl & Adler Galleries, NY, 81; New Acquisitions, Hirshhorn Mus, 83; Earthly Pleasures, Fort Wayne Mus, 88; Darkness, Guild Hall, East Hampton, 91; Irreverence, Int Monetary Fund, Washington, 94; ACA Galleries, 2001; Berrie Art Ctr, 2003; and others. *Pos:* Writer, bi-weekly column, East Hampton Star. *Teaching:* Adj prof advan painting, spring 70, 75, 77 & 81 & Master Wkshp, 85 & 94, Southampton Col; vis prof, State Univ NY, Stony Brook, 88. *Awards:* New York Times, 10 Best Garden Books, 2001; and others. *Bibliog:* An artist's garden, House & Garden, 87; Erica Lennard (auth), Madison Cox, 93; Peter Beales (auth), Visions of Roses, 96. *Mem:* Madoo Conservancy (founder & pres); Nature Conservancy (trustee); Peconic Land Trust (adv); Garden Conservancy Am (founder); NY Horticultural Soc. *Media:* Oils, Pastels. *Collection:* Am Mission to the UN. *Publ:* Notes from Madoo, Houghton-Mifflin, 2000. *Dealer:* Mark Borghi. *Mailing Add:* 618 Sagg Main St PO Box 362 Sagaponack NY 11962

DASKALOFF, GYORGY
PAINTER
b Sofia, Bulgaria, May 15, 1923; US citizen. *Study:* Acad Fine Arts, Sofia, grad. *Work:* Metrop Mus Art, NY; Nat Mus, Sofia; Royal Libr, Brussels, Belg; Butler Inst Am Art, Youngstown, Ohio. *Comn:* Mural, comn by ARA, Ann Arbor, Mich; portrait of Judge Theodor Levin, Detroit Bar Asn, 71; An American Family (mural), comn by Amos Cahan, NY, 73. *Exhib:* Bulgarian Art in Berlin, 58, Moscow, 59 & Prague, 59; Int Biennial Graphic Arts, Ljubliana, 59; Int Exhib Graphics, Leipzig, 60; Comparisons, Paris, 65-67. *Awards:* First Prize for Graphics, Bulgaria, 54 & 59. *Bibliog:* Pierre Rouve (auth), article, Arts Rev, London, 6/3/61; L L Sosset (auth), article, Les Beaux Arts, Brussels, 5/6/65; Pierre Lubecker (auth), article, Politiken, Copenhagen, 5/25/67. *Media:* Oil. *Mailing Add:* 14 Cooper Ln East Hampton NY 11937-2220

DASKALOPOULOS, DIMITRIS
COLLECTOR
b Athens, Greece, 1957. *Study:* Athens Sch Mgmt, BA, 1979; Northwestern Univ, Chicago, MBA, 1981. *Pos:* Chmn & chief exec officer, Delta Holdings (now Vivartia); chmn, Delta Dairy & Delta Ice Cream; vice chmn, Gen Frozen Foods. *Awards:* Named one of Top 200 Collectors, ARTnews mag, 2009-13. *Mem:* Fedn Greek Industries (bd mem); Fedn Hellenic Food Industries (chmn); Nat Agricultural Policy Coun; Am-Hellenic CofC (bd mem); Asn Young Entrepreneurs Greece; Greek Mgmt Asn; Greek Inst Mgmt; European Ice Cream Asn; European Round Table Industrialists. *Collection:* Contemporary art, large-scale installations; sculpture, drawings, collage, film and video. *Mailing Add:* Hellenic Federation of Enterprises Xenofontos 5 Syntagma Athens 105 57 Greece

DASS, DEAN ALLEN
PRINTMAKER, PAINTER
b Hampton, Iowa, Nov 16, 1955. *Study:* Univ Northern Iowa, Cedar Falls, BA, 78; Tyler Sch Art, Temple Univ, MFA, 80. *Work:* Va Mus Fine Arts; Kans State Univ; Univ Nebr; Univ Dallas; Brooklyn Mus Art; Philadelphia Mus Art; Walker Art Ctr, Minneapolis, Minn; Alderman Libr, Univ Va. *Exhib:* Nat Print Exhib, 81 & Artist as Printmaker, 83, Brooklyn Mus, NY; New Acquisitions, Walker Art Gallery,

Minneapolis, 86; solo exhibs, Dolan Maxwell Gallery, Philadelphia, 86 & 89, Projects & Portfolios, Brooklyn Mus, 89, Danville Mus, Va, 90 & Schmidt/Dean Gallery, Philadelphia, 91 & 96, Galleria Harmonia, Jyvaskyla, Finland, 97 & 2001, Univ Wyo Art Mus, 98, Schmidt Dean Gallery, Philadelphia, 96, 99 & 2001, 3A Gallery, San Francisco, Calif, 2000, Les Yeux Du Monde, Charlottesville, Va, 2001 & Univ Akron, 2003; Bradford Biennial, Eng, 89; Graphic Triennial, Alvar Aalto Mus, Finland, 90; 1708 Gallery, Richmond, Va, 90; Int Print Biennial, Maastricht, The Neth, 93; Univ Ala, Tuscaloosa, 95; Creativa Graphica, Alvar Aalto Mus, Finland. *Teaching:* Instr printmaking & drawing, Kutztown Univ, 83-84; asst prof, Univ Va, Charlottesville, 85-90, assoc prof, 91-, prof, 98-. *Awards:* Purchase Award, Charlotte Printmakers Soc, NC, 83; Artist's Fel, Pa Coun Arts, 85; Va Prize in Printmaking, Va Comn Arts, 88. *Bibliog:* Jukka Yli-Lassila (auth), Rakkaus, Joka Kypsyy, Keskisuomalainen, 6/1/97; Elina Puranen (auth), Uusien Ulottuvuuksien Loytoretki, Keskisuomalainen, 3/9/98; Martin Lammon (auth), Arts & Letters, fall 99; Faye Hirsch (auth), Art on Paper, 3-4/2000; Eliz Sutton (auth), 64 Mag, 4/2001. *Mem:* Mid Am Print Coun. *Media:* Oil, Print. *Publ:* Auth, Mineral Light, Journey to the Self, New Literary Hist, 95; Ed, The Land of Wandering; ed, The New World. *Dealer:* Schmidt Dean Gallery Philadelphia PA. *Mailing Add:* Univ Va 990 Allendale Dr Charlottesville VA 22901-9228

DATER, JUDY
PHOTOGRAPHER, WRITER

b Hollywood, Calif, June 21, 1941. *Study:* Univ Calif, Los Angeles, 59-62; San Francisco State Univ, BA, 63, MA, 66. *Work:* Addison Gallery Am Art, Phillips Acad, Andover, Mass; Fed Reserve Bank, San Francisco & Mus Mod Art, San Francisco; Int Ctr Photog, Metrop Mus Art & Mus Mod Art, NY; Boston Mus Fine Arts, Mass; Libr Congress, Washington, DC; and many others; Fogg Art Mus, Harvard Univ, Cambridge, Mass; Int Ctr Photog, NY. *Exhib:* Solo exhibs, Oakland Mus, Calif, 74, San Francisco Mus Mod Art, Calif, 84, Matsuya Dept Store, Ginza, Tokyo, Japan, 92, Int Ctr Photog, NY, 94, Galeries Arlesiennes, 25th Recontres Int de la Photog d'Arles, France, 94, Calif Coll Arts & Crafts, Oakland, 96 & Judy Dater Photographs, Fotogaleria del Treato General San Martin, Buenos Aires, Argentina; Photogs of Women, 72 & Mirrors & Windows (with book), Mus Mod Art, NY, traveling, 78, Photog in Am (with book), 74 & Suburban Home Life: Tracking the Am Dream (with catalog), Whitney Mus Am Art, NY, 89; Pvt Realities: Recent Am Photog (with book), Boston Mus Fine Arts, 74; Women in Photog: An Historical Survey (with book), traveling, 75, Faces Photographed (with catalog), From the Permanent Collection, 84 & Photog in California 1945-1980 (with book), traveling, San Francisco Mus Mod Art, 84; Photo Facts & Opinions (with book), Addison Gallery Am Art, Andover, Mass, 81; Subjective Vision (with catalog), The Lucinda W Bunnen Collection of Photogs, 83 & First Person Singular: Self-Portrait Photog 1840-1987 (with catalog), High Mus, Atlanta, Ga, 88; The Art of California, Selections from the Steinman Collection, 84 & Picturing California (with book), Oakland Mus, Calif, 89; Self as Subject, Honolulu Acad Art, Hawaii, 85; Reclaiming Paradise (with catalog), Tweed Mus Art, Duluth, Minn, traveling, 87; Meaning at the Crossroads: The Portrait in Photog (with catalog), Bowdoin Coll Mus Art, Brunswick, Maine, 94; Cycles (traveling show), Los Angeles Co Munic Hall, 94-95; Choices, Smith Anderson Galleries, Palo Alto, Calif, 96; A History of Women Photographers, Akron Art Mus, Ohio, 97; Collection, Int Ctr Photog, NY, 97. *Collection Arranged:* Imogen Cunningham: A Portrait Traveling Exhib, (auth, catalog), NY Graphic Soc, 79. *Pos:* Freelance artist/photogr, self-employed, currently. *Teaching:* Instr, Univ Calif, San Francisco, 66-74, San Francisco Art Inst, 74-78, 92 & 94, Int Ctr Photog, New York, 87-90, San Jose City Col, 96- & Univ Calif, Berkeley, 96-; guest instr, Kansas City Art Inst, 85; lectr & workshop leader throughout the US, Europe & Japan. *Awards:* Nat Endowment Arts Fel, 76 & 88; J S Guggenheim Mem Found fel, 78; Indiv Artists Grant, Marin Arts Coun, 87. *Bibliog:* Image, George Eastman House, Int Mus Photog & Film, vol 37, nos 1 & 2, 94; History of Photography, Kinsey Inst & Erotic Photog, vol 18, no 1, Spring 94; American Photo, vol V, no 4, 7-8/94; plus many others. *Mem:* San Francisco Camerawork; Soc Photog Educ. *Publ:* Auth, Imogen Cunningham: A Portrait, New York Graphic Soc, Boston, Mass, 79; coauth, Judy Dater: Twenty Years, Univ Ariz Press, 86; Body & Soul: Ten American Women, Hill & Co, Boston, Mass, 88; Cycles, Kodansha, Tokyo, Japan, 92; Cycles, Curatorial Assistance, Inc, Pasadena, Calif, 94; plus many others. *Dealer:* Smith Anderson Ed 440 Pepper St Palo Alto CA 94306. *Mailing Add:* 2430 5th St No J Berkeley CA 94710

DAUB, MATTHEW FORREST
PAINTER, GRAPHIC ARTIST

b New York, NY, Aug 29, 1951. *Study:* Southern Ill Univ, Carbondale, BA, 81, MFA, 84. *Work:* Metrop Mus Art & Mus City, NY; Evansville Mus Arts & Sci, Ind; Mitchell Mus, Mt Vernon, Ill; Sheldon Swope Art Mus, Terre Haute, Ind; Reading Public Mus, Pa. *Comn:* Four Seasons Hotel; Jackson, Wy. *Exhib:* Solo exhibs, Evansville Mus Arts & Sci, Ind, 83, Sherry French Gallery, NY, 84, 86, 88, 91 & 93, Jan Cicero Gallery, Chicago, Ill, 87, 89, Evansville Mus Arts & Sci, Ind, 94, Owensboro Mus Fine Art, Ky, 95, Sheldon Swope Art Mus, Terre Haute, Ind, 95, Headley Whitney Mus, Lexington, Ky, 95 & Louisville Art Asn, Ky, 95, ACA Galleries, 2011, 2013; Exactitude: New Acquisitions, Met Mus Art, NY, 87-89; Trains & Planes: The Influence of Locomotion in Am Painting, Nat Acad Scis, Washington, 89 & 90; Art and the Law, 92, 95, 96; Am Acad Arts & Lett Invitational (painting & sculpture), NY, 96; MB Mod Gallery, NY, 99; Demuth Mus, Lancaster, Pa, 2000; Reading Pub Mus, Pa, 2001; Sheltered, Lafaette Col, Easton, Pa, 2005; Imaging Industry: Pa Coal & Steel, Lebanon Valley Col, Annville, Pa, 2006; Visions of the Susquehanna, Lancaster Mus Art, 2006; ACA Galleries, 2011, 2013; Nat Acad Design, NY, 2011; Allentown Art Mus, 2013, 2014. *Teaching:* Prof fine arts, Kutztown Univ Pa, 87-. *Awards:* Purchase Awards, 35th & 36th Ann Mid-States Art Exhib, Evansville Mus, 82 & 83; Ill Arts Coun Fel, 86; Pollock-Krasner Fel, 92. *Bibliog:* Dan Wood (auth), The Craft of Drawing, Harcourt Brace Javonovich; Gerrit Henry (auth), Signs of the Times (catalog essay), American Watercolors, Engagement Calendar, Metrop Mus Art, 91; David Dewey (auth), The Watercolor Book. *Media:* Watercolor, Conte Crayon. *Publ:* Auth, The watercolor page, Am Artist, 82; Carolyn Plochmann: A Charmed Vision, Evansville Mus Arts & Sci, 90; Carolyn Plochman, Am Artist, 90. *Dealer:* ACA Gallery NY. *Mailing Add:* 237 Dreibelbis Station Rd Lenhartsville PA 19534

DAUGHERTY, MICHAEL F
EDUCATOR, SCULPTOR

b Seattle, Wash, Sept 30, 1942. *Study:* Univ Wash, Seattle, 60-62; Univ Barcelona, Spain, 64-65; Univ Wash, Seattle, BA (sculpture), 69; Univ Tenn, Knoxville, MFA (sculpture), 71. *Comn:* Outdoor fountains, comn by Walter H Stevens, Knoxville, 70, Genevieve Stoughton, Oak Ridge, 71, Alvin Rotenberg, Baton Rouge, 73, Janice Sachse, Baton Rouge, 74 & Derwood Facundus, Baton Rouge, 76. *Exhib:* 16th Joslyn Biennial, Joslyn Art Mus, Omaha, Nebr, 80; Nat Drawing and Sculpture Exhib, Del Mar Art Gallery, Corpus Christi, Tex, 81; Nat Sculpture Exhib, Westwood Ctr Arts, Los Angeles, Calif, 81; Biennial Five State Exhib, Fine Arts Gallery, Port Arthur, Tex, 81; Art for Arts Sake, Contemp Arts Ctr, New Orleans, La, 81; and many others. *Teaching:* Asst, Univ Tenn, 69-71; instr, Art Ctr, Oak Ridge, Tenn, 70; assoc prof sculpture, La State Univ, 71-. *Awards:* Purchase Award, Tenn Sculpture 1970, Tenn Arts Comn, 71; Purchase Award, 7th Ann Mobile Art Exhib, Mobile, Ala, 72; Second Place Award, Biennial Five State Exhib, Port Arthur, Tex. *Mem:* Southern Asn Sculptors; Coll Art Asn; Int Sculpture Ctr; Southeastern Coll Art Asn. *Dealer:* Adelle M Taylor Gallery 3317 McKinney Ave Dallas TX 75204

DAUN, JOSEPH
ADMINISTRATOR

b Miami, Fla, Sept 11, 1967. *Study:* Fla State Univ, BFA, 1990; Univ Texas, San Antonio, MFA, 1994. *Exhib:* Work exhibited in numerous art galleries and spaces across the United States, including Alexandre Hogue Gallery, Univ Tulsa, 2008, Legion Arts at CSPS, Cedar Rapids, 2008, Diverse Works, Houston Texas, 2009; one person exhibitions: Hallwalls Contemporary Art Ctr, Buffalo, NY, 621 Gallery, Tallahassee, Fla, Texas A&M Univ, Corpus Christie. *Collection Arranged:* University and private collections include Univ of Texas, San Antonio and the Univ of Central Oklahoma. *Pos:* Art residency, ArtPace, San Antonio. *Teaching:* New York State Col of Ceramics, Alfred Univ, NY, co-chair Freshman Found program, formerly; Georgetown Col, Kentucky, asst prof, formerly, chair art department, formerly, gallery dir, formerly; chair art department, Univ Central Oklahoma, 2003-05; department head, Art, Texas A&M Univ, Commerce, currently. *Mailing Add:* Texas A&M Univ Department of Art A104 2600 S Neal Commerce TX 75428

DAUTREUIL, LINDA TRAPPEY
PAINTER

b New Iberia, La, Mar 16, 1948. *Study:* Univ La, Lafayette, BA, 69, BFA, 84. *Work:* Univ Art Mus, Lafayette, La; Ochsner Found Collection, New Orleans Mus Art. *Exhib:* Louisiana Open, Masur Mus Art, Monroe, La, 94; Artists Alliance, Lafayette, La, 95; Artists Ann, Slidell Cult Art Ctr, Slidell, La, 98; Project Harmony, Contemp Arts Ctr, New Orleans, 98; Laredo Nat, Laredo Ctr for Arts, Laredo, Tex, 99; Living in Louisiana, Alexandria Mus Art, 99; La Women's Caucus Invitational, St Tammany Art Asn, Covington, La, 2000. *Pos:* asst to dir, Univ Art Mus, Lafayette, La, 90-92, cur of educ, 93-94. *Awards:* First Place Mixed Media, Laredo Center for Arts, 99; Best of Show, St Tammany Art Asn, 97; First Place Painting, South Cobb Arts Alliance, 98. *Bibliog:* Douglas Maccash (auth), Landscapes and Surreal Paintings, Times Picayune, 5/2000; Judith Bonner (auth), New Orleans Art Rev, 6/2000; Brian Flafaye (auth), Times of Acadiana, 9/2000. *Mem:* St Tammany Art Asn; Contemp Art Ctr; Baton Rouge Gallery; La Arts Partnership. *Media:* Acrylic. *Dealer:* Brunner Gallery 522 N New Hampshire St Covington LA 70433; Lowe Gallery 75 Bennett St Atlanta GA 30309. *Mailing Add:* 251 S Jahncke Ave Covington LA 70433

DAVENPORT, BILL
SCULPTOR

b Greenfield, Mass, 1962. *Study:* RI Sch Design, BFA (sculpture), 86; Univ Mass, MFA (sculpture), 90. *Work:* Miss Liberty on the Bayou (installation), Buffalo Bayou Artpark, Houston, Tex, 92; Leopard and Dubuffet Rocks (installation), Houston Art League Sculpture Court, Houston, Tex, 93. *Exhib:* Solo exhib, Viewing Room, Houston, Tex, 94, Inman Gallery, Houston, Tex, 94, 95, 97 & 99, Cristinerose Gallery, NY, 97, Art with Cats, Good/Bad Art Collective, Denton, Tex, 97, Sala Diaz, San Antonio, Tex, 98 & Angstrom Gallery, Dallas, Tex, 99; The Home Show (with catalog), Univ Tex Art Gallery, San Antonio, 95; Continental Discourse: Art of Mexico and the United States Today (with catalog), San Antonio Mus Art, Tex, 95; New Work III, Barry Whistler Gallery, Dallas, Tex, 95; Chateau Marmot Int Art Fair, Los Angeles, Calif, 95; Tex Art Celebration, Cullen Ctr, Houston, Tex, 96; Los Angeles Nat Art Exhib, Spanish Kitchen Gallery, 96; Buttered Side Up: 3 Houston Abstractionists, Arlington Mus Art, Tex, 96; Five Year Anniversary Exhib, Inman Gallery, Houston, Tex, 96; The Big Show, Lawndale Art & Performance Ctr, Houston, Tex, 96; The Red Hot End of Summer Show, Barry Whistler Gallery, Dallas, Tex, 96; The Incredible Shrinking Art Show, Small Projs Gallery, Univ Houston, Tex, 96; Buttered Side Up, Hallwalls Contemp Arts Ctr, Buffalo, NY, 96 & Koffler Gallery, Toronto, Ont, Can, 96; Disiptoey, Strategies For Abstraction, Angstrom Gallery, Dallas, Tex, 97; Women's Work, Arlington Mus Art, Tex, 97; Equal Pay: A Labor Exchange, Revolution Summer Art Space, Houston, Tex, 97; New Work: Gallery Artists, Inman Gallery, Houston, Tex, 97 & 98; Thread, Cristinerose Gallery, NY, 97; Material World: Artists and their Materials, Austin Mus Art, Tex, 98; Extremely Shorts, Aurora Picture Show, Houston, Tex, 98; Blunt Object, Smart Mus Art, Univ Chicago, Ill, 98; Unravelled, City Gallery at Chastain, Atlanta, Ga, 98; Nirvana, British Coun Window Gallery, Prague, Czech Repub, 98; The Texas Show, ABC No Rio, NY, 98; Artistic Centers: Houston-Galveston, Galveston Arts Ctr, Tex, 98; Hot Spots, Weatherspoon Art Gallery, Univ NC, Greensboro, 99; Threshold, Kohler Arts Ctr, Sheboygan, Wis, 99; By Design, Contemp Art Collective, Las Vegas, Nev, 99. *Awards:* Core Fel, Glassell Sch Art, Mus Fine Arts, Houston, Tex, 90-92; Individual Artist Grant, Cult Arts Coun Houston & Harris Co, 96; Louis Comfort Tiffany Grant, 97; Artadia Art Grant, 2010. *Bibliog:* Stephanie Cash (auth), Artworld: Awards, Art Am, 4/98; Jan Estep (auth), Blunt object, New Art Examiner, 12/98-1/99; Alan G Artner (auth), Blunt object works embrace popular culture, Chicago Tribune, 10/2/98. *Mailing Add:* c/o Barry Whistler Gallery 2909B Canton St Dallas TX 75226

DAVENPORT, NANCY
PHOTOGRAPHER
b Vancouver, BC, Can. *Study:* York Univ, Toronto, BFA, 1989; Sch Visual Arts, New York, MFA, 1991. *Exhib:* Solo exhibs, YYZ Artist's Outlet, Toronto, Can, 1992, Gracie Mansion Gallery, New York, 1994, Nicole Klasbrun Gallery, New York, 1995, 2001, 2004 & 2008, Linda Kirkland Gallery, New York, 1996, La Centrale, Montreal, 1997, Mercer Union, Toronto, 1998, Corchoran Gallery, NJCU, 1999, The Floating Gallery, Winnipeg, 2000, Mead Gallery, Univ Warwick, Coventry, 2005, Art Gallery Windsor, 2009; The Auto Erotic Object, Hunter College Gallery, New York, 1992; All the World's a Stage, Marsh Fogel Gallery, East Hampton, NY, 1993; More than Real, Gallery 400, Univ Ill, 1994; Desiring Authors, Enveloping Myths, Bernard Toale Gallery, Boston, 1995; Black and White, Linda Kirkland Gallery, New York, 1997; Picture/Image/World, Lemmerman Gallery, 1998; It's a Cruel World, White Columns, New York, 2000; Lifelike, Rockford Art Mus, 2001; 25th Bienal de Sao Paulo: Metrop Iconographies, Sao Paulo, 2002; Urban Dramas, de Singel International Kunstcentrum, Antwerp, 2003; Workers, JFK Performing Arts Ctr, Washington DC, 2005; 10th Int Istanbul Biennial, Istanbul, Turkey, 2007; ReConstitutions, DHC/Art Fondation pour l'art Contemporain, Montreal, 2008; Workers Leaving the Factory, Art Gallery of Windsor, Ontario, 2009. *Awards:* Can Coun Short Term Grant, 1993-94; Can Coun Visual Arts Grant, 1995 & 1999; Anonymous was a Woman Found Award, 2003; Visual Arts Writing Grant, Andy Warhol Found, 2007; DHC/Art Grant, DHC/Art, Montreal, 2008; Abigail Cohen Rome Prize, Am Acad in Rome, 2010. *Bibliog:* Elizabeth Hess (auth), Dirty Laundry, The Village Voice, 5/12/1992; Hamish Buchanan (auth), Elegant Explosion, Xtra Mag, 7/23/1993; Deborah Bright (auth), Photography on the Front Lines, Exposure, Vol 29, 1994; Kelly Devine Thomas (auth), Aftershocks, ArtNews, 11/2001; Larry Rohter (auth), A Tilt Toward the Third World at the Sao Paul Biennial, NY Times, 5/272002; John Zeaman (auth), What you See is Not Necessarily What you Get, The Record, 11/282004; Jonathan Griffin (auth), Campus, Frieze, 2/2006. *Mailing Add:* c/o Nicole Klagsburn Gallery 526 W 26th St Rm 213 New York NY 10001

DAVENPORT, RAY
PAINTER
b Rockville Centre, NY, May 5, 1926. *Study:* Pratt Inst, cert (advert design), 48; Univ SC, Columbia, 80. *Work:* SC Permanent Collection, Columbia; Ronald Reagan Libr; Stone Container Corp, Chicago, Ill; SC Nat Bank, Sumter & Columbia; Chernoff/Silver & Assocs, Columbia, SC. *Comn:* Oil painting, First Fed Savings & Loan, Sumter, SC, 75; oil painting, Black River Elec Coop, 89. *Exhib:* 14th Hunter Ann, Hunter Mus Art, 74; SC Watercolor Soc First Ann, Columbia Mus Art, SC, 78; Am Artists First Nat Art Competition, Circle Galleries, Soho, NY, 78; Allied Artists Am 70th & 72nd Ann, Nat Arts Club, NY, 83 & 85; Capricorn Galleries, Bethesda, Md, 90; JF Kennedy Ctr Performing Arts, Washington, DC, 91; Retrospective Exhib, Sumter Gallery Art, Sumter, SC, 2004; and others. *Teaching:* Central Carolina Technical College, Oil Painting Instr, 66-73. *Awards:* Atto Newer Award, Allied Artists Am 70th Ann, 83 & Gloria Benson Stacks Award, 72nd Ann, 85; Merit Award, Modern Maturity National Seasoned Eye Competition, 90; Best in Show, SC State Fair, Columbia, SC, 92; Best in Show, Milton Baline Award, 41st Mystic Art Festival, 98. *Mem:* Nat Soc Painters Casein & Acrylic; Allied Artists Am; Guild SC Artists (secy & treas, 77-78, pres, 88-89); mem with excellence, SC Watercolor Soc. *Media:* Acrylic, Oil, Lithography. *Dealer:* City Art Gallery Columbia SC; The Spencer Art Galleries Charleston SC. *Mailing Add:* 274 Keels Rd Sumter SC 29154

DAVENPORT, REBECCA READ
PAINTER, LECTURER
b Alexandria, Va, June 29, 1943. *Study:* Pratt Inst, Brooklyn, NY, BFA (with honors), 1966-70; Univ NC, Greensboro, MFA, 1970-73. *Work:* Baltimore Mus Art, Md; Corcoran Gallery Art, Washington, DC; Chrysler Mus, Norfolk, Va; Federal Reserve Bank, Richmond, Va. *Exhib:* Selected 20th Century Nudes, Harold Reed Gallery, NY, 1978; Mus d'Art Mod de la Villes de Paris, France, 1978; Taft Menagerie, Taft Mus, Cincinnati, Ohio, 1980; Images of the 70's, Corcoran Gallery Art, Washington, DC, 1980; Inside Out, Newport Harbor Art Mus, Newport Beach, Calif, 1981; Real, Really Real, Super Real, San Antonio Mus, Tex, 1981; Contemp Am Realism Since 60, Pa Acad Fine Art, Philadelphia, Pa, 1981. *Awards:* Cert of Distinction, Va Mus, Richmond, 1973; Third Gold Palette, IV Festival IX de la Peinture, Cagnes Sur Mir, France, 1977; Artist Fel, Nat Endowment Arts, 1979. *Bibliog:* Theodore F Wolff (auth), Solving the mystery of the missing subject, Christian Sci Monitor, 10/1/1980; Aubyn Kendall (ed), Real, Really Real, Super Real, San Antonio Mus Asn, 1981; Frank H Goodyear (auth), Contemporary American Realism Since 1960, New York Graphic Soc, 1981. *Media:* Oil. *Dealer:* Osuna Gallery 406 Seventh St NW Washington DC; Aberbach Fine Arts 988 Madison Ave New York NY. *Mailing Add:* 504 Scott St Beaufort SC 29902

DAVID, CYRIL FRANK
PAINTER
b London, Eng, July 13, 1920; US citizen. *Work:* Metrop Mus Art, New York, NY; Nat Mus Am Art, Washington, DC; Ark Art Ctr, Little Rock. *Exhib:* Art of Drawing, Staempfli Gallery, NY, 80, 84-89; Members Selections, Corcoran Gallery Art, Washington, DC, 80; solo exhibs, Ark Art Ctr, 84 & 93, Staempfli Gallery, NY, 86 & Mus Art, Ft Lauderdale, Fla, 96. *Awards:* Nat Endowment Arts Fel, 80; Best Miniature Work, Guild Hall Mus, 82; Creative Artists Pub Serv Fel, NY State Coun Arts, 83. *Media:* Graphite, Paper. *Mailing Add:* PO Box 100 Sag Harbor NY 11963

DAVID, IVO
PAINTER, WRITER
b St Leucio del Sannio, Italy, Nov 22, 1934; US citizen. *Study:* Lyceum, cert, 52; Inst Fine Arts, 56; Int Acad Fine Arts Paestrum, Italy, 88; Acad Fine Arts & Lit Micenei, Italy, 89; Peastum Acad Fine Arts; Acad Fine Arts and Letters Micenel; Senator of Acad Fine Arts and Literature of Micenel, IT-. *Hon Degrees:* Fine Arts Peastum Acad, Italy; Fine Arts Acad, Micenei, Italy. *Work:* Museo Storico Royal Palace, Caserta, Italy; White House; Lupoli Nikko Art Collection Air Force Inc, Roma, Italy; Pa Fed Bank, Newark, NJ; Museo Dantesco Fortunato Bellonzi, Case di Dante, Pescara, Italy; Vero Beach Township, Fla. *Comn:* Triborough Bridge, Seton Hall Univ, Ctr Ital Cult, South Orange, NJ, 67; Tompkins Park, H Rohback Art Coll Inc, NY, 75; mural, Fed & V Visceglia Corp, Newark, NJ, 75; mural, Union Ctr Realty Corp, NJ, 81; Protest Against the Wars, Union Ctr Realty Corp, NJ, 93; oil canvas, Vero Becah, Fla; and others. *Exhib:* Centenary Unification Italy, Royal Palace Gallery Mus, Caserta, Italy, 57; solo exhibs, Crespi Art Gallery, NY, 64, Les Salon des Nations a Paris, 84, Garden State Art Ctr, Holmdel, NJ, 91 & Pen & Brush Art Gallery, NY, 91; State of the Art 1993, New Eng Fine Arts Inst, Boston, 93; Les Malamut Art Gallery, NJ, 93; Fountain Ponte's Reception, NJ, 95; NY Univ, NY, 97; Musee Des Beaux Arts, D'Unet, France, 98; Inst Int D'Arts Plastiques, Bordeaux, France, 98; Biennale Int Arte Contemp, Florence, Italy, 2003, 2005, 2007, 2009, 2011; A E Backus Mus and Gallery of Art, Fort Pierce, Fla, 2007-2011; Vero Beach Art Club, Fla, 2008-2011, Special Guest Exhib: Art by the Sea, 2010-2011; Backus Mus and Gallery, 2010, 2011, 2012; Daley Co Real Estate, Orchid Island, Vero Beach, 2012. *Pos:* Planning designer, Candeub, Fleissig & Assocs, Newark, NJ, 63-65; chief art designer, Archit Fed Bus Ctr, Newark, NJ, 65-73; art consult, Williams & London, Newark, NJ, 73-75; art dir, Follia, NY, 86-94 & Ponte Mag, NJ, 92-. *Teaching:* Instr art & design, Gen Serv Admin, Air Force, Caserta, Italy, 58-61; western art, Ctr Ital Cult, Seton Hall Univ, 62-65; painting, Holy Face Monastery Ital Cult, 65-68. *Awards:* Cert Merit Award, New Art Fusionism '56, Biog Inst, Cambridge, Eng; Gold Medal & Award Cert, Acad Miceney, Italy, 92; Gold Plate Award, Acad Int Fine Arts, Micenei, Italy, 97; 1st Prize of Poster and Banner Art Competition, Hibiscus Festival, Downtown Vero Beach Farmers Market, Vero Beach, Fla, 2009; 1st prize oil on canvas, Hibiscus Festival, Downtown Vero Beach Farmers Market, Vero Beach, Fla, 2009; 1st Place Painting, Ft Pierce Yellow House, Vero Beach Mus Art, 24th Ann, 2012; 1st Place Acrylic award, Fort Pierce Yellow House, Vero Beach Art Club, 2012. *Bibliog:* Gizzi, Rossi & Tanelli (auths), the Davids fusionism, NY Mag, 83; Mario Fratti (auth), The manifest of fusionism of David, Follia Mag, 89; R Beltrame (auth), David & Dante, Reportage Art, Italy, 92; Ivo David; An Italian-American Painter in America, La Follia Di NY, 89 Ed. *Mem:* Fed Art Asn NJ; Clifton NJ Art Asn; Academie des Lettre et des Arts du Perigord, Bordeaux, France; Acad Fine Arts & Sci Paestum, Italy; Acad Arts, Letters & Sci, Italy; A E Backus Mus and Gallery of Art, Fort Pierce, Fla; Vero Beach Art Club Asn, Vero Beach, Fla; Mus Fine Art, Vero Beach, Fla; and others. *Media:* Oil, Mixed Media. *Res:* How men can be free through Art. *Publ:* Auth, Manifest of Fusionism '56, Libr Cong, Washington, DC, 89; Salvador Dali my teacher, Reportage, Italy, 92; Analysis & critique, S Scutella's Orchidea D Ponte, ItAm, USA, 92; The Fusionism of Ivo David A Search for Freedom in Art-Edition of Ponte Italo-Americano, NY; Memories of an Artist, Libr Congress, DC. *Mailing Add:* 3662 2nd Pl SW Vero Beach FL 32968

DAVID-WEILL, HELENE & MICHEL ALEXANDRE
COLLECTOR
b France, Nov 23, 1932. *Study:* Inst Scis Politiques, 1953. *Pos:* Partner, Lazard Freres & co, 1961-65, New York, 77-95, Lazard Freres & Cie, 1965-, sr partner, 1975-, chmn, Lazard Freres & co, LLC, 1995-; vchmn, Groupe Danone, 1970; bd dirs, Eurazeo, 1972-, pres, 2003; trustee, Metrop Mus Art, New York, 1985-; bd dirs, Publicis Groupe SA, 1990; bd gov, Soc NY Hosp, currently. *Awards:* Named one of Top 200 Collectors, ARTnews mag, 2004-13. *Mem:* Acad des Beaux-Arts; Academie des Beaux-Arts; Brook Club, New York; Knickerbocker Club, New York. *Collection:* 17th to 19th-century French painting; contemporary art. *Mailing Add:* Lazard Freres & Co LLC 30 Rockefeller Plaza 59th fl New York NY 10112

DAVIDEK, STEFAN
PAINTER, PRINTMAKER
b Flint, Mich, May 15, 1924. *Study:* Flint Inst Arts, with Jaroslav Brozik; Art Students League, with Morris Kantor; Cranbrook Acad, with Fred Mitchell. *Work:* Detroit Inst Arts, Mich; Flint Inst Arts, Mich; Muskegon Community Coll & Hackley Art Mus, Mich; Albion Col; McClaren Hosp, Flint, Mich; Women's League, Univ Mich; Prince Corp, Holland, Mich; Genesee Co Courthouse Murals, Flint, Mich. *Comn:* interior murals, Zehnders, Frankenmuth, Mich, 80 & 81; chapel wall, MaClaren Hosp, Flint, Mich; ceiling decoration, St Paul, Flint, Mich; Chancel mural, St Lorenz, Frankenmuth, Mich; ceiling decoration, Sunset Mem Chapel, Flint, Mich; mosaics, St Luke's, Flint, Mich; St Roberts, Flushing, Mich; Carol Church II; Pierson Childrens Mus, Sloan Mus, Flint, Mich; Genesse County Courthouse; any many others. *Exhib:* Flint Ann, 46-90; Butler Midyear Show, 59; Pa Acad Fine Art 9; Buckham Art Space, Flint, Mich; Alma Coll Print Ann, 89-94; Mich Directions, Flint Area Artists; Flint Inst of Arts. *Pos:* Artist, Printmaker, Decorative Consultant. *Teaching:* Instr Arts, Haystack Mtn Crafts, Summer Art Programs. *Awards:* Founder's Prize, 61 & Lou R Maxon Prize, Detroit Inst Art; Purchase Award, Alma Print Show, Mich, 91; Purchase Award, Alma Print Show, 93-95; Purchase Award, Flint Inst Arts. *Media:* Oil, Watercolor, Serigraphy, Silkscreen. *Dealer:* Armstrong DeGraff Fine Art Inc 403 Water St On Main PO Box 1025 Saugatuck MI 49453. *Mailing Add:* 5391 W Coldwater Rd Flint MI 48504-1025

DAVIDOVICH, JAIME
PAINTER, VIDEO ARTIST
b Buenos Aires, Arg, Sept 27, 1936; US citizen. *Study:* Nat Coll, Buenos Aires, Arg, 54-58; Univ Uruguay, 59-61; Sch Visual Arts, New York, 63. *Work:* Mus Mod Art, Buenos Aires, Arg; Mus Belas Artes, Rio de Janiero, Brazil; Dayton Art Inst, Ohio; Everson Mus Art, Syracuse, NY; Akron Art Inst, Akron, Ohio; Mus Mod Art, New York; Mus Reina Sofia, Madrid, Spain. *Comn:* Carroll Wall Proj, John Carroll Univ, Cleveland, Ohio, 71. *Exhib:* Solo exhib, Retrospective 1962-1972, Drake Univ, Des Moines, Iowa, 71, Am Mus of Moving Image, 90, Mus Modern Art, Buenos Aires, 99 & Lehman Coll, New York, 2000; Exp in Art & Technol Show, Lake Erie Coll, Ohio, 71; Five Artists, New Gallery, Cleveland, Ohio, 72; Arte de Sistemas, Mus Mod Art, Buenos Aires & Mus Fine Arts, Santiago, Chile, 72; Akron Art Inst, Ohio, 72-73; Whitney Mus Am Art, New York, 76; Long Beach Mus Art, Los Angeles, 81; Ctr

Media Arts, Paris, France, 82; Video & Television Festival, Maastrich, The Neth, 82; TV on TV, Tex Tech Univ, 84; Exit Art, New York, 86; Lecagy/Legado, The Old State House, Hartford, Conn; Zocalo 1975-98, Mus Modern Art, Buenos Aires, 98; Painting in Real Time, Lehman Coll Art Gallery, New York, 99; The End: An 18 yr History of Exit Art, Exit Art, New York, 2000. *Pos:* Rep to US, DiTella Found Art Ctr, Buenos Aires, Arg, 65; founder & mem bd dir, New Orgn Visual Arts, Cleveland, Ohio, 72-73; pres, Artists Television Network, 77-83; bd dir, Artists Television Proj, Univ Iowa, 87; res fel, Sch Art & Art Hist, Univ Iowa, 87. *Teaching:* Prof painting, Sch Visual Arts, Bahia Blanca, Arg, 61-62. *Awards:* Grand Prize, Adhesive Tape Proj, Dayton Art Inst, Dayton, Ohio, 74; Creative Artists Pub Serv Prog grants, NY State Coun Arts, 75 & 82; Visual Arts Fels, Nat Endowment Arts, 78, 84 & 90; Video 81, San Francisco Video Festival, 81; Grantee, NEA Visual Art Fel, 84 & 90; Artist-in-residence, World Trade Ctr, New York, 2001. *Bibliog:* Ellen Stern (auth), The inner tube, New York Mag, 4/17/78; TV finds its place among fine art, Plain Dealer, 5/29/80; Video artists still seek a showplace for their work, NY Times, 6-19-83; 16 Autumn, Real Life Mag, 86; and others. *Dealer:* Mitchell Algus Gallery New York NY

DAVIDOW, JOAN CARLIN
DIRECTOR, CURATOR
b New York, NY, July 27, 1940. *Study:* Jacksonville Univ, BA, 62; Univ Fla, MFA, 81. *Exhib:* Dallas Mus Art, 89; Tex Meets New York - Facing the Millennium, The Song Remains the Same, 96; Moving Pictures, 2005; Reality Bytes: digitized narratives, 2007. *Collection Arranged:* Spanish Remnants: Border Real & Imagined, 92; Digital Dramas: Computer-Generated Photog & Video, 95; Tex Meets NY: Facing the Millenium, The Song Remains the Same, 96; Space: Archit + Installation, 97; A Cool Show: abstract paintings, 98; Siting Sculpture, 2003. *Pos:* Art critic, KERA Pub Radio N Tex, 84-91; actg asst cur contemp art, Dallas Mus Art, 89-91; dir, Arlington Mus Art, 91-2000, Dallas Ctr Contemp Art, 2001-; juror, Mitchell A Wilder Pub Design Awards Competition, Tex Asn Mus, 89, 97, 42d Ann Invitational, 2002, Longview Mus Fine Arts, Tex, 2002, Mayfaire-by-the-Lake, Polk Mus Art, Lakeland, Fla, 2004; panel, Art & Design Program, DART, Victory Light Rail Sta, Design Site-Specific Com, 2000, Artist Selection, Waterworks, Dallas Cultural Affairs, Pub Works, Dallas, 2004; In the Beginning, the Women's Museum, & Jewish Women Artist's Network (JWAN), 2008. *Awards:* KATIE Award finalist, Best Specialty Reporting, Dallas Press Club, 85; Review Panelist, Tex Comn Arts, 92-93; National Lifetime Achievement Award, 2008; President's Award, 2008; Women's Caucus for Art, 2008. *Bibliog:* Sheila Taylor Wells (auth), Joan of art, Ft Worth Star-Telegram, 96; Catherine Cuellar (auth), High profile, Dallas Morning News, 98; Michael Ennis (auth), Joan of art, Tex Monthly, 98; Michael Ennis (auth), National Spotlight: Unlikely Upstart, Art News, 2000; Steve Carter (auth), The Radar Art, Dallas Modern Luxury, 2006; Perspective: Joan Davidow, Tribeza, 2007. *Mem:* Tex Fine Arts Asn (bd mem, 87-97); Dallas Artists Res & Exhib (found bd, 89-91); Emergency Artists Survival League (found bd, 92-96); Art Table. *Res:* Tex contemp art. *Publ:* Auth, Texas Figurative Drawings (exhib catalog), 89, Celia Alvarez Munoz: Abriendo Tierra Breaking Ground (exhib catalog), 90 & Harry Geffert: Bronze Allegories (exhib catalog), 90, Dallas Mus Art; Texas Realism, with a Twist: Paintings & Drawings (exhib catalog), 95 & Women's Work: Themes Associated with the Women's Realm (exhib catalog), 97, Arlington Mus Art

DAVIDSON, DAVID ISAAC
PAINTER
b Chicago, Ill, Nov, 22, 1925. *Study:* Sch Art Inst Chicago, BAE, 48; Ind State, MS, 49; Am Army Univ, Bamburg, Ger, 45-46. *Work:* Ellis Island, US Justice Dept Immigration, New York; Cole Taylor Bank, Chicago; State of Ill Gallery, Chicago. *Comn:* Portrait Mayor Richard J Daley, Daley Coll, Chicago, Ill, 77; State Capitol Mural Finalist, State Ill, Springfield, 89. *Exhib:* 54th Ann Chicago Show, Art Inst Chicago, Ill, 50; Artists for Peace, Peace Mus, Chicago, Ill, 83; Ill State Capital Murals, Ill State Mus, Springfield, Ill, 89; Solo exhibs, Artemnisia Gallery, Chicago, Ill, 84, Renner Gallery Blackburn Univ, Carlinsville, Ill, 90 & Dog House, Joy Horwitz Gallery, Chicago, Ill, 90; Images Am Immigration, Nationwide Touring Exhib, NY & Los Angeles, 91-93; Art & Law, Nationwide Touring Exhib, Chicago, Reno & Pittsburg, 95-96; Retrospective, Harper Coll, 2006. *Teaching:* Instr adv, painting & drawing, Chicago Pub Sch, Chicago, Ill, 50-85; lectr, portrait artist, Chicago Conv & Tourism Bur, Chicago, Ill, 77-83; instr, portrait, life drawing, Evanston Art Ctr, Evanston, Ill, 87-89; guest lectr, Harper Coll, 2006. *Awards:* Ill Art Fel, Fel Competition, State Ill, 85; State Capitol Mural Finalist, Murals, Ill State Mus, 89; Purchase Prize, Images of Am Immigration, Dept Justice, 91. *Bibliog:* Harold Haydon (auth), Artist for Peace, Chicago Sun Times, 5/13/83; Michael Bonesteel (auth), David Davidson Exhib, Evanston Rev Pioneer Press, 10/3/85; Lee Krantz (ed), Chicago Art Rev, Am References Inc, 89-91. *Mem:* Sch of Art Inst Chicago Alumni Asn. *Media:* Oil painting, Instructor, Educator, Watercolor. *Interests:* Golf, art history. *Collection:* Olivier d'Estaintot, France; Jack Rimland, Chicago. *Mailing Add:* 1 The Court of Harborside Apt Northbrook IL 60062

DAVIDSON, HERBERT LAURENCE
PAINTER, PRINTMAKER
b Green Bay, Wis, Sept 6, 1930. *Study:* Art Inst Chicago, Anna Raymond Foreign Traveling Fel, 56. *Work:* Kemper Ins Co; Playboy Mag; Pullman Bank of Chicago; Rahr West Mus, Manitowoc, Wis; Walter Heller Corp, Chicago; Signode Corp, Glenview, Ill. *Exhib:* Butler Inst Am Art, Youngstown, Ohio, 65; Alta Coll of Art, Calgary, 76; Mendel Art Gallery, Saskatchewan, Can, 77; Chicago Cult Ctr, 79; Syracuse Univ, Lubin Hall, 80; Sao Paolo Mus, Brazil; and others. *Bibliog:* Article, Am Artist Mag, 7/80. *Mem:* The Arts Club Chicago. *Media:* Oil; Lithography. *Dealer:* Wadle Galleries 128 W Palace Santa Fe NM

DAVIDSON, IAN J
COLLECTOR, PATRON
b Toronto, Ont, July 21, 1925. *Study:* Univ BC, BA;. *Pos:* Dir, Vancouver Art Gallery, 70-74; mem adv art comt, Can Coun, 75-; dir, Community Arts Coun, Vancouver. *Teaching:* Archit at Univ Toronto, Univ BC, Carleton Univ & Bezalel Acad, Jerusalem, Israel. *Awards:* Awards in archit in every major design award prog. *Mem:* Asn Royal Can Acad Art; fel Royal Archit Inst Can. *Interests:* Commissioning original works by major artists in the non-objective and conceptual fields. *Mailing Add:* 405-1600 Howe St Vancouver BC V6Z 2L9 Canada

DAVIDSON, MAXWELL, III
DEALER
b New York, NY, Feb 8, 1939. *Study:* Williams Col, BA (art hist), 61. *Pos:* Owner, Maxwell Davidson Gallery, 76-. *Mem:* Art Dealers Asn Am. *Specialty:* 19th & 20th century masters & contemp painters. *Mailing Add:* Maxwell Davidson Gallery 724 Fifth Ave 4th Fl New York NY 10019

DAVIES, HARRY CLAYTON
PAINTER, PHOTOGRAPHER
b Wilmington, Del, Mar 3, 1940. *Study:* Columbia Univ, BS, 66, MA, 69; Adelphi Univ, MA, 80. *Work:* Adelphi Univ, Garden City, NY; Wash Co Mus Fine Art, Hagerstown, Md; Fine Arts Mus Long Island, NY; Sci Mus Long Island; Islip Art Mus, NY. *Exhib:* Fine Arts Mus Long Island, Hempstead, 81; 2nd Invitational Show, Long Island Univ, Greenvale, 82; Eight by Ten, Wash Co Mus Fine Arts, Hagerstown, Md, 86; Heckscher Mus, Huntington, NY, 90; Manhattan Ctr Gallery, New York 96; Giordano Gallery, Dowling Coll, Oakdale, NY, 97; Islip Art Mus, East Islip, NY, 99; Adelphi Univ, Garden City, NY, 2004; Boothbay Region Art Found, 2006-2007. *Teaching:* Prof painting, drawing, & theory, chmn dept art, Adelphi Univ, 81-2004, prof emer, 2004. *Bibliog:* Long Island Looks Ahead (interview), WSNL Channel 67, Smithtown, NY, 6/82. *Mem:* William Morris Soc, London, Eng; Charles Rennie Mackintosh Soc, Glasgon, Scotland; Archit Inst Am; Royal Geographical Soc, London, Eng. *Media:* Acrylic, Oil. *Res:* Megalithic monuments of Britain & Ireland. *Interests:* Prehistoric art, archaeology. *Mailing Add:* 8 Locust Ln Brunswick ME 04011

DAVIES, HUGH MARLAIS
MUSEUM DIRECTOR, HISTORIAN
b Grahamstown, S Africa, Feb 12, 1948; Brit citizen. *Study:* Princeton Univ, AB, 1970, MFA, 1972, PhD, 1976. *Collection Arranged:* Artist & Fabricator (auth, catalog), 1975, Richard Fleischner (auth, catalog), 1977, Stephen Antonakos (auth, catalog), 1978, Sam Gilliam (auth, catalog), 1978, Al Souza (auth, catalog), 1979, John Walker (auth, catalog), 1979, George Trakas (auth, catalog), 1980, Prints of Barnett Newman (auth, catalog), 1983, Martin Puryear (coauth, catalog), 1984; at Univ Gallery, Univ Mass, Amherst; Sitings: Alice Aycock, Richard Fleischner, Mary Miss & George Trakas (auth, catalog), La Jolla Mus Contemp Art, 1986; Richard Long (auth, catalog), La Jolla Mus Contemp Art, 1989. *Pos:* Asst dir, Monumenta Int Sculpture Exhib, Newport, RI, 1974; dir & ceo, Univ Gallery, Univ Mass, Amherst, 1975-83, Mus Contemp Art San Diego, 1983-; adv coun dept art & archeology, Princeton Univ, 1989-; panel mem fed adv comt int exhibs, 1990-94; co-cur Whitney Mus Am Art Biennial, 2000. *Teaching:* Vis asst prof, Amherst Col, Mass, 1980-83. *Awards:* Nat Endowment Arts Fel, 1981-82 & 1995; Calif Arts Council Dirs Award, 2004; Panel Mem, GSA Art and Architecture Panel, 2010. *Mem:* Asn Art Mus Dirs (bd trustees 1994-2001, pres 1997-98); Coll Art Asn; Art Mus Asn Am; Friends Art & Preservation in Embassies (profl adv com 1998-). *Res:* 20th century Am & European painting, sculpture, photog, design & archit. *Publ:* Coauth (with Horton Davies), Sacred Art in a Secular Century, Liturgical Press; The Prints of Barnett Newman, Barnett Newman Found, 1983; coauth, Francis Bacon, Abbeville, 1986; auth, 25 Years of Installation Art, Mus Contemp Art, San Diego, winter 1997; Francis Bacon the Papal Portraits of 1953, 2001; and others; contribr, Interviewing Bacon, 1973, Francis Bacon-New Studies, Centenary Essay, ed Martin Harrison, Steidl, Germany, 2009. *Mailing Add:* c/o Mus Contemp Art San Diego 700 Prospect St La Jolla CA 92037-4228

DAVIES, KENNETH SOUTHWORTH
PAINTER, INSTRUCTOR
b New Bedford, Mass, Dec 20, 1925. *Study:* Mass Sch Art, Boston; Yale Sch Fine Arts, BFA, 50. *Hon Degrees:* New Eng Sch Law, Boston, Hon DFA. *Work:* Wadsworth Atheneum, Hartford, Conn; New Britain Mus Am Art, Conn; Detroit Inst Arts; Springfield Mus Fine Arts, Mass; Univ Nebr, Lincoln. *Comn:* US Postage Stamp commemorative for pharmacy, US Postal Serv, 72, chemistry, 76; Metrop Opera, 83. *Exhib:* Am Symbolic Realism, London, Eng, 50; Carnegie Inst Int, 52; Whitney Mus Am Art Ann, 52; Univ Ill Ann, 52; 25 yr retrospective exhib, New Britain Mus Am Art, 71; Retrospective at 80, Washington Co Mus Fine Arts, 2005-2006; New Bedford Whaling Mus, 2006. *Teaching:* Sr Portfolio, Paier Coll Art, Hamden, Conn, 53-81, vis prof & dean emer, 81-91. *Awards:* Louis Comfort Tiffany scholar, 50; Purchase Award, Berkshire Mus, Pittsfield & Springfield Mus, Mass, 50. *Mem:* Conn Acad Fine Arts (coun mem, 70, pres, 74-76). *Media:* Oil. *Specialty:* Realistic Painting & Sculpture. *Publ:* Auth, Painting Sharp Focus Still Lifes, 75 & Ken Davies-Artist at Work, 78, Watson-Guptill; auth, Ken Davies American Realist, 2009. *Mailing Add:* PO Box 526 Madison CT 06443

DAVILA, MARITZA
PRINTMAKER
b Santurce, PR, Apr 18, 1952. *Study:* Univ PR, BA, 74; Pratt Graphics Ctr, with Andrew Stasick & Margot Lovejoy, 74, Pratt Inst, MFA, 77. *Work:* Nat Libr France, Paris; Mus of the Univ PR; Maine Printmaking Workshop, Vinalhaven; Ateneo Puertorriqueno, San Juan; Taller Galeria Fort, Cadaques, Spain; Univ Cincinnati, Mid-Am Print Coun; Southern Graphics Coun Arch, Univ Miss; Mus of Art, Warsaw, Poland; Museo del Barrio, New York; Southern Graphics Coun, Archives, Univ of

Miss; Nat Libr Cong, Washington, DC. *Comn:* Reimpression of Thomas Hogarth plate, comn by AG Burkhart, Memphis, 85, 88 & 92; Book Art, comn by Mr & Mrs Reissman. *Exhib:* Solo exhibs, Art Ctr, Ark State Univ, 2000; Taproots Sch Arts, St Louis, Mo, 2001; Two Artists: Joysmith Gallery, Memphis, Tenn, 2003; Montreal Int Miniature Print Biennial, Can, 2002; Side by Side, Memphis Brooks Mus of Art, 2002; Mid Am Print Coun, Juried Mem Exhib, Denver Int Airport, 2002; First Contact Invitational Nontoxic Exhib, Gracefield Art Ctr, Dumfries, Scotland, 2002; Solar Plate Revolution Portfolio, Southern Graphics Coun, Gallery at First & Second Church Unitarian Universalist, Boston; Whitney Art Works, Greenport, NY, and other locations, 2003; Delta Nat Small Prints Exhib, Bradbury Gallery, Ark State Univ, Jonesboro, Ark, 2003; Memphis Coll of Arts Faculty Exhib, Memphis Tenn; SC Stare Mus, Thresholds, Expressions of Art and Spiritual Life, Columbia, SC, 2003-2004. *Pos:* Dir, Atabeira Press; mgr, Printmaking Workshop. *Teaching:* Instr art, Am Mus Natural Hist, NY, 79-81; artist-in-residence, Bd Educ, NY, 80; Prof of fine Arts, Memphis Col of Art, Tenn, 1982-; 2002-2003 bd mem, Latino Memphis, Inc. *Awards:* Purchase Award, Moravian Col, Bethlehem, Pa, 84; Award Printmaking, Ateneo Puertorriqueno, 85; Printmaking Medal Hon, Nat Asn Women Artists, 87; Prix de Dessin et Gravure Salon Int du Val d' Or a la Salle des Fetes d'Orval, France Asn Plastica Latina, 1996; Juror's Special Mention Pressed and Pulled VI Georgia Coll & State Univ, Milledgeville, 1997; Faculty Enrichment Award, Memphis Coll of Art, 1996, 1998, 2000, 2003-2004. *Bibliog:* Reuben Abruna (dir), Myths and Creations (film), New York Univ, 80; Davila to Conduct Workshop, Art Show at DSU Art Ctr, Bolival Commercial, Miss, 11/91; Fredric Koeppel Rev, Miss Coun Arts Fac Show, Commercial Appeal, 91. *Mem:* Los Angeles Printmaking Soc; Southern Graphic Coun; Mid Am Print Coun, 1998-; Memphis Childrens Adv Ctr, Visual Arts, comt for the Heart Auction. *Media:* Print Making. *Interests:* Music & Literature. *Publ:* Mario Alegre Barrios (auth), Etreel mito y la memoria, Por Dentro, SJPR El Nuevo Dia, 96; Art & Letters: Jour of Contemp Culture, Maritza Davila, Featured Artist, Georgia Coll & State Univ, Milledgeville, Georgia, Issue One Spring 1999, p 80 (cover art and eight works in color); Henkes, Robert, Latin Am Women Artists of the United States: The Works of 33 Twentieth-Century Women, 12/1998 McFarland & Co Inc, Publ. *Dealer:* Albers Fine Arts Gallery 1027 Yates Rd Suite 101 Memphis TN 38119; Galeria Botello Hato Rey Puerto Rico. *Mailing Add:* 3233 N Waynoka Circle Memphis TN 38111-3610

DAVIS, BRAD (BRADLEY) DARIUS
PAINTER
b Duluth, Minn, Apr 24, 1942. *Study:* St Olaf Col, 61; Univ Chicago, 62; Art Inst Chicago, 63; Univ Minn, BA, 66; Hunter Col, 70. *Work:* Neue Galerie, Sammlung Ludwig, Aachen, WGer; Walker Art Ctr, Minneapolis; Whitney Mus Am Art, Mus Mod Art, NY; Saarland Mus, Saarbracken, WGer; and others. *Exhib:* Biennial, 64 & two-person show, 66, Walker Art Ctr, Minneapolis; Ann Exhib, 72 & Am Drawings '63-'73, 73, Whitney Mus Am Art; solo exhibs, Holly Solomon Gallery, NY, 75, 79, 81 & 83; The New Bestiary: Animal Imagery in Contemp Art, Inst Contemp Art, Va Mus, Richmond, 81; Friends of Corcoran Gallery 20th Anniversary Exhib, Corcoran Gallery Art, 81; New Work in Black and White, 81 & A Penthouse Aviary, 81, Art Lending Serv, Mus Mod Art, NY; Decoration and Representation, Alta Coll Art Gallery, Can, 82; New Decorative Works from the Collection of Norma & William Roth, Loch Haven Art Ctr, Orlando & Jacksonville Art Mus, Fla, 83; New Decorative Art, Berkshire Mus, Pittsfield, Mass, 83; Back to the USA Traveling Exhib, Kunstmus, Lucerne, Switz, Rheinische Landesmus, Bonn & Kunstverein, Stuttgart, Ger, 83-84; Landscape/Cityscape, Art Gallery, State Univ NY Potsdam, 78; Pattern & Decoration, Sewall Art Gallery, Rice Univ, 78; Green Magic, Rutgers Univ Gallery, 79; Dekor, Kunstverein, Mannheim, Ger, 80; Am Drawings, Venice Biennale, Italy, 80; and many others. *Awards:* First Prize & Spec Jury Award, Minneapolis Inst Art Biennial, 65; Second Prize & Purchase Prize, Walker Art Ctr, 66. *Bibliog:* Alexandra Anderson (auth), Clay gardens, Portfolio, 3-4/82; Klaus Ahrens (auth), Schreie und Flustern, Stern Mag, Hamburg, Ger, 5/83; Klaus Honnef, New York Aktuelle, Kunstforum Int, 5/83. *Media:* Mixed

DAVIS, CHRISTINE
PHOTOGRAPHER
b Vancouver, BC, 1962. *Study:* York Univ, Toronto, BFA, 84. *Work:* Bibliot Nat Paris; Bruce Peel Spec Collection, Edmonton, AB; Can Mus Contemp Photog, Ottawa; Mus Beaux-Arts, Montreal; Nat Libr Can, Ottawa. *Comn:* Women's Law Asn Ont, Law Soc Upper Can, Osgoode Hall, Toronto, 2000. *Exhib:* Collectif Generation, Livres d'Artistes, Victoria & Albert Mus, 90; The Body-Le Corps (exhib catalog), Kunsthalle Bielefeld, Ger, 94; Fixing the Gaze (exhib catalog), Olga Korper Gallery, Toronto, 94, Contours, 97, New Photog, 2002; Press/Enter (exhib catalog), The Power Plant, Toronto, 95; Perspective '95 (exhib catalog), Art Gallery Ont, Toronto, 95; Rekalde Sala Expos, Bilbao, Spain, 96; solo exhibs, Macdonald Stewart Art Ctr (exhib catalog), Guelph, Ont, 93, Olga Korper Gallery, Toronto, 95, 98, 2000, Galeria Palma Dotze, Viafranca, Spain, 96 & Galeria Helga de Alvear, Madrid, 96, 99, Power Plant, Toronto, 2000, Mus des Beaux-Arts de Montreal, 2003. *Pos:* Ed collective mem, Border/lines, 84-88. *Bibliog:* News (auth), The Sibylline eye: North American women photographers, Flash Art, 1-2/91; Chantal Pontbriand (auth), De la violence et du language, Parachute, No 71, 93; Deirdre Hanna, Poetic perspective opens AGO doors to new talent, NOW, Toronto, 11/30/95. *Mem:* Founding mem, Pub Access Collective (ed, 86-); YYZ Artist's Outlet (bd dir, 89-). *Publ:* Coauth (with Nicole Brossard), Typhon Dru, Collectif Generation, Paris, 90; auth, Hyperbole, Texts, No 6, fall 91; Artists' Project, C Mag, No 33, spring 92; Work in progress, Nuevas Visiones/Nuevas Pasiones, Santander, 1999; 20thc Lexicon, ed Christine Davis & Ken Allen, PUBLIC, 19/20, 2000

DAVIS, D JACK
EDUCATOR, ADMINISTRATOR
b Canton, Tex, May 17, 1938. *Study:* Baylor Univ, BA, 59, MA, 61; Univ Minn, PhD, 66, studies with Reid Hastie, Paul Torrance & Malcolm Myers. *Pos:* Assoc dir & dir evaluation, Aesthetic Educ Prog, Arts in Gen Educ Proj, Cemrel Inc, St Louis, Mo, 69-71; dir grad progs, Univ NTex, Denton, 71-75 & chair art dept, 76-83; ed, Studies in Art Educ, Nat Art Educ Asn, 75-77; vprovost & assoc vpres acad affairs, Univ NTex, Denton, 83-93; dean, Sch Visual Arts, 93-2004; dir, N Tex Inst for Educators on Visual Arts, 2004-2011. *Teaching:* Instr art, Wayland Coll, Plainview, Tex, 61-63; prof, Tex Tech Univ, 65-69 & Univ NTex, Denton, 1971-2011, prof emeritus, 2011-. *Awards:* Distinguished Fel, 89 & Lowenfeld Award, 90, Nat Art Educ Asn; Tex Art Educator Year, 91; Nat Art Educator of the Yr, 2005; Regents Faculty lectr, Univ North Tex, 2009; Distinguished Scv with the Profession, Nat Art Edn Assn, 2010; Lifetime Achievement award, Ctr Advancement & Study of Early Tex Art, 2011. *Mem:* Life mem Nat Art Educ Asn (chmn higher educ div, 73-75); Tex Art Educ Asn (pres, 87-89). *Res:* Res trends in art educ. *Publ:* Ed, Behavioral Emphasis in Art Education, Nat Art Educ Asn, 75; The visual arts: A classroom myth or an accountable program?, Nat Asn Sec Sch Principals Bulletin, 11/79; auth, Research on Teacher Education, Teacher Education in Visual Arts, Macmillan, 90; An Experiment in School/Museum//University Collaboration, Metrop Univs, 94; coauth, Professional Conferences for Art Educators: A Pilgrimage to Excellence, 97; Doctor Study in art educ at Univ of N Tex, 2001; W Reid Hastie: A Visionary for Research in Art Educ, Studies in Art Educ, 2009; Looking Back & Looking Forward: Creativity Research in Art Edn, 2014. *Mailing Add:* 4932 Westbriar Dr Fort Worth TX 76109

DAVIS, DARWIN R
MUSEUM DIRECTOR, ADMINISTRATOR
b Goodrich, Mich, Sept 5, 1943. *Study:* Mich State Univ, BA, 65, MA, 68. *Pos:* Dir, Saginaw Art Mus, 72-74 & Art Ctr Battle Creek, 74-80; exec dir, Krasl Art Ctr, 81-. *Mem:* Am Asn Mus; Mich Mus Asn (vpres, 75-77, pres, 77-79, treas, 81-82). *Mailing Add:* 707 Lake Blvd Saint Joseph MI 49085

DAVIS, ELLEN N
HISTORIAN
b Hackensack, NJ, July 20, 1937. *Study:* Inst Fine Arts, NY Univ, with Peter H Von Blanckenhagen, PhD, 73. *Teaching:* Assoc prof ancient art hist, Queens Col, City Univ New York, 66-. *Awards:* Art Award, Coun Grad Studies. *Mem:* Archaeol Inst Am; New York Soc (pres, 80-83); New York Bronze Age Colloq. *Res:* Aegean metalworking, painting and connections with Egypt. *Publ:* Auth, The Vapheio cups: one Minoan & one Mycenean?, Art Bulletin LVI, 74; The icongraphy off the Thera Ship Fresco, In: Greek Art and Icongraphy, Univ Wis Press, 83; Youth and age in the Thera Frescoes, Am J Archaeol, 86; The Cycladic Style of the Thera Frescoes, Thera and the Aegean World, 90

DAVIS, JAMES GRANBERRY
PAINTER
b Springfield, Mo, 1931. *Study:* Wichita State Univ, Kansas, Mo, BFA, 54, MFA, 60. *Work:* Metrop Mus Art, NY; Nat Mus Am Art, Washington, DC; Univ Ariz Mus Art, Tucson; Ariz State Univ Mus Art, Tempe; Mulvane Art Ctr, Kans. *Comn:* Large painting, Container Corp Am, NY, 65. *Exhib:* Arizona's Finest, Tempe Art Ctr, 82; 38th Corcoran Biennial, Washington, DC, 83; Solo exhibs, Germans Van Eck Gallery, NY, 84, Basil Art Fair, Switz, 85, Hans Redmann Gallery, Berlin, WGer, 86, 88 & 89, Marilyn Fine Arts, Santa Fe, NMex, 87, Shoshana Wayne Gallery, Santa Monica, Calif, 87, Etherton Gallery, Tucson, Ariz, 87 & Andrea Ross Gallery, Santa Monica, Calif, 89; Modern Am Printmaking, Am-Haus, Ger, 85; The Neo-Figure, Riva Yares Gallery, Scottsdale, 85; Artists Who Teach, Nat Mus Art, Washington, DC, 87; 25 Yr Retrospective, Tucson Mus Art, 88; Evidence, San Antonio Mus Art, Tex, 89; The Hunger Project, Scottsdale Ctr Arts, 89. *Teaching:* Assoc prof, Wichita State Univ, Kans, 59-62; instr painting & printmaking, Univ Mo, Columbia, 67-69; asst prof painting, Univ Ariz, Tucson, 79-70, assoc prof, 70-. *Awards:* Purchase Award, Kans Artists Ann, 62, Topeka Art Ctr, 66, Eastern Mich Univ, 68 & Tucson Art Ctr, 74. *Bibliog:* Anita Winegate (auth), James G Davis, Artspace, 1/79; Barbara Cortright (auth), Interview with James G Davis, Phoenix Mag, 1/80; Carol Cratoza (auth), James G Davis, Art Voices S, 3/80. *Media:* Oil; Lithography, Monotype. *Mailing Add:* Linda Vista Ranch PO Box 160 Oracle AZ 85623

DAVIS, JAMES ROBERT
CARTOONIST
b Marion, Ind, July 28, 1945. *Study:* Ball State Univ. *Hon Degrees:* Ball State Univ, LHD; Purdue Univ, DFA. *Pos:* Artist, Groves & Assoc Advert, Muncie, Ind, 68-69; asst to cartoonist, Tumbleweeds (comic strip), 69-78; adv bd, Calif Mus Cartoon Art, 85-; pres & Chief Exec Officer, Paws Inc - Garfield Corp, 78-. *Awards:* Emmy Awards for Writing Best Animated Special, 85 & CBS Prime Time Specials; Distinguished Alumni Award, Am Asn State Coll & Univ, 85; Nat Cartoonist Soc, Best Humor Strip, 1981 & 1985; Elzie Segar & Reuben Award for All Round Excellence, 85 & 90. *Mem:* Nat Cartoonists Soc; Newspaper Comics Coun. *Publ:* Auth, Garfield Mix & Match Storybook, 82 & Garfield the Knight in Shining Armor, 82, Random House; Garfield Takes the Cake, 82, The Garfield Treasury, 82 & Garfield Weighs In, 82, Ballantine. *Mailing Add:* c/o Paws Inc 5440 E County Rd 450 N Albany IN 47320

DAVIS, JAMES WESLEY
PAINTER, WRITER
b Los Angeles, Calif, Oct 9, 1940. *Study:* Calif Coll Arts & Crafts, BA (educ) & BFA; Univ Colo, MA & MFA (Inst Arts & Humanities Fel), 67. *Work:* Minn Mus Art; Ill State Mus; Alberta Coll Art; Mulvane Art Mus; Laguna Gloria Mus; and others. *Exhib:* Mid-Am 4, St Louis Art Mus & Nelson/Atkins Mus, 72; Smithsonian Inst Traveling Show, 73-74; Calgary Int Biennial, Alta Coll Art Gallery, 74; Mid-Year Ann, Butler Inst Am Art, 74 & 75; 19th Mid-South Biennial, Brooks Mem Gallery, 75; Irwin Collection, Kvannert Mus, 80; Watercolor USA, Springfield Mus, 85; 6th Alabama Works on Paper, Int Auburn Art Assoc, 85; Am Watercolors, Chateau de Tours, France, 87. *Pos:* Assoc Dean, College Creative Art & prof, art dept, San Francisco State Univ, 89-. *Teaching:* Instr painting & art hist, Univ Ark, 67-69; prof painting & drawing, Western Ill Univ, 69-81; vis prof, Univ Colo, 82; head art dept, E Tex State Univ, 80-83; chmn art dept, Ind State Univ, 88-89; dir, Inter-Arts Ctr, San Francisco State Univ, 89-. *Awards:* Sworovski Int Award, Sworovski of Belg, 67;

James D Phelan Award, 73. *Bibliog:* S W Semaj (auth), Memories, Structure, Vol 2, No 3; Alfred Frankenstein (auth), Visual, surreal acrobatics, San Francisco Chronicle, 1/74; Sylvia Brown (auth), Editorial highlights, City Mag, 2/16/74. *Mem:* Coll Art Asn Am. *Media:* Acrylic, Watercolor. *Publ:* Auth, Self-actualized sculpture, Sculpture Int, Vol 3, No 2; Unified drawing by means of hybrids and grids, Leonardo, Vol 5, No 1; Some perceptual considerations on Vermeer and op art, Studies in the 20th Century, 73; Revival in the slumbering cornfield, Art J, fall 74; On mounds, Studio Int, 4/74; Hybrid Culture: Mix-Art, Kendall Hunt Publ, 2007; Image as Idea: The Arts in Global Cultures, Kendall Hunt Publ, 2007. *Mailing Add:* 1541 Union St Alameda CA 94501

DAVIS, JAMIE
INSTALLATION SCULPTOR
Study: Univ Akron, BFA (Sculpture & Metalsmithing), 2003; Univ Mass Dartmouth, New Bedford, MFA (Sculpture), 2007. *Exhib:* Solo exhibs include Sculpture Ctr, Cleveland, 2005, LUV Artspace, Karlsruhe, Germany, 2006, Cleveland Mus Contemp Art, 2008; group exhibs include Glimpse Show, Gallery 244, New Bedford, Mass, 2005, Green, 2006. The Swap Show, 2006, Sculpture Survey, 2006; Into View, Cleveland State Univ, 2006; Boston Young Contemporaries, 2007. *Mailing Add:* Sculpture Ctr 1834 E 123rd St Cleveland OH 44106

DAVIS, JERROLD
PAINTER
b Chico, Calif, Nov 2, 1926. *Study:* Univ Calif, Berkeley, BA, 53, MA. *Work:* Carnegie Inst Int, Pittsburgh; Santa Barbara Mus Art, Calif; Los Angeles Mus Art; San Francisco Mus Art; Oakland Mus Art; and others. *Exhib:* Solo exhibs, Calif Palace Legion Hon, 60-64, Flint Art Inst, 64, Newport Harbor Art Mus, Newport Beach, Calif, 73 & retrospective, Richmond Art Ctr, Calif, 80; Especially for Children, Los Angeles Co Mus, 65; Univ Ariz, 67; Lytton Ctr, Los Angeles, 67 & 68; A Sense of Place, 74; and others. *Teaching:* Instr, Univ Calif, summer 67. *Awards:* Guggenheim Fel, 58-59; Am Fedn Arts-Ford Found artist-in-residence grant, Flint, Mich, 64; Prizes, Calif Palace Legion Hon, 60 & 62; and others

DAVIS, KEITH F
CURATOR, HISTORIAN
b Middletown, Conn, June 29, 1952. *Study:* Drew Univ, 70-72; Southern Ill Univ, BS (cinema & photog), 72-74; Univ NMex, MA (art hist), 79. *Collection Arranged:* Hallmark Photog Collection (Hallmark Cards Inc), from which many exhibs & publs have been produced. *Pos:* Intern, Int Mus Photog, Eastman House, Rochester, NY, 78-79; cur, Fine Art Collections, Hallmark Cards Inc, Kansas City, Mo, 79-; vis rsch prof art history, Univ Mo, Kansas City, 1995-. *Awards:* Beaumont Newhall Hist Photog Award, Univ NMex, 77; Nat Endowment Humanities Fel, 86-87. *Mem:* Soc Photographic Educ (bd dir, 84-87). *Res:* Hist of 19th & 20th century photog. *Publ:* contribr, auth, Photography in Nineteenth Century Am, Abrams, 91; An American Century of Photography: From Dry-Plate to Digital, 2d edit, Hallmark/Abrams, 99; contrib auth, Taken by Design: Photography at the Institute of Design, 1937-1971, Art Inst Chicago/Univ Chicago, 2002; American Horizons: The Photographs Art Sinabaugh, Hudson Hills, 04; contribr auth, Art Fredrick Sommer: Photography, Drawing, Collage, Yale Univ Press, 05. *Mailing Add:* 4525 Oak St Kansas City MO 64111

DAVIS, KIMBERLY BROOKE
GALLERY DIRECTOR, ART DEALER
b Los Angeles, Calif, Nov, 25, 1953. *Study:* Pratt Inst, BFA, 75. *Pos:* Admin asst, Inst Art & Urban Res, 75; admin asst, Guggenheim Mus, 76; assoc dir, Judith Selkowitz Fine Arts, 76-79; dir, Bernard Jacobson Gallery, Los Angeles, 79-84 & New York & Los Angeles, 83; dir, LA Louver Gallery, Venice, Calif, 85-. *Mem:* Fels Contemporary Art, Dir Circle, Moca, LA. *Specialty:* Painting & sculpture by leading Am & European contemp artists, fine art prints. *Mailing Add:* LA Louver Gallery 55 N Venice Blvd Venice CA 90291

DAVIS, L CLARICE
BOOK DEALER, ART LIBRARIAN
b Akron, Ohio, 1929. *Study:* Univ Akron, BA (fine arts), 55; Univ Calif, Los Angeles, MLS, 61, MA (art hist), 68. *Pos:* Chief librn, Los Angeles Co Mus Art, 63-68; owner & mgr, Davis Art Book Store & Gallery, Los Angeles, 71-79, partner, Davis & Schorr Art Books, 79-91, L Clarice Davis, Fine & Applied Art Books, 91-; actg unit head, Art Libr, Univ Calif, Los Angeles, 73-75; art reference librn, Beverly Hills Pub Libr, 88-94. *Teaching:* Asst prof mod art hist, Calif State Univ, Northridge, 61-63 & 68-69; lectr, Otis Art Inst, Los Angeles, 69-70. *Mem:* Art Libr Soc NAm; Antiquarian Booksellers Asn Am. *Specialty:* Out of print art books and exhibition catalogues. *Publ:* Contribr bibliog catalog, R B Kitaj, 65 & Peter Voulkos, Sculpture, 65, Los Angeles Co Mus Art; contribr introd, Pornography in Fine Art From Ancient Times, Los Angeles Elysium, 69; auth, Annuals of auction sales, Art Libr Soc NAm Newsletter, 12/76. *Mailing Add:* 6131 Atoll Ave Van Nuys CA 91401

DAVIS, LISA CORINNE
PAINTER, EDUCATOR
b Baltimore, Md, 1958. *Study:* Cornell Univ, Ithaca, NY, 76-78; Pratt Inst, Brooklyn, NY, Haskell Travel Fel, 79, BFA (painting, hons), 80; Hunter Col, NY, MFA (painting), 83; apprenticeships with painters Jennifer Bartlett, 79-82, Jack Tworkov, 82 & Elizabeth Murray, 81-82. *Work:* Mus Mod Art, NY; J Paul Getty Mus; Nat Mus Women Arts, Washington; Victoria & Albert Mus, London; Art Inst Chicago. *Exhib:* Solo exhibs, Second St Gallery, Charlottesville, Va, 94, Munic Gallery, Atlanta, 94, Halsey Gallery, Sch Arts, Coll Charleston, SC, 94, Dell Pryor Galleries, Detroit, 94, Proj Rm, Bronx Coun Arts, 97-98, ALJIRA, Ctr Contemp Art, Newark, NJ, 97-98, June Kelly Gallery, NY, 98, 00, Lehman Coll Art Gallery, 01, New Work, June Kelly Gallery, NY, 2002; Allegory and Identity, Visceglia Art Ctr, Caldwell Col, NJ, 96; Dell Pryor Galleries, Detroit, 96; Artist in the Marketplace Benefit Exhib, Bronx Mus Arts, NY, 96; The Sense of Touch, Ceres Gallery, NY, 97; Waxing Poetic: Encaustic Art in America, Montclair Mus Art, NJ, 99; Book Art 12: Artist's Books from teh Library and Research Center, Nat Mus Women in Arts, Washington, DC, 2000; Paper Remix, Gallery Dieu Donne, Papermill, NY, 2001; Cultural Collaging, Univ RI, 2002. *Teaching:* Artist-in-residence & instr art, Studio in a Sch, 90-92; instr art, Lehman Col, 91-92; adj fac drawing & 3-D design, Foundation Dept, Parsons Sch Design, 92, acad adv, 92-93, coordr design studio, 93 & Col Coun, 94-; instr drawing, Outreach Prog, Cooper Union Sch Art & Archit, 93-94; lectr, Moore Col Art, Philadelphia, 94, Col Charleston, SC, 94 & Art in Gen, NY, 95; instr drawing, Yale Univ, 95, prof, 97-; vis artist & lectr, Norfolk Summer Prog, 96; asst prof, Sch Art, Yale Univ, 1998-2004; asst prof, Hunter Col, 2004. *Awards:* Mid Atlantic Arts Found Regional Fel, 92; Fac Develop Grant, Parsons Sch Design, 93; Visual Artist Fel, Nat Endowment Arts, 95-96 & NY Found for Arts; Biennial Artists Award, Louis Comfort Tiffany Found, 2001; Yaddo Residency, 2002. *Bibliog:* Nicholas Drake (auth), "Transparent Brown" requires some thought, Post & Courier, 11/94; Abby Goodnough (auth), Personal responses to a page of history, NY Times, 6/96; Ken Johnson (auth), review, NY Times, 6/98. *Mem:* Art in Gen. *Publ:* Illusr, The Red Coat, Flockophobic Press, New York, 90; Birthmark (Simon Perchik, auth), Flockophobic Press, New York, 92. *Mailing Add:* 1717 Troutman St #215 Ridgewood NY 11385

DAVIS, MEREDITH J
GRAPHIC ARTIST, EDUCATOR
b Pittsburgh, Pa, May 15, 1948. *Study:* Pa State Univ, BS, 70, Md, 74; Cranbrook Acad Art, with Katherine & Michael McCoy, MFA, 75. *Work:* Mead Libr Ideas, Dayton, Ohio; Am Inst Graphic Arts, New York. *Exhib:* Am Inst Graphic Arts, New York, 75, 82-83, 85 & 88; Mead Ann Report Competition, New York, 80; Soc Typographic Arts, Women in Design, Chicago, 81 & 88; NY Art Dir Club, 81 & 83; NY Type Dir Club, 82-85 & 88; Am Asn Mus, 84 & 87; Ryder Gallery, Chicago, 85; Cranbrook: The New Discourse (with catalog), 94. *Pos:* Cur educ, Hunter Mus Art, 75-76; partner, Communication Design Inc, Richmond, Va, 79-89. *Teaching:* Prof commun arts & design, Va Commonwealth Univ, 76-89; prof graphic design, NC State Univ, dir grad prog, currently; Dir, PhD in Design. *Awards:* Excellence in Ann Report Design, Mead Libr Ideas, 81; Excellence Visual Commun, Designers Choice, Indust Design Mag, 82 & Creativity 13, NY Art Dir, 83; Gold Medalist, Wash AA Dirs, 85; Silver & Gold Medalist, Case Cover Competition, Washington, DC, 85; Choice Award, Asn Coll & Research Libr, 99; AIGA 2005 Nat Medal & Fel. *Bibliog:* Annual reports: Business as usual?, Art Direction Mag, 81. *Mem:* Graphic Design Educ Asn (pres, 86-88 & 92-94, vpres, 90-92, bd dir, 94-96); Am Ctr Design (bd dir, 90-96, pres, 96-2000, chmn bd, 98-2000); Am Inst Graphic Arts (bd dir, 95-98). *Publ:* Contribr, The role of education in research, Design J, 83; coauth, Design as a Catalyst for Learning, Asn Supv & Curric Develop, 98; Design-Based Education, Arts Educ Policy Rev, 98; Design in Education, Int Interior Design Asn, 98; Design and Social Responsibility, Jack Williamson (ed), 98; Design In Context: An Introduction to Graphic Design Theory, Thames & Hudson (in prep); and others. *Mailing Add:* NC State Univ Box 7701 Raleigh NC 27695

DAVIS, ROBERT
PAINTER
b New York, NY. *Study:* Parsons Sch Design, cert, 55; Cranbrook Acad Art, Mich, 57; study with Ezio Martinelli. *Exhib:* Solo exhibs, Mus Northern Ariz, Flagstaff, 80, Francine Seders Gallery, Seattle, 85, 89 & Columbia Tower Club Gallery, Seattle, 91; Mich Focus Exhib Detroit Inst Arts & Flint Inst Arts, 75; Mich Artists Exhib, Univ Mich, Ann Arbor, 76; Gorden Woodside / John Breseth Gallery, 82, 83, Seattle; Still Lifes, Francine Seders Gallery, Seattle, 86; 44th Pac Northwest Prof Arts Exhib, Bellevue Art Mus, Wash, 90; McConnell Gallery, San Luis Obispo, Calif, 2003. *Media:* Acrylic, Gouache-Vinyl. *Mailing Add:* 7205 Nudoso Rd Atascadero CA 93422-7009

DAVIS, RONALD
PAINTER, PRINTMAKER
b Santa Monica, Calif, June 29, 1937. *Study:* Univ Wyo, 55-56; San Francisco Art Inst, 60-64. *Work:* Los Angeles Co Mus; Mus Mod Art, NY; Tate Gallery, London; Albright-Knox Art Gallery, Buffalo; San Francisco Mus Art. *Exhib:* A News Aesthetic, Washington Gallery Mod Art, DC, 67; Documenta 4, Kassel, Ger, 67; Whitney Mus Am Art Ann, NY, 67; Color, Univ Calif, Los Angeles Art Galleries, 69; Venice Biennial, Italy, 72; Four Contemp Painters, Cleveland Mus Art, 78; Solo exhibs, Blum Helman Gallery, NY, 79, 81, 84 & 88, Asher/Faure, Los Angeles, 82-84, Trumps, Los Angeles, 85, NY Acad Scis, 86, Sedong Art Ctr, Ariz, 87, Blum Helman Los Angeles & Santa Monica, Calif, 87, 89 & 91, DEL Fine Arts, NMex, 92 & Jaquelin Loyd Contemp, 98; Prints from Tyler Graphics, 85; Walker Art Ctr, Minneapolis, Minn; Digital Visions: Computers and Art, Everson Art Mus, Syracuse, NY, 87-89; NMex Sculpture, Stables Gallery, Taos, 91; Seven Painters, Nicholas Alexander Gallery, NY, 95. *Teaching:* Instr, Univ Calif, 67. *Awards:* Nat Endowment Arts, 68. *Bibliog:* M Fried (auth), Ronald Davis: Surface and illusion, Artforum, 4/67; R Hughes (auth), Ron Davis at Kasmin, Studio Int, 176, 12/68; B Rose (auth), American painting, Vol 2, 70. *Media:* Cel-Vinyl, Acrylic, Canvas; Computer Graphics. *Collection:* Contemporary art. *Mailing Add:* PO Box 293 Arroyo Hondo NM 87513

DAVIS, STEPHEN A
PAINTER
b Ft Worth, Tex, Apr 24, 1945. *Study:* Claremont Grad Sch, MFA, 71. *Work:* San Francisco Mus Art; Oakland Mus; Univ Art Mus, Berkeley, Calif; Addison Gallery Am Art, Andover, Mass; Mus Contemp Art, Los Angeles, Calif; El Paso Mus Art, Tex. *Exhib:* Solo exhibs, Hansen-Fuller Gallery, San Francisco, Calif, 72, 74 & 76, Hudson River Mus, Yonkers, NY, 79-80, Malinda Wyatt Gallery, New York, 85, Gallery Paule Anglim, San Francisco, Calif, 87, Jernigan Wicker Gallery, San Francisco, 92 & 95 & Mattress Factory, Pittsburgh, Pa, 90; Am Abstraction at the Addison, Addison Gallery Am Art, Andover, Mass, 91; Christiane Chassay, Montreal, 96; The Nave Mus, Victoria, Tex, 97; Harlingen Mus, Tex, 97; McAllen Mus, Tex, 97; and others. *Pos:* Cur & Four Berkeley Artist, Hansen-Fuller Gallery, 70; Lansdowne Lect, Univ

Victoria, Can, 91. *Teaching:* Lectr, Univ Santa Clara, Calif, 75-77, Univ Calif, Santa Barbara, 78, Sarah Lawrence Col, New York, 79-80, State Univ NY, Purchase, New York, 82; artist-in-residence, Wright State Univ, Dayton, Ohio, 77 & Hunter Col, 95-96; asst prof, Hunter Col, New York, 86-93; vis assoc prof, Stanford Univ, Calif, 94-95, Hunter Col, New York, 95-; vis prof, Claremont Grad Sch, Calif, 2001, The Frank Mohr Inst, Groningen, Holland, 2001. *Awards:* Gottlieb Found Award, 93-94; Joan Mitchell Found Grant, 95 & 96; Nat Endowment Arts, 75-76, 78-79 & 87-88. *Publ:* Stephen Davis (auth), Paintings, Washington Project for the Arts, (catalog), 86; Stephen Davis (auth), Jacob and His Twelve Sons, Addison Gallery Am Art, (catalog), 90; Stephen Davis (auth), 70's, 80's, 90's, Jernigan Wicker Fine Arts (catalog), 92

DAVIS, THELMA ELLEN
PAINTER
b Las Animas, Colo, Sept 1, 1925. *Exhib:* Catherine Lorillard Wolfe Art Club, NY, 82; Solo exhib, Rosicrucian Mus, San Jose, Calif, 83; Pastel Soc Am Ann, Nat Arts Club, 90; Pastel Soc West Coast Ann, Sacramento Fine Art Ctr, Sacramento, Calif, 92; Soc Western Artists Ann, Hall Flowers, San Francisco, 92; Pastel Soc Am Nat Arts Club, 95-97. *Awards:* Klimberger Mem Award, Pastel Soc Am, 93; Barnard Award, Pastel Soc West Coast, 94; Sanford Corp Award, Pastel Soc Am, 95. *Mem:* Pastel Soc Am; Pastel Soc West Coast; Soc Western Artists; Gold Country Artists. *Media:* Pastel, Oil. *Mailing Add:* 6666 Acorn Hill Placerville CA 95667

DAVIS, TIM
PHOTOGRAPHER
b Blantyre, Malawi, 1969. *Study:* Bard Coll, BA, 1991; Yale Univ, MFA, 2001. *Work:* Yale Univ Art Gallery; Whitney Mus Am Art; Walker Art Ctr; RI Sch Design Mus; Mus Mod Art, New York; Metrop Mus Art, New York; Hirshhorn Mus & Sculpture Garden; Guggenheim Mus, New York; Baltimore Mus Art. *Exhib:* Air, Julie Saul Gallery, New York, 1999; New York Now, Mus City New York, 2000; Workspheres, Mus Mod Art, New York, 2001; solo exhibs, Brent Sikkema, New York, 2002, Galerie Edward Mitterand, Geneva, 2003, Bohen Found, New York, 2004, Jackson Fine Art, Atlanta, Ga, 2005, Mus Contemp Photog, Chicago, 2006, Knoxville Mus Art, Tenn, 2007, Luckman Fine Arts Complex, Calif State Univ, 2008, Ruffin Gallery, Univ Va, 2009; Boomerang, Exit Art, New York, 2002; Office, Photographers Gallery, London, 2003; Art & Architecture 1900-2000, Genova Palazzo Ducale, Genoa, Italy, 2004; The New City, Whitney Mus AM Art, New York, 2005; The Gold Standard, PS1, Queens, 2006; The Irresistible Force, Tate Mod, London, 2007; The Leisure Suite, LeRoy Neiman Gallery, Columbia Univ, 2008. *Teaching:* Instr, Yale Univ, New Haven, 2001-2004 & Bard Coll, Annandale-on-Hudson, 2004-. *Awards:* Leopold Godowsky Jr Color Photog Award, 2005; Josseph H Hazen Rome Prize, 2007-2008. *Bibliog:* Roberta Smith (auth), Brent Sikkema Gallery, NY Times, 12/14/2001; Sarah Shmerler (auth), New York Gallery Beat, Art on Paper, 3-4/2002; Vince Aletti (auth), My Life in Politics, The Village Voice, 11/1/2004; Mia Fineman (auth), Close Up, Photograph, 56, 3-4/2005; Barbara Pollack (auth), Illuminations, Time Out New York, 82, 3/16/2006; Bas Kas (auth), Light Snow, Zeit Leben Mag, No 45, 42-48, 10/2007. *Publ:* Auth, Dailies, The Figures Press, 2000; American Whatever, Edge Bks, 2004. *Mailing Add:* Van Doren Waxter 23 East 73rd St New York NY 10021

DAVIS ELSWICK, KEINA
PAINTER
Study: Student Travel Art Prog, London, 1990; Univ Fla, Gainesville, BFA(Painting), 1996. *Work:* Retrospective Gallery & Boutique, Gainesville, Fla, 1996; Learning Through Storytelling, Fla Book Store, Gainesville, Fla, 1996; Sistas in the City, The Covered Dish, Gainesville, Fla, 1996; Dancing at the Circle, African Violet, Gainesville, Fla, 1998. *Exhib:* Solo exhibs include Treehouse Studio Atlanta, Elan Studio Gainesville, Fla, Red Door Gallery Tampa, Fla, LB Studio New York, FF Gallery San Francisco, Yin Yang Gallery Atlanta, San Francisco Aids Foundad, San Francisco, Multicultural Ctr Gallery / UC Santa Barbara, Cesar Chavez Gallery San Francisco, African Am Mus, San Francisco ; Group exhibs include Liz Long Gallery & Urban Art Retreat, Chicago; Navigating the Mainstream, St Louis Art Mus; Arts At Marks, Honolulu, Hawaii; Locus Media Gallery, New York; Noir, John Hynes Ctr, Boston; Irony, Paradox:Victory, Pen & Brush Gallery, New York; Afro Solo Genevieve Gallery San Francisco; Deconstruction & Reconstruction: Family Exprience, Mus Fine Arts, Fla State Univ; Imagining Ourselves: Global Voices from a New Generation Women, Int Mus Women, San Francisco. *Awards:* Individual Artist Grant, The Puffin Found; George Sugarman Found Grant, 2007. *Dealer:* Portfolio Gallery 3514 Delmar Blvd St Louis MO 63103. *Mailing Add:* 4644 Geary Blvd #160 San Francisco CA 94118

DAVISON, BILL
EDUCATOR, PRINTMAKER
b Burlington, Vt, Sept 23, 1941. *Study:* Albion Col, BA, 63; Univ Mich, MFA, 66. *Work:* Libr Cong, Washington, DC; Dartmouth Col, Hanover, NH; Mus Mod Art, NY; Yale Univ, New Haven, Conn; Wesleyan Univ, Middletown, Conn; and many others. *Exhib:* Boston Printmakers 20th Ann Nat Exhib, Boston Mus Fine Arts, 68; one person exhibs, The Univ Gallery, Univ S Calif, Los Angeles, 77, Fla Ctr Arts, Univ S Fla, Tampa, 77, Davison Art Ctr, Wesleyan Univ, Middletown, Conn, 78, Kathryn Markel Gallery, NY, 78, Roy Boyd Gallery, Chicago, 79, Colby-Sawyer Col, New London, NH, 83 & Albany Acad Gallery, Albany, NY, 85; Nat Print Exhib, 77 & Thirty Yrs of Am Printmaking, 77, Brooklyn Mus, NY; High Tech/High Touch: Computer Graphics in Printmaking, Pratt Manhattan Gallery, NY, 87; Int Exhib Prints, Print Club, Philadelphia, 88; Post Industrial Expression, Sordoni Gallery, Wilkes Col, Wilkes-Barre, Pa, 88; Univ Dallas Nat Print Invitational, Tex, 89; Light Aberrations: A National Exhib of Photographs & Prints, Univ Tex, San Antonio, 90; Int Symposium Electronic Art, Croningen, The Neth, 90; Exhib Electronic Art, Art Centre, Punkaharju, Finland, 91; Dakotas Int: Works on Paper, Univ S Dak, Vermillion, 91; 10th Int Conference on Computer Graphics (SIGGRAPH), Chicago, 92. *Teaching:* Assoc prof, Univ Vt, Burlington, 68-81, prof, 90-. *Awards:* Indiv Grant, Vt Coun Arts, 70-71 & 78-79; Artist's Fel, Nat Endowment Arts, 74-75; Vis Artist's Fel, Brandywine Workshop Offset Inst, Philadelphia, 88; MacDowell Colony Fel, Peterborough, NH, 89; Award of Distinction, PRIX ARS Electronica 90, Linz, Austria, 90. *Bibliog:* A Class Portrait, Arts Mag, 10/81; Print News, 12/81; New Images, Ocular, winter 82; Sculptors find new ways with wood, NY Times, 12/2/84; Bill Davison: New screenprints - John Cage: New etchings, Art New Eng, 6/90. *Publ:* Art & Technology (catalog), Lehigh Univ, Bethlehem Univ, Pa, 83; The Ways of Wood (catalog), Org of Independent Artists, Inc, New York, 84; Visual Proceedings - SIGGRAPH 1992 (catalog), Chicago, 92. *Mailing Add:* c/o Dept Art 304 Williams Hall Univ Vermont Burlington VT 05405

DAVISON, NANCY R
PRINTMAKER
b 1944. *Study:* Smith Coll with Leonard Baskin, BA, 66; Univ Mich, MA, 73; Univ Mich, PhD, 80. *Work:* DeCordova Mus & Sculpture Park, Lincoln, Mass; Mus Art, Univ Mich, Ann Arbor; Print Dept, Boston Publ Libr, Mass; Avesta Industrisdad, Sweden; IBM, Pittsburgh, Pa; Ogunquit Mus Am Art, Maine; Universiti Sains Malaysia Sch Arts, Penang, Malaysia. *Comn:* Auction 91-The Nubble, PBS Channel 10 WCBB, Portland, Maine; numerous house portraits for pvt collections. *Exhib:* Archit in Contemp Printmaking, Boston Archit Ctr, Am Inst Archit, Washington, DC & Univ NH, Durham, 94-95; Maine Printmaking 1995, Round Top Ctr Arts, Damariscotta, Maine, 95; Int Grafiks, Avesta Konst, Sweden, 97; solo exhib, Aichi Shukutoku Univ, Nagoya, Japan, 98, Franklin Pierce Law Ctr, Concord, NH, 2009; City Views: Works on paper from permanent collections, De Cordova Mus & Sculpture Park, Lincoln, Mass, 98; Maine Print Project, Ctr Maine Contemp Art; River Tree Ctr Arts, Maine Arts Comn, Kennebunk, ME, 2006-2007; 2008 Biennial Juried Exhib, Ctr Maine Contemp Art, Rockport, Maine, 2008; Field Report, Boston Printmakers Travelling Members Show, 2008-10; Showcase, Barn Gallery, Ogunquist, Me, 2006, 2012. *Collection Arranged:* Am Sheet Music Illustration (auth, catalog), Mus Art, Univ Mich, 73. *Pos:* keeper of prints asst, Boston Publ Libr, Mass, 67-70; consult & print cataloger, William L Clements Libr, Ann Arbor, Mich, 72-73; owner & operator, BlueStocking Studio, York Beach, Maine, 85-2007. *Awards:* Pittsburgh Print Group Ann Purchase Award, Westinghouse Electric Corp, 82; Purchase Award, 36th Ann Boston Printmakers Exhib, 84; Frances N Roddy Open Competition Award in paint/mixed media, Concord Art Asn, 2009. *Mem:* Boston Printmakers; Oqunquit Art Asn (pres, 88-05); Oqunquit Arts Collaborative (founder & pres, 97-); Print Alliance. *Media:* Etching, linocut. *Res:* 19th century hist prints. *Interests:* Piano, writing. *Publ:* Contribr, The grand triumphal quick-step, Prints in & of America to 1850, Univ Press Va, 70; A Jackson in cartoons, American Printmaking Before 1876, Libr Cong, 75; Bickham's musical entertainer, 18th Century Prints in Colonial America, Colonial Williamsburg Found, 79; auth, E W Clay: American Political Caricaturist of the Jacksonian Era, Univ Microfilms, 80; E W Clay & the American Political Caricature Business, Prints & Printmakers of New York State, Univ Syracuse, 86. *Mailing Add:* 1 Schooner Landing York ME 03909

DAVY, WOODS
SCULPTOR
b Washington, DC, Oct 6, 1949. *Study:* Univ NC, Chapel Hill BFA (Morehead Scholar), 72; Univ Ill, Champaign/Urbana, MFA, 75. *Work:* Palm Springs Desert Mus, Calif; Orange Co Mus Art, Calif; Fed Reserve Bank, San Francisco; Long Beach Mus Art, Calif State Univ, Long Beach; Los Angeles Co Mus Art, Armand Hammer Mus Art, Los Angeles. *Comn:* IBM, Gaithersburg, Md, 90; Sterling Drug Co, Collegeville, Pa, 92; Xerox Corp, NY, 93; Prudential Real Estate, Calif, 98; Cedars Sinai Hosp, Los Angeles, 98. *Exhib:* Solo exhibs, Security Pacific Bank Plaza, Los Angeles, 80 & McIntosh/Drysdale Gallery, Houston, 84-86; Sculpture 1975, nat traveling exhib, 75; Six Los Angeles Sculptors, Fed Reserve Bd, Washington, DC, 80; New Art of Downtown Los Angeles, nat traveling exhib, 82-84; The Forgotten Dimension, nat traveling exhib, 82; New Pub Art, Otis Art Inst, Los Angeles, 84; Monuments To, Univ Art Mus, Long Beach, Calif, 85; Arco Sculpture Garden, Am Film Inst, Los Angeles, 86; New Sculpture, Works Gallery, Long Beach, Calif; Pier Walk, Chicago, 97; Imago Gallery, Palm Desert, Calif, 98. *Pos:* Bd dir, Los Angeles Contemp Exhibs, 84-85; arts adv coun, Cedars Sinai Hosp, Los Angeles, 84-98. *Bibliog:* William Wilson (auth), How real is the downtown phenomenon? Los Angeles Times, 9/20/81; Carol Everingham (auth), Critic's choice, Houston Post, 5/3/85; JoAnn Lewis (auth), Woods Davy's sculptures, Washington Post, 2/8/86. *Media:* Steel and Stone in combination. *Dealer:* Jan Abrams Fine Art New York NY. *Mailing Add:* 562 San Juan Ave Venice CA 90291

DAW, LEILA
PAINTER, SCULPTOR
b Charleston, WVa. *Study:* Wash Univ Sch Fine Arts, MFA, St Louis, Mo; Wellesley Coll, MA, Mass. *Work:* DeCordova Mus, Lincoln, Mass; Rose Art Mus, Brandeis Univ, Waltham, Mass; Boston Pub Libr; St Louis Art Mus; Texaco Corp, Houston; AG Edwards & Sons, St Louis, Mo. *Comn:* Map Structures, Mass Tpke & Mobil Oil; Winsted on the Move, Community Coll, Winsted, Conn, 2003; Planetary Conditions, Terminal A, Bradley Int Airport, Hartford, Conn, 2004; Passages, Wilson Branch, New Haven Free Pub Libr, Conn, 2006. *Exhib:* Soho 20 Gallery, New York, 86; solo exhibs, Soho 20 Gallery, New York, 87, AIR Gallery, New York, 88 & 2006, Southampton Bldg Suffolk Community Coll, 89, Atrium Gallery, St Louis, Mo, 91, 96 & 2001, Chapel Gallery, Boston, 94 & 96, Sunrise Art Mus, Charleston, WVa, 98, Brickbottom Gallery, Somerville, Mass, 2000 & Sasaki Assocs, Boston, 2001; Atrium Gallery, 87, 89, 91, 93, 98, 2001-2002 & 2005-; AIR Gallery, 88-90, 92-95, 97-2000, 2002, 2004 & 2006-; Univ SDak Art Gallery, 90; DeCordova Mus, Lincoln, Mass, 91; Nelson-Atkins Art Mus, Kans City, 91; Univ Nev, Reno, 92; Ormond Art Mus, Fla, 94; Boston Sculptors at Chapel Gallery, 95; Kiel Triangle Park, St Louis, 96; Mystic Art Ctr, Conn, 97; Gallery at Hastings-on-Hudson, NY, 98; Bakalar Gallery, Mass Coll Art, 99; Henry St Settlement Abrons Arts Ctr, New York, 2001; Creative Arts Workshop Gallery, New Haven, 2002; Artspace, New Haven, 2003 & 2009; Galerie Fur Landschaft Kunst, Hamburg, Ger, 2003; Byrdcliffe Colony, Woodstock, NY, 2003

& 2007; Schiltkamp Gallery, Worchester, Mass, 2005; Islip Art Mus, NY, 2006; Albertus Magnus Coll Gallery, New Haven, 2006; John Slade Ely House, New Haven, 2006; Trustman Gallery Simmons Coll, Boston, Mass, 2006; Contemp Arts Ctr, Cincinnati, Ohio, 2008; Mass Mus Contemp Art, 2008. *Teaching:* Grad tchg asst, Wash Univ Sch Fine Arts, 72-74; asst prof, Tusculum Coll, Greenville, Tenn, 74-75; adj asst prof art, Maryville Coll and Forest Park Community Coll, 75-76; prof art, Southern Ill Univ, head, multimedia prog, 76-90; prof art, Mass Coll Art, 90-2002. *Awards:* Nat Endowment for Arts Fel, Mid-Am Alliance, 90; Design Arts Grant, Nat Endowment for Arts, 91; Fed Design Achievement Award for design on Metrolink Light Rail System, St Louis, 95; Fel, Mass Cult Coun/Somerville Arts Coun, 99; James & Stephiana McClennen Fel, 2000; Artists Resource Trust Grant, Berkshire-Taconic Found, 2005. *Bibliog:* Denise Markonish (auth), Badlands: New Horizons in Landscape, MIT Press, 2008; Clare Norwood (auth), Uncoordinated: Mapping cartography in contemporary art, Contemp Arts Ctr, Cincinnati, 2008; John Burnham (auth), Islands of Inspiration, Cruising World, 2/2009. *Mem:* Coll Art Asn. *Media:* Mixed Media. *Dealer:* Atrium Gallery 4729 McPherson Ave St Louis MO 63108-1918. *Mailing Add:* c/o AIR Gallery 111 Front St #228 Brooklyn NY 11201

DAWDY, DORIS OSTRANDER
WRITER, RESEARCHER, HISTORIAN
b Minn. *Study:* MacPhail Sch Music, Minneapolis; Los Angeles City Coll. *Bibliog:* Contemporary Authors; Lois Swan Jones (auth), Art Research and Resources/A Guide to Finding Art Information. *Mem:* Nat Mus Women Arts. *Res:* Am Indian paintings, arts & crafts & other furnishings; Artists of the Am west born prior to 1900. *Publ:* Auth, Annoted Bibliography of American Indian Painting, Heye Found, 68; Artists of the American West, Swallow, 74 & 80, Vol II, 81 & Vol III, 85 & 87, Ohio Univ Press; The Wyant Diary: An Artist with the Wheeler Survey in Arizona 1873, Ariz and the West, Univ Ariz Press, 80; George Montague Wheeler: The Man and the Myth, Ohio Univ Press/Swallow Press, 93. *Mailing Add:* 3055 23rd Ave San Francisco CA 94132

DAWSON, DOUG
PAINTER, INSTRUCTOR
b Oak Park, Ill, Aug 23, 1944. *Study:* Macalester Coll, St Paul, Minn, BS, 66, Drake Univ, Des Moines, Iowa, 69. *Work:* Blue Cross/Blue Shield Collection, Denver, Colo; US Senate Off, Washington; Coutts Mus Art, El Dorado, Kans; Ferrett Exploration Collection-Gibson, Dunn, Gulf cher Law Firm. *Comn:* World Relief, Mali-West Africa, Guaranty Bank, Queen Anne Inn & Littleton Med Clinic, Colo. *Exhib:* Allied Artist Exhib, NY; Palais Rameau in Lille, Paris, France; Pastel Soc SW, Tex; Pastel Soc Am, NY; Nat Arts Educ Exhib, Taipei, Taiwan; Pastel Soc Southeast; Int Pastel Painting Exhib, Spain; Art in the Embassies (Madagascar), 2005-2007; Kans Pastel Soc; Ore Pastel Soc; Southeast Pastel Soc. *Pos:* Founding bd mem, Denver Art Students League, 86-; consult, Summer Inst Linguistics, S Am, 88-. *Teaching:* Instr painting, drawing, anat, Colo Inst Art, Denver, 78-99; instr, Denver Art Students League, 86-; instr, pastels, Museo del Quijote, Guanajuato, Mexico, 90; Acad Art-Suriname, S Am; Pastel Soc Am. *Awards:* Master Pastelist, Pastel Soc Am, NY; Goldsmith Award, Am Watercolor Soc, NY; Silver Medal Excellence, Audubon Artists, NY; P Scty Southwest: Tex; Roe Award, Mc Stayaward; Int assoc Pastel Soc; Best of show, Calif; Master Circle Award, Int Asn Pastel Soc; Pastel Soc Am Hall of Fame Hon. *Bibliog:* Am Artist Mag, 7/98; Artists Mag, 2/2004-2/2005; Pastel Journal Mag, 2/2009, 6/2010, 1/2012; Masterpiece Mag, 2005; Practice Arts Mag, France, 3/2014; Am Artists Workshop Prof, 2012. *Mem:* Am Watercolor Soc; Pastel Soc Am; Pastel Soc SW; Pastel Soc Ore; Pastel Soc No Fla; Pastel Soc Colo. *Media:* Pastel, Oil. *Publ:* Capturing Light & Color with Pastel, North Light Bks, 8/91. *Dealer:* Ventana Fine Art 400 Canyon Rd Santa Fe NM 87501; Telluride Art Gallery Telluride CO; Saks Gallery Denver Colo; Total Arts Gallery Taos NMex; Shelton Smith Print America Gallery Vail Co. *Mailing Add:* 8622 W 44th Pl Wheat Ridge CO 80033

DAWSON, GAIL
ADMINISTRATOR, EDUCATOR, PAINTER
Study: Univ Calif Berkeley, BA, 79, MA, 88; Univ Tex, Austin, BFA, 97, MFA, 2000. *Work:* Nora Eccles Harrison Mus Art; Utah State Univ, Logan, Utah. *Exhib:* Solo exhibs, Possant Gallery, Houston, Tex, 2002, Gensler Design & Architecture, Houston, Tex, 2004, Women and their Work, Austin, Tex, 2004, Mark Moore Gallery, Santa Monica, Calif, 2004; Group exhibs, Salina Art Ctr, Kans, 2003, Austin City Lofts Arts Collaborative, Austin, Tex, 2004, Mark Moore Gallery, Santa Monica, Calif, 2004, and many others. *Pos:* dept chair, assoc prof, dept art, San Francisco State Univ, Calif, currently. *Bibliog:* Mike Daniel (auth) Women Painters Make Different Impressions, DallasTimes Herald, 7/31/1997; Ben Willcot (auth), Art Reviews, Austin Chronicle, 10/20/2000; Jeanne Claire Van Ryzin (auth), The Class of 2000: A Self Portrait, Austin American-Statesman, 4/23/2000, Standouts at the New American Talen Show, 6/27/2002, Art Plus Motion, 8/8/2003, A Blend of Tradition and Technology, 1/25/2004; Michael Barnes (auth), Double Exposure: Davis Highlights Post-Photographic Work of Dove, Dawson, Austin American-Statesman, 3/23/2001; Nancy Hull (auth), The Process of Art, The Salina Jour, 1/17/2003. *Mailing Add:* San Francisco State University Department of Art Fine Arts Bldg, Room 293C/265 San Francisco CA 94132

DAWSON, JOHN ALLAN
PAINTER, SCULPTOR
b Joliet, Ill, Sept 12, 1946. *Study:* Northern Ill Univ, BFA, 69; Univ NMex; Ariz State Univ, MFA, 74. *Work:* Ulrich Mus Art; Phoenix Art Mus, Ariz; Ark Art Ctr, Little Rock; Okla Art Ctr, Oklahoma City. *Exhib:* Segal Gallery, NY; Ariz Invitational 75, Phoenix Art Mus, 75; Solo exhibs, Ark Art Ctr, Little Rock, 79, Okla Art Ctr, Oklahoma City, 79, Springfield Mus Art, Mo, 80 & Sheldon Mem Collection, Univ Nebr, Lincoln, 80; Wedding Series, Elaine Horwitch Gallery, Scottsdale, Ariz, 82; James Ratliff Gallery, 99; over 50 solo exhibs. *Pos:* Artist-in-residence, Mesa Pub Schs, Ariz Comn Art, 74. *Awards:* Purchase Award, Del Mar Col, 73 & El Paso Mus Art, 75. *Bibliog:* C D Kotrozo (auth), article, Art Voices South, 5/79; A Johns (auth), The wedding series, Ariz Arts & Lifestyle, winter 82; Claude Marks (ed), World Artists, 80-90. *Media:* Oil; Bronze. *Mailing Add:* 10246 E Brown Rd Mesa AZ 85207

DAWSON, VERNE
PAINTER
b Meridianville, Ala, 1961. *Study:* Cooper Union Sch Art, New York, 1980. *Exhib:* Best of the Season, Aldrich Mus Contemp Art, 2001; Utopia Station, Venice Biennial, Italy, 2003; Interested Painting, Gallery 400, Univ Ill, 2005; Future Tense: Reshaping the Landscape, Neuberger Mus Art, Purchase, NY, 2008; Whitney Biennial, Whitney Mus Am Art, 2010. *Bibliog:* Aidan Dunne (auth), Scene Stealing?, The Irish Times, 4/2004; Martin Herbert (auth), Round and round again, Time Out London, 7/2005; Brooks Adams (auth), Report from Lyon: Time After Time, Art in Am, 2/2006. *Mailing Add:* Gavin Brown's Enterprise 620 Grenwich St New York NY 10014

DAY, BURNIS CALVIN
PAINTER, INSTRUCTOR
b Hepzibah, WVa. *Study:* Ctr Creative Studies-Coll Art & Design; Famous Artists Sch, 68; AAS, Oakland Comm Coll Art, 69. *Work:* Washington Co Mus Fine Arts, Md; Univ Utah, Mus Fine Arts; Univ Mont, Mus Fine Arts; Mus Northern Ariz, Flagstaff; Mus City New York; Detroit Inst Arts; Mus Art, Ponce, PR; Mus Art & Archeol, Univ Mo, Columbia. *Comn:* Painting, Tom Davis Agency, Detroit & Cleveland, Ohio, 70; Detroit Bus & Civic League, 78; mural of 4 sporting events, Detroit Recreation Dept, 78; painting & portrait, Detroit Bus & Civic League, 74. *Exhib:* Original Paintings by Mich Artists, Detroit Inst Arts, Mich, 76; 9th Ann Nat Small Painting Exhib, NMex Art League, Albuquerque, 79; 4th Ann Nat Am Show, Laramie Art Guild, Wyo, 79; Cult Exchange Trends, Gallery Tanner, Los Angeles, Calif, 84; Int Platform Asn, Mayflower Hotel, Washington, DC, 89; State of the Art, 93, NE Art EXPO, New Eng Fine Art Inst, Boston, Mass. *Pos:* Art assoc, Cal Summers' House of Art, Detroit, Mich, 71-77; art dir, Urban Screen Process, Detroit, Mich, 72-73; freelance artist, 77-. *Teaching:* Instr life drawing, Pittman's Gallery Inc, Detroit, Mich, 73-74; painting, Detroit Recreation Dept, Mich, 85; mixed media, Wayne Co Community Coll, Detroit, Mich, 85-98; art instr drawing & painting, UAW-Chrysler Nat Training Ctr, Detroit, Mich, 92, 95 & 98; summer art instr mixed media, St Scholastica Summer Day Camp, Detroit, 94-98. *Awards:* 1st & 2nd Place, US Tank Automotive, 77; Cert of Recognition, US Zone Comt, 77; Semi-Finalist, United Auto Workers 50th Anniversary Poster, 86. *Bibliog:* George B Eichorn (auth), Recreation center new sports mural, Detroit News, 4/78; Lora Frankel (auth), National Young Audiences Week, YAMD Newsletter, Winter 79; Marie Teasley (auth), Burnis Day in DIA Collect, Michigan Chronicle, 12/87. *Media:* Acrylic, Oil. *Publ:* Auth, A Description of Neogeometric/Burnis C Day, private publ, 85; Article, Art, artists & my paintings, Projected Int/Burnis C Day, 89; Am Artist, Survey of Leading Contemps, Am References, 89; The work book, Scott & Daughters Publ, 90. *Dealer:* 21st Century Video

DAY, E V
SCULPTOR
Study: Hampshire Coll, BA, 1991; Yale Univ, MFA (sculpture), 1995. *Work:* Whitney Mus Am Art; Smithsonian Inst Nat Art & Space Mus; San Francisco Mus Mod Art; New York Pub Libr; New Mus Contemp Art; Mus Mod Art, New York. *Comn:* Wheel of Optimism, NASA, Mars Exploration Program, Pasadena, Calif, 2005; Lovenet, The GAP-Art Production Fund, 2009; Stealth, 2004 & Bandage/Bondage, 2008, Whitney Mus Am Art. *Exhib:* Material Matters, AOI Gallery, Santa Fe, 1996; Endorphin Ladies, Sandra Gering Gallery, New York, 1997; Luster, Henry Urbach Architecture, New York, 1999; Greater New York, PS1 Contemp Art Ctr, Long Island City, 2000; solo exhibs, Whitney Mus Am Art, New York, 2001, Bellevue Art Mus, Wash, 2003, Herbert F Johnson Mus Art, Cornell Univ, 2004, G Fine Art Gallery, Washington, DC, 2005, Santa Barbara Contemp Arts Forum, Calif, 2006, Rhona Hoffman Gallery, Chicago, 2008 & New York City Opera, 2009; Open Ends, Mus Mod Art, New York, 2001; Mood River, Wexner Ctr for the Arts, Columbus, 2002; Doublures, Musee Nationale des Beaux-Arts du Quebec, Can, 2003; Needful Things-Recent Multiples, Cleveland Mus Art, 2004; Marilyn, Sean Kelly Gallery, New York, 2005; Multiple Interpretations, New York Pub Libr, 2007; Good Doll Bad Doll, Armory Ctr for the Arts, Pasadena, Calif, 2008; Sensate-Bodies & Design, San Francisco Mus Mod Art, 2009. *Awards:* Susan H Whedon Award, Yale Univ Sch Art, 1995; Sculpture fel, New York Found for the Arts, 2007. *Bibliog:* Laura Vogel (auth), Double D-Disaster, Nose, Vol 14, 1992; Erika Icon (auth), Suck on This, Coagula, 11/1999; Deborah Soloman (auth), A Role Call of Fresh Names and Faces, NY Times, 4/2000; Hilarie M Sheets (auth), The Mod Bod, Art News, 6/2001; Charles Beyer (auth), A Brief History, Frieze, 1-2/2002; Shamim M Momin (auth), Three Variations on Sculpture, Flash Art, 5-6/2003; Ellen Rutten (auth), Til Death Do Us Part, Frame Mag, 11/2007; Eric Wilson (auth), A Wrap Dress Unwinds, NY Times, 5/29/2008. *Dealer:* Deitch Projects New York NY; Carolina Nitsch Contemporary Art New York NY; G Fine Art Gallery Washington DC. *Mailing Add:* c/o Deitch Projects 76 Grand St New York NY 10013

DAY, GARY LEWIS
PRINTMAKER, PAINTER
b Great Falls, Mont, Sept 29, 1950. *Study:* Mont State Univ, BA, 1975; Fla State Univ, MFA, 1976. *Work:* Ariz State Univ, Tempe; Trenton State Col, NJ; Sheldon Mem Gallery, Lincoln, Nebr; Joslyn Art Mus, Omaha, Nebr. *Exhib:* Solo exhibs, Sheldon Mem Gallery, Lincoln, Nebr, 1984, William Jewell Coll, Kansas City, Mo, 1988; Thirty Yrs of Am Printmaking, Brooklyn Mus, NY, 1976; 62nd Ann Int Competition, Print Club, Philadelphia, Pa, 1986; Nat drawing 1987, Trenton State Col, NJ; Midlands Invitationals, Joslyn Art Mus, Omaha, Nebr, 1990. *Collection Arranged:* Drawing Invitational (auth, catalog), Univ Nebr, Omaha, 79. *Teaching:* Instr art, Metrop Tech Community Col, Omaha, 1977-79; vis lectr lithography, Creighton Univ, Omaha, 1979; assoc prof drawing, Univ Nebr, Omaha, 1979, prof art & art history, currently. *Awards:* Purchase Award, Appalachian Nat Drawing Competition, 1979; Res Fel, Univ Nebr, 1985; Purchase Award, Nat Drawing Exhib, Trenton State Col, 1987; Visual Artists Fel Grant, Nat Endowment Arts, 1987-88. *Bibliog:* The Picture Show, Nebr Educ TV doc, 1985. *Media:* Intaglio, Lithography. *Publ:* Contribr, Colleagues: An Inter-Media Anthology of Artists, Pittore Euforico, 1979; Another Normal Conception, Univ Ill, 1980; An American Portfolio, Univ Ariz, 1981

DAY, HOLLIDAY T
CURATOR, CRITIC
b Nashville, Tenn, Dec 25, 1936. *Study:* Wellesley Coll, Mass, BA, 57; Univ Chicago, MA, 79. *Collection Arranged:* Siah Armajani, 80; Martin Puryear, 80; George Sugarman retrospective (auth, catalog), 81; Jennifer Bartlett, 82; Joyce Kozloff, 82; Elyn Zimmerman, 85; New Art of Italy (auth, catalog), 85; Art of the Fantastic: Latin Am (auth, catalog), 1920-1987, 87; Power: Its Myths & Mores in Am Art 1961-1991 (auth, catalog), 91; Forefront: 23 exhibs; Poetry of Form: Richard Tuttle, 92; Felrath Hines, 95; Francesco Clemente: Indian Watercolors, 97; Kiki Smith, 99; Crossroads of Am Sculpture: David Smith, Geo Rickey, John Chamberlain, Robert Indiana, William Wiley & Bruce Nauman (auth, catalog), Indpls Mus Art, 2000. *Pos:* Writer, New Art Examiner, Chicago, 76-79, contrib ed, 79; critic, Art in Am, 79-80; cur Am art, Joslyn Art Mus, Omaha, Nebr, 80-85; cur contemp art, Indianapolis Mus Art, 85-99 & sr cur contemp art, 99-2000. *Awards:* Wellesley Scholar, 56; Nat Endowment for the Arts critic's travel grant, 78-79; Am Mus Asn Merit Award, 81. *Bibliog:* Today's Art, The Indianapolis Register, Sec B, 2/97, 113. *Res:* Surfaces of David Smith's sculpture. *Interests:* Art of 20th & 21st Centuries. *Publ:* History of Sculpture in the Midwest, Encyclopedia of the Midwest, Ohio State Univ, 2003; Biomimicry: The Art of Imitating Life, Nat Coun Educ for the Ceramic Arts, 2005. *Mailing Add:* 1207 Golden Hill Dr Indianapolis IN 46208

DAYAN, AMALIA
COLLECTOR
b Israel. *Study:* New York Univ. *Awards:* Named on of Top 200 Collectors, ARTnews mag, 2009-12. *Collection:* Contemporary art; African art; 20-century design

DEADERICK, JOSEPH
PAINTER, EDUCATOR
b Memphis, Tenn, Jan 17, 1930. *Study:* Univ Ga, BFA, 52; Cranbrook Acad Art, MFA, 54; Ind Univ, 58-59. *Work:* Kalamazoo Col, Mich; numerous pvt collections. *Comn:* Ceramic tile mural, Univ Wyo, Laramie, 68; faceted glass window, Lutheran Campus Ctr, Laramie, 68. *Exhib:* Sixth Midwest Biennial, Joslyn Art Mus, Omaha, Nebr, 60; Brooklyn Mus Biennial Print Show, 64; Drawing USA Traveling Show, St Paul, Minn, 66-68; Solo exhib, Colorado Springs Fine Arts Ctr, 67; Fedn Rocky Mountain States Traveling Show, 66-72; 20 yr retrospective, Univ Wyo Art Mus, 78. *Teaching:* Instr design, Ind Univ, Bloomington, 56-59; prof art, Univ Wyo, Laramie, 59-93, prof emer, 93-. *Awards:* First Place Award Design, Franklin Mint, 72; Nat Award Excellence in Design, Printing Indust Am Graphic Arts Competition, 72. *Media:* Multimedia. *Publ:* The Stage: A Series of Poetic Drawings by Joseph Deaderick, Univ Wyo, 78. *Mailing Add:* 24 Camino Costadino Santa Fe NM 87505-9140

DE AMARAL, OLGA
TAPESTRY ARTIST
b Bogota, Columbia, 1932. *Study:* Colegio Mayor De Cundinamarca, Bogota, Columbia, 51-52; Cranbrook Acad Art, Bloomfield Hills, Mich, 54-55. *Work:* Mus Mod Art, Metrop Mus Art, NY; Art Inst Chicago; Mus d'Art Mod de la Ville de Paris, France; Nat Mus Mod Art, Kyoto, Japan. *Comn:* Tapestry, Peachtree Plaza Hotel, Atlanta, Ga, 76; tapestry, Embarcadero Ctr, San Francisco, Calif, 79; tapestry, Miami Int Airport, Fla, 82; tapestry, Nations Bank Plaza, Atlanta, Ga, 93; tapestry, Judicial Scribeners Asn, Tokyo, Japan, 98. *Exhib:* 42nd Venice Biennial, Italy, 86; Cuatro Tiempos (with catalog), Mus de Arte Mod de Bogota, Columbia, 93; Latin Am Women Artists 1915-1995 Traveling Exhib (with catalog), Milwaukee Art Mus, Phoenix Art Mus, Denver Art Mus, Nat Mus Women Arts, Washington, DC & Ctr Fine Arts, Miami, 95-96; Nine Stelae & Other Landscapes Traveling Exhib (with catalog), Fresno Art Mus, Art Mus Americas, Wash, DC & Cleveland Inst Art, Ohio, 96-97; Retrospective 1965-1996 (with catalog), Mus de la Tapisserie Contemporaine, Angers, France, 97. *Awards:* Guggenheim Fel, 73. *Media:* Fiber. *Dealer:* Bellas Artes 653 Canyon Rd Santa Fe NM 87501. *Mailing Add:* PO Box 8010 Santa Fe NM 87504

DEAN, JAMES
PAINTER, CURATOR
b Fall River, Mass, Oct 14, 1931. *Study:* Swain Sch Design, New Bedford, Mass. *Work:* Nat Aeronaut & Space Admin, Dept Interior & Smithsonian Inst, Washington, DC; MBNA Collection. *Comn:* Contemp Christmas stamps, US Postal Serv, 85 & 87. *Exhib:* Smithsonian Inst Traveling Exhib, 72-73; Corcoran Gallery Art, Washington, DC, 74; 107th Ann, Am Watercolor Soc, NY, 74; Washington Area Art, US Info Agency Worldwide Tour, 75-76; Nat Air & Space Mus, Washington, DC, 81-83; Foster Harmon Galleries Am Art, Sarasota, Fla, 83-90; Eyewitness to Apollo II, Nat Air & Space Mus, Washington, DC, 89; Artrain-Artistry in Space, 99-2002. *Collection Arranged:* Eyewitness to Space, Nat Gallery Art, Washington, DC, 65; The Artist and Space, Nat Gallery Art, Washington, DC, 69; Inaugural Exhib, Nat Air & Space Mus, Washington, DC, 76; Apollo II-25th Anniversary, Nat Air & Space Mus, Washington, DC, 94. *Pos:* Dir fine arts prog, Nat Aeronautics & Space Admin, 61-74; cur art, Nat Air & Space Mus, 74-80. *Awards:* Cert Merit, Nat Acad Design, NY, Award of Excellence, Com Arts Mag, 76 & 77; Citation of Excellence, Am Inst Graphic Arts, 76-77. *Bibliog:* R J Williams (auth), James Dean painter of the past, Southern Living Mag, 6/73; Alice Laurich (auth), James Dean, Focus Mag, 9-10/75; Jack Perlmutter (auth), Duality of James Dean, Art Voices South, 7-8/79. *Mem:* Hereward Lester Cooke Found (bd trustees, 73-); Torpedo Factory Artists Asn (pres, 83-84). *Media:* Watercolor. *Publ:* Coauth, Eyewitness to Space, Abrams, 72, Artrain Catalog, 99; auth, Artist and space, Interdisciplinary Sci Rev; illusr, Liftoff, Grove, 88; auth, Paul Calle-An Artist's Journey, Millpond Press, 93; Splash 3, North Light, 94. *Dealer:* Torpedo Factory Art Center 105 N Union St Alexandria, VA

DEAN, KEVIN LEE
GALLERY DIRECTOR, EDUCATOR
b Evanston, Ill, Mar 19, 1950. *Study:* Western Ill Univ, BA (art & art educ), 72, MA (studio art), 76, grad art his prog, 76-77. *Pos:* Exec dir, Galesburg Art Ctr, Ill, 77-79; arts ed, Longboat Observer, Longboat Key, Fla, 80-96; dir, Selby Gallery, Ringling Sch Art & Design, Sarasota, Fla, 94-. *Teaching:* Dist specialist art, Spoon River Dist, Fairview, Ill, 73-76; adj instr art & art hist, Carl Sandburg Col, Galesburg, Ill, 77-78; instr, Ringling Sch Art & Design, Sarasota, Fla, 85-. *Mem:* Am Asn Mus; Southeastern Mus Conf; Fla Art Mus Dir Asn. *Publ:* Auth, Syd Solomon (exhib catalog), Ringling Mus, Sarasota, Fla, 90; coauth, Painting in the 80's (video script), Bus Arts Inc, 91; auth, Arlene Erdich & the Attraction of Opposites, A Erdich, 92; intro to David Budd (exhib catalog), 96 & The Third Eye (exhib catalog), 96, Ringling Sch, Sarrasota, Fla, 96. *Mailing Add:* 901 Indian Beach Dr Sarasota FL 34234

DEAN, NAT
PAINTER, EDUCATOR, ADMINISTRATOR
b Redwood City, Calif, 1956. *Study:* Calif Inst Arts, 71-76; Cooper Union Advancement Sci Art, 75; San Francisco Art Inst, BFA, 77; Capricornus Sch Bookbinding & Restoration, 77-81, Univ NMex Sch Medicine Ctr Development & Disability LEND Fel. *Work:* Fukuoka Cult Ctr, Japan; San Francisco Mus Mod Art; Aratex ARA Art Prog, Calif; San Jose State Univ, Union Gallery, Calif. *Comn:* "Box-Book", Jean Brown Archive, Tyringham, Mass, 82; ornament, White House, Washington, DC, 99-2000. *Exhib:* San Francisco/Science Fiction: SF/SF, San Francisco & NY, 83; Ruth Bachofner Gallery, Santa Monica, Calif, 90; Orange Co Ctr Contemp Art, Santa Ana, Calif, 90; Memorial/Remembrance, Ctr Gallery, Wolfson Campus, Miami-Dade Community Coll, Fla, 91; Book as Art, Boca Raton Mus Art, Fla, 91; Gods, Devils & Clowns, Los Angeles Contemp Exhibs, Calif, 91; A Tribute to AIDS, Sarasota, Fla, 94. *Collection Arranged:* Steven Watson; Robert Atkins. *Pos:* Owner/designer, Ruta Zinc Handmade, San Francisco, Los Angeles, Santa Fe, NMex, 92-; dir/owner, Artist Tools & Resources Survival, Calif, Fla, 78-, Calif, NMex, 96-; dir, career planning & placement & coop educ & internships, Calif Inst Arts, Valencia, Calif, 86-89; dir, Ctr Career Servs, Ringling Sch Art & Design, Sarasota, Fla, 89-92; columnist, Art Maker Mag, 2001; designer/producer one-of-a-kind fashions, Ruta Zinc Handmade, Santa Fe, NMex, 2001-; expert witness various legal cases, Calif, NMex, NY, 78-. *Teaching:* Instr artist survival skills & bus art, Coll New Rochelle, 80, Sch Visual Arts, 81, San Francisco Art Inst, 81 & 82, State Univ NY, Potsdam, 82, Calif Coll Arts & Crafts, 84-87 & Calif Inst Art, 88 & 89; guest lectr, Humbolt State Univ, 87 & 90, Calif Coll Arts & Crafts, 88-93, Chapman Coll, Orange, Calif, 89, Pac Northwest Col Art, Portland, Ore, 89, San Diego State Univ, Calif, 89 & Univ S Fla, Tampa, 91; sem presenter, Los Angeles Convention Ctr, 88-93; guest lectr & artist, Calif Inst Arts, Valencia, 88-93; guest lectr & consult, Savannah Col Art & Design, 88 & 89; adj fac & lectr, Ringling Sch Art & Design, Sarasota, Fla, 89-92; project dir, A Dialogue Among Peers lectr series, Santa Fe, NMex & Espanola Valley Fiber Arts Ctr, Espanola, NMex, 96-2010; disability advocate, nationally. *Awards:* Wash State Arts Comn Artist Resource Bank, 88; Fla Arts Coun Vis Artists Roster, 90-93; Ringling Sch Art & Design Prof Develop Grant, Sarasota, Fla, 90; and others. *Bibliog:* Revs, LA Times, Calif, 87 & 90; revs, LA Weekly, Calif, 88; interview, La Bete Mag, Miami, Fla, 92; and others. *Mem:* Coll Art Asn; Women's Caucus Arts; Nat Asn Artist Orgns; Nat Artists Equity Asn; Am Coun Arts; and others; Mayor's Comt on Disabilities, Santa Fe, NMex; New Vistas Legislative Action Bd & others. *Media:* Acrylic; Mixed Media, Fiber, Wood Panels, Fiber Arts. *Res:* Disability advocacy, animal assisted intervention. *Specialty:* Fine Arts. *Interests:* Sewing, design, fine arts, multi media, disability rights. *Publ:* Contribr, Whitewalls: a magazine of writings by artists (visual piece), Whitewalls, 83; Visions (column), Ringling Sch Art & Design, 89-92; For the Working Artist, 89; The Visual Artist's Business & Legal Guide, Prentice Hall, 95; and many others. *Mailing Add:* 110 Sierra Azul Santa Fe NM 87507-0188

DEAN, TACITA
VISUAL ARTIST
b 1965. *Study:* Falmouth Sch Art, 88; Slade Sch Art, 92. *Work:* Art Inst Chicago; Collection Jumex, Mexico City; Fogg Art Mus, Harvard Univ., Cambridge, Mass; Hirshhorn Mus and Sculpture Garden, Wash DC. *Comn:* sculpture project, Millennium Dome, London, 99; Sadler's Wells Theatre, London, 99; billboard, Ingleby Gallery, Edinburgh, 2009. *Exhib:* Solo exhibs: Marian Goodman Gallery, New York, 2009, Fatigues, 2013; Craneway Event, Frith St Gallery, London, Performa, New York, 2010; Line of Fate, MUMOK, Vienna, 2011; Tate Modern, Turbine Hall, London, 2011; Norton Mus, West Palm Beach, Fla, 2012; Five Americans, New Mus, NY, 2012; Group exhibs, 50th Int Art Exhib Biennale, Venice, 2003, 51st Int Art Exhib Biennale, 2005, 55th Int Art Exhib Biennale, 2013; As Long as it Lasts, Marian Goodman, New York, 2009; Moby Dick, CCA Wattis Inst, San Francisco, 2009; Performa 09, Visual Art Performance Biennial, New York, 2009; Haunted, Guggenheim Mus, New York, 2010; Displaced Fractures, Migros Mus, Zurich, 2011; The Voyage or Three Years at Sea-Part 1, Charles H. Scott Gallery, Vancouver, 2011; Documenta 13, Kassel, 2012; First Act, Museo Tamayo, Mex City, 2012; Motion Capture: Drawing and the Moving Image, Lewis Glucksman Gallery, Cork, 2012; Tacita Dean Workshop, Found Botin, Santander, Spain, 2013; Palacio de Bellas Artes, Mex City, Mex, 2013; Looking at the View, Tate Britain, London, 2013. *Awards:* Turner Prize, 98; Aachen Art Prize, 2002; Hugo Boss Prize, Solomon R. Guggenheim Mus, 2006; Name one of 10 Most Important Artists of Today, Newsweek mag, 2011; Officer of the Order of the British Empire, 2013. *Bibliog:* Brian Dillon (auth), Celestial Bodies, Sight and Sound, 6/2010; David Ryan (auth), Craneway Event, Art Monthly, 10/2010; Louise Jury (auth), Light, camera, action for Tate's Turbine Hall, Evening Standard, 12/2010; Brian Dillon (auth), Tacita Dean at the Common Guild-review, The Guardian, 2010; Adrian Searle (auth), The best visual arts for 2011, The Guardian, 1/2011. *Dealer:* Frith Street Gallery 17-18 Golden Square London W1F 9JJ; Marian Goodman Gallery 24 West 57th St New York NY 10019. *Mailing Add:* c/o Marian Goodman Gallery 24 W 57th St New York NY 10019

DE ANDINO, JEAN-PIERRE M
DEALER, COLLECTOR
b San Juan, PR, June 11, 1946. *Study:* George Washington Univ; Univ NC. *Mem:* Am Soc Appraisers (accredited sr appraiser); Appraisers Asn Am (cert sr appraiser). *Specialty:* Nineteenth & twentieth century masters & contemp art. *Collection:* Unique images on paper. *Mailing Add:* De Andino Fine Arts 2450 Virginia Ave NW Washington DC 20037

DE ANDREA, JOHN
SCULPTOR

b Denver, Colo, Nov 24, 1941. *Study:* Univ Colo Boulder, BFA, 1965. *Work:* Everson Mus Art, Syracuse, NY; Neue Galerie Stadt Aachen, Ger; Ctr Georges Pompidou, Paris, Fr; Denver Art Mus, Denver, Colo; JB Speed Art Mus, Louisville, Ky; Mus Contemporary Art, Chgo, Ill; Portland Art Mus, Ore; Scottish Nat Gallery of Modern Art, Edinburgh; Bayly Art Mus, Univ Va; Va Mus Fine Arts, Richmond; Univ Wisc, Madison; Sydney and Frances Lewis Found, Va. *Exhib:* Solo exhibs, O.K. Harris Works of Art, NY, 70, 71, 73, 76, 82, 85, 98; Wilmaro Gallery, Denver, Colo, 72; Tortue Gallery, Santa Monica, Calif, 81; Aspen Ctr Visual Arts, Colo, 82; Foster Goldstrom Fine Arts San Francisco, Calif, 82; Galerie Isy Brachot, Paris, Fr, 85, 86, 88; Carlo Lamagna Gallery, NY, 87, 89; ACA Galleries, NY, 91, 93; Denver Art Mus, Colo, 96; Ron Judish Fine Arts, Denver, Colo, 2000; Group exhibs, Whitney Mus Am Art, NY, 70, No Things but Nudes, 77; Radical Realism, MoMA, Chicago, Ill, 70, 71, The Real and Ideal in Figurative Sculpture, 74, Ten Years of Collecting, 84; Biennale, Paris, Fr, 71; Kunstmarkt, Cologne, Ger, 71; Old Realism, New Realism, Dannenberg Gallery, NY, 71; Documenta V, Kassel, Ger, 72; Sharp Focus Realism, Sidney Janis Gallery, NY, 72; Hyperrealistes Americains, Galerie des Quatre Mouvements, Paris, Fr, 72; Fogg Art Mus, Harvard Univ, Mass, 72; Art Inst Chicago, Ill, 72; Realist Revival, NY Cultural Ctr, 72; Amenkansk Realism, Lunds Kunsthall, 73; Grands Maifres Hyperrealistes Americains, Galerie des Quatre Mouvements, Paris, Fr, 73; Super-Realist Vision, DeCordova Mus, Lincoln, Mass, 73; Male Nude, Emily Lowe Gallery, Hofstra Univ, Hempstead, NY; Hyperrealistes Americains/Realistes Europeans, Ctr Nat d'Art Contemporain, Paris, 74; New Photo Realism, Wadsworth Atheneum, Hartford, Conn, 74; Living Am Artists and the Figure, Pa State Univ, 74; Photo-Realist Art, Edwin A Ulrich Mus Art, Wichita State Univ, Kans, 75; Super Realism, Baltimore Mus Arts, 76; Am Salon des Refuses, Stamford Mus and Nature Ctr, Conn, 76; The Nude: Avery and the European Masters, Borgenicht Gallery, NY, 77; Jacksonville Art Mus, Fla, 77; Art 77, Hamilton Coll, NY, 77; Contemporary Figuration, Univ Gallery of Am Art, NY, 77; Illusion and Reality, Australian Nat Gallery, Canberra, 78; Venice Biennale, Italy, 78; 20th Century Am Nudes, Reed Art Gallery, NY, 78; Seven on the Figure, Pa Acad Fine Arts, Phila, 79; Homo Sapiens: The Many Images, Aldrich Mus, Conn, 82; Documenta V11, Kassel, Ger, 82; Faces Since the 50's: A Generation of Am Portraitures, Ctr Gallery, Bucknell Univ, Lewisburg, Pa, 83; Foster Goldstrom Gallery, Dallas, Tex, 83; Games of Deception: When Nothing is as it Appears, Artisan Space, Fashion Inst Tech, NY, 84; Image, Effigy, Form: Figurative Sculpture: Univ Art Mus, Calif State Univ, Long Beach, 84; In Celebration, Tortue Gallery, Santa Monica, Calif, 84; Classic Tradition in Recent Painting and Sculpture, Aldrich Mus Contemp Art, Ridgefield, Conn, 85; Figure it OUt: Visual Body Language, Helander Gallery, Palm Beach, Fla, 88; Nude or Naked Vered Gallery, East Hampton, NY, 88; An Assessment of Contemporary Figuration, David Klein Gallery, Birmingham, Mich, 97; Feminine Image, Nassau Co Mus Art, Roslyn Harbor, NY, 97; 7 Women 7 Years Later, Andrea Rosen Gallery, NY, 99; The Photorealists, Holmes Gallery, Ctr Arts, Vero Beach, Fla, 2000; Figure it Out, Louis K Meisel Gallery, NY, 2001, The Nude in Three Dimensions, 2002, Convincing Illusions, 2004, Some Photorealism, 2004, New Bronzes, 2006, Grand Illusion, 2008; Summer of the Nude Vered Gallery, East Hampton, NY, 2002; Iperrealisti, Chiostro del Bramante, Rome, Italy, 2003; 55th Int Art Exhib Biennale, Venice, 2013; Traveling exhibs, Aspects of Realism, Rothman's of Pall Mall, Stratford Art Gallery, Ontario, 76-78; Aspects of Realism, Centennial Mus, Vancouver, 76; Reality of Illusion, Denver Art Mus, Colo, 80; Real, Really Real, Super Real, San Antonio Mus Art, Tex, 82; Fortissimo! Thirty Years from the Richard Brown Baker Collection of Contemporary Art, Mus Art RI Sch Design, 85; Images of Man: Figures of Contemporary Sculpture, Isetan Mus Art, Tokyo, 92, Daimura Mus, Osaka, Hiroshima City Mus Art, ACA Galleries, NY. *Specialty:* hyperrealism, nudes. *Publ:* The Verist Sculptures: Two Interviews: Duane Hanson and John De Andrea, with J Masheck, Art in Am, NY, 72. *Mailing Add:* c/o Louis K Meisel Gallery 141 Prince St, Ground Fl New York NY 10012

DEANGELIS, JOSEPH ROCCO
SCULPTOR, PAINTER

b Providence, RI, Apr 22, 1938. *Study:* RI Sch Design, BFA, 66; Syracuse Univ, NY, MFA, 68. *Work:* Art Gallery London, Ont; Art Gallery of Windsor, Ont, Can; Omer's Collection, Toronto, Ont; Univ Windsor, Ont, Can. *Comn:* Wood Sculpture of America's Symposium, City North Vancouver, British Columbia, 77; Fibreglass Wall Relief Sculpture, Ont Provincial bldg, Windsor, Ont, 78; Painted Wall Mural, Ciocaro Club, Windsor, Ont, 84-85; Site Specific Concrete Sculpture, Chelton Corp, City of Toronto, Toronto, Can, 88; concrete and granite sculpture fountain, Rinterzo, Windsor Sculpture Garden, Ont, 97; painted relief sculpture, First Unitarian Church Olinda, Ruthven, Ont, 97; interactive sculpture, Snake Rattle and Roll, Child's Place, Windsor, Waterfront, Ont, 97; slate, granite and terrazzo sculpture fountain, Odette Sculpture Park, Windsor, Ont, 97; 13 foot bronze sculpture, 5th Ann Int Sculpture Symposium, Chanchun, China, 2001. *Exhib:* Ontario Now (traveling), 76; Spectrum Canada, Montreal Olympics, 76; London Art Gallery, Ont, 77; Can Place, Toronto, Ont, 77; Agnes Etherington Gallery, Kingston, Ont, 81; Visual Rhythms, Toronto Sculpture Garden, Ont, 84; New Can Sculpture, The Windsor Symposium, Art Gallery Windsor, 85; Solo exhibs, Sculpture, Chatham Cult Ctr, Ont, 86, Intentions of Colour, Ten Horses and an Inch Worm, Art Gallery Windsor, Ont, 96; 24 Canadians in New York City, Amos Enos Gallery, NY, 86; The Great White North, Staten Island Inst Sciences, 88; Skulptur x 7, USA, Invitational Sculpture Exhib, Kulturforum-Meschengladbach, Ger, 91; Art For Cystic Fibrosis, Fogolar Club, Windsor, 96; RI Sch Design, 8th Ann Int Juried Exhib Woods Gerry Gallery, Providence, RI & the Boston Design Ctr, Mass, 96; Work From Italy, Galleria 3 Via Dei Albizi, Florence, 97; Art for All, Art Gallery Windsor, Ont, 97; Canadian Portraits, Artcite Gallery, Windsor, Ont, 97; Work/Site:15 Yrs at the Toronto Sculpture Garden, Art Gallery Ont, Toronto, Can, 97 (publication); Eye of Experience, BCE Place, Toronto, Can, 98; Duty Free, Exchange Exhib, Detroit Contemp Gallery, Mich, 99; New mems 2002 Part One, The Sculpture Soc Can, Can Sculpture of Can, Can Sculpture Ctr, Exchange Tower, Toronto, Can, 2002. *Teaching:* Lectr, Univ Mich, Ann Arbor, 68-69; assoc prof, Visual Art Dept, Univ Windsor, Ont, 77-; lectr, Sch Visual Arts, Univ Windsor, Ont, Can; prof emeritus, 70-. *Awards:* Sculpture Award, Art Gallery London, 75; Ont Arts Coun Grants, 77 & 84; 35th Ann Southwestern Ont Exhibs, Art Gallery Windsor, Can; 32nd Ann Western Ont Exhib, London Art Gallery, London, Ont, Can; 5th Ann Brant Open Jury Exhibitor's Art Gallery Bratford, Ont, Can. *Bibliog:* Ann Rosenberg (auth), Wood sculpture of the Americas, Capilano Review, No 12, 77; Arthur Perry (auth), Vancouver: Wood sculpture of the Americas, Art Mag, 10-11/77; David Quintner (auth), Angelic sculptural work suspends tactile senses, Windsor Star, 3/81. *Mem:* Visual Art Ont; Sculptors Soc Can; Mich Watercolor Soc Art Cite. *Media:* Miscellaneous Media. *Publ:* The Windsor Exhib, 5 Canadian Sculptors, Art Gallery of Windsor, Ont, 1985; Sculpture/Toronto An Illustrated Guide to Toronto's Historic and Contemporary Sculpture with area maps by June Ardiel, photos by Aleg Capon, 1990; Drawing/Collage, The Windsor Review J Arts, Univ Windsor, spring 97; Odette Sculpture Garden, Dept of Parks and Recereation, Windsor, Ont, 2002. *Mailing Add:* 1690 Front Rd La Salle PQ N9J 2B6 Canada

DEATS, (MARGARET)
ART DEALER, WRITER

b Houston, Tex, May 27, 1942. *Study:* Univ Houston; Univ St Thomas, Houston; Glassell Sch Art, Houston. *Collection Arranged:* Gulf Coast Invitational Sculpture Exhib, 76; Houston Festival Sculpture Invitational, 79; HJ Bott's D-O-V 20th Anniversary exhib, 92, 40th Anniv Tour, 2012; HJ Bott & Margaret Deats 30th Anniversary Exhib, 2000. *Pos:* Fine Arts writer, Galveston Daily News, 71-75; owner-pres, Loft-on-Strand Gallery, 71-78; pvt dealer, 78-; bd mem, Artlies Mag, 93-96; consult, www.glasstire.com, 2008-2010; consult, Tex Artists Today, Marquad Press, 2010; corporate consultant, Fotofest Int, 2011; fundraising cons, The Community Artists Collective, 2012-; cons, Veterans Artists Program, 2014; exec dir City ArtWorks, 2015-. *Bibliog:* Gay McFarland (auth), Living on The Strand, Sculptor & Wife Preserve Old Building, Houston Post, 5/73; Dancie Perugini (auth), Loft-on-Strand, Houston Town & Country Mag, 4/76; Clint Willour (auth), 30th Anniversary (catalog). *Mem:* Galveston Co Cult Arts Coun (bd mem, 73-74); Mus Fine Arts, Houston, 74-; Diverse Works, 90-2014; Lawndale Arts Ctr, 2005-; Contemp Arts Mus Houston, 1972-. *Specialty:* Contemp paintings, sculpture, conceptual art & process installations. *Publ:* Carol Gerhardt Photos, FOTOFEST 90 (catalog); The Abstract Expression: Houston Artists Martonette Borromeo & Jennie Couch, Mus & Art Mag, 1/93; Diverseworks celebrates ten years of exhibitions & performances, Mus & Arts Mag, 6/93; Luis Jiménez, ArtLies, 6-9/96; Paul Suttman, ArtLies, 10/12/96; Texas Artists Today, ORIGIN, 2011; HJ Bott-Rhythm and Rhetoric. *Mailing Add:* 3700 W Clay #235 Houston TX 77019

DE BACKER, KATELIJNE
ADMINISTRATOR

b Antwerp, Belgium. *Study:* Free Univ Brussels, 1980-84. *Pos:* producer & dir, MTV Europe, 1988-97; comm dir, Antwerpen Open, 1998; exec dir, The Armory Show, 2000- & Merchandise Mart Properties Inc, 2007-

DEBARRY, CHRISTINA
PAINTER

b Lviv, Ukraine. *Study:* Newark Sch Fine Arts; NY Univ, BF (arts & art educ); Art Student League, NY. *Exhib:* Pastel Soc Am, ann exhib, 90-2004; Europastel Exhib Italy, Russia; X'ian Acad Fine Art, China; Du Pastel Exhib, France; Luminous Gallery, Taiwan; Salmagundi Club, non-mem exhib, 99-2003; Catherine Lorillard Wolfe Art Club, 2002; Taiwan Exhib, 2013, 2014; Du Pastel Exhib, France, 2013. *Teaching:* instr, pastel painting in var workshops and demonstations, currently; instr, traveling workshops: China, Tex, Mich, Minn, NC, SC, Philadelphia, NY & NJ, as well as outside US; Can, Bermuda, France and Mex, formerly. *Awards:* Dianne B Bernhard Gold Medal Award, Allied Artists Am, Nat Arts Club, NYC; Gold Medal Pastel Award, Art Spirit Found, Audubon Artists, NYC; HB Holbein Award, Pastel Soc Am; Honoree, Art du Pastel en France, 2006. *Mem:* Pastel Soc Am (pres emer, 98-2001); Allied Artists Am (vpres, currently); Catharine Lorillard Wolfe Art Club; AAPL (fellow); Audubon Artists. *Media:* Pastels, Oils, Printmaking. *Interests:* Still Life, florals, animal portraits, landscapes. *Publ:* illustr, Best of Pastels, I & II, Floral Inspirations, Rockport Publ; auth, Basic Landscape, Stroking the Fires of Autumn, Joys of Summer, Artist's Mag; auth, Best of Floral Painting, North Light Books; auth, Contemporary Master Pastelists, Galerie Luminous, 94; illstr, Great Am ART WORKS, cover illus on box pastels. *Mailing Add:* 10 Harvale Dr Florham Park NJ 07932

DEBEERS, SUE
PHOTOGRAPHER

b Tarrytown, NY, Aug 9, 1973. *Study:* Parson Sch Design, NY, BFA, 95; Columbia Univ, MFA, 98. *Work:* Working in Brooklyn, Brooklyn Mus, 2004; Whitney Biennial, Whitney Mus Am Art, 2004. *Exhib:* Solo exhibs incl Heidi 2, Deitch Projs, NY, 2000, Photog/proj room: Ghost Stories Mag, Sandroni Rey, Los Angeles, 2001, Photog, Kunstlerhaus Bethanian, Berlin, 2002, Hans & Grete, Kunst Werke, Berlin, 2003, The Dark Hearts, Sandroni Rey at Statements, Basel, Miami, 2004; group exhibs at Imaginary Beings, Exit Art, NY, 95, Terra Bomba, 96, 26 Positions, Miriam & Ira D Wallach Gallery, NY, 97, Scope 3, Artist's Space, NY, 98, The Searchers, 99, Death Race, Threadwaxing Space, NY, 2000, Fresh: The Altoids Curiously Strong Collection, Int Monster League, Derek Eller Gallery, NY, 2003, SCREAM, Anton Kern Gallery, NY, 2004; SCREAM, Anton Kern Gallery, NY, 2004. *Pos:* Artist-in-residence Wexner Ctr, Ohio, 99. *Awards:* Franklin Furnace Fund for Performance Art, 98-99; Joan Sovern Award Excellence in Sculpture, 99; Philip Morris Emerging Artist Prize, AM Acad Berlin, 2001

DEBELLEVUE, LUCKY
SCULPTOR

b Lafayette, La, 1957. *Study:* Univ Southwestern La, BFA, 1983; Univ New Orleans, MFA, 1987. *Work:* Mus Contemp Art, Chicago, 1999, Dalamas Mus, Falun, Sweden, 1986, Brooklyn Mus Art, 1997, Mus D'hondt-Dhaenens, Deurl, Belgium, 2000. *Exhib:* Solo exhibs, Feature Gallery, 1997, Realismus Studio, Berlin, 1997; Group exhibs, Contemp Arts Ctr, New Orleans, 1986, Four Walls, Brooklyn, 1992, Artists Space, New York City, 1992, The Drawing Ctr, New York City, 1993, Universidad de Buenos Aires, 1995, Gasworks, London, 1997, Cornerhouse, Manchester, Eng, 1997, D'Amelio Terras Gallery, New York City, 1998, Galerie Emmanuel Perrotin, Paris, France, 1998, Stephen Friedman Gallery, London, 1999, Grand Arts, Kansas City, 1999, The Neth Gallery Art, Rotterdam, 1999, Galeria d'Arte Moderna, Bologna, Italy, 2002, Wexner Galleries, Columbus, Ohio, 2004; others. *Awards:* Joseph H Hazen Rome Prize Fel in Visual Arts, Am Acad in Rome, 2004-05. *Mem:* Coll Art Asn

DE BERARDINIS, OLIVIA
PAINTER
b Calif, 1948. *Study:* NY Sch Visual Arts, 1967. *Exhib:* Solo shows incl Erotics Gallery, New York, 1982, NY Art Expo, 1985, Tamara Bane Gallery, Los Angeles, 1987, 1989, 1991, 1993, 1995, 1996, 1997, 1998, San Francisco Art Exchange, 1992, Art Collection House, 1994, A Gallery Named Desire, New Orleans, Addi Galleries, San Francisco, 1997; group shows incl NY Art Expo, 1987, 1988, 1989, 1996, 1991, 1992, 1995; Calif Art Expo, 1987, 1988, 1990, 1991, 1992; Northeastern Comic Conv, New York, 1993; WonderCon, Oakland, Calif, 1993; DragonCon, Atlanta, 1993; Lifestyles Conv, Las Vegas, 1993; Zombie Jamboree, Pittsburg, 1993; Inkslinger's Ball at Hollywood Palldium, Calif, 1993; Nat Tatoo Conv, San Francisco, 1994; Los Angeles Tamara Bane Gallery, 1994; Fantasy Fair, Dallas, 1995; Erotic-a, New York, 1999; Robert Bane Global Gallery, 1999. *Pos:* Owner, artist, O cards, New York, Ozone Productions, Ltd. *Media:* Acrylic

DE BLASI, ANTHONY ARMANDO
PAINTER, EDUCATOR
b Alcamo, Sicily, Italy, Jan 1, 1933; US citizen. *Study:* Art Students League, with Sidney Dickenson, Univ RI, BA with Jo Cain & William Leete, Ind Univ, Bloomington, with William Bailey, James McGarrell, Henry Hope & Albert Elsen, MFA. *Work:* Golden Artist Colors, New Berlin, NY; Detroit Art Inst; Ind Univ, Bloomington; Rose Art Mus, Brandeis, Univ Waltham, Mass; Kresge Art Mus, E Lansing, Mich. *Exhib:* Midyear Show Contemp Am Art, Butler Inst, Youngstown, Ohio, 67; Mus Mod Art (Penthouse), NY, 68; solo exhibs, Spectrum Gallery, NY, 68, 69, 71 & 73, Detroit Art Inst, 72, Razor Gallery, NY, 75 & 77 & Louis K Meisel Gallery, NY, 85, 87-89, 91, 93 & 95, Fine Arts Gallery, SUNY, Oneonta, NY, 98; Hokin Kaufman Gallery, Chicago, Ill, 88; group exhibs, Hokin Gallery, Bay Harbor Islands, Fla, 90, Jaffe Baker Blau Gallery, Boca Raton, Fla, 95, Dorothy Blau Gallery, Bay Harbor Island, Fla, 97; invitational, Abstract Image Makers, Bradley Univ, Peoria, Ill, 2001; Illusionary Space & Other New Encounters, Keene State Coll, Keene, NH, 2007; NY Found for the Arts, Flash Pop, NY, 2007; Sam & Adele Golden Found, Celebrating 10Yrs, New Berlin, NY, 2007; and others; Retro-garde Pro-Jects, Invitational, Westbeth Gallery, NY, 2014. *Pos:* visiting artist, Western Mich Univ, Kalamazoo, 79, Wake Forrest Univ, Winston-Salem, NC, 80, Andrews Univ, Berrien Springs, MI, 83; artist in res, Shanghai & Jingdezhen Univ, 2007. *Teaching:* Chmn & instr, Washington & Jefferson Coll, 63-66; prof painting & drawing, Mich State Univ, 66-86; instr, Sch Visual Arts, 88-90. *Awards:* Louis Comfort Tiffany Found Grant, 66-67; Founders Purchase Prize, Detroit Art Inst, 70; Individual Artist Grant, Mich Coun Arts, 83; NY Found for the Arts Fel in painting, 2006. *Bibliog:* Emily Wasserman (auth), rev, In: Artforum, 4/68; Gene Baro (auth), The 33rd Corcoran Biennial (catalog), 73; Jonathan Goodman (auth), Tony De Blasi, Constructed Paintings (catalog), Louis Meisel Gallery, 89; and others. *Mem:* Art Students League NY; New Mus; MoMA. *Media:* Acrylic. *Res:* North African art and architecture; historical and contemporary art of Europe. *Publ:* auth, Caroline Cheng, Reinventing Subersion, Ceramics, Art & Perception, 74th Issue, 2008. *Dealer:* Louis K Meisel Gallery, NY; Hokin Galleries, Palm Beach, Fla; Hokin Galleries, Bay Harbor, Fla; Dorothy Blau Gallery, Bay Harbor, Fla; Razor Gallery, NY. *Mailing Add:* 376 Broome St 3 Flr New York NY 10013

DEBONNE, JEANNETTE
PAINTER, PRINTMAKER
b Los Angeles, Calif, Dec 2, 1937. *Study:* Univ Calif, Los Angeles, studied with William Brice, John Paul Jones & Jan Stussy, BA, 59. *Work:* Mich State Univ, Lansing; Mitsubishi Corp, Cambridge, Mass; Pepsi Cola Corp, Seattle; Xerox Corp, Honolulu; Mercedes Benz N Am, Chicago, Ill; and others. *Comn:* Oil painting, Bixby Development Corp, Los Angeles, 86; oil painting, Morris Bergreen Coll, Greenwich, Conn, 91; oil painting, Church of St Paul in the Desert, Palm Springs, Calif, 95; Mich State Univ, Lansing, Mich. *Exhib:* Mus Art Auction, Palm Springs Desert Mus, Calif, 95; Blue Mountain Small Works Invitational, Blue Mountain Gallery, NY, 95; solo exhib, Valerie Miller Fine Art, Palm Desert, Calif, 95 & 97, Miranda Galleries, Laguna Beach, Calif, 98, Reflections from the Roof of the World, Learsi Gallery, Palm Desert, Calif, 2000; Mystic Quest, Santuario de Guadalupe, Santa Fe, NMex, 96; Myths and Miracles, Miranda Gallery, Laguna Beach, Calif, 96; St Paul's Cathedral, San Diego, Calif, 97; Palm Desert Gallery, Calif, 98; Galerie Hyna, Munich, Ger, 98. *Pos:* Dir Art, Healthcare Dept at Eisenhower Med Center, Ranch Mirage, Calif. *Teaching:* Instr drawing, Village Ctr for Arts, Palm Springs, Calif, 88-90. *Awards:* East African Wildlife Soc First Prize in Painting, Whaletail Int, Nairobi, Kenya, 91. *Bibliog:* Douglas Deaver (auth), Jeannette DeBonne: Paintings, Fact Publ, 94; Judith Gross (auth), Painter finds her rhythm, The Desert Sun, 7/2/95. *Media:* Oil. *Interests:* Music (playing the harp)

DE BOSCHNEK, CHRIS (CHRISTIAN) CHARLES
PAINTER, PRINTMAKER
b Cannes, France, Apr 24, 1947; US citizen. *Study:* Cleveland Art Inst; Akron Univ. *Work:* Weiskoff, Silver & Co, NY; Newark Mus, NJ; Kelly, Drye & Warren, Stamford, Conn; US Steel Co, Pittsburgh, Pa; Sherman & Sterling, NY. *Exhib:* Solo exhibs, Akron Art Inst, Ohio, 71, Kathryn Markel Gallery, NY, 82, Queens Mus, NY, 88 & Elizabeth McDonald Gallery, NY, 88; Tibor de Nagy Gallery, NY, 73; OK Harris Gallery, NY, 79; Lerner Heller Gallery, NY, 82; Edith C Blum Art Ctr, Annandale on Hudson, 84; Hallwalls, Buffalo, NY, 85; Richard Green Gallery, NY, 86; and others. *Awards:* Yaddo Fel, 80. *Publ:* Articles in Cover Mag, spring 80 & winter 81, Arts Mag, 3/82, 9/86 & 2/88 & Artnews Mag, 4/82. *Mailing Add:* 90 S Fourth St Brooklyn NY 11211-5505

DE BRETTEVILLE, SHEILA LEVRANT
DESIGNER, EDUCATOR
b Brooklyn, NY, Nov 4, 1940. *Study:* Barnard Col, Columbia Univ, BA (art hist); Yale Sch Art & Archit, MFA (graphic design). *Hon Degrees:* Calif Coll Arts & Crafts, hon doctorate, 91; Moore Coll Art, hon doctorate, 95. *Work:* Victoria & Albert Mus, London; Design Collection, Mus Mod Art, NY; Pub Libr, Los Angeles & NY. *Comn:* 40 under 40 show, Archit League, NY, 65; spec issue design, Art Soc Wis, 70; Frederick Weisman Found Art, 85; Pub Art Proj: Biddy Mason: Time & Place, Los Angeles, 90; Path of Stars, New Haven, 94. *Exhib:* Communications Graphics, Am Inst Graphics Art, 72; 5e Biennale des Arts Graphiques, Brno Czech, 72; Color, Am Inst Graphic Arts, Whitney Mus, 74; Poster from the Vietnam Yrs, NY, 75; At Home, Long Beach Mus Art, 84; Let's Play House, Bernice Steinbaum Gallery, 86; Cooper Hewitt Mus Design Biennial, 2000. *Pos:* Typographer, Yale Univ Press, New Haven, Conn, 65-68; designer, Olivetti, Milan, Italy, 68-69; designer, Calif Inst Arts, 69-74; co-founder & pres, Woman's Bldg Community Gallery, 73-; juror, Nat Endowment Arts-Civil Serv Comn, 75; co-founder, ed & designer, Chrysalis Mag, 77-; design dir, Los Angeles Times, 78-81; chmn, Dept of Commun, Design & Illus, Otis Art Inst of Parsons Sch of Design, Los Angeles, 81-. *Teaching:* Dir inst & graphic design dept, Calif Inst Arts, 70-74; chmn, dept commun design, Otis/Parsons Univ; lectr at var cols & univs; Caroline M Street Prof, dir grad studies graphic design, Yale Univ Sch Art. *Awards:* Grand Award Excellence, Soc Publ Designers, 71; Communication Graphics Awards, 72 & five Gold Medals, Calif 2 Exhib, Am Inst Graphic Arts; IBM Fel, Int Design Conf, Aspen, 74; Gold Medal Award, Nat Design Legend, 2005. *Bibliog:* Gilles de Bure (auth), Right on Sheila, Creations Recherches Esthetiques Europeenes, 73; articles, Commun Arts, 6/83 & Eye, 93; Steven Harris, Deborah Bank (ed), Architecture of the Every Day, Princeton Archit Press, 97. *Mem:* Am Inst Graphic Arts; Internat Alliance Theatrical Stage Employees; Coll Art Asn. *Media:* Steel, Brass, Concrete and stone. *Publ:* Ed, Calif Inst Arts: Prologue to a community, Vol 7 No 2 & A reexamination of some aspects of the design arts from the perspective of the women designer, Arts Soc, 74; auth, A reevaluation of design, Icographic 6, 73; Habitability, In: Proc of the Calif Chap Am Inst Archit, 74; Feminist Design, Space & Soc, 6/83; Lure of the Local, 98. *Mailing Add:* 146 Deepwood Dr Hamden CT 06517-3452

DEBRINCAT, ALICIA
PAINTER
b Standford, Calif, May 15, 1979. *Study:* Inst Cultural Oaxaca, Oaxaca, Mex, 1998 ; Inst de Estudios Internacionales, Seville, Spain, 1999 ; Univ Ore, Eugene, Ore, BA(English Lit & Spanish), 2000 . *Exhib:* Group exhibs include A Love Supreme, Budget Gallery, San Francisco, 2005; Maitri Art Show, San Francisco, 2005; War and Peace, Frank Bette Ctr Arts, Alameda, Calif, 2005; Art of the Everyday, Subterranean Gallery, Healdsburg, Calif, 2005 ; New Work, Esteban Sabar Gallery, Oakland, Calif, 2006; Reality & Other Figments of the Imagination, Elliott Fouts Gallery, Sacramento, 2007; Everything But the Kitschen Sync, La Luz de Jesús Gallery, Los Angeles, 2007; Love and Hate, Art SF Gallery, San Francisco, 2007; Dirty Little Secrets, Altered Esthetics Gallery, Minneapolis, 2007; Heart Attack, Eclectix Gallery, El Cerrito, Calif, 2008; New Wave Feminism, Femina Potens Gallery, San Francisco, 2008. *Awards:* First Place, Painting, Ann Open Juried Show, Art Mus Los Gatos, Los Gatos, Calif, 2006; Distinguished Artist Award, Convocatoria Int de Arte, Traveling Exhib, Argentina, 2006; City of Berkeley Arts Comn Honorarium, Berkeley, Calif, 2007; George Sugarman Found Grant, 2007

DEBRITO, MICHAEL
PAINTER
b New Jersey, 1980. *Study:* Parsons Sch Design, BFA, 2003; New York Acad Art 2003-04; Salmagundi Artist Club, 2004. *Work:* Nev Mus Art, Reno. *Exhib:* Solo exhibs include Eleanor Ettinger Gallery, New York, 2008; group exhibs include Winter Exhib, Arnold & Sheila Aronson Galleries, New York, 2003; Salon Exhib, Greenhouse Gallery, San Antonio, Tex, 2004 ; Figure in Am Art, Eleanor Ettinger Gallery, New York, 2004, 2006, 2007, 2008, Int Autumn Salon, 2005, Int Winter Salon, 2005, Int Summer Salon, 2006, 2007; Immagration, Mus da Presidência da República, Viana do Castelo, Portugal, 2008. *Awards:* Gold Medal Hon, Allied Artists Am, 2005; Pollack-Krasner Grant, 2006. *Mailing Add:* c/o Eleanor Ettinger Gallery 24 W 57th St Ste 609 New York NY 10019

DEBROSKY, CHRISTINE A
PAINTER
b Kingston, NY, Dec 10, 1951. *Study:* Albert Handell, pastel workshops, 80; Woodstock Sch Art (Art Students League), 90; Wolf Kahn workshop, 93. *Work:* Key Corp Collection, Albany, NY; Standard & Poor's, NY; Renssalaer Polytechnic Inst, Troy, NY; Pfizer Chemical Corp; McGraw Hill Inc, NY. *Comn:* Residence mural project, Anderson Sch, Staatsburg, NY, 82; pastel landscape/diptych, Key Corp/Greenhut Galleries, Albany, NY, 92; Kingston Hosp, NY. *Exhib:* Pastel Soc Am, Harmon/Meek Gallery & Gallery on Venetian Bay, Naples, Fla, 92; Pastel Soc Am Ann, Nat Arts Club, NY, 93, 94, 99, 2002, 2007, 2013; Pastel Soc West Coast Int, Roseville, Calif, 98, 2000, 2001, 2003, 2005, 2006, 2009; Europastel, Italy & St Petersburg; Southern Vt Arts Ctr, 2002 & 2005; Soc Am Impressionists, 2006, 2007, 2013. *Teaching:* Pastel instr, Woodstock Sch Art, 98-; aquamedia instr, Barnett Art Ctr, 98-; instr, Led painting workshops, Tuscany & Venice, Italy, Burgundy, France, 2000-; Sedona Arts Ctr, 2010. *Awards:* Pastel Soc award, W Coast, 98, 2001 & 2003; distinguished pastellist award, Pastel Soc, W Coast, 2003; Am Impressionist Soc 2nd Place, 2006; Am Impressionist Soc Open, 2007; Best in Show, Northeast Nat Pastel, 2008; Silver Award, IAPS, 2009. *Bibliog:* Landscape Inspirations, Rockport Publ, 91; Raymond J Steiner (auth), Christine Debrosky at the Woodstock Artists Asn, Art

Times, 5/94; Janet Cassidy (auth), Combining Watercolor and Pastel for Exciting Results, Pastel Jour, 1-2/2002. *Mem:* Pastel Soc Am (signature mem); Pastel Soc West Coast (distinguished pastellist); L'Ant du Pastel, France & USA, 2006; Am Impressionist Soc; Oil Painters AM. *Media:* Pastel, Oil. *Dealer:* Gregory James Gallery Fairfield CT; Alizarin Gallery Durham NC

DE CAMPOS, NUNO
PAINTER, INSTRUCTOR
b Porto, Portugal, Nov 20, 1969; Portuguese citizen. *Study:* Univ Porto, Portugal, licensiatura, 94; Sch Mus Fine Arts, Tufts Univ, Boston, MFA, 99. *Exhib:* Solo exhibs at Clifford Smith Gallery, Boston, 1999, 2001, 2003, LFL Gallery, NY, 2003; Collection of Arthur Goldberg, Danforth Mus, Framingham, Mass, 2000; Art Cetera, Mills Gallery, Boston Ctr for Arts, 2000; Realistic Means, The Drawing Ctr, NY, 2002; She's Come Undone, Artemis, Greenberg Van Doren Gallery, NY, 2004; Private Lives, Westby Gallery, Rowan Univ, NJ, 2004; Extended Painting, Prague Biennale, 2005; The Outwin Boochever Portrait Competition Exhib, Nat Portrait Gallery, Washington, DC, 2006. *Collection Arranged:* Fogg Art Mus, Harvard Univ. *Teaching:* lectr painting, Mass Col Art, Boston, 2000; instr painting, Art in NE Summer Workshop, Bennington Col, Vt, 2000; instr painting & drawing, Sch Mus Fine Arts, Boston, 2001. *Awards:* Calouste Culbenkian Found Scholar, 96-99; Marie Walsh Sharpe Art Found Award, 2000; Grant, Mass Cult Coun, 2000; NY Found Arts, Artists Fellow-Painting, 2006. *Bibliog:* Francine Koslow-Miller (auth), Talentos para Onoyo Milenio, Elle Mag, Portugal, 1/2000, Art Forum, 2/2000, Harper's Mag, 1/2001. *Mem:* Inst Contemp Art; Coll Art Asn. *Dealer:* Clifford Smith Gallery 450 Harrison Ave Fl 3 Boston MA 02130. *Mailing Add:* 20 Jay St Ste 740 Brooklyn NY 11201-8352

DECAPRIO, ALICE
PHOTOGRAPHER, COLLAGE ARTIST
b Marshall, Mich, Feb 10, 1919. *Study:* Mich State Univ, AB; Northwestern Univ, MA;. *Work:* Ocean Co Col, NJ; US Navy; RCA Corp Hq, NY; Chatham Trust, NJ; Ringling Mus, Sarasota, Fla. *Comn:* Drawings, Ringling Mus, Sarasota, Fla, 78 & 80; US Navy-NY Harbor Oper Sail activities, 76-77; Navy Women at Work, USS Vulcan, 79; brochure, Albaz Corp, Riyadh, Saudi Arabia, 81; and others. *Exhib:* One-person shows, Nat Arts Club, 77, S Vt Art Ctr, 77, Salmagundi Club NY, 81, AT&T Hq, NJ, 80, Sarasota, Fla, Centennial Comm, 80, PlymouthHarbor, Sarasota, Fla, 91, Bird Key Yacht Club, Fla, 2009, Unity Gallery, Sarasota, 2011, Players Theatre, Sarasota, Fla, 2011. *Teaching:* Instr watercolor, Madison-Chatham Adult Sch, 68-76, instr outdoor sketching, 70-81, Creative Learning Workshop, Rockport, Mass, 77-82; instr sketching, Hilton Leech Studio Workshops & Traveling Two-Arts Workshops, 85-90; workshops, France & Portugal, 93-98. *Awards:* Naval Art Coop & Liaison Comt Bronze Medal for Achievement in Watercolor, Salmagundi Club, 78; Best in Show, Sarasota, Fla, 97; Best in Show, Longboat Key Art Ctr, 98; 1st Prize Photog, NLAPW Fla State Convention, 2011. *Mem:* Fla Watercolor Soc; NJ Watercolor Soc; Nat League Am Pen Women; Petticoat Painters, Sarasota, Fla. *Media:* Enhanced Photography, Collage. *Res:* extensive research on circus, carousels, and antique hand-carved carousel animals. *Interests:* circus, antique carousels, figures. *Mailing Add:* 3963 Country View Dr Sarasota FL 34233

DE CARVALHO, PRISCILA
PAINTER
b 1975. *Study:* City Coll, San Francisco; Arts Student League, New York. *Exhib:* Night of 1000 Drawings, Artist Space, New York, 2005; Merit Award, Cork Gallery, Lincoln Ctr, New York, 2006; Postcards from the Edge, James Cohan Gallery, New York, 2007; Emerge 10, Aljira Ctr for Contemp Art, NJ, 2009; solo exhibs, Jersey City Mus, 2009, Praxis Int Art Gallery, New York, 2010; Ain't I a Woman, Mus Contemp African Diaspora Arts, New York, 2010. *Awards:* Emerge 10 Fel, Aljira Ctr for Contemp Art, 2008; Pollock-Krasner Found Grant, 2008; Arts Fund Grant, Queens Cmty Coll, 2009; Sculpture Space Fel, NY, 2010. *Bibliog:* Nicholas Hirshon (auth), Brazilian Art Shines, NY Daily News, 8/18/2009; Benjamin Genocchio (auth), A Decade of Emergence, NY Times, 8/28/2009

DE CASTRO, LORRAINE
SCULPTOR, CERAMIST
b Rio Piedras, PR, July 19, 1946. *Study:* Univ PR, BA, 72, studied welding with John Balossi, 77; New York Univ, grad studies, 82-84. *Work:* Museo de Arte de Ponce, PR. *Exhib:* Clay and Fire: Seven Ceramists, Inst Cult, San Juan, 86; Growing Beyond, Women Artists from PR, Orgn Am States, Washington, DC, Mus del Barrio, NY & Caribe Gallery, PR, 87-88; Ceramics From PR, EuroAm Gallery, Caracas, Venezuela, 90; Women Artists: Protagonists of the 80's, Museo delas Casas Reales, Dominican Republic, Mus Contemp Art, San Juan, PR, 90; Weaving Images, Normandie Gallery, San Juan, PR, 91, 25 Anniversary: Art League of San Juan, PR, 92; and others. *Teaching:* Prof ceramics, Art Students League of San Juan, 80-; prof, Univ PR, 89-. *Bibliog:* Charlotte Speight (auth), Images in Clay Sculpture, 83. *Mem:* Mujeres Artistas de PR, Inc; Sculptors Asn PR. *Media:* Clay. *Dealer:* Botello Gallery Cristo St Old San Juan PR 00936. *Mailing Add:* G-16 Granada St Vistamar Marina Carolina PR 00983

DECELLE, PHILIPPE
COLLECTOR, CURATOR
Pos: cur, Plasticarium Mus. *Awards:* Name one of Top 200 Collectors, ARTnews mag, 2011, 2012, 2013. *Bibliog:* Andrea Dinoto (auth), Art Plastic-Designed for living, Abbeville Press, 87; Holly Wahlberg (auth), 1950s Plastic Design: Everyday Elegance, Schiffer Publishing Ltd, 99; Penny Spark (auth), Plastic Age: Modernity to Post-Modernity, Antique Collector's Club, 97. *Collection:* Plastic design; popular furniture between 1960-1973. *Publ:* auth, L'Utopie Du Tout Plastique, 60-73. *Mailing Add:* Plasticarium Museum Rue de Locquenghien 35 Brussels 1000 Belgium

DE CHAMPLAIN, VERA CHOPAK
PAINTER, PRINTMAKER
b Ger; US citizen. *Study:* Art Students League; spec studies with Edwin Dickinson. *Work:* Butler Inst Am Art, Youngstown, Ohio; Slater Mus, Norwich, Conn; Ga Mus Art, Athens; Evansville Mus Art & Sci, Ind; Smithsonian Inst Arch Am Art, Washington; NY Univ. *Comn:* Portrait, Liederkranz Found, NY, 79 & 91; pvt portraits & landscapes comns. *Exhib:* Metrop Mus Art, NY, 79; B Altman Gallery, NY, 82; Consulate Gen, Fed Republic of Ger, 86; Traveling exhib, 88-89; Broome St Gallery, Soho, NY, 91-93; Avery Fisher Hall, Cork Gallery, 94; Cornell Univ Med Libr, NY, 95, 96 & 98. *Teaching:* Art dir & instr oil painting, Emanu-El Ctr, New York, 68-. *Awards:* Twilight & Onteora Club Award, Haines Falls, NY, 65; US Investor Award, 69; First Prize-World Award, Acad Ital, Parma, 85, 87. *Bibliog:* Samuel M La Corte (auth), Creative images, Clifton Leader, 70. *Mem:* Fel Royal Soc Arts; Artists Equity Asn New York; Kappa Pi; Nat Soc Arts & Lett (art chmn Empire State, 69-); Art Students League; and others. *Media:* Oil, Watercolor; All. *Publ:* Auth, article, ArtSpeak, 3/86; article, Marketletter from Rosenthal & Co, 3/24/86. *Mailing Add:* 1801 E 26th St Brooklyn NY 11229-2437

DECHAR, PETER
PAINTER
b New York, NY, Apr 19, 1942. *Work:* Mus Mod Art & Whitney Mus Am Art, NY; Larry Aldrich Mus, Conn; Walker Art Ctr, Chicago; Fiberglass Tower Art Collection. *Exhib:* Highlights from the 1967 Season, Larry Aldrich Mus, Conn, 67; Contemp Painting & Sculpture, Krannert Art Mus, 67; Whitney Mus Am Art Ann, NY, 67 & 69; Solo exhibs, Cordier & Ekstrom Gallery, NY, 67, 69 & 75; Twentieth Century Art from the Rockefeller Collection, Mus Mod Art, NY, 69. *Media:* Oil. *Mailing Add:* 203 W Hurley Rd Woodstock NY 12498

DECIL, STELLA (DEL) WALTERS
PAINTER, INSTRUCTOR
b Indianapolis, Ind, Apr 26, 1921. *Study:* Indianapolis Acad Com Art, 38-39; John Heron Art Inst, 39-40. *Work:* Pueblo Grande Mus, Trevor Browne High Sch, Phoenix; The Veterans Admin Medical Ctr, Prescott, Ariz; Detroit Inst Arts, Mich; Banks of Rio Grande, Las Cruces, NMex; Mayo Ctr for Womens Health, Scottsdale, Ariz; Proctor Bank Vt, Great Western Bank & Trust, Phoenix; Columbia Med Ctr, Phoenix; Bench Friedlander, Cleve; Archival & Special Collections, Ariz State Univ, 62-70; Ind State Archival Libr, Indianapolis. *Exhib:* Phoenix Art Mus, Four Corners Biennial; 49th Ann Hoosier Salon, Firebird Festival, Scottsdale, Ariz; Ann FACET Woman Art Nat, Taos, NMex; Past, Present, Future, Ariz State Capitol; Southwest Contemp, Yavapai Coll; In Celebration of Women, Mayo Center, Scottsdale, Ariz; Images of Faith, Artistic Images Gallery, Prescott, Ariz, 2005. *Collection Arranged:* Mature Eye, Prescott Fine Arts Asn, 96-00. *Pos:* Art dir, Frank R Jeleff Co, Washington, DC, 50, Wm H Block co, Indianapolis, Ind, 51-61, Diamonds, Phoenix, Ariz, 62-66; art dir & free lancer; pres, Scottsdale Artists League, 73-74, Ariz Watercolor Asn, 80; cur, Mature Eye, Prescott Fine Arts Asn, 96-2001. *Teaching:* instr painting & drawing, Phoenix Art Mus, 76-78, Phoenix Parks & Recreation Dept, 80's, Workshops Art Groups, Ariz, NMex, 80's through 2005. *Awards:* Advertising Woman of the Yr, Indianapolis Ad Club, 58; 1st Mixed Media, Yavapai Co Women in the Arts, 88; 1st Mixed, Southwestern Contemp, 89; 2nd Oil, Yavapai Women in the Arts, 90; 1st Watercolor, 2nd Oil, Prescott Fine Arts Asn, 2002. *Bibliog:* Phoenix Republic, Indianapolis News & Star, Indianapolis Times, Ariz Living, Phoenix Mag, Prescott Courier, Scottsdale Progress, Carefree Enterprise and others; Prescott Woman Mag, 2007. *Mem:* Ariz Watercolor Asn (pres, 80-81). *Media:* Oil, Watercolor. *Publ:* Decil Collection on Display, Sonoran News, 97 & Arizona Senior World Art Profile, Ariz Senior World, 4/2000; PV Artist Del Decil, Prescott Courier, 97. *Dealer:* Krol Gallery 1945 Commerce Ctr Cir Prescott AZ 86301

DECKERT, CLINTON A
PAINTER, ASSEMBLAGE ARTIST
b Chicopee, Mass, May 17, 1959. *Study:* Self taught. *Work:* Univ Conn, Storrs; Naugatuck Valley Community Coll, Conn; Greater Hartford Art Coun, Conn; Northend Sr Ctr, Hartford, Conn; New Britain Rock Cats Baseball Stadium, Conn; Univ Conn Med Ctr. *Comn:* Wall mural, Univ Conn, West Hartford, 2004; various pvt collections. *Exhib:* I Dream & I was Dreaming, Artworks Gallery, Hartford, Conn, 97; Surrealist and the Poet, Univ New Haven, Conn, 2000; Gala, Wadsworth Atheneum, Hartford, Conn, 2000; Brave Destiny Int, Williamsburg Art & Hist Ctr, Brooklyn, NY, 2003; Surreal Mindscapes, Stevens Gallery, Univ Conn, Storrs, 2004; New Britain, Mus Am Art, Juried Show, Conn, 2004; Warner Theatre Atrium Gallery, Torrington, Conn, 2004; Pump House Gallery, Hartford, Conn, 2004; Winter Blues, Artworks Gallery, Hartford, Conn, 2005; Polonaise Gallery, Woodstock, Vt, 2005; Lotus Fine Art & Design, Woodstock, NY, 2005; White Heat, White Space Gallery, New Haven, Conn, 2006; Oil Drum Art Exhib, New England Carousel Mus, Bristol, Conn, 2006; Heartbeat, Aldrich Contemp Art Mus, Ridgefield, Conn, 2006; ArtSpace Hartford, Open Your Mind, Conn, 2006; New Britain, Mus Am Art, Juried Show, Conn, 2007; 64th Annual Conn Artists Exhib, Slater Mem Mus, 2007; Third Summer In, White Space Gallery, New Haven, Conn, 2007; Art Under the Big Top, Artspace Gallery, Hartford, Conn, 2008; Conjurings, White Space Gallery, New Haven, Conn, 2008; Downtown Gallery, New Britain, Conn, 2010; Gallery 101 Main, Collinsville, Conn, 2010; Harvesting the Harbinger, Paris in Plantsville, Conn, 2011. *Pos:* Pres, Artworks Gallery, Hartford, Conn, 91-92 & 97-99; pres, In Home Art Serv, Southington, Conn, 95-; judge & juror, art exhibs, 98-. *Teaching:* Lect, Conn Art Educ Asn Fall Conference, Farmington Marriott, 2004; lect, Manchester Art League, 2005, Cheshire Art League, 2005, 2007; lect, Manchester Art Asn, 2006; lectr, Hamden Art League, 2009; lectr, Warner Estate Whispering Cliffs, Tuscaloosa, Ala, 2011. *Awards:* Individual Artist Fel Grant, Grater Hartford Arts Coun, 99 & 2002; Best in Oils, 2003 & 2009 & Bank North Award, 2004, Southinghton Arts Asn; Aesthetic First Prize, 2005 & Peoples Choice Award, 2009, Oil Drum Art, ArtSpace Gallery, Hartford, Conn; Best in Oils, Southington Arts Asn, 2009; 1st pl, Bellamy-Ferriday House, Bethlehem, Conn, 2010; 2nd pl, Art League of New Britain, Conn, 2011. *Bibliog:*

Steve Starger (auth), Clinton Deckert at Art Works, Art N Eng, 97; Pat Seremet (auth), Art Works Works, Java - Hartford Courant, 2002; Will Steigerwald (auth), The Walls have Eyes and Ears, Art Is Mag, 2005; Pamela Morello (auth), Painter's award winning work balances art and function, Southington Citizen, 2005; Nancy L Rodgers (auth), Altered Awareness, Art Is Mag, 2005; Feature, Cloning the Drama, Southington's Inventive Exhibition, Kool-Record Jour, 2006; Leah Lopez Schmalz (auth), Third Summer's A Charm, Overall Complexities, Guilford Courier, Conn, 2007; Stephen Hard (auth), Surrealist Exhib, Downtown Gallery, New Britain, Hearld, 2010; Art Scuttlebutt (auth), Profl Artist Mag, 2011. *Mem:* Artworks Gallery, Hartford, Conn (pres, 91-92, 97-99, vpres, 93-96, prog chmn 2000-03, mem chmn 2004); New Britain Mus Am Art, Conn; Wadsworth Atheneum, Hartford, Conn; Real Arts Way, Hartford, Conn. *Media:* Oil on Canvas, Acrylic. *Collection:* Jack Warner Collection, Tuscaloosa, Ala. *Dealer:* White Space Gallery New Haven CT 06510; Lotus Fine Art & Design Inc 33 Rock City Rd Woodstock NY 12498; Sam Heller Fine Art 6102 N Sheridan Rd #404 Chicago IL 60660. *Mailing Add:* 55 Blossom Way Southington CT 06489-1878

DE CREEFT, LORRIE J See Goulet, Lorrie

DECTER, BETTY EVA
PAINTER, SCULPTOR, WRITER
b Birmingham, Ala, 1927. *Study:* Self taught & Otis Art Inst. *Comn:* Painting, comn by Mr & Mrs Norman, Pauma Valley, Calif, 86; portrait, Carolyn Tapp, 95-96. *Exhib:* Solo exhibs, Crocker Bank, Beverly Hills, Calif, 80, Roger Morrison Gallery, Los Angeles, Calif, 85, Bonwit Tellers, Beverly Hills, Calif, 86, Ivey's Dept Store, Gainesville, Fla, 86, Brand Libr Art Gallery, Glendale, Calif, 88, Riverside Co Mus, 89 & San Francis Gallery, Crossroads Sch Arts & Scis, Santa Monica, 92; Artists Equity Bienale Exhib, Brand Libr Art Gallery, Glendale, Calif, 87; Loyola Law Sch, SCalif Women's Caucus Art, 88; 16th Ann Multi Media Juried Art Show, Creative Arts Ctr Gallery, Burbank, Calif, 91; Laguna Mus Art, 97; Finegood Art Gallery, Woodland Hills, Calif, 98; The Grove, Pacific Grove, Calif, 99. *Pos:* Founder, Carpal Tunnel, Publishing Co, 2005. *Teaching:* Instr painting & collage, workshops; instr, workshops in studio, teaching collage and monotypes, currently. *Awards:* Cash Award, Assocs Brand Libr Award, Creative Arts Ctr Gallery, Burbank, Calif, 91; Bronze Award, Calif Discovery, 94. *Bibliog:* Women's Caucus Art, Feisty Women (video), 2/89; Mary Alice Cline (auth), Colors & Cultures Weigh in at a Ton of Kimonos, Press Enterprise, 4/16/89; Rita Townsend & Ann Perkins (coauths), Bitter Fruit, Hunter Publ Co, 92; and others. *Mem:* Women's Caucus Art; Artists Equity; NY Artists Equity; Monotypes on Etching Press. *Media:* Acrylic, Mixed Media on Canvas. *Publ:* Contribr, Contemporary Women Artists Calendar & Datebook, Cedco Publs, 92-94; Mutiny and Mainstream, Midmarch Press, 92; Contribr, Luz bilingual mag, 93. *Mailing Add:* 5412 W Washington Blvd Los Angeles CA 90016

DE CUNTO, JOHN GIOVANNI See Giovanni

DE DONATO, LOUIS
PAINTER, INSTRUCTOR
b New York, NY, Aug 29, 1934. *Study:* Art Students League, with Frank Reilly, 55-61. *Work:* Abe Sharp Found, Maine; Navy Art Combat & Laison, Washington. *Exhib:* Allied Artists Am Ann Exhib, Nat Arts Club, NY, 81 & 93; Soc Animal Artists Exhib, Acad Natural Sci, Philadelphia, 82 & Topeka, Kans, 83; Am Artists Prof League, NY, 93; SSA Exhib, Bennington, 94; Salmagundi Club, Ann Exhib, 94. *Teaching:* Instr life drawing & painting, Salmagundi Club, New York, 72-. *Awards:* Isabel Steinschneider Mem Award, Hudson Valley Art Asn, 95; Don Donaldson Award, Salmagundi Club 95 & Antonio Cirino Award, 96; Jane Impastato Award, Salmagundi Club, 94; Pres Award, Am Artists Prof League, Grand Nat Exhib, 96; Philip Shumaker Award-Marine, Hudson Valley Show, 2002; Hon mention, Salmagundi Club Annual Non-Juried Summer Show, 2002; Antonio Cirino Award, Ann Mem Combined Show, Salmagundi Club, 2003; F. Ballard Williams Fund Award, Spring Auction, Salmagundi Club, 2003. *Mem:* Salmagundi Club (bd dir, 70-90); Allied Artists Am; Soc Animal Artists (bd dir, 76-08); Am Artists Prof League; Hudson Valley Artists Asn; and others. *Media:* Oil. *Publ:* Illusr, Nat Inst Art & Design, Northwest Sch, 64. *Dealer:* Husberg Fine Arts Gallery Scottsdale AZ; Austin Galleries Austin Tex; FM Allen NY. *Mailing Add:* 400 E 77th St Apt 10 F New York NY 10075-2342

DEFAZIO, TERESA GALLIGAN
PAINTER, GALLERY DIRECTOR
b Philadelphia, Pa, May 5, 1941. *Study:* Moore Coll Art, with Paulette VanRoekins, Dolya Goutman, Ranulph Bye & Leonard Nelson, BFA, 63; Acad Fine Arts, with Louis Sloan, Seymour Remenick & Glen Rudderow, 89-90. *Work:* Rosemont Collection, Radnor Twp Sch Dist, Wayne, Pa. *Exhib:* Ann Exhib Small Oils, Philadelphia Sketch Club, 91 & 92; Ann Juried Exhib, The Plastic Club, Philadelphia, 91 & 92. *Collection Arranged:* Northern Images (Inuit & NW Coast Nat Am Art), Rehoboth Art League, Del, 98; Invitational Masters Exhib, Salisbury State Univ, Md, 99. *Pos:* Mgr, Newman Galleries, Bryn Mawr, Pa, 74-77; dir, Newman Galleries, Philadelphia & Bryn Mawr, 85-90; mgr, Art Space Gallery, Gladwyne, Pa, 90-95, regional coordr, currently. *Mem:* Fel Pa Acad Fine Arts; Philadelphia Art Dealers Asn (secy 87-89); Moore Coll Art Alumnae Asn; Rehoboth Art League; Sussex Arts Coun. *Media:* Oil. *Publ:* Coauth & ed, Moore Coll Art Alumnae J, 70s; Kenneth R Nunamaker, 1890-1957, 84, Joe Brown-A Retrospective Exhibition, 87, John Folinsbee-Following His Own Course, Newman Galleries, 90

DE GALBERT, ANTOINE
ADMINISTRATOR, COLLECTOR
b 1955. *Study:* Degree in political sci. *Pos:* past owner, Galerie Antoine de Galbert, Grenoble, France, formerly; founder & pres, La Maison Rouge-Found Antoine de Galbert, Paris, 2004-. *Awards:* Named one of Top 200 Collectors, ARTnews mag, 2004-13. *Collection:* Contemporary art, primitive art. *Mailing Add:* la maison rouge 10 blvd de la bastille Paris 75012 France

DEGETTE, ANDREA M
FILMMAKER, DIRECTOR
b Denver, Colo, Sept 6, 1962. *Study:* Univ Colo, Boulder, 80-82; Tisch Sch Art, NY Univ, BFA, 84; Duke Univ, 98-. *Work:* Duke Univ Med Ctr; Ctr Doc Studies, Durham, NC; Mint Mus Art. *Comn:* For the Sense of It, Fayetteville & Cumberland Co Arts Comn, NC, 95; Art of Community (video), Chapel Hill Pub Arts Comn, 97; NC Dir Artists, NC Arts Coun, Raleigh, 97; Wanted X-Cheerleaders, comn by Kim Irwin, Raleigh, 97; Video in the Classroom, State of NC, 98. *Exhib:* A Better Heaven, Bug Theatre, Denver, Colo, 96; Sisters from Apex, Midnight Express Theatre, Santa Monica, Calif, 97 & Mint Mus Art, Charlotte, NC, 97-98. *Pos:* Video artist in creative arts for various pub schs, 87-; video facilitator & producer, Cary Youth Proj, Page Walker Art Ctr, NC, 96-98; Adj prof, Piedmont Community Col, NC, 95-97. *Awards:* Best Dramatic Short Film, NC Film & Video Festival, 96; Emerging Artist Grant, 96; NC Arts Coun Fel, 97. *Mem:* Women Make Movies; NC Media Arts Alliance. *Publ:* Dir & filmmaker, films & videos, viewed Univ NC & NC Pub TV, 95-98. *Mailing Add:* 407 W King St Hillsborough NC 27278

DEGIULIO, LUCAS
ARTIST
b Dearborn, Mich, 1977. *Study:* Minneapolis Coll Art & Design, BFA (mixed media), 2000. *Exhib:* Midway Contemp Art, Minneapolis, 2003; 6th Ann Monster Drawing Rally, Southern Exposure, San Francisco, 2006; Day for Night, Whitney Biennial, 2006; New Langton Arts, San Francisco, 2006

DEGN, KATHERINE KAPLAN
ART DEALER
b New York, NY. *Study:* Haverford Col, Pa, BA, 86. *Pos:* Dir, Kraushaar Galleries, NY, 91-. *Specialty:* Twentieth century & Contemp Am art. *Publ:* Coauth, Kraushaar Galleries catalogs. *Mailing Add:* c/o Kraushaar Galleries 74 E 79th St New York NY 10021

DE GOGORZA, PATRICIA (GAHAGAN)
SCULPTOR, PRINTMAKER
b Detroit, Mich, Mar 17, 1936. *Study:* Smith Coll, BA, 58; S W Hayter's Atelier 17, Paris, France, 58-60; Goddard Coll, Plainfield, Vt, MA, 75. *Work:* Collection Ville de Paris (Louvre), France; Victoria & Albert Mus, London, Eng; Boston Mus Fine Arts; Provincetown Art Asn Mus, Mass; Bard Coll, Annandale-on-Hudson, NY; pvt collections of S. Tschurtz & R. Wolf. *Comn:* Tobias & the Angel (granite), Kerson, at Worcester, Vt, 87; Sun/Moon Cycle (granite), Johnson State Coll, Vt, 89; Riverbirds (large marble sculpture), Marble St Sculpture Park, W Rutland, 91; Pegasus (marble), 92, Merman & Dolphin (marble), 93, Mermaid (marble), 93, Burlington, Vt Bike Path; Tree of Life (wood polychrome), Pavilion Bldg, Montpelier, Vt, 95; cell/drum fountain, Guatamalan Green Marble, J Thompson, Morristown, VT; Alcyone (marble), T. Coates Rodney Co, New York, 2008. *Exhib:* Five Sculptors, Putney Sch, Vt, 93; Stone Sculpture Group, No Bias Gallery, North Bennington, Vt, Wood Art Gallery, Montpelier, Vt & Castleton State Coll, Vt, 93 & 97; Southern Vt Art Ctr, Manchester, 93-97; Helen Day Art Ctr, Stowe, Vt, 94-2004; West Branch Sculpture Garden, Stowe, Vt, 94-98; Manifest Poetry, Stone Sculpture Exhib, Northfield, Vt, 98; Solo exhibs, Julian Scott Gallery, Johnson State Coll, Vt, 2005 & Ox Bow Gallery, 2005, Whitewater Gallery, Vt, 2010, Whitewater Gallery, Hardwick, Vt, 2010; Vt Arts Coun Sculpture Garden, Montpelier, Vt, 2005-2007; group exhibs, Whitewater Gallery, Vt, Tamarack Gallery, Vt, summer 2007, Studio Place Arts, Barre, Vt, 2007-2008 & Five Vermont Sculptors, Marist Coll Gallery, Poughkeepsie, NY, 2009; James Gahagan Sch Retrospective, Johnson State Coll, 2009. *Pos:* Bd mem, Printmaking Workshop, NY, 70-74, Vt Coun Arts, 89-92 & Carving Studio, WRutland, Va, 90-94. *Teaching:* Bard Coll, Annandale on Hudson, NY, 66-71; Goddard Coll, Plainfield, Vt, 73-81; Univ Vt, Burlington, 81; Vt Coll, Montpelier, 88-93; vis artist, Carving Studio, W Rutland, Vt, 88-2003; instr, Vt Clay Studio, 94-97; sculpture dept, Johnson State Coll, 96; instr sculpture workshop, Akaroa, New Zealand, 99, 2003-2005; instr, VSC, 2001-2011; Johnson St MFA Prog, Vt, 2006-2007. *Awards:* First Prize Sculpture, Norwich Ann, Vt, 78 & 86; First Prize, All Vt Juried Show, Bundy Mus, Waitsfield, Vt, 82. *Bibliog:* V Watson-Jones (auth), Contemporary Women Sculptors, Oryx Press, Phoenix, Ariz, 85; Jason Kornick (auth), Creating a Life of Art, 3-5, Vt Maturity. *Mem:* Soc Am Graphic Artists; Provincetown Art Asn; Vt Women's Caucus Art; Vt Coun Arts; found Art Resource Asn. *Media:* Wood, Stone; Color Etching, Copper. *Interests:* Violinist, Vt Philharmonic, Montpelier Chamber Orchestra. *Dealer:* Clarke Gallery Stowe VT; Acme Gallery 38 Newbury St Boston MA. *Mailing Add:* 1580 Dog Pond Rd East Calais VT 05650

DE GROAT, DIANE
ILLUSTRATOR, DESIGNER, WRITER
b Newton, NJ, May 24, 1947. *Study:* Pratt Inst, 65-69, BFA. *Comn:* Children's Book Council. *Exhib:* Soc Illusr Ann Nat Exhib, NY, 72 & 75; Insides, 74 & Ann Bk Show, 77, Am Inst Graphic Arts, NY; Poster USA/74, Art Dir Club, 74 & 85; Master Eagle Gallery, NY, 81, 83-85; Southeast Ohio Arts Ctr, 90; Kimberly Gallery, NY, 90; Michelson Gallery, Amherst, Mass, 96-; Original Art, Soc Illustrators, 2000; Eric Carle Mus Picture Book Art, 2007-2012; Univ New England, 2011. *Collection Arranged:* DeGrummond Collection; Mazza Mus. *Pos:* Designer & art dir, Holt, Rinehart & Winston, NY, 69-72. *Awards:* Ark Diamond Primary Award, 98-99; NC Childrens Book Award, 98; Best Book Award, Oppenheim Toy Portfolio Platinum, 2009; Time Mag Top Ten Children's Books, 2009; New York Times Bestseller List, 2011, 2012. *Mem:* Soc Children's Bk Writers; Author's Guild; Western Mass Illusr Guild. *Media:* Watercolor, digital. *Publ:* Little Rabbit's Loose Tooth, Crown, 75; Dr Ruth Talks to Kids, Macmillan, 93; auth/illusr, Roses are Pink, Your Feet Really Stink, 97 & Trick or Treat, Smell My Feet, Harper Collins, 98; Last One in is a Rotten Egg, Harper Collins, 2007; Dogs Don't Brush their Teeth, Scholastic, 2009; illusr, Charlie the Ranch Dog, 2011; Charlie and the New Baby, 2014; and 100 other titles. *Dealer:* R Michelson Gallery Northampton Mass

DE GROOT, PAT
PAINTER
b London, 1930. *Study:* Univ Pa, Philadelphia, BA, 1953. *Exhib:* Solo exhibs, Pat Hearn Gallery, NY City, 2000, Albert Merola Gallery, Provincetown, Mass, 2001, 2003, 2005, Tibor de Nagy Gallery, NY City, 2004, Brick Walk Books & Fine Art, West Hartford, Conn, 2004, Judy Ann Goldman Fine Art, Boston, 2005; Group exhibs, Cherrystone Gallery, Wellfleet, Mass, 2000; Nielsen Gallery, Boston, 2002; Am Acad Arts & Letters, Awards Show, 2004. *Media:* Oil. *Dealer:* Tibor de Nagy Gallery 724 Fifth Ave NY City NY 10019; Judy Ann Goldman Fine Art 14 Newbury St Boston MA 02116. *Mailing Add:* c/o Albert Merola Gallery 424 Commercial St Provincetown MA 02657

DE GUATEMALA, JOYCE BUSH VOURVOULIAS
SCULPTOR
b Mexico City, Mex, Feb 25, 1938; Guatemalan citizen. *Study:* Univ Mex, 58; Univ Wis, 59; Silpakorn Univ, 60-62. *Work:* Fed Reserve Bank Pa, Philadelphia; Mus Mod Art Mex City, Chapultepec/Mexico City, Mex; Orgn Am States & Mus Mod Art Latin Am, Washington; Nat Mus Hist & Fine Arts, Escuela Nac De Bellas Artes & Guatemalan Chamber Indust, Guatemala City; Open Air Sculpture Symposium & the World Invitational Open Air Sculpture Exhib commemorating the 24th Summer Olympic Games, Olympic Park, Seoul, Korea. *Comn:* Nat Fine Arts Sch of Guatemala, Guatemala City, 75; OAS & Mus Mod Art Latin Am, Washington, 77; Exmibal-El Estor, Exmibal, Guatemala, 77; Kensington Town House Project, Redevelopment Authority of Philadelphia, Pa, 81; Elkins Park Free Lib, Pa, 85. *Exhib:* Guggenheim Mus/Olympiad of Art, Seoul, Korea, 88; Solo exhibs, Medicine Wheel, 90, Marian Locks Gallery, Philadelphia, 91, 14 Sculpture Gallery, Soho, NY, 92, Estela Shapiro Gallery, Mexico City, Mex, 92, Philadelphia Mus Art, Pa, 92 & Barbara Gillman Gallery, Miami Beach, 94 & 97; Gallery Artists, Estela Shapiro Gallery, Mexico City, Mex, 92; Books as Art, Barbara Gillman Gallery, Miami Beach, Fla & New World Sch Arts, Miami, Fla, 93; Metro-Dade Art in Pub Places, Brickell Ave, Miami, Fla, 93; Three Latin Am Artists, Barbara Gillman Gallery, 94; Centro Nac Expos, Madrid, 97; Contemp Artists Mus, Americano, Madrid, Spain, 97; State Mus Pa, 98. *Pos:* Vpres, Asociacion Tikal, 68-73; dir, Fine Art Comt, Patronato de Bellas Artes, 72-75; bd dir, Brandy Wine Work Shop, Philadelphia, Pa. *Awards:* Hon Mention for Sculpture Certamen Permanente Centro Americano, Guatemala; Miguel Gracia Granados Medal, Guatemala City, Guatemala, 76; VLI Corp Fel, Djerrasi Found Artist-in-Residence Grant, Woodside, Calif, 85 & 94. *Bibliog:* Deborah Victoria Curtis (auth), Visual Literacy, 85; Virginia, Watson-Jones (auth), Contemporary American Women Sculptors, Oryx Press, 86; Gallery Hyundai (ed), Olympic Sculpture Park Guide, Seoul Olympic Organizing Comt, 88; Ante Glibota (ed), Olympiad Art Catalogue, Seoul Olympic Organizing Comt, 88. *Mem:* Roy Soc Brit Sculptors, London; Asn Tikal; Int Sculpture Ctr, Washington, DC. *Media:* Stainless Steel, Wood. *Dealer:* Barbara Gillman Gallery The Sterling Bldg 939 Lincoln Rd, Miami Beach, FL 33139. *Mailing Add:* 320 Fairview Rd Glenmoore PA 19343

DE GUNZBURG, CHARLES
COLLECTOR
Study: Dartmough Coll, BA; Harvard Univ, Kennedy Sch Govt, MPA. *Pos:* With Seagram Co, formerly; co-founder, mem investment & mgmt comt, FdG Assocs, New York, 1995-; vchmn, First Spring Corp, New York; trustee & co-chmn, Intrepid Sea-Air-Space Mus, New York; trustee, Intrepid Fallen Heroes Fund; trustee & chmn investment comt, Jewish Mus, New York. *Awards:* Named One of Top 200 Art Collectors, ARTnews, 2007, 2008, 2012, 2013. *Collection:* Postwar & contemporary art

DE GUNZBURG, NATHALIE
COLLECTOR
Study: Inst Supérieur de Gestion. *Pos:* Mem, Int Coun Mus Mod Art, NY; trustee, Musicians on Call; mem, Dia Art Found, 2004-, chmn bd trustees, 2006-. *Awards:* Named one of Top 200 Collectors, ARTnews Mag, 2007, 2008, 2011. *Collection:* Postwar and contemporary art

DE GUZMAN, EVELYN LOPEZ
PAINTER, PRINTMAKER
b New York, NY, June 14, 1947. *Study:* City Univ New York, BA, 70; Hunter Col, Grad Sch, MA, 74; Pratt Inst; Parsons Sch Design. *Work:* Museo del Barrio & Bronx Mus, NY; Citibank Corp, NY; Museo de Ponce, PR; Mus Contemp Hispanic Art, NY; US Am Art Collection. *Exhib:* Puerto Rican Artists, Bronx Mus, NY, 81; Mus Contemp Hispanic Art, NY, 84 & 85; Project Am, Villa Taverna (traveling worldwide), NY, Washington, DC; Latin Roots, Nat Coun La Raza, Washington, DC, 90; Journeys, Martin Luther King Libr, Washington, DC, 92; Origin of Am States, Washington, DC. *Teaching:* Instr, high sch & elem syst. *Bibliog:* Grace Glueck (auth), Art: Puerto Rican show in the Bronx, New York Times, 1/26/79; Elaine Wechsler (auth), Space: The inside, the outside, Artspeak, 11/81; Juan Bujan (auth), La Geometria Dinamica de Evelyn Lopez de Guzman, La Voz, 12/3/81. *Mem:* Women Arts; Women's Caucus Art; Asn Artist Run Galleries; Brooklyn Arts Cult Asn Inc. *Media:* Acrylic, Paste; Mixed Media. *Publ:* Contribr, New York Art Yearbook, Noyes Art Books, 75-; Puerto Rico: Its people, its artists, Lightsource, 77. *Dealer:* Noho Gallery 168 Mercer St New York NY 10012; MOCHA 584 Broadway New York NY 10012. *Mailing Add:* Two Hamilton Ct Sterling VA 20165-5625

DEGUZMAN, NICOLE
DIRECTOR
b Sioux City, Iowa, Dec 16, 1977. *Study:* Univ Calif, Santa Barbara, BA, 03. *Work:* UCSB Women's Ctr Art Gallery, Santa Barbara; UCSB Univ Art Mus. *Collection Arranged:* Women Expanding their Borders, multi-media, 02; Three Women, solo-exhib, 02; The Power of Women, multi-media. *Mem:* Univ Calif Art Historians Club, pres, 02-. *Publ:* Charlotte Bocheler, Sensual Women, Santa Barbara News Press, 01. *Mailing Add:* Univ Calif Women's Center Art Gallery Bldg 434 Santa Barbara CA 93106

DE HEUSCH, LUCIO
PAINTER
b Sherbrooke, Que, 1946. *Study:* Univ Que Montreal & Ecole des Beaux-Arts Montreal, Que, 66-69. *Work:* Muse d'Art Contemporain, Mus des Beaux-Arts de Montreal, Univ Que, Montreal, PQ; Mus de Que; Calif Coll Arts & Crafts; Can Coun Art Bank; Ministry of External Affairs, Ottawa, Ont. *Exhib:* Solo exhibs, Musee d'Art Contemporain, Montreal, Que, 75, Galerie Graff, Montreal, Que, 85, 88, 91 & 92, Olga Korper Gallery, Toronto, Ont, 85, 87, 92 & 96, Ayot-de Heusch, Galerie Champlain, Universite Bishop, Lennoxville, Que, 87, Recent Paintings, Olga Korper Gallery, Toronto, 90, Art 23 '92, Basel, Switz, 92 & Centre D'Exposition des Governeurs, Sorel, Que, 93; Art 16, Bale, Switz, 85; L'Art Pense, Galerie d'Art de l'Univ de Sherbrooke, Quebec, 85 & traveling throughout Canada; Ouevres Charnieres, Galerie Graff, Montreal, 86; Graff: 20 Ans d'Affiches, Place des Arts, Montreal, 86; Parti Pris Plenture, Galerie UQAM, Montreal, Que, 93, Leslleux Incertains, 95 & Ayot-L'esplegie, Hommage, 96. *Awards:* Research Grant, Can Arts Coun, 74, 75 & 77; Ministry of Cult Affairs, Que Govt, 75 & 77; Materials Assts Grants, Can Arts Coun, 81 & 84; Accessibilite Grant, 85, Bourse du Que, 85, Que Govt. *Bibliog:* Articles, La Presse, Montreal, 84, PEI, 85; articles, Le Devoir, Montreal, 10/5/85, 1/24/86 & 1/25/86; John Bentley May (auth), article, Globe & Mail, 12/17/87. *Mailing Add:* c/o Olga Korper Gallery 17 Morros Ave Toronto ON M6R 2H9 Canada

DEITCH, JEFFREY
CONSULTANT, MUSEUM DIRECTOR
b Hartford, Conn, 1952. *Study:* Wesleyan Univ, BA, 74, Harvard Bus Sch, MBA, 78. *Collection Arranged:* Lives, Fine Arts Bldg, New York, 75; Cultural Geometry (auth), 88, Artificial Nature (auth, catalog), 90, Deste Found, Athens, Greece; Strange Abstraction, Touko Mus, Tokyo, 91; Post Human, Castello di Rivoli, Torino, 92. *Pos:* Asst Dir, John Weber Gallery, New York, 74-76; cur, De Cordova Mus, Lincoln, Mass, 78-79; vpres, Citibank art adv serv, 79-88; principal, Jeffrey Deitch Inc, 88-2010, gallery closed 2010; dir, Mus Contemp Art Los Angeles, 2009-. *Awards:* Art critics fel, Nat Endowment Arts, 79. *Publ:* Auth, Keith Haring, Stedelijk Mus, 85; Figuration Libre, Arc, Paris, 85; The Art Industry, Metropolis, Berlin, 91. *Mailing Add:* Museum Contemporary Art, Los Angeles 250 S Grand Ave Los Angeles CA 90012

DE KANSKY, IGOR
PAINTER, SCULPTOR
b Nice, France, May 19, 1926. *Study:* Ecole Nationale des Arts Appliques, dipl, 45; Ecole des Beaux Arts, Univ Paris, 46; Academie de la Grand Chaumiere, with Othon Friez, 46. *Comn:* bas relief wood, Orthopaedic Hosp, Los Angeles, 82; bas relief wood, Claremont McKenna Col, Calif, 84; City of Pasadena, 97; painting and wood carved doors, Shrine for Virgin of Guadalupe, Pasadena, 2000-01; several large paintings, Private Collector, San Diego, Calif, 2003; Mus Pacific Culture, Pasadena, Calif, 71. *Exhib:* Calif Design Show, Pasadena Art Mus, 62, 65 & 68; Otis Art Inst, Los Angeles, 65; Valley House Gallery, Dallas, 67; solo exhibs, Woodbury Univ, Burbank, Calif, 89; retrospective, Woodbury Univ, 91; Art Night, Pasadena, 2009; Sierra Madre, Calif City Hall, 2009-10. *Pos:* Guest Speaker, Plato Soc, Univ Calif Los Angeles, 96. *Awards:* Purchase Award, Calif Design Show, Oakland Art Mus, 62; Award of Merit, Am Craftsman Coun, 62. *Bibliog:* Beverly E Johnson (auth), An ancient expression in modern dress, Los Angeles Times, 62; American designer craftsmen, NY Times, 62; Architectural Digest, 64-83. *Media:* Lacquer; Wood, Watercolor. *Specialty:* Painting, sculpture. *Interests:* Drawings. *Collection:* Mr. and Mrs. Philip Verlager, Alexander Giritsky MD, Lee Main, Mr Hever Le Jenne. *Dealer:* Artitude Gallery, Paris, France. *Mailing Add:* 481 N Sunnyside Ave Sierra Madre CA 91024

DE KERGOMMEAUX, DUNCAN
PAINTER, EDUCATOR
b Premier, BC, July 15, 1927. *Study:* Banff Sch Fine Art; Inst Allende, Mex; Hans Hofmann Sch Fine Art. *Work:* Nat Gallery Can; London Regional Art Gallery; Art Gallery Ont; Study Collection, Carleton Univ, Ottawa, Ont; Ottawa Art Ctr; Mcintosh Gallery, London, Ont; Art Gallery Mus London, London, Ont. *Comn:* Exterior wall mural, Vanier Post Off, Dept Pub Works, Can, 70; Man Centennial Caravan, Dept Secy State & Man Govt, 70; shaped banners, Schoeler, Heaton Archit, Univ Ottawa, 71; mall environment, Schoeler, Heaton Archit, Garneau Sch, Orleans, Ont, 71; and others. *Exhib:* 3rd & 6th Biennials Can Art, Nat Gallery Can, Can Painting, Albright Knox Gallery, 66; DeKergommeaux-DeNiverville Touring Exhib, Nat Gallery Can, 67-68; Loranger Gallery, Toronto, 80 & 81; Take Two Touring Exhib, 80-84; An Art of Ordered Sensations, London Regional Art Gallery, 86; Process, Structure, Meaning (with catalog), London Regional Art Gallery, 95; Vanishing Icons, St John's, New Foundland, 2002; These are the Marks I Make, Ottawa Art Gallery, 2010; Mus London, London, Ontario, 2011. *Pos:* Dir, Can Pavilion Art Gallery, Expo 67, Montreal, 66-67; chmn dept visual arts, Univ Western Ontario, 81-84, prof emer, 93-. *Teaching:* Vis prof drawing & painting, Banff Sch Fine Arts, summer 74-75; prof drawing & painting, Univ Western Ont, 80-; vis prof, NS Coll Art, summer 80. *Awards:* Monsanto Can Art Competition, 57; Purchase Award, Minneapolis Biennial, Boutels, 58; Art Wall Competition, Benson & Hedges, 71. *Bibliog:* Groves (auth), DeKergommeaux at the Blue Barn, Can Art, 63; M Teitlebaum (auth), An Art of Ordered Sensations (exhib catalog), 86; Jose Barrio-Gray (auth), Process, Structure, Meaning (exhib catalog), 2010; Bonario, Falvey, Fatona (auths), These are the Marks I Make (catalog), 2011. *Mem:* Royal Can Acad Arts. *Media:* Oil. *Dealer:* Thielsen Galleries London Ontario. *Mailing Add:* 135 Springfield Rd Ottawa ON KIM IC Canada

DE LA CRUZ, CARLOS
COLLECTOR
b Havana, Cuba. *Study:* Univ Pa, BS, 1962, MBA (finance), 1963; Univ Miami Sch Law, Fla, JD, 1972. *Pos:* Chmn, CC1 Companies, Inc, currently; chmn bd dirs, United Way Dade County, 1993-1995; sr trustee & chmn bd trustees, Univ Miami, 1999-2001; bd dirs, Georgetown Univ, Belen Jesuit Prepatory Sch, Fla Int Univ, Dade

Found, Bus Assistance Ctr, Miami Partners for Progress, formerly; co-founder, De La Cruz Collection Contemp Art, Miami, Fla. *Awards:* Alexis de Tocqueville Award for outstanding philanthropy, United Way, 1997; Nat Community Serv Award, Simon Weisenthal Ctr, 1998; named one of Top 200 Art Collectors, ARTnews mag, 2004-13. *Collection:* Contemporary art, especially Latin American. *Mailing Add:* 5 Harbor Pl Miami FL 33149-1715

DE LA CRUZ, ROSA
COLLECTOR
Exhib: THAT PLACE, Moore Space, 2002. *Pos:* Co-founder, Moore Space, Fla, 2001, De La Cruz Collection Contemp Art Space. *Awards:* Alexis de Tocqueville Award for outstanding philanthropy, United Way, 1997; Nat Community Serv Award, Simon Weisenthal Ctr, 1998; named one of Top 200 Collectors, ARTnews mag, 2004-13. *Mem:* Mus Contemp Art N Miami, Fla; Miami Art Mus (acquisition comt, currently); Mus Contemp Art Chicago (exhib comt, currently). *Collection:* Contemporary art, especially Latin American. *Mailing Add:* De La Cruz Collection Contemporary Art Space 23 NE 41st St Miami FL 33137

D'ELAINE
PAINTER, LECTURER
b Puyallup, Wash, Mar 19, 1932. *Study:* Cent Wash State Univ, BA, 54; Univ Wash, MFA, 58; Univ London, research of sea hist. *Work:* Akron Art Mus, Ohio; Central Wash Univ, Wash; Edmonds City Hall, Edmonds, Wash; Byran Mawr Rehab Hosp, Pa; Edmons Community Coll, Wash; Edmonds Mus Edmonds, Wash; Green River Community Coll, Auburn, Wash; Hidetoshi Mari Art Collection, Japan; Maritime Event Ctr, Bell Harbor, Seattle, Wash; New Zealand Pvt Colelction; Nordic Heritage Mus, Seattle, Wash; Northwest Hospital, Seattle, Wash; peninsula Sch District, Harbor Ridge Middle Sch; Prince & Princess Eleski, Russia; Roche Harbor Collection of 12 paintings, Roche Harbor Island, Wash. *Comn:* Sea books illus, comn by Dept Navy for USS Bremerton submarine; Rosicrucian Order, New Zealand; Thunderbird, US Navy, Officer's Ward Room, USS Bremerton, 84. *Exhib:* Northwest Ann Exhib, Seattle Art Mus, 58-72; Frye Art Mus, Seattle, 64, 75-76, 88-89 & 91; Maritime Mus, Vancouver, BC, 75-76; Bellevue Art Mus, Wash, 89 & 92; Pac Arts Ctr Hauberg Gallery, Seattle, Wash, 92; State of the Art '93, New Eng Fine Arts Inst Nat Exhib Am Contemp Art, Boston, 93; Biennial Art Exhib Wash State Chapter Nat League Am Pen Women, Frye Art Mus, Seattle, 93; solo exhibs, Edmonds Art Mus, Wash, 94, Karshner Mus, Puyallup, Wash, 94, Ilwaco Heritage Mus, Wash, 94-95 & 2003, Northlight Gallery, Everett, Wash, 95, Myths of the Americas, Karshner Mus, Puyallup, Wash, 95, Tides of Ages, Art Ctr Gallery, Seattle Pac Univ, Wash, 95, Newark Gallery, Seattle, Wash, 95 & Contemp Northwest Artists Gallery, Maryhill Mus, Goldendale, Wash, 96; Five Indian Myth paintings, Cent Wash Univ Conv Ctr, Ellensburg, 94; Of the Nature of Water Exhib, Corvallis Art Ctr, Ore, 95; Juried World Exhib, United Nations, 2003; United Nartions Headquarters, NY, 2004; Seas of Antiquity, Odyssey Maritime Discovery Ctr, Waterway Gallery, Seattle, 2005-2008; Akron Art Mus, Ohio, 2008; over 500 others. *Collection Arranged:* The Old Steam Plant, Central Wash Univ, Ellensburg, Wash, 2008; Totem Spirit People, Bryn Maur Rehab Hospt, Malvern, Pa, 2010; Community Coll, Lynwood, Wash, 2011; and many others. *Pos:* founder, South Snohomish Co Arts Roundtable, 97-. *Teaching:* Art educator, Seattle, WA 54-78; instr drawing & painting, Mus Hist & Indust, 54-56, Edmonds Adult Classes, 57-62 & Seattle Pub Schs, 60-70; lect, various univs, community colls & asns, 58-95; art consult, Wash state area, 78-; founder, Mount Olympus Preserve for the Arts, Edmonds, Wash, 71-90. *Awards:* 1st recipient, Nat League of Am Pen Women Art Scholarship, 90; Purchase Award, Nova Scotia Art Mus, 60; 1st place, Whatcom Mus Hist & Art, 14th Ann Northwest Int Art Competition, 94; 1st place award, 10th Ann Exhib, Pa, 2006; Artist of the Year, Art Ability Exhib, Melveron, Pa, 2007; Purchase Award, Akron Art Mus, Ohio, 2008. *Bibliog:* My Art, My Life, My Love. *Mem:* Kappa Pi; Nat Artist Equity Asn; Nat Mus Women Artists; Women Painters Wash; Am Coun Arts; Nat Pen Women. *Media:* Acrylic. *Res:* researching through books, museums, writings. *Specialty:* Pisces Studio. *Interests:* Scuba diving, camping, bike, hiking, collecting sea shells, & sea artifacts, traveling, researching myths, lore, religions of sea cult, studying violin, studying psychology, writing about creativity. *Publ:* Articles include Artists of the World Waters, Beyond This Point THere Be Monsters, Cult Exchange through Spiritual Visions, Enchanted Sea Beyond, Eternal Myths, Forward, Global Art, Global Art II, Homo-sapiens, The Myth Makers, Image maker, Infinite Sea, Might of Destiny, Myth, Legends, Folklore, One Great Story, Sea of Antiquity, Sea Songs & Shanties, Sea Symphony, Sea through Iconography, Seeing the unseen Sea, Shadow of the Ancients, Spell of Myth, Symbols, Tides of Ages, Timeless Waters, We are Multi-Cultured Seaport State, What is a Myth, 71-. *Dealer:* Pisces Studio 16122 72nd Ave W Edmonds WA 98020. *Mailing Add:* 16122 72nd Ave W Edmonds WA 98026-4517

DE LAMA, ALBERTO
PAINTER
b Havana, Cuba. *Study:* Am Acad Art, Chicago, with William Mosby & Joseph Vanden Broucke. *Work:* Pullman Bank, Chicago; Talman Home Fed Savings Art Collection, Chicago; Delta Airlines, Atlanta, Ga; Galeria Vanidades, Miami, Fla; Malios, Tampa, Fla; The Hendry Corp; Ye Mystic Krew of Gasparilla, Tampa, Fla; Tampa Yacht & Country Club. *Comn:* Corp Portraits, Celotex Corp. *Exhib:* Galeria Sans Souci, Caracas, 73 & 76; Wildlife Gallery, Minocqua, Wis, 73-79; Talisman Gallery, 76; LeBlanc Wildlife Gallery, Minocqua, Wis, Talisman Gallery, Bartlesville, Okla, Galeria Sans Souci, Caracas, Univ Club Tampa, Galeria Vanidades, Miami, Tampa Yacht & Country Club, Tampa Bay History Center; and others. *Pos:* Pres, Graphic Direction Inc, Tampa Fla. *Teaching:* Instr painting & drawing, Am Acad Art, 69-74. *Awards:* Diamond Awards 70 & 71 & Gold Medal, 72-75, Palette & Chisel Acad Fine Arts; First Prize Harriet Bitterly Award, Chicago, Ill, 76. *Bibliog:* Armando Alvarez Bravo (auth), La Manera de de Lama, El Nuevo Herald, 8/96; Maria Elena Saavedra (auth), Expone Alberto de Lama, Diario de las Americas, 8/96; Esther Hammer (auth) Artist painting impressions of Tampa, The Tampa Tribune, Tampa,, 6/99; Steve Otto (auth), See Artist look at Tampa, Tampa Tribune, Tampa, Fla, 6/2010. *Media:* Oil. *Res:* Canvas Stretching; Granted Canvas Stretching Patent, 76. *Specialty:* Mr de Lama's works. *Publ:* Auth, Tercer Aniversario Puente Mariel, Cayo Hueso, 80-83. *Dealer:* Graphic Direction Inc. *Mailing Add:* c/o Graphic Direction Inc 3005 W Horatio St Tampa FL 33609

DELAP, TONY
SCULPTOR, PAINTER
b Oakland, Calif, Nov 4, 1927. *Study:* Menlo Jr Col, Calif; Calif Coll Arts & Crafts, Oakland; Claremont Grad Sch, Calif. *Work:* Mus Mod Art, Whitney Mus Am Art & Guggenheim Mus, NY; Walker Art Inst, Minneapolis; San Francisco Mus Art; Tate Gallery, London, Eng; Los Angeles Co Mus Art; and others. *Comn:* Sculpture-fountain complex, CCH Bldg, San Rafael, Calif, 70; City of Inglewood, Calif; City of Santa Monica, 91; Los Angeles Airport. *Exhib:* Whitney Mus Am Art, 64; Chicago Art Inst, 64; Mus Mod Art, NY, 64, 65 & 67; solo exhibs, Robert Elkon Gallery, 65-84, Newport Harbor, 77, Casat Gallery, La Jolla, 77, Calif State Col, Chico, 79, Janus Gallery, Venice, Calif, 79, Beatrix Wilhelm, Stuttgart, Ger, 92, Gudrun Spielvogel, Munich, Ger, 93, Mark Moore Gallery, Santa Monica, 94, 95 & 96, The House of the Magician: An Installation of Reconstructed Works 1967-1979, Calif State Univ, Fullerton, 94 & Modernism, San Francisco, 96, Charlotte Jackson Fine Art, 2010; Contemp Am Sculpture, Whitney Mus Am Art, 66; Am Sculpture of the Sixties, Los Angeles Co Mus Art, 67; Calif Painting and Sculpture: The Modern Era, San Francisco Mus Art, 76; Corcoran Biennial, 78; Art for the Pub, Dayton Art Inst, 88; Finish Fetish, Fisher Gallery, Univ Southern Calif, 91; Shape: Forming the Los Angeles Look, Calif State Univ, Fullerton, 95; Generations: The Lineage of Influence in Bay Area, Richmond Art Ctr, 96; Focus IV: Orange Co Artists, John Wayne Airport, 97; Selected Painting & Work on Paper: Modernism, San Francisco, 98. *Teaching:* Lectr fine arts, Univ Calif, Davis, 63-64; prof fine arts, Univ Calif, Irvine, 65-91. *Awards:* First Prize Sculpture, Los Angeles Dept Airports, 76; Award for Painting, Nat Endowment Arts, 83; IDM Corp Competition Sculpture Comn Award, 85. *Bibliog:* Alan Solomon (auth), Tony DeLap: The Last Five Years, Univ Calif, Irvine, 68; Gene Cooper (auth), DeLap, The Edge as Form and Metaphor, 77; Tony Delap, The House of the Magician, Calif State, Fullerton, 94. *Dealer:* Mark Moore Gallery Santa Monica CA; Modernism San Francisco CA. *Mailing Add:* 225 Jasmine St Corona Del Mar CA 92625

DE LARIOS, DORA
SCULPTOR
b Los Angeles, Calif, Oct 13, 1933. *Study:* Univ Southern Calif, BFA, 57. *Work:* Oakland Art Mus, Calif; Craft & Folk Art Mus, Los Angeles; Security Pacific Bank Collection; Am Mus Ceramic Art, Pomona, Calif. *Comn:* Ceramic mural (8ft x 40ft), Compton Co Libr, Calif, 73; cement mural (8ft x 10ft), Security First Nat Bank, 76; ceramic mural (8ft x 16ft), Norwood Co Libr, Calif, 77; ceramic mural (5ft X 20ft) & 2 ceramic panels (3ft X 6ft), Makaha Inn Resort, Oahu, Hawaii, 79; Friendship Patterns (6ft X 26ft cement mural), Cent Park Develop, Nagoya, Japan, 79; porcelain mural (7ft X 40ft), Hilton Hotel, Anaheim, Calif, 84; porcelain mural with lacquered & patina wood sects (5'6ft X 15'6ft), Huntley Hotel, Santa Monica, Calif, 85; porcelain mural (40ft x 8ft), Montage Resort & Spa, Laguna Beach, Calif, 2005; stoneware porcelain mural (10ft x 4ft), Salinas Residence, 2006. *Exhib:* Am Crafts at the White House, Renwick Gallery, Smithsonian Inst, Washington, DC, 77 & Contemp Craft Mus, NY, 77; Craft & Folk Art Mus, Los Angeles, 77; Kohler Art Ctr, Wis, 77; Everson Mus, Syracuse, NY, 77; Indianapolis Mus Art, Ind, 78; Southern Alleghenies Mus Art, St Francis Coll, Loretto, Pa 82; Western Regional Conf, Logan, Utah, 82; Solo retrospective, Wooster Coll, Ohio, 83; Los Angeles Munic Art Gallery, Barnsdall, Calif, 84. *Teaching:* Vis instr ceramics, Univ Southern Calif, Los Angeles, 58, & Univ Calif, Los Angeles, 79. *Awards:* Purchase Award for Ceramic Sculpture, Calif State Fair, 61; Certificate of Honor, Women in Design Int. *Bibliog:* Elain Levin (auth), Dora De Larios, Ceramic Monthly, Vol XXVI, No 8, 10/78; Lorelei McDevitt (auth), Art & artisan-public spaces, Designer West, Vol XXVIII, No 1, 11/80; article, Dora De Larios, Ceramica, Madrid, Spain, Vol V, No 17, 83; Lorelei McDevitt (auth), Art & artisans-the evolving mask of Dora De Larios, Designers West, Vol XXXI, No 10, 8/84; Monika Guttman (auth), An artist who needs her Space-Dora De Larios, Santa Monica Evening Outlook Newspaper, 8/85. *Mem:* Am Ceramic Soc. *Media:* Clay, Wood, Cement. *Interests:* life in all its manifestations. *Dealer:* Evalyn Daniel Laguna Beach Ca; Lois Neitar Sherman Oaks Ca. *Mailing Add:* 3914 Huron Ave Culver City CA 90232-3804

DE LA TORRE, DAVID JOSEPH
MUSEUM DIRECTOR
b Santa Barbara, Calif, June 14, 1948. *Study:* Univ San Francisco, BA, 70. *Collection Arranged:* Rockefeller Collection of Mexican Folk Art (proj dir), Mex Mus, 86; FRIDA, 87; Diego Rivera, 88; Passion with Reason: The Mex Sch, HAA, 96; The Art of Antonio Wartorell, 2000. *Pos:* Curatorial asst, Fine Arts Mus San Francisco, 77-81; develop dir, Triton Mus Art, 81-84; exec dir, Mex Mus, 84; panelist, Nat Endowment Arts, 84-89 & 92; consult, Hawaii State Found Cult & Arts, 91-; assoc dir, Honolulu Acad Arts, 91-. *Mem:* Am Fed Arts; Am Asn Mus; Western Mus Asn. *Publ:* Contribr, The Art of Rupert Garcia, Mex Mus Chronicle Books, 86; Nelson A Rockefeller Collection of Mexican Folk Art, Mex Mus Chronicle Books, 85; The Marvelous/The Real: Carmen, Lomas, Garza, 87. *Mailing Add:* Mission House Mus 553 S King St Honolulu HI 96813-3002

DE LA TORRE, EINAR
GLASS BLOWER
b Guadalajara, Mex, 1960. *Study:* Calif State Univ, BFA, 1980. *Work:* Caltrans District 11, New Campus Facility, San Diego, Caif; Plaza San Jose, Calif; San Diego New Main Pub Libr, Calif; San Diego Harbor, Calif. *Exhib:* Solo exhibs include Julie Rico Gallery, Santa Monica, Calif, 1994, William Traver Gallery, Seattle, 1997, 1999, Daniel Saxon Gallery, Los Angeles, 1997, 1999, 2002, 2003, 2004, 2005, Mex Fine Arts Mus, Chicago, 1998, Porter Troupe Gallery, San Diego, 1999, Grand Arts,

Kansas City, MO, 2001, Mus Contemp Art of Fort Collins, CO, 2002, The Salina Art Ctr, Salina, KS, 2002, Am Mus of Glass, Millville, NJ, 2004, Mus of Glass, Tacoma, WA, 2005, Koplin Del Rio Gallery, West Hollywood, Calif, 2005; Group exhibs include Monique Knowlton Returns, Monique Knowlton Gallery, New York, 1997; Spring Group Exhib, Porter Troupe Gallery, San Diego, 2000; Off Broadway, Mus Contemp Art, San Diego, 2000; Reflections of Time & Place, Latin Am Still Life in the 20th Century, Mus del Barrio, New York, 2000; Ultra Baroque-Aspects of Post Latin Am Art, Walker Art Ctr, Minneapolis, 2003, Miami Art Mus, 2003, San Francisco Mus Mod Art, 2003; Home/Land, Houston Ctr Contemp Craft, Tex, 2003; Group exhib, District Arts Gallery, Birmingham, MI, 2004; Going Global, Carnegie Mus, Oxnard, Calif, 2004; Insatiable Desires, Fisher Gallery Mus, Los Angeles, 2005. *Awards:* Louis Comfort Tiffany Found Grant, 2008

DE LA TORRE, JAMEX
GLASS BLOWER
b Guadalajara, Mex, 1963. *Study:* Calif State Univ, BFA, 1984. *Exhib:* Solo exhibs include Julie Rico Gallery, Santa Monica, Calif, 1994, William Traver Gallery, Seattle, 1997, 1999, Daniel Saxon Gallery, Los Angeles, 1997, 1999, 2002, 3003, 2004, 2005, Mex Fine Arts Mus, Chicago, 1998, Porter Troupe Gallery, San Diego, 1999, Grand Arts, Kansas City, MO, 2001, Mus Contemp Art of Fort Collins, CO, 2002, The Salina Art Ctr, Salina, KA, 2002, Am Mus of Glass, Millville, NJ 2004, Mus of Glass, Tacoma, WA, 2005, Koplin Del Rio Gallery, West Hollywood, Calif, 2005; Group exhibs include Monique Knowlton Returns, Monique Knowlton Gallery, New York, 1997; Spring Group Exhib, Porter Troupe Gallery, San Diego, 2000; Off Broadway, Mus Contemp Art, San Diego, 2000; Reflections of Time & Place, Latin Am Still Life in the 20th Century, Mus del Barrio, New York, 2000; Ultra Baroque-Aspects of Post Latin Am Art, Walker Art Ctr, Minneapolis, 2003, Miami Art Mus, 2003, San Francisco Mus Mod Art, 2003; Home/Land, Houston Ctr Contemp Craft, Tex, 2003; Group exhib, District Arts Gallery, Birmingham, MI, 2004; Going Global, Carnegie Mus, Oxnard, Calif, 2004; Insatiable Desires, Fisher Gallery Mus, Los Angeles, 2005. *Awards:* Louis Comfort Tiffany Found Grant, 2008. *Mailing Add:* Koplin Del Rio Gallery 6031 Washington Blvd Culver City CA 90232

DELAURO, JOSEPH NICOLA
SCULPTOR, EDUCATOR
b New Haven, Conn, Mar 10, 1916. *Study:* Yale Univ, BFA (Alice Kimball Fel, Tiffany Fel & Elizabeth Pardee Scholar), 41; Univ Iowa, MFA, 47; also in Italy, 53, 62, 66 & 71. *Work:* In private collections of Dr D Corradini, Quito, Ecuador, Dr B Clemente, Akron, Ohio, Rev Ralph Kowalski, Detroit & Bishop Ernest Primeau, Manchester, NH. *Comn:* Mankato stone sculpture, St Columba Cathedral, Youngstown, Ohio, 59; glass & plastic mural, Windsor Bd Educ, Ont, 64; bronze sculpture, Hiram Walker & Sons, Ltd, Ont, 67; bronze sculpture, Detroit Pub Libr, Mich, 67; bronze sculpture, Jewish Community Centre, Windsor, Ont, 70. *Exhib:* Walker Gallery, Minneapolis, 47; Mich Regional Exhib, Detroit, 48; Ecclestical Art Guild, Detroit, 50; Fine Arts Dept Fac Exhib, Art Gallery Windsor, Ont, 70-72; Biannale de Fiorino, Florence, Italy, 71. *Teaching:* Prof sculpture & drawing, Marygrove Col, Detroit, 47-59; prof, Univ Windsor, formerly. *Mem:* Fel Royal Soc Arts; Nat Sculpture Soc; Coll Art Asn Am; Mid Am Coll Art Asn; Univ Art Asn Can. *Media:* Bronze, Marble

DE LA VEGA, ANTONIO
PAINTER, DESIGNER
b El Paso, Tex, July 13, 1927. *Study:* NY Univ; Art Students League; also study in Mex, Spain, France, Italy & Port. *Comn:* Portrait, Lt Gen James Gavin, Gavin Hall, Hq 82nd AB Div, Ft Bragg, NC, 92. *Exhib:* Pintores Nuevos, Galeria Ciga, Buenos Aires, Arg, 60; Antonio de la Vega, Galeria Fuentes, Mexico City, Mex, 61; Spanish Impressions, Galeria Gran Via, Madrid, Spain, 62; Portugal Viejo, Galeria Sesimbra, Lisbon, 66; de la Vega, Galeria Botto, Rome, Italy, 68; Rockland Coll, 88; Bronx Mus Art, 89. *Pos:* Art dir & designer, Cushing & Nevell, Inc, New York, 51-62 & Persons Advert Inc, New York, 63-74; freelance art dir, designer & illusr advert, 74-76; sr art dir, Stogel co, New York, 76-88. *Teaching:* Individual advan painting tech instr. *Mem:* Nat Asn Portrait Painters; Am Artists Prof League; Am Inst Graphic Arts; Artists Guild New York (vpres, 64-65); Southwest Art Found. *Media:* Oil, Acrylic. *Mailing Add:* 702 Henderson Dr Jacksonville NC 28540-4476

DE LA VEGA, GABRIELA
PAINTER, ILLUSTRATOR
b Mexico, Oct 19, 1946. *Study:* Art Student League, 86-90; Acad San Carlos, 88-90; with Alton Tobey, NY, 90-95; Hon degrees from Centro de estudios univ Londres 80-96 & Jamar arte y literatura 85-96. *Work:* Encuentro de escritoras y pintoras, Ateneo, Madrid, Espana; Conclave de signos, Inst Politecnio Nat Mexico DF; La daza interna, Mus Franz Mayer Mexico DF; Elogio de una sospechosa, Mus de Arte Mod, Mexico DF; Inmediaciones de Van Gogh, Mus Rufino Tamayo, Mexico DF. *Comn:* Latin Am Art Show, Thorton Donnovan Sch, New Rochelle, NY, 93; Batalla de Otumba, Inst Mexiquense Cultura, Edo, Mexico, 93; Ezra Pound, Jomar arte literatura, Mexico DF; Crees saberlo todo, Bibliog Mexicana, Mexico DF 96; Si te labra prision mi fantasia, Bibliog Mexicana, Mexico DF, 96. *Exhib:* Desnudisima, Estud Churubusco, Mexico, 91 & 92; Ocho Mujeren Enel Arte, Foro Cult Delegacion Magadalena Contreras, Mex DF, 93; Chili Pepper Fiesta, Brooklyn Botanic Garden, NY, 94; De amor y desvarios, Casa del Lago, Chapultepec, Mexico DF, 94; Seven Mexican Artists, Broome St Gallery New York 94-96; La danza regional, Teatro de la danza, Mex, 2007; Les Nalbaut de Gaby, Cámara de Diputados, Mex, 2007; 45 big and medium-sized paintings, House of Representatives, Mex City, 2008; Mexican Folk Dancing, Lan Danza Regional Mexicana, 2009. *Teaching:* Instr Mex Lit & Art, Lart Lycco Jean Jacques Rousseau, Paris, 75-77; instr, Art Univ Nat Autonoma, Mexico DF, 80-84; rector, Centro de estudios Univ, Londres, 80-2007, instr literature & art, 80-2007. *Awards:* Premio Nac Cuento, Tampico Tamaulipas, 85; Premio de acuarela, Casa de la acuarela, Mexico DF, 91 & 92. *Bibliog:* Jose Luis Cuevas (auth), Rene Char, Revista Siempre, 90; Francisco Del Rio (auth), Pintores, Directorio de las artes plasticas, 93-95; Sergio Loyo (auth), Sirenas, Periodico 1990, 95. *Mem:* Students League; Artist's Equity; Amigos de los parques Mexico y Espana (pres, 92-96); Jomar aite y Literatura (du, 85-96); Centro de estudios Univ Londres (dir, 80-96). *Media:* Oil, acrylic, acuarelle, pencil. *Res:* La ópera mexicana, la danza regional mexicana, el mercado del arte en México. *Interests:* Mex art, literature & educ. *Publ:* Illusr, Inmediaciones de Van Gogh de Rene Char, 84 & Elagio de una sospechosa de Kene Char, Lince Ed, 89; La muerta de Krishna de Sitakant Mahapatra, 93 & De amor y desvaris de Patricia Vidal, 94, Jomar arte y literatura; Si te labra prision mi fantasia de Guadalupe Elizalde, Bibliofilia Mex, 96. *Dealer:* Norma Clavel M Citlaltepetl 45-302 Colonia Hipodroma Mexico DF Mexico 06100. *Mailing Add:* Col Hip Condesa Ave parque Mexico 55 PH Mexico DF 06170 Mexico

DE LA VERRIERE, JEAN JACQUES
GOLDSMITH, SILVERSMITH
b Paris, France, Mar 8, 1932; US citizen. *Study:* Ecole Nat Art Decoratifs, BA, Paris, France, 49; Escuela de Artes Suntuarias, Barcelona, Spain, 51; London Cent Col, Eng, 57; Pratt Inst, with Prof Albert, MFA, 75; Hunter Col, MA (art hist), 79. *Work:* Cooper Mus, NY; Nat Mus Design; Contemp Crafts Mus; Metrop Mus, NY; Mus Mod Art, NY. *Comn:* Monstrance, Eglise du Gesu, Montreal, 59; Masonic Jewelry, 68, Ritual pieces, 70 & commemoration medals, 75, var Masonic Lodges, Ritual Pieces, NY, Hermès NY, Arman, B Venet. *Exhib:* Solo exhibs, Pellicone Gallery, Southampton, NY, 82, Retrospective, Goldberg Gallery, NY, 85 & Pompidou Mus, Paris, 85; Caroline Corre Gallery, Paris, 83; Small Works, NY Univ, 83-85; B Fendrick Gallery, Washington, DC, 83; Alan Stone Gallery, NY, 88. *Teaching:* Instr enameling, Haystack Sch Art, 68; asst prof sculpture & electroforming, Pratt Inst, 72-75. *Awards:* First Prize Jewelry, Greenwich Village Outdoor Show, 61-80 & New York Craftsmen, 63, 68-82. *Bibliog:* Ancient Metallurgy in Art, 70; Berber Jewelry in Morocco, 89 & The Hand, 90. *Mem:* NY Craftsmen; Am Crafts Coun; Am Goldsmith Asn. *Media:* Gold, Silver, Precious and Semi-Precious Stones; Rare Woods, Ivory. *Res:* Guillotine; "Terror," part of the French Revolution; Berber tribal jewelry from North Africa. *Collection:* Arts, Hermès Collection, Paris; Schlumberger Collection, Paris; Alan Stone Collection. *Publ:* Auth, Electroforming for Jewelry & Sculpture, 70. *Dealer:* Dna. *Mailing Add:* 99 MacDougall St No 18 New York NY 10012-5031

DEL CHIARO, MARIO A
HISTORIAN
b San Francisco, Calif, Apr 22, 1925. *Study:* Univ Calif, Berkeley, BA, 50, MA, 51, PhD, 56. *Pos:* Chmn art hist, Univ Calif, Berkley, 69-70, 79-80. *Teaching:* Assoc prof, Univ Calif, 62-66, prof, 66-93, emer prof, 94. *Awards:* Metrop Mus Art Fel, 53-54; Prix de Rome, Am Acad Rome, 58-60; Nat Endowment for the Humanities Fel, 77; Order of Merit of the Ital Repub, Cavaliere Officale. *Mem:* Archeol Inst Am, Studi Etruschi ed Italici, Florence; Archeol Inst, Berlin; Archeol Inst (Ger), Rome; Europ Acad Sci & Art, Salzburg. *Media:* Archeology, etruscology. *Res:* Ancient art; archeology. *Publ:* The Genucilia Group, Berkeley, 57; auth, Etruscan Red-Figured Vase-Painting at Caere, Berkeley, 74; The Etruscan Funnel Group, Florence,74; Classical Art at the Santa Barbara Mus Art: Sculpture, 84; Studies in Honor of DA Amyx, 86. *Mailing Add:* c/o Univ Calif Dept Art Hist Santa Barbara CA 93106

DELEHANTY, SUZANNE
MUSEUM DIRECTOR
b Worcester, Mass, July 18, 1944. *Study:* Skidmore Col, BA(art hist) 65; Univ Pa, grad study (art hist), 66-68. *Collection Arranged:* Nancy Graves: Sculpture & Drawing 1970-72, 72; Agnes Martin (with catalog), 73; Six Visions (with catalog), 73; Robert Morris/Projects, 74; Cy Twombly: Paintings, Drawings, Constructions 1951-1974 (with catalog), 75; Video Art (with catalog), 75; George Segal: Environments (with catalog), 76; Pieces & Performances, 76; Improbable Furniture (with catalog), 77; Paul Thek/Processions (auth, catalog), 77; Dwellings, 78; On Sculpture/Christo, di Suvero, Irwin & Segal, 79; Richard Artschwager/Themes: The Transformation of Illusion and Reality (auth, catalog), 79; On Soundings (auth, catalog), 81; Roni Horn/Space Buttresses, 86; The Window in Twentieth-Century Art (with catalog), 86; David von Schlegell/Recent Work, 89; Fred Sandback/Sculpture (with catalog), 89. *Pos:* Curatorial asst, Inst Contemp Art, Univ Pa, 68-71, dir, 71-78; dir, Neuberger Mus, State Univ NY, Purchase, 78-88; dir, Contemp Arts Mus, Houston, 89-94 & Miami Art Mus, Fla, 95-. *Awards:* Outstanding Young Women Am, 80. *Mem:* Asn Art Mus Dir; Urban League of Greater Miami. *Mailing Add:* Miami Art Mus 101 W Flagler St Miami FL 33130

DELGYER, LESLIE
ENVIRONMENTAL ARTIST, PAINTER
b Plainfield, NJ, Sept 11, 1946. *Study:* duCret School of the Arts with Dudley V duCret & Marjorie Van Emburgh, 68. *Work:* Series of 5 Endangered Animals, World Wildlife Int Stamp Prog, Leigh Yawkey Woodson Art Mus, Wausaw, Wis; Hunterdon Med Ctr, Flemington, NJ; Ronald Reagan Presidential Mus, Calif; Hiram Blauvelt Art Mus, Oradell, NJ; W Valley Art Mus, Surprise, Ariz. *Comn:* Conserv stamp collection: New Zealand Tuatara, 90, African Mountain Zebra, 90, Egyptian Caracal, 91, Asian Goitered Gazelle, 92 & Russian Siberian Tiger, 93, World Wildlife Fund Int. *Exhib:* Cleveland Mus Natural Hist, Ohio, 99; Burpee Mus Natural Hist, Rockford, Ill, 99; Utah Mus Natural Hist, Salt Lake City, Utah, 2000; Norton Art Mus, Shreveport, La, 2000; North Mus Natural Hist and Sci, Lancaster, Pa, 2000; Nat Geographic Soc, Wash, DC, 02; Utah Mus Natural History, Salt Lake City, 03; The Canton Mus of Art, Ohio, 02; solo exhib, Blauvelt Art Mus, Oradel, NJ, 03; West Valley Art Mus, Surprise, Ariz, 04; Univ of Nebr State Mus, Lincoln, Nebr, 05; Ariz-Sonora Desert Mus, Tucson, Ariz, 06; Muscarelle Mus Art, Coll of William & Mary, Williamsburg, Va, 2006; Neville Pub Mus, Green Bay, Wis, 2006; Bergstrom-Mahler Mus, Neenah, Wis, 2007; Hickory Mus Art, Hickory, NC, 2007; Audubon Artists 66th Ann Exhib, NY, 2008 ; The Vanishings, Swain Galleries, Plainfield, NJ, 2009; 85th Anniversary Exhib, duCret Sch Arts, Plainfield, NJ, 2012. *Pos:* Bd trustees, duCret Sch, 85, vpres bd trustees, 87 & pres bd trustees, 2000; hist & paliamentarian, Soc Animal Artists, 87, asst secy exec bd, 89 & secy, 94, 2009 pres, 2004-2009, secy, 2009. *Awards:* Cert

Spec Cong Recognition, 2000; US House Reps Citation, 2000; State NJ Senate and Gen Assembly Citation, 2000; Somerset Co Comn on the Status of Women (mem); Bd of Chosen Freeholders Citation in the Field of Art (mem). *Bibliog:* Joni Kinslow (auth), Spotlight on art: Leslie Delgyer artist, Pleasure Hunt Mag, 7-8/83; NJ State of the Arts Broadcast (film), WNJN, WNYC & WHMM, 5-6/90; Tucker Commbe (auth), Art & Conservation, The Pastel Joun, 10/2009. *Mem:* Pastel Soc Am, Nat Arts Club, NY; Soc Animal Artists; Salmagundi Club, NY; duCret Sch; Nat Mus Women Arts, Wash; Pastel Soc NJ; Artists for Conservation, Canada. *Media:* Pastel. *Publ:* 30th Annual Exhibition and National Museum Tour Society of Animal Artists, US Art Mag, 11/90; The Best of Pastels 2-Collected by the Pastel Society of America & Wildlife Art, Rockport Publ, 98-99. *Dealer:* Swain Galleries 703 Watchung Ave Plainfield NJ. *Mailing Add:* 168 Westervelt Ave North Plainfield NJ 07060

DELL, ROBERT CHRISTOPHER
ENVIRONMENTAL ARTIST, EDUCATOR
b Nyack, NY, Feb 22, 1950. *Study:* NY State Univ Col, Oneonta, BS (educ), 72; NY State Univ Col, New Paltz, MFA (sculpture), 75. *Exhib:* Solo exhibs, Vorpal Gallery, Chicago, 78, NY, 81 & 88, San Francisco, 85, New Acquisitions Gallery, Syracuse, NY, 83, Blue Hill Cult Ctr, Pearl River, NY, 87 & 98, Am Cult Ctr, Reykjavik, Iceland, 88, Mid-Hudson Arts & Sci Ctr, Poughkeepsie, NY, 92, installation, Grotto & Castle Geyser Groups, Yellowstone Nat Park, 96, Akuregri Art Mus, Iceland, 99, Geysir, Haukadaker, Iceland, 99 & Reykjavid Munic Art Mus, 2001; Albert Neikan Sch of Engineering, The Cooper Union, New York City, 2004; 14 Sculptors Gallery, NY, 85 & 94; MIT Mus, Mass Inst Technol, Cambridge, Ma, 90-91; geothermal sculpture installation, Perlan, Reykjavik, Iceland, 91-; Lehigh Univ, Bethlehem, Pa, 91-92; Galleri Ofeigur, Reykjavik, Iceland, 93-94; Mass Inst Technol Mus, Ctr Advan Visual Studies, Cambridge, 94; installation, Tish Gallery, Tufts Univ, Medford, Mass, 95; installation, Carpenter Ctr Visual Arts, Harvard Univ, 95; Old Faithful, Grotto & Castle Geyser Groups, Yellowstone Nat Park, 96; Kresge Oval, Mass Inst Technol, Cambridge, Mass, 97; NJ City Univ, NJ, 98; Nassau Community Col, Garden City, NY, 99. *Pos:* Mem, Archit and Community Appearance, Bd of Review, Town of Orangetown, 79-, vice chairman, 87-; master scenic artist, One Life to Live, Am Broadcasting Co, NY, 88; res fel, Ctr for Advan Visual Studies, Mass Inst Technol, Cambridge, 93-95, res affil, 95-96; Research Fel, The Cooper Union Research Found, New York City, 2004-; Artist in Residence, The Cooper Union (sch of Engineering) 2004. *Teaching:* Guest speaker, Cooper Union Sch Art, Mass Inst Technol, Harvard Univ, State Univ NY & Nassau Community Col; vis artist, Akureyri Sch Visual Art, Iceland; Adj Prof, The Cooper Union, New York City, 2003-; Adj Prof Westchester Community Col, Valhalla, NY, 2003-2004. *Awards:* Fulbright Res Grant, 88; Coun Arts Grant, Mass Inst Technol, 97; Am-Scandinavian Found Fel, 99. *Bibliog:* review, D. Dominick Lombardi (auth),99 & Helen Harrison (auth), 99, New York Times; The Sculpture Mag review by D. Dominich Lomhard; 2001; Iceland Review, article by Jenita McCormack, Iceland, 2001. *Media:* Geothermal Sculpture, Mixed Media. *Publ:* contribr, Leonardo, MIT Press, vol 33, no 3,. *Dealer:* Galleri Ofeigur Skolavordustigur 5 Reykjauik Iceland. *Mailing Add:* 421 Washington St Tappan NY 10983

DELLA-VOLPE, RALPH EUGENE
PAINTER, EDUCATOR
b NJ, May 10, 1923. *Study:* Nat Acad Design; Art Students League. *Work:* Chase Manhattan Bank Collection, NY; Treas Bldg, Washington, DC; Slater Mus, Norwich, Conn; Pennell Collection, Libr of Cong, Washington, DC; Wichita Art Asn, Kans; and many pvt collections. *Exhib:* Pa Acad Fine Arts, Philadelphia, 52; Babcock Galleries, NY, 60-63; Butler Inst Am Art, Ohio, 63; Final, Nat Inst Arts & Lett, NY, 63 & 64; Columbia Mus, SC, 76; Seattle Art Mus, Wash; Berkshire Mus, Pittsfield, Mass; Grand Cent Galleries, NY. *Teaching:* Prof drawing & painting & artist-in-residence, Bennett Coll, 49-77; prof drawing & painting, Marist Coll, Poughkeepsie, 77-79. *Awards:* Libr of Cong Purchase Award, 52; Berkshire Mus Drawing Prize, 54; MacDowell Fel, MacDowell Art Colony, 63; Finalist, Nat Inst Arts & Letters, 64. *Media:* Oil. *Dealer:* Abby M Taylor Fine Art Greenwich CT; Vincent Vallarino Fine Art New York NY; Gregory James Gallery Kent & New Milford CT. *Mailing Add:* 241 S Rd Millbrook NY 12545

DELLER, HARRIS
ADMINISTRATOR, CERAMIST
b Brooklyn, NY, Jan 28, 1947. *Study:* Calif State Univ, Northridge, BA, 71; Cranbrook Acad Art, Mich, MFA, 73. *Work:* Ill State Mus, Springfield; Shigarnki Mus, Japan; Cranbrook Mus Mich; Everson Mus, Syracuse, NY; Am Craft Mus, NY. *Exhib:* Am Porcelain, Renwick Gallery, Smithsonian Inst, 80; solo exhibs, Int Commun Agency, Seoul, S Korea, Heroe and Icons, Mod Art Mus Ft Worth, 88, Brevard Mus Art, Fla, 98; The Service of Tea, Cooper-Hewett Mus, NY, 84; Am Clay Artist, Port of Hist Mus, Philadelphia, 85; Poetry of the Physical, Am Craft Mus, NY, 86; Crafts Today, Musee des Beau Arts, Paris; Altered States, Ctr for Visual Arts, Denver, 96; Davis Collection, Ariz State Univ, 99; Scripps Coll Ceramics Ann, 2000. *Teaching:* Vis instr Ceramics, Sch of Art Inst Chicago, 73; instr, Ga Southern Col, Statesboro, 73-75; prof ceramics, Southern Ill Univ, Carbondale, 76-, dir, Sch Art & Design, currently. *Awards:* Fulbright Hays Fel, Coun Int Exchange of Scholars, 81; Artist Fel, Ill Arts Coun, 86, 87, 89 & 99; Artist Fel, Arts Midwest, 90. *Bibliog:* Pat Degner (auth), Deller's Witty, Unpretentious Ceramics, St Louis Post Dispatch, 12/7/84; Nancy Gardner (auth), Harris Deller, American Ceramics, vol 6, no 4, summer 88; Harris Deller, Ceramics Monthly, vol 36, no 6, 88; Yih Wen Kuo (auth), Ceramic Art Mag, Harris Dellen, 94; R Zakin (auth), Ceramics, Ways of Creation, 99; The Best of Pottery 1 & 2, Rockport Publ, 96 & 99. *Mem:* Nat Asn Schs Art & Des; Nat Coun Educ in Ceramics Arts (publ chair, 94). *Media:* Porcelain. *Publ:* Is glaze dead?, The Studio Potter, Vol 24, 12/95. *Mailing Add:* Southern Ill Univ Sch Art Carbondale IL 62901

DELLIS, ARLENE B
MUSEOLOGIST, CRAFTSMAN
b Brooklyn, NY, Apr 12, 1927. *Study:* Antioch Coll; Univ NC, Greensboro, BA. *Pos:* Head lending serv, Brooklyn Mus, NY, 49-55; head traveling exhibs & registr, Solomon R Guggenheim Mus, NY, 55-63; registr, Gallery Mod Art, NY, 64, Marlborough-Gerson Gallery, NY, 64-67 & Lowe Art Mus, Univ Miami, Coral Gables, Fla, 79-82; exhib coordr, Inst of Contemp Art, Boston, 67-68; registr, ed-designer & dir traveling exhibs, Bernard Danenberg Galleries, NY, 69-72; asst to dir, La Boetie Gallery, NY, 72-77; assoc dir, Helios Gallery, NY, 78-79; fine leather designer craftsman, 76-79; exhib mgr & sr registr, Ctr for Fine Arts, Miami, Fla, 82-95, retired. *Publ:* Ed, Max Weber Drawings, 72; Kurt Seligman: His Graphic Work, 73; ed & designer, Hans Bellmer: Graphic Work, 74; auth, Kurt Seligman Graphics, Mus Fine Arts, Springfield, Mass, 74. *Mailing Add:* 14 Stoner Ave Apt 3J Great Neck NY 11021

DELLOSSO, GABRIELA GONZALEZ
PAINTER
b NY, 1968. *Study:* Nat Acad Fine Arts, NY, 99-2001; Art Students League, NY, 93-2001; Sch Visual Arts, NY, BFA, 89-92. *Exhib:* Solo exhibs include An Artist's Journey, Butler Inst Am Art, Ohio, 2006; two-person exhibs include Sundance Gallery, Bridge Hamton, NY, 98; 86th Ann Exhib, Allied Artists of Am, Nat Arts Club, NY, 99; Red Dot Exhib, Art Students League, NY, 2000; Sarah's Circle Benefit Show & Auction for Homeless Women, Swedish Am Mus Ctr, Chicago, Ill, 2001; Cork Gallery Exhib, Lincoln Ctr, NY, 2002; Ann Exhib, Butler Inst Am Art, Youngstown, Ohio, 2003; Allied Artists of Am, 2003-05, 2005; Figure in American Art, Eleanor Ettinger Gallery, NY, 2006, 2007. *Collection Arranged:* Permanent Collections, Salmagundi Club Mus, NY; Saturday Evening Post Soc; Pvt and Gallery Collections. *Teaching:* Teachers aid, Arts Students League, NY, 97-99, 93-94; teachers aid, Nat Acad Fine Arts, NY, 99-2001. *Awards:* Honorable Mention Award, Best Art of 2002, Artists Mag; Best in Show, Pen & Brush, Inc, NY, 2002; Isabel Steinschneider Mem Award, 2002; The Phil Desind Award, Butler Inst Am Art, 2003; Dianne B Bernhard Gold Medal, Art Spirit Found, 2006. *Mem:* Catharine Lorillard Wolfe Art Club, NY (bd mem, vpres, painting chmn, currently); Allied Artists of Am, NY (bd mem, news ed, 99-); Salmagundi Club, NY (juror, 2001-02); Art Soc of Old Greenwich, Conn (juror, 2001-02). *Media:* Oil, Acrylic. *Publ:* Article The Artists Mag, Dream Studio Art Competition, 95; article The Artists Mag, Annual Art Competition, 98; article Gallery & Studio Mag, Painting Review, 2002. *Dealer:* Simon & Schuster; Harper & Collins; American Girl Magazine; Random House; Willowisp Press. *Mailing Add:* 441 Albany Ct West New York NJ 07093

DELONEY, JACK CLOUSE
PAINTER, ILLUSTRATOR
b Enterprise, Ala, Nov 2, 1940. *Study:* Auburn Univ, BFA, 64. *Work:* First Nat Bank, Montgomery, Ala; First Ala Bank, Birmingham; Coca Cola Co, Montgomery, Ala; Pope & Quint Co, Mobile, Ala; Fla Gas Corp, Winter Park, Fla. *Exhib:* Seventh Juried Art Exhib, Mobile Art Mus, 72; Mainstreams 73 & 76; Hudson Valley 46th Nat, 74; WTex Watercolor Asn Nat, 75; Rocky Mountain Nat Watermedia, Colo, 76; Okla Nat Watercolor Exhib, Okla Mus Art, 76; and solo & group exhibs. *Pos:* Book designer, Methodist Publ House, Nashville, Tenn, 64-65; illusr & painter, Ft Rucker, Ala. *Awards:* Purchase Award, People's Bank & Trust, Tupelo, 72; Best Landscape, NJ Miniature Art Soc, 73; Purchase Award, Bluff Park Show, Birmingham, Ala, 77. *Mem:* Ala Watercolor Soc; La Watercolor Soc; Southern Watercolor Soc; assoc mem Am Watercolor Soc; assoc mem Allied Artists of Am. *Publ:* article, North Light, 4/78

DE LORY, PETER
PHOTOGRAPHER
b Cape Cod, Mass, Oct 2, 1948. *Study:* San Francisco Art Inst, BFA (photog), 71; Univ Colo, MFA (photog), 74. *Work:* Minneapolis Inst Art; William Hayes Fogg Art Mus, Harvard Univ, Cambridge, Mass; Mass Inst Technol, Cambridge; Nat Gallery Can, Ottawa, Ont; Addison Gallery Am Art, Andover, Mass; Nat Mus Am Art, Smithsonian Inst, Washington; Seattle Mus Art; San Francisco Mus Mod Art; Princeton Univ, NJ; Univ Washington Medical Center, Seattle; The Brookings Inst, Washington, DC, The Brainerd Found, Seattle, The Art Inst Chicago, Ill Seattle Mus Art, Washington. *Comn:* Wash State Art Comn (3' X 20' color mural), S Kitsup High Sch, Port Orchard, 85; Seattle Water Dept, 96; Seattle Arts Commission, Photographer in Residence, Seattle Public Utilities, Washington, 99; Sound Transit, Photographer in Residence, Seattle, 2000-; Wenatchee mural project, Confluence, collaberation (with Kay Kirkpatrick), 2000; Longfellow Creek, Way Findinpmankens, Seattle, 2004. *Exhib:* Solo exhib, Addison Gallery Am Art, 74; Carl Siembab Gallery Photog, Boston, Mass, 76; Sheldon Mus Art, Lincoln, Nebr, 77; The West: Real & Ideal, Univ Colo, 77; Univ Oreg, Eugene, 82; Southern Alta Art Gallery, Can, 83; Gallery Interform, Usaka, Japan, 86; Scheinder Mus Art, Ashland, Ore, 87; Santa Monica Col, Calif, 88; Blue Sky Gallery, Portland, Ore, 96; Whitman Col, Walla Walla, Wash, 2000; City Works, Bank Am Gallery, Seattle, 2001; Lisa Harris Gallery, Seattle, 2001, 2003 & 2007; Link in Process, City Hall, Seattle, 2007. *Pos:* Dir photog dept, Sun Valley Ctr Arts & Humanities, 75-79. *Teaching:* Instr photog, Ctr Eye Sch, Aspen, 69-71; asst photog, Minor White Workshop, Hotchkiss, Conn, 72-73; instr advan photog, Sun Valley Ctr Arts & Humanities, Idaho, 74-78; instr, Sch Art Inst Chicago, 80 & 84, Univ Wash, Seattle, 82, Portland Sch Art, Maine, 83, State Univ Calif, San Jose, 86-90 & San Francisco Art Inst, 91; Univ NMex, Albuquerque, 95. *Awards:* Western States Art Found Fel, Boise Art Gallery, 76-77; Nat Endowment Arts Photogr Fel, 79; Artist Fel, Calif Art Coun, 90; and others. *Bibliog:* Alex Sweetman (auth), Peter deLory Photographs, An Afterimage, Visual Studies Workshop, Rochester, NY, 11/76. *Mem:* Soc Photog Educ. *Media:* Black & white photography. *Publ:* Contribr, Aperture, Inc, 73; Creative Camera, English, 12/73; Auth, The Wild and the Innocent, Calif Mus Photog, Riverside, 87; Railwork: Rebirth of Commuter Rail, Sound Transit, Seattle. *Dealer:* Lisa Harris Gallery Seattle WA. *Mailing Add:* 1010 Portland St SW Seattle WA 98106

DELOYHT-ARENDT, MARY
PAINTER
b Independence, Mo, Mar 10, 1927. *Study:* Christian Col, AA, 46; Univ Mo, BFA, 49; Studied with Robert E Wood, Milford zorns, Robert Landry, George Post. *Work:* Empire Machinery; Valley Nat Bank; Mayo Clinic, Scott, Ariz; Giant Indust, First Interstate; Desert Caballero Mus, Wickenburg, Ariz; Booth Western Mus, Ga; Laguna Art Mus, Laguna Beach, Calif; Haggin Mus, Calif; Norton Art Mus, Wyo; Michelson Mus, Tex; Art Mus, Catalina Island, Calif; Saddleworth Mus, Saddlewood, Eng; Saddleworth New Englan; Camelback Inn, Scotts, Ariz; Biltmore Hotel, Phoenix, Az. *Comn:* Watercolors Ariz Mountains, IBM, 81-82; Michael R Ellis Inc, Phoenix, Ariz, 88; Ariz Biltmore, Phoenix, 91; Merriott's Camelback Inn, Scottsdale, 92; Mayo Clinic, Scott, Ariz; pvt collections. *Exhib:* Western Fedn Watercolor Soc, Houston, 79; Southwest Watercolor Soc, Dallas & 79, Ardmore, Okla, 80; solo exhibs, SR Brenner Gallery, Scottsdale, Ariz; Artists of the West Invitational, Ariz Bank, Phoenix, 85-90; Nat Watercolor Soc, Brea, Calif, 85-87; Plein Air Painters of Am, Avalon, Calif, 87 & 2002; Laguna Beach Mus Art, 2001-2008; SAPAP Invitational, 2010. *Collection Arranged:* US Embassy Switzerland, Mayo Clinic, Scottsdale, Ariz. *Teaching:* instr, Scottsdale Artists Sch, Ariz; Watercolor Soc Kansas, San Diego, Southwest Watercolor Soc, Dallas, Tex, Taos, NMex. *Awards:* Best of Show, Ariz Watercolor Asn, 80 & 81; Grumbacher Silver & Gold Medallion, Ariz Watercolor Soc, 84; Best of Show, Desert Plein Air, Palm Springs, 2000; Award of Excellence, Desert Plein Air, 2001-2002. *Bibliog:* In Plein View, Phoenix Mag, 92; Fresh air, Plein air, Watercolor Mag, 97 & On Location Primer, 98; Advice From Experts, Watercolor, Am Artist Mag, 11/99; The Plein Air Magazine, 1/2005; Arizona Republic, 2003. *Mem:* Ariz Artis Guild (pres, 76-78, bd dir); Royal mem Ariz Watercolor Asn (bd dir); 22 x 30 Prof Watercolor Critique Group; signature mem, Nat Watercolor Soc & Plein Air Painters of Am; Hon mem, Tucson, Plein Air Soc. *Media:* Watercolor, Oil. *Specialty:* Plein air paintings in watercolor. *Interests:* bible study, singing. *Publ:* Portal Posters, Calif; Splash 3, 5 & 7; Best of Flower Painting; Keys to Painting Flowers and Fruit; The Language of Landscape, publ Int Artist Mag; auth, Make Your Watercolors Look Professional, Painting with the White of Your Paper & The Artists Muse; Southwest Art, 1/83; Watercolor Magie, summer 98 & 2007; Artist Mag, 3/2002; Enchanted Isle, Plein Air Catalina, 2003. *Dealer:* S R Brennen, Scottsdale AZ; Millyard Gallery Uppermill Eng. *Mailing Add:* 2617 N 58th St Scottsdale AZ 85257

DE LUCA, JOSEPH VICTOR
EDUCATOR, PAINTER
b Niagara Falls, NY, Mar 1, 1935. *Study:* Bowling Green State Univ, BS, 57 & MA, 58; Mich State Univ, Clifton McChesney & Angelo Ippolito, MFA, 65. *Work:* Toledo Mus Art, Ohio; Univ Omaha, Nebr; Grand Rapids Mus, Mich; Ford Motor co, World Hq, Dearborn, Mich; Bowling Green State Univ, Ohio; Western Mich Univ, Kalamazoo; Arts Coun of Greater Kalamazoo Epic Center, Mich; Mich State Univ; Krasl Art Ctr, St Joseph, Mich; Dennos Mus Ctr, Traverse City, Mich; Uptown, Traverse City Mich, 2013. *Comn:* Cyma & Silver Square (oils & aluminum on canvas), Renaissance Ctr, Detroit, Mich, 76; Pierre Marquet Hotel, Minneapolis, Minn, 89; Northwestern Nat Life Insurance Co, Minneapolis, Minn, 89. *Exhib:* two-person exhib, Gallery Artemus, Ghent, Belg, 81, Northwestern Mich Coll, Dennos Mus Ctr, Traverse City, 94; Solo exhib, State Univ NY, Binghamton, 96; Traverse Area Arts Coun, 99; Art Below Zero, Tranverse Arts Coun, Dennos Mus Center, Transverse City, Mich, 2000; Just Touch It, 2000; Fontana Summer Festival, Kalamazoo, 2000; Participated Gallery, NorthPort, Mich, 2000 & 2001; solo exhib, Gallery 544, Transverse City, New World Order, 2002; Hatties of Suttons Bay, Mich, 2003; Little Cities Gallery, Kalamazoo, Mich, 2005; Mott Community Coll, Flint, Mich, 2005; Art Reach Gallery Mich, Mt Pleasant, 2006; Bella Galleria, Old Mission, Mich, 2006; Northwest Regional, Dennos Mus Ctr, Northwestern Mich Coll, Traverse City, 2006; Selected Works: Five Decades, Gallery Fifty, Traverse City, Mich, 2007; Belstone Gallery, Traverse City, Mich, 2007; Regional Invitational, Art Ctr, Traverse City, Mich, 2008; Richmond Ctr Visual Arts, Western Mich Univ, Kalamazoo, Mich, 2008; Belstone Gallery, Traverse City, Mich, 2009; Art of Framing & Gallery, Traverse City, Mich, 2009; Bella Galleria, Old Mission, 2010; Art Ctr, Traverse City, Mich, 2010; Art Work Alliance, Art of Framing and Gallery, Traverse City, Mich, 2011; Art Ctr, Munson Medical Ctr, Traverse City, Mich, 2011; Midtown Gallery, Kalamazoo, Mich, 2011; Center Gallery, Glen Arbor, Mich, 2011; Dennos Mus Ctr, Traverse City, 2012; Lyrain Gallery, Traverse City, Mich, 2012; Mich Artists Gallery, 2012; Suttons Bay, Mich, 2012; Selected Works, Artisans Design Network, Traverse City, Mich, 2012, 2013; Small Works Exhib, Dennos Mus Ctr, Traverse City, Mich, 2013; Invitational Exhib, Art Ctr, Traverse City, Mich, 2013; Large Paintings, Traverse City Art & Design Gallery, Mich, 2013. *Collection Arranged:* Works by George Ortman (auth, catalog), 69; Works by Angelo Ippolito (auth, catalog), 70; Works by Harry Brorby (auth, catalog), 71; Works by Clifton McChesney (auth, catalog), 72; Works by Graduates & Undergraduates, Bowling Green, Western Mich Univ, 73. *Pos:* Gallery dir (part time), Gallery Two, Western Mich Univ, Kalamazoo, 67-71; Danforth Assoc, Nat Invitational Educators Asn, 76-84. *Teaching:* Instr art, Findlay High Sch, Ohio, 58-62; instr drawing, painting & art educ, Central Mich Univ, Mount Pleasant, 62-66; prof drawing & painting, Western Mich Univ, Kalamazoo, 66-96; Art Workshop, Arezzo, Italy, 2006. *Awards:* Director's Choice Award, Kalamazoo Art Inst, 88; All Mich Regional, Muskegon Mus Art, Mich, 91; 2nd Place, Nancy's Song, All Area/All Media Statewide Exhib, 2008; People's Choice Award, Bella Galleria, Old Mission, Mich, 2008. *Bibliog:* Amy Sult (auth), Last Picture show, Kalamazoo Gazette, 96; Paul Samra (auth), On the Town Arts Mag, W Mich, 96; Artwatch, Traverse Mag, Traverse City, Mich, 96; Arts Borealis, Arts Mag, Traverse City, Mich, 96, 99, & 2002; Nancy Sundstrom Arts Ed, Traverse City Record Eagle, 2002; Christopher Young (auth), Flint J, 2004, Grayce Scholt (auth), 2006; Al Parker (auth), Express Weekly, Traverse City, Mich, 2012. *Mem:* Arch Am Art, Smithsonian Inst; Traverse Area Arts Coun; Dennos Mus Ctr, Traverse City, Mich. *Media:* Mixed. *Interests:* Contemporary Art, Sports. *Publ:* Joseph DeLuca Selected Works: Five Decades Drawings, Paintings, Contructions, 2011. *Dealer:* Bella Galleria Old Mission MI; Gallery Fifty Traverse City MI; Art of Framing & Gallery Traverse City MI; The Nines Gallery Holland Mich; Artisans Design Network Traverse City Mich; Mich Artists Gallery, Suttons Bay, Mich. *Mailing Add:* 6369 Secor Rd Traverse City MI 49684

DE LUISE, ALEXANDRA
CURATOR, LIBRARIAN
b New York, NY. *Study:* New York Univ, BA (art hist), 77; Rutgers Univ, MA (art hist), 80, MLS, 81. *Pos:* Asst librn serials, Frick Art Reference Libr, NY, 81-83; acquisitions librn, Can Ctr Arch, Montreal, 83-90; librn, European Sculpture & Decorative Arts Dept, Metrop Mus Art, NY, 90-91; art librn & cur, Queens Coll Art Ctr, City Univ NY, 91-2000, coordr, instr, 2000-. *Teaching:* instr, info literacy and grad level art librarianship. *Mem:* Art Libr Soc N Am (NY chap, vchmn, 94, chmn, 95); Libr Asn City Univ NY; Asn Coll & Res Libr (NY chap); Am Libr Asn. *Res:* Art serials and their history; electronic content retrieval, art databases; art methodology. *Interests:* Italian art between the two world wars; Dutch prints and drawings. *Publ:* Auth, A bibliography of current art journals in Eastern Europe & Soviet Union, summer 82; Architecture school publ, spring 87, & New design journals, fall 92; Art Documentation; Le Arti and intervention in the arts, RACAR, 92; Ploos van Amstel, Christian Josi & the collection d'imitations, Quarendo, summer 95; Journals of the century in the visual arts, The Serials Librarian, Vol 39, No 4, 2001; Art Documentation: Full Text of Not? All Illustrations or Not?, fall 2003; auth, chap In: Guide to the Literature of Art History 2, Max Marmor & Alex Ross (eds), Am Libr Asn, Chicago, 2005. *Mailing Add:* Queens College Benjamin S Rosenthal Library 65-30 Kissena Blvd Flushing NY 11367

DELVALLE, EDUARDO See Gomez, Mirta & Eduardo Delvalle

DEMANCHE, MICHEL S
PAINTER, PHOTOGRAPHER
b Ft Worth, Tex, Aug 16, 1953. *Study:* Univ Tex, Arlington, BFA, 75; North Tex State Univ, MFA, 80. *Work:* Wise Co Heritage Mus, Decatur, Tex; North Tex State Univ Collection, Denton; Grant Arnold Collection, State Univ Oswego, NY; Art Inst & Gallery Salisbury. *Comn:* Frito Lay Corp; Robert Crill. *Exhib:* Showdown, Alternative Mus, NY, 83; Visions of Childhood, Whitney Mus Am Art, NY, 84; Introductions, Judy Yoven Gallery, Houston, Tex, 88; Holiday Pictures, Frito Lay, Dallas, Tex, 88; Texas Women Artist, Nat Mus Women Art, Washington, 88; Artscape 90, Mount Royal Sch Art, Baltimore, MD, 90. *Pos:* Asst prof art, Univ Md, Eastern Shore; pres, Art Inst & Gallery Salisbury, 95-96; dir, Salisbury Alternative Space Gallery. *Awards:* Second Place Multi-Media, Art Quest, 86; Governor's Citation Award & Individual Artist Grant: Photography, 93. *Bibliog:* Dr Mark Thistlewaite (auth), Michel Demanche, Artspace, spring 84; Wade Wilson (auth), Captain Midnight vs the forces of evil, Dallas Arts Rev, No 20, 86; Gary McKay (auth), New Wave of Texas Artist, Ultra, 3/88. *Mem:* Wash Proj Arts; Coll Art Asn; Women in Photogr. *Media:* Mixed Media. *Dealer:* Finer Side Galleries 205 W Main St Salisbury MD 21853; Wade Wilson Gallery Chicago, IL. *Mailing Add:* c/o William Campbell Contemp Art 4935 Byers Ave Fort Worth TX 76107

DEMARTIS, JAMES J
PAINTER
b Corona, NY, Mar 30, 1926. *Study:* Acad Fine Arts, Florence, Italy, 50-54. *Work:* Pvt collections in Europe & US. *Exhib:* Solo exhibs, Ward Eggleston Gallery, Ruko Gallery, Marcaleo Gallery, Artemis East Gallery & Hicks St Gallery. *Awards:* Emily Lowe Award Painting, 61. *Mem:* Artists Equity. *Dealer:* Brownstone Gallery 76 Seventh Ave Brooklyn NY 11217. *Mailing Add:* 329 E Main St North Adams MA 01247-4427

DEMARTIS, JAMES MICHAEL
SCULPTOR
b Brooklyn, NY, Nov 22, 1968. *Study:* CW Post Col, BA, 1990; Studied wih Jerome Zimmerman, Studio Art Concentration, CW Post Col. *Comn:* Stainless Steel Outdoor Sculpture, Mitch Draizin & Fritz Brugere, Bridgehampton, NY, 2007. *Exhib:* Member's Exhib, Guild Hall, East Hampton, NY, 1995-2008; Outdoor Sculpture, Mather Hos, Port Jefferson, NY, 2005-2007; Springs Invitational, Ashawagh Hall, East Hampton, NY, 2006-2008. *Bibliog:* Donna Paul (auth), New Face of Craft, Hamptons Cottages & Gardens, 2004; Scott Gerst (auth, producer), Metal Artist (James DeMartis, film), 2005; Pat Rodgers (auth), Metal & Glass Exhib, Southampton Press, 2007; Joanne Pilgrim (auth), Feature Profile, East Hampton Star, 2007; Tom Gregory (auth, producer), East Hampton Blacksmith-film, 2008. *Mem:* East Hampton Artists Alliance; Artists Blacksmiths N Am. *Media:* Metal. *Mailing Add:* 214 Springs Fireplace Rd #6 East Hampton NY 11937

DEMATTIES, NICK
PAINTER
b Honolulu, Hawaii, Oct 19, 1939. *Study:* Calif State Univ, Long Beach, BA, 64; Inst Design, Chicago, with Misch Kohn, MS, 67. *Work:* Los Angeles Co Mus Art; Brooklyn Mus Art; Cabinet Estampes, Bibliot Nat Paris; Libr Cong; San Francisco Mus Mod Art. *Comn:* Swengle-Robbins, 87. *Exhib:* Bentley Gallery, Scottsdale, Ariz, 94; Wenninger Gallery, Rockport, Mass, 94; Montreal Int, Que, 94; Nat Painting Exhib, Albuquerque, NMex, 94; Washington & Jefferson Nat Painting Show, Washington, Pa, 94; and others. *Pos:* Founder & dir, Pac Northwest Graphics Workshop, 70-75. *Teaching:* Instr, San Diego State Col, 67-69; asst prof, Mt St Mary's Col, Calif, 69-70; vis prof, Univ Ore, 72; Asst Prof, Albion Col, Mich, 73-74; asst prof, Ariz State Univ, Tempe, 74-76, assoc prof, from 77, then prof, currently prof emeritus. *Awards:* First Place & Cash Award, Biennial, Fuller Art Ctr, Los Alamos, NMex, 91; Purchase Award, 5th Ann McNeese Nut, Lake Charles, La, 92; Cash Award, W & J Nat Painting Show, Washington, Pa, 94. *Bibliog:* Articles, Phoenix Gasette, 2/8/90, Artspace, winter 84 & 85 & Scottsdale Progress, 4/4/86; Articles, Art Voices S, 11-12/79 & 9-10/81 & Portfolio Mag, 7-8/81; and others. *Media:* Acrylic, Oil. *Dealer:* Bentley Gallery 4161 N Marshall Way Scottsdale AZ 85251

DEMETRION, JAMES THOMAS
MUSEUM DIRECTOR
b Middletown, Ohio, July 10, 1930. *Study:* Miami Univ, BS (educ), 52, Simpson Col, Hon DFA, 84, UCLA, Univ Vienna. *Collection Arranged:* Egon Schiele & The Human Form, 71; Paul Klee, 73; 25 Yrs Am Painting 1948-1973, 73; European Art: The Postwar Years 1945-1955, 78; Giorgio Morandi: Retrospective, 81; Francis Bacon, 89; Jean Dubuffet, 43-63, 93; Stanley Spencer: An English Vision, 97; Clyfford Still, 2001. *Pos:* Cur, Pasadena Art Mus, Calif, 64-66, dir, 66-69; dir, Des Moines Art Ctr, Iowa, 69-84; mem mus adv panel, Nat Endowment Arts, 73-76; mem int adv comt, Stuart Found, La Jolla, 81-90; dir, Hirshhorn Mus & Sculpture Garden-Smithsonian Inst, 84-. *Mem:* Asn Art Mus Dir (treas, 76-77, 1st vpres, 78-79, pres, 79-80). *Mailing Add:* Hirshhorn Mus & Sculpture Garden Independence Ave & Eighth SW Washington DC 20560

DEMIANCHUK, VALERIE
ARTIST
b Kiev, Ukraine, 1972. *Study:* Schevchenko Art Sch, Kiev, Ukraine, 1991; Pa Acad Fine Arts, Philadelphia; Pratt Inst, BFA, 1998. *Work:* Ark Art Ctr, Little Rock; Arnot Art Mus, Elmira, NY; The Contemp Mus, Honolulu; Dyke Coll, Little Rock; Fogg Art Mus, Harvard Univ, Cambridge, Mass; Greenville Co Mus Art, SC; Muhlenberg Coll Art Galley, Allentown, Pa. *Exhib:* Solo exhib, George Adams Gallery, NY City, 2002; Group exhibs, Tatistcheff Gallery, NY City, 1999, 2000; Nat Arts Club, NY City, 1999; Mem Art Gallery, Univ Rochester, NY, 1999-2000; The Corning Gallery, NY City, 2001; Ark Art Ctr, 2001, 2003; Arnot Art Mus, Elmira, NY, 2001; George Adams Gallery, NY, 2001, 2002, 2005-06; Martin Art Gallery, Muhlenberg Col, Allentown, Pa, 2003; Scottsdale Mus Contemp Art, Ariz, 2004; Koplin Del Rio Gallery, West Hollywood, Calif, 2004; Lyme Acad, Coll Fine Arts, 2004-05. *Awards:* Strathmore Paper Co Award, Allied Artists of Am, NY, 1999. *Media:* Pencil. *Mailing Add:* c/o George Adams Gallery 525 W 26th St 1st Fl New York NY 10001

DE MILLE, LESLIE B.
PAINTER, SCULPTOR
b Hamilton, Ont, Apr 24, 1927; US citizen. *Study:* Art Students League, NY. *Work:* Portraits, two US Pres; Death Valley 49ers Collection; Navy Art Mus, Washington, DC; Five past Pres, Whittier Coll Collection, Calif; Ronald Reagan Libr, Simi, Calif; Nat Cowboy Hall of Fame, Okla City; pvt collections, Arnold Palmer, Jack Nicklaus, Phil Mickelson, Sam Snead, Tiger Woods. *Comn:* Portrait, Ronald Reagan, Calif, 67; portrait, Richard M Nixon, Washington, DC; paintings, US Sixth Fleet, Mediterranean (naval combat artist), 72 & Pearl Harbor, Hawaii painting, 73; bronze sculpture, Pres Reagan & Gorbachev, Reagan Libr, White House, 88; bronze monument, Hillside, Sedona, Ariz, 91. *Exhib:* Death Valley 49ers Exhib, Calif, 69-84; Grand Nat Ann Exhib, Am Artists Prof League, NY, 71-; solo exhib, Hamilton Place, Ont, Can, 91; and others. *Teaching:* Organizer, dir & instr, sem for art orgn in US, 66-; portrait & still-life workshops, 66-; instr, Nat Portrait Seminar, 81; fac instr, Scottsdale Artists Sch, Ariz, 84-2010; workshop tour, Hawaii, 92, 95. *Awards:* Best Show, 71 & Gold Medals, 76, 79 & 80, Am Artists Prof League, NY; Best Show, Death Valley 49ers Inc, 80; and others. *Bibliog:* Portraits in Pastel (series of half-hour programs), Pub Broadcasting System, 81-; Feature article, SW Art Mag, 9/81; feature article, Am Artists Mag, 6/85; feature article, Art of The West Mag, 5-6/94. *Mem:* Fel Am Inst Fine Arts; fel Am Artists Prof League; LA Traditional Artists Soc (pres, formerly); Death Valley 49ers Inc (pres, formerly); Pastel Soc Am; Salmagundi Club; Pastel Soc W Coast; MyArt Tutor (founding mem). *Media:* Oil, Pastel. *Interests:* portrait commissions, golf. *Publ:* How to Draw Cats and Kittens, Walter Foster, 79; Portraits in Pastel, PBS Pub, 81; Painting with Pastels, Foster Art Libr Ser, 84; Best of Pastels, 96 & 98. *Mailing Add:* 155 Creek Rock Rd Sedona AZ 86351-7379

DEMING, DAVID LAWSON
SCULPTOR, EDUCATOR
b Cleveland, Ohio, May 26, 1943. *Study:* Cleveland Inst Art, with William McVey & John Clague, BFA; Cranbrook Acad Art, with Julius Schmidt, MFA. *Work:* Ft Worth Nat Bank, Tex; San Antonio Mus & Pub Libr Austin, Tex; Longview Mus Art, Tex; First City Ctr, Austin, Tex; Ark Art Ctr; Columbus Mus Art. *Comn:* Bronze Bust Winthrop Rockefeller for Winrock Int; Barbara Jordan Award Medallion; Harold Russell Award Medallion; Bobbit Bust, Rebecca Johnson, Libr Cong. *Exhib:* Solo exhib, Adams-Middleton Gallery, Dallas; Kouros Gallery Group Shows, NY; Int Chicago Art Expos, Navy Pier. *Pos:* Chmn, Dept Art & Art Hist, Col Fine Arts, Univ Tex, 92 & dean, 96-98; pres, Cleveland Inst Art, 98. *Teaching:* Instr sculpture, Sch Fine & Appl Arts, Boston Univ, 67-68; instr sculpture & drawing design, Univ Tex, El Paso, 70-72; prof sculpture & drawing, Univ Tex, Austin, 72-. *Awards:* Am Inst Archit Award of Honor. *Mem:* Tex Sculpture Asn; Int Sculpture Asn. *Media:* Steel, Bronze

DEMISSIE, YEMANE I
FILMMAKER
Study: L'Inst Catholique, Paris, France, diploma (French lang and lit), 85; Moorehead State Univ, Minn, BA (French), 86 & BS (mass commun), 86; UCLA, MFA (film directing & production), 92. *Exhib:* DC Int Film Festival, Kennedy Ctr, 97; London Film Festival, Nat Film Theatre, Eng, 97; House Cult, Berlin, 98; Mus Fine Arts, Boston, 98; Ger Nat Film Mus, Frankfurt, 98; Am Film Inst Film Festival, Los Angeles, Calif; Int Film Festival, Rotterdam, The Neth; Contemp African Diaspora Film Festival, NY. *Pos:* Writer, dir, producer, Treacherous Crossings, 86-; dir acquisitions, Producer Servs Group Inc, 87-92; first asst dir, Big Bang Lies, 90, Where Beans Grow, 91, That's What Women Want, 92, Genesis Pure, 94; asst dir, co-ed, res, Imperfect Journey, 94; line producer, Through the Door of No Return, 97; continuity writer, SDI Media USA, 97-; line producer, first asst dir, My Soul to Keep, 2001. *Awards:* John Simon Guggenheim Mem Found Fel, 98; Indep Film & Filmmaker Grant, Am Film Inst,; Production Grant, Montecinemaveritá Found; Film Fund, Göteborg Film Festival; Artists Fel, Calif Arts Coun; Nat Resources Fel. *Publ:* dir, Tumult, 97; auth, Gilding on the goblet, Part I, 5/2000, Part II, 9/2000, Ras Hailu's choice, 12/2000, The treasure in the Cellar, 1/2001, Educating Hiruy, 3/2001 & Goum-Goum-Shah!, 5/2001, Seleda.com. *Mailing Add:* PMB 1405 264 S LaCienga Blvd Beverly Hills CA 90211

DE MONTE, CLAUDIA
SCULPTOR, CURATOR
b Astoria, NY, Aug 25, 1947. *Study:* Notre Dame of Md Univ, BA; Cath Univ Am, MFA. *Hon Degrees:* Coll Santa Fe, LHD, 2004. *Work:* Indianapolis Mus Art, Ind; New Orleans Mus; Del Mus; Ft Lauderdale Mus; Brooklyn Mus; Tucson Mus; Flint Inst Art; Queens Mus; Miss Mus; Cocoran Mus; Tucson Mus; Boca Raton Mus; Mus Mod Art, Warsaw & Lodsz, Poland, & Salerno, Italy; Corp collections, MTV, Prudential Life Insurance, Exxon, Hyatt Rgency Hotels, Citibank, Twentieth Century Fund, Siemens. *Comn:* Brooklyn Pub Libr, NY, 90; Sch Construct Authority, NY, 93; NMex Arts Coun, Socorr, NMex, 97; New York City Percent for Art, Queens Supreme Ct, NY, 98; Univ Northern Iowa, 2003; NM Rt 66, Santa Rosa; Rockville Town Ctr, Md, 2008; Broward Co, Fla, 2008. *Exhib:* Solo exhibs, Corcoran Mus Art, Washington, DC, 76, Miss Mus Art, Jackson, 80, Ft Worth Art Mus, Tex, 80, Marion Locks Gallery, Philadelphia, 80 & Gracie Mansion Gallery, NY, 84-85 & 88-89; NY Now, Gothenburg Mus, Sweden; Biennial Paper Art, Dupen Mus, Ger; Retrospective, Chokladfabriven, Malino, Sweden, 98; Liesbeth Lips Gallery, Rotterdam, The Neth, 99; Flint Inst Art, Mich, 2000; Tucson Mus, Ariz, 2001; Mus Southwest, Midland, Tex, 2002; Contemp Art Ctr, New Orleans, La, 2005; Kunsthatle, Tallin, Estonia, 2004; Univ Md Art Gallery, 2006; Univ Md, 2006; June Kelly Gallery, New York, 2007; Makan, Amman, Jordan, 2007; Jan Colle Gallery, Ghent, Belgium, 2009; Flint Inst Art, Mich, 2009; June Jelly Gallery, New York, 2009; Miss Mus Art, Jackson, Miss, 2010; Mobile Mus, Ala, 2010; Univ Southern Mississippi Mus, 2011; Trustman Gallery, Boston, Mass, 2011; York Coll, York, Pa, 2011; June Kelly Gallery, NY, 2012, 2014. *Collection Arranged:* Women of the World: A Global Collection of Art; Real Beauty. *Teaching:* Prof Art Dept, Univ Md, Coll Park, 72-2005, prof emer, 2005-. *Awards:* Fel in Sculpture, NY Found; Agnes Gund Grant, Anchorage Found Tex; Cantor Family Found. *Bibliog:* G Henry (auth), Claudia De Monte, Art Am, 9/84; article, Claudia De Monte, NY Times, 9/27/85; Gerard McCarthy (auth), Art in Am, 12/2007; Claudia De Monte, Pomegranate, 2009; Art with Conscience, Litchfield County Times, K Boughton, p 13, 4/2014. *Mem:* EuroAm Women Coun; Art Table; NY Women's Forum. *Media:* Wood; Bronze. *Res:* Global women's art; Outsider art. *Interests:* int travel; women's issues. *Publ:* Auth, Women of the World: A Global Collection (exhib catalog), 2000. *Dealer:* Jean Albano Gallery Chicago Ill; June Kelly Gallery NY; Cole Pratt Gallery New Orleans La. *Mailing Add:* 96 Grand St New York NY 10013

DE MONTEBELLO, PHILIPPE LANNES
EDUCATOR, HISTORIAN
b Paris, France, May 16, 1936; nat US, 1955. *Study:* Harvard Coll, BA (magna cum laude), 1958; New York Univ Inst Fine Arts, BA, 1963, MA 1976. *Hon Degrees:* Lafayette Coll, LFA, 79; Bard Coll, DHL, 81; Iona Coll, DFA, 82; Dartmouth Coll, LLD, 2004; NY Univ, DFA, 2007; Savannah Coll Art & Design, HHD, 2007; Harvard Univ, DFA, 2007. *Collection Arranged:* Greek Art of the Aegean Islands, 11/79; Clyfford Still, 11/79; Horses of San Marco, 2/80; Seventeenth Century French Painting, 6/82; Cimabue, 1/82; Vatican, 1/83; Manet, 9/83; Liechtenstein: the Princely Collections, 10/85, Van Gogh in Saint-Remy and Auvers, 11/86, Zurbaran, 9/87, Degas, 10/88, Canaletto, 11/89, Velazquez, 10/89, From Poussin to Matisse: The Russian Taste for French Painting, 5/90. *Pos:* Asst cur to assoc cur Europ paintings, Metrop Mus Art, New York, 63-69, vice dir curatorial & educ affairs, 74-77, actg dir mus, 77-78, dir, 78-2008, chief exec officer, 99-2008, dir emer; dir, Mus Fine Arts, Houston, Tex, 69-74; bd trustees, Inst Fine Arts, NY Univ; mem ed bd, Int Jour Mus Mgt and Curatorship; mem adv coun depts art and archeol, Columbia Univ; bd trustees, Musée d'Orsay, Paris. *Teaching:* Scholar-in-residence, Prado Mus, 2008-; lectr curatorial studies, NY Univ Inst Fine Arts, formerly, Fiske Kimball prof hist & cult museums, 2009-, adv to Abu Dhabi campus, 2009-. *Awards:* Woodrow Wilson Fel, NY Inst Fine Arts, 61-62; Gallatin Medal & Fel, NY Univ, 81; Gold Medal Nat Inst Soc Sci, 89, Spanish Inst, 92; Rebekah Kohut award Nat Coun Jewish Women, 93; Living Landmark award NY Landmarks Conservancy, 2001; decorated chevalier Legion d' Honneur, France, Encomienda de Numero de la Orden Isabel la Catholica, Spain, officer Ordre de Leopold, Belgium, Knight Comdr, Pontifical Order St Gregory the Great, comdr Order Arts & Letts, 2001; Mayoral proclamation, 2002; Nat Medal of Arts, 2003; Amigas Museo Prado, 2004; Confederation Internat Négociants Oeuvres d'Art, 2005; Legion of Honor Medal, France, 2007; Gertrude Vanderbilt Whitney Award for Outstanding Patronage, Skowhegan Sch Painting & Sculpture, 2009. *Mem:* Asn Mus Art Dirs (mem art com); Mus Coun New York City; Am Fedn Arts (trustee exec com); Am Asn Mus. *Publ:* Auth, Peter Paul Rubens, McGraw, 1968; contribr, Metrop Mus Art Bull & others. *Mailing Add:* NY Univ Inst Fine Arts James B Duke House 1 E 78th St New York NY 10075

DE MOURA SOBRAL, LUIS
HISTORIAN, CRITIC
b Viseu, Port, June 24, 1943; Can citizen. *Study:* Univ Louvain, Belg, MA (art hist), 73, PhD, 76. *Collection Arranged:* Le surrealisme portugais (auth, catalog), Galerie UQAM, Montreal, 83; Pintura Estrangeira dos seculos XVI, XVII e XVIII da Coleccao Nogueira da Silva (auth, catalog), Nogueira da Silva Mus Minho Univ, Braga, 95-96; Bento Coelho (1620-1708), e a Cultura do seu Tempo (auth, catalog), Inst Portugues do Patrimonio Arquitectonico, Lisbon, 98; Hiver Noir de René Derouin. Construction, déconstruction, Motréal, Centré d'exposition de l'université de Montréal, 2007. *Pos:* Cur, Montreal Mus Fine Arts, 71-75; ed, Racar, 83-89. *Teaching:* Asst prof, Univ Montreal, 76-81, assoc prof, 81-87, chair, 87-95, prof 87-. *Awards:* Grand Officer, Order of the Infante Dom Henrique, Portugal, 2001; Celebrating Outstanding portuguese Canadian Achievement Award, PCNC, 2010. *Mem:* Am Soc Hispanic Art Hist Studies; elected mem Nat Acad Fine Arts, Portugal.

Res: Baroque painting; Portuguese baroque painting; Iberoamerican colonial art; surrealism; hist of prints. *Publ:* Critical study, Luis Nunes Tinoco, Elogio da Pintura, Galeria de Pintura do D Luis, 91; Vilallonga Les lieux du reve, Cloister of dreams, Ed Broquet, Montreal, 93; Pintura e poesia na epoca barroca, Lisbon, Ed Estampa, 94; Do Sentido das Imagens, Lisbon, Estampa, 96; Pintura Portuguesa do Seculo, XVII, Historias, Lenda, Narrativas, Lisbon Muse Nacional de Arte Antiga, 2004. *Mailing Add:* Dept Hist Art Univ Montreal PO Box 6128 Centreville Montreal PQ H3C 3J7 Canada

DEMPSEY, BRUCE HARVEY
MUSEUM DIRECTOR
b Camden, NJ, July 4, 1941. *Study:* Fla State Univ, BA, MFA; study exten sch, Florence, Italy; Mozarabic manuscripts with Gulnar Bosch. *Collection Arranged:* Photons-Phonons (elec sculpture), 71; Lewis Comfort Tiffany, 72; Realizations and Figurizations, 72; Karl Zerbe Mem Exhib, 73; Photo Phantisists, 73; Colors (photog exhib), 74; Talent USA, 76; Elizabethan Portraiture, Nat Portrait Gallery, London, 76; New Realism, 77; New Floridians No 1, 77; The Florida Connection: Jim Rosenquist & Robert Rauschenberg, 77; Helen Frankenthaler, 77; New Floridians No 2, 78 & No 3, 79; The Flowing Word: Chinese Calligraphy, 79; Contemporary Stained Glass, 79; Duane Hanson, 80; Currents: A New Mannerism, 81; Joseph Raffael: Recent Works, 82; Calligraphy, Ming Dynasty, 82; Arakawa: Graphic Works, 82; Master Craftsmen, 83; Empress Dowager Forbidden City, 83; Masami Teraoka, 83; Ramses II: Pharaoh & His Time, 87. *Pos:* Dir art gallery, Fla State Univ, 68-74; dir, Jacksonville Art Mus, 75-. *Teaching:* Instr fundamental art & art hist, Fla State Univ, 66-74. *Awards:* Fla Arts Recognition Award, State of Fla, 86-87. *Mem:* Am Asn Mus. *Publ:* Auth, Lewis C Tiffany-Beauty in Many Mediums, 72. *Mailing Add:* 2415 Mandarin River Ln Jacksonville FL 32223-1358

DEMSKY, HILDA GREEN
PAINTER, ENVIRONMENTAL ARTIST
b Kingston, Pa, Jul 2, 1936. *Study:* Carnegie Mellon Univ, BFA, 58; Hunter Coll, MA, 63. *Work:* Nat Gallery, Costa Rica; Fidelity Investments; US Dept Interior, Acadia Nat Park, Maine. *Comn:* Mural, Lobby walls, H Thomas Slater Ctr, White Plains, NY, 91. *Exhib:* Galeria Nacional, San Jose, Costa Rica; Gov's Mansion, Harrisburg, Pa; Fidelity Investments Corp Gallery, Boston, Mass; Mount Sinai Hosp, NY; Thomas H Slater Ctr, White Plains, NY; Westmoreland Mus Am Art, Greensburg, Pa; Hammond Mus, Salem, NY; Meridian Int Ctr, Washington, DC; Mona Ena Gallery, Mykonos, Greece; Sophia Wanamaker Gallery, Costa Rica; The Arts Ctr, Saratoga Springs, NY; The Rye Arts Ctr, NY; Pen & Brush Gallery, NY; Pleiades Gallery, NY; Fordham Univ Gallery, Lincoln Ctr, NY; Hammond Arts Ctr, Winter Harbor, Maine, 2010. *Teaching:* Art teacher, New York City Bd Educ, 59-72, White Plains (NY) City Sch Dist, 72-; prof, clinical field supv Manhattanville Coll, Purchase, NY, 2001-06. *Awards:* Arts fel painting, Coun for Basic Educ, Italy, 92; Fulbright Fel to Netherlands, Natl Endowment Arts, 92; Environ Art, Found on the Sound, Read, Puffin Found, 99; NY Found for Arts, SOS Awards & NY St Coun for Arts, 99-2000 & 2005; Saltonstall Found Arts, 2005; Henry Faurest Mem Fel, Mary Anderson Ctr Arts, Ind, 2006; Arts Alive Artist Grant, Westchester Arts Coun, 2007; Andy Warhol Fellowship, 2007; C/LL Rialaig Arts Fel, Ireland, 2010; Painting Fel, Caribbean Mus Ctr Arts, St Croix, VI, 2012; Artist Residency award, Golden Apple, Residency in ME, 2014. *Bibliog:* Roberta Hershenson (auth), Turning Beach Dross into Works of Art, NY Times, 9/4/94; William Zimmer (auth), Rocognizing Self Portraits by Americans, NY Times, 2/8/98; Eleanor Heartney (auth), Take Me to the Water (Mus catalog), 2005; Artist's Inspiration: A River Roaring with Life, New York Times, 9/2007. *Mem:* Fulbright Asn, Nat Arts Task Force (founder); Univ Coun Art Educ (bd mem, 2002-2003); Nat Asn of Astronomical Artists; Pleiades Gallery of Contemporary Art (bd mem, 2004); Pen & Brush Gallery (bd mem, 2005); Mamaroneck Artists Guild; Artists Circle NY City; Katonah Mus Artists Asn; Cue Art Found; Nat Asn Women in the Arts; Womens Caucus for Art. *Media:* Oil, Acrylic, Watercolor. *Res:* Contemp women artists; Chinese women artists. *Specialty:* Contemporary art. *Interests:* Women artists, travel & environment, tennis. *Collection:* Nat Gallery Costa Rica, US Dept of the Interior; NJ Historical Mus

DE MUSÉE, MORAN
SCULPTOR
b Bryn Mawr, Pa, 1950. *Study:* studied at El Camino Coll, Redondo Beach, Calif, Calif State Univ, Long Beach & Acad Di Belle Arti, Italy. *Work:* Il Passaggio Moresco, Fundacion Valparaiso, Rio Aguas, Spain, 95; The Parkview Collection, Fort Wayne, Indiana. *Comn:* La Vecchia Mura,Sculpture, City of Santa Monica, 2006; Art Odyssey, Intercontinental Ephemeral Sculpture Series, Bring Art to Life Found, 2006. *Exhib:* Sculpture, Calif State Univ, San Bernardino, 88; Artist Do Opera, Brand Gallery, Glendale, Calif, 2001; Klaudia Marr Gallery, Santa Fe, NMex, 2004. *Awards:* Fel, Fundacion Valparaiso, 95. *Bibliog:* Douglas Ditonto, Le Graveur (film), 75; Tom Johnson (auth), You Call This Art, Los Angeles Mag, 89; You Call This Art, Los Angeles Mag, 89; Real of Possibility, A Contemporary Portrait by Donald Anderson, 91. *Publ:* Los Angeles: Realm of Possibility, Windsor Pub, 91. *Mailing Add:* PO Box 2422 Toluca Lake CA 91610

DENES, AGNES
ENVIRONMENTAL ARTIST, CONCEPTUAL ARTIST
b Budapest, Hungary, 1931; US citizen. *Study:* City Univ New York; New Sch Social Res, New York; Columbia Univ. *Hon Degrees:* Ripon Coll, Wis, (hon) DFA 1994; Bucknell Univ, (hon) LHD, 2008. *Work:* Metrop Mus Art, Mus Mod Art, Whitney Mus Am Art, NY; Nat Mus Fine Arts, Washington; Moderna Museet, Stockholm, Sweden; John D & Catherine T McArthur Found, Chicago; Philadelphia Mus; Corcoran Gallery of Art; Smithsonian Inst, Washington; Israel Mus, Jerusalem; Wexner Ctr for the Arts, Columbus, Ohio; Honolulu Acad of Arts, Hawaii; and many others; Nat Gallery, DC. *Comn:* Circle of Megaliths with Sun Dial, Int Ctr Preserv Wild Animals, Ohio, 1990-95; Introspection I Evolution (mural), comn by Harold Wash Libr Ctr, City Chicago Pub Art Prog, 1990-91; Hot/Cold Earthship with Heartbeat (45 ft wooden barge), Mus Contemp Art, Helsinki, 1992; Tree Mountain-A Living Time Capsule, Pinsio gravel pits (400 yr proj), Ylojarvi, Finland, 1992-96; A Forest for Australia (6000 trees planted), Melbourne, 1998; Poetry Walk - Reflections: Pools of Thought, 2000; Univ Va, Charlottesville, Va, 2003; Nienwe Hollandse Waterlinie, Holland, 2000; The Golden Tree, Göteborg Internationella Konstbiennal, Sweden, 2001; Nautilus Amphitheater, Three Rivers Col, Norwich, Conn, 2008. *Exhib:* Solo exhibs incl Agnes Denes: Projects for Public Places-A Retrospective, organized by Samek Gallery, Bucknell Univ, Lewisburg, Pa (catalog, travel), 2003-2005, Chelsea Mus, NY, 2004, Ewing Gallery, Univ Tenn, 2005, Uprooted & Deified-The Golden Tree, BravinLee Programs, NY, 2007, Agnes Denes: Art for the Third Millennium-Creating a New World View, a retrospective, Ludwig Mus, Budapest, Hungary (catalog), 2008, Agnes Denes: Philosophy in the Land II, Leslie Tonkonow Gallery, NY, 2009, The Body Argument, Galerie Emanuel Layr, Vienna, Austria, 2012, Agnes Denes: Body Prints, Philosophical Drawings, and Map Projections 1969-1978, Santa Monica Museum of Art, Calif, 2012; group exhibs incl Minn Mus Art Traveling Show, St Paul, Kolnishcer Kuntsverein, Cologne, Ger, 1987; Mus Contemp Art, Helsinki, Mus Tampere, Finland, 1992; Epand La Defense, Paris, France, 1993; Staatsgalerie, Suttgart, Ger, 1997; Am Acad in Rome, 1998; Museu d'Art Contemporani, Barcelona, 2000; Venice Biennale, Italy, 2001; Markers, Venice, Biennale, Italy, 2001, Second International Art Biennial-Buenos Aires, Museo Nacional de Bellas Artes, Argentina, 2002, Contemporary Art and the Mathematical Instinct, Tweed Mus Art, Univ Minn, Duluth, 2003, Stedman Art Gallery, Rutgers Univ, Camden, NJ and Univ Mus, Univ Richmond, 2004, Six Centuries of Prints and Drawings: Recent Acquisitions, National Gallery Art, Washington, DC, 2004, Poles Apart/Poles Together, Museo Storico Navale, Venice Biennale, Italy, 2005, Drawings from the Modern, Mus Modern Art, NY, 2005, Buildings and Breaking the Grid:1962-2002, Whitney Mus American Art, NY, 2005, Green Horizons, Bates Coll Mus Art, Lewiston, Maine, 2007, Weather Report: Art and Climate Change, (Curator L. Lippard), Boulder Mus of Contemporary Art in Collaboration with Eco Arts, Boulder, Colo, 2007, Decoys, Complexes, and Triggers:Feminism and Land Art in the 1970's, Sculpture Center, Long Island City, NY, 2008, To Infinity and Beyond: Mathematics in Contemporary Art, Heckscher Mus Art, Huntington, NY, 2008, Sites, Whitney Mus American Art, NY, 2009, In Defence of Nature, Barbican Gallery, London, 2009; Travelling exhibs incl Agnes Denes: Naples Mus Art, Fla; Art for the Third Millennium, Creating a New World View (retrospective), Ludwig Mus, Budapest, Hungary; Radical Nature, Art & Archit for a Changing planet 1969-2009, Barbican Art Gallery, London, 2009; Elle, Mus Nat d'Art Mod, Ctr Georges Pompidou, Paris, 2010; Landscapes as an Idea: proj & Projections: 1960-1980, Koldo Mitzelena Kulturunea, Erakustaretoa, San Sebastian, Spain; Retrospectives, Agnes Denes: Sculptures of the Mind 1968-Now, 2012. *Teaching:* Instr fine arts, Sch Visual Arts, NY, 1974-79; instr, Skowhegan Sch Painting & Sculpture, Maine, 1979 San Francisco Art Inst, Calif, 1976, Univ Genoa, Sch Archit, Italy, 1986; guest lectr in numerous universities, museums & art centers in the US & Eur; speaker at global conf, Global Forum Environ & Develop Human Survival, The Kremlin, Moscow, USSR, 1990, Unced 92, Global Forum Parlimentary Earth Summit, Rio de Janeiro, Brazil, 1992 & Global Forum Gen Assembly, Kyoto, Japan, 1993; vis critic, Sch Archit, Univ Pa, Philadelphia, 1991, Parsons New Sch for Design, NY, 2006; scholar at large, vis critic, Bucknell Univ, Lewisburg, Pa, 2006. *Awards:* Hassam & Speicher Fund Purchase Award, Am Acad Art & Letts, 1985; Eugene McDermott Achievement Award Mass Inst Technol, 1990; Fel, Carnegie Mellon Univ, 1993, Studio for Creative Inquiry Research Fel, 1993-; Rome Prize, Am Acad Rome, 1997-98; Watson Award, Carnegie Mellon Univ, 1999; Nat Endowment Fel (4); NYSCA Grants (4); DAAD Fel, Berlin; Ctr for Advanced Visual Studies, MIT Fel; Anonymous Was a Woman, 2008; Ambassador's award for Cultural Diplomacy and strengthening the friendship between US and the Republic of Hungary through the excellence in Contemporary Art, 2008; Artist of the Year Honoree, Brower Ctr, Berkeley, Calif, 2011. *Bibliog:* J Hartz (ed), Agnes Denes A Monograph, Herbert F Johnson Mus Art, Cornell Univ, 1992; Adachiara Zevi (auth), The Visual Philosophy of Agnes Denes, L'Architettura, Rome, Italy, 10/1998; Ricardo Barreto (auth), Sculptural Conceptualism: A New Reading of the Work of Agnes Denes, Washington, DC, No 4, 1999; Krystyna Wasserman (auth), Book as Art XI - Inside the Artist's Book, Women in the Arts, 1999; Beryl Smith (auth), Lives and Works: Talks with Women Artists, vol 2, 1999; Barbara Nemitz (auth), Trans Plant: Living Vegetation in Contemporary Art, 2000; Grissim, Graham & Carpenter (auths), Nothing, 2001; Carol Kino (auth), Stretching Her Creativity as Far as Possible, NY Times, 2012; Ben David (auth), Agnes Denes: Sculptures of the Mind-1968to Now, The Week: The Best of the US and International Media, 2012; Nick Stillman (auth), Agnes Denes, Santa Monica Museum of Art, Artforum, 2013. *Media:* All Media. *Publ:* Auth, Sculptures of the Mind, Univ Akron Press, 1976; Paradox & Essence, Tau/Ma Publ, Rome, Italy, 1977; Isometric Systems in Isotropic Space: Map Projections, 1979; Book of Dust: The Beginning and the End of Time and Thereafter, 1986, Visual Studies Workshop; Notes on Eco-Logic: Environmental Art Work, visual Philos & Global Perspective, Leonardo, 1993; Artistic vision & molecular genetics, Art J, spring 1996; The Serial Attitude (catalogue), Wexner Ctr for the Arts, Ohio Univ, 1998; Light on the New Millennium - Wind From Extreme Orient (catalogue), Met Art Mus, Pusan, Korea, 1998; Afterimages: Drawing Through Process (catalogue), Mus of Contemp Art & MIT Press, 1999; Force Fields Phases of the Kinetic (catalogue), Museu d'Art Contemporani de Barcelona, Spain, 2000; Art & Mathematics 2000 (catalogue), The Cooper Union for the Advancement of Sci & Art, 2000; Kinds of Drawing (catalogue), Herter Art Gallery, Univ of Mass, 2001; auth, Living Murals in the Land, Crossing Boundaries of Time & Space, Pub Art Rev, St Paul, Minn, Fall/Winter, 2005; Manifesto, Mathematics in My Work & Other Essays, Hyperion: On the Future of Aesthetics, Vol II Issue I, Feb 2007; Notes on a Visual Philosophy, Hyperion: On the Future of Aesthetics, Vol I Issue 4, Dec 2006. *Mailing Add:* 595 Broadway New York NY 10012

DE NIKE, MICHAEL NICHOLAS
SCULPTOR, WRITER
b Regina, Sask, Sept 14, 1923; US citizen. *Study:* Nat Acad Fine Arts; also with Jean de Marco & Carl Schmitz. *Work:* Dernick Resources, Houston, Tex. *Comn:* Albert Payson Terhune Mem, Collie Fanciers Am, Paramus, NJ, 71; Medallion, Int Chef's Asn, NY, 72; Stations of the Cross, Christ Church, Pompton Lakes, NJ, 75; Bicentennial Mural, Twp Wayne, NJ, 75; Young St Francis (bronze), St David's in Kinnelon, NJ; and others. *Exhib:* Nat Acad Design, NY, 64; Audubon Artists, 65; Knickerbocker Artists, 65; Nat Sculpture Soc Ann, 66; Am Artists Prof League, 74; and others. *Pos:* Dir & founder, Am Carving Sch, Wayne, NJ, 74-90. *Teaching:* Instr woodcarving, Fair Lawn Adult Educ, 68-74; adj fac, Essex Co Col, Newark, NJ, 74-75; Am Woodcarving Sch, 74-89; Passaic Co Col, 76-80. *Awards:* Dr Ralph Weiler Award, Nat Acad Design, 64; Herald-News Award, Passaic-Clifton, NJ, 69; Allied Artists Am Award, 75. *Mem:* Am Artist Prof League; Nat Sculpture Soc; Knickerbocker Artists. *Media:* Wood, Stone. *Mailing Add:* 1241 Hart Rd Pisgah Forest NC 28768-9116

DENKER, SUSAN A
HISTORIAN, CRITIC
b New York, NY, Apr 2, 1948. *Study:* Harvard Univ, BA, 66; Wellesley Col, MA, 79; Brown Univ, ABD, 82. *Teaching:* Lectr art hist, Tufts Univ, 76-; studio fac & chmn art hist, Sch of Mus Fine Arts, Boston, 80-. *Awards:* Res Grant, French Govt, 69; Fel, Samuel Kress Found, 77-78; Russell T Smith Award, Boston Mus Sch, 92. *Mem:* Coll Art Asn. *Res:* Modern European art, 1880 to present; American art, 1940 to present; Mondrian's relationship to European and American avant-garde art; women film directors. *Publ:* Coauth, Europe in Torment: 1450-1550, 74 & French Watercolors & Drawings: 1800-1910, 75, RI Sch Design Mus Art; auth, Sandi Slone: A Retrospective Exhib 1972-1981, Watson Gallery, 81; De Stijl: 1917-1931, Visions of Utopia, Art J, fall 82. *Mailing Add:* 361 Harvard St Apt 7 Cambridge MA 02138

DENNETT, LISSY W
PAINTER, PRINTMAKER
b Vienna, Austria, May 3, 1926; US citizen. *Study:* Univ NH, 40-42; Mich State Univ, BA, 47, MA, 49. *Work:* Libr Cong, Washington, DC; Southern Ill Univ, Edwardsville; Anderson Art Ctr, Ind; Mus Contemp Art, Chicago; Portland Art Mus. *Comn:* Murals (with Raymond Pinet), Nat Youth Admin, Jr High Sch, Hudson, NH & Community Chest Bldg, Nashua, 39-40; Mural, Marshall Field Co, Chicago. *Exhib:* Butler Inst Ann, 81-83 & 90; solo exhibs, Bradley Univ, 82, Mich State Univ, 83, Chicago Pub Libr Cult Ctr, 83, Anderson Art Ctr, 83, Joy Horwich Gallery, 85, RH Love Galleries, 88 & 89 & Comus Gallery, 93; Paintings & Sculptures by Candidates for Art Awards, Am Acad Arts & Lett, 85; Archer Gallery, Clark Coll, 97; Water Resources Ctr, Vancouver, Wash, 98; Coos Bay Art Mus, 2004-2005; North Bank Gallery, Vancouver, Wash, 2006; Pan Gallery, Portland, Ore, 2008; and others. *Collection Arranged:* Am Prints, Univ Ill, Chicago; Longview Found Collection, Kalamazoo Inst Arts, Mich; Executive Collection, Upjohn Pharmaceutical Co, Kalamazoo, Mich. *Pos:* Auth, Periodical Review, Art Educ, 57-59; dir art ctr, Kalamazoo Inst Arts, Mich, 59-65. *Teaching:* Instr printmaking, calligraphy & drawing, Macalester Coll, 47-49; asst drawing, Mich State Univ, 49-50; from asst prof to assoc prof drawing, painting, printmaking & design, State Univ NY Coll New Paltz, 50-57, actg chmn art dept, 55-56; exec dir, Md Inst Coll Art, Baltimore, 57-59; chmn art dept, Univ Ill, Chicago Circle, 65-67, prof printmaking painting & drawing, 65-, assoc dean facs, 69-72, actg dean, Coll Archit & Art, 75-77, prof emer, 88-; lectr, Clark Coll, Vancouver, Wash, 2001-2006; visiting fac, Western Ore Univ, 2010-. *Awards:* Audubon Artists Medal Hon Graphics, 84; A E S Peterson Award, 2001. *Bibliog:* New Art Examiner, 11/82; Chicago Sun-Times, 6/10/83; Mizue, Japan, Spring 88. *Mem:* Nat Soc Painters Casein & Acrylic; Pastel Soc Am; Print Arts Northwest; N Bank Artists. *Media:* Acrylic; Relief Printmaking, Colored Pencil, Styrofoam Sculpture. *Res:* Louis Lozowick Prints, Fiske Boyd Prints, George Miller, Printer. *Collection:* Am women in printmaking from colonial times through 1950s; Fiske Boyd woodcuts; Winslow Homer wood engravings. *Publ:* Auth, Four Printmakers, 62; Miklos Suba, 64; Oliver Chaffee, 64; George C Miller & Son, Lithographic Printers to Artists Since 1917, Am Art Rev, 3-4/76; and numerous exhib catalogs. *Dealer:* Print Arts Northwest 17677 NW Springville Rd Portland OR 97229

DENNETT, LISSY W
SCULPTOR
b Vienna, Austria, May 3, 1926; US citizen. *Study:* Brooklyn Coll, BA, 48; Haber Sch Sculpture. *Work:* Brooklyn Col Libr; Great Neck Libr, corp & prv collection. *Exhib:* Nassau Co Mus Art, 92; Firehouse Gallery, 93; Guild Hall Mus, 94; Plandome Gallery, 95; Nat Asoc Women Artists, 96; Neshe Alpan Gallery, Roslyn. *Pos:* Pres, Sculptors Inc, Port Washington, NY, 86-; pres, Artists Network of Great Neck, 90-95. *Teaching:* Instr sculpture, Great Neck Adult Educ, 88-. *Awards:* Sculpture award, Chelsea Ctr Nassau Co Off Cult Develop, 90; Artist Network Award for Sculpture, Nassau Co Mus, 92; Sculpture Award, Great Neck Libr, 94; Artist of Distinction, Great Neck Ctr Visual & Performing Arts, 2005; Outstanding Teacher & Fac Mem, Great Neck Adult Educ Ctr, 2006; Lifetime Achievement Award, Brooklyn Coll, 2010. *Mem:* Artists Network Great Neck; Nat Asn Women Artists (Centennial Comt); Visual Arts Alliance Long Island (rec secy, 88-96). *Media:* Stone, Clay. *Dealer:* Neshe Alpan Gallery Huntington NY. *Mailing Add:* 10 Canterbury Rd No 1C Great Neck NY 11021

DENNIS, DON W
PAINTER, INSTRUCTOR
b Reading, Pa, Jan 21, 1923. *Study:* Kutztown State Col, Pa, BS (art educ), 51; Pratt Inst, Brooklyn, NY, 51-52; with Edgar A Whitney 65-68; also with Barse Miller, 69-70 & 72. *Work:* Miami Univ, Oxford, Ohio; First Nat Bank of Cincinnati, Madeira, Ohio; Reading Mus, Pa; Utstein Kloster, Norway; Bell Telephone; General Electric; Provident Bank, Cincinnati. *Comn:* 12 paintings (offshore oil rigs), Phillips Petroleum, Stavanger, Norway, 79. *Exhib:* Solo exhibs, Reading Mus & Art Gallery, Pa, 68 & Wyannie Malone Mus, Hopetown, Bahamas, 85 & 86; Am Watercolor Soc Ann, Nat Acad, NY; Cincinnati Art Mus Invitational, Ohio, 77; All-Ohio Watercolor Show, Massillon Mus, Ohio, 78; Ohio Watercolor Soc Ann, Ohio, 79, 80, 81, 82, 83, 84, 85 & 86; Group exhib, Kulturhus, Grimstad, Norway, 87. *Pos:* Art dir, Gibson Greetings, Cincinnati, 68-73; conductor watercolor workshops, Maine, Martha's Vineyard, Bahamas & Norway, 73-88; self-employed artist-teacher, 73-. *Teaching:* Guest instr, Miami Univ, Oxford, Ohio, Wine Country Workshops, Napa Valley, Calif, 87-88. *Awards:* Emily Lowe Mem Award, 80, Walser Greathouse Medal, 82, Am Watercolor Soc; M Grumbacher Bronze Medallion, Ohio Watercolor Soc, 81; and others. *Bibliog:* The Watercolor Page, Am Artist, 8/82. *Mem:* Am Watercolor Soc (Midwest vpres, 76-77); Cincinnati Art Club (pres, 71-73); life mem Ohio Watercolor Soc (trustee, 80-85); Cincinnati MacDowell Soc; assoc Nat Acad Design. *Media:* Watercolor. *Publ:* Contribr, Master Color & Design in Watercolor, Watson-Guptill Publ; Exploring Color, Light Publ; Making Color Sing

DENNIS, DONNA FRANCES
SCULPTOR, PRINTMAKER
b Springfield, Ohio, Oct 16, 1942. *Study:* Carleton Coll, BA, 64; Coll Art Study Abroad, Paris, 65; Art Students League, with Stephen Greene, 66. *Work:* Walker Art Ctr, Minneapolis, Minn; Brooklyn Mus, NY; Chase Manhattan Bank; Neuberger Mus, Purchase, NY; Indianapolis Mus Art, Ind; Microsoft Art Collection; Ludwig Forum for Internationale Kunst Aachen Germany; Martin Z Margulies Collection; and others. *Comn:* Entrance maze, Musical Theater Lab, Kennedy Ctr, Washington, DC, 77; Mad River Tunnel (outdoor sculpture), Dayton City, Ohio, 81; Moccasin Creek Cabins (outdoor sculpture), Aberdeen, SDak, 83; Steel Fence & ceramic medallions, PS 234, NY, 88; North Plaza, Klapper Hall, Queens Coll, City Univ New York, 95; fence, Wonderland Sta, MBTA, Boston, 95; fence, IS 5, Queens, 96; fence, Am Airlines Terminal, JFK Airport, NY, 98, Terminal One, 2002. *Exhib:* Solo exhibs, Holly Solmon Gallery, NY, 76, 80, 83, 98, Contemp Arts Ctr, Cin, 79, Neuberger Mus of Suny Purchase, 85, Univ Gallery, Univ Gallery, Univ Mass, Amherst, 85, Brooklyn Mus, 87, Indianapolis, Mus Art, 91-98, Sculpture Ctr, New York, 93, Dayton Art Inst, 2003 & 5 Myles, Brooklyn, NY, 2005; group exhibs, Venice Biennale, Italy, 82, 84, Whitney Mus, NY, 79, 81,Tate Gallery, London, 83, Hirshhorn Mus, Washington, 79, 84, Biennial of Pub Art, Neuberger Mus, 97, Asheville (NC) Mus Art, 98, Palazzo Ducale, Genoa, Italy, 2004; Tourist Cabins on Park Avenue, NYC Parks Dept, Park Ave, New York, 2007. *Collection Arranged:* Cue Gallery, New York, 2007; Tampa Mus Art, Fla, 2010; Neuberger Mus, Purchase, New York, 2008. *Teaching:* Instr Skowhegan Sch Art, Maine, 82, Sch Visual Arts, NY, 83-89 & Princeton Univ, NJ, 84 & State Univ NY, Purchase, 84-88; assoc prof, State Univ NY, Purchase, 90-96, prof, 96-. *Awards:* NY State Creative Artist Pub Serv Grant, 75 & 82; Nat Endowment Arts Grant, 77, 80, 86 & 94; Community Service Award for Excellence in Urban Design, Parks Coun NY, 89; Distinguished Achievement Award, Carleton Coll and Carleton Alumni Asn, 89; Bessie Award for Set Design for Quintland, 92; NY Found Arts Fel, 85 & 92; Pollock-Krasner Found Grant, 2005 & 2008; Malvina Hoffman Artist Fund Prize & Daniel Chester French Sward for Sculpture, Nat Acad Mus, New York, 2008. *Bibliog:* George Melrod (auth), Reviews: Donna Dennis at the sculpture center, Art in Am, 10/93; Roberta Smith (auth), 42nd St puts on heavy make-up and smiles a summer smile, NY Times, 7/29/94; Nancy G Heller (auth), Why Painting is Like a Pizza: A Guide to Understanding and Enjoying Modern Art, Prince Univ Press, 2002; Deborah Everett (auth), Donna Dennis Home Away from Home, Sculpture, 06/2006; Judith Collins (auth), Sculpture Today, Phaidon, 2007; Michele Cohen, Stan Ries, Michall Bloomberg (auths), Pub Art for Pub Sch, Random House, 2009; Tracy Fitzpatrick (auth), Art & the Subway, New york Underground, Rutgers Univ Press, 2009. *Mem:* NY Found Arts (bd govs, 88-91); Nat Acad, New York, 2010. *Media:* Mixed Media, Installation. *Publ:* Illusr, Hotels, Z Press, 74; auth, The presence of the past, Domus Mag, 10/80; coauth (with K Elmslie), 26 Bars, Z Press, 87; collab (with Anne Waldman), 9 Nights Meditation, Granary Books, NY, 2008. *Mailing Add:* 131 Duane St New York NY 10013

DENNISON, KEITH ELKINS
CONSULTANT, CURATOR
b Oakland, Calif, Sept 20, 1939. *Study:* San Francisco State Univ, BA; grad studies, Dr Ernest Mundt; spec training, MH DeYoung Mem Mus, San Francisco. *Collection Arranged:* Horizons, A Century of California Landscape Painting; La Pendule Francaise, A Selected Survey of French Clocks 1750-1900; Ecclesiastical Arts 13th Through 17th Centuries. *Pos:* Asst cur educ, M H DeYoung Mem Mus, 68-70; visual arts adv, Calif Arts Comn, Sacramento, 70-71; dir, Haggin Mus, Stockton, Calif, 71-86; fine arts consult, 86-. *Teaching:* Instr museology, Univ of the Pac, 74-. *Publ:* Auth, Horizons, a century of California landscape painting, 70. *Mailing Add:* PRK LDG Overbury NR Tewkesbury Gloucestershire United Kingdom GL20 7RE

DENNISON, LISA
AUCTION HOUSE EXECUTIVE
b NJ, May 13, 1953. *Study:* Wellesley Col, BA, 75; Brown Univ, MA in Art Hist, 78. *Pos:* intern, Solomon R. Guggenheim Mus, NYC, 73, asst cur, 81-89, assoc cur, 90-91, collections cur, 91-94, cur of collections exhibs, 94-96, chief cur, 96-, dep dir, 96-05, dir, 2005-07; North & S Am exec vpres Sotheby's, 2007-. *Teaching:* instr, Sch Visual Arts, NY, 83-84. *Mem:* ArtTable, NY; Société Kandinsky; bd dir, Byrd Hoffman Found, NY; Int Adv Bd, Louis T Bloudin Found; Creative Arts Adv Bd, Brown Univ. *Mailing Add:* Sothebys 1334 York Ave at 72nd St New York NY 10021

DENSON, G ROGER
CRITIC, WRITER
b Buffalo, NY, Feb 2, 1956. *Study:* New York State Univ, Buffalo, BA (arts & humanities), 78, with Paul Sharits & Hollis Frampton. *Pos:* Cur Performance, video, 78-80 & exhibs dir, 80-82, Hallwalls, Buffalo, NY; cultural critic, Artscribe Int, Parke II, Art in Am, 88-2000, Huffington Post, 2010-12. *Teaching:* Prof Criticism Recent Developments in Art Theory, Homosocial and Homoerotic Art, Grad Studies, Sch Visual Arts, New York, 2006-2008. *Mem:* Gallery Asn NY State (bd dir, 81-87); Alternative Mus (bd dir, 87-91). *Res:* Cultural studies and the critical analyses of the

languages and values of criticism, cross-cultural relations, gender and authority politics, and the development of a nomadic criticism. *Publ:* Philip Taaffe, Parkett No 26, 90; Marilyn Minter, Artscribe Int, 1/91; Robert Longo/Renee Green, Flash Art, 10/91; Capacity: History, The World and the Self, Routledge, Gordon & Breach, 96; Pat Stein, Art in Am, 11/99; Shirin Neshat, Huffington Post, 12/10, Dennis Oppenheim, 1/11, Terrence Malick, 6/11, Cindy Sherman, 3/12. *Mailing Add:* 131 W 15th St Suite 23 New York NY 10011

DENTLER, ANNE LILLIAN
PAINTER, ILLUSTRATOR
b Pittsburgh, Pa. *Study:* Pa State Univ, 74, 2002; Penn State Univ, 2002. *Work:* City of Lake Charles, La; Sowela Comm Coll. *Exhib:* Solo exhibs, Calcasieu Marine Bank, JP Morgan Chase Bank, Lake Charles, La, 97, Hibernia Bank, 98, Capital One Bank, 98-2000 & 2005, Wise Estate, Sulphur, La, 99 & McNeese Univ, 99, 2000-2002; group exhibs, McNeese State Univ, Frazer Libr, Lake Charles, La, 85-, Am Art Gallery, Hot Springs, Ark, 94-99, Agora Gallery, Soho, New York, 96, Abercrombie Gallery, McNeese Univ, Lake Charles, La, 2000-2001, Hist City Hall, Lake Charles, 2007 & Gallery by the Lake, Lake Charles, La, 2007-present; Tex Artist Mus, 2012-. *Pos:* Found, pres, secy, Associated La Artists Inc, Lake Charles, La, 84-; workshop leader, Bus of Art, 2004-; Portraiture; Art of Illus, 2010, 2011; bd dirs, Tex Artists Mus; Big Brothers, Big Sisters, 96-2010. *Teaching:* Instr, continuing educ portraiture McNeese Univ, Lake Charles, 95-; Creative Arts Ctr, Lake Charles, 2009-. *Awards:* Best of Show award, Calcasieu Mus, Calcasieu Nat Arts Festival, 86; Outstanding Artist Year award, Gateway Found, 87; Mayors Art Award, 2007; 2nd runner up, Best Artist of 2008, Times of Southwest Louisiana Poll; Imagination Award, Children's Mus, 2008. *Mem:* Assoc La Artists (found, 84, pres, 84-86, 2003-11, bd dir, workshop instr, 86-99, 2000-, secy, 90); Nat Mus Women in Arts; Arts Net; Bd of dirs, Big Brother, Big Sister; Lone Star Art Guild; Nat Soc Childrens Book Writers and Illus; Tex Artists Mus (bd dirs); Nederland Art Guild; Real Art Deridder, La. *Media:* Oil, Acrylic, Watercolor. *Interests:* Traveling, Art shows, Volunteering. *Publ:* Encyclopedia of Living Artists; Auth, Portraiture in Plain Language; illustrated 25 published books. *Dealer:* Assoc La Artists 106 W Pryce St Lake Charles La 70601

DENTZ, SHOSHANA
PRINTMAKER, PAINTER
Study: Parsons Sch Design, Paris, 1988; Brandeis Univ, BA, 1989; Bard Coll, NY, MFA (Elaine de Kooning Fel Award), 2003. *Exhib:* Solo exhibs include White Columns, New York, 1998, Nicole Klagsbrun Gallery, New York, 2002, Mixed Greens, New York, 2005, Angles Gallery, Santa Monica, Calif, 2005; group exhibs include The Stroke, Exit Art, New York, 1999; Outer Boroughs, White Columns, New York, 1999, 2001 Benefit, 2001; Brent Sikkema, New York, 2000; Abstract, Nicole Klagsbrun, New York, 2001, On Paper, 2004; I Love NY, 2001; After Matisse/Picasso, PS1 Inst Contemp Art, New York, 2003; Lower Eastside Printshop Fel Artists, Mixed Greens, New York, 2004; Playpen, Drawing Ctr, New York, 2004, Selections, 2005; New Prints, Int Print Ctr, New York, 2005; New Works on Paper, Angles Gallery, Santa Monica, Calif, 2005. *Awards:* Lower East Side Printshop Fel, 2004; NY Found Arts Fel, Drawing, 2005; Pollock-Krasner Found Fel, 2007. *Mailing Add:* 150 W96th St Apt 15B New York NY 10025-6487

DE PIÑA RAMOS, THEODORE SANCHEZ See Ramos, Theodore

DE PUMA, RICHARD DANIEL
HISTORIAN, LECTURER
b DuBois, Pa, May 15, 1942. *Study:* Swarthmore Coll, BA (art hist), 64; Bryn Mawr Coll, MA (archeol), 67, PhD (archeol), 69. *Collection Arranged:* Etruscan & Villanovan Pottery (auth, catalog), Univ Iowa Mus Art, 71; Roman Portraits (auth, catalog), Univ Iowa Mus Art, 88; Art in Roman Life: Villa to Grave (auth, catalog), Cedar Rapids Mus Art, 2003; Etruscan Gallery (auth, catalog), Metropolitan Mus Art, NY, 2007. *Pos:* Res assoc, Field Mus Natural Hist, Chicago, Ill, 84-; adv bd, Am J Archaeol, 85-98, Etruscan Studies, 91-; ed, Studies in Classics Monograph Series, Univ Wis, 93-2004. *Teaching:* Instr classical art, Univ Iowa, Iowa City, 68-69, from asst prof to assoc prof, 69-86, prof, 86-, F Wendell Miller Distinguished prof, 2000-2004, prof emeritus, 2004-. *Awards:* Nat Endowment Humanities Grant, 85, 99. *Mem:* Archeol Inst Am; Inst di Studi Etruschi ed Italici; Ger Archeol Inst; Etruscan Found. *Res:* Etruscan pottery & bronzes; Greek vase painting; mosaics; Etruscan forgeries. *Publ:* Auth, Etruscan Tomb-Groups: Ancient Pottery and Bronzes in Chicago's Field Museum of Natural Hist, Mainz, 86; Corpus Speculorum Etruscorum, USA 1 & 2, Ames, 86 & 93, USA 4, Rome, 2005; co-ed, Rome and India: The Ancient Sea Trade, Madison, 91; Murlo and the Etruscans: Art and Society in Ancient Etruria, Madison, 94; auth, Corpus Vasorum Antiquorum: J Paul Getty Mus 6 & 9, Malibu, 96, 2000; Etruscan Art in the Metropolitan Mus Art, 2013. *Mailing Add:* 409 Hutchinson Ave Iowa City IA 52246

DERBY, MARK
CERAMIST, INSTRUCTOR
b E Lansing, Mich, Jan 1, 1960. *Study:* Calif State Univ, Long Beach, BFA, 84 & MFA, 89. *Work:* Mus Ceramic Art Alfred, NY State Coll Ceramics; San Angelo Mus Art, Tex; Nora Eccles Harrison Mus Art, Utah State Univ, Logan. *Exhib:* Ameen Art Gallery, Nicholls State Univ, Thibodaux, La; Northwestern State Univ, Natchitoches, La, 96; Sylvia Schmidt Gallery, New Orleans, La, 97; Contemp Craft, La Villa Meilleur, New Orleans, La 98; Living with Tile, Wayne Art Ctr, Wayne, Pa, 98; Columbus Cult Arts Ctr, Columbus, Ohio, 1999; Erth Gallery, New Orleans, La, 2001. *Teaching:* Instr ceramics, Braille Inst, Anaheim, Calif, 87-88, Palos Verdes Art Ctr, Calif, 88, Clay Studio Sch, Philadelphia, Pa, 92-95 & Univ City Arts League, Philadelphia, Pa, 92-95; vis asst prof ceramics, Newcomb Col Art, Tulane Univ, 95-98; adj prof ceramics, La State Univ, Baton Rouge, 98. *Awards:* Individual Fel, Nat Endowment Arts, 90; Individual Fel, Ariz Comn Arts, 91; Individual Fel, La Div Arts, 98. *Bibliog:* Jimmy Clark (auth), Whimsical Clay, Ceramics: Art & Perception, issue 5, 91; Keely Coghlan (auth), Quiet Symmetry Speaks Volumes in Ceramics, San Angelo Standard Times, 4/17/92; Chris Waddington (auth), vessels apt works for sculptor's, The Times Picayune, New Orleans, La 4/20/97; Gerry Williams (auth), Louisiana Gumbo, The Studio Potter, Vol 29, No 2, June 2001; Doug MacCash (auh), Ceramics capture Feel of the City, Times Picayune, New Orleans, 9/21/2001. *Mem:* ACC; Nat Coun Educ in Ceramic Arts. *Media:* ceramic. *Dealer:* Derby Pottery & Tileworks New Orleans La. *Mailing Add:* 2029 Magazine St New Orleans LA 70115

DEREMER, SUSAN RENÉ
PAINTER, ILLUSTRATOR
b Atlanta, Ga, Jun 29, 1959. *Study:* Inst Fine Arts, Rio De Janeiro, Brazil, cert, 78; Univ Ga, BFA, 82; Art Students League NY, with Nelson Shanks, 98. *Work:* Hist Mus Smyrna, Ga; Zoo Atlanta; Tenn State Univ. *Comn:* Portrait, Tryon Publ Co, Atlanta, 97; portrait, Dr Morton S Silberman Zoo, Atlanta, 2001; portrait, Don Whitehead, Tenn State Univ, 2012. *Exhib:* Solo exhib, South Cobb Arts Alliance, Inc, Mableton, Ga, 92, Carrollton Cult Arts Ctr, 2010; Fine Arts Soc Kennesaw, Ga, 95; AAPL Grand Nat, Salmagundi Club, New York City, 97, 98 & 2003; two-person invitational, The Art Place-Mt View, Marietta, Ga, 99; solo Retrospective, Exhib Paintings Pastel & Drawings,The Cult Arts Ctr, Douglasville, Ga, 2004. *Pos:* Art dir, Exec Printing Inc, Marietta, Ga, 88-90; graphic artist, IBM, Atlanta, 92-93; pres, Deremer Studio Inc, 93-. *Teaching:* Drawing instr, Artists Atelier of Atlanta, 95; painting instr, Douglasville Sch Art. *Awards:* First Place Illustration, Ga Scholastic Press Asn, 77; First Place, Atlantic Artists Club, 94; Third Place, Fine Arts Soc Kennesaw, 95; Second Place, Summer Juried Exhib, Portrait Society of Atlanta, 2008. *Bibliog:* Suzanne Smith (auth), Susan Deremer-Spotlight, PSA Folio, 97; Master pastel artists of the world, Pastel Artist Int, Mar/Apr 2002. *Mem:* Fel Am Artists Prof League Inc; Am Soc Classical Realism; Am Soc Portrait Artists; Portrait Soc Am; Portrait Soc Atlanta Inc (treas, 95-97, pres, 97-99, 2009-11, mem of merit 2011-). *Media:* Oil, Pastel, Charcoal, Graphite, Ink. *Publ:* Auth, Atlanta An Historical Sketchbook, Tryon Publ Co, 98; auth, Folio, Portrait Soc Atlanta Newsletter, 97-2000, 2009-. *Mailing Add:* 1630 Orr Terrace The Villages FL 32162

DE RICCO, HANK
SCULPTOR
Jersey City, NJ, May 28, 1946. *Study:* William Paterson Col, 65-67; Pratt Inst, Brooklyn, NY, 67-69; Empire State Col, State Univ NY, BFA, 80; Sch Visual Art, New York, MFA, 91. *Work:* Nassau Co Mus; Reading Mus, Pa. *Comn:* Flip Flop Transit, Calif State Univ Bakersfield, 88; Here to There, Miami Univ, Oxford, Ohio, 90; Hunts Point Center Sculpture Park, New York, 90; Episode, Arts Festival Atlanta, Ga, 91; Altimeter, City Arts-Dupont St Proj Greenpoint, NY, 95. *Exhib:* Solo exhibs, PS 1, Long Island City, NY, 87, 55 Mercer St Gallery, 88-95, & New Arts Prog, Kutztown, Pa, 95; Back to the Wall, Philadelphia Art Alliance, 89; Signs, Codes & Alphabets, Tribeca 148, New York, 94; Objects & Ontology, E S Van Dam, New York, 94; Buoys: Marketing Place, Art Initiatives, New York, 95. *Pos:* Sculptor, Rockland CETA Arts Prog, 78-79; dir, A-I-R Prog, Palisades Interstate Park, 79-82; co-found & co-ed, The NY Art Intelligencer, 95-96. *Teaching:* Vis asst prof, Lawrence Univ, Appleton, Wis, 95; asst prof sculptor, Carnegie Mellon Univ, 95; instr, Jersey City State, 94-96; asst prof drawing, Pratt Inst, 95-96. *Awards:* CAPS Grant, 83; Pollock-Krasner Found Grant, 87 & 2008; Adolph & Esther Gottlieb Found Inc, 92. *Bibliog:* Phyliss Braff (auth), Sculpture inspired by site, NY Times, 5/12/85; Sculpture, Vol 6, No 4 40, 87; M Brenson (auth), Sculpture borne by earth lit by sky, NY Times, 3/8/91. *Mem:* Coll Art Asn. *Dealer:* 55 Mercer Street Gallery 55 Mercer St New York NY 10013

DERN, F CARL
SCULPTOR
b Salt Lake City, Utah, Apr 24, 1936. *Study:* San Francisco Art Inst, 1969; Univ Calif, Berkeley, 1971-1972. *Work:* In many pvt collections. *Exhib:* San Francisco Art Inst Centennial Exhib, de Young Mus, 70; New Mus Mod Art, Oakland, 70-73; 1st & 2nd Soap Box Derby, San Francisco Mus Mod Art, 75 & 78; San Jose Mus Art, 78; Syntax Corp Outdoor Sculpture Exhib, 79-80; San Mateo Arts Coun, Proarts Gallery, Oakland, 80; Richmond Art Ctr, 81; Univ Calif Nelson Art Gallery, 1988; Esprit Sculpture Park, 1990; Bolinas Mus, 1993-2003; Fresno Art Mus, 2003; and others. *Teaching:* Lectr sculpture, Univ Calif, Berkeley, 75 & Univ Calif, Davis, 83; lectr art, Sonoma State Univ, 77 & 78. *Awards:* Anne Bremer Prize in Art, Univ Calif, Berkeley, 69 & 72; First Prize, 1st Int Contemp, Jon Morehead Gallery, Chico, Calif, 71; Hand Hallow Found Fel, 82 & 83. *Mem:* Artists Equity. *Mailing Add:* 58 Park Rd Fairfax CA 94930

DERNOVICH, DONALD FREDERICK
PAINTER, EDUCATOR
b Rock Springs, Wyo, April 9, 1942. *Study:* Univ Wyo, BA (art educ), 66, MA (art), 67; Ft Hays State Univ, MFA (painting), 83. *Work:* Birger Sandzen Mem Gallery, Lindsborg, Kans; Halseth Co Community Arts Ctr, Rock Springs, Wyo; Wayne State Coll, Wayne, Nebr; Ella Carothers Dunnegan Gallery, Bolivar, Mo; Mus Nebr Art, Kearney. *Comn:* Two watercolors, Law Enforcement Acad, Douglas, Wyo, 85; painting, Chadron St Coll, Chadron, Nebr, 90; painting, Beard Oil Co, Gemini Div, 92; painting, Am First Bank, McCook, Nebr, 94 & 2000; painting, State Bank, Benkleman, Nebr, 94. *Exhib:* Arts for the Parks, Nat Wildlife Art Mus, Jackson, Wyo, 93, 96, 98-2001, 2003 & 2005; Am Watercolor Soc 128th, 135th 138th, Int, Salmagundi Club Galleries, 95, 2002 & 2005; 171 St Nat Acad Design, Nat Acad Galleries, New York, 96; Oil Painters Am, Greenhouse Gallery Fine Art, San Antonio, Tex, 96; CM Russell Art Auction, Great Falls, Mont, 97-2007; Phippin Mus Art Show, Prescott, Ariz, 97-2005; Zantman Galleries, Palm Desert, Calif, 2001; Buffalo Bill Art Show, Cody Wyo, 2004-07; Dana Gallery, Bozeman, Mont, 2006. *Pos:* Dir, McCook Area Arts Coun, 75-78; exhib bd, Asn Nebr Arts Clubs, 86-90. *Teaching:* Art dir & instr, McCook Community Coll, Nebr, 75-2004. *Awards:* Purchase Award-Best Show, Mus Nebr Art, Kearney, 89; Award for Excellence, Arts For Parks Ann-Top 100 Traveling, 93 & 98; Best Watermedia, Ann Western Spirit Art Show, Cheyenne, 94-98;

Doc Smith Award, Blackfoot Valley Art Exhib, Lincoln, Mont, 97, Silver Award, 2000; 2nd Place in Watermedia, Phippen Western Art Show, Prescott, Ariz, 99; Artists Favorite Award, Spirit of the Great Plains Invitational, Mus of Nebr Art, Kearney, Nebr, 2000; Peoples Favorite and Artists Favorite Awards, Platte River Valley Western Art Show, Saratoga, Wyo, 2000; First Place in Oil, Phippen Mus Western Art Show, Prescott, Ariz, 2002; Best of Show, High Plains Art Festival, Oberlin, Kans, 2006; Top 100 Paint Am Competition, 2008. *Bibliog:* Up the river with a paint brush, Am Artists Mag, 92; The art of Don Dernovich, Contact-News-N-Viewslett, 94. *Mem:* Am Watercolor Soc (sig mem); Oil Painters Am (sig mem); McCook Art Guild (life mem); Nat Watercolor Soc (sig mem); Kans Watercolor Soc (sig mem); Rocky Mt Plain Air Painters; IMPACT, Nebr. *Media:* Watercolor, Oil. *Publ:* Auth, Splash Four, Northlight Bks, 96; Best In Watercolor, Watercolor Places, Rockport Publ, 87 & 96; Splash Five, 98. *Dealer:* Blackhawk Gallery Saratoga Wyo; Spirits In The Wind Gallery Golden Colo; Buffalo Trail Gallery Jackson Hole WY. *Mailing Add:* 210 Taylor PO Box 163 Culbertson NE 69024

DEROSIER, DEBORAH RUSH
PAINTER, EDUCATOR
b Buffalo, NY, Oct 29, 1952. *Work:* Arabian Horse Trust-Permanent Collection, Galleries, Kentucky Horse Park. *Comn:* Mural, Town Historical, Elma Hist Soc, NY, 76; mural, Pioneer/Indian History, Canaseraga Cent Sch, NY, 86; mural, Town Historical, Elma Town Hall, 8/2003 & 6/2007; other collections 2006-present include El Adiyat Arabian Stud, Kuwait, Omar Sakr, Cairo, Egypt, Naser Moushtahu, Egypt, Jody Cruz, Rancho Bulakenyo, Calif; Ajmal Stud, Kuwait, Al Rayyan Farm, Talad Al Kharafi, Kuwait, Al Waab Farm, Qatar. *Exhib:* Allentown Art Festival, Buffalo, NY, 73; Crabbet Symposium, Denver, Colo, 84; Egyptian Event, Lexington, Ky, 84, 90, 91, 94-2012; US Nat Arabian Show, Louisville, Ky, 88, 92 & 94-98; World Cup, Tampa, Fla, 89; Mus European Art, April Group Juried Exhib (nude studies), Clarence, NY, 2004; Int Arabian Horse Show, HRH Royal Jordan Stables, Amman, 10/2005; solo exhib Fountain Arts Ctr, Belmont, NY, 9/2006; Touch of Class, Int Equine Art Exhib, Kuwait, 2010. *Pos:* DBA, Arte DeRosier, Art by Rush. *Teaching:* Creative sculpting ceramic-clay, Iroquois Cent Sch, 72-; drawings & sketching, Adult Educ Prog, Elma, NY, 75-; pvt tutor, 87-2008; premier one-day art seminar, Moshav Ha'yogev, Israel, 2005; instr, drawing, sketch, pastel painting, clay culture curriculum, Wellsville Creative Arts Ctr, NY, 2006-2007; instr drawing, sketching, the Fountain's Arts Ctr, Belmont, NY, 2010-2012, continuing instr drawing, 2012-. *Bibliog:* D Hamrick (auth), Rush's Passion--, Arabian Horse Express, 9/86; S Leadley (auth), The Easel, Arabian Visions, 2/92; Arabian Horse World, Pyramid Report, 2/2005, 4/2006 & 4/2008; Arabian Horse, Profile of the Artist, Times, 4/06. *Mem:* Lifetime honorary mem, Arabian Horse Assoc of NY, 2002. *Media:* Oil, Pencil, Acrylics. *Specialty:* Equine art, landscapes, human figure studies. *Interests:* Gardening, hiking, bible study, farming,nature studies, research, environmental science. *Collection:* Arabian House Galleries, Kentucky House Park, Lexington, Ky. *Dealer:* Arte DeRosier

DE ROTHSCHILD, ERIC ALAIN ROBERT DAVID
COLLECTOR
b New York City, NY, Oct 3, 1940. *Study:* Poly Sch, Zürich, 1963. *Awards:* Named one of Top 200 Art Collectors, ARTnews Mag, 2004-08, 2013. *Mem:* Rothschild Found, Paris (pres, currently); Nat Found, graphic & plastic Arts, Paris; Smithsonian Inst, Wash, DC (admin coun, 1996). *Collection:* Old Masters, Modern & Contemporary Art

DEROUX, DANIEL EDWARD
PAINTER, SCULPTOR
b Juneau, Alaska, Oct 25, 1951. *Study:* NS Coll Art & Design, Halifax, Can, 74-75. *Work:* Smithsonian Inst; Butler Inst AM Art. *Comn:* 3 murals, Univ Alaska, Fairbanks; 2 murals, City of Anchorage, Alaska; 5 murals, city of Juneau, Alaska; 26 paintings, Statehood Commemorative, Anchorage, Alaska; interior sculpture, Encryption Wall, Juneau High Sch, Alaska. *Exhib:* San Francisco Mus Mod Art, 79-80; 15th Ann Nat Small Sculpture & Drawing Exhib, Corpus Christi, Tex, 81; Collage & Assemblage, traveling exhib, 81-82; Los Angeles Int Art Competition, 88; NY Int Art Competition, 88; and others. *Pos:* Cur visual arts, Alaska State Mus, 78-79. *Awards:* Most Accomplished Artist, Los Angeles Int Art Competition, 81; Best of Show, Calgene W Coast Art Competition, Davis, 84; Third Place, NY Int Art Competition, 88. *Bibliog:* Margaret Firmin (auth), Only painting what he sees, Alaska Advocate, 2/79; art ed (auth), Whimsical images are his delight, Anchorage Times, 2/79; Marianna Woodward (auth), Dan DeRoux Juneau buckaroo, Alaska J, 1/80; Julie Decker (auth), Icebreakers Found & Assembled in Alaska

DERRICKSON, STEVE BRUCE
PAINTER
b Baltimore, Md, Mar 21, 1952. *Study:* Ohio Univ, BFA, 74; Tyler Sch Art, Temple Univ, MFA, 77. *Work:* Bank of Am; Principal Financial Group; Univ NC; Security Pac Bank. *Exhib:* solo exhib, Stephen Wirtz Gallery, San Francisco, 89; Sue Spaid Fine Art, Los Angeles, Calif, 90; Insect Politics, Body Horror, Social Order, Hallwalls, Buffalo, NY, 90; Invitational, Berland/Hall Gallery, NY; Eye Flower Drawings, PPOW Gallery, NY, 94; and others. *Teaching:* Instr art, Univ Tex, Austin, 77-80; asst prof art, Univ Tex, Austin, 80-84; vis artist, Ohio State Univ, Columbus, Ohio, 87. *Awards:* Installation for Text Sculpture Symp, Tex Comm Arts, Austin, 83; Fel, Nat Endowment Arts, 87-88; Residency, MacDowell Colony, Petersborough, NH, 91. *Bibliog:* Eleanor Heartney (auth), Art & the electronic fishbowl, Art News, 12/86; Kate Linker (auth), Review of cinemaobject, Artforum, 12/86; Robert Mahoney (auth), Review of a romantic distance, Arts Mag, 5/88. *Dealer:* Sue Spaid Fine Art Gallery 7454 1/2 Beverly Blvd Los Angeles CA 90036. *Mailing Add:* 572 Plutarch Rd Highland NY 12528

DE ST CROIX, BLANE
SCULPTOR, EDUCATOR
b Boston, Mass. *Study:* Mass Coll Art, BFA (sculpture); Cranbrook Acad Art, MFA (sculpture). *Work:* Laumeier Sculpture Park & Mus, Mo; Decordova Mus & Sculpture Park, Lincoln, Mass; Albrecht-Kemper Mus Art, Mo; Kohler Corp, Wis; Univ Tenn Reese Collection; numerous pvt collections. *Exhib:* Nat Sculpture Exhib, DeLand Mus, Fla, 1991; L x H x W, Mass Coll Art, Boston, 1992; solo exhibs, Margaret Harwell Art Mus, Poplar Bluff, 1992, Univ Nebr Gallery, Omaha, 1993, Los Angeles Artcore Ctr, 1997, Gasworks Alternative Gallery, London, 1998, Fla Gulf Coast Univ Gallery, Ft Myers, 2000, Coral Springs Mus, Fla, 2002, DeCordova Mus & Sculpture Park, Mass, 2003, New York Univ Galleries, 2004 & Robert Rauschenberg Gallery, Fla, 2009; 11th Bi-Ann Art Auction Benefit, Mus Contemp Art, Chicago, 1993; Art In The Law, Nev Mus Art, Reno, 1995; Hortt Ann Exhib, Mus Art, Ft Lauderdale, 1999; 2nd Ann Unaffiliated Juried Exhib, Art Basel, Miami Beach, 2002; Approaches: Sculptors from Florida, Univ Miami Dep Art, Fla, 2005; Sculpture Key West, Fort Zachary Taylor State Park, Key West, 2009. *Teaching:* Vis asst prof, Whittier Coll, formerly; vis assoc prof, Ariz State Univ, currently; assoc prof, Fla Atlantic Univ, currently. *Awards:* Sculpture award, Nat Endowment Arts, 1993; Pollock-Krasner Found Grant, 2008; Joan Mitchell Found Grant, 2009; Black & White Project Space Prize, 2009; Guggenheim Found Fel, 2010. *Bibliog:* Voelz Sandler (auth), On Art, Denver Post, 6/1996; Candice Russell (auth), Littler But Artier, City Link, 12/2000; Ivette Yee (auth), Southern Exposure, Sun Sentinel, 12/2004; Jerry Saltz (auth), Crossing the Line, NY Mag, 4/13/2009. *Mailing Add:* Florida Atlantic Univ Dept Visual Arts & History 777 Glades Rd Boca Raton FL 33431

DESANTIS, DIANA
PAINTER
b Brooklyn, NY. *Study:* Traphagen Sch Art, cert, 46; Parsons Sch Design, dipl, 49; Art Students League, with Harvey Dinnerstein & David Leffel, 91-92. *Comn:* Portrait, Brushstroke Design Asn, NY, 94. *Exhib:* Soc of Illustrators Nat, NY, 92; Catharine Lorillard Wolfe Nat, NY, 92-94; Open Juried Nat, Nassau Co Mus, 92-94; Hudson Valley Art Asn Nat, Hastings, NY, 93; Pastel Soc Am Nat, NY, 94; and others. *Awards:* Norman Rockwell Mus Award, Soc Illustrators, 92; Gold Medal, Knickerbocker Artists, 92; David & Elsie Ject Key Mem Award, Audubon Artists, 94. *Bibliog:* Article in Artspeak, 4/91; article in Williston Times, 6/93; article in News Day, 9/93. *Mem:* Knickerbocker Artists USA; Pastel Soc Am; Audubon Artists; Catharine Lorillard Wolfe Art Club; Am Artist Prof League. *Media:* Pastel, Oil

DE SANTO, STEPHEN C
PAINTER
b Louisville, Ky, May 27, 1951. *Study:* Huntington Coll, BA (art), 74; Ball State Univ, MA (art), 78. *Work:* Wichita Art Mus, Kans; Anderson Fine Arts Ctr, Ind. *Exhib:* Mid-Year Show, Butler Inst Am Art, Youngstown, Ohio, 80-82; Am Watercolor Soc Traveling Exhib, 10 mus across the US, 80, 82 & 85; 157th Ann Exhib, Nat Acad Design, New York, 82; Navy Pier Int Art Expo, Chicago, 85-88. *Pos:* Full-time fine artist. *Awards:* Ed Whitney Award, 80 & High Winds Award, 85, Am Watercolor Soc Ann Exhib; Merit Award, Watercolor USA Ann, 85. *Bibliog:* Michael Ward (auth), Letter from the editor, Artist's Mag, 1/91; Rachel Wolf (auth), SPLASH II-Watercolor Breakthroughs, Northlight Bks, 93; David Pyle (auth), The Swipe File, Artist's Mag, 7/94; and others. *Media:* Acrylic, Mixed Media. *Mailing Add:* 1325 Kensington Blvd Fort Wayne IN 46805

DESCHAMPS, FRANCOIS
PHOTOGRAPHER
b Nov 18, 1946. *Study:* Sorbonne, Paris, 64-65; Univ Ill, Champaign, BS(Phi Beta Kappa), MS, ABD (mathematics), 65-70; Ill Inst Technol, Inst Design, MS(photog), 72. *Work:* Mus Contemp Art, Chicago; Metro Mus; Houston Mus Fine Arts; Mus Mod Art, NY; Brooklyn Mus. *Teaching:* Aegean Sch Fine Arts, Paros, Greece, 73; Bradley Univ, Peoria, Ill, 72-80; teacher & dir Photog Option, State Univ NY at New Paltz, 80-; prof art dept, State Univ NY, New Paltz. *Awards:* Nat Endowment for Arts, Photog Fel, 83 & 87; Photogr's Fel, NY Found Arts, 88 & 98; Inter Arts Travel Fel, Nat Endowment Art, 94; Fel, Univ Auckland Res Found, 95; Residence Cite' des Arts, Paris, 2002; Fulbright grant, 2010. *Media:* Offset Books, Photographic Boxes. *Publ:* Auth, Life in a Book, VSW Press, 86; coauth, Particle Theory, Nexus Press, 91; auth, A Guide to Antipodia, Univ Arts, Philadelphia, 92, Memoire d'un Voyage en Oceanie, Photoforum, NZ, 95 & Sombras Rojas, USW Press, 99; Drone 1/2/3, VSW Press, 2010; Photo-Rapide, Suny Press, 2013

DESIDERIO, VINCENT
PAINTER
b Philadelphia, Pa, 1955. *Study:* Haverford Col, BA (fine arts/art history), 77, Acad di Belle Arti, Florence, Italy, 77-78, Pa Acad Fine Arts, cert, 79-83. *Work:* Sammlung Ludwig Neve Galerie, Aachen, WGer; Denver Art Mus; Everson Mus, Syracuse, NY; Metrop Mus Art, NY; Greenville Co Mus Art, SC; The Solomon R Guggenheim Mus, NY; Mus of Fine Arts, Boston, Mass; Hirshhorn Mus & Sculpture, Washington, DC; Pa Acad of Fine Arts, Phila, PA; Seven Bridges Foundation, Conn. *Exhib:* Solo exhibs, Lawrence Oliver Gallery, Philadelphia, 86, Lang & O'Hara Gallery, NY, 87, 89 & 90, Greenville Mus, SC, 88, Queens Mus, NY, 91, Marlborough Gallery, NY, 93, 97, 99, 2001, 02 & Very Spec Arts Gallery, Washington, DC, 93; Marlborough Gallery, 2004; In the Looking Glass: Contemp Narrative Painting, Mint Mus Art, Charlotte, NC, 91; On Paper, Marlborough Gallery, NY, 92, Summer Show, Marlborough Gallery, 2001, Oil on Paper, Marlborough Gallery, 2002; The Anxious Salon, Mass Inst Technol, 93; List Visual Arts Ctr, Cambridge, Mass, 93; The Seer, O'Hara Gallery, NY, 94; Queens Artists: Highlights of the 20th Century, Queens Mus Art, NY, 97; Art 1997 Chicago: 5th Ann Expo of Int Galleries Featuring Modern and Contemp Art, Navy Pier, Chicago, 97; Forma Y Figuracion: Obras Maestras De La Coleccion Blake-Purnell, Guggenheim Bilbao, 98; 1998 Collector's Show: The Ark Arts Ctr, Little Rock, Ark, 98; 1998 Collector's Show, Ark Arts Ctr, Little Rock, Ark, 98; The Cantor Fitzgerald Gallery, Haverford Coll, Pa, 2002; group exhibs, Modern

and Contemp Portraits, Forum Gallery, NY, 2003, Transforming the Commonplace, Susquehanna Art Mus, Pa, 2003. *Awards:* Pollock/Krasner Found Grant, 87; Fel, Nat Endowment Arts, 87; Grand Prize SAS Prince Rainier III, 30th Ann Show Contemp Art, Monte Carlo, Monaco, 96. *Bibliog:* David Zimmerman (auth), Art exhibit casts a critical eye at common concepts of heroism, rev, USA Today, 10/29/96; Phillipe Cruysmans (auth), Dix Artistes Couronne's a Monaco, Le Figaro, 5/14/96; Carol King (auth), realism: The new hip, ARTnews, 2/97. *Media:* Oils. *Mailing Add:* c/o Marlborough Gallery 40 W 57th St New York NY 10019

DESJARLAIT, ROBERT D
MURALIST, WRITER
b Red Lake Chippewa Reservation, Redlake, Minn, Nov, 18, 1946. *Study:* Self taught. *Work:* NDak Mus Art, Grand Forks; Meridel Le Sueur Libr, Augsburg Col, Minneapolis; Anoka-Hennepin Educ Admin Ctr, Anoka; Robbinsdale Educ Admin Ctr, New Hope. *Comn:* Illus, Anoka-Hennepin Am Indian Lang & Cult Prog, 89-90; mural, Saturn Sch Tomorrow, St Paul, 92; mural, Phillips Neighborhood Safe Art Proj, Minneapolis, 95; mural, Minneapolis Indian Educ Proj, 96; mosaic, Phillips Gateway Prog, Minneapolis, 96. *Exhib:* Homecomings, NDak Mus Art, Grand Forks, 85; Minn Chippewa Art Exhib, Am Indian Community House Gallery, NY, 86; In Defense of Sacred Lands, Harcus Gallery, Boston, Mass, 87; Pictures from Home: Minnesota Illustrators of Children's Books, Univ Art Mus, Minneapolis, 88; Metaphorical Fish, Univ Art Mus, Minneapolis, 90. *Pos:* Art dir/curric specialist, Northern Winds Arts Educ Proj, Minneapolis, 92-95. *Teaching:* Art instr, Am Indian Art Hist & Drawing, Heart of the Earth Survival Sch, Minneapolis, 89-90, Native Am Educ Serv Col, Minneapolis, 94-95, La Courte Oreilles Community Coll, 96; instr traditional arts, Am Indian OIC Col, Minneapolis, 96. *Awards:* First Place, Drawing, Ojibwe Art Expo, Minneapolis, 88; Percy Fearing Award for Illus, Minn Coun Teaching of Foreign Lang, Minneapolis, 88; CUE Award, Minneapolis Comn Arts, 95. *Bibliog:* Kathy Thornes (auth), DesJarlait depicts Ojibwe vision, Red Lake Times, 87; Interview with Robert DesJarlait (video), Northern Lights & Insights, Hennepin Co Libr, Minneapolis, 92; Beverly Slapin & Doris Seale (ed), Through Indian Eyes: The Native Experience in Books for Children, Philadelphia, 92. *Mem:* Native Cult Arts Prog/Native Arts Circle; Minn State Arts Bd Artists in Educ. *Media:* Acrylic, Graphite Pencil. *Publ:* Auth, Nimiwin, A History of Ojibway Dance, 90, Rethinking Stereotypes: Native American Imagery in Art & Illustration, Anoka-Henn Press, Coon Rapids, 93; Art of the Ojibway, Northern Winds Desktop Press, 94; auth & illusr, Nimiwin: An Ojibway Dance Curriculum Coloring Book, Northern Winds Desktop Press, 96; auth, Traditional powwow vs contest powwow and the role of the Native American community, Wicazo Sa Rev, Univ Minn Press, 96; illusr, The First American Series, 88-90, auth & illusr, Ni-mi-win: A History of Ojibway Dance, 90 & illusr, Traditional Indian Stories, 92, Anoka-Hennepin Press, Coon Rapids. *Dealer:* Art Lending Gallery 2500 Groveland Terr Minneapolis Minn. *Mailing Add:* 6024 Old Viking Blvd NW Anoka MN 55303

DESMARAIS, CHARLES JOSEPH
MUSEUM DIRECTOR
b New York, NY, Apr 21, 1949. *Study:* Western Conn State Col, 67-71; State Univ NY, Buffalo, BS, 75, MA, 77; Mus Mgt Inst, cert, 83. *Collection Arranged:* The Portrait Extended (auth, catalog), Mus Contemp Art, Chicago, 80; Mark Berghash: Jews and Germans (auth, catalog), Calif Mus of Photog, 84; Why I Got into TV & Other Stories: The Art of Ilene Segalove (auth, catalog), Laguna Art Mus, 90 Laguna Art Mus, 92; Proof: Los Angeles Art & the Photograph 1960-1980 (auth, catalog) Laguna Art Mus, 92. *Pos:* Asst ed, Afterimage, Rochester, NY, 75-77; ed, Exposure: Quart J Soc Photog Educ, 77-81; dir, Chicago Ctr Contemp Photog, Columbia Col, 77-79; dir, Calif Mus Photog, Univ Calif, Riverside, 81-88; art columnist, Riverside (CA) Press-Enterprise, 87-88; dir, Laguna Art Mus, Laguna Beach, Calif, 88-94, Robert Gumbiner Found for the Arts, Long Beach, Calif, 94-95 & Contemp Art Ctr, Cincinnati, Ohio, 95-2004; dep dir art, Brooklyn Mus, NY, 2005-11; pres, San Francisco Art Inst, 2011-. *Teaching:* Assoc prof art history, Calif State Univ, Fullerton, 94-95. *Awards:* Art Critics Fel, Nat Endowment Arts, 79. *Bibliog:* Interview, Museum dreams of future, Los Angeles Times, 7/5/81; New director focuses in on Laguna Art Mus, Orange County Register, 7/3/88; Mus chief hopes to erase narrow image, 7/10/88 & Laguna Mus job takes a good listener, (interview), 11/5/89, LA Times. *Mem:* Soc Photog Educ (bd dir, 79-83); Coll Art Asn; Am Asn Mus; Asn Art Mus Dir; Orange Co Arts Coun (chmn, 89-91); Asn Independent Coll Art & Design (bd). *Res:* Contemporary art and architecture, media arts (photography, film, video). *Publ:* Auth, Roger Mertin: Records 1976-78, 78 & Michael Bishop, 79, Columbia Col, Chicago; On Art (bi-weekly column), Riverside Press-Enterprise, Calif, 87-88; The Seventies, in: Decade by Decade (James Enveart, ed), Little, Brown, 89. *Mailing Add:* San Francisco Art Institute Office of President 800 Chestnut St San Francisco CA 94133

DE SMET, LORRAINE
PAINTER
b Passaic, NJ, May 5, 1928. *Study:* Art Students League, study with Issac Soyer, Harvey Dinnerstein, David Leffel, Hillary Holmes, Richard Goetz, 79-84; Montclair Art Mus, 86. *Work:* US Coast Guard Collection; Union Trust, Stamford, Conn; Univ Conn Health Ctr, Farmington. *Exhib:* Focus on Art, NJ, 88-90; Ridgewood Art Inst, 89-2014; Caldwell Coll, 90, 94-2009; Catherine Lorillard Wolfe, Nat Arts Club, NY; With Coast Guard on Governors Island, Hudson Valley Art Asn, NY; Am Artists Prof League; Salmagundi Club, NY; Pen & Brush Club, NY; Best of the Best, Trenton Mus, 2001; Office of the Commandant US Coast Guard, DC, 2010. *Pos:* Bd dir, Pen & Brush Club, 85-92, brush chmn, 87-89, co-chair brush sect, 94-95 & 97; bd govs, West Essex Art Asn, 92-98; bd dir, Art Ctr NJ, 94-, secy & mem chair, currently. *Awards:* Ann Waldon Award, Am Artists Prof League, 98, Merit Award, 2000 & 2002; Merit, Livingston Art Asn, 99-2002, 2009, 1st place, 2004; Millburn-Short Hills Award of Excellence, 2001, 2002, 2009, Award of Merit, 2004 & 05, Best in Show, 2007; Oakside Cult Award, 2004; 1st place, W Essex Art Assn, 2005, Merit Award, 2007; 1st place, Art Ctr NJ, 2005 & 08, 3rd place, 2011; Caldwell Progress Award, 2006, 2010; Best Still Life, 2009; Ringwood Manor Art Asn award, 2009-2011; Catherine Lorillard Wolfe award, Ridgewood Art Inst, 2011; Excellence award, West Essex Art Assn, 2013, Livingston Art Assn, 2013, 2014. *Bibliog:* Articles, Joseph Merkel (auth), Artspeak, 84, Will Grant (auth), 87, Howard Farber (auth), 90. *Mem:* Pen & Brush Club (vpres, 89-92); life mem Art Students League, NY; Am Artists Prof League (Fel, 2010); West Essex Art Asn; Art Ctr NJ; and others. *Media:* Oil. *Specialty:* Still life & portraits. *Mailing Add:* 33 Campbell Rd Fairfield NJ 07004

DESMETT, DON
CURATOR, GALLERY DIRECTOR
b Philipsburg, Pa, May 20, 1954. *Study:* Univ Mass, Amherst, MFA, 84. *Collection Arranged:* Jerry Kearns: Deep Cover (auth, catalog), Tyler Sch Art, 91; The Price of Power, (auth, catalog), Cleveland Ctr Contemp Art, 91; Michele Blondel, Tyler Sch Art, 92; Beth B (auth, catalog), 95; Mike Glier: Garden Court (auth, catalog), 95. *Pos:* Dir, Tyler Galleries, Tyler Sch Art, 90-. *Teaching:* Instr Mus Studies, Tyler Sch Art, currently

DESMIDT, THOMAS H
PAINTER, EDUCATOR
b Sheboygan, Wis, Sept 6, 1944. *Study:* Lincoln Col, AA; Layton Sch Art, BFA; Syracuse Univ, MFA. *Work:* Milwaukee Art Inst, Wis; Francis & Sidney Lewis Collection Contemp Art; F&M Corp, Richmond, Va; Miller Brewing Co, Milwaukee, Wis; Everson Mus Art, Syracuse; and others. *Exhib:* Solo exhibs, Mem Art Gallery, Univ Rochester, 72, Everson Mus, 73 & Va Mus Fine Arts, 78; James Yu Gallery, NY, 73 & 74; 19th Corcoran Biennial, Washington, 74; Va Artists, Va Mus, Richmond, 77. *Teaching:* Instr painting, Va Commonwealth Univ, 70-73, dir, Art Found, 73-76, asst prof art, 73-, asst dean, 76-. *Awards:* One-Man Exhib Award, Rochester Mem Gallery, 70; Fac Res Grant, Va Commonwealth Univ, 73. *Media:* Canvas, Acrylic. *Dealer:* James Yu Gallery 393 W Broadway New York NY 10012. *Mailing Add:* c/o Aaron Gallery 5812 Inman Park Cir Apt 210 Rockville MD 20852

DES RIOUX (DE MESSIMY), DEENA (VICTORIA COTY)
COMPUTER MONTAGE ARTIST
b Cambridge, Mass, Dec 7, 1941; French & US citizen. *Study:* RI Sch Design, 59-62; Brown Univ, 60-62; Univ Paris at Sorbonne, 61, 63-64. *Work:* New Orleans Mus Art, La; Milwaukee Art Mus, Wis; Austin Mus Art, Tex; Int Ctr Graphic Art, Ljubljana, Slovenia; Mus Art, RI Sch Design; Grand Forks Art Gallery, Vancouver, BC, Canada; Brooklyn Mus, New York; Kinsey Inst, Ind Univ, Bloomington; New York Pub Libr, Prints Division; Cent Acad Art, Kuala Lumpur, Malaysia; Hofstra Univ Mus, Hempstead, NY; Southern Ill Univ Mus, Carbondale; Ind Univ Art Mus, Boise State Univ, Idaho; Alexandria Mus Art, La; Downey Mus Art, Calif; Eastern Wash Univ; Fuller Mus Art, Brockton, Mass; Int Soc Graphic Art, Krakow; Nat Ctr Fine Arts, Cairo; Palm Springs Desert Mus, Calif; Tama Art Univ Mus, Tokyo; Univ Ala, Birmingham; Univ Pa, Philadelphia; Univ Wyo Art Mus, Laramie; Elmhurst Art Mus, Ill; Elvehjem Mus Art, Univ Wis, Madison; Mont State Univ, Billings. *Exhib:* Solo exhibs, Psychoanalytic Inst, Boston, 74, Art Inst, Boston, 75, Mus Sci, Boston, 78, Ward-Nasse Gallery, New York, 78, Helander Gallery, Palm Beach, Fla, 85, Columbia Univ, New York, 92, Univ Wyo Art Mus, Laramie, 94, Silicon Gallery, Philadelphia, 96 & 2000, Bunkier Sztuki Art Ctr, Krakow, Poland, 97, Mus Gornoslaskie, Bytom, Poland, 97, Northlight Gallery, Everett Community Coll, Wash, 98 & 2000, Kans State Univ Gallery, Manhattan, 98, Grants Pass Mus Art, Ore, 98, Cent Wash Univ, Sarah Spurgeon Gallery, Ellensburg, 98, Firehouse Gallery, Nassau Community Coll, Garden City, NY, 99, RI Coll, Bannister Gallery, Providence, 99, Wash State Univ, Tricities, Richland, 2000, Hockaday Mus Art, Kalispell, Mont, 2000, Columbia Basin Coll, Esvelt Gallery, Pasco, 2000, Herkimer Co Community Coll, Cogar Gallery, NY, 2001, Elmhurst Art Mus, Ill, 2001, Schoolhouse Hist & Art Mus, Colstrip, Mont, 2001, Mont State Univ, Northcutt-Steele Gallery, Billings, 2001, Dahl Arts Ctr, Ruth Brennan Gallery, Rapid City, SDak, 2004, Can/Grand Forks Art Gallery, Vancouver, BC, 2005, Texarkana Regional Arts & Humanities Ctr, Texarkana, Tex, 2005, Zanesville Art Ctr, Ohio, 2006-2007, Lessedra Art Gallery, Sofia, Bulgaria, 2008; invitational group exhibs, Mokotoff Gallery, New York, 86, Warwick Mus, 91, Mus Art RI Sch Design, 94, Cartier/Fifth Ave, 94, Nat Fine Arts Ctr, Egyptian Int Print Triennale, Giza, Egypt, 94, 97, 2000, 2003 & 2006, E Wash Univ, USA Mus Tour, Cheney, Wash, 94-2000, Fuller Mus Art, 95, Midwest Photog Invitational, IX, X, XI (two-yr, ten-venue) Univ Wis, Green Bay, 96-2002, Hofstra Univ Mus, Hofstra Mus at 40-Work on Paper, Hempstead, 2003, Int Print Festival Evora V & IV, Teoartis & Town Coun, Teoartis Gallery/Vimioso Palace, (Region-Lisbon), 2004 & 2007, Families & One Earth, Studio Place Arts, Barre, Vt, 2004-2006, Beyond Tomorrow, South Bend Regional Art Mus, Ind, 2005-2006, Tama Art Univ Mus, Tokyo Int Print Triennale, Tokyo, 2005-2006, Stilled Life, Islip Art Mus, Long Island, New York, 2006, Digital Technologies in Contemp Art, Novosibirsk State Art Mus, Siberia, Russ, 2007, Kinsey Confidential, Kinsey Inst Ind Univ, Bloomington, 2007 & EAM 10th Anniversary 1997-2007, Elmhurst Art Mus, Ill, 2007-, Islip Art Mus, 2008, 2010, Schneider Mus Art, Southern Ore Univ, 2010, Kinsey Inst, Ind Univ, 2010; At The Edge II, Wendy Weitman, Laguna Gloria Art Mus, Austin, Tex, 90-92, Int Triennale Graphic Art, Krakow, Poland/Nuremberg, Ger, 91-92, 94-95 & 2000-03 & 2005-2006, 26th Nat Exhib, Palm Springs Desert Mus, Calif, 95 & Franklin Inst, Philadelphia, 95; Tama Art Univ Mus, Tokyo, 95, Silvermine Guild Galleries, Spectra '97, Robert Sobieszek, New Canaan, Conn, 97, 26th Nat Exhib, Masur Mus Art, Monroe, La, 99, Int Ctr Graphic Art, Ljubljana, Slovenia, Biennale 22, 97, Pitti Immagine srl, Stazione Leopolda, Florence, Italy, 98, Brooklyn Mus Art, Digital: Printmaking Now, 2001, Museo Nacional de Bellas Arte, IV & V Salon & Colloquium of Digital Art, Havana, Cuba, 2002-2003 & Boston Printmakers N Am Print Biennial, Boston Univ 808 Gallery, Mass, 2003; Internationale Grafik Triennale Krakau, Horst-Janssen Mus, Oldenburg, Ger, 2003-2004 & 2007 & Kunstlerhaus, Vienna, 2007; Fraser Gallery, 8th Ann Georgetown Inter Kristen Hileman, Washington, DC, 2004. *Pos:* Package designer, illusr, pvt teacher, freelance artist, Boston, 62-70; founder & dir, 7 at Large, NE Women Artists' Collab, Boston, 75-78; coord exhib (grants), Art Inst, Boston, 75 & Mus Sci, Boston, 77-78; juror, Heritage Plantation Mus, Cape Cod, Mass, 77; exhib consult, Asn Artist-Run Galleries, New York, 80-82, pub relations dir, 83-84; spec

exhib cons, Mus City New York, 83-84; exhib coordr, NY Alumni Chap, RI Sch Design, 85-86, Women Exhib in Boston Inc, 73-75; guest exhib, Danvers Art and Hist Soc, Attleboro Mus, Mass & Nashua Arts and Sci Ctr, NH; co-juror, DIGITALSPLASH, Rockaway Artists Alliance, Fort Tilden, New York, 2003. *Teaching:* Guest lectr, Mass Coll Art, Boston, 75, Harvard Grad Sch Design, Lesley Coll, Cambridge, Mass, 76-77, UN Photog Soc, New York, 93, Univ Wyo Art Mus, Laramie, 94, Nassau Community Coll Firehouse Gallery, Garden City, NY, 99, RI Coll Bannister Gallery, Providence, 99, Rockaway Artists Alliance, Queens, New York, 99, Hockaday Mus Art, Kalispell, Mont, 2000, Herkimer Co Community Coll, New York, 2001 & Elmhurst Art Mus, Ill, 2001; Dahl Fine Art Ctr & Sch Mines & Technol, Rapid City, SDak, 2004. *Awards:* Named One of NY Outstanding Artists, Ethel Scull, New York, 83; Travel citation, Mid-Am Arts Alliance, 90-92; Juror/Roberta Waddell award, Boston Printmakers, Mass, 93; Grant, Duggal Color Projects Inc, New York, 92; Juror/Sachi Yanari Award in Poly Grams, Ind Univ & Purdue Univ, Ft Wayne, 99; Touring Prog Wash State Arts Comn, EWU-ETS, Cheney, Wash, 97-2001. *Bibliog:* Eileen Watkins (auth), High Tech & Myth, photo & rev, Sunday Star-Ledger, Newark, NJ, 92; Alaks & Decker (auths), solo rev, colorplate, Grants Pass Daily Courier, Ore, 98; William Zimmer (auth), Digital Exhibition Updates in the Medium, Sunday NY Times, 2000; Marilyn S. Kushner (auth), Digital Printing Now, catalog intro, Brooklyn Mus, New York, 2001; Helen A Harrison (auth), Hofstra Mus at 40: Works on Paper, Sunday NY Times, Long Island, 2003; Robert-Hirsch (auth), Exploring Color Photography, 4th ed, McGraw-Hill, New York, 2004. *Mem:* Boston Visual Artists Union (coord, 73-75); Cambridge Art Asn (juror, 73-74); RISD NY Alumni Chap; Art & Sci Collab Inc, New York; Nat Arts Club, New York. *Media:* Electronic Imaging. *Interests:* Cinema, computer animation, dance, language, psychology, robotics, science fiction, theater, travel. *Dealer:* G & O Art Inc New York Paris; Art2Art Inc Circulating Exhib New York. *Mailing Add:* 251 W 19th St Apt 3B New York NY 10011-4039

DESTABLER, STEPHEN
SCULPTOR
b St Louis, Mo, 1933. *Study:* Princeton Univ, AB, 54; Univ Calif, Berkeley, MA, 61. *Work:* San Francisco Mus Mod Art; Oakland Mus, Calif; Am Craft Mus, NY; Fine Arts Mus San Francisco; Minneapolis Inst Arts. *Comn:* Birthplace, Old St Louis Post Off, 85-87; Pieta, New Harmony Inn & Conf Ctr, Ind, 88; Winged Guardians, San Jose Conv Ctr, Calif, 93; winged figure, Grad Theological Union, 94. *Exhib:* Solo exhibs, Oakland Mus, 74, Emily Carr Coll Art, Vancouver, BC, 83, San Francisco Mus Art, 88 & Mus Contemp Religious Art, 93; CDS Gallery, NY, 94; Essential Gesture (with catalog), New Harbor Art Mus, 94; New Bronzes, CDC Gallery, NY, 95. *Teaching:* Prof art, San Francisco State Univ, 67-92. *Awards:* Am Craft Coun Fel, 94; Fourth Rodin Grand Prize Exhib, Utsukushi-gahari Open Air Mus, Japan, 92. *Media:* Clay; Metal, Cast. *Dealer:* Franklin Parrasch Gallery 20 W 57th St New York NY 10019; Paul Thiebaud Gallery 718 Columbus Ave San Francisco CA 94133. *Mailing Add:* 21 Bret Harte Rd Berkeley CA 94708

DETMERS, WILLIAM RAYMOND
PRINTMAKER, EDUCATOR
b Pontiac, Mich, June 20, 1942. *Study:* Miami Univ, Ohio, BFA, 64, MEduc, 68; Cranbrook Acad Art, MFA, 70; Univ Cincinnati, EdD, 78. *Work:* Miami Univ, Oxford, Ohio; Univ Southern Colo, Pueblo; Herron Sch Art, Indianapolis; Univ Hawaii, Manoa; Culver-Stockton Col, Canton, Mo; Univ Ark, Pine Bluff; and others. *Comn:* Drawings, Methodist Church, Fredericktown, Ohio; drawings, Methodist Church, Canton, Mo; and others. *Exhib:* Ann Midyear Show, Butler Inst Am Art, Youngstown, Ohio, 64; Solo exhibs, Bd Room, Nova Scotia Coll Art & Design, 70, Gallery, Southern Colo State Coll, Pueblo, 73, Litho Constructs, Matrix Gallery, Ind Univ, Bloomington, 79, Mabee Foundation Gallery, Culver-Stockton Col, 91 & Keokul Art Ctr, Iowa, 92; Wakonda Art Guild Group Shows, Mo, 88-92; Juried Exhib, Novinger, Mo, 89 & 90; Hannibal Arts Club, Mo, 90-92; Quad States Art Exhib, Quincy, Ill, 91-92; Images 92, Highland CC, Kans; Exhibs, 95-: Delta Art Exhib, Pine Bluff Art League, Ark Senate Offices, Little Rock, Ark Art Center, Arts & Science Center for Southeast Ark, Univ Ark, Pine Bluff, Taylor's Contemporanea, Hot Springs, Ark; and others. *Pos:* gallery dir, Culver-Stockton Col, 88-95; gallery dir, Univ Ark, Pine Bluff, 95-2002. *Teaching:* Art Teacher, Preble Co Schs, Ohio, 65-68; vis instr printmaking, Nova Scotia Col Art & Design, summer 70; instr printmaking & art educ, Southern Colo State Col, 70-73; art teacher, Fredericktown, Ohio Schs, 73-74; vis lectr, Ind Univ, Bloomington, 76; prog chmn art educ, Herron Sch Art, Ind Univ-Purdue Univ, Indianapolis, 76-80; area head art educ, La State Univ, 80-85; art educ, Univ Hawaii, Manoa, 85-88; assoc prof art, Culver-Stockton Col, 88-94; instr art, Canton R-V Sch, 94-95; prof art & coord art educ, Univ Ark, Pine Bluff, 95-. *Awards:* Educ Improvement Fund Grant, Univ Hawaii, 86-87; Fac Devt Awards, Culver-Stockton Col, 89-92; Title III Project Grant. *Bibliog:* Mildred Monteverde (auth), Art display limited to plastic and wood, Pueblo Star J, 73; Lauretta Fox (auth), Litho Constructions and other prints by Detmers, Mt Vernon News, 75. *Mem:* Nat Art Educ Asn; Mo Art Educ Asn; Wakonda Art Guild; Canton Area Arts Coun, Mo (past pres); Quincy Art Club, Ill; Pine Bluff Art League; Nat Asn Sch Art & Design. *Media:* Lithography, Intaglio. *Res:* Curriculum development & evaluation in the visual arts. *Publ:* Auth, A Conceptual Model for the Planning of Curricula for the Visual Arts in Higher Education, Dissertation Abstracts Int, 79; A Conceptual Model for Curriculum Planning and Evaluating in Visual Arts, Studies in Art Educ, 80; AV Reviews, Sch Arts, Davis Publ; Red Line Group Recommendations, Teachers Arts, La State Univ, 85; coauth (with K Marantz), The liberal education component of art teacher education: a response, Visual Arts Res, spring, 88; and others, 96-. *Mailing Add:* 2 Sutton Pl Pine Bluff AR 71603-7528

DETTWILLER, KATHRYN KING
PAINTER
b Nashville, Tenn, Dec 3, 1947. *Study:* Vanderbilt Univ, Nashville, BA, 68; George Peabody Col, 68-69; Santa Fe Inst Art, NMex, with Nathan Oliveira, 92. *Work:* Bank Nashville, Metrop Airport Authority, C A Howell & Co, Nashville, Tenn; Columbia State Community Col, Tenn; Pinnacle Bank. *Exhib:* One-woman show, Parthenon Mus, Nashville, 93 & Indivisible: New Work by Kathryn Dettwiller, Renaissance Cen, Dickson, Tenn, 2002; Tennessee: From the Mountains to the Mississippi, Cheekwood Mus Art, Nashville, 93 & About Face, 94; Scene/Unseen III Nat Exhib, Eastern NMex Univ, Portales, 94; Priva B Gross Int, Queensborough Community Col, City Univ NY, Bayside, 96; Combined Talents: The Fla National, Appleton Mus Art, Ocala, & Fla State Univ Mus, Tallahassee, 98; Interpretations, Ceramics by Bill Capshaw & Paintings by Kathryn Dettwiller, Tenn Arts Comn, Nashville, 98; A Sense of Place, Nashville Int Airport, Nashville & Belfast Waterfront Hall, Belfast, Northern Ireland, 2001; Women Beyond Borders, Frist Ctr for Visual Arts, Nashville, Tenn, 2003; Fragile Species: New Art Nashville, Frist Ctr for Visual Arts, Nashville, Tenn, 2005; Crossing Time, Sky PAC, Bowling Green, Ky. *Pos:* Asst dir educ, Tenn Fine Arts Ctr, Cheekwood, 68-69; bd mem, Metrop Nashville Arts Comn, 88-94; juror, Countdown 2001, Summer Lights Art Exhib, 91; bd mem Visual Artists Coun, Frist Ctr for Visual Arts, 99-; bd mem, Arrowmont Sch Arts & Crafts, Gatlinburg, Tenn, secy, 2005-. *Awards:* Best of Show, Northern Nat, 1991; Gallery Award, Best of Tenn, Tenn State Mus, 2001; Award of Merit, Arts in the Airport, Knoxville, Tenn, 2010. *Bibliog:* Susan Chappell (auth), Artists offer bridge to oasis, Nashville Banner, 2/24/93; Susan Knowles (auth), Changing subjects, Nashville Scene, 6/30/94; Louise Lequire (auth), Laughing with Nashville Artists, Nashville Life, 10/94; Kaaren Engel (auth), A conversation with Kathryn Dettwiller, VAAN newsletter, 11-12/2000; Encaustic art, Nashville Lifestyles, Oct-Nov/2002. *Media:* Oil, Encaustic. *Mailing Add:* 108 Savoy Cir Nashville TN 37205-5013

DEUTSCH, RICHARD
SCULPTOR
b Los Angeles, Calif, 1953. *Study:* Univ Calif, Santa Cruz, BA (art), 76. *Work:* Patrick J Lannon Foun, Los Angeles; Renwick Gallery, Smithsonian; Mill's Col, Oakland; McDonald's Corp, Chicago; Shell Oil Corp, Houston. *Comn:* Terrazza sculpture/Ocean View Park, Santa Cruz Arts Comn, Calif, 84; Marble sculpture Shelton Police Acad, Wash State Arts Comn Art in Pub Places, Shelton, 87; Terrazzo pavement medallion, San Francisco Arts Comn Pub Places, 88. *Exhib:* Renwick Gallery, Smithsonian, Washington, DC, 80; Gray Art Mus, NC, 82; Monterey Peninsula Mus Art, Calif, 82; San Jose Inst Contemp Art, Calif, 83; Art Mus Santa Cruz, Calif, 85; Jewish Community Mus, San Francisco, 87; Palo Alto Cult Ctr, Calif, 88. *Awards:* Exemplary Arts Education Residency, Calif Arts Coun, 83; Visual Artist Fel, Nat Endowment Arts, 84; Vis Sculptor, Am Acad Rome, 87. *Bibliog:* Paul Sutor (auth), Artist in the development process, Urbanland, 9/2/91; Elizabeth Broadrup (auth), Richard Deutsch: motion, Sculpture Mag, 11/12/92. *Media:* Marble. *Mailing Add:* 340 Swanton Rd Davenport CA 95017

DEUTSCHMAN, LOUISE TOLLIVER
DEALER, CURATOR
b Taylorville, Ill, Sept 6, 1921. *Study:* MacMurray Col, BA; Northwestern Univ Sch Journalism, Univ Paris, Sorbonne. *Collection Arranged:* Seven Decades of Twentieth-Century Art From the Sidney and Harriet Janis Collection, Mus Mod Art & Sidney Janis Gallery Collection, La Jolla Mus Contemp Art & Santa Barbara Mus Art, Calif, 80. *Pos:* Assoc dir, Waddell Gallery, New York, 66-74; assoc, Sidney Janis Gallery, New York, 75-78, assoc, 80-2000; dir, Alex Rosenberg Gallery, New York, 78-80; curator, Pace Wildenstein, NY, 2000-; guest cur, Nasher Sculpture Center, Dallas, Tex, 2004-2006. *Specialty:* Contemporary art; 20th century masters, American & European. *Publ:* Auth, The Women of Giacometti (essay in catalogue), Pace Wildenstein, New York, 2005, Nasher Sculpture Ctr, Dallas, 2006. *Mailing Add:* 315 W 102nd St Apt 5B New York NY 10025-8420

DEVEREUX, MARA
PAINTER, SCULPTOR
b Brooklyn, NY, Jun 9, 1925. *Study:* Great Neck, NY Studio, 50; Art Students League, 52; Otis Art Inst, MFA, 64; Liverpool Coll Art, Eng; NY Acad Art, NY. *Work:* Pvt collections, Frederick Wiseman Collection, Calif, Dr & Mrs Alex Gershman, Calif, Matthew Egan, Tex, William Brun, Calif & Dr & Mrs Victor Bekbosunov, Kazakhstan, Dr & Mrs Michel Mazouz, Calif, Delora Donovan, Kansas; Asto Mus, Calif. *Comn:* Plaster sculpture, Saks Fifth Ave, NY, 90; plaster sculpture, Bloomingdales, NY, 90; works on paper, Lipton Tea Co, Inglewood, NJ, 91; oil canvas, Canon Communications, Santa Monica, Calif, 2000; acrylic canvas, Bret Mosher Builder, Los Angeles, Calif, 2004; acrylic & oil canvas 60″x108″, comn by Dr & Mrs Alex Gershman, Beverly Hills, Calif, 2006-2008; Edward H Schreck, E Northport, NY, Elisabeth Johnson, San Luis Obispo, Calif, Guy Hithe, Los Angeles, Calif, Robert S Fink, Los Angeles, Calif, Pierre Merhl, San Francisco, Calif, Steve Dunning, Venice, Calif, Daniela Malca, Lima, Peru, Ralph Piccarelli, Las Vegas, Nev, 2013. *Exhib:* Brooklyn Mus, NY, 51; Hecksher Mus, Huntington, NY, 80; Santa Barbara Mus, Calif, 74; Jeju Int, Seogwipo Kidang, Jeju Island, 2004; Art Festival Mus, Korea, 2004-2007; Gwang Wha Moon Int Art Festival, Korea, 2006-2007; Cult Ctr, Beijing, China, 2007; Long Beach Mus Art, 2007; Gallery Asto, Los Angeles, 2007; Los Angeles Munic Gallery, 2007; Difference & Coexistence, The Contemp Art of Korea-Japan & US, Asto Mus Art, 2008; Gwangwhamoon Int Art Festival, Seoul, S Korea, 2009; Asto Int Art Festival, Asto Mus Korea, Seoul, 2009; Los Angeles Munic Art Gallery, Hollywood, Calif, 2009. *Teaching:* Instr, Grad Sch, USC, Calif, 60's. *Awards:* Otis Parsons Inst, MFA, Los Angeles, Calif; Inst Classical Art, NY. *Bibliog:* Elizabeth Gorcy (auth), An Artists Life, Film Documentary, 2003; Laurence Vittes (auth), The Invisible Made Visible, Sr Life, 2004; Tanya Shifman (auth), 10 Physicists & an Abstract Painter (film documentary), 2006; William Wilson (auth), A Critical Guide to Galleries, Los Angeles Times; Rita Riff (auth), In Philadelphia, Artists Cast a Pop Eye, NY Times; Mike Heal (auth), Nashville, Tenn, Complete Biography, 2013. *Mem:* Metrop Artist Asn, Los Angeles, Calif. *Media:* Oil, Acrylic, Clay. *Interests:* Opera, art res. *Publ:* Ed, Invisible Made Visible, Article, Calif Sr Life, 2004. *Dealer:* Gallery Asto Pearl Park 923 East Third St Los Angeles CA 90013; Asto Mus Art 3501 State Hwy 2 Wrightwood CA 92397; Art Exchange Gallery 49 Geary St San Francisco CA 94108

DEVINE, NANCY
PAINTER
b Hyannis, Mass, Feb 8, 1949. *Study:* Univ Mass, Amherst, 67-70. *Comn:* Calendar, USPS, Washington, DC, 2000. *Exhib:* Northern Arts Nat Competition, Rhinelander, Wis, 91; All New Eng Exhib, Cape Cod Art Assoc, Barnstable, Mass, 93, 95 & 2005; Homage to Norman Rockwell, Fraser Art Gallery, Washington, DC, 2001; 6x6 Exhib, Tree House Gallery, West Tisbury, Martha's Vineyard, Mass, 2007; Barebrush Calender, Barebrush Gallery, NY, 2011; Barnstable Municipal Airport, Hyannis, 2012; Post Office Gallery, North Truro Mass, 2012; Art in the Atrium, Hyannis, 2013. *Pos:* Layout artist, Rosen Textile Engraving, Agawam, Mass, 70-72. *Awards:* 2nd Place, Mashpee Arts Coun, 97-98; 1st place, BOA Artist's Challenge, Harwich, Mass, 2009. *Bibliog:* Alan Petrucelli (auth), Real Life Art of Nancy Devine, Cape Cod Times, 97; Saundra Tobins (auth), Painting Cape Cod the Devine Way, Cape Cod Mag, 2001; David Colantuono (auth), Cape Cod Life Mag, Arts Ed, 2007. *Mem:* Cape Cod Art Asn; Nat Asn Women Artists. *Media:* Acrylic, Oil. *Mailing Add:* 20 Delta St Hyannis MA 02601

DEVON, MARJORIE LYNN
ADMINISTRATOR
b Jersey City, NJ, Dec 2, 1945. *Study:* Univ Calif, Berkeley, BA, 67. *Collection Arranged:* Tamarind Impressions: Recent Lithographs (traveling), Arts Am Prog, US Information Agency, 85; Tamarind: 25 Years (traveling, with catalog), NMex Art Mus, 85; Mexico Nueve (traveling, with catalog), 87; Collaborations: Artists + Printers (traveling), Arts Am Prog, US Information Agency, 91; Tamarind: 40 Years (ed, catalog), Univ NMex Art Mus, 2000; Migrations: New Directions in Native American Art, 2006-2009. *Pos:* From asst dir to dir, Tamarind Inst, Albuquerque, 80-. *Teaching:* Pub art, Univ NMex. *Publ:* ed, Tamarind: Forty Years, Univ NMex Press, Albuquerque, 2000; ed, Migrations: New Directions in Native American Art, Univ NMex Press, Albuquerque, 2006; auth, Tamarind Techniques for Fine Art Lithography, Henry N Abrams, NY, 2008; ed, Tamarind Touchstones: Fabulous at Fifty, Univ N Mex Press, Albuquerque, 2010. *Mailing Add:* 2500 Central Ave Se Albuquerque NM 87106

DE VORE, RICHARD E
CERAMIST
b Toledo, Ohio, 1933. *Study:* Univ Toledo, Ohio, BE, 55; Cranbrook Acad Art, Mich, MFA, 57. *Work:* Yale Univ Art Gallery, New Haven, Conn; Victoria & Albert Mus, London, Eng; Philadelphia Mus Art, Pa; Los Angeles Co Mus Art, Calif; Cleveland Mus Art, Ohio; Metrop Mus Art, NY. *Exhib:* Solo exhibs, Hill Gallery, Birmingham, Mich, 87, 93, 95 & 99, Max Protetch Gallery, NY, 87, 89, 91, 94, 96 & 98 & Greenberg Gallery, St Louis, Mo, 88, Kruithuis Mus, The Neth, 99, San Francisco Mus Art, 99, Los Angeles Co Mus Art, 2000, World Ceramics Exposition, Korea, 2001; East-West Contemp Ceramics, Seoul, Korea, 88; Ten Am Ceramicists, US Embassy Exhib, Univ Hong Kong, 89; De Vore, Price, Turner, Hill Gallery, Birmingham, Mich, 90; 28th Ceramic Nat Exhib, Everson Mus Art, Syracuse, NY, 90; and others. *Collection Arranged:* Am Craft Mus, NY City; Ark Art Ctr, Little Rock; Butler Inst Am Art, Youngstown, Ohio; Contemp Mus Art, Honolulu; Detroit Inst Art; Joslyn Art Mus, Omaha, Nebr; Houston Mus Fine Arts; Metrop Mus Art; Nat Mus Am Art, Washington, DC; Newark Mus, NJ; Philadelphia Mus Art; Yale Univ Art Gallery, New Haven, Conn; Los Angeles Co Mus Art; Denver Art Mus; and others. *Awards:* Nat Endowment Arts Grant, 76, 80 & 86; Am Craft Coun Fel, 87. *Bibliog:* Garth Clark (auth), American Potters, Watson-Guptill, New York, 81; Florence Rubenfeld (auth), Pottery of Richard De Vore, Am Craft, 83; Janet Kopolos (auth), article, Art Papers, Vol VIII, No 2, 84; Sarah Bodine & Michael Dumas (coauth), Am Ceramics, 89. *Publ:* Auth, Ceramics of Betty Woodman, Craft Horizon, 78; Color, Texture & Light, Studio Potter, 86. *Dealer:* Max Protech 511 22nd St New York NY 10012. *Mailing Add:* 1617 Sheely DR Fort Collins CO 80526

DE VORE, SADIE DAVIDSON
PRINTMAKER, PAINTER
b Wheaton, Mo, Jun 12, 1937. *Study:* Mo State Univ, BS (art), 58; RI Coll, MAT (drawing); NY Univ, post grad; Skidmore, summer studies; Yale Pier Prog; Fulbright Scholar, 2009; Russian Studies, Vladimir. *Work:* Buffom, Boland, Terranova; Davidson; McMichael; Boston Pub Libr Print Collection; Boland; States Mus print. *Comn:* Padanaram, Mass; portrait, 2000. *Exhib:* Art Exhib, Springfield Mo Art Mus, 59; Lyme Acad Fine Arts, 2002-2010; NAC Gallery, Norwich, 2005-2010; Making the Mark, Slater Mus, Norwich, Conn, 2009-2010; Journey, East in the West, Laguna Ctr. *Collection Arranged:* Hoxie Gallery, Westerly; Monotype Show, Watercolor Soc, Pawtucket, RI, 2004; Emporium Gallery; Newport Art Mus. *Teaching:* Painting, printmaking, art history, Stonington, 72-2010; juror, curator; instr, monotype workshops, printmaking, RI, Conn, NY; instr, watercolor, Fla & Saratoga, NY; art hist, Mitchell Coll, Conn; instr printmaking, SCAA; watercolor instr, Mitchell Coll; int teacher, Huzhou China, Dalian, China. *Awards:* First place award, Westport Show, KC Art Dealer, 91; First place, 30 Miles of Art; Essex & Stonington Brick Gallery; MAA Triplett Award; Essex Art Asn, WHIS, ACGOW Awards; Conn Watercolor Prize. *Mem:* South Co Art Asn; Mystic Art Ctr; Monotype Guild New Eng (secy, bd, 95-2005); Lyme Art Asn; Am Marine Artists; Conn Plain Aire Painters; New Wax; Artist Cooperative Gallery of Westerly; Friends of Slater Mus (bd mem); founder, Stonington Printmaker's Soc; Norwich Art Coun (art mem); CAFA; Lyme Acad Alumni; Conn Women Artists (treasury bd). *Media:* Watercolor, Silver, Monotypes, Oil, Acrylic, Clay, Printmaking, Metals, Collage, Assemblage. *Res:* 19th Century drawing, Beardsley, Kandinsky design; Monotypes by hand and press, abstract, landscape & design; Chinese art educ; Suprematism & Constructivism in Russian Art. *Specialty:* sea side, pods, plants, New England landscapes design in color, printmaking intaglio, monotype, collograph. *Interests:* MGA, Gardening, nature, teaching, artmaking, paddling, travel, education; herbs, gardens, people. *Collection:* collections in the USA and abroad; design handbook for students. *Dealer:* Charles Gallery Water St Conn; The High Street Studio Gallery Mystic Conn; MAC; LAA; ACGOW; Mystic Fine Arts and Antiques; High Street Gallery Studio. *Mailing Add:* 137 High St Mystic CT 06355

DE WAAL, RONALD BURT
COLLECTOR, PATRON
b Salt Lake City, Utah, Oct 23, 1932. *Study:* Univ Utah, BS, 55; Mexico City Col, summer 55 & 58; Univ Denver, MA, 58. *Collection Arranged:* Beethoven in the Arts, Univ Utah, 65 & Colo State Univ, 66, 67, 70, 83 & 85. *Pos:* Humanities librn & exhibs chmn, Colo State Univ, Ft Collins, 66-88. *Awards:* John H Jenkins Award for best work of bibliography published in US during 74; Colo Libr Asn Lit Award, 87. *Mem:* Beethoven Soc; Coll Art Asn Am; Nat Sculpture Soc. *Interests:* Painting and Sculpture, Classical Music, Writing, Dancing. *Collection:* Beethoven statuary and paintings; pewter, porcelain, and wood figure sculptures; Sherlock Holmes statuary, paintings and prints. *Publ:* Auth, The World Bibliography of Sherlock Holmes and Dr Watson, NY Graphic Soc, 74; Bramhall House, 77; The International Sherlock Holmes, Shoe String Press, 80; The Universal Sherlock Holmes (5 vols), Metrop Toronto Reference Libr, 94; A Bibliography of Published and Unpublished Writings, The Shoso-in Bulletin, Tokyo, Vol 10, 8/2000. *Mailing Add:* 1435 El Rey St Salt Lake City UT 84108

DE WAN-CARLSON, ANNA
PRINTMAKER, ART DEALER
b Dec 29, 1949. *Study:* Art Inst Pittsburgh, 71; Syracuse Univ; Univ Col, Syracuse. *Work:* Carrier Corp-UTC; Print Club Albany; Onondaga Savings Bank; Onondaga Hist Asn; Maria Regina Coll. *Exhib:* Print Club Albany 17th Nat Competition, NY; Space Group Korea 6th Int Miniature Print Biennial, Seoul, Korea; Ball State Ann Drawing & Small Sculpture Exhib, Muncie, Ind; Art Ctr Grand Prairie Nat Miniature Exhib, Stuttgart, Alaska; Fine Arts Inst San Bernardino Co Mus 27th Ann Exhib, Redlands, Calif; 66th Nat Exhib, Art Asn Harrisburg, Pa. *Collection Arranged:* Proof of the Print-Syracuse Printmakers, A Retrospective Exhib, Onondaga Hist Asn, Syracuse, NY, 92. *Pos:* Exhib cur, Syracuse Printmakers; contrib writer, J of the Print World, 92; guest cur, Onondaga Hist Asn, Syracuse, NY, 92; dir, 12 RMS-4 Gallery, Syracuse, NY, 92-94, Cent NY Art Open, 95. *Teaching:* Artist-in-residence, Marie Regina Coll, 75-76. *Awards:* Best in Show-Graphics, Women's Art Gallery, NY; First Prize-Graphics, Allentown Festival Arts, Buffalo, NY; First Prize, Popular Photog Mag. *Bibliog:* Syracuse Herald Am Stars Mag, 7/94; Art & Understanding, Vol 3, No 3, Issue 12, 8/94; The Mediator-Eye on the Arts, Vol 1, Issue 9, 9/94. *Mem:* Syracuse Printmakers (pres, formerly); Print Club Philadelphia; Everson Mus; Print Club Rochester; Print Club Albany. *Media:* Serigraph; Miscellaneous Media. *Interests:* organic gardening, hybridizing hemercalis, golf, making bird houses from home grown gourds. *Publ:* Proof of the Print, J of the Printworld, Charles Stewart Lane Publ, Vol 15, No 2, spring 92. *Mailing Add:* Ravencroft Cottage 110 Clinton Rd Jordan NY 13080

DEWITT, EDWARD
PAINTER, SCULPTOR
b Jersey City, NJ, Aug 1, 1938. *Study:* Self taught. *Work:* Bronx Zoological Soc; Palisades Amusement Park. *Comn:* Am Pres Sculptures, Bass Relief Series 2003, Chesapeake Reproductions, Mappsville, Va; Sir Winston Churchill; Louis Armstrong; Babe Ruth; US Pres Gerald Ford, John F Kennedy, Dwight Eisenhower & Harry Truman; Official 3rd Millennium Commemorative Double Eagle (bronze sculpture), US Hist Soc; Lewis & Clark (sculpture), Chesapeake Reproductions, 2004; Robert Kennedy (medallion). *Collection Arranged:* Boy Scouts Am; Nat Asn Theater Collection; Anheuser-Busch, Am Series, 5 yr series, sterling silver commemorative plates; Gen Motors Fisher Body; Playboy, road to the gold medallian. *Bibliog:* Artist in Our Midst, 21st Century Pro. *Media:* Acrylic, Oil. *Publ:* Collectors Mart, 76; New Art Int, 99; Direct Art Buyer, 99. *Dealer:* CJ Mugavero 201 Farnsworth Ave Bordentown NJ 08505; Swain Galleries 703 Watchung Ave Plainfield NJ 07060

DEWITT, KATHARINE CRAMER
MUSEUM DIRECTOR
Study: Manhattenville Coll of Sacred Heart, BA. *Pos:* Docent, Cincinnati Art Mus; co-chmn, Presidential Inaugural Comt, 2001. *Mem:* Nat Coun Arts; Nat Endowment for Arts; Cincinnati Fine Arts Fund (co-chmn, Individual Gifts 85, 93, mem, Allocation Comt, 91-94). *Mailing Add:* Cincinnati Art Mus 953 Eden Park Dr Cincinnati OH 45202

DEWOODY, BETH RUDIN
PATRON, COLLECTOR
b New York, NY. *Study:* Univ Calif, Santa Barbara, studied Anthropology & Film studies; New Sch Social Res, BA. *Pos:* Pres, May & Samuel Rudin Found Inc; exec vpres, Rudin Mgt co; contrib ed, Hampton's Cottages & Garden's Mag; dir & asst dir, (TV series) Born Free; prod asst, Annie Hall, The Front & Hair; co-producer, Enter Juliet. *Awards:* Named one of Top 200 Collectors, ARTnews mag, 2006-13. *Mem:* Whitney Mus Am Art. *Collection:* Modern and contemporary art. *Mailing Add:* Rudin Mgt Co In 345 Park Ave New York NY 10154-0004

DE ZEGHER, CATHERINE
MUSEUM DIRECTOR
Pos: co-founder Kanaal Art Found., Kortrijk, Belgium, 1985; dir, Kanaal Art Found., Kortrijk, Belgium, 1987-2000; vis cur, Inst Contemp Art, Boston, 1995-97; exec dir, Drawing Center, NYC, 2000-06; dir exhibs & publs, Art Gallery Ontario, Toronto, 2008-. *Teaching:* Lectr, Univ Leeds, Royal Coll Art, London, Univ London, formerly. *Publ:* Auth: Inside the Visible: An Elliptical Traverse of Twentieth Century Art, in, of, & from the Feminine, 1996; The Precarious: Art & Poetry of Cecilia Vicuna & Quipoem, 1997; Mona Hatoum, 1997; Martha Rosler: Rights of Passage, 1997

DEZZANY, FRANCES JEAN
ASSEMBLAGE ARTIST, SCULPTOR
b Chicago, Ill, Aug 2, 1942. *Study:* Kean Univ, NJ, BA, 70; Montclair State Univ, NJ, MA, 75; Art Students League, studied anat with Anthony Palumbo, 80-85. *Work:* Bergen Community Mus, Paramus, NJ. *Comn:* Three geometric wall pieces, Interior Decorator, Livingston, NJ, 79. *Exhib:* Between Art & Craft: The Fine Line, Del Art

Mus, Wilmington, 75; Visual Interplay, Bergen Community Mus, Paramus, NJ, 77; Contemp Fiber Art, Newark Mus, NJ, 78; Leather Art/Leather Work, Montclair Art Mus, NJ, 79; Pieces in Space, Atelier Gallery/Snug Harber, Staten Island, NY, 86; Selected Works, D-Art Visual Art Ctr, Dallas, Tex, 90; Montclair State in Manhattan, Westbeth Gallery, NY, 94; La Chapelle Des Penitents, Gourdes, France, 2000; Longview Mus of Fine Arts, Longview, Tex, 2001; one-person show, Bath House Cult Ctr, Dallas, Tex, 2001. *Pos:* Dir exec bd, Double Tree - Artist Inc Gallery, 76-77; art demonstr/lectr, Mus & Schs, NJ & Tex, 76-90; sculpture juror & pub relations, Nat Asn Women Artists, New York, 81-82; art dept chairperson & asst principal, Bending Oaks High Sch, Dallas, Tex, 89-92. *Teaching:* Instr arts & crafts, Rutgers, Newark, 76, Newark Mus, 76-77. *Awards:* Cert of Excellence in Art, St John's Contemporary Relig Art, Pastor Hourihan, 86; First Place Paper City Wide, On My Own Time, Dallas Bus Com Arts, 94; Hazel Witte Collage Award, Nat Asn Woman Artist, 97. *Bibliog:* Nita Leland & Virginia Lee Williams (auth), Creative College Techniques, Northlight Books, 94; Hartly, Bellinger & Williams (auth), Bridging Time & Space, Markowitz Pub, 98; Mary Carrol Nelson (auth), Fiberarts, 3-4/99. *Mem:* Nat Asn Women Artists; Soc Layerists Multi Media; Tex Sculpture Asn. *Media:* Assemblage. *Publ:* Auth, Moth-Proofing Techniques for Weavers & Spinners, Fiberarts No 1, 80; auth & ed, Society Layerists in Multi Media Nat Newslett No 23, Soc Layerists, 89. *Mailing Add:* 5403 Ridgedale Ave Dallas TX 75206-6011

DHAEMERS, ROBERT AUGUST
SCULPTOR, EDUCATOR

b Luverne, Minn, Nov 24, 1926. *Study:* Calif Coll Arts & Crafts, BFA, 52, MFA, 54. *Work:* City San Francisco Art Comn, Calif; First Christ Lutheran Church, Burlingame, Calif; San Jose State Col; Mills Col, Oakland, Calif; St Catherine Indian Sch, Santa Fe, NMex. *Comn:* Wrought iron wall mural, Jerry's Restaurant, San Leandro, Calif, 60; sculpture crucifix, First Christ Lutheran Church, 61; fountain, Frank Hunt Archit, Oakland, Calif, 63; Sundial Cor-Ten (steel 2 ton), Sci Complex, Mills Col, 70; bronze tabernacle, Holy Cross Hosp, San Fernando, Calif, 77. *Exhib:* Am Fedn Arts Traveling Exhib of New Talent, 59; San Francisco Art Comn, Calif Palace Legion, 61; M H DeYoung Mus, San Francisco, 62; Columbia Univ, 64; Mus Contemp Crafts, Creative Casting, NY, 64; Bertrand Russell Centenary Int, Nottingham, Eng, 73; Brigham Young Univ, Utah, 76; 12th Int Sculpture Conf, Mills Col, 82; Pub Sculpture Exhib, San Francisco Art Comn, 85-86; Brigham Young Univ, Utah, 76; Am Modernist Jewelry 1940-1970, Fort Wayne Mus Art, 2008; and others. *Pos:* Adv, Kala Inst, 81-88. *Teaching:* Asst prof art, Calif Col Arts & Crafts, 51-56; assoc prof art, Mills Col, 57-75, prof, 75-, actg head dept art, 63-64, head dept, 73-76 & 79-80. *Awards:* First Award Sculpture Gold Metal, Oakland Mus Art, 52; First Award Metal Work, Calif State Fair, 62; Mellon Found Grant, 77, 80 & 83; Nat Endowment Arts Grant, 88-89. *Bibliog:* New Talent, Art Am, 66. *Mem:* Western Coll Asn (accreditation comt, 69-); Western Asn Schs & Cols; Accrediting Comn Sr Cols & Univs; Int Sculpture Asn; Bay Area Consortium Visual Arts (steering comt, 87-89). *Media:* Metal. *Res:* Linear form. *Interests:* Metal casting and fabrication. *Publ:* Coauth, Simple Jewelry Making for the Classroom, 58; contribr, Metal Techniques for Craftsmen, 68; Craftsmen of the Southwest, 65 & The Crafts of the Modern World, 68; Lunar Suite I, The Hamptons Publ Dans Papers Ltd, 7/81; Sculpture 12, Int Sculpture Ctr, 82; Calif Art Review, 88; 2004 Modernist Jewelry 1940-60; Mar Beth (auth), Wearable Art movement; Mar Beth (auth), Form & Function: American Modernist Jewelry, 1940-1970. *Dealer:* M Schon Gallery Natchez MS. *Mailing Add:* 6 Ascot Ln Piedmont CA 94611

DIAL, GAIL
METALSMITH, EDUCATOR

b Tulsa, Okla, Aug 23, 1947. *Study:* Pittsburg State Univ, Kans, MA, 71; Ind Univ, Bloomington, with Alma Eikerman, MFA, 74. *Work:* Mus Plains Ind, Browning, Mont; Idaho First Nat Bank, Boise; Ind Mus Fine Arts, Bloomington; Pittsburg State Univ, Kans. *Exhib:* Goldsmith: 74, Renwick Gallery, Smithsonian Inst, Washington, DC, 74; Forms in Metal: 275 Yrs of Metalsmith, Mus Contemp Crafts, NY, 74; Contemp Crafts Am, Colo State Univ, Ft Collins, 75; Crafts for Am, Phillipines Design Ctr, Manila, 77; Copper, Bronze & Brass, Tucson, Ariz, 77; Lake Superior Nat, Duluth Art Inst, Minn, 81. *Collection Arranged:* Marilyn Levine: Ceramics, 79; William Wiley Prints, 80. *Teaching:* Prof metal & crafts, Idaho State Univ, Pocatello, 74-. *Awards:* Cash Awards, Indianapolis Mus, 73 & Boise Art Gallery, 75 & 76. *Mem:* Prof mem Soc North Am Goldsmiths; Northwest Designer Craftsmen. *Media:* Gold, Silver. *Publ:* Contribr, Contemporary Jewelry, Holt Rinehart, 75; Contemporary Crafts of the Americas: 1975, Regnery, 75. *Mailing Add:* 533 Appaloosa Ave Pocatello ID 83201-7013

DIAMOND, CATHY
PAINTER, CONSERVATOR

b Cleveland, Ohio, Jan 7, 1960. *Study:* Univ Mich, Ann Arbor, BFA, 1982; Art Students League, 1979; NY Studio Sch, MFA, 1988. *Comn:* Portrait, Judge Gilberto Ramirez, Brooklyn Borough Hall Portrait Galleries, 2007. *Exhib:* Solo exhibs include Alena Adlung Gallery, New York, 1992, Frankel, Pariser & Rudder, New York, 1996, Bingo Hall, Brooklyn, 2000, Painting Ctr, New York, 2000, 2004, Sideshow Gallery, New York, 2003; group shows include The Figure & the Reasonable Lie, Painting Ctr, New York, 1997; Pay-Per-It, Sideshow Gallery, Brooklyn, NY, 1997, Peace, 2004, War Is Over, 2006; Raw Seeing, NY Studio Sch, 1998, Emerging Visions, 2001; BLUE, Brooklyn Brewery, 2002, RED, 2002; Faculty Exhib, Snug Harbor Cult Ctr, Staten Island, NY, 2004, 2006; 183rd Ann: Invitational Exhib Contemp Am Art, Nat Acad Mus, New York, 2008. *Teaching:* Vis prof drawing, Marymount Coll, Tarrytown, NY, formerly, NY Univ Coll Continuing Educ, 1999; instr drawing, Parsons Sch Design, 2001, 2002; instr master painting & drawing, Snug Harbor Cult Ctr, Staten Island, NY, 2002-06. *Awards:* Artists Fellowship Inc Grant; Residency Full Fel, Va Ctr Creative Arts (VCCA), 2005. *Media:* Acrylic Oil Mixed Media

DIAMOND, PAUL
PHOTOGRAPHER

b Brooklyn, NY, June 20, 1942. *Study:* Pratt Inst, BFA, 65; Purdue Univ, MA, 80. *Work:* Int Mus Photog, George Eastman House, Rochester, NY; Nat Gallery Can, Ottawa, Ont; Fogg Art Mus, Cambridge, Mass; Boston Mus Fine Arts. *Exhib:* 60s Continuum, George Eastman House, 72; Solo exhibs, Sq Bromides, Gallery Optica, Montreal, Que, 73 & Floating Found of Photog, NY, 74; Peculiar to Photog, Univ NMex, 76; Five, St Charles on the Wazee, Denver, Colo, 77; Contemp Photog, Fogg Art Mus, 77. *Teaching:* Instr photog, Calif Col Arts & Crafts, Oakland, 77-78; guest lectr photog, Univ Colo, Boulder, 77; instr, Moore Col Art, Philadelphia, currently. *Awards:* Guggenheim Found Fel, 75-76; Nat Endowment for the Arts Grant, 78. *Mem:* Soc Photog Educ. *Publ:* Contribr, Photographer's Choice, Addison House, 75, Ctr for Creative Photog, Vol 4, Univ Ariz, 77 & Grotesque in Photography, Ridge Press, 77. *Dealer:* Witkin Gallery 41 E 57th St New York NY 10022

DIAMOND, SHARI
PHOTOGRAPHER

Study: Univ Miami, BS (Educ), 1983; NY Univ, Int Ctr Photography, MA, 1988. *Exhib:* Exhibs include Imprinted Memories, Gallery at Hastings, Hastings, NY, 1988; Body Poiltics, PS 122 Gallery, New York, 1993; Live Art, Art Proj Int, New York, 1994; Universal Diversity, La Mama, New York, 1997; Women's Studio Workshop, Rosandale, NY, 2002 ; Postcards From the Edge, Galerie Lelong, New York, 2003; Body Virtual, Western Wyoming Coll, Rockspring, Wyo, 2004; The Current, AIR Gallery, New York, 2004; Mourning Rites, Galeria Atena, San Miguel de Allende, Mex, 2004. *Teaching:* Parsons Sch Design, Professor (Digital Design, Advanced Digital Design, Laboratory), 2002-Present. *Awards:* Travel Grant, Coll Art Asn, Boston, 1994

DIAMOND, STUART
PAINTER

b Brooklyn, NY, April 8, 1942. *Study:* Pratt Inst, BFA, 59-63. *Work:* Mus Mod Art, NY; Mus Contemp Art, Chicago; Samuel P Harn Mus Art, Univ Fla, Gainesville; Southwest Regional Mus, Corpus Christi, Tex; Ft Lauderdale Mus Art, Fla; Frederick R Weisman Art Found, Los Angeles; Bowdoin Mus, Brunswick, Maine; Ballinglen Archive, Ballinglen Arts Found, Ballycastle, Co Mayo, Ireland; Robert Hull Fleming Mus. *Comn:* Light & Shadow Eschlkam, Germany; installed for 50 yrs. *Exhib:* Great Wall Gallery, Toronto, 91; Japan Arts Gallery, Tokyo, 91; Baltimore Co Campus Fine Arts Gallery, Univ Md, 92; Bare Bone, curated by Nima Yankowitz, TZ Art & Co, NY, 96; After the Fall: Aspects of Abstract Painting Since the 1970s, Newhouse Ctr Contemp Art, Staten Island, NY, 97; Am Portraits, George Sherman Union Gallery, Boston Univ, Mass, 98; A Selection of Works from the Edward R Broida Collection (with catalog), Orlando Mus Art, 98; Vt Studio Ctr Press, Helen Day Art Ctr, Stowe, 98; The Children in Crisis, Invitational Benefit (with catalog), 99; Drawing in the Present Tense (with catalog), Drawing Ctr, NY, 99; ND Mus Art, Grand Forks, 2000; The Figure: Another Side of Modernism, Lily Wei, Cur, Newhouse Ctr for Contemp Art, Snug Harbor, 2000; 3 person drawing show, Western Wyo Comm Coll Art Gallery, Rock Springs, 2001; Sunshine Int Art Mus, 2008; Virus xhib, Oasis Gallery, Beijing, China, 2009; Dorothy and Herb Vogel Coll: 50 Works for Fifty States, Montclair Art Mus, 2010; Two American Masters and One Oasis Gallery, Beijing, China, 2010-2011; Gang of Four, Oasis Gallery, Beijing, China, 2011. *Teaching:* Assoc prof art, Cooper Union, NY, 88-97; instr painting, Parsons Sch Design, NY, 92-; full-time prof, Columbia Univ, 1992-2002, Univ Arts, 2003, Pratt Inst, 2003; instr art, RI Sch Design, 80-88, guest critic, Rome prog, 2000; prof, Mass Coll Art & Design. *Awards:* Nat Endowment Arts Fel, 80-81 & 87-88; Solomon Guggenheim Fel, 87-88; Ballinglen Arts Found Artist-in-residence, Ballycastle, Ireland, 97-98; Vt Studio Ctr guest artist, 98-2001; Gladys E Cook Prize in Painting, Nat Acad Design, 2002. *Bibliog:* Lois Trulow (auth), interview, Art New Eng, June-July 98; Debra Balkin (auth), essay, Drawing in the Present Tense, full color catalog, Parsons, 99; Ken Johnson (auth), Objects of Desire, 125 Views of the Human Figure, NY Times, 9/1/2000. *Mem:* Skowhegan Sch Art. *Specialty:* Int Artist. *Publ:* Joan Crowder, New York art comes to Auchincloss Gallery in a classy exhibition, Santa Barbara News-Press, 7/19/86; Dana Saulnier, Stuart Diamond, Q: A J of Art, Dept Art Coll Archit, Art, & Planning, Cornell Univ, 5/90; Painting Faculty Show (catalog), Cooper Union, 96; Bare Bones (catalog), Tex Art & Co, New York, 96; After the Fall: Aspects of Abstract Painting (catalog), 97; The Figure: Another Side of Modernism (catalog), Newhouse Ctr, 2000; Catalog of Prints, Distinguished Artists at Vermont Studio Center, Vt Studio Ctr Press, color & black/white, 99. *Dealer:* Oasis Gallery No 318 Art Canden Row 2 #1-3 West Cuigezhuang Beijing China 100020. *Mailing Add:* 60 Valley St Apt 20 Providence RI 02909-7404

DIAMONSTEIN-SPIELVOGEL, BARBARALEE
WRITER, CIVIC ACTIVIST

Study: NY Univ, Doctorate, 63; DHL (hon), Md Inst Coll Art, 90; DHL (hon), Longwood Univ, 95; DHL (hon), Pratt Inst, New York, 2010. *Hon Degrees:* Baltimore Coll Art, Hon LHD, 90; Md Inst Coll Art, Hon Dr; Longwood Col, Hon LHD, 95; Pratt Inst, Hon LHD, 2009. *Exhib:* Shutter Opened, Passives (lithograph), Norton Simon Mus, Pasadena, Calif. *Collection Arranged:* Buildings Reborn: New Uses, Old Places, traveling, 76-; Am Architecture Now (auth, catalog), Leo Castelli Gallery, NY, 80; Visions and Images, Int Ctr Photog, NY, 81-; Handmade in Am, Leo Castelli Gallery & Metrop Mus Art, NY, 83; The Landmarks of New York (auth, catalog), 88; 8 Wonders of the NY World, 92; cur, Landmarks of New York, NY Hist Soc, 98; Barbaralee's Rules of the Road: 59 Simple Ways to Cope with a Complex World, 2001; The Landmarks of New York: An Illustrated Record of the City's Historic Buildings, 2005; editor: Our 200 Years: Tradition and Renewal, 1975, MOMA at 50, 1980; traveling exhibit to 82 countries, 14 cities, Landmarks of NY, US Dept. State, 2011-. *Pos:* Staff asst, The White House, 63-66 & first dir New York City cult affairs, 66-71; writer, Sat Rev, 65-68 & Harpers Bazaar, 69-71; spec proj ed, Art News, 74-, Ladies Home J, 77-81, Int Commun Agency, 78, Partisan Rev, 78-79 & Interiors, 80;

interviewer & producer, ABC-ARTS Cable Network, CBS-TV, WNYC-TV, Manhattan Cable Television & Arts & Entertainment Network; comnr, NY Landmark Preserv Comt, 72-87, Cult Affairs Coun, 74-86, Landmarks Conservancy vice-chairperson, 83-, chmn, 87-95; assoc, Am Craft Mus, 81-; dir, Munic Art Soc, NY, 73-83 & Fresh Air Fund, 87-; adv comt hist & theory of design, Grad Sch Design, Harvard Univ, 90; bd dir, Corcoran Gallery & NY Hist Soc; mem, US Holocaust Mus Mem Coun, 90; comt mem, US Comn Fine Arts, 95; mem, NY State Hist Archives Partnership Trust, 95; chmn, Hist Landmarks Preserv Ctr, 95-; appointee, US Comn Fine Arts, 96- & Gov Pataki's Comn Hon Achievements Women, 97-; TV interviewer, prodr. ABC-TV Arts, 1980-88, A & E Network, 1980-89; TV interviewer, prodr.: CBS-TV, 1978-97; TV interviewer, prodr. (300 videotapes) Archives of Itunes, Duke U., 2008; bd mem, Trust for the Nat Mall, Wash DC, 2009; founding dir, The High Line, Elevated Park, NY, 2001-2012; Am Battle Monuments Comn, 2010-; chair, NYCLandmarks 50, 2013. *Teaching:* Adj assoc prof, City Univ NY, Hunter Col, 74-77; vis prof, New Sch-Parsons Design, 76-82, Duke Univ, 78 & 83. *Awards:* Founders Day Award, Pratt Inst, 94; Visionary in the Arts Award, Mus Contemp Crafts, 95; Good Citizens Award, Coun Sr Ctrs & Serv NYC Inc, 96; New Millenium Humanitarian Award, HELP, 99; Gen Milan R Stefanik Award, Slocak Am Cult Ctr, 2002; Aging in Am Humanitarian Award, 2003; Gold medal, Ministry of Foreign Affairs of Slovakia, 2004; Humanitarian Award, Jewish Women's Found, New York, 2005; Lifetime Achievement Award, Washington, 2007; Legend Award, Pratt Inst, 2008; Achievement Award, Citizens Commn, New York, 2010; Landmarks Lion award, Historic Districts Coun, 2011; Womens Forum Lifetime Achievement award, 2012; Bronze Medal, John Jay Heritage Soc, 2012; named chair, NYC Landmarks, 2013. *Mem:* Munic Art Soc (mem bd dir, 72-); NY Landmark Conserv (bd gov); Am PEN; Women's Forum; Art Comn NY; NY State Coun Arts (vice-chmn, 2008-); Nat Am Inst Architects; and many others. *Publ:* Auth, Women Secrets, 72; American Architecture Now, Vol I, 77; Interior Design, 3/81; American photographers on photography, 11/81; Handmade in America, Harry N Abrams Publ, 83; American Architecture Now, Part II, 84; Collaborations, Artists, and Architecture, 84; Fashion: The Inside Story, 85; Remaking America, 86; auth, The Landmarks of New York I, 89 & The Landmarks of New York III, 98, IV, 2005, V, 2011. *Dealer:* Leo Castelli Gallery 420 W Broadway New York NY. *Mailing Add:* 720 Park Ave New York NY 10021

DIAO, DAVID
PAINTER, CONCEPTUAL ARTIST
b Sichuan, China, Aug 7, 1943; US citizen. *Study:* Kenyon Col, AB, 64. *Work:* Whitney Mus Am Art, NY; San Francisco Mus; Art Gallery Ont, Toronto; Va Mus, Richmond; High Mus, Atlanta, Ga; Brooklyn Mus; Danforth Art Mus; Hirshhorn Mus; Mod Mus Art, St Etienne, France. *Exhib:* Biennial Exhib, Whitney Mus Am Art, NY, 69 & 73; Group exhibs, Postmasters Gallery, NY, 85, 86, 88, 89, 91, 93, 95, 2000, 2009, & 2012, Galeria Westersingel 8, Rotterdam, The Neth, 88, Mus d'Art Moderne, St Etienne, France, 89, Galerie Joseph Dutertre, Rennes, France, 89, Provincial Mus voor Moderne Kunst, Oostende, Belg, 90, Het Kruithuis, Musvoor Hedendaagse Kunst, s-Hertogenbosch, The Neth, 90, Claire Burrus Gallery, Paris, 90, Sidney Janis Gallery, NY, 91, Musee de Metz, France, 92, Thread Waxing Space, NY, 94, Bernard Toale Gallery, 95, Aldrich Mus Contemp Art, Ridgefield, Conn, 96, Snug Harbor Ctr for the Arts, Staten Island, NY, 97, Parrish Mus, Southampton, NY, 2000, Thomas Ammann Fine Art, Zurich, 2001, Asian Am Arts Centre, NY, 2003, Santa Monica Mus, Calif, 2004, Guangdong Mus Art, Chinca, 2005, Tang Mus, Skidmore Coll, Saratoga Springs, NY, 2007, Weatherspoon Art Mus, Greensboro, NC, 2007, Nat Acad Mus, NY, 2008, Am Univ Mus, Wash DC, 2008, Office Baroque, Antwerp, 2010, Tate St Ives, 2011, 601 ArtSpace, NY, 2012; Solo exhibs: Provincial Mus voor Mod Kunst, Oostende, Belg, 90; Het Kruithuis, Mus voor Hedendaagse Kunst, The Neth, 90; Claire Burrus Gallery, Paris, 90; Selections 1972-1991; Cherng Piin Gallery, Taipei, Taiwan, 91, 94, 99, Galeria Arsenal, Bialystok, Polar, 2005, Tanya Leighton Gallery, Berlin, 2008, Office Barqoque, Antwerp, 2010, Design Matters, Galeria Marta Cervera, Madrid, 2011, Da Hen Li House, I lived there until I was 6, MC Contemporary, Madrid, 2011, and others. *Teaching:* Independent Study Prog, Whitney Mus, New York, 70-, Cooper Union, 94-; assoc prof, Hampshire Col, Amherst, Mass. *Awards:* Guggenheim Fel, 73-74; Nat Endowment Arts, 80, 87 & 93; Gottleib Fel, 92; and others. *Bibliog:* Paul Lester (auth), I Lived there until I was 6..., Time Out New York, 2/5/2009; Nicole Pasulka (auth), Loss of Home, The Morning News, 3/2/2009; Hiram To (auth), Match Point, Harper's Bazaar, 3/2009; Elizabeth C Baker (auth), David Diao, Postermasters', p 198, Art in Am, 7/2009; Els Fiers (auth), David Diao, Metropolis M, p 198, Art in Am, 3/2011; and many others. *Mem:* Nat Acad. *Dealer:* Postmasters Gallery. *Mailing Add:* c/o Postmasters Gallery 459 W 19th St New York NY 10011

DIAS-JORGENSEN, AURORA ABDIAS
PAINTER
b Belem, Brazil, June 10, 1918; US citizen. *Study:* St Josephs Col, Brooklyn, NY, 39; Bank Street Col, New York, MA; Art Students League. *Exhib:* invitational show, Mocha Mus Contemp Hispanic Art, NY, 85; solo exhib, Broome St Gallery, NY, 93, Ceres Gallery, NY, 95, 97, 2000, Koener Gallery, West Hampton Beach, NY, 99 & 2000; group shows, Nabisco Gallery, NJ, 89, Bergen Mus Art & Sci, NJ, 90, Dupont Gallery Washington & Lee Univ, Lexington, Va, 93 & Wilkes Gallery, Wilkesboro, NC, 93; Art Students League Juried, Mus Provincetown, Mass, 93; Kunstler Forum, Bonn, Ger, 98; Midwest Mus Am Art, Elkhart, Inc, 99. *Teaching:* Art, Pub Sch 108, New York, 60-80. *Awards:* Merit Award, Annual Exhib, Nat Acad Design, New York, 79; Ralph Mayer Mem Award, Nat Asn Women Artists 98th Annual Exhib, 87; First Prize Medal of Honor & Elizabeth Stanton Blake Mem Award, Nat Asn Women Artists 103rd Annual, 92, Clara Shainess Award, 97, Gretchen Richardson Mem Award, 98, First Prize Medal of Honor Amelia Peabody Mem Award (Sculpture), 2000. *Mem:* Nat Asn Women Artists (vpres, 87-89 & 95-96); life mem Art Students League; Artists Equity, NY (bd dir). *Media:* Acrylic on Paper, Acrylic on Paper. *Dealer:* Koener Gallery

DIAZ, ALEJANDRO
INSTALLATION SCULPTOR
b 1963. *Study:* Univ Tex, BFA, 1987; Bards Coll, Ctr Curatorial Studies, MA, 1999. *Exhib:* Solo exhibs, Karen Rhymer Gallery, San Antonio, Tex, 1994, ArtPace, San Antonio, 1996, 2006, Fuller Art Mus, Brockton, Mass, 2000, Jessica Murray Proj, Brooklyn, 2001, Sala Diaz, San Antonio, 2003, Pub Art Fund, New York, 2005, Aldrich Contemp Art Mus, Ridgefield, Conn, 2009; S-Files, El Mus del Barrio, New York, 2000; Grotto, Jessica Murray Proj, Brooklyn, 2002; Open House: Working in Brooklyn, Brooklyn Mus Art, New York, 2004; The Superfly Effect, Jersey City Mus, NJ, 2005; Gift: Wrap & Set Boutique, Julia Friedman Gallery, New York, 2005; Ceci n'est pas..., Sara Meltzer Gallery, New York, 2007; What Do You Care?, Mary Goldman Gallery, Los Angeles, 2008; Phantom Sightings, Los Angeles County Mus Art, 2008. *Awards:* River Pierce Found Grant, 1993; Pub Art Fund, In the Pub Realm, New York, 2004; Louis Comfort Tiffany Found Grants, 2008; Art Matters Found Grant, 2009. *Bibliog:* Jamie Gambrell (auth), Texas State of the Art, Art in America, 3/1987; Lorna Scott-Fox (auth), Arte en su Lugar, La Jornada Semanal, 12/1990; Graciela Kartofel (auth), Arte en Capsulas, Vogue-Mexico, 5/1991; Maria Guerra (auth), Arte Tex-Mex, Poliester, 9/1992; Ann Weiss (auth), On View, New Art Examiner, 3/1995; Franklin Sirmans (auth), Cityscape San Antonio, Summer/1998; Holland Cotter (auth), Picking Out Distinctive Voices..., The New York Times, August/2000; Emma Sloley, Personal Space, Harper's Bazaar - Australia, 1/2003; Julia Herzberg, 8th Havana Biennial, ArtNexus, 4/2004; Karen Rosenberg (auth), An Afternoon in Chelsea, New York Magazine, Summer/2007. *Mailing Add:* Mary Goldman Gallery PO Box 94 New Suffolk NY 11956-0094

DIAZ, LOPE (MAX)
PAINTER, EDUCATOR
b Santurce, PR, Dec 13, 1943. *Study:* Univ PR, BA, 66; Hunter Col, New York, MA, 71. *Work:* Museo DeArte, Ponce, PR; Mus Latin Am Print, PR Inst Cult, San Juan; Glaxo, RPT, Raleigh, NC; Museo De Arte, Univ De Puerto Rico, Rio Piedras, PR; Mint Mus Art, Charlotte, NC. *Exhib:* Solo shows, Mus Univ PR, Rio Piedras, 83; Galeria Botello, Hato Rey, PR, 88-94; Greenville Mus Art, Greenville, NC, 93; Mint Mus Art, Charlotte, NC, 94; Hodges Taylor Gallery, Charlotte, NC, 94 & 97; Lee Hansley Gallery, Raleigh, NC, 97; and others. *Teaching:* Asst prof art, Sch Archit Univ PR, 84-88 & assoc prof, Sch Design, NC State Univ, 88-. *Awards:* First Prize for Watercolor, Christmas Art Festival, Ateneo, PR, 66; First Prize for Painting, IBEC Group Show, 68; Honorary Award, Second Latin Am Graphic Biennale, Int PR Cult, 73. *Bibliog:* Tom Patterson (auth), Painter Diaz turns conventional framing inside out, The Charlotte Observer, NC, 7/31/94; Enrique Garcia Gutierrez (auth), Lope Max Diaz Para Pensar y Disfrutar, Nuevo Dia, 11/5/95; Tom Patterson (auth), New works show Diaz and painting outside the box, Charlotte Observer, 1/26/97. *Media:* Acrylic, Oil. *Publ:* Contribr, Kasimir Malevich: Revolucionario, Frente, 78. *Dealer:* Maud Duquella Galeria Botello 314 FD Roosevelt Ave Hato Rey PR 00918; Hodges Taylor Gallery 401 N Tyron St Charlotte NC 28202. *Mailing Add:* PO Box 10012 Raleigh NC 27605

DIBENEDETTO, STEVE
PAINTER, PRINTMAKER
b Bronx, New York, 1958. *Study:* Parsons Sch Design, BFA, 1980. *Exhib:* Moving, Found de Appel, Amsterdam, 1993; Mus Contemp Art, Geneva, 1994; Altered States, Forum for Contemp Art, St Louis, Mo, 1995; Works on Paper, Angela Lange Gallery, New York, 1996; In-form, Bravin Post Lee Gallery, New York, 1997; Le Consortium Collection, Centre Georges Pompidou, Paris, 1998; Etre Different, Gallery Demarez, Giverny, France, 1999; Painting Zero Degree, Cranbrook Mus Art, Bloomfield Hills, 2000; Best of Season, Aldrich Mus Contemp Art, Ridgefield, Conn, 2001; Transcendent & Unrepentant, Rosenwald-Wolf Gallery, Univ Arts, Philadelphia, 2002; Unforeseen, Portland Inst for Contemp Art, 2003; PS1 Contemp Art Ctr, Long Island City, 2004; Remote Viewing, Whitney Mus Am Art, 2005; Twice Drawn, Skidmore Coll, New York, 2006. *Teaching:* Faculty, Sch Visual Arts, 1993-1999, Columbia Univ, 2001-2002, Cooper Union Sch, 2002-2004 & Rutgers Univ, 2002-2005. *Awards:* Artist-in-residence, Fondation Claude Monet, Giverny, 1999; Rosenthal Award, Am Acad Arts Letts, 2003; Guggenheim Fel, 2003; Tiffany Found Award. *Dealer:* David Nolan Gallery New York NY; Daniel Weinberg Gallery Los Angeles CA. *Mailing Add:* Harlan & Weaver 83 Canal St Ste 101 New York NY 10002

DIBERT, RITA JEAN
PAINTER, PHOTOGRAPHER
b Flint, Mich, Feb 25, 1946. *Study:* Flint Community Jr Col, AA (art), 66; Univ Mich, Ann Arbor, BFA, 69, MFA, 71; also studied with Gerome Kamrowski, Albert Mullen & Ted Ramsey; Univ Calif, Los Angeles, 67-68 & Nathan Lyons, Joan Lyons, Scott McCarney, 91-93; State Univ NY, Brockport, MFA (elec media), 94. *Work:* Detroit Inst Art; Calif Mus Photog; Munson-Williams-Proctor Inst; Polaroid Corp, Cambridge, Mass; Toledo Mus Art; Pratt Art Inst; and many others. *Comn:* Hyatt Hotels; Hayworth Furniture; Detroit Renaissance Ctr Restaurant; Blue Cross/Blue Shield, Mich; Raddison Hotels; and others. *Exhib:* One-person shows, Upper Catskill Coun Art, 91, Clausen Gallery, Chicago, 91, Cooperstown, NY, 91, Charlotte-Douglas Airport, 94, Mercer Gallery, 94, Monroe Col, Rochester, NY, 94 & Cone Univ Ctr, Univ NC, Charlotte, 94; Mich Directions Invitational, Flint Art Inst, 94; Alumni Invitational, Univ Mich Slausser Gallery, Ann Arbor, 94; New Impressions Photo Ann, Light Impressions Gallery, Rochester, NY, 94; Southern Visions Traveling Photog Exhib, 94; 25 Yr Retrospective, No Sense of Time, Quiz Gallery, 97; and others. *Teaching:* Lectr & area coordr photog & printmaking, Residential Col, Univ Mich, Ann Arbor, 72-74; asst prof, Hartwick Col, 74-79; asst prof & artist-in-residence, Pomona Col & Claremont Grad Sch, 79-86; asst prof arts, Claremont Grad Sch, 79-86; vis assoc prof, Hartwick Col, Oneonta, NY, 89-90; adj, State Univ NY at Brockport, 92-93; prof electronic media, Univ NC, Charlotte, 93-95; prin, acad tutor, head photog dept, Quay Sch Arts, Wanganui, NZ, 95-. *Awards:* Polaroid Grant, 83-92 & 98; Ruth Chenven Found Painting Grant, 90; New York State Coun Arts Decentralization Grant, 91; Grant Wanganui Regional Community Poly, 99; Top

Festival Print Festival of Photography, Wanganui Camera Club, 96 & 98; Best in Show Annual Women's Show, UNCC, Charlotte, NC, 94. *Bibliog:* Article, Trends Section, Time-Life, 82, Popular Photog Ann, 86; Series of 5 Detroit full color 24x30 Lithographs, Univ Lithoprinters, Ann Arbor, Mich. *Mem:* Coll Art Asn; Women's Caucus Art; Soc Photog Educ; Friends of the Sargeant Gallery (Whanganui, New Zealand); Artists Alliance (Auckland, New Zealand). *Media:* Acrylic. *Publ:* Illusr back cover, European Photography, Polaroid Corp, 83; infrared photog, Photo District News, 3/91; infrared photog, Pop Photo Discoveries, 7/92; James McGinnis Hand Coloring Photographs, AMPHOTO, 94; Marshalls Hand Coloring, 95. *Dealer:* Artist Trait Claremont CA; Gallery 53 Cooperstown NY

DICE, ELIZABETH JANE
CRAFTSMAN, ILLUSTRATOR
b Urbana, Ill, Apr 3, 1919. *Study:* Univ Mich, BDesign, 41, MDesign, 42; Ind Univ, MA, 66; Int Sch Art, Mex; Inst Allende, Mex; Columbia Univ Teachers Col; Norfolk Art Sch; painting with Jerry Farnsworth; Penland Sch Crafts, 71 & 73. *Comn:* Woven Hanging, Carrier Chapel, Miss Univ for Women (Gift of class of 82). *Exhib:* Miss Art Asn, 48-51, 67 & 68; Nat Crafts Exhib, Wichita, Kans, 50; Nat Watercolor Show, Jackson, Miss, 51; New Orleans Art Asn, 55; Craftsmen's Guild Miss, 75; Path of the Weaver, Memphis, 78 & 80; and many others. *Teaching:* Assoc prof art, Miss State Col Women, 45-79, prof, 80-82; retired; Weaving Workshop for Chimmneyville Weavers, Jackson, Miss, 85. *Awards:* Prizes, Jackson, Miss, 46 & 51; Miss River Craft Exhib Award, 63; Horn Lake Libr Purchase Award. *Mem:* Archaeol Inst Am; Handweavers Guild Am (state rep, 72-77); Miss Mus Art; Southeastern Coll Art Conf; Columbus Art Asn. *Media:* Weaving, Polymer Clay. *Specialty:* General; Columbus Arts Council. *Interests:* paper

DI CERBO, MICHAEL
PAINTER, PRINTMAKER
b Paterson, NJ, 1947. *Study:* Pratt Inst, BFA & MFA. *Work:* Brooklyn Mus, NY; Victoria & Albert Mus, London; Detroit Art Inst; Portland Art Mus, Ore; Brit Mus; NY Hist Society, NY; Nat Acad Art; Nat Gallery of Art, Wash DC. *Comn:* Mural, Next City Corp, 82 & In Business Corp, 82. *Exhib:* Brooklyn Mus, 78; Print Club, Philadelphia, 80 & 85; Sotheby Park Bernet, NY, 81-84; solo exhib, Union St Gallery, San Francisco, 82, Portland Art Mus, Ore, 92, Phillips Fine Art, NY, 94, Chicago Print Fair, 94-96, Int Fine Print Dealers Asn Print Fair, 93-96, Old Print Shop, NY, 94, 96, Fitzwilliam Mus, Cambridge, Eng, 94, Seton Hall Univ, South Orange, NJ, 95; World Print Coun, San Francisco, 82; Kanagawa Prefectural Mus, Yokohama, 82, 84-85, 88-90 & 92; Albany Inst Art Hist, NY, 86; De Cordova Mus, Lincoln, Mass, 86, 90, 92 & 2000; Taipei Fine Arts Mus, Taiwan, 87, 89, 93 & 2005; Schweinfurth Mem Art Ctr, Auburn, NY, 89; Aldrich Mus Contemp Art, Ridgefield, Conn, 90; Fred Baker Gallery, Chicago, 96; 2nd Int Trennial, Bitola, Macedonia, 97; Int Print Exhib, Portland Art Mus, Oreg, 97; Silvermine Guild, New Canaan, Conn, 98; Broom Street Gallery, NY, 99; Florean Mus, Carbunari, Romania, 2000; Atlantic Gallery, NY, 99-2000; The Old Print Shop, 98, 2000, 2002-2003, 2005 & 2007; Springfield Art Mus, Mo, 99, 2005, 2010, 2014; Rennsselaerville Inst, 2001; NY Hist Soc, 2004; Hollar Soc Gallery Prague, 2006; and others. *Pos:* Pres, Soc Am Graphic Artists 89-94; curator 20th, 21st century, Old Print Shop, 2000-. *Teaching:* Prof art, Seton Hall Univ, South Orange, NJ, 92-99. *Awards:* Beveled Edge Award, Saga Nat, 98; Presentation Print Award, Print Club Albany, 2001; John Taylor Arms Award, Audubon Artists', 2002; Jack Richeson, Audubon Artists, 2006; Salmagundi award, Audubon Artists, 2009; Residency Fel, Balliglew Arts Found, 2009; Vis Artist Fel, Kent State Univ, 2012. *Bibliog:* City Lights Exhib, Art & Antiques Bull, 5/2000; article, Ink Images & Impressions, Newark Star Ledger, 4/15/2001; The Opposites, Jour of the Print World, spring 2001; Loving Their Prints at Temple Bar, Irish Times, 2006; Art Seen, Uptown, Manhattan Arts, 2008. *Mem:* Soc Am Graphic Artists; Boston Printmakers & Artists Equity; Print Consort; Am Print Alliance; Nat Acad Art; Nat Acad Art. *Media:* Acrylic, Watercolor, Etching. *Publ:* Architectural Fantasies, Symmetry 2, VCH, 89. *Dealer:* Old Print Shop 150 Lexington Ave New York NY 10016; Graphic Studio Dublin Ireland; Old Print Gallery Wash DC. *Mailing Add:* 143 Bennett Ave Apt GA-3 New York NY 10040

DICKERMAN, LEAH
CURATOR
Study: Harvard-Radcliffe Coll, BA (hist & lit); Columbia Univ, PhD (art hist & archeol). *Collection Arranged:* Building the Collective: Selections from the Merrill C Berman Collection, Harvard Univ Art Mus, 1996; Aleksandr Rodchenko, Mus Mod Art, 1998; The Cubist Paintings of Diego Rivera: Memory, Politics, and Place, Nat Gallery Art, 2004; Dada, Nat Gallery Art, 2005; Henri Rousseau: Jungles in Paris, Nat Gallery Art, 2006. *Pos:* Assoc cur & acting head dept mod & contemp art, Nat Gallery Art, Washington, DC, 2001-2007; cur dept painting & sculpture, Mus Mod Art, New York, 2008-. *Teaching:* Prof art hist, Stanford Univ & Univ Delaware, formerly. *Mailing Add:* c/o Museum of Modern Art Dept Painting & Sculpture 11 W 53 St New York NY 10019

DICKERSON, BRIAN S
PAINTER
b Middleburgh, NY, May 3, 1951. *Study:* Pa Acad Fine Arts, 71-72; pvt study with Paul Rotterdam, 94-96; Beaver Col, BFA; Vt Col, MFA, 96. *Work:* US Mint, Philadelphia, public & private collections. *Exhib:* solo exhib, Nat Acad Design, NY, 80, Hahn Gallery, Philadelphia, Pa, 85-91, Del Community Col, 87, Visual Arts Gallery, Cobleskill, NY, 88 & Landscape as Mystical Metaphor, State Univ NY, Cobleskill, 89; Woodmere Gallery, Philadelphia, 80 & 81; Butler Mus Am Art, Youngstown, Ohio, 81; Hahn Gallery, Philadelphia, 82; Inst Man & Sci, Rensselaerville, NY, 83; Juried Exhib, Knickerbocker Artists Group, Salmagundi Club, NY, 87; Honorable Mem Painting Juried Exhib, Woodmere Mus, Philadelphia, Pa, 88; Fel Pa Acad Fine Arts Exhib, 88, 92-94 & 97; Woodmere Mus, Philadelphia, Pa, 88-93; Butler Inst Am Art, Pittsfield, Mass, 89; Nat Arts Club, NY, 90; Vt Col, Wood Gallery, Montpelier, 95; Family Values Rhetoric vs Reality, Wood Gallery, Vt Col, Montpelier, 96; The Unbroken Line, Centennial Exhib Fel, Pa Acad Arts, 97; NY State Mus, Albany, 99-. *Pos:* Artist, Inst Man & Sci, Rensselaerville, NY. *Teaching:* Fac mem, Art Inst Philadelphia, currently; Antonelli Inst, 94-97. *Awards:* First Prize, Woodmere Mus; Ralph Fabri Medal of Merit, Nat Soc Painters Casein & Acrylic, 80. *Mem:* Fel Pa Acad Fine Arts. *Media:* Oil, Drawing, Graphite. *Mailing Add:* 151 W Durham St Philadelphia PA 19119

DICKERSON, DANIEL JAY
PAINTER, INSTRUCTOR
b Jersey City, NJ, Dec 22, 1922. *Study:* Cooper Union Art Sch, 41-43 & 45-46; Cranbrook Acad Art, BFA, 47, MFA, 49. *Work:* Joseph H Hirshhorn Collection; Adelphi Univ Mus; Ill Wesleyan Mus; Corcoran Gallery; Weatherspoon Gallery, Univ NC. *Comn:* NVE Bank mural, Leonia, NJ; art prog, US Coast Guard. *Exhib:* Whitney Mus Am Art Ann, 47; Pa Acad Fine Arts, 53; Audubon Artists Exhib, 64; Nat Inst Arts & Lett, 68; Nat Acad Design, 74; and others. *Teaching:* Lectr art, Manhattanville Col, 65-69; chmn dept art, Finch Col, 69-78; instr, Nat Acad Design Sch Art, 77-88 & Art Students League, 78-96. *Awards:* First Prize, Springfield Art Mus, 54; Emily Lowe Award for Painting, Audubon Artists, 64; Henry Ward Ranger Purchase Award, Nat Acad Design, 74; and others. *Mem:* Artists Fel; US Coast Guard Artists; Nat Acad Design; Nat Acad. *Media:* Acrylic, Oil. *Mailing Add:* 104 High St Leonia NJ 07605

DICKERSON, VERA MASON
PAINTER, INSTRUCTOR
b Radford, Va, July 28, 1946. *Study:* Radford Univ, BFA, 68; Am Univ, MFA, 70; studied with Wayne Thiebaud, Daniel Greene (workshop), Carla O'Connor, Carole Barnes, & George James. *Work:* Miller Brewing co, Eden, NC; Gannett Publ co, Arlington, Va; Marriott Corp; Clarion Hotels; Carilion Health Care, City of Roanoke, Va. *Comn:* Portraits, Fed Judges James Hill, Atlanta, Ga, Adrian Spear, San Antonio, Tex & John Jamison, Fredericksburg, Va, comn by Bar Asn, Darlington Co, SC, 81-83; portraits, Gen Marion Kinon, Dillon, SC, 85 & Clara Black, comn by Roanoke City Schs, Va, 86. *Exhib:* Traveling Exhib, Over the Blue Ridge, Roanoke Mus Fine Arts, Va, 81; More Than Land or Sky, Nat Mus Am Art, Washington, DC, 81; Southeast Print & Drawing Show, Belle Air Gallery, Fla, 82; Va Mus Fine Arts, Richmond, 83; After Her Own Image, Salem Coll, Winston-Salem, NC, 85; Henley Spectrum, Winston-Salem, NC, 92; Nude, Lexington Art League, KY, 2001; 30 solo exhibs; and others. *Collection Arranged:* Roanoke Coll, Longwood Univ. *Pos:* Artist-in-residence pastel drawing, Va Mus Fine Arts, Richmond, 83-84; dir, Sketchbook Tour Scotland, 90, 98-99, 2003, 2007, 2010, Ireland, 2001, 2008, Wales 2006, Provence, France, 2009, 2010, Italy, 2012, Scotland, 2013. *Teaching:* Asst prof art, Va Western Community Coll, Roanoke, Va, 72-78, dept art chmn, 78-81; founded The Studio Sch, Roanoke, Va, 90-. *Awards:* Nat Endowment Arts Grant, 81; Best in show, Kaleidoscope Festival, 88 & Showcase for the Arts, 87 & 88; First Prize Bristol Community Arts, 2000; Am Watercolor Soc, 2002; Rocky Mt Nat Watermedia Exhib Award, 2002 & 2006; Nat Watercolor Award, 2007; Best in Show Award, Va Watercolor, 2007; Mid-Atlantic Watercolor Award, 2008-2010; Rocky Mt Nat Water Media Award, 2008, 2009; Silver Medal, Southern Watercolor Soc, 2010, 2015; San Diego Internat Watermedia awards, 2010-2013; Southern Watercolor award, 2013; Mid-Atlantic Watercolor Bronze Medal Award, 2015. *Bibliog:* More than Land & Sky, Nat Mus Am Art Publ, 79; Over the Blue Ridge, Roanoke Mus Fine Arts Publ, 81; A Treasury of Southern Art & Literature, MacMillan, 93; Sue St. John (auth), Journeys to Abstraction, 2012. *Mem:* Va Watercolor Soc (found mem, bd dir, pres, 98-99); signature mem, Nat Watercolor Soc; Balt Watercolor Soc; Southern Watercolor Soc; Am Watercolor Soc; Rocky Mountain Watercolor Soc. *Media:* Oil, Mixed. *Interests:* Travel & gardening. *Publ:* Bonny Views of Ireland, Ireland of the Welcomes Mag, Winter 2010. *Dealer:* Signature 9 Gallery Roanoke Va. *Mailing Add:* 148 W Arrowhead Ct Troutville VA 24175

DICKINSON, ELEANOR CREEKMORE
PAINTER, VIDEO ARTIST
b Knoxville, Tenn, Feb 7, 1931. *Study:* Univ Tenn, with C Kermit Ewing, BA, 52; San Francisco Art Inst, with James Weeks, 61-63; Univ Calif, 67, 71 & 81; Academie de la Grande Chaumiere, Paris, France, 71; Calif Coll Arts & Crafts, MFA, 82; Golden Gate Univ, 84; studied with Dr Albert Rabateau, UC Berkeley. *Work:* Smithsonian Inst; Libr Cong, Nat Mus Am Art, Corcoran Gallery Art, Washington; San Francisco Mus Mod Art; Library of Congress; Numerous private collections including Senator Edward Kennedy, Senator Herschel Rosenthal, Walter Hopps, Carolyn Huber, Roselyn Swig, Phyllis Wattis, Gretchen Weiss Berggruen, Rene Di Rosa Found and numerous others; Fine Arts Mus San Francisco; Stanford Univ Mus; Archives Am Art. *Comn:* Wall installation (bronze), Univ San Francisco, 91. *Exhib:* Solo Exhibs: San Francisco Mus Modern Art, 65, 67; Santa Barbara Mus, 66; Judah Magnes Mus, Berkely, 68; Fine Arts Mus, San Francisco, 69 & 75; William Sawyer Gallery, San Francisco, Calif, 70, 71, & 75; Knoxville Mus Art, Knoxville, 70; Corcoran Gallery Art, 70 & 74; Poindexter Gallery, NY, 72 & 74; J B Speed Art Mus, Louisville, Ky, 72; Wash State Mus, 75; Cheney Cowles Mus, Spokane, Wash, 75; Triton Mus, Santa Clara, 75 & 77; Smithsonian Inst Traveling Exhib, 75-81; Huntsville Mus Art, 77; Montgomery Mus Fine Arts, 78; Galleria de Arte y Libros, Monterrey Mex, 78; Oakland Mus, 79; Menil Mus/Screen Memories Gallery, Houston, Tex, 88; Michael Himovitz Gallery, Sacramento, 88-89, 91, 93, 98; Hatley Martin Gallery, San Francisco, 86, 89; Gallery 10, Washington, DC, 89; Diverse Works Gallery, Houston, 90; Ewing Gallery, Univ Tenn, 91; Mus Contemp Religious Art, St Louis, 95; Coun Creative Projects, NY, 96; Thacher Gallery, Univ San Francisco, 2000; Retrospective, Downtown Gallery, Univ Tenn, 2005; Retrospective, Peninsula Mus Art, Belmont, Calif, 2007; Comma Gallery, Orlando, Fla, 2007; Group Exhibs: Diverse Works Gallery, Houston, Tex, 90; California Narrative, Galerie Etmars, Brussels, 92; 20th Century Women Artists, Queensboro Community Col, NY, 90; Am Religions, Smithsonian Inst, 90-91; A Salute To Women, Nat Mus of Women in Arts, 91; Recent Acquisitions, Fine Arts Mus San Francisco, 91; Witness to Dissent, Art In General, NY, 92; 500 Yrs Since Columbus, Triton Mus, Santa Clara, 92; Images of Us, Bedford Gallery, Walnut

Creek, 92; 16th Nat Invitational Drawing Exhib, Emporia State Univ, Kansas, 92; Michael Himovitz Gallery, Crocker Art Mus, 94; New Perceptions of the Spirit, GTU Gallery, Berkeley, 95; Global Focus, UN World Conf, Women, Beijing, Moscow, 95; Searching for the Spiritual, Hope Col, Mich, 97; Mary, St Mary's Col, Moraga, Calif, 97; Radiant Object, Cheney Cowles Mus, Spokane, 97; Dorothy Gillespie's Collection, Orlando Mus, Art Mus Western Va & Art Mus Radford Univ, 97 & 98; Preserving the Past Securing the Future, Nat Mus Women in Arts, 98; Artists of Western States, Artcore Gallery, Los Angeles, 99; The Female Gaze, Ohlone Col, Fremont, 2000; Truth and Lies, Triton Mus, 2000; Art by Women, Goethe Inst, Kathmandu, Nepal, 2001; Like A Prayer, Tryon Gallery Ctr for Visual Art, Charlotte, NC, 2001; Dark Madonna, Univ San Francisco, 2001; Bay Area Figurative Art, Univ California, Berkeley, Calif, 2004; Violence Against Women/Women Against Violence, Nexus Gallery, Berkeley, 2004-5; Gender in Motion, 3 TEN HAUSTUDIO, Atlanta, GA, 2005; Ciis Gallery, San Francisco, 2005; Ohlone Col, 2006; A Model, Transformation of a Model, Lewis Pohl Gallery, Honolulu, 2005; Revisioning, Maitland Art Ctr, Fla; Artcard, Shariah Art Mus, United Arab Emirates; Highly Favored (traveling exhibit), Gordon Coll, Me, 2006-; CCA Alumni, 100 yrs, 2008; Social Justice, United Nations, Mexico City, 2009; Control, Ceres Gallery, NY, 2011. *Collection Arranged:* Howard Finster, Fine Arts Mus San Francisco, 2006. *Pos:* lectr, Academes of Art Hangzhou, Xian, Shanghai, China, 91; guest cur, currently; juror, many shows, 1977-2008. *Teaching:* Vis lectr drawing & painting, Univ Calif, 65, 70-71 & 73; prof drawing & gallery mgt, Calif Col Arts & Crafts, Oakland, 71-2001, dir galleries, 75-85; prof emerita, 2001-; vis prof, Univ Calif Ext, Davis, 83-85, Solano State Univ, 83, Fresno State Univ, 83, Davis & Eklins Col, WVa, Ark State Univ, 93, Fine Arts Mus San Francisco, 2006. *Awards:* Distinguished Alumni Citation, Nat Cathedral Sch, Wash, DC, 78; Distinguished Alumni Award, San Francisco Art Inst, 83; Master Drawing Award, Nat Soc Arts and Letters, 83; Mid-Career Award, Women's Caucus, Coll Art Asn, 95; Lifetime Achievement Award, Women's Caucus for Art, 2003; and others. *Bibliog:* R Stevens (auth), Eleanor Dickinson, La Revue Moderne, Paris, 12/1/60; Cecile McCann (auth), Dickinson's Dream Works, Artweek, 12/4/71; Walter Hopps (auth), Introduction, Revival!, Harper & Row, NY, 74; Dr Alfred Frankenstein, Celebrated Women in Art - At the Legion, San Francisco Chronicle, 10/19/75; Marsha Maguire (auth), Confirming the word: artist and social documentarian, Quarterly J Libr Cong, 81; Richard King (auth), Eleanor Dickinson: Religion and the Southern Artist, Womans Art Jour, 82; Dr Peter Selz (auth), San Francisco: Eleanor Dickinson at Hatley Martin, Art Am, 89; Martina R Norelli (auth), Allgemeines Kunstler Lexikon, 2001. *Mem:* Artists Equity Asn (nat vpres); Women's Caucus Art (Nat affirmative action off/bd mem, 2000-2006); Coll Art Asn (CAA chair Committee for Women in the Arts); Calif Lawyers Arts (state vpres, 86-2000, bd dir, 86-2012); Am for the Arts. *Media:* Oil, Pastel, Ink, All Media. *Res:* Hist of women's caucus for art; Elkmont hist; Statistical res, discrimination in the art field. *Specialty:* Contemp, figurative drawings and paintings. *Interests:* Southern revival practices. *Collection:* Drawings and prints, emotional subjects. *Publ:* Auth, Southern Revival Services, (archive of folk song, audio, & videotapes), Library of Congress, 1968-; Auth, Tennessee revival services, Libr Cong Arch Folk Song, 71; coauth (with B Benziger), Revival!, 74 & illusr, That Old Time Religion, 75, Harper & Row, Elkmont, 2005; Auth, Elkmont: The Heart of the Great Smoky Mountains National Park, 2005; Auth, The History of the W.C.A., BLAZE, Discourse on Art, Women and Feminism, Cambridge Scholars Press, UK, 2007; and others. *Mailing Add:* 406 Belmont Way San Jose CA 95125

DICKSON, JANE LEONE
PAINTER, PRINTMAKER

b Chicago, Ill, May 18, 1952. *Study:* Sch of Boston Mus Fine Arts, dipl, 76; Harvard Univ, BA (magna cum laude), 76. *Work:* Metrop Mus Art & Mus Mod Art, NY; Whitney Mus Am Art; Victoria & Albert Mus, London, Eng; Libr Cong, Washington; Art Inst Chicago, Ill; Brooklyn Mus Art, NY. *Comn:* MTA Arts for Transit Poster, New York City, 90; Radio Shack, 2004; MTA Mosaics, Times Square Station, 2006. *Exhib:* Solo shows incl Brooke Alexander Gallery, NY, 86, 88, 90 & 92, Joe Fawbush Gallery NY, 83 & Whitney Mus at Philip Morris, 96, Marlborough Gallery, NY, 2003, 05, Almost There, Jersey City Mus, NJ, 2006, Sin Titul, Galeria Petrus, San Juan Puerto Rico, 2007, Night Driving, Malborough, Chealsea, 2009, Dreamland, Gallery Saoh, Tokyo, 2012; group shows incl On 42nd Street, Whitney Mus-Philip Morris, NY, 84; Biennial Exhib, Whitney Mus, NY, 85; Pub & Pvt: Am Prints Today, Brooklyn Mus, NY, Carnegie Inst, Pittsburgh & Walker Art Ctr, Minn, 86-87; A Graphic Muse, Prints By Contemp Am Women, Yale Univ Art Gal, Mt Holyoke Coll MA & Richmond VA, 87-88; Ean Keuze/A Choice KunstRai Amsterdam, 88; Portraying the Night, Kansas City Art Inst, 88; Life Under Neon, Moore Coll Art, Philadelphia, Pa, 89; retrospective, Ill State Univ (auth, catalog), Normal (traveling), 94; Paradise Alley, Whitney Mus at Philip Morris, 96; Saints Grown Up, Temple Univ Tyler Sch Art Gallery, Philadelphia, 97; Out of Here, Ft Lauderdale Mus of Art, 01; East Village, New Mus, 2005; Downtown, Grey Art Gallery, NY Univ & Warhol Mus, Pittsburg, Pa, 2006; Caja Granada, Spain; Street as Stvdiv Kunsthalle, 2010; Neither Model Nor Muse, McNay Mus, San Antonio, Tex, 2010; Espece d'Espace, les annees 1980s Mag d'Art Contemp, France, 2008; Art in the Street, LA MoCA, 2011; The Street as Studio, Kunsthalle Vienna, 2010; Whose World is This, 2012; Out of Here, Omni Int Art Ctr, NY, 2013; Whose World is This? with Charlie Ahearn, William Paterson Univ, NJ, 2013. *Pos:* Art/Omi residency, 99; McDowell Residency, 2009; Yaddo Residency, 2011. *Teaching:* Sch Visual Arts NY 88-89, Temple Univ, Tyler Sch Art, Philadelphia Pa, 90, Cooper Union, State Univ NY, Purchase, 96; prof art Pace Univ, 2000-, Calif State Northridge, 98. *Awards:* Grants, Nat Endowment Arts, Washington & Ariana Found, 85; Dewars Young Artist Award, 90. *Bibliog:* Ken Gonzalez Day (auth), Jane Dickson at Long Beach Mus Art, Art Issues, 3-4/96; Holland Cotter (auth), A romantic haze on dead-end lives of the city, NY Times, 6/14/96; Vincent Katz (auth), Jane Dickson at Black & Herron, Art Am, 7/96; Berlind Rlot (auth), Art in Am, 04/2009; Vienna Kusthalle (auth), Street and Studio from Basquiat to Seripop, 2010; Julie Ault (auth), A Chronicle of Group Material, London, 2010; Patrick Nguyen (auth), Beyond the St Berlin, 2010; Janetta Benton (auth), Art in Culture, 4th Ed, Princeton Press, 2011. *Mem:* Century Club. *Media:* All Media. *Mailing Add:* 17 Hubert St New York NY 10013

DICKSON, JENNIFER JOAN
PHOTOGRAPHER, LECTURER

b Piet Retief, Repub SAfrica, Sept 17, 1936; Can citizen. *Study:* Goldsmith's Coll Sch Art, Univ London, 54-59; Atelier 17, Paris, with S W Hayter, 60-65. *Hon Degrees:* LLD (hon) Univ Alta, 88. *Work:* Victoria & Albert Mus, London; Nat Gallery Can, Ottawa; Metrop Mus Art, NY; Montreal Mus Fine Arts; Smithsonian Inst; Royal Acad Arts, London, Eng. *Comn:* The Secret Garden (collabr: Henry J Kahanek & Ray Van Dusen), 76 & Paradise, 80, Nat Film Bd Can; The Last Silence, Can Mus Contemp Photog, Ottawa, 93, & Palazzo Te, Mantua, Italy, 93. *Exhib:* Salon des Realites Nouvelles, Musee d'Art Moderne, Paris, 62 & 66; Biennale de Paris, Mus Mod Art, Paris, 63; Modern Prints, 65 & Contemp Prints, 66, Victoria & Albert Mus, London; Salon Int de la Gravure, Montreal Mus Fine Arts, 71; Folio Seventy Three Traveling Exhib, San Francisco Mus Art, 74; Forum 76, Montreal Mus Fine Arts, 76; Celebration of the Body, Agnes Etherington Art Centre, Queen's Univ, Ont; Tendances Actuelles au Quebec, 79 & L'estampe au Que 1970-1980, 80, Musee d'Art Contemporain, Montreal; 14th Int Biennial of Graphic Art, Ljubljana, Yugoslavia, 81; solo exhibs, Il Tempo Classica, Saidye Bronfman Centre, Montreal, 82, A Journey to Cythere, Wallack Art Ed, Ottawa, 82, Jennifer Dickson: A Continuum, Edward Monaghan Art Consult, Ottawa, 83 & Versailles: Through the Crystal Wall, Wallack Galleries, Ottawa, 83; The Thief of Time, Wallack Galleries, 2006; Romantic Idylls and Classical Dreams, Wallack Galleries, 2011. *Collection Arranged:* Imprint 76 (current Can graphic art), Ont Arts Coun; Nat Libr and Archives, Can; Can Mus Contemp Photography. *Pos:* freelance lectr & photographer. *Teaching:* Vis prof fine arts, Univ Wis, Madison, 72; vis artist fine arts, Queen's Univ, Kingston, Ont, 77-78; instr dept visual arts, Univ Ottawa, formerly. *Awards:* James A Reid Award, Can Painters-Etchers & Engravers, 73; Special Purchase Award, World Print Competition, San Francisco Mus Art, 73; Prize, 5th Norwegian Int Print Biennale, 80; and others. *Bibliog:* Michael Rothstein (auth), Frontiers of Printing, Studio Vista, 70; Anthony Gross (auth), Etching, Engraving & Intaglio Printing, Oxford Univ Press, 72; Edward-Lucie Smith (auth), Art in Seventies, Phaidon/Cornell Univ Press, 80; and others. *Mem:* Academician Royal Acad Arts; Print & Drawing Coun Can; Can Artists Representation; fel Royal Soc Painter-Etchers & Engravers. *Media:* Photography. *Res:* Syrian Orthodox monasteries in Turkey. *Specialty:* Canadian art. *Interests:* gardening, vintage fashion. *Publ:* Auth, The Hospital for Wounded Angels, Porcupines Quill Inc, 87. *Dealer:* Wallack Galleries 203 Bank St Ottawa ON K2P 1W7 Can. *Mailing Add:* 20 Osborne St Ottawa ON K1S 4Z9 Canada

DICKSON, MARK AMOS
PAINTER, PRINTMAKER

b Boulder, Colo, Mar 4, 1946. *Study:* Metrop State Univ BA, 69; Pratt Inst, 69-70; Univ Denver, MFA, 73. *Work:* Plains Art Mus, Morehead, Minn; Colo Graphic Arts Ctr, Denver, Colo; Denver Ctr Performing Arts, Colo; Amarillo Art Mus, Tex; Kirkland Mus, Denver, Colo. *Comn:* Oil on canvas, Texaco Oil, White Plains, NY; oil, American Airlines; oil, Kennedy Int Airport, NY; oil, Hakodate Hotel, Tokyo, Japan; Shopping Bag, Braodway Southwest Corp. *Exhib:* Nat Audubon, Nat Acad Design, NY, 70; Artist Exchange, Joslyn Art Mus, Omaha, Nebr, 73; Arts 80, Nat Boulder Arts Ctr, 80; Colorado Print Invitational, Colo Graphic Arts Ctr, Denver, Colo, 84; Draw 82, Boulder Arts Ctr, Colo, 82; Artist of Taos, Stables Art Ctr, Taos, NMex, 87; Downtown Ctr Visual Art, 25 Yrs, 25 Artists, Metrop State Col, Denver, Colo, 90; Near North & Northwest Art Coun Gallery, Printmakers Coop Ann Exhib, Chicago, 92; Colo Abstract Painting & Sculpture, Denver, Colo Ctr Visual Art, 2008; 528.0 Denver, Redline Gallery, Denver, Colo, 2013; LA Inaugural Exhib, KM Fine Arts, Los Angeles, Calif, 2013. *Teaching:* Instr printmaking, Univ Denver, Colo, 73; assoc prof fine art, St Thomas Col, Denver, 75-79; instr painting, Rocky Mountain Col Art, Denver, Colo, 87. *Awards:* Research & Travel Grant, Am Asn Theological Schs, 79; Award of Merit, Graphics 86, Inst Graphic Arts, 86; Award of Distinction, Creativity 86, Art Direction Mag, 86; Art Angel Award, Art Stuents League, Denver. *Bibliog:* Mystique Mag Northern NMex, 8/84; Where Chicago Mag, 9/91; Colorado Expression Mag, summer 92. *Media:* Oil, All Media, Printmaking. *Publ:* Mark Dickson Since 1967, KMD Publ, 2003; Sparrow the Cookbook (illustrations), Gem Publ, 2007; Colorado Abstract Painting & Sculpture, Fresco Fine Publ, 2009. *Dealer:* Flanders Gallery Minneapolis MN; HW Gallery Naples FL; KM Fine Arts Chicago IL Los Angeles CA

DI COSOLA, LOIS BOCK
PAINTER, DRAFTSMAN

b Brooklyn, NY, Jan 23, 1935. *Study:* Early Master classes, Mus Mod Art, NY, grant, 51, Girls Commercial, Brooklyn, NY, Fine Art Diploma, 53; New Sch, R Pousette-Dart, 60; Pratt Graphics Ctr, 73-75; State Univ NY, Bachelor of Prof Studies for life's work in art, 85. *Work:* Guild Hall Mus, East Hampton, NY; Mus Mod Art, NY; Sophia Smith Collection, Smith Coll, Northampton, Mass; Libr Cong, Washington, DC; Smithsonian Art Archives, Washington, DC; int & pvt collections. *Comn:* Sesame St Mural, comn by Henry Welt, 74. *Exhib:* Carnegie Fine Art Inst, 53; Associated Am Artist Galleries, NY, 54; Art & Design Exhib, 33rd Ann Int Art Dir Club, NY, 54; NY World's Fair, 64; Hecksher Mus, 64 & 78; Guild Hall Mus, E Hampton, NY, 63-64, Artists Select, Finch Coll Mus, Artists Select, 64, Permanent Print Exhib Coll, 80-81; X12, Pioneer Feminist Art Exhib, NY, 70; Traveling Print Exhib, Pratt Graphics Ctr, NY, 75; Provinciaal Mus, Bel, 82; Born to Survive, Mus Het Toreke, Belg, 84; Elaine Benson Gallery, Bridgehampton, NY, 89, 91 & 96; Mus Mod Art, NY, Life of the City; Mus of City of NY, 2002; 9/11 exhib, Virtual Union Square, 2002; Reactions, Exit Art, 2002; Azzociacion SIVIERA Verbania, Italy, 2007; Sewall Belmont Mus, Washington, DC, 2008; Italo Calvino Munic Libr Gallery, Torino, Italy, 2009; Ray Johnson & a Book About Death, LI Univ, Hillwood Commons Gallery, 2010; Abad, The Ties that Bind, 2nd St Gallery, Bay Shore, NY,

2011. *Pos:* Graphic artist, Norcross, 53-56, Seventeen Mag, 53-54, Sesame St, 69-70 & Time-Life Bks, 73; bd mem, vpres, Prof Artist Guild, 66 & cochair, Nat Drawing Asn, 89; arts ed, Sunstorm Arts, 82. *Teaching:* art instr, Roosevelt Integration Program, Roosevelt Sch, 65; Prof art, Hofstra Univ, Hempstead, NY, 90-. *Awards:* Augustus St Gaudens Medal for Draftsmanship, 53; Printmaking Award, Carnegie Inst Fine Art, 53; First Prize-Drawing, Seventeen Mag, Int Competition, 1953; 33rd Ann Art Dir's Club Award, 54; Painting & Drawing, Guild Hall Mus, Harold Rosenberg, Adolph Gottlieb & Larry Rivers 63, 64; Mus Mod Art Curator's award, 63; Finch Coll Mus, James Brooks' selection, 64; Guggenheim Mus Curator's Award, 64; Whitney Mus Curator's Award, 64. *Bibliog:* Art Kane (auth), We know what we like, Seventeen Mag, 6/53; Annual of Advertising & Editorial Art & Design, Farrar, Strauss & Young, 54, Artists Select, Finch Coll, Mus Cat, 64; Cindy Nemser (auth), x12' Arts Mag, 2/70; Manuel De La Torre (auth), Lois Di Cosola, 82 & 2004; Helen Harrison (auth), Best of Long Island Graphics, NY Times, 9/81; Dr Saul Levine (auth), Portrait of an Artist: Lois Di Cosola, Sunstorm Arts, 82; Elaine Booth Selig (monogr), Lois Di Cosola, Women in Arts Mus Database, 2005; Feminists Who Changed America: 1963-1975, ed Barbara Love, Univ Ill Press, pp 118, 2007; PS 1, Wack Catalog, 2007. *Mem:* Drawing Soc; Mus Mod Art. *Media:* Painting, Drawing. *Interests:* Literature, theatre, film. *Publ:* Sesame Street Book of Puzzlers, CTW, 70; Notes from the Hotel Chelsea, Art of Sewing Series, Time-Life Books, 70; Process 6, LI Poetry Mag, 80; Notes Along the Way, DiCosola, Fine Art Mag, Victor Forbes and Jamie Ellin Forbes, Spring 2010; Online portfolio includes fickr,com, brooklynmuseum.org; Feminist Online Timeline 1969-1970, Brooklyn Mus. *Dealer:* Aldona M Gobuzas 215 E 79th St New York NY 10021. *Mailing Add:* 25 Arch Ln Hicksville NY 11801

DIDOMENICO, NIKKI
CONCEPTUAL ARTIST, ASSEMBLAGE ARTIST

b Newark, New Jersey, June 8, 1948. *Study:* Douglas Col, BA, 71; d'Ecole de Beaux Art Paris, 71-72; Scuola di Torano, Carrara, Italy, Masters, 73-78. *Work:* Pagani Found, Milano, Italy; Banco di Lavoro, Carrara, Italy; pvt collections. *Comn:* Sculptures, comn by J Blum, San Francisco, 76, E Marucci, NJ, 85. *Exhib:* Salon du Mai, Palais Royale, Paris, 73; Incontri, Pietrasanta, 76; Biennale della Spezia, The City, La spezia, 75; Tentazioni, Forte di Belvedere, Firenze, 85; Expos Grup, Italy, 93. *Teaching:* Vis instr, Stockton State Col, NJ. *Awards:* Recognition, Icontri, I Noguchi, 76. *Bibliog:* Laura Grahm (auth), Avanti, 80; Mirko Puccerelli (ed), Arte Now, 84. *Mem:* Artist Equity, NY; Il Gruppo, Italy; Art Police (co-pres, 88-). *Media:* Mixed Media. *Dealer:* Stephen H Jones 357 W 54th St New York NY 10019. *Mailing Add:* 252 W 21 St No 54 New York NY 10011-3426

DIEHL, GUY
PAINTER, INSTRUCTOR

b 1949. *Study:* Diablo Valley Col, Pleasant Hill, Calif, 70; Calif State Univ, Hayward, BA, 73; San Francisco State Univ, MA, 76. *Work:* Fine Arts Mus San Francisco, Calif; Caldwell Banker, West Palm Beach, Fla; Bank of Am, San Francisco, Calif; Princeton Univ, NJ; Progressive Insurance Co, Cleveland, Ohio; and others. *Comn:* Princess Cruise Lines; Peninsula Hotel, NY; MGM Mansion, Las Vegas, Nev; Davis Mural Team Project, Davis, Calif. *Exhib:* Group exhibs, Millard Sheets Gallery, Pomona, Calif, 2001, Bank of Am, San Francisco, 2001, Anne Reed Gallery, Ketchum, Idaho, 2002, Conn Graphic Arts Ctr, Norwalk, 2002, Edith Caldwell Gallery, Sausalito, Calif, 2003, San Jose Mus Art, Calif, 2003, Gallery Henoch, New York City, 2004, Pasadena Mus Calif Art, 2004, Paula Brown Gallery, Toledo, Ohio, 2004, Hackett-Freedman Gallery, San Francisco, 2004, Piaza Gallery, San Francisco, 2004, Mendenhall Sobieski Gallery, Pasadena, Calif, 2004, Charles Campbell Gallery, San Francisco, 2005, Gallery C, Hermosa Beach, Calif, 2005, George Krevsky Gallery, San Francisco, 2005-2006, Judson Gallery Contemp & Traditional Art, Los Angeles, 2005, Bedford Gallery, Walnut Creek, Calif, 2005, Sonoma Valley Mus Art Biennial 2005, Sonoma, Calif, Sullivan Gross, Santa Barbara & Montecito, Calif, 2006, Klaudia Marr Gallery, Santa Fe, NMex, 2006, Hackette-Freedman Gallery, San Francisco, 2007, Triton Mus Art, Santa Clara, Calif, 2008, George Krevsky Gallery, San Francisco, 2009, Sullivan Goss an Am Gallery, Santa Barbara, 2010; Solo exhibs, Modernism, San Francisco, 93-94, 97, Fletcher Gallery, Santa Fe, NMex, 95, Hackett-Freedman Gallery, San Francisco, 98, 2001, 03, Hunsaker/Schlesinger Gallery, Santa Monica, Calif, 2004, Sonoma Valley Mus Art, Calif, 2007, Hackett-Freedman Gallery, San Francisco, 2007. *Pos:* Cur, Sonoma Valley Mus Art, Calif, 2007. *Teaching:* Instr painting, Diablo Valley Col, Pleasant Hill, Calif, 77-82; instr painting, Chabot Col, Livermore, Calif, 80; Las Positas Col, Livermore, Calif, 80-90; Ft Mason Art Ctr, San Francisco, 92-98. *Awards:* Purchase Award, Alameda Co Art Commission, 72; Marin Art Coun Individuaal Artists Grant, 94; Biennial Exhib Award, Sonoma Valley Mus Art, 2005. *Bibliog:* Dottie Indyke (auth), Less is more in Diehl's Seductions of light, The Santa Fe New Mexican, Pasatiempo, 7/7/95; Richard Tobin (auth), Short reviews, THE magazine, Santa Fe, NMex, 8/95; Steven Nash, Guy Diehl and History, Hackett Freedman Gallery, San Francisco, Calif, 98; Christopher Willard (auth), The Details on Details, American Artist Mag, 8/02; John D O'Hern (auth), Art Encounters On the Road, Am Art Collector Mag, Oct 2006; Susan Landauer (auth), Tradition & Innovation: The Still Lifes of Guy Diehl, Hackett-Freedman Gallery, Am Art Collector Mag, 2007. *Media:* Acrylic, Watercolor, Etchings. *Dealer:* Magnolia Editions 2527 Magnolia St Oakland CA 94607; Dolby Chadwick Gallery 210 Post St San Francisco Ca 94108

DIEHL, HANS-JURGEN
PAINTER

b Hanau, Ger, May 22, 1940. *Study:* Ecole Nationale Superieure des Beaux-Arts, Paris; Akademie der bildenden Kunste, Munich; Hochschule fur Bildende Kunste, Berlin, 59-66. *Work:* Mus Preusischer Kulturbesitz, Nat Gallery, Berlin, Ger; Ulmer Mus, Ulm, Ger; Sprengel Mus, Hannover, Ger; Kunsthalle Kiel, Kiel, Ger; Mus Witten, Witten, Ger. *Exhib:* Solo shows, Ulmer Mus, Ulm, Ger, 77, Kunsthalle, Berlin Ger, 85; Ugly Realism, Inst Contemp Arts, London, 78; Utopian Visions in Modern Art: Dreams and Nightmares, Hirshhorn Mus, Washington, DC, 83; Stationen der Moderne, Berlinische Galerie, Berlin, Ger, 89; Hugh Lane Munic Gallery Mod Art, Dublin, 91; Galerie Limmer, Köln, Ger, 99; Kesselhaus, Hannover, Ger, 2000. *Teaching:* Prof painting, Hochschule der Kunste, Berlin, 77. *Mem:* Deutscher Kunstlerbund. *Dealer:* Galerie Limmer Venloer Str 21 50672 Koln Germany. *Mailing Add:* 47 Clinton St New York NY 10002

DIETRICH, BRUCE LEINBACH
MUSEUM DIRECTOR, COLLECTOR

b Reading, Pa, Oct 10, 1937. *Study:* Kutztown Univ, BS, 60; Univ Denver, 61; Temple Univ, 62-67; Millersville Univ, 67, State Univ NY, MS, 70; George Washington Univ, 81-83; Am Legal Inst/Am Bar Asn, 81-87; Kellog Proj/Smithsonian Inst, 84, 85 & 87. *Collection Arranged:* The Sea, 76, Winter Winds, 78, Master Prints, 78, Spectrum, 78 & Director's Choice, 83, Reading Pub Mus & Art Gallery; Fractal Dimension, 88. *Pos:* Cur space sci, Reading Pub Mus & Art Gallery, 67-69, mus dir, 76-92, dir emer, 2002; dir, Reading Planetarium, 69-93; mus management consult, 92-93; retired. *Mem:* Middle Atlantic Planetarium Soc; Asn Planetariums Can; Asn Sci Mus Dirs; Am Asn Advan Sci; and others. *Mailing Add:* 1546 Dauphin Ave Wyomissing PA 19610-2118

DI FATE, VINCENT
ILLUSTRATOR, PAINTER

b Yonkers, NY, Nov 21, 1945. *Study:* Phoenix Sch Design, cert, 67; Sch Visual Arts, 68; Art Students League, 68-70; MA, Syracuse Univ, 2003. *Work:* NASA Mus, Cape Canaveral, Fla; NASM, Smithsonian Inst, Washington, DC; Soc Illusr, NY; Univ Kans; New Brit Mus, Conn. *Exhib:* Solo shows, Reading Pub Mus, Pa, 78 & Mus Sci & Natural Hist, St Louis, Mo, 82; New Brit Mus Am Art, Conn, 80; Bronx Mus Arts, NY, 80; Stadthalle Limburg, Fed Repub Ger, 80; Am Mus-Hayden Planetarium, 88. *Teaching:* Instr, Univ Bridgeport, Conn, 79 & Sci Fiction & Fantasy Illus, Fashion Inst Technol, 93-. *Awards:* Hugo Award, World Sci Fiction Asn, 78; Science Fiction Hall of Fame Induction, Science Fiction Mus, Seattle, 2011; Artistic Achievement Award, Asn Sci Fiction & Fantasy Artists, 98. *Bibliog:* George Magnan (auth), Science fiction art, Today's Art & Graphics, 3/81; Ellen Datlow (auth), Stellar technician, Omni Mag, 5/81; Brian M Fraser (auth), All the colors of space and time, Questar Mag, 10/81. *Mem:* Soc Illusr (pres, 95-97); Graphic Artists Guild; Int Asn Astronomical Artists; Am Sci Fiction/Fantasy Artists (pres, 78). *Media:* Acrylic, Oil. *Publ:* Co-auth & illusr, Di Fate's Catalog of Science Fiction Hardware, Workman Publ, 80; contribr, The Science Fiction Reference Book, Starmont House, 81; auth & ed, Infinite Worlds: The Fantastic Visions Sci Fiction Art, Penguin Studio Books, 97 & The Science Fiction Art of Vincent Di Fate, Paper Tiger, 2003. *Mailing Add:* 12 Ritter Dr Wappingers Falls NY 12590

DIFRONZO, FRANCIS G
PAINTER

Study: Calif State Univ, Fullerton, BFA, 94; Pa Acad Fine Arts, Philadelphia, MFA, 98. *Exhib:* Solo exhibs, Common Disaster, Artists' House Gallery, Philadelphia, 99, Philadelphia Cathedral, 2000, Segue, 2000, Rosenfeld Gallery, Philadelphia, 2002, 2004. *Awards:* Recipient Art in Am Scholarship Award, Liquitrex, 93; Stobbart Found Fel in the Arts, 98; Pew Fel in the Arts, 2004

DIGBY, LYNNE
PAINTER, WRITER

b Gloucester, Eng; US citizen. *Study:* Gloucester Coll Art, Eng, 56-57; Ont Coll Art, 58-59; studied with Can abstr expressionist Harold Town, 58. *Work:* McGraw Hill; Orange County Gov Ctr. *Exhib:* Mt Aramah Invitational, Orange Co Hist Soc, Clove Furnace Historic Site, 86; NE Watercolor Soc Ann Exhib, Harness Racing Mus, Goshen, NY, 95-96; 104th Ann Open Exhib, Catherine Lorillard Wolfe Art Club, 2000; solo exhib, Port of Call Gallery, Warwick, 2002 & 2004, Exec Suite Gallery, Gov Bldgs, Goshen, NY, 2005, Woodstock Artists Asn & Mus, 2007, Karpeles Manuscript Libr & Mus, NY, 2008, Greenwood Lake Libr, 2009; Woodstock Sch Art Regional 5th Juried Exhib, 2006; Woodstock Artists Asn & Mus, 2013; Seligmann Gallery, Sugarloaf, NY, 2013. *Pos:* Pres, Orange Co Sub-chap, Graphic Artists Guild NY, 82-87; vpres Graphic Artists Guild NY Inc, 85-87; pres, Digby Asn, 83-. *Awards:* Best Oil Painting, Actinolite Ann Exhib, Can, 63; Harness Racing Mus Award, Northeast Watercolor Soc Int Ann Exhib, 96; Best in Show, Orange Co, Day Exhib, 2005; Kate Mariel Diana award for Landscape Painting, Woodstock Annual Regional, 2013. *Bibliog:* Warwick Valley Dispatch, 6/2000; preview, Daily Freeman, 5/2002; Warwick Advertiser, 11/2002; Chronicle, 4/16/2004 & 6/22/2005. *Mem:* Exhib mem, Woodstock Artists Asn Mus, NY; exhib mem, Garrison Art Ctr, NY; Woodstock Artists Asn & Mus. *Media:* Oil, Acrylic, Mixed Media. *Interests:* writing fiction & poetry. *Publ:* Auth, May I Share With You?, HEP Press, Florida, NY, 2002, 2nd ed, 2004, 3rd ed, 2007; contribr, Riverine, Anthology of Hudson Valley Writers; contribr, Water Writes, Codhill Press, New Paltz, NY. *Dealer:* Flying Pig Gallery Sussex NJ; Art4business 161 Leverington Ave Philadelphia PA 19127; Woodstock Artists Asn & Mus Woodstock NY; Art Rent & Lease Gallery 16869 SW 65th Ave #308 Lake Oswego OR 97035. *Mailing Add:* 153 Montgomery St Goshen NY 10924

DI GIACINTO, SHARON
PAINTER

b 1960. *Study:* Ohio Univ, Athens, BFA, 81; Tex Woman's Univ, Denton, MFA, 83. *Work:* Hill Country Arts Found, Ingram, Tex; Glendale Pub Libr, Ariz; Paradise Valley Community Col, Phoenix, Ariz; Glendale Community Col, Ariz; Peru State Col, Nebr; City of Mesa Water Dept, Ariz. *Exhib:* solo exhib, Sun Cities Art Mus, Sun City, Ariz, 89, The Return to Animal Imagery, Visual Arts Gallery, Phoenix, Ariz, 90 & Peoria City Hall, Ariz, 95, Phoenix Col, Ariz, 2000, Heffernan Room, West Valley Art Mus, Surprise, Ariz, 2001, Fine Art Gallery, Phoenix Col, Ariz, 2000; two person exhib, Chandler Ctr Arts, Ariz, 91 & Casa Grande Art Mus, Ariz, 97; 23rd Ann Nat Exhib, San Bernardino Co Mus, Redlands, Calif, 88; 53rd Ann Nat Midyear Exhib, Butler Inst Am Art, Youngstown, Ohio, 89; Hoyt Nat Painting & Drawing Exhib, Hoyt Inst Fine Arts, New Castle, Pa, 89; Am Realism Competition, Parkersburg Art Ctr, WVa,

92; 35th Chautauqua Nat Exib Am Art, NY, 92; Stockton Nat Print & Drawing Exhib, Haggin Mus Art, Calif, 92; Beyond Drawing, Sheemer Art Ctr & Mus, Phoenix, 94; Drawn West Fourth Biennial Drawing Exhib, Norra Eccles Harrison Mus Art, Utah State Univ, Logan, 94; Primates in Art & Illustration, Univ Wis, Madison, 96; Good Night, Art After Dark, Ariz Mus Youth, Mesa, 97; Southwest Color Juried Exhib, Poway Ctr Performing Arts, Calif, 98. *Pos:* Co-chmn, Peoria Arts Comn, 88-91; juror Fine Arts Exhib, Ariz State Fair. *Teaching:* Instr, painting & color theory, Phoenix Col, 83-84; Instr, drawing & color theory, Glendale Community Col, 85-88. *Awards:* First Prize, St Hubert Giralda Animal Imagery Nat Exhib, 87; Best of Show, Don Ruffin Mem Statewide Exhib, 89; Glendale Municipal Art Gallery First Prize for Drawing and Prints, 31st Ann Juried Fine Arts Exhib, Glendale, Ariz, 94. *Mem:* Coll Art Asn of Am; Phoenix Art Mus. *Media:* Oil, Graphite, Prismacolor Pencil. *Publ:* Illusr: The Best of Colored Pencil 2, 94; The Best of Oil Painting, 96; The Best of Drawing and Sketching 98; Rockport Publ, Gloucester, Mass; Design of Dissent, Rockport Publ, 2005

DI GIACOMO, FRAN
PAINTER
b Miami, Ariz, Oct 24, 1944. *Study:* Scottsdale (Ariz) Artist's Sch, studies with Paul Leveille, 1985, David Leffel, 1995 & 96 & Howard Terpning, 2000. *Work:* Nat Ctr States Cts, Williamsburg, Va; Henry Wade Justice Ctr, Dallas; City Hall, Auburn, Maine; St Plus A Cath Ch, Dallas; Rasor Elem Sch, Plano, Tex. *Comn:* 2 portraits, Dallas Morning News, 1987 & 93; 13 telephone book covers, Area Wide Directory Co, Carrollton, Tex, 1988-94; 9 portraits, Haggar Apparel, Dallas, 1994; portrait Chief Justice Warren Burger, comn by Charles Noteboom, 1994; 3 portraits, Home Interiors & Gifts, Dallas, 1997-2001; portrait, President George W Bush, 2014; portrait, Pres George W Bush, 2014. *Exhib:* various ann exhibs, Oil Painters Am, 1992-2002; Women Artists of the West ann int, Las Vegas, 1992; ann nat, Acad Artists Asn, Springfield, Mass, 1992 & 94; Texas & Neighbors ann 5 state, Irving, Tex, 1995, 7 & 2000; ann nat, Salmagundi Club, NY, 1998. *Teaching:* pvt instruction. *Awards:* 1st Place, Asn Creative Artists, 1994, 2005, 2009; 1st Place, Plano Art Asn, 1996; 2nd Place, Richardson Civic Art Soc, 2002; Finalist, Int Artist Mag, 2009. *Bibliog:* Rasmi Simhan (auth), High profile, Dallas Morning News, 6/2002; Steve Carter (auth), Elegance articulated, Dallas Home Design, 10/2002; Charlotte Berney (auth), Gallery tour, Cowboys & Indians, 12/2002; Michael Granberry (auth), Humor is Her Weapon, Dallas Morning New, 2007. *Mem:* Am Soc Classical Realism; Oil Painters Am (signature); Asn Creative Artists (signature); Portrait Soc Am. *Media:* Oil. *Specialty:* Classical Realism. *Publ:* Contribr (book), The Best of Portrait Painting, North Light Books, 98; auth, I'd Rather do Chemo than Clean out the Garage: Choosing Laughter Over Tears, Brown Books, 2003; Contribr, Am Artist Magazine, 2004; Contribr, Am Artist, Still Life Highlights, 2005; Contribr, Heal Mag, Spring, 2008; Contribr, Beyond Mag, 2007; Coping Mag, 2007, 2008, 2009. *Dealer:* Southwest Gallery 4500 Sigma Dallas TX 75244; Gallerie Amsterdam Carmel CA. *Mailing Add:* 16806 Club Hill Dr Dallas TX 75248

DIGNAC, GENY (EUGENIA) M BERMUDEZ
SCULPTOR, ENVIRONMENTAL ARTIST
b Buenos Aires, Arg, June 8, 1932; US citizen. *Work:* Mus Mod Art, Cali, Colombia; Mus del Banco Cent Guayaquil, Ecuador; Latin Am Art Found, San Juan, PR; Fundacio Joan Miro, Barcelona, Spain; Palazzo Dei Diamanti, Ferrara, Italy. *Exhib:* Many one-women shows, 87-71 & produced 33 fire gestures, US, Europe & SAm, 1970-2000; Some More Beginnings, Exp in Art & Technol, Brooklyn Mus, NY, 68; IX Festival Art, Cali, Columbia, 69; Earth, Air, Fire, Water, Elements of Art, Boston Mus Fine Arts, 71; Arte de Sistema, Centro de Arte y Communicacion, Mus Mod Art, Buenos Aries, 71; III Biennial of Art Coltejer, Medellin, Colombia, 72. *Awards:* Uranus II (light & plastic sculpture), IX Festival of Art, Mus Mod Art, Cali, Colombia, 69. *Bibliog:* Charlotte Strifer Rubenstein (auth), American Women Artists, GK Hall & Co, 82, Del Pop Art A La Nueva Imagen; Jorge Glusberg (auth), Ediciones de Arte Gaglianome, Argentina, 85; Jules & Nancy G Heller (auths), Encyclopedia of XX Century North American Artists, Garland Publ, New York & London, 95; Douglas Davis (auth) Art and the Future, Praeger Pubs, 73; Robert Henkes (auth), Latin American Women Artists of The United States, McFarland & Co, Inc, NC & London, 99. *Media:* Light, Plastics, Fire, Temperatures. *Publ:* Kans Quart Vol 17 No 3, 85; Performance and Environmental Art, Kans Quarterly, 85. *Dealer:* Osuna Art, 7200 Wisconsin Ave, Bethesda, MD, 20814. *Mailing Add:* 4109 E Via Estrella Phoenix AZ 85028

DIKEMAN, DEANNA
PHOTOGRAPHER
b Sioux City, Iowa. *Study:* Purdue Univ, BS, 1976, MS, 1979. *Exhib:* Ninth Ann Kans City Municipal Art Comn Photog Competition, Nelson-Atkins Mus Art, 1988-89; Photospiva 90, Spiva Art Ctr, Joplin, Mo, 1990; Soc Contemp Photog, Kansas City, Mo, 1991; solo exhibs, Suburban Photographs, Baton Rouge Gallery, 1991, Rogers Gallery, 1997, Photographs, 1993, Relative Moments, Brady Commons Gallery, Columbia, Mo, 1995, Sioux City Art Ctr, 1995, Dolphin Gallery, 1996, Univ Gallery, Pittsburg State Univ, Kans, 2002, Univ Gallery, Baylor Univ, Waco, Tex, 1999, Wardrobe, Soc Contemp Photog, Kans City, 2006, Daum Mus Contemp Art, 2010; Photo Metro Tenth Ann Photog Contest, San Francisco, 1992; Baton Rouge en Blanc et Noir, Artists' Alliance, Lafayette, La, 1993; Leedy-Voulkos Art Ctr, Kans City, 1994; Southwest Mo State Univ, Springfield, 1996; Gallery of Art, Johnson Co Community Col, Overland Park, Kans, 1999; Missouri 50, Mo State Fair, Sedelia, 2000; Kansas City Flatfiles, H&R Block Artspace, Kans City Art Inst, 2001, 2004-05; Full Exposure, Trish Higgins Fine Art, Wichita, 2001; Tex Photog Soc, Austin, 2002; Sub Urbia, Hinsdale Ctr Arts, Ill, 2003; Photos@LulaMac, Lula Mac, Kans City, 2004; Domestic Diaries: Photographic Viewpoints, Rockford Art Mus, Ill, 2006; Mus Contemp Photog, Chicago, 2007-08. *Pos:* freelance photog, 1986-. *Teaching:* instr, Union Leisure Classes, La State Univ, 1992-94 & Craft Studio Classes, Univ Mo, 1995-2004. *Awards:* Individual Photogrs Fel, Aaron Siskind Found, 1996; Fel, Charlotte St Found, 2006; Fel, Visual Arts, US Artists, 2008. *Dealer:* Dolphin Gallery 1600 Liberty St Kans City Mo 64102. *Mailing Add:* Dolphin Gallery 1600 Liberty St Kansas City MO 64102

DIKER, CHARLES & VALERIE
COLLECTOR
b New York, NY. *Study:* Harvard Univ, BA, 56, MBA, 58. *Pos:* Managing partner, Diker Mgt LLC, currently. *Awards:* Named one of Top 200 Collectors, ARTnews Mag, 2004. *Mem:* Antique Tribal Art Dealers Asn Inc, George Gustav Heye Ctr (co-chmn bd, mem nat bd, currently); Nat Mus Am Indian. *Collection:* Native American Art; Modern & Contemporary Art

DILL, GUY
SCULPTOR, EDUCATOR
b Duval Co, Fla, May 30, 1946. *Study:* Chouinard Sch Art, Los Angeles, BFA, 70. *Work:* Mus Mod Art, Whitney Mus Am Art, NY; Calif State Univ, Long Beach; Long Beach Mus Art, Calif; Mus Contemp Art, Los Angeles, Calif; Newport Harbor Art Mus, Calif; LACMA; MOCA; Smithsonian Inst; Renwick Gallery; Guggenheim Mus. *Comn:* Prudential Ins Co, Canoga Park, Calif, 77; Fed Bldg, Huron, SD, 79; Pac Corp Towers, El Segundo, Calif, 86-87; Hughes Ctr, Las Vegas, Nev, 91; Sony Music Campus Arboretum in Santa Monica, Lowe Develop, Los Angeles, Calif, 92; and many pvt comns. *Exhib:* Solo exhibs include Flow Ace Gallery, Los Angeles, Calif, 82, 83, 84 & 86, Ace Contemp Exhibs, Los Angeles, Calif, 88, Ochi Gallery, Boise, Idaho, 88, Annex Gallery, San Diego, Calif, 89, San Diego Design Ctr, Calif, 89, Kay Kimpton Gallery, San Francisco, Calif, 90, Jan Turner Gallery, Los Angeles, Calif, 92, Denny Vaughn Gallery, Aspen, Colo, 95, Ellips Exhib, Brussels, Belgium, 96, 97 & 98, Bobbie Greenfield Gallery, Los Angeles, Calif, 97, 99, 2000, 2006, 2008, & Meyerovich Gallery, San Francisco, Calif, 2000, Peter Findlay Gallery, NY, 2006, Am Univ Mus, Wash DC, 2007, Greenfield Sacks Gallery, Los Angeles, Calif, Artzurd, Amsterdam, 2009, Zane Bennett Gallery, Santa Fe, NMex, 2010, Zane Bennett Gallery, Santa Fe, NMex, Meyerovich Gallery, San Fran, Calif, 212 Gallery, Aspen and Co, 2011, Miriam Shiell Fine Art, Toronto, Can, 2012; group exhibs include Guggenheim Mus, 71; Ace Gallery, Los Angeles, 71, 73 & 77; Pace Gallery, NY, 74 & 76; Biennial Show, Whitney Mus Am Art, 74; Sculpture Made in Place, Walker Art Ctr, Minneapolis, Minn, 76; Calif Sculpture Show, Bordeaux, France, 84 & Mannheim, Ger, West Bretton, Eng & Hovikodden, Norway, 85; Ooldonk Sculpture Exhib, Ooldonk Castle, Belg, 94. *Pos:* mem artists adv coun, Mus Contemp Art, Los Angeles, Calif, 81-82; mem selection panel, Calif Arts Coun, 82-83; mem adv coun arts, Cedars Sinai Med Center, Los Angeles, Calif, 85-2001; Harmon Ersner artist in res, Aspen Inst, 2010. *Teaching:* Instr, Sculpture Dept, Univ Calif, Los Angeles, 77-78 & head, 78-82; vis artist-lectr, Wright State Univ, Dayton, Ohio, 77. *Awards:* Theodoron Award, Guggenheim Mus, 71; Nat Endowment Arts Fel, 74 & 81; First Prize, Am Show, Chicago Inst Art, 74; artists award, Calif Heritage Mus, 97; Stars Design Lifetime Achievement Award, Pacific Design Center, 2000; Lifetime Achievement for Art Award, Stars of Design Lifetime, 2000. *Bibliog:* Peter Frank & Phyllis Tuchman (auths), Guy Dill, Black Innes (catalog), p 1-20; Jan Butterfield (auth), About the Collection Artists, Art Collection of Pacific Enterprises (catalog), p 36, 111 & 186; Jan Butterfield (auth), Guy Dill sculpture is about proof, Artspace, p 55-57 & 71, 9-10/92. *Mem:* Calif Art Coun; Cedars Sinai Med Ctr, Los Angeles, Calif (adv coun arts, 85-). *Media:* Mixed, Bronze, Marble, Steel, Aluminum. *Collection:* Mus Collections: Albright-Knox Mus, Buffalo, Long Beach Mus Art, Calif, LA Co Mus Art, Minneapolis Inst Art, Mus of Contemp Art, LA, MoMA NYC, Whitney Mus, NYC, MOCA, Los Angeles, Wadsworth Athenaeum, Hartford, Conn, Norton Simon Mus Art, Pasadena, Calif. *Dealer:* Peter Findlay NYC. *Mailing Add:* 1321 Innes Venice CA 90291

DILL, LADDIE JOHN
PAINTER, SCULPTOR
b Long Beach, Calif, Sept 14, 1943. *Study:* Chouinard Art Inst, BFA, 68. *Work:* Mus Mod Art, NY; Mus Contemp Art, Los Angeles; San Francisco Mus Mod Art, Calif; Smithsonian Inst, Washington; Oakland Mus Art, Calif; Chicago Art Inst. *Comn:* Glass fountain, Los Angeles Pub Libr, Cent Br, 93. *Exhib:* Solo exhibs, Pasadena Mus Mod Art, Calif, 71, Portland Univ Gallery, Ore, 71, Sonnabend Gallery, NY, 72, Calif Inst Technol, 82, Laica, 82, Charles Cowles, 83, Ochi Gallery, Sun Valley, Idaho, 89, 93, 95 & 99, Persons & Lindell Gallery, Helsinki, Finland, 89, Works Gallery S, Costa Mesa, Calif, 90 & 91, Conejo Valley Art Mus, Thousand Oaks, Calif, 92, Andrea Marquit Fine Arts, Boston, Mass, 94, Chac Mool Contemp Fine Art, Los Angeles, Calif, 96 & Bakersfield Mus Art, Calif, 99 & 2001; The Mod Era, San Francisco Mus Mod Art, 76 & Smithsonian Inst, Washington, 77; Calif Painting & Sculpture, San Francisco Mus Mod Art, 77; Painting of the 70's, Albright-Knox Gallery, Buffalo, 78-79; Corcoran Biennial, 83-84; Fredrick R Weisman Mus Art, Malibu, Calif, 97; Downey Art Mus, Calif, 98; Nev Mus Art, 98; Calif Ctr Arts, Escondido, 99; Norton Simon Mus, Pasadena, Calif, 99; Armory Ctr Arts, Pasadena, Calif, 99 & 2000. *Teaching:* Lectr painting, Univ Calif, Los Angeles, 75-88; chair visual arts, Santa Monica Col Design, Art & Archit, 90-. *Awards:* Nat Endowment Arts Grant, 75 & 82; Guggenheim Fel, 80. *Bibliog:* Robert Hughes (auth), Los Angeles, Time Mag, 71; Judy Goodman (auth), Laddie Dill new work, Arts Mag, 75; Michael Smith (auth), Laddie John Dill, Baxter Art Gallery, Calif Inst Technol, Pasadena, 78. *Media:* Cement, Polymer, Glass; Oil on Canvas

DILLOW, NANCY ELIZABETH ROBERTSON
ADMINISTRATOR, HISTORIAN
b Toronto, Ont, June 26, 1928. *Study:* Univ Toronto, BA. *Collection Arranged:* J E H MacDonald, RCA, 1873-1932 (with catalog), 65; Piet Mondrian and the Hague School of Landscape Painting (with catalog), 69; Saskatchewan: Art and Artists (with catalog), 71; Marilyn Levine-Donovan Chester (with catalog), 74; Frank Nulf (with catalog), 76; Transformation of Vision, H Eric Bergman (catalog), 83, Tony Tascona

(catalog), 84. *Pos:* From asst cur to cur exten & educ, Art Gallery Ont, 56-67; dir, Norman Mackenzie Art Gallery, 67-79; chief cur, Winnipeg Art Gallery, 80-86. *Teaching:* Prof hist Can art, Univ Regina, 72-79. *Mem:* Fel Can Mus Asn (coun, 67-70). *Res:* Canadian art history. *Mailing Add:* 99 Estelle Ave Toronto ON M2N 5H4 Canada

DI MEO, DOMINICK
PAINTER, SCULPTOR
b Niagara Falls, NY, Feb 1, 1927. *Study:* Art Inst Chicago, four year dipl, 50, BFA, 52; Univ Iowa, MFA, 53. *Work:* Art Inst Chicago; Whitney Mus Am Art, NY; Ill Bell Tel co, Chicago; Univ Mass, Amherst; Nat Collection Am Art, Smithsonian Inst; Elmhurst Coll, Elmhurst, Ill; De Paul Univ, Chicago; Smart Mus, Chicago; Hammer Mus, Los Angeles, Calif. *Exhib:* Ann Exhib Contemp Am Painting, Whitney Mus Am Art, 67-68; Fantasy & Figure, Am Fedn Arts, NY & Traveling Show, 68-69; Violence in Recent Am Art, Mus Contemp Art, Chicago, 68-69; The Crowd: Exhibit of Sculpture, Paintings & Graphics, Arts Club Chicago, 69; Visions/Painting & Sculpture: Distinguished Alumni 1945-Present, Art Inst Chicago, 76; 16th Joan Miro Int Drawing Prize Competition, Barcelona, Spain & Sala de Cult de la Caja de Ahorros de Navarra, Pamplona, 77-80; 100 Artists--100 Yrs, Alumni of the Sch of Art Inst Chicago, Centennial Exhib, Art Inst Chicago, 79-80; Momento Mori, Centro Cult/Arte Contemp, Mexico City, Mex, 86-87; Art Inst Chicago, 89-90; Pa Acad Fine Arts, Philadelphia, 2006. *Teaching:* Instr, Chicago Acad Fine Arts, 67-69; vis artist, Art Inst Chicago, 77. *Awards:* Guggenheim Mem Found Fel Graphics, 72-73; Nat Endowment Arts Sculpture Fel, 82-83. *Bibliog:* Whitney Halstead (auth), Introd, In: Di Meo, Work: 1959-1966, Galaxie, 67. *Media:* Mixed. *Dealer:* Corbett vs Dempsey Chicago. *Mailing Add:* 429 Broome St New York NY 10013

DINC, ALEV NECILE
PAINTER, DESIGNER
b Turkey; US citizen. *Study:* Inst Technol, Ankara, Turkey, 56-61; Ridgewood Art Sch, NJ, 68; Fashion Inst Technol, New York, 69. *Work:* Turkish Embassy, NY; Kismet Furniture, Paterson, NJ; NY Sch Interior Design; Clifton H S; Osterreiche Kommunal Kreditbank, Vienna. *Teaching:* Tchr art, Clifton & Wayne H S. *Awards:* First Prize, Turkey, 60; Danielle Ruebel, Mental Health Orgn, 89. *Bibliog:* Abraham Ilein (auth), Art Review, Artspeak, 87; Ernie Garcia; Robert F Lanzetti; Films by Matt Bora, Eric Rubel. *Mem:* Salute to Women in the Arts; Clifton Asn Artist; Art for Mental Health; Studio Montclair NJ. *Media:* Oil, Acrylic; Watercolor. *Publ:* Auth, Artists in the 1990's, Manhattan Arts Int Mag, 94; Art Ctr artist, interview with John Sgull, Channel 24 Cable, 93; contribr, Healing Art, Cable TV, Newark, NJ, 93; Spanish Cable TV, Channel 47, Spanish Newspaper, Secaucus, NJ, 96; N T N Network, Cable TV, NJ, 97; USA Turkish Times, 2006; Herald Newspaper, 2001; Dateline Jour. *Mailing Add:* 90 Day St Apt G-4 Clifton NJ 07011

DINGLE, KIM
PAINTER
b Pomona, Calif, 1951. *Study:* Calif State Univ, BFA, 1988; Claremont Grad Sch, MFA, 1990. *Exhib:* Solo exhibs incl Closet of Modern Art, Calif State Univ, 1991, Kim Light Gallery, Los Angeles, 1992, Jason Rubell Gallery, Miami Beach, Fla, 1993, Jack Tilton Gallery, 1994, Blum & Poe, Santa Monica, 1995, 1997, Otis Gallery, 1995-96, Gian Enzo Sperone, Rome, 1998, Sperone Westwater, NY, 1998, 2000, 2007, Galleria Cardi, Milan, 2002; group exhibs incl Richard/Bennett Gallery, Los Angeles, 1990, 1991; Parker/Zanic Gallery, Los Angeles, 1991; Sue Spaid Fine Art, Los Angeles, 1991; Asher/Faure Gallery, Los Angeles, 1992; Biennial Exhib, Corcoran Gallery Art, 1993; Mus Contemp Art, Miami, 1995; Mus Contemp Art, Chicago, 1997; La Mus Modern Art, 1997; San Francisco Mus Modern Art, 1999; Whitney Biennial, Whitney Mus Am Art, NY, 2000; Exit Art, NY, 2000; Mus Contemp Art, San Diego, 2002; Laguna Art Mus, Calif, 2003; Denver Art Mus, 2003; Lightbox, Los Angeles, 2005. *Media:* Oil on Vellum. *Dealer:* Galleria Cardi Corso di Porta Nuova 38 20121 Milan Italy; Art Resource Group 20351 Irvine Ave Santa Ana Heights CA 92707; Sperone Westwater 257 Bowery New York NY 10002. *Mailing Add:* c/o Sperone Westwater Gallery 257 Bowery New York NY 10002

DINGUS, PHILLIP RICK
PHOTOGRAPHER
b Appleton City, Mo, Jan 3, 1951. *Study:* Univ Calif, Santa Barbara, BA, 73; Univ NMex, MA, 77, MFA, 81. *Work:* Ctr Creative Photog, Tucson, Ariz; Mus Mod Art, Metrop Mus Art, NY; San Francisco Mus Mod Art; Mus Fine Arts, Houston, Tex; Buddy Holly Ctr Fine Arts Gallery, Lubbock, Tex; plus many others. *Exhib:* James Gallery, Houston Int Foto Fest, 88 & 90; Phoenix Art Mus, Ariz, 90; Dine'tah-Hajiinei: Place of Emergence, SW Mus, Los Angeles, Calif, 91; Between Home & Heaven, Smithsonian Inst, Washington, DC, 92; FotoFest, Houston Ctr for Photog, 2006; plus many others. *Teaching:* Grad Teaching asst art photogr & fundamental, Univ NMex, 76-79; lectr photogr drawing & art hist, NMex Tech, 79-81; vis lectr, Univ Colo, Boulder, 81-82; asst prof, Tex Tech Univ, 82, assoc prof, 88, prof 95-. *Awards:* Nat Endowment Art/Mid Am Art Alliance Reg Fel, 87; plus many others. *Bibliog:* Michael Costello (auth), Alternate views: A recent film by Roger Sweet and Rick Dingus, Artspace, summer 78. *Mem:* Soc Photog Educ. *Media:* Photography. *Publ:* Auth, The Photographic Artifacts of Timothy O'Sullivan, 82, Second View: The Rephotographic Survey Project, 84, Marks in Place, 88, Between Home & Heaven: Contemporary American Landscape Photo, 92, NMAA, Smithsonian, Univ NMex Press; auth, Techne: A Candid Look, Spot, 2000. *Mailing Add:* 7802 Louisville Ave Lubbock TX 79423-1726

DINKIN, LARRY
PAINTER
b Brooklyn, NY, 1943. *Study:* Pratt Inst; City Coll NY; Sch Visual Arts. *Exhib:* Solo shows incl Jamaica Plain Art Ctr, Mass, 1988, Gallery Stendhal, NY, 1999, 2001, Gallery Moos, Toronto, 2000, Westwood Gallery, NY, 2002, Flint Inst Art, Mich, 2005, Dayton Art Inst, Ohio, 2006, Lyman Allyn Art Mus, Conn, 2007; group shows incl Artwalk, NY, 1999; Gallery Stendhal, NY 1999, 2000, 2001; Expo, NY, 2000; Art Company, Ohio, 2000; Westwood Gallery, NY, 2002; 511 Gallery, NY, 2004; represented in permanent collections Flint Inst Art, Mich, Corcoran Mus Art, Wash, DC, Milwaukee Art Mus, Denver Mus Contemp Art, Rockford Mus Art, Ill, Fine Arts Mus San Francisco, The White House; Lighthouse Ctr for Arts, Tequesta, FLa, 2006. *Awards:* Clio Award; Nassau Cty Art League Juried Exhib. *Bibliog:* Article, Elements Mag, winter 2003; article, Palm Beach Daily News, 5/2004; articles, Art of the Times, 10/2004 & 10/2005; article, Art News, 4/2006; article, Art Daily, 8/2006. *Media:* Oil on Linen

DINKINS, STEPHANIE
SCULPTOR
Study: Syracuse Univ, NY, BS (Advert & Marketing), 1986; Int Ctr Photog, New York, 1995; Md Inst Coll Art, Baltimore, MFA (Photog), 1997; Whitney Mus Am Art, New York, Independent Study Prog, 1997-98. *Exhib:* Solo exhibs include Newhouse Gallery, Snug Harbor Cult Ctr, Staten Island, NY, 1994, Found & Ctr Contemp Arts, Czech Republic, 2001, Soap Factory, Minneapolis, 2005, Glyndor Gallery,Wave Hill, Bronx, NY, 2006, Jamaica Queens, NY, 2007; group exhibs include Cross Sections, Gordon Parks Gallery, New York, 1995; Kongo Criollo, Taller Boricua Gallery, New York, 1998; Tisch Sch Arts, NY Univ, New York, 2000; Face to Face, Long Island Mus, NY, 2003; Superstition, DC Arts Ctr, Washington, 2005; Diagram & Trace, Main Gallery, Univ Tex Dallas, 2005; Tuttle Gallery, Baltimore, 2007; If It Ain't Broke, Gallery 138, New York, 2007. *Teaching:* Assoc Prof Art, Stony Brook Univ, NY, 2005-Present. *Awards:* Merit Pay Award, Art Dept, Stony Brook Univ, NY, 2003, 2005. *Mailing Add:* Stony Brook Univ Dept of Art Staller Center for the Arts Stony Brook NY 11794-5400

DINNERSTEIN, HARVEY
PAINTER
b Brooklyn, NY, Apr 3, 1928. *Study:* With Moses Soyer, 44-46; Art Students League, 46-47; Tyler Art Sch, Temple Univ, cert art, 50. *Hon Degrees:* Lyme Acad Fine Arts, Old Lyme, Conn, DHL, 98. *Work:* Metrop Mus Art (Lehman Collection) & Martin Luther King Labor Ctr, New York; New Britain Mus Art, Conn; Fleming Mus, Univ Vt, Burlington; Nat Mus Am Art, Washington, DC; Butler Inst Am Art, Youngstown, Ohio; Nat Acad Design, NY; Whitney Mus Am Art, NY; and others. *Exhib:* Contemp Am Paintings, Whitney Mus Am Art, New York, 55 & Contemp Drawings, 64; Childe Hassam Award Exhib, Am Acad & Inst of Arts & Lett, New York, 74, 78 & 87; Living Am Artists & the Figure, Pa State Univ Mus Art, Univ Park, 74; 3 Centuries of Am-Nude, NY Cult Ctr, 76; Bicentennial Exhib of Am Illus, NY Hist Soc, 76; solo exhib, Sindin Galleries, NY, 83; retrospective, Butler Inst Am Art, Youngstown, Ohio, 94; Wunderlich Galleries, New York, 97; Frey Norris Gallery, San Francisco, Calif, 2003, 2005 & 2008; plus many others. *Pos:* Academician, Nat Acad Design, New York, 74. *Teaching:* Instr drawing & painting, Sch Visual Arts, New York, 65-80, Nat Acad Design, 75-92, Art Students League, 80-. *Awards:* Temple Gold Medal, Pa Acad Fine Art, 50; Purchase Award, Am Acad & Inst of Arts & Lett, 74, 78 & 87; Ranger Purchase Award, Nat Acad Design, 76; Obrig Prize, Nat Acad Design, 86; Issac N. Maynard prize, Samuel F.B. Morse Medal, Nat Acad Design, 2003. *Bibliog:* Susan E Meyer (auth), 20 Figure Painters and How They Work, Watson-Guptill, 79; How We Lived, Esquire Mag 50th Anniversary Issue, 6/83; The Seasons, Am Artist Mag, 8/83. *Mem:* Audubon Artists; Allied Artists; Nat Acad. *Media:* Oil, Pastel. *Publ:* Coauth, New look at protest, the eight since 1908, Art News, 2/58; illusr, A Portfolio of Drawings, Kenmore Press, 68; illusr & auth, Harvey Dinnerstein--Artist at Work, Watson-Guptill, 78; On pastel, Am Artist Mag, 5/88; Int Artist Magazine, 12/05-1/06; collabr (with Burt Silverman), Drawings of the Montgomery Bus Boycott 1956, Montgomery Mus Fine Arts, 2007; Underground Together, the Art and Life of Harvey Dinnerstein, Chronicle Bks, 2008; Harvey Dinnerstein-The Self Portrait, Am Artist Mag, 2011. *Mailing Add:* 933 President St Brooklyn NY 11215

DINNERSTEIN, LOIS
HISTORIAN, WRITER
b New York, NY, Oct 24, 1932. *Study:* NY Univ Wash Sq Col, BA, 53; NY Univ Inst Fine Arts, MA, 60; City Univ New York Grad Ctr, PhD, 79. *Pos:* Res cur, Benjamin Sonnenberg Collection, NY, 57-58, Daniel & Rita Fraad Collection, NY, 62-63 & Montclair Art Mus, NJ, 75-76. *Teaching:* Instr art hist, Vassar Col, 59-61, City Univ NY, Brooklyn Col, 64-77; adj prof, Brooklyn Ctr, Long Island Univ, 82-84; adj prof, Am Civilization Prog, Grad Sch Arts & Sci, New York Univ, 88; lect, Art Students League, 90-91. *Awards:* Rockefeller Found fel, City Univ New York, 77. *Mem:* Asn Historians Am Art. *Res:* Eighteenth and 19th century American art. *Publ:* Auth, Thomas Eakins' Crucifixion as Perceived by Mariana Griswold Van Rensselaer, 5/79, The iron worker and King Solomon: Some images of labor in American art, 9/79, Beyond revisionism: Henry Lerolle's The Organ, 1/80 & The industrious housewife: Some images of labor in American art, 4/81, Arts Mag; John Singleton Copley's Portrait of Elizabeth Allen Stevens (art mus catalog), Res Supplement, Montclair, 79; Artists in their studios, Am Heritage, 2/83; When Liberty was Controversial, In Support of Liberty: European Paintings at the 1883 Statue of Liberty Pedestal Fund Art Loan Exhibition (exhib catalog), Parrish Art Mus, Southampton & Nat Acad Design, New York, 86; and others. *Mailing Add:* 933 President St, 2nd Fl Brooklyn NY 11215-1603

DINNERSTEIN, SIMON A
PAINTER
b Brooklyn, NY, Feb 16, 1943. *Study:* Brooklyn Mus Art Sch, with David Levine & Louis Grebenak, 64-67; City Coll New York, BA, 65; Hochschule für Bildende Kunst, Kassel, Ger, Fulbright fel, 70-71. *Work:* Minn Mus Art, St Paul; Palmer Mus of Art, Penn St Univ; Nat Mus Am Art, Smithsonian Inst; Martin Luther King Jr Labor Ctr, Nat Acad Design, NY; and others. *Comn:* Staempfli Gallery, NY, 79 & 88. *Exhib:* Solo exhibs, Am Acad in Rome, 77, New Sch, 81 & 93; St Paul's Sch, Concord, NH, 91; An Am in Rome, NJ Ctr Visual Arts, Summit, NJ, 94; ACA Gallery, NY, 99; Bread &

Roses Gallery, NY, 99; Walton Arts Ctr, Univ Ark, 99; Gallery 1199, 85 & 99; Texarkana Regl Arts Ctr, Tex/Ak, 2000; Tenri Cult Ctr, NY & German Counsil General, New York, 2011. *Teaching:* Instr painting, Brooklyn Mus Art Sch, 71-72; instr painting & drawing, The New Sch, New York, 75-; instr, New York City Tech Col, 79-88; lectr, Am Acad Rome, 77-78, US Info Serv, Spain, 79, Pa State Univ, 84, Port Washington Pub Libr, Long Island, 90, St Paul's Sch, NH, 91 & Nassau Community Col, 94; vis prof, Pratt Inst, 86-87; Instr, drawing & painting, New Sch/Parsons Sch, NY, 75-2005. *Awards:* Fulbright Fel, Ger, 70-71; Ralph Fabri Prize, Nat Acad Design, 97 & Bertelson Prize, 98; Artists Fel, New York Found Arts, 87; Rome Prize Fel, Am Acad in Rome, 76-78; Ingram Merrill Award for Painting, 78-79; Cannon Prize, Nat Acad Design, 88; plus others. *Bibliog:* The Art of Simon Dinnerstein (monogr), Univ Ark Press, 268 pps, 140 reproductions, 90; Sandy Brooke (auth), Hooked on Drawing: Illustrated Lessons & Exercises for Grades 4 and up, Prentice Hall, 96; Cynthia Dantzic (auth), Drawing Dimensions, Prentice Hall; Roy Proctor (auth) Exploring the edge: no slave to fashion, artist draws us into other states of mind, Richmond Times, 2000. *Mem:* Soc Fel Am Acad Rome; Nat Acad Design. *Media:* Miscellaneous, Oil, Drawing, Engravings. *Specialty:* Contemporary Art. *Publ:* Auth, (monograph), The Art of Simon Dinnerstein, Univ Ark Press, 90; Anthology: Drawing from Life, Harcourt, Brace & Jovanovich, 92 & 96; Centennial Directory, Am Acad Rome, 95; Community of Creativity: A Century of MacDowell Colony Artists, Currier Gallery Art, 96; Simon Dinnerstein: A Retrospective, Ont Rev, 98; monograph, Simon Dinnerstein: Paintings and Drawings, Hudson Hills Press, 99; monograph, Simon Dinnerstein: survey of the artist's work, Hanging Loose Press, NY; St Ann's Review, 2000; Brooklyn Jews, 2001; 100 New York Painters, 2006; The Suspension of Time: Reflections on Simon Dinnerstein & the Fulbright Triptych. *Mailing Add:* 415 First St Brooklyn NY 11215

D'INNOCENZO, NICK
SCULPTOR, DIGITAL PAINTER, GRAPHIC DESIGNER
b Rochester, NY, Dec 12, 1934. *Study:* State Univ NY Buffalo, BS (art educ), 60; Cranbrook Acad Art, MFA (sculpture/design), 63. *Work:* State Univ NY Buffalo; Smith-Corona-Marchant Corp, Syracuse, NY; private collections in NY, Mich & Fla. *Comn:* 14' Welded bronze sculptures (2), State Univ NY, 12' bronze over steel sculpture, Oswego Co Savings Bank; 20', three ton clocktower, 80' fountain, State Univ NY Oswego; numerous small-scale sculptures for individual collectors. *Exhib:* Invitational Craftsmen & various juried exhibs, Munsen-Williams Mus Art, Utica, NY; Everson Mus Art (nat, juried), Syracuse, NY, 75; NY State Fairgrounds, Syracuse, 81 & 89; Pyramid Gallery, Rochester, NY, 96; Oswego Invitational, 96; Arts and Cult, 2004; Artists Pallete, 2004; Arnot Mus Art, Elmira, NY, 2005; Artists of NY State (juried), Schweinfurth Mus Art, Auburn, NY, 06; and numerous solo exhibs, 1963-2004. *Pos:* Graphic designer, Smith-Corona-Marchant Corp, Syracuse, NY, 68; designer, multi-room computer complexes with unique furniture & early ergonomic stations, State Univ NY. *Teaching:* Prof sculpture & design, State Univ NY, 63-2001. *Awards:* Chancellor's Award for Excellence in Teaching, State Univ NY, 76; Best of show, NY Oswego Invitational, 96; 1st Prize Sculpture, NY State Fair, 96 & 2nd Prize Graphics, 97; 1st Prize Graphics, Pyramid Artists, Rochester, NY, 97; Artist of the Yr, Oswego, 2004; 1st Prize, juried exhib, Rochester, Mich; 1st prize, relig art exhib, Rochester, NY. *Mem:* Int Sculpture Ctr. *Media:* Steel, Mixed Media; Computer-imagery. *Collection:* State University New York, Buffalo; Smith-Corona Corporation, Syracuse, New York. *Mailing Add:* Edwards Cir Rd 3 Oswego NY 13126

DINSMORE, JOHN NORMAN
EDUCATOR, ADMINISTRATOR
b Trenton, Mo, Jan 18, 1940. *Study:* Truman State Univ, BS, 63; Univ Northern Colo, MA, 68; Univ Kans, EdD, 78. *Work:* Sheldon Mem Art Gallery, Lincoln, Nebr; Univ Nebr at Kearney; Univ Northern Colo; Mountain State Telephone, Denver, Colo. *Comn:* Weaving, Broadway State Bank, Council Bluffs, Iowa, 75; weaving, First National Bank, Kearney, Nebr, 76; graphic design, The Cellar Shoe Store, Geneva, Nebr, 77; weaving, Nye, Hervert, Jorgensen & Watson Law, Kearney, Nebr, 79; weaving, Prof Bldg (Med), Gillette, Wyo, 83. *Exhib:* Fibers 1977, SW Mo State Univ, Cape Girardeau, Nebr, 77; Nebr Crafts Exhib, Sheldon Gallery, Lincoln, Nebr, 77; Nebr Art Educators Show, Elder Gallery, Lincoln, Nebr, 87; Nebr Crafts Coun, Mus Nebr Art, Kearney, 91; Fac Exhib, Mus Nebr Art, Kearney, 95, 19th Ann Nebr Art Educators Juried Exhib, 2001, UNK Art Dept Fac Exhb, 2003; Phelps Fine Art Gallery, Hastings, Nebr, 97. *Teaching:* Prof fibers & art educ, Univ Nebr Kearney, 68-, dept chairperson, 93-2001. *Awards:* Second Place, Midwest Weavers Conf, 74; 3-D Art Educators Award, Nebr Art Teachers Asn, 86. *Mem:* Nat Art Educ Asn; Nebr Art Teachers Asn (pres & vpres, 92-93); Nat Educ Asn; Handweavers Guild Am; Midwest Weavers Asn. *Media:* Fiber. *Res:* Exploration of patterns through weaving. *Publ:* Auth, Conceptual Crafts, Craft Range, 79; Nebraska midwife, Nebr Crafts, 83; The American avant-garde: A comparison of quilt & painting design, 83, Design influences on Hawaiian appliqued quilts, 85 & Amish quilts: A comparison of the old and the new, 89, Platte Valley Rev. *Mailing Add:* Univ Nebr Dept of Art/Art History 25th St & 9th Ave Kearney NE 68849

DINSMORE, STEPHEN PAUL
PAINTER
b Omaha, Nebr, July 7, 1952. *Study:* Univ Nebr, Lincoln, BA, 74. *Work:* Lydon Fine Art, Chicago, Ill; William Havv Gallery, Denver, Colo; Arden Gallery, Boston, Mass; Groveland Gallery, Minn; Kiechel Fine Arts, Lincoln, Nebr. *Comn:* Fairmount Hotel, Kansas City, Mo; numberous corporate and private commissions. *Exhib:* Robert Kidd Gallery, Birmingham, Mich, 2000 & 2002; William Harv Gallery, 2001; Arden Gallery, Boston, Ma, 2001 & 2005; Haydon Gallery, Lincoln, Nebr, 2001; William Harv Fine Arts, Denver, Colo, 2004; Lydon Fine Art, Chicago, Ill, 2001 & 2003 - 2005; Anderson O'Brien Gallery, Omaha, 2004. *Awards:* Artist Residency, Bemis Found, Omaha, Nebr, 92. *Media:* Oil on Canvas. *Publ:* Reproduction, Country Home Mag, 6/91; Article, Chicago Tribune, 4/2/92; Article, Rocky Mountain News, 12/4/99; New American Paintings, 97; Grand Image Poster, Seattle; Boston Globe, 7/23/01; Lincoln Journal Star, 4/18/04; Phoenix House and Garden, Fall 04. *Mailing Add:* 2303 Harrison Ave Lincoln NE 68502

DIPASQUALE, PAUL ALBERT
SCULPTOR, LECTURER
b Perth Amboy, NJ, June 29, 1951. *Study:* Univ Va, BA with hons, 73; Va Commonwealth Univ, MFA (sculpture), 77. *Work:* Va Hist Soc, Richmond; Black His Mus of Va, Richmond; Nat Air & Space Mus, Smithsonian Inst, Washington, DC; Baltimore Aquarium, Md; Billings/Rockefeller Mus, Woodstock, Vt; Verizon Inc; AT&T Inc; Dominion Resources. *Comn:* Native Am monument, Richmond Metro Authority, Va, 86; Headman monument, Va Comn for Arts, Richmond, 91; Arthur Ashe monument, Va Heroes Inc, Richmond, 96; Arthur Ashe Mem medallion, ESPN-Disney Corp, Washington, DC, 2000; Oliver Hill monument bronze bust, Richmond Convention Ctr Authority, 2001; Dr Martin Luther King Monument, King Found, Hopewell, Va; Neptune Monument, Neptune Festival, Va Beach, Va. *Exhib:* Paul Dipasquale, NC Mus Art, Raleigh, 84; Stars, Nat Air & Space Mus, Washington, DC, 91; Civil Rights - Virginia, Black Hist Mus Va, Richmond, 98; Story of Virginia, Va Hist Soc, Richmond, 99. *Pos:* vis artist, Arts Coun Richmond, Va, 89-92 & Am Acad Rome, Italy, 96 & 98; vis artist pub sculpture, Va Commonwealth Univ, Richmond, 87-98; bd dir, Black Hist Mus Va, Richmond, 96-98. *Teaching:* instr fine arts, N Va Community Col, Annandale, 79-81; vis prof sculpture, Col of William & Mary, Williamsburg, Va, 91-92. *Awards:* Fathers in Prison Grant, Fed Weed and Seed Program, 96; Richmonder of the Year, Style Mag, 96; Social Justice Award, Va Commonwealth Univ Dept Social Work, 2000. *Bibliog:* Ben Forgey (auth), Voyages of the Indian sculpture, Washington Post, 7/19/87; Scott Mason (auth), The monumental debate (doc), Cent Va Television, 96; S Driggs & RG Wilson, Richmond's monument ave, Univ NC Press, 3/1/01. *Mem:* NSS, NY; Int Sculpture Ctr, Washington, DC; Appointed mem, Urban Design Comt, Va. *Media:* Bronze. *Publ:* contribr, Working With Plastics, Time Life Books, 82; contribr, City Secrets Rome, Little Book Room, New York, 2000; contribr, City Secrets Florence, Venice and the Towns of Italy, Little Book Room. New York, 2001. *Dealer:* Addison/Ripley Fine Art 1670 Wisconsin Ave NW Washington DC 20007; Bazzanti Gallery Florence Italy; Rebecca Cross Gallery Washington DC. *Mailing Add:* 1408 National St Richmond VA 23231-1533

DIPERNA, FRANK PAUL
PHOTOGRAPHER, INSTRUCTOR
b Pittsburgh, Pa, Feb 4, 1947. *Study:* Ctr of the Eye, Aspen, Colo, with Gary Winogrand, 71; Visual Studies Workshop, Rochester, NY, with Ralph Gibson, Syl Labrot, Nathan Lyons & Alice Wells, 71-72; Goddard Col, MA (photog), 77. *Work:* Polaroid (Europa), Amsterdam, The Neth; Libr Cong, Smithsonian Inst, Corcoran Gallery Art, Washington; Bibliot Nat, Paris; Nat Mus Am Art, Washington; Metrop Mus Art, NY; Ctr Creative Photography, Univ Ariz, Tucson. *Comn:* State of Art Inc, Vancouver. *Exhib:* Solo exhibs, Bushes, 74 & Color Photographs, 77, Corcoran Gallery Art, Photographs, Diane Brown Gallery, Washington, 77 & 81, Color Photographs, Sebastian Moore Gallery, Denver, Colo, 78, Kathleen Ewing Gallery, Washington, 82 & 84, Color Landscape Photographs, Rice Univ, Houston, Tex, 86 & The Presence of Things, Kathleen Ewing Gallery, Washington, DC, 98 & 2000, In The Studio, Kathleen Ewing Gallery, 2006; Va Photogr, Va Mus Fine Arts, 73 & 75; One of a Kind (traveling exhib), Mus Fine Arts, Houston, Univ Ariz, Los Angeles Inst Contemp Arts & Art Inst Chicago; Eye of the West: Camera Vision & Cult Consensus, Hayden Gallery, Mass Inst Technol, Cambridge, 77; Washington Photog: Images of the Eighties, 82, Terra Sancta, (with catalog) 90, Corcoran Gallery Art, Washington; Light Work, Photog Over the 70s and 80s, Everson Mus Art, Syracuse, NY, 85; Comfort Gallery, Haverford Col, Pa, 86; Rice Univ, Houston, Tex, 86; Kathleen Ewing Gallery, Washington, 89 & 94; Between Home and Heaven, Contemp Am Landscape Photog, Nat Mus Am Art, Washington; Carnegie Mus Art (with catalog), Pittsburgh, Pa; Longwood Invitational, Virginia Photographers (with catalog), Longwood Ctr Visual Arts, Farmville, Va, 97; Mary, McLean (Va) Project for the Arts, 2000; Southern Exposure Contemp Photo in Virginia, Mus Western Va, Roanoke, 2002; Images of Italy Kathleen Ewing Gallery, 2004; Road Trip Gallery, Smithsonian Mus Am Art; Kathleen Ewing Gallery, 2006, 2007, 2008; Mostra, Contona, Italy, 2008; 38th Cortona Exhib, Univ Ga, 2009; 28th Gala Auction, Am Univ, Katzen Arts Ctr, DC, 2009; One Hour Photo, Am Univ, Katzen Arts Ctr, 2010; Civilian Art Projects, Wash DC, 2012; Catalyst, 35 Yrs, Washington Project for the Arts, American Univ Katzer Arts Ctr, Wash DC, 2010; Deep Element: Photography at the Beach, Corcoran Gallery of Art, Wash DC, 2012; Washington Art Matters: 1940s-1980s, American Univ, Kutzen Arts Ctr, 2013. *Pos:* artist in res, Vt Studio Center, 2002; artist in res, Coll Art and Design, San Miguel de Allende, Mex. *Teaching:* Instr photog, Northern Va Community Col, Alexandria, 73-78; instr photog, Corcoran Col Art & Design, 74-78, asst prof & chmn dept, 78-81, asst prof, 81-84, assoc prof & chmn dept, 84-87, assoc prof, 87-94, prof, 94-, prof, chmn photg dept, 99-2001; vis prof, Univ Ga, study abroad Cortona, Ital, 2005, 2008; prof photog, Ruesch Family Found, 2008. *Awards:* Cert of Distinction, Va Photog, 73; Artist-in-Residence Fel, Camargo Found, Cassis, France, Lightwork, Syracuse, NY, 82. *Bibliog:* David Taunous (auth), Frank DiPerna at the Corcoran, Mark Power at Diane Brown, Art in Am, 1-2/78; Owen Edwards (auth), SX-70: Land's painless epiphany machine, Sat Rev, 7/22/78; Jo Ann Lewis (auth), Galleries, The Washington Post, 4/89; Ferdinand Protzman (auth), Galleries, Washington Post, 9/2000; Jessica Dawson (auth), Galleries, Wash Post, 4/29/2006; Nord Wennerstrom (auth), Frank Di Perna, Artforum, 2006. *Mem:* AAUP. *Media:* Traditional & Digital Color Photographs. *Publ:* Auth, Color Photographs, Corcoran Gallery Art, 77; One of a Kind: Recent Polaroid Color Photography, Godine; SX-70, Lustrum Press, 79; contribr, Washington Photography: Images of the Eighties (catalog), Corcoran Gallery Art, 82; Between Home & Heaven: Contemporary Am Landscape Photography, Nat Mus Am Art, 92; Contact Sheet 97, 25th Anniversary Ed, Lightwork, 98; Washington Art Matters: Art Life in the Capitol 1940-1980, Washington Arts Mus. *Dealer:* Civilian Art Projects 1019 7th St NW Washington DC 20001. *Mailing Add:* 37559 Allder School Rd Purcellville VA 20132

DIRKS, JOHN
SCULPTOR, CARTOONIST
b New York, NY, Nov 2, 1917. *Study:* Art Students League, New York, 36; Boston Sch Practical Art; Yale Univ, BA, 39; Columbia Univ Painting & Sculpture, 45. *Work:* Ogunquit Mus Art. *Comn:* Over 400 pvt comns in 40 states (sculptures), 66-. *Pos:* Cartoonist assisting his father on "The Captain and the Kids" comic, better known as "Katzenjammer Kids", took over completely for father, 1958.; Dir, Ogunquit Mus Am Art, 88-98. *Mem:* Ogunquit Art Asn, Maine, 60-92; Lyme Acad Fine Arts, Old Lyme, Conn (trustee 83-91). *Media:* Non-Ferrous Metal with water. *Dealer:* Ogunquit Mus Am Art 181 Shore Rd Box 815 Ogunquit ME 03907

DI SUVERO, MARK
PAINTER, SCULPTOR
b Shanghai, China, 1933; arrived in US, 1941. *Study:* San Francisco City Coll, 1953-54; Univ Calif, BA, 1956. *Work:* Wadsworth Atheneum, Hartford, Conn; Whitney Mus Am Art; Hirshhorn Mus; Dallas Mus Fine Arts; Art Inst Chicago. *Exhib:* Solo exhibs, Hill Gallery, Birmingham, Mich, 1996, Weigand Gallery, Belmont, Calif, 1996, Galerie Jeanne-Bucher, Paris, France, 1996, Gagosian Gallery, 1997, Orange Co Mus Art, 1998 & Hiroshima Mus Contemp Art, Japan, 1998, Hiroshima Mus Contemp Art, 1998, John Berggruen Gallery, San Francisco, 1999, Danese, NY City, 2000, Gagosian Gallery, NY City, 2001, Paula Cooper Gallery, NY City, 2002, 2003, Albion, London, 2004, Tasende Gallery, 2010; Group exhib, Continuity and Change, Wadsworth Atheneum, 1962; Contemp Ann, Art Inst Chicago, 1963; Contemp Am Sculpture Section I, Whitney Mus Am Art, 1966; 1966 Ann Exhib: Contemp Am Sculpture & Prints, Whitney Mus Am Art, 1966; Park Place Show, Hayden Gallery, Mass Inst Technol, 1966; Sculpture Int, Solomon R Guggenheim Mus, 1967; Am Sculpture of the Sixties, Los Angeles Co Mus Art, 1967; 1968 Ann Exhib: Contemp Am Sculpture, Whitney Mus Am Art, 1968; Plus by Minus, ALbright-Knox Gallery, 1968; Martin Luther King Benefit, Mus Mod Art, NY, 1968-69; NY Painting and Sculpture: 1940-1970, Metrop Mus Art, NY, 1969-70; 1970 Ann Exhib: Contemp Am Sculpture, Whitney Mus Am Art, 1970-71; Works for New Spaces, Walker Art Ctr, Minneapolis, 1970-71; Am Drawings 1963-1973, Whitney Mus Am Art, 1973; Calif: 3 x 8 twice, Honolulu Acad Arts, 1978; Homage to Picasso, Walker Art Ctr, 1980; Am Sculpture/Collection of Howard & Jean Lipman, Whitney Mus Am Art, 1980; The First Show: Painting & Sculpture from Eight Collections, 1940-1981, Mus Contemp Art, Los Angeles, 1983-84; Int Exhib VII, Solomon R Guggenheim Mus, 1985; The Third Dimension, Whitney Mus Am Art, 1985; Aspects of Collage, Assemblage and the Found Object in the 20th Century, Solomon R Guggenheim Mus, 1987; Sculpture since the Sixties, Whitney Mus Am Art, 1988; "The Junk" Aesthetic Assemblage of the 1950's and Early 1960's, Whitney Mus Am Art, 1989; Akira Ikeda Gallery, Taura, Japan, 1992; Hill Gallery, Birmingham, Mich, 1992; Socrates Sculpture Park, Long Island City, NY, 1994; New Sculpture, LA Louver, Venice, Calif, 1994; The Essential Gesture, New Port Harbor Art Mus, Newport Beach, Calif, 1994; Piece Tower, Day for Night, Whitney Biennial, 2006. *Awards:* Doris C Freedman Award, 1987; Albert S Bard Award Merit in Archit & Urban Design, City Club New York, 1988; Spec Recognition Award, Art Comn City New York, 1995; Heinz Award for Arts and Humanities, 2005; Public Art Network Award, Americans for the Arts, 2006; Smithsonian Archives of Am Art Medal, 2010; Nat. Medal for the Arts, Nat Endowment for the Arts, 2010. *Bibliog:* Robert Hughes (auth), Truth amid steel and elephants, Time, 7/1971; Carter Ratcliff (auth), article, Artforum, 11/1972; EC Baker (auth), Mark Di Suvero's Burgundian Season, Art Am, 5/6/1974. *Mem:* Nat Acad Design. *Dealer:* Paula Cooper Gallery 534 W 21st St NY City NY 10011

DITOMMASO, FRANCIS
DIRECTOR
b Genoa, Italy, July 9, 1953; US citizen. *Study:* Int Univ Arts, Florence, Italy, cert, 72. *Pos:* Dir, Student Galleries, Sch Visual Arts, New York, formerly, Visual Arts Mus, 94-. *Mailing Add:* c/o Sch Visual Arts SVA Galleries 209 E 23rd St New York NY 10010

DITTMER, FRANCES R
COLLECTOR
Pos: Cur, Refco Collection, formerly; pvt consult, cur, of modern & contemp art Art Inst Chicago; bd dir, Drawing Ctr Inc, Whitney Mus Am Collectors, currently. *Awards:* Names one of the top 200 Collectors, ARTnews Mag, 2004. *Mem:* Diamond Art Found; Art Inst Chicago. *Collection:* Contemporary Art

DIVELBISS, MAGGIE
DIRECTOR
Pos: Joined Sangre de Cristo Arts & Conf Ctr, Pueblo, Colo, 1973, exec dir, 1989-; gen mgr, Broadway Theater League of Pueblo; dir, the Arts Ctr of the Capital Region, formerly. *Awards:* Pueblo Hall of Fame, 2003; Chrine of the Sun Award, El Pomar Found, 2004; Bonfils-Stanton Found Awards, 2008. *Mem:* Colo Endowment for Humanities, formerly. *Mailing Add:* Sangre de Cristo Arts Center 210 N Santa Fe Ave Pueblo CO 81003

DIVOLA, JOHN MANFORD, JR
PHOTOGRAPHER
b Santa Monica, Calif, June 6, 1949. *Study:* Calif State Univ, Northridge, BA, 71; Univ Calif, Los Angeles, MA, 73, MFA, 74. *Work:* Mus Mod Art & Metrop Mus Art, NY; Int Mus Photog, George Eastman House, Rochester; New Orleans Mus Art; Fogg Mus Art, Mass; Univ Calif & Getty Mus, Los Angeles; others. *Comn:* 11 photographs, US Info Agency, 74. *Exhib:* Solo exhibs: Blue Sky Gallery, Portland, Ore, 79; Freidas Gallery, NY, 80; New Image Gallery, Harrisonburg, Va, 80; Photographers Gallery, Melbourne, Australia, 80; Los Angeles Munic Art Gallery, Calif, 85; Galerie Niki Diana Marquardt, Paris, 90; Rena Bransten Gallery, San Francisco, 96; Edenhurst Gallery, Palm Desert, Calif, 2007; Group exhibs: 24 from Los Angeles, San Francisco Mus Art, 73; Calif Photog: Remaking Make Believe, Mus Mod Art, NY, 89; Mirrors & Windows, Mus Mod Art, NY, 78; New Presences at the Fogg, Fogg Mus Art, Mass, 78; 1981 Biennial Exhib, Whitney Mus Am Art, NY; La Jolla Mus Contemp Art, Calif, 85; Individual Realities in the California Art Scene (traveling), Sezon Mus Art, Tokyo, Japan, 91; More Than One Photog, Mus Mod Art, NY, 92; Multiple Images: Photographs since 1965 from the Collection, Mus Mod Art, NY, 93; After Art: Rethinking 150 Yrs of Photog, Henry Gallery, Seattle, 94; The Photog Condition, San Francisco Mus Contemp Art, 95; Perpetual Mirage: The Desert in Am Photog Books and Prints, Whitney Mus Am Art, 96. *Teaching:* Instr photog, Calif Inst Arts, 78-88; prof, Univ Calif, Riverside, 88-, chmn, Art Dept, 91-96. *Awards:* Nat Endowment Art Grants 73, 76, 79 & 91; Guggenheim Fel, 87; Flintridge Found Fel, 98. *Bibliog:* Photography Year 1980, Time-Life, 80; Andy Grundberg & Julia Scully (auths), Currents: American photography today, Mod Photog, 10/80; Mark Johnstone (auth), article in Camera, 11/80. *Mem:* Soc Photog Educ. *Publ:* Illusr, Three images reproduced, New West Mag, 11/6/78; John Divole, "Continuity", Smart Art Press, 97; Isolated Houses, Nazraeli Press, 2000. *Dealer:* Janet Borden Gallery 560 Broadway New York NY 10012. *Mailing Add:* University of California Riverside Art Dept 232 Arts Bldg Riverside CA 92521

DIXON, JENNY (JANE) HOADLEY
MUSEUM DIRECTOR
b Montreal, Que, Oct 1, 1950; US citizen. *Study:* Univ Colo, BFA & BA, 1972; Univ Stranieri, Perugia, Italy, 1972; Columbia Univ, MBP, 1983. *Collection Arranged:* Adminr & organizer of pub art installations by: Jean Dubuffet, Isamu Noguchi, Richard Serra and numerous others. *Pos:* Dir, Pub Art Fund, New York, 1977-86; moderator & producer of weekly radio prog, Artists in the City, WNYC-AM, 1979; exec dir, Lower Manhattan Cult Council, New York, 1986-97; exec dir, Bronx Mus Arts, 1999-2003; dir, Noguchi Mus, Queens, NY, 2003-. *Teaching:* Assoc prof, Visual Arts Admin, New York Univ, 1998 & Dept Libr Studies, Parsons Sch Design, 1998; assoc prof art hist, Cooper Union for the Advancement of Sci & Art, 94-2001. *Mem:* Asn Art Mus Dirs; Art Table. *Publ:* Ed, Walking tour guide of public art in Lower Manhattan, Pub Arts Coun, 1976; contribr to numerous exhib catalogues. *Mailing Add:* Noguchi Mus 32-37 Vernon Blvd Long Island City NY 11106

DIXON, KEN
PAINTER
b St Clair, Mo, May 30, 1943. *Study:* Drury Coll, Springfield, Mo, BA, 65; SW Mo State Univ, Springfield, 66; Univ Ark, Fayetteville, MFA, 68, with David Durst & Howard Whitlach. *Work:* Nelson-Atkins Mus, Kansas City, Kans; San Antonio Mus Art, Tex; Kalamazoo Inst Arts, Mich; Mus Mod Art, Miami, Fla; US Govt, Dept Treasury; plus others. *Exhib:* Solo exhib, Camden Inst, London, 73; Tex Fine Arts Nat, 84; Words as Images, 84 & Texas Currents, 85, San Antonio Inst; New Tex Art, Cheney Cowles Mus, Spokane, Wash, 92; Wlm Campbell Cont Art, Ft Worth, Tex 2002; Collins Gallery, Houston, Tex, 2004; Invitational, Nat Art Mus, Lima, Peru, 2007; Mus South Tex, Corpus Christi, 2006; William Campbell Contemp Art, Ft Worth, Tex, 2013; Mus Mod Art, Trujillo, Peru, 2008. *Pos:* Gallery dir, Baldwin-Wallace Coll, 69-72 & Tex Tech Univ, 77- 90. *Teaching:* Instr painting, Kalamazoo Coll, 66-69 & Baldwin-Wallace Coll, 69-72; prof painting, Tex Tech Univ, 75-2003. *Awards:* Purchase Award, Miami Graphics Inst Mus Mod Art, Fla, 77; Outstanding Emerging Artist Nat Competition, Galveston Art Ctr, 84; NEA Tex Award, 86; Artists Equity award, Tri-State Artists Equity Assn, 2013. *Bibliog:* Glen R. Brown (auth), Order & Disorder Art Papers, 63, 1/95; New Am Painting, No 30, Open Studio Press, Wellesley, Mass, 38-41, 2000; Sacred Landscapes, Art Mus S Tex, 2006. *Media:* Acrylic, oil. *Interests:* community activity. *Dealer:* Wlm-Campbell Gallery 4935 Byers Ft Worth TX 76107. *Mailing Add:* 1920 32nd St Lubbock TX 79411

DIXON, WILLARD
PAINTER
b Kansas City, Mo, Mar 31, 1942. *Study:* Cornell Univ; Brooklyn Mus Sch; San Francisco Art Inst, MFA, 69. *Work:* Metrop Mus Art, New York; Oakland Mus, Calif; Utah Mus Fine Art, Salt Lake City; San Francisco Mus Mod Art; San Francisco Int Airport, Calif. *Comn:* Storm Source (mural), Oakland Mus, Nat Hist Dept, Calif, 84; Fire Road, Trans America Corp, 88; Missouri Countryside (mural), Commerce Bancshares, Kansas City, Mo, 97; The Eastern Sierra in Fall (mural), Calif Supreme Court, San Francisco Civic Ctr, 98; Red Rock Canyon Fed Courthouse, Las Vegas. *Exhib:* SECA Centennial Exhib, San Francisco Mus Mod Art, Calif, 70; Landscape, Seascape, Cityscape, Contemp Arts Ctr, New Orleans, La, 86; Contemp Landscapes, William Sawyer Gallery, 88; The Modern Pastoral, Robert Scholekopf Gallery, NY; The Landscape in Twentieth Century Am Art, Metrop Mus Art, 92; Rediscovering the Landscape of the Americas, Gerald Peter Gallery, Santa Fe, NMex, 96; Facing Eden: 100 Yrs of Landscape Art in the Bay Area, DeYoung Mus, San Francisco; and many others; Outwin Boochever Portrait Competition, Smithsonian Nat Portrait Gallery, 2013. *Teaching:* Instr, Calif State Univ, Hayward, 71-72, Calif Coll Arts & Crafts, 73-76 & San Francisco State Univ, 89-90. *Awards:* Purchase Award, San Francisco Art Festival, 76 & 77; Fel, Nat Endowment Asn, 89. *Bibliog:* Bill Berkson (auth), Willard Dixon, Recent Landscape Paintings (catalog), Hackett-Freedman Gallery, 98. *Media:* Oil on Canvas. *Dealer:* Fischbach Gallery NY; Winfield Gallery Carmel CA; San Francisco Mus Modern Art Artists Gallery. *Mailing Add:* 5 Belloreid San Rafael CA 94901

DJURBERG, NATHALIE
VIDEO ARTIST
b Lysekil, Sweden, 1978. *Study:* Hovedskous Art Sch, Gothenburg, Sweden, 1995-1997; Malmo Art Acad, Sweden, MFA, 2002. *Work:* Sprengel Mus, Hannover, Ger; Guggenheim Mus, New York; Moderna Museet, Skeppsholmen, Stockholm, Sweden; Malmo Konstmuseum, Sweden; Kunsthaus Zurich, Switz; Hammer Mus, Los Angeles; Boras Konstmuseum, Sweden. *Exhib:* Hannover Kunstverein, Ger, 1999; Nordic Hell, Gallery Konstakuten, Stockholm, Sweden, 2002; solo exhibs, Gallery Peep, Malmo, Sweden, 2002, Gallery Flach, Stockholm, 2003, Kristinehamns Konstmuseum, Sweden, 2004, Jonkopings Mus, Sweden, 2005, Zach Feuer Gallery,

New York, 2006, Kunsthalle Wien, Vienna, 2007, Sammlung Goetz Mus, Munich & 2008, Frye Art Mus, 2009; Gallery Arnstedt & Kullgren, Bastad, Sweden, 2003; Moss Bryggeri Utstillingshall, Moss, Norway, 2004; Sala Rekalde, Bilbao, Spain, 2005; Moderna Museet, Stockholm, Sweden, 2006; Biennale of Young Artists, Tallin, Estonia, 2007; Guggenheim Mus, New York, 2007; New Mus Contemp Art, New York, 2008; 53rd Int Art Exhib Biennale, Venice, 2009. *Awards:* Silver Lion for a Promising Young Artist in the Making Worlds Exhibition, Venice Biennial, 2009. *Bibliog:* Eugenio Tassini (auth), Sei Promesse e un videotape, Io Donna, 10/15/2005; Ute Thon (auth), Hauptstrasse der Kunst, Art Mag, 4/2006; Roberta Smith (auth), Battles Rage on the Cultural Front, NY Times, 12/30/2007; Eva Wittocx (auth), Performa 07, Flash Art, 77 & 82, 1-2/2008. *Mailing Add:* Zach Feuer Gallery 548 W 22nd St New York NY 10011

DLUHY, DEBORAH HAIGH
EDUCATOR, ADMINISTRATOR
b Summit, NJ, Mar 4, 1940. *Study:* Wheaton Col, Norton, Mass, BA, 62; Karl-Ruprecht Univ, Heidelberg, Ger; Harvard Univ, Cambridge, Mass, PhD, 76. *Pos:* Develop officer, Mus Fine Arts, Boston, Mass, 78-84, asst dir, 84-86; assoc dean admin, Sch of Mus Fine Arts, Boston, 86-87, dean acad progs & admin, 87-93, dean of sch, 93-, deputy dir, 99-; trustee Cult Educ Collab Boston, 87-90; trustee Wheaton Col, Norton, Mass, 88; mem exec comt, v chair fin and facilities, 2001-2002; chair fac/staff comt, mem governance bd, 2004; vchair pres search comt; pres Wheaton Col Alumni Assoc, 94-2000; trustee ex officio; trustee 2000-, chair 2005-; visitor Walnut Hill Sch, Natick, 96; pres Pro Arts Consortium, 99-2000; bd dir Boston Arts Acad, 99; exec comt & sec, Nat Asn Shcs Art & Design, 2001-07; Wheaton material con: alumni trustee, 1988-93; pres alumni assoc & ex officio trustee, 1994-2000; trustee 2000-. *Teaching:* Lectr art hist, Wheaton Col, Norton, Mass, 75-76, Boston Col, Newton, Mass, 76-78 & Radcliffe Seminars, Radcliffe Col, 77; chair, nominating comt, 2007-08. *Awards:* Woodrow Wilson Fel, 63. *Mem:* Nat Asn Schs Art & Design; Pro Arts Consortium; Asn Ind Cols Art & Design; St Botolph Club. *Res:* Medieval art; 13th century wallpainting, Germany. *Mailing Add:* Sch Mus Fine Arts 230 Fenway Boston MA 02115-5534

DMYTRUK, IHOR R
PAINTER, EDUCATOR
b Ukraine, Feb 11, 1938; Can citizen. *Study:* Univ Alta; Vancouver Sch Art. *Work:* Alta Art Found; Univ Calgary, Alta; Ukrainian Inst Mod Art, Chicago; Art Gallery, Windsor, Ont; Art Bank, Can Coun; plus others. *Exhib:* Alta Contemp Drawings, Edmonton Art Gallery, 73; solo exhibs, Extension Ctr Gallery, Univ Alta, Edmonton, 2006; Alberta Art Found, Hokkaido Mus Mod Art, Japan, 79; Painting in Alberta: A Historical Survey, Edmonton Art Gallery, 80; Recent Acquisitions by Alta Art Found, Beaver House Gallery, 84; Mechanics of Vision: Drawing in Alberta, Ext Ctr Gallery, Univ Alberta, 2000; PULSE, A Northern Alberta traveling Drawing Exhibition, 2002-04. *Teaching:* Instr drawing & painting, Fac Exten, Univ Alta; Retired, 2002. *Awards:* All Alberta 1966 Award, Reeves & Sons Ltd; Can Coun Travel Grant, 66 & Arts Grant, 72 & 74. *Bibliog:* Myra Davies (auth), Recent work by Ihor Dmytruk, 10-11/71, Arts Can; Karen Wilkin (auth), Painting in Alberta-An Historical Survey, Edmonton Art Gallery Publ, 80; V Kubijovyc (ed), Encyclopedia Ukraine, vol 1, 84. *Media:* Multimedia. *Mailing Add:* 9801-92 Ave Edmonton AB T6E 2V4 Canada

DO, KIM V
PAINTER, EDUCATOR
b New York, NY, May 23, 1954. *Study:* New York Studio Empire State Col, 75; State Univ NY, BFA, 76; Univ Pa, MFA, 79. *Work:* Cargill Int; Johnson & Johnson, NJ; Mid Atlantic Bank, NJ; Reader's Digest, NY; Citicorp, NY; many others. *Comn:* mural, Beacon Restaurant, NY, 99; mural, Beacon Restaurant, Stamford, Conn, 2000; landscape, comn by Horace Mann Sch, 2000; portrait of Frederick Phineas Rose, Coun For Relations, 2000. *Exhib:* Bodies and Souls, Artists Choice Mus, NY, 83; 167th Ann Exhib, Nat Acad Design; Eubie Blake Nat Mus, Baltimore, MD, 93; Independence Seaport Mus, Philadelphia, Pa, 96; Colleagues in the Landscape, Paramount Ctr for Arts, 97; New Hudson River Sch, Union Col, Schenectady, NY, 99; Faces of Courage, Heroes of 9/11, touring exhib, 2002-; portrait donation, Faces of Courage, Heros of 9/11, touring exhib, 2002-04. *Teaching:* Lectr painting, State Univ NY, Purchase 82-83; dept chmn, Visual Arts, Horace Mann Sch, NY, 85-. *Awards:* Horace Mann Travel Grant, Italy, 95. *Bibliog:* Ronny Cohen (auth), Kim Do, Artforum, 4/91; M Stephen Doherty (auth), Exploring One Location, Am Artist, 7/91; Gerrit Henry (auth), Kim Do, Art In Am, 1/92. *Mem:* Coll Art Asn; Nat Art Educ Asn. *Media:* Oil, Gouache. *Interests:* landscape, portraiture, non-objective abstraction. *Publ:* Illusr, Hudson Valley Cookbook (cover), Addison Wesley. *Dealer:* Gross McCleaf Gallery 127 S 16 St Philadelphia PA 19102. *Mailing Add:* 53 Spring St New York NY 10012

DOBKIN, JOHN HOWARD
ADMINISTRATOR, CONSULTANT
b Hartford, Conn, Feb 19, 1942. *Study:* Yale Univ, BA, 64; Inst d'Etudes Politiques, Paris, France, 65; NY Univ, JD, 68. *Collection Arranged:* Paintings of the Figure, Nat Acad Design, 79; Landscape Paintings, Nat Acad Design, 80; Edwin Dickinson: Draftsman Paints, 81; Artists by Themselves, 83. *Pos:* Exec asst to secy, Smithsonian Inst, Washington, DC, 68-71; adminr, Cooper-Hewitt Mus Design, 71-78; dir, Nat Acad Design, NY, formerly; adv comt, Archives Am Art, NY; bd dir, Municipal Art Soc, Arthur Ross Found & Sch Am Ballet; pres, Historic Hudson Valley, 89-99; philanthropic cons, 99-. *Awards:* Exceptional Serv Award, Smithsonian Inst, 71

DODD, LOIS
PAINTER, EDUCATOR
b Montclair, NJ, Apr 22, 1927. *Study:* Cooper Union, with Byron Thomas & Peter Busa, 1948. *Hon Degrees:* Lyme Acad, Coll Fine Arts. *Work:* Cooper Union Mus, First Nat City Bank, Chase Manhattan Bank Collection, AT&T, NY; Kalamazoo Art Ctr, Mich; Ciba-Geigy Chem Corp, Ardsley, NY; RJ Reynolds, Winston-Salem, NC; Commerce Bank Shares, Inc, Kansas City, Mo; Security Pac Nat Bank; Nat Acad of Design; Metrop Life Insurance Co; Reader's Digest, Pleasantville, NY; Museo dell'Arte, Udine, Italy; Bowdoin Coll Mus, Maine, 2004; Colby Coll Mus Art, Waterville, Me; Farnsworth Mus, Rockland, Me; Montclair Art Mus, Montclair, NJ; Kemper Mus Contemp Art, Kansas City, Mo; Portland Mus Art, Portland, Me. *Exhib:* Solo exhibs include Tanager Gallery, NY, 1954, 1957, 1958, 1961, 1962; Green Mountain Gallery, NY, 1969-71, 1974, 1976; Thomas Col, Waterville, Maine, 1973; Cape Split Place, Addison, Maine, 1977, 1979, 1983; Colby Col, Maine, 1977; Lyman Allyn Mus, New London, Conn, 1980; NJ State Mus, Trenton, 1981; La State Univ, 1984; Anne Weber Gallery, Georgetown, Maine, 1987; Dartmouth Col, 1990; Caldbeck Gallery, Rockland, Maine, 1990, 1994, 1995, 1998, 2001, 2003, 2005, 2007, 2009, 2011 & 2012; Rider Coll Gallery, NJ, 1992; Roundtop Ctr for Arts, Maine, 1993; Paesaggio Gallery, West Hartford, Conn, 1995, 2001; Farnsworth Art Mus, Rockland, Maine, 1996; Trenton City Mus, NJ, 1996; Montclair Art Mus, NJ, 1996; Kingsborough Community Col, Brooklyn, NY, 2001; List Gallery, Swarthmore Col, Pa, 2002; Alexandre Gallery, NY, 2003, 2004, 2006-2009, 2011, 2012; Bowdoin Col, Maine, 2004; June Fitzpatrick Gallery, Portland, Maine, 2006; Reynolds Gallery, Richmond, Va, 2007; Southern Methodist Univ, Pollack Gallery, 2007, Kemper Mus Contemp Art, Kansas City, Mo, 2012, Portland Mus Art, Portland, Me, 2013; group exhibs including Childe Hassam Purchase Exhib, Am Acad & Inst Arts & Letters, NY, 1973, Paintings & Sculpture by Candidates for Art Awards, 1986, Ann Acad-Inst Purchase Exhib, 1991-94; Ann Exhib, Nat Acad Design, 1987, 1990, 1995, 1999, 2001-2003, 2005, 2007, 2009, & 2011, The Artist in the Garden, 1991, The Artist's Eye, 1994, 1997, 2002, Challenging Tradition: Women of the Acad 1826-2003; NY Studio Sch, 2003. *Pos:* Co-founder, Tanager Gallery, New York, 1952-62; bd of gov, Skowhegan Sch of Painting & Sculpture, 1980-2010, chmn, 1986-88. *Teaching:* Instr, Wagner Col, 1963-64, Philadelphia Col Art, 1963 & 1965; instr, Brooklyn Col, 1965-72, assoc prof, 1975-85, prof, 1985-92; instr, Vt Studio Ctr, Johnson, Vt, 1994, 1999, 2001, 2002, 2003, 2004, 2005, 2009. *Awards:* Ital Govt Study Grant, 59-60; Longview Found Purchase Award, 1962; Ingraham, Merrill Found Grant, 1971; Am Acad & Inst Arts & Letts Award, 1986, Hassam, Speicher, Betts & Symons Purchase Prize, 1991; Leonilda S Gervas Award, Nat Acad of Design, 1987, Henry Ward Ranger Purchase Award, 1990; Cooper Union, Distinguished Alumni Citation, 1987, Augustus St Gaudens Disting Alumni Award, Cooper Union, 2005; Benjamin West Clinedinst Medal, Artists' Fel, 2007; NA award, 2012. *Bibliog:* Madeleine Keller (ed) Bench Press Series on Art, 85; Am Artist Mag, 4/91; Yankee Mag, 4/92; Down East Mag, 6/96; Am Arts Quarterly, 2011. *Mem:* Nat Acad, 1988; Am Acad Arts & Letters, 1998; Skowhegan Sch Painting & Sculpture (bd gov). *Media:* Oil. *Publ:* Catching the Light, Kemper Mus Contemporary Art, Kans City, MO. *Dealer:* Alexandre Gallery 41 E 57th St New York NY 10022. *Mailing Add:* 30 E 2nd St New York NY 10003-8906

DODD, M(ARY) IRENE
PAINTER, EDUCATOR
b Athens, Ga, Dec 30, 1941. *Study:* Duke Univ, AB, 64; Univ Ga, with Lamar Dodd, Howard Thomas, Irving Marantz Everett Kinstler and others, MFA, 67. *Work:* Smithsonian Art & Space Mus, Washington, DC; High Mus Art, Atlanta, Ga; Macon Mus Arts & Sci, Ga; Univ Tenn, Martin; Ga Mus Art, Athens. *Exhib:* Solo exhibs, Lamar Dodd Art Ctr, LaGrange, Ga, 85 & 88, Swan Gallery, Atlanta, 87 & Valdosta Cult Gallery, Ga, 97; Hay House, Macon, Ga, 84; Fifty Outstanding Am Artists, Foster Harmon Galleries, Sarasota, Fla, 84; Woodruff Art Ctr, Atlanta, Ga, 84; Valdosta State Col, Ga, 84; Southern Watercolor Exhibition, Jackson, Miss, 85; Georgia Watercolor Exhibition, Macon Mus Arts, Ga, 86; Nat Arts Club, NY, 86-90. *Teaching:* Prof hist, painting & drawing, Valdosta State Col, 67-, dept head, 72-80. *Awards:* Prize, Ga Watercolor Exhibition, 84; Prizes, Southern Watercolor Exhibition, 84 & 85. *Mem:* Nat Arts Club; Southern Watercolor Soc; Ga Watercolor Soc; Southwest Watercolor Soc. *Publ:* Illusr, Darien, The Death and Rebirth of a Southern Town, Mercer Univ Press, Macon, Ga, 81. *Mailing Add:* 316 Oak Trace Dr Valdosta GA 31602

DODDS, ROBERT J, III
COLLECTOR
b San Antonio, Tex, Sept 19, 1943. *Study:* Yale Univ, BA, 65; Univ Pa Sch Law, LLB, 69. *Pos:* Term trustee, Mus Art, Carnegie Inst, 71-82; pres, Pittsburgh Plan for Art, Pa, 82-85; trustee, Westmoreland Co Mus Art, Greensburg, Pa, 83-91; chmn, Carnegie-Mellon Univ Art Gallery, Pittsburgh, Pa, 85-91; mem, Museums Panel, Pa Coun on the Arts, 85-88. *Collection:* Post-minimal and conceptual art and contemporary photography. *Mailing Add:* 3101 Old Pecos Tr No 687 Santa Fe NM 87505

DODGE, ROBERT G
PAINTER, SCULPTOR
b Boston, Mass, Aug 14, 1939. *Study:* Univ Pa, BA, 63, BFA, 65, MFA, 66. *Work:* McDonalds Corp, Chicago, Ill; TRW Corp, IBM & Equitable Corp, NY; James A Michener Mus. *Exhib:* Philadelphia Furniture, Pa Acad Fine Arts, 91; In Our Circle, James A Michener Mus, Doylestown, Pa, 91; New Abstraction, Rabbet Gallery, New Brunswick, NJ, 92; Sansar Gallery, Washington, DC, 92; Furniture of the 90's, Am Soc Furniture Arts, Houston & Parsons Sch Art, NY, 92. *Teaching:* Prof drawing & sculpture, Bucks Co Community Col, 68-. *Awards:* Prix de Rome Sculpture, Am Acad, Italy, 74-76. *Bibliog:* Portfolio, Am Craft, 88; Collaboration sparks creativity in wood, NY Times, 8/9/87; An exhibit fills a mansion, Philadelphia Inquirer, 8/21/87; Exhibition Review, Philadelphia Inquirer, 5/13/94. *Media:* Mixed. *Dealer:* Sansar Gallery 4200 Wisconsin Ave Washington DC 20016; Rabbet Gallery 120 Georges Lane New Brunswick NJ 08901

DODIYA, ANJU
PAINTER
b Mumbai, India, 1964. *Study:* JJ Sch Art, Mumbai, BFA, 1986. *Exhib:* Monsoon, Jehangir Art Gallery, Mumbai, 1986; Works on Paper, Gallery Chemould, Mumbai, 1990; solo exhibs, Gallery Chemould, 1991, 1996 & 2001, Max Mueller Bhavan, Mumbai, 1999, Vadehra Art Gallery, New Delhi, 1999 & 2005, Bose Pacia, New York,

2006, Bodhi Art, Mumbai, 2007 & Lukshmi Villas Palace, Baroda, 2007; In Small Format, Sakshi Gallery, Mumbai, 1993; Recent Trends in Contemp Indian Art, Vadehra Art Gallery, New Delhi, 1995; Jehangir Art Gallery, Mumbai, 1997; The Looking Glass Self, Lakeeren Gallery, Mumbai, 1998; The Fine Art Company, Mumbai, 1999; Celebration of the Human Image, Gallery 42, New Delhi, 2000; Bodied Self, Sans Tache Gallery, Mumbai, 2001; Transfiguration, India Habitat Gallery, New Delhi, 2002; Inside the Whale, Gasser & Grunert Inc, New York, 2003; Stree, Bodhi Art, Singapore, 2004; House of World Cultures, Berlin, 2005; Cymroza Art Gallery, Mumbai, 2006; Contemp Art from India, Chicago Cultural Ctr, 2007; 53rd Int Art Exhib Biennale, Venice, 2009. *Awards:* Harmony Award, Reliance Indust, 1999; Young Achiever Award, Indo-Am Society, 2001. *Media:* Watercolor. *Dealer:* Rahul & Art New Delhi India; Kings Road Gallery London UK. *Mailing Add:* Bose Pacia 163 Plymouth St Brooklyn NY 11201

DODRILL, DONALD LAWRENCE
PAINTER, ILLUSTRATOR
b Richwood, Ohio, Aug 28, 1922. *Study:* Marion Bus Coll, cert, 41; Ohio State Univ, Columbus, BFA (cum laude), 49; Syracuse Univ, MFA (illus), 75. *Work:* Schumacher Gallery, Capital Univ; Zanesville Art Ctr, Ohio; Wagnall Found Gallery, Lithopolis, Ohio; Ger Village Soc Hist Mus, Columbus; First Methodist Church, Hilliard, Ohio; St Anthony Med Ctr, Columbus. *Comn:* Union Station (painting), Ohio Bell Tel, Columbus, 78; Neil House (painting), Columbus Dispatch, 81; paintings, Huntington Bank, Washington Court House, Ohio, 81, EV Bischoff co, Columbus, 83 & Borden co, Columbus, Ohio, 83; Marysville Methodist Church, 87; Newark Advocate, Newark, Ohio, 91; Licking Co Hosp, Newark, Ohio, 92 & 96. *Exhib:* Ohio Watercolor Soc Exhibs, 74-87, 2003; Nat Watercolor Soc Exhib, Palm Springs Desert Mus, Calif, 81 & Laguna Beach Mus Art, Calif, 82; Midwest Watercolor Soc, Neville Mus, Green Bay, Wis, 84; Am Watercolor Soc, Salmagundi Club, NY, 86, 87, 88 & 92; Miss Watercolor Soc, Jackson, Miss, 91; and others. *Pos:* Partner, Dodrill Design, 54-; dir, Windon Gallery, 79-99. *Teaching:* Instr graphic design, Capital Univ, 76-83; instr watercolor, Adult Educ Prog, 77-2008, Upper Arlington, Ohio. *Awards:* Smithe Schnacke Award, Ohio Watercolor Soc, Cincinnati, 85; Hardy Gramatky Mem Award, Am Watercolor Soc, 86 & Ogden Pleisner Mem Award, 87; Karl Wolfe Award, Miss Watercolor Soc, Miss Mus Art, Jacksonville, 91. *Bibliog:* Jacqueline Hall (auth), Dodrill blends sensitivity, realism, Columbus Dispatch, 1/27/85; Susan Porter (auth), Book Dedicated to Local Cancer Victim, Worthington News, 9/27/89; Susan Stonick (auth), For Watercolor Artist Everything is a Subject, Dublin News, 9/20/89. *Mem:* Watercolor Soc, Nat, Ohio; Cent Ohio Watercolor Soc (vpres, 68, pres, 69); Upper Arlington Art League (pres, 75); Bexley Area Art Guild (pres, 80); Ohio Watercolor Soc (bd dir, 83-85); Am Watercolor Soc; Pa Watercolor Soc; Worthington Art League. *Media:* Watercolor. *Publ:* Illusr cover, Columbus Bus Forum, 75 & 76, Better Living Mag, 75 & 76 & Ohioana Libr Quart, 76-86; auth, The Transparent Touch, Watson Guptill, New York, 89; Splash 3, North Light Books, 1994; and others. *Mailing Add:* 4853 Nugent Dr Columbus OH 43220

DODSON, DONNA
SCULPTOR
b Orange, Calif, 1968. *Study:* Wellesley Coll, Mass, BA, 90. *Work:* Mus Mod Art; Franklin Furnace Artists Bk Collection, New York; Archive, Fondazione Arnaldo Pomodoro, Milan, Italy; Archives on Women Artists, Nat Mus Women Arts, Washington, DC; Artists Space Artist Files, Mus Mod Art Libr, NY. *Exhib:* Wood: Two Journeys, Jewett Art Ctr, Wellesley, Mass, 2000; Leading Lady, TZE House, Wellesley Coll, Wellesley, Mass, 2000; Carving Soul into Wood, Gallery Wright, Wilmington, VT 2002; Visual Poetry, Three Columns Gallery, Harvard Univ, Mass, 2003; Community Gallery, Lynn, Mass, 2004; Featured Artist, Artana Gallery, Brookline, Mass, 2004; New Sculpture, Concord Art Asn, Concord, Mass, 2005; She Idols, Univ Gallery, Pittsburgh State Univ, Pittsburg, Kans, 2006; Red Carpet Series, Fountainhead Gallery, New York, 2007; Elegant Elles, Mill Brook Gallery & Sculpture Gardens, Concord, NH, 2008; Sarah Dobkin & Donna Dodson, Gallery 38 Cameron Ave, Cambridge, Mass, 2008; Spring into Summer, Nat Asn Women Artists, New York, 2008. *Pos:* Guest lectr, var galleries & schs, 2002-2008. *Awards:* George Sugarman Found Grant, 2007. *Bibliog:* Carole Calo (auth), Branching Out: Explorations in Wood, Stonehill Coll, Easton, Mass, 2003; Rich Fahey (auth), Wooden Idols, The Daily Item, Lynn, Mass, 6/3/2004; Carolyn Wirth (auth), Mythic animals and real women, New Eng Sculptors, 2/2005; Nikki Patrick (auth), She Idols, The Morning Sun, Pittsburg, Kans, 12/5/2006; Barry Maloney (auth), Avian Archetypes, Dissolver Mag, Vol 16, Dedham, Mass, 2007. *Mem:* Catharine Lorillard Wolfe Art Club; Int Sculpture Ctr; Nat Asn Women Artists; Wellesly Friends of Art; Women's Caucus Art. *Media:* Wood. *Specialty:* Sculpture. *Dealer:* Boston Sculptors Gallery MA

DODWORTH, ALLEN STEVENS
ART APPRAISER, CURATOR
b Long Beach, Calif, Nov 19, 1938. *Study:* Stanford Univ, BA (fine arts & design), 62; Portland State Univ; Univ Utah. *Collection Arranged:* Ann Exhibs for Artists of Idaho, 69-75, Painters of the Idaho Scene, 72 & Am Masters in the West, 74, Boise Gallery Art; Am Abstracts, 76; The Grand Beehive, Salt Lake Art Ctr, 80; V Douglas Snow Retrospective, Utah Mus Fine Arts, 94; Looking Back, 75th Anniversary of the Salt Lake Art Ctr, 2006. *Pos:* Chmn, White Gallery, Portland State Univ, 67-69; dir, Boise Gallery Art, Boise Art Mus, 69-76; dir, Salt Lake Art Ctr, 76-81; dir, Western Colo Ctr Arts, 81-85; independent art appraiser, Salt Lake City, Utah, currently; cur of exhibs & collections, Alta Club, Salt Lake City. *Awards:* Mus Prof Fel, Nat Endowment Arts, 73. *Mem:* Utah Lawyers for the Arts; Salt Lake City (design bd); Friends of the Wagnerian Opera; Alta Club Arts Found, Salt Lake City (pres, currently); Utah Mus Fine Arts (collections committee, currently). *Publ:* Auth, To Be in this Country, Univ Utah Press, 94

DOE, WILLO
CRITIC, COLLAGE ARTIST
b Pusan, Republic of Korea; US Citizen. *Study:* Yonsei Univ, Korea, BA (philos), 79; Heidelberg Univ, Ger; E Lansing Coll, Mich, 83. *Collection Arranged:* Stonechime Images (auth, catalog), NY City Gallery, 95, Light and Darkness, 96, Across the Divide, 97 & Distinguished Criteria, 98. *Pos:* Contrib ed, Art Monthly, Seoul, Korea, 95; mus critic, Space: Archit, Art Design, 96; cur, Korean Cult Serv, NY, 98; contrib ed, NY Art World, NY, 99; contribr writer, Fiber Arts Mag, Asheville, NC, 2001-03; contribr ed, Nat Mus Contemp Art, Korea, 2003-. *Teaching:* Fac brush painting, Art Ctr Northern NJ, 94-95. *Awards:* Nat Award for Art Criticism, 95. *Res:* Independent Artists that don't belong to a specific art movement or sch, therefore easily misplaced and displaced in the history of art and the art world. *Publ:* auth, Crossing Boundaries: The Art of Lidia Syroka, Fiberarts, Fiberarts Mag, 2002; Sung Soo Kim and Ot Painting: The Korean Cultural Serv, NY, 2003; Rothko, Stamos, Vicente, and Sharf: The NY Sch, Nat Mus Contemp Art, Korea, 2004; Ethel Gittlin's Art (exhib catalogue), New York, 2006; Artists in Conversation: Renée Lerner & Susan Manspeizer (exhib catalogue), New York, 2006; Layla Fanucci's Art (exhib catalogue), New York, 2006; Florence Putterman's Art (exhib catalogue), Walter Wickiser Gallery, New York, 2007; The Art of Roseline Koener, exhib catalog, Walter Wickiser Gallery, New York, 2008. *Mailing Add:* 355 W 85th St New York NY 10024

DOEZEMA, MARIANNE
MUSEUM DIRECTOR, HISTORIAN
b Grand Rapids, Mich, Sept 8, 1950. *Study:* Mich State Univ, BA, 73; Univ Mich, MA, 75; Boston Univ, PhD (Smithsonian Predoctoral Fel, Nat Mus Am Art), 90. *Collection Arranged:* The Public Monument and Its Audience, Cleveland Mus Art, Ohio, 77-78; Am Realism and the Industrial Age, Cleveland Mus Art, 80-81 & Columbus Mus Art, 81; Davis Cone: Theatre Paintings, Ga Mus Art, 83 & Hunter Mus Art, Chattanooga, Tenn, 83; Painting Abstract: Gregory Amenoff, John L Moore, Katherine Porter, Mt Holyoke Coll Art Mus, 96, Boston Univ Art Gallery, 97, Maier Mus, 97 & Cedar Rapids Mus Art, 97; The Sporting Woman: The Female Athlete in Am Culture, Mount Holyoke Coll Art Mus, 2004; Jane Hammond: Paperwork, Mount Holyoke Coll Art Mus, 2006. *Pos:* Cur educ, Ga Mus Art, Univ Ga, 81-83, assoc dir, 83-85; prog officer, Mus, Div Pub Prog, Nat Endowment Humanities, 90-92; dir, Mt Holyoke Coll Art Mus, 94. *Teaching:* Instr & asst cur, Dept Art Hist & Educ, Cleveland Mus Art, 76-81; asst prof & adj cur art dept, Maier Mus, Randolph-Macon Woman's Coll, 92-94. *Awards:* Ralph Henry Gabriel Dissertation Prize, Am Studies Asn, 90. *Mem:* Am Asn Mus; Am Studies Asn; Coll Art Asn Am. *Res:* Life & work of Charles Dana Gibson. *Publ:* George Bellows and Urban America, Yale Univ Press, 92; The Real New York, George Bellows: Paintings, Amon Carter Mus & Los Angeles Co Mus Art, 92; Painting Abstract: Gregory Amenoff, John L Moore, Katherine Porter, Mount Holyoke Coll Art Mus, 96; ed, Reading American Art, Yale Univ Press, 98; Representing Women, In: Life's Pleasures: The Ashcan Artists Brush with Leisure, Detroit Inst Arts, 2007. *Mailing Add:* Mount Holyoke Coll Art Mus South Hadley MA 01075-1499

DOHERTY, PEGGY M
MUSEUM DIRECTOR, CURATOR
b Chicago, Ill. *Study:* Columbia Coll Chicago, BA; Sch Art Inst Chicago, MA. *Collection Arranged:* Choice Impressions, 94; Recycled & Reassembled, 94; Home: Domestic Narratives, 95; Figures, 96; Addendum, 97. *Pos:* Res asst photo collections, Art Inst Chicago, 88-89; dir, Northern Ill Univ Art Mus Gallery, 90-94, Northern Ill Univ Art Mus, 94-. *Mem:* Am Asn Mus; Ill Asn Mus; Coll Art Asn; Chicago Artists Coalition. *Res:* Contemporary art. *Mailing Add:* Northern Ill Univ NIU Art Mus Altgeld Hall Dekalb IL 60115

DOIG, PETER
ARTIST
b Edinburgh, Scotland, 1959. *Study:* Studies at Wimbledon Sch Art, 1979-80; St Martin's Sch Art, BA, 1983; Chelsea Sch Art, MA, 1990. *Exhib:* Retrospective, Tate Britain, London, Musée d'Art Moderne, Paris & Schirn Kunsthalle, Frankfurt; Solo shows, Concrete Cabins, Miro Gallery, London, 1994; Homely Gesellschaft für Aktuelle Kunst, Bremen, Ger, 1996; Blizzard seventy-seven, Kunsthalle Kiel, 1998; wing-mirror, Gavin Brown's Enterprise, NY, 1999; Almost Grown, The Douglas Hyde Gallery, Dublin, 2000; Mus Contemp Art, Miami, 2000; Nat Gallery Can, 2001; 100 Years Ago, Victoria Miro Gallery, London, 2002; Charley's Space, Bonnefanten Mus, Maastricht, 2003; Metrop, Pinakothek der Moderne, Munich, 2004; Studiofilmclub 2003-2006, Ballroom, Marfa/Tex, 2006; Group shows, New Contemporaries, ICA, London, 1982; Barclay's Young Artist Award, Serpentine Gallery, London, 1991; Twelve Stars, Barbican Ctr, London, 1993; Here & Now, 1994; Turner Prize Exhib, Tate Gallery, London, 1994; About Vision: New British Painting in the 1990's, The Fruitmarket Gallery, Edinburgh, 1998; Alpenblick, Kunsthalle Wien, Austria, 1997; Twisted: Urban & Visionary Landscapes in Contemp Painting, Can Abbermuseaum, Eindhoven, 2000; Hier ist dort, Salzburger Kunstverein, Austria, 2001; Dear Painter, paint me, Schirn Kunsthalle, Frankfurt, 2002; Days Like These, Triennial Exhib Contemp Painting British Art, Tate Gallery, London, 2003; Bearings: Landscapes from the IMMA Collection, Irish Mus Mod Art, Dublin, 2004; Day for Night, Whitney Biennial, NY, 2006. *Pos:* trustee, Tate Gallery, London, 1995-2000. *Awards:* John Moores Found Prize, 1993; Wolfgang Hang Prize, Soc Mod Art, Mus Ludwig, Cologne, Ger, 2008. *Mailing Add:* Michael Werner Gallery 4 E 77th St New York NY 10021

DOLAN, MARGO
FOUNDATION DIRECTOR, ART DEALER
b Philadelphia, Pa, Mar 19, 1946. *Study:* Conn Col, BA (art hist). *Collection Arranged:* Ballinglen Permanent Collection/Archive, Ballinglen Arts Found, Co Mayo, Ireland. *Pos:* Docent, Univ Mus, Philadelphia, Pa, 68-70; asst dir, Print Club, 70-73, dir, 73-77; dir, Asn Am Artists, Philadelphia, 78-84; co-owner, Dolan-Maxwell Gallery, Philadelphia, 84- & NY, 88-90; co-founder, Artist in Rural Ireland Fund, Pa &

Ballinglen Arts Found, Ballycastle, Co Mayo, Repub Ireland, 92-. *Mem:* Int Fine Print Dealers Asn (bd mem 2013-); Philadelphia Art Dealers Asn (bd mem, 2012-). *Specialty:* Distinguished modern & contemp works of art, WPA, NY Sch, African Am Int Contemp, Artists present ed in depth. *Mailing Add:* Dolan/Maxwell 2046 Rittenhouse Sq Philadelphia PA 19103

DOLKART, ANDREW S
HISTORIAN, EDUCATOR
Study: Colgate Univ, BA, 1973; Columbia Univ, MS (hist preservation), 1977. *Teaching:* James Marston Fitch prof, Columbia Univ Sch Archit, Planning & Preservation & dir, hist preservation program. *Awards:* Grass Roots Preservation award, Hist Dist Coun, 2004; Cult Hist award, New York City Book Awards, 2007. *Publ:* Auth, Guide to New York City Landmarks, John Wiley & Sons, 1992; Morningside Heights: A History of Its Architecture and Development, Columbia Univ Press, 1998; Biography of a Tenement House in New York City: An Architectural History of 97 Orchard St, Univ Va Press, 2006; The Row House Reborn: Architecture and Neighborhoods in New York City 1908-1929, Johns Hopkins Univ Pres, 2009. *Mailing Add:* Columbia Univ 1172 Amsterdam Ave New York NY 10027

DOLL, NANCY
DIRECTOR
b Chicago, Ill. *Study:* Mundelein Col, Chicago, BFA; Univ Iowa, Iowa City, MA; Getty Mus Mgmt Inst, Berkeley, Calif. *Exhib:* Home Show II, 97; One Word: Plastic, 2003; Manic, 2004; Jessica Stockholder: kissing the Wall, 2005; PUNCH! 2007; Achromatic, 2008; Weatherspoon Art Mus: 70 Years of Collecting; Close Relations and a Few Black Sheep. *Pos:* cur 20th Cent Art, Santa Barbara Mus Art, 86-92; exec dir, Santa Barbara Contemp Arts Forum, 92-98; dir, Weatherspoon Art Mus, 98-. *Teaching:* Instr, Univ Tenn at Chattanooga, 74-75; instr, Boston Archit Ctr, 77-78; instr, Tufts Univ, 85-86 (summers). *Mem:* AAM; SE Mus Dirs Consortium; Am Asn Coll and Univ Mus & Gal; IMLS (accreditation reviewer). *Specialty:* Contemporary Art. *Collection:* Modern & contemporary art. *Publ:* Keith Puccinelli (auth), The Wondercommon. *Mailing Add:* Univ North Carolina Weatherspoon Art Mus Spring Garden St at Tate St Greensboro NC 27402

DOLMATCH, BLANCHE
PAINTER
b New York, NY, Dec 14, 1925. *Study:* Brooklyn Coll, BA (magna cum laude), 47; Univ Wis, MA, 48; Nat Acad Design, Art Students League, 48-50. *Work:* Nat Mus Women Arts, Washington, DC; Yad Vashem (Nat Mus Israel), Jerusalem; Fed Financial Analytics, Inc, Washington, DC; Mudge Rose Guthrie Alexander & Ferdon, NY; Butler Inst Am Art, Youngstown, Ohio; Hoffman-La Roche, NJ. *Exhib:* Solo exhibs, Katonah Mus, NY, 70, Phoenix Gallery, NYC 73, Hudson River Mus, Yonkers, NY, 87, Butler Inst Am Art, Youngstown, Ohio, 2000, New York Pub Libr, 2003; Group exhibs, Spring Show, Weatherspoon Gallery, Univ NC, Greensboro, 80; Collectors Exhib, McNay Mus, San Antonio, 80; Mem Gallery Ann, Albright-Knox Gallery, Buffalo, 81-82; Archit Images Contemp Ptg, Summit Art Ctr, NJ, 82; Conversations between Cultures, Readers Digest Asn, Pleasantville, NY, 93; City/Country, Park Ave Atrium, NY, 94; Artist of Month, Artists Space, NY, 98; Westchester Arts Coun Invitational, NY, 2000; The Glory of Landscape Then and Now, Pelham Art Ctr, NY, 2008; Total Recall, Katonah Mus; Artists Assn Exhib, 2012. *Awards:* Hudson River Contemp Artist Award for Painting, 72; First Prize (Oils), Nat Asn Women Artists, 73; Top Award for Painting, 24th New Eng Exhib, Silvermine Guild, 73; Award for Painting, Katonah Mus Artists Asn, 2000; Finalist, Nat Alexander Rutsch Competition & Exhib, 2007. *Bibliog:* Helen Hennessey (auth), Interview, NEA Newspaper Syndicate, 4/20/70; Holland Cotter (auth), Review of solo show, NY Arts J, 11/12/78; William Zimmer (auth), Neighbor artists, NY Times, 10/11/92; The Vindicator (review of solo show), Youngstown, Ohio, 12/17/2000; Visions (interview), Katonah Mus Newsletter, fall 2002. *Mem:* Coun Arts Westchester; Katonah Mus Artists Asn. *Media:* Acrylic, Oil on Canvas

DOMINGUEZ, EDDIE
CERAMIST
b Tucumcari, NMex, Oct 17, 1957. *Study:* Cleveland Inst Art, BFA, 81; Alfred Coll Ceramics, MFA, 83. *Work:* Roswell Mus & Art Ctr, NMex; Albuquerque Mus Fine Art, NMex; Mus Fine Art, Santa Fe, NMex; Cooper-Hewitt Mus, NY; Kohler Arts Ctr, Sheboygan, Wis. *Comn:* Tile mural, City Tucson, Ariz; tile mural, Phoenix Airport, Ariz; tile mural, Great Brook Valley Health Ctr, Wooster, Mass. *Exhib:* New Orleans Mus Art, La, 94; solo exhibs, Firehouse Art Ctr, Norman, Okla, 94, Munson Gallery, Santa Fe, NMex, 94, 95, 99, Jan Weiner Gallery, Kansas City, Mo, 95 & 96, Joanne Rapp Gallery/The Hand and the Spirit, Scottsdale, Ariz, 95, Kavesh Gallery, Sun Valley, Idaho, 95, Munson Gallery, Santa Fe, NMex, 97, Northern Clay Ctr, Minn, 98; Margolis Gallery, NY, 95; Margo Jacobson Gallery, Portland, Ore, 96; Jane Haslem Gallery, Washington, 96; Karen Ruhlen Gallery, Santa Fe, NMex, 96; Johnson Co Community Col, Overland Parks, Kans, 96; Site Santa Fe Gallery, NMex, 96; Bruce Kapson Gallery, Santa Monica, Calif, 96; Very Special Arts Gallery, Albuquerque, NMex, 97; Joanne Rapp Gallery/The Hand and the Spirit, Scottsdale, Ariz, 97; Buddy Holly Fine Arts Ctr, Tex, 99; Qualita Gallery/Nancy Hoffman, NMex, 2000. *Pos:* Lectr, Southern Ill Univ, Carbondale, 91; Eastern NMex Univ, Clovis, 91; Cleveland Inst Art, Ohio, 92. *Teaching:* Artist in residence & lectr, Ohio State Univ, 84; Cleveland Inst Art, Ohio, 86; Univ Mont, Missoula, 88; vis artist & lectr, various US & Can Schs, Cols & Univs, 93-97; asst prof fine arts, Univ Nebr, Lincoln, 98. *Awards:* Fel, NEA, 86 & 88; Artists in Res, Roswell Mus & Art Ctr Grant, 87; Kohler Arts-in-Industry Grant, 88. *Media:* Clay, Metal. *Publ:* Contr, Ceramics Month. *Dealer:* Munson Gallery 225 Canyon Rd Santa Fe NM 87501; Joanne Rapp Gallery/The Hand & The Spirit 4222 N Marshall Way Scottsdale AZ 85251. *Mailing Add:* c/o The Munson Gallery 225 Canyon Rd Santa Fe NM 87501

DOMJAN, EVELYN
PAINTER, PRINTMAKER
b Budapest, Hungary, Mar 25, 1922. *Study:* Hungarian Royal Acad Fine Arts, BA, 45. *Work:* Birger Sanzen Mem Gallery, Linsborg, Kans; Saddleriver Valley Cult Ctr, NJ; Am Mus Folk Art, NY; Skylands, Ringwood, NJ; Hungarian Heritage Ctr, New Brunswick, NJ. *Comn:* Fish and Shells of Seven Seas, Wagstaff Residence, Tuxedo Park, NY. *Exhib:* Ringwood Manor Spring and Fall, NJ, 92-94; Skyland Centennial, NJ, 92; The Best is yet to be, Ramapo Col, Mahwah, NJ, 93; Creative Imagery, Small Work Show, Cult Ctr, Demarest, NJ, 93 & Olympia, 95; Black & White, Watchung, NJ, 95. *Teaching:* Lectr graphic arts, art hist, hist world folk art. *Awards:* Nat Endowment Arts, 68; First Prize for Wood Carved Images, Budapest Publ Gondolat, 86. *Bibliog:* Cassidy Enoch-Rex (auth), Of Gardens, Gauguin, and Greece, 1/28/2006. *Mem:* Soc Am Graphic Artist; Salute Women Arts; Ringwood Manor Asn Arts; Metrop Mus Art; Asn Int Des Arts Plastiques, UNESCO; Circle Francais Print Club, Albany. *Media:* woodcuts, exlibko, exhibitions. *Publ:* Auth, Parta, Hungarian Folk Mus, 72; Edge of Paradise, Domjan Studio, 75; Eternal Wool, Domjan Studios, 76; Woodcarved Images, Budapest, 86; Panorama of Hungarian Peasant Painting, 87; Pavologia, Domjan Studios, 88. *Dealer:* Mus Am Hungarian Found 300 Somerset St New Brunswick NJ. *Mailing Add:* 9013 Spicebrush Dr Austin TX 78759-7748

DONAHUE, PHILIP RICHARD
PAINTER, EDUCATOR
b Detroit, Mich, Apr 1, 1943. *Study:* St Peters Col, AB (art hist), 69; Spring Hill Col, MA, 72; Grad Theological Union at UC Berkeley, PhD, 83; painting and visual hermeneutics with Jay DeFeo, John Boyle & Jane Dillenberger. *Comn:* Donahue Painting Series, Soc Jesus, New Orleans, La, 70-82; St Ignatius Mural, St Charles Col, Grand Coteau, La, 72; Presidential Series, Spring Hill Col, Mobile, Ala, 74; Ordination Card Series, Jesuit Sch Theology, Berkeley, Calif, 74-82; covers (Japanese poetry bk), Tokyo, 82-83. *Exhib:* Allied Arts Competition, Metrop Mobile Mus, Ala, 74; The Holy in Art, St Alberts Col, Oakland, Calif, 75; Religious Art Ann, Grad Theological Union, Berkeley, Calif, 75-82; Emergence Art Xian Thought, Grace Cathedral, San Francisco, Calif, 76; Solo exhib, Jesuit Art Ctr, Baltimore, Md, 78; Ann US Exhib, AT Gallery, Tokyo, 82-; Grad Theological Union, Berkeley, 83; Calif Small Works, Sonoma Mus Visual Arts, Santa Rosa, Calif, 2001; Arts on Fire 5, Sanchez Art Center, Pacifica, Calif, 2001; Revealing/Concealing, Taking the Leap Heritage Square, Emeryville, Calif, 2001; 10 Artists Revealed, Sight & Insight Art Center, Mill Valley, Calif, 2001; Showcase 2002, Berkeley Art Center, Berkeley, Calif, 2002; Spring Thing, Sight & Insight Art Center, Mill Valley, Calif, 2002; Coming Together, Art Guild of Pacifica, Calif, 2003; Columbarium, Sun Gallery, Hayward, Calif, 2003; mem only, Richmond Art Ctr, Calif, 2003; Showcase 2004, Berkeley Art Ctr, 2004; Light Shows to Canvas, Cafe Galleria, 2004; Dia De Los Muertos, Sun Gallery, 2004; Showcase 2005, Berkeley Art Ctr, 2005; Paint Behaving Badly, UC Berkeley, 2005; Irohani Gallery, Sakai-Berkeley, Sakai Mus, Osaka, Japan, 2006; Dia de Los Muertos, Oakland Mus, Calif, 2006; Picasso at Lapin Agile, Bainbridge Island, Wash, 2006; Showcase, Berkeley Art Center, Calif, 2006; RTC Found Creativity Center (grand opening), Bainbridge Island, WA, 2007; Rising Sun, Alta Bates Gallery, Berkeley, Calif, 2007; Moshi Moshi, Richmond Art Center, Richmond, Calif, 2007; Showcase 2007, Berkeley Art Center, Berkeley, Calif, 2007; Oil & Water, Bainbridge Island, Wash, 2008; Bridge Artists, Ironi Gallery, Osaka, Japan, 2008; Sakai Gallery, with Junichi Hotta, Osaka, Japan, 2009; Celebration, RTC Found, Bainbridge Island Wash, 2009; Art House Gallery, Atlanta Airport, Ga, 2009; Donahue Treehouse, Bainbridge Island, Wash, 2009; Alchemy of the Abstract V, Northwind Art Ctr, Port Townsend, Wash, 2010; Open Studios, Bainbridge Island, Wash, 2010; Sakai Annual, Gallery Irohani, Osaka, Japan; Expo Culture, Gallery Irohani and HaruHakido Hall, Osaka, Japan, 2011; Open Studios, Bawbridge Island, Wash, 2011; Sakai-Berkeley, Osaka, Japan, 2012; Sakai Kyoto Berkeley, Kyoto, Japan, 2012; Open Studios Bainbridge, Wash, 2012; Mus of Kyoto, Japan, 2012; Sakai Art Mus, Japan, 2012; Corridor Gallery, Seattle, Wash, 2013; NARA Art Mus, Japan, 2013. *Collection Arranged:* Artworks 82, Int Hunger Proj, 82; Link Art Int, Tokyo, Osaka, Hiroshima, 82 & Hakuhodo, Sapporo, 83; 10 Artists Revealed, Mill Valley Art Ctr, Calif, 2001; Spring Thing, Mill Valley Art Ctr, Calif, 2002. *Pos:* Acting chmn, art hist, St Peter's Col, Jersey City, NJ, 67-68; artist-in-residence, St Charles Col, Grand Coteau, La, 70-72 & Jesuit Sch Theology, Berkeley, Calif, 74-82; dir spec events & art educ, Link Art Int Ltd, Oakland, 82-; writer, Meaning in Painting, Finearts, 91-; chief cur, studio visit, Mus of Calif, Oakland, 2003. *Teaching:* Asst instr art hist & drawing, St Peters Col, Jersey City, NJ, 64-68; asst prof painting, Spring Hill Col, Mobile, Ala, 72-74; Link Art Int, 82-. *Awards:* Full Patronage, Soc Jesus, 70-82; First Place, Asn Educ Tech, 72; First Place, Allied Artist Coun, 74; Oscar d'Italia, Academia Italia, Calvatone, Italy, 92; World Culture Prize, Centro Studio, Richerche Della Nazione, Parma, Italy, 94. *Bibliog:* C J McNaspy (auth), American Jesuits in the Arts, The Jesuit, fall 76; K G Connolly (auth), Art & belief, New Catholic World, 1-2/80; T Anzai & A Donahue (auth), Link art international, Motions, Tokyo, 11/81; Breaking all the Rules, Univ Calif Berkeley, Daily Californian, 2005. *Mem:* Am Soc Aesthetics; Int Soc Artists; Art Guild of Pacifica; Int Soc Experimental Artists; Berkeley Art Ctr, Sanchez Art Ctr & Richmond Art Ctr; Mill Valley (Sight & Insight) Art Ctr; Ctr Contemporary Art; Artist Trust; Berkeley-Sakai Artists Bridge; Nat Art Edn Asn; Link Art Int. *Media:* Oil, Mixed Media. *Res:* Iconological hermeneutics: symbolic interpretation of the levels of meanings in paintings. *Publ:* Illusr, Bom Pastor, Brazil, Catholic Voice, 77; auth, Iconological Hermeneutics, Am Acad Religion, 80; Visual Art, Society & Religion, New Catholic World, 80; Greco-Roman Influences in Early Xian Iconology, Calif Classic Asn, 81; contribr to cover, Oasis (Japanese Poetry), Tokyo, Japan, 90. *Dealer:* Gallery Irohani Sakai Osaka Japan. *Mailing Add:* 11591 Berry Patch Ln NE Bainbridge Island WA 98110

DONAHUE, THOMAS JOHN
PAINTER, INSTRUCTOR
b Memphis, Tenn, Jan 25, 1948. *Study:* Univ Memphis, 1966-1971; Memphis Col Art, 1972. *Work:* Tenn State Capitol Gov's Collection, Nashville, Tenn; Rhodes Co, Memphis, Tenn; St Jude Children's Res Hosp (ALSAC). Memphis, Tenn; Rose-Hulman Inst Tech, Terre Haute, Ind; Fairfield Univ, Fairfield, Conn. *Comn:*

Danny Thomas (portrait), St Jude Children's Res Hosp, Nashville, Tenn, 1987; Wayne Calloway (portrait), Wake Forest Univ, Winston Salem, NC, 1999; Hon James Exum (portrait), NC State Supreme Ct, Raleigh, NC, 2000; Dr William E Trout (portrait), Rhodes Co, Memphis, Tenn; Gov Don Sundquist (portrait), State of Tenn, Nashville, Tenn, 2002; Paquito D'Rivera (portrait), Nat Arts Club, NY, 2010; Lauren Bacall (portrait), The Players Club, NY, 2011. *Exhib:* Exhib Artist Members Exhib, Nat Arts Club, NYC, 1997, 1999, 2004, 2005. *Teaching:* Fac, Portraiture, Memphis Col Art, 1982-1983; fac, Portrait Soc Am, 1998-. *Awards:* Freedom Found Valley Forge Hon Cert, 1963; Medal for Arts, Germantown Arts Alliance, 2002. *Bibliog:* Chris Haywood (auth), Portrait of an Artist, Memphis Mag, July-Aug 1995; Stephen Doherty (auth), Portrait Painting Today, Am Artist, 4/1999; Kathy Martin (auth), Picture Perfect, Midsouth Living, 11/2003; Allison Malafronte (auth), Timeless Personalities, Am Artist, 9/2008. *Mem:* Portrait Soc Am (secy, treas, 1998-); Nat Arts Club; Artists Fel. *Media:* Oil on canvas. *Publ:* Auth, The Line King, Int Artist, 2003

DONEHOO, JONATHAN
ADMINISTRATOR, EDUCATOR
Study: Univ Georgia, BFA, 1977; Louisiana Tech Univ, MFA, 1980. *Exhib:* Univ Mobile, Art With a Southern Drawl; Work on Paper, San Jacinto Col, Houston, Tex; Louisiana State Univ; Tex Artists Mus, Port Arthur, Tex; 8th Annual Nat Prize Show, Cambridge, Massachusetts; Nat Compact Competition, Baton Rouge; Tex Nat, Nacpgdoches, Tex. *Pos:* Program Coordinator for communication design, Louisiana Tech Univ, 1985-2006, dir Sch of Art, 2006-. *Teaching:* Prof Graphic Design, East Tennessee State Univ, 1980-85; prof Studies Abroad Paris Program, Sch of Art, Louisiana Tech Univ, 2004-. *Mailing Add:* School of Art Louisiana Tech University PO Box 3175W VAC 113 Ruston LA 71272

DONER, MICHELE OKA
SCULPTOR
b Miami Beach, Fla, Dec 4, 1945. *Study:* Univ Mich, BA, 1966; Univ Mich, MA, Teaching Fellowship, 1968; Univ Detroit (post grad work) 1969. *Work:* Terrible Table, Art Inst Chicago, 1990; IO Cast Bench cast bronze, collection Va Mus Fine Arts, 1990; Silver Pieces for Ronaldus Shamask design collection Metrop Mus Art, NY, 1991; 18K Gold Frond Necklace, prototype, Musee Les Arts Decoratifs, Louvre Paris, France, acquired, 2004; Bronze from Celestial Plaza, Rose Planetarium. Am Mus Natural Hist, NY, 1987, reinstalled 2004; Works on Paper, Metrop Mus Art, 2006; and over 20 other pub art comns in the US. *Comn:* A Walk on the Beach, Miami Int Airport Concourse A, bronze in terrazzo, 1995; Radiant Site (11,000 stoneware gold lustre tiles), Herald Square Subway Station, NYC, 1999; Medallion: Flight, bronze in terrazzo concourse floor, Ronald Reagan Nat Airport, Arlington Va, 1996; Biblical Species, Center for Jewish Hist, NY, 1999; Lobby floor, bronze in terrazzo, US Courthouse, Gulfport, Miss, 2002; From Seashore to Tropical Garden, bronze in terrazzo, N Terminal Expansion, Miami Int Airport, Miami, Fla, 2002-. *Exhib:* Solo shows incl Michele Oka Doner: Works in Progress, Detroit Inst Arts, Detroit, Mich, 1978, Marlborough Gallery, NY, 2003, 2005, 2008, Triennial: Design Now, Cooper-Hewitt Nat Design Mus, NY, 2005, Feeding Desire, Cooper-Hewitt Nat Design Mus, Smithsonian Inst, NY, 2006; group shows incl On Growth & Form, Germans Van Eck Gallery, NY, 1984; Diane Brown Gallery, NY, 1987; Art Et Industrie, NY, 1990; Formed by Fire, Carnegie Mus Art, Pittsburgh, Pa, 1994; Debut: Selections from the Permanent Collection: Kemper Mus Contemp Art & Design, Kansas City, Mo, 1994; Body Language, Cooper-Hewitt Nat Design Mus, Smithsonian Inst, NY, 1995; Bare Witness Clothing & Nudity, Metrop Mus of Art, NY, 1996; Marlborough Gallery, NY, 2002; New Additions Outdoors, Grounds for Sculpture, Hamilton, NJ, 2003; Nat Design Triennial, Cooper-Hewitt Nat Design Mus, Smithsonian Inst, NY, 2003. *Collection Arranged:* Metrop Mus of Art, NY; Art Inst of Chicago; Am Mus of Natural Hist, NY; Va Mus of Fine Arts, Va; Children's Mus of Manhattan, NY. *Awards:* Award of Excellence, UN Soc of Artists & Writers; Distinguished Alumni Award, Univ Mich. *Bibliog:* Arthur Danto, Morris Lapidus (coauths), Michele Oka Doner, Natural Seduction, Hudson Hills Press (essays), 2003; Michele Oka Doner: Workbook, OKA Press (variety of essays by art Profs, OKA Press, 2004; Mitchell Wolfson, Jr, Alastair Gordon (coauths), Miami Beach: Blueprint of an Eden, Feierabend Unique Bks, 2005, 2nd Ed, Harper-Collins, 2007. *Mem:* Wolfsonian Mus, Miami Beach, Fla (trustee); Pratt Inst, Brooklyn, NY (trustee). *Media:* Installation Sculpture, Cast Metal, Printmaker, All Media. *Specialty:* Marlborough Gallery, NY:Contemp Fine Art, Painting, Sculpture, Works on Paper. *Publ:* auth, Glueck, Grace, Image & Object in Contemporary Sculpture (review), NY Times, 1/11/1980; auth, Floor Plan, Washington Post (p M1), 4/3/1998; auth, Glueck, Grace Michele Oka Doner: Four Decades, Four Media, Marborough Gallery (review p E46), NY Times Art in Review, 12/31/2004; Hayden-Guest Anthony, There is no Craft Here, This is About Ideas, Financial Times (p W16), 9/2006; Sandra Bloodworth & William Ayres, Along the Way: MTA Arts for Transit, NY, Monacelli Press (56, 167), 2007. *Dealer:* Marlborough Gallery 40 W 57th St New York NY 10019; Studio Stefania Miscetti Via Delle Mantellate 14 00165 Rome Italy. *Mailing Add:* 94 Mercer St 2nd Fl New York NY 10001

DONHAUSER, PAUL STEFAN
SCULPTOR, PAINTER
b Berlin, Ger, May 6, 1936; US citizen. *Study:* Univ Wis-Milwaukee, BS (art); Univ Wis-Madison, MS (art); Ill State Univ, PhD (art). *Work:* Int Mus Ceramics, Faenza, Italy; Nat Mus Art, Gdansk, Poland; Maison des Metiers d'Art Francais, Paris; Everson Mus Art, Syracuse, NY; Smithsonian Inst, Washington, DC. *Comn:* Relief mural (6ft x 15ft), Student Union, Wis State Col, Oshkosh, 71; series of five free standing outdoor sculptures, Univ Wis Campus, 78; Ceramic mural (6 ft x 40 ft), Hughes Hall, Winn City Health Ctr, 84; Paintings (4 ft x 8 ft), Columba Correctional Inst, Portage Wis. *Exhib:* Wis Directions, Milwaukee Art Ctr, 76; Landscape: New Views, Johnson Mus, Cornell Univ, Ithaca, NY, 78; Int Biennial Exhib of Ceramic Sculpture, Vallauris, France, 78; Clay & Fiber, Wustum Fine Arts Mus, Racine, Wis, 78; Donhauser Retrospective: 1957-1977, Paine Art Mus, Oshkosh, 77; Int Ceramics Exhib, Tejimi, Japan. *Teaching:* Instr ceramics, Madison Area Tech Col, Wis, 60-63; instr drawing & ceramics, Ill State Univ, Normal, 63-65; prof ceramics, Univ Wis, Oshkosh, 65-. *Awards:* Nat Award for Ceramic Sculpture, 8th Miami Ceramic Nat Exhib, Coral Gables Art Asn, Fla, 72; Grand Prize of Faenza, 35th Int Exhib of Ceramics, Int Mus of Ceramics, 76; Nat Endowment Arts, Visual Artist Fel, 84. *Bibliog:* Sergio Cavina (auth), Emilia Romagna, Regione, Bologna, Italy, 9/76; Linda Witt (auth), Donhauser wins Italy's top ceramic prize, People Weekly, 10/11/76; James Auer (auth), Uncommon clay, Milwaukee J, 9/77. *Mem:* Int Acad of Ceramics, Geneva, Switz; Am Crafts Coun; Wis Designer Craftsmen. *Media:* Acrylic, Ceramics. *Publ:* Co-auth, New Ceramics, St Martins, London, 74; auth, History of American ceramics, The Studio Potter, Kendall/Hunt, 78. *Dealer:* Ruth Volid Gallery 225 W Illinois St Chicago IL 60610; Tori Folliard Gallery Milwaukee WI. *Mailing Add:* 5724 I Ah May Tah Rd 210 Museum Pl Oshkosh WI 54901

DONLEY, RAY
PAINTER
b Austin, Tex, Dec 4, 1950. *Study:* Univ Tex at Austin, BFA, 1981; Univ Tex at Austin, MA, 1983. *Work:* Univ Tex at Austin, San Remo, Italy; Rockford Art Mus, Ill. *Exhib:* Solo exhibs, Wright Gallery, NY, 2001, Principle Gallery, Alexandria, Va, 2007, Gallery Bienvenu, New Orleans, La, 2008, Sarah Bain Gallery, Anaheim, Calif, 2008, 2010, Medici Gallery, London, Eng, 2008, Galerie Utrecht, Utrecht, The Netherlands, 2008; Principle Gallery, Alexandria, Va, 2005; Galerie Utrecht, Amsterdam, The Netherlands, 2008; The Russell Collection, Austin, Tex, 2008; Attleboro Arts Mus, Attleboro, Mass, 2008; Sarah Bain Gallery, Anaheim, Calif. *Pos:* artist in res, St Edward's Univ, Austin, Tex. *Awards:* First Prize, San Remo Biennale, 2003. *Bibliog:* Michael Barnes (auth), Last Word on the Arts, Austin Am Statesman, 2001; Jared Schroeder (auth), Exhibit: Paintings Evoke Dark Side, San Angelo Standard Times, 2003; Molly Beth Brenner (auth), A Piece of Work: A Painting by Ray Donley, Austin Chronicle, 2004; Donald Kuspit & Ryan Mihm (auths), Dancing the Inquisition Waltz: The Art of Ray Donley, Scapegoat Publ, Baltimore, Md (in prep); and others; Gail Leggio (auth), Ray Donley, Am Arts Quarterly, Spring, 2008. *Mem:* Asn Art Historians. *Media:* Oil & Mixed Media. *Dealer:* Sarah Bain Gallery Anaheim CA; Principle Gallery Alexandria VA; Gallery Bienvenu New Orleans LA; Medici Gallery London Eng; Elisa Tucci New York NY. *Mailing Add:* c/o Elisa Contemporary Art 130 Seventh Ave Ste 353 New York NY 10011

DONLEY, ROBERT MORRIS
PAINTER, EDUCATOR
b Cleveland, Ohio, July 5, 1934. *Study:* Sch Art Inst, BFA, 60, MFA, 66. *Work:* Ill State Univ, Normal; Northern Ill Univ, DeKalb; Mobil Oil Corp, NY; Smithsonian Inst, Washington, DC; Boeing Corp; and others. *Exhib:* Los Angeles Mus Ann, Los Angeles Co Mus, 59-61; Nat Traveling Exhib Chicago Artists, Crocker Mus Art, Sacramento, Calif, 76; 76th & 77th Exhib Artists Chicago & Vicinity, Art Inst Chicago, 77 & 78; New Visions, Aldrich Mus Contemp Art, Ridgefield, Conn, 81; Crimes of Compassion, Chrysler Mus, Norfolk, Va, 81; 36th Ill Invitational, Ill State Mus, Springfield, 84; Intersections: Artists View of the City, Laguna Gloria Art Mus, Austin, Tex, 86; Fetish Art: Obsessive Expressions, Rockford Art Mus, Ill, 86; Chicago Art 1945-1995, Mus Contemp Art, 96-97. *Teaching:* Prof painting & drawing, De Paul Univ, Chicago, Ill, 67-. *Awards:* Logan Prize, 77; Nat Endowment Arts Grant, 80; Pauline Palmer Prize, Chicago Show, 90. *Bibliog:* Carrie Rickey (auth), Chicago, Art in Am, 7-8/79; Judith Wilson (auth), The last detail, Village Voice, Vol XXV, No 49, 80; Michele Vishny (auth), Robert Donley, Arts Mag, 10/83. *Media:* Oil, Acrylic. *Dealer:* Corbett Us Dempsey Chicago IL

DONMEZ, YUCEL
PAINTER, SCULPTOR
b Kars, Turkey, Jan 5, 1946; US citizen. *Study:* Applied Fine Arts Acad, Istanbul, BA, 74. *Work:* UN Plaza, NY; High Flt Found, Colorado Springs, Colo; Vestel Electronics Corp, Manişa, Turkey; Truman Col, Int Press Ctr, Chicago; plus others. *Comn:* Snow paintings, Chicago Grand Park, Chicago, Ill 93; 15,000 meter square snow paintings, Fuji Film Istanbul, Mount Uludag, Bursa, Turkey, 96; Mediterranean Art Festival, Miami & Boca Raton, Fla, 1987; Turkish Art Ministry Comn. *Exhib:* Int Art Fair, Navy Pier, Chicago, 73; Sculpture Exhib, Chicago Pub Libr Cult Ctr, 74; Meditteranian Weeks, Bloomingdale Support, Miami, 87; Turkish Art Gallery, UN Plaza, NY, 87; Turkish Am Artist, Art Inst Chicago, 87; First Contemp Exhib, Topkadi Palace Mus, Turkey, 92; Istanbul Art Expo, 90, 97, 98, 99, 2000, 2002; Middletown Art Fest 2000, Middletown, Ohio; Gallery 2000 Chicago, 2002; plus others. *Collection Arranged:* Bahceschir Univ, Istanbul, Turkey, 2000. *Pos:* adviser for 21 centuries Art Rsch, Bahcesehir Univ, Istanbul, Turkey. *Teaching:* Artist workshops, Urban Gateways, Chicago, 88-97. *Awards:* 21st Century's Artist Award, North Am Turkish Asn Price Commn. *Bibliog:* Interview with Maureen Wolf, WGN TV, 7/87; Margaret Sheridan (auth), Chicago Tribune, 6/26/88; Alan G Artner (auth), Chicago Tribune, 8/24/89; Brian Clifford (auth), The Middletown Jour, 10/1/2000. *Mem:* Plastic Arts Found, Turkey; Urban Gateways, Chicago. *Media:* Acrylic, Glass, Metal, Rock, Snow, Digital Works. *Publ:* Auth, Canvas and Digital Works, Zerdust Publ, 2001. *Dealer:* Gallery 2000 Chicago 2246 N Clark St Chicago IL 60614. *Mailing Add:* 5520 N Artesian Ave Apt 3 Chicago IL 60625

DONNANGELO, DAVID MICHAEL
PAINTER, ART DEALER
b Bethlehem, Pa, Sept 3, 1957. *Study:* Studied sculpture under Italo Scanga; Moravian Col; Tyler Sch Art; Baum Sch Barnes Found. *Work:* Rome, Italy; RCA Weaversville Prog, Northampton, Pa; Musikfiest Collection, Bethlehem, Pa. *Comn:* Murals, Super Value, Laneco, Inc, Allentown, Bethlehem & Easton, Pa, 93; Catholic Oils, Wegmans. *Exhib:* Governor's Exhib, William Penn Mus, Harrisburg, Pa, 74; Art Gallery Award, Kemerer Mus, Bethlehem, Pa, 75; Lehigh Art Alliance Exhib, 80; Hazelton Art League Regional Exhib, 81; 9th Nat Print Show, Moravian Col, Payne Gallery, Bethlehem, Pa, 94. *Awards:* First Place, Bethlehem Art Show Comt, 76; Purchase Award, Pa State Univ, 81; Purchase Award, Moravian Col, 94. *Media:* Oil, Acrylic. *Dealer:* Contemporary Fine Art. *Mailing Add:* 1881 Abington Rd Bethlehem PA 18018

DONNELLY, TRISHA
CONCEPTUAL ARTIST
b San Francisco, Calif, 1974. *Study:* Univ Calif, Los Angeles, BFA, 95; Yale Univ, Sch Art, MFA, 2000. *Exhib:* Solo exhibs, Air de Paris, 2002, Casey Kaplan, NY, 2002 & 2004, Art Positions, Art Miami Beach, 2003, The Wrong Gallery, NY, 2004, Art Pace, San Antonio, Tex, 2005, Kunsthalle Zürich, 2005, Gallery Modern Art, Bolgona, 2006 & Special Project Portikus, Frankfurt a Main, 2006; group exhibs, Minty, Richard Telles Gallery, Los Angeles, 99; Found Louis-Jeantet de Médecine, Geneva, 99; Echo, Artist's Space, NY, 2000; The Dedalic Convention, MAK Mus, Vienna, 2001; Moving Pictures, Solomon R Guggenheim Mus, 2002; Hello, My Name Is..., Carnegie Mus Art, Pittsburgh, 2002; 50th Int Exhib Art, Venice Biennial, 2003; Peripheries become the center, Prague Biennial, 2003; Biennial Contemp African Art, Obrist, Dakar, 2004; Collection (or How I Spent a Year), PS1 Contemp Art Ctr, Long Island City, 2004; Moscow Biennial Contemp Art, 2005; The Imaginary Number, Kunst Werk, Berlin, 2005; 4th Berlin Biennial Contemp Art: Of Mice & Men, 2006; Documenta (13), Kassel, Ger, 2012; 54th Int Art Exhib Biennale, Venice, 2011, 55th Int Art Exhib Biennale, Venice, 2013; and many others. *Pos:* clin assoc prof art, NY Univ Steinhardt Sch Culture, Edn, and Human Develpment, 2008-. *Awards:* recipient, Central-Kuntspreis, Cologne, Ger, 2004; Prix de la Fondation Luma, Arles, France, 2010; Sharjah Biennial prize, 2011; Faber Castell Drawing award, 2011. *Media:* Photography, Drawing, Audio, Video, Sculpture, Performance. *Mailing Add:* New York University Steinhardt School of Culture 82 Washington Sq East New York NY 10003

DONNESON, SEENA
SCULPTOR, GRAPHICS ARTIST
b New York, NY. *Study:* Pratt Inst; Art Students League, with Morris Kantor; Pratt Graphic Arts Ctr, with Michael Ponce de Leon. *Work:* Mus Mod Art, NY; Phillip Morris Int, NY; Los Angeles Co Mus Art; Smithsonian Mus, Washington, DC; Ft Lauderdale Mus Art; Boca Raton Mus Art, Fla; Doris Freedman Collection, Albright Univ, Pa; Brooklyn Mus Art, New York; Cornell Univ, Med Sch, New York; USA Art in Embassies. *Exhib:* Ed prints, Touchstone Press, tapestry design, Equitable Life & Insurance Co, NY, 76, ed prints, Ft Lauderdale Mus Fine Arts, Fla, 77, outdoor sculpture, Snug Harbor Cult Ctr, Grow-Kiewit-Mk, NY, 79, outdoor sculpture, Jersey City State Col, NJ, 81; Material & Metaphor, Wm Paterson Col, Ben Shahn Gallery; Norfolk Mus Arts & Scis; Ann City Mus Art Gallery, Hong Kong; Paper Works, State Univ NY, Stonybrook, 94; The Collograph, Pratt Graphic Arts traveling exhib, NY State Coun Arts; and others. *Pos:* App mem, Nassau Co Fine Arts Comn, 70-; exhib cur coordr, Dept Parks, Recreation & Cult Affairs, NY, 71-74; jury mem, Queens Co Prog, 1995, 1998; lectr, Mod Art, NY Univ, Nassau Co, NY, 1961-1963; Art consult, Nat Exec Serv Corps, 2005-. *Teaching:* in-sch-artist, Nassau Co Cult Coun, 71-79; lectr, Nassau Co Off Cult Develop, 71-79 & New Sch Social Res, 74-; painting & drawing, New Hampshire Col, 80-83; private students; vis artist, Tamarind Lithography Workshop, Los Angeles Calif. *Awards:* Fel, MacDowell Found, 63, 64; Clayworks, NY, 81; Creative Artists Serv Prog Grant, NY State Coun Arts, 83-84; Queens Coun Arts (3 times juror, regrants), 89. *Bibliog:* John Perreault (auth), Up the river, Soho Weekly News, 78; Grace Glueck (auth), Sculpture under a city sky, New York Times, 78; Mary Anne Pennington (dir), Seena Donneson, Relief Sculpture (film), Greenville Mus Art, NC, 87; Phyllis Braff (auth), Uses of paper, New York Times, 97; Nat Asn Women Artists (photo), Newsday, 97. *Mem:* Artists Equity Asn, NY; Long Island City Artists Inc (bd dir); Nat Arts Club, NYC; New Eng Sculptors; Nat Asn Women Artists. *Media:* Metals, Paper; Collographs, Etchings. *Specialty:* Sculpture. *Interests:* Travel, Theatre, Music. *Publ:* Beata Thackeray (auth), Paper: Making-Decorating (photo, review, listing), Conran Octopus, Ltd, London, Eng, 10-97; contribr, American Printmakers, Graphics Group, 74; Women Artists in America, 75; Exploring The Visual Arts, Davis Publ, 76. *Dealer:* Quietude Sculpture Gallery Garden 24 Fern Rd East Brunswick NJ; Spring Gallery Belgrade Lakes ME

D'ONOFRIO, BERNARD MICHAEL
GLASS BLOWER, SCULPTOR
b Medford, Mass, Jan 7, 1951. *Study:* Univ Mass, Amherst, BFA, 73; Pilchuck Sch, Stanwood, Wash, 81-82; Kent State Univ, MFA, 83. *Work:* Moderne Int Glaskunst, Ebeltoft, Denmark; Pilchuck, Stanwood, Wash; Headley Whitney Mus, Lexington, Ky; Milwaukee Art Mus, Wis; Kogawezaki Glass Mus, Shizvoka, Japan; Tampa Art Mus. *Comn:* Bank One, Akron, Ohio, 82; Network World, Framingham, Mass, 90; Meditech Corp, Westwood, MA, 2004. *Exhib:* Boston Now, Inst Contemp Art, Boston, Mass, 89; Contemp Glass, Milwaukee Art Mus, Wis, 90; Solo exhibs, Snyderman Gallery, Philadelphia, Pa, 90 & Sanske Gallery, Zurich, Switz, 92; 10th Anniversary Exhibition, Helander Gallery, West Palm Beach, Fla, 91; World Glass Exhib, Gallery Nakama, Tokyo, Japan, 91; Garland Gallery, Santa Fe, NMex, 93; William Traver Gallery, Seattle, Wash, 94; Holsten Gallery, Stockbridge, Mass, 99-2000; Habatat Galleries, Boco Raton, Fla, 2000; Sofa, Chicago Navy Pier, 2000; Habatat Galleries, Chicago, 2002; Morgan Gallery, Pittsburgh, 2003. *Collection Arranged:* Bronfman Collection; Pritzker Collection. *Pos:* Dir, D'Onofrio Studio. *Teaching:* Instr design, Cranbrook Sch, Bloomfield Hills, Mich, 73-80; vis lectr glass, Mass Coll Art, Boston, 83-; vis artist glass, Tokyo Glass Art Inst, Japan, 92 & 98. *Awards:* Finalist Award, Mass Artists Fel, 89; Visual Artist Fel, Nat Endowment Arts, 90; Silver Prize International Glass Kanazawa, Japan, 92. *Bibliog:* Susan Barahal (auth), Sculptural perspectives, Art New Eng, 88; Paul Hollistr (auth), Delicate and bold, NY Times, 89; James Yood (auth), review, Glass Magazine, winter 2002. *Mem:* Glass Art Soc. *Media:* Glass. *Dealer:* Imago Art 73-970 El Paseo Palm Dessert CA 92260; Holsten Gallery Elm St Stockbridge MA 01260. *Mailing Add:* 299 Village St Millis MA 02054

DONOHOE, VICTORIA
HISTORIAN, CRITIC
b Philadelphia, Pa. *Study:* Rosemont Col, BA; Univ Pa Grad Sch Fine Arts, MFA; Pius XII Inst Fine Arts Advan Study, Florence, Italy, cert(scholar), 53; Am Fedn Arts (semester), Workshop Art Criticism, scholar(with Max Kozloff), 68. *Hon Degrees:* Villanova Univ, PhD (fine arts), 1985. *Collection Arranged:* Religious & Liturgical Art from the Eastern US, Philadelphia Civic Ctr, 63. *Pos:* Art critic, Standard & Times, Philadelphia, 59-62; art critic, Philadelphia Inquirer, 62-; guest cur, Into Storage Exhib, Univ Mus, Univ Pa, 74; corresp, Art News, 75-; dir for selection, Exhib Liturgical Art, 41st Int Eucharistic Cong, Philadelphia, 76 (for this exhib chose artists for 25 commissioned works); adv, Philadelphia Craft Show, 77; adv fac, Franklin & Marshall Col, 79; mem comt, Nat Millennium Scared Art Project. *Teaching:* Lab asst studio art & art hist, Rosemont Col, 50-52, lectr, 54-55. *Awards:* Award, Catholic Fine Arts Soc, 76; Hist Preservation Award, Hist Archit Rev Bd, Lower Merion Twp, Pa, 98; Award of Nat Register, Hist Places Status. *Mem:* Int Asn Art Critics/Am Sect; Soc Archit Historians; Irish Georgian Soc, Dublin; Medieval Acad Am; Am-Italy Soc; Lower Merion Conservaney, comt. *Res:* Late 19th & early 20th century American sculpture; figurative painting & sculpture; contemporary crafts; American architecture; cultural history; in late 19th and early 20th century Am archit and design. *Publ:* Contribr, Sculpture of a City: Philadelphia's Treasures in Bronze and Stone, 74; contribr, Knight-Ridder Newswire, 73-; also contribr to anthologies, mags, encyclopedias & Sunday supplements; contribr, Invisible Philadelphia: Community Through Voluntary Organizations, 95; contribr, From Style to Program: Evolution of Taste and Aesthetics in Liturgical Art from the Mid-19th Century to the Post-World War II Era, Stained Glass in Catholic Phila, 2002; auth (wk articles), Philadelphia Inquirer. *Mailing Add:* 34 Narbrook Park Narberth PA 19072-2124

DOO DA POST, EDWARD FERDINAND HIGGINS III
PAINTER, MAIL ARTIST
b LaCrosse, Wis, Nov 10, 1959. *Study:* Western Mich Univ, Kalamazoo, BA (art), 72; Univ Colo, Boulder, MFA, 76. *Work:* Electroworks Collection, Eastman House, Rochester, NY; US Post Off, Boulder, Colo; Univ Mich, Ann Arbor; Artists Stamps & Stamp Images, Simon Frasier Univ Gallery, Burnaby, BC; Jean Brown Arch, Shaker Seed House, Tryingham, Mass; Swiss Postal Mus, Bern, Switz; and others. *Comn:* Business Face Issue (portrait), Paul Schorr; portrait & sheets, Doo Da Stamps of Portrait, Sue Blair. *Exhib:* Fourteenth Midwest Joslyn Art Mus, Omaha, Nebr, 76; Timbres, Et Tampons, E' Artistes Cabnet des Extampes, Mus d'Art & d'Histoire, Geneva, Switz, 76; 4th Denver Metro Show, Denver Art Mus, 76; 6th New York City Doo Da Art Show & Auction, XOXO Gallery, NY, 94; Stamp Art Gallery, San Francisco, 96; Baby Jakes, NY, 96; and others. *Collection Arranged:* First New York City Stamp Invite (auth, catalog), 34 Artists' Stamp Images, 77; Commonpress Number 18 (auth, catalog), 79; Third Int Doo Da Stamp Invite (catalog in prep), 384 Artists stamps. *Pos:* 3rd Grand Poo Ba, Order Triangle-Glue (sea tech # 5). *Teaching:* Prof painting, Rivington Sch Artists, NY; prof, Elberta Sch Art, Elberta, Mich. *Awards:* CT Chew Schwendelmarken Rug Award, 96. *Bibliog:* Peter Frank (auth), Artists Stamps, Art Express 1, Vol 1, 81; Alexandra Anderson (auth), Portfolio 3, Vol 3, 5-6/81; Ronnie Cohen (auth), article, Art News, 12/81; Google up: EF Higgins III or Doo Da Postage Works. *Mem:* Rivington Sch; Knights Templar Carver Rubber-Eraser Division. *Media:* Acrylic, Color Xerox. *Publ:* Auth & illusr, To Grow an Asparagus (under pen name Sam Scotland), 70, & A Piece of Licorice and Other White Elephants, 72, Glotco; contribr, The Rubber Stamp Album, Workman Publ, 78; auth, Artists' stamps, Print Collectors' Newsletter, 11-12/79; Artistamp News, Vancouver, BC, Can, vol 1 No 2, 8/92; The 3rd International Doo Da Stamp Invite, 2000; poster/3 ft banners, Paragelrug, Art Pool, Budapest, Hungary, 2007. *Dealer:* Gracie Mansion Gallery New York City. *Mailing Add:* 153 Ludlow St New York NY 10002-2241

DOOGAN, BAILEY
PAINTER, INSTRUCTOR
b Philadelphia, Pa, Oct 24, 1941. *Study:* Moore Coll of Art, Pa, BFA, 63; UCLA, MA, 77. *Work:* Tucson Mus Art; Univ of Ariz Mus Art; Ariz State Univ Art Mus, Nelson Fine Arts Ctr, Tempe; Pensacola Jr Col, Fla; Annaghmakerrig, Tyrone Guthrie Ctr, Co Monagham, Ireland. *Exhib:* Phoenix Triennial, Phoenix Art Mus, Ariz, 90; Original Sin, Hillwood Mus Long Island Univ, 91; Mea Corpa Artists of Conscience Series, Alternative Mus, NY, 92; Int Critics Choice, Mitchell Mus, Ill, 93; Signs of Age: Representing the Older Body, Santa Barbara Contemp Art Forum, Calif, 97-98; Theatre of Self Invention: Self Portrature in Contemp Art, Speed Art Mus, Ky, 98; A Survey of Drawings 1988-98, Univ Ariz Mus of Art, 98; Picturing the Modern Amazon, The New Mus Contemp Art, NY, 2000. *Pos:* prof painting/drawing, Univ Ariz, 82-99, prof emerita, 99-. *Teaching:* visiting prof painting/drawing, Univ Nevada, 92. *Awards:* Fel in Painting Nat Endowment for the Arts, 96; Ariz Arts Award Southern Ariz Community Found, 96; Contemp Forum Grant Phoenix Art Mus, 98; Joan Mitchell Found Grant, 2009. *Bibliog:* Ann Wilson Lloyd (auth) Report from Tucson: The New West, Art in Am, 10/92; Joanna Frueh, Arlene Raven Langer (auths), New Feminist Criticism: Art Identity Action, Harper Collins, 93; Joanna Frueh (auth) Erotic Faculties, Univ Calif Press, 96. *Mem:* Coll Art Asn (bd dir national 97-). *Media:* Oil. *Publ:* contribr Conversation: Picturing the Modern Amazon, Art Journal, 2000. *Dealer:* Etherton Gallery 135 South 6th Ave Tucson AZ 85701

DOOLEY, DAVID I
PAINTER, EDUCATOR
b Olney, Ill, Jan 15, 1940. *Study:* Eastern Ill Univ, BS, 68, MS, 72; Univ Ill, post grad, 79; Am Acad Art, Chicago, 80. *Work:* Citizens Bank Collection, Evansville, Ind; George Koch Sons Inc, Evansville, Ind; Dining Oil Collection, Lawrenceville, Ill; Bristol-Myers Squibb Co, Evansville, Ind. *Comn:* Point of Purchase (illus), Berol, Brentwood, Tenn, 93. *Exhib:* Wabash Valley Exhib, Sheldon Swope Art Mus, Terre Haute, Ind, 84-94; Realism Today, Evansville Mus Arts, Ind, 84-92; Masters of Colored Pencil Nat, Massey Fine Arts, Santa Teresa, NMex, 93; New Harmony Gallery Contemp Art, Ind, 94; Lana Competition Exhib, Campbell-Thiebaud Gallery, San Francisco, Calif, 94. *Teaching:* Prof art drawing, Vincennes Univ, Ind, 82-94; workshop instr mixed media, Discover Art, San Diego, Calif, 92-94 & Nat Art Mat & Trade, 92-94. *Awards:* Purchase Award, Realism Today, Bristol-Meyers Squibb, 87; Third Place, Masters Colored Pencil Nat, Massey Fine Arts, 92; Purchase Award, Border to Border, Larson Biennial Nat Drawing, 93. *Bibliog:* Doris Replogle Porter

(auth), Illinois artist David Dooley, Ill Mag, 88; Stephen Doherty (dir), Reflections of Excellence (video), 92; Sandra Angelo (dir), Special Effects with Colored Pencils (video), 94. *Media:* Colored Pencil. *Publ:* Coauth, Isolated in the Absurd, Prairie Press Publ Co, 69; auth, Applying colored pencil over an acrylic wash, Am Artist, 89; contribr, Colored Pencil Basics, Walter Foster & Co, 94; Painting with colored pencils, Artist's Mag, 7/94; Colored-pencil artists get it together, Am Artist, 94. *Mailing Add:* RR 3 Box 384 Lawrenceville IL 62439

DOOLEY WALLER, M L
PAINTER
b Kansas City, Mo. *Study:* Rockhurst Col, Kansas City, Mo, 57; Kansas City Art Inst & Sch Design, BFA, 58; Univ Kans, MFA candidate, 71; Univ Mich, MFA, 82 (scholar Sch Art, 80). *Comn:* Lilly Research Clinic, Ind Univ Hosp, Indianapolis; Sallie Mae, 2001; Community Health Network Found, Indianapolis; Indianapolis Chamber Orchesta Comn, 2010; and many commissions for pvt individuals. *Exhib:* Solo Exhibs: Contemp Art Gallery, Kansas City, Mo, 58; Central Col, Fayette, Mo, 58; Rockhurst Col, Kansas City, Mo, 58; Kans City Art Inst & Sch Design, 58; Ruschman Gallery, Indianapolis, 93, 98, 2004 & 2008, Gallery 924, Indianapolis, 2015 ; Group Exhibs: Soc Wash Printmakers, Nat Mus Am Art, Wash, 58, Eleventh Nat Print Exhib, Brooklyn Mus, 58; Nat Mus Am Art, 58; AM Fed Arts Traveling Exhib, 58-60; Joslyn Art Mus, 58; Nelson-Atkins Mus 58-60; Gibbes Art Mus, Charleston, SC, 61-62, Detroit Focus Gallery, 80, Nina Freudenheim Gallery, Buffalo, 84, Memorial Art Gallery, Rochester, NY, 82-83, Rackham Gallery, Univ Mich, 80; Shahin Requicha Gallery, Rochester, NY, 82, 84 & 85; Rush Rhees Gallery, Univ Rochester, 85; Mulvane Art Mus, 58-59, Ruschman Gallery, Indianapolis, 92-2010; Ind Univ E, Richmond, 96; Northwest Printmakers 30th Int Exhib, Seattle Art Mus, Seattle, Wash, 1959; Artcore, Los Angeles, Calif, 90, 91, 92; The Graphics Generation 1940-1965, Indianapolis Mus Art, 93; The Act of Painting, Mem Art Gallery, Rochester, NY, 98; Collectors Vision: Selections from Collection of Edmund Pease & Nurak Israsena, Morris Mus, Morristown, NJ, 2000; Whispers to Shouts, Ind State Mus, Indianapolis, 2005; Curator's Choice, Highlighting Ind Art, Ind State Mus, 2006; Edington Gallery, Three Oaks, Mich, 2009-2013, 2014 and 2015; Celebrating 100 Years, Memorial Art Gallery, Rochester, NY, 2013; Self Portrait Show, Gallery 924, Indianapolis, 2013; Landscape Show, Gallery 924, Indianapolis, 2014. *Collection Arranged:* Mem Art Gallery, Rochester, NY.; Indianapolis Mus Art.; Ind State Mus.; Morris Mus, Morristown, NJ.; Arthur Anderson, Rochester, NY.; Bank One, Indianapolis.; Lilly Research Clinic, Indiana Univ Hospital, Indianapolis.; Citizen Gas, Indianapolis.; Community Hosp Foundation, Indianapolis.; Chermayeff & Geismar Assoc, APC Planning Consult, New York.; Kirr Maubaugh, Columbus, Ind.; McHale, Cook & Welsh, Indianapolis.; Forum Corp, Eli Lilly Co, Indianapolis. *Pos:* Bd mem, Friends of Herron, Herron Sch Art, 97, 98-99; selection comt mem, Contemp Art Soc, Indianapolis Mus Art, 97-98; juror, Arts Ind Postcard Series 15, 94, Circle Ctr Painting Project, Symphony in Color, Indpls Symphony Orch, 94 & juror, Herron Sch Art Sr Show, 2000. *Teaching:* Instr two dimensional design, Univ Mich Sch Art, 79-80; instr painting, Univ Rochester, NY, 85, Kansas City Mus, St Teresa's Acad, Plus X Sch, Kansas City, 58-59, Charleston Day Sch, SC, 62-63. *Awards:* Gernes Scholar, Kansas City Art Inst, 1957; Honorable Mention, Midwest Biennial Exhib, Joslyn Art Mus, Omaha, Nebr, 58 & 8th Mid Am Ann Exhib, Nelson-Atkins Mus, Kansas City, Mo, 58; Margaret Allen Barnett Award, Kansas City Art Inst, 1958; Diane Waldman Juror's Special Mention, Nat Midyear Exhib, Butler Inst Am Art, 83; and others. *Bibliog:* National Midyear Exhib 1983 (exhib catalog), Butler Inst Am Art, Youngstown, OH; Robert C Morgan, Art Review, Democrat & Chronicle, Rochester, NY, 84; Visions Magazine Art Quarterly, LA Artcore, Los Angeles, 92; The Graphics Generation: Am Abstract Prints (exhib catalog), Indianapolis Mus Art, 1993; Rachel Barenson Perry, (auth), Whispers to Shouts: Indian Women who Create Art (exhib catalog), Indiana State Mus, 2005; Mary Lou Dooley Waller: In the Balance, Nuvo, 2009. *Mem:* Contemp Art Soc; Friends of Herron Sch Art, Indianapolis, Ind (bd mem, 97-); Nat Mus Women Arts; Indianapolis Mus Art; IDADA. *Media:* Oil, Miscellaneous Media. *Dealer:* Ruschman Gallery 946 N Alabama Indianapolis IN 46205; Edington Gallery Three Oaks MI. *Mailing Add:* 4035 N Pennsylvania Indianapolis IN 46205

DOOLITTLE, BEV
PAINTER
b Calif. *Study:* Art Ctr Coll Design, Los Angeles, 1968. *Pos:* Art dir, advert agency, Los Angeles. *Media:* Watercolor. *Publ:* Auth, Visions: The Art of Bev Doolittle, Greenwich Workshop, 1988; auth, Bev Doolittle: New Magic, Bantam, 1995; coauth (with E MacLay), The Forest has Eyes, 1998, The Earth Is My Mother, 2000, & Reading the Wild, 2001, Greenwich Workshop. *Mailing Add:* c/o Artifacts Gallery 775 Main St Cambria CA 93428

DOPP, SUSAN MARIE
PAINTER
Study: Corcoran Sch Art, Washington, 1975; San Francisco Art Inst, BFA, 1984, MFA, 1987. *Work:* Anderson Mus of Contemp Art, Roswell, NM; NMex State Univ, Las Cruces; Roswell Mus & Art Ctr, NMex; San Jose Mus Art, Calif. *Exhib:* Solo exhibs include San Francisco Mus Mod Art, 1988, Kay Kimpton Gallery, San Francisco, 1991, Susan Cummins Gallery, Mill Valley, Calif, 1995, 1996, 1998, 1999, Hosfelt Gallery, San Francisco, 2005, 2007, New York, 2006; group exhibs include Overview, Emmanuel Walter Gallery, San Francisco, 1988, Precious Object, 1988; Worship Through the Eyes of Many, Rene Fotouhi Gallery, East Hampton, NY, 1992; Eureka Fel Exhib, San Jose Mus Art, Calif, 1993; Drawings, Triton Mus, Santa Clara, Calif, 1997; Piecing It Together, Mus Art & Hist, Santa Cruz, Calif, 2000; Unframed, Lehmann Maupin Gallery, New York, 2003; Argazzi Art, Lakeville, Conn, 2005; Preview, Hosfelt Gallery, New York, 2006, Book, San Francisco, 2006, Pattern vs Decoration, 2007; Beyond the Gift of Time, Roswell Mus & Art Ctr, 2007. *Teaching:* Painting Instr, SFAI Extension Prog, San Francisco, 1986; Vis Artist, Painting, Acad Art, San Francisco, 1989; Richmond Art Ctr, Calif, 1992; Ore Sch Arts & Crafts, Portland, 1993; Calif Coll Arts & Crafts, Oakland, 1996, 1998; Ore Coll Arts & Crafts, Portland, 2000. *Awards:* Robert Howe Fletcher Award, San Francisco Art Inst, 1984; Soc for Encouragement Contemp Art Award, Calif, 1988; Pollock-Krasner Found Inc, 2007. *Dealer:* Hosfelt Gallery 430 Clementina St San Francisco CA 94103. *Mailing Add:* 2004 E Country Club Rd Roswell NM 88201-7668

DORAY, AUDREY CAPEL
PAINTER
b Montreal, Que, June 4, 1931. *Study:* McGill Univ, Montreal with John Lyman & Arthur Lismer, BFA, 52; Atelier 17, with SW Hayter, Paris, France, 56. *Comn:* Electronic mural, Mazda Motors, Vancouver, BC, 73; two paintings, Mandarin Hotel, Vancouver, 84. *Exhib:* Solo exhib, Vancouver Art Gallery, 61; Nat Art Gallery, Ottawa, Ont, 66; Intermedia Nights, 68 & Inaugural Show, 83, Vancouver Art Gallery; Vancouver Print Show, Heidelberg, Ger, 69; Mus Contemp Crafts, NY, 72; Arteder '82, Bilbao, Spain, 82. *Teaching:* Instr painting & graphics, Vancouver Art Sch, 59-62. *Awards:* Bursary Award, Can Coun, 68-70. *Bibliog:* Tony Emery (auth), The Vancouver explosion, Art Int, 10/68; Michael Rhodes (auth), Audrey Capel Doray, Arts Can, 12/68; Doris Shadbolt (auth), Canadian Art Today, Studio Int, 70. *Media:* Acrylic on Canvas, Paper. *Dealer:* Bau Xi Gallery 3045 Granville St Vancouver BC V6H 3J9 Canada. *Mailing Add:* 4441 W First Ave Vancouver BC V6R 4H9 Canada

DORETHY, REX E
ADMINISTRATOR, EDUCATOR
b Macomb, Ill, Mar 14, 1938. *Study:* Ill State Univ, MS, 65, PhD, 72; Univ Ill, Post Grad, 68. *Pos:* Faculty & head dept, Art Ball State Univ, 72-84; chair dept of art/design, Univ Wis, 84-92; asst to dean, Coll Fine Arts, Univ Wis, 92-. *Teaching:* Asst prof, Art Educ, Ill State Univ, 67-72; prof, Ball State Univ, Muncie, Ind, 72-84; prof art, Univ Wis, Stevens Point, 84-. *Mem:* Nat Art Educ Asn; Wis Art Educ Asn; Nat Arts Policy Coun; Coll Arts Asn. *Publ:* Auth, Teacher Action-Student Response, 70 & Motion Parallax in Spatial Abilities of Young Chile, Studies Art Educ, 78; coauth, Mental Function, Perceptual Differences, Achievement in Art, Studies Art Educ, 78; auth, Research Priorities in Visual Arts Educ, Rev Res Visual Arts, 81; Questions/Positions Concerning the Gifted in Art, Viewpoints: Art Educ, 83. *Mailing Add:* 124 Maple Bluff Rd Stevens Point WI 54481-8441

DORFMAN, BRUCE
PAINTER, INSTRUCTOR
b New York, NY, Aug 15, 1936. *Study:* Art Students League, with Yasuo Kuniyoshi, Arnold Blanch, Charles H Alston; Univ Iowa, with Mauricio Lasansky, Stuart Edie, Roy Seiber, BA, 58. *Work:* Butler Inst Am Art, Youngstown, Ohio; Skirball Mus, Los Angeles; Carnegie Mus, Pittsburgh, Pa; Rockefeller Found, New York; Sewall Gallery, Rice Univ, Houston, Tex; Everson Mus, Syracuse, NY; McNay Mus, Houston, Tex; Arco Collection, Los Angeles, Calif; and others; Smithsonian Am Art Mus, Washington, DC; Atelier Mourlot, Paris, FR; Searle Collection, Chicago, ILL; Albright Knox, Buffalo, NY; Univ Iowa Mus Art, Iowa City. *Comn:* Rockefeller Found, 79; mural, NY State Coun on the Arts, 80; Stedman Collection, Houston, Tex, 88; Gov Monaco, Permanent Mission United Nations, 96. *Exhib:* Norton Mus Art, W Palm Beach, Fla, 62; NY World's Fair Invitational, 64; Butler Inst Am Art, 71-72 & 75; Arras Gallery, NY, 82, 86 & 88; Albright-Knox Art Gallery, Buffalo, NY, 87-88; Hunter Mus, Tenn, 87-88; Addison-Ripley Gallery, Washington, 90 & 94; Mus des Beaux-Arts, Mons, Belg, 94; Hal Katzen Gallery, NY, 94; Bergen Mus, NJ, 95; Korean Cult Ctr, NY, 95; Krisal Galerie, Geneva, Switz, 98; JJ Brookings Gallery, San Francisco, Calif, 98-99; Koener Gallery, Westhampton, NY, 99, 2001, 2003; The Reece Galleries, NY, 99, 2001; Process, Art Students League of NY, 2003; Kouros Gallery, NY, 2003, 2005, 2008, 2010; Galerie Dionisi, Los Angeles, 2004-2005; Fayetteville Mus Art, NC, 2007; Brunnier Art Mus, Iowa State Univ, Ames, Iowa, 2007; Broadhurst Gallery, Pinehurst, NC, 2010; Zane Bennett Gallery, Santa Fe, NMex, 2011; Heather James Gallery, Palm Desert, Calif, 2011, Heather James Gallery, Jackson, Wyo, 2011; Mus Art Univ Ky, Lexington, KY, 2011; Elizabeth V Sullivan Gallery, Art Students League Of NY, Sparkill, NY, 2013; Figge Mus, Davenport, Iowa; June Kelly Gallery, New York, NY, 2015; Art Fairs, 2015; Monmouth Univ, NJ, 2016; Elizabeth Clement Fine Art: Art Miami, Art Miami-New York, Art Southampton. Boston Int Fine Art Exhib Collection. *Collection Arranged:* Korea in Am (6 Korean Artists), Art Ctr, North NJ, 88. *Pos:* Artists Talk On Art, Panel Moderator, NY, 91; lectr, Pompidou Ctr, Musee D'Orsay, Musee Picasso and L'Orangerie, Paris, France, 94; trustee, Am Fine Arts Soc, Art Students League, NY; chair, Forum Series, Art Students League, NY, 97-98. *Teaching:* Fac, Art Students League NY, 64-; Artist-in-residence, Norton Mus, W Palm Beach, Fla, 62-64, Schenectady Mus, 65-66, Everson Mus, Syracuse, NY, 72; resident artist, Syracuse Univ, 71; mem fac, New Sch Soc Res, NY, 79-95 & Art Ctr Northern NJ, 82-96; Master Class, NY, 80-94; Int Sch Art, Loule, Portugal, 93; guest artist, Instituto de Arte Frederico Brandt, Caracas, Venezuela, 96. *Awards:* Fulbright Fel, 61; Purchase Award, Butler Inst of Am Art, 72; Arts East Found Individual Grant, 88 & 90; The Artists Fel Inc individual Grant, NY, NY, 2004; Pollock-Krasner Found Individual Grant, 2007-2008. *Bibliog:* Brian O'Doherty (auth), NY Times, 4/62; John Canaday (auth), NY Times, 10/67; Marcia Tucker, ARTnews, 10/67; David L Shirey, NY Times, 1/77; Lois Katz (auth) Exhib Catalog Text, Nightsongs and Placefields, 89; Phyllis Braff, NY Times, 8/99; Gerrit Henry (auth), article, Art in Am, 5/2000; Ingrid Periz (auth), article, ARTnews, 7/2001; Pamela Koob (auth), Process, 11/2003; Jonathan Goodman (auth), Exhib Catalog Text, 2005; Grace Glueck (auth), NY Times, 9/2005; Phyllis Braff (auth), Exhib catalog; Valerie Gladstone (auth), article, ArtNews, 7-8/2008, City Arts, New York, 4/6/2010; Kathy Winer (auth), article, Jacksonville News, Wyo, 6/2011; Lindboe Ole (auth), Magazine Kunst, Copenhagen, Denmark, 2011; James L McElhinney (auth), The Visual Language of Drawing, Sterling Pub, NY, 2012; Ira Goldberg (auth), Bruce Dorfman: An Interview, Linea- Jour Arts Students League, NY, 2013. *Mem:* Life mem Art Students League. *Media:* Mixed Media. *Publ:* Color Mixing, Grosset & Dunlap, 67; auth, Piero Della Francesca in America, Linea Journal of Art Students League; ARTNews; 9 Art Events to Attend in New York City This Week, 8/31-9/6/15. *Dealer:* June Kelly Gallery New York NY; Elizabeth Clement Fine Art Boston Mass; Broadhurst Gallery Pinhurst NC. *Mailing Add:* 215 W 57th St New York NY 10019

DORFMAN, ELISSA
PAINTER, PRINTMAKER, SCULPTOR
b Brooklyn, NY, May 12, 1950. *Study:* Fashion Inst Technol (FIT), 68-69; CUNY, 69-71, Brooklyn Mus Art Sch, with I Soyer, 69-72; Art Students League, with John Havannes & I Soyer 70-72, Pratt Graphic Ctr, 72, New Sch Social Res & Parsons, with Robert Conover, 76-79. *Work:* Museo del Banco Central de Ecuador; Autograph Mus, Poland, 2003. *Exhib:* Solo exhibs, Collector's Gallery, NY, 79, Galerie Raymond Duncan, Paris, 79, Univ Md, 80, Art Space Gallery, Hyogo, Japan, 82 & Galler Fuji, Osaka, Japan, 82, NY Carlsberg Glyptotek Mus, Copenhagen, Denmark, Galeria d'Art Zero, Barcelona, Spain, 2002, Vanderbilt Mus (Planetarium), NY, 2006, Museo del Banco Central del Equador, 2006, Iowa Biennial Exhib, 2006; Salon des Surindependents, Musee de Luxembourg, Paris, 80; Int Graphic Arts Exhib (auth, catalog), Feria Int de Muestres, Bilbao, Spain, 82; Cabo Frio Int Print Biennial, Brazil, 83; group exhibs, Tokyo Mus, 83, Mills Pond House Gallery, St James, NY, 94 & 97, Royal Castle, Poland, Facing Faces (traveling exhibs), Neth, Belg, Can, 2004, Postcards From Edge: Benefit, Robert Miller Gallery, 2005, Vanderbilt Mus (Planetarium), Centerport, NY, 2006, Post It, Atkinson Art Gallery, United Kingdom, 2006, Showdown, Saatchi Online, 2007, The Conference Board, NY, 2015-16; The Sharjah Arts Mus, United Arab Emirates, 2000; Celebrity Art Auction, Ireland, 2000; Galeria d'Art Zero, Barcelona, 2002; London Biennale 2002, 291 Gallery, London; Gallery Sigvardson, Denmark, 2008; Leopoldo Carpinteyro Gallery, Mex, 2008; Sewall-Belmont House & Mus, Washington, DC, 2008; The Tile Project, Chang Hai Int, Beijing, China & Centre for Arts, Ahmedabad, India, 2008; Showdown, Saatchi Online, 2009; NYU Langone Medical Ctr, NY, 2013; Manhattan Borough Pres Office, 2013. *Awards:* Soc of Arts Acad Award, 2001; Fine Arts Award, Art Domain, Ibiza, 2001; Digital Color Artists Award, Digital Consciousness, 2001. *Bibliog:* Olga Lomelin (auth), The Agenda, Del Arte, 96; Mantle Fielding's Dictionary of Am Painters, Sculptors & Engravers, 2001; Artprice Intl Art Market Directory, 2003; Davenport's Art Reference, 2003. *Mem:* Artists Equity; Visual Artists and Galleries Asn; Art Students League (life); Nat Mus Women in the Arts; Soc of Arts Acad UK. *Media:* Oil. *Collection:* Autograph Mus, Poland, 2003; Museo del Banco Central de Ecuador. *Publ:* Contribr, A Personal Journal with Quotes & Art by Women, Running Press, 92; How to Program Well (cover), Richard De Irwin, 92; Computer Systems Architecture, Organization & Programming (cover), 92. *Mailing Add:* 345 E 81 St No 18E New York NY 10028

DORFMAN, ELSA
PHOTOGRAPHER, WRITER
b Apr 26, 1937. *Study:* Tufts Univ, Medford, BA, 59; Boston Col, Chestnut Hill, Mass, MEd, 62. *Work:* Portland Mus Art, Maine; Wellesley Col, Mass; Mus Fine Arts, Boston; San Francisco Mus Art, Calif; Princeton Univ, NJ; Fogg Art Mus-Harvard Univ. *Comn:* numerous, 80-2003. *Exhib:* Portraits of Women, Everson Mus, Syracuse, NY, 73; Women of Photog, San Francisco Mus Art, Calif, 75; Boston Artists, Boston Mus Fine Arts, 78 & 81 & 90; Boston Now, Inst Contemp Art, Boston, 83; Self Portraits, Zurich Art Mus, Switz, 85 & Lausanne Art Mus, Switz, 85; Am Photog, Fogg Mus, 86; Decordova Mus, 2000. *Pos:* Portrait photogr at own studio in Cambridge, Mass, currently. *Teaching:* Lectr at various US universities & cols. *Awards:* Bunting Fel, Radcliffe Col, 74. *Mem:* Am Civil Liberties Union. *Media:* Portraits. *Interests:* Rare Polaroid 20x24. *Publ:* Auth, Elsa's Housebook, Godine, 74; article, Women's Rev Books, Wellesley Col, 85-90; article, Views, Photog Resource Ctr; article, Famille Granary Press, 99; En Fanukke, Nohairday, 2003. *Mailing Add:* 607 Franklin St Cambridge MA 02139

DORFMAN, FRED
ART DEALER, GALLERY DIRECTOR
b Chicago, Ill, Feb 19, 1946. *Study:* Am Univ, 69; Chicago Art Inst, 71-72. *Pos:* Owner, Dorfman Gallery, currently. *Mem:* Visual Artist & Gallery Asn; Int Art Dealers Asn. *Media:* Paintings, Sculptors. *Specialty:* International contemporary art; sculpture, drawings, paintings, multiples and graphics. *Publ:* Article, New York Arts J, 79. *Mailing Add:* 529 W 20th St New York NY 10011

DORFMAN, GEOFFREY
PAINTER, WRITER
b 1950. *Study:* Cooper Union, BFA; Syracuse Univ, MFA. *Work:* painting, Tree of Life (Henry Ward Ranger Purchase award, Nat Acad). *Exhib:* Nat Acad Mus, NY City, 2006; concerts and recitals at Weill Hall at Carnegie Hall, Columbia Univ, Westminster Choir Col, Stevens Inst Tech, Marlborough Summer Festival, England, 97; solo exhibs, Monotypes, Painting Ctr, New York, 2003 & 2005 & Ober Gallery, Kent, Conn, 2007. *Teaching:* Assoc prof painting, drawing, modern culture CUNY Col Staten Island, 78-; vis asst prof art Dartmouth Col, 2000. *Awards:* Individual Fellowship Grant, Nat Endowment for the Arts, 78. *Bibliog:* Joseph Walentini (auth), Geoffrey Dorfman: Recent Work, Abstract Art Online, 11/2005; James Kalm (auth), Geoffrey Dorfman: Recent Work at the Painting Center, Brooklyn Rail, 11/2005. *Media:* Oil on Canvas & Paper, Monotypes. *Publ:* Auth, Out of the Picture: Military Resnick and the New York Sch, MidMarch Artist Press, 2003. *Dealer:* Ober Gallery 14 Old Barn Rd Kent CT. *Mailing Add:* 232 Mercer St Trenton NJ 08611

DORMAN, JOSH
PAINTER
b Baltimore, Md, 1966. *Study:* Skidmore Coll, BA; Queens Coll, MFA. *Work:* Butler Inst Am Art; Progressvie Auto Insurance, Chicago; Meml Sloan Kettering, New York; Wellington Mgmt Co, Boston; Naples Mus, Fla. *Comn:* Murals, Clinton/Washington Subway Sta, Brooklyn, NY & Bon Secours Hosp, Baltimore. *Exhib:* Solo exhibs, Baltimore City Hall, 1996, Quincy Univ Gallery, Ill, 2003, Hunter Gallery, St George's Sch, 2003, Cue Art Found, New York, 2004, Calif State Univ, Long Beach, 2005, Craft and Folk Art Mus, Los Angeles, 2008; The Nature of Things, Islip Art Mus, NY, 2005; The Elements: Fire, Sacred Heart Univ Gallery, Conn, 2007; Bits and Pieces: The Collage Impulse, Lehman Coll Gallery, Bronx, 2008; Hebrew Union Coll Mus, New York, 2009; Mapping: Memory and Motion in Contemporary Art, Katonah Mus Art, 2010. *Teaching:* Instr, Maspeth Cmty Coll, NY, 1991-, Skidmore Coll, 1997-2003, Nightingale Bamford Sch, New York, 1998, Educational Alliance Art Sch, 1999-2001, CUNY, Brooklyn, 2000-02, Rider Univ, NJ, 2003, Spench Sch, New York, 2005-. *Awards:* Yaddo Fel, 2004, 2006, 2009; NY Found Arts Fel, 2009; Joyce Dutka Found Grant, 2009. *Bibliog:* Helen Harrison (auth), The Nature of Things, NY Times, 2005; Leah Ollman (auth), His map quest: self-discovery, Los Angeles Times, 2008; Michael Wilson (auth), New Works, Time Out New York, 2010. *Mailing Add:* c/o Mary Ryan Gallery 527 W 26th St New York NY 10001

DORN, PETER KLAUS
DESIGNER, GRAPHIC ARTIST
b Berlin, Ger, June 30, 1932; Can citizen. *Study:* Journeyman compositor, Berlin; Ont Coll Art, Toronto; Hochschule für Grafik & Buch Kunst, Leipzig. *Hon Degrees:* Distinguished Service Award, Queens Univ. *Work:* Toronto Pub Libr Fine Arts Sect; Douglas Libr, Special Collections, Kingston; Massey Col, Toronto; Carlton Univ Art Gallery, Ottawa. *Comn:* 200 Anniversary Commemorative Postage Stamp, New Brunswick; Canada, XIII Biennale di Venecia (catalogue), 86. *Exhib:* Royal Can Acad, 70; Agnes Etherington Art Ctr, Kingston, 71; Look of Books, 74, 76 & 77; Design Can, 75; Spectrum Can, 76; Group Exhib, Toronto, 79; and others; Studio 22 Open Gallery, 2007. *Pos:* Proprietor, Heinrich Heine Press, Toronto, 63; typographer, Univ Toronto Press, 66-71; dir, Graphic Design Unit, Queen's Univ, 71-95, pres, 96-; dir, Graphic Serv, King Abdulaziz Univ, Camberley, Eng, 82-83. *Teaching:* Teaching master typography, St Lawrence Col, Kingston, 78-; guest lectr, NS Col Art & Design, Univ Man, Sheridan Col, 80. *Awards:* Awards, Ont Asn Art Galleries, 80-83; Awards, Am Inst Graphic Arts, 80 & 83; Distinguished Serv Award, Queen's Univ, 91; Ont Volunteer Serv Award, 2006. *Bibliog:* Applied Arts Quart, Vol 3, No 1, spring 88. *Mem:* Royal Can Acad; Guild Hand Printers (dir); fel Graphic Designers Can (nat past pres, Kingston past pres); Am Inst Graphic Arts; Pittsburgh Hist Soc (exec); Registered Graphic Designers (emeritus). *Media:* Typography/Letterpress Printing. *Interests:* History of Printing, Gardening. *Publ:* DA, A Journal of Printing Arts, Vol 55, pg 57-60. *Mailing Add:* Graphic Design 2924 Hwy 2 East Kingston ON K7L4V1 Canada

DOROSH, DARIA
PAINTER, SCULPTOR
b Ukraine, Mar 21, 1943; US citizen. *Study:* Fashion Inst Technol, AAS, 63; Cooper-Union Sch Art & Archit, cert, 68; Smartlab, New Media Inst, PhD, Univ E London, Eng, 2007. *Work:* Libr Cong, Washington, DC. *Exhib:* Purchase Fund Exhib, Am Acad Arts & Letts, NY, 73; New Art II: Textures and Surfaces, Mus Mod Art, NY, 81; AIR Group, Kunsthalle, Lund, Sweden, 81; Patterns, San Jose Inst Contemp Art, Calif, 81; Photo Start, Bronx Mus, NY, 82; Homeless at Home, Storefront for Art Archit, NY, 86; Competition Diomede, Clocktower Gallery, NY, 89. *Teaching:* Prof fashion design portfolio, Fashion Inst Technol, 69-; instr painting, Parsons Sch Design, New York, 76-85. *Awards:* Nat Endowment Arts Grant, 86; NY State Coun Arts Grant, 88. *Bibliog:* Patricia Phillips (auth), review, Art Forum, 5/84; N F Karlins (auth), Tribeca sidwalk sculpture gets Soho Gallery preview, Battery News, 4/88. *Media:* Mixed Media, Computer Arts. *Res:* Patterning: the Informatics of art & fashion (PhD thesis), 2007. *Publ:* Auth, Art And Context: A Personal View, Leonardo J Int Soc Arts, Sci & Technol, Pergmamon Press, 88

DORRIEN, CARLOS GUILLERMO
SCULPTOR
b Buenos Aires, Arg, Oct 8, 1948; US citizen. *Study:* Univ de la Plata, Arg, 67; Lowell Technol Inst, Mass; Montserrat Sch Visual Art, Mass, BFA, 73. *Work:* Bentley Col, Waltham, Mass; John Hancock Insurance Co, Boston; Mus 20th Century, Medellin, Colombia. *Comn:* Portal (sculpture), Bentley Col, Waltham, Mass, 78; Cutting Object (marble), City Medellin, Colombia,81; Granite Ribbon, Mass Transit Authority, Porter Sq Sta, Cambridge, Mass, 82. *Exhib:* Arts on the Line, Hayden Gallery, Mass Inst Technol, Cambridge, 79; Art in Pub Places, Carpenter Ctr, Harvard Univ, Cambridge, Mass, 80; Biennial Art Medellin, Colombia, 81; Mus 20th Century, Colombia, 81; Brocton Art Mus Triennial, Mass, 83. *Pos:* Guest sculptor, City Medellin, Colombia, 81. *Teaching:* Lectr, Sch Mus Fine Arts, Boston, 80-81; instr sculpture, Art Inst Boston, 82-86. *Awards:* Traveling Grant, Partners Am, 81; Purchase Award, IV Biennial Art Medellin, Colombia, 81; WBZ-TV Fund for the Arts Grant, 83. *Bibliog:* Mary Sullivan (auth), Carlos Dorrien: An interview, Back Bay View, Vol 3, 78; Gerald Ryan (auth), Sculptures for business, Boston Today, 9/79. *Media:* Granite, Bronze. *Dealer:* Clark Gallery Lincoln Sta Lincoln MA 01773

DORSEY, DEBORAH WORTHINGTON
PAINTER
b Alexandria, Va. *Study:* Radcliffe, BA; Columbia Univ, MA, MPhil; Nat Acad Sch Design. *Work:* Commerce Bank NJ; Pfizer; Pew Charitable Found; Johnson & Johnson, NJ; Merrill Lynch. *Exhib:* Invitational Exhibition Former Prize Winners, Nat Arts Club, NY, 78; Adirondack Nat Exhib Am Watercolors, Community Arts Ctr, Old Forge, NY, 82; Am Watercolor Soc, Nat Acad Design & Salmagundi, NY, 82 & 88; Solo exhibs, Philadelphia Art Alliance, Pa, 89, Brownstone Gallery, NY, 93, Adobe Gallery, Edgewater, NJ, 95 & Educ Testing Serv, Princeton, NJ, 95; Magenta Gallery, Princeton, NJ, 91; Newman Gallery, Philadelphia, 92; Group exhibs, For Us and About Us, Nat Asn Women Artists, ARC Gallery, Chicago, 92; Three Rivers Arts Festival, Pittsburgh, 96, 98 & 2001; Audubon Artists, 97, 99, 2001, 2003, 2007, 2009, 2011, & 2012. *Pos:* Art researcher, Time Life Films, 70-73; art critic, Art News, 71-72; writer, Filmstrip House, 74-75. *Teaching:* Adj prof art hist & painting, CW Post & Long Island Univ, 74-78 & 82; instr drawing, State Univ NY-New Paltz, 82-83; instr portrait painting, Craft Students League, New York, 83-85. *Awards:* First Prize, 83 & Portrait Prize, 87, Ann Mem Exhib, Nat Arts Club, NY; Elizabeth Stanton Blake Award, 90; Solveig Stromsoe Palmer Award, Nat Asn Women Artists, 96, 99, 2003; Elias Newman Mem Award, Audubon Artists, 99; Elizabeth Horman Mem Award, Nat Asn Women Artists, 2007; Gamblin Award, Audubon Artists, 2007. *Bibliog:* Cathy Viksjo (auth), Magenta Art Gallery a gem, Trenton Times, 3/4/90;

Eileen Watkins (auth), Exploring new dimensions, Newark Star Ledger, 4/14/95; Biographical Encyclopedia of American Painters, Sculptors and Engr, Dealers Choice Bks. *Mem:* Nat Asn Women Artists; Audubon Artists. *Media:* Watercolor, Oil. *Publ:* Draw like Seurat, Artist's Mag, 2/96; Giving life to your landscapes, Artist's Mag, 2/99; River Art, Susquehanna Int Fine Art Competition, 2010. *Dealer:* Swain Galleries Plainfield NJ; Graficas Gallery Nantucket MA. *Mailing Add:* 156 E 74th St New York NY 10021

DORSEY, MICHAEL A
PAINTER, ADMINISTRATOR
b Findlay, Ohio, July 31, 1949. *Study:* Eastern Ill Univ, BS, 71; Bowling Green State Univ, MA 72, MFA, 73. *Work:* Miss Mus Art, Jackson; Meridian Mus Art, Miss; Cotton Landia Mus Art, Greenwood, Miss; Southeast Ark Arts & Sci Ctr, Pine Bluff, Ark; Bowling Green State Univ, Ohio; Univ Perugia, Italy; Burroughs Wellcome Company, NC; Greenville Mus Art, NC; Musee Gorsline; plus numerous public & pvt collections in USA, Wales, Japan, France & Scotland. *Comn:* East Carolina Univ. *Exhib:* 17th Ann Piedmont Graphics, Greenville Mus Art, SC, 81; Of On & About Paper, Columbia Mus Art & Sci, SC, 82; SPAR Nat, Barwell Art Ctr, Shreveport, La, 83; 26th Ann Delta Exhib, Ark Art Ctr, Little Rock, 84; 19th Ann Nat Exhib, Coos Art Mus, Coos Bay, Ore, 84; 9th Ann Nat Southern Watercolor Soc, Miss Mus Art, Jackson, 85; Nat Ark Exhib, Ark Arts & Sci Ctr, Pine Bluff, 85; Artists Who Teach, Fed Reserve Bldg, Washington, DC, 87; solo exhibs, Swope Art Mus, Terre Haute, In, 89, Hinds Jr Col, Jackson, Miss, 90, Albers Art Gallery, Memphis, Tenn, 90, Miss State Univ, 92, East Carolina Univ, 93 & Greenville Mus Art, 94; Greenville Mus Art, 2005; Meridian Miss Mus Art, 2006; Dorsey and Gorsline, Gorsline Mus, Burgundy, France, 2006. *Collection Arranged:* guest curator, Watercolors from the Permanent Collection, Greenville Mus Art, NC. *Teaching:* Dean & prof art, Sch Art & Design, East Carolina Univ, 91-2003-; assoc prof & dept head, Miss State Univ, 82-86, prof & dept head, 86-91. *Awards:* Outstanding Alumni, Bowling Green State Univ, 89; Outstanding Art Alumni, Eastern Ill Univ, 92; Best in Show Award, Nat Dimensions Exhib, Winston-Salem, NC, 93; Distinguished Serv Award, NC Art Educ Asn, 1996. *Bibliog:* Paul Grootkerk (auth), The beauty parlor mirror, J Am Cult, 88 & Historical permanence of Fantastic, 89; Michael Duffy (auth), The Beauty Salon Series, Greenville Mus Art, NC, 2005. *Mem:* Coll Art Asn; Miss Watercolor Soc (pres, 86-88); Nat Art Educ Asn; Miss Art Asn; NC Watercolor Soc. *Media:* Mixed Media, Drawing. *Res:* Historical influences upon beauty. *Specialty:* Internet gallery through Nicholas Dorsey. *Interests:* History & film. *Publ:* The Perceptions of Events, Joyner Libr, East Carolina Univ. *Dealer:* Nicholas Dorsey St Petersburg Fla. *Mailing Add:* East Carolina Univ Sch Art Greenville NC 27858-4353

DORST, MARY CROWE
GRAPHIC ARTIST, CRAFTSMAN
b Wis, June 5, 1927. *Study:* Bradford Coll (Scholastic award), 47; Beloit Coll, BA (art; cum laude), 49; Northern Ill Univ, MA, 66. *Work:* McDonald Corp; Vero Beach Ctr Arts; pvt collection, Edward S Curtis. *Exhib:* Colored Pencil Soc Am, 95; Int Soc Exp Artists, 94 & 97; Points of Color, 1st All-Fla Color Pencil Competition, Cornell Mus, Delray Beach, 98; Retro (with husband), Polk Community Coll Gallery, Winter Haven, Fla, 2006. *Collection Arranged:* The Other Side of the Generation Gap, Constructions in Flexible Materials & Printmakers of the Americas, Fla Atlantic Univ Art Gallery, 73-77; Florida Heritage; Contemp Women Artists of the Gold Coast; Art in Fiber and Clay. *Pos:* Gallery Dir, Fla Atlantic Univ, 73-77; art rev, Boca Raton News, Fla, 75-76 & 85-86; art dir, Palmetto Gallery, NCNB Banks, Boca Raton, 79-87; art/writer for local publ, 88-89. *Teaching:* Instr art, Marymount Coll, Fla, 65-67, & Broward Community Coll, Fla, 73-75; Palm Beach Jr Coll, 75-83; adj instr, Fla Atlantic Univ, Boca Raton Fla, 87-95. *Awards:* Hon Mention, Nat Exhib Am Painting, Soc Four Arts, 83; Spec Award, Palm Beach Watercolor Soc, 87 & 92; Broward Art Guild, 90-91. *Bibliog:* Featured artist (calendar), Broward Arts Coun, 86. *Mem:* Hon mem Fla Craftsmen (area dir, 75-78 & 82-84); Am Crafts Coun; Palm Beach Co Coun Arts; hon mem Palm Beach Watercolor Soc (pres 89-91); Soc Experimental Artists; Colored Pencil Soc Am, 93. *Media:* Pencil, Color Pencil. *Res:* Paper surfaces for the artist. *Publ:* Auth, A Day in Mino, Crafts Horizons, 6/71; contribr, art articles, local monthly mag; Revs in Art Voices, South; art critic, Boca Raton News, 77 & 87. *Mailing Add:* 618 NW High St Boca Raton FL 33432

DOUDERA, GERARD
PAINTER, EDUCATOR
b Sharon, Conn, Dec 29, 1932. *Study:* Hartford Art Sch, BFA 56; Univ Ill. *Work:* Wadsworth Atheneum, Hartford; Butler Inst Am Art, Youngstown, Ohio; New Britain Mus, Conn. *Exhib:* Solo exhibs, DeCordova & Dana Mus, Lincoln, Mass, 59, Conn Comn Arts' Showcase Gallery, Hartford, 85, Slater Mus, Norwich, Conn, 89 & 93, Pindar Gallery, NY, 89 & 90, Mus Art, Univ Conn, 90 & New Canaan Soc Arts, Conn, 93; New Britain Mus Am Art, Conn, 61; Univ Hartford, 71. *Teaching:* Prof painting, Univ Conn, 62-87, head art dept, 74-77; emer prof art, Univ Conn, 87-; artist-in-residence, Camargo Found, Cassis, France, 87; vis artist, Weir Farm Heritage Trust, 92-93. *Awards:* First CAFA Award, Conn Artists Ann, Slater Mus, Norwich, 86, First Prize, 2003. *Bibliog:* C Libov (auth), A Painter's World in Bigelow Hollow, Conn Sect, NY Times, 8/18/85; J Brodsky (auth), A Landscape Sensibility, Gerard Doudera A Retrospective (catalog), William Benton Mus, Univ Conn, 90; S Doherty (auth), Painting at the Site of American Impressionism, Am Artist, 5/93. *Mem:* Conn Acad Fine Arts (pres, 81-86). *Media:* Oil, Watercolor. *Mailing Add:* 490 Lewis Hill Rd Coventry CT 06238

DOUGLAS, EDWIN PERRY
PAINTER, INSTRUCTOR
b Lynn, Mass, June 18, 1935. *Study:* RI Sch Design, BFA; San Francisco Art Inst, MFA. *Work:* Montreal Mus Fine Arts, Can; Dayton Art Mus, Ohio; Cincinnati Art Mus; Lincoln Land Community Coll Art Mus, Springfield, Ill; Portland Mus Art. *Exhib:* San Francisco Art Inst Nat Painting & Sculpture Tour, 63; 81st Ann Spring Exhib, Montreal Mus Fine Arts, 64; 31st Ann Can Soc Graphic Art, Kingston, Ont, 64; Cincinnati Biennial, Cincinnati Art Mus, 69; Portland Mus Art, Maine, 74; Walt Kuhn Gallery, Maine, 83; Joan Whitney Payson Gallery, Maine, 84; Papendrecht Mus Contemp Art, The Neth, 85; Icon Gallery, Brunswick, Maine, 90; Greenhut Gallery, Maine, 91. *Teaching:* Instr painting, Univ Man Sch Art, 63-64; instr drawing & painting, Cincinnati Art Acad, Ohio, 64-68; vis prof art, Wash Univ Sch Fine Arts, 69-72; vis lectr painting, Univ Cincinnati, 72-73; prof, Portland Sch Art, 73-, head painting dept, 73-93; guest lectr, Joan Whitney Payson Gallery, Maine, 84 & Mt Holyoke Col, Mass, 88. *Awards:* Convocation & Commencement Addresses, 84 & 85. *Bibliog:* Dialogue on Painting (film), Miami Univ TV, 67. *Media:* Oil. *Mailing Add:* 31 Gertrude Ave Portland ME 04103-3827

DOUGLAS, LEAH
GALLERY DIRECTOR, CURATOR
b Carlisle, Pa. *Study:* Tyler Sch Art, BFA, 85. *Collection Arranged:* Gregory Botts: Villa of the Sun (paintings); Colin Chase: Alchemy of Thought (sculpture); The Impulse to Abstract: Recent Work by Ritzi Jacobi (textile; coauth, catalogue), Univ Arts, Philadelphia, 94; Renewing the Spirit: Paintings from the Harlem Horizon Art Studio (auth, catalog), Univ Arts, Philadelphia, 94; Process of Form: Drawings by Judith Shea, Univ Arts, Philadelphia, 94; Willie Cole: Iconic Structures, 95; Elaine Reichek: Guests of the Nation, 96; Jon Kessler: Unplugged, 97. *Pos:* Dir exhib, Univ Arts, Philadelphia, 90-; independent cur, 92-. *Mem:* Am Asn Mus. *Publ:* Auth, Albert Paley: Sculpture (exhib catalog), Univ Arts, 90

DOUGLAS, TOM HOWARD
PAINTER, SCULPTOR
b Lexington, Tenn, Nov 23, 1957. *Study:* Austin Peay State Univ, BFA, 80; Univ Miss Oxford, MFA, 83. *Work:* Tenn State Mus, Nashville; Parthenon Mus, Nashville; Tupelo Artist Guild Gallery, Tupelo, Miss; Univ Miss, Oxford; Austin Peay State Univ, Clarksville, Tenn; Nashville Int Airport, Tenn. *Comn:* bronze bust, Davis Center, Itawamba Community Col, Fulton, Miss, 2006. *Exhib:* Mid Am Exhib, Owensboro Fine Arts Mus, Owensboro, Ky, 80; Two Visions of Landscape, C W Woods Gallery, Hattiesburg, Miss, 85; Recent Works, Margaret F Treahorn, Clarksville, Tenn, 85; A Glimpse of the South, Brent Wood Gallery, St Louis, Mo, 86; ICC Faculty Show, Univ Ark at Littlerock, 88; Numbers Invitational, Cooper Ave Gallery, Memphis, Tenn, 88; 2 x 4, Carnegie Arts Ctr, Leavenworth, Kans, 88; Constellations, Ark State Univ, Jonesboro, 89; Oratory, Robinson-Willis Gallery, Nashville, Tenn, 89. *Pos:* Artist-in-Residence, Itawamba Co (Miss Arts Commn, NEA), 84-85. *Teaching:* Chair, dept art, painting, Itawamba Community Col, 91-, instr, 83-2013; chair, dept art, Southwest Baptist Univ, Bolivar, Mo. *Awards:* Best of Show, Crossties, Crossties Asn, 85; Best of Show, Redlands Festival, 87; Best of Show, Gum Tree Arts Fair, Gum Tree Asn, 88; Best of Show, Gumtree, 2003; Art Educ of the Year, Miss Asn Art Educ, 2004. *Bibliog:* Alec Clayton (auth), Review, Art Papers, 3-4/86. *Media:* Acrylic, Enamel on Wood, Tin, Clay, Monoprints. *Publ:* My Hearts in the High Lands, Recent Work of Ron Dale, Ceramics Monthly, 2003. *Mailing Add:* Southwest Baptist University Jester Learning Ctr Dept Art 1600 University Ave Bolivar MO 65613

DOUMATO, LAMIA
LIBRARIAN, HISTORIAN
b Aug 26, 1947; US citizen. *Study:* RI Coll, BA; Pa State Univ, MA (art hist); Simmons Coll, Boston, MLS; Boston Univ; Columbia Univ; George Washington Univ. *Exhib:* Retrospective 1972-1982, Women's Caucus for Art, Moore Coll Art, 83. *Collection Arranged:* Rhode Island Architecture, Providence Pub Libr; Raphael, Nat Gallery Art Libr, 81; Am Architecture: Hist View, Nat Gallery of Art Libr, 84; Beaux Arts et Belles Lettres, Nat Gallery Art Libr, 97; Clothing For The Soul Divine, Nat Gallery Art, 2002; Spectacles, Natl Gallery of Art, libr, 2004 & 2005; Text as Inspiration: Artists Books and Literature, Nat Gallery of Art, 2011-12. *Pos:* Art librn, Providence Pub Libr, 70-71; ref librn, Boston Univ Libr, 71-74 & Mus Mod Art Libr, New York, 74-78; reference librn, Nat Gallery Art, Washington, DC, 81-88, head of reader servs, 88-. *Teaching:* Teaching asst art hist, Pa State Univ, 70; prof & head, Art & Archit Libr, Univ Colo, Boulder, 78-81; teacher res methods, Univ Colo, 79-81. *Awards:* Coun Creative Work Grants, Univ Colo, 79-81; Robert H Smith Fel, 97-98; Bibliographical Soc of Am Fel, 99; HW Wilson Award, 2000; Arms Fel, 2001; ALSA Mellon Bruce Fel, CASVA 2001; Bibliographical Soc, Oxford, Eng, 2002; Smith Fel, 2004-2005 & 2007-2008. *Mem:* Coll Art Asn; Art Librn Soc N Am; Art Librn Soc Washington, DC; Asn Archit Librn; and others. *Res:* Production of Syriac manuscripts in 11th-13th century and the interrelations of Crusader and Indigent Artists of the Area. *Interests:* Illuminated manuscripts, architectural bibliography and women architects; History of Jewelry. *Publ:* Auth, Museum Design, Chicago Coun Planning Librn, 80; Women in literature of art, Oxford Art J, Vol 3, 4/80; contribr, The Comfortable House, Mass Inst Technol Press, Cambridge, 86; Architecture and Women, Garland Pub, 88; Architecture a Place for Women, Smithsonian Press, 89; Art of Bishop Dioscorus Theodorus, Arte Cristiana, 99; Opening the Door to Paradise, Al-Masaq, 2000; Patriarch Michael the Great, Cahiers Archeologiques, 2001; P.C. England Coll of Artists Books, 2001; auth, Pontifical of Ignatius II Arte Cristiana, 2003; In the Service of Goodness, Dawkins 58, Oxford Univ, Cahiers Archeologiques, 52, 2009; Artists Books and Literature (pamphlet), 2011. *Mailing Add:* 3001 Veazey Terr NW Washington DC 20008

DOUTHAT, ANITA S
PHOTOGRAPHER
b Cincinnati, Ohio, June 27, 1950. *Study:* Inst Design, Ill Inst Technol, BS (design), 72; Sch Art Inst Chicago, courses in video & art hist; Univ NMex, MA (art), 81, MFA (art), 86. *Work:* Albuquerque Mus Art & Hist; Univ Art Mus, Univ NMex; Columbus Mus Art, Ohio; Cincinnati Art Mus, Ohio; Mus Fine Arts, Houston, Tex. *Exhib:* Solo exhibs, Orange Coast Coll, Costa Mesa, Calif, 86, Bucks Co Community Coll, Pa, 87, Greenfield Community Coll, Mass, 89, Houston Ctr Photog, 92, Robert C May Gallery, Univ Ky, 93 & Carnegie Arts Ctr, Covington, Ky, 94, Kenyon Coll, Gambier, Ohio, 99, Barat Coll Lake Forest, Ill, 96, Indianapolis Art Ctr, 2007; group exhibs, Vertical Axis, Mus Contemp Photog, Columbia Coll, Chicago, 94; Experimental

Vision, Denver Art Mus, 94; Inside/Outside, Hood Mus, Dartmouth Col, Hanover, NH, 96; Shadows & Light, Columbus Mus Art, Columbus, Ohio, 98; The Shelf-Life of Objects, Univ Tex, Dallas, 2000; 2x2: Photographs by Anita Douthat and Cal Kowal, Cincinnati Art Mus, Ohio, 2000, Houston Ctr for Photog, 2002; Lost & Found, Weston Art Gallery, Ohio, 2003; Ross Art Mus, Ohio Wesleyan Univ, Delaware, Ohio, 2006. *Pos:* Assoc cur exhibs, John Michael Kohler Arts Ctr, Sheboygan, Wis, 83-84; cur, Photog Resource Ctr, Boston, Mass, 85-92; assoc dir, Carl Solway Gallery, Cincinnati, Ohio, 93-. *Teaching:* Instr photog, Northern Ky Univ, 93-95 & 97-99; vis artist, Ohio State Univ, 95. *Awards:* New England Found for the Arts, 91; Nat Endowment for the Arts, 92; Ky Found for Women, 2000 & 2006. *Publ:* Auth, Fabricated categories, Views, winter 88; Transforming with light, Art New Eng, 6/89; Commentary: photography at the Univ NMex, PhotoEduc, A Polaroid Newsletter for Teachers Photog, spring 90; coauth, Censorship and obscenity, Art New Eng, 11/90; auth, Fearful symmetries: the Berlin Wall reconsidered, Views, spring 92. *Mailing Add:* 6990 Reitman St Alexandria KY 41001

DOVE, DANIEL
PAINTER
Study: Univ Tex, Austin, BFA (studio art); Yale Univ Sch Art, MFA (painting). *Exhib:* Concordia Coll Gallery, Austin, 1998; solo exhibs, Rudolph-Poissant Gallery, Houston, 1999, Davis Gallery, Austin, 2001, Miami Univ, Ohio, 2004, Mark Moore Gallery, Santa Monica, 2005, Cherry & Martin Gallery, Los Angeles, 2007-08, Santa Barbara City Coll, Calif, 2010; Photo-Painting, Rudolph-Poissant Gallery, Houston, 2000; New American Talent 16, Arlington Mus Art, Tex, 2001; Five Figurative Visions, McDonough Mus Art, Youngstown, 2002; Next: New American Paintings, Bemis Ctr Contemp Arts, Omaha, 2004; I Love the Burbs, Katonah Art Mus, NY, 2006; More is More: Maximalist Painting, Fla State Univ Mus, 2007; Reflections from the Artist's Eye, Weisman Mus Art, Pepperdine Univ, Malibu, 2008. *Awards:* Kimbrough Grant, Dallas Mus Art, 2000; Vt Stuido Ctr Fel, 2004-05; William & Dorothy Yeck Award, Miami Univ, 2004; Ohio Arts Coun Artist Grant, 2005; Joan Mitchell Found Grant, 2010. *Bibliog:* Kerry Marshall (auth), Painting at Tarrytown Gallery, Austin Chronicle, 5/1998; Dan Tranberg (auth), Landmarks Reconsidered, Cleveland Plain Dealer, 11/2001; RC Baker (auth), Best in Show, The Village Voice, 3/30/2007; Christopher Knight (auth), A Wreckage in Fabrication, Los Angeles Times, 5/2/2008. *Dealer:* Cherry & Martin Gallery 2712 S La Cienega Blvd Los Angeles CA 90034

DOWD, JACK
SCULPTOR
b New York, NY, Mar 23, 1938. *Study:* Adelphi Univ, art educ, 60; Arts Students League. *Comn:* HBE Corp, St Louis; New England Biolabs, Boston; Mountain Top Mall, St Thomas, Virgin Island; David Cohen Symphony Hall, Sarasota; Rapa Nui, Inc, Hawaii. *Exhib:* Expressions, Art & Cult Ctr Mus, Hollywood, Fla, 90; Artstravaganza, Asn Visual Artists, Chattanooga, Tenn, 91; All Fla Juried Exhib, Boca Raton Mus Art, 92 & 96; The Fla Nat, Fla State Univ Mus, Tallahassee, 92; Brevard Art Mus, Melbourne, Fla, 93, Montgomery Mus Fine Arts, 92; Nat Sculpture Soc, New York City, 95, 96, 99; Ellen Noel Art Mus, Tex, 2000; High Desert Mus, Calif, 2000; Exposed Ann Outdoor Exhibit, Stowe, Vt, 2000; Ringling Mus Fine Art, Sarasota, 2001. *Pos:* Chmn, Sarasota Pub Art Comt, 91-92. *Teaching:* Artist-in-Residence, Asn Visual Artists, Chattanooga, Tenn, 92. *Awards:* Helen Gapen Oehler Award, Allied Artist Show, 93; Award Scene Unseen, East NMex Univ, 95; Visual Art Ctr, Sarasota, Fla, 99. *Bibliog:* New York Times, 99; New York Post, 99; Sarasota Herald Tribune, 96, 99. *Mem:* Sarasota Visual Arts Ctr; Sarasota Co Arts Council; Nat Sculpture Soc; Art Students League. *Media:* Wood, Clay. *Dealer:* Jack Dowd Studios 1331 10th St Sarasota FL 34236. *Mailing Add:* 6650 Gator Creek Blvd Sarasota FL 34241

DOWELL, JAMES THOMAS
PAINTER, FILMMAKER
b Greenville, Tex, Sept 11, 1949. *Study:* New York Studio Sch, 69; Southern Methodist Univ, BFA, 72; Univ Iowa, MA & MFA, 74. *Work:* Univ Iowa Mus; Southern Methodist Univ, Dallas, Tex. *Exhib:* Solo exhib, Anoka-Ramsey State Col, Minneapolis, Minn, 73, Univ Gallery, Southern Methodist Univ, Dallas, Tex, 79, Warehouse Arts Ctr, Corsicana, Tex, 82, Waco Art Ctr, Tex 83, Soho Ctr Visual Arts (with catalog), NY, 85 & Richland Coll Art Gallery, Dallas, Tex, 92; Still Life: A Selection of Contemp Paintings, Kent State Univ, Ohio, 80; In Search of the Am Experience, Jacob Javits Bldg, NY, 89; Paper Ball Section-Pavel Tchelhchew - The Landscapes of the Body, Katonah Mus Art, NY, 98; Object as Metaphor, Marymount Manhattan Col, NY; James Dowell: Portrait as Self-Portrait, McKinney Ave Contemp, Dallas, 2002; Object Lessons, Valley House Gallery, Dallas, 2003; Still Lifes, Tyler Mus Art, Tex, 2003; Sleep in a Nest of Flames, RAI network, Ital, 2006; Ned Rorem: Word & Music, Aspen Music Festival, Aspen, Colo, 2006. *Awards:* Elmer B Ischoff Award, Mus NMex SW Biennial, 70. *Media:* Oil on Canvas. *Dealer:* Valley House Gallery 6616 Spring Valley Rd Dallas TX 75225. *Mailing Add:* 777 W End No 2B New York NY 10025

DOWELL, JOHN E, JR
EDUCATOR, PRINTMAKER
b Philadelphia, Pa, Mar 25, 1941. *Study:* Temple Univ Tyler Sch Art, BFA (printmaking, ceramics), 63; John Herron Art Inst, Indianapolis, advan lithography with Garo Antreasian, 63; Tamarind Lithography Workshop, Los Angeles, artist-printer fel, 63 & sr-printer fel, 66; Univ Wash, Seattle, MFA (printmaking, drawing), 66. *Work:* Mus Mod Art, NY; Brooklyn Mus Art, NY; Boston Mus Fine Art, Mass; Art Inst Chicago; Corcoran Gallery Art, Washington, DC; and many others. *Exhib:* Solo exhibs, Venice Biennale, 70, Corcoran Gallery Art, DC, 71 & Ft Worth Art Mus Ctr, Tex, 72; Whitney Biennial, 75 & Printmaking New Forms, 76, Whitney Mus Am Art; Recent Am Drawings, Mus Mod Art, NY, 76; 30 yrs Am Printmaking, Brooklyn Mus Art, NY, 76; Three Centuries Am Art, Philadelphia Mus Art, 76; Drawings of the 70's, 35th Exhib of Soc Contemp Art, Art Inst Chicago, 77; Collectors Collect Contemp: A Selection from Boston's Collections, Inst Contemp Art, Boston, 77; A J Wood Galleries, Philadelphia, 80; and many others. *Teaching:* Assoc prof art & printmaking, Tyler Sch Art, Temple Univ, Rome, Italy, 71-74, Philadelphia, 74-76, prof, 76-82. *Awards:* Univ Ill, Champaign Fac Summer Fel, 70; Nat Endowment Arts Fel Painting, 74-75; Temple Univ Res Grant, 75-77; and others. *Bibliog:* Henry Martin (auth), Scribble, Art Int, 3/73; Donna Stein (auth), Musicianly painting, Art News, 11/73; John Dowell's sound perspective, Arts Exchange, 5/77; and others. *Mailing Add:* One Market St #239 Camden NJ 08102

DOWLER, DAVID P
SCULPTOR, DESIGNER
b Pittsburgh, Pa, Feb 1, 1944. *Study:* Syracuse Univ, BID, 69. *Work:* Leigh Yawkey Woodson Mus Art, Wausau, Wis; Corning Mus Glass, NY; Hokkaido Mus Mod Art. *Exhib:* Mus Mod Art, Kyoto, Japan, 81; Americans in Glass, Leigh Yawkey Woodson Art Mus, Wausau, Wis, 81 & Cooper-Hewitt Mus, NY, 81; Good As Gold, Smithsonian Inst, Washington, DC, 81; Production Lines, Philadelphia Coll Art, 83; Glass Now, Hokkaido Mus Mod Art, 83. *Awards:* Furniture Design Award, Progressive Archit Mag, 82. *Bibliog:* Elliot Erwit (auth), Assignment in Glass (film), 78. *Mailing Add:* 249 Pine St Corning NY 14830-3147

DOWLEY, JENNIFER
DIRECTOR
Study: Denison Univ, Granville, Ohio, BA (theater arts), 70, grad studies. *Pos:* Apprentice, Film Study Ctr, Mus Mod Art, NY, 69; asst dir, Nat Cinemas, Dublin, Ireland, 71-72; admin asst, Mus Children, Denver, Colo, 73-74; fundraising consult, Boston Ballet, Mass, 75; assoc dir, Artists Fel Prog, co-dir, Taking Care Bus Artists Found, Boston, Mass, 75-78; dir, Arts on the Line, Cambridge Arts Coun, Mass, 78-81 & Headlands Ctr Arts, Saulsalito, Calif, 86-94, formerly; coordr, Art Pub Places Prog, Sacramento Metrop Arts Comn, 81-86; dir, Headlands Ctr for Arts, Sausalito, Calif, 86-94; dir, Visual Arts & Mus Prog, Nat Endowment Arts, Washington, 94-99; Chmn Pew Fel Arts, 95-; pres, Berkshire Taconic Community Found, 99-. *Awards:* Am Inst Architects Award for Arts on the Line, 87; Distinguished Service Award, Nat Endowment for Arts, 96 & 99. *Mem:* Art Table (bd dir N Calif Chap, 88-90 & DC chap, 96-99); Alliance of Artists Communities (co-founder & chair, 91-94); Arts Advisory Bd; Civitella Found (bd dir, 2001-). *Publ:* Contribr, Money Business: Grants and Awards to Creative Artists, 1st ed, 78; Arts on the Line-a case study for the Urban Mass Transportation Administration, 80; Sculpture Sacramento (catalog), 82

DOWNEN, JILL
INSTALLATION SCULPTOR
Study: Kans City Art Inst, BFA; Wash Univ, MFA, 2001. *Exhib:* Solo exhibs, ARC Gallery, Chicago, 2002, Ninth St Gallery, 2003, COntemp Art Mus St Louis, Mo, 2004, Tarble Arts Ctr, Eastern Ill Univ, 2006, Cite Internationale des Arts, Paris, 2007, Rosenberg Gallery Hofstra Univ, 2008; Corners, Mus Contemp Art, Ft Collins, Colo, 2003; Projects 04, Islip Art Mus Long Island Carriage House, 2004; Perspectives, Brooks Mus Art, Memphis, 2007; Flat Files, Contemp Art Mus St Louis, 2007; Quad-State Biennial, Quincy Art Ctr, Ill, 2009. *Teaching:* Vis asst prof, Wash Univ, 2004-07, Wallace Herndon-Smith vis asst prof, 2007-08. *Awards:* Vt Studio Ctr Grant, 2009; MacDowell Colony Fel, Nat Endowment for the Arts, 2009; Guggenheim Found Fel, 2010. *Bibliog:* Tim Brouk (auth), Anxious Architecture, Lafayette J & Courier, 08/19/2001; David Bonetti (auth), Installation Art is Contemporary, St Louis Post-Dispatch, 08/01/2004; Jason Coates (auth), Body Talk, Style Weekly, Richmond, Va, 07/26/2006; Alan Artner (auth), Paper Now, Chicago Tribune, 09/21/2007; Hesse Caplinger (auth), Don't Think of a Construction Site, St Louis Fine Arts Examiner, 04/25/2009. *Dealer:* Bruno David Gallery 3721 Washington St Louis MO 63108

DOWNER, SPELMAN EVANS
PAINTER, PHOTOGRAPHER
b Pasadena, Calif, Aug 25, 1954. *Study:* Stanford Univ, BA (environ design), 77; San Francisco State Univ, MA (painting), 82. *Work:* Libr Congress, Washington, DC; Univ Alaska, Fairbanks; Nat Park Serv, Bettles, Alaska; Am Asn Advan Sci, Washington, DC; Brit Petroleum Corp, Anchorage. *Comn:* Petersburg Quadrants, Petersburg Sch Dist, Alaska, 87; Siberia Meets Alaska, State of Alaska & Alaska Airlines, Provideniva, USSR, 88; North Pacific Arc, Anchorage Mural Comt, 89; Cent Brooks Range, Gates of the Artic Nat Park, Bettles, Alaska, 90; Kenai Peninsula Portrait, Alaska Wildland Adventures, Cooper Landing, Alaska, 93; Geraldine R Dodge Found, Morristown, NJ, 98; Lawrenceville Sch, NJ, 98. *Exhib:* Solo-exhibs, Kenai Fine Art Ctr, Alaska, 91, Hudson River Mus, Westchester, NY, 95, Arsenal Gallery, NY, 96, Mus Hudson Highlands, NY, 97 & Mus of City NY, 98, Education Testing Svc, Princeton, NJ, 99, NJ Ctr Visual Arts, Summit, 99; Anchorage Mus Hist & Art, Alaska, 92, 94-95; Rochester Mus & Sci Ctr, NY, 94; Mesa Southwest Mus, Ariz, 94; All-of-a-Piece, Katonah Mus Art, 95; Seoul Int Art Fair, Korea, 96; New Am Talent 13, Tex Fine Art Asn, Austin, 97-98; Aerial Perspectives: Reality, Imagination and Abstraction, DC Moore Gallery, NY, 97; Landscapes Seen & Unseen, Pratt Manhattan Gallery & Pratt Brooklyn, NY, 97-98; Scale, Rudolph Poissant Gallery, Houston, 98; US Fed Reserve, New York City, 99. *Collection Arranged:* Geraldine R Dodge Found, Morristown, NJ; Lawrenceville Sch, NJ. *Teaching:* Copper Mountain Coll, Joshua Tree, Calif, 2001-2013. *Awards:* Best of Show, Int Juried Show 1996, NJ Ctr Visual Arts, 96; Dodge Found Fel Grant, Vt Studio Ctr, 97; NY State Coun Arts, Arts Educ Grant, Accessing Cult/Hist Infor, 98. *Bibliog:* Chris Farlekas (auth), Giving landscapes new form, Times Herald Record, 1/10/97; Richard Polsky (auth), Contemp Am Art, Art Market Guide, 97; Roberta Smith (auth), The Metropolis, glimpses of the first 100 years, The New York Times, 98. *Media:* Oil, Drawing; Photography. *Publ:* Auth, Second Manifesto of Maximalism, Alaska Artistic License, 94. *Dealer:* Dru Arstark Gallery 568 Broadway No 403 New York NY 10012. *Mailing Add:* PO Box 919 Joshua Tree CA 92252

DOWNES, RACKSTRAW
PAINTER
b Kent, Eng, Nov 8, 1939; US citizen. *Study:* Cambridge Univ, Eng, BA, 61; Yale Univ, BFA, 63, MFA, 64. *Hon Degrees:* Pratt Inst, DFA, 2007; NY Acad Art, DFA, 2009. *Work:* Hirshhorn Mus, Washington, DC; Pa Acad, Philadelphia; Whitney Mus Am Art, Brooklyn Mus, Chase Manhattan Bank, Metrop Mus Art, Equitable Life Insurance & Mus Mod Art, New York; Mus Fine Arts, Houston, Tex; Witherspoon Mus, NC; Carnegie Inst, Pittsburgh; Nelson Atkins Mus, Kansas City, Mo; Nat Gallery Art, Washington, DC; Cleveland Mus Art; Philadelphia Mus Art; Mus Fine Arts, Boston; Mus Art; RI Sch Design; Addison Gallery of American Art. *Comn:* Painting, US Dept Interior, 76. *Exhib:* Real Really Real, Super Real, San Antonio Mus, 81; Biennial Exhib, Whitney Mus Am Art, New York, 81; Contemp Am Realism, Philadelphia, Pa, 81; Carnegie Int, Carnegie Inst, 83; The Realist Landscape, Rutgers Univ, New Brunswick, NJ, 85; Drawing and Drawings, Hudson River Mus, Yonkers, NY, 86; solo exhib, Weatherspoon Art Gallery, 92, Chinati Found, 99 & Fresh Kills: Artists Respond, Snug Harbor Cult Ctr, Staten Island, 2001; The Artist's Eye, Colby Coll Mus Art, Waterville, Maine, 92; The Long View, Mus Mod Art, New York, 94; Reinterpreting Landscape, Maier Mus Art, Lynchburg, Va, 96; Modern Art Despite Modernism, Mus Mod Art, New York, 2000; On Site Paintings, 1972-2008 (solo), Parrish Art Mus, Southampton, NY, 2010; Solo exhib, Under the Westside Highway, Aldrich Contemp Art Mus, Conn, 2010. *Pos:* Gov, Skowhegan Sch Painting & Sculpture, 81-95. *Teaching:* Asst prof fine arts, Univ Pa, Philadelphia, 67-79; Grad Sch Fine Arts, Yale, 79-80; Harvard Univ, 97-98. *Awards:* Creative Artists Pub Serv Award, 78; Individual Grant, Nat Endowment Arts, 80; Guggenheim Found Fel, 98; MacArthur Fel Grant, 2009. *Bibliog:* Robert Storr (auth), Rackstraw Downes: Painter as Geographer, Art in Am, 10/84; Peter Schjeldahl (auth), True Views, New Yorker, 10/2004; Sanford Schwartz (auth), Rackstraw Downes, Princeton Univ Press, 2005. *Mem:* NY Artists Equity Asn; Nat Acad; Am Acad Arts & Lett. *Media:* Oil. *Interests:* Poems, essays, fiction. *Publ:* Ed, Fairfield Porter: Art in its Own Terms, 79; auth, Claude's sermon on the mount, Art News, 10/81; Impressionists vs the salon: Modern & not, Art Am, 1/96; In Relation to the Whole, Edgewise, 2000; Under the Gowanvs adn Razor-Wire Journal, Turning The Head, 2000; John Marin, Art at Colby, 2009; Nature and Art Are Physical, 2014. *Dealer:* Betty Cuningham Gallery New York NY; Texas Gallery Houston TX. *Mailing Add:* 16 Greene St New York NY 10013

DOWNIE, ROMANA ANZI
SCULPTOR
b Rome, Italy, May 9, 1925; US citizen. *Study:* Liceo Artistico Acad Belle Arti, maturita, 45; San Francisco State Univ, BA (cum laude), 61, MA, 63; Univ Calif, Berkeley. *Work:* Museo de Roma, Italy; San Francisco Libr, Mus Photog & San Francisco State Col, San Francisco; Bidwell Libr, Southern Methodist Univ, Dallas. *Comn:* Portrait, Free Masons of Rome, 45; F DeBellis (portrait), comn by DeBellis Found, San Francisco, 68; George Moscone (portrait) & Harvey Milk (portrait), comn by Joseph Dee, San Francisco, 78 & 82; mural, Herrick's Hospital, Berkeley, Calif, 81; bronze statuette, Sammy Davis Jr, comn by Joseph Dee-Brooks, Mus Photography. *Exhib:* 1st Women's Show, Palazza Brancaccio, Rome, 47; San Francisco Art Festival, 64-81; Italian Am Artists, Mus Italo Americano, San Francisco, 79-82. *Bibliog:* Michael Robertson (auth), A sculptor caught in the politics of art, San Francisco Chronicle, 7/9/82; Lucy Harris & Stephanie Johnson (auths), Artist extraordinaire, Viewpoint, Oakland, 2/84; Mark Luca (auth), Italian American artists in the Bay Area, Il Caffe, Sacramento, 2-3/86. *Media:* Clay, Wax. *Dealer:* Greenwooper Gallery & Garden Shop Elk CA 95432. *Mailing Add:* 27800 N Hwy One Fort Bragg CA 95437

DOWNS, DOUGLAS WALKER
SCULPTOR
b Pomona, Calif, May 30, 1945. *Study:* Whittier Col, BA, 67; Claremont Grad Sch, 67-68, study with Aldo Casanova & Jean Ames; Ariz State Univ, 69-70. *Work:* King Karl Gustav XVI, Stockholm, Sweden; The White House; King Don Juan Carlos I & Queen Sofia, Seville, Spain; Long Island Chess Mus, Commack, NY. *Comn:* Bust of a Scholar (bronze), Collier Art Corp, Los Angeles, 74; Abstract Family (bronze), Am Asn Marriage & Family Therapy, Washington, DC, 75; Hawk on Rock (bronze), Tor House Found, Carmel, Calif, 79; Joseph Smith (bronze), 83 & Emma Smith (bronze), 85, Monterey Sculpture Ctr, Calif; Eagle gates (bronze), Ronald M Abend Inc, 89. *Exhib:* Solo exhib, Southwestern Arts Ltd, Carmel, 78; Favell Mus, Klamath Falls, Ore, 77; George Phippen Mem Exhib, Prescott, Ariz, 77; Westerman and Downs, Galerie de Tours, San Francisco, Calif, 84; The New Masters, May Gallery, Scottsdale, Ariz, 86; Artists of the West, Trails West Gallery, Laguna Beach, Calif, 88; New works by Weers, Downs and Burns, May Gallery at Borgata, Scottsdale, Ariz, 96; Downs, Oliver and Thomas, May Gallery at El Pedregal, Ariz, 98; Worldwide Exhib of Fine Arts in Miniatures, Smithsonian Inst, Wash, DC, 2004; Downs, Meheen, and Northrop, Carmel Art Asn, Carmel, Calif, 2007. *Awards:* Best Art with Western Theme, Mont Miniature Art Soc, 15th Ann, 93; 1st Prize, Sculpture, Sage Gallery, Atlanta, Ga, 93; 1st Prize, Sculpture, 61st & 62nd Ann Int Exhibs, Washington, DC, 94 & 95; 1st Prize, Sculpture, 18th Ann North Am Exhibs, Baltimore, 2001. *Bibliog:* D W Armstrong (auth), Bronze artist Douglas Downs, Acquire, 5/74; L Longstaff (auth), Sculptor of 1000 faces, Southwest Arts, 11/77; H Sutliff (auth), Sculpture by Douglas Downs, Key, Calif Art Rev, 9/79; A survey of the state's museums, galleries and leading artists, 88; 2000 Outstanding Artists and Designers of the 20th Century, 1999; Biographical Encyclopedia of American Painters, Sculptors and Engravers of the US Colonial to 2002; Modern Masters of Miniature Art in America, 2010. *Mem:* Carmel Art Asn (bd dir, treas, 83-84, 87-88 & 93-94, 2013); sig mem, Miniature Artists Am, 96. *Media:* Bronze. *Dealer:* Carmel Art Asn Gallery CA; Caravan Bookstore Los Angeles CA. *Mailing Add:* 405 Alder St Pacific Grove CA 93950

DOWNS, LINDA ANNE
ADMINISTRATOR, CURATOR
b Detroit, Mich, May 30, 1945. *Study:* Monteith Col, Wayne State Univ, PhB, 1969; Univ Mich, MA (art hist), 1973; Mus Mgt Inst, Univ Calif, Berkeley, 1979; post grad studies, Am Univ, Washington, DC. *Collection Arranged:* Student Art Exhibs, Detroit Inst Arts, 1969-77, Barbara Chase Ribaud Sculpture, 1972, Diaghilev & Russian Stage Design, 1972, Caravaggio's Conversion of the Magdalene: An Analysis of the Painting, 1973, African Art of the Dogon, 1974; The Rouge: The Image of Industry in the Art of Charles Sheeler and Diego Rivera (auth, catalog), Detroit Inst Arts, 1978; Diego Rivera: A Retrospective (auth, catalog), Detroit Inst of Arts, 1986; The Great Am Thing: Mod Art & Nat Identity, 1915-1935, Figge Art Mus, Davenport, Iowa, 2005. *Pos:* Spec asst, Proj Outreach, Detroit Inst Arts, Mich, 1968-69, jr cur educ, 1969-73, asst cur educ, 1973-76, cur educ, 1976-89; head, education div, Nat Gallery Art, Washington, 1989-2002; bd mem, Black Mountain Coll Res Proj, 96-; bd trustee, Am Fed Arts, 1992-2004; exec dir, Figge Art Mus, Davenport, Iowa, 2002-06; exec dir, Coll Art Asn, NY, 2006-. *Teaching:* Adj asst prof art hist, Wayne State Univ, Detroit, Mich, 1976-89. *Awards:* Best Cult Film Award for Only Then Regale My Eyes, Midwest Pub Broadcasting Serv, 76; Cine Golden Eagle for the Frescoes of Diego Rivera film, 86; Arts Achievement award, Wayne State Univ, 2012. *Mem:* Am Asn Mus; Mus Educators Round Table; Art Table; Coll Art Asn (exec dir 2006-); Int Coun Mus (bd dirs 1992); Am Coun Learned Soc, (CAD 2006-); Nat Humanities Alliance (bd dir 2008-2011). *Publ:* Coauth, Gallery Activities for Unguided Groups, Mus News, 1989; Diego Rivera, International Dictionary of Art and Artists, London, 1990; A Recent History of Women Educators in Art Museums, Gender Perspectives: Essays on Women in Museums, Smithsonian Inst Press, 1994; The need for learning research in museums, In: Public Institutions for Personal Learning (John Faulk & Lynn Dierking, eds), Am Asn Mus, Washington, 1995; Diego Rivera: The Detroit Industry Murals, 1999; Ofrendas de abundancia en la época de la Depresión, Diego Rivera: Epopeya Mural, Inst Nat de Bellas Artes, Mexico, 2007; contributing auth, A Life in Museums: Managing Your Museum Career, Greg Stevens & Wendy Luke, 2012. *Mailing Add:* Coll Art Asn 50 Broadway Flo 21 New York NY 10004

DOYLE, JOE
PAINTER, EDUCATOR
b Manhattan, NY, Feb 27, 1941. *Study:* San Francisco State Univ, Calif, BA, 69, MFA, 71. *Work:* Oakland Mus, Calif. *Comn:* Dallas, Tex. *Exhib:* Option 73/30, Contemp Art Ctr, Cincinnati, Ohio, 73; Interstices, Cranbrook Acad Art, Bloomfield Hills, Mich, 75; 6 EBay Painters, Oakland Mus, Calif, 77; Aesthetics of Graffiti, San Francisco Mus Art, 78; Solo exhib, San Jose Mus Art, Calif, 79, Foster Goldstrom Fine Arts, San Francisco, 83 & 85, Route 66 Gallery, Philadelphia, J Rosenthal Fine Arts, Chicago, 86, Ill Metrop Ctr, Chicago, 86, Merging One Gallery, Santa Monica, 87 & Harcourt's Contemp Gallery, San Francisco, 88; Reality of Illusion, Denver Art Mus, Colo, 79; Three Bay Area Painters, Chico State Univ, Calif, 79; Selections from the Contemp Art Collection of the Oakland Mus, Kaiser Ctr, Calif, 80; Midwestern Mus Art, Elkhorn, Ind, 81; Icons of Contemp Art, Foster Goldstrom Fine Arts, Oakland, Calif, 83; The Gallery Collection, J Rosenthal Fine Arts, Chicago, 84; Shadows, Univ Calif, Davis, 85; Dallas Collects, Concord Bank, Tex, 86; Merging One Gallery, Santa Monica, Calif, 87; The Goldstrom Collection, Davenport Art Ctr, Davenport, Iowa, 88. *Teaching:* Instr painting, Laney Col, Oakland, Calif, 71-73; co-chmn fine arts, Acad Art, San Francisco, 75-76; adj prof fine arts, Univ San Francisco, 75-76; instr, spray painting, Calif Col Arts & Crafts Exten Prog, Oakland, 79-80, painting, drawing, figure drawing, San Francisco Acad Art, 78-79,. *Bibliog:* David Berreth (auth), Art Museum, Miami Univ, Oxford, Ohio, 9/85; Thomas Albright (auth), Art in the San Francisco Bay Area 1945-1980, Univ Calif Press, 85; Daniel E Stetson (auth), New Acquisitions, Davenport Mus Art, Davenport, Iowa, 4/88. *Mem:* Calif Fedn Art Teachers. *Media:* Mixed. *Dealer:* Harcourts Contemporary 535 Powell St San Francisco CA 94108. *Mailing Add:* 4545 Toyon Pl Oakland CA 94619

DOYLE, MARY ELLEN
PAINTER
b Hartford, Conn, Oct 8, 1938. *Study:* Vassar Col, 56-58, Boston Univ Sch Fine Arts, BFA, 62, study with Walter Murch; Columbia Sch Painting & Sculpture, 64-65, study with John Heliker. *Work:* Wadsworth Atheneum, Hartford, Conn; Ark Art Ctr, Little Rock; The Phillips Collection, Washington, DC; Achenbach Found for the Graphic Arts, Fine Arts Mus of San Francisco, Calif; Albuquerque Mus, NMex; New Orleans Mus Art, La; Nat Mus Am Art, Washington, DC; Frances Lehman Loeb Art Ctr, Vassar Coll, NY; Smith Coll Art Gallery, Northampton, Mass; Bryn Mawr Coll, Pa; Miss Mus Art, Jackson, Miss. *Exhib:* Solo exhibs, New Sch Social Res, NY, 82 & 89, Humphrey Gallery, NY, 89, Susan Conway Gallery, Washington, 92, 94, 97, 2000 & 2002, The Phillips Collection (with catalog), Washington, DC, 97, Santa Fe, 99; Towards the Horizon: Recent Works on Paper (with catalog), Montgomery Mus Fine Arts, Ala, Miss Mus Art, Jackson & Columbus Mus Art, Ga, 99-2000. *Teaching:* Instr studio art, Barnard Col, New York, 62-65; instr children's art classes, Mus Mod Art, New York, 63-71; instr drawing, New Sch Social Res, New York, 78-94, Continuous Ser Award, 95. *Awards:* Walter Biggs Mem Award, Nat Acad Design, 89; Adolf & Clara Obrig Prize, Nat Acad Design, 94; Distinguished Alumni Award, Boston Univ Sch for Arts, 2000. *Bibliog:* Janet Wilson (auth), Galleries: Mary Ellen Doyle and the beauty of the beach, Long Island Lights, Wash Post, 1/92; Weil, Rex (auth), Mary Ellen Doyle, Artnews, 12/97; Greben Deidre Stein (auth), Artist's East End Landscapes Lead to Overdue Recognition, NY Times, 11/97; Ferdinand Protzman (auth), Galleries: Geometry's Pretty Picture, Washington Post, 3/2000. *Media:* Watercolor. *Dealer:* Susan Conway Gallery 716 Acequia Madre Santa Fe New Mexico 87501. *Mailing Add:* PO Box 1421 Bridgehampton NY 11932

DOYLE, NOEL FRANCIS
PAINTER, SCULPTOR
b Kingston, Ont, Dec 18, 1961; Can & Irish citizen. *Study:* Univ Toronto; Univ Ottawa; Univ BC. *Work:* Absolute Vodka, Stockholm, Sweden; Molsons Brewing Co, Toronto, Can; Jones Brewing Co, Tenn; The Sleeman Collection, Guelph, Canada; Philips Electronics, Toronto, Can. *Comn:* The Jury (painting series), comn by Daniel

Stripinis, Ottawa, 90; Absolute Paintings, Absolute Vodka, Sweden, 94. *Pos:* Dir, Blast Gallery, 91-92, NF Doyle Gallery, 92-93; owner, Galerie Voltaire, 93-95. *Teaching:* Lectr art, Univ Ottawa, 88 & Univ Toronto, 90. *Bibliog:* Kate Taylor (auth), Noise Off, Globe & Mail, 94. *Mem:* Soc Voltaire. *Media:* Wood, Paint. *Publ:* Auth, Bounce Off-Jeff Wall, Art Focus, 92; Horoscopes of Art World, Art Focus, 94-95. *Dealer:* Lory James Gallery Voltaire 3 Rosemount Ave M6K IY4. *Mailing Add:* 196 Bathurst St Toronto ON M5T 2R8 Canada

DOYLE, TOM
SCULPTOR, EDUCATOR
b Jerry City, Ohio, May 23, 1928. *Study:* Ohio State Univ, BFA, 52, MA, 53, MFA, with Roy Lichtenstien & Stanley Twardewicz. *Work:* Carnegie Inst, Pittsburgh; Kley Collection, Ger; City Beautiful Project, Dayton, Ohio; Allentown Cedar Parkway, Allentown, Pa, 87; Cirque de Soliel Headquarters, Montreal, Can. *Comn:* Fiberglass sculpture, Pub Arts Coun, City of New York, 72; Fed Bldg & Courthouse, Fairbanks, Alaska, 80; Cooper Sq Housing, NY, 85; Queens Coll/City Univ NY, Science Bldg, Flushing, NY, 88; Jean Widmark Mem, Roxbury, Conn, 97; New Britain Mus Am Art, New Britain, Conn, 2006. *Exhib:* Vanishing Points, Moderna Museet, Stockhom, Sweden, 84; Portes Ouvertes, Foundation d'-Art De Lanapoule, Lanapoule, France, 89; solo exhibs, Allen Stone Gallery, NY, 61 & 62, Dwan Gallery, New York City, 66 & 67, Picker Art Gallery, Hamilton, NY, 76, Miami Dade Community Col, Fla, 82, Sculpture Ctr, New York City, 88, Bill Bace Gallery, 94, Longhouse Found, E Hampton, NY, 95, Mattatuck Mus, Waterbury, Conn, 96, Paris/NY/Kent Gallery, Kent, Conn, 96 & Kouros Gallery, NY, 99, Kouros Gallery, 99, Nicolaysen Art Mus & Discovery Ctr, Casper, WY, 2001, New Arts Program, Kutztown, Pa, 2001, Paessaggio Gallery, W Hartford, Conn, 2001, New Arts Gallery, 2003 & 05, Shirley/Jones Gallery, 2006; Sculptors and Their Environments, Pratt Manhattan Gallery, NY, 98; Wash, Pride and Place, The Gunn Hist Mus, Wash, Conn, 2000; Six Great Families, Paris-NY-Kent Gallery, Kent, Conn, 2000; Chesterwood Mus, Stockbridge, Mass, 2002; Sunaram Tagore Gallery, 2010, 2011; Behnke-Doherty Gallery, Washington Depot, Ct, 2012, 2013; OMI Internat Arts Ctr; The Fields Sculpture Park; Annual Summer Exhib, Ghent, NY, 2013; Purchase Award for Sculpture, Am Acad Arts & Letts, 2013, 2014. *Teaching:* Instr sculpture, Brooklyn Mus Art Sch, 60-68 & New Sch Social Res, 61-68; assoc prof sculpture, Queens Col, 70-92, prof sculpture, 82, retired. *Awards:* Guggenheim Fellow award, 82; Fel Sculpture, Nat Endowment Arts, 90-92; Jimmy Ernst Award for Lifetime Achievement, Am Acad Arts & Letts, 94; Ohioana Career Award, 96. *Bibliog:* Lucy R Lippard (auth), Tom Doyle, Kunsthalle, Dusseldorf, 65 & Space embraced: Tom Doyle's recent sculpture, Arts, 4/66; Robert Pincus-Witten (auth), Tom Doyle: Things patriotic and union blue, Arts, 9/79; Carter Ratcuff (auth), Tom Doyle, Essay, 99; Robert C Morgan (auth), Tom Doyle: Allegories of Time, Space Nature, Sculpture Mag, 2007; In Conversation: Tom Doyle with Phong Bui, Brooklyn Rail, 5/2008; and others. *Mem:* Am Abstract Artists; Nat Acad. *Media:* Wood, Bronze. *Dealer:* Kouros Gallery; NewArts Gallery; Lamoitta Fine Art; Larry Becker Contemporary Art; Sundaramtagore Gallery

DRACHNIK (CAY), CATHERINE MELDYN
PAINTER, EDUCATOR
b Kansas City, Mo, June 7, 1924. *Study:* Kansas City Art Inst, 41-42; Univ Md, BS, 45; Calif State Univ, Sacramento, MA (art therapy), 75; studied at Parsons Sch Design, NY, 45, Carmel Art Inst, Old Dominion Univ, Long Beach State Coll, Am River Coll. *Work:* Aerojet Corp Gallery, Folsom, Calif; Aerojet Corp, Collections of: Lt Gen & Mrs R Anthis, Mr & Mrs Cecil Marks, Mr & Mrs John Guirdera, Mr & Mrs Robert Trathan, Ambassador & Mrs Frederick Nolting. *Comn:* Portrait, comn by Ms Kelly Netto, 95; comn by James Jenkins, 98; comn by Mr & Mrs James Glasscock, 98; comn by Susan Baxter, 99; comn by Mrs Robert Trathen, 2000; comn by Joan Gann, 2000; comn by John Haynes, Capt USN Ret, 2003; comn by Mr & Mrs Frank Dreyer, 2007; comn by Corrine Hood, 2007; comn by CC Meyer, 2009. *Exhib:* Int Art Exhib, Saigon Art Mus, Vietnam, 62, Vietnamese Spring Exhib, 62; Capitol Area Exhib, Smithsonian Inst, Washington, DC, 64; 43rd Ann Exhib, Haggin Art Mus, Stockton, Calif, 94-98, 2002, 2003 & 2006; Calif Watercolor Asn, San Francisco, 98, 2001 & 2004-2005; Watercolor West, Brea Cult Ctr, Calif, 99; West Coast Soc Portrait Artists, Sacto Fine Arts Ctr, Sacramento, 99; Rocky Mt Nat Exhib, Colo, 99-; Biennial Statewide Watercolor, Triton Mus Art, Santa Clara, Calif, 2000, 2002, 2006 & 2008; Am Watercolor Soc, Salmagundi Club, New York City, 2000. *Teaching:* Instr art, Calif State Univ, Sacramento, 75-92 & dir Art Therapy Prog, 99; instr metaphors, Coll Notre Dame, Belmont, Calif, 75-90; instr children's art class, Sacramento Fine Arts Center, 94-95; instr fashion illustration, Sacramento City Coll, 96-2006. *Awards:* Award of Excellence, Calif State Fair, 2000 & 05; Award of Excellence, Northern Calif Artist Open, 2000; Pres award Calif Watercolor Soc, San Francisco, Calif, 2001; Most Outstanding Watercolor, Calif State Fair, 2001; Award of Excellence, Magnum Opus, Sacto Fine Arts Ctr, 2002; First Place, Watercolor, Primere Graphics, 2002; Award of Excellence, No Calif Artists, 2003; Special Award, Haggin Mus, 2003; Best of Show, Vacaville Art League, 2004, 2nd place watercolor, 2009; First Place, Watercolor, KR Gallery, 2004; 1st Place Watercolor, Calif Open, Sacto Fine Arts Ctr, 2005 & Best of Show, 2007; Merit Award, Vacaville Art League, 2005 & 2008, Second Place, Watercolor, 2009; Award of Excellence, Calif State Fair, 2005; Award of Merit, Sacto Fine Arts Center, 2006, Best of Show, 2007; Award of Merit, Calif State Fair, 2009. *Bibliog:* Holly Heyser (auth), Therapeutic Drawing, Sacramento Bee, 6/88; Chris Astone (auth), One Generation Helping Another, The Key, Spring 96; Gladys Agell (auth), Art Therapists Who Are Artists, AMC J Art Therapy, 5/99. *Mem:* Am Art Therapy Asn (hon life mem, pres, 87-89); Northern Calif Art Asn (publicity chair, 2000-2001, signature mem); Calif Watercolor Asn (signature mem); Calif State Univ Art Alumna Asn; Am Watercolor Asn; Nat Assistance League; Crocker Kinsley Art Club; Kappa Kappa Gamma Alumni Asn, Sacramento co-pres 91. *Media:* Watercolor, Acrylic. *Specialty:* Fine art. *Interests:* Swimming, movies & vis art galleries. *Publ:* Auth, The History of the Licensing of Art Therapists as Marriage & Family Counselors, Arts in Psychotherapy, 89; auth, Interpreting Metaphors in Children's Drawings, 95; auth, The Artwork of Art Therapy Pioneers, AMC J Art Theraphy, 96; contribr, Working With Images-The Art of Art Therapists, Charles C Thomas, 2001; Illustrating the Problem, Inside Arden News, 7/2003; Art for a Cause, 8/2008; Architects of Art Therapy, chap 27, Charles C Thomas, 2006. *Dealer:* Elliott Fouts Art Gallery 4749 J St Sacramento Ca 95819; CJE's Art & Fiber Gallery 10239 Fair Oaks Blvd Fair Oaks CA 95628; Doiron Gallery 1819 Del Paso Blvd Sacramento CA; Barton Gallery 1723 I St Sacramento CA. *Mailing Add:* 4124 American River Dr Sacramento CA 95864-6025

DRAEGER, CHRISTOPH
INSTALLATION SCULPTOR
b Zurich, Switzerland, 1965. *Study:* Sch Visual Arts Lucern, Switzerland, 1986-90; Ecole Nat Superieur des Arts Visuels de la Cambre, Brussels, Belgium, 1990-91. *Work:* Centre Pompidou, Paris; Whitney Mus Am Art, New York; Brooklyn Museum, New York; Kunsthaus Zurich, Switzerland; Kunstmuseum, Bern, Switzerland. *Exhib:* Solo exhibs include LiebmanMagnan Gallery, New York, 1999, Roebling Hall, Brooklyn, 2003, 2005, Galerie Anne de Villepoix, Paris, 2003, 2006, 2008, The Kitchen, New York, 2004, Catharine Clark Gallery, San Francisco, 2004, Susanne Vielmetter Projects, LA, 2005; group exhibs include Disaster & Recovery, Swiss Inst, New York, 1998; Play is the Thing, Whitney Mus Am Art, New York, 2001, Highlights from the Permanent Collection, 2001; Game Show, Mass Mus Contemp Art, North Adams, 2001; The Reconstruction Biennial, Exit Art, New York, 2003, Terrorvision, 2004; Open House: Working in Brooklyn, Brooklyn Mus, 2004; Crude Oil Paintings, White Columns, New York, 2004; Greater New York, PS1 Contemp Art Ctr, Long Island City, NY, 2004, Reprocessing Reality, 2006; The Museum as Hub, New Mus Contemp Art, New York, 2008. *Dealer:* Catharine Clark Gallery Ground Fl 150 Minna St San Francisco CA 94105; Galerie Magnusmuller Weydingerstrasse 10/12 10178 Berlin Germany; Galerie Anne de Villepoix 43 rue de Montmorency 75003 Paris France

DRAKE, JAMES
PRINTMAKER, SCULPTOR
b Lubbock, Tex, Sept 12, 1946. *Study:* Art Ctr Coll of Design, fel, BFA with Hons, 69, MFA, 70. *Work:* El Paso Mus Art, Tex; Phoenix Art Mus, Ariz; Univ NMex Art Mus, Albuquerque; Univ Tex, El Paso; Mathews Art Ctr, Ariz State Univ, Tempe. *Exhib:* New Visions, Amarillo Art Ctr, Tex, 81; Solo exhib, Galveston Arts Ctr on the Strand, Tex, 82; Southern Fiction, Contemp Art Mus, Houston, 83; New Orleans Triennial, New Orleans Mus Art, 83; and others. *Teaching:* Instr life drawing, Art Ctr Col of Design, Los Angeles, 69-70 & Univ Tex, El Paso. *Bibliog:* Barbara Cortright (auth), Sculpture & graphics, Art Week, 2/76

DRAKE, PETER
PAINTER, DRAFTSMAN
b Garden City, NY, July 29, 1957. *Study:* Pratt Inst, BFA, 79. *Work:* Mus Contemp Art, Los Angeles, Calif; Los Angeles Co Mus, Calif; Mus Mod Art Mex, Mexico City; Phoenix Mus Art, Ariz; J Patrick Lannen Found, Miami, Fla. *Exhib:* East Village Art in Berlin, Zellermayer Gallery, Berlin, 84; Nueva Pintura Narrativa, Mus Tamayo, Mexico City, 84; Blue Condition, Greenville Co Mus, SC, 85; NY/Seattle, Seattle Ctr Contemp Art, Wash, 85; Romanticism/Cyncism in Contemp Art, Haggerty Mus, Milwaukee, Wis, 86; Avant Garde in the 80's, Los Angeles Co Mus, Calif, 87; solo exhibs, Elizabeth Leach Gallery, Portland, Ore, 97 & Lowe Gallery, Atlanta, Ga, 97; The Liars (III) Frightful Paint Arti et Amicitiae, Amsterdam, 98; Small Works-The Sequel, Susan Cummins Gallery, San Francisco, Calif, 98. *Pos:* Artist/consult, Drawing Ctr, New York, 84-; staff writer, Flash Art, 86. *Awards:* Nat Endow Arts, 87. *Bibliog:* Michael Kohn (auth), Romantic Vision, Flash Art, 85; Michael Cone (auth), Peter Drake, Flash Art, 86; Michael Brenson (auth), The ink drawing of Peter Drake, NY Times, 87. *Media:* Oil. *Dealer:* Curt Marcus Gallery. *Mailing Add:* 520 Second Ave Apt 15C New York NY 10016

DRAKOPOULOS, ANGIE
PAINTER
Study: Vacalo, Athens, Greece, 1991; Corcoran Sch Art, Washington, BFA, 1994; Sch Vis Arts, New York, MFA, 1996. *Exhib:* Solo exhibs include g-module, Paris, 2002, 2006; group exhibs include Beauty & the Public, Vis Arts Gallery, New York, 1995, 1996; Perfect Plastic, g-module, Paris, 2001, Double edged abstraction, 2007; Community Word Proj Silent Auction, Nat Arts Club, New York, 2003; Between Interconnectedness, Smack Mellon, Brooklyn, NY, 2004; PS122 Gallery, New York, 2005; Local Color, Blackrock Art Ctr, Bridgeport, Conn, 2006. *Awards:* New York Found Arts Grant, 2008. *Dealer:* g-module 15 rue debelleyme paris 3e. *Mailing Add:* 5-36 47th ave Apt 3L Long Island City NY 11101

DRAPELL, JOSEPH
PAINTER, FILMMAKER
b Humpolec, Bohemia, Czech, Mar 13, 1940; Can citizen. *Study:* Cranbrook Acad Art, with Donald Willett & George Ortman, MFA, 70. *Work:* Guggenheim Mus; Mus Fine Arts, Boston; Mus Mod Art, Vienna, Austria; Brit Mus, London; Nat Gallery, Prague. *Comn:* Outdoor sculpture, Halifax, NS; mural, Cineplex Odeon Theatres, Toronto, Ont. *Exhib:* New Acquisitions, Guggenheim Mus, 72; New Abstract Art, Edmonton Art Gallery, 77; Color Abstractions, Mus Fine Arts, Boston, 79; The Threshold of Color, Edmonton Art Gallery, 82; retrospective, Art Gallery Windsor, Ont, 84 & Moore Gallery, Hamilton, Ont, 96; Island Paintings, Shippee Gallery, NY, 88; New New Painting, Galerie Gerald Piltzer, Paris; The Archetypal Figures, Gallery One, Toronto, 94; Gallery Ism, Seoul, Korea, 95; Fine Art 2000, Greenwich, Conn, 96; Flint Inst Arts, Mich, 98; New New Painters, The Real Avantgarde Armory Show, New York City, 2000; New New Painters, Nat Gallery, Prague, 2002; Anti-Drapell, Mus New New Painting, Toronto, 2005, The Unknown Drapell, 2007. *Collection Arranged:* Drapell at 65, Mus New Painters, Toronto, 2005; High Stakes the Crisis in Art, 2006. *Teaching:* Instr artistic methods, York Univ, Toronto, 70-71; vis artist-in-residence, Syracuse Univ, 73; guest artist, Triangle Artists' Workshop, Pine

Plains, NY, 84, Emma Lake Artists' Workshop, Univ Saskatchewan, 88. *Awards:* Can Coun Grant, 71; Ont Arts Coun Grants, 75 & 76. *Bibliog:* Karen Wilkin (auth), The Recent Work of Joseph Drapell (catalog essay), New York, 86; Kenworth Moffett (auth), New New Painting (book), Nouvelles Eds Francaises, Paris, 92; Donald Kuspit (auth), Painting Beside and Inside Itself (catalog essay), Art 2000, Conn, 96. *Media:* Acrylic on Canvas; Bronze; Film. *Publ:* High Stakes: A Global Crisis in Art? (dvd), 2006; auth, essays, Mus New New Painting, Toronto, 2006; and others. *Dealer:* Moore Gallery 80 Spadina Ave Toronto ON; Mus New New Painting, 128 Claremont St, Toronto, Canada. *Mailing Add:* 123 Bellwoods Ave Toronto ON M6J 2P6 Canada

DRASLER, GREGORY J
PAINTER
b Waukegan, Ill, June 7, 1952. *Study:* Univ Ill, BFA, MFA. *Exhib:* Cave Painting (auth catalog), Queens Mus Art, NY, 94. *Teaching:* Princeton Univ, Williams Col; Pratt Inst. *Awards:* New York Found Arts Fel, 91; Nat Endowment Arts Fel, 93. *Dealer:* Betty Cuningham New York NY. *Mailing Add:* 137 Duane St Apt 4B New York NY 10013

DREDGE, JILL ANN
PAINTER
b New Prague, Minn, Sept 03,1949. *Study:* Univ Ariz. *Work:* Casa Grande Mus Art, Casa Grande, Ariz; Valley Nat Bank, Casa Grande, Ariz. *Comn:* mural, Chuckwagon Scene, Frontier Insurance, Tucson, Ariz, 2006; family portrait, Connie Crosby, 2007; Drawing of Synagogue, Jewish Heritage Ctr, 2007; Cowboy Portrait, Todd Fairweather, 2009; Dog Portraits, Britta Penca, 2011. *Exhib:* 2nd Ann Masters CP Nat, Massey Fine Arts, Santa Teresa, NMex, 1993; Explore This! 4, Colored Pencil Soc Am, Brea, Calif, 2007; The Empire 100 Western Show & Sale, Tucson Ariz, 2007; Tucson Int Airport Exhib, Tucson, Ariz, 2007, 2011; Western States Horse Expo, Equine Dream Art Show, Sacramento Calif, 2010, 2011; Art at the Classic, Draft Horse Classic, Grass Valley, Calif, 2011. *Awards:* Purchase Award, Casa Grande Art Fiesta, Valley Nat Bank, 1978; Second Place, 3rd Ann Pinal Co Invitational, Casa Grande Art Mus, 1992; Second Place, Ariz Chap 212 Exhib, Ariz Colored Soc Am, 2007; 3rd place, Arizona State Fair, 2008; 3rd place, Western Horse Expo, Equine Dream Art Show, Sacramento, Calif, 2011; Cowbelles award, Judge's Choice award, 3 First Place, 1 Second Place, Fine Art and Photography Show, Willcox, Ariz, 2012, Special award, 1st Place, 2nd Place, Fine Art and Photography Show, Willcox, Ariz, 2013; 2nd Place, Celebrate the Arts, Benson, Ariz, 2013. *Bibliog:* Judy Bernas (auth), Pinal Artists Exhib Talent, Casa Grande Dispatch, 2/14/1992; Catherine Oleson, Cultural Insights, Catalina Sunrise, 6/2/1992; Alice Zientarski (auth), Color, Detail, & Design Epitomize, Northwest Explorer, 1/11/1996; Greg Crosby (auth), Catalina Artists Studio Tour, Catalina Community Arts Coun, Nov 4,5 2006; Tonya Holland (auth), Jill Dredge in Airport Show, Tucson Colored Pencil Artists News, Mar-July 2007; Carol Broeder (auth), Artist of the Month, Ariz Range News, 1/8/2013. *Mem:* Colored Pencil Soc Am; Tucson Colored Pencil Artists Asn (treas 2006-2009, Steering Comt 2006-2009); Art League of Willcox; San Pedro River Arts Council; San Pedro River Arts Council. *Media:* Acrylic, Oil, Colored Pencil, Pastel. *Mailing Add:* 1006 E Mescal Dr Pearce AZ 85625

DREIBAND, LAURENCE
PAINTER, LECTURER
b New York, NY, Nov 8, 1944. *Study:* Chouinard Art Inst, Los Angeles, 61; Art Ctr Coll Design, Los Angeles, BFA (with distinction), 67, fel & MFA, 68. *Work:* Home Savings & Loan Collection; Container Corp Am Collection; Chase Manhattan Bank. *Comn:* Great Ideas of Western Man, Container Corp Am, 70. *Exhib:* West Coast 70, E B Crocker Art Gallery, Sacramento, Calif, 70; Beyond the Actual, Pioneer Mus, Stockton, Calif, 70; Solo exhibs, David Stuart Galleries, 70-72, Los Angeles Inst Contemp Art, 80 & Allen Stone Gallery, NY, 81; California Artists, Long Beach Mus Art, 71; Galerie Quatres Mouvements, 74; Janus Gallery, 83. *Teaching:* Instr painting & photog, Art Ctr Col Design, 70-, chmn dept fine arts, 72-. *Awards:* First Prize, Fine Arts Gallery San Diego, 70; Great Ideas of Western Man Purchase Award, Container Corp Am, 70; 19th All City Festival Purchase Award, Munic Art Gallery, Los Angeles, 71. *Bibliog:* Joseph Young (auth), Los Angeles artist--Laurence Dreiband, Art Int, 70; Barbara Witus (auth), Paintings of Laurence Dreiband, Los Angeles Free Press, 3/31/72; Udo Kulterman (auth), New Realism, New York Graphic Soc, 72. *Media:* Oil, Acrylic. *Publ:* Auth, Laurence Dreiband, Paintings and Drawings, David Stuart Galleries, 72. *Mailing Add:* Art Ctr Col Design 1700 Lida St Pasadena CA 91103

DRESKIN, JEANET STECKLER
PAINTER, EDUCATOR
b New Orleans, La, Sept 29, 1921. *Study:* Newcomb Coll, Tulane Univ, with Will Henry Stevens, BFA, 42; John Hopkins Univ, med art cert, 43; John McCrady Sch, New Orleans; Clemson Univ, MFA, 73; Art Students League, New York. *Work:* Smithsonian Nat Mus Art, Washington, DC; Ga Mus Art, Athens; Greenville Co Mus Art, SC; Guild Hall Mus, East Hampton, NY; State Art Collection, SC State Mus, Columbia; Gibbes Mus, Charleston, SC; Zimmerli Mus, Rutgers Univ, NJ; Columbia Mus Art, SC. *Comn:* Seals & plaque, SC State Bd Health, Columbia, 57; McDonald Corp, Chicago, 82; painting, Nat Mus Illus, New York, 86; Fed Reserve Bank Richmond, Charlotte, 88; Greenville Hosp System, SC, 2007, 2012; Cu-icar, SC, 2009; Univ SC Medical Univ, 2012. *Exhib:* Greenville Co Mus of Art, 62, 64, 70, 75, 85, 99 & 2005; Group exhibs, Chautauqua Exhib Am Art, NY, 70; 38th Ann Mid-Yr Show, Butler Inst Am Art, Youngstown, Ohio, 74 & 83; Art in Medicine, Nat Mus Illus, NY, 86; Nat Print & Drawing Exhib, Rudolph Lee Gallery, Clemson Univ, SC, 87, 89, 91, 93, 2002, 2005, 2009, 2011; Centennial Exhib (traveling), Nat Asn Women Artists, 89-90, Invitational Drawing Exhib USA, Mid Am Arts Alliance, Kansas City, Mo, 89-91; Nat Women's Exhib, India, 89-90; Nat Works on Paper, Univ Miss, Oxford, Miss, 91; 100 Years/100 Artists, SC State Mus, 99-2012; SC State Mus, 2012; SC Biennial, Columbia, SC, 2013. *Pos:* Staff artist, Am Mus Nat Hist, New York, 43-45; staff artist, Univ Chicago Med Sch, 45-50. *Teaching:* Painting & graphics, Greenville Co Mus Sch Art, 50-52 & 62-, head sch, 68-74; adj prof art, Univ SC, 73-96, Governor's Sch, 81-2000. *Awards:* Merit Award, Int Grand Prix, Cannes, France, 73; Award, Southern Watercolor, Univ Miss, 85, 88, 97, & 08; Merit Award, San Diego Int Watercolor, 97; Am Soc Contemporary Artists Award, New York, 97, 2000 & 2002; SC Gov's Sch Arts & Humanities, Lifetime Achievement Award, 98; The Gov's Award for the Arts, 2004; Elizabeth Verner Lifetime Achievement Award, 2004; Hon award, Southern Graphics Coun, 2005. *Bibliog:* Jack A Morris, Jr (auth), Contemporary Artists of South Carolina, Tricentennial Comn, 70; Patricia Robbins (auth), Jeanet Dreskin, Art Voices S, 5-6/79; Feature, Art's the Thing, SC Educ TV, 87; Martha Severens (curator), Greenville County Museum of Art Catalogue, 99; and others; Ann Hicks (auth), Talk Mag, SC, 9/1/2009. *Mem:* Guild SC Artists (mem bd, 55-, treas, 68, vpres, 71, pres, 72); Nat Asn Women Artists (mem comt, 71-); SC Watercolor Soc (pres, 83-84); Nat Asn Med Illusr; Southern Graphics Coun (secy-treas, 74-76, treas, 88-90, mem bd, 74-92); plus others. *Media:* Goauche; Watercolor; Collage. *Publ:* Illusr, Anatomy of the Gorilla, Am Mus Nat Hist, Columbia Univ, 43-46; What's New, Abbot Labs (& Latin Am ed), 46, 47 & 49; Surgery of Repair, Lippincott, 50; Williams Obstetrics, Stander-Appleton, 50; Surgical Anatomy, BC Decker (Mosby), 90; many others. *Dealer:* Hampton III Gallery Ltd 11 Hampton Ctr Taylors SC 29687. *Mailing Add:* 60 Lake Forest Dr Greenville SC 29609

DREW, LEONARDO
SCULPTOR
b Tallahassee, Fla. *Study:* Parsons Sch Design, New York, 1981-82; Cooper Union, New York, BFA, 1985. *Work:* Metrop Mus Art; Guggenheim Mus; Hirshhorn Mus; Detroit Inst Arts; St Louis Art Mus. *Exhib:* Solo exhibs, Thread Waxing Space, New York, 1992, 1994, Herbert F Johnson Mus Art, Cornell Univ, 1994, San Francisco Art Inst, 1994, Merce Cunningham Dance Co, 1995, Pace Roberts Found Contemp Art, San Antonio, 1995, Mus Contemp Art, San Diego, 1995, St Louis Art Mus, 1996, Mary Boone Gallery, New York, 1996, 1998, 2001, Madison Art Ctr, Wis, 1999, Bronx Mus Arts, 2000, Hirshhorn Mus & Sculpture Garden, Washington, 2000, Royal Hibernian Acad, Dublin, 2001, Fabric Workshop, Philadelphia, 2002, Brent Sikkema Gallery, New York, 2005, Max Hetzler Galerie, Berlin, 2005, Existed, deCordova, Sculpture Park & Mus, Mass, 2010; From the Studio: Artists in Residence, 1990-91, Studio Mus Harlem, New York, 1991, Passages, Contemp Art in Transition, 1998; Promising Suspects, Aldrich Mus Contemp Art, Ridgefield, Conn, 1994; Carnegie Int, Carnegie Mus Art, Pittsburgh, 1995; About Place: Recent Art of the Americas, Art Inst Chicago, 1995; New Work: Words & Images, Miami Art Mus, 1997; Legacies: Contemp Artists Reflect on Slavery, NY Hist Soc, 2006; 183rd Ann: Invitational Exhib Contemp Am Art, Nat Acad Mus, New York, 2008. *Awards:* Benjamin Altman Prize, Nat Acad, 2008. *Bibliog:* Lorraine Edwards (auth), Navigating a Sea of Chaos, Sculpture 16, 2/1997; Judith H Dodrzynski (auth), Extracting metaphors from life's detritus, NY Times, 2/2000; Michael Amy (auth), Leonardo Drew at Brent Sikkema, Art in Am, 93, No 8, 9/2005. *Publ:* Threadwaxing Space, 1992; Sculpture in the age of doubt, Allworth Press, 1999; Existing Everywhere, Palazzo Delle Papesse, Siena, 2006; 30 Americans, Rubell Family Collection, 2008; Existed, Giles Publ, 2009. *Dealer:* Brent Sikkema 530 W 22nd St New York NY 10011; Chris Erck 816 Camaron No 1.2 San Antonio TX 78212

DREYFUS-BEST, ULLA
COLLECTOR
Pos: Adv bd mem, Sotheby's, currently. *Awards:* Named one of Top 200 Collectors, ARTnews mag, 2009-12. *Collection:* Old Masters, especially Mannerism; Symbolism; Surrealism; contemporary art. *Mailing Add:* Sotheby's 1334 York Ave New York NY 10021

DREZNER, A L
SCULPTOR, ARCHITECT
b Trenton, NJ, May 27, 1959. *Study:* St Lawrence Univ, BA (fine arts), 81; Johnson Atelier Tech Inst Dept Sculpture, 82; Univ Calif Los Angeles, 94; Harvard Univ Grad Sch Design, 97; Univ Calif Los Angeles,; Master in Arch UCLA, 2002. *Work:* Mass Inst Tech Visual Art Ctr, Cambridge, Mass; Rose Art Mus, Brandeis Univ, Waltham, Mass; Norton Family Found & Collection, Santa Monica, Calif; Johnson & Johnson Found, Lawrenceville, NJ. *Comn:* Proj ser, Santa Monica Mus Art, Calif, 97; Univ of Texas @ Dallas, 2005. *Exhib:* Triennial, Fuller Mus Art, Brocton, Mass, 90; solo exhib, Santa Monica Mus Art, Calif, 97; 97 Kunsthalle, Kunsthalle Lophem, Belgium, 97; Lance Fung Gallery, New York City, 2001; C Luckman Gallery Calif State Univ, Los Angeles, 2000; Univ of Tex, Dallas, 2005; Loop Show, Los Angeles, Calif, 2012, Loop Show Two, 2013; Dallas Biennial, 2012; 323 Projects, 2012; Univ Tex, Dallas, 2013; Handsome Cowboy, Los Angeles, Calif, 2013. *Collection Arranged:* Mit List @ Visual Arts Ctr, Buandeis Univ. *Teaching:* Teaching asst, Univ Calif Los Angeles, 94-95. *Awards:* Nat Endowment Arts Lottery grant, Boston Women's Installation Artist, 88; Project grant, Art Matters Inc, NY, 89; Colman Found grant, Boston Univ, 90; Pollock-Krasner Found Award, 99; Open Nat 9/11 Mem Competition, Los Angeles Int Airport, 3rd Place, 2003. *Bibliog:* Miles Unger (auth), A L Drezner, Art New England, 2/91; Amy Drezner, 1/95 & Beauty and Intrigue, 3/96, Los Angeles Times. *Media:* Installation, Sculpture, Sound Composites. *Dealer:* Marc Foxx Gallery 3026 Nebraska Ave Santa Monica CA 90404. *Mailing Add:* PO Box 49-1801 Los Angeles CA 90049

DRIESBACH, DAVID FRAISER
PRINTMAKER
b Wausau, Wis, Oct 7, 1922. *Study:* Univ Ill, Beloit Col; Univ Wis; Pa Acad Fine Arts; State Univ Iowa; Atelier 17, with S W Hayter in Paris, 69. *Work:* Seattle Mus, Wash; Dayton Art Inst, Ohio; Columbus Gallery Fine Arts, Ohio; Bibliot Nat, Paris, France; Boston Mus Fine Arts. *Comn:* Fiscal Flight (ed, 150 color etchings), Sears Roebuck Co, 67; series of bronze reliefs, Asn Am Artists, NY, 68; color intaglio ed, Checker Cab Co, Kalamazoo, Mich, 74; color intaglio, Soc Am Graphic Artists; color viscosity, Gemarts, Knoxville, Tenn. *Exhib:* Young Printmakers of America, Mus Mod Art, NY, 53; Ten Printmakers of USA, Purdue Univ, 66; solo exhib travels Yugoslavia 5 months with US Info Agency, 85; Grafica Contemporanea Americana, Venice, Italy, 77;

retrospective show, Univ Md, Baltimore Co, 79; Seventh British Int Print Biennale, Bradford, Eng, 82. *Teaching:* Prof printmaking, Northern Ill Univ, 64-91 (retired); lectr, numerous workshops on Color Viscosity at 30-35 colleges. *Awards:* Ford Found Purchase Prize for Intaglio, 60; 10th Ann Colorprint USA Purchase Prize, Tex Tech, 83; Second Int Exhib of Prints & Drawings Award, Wesleyan Col, Macon, Ga; Outstanding Printmaker, Mid Am Print Coun, 2000, Outstanding Printmaker, 2013; USA Southern Graphics Internat. *Bibliog:* Bob White (auth), David Driesbach, Chicago Art Scene, 1/68; The complex world of David Driesbach, Northern Alumnus, 3/68; David Driesbach Retrospective (catalog), Northern Ill, Univ, Dekalb. *Mem:* Midwest Coll Art Asn; Soc Am Graphic Artists; Boston Printmakers. *Media:* Intaglio. *Dealer:* Edenside Gallery Louisville KY; Sylvia Schimdt Gallery New Orleans LA; Annex Gallery Santa Rosa CA. *Mailing Add:* 500 Wyndemere Circle Apt A262 Wheaton IL 60187

DRIESBACH, JANICE
MUSEUM DIRECTOR
b Cleveland, Ohio. *Study:* Allegheny Coll, Pa, BA (Art History); Univ Iowa, MA (Art History), PhD. *Pos:* Cur, Crocker Art Mus, Sacramento, 1985-2000; dir & cur, Sheldon Mem Art Gallery, Univ Nebr, 2000-07; CEO Dayton Art Inst, 2008-. *Mem:* Board member, Sheldon Mem Art Gallery, 2000-07. *Mailing Add:* Dayton Art Institute 456 Belmonte Park N Dayton OH 45405

DRIESBACH, WALTER CLARK, JR
SCULPTOR, INSTRUCTOR
b Cincinnati, Ohio, July 3, 1929. *Study:* Sch Dayton Art Inst, 47-52, with Robert Koepnick; studio asst to Joseph Kiselewski, New York, 54-55; Art Acad Cincinnati, 55-56, with Charles Cutler. *Hon Degrees:* Sch Dayton Art Inst, diploma, 51; Art Acad of Cincinnati, Hon Dr Fine Arts, 2007. *Work:* Citizen (bronze figure), Pyramid Hill Sculpture Park & Mus, Hamilton, Ohio; Bell Tel Co; Gen Elec Co; Raymond Walters Col; Figure of a Bull, Mus Arts and Crafts, Zagreb, Croatia. *Comn:* Life of St Teresa (limestone entablature), St Teresa Church, Cincinnati, 62; The Lord's Supper (walnut relief), Good Shepherd Church, Cincinnati, 64; Firefighters' Mem (granite figure), Cincinnati, 68; Limestone portrait, (Harriet Beecher Stowe) Mercantile Libr, Cincinnati, 2002. *Exhib:* Ohio Sculptors, Akron & Canton Art Insts, 60; Northwest Territory Sculpture Show, Cincinnati Art Mus & John Herron Inst Art, Indianapolis, Ind, 61; Univ Cincinnati Regional Sculpture, 68; Invitational Exhib, Cincinnati Art Mus, Ohio, 72 & 81; Figure '82, Contemp Art Ctr, Cincinnati, 82; retrospective, Art Acad Cincinnati, 88; and others. *Teaching:* Instr drawing & sculpture, Memphis Acad Arts, 56-58, Wilmington Col, 63-66, Thomas More Col, 70-71 & 78-93; instr sculpture, Dayton Art Inst Evening Sch, 58-60 & Col Mt St Joseph, 72; instr sculpture, drawing & 3-D design, Univ Dayton, 66-72; instr sculpture, 3-D design & found, Art Acad Cincinnati, 70-87; instr wood carving, Communiv, Univ Cincinnati, 80-81; stone carving workshop, Community Educ, Art Acad Cincinnati, 90-. *Awards:* Fleischmann Purchase Prize, Zoo Arts Festival, Cincinnati, 64; First Prize, Prof Sculpture Div, Ohio State Fair Fine Arts Exhib, 66, Second Prize, 68. *Mem:* Cincinnati Carvers' Guild. *Media:* Wood, Stone. *Specialty:* Sculpture. *Publ:* Contribr, Contemporary Stone Sculpture, 70 & Creating Small Wood Objects as Functional Sculpture, 76, Crown; Masters of Wood Sculpture, Watson-Guptill, 80; Sculpture: Technique-Form-Content, Davis Publ, 89; The Sculpture Reference, Sculpture Books Publ, 04. *Dealer:* Barbara Beatrice Gallery 562-C Buttermilk Pike Crescent Springs KY 41017. *Mailing Add:* 2541 Erie Ave Cincinnati OH 45208

DRIESSEN, ANGELA KOSTA See Kosta, Angela

DRISCOLL, EDGAR JOSEPH, JR
CRITIC
b Boston, Mass, Sept 1, 1920. *Study:* Cambridge Sch Weston; Univ Iowa, with Grant Wood; Yale Univ Sch Fine Arts. *Pos:* Art critic, Boston Globe, 46-73; Boston corresp, Art News, 73-. *Mem:* Cambridge Art Asn (secy & bd dir). *Mailing Add:* 81 Joyce Kilmer Rd West Roxbury MA 02132

DRISCOLL, ELLEN
SCULPTOR, INSTRUCTOR
Study: Wesleyan Univ, BA (studio art) cum laude, 74. *Work:* Met Mus Art; Whitney Mus of Am Art; Addison Gallery of Am Art; New Sch for Social Rsch; Detroit Inst of Art. *Comn:* Mid-Atlantic States Arts Consortium Virginia Ctr Creative Arts, Sweet Briar, Va, 86; Oliver Ranch, Geyserville, Calif, 88; Ellyn & Saul Dennison, Bernardsville, 90; Mr Robert Orto, La Jolla, Calif, 91; Pub Art Comn for Grand Central Station, Metrop Transportation Authority, 92-98; As Above, So Below, 20 mosaic and glass works for Grand Ctrl Terminal North, Met Transp Authority and Met-North Railroad, 99; Circuitstream, 9'x22' sandblasted glass mural, Bank of Am, 2000. *Exhib:* A Contemp View of Nature, 86 & Innovations in Sculpture, 88, Aldrich Mus Contemp Art; Solo exhibs, Stavaridis Gallery, Boston, Mass, 87, Tim Hill Gallery, Birmingham, Mich, Whitney Mus Am Art (with catalog), 91-92, Contemp Art Ctr, Cincinnati, 92, New Work, Huntington Gallery, Mass Coll Art, Boston, 93, Threadwaxing Space, NY, 95, Univ Mich Mus of Art, Ann Arbor, 97, The African Am Mus, Fresno, Calif, 2000, Green St Gallery, Boston, 2001, Univ Mass, 2001; 1980: A New Generation, Metrop Mus, NY, 88; Totem, 89 & Am Abstraction at the Addison, 91, Addison Gallery Am Art; 55 Ferris Street Exhib, Brooklyn, NY, 93; Art en Route: MTA/Arts for Transit Paine Webber Gallery, NY & The Mus Stony Brook, Long Island, 94; Threadwaxing Space, NY, 94; Equal Rights & Justice, High Mus, Atlanta, Ga, 94; In Three Dimensions: Women Sculptors of the 90s, Snug Harbor Cult Ctr, Staten Island, NY, 95; Lehman Coll Art Gallery, Bronx, NY, 96; Paraphotography, Maier Mus of Art, Lynchburg, Va, 98; Recent Projects: Ellen Driscoll and Lesley Dill, Bernard Toale Gallery, Boston, 99; Marilyn Monroe X Times, Emily Peterson Gallery, NY, 99; Ellen Driscoll, Lesley Dill, Ambreen Butt, DNA Gallery, Provincetown, Mass, 99; Forms in Motion, Cooper Union, 2000. *Teaching:* Asst dir admissions, Parsons Sch Design, 80-83; dir, Parsons Sch Design, 85-89; vis lectr & critique, numerous museums, universities, & cols, 86-; vis artist, Univ NC, Chapel Hill, 88 & Sch Mus Fine Arts, Boston, 89; instr, sophomore & jr sculpture, RI Sch Design, 92, assoc prof sculpture, 92-98 & prof sculpture, 98-. *Awards:* Nat Endowment Arts, 84 & 86; Guggenheim Fel, 87; Grant, LEF Found, 92; Les Arques France, EEC & Local Govt, 94; Anonymous Was a Woman Fel, 98-99; Mass Cult Coun Fel in Sculpture, Pilchuck Sch of Glass Artist-in-Residence, 99; Rockefeller Found Bellagio Residency, Italy, 2001; Banff Ctr for the Arts Residency, Can, 2001. *Bibliog:* Goings on About Town/Art, New Yorker, 2/10/92; William Zimmer (auth), review, NY Times, 95; Nancy Princenthal (auth), review, Art Am, 6/95; Patricia Phillips (auth), The Proportions of Paradox, Sculpture Mag, Nov 2000; Janet Koplos (auth), Ellen Driscoll's Passages, Art in Am, June 2000; Barbara Rodriguez (auth), Autobiographical Inscription: Form, Personhood and the American Woman Writer of Color, Oxford U Press

DRISCOLL, JOHN PAUL
DEALER, ART HISTORIAN
b Madison, Minn, Oct 28, 1949. *Study:* Univ Minn, BA, 71; Pa State Univ, MA, 74, PhD, 85. *Exhib:* Hans Coper (with catalog), 94; Lucie Rie (with catalog), 94; Warren MacKenzie (with catalog), 95; Six Master Potters of the Modern Age (with catalog), 95; Gutte Eriksen (with catalog), 95; Seeking the Spiritual: The Paintings of Marsden Hartley (with catalog), 98. *Collection Arranged:* Charles Sheeler: Works on Paper (catalog), 74, Checklist of the Permanent Collection, 77, Am Paintings from Collection of Daniel J Terra, 77, Arthur B Davies from the Brill Collection, 79 & All That Is Glorious Around Us, 81, Pa State Univ Mus Art; Paintings from William H Lane Foundation, Munson-Williams-Procter Inst, 78; Contemporary British Ceramics, Fitchburg Art Mus, 82; John F Kensett: An Am Master, Worcester Art Mus, 85. *Pos:* Registr, Pa State Univ Mus Art, 75-78; cur, William H Lane Found, 78-82; guest cur, Kensett Exhib, Worcester Art Mus, 83-85; owner & dir, Driscoll & Walsh Fine Art, Boston, 83-88 & Babcock Galleries, 86-. *Teaching:* Instr, Fitchburg State Col, 79-84; adj instr, New York Univ Cont Educ, 96-. *Awards:* Alumni Achievement Award, Pa State Univ. *Bibliog:* Hilton Kramer (auth), Charles Sheeler, NY Times, 4/13/74; Outstanding exhibitions, Apollo Mag, 6/74. *Mem:* Nat Arts Club; Am Asn Mus; Am Antique Soc; Am Numismatic Asn; Archives Am Art; Nat Acad (coun). *Res:* Emphasis on American art with current focus on John F Kensett and Edwin Dickinson. *Specialty:* 19th and 20th century American painting and sculpture. *Publ:* A Marsden Hartley of 1908, Am Art J, 80; John Stuart Ingle: Paradigms of reality, Am Artist, 82; John F Kensett: An American Master, Norton, 85; All that is Glorious Around Us, Cornell Univ Press, 97; The Artist and the American Landscape, First Glance Bks, 98. *Mailing Add:* Driscoll Babcock Galleries 525 W 25th St New York NY 10001

DRISKELL, DAVID CLYDE
PAINTER, EDUCATOR
b Eatonton, Ga, June 7, 1931. *Study:* Skowhegan Sch Painting & Sculpture, with Jack Levine & Henry V Poor, scholar, 53; Howard Univ, with James A Porter & Morris Louis, BA, 55; Cath Univ Am, with Nell Sonnemann & Ken Noland, MFA, 62; Riksbureau voor Kunsthistorisches Documentatie, The Hague, Neth, cert, 64. *Work:* Corcoran Gallery Art, Smithsonian Inst, Washington, DC; Birmingham Mus Art; Corcoran Gallery Art, Washington, DC; Carl Van Vechten Gallery Fine Arts, Fisk Univ, Nashville, Tenn; Ark Fine Arts Ctr, Little Rock; and others. *Comn:* Mountain and Tile Suite (10 woodcuts-color), Tenn Arts Comn, 72. *Exhib:* Baltimore Mus Area Exhib, 65; Corcoran Area Exhib, 66; Birmingham Festival Exhib, 72; Cent South Ann, Nashville, 72; Mid-South Exhib, Memphis, 75; Painting Across the Decade, DC Moore Gallery, NY, 2006. *Pos:* Mem bd adv, Mus African Art, 67-; mem visual arts adv panel, Tenn Arts Comn, 69-, mus adv bd, 73-; guest curator, Smithsonian Inst, 72; guest curator, Los Angeles Co Mus Art, 74-76; mus adv panel, Nat Endowment Arts, 74-77; bd gov, Skowhegan Sch Painting & Sculpture, 75-. *Teaching:* Prof painting & art hist, Talladega Col, 55-62; prof painting & art hist, Howard Univ, 62-66; prof art & chmn dept, Fisk Univ, 66-76; vis prof, Univ Ife, Nigeria, 70; vis prof, Bowdoin Col, 73; vis prof, Bates Col, 73; prof art, Univ Md, College Park, 76-82, chmn dept art, 78-83. *Awards:* Model of Excellence Award in Art, Colgate-Palmolive, 93; Amistad Research Award, 93; Am Acad Arts & Letters, 93 & 94. *Mem:* Coll Art Asn Am; Nat Conf Artists; Am Mus Asn; Am Fedn Art; Nat Acad Design. *Media:* Oil, Tempera. *Res:* Role of the Black artist in American society and traditional African art, its impact on Afro-American art. *Mailing Add:* 4206 Decatur St Hyattsville MD 20781-2127

DROHOJOWSKA-PHILP, HUNTER
WRITER
b Schenectady, NY. *Study:* Ohio State Univ, Columbus, 70-72; Ariz State Univ, Tempe, 73-75; Inst Allende, San Miguel de Allende, Mex, BFA, 76. *Exhib:* Georgia O'Keeffe Honolulu Art Acad, 2006. *Pos:* Art ed, Los Angeles Weekly, Calif, 80-84; columnist, Los Angeles Herald Examiner, 83-86; W Coast corresp, Artnews, 85-; chair, Dept Libr Arts & Sci, Otis Coll Art & Design, 87-95; contribr, Los Angeles Times, 87-, KCRW radio, 2011-; cur Calif, Archives of Am Art, Smithsonian. *Mem:* Int Asn Art Critics; Author's Guild. *Res:* Los Angeles art history of the 1960's. *Publ:* Full Bloom: The Art and Life of Georgia O'Keeffe, WW Norton, 2003; Modernism Rediscovered: Architectural Photographs of Julius Shulman, Taschen, 2007; God Knows: The Prints of John Baldessar, catalog essay, The Jordan Schnitzer Collection, 2009; other articles and essays; Rebels in Paradise: Los Angeles Art Scene and the 1960s, Henry Holt, 2011; Robert Graham, Ddavid Zwirner Gallery, 2011; Craif Kauffman: Sensual Mechanical, Frank Lloyd Gallery, 2012. *Mailing Add:* 9822 Millboro Pl Beverly Hills CA 90210

DRONZEK, LAURA ANN
PAINTER
b Litchfield, Ill, Nov 14, 1961. *Study:* Univ Wis, BA, 82, MFA, 93. *Work:* Madison Art Ctr & Univ Wis Union, Madison; Gardiner Art Gallery, Stillwater, Okla. *Exhib:* The Exquisite Corpse, Transmission Gallery, Glasgow, Scotland, 94; Cimarron National Works on Paper, Gardiner Art Gallery, Stillwater, Okla, 95; Intimus, Dean

Jensen Gallery, Milwaukee, Wis, 96; Sullivan & Dronzeke, Steinway Gallery, Chappel Hill, NC, 97; Wisconsin Triennial, Madison Art Ctr, Wis, 96; Food Glorious Food, Wustum Mus, Racine, Wis, 97; Three Wise Women, Vorpal Gallery, San Francisco, Calif, 97; Undefining Painting, Detroit Artists Market, Mich, 98; Nat Ctr for Children's Illus Lit, Dallas Mus Art, Texas, 2000; Watercolor Wisconsin, Charles A Wustum Mus, Racine, Wisc, 2000; Under Light, Underlight, Dean Jenen Gallery, Milwaukee, WI, 2002; Artists & the Uncultivated Landscape, Wustum Mus, Racine, WI, 2003; A Decade of Art from the Wisconsin Acad Gallery, James Watrous Gallery, Madison, WI, 2004. *Teaching:* Lectr life drawing, Univ Wis, Madison, 94. *Awards:* Purchase Award, Cimarron Nat Works on Paper, Gardiner Art Gallery, 93; Individual Artists Grant, Wis Arts Bd, 94 & Individual Fel, 98. *Bibliog:* Nathan Gueguelerre (auth), The world around us: challenging perceptions of geography, Shepard Express, 96; N Steven Zevitas (auth), New American Painting, Open Studios Press, 97; James Aver (auth), A Feast for the eyes, Milwaukee J Sentinel, 97; Snow Business, New York Times Book Rev, 11/21/99. *Media:* Acrylic on Paper. *Mailing Add:* c/o Dean Jensen Gallery 759 N Water St Milwaukee WI 53202

DROWER, SARA RUTH
PAINTER, CRAFTSMAN
b Chicago, Ill, Oct 15, 1938. *Study:* Roosevelt Univ, BS, 59; Univ Ill, Chicago, MS, 61; Art Inst Chicago. *Work:* Ill State Mus, Springfield; Minn Mus Art, Minneapolis; Borg-Warner Corp, DePaul Univ, Standard Oil, Chicago. *Exhib:* Inedible Cakes & Souvenir Shows, 82, Am Politics, 84, Renwick Gallery, Smithsonian Inst; New Elegance, Newark Mus, NJ, 84-85; Artwear '85, Bellevue Art Mus, Wash; Designed to Wear, Ore Art Mus, Arts & Crafts, 85-86; Wearable Fibers A Revolution Bodywear, Milwaukee Art Mus, 86; plus many others. *Pos:* Sci illusr, Turtox-Biol Supply, 62-64. *Awards:* First Prize Watercolors, Union League Club, Chicago, 72; Ill Coun Grant: Crafts, 86; Best of Show, Fine Art Exhib, Artists Guild Chicago, 74. *Mem:* Surface Design; Am Crafts Coun. *Media:* Miscellaneous Media. *Mailing Add:* 127 Laurel Wilmette IL 60091-2830

DRUCKER, ZACKARY
VIDEO ARTIST, PHOTOGRAPHER
Study: Sch Visual Arts, BFA (photog), New York, 2005; Calif Inst Arts, MFA (photog and media), Valencia, 2007. *Exhib:* Solo exhibs, Westport Art Ctr, Visual Arts Gallery, New York, 2005, AERSTAR/Deitch Projects, New York, 2006, Track 16. 2007, House of Campari, 2007, Lizabeth Oliveria Gallery, 2007, Greater Los Angeles MFA/CSU Long Beach, 2007, Mackey Apts, 2007, Kreilling and Dodd, 2007, Wignall Mus, 2007, Advocatve Gallery, Los Angeles, 2007, Photo Miami, 2007, Art Chicago, 2007, UMKC, 2007, UCLA Hammer Mus, 2007, Exchange Rate/Remy's Gallery, Los Angeles, 2008, Silverman Gallery/Lexington Club, San Francisco, 2008, MIX Festival, 2008, Acuna-Hansen Gallery, 2008, Art Office for Art and Video, 2008, OUTFEST, Los Angeles, 2008, Les Recontres Internationales, Paris, Berlin & Madrid, 2008, Gender Bender VI Edition, Bologna, Italy, 2008, Homo-A-Go-Go, 2009, Platinum Festival/Phyllis Stein Gallery, Los Angeles, 2009, Jerome Zodo Contemp, Milan, 2009, Steve Turner Contemp, 2009, Sweeney Gallery, Riverside, Calif, 2009, REDCAT, Los Angeles, 2009 & Ghetto Biennale, Port-Au-Prince, Haiti, 2009. *Awards:* Alumni Scholarship Award, Sch Visual Arts, 2005; Franklin Furnace Fund Grant; Art Matters Found Grant, 2009; Emerging Artist Fel, Calif Community Found, 2009. *Bibliog:* Darin Klein (auth) Bitches Rule & Box of Books; Younger Than Jesus: Artist Directory, Taschen/New Mus

DRUICK, DOUGLAS WESLEY
CURATOR, MUSEUM DIRECTOR
Study: McGill Univ, BA, 1966; Univ Toronto, MA (English), 1967; Yale Univ, MPhil (Art History), 1972, PhD (History of Art), 1979. *Pos:* Curator prints, Nat Gallery of Canada, Ottawa, 1974-1984; Prince Trust curator of prints and drawings, Art Inst Chgo, 1985-2011, Searle curator medieval through modern European painting and modern European sculpture, currently, pres, Eloise W. Martin dir., 2011-. *Mailing Add:* Art Institute Chicago 111 S Michigan Ave Chicago IL 60603

DRUM, SYDNEY MARIA
PAINTER, PRINTMAKER
b Calgary, Alta, Nov 20, 1952. *Study:* Univ Calgary, BFA (with distinction in art), 74; York Univ, MFA, 76. *Work:* Mus Mod Art, NY; Philadelphia Mus Art, Pa; Nat Mus Am Art, Washington; Mus Am Ostwall, Dortmund, Ger; Can Coun Art Bank, Ottawa, Ont. *Comn:* Pope, Ballard, Shepard & Fowle, Chicago, 82; Zimmerli Mus, Rutgers Univ, New Brunswick, NJ, 89; Harmann-Reimer Corp, NY, 90. *Exhib:* Solo exhibs, Name Gallery, Chicago, 79, Getler/Pall Gallery, NY, 81, Hart House Art Gallery, Univ Toronto, Ont, 81 & 95 Gallery Pascal, Toronto, Ont, 81 & 83, Jan Cicero Gallery, Chicago, 82 & Mus am Ostwall, Dortmund, Ger, 94; World Print III, San Francisco Mus Mod Art, Calif, 80; Bau-Xi Gallery, Toronto, Ont, 87, 90, 92 & 95; 55 Mercer Gallery, NY, 93, 96, 98, 2000, 02, 04, 06; Woodlands Art Gallery, London, Eng, 99; Gallery Surge, Tokyo, Japan, 99; CAS Gallery, Osaka, Japan, 99; Kunstverein Alte Feuerwache, Dresden, Ger, 02; Optisches Mus, Jena, Ger, 2004; Bautzener Kunstverein, Bautzen, Ger, 2008; Phonix Gallery, New York, 2010. *Teaching:* Sessional lectr studio art, Univ Alta, Edmonton, Can, 76-77; instr studio art, Nova Scotia Col Art & Design, Halifax, Can, 77-78; asst prof studio art, Univ Ill, Chicago Circle, 78-83; univ lectr studio art, Governors State Univ, Ill, 83-84; asst prof studio art, Rutgers Univ, 84-87. *Awards:* Can Coun Arts Grant, 76-77; A-N-W Prof Prize, 55th Ann Members Show, Print Club, Philadelphia, Pa, 79; Artist Fel, Yaddo Found, 80 & 85. *Bibliog:* Joyce Zemans (auth), Beyond the border at Harbourfront Art Gallery, Artmag, 2-3/80; Liz Wylie (auth), Sydney Drum at Gallery Pascal & Hart House Art Gallery, Artmag, 5-6/81; Jonathan Goodman (auth), Sydney Drum, Exhibition Essay, 55 Mercer Gallery, New York, NY, 9-10/98; Gerrit Henry (auth), Sydney Drum, Art in America, July 2003; James Campbell (auth), Sydney Drum-Digital Painting, 9/2005. *Mem:* Coll Art Asn Am; Print Club; Printmaking Coun NJ. *Dealer:* Birch Libralato Gallery Toronto. *Mailing Add:* 138 W 120th St New York NY 10027

DRUMM, DON
SCULPTOR, CRAFTSMAN
b Warren, Ohio, Apr 11, 1935. *Study:* Hiram Col; Kent State Univ, BFA & MA. *Work:* Cleveland Mus Art; Bowling Green State Univ; Columbus Gallery Fine Arts; Pan Am Airlines; Goodyear Tire & Rubber Co; and others. *Comn:* Reliefs, walls, aluminum & steel sculpture & fountains, Alcoa Co, Pittsburgh, Episcopal Diocese, Sao Paulo, Brazil, Richard Gossar Mem Sculpture, Toledo, Ohio, Curtain Bluff Hotel, Antigua BWI & City of Akron, Ohio; 2 cement murals, Bowling Green State Univ, Ohio, 66; corten steel sculpture, Baltimore, Md & Miami, Fla, 75; corten steel sculpture, City of Miami, Fla, 75; 14 cement wall relief murals, Quaker-Hilton, Akron, Ohio, 80; and many others. *Exhib:* Group shows, 64 & 65 & Traveling Exhib circulated by Am Fedn Arts, 65-67 & 72, Mus Contemp Crafts, NY; Cleveland Mus Art, 64-68; Columbus Gallery Fine Arts, 66 & 67; and others. *Pos:* Owner, Don Drumm Studios & Gallery, Akron, Ohio, 71-. *Teaching:* Artist in residence, Bowling Green State Univ, 66-71; instr, Penland Sch Crafts, 66-79. *Awards:* Purchase Prize, Cleveland Mus Art, 64; Prize, Nat Soc Interior Design, 65; Prize, Columbus Gallery Fine Arts. *Mem:* Ohio Designer Craftsmen; Am Craftsmen's Coun; Fine Arts Comn, Akron, Ohio. *Media:* Cast Metals, Miscellaneous Media. *Res:* Investigation into the use of contemporary materials and construction techniques to create urban sculpture specializing in the use of cast aluminum and concrete. *Dealer:* Don Drumm Studios & Gallery 437 Crouse St Akron OH 44311. *Mailing Add:* Don Drumm Studio Gallery 437 Crouse St Akron OH 44311-1220

DRUMMER, WILLIAM RICHARD
GALLERY DIRECTOR
b Ottawa, Ohio, Feb 17, 1925. *Study:* Ohio State Univ, BA, 50, MA, 57. *Exhib:* Piranesi, Miss State Mus, Jackson, 80-81 & Brooks Mem Art Gallery, Memphis, 82; Pensacola Art Mus, Fla, 83; New Orleans Mus Art, La, 84; Mario Villa Gallery, New Orleans, La, 89; Maguerite Oestreicher Fine Art Gallery. *Pos:* Dir, Gallery 539, New Orleans, 75-. *Mem:* Int Fine Print Dealers Asn. *Specialty:* Japanese woodblock prints, Piranesi etchings, fine architectural prints and drawings, rare architectural books. *Mailing Add:* 539 Bienville St New Orleans LA 70130

DRUMMOND, SALLY HAZELET
PAINTER
b Evanston, Ill, June 4, 1924. *Study:* Rollins Col, 42-44; Columbia Univ, BS, 48; Inst Design, Chicago, 49-50; Univ Louisville, MA, 52. *Work:* Mus Mod Art, Metrop Mus Art, Whitney Mus Am Art, NY; Hudson's Dept Store, Detroit; J B Speed Mus Art, Louisville; Weatherspoon Art Gallery, Univ NC, Greensboro; Corcoran Gallery Art, Hirshhorn Mus & Sculpture Garden, Washington, DC; and others. *Exhib:* Solo exhibs, Tanager Gallery, NY, 60, Green Gallery, NY, 62, Fischbach Gallery, NY, 68 & 78, Aldrich Mus, 81, Artist Space, 84, Cornell Fine Arts Ctr, Rollins Col, Winterpark, Fla, 89 & Louisville Visual Arts Asn, Ky, 90, Mitchell Algus Gallery, NYC, 2003; Am Artists Ann, Whitney Mus Am Art, NY, 60; Americans 63, Mus Mod Art, NY, 63; Recent Acquisitions, Whitney Mus Am Art, 64; Albright-Knox Art Gallery, 69; Retrospective, Corcoran Gallery Art, Washington, DC, 72; A Change of View, Aldrich Mus, 75; Underknown, PS1, NY, 86; The Kentuckians 1987, Nat Arts Club, 87; 5 Points Gallery, East Chatham, NY, 94; Nat Acad Arts & Letts, NY, 95; 175th Ann Exhibn, Nat Gallery Design, NY, 2000; Armory Show, NY, 2001; Group exhib, Seeing Red, Hunter Col, NYC, 2004; 2 person show, Alexandre Gallery NYC, 2005; Nat Gallery of Design, 2007; Wash Art Asn, 2012; The Zen of Contemplation, Wash Depot, Conn, 2012. *Teaching:* Instr, Skowhegan Sch Art, 73. *Awards:* Fulbright Grant, Venice, 52; Guggenheim Grant, France, 67; Jimmy Ernst Award, Am Acad Arts & Letters, 2007. *Bibliog:* Lawrence Campbell (auth), Dotted light, Art News Mag, 4/72; Gene Baro (auth), Forward to "Retrospectives" Catalogue, Corcoran Gallery Art, 72. *Media:* Oil. *Dealer:* Philip Alexandre. *Mailing Add:* 129 Camp Creek Rd Germantown NY 12526

DRUTT, HELEN WILLIAMS
DEALER, LECTURER
b Winthrop, Mass, Nov 19, 1930. *Study:* Tyler Sch Art, Temple Univ, BFA; Barnes Found; Moore Coll Art, Philadelphia, hon DA, 90. *Collection Arranged:* Two British Goldsmiths, Ramshaw & Watkins, 73; UICA: Craft Faculty, 74; Soup Tureens: 1976 (ed, catalog), 76; Olaf Skoogfors Retrospective (ed, catalog), 79; Robert Arneson: Self-Portraits 1966-1978 (ed, catalog), 79; Ruth Duckworth & Claire Zeisler (ed, catalog), 79; Contemporary Ceramics: A Response to Wedgewood (ed, catalog); Robert L Pfannebecker (ed, catalog); Claus Bury (ed, catalog); Contemporary Arts: An Expanding View (catalog), 86; Broaching it Diplomatically: A Tribute to Madeleine K Albright (int traveling exhib), 98-99. *Pos:* Curatorial consult, Mus Philadelphia Civic Ctr, 67, 70 & 73; exec dir, Philadelphia Coun Prof Craftsmen, 67-73; mem, Acquisition Comt, Montreal Mus Decorative Arts, Can; founder & dir, Helen Drutt Gallery, 74-; gallery consult, Moore Col Art, 78; consult, Nat Endowment Arts, 79-; selected panelist & juror for numerous exhibs, 68-89. *Teaching:* Mod craft hist, Philadelphia Col Art, 72-80; prof, Moore Col Art, Philadelphia, 74-84 & prof hist art, 82 & 87; vis scholar, Am Academy, Rome, Italy. *Awards:* Award Advan Mod Ceramics, Int Ceramics Symp, 81; Grant, Pa Coun Arts, 85-88; Founders Day Award, Fleisher Art Mem, Philadelphia Mus Art, 95. *Bibliog:* Carol Saline (auth), Crafty lady, Philadelphia Mag, 75; Professional Women (film), ABC-TV, Philadelphia, 76. *Mem:* Collab 20th Century, Philadelphia Mus Art; Am Crafts Coun (Pa state rep, 75-); Pa State Coun on the Arts (crafts panel, 75-78). *Specialty:* Twentieth century work in fiber, ceramics & metal; contemporary crafts. *Publ:* Contribr, Craft Horizons, Am Crafts Coun, 70; Contemporary Jewelry: 1964-96 HWD Collection, Philadelphia Mus Arts, Stedeliek, Montreal Mus Arts; coauth, Jewelry of Our Time, Thames & Hudson, 95. *Mailing Add:* 2222 Rittenhouse Sq Philadelphia PA 19103-5505

DRUTT, MATTHEW J W
DIRECTOR, CURATOR
Study: New York Univ, BA (fine arts and Russian); Yale Univ, MA (art history). *Collection Arranged:* Vik Muniz: Model Pictures, 2002; Kazimir Malevich: Suprematism, 2003-04 (Best Monographic Exhib Organized Nationally, Internat Asn Art Critics, 2003); Olafur Eliasson: Photographs (auth, catalog), 2004; Robert Gober:

The Meat Wagon (auth, catalog), 2005-06; Marie Lorenz, 2007; Nathan Carter: The Covert Caviar Frequency Disruptor, 2007-2008; Kate Gilmore: Girl Fight, 2008; Oliver Lutz: Paint it Black, 2008; Jonathan Monk: Rew-shay Hood Proj, 2009; Jeffrey Wisniewski, 2009-10. *Pos:* Cur, Solomon R Guggenheim Mus, NY, formerly; chief cur, The Menil Collection, Houston, Tex, formerly; exec dir, Artpace San Antonio, 2006-. *Teaching:* Adj prof, Columbia Univ Grad Sch Art, formerly. *Awards:* Chevalier de l'Ordre des Arts et des Lettres, 2006. *Mem:* Int Comt Mus Mod Art; The Arts Initiative, Houston, (founding vpres, 2005-07); Am Acad Berlin, Ger, (art adv bd, 2005-07); Dokumenta Int, Kassel, Ger, (adv bd, 2006); Am Assn Mus Dirs. *Publ:* Ed, Artpace Commissions & Exhibitions 2004-2006, Artpace, San Antonio, 2009. *Mailing Add:* Artspace 445 North Main Ave San Antonio TX 78205

DUAIV
PAINTER
b France, July 26, 1952. *Study:* Beaux Arts de Paris, 69-79; Conservatoire Nat Superieur de Musique de Paris, 69-79. *Work:* Phillips Gallery, Palm Beach, Fla; Austin Gallery, Austin, Tex; Jacques Lamy Gallery, Dallas, Tex; Kavanaugh Art Galleries, W Des Moines, Iowa; Master Gallery, Greenwood Village, Colo; Trowbridge-Lewis Galleries, Middleburg, Va; Charles Hecht Galleries, La Jolla & Los Angeles, Calif; West End Gallery, Davie, Fla; Global Fine Art, Dania Beach, Fla; Baterbys Galleries, Orlando & Delray Beach, Fla; Mac Art Group, Miami, Fla. *Exhib:* Solo exhibs, Palm Beach Antique Show, Phillips Galleries, 2010-2011, Show Duaiv, Sofitel, West End Pub, New York, 2010, Baterby's Art Auction Gallery, Fla, 2010, Crown Princess Cruise Line, 2010, P & O Cruise Line Show, London to Russia, 2010; Group exhibs, Austin Galleries, Tex, 2002; Roger Weatherburn Gallery, Naples, Fla, 2003; Art Expo New York, Beyr Thyssen Ltd, 2005; Phillips Galleies, Fla, 2006, 2008; Azamara Journ Cruise Line, 2009; Oxenberg Fine Art, Chelsea Galleria, Miami, 2009; Dallas Antiques Show, Phillips Galleries, 2009. *Collection Arranged:* Mrs. Vlassevskaia Viad, M. Bernard Somja, Noosa, Australia; Kalinka & Oliver Willocq, Brussels, Belgium; Stanley Cohen, Palm Beach, Fla; Doctor Dassen, Wassenaar, Nederland. *Pos:* first cello, Orchestre de 'Unesco, Paris, 79-80; soloist, Int Career, 82. *Awards:* Chevalier Academique, Section-Art, Greci-Marino, Italian Acad Letters; Commander of the Order of the Star of Europe, European Found Prize; Lys D'or, Cannes Int Carlton. *Bibliog:* Benezit Directory International, 2006. *Mem:* Art Start Fundraiser (hon chair); Hallandale Pops Orchestra (soloist, sponsor). *Media:* Oil on canvas. *Res:* homage to impressionist artists e.g. Van Gogh, Cezannes, Le Sydaner, Utrillo, Degas, Renoir. *Specialty:* Impressionism. *Interests:* music, instruments, boating, car racing. *Collection:* paintings of the 18th, 19th, & 20th centuries; antique instruments from the 16th-19th century including cellos, violins, altos, & bass. *Publ:* auth, 40 Years of Painting, 2011. *Dealer:* Phillips Gallery; Global Fine Art; Baterbys; MAC Art Group; Image Fine Art; Park West Gallery. *Mailing Add:* Duaiv Inc 1528 Argyle Dr Fort Lauderdale FL 33312

DUBACK, CHARLES S
PAINTER, PRINTMAKER
b Fairfield, Conn, Mar 10, 1926. *Study:* Whitney Sch Fine Arts, New Haven, Conn; Newark Sch Fine & Indust Arts, NJ; Skowhegan Sch Painting & Sculpture, Maine; Brooklyn Mus Art Sch. *Work:* Corcoran Gallery Art, Washington, DC; Emory Collection, Emory Univ, Atlanta, Ga; Columbia Mus Art, SC; Butler Mus Am Art; Am Tel & Tel, New York; and others. *Exhib:* Prints & Drawings, 53, Trends in Watercolor Today, 57, 20th Biennial Int Watercolor Exhib, 59 & Print Show, 70, Brooklyn Mus, NY; Whitney Ann Exhib of Contemp Am Painting, New York, 59-60; Mus Mod Art, New York, 62; 20th Ann Exhib Contemp Am Painting, Lehigh Univ, Bethlehem, Pa, 74; Works on Paper, Weatherspoon Art Gallery, Greensboro, NC, 75; Ft Wayne Mus of Art, Ind, 76; Solo exhibs, Landmark Gallery, 79-82, Susan Gross Gallery, Philadelphia, Pa, 85, Anne Weben Gallery Georgetown, Maine, 86; New Dimensions in Drawing, Aldrich Mus, Conn, 81; Two-person exhib, Farnsworth Mus, Rockland, Maine, 84; Art in Embassies, US Govt, 85; Austin Peny State Univ, Clarksville, Tenn, 87. *Collection Arranged:* Ten Painters of Maine, Landmark Gallery, NY, 77. *Bibliog:* Connie Smith (auth), A sentimental journey, Village Voice, 4/76; Laura Pipune (auth), Window exhibit at museum, Ft Wayne Jour-Gazette, 10/76; Holland Cotter (auth), Charles DuBack, Arts Mag, 11/77. *Media:* Multimedia. *Mailing Add:* Greenhut Galleries 146 Middle St Portland ME 04101

DUBASKY, VALENTINA
PAINTER
b Washington, DC, Mar 1, 1951. *Study:* Goddard Col, BA, 74, MA, 77. *Work:* Newark Mus, NJ; Orlando Mus, Fla; HF Johnson Art Mus, Cornell; Nat Mus Women Arts, Washington; Jane Voorhees Zimmerli Art Mus, Rutgers U, NJ. *Comn:* Fuzhou Int Ctr, China. *Exhib:* New Acquisitions, Aldrich Mus Contemp Art, Conn, 81; Albright-Knox Mus, Buffalo, NY, 82, 83 & 87; Art of the 70's & 80's, Aldrich Mus Contemp Art, Conn, 85; solo exhibs, Hodges Banks Gallery, Seattle, 86, Oscarsson-Siegeltuch Gallery, NY, 86, Empire Bronze Art Gallery, Long Island, 87, Ruth Siegel Gallery, NY, 90 & 91, Rena Haveson Gallery, Pittsburg, 95, Hodges Taylor Gallery, Charlotte, NC, 97, Cheryl Pelavin Fine Art, NY, 98, Thailand Art Ctr Gallery, Silpakorn Univ, Bangkok & Friesen Fine Arts, Seattle; Documenta, 34 Raumes, Berlin, Ger, 92; Animal Imagery, Champion Paper, Hartfield, Conn, 93; ES Painting Space, NY, 93; Art in Embassy Exhib, United States Embassy, Oslo, Norway, 93; and many others. *Awards:* Pollock-Krasner Found grant, 1986 & 2001; Art Amb to the Baltics, Art in Embassies Program, 2002; Cult Exch fellow, US Dept State, Bangkok, 2001. *Bibliog:* Christian Sci Monitor, 11/23/92; Ancient Futures: Cave-wall Landscape Paintings, Bangkok Post, 2001; Elizabeth Ash (auth), The art of visual diplomacy, State Mag, 2003. *Media:* Oil on Canvas. *Publ:* Contribr, Women in Print (exhib catalog with essays), 90; Intaglio Printing in the 1980's (exhib catalog), Jane Voorhees Zimmerli Art Mus, 90 & Surface Printing in the 1980's (exhib catalog with essays), 90; photographs, Soul Survivors: Stories of Women and Children in Cambodia, Carol Wagner (auth), Creative Arts Books, 2002; Art in Embassies Exhibition, Residence of the American Ambassador, Riga, US Dept State, 2002; Toxic Landscapes: Artists Examine the Environment, Puffin Cult Forum, 2002. *Dealer:* Cheryl Pelavin Fine Arts 13 Jay St New York NY 10013; Friesen Fine Art PO Box 1613 Sun Valley ID 83353; Friesen Fine Art 1210 2nd Ave Seattle WA 98101; Hodges Taylor Gallery 401 N Tryon St Charlotte NC 28202; Galerie Timothy Tew 309 East Paces Ferry Rd # 130 Atlanta GA 30305; Robert L Kidd Gallery Birmingham MI 48011. *Mailing Add:* 463 W St Apt D1016 New York NY 10014

DUBEN, IPEK AKSUGUR
PAINTER, SCULPTOR
b Istanbul, Turkey, 1941. *Study:* Univ Chicago, MA, 65; NY Studio Sch, 4 yr cert, 76; Mimar Sinan Univ, Istanbul, Turkey, PhD, 84. *Work:* Istanbul Modern; British Mus; Bibliotheca Alexandrina; Mus Voor Volkenkune Rotterdam; Wien Mus; Ctr Book Arts NY; King Stephen Mus. *Comn:* Pvt collections in US, Turkey, United Kingdom, France, Japan. *Exhib:* New York - Istanbul, Ataturk Cult Ctr, Turkey, 92; Women Artists from the Beginning of the Republic to the Present, Istanbul Archeol Mus, 93; Ephesus, Imagination of History, Ephesus, Turkey, 95; OpPositions, Mus Voor Volkenkunde, Rotterdam, The Neth; The Fifith Sharjah International Arts Biennial, 01; Bibliotheca Alexandrina's First Int Biennial for Hand Printed Artists' Books, 04; Call Me Istanbul, ZKM, Karlsruhe, Ger, 04; Contemp Art from Turkey & Korea, Incheon Centre Contemp Art, Korea, 06; 4th Int Artist's Books Exhib, King St Stephen Mus, Hungary, 06; Substance & Light: Ten Sculptors use Cameras, Munson-Williams-Proctor Art Mus, Utica, NY, 06; Modern and Beyond, Santralistanbul Contemp Art Mus, 2007; New Works New Horizons, Istanbul Mus Mod Art, 2009; Retrospective, Akbank Art Ctr, 2009; Threads: Interweaving Textureal meanings, Ctr for Book Arts, New York, 2009; ipek Duben, A Selection 1994-2009; Istanbul Next Wave, Akademie der Kunst, Berlin, 2009; A Dream, But Not Yours, Nat Mus Women Arts, DC, 2010; Nomad, Bibliotheca Alexandrina Fourth Into Biennale for the Artists Book, 2010; Dream and Reality, Istanbul Modern, The UnFramed Photograph, Ctr for Book Arts, NY, 2011; Mail-art-book, 8th Moscow Internat Artists Book Fair; Memory Chip, Istanbul Contemporary Art Fair, 2012; The Fifth Int Artists Book Exhib, The King St Sephen Mus, Hungary, 2013; London Art Fair, 2013; 13th Int Istanbul Biennial, 2013. *Pos:* Secy gen, Asn Int des Arts Plastiques, Istanbul, Turkey, 90-91. *Teaching:* instr art hist, Bosphorus Univ, Istanbul, 86; Yildiz Univ, Istanbul, 90; adj prof, Istanbul Tech Univ, 2000-2003; instr, Istanbul Bilgi Univ, 2005; instr, Sabanci Univ, 2008. *Awards:* artists-in-residence, Sculpture Space, Utica, NY, 98; Turkish Ministry cult Exhib Grant, 01; Moon & Stars Project Exhib Grant, NY, 01 & 06. *Bibliog:* Ali Akay (auth), Sentences from a Body Multiplied, Gosteri, Istanbul, 11/94; Carol Naggar (auth), Scrolls of the Future, I Publ, 94; Beral Madra (auth), Roundtrip: cat essay, Borusan Pubs, 10/2000; Robert Morgan, Ipek Duben: Encounters Given to Art, Cat essay, 2009; Necmi Sonmez, Liberating Images: Conceptual Framework in Ipek Duben's Work, Cat esasy, 2009; Zeynap Yasa Yaman (auth), Extracted Objects, Arredamento Mimarlik, Interview with Basak Senova, #245, 4/2011; Nazli Gurlek (auth), Myth Making, Myth Taking (catalog essay), 2012. *Media:* All Media. *Specialty:* contemporary art. *Collection:* Chillie Fulton, Rabia Capa, Zorlu, Leyla Alaton, Meiz Zilberman, Robert Horton, Doltas, Dilek & Teoman. *Publ:* Numerous articles in art magazines & newspapers, 78-91; auth, Painters of Pera, Beymen Publ, 90; ed, Contemporary Thought and Art, PSD Publ, 91; auth, Turk Resmi ve Elestrisi 1880-1950 (Turkish Painting and its Criticism 1880-1950), Bilgi Univ Press, Istanbul, 2007; ed, Seksenlerde Turkiye' de Cagdas Sanat: Yeni Acilimlar, Contemporary Turkish Art in the Eighties: New Perspectives, Bilgi Univ Press, Istanbul, 2008. *Dealer:* Galeri Zilberman Istanbul. *Mailing Add:* Serdari Ekrem Sok 30 Dogan Apt A/14 Beyoglu Istanbul Turkey

DUBIEL, CAROLYN MCPEEK
COLLAGE ARTIST
b Ploesti, Romania, Aug 16, 1930; US citizen. *Study:* Okla State Univ, BS, 52; Univ Pittsburgh, MR, 54. *Work:* Mt St Marys Col, Newburg, NY; Bridgeport Hosp, Bridgeport, Conn. *Exhib:* Small Works, NY Univ, 85-90; Color Box Series, Danville Mus, Va, 87; Works on Paper, Univ Tenn, Knoxville, 90, Perkins Mus, Moorestown, NJ, 90 & Univ Tex, Tyler, 93; Nat Asn Women Artists traveling exhib, 91; Oklahomans Come Home, Oklahoma City Arts Place, 92. *Teaching:* Art, El Paso High Sch, 52-53. *Awards:* Presidents Award, North Coast Coll Soc, 88; Genius Foundation, Nat Asn Women Artists, 90. *Mem:* North Coast Coll Soc; Soc Layerists & Multi-Media; Nat Asn Women Artists; Artists Equity, NY. *Media:* Collage. *Publ:* Cover artist, Sunshine Artists, 8/91; Creative Collage, Watson-Guptill, 94; contribr, Creative Collage Techniques, Northern Lights, 94. *Mailing Add:* 4 Pine Cir Newville PA 17241-9480

DUBIN, GLENN
COLLECTOR
b. New York, NY, April 13, 1957. *Study:* Stony Brook Univ, BA, 78. *Pos:* Formerly with E. F. Hutton & Co., co-founder Dubin & Swieca, 1984, co-CEO, Highbridge Capital Management, 1992-; Co-chmn, Louis Dreyfus Highbridge Energy, LLC, bd dirs, Bogen Comm Internat Inc, Founding bd mem, bd dirs Robin Hood Found, NYC, 1988-, bd dirs, Michael J Fox Found Parkinson's Rsch, bd trustees Mt. Sinai Hosp, NYC. *Awards:* Named one of 50 Best Paid Hedge Fund Managers, Alpha Mag, 2007, Forbes 400: Richest Americans, 2009, Top 200 collectors, ARTnews mag, 2011, 2012, 2013. *Mem:* Robin Hood Foundation (founding mem). *Collection:* Modern and contemporary art. *Mailing Add:* Highbridge Capital Management 40 W 57th St, Floor 32 New York NY 10019

DUBLAC, ROBERT REVAK
PAINTER
b Farmington, Conn, Nov 28, 1938. *Study:* Hartford Art Sch, Univ Hartford, BFA (painting, cum laude), 63 & grad study, 68; Yale Univ, with Scully & Nodleman, 67; Temple Univ, Rome, Italy, with Richard Callner, Roger Anliker, Barbara LaPenta & Dmitri Hadzi, 68-69. *Work:* Vanveldon Ltd, London, Eng; Marriott Hotel Corp; Cigna Corp, Hartford, Conn; Aetna Insurance Co, Hartford, Conn; Bank of Hartford, Conn; Hartford Hosp; City First Bank, Dallas, Tex; Fleet Bank, Hartford, Conn; DCI Computers, Hartford, Conn; Conn Nat Mortgage Co, Hartford, Conn; Shipman &

Goodwin, Hartford, Conn; Marsh & McClennen, Hartford, Conn; Proctor & Gamble, Cincinnati, Ohio; Heublein Int, New York; AS Hansen Inc, Dallas, Tex; Winthrop Securities Co, Dallas, Tex; Sentinel Bank, Hartford, Conn; N Adams State Coll, Mass; and many pvt collections in US, Canada, Italy, Ger, France & Eng; St. Francis Cancer Center, Hartford, Conn; St Francis Cancer Ctr; Smilow Hospital; Yale Hospital. *Comn:* Catherine Hepburn VanVeldon, London. *Exhib:* Wadsworth Atheneum; solo exhibs, Images Art Gallery, Briarcliff Manor, NY, 85, Aires E Gallery, Brewster, Mass, 85, Portfolio Gallery, Stamford, Conn, 86, Saugatuck Gallery, Westport, Conn, 86, Unionville Mus, Farmington, Conn, 88, Hurlbutt Gallery, Greenwich, Conn, 96 & Chase/Freedman Gallery, W Hartford, Conn, 97; The Saugatuck Gallery, Westport, Conn, 86; Unionville Mus, Unionville-Farmington, Conn, 88; Images Gallery, Toledo Ohio, 89; Berkshire Mus, Pittsfield, Mass, 98; Nat Acad Design, NY; Invitational show, Hartford Art School, Curated by Paul W Zimmerman. *Pos:* Chmn art dept, Avon High Sch, Conn, 65-67 & Litchfield High Sch, Conn, 69-80; co-dir, Fortman Studio, Florence, Italy, 77-78; self-employed artist/painter, 80-; cur show for the Unionville Mus, Farmington, Conn, 2007. *Teaching:* Art instr, Avon High Sch, Conn, 65-67, adj prof art hist, 67; art instr, Litchfield High Sch, Conn, 69-80. *Awards:* Grant, Adolph & Esther Gottlieb Found, 90; Elizabeth Found Grant, New York, 95; Pollock-Krasner Found Grant, 99; Berkshire Taconic Award, 2006. *Media:* Watercolor, Oil-Gouache. *Interests:* Gardening & Garden Design; Reading. *Publ:* Limited ed 300 Prints of Summer Morning, Trig Graphics Inc, New York, 88. *Mailing Add:* Brookside 62 Cottage St Unionville CT 06085

DUBNAU, JENNY
PAINTER
b London, England, 1963. *Study:* Barnard Coll, New York, BA, 1985; Yale Univ, MFA, 1996. *Exhib:* Solo exhibs: Clifford-Smith Gallery, Boston, 2000, 2002; Bucheon Gallery, San Francisco, 2003, 2005; Bernice Steinbaum Gallery, Miami, 2007; Greenville County Mus Art, SC, 2007; group exhibs include Sense or Spit, 8th Floor Gallery, New York, 1995; Where are All the People?, DeChiara Stewart Gallery, New York, 2000; Yet Another Reality, Univ Art Gallery, Storrs, Conn, 2005; No Lemons No Melon, David Krut Proj, New York, 2006; Wild Girls, Exit Art, New York, 2006; Outwin Boochever Portrait Exhib, Nat Portrait Gallery, Washington, 2006. *Teaching:* Vis Artist, Sch Art Inst Chicago, 2003, 2004, Univ S Fla Tampa, 2003, Sch Mus Fine Arts, Boston, 2003, Boston Univ, 2004. *Awards:* Pollock-Krasner Found Grant, 2004; Guggenheim Found Fel, 2004; New York Found Arts Grant, 2008. *Dealer:* Bucheon Gallery 389 Grove St San Francisco CA 94102

DUBOIS, ALAN BEEKMAN
CURATOR, ADMINISTRATOR
b Forest Glen, NY, Dec 14, 1935. *Study:* State Univ NY, New Paltz, BS, 58; Ind Univ, MFA, 66. *Work:* Ringling Mus Art, Sarasota, Fla; New Orleans Mus Art. *Exhib:* Light Seven, Mass Inst Technol. *Collection Arranged:* Fans a la Mode, 88; Masterpieces of Am Photography, 1899-1982, 89, Good, Better & Best: Decorative Arts from Mid-Am Mus Collections, 90; European Fans 1700-1920 from the Colin Johnson Collection, 91; Color-Cut-to-Clear and Engraved Glass, 91; Elsa Freund: An Am Studio Jeweler, 91; Am Art Jewelers: 1950s, 91; National Objects Invitational, 91; Am Glass: Carder and Steuben, 92; Flights of Fancy: Audubon Prints and Porcelain Birds, 92; Working in other Dimensions: Objects and Drawings, 93; Am Arts and Crafts 1900-1920, 93; National Objects Invitational (auth, catalog), 93; Arkansas: Year of American Craft (auth, catalog), 93; Contemp Crafts from the Horn Collection, 93; Contemp Jewelry 1964-1993; Selected Works: Helen Williams Drutt Collection, 93; Connections: Objects and Drawings from the Permanent Collection, 93; Exploring Sources: Objects and Drawings from the Permanent Collection, 94; Working in Other Dimensions: Objects and Drawings II (auth, catalog), 94; National Objects Invitational, 95; Leaning into the Wind: Ceramic Works by Bennett Bean, 96; Moving Beyond Tradition, A turned-Wood Invitational, 97; Born of Ashes: Woodfired Ceramics, 99; Making Difference: Fiber Sculpture by Jane Sauer, 2000. *Pos:* Dir, Wash Co Mus Fine Arts, 64-66; asst dir, Mus Fine Arts, St Petersburg, Fla, 66-84 & Orlando Mus Art, Fla, 84-89; cur decorative arts, Ark Arts Ctr, Little Rock, 89-. *Teaching:* Adj prof photog & art hist, Eckerd Col, St Petersburg, Fla, 84-. *Awards:* Nat Endowment Arts Fel, 72 & 75. *Mem:* Coll Art Asn; Am Asn Mus. *Media:* Clay, Fiber, Glass, Metal, Wood. *Res:* contemporary objects in craft media. *Specialty:* Contemporary Objects of Craft Media. *Interests:* photography. *Publ:* Elsa Freund: An American Studio Jeweler & National Objects Invitational, Ark Arts Ctr, Little Rock, 91; Bennett Bean, Leaning into the Wind: Ceramic Works, 96; Moving Beyond Tradition: A Turned-Wood Invitational, 98; Earl Pardon: Joy in the Making, 98; Jeri Au: Works in Clay, 98. *Mailing Add:* Arkansas Arts Ctr PO Box 2137 Little Rock AR 72203

DUBOIS, DOUGLAS
PHOTOGRAPHER
Study: Hampshire Col, Amherst, Mass, BA (film & photog), 83; San Francisco Art Inst, Calif, MFA (photog), 88. *Work:* Mus Mod Art, New York; San Francisco Mus Mod Art, Calif; Victoria and Albert Mus, London, England; Ctr Documentary Studies, Duke Univ, Durham, NC; Ctr Photog at Woodstock; Columbus Mus Art, Columbus, OH; Light Work, Syracuse, NY; Mus Art, Provo, Utah. *Exhib:* Solo exhibs, Blue Sky Gallery, Portland, OR, Ctr for Photog at Woodstock, Woodstock, NY, Silver Eye Gallery, Pittsburgh, PA, Pittsburgh Filmmakers, Pittsburgh, PA, Everson Mus Art, Syracuse, NY, Columbus Mus Fine Arts, Columbus, OH, Rhode Island Sch Design, Providence, RI, New Langton Arts, San Francisco, CA, Bridge Ctr for Contemp Art, El Paso, Tex, Hampshire Coll, Amherst, Mass, Dartmouth Coll, Hanover, NH, Midtown Photography Gallery, New York, NY, SF Camerawork, San Francisco, Calif; Group exhibs, Getty Mus, Los Angeles, Calif, Johnson Mus, Cornell Univ, Ithaca, NY, Saltonstall Fellowship Exhib, Schneider Gallery, Chicago, IL, Portraits, LightWork Gallery, Syracuse, NY, LightWork Grant Recipients, Tobacco Warehouse, Brooklyn, NY, Art and Commerce: New Photography Village Roadshow Pictures, Santa Monica, Calif, The Berman Collection: Recent Acquisitions, Mus of Art, Provo, UT, Contemporary Spaces: Underlying Cultures, Louise Lawler, Doug Hall and George Rousse, Everson Mus Art, Syracuse, NY, Everson Biennial, Alan R. Hite Art Institute, Louisville, KY, Blue Star Gallery, San Antonio, Tex, ArtSource, San Francisco, Calif, SITE Santa Fe, Santa Fe, NMex, Canadian Mus of Contemporary Photog, Ottowa, Canada, Ansel Adams Ctr, San Francisco, Calif, L.A. County Museum of Art, Los Angeles, Calif, Baltimore Mus Art, Md, Mus Modern Art, NY, Rena Bransten Gallery, San Francisco, Calif, PARCO Gallery, Tokyo, Japan, Yale Univ, New Haven, Conn, San Francisco Mus Modern Art, Photo Resource Ctr, Boston, Mass, Eye Gallery, San Francisco, Calif. *Teaching:* Vis lectr, Col Marin, 87, San Francisco Camerwork, 88, Univ Calif-San Francisco, 88, San Francisco Art Inst, 89 & Calif Inst Arts, Valencia, 92; asst prof art, NMex State Univ, 89; assoc prof, program coordr, Dept Transmedia, Syracuse Univ, currently. *Awards:* Fine Arts Fel, San Francisco Found, 87; Visual Artist Fel, Nat Endowment Arts, 90; Guggenheim Fel, John Simon Guggenheim Mem Found, 2012; Arts & Sci Res Grant, NMex State Univ, 92. *Publ:* Contribr, Edge, Pub Television, 10/91; Pleasures and terrors of domestic comfort, Mus Mod Art, New York, 91 & Artnews, 2/92; Parents (catalog), Dayton Art Inst, Ohio, 92; The sun, Japan, 5/92; Flesh and Blood: Photographers' Images of Their Own Families, The Picture Project, NY, 92. *Mailing Add:* Syracuse University Dept Transmedia 221 C Shaffer Art Bldg Syracuse NY 13244

DUBROW, JOHN
PAINTER
b Salem, Mass. *Study:* San Francisco Art Inst, BFA, 1980, MFA, 1983. *Exhib:* Solo exhibs, Forum Gallery, New York, 1985, 1987, 1990, Salander-O'Reilly Galleries, San Francisco, 1993, 1996, 1998, 2000, 2003, Lori Bookstein Fine Art, 2005, 2006, 2008, List Gallery, Swarthmore Col, 2007; Nat Acad Design, New York, 1986 & 1988; Forum Gallery, 1986, 1987, & 1990; Am Acad Arts and Letts Invitational, New York, 1988, 2009; Hackett-Freedman Gallery, 1997, 1999; Salander-O'Reilly Galleries, 1994-95; Westenberg Gallery, Great Barrington, Mass, 1996; Wenham Mus, Mass, 1998; World Trade Ctr, New York, 1999; NY Studio Sch, 1999; Diamantina Gallery, Brooklyn, 2003; Sharon Arts Gallery, Peterborough, NH, 2005; Lori Bookstein Fine Art, New York, 2004-05, 2007. *Teaching:* Prof NY Studio Sch of Drawing, Painting, and Sculpture. *Awards:* Pollock Krasner Found award, 1986-87; Truman Prize, Nat Acad Design, 1990 & Carnegie Prize, 2003; Acad Award in Art, Am Acad Arts and Letters, 2009. *Mem:* Nat Acad Design. *Media:* Oil. *Mailing Add:* Lori Bookstein Fine Art 138th 10th Ave New York NY 10011-4727

DUERWALD, CAROL
PAINTER, ILLUSTRATOR
b Brooklyn, NY. *Study:* Studied with artist William C Kautz, 75-81; Parson Sch Design, 76; Huntington Art League, New York, 85-89. *Comn:* Mural, comn by Mr & Mrs B Cohen, Oyster Bay, NY, 89; portrait, comn by Mr & Mrs T Brennan, Chester, NJ, 91; portrait, comn by Mr & Mrs G Baker, Oyster Bay, NY, 92; portrait, comn by Mrs D Coleman, Charlottesville, Va, 92; portrait, comn by Mrs M Geenman, Upper Brookville, NY, 92. *Exhib:* Rochester Art Club Open Juried Exhib, Mem Art Mus, Rochester, 84; Huntington Township Art League Open Juried Exhib, Heckscher Mus, Huntington, NY, 85; Pastel Soc Am Juried Open, NY, 89-92; Am Artists Prof League Grand Nat, 91 & Salmagundi Open Juried Exhib, Salmagundi Club, NY, 92; Pastel Soc Am Open, NY, 94; Am Artists Prof League Grand Nat, 94; and others. *Pos:* Sketch & design artist, Blum Folding Paper Box, Rosedale, NY, 56-57; sketch & design artist, Cellucraft Inc, New Hyde Park, NY, 57-61; illus & design, freelance, 65-70. *Teaching:* Instr drawing, Pittsford High Sch, NY, 83-84; instr pastel painting, Pittsford Art Club, NY, 83-84; instr pastel portraits, Penny Sch, Cutchoque, NY, 88 & Somerset Art Asn, NJ, 94; instr pastel still life, Somerset Art Asn, 94-. *Awards:* Best Painting in Show, Am Artist Prof Grand Nat League, 91; George Innes Mem Award for Pastel, Salmagundi Club Open Exhib, 92; Hon Mention, Am Artist Prof NJ & others; Vera Sickenger Award (Figure in Pastel), Salmagundi Club, 2009. *Mem:* Pastel Soc Am; Am Artist Prof League; Huntington Township Art League; Somerset Art Asn; Morris Co Art Asn; Pastel Soc of Am, NY Nat Art Club, New York. *Media:* Pastel. *Publ:* Contribr, Hampton Scene, 89; Observer Tribune, 91 & 94; Currier News, 91; Star Ledger, 92; Best of Pastel II, Rockport Publ, 99. *Mailing Add:* 46 Mile Dr Chester NJ 07930

DUFF, ANN MACINTOSH
PAINTER, PRINTMAKER
b Toronto, Ont, Can. *Study:* Cent Tech Sch; Queen's Univ Summer Sch Fine Arts. *Work:* Nat Gallery Can, Ottawa; Art Gallery of Ont, Toronto, Agnes Etherington Gallery, Queen's Univ; City Toronto Arch; Ore State Univ, Corvallis; Univ Toronto Art Centre; Tom Thomson Mem Gallery, Owen Sound. *Comn:* Watercolor painting, Reader's Dig for Expo 67, Montreal. *Exhib:* Five Toronto Painters, Montreal Mus Fine Art; Can Soc Painters in Watercolor & Am Watercolor Soc Joint Exhib, 72; Fifty Yrs of Watercolour, Art Gallery of Ontario, 75; Watercolours Japan-Canada, Tokyo-Montreal, 76-77; Robarts Libr Univ Toronto, 97; On Paper, Univ Toronto Art Center, 2002; Tom Thomson Mem Gallery (Retrospective), Owen Sound, Ont, 2007; twenty-three solo exhibs in Toronto. *Awards:* Queen Elizabeth Silver Jubilee Medal, 77; Loomis & Toles Award, 84; Hon Award, Can Soc Painters Watercolour, 84. *Bibliog:* Frances Duncan Barwick (auth), Pictures from the Douglas M Duncan Collection, Univ Toronto, 75; Rebecca Sisler (auth), Passionate Spirits, Clarke Irwin, Toronto, 80; DA 41 A Journal of the Printing Arts, Porcupine's Quill Publ, Erin, Ont, 97. *Mem:* Royal Can Acad Arts. *Media:* Watercolor, Wood Engraving. *Publ:* Ann MacIntosh Duff: To Love and to Cherish, Tom Thomson Art Gallery, Owen Sound, Ontario, Canada, 2008. *Dealer:* D&E Lake Ltd 1199 Yonge St Toronto ON Canada M4T 3A8. *Mailing Add:* 133 Imperial St Toronto ON M5P 1C7 Canada

DUFF, JAMES H
RETIRED MUSEUM DIRECTOR
b Pittsburgh, Pa, Oct 11, 1943. *Study:* Washington & Jefferson Coll, BA, 65; Univ Mass, MA, 70. *Collection Arranged:* Wildlife in Art, Brandywine River Mus, Chadds Ford, Pa, 73; Maxfield Parrish: Master of Make-Believe, 74; Harvey Dunn, 74; Peter Hurd, 77; The Collection of Amanda K Berls & Ruth A Yerion, 80; An Am Vision:

Three Generations of Wyeth Art (auth, catalog), 87. *Pos:* Dir, Mus Hudson Highlands, 1966-73; consult, NY State Coun Arts, 1970-72; dir, Brandywine River Mus, 1973-2011 & Nat Mus Serv Bd, 86-95; Pres, Asn Art Mus Dirs, 96-97. *Bibliog:* various prefaces & introductions to exhibition catalogs. *Mem:* Asn Art Mus Dirs (pres, 96-97); Am Asn Mus; Mid-Atlantic Asn Mus (pres, formerly). *Interests:* American art & Chinese ceramics. *Publ:* Auth, Not for Publication: Landscapes, Still Lifes and Portraits by NC Wyeth, Brandywine River Mus, 82; An American Vision, Little, Brown, 87. *Mailing Add:* PO Box 297 Chadds Ford PA 19317

DUFF, JOHN EWING
SCULPTOR
b Lafayette, Ind, Dec 2, 1943. *Study:* San Francisco Art Inst, BFA, 67; with Manuel Neri, Paul Harris & Ron Nagle. *Work:* Kaiser Wilhelm Mus, Krefeld, Ger; Guggenheim Mus Art, Whitney Mus Am Art & Mus Mod Art, NY; Inst Contemp Art, Boston, Mass; Metropolitan Mus, NY. *Exhib:* Anti-Illusion, Procedures & Materials Show, Whitney Mus, 69, David Whitney Gallery, 70 & 71, John Meyers Gallery, 72 & 73 & Willard Gallery, 75, 76, 77 & 78, NY; Daniel Wienburg Gallery, 73, 75, 77, 79 & 81; Margo Leavin Gallery, Los Angeles, Calif, 81; Development in Recent Sculpture, Whitney Mus Am Art, 81 & Enclosing the Void, 88; Blumhelmar Gallery, 86 & 88; Solo exhib, David McKee Gallery, 93 & 95; Group exhib, David Nolan Gallery, 2010; Works from the Jenney Archive, Gagosian Gallery, 2013. *Awards:* Theodor Award, Guggenheim Mus, 77; Brandis Award for Visual Arts, 87. *Bibliog:* Barbara Rose (auth), Where we are & what we like, NY Mag, 4/72 & 4/75; John Russell (auth), current shows in NY Times, 3/75; J Tannenbaum (auth), rev in Arts Mag, 6/75. *Media:* Fiberglass, Steel. *Publ:* Contribr, Art Now: New York, 72. *Mailing Add:* 5 Doyers St New York NY 10013-5140

DUFFY, MICHAEL JOHN
PAINTER, PRINTMAKER
b Chicago, Ill, Dec 29, 1945. *Study:* Colo Col, Colorado Springs, BA, 72. *Work:* Denver Art Mus; Mesa Col, Grand Junction; Colo Col, Colorado Springs; Columbia Mus Art, SC. *Comn:* Viet Nam Vets Art Mus, Chicago. *Exhib:* Solo exhibs, Colo Coll Packard Gallery, Colorado Springs, 83, Glastonbury Gallery, San Francisco, 85 & Columbia Mus Art, SC, 90; 46th Ann, Soc Four Arts, Palm Beach, Fla, 84; Chicago Print Show, Northwestern Univ, Evanston, Ill, 85; Small Paintings & Sculpture, Univ Denver, 87; Crescent Art Centre, Belfast, Ireland, 93; and others. *Awards:* Atwater Kent Award, 46th Ann Soc Four Arts, 84; Best of Show, Colorado Springs Fine Art Ctr, 85. *Bibliog:* Irene Clurman (auth), Intensity intact, Rocky Mountaint News, 5/30/86; New prints, Print Collectors Newsletter, 7/87; Abrams (auth), The Art of the Vietnam Veterans Art Mus, 11/98. *Mem:* Chicago Art Inst; Chicago Art Coalition. *Media:* Oil. *Dealer:* A Clean Well Lighted Place New York NY; Lovely Fine Art Oakbrook Terr FL. *Mailing Add:* 400 E Randolph St #913 Chicago IL 60601

DUFOUR, PAUL ARTHUR
PAINTER, DESIGNER
b Manchester, NH, Aug 31, 1922. *Study:* Univ NH, BA, 50; Yale Univ, BFA, 52; also with Takahiko Fujita & Ikuo Hirayama, Japan, 64. *Work:* Masur Mus Art, Monroe, La; Springfield Art Mus, Mo; La State Collection, Baton Rouge; La Bicentennial Collection; Centraplex Munic Collection, Baton Rouge. *Comn:* Stained glass sculpture & mosaic, St Joseph Prep Sch, Baton Rouge, La, 68; stained glass windows, Holy Ghost Church, Hammond, La, 74; stained glass windows & bronze sculpture, Our Lady of Mercy, Baton Rouge, 74; stained glass, St Patrick Church, Lake Providence, La; glass windows & bronze doors, St Mary of Pines, Shreveport, La, 79; and many others. *Exhib:* Stained Glass Invitational, Mus Fine Arts, Jacksonville, Fla, 79; 20 Yr Retrospective, La State Univ Art Gallery, 79; Glaskunst, Int Expo of Glass, Kassel, Ger, 81; Vicointer, Glass Invitational Expo, Valencia, Spain, 83; A Rebirth of A Medium, Nat Glass Invitational, Univ Tex, San Antonio, 83; 21st through 34th Ann State Exhib Prof Artists, 66-79; Contemp Glass, Corning Mus, 79 & 80; Southeast Craft, Lemoyne Art Found, 80; Am Glass Invitational, Kansas City, Mo, 80; Int Glass Art Exposition, Kassel, Ger, 80; and many others. *Pos:* Supvr educ, Currier Gallery Art, Manchester, NH, 52-55; artist-in-residence, Viterbo Col, 68. *Teaching:* Asst prof painting, St John's Univ, 55-58; vis prof design, Sienna Heights Col, 57; prof design & stained glass, La State Univ, Baton Rouge, 58-. *Awards:* Top Award, La Int Watercolor Exhib, 69; First Purchase Award, 4th Int Watercolor, 72; Hon Mention, Vicointer, Valencia, Spain, 83. *Bibliog:* Corning Mus Glass Microfiche Prog, 78; New Glass Rev I, Corning Mus Glass, 80; Jensen & Conway (auths), Ornamentalism, Potter, 82. *Mem:* Am Glass Guild; Coll Art Asn; Am Craft Coun; La Watercolor Soc. *Media:* Multimedia. *Dealer:* Baton Rouge Gallery 205 N Fourth St Baton Rouge LA 70801; Matrix Gallery 912 W 12th St Austin TX 78713. *Mailing Add:* 20535 Narrow Rd Covington LA 70435-0424

DUFRESNE, ISABELLE COLLIN See Violet, Ultra

DU JARDIN, GUSSIE
PAINTER, PRINTMAKER
b San Francisco, Calif, Feb 19, 1918. *Study:* Univ Colo, BA; Univ Iowa, MA. *Work:* NMex Mus Art, Santa Fe; NMex Highlands Univ; Univ Iowa; Roswell Mus, NMex; Univ Colo Mus; Mus NMex, Albuquerque. *Exhib:* Butler Inst Am Art 26th Ann, 61; NMex Biennial, 71, 73 & 75; Mus NMex Southwest Biennial Exhib, 72, 74 & 76, Invitational, 78; Solo exhibs, Roswell Mus, 78, 92 & 96, Gov Gallery, NMex State Capitol, Santa Fe, NMex, 79, Western State Col, Gunnison Colo, 91, Art Inst Permian Basin, Odesa, Tex, 93, SW 96 Mus NMex & Invitational Clines Gallery, Santa Fe, 96. *Pos:* Artist-in-Residence Prog, Roswell Mus, 77-. *Awards:* First Purchase Award, Mus NMex, 61. *Media:* Acrylic, Oil. *Mailing Add:* 1403 W Berrendo Rd Roswell NM 88201

DUKE, LEILANI LATTIN
ADMINISTRATOR
b Aug 27, 1943. *Study:* Denison Univ, BA, 65; Syracuse Univ, MA, 66; Arts Admin Inst, Harvard Univ, 78; Eastman Sch, Hon Dr. *Pos:* Res asst, Onondoga City, Syracuse, NY, 66-69; staff asst, US Senate Labor & Pub Welfare Comt, Washington, DC, 68-69; fed aid coordr, Senator Jacob Javits, US Senate, Washington, DC, 69-71; exec secy, Fed Coun Arts & Humanities Nat Fdn on Arts & Humanities, 71-78; coordr, Design Educ Prog, Nat Endowment Arts, 71-76, Spec Constituencies Prog, 76-78; exec dir, Calif Confederation Arts, 79-81; prog develop officer, J Paul Getty Trust, 81-; dir, Getty Ctr Educ Arts, 83-; independent consult, currently. *Mem:* Am Craft Coun (bd mem); Coll Art Asn; Nat Art Educ Asn. *Mailing Add:* 1030 Glenhaven Dr Los Angeles CA 90272

DUNBAR, MICHAEL AUSTIN
SCULPTOR, ADMINISTRATOR
b Santa Paula, Calif, Sept 21, 1947. *Study:* Ill State Univ, Normal, BS, 71, MS, 78; Univ Ill, Springfield, MA, 74. *Work:* Flint Inst Art, Flint, Mich; Art in Public Buildings, Southfield, Mich; Krasl Art Ctr, St Joseph, Mich; Western Mich Univ, Kalamazoo, Mich; Univ Notre Dame, South Bend, Indiana; David Owsley Mus Art, Ball State Univ; Nathan Manilow Sculpture Park; Governor State Univ, Chicago Heights, Ill; Ill State Mus, Springfield, Ill; Coll Business, Univ Ill, Champaign, Ill; Oakton Community Coll, Skokie, Ill; Eastern Ill Univ, Charleston, Ill; Rockford Art Mus, Rockford, Ill; Western Ill Univ, Macomb, Ill; Soutehrn Ill Univ, Carbondale, Ill. *Comn:* Sioux City Arts Ctr, Sioux City, Iowa; Kettering Univ, Flint, Mich; Indiana State Univ, Terre Haute, Indiana; Renaissance Schaumburg Hotel and Convention Ctr, Schaumburg, Ill; Pyramind Hill Sculpture Park, Hamilton, Oh; Monticello Sculpture Gardens Godfrey, Ill; Time Equities Plaza, Dayton, Oh; Southwestern Ill Coll, Belleville, Ill; Univ Wisc, Steven's Point, Wisc. *Exhib:* Instrumental Transitions, Grounds for Sculpture, Hamilton, NJ; Three Illinois Sculptors, Northwestern Univ, Evanston, Ill, 89; Sculpture Walk, Chicago River Park, Ill, 91; Out of Time, Bloomington, Ill, 91; Abstract Works, Struve Gallery, Chicago, Ill, 91; Chicago: The Third Dimension, Ukrainian Inst Mod Art, Chicago, Ill, 94; Michael Dunbar Machinist Studies, Ill State Mus, JRT Ctr, Chicago, 96; Pierwalk, Chicago, 96-2000; Sculpture on the prairie, Wandell Sculpture Park, Urbana, Ill, 99; The Univ Notre Dame Sculpture Project, Notre Dame, Ind; Heavy Equiptment, Flint Institute of Art, Flint, MI; Six Am Sculptors in Rome, Rome, Italy; Machinist Studies, Maiden Lane Exhib Space, NY; A Measure of Time & Space, Gerald Peters Gallery, Santa Fe, NMex; Sculpture in Wood, Stone & Steel, W Mich Univ, Kalamazoo; Outdoor sculpture exhib, Purdue, Ind; Sculpture Tour, Western Mich Univ, Kalamazoo; Thea Burger Assoc Inc, New York, 2010; Spring Sculture Exhib, Gronds for Scultpure, Hamilton, NJ; Michael Dunbar Sculptures, Solo exhibits of three dimensional bronze Machinist Studies, and painted steel Machinist Studies at the Sioux City Arts Ctr., Iowa, 2013; 86th Exhib of Profl Members, Arts Club of Chgo, Ill, 2014; Art in Public Buildings, Program, Time Equities, Travelers Towers, Southfield, Mich, 2014; Genesis, Origins of an Idea, exhibit of three-dimensional bronze Machinist Studies, Kettering Univ, Flint, mich., 2015. *Collection Arranged:* Monticello Sculpture Gardens Collection; Ill Collection for the James R Thompson Ctr, Chicago, Ill; Portrait of Ill for the Ill State Libr, Springfield, Ill. *Pos:* Coordr, Art in Archit, State of Ill, 77-2011. *Teaching:* Instr, Univ Ill, Springfield, 76 & Lincoln Land Community Coll, 78 & 86. *Awards:* Pollock-Krasner Found Grant; Nat Endowment for the Arts Fel; Artist Grant & Governors Art Award Comn, Ill Arts Coun;. *Bibliog:* Suzanne Deats (auth), Michael Dunbar; Larry Shiner (auth), Machinist Studies. *Mem:* Chicago Sculpture Soc; Arts Club of Chicago. *Media:* Steel, Bronze. *Interests:* Historic preservation. *Publ:* co-auth, Ed Paschke Electronicon, Ruth Dunckworth, Clay & Bronze. *Dealer:* Gerald Peters Gallery Santa Fe NMex; Thea, Burger & Assoc, New York. *Mailing Add:* 912 S Park Springfield IL 62704-2341

DUNCAN, RICHARD (HURLEY)
DRAFTSMAN, PRINTMAKER
b Daytona Beach, Fla, Feb 11, 1944. *Study:* Southern Ill Univ, Edwardsville, BA, 66, MFA, 73; study with John Adkins Richardson, Robert Malone, and James Butler. *Work:* Aukland City Art Gallery, NZ; Springfield Civic Collection, Ill; Southeast Ctr Contemp Art, Winston-Salem, NC; Printclub Albany, Cooperstown Art Asn, NY; Dulin Gallery, Knoxville, Tenn; Barnett Bank and Sunbank, Fl. *Comn:* Two lithographs, Verein Originalgraphik, Switz, 74. *Exhib:* 35 Artists of the Southeast, High Mus & traveling, 76-78; Worldprint 77, San Francisco Mus Mod Art, 77; one-person exhibs, Hunter Mus, 77 & Ritter Art Gallery, Fla Atlantic Univ, Boca Raton, 85; 25th Nat Exhib Prints, Nat Collection Fine Arts & Libr Cong, 77-78; 100 Worldprints, Smithsonian Traveling Exhib, 77-79; Honolulu Nat Print Exhib, Hawaii, 82; 62nd Nat Print Exhib, Soc Am Graphic Artists, NY, 86-87; Printmakers 98, Pittsburgh Ctr Arts, 98; Printwork 98 Nat, Poughkeepsie, NY, 98; Best of Years Retrospective, Dulin Gallery, Knoxville, Tenn, 2004. *Pos:* Vpres, Fla Printmakers, -2004. *Teaching:* Instr printmaking, Univ South, 73-78; assoc prof printmaking & drawing, Fla Int Univ, 78-2004. *Awards:* Ford Found Grants, 74 & 77; Merit Award, 18th Nat Printmaking & Drawing Exhib, 81; Nat Endowment Arts Grant, 85; S Fla Cult Consortium Grant, 85. *Bibliog:* Coleman, Richardson & Smith (auths), Basic Design: Systems, Elements, Applications, Prentice-Hall, 83. *Mem:* Fla Print makers (bd mem, 98-); Southeast Coll Art Asn; So Graphics Coun Conf (co-chmn Miami, 2000). *Media:* Etching, Drawing & Painting. *Interests:* drawing nature from life. *Publ:* Contrib, Florida printmakers (auth), Impressions, spring-fall 95-. *Mailing Add:* 8700 SW 149th Terr Miami FL 33176

DUNHAM, CARROLL
PAINTER
b New Haven, 1949. *Study:* Trinity Coll, Hartford, Grad, 1927. *Exhib:* Solo exhibs include Daniel Weinberg Gallery, LA, 1985, 1987, 1991, 2004, Sonnabend Gallery, New York, 1989, 1990, 1993, 1994, Trinity Coll, Hartford, 1992, Nolan/Eckman Gallery, New York, 1993, 1998, 2001, 2002, 2004, Sch Mus Fine Arts, Boston, 1995, Metro Pictures, New York, 1997, 1999, 2002, White Cube, London, 1998, 2003, 2006, Weatherspoon Art Gallery, Greensboro, NC, 1999, Gagosian Gallery, Beverly Hills, 2001, New Mus Contemp Art, New York, 2002, Gladstone Gallery, New York, 2004, 2007, Brussels, 2011, Patrick de Brock Gallery, Knokke, Belgium, 2011; group exhibs include Lineup, The Drawing Center, NY, 1979, Current: Carroll Dunham, Inst of Contemporary Art, Boston, 1985, Barbara Krakow Gallery, Boston, 1988, Fall & Winter: 1991-1992, Daniel Weinberg Gallery, Santa Monica, CA, 1991, Whitney

Biennial, Whitney Mus Am Art, New York, 1995, Am Century, Part II, 1999, End Papers, Neuberger Mus Art, Purchase, NY, 2000, Remote Viewing, 2005, Collection: MOCA's First Thirty Years, Mus Contemporary Art, Los Angeles, 2009, Jr. and Son's Zach Feuer Gallery, NY, 2009, Nature, Gerhardsen Gerner, Berlin, 2010; New York Abstract, Contemp Arts Ctr, New Orleans, 1995; Carpenter Ctr Visual Arts, Harvard Univ, 1996, Some Options in Abstractions, 2001; Now on View, Metro Pictures, New York, 1997, Drawn By..., 1999; Pop Surrealism, Aldrich Mus Contemp Art, Conn, 1998; Young Americans 2, Saatchi Gallery, London, 1998; Examining Pictures, Whitechapel Art Gallery, London & Mus Contemp Art, Chicago, 1999; Open Ends, Mus Mod Art, New York, 2000, What is Painting?, 2007; We Love Painting, Mus Contemp Art, Tokyo, 2003; Remote Viewing, St Louis Art Mus, 2006; Size Matters, Hudson Valley Ctr Contemp Art, Peekskill, NY, 2007; Second Thoughts, Hessel Mus Art, Bard Coll, NY, 2008. *Awards:* Skowhegan Medal, Painting, 2004. *Mem:* Nat Acad. *Dealer:* Gladstone Gallery 515 W 24th St New York NY 10011; Barbara Krakow Gallery 10 Newbury St Boston MA 02116. *Mailing Add:* Gladstone Gallery 515 W 24th St New York NY 10011

DUNIGAN, BREON NINA
SCULPTOR
b New York, NY, Apr 13, 1961. *Study:* Atlanta Coll Art; Mass Coll Art, BFA, 84; Rutgers Univ, NJ, MFA, 86, with W Gary Kuehn. *Comn:* Sculpture, Univ Va, Charlottesville, 93. *Exhib:* Provincetown Group Gallery, 90, 91 & 92; Better Homes & Monuments Show, Brooklyn, NY, 91; Berta Walker Gallery, Provincetown, Mass, 92; Black & Herron Gallery, NY, 95; DNA Gallery, Provincetown, Mass, 95-2004; Provincetown in Hudson, Carrie Haddad Gallery, NY, 97 & The Nude, 98; Southeastern Ctr Contemp Art, Winston-Salem, NC, 98; Sex Pots, the Erotic Life of Clay, San Francisco State Univ Art Mus, San Francisco, Calif, 2002; Gregory Lind, New Field, New Territories Gallery, San Francisco, Calif, 2002. *Pos:* Freelance sculptor; carpentry. *Awards:* Nat Endowment Arts Grant, 90; Pollock-Krasner Grant, 91; New Eng Found Arts Award, 97. *Bibliog:* Sara London (auth), article, Art New Eng, 10/95. *Mem:* Provincetown Art Assoc. *Media:* Miscellaneous. *Dealer:* DNA Gallery Provincetown MA; Carrie Haddad Hudson NY. *Mailing Add:* PO Box 722 Truro MA 02666

DUNITZ, JAY
PHOTOGRAPHER
b Reading, Pa, Feb 4, 1956. *Study:* Kansas City Art Inst, 74; San Francisco Art Inst, BFA, 78. *Work:* Mus Mod Art, Int Ctr Photog, NY; Nat Mus Am Art, Corcoran Gallery Art, Washington, DC; Cornell Univ Art Mus; Indianapolis Mus Art, Ind; Cincinnati Art Mus, Ohio; Santa Barbara Mus Art, Calif; Newport Harbor Art Mus, Newport Beach, Calif. *Exhib:* New Acquisitions in Graphic Arts, Nat Mus Am Art, Washington, DC, 88; Present Tense, Los Angeles Munic Art Gallery, 88; solo exhibs, Santa Monica Coll Photog Gallery, Calif, 88 & Fitchburg Art Mus, Fitchburg, Mass, 90; Photographs from EF Hutton Collection, Contemp Art, NY, 88; Photographs from the Collection, Corcoran Gallery Art, Washington, DC, 89; Ansel Adams Gallery, Yosemite Nat Park, Calif, 92. *Teaching:* Lectr, Santa Monica Coll, Calif, Calif State, Long Beach & Rochester Inst Technol, Nat Aeronautics & Space Admin. *Bibliog:* Kathryn Livingston (auth), Making found objects, Am Photog, 9/84; Dinah Berland (auth), Dunitz zaps steel for light series, Los Angeles Times, 11/29/85; Larry Stein (rev), Arts LA, KCRW-FM, Nat Pub Radio, Santa Monica, 10/31/88. *Publ:* Auth, Pacific Light, Light Press, Inc, 89; illusr, A current affair, Confetti, 90. *Mailing Add:* 20585 Seaboard Rd Malibu CA 90265-5351

DUNKELMAN, LORETTA
PAINTER
b Paterson, NJ, June 29, 1937. *Study:* Douglass Coll, BA, 58; Acad Belle Arti, Florence, Italy, 60-61; Hunter Coll, MA, 66. *Work:* Chase Manhattan Bank; Bellevue Med Ctr, NY; Dana Art Ctr, Colgate Univ; Univ Cincinnati; Spencer Mus Art, Lawrence, Kans; Smithsonian Am Art Mus, Washington, DC. *Exhib:* Whitney Biennial Contemp Art, 73 & Am Drawings 63-73, Whitney Mus Am Art, NY; Of Paper, Newark Mus, NJ, 73; Women Choose Women, NY Cult Ctr, NY, 73; AIR Gallery, NY, 73, 74, 78, 81, 83 & 87; Waves: An Artist Selects, Cranbrook Acad Art, Bloomfield Hills, Mich, 74; Cornell Artists Past & Present, Johnson Mus, 77; NY Now, Phoenix Art Mus, 79; Structure, Narrative, Decoration, McIntosh-Drysdale Gallery, Washington, DC, 80; Konsthall, Lund, Sweden, 81; Michael Walls Gallery, NY, 89; Artist on the Edge, Mary H Dana Women Artist Series, Mabel Smith Douglass Libr, Rutgers Univ, NJ, 2005; An Electric Eye, Tucson Art Mus, Tucson, Ariz, 2007; Cool Aid, Andre Zarre Gallery, New York, 2007; 183rd Ann: Invitational Exhib, Nat Acad Mus, New York, 2008; AIR Gallery Retrospective 1972-1979, Werkstatte Gallery, NY, 2008; and others. *Teaching:* Vis artist, Univ Cincinnati, 74; asst prof art, Univ RI, 74-75; asst prof art, Cornell Univ, 77-80; vis artist, Ohio State Univ, 84; asst prof painting, Virginia Commonwealth Univ, 86-88; vis artist, Sch Art Inst Chicago, 90, Univ Calif, Berkeley, 93-94. *Awards:* Visual Artist Fel Grant, Nat Endowment Arts, 76, 82, 93-94; Adolph & Esther Gottlieb Found Individual Grant, 91; NY Found for the Arts, Artist's Fel, 91. *Bibliog:* Ellen Lubell (auth), article, Arts Mag, 5/74; Peter Frank (auth), Gifts of the imagi, Village Voice, 1/8/79; Tiffany Bell (auth), article, Arts Mag, 2/79; Robert Merritt (auth), Romantic Views: Light and dark, Richmond Times Dispatch, 10/3/87. *Mem:* Coll Art Asn. *Media:* Oil. *Mailing Add:* 151 Canal St New York NY 10002

DUNLAP, LOREN EDWARD
PAINTER, INSTRUCTOR
b Anderson, Ind, Feb 2, 1932. *Study:* Herron Art Sch, BFA; Ogunquit Sch Painting & Sculpture, Tulane Univ, MFA. *Work:* Addison Gallery Am Art, Andover, Mass; Santa Barbara Mus, Calif; Univ Calif Collection; NY Times Bk Collection, Notre Dame Univ; Fine Arts Ctr, Anderson, Ind. *Comn:* Mural, comn by Jane Blaffer Owen, Blaffer Trust, New Harmony, Ind, 65; three panel paintings, comn by Jane Arneberg, NY, 70; painting, Pfizer Chemical Co, NY, 74; mural, comn by Kenneth Owen, New Harmony, Ind, 90; mural, comn by Joan Quillin, Palm Beach, Fla, 92; portrait, New Jersey Gallery of Governors, 2010; portrait, Goldman Sachs, NY. *Exhib:* Solo exhibs, Purdue Univ, West Lafayette, Ind, 59 & Santa Barbara Mus Art, Calif, 63; Drawing Ann, Norfolk Mus, Va, 60; Albright-Knox Art Gallery, Buffalo, NY, 60; Boston Mus Contemp Arts, Mass, 60; Univ Calif Fac Show, 63; 10 Yr Retrospective, Columbia Club, Indianapolis, Ind, 85; Gebert Gallery, Scottsdale, Ariz, 2012. *Pos:* cons architecture & design. *Teaching:* Instr studio & art hist, Herron Sch, Indianapolis, 58-62; lectr studio & art hist, Univ Calif, Santa Barbara, 63-65. *Awards:* Louis Comfort Tiffany Grant, 55 & 65. *Media:* Oil, Acrylic. *Publ:* Auth, Traditions of the East, Revolutions of the West, Herron J, 60. *Mailing Add:* Box 332 Sagg Rd Sagaponack NY 11962

DUNLAP, SUSAN C
PAINTER, PHOTOGRAPHER
Exhib: Solo exhibs include Calif Polytechnic State Univ, 1988, Sheridan Coll Gallery, Wyo, 1988, Elizabeth Holden Gallery, Warren Wilson Coll, NC, 1991, Casements Cult Ctr, Ormond Beach, Fla, 1993; group exhibs include Bay Arts 90, Juried Exhib, San Mateo County Arts Coun, 1990; Contemp Surrealism, Juried Exhib, Univ Pacific, Stockton, Calif, 1990; Doorway to the Surreal, Juried Exhib, Grants Pass Mus Art, Ore, 1991; Gallery Artists, Harcourts Contemp Gallery, San Francisco, 1992; Graystone Gallery, San Francisco, 1994; Faces, Anchorage Mus Hist & Art, 1997; New Artists, Allan Stone Gallery, New York, 1997. *Pos:* Botanist, Menlo Park, Calif. *Awards:* Calif State Scholar, 1968-70; 1st Place Watercolor, Napenthe Mundi Int Competition, 1986; Merit Award Painting, Redding Mus, 1986; Pollock-Krasner Found Grant, 2007. *Mailing Add:* 220 Chester St Menlo Park CA 94025

DUNLAP, WILLIAM
ART EDUCATOR
Study: Univ Miss, MFA. *Exhib:* Solo exhibs: Corcoran Gallery Art; Nat Acad Sci; Aspen Mus Art; Southeastern Ctr Contemp Art; Mus Western Va; Albany Mus Art; Cheekwood Fine Arts Ctr; Mint Mus Art; Miss Mus Art; Contemp Art Ctr, New Orleans; In Spirit of the Land; Winding River: Contemp Painting from Vietnam, Meridian Int Ctr, Washington DC, 97-98, Outward Bound: Am Art Brink of 21st Century, writer Art & Antiques, Washingtonian, Arts Review; exhib incl, Reconstructed Recollections, Inaugural Exhib: Story of South, Ogden Mus Southern Art, New Orleans, 2003-04; What Boys Draw & Other Works, Soren Christensen Gallery, New Orleans, 2004; Panorama Am Landscape, Gibbes Mus Art, Charleston, SC, 2004-05. *Collection Arranged:* Rep in permanent collections, Metrop Mus Art, Corcoran Gallery Art, Lauren Rogers Mus, Mobil Corp., Riggs Bank, IBM Corp., Fed Express, Equitable Collection, Arkansas Art Ctr, U.S. State Department, U.S. Embassies throughout the world, Rogers Ogden Collection. *Teaching:* Prof Appalachian State Univ, NC, 70-79; Memphis State Univ, 79-80; Art Commentator, "Around Town": WETA-TV, Arlington, Va; Speaker in field: Lectr on art related subjects at coll, univ, inst, and prof conf. *Mailing Add:* WETA TV 2775 Quincy St Arlington VA 22206

DUNLOP, ANNE
ADMINISTRATOR
Study: Univ Warwick, PhD. *Pos:* Keynote speaker at the ANZAMEMS Conf, Melbourne, Australia; served on international evaluation com for Art History of the Israel Council for Higher Education; guest curator, Early Modern Faces, Newcomb Gallery, 2013-2014. *Teaching:* Assoc prof history of art, dept chair, Newcomb Art Dept, Tulane Univ, currently. *Awards:* Senior Fellow, Ctr for Advanced Study in Visual Arts, Washington, DC, 2012-2013. *Publ:* co-edit, Art and the Augustinian Order in Early-Renaissance Italy, 2007; auth, Painted Palaces: The Rise of Secular Art in Earl Renaissance Italy, 2009; Drawing Blood, RES: Journal of Anthropology and Aesthetics 63/64, 2013. *Mailing Add:* Tulane University Newcomb Art Department 315 Woldenberg Art Ctr 6823 St Charles Ave New Orleans LA 70118

DUNN, AMANDA GORDON
SCULPTOR, PAINTER
b Norman, Okla, Apr 16, 1983. *Study:* Md Inst Coll Art, BFA, Baltimore, Md, 2006. *Work:* La State Exhib Mus, Shreveport, La. *Comn:* Wall reliant Sculpture, Re/Max City Horizons, Denver, Colo, 2008. *Exhib:* Solo exhibs, Systems & Layers, Pirate Contemp Art, Denver, Colo, 2008, Untitled, 2009, Am Muscle, La State Exhib Mus, Shreveport, La, 2009, Pirate Contemp Art, Denver, 2010; Group exhibs, Space Gallery, Denver, Colo, 2007; The Nylon Show, Preston Contemp Art Ctr, Mesilla, NM, 2009; Den-Mi, Art Basel, Miami, Fla, 2009. *Awards:* Pres Scholarship, Md Inst Coll Art, 2002-2006; Dale Burton Award in fiber, 2005; Ira Basler Jr & Mary Basler Mem Scholarship, 2005; Barbara L Kuhlman Fiber Award, 2006; hon mention, Red, Core New Art Space, 2007; hon mention, Untitled, Space Gallery, 2007. *Bibliog:* The Nylon Show, Preston Contemp Art, Art in Am, 4/2009; Melissa Bolongea (auth), An Artist Named Amanda Gordon Dunn, Mod in Denver Mag, 1/2009; Michael Paglia, Art Beat, Westword, 6/2009; Tom Pace, Talk of the Town (radio interview), Shreveport, Va, 8/2009; Rick Rowe (interview),, KBS3 News, 8/2009; Michael Paglia (auth), Denver Restored, 2010. *Media:* Steel, Textiles, Plastics, Automotive Parts. *Interests:* Bug collection, rocket ships, horseback riding

DUNN, PHILLIP CHARLES
EDUCATOR, ADMINISTRATOR
b Chicago, Ill, Mar 1, 1947. *Study:* Univ Ill, BFA (art educ), 68; Inst Design, Ill Inst Techol, MS (visual educ), 70; Ball State Univ, EdD (art educ), 78. *Comn:* Sculpture, Univ SC, Spartanburg, 83, 85 & 87. *Exhib:* Photog 79, Ariz State Univ Gallery, Tempe, 79; four-person show, Presby Col, Clinton, SC, 79; two-person show, McKissick Mus, Columbia, SC, 79; Columbia Coll Gallery, SC, 80; one-person show, USC Coastal Gallery, Conway, SC, 82, McMaster Gallery, Columbia, SC, 2005. *Pos:* Prog officer, Getty Ctr Educ Arts, 88-90 (vis appointment). *Teaching:* Instr photog, Col DuPage, 71-76; vis prof photog, St Xavier Col, 74-76; prof art educ, Univ SC, 78-, dir grad studies in art, 80-85 & chmn dept art, 2002-. *Awards:* Mary J Rouse

Award, 81; Higher Educator of the Year, SC Art Educ Asn, 81; Southeastern Art Educator of Year, Nat Art Educ Asn, 87; Nat Art Educator of the Year, Nat Art Educ Asn, 99. *Mem:* Nat Art Educ Asn; Guild SC Artists; Columbia Artist Guild; SC Art Educ Asn (treas, 80-82). *Media:* Digital photography. *Res:* Curriculum develop in art. *Publ:* co-ed, A True Likeness: The Black South of Richard S Roberts, 1920-1936, Algonquin Press, 86; auth, Promoting School Art: A Practical Approach, Nat Art Educ Asn Press, 86; The Curriculum Navigator for Art: Middle Sch, 94 & The Curriculum Navigator for Art: Elementary Sch, 95, Dale Seymour Publ; Creating Curriculum in Art, Nat Art Educ Asn, 95; InFolio: An Electronic Portfolio, President Develop Group, 2000. *Mailing Add:* Dept Art Univ SC Columbia SC 29208

DUNN, ROGER TERRY
HISTORIAN
b Bethesda, Md, Feb 24, 1946. *Study:* Am Univ, Washington, DC; Pa State Univ, BA (art hist & painting); Pratt Inst, MFA (painting), 70; Northwestern Univ, PhD (art hist), 78. *Exhib:* Shanxi Teachers Univ, Linfen, China, 88; Anderson Gallery, Bridgewater, Mass, 97; Visual Arts Gallery, Boston, Mass, 99; Galerie 8, Aubeterre, France, 2006; South Shore Art Ctr, 2011. *Collection Arranged:* Quilts from the Plymouth Antiquarian Soc, 74; John J Enneking: Am Impressionist (ed, catalog), 75; The Boston Painting Invitational, 75, Michael Mazur: Vision of a Draughtsman, 76; Craftforms (ed, catalog), 76; Am Pastimes (ed, catalog), 77; On the Threshold of Modern Design: The Arts and Crafts Movement in Am (auth, catalog), Danforth Mus, 84; Terri Priest: Interactions, 2005. *Pos:* Cur, Brockton Art Ctr, Mass, 74-77; dir, Gallery at OUI, Boston, 76-80. *Teaching:* Prof art hist, Bridgewater State Univ, 80-. *Mem:* Met Mus Art; MOMA; Mus Fine Arts Boston; Fuller Craft Mus. *Res:* Monet, Rodin and their symbolist circle; exhibition research on 19th century American art. *Publ:* Auth, Lawrence Kupferman: A Retrospective Exhibition, 74; ed, Landscape and Life in 19th Century America, 74; The Ikat weavings of Joan Hausrath, Fiberarts, 11/81. *Mailing Add:* 871 Main St Hingham MA 02043-3503

DUNNIGAN, MARY CATHERINE
LIBRARIAN
b Tazewell Co, Va, May 7, 1922. *Study:* Mary Washington Col, BA; Columbia Univ, MLS. *Pos:* Librn, Col of Archit, Va Polytech Inst, Blacksburg, 66-73; librn, Fiske Kimball Fine Arts Libr, Univ Va, Charlottesville, 73-87. *Mem:* Soc Archit Historians; Art Libr Soc NAm; Asn Archit Sch Librn (pres, 80-81); Spec Libr Asn Arts & Humanities Div (chmn mus, 73-74). *Res:* Inventory-computation: Architectural drawings of University of Virginia buildings. *Interests:* Development of research library for support of art, architecture and drama curriculum. *Mailing Add:* 1643 Rugby Ave Charlottesville VA 22903

DUNNING, JEANNE
PHOTOGRAPHER, VIDEO ARTIST
b Granby, Conn, 1960. *Work:* Mus Modern Art, NY; Art Inst Chicago, Ill; Mus Contemp Art, Los Angeles, Calif; Mus Contemp Art, Chicago, Ill. *Exhib:* Venice biennial, Venice Beinnial, Italy, 95; Feminin-Maxculin, Ctr Georges Pompidou, Paris, France, 95; Sydney Biennial, Art Gallery New South Wales, Sydney, Australia, 96; Jeanne Dunning, Konstmuseet, Malmo, Sweden, 99; James Harris Gallery, Seattle, 2000; Bodybuilder & Sportsman Gallery, Chicago, 2001; Wanderings of the Mind's Eye: Photog by Ill Artists, Mus Contemp Art, Chicago, 2004. *Awards:* Comm Arts Asst Grant, Chicago Off Fine Arts, 89; Individual Artist Fel, Ill Arts Coun, 91-92; Grantee, Louis Comfort Tiffany Found, 93

DUNOW, ESTI
PAINTER, HISTORIAN
b New York, NY, June 12, 1948. *Study:* Brandeis Univ, BA, 66-70; Skowhegan Sch Painting & Sculpture, 71; New York Studio Sch, with Phillip Guston & Mercedes Matter, 70, 70-72, New York Univ-Inst Fine Arts, with Robert Goldwater, Gert Schiff, Robert Rosenblum, William Rubin, 70-81. *Exhib:* One-person show, Bowery Gallery, NY, 81, 83, 85, 87 & 90. *Pos:* Coauthor, Chaim Soutine Catalog Raisonne, 76-78, 84-. *Awards:* Ford Found Fel in Mus Work, Inst Fine Arts & Metrop Mus Art, 72; Mus Training Fel, Nat Endowment Arts, 76-77. *Bibliog:* Freddy Kaplan (auth), Regional landscapes, Artist, 2/84; Gerrit Henry (auth), New York reviews, Art News, 2/86; Jed Perl (auth), Houses, fields, gardens, hills, The New Criterion, 2/86. *Media:* Oil. *Res:* Early twentieth century painting; School of Paris, emphasis on Chaim Soutine. *Publ:* Auth, Chaim Soutine (exhib catalog) Arts Coun of Great Britain, 82; Soutive Galleri, exhib catalog, Bellman, NY, 84. *Dealer:* The Bowery Gallery 121 Wooster St New York NY 10012. *Mailing Add:* 225 W 86th St New York NY 10024-3330

DUNSKY, ANNIE
PAINTER
b Rochester, NY, April 11, 1949. *Study:* The Cleveland Inst of Art, BFA, 73; RI Sch Design, Alum '84. *Work:* Rush Rhees Rare Books & Manuscrupts Libr Watercolor Paintings for Design of the Mus House, Rochester, NY; 2 Pieces of Art, Albright Knox, Buffalo, NY; The Mushroom House. *Comn:* Interior archit design, Perinton, NY, 2001-2003. *Exhib:* Solo exhibs, Germanow Gallery, 86, Novotel Gallery, S Korea, 95, Mill Gallery, Honeoye Falls, NY, 98, Arles, France, 2000, Phillips Fine Art Gallery, Rochester, NY, 2001; Fire Angel Gallery, 93; Pyramid Arts Ctr, Rochester, NY, 93; Caelum Gallery, New York, 99, 2000; Albright Knox, Buffalo, NY, 2009; Group shows, Ward Nasse Gallery, NY, 98, Myung Sook Lee Gallery, NY; ROCO, 6x6 exhib, 2013-2014. *Pos:* artist in res, The Mushroom House, Perinton, 96. *Teaching:* TA for pastel, RI Sch Design, 83-2004. *Awards:* Rochester Art Club Award, Finger Lakes Exhib, 89; Special Opportunities Award, 97, 98, 2000; Albright Knox award, 2009. *Mem:* Hallwalls, Buffalo, NY; Rochester Contemporary Art (cultural council, 2012-2014). *Media:* All Media. *Specialty:* Contemporary art. *Interests:* all dogs, standard poodles, antiques, travel, gardens, art pottery, art glass, antiques, prints, sculptures. *Publ:* Great Homes of Rochester (showing the Mushroom House, youngest landmark house in the USA). *Dealer:* Caelum Gallery 526 W 26th St # 315 New York, NY 10001; DK Benson Design 5688 Main St Williamsville NY 14221; Megg Cook Design Buffalo NY

DUPUIS, DAVID
PAINTER
b Holyoke, Mass, 1959. *Study:* Univ Washington, Seattle, BFA, 1982, BA (in theatre), 1982. *Work:* Hammer Mus, Los Angeles; San Fran Mus Modern Art; Jane Voorhees Zimmerli Art Mus, Rutgers Univ; New Mus Contemp Art; New Sch Social Res. *Exhib:* Solo exhibs at Simon Watson Gallery, NY, 1989, Karsten Schubert, Ltd, London, 1991, Petersberg Gallery, 1991, Rubenstein/Diacono, NY, 1992, Turner & Byrne, Dallas, Tex, 1994, Mario Diacono Gallery, Boston, 1995, White Columns, NY, 1997, Derek Eller Gallery, NY, 1999, 2001, 2003, 2005, 2006, Schmidt Contemp Art, LA, Calif, 2000, Lost on the Frontiers of Heaven and Hell, Derek Eller Gallery, NY, 2007, Green, Green Grass of Home, Derek Eller Gallery, 2011, and others; Group exhibs include Outer Limits, Holly Solomon Gallery, NY, 1989; Black, White & Grey, Petersberg Gallery, NY, 1990; Synthesis, John Good Gallery, NY, 1991; Primal Abstraction, Mario Diacone, Boston, 1992; Contextures and Constructures, Rubenstein/Diacono, 1992, Summer Group Exhib, 1993; Paint Royale, Ed Thorpe Gallery, NY, 1994; Schmidt Contemp Art, St Louis, Mo, 1995, 1996; Geoffrey Young Gallery, Mass, 1997, 1998, Pencil Me In, 2004; Free Coke, Greene Naftali Inc, NY, 1999; Superorganic Hyroponic Warfare, Derek Eller Gallery, Ny, 2000, Back to Nature, 2000, Nina Bovasso, David Dupuis, Andrew Masullo, 2002, Drawings, 2003, Inaugural Group Exhib, 2006, Summer Group Exhib, 2006; Not a Lear, Gracie Mansion Gallery, NY, 2001; Drawn, Dinter Fine Art, NY, 2006; The Name of This Show is Not GAY ART NOW, Paul Kasmin Gallery, NY, 2006; Variegated Radiant Dream Plot, Gregory Lind Gallery, San Francisco, 2006; represented in collections of San Francisco Mus Modern Art, Jan Voorhees Zimmerli Art Mus at Rutgers Univ, New Mus of Contemp Art; The Tree, James Cohan Gallery, Shanghai, 2009; Other People, Hammer Mus, Los Angeles, 2008; Consider the Oyster, James Graham and Sons, NY, 2010; Salad Days, Journal Gallery, Brooklyn, NY, 2010. *Bibliog:* Mario Naves (auth), David Dupuis: Live from Deluth, New York Observer, 11/2003; Julie Caniglia (auth), David Dupuis, Art Forum, 1/2004; Tom Patterson (auth), A Profusion of Pleasure, Winston-Salem Jour, Visual Art, 12/2006; Jen Graves (auth), A Spectral Glimpse, The Stranger, Seattle, Wash, 10/2007; Douglas Britt (auth), Salt Peanuts Strikes Idiosyncratic Chord, Houston Chronicle, 2009; Roberta Smith (auth), How to Cook a Wolf: Part One, New York Times, 1/2009. *Mailing Add:* Derek Eller Gallery 615 W 27 St New York NY 10001

DUQUE, ADONAY
PAINTER, DRAFTSMAN
b Coro, Venezuela, Apr 13, 1954. *Study:* Sch Fine Arts Cristobal Rojas, Caracas, Venezuela, 72-75; Sch Fine Arts Univ Complutense, Madrid, 78-83; Atelier Hachette, Paris, 85. *Work:* Mus Fine Arts, Caracas, Venezuela; Mus Contemp Art, Caracas, Venezuela; Nat Gallery, Caracas, Venezuela; Philadelphia Mus; Studio Arts Ctr Int, Florence, Italy. *Exhib:* Nat Biennial of Art, Alejandro Otero Mus Visual Arts, Caracas, 92; The Purloined Image, Flint Inst Art, 93; Memories of Vision, Mus Contemp Art, Caracs, Venezuela, 93; New Acquisitions 20 Yrs, Mus Contemp Art, Caracs, 93; New Acquisitions, Mus Fine Arts, Caracas, Venezuela, 93; Changing Faces, Nassau Co Mus Art, Roslyn Harbor, NY, 97. *Awards:* First Prize Salon Arturo Michelena, 91; First Prize (drawing), IV Nat Biennial & Second Prize, Nat Biennial Visual Arts, Alejandro Otero Mus Visual Arts, 92. *Media:* Acrylic on Canvas. *Mailing Add:* c/o Ambrosino Gallery 769 NE 125th St Miami FL 33161

DUREN, STEPHEN D
PAINTER
b Fairfield, Calif, Apr 8, 1948. *Study:* San Francisco Art Inst, BFA, 74; Calif State Univ, Sacramento, MA, 77. *Work:* Grand Rapids Art Mus, Mich; Muskegon Mus Art, Mich; Kresge Art Mus, Mich; Dennos Mus, Mich; Van Andel Mus, Mich. *Comn:* Paintings, Steelcase Inc; drawings, Herman Miller, Inc; poster design, Grand Rapids Arts Coun, Mich. *Exhib:* Solo exhibs, Grand Rapids Art Mus, Mich; Muskegon Mus Art, Mich; Dennos Mus Center, Mich; Midland Ctr Arts, Mich; Krasl Art Center, Mich; Battle Creek Art Center, Mich; Interlochen Arts Acad, Mich; Creative Arts Center, Central Mich Univ, Mich; Byron Roche Gallery, Chicago, IL; Robert Allen Gallery, San Francisco, Calif; Patricia Carlisle Gallery, Santa Fe, NM. *Teaching:* Asst prof, Kendall Col Design, Mich, 79-84. *Awards:* Artist's Grant, Mich Coun Arts, 87; Artist Residency Fel, Ucross Found, Wyo, 88; Artist's Grant, Adolf & Esther Gottlieb Found, NY, 88. *Bibliog:* Duren, Grand Rapids Press, 12/90; Artist at work, Mich Coast Mag, 22-27, 36, 4/92; Stephen Duren/Artistic anomaly, Grand Rapids Mag, 11/94; Chicago Tribune, IL, 7/02; New City, 6/00. *Media:* Oil. *Dealer:* Art Endeavors Grand Rapids MI; Monroe Fine Art Grand Rapids MI; Byron Roche Gallery Chicago IL; Robert Allen Gallery San Francisco CA; Robert Kidd Gallery Birmingham MI. *Mailing Add:* 6087 100th St Caledonia MI 49316

DURHAM, JEANETTE R
PAINTER
b Plainfield, NJ, June 17, 1945. *Study:* Montclair State Coll, BA, 67; Art Students League with Bruce Dorfman, 71-72; Westchester Art Workshop with Gregory Lysun, 80-81; S Univ Coll Oneonta, MSEd, 91. *Work:* Kingsley Sch, Boston; Opto Generic Devices, Van Hornesville, NY; Allied Machinery, Hangzhou, China. *Comn:* Lorna Altemus (painting), 93; M/M James Wilson (painting), 96. *Exhib:* Solo exhibs, Birds of the Air and Other Phenomena, Gannett Gallery, State Univ NY, Utica, 88, Waterfalls, South Shore Arts, Little Falls, NY, 91, The Meditative Landscape, Pleiades Gallery, New York, 93, Land & Sky, Mohawk Valley Ctr Arts, Little Falls, NY, 94, Rocks, Rensselaer Polytechnic Inst, Troy, NY, 97, In Midstream: 1967-1997, Herkimer Co Comm Coll, Herkimer, NY, 97, The Meditative Landscape, Art Ctr at Old Forge, NY & Recent Work, Mohawk Valley Ctr Arts, Little Falls, New York, NY, 2004, Recent Work, Stanley Arts Ctr, NY,2010; Art of Northeast USA, Silvermine Guild, New Canaan, Conn, 86, 98 & 2006; WHMT Exhib, NY State Mus, Albany, 88; Ann Nat Exhib, Cooperstown Art Asn, 91, 94, 97, 99 & 2007; Pleiades Gallery, New York, 91-2002; 56th Ann Nat Midyear, Butler Inst Ann, 92; Mohawk-Hudson Regional, Albany Inst Hist & Art, 93 & 96; Current Works, Arts Coun Cent NY, Utica, 94; Made in NY, Schweinfurth Mem Art Ctr, Auburn, NY, 98; Gallery 210, Syracuse,

99; two-person exhib, Cazenovia Coll, 2001; Artists Who Happen to be Women, Tex A&M Univ, Coll Sta, Tex; Spring into Summer, NAWA Gallery, New York, 2008; Arkell Mus Regional, Canajoharie, 2011; NAWA Ann, Pokim Gallery, NY, 2011; Regional Mohawk Valley Ctr Arts, Little Falls, NY; Smithy-Pioneer Gallery Cooperstown, NY, 2014. *Teaching:* Instr painting, drawing, Mohawk Valley Ctr Arts, Little Falls, NY, 83; instr art, Owen D Young C S, VanHornesville, NY, 87-92; adj instr humanities, painting & drawing, Herkimer Co Comm Coll, NY, 98-2009. *Awards:* Award, Nat Asn Women Artists, 91 & 98; Award, Mohawk-Hudson Regional, Albany Inst Hist and Art, 96; SOS grant NYFA, 98; Art of Northeast USA Silvermine, 98; CNY Arts Grant Visiting Artist, Hermiker, HS, 2014. *Bibliog:* Christine Temin (auth), Discovering art off the beaten path, Boston Globe, 11/15/84; Keith Benman (auth), Artist Makes Her Mark, Herkimer Evening Telegram, 12/9/96; Jonas Kover (auth), Durham in Her Prime with a Hilly Place, Utica Observer Dispatch, 10/10/97; WKTV Utica (interview), NY, 2006; and others. *Mem:* Nat Asn Women Artists; Decentralization Grants Panel, CNYCAC, 99-2001; Mohawk Valley Ctr Arts (exhib comt, 95-2008). *Media:* Oil. *Mailing Add:* 111 Hoke Rd Jordanville NY 13361

DURHAM, JIMMIE
SCULPTOR, ESSAYIST
b Ark, 1940. *Study:* Ecole des Beaux-Arts, Geneva, BFA (sculpture), 72. *Work:* Volpinum Kunstsammlung, Vienna; MuHKA, Antwerp; Stedelijk Mus voor Actuele Kunst, Belgium; Irish Mus Mod Art, Dublin; Zerynthia Roma; Mus het Domein, Neth; Indre, Fr. *Exhib:* Souvenirs of Site-Seeing: Travel & Tourism in Contemp Art, Whitney Mus Am Art, 91; Land, Spirit, Power, Nat Gallery Can, Ottawa, 92; Crossings, 98; Antwerp Cultural Capital of Europe, 93; A Certain Lack of Coherence, Palais des Beaux-Arts, Brussels, 93-94; Original Re-runs, Inst Contemp Art, London, 93-94; Cocida y Crudo, Nat Ctr Art Mus Reina Sofia, Madrid, 94; Transformers, Illingworth Kerr Gallery, Alberta Coll Art & Design, 96; Interruptions, Nat Mus Contemp Art, Lisbon, 99; Venice Biennial, 99, 2001, 2003, 2005, 2013; Stoneheart, Ctr Contemp Art, Kitakyushu, 2000; Gallery Nordenhake, Stockholm, 2000; Int Triennial Contemp Art, Tokyo, 2001; Through a Sequence of Space, Gallery Nordenhake, Berlin, 2002; Sydney Biennial, 2004; Off Grid, Ottawa Art Gallery, 2005; Ordering the Ordinary, Timothy Taylor Gallery, London, 2005; Tirana Biennial, 2005; Guangzhou Triennial, 2005; Carnets du Sous-Sol, Galerie Michel Rein, Paris, 2006; Day for Night, Whitney Biennial, 2006; Designing Truth, Stiftung Wilheim Lehmbruck Mus, Duisburg, 2006; Saudades, Crac Alsace, Altkirch, 2006; Musee d'Art Moderne de la Ville de Paris, 2009; Glasgow Int Festival, 2010; MuHKa, Antwerp, 2012. *Pos:* writer & ed, Art & Artists Newspaper, 82-86; founder, exec dir, International Indian Treaty Coun, United Nations; exec dir, Foundation Community Artists, NY; political organizer, American Indian Movement, 73-80. *Bibliog:* Pascale Cassagnau (auth), Jimmie Durham; Calais, Vienna, Reims, Art Press, Vol 214, 96, 68-69; Joane Cardinal-Schubert (auth), In the red, in: Borrowed Power: Essays on Cultural Appropriation, Rutgers Univ Press, NJ, 97; Beverly Koski & Richard William Hill (auths), The Centre of the World is Several Places (Part 1), FUSE Magazine, Vol 21, No 3, summer 98, 24-33; Michele Robecchi (auth), Jimmie Durham, Contemporary, 2006; Laurence Bosse (auth), Jimmie Durham, Pierre Rejetees, Paris Musees, 2009; Rob Appleford (auth), Jimmie Durham and the Carpentry of Ambivalence, 2010; and others. *Publ:* auth, Stone Heart, Kitakyushu, Japan, 2001; Belief in Europe, in S Hassan & I Dadi, Unpacking Europe, Mus Boijmans Van Beuningen, Rotterdam, 2001; Situations, Contemporary Art: from Stuido to Situation, Black Dog Publishing, London, 2004; The Second Particle Wave Theory. As Performed on the Banks of the River Wear, a Stone's Throw from S'Underland and teh Durham Cathedral, Univ Sunderland, Walter Phillips Gallery, 2005; Various Element of Cowboy Life & Cherokee-US Relations, The American West, Compton Verney, Warwickshire, Compton Verney House Trust, 2005; Amoxohtli/Libro de Carretera/A Road Book, Koln, Walther Konig, 2011. *Dealer:* Christine König Gallery Vienna; Barbara Wien Gallery Berlin; Exit Art New York NY. *Mailing Add:* Galleria Sprovieri 23 Heddon St London United Kingdom W1B 4BQ

DURHAM, JO ANN FANNING
PAINTER
b Sulphur Springs, Tex, May 31, 1935. *Study:* Univ Tex, Austin, Tex A&M, BS, 56; studied with Glenn R Bradshaw, Mary Todd Beam, Ed Blackburn, Maxine Masterfield, Marilyn Hughey Phillis & Bror Utter. *Hon Degrees:* Acad Int des Arts Contemporains, Belg, Hon Dr, 94. *Work:* Huntsville Mus Art, Ala; Cannon Gallery, Bismarck State Coll, NDak; Univ N Tex Health Sci Ctr, Fort Worth; Permanent Collection, Fort Worth Women's Club, Tex; Tex A & M, Tarleton; Fort Worth Pub Libr, Tex; First United Methodist Church, Fort Worth & Sulphur Springs, Tex; Tex Pub Libr, Sulphur Springs; File in Libr. *Exhib:* Nat League Am Penwomen, Summer Art Mus, Washington DC, 92 & 96; Belgium Grand Prix, 93-96, 2004; Salon D'Automne, Grand Palais, Paris, France, 92-93 & Soc Int Des Beaux Arts, 94, 96; A Fresh Look at Tex Art, McKinney Ave Contemp, Dallas, 99; Int Soc Experimental Artists, Huntsville Mus Art, Ala, 99; Soc Layerists in Multi Media, Chapelle Des Penitents Blancs, Gordes, France, 2000; Encaustic Biennial, Kingston, NY, 2001; Salmagundi Club, NY, 2002-2003, 2005; Wales Cynon Valley Mus, Aberdare, Wales, 2004; Cardiff Wales, UK, 2005. *Pos:* Dir, Atrium Gallery, Forth Worth, Tex, 79-82; artist-in-residence, Tex Comn on Arts, 90-91 & 94-95. *Teaching:* Instr art, FWISD, Fort Worth, Tex, 68-69 & Kennedy Ctr Imagination Celebration, 90-93; instr painting, Templeton Art Ctr, Fort Worth, Tex, 86, Carrizo Lodge Art Sch, Ruidoso, NMex, 87-88 & Women's Club Art Dept, Fort Worth, 2000. *Awards:* Citation Award, John L Clardy, 86; Tom Lynch Award, 87; Best of Abstracts, Phillip Isenberg, 96; Nautilus fel, Int Soc Experimental Artists, 2000; Samuel Leitman Mem Award, Salmagundi Club, NY, 2006; Shining Star, The Arts League of Tarrant Co; Women in the Arts Recognition award, NSDAR, 2012. *Bibliog:* Art and Healing, 99; Master Painters of the World, International Artist Magazine, 2000; Splash 8, 2004; The Art of Layering Making Connections, 2004; Fort Worth Community Arts Ctr Biennial, Fort Worth Star Telegram, 2006; Visual Journeys - Art of the 21st Century, 2010; Plus many other magazine and book articles. *Mem:* Tex Fine Arts Asn, Region XV (pres & regional dir, 79-81); Soc Watercolor Artists (vpres, 89, signature); Tex Visual Arts Asn (asst vpres, 93); Int Soc Experimental Artists (pres, 98-99, signature); Salmagundi Club; Southwestern Watercolor Soc Dallas (signature); Society of Layerists in Multi Media (signature); signature, Art Dept, Womans Club of Ft Worth; Nat League of Am Pen Women. *Media:* Mixed Water Media & Encaustics, Metallics & Acrylics, Watercolor. *Specialty:* Comtemp, Abstract. *Interests:* The mysteries of the cosmos, French florals, fashions-circa 187-1909. *Dealer:* Upstairs Gallery 1038 W Abram St Arlington TX; Kens Gallery 5922 Wedgewood Dr Fort Worth TX; Your Pvt Collection Granbury Tex. *Mailing Add:* 4300 Plantation Dr Fort Worth TX 76116

DURHAM, WILLIAM
PAINTER, SCULPTOR
b Flint, Mich, Mar 14, 1937. *Study:* Mich State Univ, BA, 60; painting with Morris Kantor, Boris Margo & Abraham Rattner. *Work:* Guild Hall, East Hampton, NY; Warnaco Inc, Park Ave, NY; Mich State Univ, East Lansing; Butler Inst Am Art; Stony Brook Mus, NY; Emelin theater, Mamaroneck NY; South Hampton Hospital, NY; Woodside Church, Mich; Flint Inst Arts. *Comn:* Painting, NY World's Fair, 64. *Exhib:* Solo Exhibs: Benson Gallery, Bridgehampton, NY, 67, 71-72 & 74 & Art Placement Int, NY, 81, Blue Heron Art Ctr, New York City, 2002; Am Acad Arts & Lett, NY, 74; Heckscher Mus, Huntington, NY, 74; Artist of the Hamptons, Guild Hall, Easthampton, NY, 75; Chicago Art Inst; French Inst, New York City, 81; Kaber Gallery, New York City, 82; Vered Gallery, East Hampton, NY, 1990; Bologna Lanoi Gallery, East Hampton, NY, 83, 85, 92; 50 Yr Retrospecitve, Asawaugh Hall, East Hampton, NY, 2006. *Pos:* guest curator, Bologna Landi Gallery, East Hampton, NY, 92. *Teaching:* Grad asst, Mich State Univ, 61. *Awards:* Adolph & Ester Gottlieb Found Emergency Assistance Grant, 98; Pollack-Krasner Found Inc, 98. *Bibliog:* Article, NY Herald Tribune, 64, NY Times, 64-75 & 2006 & East Hampton Star, 2005, 2010; Art in America. *Media:* Acrylic; Aluminum. *Mailing Add:* PO Box 316 Amagansett NY 11930

DURR, PAT (PATRICIA) (BETH)
PAINTER, PRINTMAKER
b Kansas City, Mo; US & Can citizen. *Study:* Univ Kans, BA (educ), 61; Univ Southampton, 62; Kansas City Art Inst, 63; Ottawa Sch Art, with Duncan deKergommeaux, 65, with Richard Yates, 83; Univ Saskatchewan, with Nik Semenoff, 99. *Work:* Can Coun Visual Art Bank; Univ Toronto Art Gallery, Ont; Biogen Inc Cambridge, Mass; Goodwin Procter, New York; Hinshaw & Culbertson, Boston, Mass; EMC Corp, Boston, Mass; Can Embassies Kiev & Berlin; Ottawa Art Gallery, Ont; Carleton Univ Art Gallery, Ont; Nickle Art Gallery, Univ Calgary, Alberta; Robert McLaughlin Art Gallery, Oshawa, Ont; Univ Winnipeg, Manitoba; Canadian Consulate, Seoul, Korea; Fasken Martineau, DuMoulin, NY; City of Ottawa Art Collection, Can; One Constitution Pl, Boston, Mass; Univ Kansas Fine Art Collection; Partners Harvard Medical Int, Cambridge, Mass; Claridge Investment Coll, Montreal, Quebec; SEI Investments, Toronto, Ontario, Oaks, Pa; Brooklyn Art Libr, NYC; Spaulding Rehabilitation Hospital, Charlestown, MA; Nat Gallery Australia, Canberra; La Union de Escritores Y Artistas de Cuba, Holquin. *Comn:* Mural, Ottawa Sch Bd, First Ave Sch, Ont, 79; serigraph, 75th Anniversary Portfolio, Royal Trust Co, Ottawa, Ont, 80; mural, City of Ottawa Heron Rd Multiservice Ctr, 90; mural & frieze, Churchill Alternative Sch, Ottawa Bd Educ, 91; patterned concrete walkways & mural, Ottawa/Carleton Transpo Heron Rd Transitway Sta, 92-95. *Exhib:* Solo exhibs, Art Gallery Algoma, Sault Ste Marie, Ont, 90, MacLaren Art Ctr, Barrie, Ont, 92, Centre d'Exposition L'Imagier, Alymer, Que, 93, Libr Gallery, Cambridge, Ont, 94 & The Gallery, Univ Toronto, Scarborough Campus, 96, CAC Gallery, North Adams, Mass, 97, 2005, Univ Winnipeg, Manitoba, 99 & Tremaine Gallery, Hotchkiss Sch, Lakeville, Conn, 2003, Galerie St Laurent + Hill, Ottawa, Can, 2004, 2012, Traces of Chaos, 2012; Solo retrospective, Persistance of Chaos, Ottawa Art Gallery, 2012; Group exhibs, In Situ, Sightline, Univ Alta, 97 Freedom, Diversity, Pluralism, Mu de Arte Contemporaneio de la Univ de Chile, Santiago, 98, Big Impressions: the large-scale contemp print, The Art Galleries of the Fine Arts Ctr, Univ RI, 99; Pan Am Print Exhib, Site Gallery, Winnipeg, Man, Can, 99; The Spirit of Drawing, the Ottawa Art Gallery, Ont, Can; Printtypes Dickenson State Univ, Dickenson, NDak, 2004; Directors Choice, Missouri Western State Col, St Joseph, Mo, 2004; Made in NAMA, CAC, N Adams, Mass, 2005; 4th Int Juried Print Biennial, Sumei Multidisciplinary Arts Ctr, Newark, NJ, 2006; Int Print Exhib, Chinese New Year, Proof Studio Gallery, Toronto, Ont, Can, 2008-13, Muskova Art Pl, Port Carling, Ontario, Can, 2008-2012; Evidence, The Ottawa City Proj (with catalogue by Emily Falvey), Ottawa Art Gallery, Can, 2008; Stimulus, Ottawa Art Gallery, Can, 2009; The Collector's Cabinet, Ottawa City Hall & Gallery (with catalogue by Jonathan Brown), 2009; Prints Today, 2012 (catalogue by Marylynn Cherry & Renee Viau), John B. Aird Gallery, 2012; Nuit Blanche Monster Print Project, 2012; Union de Escritores y Artistes de Cuba Gallery, 2013; Art House Coop Sketchbook, Project Traveling Exhib, 2013; RCA prints, 2013; Stewart Hall Art Gallary, Point Claire, Quebec; Animalia, Milk Factory Gallery, Bowral, Australia; Shifting Ecologies, 2014; The Painting Ctr, NYC. *Pos:* Consult, Mayor's Adv Comt Arts & Cult, 79-82, Revenue Can Visual Arts Adv Bd Customs Regulations, 80-82, Ottawa Visual & Performing Arts Ctr Steering Comt, 81-84, vchmn, Health & Welfare Can Adhoc Comt Health Hazards Arts & Crafts, 82 & 86, bd mem, Can Conf of the Arts, 84-86, chmn, Jack Chambers Found, 84-86 & Munic Ottawa Visual Arts Adv Comt, 86-91; vchmn, Ottawa Arts Ctr Found, 87-88; cur, Govt Can Persons Award Exhib, 87-88; consult, Arts-Peat Marwick, 89; art comn adv, Ottawa/Carleton Regional Govt, 92-94, Cent Can Exhib Asn, 94, Can Inst Planners, 94; guest cur, Ottawa Art Gallery, 92-93; Chmn, Can Conf Arts, Art Bank Adv Com, 95; mem, RMOC Regional Arts Adv Com, 98-2000; mem, ad hoc arts adv group, City of Ottawa Transition Bd, 2000; proj mgr, CARFAC-Heritage Can Grant to Develop Serv for Artists in Nunavut & Yukon Territories, 2005-2007. *Teaching:* Fine arts coordr, Algonquin Coll Visual Art, Ottawa, Ont, 75-78, teaching master painting, 79-82; guest lectr, Univ Manitoba, NASCAD, 82, Ottawa Sch Art, 64-69, 73-75, 86, Alberta Coll Art, 87, Banff Ctr, 87, Holland Col Sch Visual Arts, PEI, 89, Georgian Coll, Ont, 92; drawing & painting inst, Alpen Sch Art, summer 87; guest lectr, Holland Coll Sch Visual Arts, PEI, 89, Yukon Art Gallery, 95, workshops at Gallery 101, Canada, 98-2002 & workshops, Carfac Ont, 2005-2008. *Awards:* Grant, Can

Coun Travel Grants, 81-82 & 99; Ont Arts Coun Grants, 85, 88, 90-96, 2002, & 2012; Banff, Alberta Leighton Colony, 88; Victor Tolgesy Award, 89; Whitton Art Award, City of Ottawa, Can, 96; City of Ottawa Senior Artist Grant, 2003; Dainon Firstwork Grant & Residency, Quebec, Calif, 2003; Artist Residency, Eclipse Mill Artist Lofts, Mass, 2006, 2007, 2008 & 2011; Keith Kelly National Arts Award, Can, 2006; Canadian Mus Asn, 2007; The Ottawa Hospital Certificate of Public Svc, 2011; CARFAC Nat Visual Arts Arts Advocacy award, 2012; Queen Elizabeth II, Diamond Jubilee medal, 2012. *Bibliog:* Heidi Geraets (auth), Pat Durr, Ottawa Art Gallery, 93 & The Library Gallery, Cambridge, 94; Judith Tolnick (auth), the Phenomenon of the Large-Scale Contemporary Print (catalog), Univ RI, 99; Jennifer Gibson (auth), Culture Trash (catalog), Univ Winnipeg, Can, 99; Julie Dault (auth), Its ok to have a crush on Art, National Post, 11/06/2003; Paul Gessell (auth), Here's the Scoop on the "...mm", The Ottawa Citizen, Arts Section, 6/14/2003; Samantha Rippner (auth), 4th International Juried Print Biennial, catalog, 2006; Peter Simpson (auth), Out of Trash Comes Art, The Ottawa Gallery, Arts & Life Section 2012; Paul Gessel (auth), The Artful Blogger: A Long Overdue Tribute to Ottwawa Art Star Pat Durr, 3/2012; Catherine Sinclair, Jen Budney, Mayo Graham (writers) Persistance of Chaos (exhib catalogue), Ottawa Art Gallery, 2014. *Mem:* Can Artists Representation-Les Front des Artistes Canadians (pres, Ottawa, 79-80, nat vpres, 80-82, nat pres, 82-84); Royal Can Acad Arts (exec coun, 85-87, 90-91 & 96-2000); Ottawa Arts Ctr Found (found mem & bd mem, 86-91); City of Ottawa Arts Adv Comt, (co-chair, 2001-2003); Can Artist Representation (nat pres, 2002-2005); Artengine Internet Collective, 2005-13. *Media:* Acrylic & Mixed Media; Printmaking. *Publ:* The not so impossible dream, Artviews, Vol 9, No 3, 83; Death & taxes, Parallelogamme, Vol 9, No 3, 2/84; The Ottawa Arts Court Project, Recreation Canada, Vol 46, No 4, 11/88; Don Wright in the National Gallery, Arts Atlantic 49, Vol 13, No 1, 94; Past, Present, Future, Arts Atlantic #66, spring 2000; Landscapes with Thighs, Charlotte Wilson-Hammond, Acts Atlantic, #73, Fall 2002; Past Present, Future, Calendar, Vol 8 #1, Spring 2005; Danny Hussey Catalogue, 2009. *Dealer:* Galerie St. Laurent & Hill 293 Dalhousie Ste 103 Ottawa ON Can K1N 7E5; Boston Art 23 Drydock Ave Boston MA 02210. *Mailing Add:* 167 First Ave Ottawa ON K1S 2G3 Canada

DURSUM, BRIAN A
MUSEUM DIRECTOR
Study: LaSalle Coll, BA (Hist), 1970; Univ Pittsburgh, MA (East Asian Hist & Cult), 1974. *Pos:* Clerk, Otto G Richter Libr, Univ Miami, Coral Gables, Fla, 1973, account clerk, 1974-75; account clerk, Lowe Art Mus, Univ Miami, Coral Gables, Fla, 1975-76, asst to dir, 1976-82, acting chief admin, 1978, cur Oriental art, 1978-, registrar, 1982-90, acting dir, 1989-90, dir, 1990-. *Teaching:* Instr, English Taiwan Normal Univ, Taipei, Taiwan, 1971-73; teaching asst history, Univ Pittsburgh, 1973-74; lectr art dept, dir, chief cur, Univ Miami, 1992-. *Awards:* Southeast Banking Corp Grant, 1979; Wilder Found Grant, 1979 & 1980; Ryder Systems Grant, 1981 & 1983; Sun Glass Hut Grant, 1989; Stiefel Labs Grant, 1989; Federated Dept Stores Grant, 1989, 1990 & 1992; MegaBank Grant, 1989; Alma Jennings Found Grant, 1989 & 1990; Manny & Ruthy Cohen Found Grant, 1992. *Mem:* AAM; Asn Art Mus Dirs; Phi Alpha Theta. *Mailing Add:* Lowe Art Mus 1301 Stanford Dr Miami FL 33124

DUSARD, JAY
PHOTOGRAPHER, WRITER
b St Louis, Mo, Feb 18, 1937. *Study:* Univ Fla, BArch, 61. *Work:* JC Penney; Eastman Kodak; Ctr for Creative Photog; Fed Reserve Bank San Francisco, Los Angeles; Snell & Wilmer, Phoenix, Tucson & Irvine; City of Scottsdale, Ariz; City of Phoenix, Ariz; Denver Art Mus, Colo; Tucson Mus Art, Ariz; Phoenix Art Mus, Ariz; Ariz Public Service, Phoenix. *Exhib:* La Frontera, Centro Cult de Tijuana, Mex, 87; Consejo Mexicano de Fotografia, Mexico City, 88; The Cowboy West: 100 Yrs of Photog, CM Russell Mus, Great Falls, Mt, 92; Art Mus S Tex, Corpus Christi, 97; Jay Dusard's West, Desert Caballeros Western Mus, Wickenburg, Ariz, 98; Int Photog Hall of Fame, Oklahoma City, Okla, 2000; Folio Gallery: Whyte Mus of the Canadian Rockies, Alberta, 05; Cattle Track Gallery, Scottsdale, Ariz, 2005; Etherton Gallery, Tucson, Ariz, 2006; Booth Mus Western Art, Cartersville, Ga, 2007; Cattle Track Gallery, Scottsdale, Ariz, 2008; Sky Harbor Airport Mus, Phoenix, Ariz, 2009; Paul Paletti Gallery, Louisville, Ky, 2010; The West Select, Phoenix Art Mus, 2011; The West Select, Phoenix Art Mus, 2012. *Pos:* Designer & draftsman, Ellery Green Archit, Tucson, Ariz, 64; designer & lithographer, Northland Press, Flagstaff, Ariz, 66-68. *Teaching:* Asst prof light graphics, Prescott Col, Ariz, 68-75. *Awards:* Four Corners Book Award for Nonfiction for La Frontera, Northern Ariz Univ, Flagstaff, 88. *Bibliog:* Michael Saltz (producer), segment, MacNeil-Lehrer News Hour (TV film), PBS-TV, 83; Sheilah Britton (producer), Arizona Artforms: The Art of Jay Dusard (TV film), KAET-TV, Tempe, Ariz, 90; Michael Markee (producer), Jay Dusard: Keeping the West Western (doc film), 2008; Jennifer McKinney (producer), Kodak Cowboy (TV film), Ch. 12, Tucson, Ariz, 2008. *Mem:* Malpai Borderlands Group, Cochise Co, Ariz & Hidalgo Co, NMex. *Media:* Photography. *Interests:* playing jazz, ranch work. *Publ:* Auth & illusr, The North American Cowboy: A Portrait, Consortium Press, 83; contribr, Photographers & Their Images, Conran Octopus, London, 88; auth & illusr, Open Country, Gibbs Smith Publ, 94; illusr, Beyond the Rangeland Conflict: Toward a West that Works, Gibbs Smith/Grand Canyon Trust, 95; illusr, Cowboy Island: Farewell to a Ranching Legacy, Santa Cruz Island Found, 2000; auth & illustr, Horses, Rio Nuevo Publ, 2005. *Dealer:* Etherton Gallery 135 S Sixth Ave Tucson AZ 85701; Mark McDowell 6105 Cattle Track Scottsdale Ariz 85250; Paul Paletti Gallery 713 E Market St Louisville Ky 40202. *Mailing Add:* 5261 N Stewart Ranch Rd Douglas AZ 85607

DUSENBERY, WALTER
SCULPTOR
b Alameda, Calif, 1939. *Study:* San Francisco Art Inst, 61; ceramics with Marguerite Wildenhain, 62-66; Calif Coll Arts & Crafts, MFA, 71. *Work:* Carnegie Inst, Pittsburgh; Columbus Mus Art, Ohio; Guggenheim Mus & Metrop Mus Art, NY; San Francisco Mus Mod Art. *Comn:* Sculpture, Justice Ctr, Portland, Ore, 83; sculpture, Dept Art, Univ Northern Iowa, in prep. *Exhib:* Metrop Mus Art, NY, 79; Int Sculpture Conf, Washington, DC, 80; Yorkshire Sculpture Park, Bretton Hall, Eng, 81-82; Hamilton Gallery, NY, 81; Grad Sch Design, Harvard Univ, 82; Anderson Gallery, Va Commonwealth Univ, 83; Laumeier Sculpture Park, St Louis, 83; solo exhibs, Univ Northern Iowa, Cedar Falls, 85, Fendrick Gallery, Washington, DC, 86 & 88, Barbara Fendrick Gallery, NY, 89; Pratt Mus Art, NY, 87; and others. *Pos:* Pres, Digital Stone Proj, Mercerville, NJ, currently. *Teaching:* Instr ceramic sculpture, Univ Calif, San Francisco, 69; vis sculptor, Sch Landscape Archit, Grad Sch Design, Harvard Univ, 79-. *Awards:* Grants, Creative Artists Pub Serv, 80 & Nat Endowment Arts, 80; Augustus St Gaudens Fel, 85. *Bibliog:* Nina French-Frazier (auth), Walter Dusenbery, Arts Mag, 6/78; David L Shirey (auth), Creations that bridge the passage of time, NY Times Long Island Ed, 9/13/81; Ann Sargent-Wooster (auth), Dusenbery at the Nassau County Museum, Art in Am, 1/82. *Mem:* Artists Equity Asn; Archit League. *Media:* Stone. *Publ:* Auth, The Story of the Bed, Natoma Soc, Santa Barbara, Calif, 70; Dusenbery interviewed by Howard Greenfeld, 57th St Rev, 1/76. *Dealer:* Eight Modern 231 Delgado St Santa Fe NM 87501. *Mailing Add:* PO Box 144 Fly Creek NY 13337

DUTTA, ANINDITA
SCULPTOR
b April 4, 1973. *Study:* Ranchi Univ, India, BA, 1994; Visva Bharati Univ, India, BFA (sculpture), 1999; Purdue Univ, MA (sculpture), 2003; Univ Iowa, MFA (sculpture), 2005. *Work:* Purdue Univ; Univ Iowa; and var pvt collections. *Exhib:* Solo exhibs, CAMAC, Marney-sur-seine, France, 2005, Project 88, Mumbai, India, 2007, Azarian McCullough Art Gallery, NY, 2007, Sakshi Gallery, Mumbai, India, 2009; Earth and Fire, Woman Made Gallery, Chicago, 2005; Queens Int Biennial, Queens Mus, New York, 2006; Material Dolorosa, Valparaiso, Chile, 2008; Hotter Than Curry, Gallery Open Eyed Dreams, Cochin, India, 2009. *Pos:* Artist-in-residence, Bharat Bhavan, Bhopal, India, 1998, CAMAC, Marnay-sur-seine, France, 2005, Skowhegan Sch Art, Maine, 2005, Sacatar Found, Brazil, 2006, Art Omi Int Art Ctr, New York, 2006, Kolkata Int Workshop, India, 2006, Sandarbh Int Artist Residency, Ga, 2008. *Awards:* UNESCO Aschberg Bursaries Artist Fel, 2005; Pollock-Krasner Found Grant, 2008

DUTTON, ALLEN A
PHOTOGRAPHER, PAINTER
b Kingman, Ariz, April 13, 1922. *Study:* Art Ctr Schs, Los Angeles; Ariz State Univ, BA, MA, 49. *Work:* Mus Mod Art, NY; Bibliot Nat, Paris; Tokyo Coll Photog Mus, Japan; Il Diaframma, Milano, Italy; Santa Barbara Mus Art; Northlight Ariz State Univ, Tempe; Ctr Photog Univ Ariz, Tucson; Univ NMex, Albuquerque; Univ Ky, Louisville; Corcoran Mus; W Valley Art Mus, Ariz State Univ. *Exhib:* Solo exhibs, Il Diaframma Gallery, Milano, Italy, 71, Northlight Gallery, Ariz State Univ, 79, 80-88, Photog Southwest Gallery, Scottsdale, Ariz, 79, Shinju Gallery, Tokyo, 79, Nagase Photo Salon, Tokyo, 84, Hayden Libr, Ariz State Univ, 85 & Hal Martin Fogle Gallery, Scottsdale, Ariz, 92. *Pos:* Art ed & photog head, Phoenix Point West Mag, 63-66. *Teaching:* Prof photog & head dept, Phoenix Col, Ariz, 61-82; prof, Tokyo Col Photog, Japan, 72-73. *Awards:* John Hay Fel, 60. *Bibliog:* A D Coleman (auth), Grotesque in Photo, Ridge Press, 78; Jim Stone (auth), Darkroom Dynamics, Curtain & London, 79. *Mem:* Soc Photog Educ. *Publ:* Auth, The Great Stone Tit, Little Wonder Press, 72; A A Dutton's Compendium, Buse Press, 74; coauth, Arizona Then and Now, AG2 Press, 82; Phoenix Then and Now, First Interstate Bank Press, 85; Mythology for the 21st Century, Zeckwough Press, 90. *Dealer:* Etherton Gallery 424 E Sixth St Tucson AZ 85705; Ratcliff Gallery Sedona AZ. *Mailing Add:* 767 W Lee Blvd Prescott AZ 86303-6728

DUVAL, JEANNE
CONTEMPORARY REALIST PAINTER
b Petersborough, NH, 1956. *Study:* Univ NH, BFA, 78; Brooklyn Coll, NY, MFA, 81. *Exhib:* Solo shows incl Jaffrey Civic Ctr, Jaffrey, NH, 80, Walt Kuhn Gallery, Cape Neddick, Maine, 81, First Street Gallery, New York, 83, Sherry French Gallery, New York, 84, 87, 91, Contemp Realist Gallery, San Francisco, 93, 95, Hackett-Freedman Gallery, San Francisco, 99, 2002; group shows incl First Street Gallery, New York, 81, 82, 84; Sherry French Gallery, New York, 83, 84, 85, 86, 88; Gallery North, Setauket, NY, 85; Contemp Arts Ctr, New Orleans, 86; Met Mus & Arts Ctr, Coral Gables, Fla, 86; Univ Art Galleries, Univ NH, 86; Int Basel Art Fair, 87; Chicago Int Art Exposition, Chicago, 88; Contemp Realist Gallery, San Francisco, 90, 92, 95, 96; Nat Acad Mus, New York, 96; Hackett-Freedman Gallery, San Francisco, 97, 98, 2000; Gallery at Sharon Arts Ctr, Petersborough, NH, 2005; represented in permanent collections EF Hutton & Co, New York, Gallery North, Setauket, NY, Carey Ellis Co, Houston, Bayly Art Mus, Va, Artspace, New York, Met Mus Art, New York. *Awards:* MacDowell Colony Fel, 81, 83, 93; Grant, Ingram-Merrill Found, 84; Grant, Pollock-Krasner Found, 87, 89; Grant, Nat Endowment for Arts. *Media:* Oil on Canvas. *Mailing Add:* c/o Hackett-Freedman Gallery 2319 12th Ave San Francisco CA 94116-1907

DUVAL CARRIE, EDOUARD
PAINTER, SCULPTOR
b Port Au Prince, Haiti, Dec 12, 1954. *Study:* Univ Loyola, Montreal, Que, BA, 78. *Work:* Miami Art Mus, Fla; Davenport Mus Art, Iowa; Detroit Inst Art, Mich; Mus de Col, St Pierre, Port-Au-Prince, Haiti. *Comn:* Jefferson Reaves, Miami Pub Health Dept, 94. *Exhib:* Sacred Arts of Vaudou, Fowler Mus, Univ Calif, Los Angeles, 95; Out of Bounds, Nexus Art Ctr, Atlanta, 96; one-man show, Musee de Col, St Pierre, Port Au Prince, Haiti, 96; From the Edge of Paradise, Polk Mus, Fla, 97; Landscapes; Real and Imagined, Bernice Steinbaum Gallery, Miami, 2000; Migrations, Installation in the New Works Room, Mus Art Of Miami, 2000, Des Migrations sous L Eau, Generous Miracles Gallery, NY, 99, Spirits, Altars & Others, Quintana Gallery, Miami, 97, From The Edge of Paradise, Polk Mus Art, Lakeland, Fla, 97, Musee du Coll St Pierre, Port-au-Prince, Haiti, 96, Silver Linings, Gutierred Fine Arts, Miami Beach, 95; Porter Troupe Gallery, San Diego, 99, Miami Dade Cult Ctr, Miami, 99, Lyle O Reitz Gallery, Santo Domingo, 99, Lakaye Gallery, Los Angeles, 98, David

Beitzel Gallery, Project Room, NY, 97. *Awards:* Southern Arts Fedn/Nat Endowment Arts Regional Arts Fel, 96. *Bibliog:* Charles Merewether (auth), Edouard Duval Carrie, Marco Mus, 92; Gerald Alexis (auth), Edouard Duval Carrie, Mus de Coll St Pierre, 96; Edward Sullivan (auth), Spirit Altered, Quintana Gallery, 97; David C Driskell (auth) African American Visual Aesthetics, 95; Richard J Powell (auth) Black Art and Culture in the 20th Century, 95; Eric Sarner (auth) La Passe Du Vent- Une histoire Haitienne, 94. *Mem:* 1996 Southern Arts Fedn, Nat Endowment Arts Regional Visual Arts Fel. *Publ:* Contribr, Vodou & Soul, Elle Decor, 90; Matters of spirit, Latin Am Art, 94; Myth magic & monsters, Art News, 95; El pintor y su Compromiso, Atlantica, 97; Edouard Duval Carrie, Artension, 98. *Dealer:* Fernando Quintana 3200 Ponce de Leon Miami-Coral Gables FL 33134; Bernice Steinbaum Gallery 3550 North Miami Ave Miami FL 33127. *Mailing Add:* 3717 Royal Palm Ave Miami FL 33140

DUZY, MERRILYN JEANNE
PAINTER, LECTURER
b Los Angeles, Calif, Mar 29, 1946. *Study:* Pvt study with Vern Wilson, Los Angeles; Calif State Univ, Northridge, BA, 74; Otis Art Inst, MFA 88. *Exhib:* Women Artists in History, Tampa Mus Art, Fla, 86; Contemp Expressions from Los Angeles, Taipei, Taiwan, 89; Of Nature & Nation Yellowstone Summer of Fire, Los Angeles, 90; Elements, Woodland Hills, Calif, 90; Women Artists in History, Platt Gallery, Los Angeles, 91; and others. *Collection Arranged:* Erotic Visions, George Sand Gallery, Los Angeles, 77; Autobiographies, Palos Verdes Art Ctr, Calif, 78; Erotica 88, Gorman Fine Arts, Santa Monica, Calif; Angels, Ancestors & Spirit Guides, Burbank, Calif; Elemental Forces, Sherman Oaks, Calif. *Pos:* Founder & pres, Fla Chapter, Women's Caucus Art, 83-84, adv bd mem, Nat Women's Caucus Art, 84-87 & vpres, new chapters, 86-88; comt Women in the Art, Col Art Asn. *Teaching:* Educator, Artspace Gallery, City of Los Angeles, 91-94; Los Angeles High Sch Arts. *Awards:* First Place, Nat Women's Caucus Art, Lehigh Univ, Pa, 84; Artists Award, Otis Art Inst, Los Angeles, 88. *Bibliog:* Linda Saul (auth), Walking through history, Tampa Mus Newlett, 5/86; Laurel Paley (auth), Merrilyn Duzy & Margaret Lazzari, Artweek, 5/90; Steve Appleford (auth), Artspace's larger view of portraits, Los Angeles Times, 91; Nancy Kapitanoff (auth), Art notebook, Los Angeles Times, 91; and others. *Mem:* Women's Caucus Art; Artists Equity; Artists Alliance; Coll Art Asn; Group Nine, Lela Clanterns of the East, Los Angeles, CA. *Media:* Oil, Pastel, Mixed media. *Collection:* Contemporary artists; Vern Wilson, Bruno Bruni, Leonor Fini, Mario Casilli, Norma Jean Squies, Emerson Woelfer & Hannah Wilke. *Publ:* Contribr, Contemporary Women Artists-Datebook, Bo-Tree, 87. *Mailing Add:* 8356 Capistrano Ave West Hills CA 91304-3319

DVERIN, ANATOLY
PAINTER
b Dnepropretrovsk, Ukraine, July 23, 1935; US citizen. *Study:* Art Coll, Dnepropetrovsk, Ukraine, BA, 50-55; Com & Indust Arts Inst, Leningrad, 55-56; Kharkov Inst Fine Arts, Ukraine, MFA, 56-62. *Work:* Paintings approved, selected & purchased by the govts & comts of the former USSR and/or Ukraine for public display at different mus & galleries, locations unknown. *Comn:* Soldiers Dream (oil), 67, Songs of the Civil War, 69, Ministry Cult USSR, Moscow, Russia; New England (oil), Delta Airlines, 87; Portrait of John Adams (oil), John Adams Venture Capital, Boston, 89. *Exhib:* Solo exhibs, Creative Art Resource & Design, Birmingham, Mich, 98 & Marin Price Galleries, Chevy Chase, Md, 98, Marin-Price Gallerie, 2000; Group exhibs, Artist Mag Nat Competition, 95 & 96; 24th Ann Open Exhib-Pastel Only, Pastel Soc Am, NY, 96; 4th Biennial Nat Exhib Pastels, Pastel Soc N Fla, 96; Pastels USA, Pastel Soc W Coast, Sacramento, Calif, 96; Madison Ave Art Gallery, 96; Marin-Price Galleries, Chevy Chase, Md, 98; Gallery 1000, Carmel, Calif, 2001. *Teaching:* Instr, workshops. *Awards:* Canson Award of Excellence, 92; Artist Mag Award, Nat Exhib Pastel, Pastel Soc N Fla, 94; Nat Exh Pastel Only, Klimberger Memorial Award, 94; Joseph V Giffuni Mem Award, Best in Show, 96; Canson Award, Best in Show, 98 & 2000. *Bibliog:* Carole Katchen (auth), 200 Great Painting Ideas for Artists, 97 & Rachel Rubin Wolf (ed), The Best of Portrait Painting, N Light Bks; Portrait Inspirations, 97 & Landscape Inspirations, 97, Rockport Publ; The Best of Pastel, Quarry Bks; auth, Anatoly Dverin, American Impressionist (bk), Book Press, 2006. *Mem:* Pastel Soc Am; Oil Painters Am; Knickerbocker Artists; Cassat Pastel Soc; Pastel Soc of N Fla. *Media:* Oil, Soft Pastel. *Interests:* Classical, Traveling, Music. *Publ:* Illusr, When Animals Used to Speak, Childrens Bks, Kiev, USSR, 67; contribr, Ron Lister, Drawing with Pastel, Prentice-Hall Inc, 82; Designing Greeting Cards & Paper Products, by Ron Lister, Prentice-Hall Inc, 84; illusr, Spirit of the Hills, Dan O'Brien (auth), Pocket Bks, 88; Getting a feel for portraits, Artists Mag, 10/98; Kenneth M Bailey (auth), The Power of Personality, Am Artist Mag, 9/2000. *Dealer:* Bayview Gallery 33 Bayview St Camden ME 04843; Gallery 1000 Ocean Ave & Dolores St Carmel-By-The-Sea CA 93921; Boston Art Mass; Gallery at Lagerfeld NH; Gallery on the Green One The Green Woodstock VT 05091; Horizon Gallery 165 N Center St Jackson WY 83001; Churchill Gallery 6 Inn St Newburyport MA 01950; Cavalier Gallery 34 Main St Nantucket MA 02554; Wildhorse Gallery Steam Boat Springs CO; Royal Gallery Providence RI; Brendon Michael Fine Art Santa Fe NM. *Mailing Add:* 9 Oak Dr Plainville MA 02762

DWYER, EUGENE JOSEPH
HISTORIAN
b Buffalo, NY, Sept 14, 1943. *Study:* Harvard Univ, BA (classics, cum laude); NY Univ Inst Fine Arts, MA, 67, PhD, 74. *Teaching:* Prof art hist, Kenyon Col, Gambier, Ohio, 73-. *Awards:* Tatiana Warsher Award for the Archaeol of Pompeii, Herculaneum & Stabia, Am Acad Rome, 73-74; Nat Endowment Humanities Fel, 80-81 & 87-88. *Mem:* Coll Art Asn Am; Archaeol Inst Am; Am Numismatic Soc. *Res:* Greek and Roman art and classical tradition. *Publ:* The subject of Durer's four witches, Art Quart, 71; Augustus and the Capricorn, Roemische Mitteilungen, 73; auth, Sculpture and its Display in Houses of Pompeii, In: Pompeii and the Vesuvian Landscape, 79; Pompeian Oscilla Collections, Roemische Mitteilungen, 81; Pompeian Domestic Sculpture, 82; The Temporal Allegory of the Tazza Farnese, Am J Arch, 92. *Mailing Add:* Dept Art Hist Bailey House Kenyon Col Gambier OH 43022

DWYER, JAMES
PAINTER, EDUCATOR
b Tulsa, Okla, Oct 24, 1921. *Study:* Art Inst Chicago, BFA, 47; Acad Grande Chaumiere, Paris, 47-48; Syracuse Univ, MFA, 50; Univ Chicago; De Paul Univ; study with Boris Anisfeld. *Work:* Everson Mus, Syracuse, NY; Munson-Williams-Proctor Inst, State Univ, Utica, NY; Syracuse Univ, NY; Ashland Col, Ohio. *Comn:* 3100 sq ft mural decoration, Onondaga Co Civic Ctr, Syracuse, NY, 76. *Exhib:* Art Inst Chicago, 47; Metrop Mus Art, NY, 51; City Ctr Gallery, NY, 55; Silvermine Guild Artists Conn, 56; Univ Maine, Portland-Gorham, 74; Lubin House, NY, 77; solo exhib, Krasner Gallery, NY, 81; and others. *Teaching:* Prof painting & drawing, Syracuse Univ, NY, 49-82; retired. *Media:* Acrylic. *Mailing Add:* 101 Harden St Columbia SC 29205

DWYER, NANCY
SCULPTOR, PAINTER
b New York, NY, Oct 7, 1954. *Study:* State Univ NY, Buffalo, BFA (cum laude), 76; NYU, MS (interactive telecommunications), 2000-2002. *Work:* Chase Manhattan Bank, NY; Israel Mus, Jerusalem; Brooklyn Mus; Albright-Knox Art Gallery, Buffalo; Memphis-Brooks Mus. *Comn:* Obsession Overruled (billboards), NY State Coun Arts, NY, 85; Its Better Live (subway posters), Pub Art Fund, NY, 89; Multiple Choice (outdoor seating), 91-95, Hallway Highways (linolium tiled flooring), New York Bd Educ, 91-95; Who's on First? & Meet Me Here (granite seating), Gateway Corp, 92-94; Word Landscapes (etched precast stone), Criminal Justice Ctr, Philadelphia, 93-95. *Exhib:* Solo shows incl Hallwalls, Buffalo, NY, 77, 80, Artists Space, New York, 80, Studio d'Arte, Cannaviello, Milan, 81, Semaphore Gallery, New York, 83, 85, Josh Baer Gallery, New York, 86, 87, 88, 90, 92, Meyers/Bloom, Santa Monica, 88, Rhona Hoffman Gallery, Chicago, 89, Gallerie Renos Xippas, Paris, 94, Cristinerose Gallery, New York, 98, Dunedin Pub Art Gallery, Dunedin, New Zealand, 2001, Sandra Gering Gallery, New York, 2006; group shows incl 1987 Biennial Exhib, Whitney Mus Am Art, NY, 87; Prospect 1989, Kunsthalle Frankfurt, Ger, 89; Word as Image, Milwaukee Art Mus, 90-91, Okla City Art Mus, 90-91 & Contemp Art Mus, Houston, 90-91; Beyond the Frame, Am Art, 1960-1990, Setagaya Art Mus, Tokyo, 91; Night Lines, Centraal Mus, Utrecht, The Neth, 91; Am Artists of the 80's, Mus D'Arte Contemp, Trento, Italy, 91; The Language of Art, Kunsthalle Wein, Vienna, Austria, 92; Bad Girls I, New Mus Contemp Art, NY, 94; Bad Girls II, Wright Gallery Univ Calif Los Angeles, 94; John Michael Kohler Arts Ctr, Sheboygan, Wis, 96; Mus Contemp Art, Sydney, Australia, 98; Cristinerose Gallery, New York, 99; Geffen Contemp at MOCA Los Angeles, 2004. *Teaching:* Sch Visual Arts, NY; asst prof visual arts, Univ Vt, currently. *Awards:* Creative Arts Pub Serv Grant, NY State Coun Arts, 80; Nat Endowment Arts Fel Grant, 82; NY State Sponsored Projs Grant, NY State Coun Arts, 85. *Bibliog:* Marcia Tucker (auth), Nancy Dwyer Makes Trouble, Artforum, 89; Ellen de Bruijne (auth), Night Lines Cent Mus, Utrecht, Neth, 91; Rosetta Brooks (auth), Lost for Words (catalog), 98. *Media:* All Media; Acrylic, Oil. *Dealer:* Artware Editions 327 W 11th St New York NY 10014; Gering & Lopez Gallery 730 Fifth Ave New York NY 10019. *Mailing Add:* University Vermont Art Dept 401 Williams Hall 72 University Place Burlington VT 05404

DYENS, GEORGES MAURICE
SCULPTOR
b Mar 18, 1932; Fr & Can citizen. *Study:* Ecole Nat Super Beaux Arts, Paris, dipl, 61, studied with painter Balthus; Concordia Univ, Montreal, MFA; Holographic Lab. *Work:* Mus Mod Art & Hotel Hilton, Paris; Mus Art Contemp, Montreal; Mus Quebec; Mus Holography, NY; Permanent outdoor installations in Montreal & Quebec City. *Comn:* Public Art Montreal, Quebec City; Repentigny, Joliette, Can. *Exhib:* Mus Rodin, Paris, 66; Int Biennial New Delhi, India, 68; solo exhib, Mus Que, 81 & 95-96; Images du Futur, Montreal, 87, 89 & 92; Alternative Mus, NY, 88; Bienniale Paris 1961-1963, Mississippi Mus Art, Jackson, 95; ART-COM Gallery, Paris, 95; and others. *Pos:* artist-in-residence, Mus Holography, NY; cur, Saidye Bronfman Ctr, Montreal. *Teaching:* Prof sculpture, Univ Que, Montreal, 69-; invited prof & artist, Univ Dauphine, Paris, 92-93. *Awards:* Grand Prix De Rome, Paris, 61; Prix Susse, Bienniale Paris, 63; Shearwater Found Award Art Holography, Ft Lauderdale, Fla, 94. *Bibliog:* Diulio Morosini (auth), La Revincita Della Vita, Paese Sera, Rome, 7/1/65; Gerald Gassiot-Talabot (auth), Dyens, Arts, Paris, 10/20/65; Frank Popper (auth), Art of the Electronic Age, Harry N Abrams, New York, 93. *Mem:* Asn Sculptors Que, Montreal; Asn Arts & Techniques Holographics, Paris; Europ Ctr Technocult, Paris; Europ Acad Sci, Arts & Lit. *Media:* Multi Media, Holography Installation. *Res:* Photonics and Holography

DYER, M WAYNE
PAINTER, DESIGNER
b Roanoke, Va, Aug 6, 1950. *Study:* Va Western Community Col, AAS (design), 70; Hollins Col, Va, 71-72; James Madison Univ, Harrisonburg, Va, BS (fine arts, paintings, drawing & printmaking), 73; Va Art Inst, with Hartwell Priest, Charlottesville, 74; Radford Univ, Va, MFA (painting & Drawing), 83: workshop, with Robert Farber, 85; Varityper Opers Training Ctr, Atlanta, 86; Arrowmont Sch Arts & Crafts, with Beverly Plummer, 88; Calif State Univ, summer arts prog, 89. *Work:* Lykes Enrichment Ctr, Lykes Hosp, Brooksville, Fla; Ctr for New Creation, Nashville, Tenn; Slocumb Galleries, ETenn Univ, Johnson City; Radford Univ Found, Va; Mary Wash Col, Fredericksburg, Va. *Exhib:* Solo exhibs, Watkins Inst Art, Nashville, 88, Tempo Gallery, Brooksville, Fla, 88, Jacksonville Univ Gallery, Ala, 90, Lincoln Mem Univ Mus, Harrogate, Tenn, 89-90, Kiosk, Johnson City, Tenn, 91, Keene Gallery, Jonesborough, Tenn, 92-93 & Libr Gallery, Wise, Va, 95; Humbolt Univ, Calif State Univ, Arcata, 91; Slocumb Galleries Fac Exhib, 94; The Land on which We Live, Oscar Howe Art Ctr, Mitchell, SDak, 94; 1st Arg Int Art Proj, Capital Fed, Buenos Aires, 94; Akim Masks USA, Sotheby's, NY, 96. *Pos:* Tenn Arts Commission, Media Panel, 85-89, chmn 87-89. *Teaching:* Assoc prof to prof, Dept Art & Design, ETenn State Univ, 83-present. *Awards:* Award of Merit, First Tenn Exhib, Johnson City Area Arts Coun, 86; Award of Merit, First Am Exhib, Kingsport, Tenn, 87; Harvey Award Industrial Advertising, 87; Best Show, Cabaret VI, Johnson City Area Arts Coun, 88;

Outstanding Art Faculty Award, 91; Tash 97' Nat Collaboration Award, 97; Pres Award, Nat Down Syndrome Congress, 98; Distinguished Faculty Award, East Tenn State Univ, 1999-2000. *Mem:* Coll Art Asn; Southeastern Ctr Contemp Art; Johnson City Area Arts Coun; Am Inst Graphic Design. *Media:* Acrylic, Oil. *Mailing Add:* Dept Art Box 70708 1809 Oakland Ave Johnson City TN 37601

DYSHLOV, VALERIY
PAINTER, INSTRUCTOR
b Novosibirsk, Russia 1950; US citizen. *Study:* Art Studio, Kharkov Cert, 1970-1974; Kharkov Art Sch, MFA, 1974-1979; Special study with Vladimir Nenado (experimental graphics lab), 1976-1978. *Hon Degrees:* Union Artists of Former USSR (exhibiting mem), 1982. *Work:* Collection Ministry Cult, Kiev, Ukraine; Odessa Mus Art, Odessa, Ukraine; Kharkov Mus Art, Kharkov, Ukraine; Zimmerli Art Mus Rutgers Univ, New Brunswick, NJ; Norton Dodge Collection, Pa; Artist House, Moscow, Russia. *Comn:* Murals for pub buildings in Ukraine. *Exhib:* Manege Hall, Nat Shows, Moscow, Russia, 1980-1987; Solo exhibs, Gallery Mod Art, Munich, Ger, 1992, Artzania, Tallahassee, Fla, 2002, Clifton Munic Gallery, NJ, 2007 & Interart, Chelsea, New York, 2006; Les Decourtenau Gallery, Belgium, 2005; HR Giger Mus, Gruyeres, Switz, 2006; Biennale Miniature, Poland, 2006; Noyes Mus Art, NJ, 2007-2009; Science Meets Art, Pa Coll Technol, Williamsport, Pa, 2007; Doors of Perception, Inter Art Gallery, Chelsea, NY, 2007; Art of Imagination, Mall Galleries, London, Eng, 2007; Art of Vision, SEED, Newark, NJ, 2009; Paradise Lost, Williamsburg, NY, 2009; Dante Show, Saeby, Denmark & Viechtach, Ger, 2009; 5 Decades of Fantastic, Murphy Hill Gallery, Chicago, 2010; Quadrant Fantasy, Strychnih Gallery, Denmark, 2010; Fantasmus Gallery, Denmark, 2010; Butterfly Fine Art, Red Bank, NJ, 2010-11. *Teaching:* Asst prof drawing & graphics, Sch Art, Kharkov, Ukraine, 1980-1990; instr drawing, painting, Art Studio, 1995-2012. *Awards:* Award Excellence, Manhattan Art, NY, 2002; Perkins Juried Watercolor Show, Moorestown, NJ, 2002; 1st Place, Artist's Mag Art Competition, 2002; Excellence Award, Arts Festival, 2004; Freedlander Award, 13th Ann Open Juried Show, Shrewsbury, NJ, 2005; Achievement in Painting Award, Open Juried Show, Shrewsbury, NJ, 2007; Brookdale Gallery Juried Show, 2009; People's Choice Award, Guild Creative Art, Shrewsbury, NJ, 2009. *Bibliog:* The Paths of Art in the Kharkov Region, Ukraine, 1998; K G Saur (auth), World Biographical Dictionary of Artists, Munich, Ger, 2002; New Art International, Bk Art Press, NY, 2005; NJ Art Annual Catalog, Noyes Mus Art, 2007; Famous 100 Contemporary Artists, Woa Bks, London, UK, 2007; The World of Levkas, Ukraine, 2007; Dante: The Divine Comedy, Fantasmus-Art Bks, Denmark, 2009; Imaginaire III, Fantasmus Art, 2010, Imaginaire IV, Fantasmus Art, 2011. *Mem:* Soc for Art of the Imagination, UK; Noyes Mus Art, NJ. *Media:* Oil, Acrylic, Etching, Drawing. *Mailing Add:* 10 Longfellow Ter Morganville NJ 07751

DYSON, TORKWASE
COLLAGE ARTIST, VIDEO ARTIST
Study: Tougaloo Coll, Miss, BA (sociology), 1996; Va Commonwealth Univ, Richmond, BFA (painting/printmaking), 2001; Yale Univ, MFA (painting/printmaking; Barry Cohen Scholar), 2003; Spelman Coll Summer Art Colony, Fel, 2002 & 2005. *Exhib:* Solo exhibs include Dillard Univ, New Orleans, 2004, Tougaloo Coll, Miss, 2005, Northwestern Univ, Evanston, Ill, 2005, Ty Stokes Gallery, Atlanta, 2006, State Univ NY, Purchase, 2006, Inst Res African-Am Studies, Columbia Univ, 2006, Gallery 31, Corcoran Coll Art & Design, Washington, 2007; group exhibs include A New Day Begun: African-Am Artists Entering the Millennium, Lyndon B Johnson Libr & Mus, Houston, 1999; Just Beyond the Tip of the Tongue, Pa State Univ, 2001; All of Us: Accessing Multiple Identities in New Media, Temple Univ, Philadelphia, 2005; Gallery Artists, Ty Stokes Gallery, Atlanta, 2005; Not by Art Alone, Corridor Gallery, Spelman Coll, Atlanta, 2005; She's So Articulate, Arlington Arts Ctr, Va, 2008. *Awards:* Nat Women's Studies Asn Travel Grant, 2005

DYYON, MARIO
PAINTER, SCULPTOR
b Ft Meyers, Fla, May 2, 1946. *Work:* Mus Mod Art, Whitney Mus Am Art, NY; Larry Aldrich Mus, Conn; Case Western Reserve Univ. *Exhib:* Cleveland Top Artists, In Town Club, 69; Int Exhib Art, Cleveland, 70; Whitney Mus Am Art Ann, 72; Reflections, Larry Aldrich Mus, 72-73; solo exhib, Mather Gallery, Case Western Reserve Univ, 83. *Awards:* Printmaker Workshop Bd Scholar, New York, 82. *Mailing Add:* 155 W 73rd St New York NY 10023

DZAMA, MARCEL
PAINTER, SCULPTOR
b Winnipeg, Canada, 1974. *Study:* Univ Manitoba, Winnipeg, Canada, BFA, 1997. *Work:* Andy Warhol Found, New York; Corcoran Gallery Art, Washington; Mus Mod Art, New York; RI Sch Design Mus, Providence. *Exhib:* Solo exhibs include Artpace, San Antonio, 1998, Timothy Taylor Gallery Ltd, London, 2002, 2007, Susan Inglett Gallery, New York, 2004, Ikon Gallery, Birmingham, England, 2006, Galleri Magnus Karlsson, Stockholm, 2007, David Zwirner Inc, New York, 2008; group exhibs include Selections Spring, Drawing Ctr, New York, 1998; Biennale de Montréal, Quebec, Canada, 2002; Fantasy Underfoot, Corcoran Gallery Art, Washington, 2002; Compulsive Line, Mus Mod Art, New York, 2005; Into Me Out of Me, Mus Contemp Art Rome, 2007; Houldsworth Gallery, London, 2007; Comic Uncanny, Shaheen Mod & Contemp Art, Cleveland, 2007; COMIX, Kunsthallen Brandts Kladefabrik, Odense, Denmark, 2007. *Awards:* Watercolor Award, Univ Manitoba, Winnipeg, Canada, 1997, Namta Award, 1997; New Artist Award, Art Cologne, Germany, 2000; Sobey Art Award, Sobey Art Found, Halifax, Nova Scotia, Canada, 2004. *Media:* Watercolor. *Dealer:* David Zwirner Inc 519 W 19th St New York NY 10011; Richard Heller Gallery 2525 Michigan Ave B-5A Santa Monica CA 90404. *Mailing Add:* c/o Richard Heller Gallery 2525 Michigan Ave B-5A Santa Monica CA 90404

DZIERSKI, VINCENT PAUL
PAINTER, DESIGNER
b Pittsburgh, Pa, Jan 1, 1930. *Study:* Studied drawing & painting with Armando Del Cimuto, 48-52. *Pos:* Creative dir, Town Studios, Inc, 70-. *Media:* Egg Tempera, Alkyds. *Mailing Add:* 1229 Parkside Dr Bridgeville PA 15017

E

EADES, LUIS ERIC
PAINTER, EDUCATOR
b Madrid, Spain, June 25, 1923; US citizen. *Study:* Bath Sch Art, Eng; Slade Sch, Univ London; Inst Polytech Nac, Mexico City, Mex; Univ Ky, Lexington, BA. *Work:* Whitney Mus Am Art, NY; Mus Fine Arts, Houston; Dallas Mus Fine Arts; Ft Worth Art Ctr; Mus Fine Arts, Holyoke, Mass; Denver Art Mus; US West, Denver; Kaiser Permanente; Amoco. *Comn:* Airport mural, Govt Honduras, Toncontin, Tegucigalpa, 48; mural, Mesa Col, Grand Junction, Colo, 79; mural, US W Communications, Denver, Colo, 89. *Exhib:* Recent Painting USA: The Figure, Mus Mod Art, NY, 62; Forty Artists Under Forty, Whitney Mus Am Art, 62; State of Man, New Sch Social Res, NY, 64; 2nd Intermountain Biennial Exhib, Salt Lake Art Ctr, Utah, 65; Colorado Springs Fine Arts Ctr, 69; Purdue Univ, West Lafayette, Ind, 1992; Awada Ctr for Arts and Humanties, Colo, 93; Lincoln Ctr, Foot Collins, Colo, 93; 20/20 Vision, Arvada (Colo) Ctr for the Arts & Humanities, 1996; Digital Images, Regis Univ, Denver, 1996; Egypt of the Mind, Denver Art Mus, 98. *Teaching:* Prof painting & drawing, Univ Tex, 54-60; prof painting & drawing, Univ Colo, 61-90, prof emer, 90-. *Media:* Oil, Acrylic, digital prints. *Publ:* Illusr, The Precipice, Univ Tex, 69

EAGEN, CHRISTOPHER T
DIRECTOR
b Ohio, Feb 18, 1956. *Study:* Kansas City Art Inst, BFA, 78. *Collection Arranged:* Beyond the Surface: Abstract Illusionists, 82, Art of the Emotionally Disturbed Adolescents, 83, Sculpture from the Ceiling, 84, Live TV: Television as It Happened, 86, Tangeman Fine Arts Gallery, Cincinnati, Ohio. *Pos:* Dir publicity, Contemp Art Ctr, Cincinnati, 78-79; pres, Cincinnati Artists Group Effort, 79-80; asst dir, Tangeman Fine Arts Gallery, Cincinnati, 80-81. *Teaching:* Instr & gallery internship art appreciation, Univ Cincinnati, 82-86. *Publ:* Contribr, Fragments, 83-84, coauth, Contemporary African Sculpture, 84, contribr, Emeritae, 85 & Art Deco Cincinnati, 85, Univ Publ, Univ Cincinnati

EAGERTON, ROBERT PIERCE
PAINTER
b Florence, SC, Mar 17, 1940. *Study:* Atlanta Sch Art, BFA; Acad Fine Arts, Vienna, Austria; Cranbrook Acad Art, Bloomfield Hills, Mich. *Work:* Nat Collection Fine Art, Smithsonian Inst, Washington, DC; Art Inst Chicago; Lessing J Rosenwald Collection, Jenkintown, Pa; Sheldon Swope Gallery Art; Norman McKenzie Mus Art, Regina, Sask; Lincoln Conf Ctr, Indianapolis, Ind. *Exhib:* Solo exhib, Norman McKenzie Mus Art; Lithographs de la Collection Mourlot, PR, 71; Prints: USA 1974, Univ Pittsburgh; Image South Gallery, Atlanta, Ga, 81; Ruschman Gallery, Indianapolis, Ind, 88 & 90; and others. *Pos:* Co-founder, Transfigurations Press, Sarasota, Fla, 64-66. *Teaching:* Prof painting, Herron Sch Art, Ind-Purdue Univ, Indianapolis, 66-88; guest artist printmaking, Univ Ill, Champaign, 70; vis prof printmaking, Tyler Sch Art, summer 72; vis artist, Univ Sask, Regina, 73, Univ Mich, Ann Arbor, 77, Louisville Sch Art, Ky, 79, Cincinnati Sch Art, Ohio, 81 & Emma Lake Wkshp, Regina. *Bibliog:* Robert Eagerton (video), Indiana Univ, 90. *Media:* Oils. *Publ:* Contribr, Horizon, 87. *Mailing Add:* 7010 Wildridge Dr Indianapolis IN 46256-2130

EARDLEY, CYNTHIA
SCULPTOR
b Trenton, NJ, Mar 18, 1946. *Study:* Douglass Col, Rutgers Univ, New Brunswick, NJ, BA (with honors), 68; Sch Visual Arts, New York, 68-69. *Exhib:* Hope (Nov-Dec), Crossroads (May-June), Access: A Feminist Perspective (Jan-Feb), Rhonda Schaller Studio, NY, 2007; Cynthia Eardley: Sculpture, Ceres Gallery, 2010; Independent Visions: A Feminist Perspective, Sidney Mishkin Gallery, Baruch Coll, NY, 2008; Eternal Idol, NY Acad of Art, 2009; Art You Can Touch, Straube Ctr, Sculpture Garden, Pennington, NJ 2009; Sideshow Gallery, Brooklyn, NY. *Pos:* Co-dir, Site Inc, NY, 69-73. *Teaching:* Asst prof, Pratt Inst, Brooklyn, 72; instr sculpture, Newark Mus Sch, 74, Philadelphia Col Art, 89; adj prof figure sculpture, anatomy, art hist; instr grad and continuing educ div, NY Acad Art, 94-2013. *Awards:* First Place Award, Enviro-Vision, Everson Mus, 72; Semi-finalist, Municipal Servs Bldg Plaza Competition, Philadelphia, 92. *Bibliog:* Roberta Smith (auth) Sculpture in the City:; Blankets to Bronze, The New York Times, 4/20/90; Cynthia Nadelman (auth), Middle-Aged Gods and Giant Babies, ART News Mag, 12/04; Site: Identity in Density, Images Press, Melbourne, Aust, 2005. *Mem:* Women's Caucus for Art. *Media:* Bronze, Ceramic. *Publ:* Auth, Editor's Choice: Helga von Eichen, Bomb Mag, summer 2004; Santiago Calatrava: Sculpture into Architecture, The Brooklyn Rail, pp 30-31. 2/06; Zaha Hadid: 30 years in Architecture, The Brooklyn Rail, 9/06; Gordon Matta-Clark: You Are the Measure, The Brooklyn Rail, 4/07; Does Hard Work Translate into Genius?, Letters to the Editor, NY Times, 5/5/09. *Dealer:* Ceres Gallery 547 West 27th St Suite 201 New York NY 10001. *Mailing Add:* 115 W Broadway New York NY 10013

EARLE, EDWARD W
CURATOR, HISTORIAN
b New Orleans, La, Aug 19, 1951. *Study:* Univ Notre Dame, BA, 74; Visual Studies Workshop, State Univ NY, Buffalo, MA (mus studies), 78. *Collection Arranged:* Points of View (ed, catalog), 79; Hand Camera in History, 82; The Orient Viewed, 82; Philip Brigandi, Photographer, 83; Prof Joseph Jastrow, 84. *Pos:* Cur, Visual Studies

Workshop, Rochester, NY, 77-79; librn & archivist, Photog Resource Ctr, Boston, 80-82; cur, Calif Mus Photog, Univ Calif, Riverside, 82-. *Teaching:* Instr photog, Swain Sch Design, New Bedford, Mass, 79-80; instr hist photog, Boston Col, Chestnut Hill, 82-83. *Mem:* Coll Art Asoc; Soc Photog Educ; Am Cult Asn. *Res:* History of photography, relating aesthetic trends to social and cultural conditions. *Publ:* Contributing articles in Afterimage and New England J Photog, 77-; Points of View, The Stereograph in America: A Cultural History, VSW Press, 79; ed, Philip Brigandi, Calif Mus Photog Bulletin, 83; contribr, The Photographic Vision (TV ser), KOCE-TV for PBS. *Mailing Add:* Senior Cur UCR-Calif Museum of Photography Univ of Calif Riverside Riverside CA 92521

EARLS-SOLARI, BONNIE
CURATOR
b Fallbrook, Calif, Oct 4, 1951. *Study:* Univ Calif, Berkeley, BA, 73. *Pos:* Asst cur, Univ Art Mus, 74-77; prog coordr, Cooper Hewitt Mus, 77-78; cur, dir, art prog, Bank Am Corp, 79-. *Mem:* Asn Prof Art Adv; Graphic Arts Coun; Foto Forum; Art Table (Women Visual Arts)

EASTCOTT, R. WAYNE
PRINTMAKER, PAINTER
b Trail, BC, July 20, 1943. *Study:* Emily Carr Coll Art & Design, (Vancouver Sch Art), with J Shadbolt, D Jarvis & R Kiyooka, Senior Cert (painting & printmaking, hons), 66. *Work:* Nat Gallery, Ottawa; Art Gallery Greater Victoria, BC; Winnipeg Art Gallery, Man; Robert MacLaughlin Gallery, Oshawa, Ont; Kanagawa Prefectural Gallery, Yokohama, Japan. *Comn:* Portfolio of 5 editions, Generation 84 Youth Soc, Vancouver, BC, 83; portrait of Mr Belzberg (serigraph), New Play Ctr, Vancouver, 83; Edition of 125 (serigraph), Adovocat Structured Settlements; wall relief on riveted aluminum, Rienhard Derreth Graphics Ltd, Vancouver, BC, 89. *Exhib:* Solo exhibs, Can & Japan, 69-91, Crown Gallery, Vancouver, BC, 97, Wayne Escott: The Printed Painting, Burnaby Art Gallery, BC, 98, Generation-Before and After, Lookout Gallery, Regent Col, Univ BC, Vancouver, 98; Burnaby Art Gallery (with catalog), BC, 88; North of the Border-Contemp Canadian Art, Watcom Co Mus, Wash, 90; Triennale (catalog), Krakow, 94, 97, 2000, 2003; Int Print Triennial, Kanagawa Perfectural Gallery, Yokohama, Japan, 98; Printmaking at the Edge, Gustav Klimt Villa, Vienna Austria, 2007; Falun Thiennial 2007, Contemp Print Art, Dalarnas Mus, Falun, Sweden. *Pos:* Founding mem & pres, Dunderave Print Soc, 71-76; Art Inst Printmaking, Capilano Univ, BC, 83. *Teaching:* Instr painting, Vancouver Sch Art, BC, 65-70; head dept printmaking, Capilano Univ, NVancouver, BC, 71-. *Awards:* Can Coun Grant, 68. *Bibliog:* A Perry & K Kritzweiser (auths),Wayne Eastcott, Okui Assoc, Tokyo, Japan, 79; Printed Painting-Ted Lindberg Burnaby Art Gallery, 88; Ted Linberg (auth), The curator's statement, Capilano Rev, 88; Richard Noyce (auth), Printmaking at the Edge, 2006. *Mem:* Royal Can Acad Arts; Dunderave Print Soc; World Print Coun; Can Print & Drawing Soc; Malaspina Printmakers. *Media:* Silkscreen, Acrylic, Enamel. *Interests:* Japanese Culture. *Dealer:* Bellevue Gallery

EASTERSON, SAM PETER
VIDEO ARTIST, CONCEPTUAL ARTIST
b Hartford, Conn, Jan 24, 1972. *Study:* Cooper Union, with Tony Ourster, BFA (scholar), 94; Univ Minn, with Lance Neckar, MS, 99. *Comn:* Video, Walker Art Ctr, Minneapolis, 98. *Exhib:* 1997 Biennial Exhib (with catalog), Whitney Mus Am Art, NY, 97; Station to Station, Artists Space, NY, 97; Dialogues, Walker Art Ctr (with catalog), Minneapolis, 98; Scope, Artists Space, NY, 98; Pandaemonium (with catalog), London Electronic Arts, Eng, 98; World Wide Video Festival (with catalog), Sledeljk Mus Modern Art, 99; Art in General (with catalog), NY, 2000; Ecotopia (with catalog), Int Ctr Photography, New York, 2005. *Awards:* Tiffany Prize, 99. *Media:* Video. *Publ:* auth, various articles in NY Times, Village Voice, Flash Art & Timeout NY

EASTMAN, GENE M
PAINTER
b Council Grove, Kans, Jan 1, 1926. *Study:* Univ Kans, BFA; Art Inst Chicago; Univ Iowa, with Stuart Edie, MFA. *Exhib:* Houston Mus Fine Arts, Tex, 58 & 61; Dallas Mus Fine Arts Ann, 59, 63 & 66; Seven States Artists Ann, Delgado Mus, New Orleans, 61; Watercolor USA, Springfield, Mo, 64; 24-64 Nat Exhib Small Paintings, Purdue Univ, 64. *Teaching:* Prof drawing & painting, Sam Houston State Univ, 58-, chmn art dept, 72-79; guest instr drawing & painting, Mus Fine Arts Sch, Houston Mus Fine Arts, Tex, 68-70. *Awards:* First Prize, Painting, Tex Fine Arts Asn, 58; Purchase Award, Okla Printmaker Soc, 64; First Prize, Painting, Tri-State Exhib, Beaumont Mus, Tex, 67. *Media:* Oil, Watercolor. *Mailing Add:* 7191 Hwy 75 South Huntsville TX 77340-7283

EASTMAN, MICHAEL DOUGLAS
PHOTOGRAPHER
b. Jan 31, 47. *Study:* Univ Wis, BA, 69; self taught photogr. *Work:* Metropolitan Mus Art, NY ; Chicago Art Inst; Los Angeles Co Mus Art, Calif; Mus Fine Arts, Boston, Mass; Int Ctr Photog, NY. *Exhib:* Recent Landscapes, St. Louis Art Mus, MO, 2006; Grandeur Saved: Aiken Rhett House, Gibbs Mus, Charleston, NC, 2007; Contemporary, Cool, and Collected, Mint Mus, Charlotte, NC, 2007; Elusive Light, St. Louis Univ Mus, MO, 2008; The Notion of Space, George Eastman House, Rochester, NY, 2009; Paris Photo, Barry Friedman Ltd, NY, 2010; Faded Elegance-Havana, Okla City Mus Fine Art, Okla, 2011. *Publ:* Forgotten Forest, Witkin Gallery, 87; Horses, Knopf, 2003; August Rodin, Archipelgo, 2004; Vanishing America, Rizzoli, 2008; Havana:The Photographs of Michael Eastman, Prestel, 2011. *Dealer:* Barry Friedman Ltd 515 West 26th St New York NY 10001. *Mailing Add:* 6305 Westminster Pl Saint Louis MO 63130

EATON, TOM
CARTOONIST, WRITER
b Wichita, Kans, Mar 2, 1940. *Study:* Univ Denver, 58; Univ Kans, BFA, 62. *Comn:* Mag covers, Boy's Life, Scholastic Voice, Scholastic Scope, Child Life, and others; posters, Scholastic Mag Inc, 74-79; plus others. *Pos:* Artist-writer Contemp Cards dept, Hallmark Cards Inc, Kansas City, Mo, 62-66; art ed, Scholastic Mag Inc, New York, 66-68; freelance cartoonist & writer, 68-; regular contrib comic features Dink and Duff, Webelos Woody, Tiger Cubs, The Wacky Adventures of Pedro, Mazes & More, Boys' Life Mag, 84-. *Awards:* Cert of Excellence for Cover, Catch the Eye, 75, Am Inst Graphics Arts. *Bibliog:* Eleanor Van Zandt (auth), A cartoonist looks at the comics, Practical Eng Mag, 68. *Mem:* Am Mensa; Am Anti-Vivisection Soc; Sierra Club; Green Peace. *Media:* Pen, Ink. *Publ:* Auth & illusr, Flap, Delacorte Press, 72; Tom Eaton's Book of Marvels, 76, Holiday Greeting Cards, 78 & Super Valentines, 79, Scholastic Bk Serv; Rufus and the Earth Patrol, Sat Eve Post, 78; Captain Ecology, 74; Otis G Firefly's Phantasmagoric Almanac, 74; and others. *Mailing Add:* 911 W 100th St Kansas City MO 64114

EBERLE, EDWARD SAMUEL
CERAMIST, DRAFTSMAN
b Tarentum, Pa, Oct 3, 1944. *Study:* Edinboro State Col, BS, 67; NY State Coll Ceramics, Alfred Univ, MFA, 72. *Work:* Carnegie Mus Art, Pittsburgh, Pa; Los Angeles Co Mus Art; Newark Mus Art; Nat Gallery Australia, Canberra; Fine Arts Mus San Francisco; Nelson-Atkins Mus Art, Kansas City. *Exhib:* Solo exhibs: Columbus Mus Art & Carnegie Mus Art. *Teaching:* From instr to asst prof ceramics, Philadelphia Col Art, 71-75; from asst to assoc prof, Carnegie-Mellon Univ, Pittsburgh, Pa, 75-85. *Awards:* Fel, Nat Endowment Arts, 87; Fel, Pa Coun Arts, 86 & 89. *Bibliog:* Gary Wells (auth), A mythic realm in black and white, Am Ceramics, 6/1/87; Michael Odom (auth), Edward Eberle: in the realm of myth, Am Craft, 5-6/92. *Media:* Ceramic, Clay. *Dealer:* Perimeter Gallery 210 W Superior Chicago IL 60654

EBERLY, VICKIE
PAINTER
b Washington, DC, May 28, 1956. *Study:* Md Inst Coll Art, BFA (painting), 78; City Univ New York, Queens Col, NY, MFA (painting), 81. *Work:* Image Communications Inc, NY. *Exhib:* Queens Community Mus, NY, 81; Queens Coll Gallery, City Univ NY, 81; Ball State Univ Art Gallery, Ind, 82; El Paso Mus Art, Tex, 82; Barrett House, Poughkeepsie, NY, 85; Central Hall Gallery, NY, 86; 22 Wooster Gallery, NY, 87; Tradition 3 Thousand Gallery, NY, 87. *Media:* Oil on Canvas, Mixed Graphics. *Dealer:* Tradition 3 Thousand Gallery 273 E 10th St New York NY 10009. *Mailing Add:* 8421 110th St Jamaica NY 11418-1243

EBERT, LESLIE JEAN
PHOTOGRAPHER, PAINTER
b Oregon City, Ore, Sept 20, 1962. *Study:* Univ Ore, BARCH, Minor Art Hist, 1987. *Work:* Crane Mus, Dalton, Mass; Good Samaritan Hos, Portland, Oregon; West Coast Bank; ESI Corp; Avista Energy; Allison Inn, Newberg, Ore; Portland Dermatology, Portland, Ore, Cascaid Aids Proj, Portlands, Ore. *Comn:* Many pvt commissions for homes and offices since 1994. *Exhib:* 74th Nat Exhib, Mus Fine Art, Springfield, Mass, 1993; Contrasts, Edmonds Art Mus, Edmonds, Washington, 1995; Retrospective, Willamette Gallery, West Linn, Ore, 2001; Celebration of American Paper Arts, Crane Mus, Dalton, Mass, 2003; Paper Mosaic, Southwest Sch of Art & Craft, San Antonio, Tex, 2004; Leslie Ebert, Wash State Univ Gallery, Vancouver, Washington, 2005; On the Edge 2005, Peninsula Fine Arts Center, Newport News, Va, 2005; CAM Biennial - Artist of Ore, Coos Art Mus, Coos Bay, Ore, 2006; Illuminations, Sidney and Berne Davis Arts Center, Fort Meyers, Fla, 2008; Soul to Soul, Microcosm Gallery, NY, 2008; Art Etc, Portland, Ore, 2009; Portland Art Mus Rental Sales Gallery, 2010; New Vibrations in Art, ADP Studios, Shelton, Wash, 2011; Sketch Book Project, ArtHouse Co-Op, Brooklyn, NY, 2011; Exploring Experimental Art, ISEA 20th Anniversary Exhib, ADP Studios, Shelton, Wash, 2011; All Oregon Art, Hart Pavillion, Salem, Ore, 2011; Exit Winter, Gallery 114, Portland, Ore, 2012; Oregon Artist Showcase, Cultural Ctr, Newberg, Ore, 2012; Experimental Art, North Shore Art Asn Gloucester, Mass, 2012; Pentimento, Waterston Gallery, Portland, Ore, 2012. *Collection Arranged:* Cur, Layerist Art' Washington State Univ, Vancouver (assembled, arranged) 6/2006. *Pos:* Curatorial Adv Bd, AIA Gallery (18 exhibs), Portland, Ore, 1991-1993; publicity chair, Artisan Center co-operative Gallery, 1993-1996; found bd mem, Art in Pearl, Portland, Ore, 1996-1997; summer regional coordr, 2004-, juror mem comt, 2006-2009, Portland Art Mus, volunteer, 2009. *Awards:* Jurys top 10, Am Design in Japan, Catalog, Mitsubishi Corp, 1993; Best of Show in mixed media, Art in the Park, West Linn Arts Comn, 1994; Mayors Choice, Art in the Park, West Linn Arts Comn, 1995; Second Place, Edmonds Arts Festival, Edmonds Art Mus, 1997. *Bibliog:* Donna Hand-Lee (auth), Artist Profile (Periodical), Art now/Gallery guide, 10/1999; Janet Goetze (auth), Finding Textures of Peace in Paper (Periodical), The Oregonian, 1/2002; Nelson/Dunaway (coauths), The Art of Layering (Bk), Soc Layerist Publ, 2004; Diane Maurer-Mathison (auth), Paper in three dimensions (Bk), Watson-Guptill publs, 2006; Gwen Heffner, Cheryll Frank (coauths), Connections: we are all one, Exhib catalog produced by Ky Arts Coun, 2006; The Portland Art Mus Rentaal Sales Gallery, The First 50 Years 1959-2009, 2009; Art of Allison Collection (catalog), 2010; Visual Journey, Art of the 21st Century, Mary Nelson & Nina Mihm, 2010; Int Soc Experimental Art (catalogue), 2011. *Mem:* Northwest Print Coun (mem 1995-2003); Am Crafts Coun (mem 1996-2005); Nat Oil & Acrylic Painters (mem 2006-); Int Soc Experimental Artists (mem 2006-); Soc of Layerist in Multi Media. *Media:* Digital Photography, Acrylic Painting, Mixed media collage. *Res:* The importance of fostering creativity in an evolving culture; How current ideas in theosophy and theoretical physics are influencing contemp art. *Interests:* Shamanism, theosophy, writing, energy medicine. *Publ:* Contribr, illusr, Art Calender, Feb Vol 15, Art Calender, Turnstile Publ, 2001; auth, Somerset Studio, Art of the Greco-Roman Era, Somerset Studio/ Stampington, 2001; contribr, illusr, Somerset Studio, Return to Asia Special Edition, Somerset Studio, Stampington, 2001; auth, Somerset Studio, Tea in the Secret Garden, Somerset Studio, Stampington, 2003; contribr, illusr, The Art & Craft of Handmade Cards, Watson, Guptill Publs, 2003; The Guild Sourcebook of Architectural and Interior Art, Number 23, 2008; Thresholds, Literary Journ, Spring 2009; Studio Visits, Vol 13, Open Studio Press, 2011. *Dealer:* Catherine Stacy 412 NW Couch St Suite 204 Portland OR 97209; Jennifer Zika 1219 SW Park Ave Portland OR 97205. *Mailing Add:* PO Box 68604 Portland OR 97268

EBIN, CYNTHIA
SCULPTURE, PAINTING
b Brookline, Mass. *Study:* Boston Univ, MA (fine arts), 1960-1963; Studied with Irving Marantz group, 1964-1967; Calif State Univ, Northridge, Calif, BA (sculpture), 1981; MA (sculpture), 1983; Calif State Univ, Long Beach, LB CA, MFA (sculpture), 1989; Univ Calif, Los Angeles, LA Calif (creative arts teaching credential), 2001. *Work:* US Holocaust Mus, Wash DC. *Exhib:* Solo & Two Person Exhibs: Finegood Art Gallery, West Hills, Calif (invitational), 1988; 14 Sculptor's Gallery, SoHo, NY (invitational), 1990; Brand Libr Art Gallery, Glendale, Calif (invitational), 1991; Upstairs Gallery, Ventura, Calif (invitational), 2003; Tracy Park Gallery, Malibu, Calif, 2010, Tracy Park Barry, Malibu, Calif, 2010, and others; Group Exhibs: Mats Bergman Gallery, Stockholm, Sweden, 2002-2006; Finegood Gallery, West Hills, Calif, 2003; Channel Islands Art Exhib, Camarillo, Calif, 2004; Joseph Wahl Art Gallery, Woodlands Hill, Calif, 2005-2006; Founders Award 3rd Ann Art Exhib, Hollywood, Calif, 2006; and others; Craft & Folk Art Mus, Los Angeles, Calif, 1984; Purim Mask Invitational, Jewish Community Mus, San Francisco, Calif, 1989, 1991, 1993; Invitational (dir Scott Ward), Downey Mus, Los Angeles, 1991; Los Angeles Co Mus Rental, Sales & Exhib Gallery, Los Angeles, Calif, 1999-2001; Orlando Gallery, Reseda, Calif, 2010; US Holocaust Mus, Wash DC, 2013. *Pos:* Instr private & group, studio, Woodlands Hills, Calif, 1990-2001; instr painting & drawing, Pierce Coll, Woodland Hills, Calif, 1997-2000; adj prof painting, Pepperdine Univ, Malibu, Calif, 2001; instr creative arts, Los Angeles Unified Sch Dist, 2001-2003. *Bibliog:* Images & Reflections of Women Artists (catalogue), Los Angeles City Hall Bridge Gallery & Rotunda, Mar 1990; Caffyn Kelly (auth), Cynthia Ebin, Gallery Women Artists, Number 8 Vol II, page 35, Apr 1990; M Davidson (auth), Women's History Honored with Convocation, ArtSpeak, Ventura, Calif, Vol 2, pages 3-4, Feb-Mar 1990; Cathy Viksho (auth), Exhibits, Times-Trenton Metro Sunday, Sec cc4, 3/35/1990; Gallery Guide, W Coast, Sept 2004; Collector's Ed, Sept 2004; Outstanding People in the Arts Today, 2014; Included in Outstanding People in the Arts Today, 2014. *Media:* Mixed Media, Clay, Installation Sculpture. *Interests:* nature, hiking. *Mailing Add:* 6200 Platt Ave Woodland Hills CA 91367

EBITZ, DAVID MACKINNON
MUSEUM DIRECTOR, HISTORIAN
b Hyannis, Mass, Oct 5, 1947. *Study:* Williams Col, BA, 69; Harvard Univ, AM, 73, PhD, 79. *Collection Arranged:* The Baroque Print, Univ Art Collection, 85; Art of Fixing a Shadow, J Paul Getty Mus, 89; Maiolica to Monstrance, Ringling Mus, 94; A Heritage of Collecting, Mus Fla Hist, 95. *Pos:* Interim dir, Univ Art Collection, Univ Maine, 86-87; head dept educ & acad affairs, J Paul Getty Mus, 87-92; dir, John & Mable Ringling Mus Art, 92-. *Teaching:* Asst prof art hist, Univ Maine, 78-84, assoc prof, 84-87. *Mem:* Asn Art Mus Dirs; Fla Art Mus Dirs Asn; Coll Art Asn; Am Asn Mus; Int Ctr Medieval Art. *Publ:* Auth, Secular to sacred: The transformation of an oliphant in the Musee de Cluny, Gesta, 86; Fatimid style and Byzantine model in a Venetian ivory carving workshop, Studies in Medieval Culture, 86; The oilphant: It's function and meaning in a courtly society, Houston German Studies, 86; Connoisseurship as practice, Artibus et Historiae, 88; DBAE: Opening a bridge between art history and art education, Alaska J Art, 89; Four Sculptors, Univ Art Collection, 87. *Mailing Add:* c/o John and Mable Ringling Mus Art 5401 Bay Shore Rd Sarasota FL 34243

EBNER, SHANNON
PHOTOGRAPHER
b Englewood, NJ, 1971. *Study:* Bard Coll, BA, 93; Yale Univ Sch Art, MFA, 2000. *Exhib:* Solo exhibs include Margo Victor Presents, LA, 2003, Wallspace, New York, 2005, 2007, PS1 Contemp Art Center, Long Island City, NY, 2007; group exhibs include Anti-Form, Soc Contemp Photog, Kansas City, 2002; High Desert Test Site 3, Josha Tree, Calif, 2003, High Desert Test Site 4, 2004; Strange Animal, LA Contemp Exhibs, 2004, Shared Women, 2007; Manufactured Self, Mus Contemp Photog, Chicago, 2005; Post No Bills, White Columns, New York, 2005, Monuments for the USA, 2006, Looking Back, 2007; Trace, Whitney Mus Altria, New York, 2006; Calif Biennial, Orange County Mus Art, Calif, 2006; Uncertain States of America: Am Art in the 3rd Millennium, Serpentine Gallery, London, 2006, traveling to France & Poland, 2007; Learn to Read, Tate Mod, London, 2007; Whitney Biennial, Whitney Mus Am Art, New York, 2008; 54th Int Art Exhib Biennale, Venice, 2011. *Dealer:* Wallspace 619 W 27th St Ground Fl New York NY 10001. *Mailing Add:* 6413 Crescent St Los Angeles CA 90042

EBONY, DAVID
EDITOR
Pos: Writer, ArtNet Mag; assoc managing ed, news ed, Art in America Mag, currently managing ed. *Publ:* Auth, Curve: The Female Nude Now, Carlo Maria Mariani, 2003. *Mailing Add:* Art in America Brant Art Publications 575 Broadway New York NY 10012

ECCLES, TOM
ADMINISTRATOR, CURATOR
Study: Glasgow Univ, Scotland, MA (philos and Italian); Bologna Univ, Italy, studied with Umberto Eco. *Pos:* Devel dir, Proj Ability, Scotland; pub art consult & proj mgr, Art in Partnership, Edinburgh, Scotland; dir & cur, Pub Art Fund, New York, 96-2005, founder, In the Pub Realm & Tuesday Night Talks; exec dir, Ctr for Curatorial Studies, Bard Coll, 2005-. *Teaching:* Instr moral philos, Univ Glasgow, Scotland; instr critical theory, Glasgow Arts Sch, Scotland, 90-92. *Awards:* Recipient Award for Best Show in an Alternative or Pub; Space as cur of Janet Cardiff: Her Long Black Hair, Int Asn Art Critics/USA, 2005. *Publ:* Coauth, Plop: Recent Projects of the Public Art Fund, Merrell Publ, 2004; written articles and reviews for Art in Am. *Mailing Add:* Pub Art Fund 1 E 53rd St New York NY 10022

ECHELMAN, JANET
SCULPTOR, PAINTER
b Tampa, Fla, Feb 19, 1966. *Study:* Harvard Col, Harvard Univ, AB (magna cum laude), 87; Milton Avery Sch Arts, Bard Col, MFA, 95. *Work:* Mus Centre Europe/Europas Parkas, Vilnius, Lithuania; Tampa Mus Art, Tampa, Fla; Harvard Univ Film Arch, Cambridge, Mass; Fields Sculpture Mus and Park, Omi, NY; John Michael Kohler Art Center, Sheboygan, Wis. *Comn:* sculpture, Harvard Univ Art Mus, 98; sculpture, Buffalo Bayou Art Park, Houston, Tex, 2000; sculpture, Florence Lynch Gallery at IFEMA, Madrid, Spain, 2001; sculpture, Casa del Cordon, Burgos, Spain, 2001; Armory Show, New York, 2002; Art Rotterdam, Netherlands, 2004; Praca Cidade Salvador, Porto/Matosinhos waterfront, Portugal, 2005; William F Poe Garage, Lights on Tampa Commission, Tampa, FL, 2006; Civic Space Park, Phoenix, Ariz, 2009; Richmond Olympic Oval, Richmond, British Columbia, 2010. *Exhib:* Solo exhibs, Works from Bali, Fung Ping Shan Art Mus, Hong Kong Univ, 90, New Vision, Tampa Mus Art, Tampa, Fla, 93, Bellbottoms: Sculpture Combining Net and Bronze, Birla Art Mus, Calcutta, India, 97; Wax Hands, Sackler Art Mus, Harvard Univ, Cambridge, Mass, 96; Trying to Hide with Your Tail in the Air, Mus Centre Europe, Vilnius, Lithuania, 98; Inside-Outside, Fogg Art Mus, Harvard Univ, Cambridge, Mass, 98; Open Spaces, ARCO, Madrid, Spain, 2001; Art Proj, Art Basel, Miami Beach, Fla, 2002; William Benton Mus Art, Univ Conn, 2004; Ctr Contemp Non-Objective Art, Belgium, 2004; Mus Art & Design, New York, 2007; Ind State Mus, 2008; Scottsdale Mus Contemp Art, Ariz, 2009. *Pos:* southeast asia regional coordr, Rauschenberg Overseas Culture Interchange, 89-91; pres, Janet Echelman, Inc, 2002-. *Teaching:* instr visual studies, Harvard Univ Grad Sch Design, 92-96; resident tutor fine arts, Harvard Col, Harvard Univ, 93-2000; senior lectr, adj prof, Lesley Univ, 98-; dir, Adams Artspace & Studio Art Prog, Harvard Coll, 93-2001; adj fac, New Sch Univ, New York, 2001-2007; fel, Harvard Grad Sch Design, Cambridge, Mass, 2008-2009. *Awards:* artist grant, Pollock-Krasner Found, 99; artist grant in sculpture, Mass Cult Coun, 99; artist fel, Japan Found, 2001; winner, 9-11 Mem Design Competition, Hoboken, NJ, 2003-2004; Year in Rev Award, Pub Art Network, 2005; Elected to PAN Coun, Pub Art Network, 2005-2008; Lily Auchincloss Fel, NY Found Arts, 2006; Int Achievement Award Excellence in Archit Structures for She Changes, 2006; Henry Crown Fel, Aspen Inst, 2006-2009; Award for Excellence in Structural Engr, Ariz Structural Engr Asn, 2008; Artist Fel Crafts & Sculpture/Installation, Mass Cult Coun, 2009; Environmental Excellence Award, Crescordia Award Art in Pub Places, Valley Forward Asn, 2009; Readers' Choice Award, Best Pub Art, Phoenix New Times, 2009. *Bibliog:* Stephen Westfall (auth), Janet Echelman: New Vision, Tampa Mus Art, 93; Adrian Randolph and John Welchman (auths), Two Essays on the Painting of Janet Echelman, Harvard Univ Bow and Arrow Press, 95; Esther David (auth) Janet Echelman (contribr), Bellbottoms: Sculpture Combining Bronze and Net by Janet Echelman, Nat Inst Design India, 97; JametEchelman: Sculpture, Florence Lynch Gallery, 2002. *Mem:* Int Sculpture Center; Coll Art Asn. *Media:* Fibers, Water, Glass, Steel, Wind, Air Space. *Publ:* auth, An Artists Journal from Bali, Hong Kong Univ Dept Fine Arts, 88; auth, Radcliffe Quarterly, Radcliffe Inst Harvard Univ, 92. *Dealer:* Florence Lynch Gallery 147 W 29th St New York NY 10001

ECHOHAWK, BRUMMETT
PAINTER, ILLUSTRATOR
b Pawnee, Okla, Mar 3, 1922. *Study:* Sch Arts & Crafts, Detroit, 44; Art Inst Chicago, 44-48. *Work:* Gilcrease Mus Am Hist & Art, Tulsa. *Comn:* Truman Mem Libr (mural, with Thomas Hart Benton), Independence, Mo, 59-60. *Exhib:* Gilcrease Mus, Tulsa; Amon Carter Mus, Ft Worth, Tex; M H De Young Mem Mus, San Francisco; Imperial War Mus, London; Karl May Theater Mus, Bad Segeberg, WGer; Art Through the Embassies, US State Dept, Pakistani, India. *Pos:* Auth & illusr, articles in Western Horseman, Colorado Springs, 50-, Tulsa Sunday World, 50- & Okla Today, 60-; bd mem, Gilcrease Mus Am Hist & Art, Tulsa, 80-. *Bibliog:* Whose Children Are These (film), ABC-TV Network, NY. *Media:* Oil, Tempera. *Publ:* Auth & illusr, Blue book, McCalls Mag, 49. *Mailing Add:* 2525 W Easton Tulsa OK 74127

ECKART, CHRISTIAN
PAINTER
b Calgary, Alta, Can, Jan 9, 1959. *Study:* Hunter Col, City Univ New York, MFA, 86. *Work:* Mus Mod Art, NY; Chicago Art Inst; List Visual Art Ctr, Mass Inst Technol; New Sch Soc Res, NY. *Exhib:* Galerie Tanit, Munich, Ger, 89 & 92; Galerie 'T Venster, Rotterdam, The Neth, 88; Galerie Thaddaeus Ropac, Paris & Salzburg, 90 & 91; Rubin Spangle Gallery, NY, 90 & 92; Eli Broad Family Found, Santa Monica, Calif, 92; Thaddaeus Ropac Gallery, Salzberg, Austria, 95 & Paris, 95; Sidney Janis Gallery, NY, 95; Ten-Year Survey Show (traveling), Univ Western Ont, 96-98. *Teaching:* Nova Scotia Col Art & Design, Halifax, NS, Can, 89, Art Ctr Col Design, Pasadena, Calif, 90, Univ Hartford Dept Art, Conn, 91, Alta Col Art, Calgary, Can, 91, Int Art His Conf, NY, 91, Aldrich Mus Contemp Art, Ridgefield, Conn, 92, Univ RI, 92, Sch Visual Arts, NY, 92; studio instr, Sch Vis Art, 94; studio instr, Sch Visual Art, 94-. *Bibliog:* Alexander Puhringer (auth), 9 Fragen am Christian Eckart, Noema Mag, 4/91; Hiromi Honda (auth), Christian Eckart, Agora Mag, 6/91; Balcon Mag, Andachtsbild Studies, No 7, 12/91. *Dealer:* Sidney Janis 110 W 57th St New York NY 10019. *Mailing Add:* 5215 Chenevert St Houston TX 77004

ECKE, BETTY TSENG YU-HO See Yu-ho, Tseng

ECKER, ROBERT RODGERS
PAINTER, PRINTMAKER
b Waynesboro, Pa, Apr 30, 1936. *Study:* Pa State Coll, Shippensburg, BS, 58; Pa Acad of Fine Arts, 59-61; Pa State Univ, MFA, 65. *Work:* Denver Art Mus, Colo; Smithsonian Am Art Mus, Washington, DC; Libr Cong, Washington, DC; NY Pub Libr, New York; Crocker Mus, Sacramento, Calif. *Comn:* Benzinger Winery Imagery Series Label. *Exhib:* Am Cult Ctr, Belgrade, 81; Denver Art Mus, Denver Colo, 91; Int Print Exhib, Portland Art Mus, Portland, Ore, 97; Int Meszzotint Exhib, Davidson Galleries, Seattle, Wash, 99; Wash State Univ Art Mus, Pullman, Wash, 2003; Artist

House Gallery, Philadelphia, 2004 & 2006; Washington Co Mus Fine Arts, Hagerstown, Md, 2008; Traveling Mezzotint Exhib, Russia, William Havu Gallery, Denver, 2009; William D Cannon Art Gallery, Carlsbad, Calif, 2012. *Teaching:* Asst prof drawing and printmaking, Wash State Univ, 65-72; prof, drawing and painting, Univ of Colo, Boulder, 72-2001. *Awards:* DH Lawrence Fel, Univ of NMex, 76; Artists Fel Nat Endowment for the Arts, 81-82; Recognition Award in Painting, Colo Coun Arts, 95; Fel Pa Acad Fine Arts Award, Philadelphia, Pa, 2011. *Mem:* Soc of Am Graphic Artists (SAGA). *Media:* Acrylic, Oil, Mezzotint Printmaking. *Res:* Mezzotint prints. *Interests:* All phases of art. *Publ:* Patirck Frank (auth), Robert Ecker, Denver Art Mus, 91; Susan Edwards (auth), Contemp Icons, Hunter Coll NY, 92; Richard Nalley (auth), Rear Window, Forbes FYI Mag, 2004; Bob Nugent (auth), Imagery: Art for Wine, 2006. *Dealer:* William Havu Gallery Denver CO. *Mailing Add:* 2143 Royal Lytham Gln Escondido CA 92026-1089

EDDY, DON
PAINTER
b Long Beach, Calif, Nov 4, 1944. *Study:* Univ Hawaii, Honolulu, BFA, 67, MFA, 69; Univ Calif, Santa Barbara, 69-70. *Work:* Cleveland Mus Art, Ohio; Toledo Mus Art, Ohio; St Etienne Mus, France; Neue Galerie, Aachen, Ger; Williams Coll Mus Art, Williamstown, Mass. *Exhib:* Fogg Art Mus, Harvard Univ, Cambridge, Mass, 73; Storm King Art Ctr, Mountainville, NY, 73; NY Avant-Garde, Saidye Bronfman Centre, Montreal, Que, 73; Hyper-realisme Americaine, Realism Europ, Centre Nat d'Art Contemporain, Paris, 74; Wadsworth Atheneum, Hartford, Conn, 74; Tokyo Biennial, Japan, 74; Baltimore Mus Art, Md, 76; Realist & Illusionist Art Traveling Exhib, Australia, 77; and others. *Teaching:* Sch Visual Arts, NY. *Bibliog:* Udo Kulterman (auth), New realism, NY Graphic Soc, 72; Peter Sager (auth), Realismus, Verlag M DuMont Schauberg; Virginia Bonito (auth), Don Eddy - The Resonance of Realism in the Art of Post War America. *Media:* Acrylic. *Dealer:* Nancy Hoffman Gallery 500 W 27th St NY 1001. *Mailing Add:* 543 Broadway New York NY 10012

EDELL, NANCY
PAINTER, PRINTMAKER
b Omaha, Nebr, Nov 12, 1942; Can citizen. *Study:* Univ Nebr, Omaha, BFA, 64; Univ Bristol, Eng, studied film with George Brandt, 68-69. *Work:* Can Coun Art Bank, & Nat Gallery of Can, Ottawa, Ont; Art Gallery Nova Scotia, Halifax; Robert McLaughlin Art Gallery, Oshawa, Ont; Winnipeg Art Gallery, Man; Mt St Vincent Univ Art Gallery, Halifax, NS; Dalhousie Univ Art Gallery, Halifax, NS. *Comn:* Survivors in Search of a Voice, Royal Ont Mus, 95; Mid Northumberland Arts Group, Ashington, Eng, 97. *Exhib:* Innovation: Subject & Technique, Univ Toronto, Scarborough, Ont, 87; 80/20: 100 Yrs of NSCAO, Art Gallery Nova Scotia, Halifax, 88 & Subject Matter: Contemp Painting & Sculpture in NS, 92; solo shows, Univ Nebr Omaha Art Gallery, 88, Univ Moncton Art Gallery, NB, 89, Art Nuns: Recent Work by Nancy Edell, Art Gallery NS (touring), 91, Bemidji Arts Ctr, Minn, 97 & Bricabra, Dalhousie Univ Art Gallery, Halifax, 98, Bricabra, Dalhousie Univ Art Gallery, Art Gallery of Southwestern Manitoba, Mus for Textiles, Toronto, Confedn Ctr, Charlottetown, PEI, 99, plus others; 4th Int Biennial Print Exhib, Taipei, Taiwan, 90; Boston Printmakers, 42nd NAm Print Exhib, Fitchburgh Art Mus, 90; Subversive Crafts, Mass Inst Technol Visual Arts Ctr, Cambridge, 93; The Female Imaginary, Agnes Etherington Art Ctr, Kingston, Ont, 94; On Paper of Paper, Kupio, Finland, 96 & Pforzheim, Ger, 97; Layers of Meaning, Woodhorn Colliery Mus, Ashington, Eng, 97, Bradford Industrial Mus, 98, Collins Gallery, Glasgow, 98, & Cleveland Arts Centre, Eng, 98. *Teaching:* part-time fac, Nova Scotia Col Art & Design, Halifax, NS, 82-2000; vis artist printmaking, St Michael's Printshop, St Johns, Nfld, 87; vis fac visual art, Banff Sch Fine Arts, Alta, 88; vis artist, Univ Windsor, Ont, 92, Alta Col Art, Calgary, 92, Mid Northcumberland Arts Group, Ashington, Eng, 97 & Mus Civilization, Hull, Que, 98. *Awards:* Can Coun grant, 74, 80, 84, 87, 88, 90, 92, 94 & 97,99; Manitoba Arts Coun Grant, 77 & 78; Can Coun, Paris Studio, 90; Nova Scotia Arts Coun Grants 97, 2000. *Bibliog:* Bricabra (exhib catalog) Dalhousie Univ Art Gallery. *Mem:* Can Artists Representation (secy, 84-85); Visual Arts NS; NS Printmakers Asn (secy-treas, 87-88). *Media:* Miscellaneous Media. *Publ:* Auth, Art Gallery of Nova Scotia (exhib catalog) 91; Subversive Crafts (exhib catalog), MIT Vis Arts Ctr, Cambridge, Mass, 93; The Female Imaginary, Agnes Etherington Art Ctr (exhib catalog), Queens Univ, Kingston, Ont, 94; Uses of the Vernacular in Contemporary Nova Scotian Art (exhib catalog), Dalhouse Univ Art Gallery, 94. *Mailing Add:* RR 1 Hubbards NS B0J 1T0 Canada

EDELMAN, ANN
PAINTER, LECTURER
b New York, NY. *Study:* Brooklyn Col, NY; Am Univ, Washington, DC; spec study with Leon Berkowitz & Jacob Kainen. *Work:* US Dept Transportation. *Exhib:* Area Show, Corcoran Gallery Art, Washington, DC, 56; Society of Washington Artists, Smithsonian Inst, Washington, DC, 59; Maryland Artists, Baltimore Mus Art, Md, 70 & 71; Corcoran Gallery Art, Washington, DC, 73. *Teaching:* Lectr contemp art, Exten Course, Univ Md, 72-78, Am Univ, Washington, DC, 79. *Awards:* First Prize, Soc Washington Artists, 72. *Mem:* Artists Equity; Washington Womens Art Ctr. *Media:* Acrylics, Oil. *Mailing Add:* 12919 Crisfield Rd Silver Spring MD 20906-5135

EDELMAN, JANICE
WATERCOLOR, WRITER
b Philadelphia, Pa, Apr 13, 1933. *Study:* Art Inst Philadelphia, AA, 57; Thomas Edison State Coll, BA, 2006, Dr Boris Blai and Henry Hensche; Gotham NY Writers. *Work:* Woodmere Art Mus, Philadelphia. *Comn:* Watercolor Portrait, Philadelphia, 99; Watercolor Portrait, Fall River, Mass, 2000; Watercolor Portrait, Elkins Park, Pa, 2002. *Exhib:* Solo exhibs, Woodmere Art Mus, 97-98, Congregation Beth Ore, 2003, Kremp's, 2008. *Pos:* Advert, illus, designer, Art dir, Philadelphia, Pa, 58-78. *Teaching:* Dept Head, Montgomery Co Vocational Sch, 78-80; instr, watercolor, Woodmere Art Mus, Philadelphia, Pa, 91-2005; lectr, 98-2007. *Awards:* Grumbacher award, 68; Award of Excellence, 39th Ann, Art Dirs Club of Philadelphia, 79; Salmagundi Club NY award, 88; Merit Award, 77th Writers Digest Competition, 2008; Philadelphia Watercolor Society, Int Exhib, 2010; Keystone Nat, 2009. *Mem:* Philadelphia Watercolor Soc; Pa Watercolor Soc; Int Women's Writers Group; Story Circle Network. *Media:* Watercolor. *Interests:* Painting, lecturing & writing. *Collection:* Pvt collection, 75 books on Pablo Picasso. *Publ:* Schlemm & Nicholas, The Best of Watercolor, Rockport, 95; Why I Paint, Artist Mag, 99; Fresh Literature Mag, 2010. *Mailing Add:* 3505 Hale Rd Huntingdon Valley PA 19006-3230

EDELMAN, RITA
PAINTER
b New York, NY, 1930. *Study:* Traphagen Sch Design, cert, 51; Silvermine Coll Art, 67; also with Victor Candell, Leo Manso & Robert Reed. *Work:* General Electric, Fairfield, Conn; Fairfield Univ, Conn; Gen Foods, White Plains, NY; Deloitte Haskins & Sells, Stamford, Conn; Wichita State Univ, Kans; Fitchburg (Mass) Art Mus; Brigham and Woman's Hospital, Boston, Mass; Hampshire Coll, Amherst, Mass. *Exhib:* Stamford Mus, Conn, 73, 77, 78, 82, 90 & 91; solo exhibs, Silvermine Guild Galleries, New Canaan, Conn, 76 & 81, Pindar Gallery, NY, 78, 80, 82, 85 & 87, Stamford Mus, Conn, 90 & Univ Mass, Amherst, 99; Grey Galleries, NY, 80; Aldrich Mus Contemp Art, Ridgefield, Conn, 81; Hampshire Col, Amherst, Mass, 2003; Forbes Libr, North Hampton, Mass, 2005; Lascano Gallery, Great Barrington, Mass, 2007; Springfield Col, 1/09; Bratteboro Mus, 2005, 2011; Hampshire Coll, 2013; Newton Free Library, Newton, Mass, 2013. *Awards:* Judges Choice, Greenwich Art Soc, 72; First Prize, New Haven Paint & Clay Club, 75; Painting Award, New Eng Exhib Painting & Sculpture, Silvermine Guild Artists, 80. *Bibliog:* George Albert Perret (auth), essay, 10/80 & Robert Yoskowitz (auth), review, 12/80, Arts Mag; Cynthia Nadleman (auth), rev, Art News Mag, 1/81. *Mem:* Westport Weston Arts Coun; New Haven Paint & Clay Club; Silvermine Guild Artists. *Media:* Oil, Acrylic, All Media. *Dealer:* Oscar Edelman, Hadley, Mass, 01035. *Mailing Add:* 18 Shattuck Rd Hadley MA 01035-9659

EDELSON, GILBERT S
ADMINISTRATOR, LECTURER
b New York, NY, Sept, 15, 1928. *Study:* NY Univ, BS, 49; Columbia Univ Sch Law, LLB, 55. *Pos:* Officer, Art Dealers Asn Am, vpres and counsel, currently; mem, com on art law, Asn Bar, City NY, 64-67, 72-75, 84-87 & 89, chmn, 92; dir, Col Art Asn, 69-89, Artforum Mag, 70-77 & Art Quart, 78-80; trustee & mem exec comt, Am Fedn Art, 82-93; trustee, Archives Am Art, Int Found Art Res & NY Studio Sch. *Mem:* Am Fedn Art; Archives Am Art; Int Found Art Res; NY Studio Sch

EDELSON, MARY BETH
CONCEPTUAL ARTIST, PAINTER
b East Chicago, Ind, 1933. *Study:* DePauw Univ, BA, 55; NY Univ, MA, 59. *Hon Degrees:* DePauw Univ, DFA, 92. *Work:* Guggenheim Mus, Mus Mod Art, NY; Walker Art Ctr, Minneapolis, Minn; Corcoran Gallery Art & Nat Collection, Washington, DC; Indianapolis Mus Art; Seattle Art Mus; Malmo Museum, Sweden; Mod Women, Art by Women Artist in Mus Mod Art Collection, New York; Mus Modern Art, NY. *Comn:* Mural, Danforth Mus, 86; mural, Musee du Quebec, Can 87; mural, London Regional Gallery, 87; mural, Mendel Gallery, 88; mural, WPA, 89; mural, Gilford Col, 90. *Exhib:* Solo exhibs, Washington Proj Arts, 89, Nicole Klagsbrun & A/C Proj Room, NY, 93, Creative Time, NY, 94, Nicolai Wallner Gallery, Copenhagen, Denmark, 96, Trickster, The Agency, London, 98, Home-made Root Beer, Malmo Museer, Sweden, 2000 & Re-scripting the Story, Traveling Exhibition, 2000-02, There's Never Only One Game in Town, The MAC Contemporary, Dallas, Tex, 2010, Players: Selected Works by Edelson from the 70s-90s, VIP Armory Week, St Regis Hotel, NY, 2011, Burn in Hell, NY, 2011, Beasts of Revelation, DC Moore Gallery, NY, 2012, Hail to the Feminists Who Produced the Revolution, Accola & Griefen, NY, 2012, Female Power: Mus Voor Moderne Kunst, Arnhem, Netherlands, 2013, NYC 1993: Experimental Jet Set, Trash, and No Star, New Mus, NY, 2013; In-Significance, The Agency, London, 95; Sniper's Nest: Art That Has Lived with Lucy R Lippard, Bard Coll Travels, 95-97; Vraiment Feminisme et Art Magazen, Ctr Nat d'Art Contemp, Grenoble, France, 97; Original Visions, McMullen Mus Art, Boston, 97; Contemp Classicism, Neuberger Mus Art & Tampa Mus, 99-2000; Picturing the Modern Amazon, New Mus, 2000; Century City: Art and Cult in the Modern Metropolis, Tate Mod, London White Columns, NY, 2001; Goddess, Lelong Galerie, New York City, 2002; Personal and Political, Guild Hall Mus, LI, NY, 2002, Chelsea Mus, 2003; Making Peace, Shedhalle, Zurich, 2003; Mothers of Invention, Mumok Mus of Contemp Art, Vienna, Austria, 2003; A Life Well Lived, A Retrospective of Mary Beth Edelson's Work, Malmo Mus, Sweden, 2006; It's Time For Action, Migros Mus, Zurich, Switz, 2006; traveling exhib, Wack! Art of the Feminist Revolution, Mus Contemp Art, Los Angeles & NY, 2007; The End, Andy Warhol Mus, Pittsburgh, Pa, 2009; Pictures by Women: A History of Modern Photography, MOMA, NY, 2010. *Teaching:* Instr, Corcoran Sch of Art, 71-76; lectr in 70 cols and universities in the US, Can, Europe & Iceland, 73-2012, Danish Royal Acad, 2001-2004; artist-in-residence, Univ Ill, Chicago, 82 & 88, Univ Tenn, 83, Ohio Univ, Columbus, 84, Md Inst Art, 85 & KC AI, Kansas City, 86, Danish Royal Acad, Copenhagen, 2000, 2003. *Awards:* Nat Endowment for the Arts, 1999-2000; Andy Warhol Found for the Visual Arts, 2001-2002; Int Artists Studio Prog in Sweden (IASPIS), 2006. *Bibliog:* The Shaman as a Gifted Artist, High Performance, autumn 1988; Open Letter to Thomas McEvilley, New Art Examiner, 1989; Politiken, Review of Malmo Exhibition, 2000; Laura Cottingham, The Art of Mary Beth Edelson, 2002; 19 Reviews in Sweden of Retrospective Exhibition at Malmo Museum, 2006. *Mem:* Founder Conf Women in Visual Arts, Washington, DC; Original Collective Mem Heresies; Women Artists Coalition; Women's Action Coalition, New York; Founding Mem Int Team to Provide an Artists Contract. *Media:* Photography, Mixed Media, Performance, Community as a medium. *Res:* Domestic violence, utopia as a short term experiment. *Interests:* Political action, film, living as an ongoing experiment, international commune of artists. *Publ:* auth The Politics of Women's Spirituality: Essays on the Rise of Spiritual Power Within the Feminist

Movement, 1982; Firsthand: Photographs by Mary Beth Edelson 1973-1993, 1993; Women's Culture: New Era of Feminist Revolution?, Scarecrow, 2005; and others; Wack! Art of the Feminist Movement, 2009; Art of Mary Beth Edelson, 2002. *Dealer:* Balice & Herling Paris; Accola & Griefem NY; Suzanne Geiss Co. *Mailing Add:* 110 Mercer St New York NY 10012

EDELSTEIN, TERI J
MUSEUM DIRECTOR, HISTORIAN
b Johnstown, Pa, June 23, 1951. *Study:* Univ Pa, BA, 72, grad fel, Stouffer Coll House, 72-74, teaching fel hist art, 73-75, Penfield scholar, 75-76, MA, 77, PhD, 79. *Pos:* Asst dir dept acad prog, Yale Ctr Brit Art, New Haven, Conn, 79-83; dir, Mt Holyoke Col Art Mus, 83-90; dir, David & Alfred Smart Mus Art, Univ Chicago, 90-92; deputy dir, Art Inst Chicago, 92-2012. *Teaching:* Lectr art hist, Univ Guelph, Ont, 77-79, Yale Univ, 79-83, Mt Holyoke Col, 83-90, Sr lectr, Univ Chicago, 90-. *Awards:* Fel Mus Prof, Nat Endowment Arts, 88; Resident Fel, Yale Ctr for British Art, 88; Trustee, Williamstown Regional Conserv Lab, 89-91 & Am Fed Arts, 97. *Mem:* Coll Art Asn; Chicago Network. *Res:* Iconology of British art. *Publ:* Auth, Berthe Morisot-The Forgotten Impressionist (video), Electronic Field Serv Productions, 89; Colin's Masaniello: Revolutionary Hero, Mt Holyoke Coll Art Mus Newsletter, 90; Vauxhall Gardens, Cambridge Guide to the Arts in England, Cambridge Univ Press, 90; Dorothea Hoffmann: Drawings, Philadelphia, 91; ed & contribr, Imagining an Irish Past: The Celtic Revival 1840-1940, Univ Chicago Press, 92; auth, The Stage Is All The World: The Theatrical Designs of Tanya Moiseiwitsch (exhib catalog), David & Alfred Smart Mus, Univ Chicago, 94

EDEN, F(LORENCE) BROWN
COLLAGE ARTIST, PAINTER
b Jericho Center, Vt, Oct 10, 1916. *Study:* Univ Fla, 53-55; Univ Mich, spec studies with Frank Cassara, 62-63. *Work:* Jacksonville Art Mus & Southern Bell Collection, Jacksonville, Fla; Fed Reserve Bank of Atlanta; Coopers and Lybrand, Jacksonville, Fla; Barnett Banks Collection, Fla. *Comn:* Collage & collage triptych Edwin & Ruth Kennedy Mus Am Art, Ohio Univ, 44; landscape watercolor pair, Touche Ross, Jacksonville; landscape watercolor, Atlantic Nat Bank, Jacksonville; collage painting, Designers Showhouse, Ponte Vedra, Fla, 44. *Exhib:* Solo exhibs, Ga Inst Technol, Atlanta, 72, Le Moyne Found Art, Tallahassee, Fla, 75, Alexander Brest Mus, Jacksonville, Fla, 69, 70, 71 & 78, Daytona Art Ctr, Daytona Beach, 80 & Gallery Contemporanea, Jacksonville, 85; Am Painters in Paris, Ctr Int Paris, France, 75; Contemp Am Paintings, Soc Four Arts, Palm Beach, Fla, 77; Nat Soc Painters in Casein & Acrylics, Nat Arts Club, NY, 80; Betty Parsons Exhib, City Hall, Naples, Fla, 80; Mus Arts & Sci, Macon, 82 & 86 & Mem Art Ctr, Atlanta, 83, Ga Nat Watercolor Exhibs IV, V & VII; Major Fla Artists, Harmon Galleries of Am Art, Sarasota, 83, 86 & 88; Audubon Artists 42nd Ann Exhib, Nat Arts Club, NY, 84; Southeastern Watercolorists, Deland Mus, Fla, 84 & 89; The Mus Collection, Jacksonville Art Mus, Fla, 85; Barnett Banks Collection, Polk Mus, Winter Haven, Fla, 86; Fla Competitive, Ctr Arts, Vero Beach, Fla, 87; Ala Nat Watercolor Exhib, 89. *Pos:* Judge of paintings, area shows; Chmn Northeast Fla Artist Group. *Teaching:* Painting, City Club, Ann Arbor, Mich, 62-63 & Art Mus, Jacksonville, Fla, 63-68; instr printmaking, Art Mus, Jacksonville, 68-69. *Awards:* First Award, Ann Juried Exhib, Fla Artist Group, 71 & 79; McDaniel Painting Award, Major Fla Artists, Harmon Galleries, 79. *Bibliog:* Elihu Edelson (auth), JU show classy and complete, Fla Times Union, 12/14/79; Rex Allyn (auth), Works by a dozen women artists, Sarasota Herald Tribune, 8/21/83; Ann Hyman (auth), Well-done exhibits can be evocative, Fla Times Union, 3/18/88. *Mem:* Audubon Artists Am; Ga Watercolor Soc; Fla Watercolor Soc; Soc Painters in Casein & Acrylics; Fla Artist Group (area chmn, 68-85). *Media:* Polymer Collage; Watercolor. *Dealer:* Hodgell Gallery 46 Palm Ave South Sarasota Fl 34236; Gallery Contemporanea 11 Aviles Street St Augustine FL 34236. *Mailing Add:* 2929 Parramore Shores Rd Tallahassee FL 32310-9473

EDEN, GLENN
DRAFTSMAN, PAINTER
b Atlanta, Ga, 1951. *Study:* DeKalb Community Col, AA, 71; Ga State Univ. *Work:* High Mus, Atlanta, Ga; Gibbes Mus, Charleston, SC; Columbia Mus, SC; Huntsville Mus, Ala; Mus Arts & Sci, Macon, Ga. *Comn:* Painting, Mariott Marquis, Atlanta, Ga, 85; drawing, Coca-Cola Co, Atlanta, Ga, 86; painting, Wilma, Atlanta, Ga, 87. *Exhib:* Wizard of Oz Drawings, Mint Mus, 76; Artists in Ga, High Mus Art, Atlanta, 81; The Human Figure, New Orleans Contemp Art Inst, La, 82; Ten Pens, Southern Arts Fedn, Atlanta, Ga, 82; Narrative Drawings, Nexus Gallery, Atlanta, 83. *Awards:* Atlanta Bureau of Cult Affairs Grant, 82; Outstanding Alumnus, Dekalb Col, 85; Artists Fel Southeastern Ctr Contemp Art, Winston-Salem, NC, 87-88. *Bibliog:* Jeff Kipnis (auth), Glenn Eden at the Gibbes, Art in Am, 81; Jeff Kipnis (auth), Profile, Art Voices, 81. *Media:* Ballpoint Pen, Prisma Color; Oil on Canvas. *Mailing Add:* 173 Middlesex Ln Marietta GA 30064-1729

EDER, JAMES ALVIN
PRINTMAKER, PAINTER
b Buffalo, NY, Jan 9, 1942. *Study:* State Univ NY, Buffalo, BS, 63; Univ Nebr, Lincoln, MS, 66; Northern Ariz Univ, Flagstaff, MA, 75. *Work:* Valley Nat Bank, Mesa, Ariz; First Interstate Bank, Honeywell Corp & Talley Industries, Phoenix, Ariz; Quanex Corp, Houston, Tex; Monoprint, Heritage Art Collection, City Tempe, 96; Nelson Art Ctr, Ariz State Univ; Hunt Inst Botanical Doc, Carnegie Mellon Univ; Sky Harbor Airport, Phoenix, Ariz; US Embassies, Moscow & Conakry & Guinea. *Comn:* Zona Mona (anamorphic mural on roof), City of Tempe, Tempe Arts Ctr, Ariz, 94. *Exhib:* Solo exhibs, Univ Ariz, Tucson, 80 & Scottsdale Community Col, Ariz, 81, Ariz State Capitol, Phoenix, 90, Sedona Arts Ctr, 91, Scottsdale Col, 91; Eder-Kollasch, touring southwest, 86-88; Contemp Nature (travelling), Tempe Arts Ctr, 89-90; Northern Ariz Images, Coconino Arts Ctr, Flagstaff, 90; 7th Int Exhib Botanical Art & Illustr, Hunt Inst Botanical Doc, Carnegie Mellon Univ, 92; Jurors Choice, Shemer Art Ctr, Phoenix, Ariz, 95. *Teaching:* Instr art, Evening Div, Phoenix Col, 78-81 & Scottsdale Community Col, 87-92. *Awards:* First Place Printmaking, Ariz State Fair, 76, 77 & 81; Relief Print, Selected Prize, Governors Art Awards, 96. *Bibliog:* Jim Eder: A unique western artist, Sedona Life Mag, winter 78; Mary Carroll Nelson (auth), James A Eder (profile), Art Voices, 9-10/81; Mary Carroll Nelson (auth), Jim Eder: Making woodcut prints, Am Artist, 11/81; The Geologic Art of Eder & Kollasch, Ariz Highways, 11/87. *Media:* Woodcut, Collagraph; Acrylic. *Publ:* Auth, Capturing the Realism of Rocks, Artists Mag, 3/85; A puzzling approach to printmaking, Am Artist Mag, 8/94. *Dealer:* Agnisiuh Gallery Box 910 Hillside Ctr Sedona AZ 86336

EDGE, DOUGLAS BENJAMIN
SCULPTOR, PAINTER
b Fennimore, Wis, Aug 4, 1942. *Study:* San Fernando Valley State Col, BA. *Work:* Mus Mod Art, NY; Arco, Washington, DC; Security Bank, Los Angeles; Patrick Lannon Mus, Fla. *Comn:* Constructionist Pagoda, Imperial Bank, Costa Mesa, Calif, 79. *Exhib:* West Coast Now, Seattle Art Mus, 68; Violence in Am Art, Mus Contemp Art, Chicago, 69; Continuing Surrealism, La Jolla Mus Art, 71; Calif Prints, Mus Mod Art, NY, 72; Separate Realities, Los Angeles Munic Art Gallery, 73; Santa Barbara Mus, 77. *Teaching:* Instr sculpture, Calif Inst Art, Valencia, 70-72; instr painting workshop, Art Ctr Sch Design, Los Angeles, 73-74; lectr sculpture & drawing, Univ Calif, Santa Barbara, 75-76. *Awards:* Cassandra Found Grant, 70. *Bibliog:* Thomas Garver (auth), rev, 10/69 & Peter Plagens (auth), rev, 11/73, Artforum; Milinda Terbell (auth), Art News, 10/73. *Mailing Add:* 237 Bernard Ave Venice CA 90291-2704

EDGERTON, DEBRA
PAINTER, EDUCATOR
b Junction City, Kans, Mar 15, 1958. *Study:* Am Acad Art, 79; Univ Kans, BFA, 81; Vt Col, 2001; Vt Coll, MFA, 2003; San Francisco Art Inst, MFA, 2005. *Work:* Kans Gas and Electric, Wichita; Northern Ariz Univ, Flagstaff. *Comn:* Great Kings and Queens of Africa, Anheuser Bush 84 Worlds Fair, New Orleans, La, 84. *Exhib:* Impressions of China, Old Main Mus, Flagstaff, Ariz, 95; Adirondacks Nat Exhib Am Watercolors, Old Forge, NY, 96; State of the Art Int Invitational, Parkland Coll, Ill, 97; Interpreting Surroundings: Works by 4 African Am Artist, Parkland, Ill, 98; Midwest Watercolor Soc 20th Ann Nat Exhib, 99; Allied Artista Am Juried Exhib, NY, 99; Reel Sisters of the Diaspora Film Festival, Brooklyn, NY, 2006; Cinema Remixed & Reloaded: Black Women Artist & the Moving Image Since 1970, Spellman Coll Mus Art, Atlanta, Ga, 2007; Contemp Art Mus, Houston, Tex, 2008; NAU Mus, Flagstaff, Ariz, 2007; New Power Generation Exhib, Hampton Mus, Hampton, Va, 2008; Contemporary Forum Exhib, Phoenix Art Mus, Ariz, 2011; If I Didn't Care: Multigenerational Artists Discuss Cultural Histories, Richman Gallery, Baltimore, Md, 2009. *Pos:* Pres, Lawrence Art Guild Asn, 91-92; mayoral appointee, Lawrence Art Commn, Kans, 92-93. *Teaching:* Instr watermedia, painting, figure painting, Northern Ariz Univ, Flagstaff, 93-; instr painting, Lawrence Art Ctr, Kans, 91-; lectr, Northern Ariz Univ, 2013. *Awards:* Dolan Found scholar, 2001-03; Elizabeth Graham Found Grant, 2006; Ariz Art Comn Artist Project Grant, 2006; Ariz Art Comn Career Advan Grant, 2006; Contemp Art Forum Artist Gallery, 2010; Van Denburg grant, NAV, Flagstaff, 2012; AASCU JSI Fellowship, San Diego, Calif, 2012; PLC MicroGrant, NAU, Flagstaff, 2013; Provost award for Faculty Excellence in Global Learning, Northern Ariz Univ, Flagstaff, 2013. *Bibliog:* Erik Schutz (auth), Mastering the Moment, Topeka Capital Jour, 4/93; Brian Johnson (auth), China Inspires Art Teacher, Ariz Daily Sun, 10/93; Betsey Bruner (auth), Exploring Connections of Heritage, Home, Ariz Daily Sun, 4/2006; Penelope George (auth), Reconstructing Home, Flagstaff Live, 2/2007. *Mem:* Am Watercolor Soc; Nat Watercolor Soc; Midwest Watercolor Soc; Allied Artists Am; Transparent Watercolor Soc. *Media:* Watercolor, Oil, Video. *Publ:* Auth, article The Watercolor Page, Am Artist Mag, 91; contrib, book Transparent Watercolor Wheel, Watson-Guptill, 94; auth, article in Ariz Comn on the Arts Bull, 2006; auth, article, Art as Pedagogy for self and a Substainable World, NAU Global, 2010. *Dealer:* Arte-Misia Gallery Sedona Ariz. *Mailing Add:* 3000 W Brenda Loop Flagstaff AZ 86001

EDGREN, GARY ROBERT
PAINTER, CRAFTSMAN
b Chicago, Ill, Jan 27, 1947. *Study:* Southern Ill Univ, BA 70, MFA, 72. *Work:* State of Ill Ctr, Chicago; Byer Mus Art & Nat Hist, Evanston, Ill; Ill Art Mus, Springfield; Univ Galleries, Southern Ill Univ, Carbondale; Kemper Insurance Corp, Chicago, Ill. *Exhib:* Painting & Sculpture, mid-west fac, Univ Ill, Champaign, 76; Solo exhibs, Deson-Zaks Gallery, Chicago, 75, Krannert Art Gallery Univ Ill, 76, Zaks Gallery, Chicago, 79 & 83 & Univ Galleries Southern Ill Univ, 84; George Irwin Collection, Krannert Art Mus, 79; 29th Ill Invitational, Ill State Mus, Springfield, 79; Survey of 16 Abstract Artists, Springfield Art Asn, 84. *Pos:* Self employed artist, 72-; owner, Special Effects Painting. *Teaching:* Consult acquisition, Univ Galleries Southern Ill Univ, 74-75, vis artist painting & drawing, 77, instr, 77-78. *Media:* All. *Dealer:* Sonia Zaks-Zaks Gallery 620 N Michigan Ave Chicago, IL. *Mailing Add:* 1785 Cedargrove Buncombe IL 62912

EDISON, DIANE
PAINTER, EDUCATOR
b Piscataway, NJ, Sept 3, 1949. *Study:* Sch Visual Arts, NY, BFA, 76; Skowhegan Sch Painting & Sculpture, 84; Grad Sch Fine Arts, Univ Pa, Philadelphia, MFA, 86. *Work:* Ark Art Ctr, Little Rock; Am Embassy, Moscow; Dana Gallery, Agnes Scott Col, Decatur, Ga; Leeway Found, Philadelphia, Pa, 00. *Exhib:* Solo exhibs include Univ Ga, Athens, 94, Chattahoochee Valley Art Mus, Lagrange, Ga, 95, Nexus Contemp Art Ctr, Atlanta, 97, George Adams Gallery, 97 & Macon Mus Arts & Sci, Ga, 98; A Second Look, George Adams Gallery, NYC, 2000, 2003; Diane Edison: Drawings, Lamar Dodd Sch Art, Univ Ga, Athens, 2002, George Adams Gallery, NY, 2007; group exhibs include SAF/Nat Endowment Arts Fel Exhib, Southeastern Ctr Contemp Art, Winston-Salem, NC, 94; Around the House, Frumbkin/Adams Gallery, NY, 94; Reaffirming the Media, Art Gallery, Univ Mo, Kansas City, 94; Figurative Drawing, Charles More Gallery, Philadelphia, 94; Frumkin/Adams Gallery, NY, 95; Portraits and Self-portraits, George Adams Gallery, 96; Large Drawings and Objects, Ark Art

Ctr, Little Rock, 96; Illumination, George Adams Gallery, 98; In Her Voice: Self Portraits by Women, Phillip & Muriel Berman Mus Art, Ursinus Col, Pa, 98-99; The Likeness of Being: Contemp Self-Portraits by 60 Women, DC Moore Gallery, NYC, 2000; About Face: The Collection of Jackye & Curtis Finch, Jr, Arkansas Art Center, Little Rock, 2001; The Art of Collecting, Flint Inst Arts, Flint, Mich, 2002; Refusing to Dance Backwards, Spruill Gallery, Ga, 2005; The Figure in American Painting & Drawing 1985-2005, Ogunquit Mus Am Art, Maine, 2006. *Pos:* Lectr, Telfair Acad Arts & Sci, Savannah, 1991; assoc dir, Univ Ga, Athens, 97-. *Teaching:* Asst prof Art, Savannah Col Art & Design, 1990-1992; prof painting/drawing, Univ Ga, Athens, 92-97, assoc prof, 97-; prof Painting & Watercolor Studies Abroad Prog (Cortona, Italy), Univ Ga, fall 1993-. *Awards:* Ga Artist Grant, Ga Coun Arts, 93; Nat Endowment Arts Fel, 94; Residency Millay, Milton Avery Found, 95. *Bibliog:* Robert W Duffy (auth), Beyond the innocence, St Louis-Dispatch, 92; Townsend Wolfe (auth), National Drawing International, Ark Art Ctr, 94; Arlene Raven (auth), Diane Edison, Ark Art Ctr, 95; Edward Sozanski (auth), Viewing Women Artists Looking at Themselves, Philadelphia Inquirer, 1/1999. *Mem:* Coll Art Asn; Womens Caucus Art; Southeastern Coll Art Conf; Am Asn Univ Prof. *Media:* Acrylic, Oil. *Publ:* Kathleen Baxter (auth), Drawing Attention to Museum Collections, Am Artist, 1/2000. *Dealer:* George Adams Gallery 41 W 57th St New York NY 10019. *Mailing Add:* c/o George Adams Gallery 525 W 26th St New York NY 10001

EDLIS, STEFAN T
COLLECTOR
Pos: Pres, Apollo Plastics Corp, Chicago, currently; trustee, Mus Modern Art, New York, currently. *Awards:* Named one of Top 200 Collectors, ARTnews Mag, 2004-12. *Mem:* Whitney Mus Am Art (nat comt, currently). *Collection:* Contemporary art. *Mailing Add:* Apollo Plastics 5333 N Elton Ave Chicago IL 60630

EDMINSTON, SCOTT
DIRECTOR, EDUCATOR
Work: Dir: (plays) Brian Friel's Molly Sweeney, 1998 (Elliot Norton Award Outstanding Dir), Harold Pinter's Betrayal, 2003 (Elliot Norton Award Outstanding Prod, 2003), Jacques Brel is Alive & Well & Living in Paris, 2003. *Pos:* Dir, off of arts Brandeis Univ, 2003-; artistic assoc, Huntington Theatre Co, Boston. *Teaching:* Asst prof - dramatic lit Boston Univ Col Fine Arts, chrmn MFA Dir Pro. *Awards:* Named one of region's ten best theatre dir, Boston Herald. *Mem:* Alliance Boston Theatre Artists & Producers (pres bd, StageSource 98—). *Mailing Add:* Brandeis Univ Dir Off of Arts MS 051 Waltham MA 02454

EDMISTON, SARA JOANNE
EDUCATOR, DESIGNER
b Independence, Mo, June 21, 1935. *Study:* Univ Kans, BAE; ECarolina Univ, MA. *Work:* NC Mus Art, Raleigh; NC Nat Banks, several cities in NC; Wachovia Banks, several cities in NC; Duke Univ. *Comn:* Door knocker, NC Nat Bank, Charlotte, 74; and others. *Exhib:* NC Mus Art, Raleigh, 65-67, 71, 73 & 76; Enamels 70 Nat, Crafts Alliance, St Louis, Mo & William Rockhill Nelson Gallery Art, Kansas City, Mo, 70; Piedmont Crafts, Mint Mus Art, Charlotte, 70-73; Crafts Invitational, Jacksonville Mus, Fla, 72; Southeastern Crafts Exhib, Greenville Co Mus, SC, 74; New Directions in Fabric Design, Fine Arts Gallery, Towson State Univ, 76; and others. *Teaching:* Prof textiles & design, ECarolina Univ, 66, prof emerita. *Awards:* Purchase Award, 5th Ann Piedmont Graphics Exhib, Mint Mus Art, 69; Purchase Award, 39th Ann NC Artists Exhib, NC Art Soc, 76. *Mem:* Surface Design Asn (treas & nat mem chmn, 76-80); Am Crafts Coun; Piedmont Craftsmen Inc; Carolina Designer-Craftsmen; NC Crafts Asn (mem bd dir, 76-79). *Media:* Dye, Enamel. *Dealer:* Piedmont Craftsmen Inc Sales Gallery 936 West Fourth St Winston-Salem NC 27101

EDMONDS, TOM
MUSEUM DIRECTOR, PAINTER
b Lawrence, Kans, July 29, 1956. *Study:* Ohio State Univ, BFA, 78; Art Inst Chicago, MFA, 80; postgrad, NY Univ, 93. *Pos:* curator, Monroe Co Hist Soc, Stroudsburg, Pa, 92-93; curator, Andover Hist Soc, Andover, Mass, 93-99; exec dir, Whister House Mus Art, Lowell, Mass, 99-2000. *Bibliog:* Articles in Boston Globe and Lowell Sun, 2000. *Mem:* Northeast Mass Regional Libr Asn (bd mem, 96-2000); Am Asn Mus. *Media:* Oil. *Specialty:* co-dir, Off Broadway Coop Gallery, Lawrence, Mass. *Mailing Add:* 243 Worthen St Lowell MA 01852

EDMUNDS, ALLAN LOGAN
PRINTMAKER, ADMINISTRATOR
b Philadelphia, Pa, June 7, 1949. *Study:* Tyler Sch Art, Temple Univ, Philadelphia & Rome; also with Romas Viesulas & John Dowell, BFA & MFA, Cardiff Art Sch, Wales, UK. *Work:* Philadelphia Mus Art; Nat Collection of Fine Art, Libr of Cong; Pa Acad Fine Arts; Yale Univ; Studio Mus Harlem. *Comn:* Photosilkscreen ed, Philadelphia Mus Art, 71-72. *Exhib:* Silkscreen: History of a Medium, Philadelphia Mus Art, 71-72; Expanded Photograph, Philadelphia Civic Ctr Mus, 72; Solo exhibs, Univ Md, Baltimore, 72, Alternative Mus, NY, Klein Gallery, Univ Calif, Santa Clara, 98; Inst Contemp Art, Philadelphia, 92; Beyond Aesthetics, Alternative Mus, NY, 93. *Pos:* founder-pres, Brandywine Graphic Workshop, Inc, 72-; visual arts panelist, Ohio, Fla, Md & Pa Coun Arts, 82-91; vis artist, Bloomsburg State Col, 80-, Ariz State Univ, 92; mem adv panel, William Penn Mus Fine Arts Collection, 81; Assoc, A L Edmunds Assoc, 81. *Teaching:* Instr graphics, Haystack Mountain Sch Crafts, Maine, 74; lectr printmaking, Philadelphia Col Art, 75; art coordr, Parkway Prog Sch Dist Philadelphia, 72-. *Awards:* Visual Artist's Fel, Pa Coun, 90; Nat Endowment Arts Fel, 90; Arts Mgt Award, Drexel Univ Int Forum, 94. *Bibliog:* Choosing Mus Sci and Industry, Chicago, 86; Int Rev African Am Art Vol 7, No 4, 88; Artists Choose Artists, Contemp Art, Philadelphia, 91. *Mem:* Brandywine Workshop, Greater Philadelphia Cult Alliance; Arts & Cult Coun, Greater Philadelphia CofC; Mayor's Cult Adv Coun; Pa Acad Fine Art. *Media:* Lithography, Serigraphy. *Res:* Continuous research project on the history of the Black graphic artist; collection of slides, manuscripts and original works as well as developing video documentation. *Publ:* Family Album Series, Univ Calif, Santa Cruz, 98. *Dealer:* Hahn Gallery 8439 Germantown Ave Philadelphia PA 19118. *Mailing Add:* 1520 Kater St Philadelphia PA 19146

EDOUARD, PIERRE
PAINTER, SCULPTOR
b Oct 28, 1959; French citizen. *Study:* Ecole nationale superieur des Arts decoratif, Dipl, 81; study painting with Zao Wouki. *Exhib:* Musee des arts Decoratif, Paris, France, 84; Autoportraits, Musee de la Seita, Paris, France, 86; Galerie Claude Bernard, 94 & 2000; Galerie Ditesheim, 2011. *Awards:* Pride dessin des Salon de Montrouge, 80; Prie du Prince Rainier du Monacó, 2004; elu Membre de e Institute en toute que sculptur, 2008. *Bibliog:* Pierre Cabanne (auth), Gravite et intersite, Elle, 3/89; Jean Marie Tasset (auth), Le style des cimes, Le Figaro, 3/89. *Media:* Oil, Egg Tempera, Bronze, Charcoal. *Mailing Add:* c/o Claude Bernard 7 Rue des Beaux Arts Paris 75006 France

EDSON, GARY F
MUSEOLOGIST, MUSEUM DIRECTOR
b Bethany, Mo, Sept 5, 1937. *Study:* Kansas City Art Inst, BFA (sculpture), 60; Newcomb Art Sch, Tulane Univ, MFA (ceramics), 62. *Work:* Stifel Fine Arts Ctr, Wheeling, WVa; WVa Univ, Morgantown; Newcomb Art Sch, Tulane Univ, New Orleans. *Comn:* Ceramic art, Ft Benjamin Harrison Hosp, Indianapolis, 73; sculpture, Robert Borns Assocs, Indianapolis, 74; ceramic art, Fairmont Hotel, New Orleans, 74; sculpture, Pickwick Place Development, Indianapolis, 75; ceramic art, Mignon Faget Ltd, New Orleans, 75-78. *Exhib:* Crosscurrents, Stifel Fine Arts Ctr, Wheeling, WVa, 83; Texas Tech Univ Mus, Lubbock, 85; Univ North Dakota, Grand Fork, 85; Gallery Eighty-Six, Belfast, Maine, 85; Texas 2-D Competition, Tex A&M Univ, Coll Station, 85; Univ NMex, Albuquerque, 85; Edson, Kreneck & Murrow, Lubbock Fine Arts Ctr, Tex, 86. *Collection Arranged:* Mochaware: Indian Pottery, Gatlinburg, Tenn, 72; Mexican Market Pottery, Indianapolis, 77 & Morgantown, WVa, 81. *Pos:* Chmn, div art, WVa Univ, Morgantown, 80-84; chmn, dept art, Tex Tech Univ, Lubbock, 84-86; exec dir, the Mus Tex Tech Univ, Lubbock, 86-. *Teaching:* Prof art & ceramics, Herron Sch Art, Indianapolis, 70-80; prof art, WVa Univ, 80-84; prof art, drawing & printmaking, Tex Tech Univ, Lubbock, 84-86, prof mus sci, museology & mus admin, 86-. *Mem:* Am Asn Mus (bd mem, 93-); Int Coun Mus (bd mem, 93-); Tex Asn Mus; Art Mus Asn Am; Nat Asn Sch Art & Design (bd mem, 86-). *Publ:* Auth, Open pit firing, 72 & Silla pottery, 73, Ceramics Monthly; Mexican Market Pottery, Watson-Guptill, 79; Handbook for Museums, Routledge, 94; International Directory of Museum Training, Routledge, 95; Museum Ethics, Routledge, 97

EDWARDS, BENJAMIN
PAINTER, LITHOGRAPHER
b Iowa City, 1970. *Study:* Univ Calif, Los Angeles, BA, 1992; San Francisco Art Inst, 1992; RI Sch Design, MFA, 1997. *Exhib:* Solo exhibs include Greenberg Van Doren Gallery, NY City, 2001, 2004, 2006, Galerie Jean-Luc & Takako Richard, Paris, 2007; group exhibs include Southern Exposure Gallery, San Francisco, 1992; OK Harris, NY City, 1995; Sol Koffler Gallery, Providence, RI, 1996; Bernard Toale Gallery, Boston, 1996; RI Sch Design Mus Art, 1997; White Columns, NY City, 1998; Kohn Turner Gallery, Los Angeles, 1999; Greenberg Van Doren, NY City, 1999, 2000, 2004, 2005; Exit Art, NY City, 2000, 2001; Beth Urdang Gallery, Boston, 2000; Elias Fine Art, Allston, Mass, 2001; Howard House, Seattle, 2001; Stedelijk Mus Voor Actuel Kunst Gent, Belgium, 2001; Am Acad Arts and Letters, NY City, 2002; Busan Bienale, 2002; Norman Dubrow Biennial, Kagan Martos Gallery, NY City, 2002; Artists Space, NY City, 2002; Cranbrook Art Mus, Bloomfield Hills, Mich, 2002; Cleveland Art Mus, 2003; Sandra Gering Gallery, NY City, 2003; Chelsea Art Mus, NY City, 2004; Gorney Bravin Lee Gallery, NY City, 2004; Lehman Coll Art Gallery, Bronx, 2005; Phiilips de Pury & Company East Gallery, NY City, 2005; Richard Tuttle, NY City, 2005; Martin Gallery, Radford Univ, 2006. *Teaching:* vis artist, lectr, Columbia Univ, 2001, Univ Wis, 2002, Columbus Col Art & Design, Ohio, 2002, Yale Univ, 2003, Ga State Univ, 2005, Brigham Young Univ, 2005, Univ Wis, Madison, 2005, RI Sch Design, 2005; lectr, Columbia Univ Sch Archit, NY City, 2004, Archit Lab, Denver, 2005, Georgetown Univ, Washington DC, 2006, RI Sch Design, 2006. *Awards:* RISD/Target Emerging Artist Award, 2006. *Bibliog:* Levin, Kim, Voice choice: Benjamin Edwards, The Village Voice, 9/25/2001; Johnson, Ken, Benjamin Edwards, The NY Times, 11/19/2004; Hall, Emily (auth), Benjamin Edwards, Artforum, 2/2007; Lindquist, Greg (auth), Benjamin Edwards: We, artcritical.com, 2/2007. *Media:* Oil, Acrylic, Graphite. *Dealer:* Tandem Press 201 S Dickinson St Madison WI 53703; Greg Kucera Gallery 212 Third Ave S Seattle WA 98104-2608; Diaz Contemporary 100 Nigara St Toronto Ont Can M5V 1C5. *Mailing Add:* c/o Van Doren Waxter Gallery 23 E 73rd St New York NY 10021

EDWARDS, GARY MAXWELL
ART DEALER, WRITER
b Southampton, NY, June 11, 1934. *Study:* Tufts Univ, BA, 56. *Mem:* Asn Int Photog Art Dealers. *Media:* Vintage Photography. *Specialty:* Nineteenth century photographs. *Publ:* Contribr, Athens 1839-1900, A Photographic Record, Benaki Mus, Athens, 85; auth, W J Stillman, an American philhellene, Dialogos, Athens, 87; International Guide to 19th Century Photographers, G K Hall, Boston, 88; Early photographers of Greece in the Musée d'Orsay & BN, Hist Photog, 90. *Mailing Add:* 1711 Connecticut Ave NW Washington DC 20009

EDWARDS, JAMES F
PAINTER, EDUCATOR
b New York, NY, July 25, 1948. *Study:* Univ Calif, Santa Barbara, BA, MFA. *Work:* Everson Mus Art, Syracuse, NY; SC State Arts Collection; Am Consulate, Osaka, Japan; Am Embassy, Ahman, Jordon; IBM Corp, Gaithersburg, Md. *Comn:* Collage, Huntsville Mus Art; mural, Atlanta Festival of Art, Atlanta Legal Aid, 88; painting, Embassy Suites Corp, Deerfield, Mich. *Exhib:* Solo exhibs, Greenville Co Mus Art, SC, 76 & Everson Mus Art, Syracuse, 77; Huntsville Mus Art, Ala, 81; Southeastern Ctr Contemp Art, Winston-Salem, NC, 81; Heath Gallery, Atlanta, 85; Hodges Taylor Gallery, Charlotte, 86; Southern Exposure, The Alternative Mus, NY, 85; Portrait of the South, Palazzo Venezia, Rome; and others. *Teaching:* Prof drawing & painting, Univ SC, 72-. *Awards:* Nat Endowment Arts Fel, 74-75; Proj Grant, SC Arts Comn,

76-77; Individual Artist Fel, SC Arts Comn, 81; and others. *Bibliog:* Kenneth Friedman (auth), James Edwards video tapes, Grossmont Col, El Cajon, Calif; Jane Kessler (auth), James Edwards: Profile, Art Papers, Atlanta, 1-2/82. *Mem:* Southeastern Coll Art Asn. *Media:* Miscellaneous, Computer. *Publ:* Auth, Getting into video, Contemp Art-Southeast, 77; Art, language and criticism, Contemp Art-Southeast, Vol II, Number 4-5. *Mailing Add:* Univ SC Dept Art Columbia SC 29208

EDWARDS, JONMARC
PAINTER, CONCEPTUAL ARTIST
b Leavenworth, Kans, Mar 11, 1959. *Study:* Minneapolis Coll Art & Design, BFA, 83. *Work:* AT&T, Chicago; First Bank System, General Mills, Walker Art Ctr, Minneapolis, Minn; Consulate General of Ger, Los Angeles. *Exhib:* Consumerism & Am, Univ Art Mus, Minneapolis, Minn, 90; 42nd Ann Int Juried Exhib, San Diego Art Inst, 98. *Pos:* Gallery dir, Medium West Gallery, 84-88. *Awards:* Louis Comfort Tiffany Found Award, 87; Jerome Emerging Artist Award, Jerome Found, 88; Bush Found Artist Fel, 89-90. *Bibliog:* Ned Rifkin (auth), Jerome Group Exhibit, Jerome Found, 88; Mason Riddle (auth), Initial View, Ctr Contemp Art, 89; Susan Kandel (auth), Word painting, Los Angeles Times, 95. *Media:* Acrylic, Mixed Media. *Publ:* Contribr, Louis Comfort Tiffany Catalog, Louis Comfort Tiffany Found, 87; coauth, How we talk about abstraction, Artweek, 95. *Mailing Add:* 2337 Observatory Ave Los Angeles CA 90027

EDWARDS, SUSAN HARRIS
DIRECTOR
b Baltimore, Md, Sept 26, 1948. *Study:* Univ SC, BA, 79, MA, 83; Grad Ctr, City Univ NY, MPh, 90, PhD, 95. *Collection Arranged:* Hunter Coll Permanent Collection, 87; Systems and Abstraction, 88; NY Area MFA Exhibition, 90; Formulation & Representation, 90; Physical Relief, 91; Contemporary Icons, 92; Ben Shahn and the Task of Photog in Thirties Am, 95. *Pos:* Managing ed, Sheep Meadow Press, Riverdale, NY, 84-85; asst dept paintings & sculpture, Brooklyn Mus, NY, 82-84; cur, Hunter Coll, City Univ NY, 87-98; dir, Katanah Mus Art, 98-2004; exec dir & ceo, First Ctr Visusal Arts, Nashville, Tenn, 2004-. *Teaching:* Instr art hist, Newberry Coll, SC, 81; instr, Queens Coll, City Univ NY, 86-89 & NY Univ, 90-98; adj assoc prof, Vanderbilt Univ, 2006-. *Bibliog:* Joshua Dector (auth), Systems & Abstraction, Arts Mag, 3/89; Roger, Denson (auth), A Feminism without Men, Tema Celeste 4-5/92. *Mem:* AAMD; AAM; CAA. *Publ:* Auth, A Debate on Abstraction, 88, Formulation and Representation in Recent Abstract Art, 90, Hunter Coll; Ben Shahn: Focus on America, 95; Horses, la Focus, In: Horse Tales, American Images & Icons 1800-2000, Taonah Mus of Art, 2001; Hiraki Sawa, Going Places Sitting Down, Frist Ctr, Nashville, 2007; The Anxiety of Influence: American Painting 1950-75, Vanderbilt Univ Press, Nashville, 2008; Oliver Herring: Common Threads (FCVA), 2009. *Mailing Add:* 401 Bowling Ave # 23 Nashville TN 37205

EDWARDS-TUCKER, YVONNE LEATRICE
CERAMIST, EDUCATOR
b Chicago, Ill, Jan 19, 1941. *Study:* Univ Ill, Urbana, BFA (art educ; summa cum laude), 62; Univ Calif, Los Angeles, 62-64; Otis Art Inst, BFA, MFA, 68; studied with Charles White, Michael Frimkess & Helen Watson; numerous other workshops. *Work:* Fisk Univ, Nashville, Tenn; Otis Art Inst; Hampton Univ, Va; Syracuse Univ, NY; Fla A&M Univ, Tallahassee. *Exhib:* Contemp African-Am Crafts, Brooks Mem Art Mus, 79; Power Objects: Ancient & to the Future, Howard Univ Art Gallery, 80; Dimensions & Directions: Black Artists of the South, Miss Art Mus, 80; Forever Free: Art by African-Am Women, 1862-1980, Joslyn Art Mus, Montgomery Mus Fine Arts, Indianapolis Mus, & Univ Md, 81-82; Magic of Clay, Calif Mus Afro-Am Hist & Cult, Los Angeles, 82; Traditional Crafts, Mus Nat Ctr Afro-Am Artists, Boston, 82; Surrealism and the Afro-Am Artist, Evans-Tibbs collection, Washington, DC, 83; Voices: Afro-American Ceramics, Syracuse Univ, 88; JB Speed Mus, Louisville, Ky, 88; Ceramic Traditions, NCECA, Contemp Art Ctr, Kansas City, Mo, 89; African Images in Am Craft, Folk Art Ctr, Asheville, NC, traveling, 92-93. *Collection Arranged:* Florida Craftsmen, 73, Impact 79: Afro-Am Women Artists, 79 & Tallahassee Tribute, 81, Fla A&M Univ Art Gallery; Harambee at Lemoyne, 85; Harambee Invitational II, 86; Fla A&M Univ Centennial Art Exhib, 87; Celebration of African-Am Art. *Teaching:* Asst prof ceramics & drawing, Miami-Dade Community Col, 68-73; adj prof art, Miami Exten, Shaw Univ, 72-74; prof ceramics & art, Fla A&M Univ, 73-. *Awards:* Award Ceramic Sculpture, Fiftieth Anniversary Exhib, Otis Art Inst, 69; Best in Show, Clay Works 72, Grove House Gallery, Miami, 72; Purchase Award, Syracuse Univ Ceramics Collection, New York, 87. *Bibliog:* Ellen A Ashdown (auth), Afro-Raku: The ceramics of Yvonne & Curtis Tucker, Black Art Int Quart, winter 79 & The ceramics of Yvonne & Curtis Tucker, Art-Craft, 2-3/80; Arna Bontemps (ed), African-American Art History: The Feminine Dimension, In: Forever Free, Stephen Sun Inc. *Mem:* Nat Conf Artists; Nat Conf Educ Ceramic Arts; founding mem Harambee Arts Coun; Fla Folk Life Coun; Fla Craftsmen. *Media:* Clay, Raku Clay, Mixed Media. *Res:* African and Afro-American folklore; Black Art of the South; Black aesthetics; folk art. *Publ:* Illusr, Le theme de la violence, African Arts, Arts d'Afrique, Vol 1, No 1, 67; auth, African, Indian & Oriental Influences in the Aesthetics of Two Contemporary Craftspeople: First National African-American Crafts Conference: Shelby State Community Col, 80; John T Scott & the black aesthetic, Int Review African Am Art, Vol 6, No 2, 85; Afro-Raku Ceramics & Y&C Tucker, NCECA J, Vol 10, 51-54, 89-90. *Dealer:* Gallery Antigua 5138 Biscayne Blvd Miami FL 33134. *Mailing Add:* 3007 Kevin St Tallahassee FL 32301-6915

EFRAT, GILAD
PAINTER
b Israel, 1969. *Study:* Bezalel Acad Art & Design, Jerusalem, BFA, 1995, post-grad prog, 1998; Cooper Union, New York, 1995; Hebrew Univ, MFA, 2003. *Exhib:* Solo exibs include Morasha Art Ctr Gallery, Jerusalem, 1995, Hakibbutz Gallery, Tel Aviv, 1997, North Gallery, Copenhagen, 1998, Herzliya Mus Art, 1998, Noga Gallery Contemp Art, Tel Aviv, 2000, 2002, 2004, Oredaria Gallery Contemp Art, Rome, 2004; group exhibs include Arad Mus Art, Israel, 2000; Focus on Painting, Haifa Mus Art, Israel, 2002; Landscapes, Israel Mus, Jerusalem, 2002; Time Capsule, Art in General, New York, 2003; Out of Conflict, Leroy Neiman Gallery, Columbia Univ, New York, 2004; Artists in Residence, Glassell Sch Art, Mus Fine Arts, Houston, 2005 & 2006. *Pos:* Cur Fine Art Dept Gallery, Bezalel Acad Art & Design, Jerusalem, 1999-02. *Teaching:* Lectr fine arts, Bezalel Acad Art & Design, Jerusalem, 1997-2003; lectr fashion design, Shenkar Coll, Ramat-Gan, Israel, 1998-2004; lectr, Glasses Sch Art, Mus Fine Arts, Houston, 2004-06; lectr visual arts, Rice Univ, Houston, 2005. *Awards:* Pollock-Krasner Found Grant, 2007. *Mailing Add:* Inman Gallery 3901 Main St Houston TX 77002

EGAN, LAURY AGNES
PHOTOGRAPHER, INSTRUCTOR
b Long Branch, NJ, June 29, 1950. *Study:* Carnegie Mellon Univ, BFA, 1972; Color Photog Workshop, Sam Abell, Princeton, NJ. *Work:* Montclair Art Mus (permanent collection), Montclair, NJ; Metropolitan Opera Archives, NY; Graphic Arts Collection, Princeton Univ, Princeton, NJ; Southern Methodist Univ Archives, Dallas, Tex; Opera co of Philadelphia Archives, Philadelphia, Pa; Philip Glass Archives, The Voyage, world premiere opera, NY; Monmouth Co Hist Asn, Freehold, NJ. *Comn:* Photos of Southern Methodist Univ, SMU Press, 91. *Exhib:* Views of Princeton, Graphic Arts/Rare Books, Princeton Univ, Princeton, NJ, 84; Mercer Co Photographic Show, Trenton State Coll Mus, Trenton, NJ, 85-88; Three-Person Show, Stuart Co Day Sch, Princeton, NJ, 86; Greek Images, Alkit Digital Collection Inc, NY, 2000; Three-Person Show, Williams Gallery (representation), Princeton, NJ, 2001-2006; The Frederick Gallery (multiple shows), Allenhurst, NJ, 2004-2008; The Guild of Creative Art, Shrewsbury, NJ, 2008, 2009; McKay Imaging, Red Bank, NJ, 2009; Sandy Hook Lighthouse, 2009, 2010; Frame to Please, 2011; Two Woman Show, Middletown Art Ctr, 2011. *Pos:* Book designer/photo illusr, Princeton Univ Press, Princeton, NJ, 72-85 & Laury A Egan Design & Photog (various addresses), 84-2011; freelance photogr, Opera Company of Philadelphia & all Lincoln Center Orgns, 91-99. *Teaching:* Guild of Creative Art, Shrewsbury, NJ, 99; instr, Brookdale Community Coll, Lincroft, NJ, 2000-2006; instr/private lectr photog, Highlands, NJ (private assignments & portfolio reviews), regional & int (Venice) workshops, 99-2011. *Awards:* Guild of Creative Art, ann photo, 83-2006; Purchase Award, Mercer Co Photog Show, Mercer Co, 86-1987; best in show, Eyesights Show, Guild of Creative Art, Shrewsbury, NJ, 2009; Hon Men, B&W, 2010; Hon men, Juried Show, Guild of Creative Art, Shrewsbury, NJ, 2009. *Mem:* Guild Creative Art, Shrewsbury, NJ (pres, bd dir, 2010). *Media:* Photography, Fine Arts. *Interests:* Writing, Poetry. *Publ:* Illusr, approx 35 book jackets/covers for 20+ univ presses, Ohio, Princeton, Johns Hopkins, 77-2003; particpating illusr, Princeton Reflections, Princeton Univ Press, 90; participating illusr & designer, SMU Reflections, SMU Press, 91; illusr brochures & publicity, Opera Company of Philadelphia, Lincoln Center Orgns, 92-2000; illusr & solo photog, Wines & Wineries of the Hudson River Valley, Countryman Press, 93; illusr, The Centrifugal Eye, 2008-11; illusr, Sea Stories, 2008-9; auth, Snow, Shadows, a Stranger (poetry), 2009; auth, Beneath the Lion's Paw, Foot Hills Pub, 2011; auth, Fog and Other Stories, Stone Garden, 5/2012; auth, Jenny Kid (novel), Vagabondage Press, 9/2012; auth, The Sea & Beyond (poetry), FootHills, 2013; The Outcast Oracle (novel), Humanist Press, 2013. *Dealer:* Guild of Creative Art 620 Broad St Shrewsbury NJ 07702. *Mailing Add:* 8 Mountain St Highlands NJ 07732

EGELI, CEDRIC BALDWIN
PAINTER, INSTRUCTOR
b Shady Side, Md, Aug 10, 1936. *Study:* Principia Col, AA, 55; studied with Bjorn Egeli, 55-84; Corcoran Sch Art with Edmund Arden, 56; Art Students League, New York with Sidney Dickenson, Frank Mason & Frank Reilly, 57-60; Cape Sch with Henry Hensche, summers 78-87. *Work:* Pentagon, Alexandria, Va; Johns Hopkins Hosp, Baltimore, Md; State Capitol, Annapolis, Md; US Dist Court, Washington. *Comn:* Portrait, Arleigh Burke, Am Ordinance Asn, Washington, 67; portrait, Stanfield Turner, CIA, Washington, 79; portrait, Jackie Presser, Teamsters Union, Washington, 83; portrait, Morris Abrahm, Brandeis Univ, Boston, 84; portrait, H Keith Brody, Duke Univ, Durham, NC, 90. *Exhib:* Nat Portrait Sems, NY, Washington, DC & Chicago hotels, 80-83; Egeli Family Exhib, Md Life Bldg, Baltimore, 86; Wohlfarth Galleries, 97-2005, yr show. *Pos:* Pres, Md Portrait Soc, 83-86 & 90-92; Coun Leading Am Portrait Painters, 96. *Teaching:* Portrait painting & figure drawing, Egeli Studios Fall Session, 79-2005; outdoor portrait painting, Cape Sch Art, Provincetown, Mass, summers, 89-2002; Honorary Portrait Instr Nat Portrait Soc, Chicago, 2000. *Awards:* Best Show, Grand Prize, Nat Portrait Sem, John Howard Sanden, 79; Gold Medal for Oil, 80 & Grumbacher Award, 81, Am Artists Prof League; Annie Award, Anne Arundel Co Cult Award, 2001. *Bibliog:* Papperfuse (auth), History of Maryland, State of Md, 78; Steven Doherty (auth), Artists & sons, Am Artist, 88; Portraits as Art, Dossier, 89. *Mem:* Md Portrait Soc (pres, 84-86 & 90-92); Am Artists Prof League; Art Students League; Charcoal Club, Baltimore; Beachcomers Club, Provincetown, Mass. *Media:* Oil. *Specialty:* Portrait Painters of Am in Birmingham, Ala; impressionistic (outdoor), Wohlfarth Gallerie Portraits. *Interests:* Figure & Landscape. *Publ:* Auth, Impressionist Outdoor Painting, 95. *Dealer:* Wohlfarth Gallery 3418 Ninth St NE Washington DC 20017. *Mailing Add:* 111 Fiddlers Hills Rd Edgewater MD 21037

EGELI, PETER EVEN
PAINTER, ILLUSTRATOR
b Miami, Fla, Apr 19, 1934. *Study:* Corcoran Sch Art; Md Inst, BFA; Art Students League; George Washington Univ; 3 yrs study with Jacques Maroger. *Work:* US Dept Agriculture; US State Dept; US District Court, Washington; Md State Capitol; US Navy Dept; US Dept Energy; Embassy of USA, London; Colonial Williamsburg Found; plus numerous other collections. *Comn:* Portrait of Judge Robert Bork, US District Ct, 95; portrait of Richard Cheney, US Dept Defense, 95; portrait of William Richardson, Johns Hopkins Univ, 96; portrait of Charles Corry, 96; portrait of Daniel Nathans, Johns Hopkins Univ, 96; portrait of Lloyd Bentsen, US Dept Treas, 97; portrait Donald Coffey, Patrick Walsh, Johns Hopkins Hosp, 99; Royal Norwegian

Embassy, DC, 01; Whitten Peters, Sec Air Force, 2001; William Cohen, Sec Defense, 2002; Lawrence Silberman, US Court Appeals, Washington, DC, 2003; Jacob Handlesman, Johns Hopkins Hosp, 2004; John Jumper, USAF, 2005; portrait, Gen Michael Hagee, USMC, 2006; portrait, Bishop Michael Bransfield, WVa, 2006; Sidney Kimmel, Johns Hopkins Hosp; Dr & Mrs David Roselle, Univ Del, 2008; Raymond A Mason, Johns Hopkins Univ, 2008; Dr Martin Abelhoff, Johns Hopkins Hosp; Thomas Usher, USX, 2008; Michael Wynne, Secy USAF, 2008; Gen Michael Moseley, USAF, 2008; Peter Pace, USMC, CJCS, 2008; portrait of Dr William Brody, JHU, 2008; portrait of Adm Michael Mullen, CNO, 2009; Dr Paul N Manson, JHH; Judge Judi-Peter Messite, District Ct, Md, 2009; Dr David Ramsay Univ Md, 2010; Dr Margaret Jane O'Brien, St Mary's Coll Md, 2010; Tom McLeay, Nat Life Ins; Admiral Gary Roughead, USN; Judge Raymond Randolf, US Court of Appeals; J Richard Thomas Jr; Maryland Club; Hon Michael B Donley, Sec USAF JM Wilson, Elkridge Club, Dr Harold Fox, JHH; Dr. David M. Paige, JHH, Dr. Paul M. Colombani, JHH. *Exhib:* Mystic Int Marine Art Shows, Mystic, Conn, 81-84; Mariners Mus, Newport News, Va, 85; Md Hist Soc, Am Soc Marine Artists, 89; Mystic Seaport Schaefer Gallery, Am Soc Marine Artists, 92; solo exhibs incl Md Fedn Art, Annapolis, 72, Grand Gallery, Wilmington, Del, 78, South Street Seaport, NY, 80; Cummer Mus & Gardens, Jacksonville, Fla, 97; Grand Central Gallery, NY, 80; Md Hist Soc, Baltimore, 88; Frye Mus, Seattle, Wash, 97; Cape Mus Fin Arts, Dennis, Ma; Del Art Mus, Downtown Gallery, Wilmington, Del, 01; Vero Beach, Mus Art, Vero Beach, Fla, 2004; Chase Ctr on the Riverfront, 2008; Cult Ctr, Cape Cod, Mass, 2008; Maine Maritime Mus, 2008; Chesapeake Bay Maritime Mus, St Michaels, Md, 2008; Noyes Mus Art, Oceanville, NJ, 2008-2009; Buffalo Naval park Mus, 2010; Hagerstown, Md Mus Fine Arts, 2010; Mus Am Art, Dover, Dela, 2010; Wis Maritime Mus, 2010; Minn Marine Art Mus, 2010; Cornell Mus Art and Culture, 2011-12; Mobile Mus Art, 2012; Art Mus S Tex, 2012; Mus Southwest Tex, 2012; Mus Southeast Tex, 2012; Coos Art Mus, Ore, 2013; Minn Mus Art, 2013; Lake Champlain Maritime Mus, 2013, Conn River Mus, 2013, Detroit Public Library, 2013, Flag House, 2013, Baltimore Nature/Nurture Exhib (with daughter Lisa Egeli), Maryland Hall of the Creative Arts, Annapolis, 2015. *Pos:* Illusr, Marine Corps Inst, Washington, 53-56; pres, Am Soc Marine Artists, 86-89, fel, 95; pvt critiques, 77-, pvt classes 67-77. *Teaching:* Instr painting, St Mary's Col of Md, 61-67; lectr, NC Ctr Advan Teaching, Portraits & Profiles, 92. *Awards:* Best of Show, Mystic Int Marine Art Show, 81; Iron Man Award, Am Soc Marine Artists, 02. *Bibliog:* Ann Powell (auth), Artists Home on the St Mary's River, Mid-Atlantic Country Mag, 6/88; Amiad J Finkel (auth), Captured on Canvas, Chief Exec, Nov/Dec 88; Geoffrey Loftus (auth), Your Best Shot, For a Really Lasting Impression Across the Board, 10/94; Peter J Wrike (auth), Westbank, Egeli and Art, Pleasant Living, 10/96; Rachel Rubin Wolf (auth) Painting Ships, Shores and the Sea, North Light Books, 97; plus others. *Mem:* Am Soc Marine Artists (pres, 86-89, fel, 95). *Media:* Oil, Pastel, Watercolor, Charcoal. *Res:* 17th century English ships, 19th and early 20th century Chesapeake Bay craft. *Specialty:* Maritime Art. *Interests:* Sailing, history, antiques. *Publ:* Auth/Illusr of seven prints of maritime subjects; Bjorn Egeli: A Life in Images, 2014. *Dealer:* Allen David Gallery, Boothbay Harbor, ME. *Mailing Add:* 47270 W St Mary's Manor Rd Drayden MD 20630

EGER, MARILYN RAE
PAINTER, EDUCATOR
b Offett AFB, Nebr, Jan 2, 1953. *Study:* Chapman Coll, Single Subject Teaching Credential (art), 90; Calif State Univ, Stanislaus, BA (art), 87; Kansas City Art Inst, 78-80; MFA, Acad Art Univ, San Francisco, Calif, 2006-2013. *Work:* Kaiser Permanente, Stockton & Modesto, Calif; Gulf Oil Chemicals, Pittsburg, Kans; KCRA Channel 3, Sacramento, Calif; Dragonlady Gallery; UC Davis Med Ctr, Sacramento, Calif; Lodi Mem Hosp, Lodi, Calif. *Comn:* Wine Country (oil painting), comn by Susan Mitchel, Stockton, Calif, 94; Elk Creek Spring (oil painting), comn by Hazel Cottrel, Lodi, Calif, 94; The Fox Theater & The Buena Vista, comn by Diane Dyer, 2007-2008; 21 pieces, Lodi Meml Hosp. *Exhib:* Realism '93, 5th Ann Exhib, Parkersburg, WVa, 93; SAL Ann, Haggin Mus, Stockton, Calif, 93; State of the Art '93, Woburn, Mass, 93; Nat League Am Pen Women, Redwood City, Calif, 93; 98th Ann, Catharine Lorillard Wolfe, New York, 94; Calif State Fair, 2006. *Pos:* Gibson Greetings Inc, Cincinnati, Ohio, 92-96. *Teaching:* Advanced placement art, advanced ceramics & introd to art, Bear Creek High Sch, 90-, art dept head, 2009-. *Awards:* Mellon Grant, Nat Coll Bd, 94; Awards of Merit, Calif State Fair, 2006; Award of Excellence, Calif State Fair, 2007. *Bibliog:* Les Krantz (auth), Calif Art Review, 89; Brian Gold (auth), Art is life for Marilyn Eger, Lodi News-Sentinel The Entertainer, 9/30/94; Greg Schaber (auth), Playing your cards right, Artist Mag, 2/95; Tricia Tomiyoshi (auth), A Life in Art, Lodi News-Sentinel Lodi Living, 10/1/2005. *Mem:* Calif Art Educators Asn; Lodi Art Center; Stockton Art League; Pastel Soc West Coast; Am Pastel Soc. *Media:* Oil, Acrylic, Pastels & Miscellaneous Media. *Interests:* Antique art glass, French cameo glass, tiffany & antique lamps, grape & olive agriculture. *Collection:* High-end antique & contemporary art glass. *Dealer:* Knowlton Gallery 115 S School St #14 Lodi CA 95240; Gallery 10 SutterCreek Ca 95685. *Mailing Add:* 1295 E Peltier Rd Acampo CA 95220

EGGLESTON, WILLIAM
PHOTOGRAPHER
b Memphis, Tenn, July 27, 1939. *Study:* Vanderbilt Univ; Delta State Col; Univ Miss. *Work:* The Streets are Clean on Jupiter, 1980; English Rose, 1988. *Comn:* Election Eve (photograph series), Rolling Stone Magazine, 1976; Gulf States (photograph series), AT&T, 1978; The Louisiana Project, 1980; Egypt (photograph series), Memphis Brooks Mus Art, 1986. *Exhib:* Solo exhibs include The Color Tradition, J Paul Getty Mus, Los Angeles, 199, Michael Hue-Williams, London, 2000, Thomas Zander, Koln, Switzerland, 2001, Xavier Hufkens Gallery, 2001, Hayward Gallery, London, 2001, Cheim and Read Gallery, NY, 2001, PreColor The Black and White Photographs, 2004, Nightclub Portraits, 2006, Galleri Riis, Oslo, Norway, 2002, Yancey Richardson Gallery, NY, 2002, Documenta XI, Kassel, Germany, 2002, Galeri Monika Spruth, Cologne, Germany, 2002, The Dallas Mus Art, 2003, Louisiana Mus Modern Art, Copenhagen, Denmark, 2002, Mus Ludwig, Germany, 2002, Victoria Miro Gallery, London, 2004, Galerie du Jour, Pairs, 2006; group exhibs include The American Century Part II, Whitney Mus Am Art, NY, 1999, American Pictures, 2005, Full House: Views of the Whitney's Collection at 75, 2006; The American Century, The Final Victory, Part III, James Danziger Gallery, NY, 1999; Summertime, Fay Gold Gallery, Atlanta, Ga, 1999; 25 Photographers 25 Years, Carol Ehlers Gallery, 2000; How you look at it - Photographs of the 20th Century, Sprengel Mus, Hannove, 2000; Open City: Street Photographs since 1950, Mus Modern Art, Oxford, 2001; Settings & Players: Theatrical Ambiguity in American Photography, White Cube, London, 2001; The Alchemy of Light, Cumberland Gallery, Nashville, 2001; Documenta XI, Kassel, Germany, 2002; Cruel & Tender, Tate Modern, 2003; In America, Sutton Lane, London, 2004; Colour after Kline, Barbican Art Gallery, London, 2005; Photographs of Las Pozas: The Fantastical Garden of Edward James in Xilitla Mexico, Texas Gallery, Houston, 2006. *Teaching:* Lecturer visual and environmental studies, The Carpenter Ctr, Harvard Univ, 1974; researcher in color video, Mass Inst Tech, 1978. *Awards:* Guggenheim Fellowship, 1974; Nat Endowment for Arts Photographer's Fellowship, 1975, 1978; One of 54 Master Photographers of 1960-1979 Award, Photographic Soc Japan, 1989; Distinguished Achievement Award, Univ Memphis, 1996; Getty Images Lifetime Achievement Award, Infinity Awards, Int Ctr Photography, 2004; Photoespana Award, Madrid, 2004. *Publ:* Auth, Election Eve, Caldecot Chub, 1977; Morals of Vision, Caldecot Chubb, 1978; Flowers, Caldecot Chubb, 1978; Wedgewood Blue, Caldecot Chubb, 1979. *Mailing Add:* Cheim and Read Gallery 547 W 25th St New York NY 10001

EGLESTON, TRUMAN G
PAINTER
b Westfield, Mass, Oct 14, 1931. *Study:* Mass Coll Art, BFA, 58; Calif Coll Arts & Crafts, MFA, 59. *Work:* Mus Fine Arts & Wellington Collection, Boston; Framingham State Col, Mass; Salem State Col. *Exhib:* Painting & Sculpture, 58 & Drawing, 59, San Francisco Mus Fine Arts; Boston Arts Festival, Boston Common, 64; Boston Now, Inst Contemp Art, 83; Solo exhib, Ann Plumb Gallery, 89; 3-man exhib, Space Attitudes, Holly Solomon Gallery, 91. *Teaching:* Asst prof drawing & painting, State Univ NY, Fredonia, 60-63; prof, Boston State Col, 64-82 & Univ Mass, Boston, 82-87. *Bibliog:* Erik Saxon (auth), Truman Egleston at Ann Plumb, Art in Am, 4/90; Rick Kreiner (auth), Points of Contact, Metroland Mag, 4/94; Light, Geometry and Color, a conversation with the Artist, Home & Style Mag, 98. *Media:* Oil. *Specialty:* 5 Points.com, Art&Sciencewebsite-includesimages (digital exhib) Plus Conversation. *Collection:* BASS MANOR MUS-Malth, NY; Private Mus Dedicated to my Art 1970's Collection, and 1990 Collection. *Mailing Add:* 3044 Rte 9 East Chatham NY 12060

EGUCHI, YASU
PAINTER
b Japan, Nov 30, 1938. *Study:* Horie Art Acad, Japan, 58-65. *Work:* Frye Art Mus, Seattle; Heidenheim, Fed Repub Ger; Giengen, Fed Repub Ger; Am Embassy, Paris; and others. *Comn:* Paintings & relief, Sandpiper Golf Course, Santa Barbara, Calif, 72; painting, Deer Valley, Park City, Utah, 81; collage, Eye Bank Sight Restoration Inc, 81. *Exhib:* Austin Gallery, Scottsdale, Ariz, 68-86; Santa Barbara Mus Art, 72-74 & 85; Frye Mus, Seattle, Wash, 74, 84 & 98; Hammer Galleries, New York, 77, 79, 81 & 93; City of Heidenheim, Fed Repub Ger, 80 & Ger, 2000; Everson Mus Art, Syracuse, NY, 80; Nat Acad Design, New York, 80-87; Artique Ltd, Anchorage, Alaska, 81-2006; Forest Lawn Mus, 2006; and many others. *Awards:* Artist of the Yr Award, Santa Barbara Arts Coun, 79; Honorary City Award, Heidenheim, Fed Repub Ger, 80; Adolph & Clara Obrig Prize, Nat Acad Design, 83; The Adolph and Clara Obrig prize, 83 & Cert of Merit, 85 & 87, Nat Acad Design. *Bibliog:* America's sunset coast, Nat Geographic, 78; article, Arts Mag, 78; article, Santa Barbara Mag, 78; article, American Artist, 80. *Mem:* Nat Acad. *Media:* Watercolor, Oil. *Publ:* Auth, Der Brenz Entlang, City of Heidenheim and Austin Gallery, 80; Yasu Eguchi, Kunsmuseum Heidenheim, 2000; contribr to J's in field. *Mailing Add:* PO Box 30206 Santa Barbara CA 93130

EHRENKRANZ, JOEL S & ANNE
COLLECTOR
b Newark, NJ, Mar 25, 1935. *Study:* Univ Pa, BS, 56, MBA, 57; NY Univ, LLB, 61, LLM, 64. *Pos:* founding partner, Ehrenkranz & Ehrenkranz, Atty at Law, 62-, Bylthedale Children's Hosp (trustee & treas, 66-74), Fedn Jewish Philanthropies (trustee & mem distrib comt, 79-83), Whitney Mus Am Art (trustee, 73-10, pres 98-02, hon trustee, 2011-); trustee NYU Law Sch, 92-, chmn inv comt, 2003-2005, grad be, Wharton Sch Univ, Pa, 85-2004, Archives Am Art (trustee, 73-92, pres, 84-86, trustee, vchmn, mem exec comt, Mt Sinai Med Ctr, NY, 87-, trustee, NYU, 98-10, 2003-; bd overseas, Calif Inst Arts, 2001-2005, trustee, Lincoln Ctr Performing Arts, 2004-, trustee, Mus Modern Art, 2009-, mem, Coun Foreign Rels. *Awards:* Named one of Top 200 Collectors, ARTnews Mag, 2004. *Mem:* Century Club (White Plains, NY). *Collection:* Contemporary art. *Mailing Add:* 375 Park Ave New York NY 10152

EHRLICH, GEORGE
HISTORIAN
b Chicago, Ill, Jan 28, 1925. *Study:* Univ Ill-Urbana, BS, 49, MFA, 51, PhD, 60. *Pos:* Chmn dept art & art hist, Univ Mo-Kansas City, 64-75. *Teaching:* Prof art hist, Univ Mo-Kansas City, 54-92. *Mem:* Hon mem Inst Architects, Kansas City; Soc Archit Historians (pres, Mo Valley chap, 71 & 72). *Res:* Architectural history of Kansas City, Missouri; interrelationship of art to science and technology. *Publ:* Auth, Kansas City, Missouri: An Architectural History, 1826-1990, Univ Mo Press, rev ed, 92; Partnership practice & the professionalization of architecture in Kansas City, Mo, Mo Hist Rev, 7/80; The Bank of Commerce by Asa Beebe Cross: A building of the latest architecture, J Soc Archit Historians, 5/84; The 1807 Plan for an illustrated edition of the Lewis & Clark expedition, The Pa Mag Hist & Biog, 1/85; coauth (with Sherry Piland), The Architectural Career of Nelle Peters, Mo Hist Rev, 10/89; coauth, Guide to Kansas Architecture, 96. *Mailing Add:* 5505 Holmes Kansas City MO 64110

EICHEL, EDWARD W
PAINTER, VIDEO ARTIST
b Brooklyn, NY, June 8, 1932. *Study:* Art Inst Chicago, BFA (G & I Brown Fel), 58; Oskar Kokoschka Acad, Salzburg, Austria, 59; NY Univ, MA. *Hon Degrees:* Medical Univ Americas, LHD. *Work:* Lyman Allyn Mus, New London, Conn; New York Drawing Soc; Detroit Inst Art; New York Metrop Mus. *Exhib:* Young Painters Int Biennale, Mus Mod Art, Paris, France, 61; Animal Drawings from the 15th to 20th Centuries, Seiferheld Gallery, New York, 62; Drawing & Print Club Exhib, Detroit Inst Art, Mich, 66; Painters & Sculptors 27th Ann, Jersey City Mus, NJ, 68; Drawings: A Reinvestigation, Joseloff Gallery, Univ Hartford, Conn, 75; 156th Ann Exhib, Nat Acad Design, New York, 81; 43rd Anniversary Exhib, Fedn Mod Painters & Sculptors, 83; Art Bizaar, 2011; Trial of Adolf Eichmann, 50th Anniversary Exhib, Dallas Holocaust Mus, 2011. *Teaching:* Instr painting & drawing, Eastern Mich Univ, Ypsilanti, 65-66; instr drawing & illustration, Hartford Art Sch, Univ Hartford, Conn, 81-82. *Awards:* Tiffany Found Grant, 67; 27th NJ Ann Medal Merit, Syndicate Mag, 68. *Bibliog:* Sketches of a journey: Israel on the line of a pen, L'Arche, Paris, 7/61; Stuart Hilton (auth), Medal of merit in New Jersey Annual, Today's Art, 12/68. *Mem:* Fedn Mod Painters & Sculptors; Westbeth Artists Community; Am Asn Artist-Therapists. *Media:* Oil, Watercolor, Drawing (Pen & ink/Pencil). *Collection:* Metrop Mus of Art, New York; The Detroit Inst. *Publ:* Illusr, The Glass Cage: The Eichmann Trial, Hakibbutz Hameuchad, 62; Israel Sketchbook, Dvir, 62; The Beast Book, Harper & Row, 64; The Perfect Fit: How to Achieve Mutual Fulfillment and Monogamous Passion through the New Intercourse, Donald I Fine Inc, 92 & Signet, 93; videos, The Coital Alignment Technique, 2000 & Monhegan Island, 2007. *Dealer:* Allan Stone Gallery 48 E 86th Street New York NY 10028. *Mailing Add:* Studio A-1106 463 W St New York NY 10014

EICKHORST, WILLIAM SIGURD
EDUCATOR, CURATOR
b Hackensack, NJ, Mar 4, 1941. *Study:* Parsons Sch Design, BFA (advert graphics), 62; Montclair State Univ, BA (art educ), 69, MA (art educ), 70; Ball State Univ, EdD (art educ), 72; Univ Mo, Kansas City, 85; Kansas City Art Inst, 86 & 87. *Work:* Nelson-Atkins Mus Art, Kansas City, Mo; Albrecht-Kemper Art Mus, St Joseph, Mo; Portland Mus Art, Ore; Spencer Mus, Lawrence KS; Quincy Art Ctr, Quincy I. *Exhib:* Art Horizons, Art 54 Gallery, NY, 88; 41st Ann Midstates Exhib, Evansville Mus Art, 88; 19th Biennial Jury Show, Muscatine Art Ctr, 88; 18th Nat Works on Paper, Minot State Univ, 88; 3rd Ann Fla Nat, Fla State Univ, 88; Kansas 13th Nat, Fort Hays State Univ, 88; 5th Ann Maritime Nat, Univ Maine, 88; William Eickhorst, Albrecht Art Mus, 89. *Pos:* Founder & exec dir, Print Consortium, Kansas City, Mo, 83-2009; vpres, Gallery on the Square, Kansas City, Mo, 85-86. *Teaching:* Prof art educ & studio art, Frostburg State Univ, Frostburg, Md, 72-75; head, grad & undergrad art educ progs, Univ Maine, Orono, 75-78; prof art theory & criticism, Mo Western State Univ, St Joseph, Mo, 78-206. *Awards:* Juror's Award, 38th Spiva Ann Competitive, 88; Cert of Excellence, Int Art Competition, 88; Mus Purchase Award, Central States Exhib, 89; and others. *Mem:* Boston Printmakers; Nat Art Educ Asn; Mo Art Educ Asn; Mo Alliance Arts Educ (bd dir, 81-82); Soc Am Graphic Artists; and others. *Media:* Mixed Media, Photography. *Specialty:* Contemporary American graphics by established and emerging artists. *Publ:* Auth, rev of Children's Art Judgment by Gordon S Plummer, Art Teacher, 75; Art education and the seventeen years war, 77, Science explains modern art, 85, rev of Art Law by Leonard DuBoff, 85 & From abacus to art, 86, Art Educ-Nat Art Educ Asn. *Mailing Add:* 6121 NW 77th St Kansas City MO 64151

EICKMEIER, VALERIE
EDUCATOR
Study: Kansas City Art Inst, BFA; Washington Univ, MFA. *Pos:* acting dean, assoc dean, divsn coordinator 3D fine arts, faculty pres, Herron Sch Art and Design, Ind Univ-Perdue Univ, formerly, dean, 1999-. *Awards:* Nat Endowment for the Arts Special Project Grants; Individual Artist Fellowship; Creative Renewal Grant from the Indiana Arts Comn; One of Midwest's Top 25 Most Influential People in the Arts, Dialogue Magazine, 2005. *Mailing Add:* Herron School of Art & Design Eskenazi Hall HR224K 735 W New York St Indianapolis IN 46202

EIDELBERG, MARTIN
HISTORIAN
b New York, NY, Jan 30, 1941. *Study:* Columbia Univ, BA, 61; Princeton Univ, PhD, 65. *Pos:* Ed, Decorative Arts Soc Newslett (quart mag), 78-80. *Teaching:* Prof art hist, Rutgers Univ, New Brunswick, 64-2002, prof emeritus; Sothebys Works of Art Prog, New York, 87-2007. *Awards:* Robert C Smith Award, Decorative Arts Soc, 82; Charles F Montgomery Prize, Decorative Arts Soc, 84; George Wittenborn Mem Award, Art Libr Soc NAm, 91; Henry Allen Moe Prize, 2007; American Ceramic Circle, 2011. *Res:* 18th century French painting and drawing; modern decorative arts. *Publ:* coauth, Masterworks of Louis Comfort Tiffany, Thames & Hudson & Abrams, 89; ed & coauth, Design 1935-1965; What Modern Was, Musee des Arts Decoratifs de Montreal, Abrams, 91; coauth, The Dispersal of the Last Duke of Mantua's Paintings, Vol 123, Gazette des Beaux-Arts, 94; auth, Watteau's Italian Reveries vol 126, Gazette des Beaux-Arts, 95; ed, Messengers of Modernism: American Studio Jewelry, 1940-1960, 96 & Designed for Delight, Alternative Aspects of Twentieth-Century Decorative Arts, 97, Flammarion & Montreal Mus Decorative Arts, Paris & New York; ed, Design for Living, Furniture and Lighting, 1950-2000, Flammarion & Montreal Mus Decorative Arts, Paris and NY, 2000; auth, The Ceramic Forms of Leza McVey, Philmark, 2002; coauth, Watteau et la fête galante, Réunion des musées nationaux, 2004; coauth, The Lamps of Louis Comfort Tiffany, Vendome, 2005; coauth, The Eames Lounge Lounge Chair, Merrel Press, 2006; coauth, A New Light on Tiffany: Clara Driscoll & the Tiffany Girls, Giles, 2007; auth, Tiffany Favrile Glass & the Quest of Beauty, Lillian Nassau LLC, 2007; coauth, Beauty in Common Things, Am Arts & Crafts Pottery, Two Red Roses Found 2008; coauth, Louis C Tiffany, A Passion for Color, Flammarion, 2009; auth, Tiffany Favrile Pottery and the Quest of Beauty, Lillian Nassau, 2010; coauth, Watteau, The Drawings, London, Royal Acad, 2011

EILAND, WILLIAM U
MUSEUM DIRECTOR
Study: Birmingham-Southern Coll, BA (summa cum laude); Univ Va, MA & PhD. *Pos:* Interim dir, dir pubs & pub relations, Ga Mus Art, Univ Ga, formerly, dir, 1992-. *Awards:* Mus Prof Yr, Ga Asn Mus & Galleries, 2000, Lifetime Achievement Award, 2007; Danforth Teaching Fel, Mus Prof Grant, Nat Endowment Arts; Woodrow Wilson Fel. *Mem:* Asn Art Mus Dirs (trustee); Ga Asn Mus & Galleries (bd dirs); Southeastern Mus Conf; AAM (vchmn, 2004-05). *Mailing Add:* Ga Mus Art Univ Ga 90 Carlton St Athens GA 30602

EINARSSON, GARDAR EIDE
INSTALLATION SCULPTOR, CONCEPTUAL ARTIST
b Oslo, Norway, Jan 1, 1976. *Study:* Nat Accad Fine Art, Bergen, Norway, 1996-2000; Staatliche Hochsch Bildende Künst, 1999-2000; Whitney Mus Am Art Independent Study, Studio Prog, 2001-02, Cooper Union, 2002-03. *Work:* Mus Contemp Art LA; Astrup Fearnley Mus Mod Art, Oslo; Malmo Art Mus, Stockholm; Norwegian Nat Mus Art. *Exhib:* Solo & two-person exhibs: Galleri 21:25, Oslo, 99; Nordic Inst Contemp Art, Helsinki, Finland, 2001; Oslo Kunsthall, 2002; White Box, 2002; Am Fine Arts, New York, 2002; Kunstlerhaus Bethanien, Berlin, 2003; Nils Staerk Contemp Art, Copenhagen, 2004, 2006; Bergen Kunsthall, Norway, 2004; UKS Gallery, Oslo, 2004; Galerie Loevenbruck, Paris, 2005; Team Gallery, New York, 2005, 2007; Gallery.Sora, Tokyo, 2006; Sorry We're Closed, Brussels, 2007; Kunstverein Frankfurt, 2007; Honor Fraser, LA, 2008; Michael Benevento, LA, 2008; group exhibs include Nordic Festival Contemp Art, 2000; Coal by Any Other Name, Am Fine Arts, 2000; Where am I Now 2, Nat Mus Contemp Art, Oslo, 2002; Between the Lines, Apex Art, New York, 2003, Adaptations, 2004; Nils Staerk Contemp Art, Copenhagen, 2004, To Be Continued, 2005; Art Film Basel, 2004; Team Gallery, New York, 2005; Greater New York, PS1 Contemp Art Center, New York, 2005, Defamation of Character, 2006; Samle Sammen, Nat Mus Art, Archit & Design, Oslo, 2006; Mafia, STANDARD (OSLO), 2006 & Gagosian Gallery, New York 2007; In Practice Projects, Sculpture Center, New York, 2007; My Sweet Sixteen Party, Galerie Rodolphe Janssen, Brussels, 2007; Whitney Biennial, Whitney Mus Am Art, New York, 2008. *Mailing Add:* care Honor Fraser 2622 S La Cienega Blvd Los Angeles CA 90034

EINS, STEFAN
CONCEPTUAL ARTIST, CURATOR
b Prague, Czech Repub; Austrian citizen; permanent resident, US. *Study:* Univ Vienna, Austria, MA, 65; Acad Fine Arts, Vienna, BA, 67. *Work:* Nat Galerie, Vienna; New Mus, NY; Landesmuseum, St Pölten; City of Vienna, Austria; Mus Mod Art, Vienna, Austria; Fed Govt, Austria; and numerous installations, 72-. *Comn:* Project Vertebrae, comn by Gresten Initiative, Gresten, Noe, Austria. *Exhib:* 112 Greene St, New York, 71-72; Liquid Steel/Life, NY, 72 & 2004; 3 Mercer St, New York, 73-76; PS 1, 76; Documenta 6, 77, Documenta 7, 82; Fashion Moda, 78, 81, 85 & 91-92; ABC Times Sq Show, 80, 86, 89, 2001; New Mus, New York, 80-81; Now Gallery, New York, 87-88; Gallery Ariadne, Vienna, 87; Nat Gallery, Oesterreichische Galerie, Vienna, 91; Trees, NY, 99; Gallery X, New York, 2000; Pfaffmen Gallery, New York, 2001; Lelong Gallery, NY, 2003; Columbia Univ, NY, 2003; Lust/Pain-Pain/Lust, NY, 2004; Deitch Projects, NY, 2005; The Downtown Show, Grey Art Gallery, NY, 2006; Andy Warhol Mus, Pittsburgh, 2006; Austin Mus, 2006; Haven Gallery, New York, 2006; Modernist, Istanbul, 2006; Mus Mod Art, PS1, New York, 2007; Kyrgyz Nat Fine Arts Mus, Bishkek, Kyrgyz Repub, 2007; Emergencies, Mus Mod Art, PS1, NY, 2007; Picture Generation, Metrop Mus Art, New York, 2008; Looking at Music, Mus Mod Art, New York, 2009; Fashion Moda, Neuberger Mus, Purchase, NY, 2012; The Cutting Edge, Fashion Moda, NY, 2012; The 5th Dimension, Fashion Moda, NY, 2013. *Collection Arranged:* Cur, Geoffrey Hendricks, 76, Sherrie Levine, 77, Fashion Moda Inaugural, 78, Robert Cooney, 78, End of Modernism, 78, Art/Fashion Inter Mix, 78, Multiculturalism, 78, Jenny Holzer, 79, John Ahearn, 79, David Wells, 79, Christy Rupp, 79, David Reed, 80, Jane Dickson, 80, Wally Edwards, 80, Haim Steinbach, 80, Marianne Edwards, 80, Elizabeth Clark, 80, Ilona Granet, 80, Paulette Nenner, 80, Calif Billboards, New York, 80, Graffiti in the Arts/Grafitti Art Success Am, 80, Sophie Calle, 80, Rebecca Howland, 80, Justen Ladda, 80, Keith Haring, 81, Paul Koenigsberg, 80, Dona McAdams, 82, Tom Warren, 82, Judy Glantzman, 83, David Finn, 83, Joy Walker, 83, Dragan Ilic, 83, Alyson Pou, 83, Paolo Buggiani, 84, Nancy Drew, 86, Barbara Smith, 88, Norbert Brunner, 93, Scott Pfaffman and Frank Shifreen, Counting Coup, Undo, Democracy at Stake, Theatre for the New City, NY, 2001, The Global Contemporary Osh Artists Union Osha and Artex, Bishkek, Kyrgyzstan, 2007; co-cur (with Joe Lewis), Fashion Moda, New Mus, New York, 80-81, (with Jenny Holzer), Fashion Moda, documenta 7, 82 and others; co-cur (with Shaaebek Amankul), South Pole, Artists Union, Osh, Kyrgyzstan, 2006; The Cutting Edge (with Brooke McGowen), Fashion Moda, NY, 2012; The Fifth Dimension (with Brooke McGowen), Fashion Moda, NY, 2013. *Pos:* Founder, exec dir & cur, 3 Mercer St, New York, 72-79 & Fashion Moda, Bronx, 78-84 & 88-93; pres, Collab Proj Inc, 88-89, 2001-. *Awards:* Nat Endowment Arts Fel, 80 & 87; CAPS Fel, NY, 70; NY Found for the Arts, 2002; Adolph and Efther Gottlieb Found, 2004. *Bibliog:* ed, Some Posters from Fashion Moda by Ingrid Sischy, Artforum, 1/81; auth, Francesca Alinovi-Arte di Frontiera (italian ed), Flash Art, 2/82; Gabriele von Arnim-Atelier in Den Slums, Art, Ger, 4/82; Lucy Lippard-Get the Message, Dutton, 84; Suzi Gablik, Has Modernism Failed?, Thames & Hudson, 84; Carey Lovelace (auth), S Bronx Art, Los Angeles Times, 9/2/84; Alan Moore & Marc Miller (auth), ABC No rio Dinero, ABC No Rio, 85; Karin Kuoni (auth), Stefan Eins: Fashion Moda, Kunstforum, 3/4/91; Coming from the Subway, Groningen Mus, Benjamin & Ptnrs, 92; Lisa Phillips (auth), The American Century 1950-2000, Whitney Mus, 99; David Ebony (auth), Eloquent Corrosions, Art in America, 7/2000; Chris Twonsend, Rapture, Arts Seduction by Fashion, Thames & Hudson, 2002; The Downtown Book, The NY Art Scene 1974-1984, Princeton Univ Press, 2006; David Gonzales (auth), In a Conspiracy of Paint Blotches and Shadows, Meaning Art, NY Times, 8/27/2009; Doug Eklund, The Picture Generation 1974-1984, Metrop Mus Art, 2009. *Mem:* Collab Proj Inc. *Media:* Ideas, Liquids, Time/Space. *Res:* Liquid formation processes;

other dimensions, pattern repeition; Stone Age Artifacts. *Interests:* Voting rights (electronic voting machines and their accuracy). *Publ:* One/Stefan Eins Exhibitions Catalog, Nat Galerie, Vienna, 91; Peter Rosenstein, Brau Madden, Tatooed Walls, Univ Press Miss, 2006. *Mailing Add:* PO Box 33 Canal St Station New York NY 10013-0033

EISENBERG, JEROME MARTIN
DEALER, COLLECTOR
b Philadelphia, Pa, July 6, 1930. *Study:* Boston Univ, AB, 51; Columbia Univ, with Otto Brendel, Edith Porada & Henry Fischer, 60-63; Pa State Univ, with Jiri Frel, 69-71, PhD, 83. *Pos:* Dir, Royal-Athena Galleries, 58-; founder, Eisenberg Mus Biblical Archeol, Louisville, 61; chmn, Herodium Archeol Expedition Fund, 62; founder, publ, editor-in-chief, Minerva, 1990-. *Teaching:* Lectr forgery & fraud in ancient art, NY Univ, 69-70; vis prof, forgery & fraud in ancient art, Univ Leipzig, 1996. *Bibliog:* Barbara Polláck (auth), Royal-Athena: Access to antiquities, Collectors Quart, 63. *Mem:* Archeol Inst Am (life mem); Appraisers Asn Am; Am Numismatic Soc (life mem); Int Asn Dealers Ancient Art; fellow Royal Numismatic Soc; Int Asn Egyptologists; Int Asn Classical Archaeology. *Specialty:* Egyptian, Near Eastern, Greek, Roman, Etruscan art. *Collection:* Ancient Egyptian faience figurines; Egyptian stone vessels; Green & South Italian pottery; Roman glass; Pre-Columbian and tribal art. *Publ:* Auth, A Guide to Roman Imperial Coins, 57; Art of the Ancient World, 65, 67 & 85; The Age of Cleopatra, 1988; Gods and Mortals: Bronzes of the Ancient World, 1989; 1000 Years of Ancient Greek Vases, 1990; Art of the Ancient World, 1992, 1995, 1997, 1999-2006; Gods & Mortals II, 2004; Images of Warfare, 2004; Mythologies of the Classical World & Ancient Egypt, 2005. *Mailing Add:* c/o Royal-Athena Galleries 153 E 57th St New York NY 10022

EISENBERG, MARC S
PAINTER, SCULPTOR
b New York, NY, Feb 17, 1948. *Study:* Sch Visual Arts, BFA, 71. *Work:* Chase Manhattan Bank, NY; Prudential Life Insurance Co, Edison, NJ; Equitable Life Insurance Co, NY; Berley & Co, NY; Weatherspoon Art Gallery, Greensboro, NC. *Exhib:* 19th Nat Print Exhib, 76 & Decade of Am Drawing, 81, Brooklyn, NY; Paper as Medium, Smithsonian Inst, Washington, DC, 78; Painting & Sculpture Today, Indianapolis Inst Art, Ind, 79; Art on Paper, Weatherspoon Mus, Greensboro, NC, 86. *Bibliog:* Corrine Robbins (auth), Works of Marc Eisenberg, Arts Mag, 76; Ronnie Cotrone (auth), Spotlight, Interview Mag, 76; Charles Gatewood (auth), Outlaw artists, Gallery Mag, 85; Lorraine O'Grady (auth), The Black and White Show, ArtForum Mag, 5/2009. *Media:* Miscellaneous

EISENBERG, MARVIN
EDUCATOR, HISTORIAN
b Philadelphia, Pa, 1922. *Study:* Univ Pa, BA, 43; Princeton Univ, MFA, 49, PhD, 54. *Hon Degrees:* Dlitt honorary, Univ St Andrews, 2003. *Pos:* Pres, Col Art Asn, 68-69; mem, Inst for Advan Study, winter 70; mem vis comt, Freer Gallery Art, Washington, DC 70-96, Dept Fine Arts, Harvard Univ, 75-80 & Ga Mus Art, 97-2003; ed, Bulletin Mus Art & Archeol, Univ Mich, 78-88; mem adv comt, Ctr Advanced Study Visual Arts, Nat Gallery, Washington, DC, 79-83. *Teaching:* Instr art hist, Univ Mich, 49-53, from asst prof to assoc prof, 54-61, prof, 61- & chmn dept, 61-69, prof emer, 89; vis prof, Stanford Univ, 73; Berg prof, Colo Col, 90, 93, 95 & 97; lectr, McMaster Univ, 94, Mt Holyoke Col, 94, St Andrews, 98, Gakushuin Univ, Tokyo, 98 & Kyoto Univ, 98. *Awards:* Guggenheim Fel, 59; Star of Solidarity, Ital Govt, 69; Distinguished Teaching in Art History, Coll Art Asn Am, 87. *Res:* Italian late medieval and early renaissance painting. *Publ:* Auth, articles on early Italian painting in journals and museum bulletins; Lorenzo Monaco, Princeton Univ Press, Princeton, 89; Confraternity Altarpiece by Mariotto di Nardo, Tokyo, 98. *Mailing Add:* Univ Mich Dept Hist Art Ann Arbor MI 48109

EISENBERG, SONJA MIRIAM
PAINTER
b Berlin, Ger; US citizen. *Study:* NY Univ, BA, 54; Nat Acad Sch Fine Arts, with Leon Kroll, 61; also with Daniel Dickerson, 62-68 & Sidney Delevante, in 60's. *Work:* Palm Spring Desert Mus; Fordham Univ Mus, NY; Archives Am Art, Smithsonian, Washington, DC; The Cathedral St John the Divine, NY; United Nations Headquarters, NY; The Jewish Mus, NY; Fordham Univ Mus, NY; Huntsville Mus Art, Ala; Anglo-Am Art Mus, Baton Rouge, La; Omega Inst, New Lebanon, NY. *Comn:* Designer cachet for United Nations, Int Year Disabled Persons; book, Seeing the Gospel According to St John, (text & 41 paintings), The Cathedral St John the Divine, NY; Die Kristall Nacht (painting), Briefmarkenhaus Krüger, Munich, Ger, 93; AKIM-USA, NY, 96. *Exhib:* One-woman shows, Galerie de Sfinx, Amsterdam, 74 & Am Mus Hayden Planetarium, NY, 80, Berlin, Germany, 2009, Leonard Towne Gallery, 2012; Archives of Am Art, Smithsonian Inst, 78; The 14th Int Art Friendship Exhib, Tokyo Metrop Art Mus, Tokyo, Japan, 89; Gallery Park Hotel, Vitznau, Switz, 94; Park Hotel Bürgenstock, Switz, 95; Park Ave Armory, NY, 96; Dussman Kulturhaus, Berlin, 98; Horton Gallery, Philadelphia, 2001; Jaffa Mus, Tel Aviv Israel, 2010; Spirit of Art, Galleria Pall Mall, London, 2011; Insel Galeria, Berlin, Germany, 2011; Spirit of Art in Vienna, Int Exhib Contemp Art, 2012; Symphony of Colors, Pall Mall, London, 2012; Leonard Tourne Gallery, 2013. *Pos:* Artist-in-residence, Cathedral St John the Divine. *Awards:* Accademia Italia delle Arti e del Lavoro, Medaglio d'Oro, 81; Gold Medal for Artistic Merit, Int Parliament Safety & Peace, 83; World Prize for Culture; Palma d'Oro d'Europa, 86; and many others. *Bibliog:* Jan deCarpentier (auth), Kijk's kunst, De Typhoon, 6/74; Gordon Brown (auth), Sonja Eisenberg, Art Mag, 4/75; Nina Brodsky (auth), Miniature Collector, 4/82; Ray Fashora (auth), Taconic Newspapers, 6/89; Peter Schmalz (auth), Die Welt, 97; Berliner Zeitung, Stefan Elfenbein (auth), New York!, 2002; Ralph Gardner (auth), article, The Wall St Jour, 2012. *Mem:* Res Bd Adv, The Am Biog Inst. *Media:* Oil, Watercolor; Pastel; Collage. *Specialty:* Leonard Towne Gallery, New York, NY. *Interests:* music; wood work miniatures; writing; poetry. *Collection:* Prin2 von Arhalt, Denise Rich, Thomas Buchanan, Von Wachmar Dussman, Heather Higgins, Poling Van Schijindel, Haars Synesteisn. *Publ:* auth, Poems and Paintings, 2001; auth, The Red Painted House, 2002; auth, Seeing the Gospel according to St John, 2003; auth, There will be no War, 2004; auth, On Its Way, 2005; auth, Poems & Paintings Nov 2, 2007. *Dealer:* Cathedral St John the Divine New York NY 10025; Leonard Tourne Gallery New York NY 10065. *Mailing Add:* 1020 Park Ave New York NY 10028

EISENSTAT, JANE SPERRY
PAINTER
b New York, NY, Mar 2, 1920. *Study:* Sculpture Studio Antonio Cortizas, 34-37; Penn Acad Fine Arts, 37-40. *Work:* William Penn Charter Sch & Pub schs & bldgs, Philadelphia; James Michner Mus, Doylestown, Pa. *Comn:* Murals & illus, William Penn Asn Art Proj, Pa, 38-40; Gimbel Brothers, Philadelphia, 40; murals, Santa Clara Asn League, 96. *Exhib:* Philadelphia Acad Fine Arts, 30-50; Juried Exhib, Art Inst Chicago, Detroit Inst Art & Rutgers Univ, Camden, NJ, 60-80; solo exhib, Philadelphia Art Alliance 50-80; Downtown Gallery, Delaware State Mus, Willington, Del, 80; Euphrate Gallery, DeAnza Col, Cupertino, Calif, 88; Triton Mus Bi Ann, Triton Mus Art, Santa Clara, Calif, 98. *Teaching:* Instr & asst prof painting, Philadelphia Col Art, 50-85; assoc prof painting, Moore Col Art, Philadelphia, 67-69; assoc prof drawing, Glassboro Univ, NJ, 72-82. *Awards:* Mary Smith Prize, 60 & Thornton Oakley Medal, Penn Acad Fine Arts, 70; Council Grant, State of NJ, 80; Penn Acad Fine Arts Fel. *Bibliog:* E T Wherry (co-illus), Wildflower Guide, Double Day Publ, 48; Charles LeClair (auth), Art of Watercolor, Prentis Hall, 85; Reproductions, Japanese Idea Art Mag, 92. *Mem:* Philadelphia WC Club. *Collection:* 1000 original Am & Eng illustrations from Darley Rowlandson to Sloan and Rockwell. *Publ:* Auth & illusr, The Challenge of AAB, Harper & Row, Almquist, Sweden, 67; coauth, Jessie W Smith-Step By Step Graphics, Dell Yearling, 87; Illustration In America, Graphis, 90. *Dealer:* Newman Gallery 1625 Walnut St Philadelphia PA 19103

EISENSTEIN, (MR & MRS) JULIAN
COLLECTORS
b Warrenton, Mo, Apr 3, 21 (Mr Eisenstein). *Study:* Mr Eisenstein, Harvard Univ, BS, 41, MA, 42, PhD, 48. *Pos:* Mr Eisenstein, Nat res fel, Oxford, 52-53; physicist, Nat Bureau Standards, 57-66; pres & trustee, Washington Gallery Mod Art, 61-65. *Teaching:* Mr Eisenstein, instr, Univ Wis, 48-52; from asst prof to assoc prof, Pa State Univ, 53-57; prof, George Washington Univ, 66-. *Collection:* Contemporary art. *Mailing Add:* 82 Kalorama Cir NW Washington DC 20008-1616

EISENTRAGER, JAMES A
PAINTER
b Alvord, Iowa, Sept 3, 1929. *Study:* Augustana Col, Sioux Falls, SDak, BA, 51; Univ Md in Wiesbaden, Ger, 52-53; Univ Northern Iowa, 55; Univ Iowa, Iowa City, MFA, 61; with Stewart Edie, Byron Burford & Mauricio Lasansky. *Work:* Univ Iowa, Iowa City; Sheldon Mem Art Gallery, Lincoln, Nebr; Millersville State Univ, Pa. *Exhib:* Ann Exhib, Springfield Art Mus, Mo, 64-72; Solo exhibs, Sheldon Mem Art Gallery, 66, Univ Del, Newark, 75 & Northern Ariz Univ Art Gallery, Flagstaff, 77; 31st Mid-Yr Show, Butler Inst Am Art, Youngstown, Ohio, 66; Mid-Am Exhib, William Rockhill Nelson Gallery of Art, Kansas City, Mo, 66 & 70; Mid-W Biennial, Joslyn Art Mus, Omaha, Nebr, 66 & 70; Ten Artists W of the Mississippi, Colorado Springs Fine Art Ctr, 67. *Teaching:* Prof painting, Univ Nebr-Lincoln, 61-; prof & lectr, Vail Summer Workshop, Colo, 71-76; vis prof art, Univ Colo, Boulder, summer 67. *Awards:* Purchase Award, May Show, Sioux City Art Ctr, Iowa, 63; Best Painting Purchase Award, Images on Paper Nat Competition, Springfield Art Asn, Ill, 73; Jesse Loomis Award, Waterloo Ann, Waterloo Munic Gallery, Iowa, 73. *Mem:* Mid-Am Coll Art Asn; Coll Art Asn. *Media:* Polymer, Oil. *Mailing Add:* Univ Nebr at Lincoln 7501 Whitestone Dr Lincoln NE 68506-1774

EISINGER, HARRY
PAINTER
b Berlin, Ger, Apr 23, 1932; US citizen. *Study:* Calif Sch Fine Arts, San Francisco, 57-59; also with Ralph Putzker, Nathan Oliveira & Wayne Thiebaud. *Work:* Slides, Whitney Mus, NY. *Comn:* Drawings, Territorial Gazette, San Francisco, 59; posters, Marin Co Art Ctr, Calif, 60. *Exhib:* Solo exhibs, Panoras Gallery, NY, 73 & Gallery 84, 77; 32nd & 33rd Nat Audubon Exhibs, Nat Acad Galleries, 74 & 75 & Allied Artists Am Exhib, 75; Gallery 84, NY, 75 & 77. *Awards:* Spinaker Award, Sausalito Mayor, Calif, 60. *Bibliog:* Herb Caen (auth), article, San Francisco Chronicle, 60. *Mem:* Allied Artists Am; Audubon Artists. *Media:* Oil. *Dealer:* Gallery 84 30 West 57th St New York NY 10019. *Mailing Add:* 90 Eaton St Stratford CT 06497-3704

EISNER, CAROLE SWID
PAINTER, SCULPTOR
b New York, NY, Oct 30, 1937. *Study:* Syracuse Univ, AB, 58; Int Sch Photog, 76-78. *Work:* Guggenheim Mus & Knoll Int, NY; Syracuse Univ; Southeast Banking Corp, Miami; Northstar Reinsurance Co, Seattle; Nat Assocs Inc; and others. *Comn:* Set designs for four plays, Theater XII, NY, 78. *Exhib:* Art of the Northeast, Silvermine Guild, New Canaan, Conn, 83; Recent Acquisitions, Guggenheim Mus, NY, 86; Images Gallery, Norwalk, Conn, 86; Sculpture by Guild Artists, Silvermine, Conn, 88; New Am Art Invitational, London, 88; First Womens Bank, 88; David Findlay Galleries, NY, 90; Gallery Sagan, Tokyo, 92; Gallery Tanishima, Tokyo, 92; River Park Atrium, Norwalk, Conn, 97; Norwalk City Hall, 2000-2008; Fordham Univ at Lincoln Ctr Campus, NY, 2000; Veterans Park, Norwalk, Conn, 2001; Heritage Park, Norwalk, Conn, 2002-2008; Shakespeare & Co, Lenox, Mass, 2006-2008; Chateau de Fontaine-Henry, Clavados, France, 2007; Abbaye de la Cambre, Brussels, 2008; The Broadway Malls, 2009-2010; Univ New Haven, Conn, 2011; Geometric Abstract Paintings, Manhatten, NY, 2013. *Awards:* Rosenthal Award, Outdoor Sculpture, All New Eng Show, Silvermine, Conn, 78; Sculpture Award, Champion Int, 80; Finalist, Johnson Atelier Nat Sculpture Competition, Princeton, NJ, 80; George Arents award, Syracuse Univ, 2013. *Bibliog:* William Pellicone (auth), article, Artspeak, 5/21/81; Jacqueline Moss (auth), article, Arts Mag, 10/84; Will Grant (auth), article, Artspeak,

7/1/86. *Mem:* Silvermine Guild Artists; Weston-Westport Arts Coun. *Media:* Acrylic; Welded Metal. *Publ:* Contribr, Contemporary Women Artists Calendar, Bo Tree Productions, 67 & 87; The Antiques J, 6/79 & 2/80. *Dealer:* David Findlay Gallery 984 Madison Ave New York NY 10021. *Mailing Add:* 1107 5th Ave New York NY 10028-0145

EISNER, ELLIOT WAYNE
EDUCATOR
b Chicago, Ill, Mar 10, 1933. *Study:* Roosevelt Univ, BA; Ill Inst Technol, MS; Univ Chicago, MA, PhD. *Teaching:* Instr art educ, Ohio State Univ, 60-61; asst prof educ, Univ Chicago, 61-65; prof educ & art, Stanford Univ, 65-. *Awards:* Hon Dr, Univ Oslo, 86; Hon Dr, Hofstra Univ, 88; hon Dr, Maryland Inst Coll Art, 89. *Mem:* Hon fel Nat Art Educ Asn (pres, 77-79); Am Educ Res Asn; Int Soc Educ Through Art (pres, 87-90); Am Educ Res Asn (pres, 92-93). *Res:* Children's artistic development; the uses of art criticism for the study and evaluation of educational practice. *Publ:* Auth, The Educational Imagination, MacMillan, 78; Cognition and Curriculum, Longmans, 82; The Art of Educational Evaluation, Falmer, 85; Qualitative Inquiry: The Continuing Debate (with Alan Peshkin), Teachers Coll Press, 90; The Enlightened Eye: Qualitative Inquiry and the Enhancement of Educational Practice, Macmillan, 91. *Mailing Add:* Stanford Univ Sch of Educ Stanford CA 94305-3096

EISNER, GAIL LEON
PAINTER, SCULPTOR
b Detroit, Mich, Oct 17, 1939. *Study:* Wayne State Univ, BFA, Sch Art Inst Chgo, Ill, 67; Art Students League New York with Xavier Gonzalez, 83. *Work:* 47th Dist Ct, Farmington Hills, Mich; DOC, Pontiac, Mich; Resurrection Hosp; Sch Art Inst Chicago, Ill; Rabobank Netherland, Chicago, Ill. *Exhib:* XXI Ann Mich Artists, Art Ctr, Mt Clemins, 93; All Mich/All Media, Krasl Art Ctr, St Joseph, 93; Fantasy and Reality, Art Ctr Battle Creek, Mich, 93 & 94; Cheekwood Mus Art, Nashville, 94; 10,000 Plus Exhib, Art Inst Chicago, 94; solo exhibs, Sinclair Coll, Dayton, Ohio, 95, Univ Mich, Ann Arbor, 97, Collin Co Col, Plano, Tex, 97, The Art Ctr, Mt Clemens, Mich, 98, Bus Relief Oils, Collin Co Coll, Plano, Tex, OK Harris, David Klein Gallery, Birmingham, Mich, Stark Weather Art Cen, Romeo, Mich, Shiawassee Art Cen, Owosso, Mich, Fantasy & Frolic, Art Cen Mt Clemens, Mich, Griswold Art Cen, Worthington, Ohio & Go Figure, Sinclair Col, Dayton, Ohio; The City Gallery, WM Costick Ctr, Famington Hills, Mich, 2004; Collages-City Halls Walls, Farmington Hills, Farmington, Mich, 2006; Donald Gallery, Dobbs Ferry, NY; Hopper House, Nyack, NY. *Pos:* artist-in-residence, Farmington Area Arts Comn, 2005. *Teaching:* collage instr, Bronxville Womens' Club, NY, 2011. *Awards:* Adrian Zahn Nat Arts Club Award, Pastel Soc Am, 87; Sara Winston Mem Award, Nat Asn Women Artists, 92 & Epstein Mem Award, 97; Epstein Mem Award, Nat Asn Women Artists, 97; Detroit Soc Women Sculptors & Painters Award of Merit; Sidney Dickinson Mem Award. *Bibliog:* Mary Klemic (auth), Dark side is bright, folded scenes open up, Eccentric, 2/95; David Grayson (auth), A new dimension on still life, Artists Mag, 12/96; Ellen Piligan (ed), Artist in focus, Metrop Woman Mag, 10/97; Cheryll Warren, Artist Exhibits Work at Shiawassee Art Cen, 3/2002; Rashun Rucker (auth), Folded Art, The Detroit News, 7/18/2004. *Mem:* Nat Asn Women Artists; New York Artist Equity Asn; Art Students League New York; Michigan Soc Painters & Sculptors. *Media:* Oil, Collage. *Publ:* Illusr, Making a Living as an Artist, Art Calendar, 92; Am Artists of the Bookplate, James P Keenan, 96, Cambridge Bookplate, Mass. *Dealer:* Outside the Lines 8410 Macomb St Ste 108 Grosse Ile MI 48138; Gwenda Jay Gallery N Wells Chicago IL. *Mailing Add:* 145 Palisade St #403 Dobbs Ferry NY 10522-1627

EISWERTH, BARRY
ARCHITECT, EDUCATOR
b Williamsport, Pa, Sept 16, 1942. *Study:* Pa State Univ Park, BArch, 65. *Comn:* Archit works incl Children's Hosp, Philadelphia, bldgs. Philadelphia '76 Bicentennial, Philadelphia Bourse Bldg, Cypress Sq. Townhouse Complex Philadelphia (recipient Design award Old Philadelphia Devel Corp, Preservation Alliance award for Design Offices and Montgomery McCracken Warker & Rhodes), Constitutional Pavillion for We The People 200, Master Plan and New Classroom Admin Bldg Cairo Am. Col, Engineering and Computer Sci Campus-Am. Univ Cairo, Master Plan Am. Int Sch, Tel Aviv, Master Plan and New Classroom Bldgs, Am Embassy Sch, New Delhi, Master Plan and Design new campus Am, Sch of Warsaw, Brit Int Sch, Cairo; Master Plan and Expansion Am Sch Paris; design of hdqrs Arab Bank, Cairo. *Pos:* Assoc, H2L2 Archits/Planners, Philadelphia, 67-77, partner, 77-88, sr partner, 88-; pres H2L2 Design Co, 80-. *Teaching:* asst prof, archit design Drexel Univ, 75-81; mem fac, thesis advisor Philadelphia Col Art. *Awards:* Recipient awards for archit designs, Alumni Achievement award Pa State Univ, 2000. *Mem:* Am Inst of Archits; Pa Soc Archits; Nat Acad; Philadelphia Club

EKDAHL, JANIS KAY
LIBRARIAN
b Topeka, Kans, Dec 7, 1946. *Study:* Occidental Col, BA, 68; Columbia Univ, MLS, 69. *Pos:* Art librn, Vassar Col, Poughkeepsie, NY, 71-81; asst dir, Mus Mod Art Libr, New York, 81-94, actg dir, 94-96, chief libr adminr, 96-. *Mem:* Art Libr Soc North Am (Eastern regional rep, 81-83); Art Libr Soc New York; Coll Art Asn; Am Libr Asn. *Interests:* Modern and contemporary art; sculpture; American art and architecture. *Publ:* Auth, American sculpture: A guide to information sources, Gale, 77. *Mailing Add:* 107 W 86th St New York NY 10024-3409

ELDER, DAVID MORTON
SCULPTOR
b Windsor, Ont, July 3, 1936; US citizen. *Study:* Wittenberg Univ, BA, 57; Ohio State Univ Grad Sch, MA, 61. *Work:* Denver Art Mus, Colo; Long Beach Art Mus, Calif. *Comn:* Sculpture (metal), Gloria Christi Chapel, Valparaiso Univ, 62, St Paul Lutheran Church, Glenn Bermie, Md, 63, Coconut Grove Ambassador Hotel, Los Angeles, 69 & Barnsdall Park, Los Angeles, 74; sculpture (resin), Pac Home Burbank, 74. *Exhib:* Long Beach Mus Art, 66, 70 & 71; Calif Sky Scape Show, Calif Coll Arts & Crafts, Oakland, 69; Calif Landscape Show, La Jolla Mus Art, 69; San Francisco Centennial Show, De Young Mus, 71; Last Plastics Show, Calif Inst Arts, Valencia, 72. *Teaching:* Asst prof sculpture, Calif State Univ, Los Angeles, 68-71; prof sculpture, Calif State Univ, Northridge, 71-, chmn dept 3-d art, formerly assoc dean sch arts, formerly, prof, currently. *Awards:* Fourth Ann Long Beach Mus First Prize, 66; Purchase Award Comn, Southwestern Col, 67; Artist of the Year, Pasadena Arts Coun, 71. *Media:* Bronze, Polyester Resin. *Dealer:* Orlando Gallery 17037 Ventura Blvd Encino CA 91316. *Mailing Add:* California State University Dept Art 3-D Media 18111 Nordhoff St Northridge CA 91330-8300

ELDER, GENE WESLEY
COLLAGE ARTIST, WRITER
b Dallas, Tex, Jul 4, 1949. *Study:* Trinity Univ, BA, 73; Maverick, MFA, 92. *Work:* San Antonio Mus Art, Tex; Bonham Exchange, San Antonio, Tex; Alamo Videos, San Antonio, Tex. *Comn:* Time Capsule 2181AD, San Antonio Mus Art, Tex, 84. *Exhib:* San Antonio Mus Modern Art, San Antonio, Tex, 76; Theatre in a Can, 2011; History Plates, 2014; The Pi in the Sky, 2014. *Collection Arranged:* Artist As Administrator, 87; Power to the Pulp, Artist made paper, 89. *Pos:* Property Mgr, Blue Star Art Complex, 85-93; cur, San Antonio Mus Contemp Art, 87-2005; archives dir, Happy Found, 88-2014. *Teaching:* instr, handmade paper, Southwest Craft Ctr, 85-93. *Bibliog:* Party Party 1979: artists' Political ticket; Nat Political Art Month, July 2010, July 2011, & 2012. *Mem:* Blue Star Art Ctr (bd mem, 88-90); Knights of Isosceles Triangle (green knight, 2000-2010). *Media:* Collage, found objects. *Res:* A View of Reality From a Chartreuse Couch, 2008-2010. *Interests:* MUD underground: Artists Taking Over The World, 2000, 2010; Wedding Cake Liberation Front, 2005-2010. *Publ:* article, Wall Street J, 8/20/99; Auth, Murder by Collage with Found Object, Artist Edition, 2000; contribr, MUD Underground, Covert Internet, 2000-2005. *Dealer:* Joan Grona Gallery 116 Blue Star San Antonio TX 78210. *Mailing Add:* 411 Bonham San Antonio TX 78205

ELDER, R BRUCE
FILMMAKER, CRITIC
b Hawkesbury, Ont, June 12, 1947. *Study:* McMaster Univ, Hamilton, Can, BA (hons), 69; Univ Toronto, Can, MA, 70; Ryerson Polytechnic Inst, Toronto, BAppArt, 72-76; Univ Film Studies Ctr, Amherst, Mass, with Ed Emshwiller, Shirley Clarke & Standish Lawder, summers 73-75; modern dance with members of Merce Gunningham Co; political theology of language, with Jacques Derrida, summer 86, courses in mathematics & computer prog, Ryerson Polytech Univ & York Univ, 87-98. *Work:* Numerous prints of films in public lending libraries, schools & universities. *Exhib:* The Art of Worldly Wisdom, Mus Mod Art, NY, 81; retrospectives, Art Gallery Ont, Toronto, 85 & La Cinematheque Quebecoise, Montreal, 86, Can, Anthology Film Archives, 88 & 95, Senzatitolo, Trento, Italy, 96, Images 97, Toronto & Antechamber, Regina, 2000; Illuminated Texts, Mus Mod Art, NY, 86; Toronto Festival of Festivals, 88 & 91; Museo Reina Sofia, Madrid, 90; Exultations, George Eastman House, 94; Et Ressurrectus Est, Stadt Mus, Munich, 95; Anthology Film Archives, NY & Festival International Nouveau Cinema, Montreal, 2000; Cinematheque Ontario, Toronto, 2003; Eros & Wonder, Cinema Nouvelles Ecritures, Paris, 2005; Crack, Brutal, Grief, Festival des Toutes les Cinema, Paris, 2005 & Winnipeg Cinematheque, 2006; and numerous solo exhibs in Europe, US & Can; Retrospective (The Book of all the Dead 1974-1994), 2008; Exis, Seoul, Republic Korea, 2010. *Collection Arranged:* The Photographic Image (auth, catalog), Toronto World Film Festival, 84; Film from Three Continents, Art Gallery Ont, 86; Osnabruck Experimental Media Festival, 88; Int Experimental Film Cong, Toronto, 89; and others. *Pos:* Independent critic aesthet, photog & film, 78-; independent cur avant-garde film, 80-. *Teaching:* Prof human figure & film, Ryerson Polytechnic Univ, Toronto, Can, 72-; dir, grad prog communications & culture, Ryerson Polytechnic Univ; adj prof, Grad Prog Film & Video, York Univ, 98. *Awards:* Best Experimental Film, Can Film Awards Found, 76; Best Independent Film, Los Angeles Film Critics Asn, 81; Study Tour Award, Auswartiges Amt, Govt Fed Repub Ger, 86; New Media Initiative Grant, Can Coun INSERC, 2003; Ryerson Univ Research Ch, 2004; SSHRC Creation Fine Arts Grant, 2004; Governor General's Award Visual & Media Arts, 2007; Royal Soc Can, 2007; Robert Motherwell Book Award for Outstanding Pub in the Hist & Criticism of Modernism in the Arts, 2009; Choice Outstanding Acad Book Award, 2009; 1st prize, Short listed Raymond Klbisansky, 2010. *Bibliog:* Lianne McLarty (auth), The films of R Bruce Elder, Take Two, Irwin Publ, 84; Loretta Czernis (auth), Elder: Artaud after Telsat, Can J Political & Social Theory, Vol X, No 1-2, 86; Bart Testa (auth), monograph, Bruce Elder Anthology, Film Archives, 88; Aysegul Koc (auth), Interview with R. Bruce Elder, Cineaction, No 61, 2003; Brett Kashmere (auth), R. Bruce Elder: In the Realm of Mystery & Wonder, Take One, Vol 12, No 45, 2004; Scritture per R Bruce Elder, No 19, 2009. *Mem:* Film Studies Asn Can (exec comt, 76 & 83-85); Forth Interest Group; Toronto Semiotic Circle. *Res:* Art and technology; Canadian film, especially the avant-garde in its philosophical context; aesthetics; international avant-garde cinema; the image of the body. *Publ:* Auth, Image and Identity Reflections on Canadian Film and Culture, WLU Press; The Body in Film, Art Gallery Ont, 89; On Sound, Sound Recording, Making Music of Recorded Sound, A dialogue between Bruce Elder and Michael Snow, the Michael Snow Prog, Art Gallery Ont, 94; A Body of Vision: Representations of the Body in Recent Film and Poetry, WLU Press, 98; The Films of Stan Brackhage in the American Tradition of Ezra Pound, Gertrude Stein and Charlie Olson, 98; Harmony and Dissent: Film and Avont-Garde Art Movements in the Early Twentieth Century, 2008. *Dealer:* Canadian Filmmakers Distribution Ctr Toronto 401 Richmond St W #119 Toronto ON Can M5C 3A8; New York Film-makers 475 Park Ave S 6th Fl New York NY 10016. *Mailing Add:* 692 St Clarens Ave 5 Toronto ON M6H 3X1 Canada

ELDERFIELD, JOHN
HISTORIAN, CURATOR
b Yorkshire, Eng, Apr 25, 1943. *Study:* Univ Leeds, BA & MPhil; Courtauld Inst Art, Univ London, PhD. *Hon Degrees:* Univ Leeds, Hon Dr Letters, 2006. *Collection Arranged:* Morris Louis (auth, catalog), London Arts Coun Gt Brit, 1974; The Wild Beasts: Fauvism and Its Affinities (auth, catalog), 1976, European Paintings from

Swiss Collections: Post-Impressionism to World War II (auth, catalog), 1976, Matisse in the Collection of the Mus of Modern Art (auth, catalog), 1978, The Masterworks of Edvard Munch (auth, catalog), 1979 & New Work on Paper (auth, catalog), 1981, Mus Mod Art, New York; Contrasts of Form: Geometric Abstract Art 1910-1980, 1985-86; The Heroic Century: The Mus of Mod Art Masterpieces, 200 Paintings & Sculptures, Mus Fine Arts, Houston, Tex, 2003-2004; rev ed, Das MoMA in Berlin, Neue Nationalgalerie, Berlin, 2004; Painting & Sculpture: Inaugural Installation, 2004-08; Manet & the Execution of Maximillian, 2006; and many others. *Pos:* Contrib ed, Artforum, 1972-74 & Studio Int Mag, 1973-75; cur painting & sculpture, Mus Mod Art, New York, 1975-93, dir dept drawings, 1979-93, chief cur at large, 1993-2003, dep dir curatorial affairs, 1995-98, chief cur painting & sculpture, 2003-. *Teaching:* Lectr hist art, Winchester Sch of Art, Eng, 1966-70; instr art hist, Univ Leeds, Eng, 1973-75; adj prof, Inst Fine Arts, New York Univ, 1995-. *Awards:* Harkness fel, Yale Univ, 1970; Guggenheim Fel, 1972; Mitchell Prize, 1986; Walter Neurath Award, 1995; Chevalier des Arts et Lettres, Fr Govt, 1989; 100 Most Influential People of the Year, Time Magazine, 2005; Officier dans l'Ordre des Arts et des Lettres, 2006. *Bibliog:* Hugo Ball (auth), The Flight from Time--A Dada Diary, Viking, 1975. *Mem:* Int Asn Art Critics; Coll Art Asn; Fel Royal Soc Arts. *Res:* Twentieth century art. *Publ:* Auth, The Cutouts of Henri Matisse, Braziller, 1978; Drawings of Richard Diebenkorn, 1988; Helen Frakenthaler, 1988; coauth, Matisse in Morocco, A Retrospective, 1992; coauth, Modern Starts: People, Places, Things, Mus Modern Art, New York, 1999; coauth, Matisse.Picasso, Mus Modern Art, New York, 2002; coauth, Manet & the Execution of Maximillian, Mus Mod Art, New York, 2006

ELDREDGE, BRUCE B
MUSEUM DIRECTOR, ADMINISTRATOR
b Van Wert, Ohio, July 1, 1952. *Study:* Ohio Wesleyan Univ, Delaware, BA, 74; Tex Tech Univ, Lubbock, MA (mus admin), 76; State Univ Albany, NY, 80-81. *Pos:* Dir, Geneva Hist Soc, 76-78, Schenectady Mus, 78-80, Frederic Remington Art Mus, Ogdensburg, NY, 81-84, Muskegon Mus Art, Mich, 84-87, Tucson Mus Art, Ariz, 87-90, Portsmouth Mus, Va, 91-92, Stark Art Mus, Tex, 92-96 & Mus Horse, NMex, 96; coordr arts & humanities, Capitol Dist Humanities Prog, State Univ Albany, NY, 80-81; chmn, Art Comn, Ruidoso, NMex, 96-98; ceo, exec dir, NW Mus Arts & Cult, current bd trustee, Group Health, 2006-. *Mem:* Am Asn Mus; Tex Asn Mus; NMex Mus Asn; Asn Youth Mus (treas, 92-93). *Publ:* Ed, Sourcebook, Tex Asn Mus, 93-96. *Mailing Add:* 2316 W First Ave Spokane WA 99204

ELDREDGE, CHARLES C, III
HISTORIAN
b Boston, Mass, Apr 12, 1944. *Study:* Amherst Coll, BA, 66; Univ Minn, PhD, 71. *Collection Arranged:* Gene Swenson: Retrospective for a Critic (contribr & ed, catalog), 71; Marsden Hartley Lithographs & Related Works (auth, catalog), 72; The Arcadian Landscape: Nineteenth Century Am Painters in Italy (coauth & ed, catalog), 72; John Ward Lockwood, 1894-1963 (auth, catalog), 74; Am Imagination & Symbolist Painting (auth, catalog), 79; Charles Walter Stetson: Color and Fantasy (auth, catalog), 82; Helen Foresman Spencer Mus Art, Univ Kans, Lawrence; Art in New Mexico, 1900-1945 (co-auth, book), Nat Mus Am Art, 86; Pacific Parallels: Artists and The Landscape In New Zealand (auth, catalog), NZ-US Arts Found, 91; Georgia O'Keeffe: Am & Modern, 93; Tales from the Easel: Am Narrative Paintings from Southeastern Mus, Circa 1800-1950 (auth, catalog), 2004. *Pos:* Cur asst, Minn Hist Soc, St Paul, 66-68; Cur collections, Univ Kans Mus Art, Lawrence, 70-71, dir & chief cur, Helen Foresman Spencer Mus Art (formerly Univ Kans Mus Art), 71-82; mem ed bd, Mid-Continent Am Studies Asn, 71-77; assoc ed, Art J, 79-81; dir, Nat Mus Am Art, 82-88; mem ed bd, Am Art, 87-2007; trustee, Amherst Coll, 87-93; prof Am Art, Hall distinguished, Univ Kans, 88-; dir, Georgia O'Keeffe Found, 89-95; Smithsonian res assoc, 88-; bd trustees, Amon Carter Mus, 2003-06 & Terra Found Am Art, 2008-. *Teaching:* Prof art hist, Univ Kans, 70-82 & 88-; vis fel, Univ Auckland, 93; vis prof, Buffalo Bill Hist Ctr, Cody, Wyo, 96. *Awards:* Smithsonian Fel, 79 & 95; Fulbright Scholar-New Zealand, 83; Outstanding Achievement Award, Univ Minn, Minneapolis, 86; WT Kemper Fel for Teaching, excellence award, 2003; Balfour Jeffrey Res Achievement Award, Humanities & Social Sci, 2008. *Bibliog:* Marsden Hartley (auth), Lithographs and Related Works, 72; Ward Lockwood (auth), 1894-1963, 1974, American Imagination and Symbolist Painting, 79. *Mem:* Asn Art Mus Dirs (treas, 81-82, trustee, 87-88, hon mem, 90-); Coll Art Asn; Mid-Continent Am Studies Asn; Am Studies Assoc. *Res:* American art. *Publ:* Contribr, Georgia O'Keeffe: Natural Issues 1918-1924, Williams Coll; Georgia O'Keeffe, Abrams, 91; Georgia O'Keeffe, American and Modern, Yale, 93; Life Cycles: The Charles E Burchfield Collection, Buffalo State Coll, 96; Reflections on Nature: Small Paintings by Arthur Dove 1942-43, AFA, 97; Tales from the Easel; American Narrative Paintings circa 1800-1950, Ga, 2004; auth, John Steuart Curry's Hoover and the Flood: Painting Mod Hist, NC, 2007; co-auth, The Legend of Rex Slinkard, Stanford, 2011. *Mailing Add:* Univ Kans Dept Art Hist 209 Spencer Mus Art 1301 Mississippi St Lawrence KS 66045-0001

ELDREDGE, MARY AGNES
SCULPTOR
b Hartford, Conn, Jan 21, 1942. *Study:* Vassar Coll, with Concetta Scaravaglione & Juan Nickford, BA; Pius XII Inst, Florence, Italy, with Josef Gudics, MFA. *Work:* Hood Mus Art, Dartmouth Coll. *Comn:* Mary the Mother of us All, Our Lady of the Snows Church, Woodstock, Vt, 90; Mary and Child, Christ the King Cath Community, Las Vegas, Nev, 91; Our Lady of Peace, St Joseph and Christ Child, Blessed Sacrament Church, Greenfield, Mass, 92-97; Processional Candlesticks, Paschal Candlestand, St Vincent Ferrer Church, New York, 97 & 2001; Processional Cross, SS Mary and Joseph, Presentation Relief, Church of Presentation, Stockton, Calif, 2001-03; Creche Mepkin Abbey, Moncks Corner, SC, 2006-2010. *Exhib:* Nat Arts Club Religous Art Exhib, New York, 66; Acad Artists Asn Nat Exhib, Springfield, Mass, 67; Modern Art and the Religious Experience, Fifth Ave Presby Church, New York, 68; 6th Biennial Nat Religious Art Exhib, Cranbrook Acad Art, 69; 42nd Nat Interfaith Conf Relig, Art and Archit, Chicago, 81; 42nd Nat Fall Exhib, Southern Vt Art Ctr, Manchester, 98. *Pos:* Dir, Springfield Art & Hist Soc, Vt, 88-90. *Awards:* 16th Ann Bldg Awards Prog Award of Excellence, Staten Island CofC, 77; Miller Award Best Sculpture, Southern Vt Art Ctr, 90; Bene Award, Permanent Visual Arts, Modern Liturgy, 92; and others. *Bibliog:* Virginia Watson-Jones (auth), Contemporary American Women Sculptors, Oryx Press, 86. *Media:* Copper, Stone, Wood. *Dealer:* Garden Gallery Rte ll Londonberry VT 05148. *Mailing Add:* 408 Parker Hill Rd Springfield VT 05156

ELECTROS See Vekris, Babis A

EL HANANI, JACOB
PAINTER
b Casablanca, Morocco, Mar 14, 1947. *Study:* Aveni Sch Arts, Tel Aviv, Israel, 66-69; Ecoles des Beaux Arts, Paris, 69-71. *Work:* Guggenheim Mus, Mus Mod Art, Metrop Mus Art, NY; Centre Georges Pompidou, Paris, France; Nat Gallery Art, Washington, DC. *Exhib:* New Acquisitions, Guggenheim Mus, NY, 77; Constructivism and the Geometric Tradition, Albright Knox Gallery, 77; Micrography, Israel Mus, Jerusalem, 81; Printing and Writing, Cooper-Hewitt Mus, NY, 82; New Acquisitions, Hirshhorn Mus, Washington, DC, 86; Trends in Geometric Abstract Art, Tel Aviv Mus, 87. *Awards:* Louis Comfort Tiffany Found Award, 97. *Media:* Ink. *Dealer:* Yoshii Gallery 20 W 57th St New York NY 10019. *Mailing Add:* 473 Broadway New York NY 10013

ELIAS, SHEILA
PAINTER
b Chicago, Ill. *Study:* Art Inst Chicago, 60-68; Columbus Coll Art & Design, BFA, 74; Calif State Univ, Northridge, MA, 78. *Work:* Brooklyn Mus, NY; Chase Manhattan Bank, New York; First Los Angeles Bank; Kunsan Contemp Mus, Korea; Laguna Beach Mus Art, Calif. *Comn:* Beverly Ctr, Los Angeles; Jeffries Residence, comn by Pasqualle Vazzana, Laguna, Calif, 74; Hilton Hotel, Barbara Dorn & Assoc, Newark, Calif, 83; Exec Life Corp, Los Angeles Co Mus Art Rental & Sales, 84; Spago Restaurant, comn by Wolfgang Puck & Barbara Lazaroff, Tokyo, Japan, 85; Segerstrom Residence, Balboa, Calif, 85. *Exhib:* Group exhibs, Liberty: The Official Exhib Commemorating the Centenary of the Statue of Liberty, NY Pub Libr & Louvre, Institude des Decoratifs, Paris, France, 86; The Embellishment of the Statue of Liberty, Cooper-Hewitt Mus, New York, 86, Los Angeles Center for Digital Art, Los Angeles, Calif, 2008, Arc Gallery, London, 2010; solo exhibs, New Eng Ctr Contemp Art, Capital Bank, Miami, 94, Metro Dade Cult Resource Ctr, Miami, 94, Lowe Mus, Univ Miami, Fla, 97, Edison Comm Coll, Ft Myers, 98 & Art & Public Places, Orlando, 98; Kim Foster Gallery, New York, 2001; Bass Mus, Miami Beach, 2002; Michelle Rosenfeld Gallery, New York, 2002; Chelsea Galleria, Miami, 2005-2006, 2008-2009; Farmani Gallery, Los Angeles, 2007; Frost Art Mus, Univ Miami, Fla; Multicultural Arts Ctr, Cambridge, Mass, 2009; Museo Vault, Miami, Fla, 2009; Coral Springs Mus Art, Fla, 2009; Nova Southeastern Univ, Fla, 2010; Frost Art Mus, Fla Int Univ, Miami. *Pos:* Bd mem, BASS Mus, Miami Beach & MoCA Mus, Miami, Fla. *Awards:* Metro Art Int Medal, New York, 86; Women of Yr, CofC, Tarzana, Calif, 86. *Bibliog:* Armando Alvarez Bravo (auth), Nuevo Herald, Sheila Elias y la Alegria de Pintar, 99; Peter Frank and Robert C Morgan (auths) Sheila Elias Somewhere-Anywhere, Mid Career Retrospective, 144 color pgs, Nova Southeastern Univ, 2011. *Mem:* Artists Equity (mem bd dirs, 81); Coll Art Asn; Women's Caucus Art. *Media:* Miscellaneous. *Interests:* Digital photography. *Publ:* Art News, New York Reviews, 157-58, 10/02. *Dealer:* Michelle Rosenfeld Gallery 16 East 79. *Mailing Add:* 9999 Collins Ave Ph 1D Bal Harbour FL 33154

ELIASOPH, PHILIP
HISTORIAN, CRITIC
b New York, NY, 1951. *Study:* Adelphi Univ, BA, 72; State Univ NY, Binghamton, MA, 75, PhD, 79, study with Kenneth C Lindsay. *Collection Arranged:* Paul Cadmus: Yesterday and Today (auth, catalog), Miami Univ & traveling, 81; Robert Vickrey: Lyrical Realist, ACA Galleries & traveling, 82; Stevan Dohanos: Images of Am, New Britain Mus Am Art, 85; Am Art: Past & Present, Kennedy Galleries, 88; Mark Balma: Drawing From Tradition, Electa, Milan, 93. *Pos:* Educ consul, Art of the Western World (TV ser), Pub Broadcasting System, 87-; Conn ed, Art New England (mo) 84-87; alternate mem & art adv comt, Stamford, Conn, Pub Arts, 86-88; dir, Open Visions Forum, 1996-2009. *Teaching:* From instr to prof art hist & art criticism, Fairfield Univ, Conn, 75-, chmn fine arts dept, 84-89; dir, Walsh Art Gallery, Quick Ctr Arts, 89-97. *Awards:* Fac Res Grant, Fairfield Univ, 84; CINE Golden Eagle (Robert Vickrey: Lyrical Realist), Int Film Jury, 86. *Mem:* Coll Art Asn Am; Int Asn Art Critics; New Eng Appraisers Asn. *Res:* 20th century American art; Italian renaissance painting; propaganda; art & politics; mass media & criticism; American figurative painting. *Publ:* Producer, Robert Vickrey: Lyrical Realist and Steven Dohanos: Images of America (doc films), 86; Valor & Vainglory: French Military Art, Forbes Mag Collection, 87; Mastering egg tempera-techniques of Robert Vickrey, Artist's Mag, 11/87; co-auth, Art of the Western World Faculty Guide, Pub Broadcasting System & Annenberg Found, 89; Robert Cottingham: Rolling Stock Series (exhib catalog), Harcourt's Contemp Art, San Francisco, 91; contribr, Am Arts Quarterly, Am Art Jour, Smithsonian, Antiques & Fine Art Magazine, 2000-; Robert Vickrey: The Magic of Realism, Hudson Hills Press, Jan, 2009. *Mailing Add:* c/o Dept Visual & Performing Arts Fairfield Univ Fairfield CT 06824

ELIASSON, OLAFUR
INSTALLATION SCULPTOR, PHOTOGRAPHER
b Copenhagen, 1967. *Study:* Royal Danish Acad Art, Copenhagen, 1989-95. *Work:* Blind Passenger, 2010, Harpa, 2011, Rainbow Panorama, 2011, Moon, 2013, Contact, 2015. *Comn:* Movement Meter for Lernacken, City of Malmö, Sweden, 2000; Windspiegelwand, German Inst Technol, Berlin, 2001; Sun Reflector, Stockholm Univ Physics Ctr, 2003; Sphere, Munich, 2003; Rewriting, KPMG, Munich, 2004; Opera House Chandeliers, Moller Found, Copenhagen Opera House, 2004; New York City Waterfalls, 2008. *Exhib:* Solo exhibs include Galerie Lukas & Hoffmann, Cologne, 1994, Stalke Galleri, Copenhagen, 1994 & 1997, Tommy Lund Galerie, Odense, 1995,

Neugerriemschneider, Berlin, 1995, 1998, 2001 & 2006, Galleria Emi Fontana, Milan, 1996, 1999 & 2003, Tanya Bonakdar Gallery, NY, 1996, 2003, 2006 & 2007, Kunsthalle Levyn, Vienna, 1997, Marc Foxx Gallery, LA, 1997 & 1999, Kunshtalle Basel, 1997, Reykjavik Art Mus, 1998 & 2004, Bonakdar Jancou Gallery, NY, 1998 & 2000, i8 Gallery, Reykjavik, 1999 & 2002, De De Appel Found, Amsterdam, 1999, Masataka Hayakawa Gallery, Tokyo, 2000, Gallery Koyanagi, Tokyo, 2000 & 2006, Irish Mus Mod Art, Dublin, 2000, Art Inst Chicago, 2000, Reykjavik Art Festival, 2001, Mus Mod Art, NY, 2001, Overgaden, Copenhagen, 2002, Sofia, Madrid, 2003, 50th Biennale Venice, 2003, Tate Mod, London, 2003, Kunnsthaus Zug, Switzerland, 2003, 2004, 2005, 2006 & 2007, Aspen Art Mus, Colo, 2004, San Francisco Mus Mod Art, 2007, PS1 Contemp Art Ctr, New York, 2008, Dallas Mus Art, 2008; group exhibs include Summer Show, Tanya Bonakdar Gallery, NY, 1996, Frankenstein, 2003, Controlled, Contained & Configured, 2005; Berlin Biennial, 1997; Trade Routes, Johannesburg Biennale, 1997; On Life, Beauty, Translations & Other Difficulties, Internat Istanbul Biennial, 1997; New Photog, Mus Mod Art, NY, 1998, Landscape, 2006, Eye on Europe, 2006; Waterfall, Sydney Biennial, 1998; Stalke Anniversary Show, Stalke Gallery, Copenhagen, 1998, On Paper, 2000; Venice Biennial, 1999, 2001 & 2005; Solomon R Guggenheim Mus, NY, 1999, 2002 & 2007; Carnegie Internat, Carnegie Mus Art, Pittsburgh, 1999; Internat Triennale Contemp Art, Yokohama, Japan, 2001; Imperfect Marriages, Galleria Emi Fontana, Milan, 2003; The Straight or Crooked Way, Royal Coll Art, London, 2003; Sitings, Mus Contemp Art, Los Angeles, 2003; Reykjavik Arts Festival, 2005; Geffen Contemp, Los Angeles, 2005; Contemp Art Biennale, Lyon, 2005; Between Art & Life, San Francisco Mus Modern Art, 2006; Peace Tower, Whitney Mus Am Art, NY, 2006; Surprise, Surprise, Inst Contemp Arts, London, 2006; Internat Archit Exhib, Venice, 2006; Kunsthaus Zug, Switzerland, 2007. *Pos:* founder, Little Sun. *Awards:* Wolf Prize in Painting and Sculpture, Israel, 2014. *Dealer:* Tanya Bonakdar Gallery 521 W 21 St New York NY 10011; Neugerriemschneider Linienstr 155 D-10115 Berlin Germany

ELIOT, LUCY CARTER
PAINTER
b New York, NY. *Study:* Vassar Col, BA; Art Students League with Bridgman, Brackman, Raphael Soyer & Kantor; Columbia Univ, with Ralph Mayer; studied with William Von Schlegell, Ogunquit, Maine. *Work:* Rochester Mem Art Gallery, NY; Munson-Williams-Proctor Inst, Utica, NY. *Exhib:* Pa Acad Fine Arts, Philadelphia, 46, 48-50, 52 & 54; Va Biennial, 48; Corcoran Biennial, Washington, DC, 47 & 51; Ringling Bros Mus, Sarasota, Fla, 58; Nat Acad Design, NY, 71, 78 & 90; Butler Inst, Youngstown, Ohio, 65, 67, 69, 70, 72, 74 & 81; Upland Idyll, Everson Mus, Syracuse, NY, 76; Cooperstown Art Asn, 78, 81 & 90. *Pos:* Mem bd, Artists' Tech Res Inst, 75-79. *Teaching:* Instr painting & drawing, Dept Occupational Therapy, Bronx Vet Hosp, NY, 50-52. *Awards:* Moore-Greenblatt Mem Award, Nat Asn Women Artists, 93; Michael M Engel Mem Award, 94; Robert Philipp Mem Award, 95. *Mem:* Artists Equity Asn; Audubon Artists; Am Soc Contemp Artists; Nat Asn Women Artists; NY Soc Women Artists; and others. *Media:* Oil, Casein. *Mailing Add:* 131 E 66th St New York NY 10021

ELKINS, LANE
EDUCATOR, CERAMIST
b McDonald Co, Mo, Mar 26, 1925. *Study:* Southwest Mo State Col, BSEd(with hon), 49; Columbia Univ, MAFA & FAEd, 50; with Marquerite Wildenhain, 56 & 63; Cranbrook Acad Art, MFA, 62. *Work:* Springfield Art Mus, Mo. *Comn:* Pottery and jewelry comns for individuals. *Exhib:* Springfield Art Mus Ann Regional Show, 53-72; Wichita Art Asn Galleries Decorative Arts & Ceramics Exhib, 60 & 62; Ann Drawing & Sculpture Show, Ball State Univ Art Gallery, 63; Am Jewelry Today, Ala Mus Fine Arts, 64; Am Craftsmen Show, Smithsonian Inst, 70. *Teaching:* Prof ceramics, Southwest Mo State Univ, 50-82, prof art, 62-87; retired. *Awards:* Protective Image (cast bronze) Award, Edmund F Ball, Nat Sculpture Show, 63. *Mem:* Am Craftsman Coun; Mo Craftsman Coun. *Media:* Clay, Metals. *Publ:* Contribr, Walker Art Quart, spec issue, 59

ELKINS, TONI MARCUS
PAINTER
b Tifton, Ga, Feb 22, 1946. *Study:* Boston Univ, 65-66; Univ Ga, ABJ, 68; Columbia Coll, 78-80. *Work:* Springfield Art Mus, Mo; Randolph Macon Woman's Coll, Lynchburg, Va; Richland NE High Sch; Clemson Univ; Asheville Mus Art, NC; Cent Carolina Community Found, Columbia, SC. *Exhib:* SC First Miniature Show (auth, catalog), Cameo Gallery, 80; Rocky Mt Nat, Foothills Art Ctr, Golden, Colo, 83; Watercolor W, 84-2000; San Diego Watercolor Soc Int, 84-2000; SC State Mus traveling exhib, 85; Nat Watercolor Soc, Brae, Calif; Watercolor USA Honor Soc, Springfield, Mo; Eastern Wash Watercolor Soc, 2000; Northeast Watercolor Soc, NY, 2000; Southern Watercolor's 24th Ann, McKissick Mus, 2001. *Pos:* Supt fine arts, SC State Fair; exec dir, SC Crafts Asn, 86-96; chmn, Sculpture Pub Places, 95-97; Wine Festival adv Coun, Columbia, SC. *Awards:* President's Award, Soc Watercolor Painters, Joshua, Tex, 92; Meyer Hardware Award, Rocky Mt Nat, Golden, Colo, 92; Howard B Smith Award, SC Watercolor Ann, Marion, 92; Elizabeth O'Neill Verner Award for Contrib to SC Art, 99; John Richeson Award, San Diego Watercolor Soc, Linda Doll Purchase Award, Golden Artists Colors Merit Award, 2000; Toni Milyard REMAX Merit Award, Western Colo Watercolor Soc, 2000; 2000 Women of Distinction Award, Congaree Girl Scouts Inc, 2000; Merit Award, Western Fedn Watercolor Socs, 2007; 2nd Place, Hilton Head Art League, 2008. *Mem:* Cult Coun Richland & Lexington Counties; Southeastern Arts & Crafts Expos (adv bd coun); Cent Carolina Community Found; SC Watercolor Soc (pres 2005-06); EdVenture Mus (bd trustees 2007-). *Media:* Acrylic, Oil, Mixed Media. *Publ:* Contribr, Miles Batl's Complete Guide to Creative Watercolor; Les Krantz (auth), The New York Art Rev, 89; Community Tour Mag (cover), SC Arts Comn, 92; Lake Murray Mag, 8/2006; and others. *Dealer:* Paul Sloan Designer Columbia SC 29201. *Mailing Add:* 1511 Adger Rd Columbia SC 29205-1407

ELLENZWEIG, ALLEN BRUCE
WRITER, CRITIC
b New York, NY, Nov 4, 1950. *Study:* Cooper Union, with Dore Ashton, BFA, 1973; New York Univ, MFA (dramatic writing), 1985. *Collection Arranged:* Private Myths: Unearthings of Contemporary Art (auth, catalog), Queens Mus, NY, 78; Visual Diaries: A Personal Use of Words and Images (auth, catalog), Alex Rosenberg Gallery, 80; Prejudice & Pride: The New York City Lesbian & Gay Community, World War II-Present (auth, catalog), Tweed Gallery, City Hall, NY, 88. *Pos:* Contrib ed, Arts Mag, NY, 74-79; contrib reviewer, Art Am, 80-86; lectr & panelist, The History of Homoerotic Themes in Photography, Ethics & Evidence in Lesbian & Gay Studies, Ctr for Lesbian & Gay Studies, City Univ NY Grad Ctr, 89; moderator & panelist, The Homoerotic at Risk: Censorship of Gay Sensibility in Photography, 4th Ann Lesbian, Bisexual & Gay Studies Conf, Harvard Univ, 90; Queering the Movies, Outwrite, 6th Ann Gay & Lesbian Writers Conf, 96; lectr, G.P. Lynes: Paris, NY, and Gay Life before Stonewall, City Coll of City Univ NY, spring/2014; NY corresp, PASSION: Mag of Paris, 83-85, contrib ed, 85-85; Paris corresp, NY Native, 85; contrib writer, critic, Gay & Lesbian Rev Worldwide, 95-; pres, bd of dirs, The Robert Giard Found, 2003-2009. *Teaching:* Part-time lectr expository writing, Rutgers Univ, 99-2000, fall/2007, fall/2014 & 2015; educator guide, NY Hist Soc, fall/2004; adj prof, Writing for Coll, Coll Mt Saint Vincent, 2009-2013. *Awards:* Writer in residence, Michael Karolyi Mem Found, Vence, France, 72 & Edward Albee Found, Montauk, NY, 79; Writing Fel, Vt Studio Ctr, 98; Writing fel, Vt Studio Ctr, 2003; Rsch Fel, Harry Rausom Center, Univ Tex, Austin, 2011. *Bibliog:* John Russell (auth), When art imitates anthropology, 4/9/1978 & Grace Glueck (auth), Visual diaries, 2/22/1980, NY Times; Robert Julian (auth), Bodies of Evidence, Bay Area Reporter, 10/15/1992; Julian Bell (auth), Decency and Delusion, Times Literary Supplement, 3/19/1993. *Mem:* Nat Writers Union; Publishing Triangle; The Authors Guild. *Res:* The life and career of 20th century photographer George Platt Lynes. *Publ:* Auth, The Homoerotic Photograph: Male Images from Durieu/Delacroix to Mapplethorpe, Columbia Univ Press, 1992, 2012; Anne Frank: The Secret Annex and the Closet, Response: Contemporary Jewish Rev, winter/spring 1997; Picturing the Homoerotic, in: Queer Representations, NYU Press, 1997; The Athena Galleria, in: Men on Men 7, Dutton/Signet, 1998; A Fine Point, in: Kosher Meat, Sherman Asher Publ, 2000; Sarah Bernhardt at the Jewish Mus, Studies in Gender & Sexuality, winter/2007; The Private Utopia of George Platt Lynes, George Platt Lynes:The MaleNudes, Rizzoli, 2011; Wounded by Beauty, Storyteller: Duane Michals, Presel & Carnegie Mus of Art, 2014. *Mailing Add:* 200 W 15th St New York NY 10011

ELLER, EVELYN ELLER ROSENBAUM
COLLAGE, ARTISTS BOOKS
b New York, NY, Apr 17, 1933. *Study:* Art Students League, New York, with Morris Kantor & W Barnet, 51-54; Acad De Belle Arte (Fulbright Fel Grant), Rome, Italy, 54-55; Sch for Visual Arts, New York, 89. *Work:* Indianapolis Mus Fine Art; Nat Mus Women Arts, Washington, DC; Libr Mus Mod Art, NY; King St Stephens Mus, Hungary; Libr Brooklyn Mus, NY; Yale Univ, Arts of the Book Collection; Univ Western Mich; Newark Public Libr, NJ; Tyler Mus of Art, Tex; Univ of Vt; Queens Mus, NY; Mus of the City, NY; Univ Calif, Los Angeles; Rutgers Univ Libr, NJ; Special Collections, NY Hist-Soc; George Mason Univ Lib, Va; Godwin-Ternbach us; Owens Coll, New York; Yeshiva Univ Mus, New York; Oberlin Coll Lib, Ohio; New York Pub Lib, New York; Duke Univ, NC; Mishkin Gallery, Baruch Coll, CUNY; collage for language & cognitive development ctr. *Exhib:* Juried Ann, Queens Mus, NY, 74-75 & 89; Works on Paper, Brooklyn Mus, NY, 75; Ctr for Book Arts, NY, 85, 87, 89, 91, 95, 2003-2004, 2007, & 2012; Int Book Exhib, King St Stephens Mus, Hungary, 87, 94, 2000, 2006, & 2013; Book as Art IV, Nat Mus Women Arts, Washington, DC, 91 & 96; Artist Book, Islip Art Mus, Long Island, NY, 91; My Vision, Sumner Sch Mus, Washington, DC, 91; Corcoran Gallery Art, Washington, DC, 93, 97 & 99; Art of the Book, Univ Indianapolis, Ind, 2002; Flushing Town Hall Biennial, 2002; Krasdale Gallery, NY, 2003 & 2007; New York City Health & Hospital Corp, 2003; Queens Mus, 2005-2006; Brooklyn Pub Libr, 2006; Brooklyn Coll Libr, 2007; Galerie 1816, Bretonneux, France, 2007; Minn Ctr for Book Arts, Minn, 2009; Free Lib Philadelphia, Pa, 2009; Park Sch Baltimore, 2010; Dana Lib, Rutgers Univ, Newark, NJ, 2011; Fla Atlantic Univ, Miami, Fla; Ga Coll Mus, Milledgeville, Ga, 2011; Kalamazoo Book Arts Ctr, Kalamazoo, Mich, 2012; Pace Univ, Westchester, NY, 2013; Kalamazoo Booth Art Ctr, 2012, 2013. *Pos:* Artist-in-residence, Yaddo, Saratoga Springs, NY, 57; admin asst, Art Sch Mus Mod Art, NY, 58-59. *Teaching:* Workshop & sem instr, Alliance Queens Artists, NY, 89-99. *Awards:* Juror Award, Small Works Ann, 83; Showcase Award, Queens Borough Pub Libr, New York, 85; Lever House Lobby Gallery Award, New York, 96. *Bibliog:* John Arthur Shanks (auth), Evelyn Eller, Techniques of Landscapes Collage, Artists Mag, 4/84; John & Joan Digby (auth), The Collage Handbook, Thames & Hudson, 85; B Ommerman (auth), Around Town, Newsday, 4/7/91; Shreen La Plantz (auth), The Art and Craft of Handmade Book, Lark, 2001; Orísolties (auth), Fixing the World, Brandies Univ Press, 2002; Covers of 4 jours, 2000, Am Speech-Language Hearing Asn; Orisolties (auth) Fixing the World, Jewish American Painters in the 20th Century, 2003; Artist Has the Gift, The Queens Courier, 2006; The Eye of the Collector (exhib catalog), Hebrew Union Coll, 2006; Suzanne Tourtillott (auth), 500 Handmade Books, Lark Publs, 2008; Tikkon Olam & the Am Left, an Interview with Evelyn Eller, Krasdale Galleries, New York, 2010; 100 Handmade Books, Lark Publs, 2010; 1000 Artists Books, Quarry Book, Rock Port, 2012; Jewish Studies Jour, Queens Coll, Spring, 2012; 500 Handmade Books, Vol 2, Lark Publishers, 2013. *Mem:* Ctr Bk Arts. *Media:* Handmade Papers, Acrylic, Book Artist. *Specialty:* Artist's Books. *Interests:* Music, literature. *Dealer:* Vamp & tramp Books Dealer LLC Birmingham AL. *Mailing Add:* 165 W End Ave Apt 16R New York NY 10023

ELLINGER, ILONA E
PAINTER, EDUCATOR
b Budapest, Hungary, June 12, 1913. *Study:* Royal Hungarian Univ Sch Art, MFA; Royal Swedish Art Acad; Johns Hopkins Univ, with David M Robinson & W F Albright, PhD; Univ Freiburg, Phi Beta Kappa; Univ Wis. *Work:* Pvt Collections, Illus of Book Hindu Mythology in Art. *Exhib:* Soc Washington Artists; Solo exhib, Am-Brit

Art Ctr, George Washington Univ, 50; Silver Spring Art Gallery, 51; Corcoran Gallery Art, 58; Batiks, Gallery N, Setauket, 77; State Univ of NJ Faculty Show, 2001; and others. *Teaching:* Prof art & head dept, Trinity Col, Washington, DC, 43-78, Fulbright prof hist art & archit, Nat Col Arts, Lahore, W Pakistan, 63-64; vis prof, State Univ NY Stony Brook, 69-79, prof emer; prof, SUNY, 79-85, Emer, currently. *Awards:* Cornelia Harcum Award, Johns Hopkins Univ; Fulbright Award, 63-64. *Mem:* Soc Washington Artists; Archaeol Inst Am. *Media:* Oils, Watercolor, Pen. *Res:* Hindu mythology as depicted in sculpture & painting. *Interests:* Hindu and Buddhist Art history. *Publ:* Auth, Hindu Mythology in Art; Hindu Divinities, 2002. *Dealer:* Trafford 2333 Government St Victoria BC Canada. *Mailing Add:* 67 Quaker Path Stony Brook NY 11790

ELLIOT, CATHERINE J
PAINTER, GRAPHIC ARTIST
b New York, NY, July 26, 1947. *Study:* Sarah Lawrence Col, BA, 69; Creative Arts Workshop, New Haven, Conn, 73; Otis Art Inst, Los Angeles, 76-77; Univ Coll Los Angeles, 80. *Work:* BBDO Advert; Cutter's Restaurant; New West Corp; Scitex America. *Comn:* Large outdoor sculpture, comn by Keith Williamson, Los Angeles. *Exhib:* Moon St Gallery, Westport, Conn, 74; Am Ceramics Soc, Brand Art Gallery, Los Angeles, 75 & 88; Otis Art Inst Group Show, Los Angeles, 77; Solo exhibs, RGA Gallery, Los Angeles, 77 & 26th St Gallery, Santa Monica, Calif, 79; 4th Ann Great Lakes Show, Chicago, Ill, 90; The Fifth Monarch Tile Nat Ceramic Competition, San Angelo Mus Fine Arts, Tex, 90. *Teaching:* Instr ceramics, Moon St Pottery, Westport, Conn, 73; instr pvt ceramics lessons, 74-77; instr, The Color Ctr, Los Angeles, 93-94. *Awards:* Purchase Award, Am Ceramic Soc Group Show, 75. *Bibliog:* Carole Katchen (auth), Artist's Mag, 90; Sara Scribner (auth), Faces, Designer's West Mag, 90. *Mem:* Am Ceramic Soc; Artists Equity Asn. *Media:* Miscellaneous Media; Computer Graphics. *Publ:* Macdigest Mag, 2/94, 4/94, 6/94, 9/94 & 11/94

ELLIOT, JOHN
PAINTER, FILMMAKER
b London, Eng, May 25, 25; US citizen. *Study:* Acad Fine Arts, Italy, 47-50; NY Univ, Film Sch, 51-54; Sch Visual Arts, 58-59; also pvt study in Europe. *Work:* Chesterwood Mus & Naumkeag, Trustees of Reservations, Stockbridge, Mass; Ala Space Ctr, Huntsville; Nat Trust Hist Preserv, Washington, DC. *Comn:* Hist Preserv, comn by Mrs Onassis, K Hepburn, A Baxter & Nat Trust, NY, Los Angeles & DC; murals, Village of Nyack & Haverstraw, NY; Pres Ronald Reagan Portrait, Republican Party; cards, BAI Int, 96-97; Finkelstein Libr Mem Portrait; portrait, Nathan S Kline Inst. *Exhib:* French Retrospective, Metrop Mus Art, NY, 76, Nat Collection Fine Arts, Smithsonian Inst, 77, Detroit Inst, Mich, 77 & Fogg Art Mus, Cambridge, Mass, 78; 20th Ann Int, Soc Illustr, NY, 77; Knickerbocker Nat, Nat Arts Club, NY, 79; Pastels Only, Copley Soc, Boston, 79; solo exhib, Retrospective, Hopper House Art Ctr, Nyack, NY, 2008. *Pos:* Pres visual commun, Graphics for Industry Inc, Dover, Del & Tenafly, NJ, 67-2000, JE-GFI Ince, NY; vpres, Hist Soc Nyacks, 99-2008. *Teaching:* Workshops and videos, The Total Pastelist, Art & Design in Action & Tools of the Trade. *Awards:* Gold Medal, Freedoms Found Valley Forge, 70; Ten Best Awards, Soc Illustrators, 77; numerous nat exhib awards. *Bibliog:* Freedom to innovate, Indust Photog, 7/70; Hudson Valley Mag, 98. *Mem:* Pastel Soc Am; Soc Illustrators; PSA Nat Arts Club; Salmagundi Club; Oil Pastel Asn Int Ltd. *Media:* Oil Pastel, Oil. *Publ:* The Night the Animals Talked, Am Broadcasting Co, 75; American Phenomenon, Nat Found, 77; Learning from the Pros, Watson-Guptill, 84; Introduction to Oil Pastels, 87; Pastels & the Portrait, 88; Painting Solutions, Hands, Faces & Figures, Quarto, 90; Pastels & the Landscape, 90; Painting Solutions, Hands, Faces & Figures, Quarto, 90; contrib ed, numerous articles, The Artist's Mag; Oil Pastel for the Serious Beginner, Watson-Guptill, 2002. *Mailing Add:* 1720 N Congress Ave Unit B209 West Palm Beach FL 33401

ELLIOT, SHEILA
WRITER, ADMINISTRATOR
b Philadelphia, Pa, Mar 25, 1946. *Study:* Vassar Coll, AB, 67; Fairleigh Dickenson Univ, MA, 79; studied and New York Univ & Columbia Univ, NY. *Work:* Oil Pastel for the Serious Beginner, Watson-Guptill, 2002. *Pos:* Dir pub relations, Pastel Soc Am, NY, 81-83; exec dir, Oil Pastel Asn NY, 83-86; ed, Art & Artists USA, 83-86; contrib ed, The Artist's Mag, 86-; publicity dir, Pen & Brush Inc, NY, 87-90; webmaster, OPAI.org, 2001-2004; Managing Ed & Staff writer on Art The Hook Mag, 2005-; publicity dir & trustee, HSN & NCAC, Hopper House Art Ctr, NY, 2006-, pres bd trustees, 2007, vpres mktg, 2008, cur, 2009-, consultant; publicity dir, Art in the Everglades Day Festival, 2009-; Palm Beach County ad exec; Antiques & Art Around Fla Mag; Antique Shoppe newspaper, 2009-; Mgr, Abbott Design Ctr, W Palm Beach, 2009-2013; bd mem, publicity chair, Audubon Soc Everglades, 2009-. *Bibliog:* Oil Pastel for the Serious Beginner, Watson-Guptill, 2002; Chinese Art & Architecture, Mason Crest Publ, 2004; Ancient History of China, Mason Crest Publ, 2005; numerous articles, The Artists Mag, American Artists, Pastel J, etc, 2001-2008. *Mem:* Oil Pastel Asn Int (treas 2001-2004. *Res:* Working methods and procedures of current American artists. *Publ:* Contribr, Painting for the Pros, Watson-Guptill, 83; coauth, Introd to Oil Pastel, Holbein, 86 & Pastels & the Portrait, 88; numerous articles, The Artists' Mag, 85-; Decorative Artist's Workbook, 90; Pastels & the Landscape, 90; Fine Arts Connoisseur, 2007; Antiques & Art Around Fla, 2014. *Mailing Add:* 1720 N Congress Ave Unit B209 West Palm Beach FL 33401

ELLIOTT, ANNE
SCULPTOR, PAINTER
b Pittsburgh, Pa, Aug 9, 1944. *Study:* Sarah Lawrence Col, BA, 66; Art Students League, 67; Parson Sch Design, 69; Pratt Inst, Cert, 92. *Work:* Westmoreland Mus, Greensburg, Pa; Alternative Mus, NY. *Exhib:* One-person exhibs, Graham Gallery, NY, 78 & 80, Westmoreland Mus Art, Greensburg, Pa, 82, Summerfare, Ctr Arts, State Univ NY, Purchase, 83 & 84, Pittsburgh Pub Theater, Installation for Production of K2, 84, Hewlett Gallery, Carnegie-Mellon Univ, 84, Johnston Art Mus, Johnstown, Pa, 88 & Blair Art Mus, Hollidaysburg, Pa, 88; Originals, Graham Gallery, NY, 80 & Selections from Gallery Artists, 83; Exchanges III, Abrons Art for Living Ctr, Henry St Settlement, NY, 81; Candidates for Awards, Am Acad & Inst Arts & Letts, NY; Nature: Images & Metaphor, Views by Women Artists, Greene Space Gallery, NY, 82; Papyrus Abstractus, Westport-Weston Art Alliance, Westport, Conn, 82; The New Explosion: Paper Art, Fine Arts Mus Long Island, Hempstead, NY, 82, Byer Mus Arts, Evanston, Ill, 83; Seven New Artists, Pittsburgh, Today, Carnegie, Pittsburgh, 84; Sculpture by Women in the Eighties, UP Gallery, Pittsburgh, 85; Columns by Artists, 14 Sculptors' Gallery, NY, 86; Paper: Form & Substance, NJ Ctr Vis Arts, Summit, NJ. *Teaching:* Col NJ, 93-94. *Awards:* Fel, Pa Coun Arts, 85. *Bibliog:* Hilton Kramer (auth), Art at Guggenheim: Niche for Favorites, NY Times, 5/31/80; John Perrault (auth), Anne Elliot, Westmoreland Mus, Gettysburg, Pa, 82; John Caldwell (auth), Seven New Artists, Pittsburgh Today, Carnegie, 84. *Mem:* Coll Art Asn; Nat Sculpture Ctr. *Media:* Aluminum Mesh & Paper; Acrylic, Oil. *Dealer:* Leslie Ava Shaw 110 W 87th St New York NY. *Mailing Add:* 2775 Main St Trenton NJ 08648

ELLIOTT, GREGORY
ADMINISTRATOR, EDUCATOR
Study: Southern Methodist Univ, MA, 80, MFA, 88. *Pos:* head sculpture, grad coord, LA State Univ, Baton Rouge, 98-2002; chair dept art, Univ Tex El Paso, 2003-2008, Univ Tex San Antonio, 2008-. *Mailing Add:* University of Texas at San Antonio Dept Art & Art History One UTSA Cir San Antonio TX 78249

ELLIOTT, LILLIAN
WEAVER, TAPESTRY ARTIST
b Detroit, Mich. *Study:* Wayne Univ, BA; Cranbrook Acad Art, Bloomfield Hills, Mich, MFA. *Work:* Mus Contemp Crafts, NY; Detroit Inst Arts; San Francisco City Art Collection; Objects, USA--Johnson's Wax Collection, Smithsonian Inst Traveling Exhib, 70-72; Univ Art Collections, Ariz State Univ, Tempe. *Exhib:* Calif Design Exhibs, Pasadena Art Mus, 62-71; Fabric Collage Invitational, Mus Contemp Crafts, NY, 65; Collagen--Collage Invitational Exhib, Kunstgewerbe Mus, Zurich, Switz, 68; Objects, USA--Johnson's Wax Collection, Smithsonian Inst Traveling Exhib, 70-72; Tapestry, Tradition & Technique Invitational, Los Angeles Co Mus Art, 71. *Pos:* Fabric designer, Ford Motor Co Styling Div, Dearborn, Mich, 56-59. *Teaching:* Instr art, Univ Mich Col Archit & Design, Ann Arbor, 59-60; lectr textiles, Univ Calif, Berkeley, 66-76. *Awards:* San Francisco Art Festival Purchase Award, 65 & 69; Founder's Soc Purchase Award, Mich Craftsmen's Show, Detroit Inst Arts, 69; Calif Arts Coun Grant/Artist in Residence, 79-80. *Media:* Textile. *Publ:* Auth, Chap, In: The New American Tapestry, Van Nostrand Reinhold, 68. *Mailing Add:* 1775 San Lorenzo Ave Berkeley CA 94707-1824

ELLIS, ANDRA
PAINTER, CERAMIST
b New York, NY, Mar 3, 1948. *Study:* Queens Col, City Univ New York, BFA, 71. *Work:* Mint Mus Art, Charlotte, NC; Karen Johnson Boyd, Racine, Wis; Sanford Besser, Little Rock, Ark; Luwa Corp, Charlotte, NC; Nations Bank, Charlotte, NC. *Exhib:* The Collector's Eye, Am Craft Mus, NY, 91; one-person exhib Hodges Taylor Gallery, Charlotte, NC, 92 & 95; B'nai B'rith Klutznick Mus, Washington, DC, 95; Miriam Cup, Hebrew Union Coll Skirball Mus, Exhib, 97; Helander Gallery, Palm Beach, Fla, 92; Works Southern Women, Fay Gold Gallery, Atlanta, Ga, 92; Spotlight, Miss Mus Art, Jackson, 91. *Pos:* Dir, Ceramics Dept, West Side YMCA, NY, 74-82, dir/producer, Int Clay Film Festival, Greenwich House Pottery & traveled to NY State Col Ceramics, Alfred, NY, 81-85; spec projs coord, Greenwich House Pottery, NY, 82-84; proj designer & dir, Children's Mural/Children's Law Ctr, Charlotte, NC, fall 91. *Teaching:* Instr Intermediate to advanced ceramics, two dimensional design, mixed media sculpture & apprenticeship progs in clay, 74-82; lectr, Viewpoints: Four Artists on Art, Mint Mus Art, Charlotte, NC, 91; lectr, Surface Exploration in Clay, Sawtooth Ctr Visual Arts, Winston-Salem, 91-92 & Queens Col, Charlotte, NC, 91-92; Philadelphia Sch Dist, currently. *Awards:* Nat Endowment Arts Visual Artists Fel, 90-91; NC Arts Coun Artist Proj Grant, 92-93. *Bibliog:* Vanessa Lynn (auth), Andra Ellis, Am Ceramics, winter 89; Pamela Blume Leonard (auth), Figurative clay, Art Papers, 11-12/91; John Rodgers (auth), Andra Ellis, Art Papers, 9-10/92. *Dealer:* Hidges Taylor Gallery 401 N Tyron St Charlotte NC 28202

ELLIS, DAVID
PAINTER
b Raleigh, North Carolina, 1971. *Study:* Cooper Union, New York, BFA, 1994. *Exhib:* Solo exhibs include 222 Gallery, Philadelphia, 2004, Jessica Murray Projs, New York, 2005, Rice Univ Gallery, Tex, 2006, New Image Art, Los Angeles, 2007, Roebling Hall, New York, 2008; Group exhibs include Clocktower Show, PS 1, New York, 2001; No Condition is Permanent, Smack Mellon, Brooklyn, 2001; One plant Under a Groove, Bronx Mus; Beautiful Losers, Contemp Art Ctr, Ohio, 2004; Grotto 2, Jessica Murray Projs, New York, 2004; Paint on Trucks in a World in Need of Love, Mus Mod Art, Queens, New York, 2004; GADGET: Mechanics and Motion in Contemp Art, Contemp Art Ctr, Ohio, 2005; Greater New York 2005, PS 1, Long Island City, New York, 2005; BMG Artists' Annual '07, Black Market Gallery, Los Angeles, 2007; Animated Painting, San Diego Mus Art, Calif, 2007; Ensemble, Inst Contemp Art, Philadelphia, 2007; 50,0000 Beds, Aldrich Contemp Art Mus, Conn, 2007

ELLIS, GEORGE RICHARD
MUSEUM DIRECTOR
b Birmingham, Ala, Dec 9, 1937. *Study:* Univ Chicago, BA & MFA, Univ Calif, Los Angeles, candidate in PhD prog. *Pos:* Art supvr, Jefferson Co Schs, 62-64; former asst dir, Birmingham Mus Art; dir develop & asst dir, Mus Cult Hist, Univ Calif, Los Angeles, presently; dir, Honolulu Acad Arts. *Mem:* Los Angeles Ethnic Art Coun; Am Mus Asn; Art Mus Dirs Asn; Hawaii Mus Asn; Pac Arts Asn. *Mailing Add:* Honolulu Acad Arts 900 S Beretania St Honolulu HI 96814

ELLIS, LOREN ELIZABETH
PAINTER, PHOTOGRAPHER
b Binghamton, NY, Dec 12, 1953. *Study:* Univ SFla, BA, 74; Fla State Univ, MFA, 77. *Work:* Eastman Kodak Collection, Pharmaceutical Br, Philadelphia, Pa; House of Reps, Capitol Bldg, Tallahassee, Fla; Mus of Modern Art; NY Public Libr; 13 Mus Szcerin, Poland; Queens Mus; Park Ave Bank, NY NY; Mus Photog Krakow, Poland; Santa Barbara Mus Art. *Comn:* Mural, Hillsborough Parks Dept, 82,; mural, Johnson & Johnson Co, 83; mural, Tampa Electric Co, 83; mural, Fund for Dance, 20th Anniversary, NY; mural, Lee Co Electric Co, Ft Myers, Fla, 84; mural, My Yankees; Joyce Theatre Dance, New York; Yar Mural Russ Adv, New York. *Exhib:* Solo exhibs, Hillsborough Co Mus, Tampa, Fla, 74, M Ingban Gallery, Soho, NY & Chasama Times Sq 9/11, Spiritual Ctr: Status Clslard My, 2008, Soho Photo Gallery, 2009, Garibaldi Meucci Mus, 2010; Professional Women Artists, Lowe Art Mus, Miami, Fla, 74; Tampa Mus Art, 79, 80 & 82 & Nostalgia, Tampa Mus W, Fla, 84; Mus Choice, Lock Haven Arts Ctr, Orlando, Fla, 81; Phoenix Gallery Invitational, Soho, 95; group exhib, Exit Art 9/11; Ryan Group, Chelsea Med Ctr, New York, 2008, 2015. *Pos:* Art cur, Photo Exhib, Youth Mus Charlotte Co, Fla, 77 & Womens Survival Ctr, 82-83; dir & founder, Art for Healing Inc, NY, photo workshops; cur, Great Neck Art Center (found by NY Arts Coun). *Teaching:* Inst art & photomontage, Parsons Sch Design, NY, 89-96; Columbia Prep Sch. *Awards:* Fine Arts Coun Fel, Fla, 77; Merit Award, Tampa Mus, 78; Grants, Arts Coun Tampa & Hillsborough Com 90; Grant, Puffin Found Ecology Works; Centrum Port Townsend Residency, WA; Grant, Lower Manhattan Cultural Council, book on 9/11; Awards Grant, Arts & Humanities of Staten Island, New York Dept Cult Affairs, 2008. *Bibliog:* Articles in Art South, Tampa Times, Photo Dist News, Szicine News & Full Page in Poland; 2-page rev, USF Alumni Mag, 2008; interview (tv), Art & Living, Times Sq, New York & Dallas, Tex, 2008. *Mem:* Prof Women Photogrs; Photog Administrators Inc; Puffin Found NY; PAI; Fla State Alumni. *Media:* Photographic Painting. *Res:* Chernobyl for ecology series, 98-; Holocaust for project, 2000-. *Specialty:* Photog; Mixed Media; Murals; Corp Identity Art. *Interests:* Ice Skating, Music, Dance, Drama. *Publ:* Contribr, cover art, Tampa Bay Mag, 79 & Organic Mag, 89. *Mailing Add:* 2350 Broadway New York NY 10024

ELLIS, RICHARD
AUTHOR, ILLUSTRATOR
b New York, NY, Apr 2, 1938. *Study:* Univ Pa, BA. *Work:* New Bedford Whaling Mus, Mass; Philadelphia Zoological Garden; Denver Mus Natural Hist; Kendall Whaling Mus; Sea Life Park, Hawaii. *Comn:* Mural of whales, Denver Mus Natural History, 78; mural of Moby Dick, New Bedford Whaling Mus, Mass, 86; mural of blue whale, New Bedford Whaling Mus, 2000. *Exhib:* Whale paintings, New Bedford Whaling Mus, 75, Mystic Seaport, 75 & Am Mus Natural Hist, 76; Animal Art Show, Los Angeles Co Mus, 77; shark paintings, Am Mus Natural Hist, 78; Acad Natural Sci, Philadelphia, 81; Museo del Mare, Genoa, Italy, 2005. *Collection Arranged:* Sharks in Art, Fort Lauderdale Mus Art, 2010-12. *Pos:* Exhib designer, Am Mus Natural Hist, 65-68 & res assoc, 2002-; Cur, Mythical Creatures, Am Mus Nat Hist, 2007; Cur, Shark! Fort Lauderdale Mus Art, 2011. *Teaching:* Lectr, Am Mus Natural Hist, 82-83. *Awards:* Explorers Club Communications Medal, 2012. *Bibliog:* T Walker Lloyd (auth), Richard Ellis, Am Artist Mag; Steve Blount (auth), Richard Ellis, Sport Diver Mag; Derek S B Davis (auth), Richard Ellis, Pa Gazette. *Mem:* Soc Animal Artists; Explorers Club. *Media:* Mixed. *Interests:* Photography, Conservation. *Publ:* Auth & illusr, The Book of Whales, Knopf, 80; Dolphins and Porpoises, Knopf, 82; Men and Whales, 91; Great White Shark, 91; Monsters of the Sea, 94; Deep Atlantic, 96; Search for the Giant Squid, 98; Imagining Atlantis, 98; Encyl of the Sea, 2000; Aquagenesis, 2001; The Empty Ocean, 2003; Sea Dragons, 2003; Tiger Bone & Rhino Ham, 2005; Singing Whales & Flying Squid, 2006; Tuna: A Love Story, 2008; On Thin Ice: The Changing World of the Polar Bear, 2009; The Great Sperm Whale, 2011; SHARK: A Visual History, 2012. *Mailing Add:* 42 W 15th St New York NY 10011

ELLIS, ROBERT M
PAINTER
b Cleveland, Ohio, 1922. *Study:* Western Reserve Univ, Sch Archit, Cleveland, Oh, 40-42; Cleveland Sch Art, Cleveland, Oh, 46-48 (grad); Mexico City Col, Mexico City, BA, 49; Univ Southern Calif, MFA, Los Angeles, Calif, 52. *Work:* Amoco Production Co, Houston; Mus Albuquerque; Mus Fine Arts, Santa Fe, NMex; Robert Walz & Assocs, Hollywood, Calif; numerous pvt collections. *Exhib:* Occidental Coll Art Gallery, Los Angeles, 57; Solo exhibs, Pasadena Art Mus, Pasadena, Calif, 61, Hollis Gallery, San Francisco, Calif, 64, Greenhill Gallery, Fort Lauderdale, Fla, 73, James Yu Gallery, New York, NY, 75, Hills Gallery, Santa Fe, NMex, 77, Santa Barbara Mus Art, Santa Barbara, Calif, 79; Wildine Gallery, Albuquerque, NMex, 81, Kauffman Galleries, Houston, Tex, 86, Retrospective, Univ NMex Art Mus, Albuquerque, NMex, 91, Cafe Gallery, Albuquerque, NMex, 91.; Philip Bareiss Fine Arts, Taos, NMex, 91,; Jill Youngblood Gallery, Los Angeles, Calif, 84; Jacqueline Lloyd Contemporary Gallery, Taos, NMex, 00, Dwight Hackett Projects, Santa Fe, NMex, 06, Bob Ellis Recent Work, Woodcuts/Works on Wood, Exhibit 208, Albuquerque, NMex, 10, Statements, A Perspective on Contemp Art in NMex, Albuquerque, NMex, 85 & 86, Landscape Invitational, Kron/Reck Gallery, Albuquerque, NMex, 86, Modern Monoprints, An Exhibit of Monotypes, Kimo Gallery, Albuquerque, NMex, 98, The Taos Exhibition of American Watercolor IV, Taos, NMex, 98, En Celebracion de Muerte, Taos Historic Museum, Taos, NMex, 03; New Mexico Cancer Center Foundation Spring Exhibit, Albuquerque, NMex, 04, Friends! Exhibit at UNMH Gallery, Albuquerque, NMex, 08, Alcove 12.2. Museum of NM, Santa Fe, NMex, 12, Art Centennial, Thinking NM, NMSU Art Gallery, Las Cruces, NMex, 12. *Pos:* Cur educ, Pasadena Art Mus, Pasadena, Calif, 56-64; asst dir, Univ Art Mus, Univ NMex, Albuquerque, NMex, 64-68, dir, 68-71; interim dir, The Harwood Found, Taos, NMex, formerly, dir, currently; award juror, Nat Exhib Am Watercolor IV, Taos, NMex, 98; mem, Site Santa Fe Advisory bd, 98; Oversaw renovation & expansion and endowment campaign of The Harwood Mus, Supervised permanent collection, 95-98. *Teaching:* prof dept art & art hist, Univ NMex, 64-87, prof emer, currently. *Awards:* Special Recognition Award, Univ NMex, Taos, 97; Regents Meritorious Service Medal, Univ NMex, 97; NMex Governor's Award, Individual Support of the Arts, 98; Wurlitzer Found Residency program, Taos, NMex, 2008. *Bibliog:* Joanne Forman (auth), Ellis Comes Home, The Taos News, March 28, 91; James A. Moore (auth), Robert M. Ellis/A Painter's Space, Paintings and Works on Paper 1951-1990, Univ NMex Art Mus catalog, 91; Melody Romancito, Review, Robert Ellis in Taos, Tempo: The Arts & Entertainment Magazine of The Taos News, October 5, 2000; Virginia L. Clark (auth) Many Will Missss Robert Ellis: Harwood Museum Director Looks Forward to Retirement, Tempo: The Arts & Entertainment Magazine of The Taos News, (review), May 31 2001. *Publ:* Viewpoints, poster for benefit art auction, Dept Art & Hist,.Univ NMex, 87

ELLIS, SALLY STRAND See Strand, Sally Ellis

ELLIS-TRACY, JO
ARTIST
b Tulsa, Okla. *Study:* Univ Southern Calif, BFA; Stanford Univ, 64. *Work:* Philbrook Art Mus; Exquisite Visions on a Theme of Balanchine, Harvard Univ Theatre. *Comn:* 20 Drawings for Apollo 17 Mission, CBS, NY; Female Athlete (sculpture), Calif Sports Inc, The Forum, Los Angeles; Bronze Man Walking (sculpture), Conn Gen Life Insurance, Hartford; Space Life (painting & film), Nat Aeronautics & Space Admin, Goddard Space Ctr, Md; Commemorative Award (steel plaque), Armco Steel Corp, Ohio; Corp Imagery & Commun Proposals & Models. *Exhib:* Calif Design Show, Pasadena Art Mus; Calif Artists Group, Newport Harbor Art Mus, Newport Beach; Fisher Gallery, Univ Southern Calif, Los Angeles; Philbrook Art Mus, Tulsa, Okla. *Pos:* Founder, Jet-Art, NY; critic, Pasadena Star News; pres & creative dir, The Eye Int Group, Inc, NY, Eye Int Gallery, Fine Arts Bldg, 89, Eye Int Gallery, Fine Arts Bldg, Los Angeles, 92; pres & ceo, Fine Art Educational & Entertainment Vision. *Bibliog:* Jo Ellis Tracy-Variations on a theme of the dance, KCET Television, Los Angeles; Jo Ellis Tracy-Artist, Pasadena Mag; Jo Ellis Tracy-American Artist, London Times. *Media:* Mixed Media, Oil, Drawing. *Specialty:* Specific projects; commissions in painting & sculpture; decorative items of unusual design. *Publ:* Illusr, Exquisite visions on a theme of Balanchine, Forbes Mag, 86 & American Business & the Arts, brochure, Forbes, 86. *Dealer:* The Eye International Group Inc New York NY. *Mailing Add:* 30 E 70th St New York NY 10021

ELLISON, ROBERT W
SCULPTOR
b Detroit, Mich, Dec 13, 1946. *Study:* Mich State Univ, BFA, 69, MFA, 71. *Work:* Tweak 360, Jordan Skateboard Park, Salt Lake City Govt, Salt Lake City, Utah, 2005; Sprouting Seed Bench, Big Tree at Country Estates, City & Co of Broomfield, Colo, 2006; Zig Zing, Aurora Senior Ctr, Aurora, Colo, 2007; Bounce, Dunedin Community Ctr, Dunedin, Fla, 2008. *Comn:* Sculpture, Untitled, Universal Steel Corp, Lansing, Mich, 69; sculpture, Point to the Time, Kincaid Elementary Sch, Municipality of Anchorage, Anchorage, Alaska, 96; sculpture, Mr Zebra & Friends, Alameda Co Recorders Off, Oakland, Calif, 99; sculpture, Impact, Stockton Teen Ctr, Calif, 2005; Bay Area Rapid Transit, Enbarcadero Sta, San Francisco, Calif. *Exhib:* Bourborbygmi, 28th Ann San Francisco Art Festival, 74; Grey Streak, 21st Ann Calif Show, 74; Solo exhibs, James Willis Gallery, San Francisco, Calif, 76, San Francisco State Univ, Calif, 88, Victor Fischer Galleries, San Francisco, 91, Am Pres Lines Hq, Calif, 92, Contract Design Ctr, San Francisco, 95 & Sculptural Invitational, Meuso Valle D' Aosta, Torino, Italy, 95; Riccochet, Palo Alto Outdoor Sculpture Exhib, 77; Four Times Daily, San Francisco Civic Ctr Plaza, 79; Arch Tworain, Donut Diorama, San Francisco Redevelop Agency, 81; People's Choice Proj, Concord, Calif, 90; Oakland City Ctr, Calif, 90; Fermi Lab, US Dept Energy, Batavia, Ill, 91; group exhib, Oakland City Ctr, Calif, 92; Northshore Sculpture Park, Skokie, Ill, 93; City of Palm Desert, Calif, 94; La Quinta Sculpture Park, Calif, 94; Mt View City Hall, Calif, 94; Olive Grove Sculpture Garden, Calif, 98; William Zimmer Gallery/Stevenswood, Calif, 98; Mill Valley Sculpture Garden, Mill Valley, Calif, 2002; Art Downtown, Santa Rosa, Calif, 2007; Paradise Ridge Winery, Santa Rosa, Calif, 2008. *Pos:* Pres, Lookout Sculpture Park West. *Teaching:* Instr sculpture design & drawing, Mich State Univ, 70-71; Lansing Community Coll, Mich, 71-72; Coll Marin, Kentfield, Calif, 72-77; San Francisco Acad Art Coll, Calif, 96. *Awards:* First Place, 21st Ann All Calif Show, 75; Feature Exhib, Bicentennial San Francisco Art Festival, 76; Purchase Recommendation, People's Choice Proj, Concord, Calif, 90. *Bibliog:* Diane Peterson (auth), County's Artists Make Lives an Open Studio, Press Democrat, 10/10/99; Public Art, The Guild, Vol 13, 202, 98; Chris Robson (auth), Donut Diorama (film doc), Sausalito, Calif; 4 Times Daily (film doc), Bravura Films, San Francisco, Calif. *Mem:* Pacific Rim Sculpture Group; Sonoma Co Cult Arts Coun; Int Sculpture Ctr, Petaluma Arts Coun. *Media:* Welded Steel Painted, Aluminum. *Specialty:* Sculpture, Contemp. *Interests:* Growing cactus and succulents. *Dealer:* Alison Bies Fine Art

ELLOIAN, PETER
GRAPHIC ARTIST
b Cleveland, Ohio, Apr 20, 1936. *Study:* Cleveland Inst Art, BFA; Univ Iowa, MFA; Pratt Graphic Ctr. *Work:* Toledo Mus Art; Libr Cong, Washington; Philadelphia Mus Art; Mus Mod Art Gallery, Yerevan, Armenia; Yugoslav Portrait Gallery, Tuzla, Bosnia; House of Humor & Satire, Gabrovo, Bulgaria. *Exhib:* Nat Exhib Prints, Libr Cong, 71, 73 & 77; Drawings & Prints, Am Cult Ctr Gallery, Belgrade, Yugoslavia, 86; Inst per la Cult e l'Art, Catania, Sicily, 87; Int Print Biennale, Varna, Bulgaria, 89, 91 & 93; Kochi Int Triennia Exhib Prints, Japan, 90; Int Invitational L'Utopie, Sans Illusion, Atelier Contrast, Fribourg, Switz, 92; Int Exhib, Portland Art Mus, Ore, 97; Nat Print Biennial, Univ, Minn, 98; McNeese Nat Works on Paper, 2000; Int Biennial of Mini Prints, Tetovo, Republic of Macedonia, 2001; Master Exhib, Minsk, Belarus, 2002; Int Small Engraving, Salon Carbunari, Romania, 2003; Pacific Rim Int Print Exhib, Univ Hawaii, Hilo, Hawaii, 2005; Mini Print Int, Cadaques, Spain, 2005; Donated with Love Exhib, House of Humor & Satire, Gabrovo, Bulgaria, 2007; un Monde en noir et Blanc, Exposition Internationale de Gravures Petit Format, Maison des Arts et de la culture de Brompton, Sherbrooke, Que, 2007; 20th Int Biennial

Humor and Satire in the Arts, Gabrovo, Bulgaria, 2011. *Teaching:* Instr, Toledo Mus Art, Sch of Design, 66-87; Instr, Village des Arts en France, Lacoste, France, 84 & 87; prof printmaking & drawing, Art Dept, Univ Toledo, Ohio, 87-2001. *Awards:* Ismet Mujezinovic Award, Fourth Int Biennial Portrait Drawings & Graphics, Tuzla, Yugoslavia, 86; Lynd Ward Mem Award, Print Nat, Hunterdon, NJ, 92; Gascar Award, House of Humor & Satire, Gabrovo, Bulgaria, 95; and others. *Mem:* Soc of Am Graphic Artists; Boston Printmakers. *Media:* Drawing, Printmaking. *Mailing Add:* 26114 W River Rd Perrysburg OH 43551

EL MAE See Lorelli, Elvira Mae

ELOWITCH, ANNETTE
DEALER
b Portland, Maine, Dec 24, 1942. *Study:* Boston Univ, 61; Westbrook Col, Portland, Maine, AA, 63;. *Pos:* Co-owner, Barridoff Galleries, 75-. *Specialty:* Nineteenth and twentieth century paintings. *Mailing Add:* Barridoff Galleries PO Box 9715 Portland ME 04104-5015

ELOWITCH, ROBERT JASON
DEALER, PATRON
b Portland, Maine, Apr 8, 1943. *Study:* Amherst Col, BA. *Pos:* Drama/film critic, Portland Press Herald & Eve Express, 67-69, Maine Times, 70-75; owner & pres, Barridoff Galleries, 75-. *Mem:* Maine State Comn Arts & Humanities (comnr, 73-75); Skohegan Sch Painting & Sculpture (dir, 68-80); Portland Sch Art (sch comt mem, 74-75); United Portland Regional Orgn of Arts Resources (vchmn, 74). *Specialty:* 19th and early 20th century American oils and contemporary regional oils, watercolors, etc. *Interests:* Promotion and support of the arts in the state of Maine; purchase and sale of American and European art of the 18th, 19th & 20th centuries

ELSAYED, DAHLIA
PAINTER
b New York, 1969. *Study:* Ctr Book Arts, New York, 1991; Barnard Coll, New York, BA (English), 1992; Columbia Univ Sch Arts, MFA (Creative Writing), 1994. *Comn:* Morris Mus; Newark Pub Libr; Zimmerli Art Mus; Jersey City Mus; Newark Mus. *Exhib:* Solo exhibs include Armenian Libr & Mus Am, Watertown, Mass, 2002, Jersey City Mus, NJ, 2003, Johnson & Johnson Corp Art Gallery, New Jersey, 2003, Lafayette Coll, Easton, Penn, 2008; Group exhibs include New Members Show: City Without Walls Gallery, Newark, NJ, 1999; Passion, Richard Anderson Fine Arts, New York, 1999; 3rd Int Gyumri Biennial, Armenia, 2002; Unveiling the Image, NJ Ctr Visual Art, Summit, NJ 2004; Synopsis 10, Pierro Gallery, South Orange, NJ, 2004; Drawing, Green Barn, Sagaponack, NY, 2004; Phantom Limb, Unit B Gallery, Chicago, 2004; Six Degrees of Separation, Black Maria Gallery, Los Angeles, 2005; Viewfinder, Moti Hasson Gallery, New York, 2005; 100 NJ Artists Make Prints, Traveling exhib, Rutgers Ctr Innovative Print & Paper, Rutgers Univ, NJ, 2006; Personal Geographies, Hunter Coll Times Sq, New York, 2006; Sprawl, Jersey City Mus, NJ, 2008. *Awards:* NJ State Council Arts Artist Fel, 1999, 2004; ArtReach Ed Prog Grant, Newark, NJ, 2001; ArtsLink Grant Individual Artists, 2003; Artist Fel, Rutgers Ctr Innovative Printmaking, NJ, 2005; Joan Mitchell Found Grant, Painters & Sculptors, 2007. *Mailing Add:* 429 Bergen Blvd Palisades Park NJ 07650

ELY, TIMOTHY CLYDE
BOOK ARTIST
b Snohomish, Wash, Feb 9, 1949. *Study:* Western Wash Univ, Bellingham, BA (drawing & printmaking), 72, Univ Wash, Seattle, MFA (design), 75. *Work:* Victoria & Albert Mus, London, Eng; Libr Cong, Washington, DC; John Paul Getty Mus, Los Angeles, Calif; Spencer Collection, New York Pub Libr, NY; Rijksmuseum Meermanno-Westreenianum Den Haag, Neth; Mus Mod Art, Brooklyn Mus, The Grolier Club, NY; Yale Univ, Princeton Univ & Harvard Univ. *Comn:* Artist Book, Polar Rare Book Rm, Univ Alaska, Fairbanks, 84; Book of Roses, Sony Music, NY. *Exhib:* Solo exhibs, Eaton/Shoen, San Francisco, 84, NY Acad Sci, 87, Contemp Crafts Gallery, Portland, Ore, 88, Granary Bks, NY, 89, 91, 92 & 93, Minn Ctr Bk Arts, Minneapolis, 89 & Victoria & Albert Mus, London, Eng, 89; Folger Libr, Washington, DC, 87; Univ Arts, Philadelphia, Pa, 88; Ctr for Bk Arts, NY, 88-92; Maison du Livre de l'Image et du Son, Ville de Villeurbanne, France, 88; Am Craft Mus, NY & Boston Athenaeum, Mass, 88; Cult Ctr, Boulogne-Billancourt, France, 89; Biblioteque de l'Arsenal, Paris, France & Bibliotheca Wittocklana, Brussels, Bel, 90; Grolier Club, NY, 91; Anchorage Hist & Fine Arts Mus, Alaska, 91; Princeton Univ, NJ, 92; Gallery Tinka, San Jose, Costa Rica, 92; Nat Coll Art & Design, Bergen, Norway, 92; The World of Maps, Mus Art, Anchorage, Alaska, 94; Smithsonian Inst Libr, Science & Artists Book, Washington, DC, 95; The New Storytellers: One-of-a-Kind artists' books in Boston Libr Mus, Wildener Libr, Harvard Univ, 96; Alphabet Book II Chicago, Ill, 97. *Teaching:* Instr book art, Ctr for Book Art, NY, 84-. *Awards:* Pollack-Krasner Found Grant, 86; Art Matters Grant, 88 & 90; Nat Endowment Arts Reg Grant, West States Art Fedn, 94. *Bibliog:* Roy Harley Lewis (auth), Fine Bookbinding in the Twentieth Century, Arco Publ, 85; Martha Bergman (auth), An interview with Timothy C Ely, The New Bookbinder, UK, 87; Lois Allan (auth), Complex and simple mysteries, Artweek, 5/88. *Mem:* Designer Bookbinders, Eng. *Media:* Painting, Drawing. *Publ:* Auth, Portfolio (article), Am Crafts Mag, 6/86; Martina Margetto (auth), International Crafts, Thames & Hudson, 91; Synesthesia, Granary Bks, 93; The Flight into Egypt, Chronicle Bks, 95. *Mailing Add:* 504 N Mill Stn Colfax WA 99111

ELYASHIV, YIZHAK
PRINTMAKER, DRAFTSMAN
b Israel, 1964. *Study:* Bezalel Acad Art & Design, Israel, BFA, 1990; RI Sch Design, MFA, 1992. *Work:* Mus Fine Arts, Boston; British Mus; Yale Univ Art Gallery; Fogg Art Mus; Cleveland Mus Art; Brooklyn Mus; Israel Mus. *Comn:* print ed, Tamarind Inst, 99; print ed, Island Press, Wash DC, 2000; print-club ed, Cleveland Mus Art, 2001. *Exhib:* Tel Aviv Mus, Israel, 1989; Contemp Art Mus, Israel, 1990; Mus fur kunsthandwerk, Frankfurt, Ger, 1991; Talentborse Handwerk, Ger, 1992; Bezalel Acad Gallery, Israel, 1994; Bannister Gallery, RI Coll, Providence, 1995; List Art Ctr, David Winton Bell Gallery, Brown Univ, 1997; solo exhibs, Betsy Senior Gallery, New York, 1998, Virginia Lynch Gallery, RI, 1998-99, Univ Wyo Art Mus, 1998, Wheeler Gallery, Providence, RI, 2000, Del Ctr for Contemp Art, 2000, NAGA Gallery, Boston, 2003, 2005, 2009, Reeves Contemporary, New York, 2005 & 2008, Montserrat Coll Art, 2006, Spheris Gallery, Vt, 2006, Lenore Gray Gallery, RI, 2007, RI Coll Bannister Gallery, 2009; N AM Print Exhib, Emmanuel Coll, Boston, 1999; Matrix, Clark Univ Art Gallery, Worcester, Mass, 2001; The American River, Florence Griswold Mus, Lyme, Conn, 2003; Tweed Mus Art, Univ Minn, Duluth, 2004; Drawing Now, Bristol Cmty Coll, Fall River, Mass, 2007. *Teaching:* Instr, RI Sch Design & RI Coll, formerly; instr drawing & printmaking, Clark Univ, Mass, 1999-. *Awards:* MacColl Johnson Fel, RI Found, 2007; Howard Award Fel, Brown Univ, 2007; Pollock-Krasner Found Grant, 2008. *Mailing Add:* 149 5th St Providence RI 02906

EMBIRICOS, EPAMINONDAS GEORGE (PANDY EMBIRICOS)
COLLECTOR
b Athens, Greece, July 15, 1943. *Study:* MIT, BS, MS, 65. *Pos:* Chmn Embiricos Shipping Agency, Ltd, London, 69-91; vchmn, Greek Shipping Coop, Com NTERCARGO, 86-99; Embiricos Shipbrokers Ltd, London, 91-; chmn, Greek Shipping Coop Com, 99-. *Awards:* Named one of top 200 collectors, ARTnews Magazine. *Collection:* Old masters, impressionism & modern art. *Mailing Add:* Embiricos Shipbrokers Ltd 1-19 New Oxford St London United Kingdom WC1A 1NU

EMBREY, CARL RICE
PAINTER, INSTRUCTOR
b Hamilton, Tex, Oct 28, 1938. *Study:* Univ Tex, Austin, BFA, 63, MFA, 64, with Everett Spruce. *Work:* Marion Koogler McNay Mus, San Antonio; San Antonio Art League, Tex; Ark Arts Ctr, Little Rock; Emerson Gallery, Hamilton Coll, Clinton, NY. *Exhib:* Am Arts Nat Exhib, Butler Inst, Youngstown, Ohio, 65; Artists of the Southeast & Tex, Isaac Delgado Mus, New Orleans, 67; 60 Tex Artists, Inst Texan Cult, San Antonio, 68; Tex Artists Invitational, Longview Mus, Tex, 68-70; Art Teachers, Witte Mem Mus, 77; Solo exhibs, Marion Koogler McNay Art Inst, San Antonio, 74 & fifteen-year survey, San Antonio Art Inst, 88; and others. *Collection Arranged:* Paintings of Carl Embrey (auth, catalog), Five Year Retrospective, 74; The Work of Carl Embrey Retrospective (with catalog), McNay Art Mus, San Antonio, 97; Carl Embrey, The Artist and the Am Landscape, McNay Art Mus, San Antonio, Tex, 2004; The Work of Carl Embrey, Forty Years, 1965-2005, Art Ctr Waco, Tex, 2005; Carl Rice Embrey and Andrew Wyeth, McNay Art Mus, 98; Traveling, The Countryside in Art and Southern Literature. *Teaching:* Prof painting & drawing, San Antonio Art Inst, 64-93. *Awards:* Onderdonk Mem Award, San Antonio Art League, 65; Honorable Mention, Arts Nat, Tyler Mus, 67; Merit Award, Tex Artists Invitational, Longview Art League, 72; Artist of the Year, State of Tex, 98-99. *Bibliog:* Gail Falbo Smith (auth), Embrey--A Documentary, Trinity Univ, 78; Nanette Simpson (auth), Carl Embrey, Southwest Art, Houston, 79; Dan Goddard (auth), Carl Embrey, Southwest Art, Houston, 89; Steve Bennet (auth), Southwest Art: Carl Embrey, 97; Michael J. Smith (auth), A Point of Origin, Carl Rice Embrey, doc, Pub Svc Television. *Media:* Acrylic Emulsion, Watercolor, Graphite Pencil, Silverpoint, Egg Tempera. *Res:* silverpoint and painting panel construction. *Interests:* Art history, painter's materials and techniques. *Publ:* John Driscoll & Arnold Skolnick (auths), The Artist and the American Landscape, Chameleon Bks Inc, 98. *Dealer:* David Findlay Jr Fine Art 724 Fifth Ave NY 10019; Parchman Stremmel Galleries LLC San Antonio TX. *Mailing Add:* 9319 Nona Kay Dr San Antonio TX 78217-5020

EMERY, LIN
KINETIC ARTIST, SCULPTOR
b New York, NY. *Study:* Ossip Zadkine Studio, Paris; Sculpture Ctr, NY. *Hon Degrees:* Loyola Univ, New Orleans, 2004, Doctor of Letters. *Work:* Nat Collection Am Art, Washington, DC; New Orleans Mus Art; Norton Art Galleries, West Palm Beach, Fla; Huntington Mus Art, WVa; Walter P Chrysler Mus, Norfolk, Va; Mus Foreign Art, Sofia, Bulgaria; Fine Arts Mus South, Mobile, Ala; Brevard Art Mus, Melbourne, Fla; Ogden Mus Southern Art, New Orleans. *Comn:* Kinetic sculpture, City of Virginia Beach, 89; City of Oxnard, Calif, 90; Hofstra Univ, NY, 90; Sterling Drug Co, Collegeville, Pa; Daytona Beach Airport, Fla; Financial Guaranty Insurance Co, NY; Neiman Marcus, Short Hills, NJ; L R Nelson Corp, Peoria, Ill, 95; Menorah Hosp, Kansas City, Mo, 96; Izumisano Hosp, Japan, 96; Osaka Dome, Japan, 97; Stirling Corp, Irving, Tex, 2000; Mitre Corp, McLean, Va, 2001; Knight Oil Co, Lafayette, La, 2005; Order of St Lazarus, New Orleans, 2007; Kinetic Sculpture, Terminus Circle, Atlanta, 2008; Kinetic Sculpture, Univ Houston, 2011; Sandler of Performing Arts, Virginia Beach, 2011; LSU Bus Sch, Baton Rouge, 2012. *Exhib:* Solo Exhibs: Contemp Arts Ctr, New Orleans, 78, 81; Max Hutchinson Gallery, NY, 82; retrospective, New Orleans Mus Art, 96; Imperial Calcasieu Mus, Lake Charles, La, 97; Arthur Roger Gallery, New Orleans, 99, 2003, 2005; Kouros Gallery, New York, 2000, 2006; Masur Mus, Monroe, La, 2001; Meadows Mus, 2002; Pensacola Mus Art, 2007; Arthur Roger Gallery, New Orleans, 2008; Group exhibs, Int Sculpture Conf Exhib, 80; GSA Art in Archit, Nat Collection Fine Art, 80; World Expo, Brisbane, Australia, 88; Alexandria Mus, La, 89; Mus SE Tex, Beaumont, 91; Brevard Art Mus, Melbourne, Fla, 92; Kouros Gallery, NY, 2000, 2006; Meadows Mus, Shreveport, La, 2001; Masur Mus, Monroe, La, 2001; Arthur Roger; Kouros Gallery, 2005; Pensacola Mus Art, Fla, 2007; Century Asn, NY, 2007; Leepa-Rattner Mus, Palm Harbor, Fla, 2010-11; Ogden Mus Southern Art, 2012; Int Kinetic Exhib, Boynton Beach, 2012; Gallery North, Long Island, NY, 2013; Int Sculpture Exhib, WUHU, China, 2014. *Pos:* Vis critic, Tulane Univ Sch Archit, 67-68; fel, Va Ctr Creative Arts, 81. *Teaching:* Vis artist, Newcomb Art Sch, Tulane Univ, 81 & Univ Maine, 88. *Awards:* Mayor's Award Excellence in the Arts, New Orleans, 80; Young Womens Club Am Role Model Award, 89; Lazlo Aranyi Award, Pub Art, 90; Grand Prize, Pub Art, Osaka Prefecture, Japan, 97; Gov's Arts Award, 2001; Role Model

Award, Young Leadership Coun, New Orleans, 2003; Order St Lazarus companionate of Merit, 2004; S Simon Sculpture Award, Nat Acad Mus, NY, 2005; Opus awards, Ogden Mus of the South, 2012; Anniversary award, N.O. Mus Art, 2013. *Bibliog:* Pierce (auth), Lin Emery's aquamobiles, Art Int, 69; Roger Green (auth), The kinetic sculpture of Lin Emery, Arts Mag, 12/79; Bill Goliantly (auth), Tubular Bells, Horizon, 4/85; Josef Marker (auth), Lin Emery, InSite, 90; V Watson-Jones (auth), Contemp Am Woman Sculptors; Charlotte Rubenstein (auth), Am Women Artists; Edward Lucie-Smith (auth), Lin Emery: Borrowing the Forces of Nature, 96; Judy Collischan (auth), Welded Sculpture of 20th Century, 2000; Philip Palmedo (auth), The Life & Sculpture of Lin Emery, 2011. *Mem:* Sculptors Guild NY; Int mem Royal Soc Brit Sculptors; Century Asn NY; Int Women's Forum; Nat Acad. *Media:* Kinetics, Metals, Installations. *Interests:* Archeology. *Publ:* Co-auth, Kinesone I, Leonardo, Vol 19, Issue No 3. *Dealer:* Kouros Gallery 23 E 73rd St New York NY 10021; Arthur Roger Gallery 432 Julia St New Orleans LA 70130. *Mailing Add:* 7520 Dominican St New Orleans LA 70118

EMMERT, PAULINE GORE
PAINTER, EDUCATOR

b Marks, Miss, July 1, 1923. *Study:* Long Island Univ, BA, 70, MA, 78. *Work:* Long Island Univ, Greenvale, NY; New York Univ Hosp, NY; Daniel Gale, Sotheby Parke Bernet; Coldwell-Banker Realty, Cold Spring Harbor, NY; Lloyd Harbor Village, NY. *Comn:* Lloyd Harbor (painting), comn by Mrs D Kent Gale, Huntington, NY, 78; Centerport Harbor (painting), comn by Capt & Mrs Victor Grubbs, Monroe, Ga 83; Cold Spring Harbor (painting), comn by Dr & Mrs Richard H Sand, Huntington, NY, 89; No--Five Cordwainer Lane, comn by Mr & Mrs Harold Paul family; Cordwainer Lane (painting), comn by Harold Paul Family. *Exhib:* Cold Spring Harbor Whaling Mus, 81 & 93; Nat Asn Women Artists-Jacob Javits Fed Bldg & Nationwide Tours, 88-96; Cold Spring Harbor Community Room, 90 & 92; Miss Mus Art, 91; Long Island MacArthur Airport Terminal, 95. *Pos:* Lectr, Art Relig-Cult, Nat Asn Univ Women, 86, Huntington Art League & Huntington Methodist Church, 78-79; Cur, TianJin Art Col, Huntington, NY, 83; Lectr, Nat Asn Univ Women, Huntington, NY, 84. *Teaching:* Mux Lane Studio, Huntington, NY Pub Schs, Cold Spring Harbor Dist 2, Huntington Dist 3. *Awards:* William Meyerowitz Memorial-Award, Nat Asn Women Artists, 94; Heckscher Mus Long Island Show Award; Silver Brush Award, Nassau Co Mus Art, 94. *Bibliog:* David Shirey (auth), Nuances of Seasons, NY Times, 8/21/81; Ronald Pisano (auth), Long Island Paintings of the 20th Century, 90; Diane Ketchum (auth), Emmert Paintings in Airport Terminal, NY Times, 8/13/95. *Mem:* Nat Asn Women Artists (judge oils, 86-88); NY Artists Equity; Suburban Art League; Art League Long Island. *Media:* Oil, Watercolor. *Res:* Art religion and culture in 70 countries. *Mailing Add:* 61 Preston St Huntington NY 11743-2054

ENCINIAS, JOHN ORLANDO
PAINTER

b San Miguel Co, NMex, Nov 24, 1949. *Work:* Millicent Rogers Mus, Taos, NMex; Frye Art Mus, Seattle, Wash; US W Direct Corp Collection, Denver, Colo; United Mo Bank, Kansas City, Mo; Wichita Art Asn, Kans. *Exhib:* Solo exhibs, Frye Art Mus, Seattle, Wash, 93-; Govs Invitational, Loveland Mus, Colo; Am Art in Miniature, Gilcrease Mus, Tulsa, 92-94; Nat Acad Western Art, Nat Cowboy Hall Fame, Oklahoma City, 85-94 & Prix de W Invitational, 95-; Western Visions Miniature Show, Nat Mus Wildlife Art, Jackson Hole, Wyo, 92-98; Albuquerque Mus Miniature, NMex, 95-98. *Bibliog:* Walter Gray (auth), Metrop Library System, The Quiet Paintings of John Encinias, 86 & Painting on Location, 87. *Media:* Oil. *Publ:* Contribr, John Encinias, Artists Rockies, fall 79; coauth, Masterworks of Impressionism, Masterworks Art Publs, 85; contribr, Introduction-John Encinias, SW Art, 4/87; Beyond reality, Art of the W, 9-10/88; Six colors & white, Am Artist, 8/98. *Mailing Add:* 2081 W 52nd Ave Denver CO 80221

ENDE, ARLYN
STUDIO ARTIST

b New Orleans, La. *Study:* La State U, 49-51; Tulane Univ, 51; Art Inst Chicago, 53. *Comn:* Tapeta, Bridgestone-Firestone Nat Hdqs, Nashville, 91; Tapetas, West End Eynagogue, Nashville, 00; Fabric Collages, IBM, Atlanta, 98; Tapeta, Mid-IN Med Ctr, 2010. *Exhib:* Uncommon Thread, Spruill Ctr Gallery, Atlanta, 99; Side By Side, Nashville, Belfast, Ireland Airports, 01; Am Women in the Arts, Art in Embassies, Lima, Peru, 00-02. *Collection Arranged:* Full Bleed, Works of Brad Thomas, 01; Tradition in Transition, Tapestries and Constructions, 01; Mining the Surface, Works of George Dunbar, 01; Vanderbilt Univ, Nashville; Little Havana Community Ctr, Miami; Shalom Theatre, Nashville; Bradley Mem Hosp, Cleveland, Tenn. *Pos:* partner, Deepwoods Studio, 94-; exec dir and cur, Art Ctr of Cannon Co, Tenn, 90-95; dir, Univ Art Gallery, Univ of the South, 99-2000. *Awards:* Grand Prize, Am Crafts Awards, NY, 1989; Best of Show, Fiber Art in the 90's, Sawtooth Ctr for Visual Arts, Winston-Salem, NC, 89. *Bibliog:* Anna Fariello, Three Approaches to Contemporary Hooking, Fiber Arts Mag, 91; Fiberarts Design Books 1,3, and 6; Guild 4 and Guild 5; A Celebration of Hooked Rugs; Contemporary Crafts for the Home; Surface Design Jour; Am Craft; Fiberarts; Interior Design. *Mem:* Tenn Asn Craft Artists; Surface Design Asn; ACC. *Media:* Textiles, Collages. *Dealer:* Tinney Contemporary Nashville TN; Sixty-One Main Gallery Andes NY. *Mailing Add:* Deepwoods Studio 464 Wildwood Lane Sewanee TN 37375

ENDERS, ELIZABETH
PAINTER

b New London, Conn. *Study:* Conn Col, BA, 62; New York Univ (MA), New York, NY, 87. *Work:* Addison Gallery Am Art, Andover, Mass; Dow Jones Art Collection; Florence Griswold Mus, Old Lyme, Conn; Lyman Allyn Art Mus, New London, Conn; Pfizer Inc; Wadsworth Atheneum, Hartford, Conn; Art Gallery Nova Scotia, Halifax; The Brooklyn Mus Art, New York; Int House, New York; New Britain Mus Am Art, New Britain, Conn, 2010; Smith Coll Mus Art, Northampton, Mass, 2010; Mus Fine Art Boston, 2010; Whitney Mus Am Art, NY. *Exhib:* Solo exhibs, Paul Schuster Gallery, Cambridge, Mass, 66, Ulysses Gallery, NY, 92 & 94, Lyman Allyn Mus, New London, Conn, 94, 2009, Cowles Gallery, NY, 95, 2009, Norbert Considine Gallery, Princeton, NJ, 97 & UNTITLED / FOLIO, Artists Space, New York City, NY, 2001, Look at Art, Charles E Shain Libr, Conn Coll, New London, Conn, 2004 & 2006, Real Art Ways, Hartford, 2004, Alva Gallery, New London, Conn, 2006 & Chester Art Ctr, Nova Scotia, 2007, Diane Birdsall Gallery, Old Lyme Conn, 2011, Life Lines: The Art of Elizabeth Enders, Addison Gallery Am Art, Andover, Mass, 2012, Place...Painting Elizabeth Enders, Art Gallery Nova Scotia, Halifax, Nova Scotia, 2012; Artists Space Multiple, 95; Human/Nature, New Mus Contemp Art, NY, 95; Image & Eye, NY Studio Sch Benefit Exhib, 95; New Talent, New Ideas, Charles Cowles Gallery, NY, 96, 2000, 2002, 2005, 2006, 2009; Nightmare on Broome St, Dieu Donne, NY, 97; The Winter Show, Works on Paper & Gotham Group, Charles Cowles Gallery, 98; Painterly Abstraction, Lyman Allyn Art Mus, 98; Femme Brute, Lyman Allyn Art Mus, New London, Conn, 2006; A Collective Endeavor, Florence Griswold Mus, Old Lyme, Conn, 2006; Growing the Addison, Addison Gallery Am Art, Andover, Mass, 2006; Holiday Cheer, Art Gallery Nova Scotia, Halifax, 2006; March Madness, Robert Brown Gallery & Brand X Projects, New York, 2007; Other Ideas, Charles Cowles Gallery, New York, 2008; Making Their Mark, Chester Art Ctr, Chester, Nova Scotia, 2009; A Contemp Look, Lyme Art Asn, Old Lyme, Conn, 2010; An Exchange with Sol Lewitt, Mass MoCA, N Adams, Mass, 2011; Robert Brown Gallery Celebrates the First 30 Yrs, Robert Brown Gallery, Wash DC, 2012; A Contemporary Look, Lyme Art Assn, Old Lyme, Conn, 2013; INCOGNITO, Santa Monica Mus Art, Santa Monica, Calif, 2013; Blue, Art Gallery of Nova Scotia, Yarmouth, Nova Scotia, 2014. *Awards:* Medal, Conn Col, 93. *Bibliog:* Janet Purcell (auth), Abstract Language at Stuart, Trenton Times, 3/14/97; Peter Slatin (auth), Elizabeth Enders/Ulysses, ARTnews, 10/94; Patricia Harris & David Lyon (auths), Connecticut, The Spirit of America, Harry N Abrams Inc Publ, New York, 2000; Elizabeth Enders Measures Art & Language, Connecticut College Alumni Magazine, 9/2004; Elizabeth Enders, The Buzz, Kathleen Edgecomb (auth), The Day, New London, CT, 2004; Pat Serenet (auth), JAVA, The Hartford Courant, 11/22/2004; Alva gallery to present recent work by Elizabeth Enders in Attachment, Antiques and the Arts Weekly, 3/10/2006; Stephen Vincent Kobasa (auth), Women's Work, Some Brutal Truths Behind the Cliches", The New Haven Advocate, New Haven, Conn, 1/25/2007; Alumna Artist Comes Home to Lyman Allyn, Conn Coll Mag, 2009; Lyman Allyn Host Retrospective, Elizabeth Enders: Landscape/Line, Antiques & the Arts Weekely, June 5, 2009; Stephen Vincent Kobasa (auth), Words, Words, Words and Pictures: Three Variations on a Theme", Hartford Advocate, April 28, 2009; Conn Calendar, NY Times, 2006, 2009, 2011; Summer Art, The Boston Phoenix, Summer Guide, 6/8/2012; Addison Gallery Features Art of Elizabeth Enders, Antiques and the Arts Weekly, 6/8/2012; Elissa Barnard (auth), Enders Expresses the Wildness of a Chosen Place by the Sea, Chronicle Herald, Halifax, Nova Scotia, 2012. *Mem:* Artists Space (bd trustees, 86-95). *Media:* Oil, Acrylic. *Publ:* Co-auth, Elizabeth Enders, John Sailer Ulysses, 92; Ulysses Gallery, Lyman Allyn Mus, 94; Landscape/Language/Line (catalog), Essay by Charlotta Kotik, Interview by Irving Sandler. *Dealer:* Robert Brown Gallery Washington DC; Susan Frei Nathan Millburn NJ; Diane Birdsall Gallery Old Lyme CT. *Mailing Add:* 530 E 86th St New York NY 10028

ENGELBERG, GAIL MAY
PATRON

Pos: Trustee, Engelberg Charitable Found; bd trustee, Solomon R Guggenheim Mus, New York City; bd dir, Jazz at Lincoln Ctr. *Mailing Add:* Engelberg Found 30 W 68th St New York NY 10023

ENGELHARDT, THOMAS ALEXANDER
EDITORIAL CARTOONIST

b St Louis, Mo, Dec 29, 1930. *Study:* Denver Univ, 50-51; Ruskin Sch Fine Arts, Oxford Univ, 54-56; Sch Visual Arts, New York, 57. *Work:* State Hist Soc Mo, Columbia. *Comn:* Mural (humorous animals), Pediat Assoc, Mo, 73. *Exhib:* Solo exhibs, Fontbonne Col, Mo, 72 & Decade of the Environment 1970-1980, Old Courthouse, St Louis, 81 & Mark Twain Bank, St Louis, 88; Sch Visual Arts Alumni Exhib, Hansen Gallery, NY, 75; plus numerous group exhibs. *Pos:* Free-lance cartoonist, New York, 57-60 & 98-; ed cartoonist, Newspaper Enterprise Asn, Cleveland, Ohio, 60-61 & St Louis Post-Dispatch, 62-97. *Awards:* Ethical Humanist of the Year, St Louis Ethical Soc, 87. *Media:* Pen & Ink, Crayon. *Publ:* Auth, Cartoonist Profiles, 69; Dateline 1976, Overseas Press Club, 76; Cartoonist Profiles, 91. *Mailing Add:* 900 N Tucker Blvd Saint Louis MO 63101

ENGELSON, CAROL
PAINTER

b Seymour, Ind, 1944. *Study:* Carnegie-Mellon Univ, Pittsburgh, Pa, BFA, 66. *Work:* Calouste Gulbenkian Found, Lisbon; Aldrich Mus, Ridgefield, Conn; Found Art This Century, Paris; San Diego Art Ctr; Chase Manhattan Bank, NY; Carnegie-Mellon Univ, Pittsburgh, Pa. *Exhib:* Solo exhibs, 112 Workshop, Inc, NY, 77, Ruth Schaffner Gallery, Santa Barbara, Calif, 78, Oscarsson-Hood Gallery, NY, 80 & Univ Conn, Hartford, 85; Third Ann Contemp Reflections, Aldrich Mus, Ridgefield, Conn, 74; Selections from the Aldrich Mus, Am Fedn Arts Traveling Exhibition, 74-77; New Dimensions in Drawing, 1950-1980, Aldrich Mus, Ridgefield, Conn, 81; Nat & Int tour, Am Painting the 80's, 79-83; Color Abstraction in the 1980's, Baruch Coll Gallery, NY, 85; Minus 40 Plus, Haenah Kent Gallery, NY, 91. *Teaching:* Vis lectr painting, Carnegie-Mellon Univ, 78, Univ Wis-Milwaukee, 82, Univ Conn, Hartford, 85, Pratt Inst, 87 & Parsons Sch Design, 88. *Awards:* Edward MacDowell Colony Fel, 71, 72, 74 & 75; Grant, Comt Visual Arts, New York, 74; Nat Endowment Arts Grant, 77-78; Am Acad Arts & Lett Grant, 83. *Bibliog:* Annette Nachumi (auth), Carol Engelson, Arts Mag, 11/80; John Yau (auth), Carol Engelson and Rick Klauber at Oscarsson-Hood, 3/81 & Deborah Rosenthal (auth), First underground show, fall 84, Art in Am; Vivien Raynor (auth), The gathering of the avant-garde: The Lower East Side, NY Times, 85; Claire Gravel (auth), A Baie Saint-Paul, l'Art Contemporian Descend dans l'Arene, Le Soleil, 8/20/88; Barbara Rose (auth), Autocritique, 88; Hilton Kramer (auth), American painting the eighties, NY Times, 1/90; Grace Gluck (auth), New Debates on Jackson Pollock, New Biography. *Media:* Oil on Canvas, Pastel on Paper. *Publ:* Auth, Jackson Pollock, The Man and the Myth, J of Art, Vol 2, No 3, 12/89, 28. *Dealer:* David Anderson Gallery Martha Jackson Pl Buffalo NY 14214. *Mailing Add:* 131 Allen St New York NY 10002

ENGERAN, WHITNEY JOHN, JR
PAINTER, EDUCATOR
b New Orleans, La, Feb 1, 1934. *Study:* Spring Hill Col, BA & MA; St Louis Univ, STL; Art Students League. *Work:* Cunningham Mem Libr, Terre Haute, Ind; Vincennes Univ; Harold E Simon Collection; Michael Gardes Collection; La State Univ, Lafayette. *Comn:* Fire ritual mural, St Marys Col, 62; suffering servant mural, Martin Army Hosp, Columbus, Ga, 66; Terre Haute First Nat Bank, 74; sci ctr mural, WVa Inst Technol, 88; Dr & Mr. Charles Pate, Cincinnati, Oh. *Exhib:* Ind State Univ Art Gallery, Terre Haute, Ind, 71-2002; Circling the Apocalypse, Tondi paintings, Pierce Gallery, Montgomery, WVa, 88; painting, Wholely, Holy, Wholely, Bicentennial Art Mus Paris, 90; Grapevine Gallery, 98-99 & Swope Art Mus 98, Terre Haute; Disking Millennium Prints Paintings, Univ Art Gallery, Terre Haute, Ind, 2001; Millennial Pulses, Drawings Prints, Pierce Gallery, Montgomery, WVa, 3/2000; Hulman Union Gallery, 2001; Farrington Gallery, 2006-2007; Univ Art Gallery, Terre Haute, Ind, 2007; Halcyon Gallery, 2007; Acadian Rhythms, Gumbo Retro-54 Years of Art, Pierce Art Gallery, Montgomery, W Va, 2008; Bayou Baroque paintings & prints, Halcyon Gallery, 2009; Gaslight Art Colony Gallery of Marshall, Ill, 2010. *Collection Arranged:* Ida Kohlmeyer Retrospective, 72, Images of Our Time, 73 & Am 6 Pak: Six Bicentennial Exhibits, 74-75, Turman Gallery, Terre Haute; I Kohlmeyer Retrospective, Mint Mus, 82-84. *Pos:* Cur permanent collection & dir, Turman Gallery, 71-75; Asst prof aesthet & chair person dept art, Loyola Univ, 66-68; prof art theory & criticism, Ind State Univ, Terre Haute, 71-2002, chmn dept, 71-78 & prof emer, 2002-. *Teaching:* assoc prof aesthet, Stephens Col, 68-71. *Awards:* First Prize Watercolor, Kans Artists' Exhib, 62 & 65. *Bibliog:* Margaret Harold (ed), Prize Winning Watercolors of America, Allied Publ, 63; Jason Berry (auth), Rev, Ida Kohlmeyer: 30 years, New Orleans Mag, 19-20, 1/85; David Kiehl (auth), Ida Kohlmeyer: Recent Works, Morris Mus, 96. *Mem:* Coll Art Asn Am; Nat Coun Art Adminr; Mid-Am Coll Art Asn. *Media:* Enamel, Acrylics, Serigraphy. *Specialty:* Regional artists of the Midwest, all media. *Interests:* Cinema 1950-2011, pop-culture, cajun hist/cult. *Publ:* article in Arts Update, 2/83; Ida Kohlmeyer 30 Yr Monograph, Mint Mus, 12/83; article, Full circle for Dick Hay--sculptor in clay, Butlleti Informatiu de Ceramica, Barcelona, Spain, 86; articles in Ceramic Art Monthly, 12/97. *Dealer:* Halcyon Contemporary Art at the Swope Ed Center 25 S 7th St Terre Haute In 47807. *Mailing Add:* 1509 S Center St Terre Haute IN 47802

ENGLER, KATHLEEN GIRDLER
SCULPTOR
b Indianapolis, Ind, Jan 30, 1951. *Study:* John Herron Sch Art, Ind Univ, 69-70; Univ Ga, 80; Med Coll of Ga, 80; Augusta Col, BFA, 81. *Work:* Southern Bell Corp Collection, AFCO Corp Collection, Atlanta, Ga; Osbon Med Syst Int; So Bell, Atlanta Ga; Creative Arts Guild, Dalton, Ga; plus others. *Comn:* Cultural Triad (bronze fountain), Maxwell Performing Arts Theater, Augusta, Ga, 86; Bronze Women of Excellence Awards, 88-98; The Graduate (bronze), Med Coll of Ga, 89; Life's Advocate, Univ Hosp Women's Ctr, Augusta, Ga, 98; 3 piece monumental bronze, Children's Med Ctr, Augusta, Ga, 99. *Exhib:* Mobile Mus Art, Ala, 96; Celebrating the Torch; A Run of Grecian Images Phorum, Augusta, Ga, 96; Red Clay Survey, Huntsville Mus Art, Ala, 98; Resurrected Forms, Spartanburg Mus Art, SC, 99 & Gertrude Herbert Art Inst, Ga, 99; Mother/Nature, B Rust and K Groler Engler, 2002; Mary Pauline Gallery, Augusta, Ga, 2002; The Nature of Change, Oconee Cult Arts Found, Watkinsville, Ga, 2003. *Teaching:* artist in res, Children's Med Ctr, Med Col of Ga. *Bibliog:* Jeffrey Day (auth), Powerful sculpture: The State, 8/93; Rich Coply (auth), Sculptor inspired by nature, Augusta Chronical, 9/94; The Source Book of Artists: Architects, Ed 10, The Guild, 95; On the Outside: Public Sculpture, Augusta Chronicale, 2/2000. *Media:* Bronze, Paper, Pulp. *Dealer:* The Mary Pauline Gallery, Augusta, Ga, 30901. *Mailing Add:* 753 Aumond Rd Augusta GA 30909-3258

ENGLER, SHERRIE LEE
PAINTER, ILLUSTRATOR
b Paducah, Ky, July 9 1962. *Study:* Ark State Univ, BS, 1985. *Exhib:* Equine Art Guild 4th Ann Art Exhib (online exhib), Mustard Creek Art Gallery, LaCrosse, Wis, 2002. *Pos:* Graphic Artist Illusr, Carson Graphics, Jackson, Tenn, 1985-1987; Illusr, Equine Res Inc, Tyler, Tex, 1999-2001; Equine Artist, Headed W Studios, Tenn, 2001-2005-. *Teaching:* Instr Art, Univ Sch Jackson (Col Prep Sch), 1991-1996. *Awards:* Top 3 Selling Items, Am Horse Publ, Horseman's Corral, 2002; Cover Artist (22 covers), Horseman's Corral, Sherrie Engler, 2000-2005. *Mem:* Nat Mus of women in the Art, Wash, DC; Blue Book of N Am Artists; Equine Art Guild; Equine Arts Protection League (pres). *Media:* Mixed Media, Paint Pencil/Watercolor. *Publ:* (Ed), Todays Horse Trader Design Assoc Inc NMex, 2002; (ed), Equine Marketeer, The Equine Marketeer, Pa, 2003; (ed), Mid-South Horse Review, Apr 2003 Review, Horse Review, Somerville, Tenn, 2003; (illus), Photos & Drawings for Conformation & Anatomy (496 pgs), 1999; (illus), True Horse Stories, Equine Res Inc, 2001. *Mailing Add:* 2797 Stafford Stone Rd Greenfield TN 38230

ENGLISH, HELEN WILLIAMS DRUTT See Drutt, Helen Williams

ENGLISH, MARK
PAINTER
b Hubbard, Tex, 1933. *Study:* Art Ctr Col, Los Angeles, 1960. *Hon Degrees:* Acad Art Col, San Francisco, LHD, 2005. *Exhib:* Solo exhibs, Johnson County Mus, Kans City, 92, Am Legacy Gallery, 99, 2002, 2004, Richard McDonald Gallery, Santa Fe, 2001, Laguna Beach, Calif, 2001, Eleanor Ettinger Gallery, New York City, 2001, 2002, 2005; Hanson Gallery, New Orleans; Telluride Gallery, 99, 2001, 2004; Linda Beutner Gallery, Denver; Eleanor Ettinger Gallery, New York City, 1999-2000, 2003-04, 2007; Albemarie Gallery, London, 2003-04. *Awards:* Artist of Yr, Guild of NY, 67; Hamilton King Award, SI, 67, Hall of Fame, 83. *Bibliog:* Jill Bossert (auth), Mark English, Madison Square Press, 2002. *Mem:* SI. *Media:* Miscellaneous. *Mailing Add:* c/o Eleanor Ettinger Gallery 24 W 57th St Ste 609 New York NY 10019

ENGLISH, SIMON RICHARD BATHURST
PAINTER, DRAFTSMAN
b Berlin, Germany, May 16, 1959. *Study:* Central Sch Art, BA, 81. *Work:* Louisiana Mus Art, Copenhagen, Denmark; Essl Mus, Vienna, Austria; Israel Mus, Jerusalem, Israel; Arts Coun Collection, London; Falckenberg Mus, Hamburg, Germany; Tate Collection, London; British Mus Collection, London; Paisley Mus, Scotland; UK Gov Art Collection. *Exhib:* Young British III, Saatchi Collection, London, 94; Erotic Drawing, Aldrich Mus, Conn, 2005; Recent Aquisitions, Louisiana Mus, Denmark, 2006,2009; Falckenberg Collection, Falckenberg Mus, Germany, 2007; Aspects of Collecting, Essl Mus, Vienna, Austria, 2009; Directors Choice, Arken Mus Mod Art, Denmark, 2010. *Awards:* Live Arts Award, Drawing Out Loud, Chisenhale Dance Space, 99; Grant, Blackdog Publ, Art Counc of GB, 2004; Meissen Art Campus, Dresden, Germany, 2010. *Bibliog:* Stella Santacatterina & Bill Arning (auth), The Army Pink Snowman, Blackdog Publ, 2005; Nicholas Weis (auth), In Conversation, NY Arts Mag, 2008; Mark Rappolt (auth), Simon English, Artreview, 2/2008; Scott Indrisek (auth), Artinfo Modern Painters, 5/2010. *Publ:* auth, Shark Infested Waters, Saatchi/Zwemmer, 94; auth, Simon English & the Army Pink Snowman, Blackdog Publ, 2005; auth, Contemporary Erotic Drawing, Aldrich Mus, 2005; auth, Collection Agnes B, JRP Ringier, 2009; auth, Aspects of Collecting, Essl/Herausgeber, 2009. *Dealer:* Robert Goff Gallery 537 B West 23rd St New York NY 10011; Galerie Volker Diehl Berlin Germany; Galerie du jour Agnes b Paris France

ENOS, CHRIS
PHOTOGRAPHER
b Calif, Aug 21, 1944. *Study:* Foothill Col, AA, 65; Univ Am, Mexico City, 67; San Francisco State Univ, BA (sculpture), 69; San Francisco Art Inst, MFA (photog), 70. *Work:* George Eastman House, Rochester, NY; Bibliot Nat, Paris; Shaklee Corp, Calif; Seagrams Collection, NY; DeCordova Mus & Sculpture Park, Lincoln, Mass; Yale Univ Art Galleries; Fogg Mus; Harvard Univ; and many others; Mus Fine Arts, Boston; Santa Barbara Mus Art; Los Angeles Co Mus Art; Denver Art Mus; J Paul Getty Mus; Smith Coll; Addison Gallery of Am Art. *Exhib:* Mass Inst Technol, Cambridge, 71, 73 & 80; San Francisco Mus Art, 71 & 80; Fogg Art Mus, 74, 76, 78 & 80; one-person shows, Somerville Community Access Ctr, Somerville, Mass, 90, Barn Gallery, Oqunquit, Maine, 90 & Pagosa Springs Art Ctr, Colo, 92; Recent Acquisitions, Boston Mus Fine Arts, 76; Univ Vt, Burlington, 80; Int Ctr Photog, NY; Inst Contemp Art, Boston, 81 & 83; Sonnabend Gallery, NY, 81; Artist Found Gallery, Boston, Mass, 91; Photog Resource Ctr, Boston, Mass, 91; Robinson Gallery, Denver, Colo, 93; Denver Art Mus, Colo, 93; Etherton Gallery, Tucson, Ariz, 2007; Yale Univ Art Gallery, 2008; Singapore Art Fair, 2009; Photographic Resource Center, Boston Univ, 2010; WM Siegal Gallery, Santa Fe, NMex, 2010; Santa Barbara Mus Art, 2011. *Pos:* Founder & pres, Photog Resource Ctr, Boston, 76-81; Gallery dir & coordr lect series, New Eng Sch Photog, 77-78; artist-in-residence, Lightwork Workshop, Syracuse Univ, 78 & Int Ctr Photog, NY, 80. *Teaching:* Instr photog, Sonoma State Univ, 71-73, San Francisco Acad Art, 72-73, Univ Calif, San Francisco, 72-73 & New Eng Sch Photog, 77-78; asst prof, Windham Col, 74 & Hampshire Col, 74-75; instr, Harvard Univ, 77 & MA prog, summer 80; vis artist, Univ Colo, Boulder, 80 & Smith Col, Northampton, Mass, 82-83; vis lectr, Univ Calif, Los Angeles, 83; assoc prof, Univ NH, 86-2008 (retired); lectr, Tufts Univ, Medford, Mass, 91; lectr, Pagosa Springs Art Ctr, Colo, 92; prof emer, Univ New Hampshire, 86-2004. *Awards:* Liberal Arts Fac Summer Res Fel, Univ NH, 91; Mass Cult Coun Fel, 98; Lifetime Achievement Award, Photographic Resource Center, Boston Univ, 2010. *Bibliog:* Alfred A Knopf (auth), Legacy of Light, NY, 87; Simon & Schuster (auths), Flora Photoraphicia, NY, 91; Photography in Boston 1955-1985, MIT Press, 2001. *Mem:* Soc Photog Educ; Photog Resource Ctr Boston; and others. *Media:* Mixed Media. *Publ:* Contribr, Camera 35 Mag, New York, 73; Camera Mag, Bucher/Switz, 75; Horticulture Mag, Boston, 77; Women See Women, Crowell, 77; auth, Landscape as Photograph, Yale Univ Press, New Haven, Conn, 85

ENRIGHT, JUDY A
PAINTER, PRINTMAKER
b Canton, Ohio, May 16, 1939. *Study:* St Mary's Col, Notre Dame, Ind, BA, 61; Univ Mich, with Jerome Kamrowski & Rudolf Arnheim, BFA (cum laude), 85; Kyoto Seika Univ, Japan, 90. *Work:* Capital Commons Ctr, Lansing, Mich; R P Scherer Corp, Troy, Mich; Spectrum Health Hosp, Grand Rapids, Mich; Swords into Plowshares Mus, Detroit; Bank of Ann Arbor. *Exhib:* Award Show, Saginaw Art Mus, Mich, 78; Ann Show, Massillon Art Mus, Ohio, 91-92; Ann Award Show, Art Ctr Battle Creek, Mich, 92-94; Ann Award Show, Ella Sharp Mus, Jackson, Mich, 93; Galeria Biegas, Detroit; Shiawasee Arts Coun. *Teaching:* Pvt art tchr. *Awards:* Bob Typsinski Mem Award, Gold Medal Exhib, Scarab Club, 86; Pauline Angle Award, All Media Show, Left Bank Gallery, Flint, Mich, 94; Outstanding Achievement Award Visual Arts, Livingston Arts Coun, 94. *Bibliog:* Robert Romaker (auth), Brighton artist puts visual questions on big canvases, Ann Arbor News, 1/91; Joy Hakanson Colby (auth), Enright exotica, The Detroit News, 4/21/94; John Carlos Canto (auth), Cleared for takeoff, Ann Arbor News, 7/17/94. *Mem:* Ann Arbor Women Painters (treas, 86); Brighton Art Guild. *Media:* Oil. *Publ:* Auth, Environment & Art Letter, Chicago, IL, 1/97; Metropolitan Women Mag, Detroit, 95, 96. *Mailing Add:* 5620 Bauer Rd Brighton MI 48116

ENRIQUEZ, GASPAR
PAINTER, METALSMITH
b El Paso, Tex, July 18, 1942. *Study:* East Los Angeles Jr Col; Univ Tex, El Paso, BA; printmaking with Loren Janzen & jewelry with Walt Harrison; NMex State Univ, metalsmithing with Kate Wagle & Peter Voris, MA. *Work:* State Nat Bank; Univ Tex, El Paso; NMex State Univ Gallery; Southwestern Bell. *Exhib:* Fresno Art Mus, 91;

San Francisco Mus Art, 91; Albuquerque Mus, 91; Denver Art Mus, 91; Plains Art Mus, Fargo, NDak; Univ Minn Art Mus, Minneapolis; Nat Mus Am Art, Washington, DC; El Paso Mus Art, La Rosa Dolorosa, 95; The Coll Santa Fe 1995 Sculpture Proj, 95; Assistance League of Houston, Celebrates Texas Art, 95-96; Figurative Foundation, Martin-Rathburn Gallery, San Antonio, Tex, 96; Texas Dialogues, Blue Star Art Space, San Antonio, Tex, 97; Tres Proyectos Latinos, Laguna Gloria, Austin, Tex, 97; Una Pagina Mas, Adair Margo Gallery, 99; and others. *Awards:* Hon Mention, El Paso Int, 85; Juniors Award, Tex Fine Arts Asn Exhib, 87; Siqueiros-Pollock Award, 96. *Mem:* Juntos Art Asn (pres); Int Designers Craftsman; Am Craft Coun. *Media:* Acrylic, Oil; Precious Metals. *Dealer:* Mi Casa Studio Gallery San Elizario TX 79849; Janson-Perez Gallery 417 8th St San Antonio TX 78215. *Mailing Add:* PO Box 1432 San Elizario TX 79849

ENSRUD, WAYNE
PAINTER, PRINTMAKER
b Albert Lea, Minn, Apr 4, 1934. *Study:* Minneapolis Coll Art & Design, BFA, 56; with Oskar Kokoschka, 56-79; with Ben Shahn, Joseph Albers & Vaclav Vitlacyl. *Work:* Bristol Mus Art, RI; New Eng Ctr Contemp Art, Brooklyn, Conn; French Inst Gallery, NY; Gallery Collection of Gov Trinidad, West Indies; Galleria of Contessa Borghese, Rome, Italy. *Comn:* Seagram's Taste of the Nation (poster), 93, 94 & 95; Domaine del la Romanee-Conti, France, 95; Domaine Le Flaive, France, 95; Sassicaia, Italy, 97; Robert Mondavi, 2001; and many others. *Exhib:* Solo exhibs, Oakland Art Mus, Bristol Art Mus, French Inst, NY Galerie Esmeralda, Paris, Galerie Damien, Paris, Sansio Gallery, Tokyo, Artistic Galleries, Scottsdale, Ariz, 93, Paintings of Paris bistros, 93, Grand Fetes Medoc, 94, Celebration of Burgundy, 95, Top NY Ital Restaurants, 96 & Famous Grand Cru Chateaux Medoc, 97, many others; Washington Ave Gallery, Minneapolis, Minn, 93; Beard Gallery, Minneapolis, Minn, 93; French Vineyard Series, Horseneck Inc, Greenwich Conn, 93; Gallery & Co, Tokyo, Japan, 93; Famous Ital Vineyards, 97; Art Collection Inc, Miami, Fla, 98; Federation of Chateauneuf du Pape, Fr, 99; Ravsen Fine Art, New Canaan, Conn, 2000; Galleria Luna, Half Moon Bay, Calif, 2005; Galerie des Artistes, Puerta Vallarta, Mex, 2006; Louis Aronow Gallery, San Francisco, Calif, 2007; Gardens Gallery Ctr, Palm Beach Gardens, Fla, 2007; Duboeuf Cultural Mus, Romaneche-Thorins, Fr, 2007; Robert Mondavi Gallery, Napa Valley, Calif, 2007; Great Neck Arts Ctr, NY, 2008; High Line Open Studios, NY, 2011; New Art Ctr, NY, 2012. *Collection Arranged:* Lever House Coll, New Eng Ctr for Contemp Art; Bristol Art Mus; Musee D'Art, Callionoe, France; Kokoschka in Minnesota, St Johns Univ, St Cloud, Minn, 90; Creative Process, Minneapolis Coll Art and Design, 2003; Duboeuf & Ensrud: 20 Yrs Friendship, Hameau du Vin, Romaneche-Thorins, Fr, 2007. *Pos:* Art dir, Univ Calif, Berkeley, 58-61; exec art dir, Channel 13 TV, New York, 64; art dir, Gemini Space Program, ABC, New York, 65-66. *Teaching:* Instr film animation, Pratt Inst, New York, 67-72; painting & drawing, Cumberland Sch, Great Neck, NY, 67-79; guest prof figure painting, Simon's Rock Early Col, Great Barrington, Mass, 78. *Awards:* permanent marble plaque, Hotel de Medicis, Paris, 87; Soc of Grappileurs of Beaujolais, France, Inductee, 90; Commanderie du Bontemps de Medoc et des Graves, France, Inductee, 97. *Bibliog:* Monika Pichler (auth), Wayne Ensrud: Life of an artist, In: Work in Progress, 81; Lisa Doherty (auth), Wayne Ensrud: Life of an Artist, In: Work in Progress, 96. *Mem:* Coffee House Club. *Media:* Oil, Acrylic, Watercolor, Lithography, Etching, Sculpture, Mixed Media. *Specialty:* abstractions, figures, nudes, landscapes, seascapes, cityscapes, still lifes, floral, portraits. *Interests:* painting, animation, sculpture, drawing. *Collection:* paintings on canvas and works on paper including abstraction, figures, landscapes, cityscapes, still life, portraits, mythological themes, animals. *Publ:* Contribr, Wine J; auth, Wine Journal with Paintings by Wayne Ensrud, Galison Press, New York, 96. *Dealer:* Peter Hastings Falk 61 Beekman Pl Madison Ct 06443. *Mailing Add:* 65 Central Park W New York NY 10023

ENSTICE, WAYNE
ASSEMBLAGE ARTIST, WRITER
b Irvington, NJ, Dec 16, 1943. *Study:* Pratt Inst, BFA, 65; Univ NMex, MA, 69. *Work:* Univ NC, Chapel Hill; Univ Ark, Art Gallery, Fayetteville; Roswell Mus & Art Ctr, NMex; Ariz Comn on Arts, Phoenix; Yuma Art Mus; Univ NMex, Albuquerque; Univ Ariz, Mus Art. *Exhib:* Alternative Mus, New York City; Drawing Ctr, New York City; Diverse Works Gallery, Houston, Tex; Getler, Pall, Saper Gallery, New York City; SPACE Gallery, Los Angeles. *Pos:* Producer/host "Just Jazz", KUAT-FM, Tucson, 1975-82; jazz columnist, Tucson Weekly News, 1980. *Teaching:* assoc prof, Univ Ariz, 1970-1990; Prof, chmn, Dept Art, Ind State Univ, Terre Haute, 90; prof, dir, Sch Art, Univ Cincinnati, Ohio, 95-2000; prof, Univ Cincinnati, 2000-. *Awards:* Artist-in-Residence Grant, Roswell Mus & Art Ctr, 84-85; grant Summerfair, Inc, 2001. *Bibliog:* Robert Murdock (auth), essay, Univ Ark Press, 79; William Peterson (auth), article, Artspace, 80; John Perreault (auth), Art in Am, 81; The New Yorker (art exhib capsule review), 84; Peter Frank (auth), essay, Roswell Mus & Art Ctr Catalog, 85; Nat Hentoff (auth), The Wall Street Journal, 9/22/2005; Ohioana Quarterly, 2006; Interdisciplinary Humanities, 2009. *Publ:* Auth, Performance Art's Coming of Age, Performance Art, Dutton Press, 84; coauth, Drawing/Space, Form and Expression, 90, Prentice-Hall, ed, 96, 2003; co-auth, Jazz Spoken Here, La State Univ Press, 92 (hard cover), Da Capo Press, NY, 94 (soft cover); Reading Jazz, Robert Gottlieb (auth), Pantheon Books, NY, 96; co-auth, Jazzwomen, Indiana Univ Press, 2004; Drawing/Space, Form, and Expression, 4th Ed, Peason, 2011. *Mailing Add:* 7310 Kirby Dr Burlington KY 41005-9687

ENWEZOR, OKWUI
EDUCATOR, CURATOR
b Calabar, Nigeria, 1963. *Study:* Jersey City State Coll (NJ City Univ), BA (polit sci). *Pos:* Founder & ed, Nka: J Contemp African Art, African Studies & Rsch Ctr, Cornell Univ, 1994-; artistic dir, 2nd Johannesburg Biennale, 1996-1997 & Documenta 11, Kassel, Ger, 1998-2002, Bienal Internacional de Arte Contemporaneo de Sevilla, Spain; adj cur contemp art, Art Inst Chicago, 1998-2000. *Teaching:* Dean acad affairs & sr vpres, San Francisco Art Inst; vis prof art hist, Univ Pittsburgh, Columbia Univ, Univ Ill & Univ Umea, Sweden. *Awards:* Prince Claus Fund for Cult & Develop grant; Ford Found grant; Rockefeller Found grant; Int Art Critics Asn award; Peter Norton Curatorial award. *Publ:* Auth, Reading the Contemporary: African Art from Theory to the Marketplace, MIT Press, Cambridge; Mega Exhibitions: Antinomies of a Transnational Global Form, Wilhelm Fink Verlag, Munich, Ger

ENYEART, JAMES LYLE
HISTORIAN, DIRECTOR
b Auburn, Wash, Jan 13, 1943. *Study:* Kansas City Art Inst, BFA, 65; Univ Santiago, Chile, cert (Orgn Am States Fel), 66-67; Univ Kans, MFA, 72. *Work:* Int Mus Photog, George Eastman House, Rochester, NY; Bibliot Nat, Paris, France; Sheldon Mem Gallery, Univ Nebr, Lincoln; Albrecht Mus Art, St Joseph, Mo; Nat Mus Am Art; Center for Creative Photography, Univ Ariz; Spencer Mus Art, Univ Kans. *Comn:* Nineteenth Century archit of St Joseph, 74 & stained glass windows of St Joseph, 75, Albrecht Mus Art, St Joseph, Mo. *Pos:* Staff photog, Nelson Gallery Art, Kansas City, Mo, 65-66; charter dir, Albrecht Gallery Art, St Joseph, Mo, 67-68; cur photog, Helen Foresman Spencer Mus Art, Univ Kans, Lawrence, 68-76; comnr, Kans Arts Comn, 73-74; dir, Ctr Creative Photog, Univ Ariz, 77-89, ed, The Archive, 77-89, George Eastman House: Int Mus Photog & Film, Rochester, NY, 89-95; leader hist sect, Rencontres Int de la Photog, Arles Festival, France, 79; visual arts rev panel, Nat Endowment for Arts, 79, panel mem design excellence proj, 84, grants panel spec exhibs category, 85, visual arts consult, 86, challenge grants/spec projs panel, 86 & 93 & peer panel mus challenge grants, 93; rev panel, 1980 Bush Found Fels, St Paul, Minn, 80; nominating comt, MacArthur Found, 82-; consult, Polaroid Corp, 83-89; adv comt, W Eugene Smith Mem Fund, 83-89 & Site Santa Fe, NMex, 98-; selection comt, Ariz Gov's Arts Awards, 84; ed, Image, 89-; mem creative arts award comn, Brandeis Univ, 90-95; adv bd Aaron Siskind Found, 91, Am Photog Inst, New York Univ, 91-, ITP & Columbia Univ, 92; adv panel, Eliot Porter Arch, Amon Carter Mus Art, 91 & Ctr for Am & Commonwealth Arts & Studies, Univ Exeter, Eng, 86-93; sr adv, Harold & Esther Edgerton Estate, Boston, Mass, 95-; dir, Marion Ctr, Col Santa Fe, 95-. *Teaching:* Instr drawing & design, Mo Western State Col, Univ Mo, 67-68; lectr art hist, Univ Kans, 68-70, asst prof, 70-72 assoc prof, 72-73, prof tenure, 73-76; adj prof art, Univ Ariz, 77-89; consult, dept art, Cornell Univ, 93; Anne & John Marion prof photog arts, Coll Santa Fe, 95-2001. *Awards:* Nat Endowment for Arts Grant, 73, 74, 75, 76-94 & 95; Photokina Obelisk Award for photog contrib, Cologne, WGer, 82 & 94; John Simon Guggenheim Mem Fel, writing, 87; many others. *Bibliog:* profile, Ariz Highways, 1/86; Tamara Scalera (auth), Interview with James Enyeart, Photo Metro, 12/87; The 100 Most Important People in Photography, Am Photo, 5-6/98. *Mem:* Nat Soc Photog Educ (bd dir, 78-82, publ comt, 73-76, nat conf chair, 76); Friends Photog (exec dir, 76-77, vpres, 78-81); hon corresp mem Deutschen Gess für Photog; Japan Photographic Soc (hon mem, 94). *Res:* Conservation and restoration of photographs; nineteenth and twentieth century photographers. *Publ:* Ansel Adams Legend and Legacy: Ansel Adams and Nineteenth Century Landscape Photographers, Pacific ress Serv, Japan, 93; The Nature of Photographs, Johns Hopkins Univ Press, 98; Land, Sky and All That Is Within: Visionary Photographers of the Southwest, Mus NMex Press, 7/98; William Christenberry: Absolute Essence (essay), in: William Christenberry:Adams House in the Black Belt, Landfall Press, 99; Mirrors of Marginal Thought (essay for Jim Dine exhib), PaceWildenstein Gallery, New York, 9/99; 140 published essays and books. *Mailing Add:* 46 Bonanza Trail Santa Fe NM 87505

EPSTEIN, YALE
PAINTER, PRINTMAKER
b New Haven, Conn, Jan 26, 1934. *Study:* Brooklyn Mus Art Sch, 55-58 & Rosenthal Scholar, 59; Brooklyn Coll with AD Reinhardt & Marc Rothko, MFA, 58; Pratt Graphics Ctr, 72-75. *Comn:* Hyatt Hotel, NY; Marriot Hotel, Palm Springs, Calif; Pfizer Corp, NY; Royal Caribbean Cruise Lines. *Exhib:* Art 14, Basel Int, Switz, 83 & 90; Prints USA, Univ Wis, La Crosse; Woodstock Artists Asn; Hudson River Mus, Yonkers, NY; Brooklyn Col. *Collection Arranged:* Brooklyn Mus, NY; Albright-Knox Gallery, Buffalo, NY; Bibliot Nat, Paris, France; City of Chicago; Univ Wis; Yale Univ. *Teaching:* Instr art, Brooklyn Col, NY, 76-83 & Sch Visual Arts, 82-90. *Awards:* First Prize Graphics, Hudson River Mus, 84. *Bibliog:* Rev, Print Collector's Newslett, 9/81. *Mem:* Nat Art Educ Asn; Coll Art Asn; Artists Equity; Woodstock Artists Asn; Soc Am Graphic Artists. *Media:* Pastel; Etching, Monoprint, Painting. *Interests:* travel. *Publ:* Auth, article, Art J, Coll Art Asn, winter 67-68; Tom Boutis, rev, Arts Mag, 6/80; Artspeak, 6/16/88; Aspects of Nature, Domberger Stuttgart Ger Publ, 90. *Dealer:* Somerhill Gallery 3 Eastgate E Franklin St Chapel Hill NC 27514; Suma Gallery 527 Amsterdam Ave NY NY 10024; Michele Birnbaum Fa PO Box 286232 NY NY 10128. *Mailing Add:* 20 Wiley Ln Woodstock NY 12498

EPTING, MARION AUSTIN
PRINTMAKER, EDUCATOR
b Forrest, Miss, Jan 28, 1940. *Study:* Los Angeles City Col, AA; Los Angeles Co Art Inst, Otis, MFA, 69; also with Ernest Freed, Lee Chesney, Shiro Ikegawa & Charles White. *Work:* Oakland Mus, Calif; Seattle Art Mus; Libr Cong, Washington, DC; Achenbach Found, DeYoung Mus, San Francisco; Whitney Mus, NY; Smithsonian Inst; and others. *Comn:* Intaglio prints comn by John Wilson, Lakeside Studios, Mich, 72 & 74. *Exhib:* 1st Nat Print Exhib, San Diego Fine Arts Soc, 69; Northwest Printmakers, Seattle Art Mus, 69; Oakland Art Mus, 73; traveling exhib, Western Asn Art Mus, 73-75; Smithsonian Inst Traveling Exhibs, 80-84. *Collection Arranged:* Black Untitled III, Western Asn Art Mus; Chico Group, Old Bergen Art Guild, NJ. *Pos:* Resident artist, Lakeside Studios, Mich, 70-; art dir, J-Squared B-Squared Consult, Los Angeles, 71-. *Teaching:* Prof art, Calif State Univ, Chico, 69-. *Awards:* Calif South 7 Best of Show, San Diego Fine Arts Guild, 69; Northwest Printmakers Purchase Award, Seattle Art Mus, 69; First Place for Graphics, Cal Expo, Del Mar, Calif, 69. *Bibliog:* J Edward Atkinson (auth), Black Dimensions in Contemporary American Art, Times Mirror, 71; Theresa Dickason Cederholm (auth), Afro American Artists, Boston Pub Libr, 73; Waddy/Lewis (auth), Art: African American, Harcourt Brace Jovanovich, 78. *Media:* Intaglio, Serigraphy. *Mailing Add:* Calif State Univ Art Dept Chico CA 95929-0820

ERBE, CHANTELL VAN
GRAPHIC ARTIST, PAINTER
b Jersey City, NJ, Dec 31, 1968. *Study:* BA. *Comn:* Computer presentations, computer illus & graphic art pvt comns. *Exhib:* Nat Arts Club, NY, 95, 96, 98, 99, 2000-2004; Salmagundi Mus, NY, 2000; Butler Inst Art, Youngstown, Ohio, 2001; Audubon Artists Inc, 2000, 2001, 2002; Nat Arts Club, 2001, 2002; Catharine Lorillard Wolfe Art Club, Broome St Gallery, New York, 2001-2002 & 2009; J Wayne Stark Gallery, College Station, Tex, 2003; Mus Tex Tech Univ, Lubbock, 2003; McInich Art Gallery, 2006; The Art of Colored Pencil, Gallery 297, Bristol RI, 2007; H20, The Colored Pencil Soc Am, Spring Bull Gallery, Newport, RI, 2008. *Awards:* Art Award most creative artist, Ramapo Co, 87; Am Biog Award, 2000; Merit Award, Gallery 297, Bristol, RI, 2007; Certificate of Merit, Salmagundi Club award for Graphics, 2001; Viewer's Choice Award for painting Island, TheArtList.com, 2014. *Bibliog:* Martin Parsins (auth), Allied artists, a plethora of pleasures, Artspeak Mag, 95-96. *Mem:* Allied Artists Am (exec sec, 95-98, bd dir, 99-2001); Catharine Lorillard Wolfe Art Club. *Media:* Colored Pencil, Mixed Media, Pen & Ink, Make-Up Artistry. *Interests:* photography, writing, culinary arts. *Publ:* Brian H Peterson (auth), The Cities, The Towns, The Crowds: The Paintings of Robert Spencer, 2004; Jessic Salisbury (auth), Exhibit Proves Fine Art Can Spring from the Humble Colored Pencil, Tel News, 4/2004; Nikki Moustaki (auth), Parrots for Dummies, 2005; Anton Souza (auth), Top 3 Friendliest Birds, Bird Talk Mag, 8/2005; Samuel Buckle (auth), Escape from Samsara, Cancer of the Tribe, Island, Revolve Mag, 2005

ERBE, GARY THOMAS
PAINTER
b Union City, NJ, Sept 2, 1944. *Study:* Self-taught. *Work:* Montclair Art Mus, NJ State Mus, NJ; Arch Am Art, Wash, DC; Phoenix Art Mus, Ariz; Springfield Art Mus, Mo; Nat Arts Club, NY; Salmagundi Club, NY; Boca Raton Mus, Fla; Butler Inst of Am Art, Oh; Woodmere Art Mus, Pa; New Britain Mus Am Art, CT; Brandywine River Mus, Pa; Peto Mus, NJ; Brinton Art Mus, WY; Canton Art Mus, OH. *Comn:* Butler Inst Am Art, Ohio. *Exhib:* Solo exhibs, Summit Art Ctr, NJ, 76, New Britain Mus Am Art, Conn, 76, Alexander Gallery, New York, 82 & 85, NJ State Mus, Trenton (with catalog), 83, Butler Inst Am Art, Youngstown, Ohio (with catalog), 85, Sordini Art Gallery, 85, ACA Gallery, NY, 98 & Harmon-Meek Gallery, Fla, 2003; Baseball Hall Fame, Cooperstown, NY, 91; NJ Fine Arts Ann, Noyes Mus, Oceanville, 92; traveling retrospective (with catalog), New Brit Mus Am Art, Conn, Butler Inst Am Art, Ohio, James A Michener Art Mus, Pa & Boca Raton Art Mus, Fla, 95; Boca Raton (Fla) Art Mus, 95; Springfield Art Mus, 99; Nat Arts Club, New York, 2000; 40 Yr Retrospective, Albuquerque Mus, NMex, 2008-09; Butler Inst Am Art, Oh, 2009; Salmagundi Club, NY, 2009; Boca Raton Mus, Fla, 2009; Canton Art Mus, OH, 2015. *Awards:* Gold Medal, Allied Artists Am, 75, 84, 92, 2006, 2007; First Prize, Nat Arts Club, 97; Gold Medal, Audubon Artists, 98; The Salzman Award, Nat Arts Club, 98; Lifetime Achievement Award, The Butler Inst Am Art, 2003; Salmagundi Club Medal of Hon, Salmagundi Club, 2007; Gold Medal, Allied Artists Am, 2010; Gold Medal, Nat Mus Sports, In, 2010; First Prize, Peto Mus, 2013. *Bibliog:* Levitational realism, Am Artist, 74; Gary T Erbe, Arts Mag, 82; An artist who captures the eye, then the mind, NY Times, 83; Local heroes, NJ Monthly, 84. *Mem:* Allied Artists Am (pres, 94-); Assoc Artists NJ; Conn Acad Fine Arts; Audubon Artists; Nat Arts Club; Salmagundi Club (artists fel); Trompe L'Oeil Soc Artists. *Media:* Oil. *Publ:* NY Art Rev & Am Artists, Krantz Publ; Int Artists Mag

ERBES, ROSLYN MARIA See Rensch, Roslyn

ERDLE, ROB
PAINTER, EDUCATOR
b Selma, Calif, Aug 17, 1949. *Study:* Reedley Col, Calif, AA; Calif State Univ, Fresno, BA; Bowling Green Univ, Ohio, MFA. *Exhib:* Ala Nat Watercolor Exhib, Birmingham Mus Art, 75-76; Toledo May Show, Toledo Mus Art, Ohio, 75-76; Southern Watercolorist Nat Exhib, Cheekwood Arts Ctr, Nashville, Tenn, 77; Rocky Mountain Nat Watercolor Exhib, Foothills Arts Ctr, Golden, Colo, 77; Solo exhib, Del Mar Coll, Corpus Christi, Tex, 77; Tex Fine Arts Nat Exhib, Laguna Gloria Art Mus, Austin, 77; and others. *Pos:* Dir, Chautauqua Inst Art Gallery, Chautauqua, NY. *Teaching:* Asst prof watercolor works on paper, NTex State Univ, 76-80, assoc prof, 80-. *Awards:* Outstanding Painting Award, May Show, Toledo Mus Art, 75 & 76; First Prize Purchase Award, Ala Nat Watercolor Exhib, Birmingham Mus Art, 76; Watercolor USA, Springfield Art Mus, 77. *Mem:* Nat Watercolor Soc, Los Angeles; Tex Watercolor Soc, San Antonio; Watercolor Soc Ala, Birmingham; Southern Watercolor Soc, Memphis; Southwestern Watercolor Soc, Dallas. *Media:* Mixed. *Mailing Add:* 1701 Greenwood Dr Denton TX 76201

ERENBERG, SAMUEL JOSEPH
PAINTER, PRINTMAKER
b Los Angeles, Calif, 1943. *Study:* Univ Calif, MFA, 76. *Work:* Mus Fine Arts, Kunstmuseum, Bern, Switzerland; Univ Calif Berkeley Art Mus; San Diego Mus Art; Santa Barbara Mus Art; Kuns Mus Lucern, Switzerland. *Comn:* Tabernacle, Skirball Cult Ctr Mus, Los Angeles, 85; Photo Light Box Project, LA Metro, 2003-2006; Lightbox Proj, MTA, Los Angeles, 2007; Roscoe Blvd Station, Orange Line Extension, LA Metro, 2012. *Exhib:* Sam Erenberg, Univ Art Mus, Santa Barbara, Calif, 75; Maxwell's Law, Santa Barbara Mus Art, 78; Sam Erenberg: Recent Work, Santa Barbara Contemp Arts Forum, Calif, 84; PLANETSprocketpaintings, Skirball Cult Ctr Mus, Los Angeles, 89; Die Sammlung Toni Gerber, Mus Fine Arts, Kunstmuseum, Bern, Switz, 96; Invitational, The Jewish Mus San Francisco, 97; In Search of the Absolute, Sheldon Mem Art Gallery, Lincoln, Nebr, 97; Sam Erenberg: Painting, Nora Eccles Harrison Mus, Logan, Utah, 2000; Craig Krull Gallery, Santa Monica, Calif, 2003; Planets Pocket Paintings, Santa Barbara Mus Art, 90; Skirball Cult Ctr, Los Angeles, 85; Invitational, Contemp Jewish Mus, San Francisco, 96; Experimental Film in Los Angeles, Pacific Standard Time, La Film Forum, Egyptian Theatre, Calif, 2012; Tricky Poses and Taxing Positions: Performance and Media, Moca, Los Angeles, 2012; Toni Gerber Collection, Kunst Mus, Luzern, Switzerland, 2013; Sam Erenberg: AWA, Coll Canyons, Santa Clarita, Calif, 2014. *Teaching:* Vis artist, The Ohio State Univ, Columbus, 78-79. *Awards:* Artists fel Calif Arts Coun, 99; Artists fel Durfee Foundation, 2003; Individual Artist Grant, City of Los Angeles, 2010. *Bibliog:* Barbara Gilbert (auth), Tabernacle, 87; Rosanna Albertini (auth), The Complete Works of R B, 99; Frances Colpitt (auth), The Ash Paintings, catalog for exhib at Craig Krull Gallery, Santa Monica, Calif, 2004; Matthew Baigell (auth), Jewish Art in Am: An Introduction, Rowman and Littlefield Pub, NY, 2007; Lyn Keinholz (auth), La Rising: So Cal Art Before 1980, Calif Int Art Found, Los Angeles, 2010. *Mem:* Am Asn Mus. *Media:* Painting, Film, Book Arts, Photography, Printmaking. *Specialty:* Painting, Photography. *Interests:* archit, hist of religion, political hist. *Publ:* White Owls: Artists I Found in Los Angeles, Rosanna Albertini, Oreste & Co, 94-2001, 2011; Binding Desire & Unfoldiing Artists' Books, Otis Coll Art & Design, Los Angeles, Calif, 2014. *Mailing Add:* 947 25th St Santa Monica CA 90403-2109

ERES, EUGENIA
PAINTER
b Winiza, Ukrania, Apr 28, 1928; US citizen. *Study:* Fine Art Sch, Sao Paulo, Brazil, with Prof Murillo, 54-58; Famous Artists Sch, Westport, Conn, with Norman Rockwell, Fletcher Martin & Doug Kingman, 66-69; Nat Acad Fine Arts, New York, with Hugh Cumpel, 70-71. *Work:* Galleria de Artes IV Centenario, Sao Paulo; Russian Am Hist Mus, Lakewood, NJ; pvt collection of Jacqueline Kennedy-Onassis, H Bartow Farr Jr Dep Gen Counsel, and others. *Exhib:* Solo exhib, Galleria de Artes IV Centenario, Sao Paolo, Brazil, 56-58, Int Art Expo NY Coliseum, 83-85, Int Art Expo, Wash, DC, 83, Hommond Mus North Salem, NY, 68; Am Artists Prof League Grand Nat, 68-94; Nat Art League, NY, 74-81; Knickerbocker Artists, 74-81; Hudson Valley, 76-94; Pen & Brush, 77-79; Salmagundi Club, 77-78; Custom House Mus Area, World Trade Ctr, NY, 79-81; Le Salon des Nations, Paris, 83. *Awards:* First Prize, Russian Am Soc, 75-78; Gold Medal of Honor, Nat Art League, 77; Gold Medal, Accademia Italia, 79; and others. *Mem:* Life fel Am Artists Prof League; Knickerbocker Artists; Nat Art League; Catharine Lorillard Wolfe Art Club; Accademia Italia; Hudson Valley Art Asn. *Media:* Oil, Lithographs. *Interests:* Traditional impressionist. *Mailing Add:* 109-10 Park Line S No A-10 Richmond Hill NY 11418

ERICKSON, MARGARET JANE See Goodwill, Margaret

ERICKSON, MARSHA A
DIRECTOR, ADMINISTRATOR
b Ancon, Panama, Feb 1, 1945; US citizen. *Study:* Univ Hawaii, Manoa, 63-65. *Exhib:* Hawaiian Quilts, Mus Am Folk Art, NY, 78. *Pos:* Founder, Volcano Art Ctr, Hawaii, 74, prog dir, 74-81, exec dir, 81-86; Kokee Natural Hist Mus, 87-. *Bibliog:* Thelma & Jay Newman (auths), Container Book, 77 & Barbara Stephan (auth), Decorations for Holidays & Celebrations, 78, Crown Publ. *Mem:* Arts Coun of Hawaii (mem bd, 85-86); State Found on Cult & Arts (comt mem, 80-86); Nat Asn Interpretation; Hawaii Environ Educ Asn (co-founder). *Res:* Intersection of arts and sciences. *Specialty:* Hawaiian landscapes, cultures and world views. *Publ:* Ed, The Volcano Gazette, Volcano Art Ctr, 74-84; At Canyons Edge, Kokee Mus, 88-

ERIKSEN, GARY
SCULPTOR, MEDALIST
b Jackson, Mich, Sept 11, 1943. *Study:* Oberlin Coll, BA, 66; Kent State Univ, MA, 68; Univ Chicago, 71-73; Acad Belle Arti Roma, 73-77; Scuola Dell'Arte Medaglia, Rome, dipl licenza, 77. *Work:* Nat Gallery Art, Budapest; Smithsonian Inst Numismatics Collection; Cooper-Hewitt Mus; Zecca Roma, Italy; Am Numismatic Soc, New York. *Comn:* American Eagle, Kurt Wayne Inc, New York, 80; Church God in Christ, New York & Memphis, 81; thirty bas-relief portraits, Basketball Hall Fame, Springfield, Mass, 85; Gate Relief, Erasmus Hall High Sch, Brooklyn, NY, 87. *Exhib:* First Ann Open Sculpture Exhib, Salmagundi Club, NY, 82; Fedn Int Editeurs Medailles Int Biennial, Palazzo Medici Riccardi, Florence, 83; Carnegie Mansion Embellishments, Cooper-Hewitt Mus, NY, 83; Am Numismatic Asn, Colorado Springs, 87. *Pos:* Consult hand tools design, Sculpture House Inc, New York, 81-82. *Awards:* First Prize, Salmagundi Club First Ann Open Sculpture Exhib, 82; NYSCA award, 83. *Bibliog:* Ed Reiter (auth), article, NY Times, 8/15/82; Arthur Williams (auth), The Sculpture Reference Illustrated, 2005. *Media:* Bronze, Terra Cotta. *Publ:* Econoclastic Controversies, 80-; Illus, Village Voice, 5/1/84; auth, Alex Ettl, master artisan, Sculpture Rev, Fall 84; co-auth, Medals to the fore, Sculpture Rev, Fall 86; This Book is Long Past Due Too, Ad Hominem Press, NY, 89; Iconoclastic Controversies (1980-present); This Book is Long Past Due Too, Ad Hominem Press, NY, 89

ERIKSON, CHRISTINE
EDUCATOR
Study: Parson Sch Design; Bank St Coll Ed, BS (arts admin), 89. *Teaching:* Asst prof art, Univ Alaska Anchorage, 81-. *Mailing Add:* Dept Art Univ Alaska Anchorage 3211 Providence Dr Anchorage AK 99508

ERLEBACHER, MARTHA MAYER
PAINTER, EDUCATOR
b Jersey City, NJ, Nov 21, 1937. *Study:* Gettysburg Coll, Pa, 55-56; Pratt Inst, Brooklyn, New York, BID, 60, MFA, 63. *Hon Degrees:* NY Acad Art, Hon Dr Fine Arts, 2006. *Work:* Philadelphia Mus Fine Art, Pa; Pa Acad Fine Arts; Art Inst Chicago, Ill; NJ State Mus, Trenton; Libr Cong, Washington, DC. *Comn:* Portrait, Most Reverend Joseph McShea, Allentown, Pa, 80; portrait, Dr William Hagerty, Drexel Univ, Philadelphia, Pa, 84; portrait, Dr Willys Silvers, Univ Pa Med Sch, Philadelphia, 90; portrait, James Bennett Straw, Pres, Union League Club of Philadelphia, 2000; Dr Carlo Croce, Kimmel Cancer Ctr, Jefferson Univ, Phila, Pa. *Exhib:* Group shows incl Philadelphia-Three Centuries Am Art, Philadelphia Mus Art, Pa, 76; Contemp Am Realism Since 1960, Pa Acad Fine Arts, Philadelphia, 81; Representational Drawing

Today: A Heritage Renewed, Univ Art Mus, Santa Barbara, Calif, 83; Am Realism: 20th Century Drawings & Watercolors from the Glenn C Janss Collection, San Francisco Mus Mod Art, Calif, 85-86; Philadelphia Collects Art Since 1940, Philadelphia Mus Art, Pa, 86; Modern Myths, Boise Gallery Art, Idaho, 87; Realism Today: Am Drawings from the Rita Rich Collection, Nat Acad Design, NY, 87-88; The Figure, Ark Arts Ctr, Little Rock, 89-90. *Teaching:* Univ Arts, Philadelphia, 66-94; Grad Sch Figurative Art, NY Acad Art, 93-2006. *Awards:* Ingram Merrill Found Grant, 78; Sr Fel, Nat Endowment Arts, 82; Pa Coun Arts, Fel visual arts, 88; 12th Ann for Excellence in the Arts, Newington-Cropsey Cult Studies Ctr, New York, 2010. *Bibliog:* Anne D'Harmoncourt (auth), Philadelphia: Three Centuries Am Art, Philadelphia Mus Art, Pa, 76; Frank H Goodyear, Jr (auth), Contemp Am Realism Since 1960, NY Graphic Soc, 81; Charles Jencks (auth) Past Modernism, the New Classisism in Art and Achit, Rizzoli, NY, 87. *Media:* Oil. *Dealer:* Sullivan-Goss Gallery 7 E Anapamu St Santa Barbara CA 93101; Seraphin Gallery 1108 Pine St Philadelphia Pa 19104; Rosenthal Fine Art Inc 3 E Huron 2nd Fl Chicago IL 60611. *Mailing Add:* 7733 Mill Rd Elkins Park PA 19027

ERMAN, BRUCE
PAINTER, EDUCATOR

b Los Angeles, Calif, Mar 14, 1945. *Study:* Univ Calif, Berkeley & Los Angeles, with James Melchert & Ibram Lassaw, BArch, 63-69; San Francisco Art Inst, with John Komisar, 74-75; Calif Coll of Arts (CCAC), Oakland, with Arthur Okamura, Jason Schoener, Jack Mendenhall & Ronald Dahl, MFA, 74-79. *Work:* Calif Coll of Arts(CCAC), Oakland; Davidson Coll, NC; Pvt collections of Peter MacLaird, Dillon Beach, CA, Bill and Elizabeth Shea, San Francisco, CA, Scott Glickenhaus, Sandpoint, Idaho. *Comn:* Favorite Toy & Under the Sea (murals), San Francisco Sch, Calif, 81; Nicacio Elementary School Mural, 82 & Black Mountain Theatre (mural), Point Reyes Station, 83, Youth-in-Arts, Greenbrae, Calif; Alamo Square Victorians (mural), Synergy Sch, San Francisco, 90-91; An Alvarado Alphabet (mural), Alvarado Arts Workshop, Alvarado Elem Sch, San Francisco, 96-97. *Exhib:* Solo exhibs: Time Pieces, Calif Coll of Arts (CCAC), Oakland, 77; New Work, Davidson Coll Chambers Art Gallery, NC, 80; Dwellings and Details, San Mateo Co Arts Coun, Belmont, Calif, 81; New Work-The Same Old Paintings, Art Space, Univ Nev Community Coll Southern Nev, Las Vegas, 83; New Work, Valley Art Gallery, Walnut Creek Art Ctr, Calif, 85 & Unreal Estate, Christa Faut Gallery, Davidson, NC, 91; group exhibs: Rainbow Show (with catalog), de Young Mus Art, San Francisco, Calif, 75; All California '84, Laguna Beach Mus Art; Layering/Connecting, Zanesville Art Ctr, Ohio & Stifel Fine Arts Ctr, Wheeling, WVa, 87; 27th Ann, Fairfield, Calif, 89; Gallery Artists, Christa Faut Gallery, Davidson, NC, 92-99, Cornelius, NC, 2000-04; Calif Coll of Arts (CCAC), Alumni Exhib, Oakland, Calif, 98; Drivers Art, Garage Gallery, San Francisco, Calif, 2007; Inaugural Art Exhibit & 1970's Retrospective, Garage Gallery San Francisco, Calif, 2009. *Pos:* Guest cur, Calif Coll of Arts (CCAC), Oakland, 77 & Chabot Coll, Hayward, 80, Calif; mem, Univ Calif Berkeley Art Alumni Group 2009-2011, treasurer 2010-2011. *Teaching:* Lectr painting, Calif Coll of Arts (CCAC), Oakland, 79 & 85, lectr exten fac, dept painting, 83-87; lectr painting, artist-in-residence, Alvarado Arts Workshop, Alvarado Elem Sch, San Francisco, 96-97. *Awards:* First Prize Painting, Univ Calif Los Angeles, Westwood, 64; Jurors Award, Fairfield, Calif, 27th Ann, 89. *Bibliog:* Thomas Albright (auth), At the end, Currant Mag, 75; Cathy Curtis (auth), Undeveloped premises, Artweek, 82; Jill Santuccio (auth), Unreal estate at Christa Faut Gallery, Mecklenburg Gazette, 91. *Mem:* Coll Art Asn, NY; San Mateo Co Arts Coun, Belmont, Calif; Univ Calif Berkeley Art Alumni Group. *Media:* All. *Res:* Materials, Methods & Techniques of Painting. *Publ:* Art Workshop, Berkeley Monthly, 74; Introduction to Woodcarving Tools, Whole Earth Epiloque & Co-Evolution Quar, 74. *Dealer:* Christa Faut Gallery Cornelius NC 28031. *Mailing Add:* 546 Shotwell San Francisco CA 94110

ERNSTROM, ADELE MANSFIELD
HISTORIAN

b Scranton, Pa, June 25, 1930; Can citizen. *Study:* Univ Utah; Univ Calif, Los Angeles, BA, PhD. *Pos:* Co-ed, RACAR (Revue d'art Canadienne/Canadian Art Review), 90-93; bd mem, Can Fedn Humanities, 94-95; mem gen assembly, Humanities & Social Sci Fedn Can, 95; pres, Univ Art Asn, Can, 94-97, adv bd mem, 98-2000; English lang book review ed, Racar, 2000-2004. *Teaching:* Asst prof, Hamline Univ, St Paul, Minn, 66-68 & State Univ NY Col, Brockport, 68-71; asst & assoc vis prof, Univ Guelph, Ont, Can, 75-77; assoc prof & chairperson, Bishop's Univ, Lennoxville, Que, 77-82, chairperson, 82-88 & 90-92, prof, 82-96,. *Awards:* Am Coun Learned Soc One-Yr Res Fel, 71-72; Res Grants, Bishop's Univ, 79 & 80; and others. *Mem:* Coll Art Asn; Univ Art Asn Can (pres, 94-97); Table Régional Dupartrimoine Religiux (Estrie). *Res:* Interconnections of Art Hist as practiced inside and outside institutions; Women Art Hist as Outsiders; Elizabeth Eastlake & the Historiography of Christian Art. *Publ:* Equally Lenders and Borrowers in Turn: The Working and Married Lives of the Eastlakes, Art Hist, 92; Anna Jameson and George Eliot, RACAR, 93; The Afterlife of Mary Wollstonecraft & Anna Jameson's, Winter Studies & Summer Rambles in Canada, Women's Writing, 97; Why Should We Be Always Looking Back?, "Christian" Art in Nineteenth Century Historiography in Britain, Art History, 99; Art Hist Inside and Outside the Univ, (guest ed and contribr auth), RACAR XXVIII, 2001-03

ESAKI, YASUHIRO
PAINTER, PRINTMAKER

b Omuta, Japan, June 8, 1941. *Study:* Acad Art Col, BFA, 72; Lone Mountain Col, MFA (painting), 75, MFA (printmaking), 78. *Work:* Achenbach Found, Fine Art Mus, San Francisco; Boston Mus Fine Arts; Brooklyn Mus; Cincinnati Art Mus; Metrop Mus & Art Ctr, Miami, Fla. *Comn:* Etching, Mark Hopkins Hotel, San Francisco, 78. *Exhib:* MIX Graphic I, San Francisco Mus Mod Art, 73; Acquisition Shows, Achenbach Found, Fine Art Mus, San Francisco, 75, 78 & 79; Nat Drawing Exhib, Rutgers State Univ, Camden, 77; Third Int Graphic Biennial, Metrop Mus & Art Ctr, Miami, Fla, 77; Contemp Am Artist Exhib, Cent Mus, Tokyo, 78; 2nd Nat Drawing Competition, Miami Univ Mus, Oxford, Ohio, 78; solo exhibs, Lone Mountain Col, San Francisco, 78, Monterey Peninsula Mus Art, Calif, 80, Collectors Gallery, Oakland Mus, Calif, 87-91, Gallery Azuchi, Osaka, Jap, 88-97, Gallery Asuka, Tokyo, Jap, 89-91; 21st Nat Print Exhib, Brooklyn Mus, 79; Am Print Survey, Truman State Univ, Kirksville, Mo, 97 & World Print Survey, 98; Print Types, Abeline Tex Univ, 97 & Indian Hills Community Col, Ottumva, Iowa, 98; Mixed Media 97, Stage Gallery, Merrick, NY, 97. *Teaching:* Instr printmaking, Acad Art Col, San Francisco, 78-91. *Awards:* Purchase Prize, Belknap Mem Int Print Competition, Columbia-Greene Community Col, 78; Purchase Prize, Stockton Nat '78, Univ Pac & Pioneer Mus & Haggin Art Gallery, 78; Purchase Award, 17th Bradley Nat Prints & Drawing Exhib, Bradley Univ, Peoria, Ill, 79. *Bibliog:* Robert McDonald (auth), Drawing by Yasuhiro Esaki, Artweek, 77; Nancy C Pierce (auth), Third Miami graphic biennial, Graphics, 78; Gene Baro (auth), Twenty-First National Print Exhibition, Brooklyn Mus, 79. *Mem:* Calif Soc Printmakers. *Media:* Acrylic, Color Pencil; Etching. *Mailing Add:* 11 San Antonio Ct Walnut Creek CA 94598

ESBER, JAMES
PAINTER

Study: Studio Art Ctrs Int, Florence, Italy, 1982; Temple Univ Abroad, Rome, 1983; Cleveland Inst Art, BFA, 1984; Skowhegan Sch Painting & Sculpture, Skowhegan, Maine, 1984. *Work:* West Collection, Oaks, Pa. *Exhib:* Solo exhibs include Hudson D Walker Gallery, Provincetown, Mass, 1992, Herter Art Gallery, Univ Mass, Amherst, 1996, Pierogi 2000, Brooklyn, NY, 1997, PPOW, New York, 1998, 2000, 2003, Bernard Toale Gallery, Boston, Mass, 2004; two-person exhibs include Hudson Walker Gallery, Provincetown, Mass, (With Mary Behrens), 1993; group exhibs include Archeology, Rutgers Univ, New Brunswick, NJ, 1987; 4 Walls Benefit Exhib, David Zwirner Gallery, New York, 1993; Current Undercurrent, Brooklyn Mus Art, NY, 1997, Open House, 2004; Hide & Seek, Bucknell Univ, Lewisburg, Pa, 1998; Brooklyn, Contemp Art Ctr, Cincinnati, 1999; Endless Love, DC Moore Gallery, New York, 2004; Drawn Page, Aldrich Contemp Art Mus, Ridgefield, Conn, 2004; Pierogi Flatfiling, Artnews Projs, Berlin, 2007; Ornament, BravinLee Progs, New York, 2007; J Fiber, Pierogi Brooklyn, NY, 2008. *Awards:* Fel, Art Matters Inc, 1989; New York Found Arts Fel, 2002, Grant, 2008. *Dealer:* Pierogi Leipzig Spinnereistr 7 04179 Leipzig Germany; Bernard Toale Gallery 450 Harrison Ave Boston MA 02118. *Mailing Add:* Pierogi Brooklyn 177 N 9th St Brooklyn NY 11211

ESCALET, FRANK DIAZ
PAINTER, SCULPTOR

b Ponce, PR, Mar 16, 1930. *Study:* Self taught. *Work:* Naprstek Mus, Nat Gallery, Prague, Czech; SE Mus Fine Arts, Beaumont, Tex; Bratslavia Primitive Mus, Slovakia; Frydek-Mistek Mus, Northern Moravia; Orgn Am States Art Mus, Washington; Art Mus of SE Tex, Beaumont; Ellen Noel Mus of the Permian Basin, Odessa, Tex; History Mus of New York City; New Britain Mus Am Art, Conn; Union of Artists, Moscow; Museo Chicano, Phoenix; Archit M Huntington Gallery, Austin, Tex; Housatonic Mus, Bridgeport, Conn; Maryknoll Sisters Ctr, NY; Museum City NY; Dowd Fine Arts Mus, Cortland, NY. *Exhib:* Solo exhibs, Naprstek Mus, Prague, 90-91, Union Artists, Moscow, 91-92, Mus Chicano, Phoenix, 96; Solo exhibs (traveling), Czechoslovakia, Russia, Poland, Yugoslavia, Hungary, Ukraine, 91-. *Pos:* Owner, operator Talent Shop, New York City, 1955-58; House of Escalet, New York City, 1958-71; Pandora's Box, Eastport, Maine, 1971-73; Cobbler's Bench Art Gallery, Pembroke, 1973-82; House of Escalet Gallery, Kennebunkport, 1982-84, House of Escalet Studios, Kennebunkport, 1984-. *Teaching:* instr leathercraft, Pasamaquoddy Reservation, Perry, Maine, 1971-72; instr, Vocational Sch, Maine, 1972-73. *Awards:* Award of Excellence, Manhattan Arts Mag, 92; Represented USA at the Meeting of Two Worlds Exhib, Prague, Czech, 92. *Bibliog:* Subject of numerous television progs, 78-89; Manhattan Arts Mag, Rene Phillips Assoc, 91; featured on pub TV, 78, 82 & 89. *Mem:* World Peace Advocates. *Media:* Paintings; Sculpture. *Publ:* Contribr, New York Art Review, An Illustrated Survey of the City's Museums Galleries & Leading Artists, Les Krantz Publ, 90

ESCALLON, ANA MARIA
MUSEUM CURATOR

b Columbia. *Exhib:* curator exhibs: 18 sculptures by Colombian artist Fernando Botero positioned along Constitution Ave in Wash, DC, 1996; An Architect of Surrealism, works by Roberto Matta, 2004; (with Twylene Moyer), Sculpture in Four Dimensions, Mus of the Americas, 2004. *Pos:* dir Art Mus of the Ams, Washington, 95-2004. *Publ:* auth, Gerchman, 94, Mejla-Guinand, 02. *Mailing Add:* Art Museum of the Americas OAS 1889 F St NW Washington DC 20006

ESCOBAR, MARISOL See Marisol

ESCOBEDO, HELEN
ENVIRONMENTAL ARTIST

b Mexico City, Mex, July 28, 1936. *Study:* Univ Motolinia, BA (humanities); ARCA, 3 yr scholar. *Hon Degrees:* Asn Royal Coll of Art. *Work:* Mus Mod Art, Mex; Prague Nat Gallery, Czech; Palacio de Bellas Artes, Mexico City; also in pvt collection of Stanley Marcus, US; Ordrup Samlung, Copenhagen. *Comn:* Coatl (steel), Univ Mex, 80; Reaseguradora Patria Bldg, 80; Barda Caida, Univ Mex, 81; The Great Cone (steel), City of Jerusalem, Israel, 86; El Reposo del Sol, Santiago, Cuba, 88; Seaview, Arlington House Lobby, London, Eng, 89. *Exhib:* Solo exhibs, Prague Nat Gallery, 69, Park Lazienkowsky, Warsaw, Poland, 70, Mus Mod Art, Mexico City, 75, Helsingin Kaupungin Taidemuseo, Helsinki, Finland, 91, Balliol Col, Univ Col, St Johns Coll & Mus Mod Art, Oxford, Eng, 92; Kunstindustri Mus, Oslo, Norway, 70; Middelheim Sculpture Bienale, Antwerp, Belg, 71; Ordrupgaard Mus, Copenhagen, 90; Mus du Que, Can, 92; The Artists Studio Gallery, Tel Aviv, Israel, 93; Sculpture Park, Isla Mujeres, 2001 & Chetumal, Quintana, Roo, Mexico, 2003; Nieheim Holzhausen, Sculpture Park, Germany, 2003; Museo Nacional del Ferrocarril, Puebla, Mex, 2006. *Pos:* Dir, Dept Mus & Galleries, Nat Univ Mex, 61-77; tech dir, Mus Nat Arte, Mex, 82; dir, Mus Arte Mod, Mex, 83. *Teaching:* Artist-in-residence, Tulane

Univ, 76, Hartnell Col, 77, Newcomb Col, 81, Kunsterhaus Betanien, Berlin, 81, Scripps Col, 83; res fel, Fac humanities, Ctr Sculptural Space, Univ Mex, 78; pentiment, Fachhochschule, Hamburg, Ger, 94; Centro Nacional para las Artes, Mexico, 98, Mus Posada Ags, 99 & Anderson Ranch, Aspen, Colo, 2007. *Awards:* Guggenheim Fel, 81; Acad Sci Letts et Beaux Arts, Belgium, 88; FONCA Fel, Mexico, 90; Nat Univ Mexico, Hommage as artist & cultural promoter, 2006. *Bibliog:* Alfredo Gurrola (dir), Helen Escobedo - Ambients Totales (film), Color Mex; Rita Eder (auth), Helen Escobedo, Nat Univ Mex; Escobedo Derouin, Mus Du Que, Can; Graciela Schmilchuk (auth), Helen Escobedo - Pasos en la Arena, Turner Libros, Madrid. *Mem:* Int Nat Sculpture Ctr, Washington, (mem bd, 71-); Int Coun Mus (mem bd, 75-); Sculptor's Guild, NY; Academie Royale de Sciences Lettres et Beaux Arts, Belgium. *Media:* Multimedia. *Publ:* Auth, Helen Escobedo, Footsteps in the Sand, Graciela Schmilchuk updated in English, Turner Libros, Madrid, 2005. *Mailing Add:* la Cerrada de San Jeronimo 19 Mexico DF 10200 Mexico

ESHOO, ROBERT
PAINTER
b New Britain, Conn, 1926. *Study:* Boston Mus Fine Arts Sch Mass, cert & dipl; Vesper George Sch Art, Boston; Syracuse Univ, BFA & MFA. *Work:* Wadsworth Atheneum, Hartford, Conn; Currier Mus Art, Manchester, NH; Munson-Williams-Proctor Inst, Utica, NY; Addison Gallery Am Art, Andover, Mass; New Britain Mus Am Art; Taft Sch, Watertown, Conn; Hood Mus, Dartmouth Col, Hanover, NH; De Cordova Mus, Lincoln, Mass. *Exhib:* Recent Drawings USA, Mus Mod Art, NY, 56; Chicago Art Inst Ann, 57; Young Artists, Whitney Mus, 57; Selections 1959, 59 & View 1960, 60, Inst Contemp Art, Boston; Am Painting 1962, Va Mus Fine Arts, Richmond, 62; The Dana Collection, 62 & Potlatch, 63, Inst Contemp Art, Boston; 28th Biennial, Corcoran Gallery, Wash, DC, 63; Northeastern Regional: Art Across Am, 65 & Art for Embassies, 66, Inst Contemp Art, Boston; Solo exhibs, Rigelhaupt Gallery, 68, Pucker-Safrai Gallery, Boston, 72 & 75, Manchester, NH, 76 & 79, Currier Mus Art, 81 & 86 & 94, Dartmouth Col, 86, St Paul's Sch, 88, New England Col, 89 & 94, Hatfield Gallery, Manchester, NH, 90, Century of Mac Dowell, Colony Artist, Nat Acad Design, New York, 96, De Cordova Mus, Lincoln, Mass, 2005; New Britain Mus Am Art, 2004; Pucker Gallery, Boston, 2004, 2007, 2010; Taft Sch, Watertown, Conn, 2007 & 2008; New Britain Mus Am Art, 2010; Currier Mus Am Art, 2010; Pucker Gallery, 2012. *Teaching:* Sch Mus Fine Arts, Boston, 54-55, Syracuse Univ, 56-57, Phillips Acad, Andover, 60 & 62-64 & Derryfield Sch, 65-80; supvr, Currier Art Ctr, 58-95. *Awards:* McDowell Colony. *Bibliog:* New Talents USA, Art in Am, 2/56; American artists coming to the fore, Harper's Bazaar, 3/60; Emerging reputations, Art in Am, summer 62. *Media:* Watercolor & Constructions. *Specialty:* paintings, sculpture, ceramics. *Dealer:* Pucker Gallery Boston MA

ESPENSCHIED, CLYDE
PAINTER
b St Louis, Mo. *Study:* With Valentine Vogel portrait painter, 44-46; St Louis Sch Fine Arts, Washington Univ, 46-49; Manhattan Graphics, New York, 93. *Work:* Peat Marwick Montvale Art Collection, Montvale, NJ; Bulgari, NY; MoMA. *Exhib:* St Louis Mus, Mo, 49; Omaha Mus, Nebr, 60; Audubon Show, Nat Acad, NY, 62; Trenton Mus, NJ, 66, 68 & 74; Millhouse-Bundy Arts Ctr, Waitsfield, Vt, 83; Heidi Jones Gallery, NY, 84; solo exhibs, Noho Gallery, NY, 84, 86, 88, 91 & 93, Mukaida Fine Arts Gallery, 91; Three Rivers Art Festival, Pittsburgh, Pa, 86 & 88; Morris Mus Fel Show, NJ, 87; Myungsook Lee Gallery, NY, 95; Westbeth Invitational, NY, 99; Drawing Exhibition (Alternative Space), Noho Gallery, 2000; Emily Harvey Found Gallery, NY, 2009. *Awards:* Nat Endowment Arts Fel Grant, 85; NJ Coun Arts Grant, 85; Honorable Mention, Three Rivers Art Festival, Pittsburgh, Pa, 86. *Bibliog:* Vivien Raynor (auth), article, Arts Mag, 60; Frederic Schwartz (auth), article, Artspeak, 84; Mark Brennan (auth), article, Art & Oxygen, 84; Sanford Sivit Shaman (auth), Pa State Univ, 87. *Media:* Oil on Canvas, Pastel on Paper, Ink on Paper & Acrylic. *Mailing Add:* 265 Main St Spotswood NJ 08884

ESQUIVIAS, PATRICIA
VIDEO ARTIST
b Caracas, 1979. *Study:* Chelsea Coll Art & Design, 1997-98; Cent Saint Martins Coll Art & Design, BA (Art & Design), 1998-2001; Skowhegan Sch Painting & Sculpture, 2006; Calif Coll Arts, MFA (Fine Arts), 2007. *Exhib:* Solo exhibs include Espacio F, Madrid, 2002, Ler Devagar, Lisboa, 2003, Ctr Arte Joven Av de América, Madrid, 2004, Arte Contemporanea, Santiago de Compostela, 2006, Maisterravalbuena Galería, Madrid, 2007, Silverman Gallery, San Francisco, 2008, White Columns, New York, 2008, Murray Guy, New York, 2008; Group exhibs include Air Container, Mus Raúl Anguiano, Guadalajara, Mex, 2005; Barclay Simpson Award, Oliver Ctr, Oakland, 2007; A Kingdom for a Horse, Peles Empire, Los Angeles, 2007; EASTInt, Norwich, United Kingdom, 2007; Self Storage, Calif Coll Arts, San Francisco, 2008. *Awards:* Merit Scholar, Calif Coll Arts, 2006; Skowhegan Sch Painting & Sculpture Fel, 2006; Barclay Simpson Award, 2007; EASTInt Fel, 2007; East Award, 2007; East Award, 2007; Artissima Present Future Illy Award, 2007. *Mailing Add:* Murray Guy Gallery 453 W 17th St New York NY 10011

ESSENHIGH, INKA
PAINTER
b Belfonte, Pa, 1969. *Study:* Columbus Coll Art and Design, Ohio, 1991; Sch Visual Arts, NY City, 1993. *Exhib:* Solo exhibs include Recent Paintings, Stefan Stux Gallery, NY, 1998, Deitch Projects, NY, 1999, Mary Boone Gallery, NY, 2000, 2001, Victoria Miro Gallery, 2000, 2002, 2005, 303 Gallery, NY, 2002, 2006, Mus Contemp Art, Miami, 2003, Michael Steinberg Fine Art, NY, 2004, Sint-Lukas Galerie, Brussels, Belgium, 2004, DA2 Domus Artium, Spain, 2005; group exhibs include Pleasure Dome, Jessica Fredericks Gallery, NY, 1999; To Infinity and Beyond, Brooke Alexander, NY, 2000; Hybrids, Tate Gallery, Liverpool, England, 2001; Berline Biennale, Germany, 2001; Go Figure, Luxe Gallery, NY, 2002; Drawing, G Gallery, Washington, DC, 2003; Heaven & Hell, Barbara Mathes Gallery, NY, 2003; Dienal de Sao Paulo, Brazil, 2004; Perspectives at 25, Contemp arts Mus, Houston, Tex, 2004; Life and Limb, Feigen Contemp, NY, 2005; Painting Codes, GCAC, Monfalcone, Italy, 2006; Cult Fiction, Hayward Gallery, London, 2007; The Triumph of Painting Part III, Saatchi Gallery, London, 2007; Comic Abstraction, Mus Modern Art, NY, 2007. *Dealer:* Victoria Miro Gallery 16 Wharf Rd London N1 7RW. *Mailing Add:* c/o 303 Gallery 525 W 22nd St New York NY 10011

ESSER, JANET BRODY
HISTORIAN
b New Haven, Conn. *Study:* Univ Iowa, with John Rosenfield & William Heckscher, BFA, 51; Kent State Univ, BS, 53; Calif State Univ, Long Beach, MA, 70; Univ Calif, Los Angeles, with Rubin & Nicholson, PhD, 78. *Collection Arranged:* San Diego Collects: African Art, 78; Faces of Fiesta: Mexican Masks in Context, 80; sr consult, Behind the Mask in Mexico, Mus Int Folk Art, Santa Fe, 88-90. *Teaching:* From asst prof to assoc prof, San Diego State Univ, 75-83, prof, 83-. *Awards:* Nat Endowment Humanities Summer Inst Fel, 78, 92; Hubert B Herring Mem Award for Best Scholarly Bk on Latin Am, 88. *Mem:* Coll Art Asn Am; Latin Am Studies Asn; Latin Am Art Historians Asn; African Studies Asn; Ethno-Hist Soc; Pac Coast Coun on Latin Am Studies. *Res:* Pre-Columbian, European and African antecedents of masking traditions in contemporary rural Mexican communities; African imagery in Iberia; Social History of Mexican Folk Art. *Publ:* Mask Making and Mask Use in Michoacan, Mex Fine Arts Ctr Mus, Chicago, 90; Auth, Mascaras rituales de la sierra tarasca, Michoacan, Inst Nac Indigenista, Mex; Tarascan Masks of Women as Agents of Social Control, Univ BC Press, Vancouver, 83; The Functions of Folk Art in Michoacan, Memphis State Univ, 84; ed, Behind the Mask in Mexico, Mus NMex, Santa Fe, 88. *Mailing Add:* Ctr Latin-Am Studies San Diego State Univ San Diego CA 92182-4446

ESSL, AGNES & KARLHEINZ, SR
COLLECTOR
b Hermagor, Austria, Apr 16, 1939. *Pos:* With Schömer co, 1959-73, Schömer L+S 1973-76, pres, 1976-99. *Awards:* Named one of Top 200 Art Collectors, ARTnews mag, 2004-13. *Collection:* Contemporary art, especially Austrian painting. *Mailing Add:* bauMax AG Aufeldstrasse 17-23 Klosterneuburg A-3400 Austria

ESSLEY, ROGER HOLMER
PAINTER, GRAPHIC ARTIST
b Rochester, NY, Jan 11, 1949. *Study:* Syracuse Univ, 66-69; Goddard Col, MA, 81. *Work:* Metrop Mus Art, NY; Indianapolis Mus Art, Ind; Joslyn Art Mus, Omaha, Nebr; Ind Univ Mus Art, Bloomington; Mem Art Gallery, Rochester, NY. *Exhib:* Solo exhib, Southeastern Ctr Contemp Art, Winston-Salem, NC, 84; Large Figurative Drawing, Va Mus Fine Arts, Richmond, Va, 85; The Figure in 20th Century Art, Nat Acad Design, NY, 85-86; Motion & Arrested Motion Contemp Figure Drawing, Chrysler Mus, Norfolk, Va, 87; Contemp Wing, Metrop Mus Art, NY, 87-88; Uncommon Ground, Va Mus Fine Arts, Richmond, 90. *Awards:* Regional Fel, Works on Paper, Mid Atlantic Arts Found, 88; Va Prize for the Visual Arts, 90. *Bibliog:* Paul Richard (auth), Together again, Washington Post, 84; Edward Lucie-Smith (auth), Am Art Now, Phaidon Pr, 85. *Publ:* Illus, Appointment, Simon & Schuster/Green Tiger, 93; auth/illus, Reunion, Simon & Schuster, 94; Under the Pear Tree, Cobblehill, 97; Angles in the Dust, Troll/Bridgewater, 97. *Dealer:* Reynolds Gallery 1514 W Main St Richmond VA 23220. *Mailing Add:* 30 N Main St Newmarket NH 03857-1210

ESTABROOK, REED
PHOTOGRAPHER, INSTRUCTOR
b Boston, Mass, 1944. *Study:* RI Sch Design, BFA, 69; Art Inst Chicago, MFA, 71. *Work:* Mus Mod Art, NY; Art Inst Chicago; Int Mus Photog, Rochester, NY; J Paul Getty, Santa Monica, Calif; Minneapolis Inst Arts, Minn; Art Inst Hawaii. *Comn:* San Jose Mus Mod Art. *Exhib:* Mirrors & Windows, Mus Mod Art, NY, 78; Solo exhibs, Sioux City Art Ctr, Iowa, 81, Klein Gallery, Chicago, 82 & James Madison Univ, Harrisburg, Va, 83; Recent Color, San Francisco Mus Mod Art, Calif, 82 & 84; Recent Aquisitions, Fogg Art Mus, Harvard Univ, Cambridge, Mass, 83; Road & Roadside: Am Photographs 1930-1986, Ill State Univ Art Gallery, Art Inst Chicago, San Francisco Mus Mod Art, 87; Big Pictures, San Francisco Mus Mod Art, Calif, 90; Translations, Mappin Art Gallery, Sheffield, Eng, 91; Three Decades of Midwestern Photog, Davenport Art Mus, Iowa, 92; Am Made: The New Still Life, Isetan Mus Art, Tokyo, Japan, Hokkaido Obihito Mus Art, Japan, 93, Royal Coll Art, London, Eng, 94; Forecast: Shifts in direction, Mus Fine Arts, Santa Fe, NMex, 94; Picturing Modernity, San Francisco Mus Mod Art, 96; Location-Location, San Jose Inst Contemp Art, 96; Image & Object, Sheppard Fine Art Gallery, Reno, Nev, 2001. *Teaching:* Instr photog, Univ Ill, Urbana-Champaign, 71-74; asst prof photog, Univ Northern Iowa, 74-78, assoc prof, 78-83; photog chmn, Kansas City Art Inst, 83-84; prof & coordr photo, Sch Art Design, San Jose State Univ, 84-. *Awards:* WR French Fel Competition, Art Inst Chicago, 71; First Place, Am Photographics, Andromeda Gallery, Buffalo, 76; Photog Fel, Nat Endowment Arts, 76; Honored Educator, Soc Photographic Educ, 2012. *Mem:* Soc for Photog Educ. *Media:* Photography. *Collection:* The Art Institute Chicago, Ill; Boise Gallery Art, Boise, Idaho; National Museum of American Art, Washington, DC; International Museum of Photography, Rochester, NY; Walker Art Center, Minneapolis, Minnesota. *Publ:* Contribr, New American Nudes, Morgan & Morgan, 81; Picture Mag No 17, 81; American Photography, 83; New Directions, Weston Naef, 84; The Making of a Collection: The Minneapolis Institute of Arts, Aperture, Millerton, 85; Photokina 1986, Cologne, W Ger, 86; Peninsular Mag, Vol 10, 87. *Mailing Add:* 4838 Proctor Rd Castro Valley CA 94546

ESTERN, NEIL CARL
SCULPTOR
b New York, NY, Apr 18, 1926. *Study:* Barnes Found, 1946-47; Tyler School Fine Arts of Temple Univ, BFA & BS (educ), 1947. *Work:* Nat Acad; Brooklyn Mus. *Comn:* Portraits, J Robert Taft, Danny Kaye, John F Kennedy, J Edgar Hoover, Pres Carter, Prince Charles, Lady Diana, Jack Nicholson, Eleanor Roosevelt, 6'7 Statue of Fiorello

La Guardia, La Guardia Memorial, Greenwich Village, NYC, Miguel de la Madrid, David Levine; life & half size portrait bust of John F Kennedy, Kennedy Mem, Grand Army Plaza, Brooklyn, 1965; Franklin D Roosevelt & Eleanor Roosevelt (life & a half size figures), FDR Mem, Washington, DC, 30 ' figure, Eleanor Roosevelt at Nat Cathedral, Washington, DC; Irving Berlin (relief portrait), Muxic Box Theater & Nat Portrait Gallery, Washington, DC. *Exhib:* Numerous solo and group exhibs in Conn, NY, NJ, Philadelphia, NH & Italy; 8'6 statue of Claude Pepper, Tallahasse, Fla; Lady Bird Johnson (life-size-proposed standing figure), Austin, Tex; Frank Sinatra, proposed for Broadway and 44th St. *Pos:* Pres, Nat Sculpture Soc, 1994-96 & 2005-2006. *Awards:* Lindsey Morris Prize, Nat Sculpture Soc, 1984, Mildred Vincent Prize, 1988 & 1992; Greenwich Village Soc Hist Preserv Award, La Guardia Statue, 1996; Nat Acad Award, Franklin D Roosevelt Scale Model, 1998; Pres Design Award, FDR Mem, 2000; Nat Sculpture Society, 2008; Friends of La Guardia, 2008. *Mem:* Fel Nat Sculpture Soc (pres 1994-97, 2005-2007); Nat Acad; Century Asn. *Media:* Clay, Bronze. *Interests:* Theater, Museums. *Collection:* Private Collections. *Dealer:* Nat Sculpture Soc

ESTEROW, MILTON
EDITOR, PUBLISHER
b New York, NY, July 28, 1928. *Study:* Brooklyn Coll, NY. *Collection Arranged:* donated collection of approximately 7,600 art books to Brooklyn Coll Libr. *Pos:* former New York Times reporter and assistant to cultural news ed; Owner, ed & publ, ARTnews, 1972-2014; publ, ARTnewsletter, 1975-2012. *Teaching:* Lectr art, mus, coll & univ. *Awards:* Soc Silurians Award, 1978, 1990, 1994-96, 1998, 2003 & 2006-2009, 2011, 2012, 2013; George Polk Award, 1981 & 1992; Nat Mags Award, 1981; Clarion Award, 1981, 1984, 1998 & 2000-2009; Investigative Reporters & Editors Award, 1984; Page One Award, 1985; Nat Headliner Award, 1985 & 1994; America Award, Overseas Press Club, 1991; Com for Jewish Claims on Austria award, 1996; Lifetime Achievement Award, Coll Art Asn, 2003; EMIPS Art Award, NY County Lawyers' Asn, 2008; Icon Award, Bruce Mus, 2010; NY State Art Teachers Asn special citation; Deadline Club, 2013. *Publ:* The Art Stealers, 1966

ESTES, RICHARD
PAINTER
b Kewanee, Ill, 1932. *Study:* Chicago Art Inst, 52-56. *Work:* Whitney Mus Am Art & Mus Mod Art, NY; Rockhill Nelson Mus, Kansas City, Mo; Toledo Mus, Ohio; Art Inst Chicago; Des Moines Art Ctr; Hirshhorn Mus, Washington, DC; and many others. *Exhib:* Solo Exhibs: include Carpenter Ctr Vis Arts, Harvard Univ, Cambridge, 90, Richard Estes 1990, traveling exhib, Mus Art, Kinetsu, Osaka & Hiroshima City Mus Contemp Art, Japan, 90, Richard Estes: Urban Landscapes, Portland Mus Art, Maine & Foster Goldstrom Gallery, NY, 91, Richard Estes: The Complete Prints, Canton Art Inst, Ohio, Los Angeles Arts & Sci Mus, Baton Rouge, Columbia Mus Art, SC, Huntsville Mus Art, Ala, 92, Marlborough Gallery, NY, 93, 95, 97, 98, 2001 & 2006 & Galleria Marlborough, Madrid, Spain, 98 & AMS Marlborough, Santiago, Chile & Monaco, 2003, Prints, Susan Sheehan Gallery, 2006; Group Exhibs include On Paper, galleria d'arte il gabbiano, Rome, Italy, 96; La Ville Moderne en Europe: Visions Urbaines d'Artistes et d'Architectes, 1870-1996, Mus Contemp Art, Tokyo, 96; Realism After Seven Am, Hopper House, NY, 96; Art 1997 Chicago: 5th Ann Expo of Int Galleries Featuring Modern and Contemp Art, Navy Pier, Chicago, 97; City Scapes, Marlborough Gallery, NY, 97; Landscape: The Pastoral to the Urban, Ctr for Curatorial Studies & Art in Contemp Cult, Bard Col, NY, 97; NY Perspectives, MB Modern, NY, 98; Le Futur du Passe, Lieu d'Art Contemporain Corbieres Maritimes, France, 98; Transforming the Commonplace: Masters of Contemp Realism, Susquehanna Art Mus, Pa, 2003; Printed Light, Nat Gallery of Australia, Canberra, 2004; American Photorealism, Galerie Patrice Trigano, Paris, 2005; Albrecht Dürer to Richard Estes: Line & Shadow in Six Centuries of Drawings & Print, Tunick townhouse, NY, 2006; Palazzo Magnani, Italy, 3-5/2007; and many others; Museo Thyssen, Bornemisza, Madrid, 6-9/2007. *Awards:* MECA Award for Achievement as a Visual Artist, Maine, 96. *Bibliog:* Carol King (auth), Realism, The new hip, ARTnews, 2/97; Jaime Fernandez (auth), Sauray Estes, doe visiones diferentes del arte actual, Ya de madrid, 1/16/98; Jose Luis Gallero (auth), Richard Estes la otra orilla de la realidad, ABC Cutl, 1/16/98. *Mem:* Nat Acad. *Media:* Oil. *Publ:* Meisel Lars (auth), Richard Estes The Complete Painting 1966-1985, Harry Abrams Inc, 1986; John Arthor (auth), Richard Estes Paintings & Prints, Chameleon Books, San Francisco, CA, 1993; John Wilmerding (auth), Richard Estes, Rizzoli Intenat Publ, NYC, 2006. *Dealer:* Marlborough 40 W 57th St New York NY 10019

ETCHISON, BRUCE
CONSERVATOR, PAINTER
b Washington, DC, Dec 19, 1918. *Study:* Am Univ, BA; Yale Univ Sch Fine Arts, BFA & MFA. *Work:* Washington Co Mus Fine Arts, Hagerstown, Md; Chesapeake Bay Maritime Mus, St Michaels, Md; Merrick Art Gallery, New Brighton, Pa. *Exhib:* Merrick Art Gallery, New Brighton, Pa; Washington Co Mus Fine Arts, Hagerstown, Md. *Pos:* Dir, Washington Co Mus Fine Arts, 50-64 & Abby Aldrich Rockefeller Folk Art Collection, 64-66; conservator for pvt collectors mus, univs, cols, hist soc & the State of Pa, formerly; currently retired. *Mem:* Int & Am Insts Conserv Hist & Artistic Works; Washington Conserv Guild. *Media:* Oil, Etching, Sculpture. *Publ:* Coauth, Roentgen Examination of Painting, 60; auth, Radiant Heat for Vacuum Tables, 69

ETHRIDGE, ROE
PHOTOGRAPHER
b Miami, 1969. *Study:* Coll Art, Atlanta, BFA (Photog), 95. *Exhib:* Solo exhibs include Block Candy Art Gallery, Atlanta, 95, Scalo Galerie, Zurich, 97, Anna Kustera Gallery, New York, 98 & 99, Vankin Schwartz Gallery, Atlanta, 99, Galerie Oliver Schweden, Munich, 1999, Rogert Pearre Gallery, Tucson, Ariz, 2000, Andrew Kreps Gallery, New York, 2000, 2002, 2004, 2005 & 2008, Greengrassi Gallery, London, 2003 & 2007, Gagosian Gallery, LA, 2006, Mai 36 Galerie, Zurich, 2007; group shows include Atlanta Biennial, Nexus Contemp Art Center, Atlanta, 97, From Your House to Our House, 99; Greater New York, Mus Mod Art/PS1, New York, 2000; Rocks & Trees, Photog Resource Center, Boston, 2001; The Americans, Barbican Center, London, 2001; Hello, My Name Is, Carnegie Mus Art, Pittsburgh, 2002; The Bow, Cheekwood Mus Art, Nashville, 2002; For the People of Paris, Sutton Lane, Paris, 2007; Artist in & Out of Cologne, Henry Art Gallery, Seattle, 2007; Whitney Biennial, Whitney Mus Am Art, New York, 2008. *Mailing Add:* care AFG Management Ste 5W 515 W 20th St New York NY 10011

ETTENBERG, FRANKLIN JOSEPH
PAINTER, PRINTMAKER
b Brooklyn, NY, May 7, 1945. *Study:* Univ Mich, BS (design), 66, with Milton Cohen, Fred Bauer & John Stephenson; Univ NMex, MA, 71, with John Kacere. *Work:* Detroit Inst Art; Roswell Mus & Art Ctr, NMex; Fine Arts Mus, Santa Fe; Minnesota Mus Art, St Paul; Anderson Mus Art, Roswell, NMex. *Comn:* Paired Paintings, NMex Arts Comn, 78; Taos Watershed Mural, Mary Medina Bldg, Taos, NMex, 78. *Exhib:* Solo exhibs, Janus Gallery, Santa Fe, 86 & 88 & Wright Gallery, Dallas, 84 & 85; Conlon Gallery, Santa Fe, 89; Artists Discover Columbus, Castillo Ctr, NY, 92; Galerie Rondula, Vienna, Austria, 94; Austria Tabakmus, Vienna, 97; Five Allies, NMex State Capitol, 2002; Kunst Forum, Hallein, Austria, 2004. *Pos:* Exec comt, Advocates for Contemp Art, Santa Fe, 73-75; cert graphoanalyst, Int Graphoanalysis Soc, Chicago, 77. *Teaching:* Instr, Santa Fe Workshops of Contemp Art, 74; pvt painting instr, 79-. *Awards:* Roswell Mus Artist-in-Residence Grant, NMex, 71; Southwest 85, Purchase Award, (monotype), Merit Award, (painting), Mus Fine Art, Santa Fe, 85; Contemporary '98 Best in Show, Fuller Lodge, Los Alamos, NMex, 98; Certificate of Recognition, State Legis, NMex, 2002. *Bibliog:* W Peterson (auth), Critique of painted low-reliefs, spring 82, W Peterson (auth), review, fall 86, Abstract painting in New Mexico, fall 88, Artspace; W Clark (auth), Artist profile, Sunday Arts, Albuquerque Journal, 3/6/88; Dr Miro Klivar (auth), FE-Master of Gestural Meditatiion (essay), Am Soc Aesthetics, Prague, CZ, 2005. *Media:* Acrylic, Linen; Monotype on Rives BFK. *Collection:* Capital Art, Santa Fe, NMex, Anderson Mus, Roswell, NMex. *Publ:* Contribr, Santa Fe Fine Arts Calendar, 93 & 94. *Dealer:* Silvia Stenitzer Santa Fe NM Tel #505-983-6934. *Mailing Add:* c/o Frank Ettenberg Studio 2001 Ft Union Dr Santa Fe NM 87505

ETTL, GEORG
PAINTER, SCULPTOR
b Nittenau, Ger, Mar 3, 31. *Study:* Sorbonne, Paris, France, 63-65; Wayne State Univ, BA, 65, MA, 67, MFA, 68. *Work:* Mus Abteiberg, Möchen Gladbach, Ger; Kaiser Wilhelm Mus, Krefeld, Ger. *Comn:* Amphitheater, 81 & Murals for City Co Bldg, Vierson, Ger, 83-84. *Exhib:* All Mich Exhib, Flint Inst Arts, 72; solo exhib, Mus Abteiberg, Mönchen Gladbach, Ger, 77-78; With a Certain Smile, Zurich, Switz, 79; Kick Out the Jams: Detroit's Cass Corridor 1963-77, Detroit Inst Arts & Mus Contemp Art, Chicago, 81; With a Certain Smile, Krefeld, Ger, 83. *Awards:* Purchase Prizes, 58th Exhib Mich Artists, Detroit Inst Arts, 70 & All Mich Exhib, Flint Inst Arts, 72. *Bibliog:* Johannes Cladders (auth), Georg Ettl, Städtisches Mus Mönchen Gladbach, 77; Julian Heyden (auth), Georg Ettl: Hausordnung, Krefelder Kunstmus, 83; Nena Dimitrijevic (auth), Sculpture and Its Double, Sculpture Show, Greater London Coun, 83. *Media:* All

ETZOLD, ECKHARD
PAINTER
b Bremen, Germany, 1965. *Study:* Slade Sch Fine Art, London, 1988; Art Inst Chicago, 1990; Hochschule der Künste, Berlin, 1992. *Exhib:* Solo exhibs include Mittelstrasse Gallery, Potsdam, Germany, 1996, Bucheon Gallery, San Francisco, 2000, 2004, Seippel Gallery, Cologne, Germany, 2001, Gallery Wachs, Berlin, 2005; group exhibs include Altarbild Geist & Körper, Mus deutsche Geschichte, Berlin, 1990; De Vonk Kunstverein, Bussum, Netherlands, 1992; Ann Exhib Inst Contemp Art PS1, Clocktower, New York, 1997; Size Matters, Gale Gates et al, Brooklyn, New York, 1999; Twilight Zone, Carrie Haddad Gallery, Hudson, New York, 2006; Natural Selection, Albany Int Airport Gallery, NY, 2007; Täglich Geöffnet, Mus Goch, Germany, 2007. *Awards:* Pollock-Krasner Grant, 1998; New York Found Arts Grant, 2008. *Dealer:* Galerie Seippel Zeughausstrasse 26 50667 Cologne Germany

EUREN, BARRY A
PAINTER, ILLUSTRATOR
b Sacramento, Calif, Oct 4, 1948. *Study:* Calif State Univ, BA, 72-73; Calif Community Coll. *Work:* White House Collection, Washington, DC; CM Russell Mus, Great Falls, Mont; Oakland Mus, Calif; Calif State Univ, Sacramento; Calif State Archives, Sacramento; Mus Religious Arts, Logan Iowa; War in Heaven, 2011. *Comn:* Bicenntenial 1976, Bur Indian Affairs, Washington, DC, 76; Book of Healing, Jesus Christ, Worldwide, 2005. *Teaching:* Instr, Community Coll. *Awards:* Crystal Award, Calif State Fair, 2005. *Bibliog:* Constance Smith (auth), Living Artists, Art Network Press, 2003. *Mem:* Am Inst Fine Art; Am Asn Printing House Craftsman; Print Club Albany. *Media:* Etching, Oil. *Interests:* Painting under the pseudonym, Nerue, inventor. *Publ:* Illusr, A Pirates Tale. *Dealer:* Wills Gallery 222 N Locust St Carlisle KY 40311. *Mailing Add:* 1801 Eureka Rd Apt 414 Roseville CA 95661-7707

EURICH, JUDITH
APPRAISER
Pos: Cur asst, 19th Century Photography, San Francisco Art Mus. *Teaching:* Teacher, Acad Art College, Hearst Art Gallery, St Mary's College, Moranga, Calif. *Mailing Add:* Bonham & Butterfields 220 San Bruno Ave San Francisco CA 94103

EVANGELINE, MARGARET
PAINTER, COLLAGE ARTIST
b Baton Rouge, La. *Study:* La State Univ, 61-63 & 65; Univ New Orleans, BA, 75, MFA, 78. *Work:* Texaco, Houston, Tex; Simone, Peregine, Smith & Redfern, New Orleans; IBM, Tenn; Bank of the South, Atlanta, Ga; Pensacola Mus, Fla. *Comn:* Painting, Entergy Collection, Jackson, Miss, 94. *Exhib:* Solo exhibs include Pensacola Mus Art, Fla, 91, Res Nova, NY, 92, Byron Roche Gallery, Chicago, Ill, 2000, Alva

Gallery, New London, Conn, 2001, Palm Beach Inst Contemp Art, Palm Beach, Fla, 2001, ACA Galleries, NY, 2001, Galerie Simonne Stern, New Orleans, La, 93, 94, 96 & 99, HP Garcia Gallery, NY, 2007; group exhibs include Galerie Simonne Stern, New Orleans, La, 93; Nave Mus, Victoria, Tex, 98; Howard Scott/M13, NY, 99; The Drawing Ctr, NY, 2000, Fluid Flow, James Graham Gallery, NY, 2000, Fall Group Show, Betty Wasserman Art & Interiors, NY, 2000 & Younger Artists, Anita Shapolsky Gallery, NY, 2001. *Awards:* Artist-in-Residence, Villa Montalvo Found, Saratoga, Calif, 91; Painting Fel, NY Found for the Arts, 96; Artist-in-Residence, ART/OMI Found, Omi, NY, 99. *Bibliog:* Dominique Nahas (auth), Margaret Evangaline, New Art Examiner, 57-58, 9/98; Michael Rush (auth), The Confessions of MLLE G (catalog), The Drawing Ctr; Lilly Wei (auth), Margaret Evaneline, Galerie Simonne Stern, Art in Am, 1/2000. *Media:* Acrylic, Oil; Found Objects. *Publ:* Illusr, cover, The critical state of visual art in New York, Review Mag, 12/1/98. *Mailing Add:* NY Studio 601 W 26th St #1385 New York NY 10001

EVANS, BOB
PAINTER, PHOTOGRAPHER
b Chicago, Ill, May 2, 1944. *Study:* Parsons Col; Univ Iowa; Northeast Mo State Univ, BEd; Drake Univ; Southern Ill Univ, Carbondale, MFA. *Work:* Southern Ill Univ, Carbondale; Western Ill Univ, Macomb; Ill State Univ, Normal; Quincy Art Club; Lakeview Mus Arts & Sci; Rockford Art Mus, Ill; Block Gallery, Northwestern Univ; Ill State Mus. *Comn:* Subscription print series, Plucked Chicken Press, Evanston, Ill, 86. *Exhib:* 16th Midwest Biennial, Joslyn Art Mus, Omaha, Nebr, 80; Irwin Collection, Krannert Art Mus, Univ Ill, 80; Watercolor USA, Springfield Art Mus, Mo, 80; Solo exhibs, Zaks Gallery, Chicago, Ill, 81 & 84; Chicago Int Art Expos, 82-87; Fabrications, Chicago Sculpture Soc, 83; Sound/Light, ARC, Chicago, 87; Solo exhibs, Endicott Coll, MA, 97, Hess Gallery, Pine Manor Coll, 2004; Fountain St Fine Arts, Framingham, Mass 2012-2013; Newton Public Library Gallery, Mass, 2011. *Collection Arranged:* Emergence of Modernism in Illinois 1914-1940, 76; Illinois Photographers 1978, 80; Illinois Invitationals, 71-84; Contemporary Am Photography, 88; White Mountain Painters, 92; Art Forms in Nature: The Prints of Ernst Haeckel, 2000. *Pos:* Res asst, Univ Galleries, Southern Ill Univ, Carbondale, 69-70; cur art, Ill State Mus, Springfield, 70-, head dept art, 81-85; gallery dir & dept chmn, Rockford Col, 85-88; dir, Danforth Mus Art, Framingham, Mass, 88-95. *Teaching:* Instr drawing & painting, Springfield Art Asn, Ill, 71-76; adj asst prof arts mgt, Sangamon State Univ, 73-78; assoc prof, Rockford Col, 85-88; adj fac, Framingham State Col, Mass, 88-95; prof visual commun, Endicott Col, Beverly, Mass, 95-2000, chmn visual comm, 95-98; prof visual art, Pine Manor Col, Chestnut Hill, MA, 2001-2007. *Awards:* Merit Award, Miss Corridors, Davenport Art Mus, Iowa, 81; Gov Art Award, Ill Arts Coun, 80; Best in show, Springfield Old Capital Art Fair, Il, 80. *Bibliog:* David Elliott (auth), article, Chicago Sun Times, 6/21/81; Alan G Artner (auth), article, Chicago Tribune, 7/3/81. *Media:* Mixed, Painting. *Publ:* Auth, articles in Living Mus, 70- & Craft Horizons & Mus News; plus numerous exhib catalogs. *Mailing Add:* 11 Willowbrook Dr Framingham MA 01702

EVANS, BURFORD ELONZO
PAINTER, LECTURER
b Golinda, Tex, July 20, 1931. *Study:* Sorbonne Univ, cert 55; Echole de Beaux Arts, Paris, France. *Work:* Mus Fine Arts, Lubbock, Tex; Black Arts Ctr, Waco, Tex; Northwood Inst, Midland, Mich; Bishop Col, Dallas, Tex. *Comn:* Josephite Black Arts Calendar, Josephite Pastoral Ctr, Washington, DC, 74. *Exhib:* Mobile Arts Festival, Ala, 70; Discovery 70, Nat Black Arts Festival, Cincinnati, Ohio, 70; Nat Black Arts Festival, Normal, Ill, 73; solo exhib, State Capitol, Austin, Tex, 73, Abajan Ivory Coast, Africa, 95, Southside Cult Ctr, Chicago, Ill, 2001; Tex Fine Arts Festival, Houston, 74. *Awards:* Second Award, Dimension IV Houston Art League, Humble Oil Co, 68; Betty McGowan Award, Mobil Arts Festival, 70; Distinguished Artist Award, Nat Coun Negro Women, 72. *Bibliog:* James Kennedy (auth), Ethnic American Art, Slide Libr, Univ Ala, 70-75; Charolette Phelen (auth), Evans remembers June tenth, Houston Chronicle, 71; Theresa Dickason Cederholm (auth), Afro American Artist, Boston Pub Libr, 73. *Mem:* Art League Houston; Tex Fine Arts Asn; Contemp Arts Asn. *Media:* Multimedia. *Specialty:* Contemporary. *Interests:* Impressionist. *Dealer:* Claude Smith 3917 Art Gallery Houston TX. *Mailing Add:* 5327 Knotty Oaks Tr Houston TX 77045-4018

EVANS, DICK
PAINTER, SCULPTOR
b Roswell, NMex, July 10, 1941. *Study:* Tex Tech Univ, Lubbock, 59-62; Univ Utah, Salt Lake City, BFA, 64, MFA, 66. *Work:* Nat Mus Am Art, Smithsonian Inst; Sheldon Mem Art Gallery, Univ Nebr, Lincoln; Milwaukee Art Mus; Ariz State Univ, Tempe; Herbert F Johnson Mus Art, Cornell Univ, Ithaca, NY; and others. *Comn:* Ceramic murals, Deloitte, Haskins & Sells, 86, Warshafsky, Rotter, Tarnoff, Gesler & Reinhardt, 86 & Milwaukee Art Comn, 88, Milwaukee, Wis; RTE Corp, 87; Firstar, 87. *Exhib:* Landscape: New Views, Johnson Art Mus, Cornell Univ, Ithaca, NY, 78; Poetic Image, Elements Gallery, NY, 80; Sheldon Mem Art Gallery, Univ Nebr, Lincoln, 82; solo exhibs, Michael H Lord Gallery, Milwaukee, Wis, 84 & 89, Elaine Horwitch Galleries, Santa Fe, NMex, 90, Tory Folliard Gallery, Milwaukee, Wis, 93, 95 & 2006, Robins Hyder Gallery, Santa Fe NMex, 96; Joyce Robins Gallery, Santa Fe, NMex, 97-2006 & 2008; Shadid Fine Art, Edmond, Okla, 2003-2009; New Ground, The Edge Gallery, Santa Fe, NMex, 2010; Indications, Winterowd Fine Art, Santa Fe, NMex, 2011; Group exhib, Out West, The Great Am Landscape (traveling), China, 2007. *Teaching:* Instr art, Texas Tech, Lubbock, 66-70; asst prof art, Univ Tenn, Knoxville, 71-72 & Univ NMex, Albuquerque, 72-75; prof art, Sch Fine Arts, Univ Wis, Milwaukee, 75-87, assoc dean, 81-83. *Awards:* NMex Disting Artists Calendar Award, NMex Mag, 99. *Bibliog:* Margaret L Brown (auth), The abstracted landscape, Southwest Art, 9/97; Susan Hallsten McGarry (auth), Inside Out: The landscape of memory, 6/99; Marsha McEuen (auth), Art Pairs, Santa Fean Mag, 5/99; Dotte Indyke (auth), Dick Evans National Reviews, Art News, 9/2/2002; Kristen Buckner (auth), Best of the West- Exploring Nature's Enigmas & Mellow Yellow, Southwest Art, 5/2004; Judith Fein & Paul Ross (auths), Emerging Artists, Art 7 Antiques, 4/2005. *Media:* Acrylic. *Dealer:* Tory Folliard Gallery 233 N Milwaukee St Milwaukee WI 53202; Winterowd Fine Art 701 Canyon Rd Santa Fe NMex 87501. *Mailing Add:* 47 Coyote Mountain Rd Santa Fe NM 87505

EVANS, GARTH
PAINTER, EDUCATOR
b Stockport, Cheshire, Eng, Nov 23, 1934; arrived in US, 79. *Study:* Studied at Manchester Jr Coll Art, 51; Manchester Regional Coll Art, 57; Univ Coll London, diploma fine art, 60. *Exhib:* Solo exhibs include Rowan Gallery, London, 62, 64, 66, 68, 69, 72, 74, 76, 78, 80, Minneapolis Inst Arts, 79, Mt Holyoke Coll Art Mus, South Hadley, Mass, 83, Robert Elkon Gallery, NY City, 83, Tibor de Nagy Gallery, NY City, 84, Robert Brown Contemp Art, Washington, 88, Compass Rose Gallery, Chicago, 89, Hill Gallery, Birmingham, Mich, 90, Wrexham Mus and Art Ctr, Rhyl, Wales, 91, Rosemary Hall, Wallingford, Conn, 93, Dana Arts Ctr, Colgate Univ, Hamilton, NY, 95, Korn Gallery, Drew Univ, Madison, NJ, 96, Claudia Carr Gallery, NY City, 97, Watercolors, Lori Bookstein Fine Art, NY, 2004, Little Dancers BCB Art, Hudson, NY, 2008, Sculpture from the Late 1980's, Lori Bookstein Fine Art, NY, 2009, Red Clay Drawings, Julian Scott Memorial Gallery, Johnson State Coll, VT, 2009, 1980s Plywood Wall Sculptures, Lori Bookstein Fine Art, NY, 2010, Evolving Constructions, 159-80, Poussin Gallery, London, 2012, Same Difference, Sculpture Drawings and Watercolors, BCB Fine Art, Hudson, NY, 2013, Little Dancers, NY Studio Sch, 2013, A Selection from the Studio, William Benton Mus, Univ Conn, 2013, Garth Evans, Sculpture, 1960-1979, Longside Gallery, Yorkshire, Eng, 2013; group exhibs include Air Gallery, London, 62, Stone Gallery, Newcastle Upon Tyne, Eng, 64, Camden Arts Ctr, London, 66, Whitechapel Art Gallery, London, 68, Hayward Gallery, London, 71, 75, Redfern Gallery, London, 77, Oporto Sch Fine Art, Portugal, 80, Robert Elkon Gallery, NY City, 81, Newhouse Gallery, NY City, 83, John Davis Gallery, Akron, 86, NY Studio Sch, NY City, 89, Charles Cowles Gallery, NY City, 91, PMW Gallery, Stamford, Conn, 92, Skidmore Col, Saratoga Springs, NY, 93, Am Acad Arts and Letters, NY City, 96, Artists of Yaddo, Claudia Carr Gallery, NY, 2000, Watercolors, Kouros Gallery, NY, 2003, In Black and White, Lori Bookstein Fine Art, NY, 2005, Ten Great Works from the Sixties and Seventies, Poussin Gallery, London, 2008, Personal Geometry, Lori Bookstein Fine Art, NY, 2009, Coincidence, Spektre Gallery, Brooklyn, NY, 2010, Group 2011, Lori Bookstein Fine Art, NY, 2011, United Enemies, Henry Moore Inst, Leeds, Eng, 2012, Sculptures, Drawings, Pangolin Gallery, London, Eng, 2012, The Individual and Organization: Artist Placement Group 1966-1979, Raven Row, London, Eng, 2012; represented in public collections Tate Gallery, London, Welsh Art Council, Brooklyn Union Gas, Merthyr Tydfil Art Gallery, Wales, Victoria & Albert Mus, London, Mus Modern Art, NY Metrop Mus, NY City, Brooklyn Mus, Joseph H Hirshhorn Mus, Washington, DC, Nat Mus Modern Art, Brazil, Power Gallery Contemp Art, Sydney, Gulbenkian Found Lisbon, Portugal, Yale Ctr British Art. *Pos:* bd governors NY Studio Sch of Drawing, Painting and Sculpture, 1995-. *Teaching:* Vis lectr Central Sch Art, London, 60-65, Camberwell Sch Art, London, 60-69, St Martin's Sch Art, London, 65-79, Chelsea Sch Art, London, 78-79, Yale Sch Art, Yale Univ, 83, 85, 86; vis prof Minneapolis Col Art and Design, 73; external examiner Maidstone Col Art, Kent, Eng, 77-79, Nat Col Art and Design, Dublin, Ireland, 78, Goldsmiths Col, Univ London, 78-81; vis tutor Slade Sch Fine Art, Univ Col, London, 70-81; vis artist sculpture dept Royal Col Art, 70-81; vis artist Mt Holyoke Col, South Hadley, 79-81, Manchester Poly, 78-83; assoc lectr in sculpture Camberwell Sch Art, London, 71-83; faculty mem NY Studio Sch, NY City, 88-. *Awards:* Sabbatical Awrd, Arts Council Great Britain, 66; Major Prize, 75; Film Bursary Award, 79; Bursary Award, Greater London Arts Asn, 78; Pollock-Krasner Found Award, 96; Newcastle Cruddas Park Sculpture Competition, 61; British Steep Corp Fellow, 69; John S Guggenheim Memorial Found Fellow, 86; British Council Exhib Abroad, 79; Artist's Fellowship award, 1999. *Mem:* Nat Acad. *Mailing Add:* NY Studio Sch 8 W 8th St New York NY 10011

EVANS, JUDITH FUTRAL
PAINTER
b Ft Smith, Ark. *Study:* Univ Ark, Fayetteville, BA, 61; Univ Iowa, Iowa City, MFA, 64. *Work:* Columbia Presbyterian Med Ctr, NY; Shearson Lehman Hutton, New York; Avon Corp, New York; US Air, Philadelphia, Pa; Towers Perrin, Stamford, Conn; Giro Credit Bank, Vienna, Austria & New York; and numerous other pub & pvt collections; Mt Sinai Med Ctr, New York; McCown & Evans LLP. *Comn:* After Diego Rivera, comn by Al Solokov & Co, New York, 86; Golden Gate with Wildflowers Comn, Tafapolsky & Smith LLP, San Francisco, 2002; Portrait, Sylvia Barker Comn, Mt Sinai Medical Ctr, New York, 2004; Gumbel Memorial Fountain, painting, Audubon Park, New Orleans, La, comn by John Ormond, 2007; Sunrise, Noon, Sunset triptych, painting, comn by Dr Michael Carey, 2007; portrait, Philip O Alderson, Columbian Presbyterian Med Ctr, NY; portrait Isabel, Michael Carey; portrait Sarah and Mack, Michael Carey; portrait Marley, Ryley and Max, comn by Emily Buckingham; portrait Lily and Camille, comn by Elizabeth Futral. *Exhib:* Blue Mt Gallery, New York, 80-94, 30th Anniv Exhib, 2010; Nat Mid-Year Am, Butler Inst Am Art, Ohio, 85, 88, 92, 2009, 2014; Nat Soc Painters Casein & Acrylic, New York, 89-2013; Park Avenue Atrium, New York, 96; Heckscher Mus Art, New York, 96; Gatehouse Gallery, Glasgow, Scotland, 97; Ethel Sergeant Smith Gallery, Wayne, Pa, 97; Sherry French Gallery, New York, 97-2007; Ark Art Ctr, Little Rock, 97; Hurlbutt Gallery, Greenwich, Conn, 98; New London Art Soc, Conn, 98; Ctr for the Arts, Vero Beach, Fla, 98; Albright Knox Gallery, Buffalo, NY, 99; Doran Gallery, Tulsa, Okla, 2002-06; JRB Art, Oklahoma City, Okla, 2004-06; Pastel Soc Am, NY, 2006, 2008, 2009, 2010, & 2011 Selections from the Pastel Soc Am, 37th Ann, Butler Inst Am Art, Youngstown, Oh, 2009; 11th Ann, Catherine Lorillard Wolfe Art Club, New York, 2007, 2010, 2012; Aububon Artists 65th Ann, Nat Arts Club, NY, 2007; Katonah Mus Art, Katonah, NY, 2009; Allied Artists of Am, New York, 2009; 83rd Nat, Am Artists Prof League, Salmagundi Club, NY, 2011; 20th Nat Roundtable, Nat Arts Club, NY, 2011; One Person Show, Oils and Pastels, Thos. Moser, NY, 2012. *Pos:* Founder, Blue Mt Gallery, New York, 79-; scenic artist, Major Motion Pictures, Network Television, Broadway Shows & Metrop Opera, New York, 84-2013. *Awards:* 34th Ann Nat Arts

Club, Pastel Soc Am, New York, 2006; Pastel Soc Am Award, 2009; Catharine Lorillard Wolfe award, 2013; Nat Soc Painters in Casein and Acrylic award, 2013, Salmagundi Club, NY, Joseph A. Cain Memorial award, Mark Freeman Memorial award, 2014; 41st Ann Nat Arts Club award, Pastel Soc Am, 2013; 42nd Ann Jack Richeson & Company Silver award, Pastel Soc Am, 2014. *Bibliog:* Jeff Stinson (auth), Arkansas puts works on display, Wash Gazette, 5/91; Diane Freedman (auth), Artists celebrate their environment, Artspeak, 3/16/96; Paulette Weiss (auth), French's American on 57th, Where Mag, 7/99. *Mem:* United Scenic Artists, Local 829, New York; signature mem, Pastel Soc Am, NY. *Media:* Acrylic, Oil; Pastel. *Specialty:* realism. *Publ:* Best of Acrylic Painting, 96, Best of Oil Painting, 96 & Landscape Inspirations, 97, Rockport Publ Inc, 97. *Mailing Add:* 34 Plaza St Apt 808 Brooklyn NY 11238

EVANS, KENYA
ARTIST
b Sumter, NC, 1974. *Exhib:* Hannah Höch, Mit Pinsel, Feder und Schere, Galerie Remmert und Barth, Duesseldorf, 98; Day for Night, Whitney Biennial, NY, 2006. *Pos:* gallery supv, Contemp Arts Mus, Houston, Tex; mem, Otabenga Jones & Assoc. *Mailing Add:* Contemporary Arts Museum Houston 5216 Montrose Blvd Houston TX 77006

EVANS, NANCY
PAINTER
b Los Angeles, Calif, 1949. *Study:* Univ Calif, Berkeley, BA (Art). *Exhib:* Solo exhibs include Sue Spaid Fine Art, Los Angeles, 1991, 1992, 1994, Rosamund Felsen Gallery, Los Angeles, 1997, Sweetney Art Gallery, Univ Calif, 1997, Cirrus Gallery, Los Angeles, 1998, POST Gallery, Los Angeles, 1999, Dangerous Curve, Los Angeles, 2006, Cardwell Jimmerson Contemp Art, Los Angeles, 2008; Group exhibs include Fever Drawings, Los Angeles Inst Contemp Art, 1985; LA Post Cool, San Jose Mus Art, Calif, 2002; Immodesty, Another Year in LA Gallery, Calif, 2006; Drawin In: Drawing in Residence Phase III, Torrance Art Mus, Calif, 2007; Some Paintings, Track 16 Gallery, Los Angeles, 2008; Good Doll/Bad Doll, Armory Ctr Arts, Pasadena, Calif, 2008. *Awards:* Joan Mitchell Found Grant, 2007

EVANS, ROBERT GRAVES
EDUCATOR, SCULPTOR
b Rawlins, Wyo, Nov 19, 1944. *Study:* Atlanta Sch Art, BFA; French Govt Fel, Paris, 69; with Stanley Hayter; Tulane Univ, with Julius Struppeck, MFA. *Work:* Evansville Mus Arts & Sci, Ind; Sheldon Swope Art Mus, Terre Haute, Ind; Ind State Univ, Terre Haute; Central Mich Univ, Mt Pleasant; The Univ of the South, Swanee, Tenn. *Comn:* Man of Year Award (sculpture), Atlanta, Ga, 69; Film Festival Award (sculpture), Atlanta, Ga, 69; bronze bust of Pres Rankin, Ind State Univ, 75; outdoor sculpture, Cent Mich Univ, 75; outdoor monumental sculpture comn, Indianapolis, Ind, 82. *Exhib:* Mid-States Art Exhib, Evansville Mus Arts & Sci, Ind, 78; New Harmony Gallery of Contemp Art, New Harmony, Ind, 82; Wabash Col, Outdoor Sculpture Exhib, Crawfordsville, Ind, 85; Solo Sculpture Exhib, Herr-Chambliss Fine Arts Gallery, Hot Springs Nat Park, Ark, 90; Sculpture Exhib at Mid-Am Mus, Hot Springs Nat Park, Ark, 91. *Pos:* Prof of Art. *Teaching:* Prof sculpture, Ind State Univ, Terre Haute, 72-78, assoc prof art, 78-84, prof art, 84-. *Awards:* Sculpture Acquisition, Swope Art Gallery, 77; Mus Guild Purchase Award, Evansville Mus Arts & Sci, 78; Beautification Award, Terre Haute CofC, 81. *Mem:* Southern Sculpture Asn; Arts Illiana; Coll Art Asn. *Media:* Bronze, Aluminum. *Mailing Add:* Ind State Univ Dept of Art Terre Haute IN 47809

EVANS, ROBERT J. See Evans, Bob

EVANS, STEVEN
GALLERY DIRECTOR, ADMINISTRATOR
b Key West, Fla. *Study:* Atlanta Coll Art, BFA (photog); Nova Scotia Coll Art & Design, MFA (fine art). *Pos:* Freelance cur & writer, formerly; asst dir, Dia Art Found Beacon, 2003-2010; exec dir & cur, Linda Pace Found, 2010-; bd mem, Dutchess County Econ Devel Corp; bd mem & vice chmn for allocations, Dutchess County Arts Coun. *Mailing Add:* Dia Beacon 3 Beekman St Beacon NY 12508

EVANS, TOM R
PAINTER
b St Paul, Minn, June 4, 1943. *Study:* Univ Minn, BA, 65, MFA, 68. *Work:* Grey Gallery, New York Univ; Chase Manhattan Bank, London, Eng; Gen Mills, Minneapolis, Minn; IBM, White Plains, NY. *Exhib:* Walker Biennial, Walker Art Ctr, Minneapolis, Minn, 68; Contemp Reflections, 71 & Best of Contemp Reflections, 73, Aldrich Mus, Ridgefield, Conn; one-person exhibs, John Bernard Myers Gallery, NY, 73 & 74 & Max Hutchinson Gallery, NY, 79; New Work-NY, New Mus, NY, 81; Gimpel & Weitzenhoffen Gallery, NY, 86; Paint as Primal Substance, Painting Ctr, NY, 97; Marymount Col, NY, 97; Solo: 55 Mercer Gallery, 2004; 55 Mercer Gallery, 2005; Group: Looking Back & Moving Forward, Univ of Minn; Bill Bollinger-Tom Evans, Mitchell Algus Gallery, NYC, 2007. *Teaching:* Asst prof, Fashion Inst Tech. *Media:* Oil on Canvas or Linen. *Mailing Add:* 115 W Broadway New York NY 10013

EVAUL, WILLIAM H, JR
PAINTER, PRINTMAKER, CURATOR
b Philadelphia, Pa, July 2, 1949. *Study:* Fleischer Mem Sch Art, Syracuse Univ, Pratt Inst, BFA, 81; Whitney Mus Am Art, Grad Studies, 81. *Work:* The Library of Congress, Provincetown Art Asn & Mus, Mass; Printmaking Workshop, NY; Jane Vorhees Zimmerli Art Mus, New Brunswick, NJ; Cape Cod Mus Art. *Comn:* Arts Found of Cape Cod-Pops-by-the-Sea Artists-Original painting and limited print edition commissioned 2002; Provincetown Tennessee Williams Theater Festival - 2013, Tennessee Williams & Women, 2012, Tennessee Williams & Music. *Exhib:* Provincetown & the Art of Printmaking, Smithsonian Inst Traveling Exhib, 90-92; Int Fine Print Dealers Asn Ann Print Fair, 90-2016; solo exhibs, Printmaking Coun, NJ, 94 & Inter-active Virtual Painting, SMA Real Time, NY, 98, The Fine White-Line, Faces Behind the Prints, Provincetown Mus 2015, Extending the White-Line Woodcut Tradition, Curator: Ron Shuebrook, Provincetown Art Asn & Mus, 2016; Modernism, Park Ave Armory, NY; Innovative Printmaking from an Am Art Colony, Zimmerli Art Mus; Int Miniature Print Exhib, 2001, Conn Graphic Arts Ctr, Norwalk, Conn; Southcoast New Eng Printmaking 1939-2003, Univ of Mass, Dartmouth; North Am Print Biennial 2005, Boston Univ; Soc of Am Graphic Artists 80th Ann 2013, SAGA Ann Nat Arts Club, New York, 2006. *Pos:* Dir/cur, Provincetown Art Asn & Mus, 86-90; guest cur, Cape Mus Fine Arts, 92, Carmen Cicero, Provincetown Art Asn & Mus, 2012, Pilgrim Monument and Provincetown Mus, 2015. *Teaching:* Asst inst lithography, Pratt Graphics Ctr, 80-82; instr printmaking, Truro Ctr Arts, 92-; guest lectr, Ga Mus Art, Ogleby Inst & others; tchr Penn Acad Fine Art, Charles Demuth Found, Zimmerli Art Mus. *Awards:* SAGA 80th Annual Exhibition Purchase Prize. *Bibliog:* Ann Brigham (auth), Contemporary artists, Orthodox traditions, Antiques & Arts, 1/90; Joe Burn (auth) Block printing undergoes an Evaul-lution The Provincetown Banner, Nov 98; Scott Dalton (auth) White-Line Woodcut Artist Bill Evaul Carves Out More Than a Niche A-Plus-Art/Antiques/Design, July, 2002; Virginia Reiser (auth), The Kindest Cut-White-Line Woodcuts, Cape Arts Review Annual 2002; Deborah Minsky, Bill Evaul a Dynamo in Motion, Provincetown Banner, 9/12; Deborah Forman (auth) Contemporary Cape Cod Artists, pub. Schiffer 2013; Jane Anderson (producer/writer) 2015 HBO Documentary Packed in a Trunk; 2015 Chronicle, WBZ-TV, Boston; Lisa Leigh Connors (auth) Carving Out a Niche, Cape Cod Magazine 7/15; Rory Marcus. *Media:* Oil, Woodcut, Watercolor, Drawing. *Res:* American Art-Provincetown White-Line Color Woodblocks. *Publ:* Auth, Print Review - The Genesis of a unique woodcut tradition, Pratt Graphics Ctr, 84; Art Guide, Provincetown in the 70's; Provincetown Arts, The Provincetown Art Asn & Mus, 1987; The Eye of the Collector, Cape Mus Fine Art, 92; Provincetown Arts - Carmen Cicero The Color of Sound 2012, 2014. *Mailing Add:* 347 Commercial St Provincetown MA 02657

EVEN, ROBERT LAWRENCE
EDUCATOR
b Breckenridge, Minn, June 7, 1929. *Study:* Valley City State Col, BS; Univ Minn, MA & PhD; Art Inst Chicago; Minneapolis Coll Art & Design. *Teaching:* Instr art, Univ Minn, 52-54; prof art, Northern Ill Univ, 63-, chmn dept, 74-91. *Awards:* Res Grant, State Ill, 64 & Dean's Fund, Northern Ill Univ, 65 & 73. *Mem:* Coll Art Asn Am; Mid-Am Coll Art Asn; Nat Coun Art Adminr; Nat Asn Sch Art. *Mailing Add:* 413 Fairmont Dr Dekalb IL 60115-2336

EVERETT, GWENDOLYN H
ADMINISTRATOR
Study: Howard Univ, degree African American Art History; Corcoran Col of Art and Design, degree African American Art History. *Pos:* Bd dirs, Arts Council of Fairfax County, secy, currently; comnr Fairfax, The Va Comn for the Arts, 2008-2013. *Teaching:* asst prof, adj prof, prof art history, Corcoran Col of Art and Design, formerly; immediate past chair dept art, Howard Univ, 2007-2012, assoc prof art history program, currently, assoc dean div fine arts, currently. *Mailing Add:* 9310 Ludgate Dr Alexandria VA 22309

EVERGON
PHOTOGRAPHER
b Niagara Falls, Ont, Dec 28, 1946. *Study:* Mt Allison Univ, Sackville, NB, BFA, 70; Rochester Inst Technol, MFA (photog), 74. *Work:* Nat Gallery Can, Can Mus Contemp Photog & Can Art Bank, Ottawa, Ont; Found Cartier pour l'Art Contemp, Jouy-en-Josas, France; Mus de Que, Quebec City. *Exhib:* Solo exhibs, Galerie Séquence, Chicoutimi, Québec, Can, 89, Recent Works by Evergon, Glenn/Dash Gallery, Los Angeles, 89, Evergon 1971-1987 Traveling Exhib, 89-90, Richard Feign Gallery, Chicago, Ill, 90, Art 45, Montreal, Que, Can, 90, Recent Polaroids, Jack Shainman Gallery, NY, 90; The Photog of Invention: Am Pictures of the 80's, Nat Mus Am Art, Washington, DC, 89; Prospect Photographie, Frankfurt Kunstverein, Frankfurt, WGer, 89; Andreas Serrano, Andrea Rugieri Gallery, Washington, DC, 90; Selection III, Polaroid Collection, Houston Foto Fest, Tex, 90; Selections V, Polaroid Collection, Photokina, Stuttgart, Ger, 90; PRET, Collection D'Oeurves D'Art, Mus du Que, Can, 90; Photographies: Pour célébrerle 150e anniversaire de la naissane de la photographie, Found Cartier pour l'art contemporain, Jouy-en-Josas, France, 90; and others. *Teaching:* Lectr photog, Louisville Sch Art, Ky, 72-73; part-time lectr photog, drawing & design, Univ Ottawa, 74-90. *Awards:* Ont Arts Coun Grants, 80 & 89; Can Coun Arts Grants, 82-90; Can Coun Art A Grant, 90. *Bibliog:* Peter Weiermair (auth), Evergon-Homo Barocco, Cliches, No 48, Belg, 88; Christie Day (auth), The wit and wisdom of a remarkable Canadian artist, Can Photog, No 1, Toronto, Can, spring 90; Martin B Pendersen (auth), Graphis Photo 90, Graphis Corp, Zurich, Switz, 90. *Mem:* Can Artists Representative, Ont & Ottawa; Visual Arts Ont. *Media:* Polaroid, Holography. *Publ:* Contribr, Artifacts at the End of a Decade, 80; Canadian Portfolio, 80; Ottawa Portfolio 1983, The Company of Artists and Patrons, 83; The New Photography: A Guide to New Images, Processes and Display Techniques, Prentice-Hall, 85. *Dealer:* Art 45 2155 Guy St Montreal PQ H3G 1K4 Canada. *Mailing Add:* c/o Jack Shainman Gallery 513 W 20th St New York NY 10011-2819

EVERHART, DON, II
SCULPTOR, MEDALIST
b York, Pa, Aug 19, 1949. *Study:* Kutztown State Univ, BFA (painting), 72. *Work:* Smithsonian Inst; Brit Mus; Nat Sculpture Soc; Georgetown Univ; Am Numismatic Soc; Brookgreen Gardens. *Comn:* The Dance of the Dolphins (art medal), 106th Issue Soc Medallists, 82; Hermit Crab (art medal), Brookgreen Gardens, SC, 91; 24 installed sculptures, (Sports Hall of Fame) Georgetown Univ, Washington, 92-; The Fossil Collection (6 art medals), 128th Issue Soc Medallists, 94; 1997 Off Inaugural Medal for Clinton/Gore, Medallic Art Co, 96; Sculpted Obverse, Buffalo Nickel, 2005; California State Quarter Reverse, 2005; Reverse, Jackie Robinson Congressional Medal, 2005. *Exhib:* Reliefs & Medals Expos, Nat Sculpture Soc, NY,

85; Am Medallic Sculpture Asn, Newark Mus, NJ, 90; Expos Fedn Int de la Medaille, British Mus, London, 92, Hungarian Nat Gallery, Budapest, 94; Traveling Show, New Medal, Am Medallic Sculpture Asn, Franklin Mint Mus, Nat Sculpture Soc, NY, Am Numismatic Soc, Colorado Springs, 94; FIDEM 94, Hungarian Nat Mus, Budapest, 94 & FIDEM 98, The Hague, Amsterdam, 98; and many others. *Pos:* Illusr, Int Design Orgn, Moorestown, NJ, 72-73; sculptor-in-residence, Franklin Mint, 73-80; freelance sculptor & medalist, 80-2004; Sculptor-Engraver, US Mint, 2004-, sculpted: Calif state quarter, 2005, nickel obverse, 2006, sculpted & designed: Nevada state quarter, 2006, Franklin the Elder silver dollar, 2006, Jamestown Silver Dollar obverse, 2007, James Madison Pres Dollar obverse, 2007, Little Rock Silver Dollar reverse, 2007, First Spouse Andrew Jackson reverse, 2008, NMex State Quarter reverse, 2008, Hawaii State Quarter reverse, 2008 and numerous other designs.; design & sculpture: Martin & Coretta King, Tuskegee Airmen, Cong Gold Medals, 2006; reverse design & sculpture, presidential dollar, 2007; reverse sculpture (Idaho & Mont), state quarter, 2007. *Teaching:* Instr sculpture, Chester Co Art Asn, 85-88 & W Chester Univ, 97-98. *Awards:* First Prize, Nat Sculpture Soc, 85; Numismatic Art Award for excellence in Medallic Sculpture, Am Numismatic Soc, 94; Best of Show, The New Medal Traveling Show, Franklin Mint, 94; Nev State Quarter reverse finalist coin of the yr, 2006; Franklin the Elder Silver Dollar obverse coin of the yr finalist, 2006; and others. *Bibliog:* Robin Salmon (auth), The 1991-1992 Brookgreen Gardens Membership Medal: The Hermit Crab, Brookgreen J, 1991; Kari Stone (auth), Opening up to medals, Coinage, 5/94; George Cuhaj (auth), Don Everhart II: A natural talent for Medallic art, The Numismatist, 10/94; Kari Stone (auth), Dinosaur medals, Coinage, 11/94; Christopher Batio (auth), Don Everhart's Sculpture, Medallic Art in Demand, Numismatic News, 1-25 1994; Everhart's Artistry Earns Recognition, Coin World Mag, page 45, 8-15 1994. *Mem:* Am Medallic Sculpture Asn (pres, 92-94); Fedn Int de la Medaille; Nat Sculpture Soc; Knickerbocker Artists; Am Artists Prof League; and others. *Media:* Bronze, Clay; Plaster, Urethane. *Interests:* bicycling, tropical fish. *Mailing Add:* 1047 Niels Ln W West Chester PA 19382-7176

EVINS, PATSY JEAN
PAINTER
b Port Lavaca, Tex, Mar 10, 1952. *Study:* North Tex State Univ, Denton, BFA, 75; Lyme Acad Fine Art, Old Lyme, Conn, 85-86; Silvermine Sch Art, New Canaan, Conn, 87-88. *Work:* John Marlor Arts Ctr, Milledgeville, Ga; Gen Electric Capital, Atlanta, Ga; St Joseph Hosp, Augusta, Ga; Univ Hosp, Augusta, Ga; NBC, NY. *Comn:* Painting, Ritz Carlton, San Juan, 97; painting, Hyatt Regency, Wichita, Kans, 97. *Exhib:* Am Watercolor Soc Traveling exhib, 91-92; solo exhibs, Gertrude Herbert Inst, Augusta, Ga, 92, John Marlor Art Ctr, Milledgeville, Ga, 93 & Chattahoochee Valley Art Mus, La Grange, Ga, 94; Takarazuka Int & Cult Ctr, Japan, 94, 96 & 98; Davidson Co Mus Art, Lexington, 95; Artexpo, NY, 95; Madison Showcase at Mercy Ctr, Conn, 95. *Teaching:* Expanding Art Boundaries, Gertrude Herbert Inst Art, Augusta, Ga, 94 & Pushing Beyond Your Boundaries, 98. *Awards:* 12th Exhib-Ga Watercolor Soc Award, 1st Union Nat Bank, 91; 14th Ann SC Watercolor Soc Award, Dutch Door Art Express, 91. *Bibliog:* Painter strives to convey positive images in works, Augusta Chronicle, 2/21/91; Through the eyes of the artist, Augusta Mag, 2-3/92; Jennifer Gipson (dir), Femme Nouvelle, Charlotte Soutter Roe, 94. *Mem:* SC Watercolor Soc; Gertrude Herbert Inst Art; Arts & Healing Network. *Media:* Two-D Casein; Oil, Pastel. *Mailing Add:* 27 County Rd 379A Hallettsville TX 77964-5636

EWALD, ELIN LAKE
ART APPRAISER
b Raleigh, NC. *Study:* Art Students League with Edwin Dickinson; Am Acad Art; Art Inst Chicago; grad prog, NY Univ & Metrop Mus Art; Nat Acad Design, NY; NY Univ, PhD (Phi Beta Kappa). *Pos:* Lectr in field; appraiser, O'Toole-Ewald Art Assoc Inc, 74-78, ASA sr appraiser, vpres, partner, 78-82, pres, 82-; adv cur Am Mus Nat Hist, NY, Walters Art Gallery, Baltimore, Md, Afro-Am Mus, Philadelphia; art adv, US Army Corps Engineers, Off Pub Adminr, Manhattan & Albany, Off Atty Gen & Dist Atty, NY & Westchester, FBI, Govt Can, Tax Revenue. *Mem:* Am Soc Appraisers (pres, 92-93, sr appraiser, bd dir, NY Chap, ed/columnist, NY Chap Newsletter); Am Asn Mus; Int Coun Mus; Costume Soc Am; Am Arbitration Asn; Am Bankruptcy Inst; Corp Art Mgt; plus others. *Specialty:* Consultants and fine art/antiques appraisers, specialists in damage/loss/fraud cases involving fine/decorative art. *Interests:* For over 60 years, firm has appraised and assembled private collections for individuals, corporations and museums; additionally, it has arranged donations of individual works of art and collections to museums; specialists in damage/loss reports and appraisals of corporate collections, expert witness testimony. *Publ:* Auth, Hester Bateman and English Women Silversmiths of the 18th Century, Ms Mag, 76; articles In: Valuation Mag, Fairshare, Ms Mag, Evaluation, CPPC Newsletter; contrib ed, Personal Property J. *Mailing Add:* 1185 Park Ave New York NY 10128-1308

EWALD, WENDY T
CONCEPTUAL ARTIST, EDUCATOR
b Detroit 1951. *Study:* Antioch Col, BA (art), 74; New Sch Social Rsch Vera List Ctr Art & Politics, Sr Fel, 2000-2003. *Hon Degrees:* Doctorate Bank St Sch of Education, 2005. *Work:* Int Ctr Photog, Metrop Mus, NY; Addison Gallery Am Art, Andover, Mass; Polaroid Collection, Cambridge, Mass; Hallmark Collection; Cleveland Ctr Contemp Art; RISD Mus, RI. *Comn:* Constructing Identity, Mondrian Found, Amsterdam, Holland, 96; World Faiths Proj, Ackland Mus, Chapel Hill, NC, 97; Artist in an Archive, Am Joint Distribution Comn, 98. *Exhib:* Solo Exhibs: George Eastman House, Rochester, NY, 93; Ansel Adams Ctr, San Francisco, 93; Ctr Creative Photog, NY, 94; Southeast Mus Photog, Daytona Beach, Fla, 94 & Addison Gallery Am Art, NY, 96; Partobject Gallery, NC, 2000; Stills Gallery, Edinburgh, 01; Museet for Fotokunst, Odense, Denmark, 01; Corcoran Gallery of Am Art, 02; RI Sch Design Mus, 02; Kemper Mus of Contemp Art, Kansas City, 02; Queens Mus of Art, New York City, 03; Yossi Milo Gallery, New York City, 03; Morocco Scalo Gallery, New York City, 03; Addison Gallery, 2006; John Hope Franklin Center, 2007; Biennial, Whitney Mus Am Art, NY, 97; Fotomus, Winterthur, Switz, 2000; Addison Gallery Am Art, 2001; group exhibs, Miami Mus Art, 99, Art Gallery, New South Wales, Australia, 2000, Ctr for Art and Vis Cult, Univ Md, 03; Handworkshop, Richmond, Va, 04; Art Angel, Toward A Promised Land, London, England, 04-06; This Place, DOX, Prague, Tel Aviv Mus, Norton Mus of Art, Palm Beach, Brooklyn Mus of Art, NYC. *Collection Arranged:* Detroit Art Inst; Addison Gallery of Am Art; Metrop Mus Art; Hallmark Collection; Int Ctr Photog; Polaroid Corp; Libr Congress; Franklin Ctr, Duke Univ; RI Sch Design Mus. *Pos:* Creator & dir, Literacy through Photog, Durham, NC, 90-. *Teaching:* Sr res assoc photog educ, Duke Univ, 91-; vis assoc prof photog, Bard Col, 96. *Awards:* Nat Endowment Arts Fel, 88; NY Found Fel, NY Found Arts, 90; MacArthur Found Fel, 92-97; Artist Residency, Cleveland Ctr for Contemp Art, 2000; Comn, RI Sch Design Mus, 02. *Bibliog:* Vicki Goldberg (auth), Family Circle Mag, 89; Anne Higgonet (auth), Pictures of Innocence, Thames & Hudson, 97; Penny Woolcock (dir), Kids, Channel 4-Britain, 97; Mary Warner Marien (auth), Photography: A Cultural History. *Media:* Photography, Video. *Publ:* Ed & contribr, Appalachia: A Self-Portrait, Gnomon, 79; auth, Portraits & Dreams, Writers & Readers, 85; Magic Eyes: Scenes from an Andean Girlhood, Bay Press, 92; I Dreamed I Had a Girl in My Pocket, W W Norton, 96; contribr, Constructing Identity/Photoworks in Progress, Snoek-Ducajut Zoon, 97; Wendy Ewald Secret Games, Scalo, Berlin, Zurich & New York, 00; American Alphabets Scalo, 05; In Peace & Harmony: Carver Portraits, Handworkshops, 05; Towards a Promised Land, Artangel & Steidl, 2006; The Transformation of This World Depends on You, Steidl, 2014; This is Where I Live, MACK, 2015. *Mailing Add:* Yossi Milo c/o 525 W 25th St New York NY 10001

EYRE, IVAN
PAINTER
b Tullymet, Sask, 1935. *Study:* Univ Sask, 52; Univ Man, BFA, 57; Univ NDak, 58. *Hon Degrees:* Univ Manitoba, LLD. *Work:* Nat Gallery Can, Ottawa, Ont; Mackenzie Art Gallery, Regina, Saskatchewan; Edmonton Art Gallery, Alta; Winnipeg Art Gallery, Man; Pavilion Gallery, Assiniboine Park, Winnipeg; McMichael Canadian Art Coll, Kleinburg, Ont. *Comn:* Resurrection, (painting) Can Cath Conf, Ottawa, Ont, 76; Black Arrow Plain, (painting) Can Indust & Com Bank, Edmonton, Alta, 80; North Northwest (painting) Teron Int, Ottawa, Ont, 86; The Canadian Art Portfolio comn for the Nfld Hist Parks Asn, 95. *Exhib:* Solo exhibs, Nat Gallery Can, Ottawa, Ont, 78 & 88, Robert McLaughlin Gallery, Ivan Eyre Expos, Oshawa, Ont, 80 (travelled To Paris, London & Edinburgh) 81, Art Gallery Greater Victoria Traveling, 82 & Winnipeg Art Gallery, Winnipeg, 82 & 88; Mira Godard Gallery, Toronto, 78-79, 81, 90, 92, 94, 96 & 99; Ivan Eyre: Personal Mythologies: Images of the Milieu Nat, Gallery Can, Ottawa, Ont, 88; Pavilion Gallery, Winnipeg, 98-2000, 2002 & 2004; Ivan Eyre, Loch Mayberry Fine Art, Winnipeg, 2000. *Teaching:* Prof design, Univ NDak, 58-59; prof drawing & painting, Univ Man, Winnipeg, 59-93, prof emer, 94-; prof painting, Banff Centre, Alta, summer 72. *Awards:* Sr Arts Awards, Can Coun, 66 & 78; Queens Silver Jubilee Medal, Gov Gen Can, 77; Univ Man Jubilee Award, 82; Queen's Golden Jubilee medal, 2002; Order of Man, 2007. *Bibliog:* E Zuk (producer), Visual Thinker (film), CBC, Winnipeg, 81; George Woodcock (auth), Ivan Eyre, Fitzhenry & Whiteside, 81; Visions (film), TV Ont, 83; Terrence Heath (auth), Beginning with One Work, Personal Mythologies/Images of the Milieu-Ivan Eyre, Winnipeg Art Gallery, 88; Tom Lovatt (auth), Ivan Eyre Drawings, Pavilion Gallery, 2003; and many other films & articles in various mags. *Mem:* Royal Can Acad Arts. *Media:* Acrylic, Drawing; Sculpture. *Publ:* Auth, Ivan on Eyre, Pavilion Gallery, 2004. *Dealer:* Loch Gallery 306 St Mary's Rd Winnipeg Manitoba Canada R2H 1J8. *Mailing Add:* 306 St Marys Rd Winnipeg MB R2H1J8 Canada

F

FABBRIS, VICO
PAINTER, ENVIRONMENTAL ARTIST
b Northern Italy, 1950. *Study:* Scuola Regionale Toscana, Florence, Italy, dipl, 73; L'Academia di Belle Arti, Florence, Italy, MFA, 78. *Work:* De Cordova Mus and Sculpture Park, Lincoln, Mass; Provincetown Art Asn and Mus, Mass; Suffolk Univ, Boston; Fidelity Investment Corp, Boston. *Comn:* mural, Univ Florence, Italy, 77, Psychiatric Hosp San Salvi, Florence, 78; outdoor floor mosaic, Judith Thurman, NY, 97; monoprint marathon, Fine Arts Work Center, Provincetown, Mass, 99; print project, Muka Studio, Aukland, New Zealand, 2000; Botanica, Cape Mus Fine Art, Dennis, Mass, 2002. *Exhib:* Juried Mem Exhib, Provincetown Art Asn and Mus, Mass, 79-91; Exploring The Corners: Box Works, Islip Art Mus, NY, 93; The Artist's Garden, Boston Ctr for the Arts, 97; Botanica, Truro Ctr for the Arts, Mass, 98; Annual Exib, De Cordova Mus, Lincoln, Mass, 98; Forum Gallery, New York City, 2001-. *Teaching:* adj fac in drawing and painting, New Eng Sch Art and Design, Boston, 95-, Lorenzo de Medici, Florence, Italy, 96, The Art Inst Boston, 96-98, 2000-. *Awards:* finalist, Blanche Coleman Award, 97, 2000; Mass Cult Council Award, 2000. *Bibliog:* Mary Behrens (auth), Botanical Unknown, Artsmedia, 96; Christine Temin (auth), Bold De Cordova Annual, Boston Globe, 98; Patricia J Williams (auth), Fresh Eggs, Fried Baloney, The Nation, 4/5/99; Botanical Unknown, Our Place, HGTV, 6/2001. *Media:* Watercolor. *Publ:* New American Paintings, Northeast vol 20, 1999. *Dealer:* Forum Gallery, 745 Fifth Ave, NYC. *Mailing Add:* c/o Rice Polak Gallery 430 Commercial st Provincetown MA 02657

FABIANO, DIANE FABIAN
PAINTER
b Winthrope, Mass, Oct 7, 1952. *Study:* Calif Coll Arts & Crafts, BA (summa cum laude, painting), 76; Calif State Univ, Northridge; Boston Univ, Mass; Worcester Art Mus Sch, Mass; Sch of Mus Fine Arts, Mass. *Work:* Ventura Mus, Calif; Laser Inst, Van Nuys, Calif; San Francisco Arts Comn Gallery, Calif; Calabasas Art Pub Places Gallery, Calif; Mass Gen Hosp, Boston. *Comn:* Site specific painting, Trade Wind Tours Hawaii, Las Vegas, Nev, 80; six site specific paintings, Benjamin Jay Stores & Salons, Woodland Hills, Calif, 90-91. *Exhib:* Dangerous/Endangered Animals, Circa 9

Gallery, San Diego, Calif, 91; Endangered Species & Rainforests, Calabasas Art Pub Places Gallery, Calif, 92; Conejo Valley Art Mus, Thousand Oaks, Calif, 94; solo exhib, Alley Gallery, Santa Barbara, Calif, 94, Paris Sketches & Paintings, Sweet Art Gallery, Oja, Calif, 97, Universal Languages, Bova Gallery, Los Angeles, 98 & BGH, The Loft Gallery, Santa Monica, Calif, Major & Minor, BGH Loft Gallery 4, Bergamot Station, Santa Monica, Calif, 2002; Downey Mus Art, Calif, 96; group exhib, Bova Gallery, Universal Language, Los Angeles, Calif, 98, Art Share Los Angeles, 40th Ann Art Exhib, Los Angeles, Calif, 2001, SCWCA Gallery, Small Works, Los Angeles, Calif, 2003, Long Beach Arts Gallery, Summer Group Exhib, Calif, 2004, Gallerie Yoramgil, Group Photog Exhib, Beverly Hills, Calif, 2005. *Pos:* Art dir, Eara Advert Resources, 90-91, gallery dir, 99-; Lectrs: South Pacific, Aboriginal Art; Central Am, Dangerous & Endangered Animals & Biodiversity Art of Region. *Teaching:* asst prof, Art & Language, Plymouth Univ, NH; prof, Art Dept, Plymouth Univ, NH, 2006. *Bibliog:* Lisa McKinnon (auth), Planet myths, symbols mix (2 page interview), Press-Courier, 2/91; Beth Farnsworth (interviewer), Art & the Endangered, Midday News Show, KEY TV, Santa Barbara, Calif, 10/6/94; Ron Soble (auth), An artist's odyssey with the LA Philharmonic, Ojai Valley Times, 6/5/97; Marianne Farr (auth) East side West Side, The Bridge Weekly, 7/2006. *Mem:* City of Calabasas, Parks, Rec & Cult Comt (arts coun liaison, 91); Artist Equity Asn; Womens Caucus Arts; Los Angeles Arts Coun; Nat Asn Women Bus Owners. *Media:* Miscellaneous Media. *Specialty:* Calif artists. *Publ:* Contribr, Encyclopedia of Living Artists, Dirs Guild Publ, 87; California Artists Review, Am References, 89; auth, The Planets, The Queens of Space, Golden Era Legacy Prod, 92; contribr, Art/Life Mag, Art/Life Eds, 2/92, 1/94 & 1/96. *Dealer:* East Side/West Side Art 597 Route 118 Warren NH 03279

FABING, SUZANNAH J
DIRECTOR
b Cincinnati, Ohio, Oct 1, 1942. *Study:* Wellesley Col, BA, 64; Harvard Univ, MA, 65. *Pos:* head division of research on collections, Nat Gallery of Art, Washington, DC, 83-92; vis comt Wellesley Col Mus, 1988-; Mem Art Info Task Force, Getty Art Info Prog, 1990-94; surveyor, AAM Mus Assessment Prog, 1991; dir & chief cur, Smith Col Mus of Art, Northampton, Mass, 92-2005; reviewer, Nat Endowment of the Humanities, 1992-94; Overview panel, Nat Edu Assoc, 1993-94; Fitchburg Art Mus, chrmn, 1983-88; trustee, Fitchburg Art Mus, 1975-82, Revels, Inc, 1981-82, 88-92), others; dir, Summer Inst in Art Mus Studies, Smith College, 2006. *Mem:* Asn Art Mus Dirs; Art Table; Am Asn Mus; Coll Art Asn; Archaeological Inst Am. *Publ:* The Gods Delight, Cleveland Mus Art, 88; Nat Gallery of Art, Cambridge Univ Press, 87; Image and Word: Art and Art History at Smith Col, 03. *Mailing Add:* Smith Coll Hillyer Hall 114 Northampton MA 01063

FACCINTO, VICTOR PAUL
PAINTER, FILMMAKER
b Albany, Calif, Oct 30, 1945. *Study:* Calif State Univ, Sacramento, BA, 69, MA, 72; Creative Artists Pub Serv Prog Fel, New York, 77, NC Visual Artist Fel, 80-81, 86 & 2000. *Work:* Film Study Collection, Mus Mod Art Collection, NY; Wake Forest Univ, Winston-Salem, NC. *Exhib:* New Am Filmmakers, Whitney Mus Am Art, New York, 72-74; Circulating Film Program, Am Fedn Arts, New York, 72-; Cineprobe, Mus Mod Art, New York, 75; Am Experimental Cinema 1905-1984, Pompidou Ctr, Paris, 85; Luise Ross Gallery, New York, 2008, 2009, 2010; solo exhibs, NC Mus Art, 86, Phyllis Kind Gallery 80, New York, 82 & 2004, Bruce Helander Gallery, New York, 90, New Films, Millennium, New York, 96 & 2003, Southeastern Ctr Contemp Art, NC, 2000 & Madison Art Ctr, Wis, 2000. *Collection Arranged:* Gladys Nilsson Retrospective, Wake Forest Univ Art Gallery, 79 & Video Sculpture, 95; Optical Allusions, WFU Gallery, 2007. *Pos:* Gallery dir, Wake Forest Univ, 78-2012. *Teaching:* Instr multi-media, Wake Forest Univ, Winston-Salem, NC, 81-82; lectr art, painting & drawing, 84-. *Bibliog:* Grace Glueck (auth), NY Times, 4/4/80; Kay Larson (auth), Village Voice, 4/7/80; Victoria Lautman (auth), exhib rev, Chicago Sun Times, 4/17/87. *Media:* Oil Acrylic; Film, Video & Digital Photography. *Publ:* Co-producer & photogr, Howard Finster: Stranger from Another World, Abbeville Press, New York, 89. *Dealer:* Luise Ross Gallery New York NY. *Mailing Add:* 1950 Cliffside Dr Pfafftown NC 27040

FACEY, MARTIN KERR
PAINTER, EDUCATOR
b Colorado Springs, Colo, Apr 25, 1948. *Study:* Univ Calif, Los Angeles, with William Brice & Charles Garabedian, BA, 71, with Richard Diebenkorn, MA, 73, MFA, 74. *Work:* Security Pacific Bank Collection, Los Angeles, Calif; Bank Am Collection, San Francisco, Calif. *Exhib:* Solo exhib, Los Angeles Munic Gallery, 79, Ivory-Kimpton Gallery, San Francisco, 81, 83-85, 87, Tortue Gallery, Santa Monica, 80, 82-83, 86 & 88, Univ Art Mus, Albuquerque, NMex, 87; two-person show, Claremont Grad Sch Gallery, 85; Jean Albano Gallery, Chicago, 88 & 91; Zimmerman-Saturn, Nashville, Tenn, 89; Sena East Gallery, Santa Fe, NMex, 90. *Teaching:* Instr painting & drawing, Santa Monica Col, Calif, 78-85; vis lectr painting & drawing, Univ Calif, Los Angeles, 83-85; assoc prof painting & drawing, Univ NMex, 86-. *Awards:* Guggenheim Fel in Painting, 82-83; Burlington Northern Found Award for Meritorius Teaching, Univ NMex, 87. *Bibliog:* Judith Spiegel (auth), Revitalizing abstraction, Artweek Mag, 6/25/88; Michael Laurence (auth), Martin Facey at Tortue, Artscribe Int, 10/86; David Winter (auth), Martin Facey at Ivory-Kimpton, Art News, 1/86; Peter Frank (auth), Pick of the Week, Los Angeles Weekly, 6/16/88; Sandy Ballatorxe (auth), Painter Centers Himself in Images. *Mem:* Coll Art Asn; Los Angeles Contemp Exhib; Albuquerque United Artists. *Media:* Oil. *Dealer:* Sena East Gallery 125 East Pl Santa Fe NM 87501; Works Gallery 106 W 3rd St Long Beach CA 90802. *Mailing Add:* c/o Jean Albano Gallery 215 W Superior St Chicago IL 60610-3528

FADEN, LAWRENCE STEVEN
PAINTER, PRINTMAKER
b Brooklyn, NY, Oct 21, 1942. *Study:* Brooklyn Mus student scholar; Sch Visual Arts; NY Studio Sch; and with Nicholas Carone. *Work:* Chase Manhattan Bank, NY; Smith Kline Beecham Corp, NJ; The Educ Allianco Art Gallery, NYC, 98; New Orleans Mus, L-Anna; Amoco Productions. *Comn:* Painted porcelain mask of James Ensor Akim Masks, Southerbys, NY, 96; Alumni Exhib, Bill Jensen: Juried NY Studio Sch, 2003; The Continuous Mark: 40 years of the NY Stud Sch, 2005, Juried by Jennifer Sachs Samet. *Exhib:* Solo exhibs, GW Einstein Gallery, 80, 85, 92 & 96; The Mask in Contemp Art, Sewall Art Gallery, Rice Univ, 93; Conviviality and Confetti, The Noyes Mus of Art, NJ, 99, Feast for the Eyes, 99; Aspects of Realism, Main St Gallery, Dobbs Ferry, NJ, 11/2000; Holiday Invitation, Broom St Gallery, 2009; Federation of Modern Painters and Sculptors, Westbeth Gallery, 2012. *Teaching:* Instr, Educ Alliance Art Sch, 82-84; vis artist, Parson Sch Design, 92. *Bibliog:* Brett Busang (auth), Am Artist Mag, 92; Gail Levin (auth), His Legacy For Artis; Edward Hopper The American Imagination, Whitney Mus Am Art, 95. *Mem:* Alliance Figurative Artists (prog dir, 75); Fedn Mod Painters & Sculptors. *Media:* Windsor Newton Oil, Watercolor; Etching, Lithography. *Dealer:* Gilbert W Einstein Co 98 Riverside Dr New York NY 10025. *Mailing Add:* 184 E Seventh St No 7 New York NY 10009

FAEGENBURG, BERNICE K
PAINTER, PRINTMAKER
b Philadelphia, Pa. *Study:* Tyler Sch Fine Arts, Temple Univ, Philadelphia, BS; Nat Acad Design; CW Post Col, Long Island Univ, Brookville, NY, MS (art educ), 72. *Work:* Jane Voorhees Zimmerli Art Mus, NJ. *Comn:* Seascape (triptych), Nature's Bounty, Bohemia, NY. *Exhib:* Reflections of Winter, Nassau Co Mus Fine Arts, Roslyn Harbor, NY, 78; 37th Ann Exhib, Audubon Artists, NY, 79; 28th Ann Exhib, Parrish Art Mus, Southampton, NY, 81; traveling painting exhib, Mus Southwest, Midland, Tex, 91; traveling painting exhib, Richmond Art Mus, Ind, 91; Art of the Northeast, Silvermine Guild of Artists, New Canaan, Conn, 92; Fine Arts Mus Long Island, Hempstead, NY, 92; A View of One's Own, Zimmerli Art Mus, New Brunswick, NJ, 94; Tokyo, Japan, Onward Gallery, 2001; NY Coll Insights, 2003. *Awards:* First Prize, Manhasset Art Asn, 79; Molly Canaday Mem Award, Nat Asn Women Artists, 87 & Beatrice Jackson Mem Award, 94; Best Show, Visual Artists Alliance Long Island, 95. *Bibliog:* M Milet (auth), L'Art A L'Etranger, La Revue Mod, 4-5/80; Helen Harrison (auth), In pursuit of meaning, NY Times, 12/13/92; East Hampton Star, Aug 5, 99, Sanscgundc, Sheridan; TV Thursday, Dec 11, 2003, Wigren's Crib, Ch 56. *Mem:* Nat Asn Women Artists (prog chair, 87-89, vpres, 89-91 & pres, 91-93); Viridian Gallery Artists (treas, 81-83); Hempstead Harbor Artists Asn; Jimmy Ernst Artists Alliance. *Media:* Acrylic, Oil; Serigraphy, Silkscreen. *Collection:* Zimmerli Art Mus, Rutgers Univ, NJ; Queensboro Community College, New York City; Steelcase Inc, New York City; Nature's Bounty, Bohemia, NY. *Mailing Add:* 31 Canterbury Ln Roslyn Heights NY 11577

FAFARD, JOE (JOSEPH) YVON
SCULPTOR
b Ste Marthe, Sask, Sept 2, 1942. *Study:* Univ Man, BFA; Pa State Univ, MFA. *Hon Degrees:* Univ Regina, LLD, Hon Doctorate, 1989; Univ Manitoba, LLD, Hon Doctorat, 2007. *Work:* Winnipeg Art Gallery, Man; Glenbow Mus, Calgary, Alta; Brock Collection, Vancouver; Montreal Mus Fine Arts; Nat Art Gallery Can, Ottawa; Douglas Udell, Vancouver, Edmonton, Calgary; Galerie de Bellefeuille, Montreal; and others. *Comn:* The Pasture (7 bronze cow sculptures), Toronto Dominion Ctr, 85; Shaw Court, Calgary. *Exhib:* Joe Fafard's Pensee, Winnipeg, Calgary, Vancouver, Regina, 73; Solo Exhibs: Edmonton, Calgary, Saskatoon, Surry, Lethbridge, Kingston, Hamilton, Banff, Oshawa, Charlottetown & Regina, 79; Susan Whitney Gallery, 2000, 2002; Mira Godard Gallery, 2000, 2004, 2007; Galerie de Bellefeuille, 2001, 2005, 2007; Douglas Udell Gallery, 2003, 2006; Mayberry Fine Arts, 2006, 2009, Kanata with Kanata Bella Futura, 2009, Evangeline & Flowers, Bayshore Developments, Vancouver, BC, 2004, and numerous others. *Teaching:* Univ Regina, 68-74; Univ Calif Davis, 80-81. *Awards:* Order of Can, 81; Royal Archit Inst Allied Award of Canada, 87; Saskatchewan Order of Merit, 2002; Lieutenant Governor's Award, Centenniel Merit, 2003; Lieutenant Governor's Award Lifetime Achievement, 2006. *Bibliog:* Mike McKinnery (auth), I Don't Have to Work that Big, Nat Film Bd, 73; and many more. *Mem:* CARFAC. *Media:* Mixed. *Dealer:* Douglas Udell Gallery 10332-124th St Edmonton AB; Galerie de Bellefeuille 1367 Ave Green Westmount Montreal Quebec; Darrell Bell Gallery 3 Ave S Saskatoon SK; Mira Godard Gallery 22 Hazelton Ave Toronto ON; Mayberry Fine Arts 212 McDermot Ave Winnipeg MB. *Mailing Add:* Box 540 Lumsden SK S0G 3C Canada

FAGALY, WILLIAM ARTHUR
CURATOR, HISTORIAN
b Lawrenceburg, Ind, Mar 1, 1938. *Study:* Ind Univ, Bloomington, BA, 62, MA, 67. *Collection Arranged:* He's the Prettiest: A Tribute to Big Chief Allison "Tootie" Montana's Fifty Years of Mardi Gras Indian Suiting, New Orleans Mus Art, 97; Preacher Art, Phyllis Kind Gallery, New York, 97; Watercolor USA 99, Springfield Art Mus, Mo, 99; Nat Works on Paper, McNeese State Univ, Lake Charles, La, 99; Its a Wonderful World, Contemporary Art Ctr, New Orleans, 2003; Speculative Grammar Artistides Logothetis, CUE Art Found, New York, 2003; Tools of Her Ministry: Art of Sister Gertrude Morgan, Am Folk Art Mus, New York, 2004; Resonance from the Past: African Sculpture from the New Orleans Mus Art, Mus African Art, New York, 2005; In the Congo: An Introduction to the Field Research Archives of Frere Joseph Cornet, Loyola Univ and New Orleans Mus Art, 2006; and many others. *Pos:* Registrar, New Orleans Mus Art, 66-67, cur collections, 67-72, Francoise Billion Richardson cur African Art, 67-, chief cur, 73-80, asst dir art, 81-2001. *Teaching:* Assoc prof art hist, Delgado Coll, 67-69; vis assoc prof, Univ New Orleans, 80. *Awards:* Mayor's Art Award, City of New Orleans, 97; Gov's Arts Award, La State Arts Coun, 97; Charles E Dunbar Jr Career Svc Award, La Civil Svc League, 99; Isaac Delgado Mem Award, The Fel New Orleans Mus Art, 2001; Chevalier de l'Ordre des Arts et des Lettres, Republique Francaise, 2006. *Bibliog:* Profile, Start to Finish Prog,

Discovery Channel, 94; Marda Burton (auth), Every Nook & Cranny, Veranda, 95. *Mem:* Arts Coun of African Studies Asn; Ctr African & African American Studies (adv bd); Southern Univ, New Orleans; Prospect l and Prospect 2: US Biennial Inc (bd dirs, 2007-). *Res:* Art and life of self-taught artists Sister Gertrude Morgan and Roy Ferdinand; Pierre Joseph Landry. *Collection:* Contemporary American self-taught art; Northwest Coast Native American baskets; Japanese ikebana baskets; African art. *Publ:* The gifted amateur: The art and life of Charles Woodward Hutson, Folk Art Mag, fall 97; Sister Gertrude Morgan, Self-Taught Artists of the 20th Century: An American Anthology, San Francisco Chronicle Bks, 98; Sister Gertrude Morgan, Charles W Hutson, Encyclopedia of American Folk Art, New York Am Folk Art Mus, 2003; Perfect Greek Island, New Orleans Times-Picayune, 2003; Gumbo Ya-Ya and Hey Pockey Way, 2004 & Jesus is my Airplane: Life and Art of Sister Gertrude Morgan, 2004, Louisiana Cult Vistas; Ancestors of Congo Square: African Sculptures from the New Orleans Museum of Art, Art Tribal, 2004; Ancestors of Congo Square: African Art in the New Orleans Mus Art, Seala Publishers, 2011. *Mailing Add:* New Orleans Mus Art PO Box 19123 City Park New Orleans LA 70179

FAGAN, ALANNA
PAINTER, PRINTMAKER
b New Bedford, Mass, 1939. *Study:* Silvermine Guild Sch Art (painting & sculpture), New Canaan, Conn; Critique Seminar, Prof Robt Reed, New Haven, Conn, 2003-2004. *Comn:* Portrait, pres, Istituto Geografico de Agostini, Novara, Italy, 81; portrait, founder, Cohen & Wolf, PC, Bridgeport, Conn, 83; portrait, Ctr Creative Leadership, Wilmington, NC, 84; portrait, former dean, New Eng Sch Law, Boston, Mass, 84; portrait, retired pres, Harvard Club, NY, 91. *Exhib:* Art of the Northeast, 95, 99 & 2000; Ctr for Contemp Printmaking, 2001-2013; Silvermine Guild, 2003-2013, solo exhib, 2009; Ridgefield Guild, 2007-08; Solo exhib, Curtis Gallery, New Canaan Libr, 2010; Kehler Liddell Gallery, New Haven, Conn, 2010; Flinn Gallery, Greenwich Libr, 2011; Westport Arts Ctr, 2011, 2012. *Teaching:* Instr portrait & pastels, Silvermine Guild Sch, 77-81. *Awards:* Best in Show, Ridgefield Guild of Artists 30th Exhib, 2007; People's United Bank Award, New Haven Brush & Palette Club, 2008. *Mem:* Silvermine Guild Artists; Ctr Contemp Printmaking; New Haven Paint & Clay Club; Westport Arts Ctr Conn. *Media:* Oil, Pastel, drypoint, monotype. *Publ:* Timeless Reveries in Interior Arts, House Enthusiast (online mag), 5/2011; On the Wings of Love, Conn Post Newspaper, 9/2011. *Mailing Add:* 73 Housatonic Dr Milford CT 06460

FAGER, CHARLES J
CERAMIST, SCULPTOR
b Osage City, Kans, Feb 3, 1936. *Study:* Kans State Univ, Manhattan, BArch, 59; Univ Kans, Lawrence, MFA (ceramics), 63. *Work:* Nat Collection Fine Art; Nat Mus Am Art, Smithsonian Inst. *Comn:* Ceramic installation, Tampa Pub Libr, 70; ceramic wall, Arbor Off Ctr, Clearwater, Fla, 73; hanging sculpture installation, GTE Fla, Tampa, 83; sculpture, Fla Dept of Law Enforcement Regional Crime Lab, Jacksonville, Fla, 87; hanging sculpture installation, Opus South Corporation, Tampa, Fla, 89. *Exhib:* Piedmont Craftsman, Mint Mus, Charlotte, NC, 76; Ceramics Conjunction, Long Beach Mus Art, Calif, 77; Craftsmen of the Southeast Invitational Exhib, Birmingham Mus Art, Ala, 78; Am Porcelain: New Expressions in an Ancient Art, Renwick Gallery, Smithsonian Inst, 81; Cast Clay, Nat Invitational Exhib, Pinch Pottery, Northhampton, Mass, 85; Tampa Triennial, Tampa Mus Art, Fla, 85; and numerous other solo & group exhibs. *Pos:* Consult archit, Rowe Holmes Assoc Archits Inc, Tampa, Fla, 73-74. *Teaching:* Art instr, Kans State Univ, Manhattan, 60-61; grad asst instr, Univ Kans, Lawrence, 61-63; prof art, Univ S Fla, Tampa, 63-. *Awards:* Irving Hill First Award for Ceramics, Ninth Ann Kans Designer-Craftsman Exhib, Lawrence, 62; Ceramics Purchase Award, Wichita Nat Decorative Arts & Ceramics Exhib, Wichita, 62; Award of Excellence, Ann State Fla Craftsmen Exhib, 76; Fla Individual Artist Fel Award, 87-88. *Bibliog:* Lloyd E Herman (auth), American Porcelain: New Expressions in an Ancient Art, 80; Charlotte F Speight (auth), Images of Clay Sculpture, 83; Donald Frith (auth), Mold making for ceramics, 85. *Media:* Clay, Metal. *Res:* Application of industrial clay form processes to art; slip casting ceramic figures from life; photoceramics. *Mailing Add:* c/o Albertson-Peterson Gallery PO Box 1900 Winter Park FL 32790

FAHLMAN, BETSY LEE
HISTORIAN
b Wolfeboro, NH, July 18, 1951. *Study:* Mt Holyoke Col, Mass, BA, 73; Univ Del, Newark, MA, 77, PhD, 81. *Teaching:* Lectr art hist, Franklin & Marshall Col, 77-79; asst prof art hist, Old Dominion Univ, Norfolk, Va, 80-88; assoc prof art hist, Ariz State Univ, 88-. *Mem:* Coll Art Asn; Soc Indust Archaeol; Soc Archit Historians; Victorian Soc Am. *Res:* American Art, 1850-1930, architecture, painting, sculpture and photography. *Publ:* From Connecticut to France: New Haven Painters in Paris, Barbizon, Brittany and Giverny, J New Haven Colony Hist Soc, Vol 41, No 1, fall 94; Guy Pene du Bois: The Twenties at Home and Abroad (exhib catalog), Wilkes Univ, Sordoni Art Gallery, Wilkes-Barre, Pa, 95; Arnold Ronnebeck and Alfred Stieglitz: Remembering the Hill, Hist Photog, Vol 20, No 4, Winter 96; Cotton Culture: Dorothea Lange in Arizona, Southeastern Coll Art Conf Rev 13, No 1, 96; John Ferguson Weir: The Labor of Art, Newark: Univ Del Press, 97. *Mailing Add:* Sch Art Ariz State Univ PO Box 871505 Tempe AZ 85287-1505

FAILLACE, RACHAEL
ARTIST
Study: RI Sch of Design, BFA,; Mason Gross Sch of the Arts, MA. *Exhib:* Life with Pocket Change & Pleasures, Ben Shahn Galleries at William Paterson Univ, Wayne, NJ, 2002; First Year Graduate Exhib, Mason Gross Galleries, New Brunswick, NJ, 2003; Prints & Drawings, MPG Contemp, Boston, Mass, 2004; Diagram & Scribble Archive, SAC Gallery, Stony Brook, NY, 2005; Structural Integrity, Arts Guild of Rahway, NJ, 2006. *Mailing Add:* 95 Hillside Ave Berkeley Heights NJ 07922

FAIMON, PEG
ADMINISTRATOR, EDUCATOR
Study: Indiana Univ, BFA; Yale Univ, MFA. *Pos:* Designer for corporate and small firm offices; design consultancy, currently; blogger, www.pegfaimondesign.com, currently. *Teaching:* Chair Dept Art, dir Miami Design Collaborative, prof graphic design, Miami Univ, currently; affiliate facility mem, Armstrong Inst for Interactive Media Studies. *Awards:* Named the Miami Univ Sch of Fine Arts Crossan Hayes Curry Distinguished Educator, 2000; Naus Family Faculty Scholar, 2008. *Publ:* Auth, designer, Design Alliance: Uniting Print and Web Design to Create a Total Brand Presence, 2003, The Designer's Guide to Business and Careers: How to Succeed on the Job or on Your Own, 2009; Co-auth, The Nature of Design: How the Principles of Design Shape Our World-from Graphics and Architecture to Interiors and Products, 2003. *Mailing Add:* Miami University 124 Art Building 501 E High St Oxford OH 45056

FAIRBANKS, JONATHAN LEO
CURATOR, PAINTER
b Ann Arbor, Mich, Feb 19, 1933. *Study:* Brigham Young Univ & Univ Utah, BFA, 53; Univ Pa & Acad Fine Arts, MFA (Teaching Fel), 57; Univ Del, MA (Winterthur Fel), 61; Inst Patologia Libro, Rome, cert conservation, 68. *Work:* Acad Nat Sci, Philadelphia; Springville Mus Art, Utah; Nat Portrait Gallery, DC; Utah Valley Univ; Boston Pub Libr; Alhambra, Spain; Mus Fine Arts, Hagerstown, Md. *Exhib:* North Point Gallery, San Francisco, 99; Tivioli Galleries, Salt Lake City, 99; The Crane Collections, Wellesley, Mass, 2000; Washington Co Mus Fine Arts, Hagerstown, MD, 2004-2005. *Collection Arranged:* WyeHouse, Alhambra, Spain; Acad Nat Sci, Phila; Nat Portrait Gallery; Boston Pub Libr; Mus Fine Arts, Boston; Washington Co Mus Fine Arts, Hagerstown, MD; also pvt collections. *Pos:* Mural painter, Acad of the Natural Sci, Philadelphia, 55-57; cur asst, Winterthur Mus, 61-62, asst cur, 62-67, assoc cur, 67-70; Katharine Lane Weems Cur, Am decorative arts & sculpture, Mus Fine Arts, Boston, 70-99, cur emer, currently; app Comt Preservation The White House; vp research, Artfact, 2002-, sr vp research; ed-at-large, The Catalogue of Antiques and Fine Art, 2002. *Teaching:* Teaching fel, Pa Acad Fine Arts, 55-57; lectr, art & art hist, Brigham Young Univ, 57-59; lectr, Haystack Mountain Sch of Crafts, Deer Isle, Maine, 65, 67 & 81; lectr & symposium chmn, Houston Baptist College Preservation Conf, 66-69; lectr, art hist dept, Univ Del, 68-69; adj prof, Am & New England studies, Boston Univ, 71-82 & Am art, Wellesley Coll, 81; research assoc, art hist, Boston Univ, 99-2001. *Awards:* Mural Award, Acad Natural Sci; Robert G Lord Award Excellence Hist Studies, Emmanuel Coll, 83; Charles F Montgomery award, Decorative Arts Soc, 83; Urban Glass Award; Ellen Banning Ayer Award; Lifetime Achievement Medal, Soc of Arts & Crafts, Boston; Luminaries Award, Fuller Craft Mus, 2009; Excellence Award, Dec Arts Trust, 2009. *Bibliog:* Jean Woods (auth), The Fairbanks Artistic Legacy & Julie Carlson (auth), Inner Life and Material Being: The art of Jonathan Fairbanks, both In: Jonathan Leo Fairbanks, A Painter's Journey 1952-2004, Hagerstown, 2004. *Mem:* Hon mem New Eng Chap, Am Soc Interior Designers; Soc Archit Historians; fel Am Inst Conserv; fel Pilgrim Soc; Colonial Soc Mass; hon fel, Am Crafts Coun, 86; Am Antiquarian Soc; Mass Hist Soc; Hist New Eng. *Media:* All Media. *Res:* Early Am arts & decorative archit & arts, preservation works of art. *Interests:* natural hist; collecting art antiques. *Publ:* Auth, forward, Art and Commerce: American Prints of the Nineteenth Century, Univ Press Va, 78; ed, Boston Furniture of the Eighteenth Century, Colonial Soc Mass, Vol 48; coauth (with Elizabeth Bidwell Bates), American Furniture 1620 to the Present, Richard Marek Inc, New York, 81; auth introd & contrib, New England Begins, The Seventeenth Century, Boston Mus Fine Arts, 82; auth introd, Sam Maloof, Woodworker, New York, 83; auth introd & contrib, American Figurative Sculpture in the Museum of Fine Arts, Boston, 86; auth introd, Paul Revere - Artisan, Businessman & Patriot: The Man Behind the Myth, Boston, 88; auth, Becoming a Nation, Americana from the Diplomatic Reception Rooms, US Dept of State (exhib catalog), Rizzoli, New York, 2003. *Mailing Add:* 247 Nahatan St Westwood MA 02090

FAIREY, SHEPARD
PRINTMAKER
b Charleston, SC, Feb 15, 1970. *Study:* RI Sch Design, BA (illus), 1992. *Exhib:* Solo exhibs include Tin Man Alley Gallery, New Hope, Pa, 2001, 1300 Gallery, Cleveland, Milk, San Francisco, 2003, Merry Karnowsky Gallery, Los Angeles, 2004, 2005, 2007, Toy Room Gallery, Sacramento, 2004, 2005, 2007, Black Floor Gallery, Philadelphia, 2005, White Walls Gallery, San Francisco, 2006, 2008, Jonathan LeVine Gallery, Brooklyn, 2007, Stolen Space Gallery, London, 2007, Inst Contemp Art, Boston, 2009. *Pos:* Founder, Obey Giant campaign, Los Angeles, 1990-. *Awards:* Named one of GQ Mag's Men of the Yr, 2008. *Dealer:* Merry Karnowsky Gallery 170 S La Brea Ave 1st Floor Los Angeles CA 90036 ; Jonathan LeVine Gallery 529 W 20th St 9E New York NY 10011. *Mailing Add:* Obey Giant Art PO Bx 26897 Los Angeles CA 90026

FAIRFIELD, RICHARD THOMAS
PRINTMAKER, EDUCATOR
b Peoria, Ill, Aug 7, 1937. *Study:* Bradley Univ, BFA, 61; Univ Ill, MFA, 63. *Work:* Howard Univ, DC; St John's Univ, Jamaica, NY; B Carroll Reece Mem Mus, E Tenn Univ, Johnson City; Ball State Univ, Muncie, Ind; Albion Col, Mich. *Exhib:* Northwest Printmakers, Seattle Art Mus, 70; Ball State Small Sculpture & Drawings, Ball State Univ, Muncie, Ind, 73; Am Miniature Printmaker, San Diego State Univ, Calif, 88; Interprint LVIV 90, LVIV Mus Hist Relig & Atheism, USSR, 90-92; Int Independents Exhib Prints, Kanagawa, Japan, 90; Paper Invitational, John F Kennedy Mem Union Art Gallery, Univ Dayton, Ohio, 90; solo exhib, Albion Coll, Mich, 91; and others. *Teaching:* Prof printmaking, Eastern Mich Univ, Ypsilanti, 63- & Santa Reparata, Florence, Italy, spring 74, prof emer; Paris, France, spring 87, 89 & 98; Florence, Italy, spring 90 & 95; Madrid, Cardoba, Barcelona, Spain, spring 92 & 96, London, Eng, 94 & Athens, Greece, 97. *Awards:* Purchase Awards, NDak Ann, Univ NDak, 66, Imprint, Kutztown State Coll, 67 & Drawing USA, St Paul Art Ctr, 67; Alma Coll, 88. *Media:* Etching, Screen. *Res:* high relief screens. *Dealer:* River Gallery Chelsea MI 48118. *Mailing Add:* 6226 Schuss Crossing Ypsilanti MI 48197

FAIRLIE, CAROL HUNTER
EDUCATOR, PAINTER
b White Plains, NY, Dec 14, 1952. *Study:* Pa Acad Fine Arts, with Lois Sloan & Dan Miller, 1974; Tex Woman's Univ, BFA, 1990; Sch Visual Arts, Univ N Tex, with Vernon Fisher & Rob Erdle, MFA, 1993. *Work:* Sul Ross State Univ, Alpine, Tex; Tetra Pak Co, Sweden; Merrill Lynch Co; Mary Kay Family. *Comn:* Mural, Tex Woman's Univ, Denton, Tex, 1986; interior, Tetra Pak Co, Denton, Tex, 1996; interior, SOHO Salon, Denton, Tex, 1996; mural, Alpine Pub Libr, Tex, 2003; portrait, comn by Jean Hardy, Alpine, Tex, 2004. *Exhib:* Watercolor USA, Springfield Mus Art, MO, 1992 & 2005; Arizona Aqueous, Tubac Ctr Arts, Mesa, AZ, 1994; Side by Side, Berman Mus, PA, 2002; Noyes Mus, Oceanville, NJ, 2003; Watercolor MO III, Winston Churchill Mus, Fulton, Mo, 2003; 15 Exposures, Pa Acad Traveling Exhib, PA, 2004. *Teaching:* Adj prof art (painting & drawing), Univ N Tex, Denton, Tex, 1993-1995; lectr, 1995-1996; prof painting & drawing, Sul Ross State Univ, Alpine, Tex, 1996-. *Awards:* Rita Phoenix Mem, 1993; Barnet Mem, Philadelphia Watercolor Soc, 2002; Fac of Yr, Sul Ross State Univ, 2009; Golden Merchandise Award, Watercolor USA, 2010. *Mem:* Nat Watercolor Soc (newsletter ed, 2002-2004); Philadelphia Watercolor Soc (signature mem); Watercolor Art Soc, Houston (signature mem); College Arts Assoc; Tex Art Educ Assoc (VASE juror, 2003-2005); Watercolor Hon Soc (signature mem); Tex Watercolor Soc; Tex Asn Sch Art. *Media:* Oil, Watercolor, Pastel, Print (Lino). *Mailing Add:* 502 E Ave 1 Alpine TX 79830

FAIRWEATHER, SALLY H
ART DEALER, CONSULTANT
b Chicago, Ill, Sept 29, 1917. *Study:* Art Students League, 36; Art Inst Chicago, BA, 39. *Pos:* Co-dir & owner, Fairweather-Hardin Gallery, Chicago, 47-91, Art Dealers Asn Am, 62-63 & Found Arts Scholar, Chicago, 64-; co-founder, Chicago Art Dealers Asn, 66. *Teaching:* Instr life drawing, Katherine Lord Sch, Evanston, Ill, 39-43. *Specialty:* Modern paintings, graphics and sculpture. *Publ:* Auth, Picasso's Concrete Sculpture, Hudson Hills Press, 82. *Mailing Add:* 294 Colonel Greene Rd Yorktown Heights NY 10598-6022

FALCHOOK, JASON
PHOTOGRAPHER
b 1976. *Study:* Corcoran Coll Art and Design, Washington DC, BFA, 1998. *Exhib:* Solo exhibs include Lightly Scratching a Trajectory, Fusebox, Washington, DC, 2002, Behind the Shine, 2004; group exhibs include Fort Lauderdale Mus Art, 1998; Martin Luther King Libr, Washington, DC, 1999; Instituto De Arte Fotographico, Lima, Peru, 1999; Arlington Arts Ctr, 2000; Signal 66 Art Space, Washington, DC, 2000; Fusebox, 2001, 2003, 2005; Artpoint, Art Basel Miami, US Embassy Brasilia, Brazil, 2002; Corcoran Gallery Art, Washington, DC, 2003; Nat Acad Sci, 2004; Shade Projs and Monorchid Gallery, Phoenix, 2005; SCOPE Miami, 2006; Civilian Art Projs, Warehouse Complex, Washington, DC, 2006; Katonah Mus Art, NY, 2006; Civilian @ G, G Fine Art, Washington, DC, 2007. *Awards:* Young Artist Grant, DC Comn on Arts and Humanities, 2001; Trawick Prize Finalist, 2003. *Mailing Add:* Civilian Art Projects 1019 7th St NW Washington DC 20001

FALCKENBERG, HARALD
COLLECTOR
b 1943. *Study:* Freibourg Univ, Geneva, JD. *Pos:* Managing dir, Sammlung Falckenberg, 1979-; hon judge, Hamburg Constl Ct, currently; pres, Hamburg Kunstverein Art Asn, currently; creator, Phoenix Art Cult Found, Hamburg, 2001-. *Awards:* Named one of Top 200 Art Collectors, ARTnews mag, 2004-13. *Collection:* Contemporary German & American art. *Mailing Add:* Sammlung Falckenberg Phoenix Fabrikhallen Tor 2 Wilstorfer Strasse 71 Hamburg 21073 Germany

FALCONER, MARGUERITE ELIZABETH
PAINTER, INSTRUCTOR
b Boston, Mass, July 5, 1919. *Study:* Mus Fine Arts, Boston, 28-30; studied with Emile Gruppe, Roger Curtis & Robert Douglas Hunter, 63-70, with George Dergalis, 68-70; DeCordova Mus, Lincoln, Mass, 68, 69 & 70. *Work:* Cape Cod Mus Fine Art, Dennis, Mass; St Christopher's Episcopal Church Libr, Eldredge Pub Libr, Chatham, Mass; Fleet Banks, Cape Cod, Mass; Nat Mus Am Art, Smithsonian Inst, Washington; Nat Mus Women in Arts, Washington, DC; Bank of Am, Cape Cod & Boston, Mass; Rockland Trust Co, Cape Cod, Mass. *Comn:* Sea & Sand, comn by Mrs William Gale Curtis Jr, Grosse Pointe, Mich, 73; Old Mill Point, comn by Mr & Mrs Paul McAdams, Chatham, Mass, 86; For the retiring speaker of the House, Thomas "Tip" O'Neil, Chatham Fish Pier, comn by Mr & Mrs Dellapenta, Rye, NY & Chatham, Mass, 93; Summer View of Mill Pond, comn by Mr & Mrs Henry Weintraub, Stamford, Conn, 94; Pleasant Bay Shore, Lower Cape Outreach Coun, Orleans, Mass, 97. *Exhib:* One-person shows, Brockton Pub Libr, Mass, 63, Forge Art Gallery, Quincy, Mass, 66, Thomas Crane Pub Libr, North Quincy, Mass, 67 & Club House Gallery, West Hartford, Conn, 92; Nyack Gallery, NY, 75-82; Christmas Juried Show, Los Angeles Contemp Gallery, Los Angeles, 86; An Exhib of Paintings by Marguerite Falconer, Churchill Gallery, Newburyport, Mass, 88, 2004-05; Reflections, Cahoon Mus Am Art, Cotuit, Mass, 90; Salmagundi Artists, Beacon Hill West Gallery, Carmel, Calif, 95. *Pos:* Judge for numerous exhibs, 65-2001; co-proprietor, McElwain-Falconer Gallery, Chatham, Mass, 68-87; bd dir, Creative Arts Ctr, Chatham, Mass, 83-85; proprietor, Falconer Gallery, Chatham, Mass, 87-93. *Teaching:* Instr oil painting, Brockton & Bridgewater YWCA, 65-71, Quincy Evening Practical Arts, 67-71 & var art asn, 68-89; instr, demonstr workshops for art asns on south shore Boston, Cape Cod, corp programs, 68-2000. *Awards:* Represented the Creative Arts Ctr as Founding Mem in the July 4th Parade in Chatham, Mass, 2009, 2010. *Bibliog:* Barbara W Foote (auth), Marguerite E Falconer-Painting Cape Cod, Nauset Calendar, 90; Barbara W Foote (auth), Painting Her Beloved Cape Cod for the Past 35 Years, Nauset Calendar, 91; Edward F Maroney (auth), A gallery is passed on as an artist focuses on her canvas, Cape Cod Chronicle, 93; Wisdom of the Eighties (documentary film), Woods Hole Film Festival, Falmouth, Mass, 2007. *Mem:* Am Artists Prof League; Cape Cod Mus Fine Arts; Creative Arts Ctr, Chatham, Mass (founder, 69); charter mem Nat Mus Women in Arts; Copley Soc Boston; Mus Fine Arts Boston. *Media:* Oil. *Interests:* travel, music, writing. *Collection:* paintings, sculpture; Dr & Mrs David Knauss, Chatham, M&M Robit Dubis, Chatham, M & Mrs Mark Kerwin, Boston, MA, Judge Philip Zandt, New Paltz, NY, Mr Robert Redford, Provo, Utah & Mr & Mrs Gil Sparks, Del, Julie Harris, Chatham, Mass & Los Angeles, Calif, Mr & Mrs Robert Tarnow, Chatham, Mass & Naples, Fla. *Publ:* An African Quest, Soundings, St Christopher's Church, 88. *Dealer:* Falconer's Chatham MA

FALSETTA, VINCENT MARIO
PAINTER, EDUCATOR
b Philadelphia, Pa, Nov 5, 1949. *Study:* Temple Univ, Philadelphia, Pa, BA, 72; Tyler Sch Art, Philadelphia, Pa, 72-73; Tyler Sch Art, Rome, Italy, MFA, 74, special study with prominent profs John Wade, David Pease, and Stephen Greene. *Work:* El Paso Mus Art, Tex; United Bank Denver, Los Angeles; Utah Mus Fine Arts, Salt Lake City; Mus Fine Arts, Houston, Tex; Mus SE Texas, Beaumont, Tex; Philadelphia Mus Art; Tyler Mus Art, Tyler, Tex; Omni Hotel, Dallas. *Comn:* Neiman Marcus, Newport Beach, CA. *Exhib:* Solo exhibs: Amarillo Art Ctr, 83, OK Harris Works of Art, New York, 86-87, 90, 96; Longview Mus, Tex, 92, 2008; San Angelo Mus Fine Arts, Tex, 93; Univ N Tex Denton, 93; Conduit Gallery, Dallas, Tex, 95, 98, 2000, 2002, 2004, 2008, 2010; Galveston Arts Ctr, 96; Vincent Falsetta-Field of Vision (with catalog), El Paso Mus Art, 96; Art Ctr, Waco, Tex, 96; Univ Texas, Arlington, Tex, 2002; Mus E Tex, Lufkin, Tex, 2003; Art Mus Southeast Tex, Beaumont, Tex, 2007; Anya Tish Gallery, Houston, Tex, 2007, REM Gallery, San Antonio, Tex, 2009, Tex State Univ, Tex, 2010, The Reading Room, Tex, 2012; group exhibs, Works on Paper: Southwest, Dallas Mus Fine Arts, Tex, 78, Gateway Exhib, Dallas Mus Art, 84 & Laguna Gloria Art Mus, Austin, Tex, 84; Mostra 91: Six Ital Am Artists, Mus Italo Americano, San Francisco; Chaos to Order, Art Mus Southeast Tex, Beaumont, 92; Signs and Symbols (traveling exhib in Africa & Near East), 94-96; Art Patterns, Austin Mus Art, Tex, 97, Committed to Abstraction, 97; Contemporaries of the Great Southwest, El Paso Mus Art, Tex, 99; A Hot Show: Abstract Paintings, Arlington Mus Art, Tex, 99; Univ Texas, Dallas, Tex, 2001; Texas Works, Buddy Holly Ctr, Lubbock, Tex, 2002; The Grid Unlocked, Fort Worth Community Art Ctr, Fort Worth, Tex, 2003; Haley Martin Galleries, San Francisco, Calif, 2004; Texas 100, El Paso Mus Art, Tex, 2006; Texas Paint: Out of Abstractions, Arlington Mus Art, Tex, 2006; Slow Magic, The Bluecoat, Liverpool, Eng, 2009; Obsessive Worlds, Art Mus Southeast Tex, Beaumont, Tex, 2011; Nancy Margolis Gallery, NY, 2011; Alexandria Mus, Alexandria, Louisiana, 2012; Full Spectrum, Prints from the Brandywine Workshop, Phila Mus Art, 2012; Tex Biennial, San Antonio, Tex, 2013. *Teaching:* Asst prof painting & drawing, Ind Univ, Bloomington, 74-75; instr, Univ Utah, Salt Lake City, 75-77; asst prof, Univ N Tex, Denton, 77-84, assoc prof, 84-92, prof, 92-. *Awards:* Vis Artist Fel Brandywine Workshop, Philadelphia, Pa, 83 & 89; Pollock-Krasner Found Grant, 92-93; Mid Am Arts Alliance Grant, Nat Endowment Arts, 96; Artist in Res, The Bluecoat, Liverpool, 2011; fel, Inst Advancement Arts, Univ N Tex, 2012, 2013. *Bibliog:* Michael Odom (auth), Art Papers, 11/2002-12/2002; John Zotos (auth), Art Lies, summer 2002; John Zotos (auth) Artlies, Winter 2003-2004; Three Decades of American Printmaking (The Brandywine Workshop Collection), Hudson Hills Press, 2004; New American Paintings, Open Studio Press, 1998, 1995 2005, 2008; Titus O'Brian (auth), Glasstire, Tex, 2008; June Mattingly (auth), The State of the Art, Contemp Art in Tex, 2012; Betsy Lewis (auth), Glasstire, Tex, 2012; Ben Lima (auth), D Mag, Dallas, 2012. *Media:* Acrylic, Oil. *Dealer:* Nancy Margolis Gallery 523 W 25th St New York NY 10001; Conduit Gallery 1626 C Hi Line Dr Dallas TX 75207; Anya Tish Gallery Houston TX; REM Gallery San Antonio Tex; Wade Wilson Art Santa Fe NM; Sherry Leedy Gallery Kans City Mo. *Mailing Add:* 202 Forest St Denton TX 76209

FALSETTO, MARIO
EDUCATOR
b Italy, May 17, 1950; Can citizen. *Study:* Carleton Univ, Ottawa, Can, BA, 71; NY Univ with Jay Leyda, Annette Michelson, Stan Brakhage, Manny Farber, VF Perkins & P Adams Sitney, MA, 76, PhD, 90. *Pos:* Chmn dept cinema & photog, Concordia Univ, 81-84, asst dean, Fac Fine Arts, 84-87 & chair, Cinema Dept, 96-97, assoc & acting dean, Fac Fine Arts, 87-90, grad prog dir, 98-2001. *Teaching:* Lectr film studies, Univ Manitoba, Winnipeg, Can, 77-78; lectr film studies, Concordia Univ, Montreal, Can, 78-82, asst prof, 82-87, assoc prof, 87-99, prof 99-. *Awards:* Social Scis and Humanities Res Coun Award, 2002-. *Mem:* Film Studies Asn Can (pres, 85-87); Soc for Cinema Studies; L'Association Quebecois des Etudes Cinematographiques. *Media:* Writer. *Res:* Recent American and experimental films; Films of Stanley Kubrick & Nicolas Roeg; Independent narrative film; Films of Gus Van Sant. *Publ:* Stanley Kubrick: A Narrative & Stylistic Analysis, Greenwood Press, 94; ed, Perspectives on Stanley Kubrick, GK Hall, 96; Personal Visions: Conversations with Contemporary Film Directors, Silman-James Press, 2000; Stanley Kubrick: A Narrative & Stylistic Analysis, 2d edit, 2001; auth, The Making of Alternative Cinema, Vol I: Dialogues with Independent Filmmakers, Praeger Press, 2007. *Mailing Add:* Hoppenheim Sch of Cinema Concordia Univ 1455 De Maisonneuve Montreal PQ H3G 1M8 Canada

FANARA, SIRENA
PAINTER, LECTURER
b White Plains, NY. *Study:* Self taught. *Work:* Mus Campidoglio, Mus Mod Art, Rome, Italy; Mus Castello Sforzesco, Milano, Italy; Mus Eureka, Ill; Regione Fruili Venezia Giulia, Regione Siciliana; Regione Sarda; Voorhees Zimmerli Art Mus, NJ; New England Ctr Mus; Mus Art & Sci, Daytona, Fla. *Comn:* Paintings for Federico Fellini, Frankie Laine, Gina Lollobrigida, Vittorio de Sica, The Vatican, Pope Paul XI & Pope John Paul II, Vatican Mus; 3 paintings, Family Bible Encycl, Vol 19-20, Curtis Bks & Copylab, 72. *Exhib:* Solo exhibs, Gallerie Andre Weil, Paris, 68, Mike Douglas TV Show Exhib, 68, Palazzo delle Esposizioni, Comune di Roma, Rome, 69 & State Gallery in Teatro Massimo, Palermo, Sicily, 70; C W Post Univ Gallery, 77; Lowenstein Gallery, NY, 83; Wapner Gallery, NY, 86; Wash Mus Fine Art, 66; Hostra Mus, 87; Pace Univ, 89. *Pos:* Dir, Sirena Art Studios, New York, formerly. *Teaching:*

Lectr, Fordham Univ, NY, 85-. *Awards:* Gold Medal Award, Acad of Paestum; Medal of Vatican, Pope John Paul II, Vatican Mus, 84; Artist of Love Trophy, 86. *Bibliog:* Guilio Bolaffi (auth), Bolaffi on modern art, Torino, Italy, 70 & 72. *Mem:* Acad of Paestum; Acad dei 500; Acad Tiberina; Int Comt Cult, Rome; Metrop Mus Art; Acad Burgkart, Rome (deleg for USA, 90). *Media:* Acrylic, Oil. *Publ:* Illusr & auth, autobiography, MPH Publ, 76; The Roses and the Thorns, pvt publ, 89; Visions of Women Artist, pvt publ, 89

FANTAZOS, HENRYK MICHAEL
PAINTER, PRINTMAKER
b Kamionka Strumilowa, Poland, Jan 18, 1944; US citizen. *Study:* Acad Fine Art, Cracow, Poland, MA (painting), 69. *Work:* Nat Mus, Poznan, Poland; Mus Gornoslaskie, Bytom, Poland; Nat Mus, Lublin, Poland; Kosciuszko Found, NY; George Washington Univ, DC. *Exhib:* The Eccentrics, Southeastern Ctr Contemp Art, Winston-Salem, NC, 83; Southeast VIsual Art, Ga State Univ, Atlanta, 86; Fantasy Landscape, Tampa Mus Art, Fla, 87; Fact, Fiction, Fantasy (traveling exhib), Univ Tenn, 87-88; solo exhibs, Philadelphia Art Alliance, Pa, 89, Waterworks Art Ctr, Salisbury, NC, 96, Weems Gallery, Meredith Col, Raleigh, NC, 97, Mus Art, Greenville, NC, 97. *Awards:* Best of Show Durham Art Guild Competition, 87; Int Print Competition Winner, San Diego Art Inst, 94; Artist Fel Award, NC Arts Coun, 97. *Bibliog:* Olga Wickerhauser (auth), Describing the incessant obstinate sight, Charleston Gazette, 1/83; Deborah Winsteadman (auth), Fantazos: Artist follows visionary muse, Durham Sun, 5/18/89; Max Halperen (auth), Fantazos at Meredith, Spectator, 3/26/97. *Mem:* Art Space Artist Asn, NC. *Media:* Oil, Egg Tempera; Copper. *Mailing Add:* 227 W Hill Ave Hillsborough NC 27278

FARAGASSO , JACK
PAINTER, INSTRUCTOR
b Brooklyn, NY, Jan 23, 1929. *Study:* Art Students League, with Frank J Reilly, 48-52. *Work:* George Washington Carver Mus, Tuskegee Inst, Ala; The Nat Mus of Am Art, Newport, RI. *Comn:* Peter Marcelle, Clare Booth Luce, Judy Goffman, James Rodgers & Charles Osgood. *Exhib:* Gallery Mod Art, NY, 69; Am Artists Prof League, 69-71 & 73-79; The Nude in Fine Art, O'Brien's Emporium, Scottsdale, Ariz, 91-92; Modern Masters of Figuative Painting, Leslie Levy Gallery, Scottsdale, Ariz, 92; Fletcher Gallery, Woodstock, NY, 2002. *Pos:* Illusr, many book co, 57-. *Teaching:* Instr drawing, painting & illus & dir, treas & trustee, Frank Reilly Sch Art, NY, 67-68; instr drawing, painting & illus, Art Students League, 68-; instr drawing & painting, Woodstock Sch Art, 81 & Scottsdale Artist Sch, Ariz 84-86. *Awards:* Distinguished Educ Medal in honor of Frank Reilly, Soc Illustractors of NY, 2010. *Bibliog:* Kent Steine (auth), The Art of Jack Faragasso, Illus Mag, No 1, 2002; articles in NY Daily News & Am Artist Mag. *Mem:* Art Students League; fel Am Artists Prof League; Am Portrait Soc; Artists Fel Inc; Am Renaissance 21st Century. *Media:* Oil, Gouache. *Interests:* writing articles & books on art & photography. *Collection:* early 20th century Am fine artists & illustrators. *Publ:* Auth, The Students Guide to Painting, North Light Publ, 79; Biog Dict Science Fiction Fantasy Artists, Greenwood Press Inc, 1988; For Edward Munch Aquaoil, Watercolor Magic, fall, 97; On choosing an art insturctor, Art Ideas, Vol 4, No 4, 98, article on Mastering drawing the human figure from life, memory, imagination, spring 2000; Mastering Drawing the Human Figure from Life, Memory, Imagination, Stargarden Press, 99; The Legacy of Frank J. Reilly, Linea, Vol 10 No 1, 2006; The Early Photographs of Betty Page, American Icon, Binary Publications, 2013. *Mailing Add:* 340 E 55th St New York NY 10022

FARBER, MAYA M
PAINTER
b Timisoara, Romania, Jan 24, 1936; US citizen. *Study:* Pratt Inst, privately with Edwin Oppler; Hunter Coll; Hans Hoffman Sch; Art Students League, with Reginald Marsh. *Work:* Butler Inst Am Art, Youngstown, Ohio; Int Tel & Tel, NY; Columbia Mus Art, SC; Ga Mus Art, Athens; Jacksonville Art Mus, Fla; Primex Plastics Corp, Richmond, Ind. *Exhib:* Solo exhibs, Rockefeller Ctr, NY, 79, Mountain Top Gallery, 80, Ugarit Gallery, Tel Aviv, Israel, 80, NY State Fair, 84-85, River House, NY, 84 & 86, Nelli Aman Gallery, Tel Aviv, Israel, 92; Group exhibs, Great Expectations, Madison Ave, 78, Mountain Top Gallery, Windham, NY, 79 & 94, & Twilight Part Art Asn, Collage, 79 & Northcoast Collage Soc, 94; Small works show, Catskill Gallery, 2000; Collage & Assembledge Soc, 2000-05; Charlotte Fin Gallery, Vero Beach, Fla, 2004; Liman Studio Gallery, Palm Beach, Fla, 2005; Windham Fine Arts, NY, 2005; Louisa Gould Gallery, Vineyard Haven Mass. *Awards:* Second Prize, Jamaica Festival Art, 67; Judges Special Merit, Nat Collage Soc, 88; Judges Special Merit, 16th Annual Exhib, Nat Collage Soc, 2000. *Bibliog:* Nita Leland & Virginia Williams (auths), Creative Collage Techniques, 94; B Bierbaum & Petrina Gardner (auths) Collage in all Dimensions, 2005. *Mem:* Nat Collage Soc. *Media:* Acrylic, Oil. *Publ:* Catskill Mountain Guide (Artist Feature) June, 2007; Winner of Artists Over 60, Artists Mag, 2012. *Dealer:* Chase Gallery Inc 31 E 64th St New York NY 10021; Windham Fine Arts Windham NY 12424; Louisa Gould Gallery Vineyard Haven Mass. *Mailing Add:* 435 E 52nd St New York NY 10022

FARES, WILLIAM O
PAINTER
b Compton, Calif, July 16, 1942. *Study:* San Francisco Art Inst, BA & MFA. *Work:* Chase Manhattan Bank; Va Mus Fine Arts; State Univ NY Coll Purchase; Yale Art Gallery; Muhlenberg Ctr for the Arts, Allentown, Pa; Guggenheim Mus & Mus Mod Art, NY. *Exhib:* Biennial, Whitney Mus Am Art, NY, 75; Albright-Knox Art Gallery, Buffalo, NY, 75; Paperworks, Mus Mod Art, NY, 76; Am Drawing 1927-1977, Minn Mus Art, St Paul, 77; Solo exhib, Zolla/Lieberman Gallery, Chicago, 77; Stamford Mus, Conn, 78; Va Mus Fine Arts, 79; Jefferson Co Hist Soc, Watertown, NY, 79; Tex Gallery, 79; and many others. *Awards:* Nat Endowment Arts Grant, 79-80. *Bibliog:* David Bourdon (auth), article, The Village Voice, 12/6/76; Barbara Cavaliere (auth), article, Arts Mag, 2/77; Kenneth Whal (auth), On abstract literalist works, Arts Mag, 4/77; articles in: Art in Am & Art Forum. *Media:* Acrylic. *Dealer:* Dannenburg 44 Broome St New York NY 10012. *Mailing Add:* 110 W 26th St 5th Flr New York NY 10001

FARLEY, KATHERINE G
COLLECTOR
b 1950. *Study:* Brown Univ, BA, 1971; Harvard Grad Sch Design, MA (archit), 1976. *Pos:* Mgr bus develop for East Asia, Turner Construction, formerly; sr mng dir Latin Am & global corp mktg, Tishman Speyer Properties, New York, 1984-; exec comt mem, NY Philharmonic, Brearley Sch; bd mem, Lincoln Ctr Performing Arts, Lincoln Ctr Theater, Alvin Ailey Dance co. *Awards:* Named one of Top 200 Collectors, ARTnews mag, 2004-13; named one of 100 Most Influential Women in New York Business, Crain's New York Business, 2007, The 50 Most Powerful Women in NY, 2009, 2011. *Collection:* Contemporary art. *Mailing Add:* Tishmanspeyer Properties 45 Rockefeller Plz Fl 12 New York NY 10111-1299

FARM, GERALD E
PAINTER, SCULPTOR
b Grand Island, Nebr, Mar 8, 1935. *Study:* Famous Artist Sch, Westport, Conn; Nebr State Col, BA (educ). *Work:* Deming Fed Savings, NMex; Olney Savings & Loan, Tex; Bank Beaver City, Okla; plus many pvt collections. *Comn:* First Nat Bank, Uvalde, Tex. *Exhib:* CM Russell Auction, Great Falls, Mont, 73 & 75; Real Show, Grand Cent Art Galleries, NY, 79; Mus Nebr Art, Kearny, Nebr, 88; Nat Finals Art Auction, Las Vegas, Nev; Cheyenne Frontier Days Art Show, Wyo, 91-98; Miniatures, Fine Arts Mus, NMex, 92; Celebrate Am Realism, San Diego, 92; Western Rendezvous of Art, Helena, Mont, 92. *Awards:* Peter Hassrick Merit Award, Western Rendezvous Art, 92. *Bibliog:* Byron Jones (auth), The story teller's art of Gerald Farm, Southwest Art, 79; Patti Jones Morgan (auth), G Farm, tinged with nostalgia, Southwest Art, 88; Patricia O'Connor (auth), Gerald Farm-Accentuating the Positive, Art West, 92. *Media:* Oil. *Dealer:* Settlers West Gallery Tucson AZ; Trailside Galleries Scottsdale AZ & Jackson WY. *Mailing Add:* 5609 Foothills Dr Farmington NM 87402

FARNHAM, ALEXANDER
PAINTER, WRITER
b Orange, NJ, May 5, 1926. *Study:* Art Students League, with George Bridgman, W C McNulty & Frank Vincent DuMond; also with Van Dearing Perrine & Anne Steel Marsh. *Work:* Newark Mus, NJ; Nat Arts Club, New York; Monmouth Coll; James A Michener Collection; Morgan Guaranty Trust Co, NY. *Comn:* Murals, Naval subjects, Naval Repair Base, New Orleans, 45; portrait of dir, Am Found for Blind, 50; painting of off bldg, NJ Mfrs Insurance co, Trenton, 69, 83, 2006; Washington Crosses the Delaware (pewter plate design), Franklin Mint, 76. *Exhib:* Methods and Materials of the Painter, Montclair Art Mus, circulated in Can, 54; Nat Acad Design 135th Ann Exhib, NY, 60; Eastern States Art Exhib, Springfield, Mass, 65-67; NJ Award Artists Exhib, Montclair Art Mus, 66; NJ Artists, Newark Mus Invitational, 68. *Pos:* Artist, US Navy, 45-46; pres, Associated Artists NJ, 72-77; writer, Maine Antique Digest, 76-2005. *Teaching:* Taught classes in painting The Hunterdon Art Center, Clinton, NJ, 1979; Rider College, Lawrenceville, NJ, 1989. *Awards:* Best in Show, Monclair Art Mus, 50; Purchase Award, Newark Mus, 68; NJ State Coun Arts Fel, 80; First Award, Summit Art Ctr Nat Exhib, 81. *Bibliog:* Diane Hamilton (auth), Painters of the Valley, Country Mag, 12/81; Palette Talk #51, M Grumbacher, Inc, 82; Dorris Brandes (auth), Artists of the River Towns, 2002; Jim Alterman (auth), Alexander Farhham Brought to Light, 2008. *Media:* Oil. *Publ:* Auth & illusr, Tool collectors handbook, 70, 72 & 75; auth, Architectural patterns, subjects for the artists brush, 74; Early Tools of NJ & the Men Who Made Them, 84; Search for Early New Jersey Toolmakers, 92. *Dealer:* Jims of Lambertville Lambertville NJ. *Mailing Add:* 78 Tumble Falls Rd Stockton NJ 08559

FARRELL, PATRICK
PAINTER, PRINTMAKER
b Escanaba, Mich. *Study:* Self-taught. *Work:* Rahr-West Art Mus, Manitowoc, Wis; Charles A Wustum Mus Fine Arts, Racine, Wis; Milwaukee Pub Libr, Wis; Univ Wis, Stevens Point; Miller Art Ctr, Sturgeon Bay, Wis; Woman's Club Wis, Milwaukee, Wis. *Exhib:* Solo exhibs, Bergstrom-Mahler Mus, Neenah, Wis, 74, Oshkosh Pub Mus, Wis, 77, Rahr-West Art Mus, Manitowoc, Wis, 86, John Michael Kohler Arts Ctr, Sheboygan, Wis, 87, Tory Folliard Gallery, Milwaukee, Wis, 2000, 2003, 2005, 2008 & 2012. Craven Gallery, West Tisbury, 2002, Martha's Vineyard, Mass, Hidell Brooks, Charlotte, NC, 2001, RiverEdge Galleries, Mishicot, Wis, 2004, Grace Chosy Gallery, Madison, Wis, 2006 & Marin-Price Galleries, Chevy Chase, Md, 93, 94, 96, 99, 2002, 2007; Wisconsin Impressions, Milwaukee Art Mus, 82; Allied Artists Am, Nat Arts Club, New York, 97, 2011; Patrick Farrell Retrospective, Wis Acad Sci, Arts & Lett, Madison, 92 & Charles Allis Art Mus, Milwaukee, 98; Allied Artists Am Invitational Exhib, Bennington Ctr Arts, Bennington, Vt, 2007; Edgewood Orchard Galleries, Fish Creek, Wisc. *Awards:* Festival of Art Purchase Award, Friends Milwaukee Art Mus, 73; Milwaukee Art Comn Award of Excellence, 84; John Young - Hunter Mem Award, 84th & 97th Allied Artists Am, New York. *Bibliog:* James M Auer (auth), The Magic World of Patrick Farrell (film), Auer Art Films, 77; Scott S Stewart (auth), The Art of Patrick Farrell, Ivy House Publ, 80; Margaret Fish Rahill (auth), Patrick Farrell Paintings, Charles Allis Art Mus, 84; Heidi Levy (auth), Famous Wis Artists & Architects: Patrick Farrell, Badger Bks, 2004; Ashley E. Rooney (auth), 100 Midwestern Artists, Schiffer Pub, 2012. *Mem:* hon mem, Allied Artists Am, New York. *Media:* Oil. *Publ:* Contribr, Oil Paintings of Patrick Farrell, Tre Art Publ, 72; Painter Patrick Farrell reveals best secret, Milwaukee Sentinel, 77; Milwaukee 1980, New Art Examiner, 80; Exhibit unveils the fruit of Farrell's labor, 95 & The artful survivor, 98, Milwaukee J Sentinel; auth, Master of Illusion: Patrick Farrell, Milwaukee Mag, 2006. *Dealer:* Marin-Price Galleries 7022 Wisconsin Ave Chevy Chase MD 20815; Tory Folliard Gallery 233 N Milwaukee St Milwaukee WI 53202; Carol Craven New York NY; RiverEdge Galleries Mishicot WI; Grace Chosy Gallery 1825 Monroe St Madison WI 53711; Edgewood Orchard Galleries Fish Creek, WI. *Mailing Add:* 2752 N Summit Ave Milwaukee WI 53211

FARRENS, JUANITA G
PAINTER, SCULPTOR
b Philippine Republic; US citizen. *Study:* Bukidnon Inst, Mindanao, Philippines, BSE, 39; Md Univ Exten, Ankara, Turkey, 53-54; La Tech Univ, 83-86, 87 & 88; Univ New Orleans, 88-92; Delgado Community Col, 88-92. *Work:* Westminster Abbey, Spencer, Mass; St Alphonso Church, Philippine Republic; St Dominic Church, Mother Cabrini High Sch & Knights of Columbus, New Orleans; Colo Gold Mine Sch, Golden; New Orleans Mus Fine Arts. *Comn:* Garden scene, comn by Joe Barhill, Boulder, 60; landscape, Shepherd Ctr, Mt Carmel Acad, New Orleans, 82; Knight Columbus, New Orleans, La, 84; Joseph Clementine, New Orleans, 85; William Sork, New Orleans, 85; The Crucifixion (life size sculpture), Courtland, Minn, 94. *Exhib:* Biennial Exhib Piedmont Painting & Sculpture, Mint Mus Art, 77-79; Joslyn Art Mus Ann, 78; Pastel Soc Am Ann, Nat Arts Club, NY, 78-80 & 83; Ga Second Ann Exhib, Columbus Mus Arts & Sci, 81; Aqueous, JB Speed Art Mus, 82; First Patron Watercolor Gala, Kresge Fine Art Ctr, Oklahoma City, 83; Springville Mus Fine Art, Utah, 84-85; 47th Contemp Am Art, West Palm Beach, Fla, 85; Kans Pastel Soc Nat, 85-86; Degas Pastel Soc First Open Nat, New Orleans, La, 86; 45th Nat Watercolor, Birmingham Mus Art, Ala, 86. *Teaching:* Instr art, Farrens Art Sch, New Orleans, 60- & Sheperd Ctr, Mt Carmel Acad, New Orleans, 78-83; lectr & demonstr painting, New Orleans Art Asn, 64-83 & Holy Cross Col, 68. *Awards:* Merit Award, Tenth Nat New Orleans Art Asn, 84; Pastel Soc Award Excellence, 86. *Mem:* Allied Artists Am; Am Portrait Soc; founding mem La Watercolor Soc (vpres, 71-72); New Orleans Art Asn; Am Pastel Soc. *Media:* Watercolor, Pastel. *Publ:* NY Art Review, American Publishing Corp, 10/88; article, Times Picayune, 85-86 & 94. *Dealer:* Archives Nat Found New York NY; Art South Inc PA

FARRIS, GREER
SCULPTOR
b Ft Smith, Ark, June 24, 1942. *Study:* Western State Col, Colo, BA, 1965; Pratt Inst, studied with Robert Natkin, 1965-66; Northeastern State Col, MEd, 1970; Southern Ill Univ, MFA, studied with Nick Verqette, 1972. *Work:* Joslyn Art Mus, Omaha; Ark Arts Ctr, Little Rock. *Comn:* ferro/cement sculpture, Ark Arts Council, Mountainburg, Ark, 1981; steel sculpture, VA Hosp, Little Rock, 1982-83; wood sculpture, Ozark Woodland Sculpture Garden, Univ Ozarks, Huntsville, Ark, 2000; welded steel sculpture, Crossroads, New Orleans, 2015; aluminum sculpture, Tossed About, Univ Ark, Fort Smith, Ark, 2015. *Exhib:* 6th Biennial Beau Arts, Columbus, Ohio 1972; La Bicentennial, Old State Capitol, Baton Rouge, 1973; Texas Ann, Laguna Gloria Mus, Austin, 1973; Craft Invitational, Univ NMex, Albuquerque, 1973; Baroque '74, Mus Contemp Crafts, NY, 1974; Looking at Earth, Smithsonian Inst, Washington, 1986-87. *Teaching:* instr art & clay, Tulane Univ, 72-76, Westark Community Col, 77-87. *Awards:* Fel, Ark Arts Coun, 1985. *Dealer:* Diamond G Gallery 200 N 21 St Fort Smith AR 72901. *Mailing Add:* 200 N 21st St Fort Smith AR 72901

FARVER, JANE
CURATOR, MUSEUM DIRECTOR
Work: Curator Global Conceptualism: Points of Origin, 1950s-1980s. *Pos:* Dir, Lehman Col Art Gallery, City Univ of NY, 1989-1992; dir exhib Queens Mus Art, 1992-1997; dir, List Visual Arts Ctr, Mass Inst of Technol, 1999-. *Mailing Add:* List Visual Arts Ctr 20 Ames St Bldg E15 Cambridge MA 02139

FARVER, SUZANNE
ADMINISTRATOR, COLLECTOR
b Pella, Iowa, Feb 22, 1955. *Study:* Grinnell Col, BA (Phi Beta Kappa), 78; Univ Denver, JD, 83. *Pos:* Trustee, Denver Art Mus, 88-93; dir develop & pub affairs, Anderson Ranch Arts Ctr, Snowmass Village, Colo, 90-92; dir, Aspen Art Mus, Aspen, 92-; collections comt, Denver Art Mus, 93-. *Mailing Add:* Aspen Art Mus 590 N Mill St Aspen CO 81611

FASNACHT, HEIDE ANN
INSTALLATION SCULPTOR
b Cleveland, Ohio, Jan 12, 1951. *Study:* RI Sch Design, BFA, 73; New York Univ, MA. *Work:* Brooklyn Mus Art; Dallas Mus Art; Fogg Mus Art, Harvard Univ; High Mus Art, Atlanta; Weatherspoon Mus Art; Walker Art Ctr; Columbus Mus Art; Tang Teaching Mus; Skidmore Coll; and others. *Comn:* Lower East Side Print Shop, 2012, 2013. *Exhib:* Solo exhibs include These Things Happen, Bill Maynes Gallery, NY, 1998, Galeria Trama, Barcelona, Spain, Galeria Trama, Barcelona, 2003, Strange Attractors, Richmond, 2004, Bernard Toale Gallery, Boston, 2005 & 2007, Pan-Am Gallery, Dallas, 2006, Kent Gallery, NY, 2005 & 2007, Preview Berlin, 2009, Kent Fine Art, NY, 2012; Group exhibs include Sculpture on the Wall, Aldrich Mus Contemp Art, Ridgefield, Conn, 1986-87; Figurative Impulses: Six Contemp Sculptors, Santa Barbara Mus Art, Calif, 1988; Enclosing the Void, Whitney Mus Am Art at Equitable Ctr, 1988; Making Their Mark: Women Artists Move Into the Mainstream 1970-1985, Cincinnati Art Mus, New Orleans Mus Art, Denver Art Musw & Pa Acad Fine Arts, 1989; Contemp Collectors, San Diego Mus Contemp Art, Calif, 1990; Breaking Ground, Contemp Arts Ctr, Cincinnati, Ohio, 1987; Mapping, Mus Mod Art, New York, 1994; Suspended Instants, Sculpture Ctr, New York, 1997-98; Yale Univ Art Gallery, Looking at Am, New Haven, Conn, 2002; NC Mus Art, Defying Gravity (with catalog), 2003; Tableau Ecrans, Galerie les Filles du Calvaire, Paris & Brussels, 2005; Invitational, Nat Acad Design, New York, 2006; Blown Away, Krannert Art Mus, Chicago, 2008; Invitational, Am Acad Arts & Letters, New York, 2008; Qbox Gallery, Athens, Greece, 2009; Impermanent Collections, Kent Gallery, NY, 2009; The Err Proj, 2009; Impermanent Collection, A Box Gallery, Athens, Greece; Impermanent Coll, QBox Gallery, Athens 2009; Mind the Gap, Kent Fine Art, NY; Drawing: A Broader Definition; Styrofoam; Hearing Pictures, Tang Mus, Saratoga Springs, NY; QBox Gallery, Athens, Greece. *Pos:* part-time asst prof, Parsons, The New Sch for Design. *Teaching:* Adj prof sculpture & drawing, State Univ NY, Purchase, 81; artist-in-residence, Bennington Col, Vt, 81 & 86; lectr, Yale Univ, 81, RI Sch Design, 87, 91 & 92, Parsons Sch Design, 89- & Whitney Mus Am Art, 90; vis artist & lectr, Cleveland Inst Arts, 81, Md Inst Col Art, 85 & RI Sch Design, 85; vis lectr, Princeton Univ, 87 & 92; asst prof sculpture, Harvard Univ, 94- & instr, 96-; assist prof, Parsons Sch Design. *Awards:* Guggenheim Grant, 90; Nat Endowment Arts, 94; Pollock-Krasner Grant, 99, 2010; Rockefeller Fndtn Fel, Bellagio, Italy, 2003 & Montalvo Ctr Arts, 06; NYFA Sculptures Fel, 2007. *Bibliog:* N Princenthal (auth), Drawing to Sublime, Kent Publs, 2003; R Rubenstein & Edward Albee (auths), Strange Attractors, Va Commonwealth Univ, 2003; Harper Glenn & Twylene Moyed (editors), A Sculpture Reader, Contemporary Sculpture Since 1980, 2006; Ian Berry (auth), Twice Drawn: Modern & Contemporary Drawings, 2011. *Media:* Photo Based Mixed Media. *Specialty:* Modern and contemporary art. *Dealer:* Kent Fine Art New York NY; Bernard Toale Gallery Boston MA; Qbox Gallery Athens Greece. *Mailing Add:* 4 White St New York NY 10013

FASOLDT, SARAH LOWRY
ADMINISTRATOR, CURATOR
b Evanston, Ill, Feb 7, 1950. *Study:* Ecole du Louvre, Paris, 69; Univ Colo, Boulder, BA, 72. *Pos:* Cur Homstead, Farnsworth Art Mus, Rockland, Maine, 83; dir, Maine Coasts Artists, Rockport, 84-89; assoc dir, Farnsworth Art Mus, Rockland, Maine, 94-. *Mem:* Maine Community Cult Alliance. *Publ:* Auth, But is it art?, 1/81 & Monhegan: 100 years of island painting, 8/84, Down East Mag. *Mailing Add:* Farnsworth Art Mus 356 Main St Rockland ME 04841

FAST, OMER
FILMMAKER
b Jerusalem, Israel, 1972. *Study:* Tufts Univ, Sch of the Mus of Fine Arts, BFA, 1995; Hunter Coll, CUNY, MFA, 2000. *Work:* Whitney Mus Am Art, New York; Guggenheim Mus Art, New York; Metrop Mus Art, New York; Tate Mod, London. *Exhib:* Solo exhibs include Frankfurter Kunstverein, Frankfurt, Germany, 2003, 2004, Ctr for Contemp Art, Fribourg, Switzerland, 2003, Postmasters Gallery, New York, 2003, 2005, Nat Ctr of Photog, Paris, 2004, Pinakothek der Moderne, Munich, Germany 2004, Int Inst for Visual Arts, London, 2005, Carnegie Mus, Pittsburgh, 2005, gb agency, Paris, 2006, Vox Contemp, Montreal, 2007, Mus Mod Art, Vienna, 2007; two-person exhibs include Two-person Exhib, Momenta Art, Brooklyn, (with Akiko Ichikawa), 2000; group exhibs include Hidden in Daylight Foksal Gallery Found, Cieszyn, Poland, 2003; Contemp Art/Recent Acquisitions, Jewish Mus, New York, 2003; Storytelling George Eastman House, Rochester, New York, 2004; Fair Use: Appropriation in Recent Film and Video Hammer Mus, Los Angeles, 2005; Why Pictures Now: New Media Acquisitions Mus Mod Art, Vienna, 2006; Visite: Contemp Art in Germany Ctr for Fine Arts, Brussels, 2007; Closed Circuit: New Media Acquisitions, Metrop Mus Art, New York, 2007; 54th Int Art Exhib Biennale, Venice, 2011. *Awards:* Peter J Wade Award Studio Work, Tufts Univ, 1995; Boit Award, Boston Mus Sch Fine Arts, 1995; Sch Fine Arts Alumni Travel Grant, Boston Mus Fine Arts, 2000 ; Found Prize, Louis Comfort Tiffany, 2003; Bucksbaum Award, Whitney Mus Am Art, 2008; SMFA Medal Award, Sch Mus Fine Arts Boston, 2010. *Dealer:* GB agency 20 rue Louise-Weiss Paris France 75013; ARRATIABEER Holzmarktstrasse 15 - 18 - S-Bahnbogen 47 Berlin Germany 10179; Postmasters Gallery 459 W 19th St New York NY 10011

FAUBION, S MICHAEL
ADMINISTRATOR
b Tex, May 10, 1952. *Study:* Univ Tex, BA, 74, LBJ Sch Pub Affairs, MPA, 76. *Pos:* Asst dir visual arts, Nat Endowment Arts, Washington, DC, 85-88, coordr, 98-. *Mailing Add:* 4016 18th St NW Washington DC 20011-5325

FAUDE, WILSON HINSDALE
DIRECTOR, CURATOR
b Hartford, Conn, Feb 20, 1946. *Study:* Hobart Col, BA, 69; Trinity Col, MA. *Work:* Wadsworth Mus, Hartford, Conn; Mark Twain Memorial, Hartford, Conn; Old State House, Hartford, Conn. *Pos:* Exec dir, Old State House, 85-; cur, Mark Twain Mem, 71-79. *Mem:* Century Asn; Nat Arts Club. *Mailing Add:* 42 Fulton Pl West Hartford CT 06107

FAUDIE, FRED
PAINTER, ILLUSTRATOR
b DuBois, Pa, May 29, 1941. *Study:* Cornell Univ, AB (art hist), 63; Univ Iowa, Iowa City, MA (painting), 65, photog with John Schulz, 67-68; Syracuse Univ, MFA (illus), 79. *Work:* Addison Gallery Am Art; Lincoln Co Heritage Trust; Lincoln State Monument. *Exhib:* Brockton Triennial, Brockton Art Mus, Mass, 81 & 84; Billy the Kid, Lincoln Co Heritage Trust, 84; Something Human, Univ Mass, 87; Ninth Ann Boston Drawing Show, 88; Black in the Light, Genovese Gallery, Boston, 88; New Eng Impressions, Art of Printmaking, Fitchburg Art Mus, Mass, 88. *Teaching:* Prof painting & drawing, Univ Mass Lowell, 68-, chairperson art dept, 80-83. *Bibliog:* Allara (auth), New Editions, Vol 81, No 9, Art News, 9/82; Billy, the myth and image, Print Collectors Newsletter, Vol 13, No 3, 83; Erdman (auth), Fred Faudie: Mixed themes, Art New Eng, Vol 9, No 2, 2/88. *Mem:* Boston Visual Artists Union; Lowell Art Asn. *Media:* Oil, Acrylic. *Mailing Add:* Dept Art Univ Mass Lowell 1 University Ave Lowell MA 01854

FAULCONER, MARY (FULLERTON)
PAINTER, DESIGNER
b Pittsburgh, Pa. *Study:* Pa Mus Sch Art; also with Alexei Brodovitch. *Work:* Paul Mellon pvt collection; Duchess of Windsor pvt collection; plus many others. *Comn:* Paintings, Steuben Glass; designed six stamps, US Postal Serv, 74; designed Rose stamp, US Postal Serv, 78; designed Love stamp, US Postal Serv, 82; Franklin Mint, 84; Katherine Hepburn; Jacquine Kennedy. *Exhib:* Alex Iolas Gallery, NY, 55, 58 & 61; Philadelphia Art Alliance, 62; Bodley Gallery, NY, 64, 66, 69 & 72; Tenn Fine Arts Ctr, Nashville, 67; De Mers Gallery, Hilton Head, SC, 71-72; Ursus, Hotel Carlyle, NY. *Pos:* Art dir, Harper's Bazaar Mag, 40; art dir, Mademoiselle Mag, 45. *Teaching:* Instr advert, Philadelphia Mus Sch Art, 36-40. *Awards:* Distinctive Merit Award, 54, 57 & 61, Silver Medal, 58 & 59, Art Dir Club; Gold Medal, Am Rose Soc, 78. *Media:* Gouache. *Dealer:* URSUS Art Dealer Madison Ave NY City

FAULDS, W ROD
ADMINISTRATOR, DESIGNER
b Rexdale, Ont, May 28, 1953; US citizen. *Study:* Humbolt State Univ, BA, 77; Calif State Univ, Fullerton, MA, 80; Williams Coll Grad Studies, Art Hist, 1989-1992. *Exhib:* Numerous exhibs rated at all prof positions. *Pos:* Dir, Brattleboro Mus & Art Ctr, 81-84; assoc dir, Williams Col Mus Art, 84-92; asst dir, Guggenheim Mus, 93-94; chief designer, Brooklyn Mus Art, 95-96; dir, Univ Galleries, Fla Atlantic Univ, 96-97. *Teaching:* Mus Studies, Fla Atlantic Univ, 96-97. *Mem:* Am Asn Mus; Asn Coll Univ Mus Galleries (NE rep, 86-89). *Res:* Contemporary art with emphasis in sculpture and photography. *Publ:* Coauth, Object/Illusion/Reality-12 American Photographers, Calif Univ, Fullerton, 79; contribr, Mary Cassatt: The Color Prints, Abrams, 89; Black Photographers Bear Witness: 100 Years of Social Protest, Williams Coll Mus Art, 89; Stitching Memories: African American Story Quilts, Williams Coll Mus Art, 89; Sites of Recollection: Four Altars and a Rap Opera, Williams Coll Mus, 92, Nu Art South Fla, 2000, South Fla Cultural Consortiumn Visual and Media Artists Fellowship Winners, 2000. *Mailing Add:* 722 SW 27th Wy Boynton Beach FL 33435

FAULHABER, PATRICK
PAINTER
b Dallas, Tex, 1946. *Study:* North Tex State Univ, BFA, 80. *Exhib:* Solo exhibs at Eastfield Coll Gallery, Dallas, 80, Tex Wesleyan Univ Gallery, 84, Conduit Gallery, Dallas, 94, Art Mus South Tex, 96, Amarillo Mus Art, 97, Dallas Mus Art, 98, John Berggruen Gallery, San Francisco, 99, The Old Jail Art Ctr, Albany, Tex, 2000, Danese, NY, 2004, 2007; group exhibs include Conduit Gallery, 92, 93, 94; Amarillo Art Ctr, Tex, 92; Trammell Crow Ctr, Dallas, 92; Gray Matters, Dallas, 92; Bathouse Cultural Ctr, Dallas, 93; Laguna Gloria Art Mus, Austin, Tex, 94; Dallas Visual Arts Ctr, Tex, 95; Slover McCutcheon Gallery, Houston, 95; Fletcher Gallery, Santa Fe, 95; Arlington Mus Art, Tex, 95; Tyler Mus Art, 96; van de Griff Gallery, Santa Fe, 96; Inman Gallery, Houston, 97; John Berggruen Gallery, 2000, 2001; Danese, NY, 2005

FAULKNER, FRANK
PAINTER
b Sumter, SC, July 27, 1946. *Study:* Univ NC, Chapel Hill, BFA, 68, MFA, 72. *Work:* Hirshhorn Mus, Washington, DC; Nat Collection of Fine Arts, Washington, DC; Albright-Knox Art Gallery, Buffalo, NY; Smith Col, Northampton, Mass; Chase Manhattan Bank, NY. *Comn:* Urban wall proj, South Eastern Ctr Contemp Arts-Nat Endowment Arts, Winston-Salem, NC, 74; Orlando Int Airport, 81. *Exhib:* Whitney Mus Am Art Biennial, NY, 75; Slocumb Gallery, Univ Tenn, 76; Solo exhibs, Knowlton Gallery, 76-81; Material Dominant, Univ Pa, Philadelphia, 77; Southeast 7, Southeastern Ctr Contemp Art, Winston-Salem, NC, 77; Painters & Sculptors SE, High Mus Art, Atlanta, Ga, 77. *Awards:* Individual Artist Grant, Nat Endowment Arts, 75; Regional Artist Grant, South Eastern Ctr Contemp Arts-Nat Endowment Arts, 76; NC Architects Award, 76. *Bibliog:* William Zimmer (auth), Frank Faulkner, Arts Mag, 10/76. *Media:* Acrylic, Mixed Media. *Dealer:* Monique Knowlton Gallery 19 E 71st St New York NY 10021. *Mailing Add:* c/o Arden Gallery 129 Newbury St Boston MA 02116

FAUSEL, ALAN
APPRAISER
Study: UCLA, BA (art hist); Stanford Univ, MA (art hist). *Pos:* Asst cur, European sculpture, decorative arts Fine Arts Mus, San Francisco, 86-89; cur, Frick Art Mus, Pittsburgh, 89-91; dir, European painting dept & mus serv's dept Butterfield & Butterfield, San Francisco, 91-94; sr vpres, dir, painting & drawing dept Doyle, NY, 94; lectr, Appraisal Asn Am, currently. *Teaching:* adj lectr, NYU Grad Sch Educ, currently. *Mailing Add:* Doyle NY 175 E 87th St New York NY 10128

FAUST, JAMES WILLE
PAINTER, SCULPTOR
b Lapel, Ind, May 22, 1949. *Study:* Herron Sch Art, Indianapolis, Ind, BFA, 71, Univ Ill, Champaign-Urbana, MFA, 74. *Work:* Minn Mus Art, St Paul; Snite Mus Art, South Bend, Ind; Ind Univ Art Mus, Bloomington; Indianapolis Mus Art, Ind; Emporia State Univ, Kans. *Comn:* Absolut/Carillon Importers Ltd; Herb & Diane Meyer Simon; Melvin Simon & Assocs; Eli Lilly & Co; structured steel sculpture, SMT Realty/Allison Pointe, Indianapolis, Ind. *Exhib:* Brazil Works on Paper Partnership Int, Mus De Arte Do Rio Grande Do Sul, Porto Allegre, S Am, 84; solo show, Indianapolis Mus Art, 85 & 92; Contemp Am Drawing, Wichita Mus Art, Kans, 87; Am Drawing Biennial, Muscarelle Mus Art, Williamsburg, Va, 88; Chicago Int New Art Forms Expos, Navy Pier, Ill, 89; and others. *Awards:* Krannert Creative & Performing Arts Fel, Univ Ill, 73; Purchase Awards, 28th & 31st Ann Drawing & Small Sculpture Show, Ball State Univ Art Mus, 82 & 85; John Gordon Mem Award, 45th Ann Exhib Contemp Am Paintings, 83. *Bibliog:* A Conversation with James Faust (documentary), Indianapolis Art League; Absolut Indiana, Absolut Statehood Campaign, USA Today, 7/23/91. *Media:* Acrylic, Graphite & Prismacolor Pencils. *Publ:* Illusr, The American Story, Sat Evening Post, 75; Sat Evening Post Cover 3/76; Rock & Romance (record album), Faith Band, Village Records, Inc, 78; Arts Indiana (magazine cover), 6/88. *Dealer:* Martha S Faust 8457 Union Chapel Rd Indianapolis IN 46240. *Mailing Add:* 8457 Union Chapel Rd Indianapolis IN 46240-4331

FAVRO, MURRAY
SCULPTOR
b Huntsville, Ont, Dec 24, 1940. *Study:* H B Beal Tech Sch, London, Ont, 58-64. *Work:* Art Gallery Ont, Toronto; Nat Gallery Can, Ottawa, Ont; Can Coun Art Bank, Ottawa, Ont. *Comn:* Sculpture, Ministry Transport Bldg, Cornwall, Ont, 78. *Exhib:* Solo shows, Carmen Lamanna Gallery, 68, 71-73, 76, 77, 80, 82 & 83; Musee d'Art Mod Ville, Paris, 73; Mt Allison Univ & Rutgers Univ Art Gallery, 75; Changing Visions: The Canadian Landscape (with catalog, travelling show), Europe, 80; London Art Gallery, Ont, 76; Ten Canadian Artists in the 1970's (with catalog, traveling exhib), Europe, 76; A Retrospective, Art Gallery Ont, 83; Outdoor Sculpture Exhib, Quebec City, 84; 49th Parallel, NY, 86; Havana, Cuba, 89; McKenzie Gallery, Saskatoon, Sask, 91; Obscure Gallery, Quebec City, Que, 92. *Awards:* Can Coun Grants, 68-72; Can Coun Senior Grant, 74, 78, 80 & 83. *Bibliog:* France Morin (auth), Icarus: The Vision of Angels, 86. *Mem:* Can Artists Representation; Royal Canadian Acad. *Publ:* Auth, Heart of London, Ottawa, 68; Biographical Information About the Influences on My Work, 71, Windmill Electric Generator, 75 & The Flying Flea and Henri Mignet Its Designer, 77, Carmen Lamanna Gallery, Toronto. *Mailing Add:* 783 Queens Ave London ON N5W 3H7 Canada

FAY, MING G
SCULPTOR, EDUCATOR
b 1943. *Study:* Columbus Coll Art & Design, dipl, 65; Kansas City Art Inst, BFA, 67; Univ Calif, Santa Barbara, MFA, 70. *Work:* Columbus Art Mus, Ohio; Hong Kong Mus Art; Sidney Lewis Found, Va; Mobile Hq, NY; Justice Ctr, Philadelphia; Teipei Mus Art, China; Economic Development Corp, NY; Dept Transportation & Pub Works, Puerto Rico, 2003; City of Chicago, O'Hara Int Airport, 2010. *Comn:* Conrad Hilton, Hong Kong, 90. *Exhib:* Solo exhib, Keen Gallery, NY, 93, Alisan Fine Arts Ltd, Hong Kong, 94, Butters Gallery, Portland, Ore, 94, Kim Foster Gallery, NY, 94 & 96, Broadway Windows, NY, 96 & Stone Quarry Hill Art Park, Cazenovia, NY 97, Alisan Fine Arts, Hong Kong, 2002, Montalvo Gallery, Calif, 2004, Ramapo Coll, NJ, 2005, Two Times Thirteen Gallery, Ne w york, 2006, Eight Mod Gallery, NMex, 2008, Gallery 456, New York, 2010, Leslie Heller Workspace, New York, 2010; Elusive Source, Corcoran Gallery Art, Washington, DC, 95; Feast for the Eyes (with catalog), John Michael Kohler Art Ctr, Sheboygan Arts Found, Wis, 96; Lings, Bulova Corp Ctr, Queens Mus Art, NY, 97; Biennial Exhib Pub Art, Neuberger Mus Art, State Univ NY, Purchase, 97; Ancient Emblems, Contemp Signifiers, Jersey City Mus, NJ, 97; Gardens of Urban Delight: The Lower East Side, Henry Street Settlement Art Ctr, NY, 97; Garden of Quin, Whitney Mus at Phillip Morris, NY, 98; Paper: The State of Connection, Bergstrom Mahler Mus, Neenah, Wis, 98; Sculpture Leedy Voulkos Art Ctr Gallery, Kansas City, Mo, 98; Contemp Art Ctr Va, 2001; Katonah Mus Art, New York, 2003; Laumeier Sculpture Park, St Louis, Mo, 2005; Laumeier Sculpture Park, St Louis, Mo, 2005; Leslie Heller Gallery, New York, 2007; Hong Kong Mus Art, 2008; China Square Gallery, 2009; Mus Chinese in Am, New York, 2009; Hillwood Art Mus, 2010. *Pos:* Adv bd, Asian Am Art Ctr, NY, 88-92; artist adv bd, New Mus, NY, 89-92; bd, Alternative Mus, NY, 91 & Chinese Am Arts Coun, NY, 92. *Teaching:* Inst, Chinese Univ Hong Kong, 68-69; Columbus Col Art and Design, Ohio, 70-71; Univ Pittsburgh, Pa, 71-74; Hong Kong Polytechnic, Hong Kong, 75; Pratt Inst, Brooklyn, New York, 78-80; Semester at Sea, UCIS, Univ Pittsburgh, 82; William Paterson Univ, Wayne, NJ, 83-99. *Awards:* Per Cent for Art, Criminal Justice Ctr, 93; New York Experimental Glass Workshop, Vis Artist Residency, 94; Mid-Atlantic Arts Found, Visual Residency Prog, Rutgers Ctr Printmaking, 94. *Bibliog:* Kathleen Finley Magnan (auth), The alchemist of spirits, Asian Art News, 7-8/94; Fay Hirsch (auth), Ming Fay - A Feast for the Eyes, John Michael Kohler Arts Ctr, 96; John Yau (auth), The Garden of Earthly Delights, The Work of Ming Fay, Whitney Mus Am at Philip Morris, NY, 98; Brook Barrie (auth), Contemporary Outdoors Sculpture, Rockport Pub, 99; A Wonderful Garden, All Art Mag, March 2007; Jonathan Goodman (auth), Ming Fay & Chihung Yang at 2x13, Art in Am, 2007. *Mem:* Epoxy Art Group. *Media:* Mixed Media; Metal. *Res:* fantasy gardens. *Dealer:* Butters Gallery Portland OR. *Mailing Add:* Power Art Ctr 25 Power Ave Wayne NJ 07470

FEAR, DANIEL E
CONSULTANT, EDITOR
b Tacoma, Wash, Mar 28, 1949. *Pos:* Dir & pres, The Silver Image Gallery Inc, 73-93; dir, Art Support, 96-. *Mem:* Founding mem Asn Int Photog Art Dealers Inc. *Media:* Photography. *Publ:* Ed, Northwest Photographer's Resource Guide, 90; Creating a Successful Career in Photography, 92; Creating a Successful Career in Visual Art, 97. *Mailing Add:* Art Support 1619 E Wright Ave Tacoma WA 98404

FEATHERSTONE, DAVID BYRUM
CRITIC, CURATOR
b Iowa City, Iowa, Jan 23, 1945. *Study:* Univ Calif, Berkeley, AB, 67; Univ Ore, Eugene, MA, 71. *Exhib:* Celebrations, Hayden Gallery, Mass Inst Technol, Cambridge, 74; Northwest Invitational, Seattle Art Mus, Wash, 75; Attitudes: Photog in 70's, Mus Art, Santa Barbara, Calif, 80. *Collection Arranged:* Bernard Freemesser, A Retrospective Exhib, 78; Photographs by Vilem Kriz (auth, catalog), 79; The Diana Show, Pictures Through A Plastic Lens (auth, catalog), 80; Aerial Photographs by William Garnett, 80; Photographs by Marsha Burns (auth, catalog), 81; Mount St Helens, the Photographer's Response, 83; Point Lobos: Place as Icon, 84; The Painted Image: Applied Color in Photography, 85; Edward Weston: A Mature Vision, 86; Holly Roberts - Painted Photographs (auth, catalog), 90; Yosemite: A Lifetime, Photographs by Ansel Adams, 90; Reagan Louie, Photographs of China 1980-1190, 91; This Is The Am Earth, 92. *Pos:* Cur photog, Historical Photog Collection, Univ Ore Libr, Eugene, 74-76; exec assoc, The Friends Photog, Carmel, Calif, 77-87, dir publs, 87-91; independent cur & ed, 1991-2000; mus grant writer (contract), 2000-. *Awards:* Residency Fel, Wurlitzer Found, Taos, NMex, 82. *Mem:* Am Asn Mus. *Res:* Contemporary photography. *Publ:* Auth, Doris Ulmann: American Portraits, Univ NMex Press, 85; Photographs of Mother Teresa's Mission's of Charity in Calcutta, Friends of Photog, 85; ed, Close to Home, Seven Documentary Photographers, 89 & Of Time and Place: Walker Evans and William Christenberry, 90, Friends of Photography; Holly Roberts, Photographs, Friends of Photography, 90. *Mailing Add:* 4317 21st St Apt 4 San Francisco CA 94114-2753

FEBLAND, HARRIET
SCULPTOR, PAINTER
b New York, NY. *Study:* Pratt Inst; New York Univ; Art Students League; Am Artists Sch; Atelier 17, Paris. *Work:* Westchester Co Courthouse, Civic Plaza, White Plains, NY; Cincinnati Art Mus, Ohio; Emily Lowe Mus, Coral Gables, Fla; Jane Voorhees Zimmerli Art Mus, Rutgers Univ, NJ; Hempstead Bank Long Island Collection Am Art; Pepsico Corp, Somers, NY; State Univ NY, Potsdam, NY; Hudson River Mus, Yonkers, NY; State Hawaii Arts & Cult Found, Hilo, Art in Pub Places Collection;

Gibson Mus, Potsdam, NY; Grounds for Sculpture Mus, Hamilton, NJ; Libr Cong, DC; Tweed Art Mus, Univ Minn, Minn; Agnes K Harverly Found, St Augustine; Mercy Coll, Dobbs Ferry, NY; New Sch Art Ctr, New York; John Kluge Coll Am ARt, Metromedia, Los Angeles, Calif; Seward Johnson Center for the Arts; Lessedra Gallery, Sofia, Bulgaria; Prahova Co Art Mus, Romania; Henry Ford Hosp, Detroit, Mich; Horace Mann Sch, NY. *Comn:* Sculpture, Haverly Collection, New York; sculpture, comn by Hon & Mrs Irwin Davidson collection, New Rochelle, NY; Metromedia HQ, Los Angeles. *Exhib:* Retrospectives, Hudson River Mus, NY, 63, Silvermine Guild, Conn, 73, Bridge Gallery, Munic Art Ctr, White Plains, NY, 76, Brainerd Art Gallery, State Univ NY, 86, Va Ctr Creative Arts, Camp Gallery, Va, 91 & Berkeley Coll Gallery, New York, 2006; Solo Exhibs: Katonah Gallery, 70 & 80, Vincent Price Gallery, Chicago, 71, Rutgers Univ Gallery, NJ, 75, Va Ctr Creative Arts, 91, Contemp Illusr Gallery, 98, Janer 81 Gallery, 98, Nat Space Soc, Houston, 99, UAHC Galleries, 2000, Donnell Libr Ctr, New York, 2003, Interchurch Ctr Galleries, NJ, 2004, Berkeley Coll Gallery, New York, 2006 & Just Sculpture, Nat Asn Women Artists Gallery, New York, 2007, Intercurch Ctr Galleries, New York, 2010, Narimal Assn Women Artists, NY, 2013; Group Exhibs: Cincinnati Art Mus, 68, Mus d'Art Mod, Paris, 70, Alwin Gallery, London, 70, Hudson River Mus, 70-83, Woman Choose Women, NY Cult Ctr, 73, Potsdam Plastics, State Univ NY, 74 & Carnegie Inst, Pittsburgh, Pa; Krasdale Gallery, White Plains, NY, 97-98; Zimmerli Art Mus, New Brunswick, NJ, 98, 2009; Univ Hawaii, Hilo; Sarah Lawrence Coll Gallery, 2000; Jamison-Carnegie Heritage Mus, Talladega, Ala, 2001; Hunterdon Mus Art, Clinton, NJ, 2002; UN Gallery, New York, 2002; Grounds for Sculpture Mus, Hamilton, NJ, 2002; Stephen Gang Gallery, New York, 2002; Binney and Smith Gallery, Banana Factory, Bethlehem, Pa, 2002; Univ Wis, Kenosha, 2003; Heuser Art Ctr, Bradley Univ, Peoria, Ill, 2003; Valdosta Fine Arts Gallery, Valdosta State Univ, Ga, 2003; Springfield Art Mus, Mo, 2003; Univ Nebr, Lincoln, 2004; Poughkeepsie Art Mus, Poughkeepsie, NY, 2004; Grounds for Sculpture Mus, Hamilton, NJ, 2005; New Arts Prog, Invitational Salon Exhib Small Works, Lehigh Valley & Berks, Pa, 2006-2007; Nat Asn Women Artists (NAWA), 117th Ann Exhib, Goggle Works Ctr Arts, Reading, Pa, 2006; Personal Landscapes, Longview Mus Fine Arts, Tex, 2007, SAGA 74th Ann Mem Show, The Old Printshop, New York, 2007, Summertime Concepts, Berkeley Coll Gallery, White Plains, NY, 2007, Contrasts: Action Inaction, Venezeula Consulate Gallery, New York, 2007 & Am Soc Contemp Artists 89th Ann, Broome St Gallery, New York, 2007; ASCA, Manhatten Borough Pres Gallery, NYC, 2007, 2008; New Arts Invitational, 2008; NY Hall of Science Mus, 2008; Purdue Univ Gallery, 2008; Saga, Ormond Mem Art Mus, Fla, 2008; John Cotton Dana Gallery, Rutgers Univ, Newark, NJ, 2008; Art Link Gallery, Ft Wayne, Ind, 2008; Google Works Ctr Arts, Reading Pa, 2008; Visual Art Ctr NJ, Summit, NJ, 2009; Roland Gibson Mus, State Univ NY, Potsdam, NY, 2009; NAWA, Salmagundi Club, New York, 2009; New Arts Prog, Kutztown, Pa, 2009; UBS Gallery, New York, 2009; Grounds for Sculpture Mus, 2010; Boxheart Gallery, Pittsburgh, 2010; Phillippine Ctr, New York, 2010; Synagogue for the Arts, ASCA, 2010; Perth Amboy Gallery, NJ, 2010; New Arts Prog, Lehigh Valley, Pa, 2010; Lessedra Gallery, Sofia Bulgaria, 2010; Howland Cult Ctr, Beacon, NY, 2010; SAGA, Prince St Gallery, NY, 2011; NAWA, Sylvia Wald and Po Kim Gallery, NY, 2011; Ebo Gallery, SAGA, Millwood, NY, 2011; New Arts Program, Kutztown, Pa, 2011; ASCA Ann, NY, 2011; Small Wonders, Maryland Fed Art, Md, 2011; Prints USA, Springfield Art Mus, MO, 2011; Berkely Coll Gallery, Brooklyn, NY, 2011; Noho Gallery, NY, 2011; Iosif Iser, Internat Contemporary Engraving Biennial, Romania, 2011; World Art Print, Lessedra Gallery, Bulgaria Art, 2012; Phyllis Lucas Gallery, NY, 2012; Old Print Ctr, NY, 2012; Betty Baker Gallery, Carriage Barn Arts Ctr, New Canaan, Conn, 2012; Eye of the Beholder, Md Fed Art, 2012; Soc American Graphic Artists, 2012; New Arts Program, Small Works, 2012; NAWA, Sylvia Walk and Pokim Gallery, NY, 2012; NAWA Gallery, 2013; Highline Loft Gallery, ASCA, 2013; New Sch Social Rsch, Anna Marie and Stephen Keller Gallery, 2013; Soc American Graphic Artists, SAGA, Delind Gallery of Arts, Milwaukee, 2013; NAWA 124th Annual, Sylvia Wald & Pokim Gallery, 2013; Phyllis Lucas Gallery, NY, 2013. *Pos:* Dir, Harriet FeBland Art Workshop (painting), 62-93, Chelsea Sch Art, London Univ, summer 85; artist-in-residence (printmaking), State Univ NY, Potsdam, 86; Bennington Coll, 88 & Santa Fe NMex, 93. *Teaching:* Instr & lectr, New York Univ, 60-62; instr & dir, Harriet FeBland Art Workshop, 62-93, Pelham Art Ctr, New York, 83-95; instr, Westchester Art Workshop, White Plains, 65-72 & Chelsea Sch Art, London Univ, 85. *Awards:* fel, Va Ctr Creative Arts, 83 & 87; Andrew Nelson Whitehead Award, Am Soc Contemp Artists, 85, 87, 89, 93-94, 96-97 & 99-2007; Agnes K Haverly Found, Award Video for TV, 86, Publ full color 16 page brochure,re released DVD of 86 TV film, 2009; Elizabeth Morse Genius Found Award, Nat Asn Women Arist, 86-98; fel, Tyrone Guthrie Ctr, Ireland, 87; fel, Woodstock Sch Art, NY, 89; Gretchen Richardson Freelander Mem Award, 97; Robert Conover Award, Soc Am Graphic Artists, 99; The Donald Pierce Mem Award for Sculpture, ASCA 87th Annual, 2005; The Joseph Lubrano Memorial Award, ASCA 89th Annual, 2007; Purchase Award, Lessedra Gallery, 2011; Renaissance Graphic Award, So Amer Graphic Artists, 2011. *Bibliog:* Newman (auth), Plastics as sculpture, 74 & Plastics as an art form, Chilton; Dona Meilach (auth), Collage and Assemblage, Doubleday, 75; Harriet FeBland (film), AK Haverly Found, 86; Charlotte S Rubinstein (auth), Women in Am Sculpture; World of Best Art, Sorrell Publishing co, 2007; Impressions in Continuity, Sorrell Publishing co, 2007; and others; Int Contemp Artists, 2010. *Mem:* NY Artists Equity Asn (vpres, 70-76, pres, 89-90, chmn & prog dir); Int Art Asn UNESCO, United Nations (secy, 80-82); Am Soc Contemp Artists (pres, 81-83, 2005-2007, pres emer, 83-current, ed 2003, hon chmn exec board comt, 2008-2009); Nat Asn of Women Artists; Soc Am Graphic Artists; Womens Inst Art; and others; ABI Int Women's Rev bd (found mem). *Media:* Plastic, Wood, Acrylic. *Specialty:* Paintings, Sculpture, Prints. *Interests:* Space, sci & astronomy. *Publ:* Encyclopedia of Polymer Science, 69-; and many others (35 bks). *Dealer:* Phyllis Lucas Gallery NY. *Mailing Add:* 245 E 63rd St Apt 1803 New York NY 10065

FECHTER, CLAUDIA ZIESER
CURATOR, WRITER

b New York, NY, Mar 14, 1931. *Study:* Case Western Reserve, AB, 52; Columbia, MA, 54. *Collection Arranged:* The Loom and the Cloth, Fabrics of Jewish Life (catalog), Temple Mus, 88; Sacred Landmarks, Cleveland State Univ Gallery, 90; For Everything a Season, Cleveland State Univ, 02. *Pos:* Dir, Temple Mus, 84-97; cur, Cleveland State Univ, 97-. *Awards:* Northern Ohio Live - Cult Exhibs, 01. *Mem:* Coun Am Jewish Mus (steering comt); Northeast Ohio Mus Coun. *Res:* Judaic ritual fabrics. *Interests:* Judaica and antiquities of the Holy Land region. *Publ:* Auth, The Loom and the Cloth, Temple Mus, 88; Custom, costume & ceremonial cloth, Creative Needle, 9/88; The fabric of Jewish Life, Vol XVIII, No 1, Coun Am Embroiderers, 2/89; From Generation to Generation: Fabrics of Jewish Life, 88; For Everything a Season, 2000. *Mailing Add:* 2541 Richmond Rd Cleveland OH 44122

FEDER, BEN
DESIGNER, PAINTER

b New York, NY, Feb 1, 1923. *Study:* Parsons Sch Design; Vet Ctr, Mus Mod Art, with Prestopino. *Exhib:* Stamford Mus Art, Conn, 60; Bodley Gallery, NY, 64; Inst Allende, San Miguel Allende, Mex. *Pos:* Designer & graphic arts consult, New Bk Knowledge, Grolier Inc; pres, Ben Feder Inc, NY; owner & design consultant, Clinton Vineyards Dutchess Co, NY. *Mem:* Am Soc Enologists. *Media:* Gouache, Acrylic. *Mailing Add:* 65 E 76th St Apt 9E New York NY 10021

FEDER, PENNY JOY
PRINTMAKER, ILLUSTRATOR

b New York, NY, Oct 13, 1949. *Study:* CW Post Col, Long Island Univ, Brookville, NY, with James Lewicki & Harry Hohen, BA (art educ), 71 & with Arthur Leipsig & Alfred van Loen, MA (printmaking), 75; Brooklyn Mus Art Sch, printmaking, 72. *Work:* Nynex Corp; Cunard Lines Int; Holland Am Shipping Lines Int; Nat Mus Am Art; Nat Mus Art, Smithsonian Inst. *Comn:* Catalog cover & poster design, Wash Sq Outdoor Art Exhib, NY, 75; woodcut, Collectors Guild, NY, 76; woodcut, Calhoun's Collectors Soc, Minneapolis, 81. *Exhib:* Ann, Audubon Artists Soc, Inst Arts & Letts, 80; Nat Acad Design, 81; Knickerbocker Artists, Nat Arts Club, NY, 81; Brooklyn Mus, 85; Fed Plaza, NY, 86; Lever House Gallery, NY, 96; James Beard Gallery, NY, 96. *Teaching:* Lectr-demonstr, Suffolk Co Sch System, NY, 70 & Salmagundi Club, New York, 79; and at various other art groups in NY. *Awards:* John Taylor Arms Award, Audubon Artists 39th Ann, 81; Knickerbocker Award, 32nd Knickerbocker Artists Ann, 83; Gold Medal, Salmagundi Club, 83. *Bibliog:* Jeanne Paris (auth), Diaries of creativity & Malcolm Preston (auth), Flourishing symbiosis, Newsday Newspaper, Long Island, NY, 2/77. *Mem:* Philadelphia Print Club; Audubon Artists Soc. *Media:* Woodcuts, Etchings. *Publ:* Auth, Original Printmakers, Art Expo Preview Mag, 1-2/93; article in Art Business News; article in Decor Mag. *Mailing Add:* 80-90 Dumfries Pl Jamaica NY 11432

FEDERHEN, DEBORAH ANNE
CURATOR, HISTORIAN

b Shirley, Mass, June 19, 1954. *Study:* Coll William & Mary, BA (art hist), 76; Univ Mo-Columbia, MA (art hist), 81; Univ Del, MA (Am cult, Lois F McNeil Fel), 85. *Collection Arranged:* Accumulation & Display: Mass Marketing Household Goods in Am, 1880-1920 (coauth, bk), Winterthur Mus, 86; Classical Taste in Am, 1800-1840, Baltimore Mus Art, 93; Extinct Specie: Money in Maine from Colony to Capitalism, York Inst Mus, 93; Garden of the East: Life in Maine - 1604-1713, York Inst Mus, 94; Memory is a Painter: The Art of Grandma Moses (traveling exhib), Richard Nixon Libr, Calif, Gerald Ford Mus & Libr, Mich, New Britain Mus Am Art, Conn, Newport Art Mus, RI, Soc Four Arts, Fla & LB Johnson Libr, Tex, 98-99. *Pos:* Cur, Soc Preserv Long Island Antiquities, Setauket, NY, 87-88; res assoc, Baltimore Mus Art, 88-91; cur, York Inst Mus, Saco, Maine, 92-96; cur collections, Bennington Mus, Vt, 96-99. *Teaching:* Instr decorative arts, Winterthur Mus, Del, 85-87. *Awards:* McCormick Scholarship, Victorian Soc, 82; Nat Mus Act Internship, Yale Univ Art Gallery, 82-83. *Mem:* Soc Winterthur Fels; Decorative Arts Soc. *Res:* American Decorative arts and material culture; specializing in furniture; silver, quilts and ceramics. *Publ:* Coauth, Paul Revere - Artisan, Businessman & Patriot, Paul Revere Mem Asn, 88; contribr, Decorative Arts & Household Furnishings in America, 1650-1920: An Annotated Bibliography, (book), Winterthur Mus, 89; Politics & furniture: The patrons & products of Jonathan Gostelowe & Thomas Affleck, Winterthur Mus, 94; coauth, Colonial Massachusetts Silversmiths: A Biographical Dictionary, Yale Art Gallery, 98; co-auth (with Ellen Denker), The Bennington Porian Project: An analytical reevaluation of the Bennington Museum Collection, Antiques Arts Weekly, 10/23/98. *Mailing Add:* Bennington Mus W Main St Bennington VT 05201

FEDERICO, FRANK
PAINTER

b New Orleans, LA, July 3, 1928. *Study:* Southwest LA Inst; New Orleans Acad of Art; John McCrady Art School. *Work:* John Hopkins Univ; Gulf Oil Corp; IBM; Hart Develop Corp. *Comn:* New Orleans Vista, YWCA, New Orleans, LA, 1964; Scenes of Yesteryear, Gortons Seafood, Gloucester, Mass, 1973; Transcendence, Univ of Conn, 1994. *Exhib:* Solo exhibs, Club House Gallery, Conn. *Pos:* Pres, Kent Art Asn, Kent, Conn, 1990-1992; pres, CT Pastel Soc, 1998-2000. *Teaching:* Instr watercolor, oils, figure, Fl Gulf Coast Art Ctr, Clearwater, 1976-1980; instr, W Hartford Art League, W Hartford, Conn, 1985-2006; instr pastel, many local & abroad workshops. *Awards:* Nat Watercolor Soc Open Juried (2nd prize), Best in Show, PSA Ann, Hahnemuhle Co, 2000; CPS Renaissance, JR Reeves, 2002. *Bibliog:* Colin Fry (auth), Make Color Work for You, Am Artist Mag, 2004. *Mem:* Pastel Soc Am (master pastelist); Int Asn Pastel Painters (master circle); Allied Artists Am (signature); Nat Watercolor Soc (signature); Am Watercolor Soc (mem); Nat Acrylic & Casein (signature); New England Watercolor Soc (signature mem). *Media:* Watercolor, oil, acrylic, pastel. *Res:* Conduct painting workshops locally & abroad. *Interests:* Art interest is having a cognizance of the world I live in. *Publ:* Ed, U Conn Mural Marks Change, Hartford

Courant, 1992; ed, Profile of an Artist, Litchfield Living, 1994; auth, A Workshop Experience; A Colorist Approach to Pastel, Pastel J, 1999; auth, Plein Air Painting, Pastel Soc Am, 2000. *Dealer:* The Gallery 309 Primrose Rd Burlingame CA 94010. *Mailing Add:* PO Box 363 Goshen CT 06756

FEENEY, BRENDAN BEN
EDUCATOR, VISUAL ARTIST
b 1967. *Study:* Boston Coll; Emerson Coll; Tufts Univ; master classes, Fine Arts Work Ctr, Provincetown, Mass, Boston Univ, Castle Hill Ctr Arts, MassArt, Boston. *Work:* Provincetown Art Asn Mus, Mass. *Exhib:* Provincetown Art Asn Mus, Cape Cod; 40th Ann Retrospective Show, Mass Coll Art. *Pos:* bd mem, Mus Fine Arts, Boston Educ Adv Bd. *Mem:* Provincetown Art Asn Mus, Mass

FEHER, TONY
ARTIST
b Albuquerque, 1956. *Exhib:* Solo exhibs include Wooster Gardens, NY, 93, Gramercy Int, NY, 94, Acme, Santa Monica, Calif, 95, New Mus Contemp Art, NY, 96, Zilkha Gallery, Wesleyan Col, Conn, 97, Richard Telles Fine Art, LA, 98, Numark Gallery, Washington, DC, 99, Anthony Meier Fine Arts, San Francisco, Calif, 2000, Red Room and More, Ctr Curatorial Studies, Bard Coll, NY, Univ Calif, LA Hammer Mus, 2001, Maybe/Enjoy, Worcester Art Mus, Mass, 2002, I'm Tired of Toast, Univ Calif Berkeley Art Mus, 2002; group exhibs include Foundation Show, Art Mus, Southern Tex, Corpus Christi, 80; Atomic Art, Max Fish, NY City, 89; AIDS/SIDA, Real Art Ways, Hartford, Conn, 90; Gulliver's Travels, Gallerie Sophia Ungers, Koln, Ger, 91; Queer Show, Minor Injury, Brooklyn, NY, 91; The Auto-Erotic Object, Hunter Col, NY City, 92; Art Around the Park, Tompkins Square Park, NY City, 93; Gramercy Int, NY, 94; Inaugural Exhib, Paul Morris Gallery, 95; Simple Matter, Numark Gallery, Washington, DC, 98; Beyond Minimalism, Koyanagi Gallery, Tokyo, 98; Hindsight, Whitney Mus Am Art, NY, 99; Deja Vu, Art Miami, 2000; New Work, Addison Gallery, Am Art, Andover, Mass, 2001; Leisure Theory, Coleccion Jumex, Mexico City, 2002; Basic Instinct, Mus Contemp Art, Chicago, 2003; Poetic Justice: 8th Int Istanbul Biennial, Turkey, 2003; State of Play, Serpentine Gallery, London, 2004; Nat Acad Mus, NY City, 2006; represented in permanent collections of Addison Gallery Am Art, Andover, Mass, Art Inst Chicago, Baltimore Mus Art, Henry Art Gallery, Seattle, Israel Mus, Jerusalem, La Collection Jumex, Mexico City, Modern Art Mus, Ft Worth, Tex, Mus Fine Arts, Houston, San Francisco Mus Modern Art, Solomon R Guggenheim Mus, NY City, Walker Art Ctr, Whitney Mus Am Art, NY City

FEIGEN, RICHARD L
COLLECTOR, DEALER
b Chicago, Ill, Aug 8, 1930. *Study:* Yale Univ, BA, 52; Harvard Univ, MBA, 54. *Pos:* Chmn & dir, Richard L Feigen & Co, Inc, 57-; trustee, John Jay Homestead, Katonah, NY & Lincoln Univ, Pa, 82-90; dir, Art Dealers Asn Am, 74-78, 86-91 & 97-99, 2001-2004. *Mem:* Life fel Metrop Mus Art; life fel Minneapolis Soc Fine Arts; gov life mem & major benefactor, Art Inst Chicago. *Specialty:* European and American paintings, drawings and sculpture, 1300 to the present. *Collection:* Old Master paintings and drawings; Beckmann, Ernst, Tanguy, Cornell, Dubuffet, Rosenquist. *Publ:* auth, Dubuffet and the Anticulture, 69; contribr, Office Design, 70; auth, George Grosz: Dada Drawings, 72; auth, Tales from the Art Crypt, Knopf, 2000; auth, Tales from the Art Crypt, Alfred A Knofpf, New York, 2000. *Mailing Add:* 34 E 69th St New York NY 10065

FEIGENBAUM, HARRIET
SCULPTOR, ENVIRONMENTAL ARTIST
b Brooklyn, NY, 1939. *Study:* Nat Acad Sch Fine Arts, New York, 59-61; Sch Gen Studies, Columbia Univ, 68-71; study art hist with Howard Hibbard, 73-74. *Work:* Nat Mus Women in Arts, Corcoran Gallery Art, Washington; Herbert F Johnson Mus, Cornell Univ, Ithaca, NY; Andrew Dickson White Mus, Colgate Univ, Hamilton, NY; Hillwood Art Mus, Long Island Univ, Brooksville, NY; Holocaust Mem, Appellate Courthouse, 1st Dept, NY. *Comn:* Willow Rings, Reclamation Proj, 85, The Greenwood Colliery Sundial, 88, Scranton Chamber Com, Pa; Holocaust Mem, Appellate Courthouse, NY, 90; relief sculpture, Dormitory Authority, NY, 94. *Exhib:* Land Structures Built Where the Petroglyphs are Made by Children, Artpark, Lewiston, NY, 77; Women in Am Archit: A Historic & Contemp Perspective, Brooklyn Mus, NY, 77; Dwellings, Inst Contemp Art, Philadelphia, Pa, 78; The Presence of Nature, Whitney Mus Am Art, NY, 78; Dwellings Travels to, Neuberger Mus, Purchase, NY, 79; Art and the Law, Am Bar Asn, traveling US, 87-89; solo exhib, Pa Acad Fine Arts, Philadelphia, 86; Office of the Dead, Wheaton Col, Norton, Mass, 97, Women of Stone, Neuberger Mus, Purchase, NY, 2000-01; Artpark: 1974-1984, Univ Buffalo Art Gallery, Ctr Arts, NY, 2010, 2013; Artpark 40, Lewiston, NY, 2013. *Teaching:* Pratt Inst, 1981-1982. *Awards:* Excellence in Design Award, Art Comn of City New York, 91. *Bibliog:* Lucy Lippard (auth), Architectural complexes in nature, Art in Am, 1-2/79; Michael Brenson (auth), The state of the city as sculptors see it, New York Times, 7/27/90; Joan Marter (auth), Nature redox: Recent reclamation art, Sculpture, 11-12/94; Gilles Tiberghien (auth), Land Art, Editions Carre, Paris, 95; Ann H Murray (auth), Artin America, Harriet Feigenbaum at the Neuberger Mus, 7/2001. *Media:* Stone, Mixed Media. *Collection:* City of NY (Holocaust Mem, Appellate Courthouse, 1st Dept New York City). *Publ:* Auth, The influence of Galileo on Bernini's Saint Mary Magdalen and Saint Jerome, Art Bull, 3/77; Where should land art go?, No 13, 81 & Reclamation art, No 22, 88, Heresies. *Mailing Add:* 49 W 24th St 11th Fl New York NY 10010

FEIN, B(ARBARA) R
EDUCATOR, PAINTER
b Brooklyn, NY, Dec 11, 1941. *Study:* Brooklyn Col, BA, 62; Univ Md, 64-66; City Univ New York, MA, 67, PhD, 69; Univ NH, 70-80. *Work:* NY Pub Libr; Seacoast Regional Coun Ctr, Portsmouth, NH; York Co Coun Ctr, Sanford, Maine; Deaconess Hosp, Boston; Kittery Art Asn, Maine; Harber Home, Maine. *Comn:* Child at a Circus (mural), USN Hosp, Portsmouth, 71. *Exhib:* Copley Soc, Boston, 69-75, Walt Kuhn Mem-Norton Hall Gallery, Cape Neddick, Maine, 69-76; Drawings '71, Minn Mus Art, Minneapolis, 71; 6th Ann Drawing & Small Sculpture Exhib, Del Mar Col, Corpus Christi, Tex, 72; Wadsworth Atheneum, Conn Acad Fine Arts, Hartford, 72; 33rd & 34th Ann Nat Art Exhib, Southern Utah State Col, Cedar City, 73 & 74; Mike Levitan Gallery, NY, 86. *Pos:* PS Gallery, Ogunquit, Maine, 87 & 88. *Teaching:* Guest lectr abstract painting, Univ Maine, Orono, 71; vis lectr drawing, oil painting & watercolor, Univ NH, Durham, 73-87; prof visual studies, NH Vocational Technol Col, Stratham, 82-. *Awards:* Third Place Prof, Manchester Art Asn, NH, 70; First Place Oil-Acrylic & Hon Mixed Media, Newbury Port Art Asn, Mass, 71; Graphics Award, York Art Asn, Maine, 71, 73, 76 & 79. *Mem:* Maine State Art Asn (bd dir, 73-74); Copley Soc; York Art Asn (pres, 88-90). *Media:* Watercolor; Pencil. *Publ:* Illusr, Dora Young's Tatting Manuals, 74 & 75; Single's Circle, 74; MCAT: New Medical Admissions Test, Barnes & Nobles, 81. *Dealer:* Kennedy Gallery New York NY; Fry Gallery York ME. *Mailing Add:* 320 Corporate Dr Portsmouth NH 03801-2887

FEIN, STANLEY
PAINTER, DESIGNER
b Brooklyn, NY, Dec 21, 1919. *Study:* Parsons Sch Design; NY Univ. *Work:* NY Univ Collection; pvt collection Dr Timothy Costello, Pres Adelphi Univ; The Bank of NY Collection; Bank of NY; NY Univ. *Comn:* NY Hist (paintings), 71, Cities of NY (paintings), 72, Historic Interiors (paintings), 78 & Cols of NY (paintings), Bank NY. *Exhib:* Phoenix Gallery, 1963; Nat Acad Design, 2000 & 2001; 55 Mercer Gallery, 2005 & 2006. *Pos:* Art dir, Doremus & Co, formerly; creative dir, Pesin Sydney & Bernard, formerly, Stanley Fein, Advertising, currently. *Teaching:* Instr design & color, Pratt Inst, 56-58. *Awards:* Art Dirs Club NY, 56-65; Wall Street Art Asn, 60; Soc Illusrs, 70 & 71. *Mem:* Fedn of Mod Painters & Sculptors. *Media:* Multimedia

FEINBERG, ELEN
PAINTER
b New York, NY, Jan 22, 1955. *Study:* Cornell Univ, Ithaca, New York, BFA, Class Marshall, 76; Indiana Univ, Bloomington, MFA, 78. *Work:* Los Angeles Co Mus Art; Israel Mus, Jerusalem; Milwaukee Mus, Wis; Univ Calif, Santa Cruz Art Mus; Fresno Art Ctr, Calif; Morgan Guarantee Trust, NY; IBM, Atlanta, Ga; Ariz State Univ Mus, Tempe; Albuquerque Mus, NMex; Roswell Mus, NMex; Anderson Mus Contemp Art, NMex; Washington & Jefferson Coll Art Mus, Pa; corp collections incl Morgan Guarantee Trust, NY, IBM, Atlanta, Ga, Northern Trust Bank, Chicago, Madison Financial Services, Nashville, Houston, Bank of Tex, Houston, Nat Economic Res & Assoc, New York, Pittman & Moore, Chicago, Tex Commerce Bank, Houston, Kaiser-Permanente, Denver, Bass, Berry & Simms, Nashville, Champion Int Corp, Chicago, Shell Oil Company, Houston, Stephen Sprouse & assoc, San Francisco, Art Environments of Chicago, Gullet, Sanford & Robinson, Nashville, The Arbor Group, New York, Chadwick, Saylor & Co Century City, Calif, Skaddenm Arp, DC, and more pub & pvt collections in the US and abroad. *Comn:* Standard & Poore, NY; Delta Airlines, Fla; var pvt collections. *Exhib:* Solo exhibs, Roger Ramsay Gallery, Chicago, 87, Mekler Gallery, Los Angeles, 89, Bill Bace Gallery, NY, 90, Mulvane Art Mus, Topeka, Kans, 93, Locus Gallery, St Louis, Mo, 96 & 98, The X Prize, St Louis Sci Ctr, Mo, 96, Impost Gallery, Albuquerque, NMex, 97, Dist Fine Arts, Washington, DC, 99, Ruth Bachotner Gallery, Los Angeles, Calif, 99 & Sarah Morthland Gallery, NY, 99, Plains Art Mus, 2000, Lost City Arts, NY, 2002, District Fine Arts, Washington, DC, 2003, 05, Chiaroscuro Gallery, Santa Fe, 2004, Scottsdale, Ariz, 2005, Price Dewey Contemp, Santa Fe, NM, 2006, Krasdale Gallery, White Plains, NY, 2008, KFG Gallery, Bronx, NY, 2009; Group exhibs, Gallery A, Chicago, 95; Pleasure, Artemisia Gallery, Chicago, 96; Cedar Rapids Mus Art, Iowa, 96; Inferno, Iowa Cedar Rapids Mus Art, 96; The Smallest Show on Earth, Richard Levy Gallery, Albuquerque, NMex, 97; Locust Gallery, St Louis,Mo, 97 & 99; Albuquerque Mus, NMex, 97; Holter Mus Art, Helena, Mont, 97; Ruth Bachofner Gallery, Santa Monica, Calif, 97 & 98; US Dept of State, Art Embassies Prog, Lilongwe, Malawi, 98; Preview/Review, Byran Cohen Gallery Contemp Art, Kansas City, Mo, 98; District Fine Arts Contemp Art, Washington, DC, 98; Remembering Beauty: Am Landscape, South Bend Regional Mus Art, Ind, 98; Albuquerque/Santa Fe, Cedar Rapids Mus Art, 98; Metaphor Contemp Art, Brooklyn, NY, 2002; Johnson Gallery of Fine Arts Mus, Univ NMex, 2003; Ruth Bachofner Gallery, Santa Monica, Calif, 2004; Gallery 101, Palm Springs, Calif, 2006; Vizivarosi Gallery, Budapest, Hungary, 2007; SCA Gallery, Albuquerque, NMex, 2008; Lost City Arts, New York, 2008; The Starry Messenger: Galileo's Vision and 21st Century Art, La Art & Sci Mus, Baton Rouge, La, 2009; The Inspiration of Astronomical Phenomena, Instituto de Scienze, Lettere ed Arti, Venice, Italy, 2009; Utopia/Dystopia, Bushwick/Storefront Gallery, Brooklyn, NY. *Collection Arranged:* Champion Int Corp, Chicago; Shell Oil Co, Houston; Delta Airlines, Orlando; Arbor Group, NY; Madison Financial Svcs, Nashville; OCI Chemical Corp, Shelton, Conn. *Pos:* guest artist, Tamarind Inst, Albuquerque, NMex, 84 & 89; Regents prof art, Dept Art & Art Hist, Univ NMex, 94-97; rep for NMex, Friends of Art & Preservation in Embassies, 2000; regents prof of Art, presidential teaching fel, Burlington Research Scholar. *Teaching:* Vis assoc prof, Art Wash Univ, 86-87; vis lectr, St James Calvier Ctr for Creativity, Valletta, Malta, 2001, Int Soc Cult Economists, Rotterdame, The Netherlands, 2002, Coll Archit, Art & Planning, Cornell Univ, 97, Herron Sch Art, Indianapolis, 95, Univ Mich, Inst Humanities, 97, Princeton Univ, 99, Vienna Int Sch, 2002, Inst Veneto di Scienze, Lettere ed Arti, Venice, Italy, 2009, Arts Club Wash, Wash DC. *Awards:* Bundeskanzleramt Fed Chancellery Fel in Painting, Vienna, Austria, 98; Fulbright Scholar Award, Ger, 2000; Fulbright Scholars Award, Ger, 2000; Fel in painting, St James Cavalier Ctr for Creativity, Valletta, Malta, 2001; Presdl Tchg Fel, Univ NMex, Albuquerque, 2002; Fel in painting, Hungarian Multicult Ctr, Balfound; Ruth Chenven Found Award in painting, New York, 91; Ingram Merrill Found Award in painting, New York, 89; Nat Endowment for the Arts Fel in Painting, 87; Artist-in-residence, Montalvo Ctr for Arts, Saratoga, Calif, 81 & 82, Hambidge Ctr for Creative Arts & Scis, Rabun Gap, Ga, Roswell Mus & Art Ctr, NMex, 85-86, 93, MacDowell Colony, 86 & Va Ctr for Creative Arts, Sweet Briar, 98. *Bibliog:* B Waterman Peters (auth), New Art Examiner, Chicago, 94; C F Shepley (auth), St Louis Post Dispatch, 96; H Glick (auth), New American Paintings, Open Studio Press, Wellesley, Mass, 97; P Zelinsky (auth), Elen Feinberg,

Arts Magazine, New York, 84; W Peterson (auth), Particular Attractions, Artspace Magazine, Los Angeles, 91; D Adams, Printmaking in New Mexico, Univ New Mexico Press, Albuquerque, 91; P Frank & E Kass (auth), Elen Feinberg, Mekler Gallery, Los Angeles, 88; L Krantz (ed), American Artists: An Illustrated Survey of Leading Contemporaries, Chicago, 91; W Peterson, Artspace Mag, Los Angeles, 91; C Adams, Printmaking in New Mexico, Univ NMex Press, 91; Erwin Wagenhofer, 6 Artists in Vienna, A Moving Forward Movie, Bundeskanzleramt, Austria, 2000; Peter Frank(auth), A Decade of Light, Plains Art Mus, 2000; INSAP VI, Univ Padua, Italy, 2010. *Mem:* Am Asn of Univ Profs. *Media:* Painting. *Publ:* Elen Feinberg, The Independent, Valetta, Malta, 2001; Elen Feinberg, Image and Analog: The Nature of Space, The Inspiration of Astronomical Phenomena: Edition Malta, 2002; Michael Conis (auth), Aa Reinhardt, a monogr, Reaktion Bks, London, 2003; Salvatore Serio (ed), Memorie della Societa Astronomical Italiana, The Architecture of the Ethereal, Inst Editoriali e Poligrafici Int, 122-124, 2004; Central Europe through the Eye of International Artists, Keki Gallery & HMC, Budapest, Hungary, 2007; Albert Feygold (auth), Elen Feinberg, Krasdale Galleries, White Plains, NY, 2008. *Dealer:* Lost City Arts New York NY. *Mailing Add:* 613 Ridge Pl NE Albuquerque NM 87106

FEINBERG, JEAN
PAINTER, EDUCATOR
b New Rochelle, NY, 1948. *Study:* Skidmore Col, BS (Fine Arts), 70; Hunter Col, MA (Painting, MacDowell Colony Fel), 77. *Work:* Best Products Co; IBM Corp; Amerata-Hess Corp; Rich & Tang Investment Banking, Inc; Peat, Marwich, Main & Co; Weatherspoon Art Gallery; Guess Jeans, Inc; and others. *Exhib:* Cadavre Exquis, Drawing Ctr, NY, 93; Remotion, ES Vandam NY, 94; Sculpture Ctr, Benefit, NY, 94; solo shows, Rosa Esman Gallery, NY, 81, 84, John Davis Gallery, Akron, Ohio & NY, 84, 85, 87, Stux Gallery, 94 & Beth Urdang Gallery, Boston, 94, John Davis Gallery, Hudson, NY, 2008; 10th Anniversary Celebration, Beth Urdang Gallery, Boston, 99; Materializing, Fashion Inst Tech, NY, 99; Yaddo Benefit, NY, 2002; Works on Paper, Fashion Inst Tech Art and Design Faculty, Mus at Fashion Inst Tech, NY, 2002; Finely Drawn: A Recent Gift of Contemp Drawings, Weatherspoon Art Gallery, Greensboro, NC, 2002; Beth Urdang Gallery, Boston, Mass, 2007; 183rd Ann: An Invitational Exhib of Contemp Am Art, Nat Acad Art, New York, 2008; and others. *Teaching:* Adj fac, Parsons Sch Design, 80-99, Fashion Inst Technol, 85-; artist-in-residence, MFA Prog, Bard Col, 84-94; vis lectr, artist RI Sch Design, Princeton Univ, Art Inst Chicago, Univ RI, Brown Univ, Kent State Univ, Syracuse Univ, Pratt Inst, Sch Visual Arts, SUNY, Fredonia, 81-97; asst prof fine art, Fashion Inst Tech, 2006-. *Awards:* Nat Endowment Arts, 78, 83 & 89; Edward Albee Found Residence, 79 & 95; Yaddo Fel, 97. *Bibliog:* Barry Schwabsky (auth), Jean Feinberg at John Davis, Arts Mag, 5/87; John Yau (auth), Jean Feinberg, Victoria Munroe Gallery, Artforum, 3/90; Vivien Raynor (auth), For a Sophisticated Audience, NY Times, 9/27/92; Jeanette Fintz (auth), Departures, Arrivals, Pit Stops- Three Artists at ADD Gallery, The Artful Mind, 1-2/03; D. Dominick Lombardi (auth), Keeping It Simple, in Color and Form, NY Times, 2/16/03; Cate McQuaid (auth), Brushstrokes Loaded with Intent, Boston Globe, 3/8/2007; and others. *Media:* Oil, Mixed Media. *Publ:* Heresies Mag, winter 78; 54 Pages, New York, 78; Roof X, A Quarterly Journal of Poetry, summer 79. *Mailing Add:* 10 Leonard St New York NY 10013-2962

FEINBERG, LARRY J
MUSEUM DIRECTOR, CURATOR
b Jan 1, 1955. *Study:* Northwestern Univ, BA (with distinction; Phi Beta Kappa), MBA; Harvard Univ, MA, PhD. *Exhib:* Girodet: Romantic Rebel; The Medici Michelangelo and the Art of Late Renaissance Florence; Gustave Moreau: Between Epic and Dream. *Pos:* Cur, Allen Mus Art, Oberlin Coll, Ohio, Frick Collection, New York & Nat Gallery Art, Washington, formerly; with Art Inst Chicago, 1991-2007, Patrick G & Shirley W Ryan cur, 1997-2007; bd dirs, Art Resources in Teaching, Chicago, 1998-2000, chmn, 2000-06; asst to UN under-secy-gen Olara Otunnu, 2004, 2005; exec dir, Santa Barbara Mus Art, Calif, 2008-. *Mem:* Old Masters Soc; Phi Beta Kappa; Asn Art Mus Dir; Art Resources in Teaching (bd chmn 99-2005). *Publ:* auth, The Young Leonardo: Art and Life in Fifteenth-Century Florence (book), Cambridge Univ Press, 2011. *Mailing Add:* Santa Barbara Mus Art 1130 State St Santa Barbara CA 93101

FEINGOLD, KEN
ARTIST
Study: Studied, Antioch Col, 70—76; Studied, Calif Instit of Arts. *Work:* One-man shows incl Whitney Mus, 79, exhibs incl Signs, The New Mus Contemp Art, 85, Contemp Art in Context, Mus Mod Art, 88, Between Word and Image, 93, 2002 Biennial Exhib, Whitney Mus Am Art, 2002, Art, Lies, and Videotape: Exposing Performance, Tate Liverpool, 2004, digital works, Subject with Four Footnotes, 1975, Jimmy Charlie Jimmy, 1992, Eros and Thanatos at Sea, 2004; auth: New Screen Media: Cinema/Art/Narrative, 2002. *Exhib:* Solo exhibs incl Whitney Mus, 79; Exhibs incl Signs, The New Mus Contemp Art, 85; Contemp Art in Context, Mus Art, 88; Between Word and Image, 93, 2002; Biennial Exhib, Whitney Mus, Am Art, 2002; Art, Lies and Videotape: Exposing Performance, Tate Liverpool, 2004; digital works, Subject with Four Footnotes, 75; Jimmy Charlie Jimmy, 92; Eros and Thanatos at Sea, 2004; auth: New Screen Media: Cinema/Art/Narrative, 2002; Recipient Bonn Videonalle, Videonale-Preis, 92; fel Guggenheim Mem Found, 2004; grantee NEA, 79, NY Found for Arts, 88, Rockefeller Found; Media Arts fel, 2003. *Pos:* Assoc prof fine arts Minneapolis Col Art & Design, 77-85; adj assoc prof, Princeton Univ, Visual Arts Prog 89-94, Cooper Union Sch of Arts, 1993-94; prof computer art Sch Visual Arts, NY, 1993-98; Vis artist Bard Col, 2001; guest fac The Royal Univ Col Fine Arts, Stockholm, 2002; Adj assoc prof Princeton Univ; Visual Arts Prog, 89-94; Cooper Union Sch of Arts, 93-94; prof computer art sch; Visual Arts NYC, 93-98; Vis Arts Bard Col, 2001; guest fac, The Royal Univ Col Fine Arts, Stockholm, 2002. *Awards:* Recipient Bonn Videonalle, Videonale-Preis, 1992; fel Guggenheim Mem Found, 2004; grantee Nat Educ Assoc, 79, NY Found for Arts, 88, Rockefeller Found Media Arts Fel, 2003

FEINMAN, STEPHEN E
DEALER, PUBLISHER
b New York, NY, Sept 29, 1932. *Collection Arranged:* Cur, Andre Masson, Johnny Friedlander, Miljenko Bengez, Felix Sherman, Nick Kosciuk. *Pos:* Pres, Gary Arts Ltd, 65-72, Multiple Impressions Ltd, 72-93, S E Feinman Fine Arts Ltd, 93- & GSL Arts Corp, 2004. *Mem:* Fine Arts Retail Trade Syst; Panther Org. *Specialty:* Twentieth Century European and American prints, drawings and paintings. *Collection:* Andre Masson, Johnny Friedlander. *Mailing Add:* 1169 Plymouth Ct #412 Chicago IL 60605

FEINSTEIN, ROCHELLE H
PAINTER, PRINTMAKER
Study: Pratt Inst, BFA, 75; Univ Minn, MFA, 78. *Work:* Mus Mod Art, NY; Libr Cong, Washington, DC. *Exhib:* Solo exhibs include Emily Sorkin Gallery, 87, 89, David Beitzel Gallery, 93, Max Protetch Gallery, NY, 94, Paintings, Halsey Gallery, Charleston, NC, 95, Copycats, BillMaynes Gallery, NY, 96, The Wonderfuls, Jersey City Mus, NJ, 96, Men, Women and Children, Max Protetch Gallery, 96, Pictures, Ten in One Gallery, NY, 2002; group exhibs include Exit Art, NY, 86; To Make the Visible Seen, Studio Sch, NY, 87; The Debate on Abstraction: The Persistance of Painting, Hunter Col, NY, 89; The Painting Project, 91; Abstraction, Schmidt Contemp, St Louis, 92; Works on Paper/Faculty, Yale Univ Sch Art, 95; Just What Do You Think You're Doing, Dave? Williamsburg Art & Historical Soc, NY, 97; The Drawing File, Pieroji, 2000; The Gasworks, London, 97; Conversation, Art Resources Transfer, NY, 99; Liste Art Fair, Basel, Switzerland, 2002; A More Perfect Union, Max Fish, NY, 2004; Nat Acad Mus, NY City, 2006. *Pos:* Pub Arts Proj, CETA/NY Artists Prog, 78-79. *Teaching:* Instr, Bennington Col, 79-94; assoc prof painting & printmaking, Yale Univ, Conn, 94-98, prof painting & printmaking, 98-. *Awards:* Nat Endowment Arts Grant, 90; Joan Mitchell Found Grant, 94; John Simon Guggenheim Mem Found Painting Fel, 96; Biennial Competition, Louis Comfort Tiffany Found, 97; Found Contemp Performance Art Grant, 99; Teseque Found Grant, 2000; Civitella Raineri Residency, 2001; Marie Walsh Sharpe Found, 2002; Giverny Artists Residency, 2003. *Dealer:* Max Protech Gallery 245 8th Ave New York NY 10011. *Mailing Add:* c/o Max Protetch Gallery 245 8th Ave New York NY 10011

FEIST, HAROLD E
PAINTER, SCULPTOR
b San Angelo, Tex, 1945. *Study:* Univ Ill, Champaign-Urbana, BFA, 67; Coll Art, Md Inst, MFA, 69. *Work:* Mus Fine Arts, Boston; Edmonton Art Gallery, Alta; Art Gallery Hamilton, Ont; Mendel Art Gallery, Saskatoon, Sask; Mem Univ Newfoundland Arts & Cult Ctr. *Exhib:* 25 Canadians, Birmingham Arts Festival, Ala, 79; The New Generation: A Curator's Choice, Andre Emmerich Gallery & traveling, 80-82; The Hines Collection, Univ Place, Boston, 84; Abstraction X Four, Can House, Can High Comn, London, toured Europe, 85; Toronto 3, Eva Cohon Gallery, Highland Park, Ill, 86; Curator's Choice: A Ten Yr Retrospective--Feist, Drapell, Sutton, Buschlen-Mowatt Gallery, Vancouver, 88; solo exhibs, Virginia Christopher Gallery, Calgary, 82 & 90, Gallery One, Toronto, 82-91, Galerie Elca London, Montreal, 83-86, 88 & 90, Buschlen-Mowatt Fine Art, Vancouver, 84 & 90, Eva Cohon Galleries, Chicago & Highland Park, Ill, 88, Agnes Etherington Art Centre, Queens Univ, Kingston, Ont, 88-90 & Kathleen Laverty Gallery, Edmonton, 90. *Teaching:* Mem fac, Alta Col Art, Calgary, 68-74, Univ Saskatchewan, Regina, 74-75 & Mt Allison Univ, Sackville, NB, 75-78, Univ Guelph, Ont, 78-80, Sheridan Col, Brampton, Ont, 79-80. *Bibliog:* Gary Michael Dault (auth), Paint, Can Art, fall 84; Karen Wilkin (auth), Harold Feist: Genesis of an image, Artpost, spring 88; Karen Wilkin (auth), Harold Feist: Genesis of an Image (exhib catalog), Agnes Etherington Art Centre exhib, 88. *Media:* Acrylic on Canvas; Acrylic Sheet, Wood. *Dealer:* Gallery One 121 Scollard St Toronto ON; Galerie Elca London Montreal. *Mailing Add:* 374 Delaware Ave Toronto ON M6H 2T8 Canada

FELD, AUGUSTA
PAINTER, PRINTMAKER
b Philadelphia, Pa, Apr 18, 1919. *Study:* Fleisher Art Mem & Music Settlement Sch, Philadelphia; Philadelphia Coll Art, BA; Tyler Sch Fine Arts, Temple Univ; Pa Acad Fine Arts, MA. *Work:* Acad Fine Arts, Hahnemann Hosp, Sch Dist Permanent Collection, Woodmere Art Mus, Philadelphia; Marple-Newtown Libr, Broomall, Pa; Widerner Col, Chester, Pa; and others. *Comn:* Tree of Life (mural of wood inlays, gold paint and vinyl, with Joseph Brahim), Delaware Co Community Ctr, Springfield, Pa, 64; dance mural (oil painting), Melita Dance Studio, Philadelphia, 68; also portraits & murals comn by individuals. *Exhib:* Woodmere Art Mus, 61-88; Artist Equity Asn, Philadelphia, 74; Philadelphia Art Alliance, 74-75; Philadelphia Civic Ctr, 74 & 80; Cheltenham Art Ctr, Pa, 79-88; Abington Art Ctr, Jenkintown, Pa, 79-88; Beaver Col, Glenside, Pa, 84-85; Philips Mill Art Ctr, New Hope, Pa, 87-88; and others. *Pos:* Dir art, Hillview-Trout Nursery Sch, Broomall, Pa, 61-; art coordr, Abington Art Ctr, Jenkintown, 79-87. *Teaching:* Instr art, Philadelphia Sch Dist, 54-65, Wallingford Art Ctr, Pa, 63-64 & Haverford, Pa, 63-65. *Awards:* First Prize for oils, Atlantic City C of C, 68; First Prize, print exhib, Cheltenham Art Ctr, 71; First Prize in Portraiture, La Lomita Mus, Mission, Tex, 79; Best in Show, Perkiomen Valley Art Ctr, 84; First Prize in Oil Painting, Cheltenham Art Ctr, 85; Painting Award, Phillips Mill Art Exhib, New Hope, Pa, 88; First Prize (graphics), Doylestown Art Ctr, 90. *Bibliog:* Article, La Rev Mod, 64. *Mem:* Philadelphia Watercolor Soc; Philadelphia Watercolor Club; Doylestown Art League; Woodmere Art Mus; fel Pa Acad Art. *Media:* All Media. *Mailing Add:* 102 Berlin-New Freedom Rd Berlin NJ 08009

FELD, STUART P
ART DEALER
b Passaic, NJ, 1935. *Study:* Princeton Univ, AB, 57; Harvard Univ, AM, 58. *Exhib:* Three Centuries of Am Painting, 65 (auth with Albert T Gardner, collection catalog), 200 Yrs of Watercolor Painting in Am (auth), 66, Metrop Mus Art; Am Paintings & Historical Prints from the Middendorf Collection (auth), Metrop Mus Art & Baltimore

Mus Art, 67; Neo-Classicism in Am Inspiration and Innovation 1910-1840 (auth, catalog), Hirschl & Adler Galleries, New York, 91; Boston in the Age of Neo-Classicism 1810-1840 (auth, catalog), Hirschl & Adler Galleries, New York, 99; Of the Newest Fashion Masterpieces of Am Neo-Classical Decorative Arts (auth, with Elizabeth Feld, catalog), Hirschl & Adler Galleries, New York, 2001; In Pointed Style: The Gothic Revival in America, 1800-1860 (auth, with Elizabeth Feld), Hirschl & Adler Galleries, New York, 2006; The World of Duncan Phyte, The Arts of NY, 1800-1847, Hirsch & Adler Galleries, NY, 2011; Very Rich and Handsome: Am Neo-Classical Decorative Arts (auth, with Elizabeth Feld, catalog), Hirsch & Adler Galleries, 2014. *Pos:* teaching fel to the asst dir, Addison Gallery Am Art Phillips Acad, Andover, Mass, 57-58, Harvard Univ, 57-61; mus fellow, curatorial assistant, assistant curator, assoc curator in charge, dept Am paintings & sculpture, Met Mus, NY, 61-67; ptnr, Hirschl & Adler Galleries, NY, 67-, pres, 82-. *Awards:* Icon award, Bruce Mus, Greenwich, Conn, 2014. *Mem:* Am Antiquarian Soc; Bryant fel, Metrop Mus Art. *Specialty:* American and European art of 18th, 19th and 20th centuries, American decorative arts of the 19th century. *Collection:* American neo-classical furniture and silver. *Publ:* Coauth (with Albert Ten Eyck Gardner), American Paintings: Painters Born by 1815 (Catalogue of the Permanent Collection of the Metropolitan Mus of Art), Vol 1, NY Graphic Soc, 65; and more than fifty exhibition catalogues and articles about American paintings, decorative arts, and architecture including; Boston in the Age of Neo-Classicism, 1810-1840, Hirschl & Adler Galleries, NY, 99; with Elizabeth Feld, Of the Newest Fashion, Masterpieces of American Neoclassical Decorative Arts, Hirschl & Adler Galleries, NY, 2001; with Elizabeth Feld, In Pointed Style, The Gothic Revival in America, 1800-1860, Hirschl & Adler Galleries, NY, 2006; with Elizabeth Feld, The World of Duncan Phyfe: The Arts of New York, 1800-1847 Hirschl & Adler Galleries, NY, 2011. *Dealer:* Hirschl & Adler Galleries 730 5th Ave 10019. *Mailing Add:* Hirschl & Adler Galleries 730 5th Ave Fl 4 New York NY 10019

FELDMAN, ALINE M
PRINTMAKER, PAINTER
b Leavenworth, Kans, May 11, 1928. *Study:* Washington Univ, St Louis, Mo, with Werner Drewes, 46-49; Indiana Univ, BS, 51; Studied woodcut & sumi painting with Unichi Hiratsuka, 62. *Work:* Nat Mus Am Art, Washington, DC; Worcester Art Mus, Mass; McNay Art Mus, San Antonio, Tex; Contemp Mus, Honolulu, Hawaii; UCLA Art Mus, Los Angeles. *Comn:* woodcut mural panel, Mutual of NY, Purchase, NY, 85; woodcut murals, Hyatt Regency Hotel, Kauai, Hawaii, 90. *Exhib:* 22nd Area Exhib Works on Paper, Corcoran Gallery of Art, Washington, DC, 80; Nat Print & Drawing Exhib, Haggin Mus, Stockton, Calif, 85; Earth Views, Nat Air & Space Mus, Washington DC 86; Grabadores USA, Museo de Arte Moderno, Buenos Aires, 87; A Graphic Muse, Santa Barbara Art Mus, Calif, 87-88; New Acquisitions, Nat Mus Am Art, Washington DC, 88; Press Work: Art of Am Printmakers, Nat Mus Women Arts, Washington DC, 91; A World of Maps, Anchorage Mus Hist & Art, Alaska, 94-95. *Awards:* Purchase Prize, Duxbury Art Mus, Mass, 97; Woodcut Award, World Print Festival, 98; Veloric Award, Cynthia & Michael Veloric, 99. *Bibliog:* Capital Edition, A Cut Above, CBS-TV, 4/29/90; Various art reviews in Washington Post. *Mem:* Southern Graphics Coun; Boston Printmakers; Los Angeles Print Soc; Washington Print Club; Mid-America Print Coun. *Media:* Woodcut; Pastel. *Dealer:* Mary Ryan Gallery 24 W 57th St New York NY 10019; Marsha Mateyka Gallery 2012 R Street NW Washington DC 20009; Locus Gallery 7700 Forsyth Blvd St Louis MO 63105. *Mailing Add:* 5013 Eliots Oak Rd Columbia MD 21044

FELDMAN, ARTHUR MITCHELL
MUSEUM DIRECTOR, ART AND ANTIQUES DEALER
b Philadelphia, Pa, Dec 22, 1942. *Study:* Villanova Univ, BS, 64; Univ Pa with George Tatum; Univ Mo, MA (art hist & archaeol), 70. *Pos:* Vis cur, Victoria & Albert Mus, London, Eng, 70-71; assoc cur & asst adminr, Renwick Gallery, Smithsonian Inst, Washington, DC, 71-73; dir, Spertus Mus of Judaica, 73-85; exec dir, Jewish Mus Chicago, 86-; pres, Arthur M Feldman Gallery, Highland Park, 86-. *Teaching:* Lectr, Col Lake Co, 86-92. *Specialty:* Antique & contemporary Judaica. *Publ:* Auth, Jewish Artists of the 20th Century, 75, The Hill Page Collection, 75, The Jews of Yemen, 76 & Faith and Form: Synogogue Architecture of Illinois, 76, Spertus Coll Press; The Sons of Zebulan: Jewish Maritime History, 79

FELDMAN, BELLA
SCULPTOR, EDUCATOR
b New York, NY. *Study:* Queens Col, City Univ New York, BA; Calif Coll Arts & Crafts; Calif State Univ, San Jose, MA. *Work:* Oakland Mus, Calif; Berkeley Art Mus, Univ Calif. *Comn:* Sculptures, Marshal Tulin, Hydronautics Inc, Silver Spring, Md, 64, Sasaki-Walker Landscape Architects, Newport Shopping Ctr, Newport Beach, Calif, 65, Royston Hanamoto Landscape Architects, Potrero Park, Richmond, Calif, 66 & Fountain Fed Home Loan Bank, San Francisco, Calif, 90. *Exhib:* Palace Legion Honor, San Francisco, 61; Summer Series, San Francisco Mus, 64; San Francisco Art Inst, 75; San Jose Mus Art, 82; Jan Baum Gallery, 2000; Bryan Ohno Gallery, Seattle, WA, 2004; Habatat Gallery, Chicago, IL War Toys Redux, Aug-Oct, 2004. *Pos:* Cult specialist, US Info Agency to Uganda, 90. *Teaching:* Prof, Calif Col Arts & Crafts, 64-, grad dir, 75-79, prof emer, 2000; lectr art, Makerere Univ Col, Fine Art Sch, Uganda, 68-70. *Awards:* Calif Mus Trustees Award, 67; First Prize, San Francisco Women Artists, 67; E L Cabot Trust Fund Award, Harvard Univ, 75; Nat Endowment Arts Grant, 86-87; Florsheim Grant, 96. *Bibliog:* Gloria Frym (ed), Second Stories, Chronicle Bks; Kate Regan (auth), Possibility and paradox, Mus of Calif Mag, 9/87 & 10/87. *Mem:* Women's Caucus Art; Committee-West, East Bay; Coll Art Asn. *Media:* Welded Metal, Cast Metal, Glass. *Dealer:* Habatat Gallery 222 W Superior St Chicago IL 60610; Sculpture Site San Francisco Calif. *Mailing Add:* 12 Summit Ln Berkeley CA 94708

FELDMAN, EDMUND BURKE
EDUCATOR, CRITIC
b Bayonne, NJ, May 6, 1924. *Study:* Newark Sch Fine & Indust Arts, with John R Grabach & Emile Alexay, dipl, 41; Syracuse Univ, BFA, 49; Univ Calif, Los Angeles, with Karl With, Stanton MacDonald Wright & Abraham Kaplan, MA (art hist), 51; Columbia Univ, with Lyman Bryson & George Counts, EdD, 53. *Pos:* Cur paintings & sculpture, Newark Mus, 53. *Teaching:* Assoc prof art, Livingston State Col, 53-56; assoc prof painting, sculpture & design, Carnegie-Mellon Univ, 56-60; chmn art div, State Univ NY Col New Paltz, 60-66; prof art, Ohio State Univ, summer 66; prof art, Univ Ga, 66-92; vis prof, Univ Calif, Berkeley, winter 74. *Awards:* Named Alumni Found Distinguished Prof Art, Univ Ga, 73. *Mem:* Kappa Pi; Coll Art Asn Am; Nat Art Educ Asn (pres-elect, 79-81 & pres, 81-83). *Res:* Art history and criticism. *Interests:* Visual literacy. *Publ:* Auth, Art as Image and Idea, 67, Becoming Human Through Art, 70, Thinking About Art, 85 & Practical Art Criticism, 94, Prentice-Hall; Varieties of Visual Experience, Prentice-Hall & Abrams, 72, second ed, 81, third ed, 87, fourth ed, 93; The Artist: A Social History, 95; Philosophy of Art Education, 96. *Mailing Add:* 140 Chinquapin Pl Athens GA 30605

FELDMAN, FRANKLIN
PRINTMAKER, WRITER
b New York, NY, 1927. *Study:* Columbia Law Sch, LLB, 51; Art Students League (study with Howard Trafton, Ivan Olinsky & Byron Browne); New Sch Soc Res, Parsons Sch Des (study with John Ross & Herman Zaage). *Work:* Princeton Univ, Rare Book Libr; Brown Univ, John Hay Libr; Dance Collection & the Jewish Div, NY Publ Libr; Harvard Univ, The Houghton Libr; Yale Univ, Sterling Mem Libr; British Mus; Victoria & Albert Mus; Univ Tex at El Paso; Univ Southern Calif, Doheny Libr; Scripps Col, Denison Libr; Univ Denver, Pennose Libr; Brigham Univ, Harold B. Lee Libr (spec collection); Green Libr, Stanford Univ; Scribner Libr, Skidmore Coll; The Jewish Theological Seminary of Am. *Exhib:* Silvermine, Prints Int, 90; Int Miniature Show, 90; Contemp Am Printmakers, Thomas J Walsh Gallery, Fairfield Univ, 94; East/West Printmakers Show, 96; Nat Print Show, Club Albany Exhib, 98; Fifty Yrs of Books, Prints & Drawings, The Century Asn, 2007. *Pos:* Vis artist, The Am Acad in Rome, 2006. *Teaching:* Lectr law, Columbia Law Sch, 79-2002. *Awards:* Fel, Yaddo, Saratoga Springs, NY, 83; Ledyard Cogsworth Purchase Prize, Nat Print Show, Print Club Albany, 98. *Mem:* Int Found Art Res (pres & dir 71-96); Grolier Club; Century Asn; Soc Am Graphic Arts; Artists Fel (dir). *Media:* Etching, Lithography, Transferred Prints. *Res:* Legal aspects of art. *Publ:* Coauth, Art Works: Law, Policy, Practice, Practicing Law Inst, 74; Art Law, Little, Brown & Co, 86; Poetry by David Giannini, Indian Mountain Press, 98; also, various articles in legal publications relating to art & law. *Mailing Add:* 15 W 81st St New York NY 10024

FELDMAN, JOEL BENET
PRINTMAKER, EDUCATOR
b Richmond, Va, Dec 9, 1942. *Study:* Carnegie Inst Technol, with Robert Gardner, BFA, 65; Ind Univ, with Rudy Pozzati & Roy Sieber, MFA, 67. *Work:* Mary & Leigh Block Gallery, Northwestern Univ, Evanston, Ill; New York Pub Libr Print Collection; Brooklyn Mus, NY; Grunwald Collection, Univ Calif, Los Angeles; Spertus Mus, Chicago. *Exhib:* Under Her Brothers Eyes, Contemp Arts Ctr, New Orleans, 88; Mid Am Print Coun Figurative Show, Purdue Univ Gallery, West Lafayette, Ind, 93; 69th Int Competition, Print Club, Philadelphia, 94; one-person show, Ill State Mus, 94 & Forum Continuing Art, St Louis, 94. *Teaching:* Instr printmaking, Univ Ga, Athens, 67-70; vis instr, Ohio Univ, Athens, 72-73; prof, Southern Ill Univ, Carbondale, 73-. *Awards:* Ill Arts Coun Visual Arts Fel, 91-92; Arts Midwest Visual Arts Fel, Nat Endowment Arts, 92-93; Visual Arts Fel, Nat Endowment Arts, 93-94. *Bibliog:* Michael Bulka (auth), Review, Art in Am, 4/91; Hamza Walker (auth), Review, New Art Examiner, summer 93. *Mem:* Mid Am Print Coun; Paint Club Ctr Prints & Photographs. *Media:* Woodcut, Drawing. *Dealer:* R Duane Reed Gallery 1 N Taylor St Louis MO 63108; SK Josefsberg 403 NW Eleventh Ave Portland OR 97209. *Mailing Add:* 116 Hamilton Park Lexington KY 40504

FELDMAN, KAYWIN
MUSEUM DIRECTOR, CURATOR
b Boston, 1966. *Study:* Univ Mich, BA (classical anthrop, Phi Beta Kappa), 88; Univ London, Inst Archeol, MA (mus studies), 90; Courtauld Inst Art, London, MA (art hist), 91; doctoral study, Antwerp, Belgium, 91-93. *Pos:* Educ cur, British Mus Art; dir exhibs, cur art, exec dir, Fresno Metrop Mus Art, Hist and Sci, Calif, 1996-1999; dir, Memphis Brooks Mus Art, Tenn, 1999-2007; dir & pres, Minneapolis Inst Arts, 2008-. *Awards:* Cent Calif Excellence in Bus Award, 1996; Thomas W Briggs Community Serv Award, 2005. *Mem:* Phi Beta Kappa; Asn Art Mus Dirs (sec bd trustees, 2007-08, pres, 2010-). *Mailing Add:* Minneapolis Inst Arts 2400 3rd Ave S Minneapolis MN 55404

FELDMAN, ROGER LAWRENCE
SCULPTOR, EDUCATOR
b Spokane, Wash, Nov 19, 1949; US citizen. *Study:* Univ Wash, Seattle, BA, 72; Fuller Theological Seminary, 72-73; Regent Coll, Vancouver, BC, studied with Hans Rookmaaker; Claremont Grad Univ, Calif, MFA, 77. *Work:* Wash State Arts Comn, 1989; Union Univ, Jackson, Tenn, 2000; Barrington Ctr for Arts, Gordon Col, Wenham, Mass, 2002; Schloss Mittersill, Austria, 2005; Beyond Malibu, Princess Louisa Inlet, British Columbia, Can, 2007. *Comn:* Bronze sculpture, East Hill Community Ctr, Gresham, Oregon, 79-80; Site spec steel sculpture, Wash State Arts Comn Renton Vocational Tech Inst, Renton, 87-89; Write Stuff, Margery Wheaton, Pasadena, Calif, 99; Freswick Castle, Caitnness, Scotland, 2011-2012; H.E. Butt Found Camps, Near Leakey, Tex, 2013. *Exhib:* Cornerstone, Bushnell, Ill, 96; Los Angeles Munic Gallery, Barnsdall Park, Hollywood, Calif, 96; Gallery W, Sacramento, 96; Roberts Wesley Col, Rochester, NY, 97; Bethel Col, Ind, 98; Tacoma Art Mus, Wash, 2004; Rock Suyama Space, 2005; Mittersill, Austria, 2005; Friesen Gallery, NNU, Nampa, Idaho, 2008; Calvin Coll, Grand Rapids, Mich, 2009; Taylor Univ, Upland, Ind, 2009; Confluence Gallery, Twisp, Wash, 2010; Whitworth Univ,

Spokane, Wash, 2010; Wheaton Coll, Wheaton, Ill, 2011; Fundacion Pons de Madrid, Spain, 2011; Caceres, Spain, 2011-2012; Trujillo, Spain, 2012; Belmont Univ, Nashville, Tenn, 2012; Galeria Municipal da Sala do Risco, Lisbon, Portugal, 2012; Regent College, Vancouver, BC, 2012. *Pos:* Chmn Art Dept, Seattle Pac Univ, 2006-2009, Fac chair, 2009-2012. *Teaching:* Prof sculpture & design, Biola Univ, La Mirada, Calif, 89-2000, Seattle Pacific Univ, Wash, 2000-. *Awards:* Fel, Nat Endowment Arts, 86; Fel, Connemara Found, 91; Artist Residency, Yaddo, Saratoga Springs, NY, 93; Prescott award, Sculpture; Artist in Res, Jentel, Sheridan, Wyoming, 2011; Artist in Res, Brush Creek, Wyo, 2013. *Bibliog:* Karen Mulder (auth), The art of true inquiry, a profile of Roger Feldman, Mars Hill Rev, winter/spring, 96; Cathy Curtis (auth), To have and have not, Los Angeles Times, 4/97; Theodore Prescott (auth), Nature and nature's God in late twentieth century American art, Cresset, 98; Theodore Prescott, David Morgan, Terrence Dempsey & Z Ori Soltes (coauths), Like a prayer: A Jewish and Christian presence in contemporary art, Tryon Ctr for Visual Art, Charlotte, NC, 2001; Sheila Farr (auth), How Spaces we Live in Come to Inhabit us, The Seattle Times, 04; Patricia Pongrancz & Wayne Roosa (coauths), The Next Generation, 2005; Rachel Hostetter Smith (auth) Charis, Boundary Crossings: Neighbors, Strangers, Family Friends, 2009; Art and Faith (exhib catalogue) Fundacion Pons de Madrid, Spain, 2011. *Mem:* Christians in Visual Arts; Int Sculpture Ctr; Seattle Art Mus; Tacoma Art Mus; Coll Art Asn. *Media:* Metal, Welded; Wood, Concrete, Stone, Installation. *Interests:* hiking, reading, exercise. *Publ:* auth, Off-Centered Consequences,Image: J of Arts & Religion, 2001; auth, The Point of Mass, It Was Good Making Art to the Glory of God, 2006; auth, Juxtapositions, Image, J of Arts & Religion, 2010

FELDMAN, WALTER (SIDNEY)
PAINTER, PRINTMAKER
b Lynn, Mass, Mar 23, 1925. *Study:* Yale Univ Sch Fine Arts, BFA, 50, Sch Design, MFA, 51; also with W de Kooning, Stuart Davis & Josef Albers. *Hon Degrees:* Brown Univ, Hon MA, 56. *Work:* Addison Gallery Am Art, Andover, Mass; Metrop Mus Art, NY; Fogg Art Mus, Cambridge, Mass; Israel Mus, Jerusalem; Mus Mod Art, NY; Bezalel Nat Mus; Decordova & Dana Mus; Gulbenkian Found, Lisbon, Portugal; Victoria & Albert Mus, London; and many others. *Comn:* Color woodcut, Int Graphic Arts Soc, 57; mosaic pavements, Temple Beth-El, Providence, RI, 57; stained glass windows, Sugarman Mem Chapel, Providence, RI, 61; World's Fair poster, IBM Corp, 63; Quezalcoatl (mural), Pembroke Col, Brown Univ, 66; 32 panel mural, Temple Emanu-El, Providence, RI, 68; commemorative silver plate, Gorham Silver Co, 73; mosaic mural, Temple Beth-El, Providence, RI, 99; portrait, Barnaby Keeny; portrait, Robert Warren Morse. *Exhib:* Am Watercolors, Drawings and Prints, Metrop Mus Art, 52; Recent Drawings USA, Mus Mod Art, NY, 55; Mostra Int, Milan, Italy, 57; 26th Biennial, Corcoran Gallery, Washington, DC, 59; Nat Inst Arts & Lett, NY, 61; Solo exhib, Hopkins Ctr, Dartmouth Col, 78; Mus Mod Art, NYC; Victoria & Albert Mus, London; Yale Univ Art Gallery; RISD (RI School Design): Mus Art, Providence; Phoenix Art Mus; and others. *Pos:* Dir, Brown/Ziggurat Press, 90. *Teaching:* Instr painting & design, Yale Univ Sch Design, 50-53; prof painting & printmaking, Brown Univ, 53-2007; vis prof drawing, Harvard Univ, 68; artist-in-residence, Hopkins Ctr, Dartmouth Col, 78; John Hay prof bibliography, Univ Calif, Riverside, 75, Brown Univ, 93-2007. *Awards:* Metrop Mus Art Award, 52; Gold Medal, Mostra Int, Milan, Italy, 57; First Painting Award, Boston Arts Festival, Mass, 64; Governor's Award for Art, RI, 80. *Bibliog:* G Y Loveridge (auth), Providence practitioner of ancient art, The Rhode Islander, 4/25/54; Michael Forster (auth), The color of Mexico is black, Nivel 41, German P Garcia (Mexico City), 5/25/62; Jane Shelton (auth), Walter Feldman, Harvard Art Rev, spring 66. *Mem:* Am Color Print Soc; Providence Art Club. *Media:* All, Painting, Printmaking. *Publ:* Coauth (with J Schevill), Ghost Names, Ghost Numbers (woodcuts), Handmade Bks. *Dealer:* Joshua Heller Washington DC; Bromer Booksellers Boston MA; Vamp & Tramp Book Sellers Birmingham AL

FELGUEREZ, MANUEL
PAINTER, SCULPTOR
b Zacatecas, Mex, Dec 12, 1928. *Study:* Academia de la Grande Chaumier, with Ossip Zadkine, Paris, 49-50. *Work:* Museo de Arte Moderno, Mex; Museo Tamayo, Mex; Museo Espanol de Arte Contemporaneo, Madrid; Museo de Arte, San Antonion, Tex; Biblioteca Miguel Arango, Bogota, Colombia. *Comn:* Mural de Hierro, Cine Diana, Mexico City, 61; escultura, Espacio Escultorico UNAM, Mexico City, 78; mural policromado, Centro Cult Alfa, Monterrey, NL Mex, 82; El Cerro Nultivara (escultura), Gobierno de Colombia, Medellin, Colombia, 83; escultura metal policromado y vidrio, Gobierno de Corea, Seoul, Korea, 88. *Exhib:* Troix Artistes Mexicains d'Aujourd'hui, Palais de Beaux Arts, Bruselas, Belgica, 75; XIII Bienal de Sao Paulo, Brazil, 75; La Maquina Estetica, Carpenter Ctr Visual Arts, Cambridge, 76; solo exhibs, Museo Espanol de Arte Contemporaneo, Madrid, Spain, 80, Fundacion Calouste Gulbenkian, Lisboa, Port, 81, Lalit Kala Acad, Neuva Delhi, India, 83; XLII Bienal, Pabellon Mexicano, Venecia, Italy, 86. *Teaching:* Instr visual arts, Univ Iberoamericana, Mex, 56-61, Univ Nat Autonoma Mex, 69-92. *Awards:* Premio de Pintura, Trienal de India, Nueva Delhi, 68; Gran Premio de Honor, XIII Bienal, San Paulo, Brazil, 75; Premio Nacional de Artes, Mex Govt, 88. *Bibliog:* Damian Bayon (auth), America Latina en sus Artes, Siglo XXI-UNESCO Paris Barcelona, 74; Octavio Paz (auth), Los Privilegios de la Vista, Centro Cult de Arte Contemoraneo, 90; Juan Garcia Ponce (auth), Manuel Felguerez, Ediciones del Equilibrista, 92. *Mem:* Acad Artes Mex; Sistema Nacional de Creadores de Arte. *Publ:* Auth, El Espacio Multiple, UNAM, Mex, 78; coauth, Diferencia y continuidad, Multiarte, Mex, 82; La Maquina estetica, UNAM, Mex, 85. *Dealer:* Galeria Ramis Barquet Av Real San Agustin No 304-L-2B Residencial San Agustin Garza Garcia Mexico 66260. *Mailing Add:* Calle 10 de Mayo No 15 Olivard de los Padres Mexico City Mexico DF 01780

FELISKY, BARBARA ROSBE
PAINTER, PRINTMAKER
b Chicago, Ill, Mar 24, 1938. *Study:* Univ Mich, studied drawing under Frederick O'Dell, BA, 60; Laguna Sch Art, with Hans Burchardt, 75, Calvin Goodman, 1982. *Work:* City of Orange Civic Ctr, Calif; City of Brea Civic Ctr, Calif. *Comn:* Murals, Home Savings & Loan, Los Angeles, 84, Gen Tel Co, Sacramento, 84, Breakers Hotel, Long Beach, 85, Off Nat Educ, Irvine, 86; Folding Screen, New Seoul Hotel, Los Angeles. *Exhib:* California Traditionalist, Redlands Mus, Calif, 80; Catharine Lorillard Wolfe, Nat Arts Club, NY, 82; The Traditionalist's Exhib, Brea Civic Ctr Gallery, Calif, 84; 51st Int Exhib, Arts Club, Washington, 84; Int Miniature Art Shows, Min Art Soc, Fla & NJ, 85. *Teaching:* Oil painting, YWCA, Santa Ana & Orange, Calif, 74-80; teacher & consult, pvt studio, 76- & City of Orange Sch Dist, 76-84. *Awards:* First Place Still Life, In Miniature Ann Exhib, 79; First Place Landscaping, Nat Western Small Painting Show, NMex, 83; Purchase Award, City of Brea, 84. *Bibliog:* Searching for Levitan, Am Artist, 7/88; Am Artist, 5/84. *Mem:* Artist mem Laguna Mus; California Art Club; Los Angeles Co Art Mus. *Media:* Oil, Monotype. *Interests:* Travel, photography. *Collection:* City of Brea, Calif; City of Orange, Calif; Nordstrom's Private Collection; ATT Corp Collections, Sacramento, Calif. *Publ:* Contribr, Flower painting then and now, Am Artist, 5/84; illusr, Los Angeles Times Home Mag, 4/28/85; auth, The Search for Levitan, Am Artists, 7/88; contribr, Painting Gardens, Art Trends Mag, 3/96. *Dealer:* Chermers Gallery 17300 Seventeenth St Tustin CA 92680; Simic Gallery P O Box 5687 Carmel CA 93921; Bev's Fine Art, Raleigh, NC; Sher Galleries, 135 NE First, Hallandale, Fla. *Mailing Add:* 2942 Lake Hill Dr Orange CA 92667

FELKER, DAVID LARRY
SCULPTOR, GALLERY DIRECTOR
b Spokane, Wash, July 6, 1940. *Study:* Eastern Wash Univ, BA, 75; Wash State Univ, MFA, 78. *Work:* Anchorage Mus Hist & Art, Alaska; Mus Judetean, Bistrita, Romania. *Exhib:* Solo exhibs, Intersections of Time & Space, 82, Three Coordinates Plus Time, 86, The Arc, Anchorage Mus Hist & Art, 87, Arc of the Alembic Current, Goldsmith's Mus, London, Eng, 90, Generator Bistrita, Mus Judetean, Generator Bucharest, Univ Bucharest Mus, Romanis, 90 & Alaska Generator, Visual Arts Ctr, Anchorage, 92; US Cult Exhib, Magadan Mus Art, Russ, 92-93; Anchorage Mus Hist & Art; Int Gallery Contemp Art, Minneapolis, 96; Brighton Festival/Tichborn Gallery, Eng, 2001; Emerald Tablet Communique, Wallingford Gallery, 2008-09. *Collection Arranged:* International (sculpture), 84; Dennis Oppenheim (drawing/sculpture), 85; Colour (paintings), 86, Altered Images, Eng, 92; Interaction 20 (paintings/sculpture), Europe, 90; Diva Galleries, Seattle, 2003. *Pos:* Dir sculpture, Visual Arts Ctr Alaska, 81; dir, Int Gallery Contemp Art, Minneapolis, Minn, 95-98; cur, Kerf Int Exhib, Seattle, Wash, 2003-05, dir, 2003-07, 09. *Teaching:* Instr drawing, Chapman Col, Alaska, 79-86; asst prof painting, drawing & sculpture, Univ Alaska, Anchorage, 86, adj fac, 91-93; instr, 3-dimensional, Col St Catherine, St Paul, Minn, 99; instr, 3-dimensional design, Shorline Community Col, Seattle, Wash, 2005. *Awards:* Nat Endowment Arts Fel 89 & 91, Arc Alembic Current Goldsmith's, London, 90, Theurgic Helmet, VACA, 92; Ken Gray Contemp Arts Award, 94; The Minneapolis Award, 96. *Bibliog:* Ron Glowen, We Work in the Dark, Anchorage Mus, 93; J Decker(auth), Ice Breakers-Alaska's Most Innovative Artists, Book Publ, 99; Julie Decker (auth), Found And Assembled in Alaska, 2001. *Media:* All. *Specialty:* Contemporary art

FELLER, DEBORAH
PAINTER, DRAFTSMAN
b New York, NY. *Study:* Pratt Inst (art therapy & creative develop), MPS, 77; Hunter Coll Sch Social Work, 85; NY Acad Art (figurative studies), MFA, 2004; Studied with Vincent Desiderio & Wade Schuman, NY Acad Art, MFA, 2004. *Exhib:* 18th Ann Sept exhib, Alexandria Mus Art, Alexandria, La, 2005; Ann Juried Exhib, Salmagundi Club, New York, 2006-2009; Art & Addiction exhib, Innovators Combating Substance Abuse, Baltimore, Md, 2007; Summer exhib, NY Acad Art, New York, 2006; Take Home a Nude, NY Acad Art, 2006; Blanche Ames Nat Art Competition, Ames Mansion at Borderland State Park, Mass, 2006. *Awards:* Award of Excellence, Light Effects, Firehouse Art Gallery, 2004; Top 10 Viewers' Choice, Literartcy, Anderson Gallery, Provo City Libr, 2004; Gold Palette Award, Ann Juried Exhib, Jack Richeson & Co Inc, 2006; Cerf Merit, Ann Juried Exhib, Salmagundi Club, 2007; Top five, Art & Addiction, Innovators Combating Substance Abuse, 2008; CLW Art Club, Gold Medal Painting, 2010. *Bibliog:* Patricia Santora (ed), Addiction & Art, Johns Hopkins Univ Press, 2010; Drawing Mag, Am Artist, 2006. *Mem:* Coll Art Assn. *Media:* Oil paint on linen, Black & White Chalk Pencils, Ballpoint Pen on Paper

FELLER, ROBERT L
CONSERVATION SCIENTIST
b Newark, NJ, Dec 27, 1919. *Study:* Dartmouth Coll, AB, 41; Rutgers Univ, MS, 43 & PhD, 50. *Pos:* Head, Nat Gallery Art Res Proj, Carnegie-Mellon Inst Res, Pittsburgh, 50-76, dir, Ctr on the Materials of the Artist & Conservator, 76-88 & dir emer, 88-; ed, Int Inst Conserv Hist & Artistic Works, Am Group Bull, 60-74. *Teaching:* Vis scientist, Conserv Ctr, NY Univ Inst Fine Arts, spring, 61. *Awards:* Pittsburgh Award, Am Chemical Soc, 83; Coll Art Asn/Nat Inst Conserv Award, Distinction in Scholar & Conserv, 92; University projects Award for Distinguished Achievement in Conservation, 2000. *Mem:* Fel Int Inst Conserv Hist & Artistic Works (pres, Am Group, 64-66); Int Coun Mus, Comt Conserv (pres, 69-78); Nat Conserv Adv Coun (pres, 76-79); Inter Soc Color Coun; Fedn Soc Paint Technol; and others. *Res:* Picture varnishes; effects of light on museum objects; analysis of pigments in works of art. *Publ:* Coauth, On Picture Varnishes and Their Solvents, 59, rev ed, 71; ed, Artists' Pigments, Vol I, Cambridge Univ Press, 85; coauth with M Wilt, Evaluation of Cellulose Ethers for Conservation, J Paul Getty Trust, 1990; auth, Accelerated Aging: Photochemical & Thermal Aspects, J Paul Getty Trust, 94. *Mailing Add:* 220 N Dithridge St Pittsburgh PA 15213

FELLOWS, DEBORAH LYNNE See Copenhaver-Fellows, Deborah Lynne Fellows

FELLOWS, FRED
PAINTER, SCULPTOR
b Ponca City, Okla, Aug 15, 1935. *Comn:* Portfolio of prints, Winchester on the Frontier, Winchester Firearms; Paintings/Bronze Sculptures for Nat Finals Rodeo, Pro Rodeo, Hesston Corp. *Exhib:* Cowboy Artists Am Show, Phoenix & Okla, 68-; Cowboy Hall of Fame; Whitney Gallery; Grand Palais, Paris; First Western Art Show,

China; Los Angeles Co Mus Art; Cowboy Artists Am Mus, Kerrville, Tex. *Pos:* Commercial artist & art dir. *Teaching:* Painting workshops for Cowboy Artists of Am Mus. *Awards:* Award for Contrib to Fine Art in Am, Grumbacher, 76; Silver Medal, Cowboy Artists of Am, 78; Gold Medal Sculpture and Best of Show, Cowboy Artist Asn Ann Exhib, 91. *Bibliog:* Brave New Cowboy (doc), Nat Pub TV; Great Plains Massacre (doc), BBC; article, Southwest Art, 10/82. *Mem:* Cowboy Artists Asn (secy-treas & vpres, 74-75, pres, 75-76 & 94-95, dir, 92-94). *Publ:* Auth, Saddles of the early west, Mont Hist Soc Mag, 68; Art of the West, 6/92. *Mailing Add:* PO Box 2454 Bigfork MT 59911

FELSEN, ROSAMUND
ART DEALER, GALLERY DIRECTOR
b Pasadena, Calif, Feb 28, 1934. *Pos:* Owner, Rosamund Felsen Gallery, Santa Monica, Calif, currently. *Specialty:* Contemporary art. *Mailing Add:* Bergamot Station B-4 2525 Michigan Ave Santa Monica CA 90404-4014

FELTER, JUNE MARIE
PAINTER, PRINTMAKER
b Oakland, Calif, Oct 19, 1919. *Study:* Oakland Art Inst, Calif, 37-40; Calif Sch Arts & Crafts, Oakland, 37-40, Calif Sch Fine Arts, San Francisco, with Richard Diebenkorn, 60-61. *Work:* Crown Point Press Archives, Nat Mus Am Art, Washington, DC; San Jose Mus Art, Calif; Oakland Art Mus; San Francisco Art Comn; Am Fedn Arts, NY; Kaiser Hosps, San Francisco Bay Area, Calif; Yale Univ Art Gallery, New Haven, Conn; Bank Am Computer Ctr, San Francisco, Calif; Univ Hawaii. *Comn:* Suite of six etchings, comn by Dana Reich & Brian Jones, San Francisco, 81; three ed lithographs, Meridien Hotel, San Francisco, 83; plus 200 portraits comn by various individuals 54-58 & stage sets for various school programs in the 50's. *Exhib:* De Young Mus, San Francisco, 59; The Painted Flower, Oakland Mus, Calif, 60; Calif Soc Etchers, San Francisco Mus Mod Art, 63; Nat Drawing Show, San Francisco Mus Mod Art, 70; Elegant Miniatures, San Francisco Mus Mod Art, 84; 871 Fine Arts Gallery, San Francisco, 89, 90, 92 & 96; Art in Embassies Program, Washington for Vienna, Austria, 94. *Teaching:* Instr watercolor, painting & figure drawing, San Francisco Mus Mod Art, 64-79; instr painting, Univ Calif, San Francisco, 79-80. *Awards:* Purchase Award, Oakland Art Mus, 60; Purchase Award Oil Painting, San Francisco Art Comn, 64. *Bibliog:* Susan Felter (dir), June Felter, A Painter (film), Univ Calif, Los Angeles, 69-70; Arthur Bloomfield (auth), A stir at the beach, San Francisco Chronicle, 8/3/78; Thomas Albright (auth), Art in the San Francisco Bay Area 1945-80, Univ Calif Press, Berkeley, 85; Kathan Brown (auth), Why Draw a Live Model, Crown Point Press, San Francisco, Calif; Barbara Guest (auth), Confetti Trees (poetry); G T McClelland & J T Last (coauths), California Watercolors, Hillcrest Press, 2002; Barbara Guest (auth), Durer in the Window: Reflections on Art, Roof Bks, 2003. *Mem:* Calif Soc Printmakers (coun mem, 83-84). *Media:* Acrylic, Watercolor, oil painting. *Specialty:* Fine arts; books and paintings, art works. *Interests:* History & current news. *Publ:* Contribr, Prize Winning Paintings, Allied Publ, 66; Auth, Musicality with poet Barbara Guest & illusr June Felter, Kelsey St Press, Berkeley, Calif, 88; illust, The Confetti Trees with poet Barbara Guest, 99, Sun & Moon Press, Los Angeles; Calif Watercolors 1850-1970, Hillcrest Press. *Dealer:* 871 Fine Arts Gallery 49 Geary St San Francisco CA 94168. *Mailing Add:* 1046 Amito Ave Berkeley CA 94705

FELTUS, ALAN EVAN
PAINTER, EDUCATOR
b Washington, DC, May 1, 1943. *Study:* Tyler Sch Fine Arts, Temple Univ, Philadelphia, 61-62; Cooper Union, NY, BFA, 66; Sch Art & Archit, Yale Univ, MFA, 68. *Work:* Univ Va Art Mus; Nat Mus Am Art, Am Med Asn & Hirshhorn Mus, Washington, DC; NJ State Mus; Nat Acad Design, New York City; Corcoran Gallery Art, Washington, DC; Huntington Mus Art, WVa; Wichita Art Mus, Kans; Okla Art Ctr, Okla City. *Comn:* Murals, Am Med Asn, 85. *Exhib:* Wash Figurative Painters, Corcoran Gallery Art, Washington, DC, 73-74; Forum Gallery, NY, 76, 80, 83, 86, 91, 94, 96, 98, 2002, 2005, 2010; Nat Acad Design, 77-78, 82, 86, 88, 90, 95, 97, 99, 2001 & 2005; Am Acad & Inst Arts & Lett, NY, 77, 79, 81 & 94; Okla Art Ctr, 78; Wash Painting, Corcoran Gallery Art, 82; Wichita Art Mus, 87; Ann Nathan Gallery, Chicago, Ill, 94, 98, 2000 & 2003; Huntington Mus Art, WVa, 2000; Hemphill Fine Arts, Washington, DC, 2001-; Boulder Mus Contemp Art, Colo, 2007; Gallery Camino Real, Boca Raton, Fla, 2007. *Pos:* artist, 1984-. *Teaching:* Instr art, Dayton Art Inst, Ohio, 68-70; assoc prof art, Am Univ, Washington, DC, 72-84; Md Inst Coll Art, Baltimore, 2006, 2009, 2010. *Awards:* Rome Prize Fel Painting, Am Acad Rome, 70-72; Tiffany Found Grant, 80; Nat Endowment Arts Individual Grant, 81; Pollock-Krasner Found Grant, 92 & 2005. *Bibliog:* Charles Jencks (auth), Post-Modernism, New York, Rizzoli, 87; Alan Feltus (auth), Inside the painter's mind, the Artist's Mag, 1/92; Alan Feltus (auth), Living and working in Italy, Am Artist Mag, 8/92; Howard DaLee Spencer (auth), Alan Feltus in Italy, Am Arts Quart, winter, 92; Edward Lucie-Smith, Am Art Now, William Morrow & Co, NY, 85, London, 95; Edward Lucie-Smith, Art Today, Phaidon Press, 95; Edward Lucie-Smith, Art Tomorrow, Editions Pierre Terrail, Paris, 2002. *Mem:* Nat Acad. *Media:* Oil. *Dealer:* Forum Gallery 745 Fifth Ave New York NY

FENDRICH, LAURIE
PAINTER
Study: Mt Holyoke Col, BA (magna cum laude), 70; Sch Art Inst Chicago, MFA (painting), 78. *Exhib:* Solo exhibs: Frans Wynans Gallery, Vancouver, Can, 82; Coll Notre Dame Maryland, Baltimore, 82; John Davis Gallery, NY, 90; Jan Cicero Gallery, Chicago, 81, 83, 86, 93; The Galbreath Gallery, Lexington, Ky, 94; EM Donahue Gallery, NY, 95; Linda Schwartz Gallery, Cincinnati, 2000; Hatton Gallery, Colorado State Univ, 2002; Gary Snyder Fine Art Gallery, NY, 2003; Katharina Rich Perlow Gallery, NY, 2006, Ruth Chandler Williamson Gallery, Scripps Coll, 2010; Group exhibs: Watson-Willour Gallery, Houston, Tex, 79; Guggenheim Gallery, Orange, Calif, 80; Squibb Corp Gallery, Princeton, NJ, 82; Critical Perspectives, PS 1 Mus, NY, 82, Slow Art: Painting in NY Now, 92, After Matisse/Picasso, 2003; 239 S Los Angeles St, LA, Calif, 84; Condeso/Lawler Gallery, NY, 86; John Davis Gallery, NY, 89, 90; The Mask Project, Los Angeles County Mus Art, 92; Emily Lowe Mus Art, Hempstead, NY, 91, 94, 98; Donahue/Sosinski Gallery, NY, 96; Affinities, Snyder Fine Art, NY, 96, Geometric Abstraction, 1937-97, 97, The New Naturalism, 97, Inaugural Exhib at gallery in Chelsea, 2001; Gramercy Int Art Fair, NY, 97; Earl McGrath Gallery, NY, 98; Jan Cicero Gallery, Chicago, 79, 82, 84, 87, 99, 2000; N-3 Gallery, Brooklyn, 99; Women and Geometric Abstraction, Pratt Gallery, NY, 99; Linda Schwartz Gallery, Cincinnati, 2000, 2001; Eaton Fine Art, West Palm Beach, Fla, 2002; Drawing Conclusions II, NY Arts, 2003; Nat Acad Design, NY, 2004; NY Arts Gallery, 2005; The Painting Ctr, NY, 2005; Order(ed), Gallery Siano, Philadelphia, 2005; Loosely Defined, Katharina Rich Perlow Gallery, NY, 2006, Summer Show, 2006. *Pos:* Exhib editor, ARTS Magazine, 90-93. *Teaching:* Instr, Univ Houston, Tex, 78-79, Univ Southern Calif, LA, 79-80; mem painting faculty, Art Ctr Col Design, Pasadena, Calif, 80-85; adj faculty, Dept Fine Arts, Hofstra Univ, NY, 89-95, assoc prof, 1995-2001, prof fine arts, 2002-; visiting artist, Emily Carr Col Art, Vancouver, 81, East Carolina Univ, Greenville, NC, 83, Claremont Grad Sch, Calif, 84, Sch Art Inst, Chicago, 93, Triangle Workshop, summer 97, Univ Del, 98, Pratt Inst, 99, Colo State Univ, October 2002, Irish Arts Council, Dublin, Ireland, May 2003

FENG, YING
PAINTER, PHOTOGRAPHER
b Chengdu City, Si Chuan Province, China. *Study:* Si Chuan Norman Univ, BFA (art), 1986-94; Pastel School/Nat Art Club with Jason Chang, 1999-2002. *Work:* Su Zhou Pastel Mus, China; Amerasia Bank Gallery, Flushing, NY; Chengdu Arts Mus, China; Queens Art Inst, Flushing, NY; Si Chan Mus of Art, China. *Comn:* Portrait of Mr. Wu, Chinese Culture Ctr, Flushing, NY, 2000; Portrait of Bank President, Lin's Gallery, Hong Kong, 2001; Portrait of Actor, Lin's Gallery, Hong Kong, 2001; Portrait of Musician, Taiwan Ctr, Flushing, NY, 2001; Mural of Chinese Culture, Lin's Gallery, Hong Kong, 2002. *Exhib:* 89th Allied Artists Am (juried), Nat Art Club, New York City, 2002; 74th Am Artists Prof League, Salmagundi Club, New York City, 2002; Collected Works of China 1st Pastel Exhib, Suzhou Art Mus, Su Zhou, China, 2003; 61st Audubon Artists (juried), Salmagundi Club, New York City, 2003; 63rd Audubon Artists Show (juried), Salmagundi Club, New York City, 2005; Joyce Duka Arts Found, Nat Art Club, New York City, 2005; 33rd Pastel Soc of Am Show (juried), Nat Art Club, New York City, 2005; 1st & 2nd Int Pastel Exhib (juried), Taiwan Ctr, Flushing, NY, 2005 & 2006. *Pos:* Prog dir, North Am Pastel Artists Asn, Flushing, NY, 98-; program dir, N Am Pastel Artists' Assoc, Flushing, NY; owner & operator, Ying Feng's Art Studio, Flushing, NY, currently. *Teaching:* Instr pastel, Golden Eagle Inst, Flushing, NY, 2004-; instr pastel & oil, Ying Feng's Art Studio, Flushing, NY, 2004-; prof, Golden Eagle Inst, Flushing, NY. *Awards:* Silver Metal, 89th Allied Artists of Am, Dianne B Barnhard, 2002; Gold Metal, 61st Audubon Artists, 2003, 63rd Audubon Artists, 2005; Vera Sickinger Award, Figure in Pastel, Am Artists Prof League, 2006. *Mem:* Audubon Artists Inc; The Am Artists Prof League Inc; Pastel Soc of Am; North Am Pastel Artists Assoc (prog dir, 97); The Allied Artists of Am Inc. *Media:* All Media. *Publ:* Ed, Allied Artists Award Winer: Ying Feng, World Jour, 2002; contribr, Collected Works of China Pastel Exhib, Gu Wu Xian Pub, 2003; ed, Art Times: Audubon Artist Award Winner, Art Time, 2003; ed, Excellent Pastelist: Ying Feng, World Journal, 2005; L'Art du Pastel, Art Du Pastel En France, 2006. *Mailing Add:* 141-25 Northern Blvd Apt C11 Flushing NY 11354

FENG, Z L
PAINTER, EDUCATOR
b Shanghai, China, Oct 23, 1954. *Study:* Shanghai Teacher's Univ, BFA, 82; Radford Univ, MFA, 89. *Work:* Springfield Art Mus, Mo; Art Mus, Radford Univ, Va; Walt Disney World, Orlando; Gulfstream Aerospace Ctr; Orlando Int Airport. *Comn:* Maya Angelou (portrait), Radford Univ, 90; Mr Ferlin (portrait), Va Tech, Blacksburg, 92; Judge Jame Sprouse (portrait), Fed Ct House, Richmond, Va, 97; portrait, CarilionHealth System, Radford, Va, 99; portrait, Dr Douglas Covington, pres Radford Univ, 2005. *Exhib:* Shanghai Mus Fine Arts, 81; Contemp Chinese Artists, Mod Art Mus, Paris, 82; Nat Mus Fine Arts, Beijing, 86; The Face of Am, Arts Ctr Galleries, Old Forge, NY, 94; Tresors, World Trade Ctr, Singapore, 94; Nat Art Club, NY, 99; Salmagundi Club, NY, 1999, 2000; one-man show, The Art of Feng, Art Mus Radford Univ, 2000; 1st Int Exhib Int Watermedia Masters, Nanjing, China, 2007; Invitational Watercolor Masters Exhibition, JinJiang, China, 2008; Shanghai Zhujiajiao Int Watercolor Biennial Exhib, Shanghai, China, 2010; Invitational exhib Contemp Int Watermedia Masters, Nanjing, China, 2010, 2012, 2013. *Pos:* Master panelist, PSA, NY, 95-. *Teaching:* Asst prof studio art, Shanghai Teacher's Univ, 82-86; prof, Radford Univ, 91-. *Awards:* Best Show award, Grand Nat Watercolor Exhib, Mississippi Mus Art, 2002; Best in Show Award, Int Juried Competition, Soc Watercolor Artist, Ft Worth, Tex, 2003; AAPL Award, Allied Artists Am, NY, 2004; Best in Show Award, Hilton Head Art Festival, SC, 2005-2006; 2nd Place Award, Watercolor Soc Ala, Nat Exhib, Birmingham, Ala, 2007; Cash Award & Patron Purchases Award for watercolor, Springfield Art Mus, Springfield, Mo, 2009; Best in Show, Red River Valley Mus Int, Juried Art Exhib, Vernon, Tex, 2010; Who's Who in Am Art References Award in aquamedia, Audubon Artists, New York, 2010; Best in Show, Watercolor Soc Ala. Nat Exhib, Tuscambia, Ala, 2011; 1st Place Award, Northwest Watercolor Soc, Nat Exhib, Mercer Island, Wash, 2011; Best in Show, KY w/c Soc, 2011, Best in Show, MT w/c Soc, 2011, W/C Honor award, Academic Artists Assn, MA, 2012; Third award, Adirondacks Nat Exhib, Am Watercolors, Old Forge, NY, 2012; First Place award, Northwest Watercolor Soc, Int Exhib, Seattle, Wash, 2013; First Place award, Rockies West Nat Grand Junction, Colo, 2013; Third award, World of Watercolor, Signature American Watermedia Exhib, Fallbrook, Calif, 2013; First Prize, La Watercolor Soc, 2013; Best in show, Soc Watercolor Artists Int Juried Art Exhib, Fort Worth, TX, 2013; Silver award, Mid Atlantic Regional Watercolor Exhib, Baltimore Watercolor Soc, Stevenson, MD, 2013. *Bibliog:* Phil Eastey (auth), West Meets East, PBS-TV Sta, Harrisonburg, Va, 91. *Mem:* AWS; Allied Artists Am; Audubon Artists; Nat Watercolor Soc; PSA; Watercolor USA Honor Soc. *Media:* Oil, Watercolor, Pastel, Egg Tempera. *Publ:* Illusr, Creative Watercolor, 95, Best of Watercolor-Painting Texture, 97 & The Best of Watercolor 2, Rockport Publ Inc, 97;

illusr, The Artistic Touch 2, The Artistic Touch 3, Creative Art Press, 99 & China-Watercolor, 2001; Watercolor Mag (featured article), 2010; Watercolor Artist Mag (cover art & featured article), 8/2011; Pastel Jour Human Nature: A Demo by Z.L Feng, 2013. *Dealer:* Little Gallery on Smith Mt Lake 30 Booker T Washington Hwy Moneta VA 24121. *Mailing Add:* 1006 Walker Dr Radford VA 24141

FENSCH, CHARLES EVERETTE
ADMINISTRATOR, EDUCATOR
b Mansfield, Ohio, Dec 11, 1935. *Study:* Kent State Univ, Ohio, BS (art), 58; Wayne State Univ, Detroit, Mich, MAE, 65; Univ Mich, Ann Arbor, Mich, MA, 75. *Work:* Univ Tex, El Paso. *Comn:* Mural series, Kent State Univ, Ohio, 58. *Exhib:* Mich Craftsmen, Detroit Inst Art; Fourth Invitational, Henry Ford Col, Dearborn, Mich; 16th Regional Exhib, Univ Mich, Ann Arbor; 15th Ann Exhib, Canton Inst Art, Ohio; Mich-Ind exhib, Nazareth Col, Ind; Brigham Young Univ, Provo, Utah; Museo de Arte, Mex; Univ Texas, El Paso, Tex. *Teaching:* Prof art, Eastern Mich Univ, 65-81; prof & chmn, Dept Art & Theatre Arts, Univ Tex, El Paso, 82-, assoc dean. *Awards:* Artist Teacher Yr, State Mich, 73; Best in Show, Mich Artists Exhib, Mich State Comn, 74; Kennedy Art Ctr Fel, 2001. *Mem:* Nat Art Educ Asn (vpres); Mich Art Educ Asn (pres); Tex Asn Sch Art (bd dir); Nat Coun Arts Adminr (sec, treas & pres, 94); Coll Art Asn; Texas Art Ed. *Publ:* Auth, Art, a return to structure, E'lan; Art conference proposals, Art Educ, Nat Art Educ Asn. *Mailing Add:* Univ Tex Dept Art El Paso TX 79968

FENTON, JULIA ANN
CURATOR, CONCEPTUAL ARTIST
b Tupelo, Miss, Feb 11, 1937. *Study:* Millsaps Coll, Jackson, Miss, BA (relig), 58; Pa State Univ, grad study in philos & visual arts, 62-65; Atlanta Coll Art, 70-74. *Exhib:* Transcripts for Justine, High Mus Art, Heath Gallery, 77; Encuentro Int de Video 1977, Mus de Arte Contemporaneo de Caracas, Venezuela, 76-77; The Avant-Garde: 12 in Atlanta, High Mus Art, 79; solo exhibs, Reductions, Atlanta Women's Art Collective, 80; You Are Here, Callanwolde Art Ctr Gallery, Atlanta, Ga, 90; Baby, Blackfish Gallery, Portland, Ore, 99; Foul is Fair, Calif State Univ, Chico, 2001; Trench, Mark Woolley Gallery, Portland, Oreg, 2001; Devices and Desires, Mark Woolley Gallery, 2003; In the Garden, Adams St Univ, Alamosa, Colo & Emory Univ, Atlanta, Ga, 2006; Emerging Artists 2006, Spruill Gallery, Atlanta, Ga, 2006; Change: Works by Lucinda Bunnen, Anette Cone-Skelton, Donald Locke and Rocio Rodriguez, Spruill Gallery, Atlanta, Ga, 2006. *Pos:* Ed, Contemp Art-Southeast Mag, 75-77 & Atlanta Art Workers Coalition Newspaper, 77-78; ed & vpres ed affairs & mem bd dir, Contemp Art/Southwest, 76-77; dir activities & ed newspaper, Atlanta Art Workers Coalition, 77-78, dir info resources & bd dir, 79-80, Southeastern Women's Caucus Art (prog chairperson, 79); acting co-dir, Nexus Contemp Art Ctr Gallery, Atlanta, Ga, 89-90; dir, Chastain Gallery, Atlanta, Ga, 90-93; gallery dir, Nexus Contemp Art Ctr, Atlanta, Ga, 93-95; dir, Newport Visual Art Ctr, Ore, 96-98; mem, City Coun, Toledo, OR, 2004-2006; exhibs dir, Spruill Gallery, Atlanta, Ga, 2006-2007. *Awards:* Named Outstanding Woman in the Arts, Atlanta Women Film, 82; Named Outstanding Woman in the Arts, Ga Soc Hist Preserv, 96. *Bibliog:* John Howett (auth), Julia Fenton at the Atlanta women's art collective, Art in Am, 4/81; Lois Allan (auth), Julia Fenton at Blackfish Gallery, Artweek, Vol 30, No10, 10/99; Sue Taylor (auth), Trench, Art In America, 2/2002. *Mem:* Coll Art Asn; Ga Asn Mus & Galleries; Am Asn Mus. *Media:* Multimedia and Site Specific Installations. *Publ:* Contribr, John Y Fenton (ed), Theology and Body, Westminster, 74; ed, Contemporary art Vol 1, No 1 & 2, Southeast Mag, 76; ed, Thirty-Six Women Artists, Atlanta Women's Art Collective, 4/6/78; Annette De Meo Carlozzi and Julia A Fenton, Out of Bounds: New Work by Eight Southeastern Artists, Nexus Contemp Art Ctr, Atlanta, 96. *Dealer:* Mark Woolley Gallery Portland OR. *Mailing Add:* 2367 Autumn Dr Snellville GA 30078

FENWICK, ROLY (WILLIAM ROLAND)
PAINTER, EDUCATOR
b Owen Sound, Ont, Feb 4, 1932. *Study:* Mt Allison Univ, NB, with Alex Colville & Lawren Harris Jr, scholar, 54. *Work:* McIntosh Gallery, Univ Western Ont; Owens Mus, Mt Allison Univ, NB; London Regional Art & Hist Mus, London Free Press, Ont; Sir George Williams Univ, Montreal; Art Gallery Hamilton. *Comn:* President portrait, Univ Western Ont, 94. *Exhib:* Montreal Spring Exhib, Montreal Mus Fine Arts; solo exhibs, Nancy Poole Studio, London, Ont, 70, 72 & 76, London Regional Art Gallery, Ont, 78, Bau-Xi Gallery, Toronto, 84, 86, 88, 89, 90, 91, 92 & 95, Gairloch Gallery, Oakville, Ont, 90, Tom Thomson Gallery, Owen Sound, Ont, 90 & Thielsen Galleries, London, Ont, 92 & 95; Experiencing Drawing, McIntosh Gallery, Univ Western Ont, London, 87; Landscape, Bau-Xi Gallery, Toronto, 87; Personal Visions, Bau-Xi Gallery, Toronto, 89; Love for the Land, Homer Watson Gallery, Kitchener, Ont, 94; Watermarks, Bau-Xi Gallery, Toronto, 97; Oil and Water Works, Michael Gibson Gallery, London, Ont, 98; James Baird Gallery, Newfoundland, 98; Art Mart 98, with Tony Urquhart, London Reg Art Gallery, London, Ont, 98; Scanning the Contemp Landscape, Gallery Lambton, Sarnia, Ont, 98. *Pos:* Art dir, Simpsons-Sears, Toronto, 56-66. *Teaching:* Prof visual arts, Univ Western Ont, 68-89, prof emer, 90-. *Mem:* Univ Art Asn Can; Royal Can Acad; Ont Soc Artists. *Media:* Oil, Watercolor. *Publ:* Illusr, War and Other Measures, House Anansi, 77; Wintering Over, Quadraut Ed, 80. *Dealer:* Bau-Xi Gallery 340 Dundas St W Toronto ON M5T 1G5; Michael Gibson Gallery Carling St London ON. *Mailing Add:* 755 Maitland St London ON N5Y 2W4 Canada

FEODOROV, JOHN
ARTIST
b Los Angeles, Calif, 1960. *Study:* Calif State Univ, Long Beach, BFA (drawing & painting); Vt Col, Montpelier, MFA. *Work:* Road to Heaven, 2004; Heaven, 2004; Origin of Religion, 2005; Chose One, 2005; Breath of Life, 2005; Myth Today, 2005; Office Shaman, 2005; Gods Feeding, 2005; Sucrement, 2006; Temple, 2006; Alphabet, 2006. *Exhib:* What Makes the Red Man Red?, King Co Art Comn, 95; Here/After, SOIL, Seattle, 99; Office Shamans & Other Mythologies, Sacred Circle Gallery, Seattle, 2001; Myths & Prophesies, Howard House, Seattle, 2002; Four Sacred Spaces, 911 Media Arts Ctr, Seattle, 2005. *Pos:* arts comnr, Seattle, 2000-2003. *Teaching:* art teacher, Fairhaven Col, Western Wash Univ, Bellingham; arts educator, Arts Corps, Seattle, 2001-. *Awards:* Sheldon Bergh Award, Basil H Alkazzi Found, NY, 95; GAP Grant, Artist Trust, Seattle, 2000; Artist Assistance Award, Jack Straw Found, Seattle, 2002. *Mailing Add:* Fairhaven College Western Washington University 516 High St Bellingham WA 98225-9118

FERBER, LINDA S
CURATOR, HISTORIAN
b Suffern, NY, May 17, 1944. *Study:* Barnard Col, New York, BA, 66; Columbia Univ, New York, MA, 68 & PhD (Wyeth Endowment Am Art fel), 80. *Pos:* Cur Am painting & sculpture, Brooklyn Mus, New York, 76-85, chief cur, 85-99; Andrew W Mellon cur Am art, 99-. *Teaching:* Adj prof art hist, Columbia Univ, 78-98 & CUNY, 2003. *Awards:* Phi Beta Kappa, 66; Fleishman Award, Smithsonian Archives Am Art, 2002. *Mem:* Coll Art Asn; Am Asn Mus; Int Found Art Res; Archives Am Art; Asn Art Mus Cur; Am Studies Asn. *Res:* Am art with a special interest in painting and sculpture of the nineteenth century. *Publ:* Coauth, The New Path: Ruskin and the Am Pre-Raphaelites, The Brooklyn Mus, 85; auth, Never at Fault: The Drawings of William Trost Richards, The Hudson River Mus, 86; coauth, Albert Bierstadt: Art & Enterprise, The Brooklyn Mus in assoc with Hudson Hills Press, Inc, 91; coauth, Masters of Color and Light: Homer, Sargent and The American Watercolor Movement, Brooklyn Mus in assoc with Smithsonian Inst Press, 98; coauth, America: The New World in 19th Century Painting, Prestel Verlag, 99, Pastoral Interlude: William T Richards in Chester County, 2001 & In Search of a National Landscape: William T Richards in the Adirondacks, 2002

FERBERT, MARY LOU
PAINTER
b Cleveland, Ohio, Sept 21, 1924. *Study:* Duke Univ, BA, 45; Cleveland Inst Art, 68-78 & 95. *Work:* Cleveland Mus Natural Hist; Cleveland State Univ, Ohio; Nat Mus Women Arts, Washington, DC; Zimmerli Art Mus, Rutgers Univ; Am Numismatic Soc, NY; El Paso Mus of Art; Butler Inst Am Art, Youngstown, Ohio; Fed Res Bank of Cleveland; Cleveland Artist Found, CARTA, Cleveland. *Comn:* Painting 45 x 30, Huntington Bank, 86; painting 641/2 x 421/2, Richard E Jacobs Group, 87; painting 48 x 96, Cleveland-Cliffs Inc, Cleveland, Ohio, 88; three paintings 60 x 36, Key Bank, Cleveland, Ohio, 92; 75th Anniversary Commemorative Medal, Cleveland Mus Natural Hist, 95; painting, 34 3/4 x 53 1/2, RPM Inc, 97; painting 36 x 96, Rocky River Pub Libr, Ohio, 98; painting 40 x 32, Rocky River Pub Libr, Ohio, 2002; painting 48 x 48, Am Diabetes Asn, Celebrity Art Auction, Cleveland, 2002; painting, Cleveland Cliffs Inc, Cleveland, Ohio, 88; painting 84x 47 3/8, Lakewood Hosp, Ohio, 90; painting 48 x 96, Cleveland Cliffs Inc. *Exhib:* solo exhibs, Gallery Madison, go, NY, 87, Butler Inst Am Art, Youngstown, Ohio, 93, Bonfoey Gallery, Cleveland, 2001, 2005, 2013, The Gathering Place, Cleveland, 2008, Old Stone Church, Cleveland, 2009, Intown Club, Cleveland, 2010, Howser Gallery, 2010, Judson Park, Ohio, 2010, Bennett Galleries, Knoxville, Tenn, 97, Howser Gallery, Ohio, 2010; Group exhibs, Catherine Lorillard Wolfe Art Club Ann, 82-90, 92-93, 95-2011; Watercolor USA, Springfield Art Mus, Mo, 94; Nat Asn Women Artists, Athens, Greece, 96; Gallery BAI, Barcelona, Spain, 98; Bonfoey Gallery, Cleveland, 2001, 2005, 2013; State of the Art Biennial Watercolor Invitational, 1st Venue Siena Hts, Ill, 2003, 2nd Venue Parkland Coll, Champaign, Ill, 2004; NEO Show, Cleveland Mus Art, 2005; Zimmerli Mus Art, Rutgers Univ, 2009; 30 Mem Watercolor Hon Soc juried, Nat Art Ctr, Japan, 2010; Bontoeg Gallery, Cleveland, 2013. *Teaching:* Instr watercolor, Cleveland Inst Art, 86 & 89-98. *Awards:* Bronze Medal of Hon, 120th Ann Exhib, Am Watercolor Soc, 87; Special Mention for Painting, 69th Ann Exhib, May Show, Cleveland Mus Art, 88; Medal Hon, 93 & Hon mem, 98, Catharine Lorillard Wolfe Art Club; Golden Achievement Award, Golden Age Ctrs of Greater Cleveland Inc, 99; Award NJ Watercolor Soc, 2000, 2002; Honored Guest, Cleveland Artists Found, 2005; plus others. *Bibliog:* Rachel Wolf (auth), Splash 1, 91, Splash 2, 93, Splash 4: The Splendor of Light, 96, Splash 5: Best of Watercolor, 98, Splash 7, 2002 & Splash 10, 2007, Splash 13, 2012, N Light Bks, Cincinnati; Elizabeth McClelland (auth), The Art of Mary Lou Ferbert, Ohio Artists Now, Cleveland, 93; Katheryn Kipp (auth), the Best of Flower Painting, N Light Bks, Cincinnati, 97; Adelene Flethcer (auth) The Flower Painter Pocket Palette Book 2, Chartwell Bks, Inc, Edison, NJ, 2000; Glencoe Lit Readers Choose, Glencoe/McGraw-Hill, NY, 2000; Nina Gibans (auth), Creative Essence: Cleveland's Sense of Place, Kent State Univ Press, 2005. *Mem:* Am Watercolor Soc; Catharine Lorillard Wolfe Art Club, Inc; Nat Asn Women Artists; charter mem Watercolor USA Honor Soc; Artists Archives of the Western Reserve; Nat Watercolor Soc; Transparent Watercolor Soc Am; Ohio Watercolor Soc; Cleveland Artists Found. *Media:* Transparent Watercolor. *Interests:* The natural science, archit, sports. *Publ:* Auth, Nature in the City, Cleveland Mus of Nat Hist, 79 & Book of Hearts, 4-Chamber Press, 2008. *Dealer:* Bonfoey Gallery 1710 Euclid Ave Cleveland OH 44115. *Mailing Add:* 334 Parklawn Dr Cleveland OH 44116

FERGUSON, ALICE C
PAINTER
b New Brunswick, NJ, Feb 7, 1947. *Study:* Rutgers Univ, 65-66; various workshops for oil painting, 94-95. *Exhib:* Art by the Sea, Bethel Creek House, Vero Beach, Fla, 94-98; Grand Nat Exhibs, Salmagundi Club, NY, 95-97, 99; Allied Artists Ann, Nat Arts Club, NY, 96 & 98; Am Artists Prof League Invitational; Regional Exhib Fine Art, Martin Co Cult Ctr, Stuart, Fla, 97; Phillips Mill (juried), New Hope, Pa, 2006. *Awards:* Best in Show, Martha Lincoln Gallery, 97; 1st Place Award, Vero Beach, 2000, 2nd place oils, 2009. *Mem:* Fel Am Artists Prof League; assoc mem Allied Artists Am; Vero Beach Art Club. *Media:* Oil. *Mailing Add:* 1221 W Island Club Sq Vero Beach FL 32963

FERGUSON, CHARLES B
MUSEUM DIRECTOR, PAINTER
b Fishers Island, NY, June 30, 1918. *Study:* Williams Col, AB; Art Students League, painting with Frank Dumond & graphics with Harry Sternberg; Trinity Col, MA. *Work:* New Britain Mus Am Art, Conn; Mattatuck Mus, Waterbury, Conn; DeCordova Mus, Lincoln, Mass; Amerind Found, Ariz; Scoville Corp, Waterbury, Conn. *Comn:* Stained glass window, Fishers Island, 71; murals, Williston Acad, East Hampton, Mass, Renbrook Sch, West Hartford, Conn, pvt home, Fishers Island, NY & Henry L Ferguson Mus, Fishers Island, NY; 7 murals, Fishers Island, NY, 94. *Exhib:* Conn Acad Fine Arts; Conn Watercolor Soc; Greater Hartford Civic Arts Festival; Williams Coll Mus, Williamstown, Mass, 91; Red Barn Gallery, Fishers Island, NY; Solo exhibs, New Britain Mus, Conn, Mattatuck Mus, Conn & Farmington Mus Village Libr, Seabury, Bloomfield, Conn. *Collection Arranged:* Aaron Draper Shattuck, 70; Robert B Brandegee, 71; William T Richards, 73; Dennis Miller Bunker, 78; Three Generations of Wiggins, 1870's-1970's, 79; Three Centuries of Connecticut Art, 81; Allan Butler Talcott, Painter of Landscapes, 83; paintings & etchings in many pvt collections in US, Eng, the Caribbean & Beijing, China. *Pos:* Dir, New Britain Mus Am Art, Conn, 65-84; trustee, Hillstead Mus, Farmington, Conn, currently; pres, Henry L Ferguson Mus, Fishers Island, NY, currently; art adv, Hartford Steam Boiler Insurance Co, Conn. *Teaching:* Instr hist art & studio painting, Trinity Col & Loomis Sch, Eaglebrook Sch, Mass & The Hillschool, Pa. *Awards:* New Britain Herald Prize, 70; Sanford Low Prize, Conn Acad Fine Arts, 71; First Place in Oil, Int Maritime Exhib, Mystic, Conn, 78; First Prize for Oils, Mystic Marine Exhib, Conn, 81. *Mem:* Conn Acad Fine Arts; Art Guild Framington; New Britain Mus; HL Ferguson Mus New York; Hill-Stead Mus Conn. *Media:* Acrylics; Watercolor. *Publ:* 67 years of the Fishers Island Golf Club Links, pvt publ, 94; 27 Views of Rare Rock Lighthouse in the Four Seasons, 2000. *Mailing Add:* 200 Seabury Dr Bloomfield CT 06002

FERGUSON, LARRY SCOTT
PHOTOGRAPHER, CURATOR
b North Platte, Nebr, May 16, 1954. *Study:* Univ Nebr, Lincoln, BFA, 77; Rochester Inst Technol, NY, sem 78. *Work:* Sheldon Mem Art Gallery, Lincoln, Nebr, Libr of Cong, DC; Western Heritage Mus, Omaha, Nebr; Univ Okla, Norman; Murray State Univ, Ky; and others. *Comn:* Photograph, collab Sachio Yamashita, Metrop Arts Coun, Omaha, Nebr, 79 & photograph, murals & sculpture, 79; photograph, Bldg Reborn, Smithsonian Inst, DC, 79; photograph, Tube Walkway, Omaha Airport Auth, Nebr, 80. *Exhib:* Am Vision, Nat Artists Alliance, NY Univ, 79; Juried Exhib, Friends of Photog Gallery, Carmel, Calif, 79 & Diana Camera Show, 80; Omaha: Then & Now, Western Heritage Mus, 79, Omaha: Then & Now II, 80 & Omaha: Then & Now III, 81; Solo exhibs, Sheldon Mem Art Gallery, Lincoln, Nebr, 79 & Southern Light Gallery, Amarillo, Tex, 80; Walker Art Ctr, Minneapolis, 81; and others. *Pos:* Cur photog, Adams Co Hist Soc, Hastings, Nebr, 77-78, Nebr Arts Coun & Nat Endowment for Arts artist-in-residence grants & cur photographs, Bostwick-Frohardt Collection, Western Heritage Mus, Omaha, 78-81. *Teaching:* Instr photog, Univ Nebr, Omaha, 81-, Bellevue Col, 82-. *Awards:* Jurors Award, Nat Artists Alliance, 79; Jurors Award, 2nd St Gallery, Charlottesville, Va, 80; Artist in residence Grant, Nebr Arts Coun, 81-82. *Bibliog:* Shawn P Leary (auth), Arts scan, 79 & Art Simmering (auth), Dodge Street, 80, Omaha Mag; Joanne Stanwick (auth), Suitable for framing, Omaha Mag, 81; article, Artweek, 9/5/81; and others. *Mem:* Soc Photog Educ; Friends of Photog; Visual Studies Workshop, Rochester, NY. *Publ:* Contribr, Twelve Photographers: A Contemporary Mid-America Document, Mid-Am Arts Alliance, 78; contribr, Self-Portrayal: The Photographers Image, 79 & Untitled Number 21, by Jim Alinder, 80, Friends of Photog; Object and Image, by George Craven, Prentice-Hall, 82. *Mailing Add:* 1701 Vinton St Omaha NE 68108-1432

FERGUSON, MAX
PAINTER, PRINTMAKER
b New York, NY, 1959. *Study:* New York Univ, BS, 80. *Work:* Metrop Mus Art, NY; Forbes Mag Collection, NY; NY Hist Soc; The British Mus; City Amsterdam, Holland; Toledo Mus Art, Ohio. *Comn:* Richard Brown Baker, Estate of H W Janson, Mus City New York, Staatliche Museen Zu Berlin, Graphische Sammlung Albertina, Vienna, Martin Margulies. *Exhib:* Solo exhibs, Gallery Henoch, New York, 84, Coney Island, Gallery Henoch, New York, 90, ACA Galleries, New York, 2003, Paintings of Urban Intimacy, Gallery Henoch, New York, 2010; Starved for Art, Sch Visual Arts Mus, NY, 85; Urban Visions: The Contemp Artist, Adelphi Univ, Garden City, NY, 87; Pratt/Silvermine Int Print Competition, New Canaan, Conn, 86; New York Realism-Touring Exhib, Japan, 94; 20th Century realism, Ogunquit Mus Am Art, Maine, 97; Realism, Amarillo Mus Fine Arts, Tex, 98; Beauty & the Book, Israel Mus, Jerusalem, 2005; Impressions of New York, NY Hist Soc, 2005. *Bibliog:* John Loughery (auth), Arts Mag, 11/86; Patrick Pacheco (auth), The New Faith in Painting, Arts & Antiques, 5/91; Vivien Raynor (auth), New York Times, 3/92; William Zimmer (auth), New Yrok Times, Feb 86; Nocturnes & Nightmares, Alys Palladino-Craig (auth), Fla State Univ Mus, 87; Vivien Raynor (auth), 8/87; Richard Levine (auth), New York Times, 12/87; Joan Schwartz-Michel (auth), Hadsassah Mag, 3/94; Milton Esterow (auth), Artnews, 4/98; Jan Seidler Ramirez(auth), Painting the Town, Mus City New York, 2000; Marilyn Symmes (auth), Impression of New York, NY Hist Soc, 2005; Joseph Jacobs (auth), Art & Antiques Mag, 12/2007; Dario Lodi (auth), Intorno Alla Piturra, Italy, 2008. *Media:* Pil on Panel, Pencil, Watercolor, Intaglio Etching

FERGUSON, RUSSELL
EDUCATOR, CURATOR
Study: Univ Stirling, Scotland, BA; Hunter Col, City Univ of NY, MA. *Collection Arranged:* In Memory of My Feelings: Frank O'Hara and American Art, Mus of Contemporary Art, 1999, The Undiscovered Country, Hammer Mus, 2004. *Pos:* Editor, then as assoc curator, Mus of Contemporary Art, Los Angeles, 1991-2001; dep dir exhibitions and programs, chief curator, Hammer Mus, Los Angeles, 2001-07, adj curator, 2007-. *Teaching:* Prof, Dept of Art, Univ Calif Los Angeles, 2007-, chair, 2007-2013. *Publ:* (ed) Discourses:Conversations in Postmodern Art and Culture; (ed) Out There:Marginalization and Contemporary Cultures. *Mailing Add:* UCLA Department of Art Broad Art Center, Suite 2275 240 Charles E Young Dr Los Angeles CA 90095-1615

FERGUSON-HUNTINGTON, KATHLEEN E
PAINTER
b Chicago, Ill, Jan 31, 1945. *Study:* Stephens Col, Columbia, Mo, 63-64; Layton Sch Art, Milwaukee, Wis, BFA, 69; RI Sch Design, Providence, MFA, 71; Md Inst Coll Art, Digital Arts, 99. *Work:* Russell Courthouse, Atlanta. *Comn:* J B Speed Mus, 87; Honeywell Corp, Minneapolis, Minn. *Exhib:* One-person shows, Univ Cincinnati, 81, Graham Mod Gallery, NY, 85, High & Mus Art, Atlanta, Ga (with catalog), 86, Kozmic Kingdom, An Environmental Installation, JB Speed Mus, Louisville, Ky, 87, Southeastern Ctr Contemp Art, Winston-Salem, NC, Sun Cities Art Mus, Ariz, 92, Angeles Gate Art Ctr, Los Angeles, 94, Milwaukee Inst Art & Design, 97, Mus Modern Art, Machynlleth, Wales, 2002, Centre Culture Francais, Doha, Qatar, 2002, Higher Bridges Gallery, Clinton Ctr Enniskillen, Northern Ireland & UK, 2009, County Cavan, Ireland, 2010; Va Mus Fine Arts, Richmond, 73; Biennial of Contemp Am Art, Whitney Mus Am Art, NY, 75; Southern Abstractions, traveling to Contemp Arts Ctr, New Orleans; The Santa Fe Sculpture Project 1993, NMex, 93; New Mexico 93, Mus Fine Arts & Mus NMex, Santa Fe, 93; Ernesto Mayans, Santa Fe, NMex, 96; 40 American Artists, Mus de Arateau de Rochefort-En-Terre, France, 2003; Women & Art, A Global Perspective, Sharjah, UAE, 2005; Summer at Home, Wakif Art Ctr, Doha, Qatar; Higher Bridges Gallery, County Fermanagh, UK, 2009; Brit Al Boranda Mus, Muscat Oman, 2008. *Teaching:* Vis artist, Conn Col, 79; asst prof, Univ Ky, 80-82; teaching fac, Va Commonwealth Univ, Doha, Qatar, 2000-2011. *Awards:* Ky Arts Coun Grant; Fel, Helene Wurlitzer Found, Taos, NMex; Ky Found for Women Grant, Sally Bingham, La; Harwood Found, Univ NMex, Taos, NMex; VCUQ Fac Rsch Grant, 2004-06, 2008-2011. *Bibliog:* John Yau (auth), article, Art Am, 79; William Zimmer (auth), article, Soho Weekly News, 79; Grace Glueck (auth), article, NY Times, 85; Peter Frank (auth), article, Press-Telegram, 5/94. *Mem:* Coll Art Asn Am Int Sculpture Ctr; Founds in Art Theory & Educ. *Media:* Mixed Media. *Res:* The Silk Road. *Publ:* Contribr, Milton Klonsky (auth), Speaking Pictures, Crown, 74; auth & illusr, Natti's Navigations, pvt publ, 78

FERHOLT, ELEANORE HEUSSER See Heusser, Eleanore Elizabeth Heusser Ferholt

FERN, ALAN MAXWELL
MUSEUM DIRECTOR
b Detroit, Mich, Oct 19, 1930. *Study:* Univ Chicago, AB, 50, MA, 54 & PhD, 60; Courtauld Inst, Univ London, res scholar. *Collection Arranged:* Diverse print, poster & photo shows, Libr Cong, 62-82; Leonard Baskin, Nat Collection Fine Arts, Smithsonian Inst, 70; var exhibs at Nat Portrait Gallery, 82-2000. *Pos:* From asst cur to cur, asst chief to chief, Prints & Photographs Div, Libr Cong, 61-76, dir, Res Dept, 76-78, dir, spec collections, 78-82; dir, Nat Portrait Gallery, Smithsonian Inst, 82-2000. *Teaching:* From asst to asst prof, Univ Chicago, 52-61. *Awards:* Chevalier, Ordre de la Couronne, Belgium, 80; Chevalier, Ordre des Arts et des Lettres, France, 85; Commander, Royal Order of Polar Star, Sweden, 88. *Mem:* Print Coun Am (dir, 63-69, pres, 69-71); Coll Art Asn Am (dir, 84-88); Am Antiquarian Soc; Double Crown Club, London; Grolier Club, New York; Cosmos Club, Washington, DC. *Res:* History of prints, posters, book design, 19th and 20th century art. *Publ:* Auth, A note on the Eragny Press, Cambridge Univ Press, 57; coauth, Art nouveau, 60 & Word and image, 69, Mus Mod Art, NY; Leonard Baskin, Smithsonian Press, 70; Revolutionary Soviet film posters, Johns Hopkins Press, 74; Arnold Newman's Americans, Little Brown, 92. *Mailing Add:* 3605 Raymond St Chevy Chase MD 20815

FERNANDEZ, JAKE
PAINTER; PHOTOGRAPHER
b Havana, Cuba, May 13, 1951. *Study:* Univ Fla, BA, 76; Univ S Fla, MFA (Grad Teaching Fel), 79. *Work:* Ringling Mus Art, Sarasota, Fla; Fla State Capitol Bldg, Tallahassee; Contemp Art Mus, Univ S Fla, Tampa; St Petersburg Community Col, Fla; Am Express Corp, Jacksonville, Fla; Lawton Chiles Foundation, Annamarie Is, Fla. *Exhib:* Ann Exhib Contemp Am Painting, Soc Four Arts, Palm Beach, Fla, 75, 76, 78; The New Floridians, Jacksonville Art Mus, Fla, 77, 78; Seven Realists from the Southeast, Southeastern Ctr Contemp Art, Winston-Salem, NC, 78; Selection from Fla Collections, Dunedin Art Ctr, Fla, 91; Screen Plays, Ormond Meml Art Mus, Ormond Beach, Fla, 95, Fla Craftsman Gallery, St Petersburg, 95, Appleton Mus, Ocala, Fla, 95, Ctr Arts, Vero Beach, Fla, 96; solo exhibs, Frances Wolfson Art Gallery, Miami Dade Co Community Col, 98, Mus Art, Ft Lauderdale, Fla, 2000. *Teaching:* Instr pastel, Armory Art Ctr, West Palm Beach, Fla, 2000. *Awards:* Merit Award, Sarasota Art Asn, 79; State Fla Individual Artist Fel, Fla Div Cult Affairs, 99. *Bibliog:* Sheldon Lurie (auth), Abstraction: Four From Latin America, Miami Dade Community Col, 86; Juan Martinez (auth), Jake Fernandez, Sites & Composites, Miami Dade Community Col, 98; Allys Palladino-Craig (auth), Jake Fernandez: Etheral Journeyman, Mus Art, Ft Lauderdale, 2000. *Media:* Oil, Pastel. *Dealer:* Cole Pratt Gallery 3800 Magazine St New Orleans LA 70115; Peter Marcel Fine Art NY; Timpson Gallery Ga; ACA Galleries NY

FERNIE, JOHN CHIPMAN
SCULPTOR
b Hutchinson, Kans, Oct 22, 1945. *Study:* Colo Col, 63-65; Kansas City Art Inst, BFA, 68; Univ Calif, Davis, grant, 69, teaching fel & MFA, 70. *Work:* San Francisco Mus Art; Univ Calif Mus, Berkeley. *Exhib:* Solo exhibs, Nova Scotia Coll Art, 74 & John Gibson Gallery, 77; Group exhibs, Documenta 5, Kasel, Ger, 72; 8th & 9th Biennale de Paris; Israel Mus, 76; Houston Mus of Contemp Art, 77; Whitney Mus, NY, 78; Denver Art Mus, 78; Boulder Art Ctr, Colo, 79; and others. *Pos:* Bd dirs, The Children's Hosp Found. *Teaching:* Asst, Univ Calif, Davis, 69; instr sculpture, Calif

Col Arts & Crafts, 70-72, Stephens Col, 72-75 & Nova Scotia Col Art & Design, 75-. *Bibliog:* Richardson (auth), article in Arts Mag, 2/71; Albright (auth), Exciting, compelling show, San Francisco Chronicle, 7/1/71; Jochimsen (auth), Magazin Kunst, 7/74. *Media:* Wood, Cardboard, Photo, Plaster. *Publ:* Auth, Petit trianon, twikkel, I worship you, God bless your symmetry, 70; Masters survey, 70; The Billy and Abdul Letters

FERO, SHANE
GLASS BLOWER, COLLAGE ARTIST
b Chicago, Ill, Sept 10, 1953. *Study:* Plattsburg State Univ, 74-76; Penland Sch Crafts, NC, with Stephen Dee Edwards, Fred Birkhill & Paul Marioni, 88-89; Pilchuck Glass Sch, Seattle, Wash, with Kurt Wallstab, 91. *Work:* Mus Am Glass, Wheaton Village, Millville, NJ; Glasmuseum, Ebeltoft, Denmark; New Orleans Mus Art; Huntsville Mus Art, Ala; Ashville Mus Art, NC. *Exhib:* Craft of the Carolinas, Gibbes Mus Art, Charleston, 93; solo exhib: Ariodante Gallery, New Orleans, 1993, 1995 & 1997, Blue Spiral 1, Asheville, NC, 2001 & 2004, erl originals, Winston-Salem, NC, 2001, R Duane Reed, St Louis, MO, 2002, Featured Artist, Vetri, Seattle, Wash, 2004, Vespermann Gallery, Atlanta, Ga, 2005, Philabaum Glass Gallery, Tucson, Ariz, 2005, Marta Hewett Gallery, Cincinnati, Ohio, 2007, Huntsville Mus Art, Ala, 2008, Georgia State Coll & Univ, Milledgeville, Ga, 2008; Breaking the Mold: New Directions in Glass (with catalog), Huntsville Mus Art, 96; The Glasmuseum-The First Ten yrs, Ebeltoft, Denmark, 96-97; Contemp Flameworked Glass, Mus Am Glass, Millville, NJ, 97; 15th Int Glass Invitational, Habatat Galleries, Boca Raton, Fla, 97; Venezia Biennial of Glass, Centro Studio Vetro, Venice, Italy, 98; Sofa: Chicago, 1995-2000; Mint Mus Craft & Design, Charlotte, NC; Kentucky Mus Craft & Design, Louisville, Ky; Hunter Mus Am Art, Chattanooga, Tenn; Mus Am Glass at Wheaton Village, Millville, NJ. *Teaching:* Penland Sc Crafts, NC, 90-99; Urban Glass, Brooklyn, 96-98; instr flameworking glass, Corning Mus Glass, NY, 97-; Pilchuck Glass Sch, Stanwood, Wash, Pittsburgh Glass Ctr, Pa, Eugene Glass Sch, Eugene, OR, Pratt Fine Arts Ctr, Seattle, Wash, Int Nat Glass Ctr, Niijima, Japan, Int Glass Festival, Stourbridge, UK, Creative Glass, Rochester, Kent, UK, formerly. *Bibliog:* Joan Falconer Byrd (auth), Glass from North Carolina, Glasmuseum, Ebeltoft, Denmark, 95 & Shane Fero: Myth, Magic & Spirit, Urban Glass Mag, 97/98. *Mem:* Piedmont Craftsmen; Am Craft Coun; Glass Art Soc. *Media:* Glass, Mixed Media. *Dealer:* Albertson-Peterson Gallery 329 Park Ave S Winter Park FL 32789. *Mailing Add:* c/o Penland Sch PO Box 266 Penland NC 28765

FERRARA , ANNETTE
EDITOR, EDUCATOR
Study: Sch of Art Inst, MA. *Pos:* Found ed, writer TENbyTEN, Chicago, 99-. *Teaching:* Lectr, Columbia Col, DePaul, SAIC; teacher, art hist Mus of Contemp Art. *Mem:* Chicago Art Critics Asn. *Publ:* Co-auth: Xtreme Interiors, 2003; contributor writings to Artforum, zingmagazine, provinceton Arts

FERRARA, JACKIE
SCULPTOR
b Detroit, Mich. *Work:* Chase Manhattan Bank, Solomon R Guggenheim Mus, Whitney Mus Am Art, Mus Mod Art & Metrop Mus Art, NY; Los Angeles Co Mus of Art; Dallas Mus Fine Art; High Mus Art; Nat Mus Am Art, Washington. *Comn:* Wash Conv & Trade Ctr, Seattle, 89; Stuart Collection, Univ Calif, San Diego, 91; Pittsburgh Int Airport, 92; Tang Ctr, Mass Inst Technol, 95; MTA Arts for Transit, Grand Central Subway, NY, 2000; Univ Conn; Baruch Coll, New York; Univ Houston; Tuft Univ, Medford, Mass; Mus Art & Design, New York. *Exhib:* Biennial Exhib, Whitney Mus, 73 & 79; Recent Acquisitions, Mus Mod Art, NY, 83; Solo exhibs, Moore Coll Art, Philadelphia, 87, San Antonio Art Inst, 87, Genovese Gallery, Boston, 90, Michael Klein Inc, NY, 91, 94 & 96, Hudson River Mus Westchester, Yonkers, NY, 93 & Freedman Gallery, Albright Coll Ctr Arts, Reading, Pa, 93, In Focus: Jackie Ferrara, Mus of Contemp Art, Chicago, 98, Univ Conn, Storrs, 2000; More Than Minimal: Women's Work in the 70s, Rose Art Mus, Brandeis Univ, 96; Max's Kansas City, 65 Thompson Street, NY, 96; Constructions, Michael Klein Gallery, NY, 96; Outdoor Exhibition, Woodson Art Mus, Wausau, Wis, 96; Red Arches, Frederieke Taylor/TZ Art, NY, 98; Solo retrospective, Frederieke Taylor/TZ' Art Gallery, NY, 2000; Sculptures and Drawings, Frederieke Taylor Gallery, 2002; Long-Bin Chen: Redaing Sculpture, Frederieke Taylor Gallery, 2003; Federieke Taylor, Tuft Univ, 2007. *Awards:* Grants, NY State Coun Arts, 71 & 75 & Nat Endowment Arts, 73, 77 & 87; Guggenheim Found Fel, 76; Award for Excellence in Design, Art Comn City NY, 88; Inst Hon, Am Inst Architects, 90; Tucker Award for Design Excellence, Building Stone Inst, 91. *Bibliog:* Kirby Gookin (auth), Jackie Ferrara, Artforum, 9/94; Davie Rimanelli (auth), Constructions, New Yorker, 2/12/96; Nancy Stapen (auth), Feminism meets minimalism, Boston Globe, 4/30/96. *Publ:* Jackie Ferrara Drawings, 6 & 7/77, Lapp Princess Press, New York, 77; Jackie Ferrara Sculpture, A Retrospective, Ringling Mus, Sarasota, 92. *Dealer:* Frederieke Taylor 535 W 22d St New York NY 10011. *Mailing Add:* 121 Prince St New York NY 10012

FERRARI, DOUGLAS
ARTIST
Study: Rutgers Univ, BA, 1992; Montclair State Col, MA, 1994; Brooklyn Col, MFA, 1997; Drew Univ, Dr of Letts in Contemp issues, 1999-. *Exhib:* Solo exhibs, Relic Quarries, Chuck Levitan Gallery, NY, 1997, Exhib of Sculpture & Prints, Lockjaw Gallery, Philadelphia, Pa, 1998, Rittenhouse Gallery (Rittenhouse Hotel), Philadelphia, Pa, 1999, Thompson Park Gallery, Middletown, NJ, 2000. *Pos:* Exec dir & pres, Shore Inst of the Contemp Arts. *Teaching:* Grad Asst, Art dept, Montclair State Univ, 1993-1994; Adj fac, Art Dept, Brookdale Community Col, 1994-; Adj fac, Bloomfield Co, spring, 1997; Adj fac, Ocean Co Community Col, fall, 1999-2002. *Mailing Add:* 610 Sewall Ave Apt 15L Asbury Park NJ 07712

FERRARI, VIRGINIO LUIGI
SCULPTOR, EDUCATOR
b Verona, Italy, Apr 11, 1937. *Study:* Scuola d'Arte N Nanni, Verona, Italy; Acad Cignaroli, Verona, Italy. *Hon Degrees:* Master of Art/Sculpture. *Work:* Biennale Nazionale di Verona; High Mus Art, Atlanta, Ga; Univ di Parma Mus, Italy; Ravinia Park, Highland Park Ill; City of Verona Public Gardens; City of Chicago, Corner of State and Washington St. *Comn:* Bronzes, Pick Hall for Int Studies, Univ Chicago, 71; Vanderbilt Univ Med Ctr Hosp, 80; Being Born(sculpture), City of Chicago, 83; Revenue Bldg, Springfield Ill, 85. *Exhib:* Brooklyn Mus, 68; Art Inst Chicago, 68; traveling exhibs, State Ill Arts Coun, 69, Ill Bronzetto Ital, 71, Int Art Expo, Chicago, 81-86 & Mile of Sculpture, 82-84; Sears Tower Bank, Chicago, 77; Seven Sculptors, DePaul Univ, 78; retrospective, Paris Art Ctr, France & Cult Ctr, Ill, 85; V Ferrari - 1959-2003 Ombre della Sera, Gallery d'Arte Moderna, Verona, Italy, 2003; and many others. *Collection Arranged:* 6 Sculturi Americani Dall'Illinois in Europa, Baur, Dunbar, Emser, Ferrari, Rojek, Scarff, EUR Lake and park, Rome, 2000. *Pos:* Sculptor-in-residence, Univ Chicago, 66-76; Liceo Artistico, Verona, 63-66; Loyola Univ, Rome Ctr, 99-01. *Teaching:* Asst prof sculpture, Univ Chicago, 67-76. *Awards:* Nostra Ministero Publica, Istruzione Roma, Italy, 64; Biennale Nazionale di Verona, 65; Ill Coun of Am Inst Architects Award, 77; Man of the Yr, Ital Cult Ctr, Ill, 86; Cavaliere Officiale Republica Italiana, Official Knight of the Italian Republic, 93; Ill Governors Award, IAC, 2003. *Bibliog:* Arturo Quitavalle (auth), Ferrari Gocce d'Amor Pop, Univ di Parma, 70; article, Cimaise Mag, 82; V Ferrari sculpture, Paris Art Ctr, Rizzoli Publ, 85. *Mem:* Sindacato Artisti; Arts Club Chicago; Hyde Park Art Ctr (bd mem). *Media:* Metal, Marble. *Mailing Add:* 5429 S Eastview Park Chicago IL 60615-5980

FERREIRA, ARMANDO THOMAS
EDUCATOR, SCULPTOR
b Charleston, WVa, Jan 8, 1932. *Study:* Chouinard Inst; Long Beach City Col; Univ Calif, Los Angeles, BA & MA. *Work:* Wichita Art Mus; State Calif Collection; Univ Utah Art Mus. *Exhib:* Los Angeles Co Mus, 58, 60 & 66; Pasadena Mus Art, 68; Univ Calif, Santa Barbara, 73; Northern Ill Univ, 86; Beckstrand Gallery, Palos Verdes, Calif, 87; Univ Madrid, 92; and other solo & group exhibs. *Teaching:* Prof ceramic sculpture, Calif State Univ Long Beach, 57-85, assoc dean, Sch Fine Arts, 85-91, acting dean, Col Arts, 91-; Fulbright lectr, Brazil, 81. *Awards:* Purchase Awards, Calif Expos, 61 & Wichita Art Asn, 66; Fel, Nat Asn Schs Art & Design. *Mem:* Nat Asn Schs Art Comn Accrediting; Int Video Art Network. *Media:* Clay, Mixed. *Mailing Add:* c/o State Univ Dept Art 1250 N Bellflower Blvd Long Beach CA 90840-0006

FERRELL, CATHERINE (KLEMANN)
SCULPTOR
b Apr 27, 1947; US citizen. *Study:* Fla Atlantic Univ, BA (sculpture), 69; Univ Miami, MA (sculpture), 72; further study, Pietrasanta, Italy; apprenticeship, Montoya Intl Art Studios; studied with Blair Buswell, Stanley Bleifield, Jill Burkee, Lincoln Fox, Jerry Balciar, Kirsten Kokkin, Jo Saylors, Zahourek & Veryl Goodnight; further study, Pietrasanta, Italy; apprenticeship, Montoya Int Art Studios. *Work:* Brookgreen Sculpture Gardens, SC; Norton Mus Art, Fla; Cornell Mus Art & Hist, Fla; Bennex Int, Oslo; Armand Hammer United World Coll, NMex. *Comn:* Black African Stone Fish, John H Surovek Fine Arts, Palm Beach, Fla, 82-83; Alabaster Self-Portrait, comn by Artine Artinian, Palm Beach, Fla, 83; Mythical Fish, comn by Mr & Mrs Gunter Schulz-Franke, Osnäbruck, WGer, 83; archit sculpture & wall reliefs, comn by Sally Gingras, West Palm Beach, Fla, 83 & 84; sculpture, comn by Mr & Mrs Marshall Brumer, Bellevue, Wash, 98; United World Col, Montezuma, NMex, 2002. *Exhib:* 105th Ann Exhib, Catharine Lorillard Wolfe Art Club, New York, 2001; 51st Nat Exhib Contemp Realism Art, Acad Artists Asn, 2001; Nat Sculpture Soc Ann Awards Exhib, SC & New York, 2001; Angels, Cupids & Winged Creatures of Fantasy, Nat culpture Soc, New York, 2002; A Magnificent Menagerie: Animals in Sculpture, Brookgreen Gardens, SC, 2001; Art in the Atrium, Nat Sculpture Soc, New York, 2002; Nine Exceptional Artists, Cheryl Newby Gallery, SC, 2005; Am Soc Marine Artists, Vero Beach Mus Art, Fla, 2005; Art of the Animal Kingdom, Bennington Ctr Arts, Vt, 2001-2001, 2004, 2006-2007; Salmagundi Club Ann Combined Exhib, New York, 2000-2008; Am Soc Marine Artists 30th Ann Nat Exhib, Chase Ctr, Wilmington, Dela, 2008; Nat Sculpture Soc 75th Ann Awards Exhib, 2008; Solo exhibs, Pen & Brush, New York, 2002, Cheryl Newby Gallery, SC, 2003, Masters Gallery Fine Art, Colo, 2007, Gallery 14, Vero Beach, Fla, 2007, Crest Theatre Galleries, Delray Beach, Fla, 2009-2010; American Women Artists, Sonoran Desert Mus, 2012; Allied Artists, 2013; The Sea of Cortez, Ariz Sonoran Desert Mus, 2013. *Pos:* Sculptor in residence, Brookgreen Garden, 2000-01; owner & pres, Art Equities Inc; artist in res, Brookgreen Gardens, 2000-1. *Awards:* Silver Medal of Honor, Audubon Artists of Am, 99. *Bibliog:* Pam Harbaugh (auth), Art from the Heart: Catherine Klemann Ferrell, Cornell Mus Art & Hist, Fla, 99; Gail Hyer (auth), The Serendipity of Sculpting, Catherine Ferrel's Charmed Career, Wildlife Art, 99; Julie Tarasovic (auth), Portrait of the Artist, Indian River Mag, Jan/Feb 2008. *Mem:* Fel, Am Artists Prof League, New York; Am Soc Marine Artists (signature mem); Pen & Brush, New York (prof mem); Salmagundi Club, New York; Catherine Lorillard Wolfe Art Culb, New York; Soc Animal Artists (assoc); Allied Artists Am; Am Women Artists (signature mem). *Media:* Bronze, Stone. *Interests:* Traveling, reading, painting & sketching. *Dealer:* Art of the Sea Gallery S Thomaston ME; Cheryl Newby Gallery Pawleys Island SC; Gunnar Nordstrom Gallery Bellevue WA; JM Stringer Gallery Bernardsville NJ; Cheryl Newby Gallery. *Mailing Add:* 12546 N Hwy A1A Vero Beach FL 32963-9411

FERRELL, HEATHER A
MUSEUM DIRECTOR
b Boise, Idaho, Aug 15, 1970. *Study:* Utah State Univ, BFA, 1994; Case Western Res Univ, MA, 1997. *Work:* Dir, Snapshots: Lives in Transition. *Exhib:* The Allegorical Figure, CWRU Mather Gallery. *Pos:* Dir & adj art fac, Roland Dille Ctr for the Arts Gallery, Univ Minn, 1998-1999; collections mgr/registrar, Plains Art Mus, Fargo, NDak, 1997-1999; assoc cur of art, Boise Art Mus, 1999-2005; dir, Salina Arts Ctr,

Salina, Kans, 2005-2008; exec dir, Salt Lake Art Ctr, 2008-. *Awards:* Best of Boise: Arts Prof, Boise Weekly, 2004; Mus Leaders the Next Generation, Getty Leadership Inst, 2004; 1997 Dorothy Zieburtz Buckhold Teaching Asst, Case Western Res Univ, 1997. *Mem:* bd mem, newsletter editor, Mus in NDak, 1998-1999; bd mem, exec com, Western Mus Asn, Berkeley, Calif, 2003-; bd mem, Idaho Asn of Mus, Boise Idaho, 2003-. *Mailing Add:* Salt Lake Art Center 20 South West Temple Salt Lake City UT 84101

FERRI-GRANT, CARSON
PAINTER, FILMMAKER
b Pawtucket, RI, Dec 17, 1950. *Study:* RI Sch Design, 1962; Hunter Col, Psychology (cum laude & Psi chi), 1979; Univ Conn, Sociodrama (summa laude), 1984; Pratt Sch Art & Design (continuing Ed), 1985; Columbia Univ; Actor's Studio with Lee Strasberg (1970-1974). *Work:* Jerome Robbins Found Collection, 1976; Robert Stigwood (SRO) Found Collection, 1977; Fun Gallery, 1978; Jack Morris Gallery, 1979; Helena Segy Found Collection, 1991. *Comn:* Nature-Nuclear Installation, Am the Beautiful Fund, NYC, 1978; Alternative Energy Installation, Avon Found, NYC, 1979; Coney Island Bathing Beauties, Coney Island Show, Am Express, NYC, 1979; Times Sq Show, Times Sq Restoration Fund, NYC, 1979; Harmony Mountain, SIGGRAPH 1990 Convention, 1990. *Exhib:* In the City Environment, Chicconelli Gallery, NYC, 1978; Art in the Parks, NJ Coun Arts, Fort Lee, NJ, 1980; NYC Project, Charas Mus, NYC, 1981; Historical Venues, Conn Coun Arts, Hartford, Conn, 1984; Spring 1987, UFT Fed Plaza, NYC, 1987; No 1 Kodak 1888, Eastman Kodak 160 Ann Javit Ctr, New York, 88; Shade of Winter, Symphony Space Broadway Ctr, NYC, 2007; Evolving Spirit, WSAC, New York, 2008; 36 Ann Salon Show, WASC, New York, 2009. *Teaching:* Adj Fac: Video Arts, Univ Conn, 1983-1984; Mixed Media Painting, Col New Rochelle, 1986-1988; Computer Animation, Pratt Sch Art & Design, 1988-1990. *Awards:* Gold Key Artisan Award, RI Youth Exhib, RI Coun Arts, 1963; Vision in Art, 1990 SIGGRAPH Convention, SIGGRAPH, 1990; GIAA: Italian Am Heritage 2007, GIAA Film Festival, Guild Italian Am Actors, 2007. *Bibliog:* James Dalton (auth), How Does a Man Imagine Post Nuclear, Times, 11/30/1979; Cathy Taylor (auth), Gratis Ads Light Great White Way, Ad Wk, 2/25/1991; Leesa Davis (auth), Who Got the Part, Backstage, 11/9/2006; Denise Kaminsky (auth), A Lifetime of Arts, Denise's Media Interviews, 4/2006; Cindy Van Schalkwyk, Native Son's Heart is in the Arts, Warren Times Gazette, 1/11/2007; Byron Colman (auth), The Creative Spirit, Gallery & Studio Mag, Vol II, Feb 2009. *Mem:* Actors Equity Asn (1970-2008); Am Fed Television & Radio Asn (1970-2008); Screen Actors Guild (1970-2008); Westside Arts Coalition (founder, bd dirs, 1976-2008); Environmental Artists United (founder, 1977-2008). *Media:* Mixed Media. *Mailing Add:* 255 W 90 St #PH-12D New York NY 10024

FERRIS, DANIEL B
GALLERY DIRECTOR, CURATOR
b Columbia, SC, Sept 10, 1947. *Study:* Univ SC, BS, 69; Alliance Francaise, Paris, 73. *Collection Arranged:* Spirit of the Object, Humphrey Fine Arts, 92. *Pos:* Dir, Amos Eno Gallery, New York, 90-; cur, YWCA Gallery, Brooklyn, NY, 90-91. *Bibliog:* The Amos Eno Performance Arm, Downtown, 3/91; Plenty of Energy, The Villager, 2/28/91; Downtown Essentials, Best of the Week - Spirit of the Object; Downtown Express, 4/26/92. *Mem:* Asn Artist Run Galleries; Coalition Independent Artists (exec dir, 85-); BWAC, 91-. *Specialty:* Contemporary. *Mailing Add:* 210 E 15th St No 11A New York NY 10003

FERRIS, (CARLISLE) KEITH
ILLUSTRATOR, PAINTER
b Honolulu, Hawaii, May 14, 1929. *Study:* Tex A&M Col; George Wash Univ; Corcoran Sch Art; spec study with Tad Crawford & Gerald McConnell, Pratt Inst, 79. *Hon Degrees:* Daniel Webster Col, Hon DHL, 95. *Work:* USAF Art Col, Pentagon; Nat Air & Space Mus, Smithsonian Inst; US Airforce Mus, US Airforce Acad. *Comn:* Boeing; Gen Electric; Lockheed Martin; Pratt & Whitney; Mural (25ft x 75ft), Fortresses Under Fire, World War II Gallery, 76, & mural (20ft x 75ft), Evolution of Jet Aviation, 81, Nat Air & Space Mus, Smithsonian Inst, Washington DC; Painting of Mem, USAF Mem Found, 2006; and others. *Exhib:* USAF Exhib, NY Soc Illusr, 61-; Solo exhibs, Nat Air Space Mus, Smithsonian Inst, Washington, 69-70, NY Soc Illusr, 70 & 79, US Air Force Mus, 83, US Air Force Acad, 83, Am Airlines C R Smith Mus, Ft Worth, 95, Simuflite, Ft Worth, 96, 03-08, Mighty Eighth Air Force Heritage Mus, Savannah, 98 & CR Smith (Am Airlines) Mus, Ft Worth, 08, Air Force Gallery, Pentagon, 2012, 2013; ASAA Ann Exhibs, 86-2013; Colo Springs Fine Art Mus, 90; Royal Air Force Mus, 91; Daniel Webster College, 2000; Pacific Air Forces, Royal Hawaiian Hotel, Honolulu, 2002; George Bush Pres Libr, Tex A&M Univ, Coll Station, Tex, 2003; US Air Force Mus, 2003; Soc Illustrators, New York, 2003; The Mighty 8th Air Force Mus, Savannah, Ga, 2003; Aviation Art Invitational Exhib, Art Mus Battle Creek, Battle Creek, Mich, 2009. *Pos:* Art dir-prod mgr, Cassell Watkins Paul Art Studio, St Louis, 52-56; freelance artist/illusr, 56-; chmn, Air Force Art Comt, Soc Illusr, 68-70 & 79-91, hon chmn, 91-; pres, Am Soc Aviation Artists, 88-90. *Teaching:* Workshop, in conjunction with Am Soc Aviation Artists Ann Forum, 89, 90, 92, 94, 95 & 96, 99, 2000, 2002, 2004, 2005, 2006, 2007, 2009, 2010, 2011, 2013; Brookdale Community Coll, Lincroft, NJ, 2004. *Awards:* Citation of Hon, Air Force Asn, 78; Dean Cornwell Recognition Award, Soc Illusr, 92; Best Show, Am Soc Aviation Artists, 95 & 96; Laureate for Life Time Achievement, Aviation Week & Space Technol Laureate Hall Fame, Nat Air & Space Mus, 2004; Laureate, Illusr Hall Fame, Soc Illustrators, NY, 2006; Nat Aviation Hall of Fame, 2012; Distinguished Statesman, National Aeronautics Assn, 2012. *Bibliog:* Putting the Brush to Art History, NY Times, 1/29/1989; Flight of the Imagination, Sunday Star Ledger, Newark, NJ, 1/16/1994; A Life of Turning Aviation into High Art, NY Times (Arts and Entertainment Section), 1/21/2001; Air Power on Canvas, Air Force Mag (cover story), 9/2008. *Mem:* Life mem NY Soc Illusr; founding mem Am Soc Aviation Artists; Air Force Assn (life mem); United States Naval Inst, (life mem). *Media:* Oil. *Res:* Specific events in military history, military & aircraft camouflage, technical aspects of aviation, art, art history, artists' rights and copyright law, and high visibility paint systems . *Specialty:* Prints, posters, aviation art. *Interests:* Aviation technology & history. *Collection:* Over 2,000 books, tech manuals, drawings, & slide/photog reference files. *Publ:* The Aviation Art of Keith Ferris, Peacock Press, Bantam Bks, 78; Real trouble, Aviation Art Mag, Vol 2, 94; Global workhorse, Flight Mag, 11-12/96; auth, Life, Flight and Art, Air Power History, Vol 52, No 1, Spring 2005; Waikiki Sunrise, Aero Brush, Vol 20, Number 20, Spring, 2007. *Dealer:* Keith Ferris Galleries. *Mailing Add:* 50 Moraine Rd Morris Plains NJ 07950

FERRIS, MICHAEL
SCULPTOR
Study: Kans City Art Inst, Mo, BFA, 1991; Ind Univ, Bloomington, MFA, 1996. *Exhib:* Solo exhibs, Pittsburg State Univ, Kans, 2001, Western Ill Univ, 2002, Ill Inst Art, 2002, Chicago Cult Ctr, 2002, Quincy Art Ctr, Ill, 2003, Roswell Mus & Art Ctr, 2003, Ctrl Mich Univ, 2009, Hope Coll, 2009, Edinboro Univ, 2009; Painting and Sculpture Exhib, Am Acad Arts & Letts, 2005; Shot in the Arm, Northern Ill Univ Mus, 2006; Besser Collection, de Young Mus, San Francisco, 2007; The Poetic Dialogue Project, Bowling Green State Univ, Ohio, 2009; The Figure Five Ways, Schick Gallery, Skidmore Coll, 2010. *Awards:* Ill Arts Coun Fel, 1999; Marie Walsh Sharpe Space Prog Grant, 2003; George Sugarman Found Grant, 2005; BRIO Sculpture Grant, Bronx Coun Arts, 2009; NY Found Arts Fel, 2009. *Bibliog:* Lisa Stein (auth), These Sculptures Tell Tales, Pioneer Press, 5/28/1998; Lydia Gibson (auth), Spiritualizing the World, Chicago J, 11/13/2003; Lauren Weinberg (auth), Monsters and Immortals, Time Out Chicago, 10/17/2005

FERRISO, BRIAN J
MUSEUM DIRECTOR
b Brunswick, Maine, Jan 25, 1966. *Study:* Bowdoin Coll, AB (economics), 1988; NY Univ, MA (visual-arts administration), 1994; Univ Chicago, AM (medieval Italian art history), 1999. *Pos:* Assoc dir develop Newark Mus, NJ, formerly; asst dir Smart Mus Art, Univ Chicago, 1997-2000; deputy dir and sr dir curatorial affairs Milwaukee Art Mus; exec dir and chief exec officer Philbrook Mus Art, 2003-06; exec dir Portland Art Mus, 2006-. *Mem:* AAM; Asn Art Mus Dirs; Phi Delta Kappa. *Mailing Add:* Portland Art Museum 1219 SW Park Ave Portland OR 97205

FERTITTA, FRANK J, III
COLLECTOR
b Las Vegas, 1946. *Study:* Univ Southern Calif, BA. *Pos:* Gen mgr, Station Casinos, Las Vegas, 1985-86, dir, exec vpres & chief operating officer, 1986-89, pres, 1989-2000, chief exec officer, 1992-, chmn, 1993-; co-owner, Ultimate Fighting Championship, 2001. *Awards:* Named one of Top 200 Collectors, ARTnews mag, 2008-13. *Collection:* Modern and contemporary art. *Mailing Add:* Station Casinos Inc 2411 W Sahara Ave Las Vegas NV 89102

FERTITTA, LORENZO J
COLLECTOR
b Las Vegas. *Study:* Univ San Diego, BA, 1991; Stern Sch, New York Univ, MBA, 93. *Pos:* Pres & chief exec officer, Fertitta Enterprises, Inc, 1993-2000; comnr, Nev State Athletic Comn, 1996-2000; pres, Station Casinos, Las Vegas, 2000-2008, bd dirs, currently; co-owner & chmn, Ultimate Fighting Championship, 2001-, chief exec officer, 2008-; chair & CEO, Ultimate Fighting Championship, 2008-. *Awards:* named one of Top 200 Collectors, ARTnews mag, 2011, 2012, 2013. *Collection:* Modern and contemporary art. *Mailing Add:* Zuffa/UFC 2960 West Sahara Ave Las Vegas NV 89102

FESSLER, ANN HELENE
FILMMAKER, WRITER
b Toledo, Ohio, Oct 2, 1949. *Study:* Ohio State Univ, Columbus, BA, 72; Webster Col, St Louis, MA (media), 75; Univ Ariz, MFA (photog), 82. *Work:* Whitney Mus Am Art; Ctr Creative Photog; Mus Contemp Art, Chicago; Franklin Furnace Book Arch, NY; Mus Mod Art. *Comn:* MAPTAP, Maryland Arts Place, 85; billboards, Art Against Aids, NY, 90; roadside installation, She Rode Horses, Washington Proj Arts, DC. *Exhib:* Going for Baroque, Walters Art Mus, Baltimore, Md, 95; Ex/Changing Families, Calif Mus Photog, Riverside, Calif, 97; Close to Home, Bell Gallery, List Ctr, Brown Univ, Providence, RI, 2001; Everlasting, Md Inst Coll Art, Baltimore, Md, 2003; Everlasting: New Eng, Radcliffe Inst, Harvard Univ, Cambridge, Mass, 2004. *Collection Arranged:* Expanding Commitment: Diverse Approaches to Socially Concerned Photography, Meyerhoff Gallery, MD Inst Coll Art, 86. *Teaching:* Instr photog & video, Webster Col, St Louis, 74-79; vis artist photog, Tyler Sch Art, 81-82; instr photog & books, Md Inst Col Art, 82-92; head, Photography Dept, RI Sch Design, 93-97, 2007-2008, 2009-2011, 2013-; prof, photog dept, RI Sch Design, 97-. *Awards:* Artist's Fel, RI State Arts Coun, 2002, 2013; Artist's Fel, Nat Endowment Arts, 89; Production grant, LEF Found, 2002, 2003; Radcliffe Fel, Radcliffe Inst, Harvard Univ, 2003-2004. *Bibliog:* Bella English (auth), The Girls Who Went Away, The Boston Globe, 7/28/2003; Robert Speer (auth), Deprived of a chance to be Mothers, San Francisco Chronicle, 5/7/2006; Kathryn Harrison (auth), In Trouble, NY Times Book Review, 6/11/2006. *Media:* Video, Audio. *Res:* Current work addresses the long-term impact of surrendering a child for adoption. Writing & artwork gives voice to the surrendering mothers. *Publ:* Auth, Guide to Coloring Hair, Tyler Offset Press, 82; First Aid for the Wounded, 87, Life Saving & Water Safety, Visual Studies Workshop, 89; Art History Lesson, copublished with Nat Mus Am Art, Washington, DC, 91; Genetics Lesson, Nexus Press, Atlanta, 92; auth, The Girls Who Went Away: The Hidden History of Women Who Surrendered Children for Adoption in the Decades Before Roe v Wade, The Penguin Press, 2006; prodr, dir A Girl Like Her (documentary film), Women Make Movies, 2011. *Mailing Add:* RI Sch Design 2 College St Providence RI 02903

FETCHKO, PETER J
MUSEUM DIRECTOR
b Yonkers, NY, July 3, 1943. *Study:* Westminster Col, Fulton, Mo, BA, 65; George Washington Univ, Washington, DC, MA, 72; Univ Paris, Sorbonne, 72. *Collection Arranged:* Stone Age New England (coauth, catalog), 75; Japan Day by Day (coauth, catalog), 77; Christian Art of an African Nation, Ethiopia (coauth, catalog), 78. *Pos:* Cur, Peabody Mus, Salem, 68-80, dir, 80-. *Mem:* Japan Soc Boston; Tatooing Club Japan; Am Ceramic Circle. *Res:* New Guinea and Pacific material culture; Japanese crafts. *Publ:* Auth, Pacific Collections of the Peabody Mus, S Pac Bull, 74; Salem Trading Voyages to Japan During the Early Nineteenth Century, Peabody Mus, 86; ed, Salem: To the Farthest Part of the Rich East, Maritime America, Peter Neill, 88

FETTING, RAINER
PAINTER
b Wilhelmshaven, Ger, Dec 31, 1949. *Study:* Hochschule der Kûnste, Berlin, Meisterschûler, 77; Columbia Univ, New York, 78-79. *Work:* Mus Gegenwartskunst, Basel, Switz; Portland Art Mus, Ore; Mus Contemp Art, Sydney, Australia; Musée des Beaux Arts, Toulon, France. *Exhib:* A New Spirit in Painting, Royal Acad Arts, London, Eng, 81; Image Innovations, Va Mus, Richmond, 83; An Int Survey of Recent Paintings, Mus Modern Art, NY, 84; Origen y Vision, Museo de Arte Moderno, Mexico City, 84; States of War: New Am Painting, Seattle Art Mus, Wash, 85; 1945-1985 Kunst in BRD, Nat Galerie Berlin, WGer, 85; solo exhibs, Kunsthalle Basel, Switz & Mus Folkwang, Essen, WGer, 86. *Bibliog:* Christo Joachimides (auth), Zeitgeist, Katalog, 82; Giovanni Testori (auth), Rainer Fetting, Flash Art, Italy, 4/86; Jean Christopher Ammann (auth), Rainer Fetting, Kunsthalle Basel Katalog, 86. *Dealer:* Marlborough Gallery 40 W 57th St New York NY. *Mailing Add:* c/o de Andino Fine Arts 2450 Virginia Ave NW Washington DC 20037-2679

FEUERHERM, KURT K
PAINTER
b Berlin, Ger, Mar 22, 1925. *Study:* Albright Art Sch; Univ Buffalo, BFA; Cranbrook Acad Art, MFA; Yale Summer Sch, Norfolk, Conn, with NaumGabo, Peter Blume & Ben Shahn; Yale Univ, with Josef Albers, Stuart Davis & Abraham Rattner. *Work:* Cranbrook Art Mus, Bloomfield Hills, Mich; Mem Art Gallery, Rochester, NY; Albright-Knox Art Gallery, Buffalo, NY; Henry Gallery, Univ Wash, Seattle; Am Fedn Art. *Comn:* Ceramic abstract mural, Midtown Plaza, Rochester, NY, 64; Stations on the Cross, Our Lady of Mercy Church, Rochester, 64; St John's the Evangelist Church, Rochester, 65; Liberty Pole (consult designer), City of Rochester, 66. *Exhib:* Am Painting Today, Metrop Mus Art, NY, 50; Cranbrook Painting Exhib, Bloomfield Hills, Mich, 52; Columbia Mus of Art Painting Biennial, SC, 57; Everson Mus Art, Syracuse, NY, 57-70; solo exhib, Henry Gallery, Univ Wash, Seattle, 69; NY Crafts, Munson-Williams-Proctor Inst, Utica, NY, 61; four-man show, Mem Art Gallery, Univ Rochester Fac Show, 70; and others. *Pos:* Conservator, Intermuseum Lab, Oberlin, Ohio, 71-72. *Teaching:* Asst prof painting, Univ Rochester, NY, 60-71; assoc prof studio arts, Empire State Col, Rochester, 73-87; design instr, Polimoda Fashion Sch, Firenze, Italy, 95-97. *Awards:* Purchase Awards (painting & watercolor), Cortland Art Mus, 53; Award of Merit, Columbia Painting Biennial, 57; Henri Projansky Award, Rochester Finger Lakes Exhib, 69. *Media:* Collage, Acrylic. *Dealer:* Malton Gallery 2709 Observatory Ave Cincinnati OH 45208. *Mailing Add:* 3199 Redman Rd Brockport NY 14420-9465

FEW, JAMES CECIL
PAINTER
b Orangeburg, SC, Aug 24, 1930. *Study:* Clemson Col, BS (elec eng), 53; Univ Chicago, MBA, 64; also workshops with Albert Handell, PSA, 88 & 90, Ben Konis, PSA, 89, Marilyn Simpson, PSA, 83, 84 & 85 & William Hook, 99. *Work:* USAF Art Collection, Washington; Air Force Armament Mus Art Collection, Eglin AFB, Fla. *Comn:* Acrylic painting, comn by Richard Pike, Lynn Haven, Fla, 90; pastel, USAF Art Collection, 92; acrylic, US Air Force Art Collection, 97. *Exhib:* Pastel Soc Am Ann Open Exhib, Nat Arts Club, NY, 88, 90, 91, 92 & 94; Knickerbocker Artists USA Nat Open Exhib, NY, 89, 92, 95 & 96; Am Artists Prof League Grand Ann Exhib, 90, 91 & 92, Salmagundi Club, NY, 90, 91 & 92; Allied Artist Am 76th & 78th Ann Exhib, Nat Arts Club, NY, 89 & 91; Salmagundi Nat Open Exhib, Salmagundi Club, NY, 93. *Teaching:* Pvt lessons. *Awards:* Award Merit, Degas Pastel Soc 2nd Biennial Nat Exhib, Degas Pastel Soc, 88; Art Student's League-NY Award, Knickerbocker Artists 39th Nat Open Exhib, Art Student's League, 89; Ballin Award, Salmagundi Nat Open, Salmagundi Club, 93. *Mem:* Pastel Soc Am; Knickerbocker Artists, USA; Degas Pastel Soc; Pastel Soc NFla (bd dir, 88-); Am Artists Prof League. *Media:* Pastel, Acrylic. *Publ:* Pastels with Zing, Artist's Mag, 06/95. *Mailing Add:* 9620 Sunnybrook Dr Navarre FL 32566-2530

FICHERA, JEFFREY
PAINTER
b Cambridge, Mass, Feb 9, 1976. *Study:* Univ Mass, Amherst; Mass Coll Art, Boston, BFA, 2000; Pont-Aven Sch Art, Brittany, France; Univ Pa, Philadelphia, MFA, 2007. *Work:* Ogunquit Mus Am Art. *Exhib:* Solo exhib, Ogunquit Mus Am Art, 2004; two-person exhib with Carol O'Malia, Powers Gallery, Acton, Mass, 2003; group exhibs include Salon Show, Clark Gallery, Lincoln, Mass, 2003, Dir's Choice, 2005 & The Comfort of Home, 2006; New Works 2005, Powers Gallery, Acton, Mass, 2005; The Architecture of Art, Arlington Ctr Arts, Mass, 2006 & Tufts Univ Art Gallery, 2007; 183rd Ann: Invitational Exhib Contemp Am Art, Nat Acad Mus, New York 2008. *Awards:* Gamblin Painting Prize, 1999; Elizabeth Greenshields Found Grant, 2001, 2002 & 2007; Jean Koch Mem Prize for Best in Show, Concord Art Asn Mems Juried Show, 2003; Blanche E Coleman Award, 2003; Best In Show, 6th Ann Newburyport Art Asn Open, 2003; Painting Prize, Frances N Roddy Open, Concord Art Asn, 2003; Hugh & Marian Scott Prize, Woodmere Art Mus Ann Juried Exhib, 2007

FICHTER, ROBERT W
EDUCATOR
b Ft Myers, Fla, Dec 30, 1939. *Study:* Univ Fla, BFA (printmaking & painting), 63; Ind Univ, MFA, 66. *Work:* Int Mus Photog, George Eastman House, Rochester, NY; Pasadena Art Mus, Calif; Nat Gallery of Can, Ottawa; Mus Fine Arts, Boston, Mass; Princeton Univ, NJ; and others. *Exhib:* Contemp Photog from the Collections, Boston Mus Fine Arts, 74; The Art of Offset Printing, Sch Art Inst Chicago, 78; Northern Ky State Col, 81; Whitney Biennial, Whitney Mus Am Art, 81; Robert Freidus Gallery, NY, 81; Photog in Calif 1945-1984, San Francisco Mus Mod Art, Calif, 84; Extending the Perimeters of Twentieth-Century Photog, San Francisco Mus Mod Art, 85; Photog & Art: Interactions since 1946, Los Angeles Co Mus, Calif, 87; Capturing an Image: Collecting 150 Yrs of Photog, Mus Fine Arts, Boston, Mass, 89; The Cherished Image: Portraits from 150 Yrs of Photog, Nat Gallery Can, Ottawa, 89; Graphic Studio, Contemp Art From the Collaborative Workshop at the Univ S Fla, Nat Gallery Art, Washington, DC, 91; one-person exhib, Photog & Other Questions, Int Mus Photog, Rochester, NY, 82 traveled to FSU Fine Arts Gallery, Tallahassee, Fla, 83, Frederick White Gallery, UCLA, 84, Mus Contemp Photog, Columbia Col, Chicago, Ill, 84, Mus Mod Art, San Francisco, Calif, 84, Univ NMex, Albuquerque, 84 & Brooklyn Mus, NY, 85 & New Work, Univ Gallery, Memphis State Univ, 89. *Teaching:* Prof art, Fla State Univ, 1972-2006, prof emeritus, 2006-. *Awards:* Fels, Nat Endowment Arts, 79 & 84; Fla Visual Arts, 81. *Mem:* Coll Art Asn Am; Soc Photog Educ. *Publ:* Auth, Robert Fichter, Photography and Other Questions (exhib catalog), Univ NMex Press & George Eastman House Mus; contribr, Graphics Studio, Univ S Fla, Tampa, 12/10/84; Tamarind Inst, Albuquerque, NMex, 11/9/87; Rolling Stone Press, Atlanta, Ga, 88-90; illus, James Huginin, (auth) A-X Cavation, Dept Art, Univ Colo, 88. *Mailing Add:* 710 Waverly Rd Tallahassee FL 32313

FIDLER, SPENCER D
PRINTMAKER
b Detroit, Mich, Nov 20, 1944. *Study:* Calif State Univ, Northridge, BA, 66; Univ Iowa, MA, 76 & MFA, 78. *Work:* Univ Iowa; Hallmark Fine Art Collection; Musee de Petit Format, Couvin, Belg; Bibliotheque Nationale, Paris; El Paso Mus Art, Tex; NMex State Univ Art Gallery. *Exhib:* Premio Internazionale Biella per l'Ineisione, Bienale, Italy, 97; Fresh Ink, Austin Mus Art, Tex, 97; Liberte, Egalite Fraternite, Mus Arts, Los Angeles, 98; 15th Nat LAPS, Los Angeles, 99; 22nd Int, Kyoto City Mus, Japan, 2002. *Teaching:* Prof printmaking, N Mex State Univ, Las Cruces, 78-. *Bibliog:* Clinton Adams (auth), Printmaking in New Mexico, Univ NMex Press, Albuquerque, 91. *Mem:* Coll Art Asn; Boston Printmakers; Southern Graphics Coun. *Dealer:* Spencer Fidler Las Cruces NM; Flatbed Austin Tex; 416 West Gallery Denison Tex. *Mailing Add:* NMex State Univ Dept Art Las Cruces NM 88003

FIELD, PHILIP SIDNEY
PAINTER, PRINTMAKER
b Brooklyn, NY, Sept 17, 1942. *Study:* Art Students League, with Arnold Blanch; Yale Norfolk Summer Sch Music & Art, 62; Syracuse Univ, BFA, 63; RI Sch Design, with Michael Mazur, MFA, 65; Vienna Acad Fine Arts, Fulbright Grant, 65-67. *Work:* Hunterdon Art Ctr, Clinton, NJ; Syracuse Univ; Univ Dallas; Tulsa City-Co Libr, Okla. *Exhib:* Solo exhibs, Shunjyo Gallery, Tokyo, Japan, 78, Tex Women's Univ, Denton, Tex, 82, Pan Am Univ, Edinburg, Tex, 86 & 88, Robinson Galleries, Houston, Tex, 90, Tex A&M Kingsville, 2003, Univ Tex Pan Am, 97, 98, 99, 2000; Texas Printmakers, N Tex State Univ, Denton, 81; Xochil Art Inst, Mission, Tex, 82; Kansas Eight Nat Small Painting, Drawing & Print Exhib, Fort Hayes State Univ, 83; Across Texas, Patrick Gallery, 84; Dia de los Muertos Exhib, Xochil Art Inst, Mission, Tex, 87 & 88; Arte Rio Grande, McAllen Int Mus, McAllen, Tex, 2001; Native Spirits, Palawan Island, Philippines, 2002; Digital Interactions, Waseda Univ, Tokyo, 2002; Int Fac Exhib, Embassy of Philippines Kuala Lumpur, Malaysia, 2002; Art on the Move, McAllen Int Mus, 2002; Digitally Propelled Ideas, Pomona, Calif, 2002; Siggraph, San Diego, Calif, 2003. *Pos:* Critic, For Art's Sake, column, McAllen Monitor, 80-81. *Teaching:* Instr art studio, Juniata Col, Huntingdon, Pa, 69-70; from instr to assoc prof, Univ Tex, Pan Am, 71-90. *Awards:* Augusta Hazard Award, Lowe Art Ctr, Syracuse Univ, 63; Merit Award, McAllen Int Mus, Tex, 88, Best of Show, 89 & 91; Art Fac of STex, McAllen Int Mus, 88. *Bibliog:* Al Brunelle (auth), article, Art News, 5/73; Maurice Schmidt (auth), Reflections on art, 1/76 & Art, light and history 6/76, Corpus Christi Caller. *Mem:* Coll Art Asn. *Media:* Intaglio; Oil. *Mailing Add:* Dept Art Pan Am Univ 1201 W Univ Dr Edinburg TX 78539

FIELD, RICHARD SAMPSON
CURATOR, HISTORIAN
b New York, NY, Aug 26, 1931. *Study:* Harvard Univ, AB, AM & PhD. *Collection Arranged:* 15th Century Woodcuts & Metalcuts from the National Gallery of Art (with catalog), 65; Jasper Johns: Prints 1960-1970 (with catalog), 70 & Silkscreen: History of a Medium (with catalog), 71, Philadelphia Mus Art; The Fable of the Sick Lion: A Fifteenth Century Blockbook (with catalog), 74, Gabriel de Saint-Aubin (with catalog), 75, Jasper Johns: Prints 1970-1977, 78, Prints Drawings and Paintings by Philip Pearlstein, 79 & The Prints of Armand Seguin (1869-1903), 80, Davison Art Ctr, Wesleyan Univ; Fifteenth Century Woodcuts, Metrop Mus Art, 77. *Pos:* Asst to dir, Fogg Art Mus, Cambridge, Mass, 61-62; asst cur of prints, Alverthorpe Gallery-Nat Gallery Art, 62-68 & Philadelphia Mus Art, 69-72; cur, Davison Art Ctr, Wesleyan Univ, Middletown, Conn, 72-79; cur prints, drawings & photographs & assoc dir, Art Gallery, Yale Univ, New Haven, Conn, 79-. *Teaching:* Assoc prof art, Wesleyan Univ, 72-79. *Awards:* Fulbright Grant, France, 59-60; Finley Fel, Nat Gallery Art, 65-67. *Mem:* Print Coun Am (dir, 70-72). *Res:* Fifteenth century woodcuts; Gauguin; contemporary prints. *Publ:* Auth, Gauguin's Noa Noa suite, Burlington Mag, 68; auth, Woodcuts from Altomunster, Gutenberg-Jahrbuch, 69; auth, Gauguin's Monotypes, 73; auth, The Prints of Richard Hamilton, 73. *Mailing Add:* 46 Mountain View Terr North Haven CT 06473

FIERO, GLORIA K
EDUCATOR, HISTORIAN
b New York, NY, May 19, 1939. *Study:* Univ Miami, Coral Gables, AB, 60; Univ Calif, Berkeley, MA, 61; Fla State Univ, Tallahassee, PhD, 70. *Exhib:* Acadiana Ctr for the Arts, 2012. *Teaching:* Prof hist, Univ La at Lafayette, 69-96, emer, 96-. *Awards:* Fulbright Fel to Belg, 66-67; Amoco Found Award Outstanding Teaching, 83; Honoree, Gloria K Fiero Friends of the Humanities Arts Series, 96; Lifetime Contribution award, La Endowment for the Arts, 2010. *Mem:* Coll Art Asn Am; Southeastern Coll Art Conf; Nat Asn Humanities Educ; South-Central Renaissance Conf (pres, 85-86). *Res:* Late Medieval, northern Renaissance painting and manuscripts; early 20th century painting. *Publ:* Courtier and commoner: Two styles of fifteenth century manuscript illumination, Explorations Renaissance Cult, 77; Geertgen tot Sint Jans & the Dutch manuscript tradition, Oud Holland, 82; Death Ritual in Fifteenth Century Manuscript Illumination, J Medieval Hist, 84; Three Medieval Views of Women, Yale Univ Press, 89; The Humanistic Tradition, 6 vols; 6/e, McGraw-Hill, 98, 2006, 2010; Landmarks in Humanities, 3/e McGraw Hill, 2013, 7th ed, 2015

FILIPACCHI, DANIEL
COLLECTOR
b Paris, France, Jan 12, 1928. *Pos:* French corresp, Ebony Mag, Paris, formerly; photographer, Paris Match mag, formerly, chmn & principal owner, currently; jazz disc jockey & radio producer, Europe 1, Paris, 1955-60; chmn & principal owner, Publs Filipacchi, Paris, 1960-; chmn & chief exec officer, Warner-Filipacchi Music, SA, Paris, 1970-85; chmn, Hachette Filipacchi Mags, New York, 1990-; co-artistic dir, Sidney Bechet Centennial, New Orleans, 1997; producer, Musicsoft/Masters of Jazz; trustee, Guggenheim Mus, currently. *Awards:* Named one of Top 200 Collectors, ARTnews Mag, 2004-12. *Collection:* Modern art, especially Surrealism. *Publ:* Ed, Surrealism: Two Private Eyes, The Nesuhi Ertegun & Daniel Filipacchi Collections, 1999. *Mailing Add:* Hachette Filipacchi Mags 1633 Broadway 40th fl New York NY 10019-6708

FILLERUP, MEL
PAINTER
b Lovell, Wyo, Jan 28, 1924. *Study:* Art Students League; study with Paul Bransom, Serge Bongart, William Reese, Conrad Schwiering, Robert Meyers & Robert Lougheed. *Work:* Nat Cowboy Hall Fame, Okla City; Northwest Community Coll, Powell, Wyo. *Comn:* Husky dogs, Husky Oil Co; mural, Vis Ctr, Cody, Wyo; 2 murals, Utah Valley State Col, Heber City. *Exhib:* Western States Show, Cody Country Art League, 65-75; Springville Art Mus Show, 70-2003; CM Russell Auction, Great Falls, Mont; Wind River Artists Asn; NY Life Ann Calendar Competition; Nat Cowboy Hall Fame, Wild Animal Art Exhib, 79; Western Rendezvous of Art, Bozeman, Mont; Buffalo Bill Art Show, Cody, Wyo. *Teaching:* Oil painting, North West Community Col, 74-75. *Awards:* Best of Show, Cody Country Art League Western Show, 91; Nick Eggenhoffer Award, 92 & 94; Peter Hassrick Merit Award, Western Rendezvous of Art, 92; Artist of the Yr Award & William Wiess Award, Buffalo Bill Art Show, 2005; Gold medal Award, AICA, San Dimas, Calif; Best of Show, Audubon Wildlife Show, Dubois, Wyo. *Bibliog:* Carl Belhtold (auth), The Artistry of Melvin M Fillerup. *Mem:* Cody Country Artist Asn (pres, 68-70); Soc Animal Artists. *Media:* Oil, Watercolor. *Specialty:* Western art. *Interests:* Drawing, painting, hunting, fishing. *Publ:* Auth & illusr, Sidon: The Canal that Faith Built; articles, Southwest Art, 9/80 & Palette Talk, No 54; Art of the West, The Studio, 7-8/93; Am Artists, 2/2000. *Dealer:* Big Horn Gallery Cody Wyoming & Tubac Arizona; Ericson Gallery Salt Lake City UT. *Mailing Add:* 2007 Kerper Blvd Cody WY 82414

FILLIN-YEH, SUSAN
MUSEUM DIRECTOR, CURATOR
b New York, NY. *Study:* Grad Ctr, City Univ New York, PhD, 81. *Collection Arranged:* Charles Sheeler: Am Interiors, The Technological Muse & Am Art in the 1950's (auth, catalog), 87. *Pos:* Cur, Douglas F Cooley Mem Art Gallery, Reed Col, Portland, Ore, 91-92, dir, 92-. *Teaching:* Asst prof, Yale Univ, New Haven, Conn, 82-89; adj prof, Hunter Col NY, 91. *Awards:* Ann Achievement Award, PhD Alumni Asn City Univ NY, 92. *Mem:* Coll Art Asn Am; Alliance of Independent Cols Art. *Publ:* Auth, The Serpentine Lattice, Herbert Newton Cooley Gallery, 93 & Modern Art in America, 96, Reed Col. *Mailing Add:* Douglas F Cooley Mem Art Gallery Reed Col 3203 SE Woodstock Blvd Portland OR 97202-8199

FILMUS, MICHAEL ROY
PAINTER
b New York, NY, May 12, 1943. *Study:* Boston Univ, BA, 66; Art Students League. *Work:* Berkshire Mus, Pittsfield, Mass; Minneapolis Inst Art; Art Inst Chicago; Denver Art Mus; Hunter Mus Art, Chattanooga, Tenn. *Exhib:* Drawings USA, Minn Mus Art, 75; Solo exhibs, Hirschl & Adler Galleries, NY, 75, 77 & 79, David Findlay Jr, NY, 84, 96 & 98, Welles Gallery, Lenox, Mass, 90; Albrecht Mus Art, 76; 200 Yrs of Am Art, Berkshire Mus, Pittsfield, Mass, 76; Flint Inst Arts, Mich, 77; Art of the State, Rose Art Mus, Waltham, Mass, 79; Contemp Naturalism, Nassau Co Mus Fine Art, Roslyn Harbor, NY, 80. *Awards:* Purchase Prize, 40th Ann Midyear Show, Butler Inst Am Art, 76. *Bibliog:* John Arthur (auth), The temperament of nature: Recent paintings by Michael Filmus, Arts Mag, 4/84; Michael Brenson (auth), Michael Filmus, NY Times, 4/84; Eunice Agar (auth), The Filmus Family, Am Artist, 12/95. *Mem:* Life mem Art Students League. *Media:* Oil, Pastel. *Mailing Add:* 221 Castle Hill Ave Great Barrington MA 01230

FILMUS, STEPHEN I
PAINTER
b New York, NY, Feb 4, 1948. *Study:* Univ Pittsburgh, BA, 70; Columbia Univ, MA, 71; Art Students League, 72. *Work:* Ball State Mus, Muncie, Ind; Bank New Eng, Springfield, Mass; Berkshire Mus, Pittsfield, Mass. *Exhib:* Solo exhibs, Still-Lifes, Berkshire Mus, Pittsfield, Mass, 80, 84; Welles Gallery, Lenox Mass, 89, 2004-06; Lenox Gallery of Fine Arts, 2002-2006, 2008; Still Life: Five Visions, David Findlay Jr, NY, 84; Works on Paper, David Findlay Jr, NY, 85; 2 plus 4 Artists Working, Clark-Whitney Gallery, Lenox, Mass, 86; Berkshire Art Gallery & Art Ctr, Great Barrington, Mass, 96; Norman Rockwell Mus, Stockbridge, Mass, 2001, 2004. *Pos:* Trustee, Becket Arts Ctr. *Bibliog:* Gerrit Henry (auth), Still Life: Five Visions, Arts Mag, 9/84; Charles Bonenti (auth), Filmus, Works on Paper, Arts Mag, 6/85; Eunice Agar (auth), The Filmus family, Am Artist, 12/95. *Media:* Oil. *Dealer:* Lenox Gallery of Fine Arts 69 Church St Lenox MA 01240. *Mailing Add:* 4 Fern Hill Rd Great Barrington MA 01230

FILOMENO, ANGELO
TAPESTRY ARTIST
b Ostuni, Italy, 1963. *Study:* Acad Fine Arts, Lecce, Italy, MFA, 1986. *Exhib:* Solo exhibs include Massimo Audiello, New York, 2001, 2003, Claudia Gian Ferrari Arte Contemp, Milan, 2003, Galerie Anne de Villepoix, Paris, 2004, 2007, Frist Ctr Visual Arts, Nashville, 2008, Galerie Lelong, New York, 2008, 2010; group exhibs include NY State Biennial, NY State Mus, Albany, 1998; Le Jardin, Villa Medici, Acad France à Rome, 2000; Officina America, Galleria d'Arte Mod, Bologna, Italy, 2002; 100% Acid Free, White Columns, New York, 2004; Think with the Senses-Feel with the Mind: Art in the Present Tense, Venice Biennale, 2007; Senso Unico, PS1 Contemp Art Ctr, Long Island City, NY, 2007; Pricked: Extreme Embroidery, Mus Arts & Design, New York, 2007. *Dealer:* Galerie Lelong 528 W 26th St New York NY 10001. *Mailing Add:* 6905 18th Ave Brooklyn NY 11204-5049

FINCH, RICHARD DEAN
PRINTMAKER, EDUCATOR
b Springfield, Mo, Apr 16, 1951. *Study:* Southern Ill Univ at Edwardsville, BA, 74, MFA, 76. *Work:* Brooklyn Mus; Detroit Inst Art; Ill State Mus; Lakeview Mus Arts & Sci, Peoria, Ill; Luxun Acad Fine Arts, Sheyang, China; Sakimi Art Mus, Okinawa, Japan. *Exhib:* Drawings: 81st Exhib, Art Inst Chicago, 85; solo exhibs, Sheldon Swope Art Mus, 89, Univ Mass, 93, The Ohio State Univ, Marion, 99, Kansas State Univ, 2001; Contemp Ill Artists, Lakeview Mus, Peoria, Ill, 94; Telling It Like It Is, Peltz Gallery, Milwaukee, Wis, 94; 19th Ann Art on Paper, Md Fedn Art, 96; Delta Nat, Ark State Univ, 2004; Inklandia, Purdue Univ, 2006; Janet Turner 7th Nat, Calif State Univ, 2008. *Pos:* Dir, Normal Editions Workshop, Ill State Univ, Normal, 77-. *Teaching:* Prof printmaking, compos & life drawing, Ill State Univ, Normal, 77-. *Awards:* Artist Fel, Nat Endowment Arts, 83; Artist Fel, Ill Arts Coun, 92; Normal Outstanding Univ Researcher Award, Ill State Univ, 2006; Independent Publ Bk Awards, 2008. *Bibliog:* Robert Malone, Zuo Yingxue & Scott Wampler (co-eds), Contemporary American Printmaking, Jilin Fine Arts Publ House, China, 99. *Mem:* Mid Am Print Coun; Print Consortium; Fla Printmaking Soc. *Media:* Printmaking, Drawing, Painting. *Interests:* Figurative and still life art. *Publ:* Coauth, Experiments in affordable custom lithography, Print News, Vol 3, 81; Lithography Lab Manual, pvt publ, 91; Lithography & Monotype: A Manual of Simplified Techniques for Student Use, pvt publ, 94 & 97; Coauth (with Veda M Rives), Ed Marks from the Matrix, Normal Eds Workshop Collaborative Ltd Ed Prints, 1976-2006, Normal Eds Workshop, 2007; Contemporary Impressions: The Journal of the American Print Alliance, 15, 26-29, No 1, spring, 2007. *Dealer:* Peltz Gallery 1119 E Knapp Milwaukee WI 53202. *Mailing Add:* 12 Swan Lake Rd Bloomington IL 61704-1297

FINCH, SPENCER
PAINTER, SCULPTOR
Study: Doshisha Univ, Kyoto, Japan, 83-84; Magna Cum Laude, Hamilton Col, NY, BA (comparative lit), magna cum laude, 85; RI Sch Design, MFA (sculpture), 89. *Work:* Whitney Biennial, Whitney Mus Am Art, 2004. *Exhib:* Solo exhibs, Postmasters Gallery, NY, 1994-95, 1997-98, 2000, 2002 & 2004, Matrix 133, Wadsworth Atheneum, Hartford, Conn, 1997, Rhona Hoffman Gallery, Chicago, 2001, Artpace, San Antonio, Texas, 2003; Two-person exhib (with Paul Ramirez), Literal Truth, Real Art Ways, Hartford, Conn, 1993; Group exhibs, Home for June, Home of Contemp Theater & Art, NY, 1991, Vacation Show, Four Walls, Brooklyn, 1992, Part II, Sandra Gering Gallery, NY, 1994, Four Views From Earth, Ctr Arts, San Francisco, 1995, Between the Acts, Ice Box, Athens, Greece, 1996, Paradise 8, Exit Art, 1999, Conceptual Art As Neurobiological Praxis, Thread Waxing Space, NY, 1999, Made You Look, Austin Mus Art, Tex, 2000, Art on Paper, Weatherspoon Art Gallery, NC, 2000, NY Paper Sculpture Show, Sculpture Ctr, NY, 2003, Indivisible Cities, Bill Maynes Gallery, NY, 2004, Nothing Compared to This, Contemp Arts Ctr, Cincinnati, 2004, 53rd Int Art Exhib Biennale, Venice, 2009 . *Mailing Add:* Postmasters Gallery 54 Franklin St Ground Fl New York NY 10013

FINCHER, JOHN H
PAINTER, ASSEMBLAGE ARTIST
b Hamilton, Tex, Aug 4, 1941. *Study:* Hardin-Simmons Univ, Abilene, Tex Tech Col, BA, 64; Univ Okla, MFA, 66. *Work:* Dallas Mus Fine Arts; Univ Okla Mus Fine Arts; Wichita Mus Art; Albuquerque Mus, NMex; St Louis Art Mus; and others. *Exhib:* Second Western States Exhib, Corcoran Gallery, Washington, DC, 83; Cold Springs Fine Arts Ctr, 86; Elaine Horwitch Gallery, 87; Albuquerque Mus, NMex, 88; J Cacciola, NY, 90; Elaine Horwitch, Santa Fe, 91; Collages, Monotypes and Paintings, Gerald Peters Gallery, Santa Fe, 2006. *Teaching:* Assoc prof art, Wichita State Univ, 66-77. *Awards:* Wurlitzer Found Grant, Taos, NMex, 72. *Media:* Oil. *Publ:* Auth, articles in Art Space, Arts, Art News & Art in Am; plus various catalogs. *Mailing Add:* 610 Don Canuto St Santa Fe NM 87501-4269

FINDLAY, DAVID B, JR
DEALER
b Kansas City, Mo, June 30, 1933. *Study:* Cornell Univ, BME & MBA. *Pos:* Pres, David Findlay Jr Gallery, currently. *Awards:* New York Artists Equity Asn Award, 2002. *Mem:* Art Dealers Asn Am. *Specialty:* American 19th and 20th Century paintings and sculpture including Hudson River Sch; Impressionism; 1920s, 1930s, 1940s Modernism; contemporary Realism. *Publ:* The Origin and Development of Modernist Painting in America, 1910-1948, 1/2005. *Mailing Add:* David B Findlay Jr Gallery 724 5th Ave 8th Fl New York NY 10019

FINDLAY, JAMES ALLEN
LIBRARIAN
b Saginaw, Mich, Aug 13, 1943. *Study:* Wayne State Univ, BA, 70, MSLS, 72; Univ Calif, Los Angeles, MA, 75. *Pos:* Reference & cataloging libr, Univ Calif, Los Angeles Art Libr, 75-79; Latin Am archivist, Mus Mod Art Libr, New York, 79-82; dir, RI Sch Design Libr, 82-87; dir, Fashion Inst Tech, New York City Libr, 87-89; head librn, The Wolfsonian Found, Miami Beach, Fla, 89-95 & Broward Co Libr, Bienes Ctr Lit Arts. *Mem:* Art Libr Soc NAm. *Res:* Modern Latin American art; design; decorative arts; propaganda arts; rare books & special collections. *Interests:* Modern art; architecture; fashion; decorative arts; propaganda arts, commercial art, typography. *Publ:* Dorothy Porter Wesley (1905-1995), 2001; Pop-up, Peek, Push, Pull, 2001; Auth, Florida, The Making of a State, 2002; Big Little Books, 2002; Modernism for the Masses: Artist-Designed Postcards, 2003. *Mailing Add:* 702 13th St No 305 Miami Beach FL 33139

FINDLAY, MICHAEL
GALLERY DIRECTOR
b Innellan, Scotland, May 13, 1945. *Study:* York Univ, BA, 1963. *Pos:* Vpres, dir exhibitions, Richard L Feigen and Co, Ltd, NYC, LA, Chicago, 1964-70; founder, owner, dir, JH Duffy and Sons, Ltd, NYC, 1970-77; dir, William Beadleston Gallery, NYC, 1977-84; sr dir, Christie, Manson and Woods, NYC, 1984-94, sr dir, 1994-97, int dir, 1997, dir fin, 1997-2000; dir, Acquevella Galleries, Inc, NYC, 2000-. *Teaching:* Lectr, Moore Coll Art, 1970-80. *Publ:* auth, The Value of Art. *Mailing Add:* Acquavella Galleries, Inc 18 E 79th St New York NY 10075

FINE, ELSA HONIG
ART HISTORIAN, EDITOR
b Bayonne, NJ, May 24, 1930. *Study:* Syracuse Univ, BFA, 51; Tyler Coll Fine Arts, MEd (art), 67; Univ Tenn, EdD (art hist), 70. *Pos:* founding ed, publ, Woman's Art J, Glenside, Pa, 80-2006, retired. *Teaching:* Asst prof, art Knoxville Tenn Col, 70-75; adj prof, various univs & col, Knoxville Coll, Tenn, 75-80; retired 2006. *Awards:* Alumni Award, Tyler Col, 2002; Woman's Caucus for Art Hon Award, 96; Recognition Award, Comt Women in the Arts, Coll Art Asn, 2001. *Publ:* Auth, The Afro-American Artist: A Search for Identity, 73, Women and Art: A History of Women Painters & Sculptors from the Renaissance to the 20th Century, 78

FINE, JANE
PAINTER
b New York, New York, 1958. *Study:* Harvard Univ, BA, 1980; Sch Mus Fine Arts/Tufts Univ, Boston, MA, 1983; Skowhegan Sch Painting & Sculpture, Skowhegan, Maine, 1989. *Work:* West Collection, Oaks, Pa. *Exhib:* Solo exhibs include White Columns, New York, 1992, Casey Kaplan, New York, 1995, 1996, Domo Gallery, Summit, NJ, 2004, Bernard Toale Gallery, Boston, 2005, Barbara Davis Gallery, Houston, 2006; group exhibs include Selections 42, Drawing Ctr, New York, 1988; Current Undercurrent, Brooklyn Mus, NY, 1997, Open House, 2004; Flat Files, Rosenwald-Wolf Gallery, Univ Arts, Philadelphia, 1999; Paintings Drawings Sculptures, Greener Pastures Contemp Art, Toronto, Ontario, 2003; Vacation Nation, Pierogi, Brooklyn, NY, 2004; Opening Bloom, Barbara Davis Gallery, Houston, 2005; Pie Fight, AR Contemp Gallery, Milan, Italy, 2005; Pierogi, Leipzig, Germany, 2006. *Awards:* New York Found Arts Fel, 1994, Grant, 2008; Pollock-Krasner Found Grant, 2001. *Dealer:* Stephanie Theodore-Pointie Dog Press PO Box 348 New York NY 10012; Pierogi 177 N 9th St Brooklyn NY 11211; Bernard Toale Gallery 450 Harrison Ave Boston MA 02118; AR Contemp Gallery Via Vespucci 5 20124 Milan Italy; Pierogi Spinnereistr 7 04179 Leipzig Germany. *Mailing Add:* Barbara Davis Gallery 4411 Montrose Houston TX 77006

FINE, JUD
SCULPTOR, EDUCATOR
b Los Angeles, Calif, Nov 20, 1944. *Study:* Univ Calif, Santa Barbara, BA, 66; Cornell Univ, MFA, 70. *Work:* Minneapolis Inst Art; Los Angeles Co Art Mus & Mus Contemp Art, Los Angeles; Mus Stuki, Lodz, Poland; Art Inst Chicago & Mus Contemp Art; Power Inst Fine Arts, Sydney, Australia; Guggenheim Mus, NY; Yale Univ Art Mus, New Haven, Conn; San Diego Mus Contemp Art, Calif. *Comn:* Security Pac, Costa Mesa Gallery, Calif; Mem Garden Carnation Co, Glendale, Calif; Spine, Los Angeles Cent Libr, 93; Scan, Culver City, Calif, 96; Mission Trail, San Antonio, Tex, 97; Venice Beach, Civic Plaza, Modesto, Calif, 98; San Francisco Zoo, 98. *Exhib:* Solo exhib, Ronald Feldman Gallery, 72, 73, 76, 78 & 81, Margo Leavin Gallery, Los Angeles, 77, 79, 81 & 84, Anderson Gallery, Va Commonwealth Univ, Richmond, 82, Thomas Segal Gallery, 83 & Los Angeles Munic Art Gallery, 85, and many others; Los Angeles Co Mus, 72; San Diego Mus Contemp Art, 73 & 88; 71st Am Exhib, Art Inst Chicago, 74; Inst Contemp Art, Boston, 74; Indianapolis Mus Art, 76; Santa Barbara Mus Art, 78; San Diego Mus Contemp Art, 93 & 98; Univ Calif Fine Arts Gallery, Irvine, 87; and others. *Teaching:* vis prof, Ohio Univ, Athens, 75; prof art, Univ Southern Calif, 88-. *Awards:* Contemp Art Coun New Talent Grant, Los Angeles Co Art Mus, 72; Laura Slobe Mem Award, Art Inst Chicago, 74; Individual Artist Fel, Nat Endowment Arts, 82; Grant, Calif State Arts Coun, Sculpture Comn, Exposition Park, Los Angeles, 83; 53rd Ann Western Bks Award. *Bibliog:* Arts Mag, 5/72, 10/73, 9/74 & 3/75; Articles, Arts Mag, 9/74 & 3/75 & Artforum, 4/75; Robert McDonald (auth), Poles Remain as Theme in Sculptures by Fine, Los Angeles Times, 2/24/87. *Media:* Mixed. *Publ:* Auth, Or: An Introduction, 74 & Walk, 75, pvt publ; Walk, Chicago, 76; Revolutions, the Art Record, Green St Recording & Ronald Feldman Fine Arts, NY, 81; Judd Fine, La Jolla Mus Contemp Art, Calif, 88; coauth, Spine, Los Angeles Libr Asn, 94. *Dealer:* Ronald Feldman Gallery 31 Mercer St New York NY 10013. *Mailing Add:* 1366 Appleton Way Venice CA 90291

FINE, RUTH E
CURATOR, PRINTMAKER
b Philadelphia, Pa, May 10, 1941. *Study:* Skowhegan Sch Painting & Sculpture; Philadelphia Coll Art, BFA, 62; Univ Pa, MFA, 64. *Work:* Philadelphia Mus Art; Nat Gallery Art, Washington, DC; Fleming Mus, Univ Vt, Burlington; Hunterian Art Gallery, Glasgow Univ, Scotland. *Collection Arranged:* Lessing J Rosenwald: Tribute to a Collector (auth, catalog), 82 & Gemini GEL: Art & Collaboration (auth, catalog), 84-, Nat Gallery Art, Washington, DC; Drawing Near: Whistler Etching from the Zelman Collection (auth, catalog), Los Angeles Co Mus Art, 84-; The 1980's: Prints from the Collection of Joshua P Smith, Nat Gallery, 89; The Art of John Marin, Nat Gallery, 90. *Pos:* Cur, Lessing J Rosenwald's Collection, Alverthorpe Gallery, 72-80; cur modern prints & drawings, Nat Gallery Art, Washington, DC, 80-. *Teaching:* Lectr, Philadelphia Col Art, 65-69, Beaver Col, 69-72 & Univ Vt, 76 & 77. *Awards:* Ingram Merrill Found Grant. *Mem:* Coll Art Asn; Print Coun Am (mem bd dir, 85-88). *Media:* Etching, Watercolor. *Res:* American and British graphic arts, 18th-20th centuries. *Publ:* Coauth, The Prints of Benton Spruance: A Catalogue Raisonné (with R Looney), Pa Press & Free Libr, Philadelphia, 86; contribr, In Honor of Paul Mellon: Collector & Benefactor, Nat Gallery Art, 86; ed, James McNeill Whistler: A Reevaluation, Nat Gallery, 87; coauth, The Drawings of Jasper Johns, Nat Gallery Art, 90. *Dealer:* Dolan Maxwell Gallery Philadelphia Pa. *Mailing Add:* Curator Mod Prints & Drawings Nat Gallery Art 6th St & Constitution Av Washington DC 20565

FINE, SALLY S
SCULPTOR, PAINTER
b Aurora, Ill, Jul 20, 1948. *Study:* Ohio Univ, BFA (graphic design), 70; Boston Univ, MFA, 85. *Work:* DeCordova Mus, Brandeis Univ; AIR Vallauris, France; Danforth Mus, Framingham, Mass; Fed Reserve Bank, Boston; Hamilton Coll, NY; Rose Art Mus, Brandeis Univ, Mass; Altos de Chavon, Dominican Rep. *Comn:* Dr & Mrs Rudolpho Llinas, Falmouth, Mass; Sandoz Pharmaceutical Corp, NJ. *Exhib:* Solo shows incl Buckingham, Browne & Nichols Sch, Cambridge, Mass, 92, Boston Sculptors at Chapel Gallery, W Newton, 94, 96, 98, 2000; group shows incl Fed Reserve Bank Gallery, Boston, 95, 99; 8th Triennial Regional Exhib Women's Caucus for Arts, Fuller Mus, Brockton, Mass, 96, Craft Transformed, 2003; DeCordova Mus & Sculpture Park, Lincoln, Mass, 96, 98, 2001; Cité Int Gallerie, Paris, 98; Children's Mus, Boston, 99; Viridian Gallery, New York, 2000; Provincetown Art Asn, 2004; Mt Ida Coll, 2005; Altos de Charon, LaRomano, Dominican Repub, 2008; Galerie Aqui Ben Siam, Vallauris, France, 2009. *Collection Arranged:* Centennial Celebration, Univ Mass, Dartmouth, 95; High-Tech, Lo-Tech: Art from Bradford Coll, Essex Art Ctr, Lawrence, Mass, 97; Digital Atelier: Three Women Digital Printmakers, Laura Knott Gallery, Bradford Coll, Haverhill, Mass, 99, Hound of Heaven: Painter Ives Gammell, 99, Creative Arts, 99, Student Shows, 99, 2000, Rejoice When You Die: New Orleans Jazz Funeral by Leo Touchet, 2000, Affinities: Boston Women Artist, 2000, Witness: Art of the Conscience, 2000. *Pos:* Graphic designer, Publications Dept, Mus Sci, Boston, 70-73; freelance graphic designer, SS Fine Design, 70-. *Teaching:* Lectr, creative arts div, Bradford Coll, Haverhill, Mass, 82-85, asst prof, visual arts, 1996-2000; instr, graphic design, Art Inst Boston, 85, sculpture workshops, Truro Ctr for Arts, Mass, 91-97; adj sculpture fac, Univ Mass at Dartmouth, 93-95; fac, Art New Eng, Bennington Coll, Mass, 95; assoc prof, visual art, Regis Coll, Weston, Mass, 2000-2006; tchr, online, Art Inst Pittsburg, 2005; adj fac, sch design, Mt Ida Coll, Newton, Mass, 2005-2006; Curry Coll, Mitton, Mass. *Awards:* Art in the Landscape Award, Mass Horticulture Soc, 90; Grant, Mass Coun for Arts, 92, Visual Artists Grant, 95; New Firms Initiative Grant, New Eng Found for Arts, 92; CA Johnson Grant, Bradford Coll, 97. *Mem:* Am Asn Univ Profs; Am Inst Graphic Arts, Boston Chap; Coll Art Asn, New York. *Media:* Miscellaneous Media, Watercolor. *Interests:* Landscape design. *Dealer:* Boston Sculptors Gallery 516 E 2nd St Unit41 South Boston MA 02127

FINEBERG, GERALD S
COLLECTOR
Pos: Founder, mgr, The Fineberg Companies, Wellesley, Mass, currently, chmn bd; mem bd overseers. Rose Art Mus, 97, chmn, 2001; chmn, Fine Hotels Co. *Awards:* Gerald S and Sandra Fineberg Gallery, The Rose Art Mus, Brandeis Univ, named in their honor, 2002. *Collection:* Modern & Contemp Art. *Mailing Add:* The Fineberg Companies 1 Washington St Ste 400 Wellesley MA 02481

FINK, ALAN
ART DEALER
b Chicago, Ill, July 17, 1925. *Study:* Univ Ill, BA. *Pos:* Dir, Alpha Gallery Inc. *Mem:* Art Dealers Asn Am; Boston Art Dealers Asn. *Specialty:* Twentieth century painting, sculpture and graphics; modern master prints. *Mailing Add:* c/o Alpha Gallery 37 Newbury St Boston MA 02116

FINK, JOANNA ELIZABETH
ART DEALER, GALLERY DIRECTOR
b Boston, Mass, Aug 8, 1958. *Study:* Wellesley Col, Mass, 76-78; New York Univ, BA, 80; Inst Fine Arts, New York Univ, MA, 83. *Pos:* Admin asst & photogr, Dept Fine Arts, New York Univ, 80-82; res consult, art prog, Chase Manhattan Bank, New York, 83; dir, Alpha Gallery, Inc, Boston, Mass, 83-; pres, Boston Art Dealers Asn, 2009-. *Teaching:* Teaching asst, art hist, New York Univ, 82. *Bibliog:* Eleanor Heartney (auth), Aaron Fink: Out of the Ordinary, pp. 196 & 197, West Stockbridge: Hard Press Ed, 2002; William Corbett (auth), Material Boy, p. 40-41, The Boston Phoenix, 10/2005; Cate McQuaid (auth), Galleries, p. E3, The Boston Globe Calender, 2002, Calling Coast to Coast, pp. 40-41, American Art Collector, 10/2006, Trying Times for Local Galleries, p. N1, The Boston Globe, 1/2012, As Boston Museums Surge, Galleries Struggle to Keep Up, 2012; Geoff Edgers (auth), Art Bus Struggles to Pick Up, p. N1, The Boston Globe, 5/2011; and many more. *Mem:* Art Dealers Asn Am; Boston Art Dealers Asn (pres); Art Table. *Specialty:* Contemporary Art; 20th century American and European works; modern master prints. *Publ:* Auth, Georg Baselitz: Selected Prints, 1963-1985 (exhib catalog), Alpha Gallery, Boston, 85; auth, The Orphic Art of Varujan Boghosian, Provincetown Arts, 95; auth, various book rev, AA New Eng, 92-95; auth, Gideon Bok (exhib catalog), Alpha Gallery, Boston, Mass, 2007; auth, Wlodzimierz Ksiazek & Rainer Gross (brochure essay), Alpha Gallery, Boston, Mass, 2010; auth, Letters to the Editor, The Boston Globe, 2011, Sunday Letters, 2011; auth, Hyman Bloom (brochure essay), Alpha Gallery, Boston, Mass, 2012; and many more. *Mailing Add:* Alpha Gallery Inc 37 Newbury St Boston MA 02116

FINK, LOIS MARIE
HISTORIAN, CURATOR
b Michigan City, Ind, Dec 30, 1927. *Study:* Capital Univ, BA, 51; Univ Chicago, MA, 55, PhD, 70; Capital Univ, Hon Dr Humanities, 82. *Collection Arranged:* Academy: The Academic Tradition in Am Art (auth, catalog); Nat Collection Fine Arts, 75. *Pos:* Cur res, Nat Mus Am Art, 70-93, emer cur, 93-. *Teaching:* Instr art hist & sociology, Lenoir Rhyne Col, 55-56; instr art hist & educ, Midland Col, 56-58; instr, Roosevelt Univ, 58-64, asst prof, 64-70. *Mem:* Coll Art Asn; Am Studies Asn; Soc Arts, Relig & Contemp Cult. *Res:* Nineteenth and early twentieth century American art; relationship of French art to American art. *Publ:* Auth, American artists in France, 1850-1870, Am Art J, 73; coauth, Academy: The Academic Tradition in American Art, Smithsonian, 75; auth, French art in the United States, 1850-1870, Gazette Beaux Arts, 78; American participation at the Paris salons, 1870-1900, Int Comt Hist Art 24th Cong, 82; contribr, Elizabeth Nourse, 1859-1938: A Salon Career, Smithsonian, 83; Am Art at the Nineteenth Cent Paris Salons, Cambridge Univ Press, 90; contribr, New Mus Theory and Practice, Blackwell, 2006; contribr, Am Artists and the Louvre, Louvre, 2006; auth, A History of the Smithsonian Am Art Mus, Univ Mass Press, 2007; contbr, The Weir Family, 1820-1920, Univ Press New England, 2011. *Mailing Add:* 3128 Gracefield Rd #313 Silver Spring MD 20904

FINKE, LEONDA FROEHLICH
SCULPTOR, DRAFTSMAN, EDUCATOR
b Brooklyn, NY, 1922. *Study:* Art Students League, New York, 45. *Work:* Butler Inst Am Art, Youngstown, Ohio; Nat Portrait Gallery Smithsonian Inst, Washington, DC; Brookgreen Gardens, SC; Brit Mus, London, Eng; Bates Coll Mus, Lewiston, Maine; Sculpture Garden; Grounds For Sculpture 2001, Hamilton, NJ; British Mus, London, Eng; Grounds for Sculpture, Hamilton, NJ; City Univ New York, Kingsboro Community Coll, Brooklyn; The Century Assocs, New York; Nat Acad Design, New York; Chrysler Mus, Norfolk, VA; Mus Foreign Art, Sofia, Bulgaria; Princeton Univ Collection Art Libr. *Comn:* Soc Medalists, The Prodigal Son, 88; Three 6 ft figures (sculpture), Women in the Sun, Atlanta, Ga, 88; Virginia Woolf, British Art Medal Soc, 89; 7 ft figure bronze (sculpture), pvt collection, Conn, 90; Max Som Medal, Otolaryngology Dept, Montefiore Hosp, NY, 92; Centennial medallic sculpture, Am Acad Otolaryngology; Aiken Taylor Award Sewahee Rev, 2002; Brookgreen Gardens 75th Anniversary Medal, 2007. *Exhib:* Images of Am, US Info Agency (traveling exhib bronze figure sculpture selected); NY Botanical Gardens, 81; Int Fedn Medalists, Stockholm, 85 & Brit Mus, London, 92; Port Hist Mus, Philadelphia, Pa, 87; Sculpture Garden, Stamford Mus, Conn; FIDEM, London, 92; Stages of Creation Pub Sculpture, Nat Acad Mus, New York, 98; FIDEM 2000, Goethe Nat Mus, Weimar, Ger; Contemp Sculpture at Chesterwood, Stockbridge, Mass; Mus Contemp At, Los Angeles; Megaro Mus Art Tokyo Japan, 2001; Grounds for Sculpture Hamilton NJ, 2002; 200 Years of Art Figure, Art by Artists, Long Island Mus, Stony Brook, NY, 2003; Challenging Tradition Women Acad, Nat Acad Design, 2003; Outdoors exhib, Sculptors guild, White Plains, NY, 2004 & 2006-2007; Century Masters, Invitational 50 Years Retrospective, Sculpture Relief, drawings, Medallic Works, Tribute by the Century Asn, New York, 2009; Garrison Art Ctr, Sculpture, drawings, Garrison, New York, 2010; Current, Summer Sculpture Outdoors, Boscobel, Garrison, New Yor, 2010; FILEM Medals, Temperey, Finland, 2010; Featured Artist, Chesterwood, Mass, 2011. *Pos:* Adj prof. *Teaching:* Adj prof sculpture & drawing, Nassau Community Coll, 70-95; vis lectr, Hartford Univ Conn, Fordham Univ, NY, Brookgreen Gardens, SC & Brit Art Medal Soc, Loughborough (Eng) Univ, 89. *Awards:* Gold Medal, Nat Sculpture Soc, 89; Agop Agapoff Award, Nat Sculpture Soc, 93; Silver Medal, Nat Sculpture Soc, 94; J Sanford Saltus Award, Am Numismatic Soc, 97; Sculpture House Award-Lifetime Adievement, Nat Sculpture Soc, 2005; FIDEM 70, (Commemorative Exhib, Honored Distinguished Artist US), 2007. *Bibliog:* Watson Jones (auth), Contemp Am Women Sculptors; Stella Pandell Russel (auth), Art in the World; Arthur Williams (auth), Sculpture, Davis Publ. *Mem:* Sculptors Guild; British Art Medal Soc; fel Nat Sculpture Soc; Am Medallic Sculptors Asn; Nat Acad; Century Asn. *Media:* Wet Plaster for Bronze, Wood, Silverpoint, Drawing. *Interests:* Reading, plants, gourmet food, dance performances. *Publ:* Nat Sculpture Rev, 93; Brooklyn J, 2004; auth, Leonda Finke (photos by David Finn, 50 yrs of works, 170 photos), Ruder Finn Press, 2006; Work & Love, A Sculptor's Life, A Beloved Wife (memoir), 2013. *Dealer:* Oxford Gallery Rochester NY; Gallery North Setauket NY. *Mailing Add:* 10 The Locusts Roslyn NY 11576

FINKELPEARL, TOM
MUSEUM DIRECTOR
Study: Princeton Univ, BA; Hunter Coll, MFA. *Pos:* Cur dir, PS 1's Clocktower Gallery, 1982-90; exec dir, Percent for Art Progressive, Dept Cultural Affairs, New York, 1990-96; dir, artist colony Maine, 1996-99; dep dir, PS 1 Contemp Art Ctr, Long Island City, 1999-2002; exec dir, Queens Mus Art, 2002-2014; commr, NYC Dept Cultural Affairs, 2014-. *Publ:* Auth, Dialogues in Public Art, 2000; auth, What We Made: Conversation on Art and Social Cooperation, 2013. *Mailing Add:* NYC Dept Cultural Affairs 31 Chambers St #2 New York NY 10007

FINKELSTEIN, HENRY D
PAINTER, EDUCATOR
b Bar Harbor, Maine, Sept 3, 1958. *Study:* Cooper Union, with Reuben Kadish & Nicolas Marsicano, BFA 1976-80; Yale Sch Art, with Lester F Johnson, MFA 1981-83. *Exhib:* Solo exhibs, Prince Street Gallery, NY, 86, 88 & 91, Andrews Gallery, Williamsburg, Va, 89, Parkerson Gallery, Houston, Tex, 89, Wash Art Asn, Conn, 91, Mus du Chateau de Rochefort en Terre, France, 93, Bengert MacRae Gallery, Wyckoff, NY, 93, Gleason Fine Art Gallery, Portland, Maine, 93, Simon Gallery, Morristown, NJ, 2000, Valley House Gallery, Dallas, Tex, 2002, 04 & Kraushaar Galleries, NY, 2001, 03, 05; group exhibs, On the Edge: 40 Yrs of Maine Painting, Portland Mus Art, Maine, 92-93 & Mostly Maine, Tibor de Nagy Gallery, NY, 93; Bengert MacRae, Wyckoff, NJ, 93; Gleason Art Gallery, Portland, Maine, 93. *Teaching:* Asst prof, Hartford Art Sch, 84-92; vis asst prof, Pratt Inst, NY, 86-87; vis artist, Col William & Mary, Williamsburg, Va, 89; instr, Nat Acad Design, NY, 96-; Lyme Acad, Old Lyme, Conn, 2003. *Awards:* Fulbright Fel, Italy, 83-84; Julius Hallgarten Prize, Nat Acad Design, 88; Klots Found Residency Grant, Chateau de Roche Forten Terre, France, 92 & 2000; Carnegie Prize, Nat Acad Design, 03. *Bibliog:* Jean-Pierre Chedaleux (auth), Ouest France, 7/28/92; Philip Isaacson (auth), Maine Sunday Telegram, 5/30/93; Carl Little (auth), Art New Eng, 10/93. *Mem:* Nat Acad. *Media:* Oil. *Dealer:* Kraushaar Galleries 724 Fifth Ave New York NY 10019; Valley House Gallery 6616 Spring Valley Rd Dallas TX 75254

FINKELSTEIN, MAX
SCULPTOR, PAINTER
b New York, NY, June 15, 1915. *Study:* Los Angeles City Col; Sculpture Ctr, New York; Calif Sch Art, Los Angeles; Univ Calif, Los Angeles. *Work:* Krannert Art Mus, Univ Ill, Champaign; Hirshhorn Mus, Washington, DC; Univ Calif Mus, Berkeley; Santa Barbara Mus Art, Calif; Los Angeles Co Mus Mod Art; and others. *Exhib:* Highlights of the 1967-1968 Art Season, Larry Aldrich Mus Contemp Art, Ridgefield, Conn, 68; Solo exhibs, La Jolla Mus Art, Calif, 68 & Esther Robles Gallery, 70; Microcosm, Long Beach Mus Art, 69; Painting & Sculpture Today, Indianapolis Mus Art, Ind, 70; and many others. *Teaching:* Instr sculpture, Univ Judaism. *Awards:* Los Angeles Munic Gallery, 65; Long Beach Mus, 65 & 67; Krannert Mus, Univ Ill, Champaign, 67. *Bibliog:* Ray Faulkner & Edwin Ziegfield (auths), Art Today, Holt, 69. *Media:* Metal, Wood Construction. *Mailing Add:* 621 N Curson Ave Los Angeles CA 90036-1811

FINLEY, DONNY LAMENDA
PAINTER, ILLUSTRATOR
b Goodwater, Ala, Oct 7, 1951. *Study:* Jacksonville State Univ, BS, 75. *Work:* Birmingham Mus Fine Arts, Ala; Columbus Mus Arts & Sci, Ga; Fine Arts Mus of the South, Mobile, Ala; LaGrange Mus Fine Arts, Ga; Fayette Mus Fine Arts, Ala; Isabel Anderson Cooper Mus. *Comn:* Painting, Ala Cattleman's Asn, Talladega, 76; Ala Federated Farmers Assn, Montgomery, Ala, 2008. *Exhib:* Am Watercolor Soc, Nat Acad Design, NY, 78, 80 & 82; Alabama Art, US Senate Bldg, 79; Watercolor USA, Springfield Art Mus, Mo, 80; Rocky Mountain Nat, Foothills Art Ctr, Golden, Colo, 81; Nat Watercolor Soc, Palm Springs Desert Mus, 83 & 84; Salmagundi Club, NY, 85; Nat Acad Design, 88, Sonat, Birmingham, 90. *Awards:* Larry Quackenbush Mem Award, Am Watercolor Soc, 80; Strathmore Award, Nat Watercolor Soc, 83; Charlotte Livingston Award, Salmagundi Club, NY, 85; Walter Biggs Mem Award, Nat Acad Design, NY, 90. *Bibliog:* Marda Kaiser Burton (auth), Just a country boy, Southwest Art, 79; Joyce Deaton (auth), Down home Donny, Birmingham Mag, 79; Nell Luter (auth), Donny Finley's Moments Captured, Royal Publ, 87. *Mem:* Am Watercolor Soc. *Media:* Egg Tempera, Watercolor. *Interests:* Realism, Impressionism. *Publ:* Contribr, The Tennessee Conservationist, Tenn Dept Conserv, 78, Southwest Art, Art Mag, 79 & Birmingham Mag, 79; illusr, A Catalogue of the South, Oxmoor House, 79; Watercolor page, Am Artist Mag, 81; auth, He Restores My Soul, Harvest House Publ, 2000; contribr, Peace Like A river, 2001, The Heart of Loveliness, 2001, Harvest House Publ; A Passion for Game, Bronze Bow Publishers, 2006. *Dealer:* Marin Price Galleries Bethesda MD; Trees Place Orleans MA; Debruyne Fine Art Naples Fl; Haynes Galleries Nashville Tn; Haynes Galleries Thomaston Ma. *Mailing Add:* 5057 Greystone Way Birmingham AL 35242-6476

FINLEY, GERALD ERIC
HISTORIAN
b Munich, Ger, July 17, 1931; Can citizen. *Study:* Univ Toronto, BA, MA; Johns Hopkins Univ, PhD. *Exhib:* Turner and George IV Edinburgh, Tate Gallery, London & Nat Gallery Scotland, Edinburgh, 81; George Heriot, Painter of the Canadas, Nat Gallery Can, Ottawa, 78. *Teaching:* Lectr art & archeol, Univ Toronto, 59-60; lectr art, Univ Sask, Regina, 62-63, actg dir, Norman Mackenzie Art Gallery, 62-63; from asst prof to prof art hist, Queen's Univ, 63-95. *Awards:* Gustav Bissing Rotating Fel, Johns Hopkins Univ, 61; Inst Advan Studies Humanities Fel, Edinburgh Univ, 79-80. *Mem:* Royal Can Acad Art; fel Royal Soc Canada, 84. *Res:* British late eighteenth and early nineteenth centuries painting; landscape, especially J M W Turner; history of ideas. *Publ:* Auth, Landscapes of Memory: Turner as Illustrator to Scott, 80; Turner and George the Fourth in Edinburgh, 1822, 81; George Heriot: Postmaster Painter of the Canadas, 83; The Deluge Pictures: Reflections on Goethe, JMW Turner and Early Nineteenth-Century Science, Zeitschrift fur Kunstgeschichte, 97; Angel in the Sun: Turner's Vision of Hist, 99; and others. *Mailing Add:* 52 Earl St Kingston ON K7L 2G6 Canada

FINN, DAVID
PHOTOGRAPHER
b New York, NY, Aug 30, 1921. *Study:* City Coll Univ New York, BA. *Exhib:* Oceanic Sculptures, Metrop Mus Art, NY, 74; Henry Moore Photographs, l'Orangerie, Paris, France, 77. *Collection Arranged:* Exploring Sculpture, Canova (auth, catalog) & Cellini, Andrew Crispo Gallery, NY; Henry Moore Sculpture and Environment (photographs), Fischer Fine Art Ltd, London, 77; Large Two Forms (auth, catalog), Fairweather-Hardin Gallery, Chicago; Henry Moore, Am Cult Ctr, Madrid. *Awards:* Herbert Adams Mem Medal, Nat Sculpture Soc. *Mem:* MacDowell Colony; Artists for Environ Found; Int Ctr of Photog; Parsons Sch of Design. *Publ:* Auth, Sculpture at Storm King, 79 & New Rochelle, Portrait of a City, 80, Abbeville Press; The Florence Baptistery Doors, Viking Press, 80; Henry Moore at the British Museum, Brit Mus Publ Ltd, 81; Monumental Greek Bronze Sculpture, Abbeville Press, 83. *Mailing Add:* c/o Ruder & Finn 301 E 57th St 3rd Flr New York NY 10022

FINN, DAVID
SCULPTOR
b Urbana, Ill, 1952. *Study:* Cornell Univ, Ithaca, NY, BS, 74; Mass Coll Art, Boston, MFA, 82. *Work:* Fondation Cartier, Paris, France; Weatherspoon Art Gallery, Univ NC, Greensboro; Leeds City Art Gallery, Eng; Herbert F Johnson Mus Art, Cornell Univ, Ithaca, NY; Bemis Found, Omaha, Nebr; Mint Mus Art, Charlotte, NC. *Comn:* New Works, Pub Art Fund, NY, 85; Diggs Tower, Winston Salem, NC, 2005;

Sculptural Wall, Chapel Hill, NC, 2009; Fictions Mobiles, Greensboro Pub Libr, NC, 2009. *Exhib:* Solo exhibs, Weatherspoon Art Gallery, Univ NC, Greensboro, 90, Atrium Gallery, Univ Conn, Storrs, 91, Watermans Art Ctr, Brentford, W London, Eng, 92, Leeds City Art Gallery, Eng, 92, NDak Mus Art, Grand Forks, 93 & ES Vandam Gallery, NY, 97; Atlantic Sculpture, Art Ctr, Coll Design, Pasadena, 87; Art on Paper 1989, Weatherspoon Art Gallery, Univ NC, Greensboro, 90; Lost and Found, Sculpture Ctr, NY, 91; de'Persona, Oakland Mus Art, Calif, 91; Disjunctive, Valencia Community Coll Gallery, Orlando, Fla, 91; Depersona, Oakland Mus Art, Calif, 91; Assemblage, Southern Ctr Contemp Art, Winston-Salem, NC, 92; Resurrections: Objects with New Souls, William Benton Mus Art, Univ Conn, Storrs, 94; Body and Soul, ES Vandam Gallery, NY, 96; Thresholds: Spiritual Art, 2003-2006, South Carolina Mus Art, Columbia, SC. *Teaching:* Vis asst prof sculpture, Wake Forest Univ, Winston-Salem, NC, 88-91 & 95-98 & assoc prof, 98-; asst prof sculpture, Kutztown Univ Pa, 94; vis artist, Univ NC, Chapel Hill, 94; asst prof, Wake Forest Univ, Winston-Salem, NC, 2000-2008, prof art, 2008-; prof Art, Wake Forest Univ, 2008-. *Awards:* Fel, New York Found Arts, 88; Fel, Nat Endowment Arts, 90; Fel, ZS Reynolds Found, 2001-2005; Fel, NC Arts Coun, 2006-2007; Fel, Robin Faculty, 2009-2012. *Bibliog:* Greg Booth (auth), Artist's Children carry a weight beyond their lightness of being, Grand Forks Herald, NDak, 11/12/92; Tom Paterson (auth), Sculptor's works is highlight of faculty exhibit at WFU, Winston-Salem J, 12/10/95; Bill Arnig (auth), David Finn (rev), Time Out, New York, 1/23/97. *Mem:* S Eastern Ctr Contemp Art, Winston-Salem, NC (mem bd dir, 2000). *Media:* Trash, Marble, Newspaper, Pub Art, Installation. *Publ:* Auth, David Finn, Salvatore Ala Gallery, New York, 86; David Finn: Newspaper Children, Third Eye Centre, Glasgow, 88; David Finn Masked Figures, Weatherspoon Art Gallery, Univ NC, Greensboro, 90; Newspaper Children, Watermans Art Centre, Brentford, Gr Brit, 92. *Mailing Add:* 716 S Hawthorne Rd Winston Salem NC 27103

FINNEGAN, SHARYN MARIE
PAINTER
b New York, NY, Aug 16, 1946. *Study:* Acad de Belli Arti, Rome, Italy; Marymount Col, Tarrytown, NY, BFA; NY Univ, studied with Esteban Vicente, MA. *Work:* Anderson Mus Contemp Art, Roswell, NMex; Rowan Univ, NJ. *Exhib:* Report from Soho, Grey Art Gallery, NY, 75; Artists' Choice: Figurative Art in NY, Bowery Gallery, and four others, NY, 76; Solo Exhibs: Roswell Mus & Fine Arts Ctr, NMex, 77; Prince St Gallery, 74, 75, 77, 80, 86 & 89; Blue Mountain Gallery and SVAC, Manchester, Vt, 2008; Interiors, One Penn Plaza, 86; NY, Long Island Univ, NYC, 2006; Blue Mountain Gallery, 2008; Painted Light, Queens Mus, 83; Am Women Artists, Cornwall Painting Ctr, New York City, 2003; Landscape Drawings, Long Island Univ, NY, 2006; Dishman Art Mus, Beaumont, Tex, 2009; Rowan Univ Art Gallery, NJ, 2009; Blue Mountain Gallery, 2011-2014. *Collection Arranged:* cur, Better Than Ever, Long Island Univ, NY, 2009; Dishman Art Mus, Tex, 2009. *Pos:* Gallery coordr, Prince St Gallery, NY, 74-75 & 77-79; Artist in Residence: Hollufgard, Denmark & Hirsholmene Denmark, 2006; Sim, Reykjavik, Iceland, 2007. *Teaching:* Assoc prof art & art hist, Parsons Sch Design, NY. *Awards:* Artist-in-residence, Roswell Mus & Fine Arts Ctr, 76; Palisades Artist-in-Residence, NY, summer 79; Residency, MacDowell Colony, Peterborough, NH, 79; Artist-in-residence, Brisons Veor, Cornwall, Eng, 2000-02, 2004, & 2011; AIR, Seydisfjordor, Iceland, 2003; AIR, Gullkistan, Iceland, 2010. *Bibliog:* J Mellow (auth), Rev, New York Times, 1/74; P Frank (auth), Rev, Soho Weekly News, 1/74; J Dreiss (auth), Rev, Arts Mag, 4/74, 3/78 & 4/81; Ellen Lubel (auth), Views by Women Artists, NY Women's Caucus for Art, 82; and others; Ed McCormack (auth), Women Artists at Cornwall Gallery & Studio, 9/2003. *Mem:* Women in the Arts, NY; Coll Art Asn. *Media:* Oil, Charcoal. *Publ:* Claire Moore, Women's Art Jrnl, Spring/Summer 81; Better Than Ever (catalog), Long Island Univ, NY, 2009; Juanita McNeely, Art and Life Entwined, Womens Art Jour, 2011. *Dealer:* Blue Mountain Gallery 530 W 25th St NYC 10001. *Mailing Add:* 5550 Fieldston Rd No 9E Bronx NY 10471-2532

FINOCCHIARO, PINO
PRINTMAKER, PAINTER
b Catania, Italy. *Study:* Inst Art Catania, Italy; Inst Art Urbino, Italy. *Work:* Sassoferrato Mus Art Cont-Nea, Sassoferrato, Italy; Exlibris Mus, Corsico Milan, Italy; Gabinetto Stampe Mod & Antique, Baenacaualło, Italy. *Comn:* Mural, BPA, NY, 86; mural, PS, Catania, Italy, 87; mural, SB, Albissola, Italy, 90; mural, SJ Ex Convento 1600, Donnalucata, Italy, 93. *Exhib:* Int Exlibris, Comunedi Pescara, Italy, 88; Grafica Originale, Casanatale Raffaello, Urbino, Italy, 91; Incisione Ital, New Art, S Benedetto Del Tronto, Italy, 92; Repertorio Incisori Italini, Comune Di Baenacauallo, Baenacauallo, Italy, 93. *Awards:* Ambrogino Artistic Merit, City Milan, Italy. *Bibliog:* Capoferri (auth), Incisione Italiana, New Art Capoferri, 92; Mariani (auth), Trompe L'Oeil, Devecchi, 93. *Mem:* Presidente Associazione Italiana Graf Originale. *Media:* Etching. *Mailing Add:* c/o John Szoke Editions 24 W 57th St Ste 304 New York NY 10019

FINTZ, JEANETTE
PAINTER
b Brooklyn, NY. *Study:* Queens Coll, City Univ NY, BA, 1972; NY Studio Sch, 1972-73; Boston Univ Sch Fine Arts, BFA, 1975; Skowhegan Sch, 1975. *Work:* Rabobank, NYC; Commerzbank, NYC; Wilmer Cutler Pickering & Hale, Boston, Mass; Nat Television 7; Hobart & William Colls, Geneva, NY; Capital G Bank. Hamilton, Bermuda; Brigham & Women's Hops, Foxboro, Mass. *Exhib:* Solo exhibs include Hobart & Wm Smith Colls, 1979, 1984, Prince St Gallery, New York, 1979, 55 Mercer St Gallery, New York, 1985, Ohio State Univ, 1986, Five Points Gallery, East Chatham, NY, 1992, Gallerie Taksu, Kuala Lumpur, Malaysia, 1997, Carrie Haddad Gallery, Hudson, NY, 1999, ADD Gallery, Hudson, NY, 2000 & 2004, Gallery 1708 Richmond, Va, 2001, Southern Vt Arts Ctr, Manchester, Vt, 2001, Hudson Opera House, NY, 2002; Invitational, Art in General, New York, 1992; Nature Abstracted, Painting Ctr, New York, 2004 & 13th Anniversary Show, 2006; Informed Color, BRIK Gallery, Catskill, NY, 2006, Cowgirls of the Hudson Valley, 2006 & Cowgirls of the Hudson Valley 2, 2007; The End Up, Windham Fine Arts, Windham, NY, 2007; Peace, Sideshow Gallery, New York, 2008; 183rd Ann: Invitational Exhib Contemp Am Art, Nat Acad Mus, New York, 2008; Locally Grown, Albany Int Airport Gallery, 2008; Surface Tension, Albany Int Airport Gallery, 2009; Affordable Affair, New York, 2009. *Teaching:* Instr painting & drawing, State Univ NY, Purchase, formerly; instr, foundations in core studies, Parsons, New Sch Design, New York, currently. *Awards:* Ingram Merrill Award, Painting, 1980; Artist Space Exhib Grant, 1984; Ludwig Vogelstein Grant, Painting, 1984; ED Found Award, Painting, 1990; NY State Individual Artist Fel, Works on Paper, 1993; Emil & Dines Carlsen Award for Painting, Nat Acad Design, 2008. *Bibliog:* S Westfall (auth), Reviews, Art Mag, 1985; R Cohen (auth), catalogue, Structure & Metaphor, 1986; catalogue, Jeanette Fintz, Paintings, Dec 1994; Thomas Lail (auth), Cross & Fintz Display Artists' Process, Times Union, Aug 1992; Jaeger (auth), Fintz's Paintings Not Only Pretty, Dec 1994; P Barton (auth), The Artful Mind, True Colors, Aug 2002. *Dealer:* Nicole Fiacco Hudson NY; Erdriech White Fine Art Boston MA; Windham Fine Art Windham NY. *Mailing Add:* Surprise Result Rd Surprise NY 12176

FIORANI, FRANCESCA
EDUCATOR, ADMINISTRATOR
Study: Univ Rome-La Sapienza, BA (Art History), 1986, MA (Art History), 1990, PhD (Art History), 1994. *Pos:* Assoc curator for special exhibitions and programs, Galleria Nazionale d'Arte Moderna e Contemporanea, Rome, 1988-1992; guest curator, Bartolo di Fredi's Adoration of the Magi: A Masterpiece Reconstructed, Charlottesville, Univ Virginia Art Mus, 2012; mem internat com, Col Art Assn, 2013-; invited lectr and presenter in the field. *Teaching:* Asst. prof, McIntire Dept of Art, Univ Virginia, 1997-2005, assoc prof art history, 2005-, chair art dept, 2013-; dir, Univ Virginia in Italy: The Art and Architecture of Rome, Summer Term, 2005-2009, Renaissance Art on Site, January Term, 2004-2010; vis prof, The Interdisciplinary Center at Hertzlya, Israel, Law School, 2007, The Hebrew Univ of Jerusalem, The European Forum, 2008. *Awards:* Accademia Nazionale di San Luca, Rome, Italy, Research Fellowship, 1988; Consiglio Nazionale delle Ricerche, Italy, Research Fellowship, 1989; Ministero dell'Universita e della Ricerca Scientifica, Italy, PhD Fellowship, 1990-1993; Warburg Inst, Univ London, Francis Yates Fellowship, 1993; Herzog August Bibliotek, Germany, 1994; John Carter Brown Library, Brown Univ, Research Fellowship, 1994; Folger Inst, The Folger Shakespeare Library, Research Fellowship, 1995; Nat Endowment for the Humanities, Research Fellowship for Univ Professors, 1997; American Council for the Learned Societies, Research Fellowship, 1997, Frederick Burckhardt Residential Fellowship, Villa I Tatti, Florence, 2009-2010; Getty Center, Postdoctoral Fellowship in the History of Art and the Humanities, 2000-2001; Sesquicentennial Fellowship, Univ Virginia, 2001-2002, 2013; John Simon Guggenheim Memorial Foundation Fellowship, 2009-2010; Inst for Advanced Study, Princeton Univ, fellowship alternate, 2013-2014. *Mem:* Soc of Fellows. *Publ:* auth, The Marvel of Maps-Art, Cartography and Politics in Renaissance Italy, 2005; articles in peer-reviewed journals and exhibition catalogues. *Mailing Add:* McIntire Department of Art University of Virginia PO Box 400130 Charlottesville VA 22904

FIORAVANTI, JEFFREY PAUL
ARTIST
b Saugus, Mass. *Study:* Salem State Coll, BSBA, 80; Clark Univ, 2000. *Work:* Cape Ann, North Shore Hist Mus, Gloucester, Mass; Bank of NH, Manchester, NH. *Comn:* Painting, Carroll Ray, N Andover, Mass, 2004; Payne Bouchier co, Boston, 2005. *Exhib:* Images of Civil War Battlefields, Nat Mus of Civil War Medicine, Frederick, Md, 2003, Am Landscape, 2004; Story Telling, Art Three Gallery, Manchester, NH, 2003; In Memory of Deeds Past, Lynn Hist Mus; History Meets the Arts, Gallery 30, Gettysburg, Pa, 2004; Painting the Soul of Am, ARA Gallery, S Hamilton, Mass, 2004; Impressions of New Eng, Bennington Ctr Arts, Bennington, Vt, 2004; 7th Ann Juried Exhib, For Pastels Only, Pastel Soc ME, Kennebunk, ME, 2006; 11th Ann Juried Exhib, For Pastels Only Cape Cod, Soc of Cape Cod, Chatham, Mass, 2006; Renaissance In Pastel, Ann Nat Juried Exhib, West Hartford, Conn, 2006-2007; Impressions of New Eng, Bennington Ctr Arts, Vt, 2007-2011; Pastel Soc of Am Signature Exhib, Bennington, Vt; Conn Pastel Soc Signature Exhib, New Milford, Conn; Pastel Society of New Hampshire, 2009-2012; Pastel by Invitation, Creative Arts Ctr, Chatham, Mass 2010, 2011, 2012, 2013. *Pos:* Sr materials planner, Teradyne Inc, Boston, 84-96; production scheduler, Compensated Devices Inc, Melrose, 97-99; web specialist Attunity Inc, Burlington, 2000-01; graphic designer, advertising copywriter TK Keith co, Wakefield, 2001-; prin, owner Fioravanti Fine Art, 2003-. *Teaching:* Instr, pastel painter, Chelmsford Ctr Arts, Mass, 2003. *Awards:* Olympian Corp award, Pastel Soc W Coast Int Open Exhib, 2000; Best in Show award, Con Pastel Soc, 2000; Terry Ludwig Gold Award, 2006; Mutating the Signature(with poet Tim Sheehan), 2009; Pastel 100 Competition- Landscape category, Pastel Journal, 2009, 3rd pl, 2010; Allied Artists Award, 2008; Richardson Award, 2009; PSA Award, 2009. *Bibliog:* Master Pastelist of the World USA Showcase, Pastel Artist Int, 5-7/2000; This Hallowed Ground, North Shore Sunday, 2003; Lynn Artist Recreates Civil War Battlefields, The Boston Globe, 2003; Help is on the Way, Art Bus News, 2004; Inspired by Historic Landscapes, Am Artist Magazine, 11/2005; Best of America Pastel Artist Volume II, Kennedy Publications, 2009; Best of Worldwide Charcoal, Pastel & Pencil Artists Volume I, Kennedy Publications, 2009. *Mem:* Pastel Soc Am (signature), NY; Conn Pastel Soc (signature), Conn; Pastel Painters Soc Cape Cod (signature mem); North Shore Art Asn, Mass; Degas Pastel Soc, LA; Pastel Painters of Me; Pastel Soc New Hampshire (signature mem). *Media:* Pastel. *Dealer:* Art Res Assoc Gallery 300 at Main S Hamilton MA 01982; Art Three Gallery 44 South St Manchester NH; Just Jennifer Gallery 33 York St Gettysburg PA 17325. *Mailing Add:* 49 Pennybrook Rd Lynn MA 01905

FIORE, ROSEMARIE
PAINTER
Study: Univ Va, BA, 1994; Sch Art Inst Chicago, MFA, 1999. *Work:* Anderson Mus Contemp Art, NMex; Capital One, Richmond, Va; Franklin Inst Sci, Pa; Neuberger Berman, New York; Lower East Side Printshop, New York. *Exhib:* Solo exhibs, Va Commonwealth Univ, Richmond, 2000, Midway Contemp Art, Minn, 2001, Roswell

Mus Art Ctr, NMEx, 2002, Grand Arts, Kans City, 2004; New Prints/Autumn, Int Print Ctr, New York, 2003; All About Drawing, Univ Nebr, Lincoln, 2004; Sir Issac's Loft, Franklin Inst Sci, Philadelphia, 2005; Sosabeol Int Art Expo, Lake Pyungtaek Art Mus, South Korea, 2007; Anthem: An All-American Dystopia, Longwood Art Gallery, Bronx, 2009. *Pos:* Window dresser, Bergdorf Goodman, NY, 2000-02; vis artist, Univ Ill, 2002, Sch Art Inst Chicago, 2004, Univ Nev, 2007, SUNY Purchase, NY, 2007, Univ Va, 2008, Vt Studio Sch, 2002-. *Teaching:* Adj prof, Univ Va, 1999-2000, Univ NJ, 2001, Va Commonwealth Univ, 2001, Parsons Sch Design, NY, 2001-04; instr, Gallery Studio Program, Brooklyn Mus, 2000-09. *Awards:* Ragdale Found Grant, Ill, 2000; Workspace Grant, Dieu Donne Papermill, New York, 2001; Found Grant, Anderson Mus Contemp Art, 2002; MacDowell Colony Fel, 2002; NY Found Arts Buitoni Fel, 2009

FIRER, SERGE
PRINTMAKER, GRAPHIC ARTIST
b Gorky, Russ, Oct 26, 1954; Can citizen. *Study:* Gorky Art Sch, MA, 73. *Work:* Pushkin Mus, Moscow; Altai Mus, Barnaul, Russ; Gorky Art Mus, Russ; State Mus Israel, Jerusalem. *Comn:* Old Gorky Etchings, Artist's Union, Moscow, 82; The Portrait Gallery of Underground Workers, Artist's Union, Moscow, 87. *Exhib:* Solo exhibs, David Gallery, Jerusalem, Israel, 92, Klim Gallery, Toronto, 96; Art Expo, NY, 95; Art Multiple, Dusseldorf, Ger, 95-96. *Teaching:* Instr etching print, Bezalel, Jerusalem, Israel, 92-94. *Bibliog:* Young Artists of 80 in Russia, Ministry Cult Russ, 89; Jerusalem Post, 92. *Media:* Etching. *Mailing Add:* c/o Klim Art Publ Ltd 1238 Centre St Thornhill ON L4J 3M9 Canada

FIRESTEIN, CECILY BARTH
PAINTER, AUTHOR
b Brooklyn, NY, Apr 25, 1933. *Study:* Art Students League, Adelphi Univ, BA, 53; with Hans Hofmann, New York, 54; New York Univ, cert advanced study, 58, MA, 55; Sch of Chinese Brushwork, New York; cert, New York Sch Interior Design. *Work:* Corcoran Gallery Art, Washington, DC; Yale Univ Art Gallery, New Haven, Conn; Rose Art Mus, Waltham, Mass; Skirball Mus, Los Angeles, Calif; Brooklyn Mus, NY; Delaware Mus, Wilmington, Del; Jane Voorhees Zimmerli Mus, NJ; Freud Mus, London & Vienna; Art in Embassies Program, Kuwait, San Jose, Costa Rica, Dhaka, Bangladesh, Damascus, Syria, Ansuncion, Paraguay, Islamabad, Pakistan; Johnson & Johnson, NJ; Midwest Mus Am Art, Elkhart, Ind; Lance Armstrong Found, Austin, Tex; US Embassy, Astana, Kazakhstan. *Comn:* Illustrations for handbook, The Central Synagogue, NY, 78 & 79; rubbing of monument, Tarrytown Historical Soc, NY, 79; art deco door, Miami Design Preservation League, Miami, Fla, 80; rubbing illus for notepapers, South Street Seaport Mus, NY, 81; Jewish Calendar, Nat Jewish Mus, 99; US Dept of State, Bishkek, Kyrgyzstan; 4 paintings, US Consulate, Fiji, 2009. *Exhib:* Solo exhibs, Phoenix Gallery, NY, 1962-2012, Joseph Wahl Gallery, Calif, 2006, In Loving Memory, Mus City NY, 78, South St Seaport Mus, NY, 81, Spanish Inst, NY, 83, Farleigh Dickenson Univ, 92, Anthony Curtis Gallery, Boston, 2008, Nat Asn Women Artists, New York, 2008, Mona Lisa Gallery, Maplewood, NJ, 2009 & Osi Gallery, NY, 2009; Galerie Meissner, Hamburg, Ger, 83; UMA Gallery, NY, 2004; Adelphi Univ, Manhattan Center, NY, 2005; Gallery Anthony Curtis, Boston, Mass, 2007; Mona Lisa Gallery, NJ, 2007; Gwangji Biannual, Korea; Nat Asn of Women Artists, 2008; Am Consulate, Suva, Fiji, 2010; NY Phoenix Gallery, 2012, 2014; art cart, Kimmel Gallery, NY Univ, 2013. *Pos:* Printmaker & art consult, District 24, Valley Stream, NY, 53-60; arts coordr, Cent Synagogue NY, 75-78; critic, Artspeak, 82-90. *Teaching:* Lectr, many univ, 72-; instr/lectr rubbings, Cooper Hewitt Mus, NY, 80, South St Seaport Mus, NY, 2002 & Parsons Sch Design, NY, 83, Univ SC, 89, YMCA NY, 90, Montclair State, NJ, 92 & Connecticut Graphics Art Center, Norwalk, Conn, 96, Mus City NY, 2000, Ctrl Park Conservancy, 2002, Creative Center, NY, 2007 & Creative Ctr for People with Cancer, 2008, 2009, 2010, 2011, 2012. *Awards:* Traveling Exhib Am Art, Am Fedn Arts, 68; Grant, Unique New York, Nat Coun Arts, 74; Artist-in-Residence, Bronx Co Hist Soc, 75-81; Medal of Honor for Printmaking, Nat Asn Women Artists, 2000; Elizabeth Stanton Lake Memorial Award for Printmaking, 2000; Md Fedn Art (hon mention), Art on Paper Show, 2007; Am Consulate in Fiji; Grant, Art Cart Research Ctr Arts & Culture, Nat Ctr Creative Affairs, 2012-2013. *Bibliog:* Angela Taylor (auth), She teaches a modern form of an ancient art, NY Times, 76; Jerry Talmer (auth), Art among the headstones, New York Post, 78; Barbara B Buchholz, article, House & Garden Guides, 79; Gallery & Studio Notebook, Mar, 2003; interview, Paintingsdirect.com, Mar, 2000; Md Fed Art, Art on Paper, 2007; Nat Ctr Creative Aging, Wash DC, 2013; Academic Commons, Columbia Univ, NY, 2013. *Mem:* Life mem Art Students League; NY Soc Women Artists; Baltimore Printmakers; Soc Am Graphic Artists; Nat Soc Women Artists; Pi Lambda Theta (Nat Hon Kappa Delta Pi); Graphic Arts Counc, NY; Monumental Brass Soc, Eng; Am Print Alliance; Nature Printing Soc. *Media:* Monotype with Collage, Works on Paper. *Interests:* antiques, oriental arts. *Publ:* Auth & illusr, Rubbing Craft, Quick Fox, NY, 77; Rub a Landmark, Nat Trust Hist Preserv, 78; Rubbing brass & stone, New World Book of Knowledge, Grolier, Inc, 80; The Art of making rubbings, Seaport Mag, 80; Reach Out and Touch Something, New York Daily News, 88; Making Paper and Fabric Rubbings, Lark Bks, 2000. *Dealer:* Phoenix Gallery New York; Creative Ctr New York. *Mailing Add:* 8 E 96th St New York NY 10128

FIRESTONE, EVAN R
ADMINISTRATOR, HISTORIAN
b Richmond, Va, Nov 21, 1940. *Study:* Kent State Univ, BA, 62; Univ Wis-Madison, MA, 65, PhD, 71. *Teaching:* From instr to assoc prof, Univ Mass, Dartmouth, 68-77, chmn, dept art hist, 73-77; prof & head, dept art, Western Carolina Univ, 77-83; prof & chmn, dept art & design, Iowa State Univ, 83-90; prof & dir, Lamar Dodd Sch Art, Univ Ga, 90-97 & prof art hist, 97-. *Awards:* Throne-Aldrich Award, State Hist Soc Iowa, 92. *Mem:* Coll Art Asn. *Res:* Twentieth century art, especially abstract expressionism. *Publ:* Auth, John Linnell: The eve of the deluge, Cleveland Mus Art Bull, Vol 62, 4/75; Herman Melville's Moby Dick and the abstract expressionists, Vol 55, No 7, 3/80, Color in abstract expressionism: sources and background for meaning, Vol 55, No 7, 3/81, James Joyce and the first generation New York school, Vol 56, No 10, 6/82 & In praise of steel: Notes on some recent direct-metal sculpture, Vol 60, No 4, 4/86, Arts Mag; Fritz Bultman (auth), The case of the missing Irascible, Arch Am Art J, Vol 34, No 2, 94; The death of Moby Dick: Vincent Desiderio's The Progress of Self Love, Am Art, Vol 10, No 2, summer 96; Fritz Bultman: Collages, exhib at Georgia Museum of Art, 97; Fritz Bultman (auth), Actaeon paintings: sexuality, punishment, and oedipal conflict, Genders 34, Fall 2001; Barnett Newman's Onement I: the way up and down is one and the same; source, Vol 24, No 1, Fall 2004. *Mailing Add:* Univ Ga Lamar Dodd Sch Art Athens GA 30602-4102

FIRSTENBERG, JEAN PICKER
DIRECTOR
Study: Boston Univ, BS (summa cum laude), 58. *Pos:* Dir, Am Film Inst, 80- & Trans-Lux Corp, currently; adv bds, Big Sisters of LA, Will Rodgers Inst & Scott Newman Found, currently; trustee, Boston Univ. *Awards:* Alumni Award, Boston Univ, 82; Women in Film Crystal Award, Women in Film, Los Angeles, 90. *Mem:* Acad Motion Picture Arts & Sci; Women in Film; Women's Trusteeship for Betterment of Women. *Mailing Add:* American Film Inst 2021 N Western Ave Los Angeles CA 90027

FISCH, ARLINE MARIE
JEWELER, EDUCATOR
b Brooklyn, NY. *Study:* Skidmore Col, BS (art); Univ Ill, Urbana, MA (art); Fulbright student grant to Denmark, 56-57; Fulbright res grant to Denmark, 66-67; Sch Arts & Crafts, Copenhagen, Denmark; also with Bernhard Hertz Guldvaerefabrik, Copenhagen. *Hon Degrees:* Doc Humane Letters, Skidmore Col. *Work:* Victoria & Albert Mus, London; Vatican Mus, Rome; Mus Arts & Design, NY; Royal Scottish Mus, Edinburgh; Schmuckmus, Pforzheim; Houston Mus Fine Arts; Nat Gallery Australia; Danner Collection, Munich; and many other public & pvt collections. *Comn:* Creatures from the Deep Proj, Racine Art Mus, 2008-2009; Sea Vellies, Monterey Art Mus, 2012. *Exhib:* Schmuck-Objekte, Mus Bellerive, Zurich, Switz, 71; Goldsmith, 74, 76 & 79; Tokyo Int Jewelry Art Exhib, 77, 80 & 83; Mus Für Angewandt Kunst, Vienna, 82; Jewelry USA, 84; Solo Retrospective, Elegant Fantasy, 2000; Fisch Out of Water, Mingei Mus, 2009-2010; Creatures from the Deep, Bellevue Mus, 2010. *Pos:* Trustee, Am Craft Coun, 72-75 & 94-2000; bd dir, Haystack Mt Sch Crafts, 73-82 & 91-2000; vpres, World Crafts Coun, 77-81; pres, SNAG, 82-85. *Teaching:* Instr design & weaving, Skidmore Col, 58-61; prof jewelry & weaving, San Diego State Univ, 61-2000; guest lectr design, Guldsmedshojskole, Copenhagen, Denmark, 67 & 71; vis lectr, Crafts Coun of Australia, 75; vis prof, Boston Univ, 75-76; Fulbright lectr, Inst Applied Arts, Vienna, Austria, 82; Fulbright lectr, Mus Fine Arts, Montevideo, Uruguay, 89. *Awards:* Gold Medal, Int Handicraft Fair, Munich, 71; Distinguished Alumni Award, Skidmore Col, 86; Living Treasure of Calif Declaration, 85; Outstanding Prof, San Diego State Univ, 96; Distinguished Craft Educator Award, James Renwick Alliance, 2000; Gold Medal, Am Craft Coun, 2001; US Artist Grant, Target Fel, 2006; Artist Residency, Alaska, 2010; San Diego Art prize, 2012; Women Artist of the Year, Fresno Art Mus, Calif, 2012. *Bibliog:* J Keefer Bell (auth), Metalsmith, summer 88; Dormer & Turner (auth), The New Jewelry, 85; Elegant Fantasy: the Jewelry of Arline Fisch, publ Arnoldsche Art Publishers; and others; Sharon Church (interview), Archives Am Art (craft documentation prog), 2003. *Mem:* World Crafts Coun (dir, 74-76, vpres for NAm, 76-81); founding mem Soc NAm Goldsmiths (pres, 82-85); fel Am Crafts Coun (Calif rep, southwest regional assembly, 69-72, craftsman-trustee, 72-75); Allied Craftsmen San Diego. *Media:* Jewelry. *Res:* Textile structures in metal including weaving, braiding, knitting & crochet. *Interests:* Travel, reading & opera. *Publ:* Auth, Textile Techniques in Metal, Van Nostrand Reinhold, 75, 2nd ed, Lark Books, 96; Contemporary Dutch Jewelry, 4/91 & Ronald Pearson, Silversmith, 6/92, Am Craft; auth, Crocheted Wire Jewelry, Lark Books, 2006. *Dealer:* Mobilia Gallery, Cambridge, MA; Taboo Studio San Diego CA. *Mailing Add:* 4316 Arcadia Dr San Diego CA 92103

FISCHER, HAL (HAROLD) ALAN
ADMINISTRATOR, CONSULTANT
b Kansas City, Mo, Dec 18, 1950. *Study:* Univ Ill, Champaign-Urbana, BFA, 73; San Francisco State Univ, with Jack Welpott, MA, 76; Univ Calif, San Diego, with David Antin, MFA, 88. *Work:* San Francisco Mus Modern Art. *Exhib:* Photo-Linguists, Santa Barbara Mus Art, Calif, 77; Camerawork Gallery, San Francisco, 78; Photographs and Words, San Francisco Mus Mod Art, 81; Photog in Calif, 1945-1980, San Francisco Mus Mod Art, 84; Made in Calif, Los Angeles Co Mus Art, 2000-01; Under the Big Black Sun, 1974-81, Calif Art, Mus Contemporary Art, Los Angeles, Calif, 2011. *Collection Arranged:* Goldsworthy, Presidio, San Francisco, 2008-2009; Presidio Habitats, Prsidio, San Francisco. *Pos:* Contrib ed, Artweek, 77-83; reviewer, Artforum, 78-82; develop assoc, Fine Arts Mus, San Francisco, 82-84; dir exhib, Timken Mus Art, 85-2007; develop planner, Balboa Art Conservation Ctr, 92-; dir for special projs, For Site Found, 2004-10; principal, Hal Fischer Assoc, 2007-; dir, San Francisco, Camerawork, 2010-2011. *Teaching:* Lectr photog, Calif Coll Arts & Crafts, Oakland, 78-80; instr, City Coll San Francisco, 79-82. *Awards:* Art Critics Fel, 77, Photogr Fel, 80, Critic-in-Residence Grant, 81, Art Writers Fel, 84, Nat Endowment Arts. *Bibliog:* Joan Murray (auth), Reading the structure of a subculture, 8/13/77 & Judith Dunham (auth), Messages on the skyline, 10/6/79, Artweek; Jeff Perrone (auth), Hal Fischer, Artforum, 10/19/77; Stephen Hannock (auth), Space & Time, 98. *Mem:* Int Asn Art Critics. *Res:* Contemporary photography and art. *Publ:* Auth, Gay Semiotics, 78; 18th Near Castro, 79; contribr, The Still Photograph: The Problematic Model, NFS Press, 81; auth, Don Worth: Photographs 1955-1985, Friends of Photog, 86; Stephen Hannock: Space & Time, The Dayton Art Inst, 98; contribr, Timken Mus Art, Acquisitions, 1995-2005, Putnam Found, 2006. *Mailing Add:* 117 Pierce St San Francisco CA 94117

FISCHER, JOHN
PAINTER, SCULPTOR, PIANIST
b Antwerp, Belg, Aug 11, 1930; US citizen. *Study:* City Univ New York, 48-49. *Work:* Fond De Decoration Du Canton De Genève, Geneva, Switz; Univ Ky, Louisville; Everson Mus, Syracuse, NY. *Comn:* Decorative mural (20 ft), Keebler Co, Chicago, 69. *Exhib:* Jewelry by Contemp Artists, Mus Mod Art, NY, 67; The Baker's Art, Mus Contemp Crafts, NY, 68; solo shows, Everson Mus, Syracuse, 72, NY Cult Ctr, NY, 73 & Musée Cantonal, Lausanne, Switz, 87; one-man retrospective, Scholoss Hardenberg, Velbert, Ger, 83; Community Arts Special Events Festivals at various galleries, mus, parks & many other locations, 1960-70; Digital Art (Electronic Paintings), Oberhessiches Mus, Giessen, Germany, 2008; Artmus Studio, New York, 2009, 2010, Kunstverein, Landau, Germany, 2010; Community arts special events include Loafers Homebakers Festivals, NEA, NY State Coun Arts, New York Dept Cult Affairs, New York Central Park, Brooklyn Mus, NY, Art Park, Lewiston, Maine, and other venues in parks, mus, galleries, NY state fairs, etc. *Pos:* Create & dir, ENVIRON, featuring the Loft Jazz Festivals, New York, 75-78. *Media:* Oil, Computer; Bread. *Dealer:* Brö & Kase Galerie L'Anciene Laiterie Soral Geneva Switz; Adrianna Schmidt Stuttgart Germany; Artmus Studio New York. *Mailing Add:* 75 Warren St Apt 1 New York NY 10007

FISCHER, ROBERT A
SCULPTOR
b Minneapolis, 1968. *Study:* Escuela Salmintina, Spain, degree, 1989; Minneapolis Coll Art & Design, Degree Interdisciplinary Studies (Hon) Prog, 1993. *Exhib:* Solo exhibs incl Hiding Places for a Dense City, Art in General, NY, 1999; New Work, Conductor's Hallway Gallery, London, 1999; Light/House, Franklin Art Works, Minneapolis, 2000; My Winnebago Travels, Vox Populi Gallery, Philadelphia, 2000; Mirrored Boat, Macalester Coll Art Gallery, St Paul, 2000; In Site, Madison Art Ctr, Wis, 2000; Dee/Glasoe, NY, 2001; Elizabeth Dee Gallery, NY, 2002; Mary Goldman Gallery, Los Angeles, 2004; Cohan and Leslie, NY, 2005; group exhibs at Five Jerome Artists, Minneapolis Coll Art & Design, 1996, Reimaging the Landscape, Katherine E Nash Gallery, Minneapolis, 1997, One Hundred Yrs of Sculpture, Walker Art Ctr, Minneapolis, 1998, Interval, Sculpture Ctr, NY, 1999, Door as Metaphor in Contemp Art, NJ Ctr Visual Art, 2002, Druid: Wood as a Superconductor, Space 101, Brooklyn, 2003, Soft Cell, Foxy Productions, Brooklyn, 2003, I Feel Mysterious Today, Palm Beach Inst Contemp Art, Fla, 2004. *Awards:* Grantee Visual Arts Fel, Minnesota State Arts Board, 1996; Jerome Found Fel, 1995; Visual Arts Fel, Bush Found, 1999. *Mailing Add:* 131 Imlay St Apt 1F Brooklyn NY 11231

FISCHER, THOMAS JEFFREY
PHOTOGRAPHER, EDUCATOR
b Glendale, Calif, May 7, 1946. *Study:* Calif State Univ, Northridge, BA, 73; Stanford Univ, MFA, 87. *Work:* Savannah Coll Art & Design, Ga; Greenwood Mus, SC; Libr Cong, Washington; Interlochen Ctr Arts, Mich; Nat Maritime Mus, Norfolk, Va. *Exhib:* Photograph as Document, Downey Mus Art, Calif, 88; Recent Landscapes, Stanford Univ Photo Gallery, Calif, 89; Nat Landscape Exhib, Mus Rockies, 89; Contemp Southeastern Photog, Crealde Inst Art, Orlando, Fla, 93; Southern Landscapes, Mobile Townhouse, Univ Southern Ala, 96; Waters of the Southeast, Nat Maritime Mus, 96; Jewels in the Crown, Nat Gallery, Washington, 2001; Paradise/Paradox, Nathan Wilson Ctr for Arts, Jacksonville, Fla, 2002; G-8 Summit, 2003; Mem Univ Gallery, 2006; Univ Notre Dame, 2007; Creative Arts Ctr, Hong Kong, 2009. *Pos:* Dean, Sch Media Art, Savannah Col Art & Design, 1998-, Chief Academic Officer, 2007-; Prof of photog, 1990-present; chmn, photog dept, 2006-. *Teaching:* Instr fine art, Lucia Mar Unified Schs, Arroyo Grande, Calif, 1973-85; lectr photog, Stanford Univ, Calif, 1986-88; prof, Savannah Col Art & Design, Ga, 1990-, ch photog dept, 2006-. *Awards:* Designation Award in Art, Cult Olympiad, US Olympic Comt, 95; James Borelli Fel, Stanford Univ, 96; Prof of Yr, Savannah Coll Art & Design, 97 & 98; US Prof of the Yr Selection, 2004. *Mem:* Soc Photog Educ; Coll Art Asn; Nat Art Educ Asn; Soc Photog Educ (nat bd mem). *Media:* Photography. *Specialty:* Photography. *Interests:* Sculpture, fishing. *Publ:* Illusr, Rodin J, Stanford Univ Press, 88; illusr & auth, Waters of the Southeast, Savannah Coll Art & Design, 96; Paradise/Paradox, Legends Press, 2007 & 2008. *Dealer:* Gallery Lumiere 124 Oglethorpe Ave Savannah GA 31401. *Mailing Add:* 307 Washington Savannah GA 31405

FISCHER, URS
SCULPTOR
b Zurich, Switzerland, 1973. *Study:* Schule für Gestaltung, Zurich, Photography. *Exhib:* Solo exhibs include Galerie Walcheturm, Zurich, 1996, 1997, Inst Contemp Art, London, 2000, Contemp Fine Arts, Berlin, 2002, Proj Room, Santa Monica Mus, Los Angeles, 2002, Gavin Brown's Enterprise, New York, 2003, 2005, 2007, Blaffer Gallery, Houston, 2006; Group exhibs include Cobra Mus Mod Art, Amsterdam, 2005; Vincent 2006, Stedelijk Mus, Amsterdam, 2006 ; Studio, Hugh Lane Mus, Dublin, Ireland, 2006; Day for Night, Whitney Biennial, Whitney Mus Am Art, New York, 2006 ; Where are we going?, Palazzo Grassi, Venice, 2006; Vanhaerents Art Collection, Disorder in the House, Brussels, Belgium, 2007; Biennale de Lyon, 2007; Traum & Trauma, MUMOK und Kunsthalle, Vienna, 2007 ; Hamster Wheel, Tese della Novissima, Arsenale di Venezia, Venice, 2007 ; Unmonumental: The Object in the 21st Century, New Mus, New York, 2007 ; 54th Int Art Exhib Biennale, Venice, 2011. *Awards:* Bundeamt für Kultur Grant, Zurich, 1995; Kiefer-Hablitzel Grant, 1997; Providentia Prize, YoungArt, 1999. *Mailing Add:* Gavin Brown Enterprise 620 Greenwich St at Leroy St New York NY 10014

FISCHLI, PETER
SCULPTOR, PHOTOGRAPHER, INSTALLATION SCULPTOR
b Zurich, Switzerland, 1952. *Study:* Acad di Belle Arti, Urbino, 1975-76; Acad di Belle Arti, Bologna, 1976-77. *Exhib:* Solo retrospectives include Tate Modern, London, 2006, Deichtorhallen Hamburgh, Germany, 2008; Solo exhibs include PS 1, Long Island City, NY, 1987, Sonnabend Gallery, New York, 1989, 1994, Venice Biennale, Venice, 1995, Matthew Marks Gallery, New York, 1999, 2002, 2003, 2007, Mus Mod Art, Paris, 2000, Swiss Inst, New York, 2007; Group exhibs include An Int Survey of Recent Painting and Sculpture, Mus Mod Art, New York, 1984; Carnegie Int, Pittsburgh, 1988, 2008; Venice Biennale, Venice, 1988; Micromegas, Am Ctr, Paris, 1995; Freie Sicht aufs Mittelmeer, Mus Mod Art, Gunma, Japan, 1998; Sydney Biennal, Sydney, 1998, 2008; Real Stories II, Fredich Petzel Gallery/ Marianne Boesky Gallery, New York, 1999; Ellsworth Kelly, Brice Marden, Mathew Marks Gallery, New York, 1999; Staged Constructions of Reality in Contemp Photography, Bankadar Jancou Gallery, New York, 2000; Europeans, Zwirner & Wirth, New York, 2000, Conceptual Photography: 1964-1989, 2007; Restaging the Everyday: Recent Work by Beat Streuli and Fischli/Weiss, San Francisco Mus Mod Art, 2001; Moving Pictures, Solomon R Guggenheim Mus, New York, 2002; It's a Wild Party and We're Having a Great Time, Paul Morris Gallery, New York, 2002; Stacked, D'Amelio Terras, New York, 2003; Hard Light, PS 1 Contemp Art Ctr, Long Island City, New York, 2004; Universal Experience: Art, Life, and the Tourist's Eye, Mus Contemp Art, Chicago, 2005; Slideshow, Brooklyn Mus, New York, 2005; Makers and Modelers: Works in Ceramic, Gladstone Gallery, New York, 2007. *Awards:* Gunther-Peill-Preis, Leopold-Hoesch-Mus, Duren, 2000; 54th Int Art Exhib Biennale, Venice, 2011. *Mailing Add:* Matthew Marks Gallery 523 W 24th St New York NY 10011

FISCHMAN, BARBARA J
PAINTER
Study: City Univ, NY, MFA; NY Univ, studied; Christie's NY, studied. *Comn:* Chow Chow, Pastel Mus China. *Exhib:* Europastel, Ital, 2002; Art du Pastel, France, 2002-03; The Butler Inst Am Art, Youngstown, Ohio, 2003; St Petersburg, Russia, 2003; Suzhou, China; Pastel Soc of China. *Pos:* art appraiser & pastelist, NY, currently. *Teaching:* instr, Giffuni Atelier for Pastels, NY. *Mem:* PSA (pres, currently); AAA (recording sec). *Media:* Pastels

FISCHMAN, LISA
CURATOR
Study: Univ Chicago, BA (art hist); Univ Minn, MA & PhD (art hist). *Pos:* Cur dept new media & educ, Walker Art Ctr, formerly; assoc cur contemp art & educ, UB Art Gallery SUNY Buffalo, 1997-2000; gallery dir, Atlanta Coll Art, 2000-2005; chief cur, Univ Ariz Mus Art, Tucson, 2005-2009; Ruth G Shaprio dir, Davis Mus & Cultural Ctr, 2009-. *Mem:* Asn Art Mus Curators (gov comt). *Mailing Add:* Davis Museum and Cultural Center Wellesley College 106 Central St Wellesley Hills MA 02481-8203

FISH, JANET I
PAINTER
b Boston, Mass, May 18, 1938. *Study:* Smith Coll, BA; Yale Sch Art & Archit, MFA; Skowhegan Summer Sch. *Hon Degrees:* Lyme Acad, Conn, hon DFA. *Work:* Whitney Mus Am Art, NY; Dallas Mus Art, Tex; Metrop Mus Art, NY; Art Inst Chicago; Pa Acad Fine Arts; and others. *Exhib:* Solo shows incl Robert Miller Gallery, New York, 1979, Orlando Mus Art, 1992, Mus Arts & Scis Macon, Ga, 1993, Yellowstone Srt Ctr, Billings, Mont, 1995, DC Moore Gallery, NY, 1995, Starting with Flowers, 1996, Food for Thought: A Visual Banquet, 1998, Summer Group Show, 1999, The Likeness of Being, 2000, Recent Paintings, 2002, Reflections, Paintings, 2002, Everyday Mysteries: Mod & Contemp Still Life, 2004, 2005, 2007, John Szoke Gallery, New York, 1998, Emory and Henry Coll, Va, 1999, Chicago Ctr for Print, 1999, Marianne Friedland Gallery, Naples, Fla, 1999, Samuel P Harn Mus Art, Gainesville, Fla, 2003, Ogunquit Mus Am Art, Maine, 2004, Janet Fish Pastels, Butler Inst Am Art, Youngstown, Ohio, 2006, Janet Fish: American Master, Lehigh Univ, Bethlehem, Pa, 2007; group shows incl Art Inst Chicago, 1972 & 1974; Am Drawings 1963-1973, Whitney Mus Am Art, 1973; The Liberation, Corcoran Gallery, Washington, DC & US Info Agency Traveling Exhib, Europe, 1976-77; Am 76 (traveling exhib), Brooklyn Mus, NY & US Dept Interior, 1976-78; Eight Contemp Am Realists, Pa Acad Fine Arts & NC Mus Art, 1977; Butler Inst Am Art, 1979, 2006; Collector's Ann Contemp Art, Boca Raton Mus Art, Fla, 1990; Selections from the Glenn C James Collection, Spiva Art Mus, Joplin, Ohio; New Viewpoints, Seville World Expo, US Pavilion, 1992; Yale Collects Yale, Yale Univ Art Gallery, 1993, Alumni Choice Exhib, 2001; Yellowstone Art Ctr, Mo Traveling Exhib, 1995-97; Contemp Am Realist Drawing, Art Inst Chicago, 1999-2000; Columbus Mus, Ga, 2000; Samuel P Harn Mus Art, Gainesville, Fla, 2003; Nat Acad Design, NY, 2003; Better Still: Looking at Still Life in the Mus Collection, RI Sch Design Mus Art, Providence, RI, 2004; The Food Show: The Hungry Eye, Chelsea Art Mus, NY, 2006; Janet Fish: Colo Light, Pattern, Fed Reserve System, DC, 2010; Art of Janet Fish, Naples Mus Art, 2009-2010; Janet Fish: Into the Light, Mt Holyoke, College Art Mus, 2008. *Pos:* Bd governors, Skowhegan Sch Painting & Sculpture; artist adv bd, Marie Walsh Sharpe Art Found. *Teaching:* instr, The Marie Walsh Sharpe Art Found Summer Sessions, 1989-2000. *Awards:* MacDowell Fel, 1968, 1970 & 1972; Australia Coun Arts Grant, 1975; Am Acad Arts & Letts Award Art, 1994; Henry Ward Ranger Purchase Prize, Nat Acad Design, 2001; William A. Paton Prize for Watercolor, Nat Acad Design, 2005; and others. *Bibliog:* Garret Henry (auth), Janet Fish, Burton Skira Publ; Linda Konheim Kramer (auth), The Prints of Janet Fish, John Szoke Publ; Vincent Katz (auth), Janet Fish Paintings, Harry N Abrams Inc Publ. *Mem:* Artists Equity; Century Asn; Nat Acad. *Media:* Oil, Watercolor. *Dealer:* DC Moore Gallery 724 5th Ave New York NY 10019; Alan Brown Gallery Naples FL 34102; Gallery Camino Real 608 Banyan Trail Boca Raton FL 33431; Valerie Carberry Gallery 875 N Michigan Ave Chicago IL 60611; Derriere L'Etoile Studios 313 W 37th St New York NY 10018; Flanders Contemp Art 3012 Lyndale Ave S Minneapolis Minn 55408; J Johnson Gallery 177 4th Ave N Jacksonville Beach FL 32250; LewAllen Contemp 129 W Palace Ave Santa Fe NM 87501; Jerald Melberg Gallery 625 S Sharon Amity Rd Charlotte NC 28211; John Szoke Editions 591 Broadway New York NY 10012-3232; Tandem Press 201 S Dickinson St Madison WI 53703; Marianne Friedland Gallery 359 Broad Ave S Naples FL 34102. *Mailing Add:* 101 Prince St New York NY 10012

FISH, JULIA A
PAINTER
b Toledo, Ore, 1950. *Study:* Pac Northwest Coll Art, BFA, 76; Coll Art, Md Inst, MFA, 82. *Work:* Art Inst Chicago, Mus Contemp Art & Harold Washington Libr Ctr, Chicago, Ill; State Ore; Seattle City Light Collection, Wash; Ill State Mus, Springfield; Mus Modern Art, New York City. *Exhib:* Solo exhibs, Robbin Lockett Gallery, Chicago, 91, Amy Lipton Gallery, NY, 92, Christopher Grimes Gallery, Santa Monica, Calif, 93, 95 & 96, 2001, Feigen, Inc, Chicago, 94, Lipton-Owens Co, NY, 95, Ill Art Gallery, Chicago, 95 & Renaissance Soc, Univ Chicago, 96, Ten in One Gallery, Chicago, 98, Feigen Contemp, New York City, 99; Drawing in Chicago Now, Columbia Coll Art Gallery, 96; Mist, Hermetic Gallery, Milwaukee, Wis, 96; Art in Chicago, 1945-1995, Mus Contemp Art, Chicago, 96; New York: Drawings Today, San Francisco Mus Mod Art, 97; Zeichnungen (4)-Drawings 4, Galerie Klaus Fischer, Berlin, Ger, 97, Bauen and Bauten: Kunst in der Architektur, 98; No Ill Univ, DeKalb, 2000; Transcending Earth and Sky, Univ Art Gallery, San Diego State Univ, 2000; Entry: Plan, Fragments, Reconstructions, Christopher Grimes Gallery, Santa Monica, Calif, 2001; Out of Place: Contemp Art and the Archit Uncanny, Mus Contemp Art, Chicago, 2002; Speculative Chicago: A Compendium of Archit Innovation, Gallery 400, Univ Ill Chicago, 2003; The World Becomes a Private World: The Cooper and Rosenwasser Collection, Mills Coll Art Mus, Berkeley, Calif, 2004; Living Rooms, Anthony Grant, New York, NY, 2005; 181st Ann Invitational Exhib, Nat Acad Design, New York, NY, 2006; Figures in the Field: Figurative Sculpture and Abstract Painting from Chicago Collections, Mus Contemp Art, Chicago, 2006; Whitney Biennial, Whitney Mus Am Art, 2010. *Teaching:* Instr painting & drawing, Pac Northwest Col Art, 78-80 & 82-83; instr drawing, Mt Hood Community Col, Gresham, Ore, 82-83 & 84; vis artist & asst prof painting & drawing, Univ Iowa, 83-85; vis artist, Art Inst Chicago, 86-89; asst prof, Sch Art & Design, Univ Ill, Chicago, 89-95, dir grad studies, 91-94, assoc prof, 95. *Awards:* Louis Comfort Tiffany Found Award, 91; Visual Artist Fel, Nat Endowment Arts, 93; Robert H Mitchel/Univ Ill Scholar Award, 96; Campus Research Bd Grant, Univ Ill at Chicago, 97, Research award in Arts, Archit and Humanities, 2000-01; Individual Artist award, Richard H Driehaus Found, 2006. *Bibliog:* Susan Snodgrass (auth), Julia Fish at the Renaissance Soc, Art in Am, 4/96; John Brunetti (auth), View: Julia Fish/The Renaissance Soc, Dialogue, 4-5/96; Laurie Palmer (auth), Julia Fish/The Renaissance Soc, Frieze, 5/96; Mahoney, Robert, Julia Fish and Claudia Matzko, Time Out New York, 99; Pincus, Robert L, Landscapes Old Passion with New Darker Side, San Diego Union Tribune, 2000; numerous others. *Dealer:* Christopher Grimes Gallery 916 Colorado Ave Santa Monica CA 90401-2717. *Mailing Add:* 1614 N Hermitage Ave Chicago IL 60622

FISHER, CAROLE GORNEY
PAINTER, SCULPTOR
b Minneapolis, Minn. *Study:* Minneapolis Coll Art & Design, BFA, 64; Pa State Univ, MFA, 66. *Work:* Roanoke Fine Arts Ctr, Va. *Comn:* Print ed, Minn State Arts Coun, 70; sculpture, Univ Minn, Morris, 73. *Exhib:* Pa State Univ, 72; Two Nations, Six Artists, Minn-Can, 74; Walker Art Ctr, Minneapolis, 74; Whitney Biennial Contemp Am Art, NY, 75; Woman as Viewer Exhib, Winnipeg Art Gallery, 75. *Pos:* Comnr, Minneapolis Art Comn, 75-. *Teaching:* Instr printmaking & drawing, Minneapolis Col Art & Design, 68-69; artist-in-residence printmaking, Bemidji State Univ, 69-70; instr drawing, Col St Catherine, 73-82. *Bibliog:* Cindy Nemser (auth), Whitney Biennial, Changes, New York, 75; Amy Goldin (auth), The New Whitney Biennial, Art in Am, 5-6/75; Chris Kohlmann (auth), 1975 Whitney Biennial, Mid West Art, 5/75. *Mem:* Coll Art Asn Am. *Media:* Miscellaneous. *Dealer:* One Hundred Eighteen: An Art Gallery 1007 Harmon Minneapolis MN 55400. *Mailing Add:* 2524 Stevens Ave S Apt 2 Minneapolis MN 55404-4346

FISHER, DORIS F
COLLECTOR
b 1932. *Study:* Stanford Univ, BA (econ). *Pos:* Co-founder & bd dirs, Gap Stores, Inc, 1969, chief merchandiser, 1969-2003; trustee, Stanford Univ, 1992-2002 & Phillips Exeter Acad. *Awards:* Named one of Top 200 Collectors, ARTnews Mag, 2004-08. *Collection:* Contemporary & American art, especially German. *Mailing Add:* Gap Inc 2 Folsom St San Francisco CA 94105

FISHER, JEROME
COLLECTOR
Pos: Chmn emer, Nine West Group; Jerome & Anne C Fisher Charitable Foundation. *Awards:* Humanitarian Award, 1997; Humanitarian of the Yr, Shoes on Sale, 2003; named one of Top 200 Collectors, ARTnews Mag, 2004-08. *Collection:* Modern art. *Mailing Add:* Nine West Group 1129 Westchester Ave White Plains NY 10604

FISHER, JOEL
SCULPTOR
b Salem, Ohio, June 6, 1947. *Study:* Kenyon Col, AB; Sunderland Univ, PhD. *Work:* Mus Mod Art, NY; Stedelijk Mus Amsterdam; Victoria & Albert Mus, London, Eng; Tate Gallery, London; Ctr George Pompidou, Paris; Kunst Mus Bern, Switz; Art Coun Great Britain, London; Brooklyn Mus; Butler Inst Art, Youngstown, Ohio; Cincinnati Art Mus, Ohio; Mus Fine Art, Richmond, Va. *Exhib:* Solo exhibs stadtisches Mus Mônchengladbach, 74, Mus Mod Art, Oxford, 77, Stedleuk Mus, Amsterdam, 78, Kunst Mus Luzern, 86, Galerie Farideh Cadot, 91, Diane Brown Gallery, 92, Lawrence Markey Gallery, NY, 94; An Int Survey of Contemp Painting and Sculpture, Mus Mod Art, NY, 84; Structure to Remblance: 8 Sculptors, Albright Knox Gallery, Buffalo, 87; Four Am, Brooklyn Mus, 89; 5th Paper Biennale, Leopold Hoesch Mus, Duren, Ger, 94. *Teaching:* Goldsmiths Col, London Univ, 79, Bath Acad Art, Eng, 80-82, RI Sch Design, 85 & 90, Vt Studio Sch, 88-, Sch Visual Arts, 89-; prof, Ecole des Beaux Arts, Paris, 95-; Philadelphia Acad Art MFA prog, 93-. *Awards:* George A & Eliza Gardner Howard Found, 86-87; Fel, Pollock-Krasner Found, 93; John Simon Guggenheim Fel, 93-94; Henry Moore Fel, 2002-2004. *Bibliog:* Simon Field (auth), Joel Fisher on Paper, Art & Artists, 1/72; Lisa Bear (auth), Strong as a Spider's Web, Avalanche, 12/74; Robin White (auth), View Mag, 81. *Mem:* Coll Art Asn Am; Phi Beta Kappa. *Publ:* Auth, Double Camouflage, Mansfield Fine Arts Ctr, 70; The Berliner Book, Berlin Kunstler Prog des DAAd, 73; Instances of Change, Bonomo Diffusione, Bari, Italy, 75; Dissolution, Stadt Mus Monchengladbach, 75; An Image in Blankness, Mus Mod Art, Oxford, 77; Diagnosis, Royal Scottihs Coll Surgeons, 2006; Apographs, Centre for Recent Drawing, London, 2009. *Mailing Add:* PO Box 349 River Rd North Troy VT 05859-0349

FISHER, KIM
PAINTER
b 1973. *Study:* UCLA, BFA, 96; Otis Coll Art & Design, MFA, 98. *Work:* 21 Paintings from Los Angeles, Robert V Fullerton Art Mus, San Bernardino, Calif, 2002; Whitney Biennial, Whitney Mus Am Art, 2004. *Exhib:* Solo exhibs, China Art Objects, Los Angeles, 99, 2001, Midway Contemp Art, St Paul, 2003, John Connelly Presents, New York City, 2004, Shane Campbell, Oak Park, Ill, 2004, Modern Inst, London, 2005; Group exhibs, LA-LV-LA, Donna Beam Fine Art Gallery, Univ Nevada, 97, The Comestible Compost, Gallery 207, West Hollywood, Calif, 98, Young & Dumb, ACME LA, 2000, Platypus, Lawrence Rubin Greenberg Van Doren Fine Art, NY, 2001, Selections, Bolsky Gallery, Otis Coll Art & Design, Los Angeles, 2001, Cancelled Art Fair!, China Art Objects, Los Angeles, 2001, The Stray Show, boom, Chicago, 2002, Fair, Royal Coll Art, London, 2002, Works for Giovanni, China Art Objects, Los Angeles, 2003, Still or Sparkling?, John Connelly Presents, NY, 2003, A Red Letter Day, Fredericks Freiser Gallery, NY, 2003, such things I do just to make myself more attractive to you, Peres Projects, Los Angeles, 2004

FISHER, LEONARD EVERETT
PAINTER, ILLUSTRATOR
b Bronx, NY, June 24, 1924. *Study:* With Moses Soyer, New York, 39; Art Students League, with Reginald Marsh, 41; Brooklyn Coll, with Olindo Ricci & Serge Chermayeff, 41-42; Yale Univ Sch Fine Arts, BFA, 49, MFA, 50. *Hon Degrees:* Paier Coll Art, BFA, 98. *Work:* Butler Inst Am Art, Youngstown, Ohio; Libr Cong, Washington, DC; Mt Holyoke Coll, S Hadley, Mass; New Brit Mus Am Art, Conn; NY Pub Libr; Union Coll, NY; Smithsonian Nat Postal Hist Mus, DC; Hebrew Union Coll Mus NY; Mus Am Illustration NY; Housatonic Mus, Bridgeport Ct; Bellarmine Mus; Fairfield Univ, Ct; and others. *Comn:* Am Bicentennial (four block eight cent commemorative postage stamps), 72, Legend of Sleepy Hollow (ten cent commemorative postage stamp), 74, Liberty Tree (thirteen cent embossed envelope), 75 & Skilled Hands for Independence (four block thirteen cent commemorative stamps), 77, US Postal Serv, Washington DC; mural, Norwalk Transit Authority Admin Bldg, US Govt & Conn state, 2002. *Exhib:* Painters Panorama, Am Fedn Arts Sponsored Tour, 54-56; New Eng Painting Ann, Silvermine Guild Artists, 68-69 & 71; Butler Inst Am Art, Youngstown, Ohio, 72; retrospective, New Brit Mus Am Art, Conn, 73 & Am Mus Illus, New York, 91; Solo Exhibs: Rotunda, Free Libr Philadelphia, 76; Univ Hartford, Conn, 76; Gen Elec Corp, 76; NY Hist Soc: 200 Yrs of Am Illus, 76; Story Lines-Scratchboard Illus, AA Resources Ore, Ore Arts Comn & Nat Endowment Arts, 93-94; NY Pub Libr, 2000; Cavalier Galleries, Greenwich, Conn, 2008, 2010, Leonard Everett Fisher, 70 Years on Artist, Hebrew Union Coll Mus, NY, 2011-2012; Soc Illustr Mus Am Illus, New York, 90-92; Milk and Eggs: The Am Revival of Tempera Painting 1930-1950, Brandywine Mus, Chadds Ford, Pa, 2002. *Pos:* Illusr & auth, children's books for major publ, 54-; bd dir, Silvermine Guild Artists, 70-74; deleg-at-large, White House Conf, Librs & Info Serv, 79; Pres, Westport, Conn Pub Libr, 86-89. *Teaching:* Dean studies, Whitney Sch Art, 51-53; instr art hist, painting, life drawing & bk illus, Paier Coll Art, 66-78, dean acad affairs, 77-81, dean emer, 82-; Lifetime Learners Inst, Norwalk Community Col, Norwalk Conn, 2007-. *Awards:* Pulitzer Scholar Art, 50; Kerlan Award, Univ Minn, 91; Arbuthnot Citation, Am Libr Asn, 94-95. *Bibliog:* Charles M Daugherty (ed), Six Artists Paint a Still Life, North Light, 77; Howard Munce (ed), Magic and Other Realism, Hastings House, 81; Norman D Stevens, Patricia Cianciolo & Ellen Embargo (auths), Leonard Everett Fisher: A Life of Art, Univ Conn, 98. *Mem:* Soc Illusr; Silvermine Guild Artists; Authors Guild; Soc Children's Bk Writers & Illustr. *Media:* Acrylic, Soft Engraving, Egg Tempera. *Publ:* Auth & illusr, The Great Wall of China, Atheneum, 86; Gutenberg, 93; Kinderdike, 94, Macmillan; William Tell, Farrar Straus & Giroux, 96; Cyclops, 91; Gods and Goddesses of the Ancient Maya, Holiday House, 2000; Sky, Sea, the Jetty, and Me, Marshall Cavandish, 2001. *Dealer:* Cavalier Galleries 405 Greenwich Ave Greenwich CT 06880. *Mailing Add:* 7 Twin Bridge Acres Rd Westport CT 06880

FISHER, PHILIP C
PAINTER, ART DEALER
b Oil City, Pa, Nov 17, 1930. *Study:* Graceland Col, 50; Univ Nebr, 55; studied with Norman Rockwell, Stevan Dohanos, Albert Dorne & Al Capp, 58-61. *Work:* Sagendorf Int Dollhouse Mus. *Exhib:* Int Platform Asn Invitational Art Show, Hyatt Regency Hotel, Washington, DC, 86; The Great Colo Showcase, Denver, 89. *Pos:* Cartoonist-illusr, 'Brenda Starr' syndicated comic strips, Chicago, Ill, 77-78; portrait artist, Omaha, Nebr & Denver, Colo, 80-88; art dealer, Fisher's Master Artists, Inc, Golden, Colo, 86-88. *Mem:* Am Portrait Soc; Int Platform Asn. *Media:* Oil on Linen, Pen & Ink, Easel Painter. *Specialty:* Realist oils on canvas, portraiture, genre, landscapes, still lifes, seascapes, impressionism. *Publ:* An illustrated survey of leading contemporaries, Am Artists, Chicago, Ill, 89; An illustrated survey of the city's museums, galleries and leading Artists, New York Art Rev, 90. *Mailing Add:* 1180 S Yerba Santa Dr Pueblo West CO 81007

FISHER, SARAH LISBETH
CONSERVATOR
b Washington, DC, Nov 1, 1945. *Study:* Wellesley Col, BA (art hist), 67; Florence, Italy, with pvt painting conservator, 67-68; Inst Technol Paintings, Stuttgart, Ger, with Dr R Straub, 69-70; Swiss Inst Art Res, Zurich, Switz, with Dr T Brachert, cert in conserv, 72; with T Hermanes, Canton of Vaud, Switz, 69 & 70; Cent Inst Art Res, Amsterdam, Holland, with Dr J Mosk, 73; Inst Royal du Patrimoine Artistique, Brussels, Belg, with N Gortghebeur, cert in conserv, 75. *Pos:* Conservator & asst to

the dir, Swiss Inst for Art Res, Zurich, Switz, 72-74; conservator, Intermus Lab, Oberlin, 75-77, Balboa Art Conserv Ctr, San Diego, Calif, 77-81 & Nat Gallery Art, Washington, DC, 81-. *Teaching:* Instr painting conserv, Intermus Conserv Asn, Oberlin, Ohio, 75-77. *Mem:* Am Inst Conserv Hist & Artist Works; Int Inst Conserv Hist & Artistic Works; Western Asn Art Conserv; Washington Conserv Guild. *Publ:* Ed, Rubens' The finding of Erichthonius: Examination and treatment, Allen Mem Art Mus Bulletin, Oberlin Col, XXXVIII, No 1, 80-81. *Mailing Add:* Nat Gallery Art Painting Conserv Dept Fourth & Constitution Ave NW Washington DC 20565

FISHER, VERNON
PAINTER, CONCEPTUAL ARTIST
b Ft Worth, Tex, 1943. *Study:* Hardin-Simmons Univ, BA, 67; Univ Ill, MFA, 69. *Work:* Hirshhorn/Smithsonian Inst, Corcoran Gallery Art, Washington, DC; Guggenheim Mus & Mus Mod Art, New York; Albright-Knox, Buffalo. *Exhib:* Whitney Mus Am Art, New York, 81 & 2000; Bronx Mus Arts, NY, 84; Hirshhorn Mus & Sculpture Garden, Washington, DC, 84; New Orleans Mus Art, La, 86; Brooklyn Mus, NY, 86; Walker Art Ctr, Minneapolis, Minn, 87; Los Angeles Co Mus Art, 87; Inst Contemp Arts, London, 87; solo exhib, Asher-Faure Gallery, Los Angeles, 86, Barbara Gladstone Gallery, NY, 87, Hiram Butler Gallery, Houston, Tex, 87, Lannan Mus, Lake Worth, Fla, 87, Fred Hoffman Gallery, Buffalo, NY, 89 & Hiram Butler Gallery, Houston, 90; Dallas Mus Art, 88 & 2007; Karsten Schubert Ltd, London, 89; Mod Art Mus Ft Worth, 89 & 2001; San Diego Mus Contemp Art, 89 & 2002; Miami Art Mus, 89; Mus Contemp Art, Houston, 89, 99 & 2004; Mus Fine Arts, Houston, 90 & 2000; Mus Mod Art, New York, 90; Asher-Faure Gallery, Los Angeles, 91; Rena Bransten Gallery, San Francisco, 92; Mus Contemp Art, Chicago, 92; Glassell Sch Art, 2000; and others; Mod Art Mus, Ft Worth, Tex,2010. *Teaching:* Assoc prof art, Austin Coll, Sherman, 69-78; prof art, NTex State Univ, 78-; regents prof art, 78-2005. *Awards:* Nat Endowment Arts Fel, 74, 80 & 81; Louis Comfort Tiffany Found Grant, 80-81 & 84; Visual Artist Award Grant, SECCA, 81 & 88; John Simon Guggenheim Fel, 95. *Bibliog:* John Habich (auth), Past/imperfect Kroust marathon, Minneapolis Star & Tribune, 4/11/87; Colleen O'Conner (auth), High profile: Vernon Fisher, Dallas Morning News, 9/20/87; Gary Schwan (auth), Lannan's walls teach perspective, Palm Beach Post, 10/23/87. *Publ:* Ed, Five stories, No 2, winter-spring 79 & A childhood friend, No 4, summer 80, White Walls; The Paris Review, Paris Review Inc, Vol 23, No 80, summer 81; auth, Navigating By the Stars, Landfall Press, Chicago, 89; ed, Navigating by the stars, Neon, summer 92. *Dealer:* Charles Conles Gallery New York NY; Dunn & Brown Contemporary Dallas TX; Mark Moore Gallery Los Angeles CA. *Mailing Add:* Mark Moore Gallery 5790 Washington Blvd Culver City CA 90232

FISHMAN, BARBARA (ELLEN) SCHWARTZ
PAINTER, PRINTMAKER
b Brooklyn, NY, May 3, 1946. *Study:* Sch Fine Arts, Boston Univ, BFA, 68; NY Univ, with Chuck Close, MA (painting), 73. *Work:* Boston Univ Traveling Art Show. *Comn:* Several pvt commissions. *Exhib:* Nat Asn Women Artists For Exhib to India, Jehangir Art Gallery, Bombay, India, 89; 100 Yrs/100 Works, Kirkpatrick Ctr, Tulsa, Okla, 90; Audubon Artists, Nat Arts Club, NY, 91; The Tree An Artist's Gift, Bergen Mus Art, Paramus, NJ, 91; North By South, Nassau Co Mus Art, Roslyn, NY, 92. *Pos:* Chair scheduling, Graphic Eye Gallery, Port Washington, NY, 86-; juror painting, Nat Asn Women Artists, New York, 93-; mem & chmn, Stan Brodsky Exhib, Art Adv Coun, Port Washington, NY, 93-. *Teaching:* Teacher art, Simon Baruch Jr High, New York, 68-70. *Awards:* Louis Lozowick Award, Audubon Artists Nat Art Club, 90; Stelly Sterling Mem, Nat Asn Women Artists, 92; Long Beach Art League/Art Club Rockville Ctr Gold Award, Nassau Co Mus Art, 92. *Mem:* Nat Asn Women Artists; Manhasset Art Asn; Audubon Artists; Art Adv Coun. *Media:* Acrylic, Oil. *Mailing Add:* 4 Woodcleft Ave Port Washington NY 11050

FISHMAN, BEVERLY
PAINTER, SCULPTOR
Study: Philadelphia Coll Art, BFA; Yale Univ, Conn, MFA. *Work:* Columbus Mus Art, Ohio; Detroit Inst Arts; Istanbul Art Centre, Turkey; Miami Art Mus; Stamford Mus & Nature Ctr, Conn. *Exhib:* Solo exhibs, Cummings Art Ctr, Conn Coll, 1985, Housatonic Mus Art, 1985, Sarah Doyle Gallery, Brown Univ, 1986, Stamford Mus & Nature Ctr, 1987, Cranbrook Mus Art, Mich, 1993, McDonough Mus Art, Ohio, 1994, Elgin Community Coll Gallery, Ill, 1996, Boulder Mus Contemp Art, Colo, 1999, White Columns, New York, 2000, Daimler Chrysler Galerie, Berlin, Ger, 2005, Tarble Arts Ctr, Eastern Ill Univ, 2008; Postopia, Craft and Folk Art Mus, Los Angeles, 1999; Post-Digital Printing, Cranbrook Art Mus, 2002; Op Art: Then and Now, Columbus Mus Art, Ohio, 2007; Infinitesimal Eternity: Making Images in the Face of Spectacle, Yale Sch Art, 2009; Am Acad Arts & Letts Invitational, New York, 2010. *Teaching:* Vis asst prof, Conn Coll, New London, 1987; adj assoc prof, Grad Art Sch, Coll New Rochelle, NY, 1983-92; instr, Md Inst, Coll Art, Baltimore, 1988-92; head painting, Cranbrook Acad Art, Mich, 1992-. *Awards:* Nat Endowment for the Arts Fel, 1989; Louis Comfort Tiffany Found Grant, 1990; Guggenhiem Found Fel, 2005. *Bibliog:* Marsha Miro (auth), A Cause to Celebrate, ARTnews, 6/2001; Victor M Cassidy (auth), Beverly Fishman at Skestos Gabriele, Art in Am, 4/2006; Kelly Crow (auth), The Art World Goes Local, Wall St J, 10/30/2009. *Mailing Add:* Cranbrook Academy of Art 39221 Woodward Ave Bloomfield Hills MI 48304

FISKIN, JUDY
PHOTOGRAPHER, VIDEO ARTIST
b Chicago, Ill, April 1, 1945. *Study:* Pomona Coll, with John Mason, BA, 66; Univ Calif, Berkeley, 66-67; Univ Calif, Los Angeles, MA (art hist), 69. *Work:* Bibliot Nat, Paris, France; Dallas Mus Fine Arts, Tex; Mus Contemp Art, La Jolla, Calif; Mus Fine Arts, Houston, Tex; Mus Contemp Art, Los Angeles; Stedelijk Mus, Amsterdam; Art Gallery New South Wales; Vassar Coll Art Ctr, NY; Nat Gallery of Art, Wash DC. *Comn:* What We Think About When We Think About Ships, Los Angeles Co Mus Art, 2000. *Exhib:* Solo exhibs, Castelli Graphics, New York, 76, Curt Marcus Gallery, New York, 91 & 94, Asher-Faure Gallery, Los Angeles, 91, Mus Contemp Art, Los Angeles, 92 & Patricia Faure Gallery, 94; Los Angeles in the 70's, Ft Worth Art Mus, Tex, 77; Group Material: Democracy, DIA Art Found, New York, 88; Typologies: Nine Contemp Photogrs, Newport Harbor Art Mus, Newport Beach, Calif, San Francisco Mus Mod Art, Akron Art Mus & Corcoran Gallery Art, Washington, DC, 91; Special Collections: The Photog Order from Pop to Now, Int Ctr Photog, New York, 92; Diary of a Midlife Crisis (film), San Francisco Film Fest, Bonn Videonale, Kassel Film & Video Fest & Mus Contemp Art, Los Angeles; 50 Ways to Set the Table (video), Mus of Modern Art, New York, 2004; Anthology Film Archives New York, 2004; Angles Gallery, Santa Monica, 2004; The end of photography, 2007; Amsterdam Int Doc Festival; European Media Arts Festival, Osnaebruck, Ger; Rencontres, Paris & Berlin; Kassel Film & Video Festival; Angles Gallery, Santa Monica; Guided Tour, Angles Gallery, 2010; Under the Big Black Sun, MOCA, Los Angeles, 2011; All Six Films, Angles Gallery, 2011; Greenburg Van Doren Gallery, NY, 2012. *Pos:* Co-dir, Womanspace Gallery, 73-74; producer, My Getty Ctr. *Teaching:* Prof photog, Calif Inst Arts, Valencia, 77-, assoc dean, 79-84. *Awards:* Nat Endowment Arts Grant, 80 & 90; Lifetime Achievement Award in Photog, Los Angeles Ctr Photog Studies, 95; Silver Spire Award, San Francisco Int Film Fest, 98; Silver Award, Worldfest, Houston; Best of Festival, Berkeley Video & Film Fest; Impakt Festival, Utecht, The Neth. *Bibliog:* Richard Armstrong (auth), Judy Fiskin's Photographs JS Calif Art Mag, 9-10/79; Robert L Pincus (auth), Judy Fiskin: some questions of aesthetics visions, winter 89; Terry R Myers (auth), Judy Fiskin, Arts, 4/91; Virginia Heckert (auth), Some Aesthetic Decisions: The Photographs of Judy Fiskin (book), Getty Pubs; Roberta Smith (auth), Art in Review, NY Times, 2013. *Mem:* Soc Photog Educ; Los Angeles Ctr Photog Studies. *Media:* Black & White Photography & Video. *Dealer:* Angles Gallery Santa Monica CA. *Mailing Add:* c/o Calif Inst Arts 24700 McBean Pkwy Valencia CA 91355

FISS, CINTHEA
PHOTOGRAPHER, VIDEO ARTIST
b New York, NY. *Study:* Antioch Univ, BFA, 78; Nova Scotia Coll Art & Design, 78-80; Calif Inst Arts, MFA, 93; Independent Study Prog, Whitney Mus Am Art, 95-96. *Work:* San Francisco Arts Comn, Calif; Los Angeles Pub Libr; Ctr Creative Photog, Tucson, Ariz. *Comn:* I-Love-Mutants (video), comn by Mutants, Fillmore Auditorium, San Francisco, 2006; Sally-remiX (video), comn by Sally Webster, Womanizer Salon, Deitch Projects, New York, 2007; Dirk-remiX (video), comn by Mutants & Kathy Peck, Dirk Fest, Slim's, San Francisco, 2007; Mutants Live at Warhol Live (video), Comn by Mutants, DeYoung Mus, San Francisco, 2009. *Exhib:* Solo exhib, Side Street Gallery, Santa Monica, Calif, 94; ISP Open Studios, Whitney Mus, New York, 96; Deadly Responses: Murder & Suicide, Longwood Arts Gallery, NY, 96; Buck Stop: Pro-Vanities in the Bathroom, Spot Gallery, New York, 96; Joint Ventures, Basillico Fine Arts, New York, 96; Open Circuits, Contemp Art Mus, Tampa, 96; Colo 2000, Boulder Mus Contemp Art, 2000; Transparent Archit, Gale Gates, Brooklyn, New York, 2000; This Year's Model, Cordell Taylor Gallery, Denver, 2003; Anxiety & Desire, Ctr Visual Arts, Denver, 2004; In The Ctr of Things, Ctr Creative Photog, Tucson, Ariz, 2004; and others. *Collection Arranged:* Women Artists at Work, Eye Gallery, 90. *Pos:* Cur & bd dir, Eye Gallery, San Francisco, 84-89; facilities mgr, Headlands Ctr Arts, Sausalito, Calif, 88-89; artist-in-residence, Calif Arts Coun, 94-95; co-dir, Internet Agency, New York, 95-. *Teaching:* Vis prof photog, Univ Ariz, Tucson, 94-95; asst prof electronic media, Univ S Fla, Tampa, 95-97 & Univ Denver, 97-2002; vis artist, Univ Colo, Denver, 2002-2003; vis asst prof photog, Metrop State Coll, Denver, 2003-2011. *Awards:* Visual Artist fel New Genres, Nat Endowment Arts Regional WESTAF, 94; Artist Equip Access Award, Bay Area Video Coalition, 94; Calif Arts Coun Grant, 94. *Bibliog:* David A Greene (auth), Women at work, Los Angeles Reader, 11/25/94; C Brue and K Shields (auths), Withinsight: Visual Territories of Thirty Artists, 95; Vivien Raynor (auth), Deadly responses, NY Times, 2/11/96. *Mem:* Coll Art Asn. *Media:* Photography; Electronic Media. *Publ:* Contribr, Tradeswomen Mag, San Francisco, 85-88; Women and Work, New Sage Press, 87 & 94; Honeycakes for Cerebus, Art Press, 93; auth, Pump, Rethinking Marxism, 95; Implications of recent technological changes, API J, 96

FITCH, BLAKE
MUSEUM DIRECTOR, PHOTOGRAPHER, CURATOR
b Greensboro, NC, 1971. *Study:* Pratt Inst, BFA, 94; Art Inst Chicago, 98; Boston Univ, MS, 2001. *Work:* Cur Photobooth, Jan Staller: A Retrospective. *Pos:* Exec dir, Griffin Mus of Photog, Winchester, Mass, currently. *Mailing Add:* Griffin Mus Photog 67 Shore Rd Winchester MA 01890

FITCH, STEVE (STEVEN) RALPH
PHOTOGRAPHER, INSTRUCTOR
b Tucson, Ariz, Aug 16, 1949. *Study:* Univ Calif, Berkeley, BA, 71; San Francisco Art Inst, 77; Univ NMex, Albuquerque, MA, 78. *Work:* Mus Mod Art, NY; Mus Fine Arts, Boston; Fogg Art Mus; Oakland Mus; Houston Mus Fine Arts. *Exhib:* Solo exhib, Art Mus, Univ Calif, Berkeley, 75; The Aesthetics of Graffiti, 79 & Beyond Color, 80, San Francisco Mus Mod Art; Color as Form: History of Color Photog, George Eastman House, Rochester, NY, 82; Exposed & Developed: Photog Sponsored by Nat Endowment Arts, Smithsonian Inst, Nat Mus Am Art, 84; Marks & Measures: Linda Connor, Rick Dingus, Steve Fitch & Charles Roitz, Spencer Art Mus, Univ Kans, Lawrence, 85; Road and Roadside, Art Inst Chicago, 87; Arts '93, Fine Arts Mus, Santa Fe, NMex, 93; Perpetual Mirage, Whitney Mus Am Art, 96. *Teaching:* Instr, Asn Students Univ Calif Studio, Berkeley, 71-77; teaching asst, Univ NMex, Albuquerque, 78-79; instr, Univ Colo, Boulder, 79-85; vis assoc prof, Univ Tex, San Antonio, fall 85; vis lectr, Princeton Univ, 86-90; asst prof art, Col Santa Fe, NMex, 90-. *Awards:* Nat Endowment Arts Fel, 73, 75 & 81. *Bibliog:* Lois Fishman (auth), article, Creative Camera, 8/77; Jonathon Greene (auth), American Photography: A Critical History, Abrams, New York, 84; Rick Dingus (auth), article, Artspace Mag, spring 84. *Publ:*

Auth, Diesels and Dinosaurs, Long Run Press, 76; Highway as Habitat, Univ Art Mus, Santa Barbara, Calif, 86; Marks in Place, Univ NMex Press, 88; Night Photography: A Survey of 20th Century Night Photography, Hallmark Photog Collection, Kansas City, Mo, 89; New Dimensions, Agfa Corp, 90. *Mailing Add:* HC63 Box 5 Pena Blanca NM 87041

FITTS, MICHAEL
PAINTER
Study: Va Commonwealth Univ, Richmond, Va, BFA, 1989 . *Exhib:* Solo exhibs include Fraser Gallery, Bethesda, Md, 2007 ; Group exhibs include Higher Grounds, Charlottesville, Va, 1996; Studio Gallery, Washington, 1999; McGuffey Art Ctr, New Members Exhibit, Charlottesville, Va, 2001; Dispatches from the New Dominion: 7 Va Artists, Brooklyn, 2001; Astra Design, Richmond, Va, 2003; Corcoran Gallery Art, Washington, 2004; Second Street Gallery Group Show, Charlottesville, Va, 2004 ; The SEVEN show, Washington, 2005; Summer Group Exhibit, Fraser Gallery, Bethesda, Md, 2006. *Awards:* George Sugarman Found Grant, 2007. *Dealer:* Fraser Gallery 7700 Wisconsin Ave Suite E Bethesda, MD 20814

FITZGERALD, ASTRID
PAINTER, WRITER
b Wil, Switz, July 28, 1938; US citizen. *Study:* Coll St Agnes, Fribourg, Switz, 55; Polytechnic Sch, London, Eng, 58-59; Art Students League, New York, 62; Fashion Inst Technol, New York, 68; Pratt Graphics Ctr, New York, 72. *Work:* Aldrich Mus, Ridgefield, Conn; Wellesley Coll, Mass; Marymount Coll, Tarrytown, NY; Rockefeller Ctr Collection; Educ Mgt Ctr, Atlanta, Ga. *Comn:* Kindercare Corp, Montgomery, Ala; IBM, Boca Raton, Fla; Ashley Plaza Hotel, Tampa, Fla; Union Bank Switz, New York. *Exhib:* Albright-Knox Mus, Buffalo, NY, 73; Contemp Reflections, Aldrich Mus, 78; Pietrasanta Fine Arts, New York, 86; Galerie Neue Kunst, Wil, Switz, 93; Harmony by Design Exhib, traveling to Chicago, Washington, DC & NY, 94; Hyposwiss, Zurich, Switz, 96; Murakami Gallery, New York, 96-97; Muroff Kotler Visual Arts Gallery, SUNY at Ulster, Stone Ridge, NY, 2000; Galerie Raubach, St Gallen, Switz, 2001-2002; Artcanal, 2002; Lelanderon, Switz, 2002; Lo River Arts, Beacon, NY, 2005; Wuersch & Gering, New York, 2005-2006; The Pearl Arts Gallery, Stone Ridge, NY, 2008; Garrison Art Ctr, Garrison, NY, 2010; Unison Gallery, New Paltz, New York, 2010; The Gallery at R & F, Kingston, NY, 2011; Retrospective, Work, Wired Gallery, High Falls, NY, 2013; Biennial: Origins of Geometry, Mus Geometric and MADI Art, Dallas, Tex, 2013. *Awards:* Juror's Award, Fourth Ann Small Works Competition, NY Univ, 80; Bootcamp award, NYFA Mark 12, NY, 2012. *Bibliog:* Roger Lipsey (auth), The Art of Astrid Fitzgerald-New Images, Old Faith, 85; Richard H Pichler (auth), Swiss Artist in New York, 85; Adrian Frost (auth) Probing the mysteries, Woodstock Times, NY, 2000; Art Canal 02 Catalog, Int Sculpture Exhib, Switzerland. *Mem:* Women's Studio Workshop. *Media:* Oil, Watercolor, Encaustic, Assemblage. *Interests:* Writing, philosophy, hiking. *Publ:* Contribr, Traveler's Key to Ancient Greece, Knopf, 89; auth, Harmony by Design, Parabola, winter 91; auth, An Artist's Book of Inspiration, Lindisfarne Press, 96; auth, Being Consciousness Bliss - A Seeker's Guide, 2002; auth, Winter Break: A Luminous Journey into Wisdom and Love, 2008. *Dealer:* Ellen Price New York NY; Chrissy Glenn Stone Ridge NY; Wired Gallery Stone Ridge NY. *Mailing Add:* 650 W End Ave New York NY 10025

FITZGERALD, BETTY JO
PAINTER, PRINTMAKER
b Colusa, Calif, Jan 10, 1942. *Study:* Univ Northern Calif, Chico, BA, 63; Univ Wash, MS, 66; Evergreen State Coll (printmaking & design), 90-92. *Work:* Univ Wash Med Ctr, Seattle, Wash; Sch Admin Ctr, Hampton, Pa; North Kansas City Hosp, Mo; Wash State Ferry Comn, Seattle, Wash; City of Olympia, Wash. *Comn:* Watercolor painting, Sovrain Financial, Baltimore, Md, 88; watercolor painting, Allen Womens Ctr, Denver, Colo, 89; 2 mixed media collages, Olympia Golf & Country Club, Wash, 90; 2 paintings watercolor, Samsun Med Ctr, Santa Barbara, Calif, 90; watercolor collage, Telco Credit Union, Seattle, Wash, 91; acrylic/canvas painting, Swedish Med Found, 04. *Exhib:* Nat Watercolor Soc Ann, Brea Civic Ctr, Calif, 91; Water Music Festival Invitational, Ilwaco Heritage Mus, Wash, 93; NW Watercolor Soc Signature Mem Invitational, Wash State Conv Ctr, Seattle, 93; SW Wash 40th Exhib, State Capital Mus, Olympia, 93; 11th Ann Greater Midwest Int, Art Ctr Gallery, Cent Mo State Univ, 96; Art for Environmental Advocacy, Adell McMillan Gallery, Univ Ore, Eugene, 98; NW Expression, Coos Art Mus, Ore, 98; NW Watercolor Soc Invitational, Maryhill Mus Art, Goldendale, Wash, 97; 1st Int Exhib, Salisbury State Univ, Md, 97; Frye Mus, 60th Anniversary, Seattle, 2000; Coos Art Mus, Oreg, 2001-2004; Bellevue Art Mus, Wash, 2001; Watcom Mus History & Art, Bellingham, Wash, 2005. *Pos:* Pres, Northwest Watercolor Found. *Teaching:* La Conner Workshops, 95 & 97; Coupeville Arts Ctr, Wash, 99; print instr, Centrum Residency, Irish Cult Exchange, Pt Townsend, Wash, 2000; Spokane Watercolor Soc Workshops, 2006; instr, Extended Educ, Evergreen State Col, Olympia, Wash, 2006-2007. *Awards:* Hon Fel, Wash Native Plant Soc, 1998; Ewws Gold Award, Ea Washington Watercolor Soc, 2000; 3rd Pl Pa Art League Nat, Gig Harbor Gallery, Wa, 2003; Best of Show, PAL Nat, Gig Harbor, Wash, 2006; and others. *Bibliog:* Glenda Helbert (auth), Joy washes the artist's watercolors, Olympian, 11/3/1986; Linda Thomson (auth), Featured artist draws on childhood for inspiration, News Tribune, 4/16/2002; Cathy Woo (auth), Think Like an Artist, Artist Mag, July 2004. *Mem:* Women Painters Wash (pres, 92-93, treas, 96-2001); Nat Watercolor Soc; Arts Olympia (treas, 95 & 96-98); NW Watercolor Soc (signature mem, vpres, 98-99, pres, 1999-2000); NCoast Collage Soc (signature mem). *Media:* Watermedia, Monotypes, Acrylic, Collage. *Specialty:* Contemporary mixed media & monotype. *Interests:* Travel, native plants, art advocate in the community. *Publ:* Auth, Abstracts in Watercolor (ed by Lou Schlemm), Rockport Publ, Mass, 96; Road Tableaux, catalogue of watercolor paintings, 2002; Journeys to Abstraction, Northlight Books, 2012. *Dealer:* Childhood's End Gallery Olympia WA; Bank Left Gallery Palouse WA

FITZGERALD, JOAN V
PAINTER, WRITER
b Batavia, NY, Jan 24, 1930. *Study:* Rochester Inst of Tech, 48-49; Buffalo State College, BS (Art Educ), 64; MS (Art Educ), 69. *Work:* Canisius Coll, Buffalo, NY; Marble House Editions Publ Co, New York, NY; Harry & Jeanette Weiberg Campus, Getzville, NY; Roswell Park Cancer Inst, Buffalo, NY; Carolyn House (Niagara Falls YWCA), Niagara Falls, NY; Women & Children's Hosp, Buffalo, NY; Hamburg Counseling Svcs, Hamburg, NY; Orchard Park Town Hall, NY; Art Dialogue Gallery, Buffalo, NY; Stony Dental Care, Lancaster, NY; Kent State Teaching Coll, Kent, Oh, 2010. *Exhib:* Summer Salon Series Invitational Exhib, Broome St Gallery, New York, NY, 2000; Collage Artists of America Juried Exhib, Brand Exhib Ctr, Glendale, CA, 2003; Recent Paintings by Joan Fitzgerald, Peter & MaryLou Vogt Gallery, Canisius College, Buffalo, NY, 2003; Viridian Artist's 15th National Juried Exhib, Viridian Gallery, New York, NY, 2004; Catherine Lorillard Wolfe Nat Juried Exhib, Nat Arts Club, New York, NY, 2005; Nat Coll Soc 21st Annual Juried Exhib, Butler Inst of Am Art, Salem, OH, 2005; First Frontier Collage Soc, Austin, Tex, 2005 & 2007; Quartet, Insite Gallery, Buffalo, NY, 2007; Masur Mus Art, Monroe, La, 2007; Tubac Art Ctr, Ariz, 2007; Joan Fitzgerald- A Retrospective, Art Dialogue Gallery, Buffalo, NY; Nat Collage Soc, Mesa, Ariz, 2012; Western NY Artists Group Modern Exhib, Art Dialogue Gallery, Buffalo, NY, 2013; Signature Mems Exhib, Nat Collage Soc, Mesa Contemporary Arts Mus, Ariz, 2013. *Pos:* Pres, Buffalo Soc of Artists, Buffalo, NY, 80; chmn, Western NY Artists Group, Buffalo, NY, 2002-2003. *Teaching:* asst prof, Humanities drawing/painting, 85-92 (PT), Erie Community Coll, Buffalo, NY, 92-98, acting asst academic dean, 90-92, instr, drawing/painting, 92-98. *Awards:* Dir Choice, Small Juried New Eng Regional, Main St Gallery, Groton, NY, 2004; Spec Recognition Award, Landscape V & Abstract VI (Int Juried Internet Exhibs), Period Gallery, Lincoln, Nebr, 2005; Winnie Borne Sherman Award, Katherine Lorillard Exhib, Nat Arts Club, New York, 2006; Spec Recognition Award, Collage & Digital, Upstream People Int Internet Exhib, Omaha, Nebr, 2007; Membership Award, First Frontier Collage, Nat Exhib, 2007; 2nd prize, Modern Exhibitions Art Dialogue Gallery, Western NY Artist Group, Buffalo, NY; Silver medal, Buffalo Soc, Artists Anderson Gally, Univ Buffalo Installation Exhib, 2011. *Bibliog:* Larry Bradshaw (auth), Period Gallery Summer Nat Invitational Exhib, Period Gallery Newsletter, Lincoln, Nebr, 2000; profile, Buffalo State Coll Alumni Mag, 2007; Artist drawn to historical site, Buffalo News, 2007; Josh B'Gosh(auth), Swash, Marble House Editions, 2010; J Tim Raymond (auth), Installations Art Voice, 2011. *Mem:* Buffalo Soc of Artists, Buffalo, NY (pres 80); Western NY Artist's Group, Buffalo, NY (chmn 2002-2003); Nat Collage Soc, Hudson, Ohio, (signature mem). *Media:* Acrylic, Collage. *Publ:* auth, Small Works/Big Show (Small Works New Eng Regional Exhib), Syracuse Post Standard, Syracuse, NY, 2003; Good Things in Small Packages (Small Works New Eng Regional Exhib), Syracuse Post Standard, Syracuse, NY, 2004; The Magic Lunch Box, Marble House Eds (in press), 2004; Not Another Christmas, Marble House Eds (in press), 2004; Glamour (poetry chapbook), Word Runner Press (in press), 2004; The Iris House, Marble House Eds (in press), 2005; The Sweet Life (poetry chapbook), Windrunner Press, 2007; Darktowers, Marble House Eds, 2007; Merry-Go-Round, Marble House Eds, 2008; The Long Way Home, Marble House Eds, 2012; Joan Fitzgerald Selected Works, Buffalo Art Publishing Co, Len Viagelmacher, editor, 5/2013; Theres a Moore in my Juice, Buffalo Arts Publishing Co, 2013. *Dealer:* Donald J. Siuta Art Dialogue Gallery One Linwood Ave Buffalo NY 14209-2203. *Mailing Add:* Box 245 Athol Springs NY 14010

FITZGERALD, JOE
PAINTER, PRINTMAKER
b Washington, DC, 1950. *Study:* Univ Md, College Park, BA, 72; State Univ NY, Oswego, studied printmaking with George O'Connell, 73. *Work:* US Embassy, Ankara, Turkey; US Embassy, St George's, Granada; Montgomery Co, Rockville, Md; US Embassy, Bahrain; Designs chosen by US Mint for Obverse & Reverse 2005 Nickel. *Comn:* Mural, Hyatt Hotel, Pittsburgh, Pa, 90. *Exhib:* Benefit Auction, Corcoran Gallery, Washington, DC, 85; solo exhibs, Studio Gallery, Washington, DC, 87, 89 & 93, Audubon Soc, Chevy Chase, Md, 89, Franz Bader Gallery, Washington, DC, 94, Studio Gallery, Washington, DC, 96, Galerie Ingrid Cooper, Kensington, Md, 98 & George Meany Int Ctr, Silver Spring, Md, 98; Heart Works, Washington Proj Arts, Washington, DC, 90; Eight DC Artists, Nat Press Club, Washington, DC, 91; invitational show, George Meany Int Ctr, Silver Spring, Md, 94; Foxhall Gallery, Washington, DC, 1999, 2001, 2002, 2005, 2008, 2010. *Pos:* Illusr, US Consumer Proj Safety Comn, 72-80; art dir, Nat Libr Med, Bethesda, Md, 80-2005. *Awards:* Honarium, US Mint, for 2005 Coin Design; Finalist, Nat Self-Portrait Competition, Am Artist Mag. *Bibliog:* Michael Welzenbach (auth), Paint for paint's sake, Washington Post, 3/4/89; Mary McCoy (auth), Dark and lovely, Washington Post, 11/24/90; Lee Fleming (auth), Joe Fitzgerald at studio, Washington Post, 3/6/93; Karen Schafer (auth), Jack of all Trades, Montgomery Gazette, 7/3/98; William L Hamilton (auth), His 5 Cents' Worth, NY Times, 3/24/05. *Media:* Oil, Pastels & woodcuts. *Dealer:* Foxhall Gallery Washington DC. *Mailing Add:* 828 Sligo Ave Silver Spring MD 20910

FITZPATRICK, ROBERT JOHN
GALLERY DIRECTOR
b Toronto, Ont, May 18, 1940; naturalized, 62. *Study:* Spring Hill Col, BA, 63, MA, 64; Woodrow Wilson Fel, Johns Hopkins Univ, 64-65. *Collection Arranged:* Roy Lichtenstein at CalArts--Drawings and Collages from the Artist's Collection, 77; Roy Lichtenstein: Interiors, Mus Contemp Art, Chicago, 99. *Pos:* Mem, Md Democratic State Cent Comt, 70-74 & Balt City Coun, 71-75; pres, Calif Inst Arts, Valencia, 75-87; trustee, Archeworks, Chicago, Am Ctr Fedn Paris, Craft and Folk Art Mus, Los Angeles, 76-82, Dunn Sch, Los Olivos, Calif, 80-84, Bennington Coll, Vt; vpres cult affairs, Los Angeles Olympic Organizing Comt, 81-84; dir, Olympic Arts Festival, Los Angeles, 84, Los Angeles Festival, 85-87; pres, EuroDisney, Paris, 87-93; chief exec officer, Reconstruct Finance Corp, Paris, 93-95; Pritzker dir & chief exec officer, Mus Contemp Art, Chicago, 98-2008; int mng dir, Haunch of Venison, 2008-. *Teaching:*

Chmn dept modern languages, Gilman Sch, Balt, 68-72; dean of students, John Hopkins Univ, 72-75; dean sch of arts Columbia Univ, New York City, 95-2001. *Awards:* Officer, l'Order des Arts et des Lettres, France; chevalier, Ordre National de Merite, France. *Mailing Add:* 2 5th Ave Apt 19H New York NY 10011

FITZSIMONDS, CAROL STRAUSE
PRINTMAKER, GALLERY DIRECTOR

b Richmond, Va, Mar 13, 1951. *Study:* Hollins Coll, Va, BA, 73; Art League Sch, Torpedo Factory Art Ctr, 84-85. *Work:* Libr Cong, Nat Mus Am Hist, Smithsonian Inst & Nat Mus Women in Arts, Washington, DC; Jane Voorhees Zimmerli Art Mus, New Brunswick, NJ; Newport Art Mus, RI; New Britain Mus Am Art, New Britain, Conn; Federal Reserve Bd, Wash DC; Slater Art Mus, Norwich, Ct. *Comn:* Pressing Matters in Printmaking Invitational, Asheville, NC, 2008. *Exhib:* Silvermine Guild 23rd Nat Print Biennial, New Canaan, Conn, 2000; Audubon Artists 64th Nat Exhib, NY, 2006; 19th Parkside Nat Small Print Exhib, Univ Wis, 2006; SAGA Mems' Exhib, Prague, Czechoslovakia, 2006; solo exhib, Newport Art Mus, 2007. *Collection Arranged:* Under Pressure Print Porfolio & Exhibit, Providence Art Club, RI, 2007; The Art of Printmaking, ACPS & PNSNE at Spring Ball Gallery, Newport, RI, 2006; PNSNE, Strathmore Art Center, Bethesda, MD, 2005; Time Pieces, Original Print Portfolio Exhibit, Printmakers Inc, Newport Art Mus, RI, 2000; Art of Colored Pencil Exhibit, Gallery 297, Bristol, RI, 2007; Micro/Macro Print Portfolio and Exhib, PNSNE at Newport Art Mus, Newport, RI, 2011; Impressions Print Portfolio and Exhib, Providence Art Club, 2011; Travel and Exhib, PNSNE, Bristol Art Mus, 2010. *Pos:* Partner, Spectrum Gallery, Washington, 85-87, Printmaker's Inc, Alexandria, Va, 86-87 & 92-2001 & Spring Bull Gallery, Newport, RI, 99-2006; dir & cur, Gallery 297, Bristol, RI, 2004-2010 & Cong St Gallery, Portsmouth, NH, 2007-2010. *Teaching:* Instr monotype, Providence Art Club, 2002; printmaking, Newport Art Mus Sch, 2002, 2011 & Providence Art Club, 2003-; bookbinding for artists, Newport Art Mus Sch, 2003. *Awards:* AAPL Leila Gardin Sawyer Mem Award, 2000; Bruce Crane Mem Award, 99; Art Students League NY Award Graphics, 63rd Audubon Artists Nat Exhib, NY 2005; Joseph Caultieri Prize, Katherine Forest Crafts Found, 2010; Providence Art Club medal, 2012, 2013. *Bibliog:* John Pantalone (auth), Artistic life of a traveling printmaker, Newport this Week, 5/4/89; The Best of Printmaking, An Int Collection, Rockport Publ Inc, 97; Mark St. John Erickson (auth), Printmaking, Daily Press, 12/10/2000; Rebecca Ronstadt (ed), A Printmaker & Her Work, Journ Print World, July 2010; Ashley E Rooney (auth), 100 Artists of New England, 2011. *Mem:* Catharine Lorillard Wolfe Art Club Inc; Am Artists Prof League; Boston Printmakers; Soc Am Graphic Artists; Audubon Artists Inc. *Media:* Aquatint Etching. *Publ:* Auth, Imagined journeys, J Print World, fall 89 & Eye Wash, 10/89; Exploring Aquatint, Artists Mag, 99; The Art of Printmaking, J Print World, spring 2006; auth, Micro/Macro Exhib, Jour of the Print World, 2011. *Dealer:* Walsingham Gallery 47 Merrimac St Newburyport MA 01950; Arnold Art 210 Thames St Newport RI 02840; Donovan Gallery 3895 Main Rd Tirerton Four Corners RI 02878; Cove Galleries 15 Commercial St Wellfleet MA 02667. *Mailing Add:* 251 Water St Portsmouth RI 02871

FIX, JOHN ROBERT
SCULPTOR, SILVERSMITH

b Pittsburgh, Pa, Oct 31, 1934. *Study:* Rochester Inst Technol, Sch Am Craftsmen, BFA; Conn Col, MAT; study with Lawrence G Copeland, Hans Christianson, William A McCloy & Frances Felten. *Comn:* Host box, Glenwood Lutheran Church, Minn, 57; chalice, St Andrew's Episcopal Church, New Kensington, Pa, 62; chalice, 68 & menorah, 71, Harkness Chapel, Conn Col, New London; altar set, St Paul's Episcopal Church, Westbrook, Conn, 79; plus many pvt comn in sculpture & metalsmithing. *Exhib:* Assoc Artists Pittsburgh Ann, Carnegie Mus, 57-80; New Eng Invitational, De Cordova Mus, Lincoln, Mass, 62; RI Arts Festival, Providence, 64; Soc Conn Craftsmen Traveling Show, 66; Three Rivers Arts Festival, Pittsburgh, 71, 73 & 74; 25th Anniversary Exhib, Brookfield Craft Ctr; solo exhibs: Metal Works, Lyman Allyn Art Mus, New London, Conn, 90; Metalsmithing & Sculpture, Lyman Allyn Art Mus; Katheryn Forrest Trust Ann Exhib, Slater Mus, Norwich, Conn, 85-2000. *Teaching:* instr, David B. Oliver High Sch, Pittsburgh, Pa, 57-60; Metalsmithing, Norwich Art Sch, The Norwich Free Acad, Conn, 60-92 (retired), head art dept, 89-92; instr sculpture & art hist, Upward Bound, Conn Col, 69; dir young peoples art prog, Lyman Allyn Art Mus, New London, 74-82; jewelry workshops, Guilford Handcraft Ctr, Conn, Wesleyan Potters, Brookfield Craft Ctr, Conn; adj fac, Three Rivers Community Col, Norwich, Conn, 96-; Adult metals & jewelry, Norwich Art Sch, 1960-. *Awards:* First Prize in Crafts, 58, Mrs Roy A Hunt Award, 61 & Jury Award for Distinction in Crafts, 68, Assoc Artists Pittsburgh; Award for Excellence in Silver, Katheryn Forrest Trust Crafts Invitational, Slater Mus, Norwich, Conn, 86; Award in Sculpture, Mystic Art Asn, juried exhib, 86; Purchase Prize, Katheryn Forrest Trust, 89, 92 & 2000; Gibson Prize, Katherine Forest Craft Found, 2009; Mabel Kingsbury Fentras prize, Mystic Art Asn, 2012. *Bibliog:* John D Morris (auth), Creative Metal Sculpture, Bruce Pub Co, NY, 71; Shirley Charron (auth), Modern Pewter, Van Nostrand Reinhold Co, 73; Gold Smiths J, 79. *Mem:* Mystic Art Asn Inc (pres, 74); Assoc Artists Pittsburgh; Lyman-Allyn Art Mus (bd dir, 88-94), New London, Conn. *Media:* Silver, Gold, Pewter. *Mailing Add:* PO Box 362 Stonington CT 06378

FLACH, VICTOR H
DESIGNER, WRITER

b Portland, Ore, May 31, 1929. *Study:* Univ Ore, Sch Archit & Allied Arts, with Jack Wilkinson, BS & MFA; Univ Pittsburgh, Henry Clay Frick Fine Arts Dept, with Walter Read Hovey; also with R Buckminster Fuller, 53 & 59. *Comn:* 4 multi-walled murals in public bldgs 1952-68 including 3-wall collage mural with John Otto, Erb Mem Union, Univ Ore, 52, 3-wall mural, Clearlake Sch, Eugene, Ore, 56, 2-wall, 3-story mosaic tile mural, sci ctr, Univ Wyo, 67-68;Heritage Series, Interview with American Painter, Ben Shahn, PBS-TV, 65; The Arts in Practice, TV prog, with Richard Evans, UW-TV, 71; hand-sculpted relief ceramic-tile mural sect, Springcreek Sch, Laramie, 95. *Exhib:* Solo, group & traveling exhibs, incl: Portland Art Mus, 52, Denver Art Mus, 71, Contextualist Arts Gallery, Palm Springs, Calif, 84-85 & Univ, Mus & Galleries from various cities across US; 40-yr Photo Retrospective, Black Hills State Univ, SDak, 89. *Pos:* Ed, In/sert: Active Anthology for the Creative, 4 vols, 55-62; cur, Cathedral of Learning-Frick Fine Arts Gallery, Pittsburgh, 59-64. *Teaching:* Prof painting, design, theory & iconography, Univ Wyo, 65-92, prof emer, 93. *Res:* Toward a comprehensive tetradic typologic systems programming as model for archetypal-prototypal iconographic and colorfielding structural morphology. *Publ:* Auth, Gloss of the Four Universal Forms, The Eyes' Mind, Anatomy of the Canvas: R Wells Paintings, Univ Pittsburgh; By These Presents: Richard Evans Retrospective, 76, 2 vols Jos Deaderick, The Stage: Poetic Drawings with Theatre of Life Retrospective, 78, Indigenous Image, 79, Contextualist Manifesto, 82, Uni Wyo; Displacings & Wayfarings, North Atlantic Bks, 2nd Ed, 88; Iconography of Wilkinson's Orientation Mural, Univ Ore, 90; History & Nextory, 2000; On Fuel & Village in Matter 9-10, Ft Collins Co, 2006-07; Print as Portal: J Jereb Retrospective, Truman State Univ, 2007; Verse Diptych in G Ricci: The Mind of Artist, Winter Park, Fla, 2014; 10 Verse Broadsides Series 1995-2015, Flying Turtle Press, Kirksville, Mo. *Mailing Add:* 1618 Custer Laramie WY 82070

FLACKMAN, DAVID J
PAINTER

b New York, NY, Mar 3, 1934. *Study:* Stanford Univ, BA, 55; Art Students League, 56-58; studied with Maestro Pietro Annigoni & Nerina Simi, Florence, Italy, 58-67. *Work:* Washington Nat Gallery; Bruce Mus, Greenwich; Parish Mus, Southampton, NY. *Comn:* Portrait of Richard Nixon, Time Mag, NY, 68; Apollo 8 Astronauts, NASA, Orlando, Fla, 69; portrait of Carlos Montoya, comn by Carlos Montoya, NY, 75; portrait of St Agnes, St Agnes Church, Greenwich, Conn, 80; portrait of St Lucy, St Ignatius Church, Tarpon Springs, Fla, 94. *Exhib:* Apollo 8, Washington Nat Gallery, DC, 70; Weiner Gallery Artists, Weiner Gallery, NY, 74; Nat Arts Club Show, NY, 74-75; Salmagundi Club Show, NY, 74-75; solo exhib, Bruce Mus, Greenwich, Conn, 77 & Tarpon Springs Cult Ctr, Fla, 94. *Bibliog:* Gordon Schmidt (auth), David Flackman, Artist, Bruce Mus, Conn, 77; Marion M White (auth), Artist cultivates then paints, Greenwich Time, 9/11/89; Ann Bakkalapulo (auth), Still life, Tampa Tribune, 1/10/94; Bruce Hosking (auth), Work of a saint, Tampa Tribune, 11/23/94. *Media:* Oil. *Mailing Add:* 4600 Riverview Blvd Bradenton FL 34209

FLAHAVIN, MARIAN JOAN
PAINTER, SCULPTOR

b Colton, Wash. *Study:* Holy Names Coll, BA (art), 59. *Work:* Deaconess Hosp, Ronald MacDonald House, St Anne's Children's Home, Valley Gen Hosp, Spokane, Wash; Leanin' Tree Publs, Boulder, Colo; Sacred Heart Children's Hosp; St John the Baptist Church, Salt Lake City. *Comn:* Plate/figurine series, comn by Goebel, Ger, 84; garden sculpture & fountain series; and many portraits throughout US. *Exhib:* Salmagundi 14th & 18th Ann, New York, 91 & 95, 2009; Pastel Soc Am 22nd Ann, New York, 94 & San Francisco, 96; Conn Pastel Soc Ann, Wallingford, 94; Int Asn Pastel Soc, Denver, 95; Am Artists Prof League, New York, 95, 97 & 2006, 2007, 2012, 2013; Pastel Soc W Coast, 2002, 2007 & 2010; Catherine Lorillard Wolfe 106th Ann, New York, 2002, 2010, 2012; Butler Inst Am Art, 2003; Portrait Soc of Am Membership Competition, 2010, 2012; and others. *Teaching:* Instr, pastel, portraiture & sculpture, currently. *Awards:* Best of Show/People's Choice, Northwest Pastel Soc Ann, 89; Merit/People's Choice, Md Ann, 90; Merit Award, Salmagundi Ann, 91; Am Artists Prof League, 2006; Merit Award, Northwest Pastel Soc, 2007; Art Spirit Gold Medal Pastel, Am Artists Prof League, 2007; Portrait Sóc Am for Sculpture, Mem Show, 2010, 2012. *Mem:* Pastel Soc Am (signature mem); Am Artists Prof League (fellow maxima cum laude); Catherine Lorillard Wolfe Art Club (full mem); Pastel Soc W Coast (signature mem); Northwest Pastel Soc (signature mem); Women Artists Am W (mem emeritus); Portrait Soc of Am (ambassador). *Media:* Pastel, Oil; Bronze. *Publ:* Contribr, Southwest Art Mag, 82; Collectors Mart Mag, 84; Art Talk mag, 84; Midwest Art Mag, 85. *Dealer:* The Painters Chair 330 Sherman Coeur D'Alene ID 83814; Garden Accents Philadelphia PA. *Mailing Add:* 4714 S Schafer Branch Rd Spokane WA 99206

FLAM, JACK D
HISTORIAN, EDUCATOR

b Paterson, NJ, Apr 2, 1940. *Study:* Rutgers Univ, BA, 61; Columbia Univ, MA, 63; New York Univ, PhD, 69. *Collection Arranged:* Henri Matisse Paper Cut-Outs (auth, catalog), Nat Gallery, 77; Matisse Image into sign, St Louis Art Mus, 93; Matisse The Dance (catalog), Nat Gallery, 93; Judith Rothschild, An Artist's Search, Metrop Mus, New York City, 98; Matisse-Derain, Collioure, Musée d'Art Moderne de Ceret, 2005; Matisse in Transition: Around Laurette, Norton Mus Art, West Palm Beach, Fla, 2006. *Pos:* Ed, The Documents of 20th Century Art, 81-; art critic, Wall Street J, 84-92; Pres, Dedalus Found, 2002. *Teaching:* Instr art hist, Rutgers Univ, 62-66; assoc prof art hist, Univ Fla, 66-70; prof art hist, Brooklyn Col & Grad Ctr, City Univ New York, 75-91, prof emeritus, 2010-; distinguished prof, City Univ New York, 91-2010. *Awards:* Guggenheim Fel, 79-80; Nat Endowment Humanities Fel, 87-88; Charles Rufus Morey Award, Coll Art Assoc, 88; and others. *Bibliog:* Eric de Chassey (auth), Jack Flam à la Source de l'Art, Beaux-Arts, 3/94. *Mem:* Int Asn Art Critics; Coll Art Asn. *Res:* Catalogue raisonné of Robert Motherwell, 2008-. *Publ:* Auth, Matisse on Art, Phaidon, 73, Dutton, 78 & Calif, 95; Matisse, The Man & His Art, Cornell Univ Press, 86; Motherwell, Rizzoli, 91; Richard Diebenkorn, Rizzoli, 92; Robert Smithson: Collected Writings, Calif, 96; and others; Judith Rothschild: An Artist's Search, Hudson Hills, 98; The Modern Drawing, Morgan Libr, 99; Matisse and Picasso: The Story of Their Rivalry and Friendship, Westview, 2003; Primitivism and Twentieth-Century Art: A Documentary History, 2003; Matisse in Transition: Around Laurette, 2006; Robert Maxtherwell Paintings and Collages: A Catalog Raisonne, 1941-1991, 2012. *Mailing Add:* 35 W 81st St New York NY 10024

FLANERY, GAIL
PAINTER, PRINTMAKER

b Cleveland, Ohio, May 7, 1947. *Study:* Cooper Union, New York, BFA, 72. *Work:* Citicorp, Chemical Bank, Lehman Bros & Solomon Bros, NY; IBM Collection, Fla. *Exhib:* Kornblee Gallery, NY, 77; Tanglewood Gallery, NY, 78; Nat Drawing Show, Holman Gallery, State Col, Trenton, NJ, 79; Landscapes, 83 & Invitational, 86,

Painting Space 122, NY; Contemp Am Landscapes, Hudson River Mus, Yonkers, NY & Tucson Mus Art, Ariz, 84; K Caraccio Collection, Montgomery Col, Rockville, Md, 85. *Bibliog:* Rev, Arts Mag, 10/76; Today's Landscape, NY Times, 2/84; Contemp American Landscapes, New Vistas, Hudson River Mus, 84. *Media:* Oil; Miscellaneous. *Dealer:* Orion Editions 270 Lafayette St New York NY 10012. *Mailing Add:* 511 Eighth St Brooklyn NY 11215

FLATTAU, JOHN W
PHOTOGRAPHER
b New York, NY, Nov 26, 1940. *Study:* Brown Univ, AB, 62; Harvard Univ, LLB, 65. *Work:* Int Ctr Photog, NY; Tour de Paris, Villeneuve-Sur Lot, France. *Exhib:* Photographs, Gallerie Agathe Ballard, Gaillard, France, 90; Witkin Gallery, NY, 91; Athens Ctr, Greece, 97; Havana, Cuba, 2000; Leica Gallery, NY, 2002 & 09. *Specialty:* Photography. *Publ:* Auth, Bridges, Lustrum Press, 85; Photographs, Witkin Gallery, 93; coauth, Les Rendez-vous de Margaret, Lustrum Press, 94; auth, Rue Obscure-Vague Regret, Ianda, 96; Recent Memories, Ianda, 2002; The Similarity of Matter, Ianda, 2008; When All Else Fails, Ianda, 2008. *Dealer:* Leica Gallery, 670 Broadway, NY, 10012. *Mailing Add:* 714 Broadway New York NY 10013

FLATTMANN, ALAN RAYMOND
PAINTER, INSTRUCTOR
b New Orleans, La, Aug 6, 1946. *Study:* John McCrady Art Sch, 64-66. *Work:* Okla Art Ctr, Oklahoma City; Lauren Rogers Mus Art, Laurel, Miss; Miss Mus Art, Jackson; Longview Mus Art, Tex; New Orleans Mus Art; Butler Inst Am Art; Ogden Mus Southern Art. *Comn:* Murals, Old Zion Baptist Church, New Orleans, 67 & Grace Episcopal Church, 72. *Exhib:* Solo exhibs, Lauren Rogers Mus Art, 70, 75 & 81 & Okla Arts Ctr, 79; Pastel Soc Am, New York, 76-2010, 2013; Degas Pastel Soc, New Orleans, 83-2008; Soc des Pastellistes de France, Lille, France, 87 & Feytiat, France, 2008; Southeastern Pastel Soc, Atlanta, 92-2010; Butler Inst Am Art, PSA Invitational Exhib, 2006, IAPS Exhib, 2010; Int Pastel Artists Invitation Exhib, Taiwan, 2007; Art Asn, Lake Charles Art Ctr, 2012; Barnwell Garden Art Ctr, Shreveport, La, 2012. *Teaching:* Instr painting & drawing, John McCrady Art Sch, New Orleans, 67-82; pvt workshops in oil, pastel, watercolor. *Awards:* Elizabeth T Greenshields Found Grant Award, 73; Master Pastelist Designation, Pastel Soc Am, 91 & 1st Place Landscape Award for Worldwide Pastel Excellence, 2000; Hall of Fame Honoree, Pastel Soc Am, 2006; Gold Award, IAPS Exhib, Von Liebig Art Ctr, Naples, Fla, 2007; Master Circle Honoree, IAPS, 2007. *Bibliog:* Joyce Kelly (auth), The Poetic Realism of Alan Flattmann, ACM Publ Co, 80; Linda Price (auth), Learning from Today's Art Masters, Am Artist, 6/96; John R Kemp (auth), Alan Flattmann's French Quarter Impressions, Pelican Publ, 2002; John R Kemp (auth) An Artists Vision of New Orleans: The Paintings of Alan Flattman, Pelican Publ, 2014. *Mem:* Pastel Soc Am; Degas Pastel Soc; Southeastern Pastel Soc. *Media:* Pastel, Oil, Watercolor. *Publ:* Auth, The Art of Pastel Painting, Watson-Guptill, 87 & Pelican Publ Co, 2007; Combining sketching and watercolor painting, Watercolor, winter 95; Impressions of the City, Pastel Artist Int, 8-10/99; Heightened Atmosphere, Pastel J, 6/2006. *Dealer:* Windsor Fine Art Gallery 221 Royal St New Orleans LA 70130. *Mailing Add:* 822 Heather Hollow Covington LA 70435

FLAX, FLORENCE P (ROSELIN POLINSKY)
PHOTOGRAPHER, WRITER
b Brockton, Mass, June 23, 1936. *Study:* Chandler Sch Women, Boston, cert, 55; Northeastern Univ, Boston; Adult Educ Ctr, Boston. *Work:* Smithsonian Inst, Smithsonian Castle, Nat Arboretum, Smithsonian Nat Mus Am Hist, Supreme Court & Nat League Am Pen Women, Washington, DC, Smithsonian Library of Archives, Georgetown Univ, United States Botanical Gardens, Historical Soc of Washington, DC, Capital Historic Trust; Towson Univ-2 Charcoal Drawings of Pandas in the Asian Dept; Works on File, Eastman Kodak Olympus Am. *Exhib:* Int Platform Asn Art Group Exhibs, Washington, DC, 92-2001; An Odyssey into Infrared, Washington, DC, Home of Steward Mott, Washington, DC, 96 & The World as Seen Through Infrared, 98; US Nat Arboretum, Washington, DC, 99; Flowers Forever--The Washington Home of Stewart Mott, The Invisible World of Infrared Photog, 2000; Chrome Inc, Washington, DC, 2003-. *Collection Arranged:* Photog (black & white), Capital Hill Art League, Washington, DC, 96; M Frisby (photog), Wall St J (corresp to White House), Northeastern Univ, Boston, 98; infrared photogs, Nat Arboretum, Washington, DC, 98. *Pos:* Photo ed, contribr, Old Dominion, Sierra Club, 94-96; contribr, photo column, Times Community Newspaper, 98-. *Teaching:* Var workshops; seminar on infrared film. *Awards:* Judge's Choice 1st Prize, Int Platform Asn Ann Art Show, 93, 1st & 2nd Prize, 94-95, 97-98, 1st Prize, 99, 2001; Best in Show Award, Capitol Hill Art League, 96. *Bibliog:* Carole Lee Morgan (auth), Fantasy of Infrared, Hill Rag, 95; Gwen Landry Impson (auth), Simply flowers, Hill Rag, 97; Amy Guerrero (auth), Hot images - photographer focuses in on hidden world, Enterprise, 98; Baltimore Sun; Washington Post. *Mem:* Am Soc Med Photogs (bd mem, 95-96); Nat League Penn Women Am; Int Platform Asn (adv com, 92-98); Capitol Hill Art League; Washington Ctr Photog; Rocky Creek Art League. *Media:* Infrared Photography, Macro Photography. *Res:* Infrared film examples, black & white infrared as a tool for portraits & color infrared as tool to detect plant disease. *Interests:* Music, modern jazz, classic films, figure skating, reading, trivia. *Collection:* Charcoal Portrait of Frank Sinatra. *Publ:* Auth, Ektachrome infrared photography, ASMP Mag, 95; Washington Beyond the Monuments, Capital Hill Art League, 96. *Mailing Add:* 13430 Coppermine Rd Apt 432 Herndon VA 20171

FLEISCHER, ARTHUR, JR
PATRON
b Harford, Conn, Jan 27, 1933. *Study:* Yale Univ, BA, 53. *Work:* Yale Univ; Whitney Mus; Mus of Modern Art; Metropolitan Mus Art; Jewish Mus Art. *Pos:* Assoc Strasser, Spiegelberg, Fried & Frank, New York City, 58-61; legal asst, Securities & Exchange Comn, Wash, 61-62, exec asst to chmn, 62-64; assoc, Fried, Frank, Harris, Shriver & Jacobson, New York City, 64-67, partner, 67-, chmn, 89-97, sr partner, 97-2012, sr councel, 2012-; adv to adv, comt Fed Securities Code Proj, Am Law Inst, 70-78; legal adv com, bd dir, NY Stock Exchange, 87-91. *Teaching:* Vis lectr, law Columbia Univ, New York City, 72-73, adj prof, NYU Sch Law, 2009-. *Mem:* Am Bar Asn (mem comt on fed regulation of securities regulation 69-); Asn Bar City New York (mem special comt on lawyers role in securities transactions 73-77, chmn comt securities regulation 72-74); Century Country Club (New York City); Ind Cur Int, (trustee, 90-2002); Whitney Mus Art, (formerly, trustee). *Collection:* Primarily photography, drawings & prints. *Publ:* Coauth, Tender Offers, 78, 7th edition, 2012, Board Games, 88; co-ed, Ann Inst on Securities Regulation, 70-81; contribr, articles to prof jours. *Mailing Add:* Fried Frank Harris One New York Plaza Fl 27 New York NY 10004-1980

FLEISCHER, ROLAND EDWARD
HISTORIAN, EDUCATOR
b Baltimore, Md, Feb 12, 1928. *Study:* Western Md Coll, BA, 52; Johns Hopkins Univ, MA, 54, PhD, 64. *Hon Degrees:* Western Md Coll, Hon DFA, 93. *Teaching:* Assoc prof art hist, Univ Miami, Fla, 56-66; prof art hist, George Washington Univ, 66-74; prof art hist, Pa State Univ, 74-96, prof emer, 96-. *Mem:* Historians Netherlandish Art; Historians Am Art; Fel emer, Penn State Inst, Arts & Humanities. *Res:* Colonial painting in America; Dutch painting of the 17th century. *Publ:* Auth, Ludolf de Jongh and the Early Work of Pieter de Hooch, Oud Holland, 78; co-ed & contribr, The Age of Rembrandt: Studies in Seventeenth Century Dutch Painting, In: Vol III, Papers in Art History from The Pennsylvania State University, Univ Park, Pa, 88; auth, Gustavus Hesselius: Face Painter to the Middle Colonies, NJ State Mus, Trenton, 88; Emblems & Colonial Am Painting, The Am Art J, Vol XX, No 3, 88; Ludolf de Jongh (1616-1679): Painter of Rotterdam, Davaco Publ, 89; and others. *Mailing Add:* 30355 Falcon Ln Big Pine Key FL 33043

FLEISCHMAN, AARON I
COLLECTOR
Study: Trinity Coll, Conn, BA, 1960; Harvard Law Sch, LLB, 1963. *Pos:* Bd dirs, Whitney Mus Am Art; trustee, Miami Art Mus; sr partner, Fleischman & Walsh LLP, 1976-. *Awards:* Named one of Top 200 Collectors, ARTnews mag, 2003-13. *Collection:* Modern & contemporary art. *Mailing Add:* Fleischman & Walsh 1255 23rd St NW 8th Fl Washington DC 20037

FLEISCHMAN, STEPHEN
MUSEUM DIRECTOR, CURATOR
b Newton, Mass, July 7, 1954. *Study:* Univ Wis-Madison, BS (fine arts), 77; MA (arts admin), 83. *Collection Arranged:* Highlights from the Permanent Collection, 91; Self-Portraits from the Permanent Collection, 92; Sculpture by Mark Lorenzi, 92; Jim Dine: Drawing from the Glyptothek (auth, catalog), 93; Deborah Butterfield: Sculpture 1980 to 1992, 94; Wisc Trienial, 96, 99, 2002, 2010, & 2013; Claes Oldenburg: printed stuff, 97; Ursula von Rydingsvard: sculpture, 98; Donald Lipski: A Brief History of Twine, 2000; Truman Lowe: Remembrance, 2001; Between the Lakes, 2006; George Segal: Street Scenes, 2008; Rob & Christian Clayton: Inside Out, 2010; Chic Imagists at the Madison Mus Contemp Art, 2011; Cecelia Condit: Within a Stones Throw, 2012. *Pos:* Spec asst dir, Walker Art Ctr, Minneapolis, 83-86, dir prog planning, 86-90; dir, Madison Mus of Contemp Art, Wis, 91-; reviewer, Accreditation prog of Am Asn Mus. *Mem:* Am Asn Mus (2009-); AAMD (2009-). *Publ:* Auth (catalog) Drawing from the Glyptothek, 93, Ursula von Rydingguard, Sculpture, 98, Donald Lipski: A Brief History of Twine, 2000; Between the Lakes, 2006; George Segal: Street Scenes, 2008; Chicago Imagists, 2011. *Mailing Add:* Madison Museum of Contemporary Art MMOCA 227 State Street Madison WI 53703

FLEISCHNER, RICHARD HUGH
ENVIRONMENTAL ARTIST, SCULPTOR
b New York, NY, July 1, 1944. *Study:* RI Sch Design, BFA, 66, MFA, 68. *Work:* Albright-Knox Art Gallery, Buffalo, NY; Whitney Mus Am Art, Guggenheim Mus, NY; Dallas Mus Art, Tex; Mus Art, RI Sch Design; Los Angeles Mus Contemp Art; and others. *Comn:* Mass Inst Technol, 85; MBTA, Arts on the Line, Cambridge, 85; Temple Univ, Philadelphia, 85; General Mills, Minneapolis, 85-87; Becton Dickinson Project, Franklin Lakes, NJ, 87; East Capital Plaza, St Paul, Minn, 91; and many others. *Exhib:* Drawings/Structures, Inst Contemp Art, Boston, 80; The Figurative Tradition, 80, Whitney Biennial, 81, New Am Art Mus, 82, Whitney Mus Am Art, NY; Form and Funtion--Proposals for Pub Art for Philadelphia, Pa Acad Fine Arts, 82; Artist as Social Designer, Los Angeles Co Mus Art, 85; solo exhibs, Harcus Gallery, 86, MacIntosh Drysdale Gallery, Washington, 87, Gerald Peters Gallery, Dallas, Tex, 91 & 95, Des Moines Art Ctr, 92 & Bell Gallery, Brown Univ, RI, 95; Individuals, A Selected Hist of Contemp Art-1945-86, Mus Contemp Art, Los Angeles, 86-88; Vanguard Gallery, Philadelphia, Pa, 87; Ten Sites, Laumeier Sculpture Park, St Louis, Mo, 91; Things for the Home, 92, & Summer Stock 1993, 93, Gerald Peters Gallery, Dallas; Différentes Natures-Visions de l'art contemporain, La Défense de Paris, France, 93. *Teaching:* Asst prof art, Brown Univ, Providence, 70-74; vis guest lectr & critic, many schs & museums throughout US. *Awards:* Am Acad Art & Letts Grant, 74-75; Nat Endowment Arts Fel, 74, 80 & 90; Gov's Award Art, RI Gov Edward Di Prete, 86. *Bibliog:* Ann Jarmusch (auth), La Jolla Institution discovers life downtown, San Diego Union Tribune, 2/7/93; Regina M Flanagan (auth), That beauty problem: four artists on 'beauty' in public art, Pub Art Rev 6, fall/winter 94; Julia Brown Turrell (auth), Richard Fleischner: Works on Paper, Gerald Peters Gallery, 95. *Media:* Miscellaneous. *Mailing Add:* 224 Williams St Providence RI 02906

FLEISHER, PAT
DESIGNER, CURATOR
b Toronto, Ont. *Study:* Univ Toronto, BA; painting, Skowhegan, Maine; Ont Coll Art; St Adele, Quebec; printmaking, York Univ, 71. *Work:* Palm Springs Desert Mus, Calif; Harbourfront Art Gallery, Toronto; Robert McLaughin Art Gallery, Oshawa; Univ Coll Cape Breton, Niagara Col. *Exhib:* Aaron Berman Gallery, NY; Arnold Gottlieb Gallery, Toronto, Ont; Roschar Gallery, Toronto, 89; Forsyth Gallery, Toronto, 89; 291 Gallery, Toronto, 90. *Collection Arranged:* Toronto Women Artists: Three Decades,

83; Horoscope Paintings by Noel F Doyle, Absolut Vodka, Can, 94; Angel Orensanz, Beta Shee Mus, 95. *Pos:* Founder-ed, Art Mag, 69-82, Toronto Int Art Fair, 80, Art Expo, Toronto, 83, Discovery, 85 & Artfocus Mag & Toronto Indoor Art Show, 92-; pres, Art Mag, Inc, 74-87; publ & ed, Art Post, 83-92; dir, 291 Gallery, Toronto, 89-92; pres, Fleisher Fine Arts Inc, 92-. *Teaching:* Lectr & art guide, Toronto & NY galleries & studios, 71-; Toronto bd educ, Koffler Art Gallery. *Awards:* Merit Award, Art Mag, Soc Publ Designers New York, 75; Queen Elizabeth Silver Jubilee Medal, awarded by Jules Leger, Gov Gen of Can, 78; Ont Asn Art Galleries Design Award, 80. *Bibliog:* Joan Murray (auth), Pat Fleisher: Photoartist, Canadian Women's Studies, 81. *Mem:* Int Asn Art Critics; Can Periodical Pub Asn; Friends Can Mus Asn; Ont Periodicals Artistic Expression & Criticism. *Media:* Cibachrome and Colour Xerox Photography. *Publ:* Auth, A western pilgrimage, 77 & The mystery of the Maya, Art Mag, 79; The woman as artist, Ave Mag, 83; Artist Rose Lindzon: A profile, City & Co Home Mag, 84; Botero review, Latin Am Art, USA, 90; Daniel Bartridge, Pastel Paintings, Allmart Ltd, 95. *Mailing Add:* 15 McMurrich St Apt 706 Toronto ON M5R 3M6 Canada

FLEMING, ERIKA
ADMINISTRATOR
Study: Boston Univ, BA; St Thomas Univ, MA. *Pos:* pres, Miami Int Univ Art & Design, 2002-. *Awards:* Outstanding Person of Yr, Puerto Rican Chamber of Commerce, 2004, Outstanding Contributions in Edn, 2005. *Mem:* Am Council on Edn; Commission on Women in Higher Edn. *Mailing Add:* 1501 Biscayne Blvd #100 Miami FL 33132

FLEMING, FRANK
SCULPTOR
b Bear Creek, Ala, June 17, 1940. *Study:* Univ Ala, BS, 62, MA, 69, MFA, 73. *Work:* City of Birmingham, Five Points South; Montgomery Mus Art, Ala; Nat Mus Am Art, Smithsonian Inst; Nelson Rockhill Mus, Kansas City, Mo; Utah Mus Fine Art, Salt Lake City. *Comn:* rabbit sculpture, 90, porcelain sculpture, 92, Birmingham Botanical Gardens, Ala; Five Points South Fountain, City of Birmingham, Ala, 91; bronze sculpture, Barney Ellis Plaza, Kansas City, Mo, 95; bronze deerman, Buckhead Park, Atlanta, 98; eagle sculpture, Assurance Corp, Miami, Fla, 98. *Exhib:* Contemp Crafts of the Americas, Ft Collins, Colo, 75; Am Porcelain, 81 & Animal Imagery, 81, Renwich Gallery, Smithsonian Inst; Art from Appalachia, Nat Mus Art, Washington, 81; solo exhibs, Birmingham Mus Art, Ala, 82 & Montgomery Mus Art, Ala, 83; Poetry of the Physical, Mus Am Crafts, NY, 86; Fourth Int Shoebox Sculpture Exhib, Univ Hawaii Art Gallery, 91. *Awards:* Harriet Murray Award, Birmingham Mus Art, 90; Ala State Arts Coun Fel, 90; Southern Arts Fedn Sculpture Fel, 91. *Bibliog:* R M N McAusland (auth), Frank Fleming's fantasy in porcelain, Am Artist, 4/79; Annette Hatton (auth), Frank Fleming, Ga Rev, summer 85; Janet Kopolos (auth), Frank Fleming, Am Ceramics, 4/2/85. *Media:* Clay, Bronze. *Mailing Add:* 2705 Scenic Dr SE Huntsville AL 35801-2862

FLEMING, JEFF
MUSEUM DIRECTOR
b 1956. *Study:* E Carolina Univ, Greenville, NC, BA (Painting); Pratt Inst, Brooklyn, MFA. *Pos:* Chief Cur of Exhib, Southeastern Ctr Contemp Art, Winston-Salem, NC, formerly; with Des Moines Art Ctr, Iowa, 1999-, sr cur, dep dir, acting dir, formerly, dir, 2005-. *Awards:* Asn Art Mus Dirs. *Mailing Add:* Des Moines Art Center 4700 Grand Ave Des Moines IA 50312

FLEMING, LEE
WRITER, CURATOR, CRITIC
b Philadelphia, Pa, Jan 26, 1952. *Study:* Yale Col, BA, 72; Univ Toronto, MA, 74. *Exhib:* Strange (auth, catalog), Rockville Arts Place, Md, 91. *Collection Arranged:* Critics Picks, Md Art Pl, 92; Family Matters, Tartt Gallery, Washington, DC, 92. *Pos:* Sr ed, Mus & Arts Mag, formerly; Art & film ed, Washington Rev Arts, 79-89; Washington Correspond, Artnews, 83-88; visual arts commentator, Nat Pub Radio, 88-; sr ed, Garden Design Mag, formerly; art critic, Washington Post, currently; managing ed, Landscape Architecture, currently. *Awards:* Washington, DC Comn Arts & Humanities Fel Lit & Criticism, 81 & 84; Ucross Found Residency Fel, 85; Larry Neal Writer's Award, 89. *Publ:* On metaphor, Washington Rev, 82; Biennial directions: Direction 1983, ARTNews & What's at issue is the issue, Artnews, 83; Art, Am Quart, 83; Manon Cleary (Gulbenkian Indth, Lisbon), 84. *Mailing Add:* WETA TV 2775 S Quincy St Arlington VA 22206

FLEMING, MARGARET NIELSEN
GRAPHIC ARTIST, ILLUSTRATOR
b Brooklyn, NY, May 10, 1924. *Study:* Parsons Sch Design, with John Rogers, Stuart Klonis & Edgar Whitney, 43. *Comn:* JW Red & JW Black Packaging, Nat Distillers, London, Eng, 74-84; Christmas card designs, Am Artists Group, NY, 75-85; portrait of Bryant Park, Deloitte, Haskins & Sells, NY, 86; credit card designs, Affinity Marketing, Rye, NY, 87-95; admin off & pavilion, US Merchant Marine Acad, Kings Point, NY, 91. *Exhib:* Catharine Lorillard Wolfe Art Club, Nat Arts Club, NY, 80; Am Watercolor Soc Ann, Nat Acad, NY, 81 & 83; Art League Nassau Co Members, CW Post Col, Westbury, NY, 85, Lever House, 88, Molloy Col, Rockville Ctr, NY, 91; Visual Art Alliance Long Island, Nassau Co Mus, Roselyn, NY, 89; Chelsea Art Ctr, 98. *Pos:* Illusr, Lester Beall Inc, NY, 43-47, Hanzl & Hanzl Inc, NY, 47-60; free lance illusr, 60-96. *Awards:* Award of Excellence, Art League Nassau Co Member's Show, 91; Grumbacher Medal, Floral Park Art League, 92; Award of Excellence, Village Art Club Rockville Ctr, 96. *Mem:* Art League Nassau Co, NY; Village Art Club Rockville Ctr, NY; Tri-Co Art League, NY. *Media:* Watercolor, Acrylics. *Publ:* Illusr, Hotel, Doubleday, 65; Cooking for Two-Betty Crocker, Western Publ, 75; Skill Builders & Condensed Books, Readers Digest, 75-85; Holidays & Special Occasions, Food Borders, Dover Publ, 93-96; and others. *Mailing Add:* 15 St Paul's Pl Garden City NY 11530

FLEMING, MARY MARGARET
GALLERY DIRECTOR
b Oct 18, 1929. *Study:* Art Inst of Chicago, 1948-1953; studied with Mohamed Dvisi. *Exhib:* 72 exhib, Artists of Chicago & Vicinity, Art Inst Chicago, 1969; Artist Guild of Chicago, 1970; Sanscriti, New Delhi, India, 1999-2000. *Pos:* owner, Studio I, Palos Heights, Ill, 1967-1969; owner, Studio II, Oak Lawn, Il, Carmel, Calif, 1976-1982; owner, Letter Perfect/Studio II, Carmell, Calif, 1988-. *Awards:* Community Gold Feather Award, United Way/ Community Fund, Evergreen Park, Ill, 1969; Nat Philantropy Day, Monterey Bay Chapter, 2001; Publisher's Community Spirit Award for Rotary Serv, Tulare, Calif, 2000; Outstanding Women of Monterey Co, Calif, 2005; Nat Women's Hall of Fame, 2006. *Mem:* Rotary Internat, 1988-; Comm of Status of Women, Monterey Co; Carmel Mission Basilica Altar Soc

FLEMING, RONALD LEE
DESIGNER, ADMINISTRATOR
b Los Angeles, Calif, May 13, 1941. *Study:* Pomona Col, BA (cum laude), 63; Harvard Univ, MCP, 67. *Comn:* Developed art plans & strategies, Carriagetown & Flint, Mich; James Ctr, Richmond, Va; Bethesda Meridian, Prince Georges Co, Md; highway corridor megalithic landscape with sculptor William P Reimann, Radnor, Pa; cultural landscape with artist Greg Lefeure, Smith Students Center, Pomona Col, Claremont, CA. *Exhib:* On Common Ground, 81; What So Proudly We Hailed: America's Threatened Cult Landscapes, 90-92. *Pos:* First chmn, Cambridge Arts Coun, 75-79, Cambridge One Percent Pub Art Comn, 79-85; pres, Townscape Inst, 79-. *Teaching:* Lectr, Columbia Univ, Harvard Univ, Yale Univ & Univ Calif, Los Angeles. *Awards:* Merit Award, Am Soc Landscape Architects, 80; Commendation Design Excellence, Dept Transportation-Nat Endowment Arts, 81. *Mem:* Founding mem Cambridge Arts Coun (chmn, 74-79); fel Royal Soc Arts, London; Tavern Club, Boston; Century Asn, NY; Knickerbocker Club, NY; Somerset Club; Sprouting Rock Beach Asn, Newport, RI. *Publ:* Coauth, Place Makers, Creating Public Art that Tells You Where You Are, 81, second revised ed, 87; On Common Ground, Harvard Common Press, 82; auth, Facade Stories, Hastings House, 82; New Providence: A Changing Cityscape, Harcourt Brace Jovanivitch, 87; Saving Face, How Corporate Franchise Design Can Respect Community Identity, 94; auth, Art of Placemaking Interpreting Community Through Public Art & Urban Design, Merrell, London. *Mailing Add:* 8 Lowell St Cambridge MA 02138-4726

FLEMING, THOMAS MICHAEL
SCULPTOR, PAINTER
b Philadelphia, Pa, May 12, 1951. *Study:* Harrisburg Area Community Col, AA (with honors), 72; Pa State Univ, BFA (with honors), 75; Univ Minn, MFA, 78. *Work:* Musee des Arts, Lausanne, Switz; Int Glasmuseum, Ebeltoft, Denmark; Univ Minn Art Mus, Minneapolis; Corning Mus, NY; Ga State Univ, Urban Life Plaza, Atlanta, Ga. *Comn:* Ceramic sculpture, Wausau Insurance Cos, Wis, 83; sculpture, McDonald's Corp, Houston, Tex, 87. *Exhib:* Americans in Glass 1981, LY Woodson, Wis & Cooper-Hewitt Mus, NY; Int Directions Glass, Art Mus W Australia, Perth, 82; Order/Chaos, Minn Mus Art, St Paul, 83; Directions IV, Milwaukee Art Mus, Wis, 84; Glass from USA & Japan, Mus Basel, Switz, 86; Expressions En Verre, Musee des Arts, Lausanne, Switz, 86. *Pos:* Co-founder & dir, SoHo Studio Ctr, NY, 87-99; pres, Art Shoot, NY, 88-92; artistic prog consult, Anglo-Am Workshops, NY, 88-89; founder, www.artnyc.com, 96-. *Teaching:* Prof art, Univ Wis Marathon, Wausau, 78-; inst, Anglo-Am Workshops, London, Eng, 88. *Bibliog:* Robert Silberman (auth), Americans in Glass: A Requiem?, Art in Am, 3/85; Dan Klein (auth), Glass: A contemporary art, Rizzoli Int, 90; Olivier Royant (auth), Les Milliardaires Americans: Scope 90, Didier Hatier, 90. *Mem:* Int Sculpture Soc; Glass Art Soc; Nat Coun for Educ in Ceramic Arts. *Media:* Miscellaneous; Acrylic, Oil. *Publ:* coauth, Recyclable Ceramics, 78 Coun Educ Ceramic J, 87; Auth, Studio Molds--Three Approaches, 83, Interview with artist Ron Nagle, 87, Nat Coun Educ Ceramic J. *Mailing Add:* 518 S Seventh Ave Wausau WI 54401

FLEMINGER, SUSAN N
ADMINISTRATOR, EDUCATOR
b New York, NY, Nov 23, 1941. *Study:* Hofstra Univ, BA, 65; Hunter Col, MA, 67. *Collection Arranged:* Riding on a Blue Note; In-Site Series (designs for community improvement project); Exchanges I, II & III, Artists Select Artists; and many others. *Pos:* Consult, NY State Coun Arts; freelance cur, Harper Collins Gallery, Fordham Univ/Lincoln Ctr, Dittengass Gallery, Brooklyn Mus/Community Gallery, Educational Alliance, Craft Students League; educ dir, Yeshiva Univ Mus, NY, 78-80; dir, visual arts & arts in educ, Henry St Settlement Arts Ctr, NY, 85-; arts ed, Prospect Press, Brooklyn, NY, 84-85; Deputy Dir /Dir of Visual Arts & Art in Education. *Teaching:* Instr art hist & arts educ, NY Community Col, Kingsborough Community Col, Stern Col & Yeshiva Univ. *Awards:* Sch & Culture Award, NY Comn Cult Affairs, 88; Very Special Arts Award, Educator Yr, Doctoral Asn, 92; Coming up Taller from Presidents Committee on Arts and Educations, 2002. *Mem:* Art Table; Nat Art Educ Asn; Nat Alternative Arts Orgns; Arts in Educ Roundtable. *Specialty:* Contemporary art. *Interests:* Creating artists books. *Publ:* Auth, Art Reviews, Prospect Press Newspaper, 82-85; Joseph Delaney: An Interview, Arts & Artists, 3/82; Laura Schechter, 86 & Bert Hasen (monogr), 87, Arts Mag; Emilio Cruz: Spilled Nightmares, Revelations & Reflections (catalog essay), Studio Mus Harlem, 87; Presentation on Community Arts Education, Nat Asn Art Educ, 96. *Mailing Add:* 571 Ninth St No 1 Brooklyn NY 11215

FLESCHER, SHARON
ART HISTORIAN, ADMINISTRATOR
b New York, NY. *Study:* Barnard Col, BA; NY Univ, MA; Columbia Univ, Grad Sch Arts & Sci, MA & PhD, 77. *Pos:* Exec Dir, Int Found for Art Research, NY, 98-; ed-in-chief, IFAR Journal, NY, 98-; mem, Advisory Roundtables US State Dept, 98; mem, Nat Archives and Records Admin, 2000; Mem, US Delegation, Interpol Emergency Conf on Iraq, 2003; lectr, Smithsonian Inst, Speed Mus, Cambridge Univ, Eiteljorg Mus, Hermitage Mus, Art Law Day, LA Fine Art Show, Sotheby's Inst, and

numerous other insts; mem, Columbia Univ Art Advisory Council, 2009-. *Teaching:* Adj Assoc Prof Arts, NY Univ, NY, 93-,. *Bibliog:* Amy Gale, Art Guardian:Sharon Flescher, Art & Antiques, Feb, 2003; Simon de Burton, IFAR, TRACE magazine, Feb 2003; Philip Eliosoph (auth), Art Sleuth: IFAR and its Director, Dr. Sharon Flescher, Antiques & Fine Art, 1-2/2006. *Mem:* Coll Art Asn; Am Asn Mus; ArtTable. *Res:* Ethical, legal, and scholarly issues concerning acquisition, ownership & authenticity of art; 19th & 20th Century European paintings. *Interests:* Travel, piano, opera. *Publ:* Auth, Zacharie Astruc: Critic, Artist, Japoniste (1833-1907), Garland Publ, 78; auth, More on a Name: Manet's Olympia, The Art Journal, 85; auth, Zacharie Astruc, Grove Dictionary Art, McMillan, 96; auth, Beware: Heliogravures Can Fool the Unwitting, IFAR Journal, 2002; The Intl Foundation for Art Research, Expert vs the Object, Oxford, 2004; auth, Anatomy of an Art Fraud: Ely Sakhai's Two-Decade Long Scheme, IFAR Journal, 2005; Rash of Art Thefts in France, IFAR Jour, 2010; Is this Painting by Rembrandt? IFAR Jour, 2011; The Buhrle Collections Stolen Cezanne and Degas, IFAR Jour, 2012; media appearances, ABC Nightline, WCBS News, BBC, NPR, NBC Today Show, The Learning Channel, NY Times, Wall St Jour, Time, ARTnews, Art & Auction, The Art Newspaper, and many others. *Mailing Add:* IFAR 500 5th Ave Ste 935 New York NY 10110

FLETCHER, HARRELL
EDUCATOR, FILMMAKER
Study: San Francisco Art Inst, BFA in Photog, 1990; Calif Coll Arts & Crafts, MFA, 1994; Univ S Calif, Cert in Ecological Horticulture & Sustainable Food Systems, 1996. *Work:* Mus Pieces, MH de Young Mem Mus, San Francisco, 1999, Whitney Biennial, Whitney Mus Am Art, NY, 2004. *Exhib:* Exhib incl Garage Sale, Gallery Here, Calif, 1993, Some People We Metrop, Richmond Art Ctr, Va, 1996, Anthony, McBean Project Room, San Francisco Art Inst, 1997, Wanderings & Observations, Bedford Gallery, Walnut Creek, Calif, 1998, The Boy Mechanic, Yerba Buena Ctr Arts, San Francisco, 1999, Saying I Love You or Something Like That, Inst, San Francisco, Calif, 2000, Every Sunshine, Portland Inst Contemp Art, 2001, The Sound We Make Together, DiverseWorks, Houston, 2003, Now Its A Party, Hartford, Conn, 2003, A Moment of Doubt, Christine Burgin, NY, 2004, Happiness Follows Us Like a Shadow, New Langton Arts, San Francisco, 2004 Tender Feelings, Gas Works, London, 2005; solo exhibs at Urban Renewal Laboratory, Southern Exposure, San Francisco, 1998, We're Excerpts, Andrew Kreps Gallery, NY, 2002, Street Selections, The Drawing Ctr, NY, 2003; cur (exhibs) Whipper Snapper Nerd, Yerba Buena Ctr Arts, San Francisco, 1998, Survivalist, Southern Exposure, San Francisco, 1999, A Love For All Animals, San Francisco Art Comn Gallery, 2001, Hello There Friend, Christine Burgin, NY, 2003. *Pos:* Co-found, Gallery HERE, Oakland, Calif, 1993-94; video & mag co-coord, Creativity Explored, 1994-98; guest lectr, Calif Col Arts & Crafts, San Francisco, 1999, Henry Art Gallery, Seattle, 1999. *Teaching:* guest lectr, Calif Col Arts & Crafts, 1994, San Francisco Art Inst, 1994; asst prof, Portland State Univ, Ore, 2004; instr, Beginning Sculpture Stanford Univ, 1998; guest lectr, Univ Calif- Berkeley, 1998; instr, Interdisciplinary Seminar, 1999; Salon Lect, Series Prog Headlands Ctr Arts, 1999; guest lectr, Calif Col Arts & Crafts, San Francisco, 2000, San Francisco State Univ, 2000, White Chapel Gallery, London, 2001, Yale Univ, 2002, Pratt Inst, Brooklyn, 2002, Otis Sch Art & Design, Los Angeles, 2003, Univ Calif-Irvine, 2003; instr, sculpture Cooper Union, New York City, 2004. *Awards:* Recipient Post-Grad Studio Award, Headlands Ctr Arts, 1994, Headlands Ctr Arts Residency, 1998; Residency Grant, Calif Arts Coun, 1994, Creative Work Fund Grant, 1996, 2000, Artists & Communities Millenium Grant, 1999, Creative Capital Grant, 2002, Artslink Grant, 2003, Gunk Grant, 2003

FLETCHER, LELAND VERNON
PAINTER, SCULPTOR
b Cumberland, Md, Sept 18, 1946. *Study:* Univ Minn, BS, 72. *Work:* Victoria & Albert Mus, London; Mus D'Art Mod, Barcelona, Spain; Minneapolis Inst Art, Minn; Mus Ludwig, Cologne, Ger; Mus De Arte Contemp Da Univ De Sao Paulo, Brazil; Art Mus Calf State Univ, Long Beach; Bradford Mus, Eng; Civico Museo Revoltella, Trieste, Italy; Mus Plantin-Moretus, Antwerp, Belg; Kunsthalle Bremen, Ger; Kunsthalle Hamburg, Ger; Muzeum Sztuki, Lodz, Poland; Chicago Art Inst; School Libr, Chicago; Samuel Paley Library, Temple Univ, Philadelphia; DeSaisset Mus, Univ Santa Clara, Calif. *Comn:* Art Zone Maubeuge (200' x 300' urban environmental sculpture) & Construction 1A:11 (16' x 10' x 10' painted steel sculpture), Ministry Cult & Ville de Maubeuge, France, 87. *Exhib:* Solo exhibs, San Jose State Univ Union Gallery & City San Jose, Calif, 78, Univ Art Gallery, Calif State Univ, Hayward, 89 & Lake Co Mus, 95; Electroworks, Cooper-Hewitt Mus, New York, 79; Recent Acquisitions, Wolfgang-Gurlitt Mus, Neue Galerie der Stadt Linz, Austria, 82; Intergrafik 84 Triennale, Berlin, Fed Repub Ger, 84; 9th Int Brit Print Biennale, Victoria & Albert Mus, London, Eng, 86; 11th Graphic Biennale, Krakow, Poland, 86; Exhib Diomede, Inst Contemp Art, The Clocktower Gallery, New York, 89; Books: Inside & Out, Anchorage Mus Hist & Art, Alaska, 91; 10th Biennale Int, Mus d'Art Contemp d'Eivissa, Spain, 91; 6th Am Drawing Biennial, Muscarelle Mus Art, Coll William & Mary, Williamsburg, Va, 98; Int Exhib, Sharjah Arts Mus, United Arab Emirates, 2000 & 2005; Reactions, Wiluamson Gallery, Art Ctr Coll Design, Pasadena, Ca, 2002; and others. *Pos:* Fine art specialist, City of San Rafael, Calif, 77-78; artist-in-residence, Lake Co Arts Coun, Calif, 98-99. *Awards:* Hon Mention, Minn State Fair Fine Arts Exhib, 70. *Bibliog:* Stephen Moore (auth), Leland Fletcher, Wordworks, Vol 3, No 2, 79; Carl Loeffler (auth), Performance Anthology, Contemp Arts Press, 80; Leland Fletcher, La Voix du Nord, 7/87; David Edlefsen (auth), Inside & Out, Anchorage Mus Hist & Art. *Media:* Miscellaneous Media. *Mailing Add:* 3288 Konocti Lane Soda Bay Kelseyville CA 95451

FLETCHER, STEPHEN L
APPRAISER
Pos: Partner, exec vpres, chief auctioneer, appraiser, Skinner, Inc, Boston, Mass, 75-; dir, Am Furniture & Decorative Arts, currently; appraiser, Antiques Roadshow, WGBH-PBS, currently; contribr, writer, Art & Antiquities in Estates, currently. *Teaching:* lectr, in field, currently. *Mem:* Provincetown Art Asn Mus (bd trustees, currently); Mus Fine Arts, Boston, Mass. *Mailing Add:* Skinner Inc 63 Park Plaza Boston MA 02116

FLETCHER, VALERIE J
CURATOR, HISTORIAN
b Madison, Wis, Aug 26, 1951. *Study:* Conn Col, BA, 73; Columbia Univ, MA, 77, MPh, 79, PhD, 94. *Collection Arranged:* Josef Albers, Hirshhorn Mus, 80, Barbara Hepworth, 81, Dreams & Nightmares: Utopian Visions in Modern Art (auth, catalog), 83-84, 20th Century Sculpture, 85, Surrealist Art (auth, catalog), 86-87, Alberto Giacometti 1901-66 (auth, catalog), 88-89, Crosscurrents of Modernism: Latin Am Pioneers (auth, catalog), 92, Alexander Calder, 93-94, Paul Gauguin 96-97, Henry Moore, 98, Shahzia Sikander, 2000 & Tim Hawkinson, 2001; Human Figure Interpreted (auth, catalog), Taiwan Mus Fine Art & Shiga Mus, Japan, 95. *Pos:* Res asst, Metrop Mus Art, New York, 76-78; cur sculpture, Hirshhorn Mus, Smithsonian Inst, 78-. *Teaching:* Lectr, dept educ, Mus Mod Art, New York, 77-78; vis prof Utopian art, Continuing Educ, Georgetown Univ, 86. *Res:* 19th and 20th century painting and sculpture. *Publ:* Alberto Giacometti (exhib catalog), Hiroshima Art Mus, Japan, 97; coauth, Hishhorn Mus: 150 Works, 96, Alberto Giacometti, Vienna Kunsthalle & Royal Acad, London, 96 & Julio Gonzalez (exhib catalog), Kunstmuseum Bern, 97; A Garden for Art, Hirshhorn Mus, 98; Alberto Giacometti, Montreal Mus, 98; Giacometti's Paintings, Columbia Univ & UMI, 99; coauth, Hishhorn Mus: 150 Works, 96. *Mailing Add:* c/o Hirshhorn Mus & Sculpture Garden Dept Painting & Sculpture Washington DC 20560

FLEXNER, ROLAND
PRINTMAKER
b Nice, France. *Work:* Nat Mus Mod Art, Japan; Fogg Art Mus, Mass; Wadworth Atheneum Mus Art, Conn; Mus National d'Art Moderne Centre Pompidou, France; Whitney Mus Am Art, New York. *Exhib:* Solo exhibs, PS1 Inst for Art & Urban Resources, New York, 1982, Edward Williams Gallery, Fairleigh Dickinson Univ, NJ, 1984, Cleveland Mus Contemp Art, 1997, Centre Regional d'Art Contemporain Languedoc-Roussillon, France, 1999; 400 Years of Vanitas, Flint Inst Art, Mich, 2006; The Sense of Collapse, Nat Mus Mod Art, Tokyo, Japan, 2007; 1st Poznan Biennial, Nat Mus Poznan, Poland, 2008; The End, The Andy Warhol Mus, Pittsburgh, Pa, 2009; Whitney Biennial, Whitney Mus Am Art, 2010. *Bibliog:* Roberta Smith (auth), Going the Way of All Flesh, Artistically, NY Times, 10/10/2007; Kurt Shaw (auth), End, Offers Crisis Management, Pittsburgh Tribune, 3/11/2009; Peter Plagens (auth), Eye Level, Art in Am, 5/2010. *Mailing Add:* 2 Spring St New York NY 10012

FLICK, FRIEDRICH CHRISTIAN
COLLECTOR
Pos: Founder & chmn, FC Flick Found against Xenophobia, Racism and Intolerance. *Awards:* Named one of top 200 Collectors, ARTnews Magazine, 2004. *Media:* C. *Collection:* Old masters, European sculpture, modern & contemporary art

FLICK, PAUL JOHN
ASSEMBLAGES, PAINTER
b Rock Island, Ill, Feb 5, 1943. *Study:* Univ Minn, BA & MFA (printing & printmaking); studied with Herman Cherry, Mario Valpe & Zigmuuns Priede. *Work:* Univ Minn; The Courage Ctr, Golden Valley, Minn; Univ Minn; Univ Tenn; Numerous pvt collections incl Mr Mark Juergens; Univ Minn, Aeronautical coll; Sister Kenny Rehab Ctr, Minn. *Exhib:* Univ of Minn Studio Art Gallery, 70-72; solo exhibs, Univ of Minn, 72, Twin Cities Metrop Art Alliance, 75, Northland Gallery, St Louis Park, 76, W Bank Gallery, Minn, 76 & Gallery 13, 2005-2006, Robbin Gallery, Robinsdale, Mn, 2013; group exhibs, Metamorphose/One, Minn Mus Art, 76, Minneapolis Inst Arts, 80, 90, 2000, 2010, Nature Gallery, Chicago, Ill, 81 & Washington Project Arts, Washington, DC, 83; Rochester Arts Ctr, Minn, 89; Alsadu Gallery Minneapolis, 2010-2013; Sister Kenny Rehab Ctr, Minn, 2010, 2013; Spirit Room Gallery, Fargo, N Dak, 2010; Va Hosp, 2009-2013; Robbin Gallery, Robinsdale, Mn, 2012-2013; The Spirit Show, St Paul, MN. *Pos:* Freelance artist, 69-. *Teaching:* Instr drawing & color, Bur Engraving, Art Instruction Sch, 72-83. *Awards:* VSA Grant, 2007, 2012. *Bibliog:* Syd Fossum, Anvil Mag, 73. *Mem:* Artist Equity Asn (pres, 76-77); Twin Cities Metrop Arts Alliance; Vietnam Vets Art Group. *Media:* Assemblages, Constructions, Paintings. *Res:* Encaustic art. *Interests:* Primitive African art & contemporary ceramics. *Publ:* de Novo Art Mag, 1977; Illustrator Mag, 1972. *Dealer:* LRM Designs 3317 Minnehaha Ave S Minneapolis MN 55409. *Mailing Add:* 4032 Lyndale Ave S Minneapolis MN 55406

FLICK, ROBBERT
PHOTOGRAPHER, EDUCATOR
b Amersfoort, Holland, Nov 15, 1939; US citizen. *Study:* Univ BC, BA, 67; Univ Calif, Los Angeles, MA, 70, with Robert Heinecken & Robert Fichter, MFA, 71. *Work:* Ctr Creative Photog, Tucson, Ariz; Chicago Art Inst, Ill; Hallmark Collections, Kansas City, Mo; Mus Mod Art, NY; Oakland Mus Art, Calif; San Francisco Mus Mod Art. *Exhib:* Art Inst Chicago, Ill; Ctr Creative Photog, Tucson, Ariz; Fine Arts Gallery, Univ Calif, Davis; Fine Arts Gallery, Univ BC, Can; Frederick S Wight Art Gallery, Univ Calif, Los Angeles; Henry Art Gallery, Univ Wash, Seattle; Light Gallery, NY; Los Angeles Co Mus; Min Gallery, Tokyo; Musee d'Art, Mod de la Ville de Paris, France; Mus Mod Art, Lodz, Poland; Photo-Kina, Koln, WGer; Vancouver Art Gallery. *Teaching:* Prof art, Univ Ill, Champaign-Urbana, 71-76 & Univ Southern Calif, Los Angeles, 76-. *Awards:* Nat Endowment Arts Survey Grant, 79; Nat Endowment Arts, Individual Artist Fel, 82 & 84; Nat Endowment Arts Individual

Artist Grant, 83. *Bibliog:* Article, Afterimage, Vol 8, No 5, 12/80; article, Journal, Southern Calif Art Mag No 29; Berger, Searle & Wadden (coauths), Radical, Rational, Space, Time, Idea Networks in Photography, Henry Art Gallery, Univ Wash, Seattle, 82; Van Deren Coke (auth), Facets of Modernism: Photographs from the San Francisco Museum of Modern Art, Hudson Hills Press, NY, 86. *Mem:* Soc for Photog Educ; Coll Art Asn. *Media:* Silverprint. *Publ:* Auth, Camera, Nos 2 & 10, C J Bucher Ltd, Lucerne, Switz, 72 & 81; Photographer's Choice, Addison House, Danbury, NH, 75; Robbert Flick, Selected Work: 1980-1981 (exhib catalog), Los Angeles Mun Art Gallery, Calif, 81; The Photographic Vision, Tele Course, Coast Community Col, Fountain Valley, Calif, CBS/Holt, Rinehart & Winston, 84; Robbert Flick, MIN Gallery, Tokyo, Japan, 87. *Dealer:* Photoman Inc 42 E 76th St New York NY 10021. *Mailing Add:* c/o Craig Krull Gallery Bergamont Sta 2525 Michigan Ave Bldg B-3 Santa Monica CA 90404-4014

FLORES, CARLOS MARINI
ARCHITECT, HISTORIAN
b Ciudad, Mex, May 28, 1937. *Study:* Univ Nac Autonoma de Mex, Arquitecto, 60, Histonador, 64; Univ de Roma, Italy, Restaurador, 62. *Comn:* Alcazar de Colon, Dominican Repub, 65; Antiqua, Guatemala, 72; rtagena de Indias, Columbia, 75; Portobelo - Panama Viejo, Panama, 78. *Collection Arranged:* El Quijote, Mus Iconografico, 88; Chavez Morado, Mus del Pueblo, 89. *Pos:* Dir monumentos coloniales, Inst Nac de Antropologia e Hist, 62-66; dir monumentos artisticos, Inst Nac de Bellas Artes, 77-81; dir centro hist cd Mex, Distrito Fed, 82-85. *Teaching:* Historia arquitectura, Univ Nac Autonoma de Mex, 60-90; restauracion monomentos, Univ de Roma, Italy, 70- & Univ Fla, Gainesville, 80-92. *Awards:* Academico Nacional, Acad de Arquitectura, 78 & Academico Emerito, 88 & Piemio Nacional, 96. *Bibliog:* Homenaje - F de la Mazatlan, Inv Esteticas, Univ Nac Autonoma de Mex, 74; Rest de Monumentos, Cuadernos de Arquitectura, Inst Nac de Bellas Artes, 79; Cons Pat Monumental Inst Nac Autonoma e Hist, ICOMOS Mexicano, 96. *Mem:* Int Coun Monuments & Sites, Paris; Acad de San Jorge, Barcelona; Consejo del Gran Caribe para los Monumentos y Sitios, Dominican Repub; Acad Nac de Arquitectura, Mex; Acad Mexicana de Arquitectura, Mex. *Res:* Hist de la arquitectura, restauracion de monumentos, art contemporaneo. *Publ:* Auth, Santigo Tianguitenco, 64; Casas Virreinales de la Ciudad de Mex, 70; Restauracion de Cuidades, 72; contribr, Arquitectura Mexicana del S XVI, 83; coauth, El Palacio de Iturbide, Banco Nac de Mex, 92. *Mailing Add:* Mazatlan 190 Ciudad de Mex Col Cuauhtemoc #06140 Mexico

FLORET, EVELYN
SCULPTOR
b France. *Study:* Wash Univ, St Louis, BA; Nat Acad School of Fine Arts studied with Anthony Antonios; Nat Acad Sch Fine Arts (three yr cert). *Exhib:* Nat Sculpture Soc Ann Exhibs, 98 & 2001; Allied Artists Am Ann Exhib, 99, 2004, 2007-2009, & 2011; Ann Sculpture & Medallic Art Exhib (Pen & Brush), 2000-2001, 2003-2006 & 2009; In Remembrance: Sept 11 (Nat Sculpture Soc), 2002; Audubon Artists Ann Exhib, 2003-2006, 2008-2011, & 2012. *Pos:* slide lectr for Four French Sculptors Between the Wars, Nat Acad Sch Fine Arts, 4/5/2007; Sculpture dir, Audubon Artists, 2010-2013; slide lectr for How to Photograph and Promote Artwork, Nat Acad Sch Fine Arts, 2011. *Awards:* Elliot Liskin Mem Award, Pen and Brush, 2000 & 2004; Gold Medal of Honor for Sculpture, Audubon Artists, 2003; Art Students League Award, Allied Artists, NY, 2008; Silver Medal hon, Audubon Artists, 2009. *Mem:* Audubon Artists Inc; The Pen and Brush, Inc; Am Society of Media photogrs; Soc of N Am Goldsmiths; Allied Artists of Am. *Media:* Clay, Bronze. *Interests:* Photography, computer for photographic art & printing, piano playing. *Mailing Add:* 8 E 83rd St Apt # 14D New York NY 10028

FLORIN, SHARON JUNE
PAINTER
b Brooklyn, NY, Feb 16, 1952. *Study:* Art Students League, with David Leffel, Issac Soyer, among others, 69-77; Adelphi Univ, BA, 73. *Work:* Mus City NY; Nawa Collection, Zimmerli Art Mus, Rutgers Univ, NJ. *Exhib:* Nat Asn Women Artists Ann Exhib, 90-2004, 2004-2011; Ann Nat Midyear Exhib, Butler Inst Am Art, Youngstown, Ohio, 91, 2003, 2005, 2007 & 2009; 35th Chautauqua Nat Exhib Am Art, Chautauqua Inst, NY, 92; Her Artworks, South Bend Art Ctr, Ind, 92; 11th Sept Competition Exhib, Alexandria Mus Art, La, 92; Braithwaite Fine Arts Gallery, Southern Utah Univ, 94; Drawing the Lines, NY Transit Mus, Brooklyn, 97; Int Juried Show, NJ Ctr Visual Arts, 98; Liberty Enlightning the World, Hudson Waterfront Mus, Brooklyn, NY, 98; Annual Exhib, Nat Arts Club, New York, 2000; Catharine Lorillard Wolfe Art Club, 2000-2006, 2009-2011, Ann Exhib; Poughkeepsie Art Mus, NY, 2005. *Awards:* Nat Asn Women Artists, NY, 89-90, 92, 95-96, 98, 2000 (medal hon), 2001, 2004, 2006, 2009, 2010; Catharine Lorillard, Wolf Art Club, New York, 98, 2000, 2004-2009; Georgetown Int Art Competition, Fraser Gallery, Washington, DC, 2001; Pen & Brush Club, New York, 2002; Allied Artists Am, 2007, 2009; Am Artists Prof League, 2007, 2011. *Bibliog:* New York Through Artists Eyes, The NY Times, 10/14/83; A Picturesque Neighborhood, NY Daily News, 5/19/91; Here's A Stroke of Genius, Park Slope Courier, Brooklyn, NY, 8/28/2000; Unforgettable Places to Create, Artist's Mag, spring 2006. *Mem:* Women Arts Inc; Nat Asn Women Artists; Catharine Lorillard Wolfe Art Club; Org of Independent Artists; NY Artists Equity; Allied Artists Am. *Media:* Oil. *Mailing Add:* 339 E 19th St New York NY 10003

FLOWER, MICHAEL LAVIN
ART DEALER, PHOTOGRAPHER
b Queens, NY, Aug 31, 1958. *Study:* Simon's Rock Early Col, AA, 77; Dartington Coll Art, UK, dipl, 78; Philadelphia Coll Art, BFA, 80. *Work:* Mednick Gallery, Philadelphia Coll Art. *Comn:* Balloon's at Lake Placid, Winter Olympic Games, comn by Dr Clayton Thomas, Brimfield, Mass, 80; The Mayans (photograph), comn by Gladys Carbo, Stockbridge, Mass, 81; Berkshire Landscapes (photograph), Arcadian Shop, Lenox, Mass, 83. *Exhib:* Year End, Fed Bldg, Philadelphia, 80; TV Veg, Main Gallery, Philadelphia Coll Art, 80. *Collection Arranged:* City Reception, 84, Photo & Pencil, 84, China: The People and Landscape, 84, Photographic Silkscreens, 84 & Photographic Installations, 85, Chiaroscuro Gallery, Lenox, Mass. *Pos:* Supvr dept photog, Moore Col Art, Philadelphia, 81; owner & dir, Chiaroscuro Gallery, Lenox, Mass, 83-. *Teaching:* Substitute prof experimental photog, Simon's Rock, Great Barrington, Mass, 86; internship dir, photog, Lenox Mem High Sch, Mass, 86; photo instr, Miss Ponters Sch Interim Prog, 87. *Specialty:* Fine art photography

FLOWERS, THOMAS EARL
PAINTER, EDUCATOR
b Washington, DC, Feb 17, 1928. *Study:* Furman Univ, BA; Univ Iowa, MFA. *Work:* Greenville Co Mus Art, SC; Columbia Mus Art, SC; Chase Manhattan Bank, NY; Vincent Price Enterprises, Chicago; Fed Reserve Bank Va, Charlotte, NC, Nations Bank. *Comn:* Mural, Vince Perome, Greenville, SC, 62; mural, Saad Rug Co, Greenville, 63; mace & medallion, Furman Univ, Greenville, 65; mural, City Hall, Greenville, SC. *Exhib:* Eighteenth Ann Guild SC Artists Exhib, 68; 11th Ann Southern Contemp Art Exhib, Mobile, Ala, 69; Best in Show, Springs Art Exhib, Lancaster, SC, 81; Atlanta Artists Club, Nat 1, Ga, 70; Southeastern Painter's Choice Exhib, Ga Col, Milledgeville, Ga, 71. *Pos:* Co-owner, Tate Gallery, Liberty, SC. *Teaching:* Asst prof art & chmn dept, Ottawa Univ, 56-58; instr sculpture, E Carolina Col, 58-59; assoc prof art & chmn dept, Furman Univ, 59-89; retired. *Awards:* Purchase Award, SC Arts Comn, 71; Second Award, Franklin Mint, 72; Art in Archit Award, SC Chap, Am Inst Architects, 77; Spartanburg Art Asn Bureau Award, 91. *Bibliog:* Jack A Morris (auth), Contemporary artists of South Carolina, Greenville Co Mus Art, 70; R Smeltzer (auth), article, Southern Living Mag, 12/70; M Hays (auth), article, Furman Univ Mag, spring 72. *Mem:* Guild SC Artists (pres, 61-62, bd dir, 71-72); Greenville Artists Guild (pres, 72-73); Southeastern Coll Art Asn; Am Craftsman's Coun. *Media:* Mixed. *Publ:* Illusr covers, Furman Univ Mag, winter 67, summer 68 & 5/69; illusr cover, Springs Cotton Mill Ann Report, 69; illusr, Images, Univ NC, Asheville, summer 69. *Dealer:* Hampton III Gallery Ltd 10 Gallery Ctr Taylors SC 29687. *Mailing Add:* 803 Shoals Creek Church Rd Easley SC 29640-9532

FLOYD, CARL LEO
SCULPTOR, ENVIRONMENTAL ARTIST
b Somerset, Ky, Oct 12, 1936. *Study:* Kansas City Art Inst, BFA, 64; Cranbrook Acad Art, MFA, 67. *Work:* Praltown Park, Lexington, Ky; Vt Freeway, St Albans; Hogback Nature Park, Madison, Ohio; Mand Corning Prof, Holden Arboretum, Mentor, Ohio; Univ Vt Art Mus, Burlington. *Comn:* Steel & wood sculpture, Willoughby Fine Arts, Ohio, 72; Stone Earth, Inner City, Bad Kreuznach, WGer, 75; All People's Park, Lake Co Metrop Parks, 76-77; Earth-Stone, Cleveland Pub Libr, 79; One Acre Proj, Ohio Arts Coun, Madison, 80. *Exhib:* Contemp Sculpture, J B Speed Mus Art, Louisville, Ky, 68; Environ Sculpture, Dulin Gallery Art, Knoxville, Tenn, 69; 2nd Cincinnati Biennial, Cincinnati Art Mus, 69 & Biennial Awards Exhib, 70; Sculpture of New Era, Chicago Fed Plaza, 76; Sculpture on the Green, Columbus Arts Coun, Ohio, 79; Nature Environ, Minn State Univ, Bemidji, 79. *Teaching:* Instr sculpture & archit, Univ Ky, Lexington, 67-71; instr sculpture, Cleveland Inst Art, 71-

FLOYER, CEAL
SCULPTOR
b Karachi, Pakistan, 1968. *Study:* Goldsmiths Coll, London, BA, 1994. *Work:* San Francisco Mus Mod Art, Calif; Denver Art Mus, Colo; Tate Modern, London; Mus fur Moderne Kunst, Frankfurt, Ger; Wadsworth Atheneum, Conn; Jumex Collection, Mex; Nat Gallery Victoria, Australia; FRAC Lorraine, France; Sammlung Zeitgenossische Kunst des Bundes. *Exhib:* Hit & Run, Tufton St, London, 1992; Good Work, Bonington Gallery, Nottingham, 1993; Fast Forward, Inst Contemp Art, London, 1994; 4th Istanbul Biennale, Istanbul, 1995; solo exhibs, Picture Gallery, Sci Mus, London, 1995, Anthony Wilkinson Fine Art, London, 1996, Herzliya Mus Art, Tel Aviv, 1997, Kunstlerhaus Bethanien, Berlin, 1998, Pinksummer, Genova, 2000, Inova, Inst Visual Arts, Milwaukee, 2001, Index, The Swedish Contemp Art Found, Stockholm, 2002, Waterline, Art Unlimited, Basel, 2004, Contemp Art Gallery, Vancouver, 2005, SAFN, Reykjavik, Iceland, 2006, Centre d Art Santa Monica, Barcelona, 2007, Museo d Arte Contemporanea Donna Regina, Naples, 2008 & Palais de Tokyo, Paris, 2009; A4 Favours, Three Month Gallery, Liverpool, 1996; Projects, Irish Mus Mod Art, 1997; Drawing Itself, London Inst Gallery, London, 1998; Peace, Museum fur Gegenwartskunst, Zurich, 1999; Film, Palm Beach Inst Contemp Art, Palm Beach, Fla, 2000; Ingenting, Rooseum Ctr for Contemp Art, Malmo, 2001; Tempo, Mus Mod Art, New York, 2002; Lapdissolve, Casey Kaplan Gallery, New York, 2003; Slowness, Govett-brewster Art Gallery, New Plymouth, New Zealand, 2004; Material Matters, Herbert F Johnson Mus Art, Ithaca, NY, 2005; Draw, Inst Modern Art, Middlesbrough, England, 2006; Brave New Year, 303 Gallery, New York, 2007; Reality Check, Statens Mus, Copenhagen, 2008; The Quick and the Dead, Walker Art Ctr, Minneapolis, Minnesota, 2009; 53rd Int Art Exhib Biennale, Venice, 2009. *Awards:* Philip Morris Scholar, Kunstlerhaus Bethanien, Berlin, 1997; The Paul Hamlyn Award, 2002; Working grant, Kunst & Nutzen, Bremerhaven, Ger, 2006; National Galerie Prize for Young Art, 2007. *Bibliog:* David Lillington (auth), The Infanta of Castile, Time Out, London, 6/1993; David Barrett (auth), Making Mischief, Art Monthly, No 182, 12/1994; Margaret Garlake (auth), Adrift in Venice, Art Monthly, No 188, 7-8/1995; Patricia Bickers (auth), The Young Devils, Art Press, No 214, 6/1996; Brian Muller (auth), Seeing the light, Contemp Visual Arts, No 16, 48-53, 1997; Tanya Gorucheva (auth), This Other World of Ours, Flash Art, 62, 1-2/2000; Tom Lubbock (auth), The Five Best Shows in London, The Independent, 5/25/2002; Roberta Smith (auth), review, NY Times, E13, 5/19/2006; Brian Boucher, Ceal Floyer at the Swiss Institute, Art in Am, 1/2007. *Mailing Add:* 52-54 Bell St London NW1 5DA United Kingdom

FLUDD, REGINALD JOSEPH
PAINTER, CRAFTSMAN
b New York, NY, June 10, 1938. *Study:* Ind Univ, BS (art); Queens Col, MS (art); study with Kenneth Campbell & Barse Miller; Art Inst Chicago; New York City Col. *Work:* Alcoa Aluminum Corp, NY; Norton Mus, Palm Beach, Fla; Nassau Community Col, Garden City, NY; Ocean City Cult Arts Ctr, NJ; Rose Art Mus, Brandeis Univ,

Waltham, Mass; and others. *Exhib:* Am Drawing Biennial, Norfolk Mus, 71; Okla Art Ctr, Oklahoma City, 72; Aldrich Mus, Ridgefield, Conn, 74; New Britain Mus Contemp Art, Conn, 74; Solo exhib, Hecksher Mus, Huntington, NY, 75; and others. *Teaching:* Instr art, Syosset High Sch, NY, 64-; asst prof painting, Suffolk Community Col, 74-77. *Awards:* Best in Show, Bayshore CofC, 68 & Patchoque CofC, 70; Grand Prix, Locust Valley Art Show, Operation Democracy, 73. *Bibliog:* Laurie Anderson (auth), article in Art News, 1/72; Malcom Preston (auth), article in Newsday, 3/12/75; Jean Paris (auth), article in Long Island Press, 7/6/75. *Mem:* Nat Educ Asn; Nat Art Educ Asn; Huntington Art League. *Media:* Oil, Watercolor. *Mailing Add:* 24 W Sanders Greenlawn NY 11740

FLUEK, TOBY
PAINTER, GRAPHIC ARTIST
b Czernica, Poland, Feb 20, 1926; US citizen. *Study:* Art Students League, with Robert Beverly Hale; also with Joe Hing Lowe & Irving Koenig. *Work:* David Mamet pvt collection. *Exhib:* Bronx Mus Arts Ann, New York, 72 & 74-76; Hudson Valley Art Asn Ann, White Plains, NY, 73, 75-84 & 86; Queensborough Community Coll Art Gallery, NY, 85 & 87-88; Rockland Ctr Holocaust Studies, Spring Valley, NY, 90; Yeshiva Univ Mus, New York, 94; The Holocaust Mem & Educ Ctr, Nassau Co, 96; Fla Holocaust Mus; Holocaust Mem Resource & Educ Center, Maitland, Fla, 2006; Jewish Community Ctr Metro West, NJ, 2010. *Teaching:* Instr oil painting, Woodside Jewish Ctr, NY, 72. *Awards:* Best Show, Art League Nassau Co, 79; Prix du Roman Historique, Hist Novel Prize, 91; Chosen Best Book for Young Adults 1991 by Am Libr Asn, Young Adults Servs Div; and others. *Bibliog:* Images of Life, Loss, Orlando Sentinel, Orlando, Fla, 5/18/2006; Memories of My Life in a Polish Village, Orlando Weekly, Orlando, Fla, 4/3/2006; Rakhmiel Peltz (producer, dir), Toby's Sunshine: The Life & Art of Holocaust Survivor Toby Knobel Fluek (film), 2008. *Media:* Oil, Charcoal, Watercolor. *Publ:* Auth, Memories of My Life in a Polish Village 1930-1949, Alfred A Knopf, 1990; Passover As I Remember It, Alfred A. Knopf, 94

FLYNN, JOHN (KEVIN)
PAINTER, RESTORER
b Los Angeles, Calif, Nov 7, 1953. *Study:* Pvt study with Clyde Johnson, 68-74, Art Center Coll of Design, with Lorser Feitelson, 75-76 & Harry Carmean, 75-78; Pratt Inst, with Joseph A Smith, BFA, 83; New York Univ, cert appraisal studies, 92. *Work:* Permanent Collection, Pratt Inst, Brooklyn, NY. *Exhib:* 45th Ann Nat Midyear Show, Butler Inst Am Art, 82; 15th Anniversary Exhib, Brooklyn Mus, 83; Artists in the Marketplace, Bronx Mus, 87; 1988 Stockton Natl Print & Drawing Exhib, Hagin Mus, Calif, 88; 165th Ann Exhib, Nat Acad Design, NY, 90; 28th Ann Open Exhib, San Bernadino Co Mus, Calif, 93; The 33rd Irene Leache Mem Exhib, Chrysler Mus, Norfolk, 96; 2000 Reasons to love the Eart, Milennium Exhib, The Hague, The Neth, 2000; 97-present, ongoing exhibitions of paintings & drawings by John K Flynn. *Pos:* Paintings restorer, J K Flynn Co, 74-, appraiser of paintings, sculpture & works on paper, 85-. *Teaching:* Instr painting-pastels & composition-drawing, Craft Students League, 90-94. *Awards:* David Humphries Mem Award, Allied Artists Am Inc, 82; Joseph S Isidor Mem Medal Excellence in Figurative Composition, Nat Acad Design, 90; William Henry Lowman Award, Silvermine Guild Ctr Arts, 92; Wheeler Page Memorial Award, Wayne Art Ctr, Wayne, Pa, 97. *Bibliog:* Malcom Preston (auth), Displaying works by five, Newsday, 83; Karin Lipson (auth), Artwork by prizewinners, Newsday, 86; Vivien Raynor (auth), The drive to be topical, The urge to compete, The NY Times, 92. *Media:* Oil on Linen, Charcoal/Graphite, Ink & Watercolor on Paper. *Publ:* Auth, Technical answers-discovering the oil medium of the masters, The Artists Mag, 9/92; Technical answers-keeping color mixing organized-saving premixed colors, The Artists Mag, 5/93; Seeing your way to better oils - Don Wards eight step painting process lets you push your paintings in any direction, The Artists Mag, 3/95; Technical answers-the art of scumbling-dealing with mildew and insects on canvas, The Artists Mag, 7/94; Technical answers-uncover old masters secrets for creating form with contrast, learn to keep your oil painting from cracking, The Artists Mag, 10/96. *Dealer:* JK Flynn Company 471 Sixth Ave Park Slope Brooklyn NY 11215-4020. *Mailing Add:* 471 6th Ave Brooklyn NY 11215-4020

FLYNN, PAT L
JEWELER, GOLDSMITH
b Edinboro, Pa, Oct 29, 1954. *Study:* Edinboro State Col, 73-76; State Univ Coll New York, New Paltz, BFA, 78. *Work:* Chicago Art Inst; Nordenfjeldske Kunstindustt Mus, Trondheim, Norway; Renwick Gallery, Smithsonian Inst; Am Mus Art; Mus Arts and Design, NY; RI Sch Design; also pvt collections of Mr & Mrs Ron Abramson, Mr & Mrs Malcolm Knapp & Robert Pfannebecker. *Exhib:* Silver in Service, Castle Gallery, New Rochelle, NY, 87; Goldsmithing, Louisiana State Univ, 88; 20th Century Decorative Art, Naval Pier, Chicago, 87, 88 & 89; Jewelers Work, Washington, 96; The Poetry of Passion, DeNova Gallery, Palto Alto, Calif; Falling Gracefully, Susan Cummins Gallery, Mill Valley, Calif; Pat Flynn, Gallery Materia, Scottsdale, Ariz, 2002, Patina Gallery, Santa Fe, NMex, 2003; Nat Invitational, Bowling Green State Univ, Ohio, 2002; At Arms Length, Saybains Gallery, Royal Oak, Mich; Patt Flynn: Ironic Attachment II, Patina Gallery, Santa Fe, NMex, 2009; Brooching the Subject: One of a Kind, The Ogden Mus Southern Art, Center for Southern Craft & Design, New Orleans, LA, 2010; The Weight of Black, Penland School of Crafts, Penland, NC, 2010; Jewelry Artists of the Hudson Valley, Forbes Gallery, New York, NY, 2011; Open Mind, The Sungkok Art Mus, Seoul, South Korea, 2012. *Pos:* Freelance jeweler, goldsmith & modelmaker, 82-85; owner, Pat Flynn Inc, 85-. *Teaching:* Arrowmont Sch Arts & Crafts, Ball State Univ, Boston Univ, Brookfield Craft Ctr, Chautauqua Inst, Creative Arts Workshop, Greenwood Galleries, Haystack Mountain Sch Crafts, La State Univ, 92nd St YMWHA, Northern Ariz Univ, Nova Scotia Sch Art & Design, Ore Sch Arts & Crafts, Parsons Sch Design, Penland Sch Crafts, Pa Guild Craftsman, Peters Valley, San Diego State Univ, Sch Fine Arts, Saide Brofman Ctr, Skidmore Col, Southwest Craft Ctr, Summer Vail Metalsmithing symp, Univ Houston, Univ Wis & Worchester Craft Ctr. *Awards:* Craftsman Fel, Nat Endowment Arts, 85, 88 & 94; Christofle Prize, Philadelphia Craft Show, 87; NY State Found Arts Fel, 88; Nat Ornamental Metal Mus, Master Metalsmith, 98. *Mem:* Am Crafts Coun. *Publ:* Ornament Mag, 1/93; Lapidary J, 6/93; Metalsmith Mag, fall 93 & summer, 94; 500 Gemstone Jewels, Lark Books, 2010. *Dealer:* Twist Gallery 30 NW 23rd Pl Portland Or 97210; Patina Gallery 131 W Palace Ave Santa Fe NMex 87501; Quadrum Gallery The Mall at Chestnut Hill Chestnut Hill Mass 02467. *Mailing Add:* 480 Mohonk Rd High Falls NY 12440-5301

FLYNT, ROBERT
PHOTOGRAPHER
b Williamstown, Mass, Mar 27, 1956. *Study:* Skowhegan Sch Painting & Sculpture, 74 & 76; NY Studio Sch, Paris, 75; Tyler Sch Art, BFA, 78. *Work:* Mus Mod Art, Metrop Mus Art, NY; Los Angeles Co Mus Art; Mus Fine Art, Houston; Baltimore Mus Art; Int Ctr Photog, NY; Worcester Art Mus, Mass. *Comn:* Dance set (co-collaborator), Bebe Miller Co, Brooklyn Acad Mus, NY, 89; Theatre set/projections (co-collaborator), Los Angeles Contemp Exhibs, Calif, 90; The Yellow Room, Dahghda dance co, Ireland, 2003. *Exhib:* Interactions, Inst Contemp Art, Philadelphia, 91; New Photog 8, Mus Mod Art, NY, 92; Bathers, Washington Ctr Photog, Washington, DC, 96; Bodies in Flux, Weatherspoon Art Gallery, Univ NC, Greensboro, 98; Waterproof, Centro Cult de Belem, Lisbon, Port, 98; San Francisco Camerawork, 99; Wessel & O'Connor Gallery, NY, 2000; Anatomically Incorrect, Mus Mod Art, NY, 2000; Partial Disclosures, Univ RI, Kingston, 2000 & Centro Cult de Belem, Lisbon, Portugal, 2000; solo exhib, Maus Habitos Gallery, Porto, Portugal, 2001 & 04, Clamp Art, New York City, 2004; Anxiety & Desire, Metrop State Coll Denver, Colo, 2004; Hidden Histories, New Art Gallery, Walsall, UK, 2004; New to View, Worcester Art Mus, Mass, 2006; Body Familiar, Griffin Mus Photography, Winchester, Mass, 2006; Body Lanuages, Katzen Arts Ctr, Am Univ, Washington, 2006; and others. *Pos:* Co-cur, Space Case Gallery, PS 122, New York, 89-94. *Teaching:* Univ Nev, Las Vegas, 96 & Sch Visual Arts, NY, 98-. *Awards:* Photog Fel, Blind Trust, Mid-Atlantic Arts Found, 95; Residency Fel, MacDowell Colony, 98; Peter S Reed Found Grant, 2004; and others. *Bibliog:* D Bright (auth), The Passionate Camera, Routledge, 98; Emmanuel Cooper (auth), Male Bodies, Pastel, 2004; Michael Petry (auth), HiddenHistories, Artmedia, 2004. *Mem:* Soc Photog Educ. *Publ:* Auth, Life Jacket, pvt publ, 92; coauth, Blind Trust, pvt publ with Temple Univ, 94; auth, Compound Fracture, Twin Palms Publ, 96; auth, Numbered Days, pvt publ, 2001. *Dealer:* Clamp Art 531 W 25th St New York NY 10001; GZ Gallery 4200 N Marshall Way Scottsdale AR 85751. *Mailing Add:* 383 Spring Lake Rd Red Hook NY 12571

FOGARTY, LORI
MUSEUM DIRECTOR
b 1963. *Study:* Occidental Coll, Los Angeles, grad (summa cum laude), 1984. *Pos:* Assoc dir, San Francisco Mus Mod Art, 1988-96, dep dir curatorial affairs, 1996-98, acting dir, 1997-98, sr dep dir, 1998-2001; dir, Bay Area Discovery Mus, Sausalito, Calif, 2001-06; exec dir, Oakland Mus, Calif, 2006-. *Mem:* Asn Children's Museums (bd dirs); Asn Art Mus Dirs. *Mailing Add:* Oakland Mus Calif 1000 Oak St Oakland CA 94607

FOGG, MONICA
PAINTER, EDUCATOR
b Belaire, Tex. *Study:* Washington Univ, 73; Principia Col, Elsah, Ill, BA, 74; St Cloud Univ, Minn, MA, 86. *Work:* General Mills & Honeywell, Minneapolis; Prudential Insurance Co Am, Plymouth, Minn; Principia Col, Elsah, Ill; Marathon Oil Co, Midland, Tex. *Comn:* Minn Protective Life, Eden Prairie, 75; Woodhill Country Club, Wayzata, 82; AMFAC-City Ctr, Minneapolis, 82; Univ Minn Hosp, 86. *Exhib:* Metamorphose-One, Minn Mus Art, St Paul, 76; Midwest Watercolor Ann, Tweed Mus, Duluth, Minn, 77 & 78; Northstar Soc Ann, Minneapolis, 77-83; Aqueous Open, Pittsburgh Watercolor Soc, Pa, 78; Solo exhibs, Expressive of Alaska, Artique, Anchorage, 81; Minn Artist Asn, Minneapolis, 82; Expressive Chroma on Paper, Kieale Gallery, St Cloud, Minn. *Teaching:* Instr, St Louis Watercolor Soc, 74, Northstar Watercolor Soc, 77, Univ Minn, 80-86, Edina Art Ctr, 80-81, Fogg Studio, 81-83, Art Ctr Minn, 83 & St Cloud State Univ, 84-86. *Awards:* Second Prize, Minn 77, State Arts Coun, 77; Award Excellence, Northstar Watercolor Soc Ann, 77, 80, 82 & 83; Award of Excellence, Minn Artists Asn, 82; and others. *Bibliog:* Fredric Appel (auth), Watercolor: When it's good, Minn Star & Tribune, 78; Cindy Rumsey (auth), Artist on the move (film), WCCO-TV, Minneapolis, 81; Warren Martin (auth), Watercolor-An Art (film), WTCN-TV, Minneapolis, 81. *Mem:* Minn Soc Fine Arts; Northstar Watercolor Soc (treas, 78-81 & bd mem, 78-81); Midwest Watercolor Soc; Twin Cities Watercolor Soc; Women's Caucus Arts. *Media:* Watercolor. *Mailing Add:* 3790 Pasture Ridge S Rd Afton MN 55001

FOGG, REBECCA SNIDER
PRINTMAKER, PAINTER
b Washington, DC, Dec 16, 1949. *Study:* Rochester Inst Technol, summer 72; RI Sch Design, BFA, 72. *Work:* Rochester Inst Technol, Henrietta, NY; Am Fed Savings & Loan, Sacramento, Calif; Resorts Unlimited, Atlantic City, NJ. *Comn:* Etching, Columbia Bank, Newark, NJ, 74; etchings with Michael Harris, Rickey's Calif Hyatt, Palo Alto, Calif, 83. *Exhib:* Solo exhibs, Will Tait & Rebecca Fogg, Mission Gallery, Carmel, Calif, 90, Between Water and Land, Hayward, Calif, Hayward Shoreline Interpretive Ctr, 97, In Their Element, 2011, Elemental Expression, Palo Alto, Calif, Pacific Art League, Norton Gallery, 2003, Plenty of Ocean, Merced Coll Art Gallery, Merced, Calif, 2013; Group exhibs, Marin MOCA, Speaking of Solitude, Novato, Calif, 2010, Sustainable Silicon Valley WEST Summit, Stanford Univ, Palo Alto, Calif, 2010, Landscapes: Real or Imagined, Pacific Art League Main Gallery, Palo Alto, Calif, 2010, Multiples, 2011, Earth Tones, Pacific Grove, Pacific Grove Art Ctr Gill Gallery, 2010, Water Works, Monterey Co Health Dept, Salinas, Calif, 2011, 25th Ann Emeryville Art Exhib, Emeryville, Calif, 2011, 26th Ann Emerville Art Exhib, 2012, The Water's Edge, Linus Galleries, Long Beach, Calif, 2012, Women's Work 2012 Ann, Old Courthouse Art Ctr, Woodstock, Ill, 2012, Nature 2013, Light Space & Time Online Gallery, Jupiter, Fla, 2013, Luminous Language, Foundry Art Ctr, St Charles, Mo, 2013. *Teaching:* Instr drawing & graphic design, Genesee Community Col, Batavia, NY, 75-77; instr computer graphics & design, Ohlone Col, Fremont, Calif, 91-. *Awards:* Community Prog Grant Award, Burlington in Transition, Mayor's Coun Arts, Burlington, Vt, 86. *Media:* Etching, Watercolor, Digital, Photography

FOHR, JENNY
PAINTER, PRINTMAKER
b New York, NY. *Study:* Hunter Col, BA; Alfred Univ; Univ Colo, MA; City Col. *Work:* Norfolk Mus, Va; Long Beach Island Found Arts & Sci, NJ; Dr Wardell Pomeroy, NY; Oakland Mus, Calif; Charles Suter, Ciba-Geigy, NY. *Exhib:* Solo exhibs, Chautauqua Art Asn Galleries, NY, 60 & Brooklyn Mus, 61; Nat Asn Women Artists, Chauteau de la Napoule, France, 65; Nat Asn Women Artists Traveling Show, India, 66; NJ State Mus, Trenton, 68; Am Color Print Soc Traveling Show, 72. *Teaching:* Asst instr sculpture, Brooklyn Mus, 49-51; instr art, Beekman Hill Sch, 69-81. *Awards:* Samuel Mann Award, Am Soc Contemp Artists, 71; May Granick Award, Nat Asn Women Artists, 75; Doris Kreindlr Award, 81; The Alvin & Co Award, 83. *Bibliog:* Article, New York News, 76. *Mem:* Am Soc Contemp Artists (pres, secy, bd dir); Nat Asn Women Artists (secy, jury chmn, dir); Painters & Sculptors Soc NJ (selection jury, bd); Am Color Print Soc; New York Soc Women Artists (dir, cat chmn). *Media:* Miscellaneous Media. *Mailing Add:* 165 E 32 St Apt 5E New York NY 10016

FOLDA, JAROSLAV (THAYER), III
HISTORIAN
b Baltimore, Md, July 25, 1940. *Study:* Princeton Univ, AB, 62; Johns Hopkins Univ, PhD, 68. *Teaching:* From asst prof to prof medieval art, Univ NC, Chapel Hill, 68-78, prof, 78-, chmn, 83-87 & N Ferebee Taylor prof art hist, 96-2008, prof emer, 2008-. *Awards:* Nat Endowment Humanities, 73-74, 81-82 & 98-99; Guggenheim Fel, 88-89; Nat Humanities Ctr Fel, 88-89, 98-99, 2007; Haskins Medal, Medieval Acad Am, 99. *Bibliog:* Jaroslav Folda (auth), Contemporary Authors, Gale Reference, 2007; Resources for the Study of the Crusades, Queen Mary Coll, Univ London. *Mem:* Medieval Acad Am; Coll Art Asn Am; Int Ctr Medieval Art; Soc for the Study of the Crusades and the Latin East; ASOR; US Nat Byzantine Comt. *Res:* Medieval art of the High and Late Middle Ages, especially Crusader art, 1098-1291. *Publ:* Auth, Crusader Manuscript Illumination at St Jean d'Acre, Princeton Univ Press, 76; contribr, K M Setton (ed), A History of the Crusaders, Vol 4, Univ Wis Press, 77; auth, The Nazareth Capitals and the Crusader Church of the Annunciation, CAA Monograph, 42, 86; The Art of the Crusaders in the Holy Land: 1098-1187, Cambridge Univ Press, 95; Crusader Art in the Holy Land, from the Third Crusade to the Fall of Acre: 1187-1291, Cambridge Univ Press, 2005; Crusader Art, Lund Humphries, 2008; and others. *Mailing Add:* 750 Weaver Dairy Rd #228 Chapel Hill NC 27514

FOLEY, DAVID E
PAINTER
b New Orleans, La, Mar 16, 1954. *Study:* Univ New Orleans, BA, 77; Univ Colo, MFA, 80. *Work:* ATT, Denver; USA Ins Corp, Colo Springs; Dushanbe Hall of Econ Achieuments, Tajikistan; Pinnocol Insurance, Denver; State Colo Collection, Denver; and var collections in US, Puerto Rico, Can, Mex, Australia, China, Israel, Ger, France, Eng & Tajikistand. *Comn:* Painting, Theodore Gentner, Portland, Ore, 2001; painting, Ted & Robin Haughland, Denver, 2002; painting, Pinnocol Insurance, Denver, 2002; painting, Terri Gillat, Boulder, Colo, 2006; painting, Dr Christine Koval, Rochester, NY, 2009; painting, Barbara Bellman Wash DC, 2010; painting, Karen Calvert, San Antonio, Tex, 2010; painting, Kathryn Mann, Bartlesville, Okla, 2012; painting, William Sweet, Estes Park, Colo, 2013; painting, Rhonda Low, San Antonio, Tex, 2014. *Exhib:* Colo State Art, Aspen Art Mus, 89; A Celebration of the Desert, Desert Caballeros Western Mus, Wickenburg, Ariz, 99; Paintings of the West Landscape, Arvada Ctr Arts, Colo, 94; The New West, Sangre de Christo Art Center, Pueblo, Colo, 96; Landscapes of NMex, Santa Fe, 2006; Landscapes of Colo, Denver, 2007; Toast, Univ Colo, Boulder, 2007; Landscapes of Colo, Ctr Visual Art, Metro State Coll Gallery, Denver, Colo, 2007. *Awards:* Purchase Award, 8th Nat Print & Drawing Exhib, Minot State Coll, 78. *Bibliog:* The Artist and the Am Landscape, First Glance Bks, 98; Landscapes of NMex, 2006 & Landscapes of Colo, 2007, Freco Fine Art Publ. *Mem:* Denver Art Mus; Boulder Mus Contemp Art. *Media:* Acrylic, Watercolor. *Publ:* Dr Lew Deitch (auth), Artbook of the New West, 2007; Virginia Campbell (auth), Southwest Art, 2/2007; Am Art Collector, 2010. *Dealer:* Sugarman-Peterson Gallery 130 W Palace Ave Santa Fe NMex 87501; Mary Williams Fine Art 5311 Western Ave #112 Boulder CO 80301. *Mailing Add:* 5045 Ingersoll Pl Boulder CO 80303

FOLEY, TIMOTHY ALBERT
ART DEALER
b New Orleans, La, May 11, 1947. *Study:* Loyola Univ, New Orleans; Univ New Orleans, BA (anthrop), 71. *Awards:* Distinguished Alumni, Univ New Orleans, 91. *Mem:* Am Soc Appraisers. *Specialty:* Quality contemp art as well as important 19th and 20th century art; Southern artists of the 19th and early 20th centuries

FOLK, TOM C
ART DEALER, HISTORIAN
b Oct 30, 1955. *Study:* Seton Hall Univ, with Petra Chu, BA, 1977; Rutgers Univ with Matthew Baigell, MA, 1980; City Univ NY with William Gennis, PhD, 1987. *Work:* James Michener Mus, Doylestown, Pa. *Exhib:* The Pa School of Landscape Painting: An Original America Impressionism, Allentown Art Mus & Corcoran Gallery, Wash, DC, 1983; A Woman of Genius, NJ State Mus, Trenton, 1990; Father of Neer Hope Modernism, Allentown Art Mus, 2003. *Teaching:* adj prof, Rutgers Univ, Newark, NJ, 1995-2000; adj prof, Caldwell Col, NJ, 1998-2001; adj prof, St Peter's Col, Jersey City, NJ, 2001-. *Awards:* Juror for Allied Artists Exhib, NYC, 2001. *Bibliog:* Denise M Topolnicki (auth), The Fine Art of Fraud, Money Magazine, 9/1986; Ann E Berman (auth), Bucks County Impressionists, Architectural Digest, 11/1994. *Mem:* Appraiser's Assoc of Am (assoc mem); Potteries of Trenton Soc. *Publ:* auth, The Pennsylvania Impressionists, Assoc Univ Presses, 1997. *Mailing Add:* 14 Pheasant Hill Dr Far Hills NJ 07931

FOLMAN, LIZA
PRINTMAKER, PAINTER
b New York, NY, Feb 25, 1951. *Study:* State Univ New York, BFA, 72; Boston Univ, MFA, 76. *Work:* Mus Fine Arts, Boston, Mass; Boston Pub Libr, Boston, Mass; Bibliotheque Nationale, Paris, France; The Coll Bd Collection, New York; The Reader's Digest Collection, New York; DeCordova Mus, Lincoln, Mass. *Exhib:* Collector's Gallery Exhibit, McNay Art Inst, San Antonio, Tex, 82; The Drawing Show, Boston Ctr Arts, Boston, Mass, 84 & 93; Drawings from Boston, DeCordova Mus, Lincoln, Mass, 87; solo exhibs, Randall Beck Gallery, Boston, 87, 89 & 94, Hampden Gallery, Univ Mass, Amherst, 97 & Scuola Internazionale di Gratica, Venice, Italy, 2006; 165th Ann Exhib, Nat Acad Design, New York, 90; Estampes et Livres d'Artistes du Xxeme Sicle: Enrichissements du Cabinet des Estampes, 78-88, Bibliotheque Nationale, Paris, France, 92; Women in Watercolor, Boston Pub Libr, Boston, Mass, 93, 96 & 99; Immortalized, The Art Complex Mus, Duxbury, Mass, 98; Proof in Print, Boston Pub Libr, 2001. *Teaching:* Instr etching & drawing, Mass Coll Art, Boston, Mass, 82-83 & 86-88; teaching assoc, Boston Univ, 89-91; prof, Art Inst Boston, Lesley Univ, Boston, Mass, 90-. *Awards:* Fulbright Fel, 84-85; MacDowell Colony Artist's Fel, 84-85; Blanche E Colman Award, 98. *Mem:* Boston Printmakers. *Media:* Etching, Watercolor. *Publ:* Christine Temin (auth), Perspectives, 89 & Artists share feelings, The Boston Globe, 99; Cate McQuaid (auth), Prints Charming & Significant, The Boston Globe, 97; Joanne Silver (auth), When art grieves, Boston Herald, 99; Proof in Print: A Community of Printmaking Studios, Trustees Boston Pub Libr, 2001; Michael Cochran (auth), RI Critics pic, Arts Media, Boston, 2004. *Mailing Add:* Art Inst Boston Lesley Univ 700 Beacon St Boston MA 02215

FOLSOM, FRED GORHAM, III
PAINTER, CONSERVATOR, WRITER
b Washington, DC, July 31, 1945. *Study:* Pratt Inst, NY, with Martha Erlebacher, 64-67; Sch Visual Arts, NY, 67; Corcoran Sch Art, Washington, 69. *Comn:* Fred Folsom Sculpture, Univ Colo, Boulder, Colo, 2004. *Exhib:* Md Biennial Exhib, Baltimore Mus Art, 74 & 85; solo exhibs, Gallery K, Washington, 80, 82, 84 & 88, WPA, 92 & Md Art Place, Baltimore, 93; Wash-Moscow Art Exchange, Tretya Kov-Gallery, Russia, 85; The Washington Show, Corcoran Gallery Art, 85; Black Art, Rockville Art Place, Md, 95; Gallery Stendahl, NY, 97; Artists Mus, Washington, 97; Montgomery Coll, Md, 99; Strathmore Hall, Md, 2002; Arts Club of Washington, DC, 2002; True Colors, Meridian House, DC, Atlanta, Cairo, Casablanca, Berlin, Vienna, Dallas, 2002-2006; Folsom Sculpture, Univ Colo, Boulder, Colo, 2004; Light Street Gallery, Baltimore, 2007; Momento Gallery, Washington, DC, 2009; Katzen Art Ctr, Am Univ, DC, 2010; Maryland Biennial, Univ Md, 2011; The Constant Artist, Am Univ Mus, Wash DC, 2012. *Collection Arranged:* Corcoran Gallery, Washington; Coach Fred Folsom Sculpture, Univ Colo, Boulder, Colo, 2004; Dimock Gallery, George Washington Univ; Hickory Mus Art, NC; Wells Col, Aurora, NY; Mayor of Silver Spring Sculpture, Md, 91; Superior Court, Washington, DC; George Mason Univ, Fairfaz, Va, 2004. *Pos:* Actor, Robert Wilson Theater Productions, New York, 66; conservator & owner, Art Restoration Ctr, Wheaton, Md, 73-. *Awards:* Md State Arts Coun, 81, 82, 87, 89, 96 & 2000; Mayor's Comn Arts, Baltimore, 82; Individual Grant Visual Arts, Nat Endowment Arts, 85; Md Gov's Citations, 1982, 1996, 2000; Bader Fund, 2005. *Bibliog:* Articles in Washington Post, 82, 84-85, 87, 91-92, 97, 99 & 2000, 2002, 2004, 2010, 2012, Art Internat, 79, 81, 83; Art in America, 80, 81, 93; Christians in the Arts, Art & Soul, 2000; G Wolfe (auth), Image Mag, 1992, Beauty Will Save the World, 2011. *Media:* Oil, Linen. *Publ:* Cover illusr, The poet John Pauker, Art Int, 1/79; auth, (cover story) The Man Who Made New York, Financial Hist Mag, 2000; ARTSO, Lid Mag, #4, 2007; auth, 100 DC Artists, Campello, 2011; Artiste, Kindle, 2013. *Mailing Add:* 212 Hillsboro Dr Wheaton MD 20902

FOLSOM, ROSE
CALLIGRAPHER, WRITER
b Madison, Wis, July 31, 1953. *Study:* Pvt study with Sheila Waters, 74-75; Rochester Inst Technol, calligraphy master class with Hermann Zapf, 79-80. *Work:* H M Queen Elizabeth II; Artery Orgn, Bethesda; Houghton Rare Book Libr, Harvard Univ. *Comn:* Nat Gallery Art, Washington; US Dept State. *Exhib:* Solo exhibs, Foundry Gallery, Washington, & Minn Ctr Book Arts, 96; Scene in DC, Amos Eno Gallery, NY, 88; Traditions of the Pen, Smithsonian Inst, 94; The Book as Art VIII, Nat Mus Women Arts, 96. *Collection Arranged:* Calligraphic Books, Nat Mus Women in the Arts, 92. *Pos:* Owner, Folsom Calligraphy Studio, 73-; Washington corresp, Calligraphy Rev Mag, Normàn, Okla, 85-93. *Teaching:* Instr, Washington Calligraphers Guild, 78-; lectr hist calligraphy, Nat Mus Am Art, Renwick Gallery, 90, Smithsonian Inst, 92 & 94. *Awards:* Hermann Zapf Educ Fund Scholar, 93. *Bibliog:* Jane Snow (auth), Living treasures, Washingtonian Mag, 8/88; Michael Welzenbach (auth), Bare bones beauty, Washington Post, 10/7/89; Paul Richard (auth), The soul of the scribe, Washington Post, 8/11/96. *Mem:* Washington Calligraphers Guild. *Media:* Ink on Paper. *Publ:* Illusr, International Calligraphy Today, Watson-Guptill, 82; auth, The Calligraphers' Dictionary, Thames & Hudson, 90; illusr, The Creative Stroke, Rockport, 93; Brush Lettering, Lyons & Burford, 94. *Mailing Add:* 212 Hillsboro Dr Silver Spring MD 20902-3126

FONDAW, RON
SCULPTOR
b Paducah, Ky, Apr 25, 1954. *Study:* Memphis Coll Art, Tenn, BFA, 76; Univ Ill, Champaign, MFA, 78. *Work:* Renwick Gallery, Smithsonian Inst, Washington; Columbus Mus Fine Art, Ohio; Tenn State Arts Comn, Nashville; John Michael Kohler Arts Ctr, Sheboygan, Wis; Richard & Joy Haft, Miami, Fla; Dr Carl Djerassi, Woodside, Calif; Martin Z Margulies, Grove Isle, Fla; Moving ahead, City of Greensboro, NC, 2009; Given, a device for seeing, Key West, 2010; Which is a Wheel, Kirkland Art Ctr, Decatur, Ill, 2010. *Comn:* Art in Public Places, Ghost Islands, Key Biscayne, Fla, 87; outdoor sculpture, Fragments, Southeastern Ctr Contemp Art, Winston-Salem, NC, 87; outdoor sculpture, NAOS, Coconut Grove, Fla, purchased by City of Miami, Coconut Grove Asn, 88; outdoor sculptures, Earth Structures, EHampton Ctr Contemp Art, NY, 88; Now and Never, Socrates Sculpture

Park, Long Island City, NY, 89; Ferro's Dream, Fla Int Univ, Miami, 90; The Giving Tree, St Louis Art Mus, 98; Whisper Walls, Cedarhurst Sculpture Park, Mt Vernon, IL; Who We Are, Arts in Transit, St Louis, 2003; The Langlow Brisge, Henry Lay Sculpture Park, Bowlingreen, MO, 2001; The Vertical Loop, Bi-State Development, St Louis, MO, 2003; gift to the city of Greensboro, Moving Ahead, Camela Foundation, NC. *Exhib:* Am Ceramics Now, Everson Mus Art, Syracuse, NY, traveling juried exhib: Am Craft Mus, NY & Crocker Art Mus, Sacramento, Calif, 87; Am Ceramics Now, traveling, De Cordova & Dana Mus & park, Lincoln; Birmingham Mus Art, Ala, 89; solo exhibs, Of Iron and Earth, Atlantic Ctr Arts, New Smyrna Beach, Fla, 89, Ron Fondaw, drawings, Nat Acad Sci, Washington, 90 & Fusion, Clay Studio, Philadelphia, 95; BMW Gallery, NY, 90; Twenty-Five in Miami, Miami Dade Community Col, S Campus Gallery, Fla, 90; Abstraction, Eve Mannes Gallery, Atlanta, Ga, 90; Buildings with Clay, Hoffman Gallery, Ore Sch Art & Crafts, 90; 3 Sampson Gallery, Stetson Univ, Deland, Fla, 90; Art in Industry, John M Kohler Art Ctr, Sheboygan, Wis, 90; Kansas City Artists Coalition, Kansas City, MO, 2002; Ron Fondaw, Northern Clay Ctr, Minn, MN, 2004; and others; Artist Invitational, Univ NC. *Teaching:* Vis instr art, Ohio Univ, 78; assoc prof art, Univ Miami, Coral Gables, Fla, 79-; lectr, Ohio State Univ, 83, Univ Gainesville, Fla, 84, Chicago Art Inst, Ill, 86, Ft Lauderdale Mus Art, Fla, Ormond Mem Art Mus & Tokyo Nat Univ Fine Art, Japan, 87, Chautauqua Sch Art, NY, 88 & Chicago Art Inst, Ill 89 & Hollufgard Kulturcenter, Odense, Denmark, 90; vis prof sculpture, Univ NC, Chapel Hill, 94-; prof art, Washington Univ, St Louis, currently. *Awards:* Guggenheim Fel, 85; Nat Endowment Art Fel, 88 & 89; Awards in Visual Arts 8, 89; New Forms, Fla, 90; Fla Arts Coun Fel, 92; Kranzberg Award, 98; Pollack-Krasner Award, 97; Kransberg Award, St Louis Art Mus, MO, 98. *Bibliog:* Paula Harper (auth), Sculpture-Ron Fondaw, Am Ceramics, Vol 2, 4, 84; Helen Kohen (auth), Staring and shivering, Art News, 6/81; Susan Peterson (auth), The Art and Craft of Clay, 91, Contemporary Ceramics, 2001, Prentice Hall; Julie Stevenson (auth) Weathering Change, Sculpture Magazine, Sept 2000; Paula Harper (auth), Sculpture on the Edge (pg 72), Art in America, 2006. *Media:* Ceramics. *Mailing Add:* 6760 Chamberlain Ave Saint Louis MO 63130

FONTANALS-CISNEROS, ELLA
PATRON
Pos: Founder, Together Found, 1989, bd mem; founder, Together Networks, 1995; co-founder, Cisneros-Fontanals Art Found, Miami, 2002-; founder, Miami Art Cent, 2003-; bd mem, Miami Art Mus, Am Patrons of Tate, Cintos Found, US Artist, Int Women's Forum. *Awards:* Spectrum Philosophy Award, Am Red Cross, 2003; Visionary Award, Mus Arts & Design, 2007; Women Together Award, United Nations, 2008; Top 200 Collectors, Artnews Mag, 2007, 2008, 2009. *Collection:* Contemporary art with strong representations of geometric abstract art from Latin America, video art, and contemporary photography focusing on architecture. *Mailing Add:* 5960 SW 57 Ave Miami FL 33143

FOOLERY, TOM
ASSEMBLAGE ARTIST
b Green Bay, Wis, Aug 29, 1947. *Study:* Self-taught. *Work:* Clorox Corp, Oakland; Ara Mark Corp, Los Angeles; Kaiser Permanente; Imagery Estate Winery; and others. *Comn:* Murals, St Francis Mem Hosp, San Francisco, 79-81. *Exhib:* Humor in Art, Los Angeles Inst Contemp Art, 81; solo exhibs, William Sawyer Gallery, San Francisco, 81 & Jacqueline Anhalt Gallery, Los Angeles, 82; Dobrick Gallery, Chicago, 83, Tortue Gallery, Santa Monica, 90 & 92, Fresno Art Mus, 91, Holter Art, Helena Mont, 94; Anxious Interiors, Laguna Beach Mus Art, Calif, & traveling, 84; Miniature Environments, Whitney Mus at Phillip Morris, 89; 40 Yrs of California Assemblage, Univ Calif Los Angeles, (traveling), 89; Tortue Gallery, Santa Monica, Calif, 90, 92; Napa Valley Col, 91; Fresno Art Mus, 91; Holter Mus Art, Helena, Mont, 95; Mont Arts Coun, 2001; Botanica, Bozeman, Mont, 2002; Sutton West Gallery, Missoula, Mont, 2004; Hallie Ford Mus Art, Willamette Univ, Salem, Ore, 2006; group exhibs, Paris Gibson Square Mus Art, 2001, Sutton West Gallery, Missoula, Mont, 2002, Holter Mus Art, Helena, Mont, 2002-2003, Custer Co Art Ctr, Miles City, Mont, 2003-2004; Hallie Ford Mus, Salem, Ore, 2006; Nicolayen Mus Art, Casper, Wyo, 2006; Micaela Gallery, San Francisco, 2006. *Awards:* fel, Mont Arts Coun, 2002. *Bibliog:* John Russell (auth), NY Times, 8/11/89; Andrew Olds (auth), Miniature Environments, ID, 11/89; Elaine de Mann (auth), Carrot & Schtick, Air & Space, 2/91. *Media:* All. *Mailing Add:* Ravin' Raven Rd Dillon MT 59725

FOOSANER, JUDITH
EDUCATOR, PAINTER
b Sacramento, Calif, Aug 10, 1940. *Study:* Univ Calif, Berkeley, BA, 64 & MA, 68. *Work:* Newport Harbor Art Mus, Newport Beach, Calif; Everson Mus, Syracuse, NY; Albuquerque Mus, NMex; Contemp Mus, Honolulu; Crocker Art Mus, Sacramento, Calif; Oakland Art Mus, Calif; San Diego Fine Arts Mus; Ark Arts Ctr, Little Rock; and numerous corp collections. *Exhib:* Laguna Beach Mus, Calif, 67; Calif Palace Legion Honor, San Francisco, 69; Wenger Gallery, San Francisco, 71, 73, 79-80, 82; Bellevue Art Mus, Wash, 76; M H DeYoung Mem Mus, San Francisco, 77; Oakland Mus, Calif, 81; Space Gallery, Los Angeles, 83, 85, 88, 95; Ark Arts Ctr, 90; R B Stevenson Gallery, La Jolla, Calif, 93, 95, 97, 2001, 2006; Louis Stern Fine Arts, West Hollywood, Calif, 97, 2000-2001, 2004; Carl Cherry Ctr Fine Arts, Carmel, Calif, 2003; Spheris Gallery, Bellows Falls, Conn, 2004; Gallery 276, San Francisco, 2005; Buschlen Mowatt Galleries, Palm Desert, Calif, 2006; JAYJAY, Sacramento, 2007; Hunsaker Schlesinger, Santa Monica, Calif, 2007; and many others. *Teaching:* Prof fine arts, Calif Coll Arts & Crafts, Oakland, 70-75, 77-93, 94-2001, 2003-; vis asst prof art, Univ Calif, Berkeley, 75-77; Wimbledon Sch Art, London, 93; Univ Calif, Davis, 2002. *Awards:* Yaddo Fel, Spring Residence, Saratoga Springs, NY, 83; Fel, Artist in Residence, Va Ctr Creative Arts, Sweet Briar, Va, 89. *Media:* Oil, Charcoal

FOOTE, HOWARD REED
ARTIST, PAINTER
b Richmond, Ind, Dec 15, 1936. *Study:* Toledo Mus Art, Ohio, 54-55; Sch Mus Fine Arts, Boston, 55-57; San Francisco Art Inst, BFA, 60; Stanford Univ, MA, 70; additional study with Nathan Oliveira. *Work:* Achenbach Found, Palace of the Legion of Honor, San Francisco; City of Leeds, Eng; City of San Francisco; Stanford Univ. *Exhib:* Bay Area Printmakers Soc Fourth Nat Exhib, Oakland Mus, Calif, 58; 1970 Peace Exhib, Philadelphia Mus Art, 70; San Francisco Art Inst Centennial Exhib, Palace of the Legion of Honor, San Francisco, 71; Four Printmakers, San Francisco Mus Art, 71; 18th Nat Print Exhib, Brooklyn Mus, NY, 72; San Francisco Area Printmakers, Cincinnati Art Mus, Ohio, 73; Interstices, San Jose Art Mus, Calif & Cranbrook Acad Art Mus, Bloomfield Hills, Mich, 75; Gallery Route One, Point Reyes Station, Calif, 98; Smith-Andersen N, San Rafael, Calif, 2007. *Teaching:* Instr printmaking, Acad Art, San Francisco, 70-90 Calif State Univ, Hayward, 71-72; instr printmaking, drawing & 3-D design, Coll Notre Dame, Belmont, Calif, 75-84. *Media:* Artist, Painter, Paintmaker, Woodworker. *Publ:* Contribr, Ramparts Mag, 6/70; BYTE, 9/81. *Mailing Add:* PO Box 311 Tomales CA 94971

FORBES, DONNA MARIE
MUSEUM DIRECTOR
b Albion, Nebr, Mar 19, 1929. *Study:* Mont State Univ; Pratt Inst; Eastern Mont Col, BS (art educ), 52; Harvard Summer Inst in Arts Admin; Univ Calif, Berkeley, Mus Mgt Inst, 83. *Collection Arranged:* The Christmas Story, 78, The Cowboy, 78, Using Paper, 80, Chinese Robes: 1750-1900, 82 & The William Andrews Clark Collection: Treasures of a Copper King, 88, Yellowstone Art Ctr, Billings, Mont. *Pos:* Dir, Yellowstone Art Ctr, Billings, Mont, 74- & 98-; mem, Eastern Mont Col Found Bd, 74-79 & 82-, pres, 78; mem selection comt, Downtown Redevelopment Bd, Billings, Mont, 86; mem, Downtown Coordr Coun, Billings, Mont, 86. *Teaching:* Instr design & art educ, Eastern Mont Col, 52-53. *Mem:* Art Mus Asn; Am Asn Mus; Mont Art Gallery Dirs Asn (adv exec bd, 78-, pres, 80-82); Mountain-Plains Mus Asn; Am Fedn Arts (bd dir, 87-97). *Mailing Add:* 1116 Eighth St W Billings MT 59101

FORBES, JOHN ALLISON
HISTORIAN, PAINTER
b Evansburg, Alta, Sept 19, 1922. *Study:* Univ Alta, BEd, 48, MEd, 51; Univ London, associateship, 56; Univ Iowa, MA, 67. *Collection Arranged:* Bart Pragnell-Watercolours, Univ Art Gallery, Edmonton, 67; J B Taylor-Memorial (auth, catalog), Edmonton Art Gallery, 73. *Teaching:* prof emeritus, art & design, Univ Alberta. *Mem:* Royal Soc Arts, London; Univs Art Asn Can; Friends Univ Alberta Mus & Collections; Canadian Aviation Hist Soc. *Media:* Watercolor, Acrylics. *Res:* Western Canadian landscape painters; military art. *Publ:* Coauth, Mountain landscapes of J B Taylor, Can Alpine J, Vol 57, 74; auth, Douglas Haynes (exhib catalog), Glenbow Art Gallery, Calgary, 74; Robert Sinclair (exhib catalog), Aggregation Gallery, Toronto, 76. *Mailing Add:* 11523-77 Ave Edmonton AB T6G 0M2 Canada

FORD, JOHN
PAINTER, SCULPTOR
b Washington, DC, Mar 2, 1950. *Study:* Self-taught. *Work:* Oakland Mus Art; Prudential Insurance Co, Newark, NJ; Nashville Med Corp, Tenn; Sidney Lewis Collection, Richmond, Va. *Comn:* Trap sculpture, Kenmare Sq, NY. *Exhib:* Whitney Mus Am Art Biennial, 75; Aspects of Abstract, Crocker Art Mus, Sacramento, Calif, 79; Coastal Currents, Ctr Arts, Corpus Christi, Tex, 81; Sacramento Connection, Laguna Gloria Mus, Laguna Beach, Calif, 82; Jersey City Art Mus, NJ, 82; solo exhib, State Univ NY, Purchase, 82. *Teaching:* Lectr, Bakersfield State Univ, 77, Sacramento State Univ, 78 & C W Post Ctr, Long Island Univ, 83. *Awards:* Artists Fel, Nat Endowment Arts, 82. *Bibliog:* Thomas Albright (auth), Sleepers and spectacles, Art News, 9/79; Vivien Raynor (auth), article, New York Times, 82; Thomas Albright (auth), Art in the San Francisco Bay Area, Univ Calif Press, 85. *Media:* Acrylic, Oil; All Media. *Mailing Add:* 28 Overlook Terr Simsbury CT 06070

FORD, JOHN GILMORE
COLLECTOR
b Baltimore, Md. *Study:* Baltimore City Col, degree; Johns Hopkins Univ; Loyola Col; Md Inst Coll Art, BFA. *Exhib:* Collection Indo-Asian art, Walters Art Gallery, Baltimore, 71. *Pos:* Nat vpres, Am Inst Interior Designers, 70-; Sr appraiser, specializing in Asian art, Am Soc Appraisers. *Bibliog:* P Pal (auth), Indo-Asian art, 71, Walters Art Gallery, Apollo Mag & Connoisseur Mag. *Mem:* Am Fedn Arts; Asia Soc; Am Soc Appraisers. *Interests:* Indian, Nepalese, Tibetan, Javanese, Chinese & Japanese bronzes, stone sculptures and paintings, contemp Asian art. *Collection:* Desire and Devotion: Art from India, Nepal and Tibet from the John and Berthe Ford Collection, Walters Art Mus, 2001; Exhib Santa Barbara Mus Art, 2002; Exhib Albuquerque Mus Art, 2002; Exhib Birmingham Mus Art, 2003; Exhib Hong Kong Mus Art, 2003. *Mailing Add:* 2601 N Charles St Baltimore MD 21218-4586

FORD, KIANGA K
INSTALLATION SCULPTOR
b Washington, DC, 1973. *Study:* Univ Dar es Salaam, Tanzania, Int Student Exchange Prog, 1992-93; Georgetown Univ, Washington, BA, 1994; Univ Calif, Los Angeles, MFA, 2003; Univ Calif, Santa Cruz, MA/PhD. *Exhib:* Solo exhibs include New Wight Gallery, Univ Calif Los Angeles, 2003, Lisa Dent Gallery, San Francisco, 2005, Raid Projs, Los Angeles, 2005, Occidental Coll, Los Angeles, 2005; group exhibs include What Do You See at Night, Track 16, Bergamot Station, Santa Monica, Calif, 2003; Sound Madness, Banff Ctr, Alberta, Canada, 2005; Frequency, Studio Mus Harlem, New York, 2005; Metro Pictures, Mus Contemp Art, Miami, 2006; Calif Biennial, Orange County Mus Art, Newport Beach, Calif, 2006. *Awards:* Creative Capital Found Grant, 2008. *Dealer:* Bernice Steinbaum Gallery 3550 N Miami Ave Miami FL 33127

FORD, LISA COLLADO See Collado, Lisa

FORD, ROCHELLE
SCULPTOR
b New Kensington, Pa, Jul 18, 1936. *Study:* Allegheny Col, Meadville, Pa, 54-56; Univ Pittsburgh Pa, BS, 56-58. *Work:* Abstract Sculpture, Ramsell Corp, Pleasanton, Calif; Claremont Sch, Gate to bldg entrance, Claremont, Calif; Endowed Chair, Mass Inst Technol, Cambridge, Mass; Multiple Tree Sculpture, City of Oakland, Calif; ITT, NY City; Soroka Med Center of the Aegir, Israel (2 story high tree in entrance). *Comn:* Congresswoman Barbara Lee, Oakland Calif; Dr & Mrs Bill Cosby, Santa Monica, Calif; Jim Burch, Mayor Palo Alto Calif. *Exhib:* Group exhib, Long Beach Mus Art, Calif, 98, Triton Mus Art, Santa Clara, Calif, 99, San Jose Inst Contemp Art, San Jose, Calif, 2000, San Jose Mus Art, Calif, 2000, Iris Gerald Ctr for Visual Arts, Stanford, Calif, 2001, Can Col, Cupertino, Calif, 2002-2004; Solo exhib, Palo Alto Medical Found, Palo Alto, Calif, 94, 3COM Corp, Santa Clara, Calif, 99, Stanford Univ, Calif, 2001, Gallery Blu, Santa Clara, Calif, 2004; Koret Gallery, Palo Alto, Calif, 2000; La Galerie Int, Palo Alto, Calif, 2000; Period Gallery, Omaha, Nebr, 2002; Classic Art & Design, Pacifica, Calif, 2005; Soco Gallery, Half Moon Bay, Calif, 2006. *Teaching:* Gallery Angels Camp, Calif, 95; Design Consortium, Cincinnati, Ohio, 99; Montclair Fine Art Gallery, Oakland, Calif, 99. *Awards:* Nat Art Calendar Mag Award, Sallsbury, Md, 2000; Soho Int Art Award, NY, 2001; Distillery Literary J Cover Award, Lynchburg, Tenn, 2002. *Media:* Recycled Metal, Mixed Media. *Publ:* Sitting Pretty, Sunset Mag, 98; auth, Artistic Splendor, Fine Living TV, 2003; Garden Rooms, Better Homes & Gardens, 2003; auth, Small Space Gardens, Harper Design Int, 2004; auth, Dream Decks & Patios Book, A Hacienda with Hue, 2005; auth, Pacific Horticulture, Front Gardens of Palo Alto, 2006; auth, Before & After Garden Makeovers, Sunset Bks, 2006. *Dealer:* Lillian White Shamwari Gallery 4176 Piedmont Ave Okland CA 94611. *Mailing Add:* 1155 Waverley St Palo Alto CA 94301

FORD NUSSBAUM DRILL, SHEILA
ART DEALER, CONSULTANT
b Philadelphia, Pa, Mar 9, 1940. *Study:* Univ Pa; New York Univ; New Sch Social Res, New York. *Pos:* Owner, Sheila Nussbaum Gallery, Millburn, NJ, currently; trustee, Montclair Art Mus. *Teaching:* Guest Lectr, Parsons Sch Design, NY. *Awards:* 1987 Woman of the Year, Bus & Prof Women Millburn-Short Hills, Inc; Bus Watch Award, Business J, NJ, 88. *Bibliog:* Patricia Malarcher (auth), New luster for Essex, NY Times, 11/7/82; Yolanda Cifarelli (auth), New Jersey gallery targets, Crafts Report, 1/85; Katherine Kaye (auth), Sheila Nussbaum: At Home with Art, Star Ledger, 11/17/89. *Mem:* Am Craft Coun. *Specialty:* Contemporary Art American crafts and art jewelry; young emerging artists. *Mailing Add:* 2 Claridge Dr Apt 10EW Verona NJ 07044

FOREMAN, LAURA
CONCEPTUAL ARTIST, SCULPTOR
b Los Angeles, Calif. *Study:* Parsons Sch Design, New York, ongoing studies since 1979. *Work:* Antwerp Mus, Belg; Storefront for Art & Archit, NY; Vermont Studio Colony, Vt. *Comn:* Time Coded Woman (art video), Channel 13 WNET-TV, NY, 78 & Brooklyn Acad Mus, 82; art video installation, New Sch Social Res, NY, 78; art holograms, Holographic Film Found, NY, 83; public art sculptor, 5 parks in New York City, JBR Found, 90. *Exhib:* Souyun Yi Gallery, NY, 89 & 91; Barbara Krakow Gallery, Boston, 91; Cityarts Show, Bronx Mus, 91-92; Kleinert Arts Ctr, Woodstock, 92; Wustum Mus, Wis, 93; Lookout Mountain Sculpture Park Maquette Traveling Exhib, Italy, Ger, Denmark & Bulgaria, 94-96. *Pos:* Consult, Nat Endowment Humanities, 70-75; judge, Television Emmy Awards, 79-81; visual arts juror, Ill Arts Coun, 85, Seattle Arts Comn, 95. *Teaching:* Instr conceptual art, performance art & creative thinking, New Sch Social Res, New York, 79-; performance art, Chapin Sch, New York, 92, conceptual art, 92 & 93, Metrop Mus Art, 94. *Awards:* Residency, Lookout Mountain Sculpture Park, Pa, 94; Contemp Artists Ctr, Mass, 96; Leighton Artists Colony, Banff, Can, 99. *Bibliog:* Georgia Dullea (auth), Artfully built nests await feathering, NY Times, 4/12/90; Leslie Garisto (auth), From Bauhaus to Birdhouse, Harper Collins, 2/92; Tucker J Coombe (auth), The Artists' Life, Artist's Mag, 4/92. *Mem:* Artists Talk on Art, NY. *Media:* Mixed Media. *Publ:* Confrontation, Literary Mag, fall 92; Santa Clara rev, Another Chicago Mag, fall 93; Pig Iron Anthology, spring 94; Collection of Foremans Work, Sundown Books, spring 96. *Mailing Add:* c/o Rich Keene 262 Mott St Apt 5 SR New York NY 10012-6108

FORESTA, MERRY A
CURATOR
b New York, NY, Aug 3, 50. *Study:* Cornell Univ, BA (eng lit), 71, MA (art hist), 79. *Pos:* Asst cur, painting & sculpture, Nat Mus Am Art, Smithsonian Inst, Washington, DC, 78-82, assoc cur, 83-88, cur, 88-93, sr cur, 94-; chmn, Smithsonian Comt Photog, 95-. *Teaching:* Various lectrs, symposia & conferences, 84-96. *Awards:* Smithsonian Res Opportunity Fund Recipient, spring 85; Smithsonian Workshop Grant, 2/86; Smithsonian Scholarly Studies Res Grant, 2/86, renewed 2/87 & 2/92. *Mem:* Soc Photog Educ; Coll Art Asn. *Publ:* Auth, Perpetual motif: The art of Man Ray, 12/88; Irving Penn: The Passion of Certainties, for Irving Penn: Master Images at the Smithsonian, Smithsonian Inst Press, 90; Between home and heaven: Contemporary American landscape photography, 5/92; coauth (with John Wood), Secrets of the dark chamber: The art of the American daguerreotype, 6/95; American photographs: The first century, 11/96

FORGEY, BENJAMIN FRANKLIN
ARCHITECT, CRITIC
b Ashland, Ky, July 31, 1938. *Study:* Princeton Univ, BA, 60. *Pos:* Art critic, Wash Star, 67-81, art/archit critic, Wash Post, 81-. *Awards:* Fulbright fel, Japan, 1985-86. *Mem:* Int Art Critics Asn (Am sect). *Res:* 20th century art, architecture. *Publ:* Var articles in Art News Mag, 70-, Smithsonian Mag, 75-, Portfolio Mag, 78- & Aperture Mag, 79-. *Mailing Add:* Wash Post 1150 15th St NW Washington DC 20071-0002

FORMAN, ALICE
PAINTER
b New York, NY, June 1, 1931. *Study:* Cornell Univ, with Kenneth Evett & Norman Daly, BA; Art Students League, with Morris Kantor. *Exhib:* Whitney Mus Am Art, 60; White Mus Art, Cornell Univ, 61; Phoenix Gallery, NY, 66, 68, 71, 74 & 75; Marist Col, 68 & 71; Butler Inst Exhib, 72; Kornblee Gallery, 77 & 79; Am Still Life, Contemp Arts Mus, Houston, 83; and others. *Teaching:* Lectr, Marist Col, 77; vis asst prof painting & drawing, Vassar Col, 80-81. *Awards:* Nat Student Asn Regional Awards; Daniel Schnackenberg Merit Scholar, Art Students League. *Media:* Oil. *Dealer:* Kornblee Gallery 20 W 57th St New York NY 10019. *Mailing Add:* 130 E 63rd St New York NY 10021

FORMAN, SETH MICHAEL
PAINTER
Study: State Univ NY Potsdam, BA, 1984; Skidmore Coll, Saratoga Springs, NY, 1985; Sch Vis Arts, New York, MFA, 1989. *Exhib:* Solo exhibs include Penine Hart Gallery, New York, 1993, Bernard Toale Gallery, Boston, 1996, Adam Baumgold Fine Art, New York, 1997, 2000, 2003, Miller Block Gallery, Boston, 2003; group exhibs include Time Pieces, Handwerker Gallery, Ithaca, NY, 1991; Its Raining (Wo/men), Terrain, San Francisco, 1997; Five & Ten, Rotunda Gallery, Brooklyn, NY, 1998; Picturing Mod Amazon, New Mus Contemp Art, New York, 2000; Face Paint, Bucheon Gallery, San Francisco, 2005; Harlem Art Proj, Saatchi & Saatchi, New York, 2006; Road Works, Adam Baumgold Gallery, New York, 2008. *Awards:* New York Found Arts Fel, 2004, 2008. *Dealer:* Adam Baumgold Gallery 74 E 79th St New York NY 10021

FORMICOLA, JOHN JOSEPH
PAINTER, EDUCATOR
b Philadelphia, Pa, Dec 27, 1941. *Study:* Fleischer Art Mem, 56-59; Pa Acad Fine Arts, cert (Cresson Award, Schiedt Award), 64. *Work:* Philadelphia Mus Art; Cleveland Mus Art, Ohio; Miami Mus Mod Art, Fla; Mus Art, Carnegie Inst, Pittsburgh; Prudential Insurance Co Am; Exxon Corp; Mus Philadelphia Civic Ctr; Noyes Mus, NJ. *Comn:* Brandywine Graphic Workshop, Philadelphia, 82. *Exhib:* Del Art Mus, Wilmington, 78; Contemp Drawings, Philadelphia Mus Art & Pa Acad Fine Arts, 78; solo exhibs, Frank Marino Gallery, NY, 80 & Marian Locks Gallery, Philadelphia, 80 & 84; 20th Anniversary Del Biennial Exhib, Univ Del, Newark, 82; Decades of Design, Baltimore, 88; Images and Objects, Boston, 90. *Pos:* Owner & dir, Gallery Pane Vino, 65-68; dir, Marian Locks Gallery, Philadelphia, 68-73; designer & consult, Danhart-Heim Architects, 76-77; partnr-dir, Chew and Formicola Gallery, 83-. *Teaching:* Instr design, Drexel Univ, Philadelphia, 70-; instr painting, Cleveland Inst Art, Ohio, 79-80. *Awards:* First Hallgarten Award, Nat Acad Design, 65. *Bibliog:* Frank Goodyear & Anne Percy (auth), Pa Academy Fine Arts, Contemp Drawing, 78; Patterson Sims (auth), The 20 Univ Del Biennial Exhib Introd 82. *Media:* Oil, Fabric. *Publ:* Images, Arts Mag, 69; John Canada (auth), New York Times, 70; Lenore Malen (auth), Arts Mag, 9/80; Michael Stolback (auth), Arts Mag, 10/80. *Dealer:* Chew and Formicola Gallery, Philadelphia, PA. *Mailing Add:* 725 Carpenter St Philadelphia PA 19147-3933

FORNAS, LEANDER
PRINTMAKER, INSTRUCTOR
b Gardner, Mass, June 18, 1925. *Study:* Pratt Inst, cert, 50; Kunstgewerbeschule, Zurich, 51; Ateneum, Helsinki, 51-53; Univ Mass, MFA, 73 & currently, Doctorate candidate, 90. *Work:* Mus Mod Art, NY; Ateneum, Helsinki; Libr Cong; Rockefeller Collection; NY Pub Libr. *Comn:* Developed new glass engraving methods, Steuben Glass, NY, 55; designed & instituted graphics facilities, Pratt Inst, NY, 58, Fine Arts Ctr, Univ RI, 66 & Holyoke Community Col, 72-75; graphic indust illus, portrait comns & misc design, Finland, 59-65. *Exhib:* Solo exhibs, New Talent, Mus Mod Art, 55 & Sao Paulo Biennial Prints, 59; Curator's Choice, Print Club, Philadelphia, 56; Printmakers Soc Finland Traveling Exhib, US, Europe & Far East, 59-66. *Pos:* Dir, Design & Graphics Studio, Helsinki, 58-66; chmn art dept, Holyoke Community Col, 70-74. *Teaching:* Instr printmaking & drawing, Holyoke Community Col, 70-96. *Mem:* Printmakers Soc Finland (bd dir, 59-61); Lit Soc Finland; Finno-Urgarian Soc Finland. *Media:* All Media. *Res:* Multicultural: North Eurasians (Siberia), Subarctic Cree, (Canada)

FORNELLI, JOSEPH
SCULPTOR, PAINTER
b Chicago, Ill, May 21, 1943. *Study:* Art Inst, Chicago. *Work:* Cornell Univ, Ithaca, NY; Columbia Mus, SC; Nat Vietnam Vets Art Mus, Chicago; Park Ridge Pub Libr, Ill; Alice Forrester Miniatures Collection, Leigh Yawkey Woodson Mus, Wausau, Wis. *Comn:* Dell Publ for Pres Nixon, NY, 74; Encycl Britannica for Pope Paul VI, Chicago, 74; Columbus Hosp, Chicago, 76; Ducks Unlimited, Memphis, Tenn, 89; US Hist, Richmond, VA, 91; Nat Rifle Asn, 93 & 94. *Exhib:* LBJ Mus, Austin, Tex, 83; Lincoln Ctr, Cork Gallery, NY, 84; Am Mus Fly Fishing, Manchester, Vt, 91; Southeastern Wildlife Expos, Charleston, SC, 92; Nat Vietnam Vets Art Mus, Chicago, 96; and others. *Pos:* Painter & sculptor, Richard Rush Studio, Chicago, 73-74; art dir, Monastery Hill Bindery, Chicago, 74-77; design coordr, Ducks Unlimited, Chicago, 79-83; bd dir, Chicago Munic Art League, 79-92; pres, Vietnam Veterans Arts Group, 81-, Fornelli Design Studio, 89-, Nat Vietnam Vets Art Mus, Chicago, 96-. *Awards:* Gold Medal, Chicago Munic Art League, 79; Award of Merit, Soc Animal Artists Denver Mus, 82; Blue Ribbon, Nat Wildlife Fedn, 83. *Bibliog:* Ann Keegan (auth), Art snares wild spirit, The Treasures of Vietnam, Chicago Tribune, 5/87; Art reflects Vietnam War, NY Times, 10/81; Joan Johnson (producer), Good Morning America, ABC TV, 10/81; Niki Barrie (auth), Tuesday's child, Wildlife Art News, 9/93. *Mem:* Chicago Munic Art League; Chicago Artists Guild; assoc Am Watercolor Soc; Oil Painters Am; Vietnam Vet Arts Group. *Media:* Watercolor, Oil; Bronze, Stone. *Publ:* Illusr, Moving Along with Charlie Dickey, Charles Dickey, Winchester Press, 85; Fly

Fishingest Gentleman, Keith Russel, Winchester Press, 86; The Wildfowler's Quest, George Reiger, Lyons Burford, 89; Steel Barbs, Wild Waters, Jerry Gibbs, Outdoor Life Books, 90; A Rough Shooting Dog, Charles Fergus, Lyons & Burford, 91. *Mailing Add:* c/o Fornelli Studio 1017 S Prospect Park Ridge IL 60068-4728

FORREST, CHRISTOPHER PATRICK
PRINTMAKER, PAINTER
b Trenton, NJ, Oct 2, 1946. *Study:* Va Polytechnic Inst, BS, 68; NC State Univ, MS, 74. *Work:* Nat Acad Sci, Washington, DC; NJ State Mus, Trenton; Ferrum Col, Va; Metro-Goldwyn Mayer, Los Angeles; Bausch & Lomb, Rochester, NY. *Exhib:* Easton Waterfowl Festival, Md, 96; Soc Animal Artists Exhib, Acad Nat Sci, Philadelphia; Solo exhibs, Golden Door, New Hope, Pa, Town Plaza, Brea, Calif, & Chabot Galleries, Campbell, Calif; Soc Animal Artists Ann, Denver Mus Nat Hist; Nat Wildlife Fedn Wildlife in Art Show, Vienna, Va; Sterling Fine Arts Gallery, Laguna Beach, Calif; Soc Am Artists Exhib, Cleveland Mus Natural Hist; Hang Ups, Orange, Calif. *Pos:* Gen production mgr, Evergreen Publ Inc, 80-81. *Bibliog:* Cathy Lyons Colletti (auth), All-enveloping moods, Southwest Art Mag; article, The Artist-Chris Forrest, Prints Mag; Judy Hughes (auth), Lasting impressions lithography, Wildlife Art News. *Mem:* Soc Animal Artists; Buzzard Coun Am. *Media:* Lithography, Intaglio; Acrylic, Oil. *Publ:* Duck Unltd Mag, 78, Readers Digest, 82, Outdoors, 83, & Conservationist Mag, 84. *Dealer:* Hang Ups 1319 W Katella Ave Orange CA 92667; Primrose Press PO Box 302 New Hope PA 18938. *Mailing Add:* 6 Cranberry Ln Vincentown NJ 08088

FORRESTALL, THOMAS DE VANY
SCULPTOR, PAINTER
b Middleton, NS, Mar 11, 1936. *Study:* Mt Allison Univ, 54-58, Hon DFA; Can Coun grant to travel & study in Europe, 58-59, sculpture grant, 67; King's Col, Hon Dr Civil Law. *Work:* Can Coun; Winnipeg Art Gallery; Art Gallery Windsor; Confederation Mem Gallery; Nat Gallery, Hungary; and others. *Comn:* Kennedy & Churchill Mem, Prov NB, 64; steel sculpture, Atlantic Pavilion, Expo 67; welded relief mural, Centennial Bldg Fredericton, 68; two large welded steel sculptures, Can Govt, Fed Bldg, Antigonish, NS, 70; mural abstract for playhouse, Beaverbrook Can Found, Fredericton, 72. *Exhib:* Solo exhibs, Montreal Mus Fine Arts, 72, Nat Mus Art, Bulgaria, 80, Nat Gallery Art, Romania, 81, Nat Mus Art, Transylvania, Nat Mus Art, Hungary, 81 & Bayard Gallery, NY, 81; Can Cult Centre, Rome, Italy, 83; Habema Centre Tel Aviv, 84; Nat Mus Art Prague, 85; Nova Scotia Pavilion, Expo '86 Vancouver; and others. *Pos:* Asst cur, Beaverbrook Art Gallery, 59-60. *Awards:* Can Coun Lectr Tour Grants, 77-79; Queen's Jubilee Medal, 78; Can 125 Medal, Order Can, 86. *Bibliog:* P Murphy (auth), Shaped paintings, article, Art Mag, 78. *Mem:* Royal Can Acad Arts; St Vincent De Paul Soc; Order Can. *Media:* Tempera; Steel, Iron. *Publ:* Coauth, Shapes, 72; Returning the Favor Dr N Webb, Lancelot Press. *Mailing Add:* c/o Forrestall Fine Arts Ltd 3 Albert St Dartmouth NS B2Y 3M1 Canada

FORSTMANN, ERIC
PAINTER
b Sharon, Conn, 1962. *Study:* With Barnett Rubenstein & Henry Schwartz; Sch Mus Fine Arts, Boston, BFA. *Exhib:* Solo exhibs include Eckert Fine Art, Naples, Fla, 2004, Butler Inst Am Art, Youngstown, Ohio, 2008; group exhibs include Summer Soiree, Eckert Fine Art, Naples, Fla, 2001; Palm Beach 3 Contemp Art Show, West Palm Beach, Fla, 2006 & 2007. *Mailing Add:* Eckert Fine Art PO Box 649 Millerton NY 12546

FORSYTH, ILENE H(AERING)
EDUCATOR, HISTORIAN
b Detroit, Mich, Aug 21, 1928. *Study:* Univ Mich, AB, 50; Columbia Univ, AM, 55, PhD, 60. *Teaching:* Lectr, Barnard Col, 56-58; instr, Columbia Univ, 59-61; asst prof, Univ Mich, Ann Arbor, 61-68, assoc prof, 68-74, prof, 74-84, Arthur F Thurnau prof emerita, 84-; vis prof hist art, Harvard Univ, 80; Andrew W Mellon prof, Univ Pittsburgh, 81; vis prof hist art, Univ Calif, Berkeley, 96. *Awards:* Inst Advan Study Fel, 77; Warner G Rice Humanities Award, 91; Kress Prof, Ctr Advan Study Visual Arts, Nat Gallery Art, Washington, DC, 98-99; fel, Medieval Acad Am, 2006. *Mem:* Int Ctr Medieval Art (dir, 70, vpres, 81-85); Acad Arts, Sci & Belles Lett, Dijon; Midwest Hist Soc (mem bd dir, 79-81; Coll Art Asn (mem bd dir, 80-84, mem exec comt, 82-84); Medieval Acad Am (mem bd adv, 85-). *Res:* Medieval art, especially Romanesque sculpture. *Publ:* Auth, Magi and majesty: Romanesque sculpture and liturgical drama, Coll Art Asn Bulletin, 68; Throne of Wisdom, Princeton Univ Press, 72; Ganymede capital at Vezelay, Gesta, 76; Cockfighting in Burgundian Romanesque sculpture, Speculum, 78; The Uses of Art: Medieval Metaphor in the Michigan Law Quadrangle, Univ Mich Press, 93; Narrative at Moissac: Schapiro's Legacy, Gesta, 2002; Word-Play in the Moissac Cloister, Romanesque Art & Thought, 2008. *Mailing Add:* 5 Geddes Heights Ann Arbor MI 48104

FORSYTHE, DONALD JOHN
PRINTMAKER, EDUCATOR
b Pittsburgh, Pa, July 2, 1955. *Study:* Ind Univ Pa, BS, 77; Rochester Inst Technol, MFA, 79. *Work:* Bank of NY, Wilmington, Del; Franklin Mint, Philadelphia, Pa; Graham Ctr Mus, Wheaton, Ill; Philadelphia Savings Fund Soc, Philadelphia, Pa; Rochester Inst Technol, NY; Atlantic Richfield Corp, Phila, Pa; Ballinglen Archive, Ballinglen Arts Found, Ballycastle, County Mayo, Ireland; Am Bible Soc. *Comn:* 6 choir windows, stained glass, Cathedral St Stephen, Harrisburg, Pa; 8 sanctuary windows, Mission Hills Baptist Church, Littleton, Colo. *Exhib:* La Grange National VI, CUAA Gallery, Ga, 81; 6th NC Printing & Drawing Society Exhib, Charlotte, NC, 82; Tactile Vision, William Penn Mus, Harrisburg, Pa, 84; New Drawings, Dolan/Maxwell Gallery, Philadelphia, Pa, 85; Visions of the World, Shoemaker Mus, Juniata, Pa, 86; 44th Ann Juried Exhib, Woodmere Art Mus, Philadelphia, 86; Sacred Arts IX, Graham Ctr Mus, Wheaton, Ill, 87; Christian Imagery in Contemp Art, Albany Inst Art, NY, 88; New Am Talent, Laquana Gloria Art Mus, Austin, Tx, 89; Perspectives from Pennsylvania, Carnegie Mellon Univ Mus, Pittsburgh, Pa; Art of the State, William Penn Mus, Harrisburg, Pa; Anno Domini: Jesus Through the Centuries, Provincial Mus Alberta, Edmonton, Can, 2000; solo exhibs, Burning Lights, monotype & collage, Union Univ, Jackson, Tenn, 2002, Time Uncertain Box Constructions 1986-2003, Penn Coll Gallery, Pa Coll Tech, Williamsport, 2003; The Next Generation Contemp Expressions of Faith, Mus Biblical Art, NYC, 2005. *Pos:* Dir, Louise Aughinbaugh Art Gallery, Messiah Col, 85-88 & 92-2000; pres, Christians Visual Art, 91-93. *Teaching:* Distinguished prof art, Messiah Col, Grantham, Pa, 81-. *Awards:* Best of show, Sacred Arts XII, Graham Ctr Mus; Hon Mention, New Am Talent, Tex Fine Arts Asn, 89; Artworks Award, Art of the State, Pa Juried Mus Exhib, Univ Pa Mus; First Prize, sculpture, 1995 & Second Prize, works on paper, 1999, Art of the State, Pa, Wm Penn Mus, Harrisburg. *Bibliog:* John Skillen (auth), The Reconstructive Art of Donald Forsythe, IMAGE: a journal of arts & religion, No 18, 1998; Ena Heller, Marcus Burke (auths), The Word as Art: Contemporary Renderings, 2000; Marcus Burke (auth), Why Art Needs Religion, Why Religion Needs the Arts, pp 154-157, 2004; Ena Giurescu (auth), Reluctant Partners: Art and Religion in Dialogue, 2004; Wayne Roosa (auth), The Next Generation: Contemporary Expressions of Faith, Eerdmans Pub, 2005. *Mem:* Christians in the Visual Arts (mem bd, 85-); Int Soc Christian Artists; Southern Graphics Coun; College Art Assoc. *Media:* Mixed Media, Collage. *Mailing Add:* Messiah College One College Ave Box 3004 Grantham PA 17027

FORT-BRESCIA, BERNARDO M
ARCHITECT
b Lima, Peru, Nov 19, 1951. *Study:* Princeton Univ, BA (archit), 1973; Harvard Univ, March, 1975. *Comn:* Babylon, Pacific Developers, Miami, Fla, 1977; Atlantis, Stonecrest Development, Miami, Fla, 1978; The Palace, Helmsley Enterprises, Miami, Fla, 1978; Imperial at Brickell, Harlon Group, Miami, Fla, 1979; Overseas Tower, Overseas Finance Corp, Miami, Fla, 1980. *Exhib:* New Americans, Inst Archit & Urban Studies, Rome, Italy, 1979; Work of Arquitectonica, Cooper-Hewitt Mus, NY, 1979, Pa State Univ, 1980 & Univ Va, 1981; and others. *Pos:* Principal, Arquitectonica, Coral Gables, Fla, 1977-. *Teaching:* Vis prof archit, Univ Miami, Coral Gables, Fla, 1975-77. *Awards:* Citation, Progressive Archit Ann Design Awards, 1978 & 1980. *Bibliog:* Articles, Wall St J, 7/7/1983, Archit Rec, 7/1983, Global Archit Document 7, 8/1983 & others. *Mem:* Am Inst Architects; Architectural Club of Miami (pres, 1978-80)

FORTIN, SYLVIE
EDITOR
Study: Univ Toronto, Art History; Univ Laval, Art History; Duke Univ, Art History. *Pos:* cur contemp art, Ottawa Art Gallery, Ontario, Can, 1996-2001; prog coordr, la chambre blanche, Quebec City, 1991-1994; collabr, OBORO, Montreal, Quebec, 1994-2001. *Awards:* Lexus Leader of the Arts, 2007. *Publ:* critical essay in Canadian, American & European catalogues; rev, Art Press, C Mag, Espace, Fuse, NKA: Journ Contemp African Art, Parachute. *Mailing Add:* Art papers PO Box 5748 Atlanta GA 31107

FORTSON, KAY KIMBELL CARTER
PATRON, ADMINISTRATOR
Study: Univ Tex, BA, 1956. *Pos:* pres, chmn bd trustees, Kimbell Art Found & Mus, 1975-; trustee, Tex Christian Univ; hon trustee, Modern Art Mus, Fort Worth, Tex. *Mailing Add:* Kimbell Art Found Suite 2300 301 Commerce St Fort Worth TX 76102-4123

FORTUNATO, NANCY
PAINTER, INSTRUCTOR
b Highland Park, Ill, Nov 29, 1941. *Study:* Master class with Ed Betts, 80, Dong Kingman, 85; Zhejiang Inst Fine Arts, with Lu Yanshao, Hangzhou, China, 84, Cheng Khee Chee, 84, 90. *Hon Degrees:* AAPL, elected a Fellow; Royal Coatimundi, Ariz Watercolor Assoc; Purple Sage, Texas Watercolor Soc. *Work:* Leigh Yawkey Woodson Art Mus, Wausau, Wis; Int Crane Found Mus, Baraboo, Wis; People of the Century Goldblatt Collection, Chicago; also pvt collections of Reverend Billy Graham & Winston Lord; Naval Air Mus, Pensacola, Fla. *Comn:* People of the Century Goldblatt Found. *Exhib:* Impressions in watercolor, Elliott Mus, Stuart, Fla, 89; 19th Ann Watercolor Exhib, W Riverside Art Mus, Calif, 89, 2007, 2008; Cleveland Mus Nat Hist, Ohio, 91; Soc Animal Artists, Roger Tory Peterson Inst, Jamestown, NY, 92; 1st Naval Air Mus Show, Pensacola, Fla, 93-94; Watercolor USA, Springfield Art Mus, Springfield, Mo, 2007, 2010; Am Art in Miniature, Gilcrease Mus, Tulsa, Okla, 2007-2009; Nat Watercolor Society, Riverside Art Mus, Riverside, Calif, 2007-2008; Rocky Mtn Nat, Foothills Art Ctr, Golden Colo, 2008, 2013; and others. *Pos:* Pres emeritus, Midwest Watercolor Soc, 97-99; pres emer, Int Soc Marine Painters, 2002-2004. *Teaching:* Instr beginning & advanced watercolor, Dist 211 & 214, Palatine & Arlington Heights, Ill, 75-; instr advanced watercolor Elgin Community Col, nat workshops. *Awards:* Windsor & Newton Award, Cuyahoga 4 State Nat, 85; Ill State Fair, Prof Exhib, First Place, 91; 12th Ann Miniature Exhib Award, Art Gallery Fells Point, Md, 95; Merchandise Award 60th Ann Exhib Northwest Watercolor Soc, 2000; merit, 26th Ann Nat Exhib of trans Watercolors at Midwest Watercolor Exhib, Kanakee, IL, 2002; merit, 27th Nat Exhib Midwest Watercolor Society, West Bend, WI, 2003; Grand Prize Winner, Mini Paint Am Exhib, 2007; Springfield Purchase Award, Watercolor, 2007, Merit Award, 2010. *Bibliog:* James Auer (auth), Mountaintop gave artist new outlook on her art, Milwaukee J, 87; Pam & Ed Menaker (coauths), She doesn't paint inside the lines, N Shore Mag, 88; Mark Mandernach (auth), Brush with greatness, Chicago Tribune, 96; Painting Without Brushes, Am Artist mag, 98. *Mem:* Am Soc Marine Artists; Catharine Lorillard Wolfe Art Club; Whiskey Painters Am; US Coast Guard Artist; fellow Am Artists Prof League; Acad Artists Am; Transparent Watercolor Society (master status); Western Fed Watercolor Artists; Watercolor Honor Society; and others. *Media:* Watercolor; Ink. *Res:* Watercolors of the 18th century (Eng); Impressionists. *Specialty:* seascapes, marine art, wildlife,. *Interests:* Photog, music. *Collection:* Zhejiang Academy of Fine Arts,

China; Leigh Yawkey Woodson Art Mus, WI; Rev Billy Graham; Winston Lord; The Loon Foundation, Naval Air Mus, Pensacola, Fla. *Publ:* Cover illusr, Birdwatcher's Digest, 84, 86 & 87; US Lighthouse Log Mag, Lighthouse Soc, 85-95; Wildbirds, Japan, 94; cover illusr, The US & Northeast Asia Nelson Hall, 93; auth, Capture Movement in Your Paintings, Quarto Publ, 96; The Artistic Touch III, 99; Texas 50th Anniversary Album, 99; Splash 11, 2010; Splash 12, 2011; Splash 14, 2013. *Mailing Add:* 249 N Marion St Palatine IL 60074

FOSS, CORNELIA
PAINTER
Study: Univ Indiana; Rome Univ, Italy; Kann Art Inst, Calif. *Exhib:* Solo exhibs, Ferris Gallery, Los Angeles, 59, James Goodman Gallery, Buffalo, NY, 67, Berry-Hill Galleries, NY, 81, David Barnett Gallery, Milwaukee, 82, Parsons Gallery, NY, 83, Sutton Gallery, NY, 84, McLean Gallery, London, 84, Haggerty Mus Art, Milwaukee, 86, Susan Schreiber Gallery, NY, 88, Ben Shahn Ctr for Visual Arts, NJ, 89, Tatiana Eitle, Greece, 90, Gallery 454 North, Los Angeles, 87, 91, Steven Scott Gallery, Baltimore, 91, Benton Gallery, NY, 92, St Gaudens Mus, NH, 94, Denise Bibro Gallery, NY, 94, Renee Fotouhi Gallery, NY, 95, Gallery Emmanuel, Great Neck, NY, 96, Lizan Tops Gallery, NY, 97, Elizabeth Meyers Gallery, NY, 98, DFN Gallery, NY, 99, 2001, 2003, 2005, 2007, Glenn Horowitz Booksellers, NY, 2000, Boston Univn, 2003, Horizon Gallery, NY, 2003, Clark Gallery, NY, 2003; group exhibs, DFN Gallery, 2000 & 2002-2007; Cold Spring Harbor Gallery, NY, 2000; Lizan Tops Gallery, NY, 2000, 2003; Elaine Benson Gallery, NY, 2000; Long Island Mus, Stony Brook, NY, 2000, 2005. *Teaching:* Art instr, Art Students League, NY, 93-, Kann Art Inst, 2005-, Nat Acad, currently. *Dealer:* DFN Gallery 210 11th Ave 6th Floor New York NY 10001. *Mailing Add:* c/o DFN Gallery 46 W 85th St Apt A New York NY 10024

FOSTER, APRIL
PRINTMAKER, EDUCATOR
b Berwyn, Ill, Oct 9, 1947. *Study:* Univ Ill, Champaign-Urbana, BFA, 1970, MA (art educ; fel), 1971; Tyler Sch Art, Temple Univ, MFA (printmaking; fel), 1973. *Work:* Cincinnati Art Mus, Ohio; Boston Mus Fine Art, Mass; Univ Mich Art Mus; Dayton Art Inst, Ohio; Miami Univ Art Mus. *Exhib:* Prints & Drawings, Thomas More Col, 1988; Invitational Exhib, Closson's Gallery, 1990, Coll Mt St Joseph, 1990; solo exhib, Xavier Univ, 1994, Sabbatical exhib, Art Acad, Cincinnati, Ohio, 1/2000; sabbatical exhib, Art Acad Cincinnati, Ohio, 2000. *Teaching:* Asst printmaking, Temple Univ, 1971-72, instr printmaking, summer 1973; prof printmaking & drawing, Art Acad Cincinnati, 1973-. *Awards:* Award for Excellence in Teaching, Greater Cincinnati Consortium of Cols & Univs, 1989. *Mem:* Coll Art Asn; Mid-Am Print Coun; Southern Graphics Coun. *Media:* Lithography, Egg Tempera. *Dealer:* Closson's Gallery 10100 Montgomery Ave Cincinnati OH 45242. *Mailing Add:* c/o Art Acad Cincinnati 1212 Jackson St Cincinnati OH 45202

FOSTER, STEPHEN C
HISTORIAN, WRITER
b Princeton, Ill, Dec 3, 1941. *Study:* Northern Ill Univ, BA; Univ Ill, MA; Univ Pa, PhD. *Pos:* Dir, Prog for Mod Studies, Univ Iowa, Iowa City. *Teaching:* Asst prof art hist, Bowdoin Col, Brunswick, Mass, 72-74, mem fac, Am Painting Summer Inst, 74 & 76; prof art hist & criticism, Univ Iowa, Iowa City, 74-. *Awards:* Smithsonian Fel, 85; Taipei Fine Arts Mus Grant, 87; Getty Grant, 92; and others. *Mem:* Coll Art Asn Am. *Res:* Sociology of modern art with research emphasis in the areas of Dada and Abstract Expressionism; folk art. *Publ:* The Critics of Abstract Expressionism, Ann Arbor: UMI Research Press, 85; contrib ed, Event Art and Events, Ann Arbor: UMI Research Press, 88; The World According to Dada, TFAM, 88; Franz Kline: Art and the Structure of Identity (exhib catalog), Electa, 94; Dada: The Coordinates of Cultural Politics, GK Hall & Co New York, 96. *Mailing Add:* Dept Art & Art Hist Univ Iowa Iowa City IA 55242

FOSTER, STEVEN DOUGLAS
PHOTOGRAPHER
b Piqua, Ohio, Sept 10, 1945. *Study:* Nathan Lyons Home Workshop, Rochester, 64-66; Rochester Inst Technol, AAS, 65; Inst Design, Ill Inst Technol, BS, 68; Univ NMex, MFA, 72. *Work:* Art Inst Chicago; Int Mus Photog at George Eastman House, Rochester; Univ NMex Art Mus; Mus Mod Art, NY; Huston Mus Art; Walker Art Ctr, Mus Contemp Photog, Chicago; and others. *Exhib:* Vision & Expressions, Int Mus Photog at George Eastman House, Rochester, 69; Artists in Ga, High Mus, Atlanta, 74; Wis Dirs II, Milwaukee Art Ctr, 78; Am Photog in the 70's, Art Inst Chicago, 79; Perception: Field of View, Los Angeles Ctr for Contemp Photog, 79. *Teaching:* Instr, Ga State Univ, Atlanta, 72-75; prof, Univ Wis-Milwaukee, 75-. *Awards:* Grad Sch Res Grant, Univ Wis-Milwaukee, 79; Milwaukee Co Individual Artist Fel, 90; Wis Arts Bd Individual Artist Grant, 94. *Mem:* Soc Photog Educ. *Media:* Black, White, Color and Silver Print. *Publ:* Contrib, Wisconsin Directions II, Milwaukee Art Ctr, 78; The Lake Series, Art Inst Chicago, 82; New American Photography, Chicago Ctr Contemp Photog, 81; Five Photographers, Milwaukee Art Mus, 87; Swimmers, Aperture, 88. *Dealer:* Ehler Crudill Gallery Chicago; Michael Lord Gallery Milwaukee

FOTOPOULOS, JAMES
FILMMAKER
b Norridge, Ill, 1976. *Work:* Whitney Biennial, Whitney Mus Art, 2004, and others. *Pos:* founder, Fantasma Inc, 98. *Teaching:* Guest lectr, "Film One" prod class Univ Tex, Austin, 2001 & 2003; guest lectr, NJ City Univ, 2003. *Publ:* Dir.: (films) ZERO, 1997, Migrating Forms, 1999 (Best Feature Award, NY Underground Film Festival, 2000, Made in Chicago Award, Chicago Underground Film Festival, 2000), Back Against the Wall, 2000, Consumed, 2001 (Chicago Underground Film Fund Grant, Chicago Underground Film Festival, 2001), Christabel, 2001, The Lighthouse, 2004 (No Budget Award, Cinematexas Inte Short Film & Video Festival, 2004), Spine Face, 2005; exhib include with Cory Arcangel Fotopoulos/Arcangel Part 5, NY Film Festival, 2004

FOULADVAND, HENGAMEH
PAINTER, CRITIC
b Tehran, Iran; US citizen. *Study:* Studied painting under masters of Persian art in Iran; San Jose State Univ, BA, 76, MA, 79. *Work:* Encyclopedia Iranica Found, Line & Tone Typographics, NY; Found Iranian Studies, Washington. *Exhib:* Middle Eastern Studies Invitational, NY & Mem Libr Invitational, Long Island Univ, NY, 89 & 91; Persian Artists in US, Strathmore Hall Arts Ctr, Md, 90; Long Island Artists Exhib, Heckscher Mus, NY, 90; Transcending the Immediate Surrounding, Port Washington Pub Libr, NY, 91; Essence & Attributes, Huntington Arts Coun, NY, 92 & 94; MacArthur Airport, Islip, Long Island, 97; Gallery Gora, Montreal, Can, 99; CIMA, Inc, NY, 99; Drawing the Line, La Mason Frances, Columbia Univ, 2000. *Pos:* Exec dir, Ctr for Iranian Mod Arts, 98-; ed bd, Tavoos Art Mag, 99-. *Teaching:* Vis artist, Creativity Workshop, Columbia Univ Dept Middle Eastern Cult, 96 & 97. *Bibliog:* Les Krants, New York Art Rev, 88; Encyclopedia of Living Artists, 94; Who's Who in the East, 97. *Mem:* Huntington Township Art League; Smithtown Arts Coun; Huntington Arts Coun. *Media:* Acrylic, Oil; Watercolor, Mixed Media. *Dealer:* Mir Enterprise 179 New York Ave Huntington NY 11743. *Mailing Add:* 525 Caledonia Rd Dix Hills NY 11746

FOULKES, LLYN
PAINTER
b Yakima, Wash, Nov 17, 1934. *Study:* Univ Wash, 53-54; Cent Wash Coll Educ, 54, Chouinard Art Inst, 57-59. *Work:* Whitney Mus Am Art, Mus Mod Art, Guggenheim Mus, NY; Art Inst, Chicago; Los Angeles Co Mus Art, Mus Contemp Art, Calif; Oakland Mus Art, Calif; San Francisco Mus Mod Art, Calif. *Exhib:* Solo exhibs, Kent Fine Arts, Forum, Zurich, 87, Hooks-Epstein Gallery, Houston, Tex, 88, Herter Art Gallery, Univ Mass, Amherst, 89, POP: The First Picture, Kent, NY, 90, I Space, Univ Ill, Chicago, 93, Patricia Faure Gallery, Santa Monica, Calif, 94, 96, Laguna Art Mus, Calif, 95, Gallery Paule Anglim, San Francisco, 97, Peter Blake Gallery, Laguna Beach, Calif, 2001, Kent Gallery, New York, 2004, 2005, 2007, Patricia Faure Gallery, Santa Monica, 2006; group exhibs, LA Hot and Cool, Stux Gallery, NY, 88; Art of the 70's, Manny Silverman Gallery, Los Angeles, Calif, 88; Am Pie, Bess Cutler Gallery, NY, 89; Real Allusions, The Whitney Mus Am Art, NY, 90; Helter Skelter, Mus Contemp Art, Los Angeles, 92; retrospective Between a Rock and a Hard place (traveling), 95-98; Norton Simon Mus, Pasadena, Calif, 99, 2001; Patricia Faure Gallery, Santa Monica, Calif, 99; Orange County Ctr Contemp Art, Santa Ana, Calif, 2000, Art Since the 1960s, 2007; Laguna Mus Art, 2001; Frye Art Mus, Seattle, 2001; Mus Modern Art, 2001; Los Angeles Post Cool, San Jose Mus Art, Calif, 2002; Paperwork, Patricia Correia Gallery, 2003; POP from San Francisco Collections, San Francisco Mus Modern Art, 2004; Ann Invitational Exhib, Nat Acad Mus, New York, 2006; Wallace Berman & His Circle, Grey Art Gallery, NY Univ, 2007; 54th Int Art Exhib Biennale, Venice, 2011. *Collection Arranged:* Cur, Imagination, Los Angeles Inst Contemp Art, Calif; Guggenheim Mus, NY City; Mus Modern Art; Art Inst Chicago; Whitney Mus Am Art, NY City; Musee Boymans, Rotterdam; Los Angeles Co Mus Art; Norton Simon Mus, Pasadena, Calif; San Francisco Mus Modern Art; Oakland Mus Calif; Mus Contemp Art, Los Angeles. *Teaching:* Prof painting & drawing & artist-in-residence, Univ Calif, Los Angeles, 65-71; resident painter, Painting workshop, Art Ctr Sch, Los Angeles, 71-77; vis prof art, Univ Calif, Irvine, 81-82, Santa Barbara, 83-84; prof, Otis Art Inst, Los Angeles, 86-87; vis grad instr, Univ Calif, Los Angeles, 2006. *Awards:* New Talent Purchase Grant, Los Angeles Co Mus Art, 64; Medal of France (first award for painting), 5th Paris Bienniale, Mus Mod Art, Paris, 67; Guggenheim Found fel, 77-78; Fel Grant, Nat Endowment Arts, 86; Acad Award in Art, AAAL, 2008; Artist award, Artists Legacy Found, 2009. *Bibliog:* Hilary Dole Klein (auth), Time out: sticking up the one-man band, Santa Barbara News & Rev, 1/23/88; Mark Van Proyen (auth), Navigating the semiotic mire, Artweek, 8/20/88; Robert Taylor (auth), LA hot and cool: A rewarding exhibit, Boston Globe, 1/88; Peter Frank (auth), Forty Years of California Assemblage, Wright Gallery, Sculpture, 1-2/90; Peter Plagens (auth), Welcome to Manson High, Newsweek, 3/22/92; David Pagel (auth), The Importance of Being Earnest, LA Times, F36, 3/2/2000; Bernard Cooper (auth), Vulgarian Rhapsody, LA Mag, 128-132, 12/2001. *Media:* Oil, Acrylic

FOURCARD, INEZ GAREY
PAINTER
b Brooklyn, NY. *Study:* Pratt Inst, Brooklyn, NY; McNeese State Univ, Lake Charles, La, BFA, 63. *Work:* Bertrand Russell Peace Found, London, Eng; Gallery Ancient & Mod Art, Salsomaggiore, Italy. *Comn:* Landscape with Pond, New Emanuel Baptist Church, Lake Charles, La, 75; Jesus & The Nativity, Mt Pilgrim Baptist Church, Lake Charles, 83. *Exhib:* La State Art Comn, traveling exhib, 64; Solo exhibs, Lynn Kottler Galleries, NY, 71 & Art Mus Southwest La, Lafayette, 72; Eminent Black Artist of Louisiana, Cent La Art Asn Inc, Alexandria, 76; Prominent Black Artists of Louisiana, La Black Legislators Caucus, State Capitol, 87; Black Heritage Festival, Civic Ctr, Lake Charles, La, 88; and others. *Awards:* Cash Award, First Prize, Mother & Son, La State Art Comn, 64; Gold Medal First Prize, The Connoisseur, Acad Italia dell Artie del Savro, 80; Statua della Vittoria, The Connoisseur, Centro Studie Ricerche Dalle Nazioni, 85. *Bibliog:* Herbert Lieberman (auth), Artist-USA, Artists Equity Asn, Inc, 70, 72 & 74; Bernadine Proctor (auth), Black Artist of Louisiana, 88. *Media:* Oil. *Publ:* Contribr, International Artist Directory, 75; The History of Contemporary Art, Int d'Arte Mod, 82. *Mailing Add:* 1414 St John St Lake Charles LA 70601

FOWLE, BRUCE S
ARCHITECT
Study: Syracuse Univ, Sch of Archit, BA (archit), 60. *Pos:* Assoc, Edward Larrabee Barnes, FAIA, 70-77; co-founder, senior principal Fox & Fowle Archits, Prof Corp, 78; Co-founder, Archits, Designers & Planners for Soc Responsibility, New York City, 82; chmn, Syracuse Univ Sch Archit Adv Commun; pres, Nat Acad Mus & Sch, NY, currently. *Awards:* named to Am Inst of Archits Coll of Fel, 85; recipient George Arents Pioneer Medal, Syracuse Univ, 2001. *Mem:* Fel, Inst for Urban Design; Am Inst of Archits Design Commun; Nat Acad (acad, 94). *Mailing Add:* National Academy Museum 1083 Fifth Ave at 89th St New York NY 10128

FOWLE, GERALDINE ELIZABETH
HISTORIAN
b Grand Rapids, Mich, Jan 3, 1929. *Study:* Am Univ, 53-58; Univ Mich, Ann Arbor, MA (art hist), 60, PhD (art hist), 70. *Pos:* Newslett ed, Midwest Art Hist Soc, 77-80 & Soc Archit Historians, 80-86; archivist, Midwest Art History Soc, 86-. *Teaching:* Asst lectr English art, Univ Manchester, England, 63-66; vis instr Baroque art, Univ Pittsburgh, 67; assoc prof, Univ Mo, Kansas City, 67-. *Mem:* Coll Art Asn; Soc Archit Historians; Midwest Art Hist Soc; Mid-Am Coll Art Asn (treas, 74-75). *Res:* Sebastien Bourdon, French artist of the 17th century. *Publ:* Contribr, Two pendants by Sebastien Bourdon, Bulletin, Boston Mus Fine Arts, 73; Sebastien Bourdon's acts of mercy, Hortus Imaginum, 74; The lady who got Tassi thrown into prison, Helicon Nine, 80; Crucifixion of St Peter, Mus Art, Univ Kans, 87. *Mailing Add:* 5726 Charlotte St Kansas City MO 64110-2762

FOWLER, ADAM
COLLAGE ARTIST
Study: Md Inst Coll Art, Baltimore, BFA, 2001. *Exhib:* Solo exhibs include Gallery at FlashPoint, Washington, 2005, Margaret Thatcher Projects, New York, 2006 & 2007; group exhibs include Tree Climb, Md Art Place, Baltimore, 2002; Living Room Concert for Eyes & Ears, Warehouse Gallery, Washington, 2003, Art Romp, 2004, Supple, 2006; Anonymous, Washington Project Arts/Corcoran, Gallery at FlashPoint, Washington, 2004; Select III Washington Project Arts/Corcoran Art Auction, Corcoran Gallery Art, Washington, 2005; Line/Age, Drawing Ctr, New York, 2005; The New Collage, Pavel Zoubok Gallery, New York, 2006, In Context: Collage + Abstraction, 2007; Etch a Sketch, Kenise Barnes Fine Art, Larchmont, NY, 2007. *Awards:* Young Artist Prog Grant, DC Comn Arts & Humanities, 2004; Trawick Prize Semi-Finalist, Bethesda Arts & Entertainment, 2005; Pollock-Krasner Found Grant, 2007

FOWLER, ERIC NICHOLAS
ILLUSTRATOR, PAINTER
b Morristown, NJ, Feb 14, 1954. *Study:* Syracuse Univ, NY, 72-74; illusr workshop (First Scholar award), 77; Pratt Inst, Brooklyn, NY, BFA(hons), 78. *Work:* Soc Illustrs permanent collection; Mercer Co Cult & Heritage Comn; The Princeton Junior Sch; Trenton Mus Soc. *Comn:* Comn by Robert A Black, Los Angeles. *Exhib:* Graphis Ann, Switz, 83-84; Diaz-Marciall Gallery, NY, 84; Art Dirs Club Ann, NY, 86; solo exhibs, Frenchtown, NJ, 89 & Princeton Trenton Artworks, 94; Larsen-Dulman, New Hope, Pa, 89-91; Bristol Myers Squibb, 91; and others; Farnsworth Gallery, 2004; Gallery DePaul, 2006-2009; Isadore Gallery, 2010. *Pos:* collections mgr, Soc Illusrs. *Teaching:* adj prof, Pa Coll Art and Design, Lancaster, 98-2012. *Awards:* Certificates Merit, Soc Illusr Ann Show 77, 82, 86, 89, 91 & Soc Publ Designers, 82 & 86; Print Regional Design Ann, 86 & 88; Distinguished Artist Grant, NJSCA, 90-91; and many others. *Mem:* Soc Illusr (bd dir 1990-, chmn permanent collection 1998-2009); Artworks, Trenton Artist Workshop Asn NJ; Trenton Mus Soc (bd dir, chmn acquisitions com); Philadelphia Sketch Club (2004-). *Media:* Oil on Canvas. *Interests:* Antique collecting, photography. *Publ:* The Directory of Illustrations vol 8, 92 & vol 12, 95. *Dealer:* Farnsworth Gallery Bordentown NJ. *Mailing Add:* 143 E 37th St Apt 1R New York NY 10016

FOWLER, FRANK EISON
ART DEALER, CONSULTANT
b Chattanooga, Tenn, June 2, 1946. *Study:* Univ Ga, BBA, 69. *Comn:* Produced Inaugural Portfolio, 76 & Presidential Portfolio, 80, comn by Pres Jimmy Carter. *Pos:* Mem adv bd, John F Kennedy Ctr Performing Arts, formerly & Ga Mus Art, Athens, currently. *Mem:* Appraisers Asn Am; Int Soc Appraisers. *Res:* Represent Andrew Wyeth

FOX, CARSON
SCULPTOR
b Oxford, Mass, 1968. *Study:* Pa Acad Fine Arts, 87-91; Univ of PA, BFA; Rutgers Univ, MFA. *Work:* Pa Acad Fine Arts; Hofstra Mus, Hempstead, NY; NJ Acad of Med, Princeton, NJ; Rider Univ, Lawrenceville, NJ. *Exhib:* Main Line Art Ctr, Haverford, Pa; Pa Acad Fine Arts; Mason Gross Gallery, Rutgers Univ, NJ; Artist House Gallery, Philadelphia, Pa, 2001; solo exhib, Artist House Gallery, Philadelphia, Pa, Women's Studio Workshop Gallery, Rosendale, NY, Montgomery Co Coll Gallery, Pa, OK Harris Gallery, New York City, 2001. *Teaching:* instr, screen printing, NY Univ, currently. *Awards:* Grumacher Award for Printmaking, 92; NJ State Mus Soc Award, 2000; Coun on Arts Sculpture Grant, 2001. *Media:* Miscellaneous Media. *Mailing Add:* 945 Berkeley Ave Trenton NJ 08610

FOX, CATHERINE
WRITER, CRITIC
Study: Univ Mich, BA & MA (art hist), 1972. *Pos:* Art critic, Atlanta Journal Constitution, 1981-2009; co-founder, ArtscriticATL.com, 2009-. *Awards:* Am Asn Sunday and Feature Editors award; Green Eyeshade award, Soc Prof Journalists; Criticism award, Best of Cox, 2000

FOX, FLO
PHOTOGRAPHER, LECTURER
b Miami, Fla, Sept 26, 1945. *Study:* With Lisette Model, 80-83 & Andre Kertesz, 85. *Work:* Focus Gallery, San Francisco; Brooklyn Mus, NY; Smithsonian, DC. *Comn:* Three-dimensional photography, Minn Mus Art, 86; Playboy Press Ecstacy, 76. *Exhib:* Asphalt Garden, Canon Gallery, Paris, 81, Camden Arts Ctr, Eng, 81; Auto-Focus Photog, Boston Mus Fine Art, 82 & Philadelphia Mus Art, 83; Beyond Limitations, The Nikon House, NY, 87; two-person exhib with Weegee the Famous, Agathe Gaillard Galerie, Paris, France, 87; IBM Building, Nat MS Soc, NY, 89; Times Square Hotel, 2000; Port Authority Bus Terminal New York, 2003; III Bienial Found One, Madrid, Spain, 2010. *Teaching:* Instr photog, Lighthouse for Blind, NY, 79-80, Village Nursing Home, 84 & YWCA, 85-86, NY; 18 seminars including, Philadelphia Mus Art, Boston Mus Fine Arts & Park West Camera Club. *Awards:* Cert Merit, Boston Mus Fine Art, 82 & Philadelphia Mus Art, 83. *Bibliog:* Georgia Dullea (auth), A camera does the seeing, New York Times, 4/80; Elizabeth Mehren (auth), Trades sight for insight, Los Angeles Times, 9/81; article in The Plain Dealer, Cleveland, Ohio, 6/85; Marshall Fine, Dicthology (movie), 2002; A Piece of Work, Joan Rivers, 2010. *Mem:* Park West Camera Club. *Media:* Silver Gelatin Prints. *Collection:* Capturing unique & grily sides of New York City from 1970-present. *Publ:* Photogr, The Picture Book of Greenwich Village, 85; Black & White New York & What She Wants-Women Artists Look at Men, Life Mag, 9/94; Sculpture Review Mag, spring 94; New York Mag, 2010. *Dealer:* Ron Ridinger 293 Troutman St Brooklyn NY 11237. *Mailing Add:* 135 W 23rd St No 607 New York NY 10011

FOX, JUDITH HOOS
CURATOR
b Oakland, Calif, June 13, 1949. *Study:* Bryn Mawr Col, BA, 71; Univ Minn, MA, 74. *Collection Arranged:* S & Y Ombra: An Autobiography in Form, Beverly Pepper, MIT, 88; Ericson Ziegler: The Wellesley Method, Wellesley Coll Mus, 90; The Matter of History: Selected Work by Annette Lemieux (with catalog), Davis Mus, 94; The Body As Measure (with catalog), Davis Mus, 94; Re:formations/design directions at the end of a century (with catalog), Davis Mus, 96; William de Koonings Door Cycle (with catalog), Davis Mus & Whitney Mus, 95-96; Surrounding Institutions: Views Inside the Car, Daris Mus (with Catalog), 2002; Over & Over: Passion for Process (with Catalog) Krannert Art Mus, Univ Illinois, 2005; Pattern Language: Clothing As Communicator (with catalog), Tufts Univ Art Mus, 2005. *Pos:* Cur intern, Walker Art Ctr, Minneapolis, 73-74; cur, Inst Contemp Art, Boston, 74-75; asst dir, Wellesley Col Mus, Mass, 77-82; cur painting & sculpture, Mus Art, RI Sch Design, Providence, 82-84; adj cur, 20th century dept, Mus Fine Arts, Boston, independent cur, 84-88; cur, Davis Mus & Cult Ctr, Wellesley Col; independent cur & consult. *Teaching:* Instr mus studies, Wellesley Col, 84; vis Assoc Cur in Am Art, Harvard Univ Art Mus. *Mem:* Art Table. *Publ:* Contribr, Naives and Visionaries, Walker Art Ctr, 74; The Railroad in the American Landscape: 1850-1950, Wellesley Coll Mus, 81; Handbook of the Museum of Art, Rhode Island Sch of Design, 86. *Mailing Add:* 21 Myrtle St Jamaica Plain Boston MA 02130

FOX, JUDY (JUDITH) C
SCULPTOR, CERAMIST
b Elizabeth, NJ, Feb 14, 1957. *Study:* Skowhegan Sch Painting & Sculpture, 76; Yale Univ, BA (Jonathan Edwards Art Award), 78; Ecole Superior des Beaux Arts, Paris, 79; NY Univ Inst Fine Arts, MA (art hist), 83, cert conserv, 84, RI Sch Design. *Comn:* Sculpture, City Univ NY, 94. *Exhib:* Solo exhibs, Kunst werk, Berlin, Ger, Yale Univ Art and Architecture Gallery, New Haven, Conn, 77, Bruno Fachetti Gallery, New York City, 87, Calof Lamagna Gallery, New York City, 89, PPOW, New York City, 93, 96, 2000, 2002 & 2005, Christine Konig Galerie, Vienna, Austria, 94, Rena Branston Gallery, San Francisco, Calif, 96, Gallery Joe, Philadelphia, Pa, 96, Kunsthalle Palazzo, Leistal, Switz, 97, Ace Gallery Los Angeles, Calif, 98, Rupertinum, Salzburg, Austria, 98, Galerie Thaddaeus Ropac, Paris, France, 2000, God Lover, PPOW, New York City, 2001, Love & War, John Michael Kohler Arts Center, Sheboygen, Wisc, 2001, Vigeland Mus, Oslo, Norway, 2004, Galerie im Traklhaus, Salzburg, Austria, 2005, Galerie Ropac, Paris, 2005; Portrait of Our Times, Revolution, Ferndale, Mich, 95; Herter Art Gallery, Univ Mass, Amherst, 95; Identita e Alterita, Venice Bienannle, Italy, 95; Narcissim, Calif Ctr Arts, Escondido, 96; Sphinx Chapel, PPOW, NY, 96; Premasculine, Rena Branston Gallery, San Francisco, 96; Prefeminine, Gallery Joe, Philadelphia, 96; To Be Real, Cen for Arts Yerba Buena Gardens, San Francisco, Calif, 97-98; Aldrich Mus Contemp Art, Ridgefield, Conn, 98; Twenty-Six Am Artists, Campo & Campo, Antwerp, Belgium, 99; Collector's Choice, Exit Art, New York City, 2000; Olympia Redux, The Contemp Mus, Honolulu, Hawaii, 2000; The End: An Independent Vision Contemp Art, Syracuse, NY, 2000; Oh Baby!, Exhibit A, NY, 2000; Traklhaus, Salzburg, Austria, 2005; PPOW Gallery, NYC, 2007 ; Ace Gallery, Beverly Hills, 2008; Am Acad Arts & Letts Invitational, New York, 2010. *Pos:* Vis artist, Empire State Prog, 89, Middlebury Col, 89, Tyler Sch Art, 92, Salzburg Int Summer Acad Fine Arts, Austria, 2000, 2003, 2005, Md Inst Art, Baltimore, 2002, NY Acad Art, 2002, Univ Tex, Austin, 2003. *Teaching:* Fac, Yale Univ, 90-92 & Tyler Sch Art, 92, Mus Contemp Art, Chicago, 97, RI Sch Design, 2000, NY Acad Art, 2000, others. *Awards:* Residency, NY Acad Art, 86; Individual Artist grant, Nat Endowment Arts, 88 & 94; Purchase Award, Am Acad Arts & Letts, 2002; Yaddo, MacDowell Colony, 2006; Guggenheim Award, 2006; NY Found Arts Fel, 2009. *Bibliog:* Rainer Metzger (auth), Kunstforum Int, 6/95; Christian Kravagna (auth), Art Forum, 9/95; Nancy Princenthal (auth), Art in America, 10/96; Christopher Reardon (auth), Fox's Fables, ARTnews, 6/2000; Genevieve Breerett (auth), La Corps Perdue, Dans Les Images, LeMonde, 5/2000; and others. *Media:* Fired Clay, Casein Paint. *Dealer:* PPOW Gallery 511 West 25th St Rm 301 New York NY 10001. *Mailing Add:* 270 Lafayette St No 1306 New York NY 10012

FOX, LINCOLN H
SCULPTOR
b Morrilton, Ark, June 14, 1942. *Study:* Univ Tex, Austin, with Charles Umlaf, BFA, 66; Univ Dallas, with Heri Barscht, MA, 67; Univ Kans, Lawrence, with Elden Tefft, MFA, 68. *Work:* El Paso Art Mus; Mus Southwest, Midland, Tex; Land of the Four Seasons Collection, Lake of the Ozarks, Mo; Albuquerque Int Airport; Bass Masters, Pentula, Ala. *Comn:* Child of Prague, Cistercian Prep Sch, Irving, Tex; Turn of the Century Cable Tool Workers, Permian Basin Petroleum Mus, Midland, Tex, 76; wall relief, First Christian Church, Ruidoso, NMex, 82. *Exhib:* Solo exhib, Smithsonian Inst, 75, Fine Arts Mus Albuquerque, 78 & El Paso Art Mus, 79; Nat Acad Western Art Ann, Nat Cowboy Hall Fame, Oklahoma City, 75, 79 & 80; Nat Sculpture Soc Ann Exhib, Equitable Bldg, NY, 82 & 83; Nat Western Artists First Ann Exhib, Civic Ctr, Lubbock, Tex, 82 & 83; Dressing the Bit, Odessa, Tex, 2007; Strength of One, Pentula, Ala; Jeremiah Lanpier, New York, 2007; and others. *Teaching:* Instr sculpture, Univ Kans, Lawrence, 67-68; instr sculpture & drawing, Amarillo Coll, 69-71; instr, Scottsdale Artists Sch (2 wks yr). *Awards:* Purchase Award, 60th Ann Nat

Competition Am Art, 70; Bronze Medal, Solon Borglum Mem Sculpture Exhib, Nat Cowboy Hall Fame, 75; Misner Award, 49th Ann Exhib Nat Sculpture Soc, 82. *Bibliog:* Morgan Catherine Merrill (auth), Lincoln Fox: Mood, media and idea, Southwest Art Mag, 5/80; Peggy & Harold Samuels (auths), Contemporary Western Artists, Southwest Art Publ, 82; article, Nat Sculpture Rev, summer 82. *Mem:* Nat Sculpture Soc; Nat Western Artist Asn. *Media:* Bronze, Stone; Pastel. *Publ:* Western Art Collector, 3/2008. *Dealer:* Sage Creek Galleries Santa Fe NM; J Willott Gallery Palm Desert CA

FOX, MICHAEL DAVID
SCULPTOR, PROFESSOR, PHOTOGRAPHER
b Cortland, NY, Dec 29, 1937. *Study:* State Univ NY, New Paltz, with Ilya Bolotowsky & Ken Green; State Univ NY, Buffalo, with Robert Davidson, BS (art educ), 62, MS, 69; Brooklyn Mus Sch, with Tom Doyle, Rueben Tam & Toshio Odate, cert, 64, Artist Loft, NY, 70-71. *Work:* State Univ NY, Buffalo, Cortland, Oswego & New Paltz; Brooklyn Mus; Morehead State Univ, Morehead, Ky; Pvt collections throughout the world. *Exhib:* Solo exhibs, SUNY, Buffalo, 62, Morehead State Univ, Ky, 66, SUNY, Oswego, 69, 75, 83 & 90, Visual Image Gallery, New York, 71, Univ Vt, Burlington, 77, Elmira Coll, 78, Oswego Art Guild, 78 & 88 & others in Toronto, NY & Rome; Finger Lakes Ann, Rochester Mem Art Gallery, 63-93; Ann Prof Exhib, Brooklyn Mus, 64; JB Speed Art Mus, Louisville, Ky, 65-67; Cent NY Ann, Everson Mus, Syracuse, 68-84; Artists Cent NY, Munson-Williams-Proctor Inst, Utica, 68-89 & 95; Visual Image Gallery, New York City, 70-71; OK Harris, NY, 71; State Univ Ark Nat, Univ Gallery, 73; Cooperstown Art Mus Nat, NY, 81; Mich Watercolor Nat, 85; State Univ NY Painters Invitational, Geneso, 88; Rome Art Ctr, Rome, NY, 89. *Pos:* Dir, Popular Image Gallery, Oswego, NY, 73-; proj dir, Nat Endowment Arts Grant, State Univ NY, Oswego, 78-2000. *Teaching:* Instr art, Rochester City Schs, NY, 62-65; artist-in-residence, var schs & orgns, 64-99; instr, Morehead State Univ, Ky, 65-67; prof art, State Univ, Oswego, NY, 67-2000, retired, 2000. *Awards:* Sculpture Award, Ann Exhib, Brooklyn Mus, 64; Painting Awards, Finger Lakes Exhib, Rochester Mem Art Gallery, 78 & NY State Fair, Syracuse, 78-81, 92, 93, 94 & 97; Best of Show, Art Asn Oswego; Outstanding Teaching Award, Morehead Univ, 67; Chancellors Award for Excellence in Teaching, 81; and many more. *Bibliog:* Sculpture (feature), CBS TV, 76, 78 & 80; Sculpture (feature), Can Nat Television, 79; PM Mag (feature), CBS TV, 81; Arthur Williams: Beginning Sculpture, Technique, Form & Content (feature), 95; Arthur Williams (auth), The Sculpture Reference, 2004; Arthur Williams (auth), Beginning Sculpture, Davis Press, 2005. *Media:* Plastic, Polyester Resin. *Publ:* Contrib, Evergreen Review (bk), Cavalier Sch Arts, NY Times; articles in Nat Lampoon & Scanlons Monthly. *Dealer:* Delavan Gallery 501 W Fayette St Syracuse NY 13204. *Mailing Add:* 38 W End Ave Oswego NY 13126

FOX, TERRY ALAN
CONCEPTUAL ARTIST, SCULPTOR
b Seattle, Wash, May 10, 1943. *Study:* Self taught. *Work:* Univ Art Mus, Berkeley; Mus Modern Art, San Francisco; Kuntzmuseum, Luzern, Switz; Folkwang Mus, Essen, Ger; Mus Contemp Art, Vienna, Austria. *Comn:* Sculpture (stone), Podio del Mondo di Arte, Middelberg, Holland, 78. *Exhib:* Solo exhibs, Univ Art Mus (with catalog), Berkeley, 73, Everson Mus, Syracuse, 74, Long Beach Mus Art, 75, Kunstmuseum (with catalog), Luzern, Switz, 82, Folkwang Mus (with catalog), Essen, Ger, 82, DAAD Galerie, Berlin, Ger, 82 & Kunstraum, Munich, Ger, 85. *Pos:* Artist-in-residence, DAAD, Berlin, WGer, 82-83. *Publ:* Auth, Catch Phrases & Hobo Signs, Kunstraum, Munich, Ger, 85. *Mailing Add:* c/o Ronald Feldman Fine Arts 31 Mercer St New York NY 10013

FRABEL, HANS GODO
SCULPTOR
b Jena, Ger, June 9, 1941. *Work:* Smithsonian Inst, White House & Nat Bldg Mus, Washington, DC; Wertheim Mus, WGer; Botanical Mus, Harvard Univ, Cambridge, Mass; Dusseldorf Mus, WGer; Headly-Whitney Mus, Lexington, Ky. *Comn:* Gift to Deng Xiaoping, comn by City Atlanta, Ga, 79; gift to people of Berlin, comn by VPres Rockefeller, Washington, DC; gift to Lord High Mayor, London, Delta Airlines, Atlanta, Ga, 79; gift to Pres Carter, Ga Democratic Party, Atlanta, Ga; Gardens for Peace, Moscow, 88; Queen Elizabeth II, 91. *Exhib:* Jr Art Gallery, Louisville, Ky, 75; New Glass, traveling, 79-; Contemp Glass Gallery, NY, 80; Westlake Gallery, White Plains, NY, 81; Glass Gallery, Bethesda, Md; Crystal Fox, Carmel, Calif; Global Gallery, Tampa, Fla; Foster-White, Seattle, 92. *Pos:* Bd, Ga Coun on Int Visitors. *Awards:* Phoenix Award, Atlanta Chamber of Commerce, Ga; Peoples Choice Best in Glass, Artists Soc Int, 87; Am Interfaith, Silver Award, 92. *Bibliog:* Sampling of contemporary picture, Cleveland Plain Dealer, 80; Creating art in glass, Dallas Times-Herald, 80; Frabel's glass meets the flame, Southern Living, 5/81. *Mem:* Glass Art Soc; Am Sci Glassblowers Soc. *Media:* Borosilicate Crystal. *Dealer:* 309 East Paces Ferry Rd Ste 101 Atlanta GA 30305. *Mailing Add:* 695 Antone St NW Atlanta GA 30318-7601

FRACKMAN, NOEL
CRITIC, HISTORIAN
b New York, NY, May 27, 1930. *Study:* Mt Holyoke Coll, Sarah Williston Scholar, 48-50; Sarah Lawrence Coll, BA, 52, MA, 53; Columbia Univ, 64-67; Inst Fine Arts, NY Univ, MA, 76, PhD, 87. *Pos:* Lectr, Aldrich Mus Contemp Art, Ridgefield, Conn, 67-75; participant, Art Critics Workshop, Am Fedn Arts, 68; lectr, Gallery Passport Ltd, New York, 68-; contrib ed, Arts Mag, New York, 68-92; cur educ, Storm King Art Ctr, Mountainville, NY, 73-75; contractural lectr, Metrop Mus Art, New York, 94-95. *Teaching:* Instr, Continuing Educ Div, Purchase Coll, State Univ NY, Purchase, 88-, adj assoc prof humanities, 98-. *Awards:* Mademoiselle First Prize, Coll Publ Contest, 61. *Mem:* Int Asn Art Critics; Art Table; Friends of Newberger Mus Art; Purchase Coll Found. *Publ:* Auth, Super-chair, Art Voices, fall 66; The Stein family and the era of avant-garde collecting, 2/71 & The enticement of watercolor, 6/74, Arts Mag; Jump into the New York art world, Harper's Bazaar, 2/72; auth art rev, Scarsdale Inquirer, 62-67, Patent Trader, 62-71 & Arts Mag, current issues; auth, John Storrs retrospective catalog, Whitney Mus Am Art, 86

FRADKIN, LUCY
PAINTER
Exhib: Solo exhibs include, Alternative Space, New York, 1981, Galeria Azul, Guadalajara, Mexico, 1996, Am Acad Rome, 2003, Kenise Barnes Fine Art, Larchmont, NY, 2004, 2005, Lesley Heller Gallery, New York, 2007; group exhibs include Women Valley Artists, Hampshire Coll Gallery, Amherst, Mass, 1981; Ann Juried, Queens Mus, Flushing, NY, 1986, Best of Ann Juried, 1989; China Int Arts Festival, Hong Kong Art Ctr, 1990; Rush Arts, New York, 1999; Wall Paper, Kenise Barnes Fine Art, Larchmont, NY, 1999, Recess, 2000, New Work, 2002, Botanical Gardens, 2002, Gallery Artists, 2003, 2004, A Thing of Beauty, 2006; Merry, Sideshow Gallery, Williamsburg, NY, 2003; 8th Ann Mermaid Show, Coney Island Mus, Brooklyn, NY, 2005; Art Bar Gallery, Ithaca, NY, 2006; Outwin Boochever Portrait Competition, Smithsonian Mus Nat Portrait Gallery, Washington, 2006. *Teaching:* Artist/Educator, Young Audiences, New York, 1992-Present; Artist/Lecturer, NY Pub Libr/NY Found Arts, New York, 2001, Islip Art Mus, Islip, NY, 2002, Temple Univ Rome Prog, Rome, 2002, RI Sch Design Rome Prog, Rome, 2003, Sala Convegni Camera di Commercio Cagliari, Italy, 2003, Hunter Coll, New York, 2005, Anderson Ranch, Aspen, Colo, 2006. *Awards:* Artist-in-Residence Grant, NY Found Arts, New York, 1993, 1994, 1995, 1996, 1997, Artist Fel, 2005; Gottlieb Found Grant, 2007. *Dealer:* Clark Gallery 145 Lincoln Rd Lincoln MA 01773. *Mailing Add:* Kenise Barnes Fine Art 1955 Palmer Ave Larchmont NY 10538

FRAENKEL, JEFFREY ANDREW
ART DEALER
b Shreveport, La, Jan 28, 1955. *Study:* Antioch Col, BFA, 77. *Pos:* Pres, Fraenkel Gallery, San Francisco. *Mem:* Art Dealers Asn Am; Asn Int Photography Art Dealers. *Specialty:* 19th and 20th century photographs. *Publ:* Photography in Spain in the Nineteenth Century, 83; The Kiss of Apollo: Photography & Sculpture 1845 to the Present; Seeing Things, 94; Open Secrets: Seventy Pictures of Paper 1815 to the Present, 96; Under the Sun, 96. *Mailing Add:* 49 Geary St San Francisco CA 94108

FRAILEY, STEPHEN A
PHOTOGRAPHER
b Chicago, Ill, Sept 3, 1957. *Study:* San Francisco Art Inst, 77; Bennington Col, BA, 79. *Work:* Fogg Art Mus, Harvard Univ, Boston, Mass; Chase Manhattan Bank, NY; Int Ctr Photog, NY; Mus Fine Arts, Houston; Princeton Univ Art Mus; and others. *Exhib:* Art & Advertising, Int Ctr Photog, NY, 87; Avant Garde in 80's, Los Angeles Mus, Calif, 87; Contemp Diptychs, Whitney Mus/Equitable, NY, 87; Photog Fabrications, Carpenter Ctr, Cambridge, 88; The Photog of Invention, Nat Mus Am Art, Washington, DC, 89; Thin Air, Julie Saul Gallery, NY, 99. *Pos:* Dir, Mary Boone Gallery, 80-85; artist-in-residence Chinati Found, Marfa, Tex, 2000. *Teaching:* Chmn, Photo Dept, Sch Visual Arts, NY, 85-, Int Ctr Photog, NY & Bard Col, Annandale, NY, 93-98; vis prof, Benington Col, 97, fac chiar grad photography dept, 94-. *Awards:* Macdowell Colony Fel, 88 & 95; Nat Endowment Arts, 88; Aaron Siskind Found Grant, 92. *Bibliog:* Portfolio, Paris Rev, spring 89; David Robbins (auth), Stephen Frailey, Arts Mag, 9/89; Portfolio, Art Forum, 10/90; and others; Genuine Initiation, Art on Paper, 1-2/99. *Publ:* Auth, Richard Avedon, Print Collector, 5/86; Ray Metzger, Art News, 9/87; Thin Air: The Photographs of Adam Fuss, Art Forum, 11/93; Murder, Mystery & Mayhem, Apature, 97; and others. *Mailing Add:* 10 Jay St Apt 2A New York NY 10013

FRANCE-VAZ, NANCI
PAINTER, INSTRUCTOR
b Brooklyn, NY, Sept 15, 1966. *Study:* Sch Visual Arts, BFA, 97; attended, NY Acad Art; studied with Paul W McCormack, McCormack Studios, 2006-2007, Michael Grimaldi, Art Students League, 2009-2010, James Childs. *Work:* The Masters Octava, Keyport, NJ; Union Co Coll, Cranford, NJ. *Comn:* figurative oil painting, comn by Frito Lay, NY, 2009; oil portrait Ted Miller, comn by The Masters Octava, Keyport, NJ, 2011; family oil portrait, comn by Rob Kirkpatrick, Old Greenwich, NJ, 2011; oil portrait Mary Weir, comn by Theodore J Miller, Keyport, NJ, 2012; oil portrait Dr. Cynthia Magro, comn by Dr. Magro Weill Cornell, NY, 2012; official presidential portrait, Dr McNemanin, Union Co Coll, Cranford, NJ. *Exhib:* Solo exhibs, Cinematic Impressions of Life, Masters Octava, Keyport, NJ, 2011, Rhapsody, 2012; Group exhibs, Audubon Artists Ann Exhib, Salmagundi Club, NY, 2008; The Masters Show, Huntington Art Coun, Huntington, NY, 2009; Portrait Soc Am, 2009; Nat Arts Club, NY, 2011. *Pos:* graphic artist, Vanguard Media, 2000-2001; art studio asst, James Childs Drawing Acad of the Atlantic, 2003-2004; 3D animator, Arakawa Gins Archit, 2003-2004; Nanci France-Vaz Fine Art LLC, 2005-. *Teaching:* instr, LaGuardia High Sch Music, Art, & Performing Arts, 2000-2003; instr portrait, figure painting, Art Guild Shrewsbury, NJ, 2010-; Brookdale Community Coll, Lincroft, NJ, 2012. *Awards:* 1st Place, Audubon Artists, Ray Padovano, 2005; Hon Mention, CSOPA Faces of Winter, Jeanine Jackson, 2007; 3rd Place, PSOA Mem Showcase, Gordon Wetmore, 2009; Best in Show, Huntington Arts Petite Gallery, 2009; Top 100 Finalist, ACOPAL, Paul McCormack, 2011; Finalist, Art Renewal Ctr Salon, 2012. *Bibliog:* Gordon Wetmore (auth), Art of the Portrait, Int Artist Mag, 2009. *Mem:* Allied Artists Am (assoc mem, 2009-); Audubon Artists Inc (graphics vol, 2005-); Portrait Soc Am (assoc, 2003-); Catherine Lorillard Wolfe (assoc, vol); Art Renewal Ctr (assoc, 2011-). *Media:* Acrylic, Oil. *Publ:* Int Artist Mag, 2009; Art of the Portrait, 2009; Art Renewal Ctr, Salon Catalog, 2011, 2012. *Dealer:* The Masters Octava Historic Site 300 W Front St Keyport NJ 07735; The Guild Gallery 620 Broad St Shrewsbury NJ 07702. *Mailing Add:* 1118 Rte 36 Atlantic Highlands NJ 07716

FRANCES, (SHERANA) HARRIETTE
MASTER PRINTER, PAINTER
b San Francisco, Calif. *Study:* San Francisco Sch Fine Arts, 42-45; San Francisco Art Inst, 63 & 65-66; James Weeks, Painting Instr, Tamarind Inst, Univ NMex, 88-90 & 92; Cert, prof printer, lifetime teaching credential. *Work:* Fresno Art Ctr, Calif; Charles D Clark Collection, McAllen, Tex; Achenbach Found Graphic Arts; San Francisco

Legion of Honor Fine Arts Mus; Charles & Nancy Curley Collection, Marin Cty, Calif. *Exhib:* Solo exhib, Haggin Mus, Stockton, Calif, 64 & Calif Palace Legion Hon, 68; James D Phelan Award Exhib, De Young Mus, San Francisco, 63 & Palace Legion of Honor, 65; Americana-Bicentennial, San Francisco Mus Modern Art, 76; Brandts-Klaenfabrik Mus, Funen, Denmark, 89; 8th Nat Juried Exhib, Berkeley, Calif, 92; Calif Small Works, Luther Burbank Ctr Arts, Santa Rosa, Calif, 96; Beyond Boundaries, Richmond Art Ctr, Calif, 97; Inst Franco-Am Rennes, France, 98; Contents & Contexts: Lithography After 200 Yrs - Honolulu, Hawaii; Radical Printmaking, San Francisco Comn Gallery, 2000; Int/Invitational Exh of Prints, Chung/Shan Nat Gallery, Taiwan, 2005; Printmakers Today, Somarts, San Francisco, Calif, 2006; Int Exhib, Astoria, Ore, 2007; Art Buzz: The 2010 Collection Book; Open Fine Arts, Marin Soc Arists, Ross, Calif, 2011; Gallery 888, San Rafael, Calif, 2010-2011; Marin Comm Found, 2011; Bankside Art Gallery, London, Eng; Triton Mus, Santa Clara, Calif; Marin Mus Contemp Art, Novato, Calif, 2012; Falkirk Ann, San Rafael, Calif; Image Hungry, Gary Francis Fine Art Gallery, Alameda, Calif, 2014. *Pos:* cur, Marin Arts Council, 88, 99; exhibitions chair, Calif Soc Artists, 2002. *Teaching:* Instr life drawing, Exten, Univ Pac; instr lithography & master printer, Artists Proof Graphics Workshop, Larkspur, Calif; instr monotype, Coll Marin, Kentfield, Calif. *Awards:* Calif State Fair Award, 64; James D Phelan Award in Art, 65; 2nd Biennial, Janet Turner Nat Print Competition, 97; Nat Open, Marin Soc Artists, 2009; Nat Open Award, Haggin Mus, Stockton, Calif, 2010. *Bibliog:* George Christy (auth), Are you with it, Town & Country Mag, 67; Martin Fox (ed), A graphic artist depicts her LSD trip, Print Mag, 67; Joan Lisetor (auth), Reviving an ancient art, Independent J, 75. *Mem:* San Francisco Mus Mod Art; Calif Soc Printmakers. *Media:* Lithography, Acrylic. *Interests:* Books; music. *Publ:* Contribr, Ramparts Mag, 66; Print Mag & Psychedelic Art, 67; Erotic Art of the Masters, 18th, 19th & 20th Centuries, Lyle Stewart Publ; The Spirit of Shamanism, Tarcher Publ, 90; auth, Drawing It Out, Maps Publ, Fla, 2001; auth, Drawing it OUt, Befriending the Unconscious, 2001. *Mailing Add:* 105 Rice Lane Larkspur CA 94939

FRANCESCHINI, AMY
ENVIRONMENTAL ARTIST, EDUCATOR

Study: San Francisco State Univ, BFA; Standford Univ, MFA. *Work:* Orange Co Mus Art; San Francisco Mus Mod Art. *Comn:* Kitchen Garden, Headlands Ctr for the Arts; Streaming News Wall & Zine Rack, Yerba Buena Ctr for the Arts. *Exhib:* Cooper-Hewitt Nat Design Mus, New York, 1998; Limn Gallery, San Francisco, 1998; Yerba Buena Ctr for the Arts, San Francisco, 1999-2000; Osnabruck Medai Art Festival, Ger, 2000; solo exhibs, Luggage Store Gallery, San Francisco, 2000, Sapporo Art Park, Japan, 2000, Gallery 16, San Francisco, 2000 & 2007, Electronic Orphanage, Los Angeles, 2001, Ramp Gallery, Waikato Inst Tech, New Zealand, 2002, Jack Hanley Gallery, San Francisco, 2003, Univ Pacific, Stockton, 2004, Nelson Galelry, Univ Calif, Davis, 2005, Pasadena City Coll Art Gallery, 2008 & Contemp Mus Balitmore, 2009; Nat Gallery Arts, Tirana, Albania, 2001; Calif Coll Arts & Crafts, Oakland, 2001; Stanford Univ Art Gallery, Palo Alto, Calif, 2002; Mus Fortuny, Venice, Italy, 2002; Whitney Biennale, Mus Art, New York, 2002; New Image Art, Los Angeles, 2003; Orange Co Mus, Santa Ana, Calif, 2004; RIXC Ctr for New Media, Art & Commun Festival, Riga, Latvia, 2004; Smart Mus, Chicago, 2005; Mus Mod Art, New York, 2005; Sonoma Co Mus, Santa Rosa, 2006; Ctr Pompidou, Les Yeux Ouverts, Paris, 2006; Boulder Mus Contemp Art, Colo, 2007; Clifford Gallery, Colgate Univ, 2008; Anchorage Mus, Alaska, 2009; Madison Mus Contemp Art, Madison, Wis, 2009. *Pos:* Founder, Futurefarmers, 1995; artist-in-residence, Headlands Ctr for the Arts, Sausalito, Calif, 2003, Lofoten Island, Norway, 2004, Anderson Ranch, Aspec, Colo, 2006 & Pasadena City Coll, 2008; co-founder, Free Soil, 2004. *Teaching:* Instr sculpture & digital media, San Francisco Art Inst, 2002-2007; instr new media & pub art, Stanford Univ, 2002-2006; vis artist, Grad Seminars in Social Practice, Calif Coll Arts, 2004-; prof art & archit, Univ San Francisco, 2007-. *Awards:* Eureka Fel, Fleishhacker Found, 2004; Artadia Award, Fund for Art & Dialog, 2005; SECA Art Award, San Francisco Mus Mod Art, 2006; Investing in Artists Grant, Ctr Cult Innovation, 2007; Seed Fund, Studio for Urban Projects, 2008; Victory Garden Grant, San Francisco Dept for Environ, 2008; Grant for Emerging Fields, Creative Capital Found, 2009; Guggenheim Found Fel, 2010. *Bibliog:* Marisa Olson (auth), Futurefarmers at University of the Pacific, Art Week, 2004; Zahid Sardar (auth), San Francisco Chronicle, Victory Gardens, Datebok, 89, 2007; Claire Dederer (auth), Looking for Inspiration in the Melting Ice, 35, 9/2007. *Mailing Add:* 499 Alabama St #114 San Francisco CA 94110

FRANCIS, JEAN THICKENS
ASSEMBLAGE ARTIST, PAINTER

b Laurel, Miss, Mar 15, 1943. *Study:* Millsaps Col, 61-63; Memphis Art Acad, BFA (sculpture), 66. *Work:* South Central Bell, Miss; Deposit Guaranty Nat Bank, Tupelo & Jackson, Miss; First Nat Bank, Miss; Boyle Investment CO, Memphis Tenn; Int Paper Co, Memphis, Tenn. *Comn:* N Mississippi Women's Health Ctr, Tupelo; Peoples Bank and Trust, Tupelo; Community Federal Savings & Loan, Tupelo; US Embassy, Riyadh, Saudi Arabia, 94. *Exhib:* Mississippi River Crafts Exhib, Brooks Mem Art Gallery, 77; Papermakers & Paperusers, Southeastern Artists, Southeastern Ctr Contemp Art, Winston-Salem, NC, 80; one-person shows, The 500 lb Paper Project, Miss Mus Art, Jackson, Open Gallery, Miss Mus Art, Jackson; Prints, Drawings & Crafts Show, Ark Art Ctr, Little Rock, 81; Artsite Invitational, New Orleans, La, 80; More Than Land or Sky: Art from Appalachia, Nat Mus Am Art, Smithsonian Inst & traveling, 81-84; The State of The Art: Mississippi, Contemp Art Ctr, New Orleans, La, 83; Papermakers Invitational, Western Carolina Univ, Cullowhee, NC, 85; Paper Art-New Directions, Texas Tech Univ Mus, Lubbock, Tex, 85; 100 Gloves: And Then Some, Univ Mus, Oxford, Miss, 85. *Pos:* Self-employed artist, currently. *Teaching:* Instr art, Memphis City Sch, Tenn, 66-67; instr sculpture, Memphis Acad Art, Tenn, summer 74; vis artist, Jackson City Sch, Miss, 76; guest artist, papermaking, Nat Mus Am Art, 81, Miss Mus Art, Jackson, 81, Arrowmont Sch Arts & Crafts, Gatlinburg, Tenn, 84 & Itawamba Jr Col, Fulton, Miss, 85; instr, papermaking, Appalachia Ctr Crafts, Smithville, Tenn, 83; artist-in-residence, Tupelo City Sch, Miss, 83-84, Bellazio Study Ctr, Italy, 90. *Awards:* Grand Prize, 76 & Second Prize, 77, Miss Artist Competitive Exhib, Miss Art Asn; Merit Award, Greater New Orleans Int Art Exhib, 77; Grant, Rockefeller Found, 90. *Bibliog:* Articles, Art Voices South, 5/79, Cityscape, 81 & 82 & Art Papers, 7-8/82; Annette Cone-Skelton (auth), Southeastern artists today: a cross section, Contemp Art/SE, 78; Gary Witt (auth), Ke & Jean Francis of Tupelo, Mississippi: A union of opposites, Art Voices/South, 5/79; Stephen Flynn Young (auth), A visit with Jean Thickens Francis, Art Papers, 82. *Media:* Mixed Media. *Dealer:* Albers Fine Art Gallery 1102 Brookfield Rd Suite 101 Memphis TN 38119. *Mailing Add:* 512 Magnolia Dr Tupelo MS 38801-3530

FRANCIS, MADISON KE, JR
SCULPTOR, PRINTMAKER

b Memphis, Tenn, Aug 19, 1945. *Study:* Miss State Univ, Starkville; Memphis State Univ, Tenn; Memphis Acad Art, Tenn; Cleveland Inst Art, Ohio, BFA (sculpture), 69; Cape Sch Art, Provincetown, Mass, study painting with Henry Hensche. *Work:* Southeastern Ctr Contemp Art, Winston-Salem, NC; Mint Mus, Charlotte, NC; New Orleans Mus, La; Mus Fine Arts, Boston, Mass; Rose Mus, Brandeis Univ, Waltham, Mass. *Comn:* Steel sculpture, People's Bank, Tupelo, Miss, 73; sculpture, Itawamba Jr Col, 78; time capsule sculpture, North Miss Med Ctr, Tupelo. *Exhib:* Southern Exposure: Not a Regional Exhib, Alternative Mus, NY, 85; A Sense of Place: Contemp Southern Art, Minneapolis Coll Art & Design Gallery, Minn, 86; Fact/Fiction/Fantasy: Recent Narrative Art in the Southeast, Traveling exhib, Ewing Gallery, Univ Tenn, Knoxville, 87; Southern Arts Fedn Touring Sculpture Exhib, Atlanta, Ga, 87- 89; Solo exhibs, Recent Works, Memphis Ctr Contemp Art, Tenn, 88, Recent Prints, Drawings & Sculpture, Marcia McCoy Gallery Contemp Art, Santa Fe, NMex, 89 & Reconstruction: Tornado Series, Clara Eagle Gallery, Murray State Univ, Ky, 89; Looking South: A Different Dixie, Touring Exhib, Birmingham Mus, Ala, 88; Freneticism, Valencia Community Col, Orlando, Fla, 88; The Blues Aesthetic: Black Cult & Modernism Touring Exhib, Washington Pro Arts, Washington, DC, 89; and others. *Teaching:* Instr, Cleveland Inst Art, 69-71; instr sculpture, Memphis Acad Art, summer 73; instr graphics, Penland Sch, NC, 78-79. *Awards:* SAF/NEQ Regional fel sculpture, Southern Arts Fedn, 87; Award for visual arts, Mississippi Inst Arts and Letters, 87; Rockefeller Found Grant, Bellagio Study Ctr, Italy, 90. *Bibliog:* Becky Hendrick (auth), El Paso/Las Cruces Letter, Art Space, winter 87-88; Jane Bedno (auth), Tornadoes in Beulah Land, Vol 2, No 3, winter 89; Stephen Flinn Young (auth), Post-southernism: The Southern Sensibility in Postmodern Sculpture, Southern Quarterly, Vol XXVIII, No 4, fall 89. *Media:* Miscellaneous Media; Intaglio, Silkscreen. *Dealer:* Galerie Simone Stern New Orleans La; Morgan Gallery Kansas City Mo. *Mailing Add:* 801 Temple Terr Oviedo FL 32765

FRANCIS, TOM
PAINTER

b Sheboygan, Wis, Mar 12, 1951. *Study:* Univ Wis, BS, 73, MA, 75, MFA (Henry Vilas Fel), 76. *Work:* State Wis, Madison; Chase Manhattan Bank, NY; Omni Int, Atlanta; Europco Corp, Fla; Coca Cola Corp, Atlanta, Ga; and others. *Comn:* Paintings, Made in Heaven (film), comn by Alan Rudolph, dir; Hyatt Corp, Aruba & Puerto Rico; Embassy Suites, Orlando, Fla; Omni Corp, Miami, Fla. *Exhib:* Columbia Mus, SC, 82; Atlanta in France, Paris, Toulouse France, 85; Volte del Sud, Rome, Italy, 85; Sandler/Hudson Gallery, Atlanta, 90; McIntosh Gallery, Atlanta, 92; Zinc Gallery, Bluewater Bay, Fla; Mary Pauline Gallery, 97; Montgomery Mus Art, Ala, 97; Spruell Ctr Arts, Atlanta, 98; & many others. *Teaching:* Chmn dept painting, Atlanta Col Art, 1978-94, 1995-2002, 2003-2006. *Media:* All. *Mailing Add:* Savannah College Art & Design PO Box 3146 Savannah GA 31402

FRANK, CHARLES WILLIAM, JR
WOOD CARVER, WRITER

b New Orleans, La, June 8, 1922. *Study:* BChemEng. *Exhib:* New Orleans Mus Art, 75; Hillsborough Co Mus, Tampa, Fla, 76; Univ New Orleans Fine Arts Mus, 76; Huntsville Mus Art, Ala, 76-77; West Baton Rouge Hist Asn, 76; Nat Crafts Coun, Winston-Salem, NC, 77. *Pos:* Auth & contribr, NAm Decoys, 72-77; auth, La Duck Decoys, 75-79; La Out of Doors, 77-78 & Ward Found Mag; Anatomy of a Waterfowl, Pelican Publ, 81 & Wetland Heritage, 85. *Awards:* Best of Show, Catahoula Lake Wildfowl Festival, 75 & 76; First Place, La Wildfowl Carvers Exhib, 76; La Master Craftsman, 77. *Bibliog:* Article in La Conservationist, State of La, 73 & 75; Phillips Petroleum Co (auth), Louisiana's Wetland Heritage, The Decoy, 76. *Mem:* La Crafts Coun; La Wildfowl Carvers & Collectors; Int Wildlife Carvers; Nat Wood Carvers Asn. *Media:* Wood, Polychrome. *Collection:* Definitive collection of several thousand Louisiana and world wide duck decoys. *Publ:* Auth articles, Am Shotgunner, 76 & Southern Outdoors, 77

FRANK, HELEN GOODZEIT
PAINTER, PRINTMAKER

b Jersey City, NJ, May 29, 1930. *Study:* Tyler Sch Fine Arts, Temple Univ; Cooper Union; New Sch, with Abraham Rattner & Seymour Lipton, 48; Art Students League, with George Grosz, 50. *Work:* NJ State Mus, Trenton; Newark Public Libr Print Collection, NJ; Am Mus Immigration, NY; UNICEF; Libr Congress. *Comn:* Portfolio, Grant Union Co, NJ, 80-81. *Exhib:* NJ State Exhib, Montclair Mus, 63; Am Watercolor Soc, NY, 65; Pratt Graphic Int, NY, 75 & 77; Morris Mus, Morristown, NJ; NJ Watercolor Soc, Morristown; Rutgers Univ, NJ. *Teaching:* Artist-in-residence, Springfield Pub Sch. *Mem:* Artists Equity. *Mailing Add:* 445 Meisel Ave Springfield NJ 07081

FRANK, MARY
SCULPTOR, PAINTER

b London, Eng, 1933. *Study:* Am Artists Sch with Max Beckmann, 1950; studied with Hans Hofmann, 1951 & 1954. *Work:* Hirshhorn Mus and Sculpture Garden, Washington; Metrop Mus Art, Mus Modern Art, NY; Mus Fine Arts, Boston; Art Inst Chicago; Brooklyn Mus Art. *Exhib:* solo exhibs incl Neuberger Mus, State Univ NY,

Purchase, 1978, 2000, Brooklyn Mus, 1987, DeCordova and Dana Mus and Park, Lincoln, Mass, 1988, Everson Mus Art, Syracuse, 1988, Pa Acad Fine Arts, Philadelphia, 1988, DC Moore Gallery, 1996, 1998 & 2000 & Allentown Art Mus, 2001; group exhibs incl 10 Independents, Solomon R Guggenheim Mus, NY, 1972; Whitney Sculpture Ann, 1972, Whitney Biennial, 1973 & 1979, Small Objects, Whitney Mus Am Art, NY, 1977; Drawings of the 70's, Art Inst Chicago, 1977; Contemp Women: Consciousness and Content, 1977 & Pub and Private: Am Prints Today, Brooklyn Mus, 1986; 8 Artists, Philadelphia Mus Art, 1978; Mysterious and Magical Realism, Aldrich Mus Contemp Art, Ridgefield, Conn, 1980; The Painterly Print, Metrop Mus Art, NY, 1980; The Painterly Print Traveling Exhib, Mus Fine Arts, Boston, 1980; Sculpture in the 70's - The Figure, Pratt Inst, NY, 1980; The Figurative Tradition, Whitney Mus Am Art, NY, 1980; The Clay Figure, Am Craft Mus, NY, 1981; Am Printmaker's Show, Brooklyn Mus, 1983; Contemp Am Monotypes, Chrysler Mus, Norfolk, Va, 1985; Body and Soul: Recent Figurative Sculpture, Contemp Arts Ctr, Cincinnati, 1985; Disarming Images, 1986, Standing Ground: Sculpture by Am Women, Contemp Arts Ctr, Cincinnati, 1987; The Jewish Mus Collects, Jewish Mus, NY, 1988; Committed to Print, Mus Modern Art, NY, 1988; The 1980's: Prints from the Collection of Joshua P Smith, Nat Gallery Art, Washington, 1990; Shadows of Africa, Cent Park Zoo Gallery, NY, 1992; Print and Drawing Society 25th Anniversary Exhib, Baltimore Mus Art, 1993; The Second Dimension: Twentieth-Century Sculptor's Drawings, Brooklyn Mus, 1993; Likeness of Being, DC Moore Gallery, 2000; Pasadena Col, 1995; Nielsen Gallery, Boston, 1996; Elena Zanz Gallery, Woodstock, 1995, 1998, 2002; Reynolda House Mus, Winston-Salem, 1999; Allentown Art Mus, 2001; Marsh Art Gallery, Richmond, 2003; Nat Acad Design, 2005. *Teaching:* Distinguished prof, Bard Coll, Annandale-on-Hudson, NY, 1992; grad fac, Pa Acad Fine Arts, Philadelphia, 1992-1993. *Awards:* Guggenheim Award, 1973 & 1983; Am Acad Arts and Letts Electee, 1984; Lee Krasner Award, Pollock-Krasner Found, 1993, 2007; Pollock-Krasner Found Grant, 2008. *Bibliog:* Jerry Thompson and Hilton Kramer (auth), The sculpture of Mary Frank, The Eakins Press, 1977; Margaret Moorman (auth), In a timeless world, Artnews, 5/1987; Hayden Herrera (auth), Mary Frank, NY: Abrams, 1990; Linda Nochlin (auth), Marty Franki Encounters, NY: Abrams, 2000. *Mem:* Am Acad Arts & Letts; Nat Acad. *Dealer:* Alan Brown Gallery Naples FL 34102; Don Christiansen Fine Art LLC 194 8th Ave New York NY 10011; Hudson River Editions 278 Piermont Ave South Nyack NY 10960

FRANK, PETER SOLOMON
CRITIC, CURATOR
b New York, NY, 1950. *Study:* Columbia Col, BA (art hist), 72; Columbia Univ, MA (art hist), 74. *Collection Arranged:* Artists' books section of Documenta 6, Kassel, WGer, summer 77; Artists' Books USA Traveling Exhib, 78-80 & Mapped Art: Charts Routes Regions Traveling Exhib, 81-83, Independent Curators Inc; Young Fluxus, Artists Space, NY, 82; Indiana Influence-The Modern Legacy, Fort Wayne Mus Art, 84; To the Astonishing Horizon, Los Angeles Visual Arts, 85; Earsights: Visual Scores & Musical Images, Nexus Gallery, Philadelphia and Southern Alleghenies Mus, Johnstown, Pa, 85; Southern Abstraction, City Gallery of Contemp Art, Raleigh, NC, 87 & Contemp Arts Ctr, New Orleans, 88; Line and Image, Independent Curators, Inc, 88-90; The Theater of the Object, 1958-1972, Alternative Mus, NY, 89; Visual Poetry, Otis/Parsons Art Inst, Los Angeles, 90; Los Angeles Art, Foreign Artists, Kilkenny Castle, Ireland, 92; The Sticking Place; Space & Image in Contemporary Collage, Long Beach City Col, 92; Multiple World, Atlanta Coll Art, 94; Fluxus Scores, Coll Creative Studies, Univ Calif, Santa Barbara, 94; Reconstructivism: New Geometric Painting in NY, Space 504, 95; Grins: Humor and Whimsy in Contemporary Art, Lost Angeles Co Fair, 97; Edge, Image, Informatgion, ARTernatives, San Luis Obispo, 98; Fluxus Film & Video, Museo Reina Sofia,Madric, 2002. *Pos:* Art critic, SoHo News, 73-76, Village Voice, 77-79 & Diversion Planner, 83-90, Los Angeles Weekly, 88-, Long Beach Press Telegram, Calif, 93-96 & Art Commotion, 96-98, Book Radio, 2000-, Angeleno Mag, 2003-; cur assoc, Independent Curators Inc, 74-81; assoc ed, Tracks, 74-78, Nat Arts Guide, 79-81 & Art Express, 80-81; cur sound & mus, Inst Art & Urban Resources at PS1, 79-80; cur, Exxon Nat Exhib, 19 Emergent Americans, Guggenheim Mus, 81; contrib ed, Art Economist, 81-83; ed, Re Dact, 83-87; Am cur adv, Documenta 8, Kassel, WGer, 87; Los Angeles Corresp Contemp, 88-90; ed, Visions, 90-95; contrib ed, Artspace, 90-93; gallery coordr, Long Beach City Col, Calif, 92. *Teaching:* Vis asst prof contemp arts, Pratt Inst, Brooklyn, NY, 75-76; adj assoc prof, Sch Arts, Columbia Univ, 78; adj lectr, Tyler Sch Art, Temple Univ, 83; lectr, Univ Calif, Irvine, 88-90; lectr, Claremont Grad Sch, 89 & 92-97; vis critic, Calif State Univ, Fullerton, 90-91; vis lectr, Univ Calif, Santa Barbara, 94. *Awards:* Nat Endowment Arts Grant, 78 & 81; Fluxus Res Fel, Royal Norwegian Ministry For Affairs, 87. *Bibliog:* Jacqueline Brody (auth), Peter Frank: A Case for Marginal Collectors, Print Collectors Newsletter, 6/78; Grace Glueck (auth), How emerging artists really emerge: Getting the biennials together, Art News, 5/81; Katherine Cook (auth), Talking Art: A Conversation with Peter Frank & Peter Selz, Artspace, summer 91. *Mem:* Int Asn Art Critics; Poets & Writers; Coll Arts Asn of Am; Int Künstlers Gremium. *Publ:* Something Else Press: An Annotated Bibliography (document text), MacPherson & Co, Kingston, NY, 83; New, Used & Improved: Art for the '80s, Abbeville Press, 87; Intermedia: Die Verschmelzung der Künste, Benteli Verlag, 87; Roller: The Paintings of Donald Roller Wilson, Chronicle Books, 88; Lawrence Gipe: Paintings, Karl Bornstein, 89. *Mailing Add:* PO Box 24A36 Los Angeles CA 90024-1036

FRANK, RACHEL E
SCULPTOR
Study: Kans City Art Inst, BFA, 2003; Royal Coll Art, London, 2005; Skowhegan Sch Painting & Sculpture, 2005; Univ Pa, MFA, 2005. *Exhib:* Solo exhibs include Farenheit Gallery, Kansas City, 2004; two-person show, Rapt, Farenheit Gallery, Kansas City, 2003; group exhibs include Small Sculpture Exhib, Nat Soc Arts & Letters, Opie Gallery, Leedy-Voulkos Arts Ctr, Kansas City, 2002; MFA Biennial, Del Ctr Contemp Arts, Wilmington, 2005; Outstanding Student Achievement in Contemp Sculpture Exhib, Int Sculpture Ctr, Grounds for Sculpture, Hamilton, NJ, 2005; Our Dark Heroes, Secret Project Robot, Brooklyn, 2007; This is Not the Future, Vox Populi, Philadelphia, 2007, Solid Gold, 2008; Works on Paper, Cuchifritos, New York, 2008. *Awards:* Robert Engman Award, Philadelphia, 2004; Juror's Choice Award, Fox Gallery Show, Philadelphia, 2004; Skowhegan Matching Fel, Univ Pa, 2005; Outstanding Student Achievement in Contemp Sculpture Award, Int Sculpture Ctr, 2005; Studio Grant, Marie Walsh Sharpe Found, 2005; Elizabeth Greenshields Found Grant, 2006; Studio Grant, Artist Alliance Inc, 2006; Pollock-Krasner Found Grant, 2007

FRANKEL, DEXTRA
EDUCATOR, DESIGNER
b Los Angeles, Calif, Nov 28, 1924. *Study:* Long Beach State Col. *Work:* Philadelphia Free Libr; La Jolla Art Mus, Calif; St Paul Art Ctr, Minn; Pac View Mem Park, Corona Del Mar, Calif; Kennecott Copper Co, Salt Lake City, Utah; also in pvt collections. *Exhib:* Los Angeles Co Mus Art, 59, 62 & 66; Cincinnati Art Mus; Newport Harbor Art Mus, Newport Beach, Calif; Butler Inst Am Art, Youngstown, Ohio; Calif Palace of Legion of Honor, San Francisco; Denver Art Mus, Colo; Seattle Art Mus, Wash; Portland Art Mus, Ore; San Francisco Mus Art, Calif; H M De Young Mus, San Francisco; Smithsonian Inst, Washington, DC; and many others. *Collection Arranged:* Recorded Images/Dimensional Media, 67, Intersection of Line, 67, Frazer/Lipofsky/Richardson, 68, Transparency/Reflection, 68 & others, Art Gallery, Calif State Univ, Fullerton; and numerous others. *Pos:* Dir art gallery, cur & designer exhib, Calif State Univ, Fullerton, 67-91; owner & founder, Dextre Frankel Assoc, 91-. *Teaching:* From asst prof to assoc prof art, Calif State Univ, Fullerton, 64-79, prof art, 79-91. *Awards:* 8 Nat Endowment Arts Grants, 75 & 77-82; Design Award, Soc Typographic Arts Union Bank Hist Mus, 81. *Mem:* Am Asn Mus; Am Craft Coun; Art Mus Asn. *Media:* Exhibits. *Publ:* Auth, article, Pasadena Mus, 65 & 68 & Crafts Horizons Mag, 73. *Mailing Add:* PO Box 5307 Santa Monica CA 90409

FRANKEL, STUART & MAXINE
COLLECTOR
Study: Univ Mich, BBA, 1961, AB, 1966. *Pos:* Bd dirs, Chinati Found, Marfa, Tex, & Independent Curators Int; bd dirs & exec comt, Mich Children's Hosp; nat adv bd, Storm King Art Ctr, Mountainville, NY; chmn bd govs, Cranbrook Acad Art and Cranbrook Art Mus; pres, Stuart Frankel Development Co, Troy, Mich. *Awards:* Named one of Top 200 Collectors, ARTnews mag, 2003-13. *Collection:* Minimalism; abstract & new-media art, ceramics

FRANKFORD, SHAWNA
MURALIST, RESTORER, EDUCATOR
b Bronx, NY, Mar 4, 60. *Study:* Brooklyn Coll, BA; NYU, MA. *Work:* San Francisco Mod Art, Calif; Calif Hist Soc; Int Polaroid Collection, Boston; Houston Mus Fine Arts; Int Ctr Restoration; Bronck House. *Exhib:* Am Folklife Ctr; Glass Eye Gallery; Weaping Willow Ctr; Black Phone Galla; Gambiela Gallery; Perrusal Ctr; Saral Gallery; Slocumstein Fine Art Gallery; Carnegie Arts Ctr. *Pos:* jr restorer, Ala Jenkins Art; fine art restorer, Marbox Toolbox; master restorer, Restoration Inc; master restorer, Meriks Restoration Serv. *Teaching:* adj prof, mural hist, Montclair State Univ; and many other teaching positions in the United States & worldwide. *Bibliog:* Janet Filos (auth), An Interview with Shawn, La Gazette, 2004. *Mem:* Restoration Soc Great Lakes Region. *Publ:* Auth, The Restoration Process, 2000; auth, Becoming the Master of Your Brush, 2002; auth, Perfecting Your Stroke, 2012; auth, The Art of Appreciating & Restoring the Past, 2013; auth, Let the Past Come Back to Life, 2015. *Dealer:* Mericks Gallery Hartford CT; LifeLike Gallery San Antonio TX

FRANKFURTER, JACK
PAINTER, DESIGNER
b Vienna, Austria, Mar 25, 1929; US citizen. *Study:* Cooper Union Sch Art, 50-51; Coll City NY, BS, 51; Columbia Univ, BA, 52; Acad di Francia, Villa Medici, Rome, 58-59. *Work:* Springfield Mus Fine Arts, Mass; Wichita Art Mus, Kans; Univ Cincinnati Art Mus, Ohio; Malcolm Forbes Collection, NY; Museo Mario Praz, Rome. *Exhib:* Allied Artists Am, Nat Acad Design, NY, 54 & 56; Am Artists Ann, Whitney Mus, NY, 55; Soc of the Four Arts, Palm Beach, Fla, 68; Biennial Int, Biennale Di Lignano, Italy, 70; X Quadriennale Di Roma, Galleria D'Arte Mod, Rome, Italy, 77; San Francisco Int Airport, 93; Empire State Building Galleries, NY, 94; solo shows, Galleria 88, Rome, 60-72, La Zagara, Napoli, 61, Country Art Gallery, NY, 62, 71, Alwin Gallery, London, 69, 72, Palm Beach Gallery, 70, Mus Fine Arts, Springfield, Mass, 70, Piccola Barcaccia, Cagliari, 71, Galleria Arno, Firenze, 73, Findlay Galleries, NY, 73, Findlay Galleries, Palm Beach, 74, Kama Studio, Rome, 74, Galleria Doria, Porto Ercole, 75, 80, Galleria Ca' d'Oro, Rome, 76, 77, 79, 82, 83-89, 2001, Bodley Gallery, NY, 76, Mickelson Gallery, Washington, DC, 76, Janice Throne Gallery, Springfield, Mass, 76, The Gallery, LA, 77, Galleria Cortina, Milano, 83, Tiffany & Co, NY, 92, 92, Empire State Bldg Galleries, NY, 94; Peter Findlay Gallery, NY, 2008; Galleria Le Opere, Rome, 2011, 2013. *Pos:* Designer, Tiffany & Co, New York, 56-57; stage designer, Bayrisches Schauspielhaus, Muenchen, Ger, 77-79. *Teaching:* Auburn Univ, Ala, 55-56. *Awards:* Gold Medal, Premio Campidoglio, Roma, 69; Premio Via Conndotti, Rome, 79. *Bibliog:* Sterling McIlhany (auth), American Artist in Rome, Am Artist, 6/61; Mario Praz (auth), Paintings of Frankfurter, Agraf Art Editions, 73; Antonio Porcella (auth), Frankfurter Galeria Ca d'Ora, Roma, 76. *Media:* Oil on Canvas. *Publ:* Contribr, numerous articles in NY Times, 60-71; cover art, Am Artist, 9/65 & 11/68; title page, Arts & Leisure, NY Times, 12/5/71; auth, article for UNICEF Art Calendar, 72; auth & cover art, Wichita, Wichita Chamber Commerce, 76. *Dealer:* Galleriea Ca d'Oro Plazza Di Spanga 81 Roma Italy 00187; Marcelle Fine Arts South Hampton LI; Peter Findlay Gallery NY; Simone Di Filppo Galleria Rome. *Mailing Add:* 90 Park Terrace E New York NY 10034

FRANKLIN, DAVID
MUSEUM DIRECTOR, CURATOR
b Montreal, Can. *Study:* Queen's Univ, BA; Courtauld Inst Art, Univ London, MA, PhD (European Renaissance art); Univ Oxford, Hon MA. *Collection Arranged:* Italian Drawings, National Gallery of Canada, 2001, Parmigianino, 2003, Leonardo da Vinci, Michelangelo, and the Renaissance in Florence, 2005, Bernini and the Birth of Baroque Portrait Sculpture, 2008, Caravaggio and His Circle in Rome, 2011. *Pos:* dep dir, chief curator, Nat Gallery of Canada, formerly; dir, Cleveland Mus Art, 2010-2013. *Awards:* Eric Mitchell Prize, 1995

FRANKLIN, DON
PAINTER, PHOTOGRAPHER, SCULPTOR
b Uniontown, Pa, Mar 16, 1931. *Study:* Art Inst Pittsburgh, 49-50. *Work:* Locust Hill Gallery, Pittsford, NY; Six Nations Mus, Onchiota, NY; Akwesasne Mus, Hogansburg, NY; Dick Moll's Gallery, Mendon, NY; Nan Miller Gallery, Rochester, NY; Spectrum Labs Caricature Coll, Rochester, NY. *Comn:* Period painting, Dick Moll's Gallery, 75. *Exhib:* Arts for Greater Rochester, Nazareth Arts Ctr, Pittsford, NY, 89; solo exhib, 1570 Gallery, Rochester, NY, 90; Fine Art Showcase, Wilson Arts Ctr, Rochester, NY, 90-91 & Mem Art Gallery, Rochester, NY, 92; Art Inst Pittsburgh, Pa, 2003; Little Theatre, Rochester, NY, 2009. *Collection Arranged:* Spectrum Labs Caricature Col, Rochester, NY. *Pos:* Art dir, Bausch & Lomb, 70-73 & creative dir, 77-94, self-employed, 94-. *Teaching:* Instr art, Univ Rochester Mem Art Gallery, Rochester, NY, 77-82. *Awards:* Award Excellence, Fine Art Showcase, WXXI Pub Television, 90; Award Excellence, Fine Art Showcase, Archit Inst Am, 91. *Media:* Miscellaneous Media, Watercolor, Graphite, Pastel, Acrylic, Pen and Ink. *Interests:* Art hist, photography, music, poetry. *Publ:* Pastel Artists Int, 1-2/2002; Int Artist's, 101 Ways to Paint People & Figures, How Did You Paint That, series. *Dealer:* The Mill Gallery Honeoye Falls NY. *Mailing Add:* 160 Chelmsford Rd Rochester NY 14618

FRANKLIN, HANNAH
SCULPTOR, PAINTER
b Poland, June 20, 1937; Can Citizen. *Study:* Montreal Mus Fine Art Sch, BA, 68; studied with Arthur Lismer. *Work:* Montreal Mus Art, Que; Musee d'Art Contemporian, Montreal; Musee du Quebec, Ont; Can Coun Art Bank, Ottawa; Cabinet du Quebec; Simon Fraser Univ, Vancouver, BC. *Comn:* Sculptures, Jacque Cartier, 84 & Vancouver Centenniel Comn, 86; St Jean Port Joli (sculpture), Mus Que, 84. *Exhib:* Solo exhibs, Pu Gallery, Nova Scotia, 82, Mus Quebec Gallery, 84, Samuel Lallouz Gallery, 85, Arts Sutton, 93, Gallery de la Ville, 2001, Victoria Hall Gallery, 2004, 2012; Saidye Bronfman Ctr, Montreal, 73; Biennial, Basel, Switz, 74; Fete du Fleuve, Que, 84; 3 Sculptors & 12 Sculptors, Palais de Cong Montreal, 85; Small Sculpture Biennial, Budapest, Hungary, 71; Salon CSQ, Conseil de la Sculpture du Quebec, 96; Agora Gallery, New York, 97; Gallery McLure, Montreal, Quebec, 99; Pass Art, Quebec, 2000. *Teaching:* Instr sculpture, Saidye Bronfman Ctr, Montreal, 74-76. *Awards:* First Prize Sculpture, Hadassah Wiz Exhib, 70, 72 & 74; Purchase Award Que Concour, Govt Que, 70. *Bibliog:* Guy Robert (auth), l'Art au Quebec, La Presse, 73; Art Actuel Quebec, Iconia, 83; Arthur Williams (auth),The Sculpture Reference, 2004; and others. *Mem:* Soc Sculptors Que (vpres, 72); Vancouver Sculptors Asn; Int Sculptors Asn. *Media:* Plastic, Bronze; Acrylic, Oil. *Publ:* La Sculpture et le Vent, Women Sculptors of Quebec, 2004. *Mailing Add:* 85 Holton Ave Montreal PQ H3Y 2G1 Canada

FRANKLIN, PATT
PAINTER, SCULPTOR
b 1941. *Study:* Pratt Inst, BFA, 62; Tulane Univ, MFA, 70. *Work:* Boston Libr Print & Drawing Collection & New Eng Med Ctr Lobby Collection, Boston, Mass; Int Telephone & Telegraph, NY; Colby Col, Waterville, Maine; Gilette Corp, Boston; LL Bean, Maine; Ogunquit Mus, Maine; Bowdoin Coll Mus Art, Maine; Honeck O'Toole, Maine. *Comn:* Painted murals, Doctors of Touro Hospital, New Orleans, La, 68. *Exhib:* Cranbrook Art Mus, 76; one-person shows, Varley & Stevens Gallery, Portsmouth, NH, 85, Portland Stage Co, Maine, 86, Unity Col, Maine, 89, Cong Sq Gallery, Portland, Maine, 89, Merrimack Col, N Andover, Mass, 90, Rissho Univ, Tokyo, 92, Ogunquit Mus Am Art, Maine, 94; Presence of Women, Bowdoin Mus, Brunswick, Maine, 92; O'Farrell Gallery, Brunswick, Maine, 93; June Fitzpatrick Gallery, Portland, Maine, 93, 98, 09, & 2011; Ratliff Gallery, Sedona, Ariz, 95-96; Mathias Fine Art, Maine, 2000-08; Elon Univ, Elon, NC, 2009. *Teaching:* Prof drawing & ceramics, Univ South Maine, Gorham, 70-2000; instr ceramics, Mass Col Art, summer 73 & Haystack Sch Art & Crafts, Deer Isle, Maine, 77. *Awards:* Fellar Award, Silvermine Competition, 73; Allgemeines Kunst Lerlexikon. *Bibliog:* Beem, Edgar Allen, Maine Art Now, Gardiner, Maine; Docear Press, 90, pages, 202,224-225; Jacks, Shirley, Art New England, Oct-Nov 94; Temin, Christine, Boston Globe, Nov, 84. *Mem:* Am Craft Coun; Women's Caucus Art; Nat Coun Educ Ceramic Arts; Coll Art Asn. *Media:* Oils; Clay. *Dealer:* June Fitzpatrick Gallery Portland Me. *Mailing Add:* PO Box 94 Gorham ME 04038

FRASER, ANDREA R
CONCEPTUAL ARTIST, MUSEOLOGIST
b Billings, Mont, Sept 27, 1965. *Study:* Sch Visual Arts, 82-84; Whitney Mus Am Art, independent study prog, 84-85; NYU, 85-86. *Work:* Antoni Tàpies Found, Barcelona; Mus Boymans, Rotterdam; Centre Georges Pompidou, Paris; Sprengel Mus, Hanover; Wadsworth Atheneum, Hartford. *Exhib:* Solo exhibs, Damaged Goods, Gallery Talk, New Mus Contemp Arts, NY, 86, Mus Highlights, Philadelphia Mus Art, 89, Welcome to the Wadsworth, Wadsworth Atheneum, 91, Aren't they lovely? (auth, catalog), Univ Art Mus, Berkeley, Calif, 92, A Society of Taste (auth, catalog), Kunstverein Munich, 93, The Seventh Mus, The Hague, 94, A Project in Two Phases, EA-Generali Found, Vienna, 95, White People in West Africa, Am Fine Arts Co., NY, 97, Inaugural Speech, InSITE97, San Diego, 97, Information Room, Kunsthalle Bern, Introduction to the Sprengel Mus, Hannover, 98, El Museo, 2000-2002, Official Welcome, MICA Found, NY, 2001, Arma Virumque Cano, Am Fine Arts Co, NY, 2002, Works: 1984-2003, Kunstverein, Hamburg, 2003, Friedrich Petzel Gallery, NY, 2004, May I Help You, Orchard, NY, 2005, Wexner Ctr Arts, 2006, What do I, as an artist, provide?, Mildred Lane Kemper Art Mus, St. Louis, 2007, Projection, Galerie Christian Nagel, Cologne, 2008, Centre Pompidou, Paris, 2009, You Are Here, Graz, 2010, All Change, Kunsthalle Wien, Vienna, 2010, Its a Beautiful House, Isn't It? MAK Ctr at the Schindler House, Los Angeles, 2011; Group exhibs, Whitney Biennial, Whitney Mus Am Art, 93, 2012; Venice Biennale, Austrian Pavilion, 93; A Project in Two Phases, EA-Generali Found, Vienna, 95. *Teaching:* Guest artist sculpture, Cooper Union, 90 & 96; part-time fac performance, Tyler Sch Art, 92; prof, Univ Calif Los Angeles, 2009-; workshop leader, PhDArts prog, Leiden Univ Acad Creative and Performing Arts and the Royal Acad of Arts, The Hague, 2009, 2011. *Awards:* Fel, Art Matters Inc, 87 & 89; NY Found Arts, 91; Nat Endowment Arts, 91. *Bibliog:* Marcia Tanner (auth), Inside information: aren't they lovely? in UAM, Berkeley, Artweek, 8/20/92; Hanne Weskott (auth), I provide services: Ein Gesprach mit Andrea Fraser, Artis, 5/93; Johanna Hofleitner (auth), Feldforschung in der Direktion: Andres Fraser in der Wiener EA-Generali Foundation, Neie Zuricher Zeitung, 5/30/95. *Media:* Performance, Installation. *Publ:* Auth, Woman 1/Madonna and Child 1506-1967, Andrea Frutsen, 84; In and out of place, Art Am, 85; Individual Works, John Weber Gallery, 88; Notes in the museum's publicity, Lusitania, 90; Museum highlights: a gallery talk, October, 91. *Dealer:* Colin De Land American Fine Arts 40 Wooster St New York NY 10014. *Mailing Add:* UCLA Dept Art Broad Art Ctr Ste 2275 240 Charles E. Young Dr Box 951615 Los Angeles CA 90095

FRASER, CATRIONA TRAFFORD
GALLERY DIRECTOR, PHOTOGRAPHER
b Reading, England, Jan 8, 1972. *Study:* Wallingford Sch, Oxfordshire, England, Grad, 88; Plymouth Coll Arts and Design, Diploma, Devon, Eng, 88-89. *Work:* Glamis Castle, 92; Brusque Mus, Santa Caterina Brazil, 93; Photographer Dunnottar Castle, 92; Kinnaird Castle, 92; Photography Competition, Calif, Fleur No II, 92. *Exhib:* Nat Art Competition, 96, Castlegait Gallery, Scotland, 92, Sacramento Fine Arts Ctr, 92, New Image Gallery, Va, 92, Carnegie Mus, Pittsburgh, 92, St Helena Art League, Calif, 93, Brusque Mus, Santa Caterina Brazil, 93, Art League Gallery, Va, 94, 95, Va Commonwealth Univ, 95, Eklektikos Gallery, Wash DC, 96, Fraser Gallery, Wash DC, 96, 97, 99, 2000, 2002, Infrared Gallery, Chicago, 98, Bruce Gallery, Edinboro Coll, Pa, 2001, Am Ctr Physics, Md, 2004. *Pos:* Asst photog trainee, Reading Evening Post, Reading, Eng, 87; Found, Cairn Photog, Fettercairn, Scotland, 91; Dir, Fraser Gallery, Wash, 96-2010, Bethesda, Md, 2002-; Found, Secondsight, 2003-. *Awards:* Recipient Hon Award, 42d Ann Boardwalk Int Arts Festival, 98. *Mem:* Art Dealers Asn Greter Wash, Bethesda CofC. *Specialty:* Contemp realism, photography. *Mailing Add:* Fraser Gallery 7700 Wisconsin Ave Ste E Bethesda MD 20814

FRASER, MARY EDNA
ENVIRONMENTAL ARTIST, CRAFTSMAN
b Fayetteville, NC, Mar 20, 1952. *Study:* E Carolina Univ, Greenville, NC, BS (textiles & interior design), 74; Arrowmont Sch Crafts, Univ Tenn, Gatlinburg, Tenn, 75-76; Univ Ga, Surface Design Southeast, 77, with Chungi Choo; pvt study with Fred Andrade & Dr Orrin Pilkey. *Work:* Smithsonian Inst, Nat Air & Space Mus, Washington; Nat Aeronautics & Space Admin, Washington; Am Embassy, Bangkok, Thailand; George Wash Univ; New Eng Aquarium; NASA; First Union Nat Bank; Charleston Int Airport; Roper Hosp; three framed batik prints, Contemp Carolina Collection, Med Univ SC, 2008; The Heinz Center for Science, Economics, and the Environment, Wash DC, 2008; Mus Natural Sci, Raleigh, NC, 2012. *Comn:* Charleston Waterways (74yardsx36″ silk sculpture), Charleston Int Airport, SC, 89; Ridges & Rivers (60″x144″ & two 3'x16' drapes silk sculpture), Symmes Libr, Greenville, SC, 90; Charleston Coastline (5'9″x18'9″ batik on silk), Charleston Visitors Ctr, SC, 91; East Coast USA & West Coast USA (7'x4' batiks on silk), Am Embassy of Thailand, Bangkok, 95; Global Perception (876 sq ft silk sculpture), CSC HQ, Columbia, SC, 99; Beyond Fort Johnson (three 21'x3' panel silk sculpture), Hollings Marine Laboratory, Charleston, SC, 2002; Iceberg (77'x44.5'), St. Olaf Coll, St. Louis, Mo, 2008; Palmetto Bluff, May River (7'x3'), Blufflon, SC; Hobcaw Barony 4'x12' batik on Silk, 2010; Above Bay (31″ x 30″ ship sails silk sculpture), Nat Maritime Mus of the Gulf of Mexico, Mobile, Ala, 2013. *Exhib:* Solo Exhibs: Islands from the Sky, Surroundings, NY, 82; Spoleto Festival USA, Charleston, 85; Islands from the Sky, Gibbes Mus Art, 89; A Celebration of Barrier Islands, Duke Univ Mus Art Nat Science Found, 99; Nat Acad Sci, 2001; Naturescapes, Mass Audubon Visual Arts Center, Canton, Mass, 2005; Silk Tableaus, Peabody Essex Mus, Salem, Mass, 2005; Our Earth and Beyond, Hickory Mus Art, Hickory, NC, 2007; Expanding Oceans, Flaten Art Mus, St. Olaf Col, Northfield, Mn, 2008; Polar Attractions, Peabody Essex Mus, Salem, Mass, 2008, A Celebration of the World's Barrier Islands, Barrier Island Ctr, Machipongo, Va, 2011, Our Expanding Oceans, Sciworks, Winston-Salem, NC, Mus Natural Sci, Raleigh, NC, 2011; Group Exhibs: Batik Exhib, Donnell Libr, NY, 85; Earth Views, Nat Air & Space Mus, Washington, 86; Contemp Batik Artists, Southern Ohio Mus, Portsmouth, 90; Aerial Inspirations, Nat Air & Space Mus, Washington, 94-95; Fashion is a VERB, Mus Fashion Inst Technol, NY, 95; Wax Eloquent, Mass Coll Art, Boston, 2005; Celebrating Women Artists of the Lowcountry, Wells Gallery, Kiawah, SC, 2005; Naturescapes: Silk Batiks by Mary Edna Fraser, Univ NC, Charlotte, 2005; Deltas, Barrier Islands & Beyond, Univ Okla, Norman, 2006; Silk Perspective, Hersham Regional Art Gallery, Australia, 2007; Mapping the Territory, Craft Alliance, St Louis, Mo, 2007; Inconvenient Truth, Circular Congregational Church, Charleston, SC, 2007; Celebrating the Worlds Barrier Islands, Gould Libr, Carleton Col, Northfield, Mn; TAFTA, Sinclair Gallery, Geelong, Australia, 2009; McKissick Mus Art, Univ SC, 2010; Florence Mus, Sci and History, Florence, SC, 2010; South Carolina Biennial, 701 Ctr for the Arts, Columbia, SC, 2011; Reflections on Water, Univ Minn, 2011; Our Expanding Oceans, NC, Mus Nat Sci, Raleigh, NC, 2011; Sciworks, Winston Salem, NC, 2011; Terraqueous, Duke Energy Hub, Duke Univ, Durham, NC, 2012; Aerial Perspectives, Albuquerque Internat Balloon Mus, Albuquerque, NMex, 2012. *Pos:* Design consult, City Charleston; lectr, AATCC Symp, Smithsonian Inst; plus numerous lectures at museums & conferences. *Teaching:* Instr batik, Textile Mus,

Washington, DC, summer 84 & 96; instr, World Batik Conf, Boston, 2005; instr, Gibbes Mus Art, Charleston, SC, 2006; instr, The Australian Forum for Textile Arts, Horsham & Orange, NSW, Australia, 2007; Instr batik, Smithsonian Folklife Festival, Wash DC, 2008; instr, Batik Workshop, TAFTA, Sydney, Australia, 2009; instr & key note speaker, Silk Painters Internat, Santa Fe, NMex, 2012. *Awards:* Third Place, Nat Air & Space Mus, 86; Third Place, Eros Data Ctr, 98; SC Art Coun Fel, 98. *Bibliog:* Hank Burchard (auth), A Seamless Show of Fabric, Wash Post, 9/9/94; Diane M Bolz (auth), Lofty Perspectives: The Silk Batiks of Mary Edna Fraser, Smithsonian Mag, 11/94; Aida Rogers (auth), Spiritual Link: Artists Join to Save the Earth with their Shared Creativity, Chicago Tribune, 12/17/97; Susan Haynes (auth), Artist With an Altitude, Coastal Living Mag, 9/2000; Bijal P Trivedi (auth), Flying Artist Preserves Beauty of Shifting Barrier Islands, Nat Geographic Today, 6/2003; Turner Studios (TV), Batik Artist, Southern Living, Episode 517, 10/2003; Harold Palmer (auth), A Celebration of the World's Barrier Islands, Oceanography, 8/2004; Andrew Goudie (auth), Its Not all Fun and Sun on Threatened Coastal Isles, The Times Higher Educ Supplement, Books Travel Section, 7/9/04; Margaret Wade (auth), Batiks Illustrate Climate Change, Manitou Messenger, St Olaf Col, 3/28/2008. *Mem:* Surface Design Asn. *Media:* Batik, Monotype, Oil. *Res:* Exploring climate and sea level change. *Specialty:* Batik on silk, monotypes, collectors' items. *Interests:* Music, poetry, sculpture, science & travel. *Collection:* Large scale batiks of the landscape. *Publ:* Contribr, Artcraft, 80; Art with architecture in mind, Am Inst Architects, 2/91; Textile Designs: Ideas and Applications, PBC Int, 92; Women & Flight, Bulfinch Press, 97; contribr, A Celebration of the Worlds Barrier Islands, Columbia Univ Press, 2003; coauth, What the Water Gives Me, BookSurge Publ, 2004; The Endless Reptition of an Ordinary Miracle (cover) by Marjory Wentworth; co-auth, Global Climate Change: A Primer, Duke Univ Press, 2011. *Mailing Add:* PO Box 12250 Charleston SC 29422

FRASSINELLI, HANNAH
PAINTER, INSTRUCTOR

b Conn. *Study:* BA, Sarah Lawrence Coll, Bronxville, NY 1976; MFA, Columbia Univ, New York, 1986. *Work:* Nat Acad Design Mus, New York; Schenectady Mus, NY; Elizabeth Found, Bob Blackburn Printmaking Workshop, New York; 245 East 87th St Tenants Corp, New York. *Comn:* Etching, bookplate, Nat Acad Sch Libr, 89. *Exhib:* Nat All media, Graham Horstman Gallery, Tex, 1989; Miniatrue Print Biennial, John Szoke Gallery, New York, 1989; Mini Print Internat, Taller Gallery Fort, Barcelona, Spain, 1989; Holiday Presents, Bob Blackburn Printmaking Workshop Gallery, New York, 1994; Nat Print Biennial, Silvermine Gallery, New Canaan, Conn, 1996; 29 Grafikow, Galerie Slad, Poland, 2001; Six on Tenth, Pen & Brush Gallery, 2008; Faculty Exhib, Nat Acad School, NYC, 2013. *Teaching:* head art tchr, 92nd St Y, 1986-1989; printmaking instr, Garison Art Ctr, NY, 1996-1998; figure drawing instr, Dahesh Mus, 2004; art tchr, Nat Acad Design Mus, New York, 1998-2008; painting & drawing instr, Nat Acad Design Sch, New York, 1998-; printmaking instr, RiverArts, Hastins on Hudson. *Awards:* Albert H Baldwin Prize for Printmaking, Nat Acad Design Sch, New York, 1989; Juried Scholarship for Landscape Painting, Acad Realist Art, Seattle, 1994; Cert Merit, Schenectady Mus, New York, 1995; Juried Scholarship for Painting, Art Students League, New York, 1995; Excellence in Works on Paper, Greenwich House Pottery, New York, 1996; Hon Mention in printmaking, Silvermine Gallery, New Canaan, Conn, 1996; Edward G McDowell Travel Grant, Art Students League, New York, 1996; Karen Hagerty Award for Teaching, Citizens's Advice Bureau, Bronx, NY, 2005. *Bibliog:* David Bell (auth), Small Works Show Draw Big Response, Journal North, Santa Fe, NMex, 85; Kate Jennings (auth), Guild's 40th Print Show Diverse, Wonderful, Darien News-Review, 96; Iris Hiskey Arno (auth), Workshop Stimulates Students with Artistic Variety, The Rivertown Enterprise, Vol 35, no 23, 2010. *Mem:* Art Student's League, NY; Artistes de Studio. *Media:* Oil Painting, Printmaking. *Res:* Dutch still life painting. *Interests:* still life paintings of Willem van Aelst. *Publ:* Bicycle Space, a portfolio of 6 Etchings, Acad Press, NY, 81, Etchings, 83. *Dealer:* John Raimondi Gallery. *Mailing Add:* 321 East 71st St Apt 1D New York NY 10021

FRATKIN, DAVID D
PAINTER, PHOTOGRAPHER

b Brooklyn, NY, June 16, 1951. *Study:* Williams Col, BA, 1974. *Comn:* 20 Drawings, Willkie, Farr & Gallagher, 1998. *Exhib:* Solo exhibs include 55 Mercer Gallery, New York, 1992, Painting Ctr, New York, 1995, 1998, 2000, 2003 & 2006; group exhibs include Painters Choose Painters, 55 Mercer Gallery, New York, 1985, What's in a Face, Salena Gallery LIU, Brooklyn, NY, 2008; Lever Myerson Gallery, New York, 1997; Painting Ctr, New York, 1993, The Big Abstract Show, 2003; Am Abstract Painting, Arts Actual, Barcelona, 1998; Pierogi Gallery, Brooklyn, 1999; The Sacred & Profane, Monmouth Univ, Long Branch, NJ, 2001; 40th Anniversary Show, NY Studio Sch, 2005; Dimension, Art League of Long Island, 2006; 183rd Ann: Invitational Exhib Contemp Am Art, Nat Acad Mus, New York, 2008. *Collection Arranged:* Selections, Painting Ctr, New York, 1993, 1995, 1997 & 2000. *Mem:* Bd mem, Painting Ctr, NYC; Bd mem Triangle Arts Assoc, NYC. *Media:* Mixed Media. *Mailing Add:* 285 Bleecker St New York NY 10014

FRATKIN, LESLIE
PHOTOGRAPHER

b Schenectady, NY, 1960. *Study:* State Univ New York, Albany, BA, 83. *Work:* Corcoran Gallery Art, Washington, DC. *Exhib:* Red Windows, Barney's, NY, 95; Image Workshop Series, Foster Goldstrom Gallery, NY, 95; Bosnia: The War Tour, Foster Goldstrom Gallery, NY, 95; House/Scene, traveling exhib, Ger, 97; Seeing the Other, Riverside Studios, London, Eng, 98; Volare: The Icon of Italy in Global Pop Cult, Florence, Italy, 99. *Pos:* Freelance photogr, 83-; creator & proj dir, Sarajevo Self-Portrait: The View from Inside, 95-. *Awards:* Grant, Trust for Mutual Understanding, 97, 99; Soros Found/Open Soc Inst Individual Proj Fel & Grant, 97, 2000; The Righteous Persons Found grant, 99. *Publ:* Auth, Sarajevo Self-Portrait: The View from Inside, Umbrage Ed, 2000

FRAUGHTON, EDWARD JAMES
SCULPTOR

b Park City, Utah, Mar 22, 1939. *Study:* Univ Utah, BFA, 62; studied under Dr Avard T Fairbanks & Justin Fairbanks. *Work:* Riveredge Found, Calgary, Can; Leanin' Tree Mus Western Art, Boulder, Colo; Valley Bank, Las Vegas, Nev; Nat Cowboy Hall of Fame & Western Heritage Ctr, Oklahoma City, Okla; Favell Mus Western Art, Klamath Falls, Ore. *Comn:* Mormon Battalion Monument, Sons of Utah Pioneers, Prisidio Park, San Diego, Calif, 69; Ben H Bohac (relief portrait), Talman Savings & Loan, Chicago, 70; All is Well, Family Monument, Sons of Utah Pioneers, Brigham Young Cemetery, Salt Lake City, 74; Truman O Angell Portrait, Church of Jesus Christ of Latter-day Saints, Salt Lake City, Utah, 77; Spirit of Wyo, 15 ft major monument, Capitol Grounds, Cheyenne, 80; Official Inaugural Medal, President Ronald Reagan. *Exhib:* Eiteljorg Mus, Indianapolis, Ind, 2005-2007, Joslyn Mus, Omaha, Nebraska, 2009, Gale Ctr Mus, South Hordan, Utah, 2010, Prix de West, Okahoma City, Okla, 1994-2014, Spring Solon, Springville, Utah, 2010, Utah State Capitol Bldg, 2014, Inst Classical Architecture and Art, NYC 2014, and many others. *Teaching:* Instr, Scottsdale Artist's Sch, 86. *Awards:* People's Choice award, Prix de West, Home is Where the Heart Is, 2004; Award of Excellence, Am Soc Landscape Architects, Central States Chapters, Pioneer Courage Monument, 2010; Nat Sculpture Soc, Henry Hering Memorial Medal, Pioneer Courage Monument; Director's award, Springville Spring Solon, Prairie Lullaby, 2010; Arthur Ross award for Excellence in the Classical Tradition for Sculpture, Inst Classical Architecture and Art, 2014. *Bibliog:* Pat Broder (auth), Bronzes of the American West, Abrams, 74; Peggy & Harold Samuels (auths), Contemporary Western Artists, Southwest Art Publ, 82; Profiles in American Art (film), Ken Meyer Prod. *Mem:* Inst Classical Architecture & Art; Utah Cultural Arts Found (bd dirs, 2010); Nat Sculpture Soc (bd dirs, 2002); Utah Westerners; Soc Animal Artists; Moscow Conference on Law and Bilateral Economic Development; Presidents Commission on White House Fellows; Jordan River Advisory Council; South Jordan, Utah Planning Commission; Park City, Utah Planning Commission. *Media:* Bronze & Stone Carving. *Mailing Add:* 10353 S 1300 W South Jordan UT 84095-8876

FRAZE, DENNY T
COLLAGE ARTIST, EDUCATOR

b Weatherford, Tex, May 28, 1940. *Study:* Univ Tex, Austin, BFA (studio, art hist), 62; Univ Colo, MFA (painting), 64, study with Luis Eades & Roland Reiss. *Work:* Univ Colo, Boulder; Dishman Art Gallery, Beaumont, Tex; Museo Internacional De Electro Grafica, Cuenca, Spain. *Comn:* Collage Amarillo Art Ctr, Tex. *Exhib:* Over 200, incl solo exhibs, Odessa Col, 80, Mus Art, Norman, Okla, 83, Koenig Art Gallery, Seward, Nebr, 87, Tex Tech Mus, Lubbock, Tex, 87, Art Inst Permian Basin, Odessa, Tex, 89, Meadows Gallery, Denton, Tex, 90, Tarleton State Univ, Stephenville, Tex, 99 & Tex Luth Univ, Seguin, 2002; Cent States Exhib, Pratt, Kans, 95; 1st Great Plains Nat, Fort Hayes, Kans, 95; Nat Works on Paper, Tyler, Tex, 96; Works on Paper '96, Houston, Tex, 96; Tex Lutheran Coll, 2002; and others. *Pos:* Founding mem and pres, Tex Asn Sch Art, 70-72, 84-86, bd mem 72-74 & 84-86; bd mem, Tex Coun Arts Educ, 70-72. *Teaching:* Prof art & chmn dept, Amarillo Col, Tex, 65-2000. *Awards:* Best Show, Cent States Exhib, 95; Recommended for Purchase, Amarillo Art Ctr, Tex, 93 & 95; Juror's Choice Award, Nat Works on Paper, Tyler, Tex, 96; and others. *Bibliog:* Southwest Art Review. *Mem:* Tex Asn Sch Art (pres, 70-72 & 86-88); hon mem Amarillo Fine Arts Asn; Tex Coun Arts Educ. *Media:* Collage, Drawing. *Collection:* Mr & Mrs Mauricio Aguilar, Rancho Santa Fe, Calif, Ms Lisa Brooks, New Milford, Conn, Captiva Island, Fl, Dr & Mrs Rob Chafin, Amarillo, Tex, Ms Carol Cowan, Tucson, Ariz, Mr David A Fraze, MBA-Harvard Univ, San Francisco, Calif, Ms Ann Gallagher, Minneapolis, Minn, Mr & Mrs Lonny S Fraze, Athens, Oh, Dr Hunter Ingalls, PhD Art History, Columbia Univ, NY, Amarillo TX, Mr & Mrs Stanley Marsh, Amarillo, Tex, Dr Roger Wade, PhD Sociology, Boulder, Colo. *Publ:* Auth, Denny Fraze Collages: A Retrospective Exhib (exhibit catalog), Art Ctr, Amarillo, Tex, 88. *Mailing Add:* 1511 S Lamar Amarillo TX 79102

FRAZER, JAMES (NISBET), JR
ASSEMBLAGE ARTIST, INSTALLATION SCULPTOR

b Atlanta, Ga, Oct 6, 1949. *Study:* Amherst Col, BA (cum laude), 71; Ga State Univ, MFA, 73; also with Fairfield Porter. *Work:* High Mus Art, Atlanta; Corcoran Gallery; Chase Manhattan Bank; Addison Gallery of Am Art; J Paul Getty Mus. *Comn:* Southern Bell Telephone Co, 80; Veterans Admin Med Ctr, Atlanta, 83; Omni Int Hotel, Atlanta, 85. *Exhib:* South Am Traveling exhib, Arte EUA: El Sur, US Info Agency, 76-77; 35 Artists in the Southeast, High Mus Art, 76-78; Art Patron Art, Southeastern Ctr for Contemp Art, Winston-Salem, NC, 78; solo exhibs, High Mus Art, Ga & Southeastern Ctr Contemp Art, Winston-Salem, NC, 81; Contemp Panoramic Photog, Addison Gallery Am Art, Andover, Mass, 84; Iron Bridge Show, Appalachian Environ Art Ctr, Highlands, NC, 89-90; Vital Signs, Nexus Contemp Art Ctr, 91; 20 Artists/20 Yrs, Nexus Contemp Art Ctr, 93; Avant-Garde revisited, Nexus Contemp Art Center, Atlanta, Ga, 98; Rocky Mountain Biennial, Mus Contemp Art, Ft Collins, Colo, 2002; Artists of Heath Gallery, Mocaga, Atlanta, Ga, 2002; Digital Splash, Studio 6 Gallery, Queens, NY, 2003; Inadventently, Kayo Gallery, Salt Lake City, Utah, 2005; Exposed, The Pickle Co, Salt Lake City, Utah, 2007; Curiosity Boxes, Finch Lane Gallery, Salt Lake City, Utah, 2007; Unravel, Revealed, Collaboration with Suzanne Simpson & Corinne Cappelletti, Westminister Coll, Salt Lake City, Utah,,2009; PDA Show, Collaboration with Suzanne Simpson, Nobrow Gallery, Salt Lake City, 2010; Surrounded, Collaboration with Suzanne Simpson, Finch Lane Gallery, Salt Lake City, 2011; Intercept, Collaboration with Suzanne Simpson, Westminster Coll, Salt Lake City, Ut, 2011. *Pos:* Pres, Nexus Inc, Atlanta, 73-74, mem bd dir, 73-81; dir, New Visions Gallery, Salt Lake City, UT, 2002-2004. *Teaching:* Instr photog, Atlanta Col Art, Ga State Univ, 72-76 & Mercer Univ, 77-81. *Bibliog:* Peter Morrin (auth), Jim Frazer: Hand-Colored Photographs, High Mus Art, Atlanta, 81; Laura Lieberman (auth), Jim Frazer, Southern Accents, 5-6/88. *Media:* Digital Imagery. *Publ:* Journey to the natural bridge, Belize Currents, No 16, 93;

Macal River trip, Belize Currents, No 20, 94; Jocassee Jour, River, Vol 1, No 6; Confederates in Brazil, South American Explorer, 2003; Pharmaceutical El Dorado, Fact or Fancy? South American Explorer, 2004. *Dealer:* Sandler-Hudson Gallery 1831 Peachtree Rd NE Atlanta GA 30309. *Mailing Add:* 258 N Main St Salt Lake City UT 84103

FRAZER, JOHN THATCHER
FILMMAKER, PAINTER
b Akron, Ohio, Apr 2, 1932. *Study:* Univ Tex, BFA; Yale Univ, MFA; with Joseph Albers; Wesleyan Univ, Hon MA. *Work:* Davison Art Ctr, Wesleyan Univ, Middletown, Conn; Libr Cong, Washington, DC; Cullinan Collection, Houston Mus Fine Arts. *Exhib:* Tex Ann, Dallas Mus Fine Arts, 58; New Haven Arts Festival, Conn, 60; Boston Arts Festival, Mass, 61; Flaherty Film Festival, Lakeville, Conn, 66; Am Film Festival, NY, 68; Wesleyan V Art Gallery. *Pos:* professor emeritus. *Teaching:* Prof art, motion pictures & drawing, Wesleyan Univ, 59-2000. *Bibliog:* New talent, USA, Art in Am, 62; Bernard Chaet (auth), The Art of Drawing, Holt, 70. *Mem:* Am Asn Univ Prof; Coll Art Asn Am; Am Film Inst. *Media:* Charcoal, Oil. *Res:* George Melies. *Interests:* Motion pictures, drawings. *Publ:* Auth, Documentary films & books on documentary films, Choice Mag, 69; Artificially Arranged Scenes, The Films of George Melies, G K Hall, 79. *Dealer:* Golden Gavel; E Windsor Ct. *Mailing Add:* 7 Bretton Pl 238 Washington Terr Middletown CT 06457-4108

FRAZIER, LATOYA RUBY
PHOTOGRAPHER, CURATOR
Study: Edinboro Univ Pa, BFA (Applied Media Arts), 2004; Skowhegan Sch Painting & Sculpture, 2007; Syracuse Univ, MFA (Art Photog), 2007; Whitney Mus Am Art, Independent Study, 2010-2011. *Work:* Fogg Art Mus, Harvard Univ. *Exhib:* Film festivals include Black Int Film Festival, New York, 2006, Brooklyn Underground, 2006, Women of Color Prodns, New York, 2006, Black Maria Film Festival, Jersey City, NJ, 2006, San Diego Women's Film Festival, 2007, Ecstatic Transformation & Emotional Realism, Portland, Oreg, 2007, Come on: Desire Under the Female Gaze, Warehouse Gallery, Syracuse, NY, 2007, Magic Lantern, Providence, 2008 & Aurora Picture Show, Houston, 2008, Civil Disobedience, White Box, NY, 2010, LUMEN Video and Projection Festival, Staten Island, NY, 2011, VideoStudio: Changing Same, Studio Mus Harlem, NY, 2011; Group exhibs include Ann Spring Exhib, Erie Art Mus, Pa, 2002; Spark Open, Spark Contemp Gallery Space, Syracuse, NY, 2004 & 2005; Emerging Artists, Light Work, Syracuse, 2005 & Family Lifestyles, 2006; Everson Biennial, Everson Mus, Syracuse, 2006; 183rd Ann: Invitational Exhib Contemp Art, Nat Acad, New York, 2008; Whos Afraid of America, Wonderland Artist Space, Denmark, 2008; White Lies and Black Noise, Rush Arts Gallery, NY, 2008; Generational: Younger Than Jesus, New Mus, NY, 2009; Living and Dreaming, AIM 29, Bronx Mus, NY, 2009; Piece de Resistance, Larissa Goldston Gallery, NY, 2010; Playboy Redux, Andy Warhol Mus, Pittsburgh, Pa, 2010; 50 Artists Photograph the Future, Higher Picture, NY, 2010; Lush Life, Collette Blanchard Gallery, NY, 2010; Inspired, Steven Kasher Gallery, NY, 2010; True Fiction, Phila Photo Art Ctr Gallery, Pa, 2010; The Pipe and the Flow, Galeria Espacio Minimo, Spain, 2011; The Truth is Not in the Mirror: Photography and Constructed Identity, Haggerty Mus Art, Marquette Univ, Milwaukee, Wisc, 2011; VideoStudio: Changing Same, Studio Mus Harlem, NY, 2011; Dust to Settle, Cuchifritos Gallery, NY, 2011; Always the Young Strangers, Higher Pics, NY, 2011; Commercial Break, Garage Projects, 54th Venice Biennale, Venice, Italy, 2011; After Destiny: The Contemporary American Landscape, Flanders Gallery, Raleigh, NC, 2011; Intimacies, Gallery 400, Univ Ill Chgo, Ill, 2011; Spelman Coll, Atlanta, Ga, 2011; Pittsburgh Biennial, Andy Warhol Mus, Pittsburgh, Pa, 2011; Incheon Women Artists' Biennale, Korea, 2011; Whitney Biennial, Whitney Mus Am Art, 2012. *Pos:* Asst, Richard Kelly Photog, Pittsburgh, 2002 & Kim Roberts Act 4 Studio, Pittsburgh, 2003; contrib photog, Fader Mag, New York & Newsweek, 2006; assoc cur, Civic Square Art Gallery, Mason Gross Sch Arts, Rutgers Univ, NJ, 2007-08. *Teaching:* Instr art photog, Community Folk Art Ctr, Syracuse, NY, 2005; instr intermediate black & white photog, Light Work/Community Darkrooms, Syracuse, NY, 2005; grad teaching asst & instr of record, Dept Transmedia, Syracuse Univ, 2005-07; instr, Ed Smith Elem Sch Dist, Syracuse, 2006; lectr digital photog, Rutgers Univ, New Brunswick, NJ, 2007-08. *Awards:* Winner, Cong Art Competition, Pittsburgh, 1999; Patron Purchase Award, Erie Art Mus, Pa, 2002; Juror's Award, Edinboro Univ Photog Exhib, 2003; Outstanding Achievement in Photog Award, Edinboro Univ, 2004; African Am Fel, Syracuse Univ, 2004-05, Creative Opportunity Grant, 2005-06 & Travel Grant, 2006, Master's Prize Award, 2007; Prodr's Choice Award, Women of Color Prodns, 2006; Dir's Citation Award, Black Maria Film Festival, 2006; Geraldine Dodge Fel, Coll Art Asn, 2006; Skowhegan Fel, 2007; SJ Wallace Truman Fund Award, Nat Acad, 2008; Art Matters Grant, Art Matters, NY, 2010. *Mailing Add:* Dept Visual Art Rutgers Univ 33 Livingston Ave New Brunswick NJ 08901

FRECON, SUZAN
PAINTER
b Mexico, Pa, Feb 12, 1941. *Study:* Univ Strasbourg, 1962; Pa State Univ, BFA, 1959-63; L'ecole Nat Super des Beaux Arts, Paris, 1963-66. *Work:* Mus Mod Art, Whitney Mus Am Art, NY; Nat Gallery Art, Washington, DC; Kunstmuseum, Bern, Switzerland; Fogg Art Mus, Cambridge, Mass. *Exhib:* Solo exhibs, Kunsthalle Bern, Switz, 1986, 1994, 2005, 2008, Julian Pretto Gallery, NY, 1988, Univ Art Mus, Berkeley, Calif, 1989, 1995, Lawrence Markey Gallery, NY, 1992, 1993, 1996, 1999, 2001, 2003, 2004, Hirschl & Adler Mod, NY, 1996, Hausler, Munich, 1998, Galerie Franck & Schulte, Berlin, 1999, Galerie Philippe Casini, Paris, 1999, Friedrich Gallery, Bern, Switz, 2000, Drawing Ctr, NY, 2002, Peter Blum Gallery, NY, 2005, Lawrence Markey Gallery (with catalog), San Antonio, Tex, 2007, Menil Collection, Houston, 2008; group exhibs, Undercurrents & Overtones, Oliver Art Ctr, CCAC, Oakland, Calif, 1998; Works on paper and drawings, Galerie Paul Andreisse, Amsterdam, 2000; Whitney Biennial, Whitney Mus Am Art, NY, 2000; The Fall Line, OSP Gallery, Boston, 2002; Watercolor, NY Studio Sch, 2002; Drawings of Choice from a NY Collection, Krannert Art Mus, Urbana-Champaign, Ill, 2002, Art Center, Little Rock, 2003, Ga Mus Art, Univ Ga, Athens, Bowdoin Coll Mus, Brunswick, Maine & Cincinnati Art Mus, 2003; Twice Drawn, Tang Mus, Skidmore Coll, NY, 2006; Touch-down, Galerie Friedrich, Basel, 2007; Whitney Biennial, Whitney Mus Am Art, 2010. *Collection Arranged:* Ark Arts Ctr, Little Rock; Diözesanmus, Freising, Ger; Fogg Art Mus, Harvard Univ, Cambridge, Mass; Kunstmus, Bern, Switzerland; Mus Mod Art; Nat Gallery Art, Washington, DC; Univ Art Mus, Berkeley, Calif; Whitney Mus Am Art, NY. *Bibliog:* Kenneth Baker (auth), Berkeley Art Mus, Art News, San Francisco, 10/95; Charles Dee Mitchell (auth), Suzan Frecon, Art in Am, 3/97; John Yau (auth), Suzan Frecon Paintings, Richter Verlag, 99; Ken Johnson (auth), NY Times, 3/5/99; NY Rev of Art, 2/94. *Media:* Oil, Watercolor. *Dealer:* Lawrence Markey, 311 6th St, San Antonio, TX, 78215; Peter Blum, 99 Wooster St, New York, NY, 10012; Fredrick Galerie, Grenzacher Strasse 4 CH 4058 Basel. *Mailing Add:* 228 E 13th St Apt 11 New York NY 10003

FREDENTHAL, RUTH ANN
PAINTER
b Detroit, Mich, 1938. *Study:* Philadelphia Mus Coll Art, 57; Yale-Norfolk Sch Art with Bernard Chaet, 58; Bennington Coll with Paul Feeley, Tony Smith & Vincent Longo, BA, 60. *Work:* Chase Manhattan Bank, NY & Albany; Brooklyn Mus, NY; Donazione Panza Di Biumo Museo Cantonale d'Arte, Lugano, Switzerland; Villa Menafoglio, Litta Panza, Panza Collection, Varese, Italy; Karl Ernst Osthaus Mus, Hagen, Ger; Albright-Knox Art Gallery, Buffalo, NY; MART, Rovereto, Italy. *Exhib:* Mus Cantonale d'arte, Lugano, Switz, 95; Palazzo Ducale, Gubbio, Italy, 98-2003; Galleria Valeria Belvedere, Milan, Italy, 99; Borromini Arte contemporanea, Ozzano Monferrato, Italy, 2000-01; Mart, Rovereto, 2002; Aganahuei Arte Contemp, Alba, Italy, 2004; Villa Lagarina, Port Venere, Italy, 2004; Karl Ernst Osthaus, Mus Der Stadt Hagen, Hagen, Ger, 2005; Albright-Knox Art Gallery, Buffalo, NY, 2007-2008; Galleria Michela Rizzo, Venice, Italy, 2008-2009; Vera Engelhorn Gallery, New York, 89, 90; Stark Gallery, New York, 93, 94, 95, 98, 2002; Museo d'Arte Lugano, Lugano, Switzerland, 2010; Group exhib The Perception of the Future: The Panza Collection at Perugia, Museo Civico di Palazzo della Penna, Galleria Nazionale dell' Umbria, Perugia, Italy, 2015. *Awards:* Fulbright Fel Painting & Graphic Arts to Florence, Italy, US State Dept, 60-61; Pollock-Krasner Found Grant, NY, 2008. *Bibliog:* Stephen Westfall (auth) article, Art Am, 3/90; Reegan Upshaw (auth), article, Art Am, 11/93; Donald Kuspit (auth), catalog essay, Stark Gallery, 95; David Sotnik (auth) video documentary, New York, 90-99. *Media:* Oil. *Interests:* Dance, music, travel, yoga, pilates. *Dealer:* Galleria Michela Rizzo Venice Italy. *Mailing Add:* 438 W 37th St 5B New York NY 10018

FREDERICK, DELORAS ANN
PAINTER, INSTRUCTOR
b Fletcher, Okla, Jan 25, 1942. *Study:* Central State Univ, 75; with Joseph Mugnaini, 79-80; with M Doug Walton, 79-80. *Work:* Presbyterian Hosp, Baptist Mem Hosp, Patrick Petroleum & CMI Corp, Oklahoma City, Okla; CCI Corp, Tulsa, Okla. *Exhib:* Artist Salon, Okla Mus Art, Oklahoma City, 75-80; Okla Territorial Mus, Guthrie, 78-80; Nat Small Painting Exhib, W F Mullaly Galleries, Birmingham, Mich, 78; The Miniature Painter, Sculptors & Gravers Soc, Art Club Washington, Washington, DC, 80; Ann Art Exhib, Mus Great Plains, Lawton, Okla, 80-81; and others. *Pos:* Instr watercolor, Art Supply Shop, Oklahoma City, Okla, 75-79; instr, Wkshps for Art Club in Okla, Oklahoma City, 77-81. *Teaching:* Instr water, Nichels Hills Elementary Sch, Oklahoma City, Okla, 81. *Awards:* Best of Show, Mid-Del Art Guild, 77, 79 & 80; Best Still Life Award, Founders Arts Club, Washington, DC, 80; Artist Holiday Award, Tri State Kans, 83. *Bibliog:* Deloras Frederick, Okla Art Gallery Mag, 80; Peggy Ridgeway (auth), Deloras Frederick, Art Voices, 81. *Mem:* Mid-Del Art Guild (1st vpres, 76-77); Oklahoma Watercolor (1st vpres, 77-78); Watercolor Oklahoma (1st vpres, 78-79); Oklahoma Art Guild (1st vpres, 79-80); Nat League Am Pen Women, Inc. *Media:* Watercolor, Acrylic. *Dealer:* House Gallery 5536 N Western Oklahoma City OK 73116; Studio Gallery 2020 E Eleventh Tulsa OK 74104. *Mailing Add:* RR 1 Box 19760 Porum OK 74455-9610

FREDERICK, HELEN C
PRINTMAKER, CONCEPTUAL ARTIST
b Pottstown, Pa, 1945. *Study:* RI Sch Design, BFA, 67, MFA, 69. *Work:* Fogg Mus, Cambridge, Mass; Nat Mus Am Art, Washington, DC; USA Today Nat Hq, Arlington, Va; Whitney Mus Art, NYC; Nat Gallery Art; and others; RI Sch Design. *Exhib:* Solo exhibs, Sequences, Steven Scott Gallery, Baltimore, Md, 89, Treading Water, David Adamson Gallery, Washington, 91, Collaborations on Paper, Va Polytech Univ, Blacksburg, Va, 93, Under Construction: Relay, Rewind, Record, Dieu Donne Gallery, NY, 96, Revealing Conditions, Art Ctr, South Fla, 2000, The View is Daunting, Lamardodd Gallery, Univ Athens, Ga, 2002; Innovative Prints & Paperworks, Baltimore, Mus Art, Md, 87; Object D'Art: Contemp Screens, traveling exhib, Va Mus Fine Arts & the Hand Workshop, Richmond, 90; Prints Washington, Corcoran Gallery Art, Washington, DC, 92; Seven-up, Master Printers of Pyramid Atlantic Montgomery Col, Rockville, Md, 94; Helen Frederick, Rick Hungerford & Ken Polinskie, Colombo Americano Cult Ctr, Medillin, Columbia, S Am, 95; Fine Prints, Washington Printmakers Gallery, Washington, DC, 95; Evolution of the Print, Addison Ripley Gallery, Washington, DC, 95; Graphic Legacy, Nat Mus Women Arts, Washington, DC, 95; Mountain Lake Series, Emerson Gallery Art, 96, McLean Project for the Arts, Va, 96; Group Print Show, Washington, DC, 98; Art Cnt South Fl Revealing Conditions, 2001; Southwest Craft Center Scieran Suspension, 2001; Univ of Georgia Solo Exhib The View Is Daintry, 2002. *Pos:* vis critic, Sch Design; exec artistic dir, Pyramid Atlantic. *Teaching:* Assoc prof, art & visual tech dept, Col Visual & Performing Arts; Assoc prof, George Mason Univ, Fairfax. *Awards:* Fulbright Grant & Am Scand Fel, Munch Mus, Oslo, Norway, 73-74; Mid Atlantic Arts Found Residency Fel, 88; Rutgers Ctr for Innovative Printmaking, 95; Governor's Award for the Arts as leading Maryland Artist, 2000; Recipient of Gov's Award for Excellence and Leadership in the Arts in Maryland, 2000. *Bibliog:* Mary McCoy (auth), Earthviews at RAP, Washington Post, 1/16/93; Joann Moser (auth), Paper alchemy at Pyramid

Atlantic, Handpapermaking, summer 93; Susan Davidson (auth), Profile, Art & Antiques, 5/94; Milena Kalinovska (interview), The View is Daunting, 2003. *Media:* Paper, Print Media, Digital Art Installations. *Publ:* Auth, Crossing Over/Changing Places, USIA Traveling Exhib, 1990-1995. *Dealer:* Addison Ripley Gallery Washington DC; Paul Bridgewater New York. *Mailing Add:* 8707 Reading Rd Silver Spring MD 20901

FREDERICK, ROBILEE
PAINTER, SCULPTOR
b Evansville, IN, Oct 08, 1931. *Study:* Wellesley Col, BA, 1953; Classes at Calif Coll of ARt, Oakland, Calif, 1970; Classes in welding & glass, 1990-2005. *Work:* Hess Collection (Donald Hess), Napa, Calif; Achenbach Ctr for the Graphic Arts, Fine Arts Mus, San Francisco, Calif; di Rosa Preserve, Napa, Calif; Doris & Don Fisher collection, San Francisco, Calif; The Buck Collection, Newport Beach, Calif. *Comn:* Light Pieces, Hess Winery, Donald Hess, Colome, Chile, 2002; Light Pieces, Quintessa Winery, Napa Valley, Calif, 2003; Light Pieces, Hess Collection, Napa, Calif, 2006. *Exhib:* Veiled Memories, San Francisco Arts Comn Gallery & Ariz State Univ Art Mus, 96 & 99; Toward the Millennium, Monterey Mus of Art, Monterey, Calif, 1997; An Art Odyssey, Univ Art Gallery at Sonoma State Univ, Santa Rosa, Calif, 2001; Burn, Norton Mus Art, West Palm Beach, Fla & Columbia Mus Art, SC, 2001; On the Surface: Contemp paintings by Bay Area Women, Monterey Mus, 2002; Parallel Convergence, Napa Valley Mus, Yountville, Calif, 2004; Circle of Memory, Mus of Photog Arts, San Diego, Calif, 2004; Santa Fe Art inst, Santa Fe, NMex, 2005. *Awards:* Grants, Veiled Memories, Zellerbach Family Fund, Friends of the San Francisco Pub Libr, Poets & Writers Grant, Nat Endowment for the Humanities, 1996. *Bibliog:* Donna Schumacher (auth), Veiled Memories, Sculpure Magazine, 97; Gary Brady-Herndon (auth), A Studio Built for Two, Napa Valley Register, Napa, CA, 8/2002; Stephanie Salter (auth), Stones of Sorrow for the Missing, San Francisco Chronicle, 2003; Robert Pincus (auth), Food for the Soul, San Diego Tribune, 2004; Gary Brady (auth), Along Similar Lines, Napa Valley Register, 2004; and others. *Mem:* Calif Soc of Printmakers (CSP), (vpres speaker, 1970); Art Coun of Napa Valley. *Media:* Mixed Media. *Publ:* Auth, Fie de Siecle Painting (art), Artweek, 1997; coauth, Art by Gail Chase-Bien & Robilee Frederick, Napa Valley Mus, 2004; and others. *Dealer:* Braunstein/Quay 430 Clementina San Francisco CA 94103 4107; Ruth Bachofner Gallery Bergamot Station G2 2525 Michigan Ave Santa Monica CA 90404. *Mailing Add:* 1417 Hudson St Saint Helena CA 94574

FREDMAN, FAIYA R
SCULPTOR, PAINTER
b Columbus, Ohio, Sept 8, 1925. *Study:* Calif State Univ, San Diego; Univ Calif, Los Angeles. *Work:* Chicago Art Inst, Ill; Mus Mod Art, New York; Cedars-Sinai, Los Angeles, Calif; Oakland Mus, Calif; Mus Photog Arts, San Diego; Mus Contemp Art, San Diego; Getty Ctr, Rare Bk Special Collections, Santa Monica, Calif; Banff Ctr Arts, Can; Ariz State Univ, Tempe; Athenaeum, La Jolla, Calif; La Jolla Sculpture Garden, Calif; Brandes Investment, San Diego; Nat Mus Women Arts, Washington, DC; San Franciso Mus Mod Art; Seacrest Village, Encinitas, Calif; Artist Book Collection, Univ Calif, Los Angeles & San Diego; San Diego Mus Art; pvt collections, Luce-Forward, San Diego, Peter Farrell, San Diego, Suzanne Stanford, La Jolla, Calif, Joseph & Elaine Monsen, Seattle & Dana Fayman, San Diego. *Comn:* Sardina (sculpture), comn by Robert Orton Sculpture Garden, 98. *Exhib:* Solo exhibs, La Jolla Mus Contemp Art, 68, 74 & 81, Thomas Babeour Gallery, La Jolla, 81, Univ Calif, San Diego & Irvine, 84, Ruth Bachofner Gallery, Los Angeles, 85 & 88, Univ Calif, Riverside, 85 & Pacific Beach Libr, Taylor Gallery, 2007; Mus Photog Arts, La Jolla, Calif, 88; Ruth Bachofner Gallery, Los Angeles, 90; Palomar Coll Boehm Gallery, San Marcos, Calif, 90; Athenaeum, La Jolla, Calif, 94, 2013; Porter-Troupe Gallery, San Diego, 96; Joseph Bellows Photography Gallery, La Jolla, Calif, 2010. *Teaching:* Instr, Exten, Univ Calif, San Diego, 77-. *Awards:* US Dept Housing & Urban Develop Nat Community Art Competition Award, 73; First Prize, San Diego Pub TV Prog, 78. *Bibliog:* Lucy Lippard (auth), Body, Nature & Ritual in Women's Art, Chrysalis Mag, 77; Jean Luc Bordeaux (auth), Unstretched surfaces Southern Calif, Los Angeles Inst Contemp Art J, 11/77. *Media:* Mixed Media, Computer. *Publ:* Auth, Faiya Fredman Akroteri Series Catalog, Univ Calif, 84 & Faiya Fredman Selected Works 1968-1989 (with catalog), Palomar Coll Boehm Gallery, 90. *Dealer:* Joseph Bellows Gallery. *Mailing Add:* PO Box 2735 La Jolla CA 92038

FREED, DAVID
PRINTMAKER, PAINTER
b Toledo, Ohio, May 23, 1936. *Study:* Miami Univ; Univ Iowa; Royal Coll Art, London. *Work:* Art Inst Chicago, Ill; Nat Am Mus Arts, Washington, DC; Va Mus Fine Arts, Richmond; Victoria & Albert Mus, London; Mus Mod Art, NY; and others. *Exhib:* Photog in Printmaking, AAA Gallery, NY, 68-70; solo exhibs, Franz Bader Gallery, Washington, DC, 68, 70, 73, 76 & 82 & Va Mus Fine Arts, Richmond; Albright-Knox Art Gallery, Buffalo, NY; Biennial Graphic Art, Moderna Galerija, Ljubljana, Yugoslavia; Il Bisonte, Florence, Italy, 89; Retrospective, Anderson Gallery & Cabell Libr, Va Commonwealth Univ, 2001; Common Ground, Corcoran Gallery, Washington, DC, 2005. *Pos:* prof emeritus, Virginia Commonwealth Univ. *Teaching:* Prof printmaking, Va Commonwealth Univ, 66-, prof, 78-; guest lectr etching, Cent Sch Art, London, 69-70; prof, Va Commonwealth Univ, 1966-. *Awards:* Fulbright grant, 63-64; Va Mus Fine Arts Fel, 83-84; Natie Marie Jones Fel, Lake Placid, NY, 84; Thersea Pollak award in Visual Arts, 2001; Svc Award, Va Commonwealth Univ; Award of Distinction, Southern Graphics Coun, 2008. *Bibliog:* David Freed-Printmaker; Long Art, film by David Williams. *Mem:* Soc Am Poets; Sierra Club; Southern Graphics Coun. *Media:* Works on Paper. *Res:* Studio. *Collection:* Prints & Small Sculpture. *Publ:* Collaborations and Artists Books with Poets Charles Wright, Larry Levis, Steven Lautermilch and Philip Levine. *Dealer:* Reynolds Gallery Richmond Va. *Mailing Add:* 1825 W Grace Richmond VA 23220

FREED, DOUGLASS LYNN
PAINTER, RETIRED MUSEUM DIRECTOR
b Garden City, Kans, Dec 24, 1944. *Study:* Ft Hays Kans State Univ, BS, 67, MA, 68; Rotary Int Group Study Exchange to Italy, 78. *Work:* Univ Mo Mus Art & Archeol, Columbia; St Louis Art Mus; Mildred Kemper Mus Art; Newark Mus, NJ; Wichita Ctr for Arts; Kemper Mus Contemp Art, Kansas City, Mo; Daum Mus Contemp Art, Sedalia, Mo. *Comn:* Oil painting, KEO Bldg Corp, Sedalia, Mo, 91; oil paintings, Deloitte & Touche, St Louis, 96; Emerson Electric, St Louis 2008; Sach's Properties, St Louis, 2008; Fed Reserve Bank, Kansas City, 2008; Ritz Carlton Laguna, Calif, 2009. *Exhib:* Visions, Mid Am Arts Alliance, 81 & traveling; Vorpal Gallery, NY, 81-84, 86 & 88; solo exhibs, Vorpal Gallery, San Francisco, 82 & 90, Batz-Lawrence Gallery, Kansas City, 83, 85; Zola-Lieberman Gallery, Chicago, 85; Greenberg Gallery, St Louis, 85; St Louis Design Ctr, 86; Mus Art & Archeol, Univ Mo, 92, Elliot Smith Contemp Art, St Louis, 92, 95, 96, 2000; Leedy Voulkos Arts Ctr, Kansas City, 93, 97; Sherry Leedy Contemp Art, Kansas City, 2000, 2005, 2009, 2010, 2011; Kathryn Markel Fine Arts, NY, 2004; Olsen-Larson Gallery, Des Moines, IA, 2004; ETRA Fine Arts, Miami, Fla, 2005, 2007; Lanoue Fine Art, Boston, MA, 2005; Dean Day Gallery, Houston, Tex, 2009; Loucks Gallery, Chicago, 2006, 2008, 2009; Micaela Gallery, San Francisco, Calif, 2007; Mary Martin Gallery, Charleston, NC, 2005, 2006, 2012; Daum Mus Contemp Art, Douglass Freed, Paintings 1973-2010, Sedalia, Mo. *Collection Arranged:* Works on Paper, Mo State Coun on Arts (contribr, assembled 12 sites), 80-81; Mid Am Art Alliance, 24 sites, 82-83; Missouri Painters, 12 sites, Mo Coun Arts, 85; cur, 42 solo exhib, Goddard Gallery, 1995-2000; cur, Daum Mus Contemporary Art, Sedalia, Mo, 2001-2007; cur, Betty Woodman, 2002,culpture Clay Invitation, 2002, Jun Kaneko, 2003, Awakening, 2003, Bay Area Ceramic Sculptures, 2004, Michiko, Tatani, 2004, Vera Kelment, 2004, Joyce Jablonski, 2005, Jim Sajovic, 2005, Steven Montgomery, 2006, Saint Louis Painters, 2007, Jim Sherosbry, 2006, Peter Callas, 2007, Jeffrey Moncrain, 2007, Ruth Borgenicht, 2007, Walter McConnell, 2008. *Pos:* Dir, Daum Mus Contemp Art, 2001-2007. *Teaching:* Chmn dept art, State Fair Community Col, Sedalia, Mo, 68-2001. *Awards:* Biannual Grant, Mo Art Coun, 84; Design Arts Grant, Nat Endowment Arts, 87; Creative Artists Grant, Mo Arts Coun, 90; Mo Arts Award for Leadership in the Arts, 2007. *Bibliog:* Patterson Sims (auth), catalog, Mo Artist's Exhib, 84; Nancy N Rice (auth), Doug Freed, New Art Examiner, 3/85; Jim White (auth), Douglas Freed, Abstract Painter, Dept Art Hist, Univ Mo, Columbia, 92; Elizabeth Kirsh & Robert Dufy Tom Piche (coauths), Douglass Freed Retrospective (catalog). *Mem:* Am Asn Mus. *Media:* Oil. *Specialty:* Contemporary art. *Publ:* auth catalog, Betty Woodman, 2002; auth catalog, Sculptural Clay Invitational, 2002; auth catalog, Awakenings, 2002; auth catalog introduction, Jun Kaneko, 2003; auth, catalog,Bay Area Ceramics Culpturs, 2004; auth catalogue, Michiko Itatani, 2004; auth, catalog, Joyce Jablonski, 2005; auth, catalogue, Steven Montgomery, 2006; auth catalog, Jim Shrosbry, 2006; auth catalogue, Peter Callas, 2007; auth, catalogue, Jeffrey Mongrain, 2007; auth, catalogue, Ruth Borgenicht, 2007. *Dealer:* Sherry Leedy Contemp Art Kansas City MO; Etra Fine Art Miami; Kathryn Markel Fine Arts New York; Quidley and Co Gallery Boston; Aberson Exhibits Tulsa; Dean Day Gallery Houson TX; Loucks Gallery Chicago; William Shearburn Gallery St Louis; Mary Martin Fine Art Charleston. *Mailing Add:* 110 E Main St Sedalia MO 65301-3849

FREEDBERG, DAVID
EDCUATOR, HISTORIAN
Study: Yale Univ, BA (summa cum laude), 1969; Balliol Coll Oxford Univ, DPhil, 1973. *Pos:* Founding dir & adv ed, Print Quarterly, 1983-; adv bd, Res, 1991-; ed adv bd, Italian Review 2000- & Nuncius, Florence, 2004-; ed bd, FMR, 2003-2009, Material Religion, 2003-2009, J Neuroesthetics, London, 2005- & Arts & Neurosciences, Paris, 2006. *Teaching:* Lectr in art history, Westfield Coll, 1973-76 & Courtauld Inst Art, 1976-84; chmn dept art history, Barnard Coll, 1984-86; prof art history, Columbia Univ, 1986-2007 & Pierre Matisse prof art history, 2007-; dir, Italian Acad for Advanced Studies in America, 2000-. *Awards:* Guggenheim Fel, 1989-90. *Mem:* Am Acad Arts & Sciences; Am Philos Soc. *Publ:* Auth, Rubens & Women, Sunday Times Mag, 30-36, 6/26/1977; The Hidden God: Image and Interdiction in the Netherlands in the Sixteenth Century, Art History, V, 133-153, 1982; Paintings or Prints-Experiens Sillemans and the Origins of the Dutch Grisaille Sea Piece: Notes on a Rediscovered Technique, Print Quarterly, I, 149-168, 1984; The Problem of Classicism: Ideology & Power, Art J, XLVII, No 1, 1-6, 1988; Context, Visuality, and the Objects of Art History, Art Bull, LXXVI, 1994; The Paper Museum, Natural History, 58-62, 10/1999; The Power of Wood and Stone, The Washington Post Outlook, B2, 3/25/2001; Damnatio Memoriae: Why Mobs Pull Down Statues, Wall Street J, D10, 4/16/2003. *Mailing Add:* Columbia Univ Dept Art History & Archaeology 932 Schermerhorn Hall New York NY 10027

FREEDMAN, DEBORAH S
PAINTER, PRINTMAKER
b New York, NY, May 1, 1947. *Study:* Studied Art Students League, 67 & New York Univ, BS, 70. *Work:* NY Pub Libr; NY State Facilities Corp. *Comn:* Touch Sanitation Map NY, Ronald Feldman Gallery, 84; waterfall suite folding screen, comn by Jeff Winant, Short Hills, NJ, 89; monoprint etching, KOP Finnish Bank, NY, 90. *Exhib:* Alternative Imaging Systems, Everson Art Mus, Syracuse, NY, 79; Electro Works, Int Mus Photog, Rochester, NY, 79 & Cooper Hewitt Mus, NY, 80; Artists Books, Rutgers Univ, New Brunswick, NJ, 82; Abstract Energy Now, Islip Art Mus, NY, 86; Projects & Portfolios, Brooklyn Mus, NY, 89; Works on Paper '90, Long Island Univ, Brooklyn Campus, NY, 90; Garbage Out Front, Munic Arts Soc, NY, 90; Retakes, Canadian Coun Prints & Drawings, Toronto, 90. *Awards:* MacDowell Colony fel, 90. *Bibliog:* Video Portrait, interview, Asaaiti Broadcasting, Tokyo, 88; Jack Anderson, rev, That was fast, NY Times, 88; Jackie Brody (auth), Deborah Freedman-Monoprints, Print Collectors Newsletter, 89. *Media:* Monoprint etching. *Publ:* Contribr, The great goddess, Heresies, 78; auth, Flue--a painter testifies to the glory of xerox, Franklin Furnace, 82. *Dealer:* Betsy Senior 55 Crosby St New York NY 10012. *Mailing Add:* 121 Wooster St No 5 New York NY 10012

FREEDMAN, JACQUELINE
PAINTER
Study: New Sch Social Res, New York, 65; Sch Visual Arts, 70. *Work:* Everson Mus Art, Syracuse, NY; Hudson River Mus; Queens Mus; Mus Mod Art, Art Lending Serv; Air France. *Comn:* 5 Clay Totem (50 clay paintings), pvt, 88. *Exhib:* Solo shows, Painted: Over Pages, Ctr Book Arts, NY, 82, Found Gallery, 82, Painted Photographs of Queens Streets & Neighborhoods, La Guardia Community Col, Long Island City, 85 & Recent Paintings, Flushing Gallery, Flushing Coun on Cult & Arts, NY, 87; group show, Art By The Book, Islip Mus, NY, 88; Queens Artists (with catalog), Queens Mus, 89; Works on Paper, Queensboro Community Col, 90; Long Island City Artists, Queens Coun Arts, NY, 92; OIA Benefit Exhib, Org Independent Artists, Brooke Alexander Gallery, N, 93; Women's Art, Women's Lives, Women's Issues, New York City Comn Status of Women, Tweed Gallery, 93; Open Studios, Independent Studios I, Long Island City, NY, 94-98; Henri Gallery, Washington, DC, 94-96; Cow Parade, NY Cent Park, 2000; The Garden Revisited, Islip Mus, Flowers, Petals and Seeds, Painted Book, 2000; plus others. *Teaching:* Instr painting & drawing, Jamaica Arts Ctr, 75-85. *Awards:* Nat Endwoment Arts Proj Grant, 80-81; Fel, Creative Arts Pub Serv, 82-83; Arts Apprenticeship Prog, Dept Cult Affairs, NY, 84. *Bibliog:* Helen A Harrison (auth), Work in miniature challenges the power of perception, New York Times, 11/81; Just above midtown, Black Current, vol 2, 9/82; William Peterson (auth), Jaqueline Freedman, Artspace Mag, winter 83. *Media:* Acrylic, Oil. *Dealer:* Independent Studios I 10-27 46th Ave NY NY 11101

FREEDMAN, SUSAN K
ADMINISTRATOR
Study: Brown Univ, BA (Studio Art & Am Civilization), 1982. *Pos:* Asst to Mayor Edward I Koch, New York, formerly; dir special projects & events, Art Comn City of New York, 1983-1986; pres, Pub Art Fund, New York, 1986-; mayor's rep, bd trustees, Mus Mod Art, currently; bd dirs, Munic Art Soc, Eldridge Street Project, WNYC Radio, currently; vpres bd, City Parks Found, New York, currently; mem advisory comn, New York Dept Cult Affairs, currently. *Awards:* Ann Award, Assocs Art Comn, New York, 1999; Evangeline Blashfield Award, Munic Art Soc, 2005. *Mailing Add:* Pub Art Fund 1 E 53rd St New York NY 10022

FREELAND, BILL
SCULPTOR, PAINTER
b Pittsburgh, Pa, June 16, 1929. *Study:* Philadelphia Mus Sch Art, 51-55; Hans Hofmann Sch, Provincetown, Mass, 56-. *Work:* Wilmington Mus & Soc Fine Arts, Del; Int Tel & Tel Collection, NY; Pa Acad Fine Arts; Philadelphia Mus Art, 87; Westtown Sch, Westtown, Pa; Allied Irish Bank, Dublin, Ireland; Mayo Co Coun, Castlebar Co Mayo, Ireland; Allied Irish Bank, Dublin, Ireland; American Express, NY; Arco Co, Philadelphia, Pa; Delaware Art Mus, Wilmington, Del; ITT Collection, NY; Lannan Found, Los Angeles, Calif; Montclair Mus, NJ; Pa Acad Fine Arts, Philadelphia; Philadelphia Mus Art, Pa; Univ Del, Newark, Del; Ballinglen Found, Ballycastle, Mayo Co, Ireland; Hawkswell Theatre, Sligo, Ireland. *Comn:* Sculpture, South St Develop Co, Philadelphia, Pa. *Exhib:* Color Show, Birmingham Mus, Ala, 63; Nat Watercolor Show, Pa Acad Fine Arts, Philadelphia, 69; Solo exhibs, Touchstone Gallery (with catalog, 80), NY, 78 & 80, Dolan/Maxwell (with catalog), NY, 89; From the Winston Malbin Collection Traveling Exhib (with catalog), 80; Pa Acad Fine Arts, 85; Iontas 97, Royal Hibernian Acad, (with catalog) Dublin, 99; Garrubbo/Bazan Gallery, West Chester, PA, 2004; Taylor Gallery, Dublin, Ireland, 2005; List Gallery, Swarthmore Coll, 2006; Royal Hibernian Acad Invitational Exhib, Dublin, 2007; Nat Academy Mus, New York, NY, 2008. *Teaching:* Prof emer fine arts, Moore Col Art, 69-90. *Awards:* Pa State Grant, 87; Pollock-Krasner Found Grant, 89; Ballinglen Arts Fel, Co Mayo Ireland, 92; Hereward Lester Cooke Found Grant, 78; Sculpture Award, Nat Academy, NY, 2008. *Bibliog:* Theodore F Wolf (auth), articles, Christian Sci Monitor, 3/24/81 & 1/16/84; Robert M Murdock (auth), The Sculpture of Bill Freeland, 89; Conor Fallon, Patrick Murphy (auths) Bill Freeland Process and Ritual, 99. *Media:* Miscellaneous Media, Wood, Steel, Oil, Stone, Bronze. *Collection:* Color Show, Birmingham Mus, Ala, 63; Nat Watercolor Show, Pa Acad Fine Arts, Philadelphia, 69; One-man shows, Touchstone Gallery (with catalog, 80), NY, 78 & 80, Dolan/Maxwell (with catalog), NY, 89; From the Winston Malbin Collection Traveling Exhib (with catalog), 80; Pa Acad Fine Arts, 85; Iontas 97, Royal Hibernian Acad, (with catalog) Dublin, 99; Garrubbo/Bazan Gallery, West Chester, PA, 2004; Taylor Gallery, Dublin, Ireland, 2005; List Gallery, Swathmore Gallery, 2006; List Gallery, Swathmore Col, 2006. *Dealer:* Taylor Galleries Dublin Ireland. *Mailing Add:* 1170 Valley Creek Rd Downingtown PA 19335

FREEMAN, DAVID L
PAINTER, GRAPHIC ARTIST
b Columbia, Mo, Nov 10, 1937. *Study:* Univ Mo, BA & MA; State Univ Iowa, MFA; Penland Sch Crafts & Penland Weavers. *Work:* Mint Mus Art, Charlotte, NC; Minn Mus Art, St Paul; SC Nat Bank, Columbia; SC State Art Collection; NCNB Corp, Charlotte, NC; Dupont, Atlanta, Ga; US Teledsta, Atlanta, Ga; SC State Art Collection, Columbia; Fannie Mae, Atlanta, Ga; Bank Mecklenburg, Charlotte, NC. *Comn:* Painting, RJ Reynolds Inc, Winston, Salem, 85; painting, Swanston Fine Arts, Atlanta, Ga, 86; painting, GE/Electrical Distribution & Control, 90. *Exhib:* Eleventh Piedmont Painting & Sculptor Show, Mint Mus Art, NC, 71; three-person exhib, Mint Mus Art, NC, 78; two-person exhib, Greenville Co Mus Art, SC, 81 & Asheville Mus Art, NC, 87; Three SC Painters, Waterworks Gallery, Salisbury, NC, 82; solo exhibs, High Point Theater Galleries, NC, 84 & Carlson Lobrano Gallery, Atlanta, Ga, 90; Columbia Coll, SC, 87; SC Arts Comn Triennial, 92-93. *Teaching:* Asst prof studio art, Univ Wis, Madison, 63-70; prof studio art, Winthrop Univ, Rock Hill, SC, 70-, prof emeritus. *Awards:* Purchase Awards, Drawings USA, Minn Mus Art, St Paul & 8th Ann Piedmont Graphics Exhib, Mint Mus Art, 71; Spring Mills Exhib & Traveling Show Award, New York, 78. *Mem:* Nat Coll Art Asn. *Media:* Acrylic. *Specialty:* Mod Art. *Interests:* Music, Gardening. *Dealer:* Edge Gallery Philadelphia PA. *Mailing Add:* 630 University Dr Rock Hill SC 29730

FREEMAN, KATHRYN
PAINTER, INSTRUCTOR
b Elmira, NY, Oct 28, 1956. *Study:* Univ NH, BFA 79; Brooklyn Col, MFA, 81; Skowhegan Sch Painting & Sculpture, 81. *Work:* Arnot Mus, Elmira, NY; Miller d Chevalier, Washington DC; Van Ness Feldman, Washington DC; Chase Manhattan Bank, NY; Swiss Bank, NY. *Comn:* murals, Orlando City Hall, Fla, 91; mural, Williams & Connolly, Washington, 95; murals, Jacksonville Pub Libr, 2005; and numerous pvt collections. *Exhib:* Solo exhibs, First Street Gallery, NY, 83, Rozbrat-Warsaw, Warsaw, Poland, 86, Tatistcheff Gallery & Co, NY, 86, 91 & 94 & Pepper Gallery, Boston, 95, Hanmon-Meek Gallery, Naples, Fla, 99, David Findlay Gallery, NY, 99; Bodies & Souls, Artist Choice Mus, NY, 83; The New Am Scene, Squibb Gallery, Princeton, NJ, 85; New Talent-NY, Sioux City Ctr, Iowa, 86; Artsites, Emerson Gallery Art, McClean, Va; Trees, Nat Acad Scis, Washington DC, 97; Catching the Shimmer, Nancy Hoffman Gallery, NY, 97; Dedicated to Art, Corcoran Mus Art Design, Washington DC, 2000. *Pos:* illusr, Loon Chase, 2006. *Teaching:* Instr design & color, Brooklyn Col, 82; instr painting, NY Acad Art, 82-84; adj prof painting & drawing, Corcoran Sch Art Design, Washington DC, 98-; instr, Corcoran Col of Art & Design, 98-. *Awards:* Ingram Merrill Fel, 87; Individual Artist Award, State Md, 98, 99. *Bibliog:* Susan Koslow, Kathryn Freeman, Arts Mag, 83; Ronny Cohen, Kathryn Freeman, Art Forum, 89; Michael Brenson, Kathryn Freeman, NY Times, 91. *Media:* Oil, Egg Tempera, Watercolor. *Dealer:* Lonstreet-Goldberg Art 5640 Taylor Rd Naples FL 34109; Osterville Fine Arts Osterville MA. *Mailing Add:* 6917 Woodside Pl Chevy Chase MD 20815

FREEMAN, ROBERT
PAINTER
b May 8, 1946. *Study:* Boston Univ, Mass, MA, BFA, 71, MA, MFA, 81. *Work:* Brown Univ; Nat Ctr AFO Am Artist; Mus Fine Arts, Boston. *Exhib:* Solo exhibs, Smith & Mason Gallery, Washington, 70, Nat Mus Afro-Am Artists, Roxbury, Mass, 81, Chapel Gallery, W Newton, Mass, 82, Addison Gallery Am Art, Andover, Mass, 82, Wendell St Gallery, Cambridge, Mass, 83, 86 & 87, Clark Gallery, Lincoln Mass, 83, 86, 88, 90, 2004 & 2006, Zenith Gallery, Washington, 84, Isabel Neal Gallery, Chicago, 89, June Kelly Gallery, NY, 89; Carpenter Ctr Visual Arts, Harvard Univ, Cambridge, Mass, 88; Boston Collects: Contemp Painting & Sculpture, 86, Massachusetts Masters: Afro-Am Artists, Mus Fine Arts, Boston, Mass, 88; Selections: Six Contemp African-Am Artists, Williams Coll Mus Art, Williamstown, Mass, 89. *Teaching:* Art dir, Weston Pub Schs, Mass, 73-81; artist-in-residence & painting instr, Noble & Greenough Sch, Dedham, Mass, 81-; lectr/instr, Harvard Univ, Cambridge, Mass, 88-94. *Awards:* Distinguished Alumni Award, Boston Univ, 97. *Bibliog:* Petty Peyton (auth), Portrait of the artist as a rising star, Tab, 1/17/88; Marty Carlock (auth), Electric Lady Land, Lincoln J, 1/21/88; Allan Gold (auth), Boston Curator Defends Black Artists' Exhibition, NY Times, 1/26/88; Robert Freeman's Social Season, Art New Eng, 2007. *Media:* Oil. *Dealer:* Clark Gallery 145 Lincoln Rd Lincoln MA 01773 ; Parish Gallery Georgetown 1054 31st St NW Washington DC. *Mailing Add:* 28 Seaverns Ave Boston MA 02130

FREEMAN, TINA
PHOTOGRAPHER, CONSULTANT
b New Orleans, La, May 5, 1951. *Study:* Art Ctr, Coll Design, BFA, 72; Rochester Inst Technol, 78; also with Helmet Gernsheim & Beaumont Newhall. *Work:* New Orleans Mus Art; Bibliot Nat, Paris; Nat Mus Photog, Film & Television, Bradford, Eng. *Comn:* NEA Art in Pub Places, Pascagoula, Miss. *Exhib:* Solo exhibs, Cunningham-Ward Gallery, NY, 77, Galerie Simonne Stern, New Orleans, 78, 80 & 84, Newcomb Art Gallery, Tulane Univ, New Orleans, 83 & Southeastern Ctr Contemp Art, Winston-Salem, NC, 85, Univ Ore Mus Art, 88; Contemp Art Ctr, New Orleans, 79-86; Clouds and Trees, 84 & A Tribute, 85, Witkin Gallery, NY; A Sense of Place: Contemp Southern Art, Minneapolis Coll Art & Design, Minn, 86; Arthur Roger Gallery, New Orleans, La, 92; The Academy Gallery, New Orleans, La, April 2, 2005- May 12, 2005. *Collection Arranged:* Paris After the Great War, 77; Diverse Images (auth, catalog), Photog Collection of New Orleans Mus Art, 78; Hard Times, Farm Security Administration Photography, 79; Women in Photography, 79; Deep Ocean Photography (with assistance from US Navy), 80; Lisette Model: A Retrospective (auth, catalog), Washington, DC, 81; New Acquisitions: New Directions in Black and White, 81; The Photographs of Mother St Croix (auth, catalog), 82 & Leslie Gill: A Classical Approach to Photography (auth, catalog), New Orleans Mus Art and traveling, 83-. *Pos:* Assoc cur photog, New Orleans Mus Art, 77-79, sr cur, 79-82, consultant, 82-85; vpres arts, Contemp Arts Ctr, New Orleans, 85-86. *Teaching:* Lectr, Free Univ, New Orleans, 80. *Awards:* Nat Endowment Art, Purchase Prize; Culver Artist Hall of Fame, 2004. *Bibliog:* John Lawrence (auth), monograph, Women Artists News, 80; Kathleen Moak (auth), The enduring appeal of portraits, Contemp Arts Southeast, 80; Eric Bookhardt (auth), Tina Freeman photographing artists, Uptown, 83; John Lawrence (auth), Tina Freeman: A sense of place and mortality, New Orleans Art Rev, 3-4/83. *Mem:* Soc for Photog Educ; Am Soc Media Photogrs. *Publ:* Auth, Diverse Images, Amphoto, Garden City, 78; The Photographs of Mother St Croix, New Orleans Mus Art, 82; Leslie Gill: A Classical Approach to Photography, New Orleans Mus Art, 84; contribr, Arts Quart, New Orleans; Photographer for Color, Natural Palletts for Painted Rooms, Clarkson Potts, 92

FREER, FRED-CHRISTIAN
PAINTER, ILLUSTRATOR
b Cortland, NY, Dec 17, 1956. *Study:* State Univ NY, Cobleskill, AAS, 77; studied with Ray Pierotti, 94 & 96, Paul Darrow, 95. *Comn:* Mug, KUAC TV & Radio 104-7, Fairbanks, Alaska, 94 & 2002; logo & letterhead, AK Libr Asn, 2004 & 2008; book cover, Raven's Light by Marianne Schlegelmilch, 2008. *Exhib:* Group exhibs, The Bear Gallery, Fairbanks, Alaska, 89-90, 94-95, 96, 98, 2002 & 2007, Anchorage Mus Fine Arts, Alaska, 90, New Horizons Gallery, Fairbanks, Alaska, 92-96, 98, 2001 & 2008, Yukon Arts Ctr Gallery, Whitehorse, Yukon, Alaska, 2000, Design Alaska's Wild Arts Walk, Creamer's Field Migratory Waterfowl Refuge, 2006-2009; solo exhibs, New Horizons Gallery, 93, Schweinfurth Art Ctr, Auburn, NY, 94, Bear

Gallery, 2005 & 2008, Barnes & Noble, 2007-2008. *Awards:* Made in Alaska, permit holder, 2003. *Mem:* Fairbanks Art Asn. *Media:* Acrylics, Watercolor. *Publ:* Auth, Coffee Spills, Art with Coffee in Mind, 89; Christmas Raven Series, 94, 95 & 96; Images Inspired by God, 2007; Raven Speak, 2008. *Dealer:* Full Spectrum Studio 1610 Kennedy St Fairbanks AK 99709; Expressions in Glass 1922 Peger Rd Fairbanks AK 99709; If Only...A Fine Store 215 Cushman St Fairbanks AK 99701. *Mailing Add:* 1610 Kennedy St Fairbanks AK 99709-5103

FREHM, LYNNE
PAINTER
b Yonkers, NY, 1947. *Study:* Southern Conn Univ, New Haven Conn, BS (Art Educ, Painting & Drawing), 1971; Scholar & Fel to Univ Cincinnati MFA Prog, 1971; Univ Cincinnati, Cincinnati, OH, MFA (Painting & Drawing), 1973. *Work:* Black Sails, 75-78; Clown, 76; Aquarium, Lifetime Television Corp Off, New York, 90; King Bill, 92; Wedding, 93; Secret Places, 95-96; Night Sail, 97; and many more pvt collections. *Exhib:* Solo shows include Bruce Mus., Greenwich, Conn., 1974, Ruth Siegel Gallery, NYC, 1991, Exhibit A Gallery, NYC, 2000, Andre Zarre Gallery, NYC, 1996, 2002, 2011, exhibited in group shows at Yale U., New Haven, 1968, Fed. Courthouse, NYC Orgn. Ind. Artists, 1977, Landmark Gallery, NYC, 1978, Attitude Art Gallery, NYC, 1987, Blondies Contemporary Art, NYC, 1991-94, Allan Stone Gallery, NYC, 1995, Andre Zarre Gallery, NYC, 1996-2012, Beatrice Conde Gallery, NYC, 1997, The Fanelli Show, OK Harris Gallery, NYC, 1998, 181st Ann.: An Invitational Exhbn. Contemporary Art, Nat. Acad. Mus., NYC, 2006, Andre Zarre Gallery, NYC, 1996-2012, prin. works include Black Sails, 1975-78, Life Mask, 1990, Secret Places, 1995-96, Night Sail, 1997, Grain of Rice, 2001-02, Ghosts Over Manhattan, 2001-02, NY Abstract Painter Interview, Biddington's Contemporary Art, Emerald Forest, 2010. *Teaching:* Asst to Dir Grad Prog, Univ Cincinnati, 1971-1973. *Awards:* Max Beckman Scholarship award, Brooklyn Mus Sch, 71. *Bibliog:* Jeanne C Wilkenson (auth), One-person Exhib, Andre Zarre Gallery (review), Bill Bace Publ, 1996; Ken Johnson (auth), For a Broad Landscape, An Equally Wide Survey, NY Times Review, 2006. *Mem:* Artist Equity, New York. *Media:* Oil. *Interests:* Swimming, cooking. *Dealer:* Andre Zarre Gallery NYC

FREIMARK, BOB (ROBERT)
PRINTMAKER, PAINTER
b Doster, Mich, Jan 27, 1922. *Study:* Univ Toledo, BEd; Cranbrook Acad Art, MFA; Independent study in Mex, Czech Republic, Guatemala & Cuba. *Work:* Nat Gallery, Prague, Czech; Smithsonian Inst & Libr Cong, Washington, DC; Los Angeles Co Mus, Calif; Brit Mus, London; Portland Art Mus, Ore; Bibliotheque Nat, Paris; Egyptian Mus, Cairo; and others. *Comn:* Brenton Banks, Des Moines, 74; Kundalini Found, NY, 74; Impressions Workshop, Boston, 74-75; tapestry, Olympic Games, Moscow, 80; Hotel Cosima, Tokyo, Japan, 95; Mural, Hist of San Jose, 2007. *Exhib:* Drawings of 12 Countries, Art Inst Chicago, 52; Pa Acad Fine Art Painting Ann, 52-53; Brooklyn Mus Biennial Watercolor Exhib, 64; Tokyo Munic Mus, 95 & 96; Mus Contemp Art, Sao Paulo, Brazil, 96; Nat Parliament, Praha, Czech Repub, 96; Beyond Boundaries, Richmond Art Ctr, 97; Int Print Exhib, Portland Art Mus, 97; The Art of Dissent, Mex Heritage-Plaza, San Jose, Calif, 2007; San Jose, Mus Quilts & Textiles, 2007. *Pos:* Guest artist, Joslyn Mem Mus, Omaha, Nebr, 61, Huntington Galleries, WVa, 63 & Riverside Art Ctr, Calif, 64; guest artist & lectr, Columbia Univ, 63; vis prof, Harvard Univ, 72-73. *Teaching:* Instr drawing, Toledo Mus Art, 52-55; instr painting, Ohio Univ, 56-59; resident artist, Des Moines Art Ctr, 59-63; prof graphics, San Jose State Col, 64-86, prof emer, 86-; artist-in-residence, Mus Regla, Cuba, 2001, Mus Guayasamin, Quito, Ecuador, 2002, Balatonfured, Hungary, 2002. *Awards:* New Talent in USA Award, Art in Am, 57; Ford Found Grant, WVa, 65; Spec Creative Leave, Calif State Coll Syst, 67. *Bibliog:* Roberta Loach (auth), In conversation with Robert Freimark, Visual Dialog, 76; Dan McGuire (auth), Kaleidoscope, TV video, KTEH, 79-80; David Howard (auth), Bob Freimark (video), Channel 16, New York & Channel 25, San Francisco. *Mem:* Am Print Alliance; Los Angeles Printmaking Soc; South East Conference Latin Am Studies (SECOLAS). *Media:* Painting, Lithography; Tapestry. *Res:* Mex popular cult; rehabilitation through art; environ planning for contemp living; Art Protis tapestries. *Interests:* Graphics, film and video. *Publ:* video, Arte Cubano: Contemporary Art and Culture in Cuba, 2000; video, film, El Dia Tarasco: The Day of the Dead among the Tarascan Indians; Royal Chicano Air Force; Los Desaparecidos-The Disappeared Ones, World Fest Houston, Tex. *Dealer:* Haus Wiegand Munich Ger; Windermere Gallery Seal Rock OR; Hart Gallery Palm Desert Carmel Chicago IL; Parish Gallery Washington DC. *Mailing Add:* Rte 2 Box 539A Morgan Hill CA 95037

FRELIN, ADAM
SCULPTOR, VIDEO ARTIST
Study: Indiana Univ, Pa, BFA, 1997; Univ Calif, San Diego, MFA, 2001. *Exhib:* Pulse, Contemp Art Mus St Louis, St Louis, Mo, 2004; Traffic, Exit Art, New York, 2005; Glitch, Los Angeles Co Mus Art, 2006; The Faction, Ctr for Contemp Art, Kiev, Ukraine, 2007; Evergreen Outdoor Sculpture Biennial, Johns Hopkins Univ, Md, 2008. *Teaching:* Vis artist prof, Webster Univ, Mo, 2002-03, asst prof, 2003-04; asst prof sculpture, SUNY Albany, NY, 2006-. *Awards:* Prof Develop Fel, Coll Art Assn, 2001; Pub Art Project Grant, Gunk Found, 2002; US/Japan Creative Artists Program Grant, Nat Endowment for the Arts, 2005; NY Found Arts Fel, 2009. *Bibliog:* Mary Thomas (auth), Exhibits alter view of daily life, Pittsburgh Post-Gazette, 1/22/2004; David Bonetti (auth), Great Rivers: Exhibit Gets Contemporary in the Flow, St Louis Post-Dispatch, 7/11/2004; Laura Dillon (auth), White Line, Sculpture, 6/2007

FRENCH, CHRISTOPHER CHARLES
PAINTER, WRITER
b St Louis, Mo, 1957. *Study:* Univ Calif, Davis, BA, 80. *Work:* Hewlett-Packard, NY & Atlanta; Sallie Mae Inc, Wash; Hirshhorn Mus & Sculpture Garden, Washington, DC; McNeese State Univ, Lake Charles, LA; Richard L Nelson Gallery, Univ Calif at Davis; Mus Fine Arts, Houston; Weatherspoon Mus, Greensboro, NC. *Comn:* Painting, Hewlett Packard, Atlanta, 94; painting, Goethe-Inst, Wash, 97. *Exhib:* Cité Int Arts, Paris, 96; Transformal, Wiener Secession, Vienna (with catalog), 96; Md Art Place (with catalog), 98; Galveston Art Ctr, Tex, (with catalog) 2003; Blue Star, San Antonio, Tex, 2003; solo exhibs, Bill Maynes Gallery, NY, 2000, Devin Bolden Hiram Butler Gallery, Houston, 2003; Devin Borden Hiram Butler Gallery, 2005; Marsha Mateyka Gallery, Washington, DC, 2006, 2011; Holly Johnson Gallery, Dallas, 2007; Devin Borden Hiram Butler Gallery, 2008; Holly Johson Gallery, Dallas, 2009; Drawing Room Gallery, East Hampton, NY, 2011; Devin Borden Gallery, Houston, 2012. *Pos:* Contrib ed, Artweek, 83-87 & J Art, 88-91; bd trustees, Washington Proj Arts, 94-96 & DiverseWorks, Houston, 2001-2006; contribr, ARTnews, Art Papers, FlashArt, Glasstire.com; pres, AICA-USA, 2012-. *Teaching:* Adj prof, Univ Md, College Park, 97-99; vis prof, Univ Houston, Tex, 2000-2001; tchr, Glassell Sch, Houston, 2002-2005; vis prof, Univ Tex, San Antonio, 2007. *Awards:* Fel, Nat Endowment Arts, 93; Cité Int Arts, Paris, 96; Joan Mitchell Found, 99; Grant CACCH, Houston, 2003. *Bibliog:* Brigitte Borchhardt-Birbaumer (auth), Von ästhetik und Verwandlung, Wiener Zeitung, 4/4/96; David Pagel (auth), Redefining the borders of abstraction, Los Angeles Times, 11/14/96; Ferdinand Protzman (auth), In Paris, an artist regains his touch, 11/16/96; Janet Kutner (auth), Review, ARTnews, 6/2007; Rex Weill (auth), Christopher French at Marsha Mateyka, ARTnews, 2011; Mark Jenkins (auth), Christopher French's Inventions, Washington Post, 2011; Matthew Smith (auth), Interview with Christopher French, newamericanpaintings.com, 2011; Susie Kalil (auth), Christopher French at Devin Borden Gallery, 2012. *Mem:* AICA, NY (pres). *Media:* Acrylic & Oil. *Specialty:* contemporary visual art. *Publ:* Ed, Facing History, Corcoran Gallery Art, 90; contribr, Beyond the Frame, Setagaya Art Mus, Tokyo, 91; auth, The Human Factor, Albuquerque Mus, 93; Like a Body Without a Shadow, Marsha Mateyka Gallery, 93. *Dealer:* Devin Borden Gallery Houston; Holly Johnson Gallery Dallas; Marsha Mateyka Gallery Washington DC; Drawing Room Gallery East Hampton. *Mailing Add:* 19 Fairbanks Ct Water Mill NY 11976-2341

FRENCH, STEPHANIE TAYLOR
ADMINISTRATOR
b Newark, NJ, Sept 13, 1950. *Study:* Wellesley Coll, BA, 1972; Harvard Univ, MBA, 1978. *Pos:* Bd dirs, New Mus Contemp Art, Mus Arts & Design, Parsons Dance Co, Columbia Univ Miller Theatre, PERFORMA, Works & Process, Shen Wei Dance, Metrop Mus Art Bus Com, Harvard Grad Sch Educ Arts & Educ Coun, Juilliard Sch Dance Com; dir, European Gallery, San Francisco, 1974-75; account exec, Young & Rubican, New York, 1978-79; account supervisor, Rives Smith Baldwin & Carlberg, Houston, 1980-81; mgr cult affairs & spec programs, Philip Morris Companies, Inc, New York, 1981-86, dir cult & contributions programs, 1986-90, vpres corp contribution & cult programs boards, 1990-2001; dir & chief exec officer, Byrd Hoffman Watermill Found, New York, 2009-. *Collection:* purchased Philip Morris Co collection

FRERICHS, RUTH COLCORD
PAINTER, LITHOGRAPHER
b White Plains, NY. *Study:* Conn Col, BA; Art Students League. *Work:* Thunderbird Bank, Phoenix, Ariz; First Nat Bank, Continental Bank, Valley Nat Bank, Ariz; permanent collection, Mus State Univ Southeastern Mo; and others. *Exhib:* Watercolor West Nat Exhib, Riverside, Calif, 72; Southwestern Fedn Watercolor Exhib, Mus Albuquerque, 76; Nat Watercolor Soc Ann, 76; Scottsdale Watercolor Biennial, Ariz, 78; Conn Coll Alumni Exhib, New London, 78; and others. *Mailing Add:* 321 E Pomona Rd Phoenix AZ 85020

FRESKO, COLLEENE
APPRAISER
Study: Bucknell Univ, BA. *Pos:* appraiser, Childs Gallery, Boston, currently; consult, Vespi Corp; fac, Skinner, Inc, Boston, 87, vpres, & dir, Am European paintings & prints dept, currently; appraiser, Antiques Roadshow, WGBH-PBS, currently; founder, Firewall Gallery Skinner, Inc. *Teaching:* Teacher, art hist Mount Ida Col, formerly. *Mem:* Art Table women in arts orgn. *Mailing Add:* Skinner Inc 63 Park Plaza Boston MA 02116

FREUDENHEIM, NINA
DEALER, COLLECTOR
Pos: Owner, Nina Freudenheim Gallery; art cons, Baird Music Hall, SUNY, Buffalo, 86, Rochester Swsquicentennial, Inc, 87, Buffalo and Erie Co Pub Lib, 95 & Highland Hosp Rochester, NY, 98 & others; corp art cons, Westwood Pharmaceuticals, Inc, Marine Midland arena, Buffalo, Mark IV Industries, Buffalo, Headquarter Cos/Olympic Mgt, Buffalo & others; art appraiser Albright-Knox Art Gallery, AT&T, Castellani Art Mus, Nat Gallery Can, IRS, Mem Art Gallery Univ Rocheste & others. *Awards:* Community-Univ Award Outstanding Woman in the Arts, SUNY, Buffalo, 82; Award Outstanding Individual Arts Prof, Arts Coun and Greater Buffalo CofC, 89. *Mem:* Appraisers Asn Am. *Specialty:* Contemporary, national and international art. *Collection:* Works by Pol Bury, Jules Olitski, Georges Noel, Lucas Samars, Fontana and many others. *Mailing Add:* 140 North St Buffalo NY 14201

FREUDENSTEIN, ELLIE (ELEANOR) T(ERENYI)
PAINTER, ENVIRONMENTAL ARTIST
b Detroit, Mich, Feb 4, 1936. *Study:* Univ Calif, Los Angeles, with Lucille Brown Green Jan Stussey, Rico Lebruu & Sam Amato, BFA (honors, art), 58. *Work:* Santa Barbara Bank & Trust; David Zukor Prodns, Hollywood, Calif; Transamerica Life, San Francisco; Westcap Investors Inc, Los Angeles; Cynthia Wood Found. *Comn:* EDS Unigraphics, Cypress, Calif, 96; Cynthia Wood Found; Transamerica Life, San Francisco, Calif, 2000; Santa Barbara Bank Trust, Calif, 2001; Barbie Benton, Aspen co, select personnel serv, Santa Barbara, Calif; Peppertree art show, Santa Ymez, Calif, 2006; Group show Tirage Gallery show, Pasadena, Calif, 2006. *Exhib:* Solo exhibs, Gallery Los Olivos, Calif, 93, Doubletree Gallery, Ventura, Calif, 93, Faulkner West, Santa Barbara, Calif, 93 & Waterhouse Gallery, Santa Barbara, Claif,

2000-2001, Am Impressionist Soc Nat Exhib, 2001, 2002, 2003; Watercolors, Hahn & Horn Gallery, Santa Barbara, Calif, 93-94; Women Artists of West, Gallery Liz Montana, Los Olivos, Calif, 94; Under the Oaks, Santa Barbara Natural Hist Mus, Calif, 95; Label Art Exhib, Cent Coast Wine Classic, 95; 87th Calif Art Club Gold Medal Exhib, Los Angeles Arboretum, Calif, 96; Small Painting Show, Watercolor Gallery, 98; Mission San Juan Capestrano Show, 98, 99 & 2000; Oil Painters of Am Nat Show, Americana Gallery, Carmel, Calif, 2000; 1st Ann Spring Salon, Edenhurst Gallery, 2000; Ronald Reagan Presidential Library & Mus, 2003; 7th nat AIS, Rockport, Tex, 2006; others. *Teaching:* Instr watercolor, Sea Pines Studio, 83-96. *Awards:* Bronze Award, Discovery 93, Art Calif Mag, 93; Ojai Spring Competition 3rd Prize, Cent Coast Watercolor Soc, 94; Best of Show, Santa Barbara Mus Nat Hist, 97; Award Joan Irvine Smith Competition, 99. *Mem:* Am Impressionist Soc; Calif Art Club; Oil Painters Am; Gold Coast Watercolor Soc; Women Artists West; Conservancy Painters. *Media:* Watercolor, Oil. *Specialty:* Traditional Works of Art, Oil, Watercolor. *Publ:* Women in the arts, Southwest Art Mag, 11/96; Guide book of Western artists, Art of West Mag, 97. *Dealer:* Waterhouse Gallery 1114 State St Santa Barbara CA 93110; Tirage Gallery One West California Blvd Pasadena CA; Huntsman Gallery 410 East Hyman Ave Aspen CO; Zantman Gallery Carmel & Palm Desert CA. *Mailing Add:* 4595 Via Huerto Santa Barbara CA 93110

FREUND, PEPSI
PAINTER, COLLAGE ARTIST
b New York, NY, Oct 17, 1938. *Study:* Self taught. *Work:* Citibank & Chase Bank, NY; Long Island Jewish Med Ctr, New Hyde Park, NY; Franklin Gen Hosp; St James Nursing Home; 9/11 Mem, Hofstra Univ, Hempstead, NY; and various corps; Phillippi Mansion, Sarasota Mem Light Chasers, Sarasota, Fla. *Exhib:* Long Beach Mus, Long Island; Fine Arts Mus, Long Island; Guggenheim Mus, Long Island; one person shows, St John's Univ, Oceanside Libr & W Hempstead Libr; Long Beach Celebrity Arts, Nat Art League; Collector's Corner, Venice, Fla. *Pos:* workshop instr, Watermill, NY and Sarasota, Fla. *Teaching:* Instr at var Nassau Co Schs; Boces Demonstr, Venice & Sarasota, Fla; instr, workshops, Riverhead & Watermill, Long Island, NY. *Awards:* Gold & Silver Awards (bronze), Nat Art League; Bronze Award, Nassau Mus Fine Art; Photography Awards, Metro Gallery, Greenport, NY. *Bibliog:* Articles in Mag & newspapers. *Mem:* 30 Artists; Nat Asn Women Artists Am. *Media:* Collage, Watercolor; Acrylic. *Specialty:* fine art. *Publ:* Illustrator 4 books, The spirit of Jezebel, Offenses-Diane Ford, Abuse-Theresa Duffy, God's Little Tomatoes, Joan Ann Warnell. *Dealer:* Soundview Art Gallery 35 Chandler Sq Port Jefferson New York NY; Galerie des Hamptons Hampton Beach NY; Christopher Gallery Stonybrook NY; The Gallery of Calverton Rte 25A Calverton NY; Abbacino Gallery 243 W Venice Ave Venice FL. *Mailing Add:* 3416 Montilla Ct Sarasota FL 34232

FREUND, WILL FREDERICK
PAINTER, EDUCATOR, WRITER
b Madison, Wis, Jan 20, 1916. *Study:* Univ Wis, BS, MS; Univ Mo; Tiffany Found Fel, 40 & 49. *Work:* William Rockhill Nelson Gallery Art, Kansas City, Mo; Joslyn Mus Art, Omaha, Nebr; Okla Art Ctr, Oklahoma City; Mulvane Mus Art, Topeka, Kans; Univ Nebr Art Galleries, Lincoln; and others; Gimble Collection, Milwaukee, Wis. *Exhib:* Mo Pavilion, NY World's Fair, 64; New Talent USA, Art in Am Mag, 65; Watercolor USA, Springfield Art Mus, Mo, 70 & 72; Evansville Mus Art, Ind; Denver Art Mus; Butler Inst Art; Nat Gallery Art, Washington, DC; Windsor Gallery, Stephens Col, Columbia, Mo; Columbia Art League Gallery; Southern Ill Univ, Edwardsville; and others. *Teaching:* Instr art, Stephens Col, 46-64; prof emer, fine art, Southern Ill Univ, Edwardsville, 64-81. *Awards:* First Prize Watercolor, Ruth Renfro Award, St Louis City Art Mus, 63; Purchase Prize & Bronstein Award, Evansville Mus Art, St Louis; First Prize Watercolor, Quincy, Ind 24th Ann. *Bibliog:* article, Will Freund, painter, potter, woodworker, boombass player, Wis Alumnus, 1/61; Eileen B Saarinan, New Talent USA, NY Times; La Revue Moderne, French Arts Mag; American Biographical Inst & Exhib, Personalities of the West & Mid West; Academia Italia delle Arti e del Lauoro; Palazzo Delle Manifestazioni Salsomaggiore Terme. *Mem:* life fel Int Arts and Letters; Int Inst Arts and Letters, Zurich, Switz; Int Dir Art, Berlin, Germ; Mich Artists Registry; Detroit Inst Arts; St Louis Art Mus Libr Archives. *Media:* Oil, Watercolor. *Res:* Sabbaticals: circuitous odyssey of Irish Art & the Spec Psyche of the Irish People. The Pour, Flood, Flow, Techniques of watercolor. *Specialty:* visual opportunity to share. *Publ:* featured in Art News, NY Times, New Talent USA, Art in Am, Art Moderne, paris, Life Mag. *Mailing Add:* PO Box 182 Watersmeet MI 49969

FREUNDLICH, AUGUST L
ADMINISTRATOR, COLLECTOR
b Frankfurt, Ger, May 9, 1924; US citizen. *Study:* Antioch Col, BA, 49, MA, 50; New York Univ, PhD, 60. *Collection Arranged:* All in Line (linear drawings, auth, catalog), Joe & Emily Lowe Art Gallery, Syracuse Univ & Terry Dintenfass Inc Gallery, NY, 80; Self Portraits (auth, catalog), Tampa Mus Art, 88; Robert Gwathmey (auth, catalog), Butler Inst Am Art, Mus Fine Arts, St Petersburg, Fla, Va Hist Mus, Telfair Mus, Pa Acad Fine Arts, 98-2000; and others. *Pos:* Consult, Nat Found Advan Arts; pres & exec dir, RA Florsheim Art Fund; bd, Exec Serv Corps, Tampa; trustee & pres, Richard Florsheim Art Fund, 87-; cur, Work of Richard Florsheim, Contemp Tableau (Beal, Goodman, Witkin). *Teaching:* Head art dept, Eastern Mich Univ, 54-58; chmn arts div, George Peabody Col, 58-64; dir & chmn art dept, Lowe Art Mus, Univ Miami, 64-70; dean, Sch Art, Syracuse Univ, 70; dean, Col Visual & Performing Arts, 71-82; dean, Col Fine Arts, Univ SFla, 82-86, prof fine arts, 86-91. *Awards:* Kress Found grant (2); Ford Found grant. *Mem:* Int Coun Fine Art Deans; Coll Art Asn; Am Asn Mus; Nat Art Club; Life Fel Nat Art Educ Asn. *Res:* Social commentary art, American & German; American graphics and sculpture. *Collection:* Self-portraits; 20th century prints; American drawings. *Publ:* Auth, William Gropper, Ward, Richie Press, 63; Frank Kleinholz, Univ Miami, 66; Karl Schrag, 70 & 80; Richard Florsheim, AS Barnes, 76; auth, Federico Castellon, Syracuse Univ, 78; S Rosenblum, Nogorme Press, 89; The Sculpture of James Earle Fraser, Universal Press, 2000; and others

FREY, BARBARA LOUISE
CERAMIST, EDUCATOR
b Bloomington, Ind, Apr 28, 1952. *Study:* Ind Univ, Bloomington, BFA, 76; Syracuse Univ, MFA, 78. *Work:* Diane and Sandy Besser Teapot Collection, de Young Mus, San Francisco, Calif; The Kamm Foundation Teapot Collection, Sparta, NC; Kohler Co. Permanent Collection, Kohler, Wisc; Jacqueline and Daird Charak Collection, Racine Art Mus, Racine, Wisc; San Angelo Mus Fine Arts, San Angelo, Tex. *Comn:* Ceramic tile mural, comn by Dr Karl F Frey, Harlingen, Tex, 85. *Exhib:* A Tea Party, Ferrin Gallery, Northampton, Mass, 89, 91-92, 94 & 97; The Tea Party, Am Crafts Mus, NY, 91 & 93; Teapot Invitational, Dorothy Weiss Gallery, San Francisco, 91, 93 & 94 & Craft Alliance Gallery, St Louis, 93, 94 & 96; Rituals of Tea, Garth Clark Gallery, NY, 91; The Tea Party: An Exhib of Contemp Teapots, Nat Mus Ceramic Art, Baltimore, 93; Purple Sands: 21 Western Potters in China, JBK Gallery, Amsterdam, The Neth, 97; Contemp Clay in Texas, Austin Mus Art, 97; Clay Traditions: Texas Educators and their Teachers, Dallas Mus Art, 98; Eight Texas Artists, Arlington Mus Art, 98; Confluence, Australian, Bolivian and Am Artists Exhib, Kyoto Munic Arts & Crafts Gallery, Japan, 98; Teapots: Object to Subject, Craft Alliance Gallery, St Louis, Mo, 2004; Delightful Teapot, Yeoju World Ceramic Livingware Gallery, 3rd World Ceramic Biennale, Yeoju, Korea, 2005; The Yixing Effect, Holter Mus Art, Helena, MT, 2006; American Potters Working in the Realist Tradition, Decorative Arts Mus, Ark Arts Center, Little Rock, Ark, 2003; San Angelo National Ceramic Competition, San Angelo Mus Fine Arts, San Angelo, Tex, 2002, 2004, 2006, 2008. *Teaching:* Instr ceramics, State Univ NY, Oswego, 78-80; prof, Tex A&M Univ, Commerce, 80-. *Awards:* First Prize, Read Head: Contemporary Work in Clay, Alexander Hogue Gallery, Univ Tulsa, Tulsa, Okla, 2005; Jurors Award, Materials Hard and Soft, Meadows Gallery: Center for Visual Arts, Denton, Tex, 2006; Best in Show, Univ Dallas Regional Juried Ceramic Comp, Beatrice M Haggerty Gallery, Univ Dallas, Irving, Tex, 2007. *Mem:* Nat Coun Educ Ceramic Arts; Coll Art Asn. *Media:* Ceramics. *Publ:* Contribr, Porcelain: Traditions and New Visions, Watson-Guptill, 81; Electric Kiln Ceramics, 81 & 94, 2nd ed, Ceramics: Mastering the Craft, 90 & Hand-Formed Ceramics, Chilton Bk Co, 95; The Best of New Ceramc Art, Hand Bks, Madison, Wis, 97; Contribr, Suzanne Tourtillot (auth), 500 Teapots: Contemporary Explorations of a Timeless Design, Lark Books, 2002; Contribr, Robin Hopper (auth), Making Marks-Discovering the Ceramics Surface, KP Books, Iola, Wisc, 2004; Contribr, Richard Zakin (auth), Electric Kiln Ceramics, Krause Publications, Iola, Wisc, 2004; Contribr, Marvin Sweet, The Yixing Effect: Echoes of the Chinese Scholar, Foreign Language Press, Beijing, China, 2006; Contribr, The Diane and Sandy Besser Collection, Fine Arts Mus of San Francisco, 2007. *Dealer:* Ferrin Gallery 437 N St Pittsfield Mass 01201. *Mailing Add:* 1513 Park St Commerce TX 75428

FREY, MARY E
PHOTOGRAPHER
b Yonkers, NY, Nov 25, 1948. *Study:* Coll New Rochelle, NY, BA (fine arts), 70, Yale U, MFA (photog), 79. *Work:* Art inst Chicago; Mus Fine Arts, Houston Ctr Photog, Houston, Tex; Mus Mod Art, NY; Smith Coll Mus Art, Northampton, Mass; Int Polaroid Corp & Carpenter Ctr Visual Arts, Harvard Univ, Cambridge, Mass. *Exhib:* New Photog 2, Mus Mod Art, NY, 86; Arrangements for the Camera, Baltimore Mus Art, Md, 87; solo exhibs, Northfield Mt Hermon Sch, Northfield, 89, Blatent Image/Silver Eye, Pittsburgh, Pa, 89, Ledel Gallery, NY, 89, Arno Maris Gallery, Westfield State Col, Mass, 91, Springfield Mus Fine Arts, 93, Laelia Mitchell Gallery, Boston, 95, Northlight Gallery, Ariz State Univ, 96, Springfield Tech Comm Col, Springfield, 97, Marlboro Col, Vt, 98, Donaldson Gallery, Miss Porter's Sch, Farmington, Conn, 2001; Pleasures and Terrors of Domestic Comfort, Mus Mod Art, NY, 91 & Baltimore Mus Art, 92; Los Angeles Co Mus Art, 92; Arno Maris Gallery, Westfield Col, Mass, 2001; Gameface, Arts & Industry Bldg, Smithsonian Instn, Washington, 2001. *Teaching:* prof, Hartford Art Sch, Univ Hartford, 79-; vis artist, Smith Col, 94-95. *Awards:* Fel, Nat Endowment Arts, 81, 92; Guggenheim Fel, 84; Mass Coun Cult Grant, 96; Springfield Cult Coun Artist Grant, 97, 99. *Bibliog:* Gloria Russell (auth), Photography, sculpture exhibits explore grand themes, 5/17/92 & Real life through a lens, 4/4/93, Sunday Republican, Springfield, Mass; Kathryn Marx (auth), Right Brain/Left Brain Photography, Watson-Guptill, New York, 94. *Mem:* Soc for Photog Educ. *Mailing Add:* Hartford Art School 200 Bloomfield Ave Hartford CT 06117

FRICANO, TOM S
PAINTER, PRINTMAKER
b Chicago, Ill, Oct 28, 1930. *Study:* Bradley Univ, BFA, 53; Univ Ill, Urbana, MFA, 56. *Work:* Libr Cong, Washington; Philadelphia Mus; Art Inst Chicago; Los Angeles Co Mus Art; Seattle Art Mus; Utah Mus Fine Art; Brooklyn Mus Art, NY; Univ of Tex, Austin, Tex; Univ of Lethbridge, Can; Ohio State Univ, Athens, Ohio. *Exhib:* Solo exhibs, Harmon Fine Arts Ctr, Drake Univ, Des Moines, Iowa, 77, Fresno State Univ Gallery, Calif, 78, Pepperdine Univ, Malibu, Calif, 79, Univ NDak, Grand Forks, 80, Bibo Gallery Art, Peoria, Ill, 81, Arts Place II, Okla Arts Ctr, Oklahoma City, 83, A Survey: 25 Yrs of Printmaking, Fairweather Hardin Gallery, Chicago, Ill, 88; Carnegie Art Mus, Oxnard, Calif, 94; Millard Sheets Gallery, Pomona, Calif, 95; Calif State Univ, Northridge, 96; Gilkey Ctr Graphic Arts, Portland Art Mus, Ore, 97. *Teaching:* Instr painting & printmaking, Bradley Univ, Peoria, Ill, 58-63; prof painting & printmaking, Calif State Univ, Northridge, 63-; vis artist, Ohio State Univ, Columbus, 69, Univ Utah, 71, Univ Mont, Bozeman, & Art Inst Chicago, 75, Univ NDak, Grand Forks, Cranbrook Acad Art, Bloomfield Hills, Mich & Eastern Mich Univ, Ypsilanti, 80. *Awards:* Fulbright Grant, Florence, Italy, 60-61; Louis Comfort Tiffany Res Grant, 65; Calif State Univ Found Res Grant, 66, 68, 74 & 78; Guggenheim Found Fel, 69 & 70. *Bibliog:* Lawrence C Goldschmidt (auth), Watercolor Bold and Free, NY/Pitman Publ, 80; John Ross & Claire Romano (coauths), The Complete Collagraph, Free Press, 80; Leonard Edmondson (auth), Etching, Van Nostrand Reinhold. *Mem:* Hon mem Los Angeles Printmaking Soc (vpres, 64-65). *Publ:* Auth, Thoughts Emerging, 91; Contemporary Flight, 91; Book, Thoughts Emerging,91: Portfolio, Contemporary Flight, 91; It All Adds Up, 92. *Mailing Add:* 9820 Aldea Ave Northridge CA 91325-1916

FRIED, HOWARD LEE
SCULPTOR
b Cleveland, Ohio, June 14, 1946. *Study:* Syracuse Univ, 64-67; San Francisco Art Inst, BFA, 68; Univ Calif, Davis, MFA, 70. *Work:* Cleveland Mus Art, Ohio; Syracuse Univ, NY; Univ Calif, Davis; Ft Worth Art Mus, Tex; San Francisco Mus Mod Art, Calif. *Comn:* Mural, Syracuse Univ, 66. *Exhib:* Looking West, Joslyn Art Mus, Omaha, Nebr, 70; The 80's, Univ Art Mus, Univ Calif, Berkeley, 70; Projection, Kunsthalle, Dusseldorf, Ger, 71 & Louisiana Mus, Denmark, 72; Documenta 5, Kassel, Ger, 72; and many others. *Teaching:* Instr sculpture, San Francisco Art Inst, 68-, chmn performance & video dept, 83-. *Awards:* Augusta Hazard Award, Syracuse Univ, 66; Adeline Kent Award, San Francisco Artist's Comt, 71-72; Nat Endowment Arts Grant, 75. *Bibliog:* Grace Glueck (auth), New York: Big thump on the bass drum, Art in Am, 5-6/71; Brenda Richardson (auth), Howard Fried: Paradox of approach-avoidance, Arts Mag, 6/71; Steve Davis (auth), Howard Fried installation piece, Art Week, 3/25/72. *Publ:* Auth, Inside the harlequin, Flash Art, 71; auth, Studio relocation, Breakthroughs in Fiction, 72; auth, Cheshire cat 4, Avalanche. *Mailing Add:* 1101 Georgia St Vallejo CA 94590

FRIEDBERG, M. PAUL
LANDSCAPE ARCHITECT
b Bklyn, NY, Oct 11, 1931. *Study:* Cornell Univ, BS in Landscape Archit, 54; Ball State Univ, LLD, 83. *Work:* Carver House Plz, NY; Riis Houses Plz, NY; Buchanan Sch, Wash Pub Sch 166, NY; Bedford Stuyvesant Superblock, Harlem River Bronx State Park; Jeannette Plz, NY; Worlds Fair, 1965; Winter Garden, Niagara Falls, NY; State St Mall and Concourse, Madison, Wisc; Pershing Park, Wash; Ft Worth Cultural Dist. *Pos:* landscape architect with Arthur Hoffman, Hartford, Conn, 54, Joseph Gangemi, NYC, 54, 56-58; pres, M. Paul Friedberg & Partners, NY, 60-. *Teaching:* vis critic lectr, Harvard Univ, 66, Univ Pa, 67, Syracuse Univ, 67, Carnegie Inst Tech, 67, 1st Fed Design Assendly, Wash, 73, and many others; mem faculty Pratt Inst, Columbia Univ, New Sch Social Rsch, formerly; head urban landscape archit program, City Coll, NY, formerly, prof emer, currently. *Awards:* Albert S Bard award, 65, 67; Honor award, AIA, 67, Citation, 69; Nat Landscape Asn, 71; NYC Award for Excellence, 73; IDEA Downtown Achievement award, 79; 1st Ann award, NY Art Comn, 83. *Mem:* Nat Acad; Am Landscape Architects; NY Municipal Arts Soc; NYC Coun Parks & Recreation Archit League. *Mailing Add:* M Paul Friedberg & Partners 41 E 11th St Fl 3 New York NY 10003

FRIEDBERG, RICHARD S
SCULPTOR, EDUCATOR
b Baltimore, Md, Aug 10, 1943. *Study:* Antioch Col, BA, 65; Yale Univ, BFA & MFA (Graham Found Fel), 68. *Work:* Citicorp Bank, Chase Manhattan Bank, NY. *Comn:* Sculpture, Rutgers Univ, NJ, 70; sculpture, Mobil Corp, Va, 79. *Exhib:* Whitney Ann, 71 & Whitney Biennial, 73, Whitney Mus Am Art, NY; Munson-Williams Proctor Inst, NY, 77; Storm King Art Ctr, NY, 79; Prospect Mountain Sculpture Show, Lake George, NY, 79; Alexander Milliken Gallery, NY, 81. *Teaching:* Assoc prof fine art, Fairleigh Dickinson Univ, Rutherford, 70-. *Awards:* Nat Endowment Arts Fel, 74. *Bibliog:* Ellen Schwartz (auth), Richard Friedberg, Art News, 78; Carter Ratcliff (auth), Richard Friedberg, Arts Mag, 79. *Mem:* Coll Arts Asn. *Media:* Steel, Aluminum. *Mailing Add:* 62 Green St No 5 New York NY 10012

FRIEDMAN, ALAN
SCULPTOR, DESIGNER
b Philadelphia, Pa, Sept 9, 1944. *Study:* Rochester Inst Technol Sch Am Craftsman, BFA, 67; Univ Wis, Madison, MFA (sculpture), 69. *Work:* Univ Wis, Union Galleries, Madison, 69; Ind State Univ, Terre Haute, 72; Indianapolis Mus of Art, 77. *Comn:* Entrance doors (wood), St Paul's Univ Cath Church, Madison, 68; sculpture (plywood), Cunningham Mem Libr, Ind State Univ, Terre Haute, 73; and many more pub & pvt collections. *Exhib:* Retrospective, Wis Directions, Milwaukee Art Ctr, 75; Indianapolis Mus Art Traveling Exhib & Mus Gallery Exhib, 75-76; New Handmade Furniture, Mus Contemp Crafts, NY, 79; Contradictions, Fendrick Gallery, DC, 79; Fine Arts Comt Visual Arts, Program of the XIII Olympic Winter Games, Lake Placid, NY, 80; Recent Art Furniture, Niagara Univ, 82; and others. *Pos:* Designer furniture, E A Roffman Co, NY, 72; AF Works, Mansfield Rd Studio, Hillsdale, NY, 78. *Teaching:* Vis asst prof art, Univ Wis, Madison, 69-70; assoc prof furniture design & sculpture, art dept, Ind State Univ, Terre Haute, 72-79; guest lectr, State Univ NY, New Paltz, 83; lectr, The Creative Process, NY Found Art Grant, Hudson River Mus, Yonkers, 89. *Awards:* Nat Endowment Arts Individual Fel Grant, 76-77; Design Award for Excellence, Daphne Found, NY, 82; Individual Fel Grant, NY Found Arts, 88-89. *Bibliog:* Thelma Newman (auth), Woodcraft, Chilton Bks, NY, 78; Nicholas Rookes (auth), Masters of Wood Sculpture, Watson-Guptill, NY, 80; Dona Meilach (auth), Woodworking, The New Wave, Crown, New York, 81. *Mem:* Am Crafts Coun. *Publ:* The Designer, NY, 80; Progressive Archit, 81; Archit Record, 81. *Mailing Add:* 61 Mansfield Rd Hillsdale NY 12529

FRIEDMAN, BERNARD HARPER
WRITER
b New York, NY, July 27, 1926. *Study:* Cornell Univ, BA, 48. *Pos:* Adv coun mem, Cornell Univ Arts Col & Herbert F Johnson Mus; trustee, Am Fedn Arts, 58-64 & Whitney Mus Am Art, currently; bd mem, Fine Arts Work Ctr, Provincetown, Mass, 68-82. *Teaching:* Lectr Eng, Cornell Univ, 66-67. *Awards:* Fels, Coord Coun Lit Mag, 75; Nelson Algren Award, 83. *Mem:* Century Asn. *Media:* Books, Magazines. *Res:* Art & literature. *Publ:* ed, School of New York, 1959; auth, Lee Krasner (monogr), 1965; auth, Jackson Pollock: Energy Made Visible (biog), 72; Auth, Whispers, 72; auth, Alfonso Ossorio (monogr), 73; auth, Museum, 74; auth, Almost a Life, 75; auth, Gertrude Vanderbilt Whitney (biog, with research collaboration of Flora Biddle), 78; ed, Give My Regards to Eighth Street: Collected Writings of Morton Feldman, 2000

FRIEDMAN, CHARLEY
CONCEPTUAL ARTIST
b 1991. *Study:* Macalester Coll, BFA, 1990; Sch Mus Fine Arts, Boston, MFA, 1996; Skowhegan Sch Art, Maine, 1995; Bemis Ctr Contemp Arts, Omaha, 1998 & 2001; MacDowell Colony, NJ, 2000. *Work:* NY Pub Libr; Sheldon Mem Art Gallery, Univ Nebr; Bemis Ctr Contemp Arts, Omaha; Amherst Coll, Mass. *Exhib:* Solo exhibs include CRP Inc, New York, 1998, Queens Mus, New York, 2002, White Columns, New York, 2003, Kantor/Feuer, New York, 2006, Barbara Mathes Gallery, New York, 2006, Sheldon Mem Art Gallery, Lincoln, Nebr, 2007, Gallery Diet, Miami, 2008; group exhibs include The End, Exit Art, New York, 2000, Reactions, 2002, Renegades: A History of Performance, 2006; Posers, White Columns, New York, 2000, Silent Auction, 2001; 20 Yrs of Excellence, Bemis Ctr Contemp Art, Omaha, 2001, Signal Channel, 2006; How I Learned To Stop Worrying and Love the Recession, Ten In One Gallery, New York, 2001; Reactions, Libr Cong, Washington, 2002; Enough About Me, Momenta Art, New York, 2002; B-List: Brooklyn, Angst, Desire, Hallwalls, Buffalo, 2003; Summer Exhib, Cooper Union, New York, 2005; Parts of the Whole, Vox Populi, Philadelphia, 2006; Emergency Room, PS1 Contemp Art Ctr, New York, 2007. *Awards:* Pollock-Krasner Found Grant, 2006

FRIEDMAN, LYNNE
PAINTER, INSTRUCTOR, COLLAGE ARTIST
b Panama City, Fla, Feb 26, 1945. *Study:* Queens Col, with John Ferren, BA (art), with Rosemary Beck & Louis Finkelstein, MFA, 74; Brooklyn Mus Art Sch; Columbia Univ, EdD (art), 79. *Work:* Albright Knox Gallery, Buffalo, NY; Pace Univ; IBM; Dillon Read; Pfizer Corp; Columbia Presbyterian Hosp; Robert Wood Johnson Hosp; Ritz Carlton Hotel, Naples, Fla; US Dept State Art in Embassies Program, Djibouti, W Africa; Columbo, Sri Lanka. *Exhib:* Solo exhibs, Noho, Gallery, 1996, 1998, 2001, 2005, Land's End, 2003, En Plein Air-Here & Abroad, Whistler House Mus Art, Mass, 2010, Southwest Sun, Lifebridge Sanctuary, New York, 2010, Poetry of the Flowering World, Arts Soc Kingston, New York, 2010, Northeast/Southwest, Prince St Gallery, NY, 2011; Fire & Ice, Attleboro Mus, Mass, 97; Thunder & Lightning, Salisbury State Coll, Md, 97; Visions of the Land, Del Valley Art Center, NY, 99; Dancing Ground of the Sun, 2004; Booth Western Art Mus, 2009; Artifact Gallery, 2014. *Pos:* Bd, Art Soc of Kingston, Kingston, NY; Bd, NY Soc Women Artists. *Teaching:* Prof art, Kean Col NJ, Manhattanville Col, Purchase, NY, Ulster Co Community Col, 2002; Sierra Club tups, 2004-2006, State Univ New York New Paltz, LLI, 2009-; artist-in-residence: Helene Wurlitzer Found, 2003, Va Ctr for Creative Arts, 2000, Erpf Ctr, 2001; Fundacion Valparaiso, 2005; Moulin a Nef, Auvillar, France, 2006; White Colony, Costa Rica, 2007-08; Tyrone Guthrie Centre, Ireland, 2008. *Mem:* NY Soc Women Artists (96-present). *Media:* Oil, Watercolor, Pastel. *Publ:* Deciphering the secret landscapes, Queens Courier, 11/98; Water as Metaphor, Gallery & Studio, 4/2001; US Dept State Art in Embassies Program, Djiboutii, W Africa; Plein Air Painters, Vortex, 2011; Portrait of the Artist: Lynne Friedman, Poughkeepsie Jour, 2012. *Mailing Add:* 414 Circle Ave Kingston NY 12401

FRIEDMAN, MARTIN
MUSEUM DIRECTOR
b Pittsburgh, Pa, Sept 23, 1925. *Study:* Univ Pa; Univ Wash, BA, 47; Univ Calif, Los Angeles, MA, 49; Columbia Univ, 56-57; Belg-Am Found Grant, Brussels, 57-58; Univ Minn, Am Art Fel, 58-60; numerous honorary degrees, nationally & internationally. *Exhib:* Jean Dubuffet: Monuments, Simulacres, Practicables, 73; Nevelson: Wood Sculpture, 73; Naives & Visionaries, 74; Projected Images, 74; Oldenburg: Six Themes, 75; The River: Images of the Mississippi, 76; Scale & Environ: 10 Sculptors, 77; Noguchi's Imaginary Landscapes, 78; George Segal Sculptures, 78; Picasso: From the, Musee Picasso, Paris, 80; Hockney Paints the Stage, 83; Tokyo: Form and Spirit; Jan Dibbets, 87; Sculpture Inside Outside, 88. *Pos:* Fel, Brooklyn Mus, 56-57; sr cur, Walker Art Ctr, 58-60, dir, 61-; co-chmn mus panel, Nat Endowment Arts, 77-78; mem, Nat Coun Arts, 78-84; arts adv to mus & educ inst. *Awards:* Ford Found Fel, 61-62; Intellectual Interchange Fel, 82. *Mem:* Am Fedn Arts; Nat Collection Fine Arts Comn; Asn Art Mus Dirs (pres, 78-79); Century Asn. *Publ:* Auth, Charles Sheeler, Watson-Guptill; Hockney Paints the Stage, Abbeville Press co-publ, 83; Tokyo: Form and Spirit, Harry N Abrams co-publ, 86; Jan Dibbets, 87 & Sculpture Inside Outside, 88, Rizzoli Int, co-publ; Sculpture Inside Outside, Rizzoli Int, co-publ, 88. *Mailing Add:* 18 E 12 St Apt 12 New York NY 10003

FRIEDMAN, MARVIN ROSS
DEALER
b Minneapolis, Minn. *Study:* Univ Miami, BA, 63, JD, 66. *Awards:* Guest cur, James Rosenquist Metrop Mus, Antoni Tapias Metrop Mus & Komar & Melamid Metrop Mus. *Bibliog:* Joan Kleinman (auth), The Art Market: Interview with Leading Dealers, Metrop Mus, 79; Tim Harris (auth), Great art dealers, Venture Mag, 9/83. *Specialty:* Major modern and contemporary pictures. *Publ:* Auth, Antoni Tapias (exhib catalog). *Mailing Add:* 2600 S Douglas Rd Suite 1011 Miami FL 33134

FRIEDMAN, SABRA
PAINTER
b New York, NY. *Study:* New York Univ. *Work:* Bellevue Hospital; Islip Art Mus. *Exhib:* Primordial Elementaire, Caidoz Gallery, 83; Emblems of Imaginations, Islip Art Mus, 84; Affirmations of Life, Kenkeleba House; Chain Reaction, 55 Mercer St, 85; Queens Artists Salon, Flushing Gallery, 86; Second Ann Long Island City Open Studios, 87; Laguardia Community Col, 87. *Bibliog:* Margaret Betz (auth), New York reviews: Fourteen artists, ArtNews, 12/80. *Mailing Add:* 243 W 70 St No 9A New York NY 10023

FRIEDMAN, SALLY
PAINTER
b New York, NY, Jan 21, 1932. *Study:* Queens Col, City Univ New York, BS, 53, MA, 59; Ruskin Sch Art, Oxford Univ, Eng, 62-64; Art Students League, 65-70. *Work:* Okla Art Ctr; New Eng Ctr Contemp Art, Brooklyn, Conn; Berkshire Bank & Trust Co, Pittsfield, Mass; Mitsubishi Paper Int & Warwick, Welsh & Miller Inc, NY;

Allianz Risk Transfer Inc, NY; Mus Arts & Scis, Daytona Beach, Fla. *Exhib:* Works on Paper, Brooklyn Mus, 75; Butler Inst Am Art Ann, 75 & 76; Pratt Inst, 85; Donnell Libr Ctr, NY, 87, 91, 96 & 97; Long Island Univ, NY, 92; Fairleigh Dickinson Univ, NJ, 93; Coach Gallery, East Hampton, NY, 2000; Clayton, Libertore Gallery, Bridgehampton, NY, 2002; Donnell Libr Center, NY, 2006; Guild Hall, East Hampton, NY, 2007. *Pos:* Secy, Phoenix Gallery, New York, 80-81, pres, 82-83. *Teaching:* Elem sch, New York City, 85-. *Awards:* Grumbacher Award, 80, Sara Winston Mem Prize, 82 & Erlanger-Seligson Mem Prize, 86, Nat Asn Women Artists. *Bibliog:* Artists stick to their guns, 6/90, Art values both the home and the exotic, 9/91 & Three solos of artists at their peak, 5/92, Pursuing a single concept, 10/93, Art Speaks; Behind the Walls of Artists Studios, 7/2000. *Mem:* Art Students League; Artists Alliance East Hampton. *Media:* Oil. *Interests:* Subject of my work stems from nature, the intimate & familiar settings of the home, city & country life. *Publ:* Contribr, Art Now--color slides, Vol VI, No 3 & 4, 78. *Dealer:* Paintings Direct Inc. *Mailing Add:* 255 W 88th St Apt 4D New York NY 10024

FRIEND, PATRICIA M
PAINTER
b Philadelphia, Pa, May 4, 1931. *Study:* Goucher Coll, BA, 54; Am Univ, MFA, 75; studied with Laura G Douglas. *Work:* Deke Perrerea Int Bank, New York; Fed Reserve Bank Richmond, Baltimore; Arent, Fox, Kintner, Plotkin & Kahn Collection, Washington, DC; Squires, Sanders & Dempsey Collection & Watkins Collection, Am Univ, Washington, DC; C&P Tel co, Exec off, Arlington; Wash Theology Union, Washinton DC; Henry Luce II Ctr for Relig and Artsm Wasley Theology Sem, Washington, DC; Shrine of the Most Blessed Sacrament, Washington, DC. *Comn:* Large oil painting, exec lobby, Am Physical Therapist Asn, Alexandria, 83; painting for advert, Nat Security Bank, Washington, DC, 86; Delta Airlines; reproduction of work for 91 calendar, Women Art. *Exhib:* Solo exhibs, Emerson Gallery, McLean, Va, 67, Plum Gallery, Kensington, Md, 80, 82, 84 & 86 & Franz Bader Gallery, Washington, DC, 86, 89, 91 & 92; Landscape in Art, Int Monetary Fund, Wash, 81; Painting: A Decade, Art Place, Rockville, Md, 90; Landau Gallery, Bethesda, Md, 2002; NIH, Gallery One, Bethesda, Md, 2002; Daystar Gallery, Wash, DC, 2004; Orchard Gallery, Bethesda, Md, 2005; Washington Theological Union, Wash, DC, 2006; Wesley Theological Seminary, 2008; Pope John Paul II Cult Ctr, 2010. *Pos:* Corresponding secy, Washington Soc Artists, 70-71; art in embassies prog, State Dept, 78-88. *Teaching:* Instr, co-founder, Kensington Workshop, 77-; Mt Vernon Coll, Washington DC, 79-83; pvt instr, currently. *Awards:* Master Fine Art, Nat Security Bank; Top 10 Finalist, Search for Jesus 2000 Int Competition. *Mem:* Wash Soc Artists (corp secy, 70-71); Artists Equity. *Media:* Oil, Mixed Media. *Publ:* DC Area Artists Publ, Lab Sch Washington, 89-94; and others. *Mailing Add:* 7206 45th St Chevy Chase MD 20815

FRIESE, NANCY MARLENE
PAINTER, PRINTMAKER
b Fargo, NDak, Sept 1, 1948. *Study:* Yale Univ Summer Sch Music & Art, with Louis Finkelstein Fel, summer 76; Art Acad Cincinnati, studied with Stewart Goldman, April Foster, Diploma of Art, 77; Univ Calif, Berkeley, studied with Sylvia Lark, Hassel Smith, Elmer Bischoff, One Year Grad Sch, 77-78; Yale Univ Sch Art, studied with Gabor Peterdi, Gretna Campbell, Andrew Forge & Bill Bailey, Bernard Chaet, MFA, 80. *Work:* NDak Mus Art, Grand Forks; Grunwald Ctr Graphic Arts, Univ Calif, Los Angeles; William Benton Mus Art, Storrs, Conn; Yale Univ Gallery Art, New Haven; Housatonic Mus Art; Federal Reserve Bank, Boston; Boston Public Libr; NY Public Libr; Muscarelle Mus Art; RI Sch Design Mus Art; Colby Coll Mus Art; World Art Bank, Washington DC; Spencer Mus, Lawrence, Kans; Los Angeles Co Mus Art; Portland Mus Art; Nat Mus Women in Art; Mus Fine Arts, Boston. *Comn:* Theodore Roosevelt Found; Ina Mae Rude Entrepreneur Ctr; Hotel Providence, Simmons Coll; Nordstrom Stores; BankRI, New England Corporate Office; Ctr for Innovation, Univ NDak. *Exhib:* Solo exhibs, Catholic Univ of America, 1983, Giannetta Gallery, 89, NDak Mus Art, Grand Forks, NDak, 90, Univ Mont Gallery, Missoula, 90, Cornell Univ Gallery, 92, Pepper Gallery, Boston, 94, 96, 97, 98, 2000, 2001, 2006, Prints, Korn Gallery, Drew Univ, Madison, 97 & Under Brittany Skies, Nancy Moore Fine Art, New York, 97, Trustman Gallery, Boston, 2009, Planting Fields, Oyster Bay, NY, 2009, Plattsburgh State Mus Art, 2010-2011, Monumental Watercolors Cade Tompkins Projects, Providence, RI, 2011, Gallery Talk by Amy Kurtz Lansing, Griswold Mus, 2011, A Decade of Prints, Art Acad of Cin, Pearlman Gallery, OH, 2011; two-person exhibs Nature's Spirit Erector Square Gallery, New Haven CT, 91, Landscapes, Simon Gallery, Morristown, NJ, 99, The Painting Center, NY, 2003; group exhibs, Virginia Lynch Gallery, Tiverton, RI, 95, Pepper Gallery, Boston, 98, Boston Univ Art Gallery, 2000, NDak Mus of Art, Grand Forks, 2000, Dennis Morgan Gallery, 2001, US Artists American Fine Art Show, Philadelphia, 33rd Street Armory, 1998-2002, From the Collection, William Benton Mus, Storrs, CT, 2005, Collected Prints and Multiples, Janalyn Hanson White Gallery, Mount Mercy Coll, IA, 2009, New Works, Lyme Acad Coll of Fine Arts, CT, 2010, Printed In Providence, Cade Tompkins Projects, RI, 2011; Kristina Wasserman Gallery, Providence, RI, 95; Gallery BAI, Barcelona, Spain, 96; Generations, New Bedford Art Mus, Mass, 97; PSA, New York; Pepper Gallery, Boston, Mass, 98; Jaffe-Friede & Strauss Gallery, New York, 99; Gross McCleaf Gallery, Philadelphia, 99; Mary Williamson Chandler Gallery, Claremont, Calif, 2008. *Pos:* Artist-in-residence, Millay Colony for the Arts, Austerlitz, NY, 81, Artists for the Environ Found, Walpack, NJ, fall 81, Theodore Roosevelt Medora Found, ND, summer 92, Anderson Ranch, 97, MacDowell Colony, NH, 97, I-Park, Conn, 2002-2004, Westerly Land Trust, RI, 2006-, Trustman Gallery, Boston, Mass, 2007-2009, Planting Fields, Residency Oyster Bay, NY, 2009. *Teaching:* Drawing, Bennington Coll, VT, 80-81; asst prof, Printmaking, Univ Tulsa, 83-87; vis asst prof, Visual Art Dept, Princeton Univ, NJ, 86; head, Printmaking Dept & prof, RI Sch Design, Providence, 90-; Dean of Grad Studies, Full Prof of Grad Studies, 2004-. *Awards:* Nat Endowment for Arts painting grant, 91 & 92; US-Japan Grant, Nat Endowment Arts, 93; Blanche E Colman Award, 95; Residency, City of Pont-Aven, Brittany, France, 97 & 99; George Sugarman Found Award, 2005; Pollock Krasner Found Grant, 2002; Lila Acheson Wallace Giverny Fellowship. *Bibliog:* Jude Schwendenwein (auth), article, Art New Eng, 88; Michael Jones & Betty Collings (auth), Moving the Margin Catalog, Emily Davis Gallery, Akron, 90; William Zimmer (auth), Bound By Light Catalog, 94; Cate McQuaid (auth), Friese's Wild Color, The Boston Globe, 98; Faye Hirsch (auth), Art on Paper, 2000; Arttable. *Mem:* Coll Art Asn; Women's Caucus for Art; Calif Soc Printmakers; Los Angeles Soc Printmakers; Printmakers Network Southern New Eng, (co-founder, 92); Art Table; Risd Mus Art (bd of govs); NDak Mus Art (found bd mem); First Works, Providence (bd mem); Nat Acad. *Media:* Oil, Watercolor; Etching, Woodcut, Monotypes. *Res:* Wood engraving; History of women landscape artists. *Publ:* Auth, The Poetic Etchings of Mary Nimmo Moran, Gilcrease Mus & Univ, Tulsa, 84; coauth, Prints of Thomas Moran, Gilcrease Mus, 86; New American Painting, The Open Studio, 99; Imaging Nature, Women in Art. *Dealer:* Cade Tompkins Projects Editions Providence RI; MimosaPress Tulsa OK

FRIIS-HANSEN, DANA
MUSEUM DIRECTOR
b 1961. *Study:* Carleton Coll, BA (Art Hist), 1983; Whitney Mus Art Independent Study Prog, Helena Rubenstein Fel. *Collection Arranged:* co-cur, TransCulture, Venice Biennale, 1995. *Pos:* Asst cur, cur, List Visual Arts Ctr, MIT, Cambridge, Mass, 1985-91; assoc cur, Nanjo & Assocs private curatorial serv, Tokyo, 1991-95; sr cur, Contemp Arts Mus, Houston, 1995-99; chief cur, Austin Mus Art, Tex, 1999-, interim exec dir, 2001-02, exec dir, 2002-; panelist, Pew Fel Arts, 2002. *Publ:* Auth, Abstract Painting Once Removed, 1998; co-auth, Takashi Murakami, 2000, Cai Guo-Qiang, 2002, History of Japanese Photography, 2003, Terry Allen: Dugout, 2005. *Mailing Add:* Austin Mus Art 823 Congress Ave Austin TX 78701

FRINTA, IRENA ALTMANOVA
PAINTER
b Plzen, Czech, Sept 3, 1923; US citizen. *Study:* Graphic Sch, Prague, Czech Repub, cert, 43, Coll Art, 47; Ecole Des Beaux - Arts, Paris, France, Cert, 50; Acad Andre Lhote, Paris, France, cert, 48; New York State Univ, Albany, MA, 70. *Work:* Albany Inst Hist Art, NY; State Univ New York Art Mus; Empire Blue Cross & Blue Shield, Albany, NY; Gallery Western Bohemia, Plzen, Czech Repub; Four Winds, Saratoga Springs, NY. *Exhib:* Landscapes, Int Monetary Fund, Washington, 81; Pastel Artists, Cooperstown Libr, NY, 90; Nat Asn Women Artists: 100 Yrs, Albany, NY, 90; Nature & People, Gallery J Trnka, Plzen, Czech Repub, 92; Les Urbach Gallery, Albany, NY, 96; The Arts Ctr Gallery, Saratoga Springs, NY, 2000. *Pos:* Mem, Art Coun, Schenectady Mus; pres, Graphic Artists New York, Albany, Schenectady, Troy. *Teaching:* Art instr pastel, State Univ NY, Albany, 76-81, Col at Oswego, Pisa, Italy, 78. *Awards:* Thomas Leighton Mem-Dier Award, Pastel Soc Am, 79; Guest Artist at Yaddo, Saratoga Springs, NY, 84; Honorable mention, The Pastel J, 6th Annual Pastel 100 Competition, 2005. *Mem:* Graphic Artist NY (pres, formerly); Ctr Galleries, Albany, NY; Albany Mus Hist Art; Pastel Soc Am, NY. *Media:* Pastels. *Publ:* The Pastel J, The Years Best Art, issue 37, April, 2005. *Dealer:* Rice Gallery Albany NY. *Mailing Add:* c/o Pastel Soc Am National Arts Club 15 Gramercy Park S New York NY 10003

FRINTA, MOJMIR SVATOPLUK
ART HISTORIAN, EDUCATOR
b Prague, Czech, July 28, 1922; US citizen. *Study:* Coll Fine & Appl Arts, Prague; Karlova Univ, Prague, BA, 47; Ecole des Beaux Arts, Paris, France; Ecole du Louvre, Paris, 51; Univ Mich, MA, 53, PhD (hist art), 60. *Pos:* Sr restorer, Metrop Mus Art, New York, 55-63. *Teaching:* Prof art hist, State Univ NY, Albany, 63-93, prof emer, 93. *Awards:* Bourse du government Francais, 1947-1948; Nat Endowment Humanities Grant, 77-78 & 82-84; Mellon Senior Fel, CASVA, 84-95; Fulbright Fel Yugoslavia; Publication Grant, Getty Grant Program, 92; Grant, Millard Meiss Publication Fund, 93; Grant, Samuel Kress Found, 2000. *Mem:* Coll Art Asn; Int Inst Conserv Art; Int Ctr Medieval Art; Medieval Acad Am. *Res:* Late medieval & Byzantine painting & sculpture; early Netherlandish painting; art technology. *Specialty:* Panel Painting. *Publ:* Auth, Master of the Gerona martyrology & Bohemian illumination, 64, auth, Investigation of the punched decoration of medieval Italian & non-Italian panel paintings, 65, The quest for a restorer's shop of beguiling invention: Restorations and forgeries in Italian panel paintings, 78, Art Bulletin; Genius of Robert Campin, Mouton, 66; The puzzling raised decoration in the paintings by Master Theodoric, Simiolus, 76; Punched Decoration on Late Medieval Painting (vol 1-catalog), Maxdorf, Prague, 98; History of the Punched Decoration (vol 2), Prague. *Mailing Add:* 150 Maple Ave PO Box 854 Altamont NY 12009

FRITZ, CHARLES JOHN
PAINTER
b Mason City, Iowa, Feb 20, 1955. *Study:* Iowa State Univ, BS, 77. *Work:* Denver Art Mus; Macnider Art Mus, Mason City, Iowa; Rohr-West Mus, Monitowoc, Wis, 99; CM Russell Mus, Great Falls, Mont, 02; Buffalo Bill Hist Ctr, Cody, Wy. *Comn:* Painting, Iowa Vet Hosp, Des Moines, 83. *Exhib:* Artists of Am, Colo Hist Mus, Denver, 94-96; Am Art in Miniature, Thomas Gilcrease Mus, Tulsa, Okla, 95; In the Mountains and Under the Sky, Charles H Macnider Mus, Mason City, Iowa, 95; Great Am Artists, Cincinnati Mus Ctr, Ohio, 96; Prix de West, Nat Cowboy Hall Fame, Oklahoma City, 96-2009; Western Visions Exhib, Nat Mus Wildlife Art, Jackson, Wy; Charles Fritz, An Artist with the Corps of Discovery, 2003-2006, Mont Mus Art & Cult, Missoula, Ore Hist Soc, Portland, Nat Cowboy & Western Heritage Mus, Oklahoma City, CM Russell Mus, Great Falls, Mont, Booth Mus Western Art, Cartersville, Ga, Macnider Art Mus, Mason City, Iowa; An Artist with the Corps of Discovery, Buffalo Bill Hist Ctr, 2009. *Awards:* Dale Hawkins Mem Award, Western Heritage Ctr, 90; Best of Show, CM Russell Mus, 92, 96, 97, 2000; Lee M Loeb Mem Award for Landscape, Salmagundi Club, New York, 93; and others. *Bibliog:* Nancy Gillespie (auth), A healthy tension, Art of the West, 2/92; Carol Dickinson (auth), rev, Rocky Mountain News, 4/92; Gayle Shirley (auth), Charles Fritz, Big Sky J, 3/97; Nancy Gillespie (auth), Big Country, Big Talent/Art of the West, 5/99; Vicki Stanig (auth), An Artist's Eyes: The Lewis and Clark Expedition, 11/04; Donna Healy (auth), The Art of Exploration, Billings Gazette, 8/15/04; Dan Hays (auth), Epic Adventure,

Statesman Journal, 12/26/04; Vicki Stanley (auth), Trough An Artist's Eyes, Art of the West, Nov 2004; Terry Zinn (auth), Into The West, Persimmon Hill, summer 2005; Dayton Duncan (auth), Lewis & Clark in Montana, Montana Outdoors, Mar 2005; Kevin Brooke (auth), Visions of Epic Adventure, Big Sky J Arts, 2005; Lewis & Clark in the Missouri Breaks, Smithsonian Mag, Mar 2005. *Media:* Oil, Watercolor. *Publ:* Illusr, Places of Spirit-Canyon de Chelley, Gibbs-Smith, 96; Donald Hagerty (auth), Lending the West-100 Contemporary Artists, Gibb-Smith; auth, Charles Fritz - An Artist with the Corps of Discovery, Farcountry Press, 04; auth, An Artist with the Corps of Discovery, 100 Paintings Illustrating the Journals of Lewis & Clark, Farcountry Press. *Dealer:* Stuart Johnson 6420 N Campbell Ave Tucson AZ 85718. *Mailing Add:* 8912 Susanna Dr Billings MT 59101

FRITZLER, GERALD J
PAINTER, WATERCOLOR
b Chicago, Ill, Aug 27, 1953. *Study:* Am Acad Art, Chicago, AA (graphic art), 74, AA (fine art, scholar), 76; Studied under Irving Shapiro & Bill Parks. *Work:* Am Acad Art, Chicago; Am Western Art Collection, Peking; Pvt collection of Pres & Mrs Reagan; Rocky Mountain Nat Park, Estes Park, Colo; CM Russell Mus, Great Falls, Mont. *Exhib:* A Brush with Reality, CM Russell Mus; Salon D'Arts, Artists of Am, & Colo Watercolor Soc, Colo Hist Mus,; Laguna Plein Air Painters Invitational, Laguna Art Mus; Nat Acad Western Art, Nat Cowboy Hall of Fame; Colo Governors Invitational Exhib, Loveland Mus; Am Watercolor Soc, NY; Transparent Watercolor Soc Am, Ill; Nat Watercolor Soc, Calif; Northwest Rendezvous Exhib, Mont; Maynard Dixon Country Exhib, Utah. *Pos:* Art Dealer, Historian, Juror. *Teaching:* Instr outdoor watercolor painting wkshps & figure painting & drawing, Western Colo Ctr Arts, 83-98; Jackson Hole Acad Art, 90; Western State Col, Gunnison, Colo, 90. *Awards:* Strathmore Paper Award, Am Watercolor Soc, 86; Artist in Residence, Rocky Mountain Nat Park, 90 & 94; Colo Watermedia Award, Colo Watercolor Soc, 92 & 96. *Bibliog:* Walter Gray & Dan Blanchard (auth), Gerald Fritzler, Southwest Art, 6/91; Peggy & Harold Samuels (auth), Contemporary Western Artists; Rachel Wolf (auth), Splash III, 94, Splash IV, 96 & Splash V, 98, Northlight Books, F & N Pub; Stephen Doherty (auth) The Force of Inspiration-Watercolor Mag Winter 2004; Stephen Doherty (auth), Plein Air Watercolor Techniques Based on Decades of Experience, Plein Air Mag, 2012. *Mem:* Colo Watercolor Soc; Am Watercolor Soc; Nat Watercolor Soc; Transparent Watercolor Soc Am; Plein Air Painters Am; Calif Art Club. *Media:* Watercolor. *Specialty:* Fine traditional art, watercolors, oils, bronze sculpture, ceramics, drawings, pastels. *Collection:* traditional work in oil, watercolor & pastel, as well as bronze; Raku ceramics. *Publ:* Auth, The Best of Watercolor, 95 & Marine Art, 98, Rockport Publ; Watercolor Expressions, Rockport Publ Inc, 99; The Simple Secret to better Painting, North Light Books, 2003; Enchanted Isle, a History of Plein Air Painting on Santa Catalina Island, The Soc for the Advan Plein Air Painting, 2003. *Dealer:* Claggett/Rey Gallery Vail Colo; Fritzler Fine Art Mesa Colo; Grapevine Gallery Oklahoma City OK. *Mailing Add:* PO Box 253 Mesa CO 81643

FROEHLICH, ANNA & JOSEF
COLLECTOR
Awards: Named one of Top 200 Collectors, ARTnews mag, 2009-12. *Collection:* Contemporary art, especially German & American

FROMAN, ANN
SCULPTOR, DESIGNER
b New York, NY, Apr 7, 1942. *Study:* Fashion Inst Technol, NY, AA, 61; Palace of Fontainebleau Sch Fine Art, France, cert, 61; Nat Acad Sch Fine Art, New York; Art Students League. *Work:* Radcliff Col; Butler Mus Art, Youngstown, Ohio; Richmond Libr, Wichita, Kans; Brooklyn Col, NY; Time Warner Inc, NY; Harvard Univ, Cambridge, Mass; St Patricks Cathedral, NYC; Temple Emannuel, NY; Florida Holocaust Mus, Fla. *Comn:* Queen Esther (bronze), Temple Israel, Wilkes Barre, Pa, 79; Women of the Bible (bronze), Temple DeHirsch Sinai, Seattle, Washington, 80; Swirl (bronze), Bankers Trust Co & Footwear Asn of New York, 82; Holy Family, St Raphael Church, Livingston, NJ, 83; American Bounty (bronze), Culinary Inst Am, Hyde Park, NY, 83. *Exhib:* Art of Relationships, Wisser Libr, NY Inst Technol; Fashion Inst Technol; NY Artists, Brooklyn Mus, 71; Solo exhibs, Berkshire Mus, Pittsfield, Mass, 77, Coll Misericordia, Dallas, Pa, Bennington Mus, Vt, 81 & Judaica Mus, Phoenix, Ariz, 82; US Customs Mus, NY, 80; and others; Heroes, Int Raoul Williamsberg Found, NY, 2009-2010; Biblical Arts Mus, Dallas, Tex, 2010. *Pos:* creator, The Wizart of Art (TV Show). *Teaching:* Hunter Col, 89, Fashion Inst, 80s. *Awards:* Mortimer C Ritter Award, Fashion Inst Technol, 71; Watson Guptill Award, Nat Art Club, 76; First Prize Sculpture, Salmagundi Club, Am Soc Contemp Artists, 80. *Bibliog:* Sculpture & poetry unite in Ann Froman's art, Art Speaks, NY; Images in Art, Jewish J; Richard Lesser (auth), Bronze dance from sculptor's mind, Ariz Repub, 1/30/82; Sculptor Ann Froman proves Bible relations are relevant today. *Mem:* Am Soc Contemp Artists; Artists Equity Asn. *Media:* Plastic, Cast Metal. *Dealer:* Froman Studios Anson Rd Stanfordville NY 12581-0367. *Mailing Add:* Ann Froman Gallery PO Box 367 Stanfordville NY 12581

FROMBOLUTI, SIDEO
PAINTER
b Philadelphia, Pa, Oct 3, 1920. *Study:* Tyler Coll Fine Art, Philadelphia, Pa. *Work:* Philadelphia Mus Art, Pa; Mus Art, Carnegie Inst, Pittsburgh, Pa; The Nelson Rockefeller Collection; Corcoran Gallery, Washington, DC; Allentown Mus, PA; Allegheny Coll Mus, Pa; Southern Ill Univ; Ciba-Geigy Corp, Ardsley, NY; First Nat Bank, Chicago; Boston Mutual Life Insurance Co, Mass Hyatt Hotel, NY; Fidelity Bank, Philadelphia, Pa. *Exhib:* Solo exhibs, Galerie Darthea Speyer, Paris, 70-74, Landmark Gallery, NY, 73, 75, 78, 80 & 82, Brownson Art Gallery, Purchase, NY, 83, Gross McCleaf Gallery, Philadelphia, 83, Maurice M Pine Libr, Fairlawn, NJ, 84 & Ingber Gallery, NY, 87; Art on Paper, Weatherspoon Gallery, Greensboro, NC, 75; Butler Inst Am Art, Youngstown, Ohio, 78; A Gray Day, Longpoint Gallery, Provincetown, Mass, 82; Woman Artists, Paris, France, 84; Knowing What I like, John Myers, Kouros Gallery, NY, 87; Jerald Melberg Gallery, Charlotte, NC, 87. *Awards:* Drawing Award, Acad Design Juried Exhib, NY, 84. *Bibliog:* Sandler (auth), article, Aujourd'hui; Oeri (auth), article, Quadrum; Kingsley (auth), article, Art Int. *Mem:* Century Club, NY; Nat Acad. *Media:* Oil on Canvas. *Dealer:* Barbara Ingber Gallery 415 West Broadway New York NY 10012

FROMENTIN, CHRISTINE ANNE
PAINTER, GRAPHIC ARTIST
b 1953. *Study:* Elmira Col, NY, BFA, 75; New York Univ, MFA, 77, studied figurative painting with John Kacere, realism with Don Eddie & Idelle Webber. *Work:* Gelmart Indust, NY; Cole of Calif, Los Angeles; and many pvt collections. *Comn:* Paintings, Essilor Co Inc, Joinville, France, Gellis & Mellinger Inc, NY, Prisma-Sun Bow, Inc, Los Angeles & Logo-Paris, Inc, Novato, Calif, World Market Equities, Inc, NY. *Exhib:* Martin Molinary Galleries, NY, 82; Gallerie Jean Pierre Lavignes, Paris, 83; Yve Arman Gallery, NY, 84; Vered Gallery, East Hampton, NY, 85; De Marigny Gallery, NY, 86; Joseph Bruck Artists Management, NY, 89-90; New Eng Fine Art Inst, Boston, 93; and others. *Pos:* Illusr, Joseph Bruck Artist's Rep, 84-85 & Joseph Mendola Inc, 85-86, NY; graphic designer, The Gap, NY, 89-90, Wathne Ltd, 90-92 & Polo Ralph Lauren, NY, 93-96; art dir, Bugle Boy Ind, NY, 97-98; acct mgr Christie's Auction House, Estates & Appraisals dept, 99-2002. *Awards:* Hample Ctr Scholar Prize, Contemp Paintings Exhib, Arnot Art Mus, 75; Juror's Award Pavilion, New Eng Fine Art Inst, Boston, 93. *Bibliog:* Josette Malze (auth), Christine Fromentin: The myth of women, Paris-Scope, Le Matin & Vital Mag, Paris, 83; Toni Canger (auth), Christine Fromentin, NJ Art Forum, 85. *Media:* Oil on Linen. *Publ:* Illusr, Lee Iacocca, Time Mag, Switch, Signet Bks, Allesandro, Bantam Bks, 85, Dark Side, Berkley Bks & Point of Purchase, Smirnoff Liquors, 86

FRONTZ, LESLIE
PAINTER
b Cleveland, Ohio, Aug 23, 1950. *Study:* Muskingum Coll, BA (cum laude), 72; Southern Ore State Coll, BS (summa cum laude), 81; Univ NC-Greensboro, MFA (Holderness Fel), 86. *Exhib:* Arts for the Parks, Smithsonian Inst, 87; Loveland Mus & Gallery, 90; Nat Oil & Acrylic Painters, Mo, 93; Oil Painters Am, Ill, 94; Southern Representational Exhib, Comer Mus, Ala, 95; Davidson Co Mus Art, NC, 97; Salem Coll Fine Arts Center, NC, 2003; Soc of Women Artists, London, 2005-2011; Southern Watercolor Soc Ann, Va, 2005-2011; Am Watercolor Soc, New York, 2009-2012. *Teaching:* Adj fac art hist, Front Range Community Coll, Fort Collins, Colo, 89-90; instr drawing, 2-d design & art appreciation, Wash State Community Coll, Marietta, Ohio, 91-92; instr art, Southwest Sch, Lexington, NC, 97-2003; adj fac, Davidson Co Community Coll, Lexington, NC, 2006-2008, Rowan-Cabarrus Community Coll, Salisbury, NC, 2013. *Awards:* Award of Excellence, Ohio Watercolor Soc, Ohio, 92; Best of Show, Comer Mus, 95; Canson Award, Watercolor Soc, 2006; Georg Shook Mem Award, Southern Watercolor Soc, 2007; HRH Princess Michael of Kent Watercolor Award, Soc Women Artists, 2007; Ogden & Mary Pleissner Mem Award, Am Watercolor Soc, 2009; High Winds Medal, Am Watercolor Soc, 2011; Watercolor Mag award, Am Watercolor Soc, 2012. *Bibliog:* Shelly Fling (auth), pvt showings: Leslie Frontz, US Art, 12/89; Meredith Lewis (auth), Studied Simplicity, Watercolor Artist, 2011. *Mem:* Southern Watercolor Soc (sig mem); Soc of Women Artists (sig mem); Plein Air Carolina (founding mem); Am Watercolor Soc (sig mem). *Media:* Watercolor. *Publ:* Painting for Impact, Artist's Mag, 1/95. *Dealer:* Ambleside Gallery 528 S Elm St Greensboro NC 27406. *Mailing Add:* 296 Peace Haven Dr Lexington NC 27292

FROST, STUART HOMER
EDUCATOR, PAINTER
b Arendtsville, Pa, Nov 22, 1925. *Study:* Pa State Univ, BA; Brooklyn Mus Sch; Skowhegan Sch Painting & Sculpture. *Work:* Pa Acad Fine Arts, Philadelphia; Butler Art Inst, Youngstown, Ohio; Dulin Gallery Art, Knoxville, Tenn; Mus Art, Pa State Univ, University Park; Mansfield Univ, PA. *Exhib:* Am Watercolors, Drawings & Prints, Metrop Mus Art, 62; Recent Drawings USA, Mus Mod Art, 64; Watercolor USA, 66; Butler Art Inst Mid-Yr Show, 75; 9th Dulin Nat Print & Drawing Competition, 75; Drawings from Four Decades, Stuart Frost Babcock Galleries, 88; Drawn to Constructions, Stuart Frost Babcock Galleries, 93; Recent Paintings, Penn State Univ, 2011. *Pos:* Mural Assist. to Henry Varnum Poor, Allyn Cox. *Teaching:* Emer Prof of Art, Pa State Univ, University Park, currently. *Media:* Pen, Ink. *Interests:* antique furniture, worldwide travel. *Dealer:* Babcock Galleries 725 Fifth Ave New York NY. *Mailing Add:* 139 E Hubler Rd State College PA 16801-7918

FRUDAKIS, ANTHONY P
SCULPTOR, EDUCATOR
b Bellows Falls, Vt, July 30, 1953. *Study:* Pa Acad Fine Arts, cert, 76; Univ Pa, MFA, 91. *Work:* Brookgreen Gardens Mus, SC. *Comn:* Summer (male & female runners), Tropicana Hotel & Casino, Atlantic City, NJ, 86; Otter Fountain (lifesize cold cast bronze), Bally Hotel & Casino, Atlantic City, NJ, 86; Mother & child (cold cast bronze), Atlantic City Day Nursery, Atlantic City, NJ, 88; Justice (bas relief), Cape May Ct House, NJ, 89; Dr Charles Drew (bust), Drew Ct, Atlantic City, NJ, 89; Jonah (monument), Ocean City Cult Ctr, NJ, 90; Ascension, St Mary's Cathedral, Saginaw, Mich, 99; Andromeda (monumental bronze), East Lansing, Mich, 2000; George Washington (monumental bronze statue), Hillsdale, Mich, 2003; Abraham Lincoln, Monumental Bronze, Hillsdale, Mich, 2009; Thomas jefferson, Monumental Bronze, Hillsdale, Mich, 2009; St Sebastian Life Size Bronze, St Sebastian Church, Grand Rapids, Mich, 2011; Ronald Reagan monument, Al Bronze, Hissdale Coll, Mich, 2011; Thomas Jefferson monument, bronze, Thomas Jefferson High School Council, Bluffs, Ia, 2012. *Exhib:* Nat Sculpture Soc, New York, 76-89; Brookgreen Gardens Mus, SC, 83; Accent Gallery, Northfield, NJ, 88; Aaron's Gallery, Indianapolis, 88; Philadelphia Sketch Club, Pa, 88; Image of Women in Art, Renaissance Gallery, Philadelphia, 88; Corp Art, Trammel & Crow, Philadelphia, 89; Grand Cent Art Gallery, New York, 90 & 92; Ocean City Cult Ctr, NJ, 92; Sturgis Civic Ctr, Mich, 92; Hillsdale Coll, Mich, 93, 97, 99; Toledo Art Mus, Ohio, 94; Nat Sculpture Soc, New

York, 97; Nat Acad Design Ann Show, New York, 2001-2007; Sculptors of Mich, Hillsdale Coll, 2001; and others; Cedarhurst Ctr Arts, Mt Vernon, Ill, 2008; The Old Court House Figurative League, Woodstock, Ill, 2008; Nat Acad Design, New York, 2007; Ella Sharp Mus Art, Jackson, Mich, 2007; Basilica of the Nat Shrine of the Immaculate Conception, Wash DC, 2007. *Teaching:* Instr sculpture, Frudakis Acad Fine Arts, Philadelphia, Pa, 74-77, Stockton State Coll, Pomona, NJ, 77 & Fashion Inst Technol, New York, 81-82; adj prof, Atlantic Community Coll, 90-91; assoc prof fine arts, Hillsdale Coll, 91-. *Awards:* Best Portrait, Lantz Award, 78 & 88, Gold Medal, 82, Gloria Medal, 83 & L Miselman Prize, 86, Nat Sculpture Soc, New York; First Prize for Sculpture, NJ State Art Show, 79; M B Hexter Award, Allied Artists Am, 82; finalist, NJ Vietnam Meml Competition, 90, Chatham Fishermen's Monument, Mass, 90; prize, Nat Acad Design Artist Fund, New York, 91; Daniel Chester French award, Nat Acad Design, New York, 2001; Finalist, Native Am Mus Sculpture Competition, Wash DC, 2003. *Bibliog:* Arthur William (auth), Sculpture, 93; Donald Reynolds (auth), Masters of American Sculpture, 93; Glenn Opitz (ed), Dictionary of American Sculptors; New York Art Rev, 98. *Mem:* Nat Sculpture Soc, New York; Nat Acad. *Media:* Bronze. *Interests:* Guitar, billiards. *Mailing Add:* 1489 Bishop Rd Saline MI 48176-9403

FRUDAKIS, EVANGELOS WILLIAM
SCULPTOR, INSTRUCTOR
b Rains, Utah, May 13, 1921. *Study:* Greenwich Workshop, New York, 35-39; Beaux Arts Inst Design, New York, 40-41; Pa Acad Fine Arts, Cresson, Scheidt & Tiffany Scholar; Am Acad Rome, Italy, Prix de Rome Fel, 50-52. *Work:* Pa Acad Fine Arts, Philadelphia; Smithsonian Inst; Weizmann Inst, Israel; Airlie Found, Va; Woodmere Art Mus. *Comn:* Icarus & Daedalus Fountain, Little Rock, Ark; Minute Man, Washington, DC, 91; Minute Man, Arlington, Va, 94; Reaching Found, Brookgreen Gardens, 97; bronze figure, Welcome Fountain, Nat Guard Bldg, Washington, DC; bronze memorial, Stephen F Hyde, Trump Castle, Atlantic City, NJ; Greek Relief, Greek Orthodox Archdiocese, New York & Ellis Island; bronze monument, The Signer, Independence Nat Hist Park, Philadelphia, Pa; bronze figure, Naiad Fountain, Brookgreen Gardens, SC; and others. *Exhib:* Nat Sculpture Soc Ann, 41-85; Pa Acad Fine Arts Ann, 41-62; Nat Acad Design Ann, 48-86; Philadelphia Mus Art, 59 & 62 & Twenty-three Sculptors Exhib, 72; solo exhibs, Atlantic City Art Ctr, 56 & 61, Woodmere Art Mus, 57 & 62, Philadelphia Art Alliance, 58, Pa Acad Fine Arts, 62 & Briarcliff Coll Mus Art, 74; retrospective, Hill Country Arts Found, 2007. *Teaching:* Instr, var art ctrs, NY, NJ & Pa, 41-63; instr, Nat Acad Design, Sch Fine Art, New York, 70-76, Old Church Cult Ctr, Demarest, NJ, 75-78; sr instr, Pa Acad Fine Arts, Philadelphia, 72; founder & instr, Frudakis Acad Fine Arts, Philadelphia, 76-90; instr, Loveland Academy Fine Art, 89-96 & Hill Country Arts Found, 2007-2008. *Awards:* Gold Medal, Nat Acad Design, 64, 84; Gold Medal, Nat Sculpture Soc, 72; Artists Fund Prize 75, 79 & 90; and others; Medal of Honor, Nat Sculpture Soc, 2012. *Mem:* Fel Pa Acad Fine Arts; fel Am Acad Rome; fel Nat Sculpture Soc; academician Nat Acad Design; Allied Artists Am; Nat Acad. *Media:* Bronze, Marble. *Res:* Statues of the Roman Forum; Michelangelo's Rondanini Pieta. *Mailing Add:* 3132 E Thompson St Apt 2C Philadelphia PA 19134

FRUDAKIS, ZENOS
SCULPTOR
b San Francisco, Calif, Jul 7, 1951. *Study:* Pa Acad Fine Arts, Philadelphia, 73-76; Univ Pa, Philadelphia, BFA, 81, MFA, 83. *Hon Degrees:* Acad Int L'Unita Cult, Rome, Academician. *Work:* LBJ Libr, Tex, King Ctr, Philadelphia, Brookgreen Gardens, SC; two over life size bronze figures, Utsukushi-Ga-Hara Mus, Japan; K Leroy Irvis (bust), State Mus, Harrisburg; Nat Acad Design, NY. *Comn:* Portraits, Dilworth, Paxson, & Kalish, Philadelphia, 80-81; Workers Mem, Bethlehem, Pa, 91; Reaching (monumental bronze figures), Indianapolis; Dream to Fly (monumental bronzes), Cherry Hill, NJ; bronze portrait busts, Martin Luther King Jr, Douglas MacArthur, Dinah Shore, Arnold Palmer, and many others; Pa Anthracite Miners Mem, Shenandoah; Arnold Palmer & Bobby Jones, August, Ga; Former Mayor Frank Rizzo, Philadelphia, Pa; Gov Ellis Arnall, Atlanta; Arch Bishop Cavvadas (portrait), Brookline, Mass, 96; Air Force Memorial, Arlington Nat Cemetery, Va; Four Phillies Greats: Mike Schmidt, Richie Ashburn, Robin Roberts, Steve Carlton. *Exhib:* Nat Sculpture Soc, 79-2000; Allied Artists Am, NY, 80-81; Nat Acad Design, NY, 80, 84, 86 & 90; Pa Acad Fine Arts Fel Ann, 81; Inst Contemp Art, Philadelphia, 81-83; Rutgers Univ Fac Show, 84-86; Invited artist, Utsukushi-Ga-Hara Open Air Mus, Japan, 90. *Pos:* Nat Academician, Nat Sculpture Soc; mem, ed bd, Nat Sculpture Rev Mag; Nat Academician. *Teaching:* Coadj prof sculpture & drawing, Rutgers Univ, 84-85; guest lectr anat & sculpture, Med Col Pa, Philadelphia, 86 & 87, Scottsdale Artist's Sch, Ariz, 90; invited artist, Utsukushi-Ga-Hara Open Air Mus, Japan, 1990. *Awards:* John Spring Art Founder Award, Nat Sculpture Soc, 81, Gloria Medal, 81, Tallix Award, 82, President's Prize, 85, Silver Medal Honor, 86; Liskin Award, Knickerbocker Artists, 85; Henry Hearing Art-in-Archit Award, 90; Hakone Open-Air Mus Award, Japan, 90. *Mem:* Fel Nat Sculpture Soc (bd dir, 1988-, Art-in-Archit award 1990, edit pro-tem Nat Sculpture Rev, 1991-2002); Allied Artists Am; Fel, Pa Acad Fine Arts; Knickerbocker Artists; Am Artists Prof League; Fel, Nat Acad. *Media:* Bronze. *Publ:* Drawing, Nat Sculpture Rev Mag, 86; The National Sculpture Society Celebrates the Figure, Dr Jean Henry, 87. *Dealer:* Portraits Incorporated New York NY. *Mailing Add:* 2355 Mt Carmel Ave Glenside PA 19038

FRUEH, DEBORAH K. (DEBI)
PAINTER, SCULPTOR
b St Louis, Mo, Nov 24, 1951. *Study:* St Louis Coll, AA, studied painting with George Bartko, 69-71; Fontbonne Coll, Advan Studies, studied sculpture with Rudi Torrini, 71-72; St Louis Univ, Advan Studies, studied Baroque Art, 72-73. *Work:* The White House, Washington, DC; Off of Congressman Ed Whitfield, Paducah, Ky; Waterstreet Gallery, Seamans Church Inst Hq, NY; Museu Carmin Miranda, Rio de Janerio, Brazil; Wis Barge Lines Collection, Cassville, Wis. *Comn:* Oil portrait (30″x40″), Dr Everett Lerwick, comn by friends of Dr Lerwick, Mo Baptist Hosp, St Louis, Mo, 80; Portrait (20″x24″), Dr Zemlyn, comn by Bd Dirs, Chester Mem Hosp, Chester, Ill, 89; Portrait (50″x60″), Susan Lengsfield Kasper & Children, comn by Diane Lengsfield (Paducah, Ky), Washington, DC, 93; Portrait (20″x24″), Pres Len O'Hare, comn by bd dirs W Ky Coll, Paducah, Ky, 2002; Pencil 24″x30″), M V Jayne Hougland, comn by Asn Retired Marine Personnel, Paducah, Ky, 2004; Oil portrait (25″x30″), Juliette Grumley, comn by Dr Paul Grumley & Mary Louise Miller Ezzell Katterjohn, Kenmil Place, Paducah, Ky, 2006. *Exhib:* Solo exhibs, The Art of Debi Frueh, Paducah Art Guild, Market House Mus, Paducah, Ky, 73 & Debi Frueh Paintings/Sculptures, Arts Coun Gallery, Paducah, Ky, 79; 26th Midstates Art Exhib, Evansville Mus Arts & Sci, Evansville, Ind, 16th Ann Art Exhib, Paducah Art Guild, Market House Mus, Paducah, Ky, 73; Gallantly Streaming (artists respond to 9/11), Yeiser Art Ctr Mus, Paducah, Ky, 2002; Torrit Grey, 10th Ann, Gamblin Artists Colors Co, Portland, Ore, 2003; Size Matters, Yeiser Art Ctr Mus, Paducah, Ky, 2006; Solstice, Two Street Gallery, Paducah, Ky, 2009. *Pos:* Gallery asst, St Louis Coll, St Louis, Mo, 71-72. *Teaching:* Lectr Sculpture, Paducah Art Guild Market House Mus, 73; instr sculpture, Paducah Coll, Paducah, Ky, 77-79. *Awards:* Best of Show (oil painting), 41st Ann Art Exhib, City of Paducah, 76; 1st Place (oils), Celebrating Women, Lourdes Found, 2002; Special Award for Creativity (Torrit Grey), 10th Ann Gamblin Artists Color Co, 2003. *Bibliog:* Berry Craig (auth), Artist Enjoys Reactions to Her Sculptures, Sun Democrat, 79; Erin Green (auth), Debi Frueh, Portrait Artist, Film/Interview WPSD TV, 2000; Darlene Mazzone (auth), From Wickliffe to the White House, Paducah Life Mag, 2003; Thomas B Oliverio (auth), Debbie Frueh Turns Grey into Gold, Paducah Life Mag, 2010. *Mem:* Mus Women in the Arts; Am Soc Portrait Artists; Yeiser Art Ctr. *Media:* Acrylic, Oil, All Media; Clay. *Publ:* Auth, Illusr (art), Christmas Wish, Millennium Tribute, Paducah Life Mag, 2000; auth, illusr (art), Love Lady Liberty, Paducah Life Mag, 2002; contribr, illusr (art), From the Gallery, (From Wickliffe to the White House), Paducah Life Mag, 2003; auth, illusr (art), Lets Give Thanks, Paducah Life Mag, 2003; auth, illusr (web), Torrit Grey, Allegory of Painting, Gamblin Artist Colors Co, 2004. *Mailing Add:* Debi Frueh Portrait Studio 1985 Deerfield Rd Wickliffe KY 42087

FRUEH, JOANNA
CRITIC
b Chicago, Ill, 1948. *Study:* Sarah Lawrence Col, BA, 70; Univ Chicago, MA, 71, PhD, 81. *Exhib:* Retrospective, Joann Frueh (auth), 2005; Retrospective, Tanya Augsburg, (auth), Nev Mus Art, 2005. *Pos:* Dir, Artemisia Gallery & Fund, Chicago, 74-76. *Teaching:* Asst prof mod art, Oberlin Col, Ohio, 81-; asst prof contemp art & art criticism, Univ Ariz, Tucson, 83-85; prof art hist, Univ Nev, Reno, 90-. *Awards:* Susan Koppelman Award for Feminist Art Criticism: An Anthology, 89; Artist Fel Lit Arts, Nev Arts Coun, 2001; Lifetime Achievement Award, Women's Caucus for Art, 2008. *Bibliog:* Robert Christgau (auth), Children of the Porn, Village Voice, 67-68, 7/30/96; Maria Elena Buszek (auth), Monster/beauty: building the body of love, BUST, spring 2002; Carol Siegel (auth), Practicing what they teach, Rhizomes, issue 3, 2002. *Mem:* Coll Art Asn (bd dir, 97-2001). *Media:* Performance art, photography. *Res:* Contemporary art, with a special interest in women artists and feminist art theory. *Interests:* Yoga, bodybuilding. *Publ:* Auth, Brumas: A Rock Star's Passage to a Life Re-Vamped, Freshcut Press, 83; Hannah Wilke: A Retrospective, Thomas H Kochheiser (ed), Univ Mo Press, Columbia, 89; New Feminist Criticism: Art, Identity, Action, Harper Collins, NY, 94; Erotic Faculties, 96, & Monster/Beauty: Building the Body of Love, 2001, Univ Calif Press; Picturing the Modern Amazon, Rizzoli Int, 2000; Maria Elena Buszek, Pin-Up Grrrls: Feminism, Sexuality, Popular Culture, Duke Univ Press, 2006, 14-16; Swooning Beauty: A Memoir of Pleasure, Univ Nev Press, 2006. *Mailing Add:* c/o Univ Nev - Reno Dept Art 224 Reno NV 89557-0007

FRUGÉ-BROWN, KATHLEEN
PAINTER, PRINTMAKER
Study: Inst Internat Educ, Florence, Italy; Tyler Sch Art, Temple Univ, BFA (painting); Univ Wash, MFA (painting). *Exhib:* Solo exhibs include Seattle Pacific Univ, 1982, Steven Keely Gallery, Seattle, 1985, Artefiera 88, Bologna, Italy, Davidson Galleries, Seattle, 1989, Mariane Partlow Gallery, Olympia, Wash, 1991, Bellevue Community Coll, Wash, 1992, Kinsey Gallery, Seattle, 1995, Childhood's End Gallery, Olympia, 1999, Auburn Arts Comn Gallery, 2000, Helen S Smith Gallery, Auburn, Wash, 2002, Centennial Ctr Gallery, Kent Arts Comn, Wash, 2005, 2007; group exhibs include Pacific Northwest Art Exhib, Bellevue Art Mus, 1990, 1992; The Land, Tacoma Art Mus, Wash, 1995, New Religion, 1999; Mt Rainier Centennial Invitational, Univ Puget Sound, Tacoma, 1999; Kent Arts Comn, Centennial Ctr Gallery, 2005; People & Place, Seattle Munic Tower Gallery, 2007; Pressing Matters in Printmaking, Folk Art Ctr, Asheville, NC, 2008. *Awards:* Purchase Award, Kent Arts Comn, 1999, 2002, 2003 & 2004; GAP Grant, Artist Trust, 2000; Painting Prize, Puget Sound Group Northwest Painters, 2002; Commissioned Art Award, City of Kent, Wash, 2004; Juror's Award, Carnegie Art Ctr Ann Exhib, Walla Walla, Wash, 2005; George Sugarman Found Grant, 2005; Pollock-Krasner Found Grant, 2007. *Mailing Add:* PO Box 991 Maple Valley WA 98038

FRYBERGER, BETSY G
CURATOR
b Chicago, Ill, May 7, 1935. *Study:* Bryn Mawr Col, BA, 56; Radcliffe Col, MA, 58; Harvard Univ, MA, 57-58. *Collection Arranged:* Gavarni: Prints (auth, catalog), Stanford Univ, 71, Toulouse-Lautrec: Prints and Drawings (auth, catalog), 72, Morris and Company (coauth, catalog), 75, Whistler: Themes and Variations (coauth, catalog), 78, Paul Klee: In Celebration of/50 Prints (coauth, catalog), 79 & Gwen John (coauth, catalog), 82, Two Decades of Am Prints from the Anderson Collection 1967-87 (catalog exhib), 87, Mark Tobey: Works on Paper (coauth, catalog), 90, Stanford University Mus of Art / Drawing Collection (coauth, catalog), 93, Picasso: Graphic Magician / Prints from the Norton Simon Mus, (auth, catalog), 98, The Changing Garden: Four Centuries of European and Am Gardens (auth, catalog), 2003. *Pos:* Asst cur prints & drawings, Art Inst Chicago, 60-67; cur prints & drawings, Stanford Univ Mus Art, 70-; McMurtry Cur of Prints & Drawings emerita, Cautov Arts Ctr, Standford, 2010. *Teaching:* lect in Continuing Studies, exhib, The Changing

Garden, 2003, & exhib, The Artist Observed: Portraits & Self-Portraits, 2004; lect, Gertrude Jekyll and William Morris, The Huntington, San Marino, Calif, 96; lect, Monet and the Influence of Japanese Prints on his Garden, Elizabeth F Gamble Garden, Palo Alto, Calif, 96; lect, French 17th and 18th century Gardens, Norton Simon Mus, 2002; lect, The Changing Garden, Filoli, Woodside, Calif, Elizabeth F Gamble Garden, & the Calif Garden & Landscape Hist Soc ann meeting at Standford Univ, 2003; lect, Three Garden Heriones: Gertrude Jekyll, Beatrix Jones Farrand & Vita Sackvill West, Elizabeth F Gamble Garden, Libr Assoc, Ann Arbor, Mich, 2004; lect, Versailles: Example and Influence, Univ Mich Mus Art, Ann Arbor, 2004; lect, 18th century Artists Exploring the Roman Countryside: Views of Hadrain's Villa and Villa d'Este at Tivoli by Piranesi Fragonard and Hubert Robert, Cantor Ctr for the Arts at Stanford Univ, 2005. *Mem:* Print Coun Am (bd mem, 79-, vpres, 81-); Coll Art Asn; adv bd & chair of the educ committee, Elizabeth F Gamble Garden, Palo Alto, Calif. *Interests:* Gardens

FUERST, SHIRLEY MILLER
SCULPTOR, PRINTMAKER
b Brooklyn, NY, June 3, 1928. *Study:* Brooklyn Mus Art Sch, with Reuben Tam; Pratt Ctr Contemp Printmaking; Art Students League, with Roberto DeLamonica; Hunter Coll, MFA, 71. *Work:* James A Michener Found Collection of Twentieth Century Am Art, Univ Tex, Austin; Exxon Corp, NJ; Allentown Art Mus, Pa; Portland Mus Art, Maine. *Comn:* Translucent sculpture, comn by Marcia Frazier, Beverly Hills, Calif, 84; Triple Cloud Column (translucent sculpture), comn by Michael Jacobs, Sausalito, Calif, 96-2007; Small Cloud (translucent sculpture), comn by George Van Deventer, Washington, Maine; Left, Right, Translucent Sculptures, comn by David Fuerst, Sherman Oaks, Calif, 2014. *Exhib:* 32nd Midyear Show, Butler Inst Am Art, 68; solo exhibs, Underwater Gardens, Steinhardt Conservatory Exhib Gallery, Brooklyn Botonic Garden, 90, Reef and Cloud Gardens, Broadway Windows, NY, 91, Tide Pool Series, Ednl Testing Svc Conf Ctr, Princeton, NJ, 93, Wind Spirits and Microcosms, Space Between Gallery, Bangor, Maine, 96, New/Now, New Britain Mus of Am Art, New Britain, Conn, 2000, Shirley Fuerst: Translucent Sculpture, Flinn Gallery, Greenwich, Conn, 2001 & Translucent Sculptures, St Peter's Church, Citigroup Bldg, NY, 2002, Great Harbor Maritime Mus, Maine, 2009; 24th Juried Show, Allentown Art Mus, 94; Solstice 97, Portland Mus Art, Maine; Island Invitational, Blum Gallery, Coll Atlantic, Maine, 98; Celebrating 80 Years: Eight Artists, Flinn Gallery, Greenwich, Conn, 2010; The Wingspread Legacy, Courthouse Gallery, Ellsworth, Maine, 2010; Forty Years of Women Artists at Douglass Lib, Rutgers Univ, 2012; Where Science and Art Meet, Mt Desert Biological Laboratory, Salibury Cove, Me, 2012. *Awards:* Oil Competition First Prize, Village Art Ctr, NY, 63; Merit Award with Distinction, Enjay Chem Co, NJ, 66; Eric Schwartz Graphics Award, Nat Asn Women Artists, 70. *Bibliog:* Conversation with an artist, Shirley Fuerst, Joy Goodman (videotape), Channel 31, 77; Carl Little (auth), Wind spirits and micro cosms: sculpture by Shirley Fuerst, Art New Eng, 97; Carl Little (auth), A Floating World, Bangor Daily News, 2004; George Van Deuenter (ed), Off the Coast, cover, Poetry Mag, 2010. *Mem:* Orgn Independent Artists; Am Asn Mus. *Media:* Plastic, Miscellaneous Media. *Publ:* Auth, Health hazards in art, Art Workers News, 75; videotape documentaries of women artists, 70 & Women Artists Newsletter, 76; ed, Feminism and ecology, Heresies, 80. *Mailing Add:* 266 Marlborough Rd Brooklyn NY 11226

FUGLIE, GORDON LOUIS
GALLERY DIRECTOR, HISTORIAN
b Los Angeles, Calif. *Study:* Univ Calif, Los Angeles, MA (art hist), 1991. *Collection Arranged:* Early 20th Century German Prints, Univ Calif, Los Angeles, 1982-84; Tamarind Lithography Workshop & Inst, Univ Calif, Los Angeles, 1983-85; Max Thalmann Graphics, Loyola Marymount Univ, 1991-94; LMU Art Collection, res and exhib, 2005. *Pos:* Asst cur & actg cur, Grunwald Ctr Graphic Arts, Univ Calif, Los Angeles, 1981-86; dir, Laband Art Gallery, Loyola Marymount Univ, 1989-. *Mem:* Coll Art Asn; Am Art Mus Asn. *Res:* Figurative art, 1950-2000; Contemp Art. *Publ:* Attending To the Earth: Robert Glenn Ketchum, Loyola Marymount Univ, 1990; co-auth, Burning Lights, Loyola Marymount Univ, 1994; contrib auth, The Art of Michael Schrauzer, Image, 1995; Representing LA: Recent Pictorial Currents in Southern California Art, Seattle, 2000; auth, John Frame: Enigma Variations, Long Beach, 2005

FUHRMAN, ESTHER
SCULPTOR, JEWELER
b Pittsburgh, Pa, Feb 25, 1939. *Study:* Pa State Univ, 56-57; Frick Dept Fine Arts, Univ Pittsburgh, BA, 60; also with Sabastiano Mineo & Hana Geber, NY. *Work:* Am Crafts Coun, NY; UAHC Architects Adv, NY; Deere & Co, Moline, Ill; Temple Sinai, Pittsburgh, Pa; Scott Paper Co, Phila, Pa; World Trade Ctr, NY (destroyed on 9/11); Colt Int. *Comn:* Gemstone & bronze memorial, Temple Sinai, Pittsburgh, 78; bronze memorial, Temple Keneseth Israel, Philadelphia, 79; pvt residential comns, NY, Philadelphia, Pittsburgh, Miami, NJ, Los Angeles, Paris, Sydney, 79-81; bronze figure, Scott Paper Co, Philadelphia, 81; John Deere Co, Moline, Ill; and others; Colt Int, New York City. *Exhib:* Nat Asn Women Artists, NY; Sculptors League, NY; Equitable Life Assurance, NY; Lever House, NY; Jewelers of Am, Javits Ctr, NY; and others. *Pos:* Head Designer, Outasight Jewelry Coll, 94-; EF Designs Ltd, Demika Collection, 2008-; pres, Demika Clasp Corp, 2009, Spokesperson, Clicksecure & Demika on QVC; Jewelry & Clasp Designer, EF Designs for Sculpture to Wear jewelry in Gold, Silver & Fashion metals, 93-, pres, 2012; spokesperson, Clicksecure& Demika Clasps, QVC TV. *Teaching:* lectr studio secrets, Montclair Art Mus; speaker on Living with Sculpture, Bloomingdales NY; instr Dale Carnegie course 8 years on public speaking and secy Weehawken Township Zoning Bd, 2014. *Awards:* New Designer Award, Jewelers Am; Sculpture Award, Nat Asn Women Artists; Mechanical/design patents for jewelry (5). *Bibliog:* Marilyn Goldstein (auth), Massive sculpture shapes her life, Newsday, 3/69; article, La Rev Mod, 3/72; Jewelers Circular Keystone, 6/88; Modern Jeweler, 7/88; Accent Mag, 3/89; Accessories Mag, 3/4/5-89. *Mem:* Nat Asn Women Artists; Sculptors League (vpres, currently); Women in Jewelry (WJA). *Media:* Bronze, Wood, Gold, Silver. *Dealer:* Stuller Inc LA; QVC Pa. *Mailing Add:* Rivá Pointe 600 Harbor Blvd Apt 1022 Weehawken NJ 07086

FUHRMAN, GLENN R
COLLECTOR, PATRON
Pos: Managing dir, head spec investments group, Goldman, Sachs & co, 1988-98; co-founder & co-managing partner, MSD Capital, LP, New York; chmn Am acquisitions comt, Tate Mus, London; vice chmn contemp arts coun, Mus Mod Art, New York; bd trustees, Berea Coll, Ky, Hirshhorn Mus & Sculpture Garden, Washington, DC, Inst Contemp Art, Philadelphia & Dia Ctr for Arts, New York; founder, FLAG Art Found. *Awards:* Named one of Top 200 Collectors, ARTnews mag, 2007-13. *Mem:* Fed Enforcement Homeland Security Found. *Collection:* Contemporary art. *Mailing Add:* MSD Capital LP 645 Fifth Ave 21st Fl New York NY 10022-5910

FUJITA, KENJI
SCULPTOR
b New York, NY, 1955. *Study:* Bennington Col, BA, 78; Whitney Mus Independent Study Prog, NY, 78; Queens Col, NY, MFA, 98. *Exhib:* Solo exhibs, Cable Gallery, NY, 85 & 86, Daniel Weinberg Gallery, Los Angeles, 87 & 88, Jean Bernier, Athens, 89 & Luhring Augustine, NY, 88, 91 & 92; Aldrich Mus, Ridgefield, Conn, 86; Venice, Bienniale, Italy, 88; Sculpture, Kruygier/Landau Gallery, Santa Monica, 89; Luhring Augustine Gallery, NY, 90; Drawings, Luhring Augustine Hetzler, Santa Monica, 90; Recent Acquisitions of Prints & Drawings by Contemp Artists, Brooklyn Mus, NY 92; Contemp Wood Sculpture, Brooklyn Mus, NY, 92. *Teaching:* instr, Sch Visual Arts, Bard Col, 93 & vis asst prof visual arts, 98. *Awards:* Nat Endowment Arts Fel Sculpture, 84, 88 & Works on Paper, 91; NY Found Arts Fel, 87; Pollock/Krasner Found Grant, Sculpture, 96; John Simon Guggenheim Mem Found Fel, Visual Art, 98. *Bibliog:* Joshua Decter (auth), Kenji Fujita, Arts, 4/92; Holland Cotter (auth), Kenji Fujita: Luhring Augustine Gallery, New York Times, 7/24/92; Roberta Smith (auth), Kenji Fujita: The merge of sense and nonsense, NY Times, 88. *Media:* Sculpture, Works on Paper. *Mailing Add:* PO Box 205 71 Old Post Rd Staatsburg NY 12580

FUKUI, NOBU
PAINTER
b Tokyo, Japan; US citizen. *Study:* Art Students League, 64-65. *Work:* Indianapolis Mus Art, Ind; Larry Aldrich Mus, Conn; Nat Mus Mod Art, Tokyo & Kyoto; Chase Manhattan Bank, NY; New Britain Mus American Art, Conn. *Exhib:* Solo exhibs, Daniel's Gallery, 1965, Max Hutchinson Gallery, 1970, 72, 73, 75 & 79, Patricia Hamilton Gallery, 1987 & 1988, Marisa Del Re Gallery (with catalog), NY, 1989-90 & 1993, Richard Green Gallery, Santa Monica, Calif, 1990, Hokin Gallery, Fla, 1992 & 1993; Painting & Sculpture Today, Indianapolis Mus Art, 1970, 1972 & 1974; David Klein Gallery, Mich, 1993 & 1997; Central Fine Arts, NY, 1999; Camino Real Gallery, 1991 & 2004; Stephen Haller Gallery, 2004, 2005, 2007, 2008, 2009 (with catalog), 2010, 2012, 2013, 2014; Jump Cut Pop, Haggerty Mus Art, Milwaukee, Wis; GCA Contemporary, Milan, Italy, 2009; Gallery Weisswand, Japan, 2012; Samek Art Gallery, Bucknell Univ, Pa; Incredulity, Mattatuck Mus, Waterbury, Conn. *Bibliog:* David Shirley (auth), Art downtown: Construction shifts, The NY Times, 1/15/72; Carter Ratcliff (auth), Notes on line, Art Am, 90; Priya Malhotha (auth), A Man of Spiritual Exploration, Asian Art News, Nov 2004; Grace Glueck (auth), Nobu Fukui, The NY Times, 5/14/2004; Carter Ratcliff (auth), States of Stability, Art in America, 5/2005; Michael Tysou Murphy (auth), Dizzy Superheros, The Village Voice, 6/21/2007. *Media:* Oil. *Mailing Add:* 141 W 26th St New York NY 10001

FUKUTAKE, SOICHIRO
COLLECTOR
b 1945. *Study:* Waseda Univ, BS (mechanical engineering). *Pos:* Pres, Benesse Corp, Japan, 1986-2003, dir, chmn & chief exec officer, 2003-; owner & dir, Chichu Art Mus, Naoshima, Japan, 2004-; pres, Fukutake Sci & Cult Found, Fukutake Educ & Cult Found, Naoshima Fukutake Arte Mus Found, Fukutake Found Promotion of Regional Cult; chmn, Benesse Holdings Inc, 2009. *Awards:* Named one of Top 200 Collectors, ARTnews mag, 2004-13; Top Ten Richest People in Japan, Forbes mag, 2006, The World's Billionaires, 2010. *Mem:* Naoshima Fukutake Art Mus Found (pres). *Collection:* Impressionism & contemporary art. *Mailing Add:* Benesse Holdings Corp 3-7-17 Minamigata, Kita-Ku Olcayama Japan 700-0807

FULD, RICHARD SEVERIN, JR
COLLECTOR, PATRON
Study: Univ Colo, BA, 1969; NY Univ Stern Sch Bus, MBA, 1973. *Pos:* Joined Lehman Brothers, New York City, 1969, managing dir, 1969-84; vice chmn Shearson Lehman (merger Shearson and Lehman Brothers), 1984-90; pres, co-CEO Shearson Lehman Brothers Inc, 1990-93; pres, COO Lehman Brothers Holdings, Inc., 1993-94, CEO, 1993-, chmn, 1994-; Mem PSA Govt and Fed Agency Securities Com; dir Fed Reserve Bank of NY; mem exec com Partnership for New York City, Bus. Roundtable and Bus Coun. *Awards:* Named one of Top 200 Collectors, ARTnews, 2005-08. *Mem:* Trustee Mt Sinai Med Ctr, New York City, Middlebury Coll.; former chmn Mt. Sinai Children's Ctr Found, mem exec com; bd dir Ronald McDonald House. *Collection:* Collects works on paper, especially postwar and contemporary

FULLER, DIANA
CURATOR, EDITOR
b New York, NY, Jan 14, 1939. *Study:* Sorbonne, art hist. *Exhib:* San Jose Mus Art (traveling exhib) 2004; co-cur, Transparent Reflections, Richard Pousette-Dart, Works on Paper, Los Angeles Co Mus Art, 2006; Painter as Photographer, Richard Pousette-Dart, 1940s & 1950s, 2011-2012. *Pos:* owner, co-dir, Hansen Fuller Gallery, 60-77, Hansen Fuller Goldeen Gallery, 77-80, Fuller Goldeen Gallery, 80-87, Fuller

Gross Gallery, 87-90; trustee, Headlands Ctr Arts, San Francisco Art Inst; co-founder, Bacva and 80 Langton St; pres, Performing Arts Workshop, formerly; founder & pres, Proj Sculpture Pub Site, 82-86; Prog Dir, Squaw Valley Community of Writers Screenwriting Prog, 1986-; owner/dir, Creative Arts Enterprises, 90-; dir, Greg Jubileum: Norway Celebrates the Arts, 92-94; int arts comt, Exploratoreum, 95-; bd dir, Pub Art Works, 2003; consult to the Estate of Richard Pousette-Dart, 2003-2008; Bd San Francisco Film Arts Found; bd Roxy Theatre Bd; pres of bd, Film Arts Found, 2008-2009. *Mem:* San Francisco Legion of Honor, 2006; San Francisco Mus Mod Art; San Francisco Film Soc; San Francisco Fine Arts Mus; Mus Mod Art, New York; Whitney Mus Am Art, New York; Metropolitan Mus. *Interests:* art, mediterranean hist, film & tennis. *Publ:* Co-ed, proj dir, Parallels & Intersections: The Remarkable History of Women Artists in California, UC Press, 1950-2000. *Mailing Add:* 2173 15th St San Francisco CA 94114

FULLER, EMILY RUTGERS
PAINTER
b New York, NY, Aug 9, 1941. *Study:* Garland Jr Col, Boston, Mass, Assoc BD, 62; Mus Sch Fine Arts, Boston, Mass, 62-66; Tufts Univ, BS (art educ), 66; Art Students League, New York; Sch of Visual Arts, NYC, 88-89, study with John Parks. *Work:* Mus Mod Art; Prudential Ins Corp Am; Indianapolis Mus Art, Ind; City Bank NAm, NY; Miami Dade Pub Libr System, Fla; IBM Corp, NY; Deutsche Bank, New York; Machias Art Galleries, Univ Maine. *Exhib:* Solo exhibs, 55 Mercer, NY, 72, 75, 78 & 79, Soho 20, NY, 77, Webb & Parsons, Bedford Village, NY, 77, Frank Marino Gallery, NY, 80, Cardet Gallery, Coral Gables, Fla, 81, New Materialism, Frauen Mus, Bonn, Ger, 85, Stanford Mus & Nature Ctr, Conn, 88, Maine Coast Artists, Rockport, 89, Foxhall Gallery, Washington, DC, 90 & Bergen Mus Art & Sci, Paramus, NJ, 92; Art in Transition: A Century of The Mus Sch, Mus Fine Arts, Boston, Mass, 77; Paper as Medium, Smithsonian Inst Traveling Exhib Serv, 78-79; Gifts of Drawings: European Acquisitions, Am Acquisitions, Mus Mod Art, NY, 79; Gallery One Twenty Eight, NY, 2011; Warner Gallery, Millbrook Sch, Millbrook, NY, 2012; Group shows: Carter Burden Gallery, NYC, 2015, group "Represent"; One person show: Millbrook Library, Millbrook, NY, 2015. *Pos:* Trustee, Bergen Mus Arts & Sci, Paramus, NJ, 93-94. *Bibliog:* Michael Florescu (auth), Emily Fuller, article in Arts Mag, 4/79; John Russell (auth), Art: New drawings at the Modern, New York Times, 8/10/79; Linda Rohr (auth), Emily Fuller, Bergen Mus Arts & Sci, 92. *Media:* Oil, Pastels. *Interests:* archit; antiques; glass. *Collection:* Mus Mod Art; JP Morgan Chase; Indianapolis Mus Art; Prudential Insurance Co Am; IBM; Deutsche Bank; and others. *Publ:* Contribr, Emily Fuller pioneers in art, Garland Mag, Garland Jr Col, 74. *Dealer:* Gallery One Twenty Eight 128 Rivington St New York NY 10002. *Mailing Add:* 130 W 24th St Apt 3A New York NY 10011

FULLER, JEFFREY P
DEALER, GALLERY DIRECTOR
b Chicago, Ill, May 14, 1950. *Study:* Univ Vienna, 70-71; Holy Cross Col, Worchester, Mass, BA, 72. *Pos:* Asst, Hokin Gallery, Inc, Chicago, 74-78, dir, 78-79; dir, Jeffrey Fuller Fine Art, Ltd, 79-; accredited sr appraiser, Am Soc Appraisers, 84-; dir, Fuller's Fine Art Auctions, 2007-. *Mem:* Philadelphia Art Dealers Asn (treas, 82-83, 88-89, pres, 87-88); Am Soc Appraisers (bd mem, 2008-, vpres, 2011); Philadelphia Art Alliance (bd mem, 82-85); Swedish Am Hist Mus (art adv panel, 82-85); Philadelphia Volunteer Lawyers for Arts (bd mem, 84-); Art & Bus Coun Great Philadelphia, (bd mem, 2008-11, adv bd mem, 2011-). *Specialty:* Twentieth century American and European art. *Mailing Add:* Jeffrey Fuller Fine Art Ltd 730-32 Carpenter Ln Philadelphia PA 19119

FULLER, MARY (MARY FULLER MCCHESNEY)
SCULPTOR, WRITER
b Wichita, Kans, Oct 20, 1922. *Study:* Univ Calif, Berkeley, AA, 43. *Work:* State Calif; Children's Sculpture Garden, Community Ctr, Salinas, Calif; San Francisco Art Comn; Petaluma Pub Libr; San Francisco Gen Hosp; and others. *Comn:* Santa Cruz Art Comn, 93; Berkeley, Calif, 2002; Reno, Nev, 2002; and others. *Exhib:* San Francisco Mus Art, 47-50 & 60; Gump's Gallery, San Francisco, 65; Calif State Univ, Sonoma, at Cotati, 71; Santa Rosa City Hall, Calif, 74 & 86; Fremont, Calif, 80; Lafayette, Calif, 82; Portland, Ore, 88; Carmel, Calif, 88; San Francisco, 2002. *Collection Arranged:* Period of Exploration (with catalog), Oakland Mus, 73. *Pos:* Researcher, Arch Am Art, 64-65; staff writer, Currant Mag, San Francisco, 75-76; ed & publ, Sonoma Mt Publ Co, 96. *Awards:* First Prize Ceramic Sculpture, Pac Coast Ceramic Ann, 47 & 49; Ford Found, 65; Merit Award, San Francisco Art Festival, 71; Nat Endowment Arts art critic grant, 75. *Media:* Carved concrete. *Publ:* Auth, articles In: Art Digest, 54, Artforum, 62, 63, 70-71, Art in Am, 63-64 & Craft Horizons, 73, 76-78; A Period of Exploration, 73; Robert McChesney, An American Painter, 96. *Mailing Add:* 2955 Sonoma Mountain Rd Petaluma CA 94954

FULLERTON, MARY See Faulconer, Mary (Fullerton)

FULTON ROSS, GALE
ARTIST
b Medford, MA, July 28, 1947. *Study:* Studied with: Melvin Johnson, Melvin George Sch Art, Boston, 1965-1976; Cleveland Bellow, DeYoung Mus, Oakland, Calif, 1976-1981; Pierre Parsus, France, 1993; studied, Berlin, 1996. *Work:* Am Mus African Am Artists; Calif Mus African Am Art; Forbes Gallery, NYC; Arthur Ashe Found; Thurgood Marshall Estate, NC Univ. *Comn:* Archbishop Desmond Tutu; Jackie Robinson, comn by Mrs Rachel Robinson; Dr Arthur Logan, comn by Marion Logan; Ambassador Bradlet Holmes; Gov Michael Dukakis. *Exhib:* Earth N' Arts Gallery, Oakland, 1971-1976; Black Expo, San Francisco, 1972; The Gallery, Los Angeles, 1978; Brockman Gallery, 1984; Calif African Mus, 1986; Chuck Levitan Gallery, NYC, 1996; SoBo Fine Art, Tulsa, 1999; One-women shows: Nat Coun Chas Hdqs, NYC, Castillion Fine Art, 1991; Zora Neal Hurston Mus, Monique Knowlton Gallery, NYC, 1994; Don Roll Gallery, Sarasota, African Am Mus, 1995. *Pos:* Trustee, Nat Urban League, 1976-1978; local/state judge, Miss Am Pageant, 2000; actor roles in: Blue Hill Ave & The Crucible (films). *Awards:* Atlanta Life Painters award, 1990; Nat Coalition of 100 Black Woman Artistic Achievement Award, 1995; Humanitarian award W Coast Center Human Develop, 1996

FUMAGALLI, BARBARA MERRILL
PRINTMAKER
b Kirkwood, Mo, Mar 15, 1926. *Study:* Univ Iowa, Iowa City, BFA, 48, MFA, 50, with Mauricio Lasansky; Univ NMex, 80-81, with Garo Antreasian, John Sommers & Jim Kraft. *Work:* Mus of Mod Art, NY; Nelson A Rockefeller Collection, NY; Univ Ill, Urbana; Univ Iowa, Iowa City; Hamline Univ, St Paul, Minn; St John's Univ, Collegeville, Minn; Univ Wis, Stout, Menomonie, Wis. *Exhib:* Walker Art Ctr, Minneapolis, Minn, 49, 56 & 63; Young Am Printmakers, Mus Mod Art, NY, 53; Solo Exhibs, Tweed Gallery, Univ Minn, 65, 82; Concordia Coll, Moorhead, Minn, 65; Suzanne Kohn Gallery, St Paul, 67; Hamline Univ, St Paul, 69, 84; Paine Art Ctr & Arboretum, Oshkosh, Wis, 73; St John's Univ, Minn, 84; Smithsonian Inst (traveling), 66-68; NW Printmakers, Seattle Art Mus, 66-69; One West Contemp Arts Ctr, Ft Collins, Colo, 94; Truman State Univ, Kirksville, Mo, 98; Indian Hills Community Coll, Ottumwa, Iowa, 98; Southeast Mo State Univ, Cape Girardeau, Mo, 99; Wayland Baptist Univ, Plainview, Tex, 99; Studio Channel Islands, Camarillo, Calif, 2000, 2001, 2007, 2009; Univ Cent Ark, Conway, 2001; Focus on the Masters, Ventura Calif, 2002, 2003, 2011; Mo Western State Coll, St Joseph, 2003; Ventura Co Arts Coun, 2004; Dickenson State Univ, NDak, 2004; Ashford Univ, Clinton, Iowa, 2005; Art & Jazz Festival, Studio Channel Islands Art Ctr, Calif State Univ, Camarillo, Calif, 2006, 2007; 60 Years of Engraving, Studio Channel Islands Art Ctr, Calif State Univ, Camarillo, Calif, 2007; Celebration SCIART: 10th Anniversary Exhib, Studio Channel Islands Art Ctr, Calif State Univ, 2007; Proverbs Coffee House, Camarillo, Calif, 2007; Concordia Univ, Irvine, Calif, 2008; Levitt Gallery, Sch of Art and Art History, Mauricio Lasansky and the First Generation, Univ iowa, Iowa City, 2014. *Teaching:* Instr, Univ Wis, Stout, 79 & 81. *Awards:* Post Facto Prize, City Art Mus, St Louis, Mo, 47; Purchase Prize, Univ Ill, 54; Best Show, Arrowhead Art Exhib, 63. *Bibliog:* Donald M Anderson (auth), Elements of Design, Holt, Rinehart & Winston, 61. *Media:* Engraving, Serigraphy; Oil, Watercolor. *Publ:* Illusr, Swing Around the Sun, Lerner Publ, 65. *Mailing Add:* 352 E Calle La Sombra Camarillo CA 93010

FUNDERBURK, AMY ELIZABETH
PAINTER, PHOTOGRAPHER
b Charlotte, NC, Feb 16, 1966. *Study:* Appalachian State Univ, BS, 88; Assoc Artists Winston-Salem Pastel Workshop with Wolf Kahn, 91, Vermont Studio Center, Residency, April 2005. *Work:* The Artinian Self-Portrait Collection, Appalachian State Univ, Boone, NC, 87; Babcock School for Business Management, Wake Forest Univ, Winston-Salem, NC, 97; Dubai Aerospace Enterprises Capital, Seattle, Wash, 2008. *Comn:* Portraits, Legends Entertainment Ctr, Appalachian State Univ, 88; many pvt commissions in the US and Rep of Ireland, 88-; Brighid at the Forge (oil on linen painting), Student Govt Asn Permanent Art Collection, Forsyth Tech Community Col, Winston-Salem, NC, 96. *Exhib:* Solo Exhibs: Wisdom of the Ancient Lore: Symbolic Interpretation of Spiritual Knowledge, Parsons Gallery, Spartanburg Co Mus Art, SC, 96; Durham Art Guild, Central Carolina Bank Gallery, Durham, NC, 98; Mars Hill Coll, Mars Hill, NC, 1999; Wisdom of the Ancient Lore: Symbolic Interpretation of Spiritual Knowledge, Gallery 2, Artspace, Raleigh, NC, 2001; Wisdom of the Ancient Lore: Selections from Two Symbolic Series & Related Works, Ctr Creative Arts, Yorklyn, DE, 2002; Aisling: An Artist's Vision of Ireland, Dublin Arts Council, Dublin, OH, 2005; Between the Worlds: Irish Imagery from the Seen and Unseen Realms, Flanders Gallery, Raleigh, NC, 2007; From the Beara to Sligo: Works from the W of Ireland, Timothy Nichols Gallery, Winston-Salem, NC, 2007; Images From the Otherworld: New Works and a Retrospective, Mary Holt Davis Gallery, Salem Fine Arts Ctr, Salem Coll, Winston-Salem, NC, 2012, Images from the Otherworld and Related Works, Gaston Co Mus Art and History, Bullpen Gallery, Dallas, NC, 2013, New Workds by Amy Funderbunk: Exploring Above, Beyond, and Below, Inter-Section Gallery, 2013; Group exhibs, Creating Ceremony, Main Gallery, Theatre Art Galleries, High Point, NC, 2000; NCAC Visual Artist Fel Recipients Exhib, Hickory Mus of Art, Hickory, NC and McColl Ctr Vis Art, Charlotte, NC, 2004; Two person show, Magic Casements: A Mixed-Media View of Lit, Tuttle Gallery, McDonogh Sch, Baltimore, 95-96; Two person show, Narrative Paintings, Howard County Center for the Arts, Ellicott City, MD, 2005 ; Blurring Racial Barriers, Diggs Gallery, Winston-Salem State Univ, Winston-Salem, NC, 2005, Fine Arts Ctr, Salem Coll, NC, 2006, The Periphery Arts Council of Winston, Salem, Eleanor Davis Gallery, Sawtooth Bldg, Winston-Salem, NC, 2007; Reflections: Politics & Religion in Art-Mary Holt Davis Gallery, Salem Fine Arts Ctr, Salem Coll, NC, 2008; Many Paths, One Source: The Path of the Artist & the Creative Spirit, Chalice Well Trust, Glastonbury, England, 2009; Making a Living, Making a Life, East Carolina Univ, Mendenhall Gallery, Greenville, NC, 2010; Appalachian Alumni in the Arts, Turchin Ctr for the Visual Arts, Boone, NC, 2011; Juried exhibs, The Red Clay Survey, Huntsville Mus Art, Ala, 90, Transformation: Death as Metaphor, Woman Made Gallery, Chigo, Ill, 94, Spotlight 95 Art Exhib, Davidson Co Mus Art, Lexington, NC, 95, Whose Body is it Anyway?, Mills Pond House Gallery, Smithtown Twp Arts Coun, St James, NY, 95, Holy Baloney, Woman Made Gallery, Chgo, 95. *Collection Arranged:* Journeys: Work from Artists' Intl Travels,. Milton Rhodes Gallery, Winston-Salem, NC, 2002 & 2003; Allegory, Milton Rhodes Gallery, Winston Salem, NC, 2003. *Pos:* Exhib coordr, Winston-Salem Forsyth Co Arts Coun, 92-96, Greater Winston-Salem Chamber Com, 93-2009; art reviewer, Now Mag, Winston-Salem, 94; exhib coordr, Babcock Sch of Bus, Worell Prof Ctr for Bus Mgt, Wake Forest Univ, Winston-Salem, 96-2005; exhibs coordr, Sch of Law, Worrell Prof Ctr, Wake Forest Univ, 98-2005; exhibs coordr, Davidson County Community Col, Lexington, NC, 2000-2006; exhibs coordr, Baptist Medical Center, Wake Forest Univ, Winston-Salem, NC, 2004-2009. *Teaching:* Instr art, Sawtooth Ctr Visual Art, 89-99; instr oil painting, Forsyth Tech Community Col, 89-2000. *Awards:* Emerging Artist Fel Grant, Winston-Salem Forsyth Co Arts Coun, 90-91; Solo Show Award, 6th Juried Show, Ctr/Gallery, Carrboro, NC, 91; first place, 26th Annual Spotlight, Juried Exhib,

Davidson Co Mus Art, 99; Visual Artists Fel, NC Arts Coun, 2002-2003; Full Fel Award, Vermont Studio Center, Johnson, Vt, 2004; Women in the Arts Seed Grant, Thomas S. Kenan Inst Arts, Winston-Salem, NC, 2006; Three works selected for 2 year loan to US Embassy in Estonia, 2007. *Bibliog:* Jill Doss (auth), Art features artists' friends & family, The Dispatch, 8/4/94; Tom Patterson (auth), Exhibition to highlight emerging artists who received small arts council grants, The Winston-Salem Journal, 5/14/95; Spiritual Journeys, Herald Jour, 9/25/96; State of the Art, The Fayettville Observer Times, 3/15/98; Blue Greenberg (auth), The Herald-Sun, 4/6/2001; Tom Patterson (auth), A Sampling of NC's Finest, Winston-Salem Journal, 8/15/04; Tom Patterson (auth), Provocative: Local Project Moves to Salem, Winston-Salem Journal, 4/23/06; Tom Patterson (auth), Let us Show Your Work, Winston-Salem Journal, 1/21/07; Tom Patterson (auth), The Sawtooth, Winston-Salem Journal, 6/3/07; Tom Patterson (auth), Strong Women Speak: Exhibitions in Asheville and at Salem College Address Survival in a Man's World, Facing Religious-Political Issues, Winston-Salem Jour, 1/25/2009, Andrea Brill (auth), Artists Profile: Funderburk's Creations Otherworldly, Relish, 12/15/2011, 3 Artists Show Views of Reality for Shows, Winston Salem Jour, 4/22/12; Tom Patterson (auth), 3 Artists...Artwork on display at 3 galleries, Winston-Salem Jour, 8/11/2013. *Mem:* Assoc Artists of Winston-Salem (vpres, 94-95; pres, 96), 88-2000, 2005-2006; Society for the Arts in Healthcare, June 2005-2009. *Media:* Oil, Pastels, Photography. *Publ:* Illusr, Candle Lovefeast, Old Salem, Inc, 90; auth, Imagery in Celebration of the Divine Feminine on Display, The Winston Salem Chronicle, 3/23/95; auth, "Alternative Locations: the Hidden Market," Art Calendar Mag, Jul-Aug, 2002; Art of Wellbeing (cover art), Spring, 2010. *Mailing Add:* 416 Corona St Winston Salem NC 27103-2817

FUNDORA, THOMAS
PAINTER
b Havana, Cuba, March 7, 1935; US citizen. *Study:* Candler Coll (art), 58, Escuela San Alejandro (oil painting), 59, Wash Sch Art (drawing & oil), 61, Escuela de Arte Bologna (restoration), 65, Sch Art, Bologna, Italy (art restoration), 65. *Work:* Mama Leone's Art Gallery, New York; Spanish Pavillion, New York World's Fair; Record World Art Collection, New York; J Cayre Art Exhib, New York; Coleccion Arte Latinoamericano, Rio de Janeiro, Brazil; pvt collections, Paul Ellison, Hector Cap, Raul Leal & Emilio Garcia III. *Comn:* Gran Canal, Venice, Mama Leone's Restaurant, New York, 68; Plaza Catedral de La Habana, Ital Art Gallery, Miami, Fla, 90; Jose Marti, Fundacion Cubanoamericana, Miami, Fla, 90; Balseros, Garces Com Coll, Miami, Fla, 91. *Exhib:* Bienal Latinoamericana, Instituto Arte Latino, Washington, DC, 68; Los 10 Grandes, Instituto de Puerto Rico, New York, 69; Bienal de Sao Paulo, Arte Latinoamericano, Brazil, 71; Int Art Exhib, Int Art Gallery, Miami, Fla, 89; European & Latin Masters, Martin's Art Gallery, Coral Gables, Fla, 90; CatalinaArt Gallery, Kendall, Fla, 96; Domingo Padron Art Gallery, Coral Gables, Fla, 97; Frames USA Gallery, Kendall, Fla, 97; Catalina Art Gallery, Coral Gables, Fla, 98; Izzo's Artery Gallery, Chicago, Ill, 98; Ocean Reef Art League, Key Largo, Fla, 2002. *Pos:* Dir, Fundora Art Gallery. *Awards:* Int Grand Prize, Mama Leone's Art Show, 66; Painter Year, Carteles Mag, 67; Second Prize, CCIA Art Show, 69. *Bibliog:* Don Galaor (auth), Fundora Pinta Milagros, Diario Las Americas, 10/65; Ramon Cotta (auth), Obra Pintor Cubano en NY, El Imparcial, Puerto Rico, 5/66; Efrain Hidalgo (auth), Cristo se Movio, Diario La Prensa, 11/68. *Mem:* Asn Pintores Latinoamericanos, New York; Circulo Pintores de Miami; Thomas Fund Art Ctr, Coral Gables; Monroe Coun Arts (adv bd mem). *Media:* Watercolor, Oil. *Mailing Add:* 100 Bahama Rd Key Largo FL 33037

FUNK, CHARLOTTE M
TAPESTRY ARTIST, EDUCATOR
b Milwaukee, Wis, Sept 27, 1934. *Study:* Univ Wis-Whitewater, BS, 71; Ill State Univ, Normal, MS, 75, MFA, 76. *Comn:* Passage to the Sea: Land, Sand & Sea, Corpus Christi Nat Bank, Tex, 81; Wind in the West, Lubbock Munic Bldg, 86; Sunset Winds, Mem Hosp, Midland, Tex. *Exhib:* Seventh Int Biennial Tapestry, Lausanne, Switz, 76; Clay, Fiber, Metal-Women Artists, Bronx Mus Arts, NY, 78; Contemp Tapestry, Pratt Inst, NY, 80-81; Fiber Structure Nat, 87; Nine in Texas, Houston, 89; solo exhib, Hueser Art Ctr, Bradley Univ, 90; Funk and Funk - Fired & Woven, Albany, Tex, 96. *Teaching:* Instr textiles, Tex Tech Univ, Lubbock, 78-97; instr, Arrowmont Sch Arts & Crafts, 81-88. *Awards:* Judges' Choice Award, Contemp Crafts Americas, Handweavers Guild Am, 75. *Bibliog:* Geometric Design in Weaving, Regensteiner, 86; Art Space, 1-2/90; Handwoven Mag, 5-6/94. *Mem:* Am Craftsmens Coun. *Media:* Miscellaneous Fibers. *Mailing Add:* 15422 Kid Run San Antonio TX 78232-4043

FUNK, VERNE J
SCULPTOR, EDUCATOR
b Milwaukee, Wis, July 19, 1932. *Study:* Univ Wis-Milwaukee, BS, MS & MFA. *Work:* Milwaukee Art Ctr; Mus Contemp Crafts, NY; Columbus Gallery Fine Arts, Ohio; Ariz State Univ, Tempe; Charles A Wustum Mus of Fine Arts, Racine, Wis; Mus of Tex Tech Univ, Lubbock, Tex; San Angelo Mus of Fine Arts, San Angelo, Tex; Nat Decorative Arts Mus, Riga, Latvia; Canton Art Inst, Ohio. *Exhib:* Objects: USA; Clayworks, 20 Americans, Mus Contemp Crafts, NY; solo exhibs, The Dance, W Tex Mus; The Figure in Clay, Craft Alliance, 91 & Steppin' Out, Canton Art Inst; Ceramics Now-89, Downey Mus, Calif; Third Ceramic Nat Invitational, Canton Art Inst; Verne Funk: Thirty Yr Rev, NAU, Flagstaff, Ariz; Earth and Fire: Ceramic Sculpture, San Antonio Mus Art; Tex Clay III, San Marcos, Tex; Red Heat, Univ Tulsa, Okla; Tex Mud, Dallas Ctr Continuing Art; 21st Century Ceramics, Columbus Coll Art & Design; Big Head, SW Ctr Art & Craft, Tex; 14th Ann Ceramics Compilation, San Angelo, Tex; Verne Funk-Sculpture & Drawing, Continuum Celebration, UWM, Milwaukee, Wis; Int Ceramic Art Mus, Fuping, China, 2008; NCECA Nat Biennial, 2009; IAC, Paris, France, 2010; 19th Ceramic Nat, 2012. *Pos:* Pres, Wis Designer-Craftsmen, 64-66; chmn, Visual Arts II, Wis Arts Found & Coun, 67. *Teaching:* Instr, Carthage Coll, 66-69 & Univ Wis-Whitewater, 69-73; guest artist ceramics, Calif State Univ, Fresno, 72; prof ceramics & dir art sch, Bradley Univ, Peoria, Ill, 73-77; assoc prof ceramics, Tex Tech Univ, Lubbock, 77-81 & prof, 81-97; prof emer. *Bibliog:* Donald Key (auth), Prominent Wisconsin potters, Milwaukee J, 71; Elizabeth Sasser (auth), Verne Funk: The dance, Ceramics Mo, 1/87; Gene Kleinsmith (auth), Clay's the Way, Victor Valley Press, 2nd Ed, 88. *Mem:* Am Craft Coun; NCECA; ISC; Int Acad Ceramics. *Media:* Clay. *Specialty:* Contemporary Art. *Publ:* Craft & Art of Clay, 2nd ed, 3rd ed & 4th ed; History of American Ceramics: the Studio Potter; Objects: USA; Spirit of Clay; Surface Decoration, Lark Books, 99; Working with Clay, 2nd Edition Prentice Hall, 2003; contrib, Electric Kiln Ceramics, 3rd Edition, 2004; Making Marks, Ceramics Surface, KP Bks, 2004; Ceramics: Art & Perception #69; Confrontational Clay, Schwartz, 2008; 500 Ceramic Sculptures, Lark, 2009. *Dealer:* CODA Gallery Palm Desert CA. *Mailing Add:* 15422 Kid Run San Antonio TX 78232-4043

FURINO, NANCY V
PAINTER
b Chicago, Ill, Nov 19, 1928. *Study:* Sch of Mus Fine Arts, Boston (summa cum laude, traveling fel) 51. *Comn:* Landscape painting, comn by Rosabeth Moss Kanter, Edgartown, Mass, 89; landscape painting, comn by Thomas Nessa, Mass, 92. *Exhib:* Brooklyn Mus, 50; Allied Artists of Am, Nat Arts Club, NY, 87, 88, 89; Copley Master's Show, Pittsburgh Ctr for Arts, 86, New Eng Regional, Fed Reserve Bank, Boston, 88; 12 Copley Masters, Fitchburg Art Mus, Mass, 89; Audubon Artists, Nat Arts Club, Salmagundi Club, NY, 90, 92, 97, 2000, 2005; Carol Craven Gallery, 2006, 2007, 2008, 2009; Retrospective exhib, Dragonfly Gallery, Oak Bluffs, Mass. *Teaching:* Masters Workshops for the Copley Soc of Boston. *Awards:* Originality Award, Copley Soc, 81; Beatrice Jackson Mem, Audubon Artists, 2000. *Bibliog:* Elaine Lembo (auth), Nancy Furino, Vineyard Gazette, 85; Nancy Furino, Cape Cod Life, 87; Edward Feit (auth), Am Artist, 88; Jacqueline Sexton (auth), 87-90; Marthas Vineyard Times, 2005; 2 covers of Martha's Vineyard Mag, 2006; Cover, Martha's Vineyard Times, 2006. *Mem:* Audubon Artists Inc; Copley Soc Boston. *Media:* Oil. *Specialty:* Carol Craven Gallery, American Modernist Paintings. *Publ:* Cover, Arts, Mathas Vineyard Times, 2005; Two covers, 2006 Marthas Vineyard mag. *Dealer:* Carol Craven Gallery Holms Hold Rd Vineyard Haven Ma 02568. *Mailing Add:* 46 Marthas Rd Edgartown MA 02539

FURMAN, (DR & MRS) ARTHUR F
COLLECTORS, PATRONS
b Scranton, Pa; Mrs Furman, b Hazleton, Pa. *Study:* Dr Furman, Temple Univ, DMD; Mrs Furman, Pa State Univ. *Pos:* Trustees, Furman Family Trust; pres & vpres, Found Visual Arts. *Interests:* Arranging and exhibiting items from collection in various institutions, museums, galleries and schools. *Collection:* American contemporary masters painting and sculpture; ancient Thai, Cambodian and Indian bronzes; Chinese incense burners, Oriental artifacts. *Mailing Add:* 1250 S Washington St No 611 Alexandria VA 22314-4455

FURMAN, DAVID STEPHEN
SCULPTOR, EDUCATOR
b Seattle, Wash, Aug 15, 1945. *Study:* Univ Ore, BA (ceramics), 69; Univ Wash, MFA (ceramics & glass blowing), 72. *Hon Degrees:* Escuela Nac de Bellas Artes, Hon PhD, 2000. *Work:* Univ Puget Sound Mus Art; Security Pac Nat Bank; Los Angeles Co Mus Art; World Ceramic Foundation Mus, Icheon, Korea; Fulbright Comn, Lima, Peru; Marietta Coll Art Mus; US Embassy, Lima, Peru; San Francisco Mus of Art; and others. *Exhib:* Clay (ceramic sculpture), Whitney Mus, 74; Small Scale in Contemp Art, Chicago Art Inst, 75; Hard and Clear, Los Angeles Co Art Mus, 75; Seattle Art Mus; MH De Young Mem Mus; Solo Exhibs: OK Harris Works of Art, NY, 90; Margulies Talpin Gallery, Miami, 90; Tortue Gallery, 91; Judy Yovens Gallery, 93; Sherry Frumkin Gallery, 96; S Ore State Univ, 96; Gallery 221, NY, 04; Dubnick gallery, Sacramento, Calif, 05; Univ Ore Mus Art, Eugene, Ore; Jacqueline Anhalt Gallery, Los Angeles, Calif; Gayle Weyhler Gallery, Salt Lake City Utah; Tortue Gallery, Santa Monica, Calif; J Cotter Gallery, Vail/Beaver Creek, Colo; UMKC Belger Art Center, Kans City, Mo; San Angelo Mus Art, San Angelo, Tex, Bakersfield Mus Art, Ca; Sherry Frumkin Gallery, 93; Los Angeles, 93; Dorothy Weiss Gallery, 94; Laguma Art Mus, 94; Navy Pier, Chicago, 94; Frumkin Duvall Gallery, 2000. *Teaching:* Prof art, Claremont Grad Sch, Pitzer Col, 1973-2007, prof art, Studio Arts Prog; prof emer, 2008; instr clay sculpture, Otis Art Inst, 75-; lectr, Univ Utah, Boston Univ, Ind State Univ, Univ Ga, Univ Washington, Univ Calif, Los Angeles & Irvine; Peter, Gloria Gold Endowed Prof Art prog, Pitzer Col, Claremnt, Calif, 2003-2008. *Awards:* Craftsman's Fel, Nat Endowment for Arts, 75, Interdisciplinary Fel, 86-87 & vis artist fel, 96; Fulbright Fel, Peru, 79-80, 2000 & Fulbright Sr Artist Fel, Costa Rica, 90 & Peru, 99; Fac Dev Fel, Pitzer Col, 81-83; Fulbright Sr Artist's Fel, 2000; Special Prize Winner, 2nd Int Ceramic Biennale, Icheon World Ceramic Ctr, 2003 ; Gloria & Peter Gold Endowed Chair, Pitzer Col, 2003-2008; Silver Medal 3rd Int Ceramic Biennale, Icheon, World Ceramic Ctr, 2005; juror, 1x Biennale Ceramics & Sculpture, Honduras, Calif; Fel, Office of Citizen Exchanges, US Dept State/Cultural Affairs, Honduras, Central Am, 2007. *Bibliog:* C H Hertel (auth), David Furman-Biographical Narrative Sculpture, 74; W C Hunt (auth), David Furman-miniature environments, Ceramics Monthly, 1/75; article in Am Ceramics, 8/2/90. *Mem:* World Crafts Coun; Am Crafts Coun; Nat Coun Educ Ceramic Arts; Artists Equity; Int Acad Ceramics. *Media:* Ceramics, Sculpture. *Res:* Pre Colombian History of Peru. *Specialty:* Art. *Collection:* Los Angeles County Mus Art; Long Beach Mus Art; Garland Mus Art; San Francisco Mus Mod Art; Yixing Ceramic Mus, Yixing, China; Racine Art Mus; Mus Ceramics, Faenza, Italy; US Embassy, Lima, Peru. *Publ:* Studio Potter, Vol 14, No 1, Las Lineas De Nazca. *Dealer:* Sherry Frumkin Gallery Santa Monica CA; Gallery 221 New York City; Solomon Dubnick Gallery Sacramento CA. *Mailing Add:* 4739 Glen Ivy St La Verne CA 91750

FURNAS, BARNABY
PAINTER
b 1973. *Study:* Sch Visual Arts, NY, BFA, 95; Columbia Univ, BFA, 2000. *Work:* War (What Is It Good For?), Mus Contemp Art, Chicago, 2003, Go Johnny Go, Kunsthalle Wien, Austria, 2003, Watercolor Worlds, Dorsky Gallery, Long Island City, 2004, Whitney Biennial, Whitney Mus Am Art, 2004, 179 Ann: Invitational Exhib Contemp

Art, Nat Acad Design, NY, 2004, Seeing Other People, Marianne Boesky Gallery, 2004. *Exhib:* Solo exhibs, Marianne Boesky Gallery, NY, 2002, 2003, Modern Art Inc, London, 2004; Group exhibs, Urban Romantics, Lombard Fried Gallery, NY, 1999, All Terrain, Freidrich Petzel Gallery, NY, 1999, @, PPOW Gallery, NY, 2000, Project Room, Artists Space, NY, 2000, Collector's Choice, Exit Art, NY, 2000, All Am, Bellwether, Brooklyn, 2001, The Fourth Ann Altoids Curiously Strong Collection, Los Angeles Contemp Exhib, 2002, Officina Am, Galleria d'Arte Moderna, Bologna, Italy, 2002, Drawings, Metro Pictures, 2003, Transnational Monster League, Derek Eller Gallery, NY, 2003, Funny Papers: Cartoons & Contemp Drawing, Daniel Weinberg Gallery, Los Angeles, 2003

FURR, JIM
PAINTER, PRINTMAKER
b Camden, Tenn, Aug 14, 1939. *Study:* Univ Tenn, BFA; Tulane Univ, MFA; Tamarind Inst Lithography. *Work:* Montgomery Mus Fine Arts, Ala; Equitable Life Assurance Soc US, Bank Am Corp; Kans State Univ, Lawrence; R J Reynolds Corp; IBM Corp; and others. *Comn:* Colony Sq Hotel Corp, Atlanta, 78; Loew's Anatole Hotel Corp, Dallas, 79; Cannon Chapel, Emory Univ, Atlanta, 81; Marriott Marquis, Atlanta, 87. *Exhib:* Drawings, Mint Mus Art, NC, 79; one-person show, Tex A&I Univ, Kingsville, 74 & Montgomery Mus Fine Arts, 81; Southeast Seven IV, Southeastern Ctr Contemp Art, 81; Continuum III, Dulin Gallery Art, Knoxville, Tenn, 81; Red Clay Survey: Southeastern Biennial, Huntsville Mus, Ala, 90; Southern Abstraction: Contemp Arts Ctr, Raleigh, NC & traveling, 89; Lagrange Nat Biennial, Ga, 94; and many others. *Teaching:* Sabbatical replacement printmaking, Tulane Univ, New Orleans, La, 73-74; vis artist printmaking, Tex A&I Univ, Kingsville, 74-75; prof painting & drawing, Auburn Univ, Ala, 77-. *Awards:* Southeastern Ctr Contemp Art/Nat Endowment Arts Grant, 80; Nat Endowment Arts Individual Artists Fel Grant, 81; Special Merit Award, Southeastern Exhib, Spartanburg, SC, 82. *Bibliog:* Mark Price (auth), Jim Furr, Artpapers, 3-4/81; Norman Pendergraft (auth), Southeastern Seven at SECCA, Art Voices, 7-8/81. *Media:* Oil; Charcoal, Oilstick. *Dealer:* Heath Gallery 416 E Paces Ferry Rd Atlanta GA 30305. *Mailing Add:* Auburn Univ Dept Art Auburn AL 36849

FURTH, KAREN J
PHOTOGRAPHER
b New York, NY, 1961. *Study:* Univ Pa, BA (am hist), 83; NY Univ, Int Ctr Photog, MA (photog), 88. *Work:* JP Morgan; Mount Sinai Hosp; also pvt collections of Frank & Mary Ann Arisman, Valle Furth & Dr Yael Danielli. *Exhib:* Solo exhibs, 494 Gallery, 91, 92 & 94 & Pulse Art Gallery, 97; Domestic Landscapes, Sullivan Co Mus, 95; Artwalk NY, Puck Bldg, 95; The Furor of Change, Pulse Art Gallery, 96; Play, Dance Theater Workshop, 98; A Room With a View, Golin/Harris, 98, Face Value, 2002; The Current, AIR Gallery, 2004; Artists Work, The Creative Ctr, 2005. *Collection Arranged:* JP Morgan, Mt Sinai Hosp, Frank and Valle Furth, Dr Yael Daneili; Vantagepoint 13 "Community", ICP at the Point, Bronx, NY, 2005; Still Life: A Documentary Photography Project for Cancer Survivors, The Creative Center, NY, 2006. *Pos:* Biomedical photogr, Rockefeller Univ, 88-89; photogr, Smithsonian Inst, Nat Mus Am Indian, 89-94; freelance photogr, 94-. *Teaching:* Lectr, Int Ctr Photog, 89-90, instr, 98-2005; instr/consult, Ctr Urban Community Serv, Times Sq, 94-2002; fac, New School Univ, Eugene Lang College, 99-2005; instr, The Creative Ctr: Arts for People with Cancer, 2003-. *Awards:* Int Outreach Grant, 93 & 94; Gilbert Graphic Paper Award, 93; Open Soc Inst Individual Proj Fel, Soros Found, 97. *Bibliog:* Greg Emmanuel (auth), This Week Around Town, Photography in Motion, Time Out NY, Vol 43, No 172, 1/7/99-1/14/99; Geoff Carter (auth), The Passenger's Picks for the Week, Squaring the Circle, Circling the Square, 2/17/99. *Mem:* Coll Art Asn; Soc Photog Educ. *Media:* Photography, Video. *Publ:* auth, Still Life: Documenting Cancer Survivorship, Umbrage Editions, 2006; auth, Through the Front Door, The Turtle, Vol 5, No 1, 28-33, winter 1993; plus many others. *Mailing Add:* 17 Dennett Pl Brooklyn NY 11231

FUSCO, LAURIE S
HISTORIAN, EDUCATOR
b Boston, Mass, Oct 31, 1941. *Study:* Wellesley Col, Mass, with John McAndrew & Curtis Shell, BA (art hist), 63; NY Univ Inst Fine Arts, with Colin Eisler, Ludwig Heydenreich, Craig Smyth, Richard Krautheimer & Charles Sterling, MA & PhD (art hist), 77. *Pos:* Sr lectr & head scholarly progs; J P Getty Mus, 78-. *Awards:* Fulbright-Hays Grant, 72-73; Samuel H Kress Res Grant, 74-75; Harvard Fel, Villa I Tatti, 83. *Mem:* Coll Art Asn Am; Art Historians of Southern Calif (secy-treas, 79-80). *Res:* Study of anatomy and movement by fifteenth century Italian artists; New documents for Lorenzo de Medici as a collector of antiquities. *Publ:* Auth, Antonio Pollaiuolo's use of the antique, J Courtauld & Warburg Inst, Vol 42, 257-263; The use of sculptural models by painters in fifteenth century Italy, Art Bulletin, Vol 65, 175-194; An unpublished Fra Filippo Lippi, J Paul Getty Mus J, Vol 10, 1-16; Pollaiuolo's Battle of the Nudes, In: M Natale, Scritti di storia dell'arte in onore di Federico Zeri, Vol 1, 196g, Milan, 84

FUSCO, YOLANDA
PAINTER, PRINTMAKER
b Ben Kovce, Czech, Oct 24, 1922; US citizen. *Study:* Art Students League of New York, 40-45; Pratt Inst, Brooklyn, NY; studied with Ernest Fiene, Vaclao Vytlaci & Harry Sternberg. *Work:* Michael Waldorf Asn, Los Angeles, Calif; Donald Commors Asn, Duxbury, Mass; many private and corp collections. *Comn:* Portrait, comn by Nassau Co, NY, 81; many portraits comn by various individuals. *Exhib:* Group exhibs, Columbia Univ, NY, 65, Heckscher Mus, Huntington, NY, 76, Gallery by the Sea, Port Clyde, Maine, 95, Lupine Gallery, Monhegan, Maine, 96 & Governor's Mansion-Maine Arts Coun, Augusta, 96, Backroads Gallery, Damariscotta, Maine, 2000; Traveling watercolor exhib, Butler Inst of Am Art, Youngstown, Ohio, 82; two-person shows, Hewlett_Woodmere Pub Libr, Long Island, NY, 85, Art League Daytona Beach, Fla, 86; solo exhibs, Daytona Art League Gallery, Daytona Beach, Fla, 92 & Adelphi Univ, NY, 91, Village Art Ctr Gallery, NY; Backroads Gallery, Damaroscola, Maine; Monhegan Modernists from the collection of John M Day, Susquehanna Univ, Lore Degenstein Gallery, Selinsgrove, Pa; and others. *Pos:* Dir, Washington Co Mus. *Teaching:* Pvt art teacher, Adult Ed, 60-87. *Awards:* Sadie & Max Tesser Award, Audubon Artists, Nat Arts Club, NY, 81; R W Rall Award, Daytona Beach, Fla, 90; Award for Oil, Nassau Co Mus Art, 93. *Bibliog:* reviews, Allied Publications, Art News, Herald Tribune, Newsday, Village Voice. *Mem:* Nat Asn Women Artists; NY Artists Equity; Life mem, Art Students League; Monhegan Artists; Art League of Daytona Beach, Fla. *Media:* Watercolor, Oil; Lithography. *Publ:* Prize Winning Watercolors, Allied Publ, 62; NAWA Catalog, 79; Audubon Artists Catalog, 81

FUSS, ADAM
PHOTOGRAPHER
b 1961, London; arrived in NY City 1982. *Work:* Akron Art Mus; Albright-Knox; Cincinnati Art Mus; Denver Art Mus; Los Angeles Co Mus Art; Metrop Mus Art; Mus Mod Art; Nat Gallery of Victoria, Melbourne, Australia; Victoria & Albert Mus; Whitney Mus; corp collections incl, Camera Works, Inc, Chase Manhattan Bank, US Trust co, and more; pvt collections, Mr Paul Walter, New York & Mr Thomas Walther, New York. *Exhib:* Solo exhibs include Massimo Audiello Gallery, NY, 85, 88, 89, 90, Robert Miller Gallery, NY, 90, 92, 93, 95, 2001, 2002, Thomas Soloman's Garage, Los Angeles, 90, 92, Fraenkel Gallery, San Francisco, 92, 94, 98, 2002, Akron Mus Art, 92, Nat Gallery Victoria, Australia, 92, Laura Carpenter, Santa Fe, NMex, 94, Charlotte Lund, Stockholm Sweden, 94, 97, 2000, Rhonda Hoffman Gallery, Chicago, 96, Fay Gold Gallery, Atlanta, Ga, 98, Cheim and Read, NY, 99, 2003, Galerie Karsten Greve, Milan, 2000, 2001, Galeria Leyendecker, Santa Cruz de Tenerife, 2002, Baldwin Gallery, Aspen, 2005, Timothy Taylor Gallery, London, 2005, Modern Art Mus of Fort Worth, Tex, 2006, Xavier Hufkens, Brussels, 2008; group exhibs include Atkins Mus Art, Kansas City, Mo, 2001; Some Options in Abstraction, Carpenter Ctr Visual Arts, 2001; Uncommon Threads, Herbert F Johnson Mus Art, Cornell Univ, Ithaca, NY, 2001; Affecting Invention: The Manipulated Photograph, Carrie Secrist Gallery, Chicago, 2001; The Crafted Image: Nineteenth-Century Techniques in Contemp Photography, Boston Univ Art Gallery, 2001; White Light, University Galleries, Ill State Univ, 2001; Air, James Cohan Art Gallery, NY, 2002, A Simple Plan, 2002; Fiat Lux, Robert Klein Gallery, Boston, 2002; The Antiquarian Avant-garde, Sarah Morthland, Gallery, NY, 2002; Intricacy, ICA, Philadelphia, Pa, 2003; In Your Face, Alan Koppel Gallery, 2003; Birdspace: A Post-Audubon Artist's Aviary, Contemp Art Ctr, New Orleans, 2004; Baldwin Gallery, Aspen, 2004; Fay Gold Gallery, Atlanta, 2004; Corcoran Biennial, Corcoran Gallery, Washington, DC, 2005; Richard Levy Gallery, Albuquerque, NMex, 2005; In Focus, NC Mus Art, Raleigh, NC, 2005; Alchemy, The Terrace Gallery, Leeds, England, 2006; Empty Nest: The Changing Face of Childhood in Art, 1880 to the Present, Natheran A Bernstein & co, Ltd, New York, 2007; Pretty Baby, The Mod Mus Forth Worth, 2007; Depth of Field: Mod Photog at the Metrop, Metrop Mus Art, New York, 2008; The Sume of its Parts, Cheim & Read, New York, 2008. *Awards:* ICP Infinity Award for Art, 2000. *Dealer:* Timothy Taylor Gallery 21 Dering St London W1S 1TT; Xavier Hufkens Sint Jorisstraat 6-8 Rue Saint-Georges Brussels 1050 Bruxelles; Fraenkel Gallery 49 Geary St San Francisco CA 94108. *Mailing Add:* c/o Cheim & Read Gallery 547 W 25th St New York NY 10001

FUTTER, ELLEN V
MUSEUM DIRECTOR
Study: Barnard Coll, NYC, AB, 71; Columbia Law Sch, NYC, 74. *Hon Degrees:* Hamilton Coll, LLD, 85, NY Law Sch, LLD., Hofstra Univ, DHL, 94., CCNY, DHL, 96., LI City Coll, DHL, 95., Yale Univ, DHL, 2000. *Pos:* Assoc. Milbank, Tweed, Hadley & McCloy, NYC, 1974-80; acting pres. Barnard Coll., 1980-81, pres., 1981-93, American Mus. Natural History, NYC, 1993-. Bd. dirs. Fed. Res. Bank NY, 1988-93, chair, 1992-93; bd. dirs. Consol. Edison NY, 1997-, J.P. Morgan Chase & Co., 1997-, Bristol-Myers Squibb Co., 1999-2005, Am. Internat. Group (AIG), 1999-2008, Viacom, 2006-07. *Awards:* Alexander Hamilton award, Manhattan Inst. Policy Rsch., 2002, Woman of Achievement award, Women in Devel. NY, 2006, Lawrence A. Wien prize for Social Responsibility, Columbia Law Sch., 2008, Mark Schubart award in Edn., Lincoln Ctr. Inst. Arts in Edn., 2008; named one of The 100 Most Influential Women in NYC Bus., Crain's NY Bus., 2007, The 50 Most Powerful Women in NY, 2009, 2011. *Mem:* Am Acad Arts & Sciences (fellow); ABA; Nat Inst Social Sci; Asn Bar City NY; NY State Bar Asn; Econ Club NY; Century Club; Cosmopolitan Club; Phi Beta Kappa. *Mailing Add:* Am Mus Nat Hist Central Park W at 79th St New York NY 10024

FYFE, JO SUZANNE (STORCH)
INSTRUCTOR, PAINTER
b Omak, Wash, May 8, 1941. *Study:* Wash State Univ, BA (fine arts), 64, MFA, 68; Whitworth Col, Spokane, Wash & Eastern Wash State Univ, Cheney, grad studies. *Work:* Mt Vernon Sch Dist, Wash; Oak Harbor Sch Dist, Wash; Cashmere High Sch, Wash; Wash State Univ, Pullman; 27 works, Wash State Arts Comn. *Comn:* Triptych-painting/mixed-media, Wash State Arts Comn, Cashmere, 84; sculpture, Spokane Art Comn, Spokane Fire House, 92. *Exhib:* Women in Art, Eastern Wash State Univ Art Gallery, Cheney, Wash, 81; Juried Show, Carnegie Art Ctr, Walla Walla, Wash, 83; Works on Paper, The Art Gallery, Longview, Wash, 86; Works of Heart, Cheney Cowles Mus, Spokane, Wash, 86-2003; Western Art Show, Ellensburg & Spokane, Wash, 86-88; Works on Paper, Evergreen State Col, 87-89; Past Presence, A Circle of Women's Vision, Corvallis, Ore, 87; Art on the Green, Coeur D'Alene, Ind, 90; Art Walk, Sand Point, Ind, 90; Jumping the Fence, Spokane Art Sch, Wash, 92, Play, 2000; 25th Anniversary, Gallery One, Ellensburg, Wash, 95; Interpretations: A Celebration of Native Am Heritage Month, Lewis-Clark Ctr, Lewiston, Idaho, 98; Earth Day Exhib, Chase Gallery, Spokane, 2000, 2003; Two in-Two Out, Spokane Community Col, 2002; First Night, 2007. *Pos:* acad advisor, Spokane Falls, 2007-. *Teaching:* Part-time instr design, Wash State Univ Exten, Spokane, 64-72; instr art, design, & sculpture, Spokane Falls Community Col, 65-2002, chmn dept, 75-84, 88-; retired, 2002. *Awards:* 1st Prize, acrylic, Clarkson Valley Ann, Lewis & Clark Art Asn, 81; Painting Award, Art on the Green, 90-94; Community Purchase Award, Art on the

Green, 94, 2000, 2002; Art on the Green, Coeur d'Alene Awards, 2005-2007. *Bibliog:* Dodie Murphy Wagner (auth), Painting and sculpture said good combination, Pullman Herald, 83; other newspaper articles; Julianne Crane (auth), Spokesman Review, Spokane, WA. *Mem:* Artists Trust. *Media:* Acrylic, Miscellaneous Media. *Interests:* Making art, gardening. *Dealer:* Cheney Cowles Mus W2316 First Ave Spokane WA 99204; Northwest Mus Arts & Culture Spokane WA. *Mailing Add:* S 8017 Ramona Rd Spokane WA 99224-9617

FYFE, JOE
PAINTER
b New York, New York, 1952. *Study:* Univ Arts, Philadelphia, BFA, 1976. *Exhib:* Solo exhibs include Barbara Toll Fine Arts, New York, 1983, Morehead State Univ, Ky, 1997, Nicholas Davies Gallery, New York, 1998, Jay Grimm Gallery, New York, 2002, Mai Gallery, Ho Chi Minh City, Vietnam, 2004, JG Contemp/James Graham & Sons, 2005, Galerie Pitch, Paris, 2005, Ryllega Galley, Hanoi, Vietnam, 2006; group exhibs include Painting III, N-3 Proj Space, Brooklyn, 1999; Uptown/Downtown, JG Contemp, James Graham & Sons, New York, 2003; Grisaille, James Graham & Sons, New York, 2003; Summer, Bruno Marina Gallery, Brooklyn, 2004; Field Questions, Rosenwald-Wold Gallery, Univ Arts, Philadelphia, 2005; Carton Rouge, Atelier Tampon-Ramier, Paris, 2006; Intersections, Meyers Sch Art, Univ Akron, Ohio, 2006; Paint/Not Paint, Paul Sharpe Contemp Art, NY, 2006. *Awards:* John Simon Guggenheim Mem Found Fel, 2008. *Dealer:* James Graham & Sons 1014 Madison Ave New York NY 10021; JG Contemporary 32 E 67th St New York, NY 10065. *Mailing Add:* 342 Flushing Ave Brooklyn NY 11205

G

GABELER, JO
PAINTER
b Baton Rouge, La, Feb 14, 1931. *Study:* Stephens Col, with John Pike, Ray Ellis, Fred Messersmith, Dong Kingman, Tony van Hasselt, Tom Hill, Millard Wells, Miles Batt, Al Brouillette, Christopher Schink, Judi Betts, Jeanne Dobie, Edward Betts, Charles Reid & Stephen Quiler. *Work:* Elliott Mus, Stuart, Fla; Moody Found & Rosenberg Libr, Galveston, Tex; Transco Energy Co, Houston; Allied Bank of Seabrook, Tex. *Comn:* Nine Watercolors, Lily Pulitzer, Palm Beach, Fla, 65; Commemorative plaque, Corps Diplomatic, Vientiane, Laos, 68; Christmas cards, Am Women's Club, Vientiane, Laos, 68-71; Lao Silk Pavilion, Mme Tao Peng Sananakone, Vientiane, Laos, 70; watercolor, City of Galveston, 82, presented to City of Nigata, Japan. *Exhib:* Group exhibs, Fla Watercolor Soc, Mus Arts & Sci, Daytona, 78, Brevard Art Ctr & Mus, Melbourne, 81, State Capitol, Tallahassee, 82 & Boca Raton Mus Art, 84; Watercolor Art Soc, Houston Pub Libr, 81; Galveston Art League, Rosenberg Libr, 83; Prof Artists Guild, Boca Raton Mus Art, 84-86; Solo exhibs, Elliott Mus, Stuart, Fla, 86 & Scarborough House, Savannah, Ga, 88; John Tucker Fine Arts, 2000; 2-person exhibs, Al Stine Gallery, Anderson, SC, 2002. *Teaching:* Instr, Landings Art Asn, 93, 95, 97, 98, Savannah Art Asn, 2000, 03 & 04. *Awards:* Pres Award, Fla Watercolor Soc, 81 & 82; Purchase Award, Galveston Art League, 82; Merit Award, Watercolor Art Soc Houston, 82 & Fla Watercolor Soc, 86. *Bibliog:* Eileen B Flaum (auth), Watercolorist-Jo Gabeler, Focus, 3/86. *Mem:* Salmagundi Club, NY; Signature mem Fla Watercolor Soc; Galveston Art League (pres, 81-82); Landings Art Asn Savannah, Ga (pres 90). *Media:* Watercolor. *Interests:* Ceramics, needle point design. *Publ:* Illusr, The Galley Collection, 97; illusr (with others), The Golf Courses of the Landings, 93. *Dealer:* Gallery 209 209 River St Savannah Ga; Savannah and the Dolphin and the Mermaid thunderbolt Ga. *Mailing Add:* 11 Mainsail Crossing Savannah GA 31411-2723

GABIN, GEORGE JOSEPH
PAINTER, INSTRUCTOR
b Brooklyn, NY, Apr 16, 1931. *Study:* Brooklyn Mus Art Sch; Art Students League, with Reginald Marsh, Ivan Olinsky & Will Barnett. *Hon Degrees:* Montserrat Coll Fine Art, DFA. *Work:* Bank Boston, Boston Pub Libr, Mass; Tenn Botanical Garden & Fine Arts Ctr, Cheekwood; Grunwald Ctr Graphic Arts, Los Angeles, Calif; Jane Voorhees Zimmerli Art Mus, New Brunswick, NJ; Brush Art Gallery, Canton, NY; and others; Deloitte-Touche, Boston, Mass; Samuel P Horn Mus, Gainesville, Fla; John D Merriam Collection, Boston Pub Libr; Rockport Pub Libr, Mass; Peter & Virginia Benin, Wilton, Conn, Robert & Graziella Singer, Milan, Italy. *Exhib:* solo exhibs, Carl Seimbab Gallery, 63 & 67, Guild Boston Artists, 72, Doll & Richards Gallery, 75, Montserrat Coll Art, 83, Edna Stebbins Gallery, Cambridge, Mass, 86, Pingree Sch, Hamilton, Mass, 90 & Chase Gallery (with catalog), Boston, Mass, 91, 94, 2001, 2004, 2008 (with catalog), Sherry French Gallery (with catalog), NY, 03, Chase Gallery(with catalog), Boston, Mass, 2008, Chase Young Gallery ; Nat Acad Design, Allied Artists Am & Audubon Artists, 60-91; Am Fedn Arts Nat Traveling Show, 64-65; Albright Mus, Buffalo, NY, 66; Montserrat Coll Art, Beverly, Mass, 90, 98; retrospective, 35 Yrs (with catalog), Chase Gallery, Boston, Mass, 94; Parallel Lives, Two Person Show, Montserrat Coll of Art, 98; Chase Galleries, Boston, MA, 98, 2001, 2004, 2008; Retrospective 1958-2008, Museo di San Francesco, Greve in Chianti, Italy, 2008; Ovo Sapiens, Palazzo del Fiorino, Greve in Chianti, Italy, 2009, 2010. *Collection Arranged:* Bank of Am, Boston, Mass; Davidson col, Davidson, NC; Eckard col, St Petersburg, Fla; Gruenwald Ctr Graphic Arts, UCLA Los Angeles, Calif; Honolulu Acad Art, Honolulu, HI. *Teaching:* Instr illus & drawing, New Eng Sch Art, Boston, 63-70; instr drawing & painting, Montserrat Col Art, 70-, prof, chmn, dept painting & drawing, founding fac; landscape painting, La Scoula del Vedere, Trieste, Italy, 89-95; prof emer, Montserrat Col of Fine Art. *Awards:* Grumbacher Gold Award, Holyoke Art Coun, 81; Stow Wengenroth Award, Rockport Art Asn, 82; Ralph Fabri Medal Merit, Allied Artist Am, 83; and others. *Mem:* Allied Artists Am; Guild Boston Artists; Brickbottom Artist Asn. *Media:* Oil, Pastel, Lithography. *Publ:* Auth, The World & I, monograph, Imaginary Idyll, 7/97; auth essay, Report From Boston, Art in America, 6/99. *Dealer:* Chase Young Gallery 450 Harrison Ave #57 Boston MA 02118. *Mailing Add:* Studio B554 One Fitchburg St Somerville MA 02143

GABLE, JOHN OGLESBY
PAINTER, MURALIST
b Frankfort, Ky, Mar 7, 1944. *Study:* Univ Ky; Art Ctr Coll Design, BS (indust design), 66. *Work:* Oxford Univ; Union Mutual; Charles S Payson collection; Smithsonian Inst, Peabody Mus; Bank New Eng; Princeton Univ. *Comn:* Watercolors, comn by Alan Bond, Australia, 83, Boston Classical Orch, 83, Dennis Conner, 87, Oxford Univ, 89, Philip Morris, USA, 94; Portraits: Smithsonian Inst, Washington, DC; Kennedy Family, Boston, 99; Murals: Clydes, Washington, DC, 94; Automotive Hall of Fame, Greenfield Village, Dearborn, 97, Audi Corp, Ger, 99; Volkswagen Corp, Ger, 2000; MBNA, 2001; Paintings: Clydes, Washington, DC, 2005; Series of Historical Murals, Willard Internat Hotal, Wash DC; Mural of Samuel Clemens & Alice Roosevelt Longworth. *Exhib:* 46th Nat Ann, Butler Inst Am Art, 82; 161st Ann Exhib, Nat Acad Design, New York, 86 & 88; Coe Kerr Gallery, New York, 82; Payson-Weisberg Gallery, New York, 83 & Barridoff Galleries, Portland, Maine; Portland Mus Art, Maine; Forum Gallery, New York, 86; Guild of Boston Artists, 93. *Awards:* Wurdemann Prize, Nat Watercolor Soc; William A Paton Prize, Nat Acad Design, New York; Artist Mag Award, Am Watercolor Soc. *Bibliog:* Alexander Bridge (auth), Am Artist, 83; Philip Isaacson (auth), Maine Sunday Telegram, 83; Martha Thomas (auth), Archit Digest, 07/2005. *Media:* Watercolor, Oil, Acrylic. *Specialty:* Contemp Realism. *Interests:* The Human Condition. *Dealer:* Guild of Boston Artists 162 Newbury St Boston MA 02116; Midtown Payson Gallery 11870 SE Dixie Hwy Hobe Sound FL 33455

GABLIK, SUZI
PAINTER, WRITER
b New York, NY, Sept 26, 1934. *Study:* Black Mountain Coll, NC, summer 51; Hunter Coll, BA, 55, with Robert Motherwell. *Work:* Archive of professional and personal papers placed in the archives of American Art, Smithsonian Inst, Wash DC. *Exhib:* Solo exhibs, Alan Gallery, NY, 63 & 66, Landau-Alan Gallery, NY, 67, Henri Gallery, Washington, DC, 71, Terry Dintenfass, 72 & 78 & Hester Van Royen Gallery, London, 78; Photog Image, Guggenheim Mus, NY, 66; Young & Fantastic, Inst Contemp Arts, London, 69; After Surrealism: Metaphor & Simile, Ringling Mus Art, Sarasota, Fla, 72; Women Choose Women, NY Cult Art Cts, 73; Menagerie, Mus Mod Art Lending Serv, 75. *Pos:* Vis artist & lectr, Univ Colo, Syracuse Univ, Yale Univ, Univ Wis, Boston Coll, San Francisco Art Inst, Oberlin Coll, Bard Coll & Md Inst Art, 74-75. *Teaching:* Vis prof fine arts, Univ South, Sewanee, Tenn, fall, 82 & 84, Univ Calif, Santa Barbara, spring, 85, 86 & 88 & Va Tech, Blacksburg, fall, 89 & spring, 90. *Awards:* Lifetime Achievement Award, Women's Caucus for Art, 2003. *Bibliog:* London Correspondent, article in Art in Am. *Mem:* Coll Art Asn. *Media:* Miscellaneous Media. *Publ:* Coauth, Pop Art Redefined, 69 & auth, Magritte, 70, New York Graphic Soc; auth, Progress in Art, Rizzoli, 77; Has Modernism Failed?, 84, The Reenchantment of Art, 91 & Conversations Before the End of Time, 95, Thames & Hudson; Living the Magical Life: An Oracular Adventure, Phanes, 2002. *Mailing Add:* 1191 Oakland Sq Blacksburg VA 24060

GABRIEL, JEANETTE HANISEE
CURATOR, HISTORIAN, CONSULTANT
b Long Beach, Calif, 1940. *Study:* Calif State Univ, BS, 76, MS, 78; Univ Calif - Santa Barbara, MA, 88. *Work:* Los Angeles Co Mus Art, Calif; Gilbert Collection (auth catalog), Los Angeles, Calif & London, Eng. *Pos:* Cur, LACMA, 89-92; cur, Gilbert Collection Mus, Los Angeles, 94-2000; hon cur, Somerset House, London, 2001-. *Mem:* Reform Club, London; Churchill Ctr. *Interests:* Mystery writing. *Publ:* Coauth, Mosaic tables in the Gilbert collection, 11/89 & Mosaic mementoes, 5/93, Antique Collector Mag, By judgement of the eye: The Varya and Hans Cohn collection, Los Angeles County Mus Art, 91, The World of Jade, Marg Publs, 92, Silver, gold boxes and decorative objects in the Gilbert collection, Apollo, 1/97 & The Winston Churchill portraits of Alfred Egerton Cooper, Finest Hour: The J of Int Churchill Soc, 97, Gilbert Collection, Micromosaics and Hard Stones, 2000, The Open Portrait Winston Churchill, Spring, 2003, No 118, Summer, 2003, No 119. *Mailing Add:* 3150 31 St San Diego CA 92104

GADDIS, EUGENE RICHARD
CURATOR, HISTORIAN
b Oakland, Calif. Oct 16, 1947. *Study:* Amherst Coll, AB (cum laude), 69; Univ Penn, MA (hist), 71, PhD (hist), 79. *Exhib:* Avery Memorial: The First Mod Mus, Wadsworth Atheneum, 84.; The Spirit of Genius: Art at the Wadsworth Atheneum, 92.; Sarah Goodwin Austin Mem Exhib, Allusions & Intuitions, Jeffrey Walker (co cur), Widener Gallery, Austin Arts Ctr, Trinity Coll, 94.; The Austin House, A Nat Hist Landmark, Wadsworth Atheneum, 94.; Magic Façade, The Austin House, Wadsworth Atheneum Mus Art, 2007-2008. *Pos:* Res historian, Conn State Libr, 77; asst ed, The Papers of Jonathan Trumbull Sr, 77-81; cur, Austin House, Wadsworth Atheneum, 86-; archivist, Wadsworth Atheneum, 81-. *Teaching:* Adj prof hist, Hartford Coll Women, 78-79, Univ Conn, 80-81; Vis fac, Trinity Coll, 2009, Univ Harford, 2011. *Awards:* Fel, Forris Jewett Moore Scholar in History, Amherst Coll, 69-70; Fel, Univ Penn Teaching Fel in Hist, 72-73; Fel, Luce Found Scholar Am Art, Wadsworth Atheneum, 85-86; Conn Bloomer Award, 2001; Hartford Preservation Alliance Award, 2008; Betty M Linsley Award, Magic Façade, The Austin House: Wadsworth Atheneum Mus Art, 2008; Hartford Preservation Alliance Award, Magic Façade, The Austin House: Wadsworth Atheneum Mus Art, 2008. *Bibliog:* Judith A Barter (auth), Drawings & Watercolors at the Wadsworth Atheneum: Reflections, Drawings & Watercolors from the Wadsworth Atheneum, Hudson Hills Press, 87; Linda Ayres (ed), Foremost Upon this Continent: A History of the Wadsworth Atheneum, Spirit of Genius: Art at the Wadsworth Atheneum, Hudson Hills, Press, New York, 92; Nancy Reynolds (ed), Lincoln Kirstein: Meeting the Master, Remembering Lincoln, Ballet Soc Inc, New York, 2007. *Publ:* Avery Memorial: The First Modern Museum, Hartford: Wadsworth Atheneum, 84; Foremost Upon This Continent: The Founding of the Wadsworth Atheneum, Conn Hist, Nov 85; The Austin Papers at the Wadsworth Atheneum, Hartford, Mus Archivist, Dec 87; All That Mighty Heart: William George DeLana, Hartford, Alice M DeLana, 89; The Wadsworth Atheneum: A Brief History, Goya to

Matisse: Paintings, Sculpture & Drawings from the Wadsworth Atheneum of Hartford, Conn, 91; Magician of the Modern: Chick Austin & the Transformation of the Arts in America, Alfred A Knopf, New York, 2000; Eric Zafran (auth) & Susan Hood (contribr), Dance at the Wadsworth Atheneum, Hartford, Conn, 2004; ed & principal auth, Magic Façade, The Austin House: Wadsworth Atheneum Mus Art, Hartford, Conn, 2007. *Mailing Add:* Wadsworth Atheneum 600 Main St Hartford CT 06103

GAGAN, JAMIE L.
PAINTER, PRINTMAKER
b Portland Me, July 21, 1954. *Study:* Univ Vt, BS, 76, MD, 82; Coll Santa Fe, Printmaking, Santa Reparata Sch, Florence, Italy, with Ron Porrasso & Dan Weldon. *Work:* City of Cape Elizabeth, Me; St Vincent Hospital (now Christus St Vincent Regional Medical Ctr), Santa Fe, NMex; La Famiglia Medical Ctr. *Comn:* landscape mural (6x9), Mr & Mrs Robert Hayden, Flower Mound, TX, 2005. *Exhib:* Western Federation of Watercolor, Sun Cities Art Mus, Ariz, 1996, Mus Tex Tech, Lubbock, Tex, 1998; Night Walker, Fort Collins Mus, Colo, 1998; Salsa Spirits & Souls, Georgia O'Keefe Mus, Santa Fe, NMex, 2000; War and Peace, Manitou Gallery, Santa Fe, NMex, 2003; Florence Internat Bienalle, Fortezza da Basso, Florence, Italy, 2003; Internat Biennal Artists, Luminate Gallery, Dallas, Tex, 2011, LMNT Gallery, Miami, Fla, 2012. *Awards:* Excellence in Watercolor, Artist Postcards, Dear Gallery, Taos, NMex, 1990; Artisans award, NMex Watercolor Soc, 1999. *Bibliog:* Hollis Walker (auth), ER Doc Finds Prints A Chance to Cut Loose, Santa Fe, NMex, 1998; Dottie Indyke (auth), Wowing the World, Albuquerque Jour, 2003; Jon Carver (auth) Voices Against the War, The Mag, 2008. *Mem:* NMex Watercolor Soc (signature mem); Internat Biennale Artists; Creative Santa Fe. *Media:* Mixed Media, Monotype, Solar Etching, Watercolor. *Dealer:* Luminarte Gallery 1727 E Levee St Dallas TX 75207. *Mailing Add:* PO Box 803 Tesuque NM 87574

GAGE, BEAU
SCULPTOR, PHOTOGRAPHER
b Rye, NY, Dec 3, 1945. *Study:* St John's Col, BA, 71; Art Students League, 84-87; Pacifica Grad Inst, Carpinteria Calif, Doctorate Candidate, 2009-2011. *Work:* Jacksonville Mus Sci & Hist, Fla; Interbank of NY. *Comn:* sculpture, Jacksonville Jaguars Inc, Fla, 96. *Exhib:* A Valentine For Martha Graham, Sotheby's, NY, 90. *Mem:* Orgn Independent Artists, NY; Internat Sculpture Ctr, NY; Internat Ctr Photog, NY; Poets House, NY; Fel Mus Mod Art, NY. *Media:* Bronze; Iris Prints. *Mailing Add:* PO Box 1559 Shelter Island NY 11964

GAGOSIAN, LARRY GILBERT
ART DEALER
b Los Angeles, April 19, 1945. *Pos:* Founder, owner, Gagosian Gallery, New York, Beverly Hills, London, Rome & Hong Kong; represents Andy Warhol estate; co-founder (with Peter M Brant), Contemp Art Holding Corp, Tex, 1990, pres & dir, 1990-. *Awards:* World's Greatest Art Businessman, Art Rev, 2004; Named one of Contemporary Art's 100 Most Powerful Figures, ArtReview mag, 2009. *Mailing Add:* Gagosian Gallery Inc 980 Madison Ave New York NY 10021

GAIBER, MAXINE OLIANSKY
MUSEUM DIRECTOR
b Brooklyn, May 6, 1949. *Study:* Brooklyn Coll, BA, 70; Univ Minn, MA, 72. *Pos:* Tours & curriculum serv dir, Minneapolis Inst Arts, 72-77, assoc chair educ, 77-79; consult mus educ, Field Mus, Art Inst Chicago, 79-82; prog coodr, Field Mus Natural Hist, 82-83; publ dir, Art Ctr Coll Design, Pasadena, Calif, 83-85, res dir, 85-86, campaign dir, 86-88; pub relations officer, Newport Harbor Art Mus, Newport Beach, Calif, 88-94, dir educ & publs, 94-96; dir, educ, Orange County Mus Art, 96-2000; dir educ & pub progs, San Diego Mus Art, 2000-2006; exec dir, Del Ctr Contemp Arts, Wilmington, 2006-. *Teaching:* Instr, LA County Mus Art, 85, Art Ctr Coll Design, Pasadena, 86-89, Coll DuPage, Ill, 81-83. *Mem:* Am Assn Mus (educ comn rep, 1979-1983); Art Table; Del Arts Alliance (bd pres, 2011-2013, exec com 2014-); Trustees of Color (bd mem); Forum for Exec Women (bd mem). *Mailing Add:* Delaware Center for the Contemporary Arts 200 S Madison St Wilmington DE 19801

GAINES, ALAN JAY
PRINTMAKER
b New York, NY, Aug 23, 1942. *Study:* NY Univ, BS, 65; New Sch, Parsons Sch Design, with John Ross, 72-74. *Work:* South Street Seaport Mus, Mus Gallery, NY; and others. *Comn:* Historic American Ship, Franklin Mint, Pa, 75; Nantucket Whalers & New Bedford Whalers, 77 & Develop of Am Transportation, 78, Collector's Guild, NY; Gloucester Schooners (etching), Bk of Month Club & 260 Club, 77; marine etchings, 77 & two railroad etchings, 78, Graphics Guild, Div of Doubleday, NY; spec series five important & hist Am ships, Am Express, 78; America's Maritime Heritage (four etchings), Franklin Mint, Pa, 81; and others. *Exhib:* Solo exhibs, South Street Seaport Mus, 74, Oestreicher Gallery, NY, 74, Wiseman Gallery, Newport, RI, 76, Redwood Libr & Atheneum, Newport, RI, 79 & Providence Pub Libr, RI, 81. *Bibliog:* Joseph Patrick Henry (auth), Artist of the sea, The Franklin Mint Almanac, 7/75; article, RI Mag, 9/80. *Media:* Mixed. *Mailing Add:* 40 Franklin St Newport RI 02840

GAINES, CHARLES
EDUCATOR, CONCEPTUAL ARTIST
b Charleston, SC. *Study:* Jersey City State Col, NJ, BA, 1966; Rochester Inst Technol, MFA, 1967. *Work:* Mus Mod Art, New York; Whitney Mus Am Art; Mus Contemp Art, Chicago; Los Angeles County Mus Art; Mus Contemp Art, Los Angeles; Oakland Mus; Santa Fe Mus Contemp Art; Städtishche Galerie im Lenbachhaus, Munich; Galerie der Stadt Esslingen; Villa Merkel, Esslingen. *Exhib:* Solo exhibs, State Univ NY, Oswego, 1969, Louisville Sch Art, Ky, 1971, Univ Southern Calif, 1972, 1975, Cinnque Gallery, New York, 1972, Daniel Weinberg Gallery, San Francisco, 1978, 1980, Fresno Art Ctr, Calif, 1978, Young Hoffman Gallery, Chicago, 1979, Thomas Segal Gallery, Boston, 1980, Margo Leavin Gallery, Los Angeles, 1980, Leo Castelli Gallery, New York, 1980, 1981, 1985, 1987, 1991, John Weber Gallery, New York, 1980, 1981, 1987, 1989, 1991, 1996, 2000, Los Angeles Inst Contemp Art, 1984, Brigitte March Gallery, Ger, 1988, 1997, 2006, Gallery Lavignes-Bastille, Paris, 1988, 1991, Dorothy Goldeen Gallery, Santa Monica, Calif, 1989, 1990, Fresno Art Mus, 1993, Santa Monica Mus, Calif, 1995, Phoebe Conley Art Gallery, Calif State Univ, Fresno, 1996, 2003, Richard Heller Gallery, Santa Monica, Calif, 1997, 2000, City Univ New York, 2000, San Francisco Art Inst, 2001, Luckman Fine Art Gallery, Calif State Univ, Los Angeles, 2002, Triple Candie, New York, 2004, Steve Wolf Gallery, San Francisco, 2005, Lentos Kunstmuseum, Mus Contemp Art, Linz, Austria, 2006, Kapinos Galery, Berlin, 2006, REDCAT Gallery, Los Angeles, 2006, Susanne Vielmetter Los Angeles Projects, 2006; group exhibs include Oakland Mus, Calif, 1973 & 1975; Black Artists Recent Attitudes, Calif State Univ, Fresno, 1974; Golden West Coll, Los Angeles, 1976 & 1977; Numerals: Mathematical Concepts in Contemp Art, traveling, 1978; Works on Paper, Margo Leavin Gallery, Los Angeles, 1978; John Weber Invitational, John Weber Gallery, New York, 1978, Gallery Artists Show, 1979, Paper Work, 1994 & A Selective Survey of Political Art, 2000; Santa Barbara Mus Art, Calif, 1980; Numero Quattro, Basel Art Fair, Switz, 1984; Process & Construction, Brigitte March Gallery, Stuttgart, Ger, 1985, Landscape-Cityscape, 1999, What About Hegel, 2002, The Night of the Hunter, 2003 & Hommage to Friedrich Schiller, 2005; Work from the Collection of Sol LeWitt, traveling, 1985-86; Cologne Art Fair, Ger, 1988 & 1994; The Grid, Ben Shahn Galleries, William Patterson Col, NJ, 1990; No Justice, No Peace, Calif Afro-Am Mus, Los Angeles, 1992 & Urban Aesthetics 2003, 2003; LA Next, Contemp Art Ctr, New Orleans, 1993; Earthworks & Landscapes, Fuel Gallery, Seattle, 1994; Nat Mus Art, Die Magie Der Zahl, Stuttgart, Ger, 1997; More than Meets the Eye: Triennale Photog, Deichtorhallen, Hamburg, Ger, 1999; Pictures of Other People's Bodies, Richard Heller Gallery, Los Angeles, 1999; Deep Distance, Kunsthalle Basel, 2000; Fade (1990-present): African Am Artists in Los Angeles, traveling, 2004; Kamm Gallery Anniversary Exhib, Galerie Kamm, Berlin, 2005; Greenhouse, LAX Art, Los Angeles, 2007; Am Acad Arts and Letts Invitational, New York, 2009. *Teaching:* Mem faculty, Calif Inst Arts, Sch Art, Valencia, Calif, 1989-. *Awards:* Nat Endowment Arts Grant, 1977; Adaline Kent Award, San Francisco Art Inst, 2001; Calif Inst Arts Dean's Grant, 2004; Durfee Found Grant, 2004; Purchase Prize, Am Acad Arts and Letts, 2009. *Dealer:* Susanne Vielmetter Los Angeles Projects 5795 W Washington Blvd Culver City CA 90232; Steven Wolf Fine Arts 49 Geary St Ste 411 San Francisco CA 94108. *Mailing Add:* Calif Inst Arts 24700 McBean Pkwy Valencia CA 91355

GAINES, MALIK
CURATOR, WRITER, PERFORMER
Study: Univ Calif Los Angeles, BA (hist). *Exhib:* Read Me! Text in Art, Armory Ctr for Arts, 2007; Talks About Acts, LAXART, 2007; We Want a New Object: CalArts MFA Graduate Exhibition, TELIC Arts Exchange, peres projects, Mihai Nicodim Gallery, Black Dragon Soc, acuna-hansen gallery& David Salow Gallery, 2008; Surface Sounding - Ten Curators - Ten Artists, See Line Gallery, 2008; We Want a New Object, Chinatown Galleries, Los Angeles, 2008; Dance witches Dance, Luckman Fine ARts Complex, 2009; The Night Episode, Participant Inc, 2009. *Collection Arranged:* African American Artists in Los Angeles (1990-2003); Follow Me: A Fantasy, Arena 1 Gallery, Santa Monica. *Pos:* Performer, My Barbarian. *Teaching:* Teacher, Univ Calif, Irvine & San Francisco Art Inst. *Awards:* Penny McCall Found Award, 2003; Fel, Mark Taper Forum, 2003; Art Matters Found Grant, 2008. *Mailing Add:* Calif Inst Arts 24700 McBean Pkwy Santa Clarita CA 91355-2340

GAITHER, EDMUND B
MUSEUM DIRECTOR, HISTORIAN
b Great Falls, SC, Oct 6, 1944. *Study:* Morehouse Col, BA, 66; Ga State Col; grad study, art history, 66-68, Northeastern Univ, 84, Framingham State Col, 93, RI Col, 94. *Collection Arranged:* Afro-Am Artists: NY & Boston (with catalogue), Jamaica Art Since the Thirties, Henry O Tanner, A Romantic Realist, Home Folks Africa, For Us, Abdias Do Nascimento: A Brazilian Brother, African Gods in Brazil, Our Elders, Crite & Dames, Ah Haiti, Glimpses of Voudou, Haiti-Haiti, Bannister & Duncanson, Twentieth Century Afro-Am Artists, Mus Fine Arts, Boston; Richard Yarde: Watercolors, 93; Blues Paintings of George Hunt, 93; traveling exhib, Treasures of the MNCAAA, 93; Struggles Against Racism, 94; Rashid Diab: A Retrospective, 94; A Selection of Paintings & Drawings by Afro-Am Artists, 94; Holy War in the Sudan/Relics of Mahdist Era, 94; Aspelta: A Nubian King's Burial Chamber, 94; Carlos Byron: Renaissance Artist, 95. *Pos:* Dir & cur, Mus Nat Ctr Afro-Am Artists, Boston, 69-; dir visual arts prog, Elma Lewis Sch Fine Arts, Boston, 69-; spec consult, Mus Fine Arts, Boston, 69-; curric consult, Urban Gateways, Ctr Arts Educ, 90 & Miami Pub Schs, 88. *Teaching:* Asst prof art hist, Boston Univ, 70-78; lectr art hist, Wellesley Col & Harvard Col, 71-76. *Bibliog:* An American Collector, Mus Art, RI Sch Design, Providence, 68; Robert H Glauber (auth), Black American Artists, Ill Bell Tel Co, 71; Leo Twiggs (auth), Opinion, Mus News, 5/72. *Mem:* Nat Conf Artists; Coll Art Asn; Pan-African Conf Artists; Boston Black Artists Asn. *Res:* Historical and critical discussion of Afro-American art. *Publ:* Ed, Affairs of Black Artists, 71; contribr, Artists Proofs, The Annual of Prints and Printmaking, NY Graphic Soc, 72; Afro-American Art, in: Negro Reference Book, Phelps-Stokes Found, New York, NY, 73; auth, Afro American Art in: Dialogue, John Wilson/Joseph Norman (article), Mus Fine Arts, 95; and numerous others. *Mailing Add:* c/o Mus Nat Ctr Afro Am Artist 300 Walnut Ave Boston MA 02119

GALASSI, SUSAN GRACE
CURATOR, EDUCATOR
Study: Finch Coll, BA; Wellesley Coll, MA; NYU Inst Fine Arts, Phd (art hist). *Collection Arranged:* Whistler, Women and Fashion (auth, catalog), 2003. *Pos:* Asst cur, Frick Collection, 1991-1996, assoc cur, 1996-2000, sr cur, 2000-. *Teaching:* Prof, Vassar Coll, Columbia Univ & NYU; sr lectr, Mus Mod Art. *Publ:* Auth, Picasso's Variations on the Masters: Confrontations with the Past, Abrams, 1996. *Mailing Add:* 1 E 70th St New York NY 10021-4994

GALE , ANN
PAINTER

b Baltimore. *Study:* Yale Summer Sch Art and Music, New Haven, Conn, 1987; RI Col, Providence, BFA, 1988; Yale Univ, MFA, 1991. *Exhib:* The Figure, Fleet Gallery, Providence, RI, 1987; Gabriel Laderman Selects, First Street Gallery, New York, 1991; Frederick Layton Gallery, Milwaukee Inst Art & Design, 1992 & 1994; Politics of Gender, Walkers Point Ctr for Arts, Milwaukee, 1993; solo exhibs, Dean Jensen Gallery, 1993, 1995 & 1999, Kittredge Gallery, Tacoma, Wash, 1997, Hackett-Freedman Gallery, 2000, 2004 & 2008 & APEX: Ann Galle, Portland Art Mus, Ore, 2007; Lyons Weir Gallery, Chicago, 1996-97, 1999 & 2001; Seattle Art Fair, 1997; Hackett-Freedman Gallery, San Francisco, 1998; Frye Mus Art, Seattle, 2002; About Faces: Portraits Past and Present, Staten Island Mus, 2005; Ctr Contemp Art, Sacramento, 2006; This is Not a Group Show, Jacob Lawrence Gallery, Seattle, 2007; Am Acad Arts & Letts Invitational, New York, 2009. *Awards:* Ellen Battel Stoeckel Fellowship, Yale Summer Scg of Music and Art, 1987; Green Art Gallery Prize, Conn Women Artists, 1991; Grumbacher Gold Medallion Prize, New Haven Paint and Clay Club, 1991; Old Holland Oil Color Prize, Yale Univ, 1991; Individual Artists Fel, Wis Arts Bd, 1993, Wash State Arts Coun, 1996 & 2006; Artist Trust Grant/GAP Award, 1993; WESTAF/NEA Fel, 1996; Elizabeth Greenshields Found Grant, 1997; Royal Rsch Scholar Grant, Univ Wis, 1998; Grant for Artists Projects, Artists Trust, Wash, 2000; John Simon Guggenheim Fel, 2007; Purchase Award, Am Acad Arts and Letts, 2009. *Bibliog:* Yale Literary Mag, Spring 1992; Tales in canvas, December 1993 & Quiet Dramas, April 1995, Milw Mag; Michael Duncan (auth), New American Paintings, Open Studios Press, Wellesley, Mass, 1996; Megan Dailey (auth) & Jane Harris (auth), Curve: The Female Nude Now, Universe Publishing, New York, 2004; Debra Koppman, Artweek, Palo Alto, Calif, February 2008; Peter Trippi, Three to watch: artists making their mark, Fine Art Connoisseur, New York, January 2009. *Mem:* Nat Acad. *Media:* Oil

GALE, NESSA
SCULPTOR, PAINTER

b Chicago, Ill, Aug, 2, 1937. *Study:* Studied sculpture with Brian Quinn. *Work:* Tucson Mus Art, Ariz; Ariz State Univ, Tempe; Northern Ariz Univ, Flagstaff; Univ NMex, Albuquerque; Smithsonian Nat Portrait Gallery; Mus Modern Art; Queen Elizabeth II. *Comn:* Sculpture, Western Properties, Phoenix, Ariz, 86; painting, Median Inst, Pittsburgh, 87; painting, Practice Outlook Inc, Phoenix, Ariz, 88; mural, Har Zion Temple, Paradise Valley, Ariz, 90; sculpture, IB Goodman, NY, 91. *Exhib:* Ariz Biennial, Tucson Mus Art, 80-84; Midwestern Invitational, O'Rourke Gallery, Moorhead, Minn, 84; Pedestal I, Scottsdale Art Ctr, Ariz, 93. *Dealer:* Wiseman & Gale 4015 N Marshall Way Scottsdale AZ 85251. *Mailing Add:* 7011 E Doubletree Ranch Rd Paradise Valley AZ 85253

GALE, PEGGY
WRITER, CURATOR

b Mackenzie, Guyana, May 18, 1944; Can citizen. *Study:* Univ degli Studi, Florence, Italy, 65-66; Univ Toronto, Can, BA, 67. *Collection Arranged:* Tout le Temps/Every Time, La Biennale de Montreal 2000, Centre International D'art Contemporain de Montreal, 2000; Nuit Blanche, Toronto, 2006; Analogue: Pioneering Video from the UK, Canada and Poland (1968-88), 2008; Archival Dialogues: Reading the Black Star Collection, Ryerson Image Centre, Toronto, 2012. *Pos:* Educ off, Art Gallery Ont, Toronto, 67-74; asst film & video off, Can Coun, Ottawa, 74-75; video dir, Art Metropole, Toronto, 75-79, spec proj coordr, 85-87; exec dir, A Space, 79-81; contrib ed, Canadian Art (mag), Toronto; guest cur, Nat Gallery, Art Gallery Ont, Toronto & other Can & Int mus. *Teaching:* Instr, Nova Scotia Coll Art & Design; lectr video & performance art, var schs, mus & galleries, 75-. *Awards:* Canada Coun A Grant, 83; Toronto Arts Award, 2000; Governor General's Award, Vis & Media Arts, 2006. *Mem:* Int Asn Art Critics; The Writers Union Can; Int Curators. *Res:* Media art, specializing in performance, video, installations, thematic assessment and development of critical language, 65-. *Publ:* Auth, Muntadas, Searching Between the Frames, spring 93; Videotexts, Wilfred Laurier Univ Press & The Power Plant, 95; ed, (with Lisa Steele) Video re/View the (best) source for critical writings on Canadian Artists' Video, Toronto Art Metrop, 96; Tout le temps/Every Time, Le Biennale de Montreal (catalog), Montreal Ctr Int d'art Contemporain, 2000; Artists Talk, Press Nova Scotia Coll Art & Design, 2004; ed, contbr, Archival Dialogues, Reading the Black Star Collection, Toronto Ryerson Image Ctr, 2012. *Mailing Add:* 176 Cottingham St Toronto ON M4V 1C5 Canada

GALEMBO, PHYLLIS
PHOTOGRAPHER

b New York, NY, 1952. *Study:* Univ Wisc, MFA, 77. *Work:* Metropolitan Mus Art; NY Public Libr; Rockefeller Found; Polaroid Corp; Schomburg Ctr Rsch in Black Culture; Houston Mus Art; Phila Mus Art. *Exhib:* Solo exhibs, Int Ctr Photog, NY, 93; Nat Afro-Am Mus and Cultural Ctr, Oh, 94; NY and Photogroup Ctr, Fla, 95; Brush Gallery, Mass, 95; Cavin Morris, NY, 96; Am Mus Nat History, NY, 98; Univ Mo, Kans City, 99, La Galeria Sacred Stone, Santa Fe, 99; Smithsonian Mus Nat History, Wash DC, 2001; Newark Mus, NY, 2002; Fashion Inst Tech Mus, NY, 2004; Mead Art Mus, Mass, 2004; Philip Slein Gallery, St Louis, 2005; Alkazi Coll, NY, 2005; Skidmore Coll, NY, 2007; George Eastman House Int Mus Photog and Film, NY, 2008, Steven Kasher Gallery, NY, 2008, 2011, Chazen Mus Art, Wisc, 2009, Reflex Art Gallery, Amsterdam, 2009, Three Squares Studio, NY, 2012; Group exhibs, Ctr for Photography at Woodstock, NY, 2002; Fotofest Biennial, Houston, Tex, 2004; Mean Art Mus, Mass, 2007; Halsey Inst Contemporary Art, SC, 2010; New Orleans Ctr Contemporary Art, New Orleans, 2010; Ramapo Coll Art Galleries, NJ, 2011; 55th Int Art Exhib Biennale, Venice, 2013. *Pos:* prof fine arts dept, SUNY Albany, 78-. *Awards:* Artists Fellowship, NY Found Arts, NY, 96; Catalogue Grant, NY Council Arts, 96. *Mailing Add:* Steven Kasher Gallery 521 W 23rd St New York NY 10011

GALEN, ELAINE
PAINTER

b New York, NY, July 12, 1928. *Study:* Philadelphia Mus Sch Art, dipl, 50; Univ Pa, BA, 51; Art Students League, 55-59; NY Univ, MA, 63; major study with Morris Kantor. *Work:* Brooklyn Mus; Miss Mus, Jackson; Tampa Mus, Fla; Neuberger Mus, NY; NY Pub Libr; Univ Ariz Mus; Michener Mus, Doylestown, Pa; Israel Mus, Jerusalem; Univ of Arts Libr, Nat Liberty Mus, Free Library, Philadelphia, Pa; Wellesley Coll, Mass; Pepperdine Coll, Calif; The Arts Exchange, Pfizer Coll, NY; Metro Media Corp Coll, NY; corp, pvt & univ collections; Hudson Valley Hosp, NY; Yale Univ, 2008; Smith Col, 2008; Hudson Valley Hosp, New York, 2010; Concordia Coll, NY 2011; Univ Calif Santa Cruz; Baylor Univ. *Exhib:* Whitney Mus Am Art, NY, 61; Brooklyn Mus Int, 63 & 78; Solo Exhib: Pa Acad Fine Arts, Peale House, 72, Paradise Lost & Found, Atrium Plaza, New York, 2010; Art Inst Chicago, 78; The Jewish Mus, 88; Soho 20, NY, 88, 90, 92 & 94; Rathbone Gallery, Albany, NY, 88; Neuberger Mus, Purchase, NY, 92, 94 & 2001; Tampa Mus Art, Fla, 94; Gallery 1756, Chicago, 96, 98-99 & 2002; Art in Embassies, Nicosia, Cypris, 97; Michener Mus, Doylestown, Pa, 2000; Miss Mus, Jackson, 2000; Monique Goldstrom, 2002; The Studio, NY, 2004-2006; Concordia Gallery, 2004-2005; Van Brunt Gallery, NY, 2007; Kreft Gallery, Concordia Univ, Ann Arbor, Mich, 2007; Pelham Art Center, NY, 2008; Elisa Tucci Contemp Art, NY, 2008, 2009, 2010, 2011; Flat Iron Gallery, NY, 2012; Elisa Contemp Gallery, NY, 2012, 2013; Michener Mus, Doylestown, Pa, 2013. *Collection Arranged:* The Arts Exchange, Pfizer Coll, NY City; Metro Media Corporate Coll, NY City. *Pos:* Consult Developing, NJ Schs, 68-72, lectr-instr painting & drawing, 73 & assoc prof, 84-96; vis prof, Ben Gurion Univ, Israel, 98, Kaye Coll, Israel, 99. *Teaching:* Lectr hist art, painting & drawing, NY Univ, 70-73, Prairie State Coll, Chicago Heights, Ill, 74-, Lake Forest Coll, 78-80, Manhattanville Coll, 81-88, NY, Purchase, 81-; Columbia Univ, 84-90; assoc prof drawing & design, State Univ NY, Purchase, 90-96; Ben Gurion Univ, Israel, 97-98; Kaye Col, Israel, 98-99. *Awards:* Nat Print Award, Hunterdon Ctr, NJ, 70; Am Iron & Steel Inst Award for Design Excellence, 72; Florsheim Art Fund Grant, 92; Residency Award, Rochefort-en-Terre, France, 2007; Emily & Joe Lowe Award, 62; Chautauqua 1st Prize (Painting), New York, 70. *Bibliog:* Conversation with the Artist, Channel 19, NY State Coun Arts; Gerrit Henry (auth), Art in America, 80; Cornelia Butler (auth), Inspired by Nature, 94. *Mem:* Print Club, Philadelphia (artist mem). *Media:* Oil, Multi-Media. *Res:* Ancient and biblical heroic women. *Publ:* Auth, Deborah Portfolio, Haybarn Press, 96, Miriam Portfolio, 98, Lilith Portfolio, 2004, Dinah Portfolio, 2010; The Cushite, 2008; Feminists Who Changed America by Barbara Love, 1963-75; Encyclopedia of North American Women Artists, J & N Heller (auth), 95; Artists Recall, 2013. *Dealer:* Gallery 1756 Chicago IL; Elisa Contemporary Gallery, NY; Flat Iron Gallery NY. *Mailing Add:* 512 Millwood Rd Mount Kisco NY 10549

GALINA, BRENDA MOSS
MUSEUM DIRECTOR

Pos: chair, early childhood edn, Ga State Univ, formerly; exec dir, Mus of Design Atlanta, 2007-. *Mailing Add:* Museum of Design Atlanta 1315 Peachtree St NE Ste 100 Atlanta GA 30309

GALINDO, REGINA JOSE
VISUAL ARTIST, PERFORMANCE ARTIST

b Guatemala City, Guatemala, July 27, 1974. *Work:* Fondazione Teseco, Pisa, Italy; UBS Art Collection, Zurich, Switzerland; Blanton Mus Art, Austin, Tex; Consejeria de Murcia, Murcia, Spain; Art Found, Mallorca, Spain. *Comn:* Cisneros Fontanal Art Found, Miami, 2006; ArtPace, San Antonio, Tex, 2008; Futura, Trebecise Castle, Prague/Trebecise, Czech Republic, 2009. *Exhib:* Group Exhibs: Freewaves, Mus Contemporary Art LA, 2002, Into me, Out of me, PS1, New York, 2006;The Power of Women, Galeria Civica di Trento, Italy, 2006; Venice-Istanbul, Istanbul Mod Mus, 2006; Global Feminism, Brooklyn Mus, New York, 2007; Beyond the Dust, Arqueological Mus Naples, Italy, 2007; Arte/Vida: Actions by Artists of the Americas 1960-2000, Museo del Barrio, New York, 2008; Corpos Estranhos, MAC USP Sao Paulo, Brazil, 2009; The Fear Soc, 53rd Venice Biennale, Italy, 2009; NeHooDoo, PS1 & Miami Art Mus, 2009; Fact & Fiction, Nat Art Mus China, Beijing, 2009; Indomitable Women, Ctr Contemp Cult, Barcelona, Spain, 2009; Arte no es Vida, Mus Cariillo Gil, Mexico, 2009; The Fear Soc, Arsenale, Venice, Italy, 2009; Am Latina, Mus del Palacio de Bellas Artes, Mexico, 2010; Un Rage, Hause der Kulturn der Welt, Berlin, 2010; Corpus, Arte in Arione, Mus Contemp Art, Naples, Italy, 2010; The Beauty of Distance, 17th Biennale of Sydney, Australia, 2010; Unresolved Circumstances, Video Art from Latin America, Mus Latin American Art, Long Beach, Calif, 2011; Superhuman Wellcome Collection, London, 2012; Good Girls, Memory Desire Power, Nat Mus Contemporary Art, Bucharest, Romania, 2013; Aonflict in Latin America, Art Nexus Space, Bogota, Columbia, 2014; I Am Alive, The School of Nature and Principle, EFA, Project Space, NY, 2015; Solo Exhibs: Three Actions, Prometeogallery di Ida Pisani, Milan, Italy, 2007; America's Family Prison, Artspace, San Antonio, Tex, 2008, Regina Jose Galindo: Crisis Cloth, Exit Art, NY, 2009, Urgent Issues, Mus Contemp Art, Bucharest, Romania, 2010, Marabunta, Santa Domingo, Dominican Republic, 2011, Vulnerable, Mus of Latin American Art, Long Beach, Calif, 2012, Piel de Gallina, Centro Atlantico de Arte Moderno, Las Palmas de Gran Canaria, Spain, 2013, Pecora Nera, Rave Residency, Italy, 2014, Bearing Witness, Van Every/Smith Galleries, Davidson Col, NC, 2015. *Pos:* Artist-in-residence, Le Plateau, Paris, France, Kunstlerhaus Bethanien, Berlin, Germany. *Awards:* Golden Lion, 51st Venis Beinnale, 2005; winner,Inquieta Imagen V Edition, Mus Contemp Art Costa Rica, 2007; Unique prize of poetry, Fundacion Mirna Mack, 98; Prince Claus award, The Netherlands; First Prize, Juannio, Guatemala. *Bibliog:* Francisco Goldman (auth), Bomb Mag, NY, 2006; Joseph R Wolin (auth), Time Out NY, 2009; Thomas Micchelli (auth), The Brooklyn Rail, 2009; Holland Cottter, NY Times, 2009. *Publ:* Silvio de Gracia (auth), Inter Art Actual 105, 2010; auth, Personal e Intransmisible, Colloquia Ed, Guatemala, 99; coauth, Tanta Imagentras la Puerta, U Rafael Landivar Ed, 99; coauth, Mujer Cuerpo y Palabra, Torremozas Ed, Spain, 2004; coauth, Vanilla ed, Italy, 2006; coauth, Trenta Cuentos, Casa Abierta Ed, Spain, 2009

GALINSKY, NORMAN
PAINTER, GRAPHIC ARTIST
b Charleston, WVa, Jan 28, 1942. *Study:* Univ Cincinnati, BS, 64; Columbia Univ, with Philip Guston, Stamos, Malcolm Morley & Jack Tworkov, MFA, 73; Art Students League, printmaking workshop with Bob Blackburn. *Work:* Columbia Univ, NY; Mobil Oil Corp, NY; Four Seasons Hotel, Washington, DC; IBM, Armonk, NY; Pepsico, Purchase, NY. *Exhib:* Solo exhibs, Truman Gallery, NY, 78 & Katonah Gallery, NY, 79; Five on Paper, Spencer Mus, Univ Kans, Lawrence, 78; Small Works, 6th Ann Juried Show, Washington Sq Gallery, NY Univ, 82; Paperworks '80, Hudson River Mus, Yonkers, NY; The Abstract Vision, Cork Gallery, Lincoln Ctr, NY, 85; Constructions, Wooden Tent Gallery, Vineyard Haven, Mass, 90. *Pos:* Bd dir, Rockland Ctr Arts, West Nyack, NY, 84-. *Awards:* Contemp Artist Prize, Paperworks 80, Hudson River Mus, 80; NY Tele Award, Mt Aramah Exhib, Arden, NY, 86. *Bibliog:* Gordon Brown (auth), rev, Arts Mag, 9/78; Martin Filler (auth), Remodeled house-remodeled lives, House & Garden, 5/80; Steve Bush (auth), Salon West 3, Artspeak, 2/16/86. *Media:* Miscellaneous. *Dealer:* Orions Editions 270 Lafayette St New York NY 10012; Katonah Gallery 28 Bedford Rd Katonah NY 10536. *Mailing Add:* 20 Lawrence Ln Box 636 Palisades NY 10964

GALLACE, MAUREEN
PAINTER
b Stamford, Conn, 1960. *Study:* Univ Hartford, BFA, 1981; Rutgers Univ, MFA, 1983. *Exhib:* Solo exhibs include Jualian Pretto Gallery, NY, 1990, 1991, Nielsen Gallery, Boston, 1993, 1994, 1998, Nicole Klagsbrun Gallery, NY, 1993, Jack Hanley Gallery, San Francisco, 1994, Kohn Turner Gallery, Los Angeles, 1995, 1998, Modulo Gallery, Lisbon, Portugal, 1996, Museum Schloss-Hardenberg, Velbert, Germany, 1996, 303 Gallery, NY, 1997, 2000, 2003, 2006, Tex Gallery Art, 1999, Gallery Side2, Tokyo, 2000, 2002, Kerlin Gallery, Dublin, 2001, 2005, Michael Kohn Gallery, Los Angeles, 2002, 2003, Art Inst Chicago, 2006, Maureen Paley Interim Art, London, 2007; group exhibs include 98 Made in US, Galleria Il Capricorno, Venice, Italy; The Great Drawing Show, Kohn Turner Gallery, Los Angeles, 1999; The Poetic Landscape, Barbara Mathes Gallery, NY, 2000; The Devil Is In The Details, Allston Skirts Gallery, Boston, 2001; Gravity Over Time, Melleventi, Milan, Italy, 2002; The Holiday Show, 2002; School is Out, Southfirst, Brooklyn, 2003; Now is a Good Time, Andrea Rosen Gallery, NY, 2004; The Wonderful Fund, Place Ben Youssef, Medina, Marrakech, Morocco, 2005; Whitney Biennial, Whitney Mus Am Art, 2010. *Dealer:* Nielsen Gallery 179 Newbury St Boston MA 02116. *Mailing Add:* 303 Gallery 525 W 22nd St New York NY 10011

GALLAGHER, CAROLE
PHOTOGRAPHER, WRITER
b New York, NY, July 16, 1950. *Study:* Coll New Rochelle, BA, 72; New Sch, with Philippe Halsman, 73; Hunter Col, City Univ New York, with Tony Smith, Robert Morris, Doug Ohlson & Rosalind Krauss, MA, 77. *Work:* Bibliot Nat, Paris; State Mus, Pazin, Yugoslavia; World Image Ctr Photog; Fuji Art Mus, Tokyo. *Exhib:* The Nuclear Half Century-Witnesses Testify, Hiroshima, Japan; Visa Pour L'Image, Perpignan, France, 94; Am Ground Zero, Int Ctr Photog, Midtown Gallery, NY (traveling), 94-97; Latent August: the Legacy of Hiroshima & Nagasaki, Japanese-Am Hist Soc, San Francisco, 95; From Nuclear Bombs to Nuclear Bullets, Edge Gallery, London, 95; Perpetual Mirage: Photog Narratives of the Desert West, Whitney Mus Art, 95; Future Perspectives, World Image Ctr Photog, Fuji Art Mus, Tokyo, 97. *Pos:* Dir Nuclear Towns Doc Proj, Utah State Hist Soc, 85-90; consult & researcher, ABC-News Turning Point, 93; consult, The Peoples Century, BBC Series, 94; syndicated journalist/photojournalist, SYGMA, 94; writing memoirs, Lust for Light. *Teaching:* Instr photog, Col New Rochelle, NY, 77-78 & Kingsborough Col, City Univ NY, 77-79 & Univ Utah Commun Dept, Salt Lake City, 88-90; vis prof, Univ Utah Art Dept, 88-90. *Awards:* Nev Humanities comt, 92; Pope Found Award for Investigative Journalism, 93; Fel in nonfiction literature, New York Found Arts, 93; and others. *Bibliog:* Paul Stimson (auth), Between the signs, Art in Am, 10/79; Rene Denizot & R Barry (auths), Il Est Temps--It's About Time, Yvon Lambert, Paris, 80; Carole Gallagher at Leo Castelli, Express, fall 81; Susan Lyman (auth), Fallout: picturing the downwind survivors, The Deseret News, 2/25/87; Judy Rollins (auth), Clouds of Creation, The Salt Lake Tribune, 6/19/88. *Publ:* Illusr, Muscles, 83 & Punch, 83, Avon; Nuclear Test's Legacy of Anger: Workers See Betrayal on Peril, New York Times, 12/14/89; American Ground Zero: The Secret Nuclear War, Cambridge: MIT Press, 93, Elefanten Press, Berlin, spring 95. *Dealer:* Ronald Feldman Gallery 31 Mercer St New York NY 10013; SYGMA Photo News Inc 322 Eighth Ave New York NY 10001

GALLAGHER, CYNTHIA
PAINTER, EDUCATOR
Study: Philadelphia Coll Art, BFA, 72; Queens Col, Flushing, NY, MFA, 74. *Work:* Metro Mus Art, NY; First Nat Bank of Chicago; Shearson-Lehman American Express, NY, San Francisco; also pvt collections of James & Beth Rudin DeWoody, Curt Marcus & Robin Tewes and Mary Ryan & Bruce Liebowitz; Skadden, Arps, Meagher & Flom. *Exhib:* Solo exhibs, 55 Mercer St, NY, 76 & 78, Grace Borgenicht Gallery, NY, 81, Luise Ross Gallery, NY, 88, Edward Thorden Gallery, Göteborg, Sweden, 89, Charles More Gallery, Philadelphia, 90 & 91, Mary Ryan Gallery, NY, 92 & Espace Croix Barangon, Toulouse, 94; Art on Paper, Weatherspoon Mus, Greensboro, NC, 82; Collectors Choice, Ark Art Ctr, Little Rock, 88; Parrish Art Mus Design Biennial, Southampton, Long Island, NY, 91; Fanfare, 150 Anniversary NY Philharmonic; Montclair (NJ) Mus, 97; Nabisco Gallery, E Hanover, NJ, 98; Elsa Mott Ives Gallery, New York City, 99. *Pos:* Graphics consult, NY State CAPS; vis critic, Brown Univ, RI Sch Design, 94. *Teaching:* Asst prof, Queens Col, City Univ NY, 74-89; vis critic, NY Univ, 74-75; Philadelphia Col Art, Philadelphia, Pa, 76-77; Yale Univ, Summer Sch of Music & Art, Norfolk, Conn, 80; vis critic, Brandeis Univ Alumni Asn, NY, 84; guest lectr, Stanford Univ Alumni Asn, 85; life drawing, two-dimensional painting, drawing, design, Fashion Inst Technol, NY, 88; instr, Found Dept, Parsons Sch Design, NY, 94-. *Awards:* Creative Artists Pub Serv Prog, 81; Nat Endowment Arts, 83 & 89; NY Found Arts, 89. *Bibliog:* Articles in NY Times, 1/18/87 & Philadelphia Inquirer, 4/13/90; Mary Cummings (auth), Southampton Press, 8/29/91; Edward Sosanski (auth), On galleries, Philadelphia Inquirer, 10/31/91; Kenneth Leslie, (auth book) Oil Pastel, 90. *Dealer:* Kristina Wasserman Gallery Providence RI

GALLAGHER, ELLEN
PAINTER
b Providence, RI, 1965. *Study:* Sch Mus Fine Arts, Boston, 92, student, Skowhegan Sch Art, Maine, 93; Oberlin Coll, student. *Work:* Mus Mod Art, Whitney Mus Art, Metrop Mus Art, Guggenheim Mus, NY; Mus Fine Art, Boston; Mus Contemp Art, Los Angeles; Denver Mus Art, Denver; Moderna Museet, Stockholm. *Exhib:* Solo exhibs, Akin Gallery, Boston, 92, Mario Diacono Gallery, Boston, 94, Mary Boone Gallery, NY, 96, Anthony d' Offay Gallery, London, 96, Gagosian Gallery, NY, 98, Ikon Gallery, Birmingham, 98, Galerie Max Hetzler, Berlin, 99, Anthony d'Offay Gallery, London, 2000, Watery Ecstatic, ICA, Boston, 2001, Ellen Gallagher: Preserve, Drawing Ctr, NY City, 2002, Currents 88, St Louis Art Mus, 2003, Murmur, Galerie Max Hetzler, Berlin, 2003, Orbus, Fruitmaker Gallery, Edinburgh, 2004, deLuxe, Whitney Mus Am Art, NY City, 2005, Fluidity of Time, Mus Contemp Art, Chgo, 2005-06; Whitney Biennal, Whitney Mus Am Art, New York, 95, 2010; Inside the Visible, Inst Contemp Art, Boston, 96 & Whitechapel Art Gallery, London, 96; Project Painting, Basilico Fine Arts, 97 & Irish Mus Mod Art, Dublin, 97; The Body Pointing, Mario Diacano Gallery, 97; Postcards from Black Am, De Beyerd Ctr Contemp Art, Breda, The Neth, 98; PS1 NY, Mus Mod Art, 2000; Mus Contemp Art, Chicago, 2005-06. *Awards:* Provincetown Fine Arts Fel, 95; MacDowell Colony, New Hampshire, 96; Joan Mitchell Fel, 97; Am Acad award in Art. *Bibliog:* Martin Coomer (auth), Ellen Gallagher, Flash Art, 1-2/97; Eric de Chassey (auth), La Peinture est Vivante, L'Oeil, No 489, 10/97; Roberta Smith (auth), Ellen Gallager, NY Times, 3/98. *Dealer:* Mario Diacono Gallery 207 South St Boston MA; Don Christiansen Fine Art LLC 194 8th Ave New York NY 10011; Goya Contemporary / Goya-Girl Press 3000 Chestnut Ave Baltimore MD 21211; Hauser & Wirth 196A Piccadilly London W1J 9DY United Kingdom; Jim Kempner Fine Art 501 W 23rd St New York NY 10011; Two Palms 476 Broadway New York NY 10013. *Mailing Add:* c/o Gagosian Gallery 555 W 24th St New York NY 10011

GALLAGHER, KATHLEEN ELLEN
PRINTMAKER, PAINTER
b New York, NY, Dec 18, 1949. *Study:* Marymount Manhattan Coll, New York, BA, 71; Herbert H Lehman Coll, Grad Sch, New York, with Arun Bose, MA, 75. *Work:* Brooklyn Mus, Mus Mod Art & Pratt Graphics Ctr, NY; DeCordova Mus, Lincoln, Mass; Philadelphia Mus Art, Pa; Portland Mus, Ore; Housatonic Mus Art, Bridgeport, Conn; Mus of City of NY, 2002; corp collections, Atlantic Richfield co, Citibank NA, IBM Corp, Mellon Bank, NY Times. *Comn:* Etching editions, Lyndhurst, Tarrytown, NY & Drayton Hall, Charleston, SC, Nat Trust Hist Preserv-Christie's, London & NY, 82; Surface & Diversity, Housatonic Mus Art, Bridgeport, CT, 98. *Exhib:* Grunwald Ctr, Univ Calif, Los Angeles, 86; NY Inspired: Past & Present, John Szoke Gallery, NY, 88; Lynd Ward Exhib, Soc Am Graphic Arts, NY, 92; NY Icons: Michael Ingbar Gallery, NY, 93; Thomas J Walsh Art Gallery, Fairfield Univ, Conn, 94; Lore Degenstein Gallery, Susquehanna Univ, 95; 479 Gallery, NMex, 96; Old Print Shop, NYC, 2001; Nat Taiwan Normal Univ (NTNU), Taiwan, 2004, 2008. *Collection Arranged:* Atlantic Richfield co, Citibank NA, IBM Corp, Mellon Bank, NY Times, others. *Teaching:* Instr watercolor, Elizabeth Seton Coll, Yonkers, NY, 84-88; instr printmaking & painting, Coll New Rochelle, NY, 86-92; vis artist watercolor & printmaking, Westchester Arts Coun, NY, 86-; instr printmaking, Herbert H Lehman Coll, 92 & 97-; instr art, Albert Leonard, New Rochelle, NY, 90-; instr watercolor, Herbert H Lehman Coll, 2001-02. *Awards:* Stuart M Egnal Award, 55-65, Print Club, 80; Purchase Award, Prints USA, Pratt Graphics Ctr, New York, 82. *Mem:* Printmaking Workshop; Westchester Arts Coun; Soc Am Graphic Artists NY (Adv Coun). *Media:* Etching; Watercolor. *Dealer:* Michael Ingbar Gallery Archit Art 568 Broadway New York NY 10012. *Mailing Add:* 6 Brookside Ave Pelham NY 10803

GALLANDER, CATHLEEN S
ART DEALER, REPRESENTATIVE
b San Antonio, Tex, Feb 4, 1931. *Study:* Univ Tex, Austin, BA (hist); Harvard Univ, scholar art hist; Harvard Bus Sch, Inst Arts Admin. *Pos:* Dir, Art Mus S Tex, Corpus Christi, 61-80 & Newport Harbor Art Mus, Calif, 80-83; panelist, Nat Endowment Arts; pvt consult & fine arts appraisals, currently. *Mem:* Coll Art Asn Am; Am Asn Mus; Am Fedn Arts; Western Asn Art Mus; Art Table

GALLARDA, MICHAEL
ARTIST
b Martinez, Calif, 1953. *Exhib:* Atlantic Gallery, Georgetown Univ, Washington, DC, 1991; New Masters Gallery, Carmel, Calif, 1993; Grand Nat Exhib, Am Artists Professional League, NY City, 1993, 1996; Lawrence Gallery, Sheridan, Ore, 1994; Four Contemporary Still Life Masters, Panache Gallery, Mendocino, Calif, 1994; Galeria Atenea, San Miguel de Allende, Mex, 1995; Summer Dreams, Humboldt Arts Council, Eureka, Calif, 1998; Annual Still Life Show, Albemarle Gallery, London, 1998, Annual Still Life and Trompe l'Oeil, 1999; Summer Salon, Eleanor Ettinger Gallery, NY, 2000, 2003, 2004, Figure in American Art, 2001, 2002, 2006, 2007, The Art of Still Life, 2001, Winter Salon, 2002, Autumn Salon, 2005; Still Lifes, Florals and Trompe l'Oeil, John Pence Gallery, San Francisco, 2000; Visual Deceptions, Woodson Art Mus, Wausau, Wis, 2003. *Awards:* Helen G Oehler Award, Am Artists Professional League, NY, 1993

GALLES, ARIE ALEXANDER
PAINTER, EDUCATOR
b Tashkent, Russia, Oct 2, 1944; US citizen. *Study:* Temple Univ, BFA, 68; Univ Wis, MFA, 71. *Work:* NJ State Mus, Trenton. *Comn:* Charles Allen, NY; Edgar Kaiser Jr, Vancouver, Can. *Exhib:* Solo exhibs, O K Harris Gallery, NY, 77, 79 & 82, Zolla-Liberman Gallery Chicago, Ill, 79 & NJ State Mus, Trenton, 89; Abstract,

Material, Pictorial, Illusionism, O K Harris West, Scottsdale, Ariz, 80; Contemp Painting, Del Mus, Wilmington, 80; Five Decades: Recent Works by Alumni of the Dept Art, Elvehjem Mus Art, Univ Wis, Madison, 80; Art of Fashion, Bernice Steinbaum Gallery, NY, 90; Painting: NJ Benjamin Gallery, William Paterson Col, Wayne, NJ, 92; and others. *Pos:* Dir, Madison Acad of Art & Morris Gallery, 77-80, Phyllis Rothman Gallery, Fairleigh Dickinson Univ, 88-. *Teaching:* Prof art & chmn fine arts dept, Fairleigh Dickinson Univ, Madison, NJ, 72-81, assoc prof, 81-84, prof, 84-. *Bibliog:* Article in Chicago Sun Times, 9/23/79 & Phoenix Gazett, 12/27/80; Robert Paschal & Robert Anderson (auths), Advanced Air Brush The Techniques-Art of the Dot, Van Nostrand Rineholt, 84. *Media:* Fluorescent Acrylic on Aluminum Extrusions, Caran D Ache Oil Pastel. *Publ:* Auth, Air Brush Action, Mag, 10/88. *Dealer:* O K Harris 383 W Broadway New York NY; Zolla-Lieberman Gallery 356 W Huron Chicago IL 60610. *Mailing Add:* 116 Blue Lagoon Laguna Beach CA 92651-4233

GALLO, ENZO D
SCULPTOR
b Italy, Oct 25, 1927. *Study:* San Alejandro Univ Fine Arts, Havana, Cuba, MFA; Senatus Univ Verae Arademirus, BA; study with Jose Sicri & Ramos Blanco, sculptor & Augusto Valderama, painter, Havana. *Work:* Pagani Mus, Milan, Italy; Young Circle, Hollywood, Fla; Town of Padula, Italy; Art Mus the Amercias, Washington, DC; Port Everglades Park, Ft Lauderdale, Fla. *Comn:* Sculpture & mosaic murals, Hollywood Mem Gardens, Fla; mosaic murals, Am Savings & Loan, Miami Beach; sculpture, Doral Beach Club, Miami Beach; sculpture (bronze), Hallandale Pub Libr. *Exhib:* Metrop Mus, Miami, 75; Solo exhibs, Omni Int, Miami, 78, West Palm Beach Art Gallery, 79, Inter-Am Art Gallery, Coral Gables, 80, Fedn of Cuban Teachers of Fine Arts, Miami, Fla, 86, Heller Bldg, 87; Latin Am Artist of the Southeastern US, Lowe Art Mus, Miami, 78; First Ann Art Competition, Nova Univ, 79. *Teaching:* Prof sculpture, San Alejandro Inst Fine Arts, Havana, Cuba & Broward Adult Educ, 62-65. *Awards:* Selected by US Dept of HUD for Environ Art in Pub Places, 73; First Monumental Proj Assigned by Pres Reagan for Christopher Columbus Quincentenary, Port Everglades, Fla, 88; Medallion Design Accepted as the Off Medallion of Grand Regatta Columbus 1992 Quincentenary, Wash, DC, 89. *Bibliog:* John R Thompson (auth), Traveling Tribune Reporter Pays Visit to Sculptor in Exile, The Chicago Tribune, 69; Marian Vynne (auth), Italian Artist Works, The Miami News, 2/73; Thomas Lawrence (auth), Enzo Gallo Reduces Natural Data to Pure Forms, Manhattan Arts Mag, 9/91. *Mem:* Fla Sculpture Asn; Artist Equity Asn Fla (pres, 75-78); Am Fedn Arts; Fla Artist Group; Broward Art Guild. *Media:* Marble, Bronze. *Publ:* Auth, Columbus Rediscovered, The Miami Herald, 8/87; The Man of the Mountain, The El Nuero Miami Herald, 92

GALLO, FRANK
SCULPTOR, EDUCATOR
b Toledo, Ohio, Jan 13, 1933. *Study:* Toledo Mus Sch Art, BFA, 54; Cranbrook Acad Art, 55; Univ Iowa, MFA, 59; Univ Ill, 85, sr scholar. *Work:* Mus Mod Art & Whitney Mus Am Art, NY; Art Inst Chicago; Los Angeles Mus Art; Cleveland Mus Art; plus others. *Comn:* Portrait, Daniel Pope Cook, Ill, 69; portraits, String Teachers of Am, 69-72; seven life-size concrete figures, Bicentennial Comn, Champaign, Ill, 76; stained glass wall, Harry Thoroue, 80; ed paper castings, Beethoven Found, 85. *Exhib:* Ann, Whitney Mus Am Art, 64-67, Young Am, 65; Alliance on Art, Smithsonian Inst, Washington, DC, 68; Venice Biennale, 68; Works in Paper, Art Inst Chicago, 78; retrospective, Paine Art Ctr, Oshkosh, Wis, 83; and others. *Teaching:* Prof sculpture, Univ Ill, 60-94. *Awards:* Guggenheim Found Fel, 66; Best Illus of the Year, Soc Publ Designers, 79. *Bibliog:* Peter Plagent (auth), article, Schlock Elite, New York, 12/3/78; Frank Gallo, Famous Artists Ann I (catalog), NY Hastings House, 80; Frank H Goodyear (auth), Contemporary American Realism since 1960, Archives of American Art Series, Little Brown, Boston, 81. *Publ:* Illus, cover, Raquel Welch, Time Mag, 11/69, The faint, Playboy Mag, 1/78 & Illus 21, NY Hastings House, 80

GALLO, RUBEN A
CRITIC, CURATOR
b Guadalajara, Mex, Dec 22, 1969. *Study:* Yale Univ, BA, 1991; Columbia Univ, MA, 1996. *Collection Arranged:* Video Faz, Museo Regional Guadalajara, Mex, 1996; The Conceptual Trend, Museo del Barrio, NY, 1997. *Pos:* Dir, Forum Int Art & Theory, Guadalajara, Mex, 1997-98; dir, Prog in Latin Am Studies, Princeton Univ, 2006-. *Teaching:* Preceptor humanities, Columbia Univ, NY, 1995; adj Latin Am art, Lehman Col, City Univ NY, 1997; asst prof, Span Am Lit, Princeton Univ, NJ. *Awards:* Katherine Singer Kovacs Award, 2009. *Bibliog:* Frudi Mexico, MIT Press, 2010; Mexican Modernity, MIT Press, 2005. *Mem:* Mod Language Asn. *Res:* Latin American art; contemporary art; photography. *Publ:* Auth, The Labyrinths of Mexican Art, Flash Art 186, 1996; El Intelectual Arte el Memoricidio, 1/1997 & Manuel Alvarez Bravo y el Andante con Moto, 9/1997, Vuelta, Mex; The Necessity of Revolt Interview with Julia Kristeva, Trans, 1998. *Mailing Add:* Princeton Univ 337 E Pyne Princeton NJ 08544

GALLOWAY, JULIA
CERAMIST, EDUCATOR, ADMINISTRATOR
Study: NY State Col of Ceramics, Alfred Univ, BFA, 1988; Nova Scotia Col of Art and Design, Visiting Scholar Program, 1994; Univ Colo, Boulder, MFA, 1995. *Exhib:* Solo exhibitions include Solo Flight, 1992 Image Alternative Gallery, Rugg Road Collective, Alston, Mass, 1998, Daily Odyssey, Archie Bray Gallerry, Helena, 1999, Select Artist, The Clay Studio, Phila, 2001, New Work, Huntington Mus of Art, WVa, 2003, Dulcis Domus, Trax Gallery, Iowa City, 2005, New Work, AKAR Gallery, Iowa City, 2006, 2010, Wake Robin, Harvey Meadows Gallery, Aspen, Colo, 2008, Mirth, Harvey Meadows Gallery, Colo, 2009, New Work Trax Gallery, Berkeley, Calif, 2011 and several others; group exhibitions includes Side By Side, Double O Gallery, Halifax, Nova Scotia, Can, 1995, Table Manners, Ranhorne Gallery, Peninsula Fine Arts Center, Newport News, 1997, Holiday Exhibition, Signature Shop Gallery, 1999, Teapot Exhibition, Ryan & Maclean Gallery, 2001, Bray Bash West, Univ Washington, Seattle, 2003, Mastery in Clay, The Clay Studio, Phila, 2005, Claybash!-Gallery 31 North, Hunterdon Mus, NJ, 2006, 100 Teapots III, Baltimore Clayworks, Md, 2007, Made in Clay, Greenwich House Pottery, NY, 2008, 2009, Ceramics Symposium 2010, Lawrence Arts Center, Kansas, 2010, Pot Sketch, The Clay Studio, Mont, 2011 and several others. *Collection Arranged:* Collections include The Long Beach Mus of Art, Calif, Renwick Gallery, Smithsonian Mus, Huntington Mus of Art, WVa, Archie Bray Found, Helena, Mont, Art Gallery of Nova Scotia, Clay Art Center, NY, Univ Arkansas, North Central Col, Piedmont, Ill, Col of William and Mary, Crocker Art Mus, Sacramento, and the Woodman Collection:Univ of Colo, Boulder. *Pos:* Demonstrated at the Utilitarian Clay Conference, and NCECA; taught workshops at Archie Bray Found for the Ceramic Arts, Arrowmont Sch of Arts and Crafts, Penland Sch of Crafts, Haystack Mountain Sch of Crafts, Anderson Ranch Arts Center, Cleveland Inst of Art and the Nova Scotia Col of Art and Design; studio technician, Univ Colo, Boulder, 1992; exec bd mem, Haystack Moutain Sch of Crafts, 2001-09; Artist in Residence, Anderson Ranch Arts Center, 1995-96, Archie Bray Found, 1997-99; vis scholar, Nova Scotia Col of Art and Design, Halifax; juror for several musuems and other organizations; bd dir, Archie Bray Found for the Ceramic Arts, 2010-13; participant, The Object and Making: Function and Meaning, Haystack Mountain Sch of Crafts, 2007. *Teaching:* Graduate instructor/asst ceramic hand-building, beginning sculpture, Univ Colo, Boulder, 1993-95; vis instructor, Col of William and Mary, 1996-97, North Central Col, 1997, Cleveland Inst of Art, 2000, Nova Scotia Col of Art and Design, 2001, 2005, 2008; instructor, Archie Bray Found, 1997-99; assoc prof, Sch for American Crafts, Ceramics Dept, Col of Imaging Arts and Sciences, Rochester Inst of Technology, NY, 1999-2009, chair, 2005-09; dir of the Sch, prof ceramics, Sch of Art, Col of Visual and Performing Arts, Univ of Montana, Missoula, 2009-. *Publ:* Published in Ceramics Monthly, Studio Potter, Art and Perception and Clay Times. *Mailing Add:* The School of Art College of Visual and Performing Arts The University of Montana 32 Campus Drive Fine Arts 305B Missoula MT 59812-5400

GALLOWAY, PAUL
PAINTER
b Kansas City, Mo. *Study:* Univ N Tex, Denton, BFA (painting and drawing), 2001; Univ Ga, Athens, MFA (painting and drawing), 2004; Skowhegan Sch Painting and Sculpture, 2004. *Exhib:* A New Art Group, Brickhaus, Denton, Tex, 1999; Person, Place, Machine, Union Gallery, Denton, 2000; Summer Group Show, Fay Gold Gallery, Atlanta, 2003; Selected Works, OSP Gallery, Boston, 2003; The Georgia 7: Seven Emerging Georgia Artists, Mus Contemp Art, Atlanta, 2004; Art Papers Art Auction, Mason Murer Fine Art, Atlanta, 2005; Queens Internat 2006, Queens Mus Art, New York, 2006; Out of Time, Payne Gallery, Moravian Col, Bethlehem, Pa, 2007; solo exhibs, Parallaz, Lamar Dodd Sch Art Main Gallery, Athens, 2002, Fay Gold Gallery, 2004 & 2005. *Awards:* Skowhegan Fel, 2004; Art Matters Found Grant, 2008. *Media:* Acrylic

GAMACHE, CLAUDETTE THERESA
PAINTER
b Fall River, Mass, Dec 9, 1941. *Study:* St Anne's Nursing Sch, Fall River, Mass, grad, 1962; Univ Hartford, Conn, BFA, 1984; Lesley Univ, Cambridge, MA, 1985. *Work:* Central Maine Med Hospital, Portland, Maine; Mercy Hospital, Portland, Maine. *Exhib:* Butler Inst Am Art, Ohio, 2004, 2008; Chocolate Church Art Ctr, Bath, Maine, 2004; Nat Pastel Show, Saco Mus, Saco, Maine, 2009; Ventane Art Gallery, Santa Fe, NMex, Int Asn Pastel Soc, 2009; Nat Pastel Show, Brickstore Mus, Kennebunk, Maine, 2010; BREA Art Gallery, Brea Calif, Int Asn Pastel Soc, 2010; PSA Signature Exhib, Noyes Mus Art, Oceanville, NJ, 2012. *Pos:* RN, Mt Sinai Hosp, Hartford, Conn, 1984-86; expressive therapist, Elmcrest Psychiatric Hosp, Portland, 1986-87; nurse clinician/expressive therapist, New Britain Gen Hosp, 1987-89; hospice nurse, VNA Group, Hartford, 1989-1993; hospice mgr, Portsmouth Visiting Nurses, NH, 1994-1997; artist, Glaudette Gamache Gallery, Bath, Maine, 1997-; pres, Pastel Painters of Maine, 2007-2010. *Teaching:* Pastel painting teacher, Heartwood Coll Art, Kennebunk, Maine, 2000-02, Chocolate Ch Art Ctr, Bath, Maine, 2003; vis art teacher, Wells Middle Sch, 2000; ind pastel painting teacher, Bath, 2004-; pvt instr, workshops in Maine, 2007-; mentor, Low Residency MFA Prog, Heartwood Coll Art, 2010; workshop leader, Southwest France. *Awards:* 1st place, Nat Pastel Show, Heartwood Coll Art, 2006; 5th place, Nat Pastel Show, Heartwood Coll Art, 2007; 1st place, Nat Plastel Show, Saco Mus, 2009; Merit award, Pastel Paintings of Maine, 2011; Hon mention, Master Circle Show, Int Asn Pastel Soc, 2011. *Mem:* Am Art Therapy Asn; Pastel Painters of Maine (signature mem, vpres 2006, pres 2007-2010); Pastel Soc Am (signature mem); Conn Pastel Soc (signature mem); Int Asn Pastel Soc (master circle mem). *Media:* Pastels. *Interests:* Writing, piano. *Publ:* Contrib, How Did You Paint That? 100 Ways to Paint Landscapes, Internat Artist Publ

GAMBLE, SARAH
PAINTER
b 1974. *Study:* Corcoran Sch Art, BFA, 1998; Univ Pa, MFA (painting), 2001. *Exhib:* Solo exhibs, Fleischer Art Meml, Pa, 2005, Philadelphia Art Alliance, Pa, 2006, Pageant Gallery, Pa, 2007, Bambi Gallery, Pa, 2009, Fleetwing Gallery, New York, 2010; Bad Touch, Rose Mus Brandeis Univ, Mass, 2005; Omaha Hobo Showbo, Bemis Ctr Contemp Art, Omaha, 2006; New Trends in Painting, Concordia Univ, Nebr, 2006; Philagrafika Invitational Portfolio, Univ Arts, Pa, 2008; Art of the State, Pa Mus Art, Harrisburg, Pa, 2009. *Awards:* Pew Ctr for Arts Fel, 2009

GAMMON, JUANITA L
ART EDUCATOR, GRAPHIC ARTIST
b New Orleans, La. *Study:* Univ Ill, BFA & MFA; advanced study. *Work:* Work in many pvt & pub collections. *Comn:* Many pvt comns. *Exhib:* Dream Mus, Champaign, Ill, 70; McKinley Found, Urbana, Ill, 70; Nat Acad Design, NY, 70-71; Univ Ill, 71; Parkland Col, 75, 79-2003; Quincy Art Gallery, 94; Springer Art Ctr,

2006; Artist Guild, St Louis, Mo, 2006; USA Master Gardners Art Exhib, 2010. *Pos:* Judge, local, regional & nat art exhibs, 67-; art lectr & critic & consult curric design, 67-; supvr, Champaign Co Art Show, 69-89; exhibitor, cur & spec tour guide, Nat Drawing Invitational, Parkland Gallery, 94, guest lectr garden art, 2012. *Teaching:* Prof art & chmn Fine & Applied Arts Dept, Parkland Col, Champaign, 67-; serving on many col comts, teaching specialties (painting, drawing, illus, art hist, computer graphics), workshops on drawing from nature. *Awards:* Many prof hons & awards. *Mem:* Colored Pencil Soc Am; many other prof organizations. *Media:* Acrylic, Colored Pencils; Watercolor. *Specialty:* private and public garden landscapes. *Interests:* Photography; research pub & private gardens (for artist's panoramic style garden paintings). *Publ:* Ed, Parkland Intercom, Story Shop Book; contrib (drawing), A Stroke of Genius: The Best of Drawing, 2007; Corresp writer, Savoy Star Newspaper; Ed, Artist of Savoy Garden Friends Newsletters. *Dealer:* Rocking Chair Studio 711 W Healey Champaign IL 61820. *Mailing Add:* 711 W Healey Champaign IL 61820-5026

GAMWELL, LYNN
CURATOR, HISTORIAN

b Chicago, Ill, June 24, 1943. *Study:* Univ Ill, BA, 67; Claremont Grad Sch, MFA, 70; Univ Calif, Los Angeles, PhD, 77. *Pos:* dir, Art Mus, State Univ NY, Binghamton, currently. *Teaching:* Lectr art hist, Univ Calif, Los Angeles, 72-74; asst prof art hist, Saddleback Col, Mission Viejo, Calif, 84-87; lectr, Science, Sch of Visual Arts, NY, currently. *Mem:* Coll Art Asn; Art Table. *Res:* Contemporary art. *Publ:* ed contribr, Sigmund Freud and Art: His Personal Collection, Abrams, NY, 89; coauth, Madness in America: Cultural & Medical Perceptions of Mental Illness Before 1914, Cornell Univ Press, 95; Health and Happiness in Twentieth-Century Avant Garde Art, Cornell Univ Press, 96; co-auth; Dreams 1900-2000: Science, Art and the Unconscious Mind, Cornell Univ Press, 2000; auth, Exploring the Invisible: Art, Science and the Spiritual, Princeton Univ Press, 2002. *Mailing Add:* 101 W 80th St Apt 10A New York NY 10024-7102

GANAHL, RAINER
CONCEPTUAL ARTIST

b Bludenz, Austria. *Study:* Univ Innsbruck, MA, 85; Akademie Dusseldorf, MA, 90; Whitney Independent Study Prog, 90-91. *Work:* Pompidov Collection, Ctr George Pompidou, Paris, France; Guggenheim Mus (web site project), NY; Mus Mod Art & General Found, Vienna, Austria; Mus Contemp Art, Oslo, Norway. *Exhib:* Solo exhibs, Persons Weekend Mus (auth, catalog), Tokyo, 93, Dallas Mus Art, 92, Kunsthaus Bregenz (auth, catalog), 98 & Mus Modern Art, Vienna, 99; Educational Complex (auth, catalog), General Found, Vienna, 97; Venice Biennial - Austrian Pavillion, Venice, 99; Kunstwelten Im Dialog, Mus Ludwig, Cologne, 99-2000; Vernaculars: Speaking Performances, Pompidou Ctr, Paris, 2000-2001. *Teaching:* assoc prof, Sch/Acad Fine Arts, Esav, Geneva, 96-98. *Bibliog:* Barry Schwarsky (auth), Rainer Ganahl: Windows on the World, Cambridge Univ Press, 97; George Baker (auth) Rainer Ganahl: Max Protetch Gallery, Artforum, 4/99; Roberto Costantino (auth), Broken Language, Flash Art Ital, summer 2000; Gregory Williams (auth), Artforum, summer 2001. *Media:* Video, Paper. *Publ:* Coauth, Rainer Ganahl, Imported - A Reading Seminar, Semidtext New York, 98; auth, Reading Karl Marx, Bookworks, London, spring 2001. *Dealer:* Galerie Nachst St Stephan Grunzngerg 1/2 1010 Vienna Austria; Baumgartner Gallery New York NY. *Mailing Add:* 1255 Fifth Ave Apt 3H New York NY 10029

GANDER, RYAN
FILMMAKER, INSTALLATION SCULPTOR

b Chester, UK, 1976. *Study:* Manchester Metrop Univ, Manchester, UK, BA(Hons), 1996-99; Jan van Eyck Akademie, Maastricht, Post-Grad Fine Art Res Participant, 1999-2000; Rijkasakedemie van Beeldende Kunsten, Amsterdam, Post-Grad Fine Art Participant, 2001-02. *Exhib:* Solo exhibs include Artists Space, New York, 2005, Marc Foxx, Los Angeles, 2006,Art Basel Premier with STORE, Miami, 2006, CCA Wattis Inst Contemp Arts, San Francisco, 2007, Tanya Bonakdar Gallery, New York, 2008, South London Gallery, London, 2008; Group exhibs include Romantic Detachment, PS 1, New York, 2004; Post No Bills, White Columns, New York, 2005; The Standard Hotel, The Standard Hotel, Miami, 2006; Tate Triennial, Tate Britain, London, 2006; Whitstable Biennale, Whitstable, UK, 2006; Constellations, Tanya Bonakdar, New York, 2006; Kit Bashing, Western Bridge, Seattle, 2007; Words Fail Me, Mus Contemp Art, Detroit, 2007; Loose Asns, Performa, New York, 2007; HEY HEY GLOSSOLALIA, Creative Time, New York, 2008; Wouldn't It Be Nice, Ctr d'Art Contemp, Zurich, 2008; Life on Mars: Carnegie Int Exhib, Carnegie Mus Art, Pittsburgh, 2008; 54th Int Art Exhib Biennale, Venice, 2011. *Awards:* Fel Arts Council England, 2002; Cocheme Fel, Byam Shaw Sch Art, London, 2004; Dena Found Award, 2007. *Mailing Add:* STORE 27 Hoxton Street London N1 6NH United Kingdom

GANDERT, MIGUEL ADRIAN
PHOTOGRAPHER, LECTURER

b Espanola, NMex, Jan 12, 1956. *Study:* Univ NMex, BA, 77, MA, 83. *Work:* Mus Fine Arts, Santa Fe; Phoenix Art Mus, Ariz; Mass Coll Art, Boston; Getty Ctr Hist Art & Humanities, Santa Monica, Calif; Ctr Creative Photog, Univ Ariz, Tucson. *Comn:* Martineztown/Santa Barbara, Community Photog Survey, City Albuquerque, 92; Retratos Mestizaje: A Photographic Survey of the Indo-Hispano Traditions of the Rio Grande Corridor, Rockefeller Found, 92-93; Latino Diversity, Use of 20 inch by 24 inch instant camera; Photographic collaboration with Sonaran photog Oscar Monroy (photog colonias in Nogales, Mex), Ariz Comn Arts, 94; From the West: Chicano Narrative Photography (narrative photog series), Mex Mus, San Francisco, Calif, 94. *Exhib:* Contemp-Am Photog, Galeria Licht, Oslo, Norway, 77-78; Boxers & Wrestlers, Blue Sky Gallery, Portland, Ore, 78; Let's Boogie at Okies, ASA Gallery, Univ NMex, Albuquerque, 80; Burque, Santa Fe Ctr Photogr, NMex, 84; The New Photog Survey, Mus Fine Arts, Santa Fe, 85; Statements, NMex State Fair Gallery, Albuquerque, 85 & 86; VSJ/Scenes from an Urban Chicano Experience, Nev State Mus Am Hist, Smithsonian Inst, Washington, DC, 90 & Univ NMex Art Mus, Albuquerque, 93; Hispanic Scenes from the Southwest, Kenyon Col, Gambier, Ohio, 91; La Frontera: A Way to Survive, MARS Art Space, Phoenix, Ariz, 94; Homeland/Use and Desire, Mass Coll Art, Boston, 94; From the West: Chicano Narrative Photog, Mex Mus, San Francisco, Calif, 95-. *Teaching:* Instr photogr, Univ NMex, Albuquerque, 82-83, asst prof, currently. *Bibliog:* Kathy Livingston (auth), Riding low, Am Photogr, 4/84; Bart Ripp (auth), The south valley knows the photographer, Albuquerque Tribune, 8/12/85; Hal Rhodes (dir), The Illustrated Daily, 85 & Miguel Gandeft photographer-on assignment, KNME TV. *Mem:* Hispanic Cult Found. *Publ:* Contrib, Contemporary Identities: The Phoenix Triennial, Phoenix Art Mus, 93; 1993 Biennial Exhibition, Whitney Mus Am Art, Harry N Abrams Inc, Publ, NY; Three Generations of Hispanic Photographers Working in NMex, Harwood Found Univ NMex, Taos, 93; coauth, Flow of River, Hispanic cult Found; photogr, Los Tesoros del Espiritu: Familia y Fe, Academia El Norte Publ, 94. *Dealer:* Andrew Smith Gallery 76 E San Francisco St Santa Fe NM 87501. *Mailing Add:* c/o Andrew Smith Gallery 203 W San Francisco St Santa Fe NM 87501

GANEK, DANIELLE & DAVID
COLLECTOR

Study: Franklin & Marshall Coll, grad, 1985. *Pos:* Risk arbitrage trader, Donaldson Lufkin & Jenrette, New York; partner, Strategic Air Command Capital Advisors LLC, Stamford, CT; co-founder & principal, Level Global Investors LP, Greenwich, 2003. *Awards:* Named one of Top 200 Collectors, ARTnews mag, 2004-13; Top Billionaire Art Collectors, Forbes mag, 2005 (David); Investment Mgmt Divsn award, UJA Fedn, NY, 2008 (David). *Collection:* Contemporary art & photography

GANEK, DOROTHY SKEADOS
PAINTER, DESIGNER

b Athens, Greece, Aug 8, 1946; US Citizen. *Study:* NY Sch Interior Design, 65-68. *Work:* Schering Plough Corp, NJ; Sheraton, Needham, Mass; Cigna Corp; PSE & Gas Co, Warner Lambert Inc; Caldwell Banker; Kenwood Electronics; Kessler Institute, NEC; and others. *Exhib:* Zheijiang Mus, Hangzhou, China; Nat Asn Women Artists (traveling), 88; Los Angeles Artcore Invitational, Nat Watercolor Soc, 88; Am Watercolor Soc, 91-92. *Pos:* Interior designer, Ganek Interiors. *Awards:* Silver Medal Honor, NJ Watercolor Soc; Cecil Shapiro Award, Nat Asn Women Artists, 91; John Young Hunter Award, Am Watercolor Soc, 92. *Mem:* Nat Asn Women Artists; NJ Watercolor Soc; Allied Artists Am; Audubon Artists; Am Watercolor Soc. *Media:* Mixed Media. *Publ:* Splash (watercolor book), 90; Goodlife Mag, 90; Am Artist Mag-Watercolor, spring 94; The Best of Watercolor & The Best Compositions, Rockport Publ; and others. *Dealer:* Kerygma Gallery Ridgewood NJ; Juxtapose Gallery Westfield NJ. *Mailing Add:* 125 Rynda Rd South Orange NJ 07079

GANESH, CHITRA
PAINTER, PRINTMAKER

b Brooklyn, NY. *Study:* Brown Univ, Providence, BA, 1996; Columbia Univ, MFA, 2002. *Work:* Deutsche Bank; Brooklyn Mus; Queens Mus Art; Wake Forest Univ; Devi Art Found. *Exhib:* Floorplay, Brooklyn Coll Art Gallery, NY, 2004; solo exhib, Jersey City Mus, NJ, 2005; The Gift: Building a Collection, Queens Mus Art, 2005; E7 Emerge Artist Exhib, Aljira Ctr for Contemp Art, NJ, 2006; One Way or Another, Blaffer Gallery, Univ Houston, 2007; Vital Signs, Newcomb Art Gallery Tulane Univ, 2008. *Awards:* Workspace Grant, Lower Manhattan Cult Coun, 2004; Gregory Millard Fel, 2005; NY Found Arts Fel, 2005, 2009. *Bibliog:* Daniel Kunitz (auth), Defying the Definitive Museums, New York Sun, 9/14/2006; Holland Cotter (auth), Sex in the City, NY Times, 11/23/2007; Sharon Mizota (auth), Indian art: unique yet mainstream, Los Angeles Times, 7/8/2008. *Mailing Add:* c/o Thomas Erben Gallery 526 W 26th St New York NY 10001

GANG, JEANNE
ARCHITECT

b 1964. *Study:* Univ Ill Urbana-Champaign, BS in Archit, 86; Eidgenössische Technische Hochschule, Archit & Planning, Zürich, 89; Harvard Univ, MArch with distinction, 93. *Work:* Starlight Theatre at Rock Valley Coll, Rockford, Ill; Chinese-Am Community Ctr, Chgo, Ill. *Exhib:* Marble Curtain, Masonry Variations Exhib, Wash; Venice Biennale; Nat Bldg Mus; Art Inst Chgo. *Pos:* registered archit, Ill Project Archit Office for Metropolitan Archit (OMA), Rotterdam, Netherlands, 93-95; designer, Booth Hansen Architects, 95-97; pres, Chgo Archit Club, 2000-2001; founder, prin, Studio Gang Architects, 98-. *Teaching:* adj assoc prof, Ill Inst Tech, 98-; facilitator, Archeworks; vis prof, Harvard Grad Sch Design, 2004; Louis I Kahn prof chair, Yale Sch Archit, 2005; grad design studio vis lectr, Princeton Univ, 2007. *Awards:* Acac award, Am Acad Arts & Letts, 2006; Named a MacArthur Fellow, John D & Catherine T MacArthur Found, 2011; Named One of 25 Women to Watch, Crain's Chgo Bus, 2007. *Mem:* AIA; Nat Acad. *Publ:* featured in Metropolis & Architecture Mag. *Mailing Add:* Studio Gang Architects 1212 N Ashland Ave Ste 1212 Chicago IL 60622

GANIHAR, TOMER
PHOTOGRAPHER

b Tel Aviv, 1970. *Exhib:* Solo exhibs include We Shall Live to See, Tel Aviv Mus Art, 2000; Holy Land X, Paul Rodgers/9W, New York, 2002; Sharing the Light, UN Headquarters, New York, 2003; Raving in the Desert, Contemp Arts Ctr, New Orleans, 2005; group exhibs include 90th Anniversary of Tel Aviv, Tel Aviv Mus Art, 1999; Views from Israel, Gallery Contemp Art, San Francisco, 2000; Think with the Senses, Feel with the Mind: Art in the Present Tense, Venice Biennale, 2007. *Dealer:* Paul Rodgers/9W Gallery 529 W 20th St 9th Fl New York NY 10011

GANIS, LUCY
SCULPTOR, EDUCATOR

b Plainfield, NJ. *Study:* Art Students League, 70; Lake Erie Col, BFA, 71; Pratt Inst, with Calvin Albert & George McNeil, MFA, 74. *Work:* Lehigh Univ, Westtown Sch, Pa; ARA Services. *Exhib:* May Show, Cleveland Mus Art, 74; Drawings USA, Smithsonian Inst Traveling Exhib, 76-79; solo exhib, Westchester State Col, Pa, 79;

For the Love of Drawing, Kemerer Mus, Bethlehem, Pa, 81; Del Biennial, Univ Del, Newark, 81 & 83; Installation of Drawings & Sculpture, Muse Gallery, Philadelphia, 83 & 85; Installation of Sculpture and Drawings, Lehigh Univ, 85; Allentown Art Mus, 86; Southern Vt Art Center, 86; In Her Own Words, Zoellner Art Center. *Collection Arranged:* Women's Caucus Art Nat Exhib (auth, catalog), 84. *Teaching:* Vis lectr sculpture & drawing, Lake Erie Col, Ohio, 74-75; instr sculpture, Univ SAla, 76-77; assoc prof sculpture, drawing & painting, Lehigh Univ, Pa, 81-; prof, dir design arts, Lehigh Univ, 2008. *Awards:* Art with a Social Impact Award, Bethlehem Fine Arts commission. *Mem:* Coll Art Asn; Women's Caucus Art. *Media:* Mixed Media, Paper. *Dealer:* Muse Gallery 1915 Walnut St Philadelphia PA 19103. *Mailing Add:* Dept Art & Archit Lehigh Univ 17 Memorial Dr E Bethlehem PA 18015

GANIS, WILLIAM V
EDUCATOR, ADMINISTRATOR, WRITER
Study: Univ Pittsburgh, BA (Art History, Studio Art and Business), 1993; Stony Brook Univ, MA (Art History and Criticism), 1998, PhD (Art History and Criticism), 2001. *Teaching:* Asst to Assoc prof art history, advisor, art historymajor, coordinator art history minor, dir String Room Gallery, Wells Col, formerly; prof art history, dept chair, Indiana State Univ, currently. *Publ:* Active arts writer, pens reviews and articles for national and international publications including Artforum, Scuplture, and Border Crossings, Contemporary, Glass Quarterly, and Sculpture; auth, Andy Warhol's Serial Photography, 2004; auth, Anxious Objects: Andy Warhol's Photography, 2009; auth, Photography: Andy Warhol's Social Disease, 2012. *Mailing Add:* Indiana State University Department of Art and Design 200 North Seventh St Terre Haute IN 47809-1902

GANJIAN, LINDA
SCULPTOR
b Boston, 1970. *Study:* Bard Coll, NY, BA (painting), 1992; Hunter Coll, City Univ NY, MFA, 1998. *Exhib:* Solo exhibs include Eyewash @ Gallery Boreas, Brooklyn, NY, 2006; group exhibs include Between the Acts, Art in General, New York, 1997; Armenian Ctr Contemp & Experimental Art, 1998; Open House: Working in Brooklyn, Brooklyn Mus Art, 2004; Garden of Eden, US Embassy of Armenia, 2005; Queens Int, Queens Mus Art, Flushing, NY, 2006; 183rd Ann: Invitational Exhib Contemp Am Art, 2008. *Awards:* Artslink Grant, 2001; Arpa Found Film Mus & Art Grant, 2001; Gunk Found Grant, 2002; Vt Studio Ctr Fel, 2003; Millay Colony Fel, 2004; Pollack-Krasner Found Grant, 2005; Hall Farm Ctr Fel, 2005; MacDowell Colony Fel, 2006. *Mailing Add:* 84-12 35th Ave #6F Jackson Heights NY 11372

GANLEY, BETTY
PAINTER, PHOTOGRAPHER
b Rahway, NJ, Sept 18, 1942. *Work:* Freddie Mac Corp, McLean, Va; Holy Cross Hosp, Silver Springs, Md; Oxford Town Hall, Oxford, Md. *Exhib:* Quiet Waters Gallery, Annapolis, Md, 96; 20th Ann Exhib, Southern Watercolor Soc, Delf Norna Mus, Moundsville, WVa, 97; Mid-Atlantic Regional Watercolor Exhib, Rockville, Md, 97; Va Watercolor Soc, Va, 2000 & 2004; Rocky Mt Nat Watermedia Exhib, Colo, 2000; The Manor House, Green Spring Gardens Park, Alexandria, Va, 2002; Blackrock Ctr Arts, Germantown, Md, 2003. *Awards:* Merit Award, Mid-Atlantic Regional Watercolor Exhib, 98; Best of Show, Treasury Art Show, Vienna Art Soc, 99, Rockville Art League, 97 & 2001, Potomac Valley Watercolor Soc, 6/2004 & Wash Watercolor Soc, 2005; Spec Award, Va Watercolor Soc Ann Show, 2000; Selected, Neiman Marcus Top 100 Artists of 2000; Top 100, Nat Arts for the Parks Competition, Jackson Lake Lodge, 2001; Second Place, Baltimore Watercolor Soc, Slayton Gallery Show, 2002; Best of Show & Hon Mention, Potomac Valley Watercolor Soc, Quiet Waters Gallery, 9/2004; Top Ten, Australian Artist Magazine, Still Life Competition (Int), 2004; North Light Award, Virginia Watercolor Soc, North Light Publ co, 2004; Peoples Choice Award, Vienna Art Soc, Small Works Show, 2005; D'Arches Award, Mid-Atlantic Regional Watercolor Exhib, Strathmore Hall, 2007; First Place, Watercolor Reston Art League, 2007; Gibson/Blick Award, Mid-Atlantic Watercolor Exhib, Strathmore Hall, 2009; Best of Show, League of Reston Artist's Ann Exhib, 2009. *Bibliog:* Alice Ross (auth), A Matter of Perspective, Elán Magazine, 2000. *Mem:* Southern Watercolor Soc; Va Watercolor Soc, (dir at large, 2004); Potomac Valley Watercolor Soc; Wash Watercolor Soc; Baltimore Watercolor Soc; Vienna Art Soc; Rockville Art League. *Media:* Watercolor. *Publ:* Contribr, Fresh Flowers, The Best of Flower Painting, North Lights Publ, 96; Splash 5, The Glory of Color, North Light Publ, 98; The Artists Touch III, Creative Art Press, 99; Splash 7, A Celebration of Light, North Light Publ, 2002; contribr, Splash 9, Watercolor Secrets, North Light Publ, 2006; auth & illustr, Artists Projects You Can Paint, 10 Secret Gardens in Watercolor, Int Artist, 2005. *Mailing Add:* 713 Forest Park Rd Great Falls VA 22066

GANTZ, ANN CUSHING
PAINTER, INSTRUCTOR
b Dallas, Tex, Aug 27, 1935. *Study:* Memphis Acad Art; Southwestern Univ, Memphis; Newcomb Coll Tulane Univ, New Orleans, La, BFA, 55. *Work:* Dallas Mus Fine Arts; Denver Mus; Smithsonian Inst, Washington, DC; Boston Mus; Los Angeles State Mus; Oklahoma City Mus, Okla; corp collections incl Southland Life co, Tex Instruments Inc, LTV co, Collins & Collins Law Firm; others. *Comn:* KERA-TV, 88; Trammell Crow co, 88; Alpha Omicron Pi Hq, 95; Dallas Opera, 96; Design Ctr, 96; Tex Visual Arts Asn, 2009. *Exhib:* Oklahoma City Art Ctr, 56-58; Painting & Sculpture Ann, Nat Acad Design, New York, 57 & 60; Norfolk Mus, Va, 58 & 59; Printmaking Today, Brooklyn Mus, NY, 59; Ann Shows, Ark Art Ctr, Little Rock, 59-61; Retrospective, Dallas Visual Art Ctr, 96; Tennison Gallery, 99; Valley House, 2003; David Dike Gallery, 2002 & 2003; Tex Art Collectors, 2002 & 2003; MAC Mus, Group, 2004-2006; Solo exhib, Plano Art Ctr, 2006 & Monticello Gallery, Fort Worth, 2006; and others. *Collection Arranged:* Var families. *Pos:* Pres, Cushing Galleries Inc, 63-79; owner, Cushing Studio, 79-. *Teaching:* Instr printmaking & painting, Dallas Mus Fine Arts Sch, 56-62; instr painting, printmaking & drawing, Cushing Galleries Sch Studio Art, 62-79, instr, Cushing Studio, 79-. *Awards:* TFAA Artist of Yr Award, 79; Oak Award, 81; McMurray Found Award, 83; Delta Kappa Award, 87. *Mem:* Dallas Print & Drawing Soc (pres, 58-60); YWCA Art Comt; Tex Printmakers (pres, 60-63); Dallas Art Gallery Asn (founder, 78); Cushing Atelier (founder, pres, 90-2003); TV Visual Arts Asn (hon); Dallas Arts Coalition. *Media:* Oil, Woodcut; Acrylic, Serigraphy. *Res:* Papers in Smithsonian collection and Hamon Library of Texas Art. *Mailing Add:* 4654 Edmondson Dallas TX 75209

GANZ, JULIAN, JR
PATRON
b Dec, 1929. *Pos:* Pres, McMahan Furniture Stores, Los Angeles, currently; trustee, Los Angeles Co Mus Art, currently; Nat Gallery Art, Wash, DC. *Mailing Add:* McMahans Furniture 100 N Brand Blvd Ste 516 Glendale CA 91203

GANZ, SYLVIA SQUIRES See Squires Ganz, Sylvia (Tykie)

GANZI, VICTOR FREDERICK
PATRON
b NY City, Feb 14, 1947. *Study:* Fordham Univ, BS, 68; Harvard Univ, JD, 71; NYU, LLM (taxation), 81. *Pos:* Tax accountant, Touche Ross & Co, Denver, 71-73; assoc, Rogers & Wells, New York City, 73-78, partner, 78-86; managing partner, Rogers & Wells (now Clifford Chance Rogers & Wells), 86-90; vpres, secy, gen counsel, Hearst Corp, New York City, 90-92, Chief Financial Officer, chief legal off, sr vpres, 92-97; pres, Hearst Books/Bus Pub Group, 95-99; exec vpres Hearst Corp, New York City, 97-2002, Chief Operating Officer, 98-2002, pres, Chief Exec Officer, 2002-. *Mem:* Am Bar Asn; Am Inst of CPA; Colo Soc CPAs; William Randolph Hearst Found (bd dir, currently); Whitney Mus Am Art (trustee, currently). *Mailing Add:* c/o Towers Watson 335 Madison Ave New York NY 10017

GARBUTT, JANICE LOVOOS
PAINTER, WRITER
b Dubuque, Iowa. *Study:* Chouinard Art Inst. *Comn:* Mural, comn by Mr & Mrs Walter Frey, San Clemente, Calif. *Exhib:* Los Angeles Co Art Mus; Calif Art Club; solo exhibs, Circle Gallery, San Diego, Descanso Gardens, Carol Hard's Rancho Mirage Gallery & the Gallery, Palm Springs, Calif. *Pos:* Narrator, Visions of Calif (doc film), KCOE Pub Television, 95. *Teaching:* Instr fashion promotion, Chouinard Art Inst, 47-48. *Awards:* Merit Award; First Prize for Short Story, Ann Conf Mary & Donald Decker, Royal Lit; Selected as one of Ten Living Legends Exhib, Kluglak Gallery, Miracosta Col; Svc Award Am Artists mag. *Mem:* Am Soc Composers, Authors & Publishers; Author's Guild; Dramatist's Guild Am. *Media:* All. *Res:* Archived writings on Calif art by the Smithsonian. *Publ:* Auth & illusr, Design is a Dandelion; co-auth, Making Pottery without a Wheel, Prentice Hall, in prep; many articles in Los Angeles Times, Am Artist, Westways, Christian Sci Monitor, Charm, Parade, Toledo Star News & Southwest Art; Antiques & Fine Arts. *Dealer:* ART Beasley Gallery 2802 Juan St San Diego CA 92110. *Mailing Add:* 431 Calle Empalme San Clemente CA 92672

GARCIA, OFELIA
ART ADMINISTRATOR, EDUCATOR
b Havana, Cuba, Feb 12, 1941; US citizen. *Study:* Escuela Nacional de Bellas Artes, Havana, Cuba, 58-60; Manhattanville Coll, BA, 69; Tufts Univ & Boston Mus Sch, MFA (printmaking), 72; Duke Univ, Post-Grad. *Hon Degrees:* Atlanta Coll Art, Hon Dr (fine arts), 91. *Work:* Princeton Univ Graphic Arts Coll; NJ State Mus, Trenton; Free Libr Philadelphia; Museo Grafico, Inst Puerto Rican Culture, San Juan; Barnard Coll, NY. *Exhib:* Solo exhibs, Colegio Universitario, Santurce, PR, 70, Cohen Arts Ctr, Tufts Univ, 72 & Duke Univ Gallery, 74; Third Miami Graphics Biennial, Metrop Mus & Art Ctr, Fla, 77; 53rd Ann Juried Show, The Print Club, Philadelphia, 77; NJ State Mus, Trenton, 78; Barnard Coll, NY, 79; Five Hispanic Artists, Deshong Mus, Pa, 82; A Growing Am Treasure, Pa Acad Fine Arts, William Penn Mus, 83. *Collection Arranged:* Invitational Print Exhib in honor of Lessing J Rosenwald (auth, catalog), Print Club, Philadelphia, Pa, 80; Contemp Prints from Lehigh Univ Collection (auth, catalog), Bethlehem, Pa, 80; Recent Gifts: Print at Univ Pa (auth, catalog), Grad Sch Fine Arts, 81; Printed by Women (auth, catlog), Philadelphia, Pa, 83; Int Mezzotint Competition, The Print Club & Pratt Graphic Ctr, NY, 84. *Pos:* Dir, Print Club, 78-85; critic, PAFA, 82-85; pres, Atlanta Coll Art, 86-91; pres, Rosemont Coll, 91-95; Senior Fel, Am Coun Educ, 95-97; Dean, Coll Art, 97-2006; Fac, Coll Art & Commun, William Paterson Univ, 2006-2011, retired. *Teaching:* Asst prof printmaking & drawing, Newton Coll Sacred Heart, 69-73, chmn dept, 70-73; asst prof, Boston Coll, 75-76; prof, William Paterson Univ, 97-2011. *Awards:* First Prize, All-Sch Competition, Escuela de Bellas Artes, Havana, Cuba, 59; Am Bk Builders Scholar Prize, Boston Mus Sch, 69; Kent Fel, Danforth Found, 75-80; citation, City of Philadelphia, 85; President's Award, 99 & Lifetime Achievement Award, 2011, Women's Caucus for Art. *Bibliog:* Ross Romano (auth), The Complete Collagraph, Macmillan, 80; articles in Philadelphia Inquirer, 79-95, Atlanta Constitution, 86-91 & Print Collector's Newsletter. *Mem:* Fel Soc Values Higher Educ; Woman's Caucus Art (pres, 84-86); Coll Art Asn Am (bd dir, 86-90); Haverford Coll (bd mem, 1992-2004); ArtPride NJ (mem, 2005-); Jersey City Mus (bd chmn, 2001-08); NJ State Coun Arts (mem 2007-2009, vice chmn, 2009-2011, chair, 2011-); Hudson County Arts Comn, 2009-2012; Libr Comm Phila Mus Art. *Media:* Prints, Drawings. *Interests:* Works on Paper, particularly by women artists. *Publ:* contribr, Mentoring the Profession, Career Development and Support, The Eye, The Hand, The Mind: 100 Years of Coll Art Asn, Rutgers Univ Press, 2011. *Dealer:* The Print Ctr 1614 Latimer St Philadelphia PA 19103. *Mailing Add:* 28 N 3rd St 2R Philadelphia PA 19106

GARCIA, RUPERT (MARSHALL) R
PAINTER, EDUCATOR
b French Camp, Calif, Sept 29, 1941. *Study:* San Francisco State Univ, with John Gutmann, BA, 68, with Richard MacLean & Robert Bechtle, MA, 70; Univ Calif, Berkeley, with Peter Selz, Herschel Chipp & T J Clark, MA, 81. *Work:* Nat Mus Am Art, Smithsonian Inst, Washington, DC; Oakland Mus, Calif; Univ Art Mus, Berkeley,

Calif; San Francisco Mus Mod Art, Calif; The Mex Mus, San Francisco. *Comn:* Posters and Society (poster), San Francisco Mus Mod Art, 74; posters for Amnesty Int, San Francisco, 76; Mex Mus, San Francisco, 76; Nat Chicano Coun Higher Educ, Berkeley, Calif, 79; pastel painting, Ruben Libr, Sonoma State Univ, Rohnert Park, Calif, 79. *Exhib:* Solo exhibs, Oakland Mus, 70, San Francisco Mus Mod Art, 78, Univ Art Gallery, State Univ NY, Binghamton, 81, Univ Art Mus, Berkeley, Calif, 84, Mex Mus, San Francisco, 86 & The Haggin Mus, Stockton, Calif, 88; Images of an Era: The Am Poster 45-75, Nat Collection Fine Arts, Smithsonian Inst & Corcoran Gallery Art, Washington, DC, 75; Raices Antiquas/Visones Nuevas, Tucson Mus Art, Ariz, 77; Prelude to the Fifth Sun, Univ Art Mus, Berkeley, Calif, 77; Mex-Am Artists San Francisco Bay Area, Mex Mus, 78; Das Andere Am, Staaliche Kunsthalle, Berlin, WGer, 83; The Human Condition, Mus Mod Art Biennial III, San Francisco, 84; Close Focus, Nat Mus Am Art, Washington, DC, 87; Committed to print, Mus Mod Art, NY, 88; Latin Am Presence in US, Bronx Mus Arts, NY, 88; and others. *Collection Arranged:* Arte de la Revolucion Cubana: Silkscreens by Rene Mederos, Galeria de La Raza, San Francisco, 73; Realismo Chicano: Drawings by Juan Fuentes, Chicano Students Libr, Univ Calif, Berkeley, 76. *Pos:* Artist in residence, Calif Arts Coun, 86, Inst Cult Commun EW Ctr, Honolulu, Hawaii, 87. *Teaching:* Lectr silkscreen, printmaking, painting & drawing, San Francisco State Univ, 78, 79 & summer 81; lectr art hist Mex, Univ Calif, Berkeley, 79-81, lectr graphic design, 82-85; vis asst prof art hist Mex, Wash State Univ, Pullman, 84; vis artist, Ill State Univ, Bloomington, 88; assoc prof art, San Jose State Univ, 88-. *Awards:* Printmaking, San Francisco Arts Comn, 86; Purple Globe Award, San Francisco State Univ, 86. *Bibliog:* Ramon Favela (auth), The Art of Rupert Garcia, The Mexican Mus, San Francisco, 86; Peter Selz, (auth), Rupert Garcia: The Moral Fervor of Painting and its Subjects, Arts, 4/87; Bill Berkson (auth), Rupert Garcia, The Haggin Mus, 88. *Media:* Oil, Pastel. *Res:* Art and culture of the Chicano and Mexican. *Publ:* Coauth, Recent Raza murals in the US, Radical Am, 78; auth, Politics of Popular Art, Chimearte, Los Angeles, 78; Murales Recientes de La Raza en Estado Unidos, Plural, Mex, 79; Mexican Movie Poster Art, Myth, Illusion, Deception, Galeria de la Raza, San Francisco, 79; Frida Kahlo, A Bibliography and Biographical Introduction, Univ of Calif, Berkeley, 83. *Dealer:* Iannetti-Lanzone Gallery 310 Grant Ave San Francisco CA 94108; Saxon-Lee Gallery 7525 Beverly Blvd Los Angeles 90036

GARCIA GUERRERO, LUIS
PAINTER

b Guanajuato City, Mex, Nov 18, 1921. *Study:* Escuela Nac de Artes Plasticas, UNAM, 49; Escuela de Pintura, Escultura y Grabado, INBA, 50; Taller de Tecnicas y Materiales, IPN, 51. *Work:* Galeria de Arte Mexicano, Mus Nac de la Estampa, INBA, Galeria Lopez Quiroga, Mexico City. *Comn:* Stained-glass window, Zoquiapan, Mex, 53-56. *Exhib:* Los Surrealistas en México, Mus Nac de Arte, INBA, Mexico City, 86; Divertimentos, Galeria de Arte Mexicano, Mexico City, 86; one-man show, Mus del Pueblo, Guanajuata City, 87. *Bibliog:* Luis Cardoza Y Aragon (auth), Luis Garcia Guerrero, State of Guanajuato, 82; Carlos Monsivais (auth), Garcia Guerrero, Promexa, 87; Sergio Pitol (auth), Luis Garcia Guerrero, State of Guanajuato, 93. *Media:* Oil. *Mailing Add:* c/o Galeria De Arte Mexicano Gobernador Rafael Rebollar 43 San Miguel Chapultepec 11850 Mexico

GARD, SUZANNE E
PAINTER

b Seattle, Wash. *Comn:* Benton's Heavenly Serenade, comn by FE Everett Jr, Pres DAPC, 94; Animal Portraits, comn by Dr C Hunter, OD Seattle, Wash, 94. *Exhib:* Mamaroneck 36th Ann Nat Open Exhib, Westbeth Gallery, NY, 94; Special Voices, Thunder Spirit Lodge, Jahn/Matter Arts, Minneapolis, Minn, 94; solo exhibs, Sidney Gallery & Mus, Port Orchard, Wash, 94, Moss Bay Gallery, Kirkland, Wash, 95 & Kent Arts Comn Exhib, City Hall, Wash, 95-96; Children's Hosp, Seattle, 95; AKIM, MASK's 96, Sotheby's, NY, 96. *Teaching:* Instr drawing & inks, City of Kent Cult Arts, 95-. *Awards:* Award Excellence, Manhattan Arts Int Artists 90s, 95 & 96; First & Third Places, Auburn Juried Fine Art, Wash, 96. *Bibliog:* Catherine Drillis (auth), Suzanne Gard explores natures evolutions, Manhattan Arts Int Artists in the 90's, 11-12/93; JM Lewis (auth), About the cover artist Suzanne Gard, The Entertainer, 3/94; Thomas Lawrence (auth), Suzanne Gard blends detail with drama, Manhattan Arts Int Artists in the 90's, 11/12/94. *Mem:* Catharine Lorillard Wolfe Art Club; Oil Pastel Asn/United Pastelists Am; Knickerbocker Artists USA; NW Watercolor Soc, Seattle. *Media:* Watercolor; Mixed Inks on Paper. *Mailing Add:* 24301 138th Ave SE Kent WA 98042-5185

GARDINER, HENRY GILBERT
ART APPRAISER, MUSEUM DIRECTOR

b Boston, Mass, Aug 27, 1927. *Study:* Harvard Col, AB, 50; Harvard Univ, MA, 59. *Collection Arranged:* Color & Form, 1909-1914, & Cross & Sword, 76, San Diego Mus, 76. *Pos:* Cur paintings & sculpture, Philadelphia Mus Art, 60-69; dir, San Diego Mus Art, 69-79 & Mitchell Wolfson Mus, Miami, 83-84. *Teaching:* Prof mus studies, Univ Southern Calif, 81. *Specialty:* European and American art from 1850 to 1950, with emphasis on abstract painting 1900-1915. *Publ:* Philadelphia Mus Art (bulls): Sculpture Checklist of the 19th & 20th Centuries at Philadelphia Mus Art, Vol LVI, 269, spring 1961; The Samuel S White 3rd & Vera White Collection, Vol LXIII, 296 & 297, Jan-June 1968; Arthur B Carles: A Critical & Biographical Study, Vol LXIV, 302-303, Jan-June 1970; Painter Exterior Walls of Southern California, Vol I, 2 (current), June-June 1975. *Mailing Add:* PO Box 3121 Palm Beach FL 33480

GARDNER, SHEILA
PAINTER

b Jersey City, NJ, Mar 31, 1933. *Study:* Endicott Coll, AA, 52; Art Students League, 54-57; New Sch, 56-59. *Work:* AT&T, Mobil Oil & Chemical Bank, NY; Portland Mus Art, Maine; Boise Art Mus, Idaho; Wilding Art Mus, Los Olivos, Calif. *Comn:* Arthur Anderson, Boston, Mass, 87; Westone Bank, Boise, Idaho. *Exhib:* Contemp Images: Watercolor, Allen Priebe Gallery, Univ Wis, Oshkosh, 83; Traveling Exhib, Am Realism-20th Century Drawings & Watercolors, San Francisco Mus Mod Art, Calif, 85-86, De Cordova & Dana Mus, Lincoln, Mass, 86, Akron Art Mus, Ohio & A M Huntington Art Gallery, Univ Tex, Austin, 87; The Monumental Image: Watercolor USA, Springfield Art Mus, Mo, 86; Boise Art Mus, 88-90; Univ Idaho, Moscow, 90; Green Woods and Crystal Waters: The Am Landscape Tradition Since 1950, Philbrook Mus Art, Tulsa, Okla & 3 Mus, 99-. *Teaching:* Workshops, Sun Valley Ctr Arts & Humanities, 85, 89, 90, 93-95, 2006; instr painting & drawing, Univ Maine, 86. *Bibliog:* Women Artists and American Watercolors, Abbeville Press, 88; John Arthur (auth), Spirit of Place, Bullfinch; Abrams (auth), American Realism-Janss Collection; John Driscoll (auth), The Artist and the American Landscape, Chameleon Press, 98. *Media:* Oil, Watercolor. *Dealer:* Gail Severn Gallery 400 First Ave North Ketchum ID 83340. *Mailing Add:* 748 Eastlake Dr Spring Creek NV 89815

GARDNER, SUSAN ROSS
PAINTER

b New York, NY, Oct 25, 1941. *Work:* Metrop Mus Art, NY; Southern Ill Univ; Northern Ill Univ; Atlantic Richfield Corp; Woman's Interart Ctr; Art Embassies Prog, Washington, DC; other private collections. *Comn:* Two wall murals, Pub Sch 94, Dept Cult Affairs Percent for Arts Prog, NY; Noah's Ark, St Peters Church, Citicorp, NY. *Exhib:* Seattle Art Mus, 71; De Cordova Mus, Lincoln, Mass, 71; Cook Gallery, Lincoln Ctr, 81; Brooklyn Mus, 72, 78, 79, 82 & 84; 55 Mercer St, NY, 82; one-person shows, Webb & Parsons Gallery, Conn, 82, Twinning Gallery, NY, 83, LaGuardia Community Col, 84, 94 & 97 & Saint Peter's, Citicorp, NY, 86; The Doll Show, Hillwood Art Gallery, CW Post Col, NY, 85; City Without Walls, Newark, 1986, 87, 88 & 90; Goddard Gallery, NY, 1991 & 94; Animals, Animals, Anita Shapolsky Gallery, NY, 1995; Art and the Law (traveling), univ galleries acroos USA, 1996-97; Earthquake, Mus Moving Image, Astoria, NY, 1997; Fed Reserve, NY, 1998; Outsider (invitational), Bittersweet Gallery, New Haven, Conn, 1998; Art and Humor invitational, NY, 1999; You Are What You Eat (invitational), Peekskil (NY) Art Ctr, 1999; The Dirt Show (invitational), Tobey Fine Arts, NY, 2000; SmallWorks Invitational, Blue Mountain Gallery, NY, 2001. *Teaching:* Asst prof studio & art hist, Manhattan Community Col, New York, 66-70; assoc prof, head of Art Dept, Yeshiva Univ, 75-. *Awards:* Purchase Award, Northern Ill Univ, 71. *Bibliog:* interview, NY Times, 5/27/1973; photo & article, Long Island Press, 4/27/73, East Hampton Star, 5/73 & Arts, 6/83; article, Daily News, 3/1970, 4/1973 & 10/1987. *Mem:* Coll Art Asn Am. *Media:* Acrylic, Rhoplex, Metal; Mosaic, Tiles, Beadwork. *Mailing Add:* 108 Wyckoff St Brooklyn NY 11201-6307

GAREY, PATRICIA MARTIN
CERAMIST, PAINTER

b State College, Miss, Nov 11, 1932. *Study:* Tex Woman's Univ, BS (costume design & fashion illus); Tex Tech Univ, Lubbock, MFA, with Jim Howze, Terry Morrow, Lynwood Kreneck, Hugh Gibbons, 2-Dimensional Studio & Minor Art Hist; Art Students League, 77; Villa Maria Ctr Arts, Perugia, Italy, 85. *Work:* Home Econs Dept, Tex Tech Univ, Lubbock; NMex Jr Coll, Hobbs; Black Gold Casino, NMex; NMex state capitol bldg, The Round House, Santa Fe; Broadmoor Tower, Hobbs, NMex. *Exhib:* Santa Fe Festival of Arts, 79 & 80; Sangre Cristo Art Ctr, Pueblo, Colo, 79; Solo exhibs, NMex Jr Coll, Hobbs, 81 & Univ Tex Permian Basin, Odessa, 81, Dallas Mus Fine Art, Beaux Arts Ball Art Auction & Exhib, Dallas, Tex, 86-88 & 90; Clayworkers of NMex Invitational Exhib, Governors Gallery, Round House State Capitol, Santa Fe, 95; and many others. *Pos:* Artist in sch prog, HEW Emergency Sch Aid Proj, Hobbs, 74-; artist, bd dir, Southwest Symphony, Hobbs, NMex, 88 & 90; West States rep, Villa Maria Ctr Arts, Perugia, Italy; arts comnr, NMex, 99-2002. *Teaching:* Instr drawing & painting, Coll Southwest, NMex, 67-70, instr art hist & appreciation, 74; summer workshops, Cloud Croft, NMex, 89, 91 & 92; instr, Dossant Meadows Mus Art, Dallas, Tex, 90; drawing instr, Villa Maria Ctr Arts, Perugia, Italy, 96; prof, NMex Jr Coll, 96-97. *Awards:* Cash Award, Figure Study No 1, 72; First Prize Ceramics, 74 & First Prize Graphics, 75, Llano Estacado Art Asn; Best of Show, ceramics, Llano Estacado Art Asn, 98 & Best of Show, oil painting, 2004. *Media:* Drawing; Acrylic, Oil, Clay. *Interests:* Swimming, travel, book collecting, piano. *Dealer:* De-Lis Galleries Hobbs NMex; Contemporary Arts Hobbs NM

GARFIELD, PETER
PAINTER, PHOTOGRAPHER

b Stamford, Conn, 1961. *Study:* Dartmouth Coll, BA (cum laude), 84; Ecole Nationale Superieure des Beaux-Arts, Paris, France, 85-87; Pratt Inst, Brooklyn, NY, 87. *Work:* San Francisco Mus Mod Art; Los Angeles Co Mus Art; Progressive Corp, Cleveland, Ohio; Howard Stein Collection, NY. *Exhib:* solo exhibs, Am Cathedral, Paris, France, 87, Strauss Gallery, Dartmouth Col, 93, Plerogi 2000, Brooklyn, 96 & Felgen Gallery, Chicago, 96, Feigen Contemp, NY, 98,Queens Mus Bulova Cen, NY, 98, Kaplnos Galerie, Berlin, Ger, 99, 2000, Vaknin Schwartz, Atlanta, Ga, 99, Art & Pub, Geneve, Switz, 2000; Planie-Galerie Guth & Maas, Reutlingen, Ger, 96, Feigen Contemp, NY, 98, Queens Mus Bulova Ctr, NY, 98; High Anxiety, Ctr Photog Woodstock, NY, 96; Blind Spot: The First Four Years, Paolo Baldacci Gallery, NY, 96; The Lie of the Land, Univ Art Mus, Univ Calif Santa Barbara, 96; Making it Real (traveling), Aldrich Mus Contemp Art, Reykjavik Muniç Art Mus, Iceland, Portland Mus Art, Maine, Yukon Arts Ctr, Can, Virginia Beach Ctr Arts, 97-98; Exterior/Interior: The Way I See It: Five Photographers Working in Brooklyn, Brooklyn Mus Art, NY, 98; Neighborhood Watch, Julie Saul Gallery, NY, 98; NY State Biennial, NY State Mus, Albany; MAYDAY, Cen Art, Neuchatel, Switz, 99; Threshold, Contemp Art Cen Va, Virginia Beach, 2000; WestWecheel-Zum Wert des Junstwerks, Mus Angewandte Kunst, Cologne, Ger, 2001; others. *Collection Arranged:* Bankers Trust Co, NY City; The Equitable Corp, NY City; FRAC Bourgogne, Dijon, France; Los Angeles Co Mus Art, Calif; MacArthur Found, Chicago, Ill; MIT List Visual Arts Cen, Cambridge, Mass; Progressive Corp, Cleveland, Ohio; San Francisco Mus Modern Art, Calif. *Awards:* Visual Arts Fel, Edward F Albee Found, Montauk, NY, 92 & 94; Fel, Nat Endowment Arts, 93-94; MacDowell Colony Studio Residency, Peterboro, NH, 96;

NY Found Arts Fel, 2009. *Bibliog:* Ken Johnson (auth), Peter Garfield at Feigen Contemp, NY Times, (p E38), 2/20/98; Vince Aletti (auth), Stuck Inside of Mobile: Peter Garfield, after the fall, Village Voice, 137, 3/10/98; Grady T Turner (auth), House of Shards, World Art, Issue No 18, 64-68, 9/98. *Mailing Add:* 70 Skillman Ave Brooklyn NY 11211-2209

GARHART, MARTIN J
PAINTER
b Deadwood, SDak, July 2, 1946. *Study:* student, Univ Wyo, 64-66; SDak State Univ, BA, 69; WVa Univ, MA, 70; Southern Ill Univ, Edwardsville, MFA, 72. *Work:* Libr Cong, Smithsonian Inst, Washington, DC; Brit Mus, London; Calif Palace Legion of Honor, San Francisco. *Exhib:* Drawings USA, 72; Colorprint USA, 73; Bradley Print Show 15th Nat, 74; 2nd NH Int Print Competition, 74; Davidson Nat Print & Drawing Competition, 74; group shows, Flanders Gallery, Minneapolis, Minn, 96, 98 & 99, Place of the Mind, Mansfield Arts Ctr, Ohio, 00, Purdue Univ, West Lafayette, Inc, 00, Foster Art Ctr, Peoria, Ill, 00, others. *Teaching:* From asst to assoc prof art, Kenyon Col, 72-. *Awards:* Spec Purchase Award, Davidson Print & Drawing Competition, 74; Purchase Award, Bradley Print Show 15th Nat, 74; Jurors Award of Merit, 2nd NH Int. *Mem:* Coll Art Asn Am; NH Graphic Soc. *Media:* Oil, Watercolor. *Mailing Add:* 405 W 2nd St Powell WY 82435-2301

GARNER, JOYCE (CRAIG)
PAINTER
b Covington, Ky, Dec 4, 1947. *Study:* Univ Ky, BS, 68. *Work:* University Hosp, Cincinnati, Ohio; US Mission to Europ Community, Brussels, Belg; St Lukes Hosp, Newport, Ky; Southern Progress Collection, Birmingham, Ala. *Comn:* Mural, Balke Properties; St Louis, Mo, 91; 1915 Reminiscence, Mackey/Mitchell Architects; Rain or Shine painting & poster, Asn Metrop Sewage Agencies, Washington, 95. *Exhib:* Art Forms 90, Greater Lafayette Mus Art, Ind, 90; All Ky Women's Art Exhib, Headley-Whitney Mus, Lexington, Ky, 91; solo exhib, Headley-Whitney Mus, 92, Jewish Community Ctr, Louisville, 95, Marin-Price Gallery, Chevy Chase, Md, 98; Ladies Lunch: Exploring the Tradition, New Harmony Gallery Contemp Art, Ind, 92; The Marriage Project: a midlife perspective traveling exhib, 95-96; Midwest Mus Am Art, 97. *Awards:* Alternate Visions Grant, Nat Endowment Arts, Rockefeller Found, Warhol Found & NC, SC & Ky Coun Arts, 93; Resident Fel, Hambidge Ctr, 94; The Best Oil Painting, Rockport Publ, 96, The Landscape Inspirations, 97. *Bibliog:* Judy Look (auth), That's where you'll find me, Louisville Eccentric Observer, 10/23/94; Barney Quick (auth), The big and little enchantments of Joyce Garner, Nuvo, Indianapolis, 6/27/96; Benita Heath (auth), Visual metaphors play in Joyce Garner's work, Lexington Herald-Leader, 9/13/98. *Media:* Oil. *Dealer:* Malton Gallery 2709 Observatory Cincinnati OH 45208; Hot House Gallery 546 S Meridian Suite 511 Indianapolis IN 46225. *Mailing Add:* 7300 Happy Hollow Ln Prospect KY 40059

GAROFALO, CHRIS
SCULPTOR
Study: Notre Dame, St Mary's Coll, South Bend, Ind, BFA. *Comn:* Embassy Suites Hote, St Louis, MO; 900 North Michigan, Chicago; Garfield Park Conservatory. *Exhib:* Solo exhibs include Eastwick Art Gallery, Chicago, 1993, 1994, 1998, Aron Packer Gallery, Chicago, 1991, 1992, 1994, Lionsweir/Packer, Chicago, 2000, Garfield Park Conservatory, Chicago, 2005; Group exhibs include Axis Gallery, Chicago, 1992; World Tattoo Gallery, Chicago, 1992; Peter Mars Gallery, 1993; Lanning Gallery, Columbus, OH, 1998; Galery 213 Com, Chicago, 1999; Karkula, New York, 2004; Rhona Hoffman, Gallery, 2006. *Awards:* Joan Mitchell Found Grant, 2007. *Mailing Add:* Rhona Hoffman Gallery 118 North Peoria Street Chicago IL 60607

GAROIAN, CHARLES RICHARD
CONCEPTUAL ARTIST, EDUCATOR
b Fresno, Calif, Nov 7, 1943. *Study:* Calif State Univ, Fresno, BA (art), 68, MA (art), with Allen Bertoldi, 69; Stanford Univ, with Elliot W Eisner, PhD (educ), 84. *Exhib:* SECA Exhib, San Francisco Mus Mod Art, 74; Circumstantial Evidence, Birmingham Loft, Pittsburgh, 91; Flayed Ox, Paul Robeson Cult Ctr, Penn State Univ, 92; Butt of the Media in the Face of the Publ, Cleveland Performance Art Festival & Ward-Nasse Gallery, NY, 92; Naked Controversy, Pittsburgh Ctr Arts, Kutztown Univ Art Series, 94; Requiem March, Studio for Creative Inquiry, Carnegie Mellon Univ, 94; and others. *Teaching:* Art, Los Altos High Sch, 69-86; lectr art educ, Univ Washington, Seattle, summer 77; educ dir, Palmer Mus Art, Penn State, 86-90, asst dir, 90-91, assoc prof art educ, Sch Visual Arts, 91-; lectr performance art, Deep Creek Sch, Ariz State Univ Summer Inst, 92-96. *Awards:* Teacher of the Year Mountain View/Los Altos High Sch Dist, 1976; Pa Coun on Arts grantee, 1986, 87, 88, 90, 91; recipient Creative Prog award Nat Univ Continuing Educ Assoc, 1990, 91; Interdisciplinary Arts Fel, Pa Coun Arts, 93; Fulbright Scholar to Armenia, 94; Research Grant, Getty Educ Inst Arts, 96. *Bibliog:* Paul Blaum (auth), The lonely passion of Charles Garoian, Ararat Quar, spring 91; Amy Sparks (auth), Cleveland Performance Art Fest: Community Outreach or Shotgun Wedding?, summer, 93; Frank Green (auth), Dialogue, Arts in the Midwest, 9/93. *Mem:* Nat Art Educ Asn; Coll Art Asn; Int Soc Educ Through Art. *Publ:* Coauth, The Deep Creek School: Technology, Ecology and the Body as Pedagogical Alternatives in Art Education, J Soc; Theory in Art Educ, 94; Censorship in the art classroom, Sch Arts, 1/96, 3/96 & 1/97; A Common Impulse in Art and Science, Leonardo J, 96; auth, Art Education and the Aesthetics of Land Use in the Age of Ecology, Studies in Art Educ, 97; Performance Art: Repositioning the Body in Postmodern Art Education, J Multicultural & Cross-cult Res Art Educ, 97. *Mailing Add:* Pa State Univ Sch of Visual Arts 210 Patterson Bldg State College PA 16802-2502

GARRARD, MARY DUBOSE
HISTORIAN, EDUCATOR
b Greenwood, Miss, July 25, 1937. *Study:* Newcomb Col, BA, 58; Harvard Univ, MA, 60; Johns Hopkins Univ, PhD, 70. *Hon Degrees:* Millsaps Col, PhD, 99. *Teaching:* From asst prof to prof art hist, Am Univ, Washington, DC, 64-2003, prof emeritus, 2003-; disting vis prof, Syracuse Univ, 2011. *Awards:* Mid-Career, Achievement Award, Women's Caucus for Art, 91; Lifetime Achievement Award, Women's Caucus for Art, 2005, Miss Inst of Arts & Letters. *Mem:* Women's Caucus for Art (pres, 74-76); Coll Art Asn Am (bd dir, 77-81); Am Asn Univ Prof; Miss Inst Arts & Letters. *Res:* 16th century and 17th century Italian art; feminist and gender studies, 15th-18th century. *Publ:* Auth, Artemisia Gentileschi: The Image of the Female Hero in Italian Baroque Painting, Princeton Univ Press, 89, Artemisia Gentileschi around 1622: The Shaping and Reshaping of an Artistic Identity, 2001, Brunelleschi's Egg: Nature, Art, and Gender in Renaissance Italy, 2010; co-ed, Feminism and Art History: Questioning the Litany, Harper & Row, 82, The Expanding Discourse: Feminism and Art History, Harper Collins, 92, The Power of Feminist Art, Abrams, 94, Reclaiming Female Agency: Feminist Art History after Postmodernism, 2005. *Mailing Add:* 2915 NW University Terr Washington DC 20016

GARRELS, GARY
CURATOR
Study: New Coll Fla, Sarasota, BA, 1974; Princeton Univ, doctoral prog sociology; Boston Univ, MA (art hist). *Collection Arranged:* Photog in Contemp German Art: 1960-Present, Walker Art Ctr; Sol LeWitt: A Retrospective, San Francisco Mus Mod Art, Willem de Kooning: The Late Paintings, The 1980s, Inside Out: New Chinese Art, Present Tense: Nine Artists in the Nineties; Roth Time: A Dieter Roth Retrospective, Mus Mod Art, New York, 2004; Oranges & Sardines, Hammer Mus, 2008. *Pos:* Dir, Carpenter & Hochman Gallery, New York, formerly; asst, contemp dept, Christie's, New York, formerly; dir progs, Dia Art Found, New York, 1987-91; sr cur, Walker Art Ctr, Minneapolis, 1991-93; sr cur painting & sculpture, San Francisco Mus Mod Art, 1993-2000, 2008-; chief cur drawings & cur painting & sculpture, Mus Mod Art, New York, 2000-05; sr cur, Hammer Mus, Los Angeles, 2005-08. *Awards:* AICA Award for Best Monographic Exhib in New York, 2004. *Mailing Add:* San Francisco Mus Mod Art 151 3rd St San Francisco CA 94103

GARRISON, BARBARA
PRINTMAKER, ILLUSTRATOR
b London, Eng, Aug 22, 1931. *Study:* Wellesley Col, Mass, BA, 53; Columbia Univ, MA, 56; Pratt Graphics Ctr. *Work:* De Grummond Collection, Univ Southern Miss; Mus Am Illust, NY; Mazza Collection, Univ Findley, Ohio; Mus of Am Illustration, NY; Skirball Mus, Los Angeles, Calif; and many others worldwide. *Comn:* Unicef Cards, Carnegie Hall Stage Bill (cover), Unum (Mag Cover). *Exhib:* Mini-Gravat Int, Barcelona, Spain, 84; Int Miniature Print, Seoul, Korea, 84; Int Miniature Print, Pratt Graphics Ctr, NY, 84-85; Statue of Liberty Traveling Exhib, 86; Soc Illusrs Ann, NY, 86. *Teaching:* Instr art, Spence Sch, 63-69, Nightingale-Bamford Sch, 70-78, NY. *Awards:* IAGA Award, 78; New York Times 10 Best Illus Books, 92; Ezra Jack Keets Unicef Award, 92; ALA Pick of the Lists Award, 95, 96 & 97. *Mem:* Soc Illusrs; Artists Equity NY; Graphic Artists Guild. *Media:* Etching, Collagraph. *Publ:* Only One, Cobble Hill, 92; My First Book of Jewish Holidays, Dial, 94; Josiah True & the Art Maker, Simon & Schuster, NY, 95; Look at the Moon, Mondo Publ, 96; One Room School, Boyds Mills, 97; The Frog House, Dutton, 04; Only One Neighborhood, Dutton. *Mailing Add:* 12 E 87th St No 3C New York NY 10128

GARRISON, DAVID EARL
PAINTER, MURALIST
b Jacksonville, Ill, Mar 23, 1940. *Study:* Am Acad Art, studied pastel with Daniel Green & watercolor with Irving Shapiro, 64-68; Anatomy with Bill Parks; Iowa Wesleyan Coll, BA, 87; art study in Mex. *Work:* Marriott Hotel Corp; Holiday Inn Corp; United Airlines; Iowa's Sesquicentennial Mural. *Comn:* Hist mural, Iowa Welcome Ctr; Iowa Sesquicentennial Mural. *Exhib:* Nat Artists Prof League Exhib, NY, 87-90 & 92-94; Xi'an China Exhib, Pastel Soc Am, NY, 88-98; Oil Painters Am Exhibs, Chicago, Ill, 2000 & San Antonio, Tex, 2000; Pastels toured France, 2002, Italy & Russia, 2003; Butler Inst Am Art, 2003; Pastel Soc France, 2003. *Teaching:* Instr, Iowa Arts Coun, Des Moines, 79, 94 & 98; Attitude for Artist, workshops across country; Teach the Teachers, Amana (Iowa) Colonies. *Awards:* Pastel Soc Am Award, 96-97 & 2008; Wyo Conservation Stamp, 2000; Guest of Honor, Art du Pastel en France Int Show, 2008; Societe des Pastellistes de France, 2010; 1st Pl, Soc Master Impressionists; Lead Crystal Award, Excellence in Art, Salon de Peinture, Normandie, France; Jack Richeson Award, Am Artist Prof League, NY. *Mem:* Am Artist Prof League (signature mem, award, 2000); Pastel Soc Am (signature mem); Hudson Valley Art Asn. *Media:* Oil, Pastel; Acrylic. *Publ:* Auth, The Best of Oils, The Best of Pastels, Rockport Publ, 96; article, Artist's Mag, 3/98; Best of the Best in Pastel, Kennedy Pub. *Dealer:* Henry Myrtle Gallery Cedar Falls IA; Hilligass Gallery Chicago IL. *Mailing Add:* 831 S Garfield Burlington IA 52601

GARRISON, GENE K
PAINTER, WRITER
b Aug 11, 1925. *Study:* Ariz State Univ; Phoenix Coll, AFA; Glendale Community Coll; study with Bill Ahrendt, Jason Williamson, Linae Frei, Jan Sitts, Helen del Grosso & Joella Jean Mahoney; Yavapai Community Coll. *Exhib:* Art Barn and Art Room, Cave Creek, Ariz; Conrad's Imagine & Es Posible, El Pedregal, N Scottsdale, Ariz; Cactus Shadows Fine Art Ctr, Cave Creek, Ariz; Cave Creek Mus, Ariz; Sedona Arts Ctr, Ariz; Sedona City Hall, Ariz; Sedone Area Guild of Artists; Sedona Art Mus. *Pos:* writer, artist. *Teaching:* Volunteer art teacher, spec educ handicapped children, Desert Arroyo Middle Sch, Cave Creek, Ariz; tutor The Literacy Ctr, Sedona, Ariz. *Mem:* Sedona Art Ctr; Western Writers of America; Sedona Camera Club; Int Soc Experimental Artists; Sedona Writers Salon; SAGA (Sedona Area Guild of Artists). *Media:* Photography, Oils, Acrylics, Multi-Media. *Res:* currently researching materials for a book. *Specialty:* Eclectic Galleries. *Interests:* Reading, writing, art & photog. *Publ:* Various articles on artists & art shows published in magazines such as Carefree Enterprise, Roundup, Antiques World; coauth, From Thunder to Breakfast, 77; auth, Javelina Have-uh-What?; auth, Widowhood Happens, Xlibris Corp, 2002; auth, There's Something About Cave Creek, 2006. *Mailing Add:* 495 Rodeo Rd Sedona AZ 86336-3369

GARRO, BARBARA
PAINTER, WRITER
b Camden, NJ, Feb 1943. *Study:* State Univ NY, AA, 93, BS, 93, MA, 96; studied with Morris Blackburn, Philadelphia Art Mus, 60-61; studied with Tom Vincent, 2007-2010. *Work:* Warren Co Munic Bldg, Lake George, NY; The Glen, Glens Falls, NY; Mary's Haven, Saratoga Springs, NY; Still Point, Stillwater, NY; St Joseph's Roman Cath Church, Greenfield Ctr, NY; Our Lady of Perpetual Help Roman Cath Church, Brooklyn, NY. *Comn:* Painting of Farm, Fort Miller Company, Schuylerville, NY; Three Generations with Car Mary Anne Macica, Saratoga Springs, NY. *Exhib:* Painting the Chapman, Chapman Mus, Glens Falls, NY; Clermont Barn Art Show, The Clermont, Germantown, NY; Saratoga Chic, Hyde Gift Shop, Glens Falls, NY. *Pos:* pres, Electric Envisions Inc. *Teaching:* painting, Saratoga Co Arts Coun, 2003; instr, private students, 2007-. *Awards:* Best of Show, Patriot's Daughter, 2003; Best of Saratoga Springs Award, US Commerce Asn, 2010. *Bibliog:* Maria M Bucciferro (auth), A Risk Manager Gambles, The Post Star, 1/2/2002; Kathleen Dooley (auth), Painting anew begins, Times Union, 1/24/2002; Pamela A Brooks (auth), Painting from the Heart, Post Star, 12/26/2003; Nicole A Weinstein, Renaissance Woman, Daily Gazette, 12/20/2005; Bill Buell (auth), A View from the Pews, Life & Arts/ Sunday Gazette, 3/21/2010. *Mem:* Am Watercolor Soc; Saratoga Co Arts Coun. *Media:* Mixed Media, Watercolor, Acrylic, Casein. *Res:* History of art; Classical painters; Newest methodology. *Specialty:* Flowers. *Interests:* Religious, small business, and art related subjects. *Publ:* auth, Science & Emotions, Neuroesthetics: What Makes Certain Art Famous, Art Calendar, 2004; auth, How Artists Put a Signature on their Art Enlightening Bolt, 2006; auth, From Jesus to Heaven with Love, A Parable Pilgrimage, Cambridge Books, 2010; auth, Grow Yourself a Life You'll Love, Thomas Moore, 2000; auth, The Comfort of the Shepherd: Parable Prayer and Meditation, Cambridge Books, 2012; auth, Living the Call of God, Cambridge Books, 2014; Garro Talk, monthly syndicated column for small business. *Dealer:* Ginofor Gallery 38 West Main St Cambridge NY 12816; Monitor Gallery Rome Italy; Palazzo Sforza Cesarini 4300. *Mailing Add:* Electric Envisions Inc 205 Regent St Saratoga Springs NY 12866

GARTEL, LAURENCE M
COMPUTER ARTIST, PHOTOGRAPHER
b New York, NY, June 5, 1956. *Study:* Art Students League, with Knox Martin, 75; Sch Visual Arts, with Al Brunelle, George Trakas, Bill Beckley & Cora Kennedy, BFA, 77; CW Post Coll, Grad Sch (photog), Long Island, NY, 1978-1980. *Work:* Calif State Univ, Long Beach; Polaroid Corp, Cambridge, Mass; Lending Collection, Mus Mod Art, NY; Universita Degli Studi Di Camerino, Italy; Dept Housing, City Univ New York; Masur Mus Art Louisiana; Scripps Research Inst, Jupiter, Fla; Victoria & Albert Mus, London; Australian Ctr for the Moving Image, Melbourne; Tempra mus Contemp Art, Malta. *Comn:* Absolut Gartel, Absolut Vodka; Miami Int Airport; Tesla Electric Car Co, Calif, 2010; Ferrari Scuderia Art Car, Artfellas, Italy, 2011; Sx Liquors, Ft Lauderdale, Fla, 2012; Lincoln Premiere Convertible, 1957 Art Car; Cadillac Limousine 1959 Art Car. *Exhib:* Exchange of Information, Mus Mod Art, NY, 90; Nuvo Japonica & Other Cybernetic Romances, Norton Gallery Art, West Palm Beach, Fla, 91 & Ringling Sch Art, Sarasota, Fla, 92; Masur Mus Art, Monroe, La, 94; A Cybernetic Romance, Palm Beach Int Airport, Fla, 95; Am Haus, Frankfurt & Berlin, 97; Galerie Posteria, Milan, Italy, 98; Palm Beach Photog Mus, DelRay Beach, Fla, 2001; Gallery of Fine Art, Edison Coll, Ft Myers, Fla, 2003; Coral Springs Mus Art, Fla, 2004; Gartel Erotica, World Erotic Art Mus, 2007; New Works, Bob Rauschenberg, Ft Myers, Fla, 2009; 30 Years of Digital Art, Palm Beach Photographic Ctr, 2009; Gartel at Bangtolufsen, Art Basel Miami Beach, 2011; Victoria and Albert Mus, London. *Collection Arranged:* Bibliotheque Nationale, Paris; Smithsonian Inst Mus of Am History, Wash DC. *Teaching:* Sch Visual Arts, NY, 1978-1992; Palm Beach Photographic Ctr, 1992-2009; Pratt Inst, NY, 1993-1994; Int Fine Arts Coll, Fla, 1997-1998; Miami Dade Coll, Fla, 2004-2005; Maine Media Workshops, 2000-2009. *Awards:* Residency Grant, Experimental Television Ctr, Owego, 78-92; Poster Award, Art Director's Club, NJ, 85; Artist-in-Residency Grant, NY State Coun Arts, 85. *Bibliog:* End of artistic barbarians, Computerworld, Australia, 85; Mary Ann Marger (auth), Computer art, St Petersburg Times, Tampa, Fla, 87; Helen Harrison (auth), Mod Romance, Via Computer, NY Times, 10/88; Gartel: Arte and Technologia, Edizioni Mazzotta, Italy, 98. *Mem:* Electronic Design Ast, Boca Raton, Fla. *Media:* Computer Graphics. *Interests:* Digital photog. *Publ:* Auth & illusr, The incubation of electronic imaging, Photomethods, 82; illusr, Laurence Gartel video, fantasy or future?, Camera Weekly, Eng, 82; coauth & illusr, Fantasia Ben Calcolata, PM Mag, Italy, 83; auth, Laurence M Gartel: A Cybernetic Romance, Gibbs Smith, Utah, 89; Laurence Gartel, the CD, Diamar, Seattle, 97; Gartel Arte & Technologia (introd by Pierre Restany), Edizioni Mazzotta, Milan Italy, 1998; La Storia Dell Arte, Edizioni Giunti, Florence, Italy, 2001. *Dealer:* Corporate Art Directions New York

GARVER, FANNY
ART DEALER
b Racine, Wis, Apr 3, 1927. *Study:* Univ Wis, BA, 49, BLS, 50; Middlebury Col, Vt. *Collection Arranged:* Regional Artists of Wisconsin (auth, catalog), 77 & Nineteenth Century British Watercolour Drawings, Fanny Garver Gallery, Madison, Wis; John Wilde and His Students; Harold Altman Retrospective. *Pos:* Dir, Jane Haslem Gallery, 69-72; founder, dir & pres, Fanny Garver Gallery, 72-2000; vpres, Garver Crafts, 85. *Awards:* Artful Woman of the Year, Nat Women's Political Caucus Dane Co, 96. *Mem:* Art Inst Chicago; Am Craft Coun; Madison Print Club (mem chmn); Milwaukee Art Ctr; Madison Art Ctr. *Specialty:* 19th century British, Wisconsin and regional artists; American fine arts crafts; Oil. *Publ:* Auth, Master Prints, 82 & Fanny Garver Collection of American Crafts, 85, Fanny Garver Gallery, Madison, Wis. *Mailing Add:* 230 State St Madison WI 53703

GARVER, THOMAS H
CONSULTANT, CURATOR
b Duluth, Minn, Jan 23, 1934. *Study:* Barnes Found, Merion, Pa; Haverford Coll, BA; Univ Minn, MA; Mus Mgt Inst, Univ Calif, Berkeley, 79. *Collection Arranged:* George Tooker Retrospective, Fine Arts Mus San Francisco, 74; New Photography: San Francisco & Bay Area, 74; Representations of Am (co-organized with Henry Geldzabler, coauth, catalog), traveling USSR, 77-78; Joseph Raffael, The California Years, 1969-78 (auth, catalog), San Francisco Mus Mod Art, 78 & Nathan Oliveira, 84; Sylvia Pilmack Mangold, Madison Art Ctr, 82; Corp Art Collection, Rayovac Corp, Madison, Wis, 85; Regarding Art: Artworks about Art, John Michael Kohler Arts Ctr, Sheboygan, Wis, 90; Mind and Beast: Contemporary Artists and the Animal Kingdom (auth, catalog), Leigh Yawkey Woodson Art Mus, Wausau, Wis, 92; Flora, Contemporary Artists and the world of flowers, Leigh Yawkey Woodson Art Mus, Wausau, Wis, 95; Trains that passed in the night, the Railroad Photography of O Winston Link, Sheldon Mem Art Gallery, Univ Nebr, Lincoln, Nebr, 98; Water: A Contemporary Am View, Gibbes Mus Art, Charleston, SC, 99. *Pos:* Asst to dir, Krannert Art Mus, Univ Ill, 60-62; asst dir, Seattle World's Fair, 62 & Rose Art Mus, 62-68; dir, Newport Harbor Art Mus, Newport Beach, Calif, 68-72 & 77-80 & Madison Art Ctr, Wis, 80-87; consult art gallery design, Univ Chicago, Calif Inst Arts, 69 & ARCO Ctr Visual Arts, 73; cur exhibs, Fine Arts Mus San Francisco, 72-77; site vis, Mus Accreditation Prog, Am Asn Mus; Consulting Org Cur, O Winston Link Mus, Roanoke, VA, 2002-04. *Teaching:* Hist of art & museology, Calif State Univs, Long Beach & Fullerton, San Quentin Prison, through Col Marin, Kentfield & Univ Wis, Madison. *Res:* Contemporary American art. *Publ:* Auth, Nathan Oliveira, Survey Exhib (catalog essay), San Francisco Mus Mod Art, 84; George Tooker, Clarkson N Potter Inc, Publ, 85, rev 92; Mind and Beast: Contemporary Artists and the Animal Kingdom, Leigh Yawkey Woodson Art Mus, Wausau, Wis, 92; The Last Steam Railroad in America: Photographs by O Winston Link, Harry N Abrams Inc, 95; intro to Invisible New York: The Hidden Infrastructure of the City, John Hopkins Univ Press, Baltimore, 98; intro to In The Traces: The Railroad Paintings of Ted Rose, Ind Univ Press, Bloomington, 2000; intro to Doubletake-A Rephotographic Survey of the City of Madison, Wis, 1925-2000, Univ Wis Press; intro to Joseph Goldyne, Washington, DC, The Corcoran Gallery of Art, 2003; O Winston Link The Man and The Mus, O Winston Link Mus, 2004. *Mailing Add:* 1962 Atwood Ave Madison WI 53704

GARVER, WALTER RAYMOND
PAINTER, WRITER
b Medina, NY, 1927. *Study:* State Univ NY Buffalo, BFA, 55; also with Charles Burchfield, 50. *Work:* Butler Inst Am Art, Youngstown, Ohio; Minn Mus Art, St Paul; Cincinnati Univ; Indiana Univ Pa; Burchfield-Penney Ctr, Buffalo, NY. *Exhib:* Nat Acad Design Ann, NY, 56, 60, 70-71 & 75; Chautauqua Nat Exhib, NY, 58-; Solo exhibs, Albright-Knox Art Gallery, 72 & 90; Okla Art Ctr Ann, Oklahoma City, 81 & 83; Audubon Artists Ann, NY, 83-2003; Am Watercolor Soc, 85 & 86; and many others. *Pos:* Contrib ed, Artist's Mag, 86-06. *Teaching:* Teacher art hist, drawing, painting & photog, Amherst Sr High Sch, Snyder, NY, 58-85, chmn art dept. *Awards:* Remy Award, Am Watercolor Soc Ann Exhib, 85; Gilmore-Romans Mem Award, Allied Artists Ann Exhib, 94; Gold Medal of Hon, Audubon Artists Annual Exhib, 2003. *Mem:* Buffalo Soc Artists (pres, 64); Audubon Artists; Nat Watercolor Soc; Allied Artists Am. *Media:* Oil, Watercolor. *Res:* Continued research on the lives of master watercolor painters for the Meet the Masters column in Watercolor Magic Magazine. *Publ:* Numerous articles & reviews in The Artist's Mag & Watercolor Magic; contrib ed, Watercolor Magic mag, 1999-, Artist's Mag, 1986-1999, Magic Mag, 99-2006; Children of the Forest, 2010. *Dealer:* Vern Stein Fine Arts 5747 Main St Williamsville NY 14221; Oxford Gallery 267 Oxford St Rochester NY 14607. *Mailing Add:* 4230 Tonawanda Creek Rd East Amherst NY 14051

GARY, JAN (MRS WILLIAM D GORMAN)
PAINTER, PRINTMAKER
b Ft Worth, Tex, Feb 13, 1925. *Study:* Art Ctr Sch, Los Angeles; San Antonio Art Inst, Tex; Art Students League. *Work:* Butler Inst Am Art, Youngstown, Ohio; Pensacola Art Ctr, Fla; Wis State Univ, Eau Claire; Brandeis Univ, Waltham, Mass; Rosenberg Libr, Galveston, Tex. *Exhib:* One-person show, Caldwell Col, NJ, 78; Am Acad Arts & Lett, 67-68; Four NJ Artists, Canton Art Inst, Ohio, 71; Cent Wyo Mus Art, Casper, 75; Charles & Emma Frye Mus Art, Seattle, Wash, 77; and others. *Pos:* Assoc dir, Old Bergen Art Guild, Bayonne, NJ, 62-90. *Awards:* Childe Hassam Fund Purchase Award, Am Acad Arts & Lett, 68; Dorothy F Seligson Mem Prize, Nat Asn Women Artists Ann, 75; David Soloway Mem Award, Allied Artists Am, 85. *Bibliog:* Henry Gasser (auth), article, Am Artist, 10/70. *Mem:* hon mem, Audubon Artists; hon mem Allied Artists Am; hon mem Am Watercolor Soc. *Media:* Acrylic, Casein; Woodcut. *Mailing Add:* 43 W 33rd St Bayonne NJ 07002

GARZA, CARMEN LOMAS
PAINTER, PRINTMAKER, ILLUSTRATOR
Study: Tex Arts Industry Univ, BS, 72; Juarez-Lincoln/Antioch Grad Sch, MEd, Austin, Tex, 73; San Francisco State Univ, MA, 81. *Comn:* History of Northern California Water (paintings), San Francisco Water Dept, 84; Cumpleaños y Barbacoa (painting), Fed Reserve Bank, Dallas, 93; Baile (wall sculpture), San Francisco Int Airport, 99. *Exhib:* Solo shows incl Estudios Rio Gallery, Mission, Tex, 72, Mex Mus, San Francisco, 77, 87, Laguna Gloria Art Mus, Austin, 91-92, Smith Coll Mus Art, Northampton, Mass, 92, Honolulu Acad Art, 94, Millicent Rogers Mus, Taos, NMex, 95, Whitney Mus Am Art at Philip Morris, New York, 95, Hirshhorn Mus and Sculpture Garden, Smithsonian Inst, Wash, DC, 95, Steinbaum-Krauss Gallery, New York, 96, Kemper Mus Contemp Mus Contemp Art & Design, Kans City, Mo, 97, Galeria de la Raza/Studio 24, San Francisco, 99, San Jose Mus Art, 2001, List Gallery, Swarthmore, Pa, 2003, Austin Children's Mus, Tex, 2003; group shows incl Contemp Arts Mus, Houston, 77; Galeria de la Raza/Studio 24, San Francisco, 78; Mus Fine Arts, Houston, 87; Corcoran Gallery Art, Wash, DC, 87; Wight Art Gallery, Univ Calif, Los Angeles, 90; Mex Mus, San Francisco, 92; Mex Fine Arts Ctr Mus,

Chicago, 93; MH deYoung Mem Mus, 95; Smithsonian Am Art Mus, 2000; San Antonio Mus Art, 2001; San Jose Mus Art, 2002. *Awards:* Fel in Printmaking, Nat Endowment for Arts, 81, Fel in Painting, 87; Fel in Painting, Calif Arts Coun, 90; Notable Book, Am Libr Asn, 90, Pura Belpré Hon Award, 90, 96, 2000; Tex Bluebonnet Award, 90; Children's Books of Distinction Award, Hungry Mind Review, 96; Tomás Rivera Mex Am Children's Book Award, Southwest Tex State Univ, San Marcos, 96-97; Outstanding Achievement Award, Parent's Guide to Children's Media, Inc, 2000; Carter G. Woodson Hon Book, Nat Counc Soc Studies, 2000. *Media:* Gouache on paper, Oil on Linen, Acrylic. *Publ:* Auth, Family Pictures, 93 & In My Family, 96, Children's Book Press; auth, Making Magic Windows, Tandem Libr, 99. *Mailing Add:* PO Box 881683 San Francisco CA 94188-1683

GARZA LAGUERA, EUGENIO
COLLECTOR
b Monterrey, Dec 18, 1926. *Study:* Instituto Tecnologico y Estudios Superiores de Monterrey. *Pos:* Laboratorist, Tecnica, 47, pres, 63; pres bd dirs, Visa Group, 81, bd dirs, 96; joined FEMSA, Mexico, 46, chmn, formerly, hon life chmn bd, 2001-; chmn, Bancomer, SA, formerly, hon life chmn, currently; chmn, Financiera de Credito de Monterrey, formerly, Valores Industriales, S.A., Banca Serfin; hon life chairman ITESM; pres, EISAC, currently. *Awards:* Named one of Top 200 Collectors, ARTnews mag, 2004, 2006 & 2009-11. *Mem:* Nat Fund for Cult and the Arts (exec comt). *Collection:* Contemporary and 20th-century Mexican art. *Mailing Add:* FEMSA General Anaya No 601 Pte Col Bella Vista Monterrey Nuevo Leon Mexico CP 64410

GARZIO, ANGELO C
POTTER, CRAFTSMAN
b Campobasso, Italy, July, 22, 1922. *Study:* Syracuse Univ, NY, BA, BS (libr sci), 49; Univ Iowa, MA (art hist), 54, MFA (ceramics), 55; Arabia Pottery, Helsinki, Finland, 56-57; Hochsch Keramicks, Höhr-Grenzhausen, Ger, 60-61, postgrad, Faenza, Italy, 65. *Work:* Mus Contemp Crafts, NY; Wichita Art Asn; Univ Art Mus, Hong Ik, Seoul, SKorea; Art Mus, Univ Benin, Benin; Everson Mus, Syracuse, NY; and others. *Exhib:* Biannual Nat Ceramic Exhib, Syracuse Mus Art, NY, 56, 58, 62, 64 & 66; Fiber-Clay-Metal Nat Craft Exhib, St Paul Art Mus, Minn, 57; Invitational Int Exhib, Brussel's World Fair Art Pavillion, Belg, 58-59; Smithsonian Inst, Washington, 60, 62 & 63; Ceramic Arts USA, Int Mineral Corp Mus, Skokie, Ill, 66; 24th, 25th, 28th & 31st Int Ceramic Competition, Int Ceramic Mus, Faenza, Italy, 68, 69, 72 & 75; Sargadelos Gallery, Madrid, Spain, 89. *Collection Arranged:* Syracuse Everson Mus, NY; Univ Iowa Mus Fine Art; Wichita Art Asn Collection, Kan; Utah State Univ, Logan; Univ Utah, Salt Lake City. *Teaching:* Prof ceramic art, Kans State Univ, 57-92, prof emer, 92-; vis lectr & prof ceramic art, Hong Ik Univ, Seoul, Korea, 73-74; lectr & dept head, Dept Indus Design, Ahmadu Bello Univ, Nigeria, 77-78; lectr & prof ceramic art, Univ Misiones, Arg, 92-2007. *Awards:* Faculty Res Grants, Kans State Univ, 62 & 66; USA State Dept Cult Exchange Fel, Santa Cruz & Sucre, Bolivia, July-Aug 2002. *Bibliog:* Sandra B Ernst (auth), Angelo Garzio, Ceramics Monthly, Vol 29, No 1, 81; LuAnn F Culley (auth), Angelo Garzio: Life as the ultimate art form, Kans Quart, Vol 14, No 4, 82; Antonio Vivas (auth), Angelo Garzio, Ceramica, Madrid, Spain, Vol 6, No 22, 85. *Mem:* Nat Conf Educ Ceramic Art; Kans Artist Craftsman Asn (vpres, 63-64). *Media:* Clay. *Res:* Salt Glazing Teniques at Cones; Develop 50 acre tract of grassland into a forest for educ recreational & res purposes. *Publ:* Auth, German salt glazing, Craft Horizons, Vol 13, No 3, 63; Raku (portfolio feature article), Ceramics Monthly, Vol 15, No 6, 67; Kansang Mus Collection of Koryo Celadons, Korea J, Vo 14, No 7, 74; A Man & A Kiln: Mark Zamantakis, NZ Potter, Vol 26, No 1, 84; Antonio Prieto: In retrospect, Ceramica, Spain, Vol 6, No 23, 86. *Dealer:* Pewabic Pottery 10125 E Jefferson Detroit MI 48214; Clay Pigeon Gallery Denver CO; Collections Gallery, Topeka, Kans. *Mailing Add:* PO Box 1806 Manhattan KS 66505-1806

GARZON-BLANCO, ARMANDO
DESIGNER, PAINTER
b Havana, Cuba, Feb 1, 1941. *Study:* La State Univ, BA, 66, MA (design), 68, MA (art hist), 69, PhD(theatre-art), 76; Fulbright-Hays Res Grant, Spain, 72-73, La State Univ Coun on Res & Rodriguez-Acosta Fund Grants, Spain, 74. *Work:* Centroplex, Baton Rouge; Anglo-Am Mus & Univ Libr, La State Univ, Baton Rouge; Cath Student Ctr, Baton Rouge. *Comn:* Baptistry murals, St Paul Cath Church, Baton Rouge, 70; sanctuary & chapel, Christ the King Chapel, Baton Rouge, 73-75; altarpiece, St James Lutheran Church, Gonzales, La, 77. *Exhib:* Jay Broussard Mem Gallery, State La Dept Art, Hist & Cult Preserv, 72; US Cult Ctr of Am Embassy, Madrid, Spain, 73; Fundacion Rodriguez-Acosta Banco de Granada Gallery, Spain, 73. *Teaching:* From instr to prof design, painting & art hist, La State Univ, Baton Rouge, 68-77; prof design, painting & art hist & head art dept, Nicholls State Univ, Thibodaux, 77-. *Awards:* Purchase Award, 2nd Ann Int La Watercolor Soc, 71. *Bibliog:* Miguel Rodriguez-Acosta Carlstrom (auth), Los artistas por el sureste espanol, Banco de Granada & Fundacion Rodriguez-Acosta, Spain, 73. *Mem:* La Watercolor Soc; SCent Renaissance Asn; Coll Art Asn Am; Northeastern Mod Lang Asn; Nat Coun Art Adminr. *Media:* Watercolor, Mixed Media. *Res:* Interrelation of the theatre arts and visual arts; Spanish Jesuit theatrical practice in the 16th and 17th century; Afro-Cuban art. *Publ:* Auth, Note on the authorship of the Spanish Jesuit play of San Hermenegildo, Theatre Survey, 74; The Tragedia de San Hermenegildo, Seville, 1590, Explorations in Renaissance Culture, 76; La Tragedia de San Hermenegildo en el teatro y en el arte, Estudios sobre literatura y arte dedicados al profesor, Emilio Orozco Diaz, II, Universidad de Granada, 79. *Mailing Add:* PO Box 31 Tucson AZ 85702

GASKELL, ANNA
PHOTOGRAPHER
b Des Moines, Iowa, 1969. *Study:* Art Inst Chicago, BFA, 92; Yale Univ, MFA, 95. *Exhib:* Solo shows incl Casey Kaplan Gallery, New York, 97, Mus Contemp Art, Miami, 98, White Cube, London, 99, 2002, Aspen Art Mus, Colo, 2000, Castello di Rivoli, Italy, 2001, Menil Collection, Houston, 2002; group shows incl Inst Contemp Art, London, 98; Burden Gallery, New York, 2002; Solomon R Guggenheim Mus & Guggenheim Mus Bilbao. *Awards:* Citibank Private Bank Photography Prize, 2000; Grant, Nancy Graves Found, 2002. *Dealer:* Galerie Gisela Capitain St Apern-Strasse 20-26 50667 Cologne Germany; Karolyn Sherwood Gallery 475 S 50th St Des Moines IA 50265. *Mailing Add:* c/o Karolyn Sherwood Gallery 666 Walnut St # 1830 Des Moines IA 50309

GAST, CAROLYN BARTLETT (LUTZ)
ILLUSTRATOR, ILLUMINATOR
b Cambridge, Mass, Apr 30, 1929. *Study:* Coll Practical Arts & Lett, Boston Univ, BS (bk illus), 50. *Work:* Nat Mus Natural Hist, Smithsonian Inst & US Geol Surv, US Dept Interior, Washington. *Exhib:* Seventeenth Area Exhib Corcoran Gallery Art, Washington, 65; Scientific Illus, Nat Mus Natural Hist, Smithsonian Inst, 68; Ann Exhibs Asn Med Illusr, 69-79; one-women shows, Kotor, Yugoslavia, 70 & Tyler Gallery, NVa Community Coll & Cosmos Club, Washington, 85; Nat Exhibs, Guild Natural Sci Illusr, 79 & 81-85; 30 Yr Retrospective, Nat Mus Nat Hist, Smithsonian Inst, 84; invitational exhib, Guild Natural Sci Illusr, Nat Acad Sci, 85; Nat Exhib, Calligraphers Guild, Washington, 86; Eyes on Sci: Illustrating Natural Hist, Nat Mus Nat Hist, Smithsonian Inst, 96. *Pos:* Scientific illusr, US Geol Surv, Dept Interior, 52-56 & Nat Mus Natural Hist, Smithsonian Inst, 59-85. *Awards:* Hon Mention in Sculpture, 17th Area Exhib Corcoran Gallery Art, Washington, 65; First Place, Nat Exhibs, Guild Nat Sci Illusr, 79 & 82. *Mem:* Founding mem Guild of Natural Sci Illusr (vpres, 71-73, pres, 73-75); Nat Stereoscopic Asn. *Media:* Mixed. *Publ:* numerous scientific publications and journals, 59-85; Illusr, Smithsonian Contributions to Zoology, 67-85; Mary S Gardiner's The Biology of the Invertebrates, McGraw-Hill, 72; The Guild Handbook of Scientific Illustration, New York, Van Nostrand Reinhold, 89; auth & illustr, Stero World, Vol 18, No 1, 3/4-91. *Mailing Add:* 5730 First St S Arlington VA 22204

GAST, MICHAEL CARL
PAINTER
b Chicago, Ill, June 11, 1930. *Study:* Sch Art Inst Chicago, BFA, 52; Univ Am, Mex, MFA (cum laude), 60. *Exhib:* Washington Watercolor Asn 66th Ann Nat Exhib, Smithsonian Inst, 63 & Metrop Area Exhib, Howard Univ, Washington, DC, 70; Soc Washington Artists 70th & 71st Ann Exhib, Smithsonian Inst, 63 & 64; four-man show, Mickelson Gallery, Washington, DC, 66; Foundry Gallery, Washington, DC, 80; Downtown Gallery, Del Art Mus, Wilmington, Del, 80; Portraits, Gallery 10 Ltd, Washington, DC, 85; A Tribute to Isobel MacKinnon, Sch Art Inst Chicago Gallery, 85; Art Inst Chicago Alumni Exhib, Parish Gallery, Washington, DC, 98. *Pos:* Mus technician, div ceramics & glass, Nat Mus Hist & Technol, Smithsonian Inst, 61-64 & mus specialist, Nat Collection Fine Arts, 69-71. *Teaching:* Asst prof painting, George Washington Univ, 71. *Bibliog:* Andrea O Cohen (auth), article, Washington DC Gazette, 4/19/72. *Mem:* Artists Equity Asn (chap vpres, 73-77, nat secy-treas, 75-79, nat pres, 79-81). *Media:* Polymer, Oil. *Publ:* Contribr, Fed Art Patronage Notes, 77, Ceramics Monthly, 78 & Artists Equity Asn Nat Newsletter, 77-81. *Mailing Add:* 5730 First St S Arlington VA 22204

GATES, HARRY IRVING
SCULPTOR, EDUCATOR
b Elgin, Ill, Dec 8, 1934. *Study:* Univ Ill, BFA, 58, MFA, 60. *Work:* Chase Manhattan Bank, NY; Corcoran Gallery Art, Washington; Int Art Prog Div, Nat Collection Fine Art, Washington; Washington Co Mus Fine Arts, Hagerstown, Md; Baltimore Mus Fine Art, Md; Washington & Lee Univ, Va. *Exhib:* Solo exhibs, Baltimore Mus Fine Art, 64, Western Md Col, Westminster, 95, Wash Co Mus Fine Arts, Hagerstown, 95, Japan Info & Cult Ctr, Embassy of Japan, Washington, 96 & Higgins Armory Mus, Worcester, Mass, 97; Small Sculpture Purchases for Int Art Prog, Nat Collection Fine Art, 69; New Sculpture, Corcoran Art, Washington, 70; Five Maryland Artists, Md Arts Coun, 72-73; Sculpture Invitational, Rochester Inst Technol, 75; The Object as Poet, Renwick Gallery, Washington, & Mus Contemp Crafts, NY, 77; 18 yr retrospective, Washington Co Mus Art, Md, 78; Two-person exhib, Dimock Gallery, George Washington Univ, 79. *Teaching:* Asst prof sculpture, George Washington Univ, 64-78, assoc prof, 78-98, prof, 98-. *Awards:* First Prize, 21st Ann Contemp Art, Palm Beach, Fla, 59; Artists Coun Award, 25th Ann Exhib for Sculpture, 61; Gov Prize, Md Ann, 70

GATES, JAY RODNEY
MUSEUM DIRECTOR
b Kansas City, Mo, Nov 21, 1945. *Study:* Inst European Studies, Vienna, Austria, 1967; Coll Wooster, Ohio, BA, 1968; Univ Rochester, NY, MA, 1970. *Exhib:* Mitthoefer Collection of African Sculpture, Coll Wooster Mus, Ohio, 1974; Prints & Drawings by Sculptors, Cleveland Mus Art, Ohio, 1975; Tenn Quilts, Brooks Mem Art Gallery, Memphis, 1979; Arts of Ancient Egypt: Treasures on Another Scale, Memphis & Washington, DC, 1981. *Pos:* mus cur, Coll Wooster, 1971-73; asst cur art hist & educ, Cleveland Mus, 1973-76; cur educ, St Louis Art Mus, 1976-78; dir, Brooks Mem Art Gallery, Memphis, 1979-81, Spencer Mus Art, Univ Kans, Lawrence, 1983-87, Seattle Art Mus, 1987-93, Dallas Mus Art, 1993-98 & Phillips Collections, Washington, DC, 1998-2008; asst dir & cur Am art, Nelson Gallery, Atkins Mus, 1981-83. *Teaching:* Instr art hist, Coll Wooster, Ohio, 1971-73 & Case Western Reserve Univ, Cleveland, 1973-76; prof art hist, Univ Kans, 1983-87. *Mem:* Am Asn Mus; Coll Art Asn; Asn Art Mus Dirs. *Res:* Public education in art museums; American painting. *Publ:* Auth, Television from the galleries, Mus News, 1975; coauth, Teaching advanced placement art history in a museum, Art J, 1975

GATES, JEFF S
PHOTOGRAPHER, DESIGNER
b Los Angeles, Calif. *Study:* Mich State Univ, East Lansing, BA, 71; Univ Calif, Los Angeles, MFA, 75. *Work:* Ctr Georges Pompidou, Paris; Victoria & Albert Mus, London; Los Angeles Co Mus Art; Seattle Art Mus; J Paul Getty Mus, Los Angeles; and others. *Exhib:* In Our Path, online; Solo exhibs, Midtown Y, NY, 89, Baltimore

Mus Art, 92, Grey Art Gallery, NY, 92, Sheppard Col, Sheppardstown, WVa, 93, El Camino Col, Torrance, Calif, 95, Downey Mus Art, Calif, 95 & Millersville Univ, Pa, 96; Outcry: Artists Answer AIDS (traveling), Mus Contemp Art, Baltimore, 91; Siggraph '91, Nat Siggraph Conf, Las Vegas, 91; Wit & Wisdom: Humor in Art, Forum Gallery, Jamestown, NY, 92; Multi Media Grunderziet: Computer Graphics State of the Art, Univ Wuppertal, Ger, 92; and others. *Pos:* Dir, ArtFBI, 88-. *Teaching:* Keynote speaker, Nat Conf Art Admin, Anchorage, Alaska; Instr, Md Inst, Col Art, 85-; online web design instr, Minneapolis Col Art & Design, 84-85 & 95-. *Awards:* Photog Fel, Md State Arts Coun, 91; Travel Grant, Brit Coun, Washington, 92; Photog Fel, Nat Endowment Arts, 84 & 90, Arts Admin Fel, 90. *Bibliog:* Ayofemi Folayan (auth), article, High Performance, spring 93; Blake Lange (auth), Artists on exhibit, J Washington Apple Pi, 9/94; Patricia Riedman (auth), Artists make best use of the net, Adobe Mag, 2/97; and others. *Media:* Web Design, Internet Art

GATES, MIMI GARDNER
RETIRED MUSEUM DIRECTOR
b Dayton, Ohio, July 30, 1942. *Study:* Stanford Univ, BA, 64; Univ Iowa, MA, 70; Yale Univ, PhD, 81. *Collection Arranged:* Co-cur, Stories of Porcelain, From China to Europe, 2000; Ancient Sichuan: Treasures from a Lost Civilization, 2001. *Pos:* Cur Asian Art, Yale Univ Art Gallery, 75-87, Henry J Heinz II dir, 87-94, mem gov bd, currently; Illsley Ball Nordstrom dir, Seattle Art Mus, 94-2009, dir emer, currently; chmn Fed Indemnity panel, Nat Endowment Arts, 99-2002; alumni fel, Yale Corp, 2007-; bd dirs, Downtown Seattle Asn YWCA, Northwest African Am Mus, Downtown Seattle Assn & Copper Canyon Press; mem adv bd, Getty Leadership Inst; leadership adv bd, Cascade Land Conservancy. *Teaching:* Instr Chinese art hist & mus studies, Yale Univ; adj fac Dept Art, Univ Wash. *Awards:* Wilbur Lucius Cross Medal, Yale Univ, 2006. *Mem:* Asn Art Mus Dirs (pres, 90). *Publ:* Coauth, Real & Imaginary Beings, Yale Art Gallery, 80; contribr, Bones of Jade, Soul of Ice, Yale Art Gallery, 85; ed, Communion of Scholars: Chinese Art at Yale, Chinese Inst, 87. *Mailing Add:* 5161 NE 41st St Seattle WA 98105-4955

GATES, THEASTER, JR
CERAMIST, SCULPTOR
Study: Iowa State Univ, BS, 1996, MS, 2006; Univ Cape Town, MA, 1998. *Exhib:* Solo exhibs, Dept Cult Affairs, Chicago, 2005, Inax Ceramic Mus, Japan, 2005, Tokoname Mus Ceramic Hist, Japan, 2005, Hyde Park Art Ctr, Chicago, 2007, Univ Ill, 2009, Mus Contemp Art, Chicago, 2009, Pulitzer Mus Art, St Louis, 2010, Milwaukee Art Mus, 2010; Storied Toy: The Emotional and Imaginative Relationship Between a Boy and His Toys, Univ Northern Iowa, 2007; Branded Alongside the Cabinet of Curiosities, Milwaukee Art Mus, 2008; Black Monks and the Gospel of Black, Van Abbemuseum, Neth, 2009; Black Monks of Mississippi, South Side Community Art Ctr, Chicago, 2009; Whitney Biennial, Whitney Mus Am Art, 2010. *Pos:* Dir edn & outreach, Little Black Pearl, 2005; coord, Humanities Divsn, Univ Chicago, 2007, lectr, Dept Visual Arts, 2008, dir, Arts Program Develop, 2009. *Awards:* Graham Found Archit Award, 2009; Artadia Award, 2009; Loeb Fel, Harvard Univ Grad Sch Design, 2010. *Mem:* David Logan Ctr for Creative & Performing Arts; South Side Community Art Ctr; Hyde Park Alliance for the Arts; Univ Chicago Arts Coun

GATTEN, DAVID
FILMMAKER
b Ann Arbor, Mich, 1971. *Study:* Sch Art Inst Chicago, MFA, 98. *Work:* Whitney Mus Am Art; Art Inst Chicago. *Exhib:* Whitney Biennial, 2002 & 2006; The Am Century, Whitney Mus Am Art, Art Inst Chicago; San Francisco Cinémathèque; Art Gallery of Ont; Cinémathèque Française; Helsinki Film Co-Op; Mus Contemp Cinema; Contemp Cinema, Lisbon; Millennium Film Workshop; First Person Cinema; Anthology Film Archives; Cinema Project Chicago; Filmmakers, Views from the Avant Garde, NY Film Festival, 2005. *Teaching:* assoc prof, Cinema & Photog, Ithaca Col, NY. *Mailing Add:* 14 Verona St 4C Brooklyn NY 11231

GATTO, PAUL ANTHONY
PAINTER, INSTRUCTOR
b Brooklyn, NY, Sept 19, 1929. *Study:* Self taught fine artist. *Work:* Jennings Hall, S Oaks Hosp, Amityville, NY; Kramer Lane Sch, Bethpage, NY; Garden City Inn, NY; Manhasset High Sch, NY; Methodist Church Community Ctr, NY. *Comn:* The Visitation, The Annunciation, The Parable, The Ministry & The Shepherd, (oil panels) Maria Regina RC Church, Seaford, NY, 89-. *Exhib:* Ninth Art Festival, Two Flags, Douglas, Ariz, 81; 61st Ann Nat Exhib, Ogunquit Art Ctr, Maine, 81; 59th Ann Nat Apr Salon, Springville Mus, Utah, 83; Pro Art Exhib, Utah Pageant Arts, Am Fork, 83; Artists at Work, Nassau Co Mus Art, Roslyn, NY, 90; The Morsel, Nat Mus Catholic Art & History, NY; and others. *Pos:* Pres & bd trustees, Farmingdale Pub Libr, 77-; pres, Ital Cult Soc, 75-78; art damage appraiser, Royal, Home, Aetna & Utica Mutual Insurance, 70-. *Teaching:* Lectr demonstr fine arts, painting, 67-; teacher fine arts, painting, Paul Gatto Gallery, Farmingdale, NY, 67-; teacher fine arts, painting, NY Inst Technol, Islip, 88-. *Mem:* Hechscher Mus, Huntington, NY, Artists Regist, 82. *Media:* Oils, Watercolor. *Interests:* music, piano. *Publ:* Illusr, Published prints, 11/76 & Times Square-New Years Day, 82, Paul A Gatto; poster, portrait Alexander, Fundraiser, Polish Gift Life Charity, 91. *Mailing Add:* Paul Gatto Gallery 300 Main St Farmingdale NY 11735

GATTO, ROSE MARIE
PAINTER
b Brooklyn, NY, Apr 11, 1931. *Study:* Brooklyn Col, 49; Art Students League, 80. *Work:* Cranford Pub Libr, NJ, 80. *Exhib:* Summit Art Ctr, NJ, 83; Nat Asn Women Artists, 89-90. *Teaching:* Instr, Jane Law Gallery, 86-; Teen Festival Union Col, 86-89; Westfield Adult Sch, 87-88. *Awards:* First Place, NJ Watercolor Soc, 86. *Bibliog:* Three Generations of Artists, Daily J, 82. *Mem:* NJ Watercolor Soc (asst nat chmn, 89); Nat Asn Women Artists (record secy 89). *Media:* Watercolor, Mixed Media. *Mailing Add:* 10 Claremont Pl Cranford NJ 07016

GAUCHER, YVES
PRINTMAKER, PAINTER
b Montreal, Que, 1934. *Study:* L'Ecole des Beaux Arts, Montreal, 54-56. *Work:* Mus Mod Art, NY; Libr of Cong, Washington, DC; Victoria & Albert Mus, London, Eng; Mus d'Art Contemp, Montreal; Nat Gallery of Can, Ottawa, Ont. *Exhib:* Contemp Painters as Printmakers, Mus Mod Art, NY, 64; Expo 70, Japan; Aspects of Can Art, Members Gallery, Albright-Knox Art Gallery, Buffalo, NY, 74; Thirteen Artists from Marlborough Gallery, NY, 74; Solo exhibs, Mural Installation, Nova Corp, Calgary, Alberta, 82, Centre Cult Can, Bruxelles, Belg, 83, Can House, London, Eng, 83, Centre Cult du Can, Paris, 83, Galerie Esperanza, Montreal, 86, Olga Korper Gallery, Toronto, 85-86 & 88 & 49th Parallel Centre Contemp Can Art, NY, 89; 15th Anniv Show, Olga Korper Gallery, Toronto, 88; Waddington & Gorce Inc, Montreal, 88; Montreal Painting of 1960's, Americas Soc Art Gallery, NY, 89; Living Impressions, Art Gallery, Hamilton, Ont, 89; and others. *Teaching:* Asst prof fine arts, Sir George Williams Univ, Montreal, 63-69, assoc prof, 70-; prof, Concordia Univ, Montreal, 66-. *Awards:* First Prize, Nat Print Competition, Burnaby, BC, 61; Second Prize, Int Triennale of Colored Prints, Grenchen, Switz, 64; Grand Prize, Sandage 68, Montreal Mus Fine Arts, 68. *Bibliog:* Donald Brackett (auth), Yves Gaucher & Christopher Kier, Arts Report, 3/8/88; Perceiving painting through the pores, Now Mag, 3/10/88; Norman Theriault (auth), Art: Style over story, Forces, winter 88. *Publ:* Auth, Living Impressions (exhib catalog), Art Gallery Hamilton, Ont, 89. *Mailing Add:* Dept Art Concordia Univ George Williams Campus Dept Studio A 1455 De Maissoneuve W Montreal PQ H3G 1M8 Canada

GAUCHER-THOMAS, NANCY A
PAINTER, INSTRUCTOR
b Marlboro, Mass. *Study:* New York Phoenix Sch Design, 73-75; with Paul Wood, Dorothy Watkeys Barberis, Thomas Sgouros, Irwin Greenberg & Pat Sansoucie. *Work:* Newport Hosp, RI; Bank of Newport, Middletown, RI; Newport Nat Golf Club, RI; Vis Nurse Serv, Middletown, RI; Ocean Plaza Hotel, Ocean Grove, NJ. *Comn:* Watercolor painting, Newport Nat Golf Club, RI, 94; watercolor painting, comn by Mrs M Rohrmann, Guatamala, 94; portrait, KVH, 2006. *Exhib:* Nat Asn Women Artists Showcase, Lever Gallery, NY, 95; NE Watercolor Ann, Goshe, NY, 96; Springfield Art League 78th Nat, Mus Fine Arts, Mass, 97; Newport Art Mus Mem Show, RI, 98; Acad Artists 48th Nat Exhib Contemp Realism Art, First Church Gallery, Springfield, Mass, 98; Art NE-USA 43rd Ann, Silvermine Arts Guild, New Canaan, Conn, 98; 102nd Ann Catherine Lorillard Wolfe Art Club Nat, Nat Arts Club, NY, 98. *Teaching:* Studio workshop, watercolor painting, 90-. *Awards:* JD Ayers Art Diversified-Springfield Art League 78th Nat Exhib Award, Mus Fine Arts, Springfield, Mass, 97; First Place Watercolor, Newport Art Mus, 98; Jack Richeson Merchandise Award, Northwest Watercolor Soc, 2000. *Mem:* Nat Asn Women Artists; Am Artist Prof League (pres emerita RI chap); signature mem Northeast Watercolor Soc; Nat Watercolor Soc; Acad Artists. *Media:* Watercolor

GAUDARD, PIERRE
PHOTOGRAPHER, GRAPHIC ARTIST
b Marvelise (Doubs), France, Oct 6, 1927; Can citizen. *Study:* Ecole Estienne, Paris, France. *Work:* Can Mus Contemp Photog, Ottawa, Ont; Musee Art Contemporain, Montreal, Que; Galerie FNAC, Paris, France; Bibliotheque Nationale, Paris, France; Winnipeg Art Galerie, Can; Can Coun Bank of Ottawa; Nat Art Galerie, Ottawa. *Exhib:* Solo exhibs, Les Prisons, Galerie de L'Image, Ottawa, 77, Musee d'Art Contemporain, Montreal, 80, Galerie Canon, Amsterdam, The Neth, 80, Univers Carceral, Galerie FNAC Forum, Paris, 80, En France, Galerie de L'Image, Ottawa, 82, Place des Arts, Montreal, 83 & Exercises de Style, Galerie Dazibao, Montreal, 84; Exposure, Art Gallery Ont, Toronto, 75; Tendances Actuelles au Quebec, Musee d'Art Contemporain, Montreal, 78; 66-Photographes-Actuels, Palais des Beaux Arts, Brussels, Belg, 81; Photographie au Quebec, Galerie du Rip, Arles, France, 82; Photographie Actuelle au Quebec, Galerie Quebec, Paris, France, 82; Le Mois de la Photo Á Montréal, Maisons de la Cult, (invité d'honneur), 89; and others. *Teaching:* Photo workshop, Col Bois de Boulogne, Montreal, Can, 88-. *Awards:* Medaille de la Fedn Int d'Art Photo-graphique, Montreal, 69; Carveth Award, Hamilton Camera Club, Can, 70; Medaille d'or ONF, Ottawa, Nat Film Bd, 72; Ministere des Affaires Cult du Que Grants, 82 & 86; and many others. *Bibliog:* Jacque Giraldeau (auth), La Toile d'Araignee, Films Nat Film Bd, Can, 79; Francois Caillat (auth), Pierre Gaudard, Zoom, Paris, 3/80; Serge Jonque (auth), Photo a l'Air Libre, Vie des Arts, 7/83. *Publ:* Coauth, Canada du Temps Qui Passe, ONF, 67; auth, Image-10-Les Ouvriers, Nat Film Bd, Ottawa, 72; coauth, Exposure, Art Gallery, Toronto, 75; Entre Amis, ONF, 76; auth, Les Prisons, OVO, 77. *Mailing Add:* 10255 Jeanne Manee Montreal PQ H3L 3B7 Canada

GAUDEAMUS See Jordan, John L

GAUDIERI, ALEXANDER V J
MUSEUM DIRECTOR
b Columbus, Ohio, Apr 23, 1940. *Study:* Ohio State Univ; Univ Paris, Sorbonne; Colgate Univ; Barton Kyle Yount Scholar, Am Grad Sch Int Com; Inst Fine Arts, NY Univ, with Robert Rosenblum, Sir Francis Watson & James Parker. *Exhib:* Picasso: Meeting in Montreal, 85 & Miro: Works on Paper & in Bronze, 86, Montreal Mus Fine Arts. *Pos:* Dir, Telfair Acad Arts & Sci, 76-83, Montreal Mus Fine Arts, 83-87, Locust Grove (Samuel FB Morse hist site, 94-95) & Marietta-Cobb Mus Art, 97. *Teaching:* Adj prof mus studies prog, Grad Sch Arts & Sci, NY Univ, 92-97. *Mem:* Asn Art Mus Dirs; Am Asn Mus; Soc Archit Historians; and others. *Res:* European decorative arts, wood marquetry; Develop of geometric forms into curvilinear and floral motifs from circa 1715 to mid-century; French romantic painting, the horse paintings of Alfred de Dreux and the influence of Gericault on his oeuvre. *Collection:* Decorative arts including Georges II & III furniture, silver and porcelain. *Mailing Add:* Lost Tree 926 Village Rd West Palm Beach FL 33408

GAUNTT, JEFF
INSTALLATION SCULPTOR, VIDEO ARTIST
b Houston, Tex, 1967. *Study:* Univ Houston, BFA; Pratt Inst Art, MFA. *Exhib:* Best of Williamsburg Open Studios, Brooklyn, NY, 1998; Aqua Agua, Revolution Gallery, Detroit, 1999; Greater New York, PS1, New York, 2000; Neverous System, Hayworth Gallery, Los Angeles, 2002; The Men's Room, Nassau County Mus Art, NY, 2003; About Painting, Frances Young Tang Mus, NY, 2004; Drawing Narrative, Coll Wooster Art Mus, Ohio, 2005; Still Missing: Beauty Absent Social Life, Visual Arts Mus, New York, 2006; Horizon, Elizabeth Found Galleries, New York, 2007. *Awards:* Louis Comfort Tiffany Found Grant, 1999; Pollock-Krasner Found Grant, 2008. *Bibliog:* Jerry Saltz (auth), Greater Expetations, Village Voice, 3/9/2000; Holly Myers (auth), Vaugely Out of Touch With Nervous System, Los Angeles Times, 2002; Tom Collins (auth), Hidden Depths, Albuquerque J, 7/22/2005; David Taylor (auth), The Artful World of Gauntt, Pasadena Citizen, 11/1/2006; Doug Mason (auth), Teaching-and Learning, Knoxville News Sentinal, 1/20/2008. *Dealer:* Sikkema Jenkins & Co 530 W 22nd St New York NY 10011; Inman Gallery 3901 Main St Houston TX 77002. *Mailing Add:* Sikkema Jenkins & Co 530 W 22nd St New York NY 10011

GAUTHIER, NINON
CURATOR, ART HISTORIAN
b Montreal, Que, Nov 9, 1943. *Study:* Studied with Marcel Rioux, Raymonde Moulin, Georges-Henri Riviere and Serge Lemoine; Univ de Montreal, BS (sociology), 67; MS, 68; Ecole des Hautes Etudes, en sciences humzines, Paris, 72-74; Univ Paris IV-Sorbonne, MA (contemporary art history), 95, DEA (contemporary art history), 96, PhD (art history), 2004. *Exhib:* Cur, Josef Albers Hommage au carre De la science a la magie, Galerie HEC, Univ de Mtl, (cur & auth), 1985; Of color & light drawing allusions, Century Gallery, Sylmar, LA Co Art Centre, Calif, (cur & auth, catalog), 1994; Marcel Barbeau-Mastering the accidental, Churchill Coll Art Gallery, Univ Cambridge, UK (asst-cur, coauth catalog), 1998; Marcel Barbeau-Le fleuve en escales/Episodes along the river, Mus Du Bas-St Laurent, riv-Loup, (nat traveli exhib), (cur, coauth catalog), 1999-2001; Marcel Barbeau en filigranes, Mus & jardin Domane Catraqui, Quebec City, 1999; Marcel Barbeau Derives et variations: Gatineau & Mtl, 2000; Centre d'expo, Baie St Paul (cur, coauth catalog), 2003; plus others. *Collection Arranged:* Union Vie, Drummondville, Que, Can; Gaz Metropolitain, Montreal, Que, Can; Via Rail's Transcontinental Train Art Collection. *Pos:* Asst dean, Fac Fine Arts, Univ du Que Montreal, 74-76; dir, Centre d'etude et ed communication sur l'art, 89-; corresp, Paris Sculpture, 2005-2008; art critic, France, 80-90; Le Collect; Unneur: Finance, 1980-1990; Parcours, 91-2008; Decormag, 81-84; Vie Des Arts, 2007-. *Teaching:* Lectr Dept Continuing Educ, Univ de Montreal, 1983, 1984, 1986; Lectr, Dept Art Hist & Dept Fine Arts, Univ Que, Montreal, 86, 87 & 89-90. *Awards:* Spec Collab Award, Nat Bus Writing Award, Toronto Press Club, Royal Bank Can, 87; Cult Journalism Excellency Award, Can Conf Arts, Samuel & Saydie Bronfman Found, 89. *Bibliog:* Marie-Claude Fortin (auth) Mine d'art, Voir, 12/19/90; Ann Duncan (auth), New art-book venture defying the odds, The Gazette, 2/2/91; Gerald Needam (auth) Loyal to abstraction, Books in Canada, Vol XX, No. 2, 91; Jean Dumont (auth), Marcel Barbreau: retour a Paris, Le Devoir, Montreal, 91; Theo Barbu, Marcel Barbeau a Canadian in Paris, Art Speak, New York, 6/91. *Mem:* Int Asn Art Critics Can (secy, 89-92); Art Collectors Asn Que (CA, 88-92); Centre d'etude et de communications sur l'art (pres, 88-93); Int Asn Art Critic, France, 1994-2008; Int Asn Art Critic,Can, 2009-. *Media:* Sculpture, Painting, Drawing. *Res:* Canadian art of fifties and sixties, Marcel Barbeau's comprehensive catalogue: drawings, paintings, sculptures, collages, prints, installations & performances; hist of Canadian Contemp art scene & market; interaction between critics, institutions, media & art market on artist's works, career & on the prices of art work; hist of comtemp sculpture; Marcel Barbeau's comprehensive catalogue: drawings, paintings, sculptures, collages, prints, installations & performances. *Interests:* Transdisciplinarity, post war abstraction. *Publ:* Coauth, Le marché de l'art et le statut de l'artiste, Ministere des affaires culturelles du Que, 82; Le Mecenat prive au Quebec: mythe ou realite?, Possible, 85 & 86; auth, Vivre des arts visuels, Publs du Que, 87; Code d'ethique des sculpteurs, Conseil de la sculpture du Que, 90; coauth, Marcel Barbeau: le regard en fugue, CECA, 90; plus others

GAUTHIER, SUZANNE ANITA
PAINTER
b Saint-Boniface, Man, Aug 12, 1948. *Study:* Univ Man, Winnipeg, BFA (hons), 69. *Work:* Can Coun Art Bank & Mus of Man, Ottawa; Winnipeg Art Gallery, Man; Mus Québec; Bemis Foundation, Omaha; Musée D'Art Contemporaine, Collection Lavalin, Montréal. *Exhib:* Palazza Della Esposizioni, Faenza, Italy, 85-86; 37th Salon de la Jeune Peinture, Grand Palais, Paris, 86; Jane Corkin Gallery, Toronto, 88; Exten Print & Drawing Coun of Can, Toronto, 90; Subject/Matter, Art Gallery NS, 92; and others. *Teaching:* Lectr printmaking, Sch Art, Univ Man, 77-79; asst prof painting, NS Col Art & Design, 88-92. *Awards:* B Grant, Can Coun, 87; Soutien Aux Artistes, Ministér des Affaires, Culturelles, Que, 88; Travel Grant, Can Coun, 89. *Bibliog:* Françoise Legris-Berggman (auth), L'ouevre polymorphe de Suzanne Gauthier, Vie des Arts, 88; Bernard Mulaire (auth), Chien, Les Editions du Blé, 85; Gérard Xuriguera (auth), Le dessin, le pastel, l'aquarelle dans l'art, Éditions Mayer, Paris, 87. *Mem:* Can Artists Representation/Front des Artistes Canadiens. *Media:* Encaustic Painting; Photography. *Publ:* Illusr, Canadian Artists in Exhibition, 1973-1974, Roundstone Coun, 74; Le Nu, La Lumiére et Les Ombres, Les Editions du Blé, 75; coauth & illusr, Vortex, Les Editions du Blé, 85; Figures Nomades, Migrant Images, Les Ed Ink, Inc, 89

GAUVREAU, ROBERT GEORGE
PHOTOGRAPHER, EDUCATOR
b Renton, Wash, Aug 14, 1948. *Study:* Cent Wash State Univ, BA, 70; Ariz State Univ, Tempe, MFA, 73. *Work:* Coos Art Mus, Coos Bay, Ore. *Exhib:* Phoenix Art Mus, Ariz, 73; Spectrum Gallery, Tucson, 76; Creative Eye Gallery, Sonoma, Calif, 76; Cent Wash State Univ, Ellensburg, 77; Coos Bay Mus, Ore, 78; and others. *Teaching:* Lectr photog, State Univ NY, New Paltz, 73-74; instr photog, Modesto Jr Col, Calif, 74-, dean arts, humanities & commun, currently. *Mem:* Soc Photog Educ. *Media:* Color

GAVALAS, ALEXANDER BEARY
PAINTER
b Limerick, Ireland, Jan 6, 1945; US citizen. *Study:* Sch Art & Design, dipl, 63; Manhattanville Col, 69-; Coll New Rochelle, BA, 95. *Work:* Tweed Mus Art, Duluth, Minn; and others. *Exhib:* Solo exhibs, Tweed Mus Art, Minn, 80, Western Ill Univ Libr Gallery, 81, Ft Wayne Mus Art, Ind, 82, Marycrest Coll Eberdt Art Gallery, Iowa, 82, Arnot Art Mus, NY, 82 & Queens Coll Art Ctr/Paul Klapper Libr, NY, 83. *Teaching:* Instr art & music, St Catherine of Alexandria, Brooklyn, NY, 84-86. *Awards:* Commemorative Award, Men of Achievement, IBC, 85. *Bibliog:* Matt Santoro (auth), At peace with his environment, Queens Ledger, 80; Alan Garfield (auth), Alexander Beary Gavalas Recent Paintings & Drawings, Krasl Art Ctr, 80; Idealism, serenity mark Gavalas' landscapes, Ft Wayne Sentinel, 4/82. *Mem:* Int Platform Asn. *Media:* Oil, Pen & Ink. *Publ:* Auth, articles, Irish Echo, 82 & 83; articles, New York Daily News, 82; articles, Western Queens Gazette, 82. *Mailing Add:* 185 Atlantic Ave Apt B4 Lynbrook NY 11563

GAVIN, ELLEN A
PAINTER
b Philadelphia, PA, Dec 8, 1954. *Study:* Tyler Sch Art/Temple Univ, BFA (cumlaude), 76; Art Students League, NY, NY; Mus Natural Hist, NY, NY; Studied with Kim English, Scottsdale Artist Sch, Betty Lou Schlemn, Glouster Art League, Moe Brooker Tyler Sch Art. *Work:* Bryn Mawr Hosp, Philadelphia, Pa; Ocean City Art Ctr; Nipper Leader of the Pack (pub sculpture), Moorestown, NJ. *Comn:* Art Strings, NJ Symphony Orchestra, Newark, NJ, 2002; Beacon Hill Grand Prix, comn by Frank Madden (Beacon Hill), Colts Neck, NJ, 2003-2007; Painting, US Hanoverian Soc, Rolling Stone Farm, Lexington, Ky, 2005; plus many pvt comns. *Exhib:* Am Acad Equine Art, Int Mus of the Horse, Lexington, Ky, 2001-2007; Nat Exhib, Cambridge Art Asn, Cambridge, Mass, 2002; Faber Birren Show, Stamford Art Asn, Stamford, Conn, 2002; Solo Exhib, Liriodendron Mus, Bel Air, Md, 2003; Grand Nat Exhib, Am Artist Prof League, Salmagundi Club, NY, NY, 2005; Soc Animal Artist, Wildlife Experience, Parker, Colo, 2006-2007; Pen & Brush, NY, NY, 2007; Signature Artist, Noyes Mus, Oceanville, NJ, 2007; Plein Air Easton, Md, 2008-2012; Bennington Ctr Arts, Vermont Art of the Animal, 2010; Rittenhouse Square Fine Art Show, Philadelphia, 2003-2013; Hist Yellow Springs Art Show, Pa, 2005-2013; Small Matters of Great Importance, Edward Hopper House Art Center, Nyack, NY, 2011; Wayne Plein Air, Wayne, Pa, 2012; Callaway Gardens Plein Air, Atlanta, Ga, 2012; Easels in Fredrick, Md, 2012; Cranford Plein Air, Cranford, NJ, 2012; Solo exhib, Trippe-Hilder Brandt Gallery, Easton, Md, 2012; Mt Lebonon Plein Air, Pittsburgh, Pa, 2012-2013. *Pos:* Vpres (creative), Loreal, NY, NY, 84-2001. *Teaching:* Workshops: (oils), Riverfront Renaissance Center Arts (RRCA), Millville, NJ, 2006-2007; Am Acad Equine Art, Lexington, Ky, 2006-2008; Wayne Art Ctr, 2007, 2009, 2010; Green Boots Studio, Millville, NJ, 2009-2010, Hudson River Valley Workshops, Greenville, NY, 2011, 2013, Red Barn Art Ctr, Wellsboro, Pa, 2013. *Awards:* Purchase Award, Ocean City Art Show, Ocean City Art Center, 2002; Sporting Art Award, Am Acad Equine Art (AAEA), 2003, 2005; Raymond Chow Mem, Salmagundi Club, Am Artist Prof League, 2005; Wash Miniature, Miniature Paintings of Wash, 2005; Mus Dir Award, Am Acad Equine Art (AAEA), 2007; 300th Anniversary Annapolis, Paint Annapolis, Mid-Atlantic Plein Air Painters Asn (MAPAPA) City of Annapolis, 2007; Chestnut Hill Fall Arts, Best in Show, 2008; 1st Place, Millville Plein Air, 2009; 1st Place, Noyes Mus, Hammonton Plein Air, 2010 & 2011; Hon Mention, Wayne Plein Air, Pa, 2010; Vasari oil Color Award, Easton Plein Air, Easton, Md, 2010; Best in Show, Media Fine Art Show, Media, Pa, 2011; Hon Mention, Callaway Gardens, Quick Draw, 2011; Peoples Choice, Paint Annapolis, 2011; 2nd Place, New Hope Plein Air, Pa, 2012; Grand Prize, Mt Lebanon Plein Air, Pittsburgh, Pa, 2012. *Bibliog:* Nancy H James (auth), Living the Artful Life, Down Jersey, Aug 2003; Daryl Corcoran (auth), Horse Show on Canvas, NJ Country Side, autumn 2004; Arlene J Newman (auth), Paints the Horses Soul, Equestrian Talk, Jan-Feb 2004; Rusty Pray (auth), Dog Days Come Early, Philadelphia Inquirer, June 2005; Charles Cushing (auth), Rittenhouse Fine Art Show, Rittenhouse Revue, June 2007; Amy S Rosenberg (auth), Store to Shore, Wanamakers, the Eagle, and the Memories they Evoke, Phila Inquirer, 6/2012. *Mem:* Full mem, Am Acad Equine Art, 2003-2008; Invited mem, Miniature Painters, Sculptors & Gravers Soc Wash, 2003-2008; Assoc mem, Oil Painters Am, 2005-2008; Mid-Atlantic Plein Air Painters Asn (MAPAPA), 2006-2013; Assoc mem, Soc Animal Artist, 2006-2008. *Media:* Oils. *Mailing Add:* Green Boots Studio 14 N Second St Millville NJ 08332

GAWARECKI, CAROLYN ANN See Grosse, C(arolyn) Ann Gawarecki

GAY, BETSY (ELIZABETH) DERSHUCK
PAINTER, INSTRUCTOR
b Philadelphia, Pa, Nov 27, 1927. *Study:* Sweet Briar Col, Va, BA, 49; Nat Acad Fine Arts, New York, 56; studied with Edgar A Whitney, Charles Reid, Frank Webb, Gerald Brommer, Virginia Cobb, Nita Engle & others. *Work:* George B Markle Gallery, Penn State Univ Gallery, Pardee Collection Church Gallery, Hazelton, Pa; Sweet Briar Coll Gallery, Va; Pelham Art Ctr Gallery, NY. *Comn:* Painting, Eleventh Hole, Whippoorwill Club, Armonk, NY, 72; painting, Creation, Art Comt Church Collection, Hazleton, Pa, 75; painting, Summer Delights, Bedford Gourmet, NY, 90. *Exhib:* New Eng Exhib at Silvermine, Conn; Knickerbocker Artists, NY, 76; Nat Arts

Club, NY, 78; Nat Asn Women Artists NY, Ber Community Mus, Bergen, NJ, 82; Katonah NY Mus Art. *Teaching:* Instr water media, Northcastle Adult Educ, Armonk, NY, 77-82, Pelham Art Ctr, NY, 78- & Briarcliff Continuous Educ, New York, 79-83. *Awards:* Catharine Lorillard Wolfe Art Club President's Award, 98th Ann Exhib, Nat Arts Club, NY, 94; CLW Art Club Cash Award, 98th Ann Exhib, Nat Arts Club, NY, 94; First Prize, Mixed Media, Founder's Show, Hurlbutt Gallery, Conn, 97. *Bibliog:* The Best of Acrylic Painting, Rockport Publ, 96; Creative Inspirations, Rockport Publ, Inc, 97. *Mem:* Nat Asn Women Artists; Catherine Lorrilard Wolfe Art Club, NY; Mamaroneck Artists Guild; Katonah Mus Art. *Media:* Watercolor; Mixed Media. *Interests:* Painting, teaching, golf, tennis, gardening, 9 grandchildren, love to be with and help with.

GAYDOS, TIM (TIMOTHY) JOHN
PAINTER, SCULPTOR
b New York, NY, Dec 6, 1941. *Study:* Univ Calif, Berkeley, 59-61; Acad Di Belli Arti Di Brera, Milano, Italy, 62-63. *Work:* Rutgers Univ, New Brunswick & Newark, NJ; Vets Admin Hosp, Paramus, NJ; Butler Inst of AM Art Youngstown, Ohio; Metropolitan Opera, New York City; Montclair Art Mus NJ; Jersey City Mus, NJ; Bergen Mus, Paramus, NJ. *Comn:* Painting of Richard Wagner (composer), Bloomfield Libr, NJ, 84; Lady Cow Diva, Sculpture NY, Cow Parade, 2000; The New York Palace/Le Cirque Patrons; Portrait, Jerome Hines, Metrop Opera, NYC. *Exhib:* NJ Biennial, NJ State Mus, Trenton, 83 & Newark Mus, 85; Pastel Invitational, Hermitage Mus, Norfolk, Va, 85 & 87; solo exhib, Montclair Art Mus, NJ, 88-89; Bergen Mus NJ, 98; Univ of Maine at Machias, 2000, 2005; 165th Ann, Nat Acad Design, NY, 90; NJ Arts Ann, Noyes Mus, Oceanville, NJ, 92; Butler Inst of Am Art Ann, 2001, 2003, 2004. *Pos:* Only Fine Artist-Painter & Sculptor. *Awards:* NJ State Coun Arts Fel, 93-94; Gold Medal of Honor Am Watercolor Soc, 95; Top Award Pastel Soc Am, 95; Silver Medal of Honor Am Watercolors Soc, 2002; Nat Arts Club Award, Pastel Soc Am, 2004; Fell for Painting, NJ State Coun Arts, 2006. *Bibliog:* Award Winning Watercolors of 95 by Bebe Raupe The Artist's Mag, 9/95; Guilding The Eye by Kate Bolick, AM Artist Mag, Jan, 2002; Making the Human Connection by Maureen Bloomfield Watercolor Magic, Autumn, 2002. *Mem:* Pastel Soc Am (master pastellist); Am Watercolor Soc-Dolphin Fell NJ, Watercolor Soc. *Media:* Pastel, Acrylic. *Publ:* Contribr, Pastel Interpretations, North Light, 93; Contributor Pastel Portraits, by Watson Guptill, 96. *Dealer:* Woodwind Gallery, Machias, ME

GAYLORD, FRANK CHALFANT, II
SCULPTOR, DESIGNER
b Clarksburg, WVa, Mar 9, 1925. *Study:* Carnegie Inst Technol Coll Fine Arts; Tyler Sch Fine Arts, Temple Univ, BFA. *Comn:* Firemen Mem (granite), Nyack, NY; Pioneer Family (granite), Akron, Ohio; Arthur Fiedler (granite portrait), Boston Univ Libr, 82; William Penn (granite figure), Pen Treaty Park, Philadelphia, 82; William Shakespeare (granite portrait), Old Globe Theater, San Diego, 83; Nat Korean War Mem on the Mall, Washington, DC, 93. *Exhib:* Nat Sculpture Soc Ann Exhib, 65, 79 & 90. *Bibliog:* Article, The memorial sculpture of Frank Gaylord, Stone Am Mag, 4/82; The Stone Whistle (film), Barre Granite Asn. *Mem:* Assoc Nat Sculpture Soc; Fel, Nat Sculpture Soc. *Media:* All Media. *Publ:* Auth, Why Christ? & A portrait of Hector, 68, Monumental News Rev. *Mailing Add:* 2844 Vt Route 14 Ste 1 Williamstown VT 05679-9188

GAYLORD, JIM
PAINTER
b North Carolina. *Study:* Univ NC, Greensboro, BA (Film), 1997; Univ Calif, Berkeley, MFA, 2005. *Work:* Progressive Art Collection, Cleveland; West Collection, Oaks, Pa. *Exhib:* Solo exhibs include Gregory Lind Gallery, San Francscio, 2004; two-person exhibs include PS 122 Gallery, New York, (With Eric Hongisto), 2003; group exhibs include Recent Digital Art, Ctr Elec Art, San Francisco, 2000; Monster Drawing Rally, Southern Exposure, San Francisco, 2003; Antics Road Show, Timbrespace, Los Angeles, 2004; Realms of San Francisco, Nakaochiai Gallery, Tokyo, 2005; Pierogi Flatfiling, Artnews Projs, Berlin, 2007; Its Gouache & Gouache Only, Jeff Bailey Gallery, New York, 2008; Art On Paper, Weatherspoon Art Mus, Greensboro, NC, 2008. *Awards:* Eisner Award in Art Practice, Univ Calif Berkeley, 2005; New York Found Arts Fel, 2008. *Dealer:* Alberto Matteo Torri Via L De Bernardi 1 - 20129 Milan Italy; Pierogi 177 N 9th St Brooklyn NY 11211. *Mailing Add:* Gregory Lind Gallery 49 Geary St 5th Floor San Francisco CA 94108

GEALT, ADELHEID MEDICUS
MUSEUM DIRECTOR, HISTORIAN
b Munich, Ger, May 29, 1946; US citizen. *Study:* Ind Univ, PhD, 1979. *Collection Arranged:* Italian Portrait Drawings, 1400-1800 from North Am Collections Traveling Exhib (auth, catalog), 1983. *Pos:* Cur, Ind Univ Art Mus, Bloomington, 1976-, dir, 1989-. *Awards:* Nat Endowment Arts Cur Grant, 80; Nat Endowment Arts Planning & Implementation Grant, 81; Am Philos Soc Grant, 81; Nat Endowment Humanities Grant, 85. *Mem:* Ind Arts Comn(adv panelist, 89-). *Res:* Primarily Italian painting and drawing from 1300-1800. *Publ:* Auth, Looking at Art, A Visitor's Guide to Art Museums, RR Bowker, 1983; The Punchinello Drawings of Domenico Teipolo, Braziller, 1986; coauth, Art of the Western World, Summit Bks, 1989; auth, Painting of the Golden Age: A Biographical Dictionary of Seventeenth-Century European Painters, Greenwood Press, 1993; coauth/co-cur, Giandomenico Tiepolo: Maestraia e Gioco, Electra, 1996. *Mailing Add:* Ind Univ Art Mus Bloomington IN 47405

GEAR, EMILY
MUSEUM DIRECTOR, CURATOR
Study: Kalamazoo Coll, BA (Studio Art), 2000. *Pos:* Marketing/educ asst Cinninati Art Mus, 2000-2001; gallery asst, Tanya Bonakdar Gallery, New York, 2001; cur & exec dir, Garibaldi-Meucci Mus, Staten Island, NY, 2002-. *Mem:* vpres, educ & cultural Staten Island chap, Fieri Int, 2003, secy, 2004--05, fundraising/pub rel dir, 2005-2007, mem exec bd, 2005. *Mailing Add:* Garibaldi-Meucci Museum 420 Tompkins Ave Staten Island NY 10305

GEBHARDT, ROLAND
SCULPTOR, DESIGNER
b Paramaribo, Suriname, Sept 24, 1939; US citizen. *Study:* Art Acad Hamburg, Ger, with Theo Ortner; Kuntsgewerbeschule, Zurich, Switz; also apprenticeship in stained glass, Marburg, Ger. *Work:* Art Acad, Hamburg; Brandeis Univ; Storm King Art Ctr, Mountainville, NY; City of Ludwigshafen, Ger; Neuberger Mus, Purchase, NY. *Exhib:* Solo sculpture & painting exhib, Hudson River Mus, 71, Gallery 84, NY, 73 & Robert Freidus Gallery, 78; 20th Century Sculpture in Westchester Collection, Yonkers, NY, 72; Carlton Gallery, NY, 74 & 77; Storm King Art Ctr, 75 & 76; The Minimal Tradition, Aldrich Mus, Ridgefield, Conn, 79; Pumpkins, Art Et Industry, NY, 82; Eight one-day exhibs, Kunstmuseum, Dusseldorf, Fed Repub Ger, 82. *Awards:* Annual Prize, Art Acad Hamburg, 62. *Bibliog:* Fred Salaff (auth), Roland Gebhardt--Sculptor (film), 72; Arlene Krebs (dir), Liniar Void (video), 78. *Media:* Metal, Stone; Fiberglass, Concrete. *Publ:* Auth, Fresh Sculpture, 81. *Mailing Add:* 67 Vestry St New York NY 10013-1734

GECHTOFF, SONIA
PAINTER, DRAFTSPERSON
b Philadelphia, Pa, Sept 25, 1926. *Study:* Philadelphia Mus Coll Art, BFA, 50; Ford Found Fel, Tamarind Lithography Workshop, 63; study, CSFA Lithography Studio, 52-53. *Work:* Guggenheim Mus, Mus Mod Art & Metrop Mus Art, New York; Baltimore Mus Art; San Francisco Mus Mod Art; Worcester Art Mus, Mass; Whitney Mus, NY; Menil Collection, Houston; Calif Mus Art, San Jose. *Exhib:* Calif Painting: Mod Era, San Francisco Mus of Art, 76; Drawing Acquisition Shows, Mus of Mod Art, NY, 77 & Extraordinary Women & Am Drawn & Matched, 76-77; Solo exhibs, Gruenebaum Gallery, NY, 79-80, 82-83, 85 & 87 & Kraushaar Gallery, NY, 90, 92, 95 & 98, Alex Adam Gallery, New York, 2009; New Dimensions in Drawing, 50-80, Aldrich Mus Contemp Art, Conn, 81; Am Women-Am Art, Stamford Mus, Conn, 85; Art on Paper: Weatherspoon Guild, NC, 87; 56th Nat Midyear Exhib, Butler Inst Art, Youngstown, Ohio, 92; Paper Trails, Art Mus Santa Cruz, Calif, 93; San Francisco Sch Abstr Expressionists, San Francisco Mus Mod Art, 96; Poindexter Collection, Denver Art Mus, 98-99; Stamp of Impulse - Abstract Expressionist Prints, Worcester Art Mus, Mass, 2001; The Most Difficult Journey, Yellowstone Art Mus, Billings, Mont, 2002; Expressive Impressions: 3 Decades of Am Abstract Prints, Cummer Mus Art, Jacksonville, Fla, 2003; West Coast Abstract Expressionist Art, Menil Collection, Houston, 2006; Abstract Expressionist Prints, Pollock-Krasner House, New York, 2006; The Abstract Impulse, Nat Acad Design Mus Art, New York, 2007; Then and Now (Hudson River painting), Pelham Art Center, NY, 5-6/2008; Wonder Women, Shapolsky Gallery, NY, 2008-09; Bella Pacifica Exhib, Nyehaus Gallery, NY, 2011. *Teaching:* Instr, Calif Sch Fine Art, San Francisco, 56-58; lectr art, Queens Coll, 70-74; assoc prof art, Univ NMex, 74-75; artist-in-residence, Skidmore Coll, NY, 88-90 & 95; vis artist, Chicago Art Inst, 89; artist-in-residence, Adelphi Univ, NY, 91 & 93; master drawing, Nat Acad Sch Art, NY, 2000-2003, master painting, 2003-2007, & 2009; Nat Acad Sch Art, New York, 2010. *Awards:* Mid-Atlantic Nat Endowment Arts Grant, 88; Pollock-Krasner Found Grant, 94, 98, & 2002; Richard Florsheim Art Fund, 95; Charles Eliot Norton award in graphics, Nat Acad Design Mus Art, 2001; Award of Recognition for Teaching and Sch Comt Serv, Nat Acad Sch Fine Arts, 2008. *Bibliog:* James Mellow (auth), Sonia Gechtoff: A different kind of knowledge, Arts Mag, 2/82; Michael Brenson (auth), Sonia Gechtoff's New Direction, NY Times, 11/25/83; John Loughery (auth), Sonia Gechtoff: The Theatre of the Visible Kraushaar Galleries Catalogue, 5/92 & Sonia Gechtoff: 4 Decades Works on Paper, Skidmore Coll (catalog), 95; American Abstract Expressionism of the 1950s: An Illustrated Survey, NY Sch Press, 2003; 100 New York Painters, Schiffer Press, 2006; American Abstract and Figurative Expressionism, NY Sch Press, 2009; K McKenna (editor), The Ferus Gallery: A Place to Begin, Steidl Publishing, 2009; Art in America Mag, interview by Fay Hirsh, 2/2011. *Mem:* Arch Am Art; Nat Acad. *Media:* Acrylic, Oil, Graphite. *Dealer:* Nyehaus Gallery NY. *Mailing Add:* 463 W St Apt 936 New York NY 10014

GEDEON, LUCINDA HEYEL
MUSEUM DIRECTOR, ADMINISTRATOR
b Port Chester, NY, Oct 13, 1947. *Study:* Calif State Univ, Long Beach, BA (art hist), 1978; Univ Calif, Los Angeles, MA, 1981, PhD (art hist), 1990. *Collection Arranged:* Jacob Lawrence, Collaborations & Connections: 20th Century Collaborative Bookworks (with John Risseeuw; auth, catalog), Ann Flaten Pixley, Sharokh Rezvani Workshop, Meeting Ground: Basketry Traditions & Sculptural Form (with Margo Shermeta; auth, catalog), Felice Lucero-Giaccardo: Contemporary Pueblo Painter (with Barbara Loeb; auth, catalog), Univ Art Mus, Ariz State Univ, Tempe, 1990-91; Art Detour Exhib, Artlink Inc, Phoenix, Ariz, 1990; Alison Saar: Inside Looking In (with Nancy Miller & Francis Sprout; auth, catalog), Neuberger Mus Art, State Univ NY, Purchase, 1992; Rebecca Medel: Transcendental Fiber Constructs (auth, catalog), Neuberger Mus Art, State Univ NY, Purchase, 1993; Melvin Edwards Sculpture: A Thirty Year Retrospective 1963-1993 (ed, catalog), Neuberger Mus Art, State Univ NY, Purchase, 1993; Roy R Neuberger: Patron of the Arts, Neuberger Art Mus (ed, catalog), State Univ NY, Purchase, 93; Color Options, Westchester Community Coll Art Gallery, 1993; June Wayne: A Retrospective (sculpture; auth, catalog), 1996; Elizabeth Catlett Retrospective (auth, catalog), 1997. *Pos:* Asst dir, Grunwald Ctr Graphic Arts, Univ Calif, Los Angeles, 1981-83, actg dir & cur, 1983-85; chief cur, Univ Art Mus, Ariz State Univ, Tempe, 1985-91; bd dirs, Balboa Art Conservation Ctr, San Diego, 1986-91, ArtTable, NY, 1995-98, Westchester Arts Coun, 1998-2004; chair, Temple Music Arts Comn, 1989-90; dir, Neuberger Mus Art, State Univ NY, Purchase, 1991-2004; dir, CEO, Vero Beach Mus Art, Fla, 2004-. *Awards:* Afro-Am Studies Fel & Edward A Dickson Hist Art Fel, Univ Calif, Los Angeles, 1984; Coll Fine Arts Research Grant, Ariz State Univ, Tempe, 1990; Arts Exhib Grant, Ariz Comn, 1990-91; State Univ NY Chancellor's Award, 2002; Individual Arts Award, Westchester Arts Coun, 2002. *Mem:* Am Asn Mus; Art Table; Coll Art Asn; Mus Asn

Ariz (bd mem, 88-90); Asn Art Mus Dirs. *Res:* History of American and African-American art; history of prints. *Publ:* Auth, Rebecca Medel's Transcendental Net Results, Fiberarts, 9-10/91; The Janet Taylor Studio: A Tapestry Workshop in the Arizona Desert, Fiberarts, 3/91. *Mailing Add:* Vero Beach Mus Art 3001 Riverside Pk Dr Vero Beach FL 32963

GEDEON, PETER FERENC
PHOTOGRAPHER, CURATOR
b Pecs, Hungary, May 19, 1955. *Study:* Technical Univ for Heavy Industry, MS, Miskolc, Hungary, 79; Asn of Hungarian Photoartists, cert (photographic artist), Budapest, Hungary, 81; Art Found of Hungary, cert (creative artist), 81; TUHI, Miskolc, Dr Lajos Vegvari (Hist of Art), 76-79. *Work:* Int Ctr of Photography, New York; Hungarian Mus of Photography, Kecskemet, Hungary; Dery Mus, Debrecen, Hungary; Otto Herman Mus, Miskolc, Hungary; Int Photographic Workshop, Lanslebourg, France. *Comn:* Balmazujvaros Photo-Artist Creative House; Hortobagy, Winter Hortobagy, The Second Meeting, Fairy's Garden. *Exhib:* Solo exhibs, The Dark Side of Moon, Ctr Montrsquieu de Maison-Laffitte, France, 91, Landscape & Nudes, Plaza of Nations, Vancouver, Can, 92, Carriers of My Dreams, Ferihegyi Galeria, Budapest, Hungary, 98, Marosvasarhely, Romania, 2001; Group exhibs, 7th Berlin Int Photo Exhib, Germany, 79; Great Wall Int Sportphoto Contest, Beijing, China, 85; 20th Korea Int Salon of Photography, Seoul, Korea, 99. *Collection Arranged:* Int Photography Exhib Exchange, multiple locations in Fla & Hungary, 93-94; The Women of Freddy Mary, Exposures Photo Workshop, Sarasota, Fla, 97; Hungarian Millenial Days-Eternity (with co-cur Peter L Koenig), Art Ctr, Sarasota, Fla, 2000; Un-Holy Icons by Pamela Jablonski, Green Bull Gallery, Bradenton, Fla, 2005; Banned Beauties of Bradenton by Ginger White, Green Bull Gallery, Bradenton, Fla, 2006; Delirium by Micole Bredean, Green Bull Gallery, Bradenton, Fla, 2006. *Pos:* Art dir, Diosgyor Art Circle, Miskolc, Hungary, 81-92; Founder & pres, Diosgyor Visual Art Guild Soc, Miskolc, Hungary, 89-92; founder & dir, Green Bull Gallery, Bradenton, Fla, 2004-. *Awards:* 1st Prize, My Environ- through the eyes of youth, Univ Art & Design, Tapiola, Finland, 80; Sobeka Gold Medal, 12iem Salon Int Sobeka, Belgium, 90; Best Nude Photograph, 2-0 Concurso Int d'Art Fotografica, Fabriano, Italy, 92; Gold Medal, 61st Int Photographic Salon of Japan, Tokyo, Japan, 2001; Artist of FIAP, Fed Int de l'Art Photographique, Paris, France, 2005, Excellence of FIAP, 2008. *Bibliog:* Gerhard Ihke (auth), Fotografua Academica, Fotografie, Leipzig, Germany, 79; Lajos Vegvari (auth), Gedeon Peter es Pap Zoltan Kiallitasa, Foto, Budapest, Hungary, 2/83; Lajos Vegvari (auth), Miskolci fotomuveszek, Fotomuveszet, Budapest, Hungary, 2/89; Peter Gedeon (ed), ObJetivf, Virton, Belgiu, 90; Peter L Koenig, Best of the Suncoast/Best Art Photographer, Weekly Planet, 9/20/2001. *Mem:* Diosgyor Art Circle, Miskolc, Hungary (art dir, 81-92); Asn of Hungarian Photoartists, 81-; Asn of Hungarian Creative Artists, 81-; Diosgyor Visual Art Guild Soc, Miskolc, Hungary (pres, 89-92, perpetual chmn, 2004), 89-; Nat Asn of Photoshop Prof, 2004-. *Interests:* Landscapes, nudes. *Publ:* Contribr, Photocommunication, Paperpress, Vienna, Austria, 82; contribr, Photography Yearbook, Fountain Press, Surbiton, Eng, 91-94; contribr, Here We Are, Asn of Hungarian Photoartists, 91; PSZ Parosan Szep, Asn of Hungarian Photoartists, 2003; Carriers of My Dreams, 2008. *Dealer:* Green Bull Gallery 913 12th Ave W Bradenton FL 34205

GEE, HELEN
ART CONSULTANT, CURATOR
Collection Arranged: Curated 78 exhibs, 54-88; Stieglitz & the Photo-Secession, NJ State Mus, 78; Bank Tokyo, NY; Indust Bank Japan, NY; Photography of the Fifties (catalog), Ctr Creative Photog, Tucson. *Pos:* Owner & dir, Limelight Gallery. *Teaching:* Parsons Sch Design, 80-. *Interests:* 19th and 20th century painting, sculpture and photography. *Publ:* Photography of the Fifties: An American Perspective, Univ Arizona Press, 83; Limelight: A Memoir, Univ NMex Press, 97

GEE, LI-LAN See Li-lan

GEFTER, JUDITH MICHELMAN
PHOTOGRAPHER
b Gloversville, NY. *Study:* Pratt Inst, cert; NY Univ; Univ Fla; Fla State Univ; also with William E Parker & Wilson Hicks Conf, Univ Miami. *Work:* Mint Mus, Charlotte, NC; Jacksonville Art Mus, Fla; Tampa Art Inst, Fla; Southern Bell Collection, 85; Barnett Bank, 90; Cummer Mus, Jacksonville, Fla. *Comn:* Two wood carvings, comn by Mem Hosp, Jacksonville, Fla, 84; sculpture, Art-in-Public Places, Housing Urban Develop, 85. *Exhib:* Am Soc Mag Photogr Traveling Show, 62-63; solo exhibs, Pratt Inst, 66 & 67, Breast & Face, Steiglitz Gallery, New York, 75, Phillips Gallery, Jacksonville Univ, Fla, 77, Univ Fla, 78, Computography, Neikrug Gallery, New York, 92 & Thrasher Horne Gallery, Orange Park, Fla, 2006; retrospective, Jacksonville Art Mus, 70; There is No Female Camera Traveling Show, Neikrug Gallery, New York, 75 & Univ N Fla, 81; Fabulous Photographs, Cummer Mus, Jacksonville, Fla, 92; JCA Gallery, 98-2000; Fairfax Gallery, Jacksonville, Fla, 2000; Venice Redux, Haskell Gallery, Jacksonville Airport, 2003; Thrasher Horne Gallery, Initiating Exhib, New Performing Arts Ctr, Orange Park, Fla, 2006; Merce Cunningham, Pence Gallery, Davis, Calif, 2008; Merce permanent collection, Mondavi Ctr Performing Arts, Univ Calif Davis, 2010. *Teaching:* Adj prof photogr, Fine Arts Dept, Univ N Fla, 80-81; Kodak guest artist, Ctr Creative Imaging, Camden, Maine, 92. *Awards:* Best Ann Report (2 yrs), Koger Co, Mead Paper Co, 79-80; Best Cover (photograph) Ann Reports, J Cato Ann Report Dept Cato Inst, 85; Best of Am Soc Media Photographers, 2010; Best of 2010, ASMP. *Bibliog:* Elizabeth Kaufman (auth), My life & my art, Arts Assembler, 11/75; portfolio, Charter Issue Kalliope, A Tour of Women's Art, winter 79; Challenge of Freelance Photography (audio-visual prog), Media Loft Inc, 80 & Jacksonville Mag, 10/85; Profile in Fla Times Union, March 2003. *Mem:* Life mem, Am Soc Media Photogr; Soc Photogr Commun (pres, N Fla chap, 65-70); Nat Soc Lit & Arts. *Media:* Computer Art, Photography, Digital Photography. *Interests:* Computer, fiction and memoir writing, art museums, classical music. *Collection:* André Kertesz; B Schoenfeld. *Publ:* Illusr, Jacksonville Calendar Diary Bicentennial Ed, 76; contribr, Longman Dict Mass Media & Communication, 82. *Dealer:* Pence Gallery Davis CA. *Mailing Add:* 1515 Shasta Dr #3334 Davis CA 95616

GEIER, PHILIP HENRY, JR
PATRON
b Pontiac, Mich, Feb 22, 1935. *Study:* Colgate Univ, BA, 57; Columbia Univ, MS, 58; Delta Kappa Epsilon. *Pos:* With, McCann-Erickson, Inc, Cleveland, 58-60, New York City, 60-68; chmn, McCann-Erickson Int UK Co, London, 69-73; exec vpres, McCann-Erickson Europe, 73-75; vchmn, int operations McCann Worldwide, London, 73-75; vchmn, int Interpublic Group of Cos, Inc, New York City, 75-77, pres, chief operating off, 77-80, chmn, chief exec off, 80-2001, pres, 85-2000. *Mem:* Doubles (New York City); River (New York City); Sloane (London); Hurlingham (London); Whitney Mus of Am Art (trustee, currently)

GEIGER, PHILLIP NEIL
PAINTER, DRAFTSMAN
b Ft Lauderdale, Fla, Feb 26, 1956. *Study:* Wash Univ, BFA, 1978; Yale Univ, MFA, 1980. *Work:* Chemical Bank, New York, NY; Gen Foods, Minneapolis, Minn; CSX Corp, Richmond, Va; Stevens Co, Little Rock, Ark. *Exhib:* Solo exhibs include More Gallery, Philadelphia, 1982 & 1983, Swarthmore Coll, 1987 & Tatistcheff & Co, NY, 1986, 1988, 1990, 1993 & 1995, Hollins Coll, 1989; group exhibs include Bodies & Souls, Artists' Choice Mus, NY, 1983; Drawings, Drawings, Drawings, Forum Gallery, NY, 1984; Painterly Realism, Fontbonne Coll, St Louis, 1984; Contemp Narrative Figure Painting (with catalog), Payne Gallery, Moravian Coll, Bethlehem, Pa, 1986; Am Art Today: The Figure in Landscape, Art Mus at Ft Lauderdale Int Univ, Miami, 1986; Landscape Painting (with catalog), Gibbes Mus Art, Charleston; Hacket-Freedman, San Francisco, Calif, 2000 & 2002; Reynolds, Richmond, Va, 1998, 2001 & 2003; Tibor De Nagy, NY, 2005. *Teaching:* Asst prof art, Colo State Univ, Ft Collins, 1980-83 & Univ Va, Charlottesville, 1983. *Bibliog:* Kay Larson (auth), New Fares '86, New York Mag, 3/1986; Michael Kimmelman (auth), New York Times, 2/26/1988; Ronnie Cohen (auth), Art Forum, 5/1990. *Media:* Oil. *Dealer:* Peter Tatistcheff 50 W 57th St New York NY 10019; Tibor de Nagy Gallery 724 Fifth Ave New York NY 10019. *Mailing Add:* McIntire Department of Art Univ Virginia PO Box 400130 Charlottesville VA 22904-4130

GEISERT, ARTHUR FREDERICK
PRINTMAKER, ILLUSTRATOR
b Dallas, Tex, Sept 20, 1941. *Study:* Concordia Teachers' Col, Seward, Nebr, BS, 63; Univ Calif, Davis, MA, 65; Chouinard Art Inst, Los Angeles; Otis Art Inst, Los Angeles; Art Inst Chicago. *Work:* Mus Art, Lodz, Poland; Freeport Art Mus, Ill; First Nat Bank Chicago; Standard Oil of Ind, Chicago; Calif Coll Arts & Crafts, Oakland. *Exhib:* Solo exhibs, Ill Art Coun Gallery, Chicago, 79, Foxley Leach Gallery, Washington, DC, 86, Boston Pub Libr, 86 & The Print Club, Philadelphia, 86; West 79, The Law, Minn Mus Art, St Paul, 79; 5th Univ Dallas Nat Print Invitational, Univ Dallas, 79. *Teaching:* From instr to asst prof art, Concordia Col, River Forest, Ill, 65-70; asst prof art, Concordia Col, Seward, Nebr, 70-71. *Awards:* 10 Recommended Picture Books, Time Mag, 95; Horn Book Honor Book, Boston Globe, 96; Silver Medal, Soc Illustrators, 96. *Mem:* Chicago Artists Coalition; Artists Equity Asn Inc; Boston Printmakers; The Print Club, Philadelphia; Los Angeles Printmaking Soc. *Media:* Etching. *Publ:* Auth & illsr, Oink Oink, 93; After the Flood, 94; Haystack, 95; Roman Numerals I to MM, 96; The Etcher's Studio, 97

GEKIERE, MADELEINE
PAINTER, ILLUSTRATOR, FILMMAKER
b Zurich, Switz; US citizen. *Study:* Art Students League, with Kantor; Brooklyn Mus Art Sch, with Tamayo; NY Univ, with Sam Adler. *Work:* Worcester Art Mus, Mass; Fogg Mus Art, Cambridge, Mass; NY Univ Collection; Brooklyn Mus, NY; Butler Art Inst; and others; Eric Carle Mus, Amherst Mass. *Exhib:* Univ Ga, 67; Western Carolina Univ, 72; NY Univ Loeb Ctr; many solo exhibs in NY, Babcock Galleries, film showings, Millenium & Artists Space, The Collective for Living Cinema, NY & 2nd Int Women's Film Festival, Donell Branch NY Pub Libr; Anthology Film Archives, New York, 2009; Fred Torres Collaborations, NY, 2012; Fred Torres Collaborations, 2013; Anthology Film Archives, NY, 2011. *Collection Arranged:* Schweizersche Landes Bibliothek Graphische Collection, Bern, Switzerland. *Teaching:* Assoc prof art, NY Univ, 58-67; prof art, City Col NY, 67-90; vis prof painting, Univ Ga, 67; prof Emer, City Coll of NY, currently. *Awards:* Best Ill Bk of Year, New York Times, 57, 59 & 63; Audubon Medal of Honor, 69; Childe Hassam Purchase Prize, Soc Art & Lett, 73. *Mem:* Artists Equity Asn. *Media:* Children's Books, Mixed Media. *Publ:* Auth & illusr, Who Gave Us, 53; illusr, Switch on the Night (by Ray Bradbury), 57; auth & illusr, The Princess & the Frilly Lilly, 60; illusr, The Reason for the Pelican (by John Ciardi), 60; illusr, John J Plenty and Fiddler Dan (by John Ciardi), 63. *Mailing Add:* 427 W 21st St New York NY 10011

GELBER, SAMUEL
PAINTER, EDUCATOR
b Brooklyn, NY, Mar 14, 1929. *Study:* Brooklyn Col, BA; NY Univ, MA. *Work:* Purchase Mus, NY; Farnsworth Mus, ME; Brooklyn Mus, NY. *Comn:* painting, Bellevue Hosp, 86; three sets for ballet, Overcoat, After gogol, Kirov Ballet, Mariinsky Theater, St Petersberg, Russa, 2006. *Exhib:* Brooklyn Mus Biennial, 56; solo exhibs, Green Mountain Gallery, NY, 72, 74, 76 & 79, A Sense of Place, Wichita Art Mus, Kans, 73, Springfield Art Mus, Mo, 74 & Joslyn Art Mus, Nebr, 74; Maine Coast Artists, 98, Portland Mus, ME, 2000, Farnsworth Mus, ME, 2001; and others. *Teaching:* Instr drawing, Pratt Inst, Brooklyn, 62-65; prof painting & drawing, Brooklyn Col, 62-, chmn, 88, prof emer, 91-. *Awards:* Crane & Co Award for Painting, Berkshire Mus, 66. *Bibliog:* Lee Wallin (auth), New Realism 70, St Cloud State Col,

70; Alan Gussow (auth), A Sense of Place--the Artist and the American Land, Friends of Earth, 72; Sanford Sintz Shannan (auth), An interview with Philip Pearlstein, Art in Am, 9/81; Samuel Gelber, The Season Suite, Farnsworth Mus, 10/2001. *Media:* Oil, Lithography. *Mailing Add:* 215 W 98th St New York NY 10025

GELDIN, SHERRI
MUSEUM DIRECTOR
Study: Univ Calif, LA, BA (art history), MBA (arts management). *Pos:* Intern, Cooper-Hewitt Mus, NY, formerly; assoc dir, Mus Contemp Art, Los Angeles, formerly; dir, Wexner Ctr for Arts, Ohio State Univ, 1993-; trustee, Andy Warhol Found for Visual Arts, currently, chair bd, 2006-; bd mem, Great Columbus Convention and Visitor's Bureau, currently. *Awards:* Women of Achievement Award, YWCA, 2002; Chevalier French Order Arts & Letters, 2006. *Mem:* Asn Art Mus Directors; ArtTable. *Mailing Add:* Wexner Center for Arts Ohio State Univ 1871 N High St Columbus OH 43210-1393

GELFAND, LAURA D
EDUCATOR, ADMINISTRATOR
Study: State Univ of NY at Stony Brook, BA, 1987; Williams Col, Mass, MA, 1989; Case Western Reserve Univ, Cleveland, Ohio, PhD, 1994. *Pos:* Leadership training includes 11th Annual Conference ACE Ohio Women's Network, 2009, 12th, 2010, Univ of Akron Academic Leadership Forum, 2009-10, & HERS Inst, Denver, 2010; Founding Fellow of the Executive Leadership Acad, Univ Calif, Berkeley, 2011. *Teaching:* Lecturer, John Carroll Univ, 1990-91, Case Western Reserve Univ, 1991; asst prof, Mankato State Univ, 1994-95, Univ of the Pacific, 1995-97; asst lecturer, Univ Utah, 1995; prof art history, Summer Voyage, 2004; asst prof art history, Honors Col, Univ of Akron, 1997-2002, assoc prof, 2002-08, prof art history 2008-11, assoc dean, 2009-11; prof art history, head Departments of Art and Interior Design, Utah State Univ, 2011-. *Awards:* Case Western Reserve Univ Alumni Fellowship, Dept of Art History, 1990-91, 91-92; Stony Brook Found award for Excellence in Art History, 1987; Ohio Magazine Excellence in Educ award, 2004; 2004 Northeast Ohio Council on Higher Educ award for Excellence in Teaching; Univ of Akron Outstanding Teacher of the Year, 2004; Nat Endowment for the Humanities Summer Seminars for Col Teachers, Paris and Cambridge, UK. *Res:* Presented research at numerous national and international conferences as well as organizing several symposia and chairing many sessions. *Publ:* (co-editor) Art and Material Culture in Medieval and Renaissance Europe, 2011; (co-editor) Push Me, Pull You: Imagination and Devotional Practices in Late Medieval and Renaissance Art and Push Me, Pull You: Physically and Devotional Practices in Late Medieval and Renaissance Art, 2011. *Mailing Add:* Department of Art History Utah State University FAV 122 Logan UT 84322-4000

GELINAS, ROBERT WILLIAM
PAINTER, EDUCATOR
b Springfield, Mass, Mar 1, 1931. *Study:* Univ Conn; Univ Ala, BFA & MFA; also with Lawrence Calgagno & Tatsuiko Heima. *Work:* Kelley Fitzpatrick Mus, Montgomery, Ala; Mead Corp Collection, Atlanta, Ga; Fla House of Rep, Tallahassee; Mus Fine Arts, Little Rock, Ark. *Comn:* Chapel sculpture, Wesley Found Student Ctr, Memphis, 60. *Exhib:* Art USA, 58, NY, 58; 26th & 27th Corcoran Biennials, Washington, DC, 59 & 61; Painting of the Yr Ann, Mead Corp, Atlanta, 61; Bon Marche Nat Gallery Exhib, Seattle, Wash, 63; Fla Showcase, Rockefeller Ctr, NY, 64; Soc of Four Arts Exhibs, Palm Beach, Fla, 66, 72, 77, 78 & 79. *Pos:* Art dir, Tuscaloosa News, Ala, 55-57; artist-in-residence, Maitland Res Ctr, 65 & Upham Studio, Naples, 66-69. *Teaching:* Guest artist instr, Allisons Wells Art Colony Workshops, Canton, Miss, 58-62; asst prof art, Memphis State Univ, 58-63; from assoc prof to prof art, Univ SFla, 63-98. *Awards:* First Purchase Prize, Mid South Ann, 61; 18th Ann Purchase Exhib Prize, Carrol Reese Mus, 67; Best of Show, Gulf Coast Art Exhib, Bellaire, Fla, 78. *Bibliog:* Benbow (auth), All out war, St Petersburg Times, 8/65; Gelinas the modern master, Tampa Tribune, 66. *Media:* Acrylic. *Mailing Add:* 1235 15th St Apt 2 Sarasota FL 34236-2541

GELLER, BUNNY ZELDA
WRITER, SCULPTOR
b New York, NY, May 21, 1926. *Study:* Univ Calif, Los Angeles, 44-46; studied with Alfred Van Loen & Philip Darling & Berta Margolies, 62-70; Fla Int Univ, 89-97. *Work:* Nat Mus Women Arts, Washington, DC; Broward Co Main Libr, Ft Lauderdale, Fla; Kushi Found, Brookline, Mass; Hallandale Cult Ctr, Fla. *Comn:* Two sculptures, Hallandale Cult Ctr, Fla, 98. *Exhib:* Solo exhibs, Bowery Savings Bank, NY, 78, Lynn Kottler Galleries, NY, 78 & Hollywood Art Mus, Fla, 78-79; All Broward Exhib, Ft Lauderdale, Fla, 78; Old Westbury Hebrew Congregation, NY, 78; De Ligny Galleries, Ft Lauderdale, Fla, 79 & 83-84; Int Treasure Fine Art, Plainview, NY, 78-81; Int Art Expo (with catalog), NY, 82-83 & 92; Nelson Rockefeller Collection Inc, NY, 83; First Ann Int Wildlife Expo, Atlantic City, 83; Exhibition of Fine Art, Nassau Mus Fine Art Asn, 85; United Nations Conf, Nairobi, 85; Hallandale Cult Ctr, Fla, 98; Pegasus Int Corp, NJ 81, 82, 83, 84, 85; Jockey Club, Fla, 80, 81, 83, 84; Buckeye Sweepstakes, Columbus, Ohio, 82; Bondstreet Gallery, Pittsburgh, Pa, 82; Blumka Gallery, New York, 82; Korby Gallery, Cedar Grove, NJ, 82; Wash Int, Horse Show, Md, 82. *Pos:* Judge, Fine Art & Craft Show, Ft Lauderdale, Fla, 79-81; art adv coun, Westbury Mem Libr, NY, 90-94. *Awards:* First Prize, Carrier Found Auxilary Arts Festival, 85; Ed Choice Award, Nat Libr Poetry, 95; Inductee, Int Poetry Hall Fame, 96. *Bibliog:* Town & Country Mag, 82; Art in Am Mag, 83-84; Sunstorm Arts Mag, 84. *Mem:* Nat Mus Women Arts Asn; Int Soc Poets (distinguished mem). *Media:* Bronze, Clay. *Res:* "Free Spirit" (bronze). *Publ:* Auth, Bunny Geller Original Poetry, 95; Choices, 96; contribr, Beyond the Stars, 95 & Best Poems of the 90's, 96; Kaleidoscope, 97; The Monkey and the Parakeet (A Poetic Tale for Children), 97; auth, Impressions, 99; auth, Bunny Geller: Original Bronze Sculptures, 95. *Dealer:* BZG Enterprises Hallandale Beach Fla 33009. *Mailing Add:* 400 Diplomat Pkwy Apt 711 Hallandale FL 33009-3732

GELLER, ESTHER GELLER SHAPERO
PAINTER, PRINTMAKER
b Boston, Mass, Oct 26, 1921. *Study:* Mus Fine Arts Sch, Boston, dipl; also with Karl Zerbe. *Work:* Mus Fine Arts, Boston; Addison Gallery Am Art, Andover, Mass; Brandeis Univ; Walters Gallery, Regis Col; St Mark's Sch Gallery, Southboro, Mass. *Exhib:* Art Inst Chicago Ann; US Info Serv Circulating Exhibs in the US & Far East; Solo exhibs, Am Acad Art Gallery, Rome, 71, Newton Art Ctr, 78, Artworks at the Wayne, 79 & Stonehill Col, 86; Pastel Show, Regis Col, 84; Honored Artists, Danforth Mus, 95; Passion for the Human Form, Art Space Gallery; Expressive Voice, Danforth Mus, 2012. *Teaching:* Instr painting & drawing, Sch Mus Fine Arts, Boston, 43, Boris Mirski Art Sch, 46-48, Natick Art Asn Sch, 55-61 & Wayland Art Asn, 83. *Awards:* Cabot Fel, 49; Fels, MacDowell Colony, Yaddo & Am Acad, 50-71. *Bibliog:* Pratt & Fizell (auth), Encaustic, Lear Publ, 49; Bern Chaet (auth), Artists at Work, Webb, 60; B Hayes (auth), The Layman's Guide to Modern Art; R Lister (auth), Drawing with Pastel; and others. *Media:* Watercolor, Encaustic. *Dealer:* Geller Studio 5 Summer St Natick MA 01760; Firehouse Studios. *Mailing Add:* 9 Russell Cir Natick MA 01760

GELLER, MATTHEW
SCULPTOR
b New York, NY, Sept 28, 1954. *Study:* Conn Col, BA, 76; Univ Del, MFA, 78. *Work:* Mus Mod Art, Whitney Mus Am Art, Franklin Furnace, NY; Stedelijk Van Abbemuseum, Einhoven, Moderna Musset, Stockholm; Witte de With, Rotterdam; Inst Contemp Art, London. *Comn:* Foggy Day, Lower Manhattan Cult Coun, Cortland Alley, New York, 2003; 60 Weak Knees, Arthouse, Austin, 2005; Awash, NY City Dept Parks, Lower Manhattan Cult Coun, Collect Park, New York, 2006; Open Channel Flow, Sabine St Water Pump Sta, Houston, 2008; Munic Park & Polic Sta, Austin, 2008. *Exhib:* The Times Square Show, Collaborative Proj Inc, 80, Mus Mod Art, 82, 87, 88, 94 & 2000, Int Ctr For Photog, NY, 89; Mus Mod Art, Jerusalem, 81; Long Beach Mus, 82, La Jolla Mus, Calif, 87; Whitney Mus Am Art, 83, 90 & 96; Inst Contemp Art, Boston, 84; Laforet Mus, New Orleans, 84; Your Television, Your Home, New Mus Contemp Art, NY, 90; Witte de With, Rotterdam, 99. *Pos:* VPres, Collaborative Proj Inc, NY, 81-82; co-dir, Line Asn, NY, 81-83; consult, Visual Arts, Nat Endowment for the Arts, 84, 85; co-chair media panel, NY State Coun on the Arts, 86-88. *Teaching:* Sch of Visual Arts, NY, 83-84, 86-90, Univ Calif, San Diego, 87, Princeton Univ, 88, William Col, Williamstown, Mass, 90, Pratt Inst, 94- & Parsons Sch Design, 96-. *Awards:* Nat Endowment Arts Fel Visual Arts, 87 & 89; Rome Prize, Am Acad in Rome, 91-92; Fel, Creative Capital Foun, 99-2000. *Bibliog:* Articles in Village Voice, NY Times, Artnews, Art in American & Art Forum. *Mem:* NY State Coun Arts. *Media:* Installation, Public Art. *Publ:* Contribr, Difficulty Swallowing: A Medical Chronicle, 81 & 1983 Engagements, 82, Works Press, NY; Hidden away in a musty chamber, Wedge Mag, 83; From Receiver to Remote Control: The TV Set, New Mus Contemp Art, 90. *Mailing Add:* 4 White St New York NY 10013

GELLIS, SANDY L
SCULPTOR, ENVIRONMENTAL ARTIST
b Bronx, NY, 1940. *Study:* Sch Visual Arts; City Coll New York; New Sch Social Res, FIT (AAS). *Work:* Libr Congress, Washington, DC; Brooklyn Mus, Whitney Mus & Spencer Col, NY Publ Libr; Allentown Art Mus, Pa; Fogg Art Gallery, Harvard Univ, Mass; Nat Mus Natural Hist, Washington, DC. *Comn:* River Memory, Work Wall, Children's Room, Helen B Atkinson Health Ctr; Cygnus A: Environment, Pub Libr Plaza, Bronx, NY, 92-94; River Memory, Word Wall, Children's Room, Helen Batkinson Health Ctr; and many others. *Exhib:* Adelade of Northland Glass, Nat Mus Scotland, Edinburgh; Projects and Portfolios, 25th Nat Print Biennial, Brooklyn Mus, NY, 89; Presswork: The Art of 100 Women Printmakers (traveling), Nat Mus Women Arts, Washington, DC, 91; solo exhib, Gallery Three Zero (with catalog), 92, TZArt & Co, 95 & Karen McReady Fine Art, NY, 98; Karen McReady Fine Art, NY, 97, 98 & 2000; Contemp Narratives in Am Prints, Whitney Mus Am Art at Champion, Conn, 2000; Prints & Drawings 1960-2000, Arthur M Sackler Mus, Harvard Univ Art Mus, Cambridge, 2000; River Stories, Brattleboro Mus Art, Vt, 2010. *Collection Arranged:* Northland Creative Glass, Lybster, Scotland; LA Specola Natural History Mus, Florence Italy; United States Dept of State; J P Morgan & Co, NY; Houghton Libr, Harvard Univ, Mass; Prudential Ins Co Am, NY; Mem Art Gallery, Univ Rochester, NY; Whitney Mus Am Art, NY; NY Pub Libr; Fogg Art Gallery, Harvard Univ, Cambridge, Mass; Brooklyn Mus; Northlands Glass Workshop, Scotland. *Teaching:* Instr, Sch Visual Arts, NY, 79-2000 & Fashion Instr Technol, 80-83; vis artist, Sch Visual Arts, 79-2000, Fashion Inst Tech, 80-83, Md Inst Art, Parsons Sch Art & Design, C W Post Univ, Univ Gallery Fine Arts Ctr, Univ Mass, Amherst & Univ Idaho, Moscow; guest artist, printmaking workshop, NY, 86-87 & 93, NY Experimental Glass Workshop, 84. *Awards:* Grants, Sculpture, 79-80 & 81-82 & Drawing & Printmaking, 87-88, Nat Endowment Arts; MacDowell Fel, Sculpture, 79; CAPS Fel, Sculpture, 78; and others. *Bibliog:* Articles, NY Times, 90 & 94; Zahra Partovi (dir), Footsteps (video), 97; Richard Yelle (auth), Glass Art from Urban Glass, 2000; many others. *Media:* Etching, Printmaking. *Interests:* Environment; Computers; Space; Cultures. *Publ:* Earth-Mapping Artists Reshaping Landscape, Edward S Casey; Auth, Intericon 1986 (exhib catalogs, 1 & 2), Charlottenborg, Denmark, 86; Glass (exhib catalog), Soc Arts Crafts, Pittsburgh, Pa, 89; Projects and Portfolios, 25th Nat Print Biennial (exhib catalog), Brooklyn Mus, NY, 89; Political Landscapes (exhib catalog), Hillwood Art Mus, Greenvale, NY, 90; and numerous other exhib catalogs. *Mailing Add:* 39 Bond St New York NY 10012

GELTNER, DANITA SUE
SCULPTOR, PAINTER
b Atlanta, Ga, May 19, 1952. *Study:* Studied at Sorbonne, Paris, France, certificat Francaise, 73; Univ Pittsburgh, BA, 76; Md Inst Coll Art; MFA, 78. *Work:* K & B Found, New Orleans, La; Verlain Found, New Orleans, La; Prudential Collection, Newark, NJ. *Comn:* Window installation, Charles Jordan Shoes, Trump Tower, NY, 92. *Exhib:* Art Mart Gallery, NY, 85 & 86; PPOW Gallery, NY, 87; Grace Borgenicht Gallery, NY, 88; UP Gallery, Pittsburgh, Pa, 91; Mendelson Gallery, Pittsburgh, Pa, 92. *Awards:* Art Matters Inc, Found Grant, New York, 86 & 88; Committee Award,

Biennial Exhib, Fine Arts Mus S, 87. *Bibliog:* Michael Brenson (auth), Danita Geltner, NY Times, 2/7/86; Elizabeth Hess (auth), Faux foe, Village Voice, 6/30/87; Kate Linker (auth), Review, Art Forum, 10/87. *Mem:* Orgn Independent Artists, NY; Artists in Residence, NY; Artists Equity, NY; White Columns, NY (secy bd dir, 90-92); Ringside, NY. *Mailing Add:* 80 Warren St No 19 New York NY 10007-1013

GENGER, ORLY
INSTALLATION SCULPTOR
Study: Brown Univ, BA, Providence, RI, 2001; Sch Art Inst Chicago, 2002. *Work:* Mus Mod Art; Hood Mus Art; Albright-Knox Art Gallery; Indianapolis Mus Art. *Exhib:* Solo exhibs, Elizabeth Dee Gallery, New York, 2004, Locust Proj, Miami, 2005, Aldrich Contemp Arts Mus, Conn, 2005, Larissa Goldston Gallery, New York, 2007, 2009, Lemberg Gallery, Ferndale, Mich, 2007, Cornell Fine Arts Mus Rollings Col, Fla, 2008, Indianapolis Mus Art, Ind, 2008, Gavlak, West Palm Beach, Fla, 2010; group exhibs, Rare Gallery, New York, 2003; Stefan Stux Gallery, New York, 2003; Solomon Fine Art, Seattle, Wash, 2004; Bergdorf Goodman, New York, 2005; Larissa Goldston Gallery, New York, 2006, 2009; Karin Bravin, New York, 2006; Queens Mus Art, New York, 2006; Orlando Mus Art, Fla, 2007; Bravinlee Prog, New York, 2007; La Triennale di Milano, Italy, 2009; Univ Gallery & Grinter Gallery, Univ Fla, 2009; Lyons Wier Gallery, New York, 2009; Lemberg Gallery, Mich, 2010; Mass Mus Contemp Art Mass, 2010. *Teaching:* lectr, Mus Contemp Art Denver, Indianapolis Mus Art, Coll Creative Studies, Cranbrook Acad Art, Aldrich Contemp Art Mus, Univ Penn. *Bibliog:* auth, Jerry Saltz, Rays of Light, The Village Voice, 2003; auth, Roberta Smith, A Space Reborn, With a Show That's Never Finish, The New York Times, 2003; auth, Matthew Kangas, Story weaving appears threadbares in Yarns, The Seattle Times, 2004; auth, Barbara Pollack, From Garret to Gallery, Time Out new York, 2004; auth, Black Gopnik, For Art Lovers, A Chelsea Morning, Washington Post, 2004; auth, Nick Sousanis, Orly Genger, The Detroiter, 2007; auth, Barbara MacAdams, The Shape of Things to Come, ArtNews, 2008; auth, Ana Finel Honigman, Talk Dirty to Me, Dazed Digital, 2009; auth, Liz Kwon, Orly Genger: Art in Space, bob- Int Mag of Space Design, 2010; auth, Hilarie Sheets, Rope Wrangler, Art in America, 2010. *Mailing Add:* Larissa Goldston Gallery 551 W 21st St New York NY 10011

GENIUSZ, ROBERT MYLES
PRINTMAKER, FILMMAKER
b Milwaukee, Wis, Aug 30, 1948. *Study:* Sch Fine Arts, Univ Wis, Milwaukee, BFA, 74, MFA, 76. *Work:* Kohler Art Ctr, Sheboygan, Wis; Sheboygan Pub Schs, Wis; Performing Art Ctr, Theatre Sch, Milwaukee. *Comn:* Puppet Theatre, Kohler Art Ctr, Sheboygan, Wis, 76. *Exhib:* Strange Tales, Kohler Art Ctr, Sheboygan, Wis, 76; Ann Beloit & Vicinity, Wright Arts Ctr, Beloit, Wis, 76, 77 & 79; Artists/Toys, Milwaukee Art Ctr, 77 & 79; Toys Designed by Artists, Ark Arts Ctr, Little Rock, 78 & 27th Ann Delta Invitational, 79; Form, Fun & Fantasy, Mt Mary Col, Milwaukee 78; Solo exhib, Printed Worlds, Oshkosh Pub Mus, Wis, 79; Wisconsin Artists, Cudahay Gallery, Milwaukee Art Mus, 83; Int Paper Conference, Kyoto, Japan, 83; and others. *Teaching:* Instr 3-D, 2D & drawing, Univ WisParkside, Kenosha, Jan, 78; instr filmmaking, Univ Wis-Milwaukee, Sept, 79; artist-in-residence filmmaking, Performing Art Ctr, Milwaukee, Wis, 79-80, Milwaukee Pub Schs, 81-83. *Awards:* Nat Endowment Arts Grant, Artist-in-Residence Prog, 76-77 & 79-84. *Bibliog:* Evelyn Terry Bridges (auth), Wisconsin artists make toys, Milwaukee, Vol 4, No 12, 12/79. *Mem:* Coll Art Asn Am; Artists Equity Asn. *Mailing Add:* 997 Granville Rd Cedarburg WI 53012-9379

GENKIN, JONATHAN
PAINTER
b New York, NY, 1957. *Exhib:* Solo exhibs, Damon Brandt Gallery, New York, 86-89, Galeria Bonk, Cologne, Ger, 87 & Daniel Newburg Gallery, NY, 89; Glastnost, Galeria Bonk, Cologne, Ger, 87; From the Monochrome and Beyond, Univ Maine, Orono, 88; The Colour Alone: The Monochrome Experiment, Mus St Pierre, Lyon, France, 88. *Awards:* Nat Endowment Arts Fel, 87. *Mailing Add:* 3850 Hudson Manor Ter Apt 4E Bronx NY 10453-1134

GENN, NANCY
PAINTER, SCULPTOR
b San Francisco, Calif. *Study:* San Francisco Art Inst, Calif; Univ Calif, Berkeley. *Work:* San Francisco Mus Mod Art; Mus Mod Art, Brooklyn Mus, NY; Nat Mus Am Art, Smithsonian Inst, Libr Congress, Washington; Los Angeles Co Mus Art, Calif; Mills Coll Art Mus, Oakland, Calif; and others. *Comn:* Bronze lectern & five bronze sculptures for chancel table, First Unitarian Church, Berkeley, Calif, 61 & 64; bronze fountain, Cowell Col, Univ Calif, Santa Cruz, 66; bronze menorah, Temple Beth Am, Los Altos Hills, Calif, 68; 17 murals in ceramic glazed tile & two bronze fountain sculptures, Sterling Vineyards, Caligosta, Calif, 72 & 73; bronze fountain sculpture, Expo 74, Spokane, Wash, 74; pair of mixed media paintings on paper, IBM, San Jose, Calif. *Exhib:* Solo Shows: MH de Young Mem Mus, San Francisco, 55 & 63, San Francisco Mus Art, 61, New Worlds, Oakland Art Mus, 71, Los Angeles Inst Contemp Art, 76, Harcourts Gallery, San Francisco, 91 & 96, Brendan Walter Gallery, Los Angeles, Calif, 92, Mills Coll Art Mus, Calif, 99, Leighton Gallery, Blue Hill, Maine, 2000, Ulivi Gallery, Prato, Italy, 02; Fresno Art Mus, Fresno, Calif, 2003; Bolinas Mus, Bolinas, Calif, 2003; Istituto Ital di Cult & the Chicago Art Inst, Chicago, Ill, 2004; Istituto Italiano di Cult, Los Angeles, Calif, 2004; Flatfile Galleries, 2005, 2008, Sanchez Art Ctr, Pacific, Calif, 2011, Univ Calif Santa Cruz, Cowell Coll, Calif, 2012, Vessel Gallery, Oakland, Calif, 2013; Twentieth Century Drawings, Stanford Univ, Palo Alto, Calif, 55; Winter Invitational, Calif Palace Legion Hon, San Francisco, 60-63; group show, Contemp Reflections, Aldrich Mus, Ridgefield, Conn, 72-73; group show, Works on Paper, Mus Mod Art, NY, 76; group show, Paper as Medium Smithsonian Inst Traveling Exhib, 78-80; group show, Making Paper, Am Craft Mus, NY, 82-84; group show, Paper as Image, Arts Coun Gt Brit, 83-84; Paper Works: Seven Perspectives, Tampa Mus, Fla, 86; group show, First Int-Biennale Paper Art, Leopold-Hoesch Mus, Duren, WGer, 86; solo show, Takada Gallery, San Francisco, 99, 2000, 2003, Michael Petronko Gallery, NY, 97, Fresno Art Mus, 03, Bolinas Art Mus, 03 & Leighton Gallery, Blue Hill, ME, 99 & 2000; group shows, DL Gallery, Seoul, South Korea, 02, Monique Goldstrom Gallery, New York City, 02, Portland Art Mus, Oreg, 97, JJ Bookings Gallery, San Francisco, 97, Albright-Knox Gallery, Buffalo, NY, 93-94, 95. *Collection Arranged:* Albright-Knox Art Gallery, Buffalo, NY; Aldritch Mus, Ridgefield, Conn; Am Craft Mus, NY City; Auckland Mus, New Zealand; Brooklyn Mus, NY; Cincinnati Art Mus; Indianapolis Mus Art; Internat Ctr Aesthetic Rsch, Italy; Libr Congress, Washington, DC; Los Angeles Co Mus; Mills Col, Oakland, Calif; Mus Modern Art, NY City; Nat Mus Am Art, Washington, DC; Smithsonian Inst, Washington, DC; NY Univ Art Collection; Oakland Mus, Calif; San Francisco Mus Art; Univ Calif, Berkeley; NY Public Libr; Achenbauch Foundation, Calif Palace of the Legion of Honor, San Francisco, Calif; Fresno Art Mus, Fresno, Calif; NY Public Libr; Southwest State Univ Art Mus; Univ Texas El Paso. *Pos:* Univ of Calif, Berkeley, Art Alumni, Advisory Board Member, pres, 2008-2010; Kala Art Institute, Board Member, Berkeley, Calif, 2005-2006. *Awards:* Purchase Award Painting, State of Calif, 57; Hon Award for Design Excellence, US Dept Housing & Urban Develop, 68; US-Japan Creative Arts Fel, 78-79; Visiting Artist, Am Acad in Rome, 89, 94. *Bibliog:* David Bourdon (auth), Pulp Artists Paper MOMA, The Village Voice, 106, 8/23/1976; Robert McDonald (auth), Genn and Al-Hilali - Works in Paper, Artweek, Vol VIII, 8, 2/19/1977; Deloris Tarzan (auth), Nancy Genn Grows, Seattle Times, 4/15/1977; Max Wykes-Joyce (auth), Art in London, Internat Herald Tribune, Paris, 4/21/1978; John Perreault (auth), Paperworks, American Craft, 2, 6, 8-9/1982; Alan G Artner, Artcritic-Review, Nancy Genn, Chicago Tribune, May 21. 2004. *Mem:* Univ Calif Alumni. *Media:* Mixed media on paper; mixed media on canvas, Bronze Sculpture. *Res:* lectures on handmade paper in contemporary art. *Specialty:* contemporary, modern. *Interests:* architecture, aesthetics, painting, sculpture. *Publ:* Nancy Genn, Paper Paintings, essay by Jane Farmer, 84, Andro Crispo Gallery, New York,; Nancy Genn, Places of Light, Recent Paintings essay, by Bruce Nixon, 97; Catalogue- Nancy Genn, Istituto Italiano di Cultura, Chicago, IL, Curator, Francesca, Valente, 2004; Plaines of Light, Nancy Genn, essay by Jacqueline Pilar (cur), Fresno Art Mus, Fresno, Calif, 2003. *Dealer:* Takada Gallery 251 Post St San Francisco CA; Vessel Gallery Oakland CA; Burton Marinkovich Fine Art Wash DC. *Mailing Add:* 1515 La Loma Ave Berkeley CA 94708

GENTELE, GLEN
MUSEUM DIRECTOR, CURATOR
b New York. *Study:* Fla State Univ, BFA; Md Inst Coll Art, Baltimore, MFA. *Collection Arranged:* John Henry, New Monuments, 2002; Franco Mondini Rviz, Pan in the Park, 2003; Robert Chambers, In-Sit-U, 2004; Christina Shmigel, Chinese Garden, 2005; Joseph Havel, Drinks Are Boilin (auth, catalog), 2006; Karyn Olivier, A Closer Look (auth, catalog), 2007; Deborah Ashheim, Reconsider (auth, catalog), 2008; Artistically Incorrect: The Photographs & Sculpture of John Wate, 2009; Jason Peters, Anti. Gravity. Material. Light, 2010. *Pos:* Head collections mgmt & cur exhibs, John & Mable Ringling Mus Art, 1997-2001; prof mod & contemp art, Univ Mo, St Louis, 2001-2008; dir, Laumeier Sculpture Park & Mus, St Louis, 2001-2008; dir, Oklahoma City Mus Art, 2009-2012; dir, CEO, Orlando Mus Art, 2013-. *Teaching:* Adj prof art, Fla Int Univ, Miami; adj prof, Ringling Sch Art & Design; Aronson Endowed Prof Mod & Comtemp Art, Univ Mo, St Louis. *Awards:* CORE Prog, Glassell Sch Art, Mus Fine Arts, Houston. *Mem:* OVAC; Int Sculpture Ctr; AAM; CAA; AMM; Am for the Arts; OMA. *Mailing Add:* Orlando Museum of Art 2416 North Mills Ave Orlando FL 32803

GENTILE, GLORIA IRENE
DESIGNER, SCULPTOR, PAINTER
b New York, NY. *Study:* Cooper Union, New York, 47-50; Yale Univ, 51-54, BFA & MFA; study with Josef Albers, Will Barnet, Abraham Rattner, Nicholas Marscicano, Stuart Davis, Buckminster Fuller, Philip Johnson, Frederick Kiesler, Louis Kahn, Frank Lloyd Wright & Alvin Lustig. *Exhib:* One-person shows, Art Dirs Club, NY, 68, Young & Rubican Gallery, NY, 68, Ogilvy & Mather Inc Gallery, NY, 68, William Esty Gallery, NY, 68, Batten, Barton, Burstine & Osborne Agency, NY, 69, Cooper Union Gallery, NY, 74, Caffe Latte & Double Rainbow, Calif, 94; Sculpture Happening, Mus Mod Art, NY, 72; Los Angeles Art Asn, 91-94; Contemp Images Gallery, 92; Midway Hosp, Los Angeles, 93; Computer paintings, Cyberspace, Calif, 93. *Pos:* Founder & dir, Gentile Studio Computer Graphics, 75-2005. *Teaching:* Instr concepts & promotion, Sch Visual Arts, New York, 68-74 & Parsons Sch Design, 72-; instr promotional design, Cooper Union, 74-; Queens Col, 78-79; instr, Fashion Inst Technology, 80-81 & Pratt Inst, 82-83. *Awards:* Graphic Design Desi Award. *Bibliog:* Article in New Worlds of Reading, Harcourt Brace Jovanovich, 69. *Mem:* Art Dir Club; The Creative Center. *Media:* Articulated Bronze, Ball Jointed, sculpture, Watercolors

GENTRY, AUGUSTUS CALAHAN, JR
PAINTER, PRINTMAKER
b Tyler, Tex, Feb 5, 1927. *Study:* Tyler Jr Col, AA, 48; Univ Tex, with Boyer Gonzales, Ralph White & Seymour Fogel, BFA, 52. *Work:* Am Nat Life Collection, Galveston, Tex; Shell Oil Collection, Houston; Repub Nat Bank, Dallas; First City Bank & InterFirst Bank, Tyler, Tex; Spring Valley Collection, Dallas. *Comn:* McKittrick Canyon (16 pieces), comn by Donors of McKittrick Canyon Nat Park, Houston, 70. *Exhib:* NY Int, 70; Southwest Watercolor Soc 100 Best Ann, 73 & 74; Midwest Wildlife Art Show, Kansas City, Mo, 74-75; Outdoors in Ga, Nat Wildlife Show, 76-77 & 79-82; solo exhib, Tyler Mus Fine Art, 2006. *Pos:* self-employed, Watercolorist. *Teaching:* Grad asst sculpture, Univ Tex, Austin, 52-53; instr art, Tyler Independent Sch Dist, 53-59; instr watercolor, Tyler Jr Col, 70-73; artist-in-residence, Univ Tex, Tyler, 80-, instr overseas grad studies in watercolor, 83. *Awards:* Tex State Artist, 73; Signature Mem Award, Southwest Watercolor Soc, 74. *Bibliog:* Wilkins (auth), The local gentry, Chronicles, Smith Co Hist Soc, 70; E L Enloe (auth), E Guide, 5/21/98. *Mem:* Southwest Watercolor Soc; Graphics Soc. *Media:* Watercolor; Etching. *Publ:* Illusr, Chronicles of Smith Co, Tex, 70 & 71. *Mailing Add:* 922 S Bois D Arc Ave Tyler TX 75701-1507

GENTRY, WARREN MILLER
PAINTER
b Manville, Wyo, Oct 3, 1921. *Study:* Ariz State Univ, with Tom J Harter, BA, 50, MA, 55; Univ Calif, Berkeley, with Frank Lobdell, 64. *Work:* Munic Collection, Orange, France. *Exhib:* Ariz State Fair Fine Arts Exhib, 49-63; 1st Ariz Ann, Phoenix, 59; Fresh Paint Show, MH De Young Mus, 59; Old Phoenix Art Mus. *Pos:* Founding chmn dept art, 63-68, Glendale Coll & founding dir, Art Collection, 63-69; owner & founder, The Gentry Gallery, Scottsdale, Ariz. *Teaching:* Prof art hist & painting, Glendale Community Coll, 63-83; retired. *Awards:* Valley Bank Purchase Award, 1st Ariz Ann, 59. *Mem:* Scottsdale Beautification Comn (first chmn); founding mem, Scottsdale Fine Arts Comn. *Media:* Oil, Watercolor. *Res:* Experimenting with historic painting surfaces. *Specialty:* Asian Art. *Interests:* World travel including South America, Africa, Asia & Europe. *Collection:* Asian art: Chinese cloisonne and champleve collection of 45 pieces from fifteenth century Ming through the period of Qianlong; Buddha sculpture collection of bronze, stone, and wood (16 pieces); 20 pieces of carved ivory; collection of jade. *Mailing Add:* 9200 E Pima Ctr Pkwy Ste 260 Scottsdale AZ 85258

GENUTE, CHRISTINE TERMINI
PAINTER, SCULPTOR
b Brooklyn, NY, Sept 30, 1947. *Study:* Pratt Inst, BFA; Hunter Col, study with Tony Smith & Robert Walker, MFA; Montclair Univ (learning consult & special educ), 92. *Exhib:* Long Beach Mus, NY, 80 & 81; Nat Soc Painters Casein & Acrylic, 81; solo exhib, Univ Pa, 82; Laguna Beach Mus Art, Calif, 84; Newport Harbor Art Mus, Calif, 84; EAC Gallery, NY, 85-90; Beaux Arts Gallery, Southbury, Conn, 88; Phoenix Gallery, NY, 88; Mahwah Libr, NJ, 99; Ridgewood Art Inst, NJ, 2000, 2003, 2013; Bergenfield Libr, NJ, 2001; Ridgewood Gallery, 2003. *Pos:* Art dir, Circle Galleries, New York, 76-77, Jack Gallerie, New York, 76-77, Gallerie La Grande Illusion, New York, 77, Neill Gallery, New York, 78-79, Atelier Royce Ltd, 81, Hanover Fine Arts, Mass, 83; bd mem, CHADD of Bergen Co, NJ; Learning Consult, NJ Reg Sch District, 92-2010; prvt practice, LC, 2010-. *Teaching:* Lectr galleries, New Sch, Sch Visual Arts, New York, 77-78; adj prof, La Guardia Community Col, 89-90. *Bibliog:* Chris Jones (auth), The 24 Hour Room, Am Home Mag, 5/77; New York Art Rev, 88. *Media:* Acrylic, Oil, Clay, Oil Pastel Originals. *Interests:* involvement in creative/multi-sensory/ learning as a learning Consultant. *Collection:* Ridgewood Gallery, 2/2003 Group Show. *Publ:* New York Art Review Les Krantz by American Reference. *Mailing Add:* 81 Malcolm Rd Mahwah NJ 07430

GEOFFRION, MOIRA MARTI
SCULPTOR
b Olney, Md, July 11, 1944. *Study:* Boston Univ, BFA, 1965; Southern Ill Univ, MFA, 1974. *Exhib:* Solo exhibs include Tucson Mus Art, Sonia Zaks Gallery, Chicago, Plieades Gallery, NY, 14 Sculptors Gallery, NY; Group Exhibs: include Process Space Festival; Eitel Jorg Mus, Indianapolis; BIS Altes Mus, Mönchengladbach, Germ; Gallery 10-10, St Petersburg, Russia, 1990; Chicago Navy Pier Show; principal works include River Road Expansion, Tuscon, Ariz; Tangerine Road and First Avenue Enhancement, Oro Valley, Ariz. *Collection Arranged:* Borg Warner Collection, Chicago Ill; McDonalds Collection, Chicago, Ill; Crowe Chizek Collection, South Bend, Ind; Neurosciences Center, Tucson, Ariz; Tucson Mus Art Collection, Tucson, Ariz. *Pos:* Dir, Isis Gallery, Ind, 1980s; pres, Central Arts Collective Gallery; artist in residence, Silguay Studios, Zurich, Switzerland; Process Space Festival, Balchik, Bulgaria; Rousenski Lam Conservatory, Bulgaria; Oryahovo Residency, Bulgaria; Connemara Residency, Tex. *Teaching:* Asst prof to prof art, Notre Dame Univ, 1974-86; chair Dept Art, Univ Ariz, 1986-91, prof art (distinguished faculty fellow), currently, dir sculpture area, 1991-2000; visiting artist Univ Colo, Boulder, Univ Mont, Missoula, San Jose State Univ, Univ Cincinnati, Univ Indiana, Bloomington, Univ Northern Ill, DeKalb; Stonewall Found Grant, Tuscan Mus Art Solo Exhib. *Awards:* Exxon Distinguished Scholar Grant; ICIP/Fulbright Grant for research. *Bibliog:* Robert Mahony (auth), Arts Mag, 1985; Kay Whitney (auth), 4 Arizona/4 New Mexico Artists, Sculpture Mag, 7-8/1998; Sculpture Mag (review), Zaks Gallery, Chicago, 1995. *Mem:* MACAA. *Res:* Translucent layerings: Botanical and sociological disappearances. *Dealer:* Mark Sublett Modern Tucson Ariz. *Mailing Add:* Univ Ariz School of Art PO Box 210002 1031 N Olive Rd Tucson AZ 85721

GEORGE, PATRICIA
PAINTER
b Cheyenne, Wyo. *Study:* Univ Calif, Los Angeles, BA. *Work:* Hilton Hotel, Long Beach, Calif; J C Penney Bus Systems, Dallas, Tex; Instar Corp, Montgomery, Ala. *Comn:* Four major oil paintings, Hilton Hotel Corp, Los Angeles, Calif, 91; numerous interior designs. *Exhib:* Int Invitational, Hellenic Inst, Athens, Greece, 90; Permanent Collection, Commanderie d Unet Mus, Bordeaux, France, 92; Grand Prix de France, Chapelle de la Sorbonne, Paris, France, 92; Permanent Collection, Fayette Mus, Ala, 93; Int Exhib, Int Artists Japan, Tokyo, 93; Int Artists Sapporo, Japan, 97. *Awards:* Lauret Award, Vieux de la Colombier, French Minister of Culture, 90; Spec Award of Jury, Exhib Famboyance, Musee d'Art Moderne, France, 93; Winner Cover Contest, Manhattan Arts, NY, 93. *Bibliog:* Irene Kleist (auth), Patricia George artist, Metro Mag, 89; Alexandra Shaw (auth), Patricia George captures impact of scene, Manhattan Arts, 9/92; Diana Roberts (auth), Patricia George follows the Sun, Manhattan Arts, 9/93. *Media:* Oil. *Mailing Add:* 4141 Ball Rd Studio 221 Cypress CA 90630

GEORGE, SYLVIA JAMES
PAINTER, ILLUSTRATOR
b Syracuse, NY, Oct 13, 1921. *Study:* Pratt Inst, 44; Am Univ, 53; pvt study with Robert Gates, 53, John H Sanden 77-78 & Daniel Greene, 82. *Work:* John F Kennedy Libr, Boston, Mass; Howard High Sch, Ellicott City, Md; DuFief Elementary Sch, Gaithersburg, Md; St Louis Church, Clarksville, Md; Howard Community Col, Columbia, Md; S Bauman, Elkridge Hist Soc; Dept of Agriculture, Okla. *Comn:* Portrait of Milton S Kronheim & the Hon Judge Milton S Kronheim Jr of the Kronheim Co, Alpha Gamma Rho, AB Hamilton Univ Md; eight portraits, Belgian dignitaries; portrait of Mike Cusimano, Asn Growth Enterprises Inc, 93; portrait of Nicholas B Mangione Sr, Md Health Enterprises, 94; portrait of Charles Kratz & Family, Kratz Auto Parts Inc, 94. *Exhib:* Solo exhib, Howard Community Col, Columbia, Md, 73; Baltimore Watercolor Soc Show, Turner Bldg, Johns Hopkins, 76; Slayton House Gallery, Columbia, Md, 70-88; Life of Baltimore Gallery, Baltimore, 84; Corcoran Gallery, Washington, 85; Faces: A Look Within, Shenandoah Col, Winchester, Va, 85; 100th Anniversary of the Automobile, Daimler-Benz, Stuttgard, WGer, 85; Mansion Art Gallery, Rockville, 96. *Pos:* Chmn registry, Howard Co Arts Coun, Md, 79-80; vpres, Visual Arts Alliance, 80-82; dir publicity, Md Pastel Soc, 86; chmn, art selection comt, Slayton House, Columbia, Md, currently; pres, SJG Art Studio/Gallery, currently. *Teaching:* Pvt adult instr, 70's; instr children, Glenely Co Sch, 70's; art asst, drawing & painting, Palotti High Sch, Md, 80-82; artist-in-residence, Oakland Mills High Sch, Md, 82; pvt art classes. *Awards:* Dey Brothers Award, 36; First Prize, Johns Hopkins Univ-APL Art Competition, 79. *Bibliog:* Article in The Sun, Howard Co, 9/29/93; Article in Washington Post, Howard Co, 10/7/93; Article in Columbia Mag, summer 94. *Mem:* Artists Equity; Md Pastel Soc; New Art Ctr; Nat Mus Women Arts; Md Soc Portrait Painters; Portrait Club New York; Visual Arts Alliance; Coll Art Asn. *Media:* Oil, Watercolor. *Specialty:* Commissioned portraits and paintings; composites of ideas. *Interests:* Creating customers ideas and desires. *Publ:* Illusr, covers, Guard Mag, Johnson Studios, 76-78. *Mailing Add:* SJG Art Studio/Gallery 8600 Foundry St Savage MD 20763-9512

GEORGE, THOMAS
PAINTER, DRAFTSMAN
b New York, NY, July 1, 1918. *Study:* Dartmouth Coll, BA, 40; Art Students League; Acad Grand Chaumiere, Paris; Ist Statale Arte, Florence, Italy, 49-51. *Work:* Guggenheim Mus, Mus Mod Art, Whitney Mus & Brooklyn Mus, New York; San Francisco Mus; Mus Am Art, Washington, DC; Tate Gallery, London, Eng; Mus Fine Arts, Houston; Nat Gallery, Oslo, Norway; Bridgestone Mus, Tokyo; numerous corp collections including Chase Manhattan Bank, AT&T, RCA, Ford Motor co, Portland Art Mus, Maine, Mus Contemp Art (Samtidskunst), Oslo, Norway; Princeton Univ, 2005; Rider Univ, NJ, 2006; Yale Univ Art Gallery, New Haven, Conn; others. *Comn:* Tapestry, Slatkin Art Gallery, New York, 68; poster/print, US Olympic Comt & Kennedy Galleries, New York, 74; Dodge Found, 87. *Exhib:* Whitney Mus Am Art Ann, 60-62 & 65; Betty Parsons Gallery, 68, 70, 72, 74, 76, 78 & 81; solo exhibs, Princeton Gallery Fine Art, 71, 73, 81, 83, 85, 87 & 89, Jefferson Place Gallery, Washington, DC, 74, Princeton Univ Art Mus, 75, Nat Collection Fine Arts, Washington, DC, 77, NJ State Mus, 87, Hood Mus Art, Dartmouth Coll, 90, Williams Gallery, Princeton, NJ, 97, 99, The Santa Fe Paintings, Mercer Co Coll, NJ, 2001, Rider Univ, Lawrenceville, NJ, 2006, Princeton Arts Council, Princeton Community Found, 2011 & many others; Princeton Univ Art Mus, 75; Nat Collection Fine Arts, 77; Maxwell Davidson, New York, 83 & 85; retrospectives, NJ State Mus, 87, Galleri Riis, Oslo, 84, 86, 88 & 90 & Snyder Fine Art, New York, 90-91, 93 & 96; Hood Art Mus Dartmouth Coll, 90; Julian Hartnoll Gallery, London, 90. *Pos:* Found, Thomas George Fund for young New Jersey Artists, 2005-. *Teaching:* Vis artist, Univ Tex, 78; artist-in-residence, Dartmouth Coll, 79. *Awards:* Purchase Award, Salon Int des Galeries Pilote, Lausanne, Switz, 66; Award, NJ State Mus, 71; Pres Medal Life Achievement, Dartmouth Coll, 91; Princeton Arts Coun Award, 92. *Mem:* Fel Edward MacDowell Colony. *Media:* Oil, Ink; Pastel. *Publ:* Illusr, A Line of Poetry, A Row of Trees, Jargon, 65; Kweilin's An American artist in China, 76; The Norway Series, Capellen, Oslo, 80; Inscape, 30 Gouache Paintings by Thomas George, Princeton Area Community Found, 2008

GERAN, JOSEPH, JR
SCULPTOR, DESIGNER
b 1945. *Study:* San Francisco City Col, AA, 66; Calif State Univ, San Francisco, BA, 70; Calif Col Arts & Crafts, MFA, 73. *Comn:* Prints of movie stars, Oakland Mus, 74; bronze bust of Dr Martin Luther King Jr, RI State, 87. *Exhib:* Los Angeles Co Mus, Los Angeles, 74; RI Sch Design, 75; Southeastern Mass Univ, 75; Bryant Col, 75; Univ Vt, 75; San Francisco Mus Art, 76; Ctr Art & Cult of Bedford Stuyvesant, 88; plus numerous solo & group exhibs. *Pos:* Corp vpres, Col Inc, 70-71; processing chmn, FESTAC 74, 73-74; freelance jewelry designer. *Teaching:* Instr, EOC Summer Youth Prog, 69; lectr, Calif State Univ, San Francisco, 69-71; art consult & sch aide, Galileo High Sch, San Francisco, 70; instr, Booker T Washington Community Ctr, San Francisco, 71; asst prof painting, drawing & sculpture & co-dir ethnic studies div, Calif Col Arts & Crafts, 70-74; adj fac mem, Antioch Col West, 74; dean third world prog, RI Sch Design, 74-; prof art, Community Col RI, 81-; instr, The Jewelry Inst, 85-86. *Awards:* Guy F Atkinson Found Award, 69-71; Ill State Univ Sculpture Award, 73; Distinguished Serv Award, Congressman Ron Dellums, 75. *Mem:* Nat Conf Artists; San Francisco Art Comn Screening Comt. *Media:* Bronze, Wood; Multi. *Publ:* Cover design, Black Art, Black Cult, issue, J Black Poetry, 72; photog of art work, Yardbird Reader, 73; cover design, Blacks on Paper, Brown Univ, fall 75

GERARD, CELIA
SCULPTOR
b Washington, DC, 1973. *Study:* Colgate Univ, BA (Art & Art Hist), 1995; Int Sch Art, Italy, 1996-98; Harvard Univ, EdM (Arts in Educ), 2003; NY Studio Sch, MFA (Sculpture), 2007. *Exhib:* Solo exhibs include Gutman Libr, Harvard Univ, 2003, NY Studio Sch Gallery, New York, 2006, the shala, New York, 2007, NY Studio Sch Dumbo Annex, Brooklyn, 2008, Mark Potter Gallery, Watertown, Conn, 2010, Regions of Unlikeness, Sears Peyton Gallery, NY, 2011; group exhibs include Summer Show, Int Sch Art Gallery, Italy, 1998; 68 Greenpoint Gallery, Brooklyn, 2000; LREI Auction, I-20 Gallery, New York, 2005, LREI Invitational Auction, 2007, 2008; Inaugural Show: Drawings, NY Studio Sch in Dumbo, 2007; I Wonder If You Know What it Means, Sears-Peyton Gallery, New York, 2008; Ann Invitational Exhib Contemp Art, Nat Acad, New York, 2008. *Teaching:* instr, Swarthmore Coll, Bard Coll, Sch Visual Arts. *Awards:* Cathedral St John the Divine Sculpture Fel; Seligman/Von Simson Scholar, 2005, 2006-07; LCU Found Grant, 2007; SJ Wallace Truman Fund Award, Nat Acad, 2008. *Dealer:* Sears-Peyton Gallery 210 11th Ave Ste 802 New York NY 10001

GERBARG, DARCY
PAINTER
b Baltimore, Md, May 20, 1949. *Study:* NY Studio Sch Drawing, Painting & Sculpture, 73-74, Univ Pa, BA, 76. *Work:* Siemens Mus, Ger; Insurance Co N Am; Polaroid Corp; Sierra Fed. *Exhib:* SIGGRAPH Ann Art Show, US & Int tours, 81-87; Electra, Mus Art Mod de la Ville de Paris, France, 83; Bronx Mus Art, 85, Computers & Art, IBM Mus Sci & Art, 87-89, NY; Siemans Mus, Munchen, Ger, 85; CADRE Exhib, San Jose Mus Art, Calif, 86; artware, Kunst und Elektronik, Landesmuseum Volk und Wirtschaft, Dusseldorf, WGer, 87; Solo exhib, Fine Arts Mus Long Island, 89; Everson Mus, Syracuse, NY; Smithsonian Inst, Washington, DC, 90. *Teaching:* Adj fac, Tisch Sch Arts, NY Univ, 81-84; artist-in-residence Courant Inst Mathematics, Robotics & Manufacturing Res Lab, NY Univ, 88-, founding dir MFA prog computer art, Inst Computers Arts, Sch Visual Arts, NY, 84-88; lectr, Computer Graphics Ctr, Pratt, NY & State Univ NY, Stony Brook. *Bibliog:* Digital Portfolio Computer Graphics World, 83; Dale Petersen (auth), Genisis II: Creation & recreation with Computers, Reston, 85; Computer Graphics: Village Voice, 88. *Mem:* Spec Interest Groups Graphics Siggraph Nat (art show chmn, 81); Nat Computer Graphics Asn Arts (bd dir), 85-89. *Media:* Acrylic. *Publ:* Ed, Siggraph 82 Art Show (exhib catalog), Acme Printers, 82; auth, Digital Imaging: Paint Systems, Computer Graphics World, 8/83; contrib, Computers as Artist's Tool, Springer-Verlag, 86; auth, Anniversary Spec: Reflections on a Goldan Decade: Pennwell Publ Co, 12/87. *Mailing Add:* 149 W 24th St New York NY 10011-1917

GERBER, GAYLEN
CONCEPTUAL ARTIST, PAINTER
b McAllen, Tex, June 8, 1955. *Study:* New York Studio Sch Painting, Drawing & Sculpture, 78-79; Art Inst Chicago, MFA, 80. *Work:* Neues Mus Weserburg, Bremen, Ger; Mus Contemp Art, Chicago, Ill; Domaine de Kerguehennec, Ctr D'Art Contempotain, Locmine, France; Charlottenborg Exhib Hall, Copenhagen, 2002. *Exhib:* Solo exhibs, The Renaissance Soc, Chicago, Ill, 92, High Mus Art, Atlanta, Ga, 98, Neues Mus Weserburg, Bremen, Ger, 2000; Documenta IX, Kassel, Ger, 92; 25 Americans, Milwaukee Art Mus, Wis, 95; DeadPan, Kunstverein Munich, Ger, 96; Kunst in der Stadt, Kunsthaus Bregenz, Ger, 99; Art Inst of Chicago, IL, 2002. *Teaching:* Assoc prof Sch Art Inst Chicago, 87-2000. *Awards:* NEA Arts Midwest Award, 95; Tiffany Found Award, 2000; Art Coun NY Award, 2001. *Bibliog:* J Cullum (auth), Artificially achieved perfection, Atlanta Jour, 4/10/98; M Grabner (auth), Gaylen Gerber, Frieze Issue 40, 98; G Gerber/K Bitterli (auth), Interview, La Biennale de Montreal, 2000. *Dealer:* Chicago Project Room 6130 Wilshire Blvd Los Angeles CA 90048; Galerie Susanna Kalli Davidstrasse 40 CH-9000 St Gallen Switzerland. *Mailing Add:* 1459 W Cortez St Apt 1F Chicago IL 60622

GERBRACHT, BOB (ROBERT) THOMAS
PAINTER, INSTRUCTOR
b Erie, Pa, June 23, 1924. *Study:* With Joseph Plavcan, 38-42; Yale Sch Fine Arts, with Rudolph Zallinger, Deane Keller & Josef Albers, BFA, 51; Univ Southern Calif, with Jules Heller, MFA, 52. *Work:* Triton Mus Art, Santa Clara, Calif; Univ S Calif, Los Angeles, 52; Univ Art Acad, San Francisco, Calif, 80 & 96; City of Sunnyvale, Calif, 90; Glide Ch, San Francisco, 90. *Comn:* Stations of the Cross (oil painting) & Creche (sculpture), Queen Apostles Church, San Jose, Calif, 63; portraits, notably, Mrs Bruce Jenner and children, Malibu, Calif, 80 & 82; Rev Jack La Rocca, Los Altos, Calif, 88; Rev Cecil Williams, Glide Mem Methodist Church, San Francisco, 90; Historical Portraits Competition Comn Award to paint John Hendy, City of Sunnyvale, Calif, 90; Mr Austin Warburton for the Triton Mus Art, Santa Clara, Calif; and many pvt collections; and others. *Exhib:* Solo exhibs, Fisher Art Gallery, Univ Southern Calif, 51, Laudau Gallery, Los Angeles, 52, Images West Gallery & Montalvo, Saritoga, Calif, 72, San Jose Art Ctr, 79 & 83, Montalvo, 82, Discovery Gallery, La Tarentella, Cupertino, Calif, 84 & Commonwealth Club, San Francisco, Calif, 92, Triton Mus Art, Santa Clara, Calif, 2003 & 2006; group exhib, 2nd Ann Open Exhib, Salmagundi Club, New York, 79; Pastel Soc Am Ann Nat Exhib, New York, 79, 88, 90-92 & 97-98; San Jose Mus Art, 50th Ann Celebration Exhib of San Jose Art League, 88; San Jose Art League World Without War Exhib, 88; Bedford Biennial, Regional Ctr Arts, Walnut Creek, Calif, 91; Grand Exhib, Akron Soc Artists, Cuyahoga, Ohio, 91; 78th Ann, Allied Artists Am, New York, 91; 6th Ann Open Exhib, Pastel Soc West Coast, Sacramento, Calif, 92; Figurative Paintings, John Pence Gallery, San Francisco, 97; Realism Today, Am Artists Mag Exhib, San Francisco, 2000; Pastel Soc West Coast Dist Pastelist Exhib, Carmichael, Calif, 2002; Pastel Soc Am Invitational Exhib, Butler Inst Am Art, Youngstown, Ohio, 2003; People and Places, Triton Mus Art, Santa Clara, Calif, 2003; The Group, Odd Fellows Yerba Buena Lodge # 15, San Francisco, 2003-2006; Pinole Artisans, Pinole, Calif, 2004; Bay Area Figurative Art Exhibit, Univ Calif, Calif, 2004; The Human Figure, Los Gatos Mus Art, Los Gatos, Calif, 2005; Friends of Bob Gerbracht, Epperson Gallery, Crockett, Calif, 2006; Beyond the Likeness: Self Portraits by Calif Artists, Triton Mus Art, Santa Clara, Calif, 2006; Landscapes: Rural and Urban Realities, Triton Mus Art, Santa Clara, 2007; Depth & Distance, San Francisco Lesbian Gay Bisexual Transgender Community Ctr, Calif, 2008 ; Civic Arts Instrs, Bedford Gallery, Lesser Ctr, Walnut Creek, Calif, 2008; Pastel Soc, West Coast Int Exhib, Los Gatos, Calif, 2010; Soc Western Artists Exhib, Redwood City, Calif, 2010; Pastel Society of the West Coast, Haggin Mus, Stockton, Calif, 2011. *Pos:* Vpres, Images West Gallery, Saratoga, Calif, 72; trustee, Soc Western Artists, 87-88; judge, Pastel Soc West Coast, Int Exhib, 2004, 2011; juror, Sierra Pastel Soc Exhib, 2004; judge, Los Gatos Art Fest, 2004, 2009. *Teaching:* Instr art, Coll Notre Dame, Calif, 58-60 & San Jose City Coll, 68-71; classes in portrait & figure painting, San Jose, Calif, 76-89 & San Francisco, 90-; founder & instr, Nat Ann Portrait & Figure Painting Workshops: Univ Calif, Santa Cruz, Asilomar, Pacific Grove, Pleasanton, Walnut Creek, San Jose, Crockett & Sacramento, Calif, 80-; nat sem portrait & figure painting, Calif, Mo, Nebr, Nev, NMex, Tex, Vt, Mex, NY, Colo, Fla, Mass, Ore & SC. *Awards:* Achievement Award, Pastel Teacher, Am Artist Mag, 93; Gold Medal in Pastel, Tools of Trade Show, San Francisco, 98; Lifetime Achievement Award of Sonoma Plain Air Corp, 2002; Pastel Laureate, Pastel Soc West Coast; Master Pastellist, Pastel Soc Am; Hall of Fame, Pastel Soc Am, 2015. *Bibliog:* Nat art competition winners, Am Artist Mag, 7/85; Cathy Kosier (auth), Best of show, US ART, 12/88; Pvt showings, US ART, 9/89; The Little Book About Pastel, Zandal Bks, 2002; Pure-Color, The Best of Pastel, North Light Bks, 2006; Strokes of Genius, The Beast of Drawing, North Light Bks, 2007, 2009. *Mem:* Soc Western Artists (trustee, 87-88); Pastel Soc West Coast; Pastel Soc Am; Pinole Artisans. *Media:* Oil, Pastel, Charcoal, Watercolor. *Interests:* Portrait and Figure Painting. *Collection:* Liz & Steve McNamara, Kitty & Ron Francis, Dennis & Linda Moreno, Val Bitting, Susan Hall, "Bo" Bogatin, Walter Crow, Lottie Dyhberg, Robert Joy, Maralyn & Frank Dorsa, Jean Engle, Mike Eros, Kevin & Becky Fernandez, Bob Jones, Mark Loeffler, Debbie Matlack, Nancy McDonald, Barbara Noonan, John R Peck, David Silva, Bill Vujevich, Norma Wright. *Publ:* Auth, Drawing what you see, Am Artist Mag, 82; Let go and look, Profile Mag Am Portrait Soc, spring 84; Tips on painting the head & figure, Am Artist Mag, 9/92; Realism Today, Am Artist, 10/2000; People & Places, Exhib Catalog of Triton Mus Art, 2003; A Matter of Perception, Artist's Mag, 8/2005. *Mailing Add:* 1301 Blue Oak Ct Pinole CA 94564

GERDTS, ABIGAIL BOOTH
HISTORIAN, CURATOR
b New Milford, Conn, June 20, 1937. *Study:* Radcliffe Coll, AB (fine arts), 60; Syracuse Univ, Sch Art, 62-63. *Collection Arranged:* Spec exhib, Charles Sheeler (auth, catalog), Nat Collection Fine Arts, Smithsonian Inst, 68; The Working Am (auth, catalog), Dist 1199 & Smithsonian Inst Traveling Exhib Serv, 79. *Pos:* Mem secy, Corcoran Gallery Art, Washington, DC, 59-61; res asst painting dept, Mus Fine Arts, Boston, 61-62; asst cur exhib, Nat Collection Fine Arts, 64-70, coordr bicentennial inventory Am paintings, 70-77, coordr 19th century exhibs index, 77-78; spec asst to dir, Nat Acad Design, New York, 80-87, cur paintings & sculpture, 88-89; dir, Winslow Homer Catalogue Raisonne, City Univ New York Grad Center, 90-. *Publ:* Auth, The Working American, Sites, 79; Winslow Homer in Monochrome, Knoedler Galleries, 86; An American Collection: Paintings and Sculpture, Nat Acad Design, 89; auth, Record of the Works of Winslow Homer, Vols 1-4, 2005-2012. *Mailing Add:* PhD Program in Art History/Graduate Center/ City University of New York 365 Fifth Ave New York NY 10016

GERDTS, WILLIAM H
HISTORIAN, EDUCATOR
b Jersey City, NJ, Jan 18, 1929. *Study:* Amherst Coll, BA, 49, LHD, 92; Harvard Univ, MA, 50, PhD, 66; Syracuse Univ, Hon Dr fine arts, 96. *Collection Arranged:* Thomas Birch (auth, catalog), 66; and many others. *Pos:* Dir, Myers House, Norfolk, Va, 53-54; cur painting & sculpture, Newark Mus, NJ, 54-66; dir gallery, Univ Md, 66-69; assoc with Coe Kerr Gallery, NY, 69-71. *Teaching:* Assoc prof, Univ Md, 66-69; assoc prof art, Brooklyn Coll, 71-74, prof, 74-85; prof, Grad Ctr, City Univ NY, 85-99, prof emer, 99-; lectr, Am art in mus, coll, univ & adult schs. *Awards:* Guggenheim Found Fel, 80. *Publ:* Auth, American Still-Life Painting, Praeger, 71; American Neo-Classical Sculpture: The Marble Resurrection, Viking, 73; The Art of Henry Inman, Nat Portrait Gallery, Smithsonian Inst, Washington, 87; American Impressionism, 84, Art Across America: Regional Painting in America Through 1920, 3 vols, 90, Abbeville Press; Monets Giverny: An Impressionist Colony, Abbeville Press, 93; William Glackens: Line and Work, Abbeville Pres, 96; plus others. *Mailing Add:* Dept Art Hist City Univ New York 365 Fifth Ave New York NY 10016

GERICH, BETTY A.
SCULPTOR
b Danbury, Conn. *Study:* Univ Conn, BFA, 68; Univ Hartford, MAEd, 80; Wesleyan Univ, CAS, 89. *Exhib:* Solo shows, Garrett Gallery, Am Int Col, Springfield, Mass, 80, New Britain Mus Am Art, Conn, 85, Zilka Gallery, Wesleyan Univ, Middletown, Conn, 89 & Artworks Gallery, Hartford, Conn, 91, Artworks Gallery, 9/2001, Behind the Mask, Artworks Gallery, Hartford, Conn, Face Value, Exposure, Manchester, Conn, 2004, Chasing Beauty, Sue & Eugene Mercy, Jr, Gallery, Windsor, Conn, 2005, Gallery on the Green Canton, Conn, 2010, Thicker Than Water, Gallery on the Green, Canton, Conn, 2012; Society of Conn Crafts, Slater Mem Mus, Norwich, 81; Springfield Art League, George Walter Vincent Smith, Mass; Conn Clay, Slater Mem Mus, Norwich. *Teaching:* Art teacher, Somers High Sch, 76-3003; art coordr, Somers Schs, 83-91; lectr, Art Hist Survey, Asnuntuck Community Col, 2003-. *Awards:* Individual Artist Fel, Greater Hartford Arts Coun, 99; Koenig Art Award, Conn Women Artists, 99; Beatrice G Epstein Mem Award, Nat Asn Women Artists, 2003. *Bibliog:* Heather Nann Davis (auth), Passion for Sculpture, Jour Inquirer, 1999; Indraneel Sur (auth), A Way with Clay, The Hartford Courant, 2001; Richard Guinness (auth), Artist Depicts Power of One Over Others, Jour Inquirer, 2001; Betty A. Gerich: Expressions, Artist Mag, 2005; Up Front, Ceramics Monthly Magazine, 2006. *Mem:* Conn Women Artists; New England Sculptors Asn, Boston, Mass; Artworks Gallery, Hartford, Conn; Womens Caucus for Art; Canton Artist's Guild; Art Ctr Sarasota. *Media:* Ceramic Sculpture, Watercolor. *Publ:* Contribr, Shaping Space, Holt, Rinehart & Winston, 87; photo & article, Artis Mag, winter, 2004; contribr (sculpture), 500 Figures in Clay, fall 2004; contribr (photo & article), Artis Mag, summer, fall 2005; contribr (photo & article), Up Front, Ceramics Monthly Mag, 2006. *Dealer:* Gallery on the Green PO Box 281 Canton CT 06019. *Mailing Add:* 18 Carriage Dr Enfield CT 06082

GERLACH, CHRISTOPHER S
PAINTER
b Wareham, Mass, Dec 8, 1952. *Study:* Lake Forest Col, Ill Univ Calif, BA, 74; Calif State Univ, San Diego, MA, 77; Oxford Univ, 79; Royal Acad London, 79. *Work:* Oxford Univ, England; Buckingham Palace, London; Calif State Univ, San Diego. *Exhib:* Exhibition XI, Fine Arts Mus, San Antonio, Tex, 83; Contemp Art, La Jolla Mus, Calif, 85; Art & the Law, traveling, 87-88; Utopian Visions, Mus Mod Art, NY, 88; Am Beach Paintings, Tampa Mus, Fla, 89. *Teaching:* Instr, Calif State Univ, San Diego, 75-77. *Awards:* Bank Am Award, Eggerton Coghill Landscape, Oxford Univ,

69. *Bibliog:* Abigail Wender (auth), Venice--Painting by CG, Diversion, 9/87; Jan Jennings (auth), A World in Oils--Ranch & Coast, 4/90. *Media:* Oil. *Dealer:* William Sawyer Gallery 3045 Clay St San Francisco CA 94115. *Mailing Add:* c/o Art Space/Virginia Miller Galleries 169 Madeira Ave Coral Gables FL 33134-4515

GERLOVINA & GERLOVIN, RIMMA & VALERIY
CONCEPTUAL ARTISTS, PHOTOGRAPHERS
b Mrs Gerlovina b Russ, 1951; Mr Gerlovin b Russ, 1945; US citizens. *Study:* Mrs Gerlovina, Moscow State Univ, Russ, 68-73; Mr Gerlovin, Moscow Art Theater Studio, Russ, 62-67. *Work:* Art Inst Chicago; John Paul Getty Mus, Malibu, Calif; Denver Art Mus, Colo; Int Ctr Photog, NY; Zimmerli Art Mus, Rutgers, NY. *Comn:* Changes (photo proj), Progressive Corp, Cleveland, 96-97. *Exhib:* Photems, Art Inst Chicago, 89; Photos, List Visual Arts Ctr, Mass Inst Technol, Cambridge, Mass, 89; Photog of Invention, Nat Mus Am Art, Smithsonian Inst, Washington, DC, 89; Retrospective, Fine Art Mus Long Island, Hempstead, NY, 91; Traveling Retrospective Photoglyphs (with catalog), Jacksonville Mus Art, 93, New Orleans Mus Art, 94 & Telfair Mus Art, Savannah, 96; Portraits, US Embassy, Moscow, Russ, 97-; and others. *Awards:* Best Cover & Top Ten Photographs Award, Black Book, 97; Award of Excellence, Communication Arts Mag, 97; Design Excellence, Print Mag, 97. *Bibliog:* John Jacob (auth), Photoglyphs (monograph), New Orleans Mus Art, La, 93; Phyllis Braff (auth), Photoglyphs, NY Times, Long Island Sect, 4/9/95; Linda Weintraub (auth), Art on the edge and over, Am Showcase, NY, 96. *Media:* Multimedia. *Publ:* Auth, Russian Samizdat Art, Willis Locker & Owens, NY, 86; co-ed, Collective Farm, pvt publ, 82-87; illusr cover & reproductions, NY Times Mag, 7/7/96; cover, Sciences Mag, NY Acad Sci, 5-6/97; Genesis, Doubleday, 96. *Dealer:* Robert Brown Gallery 2030 R St Washington DC 20009

GERMANO, THOMAS
PAINTER, EDUCATOR
b New York, NY, Oct 11, 1963. *Study:* Cornell Univ, Scholar, BFA, 85; Yale Univ, Scholar, MFA, 89. *Work:* Arthur Anderson & Co, Int Hq, St Paul, Ill & Melville, NY; Acad Arts, Moscow, Russia; Yale Univ Art Mus, New Haven, Conn; Cape Cod Retreat House, Mass; Am Postal Workers Union, Washington, DC; George Billis Gallery, NY. *Comn:* 1185 Park Ave proj. *Exhib:* Am Labor Mus, Haledon, NJ, 92; Michael Ingbar Gallery, New York, 92-94; Seminole Community Coll, Sanford, Fla, 93; Art/La 1993, Contemp Realist Gallery; Art & the Law, West Publ Co, 94; Mus City NY; Heike Pickett Gallery, Ky, 97-2005; Dumbo Arts Festival, Brooklyn, NY, 99-2007; Small Works Show, East Galleries, New York, 2004-2006; 179th Invitational Exhib, Nat Acad Mus, New York, 2004; solo exhibs, Heike Pickett Gallery, Lexington, Ky, 11-12/2006 & George Billis Gallery, New York, 2007; George Billis Gallery, New York, 2009; Heike Pickett Gallery, Versailles, Ky, 2010. *Teaching:* Prof, SUNY, Farmingdale. *Awards:* Traveling Grant to Russia, Int Res & Exchanges Bd, 89; Traveling Grant to Washington, DC, UUP, 2000; Traveling Grant to Amboise, France, UUP, 2001; Travel Grant to Greece, UUP, 2005; Puffin Found Grant, 2006; Travel Grant to London & Amsterdam, UUP, 2006; Travel Grant to Rome, UUP, 2007; Travel Grant to Egypt, UUP, 2009; NEH Grant, Nat Endowment for the Humanities, 2011. *Bibliog:* Lexington Herald Leader, 11/2006; Am Art Collector, 6/2007. *Mem:* Coll Art Asn; NY Metro Mus Art. *Media:* Oil. *Res:* Leonardo da Vinci. *Specialty:* Realist, urban landscapes. *Interests:* Oil Painting and Renaissance Art History. *Publ:* Auth, Labor Paintings (catalog), 92; illusr, cover, Wordsmith Mag, 93; American Icons, Lithographic Print Edition of 1500, 2000; Nat Academy Mus (catalog), 2004; Am Art Collector, June 2007. *Dealer:* Bachelier-Cardonsky Gallery Kent Conn; Heike Pickett Gallery Versaillies Ky; George Billis Gallery New York NY. *Mailing Add:* 83 Walnut Ave East Norwich NY 11732

GERNHARDT, HENRY KENDALL
SCULPTOR, CERAMIST
b Salem, Conn, Aug 3, 1932. *Study:* Norwich Art Sch, Conn; Sch Am Craftsmen, Rochester Inst Technol, NY, with Frans Wildenhain; Sch Art, Syracuse Univ, NY, BA & MFA; Sch Appl Arts, Helsinki, Finland, study with Kyllikki Salmenhaara, Fulbright Scholar. *Work:* Everson Mus Art, Syracuse, NY; Syracuse Univ; DePauw Univ, Greencastle, Ind; Chrysler Mus, Provincetown, Mass; Univ SDak, Vermillion. *Comn:* Pottery, Imperial House, NY, 60; tile mosaic, Syracuse Univ, 63; vase, State Univ NY, Cortland, 67; baptismal font, Lynnwood Reformed Church, Guilderland, NY, 69; sculpture, comn by Alexander E Holstein, Syracuse, 72. *Exhib:* Ceramic Nat, Everson Mus Art, 54-72; Int Trade Fair, Posen, Poland, 58; Contemp Crafts Exhib, Skidmore Coll, Saratoga Springs, NY, 62, 71 & 75; Int Ceramic Exhib, Silvermine Guild Artists, New Canaan, Conn, 64; 22nd Ceramic Ann, Scripps Coll, Claremont, Calif, 66. *Teaching:* Prof ceramics, Sch Visual & Performing Arts, Syracuse Univ, 60-96 & Sch Am Craftsmen, summer 71, Munson-Williams Proctor Inst, 2001. *Awards:* Merle Alling Sculpture Award, Rochester Finger Lakes Exhib, Mem Art Gallery, 63 & 71; O Hommel Prize for Pottery, Ceramic Nat, Everson Mus, 68; 1st, 2nd & 3rd Awards, NY State Expos, Syracuse, 71; Sculpture Award, 2006 & Purchase Award, 2008, Cedar Key Art Festival; Cermaic Award, CraftArt, 2006; Sculpture Award, Fernandina Beach Art Show, 2008. *Bibliog:* Lewenstein & Cooper (auth), New Ceramics, Van Nostrand Reinhold, 74; Rick Hirsch (auth), Raku, Watson Guptill, 75; article, Craft Horizons, 75; Ulysses Diete (auth), Great Pots, Newark Mus, 2003. *Mem:* Nat Coun Advan Ceramic Arts; Am Crafts Coun; New York Craftsmen; Fla Craftsmen. *Media:* Clay, Glaze. *Mailing Add:* PO Box 975 Cedar Key FL 32625

GERST, HILDE W
DEALER
Study: Ploner Acad, Italy. *Pos:* Owner, Hilde Gerst Gallery, NY. *Mem:* Am Asn Mus; Nat Soc Lit & Arts; Nat Mus Women Arts. *Specialty:* French painting from Impressionist to contemporary; sculpture. *Mailing Add:* 955 Fifth Ave New York NY 10021-1738

GERSTEIN, DAVID STEVEN
FILMMAKER
b Cleveland, Ohio, Sept 23, 1951. *Study:* Antioch Col, BA, 74; Art Inst Chicago; San Francisco Art Inst. *Exhib:* Solo exhibs, NAME to Name Gallery, Chicago, 76 & Canyon Cinematheque, San Francisco, 78, 80 & 82; High Mus Art, Atlanta, Ga, 79; Anthology Film Archive, NY, 81; Newberger Mus, Purchase, NY, 81; Arsenal Cinema, Berlin; Austrian Film Mus, Vicuna; and others. *Pos:* Bd dir, Canyon Cinema Coop, San Francisco, 77-82, Found Art Cinema, 83-. *Awards:* 3rd Place, San Francisco Art Inst Film Festival, 77; Ann Arbor Film Festival, 78; Hon Mention, Athens Int Film Festival, 78. *Bibliog:* Linda Dackman (auth), Kino-Frisco, Cinema News, Found Art Cinema, 77. *Publ:* Auth, Films of Joel Singer, 77, auth, A modest confutation, 78 & ed, Cinemanews. *Dealer:* Canyon Cinema Coop 2325 3rd St 338 San Francisco CA 94133. *Mailing Add:* c/o GALLERIA SILECCHIA 12 S Palm Ave Sarasota FL 34236

GESKE, NORMAN ALBERT
MUSEUM DIRECTOR, EDUCATOR, LIBRARIAN
b Sioux City, Iowa, Oct 31, 1915. *Study:* Univ Minn, BA; NY Univ Inst Fine Arts, MA. *Hon Degrees:* Doane Coll, DFA, 69. *Collection Arranged:* Ernst Barlach (first Am mus exhib), 55; Am Participation, 34th Venice Biennale, 68; Am Sculpture, 70; Ralph Albert Blakelock (auth, catalog), 75 & 2007. *Pos:* Asst dir, Univ Nebr Art Galleries, 50-53, actg dir, 53-56, dir, 56-83 & dir emer, 83. *Teaching:* Prof, Univ Nebr-Lincoln. *Awards:* Distinguished Service Award, Univ Nebr, Kearney, 80; Distinguished Serv Award, Lincoln Found, 91; Founders Award, Mus Nebr Art, 93; Nebraskaland Foundation, Pioneer Award, 2004; Nebraska Arts Coun, Leonard Thiessen Award, 2004. *Mem:* Hon mem Asn Art Mus Dirs; Nebr Art Asn (life trustee); Mus Nebr Art Found (trustee). *Res:* Nebraska Blakelock inventory. *Specialty:* American art. *Interests:* City of Paris; French art history. *Publ:* Auth, The Figurative Tradition in Recent American Art, 68; Rudy Pozzatti, American Printmaker, 71; Ralph Albert Blakelock 1847-1919, 75; The American Painting Collection of the Sheldon Memorial Art Gallery, 88 & Beyond Madness, The Art of Ralph Blakelock, 1847-1919, 2007, Univ Nebr Press; The Unknown Blakelock, 2008. *Mailing Add:* 128 N 13th St No 408 Lincoln NE 68508

GETLER, HELEN
ART DEALER, CONSULTANT
b New York, NY, May 30, 1925. *Study:* Bryn Mawr Coll, BA, 45. *Pos:* Co-dir, Getler/Pall Gallery, New York, formerly; consult, currently. *Mem:* Art Table. *Specialty:* Contemporary artists, works on paper, prints, paintings and drawings

GETTY, NILDA FERNANDEZ
EDUCATOR, SILVERSMITH
b Buenos Aires, Arg, June 2, 1936; US citizen. *Study:* Archit at Buenos Aires Univ, Univ NC, Raleigh & Univ Pa; Stetson Univ, Deland, Fla, BFA (art); Univ South Fla, Tampa; Univ Ga, MFA (metalsmithing & printmaking). *Work:* Deland Mus, Fla; Univ South Fla; Denver Art Mus; Minn Mus of Art, St Paul; Colo State Univ. *Comn:* St Luke's Chalice, St Luke's Episcopal Church; eleven copper emblems, Larimer Co High Sch. *Exhib:* Goldsmiths Invitational (traveling exhib), Minn Mus Art, St Paul, 74; Metals Invitational, Fullerton Gallery, Calif, 75; two-person show, Gryphon Gallery, Denver, 75 & 77; Sheldon Mem Art Gallery, Lincoln, Nebr, 76; NAm Goldsmith Invitational, Phoenix Mus, Ariz, 76-77; Metals Invitational, Henry Gallery, Seattle, Wash, 77; solo exhib, Minn Mus Art, St Paul, 74; and others. *Teaching:* From instr to prof metalsmithing, Colo State Univ, Ft Collins, 70-. *Bibliog:* Donald Willcox (auth), Body Jewelry: International Perspectives, Regnery, 73; Philip Morton (auth), Contemporary Jewelry, Holt, Rinehart & Winston, 2nd ed 76. *Mem:* Soc NAm Goldsmiths; Am Crafts Coun; World Crafts Coun. *Media:* Silver, Gold. *Publ:* Auth, Contemporary Crafts of the Americas, Regnery, 75; auth, articles, Contemporary Crafts, 75 & Ceramics Mo, 75; auth, Crafts in the Americas, Crafts Horizons, 74. *Mailing Add:* c/o Colo State Univ Dept Art Fort Collins CO 80523-1770

GEVAS, SOPHIA
DIRECTOR, PAINTER
b Athens, Ohio, Oct 3, 1954. *Study:* L'Univ D'Aix-Marseille, L'Ecole Des Beaux Arts, Aix-En-Provence, France, 74; Miami Univ, Ohio, BFA, 76; apprentice to Reuben Nakian (sculptor), 83. *Work:* Pepsi-Co Int, Purchase, NY; Epic Co, Falls Church, Va; Tower Marketing Systs, Malvern, Pa; Communication Skills Inc, Phoenix, Ariz; Energy Conservation Systs, Arlington, Va. *Comn:* Large scale oil painting, comn by Mr & Mrs Deupi, McLean, Va, 80; large scale oil painting, comn by Mr & Mrs Donald Smith, Vienna, Va, 80; large scale oil painting, comn by Thomas Murphy, Arlington, Va, 85. *Exhib:* Solo exhibs, Gloria Gallery, Nicosia, Cyprus, 86, Antinor Gallery, Athens, Greece, 86 & Adelphi Univ Manhattan Ctr, NY, 91; In the Natural World, Park Ave Atrium, NY, 87; 29th Ann Barnum Exhib, Discovery Mus, Conn, 88; That's What It's All About, Erector Square Gallery, New Haven, Conn, 88; Addressing the Margin, Ferguson Libr Gallery, Stamford, Conn, 94. *Collection Arranged:* Monuments & Memory: Reflections on the Former Soviet Union traveling exhib (auth, catalog), 94; Fictitious Icons Ann Charnow traveling exhib (auth, catalog), 99; Rough (auth, catalog) 2000; The Color Withing, Work by Artists From Luxembourg (auth catalog) 2000. *Pos:* Co-founder & vpres, Loft Artist Asn, Stamford, Conn, 84-89; dir/cur, Gallery Contemp Art, Sacred Heart Univ, Fairfield, Conn, 89-. *Teaching:* Adj instr art hist/life drawing, Sacred Heart Univ, Fairfield, Conn, 84-89; instr painting/sculpture, Stamford Mus, Conn, 87. *Bibliog:* Paris Takopoulos & Dorothy Kosinski (auths), Art news: Sophia Gevas, Political Times (Greece), 4/11/86; Glafkos Xenos (auth), The human relationship to nature (review), O Agon, 5/22/86; Janet Koplos (auth), Artist explores mythic spaces (review), Advocate/Greenwich Time, Times Mirror, 3/10/91. *Mem:* Stamford Art Asn. *Media:* Oils & Mixed Media on Paper & Masonite. *Publ:* Auth, From the Figure: In Black & White (catalog), Sacred Heart Univ, 94. *Mailing Add:* 44 Fairfield Ave Norwalk CT 06854

GHAHARY, ZIA EDIN
CONSULTANT, ART HISTORIAN
b Mar 5, 1927. *Study:* Univ Tehran, Iran, BA (lit), 45, BA (law & political sci), 46; Post Grad Studies (Persian & Islamic Art, Antiquities: South & West Asia, India, Iran, Egypt, Iraq, Lebanon, Syria & Israel), 48-49; Sorbonne Univ Paris, PhD (comparative lit & schs art), 50; Univ Rome, PhD (political sci), 53; movie director, Centro Esperimentale Di Cinemtografia, Rome with Roberto Rossellini & Vittorio DeSica; Ind Univ (cert appraiser art/antiques). *Pos:* Minister, acting ambassador Canada, Syria, and Lebanon, 73-75; ambassador in Venezuela, Brazil, Colombia, Peru, Ecuador, Trinidad & Tobago, 77-79; pres, Zighom Int Fine Arts & AAA (Art, Antique, Authentication & Appraisals, 83-; pres, int studies advisory bd, Bergen Community Col, formerly; platform speaker, Program Corp Am (topics incl, future of mus & art, China, Middle East & oil issues), currently. *Teaching:* Lectr & prof, Univ Tehran, 60-67, Nat Univ Iran, 64-70. *Awards:* Millenum of Avicenna Award; Homayoum of 2nd Order; Life Mem Award, Int Soc Appraisers; Life Mem Award, ISA. *Mem:* CAPP Int Soc Appraisers (cert appraiser); World Future Soc; Art Students League (life mem); Appraisers Asn Am (cert appraiser); Appraisers Asn Am (life mem). *Media:* Photography, Video, Movies. *Res:* Am, Oriental, Europ and Middle Eastern paintings, sculptures, manuscripts and illuminated miniature paintings; Oriental Rugs, Middle Eastern and Europ Tapestry and Carpets; Persian antiquities, Egyptian, Roman, Greek, Islamic, Judaica and Pre-Colombian artworks, decoratives and furniture. *Specialty:* Painting, Period Europ and Am Furniture. *Interests:* Rare coins, Oriental rugs. *Collection:* Am, Eng, Can, Persian and some Israelite coins; 18th & 19th Century Am and Fr furniture, paintings, sculpture; Persian rugs & tapestry collection. *Publ:* Auth, Noise of Silence, 48; Blue Letters (Surrealist Poems), 48; Series of articles on neorealism in European movies, 54-55; Third world article series (future of social, economic & political development in the world), 57; ed, Catalogues Raisonnee on painter, sculpture, Betty Gilman & Ainslie Burke (American 1922-1991), 93. *Dealer:* Sothebys New York; Christys New York. *Mailing Add:* c/o AAA Appraisals/Zighom Intl Fine Arts 240 Heather Lane Franklin Lakes NJ 07417

GHENT, HENRI
CRITIC, WRITER
b Birmingham, Ala, June 23, 1926. *Study:* US Armed Forces Inst, Honolulu, Hawaii, 45-46; New Eng Conservatory, Boston, 47-51; Marian Anderson scholar, 51 & 52; Georges Longy Sch, Cambridge, 51-53; Martha Baird Rockefeller grant, 57; Univ Paris, 58-60; also pvt study in Ger & Eng; Vogelstein Found Fel, 78; Yaddo Found Fel, 79, Cottonwood Found & Jarvil Commonwealth Found. *Hon Degrees:* Allen Univ, Hon Dr Humanities. *Collection Arranged:* The Invisible Am: Black Artists of the 1930's, 69; 10 Afro-Am Artists, Mt Holyoke Col, 69; 15 International Artists, Community Gallery, Brooklyn Mus, 69, Allusions, 2nd Anniversary Exhib, 70 & Native North Am Art: Mixed Media Works by Contemporary Am Indian Artists, 72; Afro-Am Artists: Since 1950, Brooklyn Col, 69; 8 Afro-Am Artists (catalog), Rath Mus, Geneva, Switz, 71; 1972 All-Ohio Painting & Sculpture Biennial, Art Inst, Dayton, 72. *Pos:* Consult, Nat Endowment Arts, Minn Mus Art, St Paul, Dayton Art Inst, Mt Holyoke Col, Rath Mus, Geneva & Mus d'Art Haitien, Port-au-Prince, Haiti; with Allen Univ; dir, Community Gallery, Brooklyn Mus, 68-72; corresp, Le Monde de la Musique, Paris, France, 83-. *Teaching:* Vis lectr, Col Finger Lakes Series, 70-71 & Dayton Art Inst, Ohio; Queens Col, NY, 74; lectr, Teachers Col, Columbia Univ, 75-80. *Awards:* Ford Found Res-Travel Grant, 74-75; Crane Found Res-Travel Grant, 81-82; Cottonwood Found Grant, 83. *Bibliog:* Articles in Boston Sunday Globe, 12/7/75, Village Voice, 7/19/76, Los Angeles Times, 10/10/76, Artforum, New York Times, Cleveland Plain Dealer,; plus others. *Mem:* Smithsonian Assocs; Int Soc Educ Through Art; African-American Inst; Nat Art Educ Asn; Nat Soc Lit & Arts. *Interests:* Eclectic art with emphasis on contemporary painting, sculpture and graphics. *Collection:* Contemporary painting, sculpture & graphics. *Publ:* Auth, White is not superior, NY Times, 12/8/68; Black creativity in quest of an audience, Art in Am, 5-6/70; The second generation, Art Gallery Mag, 6/74; Spanish art in transition, Art Int, 10/15/75; contribr, Le Monde de la Musique, Danser Mag, Paris; and others

GHIKAS, PANOS GEORGE
PAINTER, EDUCATOR
b Malden, Mass. *Study:* Yale Univ Sch Fine Arts, BFA, 43, MFA, 47; Akad der Bildenden Kunste, Stuttgart, Ger, with Willi Baumeister, 53-54. *Work:* Wadsworth Atheneum, Hartford, Conn; Walker Art Mus, Bowdoin Col; New Britain Mus Am Art, Conn; Colby Col; Art Mus, Waterville, Maine; and others. *Exhib:* Abstract & Surrealist Show, Chicago Art Inst, 47; 2nd Int Salon des Realites Nouvelles, Paris, France, 48; Ann Am Painting, Whitney Mus Am Art, 49; Am Painting Ann, Univ Ill, 50; Worcester Mus Biennial Contemp Am Painting, 52. *Pos:* Asst conservator, Yale Univ Art Gallery, 57-59. *Teaching:* Vis artist design, Carpenter Ctr, Harvard Univ, 64-66; vis prof drawing, Bowdoin Col, 70-71; prof painting, RI Sch Design, Providence, 71-82 & Mass Col Art, 72-. *Awards:* Fulbright Fel, 53; MacDowell Colony Fel, 67; Blanche E Colman Found Grant, 69. *Bibliog:* Chaet (auth), Artists at Work, Webb, 61. *Media:* Egg Tempera. *Publ:* Illusr, Tales of Christophilos, 54; illusr, Again Christophilos, 56; illusr, The Golden Bird, 57; illusr, The Golden Sword, 60. *Mailing Add:* Mass Col Art Boston MA 02115

GIACALONE, VITO
PAINTER, HISTORIAN
b Newark, NJ. *Study:* Montclair State Univ, BA, 60; Univ Iowa, MA, 65, MFA, 66. *Work:* Mus Univ Iowa; Guggenheim Mus; Metrop Mus Art; Smithsonian Nat Mus Am Art; Brit Mus; Prudential Insurance Co; Mus Mod Art Study Collection; New York Public Libr; Brooklyn Mus Print Collection; Princeton Univ Libr Graphic Arts Collection. *Exhib:* Howe Gallery, Kean Univ, NJ, 85-87, 90, 94-97; Albright Knox, Buffalo, NY, 87; Philadelphia Mus Art, 88; Benton Gallery, Southampton, NY, 90-91; Edwin A Ulrich Mus Art, Wichita, Kans, 92; Ben Shahn Gallery, Wayne, NJ, 93; Castrol World Hq, 93; Nabisco Corp Hq, 94; Noyes Mus, NJ, 94; Schering-Plough Corp Galleries, 94; Am Abstract Artists (auth, catalog), Kean Col, NJ, Westbeth Gallery, NY & Baruch Col, NY, 96; Guild Hall Mus, E Hampton, NY, 97; Hillwood Art Mus, Brookville, NY, 2000; Martin Art Mus, Pa, Westbeth Gallery, NY, 2002-2004, 2007, 2010; Am Abstract Artists 75th Anniversary, UK Harris Gallery, NY; Abstraction to the Power of Infinity, Am Abstract Artists, The Icebook Gallery, Phila, Pa, 2011. *Collection Arranged:* Chu Ta, Selected Paintings and Calligraphy (auth, catalog), Vassar Coll Art Gallery, 72-73 & NY Cult Ctr, 73; Style & Theme in Japanese Art: from the 13th to the 20th Centuries (auth, catalog), 88, Power of the Brush: Calligraphic Painting by Wang Fang-yu (auth, catalog), 89, James Howe Gallery, Kean Col, NJ; The Eccentric Painters of Yangzhou (auth, catalog), China House Gallery, China Inst Am, NY, 90; Bada Shanren at the Smithsonian, Oriental Art Magazine, 2004; Abstraction: American Abstract Artists, Crane Arts Phila, Pa, 2011. *Teaching:* Prof painting, Kean Univ, NJ, 66-2001, prof emer; artist-in-residence, Univ Ill, Urbana, 75-; lectr Chinese painting, China Inst Am, NY, 78-80 & 90, Inst Asian Studies, NY, 82-89; vis artist, Columbia Col, Mo, 84; instr, Detroit Art Inst, 85; adj prof, Studio Arts, Sch Visual Arts, NY, currently. *Awards:* Painting Fels, MacDowell Colony, NH, 84 & 85 & Va Ctr Creative Arts, 86 & 87. *Bibliog:* Suzanne Frank (auth), article, Arts Mag, 72; Karen Lipson (auth), article, Newsday, 86; Eileen Watkins (auth), article, Sunday Star Ledger, 96. *Mem:* China Inst Am; Am Abstract Artists; Int Asn Art Critics. *Media:* All Media. *Res:* Chinese eccentric painting of the 17th and 18th centuries. *Interests:* Am abstract painting, asian art. *Publ:* Auth, Chu Ta (1626-1705): Toward an understanding of his art, Oriential Art Mag, 75, Wen Cheng Ming exhibition, 76, Eight dynasties of Chinese painting, 81 & The John M Crawford Jr Collection of calligraphy and painting in the Metropolitan Museum of Art, Part 1, 85, Part 2, 86, Oriental Art Mag; Style and Theme in Japanese Art: from the 13th to the 20th centuries, 88; Power of the Brush: calligraphic paintings by Wang Fang-Yu, 89; The Eccentric Painters of China, 90; Wei Jing Xian, A Unique View of Chinese Art and Culture, Kean Univ, 2000. *Dealer:* Anita Shapolsky Gallery 152 E 65th St New York NY 10021; Arlene Bujese Gallery 66 Newtown Lane East Hampton NY 11937. *Mailing Add:* 463 W St B938 New York NY 10014

GIALANELLA, DONALD G
SCULPTOR, GRAPHIC ARTIST
b Plainfield, NJ, June 9, 1956. *Study:* Montclair State Col, 74-77, Cooper Union, BFA, 79, with Jim Dine, Milton Glazer & Louise Bourgeois. *Comn:* The Fire Unleashed, graphics, ABC Documentary Unit, 85; 25th anniversary, opening animation, Wide World of Sports, 86; Superbowl XIX, opening animation, ABC Sports, 87; Good Morning America, opening animation, 87 & 90; Loving, Opening Animation, 90; and others. *Exhib:* Solo shows, City Without Walls, Newark, NJ, 80, ARS Gallery, Ankara, Turkey, 95, Marcella Luiso, Bronxville, NY, 96 & Gallery 53, Cooperstown, NY, 96; Wind & Water, Smithy-Pioneer Gallery, Cooperstown, NY, 96; Luma Gallery, Colorado Springs, Colo, 98; Sommerhill Gallery, Chapel Hill, NC, 98; Icarus Int, Nags Head, NC, 99; Salmagundi Club, Audubon Artists, NY, 2000; 23rd Ann Smithsonian Show, Washington, DC, 2005. *Pos:* Art dir, ABC News, NY, 84-86, ABC Sports/Entertainment, 86-93; creative dir, Turkish Radio & Television Network, 93-95; founder, Wind & Sky Studio, Cooperstown, NY, 96-. *Teaching:* Lectr, Montclair State Col, State Univ NY, Long Island, 86-89; instr, Bilkent Univ, Ankara, Turkey, 93-95. *Awards:* Cleo Hartwig Mem Award, Audubon Artists 58th Ann Exhib, NY, 2000; Domenico Facci Award, Audubon 59th Ann New York City, 2001; Best in Show, Paradise City Arts Festival, 2004. *Bibliog:* Computer manipulation of news, Computer Pictures, 1/85; Computer graphics on television, Computer Graphics World, 4/85; The changing face of news graphics, Technol Rev, 3/87. *Mem:* Broadcast Designers Asn; Am Craft Coun; Audubon Artists, NY City. *Media:* Steel. *Publ:* Auth, Electronic wizardry, computer graphics at ABC, Capitol Cities/ABC, 86. *Mailing Add:* Liversteel Studio 7017 Darby Ave Reseda CA 91335

GIAMPIETRO, ISABEL ANTONIA
SCULPTOR, DESIGNER
b Marsicovetere, Potenza, Italy; US citizen. *Study:* Scuola Dell'Arte Della Medaglia, with G Romagnoli, dipl, 50; Fine Arts Acad, Rome, Italy, with Calori, Rivosecchi & Cataudella, degree 51, Stockholm, Sweden, glass with SE Skawonius, cert, 56; Manhattanville Coll of the Sacred Heart, BA (humanities); Manhattanville Cum Laude, graduated. *Work:* Smithsonian Inst; Corning Glass Mus; Metrop Mus Art; Mitchell Wolfson Jr collection of decorative arts, Fla; and other mus in Europe and pvt collections. *Comn:* Seal of State of Va (bas-relief), Jr CofC, Oklahoma City, 52; portrait of George Washington (bronze relief 5'x41/2'x3'), George Washington Masonic Nat Mem, Eastman Kodak (1976 Bicentennial Celebration), Alexandria, Va, 1982. *Exhib:* XI Milan Triennale, Stedelijk Mus, Amsterdam, The Neth, 57; two-person exhib, Leerdam New Glass, Utrecht Mus, The Neth, 57; Expos Int, Brussels, Belgium, 58; Glass 1959, Metrop Mus Art, NY; Corcoran Gallery, Washington; solo exhib: Alan Moss Gallery, 84; Modern Glass, Metrop Mus Art, 95-96; and others. *Awards:* Nominee of the Gold Medal, Triennale XI, 57; Grand Prix, Expo, Brussels, Belgium, 58; Environmental Design Grant, Nat Endowment Arts, 78. *Bibliog:* Renzo Marchelli (auth), Portrait of an artist, Negozi e Vetrine, 57; The Metropolitan Museum of Art: Glass 1959, Corning Mus, 59; Geoffrey Beard (auth), International Modern Glass, Charles Scribner's & Sons, 76. *Media:* Bronze, Glass. *Interests:* Photog

GIANAKOS, CRIS
SCULPTOR
b New York NY, Jan 4, 1934. *Study:* Sch Visual Arts, cert. *Work:* Mus Mod Art, NY; Moderna Museet & Nat Mus, Stockholm; Nassau Co Mus Fine Arts; Smithsonian Inst; Fogg Art Mus, Cambridge, Mass; Nat Gallery, Athens; State Mus Contemp Art, The Costakis Collection, Thessaloniki, Greece; Johnson Mus Art, Cornell Univ, Ithaca, NY; US Information Agency, Washington, DC; Malmo Mus, Sweden; Brooklyn Mus, NY. *Comn:* Gemini (steel sculpture), City Malmo, Sweden; Styx (large scale interactive sculpture), Coll Long Island Univ, 88; Zumikon Ramp, Max Bill George Vontongerloo Found, Zurich; The Victory Apartment Complex, NY; Double Cross: Umedalen Sculpture, Sweden; Wanasramp and Orion, Wanas Sculpture Park, Sweden; 2004 Olympics, Athens, Greece; Cephallonia Oracle, Cephallonia Botanica, Greece, 2010; Omega, Onassi Cultural Ctr, Athens, Greece, 2011; Two Plywood

Cubes, Berlin, 2012; Rampways & Access to Ancient Byzantine Sites, Thessaloniki, Greece, 2010-2011. *Exhib:* Mus Mod Art, NY, 71; PS 1, Queens, NY, 78; solo exhibs, Nassau Co Mus Fine Arts (with catalog), NY, Hal Bromm Gallery, NY, 79 & 81, Galerie Nordenhake, Stockholm, Sweden, 85, Univ Gallery, Univ Mass, Amherst (with catalog), 89 & Stark Gallery, NY, 90, 92, 93, 97, 2000, 2002, & 2005; Los Angeles Inst Contemp Art, 80; Brooklyn Mus, NY, 89; Wynn Kramarsky, NY; Stefan Stux Gallery, NY; Thessalonik, Cult Capital Europe (with catalog), Greece, 97; Retrospective Exhib State Mus Contemp Art, Greece (with catalog); Olive Tjaden Gallery, Cornell Univ, Ithaca, NY, 2006; Gallery Citronne, Poros, Greece, 2008; Galleri Andersson Sandstrom, Stockholm, Sweden, 2009; Illeana Tounta Contemp Art Ctr, Athens, 2013; Arevalo Gallery, Miami, Fla, 2013. *Teaching:* Prof Sch Visual Arts, New York, 65-. *Awards:* Nat Endowment Arts Award, 80; Adolph & Ester Gottlieb Found Grant, 76, 80, 89; Pollack-Krasner Found Grant. *Bibliog:* William Zimmer (auth), exhib catalog, 1980; Gianakos-4 Scandanavian Exhibitions (catalog, Steven Madoff auth), 85-86; Stephen Westfall (auth), Rev, Art Am, 87 & 89; William Zimmer (auth), New York Times, 90; Thomas McEvilley, Retrospective catalog, 1992; John Yao (auth), Exhib Catalogue, 2006; Tatiana Spineri (auth), exhib catalog, 2008. *Media:* Mixed, Wood, Stone, Steel. *Res:* Archit, ancient cult, human behavior; Explorations into geometric forms & classical proportions. *Specialty:* Contemp Art. *Interests:* Studying, working with the environment. *Publ:* Contribr, Words and Images, Mus Mod Art, New York, 70; Image of an Era: The American Poster 1945-1975, Nat Collection Fine Art, Smithsonian Inst; Architectural Sculpture, Los Angeles Inst Contemp Art, Calif, 80; Places in Our Llives, Art in Embassies Program, 2001; Culture Capital of the World, Gridlock, Thessalioniki, 1997; Modern Odysseys-Greek American Artists of the 20th Century, 1999. *Dealer:* Stux Gallery, 530 W 25 St, New York, NY; Gallery Nordenhake Berlin; Gallery Anderson Sandstrom; Alpha Delta Gallery Athens Greece; Minus Space 111 Front St Brooklyn NY. *Mailing Add:* 93 Mercer St New York NY 10012

GIANGUZZI, JOSEPH CUSTODE
SCULPTOR, PAINTER
b Bronx, NY, Mar 4, 1941. *Study:* Art Students League, NY City, 1958-59; Studied under William Zorach, Harry Sternberg, Morris Kantor. *Comn:* Unicorn, Margaret B Freeman Collection, comn by Thomas PF Hoving, NY, 1966; Athletes, 20' Terra Cotta wall, LaGuardia Community Col, Long Island City, NY, 1981; Statue Sam Levinson, Brooklyn Center Performing Arts, Brooklyn, NY, 1985; Statue Helen Kelly, City Univ NY, 1994; Statue David B Steinman, City Univ NY, 1996. *Exhib:* Group exhibs incl: Burr Galleries, New York City, 1958-61, Sagittarius Gallery, New York City, Salmagundi Club Galleries, New York, 1963-65, The Barn Gallery, Hartford, Conn, 1979; solo exhib Queensborough Community Col, 1977; commns from Thomas P F Hoving, La Guardia Community Col, Brooklyn Col, City Univ of NY; Backus Gallery & Mus, Fort Pierce, Fla, 2003; Riverbend Sculpture Beinnial, Owensboro Mus Fine Art, Owensboro, Ky, 2005. *Awards:* Gruber Award, SUNY at Purchase, Harrison Coun for the Arts, 1983. *Media:* Marble & Oil Painting. *Mailing Add:* 250 NE 40th Ct Fort Lauderdale FL 33334

GIANLORENZI, NONA ELENA
PAINTER, DEALER
b Virginia, Minn, July 20, 1939. *Study:* Queens Col, 61-65, studied color with John Ferron & Herb Aach; New Sch Social Res, 62-67, studied sculpture with T Doyle & C Guinnivar, painting with A Savelli; Brooklyn Col, 67-68, studied painting with H Holtzman & Carl Holty; studied sculpture with Lee Bonticou, 89; studied color & portraiture with Lois Dodd, 91; studied mod & contemp art hist with Mona Hadler, 92; studied techniques & theories art hist with Susan Koslow, 94; studied art connoisseurship with Jack Flam, 94. *Exhib:* Womens Internat Ctr, 72; 9th Street Survival Show; Black Velvet Erotic Arts Show, 81; Projective-Kinetic Traveling Exhib, 86, 78, 88; Asage Gallery, NY; Brooklyn Coll Exhib, 92; Outdoor Sculpture Exhib, 93; Bruce High Quality Found Exhib, 2010, 2012. *Pos:* Asst dir, Am Art Gallery, New York, 61-67; dir, ASAGE Art Gallery, New York, 77-88 & Art Space Inc New York, 89-92. *Teaching:* Art teacher, Charles Borromeo, Brooklyn & Mt Carmel & St Francis Sch Deaf, Queens, 68-71. *Awards:* Work Study Grant, St Scholastica, Duluth, Minn; Art Studio Scholar, New Sch Soc Res; Loy Scholar, Ford Found Fel, Brooklyn Col. *Bibliog:* Grace Glueck (auth), No More Raw Eggs at the Whitney, New York Times, 2/13/72. *Media:* Acrylic; Wood, Metal Detritus. *Specialty:* Three-dimensional wall painting existing in real space with movement, light and/or sound (kinetic); contemporary art masterworks, side by side with works by emerging artists. *Interests:* Philosophy, science, art history, music, theatre, nature. *Publ:* Auth, The Art Market, Jackie Fine Arts, 79; Don Jacobson: Kinetic Art (exhib catalogs), ASAGE Gallery, 81 & 84; Position paper (for an emerging gallery), ASAGE Gallery, 82; coauth, Yudel Kyler: Cool Surrealism (exhib catalog), 85 & Gerald Lindahl and the Creation of Psychological Space (exhib catalog), 86, ASAGE Gallery; Grace Glveck (auth), No More Raw Eggs at the Whithey, NY Times, 2/13/72. *Dealer:* Am State of the Art Gallery Exchange 162 W 4th St New York NY 10014; Art Space Inc 415 Rugby Rd Brooklyn NY 11226

GIBB, ANN W
PAINTER
b New York, NY, 1925. *Study:* Cornell Univ, 41-45; Art Students League; studied with Herb Olsen, Charles Reid, Christian Midjo & Glenora Richards. *Exhib:* Nat Acad Design; Audubon Artists; Allied Artists Am; Hudson Valley Art Asn; Solo exhib, Darien Libr, 57 & 96, Barbizon Gallery, New York City, Acad Our Lady Mercy, Kauffmann-Locke Gallery, Nantucket, Mass, 94. *Teaching:* instr, Silvermine Sch Art. *Awards:* Best Landscaped Award, New Canaan Ctr for Arts; Rothchild Purchase Prize, Allied Artists of Am; Landscape Prize, Art of the Northeast. *Mem:* Knickerbocker Artists; Allied Artists Am; Am Watercolor Soc; Miniature Art Soc NJ

GIBBONS, ARTHUR
SCULPTOR, EDUCATOR
Study: Ohio Wesleyan Univ, BA; Univ Pa, BFA, MFA. *Exhib:* Solo exhbits, Robert Freidus Gallery, 1977, 1979, 1980, 1982, Andre Emmerich Gallery, 1984-86, 1988, 1990, 1992, Art Acad Cin, 2001, Incident Report, Hudson, NY, 2007; group shows in NY at Guild Hall, Est Hampton, storm king Art Ctr, Neuberger mus., SUNY purchase, Albert Knox Gallery, Denver Art Mus., Chase Manhatten Bank, Prudential Insurance Co of America, Vir Mus of Fine Arts, Case Reserve Univ. *Pos:* S William Senfeld artist in residence, prof sculpture, dir, Milton Avery Grad Sch of Arts, Bard Col, currently. *Awards:* Edward F Albee Found Fellowship. *Mailing Add:* Milton Avery Graduate School of Arts Bard College, PO Box 5000 30 Campus Rd Rm 117 Red Hook NY 12504

GIBBONS, HUGH (JAMES)
PAINTER, EDUCATOR
b Scranton, Pa, Oct 26, 1937. *Study:* Pa State Univ, with Elaine de Kooning & Robert Mallary, BA (painting), 59, MA (painting), 61. *Work:* WTex Mus, Lubbock; Bucknell Univ Collection. *Exhib:* Solo exhibs, Univ Tex, Permian Basin, Odessa, Tex, 90 & Charleston Heights Gallery, Las Vegas, Nev, 90; TVAA Citation, Dallas, 91; Amarillo, Tex Competition, 93; New Am Talent, Austin, Tex, 94; 22nd Ann, Confluence, Ingram, Tex, 94; Texas Art Int, El Paso, Tex, 94; and others. *Teaching:* Prof painting & drawing & MFA coordr, Tex Tech Univ, 63-. *Media:* Oil, Pencil. *Mailing Add:* Tex Tech Univ Dept Art Lubbock TX 79409

GIBBONS, JOE
FILMMAKER
Exhib: AFI Video Festival, Los Angeles, 89; Art of the Century, Whitney Mus, 89-91; The Talking Cure, Artist's Space, NY, 90-91; Consumer Tools, Mus Mod Art, 91; The Kitchen, NY, 92; Whitney Biennial, 92, 2000, 2002 & 2006; Impakt Festival, Utrecht, Neth, 94-99; Black Maria Film & Video Festival, 95-2000; NY Video Festival, Film Soc Lincoln Ctr, 95-2002; Int Film Festival, Rotterdam, 95-2003; Viper Festival, Zurich, 98; NY Film Expo, 99; Pacific Film Archive, Calif, 2000. *Pos:* lectr, Vis Arts, MIT. *Awards:* Best Experimental Film, New Eng Film & Video Festival, 86 & 92; Award of Excellence, 27th Sinking Creek Film/Video Festival, 94; Second Prize, Black Maria Film & Video Festival, 96, 98-2001 & 2004; First Prize, Viper Video Festival, 96; and many other fellowships & grants. *Mailing Add:* MIT School of Architecture and Planning 265 Massachusetts Ave Cambridge MA 02139

GIBBS, TOM
SCULPTOR
b Dubuque, Iowa, Sept 17, 1942. *Study:* Loras Coll, BA (art); Univ Iowa, with Olivier Strabelle, MA (sculpture) & MFA; also with Walter Arno, Ger. *Work:* Tweed Mus, Univ Minn, Duluth, 89. *Comn:* Western Electric Corp, 80; Esterville Pub Libr, 81; Univ Dubuque, 88; Morningside Coll, Sioux City, Iowa, 89; Univ Central Ark, 94; Univ Northern Iowa, 95; Pyramid Sculpture Park, 2004; Flipse Bldg, Univ Miami, Coral Gables, 2005. *Exhib:* Univ Minn, Duluth, 88; Riverwalk Outdoor Invitational, Chicago, 89; Sculpture Tour 91, Walters State Coll, Tenn; Ala Biennial, Univ Ala, Tuscaloosa, 93; Pier Walk 98, Chicago, 98. *Teaching:* Instr art, Clarke Coll, 68-69; asst prof sculpture, Ariz State Univ, 70-72. *Awards:* Hon Mention, Nat Vietnam War Memorial Design Competition, Washington, DC, 81; Nominee, Second Ann Awards in the Visual Arts, 82; Creative Artists Planning Proj Task Force, Iowa, Art Coun, 88-90; Gov's Award for Service to Arts, 89. *Bibliog:* Articles, Chicago Sun Times, 6/29/80, 5/23/82 & Art News, 11/80; Joan Jeremy Hewes (auth), Worksteads, Tom Gibbs, Sculptor, 24-29 & 120, Doubleday, New York, 81. *Mem:* Int Sculpture Ctr. *Media:* Welded, Cast Metal, Stone. *Publ:* Auth, Field hearings on the reauthorization of the National Foundation for the Arts on Humanities Act J, 412-421. *Dealer:* Molly-Rose Gallery 5400 SW 99th Terr Coral Gables FL. *Mailing Add:* 2500 Corto Dr Dubuque IA 52001

GIBSON, BENEDICT S
PAINTER, EDUCATOR
b Grand Rapids, Mich, Sept 21, 1946. *Study:* Kendall Sch Design, dipl, 67; Aquinas Col, BA, 70; Univ Nebr, MFA, 73. *Work:* Albright-Knox Art Gallery, Buffalo, NY; Butler Inst Am Art, Youngstown, Ohio; Mem Art Gallery, Rochester, NY; Rutgers Univ, New Brunswick, NJ; Flint Inst Arts, Mich; and others. *Exhib:* 34th Western NY Exhib, Albright-Knox Art Gallery, 74; Nat Drawing 1994, Trenton State Col, NJ, 94; 71st Ann Spring Show, Erie Art Mus, Pa, 94; 84th Ann Juried Show, Assoc Artists Pittsburgh, Carnegie Mus Art, Pa, 94; Art Fac Exhib, Bruce Gallery, Edinboro Univ Pa, 94; 20th Ann October Evenings Exhib, Meadville Coun Arts, Pa, 94; and others. *Collection Arranged:* Drawing Invitational (cataloged), 76; First Decade, Charles B Burchfield Ctr Col, 76; Penney Collection (cataloged), State Univ NY Upstate Med Ctr, 77; Three Painters, Millersville State Col, 77; Tenth Anniversary Exhibition, Kenan Ctr, Lockport, NY, 77. *Teaching:* Prof art, Edinboro Univ Pa, 76-. *Awards:* Cash Award, 79th Ann Juried Assoc Artists Pittsburgh Show, Pa, 89; Edinboro Univ Fac Res Grant, 90; Cash Award, 71st Ann Spring Show, Erie Art Mus, Pa, 94. *Bibliog:* Edward Booth-Clibborn (ed), American Illustration 2, Harry Abrams, Inc, New York, 83; Susan Krane (auth), Wayward Muse, A Historical Survey of Painting in Buffalo, Albright-Knox Art Gallery, Buffalo, NY, 87; Harry Schwalb (auth), Catching up, state of the art in Pittsburgh, Pittsburgh Mag, 1/94. *Mem:* Asn Artists Pittsburgh, Pa; Copyist Prog, Nat Gallery Art, Washington, DC, 2004. *Media:* Acrylic, Oil. *Publ:* Michael A Tomor (ed), Artists of the Commonwealth, Realism in Pennsylvania Painting, 1950-2000, Southern Alleghenies Mus Art. *Mailing Add:* Edinboro Univ Dept Art Edinboro PA 16444

GIBSON, JOHN STUART
PAINTER, PRINTMAKER
b Northampton, Mass, Oct 14, 1958. *Study:* RI Sch Design, BFA, 80; Yale Sch Art, MFA, 82. *Work:* New York Pub Libr; Acklin Mus, Charlotte, NC; Univ Mass, Amherst; Smith Coll Mus Art; Mus Fine Arts, Boston. *Exhib:* Beyond Realism, Southern Alleghenies Mus, Loretto, Pa, 92. *Teaching:* Instr art, Smith Col, Northampton, Mass, 85-92. *Media:* Oil. *Dealer:* Miller Block Gallery Newbury St Boston Ma 02116; Wendy Hoff Perspective Fine Arts 19 E 71st St New York NY 10021. *Mailing Add:* 30 Williams St Northampton MA 01060-9703

GIBSON, MICHAEL
PAINTER
b Atlanta, Ga, 1962. *Study:* Univ Ga, Athens, BFA, 89. *Work:* Hunter Mus, Chattanooga, Tenn; NBHV, Hamburg, Ger; numerous pvt collections throughout the US & Nantes, France. *Exhib:* Contemp Int Mus Art, 92; Spotlight on Southeastern Artist Ann Exhib, 93, 94 & 95; An Am Renaissance, Lowe Art Gallery, Atlanta, Ga, 93; Nexus Contemp Arts Ctr, 95; November Show, New Mus Contemp Art, NY, 95; Atlanta Collects: Contemp Southern Art in Atlanta Collections, Consult Art, Ga, 97; Watermark, Fay Gold Gallery, Atlanta, Ga, 97; Born Again: Found Objects in Contemp Art, Art Walk, Atlanta, Ga, 98; Body and Soul: Contemp Southern Figures, Columbus Mus, Miss Mus Art, Mobile Mus Art & Cummer Mus Art, 98; Fay Gold Gallery, Atlanta, 99, 2001, 02; LPP Projects, London, Eng, 2000; Kevin Bruk, Miami, Fla, 2002; Cascade of Scales: James Graham & Sons, NY, 2002; Fresh: NoNo, Atlanta, Ga, 2002; Painting as Paradox: Artist Space, NY, 2002. *Awards:* Nat Endowment Arts Fel, Southeastern Ctr Contemp Art/Nat Endowment Arts 96-97. *Publ:* Contribr, Art & Antiques, Jezebel Mag, Atlanta Mag & New Art Examiner, 97; and many others. *Mailing Add:* c/o Fay Gold Gallery 3670 Paces Ferry Rd NW Atlanta GA 30327-3017

GIBSON, SANDRA
PAINTER, FILMMAKER
b Portland, Ore, 1968. *Study:* RI Sch Design, BFA, 1999; The Sorbonne, Paris, 1992; Ecole des Beaux Arts, Paris, 1993. *Work:* Artist Whitney Biennial, Whitney Mus Am Art, 2004. *Exhib:* Solo exhibs include Handmade Films, Kala Art Inst, Berkeley, Calif, 2000, The Matter With Film, Squeaky Wheel, Buffalo, NY, 2003, Cinema Project, Portland, Ore, 2003, Images Festival, Toronto, Can, 2004, Olympia Film Festival, Wash, 2004, Viewer, Youkobo Art Space, Tokyo, 2005, Coming Attractions, Janalyn Hanson White Gallery, Cedar Rapids, Iowa, 2005, Light Spill, Pittsburgh Filmmakers Galleries, 2006 & 2007, Holland Animation Film Festival, Utrecht, 2006; group exhibs include Black Maria Film Festival, Smithsonian Inst, Washington, 2000; Internat Film Festival, Rotterdam, The Netherlands, 2000, 2002, 2003, 2004; Calling Cards, Telluride Film Festival, 2001; Mad Cat, Pacific Film Archive, Berkeley, Calif, 2001; Toronto Internat Film Festival, Can, 2001, 2003; Animations, PS 1 Mus Mod Art, NY, 2002; Short Cuts Internat Film Festival, Cologne, Germany, 2002; Brit Film Inst, London, 2003; VideoEx, Zurich, Switzerland, 2003; Hong Kong Internat Film Festival, 2004; 2004 Whitney Biennial, Whitney Mus Am Art, NY, 2004; Busan Asian Film Festival, Busan, South Korea, 2005; Image Forum Festival, Yokohama Mus Art, Tokyo, 2005; Seoul Internat Film Festival, South Korea, 2005; Kill Your Timid Notion, Dundee Contemp Arts, Scotland, 2006; Inst Contemp Art, London Film Festival, 2006. *Awards:* Kala Art Inst Fel, Berkeley, Calif, 2000; Mus Contemp Cinema Found Award, France, 2003; Nat Endowment Arts Digital Filmmakers Internat Res, 2003; NY Found Arts Film Award, 2004. *Publ:* dir, (films) Cinematheque, ON, Pacific Film Archive, Anthology Film Archive, Rotterdam Film Festival, Ind. Exposure, Empire State Film Festival, Ann Arbor Film Festival, South Beach Animation Festival

GIBSON, WALTER SAMUEL
WRITER, LECTURER
b Columbus, Ohio, Mar 31, 1932. *Study:* Ohio State Univ, BFA, 57, MA, 60; res at Kunsthistorisch Inst Rijksuniversiteit, Utrecht, 60-61 & 64-66; Harvard Univ, PhD, 69. *Pos:* Murphy Lectureship, Univ Kans & Nelson-Atkins Mus Art, Kansas City, Mo, 88. *Teaching:* Asst prof art, Case Western Reserve Univ, Cleveland, 66-71, chmn dept & assoc prof, 71-79, Andrew W Mellon prof humanities, 78-97, Andrew W Mellon prof emer, 97-; Clark vis prof art hist, Williams Coll, 89 & 92, lectr, 2006. *Awards:* Kress Found Grant, 70; Guggenheim Found Grant, 78-79; Fel in Residence, Neth Inst Advan Study, Wassenaar, Neth, 95-96. *Mem:* Coll Art Asn Am; Int Ctr Medieval Art; Midwest Art Hist Soc; Renaissance Soc Am; Medieval Acad Am; Historians Netherlandish Art; Soc Emblem Studies. *Res:* Dutch and Flemish art, 15th-17th centuries; iconography. *Publ:* Hieronymus Bosch: Thames and Hudson, 73; Hieronymus Bosch: An Annotated Bibliography, G K Hall, 83; Bruegel: Thames and Hudson, 77; Mirror of the Earth: The World Landscape in Sixteenth-Century Flemish Painting, Princeton, 89; Pieter Bruegel the Elder: Two Studies (The Franklin D Murphy Lectures XI), Univ Kans, 91; Pleasant Places: The Rustic Landscape from Bruegel to Ruisdael, Calif, 2000; Pieter Bruegel and The Art of Laughter, Calif, 2006; Figures of Speech, Picturing Proverbs in Renaissance Netherlands, Calif, 2010. *Mailing Add:* 938 N Mason Hill Rd Pownal VT 05261-9339

GIDDENS, KATHLEEN COLETTE
PAINTER, EDUCATOR
b St. Petersburg, FL, April 20, 1949. *Study:* Univ FL, BA Fine Arts, 1971; MA Art Educ, 1979. *Work:* Danville Mus Natural Hist, Danville, Va; State of Fla Art Pub Bldgs, Tallahassee, Fla; Art in Embassies, Santiago, Chili. *Comn:* Danville Mus of Natural Hist, comn by Dir, Danville, Va, 1987; Artist in Residence Painting, SC State Parks, SC, 2005. *Exhib:* Traveling Art Show, NC Mus Art, Raleigh, NC, 1981; Nat Juried Show, Terrance Art Gallery, Palenville, NY, 1981; Nature's Embellishments, Galerie Triangle, Wash, DC, 1986; Semi Ann Competition, Milwaukee Mus Art, Milwaukee, Wis, 1992; South Works Competition, Watkinsville, Ga, 1998; Solo Exhib: Governors Gallery, Tallahassee, Fla, 1998, 2006; ABP 16 Exhib, Calif State Univ, Long Beach, Calif, 2001; AE Backas Gallery, Ann Fla Show, Fort Pierce, Fla, 2006; Group Exhib: Tampa Mus Art, Tampa, Fla, 2007; Bryn Mawr Rehab Hospital Annual Show, 2008, 2009, 2010, 2011, 2012, 2013; Fla Mus Women Artists Annual Show, 2009, 2010, 2013; Eckerd Coll, 2012. *Pos:* Teacher's Aid, Alachua Co Schs, Gainesville, Fla, 1975-1978; Advert Specialist, JC Penney Gainesville, Fla, 1978-1980. *Teaching:* Instr, art hist, Sampson Tech Col, Clinton, NC, 1980-1982; Patrick Henry Community Col, Martinsville, Va, 1983-1985; instr, painting, Rockingham Community Col, Eden, NC, 1983-1985; instr, Community Art Center, Waukesha, Wis, 1987. *Awards:* First Place, 9th Ann Competition NC Artist, 1980; First Place, Competition Danville Mus Fine Arts, 1984; Second Place, Accessible Parks, Renaissance of Promise Art Show, 1994; First Place, Juried Exhib Thomas Center Galleries, 2001, 2002; First Place, Impressions of Old South Art Show, 2004. *Mem:* Nat Mus Women in the Arts, Wash, DC; Fla Mus Women Artists. *Media:* Oil. *Publ:* Auth (calendar), Confronting Cancer, Alverno Col,,Wis 1991; auth (playbill cover), Kravis Center Performing Arts, W Palm Beach, Fla, 2003; auth (calendar), Christopher Reeve Found, 2004-2005; auth (calendar), AARP Found, Wash, DC, 2006. *Dealer:* Gateway Art Gallery Lake City Fl

GIGLIOTTI, JOANNE MARIE
ADMINISTRATOR, PAINTER
b Pittsburgh, Pa, June 12, 1945. *Study:* Carnegie-Mellon Univ, BFA, 67; Penn State Univ, MA, 78; grad courses, George Wash Univ; Trinity Coll. *Work:* The Charlotte McCormick Pvt Collection, Fla; Nat Mus Women Arts; Westinghouse Collection; Penn State Univ; The Anita Shelford Family Collection; The Embassy of the Republic of Indonesia, Wash DC. *Comn:* The McCormick Collection; Senator Strom Thurmond Info Ctr, SC; Jay & Addie Edleson Collection; Ann Burger Linden House; Mary & Michael Buckler Collection. *Exhib:* Carnegie Mus Art, Pittsburgh, Pa, 68 & 71; solo exhibs, Beautiful Batik, Arts & Sci Ctr, Nashua, NH, 74, Battle Creek Art Ctr, Mich, 75, Brigham City Mus Art, Brigham City, Utah, 75, Arnut Mus Art, Elmira, NY, 75, Abilene Fine Arts Mus, Tex, 76, Bronx Libr, Manhattan Branch, 76, Fayette Art Mus, Ala, 76; Early Childhood Enrichment Auction, Smithsonian Inst, 94 & Women's Exhib, 95; Tile Heritage Exhib, Santa Barbara, Calif, 96; Tile Artist's Today by Susan Werschkul, Tile Heritage Found Symposium, 96; Coverings, Int Tile Conf, Orlando, Fla, 97; Am Tile Artists by Richard Serving, ITC Coverings, 97; Philadelphia Artists Alliance Tile Exhib, 98; NIH Exhib, Rockville, Md, 2007; Welcome to Washington Asn, Georgetown, Washington, DC, 2007; Met Ctr for Visual Arts, Rockville, Md, 2007; Food as Art, City Hall, Gaither, Md, 2008; Am Batik Design Competition Winner Exhib, Indonesia Awards and Celebration, The Palace Hotel, San Francisco, Calif, 2011, 2012; Jakarta Convention Ctr, Adi Wastra Indonesia, Pameran Kain Tracisional, Batik dan tari Saman featuring Am Batik Exhib, The Republic of Indonesia, Jakarta, 2012. *Collection Arranged:* Etruscan Exhib, Univ Perugia/Oshna Gallery, Washington, DC, 84; Juried, 19th Ann 4 State Competition, Masur Mus Art, Monroe, La, 92; Russian Art Project Exhib & auction, Georgetown, Washington, DC, 5/2006. *Pos:* Dir, Hub Arts & Craft Ctr, Penn State Univ, 78-80; founder & dir, Fine Arts Connection, Washington, DC, 80-87; chair, Smithsonian Inst Women's Coun, 88-95, art specialist, Russian art proj/auction, 2005-06; dir, Studio Arts Dept, Smithsonian Assoc Resident Prog, dir, Discover Graphics, Smithsonian Inst, Washington, DC, 93-94; artist/owner, BatikTile.com, Gaithersburg, Md, 95-. *Teaching:* Instr, Batik-silkscreen-color-design & marketing & bus art, Smithsonian Inst - Resident Assoc Prog, 83-87; lectr, Am Univ, 84-86; guest lectr, George Washington Univ, 93-95, Smithsonian Inst, Yale Univ, 94; teacher, pvt art and computer graphics classes; teacher, mentoring for young artists, 95-; teacher, master classes ceramics; teacher, Women's Issues Project - Women's Informational Needs, 2002-2003; teacher, artist's master classes, 2005-; instr, Metropolitan Ctr for the Visual Arts, Rockville, Md, 2005-2009; Strathmore Mus Arts, Public Presentations, N Bethesda, Md, 2010-. *Awards:* Best in Category (mixed media), Big Bends Nat Art Competition, Tallahassee, 68; Creative Programming Award, Nat Univ Continued Educ Asn, 90; Smithson Soc Grant, 94-95; 1st Pl Winner, The First Am Batik Design Competition, Embassy of the Republic of Indonesisa, Wash DC. *Bibliog:* Artists World, Discovery Channel, 90; article, Wash Home Sect, 92; article with photos, Traditional Home Mag, spring 96; article, Designers Showcase, 96 & 97; article, Tile and Decorative Surfaces, 5/98; article, Traditional Buildings Mag, 95 & 98; article, Kitchen and Bath Mag, fall 98; article, Kitchen and Bath Design News, 3/98, 5/98; Serious about ceramics, Jour Newspapers, 8/99; Unique Batik, Decor Mag, 3/2001; Exploring the Art of Balik (Tile to Die for), Expression Magazine, 5-6/2002; Eloise Piper, Batik for Artists & Quilters, North Light Books, Cincinnati, Ohio, 3/2001; winning entry and related exhibs include, The Jakarta Post, Jakarta Globe, Jaring News, Kompas Female, Voice of America, AP Press, Suaramer Deka Pubs, Pikiran-Rakyat Press, Media Indonesia, ViVA News, Indonesia, North Hills Record, McKnight Jour, Carnegie Mellon Today, Good Housekeeping, etc. *Mem:* Women in Mus Network, (87-); Tile Heritage Found, (94-); Tile Coun Am; Int Tile Coun; Art Speak (World Art Asn); Tile Artists Am; Smithsonian Inst (mem Latino Working Com, 93-95); Fine Arts Network Carnegie Mellon Alumne DC Chap, (1996-2006); Strathmore Artists (2009-). *Media:* Painting on Tile, Painting on Jewelry. *Res:* Baik: Painting media of Artists from Many Cultures. *Interests:* Politicals, hospitals, mentoring. *Publ:* Coauth, Time-Life Art Ser, Time-Life Publ, 88; The Business of Art, Prentice-Hall, 89; Eloise Piper (auth), Batik for Artists & Quilters, North Light Books, 2001; Traditional Buildings Magazine, Portfolio Section, 95 & 98; Exploring the art of Batik, Expression Mag, May/June/2002; The Spirit of America in the Heritage of Batik, 2011. *Mailing Add:* 69 Bralan Ct Gaithersburg MD 20877

GILBERT, AARON J
PAINTER
Study: Pa State Univ, AS, 2000; RI Sch Design, BFA (painting), 2005; Yale Sch Art, MFA (painting), 2008. *Exhib:* Solo exhibs, Gallery Agniel, Providence, RI, 2005; Red Door Gallery, Providence, 2004; Woods-Gerry Gallery, Providence, 2004 & 2005; Gallery Agniel, 2005; Hillel Gallery, 2005; Sol Koffler Gallery, Providence, 2005; Marc Selwyn Fine Art, Los Angeles, 2007; Loop Video Art Fair, Barcelona, Spain, 2008; Met Pavilion, New York, 2008; Galerie Schuster, Berlin, Germany, 2008;

Deitch Projects, New York, 2008; Rush Arts, New York, 2009; Ramis Barquet Gallery, New York, 2009; JW Brennan Gallery, Jersey City, 2010; Am Acad Arts & Letts Invitational, New York, 2010. *Awards:* Gordon Peers Award, RI Sch Design; Rosenthal Family Found Award in Painting, Am Acad Arts & Letts, 2010. *Media:* Oil

GILBERT, ALBERT EARL
PAINTER, ILLUSTRATOR
b Chicago, Ill, Aug 22, 1939. *Work:* Am Mus Natural Hist, NY; Carnegie Mus, Pittsburgh; Ill State Mus, Springfield; Nat Audubon Soc, NY; du Pont Collection, Del Mus Natural Hist, Wilmington; Princeton Univ. *Comn:* Paintings of Am wildlife & plants, Nat Wildlife Fedn, Washington, DC, 67-74; Audubon bird proj (20 color plates of Am birds), Franklin Mint, Pa, 75. *Exhib:* Wildlife in Art, Brandywine River Mus, Chadds Ford, Pa, 73; SAm Birds, Am Mus Natural Hist, NY, 73; Solo exhib, Wildlife Portraits, Incurable Collector Gallery, NY, 74; Animals in Art, Royal Ont Mus, Toronto, 75; Bird Art Exhib, Leigh Yawkey Woodson Art Mus, Wausau, Wis, 77; and others. *Awards:* Winner, Fed Duck Stamp Competition, 78-79. *Bibliog:* B J Lancaster (auth), Gilbert's birds, Cornell Univ Lab of Ornithology Bulletin, 75; The artist--Al Gilbert, Prints Mag, spring, 79. *Mem:* Soc Animal Artists; Ridgefield Guild Artists. *Media:* Opaque Watercolors, Acrylics. *Publ:* Illusr, The Audubon Illustrated Handbook of American Birds, 68, The Red Book--Wildlife in Danger, 68, Curassows and Related Birds, 73 & Birds of New York State, 74; auth, My studio is the jungle, Int Wildlife Mag, 9-10/76; and others. *Dealer:* Blakeslee Gallery 350 Royal Poinciana Palm Beach Fl 33480; Steep Rock Wildlife Art PO Box 107 Bridgewater CT 06752. *Mailing Add:* 279 New Milford Rd W Bridgewater CT 06752-1029

GILBERT, BILL
EDUCATOR, CERAMIST
Study: Pitzer Coll, Claremont, Calif, BA, 1973; Univ Mont, Missoula, MFA, 1978. *Exhib:* Five from New Mexico, Univ Tex, El Paso, 1985; Site Specific Adobe, Univ Tex, San Antonio, 1986; solo exhibs, NMex Mus Art, 1986, Wadsworth Antheneum, Hartford, 1987, Univ NMex Art Mus, 1988, Creative Arts Gallery, 1989, Boulder Art Ctr, Colo, 1991, Mobius, Boston, 1992, Fundacion Paul Rivet, Ecuador, 1994, Art Ctr, Waco, 1995, Ctr for Contemp Art, Santa Fe, 1998, Robert Nichols Gallery, 2002, Santa Fe Clay, 2003; Small Works, Univ Art Mus, Albuquerque, 1987; 45th Scripps Invitational, Lang Art Gallery, Claremont, Calif, 1989; Southwest 90, NMex Mus, Santa Fe, 1990; Exquisite Corpse, Ctr for Contemp Art, Santa Fe, 1991; Clay Out of Context, San Diego State Univ Gallery, 1993; Clay Nat, Zoller Gallery, Pa State Univ, 1994; Sense of Place, Governors Gallery, Santa Fe, 1995; Alert, OFF-Site, Santa Fe, 1996; The Tie that Binds, Anderson Gallery, 1998; Term Limits, Mus NMex, Santa Fe, 2000; Beyond the Physical: Substance, Space & Light, Univ NC Galleries, Charlotte, 2001; Fuse, Robert Nichols Gallery, Santa Fe, 2002; I-25, Sangre de Christo Art Mus, Pueblo, 2003. *Collection Arranged:* Quichua Pottery of Ecuador, S Broadway Cult Ctr, Albuquerque, 1994; The Potters of Mata Ortiz, Univ Art Mus, Albuquerque, 1995; Juan Quezada, Univ Dallas, Nat Coun Educators in the Ceramic Arts Conf, 1998; The Potters of Mata Ortiz (auth, catalog), Southwest Craft Ctr, San Antonio, 1999; Crossing Boundaries, Transcending Categories (auth, catalog), Mus Fine Arts, Santa Fe, 2000. *Pos:* Creator & Lannan Chmn, Land Arts Am West Prog, Dept Art & Art Hist, Univ NMex, 2000. *Awards:* RAC Grant, Univ NMex, 1987, 1991 & 1997; Lila Wallace Arts Int, Ecuador, 1994; Lannan Found Grant, 2000; Elizabeth Firestone Graham Found Grant, 2003. *Bibliog:* Robert Creeley (auth), My New Mexico, Albuquerque Mus, 1982; William Peterson (auth), Santa Fe, Art News, 131, 11/1985; Owen McNally (auth), Sculptor Chooses Materials That Celebrate the Present, Hartford Courant, 6/17/1987; Dennis Fawcett (auth), On Sculpture: When Less is More, New Haven Register, 7/16/1988; Carl Hoover (auth), Installing Outdoors Indoors, Tribune Herald, 2/24/1995; Carl Hertel (auth), The Voices of Clay, Albuquerque Arts Mag, 10, 8/1998; Kay Whitney (auth), Skilled Labor, Sculpture Mag, Vol 18, No 4, 24-29, 5/1999; Meghen Jones (auth), Beyond the Physical: Substance, Space and Light, NCECA J, 142-149, 2002. *Publ:* Auth, Mata Ortiz: Traditions and Innovations, In: Ceramics Monthly, 51-56, 12/1995; Quichua Pottery: Cultural Identity and the Market, In: J Occupational Sci, Vol 3, No 2, 72-75, 1996; Juan Quezada: The Casas Grandes Revival, In: Nat Coun Educators in the Ceramic Arts J, Vol 19, 35-38, 1998; coauth (with Chris Taylor), Land Arts of the American West, Univ Tex Press, 2008. *Mailing Add:* 3358-C Hwy 14 Cerrillos NM 87010

GILBERT, HERB
PAINTER
b Brooklyn, NY, Oct 30, 1929. *Study:* Art Career Sch, 48-51; Brooklyn Mus Art Sch, with Reuben Tam, 55-58; Pratt Inst with Walter Murch, Reuben Nakian & George McNiel, 56-57; Univ Calif, 73. *Work:* Mus NMex, Santa Fe; Motorola Corp, Phoenix, Ariz; Am Republic Insurance Co, Des Moines, Iowa; Salt River Proj, Phoenix, Ariz; Bahai Nat Ctr, Wilmette, Ill; Univ Ariz Mus Art. *Exhib:* Own Your Own Regional, Denver Art Mus, 64; Southwest Fine Arts Biennial, Mus NMex, 74; Invitational, Cochise Col, Douglas, Ariz, 77; Birds Eye View Gallery, Newport Beach, Calif, 78; Cochise Fine Arts, Bisbee, Ariz, 79, 82 & 84; Lambert-Miller Gallery, Phoenix, Ariz, 81; Ariz Biennial, TMA, Tucson, Ariz, 82; Dinnerware Gallery, Tucson, Ariz, 82; Galeria Mesa-Chroma-Zone, Mesa, Ariz, 88; Davis Gallery Tucson, Ariz, 89, 90, 92, 93 & 94; Univ Ariz Mus Art, 89. *Teaching:* Instr graphics & drawing, Inst Am Indian Arts, Santa Fe, 71-75, chmn dept commun design, 74-75. *Awards:* Three Distinctive Merit Awards, Two Gold Medals & Eight Honor Awards, Art Dirs Club Denver, 59-69. *Bibliog:* Interview: Six Bisbee Artists, Artspace, winter 79; Michael Cadieux (auth), Herb Gilbert, Artspace, summer 83. *Media:* Acrylic, Collage. *Publ:* Contribr, Impressions of Arizona (painting), Art Am, 4/81. *Mailing Add:* c/o Davis Dominguez Gallery 154 E Sixth St Tucson AZ 85705

GILBERT-ROLFE, JEREMY
PAINTER
b Tunbridge Wells, Kent, Eng, Aug 4, 1945. *Study:* Tunbridge Wells Sch Art, NDD, 65; London Univ, ATC, 67; Fla State Univ, MFA, 70. *Work:* Getty Study Ctr, Santa Monica; Commodities Corp, NJ; Chase Manhattan, NY; Albright-Knox Mus, Buffalo, NY; many pvt collections. *Exhib:* One-man shows, Anne Plumb Gallery, NY, 90, Genovese Gallery, Boston, 90, 93 & 96, Stark Gallery, NY, 94, Merve Verlag, Berlin, 96 & Shoshana-Wayne Gallery, Santa Monica, Calif, 96; Critics as Artists, Andre Zarre Gallery, NY, 95; Surface/Support, Bennington Col, Vt, 96; Trans-Hudson Gallery, NY, 96; Color Field to New Abstraction, Rose Art Mus, Brandeis Univ, 96. *Teaching:* Instr, Fla State Univ, 68-71, Princeton Univ, 72-78, Parsons Sch Design, 78-80, Calif Inst Arts, Valencia, 80-86, Art Ctr Col Design, Pasadena, Calif, 86- & Yale Univ, fall 87-89. *Awards:* Nat Endowment Arts, 74, 80 & 89; Guggenheim Fel, 97. *Bibliog:* Michael Cohen (auth), Jeremy Gilbert-Rolfe (interview), Flash Art, 5-6/95; Saul Ostrow (auth), Une ensemble fragmente, la peinture abstraite apres le modernisme, Art Press, 16, 95; Charles D Mitchell (auth), Works in UNT exhibit are monochromatic but multifaceted, Dallas Morning News, 2/96. *Mem:* Int Asn Word & Image Studies; Int Asn Philos & Lit. *Publ:* Auth, Cabbages, raspberries & video's thin brightness, Art & Design, 5/96; Gehry's houses, gastarbeitenhauslich, GA (in press), spring 96; Sheer without fear, the boys can't take it, Contemp Art Issues, 19-20, 96; introd, In: Seams: Art as a Philosophical Context, Gordon & Breach Publ, Inc, 96; Eugene Kaelin, artist's philosopher, J Aesthetic Educ (in press), 97. *Dealer:* Shoshana Wayne Gallery Bergamont Sta B-1, 2525 Michigan Av, Santa Monica, CA, 90404. *Mailing Add:* 1818 Glendale Blvd Los Angeles CA 90026-1740

GILBERTSON, CHARLOTTE
PAINTER, LECTURER
b Boston, Mass. *Study:* Boston Univ, BA; Art Students League; Pratt Inst, New York; studied with Fernand Leger, Paris; other studies incl, courses in English Literature & English Usage, Cape Code Community Coll, Mass & other similar studies, Univ Dublin. *Work:* Guild Harwich Artists, Cape Cod; many pvt collections USA & Europe. *Exhib:* E A T Show, Brooklyn Mus, NY, 68-69; Erik Nord Gallery, Nantucket, 75; Bodley Gallery, 75 & 77; Irving Galleries, Palm Beach, Fla, 77; Pace Univ Mus & St Peters Coll Mus, 78; Galeria Bryna, Palm Beach, 80 & 81; Guild of Harwich Artists, Harwich Port, Mass, 98 & 99; Eissey Campus Gallery, North Palm Beach, 2000; pvt exhib, Completed Papua New Guinea Series, Harwich Port, Mass, 2002; invitational exhib, Collage Series on paper based on letters A to Z, Palm Beach, Fla, 2003; and several others. *Pos:* Dir, Iolas Gallery, NY, 62-74 & Galeria Bryna, Palm Beach, 79-80; free lance lectr, 80-; Palm Beach Mirror, Palm Beach, Fla; publ rels, Ann Norton Sculpture Gardens, West Palm Beach, Fla; asst to Cy Coleman, pianist and composer, during engagement at Regency Hotel, NY. *Mem:* Visual Arts Galleries Asn; Am Fedn Arts; Int Women's Writing Guild; life mem, Art Students League; Palm Beach Co Coun Arts; Nat League Am Pen Women; Eng Speaking Union Palm Beach. *Media:* Acrylic, Mixed Media. *Publ:* Papua New Guinea: Lik Lik Hap, Club Press, 98. *Dealer:* Art Commun Int 210 Rittenhouse Sq Suite 100 Philadelphia PA 19103; VAGA 350 Fifth Ave Ste 2820 New York NY 10118

GILCHRIEST, LORENZO
CONSTRUCTIONIST, EDUCATOR
b Thomasville, Ga, Mar 21, 1938. *Study:* Newark Sch Fine & Indust Arts, 57-58; Newark State Col, BA, 62; Pratt Inst, MS, 67; Md Inst, MFA, 75. *Work:* Newark State Col; Fairleigh Dickinson Univ; Edward & Verdi Johnson Collection, Howard Univ; pvt collections of David Driskell, Grace Parks Johnson, Dr. Benjamin Jenkins & Dr. James Tolliver. *Exhib:* Some Negro Artists, Fairleigh Dickinson Univ, 65; Solo exhibs, Univ Md, 70 & Morgan State Univ, 79; Md Regional, Baltimore Mus Art, 71; Black Art, Towson State Coll, 75; Three solo & many group exhibs, Argus Gallery; Solo sabbatical exhib, Towson State Coll, 93. *Pos:* Assoc art dir, Sen Robert Kennedy Proj, Bedford Stuyvesant Youth in Action, Brooklyn, NY, 65-67. *Teaching:* Asst prof art, Towson State Col, 67-97; guest prof sculpture, Cornell Univ, summers 72 & 73; teacher constructions, painting & drawing, Baltimore Mus Art, 73-74; guest prof print workshop, Morgan State Univ, summer 77. *Awards:* Afro American Slide Depository for Afro Americans, Samuel Kress Found, 71; Fel Int Arts Sem, Fairleigh Dickinson Univ, 62. *Bibliog:* Barbara Gold (auth), Blackmarks, Black art, Sun Paper Art Sect, 6/75. *Media:* mixed media. *Mailing Add:* 55 Pond Rd Delta PA 17314-8660

GILCHRIST, E. BRENDA
WRITER, EDITOR
b Coulsdon, Eng; US citizen. *Study:* Smith Coll, BA (art hist); Art Students League. *Pos:* Asst, Durlacher Brothers Art Gallery, New York, 54-57; art admin asst, Brussels World's Fair, Belg & New York, 57-58; fund raiser, Mus Mod Art, New York, 59-62; reporter, Show Mag, New York, 62-64; staff writer, Am Heritage Publ Co, 64; sr art ed, Praeger Publ, New York, 65-75; ed publ, Cooper-Hewitt Mus, Nat Mus Design & Smithsonian Inst, New York, 76-81; mem adv coun for continuing educ prog, Mus Collaborative Inc, 77-78, publ consult & art ed (freelance), 81-. *Awards:* Hon mention, Maine Writers & Publ Alliance's Open Writing Competition. *Mem:* Drawing Soc (mem bd dir, 60-81, mem exec comt, currently); Soc Archit Historians; Coll Art Asn; Am Asn Mus; Victorian Soc Am. *Collection:* Maine State Libr; Author Collection, Augusta, Maine. *Publ:* Gen ed, The Smithsonian Illustrated Library of Antiques, Cooper-Hewitt Mus, 76-81; auth, Yoga Mooseana Book, 2000; FlimFlam For a Nephew: A Tale of Chairs, 2001; Paws for Peace, 2002; Gabi's Guide to Maine, 2003, Leguminous Verse, 2006, Braceypoint Press, Eggemoggin Reach Rev, Vol I & II, 2004, 2006, Harbor Journ, Vol II. *Dealer:* Blue Heron Gallery Deer Isle ME. *Mailing Add:* 1 Croswell Ln Deer Isle ME 04627

GILDERSLEEVE, ALLISON
PAINTER
b New London, Connecticut, 1970. *Study:* Coll William & Mary, BFA, 1992; Milton Avery Sch Art, Bard Coll, MFA, 2005. *Exhib:* Solo exhibs include Red Mill Gallery, Johnson, Vt, 1998, Supreme Trading, Brooklyn, NY, 2004, 650 Madison Ave Exhib Prog, New York, 2005, Michael Steinberg Fine Art, New York, 2007; two-person

exhibs include Nightingale Gallery, Water Mill, NY, (With Carol Hinrichsen), 1999, PS122 Gallery, New York, (With Cynthia Innis), 2003; group exhibs include Delicate, 381G Gallery, San Francisco, 1999; Cross Point, Gana Art Space, Seoul, Korea, 1999; Bowery Gallery, New York, 2000; Bay Area Ctr Consolidated Arts, Berkeley, Calif, 2001; Warm Weather is Holding, Milton Avery Grad Sch, Red Hook, NY, 2004; Flow, Collaborative Concepts, Beacon, NY, 2004, 2005; Six, Supreme Trading, Brooklyn, NY, 2005; First Look, Hudson Valley Ctr Contemp Art, Peekskill, NY, 2005; Greater Brooklyn, CRG Gallery, New York, 2005; Red Desert, Heskin Contemp, New York, 2006. *Awards:* New York Found Arts Grant, 2008. *Dealer:* Michael Steinberg Fine Arts 526 W 26th St Suite 215 New York NY 10001. *Mailing Add:* 612 Lorimer St Brooklyn NY 11211

GILDZEN, ALEX
WRITER, COLLECTOR

b Monterey, Calif, Apr 25, 1943. *Study:* Wagner Col, with Kenneth Koch, 63; Kent State Univ, BA, 65, MA, 66. *Collection Arranged:* The Photographer's Art: An Exhibition of Prints and Books on Photography, 81; The Art of P Craig Russell, 92. *Pos:* Assoc cur, Spec Collections, Libr, Kent State Univ, 77-85, acting cur, Mus, 82-83, cur, Spec Collections, 85-93; ed, Dress: J Costume Soc Am, 82-84; volunteer, Santa Fe Inst Fine Arts, 94-95; bd dir, Santa Fe Cares, 98-. *Teaching:* Prof, Libr Admin, Kent State Univ, 85-93. *Awards:* Exhib Catalog Award, Comt Rare Bk Section, Ala; President's Medal, Kent State Univ, 93; Ohioana Citation, Ohioana Libr, 93. *Bibliog:* Roberta Berke (auth), Bounds Out of Bounds, Oxford Univ Press, 81; Dimitris Karageorgiou (ed), Gildzen at 50, Toucan Press, 93. *Mem:* Costume Soc Am (region III pres, 82-83). *Res:* Film and theater history; modern sculpture. *Collection:* Contemporary sculpture, drawings, prints and photographs. *Publ:* Ed, Six Poems-Seven Prints, Kent State Univ Libr, 71; auth, Haber's shattered landscapes: Studies in nature and time, (exhib catalog), Kent State Univ, 77; Partially buried woodshed: A Robert Smithson log, 78 & Ira Joel Haber: Poolside reflections on coming out of the box, 82, Arts Mag; The Avalanche of Time: Selected poems 1964-1984, 86; Joseph Chaikin: A Bio-bibliography, 92; A Gathering of Poets, 92. *Mailing Add:* 2328 Brother Abdon Santa Fe NM 87505

GILHOOLEY, DAN
PAINTER

Study: Hunter Col, BA, MA; Ctr Modern Psychoanalytic Studies; Boston Grad Sch, MA (psychoanalysis). *Teaching:* Prof, art, Suffolk Co Community Col, currently. *Mem:* Nat Acad. *Mailing Add:* Suffolk Co Cmty Col Asst Dean Instr 121 Speonk-Riverhead Rd Riverhead NY 11901

GILHOOLY, DAVID JAMES, III
SCULPTOR

b Auburn, Calif, Apr 15, 1943. *Study:* Univ Calif, Davis, BA, 65, MA, 67. *Work:* Philadelphia Mus Art, Pa; San Francisco Mus Mod Art; Whitney Mus Am Art; Norton Mus Art, West Palm Beach, Fla; Australia Nat Gallery, Canberra; Stedelijk Mus, Amsterdam; San Jose Art Mus, Calif; Nat Gallery, Ottawa, Can; Smithsonian, Washington, DC; and others. *Comn:* Breadwall, Govt Can Bldg, Calgary, Atla; Merfrog Fountain, Stanford Univ, Calif; and others. *Exhib:* Funk Show, Inst Contemp Art, Boston, 67; Realism '70, Montreal Mus Art & Art Gallery, Ont, 70; Whitney Mus Am Art, 70-71, 74 & 82; Matrix Gallery, Wadsworth Atheneuem, Hartford, Conn, 76; Painting & Sculpture: The Mod Era, San Francisco Mus Art & Nat Collection Fine Art, Washington, DC, 77; Mus Contemp Craft, New York, 78; Ceramic Sculpture: Six Artists, Whitney Mus Am Art, 81 & San Francisco Mus Mod Art, 82; Keepers of the Kiln Traveling Exhib, 91; San Jose Mus Art, Calif, 92; Elvis & Marilyn 2 x Immortal Traveling Exhib, Inst Contemp Art, Boston, 94; var exhibs at maj mus incl Whitney Mus, Los Angeles Co Mus Art, Philadelphia Mus Art & San Francisco Mus Art; Trashformations Traveling Exhib, Whatcom Mus Art, Bellingham, Wash; De Saisset Mus, Santa Clara Univ, 99; Halle Ford Mus, Willamette Univ, Salem, Ore, 2000; and others. *Teaching:* Instr drawings & watercolor, San Jose State Coll, 67-69; instr ceramics & sculpture, Univ Sask, Regina, 69-71 & York Univ, 71-75 & 76-77; instr ceramics & drawing, Univ Calif, Davis, 75-76. *Bibliog:* The Artist as Historian, artscanada, 75; Henry Hopkins (auth), 50 West Coast Artists, Chronicle Bks, 81; Ceramic Sculpture, Six Artists, Univ Wash Press, 82; David Gilhooly, J. Natsoulas Press, 92; The Not-so-Still Life, Univ Calif Press, 2002; Regina Clay (auth), Worlds in the Making, McKenzie Art Gallery, 2005. *Mem:* Royal Can Acad. *Media:* Plastics, Assemblage, Acrylics. *Publ:* Peter Selz (auth), Funk, Univ Calif Press, 67; David Zack (auth), Nut Art in Quake Times, Artnews, 3/70; J. Arneson (auth), David Gilhooly, Craft Horizons, 8/71; Steve Prokopoff (auth), David Gilhooly, Chicago Mus Art, 76; G.M. Dault (auth), My Beavers and I, Vancouver Art Gallery, 76; Tom Folk (auth), Plasticity & David Gilhooly, Art Magazine, 10/87; David Gilhooly, John Natsoulas Press, 94. *Mailing Add:* 4385 Yaquina Bay Rd Newport OR 97365

GILL, BRYAN NASH
SCULPTOR, PRINTMAKER

b Conn. *Study:* Tulane Univ, BFA, 1984; Calif Coll Arts & Crafts, Oakland, MFA, 1988. *Exhib:* Solo exhibs include DeCordova Mus & Sculpture Park, Lincoln, Mass, 1995 & 2003, New Britain Mus Am Art, Conn, 1996 & 2004, Paesaggio Gallery, Canton, Conn, 1996, West Hartford, Conn, 1998 & 2000, Real Art Ways, Hartford, 2001, Fairfield Arts Coun, Conn, 2007; group exhibs include Berkshire Mus, Pittsfield, Mass, 1991; New Work, New Haven '92, Artspace Gallery, New Haven, 1992, Small Works Invitational, 1992; Year-End Show, Charter Oak Cult Ctr, Hartford, 1992; RAW Space, Real Art Ways, Hartford, 1995, No England/No Amsterdam, 1996; Natural Soundings: Art, Artist & Nature, Stamford Mus & Nature Ctr, 1997; Members Exhib, Conn Graphic Arts Ctr, Norwalk, Conn, 1997, 1998, Prints from Within, 2000, Spokes & Wheels, 2001, Prints from Within II, 2002; Fel Recipients, Conn Comn Arts, Hartford, 1999; Striking Impressions, Ctr Contemp Printmaking, Norwalk, Conn, 2002, Ink From Wood, 2003, Night Vision: Printing Darkness, 2007; Int Print Ctr, New York, 2004; New England Now, Paper New England, Hartford, 2007; 18rd Ann: Invitational Exhib Contemp Art, Nat Acad, New York, 2008. *Awards:* Drawing Fel, Calif Art Coun, 1989; Best in Show, Artspace Gallery, New Haven, 1992; Individual Artist Grant, Conn Comn Arts, 1993, 1997; Individual Artist Fel, Greater Hartford Arts Coun, 1997, 2006. *Mailing Add:* 761 Steele Rd New Hartford CT 06057

GILL, GENE
PAINTER, CRAFTSMAN

b Memphis, Tenn, 1933. *Study:* Memphis State Univ; Chicago Art Inst, Ill; Chouinard Art Inst, Los Angeles, BFA. *Work:* Los Angeles Co Mus, Los Angeles; Palm Springs Desert Mus, Calif; Atlantic Richfield Corp, Los Angeles; Tee Ridder Mus Miniatures, NY; Ronald Reagan Pres Libr; Pasadena Mus Hist. *Exhib:* 9th Ann Southern Calif Exhib, Long Beach Mus Art, 71; Laguna Beach Art Mus Exhib Ten, Calif, 71; Dimensional Prints, Los Angeles Co Mus Art, 73; Laguna Beach Art Mus, 77; Los Angeles Printmakers 1960-1980, Los Angeles Co Mus Art, 81; solo exhibs, Comara Gallery, 70-71 & 74; Orlando Gallery, 95; Ronald Reagan Pres Libr, 2000. *Awards:* Purchase Award, Home Savings, 69; Purchase Award, Westside Jewish Community Ctr, 70; Jurors Award, Laguna Beach Art Mus, 70. *Bibliog:* Gatto, Porter & Selleck (auths), Exploring Visual Design, 78; George Magnan (auth), Today's Art, 79; Gerald F Brommer (auth), Discovering Art History, 81. *Media:* Acrylic, Oil; Serigraphy, Mixed media. *Mailing Add:* 3895 Valley Lights Dr Pasadena CA 91107

GILL, JEAN KENNEDY
PAINTER, JUROR

b Mass. *Study:* Mount Holyoke Coll, BA, 69, studied with Leonard DeLonga. *Exhib:* Signature Members Exhib, Nat Watercolor Soc Gallery, San Pedro, Calif, 2000, 2006, 2008, 2010, 2011, 2012, 2013, Annual Exhib, 99, 2005, 2007, 2012; Am Watercoloc Soc Int Exhib, Salmagundi Club, NY, 2002, 2004, 2006, 2013; First Shanghai Zhujiajiao Int Watercolor Exhib, Quanhua Watercolor Art Gallery, Shanghai, China, 2010; Adirondacks Nat Exhib of Am Watercolors, Arts Ctr, Old Forge, NY, 2011, 2012, 2013, 2014; Fallbrook Signature Am Watercolor Exhib, 2013, 2014. *Pos:* practicing artist, juror, Oak Hill Va, 92-2012. *Teaching:* instr watercolor, Fairfax Co Public Sch Adult & Community Educ, 92-2012. *Awards:* Watercolor West award, Nat Watercolor Soc 79th, Watercolor West, 99; Mario Cooper/Dale Myers medal, Am Watercolor Soc Int Exhib, Mario Cooper/Dale Myers, 2004; Award of Excellence, Phila Watercolor Soc, Newman Galleries, 2004, 2005; Potomac Valley Watercolor award, BWS Mid-Atlantic Regional Exhib, Potomac Valley Watercolorists, 2007; Phil Dike award, Nat Watercolor Soc, 2008; Award of Achievement, Missouri Nat Exhib, Missouri Watercolor Soc, 2008; Award of Distinction, Va Watercolor Soc, 2014. *Bibliog:* Evelyn HT Gardett (auth), Elements of Play, èlan mag, 2008. *Mem:* Am Watercolor Soc (signature mem, 2006-); Nat Watercolor Soc (signature mem, 99-); Va Watercolor Soc (signature mem, 95-, bd mem, 2004 & 2009); Western Colo Watercolor Soc (master signature mem, 2012-); Missouri Watercolor Soc (signature mem, 2005). *Media:* Watercolor. *Publ:* contbr, Splash 5: Best of Watercolor, The Glory of Color, North Light Books, 98; Watercolor 20th Anniversary Issue, VNU Business Media, 2006; Artistic Touch 4, Creative Art Press, 2010; Eyes on: Landscapes, Blaze Hill Press, 2012; Splash 14: Light and Color, North Light Books, 2013; Artistic Touch 5, Creative Art Press, 2012; Artistic Touch 6, Creative Art Press, 2014; Splash 16: Exploring Texture, Northlight Books, 2015. *Mailing Add:* 2872 Spring Chapel Ct Oak Hill VA 20171

GILL, JOHN P
SCULPTOR

b Renton, Wash, Oct 24, 1949. *Study:* Cornish Sch Allied Arts, Seattle, Wash; Kansas City Art Inst, Mo, BFA, 73; NY State Coll Ceramics, Alfred Univ, MFA, 75. *Work:* Victoria & Albert Mus, London, Eng; Brooklyn Mus, NY; Ark Art Ctr, Little Rock; Kansas City Art Inst, Mo; Los Angeles Mus, Calif; and others. *Comn:* Vase, Mus Mod Art, NY, 88. *Exhib:* One & two man exhibs, Hadler-Rodriguez Gallery, NY, 81, 83 & 85, Univ Colo, 84, DBR Gallery, NY, 84, Dorothy Weiss Gallery, San Francisco, Calif, 86, 88, 90, 92 & 94, Grace Borgenicht, NY, 83, 86, 90 & 93, Revolution Gallery, Mich, 95 & Kraushaer Galleries, NY, 96 & 98; Am Ceramics, Victoria & Albert Mus, London, Eng, 86; What's New? Am Ceramics Since 1980 (with catalog), JB Speed Art Mus, Louisville, Ky, 87; 28th Ceramic Nation, Everson Mus, 90; Borgenicht 40th Anniversary Show, NY, 91; Nat Object Invitational, Ark Art Ctr, Little Rock, 91; Chthonic Realm, Helen Drutt Gallery, Philadelphia, 92. *Teaching:* Assoc prof, NY Col Ceramics; prof, Alfred Univ, 1984-. *Awards:* Fel, Nat Endowment Arts, 79, 92 & 93; Ohio Arts Coun Individual Artists Grant in Crafts, 83 & 84; Grant, NY State Found Arts Grant, 88. *Dealer:* Kraushaar Galleries 724 5th Ave New York NY. *Mailing Add:* 149 N Main St Alfred Station NY 14802

GILLEN, JOHN
SCULPTOR, PAINTER

b Uniontown, Pa, 1947. *Study:* Univ Calif, Los Angeles, 64-68, BA, Univ Calif, Berkeley, 72-74, MA. *Exhib:* Solo exhibs, Davis Art Ctr, Calif, 72, The Clocktower, NY, 80, Wall Constructions, Paul Klein Gallery, Chicago, 87, Wall Sculptures, Laurie Rubin Gallery, NY, 87, New Work, Burnett Miller Gallery, Los Angeles, 88 & Concept Gallery, Pittsburgh, Pa, 92, Jernigan Wicker Fine Arts, 2000; Abstraction: Painting & Sculpture, Angles Gallery, Santa Monica, Calif, 86; Selections from the Berkus Collection, Long Beach Mus Art, Calif, 88; Jernigan Wicker Fine Arts, 2001; and many others. *Teaching:* Asst prof studio arts, Baruch Col, CUNY, 80-84, Univ Pittsburgh, Pa, 88-96. *Awards:* Eisner Prize for Creative Achievement in the Arts, Univ Calif, Berkeley, 74; Creative Artists Pub Serv Grant, NY State Coun Arts, 78; Artists Fel, Nat Endowment Arts, 80, 84 & 86. *Bibliog:* Joan Quinn (auth), LA, Art & Auction, 11/86; Deborah Gimelson, It's all relative, Art & Auction, 3/87; Cathy Curtis (auth), In the galleries, Los Angeles Times, 1/88. *Mem:* Coll Art Asn. *Dealer:* Concept Art Gallery Pittsburgh PA; Jernigan Wicker Fine Arts San Francisco CA. *Mailing Add:* 4 Foxglove Ln Yountville CA 94599

GILLESPIE, OSCAR JAY
PRINTMAKER
b McNary, Ariz, Dec 31, 1952. *Study:* Arizona Univ, BFA, 77; Ariz State Univ, MFA, 83. *Work:* Fogg Mus,Harvard Univ, Cambrdige, Mass; Bibliotheque Nationale de France, Paris; Kemper Group collection, Chicago, Ill; Plains Mus, Fargo Ndak; NY Pub Libr, NY. *Exhib:* Fabled Impressions, Georgia Mus of Art, Athens, 2000; ECCE Home 2000, Rudolph E Lee Gallery, Clemson Univ, SC, 2000; Prints USA, Springfield Art Mus, Mass, 2001; solo exhibs incl: Printmaking Gallery, Temple Univ, Philadelphia, Pa, 2001; Volunteer State Col, Gallatin, Tenn, 2002; Contemp Art Ctr, Peoria, Ill, 2003; New Faces Exhib, Marshall Arts Gallery, Scottsdale, Ariz, 2002; Sixty Square Inces Exhib, Purdue Univ Gallery, West Lafayette, Ind, 2004. *Teaching:* Prof art, Bradley Univ, Peoria, Ill, 86-. *Awards:* Finalist award, Artist Fel, Ill Arts Coun, 2002; Samuel Rothberg award, Prof Excellence, 2003; Purchase award, Sixty Square Inches Exhib, 2004. *Mem:* Soc of Am Graphic Artsists; Southern Graphics Coun; Mid-Am Print Coun. *Media:* Printmaking (intaglia, monotype), drawing. *Mailing Add:* 5713 N Keenland Ave Peoria IL 61614

GILLHAM, ANDREW
GRAPHIC DESIGN ARTIST, EDUCATOR, ADMINISTRATOR
Study: Albion Col, BA (Studio Art); Mich State Univ, MFA (Graphic Design). *Pos:* Designer, Detroit, formerly; freelance design business, 1988-. *Teaching:* assoc prof graphic design, department chair, Indiana Univ of Pa, currently. *Mailing Add:* Indiana Univ of Pennsylvania Art Department Sprowls Hall Room 115 470 S Eleventh St Indiana PA 15705

GILLICK, LIAM
ARTIST, WRITER
b Aylesbury, UK, 1964. *Study:* Hertfordshire Coll Art, 1984; Goldsmiths Coll, Univ London, 1987. *Work:* Albright Knox Mus, Buffalo, NY; Baltimore Mus Art; Hirshhorn Mus & Sculp Garden, DC; Mus Mod Art, New York; Solomon R Guggenheim Mus, New York. *Exhib:* Solo exhibs include Interim Art, London, 1994, Robert Prime, London, 1996, 1998, Basilico Fine Arts, New York, 1997, Air de Paris, 2000, Galerie Meyer Kainer, Vienna, 2002, Casey Kaplan, New York, 2003, 2005, 2008, 2010, Mus Mod Art, Nwe York, 2003, Milwaukee Art Mus, 2004, Baltimore Mus Art, 2004, Micheline Szwajcer, Antwerp, Belguim, 2011; group exhibs, Esther Schipper, Koln, 1992; Lisson Gallery, London, 1993; Don't Look Now, Thread Waxing Space, New York, 1994; Inst Cult Anxiety, ICA, London, 1994; New British Art, Mus Sztuki, Lidz, 1995; Departure Lounge, Clocktower, New York, 1996; Supastore de Luxe, Up & Co, New York, 1996; Heaven- A Private View, PS1, New York, 1997; Maxwell's Demon, Margo Leavin, Los Angeles, 1997; Construction Drawings, PS1, New York, 1998; Continued Investigation of the Relevance of Abstractioni, Andrea Rosen Gallery, New York, 1999; Paula Cooper Gallery, New York, 2000; Demonstration Room: Ideal House, Apex Art, New York, 2001; Collaborations with Parkett: 1984 to now, Mus Mod Art, New York, 2001; Animations, PSA1, Long Island City, 2001; No Ghost Just a Shell, San francisco Mus Mod Art, 2002; Singular Forms, Art from 1951 to the Present, Guggenheim Mus, New York, 2004; Establishing Shot, Artist's Space, New York, 2004; Grey Flags, Sculpture Ctr, New York, 2006; Eye on Europe: Prints, Books and Multiples 1960 to now, Mus Mod Art, New York, 2006; Edition Schellmann Door Cycle, Friedrich Petzel Gallery, New York, 2007; Book/Shelf, Mus mod Art, New York, 2008; theanyspacewhatever, Guggenheim Mus, New York, 2008; Unbuilt Roads, e-flux, New York, 2009; A Testbed of Futurity, Southfirst, Brooklyn, New York, 2010; Multiple Pleasures: Functional Objects in Contemp Art, Tanya Bonakdar Gallery, New York, 2010; Today I Made Nothing, Elizabeth Dee, New York, 2010. *Awards:* Paul Cassirer Kunstpreis, Berlin, 1998; Turner Prize Nom, London, 2002; Vincent Award Nom, Stedelijik Mus, Amsterdam, 2008. *Bibliog:* Saul Ostrow (auth), Liam Gillick: Practical Considerations, Art in Am, June/July 2009. *Publ:* Don't Look Now, Threadwaxing Space, New York, 1994; Lost for Words, London, Toby Mott, 1996; Designs for a four storey building, New York Open City, 1999; Intelligence, Tate, London, 2000; Parkett: Collaboration & Editions Since 1984, New York Mus Mod Art, 2001; Extreme Abstractions, Albright Knox Art Gallery, Buffalo, 2005; Art Papers Live!, High Mus Art, Atlanta, 2006; Grey Flags, Sculpture Ctr, Long Island City, NY, 2006; The Art of Lunch, The Observer, July 26, 2010. *Mailing Add:* Casey Kaplan 525 West 21st St New York NY 10011

GILLIE, PHYLLIS I DANIELSON
ADMINISTRATOR, TAPESTRY ARTIST
b Marion, Ind. *Study:* Ball State Univ, BA (art), 53; Mich State Univ, MA, 60, EdS, 66; Ind Univ, EdD, 68; Kendall Coll Art & Design, Hon DFA, 89. *Work:* Mint Mus Art, Charlotte, NC; pvt collections. *Comn:* Jewish Communtiy Ctr, Indianapolis. *Exhib:* Weatherspoon Gallery, Greensboro, NC, 69 & 70; Stitchery, Pa, 71 & Iowa, 75; Matrix Gallery, Bloomington, Ind, 72; one-person shows, Jewish Community Ctr, Indianapolis, Ind, 72 & Eye-Opener Gallery, Cincinnati, Ohio, 72; Mint Mus Art, 74; Herron Art Gallery, Indianapolis, 74; Sloane O'Stickey Gallery, Cleveland, Ohio, 74; Women in Art, West Bend, Wis, 76; Moonspace Gallery, Wis, 2002. *Pos:* Pres, Kendall Col Art & Design, Grand Rapids, formerly; consult, mus & arts orgns & non-profit orgns; pres, Danielson/Gillie & Assoc & D G Imports & Designs; pres, PDG Gallery. *Teaching:* Asst prof art, Ball State Univ, Muncie, Ind, 66-67; asst prof art educ, Univ NC, Greensboro, 68-70; assoc prof educ & art, Herron Sch Art, Indianapolis, 70-76. *Awards:* Mich Woman of the Yr Arts Award, 84. *Bibliog:* Kathleen Fisher (auth), Women in Action. *Mem:* Fair Trade Fedn; Mus Stores Asn; ArtServ Mich; Grand Valley Artists Mich; Women Made Gallery Chgo. *Media:* Fabric, Fiber, Wood. *Publ:* Auth, Art for the Second & Third Grades, Kimball/Hunt, 66; Paper mache and the elementary teacher, Arts & Activities, 12/70; Selected teacher characteristics of art student teachers, Studies Art Educ, winter 71; The woman administrator in art, Coll Art J, 76; and others. *Mailing Add:* 1707 Timberlake Dr Salisbury MD 21801

GILLINGWATER, DENIS CLAUDE
SCULPTOR, EDUCATOR
b Glendale, Calif, Feb 15, 1946. *Study:* Univ Cincinnati, BFA, 68, MFA, 70. *Exhib:* Eighth West Biennial, Western Colo Ctr Arts, 74; Southwest & Rocky Mountain States Exhib, Scottsdale Fine Arts Comn, 75; solo exhib, Scottsdale Ctr Arts, 78; Ariz Sculpture, Northern Ariz Univ Art Gallery, Flagstaff, 80 & 81; Four Corners State Biannual, Phoenix Art Mus, 81; and others. *Teaching:* Asst prof intermedia, Ariz State Univ, 73-78, assoc prof, 78-. *Awards:* Nat Endowment Arts Artist-in-Residence, Mesa, Ariz, 73; Acquisitions, Phoenix Art Mus, 77 & Scottsdale Ctr Arts, 75; and others

GILLMAN, BARBARA SEITLIN
DEALER
b Miami, Fla, Jan 14, 1937. *Study:* H Sophie Newcomb Col, 55; Univ Miami, with Dr Virgil Barker, BA (Am art), 58. *Collection Arranged:* Israel 25, contemp Israeli art (auth, catalog), Bacardi Bldg, City of Miami, 79. *Pos:* Panelist, State Fla Grant Panel. *Specialty:* Contemporary original art, paintings and sculpture; Regional artists. *Mailing Add:* Barbara Gillman Gallery 16 Island Ave Miami FL 33139

GILLMAN, DEREK A
MUSEUM DIRECTOR, ADMINISTRATOR
b Dec 7, 1952. *Study:* Oxford Univ, Eng, MA; Univ East Anglia, Eng, LLM. *Pos:* Mem Getty Trust Mus Mgt Inst, 1991; exec dir & provost, Pa Acad Fine Arts, Philadelphia, 99-2000, pres & Chief Exec Officer, 2001-06; Research Asst, British Mus; keeper (dir), Sainsbury Centre Visual Arts, Univ East Anglia, Norwich, Eng; dep dir, Nat Gallery Victoria, Melbourne, Australia; exec dir & pres, Barnes Found, 2006-. *Bibliog:* The Idea of Cultural Heritage, Inst Art and Law, 2006, 2nd ed, Cambridge Univ Press, 2010. *Mem:* Norfolk Inst Art & Design (gov 90-95). *Mailing Add:* Barnes Foundation 300 N Latches Ln Merion Station PA 19066

GILMOR, JANE E
SCULPTOR, EDUCATOR
b Ames, Iowa, June 23, 1947. *Study:* Iowa State Univ, Ames, BS (textiles), 69-70; Sch Art Inst, Chicago, 69-70; Univ Iowa, Iowa City, MA (paint), 76 & MFA (painting), 77. *Work:* Tokyo Univ Mus Art, Japan; Mus Contemp Crafts Libr, New York; Tyrone Gutherie Ctr, Newbliss, Ireland; Los Angeles Co Mus Art Libr; Ragdale Found, Lake Forest, Ill; Banff Ctr, Can; Mus Contemp Art, Chicago; Cedar Rapids Mus Art. *Comn:* Davenport Mus Art; Des Moines Art Ctr, Iowa; Faulconer Gallery, Grinnell Coll, Grinnell, Ia. *Exhib:* Minn Mus Art, Minneapolis, 86; Nat Sculpture Exhib, Cincinnati, 88; Artemesia, Chicago, 89 & 2000-2001; AIR Gallery, New York, 89-90, 92, 94, 98, 2000, 2002 & 2005; Bemis Ctr Contemp Art, Omaha, 93 & 99; Cedar Rapids Mus Art, 94; Univ Minn Gallery Art, 96; Gallerie Rufino Tomayo, Oaxaca, Mex, 96; Olson-Larsen Galleries, Des Moines, Iowa, 98; Banff Int Ctr for the Arts, Can, 2000; Platformia Revolver Gallery, Lisbon, Portugal, 2006; Solo exhibs, AIR Gallery, New York, 2007, Long ISland Univ, Brooklyn, NY, 2009; (Un)seen Work, Daulconer Gallery, Grinnell Coll, Iowa, 2010; The White Elephant: an installation, CSPS, Cedar Rapids, Iowa, 2012; Sperling Joy, Jane Gilmor: I'll be Back for the Cat, AIR Gallery, New York, 2012. *Teaching:* Prof art, Prof Emeritus, chmn Art Dept, Mount Mercy Univ, Cedar Rapids, Iowa, 1974-2012; vis prof, Sch Art, Univ Iowa, 86; Fulbright vis prof, Univ Evora Portugal, 2003-04. *Awards:* Artist's Proj Grant, Iowa Arts Coun, 95 & 2002; McKnight Found/Intermedia Arts Interdisciplinary Artist's Fel, 96; Leighton Studio resident, Banff Ctr, Can, 2000; SOS Grant, Smithsonian Inst, 2001; NEA Creativity Grant, 2002; Sr Fulbright Fel, Portugal, 2003-2004; Tanne Found Award, 2011; Artist Project Grant, IAC, 2011; NEA Art Works Grant, 2012. *Bibliog:* Hope Palmer (auth), Rev, Tractor, fall 93; Debra Leveton (auth), Three Iowa masters, Iowa Architect, spring 94; Kay Turner (auth), Beautiful Necessity, Thames and Hudson, 99; B Love (auth), Feminists Who Changed America 1963-1973, 2006; Priscilla Sage (auth), Fifty Years of Sculpture, Iowa State Univ Press, Ames, Iowa, 2008; Teresa Furtado (ed), Backing Forwards: The All-American Glamour Kitty finally meets The High Heel Sisters, ACTUp: Performance Video, 2010; Joy Sperling (auth) Jane Gilmor: I'll be Back for the Cat, A.I.R. Gallery, NY, 2012. *Media:* All Media. *Specialty:* Contemporary Art. *Publ:* Where are you From? Contemp Portuguese Art, Exhib Catalogue, Faulconer Gallery, Grinnell Col, 2008. *Dealer:* Olson-Larson Galleries Des Moines IA; AIR Gallery New York. *Mailing Add:* 358 Trailridge Rd SE Cedar Rapids IA 52403

GILMORE, KATE
VIDEO ARTIST
b Washington, DC, 1975. *Study:* Bates Coll, BA, 1997; Sch Visual Arts, New York, MFA, 2002. *Exhib:* Reconstruction Biennial, Exit Art, New York, 2003; Holiday Windows, 2005; The Studio Visit, 2006; Wild Girls, 2006; AIM 23, Bronx Mus Art, New York, 2003; solo exhibs, Plus Ultra Gallery, Brooklyn, NY, 2004, White Columns, New York, 2004, Real Art Ways, Hartford, Conn, 2005, Pierogi, Brooklyn, 2006, Contemp Art Ctr, Cincinnati, 2006, Artpace San Antonio, 2007, Tyler Sch Art, Philadelphia, 2007, Inst Contemp Art, Philadelphia, 2007, Franco Soffiantino Arte Contemp, Turin, Italy, 2008; Open House: Working in Brooklyn, Brooklyn Mus Art, 2004; Video 2005, Art in General, New York, 2005; Video Screening, Hudson Valley Ctr Contemp Art, Peekskill, NY, 2005; Greater New York 2005, PS1 Contemp Art Ctr, Long Island City, NY, 2005; Factitious, Pierogi Gallery, Brooklyn & Pierogi Leipzig, Germany, 2006; Reckless Behavior, J Paul Getty Mus, LA, 2006; Line-Up, Socrates Sculpture Park, Long Island City, NY, 2007; (Un)Natural Selection, Pierogi Gallery, Brooklyn, 2007; The Leisure Suit, Leroy Neiman Gallery, Columbia Univ, 2008; Beware of the Wolf, Am Acad in Rome, 2008; Whitney Biennial, Whitney Mus Am Art, 2010. *Awards:* Independent Proj Grant, Artists Space, New York, 2003; Manhattan Community Arts Grant, Lower Manhattan Cult Coun, 2003, Workspace Award, 2004; NY Found Arts Fel, 2005; Farpath Workspace Award, Dijon, France, 2006; Franklin Furnace Fund for Performance, 2006; Art Omi Award, 2007; Rome Prize, Am Acad Rome, 2007; Louis Comfort Tiffany Found Grant, 2009. *Dealer:* Maisterravalbuena Galeria Doctor Fourquet 1 28012 Madrid Spain; Franco Soffiantino Arte Contemporanea Via Rossini 23 10124 Turin Italy

GILMORE, ROGER
ADMINISTRATOR, CONSULTANT
b Philadelphia, Pa, Oct 11, 1932. *Study:* Dartmouth Coll, AB; Univ Chicago Divinity Sch, grad study. *Hon Degrees:* hon DFA Sch Art Inst Chicago, 93; hon DHL Main Coll Art, 2002. *Pos:* Dean, Sch Art Inst Chicago, 65-87, provost, 87-89; pres, Ox Bow Summer Sch Art, 87-89; pres, Maine Coll Art, Portland, Maine, 89-2001; trustee & 2nd vpres, Maine Historical Society, 2005-11; trustee, Maine Preservation, 2005-11. *Mem:* Nat Trust Hist Preserv; fel & life mem Nat Asn Schs Art & Design (pres, 87-90). *Publ:* Ed, Over a Century: A History of the School of the Art Inst of Chicago, 82. *Mailing Add:* 80 Lyme Rd #251 Hanover NH 03755

GILSON, GILES
SCULPTOR, DESIGNER
b Philadelphia, Pa, July 19, 1942. *Study:* Self-taught. *Work:* Metrop Mus Art, NY; Nat Collection, The Renwick, Smithsonian Inst, Washington; Detroit Inst Art, Mich; Los Angeles Co Mus Art, Calif; Contemp Mus Honolulu; and others. *Comn:* Wall sculpture, Lewis Collection, Richmond, Va, 81 & 82; Story Piece, Lipton Collection, Los Angeles, 84; Library Table, Hunter-Stieble Collection, NY, 86; Sculpture- NEC Found, Ronsselear Polytechnical Inst. *Exhib:* 20th Century Decorative Arts, Metrop Mus Art, NY, 81; Art of Woodturning, Am Craft Mus, NY, 83; Nat Wood Invitational, Craft Alliance, St Louis, Mo, 83; Polished Perfection, The Renwick, Washington, 86; Int Turned Object Show, Port of Hist Mus, Pa, 88; Out of the Woods, touring Eastern Europe, 93-97. *Pos:* Consult artist & technician, Creative Advantage, Schenectady, NY, 78-; consult artist, Gen Elec Co, Schenectady, NY, 82 & Harmony Arts Ltd, NY; tech consult, 3M Corp, St Paul, Minn, Harmony Arts Ltd, NY & Steinburger Sound, Newburgh, NY, 85; designer, Formula Honda race car body, 91; tech consult, GE (product test), 96. *Teaching:* Panelist-speaker, Conv Am Soc Interior Designers, Washington, DC, 78; instr, NAm Turning Symp, Philadelphia, 81, State Univ NY, New Paltz, 84-87, Am Asn Woodturners Conv, Gatlinburg, Tenn, 90 & State Univ NY, Purchase, 93 & Woodturning Design Conf, Saskatoon, Can, 92; workshops, Design Prog, State Univ NY; speaker & slides, Carnegie-Mellon Univ, Pittsburgh & Soc Art Craft, Pittsburgh; Am Craft Armory, NY, 87; speaker, Craft Alliance, St Louis, Mo, 88; artist-in-residence, Univ Pa, Ind, 89; guest lectr & instr, Calif State Univ, Fullerton, 90; panelist & instr, Am Crafts Coun Southeastern Conf, Jackson, Miss, 91; keynote speaker & workshops, Asn Woodturners Gt Brit Int Sem, Loughborough, Eng, 93. *Awards:* Spec Award, NAm Turned Object Show, 81; Best Dimensional Display, Upstate NY Ad Club, 85; Artist-in-Residency, Mid-Atlantic Found Arts, 88. *Bibliog:* Design Book II, Taunton Press; Albert Locolf (auth), A Gallery of Turned Objects; Lathe Turned Objects, Wood Turning Ctr; Beyond Wood-Emotional Expressions (video), KATIA-TV, Video Art Production; Speilman (auth), The Art of the Lathe; and others. *Mem:* Am Craft Coun; Am Asn Woodturners. *Media:* Wood, Metal; Plastics, Composites; Paints; Acrylics; Lacquers; Urethanes. *Publ:* Auth, Router rail, Techniques 4, Taubton Press, 82; Polychromatic Turning, Turning Points, 88; introd, Works of the Lathe: Old and New Faces, 88; contribr, Polychromatic Assembly for Woodturning, Linden Publ; Make Money from Woodturning, Guild of Master Craftsmen Publ, Eng. *Mailing Add:* 766 Albany Schenectady NY 12307

GIMBLETT, MAX(WELL)
PAINTER, SCULPTOR
b Auckland, NZ, Dec 5, 1935; US & NZ citizen. *Study:* Ont Coll Art, Toronto, 64; San Francisco Art Inst, 65. *Work:* San Jose Mus Art, Calif; San Francisco Mus Mod Art, Achenbach Found, San Francisco; Pa Acad Fine Arts, Philadelphia; Getty Ctr, Santa Monica, Calif; Mus Contemp Art, Sydney, Australia, Art Gallery New South Wales, Univ New South Wales; Art Gallery of Queensland, Brisbane, Australia; Mus Mod Art, NY; Whitney Mus Art, NY; Bodleian Library, Oxford Univ, England; Nat'l Art Gallery, Washington; Yale Univ, New Haven, CT; Nat Gallery Australia, Melbourne; Auckland Art Gallery, New Zealand; Libr Congress, Wash DC; Mus New Zealand, Wellington; Stanford Univ; Univ Calif, La Jolla, San Diego, Calif; Japan Soc, New York; Saatchi & Saatchi, New York; ICC Maine Coll Art; Christ Church Art Gallery, New Zealand. *Exhib:* Haines Gallery, San Francisco, Calif, 91, 93, 96, 97, 2000, 2003, 2005, 2006, 2007, 2008; Gow, Langsford Gallery, Auckland, NZ, 91, 93, 95, 97, 98, 99, 2001, 2003, 2004, 2006, 2007, 2008, 2009, 2010, 2011, 2012; Jan Turner Gallery, Los Angeles, 92; Jensen Gallery, Wellington, NZ, 92, 93, 95, 96, 97 & 98; Getty Ctr, Santa Monica, 92; Sherman Gallery, Sydney, 95; Margaret Thatcher Projects, NY, 99, 2003; Ethan Cohen Fine Arts, NY, 2001; Page Blackie Gallery, New Zealand, 2008-2011, 2013; Guggenheim Mus, New York, 2009; Nadene Milne Gallery, New Zealand, 2009, 2010, 2011, 2013; The Suter Nelson, New Zealand, 2010; Japan Soc, NY, 2010; Saatchi & Saatchi, NY, 2010; ICA Maine Coll Art, Portland, ME, 2010; Andy Warhol Mus, Pittsburg, 2011; Kenyon Coll, Ohio, 2011; Gary Snyder Gallery, 2012. *Pos:* Trustee, Len Lye Found, New Plymouth, New Zealand; Inaugural Vis Prof, Nat Inst Creative Arts & Industries, Auckland Univ, Auckland, New Zealand. *Teaching:* Vis artist printmaking, Ind Univ, Bloomington, 79; vis assoc prof, Pratt Inst, Brooklyn, 79-89; vis lectr, Univ Canterbury, Christ Church, NZ, 81 & 92; vis assoc prof, Int Honors Program in Japan, India & Kenya; vis artist, City Art Inst, Sydney, Australia, 86; J Paul Getty assoc, Getty Ctr Hist of Art & Humanities, Santa Monica, 91-92; artist-in-residence, Queensland Univ Technol, Brisbane, Australia, 93 & Rockefeller Found Study & Conf Ctr, Bellagio, Italy; Visiting Artist Elam School of Fine Arts, Univ Auckland, New Zealand, 2004; Vis artist printmaking, Hui Press, Maui, Hawaii, 79. *Awards:* Grant, Queen Elizabeth II Arts Coun NZ, 80, 86; Painting Fel, Nat Endowment Arts, Washington, DC, 89; Artist in Residence, Laila Foundation, Hui Press, Maui, Hawaii; Old Boy of the Year Award, Kings Sch, New Zealand; Inaugural Special Artist, Christchurch Art Gallery; Augusta Award, Auckland Grammar. *Bibliog:* Wystan Curnow, Thomas McEvilley, and Barbara Kirshenblatt-Gimblett, Max Gimblett; The Brush of all Things, Auckland Art Gallery New Zealand, 72 pgs; Wystan Curnow and John Yau Max Gimblett, Craig Potton Publishing Co and Gow Langsford Gallery, New Zealand, 172 pgs, 123 color plates, Anne Kirker, Max Gimblett The Language of Drawing; Kirshenblatt-Gimblett (auth), Art From Start to Finish. *Mem:* Jung Found, NY; Queensland Gallery Art (special patron); New Mus, NY; Auckland Art Gallery, New Zealand; Guggenheim Mus, NY. *Media:* Acrylic Polymer, All Media. *Publ:* Contribr, In the presence, Art NZ, 80; Max Gimblett and Wystan Curnow, Modernism, San Francisco, 82; Spirit Tracks, Pratt Manhattan Gallery, NY, 86; Sightings & Drawing with Color, Pratt Inst & Instituto de Estudios Norte Americanos, 88; Wystan Curnow, Objects of Alchemy, Artis Gallery, Auckland, NZ, 90; Mindfood, 2008; Tricycle: The Buddhist Review, 2011; Vogue Australia, 2011. *Dealer:* Haines Gallery 49 Geary St San Francisco CA; Gow Langsford Gallery Auckland NZ; Page Blackie Gallery Wellington New Zealand; Hui Press Maui Hawaii. *Mailing Add:* 231A Bowery New York NY 10002-1218

GINDLESBERGER, HANS
PHOTOGRAPHER
b Northwest, Ohio. *Study:* Bowling State Univ, BFA; State Univ New York, Buffalo, MFA (Photography). *Exhib:* Solo exhibs include Carnegie Art Ctr, N Tonawanda, NY, 2006, YO! Darkroom, Philadelphia, 2006, Pemberville Historic Opera House, Pemberville, Ohio, 2008 ; Group exhibs include Pinned to the Wall, 402 Gallery, New York, 2004; 87th Ann Toledo Area Artist's Exhib, Toledo Mus Art, Toledo, Ohio, 2005; Ann Member's Exhib, Big Orbit Gallery, Buffalo, 2005; Wild Unknown, Kitchen Distribution, Buffalo, 2005; Motherland, Kunstvlaai 6, Westergasfabrick, Amsterdam, Holland, 2006 ; Hey, Hot Shot! Winners' Showcase, Jen Bekman Gallery, New York, 2006; Terminal for Hallwalls Contemp Arts Ctr, Buffalo, 2007; A Field Guide to the N Am Family, The Exhib, Gallery Bar, New York, 2008; Unpacking Artspace, Artspace, Buffalo, 2008; Le Carnivale du Portrait, Big Orbit Gallery, Buffalo, 2008. *Awards:* Dimensional Scholar Award, 2003; Individual Artist Fel in Photography, NY Found for the Arts, 2008. *Mailing Add:* 6909 Township Rd 331 Millersburg OH 44654-8210

GINSBERG, ELIZABETH G
PAINTER, PHOTOGRAPHER
b New York, NY. *Study:* RI Sch Design, BFA (European hon prog); Textron Fel, Tokyo & Kyoto, Japan. *Work:* Setagaya Mus, Tokyo, Japan; Anchorage Mus Hist & Art, Anchorage, Ala; Zimmerli Art Mus, New Brunswick, NJ; Univ Mich, Ann Arbor, Mich; Castello di Roncade, Italy. *Comn:* "Balambuan" painting, Parsippany Ctr, NJ. *Exhib:* Solo exhibs, Works on Paper, Mus Hudson Highlands, NY, Salt Lake City Art Ctr, Utah, Photoworks, Pintsch Contemp Art, Germany, Spacial Coincidence, NY Acad Sci, NY, Prints & Works on Paper, Switzer Ctr Visual Art, Fla, Between Tides, Casement Cult Ctr, Ormond Beach, Fla, Paintings & Works on Paper, Kemper Ctr Arts, Fulton, Mo, Pellucid Skies, Art Ctr, Seattle Pacific Univ, Wash, Castello di Roncade, Italy, 2004, 2006, 2009, Tai Gallery, NY, 2001, 2003, 2005, Southern Light Gallery, Amarillo Coll, Tex, 2005, Marsha Mateyka Gallery, Wash DC. *Collection Arranged:* cur, 10 New York Artists, Points of View, Northcutt Gallery, Eastern Mont Coll, 92. *Teaching:* lectr, Kyoto Fujikawa Coll; instr, RI Sch Design; faculty, Parsons Sch Design, NY; assoc prof, Moore Coll Art, Pa. *Awards:* faculty res grant, Moore Coll Art, Japan & Peru; Textron fel, Textron Found, Japan; Carnegie Grant, Rome, Italy; Residency grant, Emily Harvey Found, Venice, Italy, 2009, 2011, & 2014. *Bibliog:* Joelle Bentley (auth), The Fragmented Image, Nat Acad Sci, Wash DC; Joelle Bentley (auth), Spacial Coincidence, NY Acad Sci; Japanning, Tokyo; Shukau Sankei, David Bell (auths), Albuquerque Jour; Janet Wilson (auth), The Washington Post; Richard Kostelanetz (auth), Assembling George Dibble, Salt Lake Tribune. *Mem:* Am Asn Mus; Internat House of Japan, Tokyo. *Media:* Acrylics on Canvas, Mixed Media on Folding Screens, Digital Prints, Collage. *Publ:* auth, Between Tides, Casements Cult Ctr, Fla, 96; Images & Influences, 12 Mile Press, 2013; Reflections: A Survey of Prints, 12 Mile Press, 2015. *Dealer:* Aileen Ryan Earnest New York & Jacksonville OR; Lorraine Skidmore Princeton NJ

GINSBURG, ESTELLE
PAINTER, SCULPTOR
b St Louis, Mo, Mar 27, 1924. *Study:* Univ Mo; Brooklyn Mus Art Sch; Cornell Univ. *Work:* C W Post Univ, NY; Univ Mass, Amherst; Univ Art Gallery, State Univ NY, Stony Brook; pvt collections in Europe, S Am & US. *Exhib:* Ball State Univ, Muncie, Ind, 73; solo exhibs, Cent Hall Gallery, NY, 75, 77-79, Fine Arts Mus Nassau Co, NY, 77 & Royal Acad, Stockholm, Sweden, 79; Invitational, York Coll, Pa, 77; Brentano Gallery, NY, 79, 81 & 82; Univ Stony Brook Mus (auth, catalog), NY, 96. *Pos:* Art lectr mus collections, N Shore Community Arts Ctr, NY, 70-73; instr, Five Towns Music & Art Found, NY, 73-83, Nassau Off Cult Develop, 74-77 & Art Resources Ltd, NY, 79-80. *Teaching:* Lectr art, 5 Towns Sch Dist, 80-96. *Awards:* Mixed Media Award, Heckscher Mus, NY, 72; Sculpture Award, North Shore Art Exhib, 74; Painting Award, Port Washington Libr, 75. *Bibliog:* Malcum Preston (auth), rev, Newsday, NY, 76-79; Jeanne Paris (auth), rev, Long Island Press, 77 & 78; articles, New York Times, 79, 86 & 87. *Mem:* Cent Hall Artists, NY; Prof Artists Asn NY (mem chmn, 74-76). *Media:* Wood, Paint; Mixed Media, Silkscreen. *Publ:* J Digby (auth), Collage Handbook, Thames & Hudson; News Day Women, Stonybrook Univ. *Mailing Add:* 370 Longacre Ave Woodmere NY 11598

GINSBURG, MAX
PAINTER, ILLUSTRATOR
b Paris, France, Aug 7, 1931. *Study:* Syracuse Univ, BFA; Nat Acad Design; City Coll New York, MA. *Exhib:* Allied Artists Am, 1956-2003; Am Vet Soc Artists; Audubon Artists, 1962-2003; Harbor Gallery, Cold Spring Harbor, 66, 68, 69, 71, 72, 74, 76, 78 & 80; Reyn Gallery, 80; Grand Central Gallery, 80-81; Soc Illurs, 1979-2000; NY Cult Ctr; Martin Luther King Labor Ctr; Cavalier Gallery, Greenwich, CT, 2005. *Collection Arranged:* New Britain Mus Am Art; Martin Luther King Labor Ctr; NY Cultural Ctr Mus; Soc Illustrators Permanent Collection; HJ Heinz Co. *Teaching:* Instr painting & illus, Sch Visual Arts, New York, 84-2000 & Art Students League, New York, 97-99. *Awards:* Prize, 61 & Gold Medal, 62 & 65, Am Vet Soc Artists; Allied Artists Am, 61, 72, 2000 & 2002; Nat Art Club, 63; Gold Medal, Soc Illusrs, 83; Christopher Award. *Mem:* Allied Artists Am; Audubon Artists; Soc Illusrs. *Media:* Oil. *Dealer:* Cavalier Galleries Inc 405 Greenwich Ave Grennwich CT 06830. *Mailing Add:* c/o Jenkins Johnson Gallery 464 Sutter St San Francisco CA 94108

GINZBURG, YANKEL (JACOB)
PAINTER, SCULPTOR
b Alma-Ata, USSR, Mar 23, 1945; US citizen. *Study:* Inst Art Israel, dipl, 61. *Work:* Israel Mus, Jerusalem; Hirshhorn Mus; Bat-Yam Mus, Tel Aviv Mus, Israel; Skirball Mus, Los Angeles; Holocaust Mus, Washington, DC. *Comn:* A Hope Fulfilled is a Source of Life (mural), comn by B'nai B'rith, Jerusalem, 73; Freedom Road (tapestry), comn by Bicentennial Comn; Hands & Hearts (monumental mural), Washington, DC, 79; Bicentennial Poster, comn by Pres Reagan, Air & Space Mus, Washington, DC, 83; comn to design 3 graphics commemorating the Bicentennial of the Constitution, 85; Invisible Hands (monumental sculpture), Tampa, Fla, 86. *Exhib:* Solo exhibs, Washington Gallery Art, 69, Martin Lawrence Galleries, Los Angeles, Calif, 79, 82 & 83, Arthur Charles Galleries, Washington, DC, 82 & 83, Hallowell Gallery, Philadelphia, 83, Dyansen Gallery, San Francisco, Carmel, Beverly Hills & San Diego, Calif, New Orleans, La, NY, Boston, Tokyo, Japan, 89, Bronte Contemp Arts, Boston, 92 & many others; Int Art Fair, Cologne, Ger, 75; Int Art Show, Dusseldorf, Ger, 76; Mod Masters of Israel Show, Philadelphia Mus Art Civic Ctr, 78; Works on Paper, Skiball Mus, Los Angeles, Calif, 78; Washington Light Show, Washington, DC, 80; Gallery Hawaii, 80; Gallery Virgin Islands, St Thomas, 80; Vincent Lee Fine Arts, Hong Kong, 92-94. *Teaching:* Instr, Acad Arts, Israel, 65-67. *Awards:* Silver Medal, Rome Biennale, 62; First Prize, Bat-Yam Mus Art Competition, Israel, 65; First Israeli artists to exhib in Cairo, Egypt as guest of Anwar Sadat, 79 & invited by Soviet Union to exhib in Moscow, 90; Humanitarian Award First Class, hon by Pres Yeltsin & Supreme Soviet of the Russian Fedn, 92. *Bibliog:* The Art of Yankel Ginzburg, Alef Editions, 85; Ginzburg: The Russian Collection, Russian Academy of the Arts, 92; Herman Taube (auth), The Art and Life of Yankel Ginzburg, 94. *Media:* Acrylic, Oil. *Publ:* Art book, Soc of Art Collectors, 75; Treasures of the Sea, 79

GINZEL, ANDREW See Jones & Ginzel

GINZEL, ANDREW H
ARTIST, EDUCATOR
b Chicago, July 14, 1954. *Study:* Attended State Univ NY, 81, Bennington Coll, 74. *Work:* Brooklyn Mus; Beckton Dickinson & Co, Franklin Lakes, NJ; Centro Corp, Cleveland; Prudential Life Ins, Co; Kunsthalle, Basel, Switz; Fluent, Hoboken Ferry Terminal, 2011. *Comn:* Kunsthalle, Basel, Switz, 1989; Ore Convention Ctr, Portland, 1990; Pa Convention Ctr, 1994; Battery Park City, New York, 1992; Olympic Arts Festival, Atlanta, 1996; Oculus, MTA, New York, 1999; Metronome Union Sq S Proj, New York, 99; Polarities Kansas City Int Airport, 2004; Spiraculum, Tampa Int Airport, 2005; Panopia, Chicago, 2005; Metro, St Louis, Mo, 2008; Ohio State Physics, Columbus, Ohio, 2009; Univ Colo, Boulder, Colo, 2010; Snow Coll, Utah, 2010, 2012. *Exhib:* The Drawing Ctr, New York, 93-94; Paine Webber Gallery, New York, 94; group exhibs, Contemp Artists and the Am Acad Rome, 95-96; solo exhibs, TZ'Art, NY City, 96, Acqario Romano, Rome, 95, Madison Art Ctr, Wis, 92-93, Three Rivers Arts Festival, Pittsburgh, 91, Minneapolis Coll Art and Design, 91, Damon Brandt Gallery, NY City, 90, Kunsthalle, Basel, 89; Equitable Gallery, New York, 96; Nat Acad Mus, New York, 2006; Pera Mus, Istanbul, 2009. *Pos:* Artistic consult, Hudson River Park Conservancy, New York, 97. *Teaching:* Fac mem, fine arts, Sch Visual Arts, New York, 86-. *Awards:* Yaddo Fel, 1987, 1999 & 2004-2009; MacDowell Colony Fel, 89, 91, 2000-2003 & 2007; Visual Arts Fel, Nat Endowment Arts, 1986 & 1994; Indo-Am Coun Exchange Scholars Fel, 1990; Louis Comfort Tiffany Found Award, 1991; Pollock-Krasner Found Award, 1994; Rome Prize, Am Acad Rome, 1994; Kester Award, Nat Academy. *Mem:* Fel, Am Acad Rome; Nat Acad. *Media:* Multimedia Installation; Sculpture

GINZEL, ROLAND
PAINTER, PRINTMAKER
b Lincoln, Ill, 1921. *Study:* Art Inst Chicago, BFA; State Univ Iowa, MFA; Slade Sch, London. *Work:* Univ Southern Calif; Univ Mich; Ill Bell Tel Co; Art Inst Chicago; US Embassy, Warsaw, Poland; Mus of Contemp Art, Chicago, IL; Wooster Art Mus, Wooster, MA; and others. *Exhib:* Art Inst Chicago, 69; Madison, Wis, 69; Notre Dame Univ, 69; solo exhib, Phyllis Kind Gallery, 69; Whitney Mus Am Art Biennial, NY, 75; Roy Boyd Gallery Chicago, 85-. *Teaching:* Prof printmaking, Univ Chicago, 57-58; prof prints & painting, Univ Ill, Chicago Circle, 58-69; instr painting, Univ Wis, 60; instr art, Saugatuck Summer Sch, 61-62. *Awards:* Print & Drawing Prize, 67 & Campana Prize, 69, Art Inst Chicago; Fulbright Fel to Rome, 62. *Media:* Painting, Sculpture. *Interests:* Fly Fishing. *Dealer:* Roy Boyd Gallery, Chicago, IL. *Mailing Add:* #120 Kimball Farms 235 Walker St Lenox MA 01240

GIOBBI, EDWARD GIOACHINO
PAINTER, SCULPTOR
b Waterbury, Conn, July 18, 1926. *Study:* Student, Whitney Sch Art, New Haven, 47; Vesper George Sch Art, Boston, 50; Cape Sch Art, Provincetown, Mass, 50; Art Students League, NY City, 56; Acad Fine Arts, Florence, Italy, 54. *Work:* Boston Mus Fine Arts; Whitney Mus Am Art, NY; Hirshhorn Mus; Art Inst Chicago; Albright-Knox Gallery. *Exhib:* Solo exhibs, Neuberger Mus, 77 & Gruenebaum Gallery, NY, 78 & 79; Young Am, Whitney Mus Am Art, 60; Recent Figure USA, Mus Mod Art, NY, 60; 40 Painters under 40, Whitney Mus Am Art, 62; and others. *Teaching:* Artist-in-residence, Memphis Acad, Tenn, 59-60 & Dartmouth Col, 72. *Awards:* Emily Lowe Award, 49; Ford Found Artist-in-Residence Prog, 66; Guggenheim Fel, 72. *Mem:* Westchester Coun Arts, Katonah Gallery (adv bd, currently); Nat Acad. *Media:* Oil; Mixed. *Mailing Add:* 161 Croton Lake Rd Katonah NY 10536-1201

GIOELLO, DEBBIE
PAINTER, DESIGNER
b Jan 1, 1935. *Study:* Univ State NY, 68; Oswego State Univ, BS,70; H Lehman Coll MA, 72. *Work:* Hudson River Mus, Yonkers, NY; Queens Cult Ctr, NY; Fashion Inst Tech, NY; State Office Building, Albany, NY. *Exhib:* Hudson River Mus, Yonkers, NY; Bronx Mus Arts, NY; Bruce Mus, Greenwich, Conn; Nat Asn Women Artists, NY; Dickinson State Univ, NDak; Up Front Gallery, NY ; Golden Fish Gallery, Pa; Gallery on Seventh, Pa; Artisan Exchange, Pa; The Artery, Milford, Pa; Lacawana Coll Environmental Inst, Pa; Orange Co College, NY. *Pos:* Owner, Gallery on Seventh, 113 Seventh St, Milford, Pa, 2008-. *Teaching:* Prof design, Fashion Inst Tech, 68-, chairperson fashion design dept, 89-93. *Awards:* Award Silvermine Guild, 75; Award for Excellence in Teaching NY State Chancellor, 98; Teacher of the Yr Avalon, 98. *Mem:* Nat Asn Women Artists. *Media:* Watercolor; Graphics, Acrylics. *Publ:* Coauth, Fashion Production Terms, Fairchild Publ, 79; auth, Profiling Fabrics, 80, Designer Stylist Handbook, Vol I & II and Figures, 80, & Understanding Fabrics, 82, Fairchild Publ; contribr, Random House Dictionary-Fashion & Textile Area, Random House, 83-85; auth, Design Solutions for Fashion Designer, 99; Fashion Figures for Design Solutions, 99. *Mailing Add:* 237 Van Cortland Pk Ave Yonkers NY 10705-1548

GIOIA, DANA (MICHAEL)
CRITIC, EDITOR, ADMINISTRATOR
b Los Angeles, Calif, Dec 24, 1950. *Study:* Stanford Univ, BA, 1973, MBA, 1977; Harvard Univ, MA, 1975. *Hon Degrees:* St Andrews Col, PhD in Lit, 2003; LHD, Lehigh Univ, 2003; LittD, West Chester Univ, 2003; LittD, Chapman Univ, 2005; LittD, Univ Pacific, 2005; LittD, Seton Hall Univ, 2005. *Pos:* Vpres marketing, Gen Foods Corp, White Plains, NY, 1977-92; pres, bd dirs, Story Line Press, 1992-2001; commentator, BBC Radio, 1992-2003; co-dir, West Chester Writers Conf, 1995-2002; music critic, San Francisco mag, 1997-2003; dir, Teaching Poetry Conf, 2001-02; chmn, Nat Endowment for the Arts, 2003-09. *Teaching:* Vis writer, John Hopkins Univ, Sarah Lawrence Col, Colo Col, Wesleyan Univ. *Awards:* Frederick Bock Prize Poetry, 1986; Am Book Award, 2002; Presidential Citizens Medal, 2008. *Mem:* Poetry Soc Am (vpres 1992-2003); Nat Endowment Arts, (chmn, 2003-); Nat Fed Coun on Arts & Humanities. *Publ:* Auth: (poetry) Daily Horoscope, 1986, The Gods of Winter, 1991, Interrogations of Noon, 2001, (criticism) Can Poetry Matter? Essays on Poetry an Am Culture, 1992, 2d ed, 2002; editor: The Ceremony and Other Stories, 1984, Poems from Italy, 1985, New Italian Poets, 1990; ed: The Ceremony & Other Short Stories, 1984, Poems from Italy, 1985, New Italian Poets, 1991; co-ed: Literature: An Intr to Fiction, Poetry and Drama, 2001, Longman Anthology of Short Fiction, 2000, Selected Short Stories of Weldon Kees, 2002, Twentieth-Century Am Poetry, 2003, Disappearing Ink, 2004; translator: Eugenio Montale's Mottetti: Poems of Love, 1990; contribr to periodicals includ New Yorker, Atlantic, Washington Post, Hudson Rev., Poetry; librettist for opera Nosferatu, 2001

GIORDANO, GREG JOE
PAINTER, PHOTOGRAPHER
b New York, NY, Nov 27, 1960. *Study:* Sch Visual Arts; Robert Bateman Master Class, Wausau, Wis, 86. *Exhib:* 1984 Winter Olympic Games, Int Olympic Comt Hq, Sarajevo, Yugoslavia, 84; National Art Exhib Alaskan Wildlife, Anchorage, 84 & 85; Group Miniature Exhib, Wild Wings Gallery, San Francisco, Calif, 85; Federal Duck Stamp Competition, Easton Waterfowl Festival, 85 & 86; Trailside Galleries. *Teaching:* Scottsdale Artists Sch. *Awards:* Finalist, Fed Duck Stamp Competition, 84 & 85; People's Choice Award-Best in Show, Alaskan Art Exhib, 85. *Bibliog:* Leonard Lang (auth), Artist vignette, Wildlife Art News, 9/85. *Media:* Gouache, Oil. *Publ:* Field & Stream Mag. *Mailing Add:* 76 Tally Ho Rd Ridgefield CT 06877-2818

GIORNO, JOHN
CONCEPTUAL ARTIST, PRINTMAKER
b New York, NY, Dec 4, 1936. *Study:* Columbia Univ, BA, 58. *Work:* Mus Mod Art, NY; Cen Pompidou Mus, Paris, France. *Comn:* Innovated Dial-A-Poem, 68. *Exhib:* Performance, Beacon Theatre, Ritz & Palladium, NY; Poem Print Gallery Exhibs, NY, Paris & Berlin; Galerie Agnes B, 2004; Pompidou Centre, Paris, 2008. *Pos:* Founder & pres, Giorno Poetry Systems Inst Inc, 65-. *Media:* Silkscreen, Painting, Drawing. *Publ:* Contribr, Balling Buddha, Kulchur Press, 70; Cancer in my Left Ball, Something Else Press, 73; Shit, Piss, Blood, Pus, & Brains, Painted Bride Press, 77; Grasping at Emptiness, Kulcur Press, 85; You Got to Burn to Shine, Serpents Tail Press, 94; auth, Subduing Demons in America, Selected Poems 1962-2007; Counterpoint Soft Skull, 2008. *Dealer:* Galerie Almine Rech Paris France; Nicole Klagsbrun Gallery New York NY. *Mailing Add:* 222 Bowery New York NY 10012

GIOVANNI
PAINTER, PRINTMAKER
b Laurence, Mass, March 13, 1949. *Study:* Vesper George Art Sch, 69-70; Art Inst Boston, 70-71; Boston Univ Sch Fine & Appl Arts, BFA, 87; Boston Univ Coll of Lib Arts (scholarship Renaissance study, Padera, Italy), 87-88. *Work:* Alamo Rent-A-Car headquarters, Ft Lauderdale; Nat Portrait Gallery, Washington, DC; Mus Fine Arts, Boston, Mass; Fogg Mus, Cambridge, Mass; The White House, George Bush Libr Collection, Washington, DC; Pres George Bush Libr, Houston, Tex. *Comn:* Portrait, M I T Hist Collection, Boston, Mass, 89; various canvases, Westwood Int, Caleo, Peru, 89; mural, Boston Redevelopment Authority City Hall, Padua, Italy, 89; American Flag, Bass Energy Corp, Fairlawn, Ohio, 91; The American Spirit, Republican Nat Conv, Houston, Tex, 92. *Exhib:* Dallas Design Center, 89; Ergane Gallery, NY, 91-92; one-man show, Francesco Anderson Gallery, Boston, 89-90, Pierce Galleries Inc, Hingham, Mass, 91-92, Boston Design Ctr, 91, Gallery at 4 India, Nantucket, 92; one-man retrospective, Bridgewater State Col, Bridgewater, Mass, 91; Fuller Mem Art Mus, Brockton, Mass, 96. *Pos:* Owner, Giovanni Studios, Boston, Mass, 88-. *Bibliog:* Patricia Jobe Pierce (auth), Giovanni DeCunto, Nantucket Beacon, 8/7/91; Patricia Jobe Pierce (auth), Italian-American painter makes an impact, Boston Post Gazette, 5/15/92; Patricia Jobe Pierce (auth), The leather district goes "pop" with art of Giovanni, Improper Bostonian, 5/27/92. *Media:* Acrylic, Oil, Lithography. *Mailing Add:* c/o Pierce Galleries Inc 721 Main St Rte 228 Hingham MA 02043

GIOVANOPOULOS, PAUL
PAINTER
b Kastoria, Greece, Nov 11, 1939; US citizen. *Study:* New York Univ (Dept Fine Arts Scholar), 58-59; Sch Visual Arts, New York, cert, 61. *Work:* Libr Congress, Washington; Butler Inst Am Art, Youngstown, Ohio; Harvard Univ, Cambridge, Mass; Guild Hall Mus, East Hampton, NY; Bruce Mus, Greenwich, Conn. *Comn:* Newport X 25, Lorillard Loewes Corp, NY, 93; Classic Camel, RJ Reynolds, Holland, 94; Ark Restaurant Corp, 95; Vorres Mus, Greece, 98. *Exhib:* Lower Manhattan Revisited: SoHo, NoHo & Tribeca, Maier Mus Art, Lynchburg, Va, 87; The Purloined Image, Flint Inst Art, Mich, 93; Art after Art, Nassau Co Mus Art, Roslyn Harbor, NY, 94; Food for Thought, Louis K Meisel Gallery, NY, 95; Butler Inst Am Art, 96; Jaffe Baker Gallery, Boca Raton, Fla, 96; Elaine Baker Gallery, Boca Raton, Fla, 99; Galerie Wagner, Switzerland, 2000; Galerie Sechzig, Austria, 2000. *Teaching:* Sch Visual Arts, New York, 69-70, Parsons Sch Design, 70-78 & Pratt Inst, Brooklyn, NY, 80-82. *Awards:* Chaloner Prize Found Fel, 64 & 65; Five Towns Music & Art Award, 94. *Bibliog:* Matthew Rose (auth), Honoring the Artists of the Hamptons, Dans Papers, 8/23/91; Constance Schwartz (auth), Paul Giovanopoulos, Art after Art, 9/94; David Shirey (auth), Paul Giovanopoulos (exhib catalog), Butler Mus Am Art, 10/96. *Media:* Acrylic on Canvas. *Mailing Add:* 119 Prince St New York NY 10012

GIPE, LAWRENCE
PAINTER
b Baltimore, Md, 1962. *Study:* Va Commonwealth Univ, BFA, 84; Otis Art Inst/Parsons Sch Design, MFA, 86. *Work:* Worcester Art Mus, Mass; Brooklyn Mus, NY; Orlando Mus Art, Fla. *Exhib:* Solo exhibs include Joseph Helman Gallery, NY, 96, 98 & 99, Bentley Gallery, Scottsdale, Ariz, 96, Fay Gold Gallery, Atlanta, Ga, 98, Ludwig Found, Havana, Cuba, 2000 & Alan Koppel Gallery, Chicago, Ill, 01, Joseph Helman Gallery, NY, 2003, Bentley Gallery, Scottsdale, Ariz, 2004, Atelier Richard Tullis, Santa Barbara, Calif, 2004, Hunsaker/Schlesinger Fine Art, Santa Monica, Calif, 2005, Ro Snell Gallery, Santa Barbara, 2005, Bentley Projects, Phoenix, Ariz, 2006, University Art Mus Ariz State Univ, 2006, Randall Scott Gallery, Washington, DC, 2007, Graficas, Tuscon, Ariz, 2007, Alexander Gray, NY, 2007; group exhibs include Va Mus Fine Arts, Richmond, 83; Tampa Mus Art, Fla, 96; Joseph Helman Gallery, NY, 96, 97, 98, 99 & 2000; Boston Univ Art Gallery, Mass, 97; Yoshi Gallery, NY, 99; Alan Koppel Gallery, Chicago, Ill, 2000; Modernism Gallery, San Francisco, 2004; San Jose Mus Art, Calif, 2004; Bryon Cohen Gallery, Kansas City, Mo, 2005; Laurie Frank Gallery, Santa Monica, 2005; Hunsaker/Schlesinger Fine Art, Santa Monica, 2005; Jack the Pelican Presents, Brooklyn, 2005; Randall Scott Gallery, Washington, DC, 2006, Winston-Wacter Fine Art, NY, 2006. *Pos:* Writer & critic, 85-; bd dir, Found Art Resources, Los Angeles, 86-87; co-cur, Natural Sources, Angel's Gate Cult Ctr, San Pedro, Calif, 87; cur, Cult Fetish, Pasadena City Col Gallery, 89; vis artist, Art Ctr Pasadena, 89; art hist fac, Art Ctr Sch Design, Pasadena, Calif, 96; guest lectr, Univ Calif, Santa Barbara, 99, Calif State Univ, Channel Islands, 2003. *Teaching:* Lectr & panelist, numerous col & univ in Calif. *Awards:* Fel, Nat Endowment Arts, 89 & 95; Printmaking Studio Portfolio Grant, Rutgers Archive, 92. *Bibliog:* Martha Donelan (auth), In the Studio with Lawrence Gipe, Santa Barbara News-Press, 3/99; Niki Richards (auth), Making Their Mark, The Independent, 4/99; Robert Mahoney (auth), The Last Picture Show, Time Out New York, 1/2000. *Publ:* Cover art, One Hundred Children Waiting for a Train, 2001; co-author, Color Me Arnold: The Unofficial Arnold Schwarzenegger Coloring and Activity Book, 2004

GIPS, C L TERRY
PHOTOGRAPHER, EDUCATOR
b Oneida, NY, Mar 4, 1945. *Study:* Cornell Univ, BS, 67; Yale Sch Art & Archit, MArch, 71. *Work:* Nat Mus Am Art, Washington; Picker Gallery, Colgate Univ, Hamilton, NY; State Vermont, Montpelier; Nat Mus Women in Arts, Washington. *Exhib:* One-person shows, 112 Workshop, NY, 77, Light Work Gallery, Syracuse, NY, 89, Tweed Mus Art, Duluth, Minn, 90 & Arnold Porter, Washington, 92; Ann Invitational Photog Exhib, Atrium Gallery, Conn, 83; Printed by Women, Port of History Mus, Philadelphia, 83; Selected Photographs 86, Philadelphia Print Club, Pa, 86; AIR Gallery, NY, 88; Am Artists, Deutsch-Amerikanisches Inst, Regensberg, WGer, 88. *Pos:* VPres bd trustees, VT Coun Arts, 83-84; dir, The Art Gallery, Univ Md, College Park, 92-. *Teaching:* Core fac Fine Art, Goddard Col, Plainfield Vt, 76-80; adj fac art & photog, Univ Vt, Burlington, 80-84; asst prof photog, Univ Maryland, 84-89, assoc prof photog, 90-. *Awards:* New York State Council Exhib Grant, 74; Nat Endowment Arts Artist's Fel, 86; Creative and Performing Arts Grant, Univ Md, 90, 92. *Mem:* Coll Art Asn; Soc Photog Ed; Womens Caucus Art (chair, nat honor awards comt, 84-86). *Publ:* Guest ed, Computers & Art, Art J, 90; ed, Significant Losses: Artists Who Have Died from AIDS (exhib catalog), Univ Md, 94; Joyce Scott's Mammy Nanny Series, Feminist Studies, 96; Willem de hooper, A Retrospective Exhib 1966-1996 (exhib catalog), Univ Md, 96; Terra Firma (exhib catalog), Univ Md, 97

GIRARD, BILL
SCULPTOR
b Reno, Nev, May 12, 1936. *Study:* San Diego State Univ, BS, 58; Ariz State Univ, 64; Scripps Univ, Calif, 66. *Work:* DuPage Art Ctr Mus, Glen Ellen, Ill. *Comn:* Portrait, pvt comn, Austin, Tex, 99; miniature Indian pow-wow dancers, Franklin Mint, Pa, 91; two life-size champion show dogs, pvt comn, Hillsborough, Calif, 92; earthenware Indian, Ray Tracey Gallery, Santa Fe, NMex, 92. *Exhib:* Sculpture in the Park & Invitational, Loveland, Colo, 87-97; Southwest Art in the Wine Country, Sharpsteen Mus, Calistoga, Calif, 90-93; Mountain Oyster 22nd-27th Ann Shows, Tucson, Ariz, 91-94; AICA Western Art Exhib, San Dimas, Calif, 92; Danada/Cantigny Sculpture Invitational, Chicago, 93-94; Classic-Am show, Los Angeles, 94; and others. *Teaching:* Instr, Loveland Art Acad. *Awards:* Best of Show, Heritage Am Show, Heritage Am Mus, 88; Peoples' Choice Award, Southwest Art in Wine Country, Art West Mag, 91; Purchase Award, Loveland Invitational Show & Sale, Colo, 97. *Bibliog:* Katherine Newman (auth), Bill Girard, 91 & Vicki Stavig (auth), Girard Studio, 92, Art West; Shirley Behrens(auth), Profile of Bill Girard, Art West, 94; Rita Simmons (auth), Bill Girard, Southwest Art Mag, 97. *Mem:* NMex Sculpture Guild; Albuquerque United Artists; Albuquerque Arts Alliance. *Media:* Bronze, Stoneware Clay. *Interests:* Travel, computers, family. *Publ:* Auth, Artistic News, Artistic Galleries, 92. *Mailing Add:* 1628 Sagebrush Trail SE Albuquerque NM 87123-4463

GIRARD, (CHARLES) JACK
PAINTER, EDUCATOR
b Ft Knox, Ky, May 15, 1951. *Study:* ECarolina Univ, BFA, 73, MFA, 76; Univ SC, 83. *Work:* SC Mus Comn, Columbia; Berea Coll, Ky; Appalachian State Univ; Coca-Cola Bottling Co, Atlanta; Cent Bank & Trust Co, Ky; Transylvania Univ, Ky; Eastern Kentucky Univ, Ky. *Comn:* Drawings, collab with writer Jo Carson, Lexington Alzheimers Asn, 90; Aside Show installation, collab with artist Steve Armstrong, Morlan Gallery, Lexington, NJ. *Exhib:* Univ Ky Art Mus, Lexington, 91; Ky Art and Craft Found Gallery, Louisville, 93; Chapman Friedman Gallery, Louisville, 96-99, 2001 & 2003-2004; Carnegie Ctr, Covington, 2003; Water Tower, Louisville, 2003; Vanderbilt Univ, Nashville, 2004; Morlan Gallery, Lexington, 2005; Ill Central Coll, 2006; Wofford Coll, 2007. *Pos:* Asst, Walker Gallery, Columbia, SC, 76-78, chair, Division Fine Arts, 2007-. *Teaching:* Vis artist, Carteret Tech Coll, 78-79; instr art, Berea Coll, 79-80; asst prof art, Centre Coll, Ky, 80-81; prof art, Transylvania Univ, 81-. *Awards:* Jones Develop Grant, 87, 90, 92, 94, 96, 98, 2002 & 2004-05; Lexington Arts & Cult Coun Grant, 90 & 96; Kenan Grant, 2006-2007. *Bibliog:* Steve Lyon (auth), Keeping tabs on the masquerade, J Seamus, 10/86. *Mem:* Coll Art Asn of Am (CAA). *Media:* All Media. *Publ:* Coauth (with Ann Kilkelly), Confinement and isolation in the art of Edward Kienholz, Med Heritage J, 1-2/86; Asensio Saez Garcia, Literatura de Levante, CAM Fundacion Cult, Murcia, Spain, 93; Asensio Saez Garcia: Symbiosis of word and Image, Literature Film and the other Arts in Modern Spain, Letras Peninsulares, 95. *Dealer:* Chapman Friedman Gallery Louisville KY. *Mailing Add:* 145 W Bell Ct Lexington KY 40508

GISPERT, LUIS
SCULPTOR, PHOTOGRAPHER
b Jersey City, NJ, 1972. *Study:* Sch Art Inst Chicago, BFA (film), 1996; Yale Univ, MFA (sculpture), 2001. *Work:* Fogg Art Mus; Haifa Mus Art, Israel; Hood Mus Art; Miami Art Mus; Ft Lauderdale Mus Art; Neuberger Mus Art, Purchase; New Mus Contemp Art, New York; San Diego Mus Contemp Art, San Diego; Guggenheim Mus; Univ Calif Berkeley Art Mus; Whitney Mus Am Art. *Exhib:* One Planet Under One Groove, Bronx Mus the Arts, 2001; Whitney Biennial, Whitney Mus Am Art, 2002; solo exhibs, Miami Art Ctrl, 2003, Univ Calif Art Gallery, San Diego, 2004, Hood Mus ARt, 2004, Fredric Snitzer Gallery, 2005, Santa Barbara Contemp ARts Forum, 2005, Zach Feuer Gallery, New York, 2005, Mary Boone Gallery, New York, 2008, Mus Contemp Art, N Miami, 2009; NextNext Visual Art, Bklyn Acad Music, 2003; Fade In, Contemp Arts Mus, Houston, 2004; EV, Limerick City Galelry Art, Ireland, 2005; Nominally Figured, Fogg Mus Art, 2006; Art in Am: 300 Years of Innovation, Shanghai Mus Contemp Art, China, 2007; TRANSactions, High Mus Art, Atlanta, 2008. *Awards:* Visual Arts fel, S Fla Cult Consortium; New Forms Visual Arts Grant; Art Acces Traveling Grant; Fla Individual Artist Fel; Alice Kimball Traveling Grant; Art Gant, Rema Hort Mann Found; Visual Arts Fel, Cintas Found; Emerging Am Photogr award, The Baum. *Bibliog:* Gean Moreno (auth), On View: Miami, New Art Examiner, 5/1999; Carol Vogel (auth), A Homegrown Biennial, NY Times, 11/26/2001; Peter Plagens (auth), This Man Will Decide What Art Is, Newsweek, 3/4/2002; Martha Schwendener (auth), Women Beware Women, Time Out NY, 12/4-11/2003; Ken Johnson (auth), Urban Myths PT II, NY Times, 1/9/2004; Jeff Howe (auth), Paint by Numbers, Wired, 88, 4/2005; Rob Sharp (auth), Is that a Picasso in the Pool, Guardian Observer, 9/10/2006; Christopher Knight (auth), Friskily is Best Revenge, Los Angeles Times, 8/3/2007; RC Baker (auth), Best in Show, Village Voice, 1/29/2008. *Mailing Add:* c/o Zach Feuer Gallery 548 W 22nd St New York NY 10011

GITLIN, MICHAEL
SCULPTOR, DRAFTSMAN
b Capetown, SAfrica, April 23, 1943. *Study:* Hebrew Univ Jerusalem, BA, 67; Bezalel Acad Art, Jerusalem, dipl, 67; Pratt Inst, MFA, 72. *Work:* Guggenheim Mus; Stedelijk Mus, Amsterdam; Lenbachhaus, Munich; Israel Mus, Jerusalem; Ludwig Mus, Koln; Fogg Art Mus, Cambridge; Guggenheim Mus, New York; Hirshhorn Mus & Sculpture Garden, Washington, DC; Rijksmuseum, Otterlo, Neth. *Comn:* Sculpture (Cor Ten steel), Schmela Gallery, Düsseldorf, 76; Adam's Gate (mahogany), Jerusalem Found, Israel, 83; Sequence, Tel Aviv Mus, Israel, 84. *Exhib:* Solo exhibs, Israel Mus, Jerusalem, 1977, Kunstraum, Munich, 1986, Bonner Kunstverein, Bonn, Ger, 1988, Stadtische Kunsthalle, Mannheim, Ger, 1989, Carnegie Mellon Art Gallery, Pittsburgh, 1990 & Mus Contemp Art, Antwerp, 1991; Documenta 6, Kassel, Ger, 1977; SkulpturSein, Kunsthalle, Dusseldorf, 1986; Scultura in America, 2nd Biennale Internazionale di Scultura Contemporanea, Circolo la Scaletta, Matera, Italy, 1990; Critical Mass, Yale Univ Art Gallery, 1995; The Boundaries of Language, Tel Aviv Mus Art, 2008; Minimal & Conceptual Art in Europe, Helga & Walther Lauffs Collection, Zwirner & Wirth, New York, 2008. *Teaching:* Instr art, Parsons Sch Design, 79-84; prof, Bezalel Acad Art, Jerusalem, 1985, Columbia Univ, NY, 1987, Univ Calif, Davis, 1988 & Vt Studio Sch, 2000 & 2005. *Awards:* Fel, Nat Endowment Arts, 84-85 & 85-86; Guggenheim Fel, 87-88; Pollock Krasner Found, 91-92. *Bibliog:* Stephen Westfall (auth), Humanizing Sculpture (text in Kunstraum exhib catalog), Munich, 86; Annelie Pohlen (auth), From Seeing to Feeling (text in Bonner Kunstverein exhib catalog), Bonn, 88; Maia Damianovic (auth), Silence and Reprieve (text in Muhka Mus catalog), Antwerp, 91. *Mem:* NY Artists Equity Asn. *Media:* Wood, Mixed Media, Copper, Spandex. *Collection:* Solomon R Guggenheim Mus, NY; Hirshhorn Mus & Sculpture Garden; Ludwig Mus, Köln; Stedelijk Mus, Amsterdam; Städtische Galerle, Lenbachhous, Munich. *Mailing Add:* c/o Soho Crates 810 Broadway New York NY 10003

GITTLER, WENDY
PAINTER, HISTORIAN
b Manhattan, NY. *Study:* Columbia Univ, New York, BS (art hist), 63; Hunter Col, New York, MA, 67; Brooklyn Col, MFA (painting), 73. *Work:* Pvt collections of, Prof Martin James, Brooklyn, NY, Prof Edward Casey, State Univ NY, Stony Brook, Violet Baxter, NY & Mr & Mrs Sibony, NY; Savannah Coll Art & Design, Ga; Barbara Goodstein, Queens, NY; Southeast Mo State Univ Mus; Savannah Coll Art & Design, GA. *Exhib:* Nat Exhib, Lehigh Univ, Pa, 84; The Figure Now, NY, 90; Invitational exhibs, Blue Mountain Gallery & Atlantic Gallery, NY, 1996-2010; Fedn Modern Painters & Sculptors, Fordham Univ, NY, 96, 2000-2010, 2012; Benefit Exhib, The Artist Mirrored: Self Portraits, NY Studio Sch, 1996-2006-2008; Benefit Exhib, Mckee Gallery, NY & Royal Coll Art, London, 98; Solo Exhibs: First Street Gallery, New York City, 1976, 82, 88, 95, 99, 2002, 2005, 2009, 2010, 2013; Benefit exhib NY Studio Sch, 1996-2005; Liman Studio Gall, Palm Beach, Fla, 2004-2005; West Beth Gallery, NY, 2006, 2012; Broom St Gallery, 2009; Group Exhib: Fednmod Painters and Sculptors, 2008; First St Gallery, 76-2013. *Collection Arranged:* S E Mo St Univ Mus; Savannah Coll Art & Design, Ga. *Pos:* Coordr artists meetings, Educ Alliance, NY, 72-74; moderator, Image, Symbol & Sign ann meetings, Artists Equity, 95-2012 & Paths of Narrative Today, 96, vpres; juror, Am Soc Contemp Artists, currently. *Teaching:* Lect Survey Art, Hunter Col, NY, 68-80, 19th-20th century art, Sch Visual Arts, NY, 79-86, aesthetics, Parsons Sch Design, NY, 89-96; NY Studio Sch, NY, 90-2006; Lectures & Critiques 90-2009; lect, Stony Brook Grad, 2006-2012. *Bibliog:* Albert P Ryder (auth), Under a cloud, Art News, 95. *Mem:* Coll Art Asn; Fedn Mod Painters & Sculptors; Artists Equity; Int Asn Art Critics. *Media:* Oil, Watercolor; Gouache. *Res:* Beyond the Frame; Space in the Late Paintings of Matisse, Bonnard & Braque. *Interests:* history; philosophy; archaeology. *Publ:* Auth, Image, symbol, sign, 95 & Paths of narrative today, 96, Artists Equity Bull; Wings & Anchors-Selected Paintings of John Hultberg 1949-93 (exhib catalog), Univ Art Gallery, Stony Brook, NY, 96; Art words-Bonnard & the Space of Inhabited Time, 98; Drawing Without Models, Wiegand Gallery, Belmont, Calif, 99; Provincetown Arts-A Harbor of Artists, Avery, Kraths & Maril, 2007; The Transfigured Landscape, Anselm Kiefer and John Walker, Conoscenti Mag, 2011; John Hultberg: Poet Painter, The Climate of Uncertainty, 2012. *Dealer:* First Street Gallery 524 W 26th St New York NY. *Mailing Add:* 780 W End Ave New York NY 10025

GIUFFRE, HECTOR
PAINTER, GRAPHIC ARTIST
b Buenos Aires, Arg; US citizen, Aug 5, 1944. *Study:* Escuela Superior Bellas Artes, Buenos Aires; Univ Salvador, Buenos Aires. *Work:* Mus Mod Art Buenos Aires, Arg; Mus Mod Art Bogota, Colombia; Archer-Huntington Coll, Univ Tex, Austin; Citibank NA Collection, NY; Lever Collection, London, Eng; Nat Mus Fine Arts Buenos Aires. *Comn:* portrait, comn by Alice Ryerson-Hayes, Chicago; portrait, comn by Jacques Lassaigne, Paris; portrait, comn by Marcos Curi, Buenos Aires; portrait, comn by Ignacio Pirovano, Buenos Aires; many other comn portraits worldwide, 67-. *Exhib:* 10th Biennial Paris, Mus Mod Art, 77; 2nd Biennial Havana, Biennial Bldg, 86; Abstraccion-Figuracion/Figurative-Abstract, Archer-Huntington Art Gallery, Univ Tex, Austin, 89; Solo exhibs: Mus Mod Art, Bogota, Colombia, 89; 12th Biennial-Evanston, Evanston Art Ctr, Ill, 94. *Teaching:* Instr painting & compos, studio, Buenos Aires, 70-89; workshop instr, Mus Mod Art Buenos Aires, 87-89; workshop instr, Art Ctr, Camara Comercio Bldg, Medellin, Colombia. *Awards:* Lever Art Contest First Prize, Instr Contemp Art, London, 80; 4th Biennial Medellin Critic's Award, El Colombiana newspaper, 81; Fulbright Fel, 1988. *Bibliog:* Raul Santana (auth), Hector Giuffré, an Opening to the Real, Art Editions Gaglianone, 80; Seymour Menton (auth), Magic Realism Rediscovered, Asn Univ Press, NJ, 83; Jorge Lopez Anaya (auth), History of Argentine Art, Emece, 2006. *Mem:* Chicago Artists Coalition; Coll Art Asn, NY; Soc Arg Artistas Plasticos, Buenos Aires. *Media:* Painting, All. *Publ:* Auth, On the Intimate Structure of Reality, Lirolay Gallery, 68; Guidelines to structural realism, Hitos Mag, 75; The realism in which I believe, Pluma y Pincel Mag, 76; Structural realism as a possibility of being of peinture, Artemas Mag, 78; Related and Realist Manifesto, Julia Lublin Gallery, 84. *Mailing Add:* Giuffre Art Studio 823 W Lakeside Pl #1W Chicago IL 60640

GIURGOLA, ROMALDO
ARCHITECT
b Rome Sept 2, 1920. *Study:* Scuola Di Archit Univ di Roma, graduate, (summa cum laude), 48; Columbia Univ, MS (archit), 51. *Pos:* Partner, Mitchell/Giurgola Archit, Philadelphia, New York City, from 58; chmn, dept archit Columbia Univ, 68-71. *Awards:* Gold Medal Award, Fel Am Inst of Archits, 82. *Mem:* Fel Am Inst of Archits; Nat Acad, Am Acad & Inst Arts and Letters, Acad Nazionale di San Luca (corr)

GIUSTI, KARIN F
SCULPTOR
Study: Yale Univ Sch Art, MFA (sculpture). *Comn:* The World is Your Oyster, Long Wharf Park, New Haven, Conn, 90; Pearl Necklace, pvt collection, Philadelphia, Pa, 91; Oyster-Hearts, PECO Energy Co, Philadelphia, Pa, 95; Bon Chance Baby & Par-O-Dise, PECO Energy Co, Philadelphia, Pa, 96. *Exhib:* Absolute Cow, Vt Coll Art Ctr, Montpelier, 89; On Site New Eng, Urban Arts Inc, Bank Boston Gallery, Mass, 89; Trouble in Paradise, Mass Inst Technol List Visual Arts Ctr, Cambridge & Art Gallery, Univ Md, College Park, 89; Towards 2000, RI Sch Design & Hartford Art Sch, 91-92; Contemp Sculpture, Chesterwood Mus, Stockbridge, Mass, 91-92; Challenging Utopia, 14 Sculptors, NY, 91-92; Invitational, Real Art Ways, Hartford, Conn, 91-92; Seasons: Passage and Presents (installation), Bradley Int Airport, Hartford, Conn, 93; Alumni III, Univ Mass Fine Arts Ctr, Amherst, 93; Sculpture Ctr at Roosevelt Island, Sculpture Ctr, Roosevelt Island, NY, 93; Garbage, Real Art Ways, Hartford, Conn, 94 & Thread Waxing Space, NY, 95; Contemp Installations, La Quita Open Air Mus, Calif, 94; Faculty Show, Brooklyn Col, City Univ NY, 95; Pop Up Show, Socrates Sculpture Park, Queens, NY, 95; Art in the Anchorage 1995, Creative Time, NY, 95; Investing in Dreams, Conn Comn Arts, Lyman Allyn Art Mus & Statewide Mus Collaborative by Conn Comn Art Individual Grant Recipients, 95; The White House/Green House, Real Art Ways, Hartford, Conn, 95 & Lower Manhattan Cult Coun, NY, 96; Just the Thing, Contemp Outdoor Sculpture & Object Woodson Art Mus, Wis, 98; Art Exchange Show, Anya von Gosslen Gallery, NY, 98; Gothic Distress, Trans Hudson Gallery, NY, 98; EV plus A 98 - Int Biannual Exhib, St Mary's Cathedral, Limerick, Ireland, 98. *Teaching:* Head sculpture dept, Brooklyn Col, City Univ New York, 95-. *Awards:* Nat Endowment Arts Regional Grant, New Eng Found Arts, 91; Guggenheim Fel Installation & Sculpture, 97-98; Fulbright Research Award, Ireland, 98-99. *Bibliog:* Roberta Smith (auth), Anchor and balm for restless souls, NY Times, 8/4/95; Holland Cotter (auth), Sculpture that basks in the summer sunlight and air, NY Times, 8/9/96; Josephine Gear (auth), Site specific, public sculpture by Armajani and Giusti, Rev Mag, 9/15/96. *Mailing Add:* c/o Guisti Studio 82 Wall St Ste 1105 New York NY 10012

GJERTSON, STEPHEN ARTHUR
PAINTER, WRITER
b Minneapolis, Minn, May 21, 1949. *Study:* Univ Minn, 67-70; Sch Assoc Arts, St Paul, 70-71; Atelier Lack, Minneapolis, Minn, 71-75. *Work:* Coll St Benedict, St Joseph, Minn; Christ Coll Irvine, Calif; Montclair Art Mus. *Comn:* Triptych with predellas, Nokomis Heights Lutheran Church, Minneapolis, Minn, 1979-2008; Peace, Be Still (painting), St John's Lutheran Church, Mound, Minn, 97; Newington-Cropsey Found, Hasting-on-Hudson, NY; portrait of gov Arne H Carlson, Minn State Capitol, 99. *Exhib:* Classical Realism: The Other 20th Century, traveling exhib, 82-83; Classical Realist Conf & Exhib, Heritage Art Gallery, Alexandria, Va, 86, 88 & 92; 63rd & 64th Nat Apr Salons, Springville Mus Art, Utah, 87 & 88; Newington-Cropsey Found, NY, 96, 01, 06, & 10; E Coast Ideals, W Coast Concepts (traveling exhib), 97; Biblical Arts Ctr, Dallas, 02; Distinguished Company, Bloomington Art Ctr, 2009. *Pos:* Ed adv, Classical Realism J; Pres, Am Soc Classical Realism; Ed, Classical Realism Newsletter. *Teaching:* Atelier Lack, 73-88; Atelier N, 84-93; Atelier LeSueur, 91-92. *Awards:* Juror's Award, 63rd Nat Apr Salon, Springville Mus Art, 87; Cash Award, 64th Nat Apr Salon, Friend Grand Central Art Galleries, 88; Artists Choice award, ASTA, 2012, Golden Palette awards, 2012. *Bibliog:* Annette Hathaway (auth), Stephen Gjertson, Am Artist, 10/83; Carole Katchen (auth), Creating a Joyous Beauty, Painting Faces & Figures, Watson-Guptill, 86; Annette LeSueur (auth), Timeless Treasure: The Art of Stephen Gjertson, Am Soc Classical Realism, 93. *Mem:* TRIAD: Three Am Painters; Am Soc Traditional Artists. *Media:* Oil. *Publ:* Auth, The Necessity of Excellence, Realism in Revolution/Taylor, 85; Hippolyte Flandrin-A Personal Appreciation, Classical Realism Quarterly, summer 88; contribr, Classical Realism J, Am Soc Classical Realism; auth, Richard F. Lack: An American Master, Am. Soc. Classical Realism, 01; co-auth, For Glory and For Beauty: Practical Perspectives on Christianity and the Visual Arts, 02. *Dealer:* Stephen Gjertson Studios 3855 Colfax Ave N Minneapolis MN 55412. *Mailing Add:* 3855 Colfax Ave N Minneapolis MN 55412

GLADSTONE, BARBARA
DEALER, HISTORIAN
b Philadelphia, Pa. *Study:* Univ Pa; Hofstra Univ, BA, 68, MA, 70. *Pos:* Founder, owner & dir, Barbara Gladstone Gallery, New York, 80-; bd mem, Art Dealers Asn, 90-93, 94-95, Printed Mattes, 93-94; founder, Stuart Regen Visionaries Fund, New Mus, NY, 2008. *Teaching:* Instr art hist & mod archit, Hofstra Univ, 71-75. *Mem:* Art Dealers Asn Am. *Specialty:* Contemporary painting, sculpture and photography; publisher of contemporary American prints and photographs. *Publ:* producer, The Cremaster Cycle (film); producer, Drawing Restraint 9 (film), 2006. *Mailing Add:* Barbara Gladstone Gallery 515 W 24th St New York NY 10011

GLADSTONE, M J
PUBLISHER
b New York, NY, May 4, 1923. *Study:* Harvard Univ, SB (anthrop), 44, MA (fine arts), 46. *Pos:* Ed, Print & Print Collector's Quart, 50-53, Merriam-Webster Dictionary, 53-55, Collector's Quart Report, 62-63; assoc dir publ, Mus Mod Art, New York, 63-64; consult, NY State Coun Arts, 67-73; dir, Mus Am Folk Art, New York, 69-70 & Publ Ctr Cult Resources, New York, 73-88, ed-in-chief, 88-89; publ, Furthermore Press, Germantown, NY, 91-; consult, JM Kaplan Fund, NY, 96-. *Publ:* Contribr, Britannica Encycl Am Art, 73; auth, A Carrot for a Nose, Scribner, 74; contribr, How to Know American Folk Art, Dutton, 77. *Mailing Add:* PO Box 355 Germantown NY 12526

GLADSTONE, WENDELL
PAINTER, SCULPTOR
b 1972. *Study:* Brown Univ, BA, 1995; Skowhegan Sch Painting & Sculpture, Maine, 1997; Claremont Grad Univ, MFA, 1998. *Exhib:* Solo exhibs include Kravets/Wehby Gallery, New York, 1998, 1999, 2001, 2003, 2005, 2006, Roberts & Tilton, Los Angeles, 2003, Mus Contemp Art, San Diego, 2003; Group exhibs include LA Current, Armand Hammer Mus, Los Angeles, 1997; Six Emerging Artists, Dan Bernier Gallery, Los Angeles, 1998; Los Angeles Contemp Exhibs Ann, Los Angeles Contemp Exhibs, Los Angeles, 1998; Collector's Choice, Exit Art, New York, 2000; Spring, Kravets/Wehby Gallery, New York, 2002; Split, Sandra Gering Gallery, New York, 2003; Eye of the Needle, Roberts & Tilton, Los Angeles, 2004; Phantasmania, Kemper Mus Art, Kansas City, Mo, 2007; The Incomplete, Chelsea Art Mus, New York, 2007; Against the Grain, Los Angeles Contemp Exhib, 2008. *Dealer:* Kravets/Wehby Gallery 521 W 21st St New York NY 10011. *Mailing Add:* Kravets/Wehby 521 W 21st St, Ground Fl New York NY 10011

GLANZ, ANDREA E
ADMINISTRATOR, CURATOR
b New York, NY, Oct 14, 1952. *Study:* Cornell Univ, BS (human develop & expressive arts); Stanford Univ, MA (art educ). *Pos:* Grad asst, Stanford Univ Mus Art, Calif, 74-75; cur educ, Triton Mus Art, Santa Clara, Calif, 75-77, dir, 77-78; from asst cur to cur, San Jose Mus Art, Calif, 78-79; asst dir, Continuing Prof Educ, Mus

Collab, New York, 79-80, dir, 80-85. *Teaching:* Instr, West Valley Community Col, Saratoga, Calif, 76. *Mem:* Am Asn Mus; Mus Educators Roundtable; Coll Art Asn; Nat Trust for Hist Preserv. *Publ:* Coauth, A Catalog of Paintings by Theodore Wores in the Collection of the Triton Museum of Art, 76 & Two Hundred Years of Santa Clara Valley Architecture: A Stylistic Survey, 76, Triton Mus Art; auth, The Role of Museum Management Training in Developing Effective Museum Managers & In Search of Excellence: The American Museum Experience, Scottish Mus Coun, Edinburgh, 85. *Mailing Add:* 90 Jane St Hartsdale NY 10530-1927

GLASER, BRUCE
HISTORIAN, EDUCATOR
b Brooklyn, NY, Sept 25, 1933. *Study:* Columbia Col, BA; Columbia Univ, MA. *Pos:* Dir, Howard Wise Gallery, New York, 60-61 & Gallery of Israeli Art, Am-Israel Cult Found, New York, 65-68; exec dir, Art Ctr Northern NJ, Tenafly, 68-70. *Teaching:* Instr art hist, Pratt Inst, 61-62; instr, Hunter Col, 62-65; prof art hist, Univ Bridgeport, 70-, chmn dept, 70-77, dean, Col Fine Arts, 77-81. *Awards:* Mem Found for Jewish Cult Fel, 70-72; Summer Inst, Nat Endowment Humanities, Chicago, 84; Vis Scholar, Coun for Humanities, 86. *Mem:* Coll Art Asn Am; Int Coun Mus; Am Asn Mus. *Res:* Modern and contemporary art; Israeli art. *Publ:* Ed & coauth, Oldenburg, Lichtenstein, Warhol: A discussion, Artforum, 2/66; coauth, Questions to Stella & Judd, Art News, 9/66; ed & coauth, An interview with Ad Reinhardt, Art Int, 12/66; ed & coauth, Modern art and the critics, Art J, winter 70-71; auth, Robert Natkin, Arts, 6/78. *Mailing Add:* 78 Gaybowers Ln Fairfield CT 06430-2011

GLASER, DAVID
PAINTER, SCULPTOR
b Brooklyn, NY, Sept 29, 1919. *Study:* Art Students League, scholar, with Wilhelm Von Schlegel, NY Sch Art, NY Sch Contemp Art, with Philip Evergood; Brooklyn Mus Art Sch, with Moses Soyer, Xavier Gonzales & Edwin Dickinson. *Work:* Full-color reproductions of paintings mailed throughout Long Island, NY. *Comn:* Artist: Civilian Conserv Corps, 36; Created (Giggy F Useless) World War II cartoon character, USA, 42-46; Poster ser for US Army, 43-44; 1950-1985 Fine Art and Graphic Art Promo in all New Space Age Technologies, N Am Philips (Amperex), Gen Signal (Cardion), Polytech Res and Develop, Plessey Inc, Hohner Harmonicas Corp, others. *Exhib:* Munic Galleries, Jackson, Miss, 44; Nat Art Club, 59; ACA Galleries, 60; illuminated slide series (projected art) Long Island Cmty Chorus, Warsaw Ghetto Contata, 60; three-person exhib, Heckscher Mus, Huntington, NY, 64; Nassau Community Coll, 79 & 81; Hofstra Univ, NY, 80; Adelphi Col, 80; Nassau Co Mus Fine Art, 80; Wantagh Libr, 82; Hempstead Harbor Art Asn, Glen Cove, 82; Islip Mus, 83; Levittown Libr, 86; Freeport Libr, 87; Long Beach Art League, 89. *Pos:* Inventor, art dir & designer, Mosamics Co pres, 46-48; newspaper artist, Bering Breeze, Aleutians, 45-46; treas, Comic Artists Guild, 48; art dir, 54-60; dir & designer, Studio Concepts, 60-; pres, Allied Artists Am, 85. *Teaching:* Instr, Art Ctr Island Jewish Sch, 59; spkr in field, 99. *Awards:* Grand Prize, Redesign of Levitt House, 67 & Printing Indust NY, 73 & 77; Monadnock Mills Graphic Excellence Award, 75; Cert of Merit, Vet Soc Am Artists, 79; Desi Graphics Award, 80 & 82; Inst Elec & Electronics Engrs Award, 83; Award of Excellence, Long Beach, LI, 89. *Mem:* Allied Artists Am; Huntington Township Art League; Int Soc Poets; Nat Libr Poetry. *Media:* Mixed Media; Copper, Illumination. *Res:* Experimental silk screen production for industry; developed Process Mosaic Reproduction; new approaches in advertising and media including all communication skills; architectural sculpture using copper, plastics or electricity; pictorial Map Entire Am Revolution. *Specialty:* Combining poetry, art, and music on tape to tell a complete creative story, using specific lighting/focus on human condition and environment. *Interests:* Mechanics, environment, nature, hiking, long distance swimming. *Publ:* Auth & illusr, American Indian, Crime & Punishment, Superstition & Parapsychology, 47-50; Popular Sci, Popular Mechanics & Electronics Illustrated, 61-65; My Mother Died Dancing; Cross-over, Bridges of the Mind, 93; Poetry anthologies, Nat Libr Poetry, 96-98; Two Thousand Outstanding People of the 20th Century, Cambridge, Eng, 98; 90 Years Live! Poetry, Words & Image, Int Libr of Poetry, 2009. *Dealer:* Kennedy Studios 37 Clarendon St Boston MA. *Mailing Add:* 33 Downhill Ln Wantagh NY 11793

GLASER, MILTON
DESIGNER, ILLUSTRATOR
b New York, NY, June 26, 1929. *Study:* Cooper Union Art Sch, 51; Acad Fine Arts, Bologna, Italy, with Giorgio Morandi, Fulbright Scholar, 52-53; Minneapolis Inst Art, Hon DFA; Moore Coll Art, Hon Degree; Philadelphia Mus Sch, Hon Degree; Sch Visual Arts, Hon Degree; State Univ Col, Buffalo, Hon Degree, 87, Hon Doctorate, Queens Col, City Univ NY & Londons Royal Coll Art. *Work:* Mus Mod Art, NY, Chase Manhattan Bank, NY; Israel Mus, Jerusalem; Nat Archives, Smithsonian Inst, Washington; Cooper Hewitt Design Mus, NY. *Comn:* Mural, Fed Off Bldg, Indianapolis, 74; permanent exhib, Port Authority NY, World Trade Ctr, 75; interior elements, signage & graphic theming, Sesame Park, Pa, 81-83; mural, Astor Place Subway Sta, NY, 85; Int AIDS symbol, World Health Orgn, 87. *Exhib:* Solo exhibs, Portland Visual Arts Ctr, Maine, 75, Mus Mod Art, NY, 75 & Wichita State Univ, 75, Ctr Georges Pompidou, Paris, France, 77, Lincoln Ctr, NY, 81, Carpenter Ctr Gallery, NY, 81, others; Mus Mod Art, Liege, Belgium, 82; Houghton Gallery at The Cooper Union, NY, 84; Hammer Gallery, NY, 86; Mus Bellas de Artes of Buenos Aires, Argentina, 87; Galleria d'Arte Maderna, Bologna, Italy; Univ Cent Mus, Barcelona, Spain; Errepidue Evento, Vicenza, Italy; Sch Visual Arts, NY; Nuages Gallery, Italy; Piero della Francesa Exhib, Arezzo, Italy; Creation Gallery, Japan, 95; Sawhill Gallery, James Madison Univ, 98; Pushpin and Beyond: The Celebrated Studio Transformed Graphic Design, Japan, 97; Brigham Young Univ; and others. *Collection Arranged:* Mus Modern Art, NY; Israel Mus, Jerusalem; Chase Manhattan Bank, NY; Nat Archives, Smithsonian Inst, Washington, DC; Cooper Hewitt Nat Design Mus, NY; Civic Mus, Vicenza, Italy; Mus Modern Art, Buenos Aires, Argentina. *Pos:* Pres, Push Pin Studios, NY, 54-74; chmn bd & design dir, NY Mag, 68-77; pres, Milton Glaser Inc Design Studio, 74-; vpres & design dir, Village Voice, 75-77; cofounder, WBMG Design Firm, 83-. *Teaching:* Instr design prog, Sch Visual Arts, NY, 61- & Cooper Union, NY, 94-. *Awards:* Gold Medal, Soc Illusr, 78; Fulbright Award, Metro Int, 92; Prix Savignac, World's Most Mem Poster, 96; Cooper Hewitt Lifetime Achievement Award, 2004; Nat Medal Arts award, Nat Endowment for the Arts, 2010. *Bibliog:* Linda Moss (auth), Milton Glaser at 58, Crains' NY Businessman, 7/13/87; Gael Greene (auth), Over the rainbow, the renaissance of a New York classic, NY Mag, 2/88; Ruth Reichl (auth), Heaven's plate Metrop Home, 6/88. *Mem:* Int Graphic Alliance; Cooper Union (bd trustee, vpres chmn), Art Dir's Club Hall Fame; Art Dir Club; Int Design Conf, Aspen; Soc Arts London; Soc Illusrs. *Publ:* Illusr, Art is Work, 2000, The Alphazeds, 2002, The Design of Dissent, 2004 The Big Rave, 2004 & others. *Mailing Add:* 207 E 32nd St New York NY 10016-6305

GLASGOW, VAUGHN LESLIE
CURATOR, HISTORIAN
b Apr 23, 1944; US citizen. *Study:* La State Univ, BA; Borso di Studii, Centro Int Studii Archit A Palladio, Vicenza, Italy, cert, 68; Pa State Univ, MA (Nat Defense Act Title IV Fel), 70; Inst Mus Mgt, Univ Calif, Berkeley, fel, 79; Int Partnership Among Mus, La Rochelle, France, fel, 81. *Exhib:* Solo exhib, Rocks of Ages, Central Conn State Univ, New Britain, 92. *Collection Arranged:* Permanent Collection, Anglo-Am Art Mus, La State Univ, 66-67; G P A Healy: Famous Figures and La Patrons (coauth, catalog), 76; Savoir Faire: The French Taste in Louisiana, 77; Played With Immense Success, 79; L'Amour de Maman: The Acadian Textile Heritage (auth, catalog), 80; The Sun King: Louis XIV and the New World (auth, catalog), 84; The Old State Capital, Baton Rouge, 88; and others. *Pos:* Reader youth grants, Nat Endowment Humanities, Washington, DC, 71-76; arts mgr, State Arts Coun, New Orleans, La, 73-75; chief cur, La State Mus, New Orleans, 75-83, assoc dir, 83-86; dir, spec projs, La State Mus, New Orleans, 86-. *Teaching:* Instr art hist & admin asst, Pa State Univ, 70-71; asst prof art hist, Middle Tenn State Univ, 72-73; lectr art hist, Tulane Univ, 74-79; lectr arts mgt, St Mary's Dominican Col, 81-82. *Awards:* Chevalier des Palmes Academiques, French Govt, 84; Chevalier des Arts et des Lettres, French Govt, 86; Am Asn State Local Hist Award, 92. *Mem:* Am Asn Mus; Int Coun Mus (exhib exchange comt); La Asn Mus; Am Asn State & Local Hist (awards comt); Southeastern Mus Conf. *Res:* European post-Renaissance period; Louisiana studies; architectural history; post-revolutionary French painting. *Publ:* Auth, The Sun King: Louis XIV & the New World (with S Reinhardt, R Macdonald & P Lemoine), LMF, New Orleans, 84; Planning a Traveling Exhibition: American Asn State & Local Hist Technical Report No 10; A Social History of the American Alligator, St Martin's Press, NY, 91; and others. *Mailing Add:* La State Mus 751 Chartres St PO Box 2448 New Orleans LA 70176

GLASS, BRENT D.
MUSEUM DIRECTOR
b Brooklyn, NY, Sept 27, 1947. *Study:* Lafayette Coll, BA, 69; NYU, MA, 71; Univ NC, PhD, 80. *Pos:* rsch historian, Div Archives and History, Raleigh, NC, 74-75, deputy state history preservation officer, 76-80; asst dir, S Oral History Program, Chapel Hill, NC, 75-76; exec dir, Durham Neighborhood Housing Svcs, NC, 80-83, Humanities Coun, Greensboro, NC, 83-87; Pa History & Mus Comn, Harrisburg, 87-2002; CEO, US Brig Niagara, Homeport Erie Maritime Mus, Erie, Pa; dir, Nat Mus Am History, Wash, 2002-2011, dir emeritus, 2011-; Bd advisors Capitol Area Therapeutics Riding Acad, Grantville, Pa, 1989, mem, Flight 93 Meml Comn, bd trustee Lafayette Coll, Easton, Pa. *Mem:* Nat Trust for Historic Preservation; Orgn Am Historians; Am Asn for State and Local History; Soc for Indust Archeol, Pa; Fedn Mus and Historic Orgns (secy, 87). *Interests:* reading, jogging, basketball, museums. *Publ:* auth, North Carolina's Industrial Archeology, 75; guest appearance, Oprah Winfrey Show (show theme-What Makes America America), 2008. *Mailing Add:* National Museum of American History PO Box 37012 Washington DC 20013

GLASS, DOROTHY F
HISTORIAN
b New York, NY. *Study:* Vassar Coll, BA, 64; Johns Hopkins Univ, PhD, 68. *Teaching:* Asst prof medieval art, Boston Univ, 69-74; assoc prof, State Univ NY, Buffalo, 74-81, prof, 81-, chair, 87-89. *Awards:* Rome Prize, Am Acad Rome, 85-86; Fulbright Fel, Western European Regional, 89-90; Jane & Morgan Whitney Senior Fel, Metrop Mus Art, 91-93. *Mem:* Medieval Acad Am (counr, 94-97); Coll Art Asn; Int Ctr Medieval Art (bd dir, 80-83, domestic adv & publ comt, 87-90, ed newsletter, 92-95 & vpres, 96-99); Soc Fels, Am Acad Rome. *Publ:* Auth, Romanesque sculpture in Campania: a problem of method, Art Bull, 74; Italian Romanesque Sculpture: An Annotated Bibliography, Boston, G K Hall & co, 83; Pseudo-Augustine, Prophets & Pulpits in Romanesque Campania, Dumbarton Oaks Papers 41, 87; Romanesque Sculpture in Campania: Patrons, Programs and Style, Pa State Press, 91; Portals, Pilgrimage and Crusade in Western Tuscany, Princeton Univ Press, 97. *Mailing Add:* Dept Art Hist-Rm 601 Clemens Hall State Univ NY-North Campus Buffalo NY 14260

GLASSER, NORMA PENCHANSKY
SCULPTOR
b New York, NY, Mar 6, 1941. *Study:* Leslie Coll, BS, 62; Eastern Mich Univ, MFA, 74. *Work:* Marietta Coll, Ohio; La Grange Coll, Ga; Saginaw Valley State Coll, Mich; Boone Sculpture Garden, San Marino, Calif; Pac Enterprises, Los Angeles, Calif; St Joseph's Hosp, Ann Arbor; Univ of MI, Dearborn, Mich; St Joseph's Hospital, Ypsilanti, Mich; Blue Cross, Blue Shield, Detroit, Mich; Ann Arbor Pub Libr, Ann Arbor, Mich, 2006; Restorative View Ctr, St Joseph's campus, Ypsilanti, Mich, 2006; and var pvt, state & nat collections; Pasadena Coll, Calif. *Comn:* Women Waiting, comn by Charles Givens, Oklahoma City, 84; Summer Garden, Ind Univ-Purdue Univ, Ft Wayne, Ind, 91; Martha Graham, Las Sendas, Ariz, 95. *Exhib:* 56th Ann Nat Exhib, Springville Mus, Utah, 80; 16th Ann Drawing & Small Sculpture Exhib, Del Mar Col, Corpus Christi, Tex, 82; Nat Sculpture Soc Exhib, Equitable Gallery, NY, 83; Mich Outdoor Sculpture II, Southfield Civic Ctr, 89; Taubman Gallery, Ann Arbor, Mich, 91; Power Ctr Performing Arts, Ann Arbor, 92; Nat Asn Women Artists, NY, 94; Dennos Mus, Traverse City, Mich, 96; Invitational Power Ctr Performing Arts, Ann Arbor, 2000; Bronze 2000, Park Gallery, Kalamazoo, Mich; The Figure as Landscape,

Ann Arbor Art Ctr, 2002; Pfizer Sculpture Exhib, Ann Arbor, 2002; Pivotal Space: Recent Sculpture & Drawings, Washington Gallery, Ann Arbor, 2002; Celebrating the Figure, Lansing Art Gallery, Lansing MI, 2002 (Judge Commendation Award); 15th Ann Nat Women's Art Exhib Oakland Community Coll Farmington Hills, MI, (2nd Place Award); Art Around Town- Outdoor Sculpture Inst, Saugatuck, MI, 2004; Wall to Wall, A Survey of Current Regional Sculpture, Flatlanders Galleries Blissfield, MI,2004; Equestrian Gestures Washington St Gallery Ann Arbor, Mich, 2004; From Our Perspective, Oakland Community Coll, Farmington Hills, Mich, 2006; Art Around Town, Saugatuck, Mich, 2006; Ella Sharpe Mus, 2007; Crooked Tree Arts Center, 2007; solo exhib, Washington St Gallery, Ann Arbor, Mich, 2008, WSG Gallery, Mich, 2010; Lansing Art Gallery, Lansing, Mich, 2008-09; Ella Sharpe Mus, 2009-10; Uptown Gallery, Kalamazoo, Mich, 2011; Gifts of Arts, Univ Mich, Hospital of Ann Arbor, 2011; Birmingham Bloomfield Art Ctr, Mich; solo exhib, Line & Motion, WSG Gallery, Ann Arbor, Mich, 2012; WSG Gallery, Ann Arbor, Mich, 2013, solo exhib, 2015; Book & Paper Art, 2013; Summer Collection, Joppichs Bay St Gallery, Northport, Mich, 2013; Muskegon Mus Art 87th Regional Juried Exhib, Mich, 2015. *Pos:* Staff, Ann Arbor Street Fair, 87-2002. *Teaching:* Instr sculpture-drawing, Ann Arbor Art Ctr, 73-2001; guest lectr, Univ Mich, 85 Ann Arbor Publ Schs, 86. *Awards:* First Place, Annie Achievement Award, Visual Arts Three Dimensional, Washtenaw Coun Art, Ann Arbor, Mich, 91; Shidon Bronze Gallery, Tesuque, NMex; Cleo Hartwig Award for Sculpture, Nat Asn Women Artists, NY, 94; Purchase Award Univ MI, Dearborn, MI, 2003; Jurors Commendation award, AMA Exhib, Eastern Mich Univ, 2006; Honorable Mention 3D, Great Lakes Small Works Competition, Riverside Art Ctr, Ypsilanti, Mich, 2012. *Mem:* Ann Arbor Art Asn (bd mem, 82-87); Nat Asn Women Artists; Mich Guild Artists & Craftsmen; Nat Sculpture Soc. *Media:* Metal, Cast. *Specialty:* fine art. *Publ:* Contribr, Heroic Sculpture, Western Art Digest, 86. *Dealer:* Washington St Gallery 306 S Main St Ann Arbor MI. *Mailing Add:* 2859 Gladstone St Ann Arbor MI 48104

GLASSON, LLOYD
SCULPTOR, EDUCATOR
b Chicago, Ill, Jan 31, 1931. *Study:* Art Inst Chicago, BFA, 57; Tulane Univ, MFA, 59. *Work:* New Brit Mus Am Art, Conn; George Walter Vincent Smith Mus, Springfield, Mass; Wichita Art Mus; Univ Hartford, Conn; Hartford Hosp and The Bushnell Auditorium, Hartford, Conn. *Comn:* Shapiro Mem & Herbert Portraits, Karen Horney Clin, NY, 67; Finial angels atop soldiers & sailors mem arch, Hartford, Conn, DeVane Mem, Yale Univ, Conn, 68; Fox Mem & Patterson Mem, Univ Conn Med Ctr, Farmington; Church of St Helena, West Hartford, Conn; Helen & Harry Jack Gray (portraits), Wadsworth Atheneum; ACMAT Corp, Portrait of Henry Nozko. *Exhib:* Solo exhibs, Dorsky Gallery, NY, 66 & 74, Trinity Coll, 77 & Saltbox Gallery, 85, Hartford, Conn; Univ NH, Durham, 76; Manchester Community Coll, 90; Cent Conn State Univ, 91. *Pos:* Exhib designer, Newark Mus, NJ, 60-61; co-founder, Artists Tenants Asn, 61-. *Teaching:* Prof sculpture & drawing, Univ Hartford, West Hartford, Conn, 64-2009, prof emer. *Awards:* First Prizes, Art Asn Regional, Delgado Mus, New Orleans, 59; Gold Medal, Nat Sculpture Soc, 85 & Nat Acad Design, 86; James E & Francis W Bent Award for Creativity, 89; Albert Schweitzer Humanitarian Award; Univ Hartford Medal; John G. Lee Medal. *Bibliog:* Jolene Goldenthal (auth), Adventurous Revivalist, Hartford Courant, 4/77; Anthony Padovano (auth), The process of sculpture, 81; Vernon Mays (auth), Arch has its angels again, Hartford Courant, 8/20/87; Donald M Reynolds (auth), Masters of American Sculpture, Abbevile Press, 93; Constance Neyer and John Long (coauths) Honored Service, Hartford Courant, 4/16/2000; plus others. *Mem:* Sculptors Guild; Nat Acad; Soc Conn Sculptors; Nat Sculpture Soc. *Media:* Bronze, Ceramic. *Mailing Add:* 229 Grand St New York NY 10013-4240

GLAZER, JAY M & MARSHA S
COLLECTORS, PATRONS
b Anderson, Ind (Mr Glazer); b Portland, Ore (Mrs Glazer). *Study:* Univ Wash, BS, 63-67; Ind Univ, BS (bus), 69; Univ Tex, MBA, 71. *Exhib:* Out of Site: Selections From the Marsha S Glazer Collection (24 pieces by artists such as Pablo Picasso, Roy Lichtenstein, Jasper Johns, David Hockney, Jackson Pollock and Wayne Thiebuad), Univ Art Mus, Univ Calif Santa Barbara, 2005. *Pos:* Collector's comt mem, Nat Gallery Art, 97-. *Awards:* Named one of the Top 200 Collectors, The ARTnews, 2004, 2006. *Mem:* Seattle Art Mus (bd mem, 91-94); Mus Mod Art, NY; Guggenheim Mus. *Collection:* Modern and contemporary art. *Mailing Add:* PO Box 997 Mercer Island WA 98040

GLEIM-JONAS, LISA
PAINTER, WRITER
b Boone, NC, Jul 02, 1971. *Study:* Pa Acad Fine Arts, Cert in painting, 92-96. *Work:* Div of Orthopaedic Surgery, Children's Hosp of Philadelphia, Pa. *Comn:* Atlanta Hematology & Oncology Assocs; Astra-Zeneca Pharmaceutical Company, Philadelphia, Pa; Merle Manders Conference Ctr, Stockbridge, Ga ; Merryl Lynch, Elkins Park, Pa ; Court of Chancery, Wilmington, De; City of Sandy Springs, Ga. *Exhib:* Conn Pastel Soc, 97, 98; Atlanta Fine Arts League, 2000, 2005, 2006, 2007, 2008, 2009; Catherine Lorillard Wolfe Art Club, 2007; Pa Acad Fine Arts, 2002, 2008; Northeast Nat Pastel Exhib, 2009; Southeastern Pastel Soc Mem Juried Exhib, 2006, 2007, 2008, 2009; Md Pastel Soc, 2000; The Portrait Soc of Atlanta, 2000, 2001, 2002, 2004, 2005, 2006; Pastel Soc Am, 2007; Ala Pastel Soc, 2009; Nat League of Am Pen Women, 2009. *Pos:* dir exhibs, Atlanta Fine Arts League. *Awards:* Second Place, 6th Mid-Atlantic Regional Art Exhib, 98; Mem's Choice Award, Portrait Soc Atlanta, 2005; First Place, Atlanta Fine Arts League, 1st Ann Nat Juried Exhib, 2007; 2nd Place, Southeastern Pastel Soc, Mem Juried Exhib, 2007; Merit Award Southeastern Pastel Soc, 2008; Diane Townsend Pastel Award, 5th Ann Northeast Nat Exhib, 2009 ; Golden Artist's Colors Award, Ala Pastel Soc, Mem Exhib, Merit Award, 2009; Mem of Excellence, Southeastern Pastel Soc, 2009; Hon mention, Judges Choice, 6th Ann nE Nat Exhib, 2010; 3rd Place, Va Avery Mem Exhib Atlanta Branch Nat League Pen Women, 2009; Outstanding Small Format Award, 6th Ann NE Nat Exhib, 2010; Hon mention, Atlanta Fine Arst League, 2010. *Bibliog:* Fireman's Memory: Portrait of his Smile, Journ News, 8/27/2002; Lisa Gleim; Capturing your Pet, Piedmont Rev, Vol 9, No 10, 10/2002 ; 2004 Holiday Gift Guide, Points North Mag, 11/2004; Atlanta 101:101Great Gifts 2005, Atlanta Mag, 12/2005; Lisa Gleim: Born to Paint, Southern Seasons Mag, Spring 2008 ; Commemorate Your Prized Horse In a Fine Art Portrait, Equestrian Mag, 3/2009; Drawing Praise, Northside Neighbor, 6/23/2009; Emmy Award winning segment Art From the Heart, State of the Arts, Ga Pub Broadcasting, 01/2008. *Mem:* Portait Soc of Atlanta (bd of dir-dir of exhibs), 2002-2005; Atlanta Home Improvement Mag (adv bd mem), Atlanta, Ga, 2002-2004; bd mem & found, Atlanta Fine Arts League, 2005-; Cecilia Beaux Forum of the Portrait Soc Am (exhib comt planning head), 2009-2011; Pastel Soc Am (Juried assoc mem), 1998-; Pub Artists Registry Mem, Fulton Co Arts Coun, Atlanta, Ga, 2009-; Mus of the Dog Artist Registry, 2000-; Southeastern Pastel Society, Member of Excellence, 2005. *Media:* Pastel. *Publ:* RABIES Flyer, Montgomery County, Pa Health Dept, 97 ; Stomping Ground column, Weisner Publ, Atlanta, Ga, 99; Home Grown Décor, bi-monthly column, homestore.com & aol.com, 2000-2001; Crafty Ideas, Atlanta Home Improvement Mag, monthly column, 2001- 2004; Strokes of Genius: The Best of Drawing, North Light Books, Aug 2007; Strokes of Genius 3: Fresh Perspective, The Best of Drawing, North Light Books, 2011. *Mailing Add:* Lisa Gleim Fine Art 3739 Cloudland Dr Atlanta GA 30327

GLENDINNING, PETER
PHOTOGRAPHER
b New York, NY, Sept 23, 1951. *Study:* Syracuse Univ, BFA, 76, MFA, 78. *Work:* Int Mus Photog, Rochester, NY; Everson Mus Art & Light Work, Syracuse, NY; Tweed Mus Art; Murray State Univ, Ky; Unicolor Corp; Ctr Creative Photography, Tucson, Ariz. *Comn:* Official portrait, Gov John Engler, State of Mich; Photog, State Capitol Restoration Proj, Lansing, Mich. *Exhib:* One-person shows, Lightsong Gallery, Tucson, 80, CEPA Gallery, Buffalo, NY, 81, Foto Gallery, NY, 82 & Lowe Art Gallery, Syracuse Univ, 84; Proj Art Ctr, Cambridge, Mass, 82; Contemp Photog as Phantasy, Santa Barbara Mus Art, 82; Main Street Gallery, Nantucket, Mass, 90; South African Consulate, NY, 99; South African Embassy, Washington DC, 99. *Pos:* Dir, Light Fantastic Gallery, Mich State Univ, East Lansing, 78-; portrait photogr for corp & advert, 84-. *Teaching:* Prof dept art & head photog, Mich State Univ, 78-. *Awards:* Res Grant, Mich State Univ, 81; Unicolor Artist Support Grant, 82; Individual Artist Grant, Mich Arts Coun, 89-90; Addy Citation Excellence, 94. *Mem:* Soc Photog Educ; Friends of Photog; Ctr Creative Photog; Lansing Advert Club; Photo Imaging Educ Asn (bd dir). *Media:* Color. *Publ:* Contribr, Fugitive Color (exhib catalog), Univ Mich, 82; Color Photography: History, Theory and Darkroom Technique, Prentice-Hall, 85; Michigan Quilts: 150 Years of a Textile Tradition, Mich State Univ Mus, 88; numerous magazine covers, advertisements & ann reports. *Dealer:* Photography Assocs Inc 2654 Linden Dr East Lansing MI 48823. *Mailing Add:* Art Dept Kresge Art Ctr Mich State Univ East Lansing MI 48824

GLENN, CONSTANCE WHITE
MUSEUM DIRECTOR, WRITER, CURATOR
b Topeka, Kans, Oct 4, 1933. *Study:* Univ Kans, BFA; Univ Mo, Kansas City; Calif State Univ, Long Beach, MA. *Collection Arranged:* Lucas Samaras: Photo-Transformations (auth, catalog), 75; Roy Lichtenstein: Ceramic Sculpture (auth, catalog), 77; George Segal: Pastels 1957-1965 (auth, catalog), 78; Jim Dine Figure Drawings: 1974-1979 (auth, catalog), 79; Frederick Sommer at Seventy-Five (auth, catalog), 80; Apropos Robinson Jeffers: Robert Motherwell-Renate Ponsold (auth, catalog), 81; Robert Longo (auth, catalog), 86; Eric Fischl: Scenes Before the Eye (auth, catalog), 86; Imagenes Liricas: New Spanish Visions (auth, catalog), 90; James Rosenquist: Time Dust (catalog raisonne), 93; The Great Am Pop Art Store: Multiples of the Sixties (auth, catalog), 97; Double Vision: Photographs from the Strauss Collection, 2001; Tom Wesselmann: The Intimate Images (auth, catalog), 2003; The Artist Observed (auth, catalog), 2003; Candida Höfer: Architecture of Absence (auth, catalog), 2004; and many others. *Pos:* Prof & dir, Mus Studies Cert Prog, Univ Art Mus, Calif State Univ, Long Beach, 73-2004, prof & dir emer, 2004-; chmn South Calif adv bd, Arch Am Art, 78-90; art consult, Archit Digest, 80-89; publ & ed, Artexpress, 88-2013; contrib ed, Angeles Mag, 88-90 & Antiques & Fine Art, 90-91; owner & ceo, ARTexpress Travel Newsletter, 90-2013. *Teaching:* Prof emer, 20th century art, 2004-. *Awards:* Distinguished Scholarly & Creative Achievement Award, Calif State Univ Long Beach; Outstanding Contribr to the Field, Calif Mus Photog, 86; Arts Admin of the Year, Long Beach Pub Corp Arts, 89; Woman of Distinction Award, Soroptimist, 99. *Mem:* Am Asn Mus; Assoc Art Mus Dir (trustee 2000-02, emer, 2004-); Coll Art Asn; Art Table. *Res:* American art since 1945. *Collection:* Art of the Sixties, Contemporary art & photography. *Publ:* Auth, Jim Dine Drawings, 85, Roy Lichtenstein: Landscape Sketches, 86, Lucas Samaras: Doodles, Sketches and Plans, 87, Wayne Thiebaud: Private Drawings, 88 & Robert Motherwell: The Daedalus Sketches, 88, Harry N Abrams, The Great American Pop Art Store: Multiples of the Sixties, 97; ed, Imagenes Liricas: New Spanish Visions, 90; James Rosenquist: Time Dust, The Complete Graphics 1962-1992, Rizzoli, 93; contribr auth, Dictionary of Art, 96-, Encyl Americana, 96-; co-auth, Pop Art: An International Perspective, 91; contribr auth, Carrie Mae Weems: The Hampton Project, 00; Double Vision: Photographs from the Strauss Collection, 2001; Tom Wesselmann, 2005; Beyond Pop Art: Tom Wesselman, 2012; The Small Utopia: Ars Multiplicata, 2012. *Mailing Add:* 18 Altino Newport Beach CA 92657

GLESMANN, SYLVIA MARIA
PAINTER
b Bavaria, Ger, June 8, 1923; US citizen. *Study:* Acad Fine Arts, Nurnberg, Ger; Acad Fine Arts, Munich, Ger, 44; Studied with Robert Sakson & Nicholas Reale. *Work:* Ortho Diagnostics, Bridgewater, NJ; Salmagundi Club (30 paintings). *Comn:* Many pvt comns. *Exhib:* NJ WC Soc, Morris Mus, Morristown, NJ, 80; Summer Selections, Nabisco Brands, East Hanover, NJ, 84; Salmagundi Club Gallery, NY, 88-89, 94, 2000-; Nat Asn Women Artists, NY, 91-92 & 94; Barrons Art Ctr; Solo Exhibs: Ocean Co Coll, NJ, Bridgewater Raritan Pub Libr, 96, Bridgewater Libr, NJ, Ziko's Gallery, New Hope, Pa, Jockey Hollow Gallery, Morristown, NJ; Bridgewater Creative Art

Com, NJ, 2006-2007; Trinity United Church, Warren, NJ, 2006; 3rd Annual Sylvia Maria Glesmann Members Floral Exhib, Salmagundi Club, NY, 2012. *Collection Arranged:* 12 paintings, Patrons Gallery, Salmagundi Club, NY. *Pos:* Chair, 10th chap Outdoor Art Show, Somerset Art Asn. *Teaching:* Somerville Adult Educ Classes; Bridgewater Raritan High Sch, Career Day Demo and Speech, 93-94. *Awards:* Many awards from 70-2008; Editors Choice for Poetry, Int Soc Poetry; over 60 awards in fine art. *Bibliog:* Les Krantz (auth), NY Art Review, 89. *Mem:* Raritan Valley Arts Asn (pres 76-78); Am Artist Prof League (NJ chap, pres 88-91); Nat Asn Women Artists, NY (juror for works on paper 94-96); Garden State Watercolor Soc; charter mem Nat Mus Women Arts, Washington, DC; Salmagundi Club Mem. *Media:* Egg Tempera, Watercolor. *Specialty:* Art. *Interests:* Poetry, music, painting, reading and travel. *Collection:* NFS. *Publ:* Auth, She is Hearts and Flowers, 78, From the Heart, 89, Showcase, 90, Messenger Gazette; Heart in Home, Courier News, 89; On the Towns, Star Ledger, 91. *Mailing Add:* 36 Twin Oaks Rd Bridgewater NJ 08807

GLICK, PAULA F
ART HISTORIAN, DEALER, WRITER
b Baltimore, Md, 1936. *Study:* Am Univ; George Washington Univ, BA & MA; Columbia Univ, MPhil. *Collection Arranged:* Blue Ridge Ctr Collection. *Pos:* Assoc dir, Capricorn Galleries, 74-87, co-dir, 87-97, consultant, appraiser & private dealer; consult to var mus, auction houses & dealers; art history res, lectr; Loudoun Co, Va art advisory comt, 2003-2010. *Teaching:* Instr art hist, Cath Univ, 85. *Bibliog:* Paul Sample, Ivy League Regionalist. *Mem:* Coll Art Asn Am; Art Table: Am Soc of Appraisors, Am Asn Mus; Asn Historians Am Art; and others. *Res:* Paul Sample; American technology and culture 1830-1960; architecture of Michelangelo; American art 1925-1950. *Interests:* Italian Renaissance and Baroque; American Art of the 1930's & 1940's; American contemporary realists; 19th Century American Landscape. *Collection:* Contemporary American realists from 1900 to 1990. *Publ:* Coauth, Paul Sample: Painter of the American Scene, Hood Mus Art, Dartmouth Col; First Cheureul in America, Am Art J, 96; Paul Starrett Sample, Am Nat Biography, 99; essay, Surrounded by Luxury, Objects of Desire; contribr, Sight and Insight: The Art Works of Burton Silvermann, 98; auth, Highlights of the International Personal Property Conference, Taos, N Mex, 99, Personal Property Jour, Vol 12, No 1, 2000; catalog, Made in California, LACMA, 2000. *Mailing Add:* 42842 Falling Leaf Ct Ashburn VA 20148-6928

GLIER, MIKE
DRAFTSMAN, PAINTER
b Fort Thomas, Ky, Aug 26, 1953. *Study:* Williams Col, BA, 76; Hunter Col, with Robert Morris, MA, 79. *Work:* Addison Gallery Am Art, Andover, Mass; Williams Coll Mus Art, Mass; Hartford Atheneum, Conn; Albright-Knos Mus, Buffalo, NY; Mus Mod Art, NY. *Comn:* BAM-Next Wave, set design comn by Tim Miller, Brooklyn, NY, 84; Walls, Norton Gallery Art, West Palm Beach, 86; Green (wall drawings), comn by Wave Hill, Bronx, NY, 89; Goerdler Mem (with Jenny Holzer), City of Leipzig, Ger. *Exhib:* Biennial, Whitney Mus, NY, 83; Hair Breadth: New Wall Drawings (with catalog), La Jolla Mus Contemp Art, Calif, 84; Sydney Biennial, Art Gallery New South Wales, Australia, 84; Am Ne-Expressionists (auth, catalog), Aldrich Mus, Ridgefield, Conn, 84; Ecrans Politiques, Musee d'Art Contemp de Montreal, 85-86; Wallworks, John Weber Gallery, NY, 86; South Africa Drawings, Washington Project for Arts, Washington, DC, 86; solo exhibs, Mus Mod Art, NY, 87, (auth, catalog) San Jose Mus Art, Calif, 89, Alphabet of Lili, Drawing Ctr, NY, 92, Garden Court, Tyler Galleries, Tyler Sch Art, Elkins Park, Pa, 95 & Full Moon on the Hoosick (drawing), Mass Mus Contemp Art, N Adams, 2000-01; Committed to Print, Mus Mod Art, NY, 88; Drawings from the Permanent Collection, Addison Gallery, Andover, Mass, 90; I Love My Time: Contemp Art from the Permanent Collection, Williams Coll Mus Art, Mass, 95; Cult Economies (with catalog), Drawing Ctr, NY, 96; The Flower Show, Fruitmarket Gallery, Edinburgh, Scotland, 99-2000; many others. *Pos:* Adv bd mem, Printed Matter Inc, 83; artist adv bd, New Mus, New York, 89; vis comt, Williams Col Mus Art, 90; juror, Albany Inst Hist & Art, 99. *Teaching:* Asst prof art, studio & art hist, Williams Col, Williamstown, Mass, currently. *Awards:* Nat Endowment Art Fel, 81; Award in Visual Arts 9, New Eng Region; Guggenheim Mem Found Fel, 96. *Bibliog:* Sally Yard (auth), The shadow of the bomb, Arts Mag, 4/84; Robin Carson (auth), Untamed Visitation, Garden Design, winter 89; Elizabeth Hess (auth), The equalizer, Village Voice, 6/21/89. *Mem:* Coll Art Asn. *Media:* Mixed Media. *Publ:* Auth, The 1979 dime store figurine, Art Forum 80; White Male Power, Senators, Game Show Hosts, National Monuments, pvt publ, 82; Patience observation & investigation, Art Forum, 82; Working Watteau, Art Forum, 4/88; Satisfaction, Hallwalls, San Jose Mus Art, 89. *Mailing Add:* Williams Col Spencer Studio Bldg 35 Driscoll Hall Dr Williamstown MA 01267

GLINES, KAREN
WRITER
b St Louis, MO. *Study:* St Louis Univ, BA; Webster Univ, MA. *Pos:* culture and arts writer, Online Am, St Louis, formerly; pres bd govs, St Louis Artists' Guild, Oak Knoll Park, Clayton, Mo, currently. *Teaching:* instr communication, Fontbonne Univ. *Awards:* Governor's Humanities Award for Distinguished Literary Achievement, 2009. *Publ:* auth, Painting Missouri: The Counties en Plein Air, 2008. *Mailing Add:* St Louis Artists' Guild and Galleries Two Oak Knoll Park Saint Louis MO 63105

GLOECKNER, PHOEBE LOUISE
CARTOONIST, ILLUSTRATOR
b Philadelphia, Pennsylvania, 1960. *Study:* San Francisco State Univ; Univ Tex Southwestern Med Ctr, Masters (Med Illus). *Exhib:* Solo exhibs include Cartoon Art Mus, San Francisco, 1998. *Teaching:* Asst prof, Univ Mich Sch Art & Design. *Awards:* John Simon Guggenheim Mem Found Fel, 2008. *Publ:* Illus, The Atrocity Exhibition, Re/Search, San Francisco, 1991; Encyclopedia of Unusual Sex Practices, Barricade Books, NY, 1992; The Re/Search Guide to Bodily Fluids, Re/Search, San Francisco, 1997; auth & illus, A Child's Life & Other Stories, Frog Ltd, 1998 & The Diary of a Teenage Girl in Words & Pictures, 2002; illus, The Good Vibrations Guide to Sex, 3rd ed, Cleis Press, 2002. *Mailing Add:* Univ Mich Sch Art & Design Office 2070 2000 Bonisteel Ave Ann Arbor MI 48109-2069

GLORIG, OSTOR
PAINTER, CRAFTSMAN
b New York, NY, Feb 14, 1919. *Study:* Am Art Sch, New York, with Robert Brackman, Raphael Soyer & Gordon Samstag, four yr cert. *Work:* Mark Twain Portrait, Mark Twain Libr & Mem, Hartford, Conn. *Exhib:* Solo exhibs, Lynn Kottler Galleries, 56, 59, 61, 64 & 72, Clarksville Gallery, 65 & Coll Mt St Vincent, 67; Nat Soc Arts & Lett Empire State Chap Showing, 69 & 79. *Awards:* Interior Design Cover Award, 51; Grumbacher Merit Award, 61. *Bibliog:* Elaine Israel (auth), From diamond to canvas, Long Island Star-J, 5/9/67. *Mem:* Life fel Royal Soc Arts Eng; life mem Nat Soc Arts & Lett; hon mem Kappa Pi. *Media:* Oil. *Dealer:* Lynn Kottler Galleries 3 E 65th St New York NY 10021

GLOVER, ROBERT
SCULPTOR, CERAMIST
b Upland, Calif, May 20, 1936. *Study:* Los Angeles County Art Inst, with Peter Voulkos & Helen Watson, MFA, 60. *Work:* Security Pacific Bank, First Bank of Los Angeles & Bella Lewitsky Dance Found, Los Angeles; Fluor Corp, Irvine, Calif; Everson Mus Fine Arts, NY; Oakland Mus Art, Calif. *Exhib:* Drawing Exhib, San Francisco Mus Art, 57; Ceramics National, Everson Mus Fine Arts, Syracuse, NY, 60; Design 11, Pasadena Art Mus, Calif, 71; Sculpture Invitational, San Diego Mus Art, 73; duo exhib, Munic Gallery, Los Angeles, 79; Dualism, Otis-Parsons Exhib Ctr, Los Angeles, 82. *Teaching:* Asst prof ceramics, Otis Art Inst, 62-79; instr color & design, Otis-Parson Sch Design, 79-, instr ceramics, 92. *Awards:* Ford Found Fac Grant, 78. *Bibliog:* Peter Clothier (auth), Remembrances of things past, Los Angeles Weekly, Vol 8, No 5, 12/27/84; Kristine McKenna (auth), Galleries, Los Angeles Times, 12/13/85; Mac McCloud (auth), Metamorphosis of form, Artweek, Vol 16, 12/21/85. *Mem:* Los Angeles Contemp Exhibs. *Media:* Clay, Mixed Media. *Dealer:* Space Gallery 6015 Santa Monica Blvd Los Angeles CA 90038. *Mailing Add:* Otis College of Art and Design 9045 Lincoln Blvd Los Angeles CA 90045

GLUCK, HEIDI
PAINTER, EDUCATOR
b Brooklyn, NY, Dec 30, 1944. *Study:* Bennington Col, with D Smith, T Smith, Caro, Londo, Stroud & P Feely, BA, 66; Hunter Col, New York, with E Goosen, T Smith, R Humphrey & R Morris, 66-70. *Work:* Guggenheim Mus, NY; Israel Mus, Jerusalem; State Univ Ohio, Columbus; Picker Art Gallery, Colgate Univ, Hamilton, NY; Bennington Col, Vt. *Exhib:* Sensible Exploration, Univ Gallery Fine Art, Ohio State Univ, Columbus, 70; A Painting Show, PSI Projects Studios One, Inst Art & Urban Resources, NY, 77; A Brooklyn Portfolio, Brooklyn Mus, NY, 80; Contemp Drawings & Watercolors, Mem Art Gallery, Univ Rochester, 80; Creative Artists Pub Serv Prog Grantees, Brooklyn Mus, NY, 81; 19 Artists-Emergent Am, Guggenheim Mus, NY, 81. *Teaching:* Vis artist painting, Princeton Univ, 80-91. *Awards:* Creative Artists Pub Serv Prog Grant, 78-79. *Bibliog:* Robert Pincus-Witten (auth), Entries: Glück, Stephen, Acconci, Arts Mag, 3/78; Donald B Kuspit (auth), Heidi Glück, Arts Mag, 6/79; Donald B Kuspit (auth), Stops & starts in seventies art and criticism, Arts Mag, 3/81. *Media:* Oil, Acrylic. *Mailing Add:* 414 2nd St 1st Fl Apt 1A Jersey City NJ 07302

GLUHMAN, MARGARET A
GRAPHIC ARTIST, PHOTOGRAPHER
b Bethel Park, Pa. *Study:* Univ Pittsburgh; Cleveland Inst Art. *Work:* Rutgers Univ Art Mus; Meidinger Corp, Louisville, Ky; Owensboro Mus Fine Art; Eastman Pharmaceutical, Pa; and others. *Exhib:* JB Speed Art Mus, 86; 19th Nat Works on Paper, Minot, NDak, 89; La Grange Nat, Ga, 89, 91, 92 & 94; Multi-Focus Int, State Univ NY, Plattsburgh, 95; Nat Small Works, Armory Art Ctr, Fla, 95; Tex Int, Univ Tex, El Paso, 96. *Collection Arranged:* New Works Series I-XXV, 81-87; Collectors & Collections (auth, catalog), 85; Mid-South Monotypes (auth, catalog), 86-87; New Works/New Alabamians (auth, catalog), 90-91. *Pos:* Exhib coordr, Capitol Arts Ctr, Bowling Green, Ky, 81-87. *Media:* Paper. *Mailing Add:* 2095 Evergreen Dr S Auburn AL 36830-6934

GLUSKA, AHARON
PAINTER
b Feb 26, 1951. *Study:* France Avni Inst Fine Arts, Israel, 73-76; Academie Ecole des Beaux Arts, Paris, 76-77. *Work:* Albright Knox Mus; Brooklyn Mus; Tel Aviv Mus; Cornell Univ Mus; Israel Mus, Jerusalem. *Exhib:* Solo exhibs, Bertha Urdang Gallery, NY, 83, 86 & 88, Tiro Gallery, Copenhagen, Denmark, 87, Eric Siegeltuch Gallery, NY, 88, Gordon Gallery, Tel Aviv, Israel, 88, Shoshana Wayne Gallery, Los Angeles, 90, CS Schulte Galleries, South Orange, NJ, 91, Estok/Lanza Fine Art, New York, 92 & Robert Mann Gallery, NY 95, Nat Jewish Mus, Wash DC, 98, Carole Rubenstein Associates Contemporary Art, Phila, 2001, 2002, 2004, Fla Holocaust Mus, Tampa, Fla, 2005, Total Art/Courtyard, Dubai, 2009, 2012, Art Affairs, Amsterdam, The Netherlands, 2010, Schuppenhauer Galerie, Koln, Ger, 2010, Rivera Gallery, West Hollywood, Calif, 2011, Trierweiler Contemporary Galerie, Weimar, 2013; Book, Box, Word, NMiami Ctr Contemp Art, 92; Book, Box, Word Volume II, Univ Fla, 93; Four Contemp Artists, Jewish Mus, NY, 94; Burnt Whole, Washington Proj Arts, DC, 94; Carol Rubenstein Assoc, Pitts, 99 & Phila, 2000; Park Ave Synagogue, Israeli Art Exhib, 2002; Etched Voices, Yad Vashem, Jerusalem, Israeil, 2005; Mana Fine Arts, Jersey City, NJ, 2007; Art Affaires, Amsterdam, The Netherlands, 2010; Galeria de Arte, Buenos Aires, 2010; Schuppenhauer Galerie, Koln, Ger, 2010; Anthrophysis, Rivera Gallery, West Hollywood, Calif, 2011. *Awards:* Pollock-Krasner Found Grant, 89; Nat Endowment Arts Grant, 89. *Mailing Add:* 535 Broadway New York NY 10012

GNOTT, JACQUELINE
PAINTER
Study: Ind Univ, BA. *Exhib:* Solo exhibs include Colfax Cult Ctr, South Bent, Ind, 1992, South Bend Regional Mus Art, 1994, Univ St Francis, Ft Wayne, Ind, 2002, Fernwood Botanical Garden, Niles, Mich, 2003; group exhibs include Int Exhib Botanical Art & Illustration, Hunt Inst, Carnegie Mellon Univ, Pittsburgh, 1995;

Contemp Am Realism, Ft Wayne, Ind, 2006; Small Sizes-Precious Pieces, Sherry French Gallery, New York, 2006, Flowers in February, 2007, Painting, 2007, Gallery & Invited Artists, 2007. *Awards:* Pollock-Krasner Found Grant, 2006. *Mem:* Int Guild Realism, Scottsdale, Ariz. *Media:* Watercolor. *Dealer:* Sherry French Gallery Inc 601 W 26th St 13th Fl New York NY 10001-1101. *Mailing Add:* 19327 Brick Rd South Bend IN 46637-1813

GOAD, ANNE LAINE
ART DEALER, PUBLISHER
b Nashville, Tenn. *Study:* David Lipscomb Univ, Nashville, Tenn, BA (magna cum laude), 67. *Collection Arranged:* 10 + 2, The Parthenon Mus, Nashville, Tenn, 1991; Light a Long Time After, The Parthenon Mus, 2002. *Pos:* Partner, ASID Indust. *Awards:* Industry Ptnr of Yr, Tenn Chpt ASID, 2002. *Bibliog:* Pat Swingley (auth), Italian charm, Tennessean, 5/92; Deborah Highland Collins (auth), Art dealer brings city "vibrationism", Tennessean, 7/95; Peggy Krebs (auth), Original art reflects trend among home buyers, Tennessean, 9/98. *Mem:* Visual Artists Alliance Nashville; Nat Asn Women Bus Owners. *Specialty:* Original paintings featuring mid-south regional artists since 1984. *Mailing Add:* Anne Laine Goad Art Inc PO Box 2165 Brentwood TN 37024

GOBER, ROBERT
SCULPTOR
b Wallingford, Conn, Sept 12, 1954. *Study:* Tyler Sch Art, Rome, Italy, 1974; Middlebury Coll, Vt, BA, 1976. *Work:* Whitney Mus Am Art; Mus Mod Art; San Francisco Mus Mod Art; Guggenheim Mus; Menil Collection; Tate Mod; Hirshhorn Mus & Sculpture Garden. *Exhib:* Solo exhibs, Paula Cooper Gallery, New York, 1984-85, Daniel Weinberg Gallery, Los Angeles, 1985-86, Galerie Jean Bernier, Athens, 1987, Galerie Max Hetzler, Koln, 1988, Galleria Marga Paz, Madrid, 1990, Dia Ctr for Arts, New York, 1992, Serpentine Gallery, London, 1993, LACMA, 1997, Aldrich Mus Contemp Art, 1998, San Francisco Mus Mod Art, 1999, 49th Venice Biennale, 2001, Astrup Fearnley Museet for Moderne Kunst, Oslo, 2003, Royal Hibernian Acad, Dublin, 2005 & Matthew Marks Gallery, 2008, 2012, Mus Contemporary Arts, Denver, 2010, Mus fur Gegenwartskunst, Basel, 2012; Group exhibs, Scapes, Univ Art Mus, Santa Barbara, 1985; Koons, Daniel Weinberg Gallery, Los Angeles, 1986; Avant Garde in the Eighties, LACMA, 1987; Furniture as Art, Mus Boymans-van Beuningen, Rotterdam, 1988; Horn of Plenty, Stedelijk Mus, Amsterdam, 1989; Drawings, Burnett Miller Gallery, Los Angeles, 1990; Forbidden Games, Jack Tilton Gallery, New York, 1991; The Last Days, Pabellon de Espana, Seville, Spain, 1992; Works on Paper, Galerie Ghislaine Hussenot, Paris, 1993; Desire and Loss, Carl Solway Gallery, Cincinnati, 1994; Ars 95 Helsinki, Mus Contemp Art, Finland, 1995; Model Home, Inst Contemp Art, Clocktower Gallery, New York, 1996; De-Genderism, Setagaya Art Mus, Tokyo, 1997; Wounds, Moderna Museet, Stockholm, 1998; Recent Prints, Betsy Senior Gallery, New York, 1999; Vanitas, Va Mus Fine Arts, Richmond, 2000; Body Space, Baltimore Mus Art, 2001; REACTIONS, Exit Art, New York, 2002; Air, James Cohan Gallery, New York, 2003; The Big Eat in Art, Kunsthalle Bielefeld, Bielefeld, Ger, 2004; The Shape of Time, Walker Art Ctr, Minneapolis, 2005; Artists at Work, Cranbrook Mus Art, Bloomfield Hills, Mich, 2006; Two Years, Whitney Mus Am Art, 2007; Make Art/Stop AIDS, Fowler Mus, Los Angeles, 2008; Notations: The Closing Decade, Philadelphia Mus Art, 2009; Slides of a Changing Painting, Mus Contemp Art, Denver, 2010; The Whitney Biennial, A Selection of Work by Forrest Bess, Whitney Mus Art, New York, 2012; Object Fictions, James Cohan Gallery, New York, 2012; This Will Have Been: Art, Love, & Politics in the 1980s, Mus Contemp Art, 2012; Theater of the World, Mus of Old and New Art, Hobart, Australia, 2012; Schaulager Satellite, Messeplatz Basel, Art Basel, 2012; 55th Int Art Exhib, Biennale, Venice, 2013. *Collection Arranged:* Heat Waves in a Swamp: The Paintings of Charles Burchfield, Hammer Mus, Los Angeles, Calif, 2009. *Awards:* Larry Aldrich Found Award, 1996; Skowhegan Medal for Sculpture, 1999; Artists Space Honoree, Spring Benefit, 2002. *Bibliog:* Robert Gober: Sculptures and Installations 1979-2007, 2007. *Mem:* Nat Acad. *Publ:* coauth (with Brenda Richardson), A Robert Gober Lexicon, 2008; coauth (with Elisabeth Sussman), Sculptures 1979-2007, 2009. *Dealer:* Matthew Marks Gallery 523 W 24th St New York NY 10011. *Mailing Add:* 119 E 10th St Apt 1 New York NY 10003

GOBUZAS, ALDONA M
ART DEALER, CONSULTANT
b Brooklyn, NY. *Study:* Notre Dame Coll, St John's Univ, BA. *Specialty:* Contemporary American art; Modern art; Current Artists; Lois Dicoscola, Robert Civello, Olga Sheirr, Julius Ludavicius, Arunas Kulikauskas, Estates Represented; John Curoi, Gertrude R Schwartz, Lynne Drexler. *Collection:* Contemporary paintings; sculpture; drawings, etchings; prints. *Mailing Add:* Galerie Aldonna 215 E 79th St Apt 7D New York NY 10075

GODBEE, GARY
PAINTER
b Coral Gables, FL Jan 20, 1952. *Study:* Boston Univ, Sch Fine Arts, BFA, 74; Brooklyn Coll, grad painting with Lennart Anderson, 92; Montclair Univ, grad painting with John Czerkowicz, 93; Painting Fel, NJ State Coun Arts, 93 & 2004. *Work:* Pfizer Inc Collection, NY,; Boston Univ, Boston, Mass; Whelan Collection, Washington, DC; Ethyl/New Market Corp Collection, Richmond, Va; Chase Mellon Collection, Jersey City, NJ; LMA, Toronto, Canada; NJ Dept Labor, Trenton, NJ. *Comn:* Antoine DeLaire, DeLaire Inc, New York, 91; Jack Funesti, Am Soc Perfumers, New York, 92; Two Views of Trenton (5' x 20' each), State NJ Dept Labor, Trenton, NJ, 98-2000; Newark at Dusk, Arcorp, Newark, NJ, 2000; A Tribute to Dr. Minnefore, St Barnabas Hosp, Dept Pediatrics, Livingston, NJ, 2006. *Exhib:* Nat Portrait Competition, Portrait Inst, New York, 96; NJ Mural Proposals, NJ State Gallery/NJ State Mus, Trenton, NJ, 2000-2001; 15E: Contemp Art/NJ Turnpike, Robeson Gallery, Rutgers Univ, Newark, NJ, 2001; Jersey Bound, Tomasulo Gallery, Union Co Coll, Cranford, NJ, 2003; NJ: Place of Mind/NJ Arts Ann, Montclair Art Mus, Montclair, NJ, 2005; NJSCA Fel Exhib, NJ State Mus, Trenton, NJ, 2006; Clarity of Form, Edward Williams Gallery, Fairleigh Dickinson Univ, Hackensack, NJ, 2009; Art & Artifice, NJ Arts Ann, NJ State Mus, Trenton, NJ, 2010; Acopal Exhib Contemp Am Realism, Butler Inst Am Art, 2011; Contemporary American Realism, World Art Mus, Beijing, 2012. *Teaching:* Instr figure drawing, Art Students League, 92-93; instr painting, Montclair Art Mus/Yard Sch Art, 93-; instr, Somerset Art Asn, 2001-; instr painting, Vis Arts Ctr NJ, Summit, 2008-2009. *Awards:* NJSCA Painting Fel, 94 & 2004; Exceptional Merit Award, 14th & 21st Ann Metro Shows, City Without Walls Gallery, 95 & 2002. *Bibliog:* Dan Bischoff (auth), Asphalt Artery, 2001 & Terrain Fare, 2003, Star-Ledger; Joshua Rose (auth), Gary Godbee's Panoramas, Am Art Collector Mag, 2006; Dan Bischoff (auth), Godbee at Gallery Henoch, Star-Ledger, 2011. *Mem:* Am China Oil Painting Artists League (lifetime hon mem). *Media:* Oil, Drawing Media. *Dealer:* Gallery Henoch 555 W 25th St NY; Studio 7 Gallery 5 Morristown Rd Bernardsville NJ 07924. *Mailing Add:* 210 Washington St Westfield NJ 07090

GODDARD, DONALD
EDITOR, WRITER
b Cortland, NY, Apr 16, 1934. *Study:* Princeton Univ, BA, 56; Columbia Univ, 1958-1960; NYU Inst Fine Arts, 1966-1968, 1974-1975. *Exhib:* photographer for Hannah Wilke on several works including So Help me Hannah, 1978, P.S. 1 in Long Island City and Intravenus, 1991-1993, Ronald Feldman Fine Art, NY. *Pos:* Writer & ed, McGraw-Hill Book Co, New York, 66-69; managing ed, Art News Mag, New York, 74-78, contrib ed, 78- 90; ed, Harry N Abrams Inc, 79-82 & Wildlife Conserv Soc, 82-96. *Mem:* Int Asn Art Critics. *Publ:* Auth, Mark di Suvero: An epic reach, 76 & Rothko's journey into the unknown, 79, Art News Mag; Harry Jackson, Harry N Abrams Inc, 81; Sound-Art, Sound Art Found, 83; Am painting, Hugh Lauter Levin, 90; auth, Saving Wildlife, Harry N Abrams, 1995; art rev, newyorkartworld.com, 2000-. *Mailing Add:* 463 West St New York NY 10014

GODDARD, JANET SNIFFIN
GALLERY DIRECTOR, EDUCATOR
Study: Univ Hartford, Conn; Tampa Art Inst, Fla; William Pachner Sch Art, Fla; Delatolas Marble Sculpture Studio, Tinos, Greece; Am Inst Med Educ, Fla. *Exhib:* Solo exhibs, Denise Bibro Fine Art, New York, Pindar Gallery, Rockerfeller Townhouse Gallery, Corner Gallery, Conn, Univ FLa, Arts Ctr Gallery, St Petersburg Pub Libr Gallery, Fla, Green Mountain Coll, Liturgical Conf, Vt, Marco Leo Ltd Gallery, New York, WEDU TV, Fla, Gallery 205, Southern Alleghenies Mus Art, Pa, St Petersburg Mus Fine Art, Fla, Jackson Mus Fine Art,; Group exhibs, Lever House, Broom St Gallery, 41 Union Square West Studies, New York, Soc Four Arts, Palm Beach, Fla, LeMoyne Gallery, Fla, Pindar Gallery, New York, Eckerd Coll, Rollins Coll, Fla, Edison Coll, Univ Fla, Jacksonville Mus Contemp Art, Fla, St Petersburg Mus Fine Art, Tampa Pub Libr, St Petersburg Gallery, New York, Hodgell-Hartman Gallery, Fla, Murray-Leobold Gallery, Chambers Interior & Industiral Design, Inc, Tampa Art Inst, Fla Guilf Coast Art Ctr, Sarasota Visual Art Ctr, S Allenghenies Mus Art, Pa, Women Artists in Fla, Gallery 205, Fla, Bayless Gallery, Conn, Gallery Paule Anglim, Calif, Denis Bibro Fine Art, New York, Contemp Gallery, Fla, Cornerstone Gallery Inc, Conn, Cornerstone Five, Inc, Joseoff Gallery, Beautiful Things, New York, Conn, Evelyn Cobb Gallery, Fla. *Pos:* Found & educ, Gallerist Studio 1212, Inc, Fla, Cornerstone Studio, Cornerstone Five, Inc, Conn, Cornerstone Gallery, Inc; Cofound, USA Fla; Rep, Denise Bibro Gallery, New York, 82-. *Teaching:* Instr, Pinellas Co Arts Cound, Fla, Fla Guilf Coast Art Ctr, Conn, Fla, Central Fla Community Coll

GODFREY, ROBERT
PAINTER, CRITIC
b Mt Holly, NJ, Apr 17, 1941. *Study:* Univ of the Arts, BFA, 66; Royal Acad Fine Arts, Copenhagen, post grad, 66-67; Ind Univ, MFA, 69. *Work:* Acad d'Arte Moderna, Montecatini, Ital; Asheville Art Mus, NC; Butler Inst, Ohio; Greenville Mus Art, NC; Ind Univ Mus Art; Musea d'Arte Contemporanea, Ital; Museoa Gernika, Spain; State Mus Pa; Woodmere Art Mus, Pa. *Comn:* Site Specific Installation, NC Mus Art. *Exhib:* Solo exhibs, Butler Inst Am Art, Youngstown, Ohio, 83 & 92, Zone One Contemp, Asheville, NC, 92, 95 & 97, Rutnsache Cont, Hamburg, 98, Reed Gallery, Copenhagen, 99, Goya Gallery, Melbourne, 2003, Bridget Mayer Gallery, Philadelphia, 2005, Black Mountain Center for the Arts, NC, 2007; Group exhibs, Del Art Mus, Mint Mus Art, Nat Acad Mus, State Mus Pa, Southeastern Ctr Contemp Art, Counihan Gallery, Melborne, Mus di Murlo, Italy, Museul Nat de Arta, Romania. *Pos:* Dir, Artists' Choice Mus, New York, 79-80, ed, 80-82; art critic, Asheville Citizen Times, 85-89; ed, CRITS: Discourses on the Visual Arts, 88-93. *Teaching:* Vis artist, Univ Pa, Philadelphia, 79-82; prof art, Westminster Coll, New Wilmington, Pa, 82-85; head art dept, Western Carolina Univ, Cullowhee, NC, 85-2001; MFA coordr, Western Carolina Univ, 2003-2006. *Awards:* The Butler Medal for Lifetime Achievement in Am Art; Fulbright-Hays scholar, Denmark, 66-67; Buhl Found grant, 78; Hon Research Fel, Arch Humanist Art, Melbourne, Australia, 2003. *Bibliog:* James Thompson (auth), Recent paintings by Robert Godfrey: Between the dog & the wolf (catalog essay), St John's Mus, NC, 91; E Gunn (auth), Robert Godfrey: Dreamdates (Catalog Essay) Semi-Public: A Sparefoot Cont Art (NC), 2003; Roberta Fallon & Libby Rosof (auths), Wet Daydreams (Art Blog) Philadelphia, Pa, 2005; Edward J Sozanski (auth), Godfrey in Love, Philadelphia Inquirer, 5/2005; and others. *Mem:* Int Asn Art Critics; NC Art Coun; Coll Art Asn. *Media:* Oil. *Publ:* About sentimentality, 83 & A lesson in still life painting, 84, Artists' Choice Mus J; Civilization, Education and the Visual Arts: A Personal Manifesto, Kappan Mag, 92; monograph, Kenneth Noland: Music Without Words, Greenville Mus Art, NC, 2006; auth, The Girl with the Hat, Surface Design Jour, Calif, 2007; and others. *Mailing Add:* PO Box 900 Hudson NY 12534

GODFREY, WINNIE (WINIFRED) M
PAINTER, INSTRUCTOR
b Philadelphia, Pa, Nov 21, 1944. *Study:* Marycrest Col, Iowa, 61-63; Art Inst Chicago, 62; Univ Wis, Madison, BS, 66, MFA, 70. *Work:* Ill State Mus, Springfield; Portland Mus, Ore; Rochester Art Ctr, Minn; FMC Corp, Chicago, Ill; Northern Ill Univ, De Kalb, IL; Union League Club Chgo. *Comn:* Oil painting, State Ill, Danville, 83; oil painting, Oakton Community Col, Ill, 86; oil painting, Lewis & Clark Coll, Alton, Ill, 2010; oil painting, Methodist Hospital, Houston, Tex, 2010; Prentice Womens Hosp, Chgo, Ill, 2007. *Exhib:* Two-person show, Art Inst Chicago Sales Gallery, 81; solo exhib, Chicago Botanic Garden, Glencoe, Ill, 86, 94, 2001, Rahr-West Art Mus, Manitowoc, Wis, 88, 93, Univ Penn Mus, 2004, Idaho State Hist Mus, 2006, Carnegie Mus Natural Hist, 2006, Ill State Mus, Ill, 2008, Chicago Cult Ctr, 2010; 20th Century Flower Painting, Mus Art, Ft Lauderdale, Fla, 91; Headley-Whitney Mus, Lexington, Ky, 91; Holland Mus, Mich, 96; Chgo Cultural Ctr, 2010; Renaissance Gallery, Chgo; Lewis & Clarke Col, Godfrey, Ill, 2013. *Teaching:* Artist-in-residence drawing & painting, Rochester Art Ctr, Minn, 70; vis lectr drawing, Univ Ill, Chicago, 75-76; instr portraits, Evanston Art Ctr, Ill, 80-85. *Awards:* First Prize, Milwaukee Lakefront, Milwaukee Art Ctr, 75 & 78; Best of Show, Arthur Baer Mem Competition, Beverly Art Ctr, 83; Award of Excellence, Flora Exhib, Chicago Botanic Garden, Glencoe, Ill, 86, 88; Award of Excellence for Career Municipal Art League of Chicago, 2007. *Bibliog:* Richard Waller (auth), article, New York Gallery Guide, 5/82; Jim Hatfield (producer), Two on two, CBS, 84; Am Artist Mag, 7/8/2005. *Mem:* Artists Equity; Chicago Artists Coalition; North Shore Art League. *Media:* Oil. *Interests:* Snorkeling, travel, horticulture, major culture. *Publ:* Auth, article, In: Gallery Guide, Art Now Inc, 82; contribr, The New York Art Review, Macmillan, 82; Illustrators 23, Madison Sq Press, 83; Artists Mag, F&W Publ, 86 & 91; American Painting, Open Press Studios, 95; Am Artist Mag, 2005; chicago Home & Garden, 2007. *Dealer:* Winifred Godfrey 2647 N Orchard Chicago IL 60614. *Mailing Add:* 2647 N Orchard St Chicago IL 60614-1548

GODSEY, GLENN
EDUCATOR, PAINTER
b Amarillo, Tex, June 1, 1937. *Study:* Okla State Univ; Univ Tulsa, BA & MA; and with Alexandre Hogue. *Work:* Springfield Art Mus, Mo; Okla State Art Collection, Okla Arts & Humanities Coun, Oklahoma City; Gilcrease Mus, Tulsa. *Comn:* Portrait, Univ Tulsa; portraits, Oral Roberts Univ, The Union Depot & Gilcrease Mus, Tulsa. *Exhib:* Solo exhibs, Philbrook Art Ctr, Tulsa, 71, Amarillo Art Ctr, 85 & Univ Tulsa, 85; Traveling Exhib of Okla Art, Washington, DC, 76; Saltillo, Mex, 77; Two-person exhib, Univ Tulsa, 78; Am Watercolor, Taipei Fine Arts Mus, Taiwan, 85; Aquarelles Americaines, Tours, France, 86. *Teaching:* Assoc prof painting, Univ Tulsa, 67-. *Awards:* Watercolor USA Purchase Award, SMo Mus Asn, 74; Okla Artist Ann Award, 72 & 74. *Bibliog:* Rev Blakey (auth), Delineating the mysterious, Univ Tulsa Mag; Maurice DeVinna (auth), Music & the arts, Tulsa World Mag, 71; Bill Donaldson (auth), Showcase, Tulsa Tribune, 71. *Mem:* Watercolor USA Hon Soc. *Media:* Acrylic, Watercolor. *Publ:* Auth, Hip generation, Univ Tulsa Mag, 68; illusr, Okla State Univ Lit Quart, Nimrod, Tulsa Mag & Univ Tulsa Mag. *Dealer:* M A Doran Gallery Tulsa OK. *Mailing Add:* Phillips Hall Rm 218 Sch Art Univ Tulsa Tulsa OK 74104

GODWIN, JUDITH
PAINTER
b Suffolk, Va. *Study:* Richmond Prof Inst, Coll William & Mary, Va, BFA; Art Students League, with Vaclav Vytlacil, Will Barnet & Harry Sternberg; Hans Hofmann Sch, Provincetown, Mass & New York; Va Commonwealth Univ, Hon DFA, Mary Baldwin Col, Staunton, Va. *Hon Degrees:* Virginia Commonwealth Univ, Hon DFA; Mary Baldwin Col, Hon Doc Humane Letters, VA. *Work:* Metrop Mus, NY; Milwaukee Art Ctr, Wis; San Francisco Mus Mod Art; Nat Mus Art, Osaka, Japan; Yale Univ; Nat Mus Wales, Cardiff; Vassar Coll Mus; Va Mus, Richmond; Smith Coll Mus; Utah Mus, Salt Lake City; Herbert F Johnson Mus, Cornell Univ; Amarillo Mus Art, Tex; Art Inst of Chicago, Ill; Hirsh Horn Mus and Sculpture Ctr, Washington, DC; and others; Nat Mus Women in the Arts, Washington, DC; NC Mus Art, Raleigh; Newark Mus, NJ; Greenville Co Mus, SC. *Comn:* Painter's Themes (fabric design), Bloomcraft Inc, NY, 76. *Exhib:* One-person shows, Betty Parsons Gallery, 59-60, Ingber Gallery (with catalog), NY, 77, 79, 81-82, 84, 90, 93, 94, 97, Womensbank, Richmond, Va, 81, Phoenix II Gallery, Washington, 83, Marisa del Re Gallery (with catalog), NY, 83, 90 & 92, Northern Mich Univ, Marquette, 84, Mukai Gallery, Tokyo & Lockwood Mathews Mansion Mus, Norwalk, Conn, 85; Mary Baldwin Col, Staunton, VA, 76; Am Fedn Art Traveling exhib, Hans Hofmann as Teacher, 79 & 82; Kenkeleba Gallery, NY, 85; retrospective, Va Polytech Inst, 88, Danville Mus Fine Arts, Va, 89 & Amarillo Mus Art, Tex, 95; Art Mus WVa, 97; Albany Mus Art, Ga; Rutgers Univ, NJ, 2001; Del Ctr for Contemp Art, 2001; Towson Univ, Md, 2002. *Pos:* bd trustees, Mary Baldwin Col, 84-89. *Teaching:* Lectr, May Baldwin Col, VA, 92. *Awards:* Popular Prize, Leache Mem Exhib, Norfolk, 51; Sequicentennial Medal, Mary Baldwin Col, 92; Career Achievement Award, Mary Galdwin Col, Va, 2002. *Bibliog:* Sibella Conner (auth), Judith Godwin responds gradually, Richmond Times-Dispatch, 1/31/93; Robert Hobbs (auth), Judith Godwin, Aesthetic mediations between east and west, Women's Art J, spring-summer, 93; Mark Morey (auth), Judith Godwin: an artist out of time, Amarillo Mus Art, 11/18/95. *Mem:* Am Fedn Arts; Coll Art Asn; Women's Caucus Art. *Media:* Oil, Acrylic

GOEHLICH, JOHN RONALD
EDUCATOR, PAINTER
b Chicago, Ill, Sept 29, 1934. *Study:* Bard Col, with Louis Schanker, BA, 56. *Comn:* interior watercolors, Redwood Library, Newport, RI; interior watercolors, George Herrick, Newport, RI; interior watercolors, Andrea Roselli Del Turco, Paris, France; interior watercolors, Betty Fagan, Portsmouth, RI; interior watercolors, Meg Braff Interiors, New York. *Exhib:* Newport Art Mus, 2012; Spring Bell Gallery, 2012. *Pos:* Art dir, Doyle Dane Bernbach Inc, New York, 57-64. *Teaching:* Dean admis, Sch Visual Arts, New York, 66-68; head dept visual commun, Ill Inst Art, Chicago, 69-97. *Awards:* Cert Merit, Art Dirs Club, New York, 63 & 64. *Mem:* Newport Art Mus; Redwood Library & Athenaeum, Newport, RI. *Media:* Acrylics, Watercolor, Prints. *Dealer:* Newport Restoration Foundation Newport RI. *Mailing Add:* 70 Carroll Ave Unit 302 Newport RI 02840

GOELL, ABBY JANE
PAINTER, ASSEMBLAGE ARTIST, PRINTMAKER
b New York, NY. *Study:* Art Students League, with Harry Sternberg & Charles Alston; Syracuse Univ, BA; NY Sch Interior Design, Cert; Columbia Univ, with Robert Motherwell, Stephen Greene & John Heliker, MFA (painting), 65; Attingham Park, Shropshire, UK, 63; Pratt Graphic Ctr, 65; The Yeats Summer Sch, Sligo, Ireland, 90. *Work:* Mus Mod Art, NY; Yale Univ Art Gallery; Chase Manhattan Bank Collection, NY; Kresge Art Ctr, Mich; Atlantic Richfield Oil Co; Neuberger Mus, Purchase, NY; Print Collection, NY Pub Libr; Smith Coll Art Mus; Princeton Univ Art Gallery, Grafisches Kabinet, Munich; Univ Alberta, Can, plus others; Sloane-Kettering Meml Ctr, NY; United Negro Coll Fund; Zimmerli Mus, Rutgers Univ, NJ; Newark Pub Libr Print Collection; Loeb Art Mus, Vassar col, Poughkeepsie, NY; Dartmouth-Hitchcock Med Center, Lebanon, NH. *Comn:* Original print, Pratt Graphics Ctr, 75. *Exhib:* Grey Gallery & Study Ctr, NY Univ, 77; Am Acad Arts & Letts, 77; Childe Hassam Purchase Prize Exhib, 77; US Mission, Havana, Cuba, 79-81; Sculpture Ctr, NY, 81; TAGA-PRATT Exhib, Caracas, 82; Silvermine, Conn Ann, 81-82; John Szoke Gallery, NY, 88-89; Southeastern Ohio Cult Ctr, 92; Kavehaz Gallery, SoHo, NY, 96; Fotouhi-Cramer Gallery, SoHo, NY, 96, Cooperstown, NY Art Asn Ann, 97; Hudson River Quadricentennial, Edward Hooper House, NYACK, NY, 2009. *Pos:* Founder & publ, Arcadia Press, NY; independent art appraiser, 79. *Teaching:* Instr art hist, Hunter Col, 67; lectr, Lab Inst Merchandising, 67-70. *Awards:* Yaddo Fel, Saratoga Springs, NY, 68; Fondation Samuel Buffat, Geneva, Switz, 97; artist-in-residence, The Banff Ctr for Arts, 2001; CAMAC, Marnay-sur-Seine, France, 2006 & 2007. *Bibliog:* Archive, Am Mus Women Arts, Washington. *Mem:* Life mem, Art Students League. *Media:* Acrylic, Oil; Collage, Assemblage, Silk Screens. *Publ:* Ed, English Silver 1675-1825, Ensko & Wenham, revised ed, 80. *Mailing Add:* 37 Washington Sq W New York NY 10011

GOERTZ, AUGUSTUS FREDERICK, III
PAINTER, PHOTOGRAPHER
b Greenwich Village, New York, NY, Aug 15, 1948. *Study:* High Sch of Music & Art, New York; Carnegie-Mellon Univ, Pittsburgh, Pa; San Francisco Art Inst, BFA; also with Tom Akawie, Jay Defeo, Augustus Goertz Sr, Wally Hedrick, Bruce Nauman & Jim Rienekin. *Work:* San Francisco Art Inst; Chicago Art Inst; Aldrich Mus Contemp Art, Ridgefield, Conn; Huntington Bank of Ohio; Hyatt Collection, NY; Aetna Casualty & Insurance, Harrison, NY; Siemens Electronics: Shersan Lehman, Chubb Avatav Brokerage. *Exhib:* Selections from The Collection, Aldrich Mus of Contemp Art, 78; Arte Fiera, Bologna, Italy, 78; Todd Capp Gallery, NY; Ruth Bachoffner, Los Angeles; Solo exhibs, NY Law Sch, 77 & Sarah Rentschler Gallery, 78-85; Are You Experienced, Univ Brussels, Belgium, 81; Somers Gallery, Somerstown, NY; Todd Capp 85-86; The Gallery, Bond St, NY, 90; New-Persona, NY, 90; Patricia Correa, Los Angeles; Robin Rice Photo, NY. *Collection Arranged:* Contemporary Reflections, Aldrich Mus of Contemp Art, Ridgefield, Conn, 73; Encounter, Warren Benedek Gallery, NY, 73. *Pos:* Dir, Art Time Found, NY; consultant, Downtown Ventures, NY; corresp, Viva Mag, Ger, Maire-Claire Mag, German edition. *Awards:* Spec Achievement Award, New York Taxi Drivers, Robert Scull, 65; Honor Student Award, San Francisco Art Inst, 67. *Bibliog:* J Wiessman (auth), article, Art News, 75; Ellen Stern (auth), article, New York Mag, 78; Eleanor Blan (auth), article, New York Times, 80; Ellen Handy (auth), article, Arts Mag, 87. *Mem:* Orgn of Independent Artists; NY WPA Artists Inc; San Francisco Art Inst Alumni Asn. *Media:* Oil, Acrylic; Photo Emulsion. *Publ:* Contribr, New York Art Review, 89; photographs, Viva Magazine, Ger & Bilden Suntag, Ger. *Dealer:* Patricia Correia 1355 Abbot Kinney Blvd Venice Los Angeles CA; Romy Barron 95 Horatio St New York NY 10014. *Mailing Add:* 319 Greenwich St No 2 New York NY 10013-3339

GOETZ, INGVILD
COLLECTOR
Pos: Owner & dir, Art in Progress Gallery, Zurich, Switz, 1969 & Munich, Germany, 1971; founder, Sammlung Goetz Mus, Goetz Collection, Munich, 1993-. *Awards:* Art Cologne Award, 2001; München Leuchtet Award, 2001; named one of Top 200 Collectors, ARTnews mag, 2004-13. *Collection:* Contemporary art. *Mailing Add:* Goetz Collection Oberföhringerstrasse 103 Munich D-81925 Germany

GOETZ, MARY ANNA
PAINTER, INSTRUCTOR
b Oklahoma City, Okla, Oct 7, 1946. *Study:* Okla city Univ, BA, 68; Cape Sch Art, Provincetown, Mass, 69-70; NY Acad Art, New York, 81-82. *Work:* Meyers Gallery State Univ NY, Plattsburgh; Union Pac, Union League Club, White & Case, NY; McCarter & English, Princeton, NJ; Springfield Mus, Springfield, Utah; Rittenhouse Hotel, Philadelphia, Pa; Okla State Art Collection; Woodstock Libr. *Comn:* Landscape of golf course, PGA World Hall of Fame, Pinehurst, NC; View from Olana, Hudson River Club; View from the Gold Star Bldg, Okla City Skyline, Mr and Mrs Dennis Pealor, Okla City Univ. *Exhib:* Collector's Choice, Miss Mus Art, Jackson, 86-88; Ann Nat Salon, Springfield Mus Art, Utah, 86-87; Brooklyn Bounty: Natural Splendor & Domestic Opulence, Mus Borough Brooklyn, NY, 85; solo exhibs, Grand Cent Art Galleries, NY, 91, Newman Galleries, Philadelphia, 86; Kirk Patrick Ctr, Okla City, 93; James Cox Gallery, Woodstock, NY, 94-95 & 2002-03; Howell Gallery, Okla City, 2005-2006; Nat Arts Club, 2006-2007; James Cal Gallery, Woodstock NY, 2007; Howell Gallery, Okla City, 2007. *Teaching:* Instr, landscape & still life painting, Woodstock Sch Art, 91-. *Awards:* Warren E Bower Meml award, Salmagundi Club, 84, prize, 86; Pres Award, Nat Arts Club, 2004; Art Students League award, Nat Arts Club, 2014. *Bibliog:* Stephen Douherty (auth), Survey of Outdoor Painters, Am Artist, 10/88; Joan D'Arcy (auth), The Richly Diverse Art of Mary Anna Goetz, Santa Fe

Focus, 7/92; Stephen Doherty (auth), Pursuing a Landscape Theme, Am Artist Mag. *Mem:* Nat Arts Club; Salmagundi Club (jury of awards); Nat Asn Women Artists (newsletter ed); Artists Fel; Woodstock Artists Asn; Okla Soc Impressionists. *Media:* Oil. *Publ:* Auth, Robert Shultz: In Memoriam, Portraiture, It's Two Irresistible Forces: Artist & Subject, The Illuminator, 79; Painting Landscapes in Oil, North Light, 91; Impact of Brush Strokes, Am Artist, 92; A Field Guide to Landscape Paintings (video/DVD); Techniques Revealed from Start to Finish. *Dealer:* James Cox Gallery 4666 Rt 212 Willow NY 12495; Newman Gallery Phila; Howell Gallery Okla City. *Mailing Add:* 4666 Rte 212 Willow NY 12495

GOETZ, PETER HENRY
PAINTER, LECTURER
b Slavgorod, Russia, Sept 8, 1917; Can citizen. *Study:* Waterloo Col, 45; Doon Sch Fine Art, with F H Varley; study watercolor in Japan. *Work:* Queen Elizabeth Collection, Windsor Castle, Eng; London Pub Libr & Art Mus, Ont; Sarnia Pub Libr & Art Mus, Ont; Kitchener Waterloo Art Gallery; Univ Waterloo, Ont; Arnot Art Mus, Elmira, NY; 73 paintings, New City Hall, Waterloo, Ont. *Comn:* Series of twelve paintings from around the world, Waterloo Co Health Bldg, 65; painting of Parliament bldgs, Nat Club, Toronto, 67; Peace Tower, comn by Sen John B Aird, Toronto, 69; painting of Budapest, CFTO-TV, Toronto, 69; View of Prague, Toronto Stock Exchange, 69. *Exhib:* Royal Can Acad; Ont Soc Artists; Can Soc Painters Watercolour; Nat Gallery Ottawa; Am Watercolor Soc, NY, 72. *Teaching:* Lectured and demonstrated adult educ classes throughout Ontario for Dept Educ. *Awards:* Watercolor Prize, Western Ont Exhib; First Prize, Brampton Ann Exhib; Purchase Award, Image 76, Ont Soc Artists, 76; Grand Prize, Que Nat Exhib. *Mem:* Ont Soc Artists; Canada Soc Painters Watercolour; Soc Can Artists; Centro Studi & Scambi Int, Rome; fel Int Inst Arts & Lett; Am Fedn Art. *Media:* Watercolor. *Specialty:* Watercolour paintings. *Interests:* World travel. *Mailing Add:* 784 Avondale Ave Kitchener ON N2M 2W8 Canada

GOETZL, THOMAS MAXWELL
LECTURER, EDUCATOR
b Chicago, Ill, May 31, 1943. *Study:* Univ Calif, Berkeley, AB (psychology), 65 & Boalt Hall Sch of Law, JD, 69. *Pos:* Mem bd dir, Calif Lawyers Arts, currently; assoc mem, Nat Conf State Legislatures, Arts Tourism and Cult Resources Comt, currently. *Teaching:* Prof Art Law, Golden Gate Univ, Sch of Law, San Francisco, Calif, 72-. *Mem:* Artists Equity Asn; Calif Lawyers Arts; Calif State Bar. *Publ:* Copyright & the Visual Artists Display Right, A New Doctrinal Analysis, 9 Colum VLA J L & Arts, 84; Kennedy Proposal to Amend the Copyright Law; In Support of the Resale Royalty, 7 Cardozo A & E L J 249, 89; Visual Arts and the Public: A Legislative Agenda for the 1990's, 12 Hast Comm/Ent L J 403, 90. *Mailing Add:* Dept Law Golden Gate Univ 536 Mission St San Francisco CA 94105

GOGGIN, NAN ELIZABETH
EDUCATOR, GRAPHIC ARTIST
Pos: Assoc provost fellow, Univ Ill, Urbana-Champaign, dir, Sch of Art and Design, currently, prof, currently, co-founder New Media Prog, Sch of Art Design. *Awards:* Ill Univ Scholar; NCSA fellow; Ifoundry and Ctr for Advanced Study fellows. *Mailing Add:* University of Illinois Art & Design 139 C Art Design 408 E Peabody Dr MC 590 Champaign IL 61820

GOHEEN, ELLEN ROZANNE
HISTORIAN, CURATOR
b New York, NY, Mar 30, 1944. *Study:* Univ Kans, Lawrence, BA & MA. *Collection Arranged:* Masters of 20th Century Photography, 73, Am Impressionism, 74, Friends of Art Retrospective, 76, Joseph Cornell, 77, Jasper Johns in Kansas City 1967-1977, 78, Thomas Hart Benton An Am Original, 89 & The Drawings of Ralph Barton, 91, Nelson Gallery-Atkins Mus, Kansas City, Mo. *Pos:* From asst cur to assoc cur Europ painting & sculpture, Nelson Gallery-Atkins Mus, 70-75, 20th century art, 75-81, sr lectr, 81-85; coordr, Thomas Hart Benton Proj, 85-89, admin spec exhib & collections mgt, 89-98, dir collections & spec exhibs, 98-99. *Awards:* Sir George Trevelyan Scholar, Attingham Park Summer Sch, Shropshire, Eng, 73. *Mem:* Archaeol Inst Am (pres, Kans Chap, 74-77); Nat Trust Hist Preserv; Soc Archit Historians; Libr Am Landscape Hist; Advisory Bd, Coll Liberal Arts & Sci, Univ Kans. *Res:* Twentieth century American and European art, European and American architecture. *Publ:* Contrib, Christo: Wrapped Walk Ways, 79, The Collections of the Nelson-Atkins Mus Art, Abrams, 88; Warren Rosser, Turn and Turn About Kansas City Art Inst, 89. *Mailing Add:* 6135 Overhill Rd Shawnee Mission KS 66208

GOHLKE, FRANK WILLIAM
PHOTOGRAPHER
b Wichita Falls, Tex, Apr 3, 1942. *Study:* Univ Tex, Austin, BA, 64; Yale Univ, New Haven, Conn, MA, 66; pvt study with Paul Caponigro, 67-68. *Work:* Nat Gallery Can, Ottawa, Ont; Australian Nat Gallery, Canberra; Bibliotheque Nationale, Paris, France; Mus Mod Art, NY; Cleveland Mus Art, Ohio. *Comn:* Tex Sesquicentennial (photog survey), comn by Tex Hist Found, Austin, 84; Linea di Confine della Provincia di Reggio Emilia, (photog survey), Italy, 94; Photographs of Lake Erie, George Gund Found, Cleveland, Ohio, 97; Comune di Venezia, Italy: Venezia-Marghera, 98-99; Nat Millennium Survey, Coll Santa Fe, NMex, 99-. *Exhib:* Solo exhibs, Int Mus Photog, George Eastman House, Rochester, NY, 74, Amon Carter Mus Western Art, Ft Worth Tex, 75, Mt St Helens: Work in Progress, Mus Mod Art, 83, Landscapes from the Middle of the World, Mus Contemp Photog, Chicago, 88 & Living Water: Photogs of the Sundbury River (with catalog), Mt St Helens; Photog by Frank Gohlke, 81-90; DeCordova Mus, Lincoln Mass, 93; New Topographics: Photographs of a Man-Altered Landscape, Int Mus Photogr, George Eastman House, Rochester, NY, 74; Mirrors & Windows: Am Photog since 1960, Mus Mod Art, NY, 78; An Open Land: Photographs of the Midwest 1852-1982, Art Inst Chicago, Ill, 83; Photog Now, Victoria & Albert Mus, London, 89; Photog Until Now, Mus Mod Art, NY, 92; More Than One Photog, Mus Mod Art, NY, 92; Crossing the Frontier: Photographs of the Developing West, 1849 to the Present, San Francisco Mus Mod Art, 96; Mus Mod Art, New York City, 2005. *Teaching:* Vis lectr, Colo Col, Colorado Springs, 79-88, Mass Col Art, 89-, Yale Univ, 92, Princeton Univ, 95 & Harvard Univ, 96-97. *Awards:* Guggenheim Fel, 75 & 84; Photogr Fel, Nat Endowment Arts, 77 & 86; Artists Fel, Bush Found, St Paul, Minn, 78. *Bibliog:* Robert Silberman (auth), Our town: Tulsa murals, Art Am, 7/85; Vicki Goldberg (auth), What landscapes really mean, Am Photog, 12/88; Ingrid Sischy (auth), Frank Gohlke, The New Yorker, 5/17/92. *Media:* Photography. *Publ:* Landscapes from the Middle of the World (exhib catalog), Friends of Photography, 88; auth, Bare Facts: The Photography of Wright Morris, Hungry Mind Rev, fall 86; Measure of Emptiness: Grain Elevators in the American Landscapes (monograph, with a concluding essay by John C Hudson), John Hopkins Univ Press, 92; Looking for Lee Friedlander, In: Photographs from the Real World (exhib catalogue), Die Norske Bokklubene, Lillehammer, Norway, 93; Linea di Confine Della Provincia di Reggio Emilia: Laboratorio di Fotografia 7 (exhib catalogue), Reggio Emilia, Italy, 95. *Dealer:* Howard Greenberg Gallery, New York, NY,. *Mailing Add:* 3007 N Gaia Pl Tucson AZ 85745

GOICOLEA, ANTHONY
PHOTOGRAPHER, SCULPTOR
b Atlanta, Ga, 1971. *Study:* La Universidad de Madrid, 1989; Univ Ga, BA (art hist), 1989-92 & BFA (drawing & painting), 1992-94; Pratt Inst, MFA (sculpture & photog), 1994-96. *Work:* Hirshhorn Mus & Sculpture Garden; Whitney Mus Am Art; Mus Mod Art, New York; Guggenheim Mus Art, New York; Mus Contemp Photog, Chicago; Yale Univ Art Collection; Herbert F Johnson Mus Art, Cornell Univ. *Exhib:* Solo exhibs, Rare Gallery, New York, 1999, Fabien Fryns Gallery, Marbella, Spain, 2000, Corcoran Gallery Art, 2001, Mus Contemp Photog, Chicago, 2002, Contemp Ctr Photog, Melbourne, 2003, Torch Gallery, Amsterdam, 2004, Ariz State Univ Mus Art, 2005, MAPR, San Juan, 2006, Gallery Hyundai, Korea, 2007, Monte Clark Gallery, Toronto, 2008; Good Business is the Best Art, Bronx Mus, NY, 2000; Collector's Choice, Nassau County Mus Art, Roslyn Harbor, NY, 2001; Guide to Trust No 2, Yerba Buena Ctr for Arts, San Francisco, 2002; Potential Images of the World, Speed Art Mus, Louisville, 2003; Boys Behaving Badly, Contemp Arts Mu, Houston, 2004; In Focus, NC Mus Art, Raleigh, 2005; Modern Photographs, Miami Art Mus, 2006; Contemporary Cool, Mint Mus Art, Charlotte, 2007; Badlands, Mass Mus Contemp Art, 2008; Generation, Art Gallery Alberta, Can, 2009. *Awards:* Joan Mitchell Found Grant, 1997; BMW Photo Paris Award, 2005; Cintas Fel, 2006. *Bibliog:* Joe Perreault (auth), Toe to Toe, Tongue to Tongue, New York Arts, Vol 5, No 3, 14-15, 3/2000; Ken Johnson (auth), Detention, NY Times, 6/2001; Margaret Hawkins (auth), Youth is Well-Served, Chicago Sun-Times, 7/2002; Marisa S Olson (auth), Reflections of Self, Planet, 44-47, 2003; Linda Yablonsky (auth), To thine own self be True, ART News, 143, 11/2005; Francis Morrone (auth), Darger's Disciples, New York Sun, 4/2008

GOIN, PETER
PHOTOGRAPHER, VIDEO ARTIST
b Madison, Wis, Nov 26, 1951. *Study:* Hamline Univ, BA, 73; Univ Iowa, MA, 75, MFA, 76. *Work:* Nat Mus Am Art, Washington, DC; Los Angeles Co Mus Art; San Francisco Mus Mod Art; Amon Carter Mus, Ft Worth, Tex; Minneapolis Inst Art, Minn; Whitney Mus Am Art, NY; Princeton Univ Art Mus; Libr Congress, Washington; numerous pub and pvt collections; Ctr Creative Photog, Univ Az. *Exhib:* Picturing Calif, Oakland Mus Art, 89; solo exhibs, Baltimore Mus Art, Md, 91, Phoenix Mus Art, Ariz, 92, Mint Mus Art, Charlotte, NC, 92 & Seattle Mus Hist & Indust, Wash, 92; Between Home and Heaven, Nat Mus Am Art, Washington, DC, 91; Wasteland, Fotographie Biennale, Rotterdam, 92; New Orleans Triennial, New Orleans Mus, La, 92; Mus Contemp Art, San Diego, 93; Atlanta Art Festival, 93; El Maso Mus Art, 94; Southeast Mus Photog, 95; Whitney Mus Am Art, NY, 96; Princeton Univ Art Mus, 96; San Francisco Mus Modern Art, 96; Nev Mus Art, 98, 2005, 2007; Univ Ore Mus Art, 98; Tokyo Met Mus Photog, 2000; Los Angeles Mus Art, 2000; Mus Fine Arts, Houston, 2000; Houston Fotofest, 2000; Bienal Int de Fotographia de Cordoba, Spain, 2001; Int Ctr Photog, 2002; Norsk Mus Fotografi, Orten, Norway, 2003. *Pos:* chair, Art Dept, Univ Nev Reno. *Teaching:* Prof art, Univ Nev, 84-. *Awards:* Nat Endowment Arts Fels, 82 & 90; Nathan Cummings Grant, 92; Gov's Millennium Award Excellence in the Arts, 99-2000. *Publ:* Auth, Tracing the Line: A Photographic Survey of the Mexican American Border, 87; Nuclear Landscapes, Johns Hopkins Univ Press, 91; Stopping Time: A Rephotographic Survey of Lake Tahoe, Univ NMex Press, 92; ed, Arid Waters, Univ Nev Press, 92; auth, Humanature, Univ Tex Press, 96; co-auth, A Doubtful River, Univ Nev Press, 2000; Changing Mines in America, Center for Am Places, 2004; Black Rock, Univ of Nevada, Press, 2005; Nevada Rock Art, 2009; coauth, A Field Guide to Calif Agricultrue, Univ Calif Press, 2010; Lake Tahoe: A Martitime History, Arcadia Pub, 2012; Time and Time Again, Mus in NMex Press, 2013. *Mailing Add:* 2365 Crescent Cir Reno NV 89509-3512

GOLBERT, SANDRA
ARTIST, WRITER
b San Juan, Puerto Rico, Nov 9, 1937. *Work:* Zimmerli Mus, Rutherford, NJ. *Comn:* Condado Plz Hotel, San Juan, 87; Pierre Hotel, 90; Mural, Swissotel, Chicago, 2000. *Exhib:* Paper, Silk & Shadow, InterChurch Ctr, NY, 98; Retrospective, Old Church Cult Ctr, Demarest, NJ, 97; Art From My First 1000 Yrs, Presbyterian Church, Franklin Lakes, NJ, 99; 9x9x3 Am Craft Mus, New York, 98; La Concha Hotel, San Juan, 2008; Caribana, Tropical Sights and Colors, Hess Gallery, Chestnut Hill, Mass, 2012; Fibers, Marblehead Art Asn, Mass, 2012. *Collection Arranged:* Fiber, Marblehead Art Assn, Ma, 2012. *Teaching:* Instr, Rockland Ctr for the Arts, NY, Old Church Cult Ctr, NJ, The Creative Ctr, NY, Newburyport Art Asn, Mass, Coll 4 Kids, Northern Essex Community Coll. *Awards:* Grant, Nat Endowment for the Arts, 90; Grant, Pollock-Krasner Found, 91; Grant, NY Found Arts, 98. *Mem:* Surface Design Asn; Salute to Women in Arts; Textile Study Group of NY; Marblehead Art Asn;

Newburyport Art Asn. *Media:* Paper, Silk, Fiber. *Publ:* Fiberarts; Surface Design; Vogue; Archit Digest, 8/2009; Fiber Arts Now, 2014. *Dealer:* Shidoni Gallery NM; Little Beach Gallery Hyannis Ma; NOA Gallery Boston Ma; Contemporary Craft Pittsburgh Pa; Hourglass Gallery Melrose Ma; Marblehead Arts Gallery Ma; Fuller Craft Mus Brockton Ma

GOLD, LEAH
PAINTER, PRINTMAKER
b New York, NY. *Study:* With Ruth Reeves & Hans Hofmann. *Work:* Butler Inst Am Art; Birmingham Mus Art, Ala; Slater Mem Mus, Norwich, Conn. *Exhib:* Montclair Mus, NJ, 73-75; Tirca Karlis Gallery, Provincetown, Mass, 75-; Fordham Univ at Lincoln Ctr, NY, 75; Nat Art Mus of Sports, NY, 75; Cork Gallery, Lincoln Ctr, NY, 76-. *Awards:* Mrs John T Pratt Prize for Woodcut, Nat Asn Women Artists, 57; Prize for Casein Painting, Painters & Sculptors Soc NJ 18th Ann, 59; Award for Stained Glass Sculpture, Brooklyn Soc Artists, 59. *Mem:* Artists Equity Asn NY (bd dir, 65-); Am Soc Contemp Artists; Metrop Painters & Sculptors, NY (publicity & exhib comt, 72-); Painters & Sculptors Soc NJ. *Media:* Casein, Graphics; Stained Glass, Collages

GOLD, LOIS M
PAINTER
b New York, NY, June 2, 1945. *Study:* Boston Univ, BA, 67; Columbia Univ, MA, 70; Nat Acad Design, Marymount Col, 86-89; Art Students League, 86-89. *Work:* Herbert F Johnson Mus Art, Ithaca, NY; Bristol Myers Squibb; Bed Bath & Beyond; Brooklyn Union Gas; Imperial Oil; Canyon Ranch; Boston Univ. *Exhib:* Long Island Landscape: A New Era, Lizan-Tops Gallery, 94 & Long Island Landscape Shows, 95-98; Ruzetti & Grow, NY; Solo Exhibs: Lizan-Tops Gallery, 95-97; Nat Asn Am Artists, Kiesendahl and Calhoun Gallery, 2007; Lizan -Tops Gallery, 98-2001; Martha Keats Gallery, Santa Fe, NMex, 98-2001; Rice Gallery, Denver, Colo; Ute Stebich Gallery, Lenox, Mo; Helen Jones Gallery, Sacramento, Calif; Laurel Seth Gallery, Santa Fe; Summa Gallery, NY; Claggett Rey Gallery, Denver; Berkeley Gallery, Scottsdale, Ariz; The Flinn Gallery, Greenwich, Conn, 2005; Nutmeg Gallery, Kent, Conn. *Awards:* Mixed Media Finalist, Artavita; Works on Paper, Nat Asn Women Artists, 89; Landscape Awards, Artists Mag, 91 & 93; Juried Scholarship Award, Pastel Soc Am, 94-95; Studio Finalist Award, Artists Mag, 95 & 96; Landscape Award, The Artists Mag, 2000. *Mem:* Cassatt Pastel Soc; Nat Asn Women Artists; Pastel Soc Am; Studio Ctr Artists Asn. *Media:* Pastel. *Interests:* Poetry; ballroom dancing; cooking. *Collection:* Brooklyn Union Gas; Bristol Myers Squibb; Imperial Oil; Canyon Ranch, Lenox, Mass; Pastelagram, Pastel Artist Int. *Publ:* Pastel Sch, Readers Digest; Painting Shapes and Edges, Readers Digest; Best of Flower Painting, Northlight Books; cover art, The Pastel Journal, Dan's Papers, 99, 2000, 01, 02, 03, 04; Pastel Artist Int, vol 2, 99; Southwest Art, 01; Int Book Art Press, 03; Art reproductions Romm Art; Pure Color, The Best of Pastel, North Light Books, 2006; featured artist, Tim Green (ed), Rattled, fall 2008; featured artist, The Pastel Jour, 10/2009; featured artist, Artinfo.com, 1/2009; Pratique des Arts, 2011. *Dealer:* Lizan-Tops Gallery 8 E 92nd St New York NY 10128; Martha Keats Gallery 644 Canyon Rd Santa Fe NM 87501; Ruzetti and Gow 162 E 74 St New York NY 10021; Karin Zatt Los Angeles CA

GOLD, MARTHA B
SCULPTOR, PAINTER
b New York, NY, Sept 20, 1938. *Study:* Univ Rochester; Barnard Col, Columbia Univ, BA; Columbia Univ, MA; Nat Acad Sch Fine Arts, cert; Art Students League. *Exhib:* NAm Sculpture Ann, Foothills Art Ctr, Golden, Colo, 80, 83 & 88; Allied Artists Am, Am Acad Inst Arts & Letts, 80, Audubon Artists Ann, Nat Arts Club, 81 & Nat Sculpture Soc Ann, Equitable Life Insurance Bldg, 81, NY; Philadelphia Tricentennial, 82; solo shows, Ward-Nasse Gallery, 87, 89 & 90. *Teaching:* Privately. *Awards:* Mem Award, Audubon Artists, 79; Youth Award, Nat Sculpture Soc, 79 & 80; Gold Medal Hon, Allied Artists Am, 80 & 83; Foondry Award, NAm Sculpture Exhib. *Bibliog:* Article, Nat Sculpture Rev, 80, Sculpture Mag, 87, Manhattan Arts, 87, NY Art Review, 89, Arte el dia, Argentina, 89. *Mem:* Allied Artists Am; Nat Asn Women Artists; Artists Equity. *Media:* Bronze, Clay; Ink, Oil. *Dealer:* Ward-nasse Gallery Prince St New York NY. *Mailing Add:* 315 E 91st St New York NY 10128

GOLD, SHARON CECILE
PAINTER, EDUCATOR
b Bronx, NY, Feb 28, 1949. *Study:* Hunter Col, City Univ of NY, 68; Columbia Univ, 69-70; Pratt Inst, BFA, 76. *Work:* McCrory Corp, Chase Manhattan Bank, Norsearch Indust & Chemical Bank, NY; Prudential Insurance Co Am, NJ; Best Products, Inc, Va; Rose Art Mus, Brandeis Univ, Mass; Southeast Bank, Fla; Everson Mus, Syracuse, NY. *Comn:* Painting on aluminum & fiberglass, Humbolt-Hospital Station, Niagara Frontier Transportation Authority, Buffalo, NY, 82-84. *Exhib:* Works on Paper, Mus Mod Art, Art Lending Serv, NY, 81; solo exhibs, Galerie Michael Storrer, Zurich, Switz, 81, John Davis Gallery, Akron, Ohio, 86, Stephen Rosenberg Gallery, NY, 87, 89, 91; Tyler & Penrose Galleries, Tyler Sch Art, Philadelphia, 83; Summer Show, GH Dalsheimer Gallery, Baltimore, Md, 88; Four-person Group exhib, Stephen Rosenberg Gallery, NY, 88; Painting Beyond the Death of Painting, Kuznetsky Most Exhib Hall, Moscow, USSR, 89; The Image of Abstract Painting in the 80's, Rose Art Mus, Brandeis Univ, Waltham, Mass, 90; and many others. *Pos:* Assoc ed, Re-View Mag, NY, 77-. *Teaching:* Lectr, Princeton Univ, 79-80; NY Univ, 83; vis assoc prof, Univ Tex, San Antonio, 80 & Syracuse Univ, 80-81; vis prof, Va Commonwealth Univ, 82; adj prof, NY Univ, 83; assoc prof painting & critical theory, Syracuse Univ, 85-. *Awards:* MacDowell Colony Fel; Nat Endowment Arts Painting Fel, 81-82; Distinguished Artist Award Lifetime Achievement. *Bibliog:* Joseph Masheck (auth), Sharon Gold, Arts Mag, 10/87; Stephen Westfall (auth), Review, Art in America, 1/88; and others. *Mem:* Coll Art Asn Comt (chair, 89). *Media:* Oil. *Publ:* Contribr, reviews in Artforum, 77; auth, Statement, Re-View Mag, 79; The Texas Paintings-Modernism: Forms and Concepts, Univ Tex Press (in prep); auth, Statement, Forum, 89. *Mailing Add:* 10 Leonard St New York NY 10013

GOLDBERG, ARNOLD HERBERT
PAINTER, PRINTMAKER
b Brooklyn, NY, May 16, 1933. *Study:* Univ Wis, BS (appl arts), 55; Pratt Inst, BArch, 59; Univ Houston, painting, 70-72. *Exhib:* Twelfth Midwest Biennial, Joselyn Mus, Omaha, Nebr, 72; 17th Ann Delta Art Exhib, Ark Art Ctr, 74; 16th Ann Eight State Exhib, Okla Art Ctr, 74; 52nd Exhib, Shreveport Art Guild, 74; Corpus Christi Art Found Ann Exhib, Art Mus STex, 75; Corpus Christi Art Found Ann Exhib, Art Mus STex, 77. *Teaching:* Instr desktop publ, Houston Community Col, 87-. *Awards:* Dimension VI Award, Art League Houston, 71; Eighth Jury Award Art Exhib, Jewish Community Ctr, Houston, 72; Corpus Christi Art Found Grant, Art Mus STex, 75 & 77. *Media:* Acrylic; Silkscreen. *Mailing Add:* 425 White Wing Ln Houston TX 77079-6828

GOLDBERG, CAROL
COLLECTOR
Awards: Named one of Top 200 Collectors, ARTnews mag, 2011, 2012. *Collection:* Contemporary art. *Mailing Add:* 1050 5th Ave Apt 9F New York NY 10028

GOLDBERG, GLENN
PAINTER
b Bronx, NY, Aug 31, 1953. *Study:* Queens Col, MFA. *Work:* Mus Mod Art, Metrop Mus Art, NY; The Brooklyn Mus; High Mus Art, Atlanta, Ga; Mus Contemp Art, Los Angeles; Nat Gallery Art, Washington. *Exhib:* One-man shows, Willard Gallery, NY, 85, Dart Gallery, Chicago, Ill, 86, Albany Mus Art, Albany, Ga, 89, Knoedler & Co, NY, 94 & 96, Galerie Albrecht, Munich, Ger, 94, Addison/Ripley Fine Art, Washington, 95 & Grand Arts, Kansas City, Mo, 95; retrospectives, Green Gallery (with catalog), St Louis, Mo, 90, Hill Gallery, Birmingham, Mich, 90, Knoedler & Co Inc, NY, 91 & 92, David Beitzel Gallery, NY, 92; Wacko, The Work Space, NY, 95; Galerie Albrecht, Munich, Ger, 95; Edward Hopper House, Nyack, NY, 95. *Teaching:* Fac, NY Studio Sch, 86-, Chautauqua Inst, NY, 91-93, Vt Studio Ctr, 93 & Parsons MFA Prog, NY, 93-94. *Awards:* Guggenheim Fel, 88-89; Nat Endowment Arts, 89. *Bibliog:* Marsha Miro (auth), Painter's work presents studies in contradiction, Detroit-free Press, 3/24/93; Jeff Wright (auth), Moving images: paintings that appear to have a life of their own, Cover, 3/94; Alice Thorson (auth), Space may look like a million, but exhibit is only average, Kansas City Star, 5/3/95

GOLDBERG, IRA A
ADMINISTRATOR
b Queens, NY, Sept 27, 1955. *Work:* The Art Students League of NY. *Exhib:* Nat Acad of Design Ann Exhib, 96. *Pos:* Exec dir, The Art Students League of NY, 2001-. *Awards:* Best Still-Life, Nat Acad, 96. *Mailing Add:* c/o Art Students League of NY 215 W 57th St New York NY 10019

GOLDBERG, NORMA
SCULPTOR
b New York, NY. *Study:* Sculpture instruction with Victor Trapote, 66-68; sculpture instruction with Carma Anderson, Pat Foley & Abraham Gonzalez, 68-70. *Work:* Tel-Hashomer Hosp, Tel Aviv, Israel; Mus Nat de Art, Punta del Este-Montevideo, Uruguay; Medley Distilling Co, Chicago; Int Mex-Israeli, Mex. *Comn:* Golfer, Club de Golf Bellavista, Calacoaya, Mex, 74. *Exhib:* Int Art Fair, Tel-Aviv, Israel, 77; Retrospective del Arte Judeo-Mex, Moltibanco Mercantil por Bnai Brit, Mex, 85; Lillian Heidenberg Gallery, NY, 86; Art Expo, Arte de Mex, 88; Subasta de Arte, David Alfaro Siqueiros, Mex, 90; and others. *Awards:* Art Show Second Place, Acapulco, Mex, 78; Dipl of Outstanding Merits, Ash Kenazi Community Mex, 91. *Bibliog:* Lilly Kassner (auth), Diccionario de la escultura Mex Sigloxx, Univ Aut de Mex, 84; Art Diary Int, Giancarlo Politi Editore, 92. *Media:* Metal, Stone. *Publ:* Contribr, Norma Goldberg, The News, 84; Norma Goldberg en torno al ser humano y su problematica, Endiciones Tiempos Modernos, 85; Norma Goldberg and the human presence, Novedades, 85; A Sculptress of Omnipresent Quality, Arte de Mex, 87; Arte Y Artistas, Ignacio Flores Antunez, 89. *Dealer:* Galeria Aura Amberes 38PB Colonia Juarez 06600 Mexico. *Mailing Add:* Monte Bianco 115-101 Lomas de Chapultepec Mexico #11000 Mexico

GOLDBERGER, PAUL JESSE
CRITIC, WRITER, EDUCATOR, EDITOR
b Passaic, NJ, Dec 4, 1950. *Study:* Yale Univ, BA, 72. *Hon Degrees:* Pratt Inst, LHD, 92; Ctr Creative Studies, LHD; NY Sch Interior Design, Hon Dr. *Pos:* Staff ed, The New York Times Mag, New York City, 72-73; archit critic, The New York Times, 73—; ed cult news, 90-94, chief cult corr, 94-95, freelance contribr, 1995—; archit critic, Sly Line Column The NY, 1997—; dean, Parsons Sch Design, 2004—. *Awards:* Roger Starr Journalism award Citizens Housing & Planning Coun, 87; Medal of Honor, NY Landmarks Preservation Found, 91; Preserv Achievement Award, New York City Landmarks Preserv Comn, 96. *Mem:* Soc Archit Historians (bd dir, 77-79); Am Inst of Archits. *Publ:* auth, The Skyscraper, 81; auth, On the Rise: Archit & Design in a Post-Modern Age, 83; auth, The World Trade Ctr Remembered, 2001; auth, Up From Ground Zero, 2004; contribr, articles and essays to prof publs

GOLDEN, EUNICE
PAINTER, FILMMAKER
b New York, NY. *Study:* Univ Wis; Brooklyn Coll, MFA; New Sch Social Res; Art Students League; Empire State Coll, BFA. *Work:* Hudson River Mus, Yonkers, NY; Mus Mod Art, Whitney Mus & Guggenheim Mus, NY; Guild Hall Mus, East Hampton, NY; Mus NMex, Santa Fe, NMex. *Comn:* Portrait, comn by Leon Herald, 71; murals, Dept Parks & Recreation, NY, Dept Cult Affairs, NY & Bronx Mus Art; Bronx Community Coll. *Exhib:* Palacio de Las Bellas Art, Mexico City, 72; Allan Stone Gallery, NY, 73; Nat Acad Design, NY, 73; Indianapolis Mus, Ind, 74; Bronx Mus Art, NY, 75; Works on Paper, Brooklyn Mus, NY, 75; Film exhib, Anthology Arch, 77; Whitney Mus Am Art, NY, 77; film exhib, Gemeente Mus, The Hague, The Neth, 79; Artists Space, NY, 83; Long Beach Mus, Calif, 85; Hudson Ctr Galleries,

86; Committed to Print Traveling Exhib, Mus Mod Art, 88-89; Guild Hall Mus, Easthampton, NY, 91-98, 2002; Sniper's Nest, Bard Coll Ctr Cur Studies (traveling), 95-97; Mus Fine Art, Santa Fe, NMex, 97, 2002-03; solo exhib, Mitchell Algus Gallery, New York, 2003; Steven Kasher Gallery, New York, 2006; Pollock Krasner House, East Hampton, NY, 2010. *Collection Arranged:* Hudson River Mus, NY; Bronx Mus Art, New York; Mus NMex, Santa Fe; Guild Hall Mus, East Hampton, NY. *Pos:* Dir, Walk-On Community Art Proj, Dobbs Ferry, NY, 68 & Westbeth Gallery I, NY, 80-82. *Teaching:* Lectr erotic art, New Sch Social Res, 73; instr mural painting, Guggenheim Mus Prog, NY, summer 75; artist-in-residence, Univ SDak, 76 & Cooper Union, 84; instr painting, Pratt Inst, 80-81. *Awards:* Purchase Award, Hudson River Mus, 63; One of Outstanding Women, NY State Women's Unit Exec Chamber, Albany, 68; MacDowell Colony Fel, 69 & 71; Award, Archives Am Art, Smithsonian Inst, Washington; Grant, NY Found for the Arts, 75; Medal of Honor, Veteran Feminists Am, 2003. *Bibliog:* Lucy Lippard (auth), From the Center, Feminist Essays on Women's Art, Dutton, 76 & Art in Am, 11/81; Carter Ratcliff (auth), Art Int, 3/77; Lucy Lippard (auth), Overlay, Random House, 83; Judith Fryer Davidov (auth), Women's Camera Work, Duke Univ Press, 97; Holland Cotter (auth), article, NY Times, 2003; Richard Myer (auth), Wack! Art and the Feminist Revolution, Mus Contemp Art, Los Angeles, 2007; Gail Levin (auth), Nashima, 2007-, essay, censorship, politics, sexual imagery, in the work of Jewish Am Feminist artists; East End Stories, Parrish Art Mus, Watermill, NY, 2011. *Mem:* Fel MacDowell Colony; Coll Art Asn Am; Women's Caucus Art. *Media:* Oil, Acrylic. *Publ:* Illusr, Ms Mag, 75; auth, article, Art Workers News, New York, 76; coauth, article, An Anti-Catalog, 77; auth, The male nude in womens art, Heresies, spring 81; Woman's Art Jour, Spring/Summer, 82; and others. *Dealer:* Mitchell Algus Gallery, NYC. *Mailing Add:* 463 W St Apt 332B New York NY 10014

GOLDEN, HAL
PAINTER, CONSERVATOR
b Brooklyn, NY, Dec 10, 1925. *Study:* WPA Art classes, Brooklyn, NY, 1939-40; NY Sch of Industrial Art/Sch of Art & Design NY, 1941-1943; The Art Students League, NY, with Ivan Olinsky, 45, 46; Private instr with: artist, Rolph Scarlett, 1950-53; Vladimir Lebedev, painter/conservator, 1980-83. *Work:* (Conserv) Putnam Co Mus of Art, Cold Spring, NY; (Conserv) NY Med Coll (collection, 19th century paintings), Valhalla, NY; (Conserv) Abby Aldrich Rockefeller Folk Art Mus, Williamsburg, Va. *Comn:* Landscape painting, Dr N Bruno, Providence, RI; portraits, D Waldron, Providence, RI, 2003-2005; estate painting, W Slocum, Barrington, RI, 2004; portrait, C Little, Providence, RI, 2006; landscape painting, M Lyle, Madison, Conn, 2006; portrait, David Audette, Seekonk, RI. *Exhib:* Nat Marine Art Show, Stamford Art Asn, Stamford, CT, 1999; East Southeast Regional, Oil Painters of Am Brazier Fine Art, Richmond, Va, 2002; 74th Grand Nat Exhib, Am Artists Prof League, NY, 2002; Open Non-Mem Juried Exhib, Salmagundi Club, NY, 2003-2004; Nat Open Exhib, Community Arts Asn, Ridgewood, NJ, 2003-2005; two person show, Providence Art Club, 2000 & 2005. *Pos:* Art Dir, numerous Ad Agencies. *Teaching:* New Sch Univ, New York City, pvt students. *Awards:* Certificate of Excellence (Int Poster Competition, Latham Found, 1951; Louis Kuriansky Found Award, (Stanley & Vivian Reed Nat Marine Art Show), Stamford, Conn, Art Asn, 1999. *Bibliog:* Providence (RI) Journal; E Side Monthly, Providence, RI; The Advocate and Greenwich Time, Greenwich, Conn; Sun Chronicle, Attleboro, Mass. *Mem:* Oil Painters of Am (Exhibiting Artist); Am Artists Prof League (Exhibiting Artist); Am Inst for Conserv of Hist & Artist Works (Assoc). *Media:* Oil. *Mailing Add:* 50 Park Row W Apt 908 Providence RI 02903

GOLDEN, JUDITH GREENE
PHOTOGRAPHER-MIXED MEDIA
b Chicago, Ill, Nov 29, 1934. *Study:* Art Inst Chicago, BFA, 73; Univ Calif, Davis, MFA (Regents Graduate Fel), 75. *Hon Degrees:* Moore Coll Art, Philadelphia, Pa, Hon PhD, 90. *Work:* Oakland Mus of Art; Denver Art Mus; Fogg Mus, Cambridge, Mass; Mus Photog Art, San Diego; Art Inst Chicago & Mus Contemp Photog, Chicago; Mus Contemp Art, Los Angeles; Los Angeles Co Mus Art; Tokyo Metro Mus Photog; Newport Harbor Mus, Newport Beach, Calif; Seattle Art Mus; San Francisco Mus Mod Art; Center for Creative Photog, Tuscon, Ariz; Photog Mus, Osaka, Japan; Akron Art Mus, Ohio; Avon Coll, NY; Mus Fine Arts, Santa Fe, NMex; Tucson Mus Art; Santa Barbara Mus Art; Weisman Found, Los Angeles. *Exhib:* Solo exhibs, San Francisco Mus Mod Art, Calif, 81, Mus Photog Arts, San Diego, 86, Tucson Mus Art, 87; Visual Arts Ctr, Anchorage, Alaska, 90, Scottsdale Ctr Arts, Scottsdale, Ariz, 93, Arte de Oaxaca, Mex, 95, Columbia Ctr Arts, Dallas, Tex, 97, Temple Mus Art, Tuscon, Ariz, 97 & Univ Arts, Philadelphia, Pa, 2002, Temple Music & Art, 2005, Temple of Music & Art, Tucson; Group exhib, Silver & Ink, Oakland Mus, Calif, 78; Attitudes-Photog in the 70's, Santa Barbara Mus Art, Calif, 79; Geo Pompidou, Paris, 81; Extending the Perimeters of 20th Century Photog & Photog Facets of Modernism, San Francisco Mus Mod Art, 86; Photog and Art, Los Angeles Co Mus Art, Calif, 87; Selections 5: From the Polaroid Collection, Traveled Europe/US, 90-94; Self Portraits of Contemp Women: Exploring the Self, Tokyo Metrop Mus Photog, 91; Photog Book Arts in the US Today Traveling Exhib, Univ Tex, San Antonio, 91-94; Proff: Los Angeles Art & the Photog 1960-1980 Traveling Exhib, Laguna Art Mus, Laguna Beach, Calif, 92-94; Art of This Century: 30th Anniversary 1963-93, Univ Art Mus, Univ NMex, Albuquerque, 93; The Irmas Collection of Photog Self Portraits, Los Angeles Co Mus Art, 94; Hist Women Photogrs, NY Pub Libr, 96; The Painted Photograph: Hand Colored Photog, 1830-present (traveling exhib), Univ Wyo Art Mus; History of Women Photographers (traveling exhib), Santa Barbara Mus Art, Calif & Akron Art Mus, Ohio; Our Quarter Century, Ctr Creative Photog, Univ Ariz, Tucson, 2000; Idea Photog: After Modernism, Mus Fine Arts, Santa Fe, NMex, 2002; Los Angeles Co Mus Art, 2003; Ctr for Creative Photo, 2004; Santa Barbara Mus Art, 2005; Mus of Photog Arts, San Diego, 2006; Albuquerque Mus Art, 2007; Sandy Gallery, Portland, Ore, 2008; Harwood Art Ctr, Albuquerque, NMex, 2008; Art Inst Chicago, 2008; Art Alliance, Albuquerque, NMex, Captial Bldg, Santa Fe, NMex, 2008 ; Santa Barbara Mus Art, 2010; Center for Creative Photo, 2010; New Mexico State Univ, 2010; Pence Gallery, Davis, Ca, 2011; Minneapolis Inst Arts, 2011; Univ Ariz, 2012; Millicent Rogers Mus, Taos, ND, 2012. *Pos:* Bd mem, Los Angeles Ctr Photog Studies, Calif, 77-79 & Camera Work, San Francisco, Calif, 81; established, Artists Archive Ctr Creative Photog, Univ Ariz, 96. *Teaching:* Vis lectr photog, Univ Calif, Los Angeles, 75-79 & Univ Calif, Davis, 80; assoc prof photog, Univ Ariz, Tucson, 81-89, prof, 89-96, emer prof, 96-. *Awards:* Nat Endowment Arts Individual Photogrs Fel, 79; Photog Fel, Ariz Comn on Arts, 84; Polaroid Studio Grants, 83, 84, 89, 90; Tucson Pima Arts Counil Grant, 87; Univ Ariz Deans Incentive Grant, 91 & 99. *Bibliog:* Claire VC Peeps (auth), Cycles: A Decade of Photographs by Judith Golden, Friends of Photog, 88; Naomi Rosenblum (auth), The History of Women Photographers, 94; Robert Hirsch (auth), Seizing The Light: A History of Photography, 2000; Gerry Badger (auth), The Pleasure of Good Photographs, 2010; La Rising: So Cal Artists Before, 1980, Calif Int Arts Found, 2010. *Mem:* Soc Photog Educ; Women's Caucus Arts; BAG Santa Fe; LIBROS Art Paperworks, Tucscon, Ariz. *Media:* Collage, Mixed Media, Photography. *Publ:* Thomas, 1000 Artists Books, 2012

GOLDEN, ROLLAND HARVE
PAINTER, PRINTMAKER
b New Orleans, La, Nov 8, 1931. *Study:* John McCrady Art Sch, studied with John McCrady. *Work:* Pushkin Mus, Moscow; Masur Mus; New Orleans Mus Art; Miss Mus Art; Springfield Mus Art; Ogden Mus of Southern Art; Alexandria Mus Art; Bon Encontre, France; Nat Arts Club, New York; Lauren Rogers Mus, Miss; Hist New Orleans Collection; Ark Arts Ctr; US State Dept; La State Univ Mus Art. *Comn:* Fifty watercolors, La State Hwy Dept, Baton Rouge, 59-60; four watercolors, comn by Gov John McKeithen, La, 65; mural, Furash & Co, 88. *Exhib:* Seven Am Watercolor Soc Exhibs, NY, 65-78; Watercolor USA, Springfield, 66-2003; Butler Inst Am Art, Youngstown, Ohio, 67-78; Nat Arts Club, NY, 68 & 72-03; Nat Soc Painters in Casein & Acrylics, NY, 72-88; solo exhibs, touring USSR, Moscow, Kiev, Leningrad, Odessa & Southern France, 93-94, New Orleans Mus Art, 2007-2008 & over 100 solo exhibs in USA; Hist New Orleans Collection, 2008; Springfield Art Mus, Mo, 2009; Miss Mus Art, 2010; Alexandria Mus Art, Masur Mus Art; Old State Capitol, Baton Rouge, 2011; Walter Anderson Mus Art, 2012. *Pos:* Vpres, Watercolor USA Honor Soc, formerly; adv bd, Watercolor Mag. *Awards:* Eleven Awards, Nat Arts Club, NY; Seven Awards including Thomas Hart Benton, Watercolor USA; Five Awards, Rocky Mountain; Six Awards, Nat Watercolor Soc; featured on cover of Harper's mag, July 2007; Visual Arts Award, MS Arts and Letters, 2011. *Bibliog:* John R Kemp (auth), Rolland Golden, The Journeys of a Southern Artist, Pelican Publ Co, 2005, Days of Terror, Months of Anguish-Katrina, New Orleans Mus Art, 2007; Don Lee Keith (auth), Golden boy of watercolor, Delta Rev Mag, 68 & World of Rolland Golden, Royal Publ Co, 70; Jim Keyser (auth), Rolland Golden's Southland, WDSU TV, 73; Mel Leavitt (auth), First Person, 86; Edith Long (auth), Along the Banquette, 2004. *Mem:* Nat Watercolor Soc; Nat Arts Club; Allied Artists Am (hon life mem); Watercolor USA Hon Soc (vpres, formerly); hon mem La Watercolor; Rocky Mt Nat Watermedia; Watercolor West. *Media:* Watercolor, Oil, Acrylic; Lithography, Pencil. *Publ:* Article, In: Louisiana Life Mag, 82 & 2003; article In: Miss Mag, 5/86, 9/10, 10/10; auth, Palette Talk Mag, 5-6/87 & 9-10/88; articles in Int Fine Art Collector Mag, 9/91 & Am Artist Mag, Watercolor, fall 91; article & cover watercolor, Best of Oil Painting, Best of Acrylic Painting, Splash I & America's Best Contemporary Watercolors, Watercolor (mag), Fall 95 & Spring 2000; Country Roads Mag, var covers; cover & article, Inside Northside, summer 2003, fall 2005; article & cover, LA Cultural Vistas, fall, 2006, winter, 2007-2008, 2010-11; cover, Harper's Mag, 6/2007. *Dealer:* Rolland Golden Gallery. *Mailing Add:* 215 St Charles Ave Natchez MS 39120

GOLDEN, THELMA
MUSEUM DIRECTOR, CURATOR
b New York, NY, 1965. *Study:* Smith Coll, BA (Art Hist & African Am studies), 1987. *Hon Degrees:* Hon DFA, Moore Coll Art and Design, Pa, 2003; Hon DFA, Smith Coll, Mass, 2004; Hon DFA, San Francisco Art Inst, 2008. *Collection Arranged:* Black Male: Representations of Masculinity in Contemporary American Art, 1994; Bob Thompson: A Retrospective, 1998; Julien: Vagabondia, 2000; Martin Puryear: The Cane Project, 2000; Freestyle, 2001; Black and Green, 2001; Yinka Shonibare, 2002; Black Romantic: The Figurative Impulse in Contemporary American Art, 2002; Aaron Siskind: Harlem Document, 2003; Harlemworld: Metropolis as Metaphor, 2004; Chris Ofili: Afro Muses 1995-2005; Frequency, 2005-06; Africa Comics, 2006-07. *Pos:* Visual arts dir, Jamaica Arts Ctr, Jamaica, NY, 1989-91; dir, exhib coordr, Whitney Mus Am Art at Philip Morris, 1991-93; assoc curator, dir br museums, Whitney Mus Am Art, 1993-96, cur, 1996-98; cur special projects, Peter Norton Family Found, 1998-99; dep dir exhibs & programs, Studio Mus, Harlem, NY, 2000-05, chief cur, 2000-, exec dir, 2005-. *Awards:* Crain's NY 40 Under 40, 1994; Crain's 100 Most Influential Women in NYC Bus, 2007. *Mem:* Henry Crown Fel, Aspen Inst. *Mailing Add:* Studio Mus in Harlem 144 W 125th St New York NY 10027

GOLDFINE, BEATRICE
PAINTER, SCULPTOR
b Philadelphia, Pa, Aug 17, 1923. *Study:* Studied with Jimmy Leuders, Roy Nuse & Will Barnett, 69-74; also pvt instr with Morris Blackburn, 75-80; Pa Acad Fine Arts, 5 yr cert art, 80. *Work:* Blue Cross, Philadelphia, Harrisburg, Norristown; Bell Atlantic, Philadelphia; Merck Sharp & Dohme, West Point, Pa; Philadelphia Co Med Soc; EI DuPont. *Comn:* Bust, Sir Winston Churchilll, Technion-Israel Inst Technol, Haif, 82; bust, Golda Meier, NY, 84; pastel portrait of Phillip Zinman, Phillip Zinman Found, Boca Raton, Fla, 94. *Exhib:* 71st Ann, Allied Artists Am, NY, 84; Philadelphia Watercolor Club, Art Inst, Pa, 86-94; Forms to Figure With, Glassboro State Col, NJ, 89; one-woman show, Nudes & Other Landscapes, Joy Berman Gallery, Philadelphia, Pa, 90; Cheltenham Sch Fine Arts Ann, Philadelphia, Pa, 91, 92 & 93; Fel, travel show, Pa Acad Fine Arts, Philadelphia & Pittsburgh, 91, 92 & 93. *Awards:* First Prize, Woodmere Art Mus, 79 & Pa Acad Fine Arts Ann, 93; Bok Award, Harrisburg Mus, 84; First Prize Pastel, Philadelphia Sketch Club, 85. *Bibliog:* Dr Burton Wasserman (auth), Art Matters, 87; Guide to Manhattan's Outdoor Sculpture, Art Comn & Munic Art Soc, 88; Palmer Poroner (auth), Art Speak, Monthly Gallery Rev, NY, 91. *Mem:*

Pastel Soc Am, NY; fel Pa Acad Fine Art; Philadelphia Watercolor Club; Friends Bezaiel Acad Arts & Design; Philadelphia Art Alliance. *Media:* Oil, Pastel, Clay. *Interests:* Art History, Chinese culture & history. *Publ:* The Best of Oil Painting, Rockport Publ, Inc, 96, The Best of Pastel, 96 & Portrait Inspirations, 97. *Dealer:* Joy Berman Gallery 2201 Pennsylvania Blvd Philadelphia PA 19130; Philadelphia Mus Art Sales Gallery. *Mailing Add:* 1250 Glenwood Ave Jenkintown PA 19046

GOLDFINGER, ELIOT
SCULPTOR
b New York, NY, Aug 14, 1950. *Study:* Pratt Inst, BFA, 74; Nat Acad Sch, New York, 77-78. *Work:* Am Mus Natural Hist; Metrop Opera House; Mus City of New York; Tel Aviv Cult Ctr, Israel. *Comn:* Bust of Mayor John Lindsay, 78, Mayor Abe Beame, 79, Mayor Robert Wagner, 80 & Mayor Ed Koch, Mus City New York, 81; Bust Leonid Brezhnev, comn by Newsweek for cover, 4/12/82; Bust of Judge Henry Friendly, comn by US Court of Appeals, NY, 89. *Exhib:* Ann Exhib, Allied Artists Am, NY, 78, 80 & 82-86; Ann Exhib, Nat Acad Design, NY, 79 & 86; Mem Exhibs, Salmagundi Club, NY, 79-81; Ann Exhib, Nat Sculpture Soc, NY, 80-91. *Pos:* Staff artist, Am Mus Natural Hist, NY, 74-79. *Teaching:* Instr human & animal anat, NY Acad Art, 83-86; instr human anat, Art Students League, NY, 88-90. *Awards:* Gloria Medal, 80 & Meiselman Prize, 84, Nat Sculpture Soc; Dr H Debellis Prize, Salmagundi Club, 81; Allied Artists Mem Award, 85. *Bibliog:* John David Klein, Apple Polishers (film), WOR-TV News, 81; Sculpture in the News, Sculpture Review, 81; Interview, Sculpture Rev, 1st quarter, 92. *Mem:* Nat Sculpture Soc. *Media:* Plastillene, Bronze. *Res:* Human anatomy for artists, research from life & from cadavers; anatomy of the horse; comparative anatomy for artists. *Publ:* Auth, A sculptural approach to a three-dimensional subject, Catasus J Soc Animal Artists, spring 86; Human Anatomy for Artists, Oxford Univ Press, 91. *Mailing Add:* 37 Rolling Way New Rochelle NY 10804-2405

GOLDIN, NAN
PHOTOGRAPHER
b Washington, DC, 1953. *Study:* Boston Mus Fine Arts, BFA, 77. *Work:* Folkwang Mus, Essen, Ger; Victoria & Albert Mus, London; First Bank, Minneapolis; George Eastman House, Rochester; Whitney Mus Am Art, NY; and others. *Exhib:* Solo shows incl Parco Gallery, Tokyo, 98, Jablonka Gallery, Cologne, 98, Gagosian Gallery, Los Angeles, 98, Vaknin Schwartz, Atlanta, 98, Catherine Edelman Gallery, Chicago, 98, Galleri Nordenhake, Stockholm, 98 & Galleri Fauschou, Copenhagen, 98, Contemp Art Mus, Houston, 99, Nat Gallery of Iceland, 99, Joseloff Gallery, Hartford, Conn, 99, White Cube, London, 99, Scalo, Zurich, 2000, Matthew Marks Gallery, NY 2001, Studio Casoli, Milan and Rome, 2001, Marktkirche, Hannover, Germ, 2002, Galerie Krohn, Germ, 2002, Margarete Roeder Gallery, NY, 2002, Gallery N Von Bartha, London, 2003, Matthew Marks Gallery, NY, 2007; group shows incl Rendez-vous 1 and 2, Collection Lambert en Avignon, 2000; Photog Now, Contemp Arts Ctr, New Orleans, 2000; Essenbilder, Dorrie/Priess, Hamburg, 2000; Couples, Cheim and Read, NY, 2000; 46th Biennial Exhib, Corcoran Mus of Art, Washington, DC, 2000; Angles of Incidence, Ctr for Curatorial Studies, NY, 2001; Matthew Marks Gallery, 2006; and others. *Teaching:* Grad photog, Yale Univ, New Haven. *Awards:* Nat Endowment Arts Grant, Washington, DC, 90; Louis Comfort Tiffany Found Award, 91; Brandeis Award in Photography, 94; Aaron Siskinf Found, Grant in Photog, 2001; French Order Arts and Letters, 2006; Int Award in Photog, Hasselblad Found, 2007; 53rd Edward MacDowell medal, MacDowell Colony, Peterborough, NH, 2012. *Publ:* Cookie Mueller (catalog), Pace/MacGill Gallery, New York, 91; The Other Side 1972-1992, Scalo Verlag, 92; coauth (with Joachim Sartorius), Vakat, Walther König, Cologne, 93; (with David Armstrong), A Double Life, Scalo verlag, 94; I'll Be Your Mirror, Scalo Verlag in conjunction with Whitney Mus, NY. *Dealer:* Matthew Marks Gallery 523 W 24th St New York NY 10011. *Mailing Add:* 334 Bowery New York NY 10012

GOLDMAN, BEN
PAINTER
b Philadelphia, Pa, Oct 21, 1960. *Study:* NY Studio Sch, 80; Vassar Col, AB, 82; NY Univ, PhD, 93. *Work:* Jersey City Mus, NJ. *Exhib:* Artsthma, Bronx River Arts Ctr, NY, 2002; In Response, Savannah Coll Art & Design, Ga, 2002; Artists in Residence, Newark Mus, NJ, 2002; Fragments, Urban Inst Contemp Art, Grand Rapids, Mich, 2003; Paper Ball, Jersey City Mus, NJ, 2003; Fighting Chance, Lower Manhattan Cult Coun, NY, 2003; True Colors, Allied Mus, Berlin, Ger, 2004; Super Heroine Show, Gallery 128, 2004; Emerge 6, Aljira, 2005; Urban Eviron, CB Richard Ellis, 2006. *Pos:* Exec Dir City Without Walls; Founder & CEO, United Visual Arts, LLC. *Teaching:* lectr, Artist Forum, 2005; lectr, Jersey City Mus, 2005; lectr, Post Modernism, Sch Visual Arts, 2006. *Awards:* Artist in Residence, Newark Mus, 2002; Certification, Artist in Educ, NJ State Coun on Arts, 2003; Artist Grant Vt Studio Ctr, 2003; Fel, Emerge 6, Aljira, 2004; Fel, Strategic Planning Prog, Creative Capitol, 2004. *Bibliog:* Herman Lloyd (auth), Object Lessons, Guild Publ, 2001; Catherine Carlson (auth), Urban Meets Urban Hip, Voices of Lower Manhattan, 4/4/03; Jeff Theodare (auth), Nohu Art Scene on the Rise, Jersey J, 10/30/04; Holland Cotler (auth), Emerge 5, NY Times, 12/9/2005; Ben Genocchio (auth), Renovation & Extra Security, NY Times, 6/25/2006. *Mem:* Coll Art Asn; White Columns Curated Artists Register; Artists Space. *Media:* Acrylic, Oil. *Publ:* On Every Wall: Reproduction & the Future of Art, (article, book) Forthcoming, 2005. *Mailing Add:* 53 Fulton St Weehawken NJ 07086

GOLDMAN, JUDITH
WRITER, CURATOR
b Chicago, Ill. *Study:* Bard Col, Annandale-on-Hudson, NY, printmaking with Louis Schanker, BA (Lit), 64; Inst Design Ill Inst Technol, printmaking with Misch Kohn, 64. *Pos:* Managing ed, Artist's Proof, Pratt Graphics, New York, 67-69; ed, Print Collector's Newslett, New York, 70-72; managing ed, Artnews, New York, 73-75, contrib ed, 75-; adj cur, Print Collection, Whitney Mus Am Art, 76-92; consultant, The Andy Warhol Art Authentication Bd, 1999-, mem bd, 2006-. *Teaching:* Adj instr graphics, Hunter Col, New York, 74-75; asst prof criticism, Pratt Inst, 76-78. *Awards:* Nat Endowment Arts Grant Criticism, 78. *Res:* Twentieth century graphics, painting and photography: biography. *Publ:* Auth, American Prints: Process & Proofs Jasper Johns Prints: 1977-81, Harper & Row, 81; Jasper Johns: 17 Monotypes, Universal Art Ed, 82; Frank Stella, Fourteen Prints, Princeton, 83; James Rosenquist, Viking, 85; James Rosenquist: The Early Pictures, Rizzoli, 92; The Pop Image: Prints and Multiples, Marlbourough, 94; Frankenthaler, The Woodcuts, George Braziller, 2002; The Painted Sculptures of Betty Parsons, Naples Mus Art, 2005; Robert & Ethel Seull Portrait of a Collection, Acquaveila, NY, 2010

GOLDMAN, MATT
CONCEPTUAL ARTIST, KINETIC ARTIST
b New York, NY, May 2, 1961. *Study:* Clark Univ, BA (econ), 83, MBA, 84. *Work:* New Mus Contemp Art (performance), NY; Milwaukee Art Mus (performance), Wis; Contemp Art Ctr New Orleans (performance), Fla. *Awards:* Obie, Tubes, Village Voice, 91; Drama Desk, Tubes, 92; Lucille Lortel Found Award, Tubes, 92. *Bibliog:* Alisa Soloman (auth), Pissing on propriety, Village Voice, 1/15/91; Vicki Goldberg (auth), Hi tech meets God with Blue Man Group, New York Times, 1/17/91; Thomas M Disch (auth), Blue Man Group: Tubes, Nation, 1/20/92. *Media:* Performance. *Mailing Add:* c/o Blue Man Group 434 Lafayette St New York NY 10003

GOLDNER, JANET
SCULPTOR
b Washington, DC, June 6, 1952. *Study:* Asgard Sch, Hurup Thy, Denmark, 71; Penland Sch, NC, 72; Antioch Col, BA, 74; NY Univ, MA, 81, Forum 85, United Nations Women's Conference, Nairobi, Kenya, 85. *Work:* Am Embassy, Bamako, Mali, Negelan; Islip Mus, East Islip, NY; Most of Us Are Immigrants, The Granary, Assn Segou Laben, Segou, Mali, 2002; and many other private collections. *Comn:* Sculpture, Millay Colony Arts, Austerlitz, NY, 81; sculpture, comn by Robert Mitchell, Ridgefield, Conn, 82; Europos Parkas, Vilnius, Lithuania, 2000; public sculpture in collaboration with Assn Segou Laben, Gratz High School, Phila, Pa, 2003. *Exhib:* Mus Exhibs, New Mus Contemp Art, NY, 89; WAC Collaborative, Art Anchorage & Creative Time, NY, 92; Global Sweatshop, Art in General, NY, 95; Monmouth Mus & Cult Ctr, Lincroft, NJ, 96; Noyes Mus, Oceanville, NJ, 2006, Global Africa Project (with catalog), Mus Arts and Design, NY, 2010, Multiple Exposures (with catalog), NY, 2013; One-person shows, Klutznick Mus, Washington, DC, 96, Most of Us Are Immigrants (outdoor sculpture), Sara Roosevelt Park, NY, 97, Art Resources Transfer, NY, 2002, 03, Statements in Steel, Walton Art Ctr, Fayetteville, Ark, 98, Have We Met? Colgate Univ, Hamilton, NY, 2007; Group shows, Bronx Mus Arts, NY, 96, Text and Identity, State Univ, NY, Stony Brook, 97, Suture, Rotunda Gallery, Brooklyn, NY, 97, Artemisa Gallery, Chicago, 97, Michael Petronko Gallery, NY, 97, O'Kane Gallery, Univ Houston, Tex, 97, Ctr Bk Arts, NY, 98, Susquehanna Art Mus, Harrisburg, Pa, 2003, McLean Project for the Arts, 2003, Nathan Cummings Found, NY, 2006, Ctr for Book Arts, NY, 2006, Conventions and Attitudes-Habeas Lounge, Temple Gallery, Los Angeles, Calif, City Univ NY, 2008, Sustaining Vision: A Tribute to Arlene Raven, NJ City Univ, Jersey City, 2008, Anthropology: Revisited, Reinvented, Reinterpreted, Central Booking, Brooklyn, NY, 2009, Ka Kelen Kelen Wili (May We Wake Up One by One, Brooklyn Public Lib, NY, 2009, Ill Cut Thru, Ctr Book Arts, NY, Sarah Lawrence Coll, Bronxville, NY, 2010, Interstice & Emphasis, Aljira Ctr Contemporary Art, Newark, NJ, Cur by Carl Hazelwood, 2011. *Collection Arranged:* South African Mail: Messages From Inside, UN Spec Comt Against Apartheid, 90; Artists on the Home Front (with catalog), Goddard-Riverside Community Ctr, NY, 91; Groupe Bogolan Kasobane (mudcloth costumes & paintings from Mali), Lincoln Ctr Performing Arts, NY, 98; Unbound: Reshaping Artists Books, Abrons Art Ctr, Henry St Settlement, NY, co-cur, 2000. *Pos:* Dir, S African Women Artists in Resistance, 88- & Until That Last Breath: Women with AIDS, NY, 88-89, Hambidge Ctr, Rabun Gap, Ga, 2000, Europos Parkas, Vilnius, Lithuania, Can We Heal? 2000; dir, Art & Culture in Mali, Study Abroad Program, Antioch Col, Yellow Springs, Ohio, 2002-2006; Tucson Arts Brigade, 2004, consultant, Assn Mali Women Artists, Bamako, Mali, 2004, Mich State Univ, East Lansing, Mich, 2009, Community & Family in Mali, 2009, consultant, Lalla and SeguiSo SARL, Mali, 2009; vis artist, NJ City Univ, Jersey City, NJ, 2010; Alys Ctr, Unv Ala, Birmingham, 2011. *Teaching:* Lectr, Elmira Col, NY, 84, Cornell Col, Mt Vernon, Iowa, 85 & UN Women's Conf, Nairobi, Kenya, 85; vis artist lect series, Cortona, Italy, 87 & Am Cult Ctr, Bamako, Mali, 95; panel moderator, Nat Conf, Women's Caucus Art, NY, 90, 92 & 94, Studio Mus Harlem, NY, 92, Artists Talk on Art, NY, 93 & Col Art Asn Ann Conf, NY, 94; vis artist, Am Cult Ctr, Bamako, Mali, 95; lectr, Women's Studio Workshop, 95 & 96, Women's Caucus Art, NY, 96; lectr pottery workshops, Queens Mus Art, NY & Adirondack Ctr Arts, Blue Mountain Lake, NY, 96; artist residence, COSACOSA, Philadelphia, 94 & Metal Bks workshop, Webster Univ, St Louis, 98, 99, 2000. *Awards:* Visual Artists Exchange Award, NY Feminist Art Inst, New York, 83; UN Comt Against Apartheid Exhib Grant, 89; Fulbright Sr Res Fel, Mali, Africa, 94-95; Mid-Atlantic Arts Found, Phila, Pa, 2003, 2009; Ford Found, Three Continents Textile Collaboration, Indonesia, Mali, Nigeria, 2005; Fulbright Sr Specialist Grant, Conservatory of Arts, Bamako, Mali, 2009. *Bibliog:* Vivian Raynor (auth), article, NY Times, 2/26/95; Ori Soltes (auth), Janet Goldner: Sticks & Stones (monograph), Kyultznick Mus, Wash DC, 96; Roberta Smith (auth), article, NY Times, 8/8/97; Amy Blankstein (auth), Commissions, Sculpture Mag, 12/97; Carol Lorenz (auth), Have we Met? A Portrait of Maili (monograph), Colgate Univ, Hamilton, NY, 2006; Global African Project (catalog), Mus Art and Design, NY, 2010. *Mem:* Int Sculpture Ctr; Coll Art Asn; Arts Coun Africa Studies Asn; Mande Studies Asn; Mali Watch. *Media:* Steel, Mixed Media. *Res:* West Africa & the country of Mali; cultural research, projects concerning cultural preservation and contemporary art and artists in Mali. *Publ:* Auth, South African Mail: Messages from Inside (essay, catalog), 90; Artists on the Home Front (essay, catalog), 91; Connect Mag, Arts Internat, NYC; The Language of Beads: Kandioura Coulibaly, Beadwork Mag, 4/2002; Three Countries Textile Collaboration (catalog, essay), Indonesia, Mali, Nigeria, Ford Found, 2005; The Women of Kalabougou (photo, essay), African Arts Mag, 2007; Poetics of Cloth (catalog, essay), Grey Art Gallery, New York Univ, 2008; Contemporary African Fashion (book), Indiana Univ Press, 2010

GOLDRING, ELIZABETH
WRITER, ENVIRONMENTAL ARTIST
b Forest City, Iowa, Feb 13, 1945. *Study:* Smith Col, BA, 67; Harvard Univ, MEd, 77. *Exhib:* Artransition (coordr), Mass Inst Technol, Cambridge, 75; Inst Contemp Art, Boston, 76; Centerbeam (coordr), Documenta 6, Kassel, Ger, 77 & Smithsonian Inst, DC, 78; Int Biennial Exhib Graphic & Visual Art (doc), Secession, Vienna, Austria, 79; Int Alarm (with Otto Piene), Munich, 83; Coyote for Desert Sun/Desert Moon (CAVS artists) Lone Pine, Calif, 86; Eye/Sight (with Vin Grabill) for LightsOROT, Yeshiva Univ Mus, NY, 87; Eye/Sight (with Vin Grabill) & Int Alarm (with Otto Piene) for Otto Piene and CAVS, Kunstrevien, Karlsruhe, Fed Repub Ger, 88. *Pos:* Elem educ specialist, Nat Collection Fine Arts, Smithsonian Inst, 71-72; exhib developer, Childrens Mus, Boston, 73-75; exhib & proj dir, Ctr Advan Visual Studies, Mass Inst Technol, 78-. *Teaching:* Lectr, Art & Environment, CAVS/MIT, 75-. *Awards:* Grant, Diabetes Res & Educ Found, 87. *Res:* Sky Art; Visual Language. *Publ:* Contribr, You are Here (exhib catalog), Mass Inst Technol, 76; ed, CAVS Report on Elemental Sculpture in Public-Predominantly Urban-Places, Nat Endowment Arts & Ctr Advan Visual Studies, Mass Inst Technol, 78; auth, Sky Art-Art That Flies, Flying Colors, Braniff, 79; ed & contribr, Centerbeam, Ctr Advan Visual Studies, Mass Inst Technol, 80; Laser Treatment: Poems and Two Stories, Blue Giant Press, Boston, 83; The Sky Art Conference, Lightworks, No 17, 85; The Sky Art Manifesto, (coauth with Otto Piene and Lowry Burgess), CAVS/MIT, 86; auth, Desert Sun/Desert Moon and the Sky Art Manifesto, Leonardo, Vol 20, No 4, 12/88; The Inner Eye from the Inside Out, 88. *Mailing Add:* Center for Advanced Visual Studies 265 Massachusetts Ave Cambridge MA 02139

GOLDRING, NANCY DEBORAH
VISUAL ARTIST, EDUCATOR
b Oak Ridge, Tenn, Jan 25, 1945. *Study:* Smith Col, Northampton, Mass, BA(art hist), 67, Univ Florence, with Mina Gregori (Fulbright Fel), 67-68; NY Univ, MFA (sculpture, graphics), 70. *Work:* St Louis Art Mus; Mus Fine Arts, Houston; Int Ctr Photog, NY; Bibliot Nat, Paris; Int Ctr Photog, Bombay, India; and many others. *Comn:* Set design for Ode, Nat Choreography Proj, Nat Endowment Arts & Exxon, 85; set design for Ode with Ze' Eva Cohen & dancers, Joyce Theater, NY, 87. *Exhib:* Solo exhibs: Elliot Smith Gallery, St Louis, Mo, 94, Duane Reed Gallery, St Louis, Mo, 96, SE Mus Photog, Daytona Beach Community Col, Fla, 99, 2000, Houston Ctr Photog, Tex, 99-, Alva Gallery, 2000 & Web Gallery, Univ Houston, 2000, Last Days of Print Culture, European Inst, Columbia Univ, NY, 2009, Carrie Haddad Gallery, Hudson, NY, 2010, Projections of Nancy Goldring, Sarai Found, Delhi, 2012, Vanishing Points (Punti di Fuga), The Monitor Space, Casa dell'Architettura, Rome, 2012, Galleria Martini, Ronchetti, Genoa, 2012, Punti di fuga, Altri paesaggi, Galleria Martini Ronchetti, 2012, Projections: Place Without Description, Devi Art Found, Goethe House and Thyssen-Bornemisza Mus, 2013; Group Exhibs: Inside Spaces, Mus Mod Art, NY, 83; Photog of Inventions: Pictures of the Eighties (with catalog), Nat Mus Am Art, Washington, DC, Mus Contemp Art, Chicago & Walker Art Ctr, Minneapolis, 89; Constructed Spaces, Photog Resource Ctr, Boston, 90; New Directions, Fla Int Univ Art Mus, 91; Making Pictures, Caldwell Col, NJ, 94; Seeking the Sublime: Neo Romanticism in Landscape Photography, SE Mus Photog, Daytona Beach Community Col, Fla, 95; Landscape, Tisch Sch Arts, NY Univ, 95; New in the Nineties, Katonah Mus, NY, 96; Moving On, Soho 20 Gallery, NY, 96; The Archaeology of Memory, Trinity Coll, 97; Diverse Visions, Photog Perspectives, Pittsburgh Ctr Arts, 97; The Avon Collection, Int Ctr Photog, NY, 97; Distillations, Photog as an Art Form, Nat Ctr Performing Arts, Bombay, 97; World Artists for Tibet, Jonathan Schorr Gallery, NY, 98; Fresh Work 2 (with catalog), SE Mus Photog, Daytona Beach Community Col, Fla, 98; Inst Arts, Shanghai, China, 99; PROFIL, Int month of photo, Czech Republic, 03; Lyman Allen Mus, New London, Conn, 02; Sanvitale, Comune di Parma, Italy, 03-04; Houston Ctr for Photo, Fotofest, 02; Palimpest: Nancy Goldring, Palazzo Pigorini, Bk Mazzota, ed Milan; Gakerie Z, Int month of photog, Bratislava, Slovakia, cat repro, Nov 2003; Palinsesto, Palazzo Pigorini, Parma, Feb 2005; Palimpsest, Gallery 138, New York City, Mar 2006; An Italian Sense of Place II, George Segal Gallery, Montclair State Univ, Mar-Apr, 2008; Arte in Piazzetta, International Rassegna di Arte Graphica, Cesena, Italy, Dec 2007; Miami Basel: Bridge, Dec 2007; Bridging Cultures Through Art, Les Atlassides Gallery, Marrakech, Morocco, Nov 2006; Directors Choice, William Benton Mus, Storr, Conn, Summer 2006; Paper Trails: Works from the New York Metro, Pearce Gallery, Whitecliffe Coll Art and Design, Auckland, New Zealand, 2010; Antidote, Verge Art Fair, Dylan Hotel, NY, 2010; Judische Frauen in Der Bildenden Kunst, Inselgalerie, Berlin, DE, 2011; Classical Mythology in Modern and Contemporary Art, The Benton Mus, Conn, 2012; Faculty Exhib, Montclair State Univ, 2012; Columbiart, NY, 2013; Selections from the Permanent Collection of the Southeast Mus Photography: Leah King-Smith, Nancy Goldring, Barbara Norfleet, Atlantic Ctr Arts, Smyrna, FL, 2012; Anonymous Drawing, Ufferhallen, Berlin, 2013; Galerie Delikatessenhaus Leipzig May, June aTemporary Art Ct, Eindhoven, Netherlands, 2013; After Effects, Found Arts, 2013; Berlin Sun Theatre, Whitney Mus, 2013; The Last Brucennial, NYC, 2014; Prime Matter, Senspace, NYC Drawing Mus, Laholm, Sweden, 2015. *Pos:* Co-founding dir, SITE, NY, 69-72 & Chamber, NY, 76-; vis artist & critic, Parsons Sch Design, 80, juror, 88; juror, Sch Archit, NJ Inst Technol, 81; judge, State Arts Exhib & Workshop, Ogden, Utah, 93; Corresp, Press News; Art Reviewer, Architects Newspaper; AIA, Young Architects Juried Drawing Competition, 2007. *Teaching:* prof drawing, Montclair State Univ, NJ, 72-; vis prof contemp art, RI Sch Design, Providence, 74-75; vis prof, Haverford Col, Pa, 78, Dept Environ Design, Parsons Sch Design; lectr at Art Organizations, Schools and Universities for the Past 28 Years; Facolta di Lettere, Instr English Lit & Language, Univ Pisa 67-68; Lectr, Pratt Institute, Cooper Union, New York Studio Sch, Sch of Visual Arts, Eastman House Museum, 2004-2008 and several others. *Awards:* Grant, NY State Coun Arts, 70-73, 77-79 & 86-89; Res Grant, Montclair State Col, 82-87, 92, 98, Alumni Grant, 86-87, 91, Career Develop Grant, 88-89, 97-99 & Global Educ Travel Grant, 98; Fulbright SE Asia Fel, 94-95; Disting Scholar award, Montclair State Univ, 2003; NYFA Emergency Grant, 2012; Joan Mitchell Found Grant, 2013; Curator, Am Inst Architecture, Ann Exhib, 2013; and others. *Bibliog:* Jay Tolson (auth), What's After Modern, US News & World Report, 6/7/99; PMR, Review of Reflections in a Glass Eye, 12/99; Ellen Handy (auth), Distillations: Nancy Goldring, SE Mus Photog, 2000; Compagni di viaggio, Gazetta di Parma, 9/12/2003; Tom Wolf (auth), Reviews of Palimpsest, 2006; Erasure and exchange: Nancy Goldring's palimpsest, The Architect's Newspaper, 5/2006; John Baldacchino (auth), Erasure and Exchange: Nancy Goldring's Palimpsest, Architect's Newspaper, May 2006; Tammy La Gorce (auth), Tony Soprano! No, Here's the Real Italy, New York Times, Jan 2008; Barbara Wysocki (auth), Pleasures of Parma, Arts & Antiques, 5/2009; Colomina, Beatriz and Buckley, Craig (Ed) Clip, Stamp, Fold: The Radical Architecture of Little Magazines 196x-197x, Actar, 2010; Interview with Nancy Goldring (book, DVD), Fei Ctr Contemporary Art, Shanghair, 2011; I Strati di Tempo di Nancy Goldring, Massimiliano Tomba, Daniel Balico, Manifesto, 2012; Miriam Kreinin Souccar and Theresa Agovino (auth), Crain's Time for Healing: Exhibition Will Feature Art that Is Realted to Or Was Damaged by Hurricane Sandy, Crains, 2013; Ula Ilnytzky (auth), Exhibitions Plumb Artistic Responses to Disaster, Associated Press, 2013; Exhibition Showcases Artistic Response to Disaster, Good Morning America, Yahoo News, 2013; New Show of Hurricane Sandy-Inspired Art was made Possible by the NYFA's Relief Fund, ArtInfo, 2013; Oblique Perspective, The Architects Newspaper, NY, 9/2012. *Media:* Pencil, Gouache, Projection Photography. *Publ:* Auth, rev, Deconstructive architecture, 7/88 & George Ranalli: buildings & projects, 3/89, Bldg Design, London; rev, Identity, Arts Mag, 3/89; contribr, Generation of Place, Offramp, Univ SCalif, Vol 1, No 3, fall 90; auth, Imagining Egypt, Avant Garde: J Archit & Aesthetics, Univ Colo, Denver, 7/91; Dream Stills, Avant Garde: J Archit & Aesthetics, Univ Colo, 9/93; Nancy Goldring's Installation, Antiques and the Arts Weekly, 02; Photogr, To Desire It, Mike McGregor, Portland, Univ Portland, Winter 2007; In Good Hands, Architects Newspaper, Feb 2008; On Why Artists Loved Leo Steinberg, The Brooklyn Rail, 4/2011; First Measure, The Architect's Newpaper, 2012; Raritan (featured in 4 issues), 2012-2013; Nancy Goldring on Walls: Enrichement and Ornamentation, Word Processor, Reanimation Library, 9/12; Milano Triennale, The Architect's Newspaper, 11/2013; Putting Yourself in a Palce Where Grace Can Flow To You, The Brooklyn Rail, 2/5/15. *Dealer:* Gallery 138 New York. *Mailing Add:* 463 West St A1112 New York NY 10014

GOLDSLEGER, CHERYL
PAINTER, DRAFTSMAN
b Philadelphia, Pa, Dec 16, 1951. *Study:* Tyler Sch Art, Rome, 71; Philadelphia Coll Art, BFA, 73; Washington Univ, MFA, 75. *Work:* Albright-Knox Gallery, Buffalo, NY; Tel Aviv Mus, Israel; Israel Mus, Jerusalem; RI Sch Design Mus, Providence; Mus Mod Art, NY; Yale Univ Art Gallery, New Haven, Conn. *Exhib:* Palazzo Vagnotti, Cortona, Italy, 93; Women & Geometric Abstraction, Pratt Inst of Art, NY, 99; Interiors NC, Mus Art, NC, 2000; Drawings of Choice, Krannert Mus, Ill, 2002; Improvisation, Halsey Gallery, Coll Charleston, SC, 2002; Utopia, Mus Contemp Art Ga, 2003; Nat Acad Science, Wash, DC, 2005; Divas and Iron Chefs of Encaustic Mus Arts, Richmond, Va, 2008. *Pos:* dir, Welch Sch Art and Design, Ga State Univ, Atlanta, Ga. *Teaching:* Asst prof painting, Western Carolina Univ, 75-77; chmn art dept, Piedmont Col, Demorest, Ga, 88-2001; assoc prof, Ga State Univ, Atlanta, 2001-. *Awards:* NEA Fel, 81 & 91; US/France Fel, 93; Fifth Floor Found, 99. *Bibliog:* Donald Kuspit (auth), Cheryl Goldsleger, Artforum, 11/93; Mark Daniel Cohen (auth), Cheryl Goldsleger, Review, 5/99; Tom McDonough (auth), Cheryl Goldsleger at Rosenberg & Kaufman, Art in Am, 2/00; Jerry Cullum (auth), Designing Women, Art in Am, 9/03; Rex Weil (auth), Utopia, Mus Contemp Art Ga, 2003; Karen Wilson (auth), Hudson Review, 2005. *Mem:* Coll Art Asn. *Media:* Encaustic, graphite. *Dealer:* Kidder Smith Gallery Boston Mass; Gallery Joe Philadelphia Pa. *Mailing Add:* 170 Greenwood Dr Athens GA 30606-4704

GOLDSMITH, BARBARA
WRITER, HISTORIAN
b New York, NY, May 18, 1931. *Study:* Wellesley Col, BA, 57; Pace Univ, Hon DLit, 81; Syracuse Univ, Hon DLett, 81; Lake Forest Col, LHD, 96. *Hon Degrees:* Three Hon Dr. *Pos:* Ed, NY Mag, 66-74; sr ed, Harper's Bazaar, 70-74; The New Yorker; appointee, Pres's Comn on Celebration of Women in Am History, Gov NY, NY State Coun Arts; trustee, NY Pub Libr, exec & nominating comts; Pres Comn for Preservation & Access, Permanent Paper Task Force of Nat Libr Medicine; trustee, NY Soc Libr, Am Acad in Rome; former overseer, Ctr for Res on Women, Wellesley Col; founding ed, NY Mag. *Teaching:* lectr, NY Univ, Harvard Univ. *Awards:* Penn Paper-Pres & Access Award, Am Acad Arts & Scis, 92; 2 Emmy Awards; Presidential Citation, NY Univ; many others. *Mem:* Whitney Mus Am Art; Mus Mod Art, NY; Mus City NY (pres coun, 70-); NY Coun Arts; Guggenheim Mus. *Publ:* Auth, articles The New Yorker, Esquire, Vanity Fair & contrib ed Archit Digest; The Straw Man, Farrar, Straus & Giroux, 76; Little Gloria...Happy at Last, Alfred A Knopf Publ, 80; Johnson v Johnson, 87; Other Powers, The Age of Suffrage, Spiritualism & the Scandalous Victoria Woodhull, Alfred A Knopf Publ. *Mailing Add:* Janklow/Nesbit Assocs 445 Park Ave #13 New York NY 10022

GOLDSTEIN, ANN
CURATOR, DIRECTOR
b Los Angeles, Calif, 1957. *Study:* UCLA, BFA (studio art), 1979. *Collection Arranged:* Roni Horn, 1990, Judy Fiskin, 1992, Cady Noland, 1992, Felix Gonzalez-Torres, 1994, Christopher Wool, 1998, Jorge Pardo, 1998, Barbara Kruger, 1999, Jennifer Bornstein, 2005 & Cosima von Bonin, 2007; A Forest of Signs: Art in the Crisis of Representation (with catalog), 1989; Reconsidering the Object of Art: 1965-1975 (with catalog), 1995; A Minimal Future? Art as Object 1958-1968 (with catalog), 2004; Lawrence Weiner: As Far as the Eye Can See (with Donna De Salvo), 2007; Martin Kippenberger: The Problem Perspective, 2008. *Pos:* Libr asst, Mus Contemp Art Los Angeles, 1983-1993, cur, 1993-2001 & sr cur, 2001-2009; gen artistic dir, Stedelijk Mus, Amsterdam, 2009-. *Mailing Add:* 250 S Grand Ave Los Angeles CA 90012

GOLDSTEIN, CARL
HISTORIAN
b New York, NY, June 24, 1938. *Study:* Brooklyn Coll, BA, 60; Columbia Univ, MA, 62, PhD, 66. *Teaching:* Instr art hist, Wheaton Coll, Norton, Mass, 66; asst prof, Brown Univ, 66-71; prof, Univ NC, Greensboro, 71-. *Awards:* Grants, Am Philosophical Soc, 77 & 82. *Mem:* Coll Art Asn Am. *Res:* Baroque art; twentieth century sculpture; history of academies of art. *Publ:* Auth, Visual Fact Over Verbal Fiction, A Study of the Carracci and the Criticism, Theory and Practice of Painting in Renaissance and Baroque Italy, Cambridge Univ Press, 88; Teaching Art: Academies and Schools from Vasari to Albers, Cambridge Univ Press, 96; Print Culture in Early Modern France: Abraham Bosse and the Purposes of Print, Cambridge Univ Press, 2012. *Mailing Add:* 801 Greenwood Greensboro NC 27410

GOLDSTEIN, CHARLES BARRY
ART DEALER, APPRAISER
b New York, NY, 1945. *Study:* Ohio Univ, Athens, BBA, 67; Am Univ, Washington, MPA, 75; Ind Univ Int Soc Appraisers, Certified Appraiser Personal Property in Limited Edition Prints, CAPP Dipl, 91, CAPP Recertification, 95, 2000, & 2005; independent art study in forensic appraising, signatures, art fraud & art terminology; Univ Md & Int Soc Appraisers, CAPP dipl, 2000, cert appraiser personal property in fine art; CAPP Recertification, 2005; USPAP Compliant, 2007. *Pos:* Art dealer, Charles Barry Int, Rockville, Md, 75-, art appraiser, 79-, court qualified expert witness & trial consult, 92-; arts comnr, City of Rockville, Md, 91-96, chmn Art Pub Places prog, 93-95 & chmn, Cult Arts Comn, 95-96; chair, Appraisal Studies Comt Nat Capitol Area Chap of the Int Soc of Appraisers (NCAC-ISA), 2006. *Teaching:* fac mem, Continuing Legal Educ (CLE), Visual Arts & The Law Ann Conference, Santa Fe, NMex; Lectr & forums art & appraisals, Int Soc Appraisers, Hoffman Estates, Ill Nat Confs & Seattle Nat Confs, 89-; forensic guest lectr, George Washington Univ Masters Forensic Scis Prog; lectr, Art Fraud, Misrepresentation & Gobbledygook, 8/2006. *Awards:* ISA Lamp of Knowledge Award, Outstanding Serv Cert of Appreciation, 2007; Fine Art Comt Chair, 2007-2008; Certs Appreciation, Int Soc Appraisers; Cert Appreciation, City Rockville, Md; Learned Res J Hon, Brandeis Univ Libr. *Mem:* Int Soc Appraisers, (nat fine arts comt, 90-97, designation & rev comt, 89-97, 2005-, Fine Arts Chair, 2006); Catalogue Raisonne Scholars Asn; Int Found for Art Res (IFAR). *Specialty:* Prints, paintings & sculpture. *Interests:* Art Terminology & definitions, Art Fraud, Art Misrepresentation, Expert Witness, Trial Consulting & Litigation Support. *Publ:* Stretching the Limits of a Limited Edition Print, PrintThoughts (reprinted in Wash Print Club Quart fall 1999), 11/1995; The Original Print Debacle, PrintThoughts (reprinted in Wash Print Club Quart, winter 1999-2000), 1/1995; The Importance of the Artist's Signature in Contemporary Paintings & Prints, Art Calendar (reprinted in ISA's PAIE), Jul, Aug 1998; Auth, Art Fraud, Misrepresentation & Gobbledygook, 1999; auth, Commentary on Art & Appraisal Matters, quart column in ISA's Prof Appraisers Info Exchange, 12/2005; auth, Toulouse Lautrec Moulin Rouge: La Goulue-Lithograph or Reproduction, Int Found Art Res (IFAR) jour, 2005-2006; auth, Strokes of Genius-Rembrandt's Prints & Drawings, J of the Print World, winter 2006-2007. *Mailing Add:* c/o Charles Barry International 8 Hardwicke Place Rockville MD 20850-3010

GOLDSTEIN, DANIEL JOSHUA
KINETIC ARTIST, SCULPTOR
b Mt Vernon, NY, June 19, 1950. *Study:* Brandeis Univ; Univ Calif, Santa Cruz, BA; St Martin's Col, London, Eng. *Work:* Brooklyn Mus, NY; Chicago Art Inst; Achenbach Found, San Francisco, Calif; Oakland Mus Art, Calif; Carnegie Inst; and others. *Comn:* Sculpture, City of Mountain View, Calif, 93; sculpture, Synoptics, 93; sculpture, Colma BART Sta, Colma, Calif; sculpture, Norcal Waste, San Francisco, Calif, 2001; sculpture, Astra Zeneca, Wilmington, Del, 2002. *Exhib:* Achenbach Found, 72; Prints Calif, Oakland Mus Art, 75; Nat Print Exhib, Brooklyn Mus, NY, 76 & 80; Solo exhibs, Getler-Pall Gallery, NY, 77, ADI Gallery, San Francisco, 77 & Brooklyn Mus, 83; Calif Palace Legion Hon, San Francisco; Foster Goldstrom Gallery, NY, 93; Mus Contemp Relig Art, St Louis, Mo, 94; Richmond Art Ctr, Calif, 94; Nat Gallery Victoria, Melbourne, Australia, 98; Durke Chang Gallery, San Francisco, Calif, 2002. *Bibliog:* Barry Walker & Richard Howard (coauths), Daniel Goldstein: Woodblocks & Paper Cut-Outs, Brooklyn Mus, 83; Robert Flynn Johnson (auth), Beyond Belief, Nat Gallery Victoria, 98; Richard Howard, Robert Atkins & David Maxim (coauths), Reliquaries, Foster Goldstrom Gallery, NY, 94. *Media:* Aluminum, Leather. *Mailing Add:* 224 Guerrero San Francisco CA 94103

GOLDSTEIN, ELEANOR
PAINTER
b New York, NY, May 2, 1935. *Study:* Bennington Coll, BA, 57. *Work:* US State Dept Art in Embassies; IBM, Armonk, NY; Standard & Poors, Pfizer Co, NY; Pepsico, Purchase, NY; Center for Contemporary Printmaking, CT. *Comn:* Mural, Cathedral St John Divine, NY, 96. *Exhib:* 12th Ann Art Exhib, Salmagundi Club, NY, 89 & 2000; 11th Ann Pastel Exhib, Pen & Brush Club, NY, 92; HRCA at the Hammond, Hammond Mus, Salem, NY, 92; Allen Sheppard Gallery, New York, 2001; Art of Northeast, Silvermine, Conn, 2002; River Rock Gallery, Woodstock, NY, 2005; Rockefeller Preserve Art Gallery, Pocanitico Hills, NY, 2006; The Noyes Mus Art, Ocreanville, NJ 2009, 2012; Katonah Mus, Katonah, NY, 2012; Monmouth Mus, NJ, 2013; Butler Inst Am Art, Oh, 2013. *Teaching:* Instr, Long Beach Island Art Found, Loveladies, NJ, 2004-07. *Awards:* Norman Wenig Purchase Prize, Pastel Soc Am, 91; Philip Glasser Mem Award, Mamaroneck Artist Guild Nat, 94; Nat Arts Club Award, 97; Seascape Award, Salmagundi Club, 2000. *Mem:* Nat Asn Women Artists; Pastel Soc Am; N Artist Equity Asn. *Media:* Pastel, Oil. *Mailing Add:* 1 Chester Terr Hastings On Hudson NY 10706

GOLDSTEIN, GLADYS
PAINTER, COLLAGE ARTIST
b Newark, Ohio. *Study:* Md Inst Art; Art Students League; Columbia Univ, New York; Pa State Univ, Univ Park; study with Hobson Pittman. *Work:* Baltimore Mus Art, Md; Pa State Univ; Univ Ariz; Goucher Col, Baltimore; Univ Md; Fed Reserve Bank; and others. *Exhib:* Solo exhibs, Baltimore Mus Art, Goucher Col, Duveen-Graham Gallery, NY, Galerie Philadelphia, Paris, IFA Gallery, Washington, DC, Western Md Col, Newark Gallery, Del, Richter Gallery, Weisbaden, Ger, 65-75. *Pos:* Co-chmn art festival, City Baltimore, 71-74; art comt, Mayor's Ball, 73-74; exec comt, Mayor's Adv Comt for Arts & Cult, 74-. *Teaching:* Instr painting, Md Inst Col Art, 60-65; instr art, Col Notre Dame, Md, 65-85. *Awards:* Third Award, Md Art Today, H K & Co, 72; First Award, 25th Ann of Israel, JCC, 74; Awards, Baltimore Mus Art & Pa State Univ. *Media:* Oil; Paperwork, Acrylic

GOLDSTEIN, SHELDON (SHELLY)
PAINTER
b St Louis, Mo, 1951. *Study:* Univ Mo; studied with James Harmon, St Louis & Val Dunnett, London. *Work:* Off Secy Interior, Washington. *Comn:* Landscapes, portraits & still-lifes, Italy, Ireland & US. *Exhib:* Bibliot Provinciale, Arezzo, Italy, 93; Palazzo Casali, Cortonra, Italy, 93; Embassy Repub SAfr, 94; Royal Geographical Soc, London, Eng, 95; Hotel Martinez, Cannes, France, 95. *Awards:* Artistic Ambassador, People to People Int, Hq, Kansas City, Mo, 94-95. *Bibliog:* Victoria Fowler (auth), Sheldon Goldstein: Paintings 1980-1989 (monogr), 89; Victoria Fowler (auth), Sheldon Goldstein: Un Pittore in Toscana, The Region of Tuscany (catalog), 90; The Zulus and Landscapes of South Africa, Pts I & II (catalog). *Mem:* Fel Royal Geographical Soc, London, Eng. *Dealer:* Kertesz Gallery 521 Sutter St San Francisco CA 94102; Max Bollag Gallery Werdmuhlestrasse 9 Zurich Switzerland

GOLDSTON, BILL
PRINTMAKER, DIRECTOR
Pos: Printer, Universal Limited Art Editions, 1969-1982, dir, 1982-. *Mailing Add:* ULAE 1446 N Clinton Ave Bay Shore NY 11706

GOLDSZER, BATH-SHEBA
PAINTER, GRAPHIC ARTIST
b Warsaw, Poland, Jan 26, 1932; US citizen. *Study:* Hertzeliah Teachers Sem, BA (educ), 56; Art Students League, with Gustav Rehberger; also with Joe Hing Lowe & Ludmila Morosova. *Work:* Many pvt collections, US, Israel, Poland & Argentina. *Exhib:* Hudson Valley Art Asn, Westchester Co Ctr; Catharine Lorillard Wolfe Arts Club, Nat Arts Club Gallery; Am Artists Prof League, Salmagundi Club, NY; Chung-Cheng Art Gallery, Sun Yat Sen Hall, St John Univ; and others. *Awards:* First Prize in Oil, Nat Art League, 74 & 82, Queensboro Soc Arts, 74-77 & Art League Nassau Co, 78 & 79; 7 first prizes in oil and numerous others. *Bibliog:* Jack Besterman (auth), Big Six Art League, Chapel & Pension News, 2/72, An accomplished artist, 2/73 & Coop art scene, 4/74 & 5/79, Towers Reporter. *Mem:* Life fel Am Artists Prof League; Hudson Valley Art Asn; Catharine Lorillard Wolfe Arts Club; Nat Art League; Art League Nassau Co; and others. *Media:* Oil. *Mailing Add:* 7583 Granville Dr Bldg F Fort Lauderdale FL 33321

GOLEMBESKI, BEVERLY L
PAINTER, INSTRUCTOR
b Camden, NJ, Oct 20, 1940. *Study:* Montclair Univ, BA (art educ), 62; studied with L Geiser, Chas Reid, F Webb, S Szabo, F Peitre, Judi Betts, RC Clark, A Westerman, Don Getz, Nita Engles, Dom DiStefano, M Ahern, N Barch, V Spicer, Roberta Carter Clark. *Work:* Islands Heights Cult Heritage, NJ; paintings, GTECH Int, Mexico City, Mex; paintings, GTECH Int, Buenos Aires, Arg; sports mural, Cent Regional High Sch, Bayville, NJ; watercolor, Baltimore Art Mus, Md; mural, Shore Community Bank, Toms River, NJ. *Comn:* Bathroom/bedroom design, comn by R Efel, Bayville, NJ, 93; rm design, comn by Paul Orni, Seaside Park, NY, 96; mural, Shore Community Bank, Toms River, NJ, 97; nautical design, comn by B Gollob, Basking Ridge, NJ, 99; portraits, comn by Di Santi family, Rutherford, NJ, 2000. *Exhib:* Monmouth Mus, NJ, 80-82, 98, 2000, 2001 & 2002; Allied Artists Nat Juried, Nat Arts Club, NY, 85 & 2002; Adirondack Nat Exhib, Old Forge, NY, 88-89, 92-99; Baltimore Nat Exhib, Johns Hopkins Univ, 88-89, 91-92; Jane Law Int Miniature Exhib, Surf City Gallery, NJ, 89-90; Salmagundi Club, NY, 89-92, 99-2000 & 2002; Trenton Mus Art, NJ, 89-90; Rider Col, NJ, 2002; Johnson & Johnson, Princeton, NJ, 2002; Georgian Ct Col, Lakewood, NJ, 2002; Muriel Berman Mus Art, Collegeville, 2002. *Collection Arranged:* Office Design, GTech, Mexico & Argentina; Murals, Shore Comm Bank, Prof Buildings, Libr, NJ & PA. *Teaching:* Instructor of classes, demonstrations and workshops from Maine to Fla & Tuscany, Italy. *Awards:* J Bermingham Award, NJ Watercolor Soc, 89; Merit Awards Pine Shores Ann Juried Show, 99; Fel Nat Artists Prof League, 99; Nat Am Art Prof League, 2000 & 2002; Dick Blick Award, Audubon Artist Inc, 2004; AG Edwards Award, NJ Water Color Soc, 2004; Merit Award, RI Water Color So, 2004. *Bibliog:* Susan Ecord (auth), A Watercolor Demo, NJ Cable TV, 91; Wanda Callagy (auth), Local Scenes at Mural, Del Times, NY, 96; Doug Hood (auth), Daily Observer, Toms River, 99. *Mem:* NJ Watercolor Soc (mem bd, 97-99); Pa Watercolor Soc; Garden State Watercolor Soc; Philadelphia Watercolor Club (signature mem); Ocean Co Artists' Guild (pres, 97-99); fel, Am Artists Prof League; Guild of Creative Art, Shrewsbury, NJ (exhibiting mem); Audubon Artist Inc. *Media:* Watercolor, Acrylic. *Res:* Local art publications & writing articles. *Specialty:* Orginals & prints in all medias covering diverse subject matter. *Collection:* NJ shore scenes, boats, ocean, boardwalks, fish, florals, people, race horses, snow scenes, carousels, tropical parrots. *Publ:* Illusr, Central region sports design, Bayville Press, 81-85; illusr, Lifeguard Book, Art Works, 87, 88, 89; auth, illusr, Calendar, Garden State Publ, 88; illusr, contribr, Art Dialog, NJ Watercolor Soc, 99; illusr, To The Shore Once More, Jersey Shore Publs, 2000; fall cover, Jersey Shore Mag, 2002. *Dealer:* Annex Gallery Surf City NJ; Forked River Framing Forked River NJ; Erickson's Gallery Toms River NJ; Anchor & Palette Gallery Bayhead NJ; Watermark Gallery Tuckerton NJ; Jane Law Studio & Gallery Surf City NJ. *Mailing Add:* 16 I St Seaside Park NJ 08752

GOLEY, MARY ANNE
ART HISTORIAN, DIRECTOR
b Washington, DC, July 1, 1945. *Study:* Univ Md, asst to Dr William H Gerdts, BA, 67; Oberlin Coll, 70-71; Case Western Reserve Univ, with Wolfgang Steckow & Karal Ann Marling, MA, 73; Cleveland Mus Art, cert, 75. *Exhib:* John White Alexander: 1856-1915, SI Mus Am Art, 76-77; The Hague Sch & its American Legacy, Fed

Reserve Bd & Norton Gallery, West Palm Beach, Fla, 82; The Office as Art: Furnishings & Fixtures, Arlington Art Ctr, 86; Paintings of Edward Steichen, 88 & Samuel Halpert, 91, Fed Reserve Bd; Show Me the Money, Trust for Mus Exhibs; Graham Williford's America, Tyler Mus, Tex, 2008. *Collection Arranged:* Permanent collections of Fed Reserve Bd, 75 & Fed Reserve Banks, Miami, 79, Jacksonville, 86 & Dallas, 92, Atlanta, 2003 & Detroit, 2007. *Pos:* Asst registrar, SI Mus Am Art, 68-71; dir, Fine Arts Prog, Fed Reserve Bd, 75-2006; guest cr, JW Alexander Survey, Milwaukee Art Mus, 2013-. *Awards:* Lady of the House of Orange-Nassau, Queen of Neth, 82; House of Nassau, Grand Duke of Luxembourg, 88. *Mem:* Am Asn Mus; Asn Prof Art Advisor (Pres, 94); Arlington Arts Ctr (bd pres, 87-90); Mus Trustee Asn (dir comt, 2006). *Res:* Late 19th century American artists in the context of their European influences; J W Alexander, Frank Duveneck, Eduard J Steichen & Victor Dubreuil. *Publ:* Auth, The Hague School and Its American Legacy, Fed Reserve, 82; Gerald Murphy: Toward an Understanding of his Art and Inspiration (exhib catalog), Fed Reserve Bd, 83; Panel for Music Room by John White Alexander, Detroit Inst Arts Bull, 89; Arquitect ura y Pinturos del Consejo de la Reserva Federal, Banco de Espana, 99; auth, The Influence of Velasquez on Modern Painting, The American Experience, Fed Res, 2000; Circuit: America-Europe, European Cent Bank, 2006; Graham Willifords America, Am Art Rev, 3-4/2008; auth, Kindred Spirits: John White Alexander and Auguste Rodin, Antiques Mag, 2011; auth, The Tribute of Isabella, Apollo, 2012; What Fed Chiefs Like WSJ, 3/16/2010; John White Alexander's Industrial Lunettes for the Pa State Capital, Jour for Industrial Archaeology, Vol 34, nos 1 & 2, 2008; Portrait of Mrs. Ashton Potter, John White Alexander, Style and Grace, Mennello Mus Amer Art, 2012; Tuscan Light, Apollo, 5/2012. *Mailing Add:* 4909 Washington Blvd Arlington VA 22205

GOLICI, ANA
ARTIST

b Romania, 1955; arrived in US, 87. *Exhib:* NY Hall of Science; Hunter Coll Times Square Gallery; East-West Gallery, NY; Int Print Ctr, NY; Holiday Show, Gallery 49, NY City, 2003-2004; Nat Acad Mus, NY, 2006. *Pos:* With Podul Printmaking Workshop, Romania. *Teaching:* Mem faculty continuing educ Hunter Col, NY City

GOMEZ, MIRTA & EDUARDO DELVALLE
PHOTOGRAPHER

b Havana, Cuba, Dec 20, 1953 (Gomez); b Havana, Cuba, Sept 14, 1951 (Eduardo Delvalle). *Study:* both: Fla Int Univ, BFA, 76; Brooklyn Col, MFA, 81. *Work:* Mus Mod Art, NY; New Orleans Mus Art, La; Brooklyn Mus, NY; Art in Pub Places, Miami, Fla; Bibliot Nat, Paris. *Exhib:* Viva Nada, Blue Sky Gallery, Portland, Ore, 91; Contemp Southern Photog, New Orleans Tri-Annual Exhib, 92; Mayan Dwellings, Univ Calif, San Francisco, 94; Mayan Dwelling, OK Harris Gallery, NY, 97. *Teaching:* Assoc prof art, Fla Int Univ, Miami, 83-. *Awards:* Individual Artist Fel Photog, Nat Endowment Arts, 76 & 90; Oscar B Cintas Fel, 89 & 96; S Fla Cult Consortium Award, 92; John Solomon Guggenheim fellowship, 97

GOMEZ-QUIROZ, JUAN MANUEL
PAINTER, PRINTMAKER

b Santiago, Chile, Feb 20, 1939; US citizen. *Study:* RI Sch Design, Fulbright Fel, 62-63; Yale Univ, Fulbright Fel, 63-64; Pratt Graphic Art Ctr, 64-65; Workshop with Justo Mellado, critic, art curator and Claudio Gianconi, writer, author, poet, 89-90. *Exhib:* Solo exhibs, Schubert Gallery, Marbella, Spain, 77, Sutton Gallery, NY, 80, 83 86 & 88, Held-Koupernikoff Gallery, Boston, 82, Omar Rayo Mus, Rodalnillo, Colombia, 84 & Todd Capp Gallery, NY, 86; The Latin Am Spirit: Art and Artists in the United States 1920-1970, Bronx Mus Art, NY, 88; ST LIFER, Art Exchange, NJ, 89; The Dead Blimpee Show II, NY, 89; IX Biennal Int De Arte, Valparaiso, Chile, 89; Efectos de Viaje, Mus Nat de Bellas Arts Santiago de Chile, 91; printmaking workshop traveling show to Africa, 94; Paula Rieloff Gallery, NY, 96; group exhib, Primer Festival del Grabado, Mus de la Nac, Lima, Peru, 2004; La Trascendencia del deseo de expresar la forma, la linea y el color en la cuarto dimension, Museo de la Nacion, Lima, Peru, 2006; Works on Paper 1968-2004, Museo de Arte Contemporaneo, Santiago, Chile, 2007-. *Pos:* pres, HH Silverman Publishing Co, Fine Art Printing, 86-88; Cur & admin asst, Mus Contemp Spanish Art, NY, 90; auth; jury, Premio Internacional de Novela, Casa de la Cultura Dominicana, NY, 2002. *Teaching:* Lectr studio art, Univ Calif, Santa Barbara, 67-68; dir, NY Univ, Photo Etching Workshop, 69-70; adj prof, art dept, NY Univ, 69-76; lectr, Summit Art Ctr, Summit, NJ, 72-77; Escuela de Bellas Artes, Lima, Peru, 75; NJ Ctr Visual Art, 87; Fla Inst Technol & Printmaker Workshop, 88. *Awards:* Second Prize, Painting, Salon de Primavera, Santiago, Chile, 61; Grand Prize, VI Biennial Printmaking, San Juan, PR, 79; Prize Bienal Maracaibo Venezuela, 82; Hispanic Achievers Feria Mundial Hispana, NY, 85; and many others. *Bibliog:* David Shirley (auth), article in NY Sunday Times, 78; Joseph Merkel (auth), The flexibility of sculpture, Artspeak, 86; article in IBM Nachrichten, 6/89, Ger; Javier Martinez de Pinson (auth), La pintura Multidimensional de Gomez-Quiroz, Medico Interamerico, Vol 17, 4/98; and many others. *Mem:* Sociedad de Escritores de Chile. *Media:* Oil, Acrylic; Intaglio. *Collection:* Solomon Guggenheim Mus, New York City; Metrop Mus Art, New York City; Mus Mod Art, New York City; De Menil Collection, Houston, Tex; Mus Fine Arts, Boston, Mass. *Publ:* auth, Crónicas de Literatura Hablada, Novel, Latino Press; auth, Anthology, Plain View Press, Austin, Tex; auth, Hybrido, Arte y Literatura Ano II Numero 2, 98; auth, La Palabra, Revista de Literatura, 98; and many others. *Mailing Add:* 44 Grand St Apt 2 New York NY 10013

GONZALES, WAYNE
PAINTER

b New Orleans, La, 1957. *Study:* Univ New Orleans, BA, 1985. *Work:* Whitney Mus Art, NY; Solomon R Guggenheim Mus, NY; Hirschorn Mus, Washington, DC; Dallas Mus Art, Tex; Maramotti Collection, Italy; Mus Fine Arts, Boston; Albright-Knox Art Gallery, Buffalo, NY. *Exhib:* Solo Exhibs: include Galerie Art & Public, Geneva, 1995; Lauren Wittels Gallery, NY, 1997; Mary Boone Gallery, NY City, 1998; Derek Eller Gallery, NY City, 1998; Reali Arte Contemporanea, Brescia, Italy, 2000; Paula Cooper Gallery, NY City, 2001, 2003, 2005, & 2007; Le Consortium, Dijon, France, 2002-03; Mario Diacono, Boston, 2003; Galerie Almine Rech, Paris, 2004-05;l Patrick de Brock, Knokke, Belgium, 2004-05; Conner Contemp Art, Wash, DC, 2005; QED, Los Angeles, 2006; Steven Friedman Gallery, London, Eng, 2/1/2008-3/1/2008, Seomi Gallery, Seoul, Korea, 2008, Wayne Gonzales, Paula Cooper Gallery, New York, Stephen Friedman Gallery, London; Group Exhibs: include Contemp Art Ctr, New Orleans, 1987; Four Walls, 1992; Terrain, San Francisco, 1994; Arthur Roger Gallery, New Orleans, 1994; Momenta Art, Brooklyn, 1995; Mus Fine Arts, Boston, 1996; Tomio Koyama Gallery, Tokyo, 1997; Islip Art Mus, NY, 1998; Galerie Art & Public, Geneva, 1999; Paula Cooper Gallery, NY City, 2000, 2002, 2004, 2006 & 2009; Aldrich Mus Contemp Art, Ridgefield, Conn, 2000; Albright-Knox Art Gallery, Buffalo, NY, 2001; Anton Kern Gallery, NY City, 2003; Roebling Hall, Brooklyn, 2004; Sandra Gehring Gallery, NY City, 2004; Max Henry, Apex Art, NY, 2005; PS 1 Contemp Arts, Queens, NY, 2006; Whitney Mus Am Art, NY, 2007; Layr Wuestenhagen Gallery, Vienna, 2007; White Columns, NY, 2008; Seiler & Mosseri, Marlio Galeriem Zurich, Switzerland, 2008; Janies Graham and Sons, NY, 2009; Every Revolution is a Roll of the Dice, Paula Cooper Gallery, New York, 2009; Reprise, Paula Cooper Gallery, New York, 2010. *Pos:* vis artist, Cooper Union, NY, 2004-05; cove critic, Yale Univ Grad Program, New Haven, Conn, 2009. *Teaching:* Vis asst prof, grad prog, Hunter Coll, NY, 2003-06. *Publ:* Art Works: The Progressive Collection, Art Publ, NY, 2007. *Dealer:* Conner Contemp Art 1730 Connecticut Ave NW Washington DC 20009; Patrick De Brock Gallery Strandstraat 11 B-8300 Knokke Belgium; Editions Fawbush 448 West 19th St NY City, NY 10011; Paula Cooper Gallery 534 W 21st St New York NY 10011. *Mailing Add:* c/o Paula Cooper Gallery 534 W 21st St New York NY 10011

GONZALEZ, MAURICIO MARTINEZ
ADMINISTRATOR, GALLERY DIRECTOR

b Mexico City, Mexico, Sept 30, 1945. *Study:* Univ Tex at Arlington, BFA, 73; Univ of Americas, MA, 76; Fla State Univ, PhD, 88. *Exhib:* Rio Azul: City of the Storm God, traveling exhib, Univ Tex San Antonio Art Teaching Gallery, Tex, 89, Denver Mus Nat Hist, Colo, 90, Nat Geographic Soc Explorers Hall, Washington, DC, 90, Nat Hist Mus Los Angeles, Calif, 90, Museo Nac de Arqueologia Etnologia, Guatemala City, 91. *Pos:* Gallery dir, Univ Tex, San Antonio, 82-; asst dean, Col Fine Art & Humanities, Univ Tex, San Antonio, 88-; asst vpres, Off of Multicultural Student Develop, Univ Toledo, Ohio, 90-. *Awards:* Fel Nat Endowment Art, 79; Award for minority mus prof, Smithsonian, 88; Grant, USIA, 89. *Mem:* Am Fed Arts; Am Asn Mus. *Publ:* Coauth, The Museum as a field setting for Teacher Education, J of Mus Educ, 87; InterAmerican Cultural Development, Fla State Univ, Ctr Arts Admn, 88. *Mailing Add:* Office Multicultural Student Develop Student Union Rm 2500 2801 W Bancroft Toledo OH 43606-3390

GONZALEZ, TONY
PHOTOGRAPHER, EDUCATOR, ADMINISTRATOR

Study: Cooper Union Sch of Art, BFA, 1987; Yale Univ Sch of Art, MFA, 1989. *Exhib:* group shows Trenton City Mus, 1990, Aljira Fine Arts, Newark, NJ, 1992, La Mama La Galleria, NY, 1994, Bronx Mus of Arts, 2000, Cheryl McGinnis Gallery, NYC, 2000, 2006, Urban Ctr, NYC, Soho Photo, NYC, 2006, Town Hall in Flushing, 2006, Longwood Arts Gallery, Bronx, 2007 and several others; solo exhibits Sam Houston State Univ, Tex, 1996, View Point Gallery, Calif, 1997, Numina Gallery, Princeton, NJ, 2001, Ill Central Col, Peoria, Ill, 2006, Queens Col Art Ctr, Flushing, 2006, Cheryl McGinnis Gallery, NYC, 1999, 2007, 2010, David Bruner Gallery, 2008, Park Row Gallery, Chatham, NY, 2008, The Gallery at Kinderhook Group, Conn, 2009 and several others. *Collection Arranged:* Permanent collections include Ctr for Photography, Woodstock, NY, Mercer County Cultural and Heritage Commission, Trenton, NJ, Numina Gallery, Princeton, NJ and En Foco Inc, Bronx, NY. *Pos:* Photography consultant, Ford Found, NY, Photography, 1995-98, Edna McConnell Clark Found, NY, 1996-97, American Indian Coll Fund, 1996-98; BRIO award panelist, Bronx Council of the Arts, 2005; vis artist, Pratt Inst, Brooklyn, NY, 1998-2002. *Teaching:* instructor, Burlington County Col, Pemberton, NJ, 1989-91; adjunct asst prof, Cooper Union, NY, 1991-2001; adjunct asst prof, NY Univ, 1999-2002; full-time teaching, assoc prof Queens Col, City Univ of NY, 2000-, chair art dept, 2002-. *Awards:* Ford Found Fellowship, 1987-89, Ward Cheney Memorial Award, 1989, and others. *Publ:* The Futurist Magazine, 1997, The Edna McConnell Clark Found: Annual Report, 1996-97, Marie Claire Magazine, 1999, Series on the NJ Shore appeared in Professional Photographers of America, 2000, The Landmarks of NY, Vol IV, 2005, Book of Alternative Photographic Processes, 2nd edit, 2008 and others. *Mailing Add:* The City University of NY-Studio Art Klapper Hall 172 65-30 Kissena Blvd Flushing NY 11367

GONZALEZ-TORNERO, SERGIO
PAINTER, PRINTMAKER

b Santiago, Chile, May 22, 1927; US citizen. *Study:* Slade Sch, London, Eng; Atelier 17, Paris, with S W Hayter. *Work:* Metrop Mus Art, New York; Mus Mod Art, New York; Libr Cong, Washington, DC; Mus Fine Arts, Santiago, Chile; Smithsonian Inst, Washington, DC. *Comn:* Whatzits, Steel Outdoor Sculpture, comn by Silverbow Art Found, Butte, Montana, 2014. *Exhib:* High Mus, Atlanta, Ga, 64; Printers & Sculptors as Printmakers, Mus Mod Art, New York, 64; Retrospective Exhib, Nat Mus Fine Arts, Santiago, Chile, 93; Westchester Community Coll, Valhalla, NY, 94-2006; Homage Exhib, XII Biennial Prints, Latin Amer & Caribbean, San Juan, PR, 96; Haida Gwaii Mus, Qay'llnagaay, Skidegate, BC, 96; Gallery Tribal Art, Vancouver, BC, 96; Mus Northern BC, Prince Rupert, 97; Greenhill Invitationals, Yorktown, NY, 2008; White Gallery, Lakevine, Conn, 2010; Silvermine Guild, New Canaan, Conn, 2011; Marina Gallery, Cold Springs, NY, 2012; MAC, San Juan, 2014. *Teaching:* Vis artist, Concordia Univ, Montreal. *Awards:* NY State Coun Arts Fel, 87; Grant, Adolph & Esther Gottlieb Found, 90; First Prize, 10th Biennial Prints, Latin America & the Caribbean & San Juan, Puerto Rico, 93; Trustees' Award, Art of the Northeast, Silvermine Arts Ctr, New Canaan, Conn, 2010. *Bibliog:* S W Hayter (auth), About

Prints, 62 & New Ways of Gravure, 66, Oxford Univ Press; Fritz Eichenberg (auth), The Art of the Print, Abrams, 76. *Mem:* Soc Am Graphic Artists; Philadelphia Print Club; Boston Printmakers. *Media:* Oil, Intaglio. *Interests:* Art of Haida Gwaii. *Dealer:* Eden Gallery 1903 Eden Ln Wichita Falls TX 76306; Annex Galleries 604 College Ave Santa Rosa CA 95404; A Clean Well-lighted Place 363 Bleeker St NY NY 10014; The Studio 2 Maryland Ave Armonk NY 10504. *Mailing Add:* 30 Highridge Rd Mahopac NY 10541

GOODACRE, GLENNA
SCULPTOR
b Lubbock, Tex, Aug 28, 1939. *Study:* Colo Coll, BA; Art Students League, NY. *Hon Degrees:* Colo Coll, Hon Dr; Tex Tech Univ, Hon Dr. *Work:* Tex Tech Mus, Lubbock; Presby Hosp, Denver, Colo; Brigham Young Univ Art Gallery, Provo, Utah; Cleveland Clinic Children's Hosp, Ohio; Denver Mus Natural Hist, Colo; Vietnam Women's Mem, Washington, DC; Nat College Football Hall of Fame; Irish Memorial, Penn's Landing, Philadelphia. *Comn:* Dr Harvie Pruitt, Lubbock Christian Coll, 1982; Patrick Haggerty, Tex Instruments, 1982; Eric Sloan, 1983; Erik Jonsson & Cecil Green, Tex Instruments, 1983; William B Travis, Sea World, San Antonio, Tex, 1988; Sacagawea, US Mint, 2000. *Exhib:* Solo shows incl Read-Stremmel Gallery, San Antonio, Tex, 1988; group shows incl Fifth Ann Sculpture Park, Loveland, Colo, 1988; Eighth Ann Artists Am Show, Colo Heritage Ctr, Denver, 1988; Twentieth Anniversary Invitational Exhib, NAm Sculpture Exhib, Foothills Art Ctr, Golden, Colo, 1988; Borderlands, Second Ann Exhib, Americana Mus, El Paso, Tex, 1988; Fifty-fifth Ann Exhib, Nat Sculpture Soc, NY, 1988; two-person show, O'Brien's Art Emporium, Scottsdale, Ariz, 1988; Artists Choice Show, Nat Acad Western Art, Oklahoma City, 1988; Am Art in Miniature, Thomas Gilcrease Mus, Tulsa, Okla, 1988; Prix de West Exhib, 2003. *Teaching:* Scottsdale Artists Sch. *Awards:* Leonard J Meiselman Award, Nat Sculpture Soc, 1983; James Earl Fraser Sculpture Award, Prix De West Exhib, 2002; Inductee, Cowgirl Hall of Fame, 2003; Recipient Tex Medal Arts, 2003; Tex Medal of Arts, 2003; NMex Governor's Award, Excellence in Arts, 2005. *Mem:* Allied Artists of Am; fel, Nat Sculpture Soc; Catharine Lorillard Wolfe Art Club; fel, Nat Acad Western Art; Nat Acad Design (acad, 1994-); Nat Acad. *Media:* Bronze. *Publ:* Illusr, bronze relief for jacket, The Flamboyant Judge, 1973 & Trank Tenny Johnson, 1975; illusr, silver relief for jacket, Robbing Banks was My Business, 1974. *Dealer:* Altermann Galleries & Auctioneers 225 Canyon Rd Santa Fe NM 87501; JN Bartfield Galleries 30 W 57th St New York NY 10019; Nedra Matteucci Galleries 1075 Paseo de Peralta Santa Fe NM 87501; Trailside Galleries Box 1149-Town Sq Jackson Hole Wyoming 83001. *Mailing Add:* c/o Galleria Silecchia 12 S Palm Ave Sarasota FL 34236

GOODE, JOE
PAINTER
b Oklahoma City, Okla, Mar 23, 1937. *Study:* Chouinard Art Inst. *Work:* Mus Mod Art & Whitney Mus Am Art, NY; Pasadena Art Mus, Calif; Los Angeles Co Mus Art; Victoria & Albert Mus, London; Ft Worth Art Mus, Tex. *Exhib:* Solo exhibs, Contemp Arts Mus, Houston, 73, Arco Ctr Visual Art, 82, James Corcoran Gallery, Santa Monica, Calif, 86, 89, 90 & 92, Karsten Greve Gallery, Paris, 92, Takada Fine Arts, San Francisco, 93, Bobbie Greenfield Gallery, Venice, Calif, 94 & LA Louver, Venice, Calif, 94; American Pop Art, Whitney Mus Am Art, 74; Chicago Art Inst, 74; Calif Painting and Sculpture: The Modern Era, San Francisco Mus Art, 76; Black and White Art Colors, Scripps Col, 78; Am Painting in the Seventies, Albright-Knox Art Gallery, 78; Aspects of Abstract, Crocker Mus, 78; Art Park, Los Angeles/Brazil Projects 90, Los Angeles, Calif, 90; Takada Fine Arts, San Francisco, Calif, 91; Los Angeles Co Mus Art, Calif, 92. *Awards:* Copley Found; Nat Endowment Arts; Maestro Grant, Calif Arts Coun. *Bibliog:* T Henry (auth), Introduction (exhib catalog), Oklahoma City Art Mus, 89; Nora Halpern Brougher (auth), Looking Through the Work of Joe Goode (exhib catalog), James Corcoran Gallery, Santa Monica, Calif, 90. *Media:* Wood; Oil

GOODELL, ROSEMARY W
PAINTER, EDUCATOR
b Burbank, Calif, May 20, 1945. *Study:* Boston Mus Sch; Univ Calif Los Angeles; Univ Calif Berkeley, BA, MA. *Work:* Int House, New Orleans, La; Harmony Oaks, New Orlean, La; Baton Rouge Gen Hosp. *Comn:* Large paintings (2), WBRZ-TV, Baton Rouge, La, 90. *Exhib:* Solo exhib, Ziegler Mus, 82; Group exhibs, Women in the Arts, New Orleans World's Fair, 83; Artists in Action, La Arts & Sci Mus, Baton Rouge, La, 86; Off The Walls, Art in Transit, Contemp Art Ctr, New Orleans, 88; Through Her Eyes, Delgado Coll, New Orleans, 95; Baton Rouge Gallery, 2004-2010; Galerie Eclaireuse, 2008; In the Garden, Royal Caleasieu Mus, 2004; Mansur Mus, 2005; Henry Hood Gallery, Covington, 2010; Artists Showcase, Univ Southeast, Louisiana, Hammond, 2011; Gravity Prints, Baton Rouge Gallery, 2013; Contemporary Art Gallery, Univ Southeast La, 2013; Quirky Gardens', Baton Rouge Gallery, 2014; Henry Hood Gallery, 2015; Capital City Contemporary, La Arts and Sci Mus, 2015. *Teaching:* Vis artist, E Baton Rouge Parish Schs, 90-91; artist-in-residence, Glasgow Sch, Baton Rouge, La, 93; art instr, Episcopal Sch, Baton Rouge, La, 93-; assoc prof, Art Dept, Baton Rouge Community Coll, 93-2010. *Awards:* Painting fel, Skidmore Coll, 96; Fullbright Mem Fel, Japan, 98; La Div Arts, minigrant, 98 & 2000; La Div Arts, Visual Art Fel, 2003. *Bibliog:* Rosemary Goodell, Merci, 76; 30 minute doc, WYES-TV, 96. *Mem:* Coll Art Asn; Phi Beta Kappa. *Media:* Acrylic, Oil. *Interests:* Art hist, poetry & jazz. *Publ:* Sch Arts, 4/93; The Louisiana Review, vol 13, 2015. *Dealer:* Baton Rouge Gallery 1442 City Park Ave Baton Rouge LA 70816; Caffery Gallery 4016 Government St Baton Rouge LA 70806; Henry Hood Gallery 325 East Lockwood Covington LA 70433. *Mailing Add:* 16720 Caesar Baton Rouge LA 70816

GOODINE, LINDA ADELE
PHOTOGRAPHER, SCULPTOR
b Watkins Glen, NY, July 29, 1958. *Study:* Univ Rochester, NY, 80; Ithaca Col, NY, MS, 81; Fla State Univ, Tallahassee, MFA, 83. *Work:* Light Work, Menschel Gallery, Syracuse Univ, NY; Frederick R Weisman Collection, Los Angeles, Calif; Aaron Siskind Found; Int Sch Photog, Arles, France. *Exhib:* Personal Icon, Los Angeles Ctr Photog Studies, Calif, 86; The Manipulated Environment, Houston Ctr Photog, Tex, 87; Looking South: A Different Dixie, Birmingham Mus Art, Ala, 88; Vernon Fisher & Linda Adele Goodine, Pensacola Mus Art, Fla, 89; New Southern Photog, Burden Gallery, NY, 89-92; traveling shows, Selections from Weisman Collection, Frederick Weisman Found, Los Angeles & Linda Adele Goodine, Southeastern Ctr for Contemp Art, Winston-Salem, NC; Montgomery Bienial, Indianapolis Mus Art, 92; Cibachromes 1982-1992, Linda Adele Goodine, Ind State Mus, 92. *Teaching:* Artist in residence, photog, Lightwork Community Darkrooms, Syracuse, NY, 86; instr 3-D, Delgado Community Col, New Orleans, La, 88-89; vis artist & assoc prof, Herron Sch Art, Indianapolis, Ind, currently. *Awards:* Nat Endowment Arts, Rockefeller Found, 90; Southern Arts Fedn, 91; Aaron Siskind Found Grant. *Bibliog:* Marcia E Vetrocq (auth), Linda Adele Goodine at Res Nova, Art in Am, 88; Jay Murphy (auth), Linda A Goodine & Vernon Fisher, Art papers, 89; Donald Kuspit Art papers, summer 92. *Mem:* Coll Art Asn. *Publ:* Illusr, Exploring Color Photography, Wm C Brown, 89; Louisiana Artist's Pages: Love in the Ruins, Contemp Art Ctr, 89; article for Aperture, No 115, Aperture Found, 89; article for Red Bass, No 13, 89; North of Wakulla: An Anhinga Anthology Anhinga, Press, 90. *Mailing Add:* c/o Herron School Art and Design 735 W New York St Indianapolis IN 46202

GOODMAN, CALVIN JEROME
CONSULTANT, WRITER
b Chicago, Ill, Mar 1, 1922. *Study:* Harvard Univ, AB (hon), 49. *Pos:* Mgt consult to artists & art dealers, 58-; vpres, Tamarind Lithography Workshop, 59-76; nat consult, Artists Equity Asn, 74-76; nat adv bd Portrait Soc Am, 98-. *Teaching:* Instr bus methods for artists & artisans, Tamarind Lithography Workshop, 61-71; instr prof practices, Calif Inst Arts, 67-71 & Otis Art Inst, 68-71; lectr, seminar & workshops in marketing art for San Francisco Art Inst, Scripps Grad Sch of Art, Pratt Inst, Portrait Soc Am, Washington, DC, 99- & Art Students League, New York, 2007. *Awards:* Lifetime Achievement Award, Portraits Inc, 2008. *Bibliog:* B Fredericks (auth), The Art of Creating Monotypes, HR Productions, 90; S Doherty (auth), The Art of G Wetmore, Am Artist, 6/2000; L Moss Perricelli (auth), Review Art Marketing Handbook, Am Artist, 10/2004. *Mem:* Portrait Soc Am (nat bd, 98-); Mrs Grossman's Paper co (exec bd, 70-). *Res:* Fine art market; operations of specialized schools of art and music; original print market; making/marketing monotypes; paper specialties, murals & giclée prints market. *Interests:* Portraiture, contemp art. *Publ:* Auth, Art Marketing Handbook, GeeTeeBee, 7th ed, 2003; Wilson Hurley's Color Theory and Practice, 5/86; Thomas Hart Benton, 12/89 & 1/90; Advice for Portraitists, 6/2000; Art Fraud, Am Artist, 9/2007; Gorden Wetmore, My Painting Process, DVD: Calvin Goodman Portrait Marketing, 2008; and others. *Mailing Add:* 11901 Sunset Blvd Suite 102 Los Angeles CA 90049

GOODMAN, CYNTHIA
WRITER, CURATOR
b Cincinnati, Ohio. *Study:* Univ Pa, PhD (art hist). *Collection Arranged:* InfoARt Pavilion, Kwangju Biennale, Korea; The Art of Caring, New Orleans Mus Art, 2009. *Pos:* Dir, IBM Gallery Sci & Art, formerly; creative dir & prodr, Exhibits & Attractions, Millennium Monument; dir exhibit technologies, Rutt Video Interactive; adv, IBM, Polaroid & Time Warner; acting dir & chief cur, Contemp Arts Ctr, Cincinnati; guest cur, Mus Fine Arts, Houston. *Bibliog:* Auth, Hans Hofmann as Teacher: Drawings by His Students, Met Mus Art, 1979; Hans Hofmann, Abbeville Press, 1986; Digital Visions: Computers and Art, 1987; The Digital Revolution: Art in the Computer Age, Coll Art J, 1990; Thomas Shannon, Contemp Arts Ctr, 1993; InfoART: The Digital Frontier from Video to Virtual Reality. *Mem:* MIT Ctr for Advanced Visual Studies (fel); Adv Comt for Women and the Art of Multimedia, Nat Mus Women in the Arts

GOODMAN, GWEN DUCAT
MUSEUM DIRECTOR
Study: Univ Pa, BA (Educ), MA (Educ), 1957. *Hon Degrees:* Cert in Fundraising, Univ Pa. *Pos:* Regional dir, US Holocaust Mem Mus, Pa, Del, NJ; exec dir, CEO, Nat Mus Am Jewish Hist, 2002-. *Mem:* bd trustees, Nat Mus Am Jewish Hist. *Mailing Add:* National Museum of American Jewish History Independence Mall East 55 North 5th Street Philadelphia PA 19106

GOODMAN, HELEN
HISTORIAN, CRITIC
b Detroit, Mich, May 18, 1939. *Study:* Univ Mich, BA, 60; Wayne State Univ, MA, 66; New York Univ, PhD, 75. *Exhib:* The Art of Rose O'Neill (auth, catalog), The Brandywine River Mus, 89. *Collection Arranged:* Art Rose O'Neill, Brandywine River Mus, Chadds Ford, Pa, 89. *Pos:* guest cur, Brandywine River Mus, 1989. *Teaching:* Asst prof art hist, Stern Col Women, New York, 66-72; asst prof, Fashion Inst Technol, New York, 68-. *Awards:* Research Found Grant, State Univ NY, 83; Nat Endowment Humanities Grant, 85, 89 & 91; John Sloan Mem Found Grant; Swann Found Caricature & Cartoon Grant, 85. *Bibliog:* Elizabeth Buehrmann (auth), History of Photography, Vol 19, No 4, 338-342, 95; Louise Dahl Wolfe, Dictionary of Women Artists, 427-428, Fitzroy Dearborn Publ, London, 97; Frances Benjamin Johnson (auth), Dictionary of Women Artists, 444-447, Fitzroy Dearbourn Publ, 97. *Mem:* Coll Art Asn; Asn Hist Am Art. *Res:* American late 19th and early 20th century art. *Publ:* Auth, essay, In: America's Great Women Illustrators: 1850-1950 (exhib catalog), Madison Sq Press, 85; Women illustrators of the golden age of Am illustration, Woman's Art J, spring/summer 87; The Art of Rose O'Neill, Brandywine Riv Mus, Chadds Ford, Pa, 89; Emily Sartain, The Sartain Family and the Philadelphia Cultural Landscape, Barra Found, Univ Press, 97 & 98; numerous articles in Arts Mag, 1977-87. *Mailing Add:* c/o Fashion Inst Technol 227 W 27th St New York NY 10001

GOODMAN, JAMES NEIL
DEALER, COLLECTOR
b Rochester, NY, Apr 11, 1929. *Pos:* Dir, James Goodman Gallery. *Specialty:* Modern American and European masters, including Calder, Cornell, de Kooning, Klee, Leger, Lichtenstein, Matisse, Moore, Picasso and Tanguy. *Mailing Add:* c/o James Goodman Gallery 41 E 57th St New York NY 10022-1908

GOODMAN, JANIS G
PAINTER, DRAFTSMAN
b New York, NY, Oct 21, 1951. *Study:* Queens Col, NY, BA, 72; Corcoran Sch Art, Washington, DC, 73-74; Etruscan Found, Siena, Italy, 74; George Washington Univ, MFA, 75. *Work:* Hirshhorn Mus & Sculpture Garden, Corcoran Gallery Art, Washington, DC; Hunter Mus Am Art, Chattanooga, Tenn; Knoxville Mus Art, Tenn; Univ Va, Charlottesville; Allen Mem Art Mus, Allen Meml Art Mus, Oberlin, Ohio; Dept Interior, Acadia Nat Park, Mt Desert Island; Miss Mus Art, Jackson; Epson Europe, Amsterdam, Neth; IDTV, Amsterdam, Neth; John A Wilson Bldg, City Hall, DC. *Comn:* paintings, Westin Hotel, Ft Worth, Tex. *Exhib:* Corcoran Gallery Art, Washington, DC, 80; solo exhibs, Jane Haslem Gallery, Wash, 88, 89 & 93, Steven Scott Gallery, Baltimore, 90, Galerie Maas, Rotterdam, The Neth, 94, The Contents of History (with catalog), B'Nai B'rith Klutznick Nat Jewish Mus, Wash, 95, Gordon Fennell Gallery, Coe Col, Cedar Rapids, 96, Kunstler Werkstatt Bahnhof Westend, Berlin, Ger, 97, Wash Project for Arts, DC, 99, Weatherspoon Art Gallery, Greensboro, NC, 99, Peruvian North Am Cult Inst, Lima, Peru, 2000 & Dist Fine Arts, Wash, DC, 2000; Faculty II, Corcoran Gallery Art, 93; Personal Vision, Five Women Artists, Tatem Art Gallery, Hood Col, Md, 94; Three Am Artists, Galerie Witteveen, Amsterdam, 95; Drawing on Washington, Marsha Mateyka Gallery, 95; Indianapolis Jewish Community Ctr, Ind; Dist Fine Arts & Proj Space, Washington, DC, 98; AVC Contemp Art, New York City, 2002; Hay Gallery, Portland, Maine, 2002; 2004 Biennial, Ctr Maine Contemp Art, Rockland, 2004; Massillon Mus Art, OH, 2006; Butte Silver Bow Arts Found, Mont, 2006; Thomas Deans Fine Arts, Atlanta, 2008; JK Gallery, Los Angeles, 2009; Reyes & Davis, DC, 2008; Cohn Drennan Contemp Art, Tex, 2010; Flashpoint Gallery, DC, 2007; Delaplane Visual Arts Ctr, Md, 2008; Bradley Univ, Heuser Arts Ctr, Ill, 2008; Mitchell Gallery, St John's Coll, Md, 2009. *Pos:* arts reviewer, Around Town, WETA/TV, 2003-; faculty develop, Corcoran Mus, 2003 & 2006; artist in res, St Mary's Col of Md & Butte Silver Bow Artist Residency (mem of workingman collective), Mont, 2006. *Teaching:* Instr drawing, Smithsonian Inst, 77-87; instr color theory, Parsons Sch Design, NY, 85-86; assoc prof fine arts & drawing, Corcoran Sch Art, Washington, DC, 87-, Santa Reparata, Florence, Ital, 2002, St Mary's, Md, 2005, Univ Ga, Cortona Ital Prog, fall 2006. *Awards:* Washington Comn Arts Grant, 81 & 90; Montpelier Cult Award, Md State Drawing, 83; Grant to Individual Artists, DC Comn Arts, 95-96; NEA Exhib Support Grant, 98; DCCAH Award, 2007. *Bibliog:* Morris Yarowsky (auth), The Contents of History, Art Papers, Atlanta, 95; Norma Broude & Mary D Garrand (eds), The Power of Feminist Art, The American Movement of the 1970s, History & Impact; Leslie Wright (auth), Art Papers, Janis Goodman, 97; Erin Pustay (auth), The Independent Weekender, Massillon, OH, 5/6/2006; Roberta Forsell Stauffer (auth), Montana Standard, 5/16/2006; and many others. *Media:* Oil, Mixed Media, Graphite. *Publ:* co-auth (with Dennis Weller), Is Seeing Believing, The Real, The Surreal, The Unreal in Contemporary Photography, NC Mus Art, 2000. *Dealer:* Thomas Deans Fine Art Atlanta GA; Lee Hansley Raleigh NC; AVC Contemporary Art NY; Turtle Gallery Deer Isle ME; Reyes & Davis DC; Cohn Drennan Contemp Art Dallas TX. *Mailing Add:* 512 8th St NE Washington DC 20002

GOODMAN, MARK
PHOTOGRAPHER
b Boston, Mass, May 19, 1946. *Study:* Boston Univ, BA, 70; also with Minor White, 70. *Work:* Mus Mod Art, NY; Mus Fine Arts, Boston; George Eastman House, Rochester, NY; Mus Fine Arts, Houston; Samuel A Dorsky Mus, SUNY, New Paltz. *Exhib:* Recent Acquisitions, Mus Mod Art, NY, 78-79; solo exhib, George Eastman House, Rochester, NY, 80-81; Am Children, Mus Mod Art, NY, 81; Contemp Photogrs IX, George Eastman House, Rochester, NY, 82; Capital Improvements, Austin Hist Ctr, Tex, 86; A Kind of History, The Tremaine Gallery, The Hotchkiss Sch, Lakeville, Conn; plus others; Picturing What Matters, George Castman House Traveling Exhib, 2005-. *Teaching:* Artist-in-residence photog, Apeiron Workshops Inc, Millerton, NY, 72-76; asst prof, Univ Tex, Austin, 80-86, assoc prof, 86-02, prof, 2002-, grad advisor studio art MFA program, 2005-. *Awards:* Nat Endowment Arts Fel, 73; Guggenheim Fel, 77. *Bibliog:* Julia Scully & Andy Grundberg (auth), Currents: American photography today, Mod Photog, Vol 44, No 2, 80; James Kaufmann (auth), Works of love: The photographs of Mark Goodman, Exposure, Vol 20, No 1, 82; Jeanne Clare van Ryzin (auth) Portrait of a small town, Austin Am-Statesman, 3/2000; Timothy Cahil (auth) Photographer's book takes heartfelt look at a small town, Albany New York Times Union, 11/5/2000; Vince Aletti (auth), Open Book, Village Voice, 4-5/2000. *Publ:* Contribr, Photographs of Millerton, NY, 1971-1975, Aperture, Vol 19, No 4, 75; Kansas Album, Addison House, 77; Photographing Children, Time-Life Books, 83; A Kind of History, Millerton, NY: 1971-91, Markerbooks, 99; Mark Goodman (auth), Second Thoughts On Questions I Was Asked Twenty Years Ago, SPOT, spring/summer, 2001

GOODRIDGE, LAWRENCE WAYNE
PAINTER, SCULPTOR
b Cincinnati, Ohio, Mar 18, 1941. *Study:* Univ Cincinnati, BFA (with hon), 63; Univ Cincinnati & Art Acad Cincinnati, MFA, 67. *Exhib:* All-Ohio Painting & Sculpture Exhib, Dayton Art Inst, 67; Mid-States Art Exhib, Evansville Mus Arts & Sci, Ind, 70; Solo exhib & Louisville Biennial, J B Speed Art Mus, Ky, 71; 17th Ann Drawing & Sculpture Show, Ball State Univ, Muncie, Ind, 71. *Pos:* Toy designer, Kenner Prod Co, 63-65. *Teaching:* Instr found design & color theory, Art Acad Cincinnati, 69-, co-dean, 72-. *Awards:* Second Prize, Eastern Fine Paper Graphic Design, 65. *Publ:* Auth & illusr, European diary, 70 & Truck stop, 71, Cincinnati Mag. *Dealer:* Richard Feigen Gallery 226 E Ontario St Chicago IL 60611. *Mailing Add:* 29 Kathryn Ave Florence KY 41042-1535

GOODSPEED, BARBARA
PAINTER
b Gardner, Mass, Sept 1, 1919. *Study:* Famous Artists Sch, Westport, Conn, cert; studied with Edgar A Whitney & Frank Webb. *Exhib:* Hudson Valley Art Asn, Hastings-on-Hudson, NY, 83-93; Am Artists Prof League, NY, 84-94; Salmagundi Club, NY, 86-94; Catharine L Wolfe Art Club, NY, 87-94; Allied Artists Am, NY, 88, 94 & 96; others. *Pos:* Dir & trustee, Kent Art Asn, 72-2005; dir, Catharine L Wolfe Art Club, 90-93 & 98-, Soc Creative Arts, Newtown, Conn, 90-94, vpres painting; Hudson Valley Art Assoc- Board, 2001. *Teaching:* Instr watercolor, Washington Art Asn, Conn, 89-93, Wooster Community Arts, Danbury, Conn, 90-93, Soc Creative Arts, Newtown, Conn, 91-93 & Heritage Village, Southbury, Conn, 95-96. *Awards:* Jane Peterson Award, Salmagundi Club, 93; Corp Award, Catharine L Wolfe Art Club, 93; Claude Parsons Award, Am Artists Prof League, 93; others. *Bibliog:* Denise Matteau (dir), Watercolor Demo, Pittsfield Community TV, Mass, 92. *Mem:* Fel Am Artists Prof League; Catharine L Wolfe Art Club; Acad Artists; Kent Art Asn (pres, 85-88 & 89-92, 2004-2005); Conn Watercolor Soc. *Media:* Oil, Watercolor. *Publ:* Illusr, Forever Flowers, Scribners, 79; The Best of Oil Painting & The Best of Watercolor, Light & Shadow/Landscape Inspirations, Rockport Publ; Best of Watercolor, vol 3. *Dealer:* The Lenox Gallery of Fine Art Lenox MA; Fine Line Art Gallery, Woodbury, CT. *Mailing Add:* c/o Oxford Gallery 267 Oxford St Rochester NY 14607

GOODWILL, MARGARET
PAINTER, DESIGNER
b Los Angeles, Calif, Sept 27, 1950. *Study:* Carnegie Mellon Inst, cert, 66; Univ Calif, Santa Barbara, 68-70; Calif Coll Arts & Crafts, Oakland, BFA (cum laude), 72. *Work:* Oakland Mus Collectors Gallery, Calif; Triple Crown Hall-Hilton Resort Hotel, Pleasanton, Calif; Tamarack Beach Resort, Carlsbad, Calif; Na Hoola Spa, Hyatt Regency, Waikiki, Hawaii, 2000; Del Monte, Kunia, Hawaii, 2000; Plantation Spa, Kaaawa, Hawaii, 2002; Hui No'eau, Maui, Hawaii, 2002. *Comn:* Wave Waikiki (mural, 30' x 90'), Honolulu, Hawaii, 91; catalog cover, Benjamin Cummings Publ, Calif, 91; The Breaks (TV show), Pub Television, Hawaii; concept, design, murals & 3 dimensional sculptures, The Pyramids Restaurant, Honolulu, 96; and others; illus, Forest Solutions, Big Island, Hawaii; mural, Curves, Haleiwa, Hawaii, 2003. *Exhib:* Puna hoe Invitational, Honolulu, Hawaii, 2000; Polynesian Cult Ctr, Hauula, Hawaii, 2000; Boutiki, Pearl Harbor, Hawaii, 2000; Garden Biersch Mardi Gras, 2000; Haleiwa Arts Festival, 2003; many others. *Pos:* Graphic artist, City Arts, Oakland, 70-71; creative art dir, Am Analysis Corp, San Francisco, 74-76; dir, Lone Wolf Gallery, 82-84. *Awards:* First Prize, Ossining Woman's Club Competition & Poughkeepsie Art Ctr, 68; Merit Award, Delta Art Show, 71. *Bibliog:* Wayne Herada (auth), Waikiki's new look, Honolulu Advertiser, 7/20/91; Kristine Bucar (auth), A Couple of artists, The East Honolulu Newspaper 12/93; Kristine Bucar (auth), When art goes online, Honolulu Advertiser, 10/18/94. *Mem:* Historic Hawaii Found; Natural Found Materials; Bishop Mus; Contemporary Mus Art; Acad of Art. *Media:* Acrylic on Canvas, Oil Pastel on Handmade Paper. *Publ:* Illusr, Wit and Wisdom of The Coachella Valley, Desert Discoveries Pubs; Palm Parade (poster), publ by Portal, 92; Greeting cards, calendars, gift bags, etc, publ by Island Heritage; shower curtains, publ by The Springs; plus 18 other posters, 1986-93 calendars & t-shirts. *Mailing Add:* 68-234 Au St Waialua HI 96791-9304

GOODWIN, DANIEL
EDUCATOR, ADMINISTRATOR, PHOTOGRAPHER
Study: School of Art, Univ North Texas, Sch of Visual Arts, BFA (Photography), 1989; Hunter col, MFA (Combined Media), 1992. *Exhib:* Solo exhibitions Art Resources Transfer Inc, NYC, 2000, Jack the Pelican Presents, Brooklyn, 2003, PhotoNewburgh Gallery, NY, 2006, Schenectady Mus & Suits-Bueche Planetarium, NY, 2007, Atrium, Albany NanoTech Complex, Col of Nanoscale Sci and Engineering, Univ Albany, SUNY, 2010-, and several others; group exhibitions North Texas Photographers, 500X Gallery, Dallas, 1987, Inaugural Exhibition, Momenta Art, Brooklyn, NY, 1995, In Our Sights: Artists Look at Guns, Calif Mus of Photography, Riverside, 1996, Current Undercurrent: Working in Brooklyn, Brooklyn Mus of Art, 1997, One Less Than Nine, Proposition Gallery, Belfast, Ireland, 1998, Night of 1000 Drawings, Artists Space Gallery, NY, 2002, 2005, Model Citizen, Cambridge Arts Council, 2006Bad Moon Rising 4, Galerie Sans Titre, Belgium, 2009, No Longer the Property of, Lost Coast Culture Machine, Fort Bragg, Calif, 2011 and several others. *Teaching:* Technician photography, Hunter Col, City Univ of NY, 1992; technical supervisor photography, The Cooper Union Sch of Art, NY, 1992-97, mem portfolio review panel, 1995-97, instructor, 1994-97, interim dept coordinator photography, 1996-97; vis asst prof art, Purdue Univ Dept of Visual and Performing Arts, West Lafayette, Ind, 1997-98, asst prof of art and design, 1998-99; asst prof art, photography and digital media, Univ Albany, State Univ of NY (SUNY), 1999-2005, assoc prof art, photography and digital media, combined media program dir, 2006-, chair Dept of Art (studio art, art history, mediterranean art and archaeology, religious studies), 2007-. *Awards:* Artists' Fellowship Recipient of the NY Found for the Arts. *Mem:* Col Art Asn; Soc for Photographic Educ; Ctr for Photography at Woodstock; Rhizome at the New Mus of Contemporary Art; United Univ Professions. *Publ:* Publications include Influence Magazine, Details Magazine, i-D Magazine, Pierogi Press, Brooklyn Rail, NY Daily News, Washington Post, Seattle Times, Fort Worth Star Telegram, and Albany Times Union. *Mailing Add:* 29 Western Ave Delmar NY 12054

GOODWIN, GUY
PAINTER
b Birmingham, Ala, June 19, 1940. *Study:* Univ Ala; Auburn Univ, BFA, 63; Univ Ill, MFA, 65. *Work:* Patrick Lannen Mus, Palm Beach, Fla; Chase Manhattan Bank, NY; Philadelphia Acad of Fine Arts. *Exhib:* Solo shows, Area X Gallery, NY, 84, Dolan/Maxwell Gallery (with catalog), Philadelphia, Pa, 86, Daniel Weinberg Gallery, Los Angeles, 87, Dolan/Maxwell, New York, 89 & 90, Seigfred Gallery, Ohio Univ, 95, Bill Maynes Gallery, New York, 98, Lindsey Brown Gallery, New York, 2002, Art Resource Transfer, New York, 2003; group shows, Abstract Issues (with catalog), D Hood, S French & Tibor Denage Galleries, NY, 85; Drawing with Respect to Painting II, NY Studio Sch Gallery, 86; Thorden/Wetterling Gallery, Sweden, 87, 90; Suzanne Hilberry Gallery, Mich, 91, 93 & 97; Masters of Masters, Butler Inst Am Art,, Youngstown, Ohio, 98; Conversation with Amy Pryor, Art Resource Transfer, New York, 1999 & Benefit Show, 2002; 100 Artists 100 Watercolors, Jeannie Freilich Fine

Art, 2006; Nat Acad Mus, New York, 2007. *Pos:* Mem bd govs, Skowhegan Sch Painting & Sculpture, Maine, 89-. *Teaching:* Vis artist painting, Wayne State Univ, Detroit, Mich, 78 & Art Inst Chicago, Ill, 80; instr painting & drawing, Bennington Col, Vt, 80-85; artist in residence, Skowhegan Sch Painting & Sculpture, Maine, 88 & 92; distinguished vis prof, Univ Calif, Davis, 1980; adj instr painting & drawing, Cooper Union, 91-94; grad instr, Sch Visual Arts, New York 93-94; assoc prof painting, Ohio Univ, 1994-2005. *Awards:* Nat Endowment Arts, 74 & 80; Creative Artists Pub Serv, 76; Pollock Krasner Fel, 97; Adolf & Esther Gottlieb Found, 94; Guggenheim Found, 93; Joan Mitchell Found Grant, 2007. *Bibliog:* Michael Brenson (auth), Drawing with respect to painting, New York Times, 5/2/86; Tiffany Bell (auth), Drawing with respect to painting, 6/86 & Margaret Berensen (auth), Guy Goodwin, 10/86, Arts Mag; Edward Suzanski (auth), rev, Philadelphia Inquirer, 9/25/86; Robert Murdock (auth), Guy Goodwin, Chauncey Flats, Review Mag, Feb, 98; Tiffany Bell (auth), Guy Goodwin at Bill Maynes Gallery, Art in America, Oct, 98. *Media:* Oil, Watercolor. *Mailing Add:* 83-10 35th Ave #5F Jackson Heights NY 10013-2911

GOODYEAR, FRANK H, JR
ADMINISTRATOR, HISTORIAN

b New York, NY, Jan 5, 1944. *Study:* Yale Univ, BA, 66; Univ Del, Winterthur Prog, MA, 69. *Collection Arranged:* Pennsylvania Academicians (with catalog), Pa Acad of Fine Arts, 73, The Beneficent Connoisseurs, Gibson, Harrison (with catalog), 74 & In This Academy: The Pennsylvania Academy of the Fine Arts, 1805-1976 (with catalog), 76; Thomas Doughty: An Am Pioneer in Landscape Painting, 1793-1856 (with catalog), Pa Acad, Corcoran Gallery of Art & Albany Inst, 73-74; Am Paintings in the Rhode Island Historical Soc, 74; Cecilia Beaux (1855-1942): Portrait of an Artist (with catalog), Pa Acad & Indianapolis Mus of Art, 74-75; Am Art: 1750-1800 Towards Independence, Yale Univ Art Gallery, 76; Eight Contemporary Am Realists: Philip Pearlstein, Alfred Leslie, Stephen Posen, Janet Fish, Duane Hanson, Joseph Raffael, Neil Welliver & Sidney Goodman, 77; Seven on the Figure (with catalog), Pa Acad Fine Arts, 79; A Man of Genius: The Art of Washington Allston, Pa Acad Fine Arts & Mus Fine Arts, Boston, 80; Contemp Am Realism since 1960 (with catalog), Pa Acad Fine Arts, 81. *Pos:* Cur, RI Hist Soc, 69-72; cur & ed exhib catalogs, Pa Acad Fine Arts, 72-82, pres, 83-; actg cur, Am Painting & Sculpture, Yale Univ Art Gallery, 74-75. *Teaching:* Guest lectr, Univ Tex, Austin, 91. *Mem:* Am Asn Mus (mem, Legislative Comt, currently); Fairmount Park Art Asn (dir, currently); Conserv Ctr Art & Hist Artifacts (dir); Yale Univ Coun Comt on the Art Gallery & Brit Art Ctr (chmn). *Publ:* Auth, Welliver, Rizzoli Int Publ Inc, 85. *Mailing Add:* c/o Buffalo Bill Hist Ctr 720 Sheraton Ave Cody WY 82414

GOODYEAR, JOHN L
SCULPTOR, PAINTER

b Los Angeles, Calif, Oct 22, 1930. *Study:* Univ Mich, BD, 52, MD, 54. *Work:* Guggenheim Mus, Whitney Mus Am Art, Metrop Mus Art & Mus Mod Art, NY; Bibliot Nat, Paris; Brit Mus, London. *Comn:* State NJ, 81 & 90; Chiron (plaza), Univ Medicine & Dentistry, NJ, 83; Drawn from the Water (stone reliefs), Jewish Ctr, Princeton, NJ, 84; Dawn of Law (marble relief), State House, Trenton, NJ, 91. *Exhib:* solo exhibs, Amel Gallery, NY, 66, Mass Inst Technol Ctr Advan Visual Studies, Cambridge, 76, Pyramid Gallery, NY, 89, Snyder Fine Arts, NY, 92, Muhlenberg Col, 95, Michener Mus, Doylestown, Pa, 2000 & Ericson Gallery, Philadelphia, Pa, 2000, Hunterdon Mus Art, Clinton, NJ, 2005, Rider Univ Art Gal, 2005; Plus By Minus, Albright-Knox Art Gallery, Buffalo, NY, 68; Boston Mus Fine Arts, 71; Mus Mod Art, NY, 72; Geometric Abstraction 1937-1997, Snyder Fine Art, NY, 97; Six Artists in the '90s, NJ State Mus, Trenton, 96; Trace, Rosenwald-Wolf Gal, Phila, PA, 2004; Twister, Blanton Mus Art, Austin, Tex; Conceptual Objects & Demoiselles Revisited, Francis M Naumann Fine Art, NY, 2007; In Suspension, Mason Gross Galleries, Rutgers Univ, NJ, 2008; Reinventing the Wheel, Tatlin Gallery, Princeton, NJ, 2010; 1960s Revisited, David Richard Contemporary, Santa Fe, NMex, 2010; 75th Anniversary, Am Abstract Artists, Harris Gallery, NY, 2011; Shifting Views, Visual Art Ctr, Summit, NJ, 2012; John Goodyear, David Hall Fine Arts, Wellesly, Mass, 2012; Boomerang, NJ State Mus, Trenton, NJ, 2013; Ham and Eggs, Hunterdon Mus Art, Clinton, NJ, 2013; Noise at Noyes, Noyes Mus, Oceanville, NJ, 2013; John Goodyear, David Hall Fine Arts, Wellesley, Mass, 2015; group exhibs, 10 Ways, Clement & Schneider Gallery, Bonn, Germany, 2015. *Collection Arranged:* Iron Works, Univ of Arts, Rosenwald Wolf Gallery, Philadelphia, Pa, 2003. *Pos:* Prof emeritus, Rutgers Univ. *Teaching:* Instr, Univ Mich, Grand Rapids, 56-62 & Univ Mass, Amherst, 62-64; prof art, Mason Gross Sch Art, Rutgers Univ, 64-97, prof emer, 97-. *Awards:* Graham Found Fel, 62 & 70; Ctr Advan Visual Studies Fel, Mass Inst Technol, 70-71. *Bibliog:* Stephen Westfall (auth), Thinking into Form, (catalog essay), Michener Mus Art, Bucks Co, Pa, 2000; John Yau & Mary Birmingham (auths) Shifting Views (catalog essays), Visual Art Ctr NJ, 2012; Carl Belz (auth), Rewind & Reflect (catalog essay), David Halle Fine Art, Wellesley, Mass. *Mem:* Am Abstract Artists; MOVIS Artist Group. *Media:* Mixed. *Res:* Sculpture & painting; Kinetic Painting. *Interests:* New Ideas. *Collection:* Prints. *Dealer:* David Hall Fine Art Wellesly Mass. *Mailing Add:* 167 Seabrook Rd Lambertville NJ 08530

GORBATY, NORMAN
PAINTER, SCULPTOR

b New York, NY, Oct 5, 1932. *Study:* Amherst Coll, BA, 53; Yale Univ, MFA, 55. *Work:* Yale Mus Fine Arts, New Haven, Conn; Baruch Coll, New York; Glucksman Ireland House, New York Univ; Mead Art Mus, Amherst Coll, Amherst, Mass; Nat Portrait Gallery, Smithsonian, Washington, DC. *Exhib:* Young Am Print Makers, Mus Mod Art, New York, 53; Nat Print Exhib, Brooklyn Mus, New York, 54. *Pos:* Designer, James Eng Assoc, 55-56; designer, L W Frohlich, 56-58; vpres art group supervisor, Benton & Bowles Inc, 59-68; pres designer, Norman Gorbaty Design Inc, 68-. *Teaching:* Teaching fel printmaking, Yale Univ, New Haven, Conn, 53-55; adj prof advan graphic design, Cooper Union Sch Art, New York, 61-70; instr graphic design, Silvermine Sch Art, New Canaan, Conn, 71. *Awards:* Heisey Award, Corning Glass; Yale-Norfolk Art Sch Scholar; 50 Best Books Award, AIGA; Award of Distinctive Merit; and others. *Bibliog:* Gabor Peterdi (auth), Printmaking Methods Old & New, MacMillan, 59; Print Making with a Spoon, Reinhold, 60. *Media:* All Media. *Publ:* Contribr & designer, Time Mag, US News & World Report, Fortune Mag, CA Mag (Cancer Soc J), Impact 21, Maine Mag, and others. *Mailing Add:* 42 Meadowwoods Rd Great Neck NY 11020

GORCHOV, RON
PAINTER

b Chicago, Ill, Apr 5, 1930. *Study:* Art Inst Chicago, 47-50; Univ Ill, 50-51. *Work:* Whitney Mus Am Art, Mus Mod Art, Metrop Mus Art, Guggenheim Mus, NY; Chicago Art Inst. *Teaching:* Prof art, Hunter Col, formerly. *Awards:* Guggenheim Fel, 94; Skowhegan Medal in Painting, Skowhegan Sch Painting & Sculpture, 2010. *Media:* Oil on Canvas, Watercolor. *Mailing Add:* 113 Nelson St Brooklyn NY 11231

GORDIN, MISHA
PHOTOGRAPHER, VIDEO ARTIST

b Riga, Latvia, Russia, Mar 12, 1946. *Study:* Self taught in art; Aviation Inst, Russia, MEng, 72. *Work:* Nat Mus Mod Art, Georges Pompidou Ctr, Paris, France; Art Inst Chicago; Detroit Inst Art; Int Mus Photog at George Eastman House, Rochester, NY; Toledo Mus Art, Ohio. *Exhib:* Klein Art Works, Chicago, 91-94; solo exhibs, Mark Masouka Gallery, 90 & 91, New Gallery, Bemis Proj, Omaha, Nebr, 90, Klein Art Works, Chicago, 91 & 94, Bentley Gallery, Scottsdale, Ariz, 92 & 95, Dennas Mus Ctr, Northwestern Mich Univ, Traverse City, 93, Morgan Gallery, Kansas City, Mo, 94 & NDak Mus Art, Grand Forks, 94, JJ Brookings, San Francisco, 2000, Lewalen Contemp, Santa Fe, 2000; Thomson Gallery, Minneapolis, 95; Cedar Rapids Mus Art, Iowa, 96; traveling group exhib, West Publ Corp, Eagan, Minn, 96; and others. *Awards:* Visual Arts Fel, Nat Endowment Arts, 86; Mich Arts Award, Art Found Mich, 87; Creative Artist Grant, Mich Coun Arts, 88; Minn Art Bd Photog Grant, 2000. *Bibliog:* C Reeve & M Sward (auth), The New Photography, Spectrum Publ, 89; Afterimage, Vol 15, Visual Studies, 1/88. *Publ:* Cover Story, black & white Photo Metro, Vol 18 2000, Issue II, 2001. *Mailing Add:* 15257 Fruit Farm Rd Saint Joseph MN 56374

GORDLEY, MARILYN CLASSE
PAINTER, PRINTMAKER

b St Louis, Mo, Aug 4, 1929. *Study:* Washington Univ, BFA; Univ Okla, MFA; Ohio State Univ. *Work:* Greenville Mus Art, NC; Spring Mills, Lancaster, SC; Univ Okla; Bank of Am, Greenville; James Michener Mus, Doylestown, Pa. *Comn:* Portraits of Gov Kerr Scott, Arthur Tyler, Henry Belk, Elmer Browning & Weldell Smiley, E Carolina Univ, 64-74. *Exhib:* Cent South Exhib, Nashville, Tenn, 69; Nat Drawing Exhib, Southern Ill Univ, Carbondale, 75; Miss Mus Art, Jackson, 78; Fayetteville Mus Art, NC, 79; Southern Exposure, Hanson Gallery, New Orleans, 80; Now & Then, Mus York Co, Rockhill, SC, 90; Arlington Hall, Greenville, NC, 90; The Contemp Eye, James Michens Art Mus, New Hope, Pa, 05; and numerous two person shows. *Collection Arranged:* Greenville Mus, NC; Luwisburg Coll, NC. *Teaching:* Assoc prof drawing & painting, ECarolina Univ, 64-93; retired. *Awards:* 18th Irene Leache Award, Norfolk Mus, 66; Spring Mills First Prize, 67; Cent South Exhib Award, 69; Innovative Printing Award, Noyes Mus, NJ, 2001; Best in Show, Atlantic City Art Ctr, NJ, 2003. *Mem:* Am Asn Univ Women; Woodmere Art Mus; Phila/Tri State Artist Equity; Philadelphia Art Mus; Michens Art Mus. *Media:* Acrylic, Woodcut. *Dealer:* Riverbank Arts Stockton, NV. *Mailing Add:* 5802 Belmont Manor Pipersville PA 18947-1126

GORDLEY, METZ TRANBARGER
PAINTER

b Cedar Rapids, Iowa, May 24, 1932. *Study:* Wash Univ, BFA; Univ Okla, MFA; Ohio State Univ; Univ NC, Chapel Hill. *Work:* Greenville Mus Art, NC; E Carolina Univ; NC Print & Drawing Soc; Univ Okla, Norman; Louisburg Col, NC; Bank of Am; Glaxco; Smith Kline Corp. *Comn:* Aycock portrait for E Carolina Univ. *Exhib:* Ball State Univ Art Gallery, 75; Biennial Exhib Piedmong Painting & Sculpture, Mint Mus, Charlotte, NC, 75; Solo exhib, Mint Mus, Charlotte, 78; Razor Gallery, NY, 79; 44th Ann, Butler Inst Am Art, Youngstown, Ohio, 80; Two-person exhibs, Greenville Mus Art, 82, Bank of the Arts, New Bern, 84 & Arlington Hall Gallery, Greenville, 85 & 90, Coll Albemarle, Elizabeth City, NC, 90, Gaston Col, Dallas, NC, 91, QLM Assocs, Princeton, NJ, 93 & Stover Mill Gallery, E Pa, 94; 30th Irene Leache Mem, Chrysler Mus, Norfolk, Va, 90; 53rd-62nd Ann Exhib, Woodmere Art Mus, Philadelphia, 93-2005, 55th-63rd Ann Mem Exhib, 95-2002; Tri-State Artist Equity Shows, 2001-06; Riverbank Arts, Stockton, NJ, Langman Gallery, Willow Grove, Pa; Innovare Gallery, Easton, PA, 2004; Atlantic City Art Ctr, Atlantic City, NJ, 2004. *Teaching:* Prof painting, E Carolina Univ, 59-92, retired. *Awards:* Award Excellence, Art with a Southern Draw, Univ Mobile, Ala, 98; Second Prize for Watercolor & Second Prize for Oil, Kinston Art Show, 68; Merit Award, Wake Visual Arts Asn, Raleigh, 86; Cash Sculpture Award, 35th Tenn, All-State Art Exhib, 96; Artist Equity, Cheltasham, PA, 03; Woodmere Art Mus Members Show, Best in Show, Philadelphia, 2003. *Bibliog:* Emily Farnham (auth), Behind a Laughing Mask, Charles Demuth; SECAC Review, Vol V, No 2, 4/72; Philip Fehl, The Classical Monument, SECAC, Vol VII, No 1, spring 74; Lucy Lippard, Overlay: Contemporary Art and Art of Prehistory, SECAC, Vol XI, No 1, spring 86. *Mem:* Philadelphia TriState Artists Equity (vpres). *Media:* Oil. *Dealer:* Riverbank Arts Stockton NJ; Howard Gallery, New Hope, PA

GORDLEY, SCOTT MATTHEW
EDUCATOR, ADMINISTRATOR, ILLUSTRATOR

Study: Bowling Green State, (painting), 1974; Ringling Sch of Art, BFA (graphic design), 1977; Tufts Univ, MFA, 1998. *Hon Degrees:* Work appears in many public and private collections. *Work:* Documentary work, Tennessee, 1995, Bledd White, Revealed, 1995; art and experimental work includes Angel, 1994, Building Apollo, 1997, Overdrive, 1995, Fear of Dancing, 1997, Video Dolls, 1998, Doll Boys, 1998, Dance, Dance, Dance, 2003; Music recordings (Tenor, Baritone, and Alto Saxophone) include Can't Take It, Little Anthony and the Loco-motives, 1991; Blues on My Side, Johnny and the East Coast Rockers, 1995, Rock'em Dead All Night, 1997, Live & Swingin', 1998, Rock that Beat, 2000; Ride the Rocket, The Gamma Rays, 2001; Train to New Orleans, John MacLeod, 2005; Off the Cuff, Scott Gordley Trio, 2006. *Comn:* Portrait commissions include Ms Edith Oliver, 1990, Mr Lloyd Richards, 1991, Admiral Thomas Matteson, 1992, 1998, Admiral Douglas Teeson, 2000, Betrand Clifford, 2003 and Madonna for Esquire Magazine; New York City Jazz: Bebop and Beyond, 16 painting for publication and permanent exhibition commissioned by Adagio Jazz, Inc, 2005; Pub Master, Hanafin Corporation, New London, 2006, The Jazz Series, Adagio Jazz, Inc, published in 48th Annual Best of American Illustration, Soc of Illustrators, NYC, 2006, Thanksgiving at the Clearview Motel, 2006. *Exhib:* Solo exhibitions Anderson Marsh Gallery, Fla, 1978, 1979, 1985, Galerie Macler, Fla, 1980, 83, 84, H Pelham Curtis Gallery, New Canaan, 1995, Lincoln Ctr for the Arts, Maine, 2003 and others; Group Invitational, Nat Arts Club, NYC, 1978; Best of American Artists, Grand Central Galleries, NYC, 1985; Connections, International Exchange Exhibition with Kunstlerbund Graz, Austria, 2003; Critical Mass, 1708 Gallery, Richmond, Va, 2004; American Educators Exhibition, Mus of American Illustration, Soc of Illustrators, NYC, 2004; Soc of Illustrators 48th Annual American Illustration Exhibition, 2004; Soc of Illustrators Group Exhibition, Mus of American Illustration, NYC, 2005; The Family Experience:Deconstruction and Reconstruction, Fla State Mus of Fine Arts, 2006; 17th Annual Illustrators Show, Mus of American Illustration, NYC, 2006. *Collection Arranged:* Work in several private and public collections including President and Mrs. Ronald Reagan, President and Mrs. George H. Bush, Jason Robards, Geraldine Fitzgerald, & Dina Merill; permanent public collections include American Soviet Theater Initiative, Moscow, Swedish Royal Theater, HUD headquarters, Washington, DC, Ringling Sch of Art, Eugene O'Neill Theater Ctr. *Pos:* Illustrator for clients including Time, Esquire, Reader's Digest, Newsday, Spy, Morrow Publishing, Viking Penguin, Saatchi & Saatchi International, London Times, and Ogilvy & Mather, formerly; invited lecturer in the field. *Teaching:* Faculty, art department, Mitchell Col, New London, Conn, 1986-2001, department head/coordinator graphic design department, 1996-2001; prof Fine Arts, Montclair State Univ, NJ, 2001-, chair, Art and Design, currently. *Awards:* Soc of Illustrators award; Silvermine Found award, Print Magazine award and others; Dir, chief editor, Nat Endowment for the Arts grant in conjunction with the the Connecticut Commission on the Arts to produce a documentary on the civil rights movement entitled Voices of Change with participation from Julian Bond and Rev Jesse Jackson, 1998. *Publ:* (Auth) Painting from Life, Freepress, 2003, I'm Jay McInerney: A Transmutational Fantasy, Hartford Monthly Magazine, 1993, Reunion, The Journal Herald, 1992, Sacrifice, Dayton Daily News, 1991, Painting What You Feel, American Artist Magazine, 1984. *Mailing Add:* 22 Moss St Pawcatuck CT 06379

GORDON, ALBERT F
ART DEALER
b Antwerp, Belg, June 18, 1934; US citizen. *Study:* Sorbonne, Univ Paris; Columbia Univ, MA, 60. *Collection Arranged:* Aspects of the Doubled Image in African Art (auth, catalog), 76; Beauty and the Beast: A Study in Contrasts (auth, catalog), 77; Ekon Soc Puppets: Sculptures for Social Criticism (auth, catalog), 77. *Pos:* Pres, Tribal Arts Galleries, Inc, New York, 68-. *Bibliog:* Terry Trucco (auth), Primitive art, Art News, 4/81. *Mem:* Am Appraisers Asn; Explorers Club. *Specialty:* African art. *Publ:* The Tribal Bead, Tribal Arts Gallery Publ Inc, 74. *Mailing Add:* c/o Tribal Arts Gallery 155 Round Mountain Rd Stephentown NY 12168

GORDON, COCO
ENVIRONMENTAL ARTIST, WRITER
b Genoa, Italy, Sept 16, 1938; US citizen. *Study:* Univ Mich, 55-57; Adelphi Univ, BA (art), 59; Gaia Univ, MSc, 2012. *Work:* Vassari Futurist Collection, Messina, Italy; Getty Ctr Arts & Humanities, Santa Monica, Calif; Am Craft Mus, NY; Smithsonian Mus, Washington; Visual Art Mus, Beer Sheva, Israel; Whitney Mus; MoMA (Books). *Comn:* Culture project (hops for beer), Kulturverein Schreams, Steiermark, Austria, 93; Sculpture, Bonotto Collection, Italy, 98-2000. *Exhib:* Solo exhib, Heckscher Mus, Huntington, NY, 78, Real Art Ways, Hartford, Conn, 86, Foro Boario, Reggio Emilia, Italy, 89, World Fair Pavillion, Messina, Italy, 91, Kunstkanzlei, Vienna, Austria, 93, V-Idea, Genoa, Italy, 95 & Gallery One Twenty Eight, NY, 98; group exhib, Am Craft Mus, NY, 81, Fine Arts Mus Long Island, Hempstead, NY, 81-82 & Sandra Gering Gallery, NY, 97, Instituto De Artes Graficas, De Axaca, Mex, 98, elevator audio work, Art-in-General, NY, 2000, Deep Listening Space, Kingston, NY, 2003, Corallo, Napoli, Italy, 2005. *Pos:* Publ, W Space Books & Water Mark Press, 78-; instr permaculture, Willow Way, Niwot Colo. *Teaching:* art residency, Vienna Pub Sch, 93; residency Oreste, Italy, 98-2000. *Awards:* Susan B Anthony award, NYC, 86; Women Studio Workshop Grant, Rosendale, NY, 87; Harvestworks Grant for Audio Production, Studio Pass, 93; Djerassi Found Residency, 96. *Bibliog:* Jerome P Frank (auth), Making handmade paper perform, Small Press Mag, 86; Henry Martin (auth), Il sogno del tempo, Apeiron Mag, Messina, Italy, 91; Marie-Therese Pfeiffer, Coco Gordon-radical food, Vernissage Mag, Vienna, Austria, 93. *Mem:* Poetry Soc Am; Poets & Writers; Acad Am Poets and IAWA; Front Range Permaculture Guild. *Media:* Installation, Artist Books, Art & Poetry Performance Events. *Specialty:* Eco Arts, Fluxus Art. *Interests:* Bioregionalism, Permaculture. *Collection:* Dittadi, Italy. *Publ:* Auth, ed & illusr, Radical Food, Kunstkanzlei, 93; Hip-Hop Solarplexus, Kulturverein Schreams, 93; Superskywoman, V-Idea, 95 & New Observations, 97; TIKYSK (things I know you should know), 96; Visioning Life Systems, 2003; Chap books: translation of Rita degli Esposti Poesie per Clunk!, What Opens Stays forever, Clunk!, and Conflu-Essence, 2008; Chapbook of tibetan inspired poems by Coco Gordon, Anne Waldman, John Gian and Rita degli Esposti, 2008; Interactiv#14 Lyons Creating Champions, A Blueprint for Recovery and Risk Mitigation, TIKYSK Press, Il Vento La Pioggia, 1/31/14; Politically Correct? collaboration between Luc Fierens (Belgium) and Coco Gordon (USA), Extra Postfluxpost, May, 2015. *Dealer:* Rosa Leonardi V-Idea P'zza Campetto 8A/9 16123 Genova Italy; Christine Jones Kunstkanzlei Riemergasse 14/29 Al0l0 Vienna Austria; Rosanne Chiessi Pari Dispari Gallery RE Italy. *Mailing Add:* PO Box 225 Lyons CO 80540-0225

GORDON, DAVID S
CONSULTANT
b London. *Study:* Grad, Balliol Coll, Oxford; studied at London Sch Econ & Harvard Business Sch. *Pos:* Financial journalist; asst editor, The Economist, CEO, 81-93; gov, British Film Inst, 82-92; bd mem, South Bank Ctr, 88-96; trustee, Architecture Found, 91-2001, Tate, 93-98; chmn, Contemp Art Soc, 92-98; sec, Royal Acad Art, 96-2002; dir, Milwaukee Art Mus, 2002-08; principal, Gordon Adv LLC; bd dirs, Profile Bks Ltd; Dice Holdings Inc. *Mem:* Chevalier des arts et des Lettres

GORDON, DOUGLAS
SCULPTOR
b Glasgow 1966. *Study:* Glasgow Sch Art, 84-88; Slade Sch Art, London, 88-90. *Work:* Guggenheim Mus, New York; Mus Mod Art, New York; Mus Mod Art, San Francisco; Tate Collection, London; Mus fuer Moderne Kunst, Frankfurt; Centre George Pompidou, Paris; Mus d'Art Moderne de la Villede Paris; Hammer Mus, Los Angeles; Kunstmuseum Wolfsburg; Hirshhorn Mus, DC; Van Abbe Mus, Eindhoven. *Exhib:* Solo exhibs, Mus d'Art Moderne de la Ville de Paris, 2000, What Have I Done, Hayward Gallery, London, 2003, Letters, telephone calls, postcards, miscellaneous, Van Abbemuseum, Eindhoven, 2004, What You Want Me to Say, I am Already Dead, Fundacio Joan Miro, Barcelona, 2006, Superhumanatural, Royal Scottish Acad Bldg, Edinburgh, 2006, The Mus Mod Art, 2006, MART, Trento, Italy, 2006, Between Darkness & Light, Kunstmuseum Wolfsburg, Wolfsburg, 2007, Zidane: A 21st Century Portrait, daadgalerie, Berlin,2008, La Collection Lambert en Avignon, 2008; Group exhibs, Royal Botanic Garden, Edinburgh, 2005; New British Art, Tate Britain, 2006; Irish Mus Mod Art, Dublin, 2006; The Fruitmarket Gallery, Edinburgh, 2008; Pergamonmuseum, Berlin, 2008; Mus d'Art Contemp de Montreal, 2009; Louisiana Mus, Denmark, 2009-2010. *Teaching:* Prof, Glassgow Sch Art, Univ Edinburgh. *Awards:* Turner prize, 96; Premio 2000 award, Venice Biennale, 97; Hugo Boss Prize, Guggenheim Mus, New York, 98; Roswitha Haftmann Prize, Kunsthaus, Zurich, 2008; Kathe Kollwitz prize, Acad Arts Berlin, 2012. *Bibliog:* Russell Ferguson (auth), Douglas Gordon, MIT Press, Cambridge, Mass, 2001; Nancy Spector, Francis McKee & Alison Gineras (auths), Douglas Gordon's The Vanity of Allegory, Solomon R Guggenheim Found, Berlin, 2005; Klaus Biesenbach (auth), Douglas Gordon: Timeline, Mus Mod Art, New York, 2006. *Mem:* Groucho Club, London; Soho House, New York. *Interests:* eating, drinking, sleeping. *Publ:* Douglas Gordon: From God to Nothing, Beatrice Schaechterle, Noema Art Journ, 98; 21st Century Portrait, Hans Ulrich Obrist, Spike Art Quarterly, 2006; Processus Gordon, Ingrid Brochard, bc be contemp, 2008; Feuer und Flamme, Jenny Schlenzka, Monopol Mag fuer Kunst und Leben, Nr, 2008. *Dealer:* Gagosian Gallery; Yvon Lambert Paris; Galerie Eva Presenhuber. *Mailing Add:* c/o Gagosian Gallery 555 W 24th St New York NY 10011

GORDON, JAMES A
PATRON
Study: Northwestern Univ, BA (summa cum laude). *Pos:* Fac, Gordon's Wholesale, 71-86; founder, managing partner,Edgewater Growth Capital Partners, currently; treas, Whitney Mus Am Art, trustee currently; bd dir, Des Moines Ballet; bd dir, Chicago Mus Am Art, Northwestern Mem Found, John F Kennedy Ctr Performing Arts, Chicago Cares Inc, Bankers Trust Co, Methodist Medical Adv; bd dir & former pres, Des Moines Art Ctr; bd dir, Iowa Soc to Prevent Blindness, Des Moines Opera; mem bd, Grinnell Col, chmn, investment comt; trustee, Art Inst Cihcago, Mus Contemp Art Chicago. *Mailing Add:* Edgewater Funds Growth Capital Partners 900 N Michigan Ave Ste 1800 Chicago IL 60611

GORDON, JOHN S
SCULPTOR, EDUCATOR
b Milwaukee, Wis, Nov 16, 1946. *Study:* Antioch Col, BA, 70; Claremont Grad Sch, MFA, 73. *Work:* Prudential Insurance Co. *Exhib:* Whitney Mus Am Art, Biennial Contemp Am Art, NY, 75; solo exhibs, Los Angeles Louver Gallery, Venice, Calif, 77 & Artists Space, NY, 79; USC Atelier, Santa Monica, 88; Shidoni Contemp Gallery, Santa Fe, NMex, 91; Jan Weiner Gallery, Kansas City, Mo, 94; Tinsletown Too, Domestic Setting, Los Angeles, 2004. *Pos:* Consult, Community Redevelop Agency, Los Angeles, 84; Southern Calif Rapid Transit Dist Metro Rail Art-in-Transit Comt, 85-90; mem, Mayor's Task Force Arts, 87-88; consult, Los Angeles Co Transportation Comn, 90-91; bd trustees, Santa Fe Chamber Music Festival, 92-93; consult, Metrop Transit Authority, NY, 97-99; mem, Comn on Accreditation, Nat Asn Schs Art and Design, 2000-; moderator, The Work of 20th Century Self-Taught Artists, John Michael Kohler Arts Ctr, Sheboygan, Wis, 5/2000, Aspects of Henry Darger, Mus Am FolK Art, NY, 2001; mem pub art com, Port of San Diego, 2002-04; mem art selection com, N Embarcadero Visionary Plan, San Diego, 2003-05; mem Deans Steering Comt, Asn Independent Colls Art & Design, 2006-; moderator, Night Conversations, Los Angeles Co Natural Hist Mus, 2006; coordr, The Sims in the Hands of Artist, exhib, Ben Maltz Gallery, Los Angeles, 2007. *Teaching:* instr ceramics, Mt St Mary's Col, Los Angeles, 73; assoc prof sculpture & ceramics, Univ Southern Calif, 73-, assoc prof, Sch Fine Arts, 89-91; vis asst prof, Claremont Grad Sch, fall 79; dean, Sch Fine Art, Univ Southern Calif, 81-87; acad vpres, Calif Col Arts & Crafts, 88; dean fine arts & cult studies, Inst Am Indian Arts, 91-93; Kansas City Art Inst, 93-96; dean, Sch Art and Design, Pratt Inst, Brooklyn, 96-99, provost, 99-02; dir, Sch of Art, Design, and Art History, San Diego State Univ, 2002-04, 2012-2013, emeritus, 2013; provost, Otis Col Art & Design, 2004-2009; pres, Col of Santa Fe, 2010-2011. *Awards:* Nat Endowment Arts Grant, 76; Mayor's Cert Appreciation, City of Los Angeles, 84. *Bibliog:* Susan C Larsen (auth), John S Gordon, Arts Mag, 3/77; Peter Frank (auth), On the trail of the emergent American, The Nat Gallery Guide, 1/81; Margaret Lazzari (auth), Delving into minor works, Artweek, 2/6/88. *Mem:* Coll Art Asn Am; Int Coun Fine Arts Deans. *Media:* Mixed Media. *Publ:* How about some art

in next year's Los Angeles festival, Los Angeles Herald Examiner, 10/6/87; References to Political Climate, Fragility of Human Emotions, Santa Fe New Mex, 10/11/91; New Mexico: Growing internationalism, Art News, 4/92; Authenticity and the curatorial dilemma, The Mag, 7/92; National endowments are not as critics see them, Kansas City Star, 8/4/95; The Practical Handbook for the Emerging Artist (2nd ed), 2002. *Mailing Add:* Sch of Art, Design Art and History San Diego State University 5500 Campanile Dr A-505 San Diego CA 92182-4805

GORDON, JOY L
CURATOR, DIRECTOR
b New York, NY, Jan 31, 1933. *Study:* NY Univ, BA, 57, MA, 72. *Collection Arranged:* Contemp Latino Americano Art, 72; Prints from the NYU Art Collection, Hudson River Mus, Yonkers, 73; Paintings & Sculpture from the NYU Art Collection, Art Gallery, Univ Notre Dame, 73; William Benton Mus Art, Univ Conn, 73; Contemp Asian & Middle Eastern Art from the Grey Found Collection, 75; Report from Soho, 75; Aspects of Am Realism, 76; Prints & Techniques (with catalog), 76; Drawing & Collage (with catalog), 76; Contemp Israeli Crafts, 77; Am Impressionist Painting, 77; Am Still Life Paintings, 19th & 20th Centuries, 78; Containers, Mass Crafts, 79; Art in Process, 79; Directions in Realism: Boston, 80; Am Artists in Dusseldorf, 82 & On the Threshold of Mod Design, The Arts & Crafts Movement, 84, Danfort Mus. *Pos:* Cur & researcher pvt collections, NY Univ Art Collection, 72-74; cur, Grey Art Gallery & Study Ctr, NY Univ, 74-77; dir, Danforth Mus, Framingham, Mass, 77-88 & Guild Hall, East Hampton, NY, 88-93; independent cur, 94-. *Teaching:* Adminr mus studies, NY Univ, 72-77 & Framingham State Coll, 78-88. *Mem:* Coll Art Asn; Am Asn Mus; Art Table. *Mailing Add:* 28 Sandra Dr East Hampton NY 11937

GORE, DAVID ALAN
PAINTER, PHOTOGRAPHER
b Ann Arbor, Mich, May 6, 1947. *Study:* Tyler Sch Art, Philadelphia, BFA, 68; Acad Fine Art, with Joseph Amerotica, 72; Philadelphia Mus Art, with Theodore Segal, 72-74, Fortessa Di Basso, Florence, Italy, with Umberto Baldini, 73. *Comn:* Empire & Flute Player (murals), comn by Wilbur Pierce, 85; Pompeian Room, comn by Dr James Sullivan, 85; sculpture, comn by Dr R Shafto, 91; conservation mural (6 ft x 19ft), Bur Mus Delaware; mural (10 ft x 76 ft), Sports Club Woodlyn, Pa. *Exhib:* British & Australian Embassy, 85; Very Victorian, Del State Mus, Dover, 88-89; Mixed Media by David Gore, Widener Univ Mus, Chester, Pa, 90; Afterwords, Philadelphia, Pa, 93; Roam, Wilmington, Del, 94. *Pos:* Chief conservator, Bureau of Mus Del, 74-, Henry M Flagler Mus, 75-80, Widener Univ Mus, 87-94 & Classic Conservation, Chester, Pa. *Teaching:* Instr painting, drawing & design, Bucks Co Community Col, Pa, 71-73. *Awards:* French Int Poster Contest, Paris, 63; Nat Designers Award, 68. *Bibliog:* Art Carey (auth), Restoring Masterpieces, Philadelphia Inquire, 81; Rita Beyer (auth), David Gore Works Shown at Schwartz Gallery, Chestnut Hill Local, 92; Patty Mengers (auth), High Tech Endeavor for Chester Artist, Delaware Co Daily Times, 94. *Media:* Oil, Photographer. *Mailing Add:* 3900 N Washington St Wilmington DE 19802-2148

GORE, JEFFERSON ANDERSON
CURATOR
b Selma, Ala, April 25, 1943. *Study:* Harvard Col, BA (visual studies), 65; Skowhegan Sch Painting & Sculpture, 66; Grad Sch Fine Arts, Univ Pa, MFA (sculpture), 70. *Collection Arranged:* Sesquicentennial of Railroad in the Arts (auth, catalog), 79; Exquisite Nomads: Seashells Real and in Art (auth, catalog), 80; Season of Mists (auth, catalog), 81; Spacetoys: Fifty Years of Fantasy, 82; Painted Light (auth, catalog), 83; Mushroom Magic: The R Gordon Wasson Collection of Mycological Art. *Pos:* Cur fine arts, Reading Pub Mus, Pa, 78-. *Teaching:* Asst sculpture, Grad Sch Fine Arts, Univ Pa, 68-70; instr, Albright Col, Pa, 70-74. *Mem:* Citizens Arts in Pa; Philadelphia Art Alliance. *Res:* Cross-cultural influences between Europe and Asia in art and philosophy. *Mailing Add:* 73 Hardwood Ln Mohnton PA 19540-7720

GORE, PAUL M See Goreniuc, Mircea C Paul

GORE, SAMUEL MARSHALL
PAINTER, SCULPTOR
b Coolidge, Tex, Nov 24, 1927. *Study:* Atlanta Coll Art, BFA, 50; Miss Coll, BA, 52; Univ Ala, MA, 56; Ill State Univ, EdD, 69. *Work:* Hull Gallery, Hinds Community Coll, Raymond, Miss; Ill State Univ; Miss Univ Women; Samuel Marshall Gore Galleries, Miss Coll; Miss Mus Art. *Comn:* Mural, Van Winkle Methodist Church, Jackson, Miss, 74; portrait bust (bronze), US Sen John Stennis, Lt Col SQDR CDR, Miss Wing, Civil Air Patrol, Air Force Cap, 74 & William Faulkner, Sta WJTV, Howard Lett, Jackson, Miss, 74; bronze sculpture, Nurse, Miss Baptist Hosp, 88; bronze sculpture, Working Man, Miss Mus Agr & Forestry; sculptures, Student Nurse, Miss Baptist Med Ctr & Harlington, Tex; Christ the Healer, Miss Baptist Med Ctr; Citizen Soldier, State Miss Woolfolk SS Office Bldg; Jesus with Children, First Baptist Church, Clinton, Miss; Servant Savoir, Miss Coll; Mary & Christ Child, CHapel of the Cross, Madison, Miss & Samuel Marshall Gore Galleries, Miss; Moses Giver of the Law, Miss Coll, Sch Law, Jackson, Miss. *Exhib:* Solo exhibs, Miss Art Asn, 57 & House Admin Off Suite, US Capitol Bldg, 75; Nat Oils Show & Mem show, Miss Art Asn, Jackson 58; Sears Traveling Show, 63. *Teaching:* Prof drawing, painting & sculpture & head art dept, Miss Col, 51-, ettl endowed prof, currently. *Awards:* Nat Merit Service Award, Air Force Civil Air Patrol, 77; GOvs Award, Career in Art, 97; Citizen of the Year, Clinton Miss CofC, 2000; Ageless Heroes, Blue Cross-Blue Shield, Miss, 2001. *Bibliog:* Ruth Campbell (producer), Conversation with Sam Gore (video tape), Miss Educ TV, 11/75. *Mem:* Miss Art Educ Asn (secy, 61, vpres, 62, pres 63); Nat Art Educ Asn; Southeastern Art Educ Asn; Med-Art USA (bd dir); Christians in Visual Arts. *Media:* Oil, Watercolor; Terra Cotta, Bronze. *Publ:* Illusr, Mississippi Game and Fish, 58-59; Freshwater species of Mississippi, 59; Christianity and the Arts. *Mailing Add:* Miss Coll Art Dept PO Box 4205 Clinton MS 39058

GORE, TOM
PHOTOGRAPHER, EDUCATOR
b Victoria, BC, Aug 7, 1946. *Study:* Univ Victoria. *Work:* Prov Collection, Parliament Bldgs, Victoria; Vancouver Art Gallery, BC; Univ Victoria, BC; City Seattle. *Comn:* Illusr, Earth Meditations, Mike Doyle, 70 & Vancouver Island Poetry Soft Press, 74. *Exhib:* Sask Cult Exchange, 86 & 87; Escuela Artos Aplicadas, Ibiza, Spain, 88; Applied Art Sch, Soria, Spain, 91; Ctr of Cult Brno, Czech Repub, 94 & 95; Joigny, France, 94; Rogue Art, Victoria, 95; Bologna, Italy, 95; Sooke Fine Arts, 2007-2012; Sidney Fine Arts, 2008-2013; UCC, 2012; LOOK, 2010-2014; Eros, 2014. *Collection Arranged:* Victoria & Victoria Five, Secession Gallery; Polaroid Collaboratory, 78 & The Stereo Show, 80, Open Space; Latitudes and Parallels, Winnipeg Gallery, 81. *Pos:* Ed art mag, Tryste, 66-68; com photogr, 69-71; cur photog, Open Space, Victoria, 75-84; ed, Rhino Press, 79-90; consult, Winnipeg Art Gallery, 81-; photo ed, Malahat Rev 92. *Teaching:* Lectr photog, Univ Victoria, 77-2012; instr photog, Camosun Coll, Victoria, BC, 73-78. *Awards:* Hon Mention, BC Photogr Show, Simon Fraser Art Gallery, 73; First Prize, Vancouver Island Juried Show, Art Gallery of Greater Victoria, 74; Can Coun Grants, 77, 78 & 90; Dept Communications Grant, Photographic Soc Am, 90; Comm Art Corner, 2013, 2014. *Bibliog:* Glen Howarth (auth), Bio-article, Victoria Press, 70; Carolyn Leier (auth), Bio-article, Arts W, 76; Contemporary Personage, Padua, Italy, 80; Photographic Artists & Innovators, 84; International Catalog Of Contemporary Art, 89; Robert Amos (auth), Bio Article Times Colonist, 2011; Full of Sound & Fury, 1/2012. *Mem:* Open Space Arts Soc (pres, 78-); Soc for Photog Educ, NW Region (chmn, 78-81); Victoria Civil Liberties Asn (pres, 88-); Can Federation of Rights & Liberties (bd, 92-94), 2012; BC Civil Liberties Asn (bd, 96). *Media:* Collage, Photography, Digital Photography. *Res:* Criticism of photography; John Thomson biography; the photograph as theatre; evolution of photographic landscape; Contexts of the Portrait. *Publ:* Contemporary Photography in British Columbia, Ryerson, 79; auth, In perspective: Vancouver art, Arts W, 1/79; Collecting the paradoxical magic mirror, Photo Communique, PI, 5/79; Portfolio, Camera Mainichi, Tokyo, 10/81 & 3/83; Portfolio, Camera Canada, Toronto, 84; An Admirable View, Rhino Press, Victoria, 86; George Craven's Objects and Images, New York, 88; Robert Hirsch's Photographic Possibilities, New York, 90; Building Consensus, Democrat, 92; Close Up, 2012, 2013. *Mailing Add:* 1653 Dean Park Rd North Saanich BC V8L 4Y7 Canada

GOREE, GARY PAUL
INSTRUCTOR, PAINTER
b Jackson, Miss, Apr 8, 1951. *Study:* Southwestern Okla State Univ, BFA, 72; Tex Tech Univ, MA (educ), 80. *Work:* Williams Co, Tulsa, Okla; Presby Hosp, Oklahoma City, Okla. *Exhib:* Greater Fall River Nat, Mass, 78; Nat Cape Coral Ann, Fla, 79; Okla Art Ann, Tulsa, 80; Okla 81, Univ Okla, Norman, 81; Solo exhibs, Odessa Col, 94 & Rogers State Col, 96. *Pos:* Art supervisor, Tulsa Pub Schs, 82-86, fine arts coordr, 86-. *Teaching:* Instr art, Tulsa Pub Schs, 73-81; teaching asst art, Tex Tech Univ, 77 & vis prof art, 85-95; instr watercolor, Tulsa Jr Col, Okla, 74- & Philbrook Mus Sch, Tulsa, 94-96. *Awards:* Okla Art Educr of Yr, 83; Nat Western Region Art Supervisor of Yr, 87; Gov's Art Award, 99. *Bibliog:* Peg Ridgeway (auth), article, Art Voices Mag, 9-10/81. *Mem:* Nat Art Educ Asn; Okla Art Educ Asn; Southwestern Art Asn; Okla Art Guild; Tulsa Artist Guild. *Media:* Watercolor. *Publ:* Coauth, Found Object Design in Jewelry, 76, Weaving, Soft Sculpture & Natural Dyes, 77 & Plans, Projects and Processes, 80, Tulsa Pub Schs. *Dealer:* Margo Shorney 6616 N Olie Oklahoma City OK 74128. *Mailing Add:* 1541 S Florence Ave Tulsa OK 74104-5208

GORENIUC, MIRCEA C PAUL
SCULPTOR
b Bucharest, Romania, Dec 12, 1942; US citizen. *Study:* Fine Art Acad, Munich, WGer, 70-72; San Francisco State Univ, BA, 75; San Jose Univ, Calif, MA, 76, MFA, 78. *Work:* Palo Alto, San Jose, Concord, Los Altos & Los Gatos, Calif; pvt collections, Romania, Ger, Sidney, Australia, USA, Paris-France, Norway, Finland, Sweden, Denmark & China. *Comn:* Space Dance for Peace, Wolfe-Sesnon & Buttery, San Jose, Calif, 82, Syntex Corp, (outdoor permanent collection), Palo Alto, 83, City of Los Gatos, 87; Homage to the Challenger, Lyncoln Park, Los Altos, Calif, 86; Rock and Roll for Peace, Art in Pub Places, City of Concord, Calif, 90; pub art collection, City Palo Alto, 94; China Int City Sculpture Exhib & Symposium, Beijing, 2002; Intl Sculpture Park, Beijing, China, 2002. *Exhib:* Grands et Jeunes D'au Jourd' Hui-Grand Palais de Champs Elysee Salon, 85; Orgn Am States, Washington, DC, 99; XIV Int Sculpture Biennale, Ravenna Italy, 2003; Int City Sculpture Exhib & Symposium, Beijing, China, 2003; Beijing Exhib Hall, 2005; One Show Show, Romania, Beijing, China, 2006; Exhib Seoul, S Korea, 2006; 5th Int Art Biennale; China Nat Mus Fine Arts, Beijing, 2010. *Pos:* VPres, IAA/UNESCO US chap, W Coast. *Teaching:* Instr sculpture, West Valley Col, Saratoga, Calif, 80-82. *Awards:* Most Controversial Pub Sculpture, Sunnyvale, Calif, Metro News, 89; Phi Kappa Phi, First Prize & People's Choice Concord 1 percent Art in Pub Places Prog, 91; First Prize, Redding Mus, 1983. *Bibliog:* Art reviews in numerous publs; Vol V, Enciclopedy of Contemporary Romanian Personalities in America, 2003. *Mem:* Int Art Asn, USA Chap (vpres 87-91); Artist Equity Asn; Calif Confederation for the Arts; Union Plastic Artists Romania; Phi Kappa Phi Nat Hon Soc (Lifetime Mem); Artists Rights Soc. *Media:* Cast Metals, Granite. *Res:* New methods in bronze casting, lost wax. *Interests:* Piano, classical music, beekeeping, gardening, fishing & swimming. *Publ:* American Romanian Academy Journal, 86; Architectural Arts and Sculpture, vol 14& 15, 99; Int Sculpture Mag, 2011-2012; NY Art Expo, 2011, 2012. *Mailing Add:* 1251 Phelps Ave San Jose CA 95117

GORI, GIULIANO
COLLECTOR
b Prato, Italy, 1930. *Pos:* Founder, Gori Collection Site-Specific Art, Santomato di Pistoia, Italy. *Awards:* Named one of Top 200 Collectors, ARTnews mag, 2003-10. *Mem:* Florence Acad Fine Arts. *Collection:* Modern & contemporary art; site-specific art. *Mailing Add:* Fattoria di Celle Gori Collection Site-Specific Art Via Montalese 7 Santomato di Pistoia 51030 Italy

GORING, TREVOR
PAINTER, WRITER
b London, Eng, Nov 28, 1949; Can & Europ citizen. *Study:* Ecole Des Beaux Arts, Montreal, BA, 70; Univ Que, Montreal, BFA, 72; St Martins Coll Art, London, MFA (painting), 74. *Work:* Can Coun Art Bank, Ottawa; NY State Trial Lawyers Asn, New York; Rotunda Gallery, London, Eng; Georgia Supreme Court Body, Atlanta, GA; Osgoode Hall, Toronto, ON; and others. *Comn:* Mural, Univ du Que, Montreal, 71; street installation, Olympic Comt, Montreal, 76. *Exhib:* Forum 76, Montreal Mus Fine Arts, 76; Quebec Drawings Traveling Show, Nat Mus Can, 76-78; Vehicule Artists, Arte Fiera, Bolonga, Italy, 78-79; Art for the Earth, Bonhams Fine Art, London, Eng, 86; Research in Progress, Concordia Art Gallery, Montreal, 91; Boreale Blues, Musee Du Bas St-Laurent, Que, 91; over 300 exhibs at legal confs in Europe & NAm. *Pos:* Pres, Vehicule Art Ctr, Montreal, 75-82; co-founder & treas, Asn Nat Non-Profit Artist Ctr, Can, 76-78; co-founder & art dir, Parallelogram Arts Mag, Can, 78-81; co-founder & publ, Virus Arts Mag, Montreal, 78-83; publ, Just Art Int, 94-. *Bibliog:* Dale McConathy (auth), Instant archaeology in Montreal, Artscanada, 7/76; Marie Michel Cron (auth), Entre l'hallucination et la douceur, Le Devoir, 9/19/92; Michael Molter (auth), Des forets et des hommes, Vie Des Arts, No 157, 95; Randy Chapnick Myers, (auth) A Tapestry of Law, Lawyers Weekly, 2/4/2005. *Mem:* Hon Fel Roscoe Pound Inst. *Media:* Acrylic on Canvas/limited edition prints. *Res:* Visual history of the legal profession and world judicial systems from earliest times. *Publ:* Ed, Real Live Art, Vehicule Art Inc, 75; contribr, Hommage to Marco Duchamp, Forest City Gallery, 87; auth, Boreal Blues, Trevor Goring, 91; Images of Justice - Women In-Law, Justart Int, 96; Images of Justice - Judges in Time, Justart Int, 97

GORNEY, JAY PHILIP
GALLERIST
b Brooklyn, NY, Sept 26, 1952. *Study:* Oberlin Col, with Ellen H Johnson, BA (art hist), 73; Whitney Mus Independent Study Prog, fall 72. *Pos:* Dir, Contemp Art, Mitchell-Innes & Nash, NY. *Bibliog:* New York Mag, 6/25/90; Flash Art Int, No 154, 10/90; and others. *Mem:* ADAA. *Res:* Contemporary painting, drawing, sculpture, photography, video. *Specialty:* Contemp & mod masters. *Mailing Add:* 534 W 26th St New York NY 10001

GORNIK, APRIL
PAINTER, PRINTMAKER
b Cleveland, Ohio, Apr 20, 1953. *Study:* Cleveland Inst Art, 71-75; NS Coll Art & Design, BFA, 76. *Work:* Chase Manhattan Permanent Collection, London, Eng; Metrop Mus Art, NY; Whitney Mus Am Art; Fort Worth Mus, Tex; High Mus Art, Atlanta. *Exhib:* Solo shows, Mary Ryan Gallery, NY, 93, Frederick R Weisman Mus Art, Pepperdine Univ, Malibu, Calif, 93, Offshore Gallery, East Hampton, NY, 94, Guild Hall Mus, East Hampton, NY, 94, Edward Thorp Gallery, NY, 94, 96 & 2000, Kohn Turner Gallery, Los Angeles, 95, Turner & Runyon Gallery, Dallas, 97, Mus of Am Art of Pa Acad of Fine Arts, Phila, 98, Glenn Horowitz Booksellers, East Hampton, NY, 99 & Harley Baldwin Gallery, Aspen, Colo, 99, Danese, NY, 2001, 2003, 2005, Huntington Mus of Art, WVa, 2002, Allen Mem Art Mus, Oberlin, Ohio, 2006; Pub and Pvt: Am Prints Today, 24th Nat Print Exhib, Brooklyn Mus, 86; Spectrum, Natural Settings, Corcoran Gallery Art, 86; A View of Nature, Aldrich Mus Contemp Art, 87; The New Romantic Landscape, Whitney Mus Am Art, 87; Nocturnal Visions in Contemp Painting, Whitney Mus Am Art, 89; Biennial Exhib, Whitney Mus Am Art, 89; Harmony & Discord: Am Landscape Today, Va Mus Fine Arts, 90; Four Friends, Aldrich Mus Contemp Art (traveling), 92; Landscape as Metaphor, Whitney Mus Am Art, 93; Timely and Timeless, Aldrich Mus Contemp Art, 94; Guild Hall Mus, E Hampton, NY, 94; Kohn Turner Gallery, Los Angeles, 95; Turner and Runyon Gallery, Dallas, 97; Univ Arts & Mus Am Art, Philadelphia, 98; Water: A Contemp Am View, Gibbes Mus of Art, Charleston, SC, 99 & Mobil Mus of Art, Ala, 2000; Why Draw A Landscape, Crown Point Press Gallery, San Francisco, 99 & Karen McCready Gallery, New York City, 99; A Place in the Sun, Steven Scott Gallery, Balt, 99; As Far as the Eye Can See, Atlanta Coll of Art Gallery, 99; The Perpetual Well: Contemp Art from the Collection of the Jewish Mus, Harn Mus of Art, Gainesville, Fla, 2000; Works on Paper 2000, Am Ambassador of Slovak Rep, 2000; Group Landscape Exhib, Winston Wachter Fine Art, Seattle, 2000; Art of the 80s, Winston Wachter Mayer Fine Art, New York City, 2000; Drawings 2000, Barbara Gladstone Gallery, New York City, 2000; Univ Gallery, Fine Arts Ctr, Univ of Mass, Amherst, 2001, Danese, NY, 2001, Michael Kohn Gallery, Los Angeles, Calif, 2001, The Parrish Art Mus, NY, 2001, Carrie Secrist Gallery, Chicago, Ill, 2001, Elizabeth Harris Gallery, NY, 2001; Hunter Mus Am Art, Chattanooga, Tenn, 2004; Cleveland Mus Contemp Art, 2005; Nat Mus Gdansk, Gdansk, Poland, 2006; Herbert F Johnson Mus Art, Ithaca, NY, 2007; Am Acad Arts & Letts Invitational, New York, 2009. *Bibliog:* John Russell (auth), Making pen and ink seem passe: the proliferation of new ways to draw, NY Times, 8/11/2000; Ken Johnson, Art in review: April Gornik, NY Times, 10/6/2000; Nancy Grimes, April Gornik, ARTnews, 11/2000. *Media:* Oil. *Dealer:* Danese Gallery 535 W 24th St New York NY 10011. *Mailing Add:* 41 Greene St No 4A New York NY 10013-5917

GORSKI, DANIEL ALEXANDER
PAINTER, SCULPTOR
b Cleveland, Ohio, Oct 26, 1939. *Study:* Cleveland Inst Art, dipl, 61; Yale Univ Sch Art & Archit, with Jack Tworkow & Al Held, BFA, 62 & MFA, 64. *Work:* Yale Univ. *Comn:* Mural, comn by Mr & Mrs Barney Kogen, 92; mural, comn by Mr Scott Johnson; mural, comn by Mr & Mrs Jack Berridge, 94; installation, comn by Ms Bebe Woolley, 96. *Exhib:* Primary Structures, Jewish Mus, NYC, 1966; Cool Art, Larry Aldrich Mus, Ridgefield, Conn, 68; Hanging and Leaning, Emily Lowe Gallery, Hofstra Univ, 70; 26 x 26, Vassar Coll Art Gallery, 71; Md Biennial Exhib, Baltimore Mus of Art, 76; Sculpture Outdoors, Temple Univ, Ambler, Pa, 77-80; Elements Style Artscape, Baltimore, Md, 86; Themes and Variations: Cubism, Artscape, Baltimore, Md, 87; Franz Bader Gallery, 88; Davis McClain Gallery, 95; Yaddo/Residency, 2000; Wade Wilson Gallery, 2014. *Pos:* Dir, Glassell Sch Art, Mus Fine Arts, Houston, Tex, 90-96. *Teaching:* Artist/adminr, Glassell Sch Art; instr & dir, Mus Fine Art, Houston, Tex, 90-96; artist/adminr, Maryland Inst Col Art, Baltimore, 1971-90. *Awards:* Mr & Mrs Jules Horelick Award, Baltimore Mus of Art, 76; Ford Found Grant, Shelter Inst, summer 79; A Mellon Grant, 84; AICA Grant, 85; City Arts Grant, 87. *Bibliog:* L Lippard (auth), Recent sculpture as escape, 2/66 & Escalation in Washington, 1/68, Art Int; U Kalterman (auth), The New Sculpture, Praeger, 68; Meyer (auth), Minimalism, Yale Univ Press, 2001. *Interests:* Antique and Ethnic Textiles, Lap Steel Guitars, 60s Japanese Guitars. *Mailing Add:* 13 Bayou Shadows St Houston TX 77024

GORSKI, RICHARD KENNY
EDUCATOR, GRAPHIC ARTIST
b Green Bay, Wis, Apr 20, 1923. *Study:* Northern Ill Univ, De Kalb, 62-65; Univ Wis, Milwaukee & Madison, MS (art educ), 50. *Work:* Milwaukee Pub Schs collection Wis Artists. *Exhib:* Wisconsin Painters & Sculptors, Wis Union Gallery, Madison, 39, 47, 49 & 53-56; Milwaukee Art Inst, 40, 46, 47, 49, 50, 53, 55-57 & 60; Walker Art Inst, 47 & 49. *Pos:* Cur & dir, Rahr Civic Ctr & Mus, Manitowoc, Wis, 50-53; illusr & designer, John Higgs Studios, Milwaukee, Wis, 56-57; art dir, United Educators Publ Inc, Lake Bluff, Ill, 60-61; dept head, art & design, Northern Mich Univ, Marquette, 65-75. *Teaching:* Instr art educ, Nat Col Educ, Evanston, Ill, 57-60; assoc prof art educ, Northeastern Ill Univ, Chicago, 61-65; prof graphic design, visual commun, Northern Mich Univ, Marquette, 65-94, emer prof, 95-. *Awards:* Special Merit Award, Wis Gimbels Salon, Gimbels Inc, 47; J Purchase Award, Wis Painters Ann, Milwaukee J Pub Schs Collection, 55. *Mem:* Semiotic Soc Am. *Media:* Oil, Pastel. *Res:* Structural basis of visual communication, and the semiosis of sight. *Interests:* Sensory structure. *Publ:* Auth, Color; article, United Educators Encycl & auth, Painting; article, The Wonderland of Knowledge Encycl, United Educ Publ, 60. *Mailing Add:* 2235 Rockwood Ave, Apt 604 Saint Paul MN 55116

GORVY, BRETT
ART APPRAISER
b London, England. *Pos:* Int co-head post-war & contemp art, Christie's, 2001-. *Mailing Add:* 20 Rockerfeller Plaza #6 New York NY 10020-1514

GOSSAGE, JOHN RALPH
PHOTOGRAPHER
b New York, NY, Mar 15, 1946. *Study:* Walden Sch, 67-69. *Work:* Mus Mod Art, NY; Houston Mus Fine Art; San Francisco Mus Art; Philadelphia Mus Art; George Eastman House, Rochester, NY. *Comn:* Nation's Capitol in Photographs, Corcoran Gallery, 76; Photography in America, AT&T, NY, 78; Photography and the City, Seattle Art Comn, 79. *Exhib:* 14 Am Photogrs, Baltimore Mus & traveling, 75; solo exhibs, Castelli Gallery, NY, 76 & Lunn Gallery, Washington, DC, 80; 10th Biennale Paris, Mus Mod Art, France, 77; Contemp Photog Works, Houston Mus Fine Arts, 77; Gardens, Werkstalt Photog, Berlin, 78; Photog & Sense of Order, Inst Contemp Art, Philadelphia, 81; History of Portrait Photog, Mus Art, Bonn, Ger, 82. *Pos:* Vpres, Columbia Arts Inc, 82-. *Teaching:* Assoc prof photog & art, Univ Md, 77-89. *Awards:* Grants, Stern Fund, 74 & Nat Endowment Arts, 74 & 78; Pratt Mem Award, 96. *Bibliog:* Renato Dansse (auth), American Images, McGraw Hill, 79. *Publ:* Auth, Gardens, Castelli Graphics, 78; The Pond, Aperture Publ, 84; Stadt des Schwarz, Loessstrife Ed, 89; There & Gone, Nazraeli Press, 96. *Dealer:* Castelli Uptown 4 E 77 St New York NY 10021; Ram Gallery Los Angeles Tokyo. *Mailing Add:* 2070 NW Belmont Rd Washington DC 20009

GOSSEL, GREG
PAINTER
b Baldwin, Wis, 1982. *Study:* Univ Wis, Eau Claire, BFA (graphic design), 2005. *Exhib:* Solo exhibs include Drunknbutterfly, Madison, Wis, 2007, Gallery Three, San Francisco, 2007, Dirty Pilot, Boston, 2008, Shooting Gallery, San Francisco, 2008; group exhibs include Fallout Art Festival, Fallout Urban Art Ctr, Minneapolis, 2006; Art of Design: The Future, Density Studios, Minneapolis, 2006; Party, Suite 100 Gallery, Seattle, 2007, Sweet 100, 2007; Festival of Appropriation, Soap Factory, Minneapolis, 2007; Pleased to Meet You, Tag Art Gallery, Nashville, 2008; Groundwork II, Foundation One Gallery, Atlanta, 2008

GOTTESMAN, GERALDINE & NOAM
COLLECTOR
b May 24, 1961. *Study:* Columbia Univ, BA. *Pos:* Fund mgr, Goldman Sachs Private Client Services, 1985-95; co-founder & mng dir US equities, Lehman Bros Int GLG Partners, 1995-2000; mng dir US equities & sr fund mgr, GLG Partners LP, 2000-2012, non-exec chmn, 2012-. *Awards:* Named one of Top 200 Collectors, ARTnews mag, 2006-2009, 2013. *Mem:* Tate Gallery (mod art coun); Dia Ctr for Arts (coun mem). *Collection:* Postwar and contemporary art. *Mailing Add:* GLG Partners LP 1 Curzon St London United Kingdom W1J 5HB

GOTTSCHALK, FRITZ
DESIGNER, LECTURER
b Zurich, Switz, Dec 30, 1937. *Study:* Kunstgewerbeschule, Zurich, Switz, dipl; Art Inst Orell Fussli, Zurich, dipl; Allgemeine Gewerbeschule, Basel, Switz, post-grad dipl, with E Ruder & A Hofmann. *Exhib:* The Visual Image of the Montreal Mus, Montreal Mus Fine Arts, Que, Can, 68; Swiss Design, Mus du Louvre, Paris, France, 71; Alliance Graphique Int: 107 Int Designers, Milan, Italy, 74; The Work of Gottschalk & Ash Ltd, Ryder Gallery, sponsored by Container Corp of Am, Chicago, 76; Coninx Mus, Zürich, Switz, 95. *Pos:* Designer art & design dir, Gottschalk & Ash Int, Meilen, Zurich, Switz, 77-; dir design & quality control off, Organizing Comt of 1976 Olympic Games, 74-76. *Awards:* Award of Excellence, Swiss Contemp Design, Dept of Interior, Swiss Govt, 62; two Awards of Excellence, Soc Publ Designers, New York, 70; Bronze Medal, Foire Int du Livre, Leipzig, EGer, 77; Lifetime Achievement Award, Canadian Soc Graphic Designers. *Bibliog:* Adrian Gatrail (auth), The Image Makers, The Gazette, Can, 70; Bill Bantey (auth), Gottschalk & Ash Ltd, Graphis, Switz, Vol 148 (1972); Midori Imatake (auth), Gottschalk & Ash Ltd, Idea (Japan), Vol 115 (1973). *Mem:* Que Soc Graphic Artists; Royal Can Acad; Asn of Swiss

Graphic Artists; Alliance Graphique Inter; Graphic Designers Can. *Media:* Graphic Design, Books and Corporate Images. *Publ:* Auth & illusr, article, Idea, Seibundo Shinkosha Publ Co, Japan, Vol 115, 72; ed, article, Revue Suisse de l'Imprimerie, Zollikofer AG, Switz, 74; illusr & contribr, article, Communication Arts, Coyne & Blanchard, Inc, 75; ed, article, Graphis, Vol 185, 77. *Mailing Add:* 26 Bocklingerstrasse Zurich 8032 Switzerland

GOUGH, GEORGIA BELLE LEACH
CRAFTSMAN, EDUCATOR
b Oklahoma City, Okla, Dec 21, 1920. *Study:* Central Okla Univ, BS, 41; Univ NTex, MS, 47; with Carlton Ball, 48; with Daniel Rhodes, 54; Univ Okla, PhD, 60. *Work:* Campbell Mem Collection, Am Craft Mus, NY; Visual Art Ctr, Denton, Tex. *Comn:* Wall hanging, comn by Greater Denton Arts Coun, Festival Hall Ctr Visual Arts. *Exhib:* Wichita Decorative Arts & Crafts, Wichita Mus, Kans, 50, 51 & 53; Syracuse Mus, NY, 51 & 56; Miami Nat Ceramic Exhib, Fla, 56; Dallas Craft Market, Tex, 81 & 82; Handmade in Tex, 87; A Decade of Dallas Crafts, 88; solo exhibs, Earth, Water, Fire, Air, 96 & Family Reunion, 2000. *Collection Arranged:* Materials Hard & Soft, (ann exhib) Greater Denton Arts Coun, 86-. *Teaching:* Prof ceramics, N Tex State Univ, 47-75, emer prof Coll Visual Art & Design. *Awards:* Third Place, Tex Fine Arts Asn, 53; Community Arts Recognition Award, Denton, Tex, 95; Community Gallery named: Georgia & Ray Gough Gallery, 2008. *Mem:* Nat Coun Educ Ceramic Arts (secy, 70-73); Am Craft Coun (trustee, 76-80); Am Ceramic Soc Design Sect Southwest Region (pres & secy); World Crafts Coun (US delegate, 78 & 80); hon mem Tex Designer-Craftsmen. *Media:* Ceramics. *Publ:* Auth, Use of native clays in high-grade pottery, Ceramic Industry, 53; Computer data processing system calculations of glaze formulae, Am Ceramic Soc Bulletin, 65; coauth, Fine Arts in Texas Colleges & Universities, 65. *Mailing Add:* 1813 Willowwood Denton TX 76205-6992

GOUGH, ROBERT ALAN
PAINTER
b Quebec, PQ, Aug 13, 1931; US citizen. *Study:* Am Acad Art, Chicago, with William H Mosby & J Allen St John. *Work:* Am Fedn Arts; Butler Inst Am Art; Univ Nebr; Sheldon Swope Art Gallery; Battelle Inst. *Exhib:* Painting & Sculpture Today, Herron Mus Art, 66; solo exhibs, Gilman Galleries, Chicago, 67 & 69; 35 Yrs in Retrospect, Butler Inst Am Art, 71; Mainstreams, Marietta Coll, 74, 75 & 77; Art from Appalachia Traveling Exhib, Smithsonian Inst, 81-; and others. *Awards:* Henry Ward Ranger Purchase Prize, Nat Acad Design, 62; Judges Award, Marietta Nat, 78; Ohioana Libr Asn Citation, 81. *Bibliog:* Doc, WBNS-TV, Columbus, Ohio, 70. *Media:* Oil. *Dealer:* Keny Galleries 300 E Beck St Columbus OH 43206. *Mailing Add:* 220 Brookside Dr Chillicothe OH 45601

GOULD, CLAUDIA
MUSEUM DIRECTOR
Study: Boston Coll, BA (Art Hist); New York Univ, MA (Mus Studies). *Pos:* cur, proj dir, cur exhibs Wexner Ctr Arts Ohio State Univ, 1989-91; independent cur, New York City, 1992-94; exec dir, Artists Space 1994-99; Daniel W Dietrich II dir, Inst Contemp Art, Philadelphia, 1999-2011; Helen Goldsmith Menschel dir, Jewish Mus, NY, 2011-. *Mailing Add:* Univ Pennsylvania Inst Contemporary Art 118 S 36th St Philadelphia PA 19104-3289

GOULD, KAREN
WRITER, HISTORIAN
b Austin, Tex, Sept 26, 1946. *Study:* Univ Tex, Austin, BS, 68, MA, 70, PhD, 75. *Teaching:* Vis asst prof art hist, Univ Ore, 80; Mellon Fel, Duke Univ, 80-81; lectr hist, Univ Tex, Austin, 81-89. *Mem:* Int Ctr Medieval Art (mem adv bd, 81-83); Southeastern Medieval Asn (mem exec coun, 81-83); Medieval Acad Am. *Res:* art and emotion. *Publ:* The Psalter and Hours of Yolande of Soissons, Medieval Acad, 78; Sequences De Sanctis Reliquiis as Sainte-Chapelle Inventories, Medieval Studies, 81; Terms for book production in a Latin-English nominale, Papers of the Bibliog Soc Am; The Recovery of a Fifteenth-Century Book of Hours, HRC 2, Scriptorium, 89; Jean Pucelle and Northern Gothic Art, Art Bull, 92

GOULD, PHILIP
CURATOR, COLLECTOR
b New York, NY, Oct 17, 1922. *Study:* NY Univ, BA, 49; L'Univ Paris, Dr Univ, 53. *Exhib:* Exhib African Ornaments, Donnell Libr Center, NY Public Libr, 2/2007. *Collection Arranged:* Traditional Anatolian Kilims (coauth, catalog), Sarah Lawrence Coll Art Gallery, 86; Artists from China - New Expressionism, Sarah Lawrence Coll Art Gallery, 87; The Art of Kuba Weaving (textiles from Zaire), Columbia Univ, 98; Africa's Iron and Copper Currency in the Rotunda, Low Mem Libr, Columbia Univ, 2000; Africa's Copper Currency, Uticia Coll, 2002; Exhib of African Ornaments, Donnell Libr Ctr, New York, 2007. *Pos:* Vis cur, Nat Mus Cath Art & Hist, New York, 2006; guest spkr, NY Historial Soc, 2013. *Teaching:* Instr art hist, Columbia Univ, 54-59, lectr, 56-62; prof, Sarah Lawrence Coll, 59-92, retired; vis prof, Fordham Univ, spring 68, Pratt Inst, fall 73 & Coll Chinese Cult, Taipei, Taiwan, 75-76; lectr, New York Coun Humanities, 95-, speaker, 2007-; lectr, NY Coun Humanities, 2010, 2012. *Awards:* Sapirstein lect, Cooper-Hewitt Mus, Smithsonian Inst, 87; UN Develop Prog, Sr Tech Adv, Beijing Teacher's Coll, China, 89; Elected Assoc Mem, Columbia Univ Sem: Traditional China, 92-95 & Africa, Pacific Asian & Latin Am Art, 99-2006. *Bibliog:* Nick Natanson (auth), The craft of teaching, Sarah Lawrence Coll Bull, spring 83. *Mem:* Soc Archit Historians; Am Soc Aesthet; AAM; ICOM; Textile Conserv Group; Textile Mus, Wash, DC. *Res:* Chinese art in general and comparative occidental and Oriental iconography in particular; Ancient & Modern African material cultures. *Publ:* Auth, Exhibition of Chinese Painting, Ming & Ch'ing (catalog), 73 & Exhibition of Chinese Folk & Provincial Ceramics (catalog), 76, Sarah Lawrence Coll; contribr, Acad Am Encyl, 80; auth, Jan van Eyck's Arnolfini Wedding Portrait: The mirror image, In: Iris, Notes Hist Art, Vol 2, 12/83; preface, In: Book of Paintings by Yu Chit-Fu; Rita Reif (auth), The Precious and Proverbal Art of African Money, Sunday, 3/12/2000; auth, an E-book of 50 short stories. A New Yorker's Stories, Boson Books, 2010; A Case for Identity, 2013. *Mailing Add:* 15 Claremont Ave New York NY 10027

GOULET, LORRIE
SCULPTOR, PAINTER
b Riverdale, NY, Aug 17, 1925. *Study:* Inwood Potteries Studios, NY, 32-36, with Amiee Voorhees; Black Mountain Col, drawing & painting with Josef Albers; sculpture with Jose de Creeft, 43-44. *Work:* Sarah Roby Found; Joseph H Hirshhorn Mus & Sculpture Garden, Washington, DC; NJ State Mus; Nat Mus Women in the Arts, DC; Ball State Univ Art Gallery; Asheville Art Mus, 2008. *Comn:* Ceramic relief, NY Pub Libr, Grand Concourse, Bronx, 58; ceramic relief, Nurses' Residence & Sch, Bronx Munic Hosp, 61; stainless steel relief, 48th Precinct Police & Fire Sta, Bronx, 71; portrait of King Juan Carlos, National Palace, Madrid, Spain, 2008. *Exhib:* Dimensions 69, Temple Emeth, NJ, 69; Outdoor Sculpture Show, Van Saun Park, NJ, 71; Solo exhibs, Contemporaries Gallery, NY, 59, 62, 66 & 68, Kennedy Galleries, NY, 71, 73-75, 78, 80 & 83-86 & Retrospective, Carolyn Hill Gallery, 88, 50 Yr Retrospective, Nat Mus Women Arts, Wash, DC, 98, David Findlay Jr Gallery, NY, 2004-2005, 2009, 2011, 60 Yrs of Sculpture, 2007, Harmon Meek Gallery, Naples, Fla, 2009; Black Mountain - Una Aventura Am, Museo Nat Centro DeAste Reina Sopha, Madrid, Spain, 2002; Group exhibs: Mus Nat Hist, 36, Whitney Mus Am Art, NY, 48-50, 53, 55, Metrop Mus Art, 51, Detroit Inst Art, 60, Pa Acad, 1950-52, 54, 59, 64, AD, NY, 66, 75, 77, Corcoran Gallery, Wash, 66, Summit Art Ctr, NJ, 78; Nat Arts Club, NY, 78, Hofstra Mus, NY, 90, McNey Mus, 90, Copley Soc, Boston, 91, Spanish Inst, 92, Lehigh Univ Art Gallery, 92, Iowa State Univ Brunne Gallery, 92, Paine Art Ctr, Oshkosh, Wis, 92, Mitchell Art Gallery, St John's Col, Annapolis, Md, 92, Erie (Pa) Art Mus, 95, Nat Sculpture Soc, 01, Art Students League, New York City, 2003; An Archicaval Materialto Smithsonian Am Art, 2010; An Archicaval Materialto Smithsonian Am Art, 2010; Public Coll, Childrens Mus Naples, Florence, 2011. *Collection Arranged:* Rep in permanent collections Hunter Mus, Chattanooga, NJ State Mus, Wichita Mus Art, Hirshhorn Sculpture Mus, Wash, The Philharmonic Center, Naples, Fla, Art Students League, NY, Savannah Coll Arts. *Pos:* Guest demonstr, Around the Corner, NY Dept Educ, CBS-TV, 64-65; pres, NY Artists Equity Inc, 97 & Fine Arts Fedn, NY, 97, 2011. *Teaching:* Instr sculpture-var media & staff mem, Mus Mod Art, NY, 57-64; sculpture staff mem, Scarsdale Studio Workshop, 59-61 & New Sch Social Res, 61-75; staff instr sculpture, Art Students League, NY, 81-2006. *Awards:* First Sculpture Prize, Norton Gallery, 49 & 50 & Westchester Art Soc, 64; Soltan Engel Mem Award, Audubon Artists, 67; The Malvina Hoffman Award, Nat Acad Design, 2001; Fleichman grant, 2009. *Bibliog:* Cole Thompson (interviewer), Goulet at Inwood Potteries, 2012. *Mem:* NY Artists Equity (pres, 98-2002); Fedn Fine Arts (pres, 98-2002, hon vpres 2003); founding mem Visual Artists & Galleries Asn; Nat Acad (acad 89, mem coun 94); Art Bank (trustee). *Media:* Stone, Wood; Acrylic. *Specialty:* Modern Artists. *Publ:* Contribr, 20th century sculptors look at their work, The Palette; auth article on greenstone, In: Slate & Soft Stones, 71. *Dealer:* Harmon-Meek Gallery Naples Fla; David Findley Jr Gallery, New York City NY

GOUREVITCH, JACQUELINE
PAINTER
b Paris, Oct 28, 1933; US citizen. *Study:* Black Mountain Col, NC, 50; Art Students League, 52; Univ Chicago, BA, 54; Art Inst Chicago, 54-55. *Work:* Wadsworth Atheneum, Hartford, Conn; The Menil Collectin, Houston, Tex; De Cordova Mus, Lincoln, Mass; Univ Art Mus, Berkeley, Calif; Charles A Wustum Mus, Racine, Wis; Univ NMex, Albuquerque; Wesleyan Univ, Middletown, Conn; Yale Univ Art Gallery, New Haven, Conn; Mus City New York; Morgan Lib and Mus, NY; Ashville Mus Art, NC; Vassar Coll Mus, Poughkeepsie, NY; Nat Acad Mus, NY. *Comn:* Conn Comn Arts, Western Conn State Univ, Danbury, 83. *Exhib:* Solo exhibs, Tibor de Nagy Gallery, NY, 71, 72 & 73, Wesleyan Univ, Conn, 74, 77 & 83, Wadsworth Atheneum, Matrix Gallery Hartford, Conn, 75, Condeso-Lawler Gallery, NY, 80, 82 & 84, Aerial Notations, New Brit Mus Am Art, Conn, 93, Paesaggio Gallery, Conn, 93, 96 & 99 & DFN Gallery, NY, 2000, 2002, Mary Ryan Gallery, 2005, William Siegal (with catalog), Santa Fe, NMex, 2008; group exhibs, De Cordova Mus, Lincoln, Mass, 71 & 78; Painting & Sculpture Today, Indianapolis Mus Art, 72; Whitney Mus Art Ann, 73; Acad Arts & Letts, 73, 94 & 2004; Maxwell Davidson, NY, 90; Paesaggio Gallery, Conn, 93, 96 & 99; Nat Acad of Design, New York, 2002, 06; NY Studio Sch, 2002; Pierogi, NY, 97-2004; 181st Ann: An Invitational Exhib Contemp Art, Nat Acad Mus, NY City, 2006. *Teaching:* Wesleyan Univ, 67-71 & 78-88; Hartford Art Sch, Univ Hartford, 73-78; Univ Calif, Berkeley, 74, Vassar Col, 77, Univ Houston, 78 & Yale Univ, 82; Cooper Union, 89-92; Mt Holyoke Col, 95. *Awards:* Purchase Award, Am Acad Arts & Letts, New York, 73; grants, Nat Endowment Arts, 76 & Conn Comn Arts, 76; Richard Florsheim Art Fund, 95; Obrig Watercolor, Nat Acad of Design, 2002; Acad award, American Acad of Art & Letters, NY, 2004. *Bibliog:* Annie Dillard & Deborah Frizzell (auths), catalogue, New Britain Mus Am Art, Conn, 94; Jude Schwendenwein (auth), article, Hartford Courant, 6/9/96; Patricia Rosoff (auth), article, Hartford Advocate, 6/13/96; Ken Johnson (auth), NY Times, 4/28/2000. *Mem:* Nat Acad Mus and Sch, NY. *Media:* Oil, Watercolor. *Publ:* Auth, article, Art Now: New York, fall 71. *Dealer:* DFN Gallery 74 E 79th St New York NY 10075. *Mailing Add:* 120 Duane St Apt 6 New York NY 10007-1113

GOVAN, MICHAEL
MUSEUM DIRECTOR
Study: Williams Coll, BA (art hist); studied at Univ San Diego; studied Renaissance art in Italy. *Collection Arranged:* Cur, Picasso and Rembrandt, Williams Coll Mus Art, 86; co-cur, Dan Flavin: A Retrospective. *Pos:* Acting cur, Williams Coll Mus Art; dep dir, Solomon R Guggenheim Mus, 88-94; dir, Dia Art Found, 94-2006, instrumental in establishment of Dia: Beacon, 2003; CEO & Wallis Annenburg dir, Los Angeles County Mus Art, 2006-. *Publ:* The Great Utopia: The Russian and Soviet Avant-Garde, 1915-1932. *Mailing Add:* LA County Museum of Art 5909 Wilshire Blvd Los Angeles CA 90036

GOVER, KEVIN
MUSEUM DIRECTOR
b Lawton, Okla, Feb, 16, 1955. *Study:* Princeton Univ, AB, 78; Univ NMex, JD cum laude, 81. *Hon Degrees:* Princeton Univ, LLD, 2001. *Pos:* judicial clerk, US District Court, Albuquerque, 81-83; assoc atty, Fried, Frank, Harris, Shriver, & Kampelman, Washington, 83-86; partner, Gover, Stetson, & Williams, PC, Albuquerque, 86-87, Steptoe & Johnson, LLP, Wash, 2001-2002, counsel; asst secy Indian affairs US Dept Interior, Wash, 97-2000; dir, Nat Mus Am Indian, 2007-; Bd dirs Southwestern Asn Indian Art, 1995-97, co-exec dir, Am Indian Policy Inst Ariz State U, assoc judge Tonto Apache Tribal Ct Appeals, Payson, Ariz, 2005-07, San Carlos Apache Tribal Ct Appeals, Ariz, 2005-07. *Teaching:* prof Indian law, Sandra Day O'Connor Coll Law, Ariz State Univ, Tempe, 2003-2007. *Mem:* ABA (chmn comn on Native Am natural resources law 89-90, v chmn comn on Native Am Rights 2002); FBA; DC Bar Asn. *Interests:* gardening, history. *Mailing Add:* National Museum of the American Indian 4th St and Independence Ave SW Washington DC 20560

GOWDY, MARJORIE E
MUSEUM DIRECTOR
Study: Univ NC, Greensboro, Masters (Lib Scis). *Pos:* Exec dir, Ohr-O'Keefe Mus Art, Biloxi, Miss, 1992-. *Mem:* Rotary Club

GOWIN, ELIJAH
PHOTOGRAPHER
b Dayton, Ohio, 1967. *Study:* Davidson Coll, BA Art History, 1990; Univ New Mexico, MFA, 1996. *Work:* Corcoran Gallery Art, Washington; Princeton Univ Mus Art, NJ. *Exhib:* Solo exhibs include Silver Eye Ctr Photog, Pittsburgh, PA, 2000, Robert Mann Gallery, New York, 2001, 2007, Dolphin Gallery, Kansas City, 2001, Houston Ctr Photog, Tex, 2001, Light Factory, Charlotte, NC, 2001, Photo Gallery Int, Tokyo, 2004, Vermont Ctr Photog, Brattleboro, Vt, 2006, Contemp Art Ctr Virginia, Virginia Beach, 2006, Ellen Curlee Gallery, St Louis, Mo, 2006, Page Bond Gallery, Richmond, Va, 2006; group exhibs include Backyards, Robert Mann Gallery, New York, 1997; Common Ground, Corcoran Mus Art, Washington, 2004; Photog Now & Next 30 Years, Photog Resources Ctr, Boston Univ, 2006; Duscubrimientos, Mus Municipal Arte Contemp, Madrid, 2007; Act of Faith, Noorderlicht Photogallery, Groningen, Holland, 2007. *Teaching:* Asst Prof Photog Studies, Univ Missouri-Kansas City, 2002. *Awards:* Fel, Silver Eye Ctr Photog, Pittsburgh, 2000; John Simon Guggenheim Mem Found Fel, 2008. *Dealer:* Dolphin Gallery 1600 Liberty Kansas City MO 64102. *Mailing Add:* Robert Mann Gallery 210 11th Ave New York NY 10001

GRABARSKY, SHEILA
PAINTER
b Brooklyn, NY. *Study:* NJ Ctr Visual Arts, with Philip Sherrod, spec accreditation; Syracuse Univ; Shrewsbury Art Guild, with Georgette Pettit. *Work:* Cooper Cancer Care Hosp, Camden, NJ. *Comn:* numerous pvt collections. *Exhib:* Solo Exhibs: Monmouth Univ, West Long Branch, NJ, 94; Johnson & Johnson, New Brunswick, NJ, 2002; Atlantic City Art Ctr, NJ, 2007, Jersey Arts.com, 2009, Park Ave Club, Florham Park, NJ, 2010; Imaging/Aging, Bucknell Univ, 92; Ellarslie Open XI, Trenton Mus, NJ, 92; Painting Today, Fairleigh Dickinson Univ, 91; Selected Juried Exhibs: Flim Flam & Fins, Clymer Mus, Ellensburg, WVa, 96; Masur Mus, Monroe, La, 2002; Noyes Mus, Oceanville, NJ, 2007; Int Society Acrylic Painters, 2008; George Segal Gallery, Montclair Univ, 2009; Abstract Expressions Gallery, Mt Holly, NJ, 2008, 2009; Ellarslie Open, Trenton Mus, 2010; Monmouth Co Arts Co, 2010; Period Gallery, Omaha, Neb, 2010; Fredericksburg Ctr Creative Arts, Fredericksburg, Va, 2010; Governors State Univ, Illinois, 2011; Farmington Mus, Farmington, NMex, 2011; Aljra Gallery, Newark, NJ, 2011; Caladan Gallery, 2011; Cape Fear Studios, Fayetteville, NC, 2011; 3rd St Gallery, Phila, Pa, 2012; Noyes Mus, Oceanville, NJ, 2012, 2013; Monmouth Mus, 2013. *Awards:* Best in Show, 36th Regional Juried, Hudson Artists, 89; Hon Mention, Bergen Mus Arts & Sci, 89; Award of Merit, Int Cover Art Competition, Manhattan Arts, 95; Best in Show, N Calif Arts Int Juried Show, 2000; Best Art, Tulane Univ Literary Review, 2000; Townsend Award, Art Alliance, Red Bank, NJ, 2002; Merion Award, 3rd St Gallery, Philadelphia, 2002; Daler-Rowney Award, Int Society Acrylic Painters, 11th Int Exhib, 2008; First Place Award, Park Ave Club, Florham Park, NJ, 2008; 14th Int Soc Acrylic Painters, 2011; Richardson Award, 2011; 12th Ann Abstraction Online Exhib; Special Recognition award, Upstream People Gallery, 2013. *Bibliog:* Numerous reviews, Artspeak, 90; Renee Philips (auth), Artists of the 90s, Manhattan Arts, 91; Paul Haupt (auth), Breathing Life Into Canvas, The Herald, 93; Abstract Artist Takes the Inside Track to Discovery, Sandpaper, 18, 10/2006; Julie Basello-Holt (auth), Color Your World, Fusion Mag, 2006; Ellarslie Open XXVIII Calendar, Trenton Mus Soc, NJ, 6/2011. *Mem:* Nat Asn Women Artists; Soc Experimental Artists; NY Artists Equity Asn; Org Independent Artists; Nat Women's Caucus for Art; Shrewsbury Art Guild; Art Alliance; Ocean Co Artists Guild; Sig mem, Noyes Mus Art, Oceanville, NJ; Sig mem, Int Society Acrylic Painters; Catherine Lorillard Wolfe Art Club, New York; Nat Soc Painters in Acrylic & Casein; Manhattan Arts Int, NY (featured mem). *Media:* Acrylic, Mixed media. *Specialty:* Contemp organic, abstraction. *Interests:* Music, reading, the ocean, yoga, cycling. *Publ:* Life's Tango, CD cover, Rae Perrigo, Toronto, 2000; Tulane Univ Ann Literary Rev, Vol XII, New Orleans, 2000; background art for video: Impact of Disaster on Children in our Schools: A Program for School Nurses, Rutgers Univ, Johnson & Johnson Pharmaceutical, 2002; Eyes on: Abstracts, edited by Joe Guimera, Blaze Hill Press, 2012. *Dealer:* MT Burton Gallery Surf City NJ; Soma Gallery Cape May NJ; Boxheart Gallery Pittsburgh Pa; 3rd St Gallery Philadelphia Pa; Noyes Mus Gift Shop Hammonton NJ

GRABEL, SUSAN
SCULPTOR, PRINTMAKER
b Brooklyn, NY, June 5, 1942. *Study:* Brooklyn Mus Art Sch, with Joseph Konzal & Tom Doyle, 61-65; Brooklyn Coll, New York, BA, 63. *Work:* Staten Island Mus; Rowan Univ Art Gallery. *Comn:* Ceramic mural, Staten Island Children's Mus, 91; Regarding Women, (installation), A Public Work of Art, Ctr Women's Health, Staten Island, New York. *Exhib:* Solo exhibs, Venus, Wagner Coll Gallery, Staten Island, New York, 2001, Venus Emerging, SoHo 20, Chelsea, 2006, Constructions of Conscience: The Social Art of Susan Grabel, Staten Island Mus, Staten Island, 2012, Venus Comes of Age, Ceres Gallery, NY 2013, Faces of Alienation, Georgia Coll Mus, Milledgeville, Ga, 2014; Group exhibs, In Three Dimensions: Women Sculptors of the '90s, Newhouse Ctr Contemp Art, Staten Island, New York, 95; Nude Int 2005; Lexington Art League, Lexington, Ky, 2005; Fabulous Fiber, Monmouth Mus, Monmouth, NJ, 2008; Chautauqua, a Continuim of Creativity, Denis Bibro Gallery, New York, 2010; 100 Years of Women Rockin the World, Artrage Gallery, Syracuse, NY, 2011. *Teaching:* Instr, art hist survey, Wagner Coll, 2002-03; life modelling, Chautauqua Sch Art, 2001-2009. *Awards:* NY Sculpture Artists Grant, Snug Harbor Cult Arts, 96; Encore Grant, Coun Arts & Humanities for Staten Island, 2000; Original Works Grant, Coun Arts & Humanities for Staten Island, 2004; Jentel Artists Residency Fel, Banner, Wyo, 2007. *Bibliog:* William Zimmer (auth), Mansion and former factory offer varied views of women, NY Times, 90; Vivien Raynor (auth), Color relationships in Valhalla, Family ties in Krasdale, NY Times, 93; Michael J. Fressola (auth), Staten Island Advance, 2012; How Many Wrongs Make a Right? 2012. *Mem:* Women's Caucus Art (pres, NY chap, 92-95); New York Artist Circle; Ceres Gallery. *Media:* Cast Paper, Ceramics; Collagraph, Monoprints. *Publ:* Art as Activism issue, Woman of Power Mag, spring/87. *Dealer:* Ceres Gallery 547 W 27th St New York NY 10001. *Mailing Add:* 257 Oakland Ave Staten Island NY 10310

GRABER, STEVEN BRIAN
GRAPHIC ARTIST, PAINTER
b Newton, Kans, Nov 14, 1950. *Study:* Univ Redlands, BA, 72. *Work:* Butler Inst Am Art, Younstown, Ohio; State Ala Capitol Bldg, Montgomery, Ala; S Bend Regional Art Mus, Ind; Fine Arts Mus S, Mobile, Ala; Disney World, Orlando, Fla; Spencer Art Mus, Univ Kans, Lawrence; Wichita Art Mus, Kans. *Exhib:* Getting Real, S Bend Regional Mus, Ind, 96; Landscape Exhib, Riverside Art Mus, Calif, 96; solo exhib, Butler Inst Am Art, Youngstown, Ohio, 99; Arnot Art Mus, Elmyra, NY, 99; The Am River, Great River Arts Inst, Walpole, New Hampshire, 2002; Celebrating 25 Yrs of Art, Spencer Mus Art, Lawrence, Kans, 2003; solo exhib, Wichita Art Mus, Kans, 2006. *Bibliog:* Bill Machomer (auth), In the galleries, Art Talk Mag, 1/98; Kristin Bucher (auth), Best of the west, Southwest Art, 2/98; Stephen Doherty (auth), Steven Graber, Am Artist Mag, 1/99; Joseph C Skrapits (auth), Realists & Romantics, Am Artist Magazine, 5/2000; Gussie Fauntleroy (auth), Mysteries & Possibilities, Southwest Art Mag, 5/2001; New Am Paintings, Juried Exhib in Print Number 36, The Open Studios Press, 11/2001. *Media:* Charcoal. *Publ:* Int Artists Mag, fall/2000; Art Review, The NY Times, 10/2003; Am Art Collector Mag, 10/2005. *Dealer:* M B Modern 41 E 57th 8th Flr New York NY 10022; Bryant Galleries 316 Royal St New Orleans LA; David Findlay Jr Fine Arts 41 E 57th St New York NY 10022; and others. *Mailing Add:* 938 E 1700 Rd Baldwin City KS 66006

GRABILL, VIN (E VINCENT, JR)
VIDEO ARTIST, ENVIRONMENTAL ARTIST, EDUCATOR
b Boston, Mass, Apr 4, 1949. *Study:* Oberlin Col, BA (studio art), 71; Mass Inst Technol, Ctr Advanced Visual Studies, SM (visual studies; Mass Artists Found Fel & St Botolph's Grant), 81. *Work:* De Cordova Mus (paintings), Lincoln, Mass; Kunsthaus (videotape), Zurich, Switz; and others. *Comn:* Mural painting, State St Bank, Quincy, Mass, 73; mural painting, Houghton Chemical Co, Cambridge, Mass, 74; Vermont Story (videotape), WGBH-TV, Boston, Mass, 81; and others. *Exhib:* Sculpture in the Park, De Cordova Mus, 73; Video Nu, Stockholm Mus Art, Sweden, 81; Centervideo, Kunsthaus, Zurich, Switz, 81 & Kolnischer Kunstverein, Cologne, Ger, 81; Boston Now, Inst Contemp Art, Boston, 83; San Paolo Biennale, Brazil, 83; and others. *Pos:* Chief designer, Akko Inc, Lawrence, Mass, 74-79; fel, Ctr Advanced Visual Studies, Mass Inst Technol, 81-83. *Teaching:* instr visual art, Mass Coll Art & Design, 84-88; joined faculty Univ Md Baltimore Co, 84, assoc chair, formerly, interim chair, 98-2000, imaging & visual art MFA grad program dir, 2001-2007, assoc prof film & video, chair dept visual arts, currently. *Awards:* New Stagings/Video Performance Grant, Coun Arts, Mass Inst Technol, 81. *Bibliog:* Florence Gilbard (auth), Interactive cable, In: Visions, Boston Film/Video Found, 81. *Media:* Video. *Publ:* Ed, Centervideo, 81 & Centerdisk/Skydisk (electronic videodisk catalog), 83, Ctr Advanced Visual Studies, Mass Inst Technol; ed, Communicodes, d'Video Reality, 81. *Mailing Add:* University of Md Baltimore County 1000 Hilltop Cir Baltimore MD 21250

GRABSKI, JOANNA
EDUCATOR
Study: Indiana Univ, MA & PhD (art hist & African studies). *Teaching:* Assoc prof art hist, Denison Univ. *Awards:* Fulbright-Hays Res Abroad Fel, US Dept Educ, 1998 & 2009; Art J award, Coll Art Asn, 2010. *Publ:* Contribr, African Arts, Art J, NKA, Fashion Theory & Africa Today; auth, Urban Claims and Visual Sources in the Making of Dakar's Art World City, Art World J, 2009. *Mailing Add:* Denison Univ Art History Program 510 Cleveland Hall Granville OH 43023

GRACHOS, LOUIS
GALLERY DIRECTOR
b Toronto. *Study:* Univ Toronto, BA (art hist); John F Kennedy Univ, San Francisco, Cert Mus Studies. *Pos:* Curatorial intern, Whitney Mus Am Art, New York, 82; asst dir, Ctr Fine Arts, Miami, formerly, interim dir, formerly; cur, Mus Contemp Art, San Diego, 94-96; dir & cur, SITE Santa Fe, 96-2003; dir, SITE Santa Fe Int Biennial, 97, 99 & 2001; dir, Albright-Knox Art Gallery, Buffalo, 2003-2013; exec dir, AMOA-Arthouse, Austin, Tex, 2012-. *Mailing Add:* Albright-Knox Art Gallery 1285 Elmwood Ave Buffalo NY 14222-1096

GRADE, JOHN
INSTALLATION SCULPTOR
Study: Pratt Inst, BFA, 1992. *Comn:* installation, City of Seattle/SPU, Bitterlake Reservoir, Seattle, 2009. *Exhib:* Solo exhibs, Davidson Galleries, Seattle, 2000, 2002-07 & 2009, Laura Russo Gallery, Portland, Ore, 2000, Boise Art Mus, 2004, Seattle Art Gallery, 2007, Suyama Space, Seattle, 2008, Bellevue Arts Mus, 2008, Whatcom Mus, 2009, Univ Wyo Gallery, 2009, Fabrica, Brighton, United Kingdom, 2009, Cynthia-Reeves Gallery, New York, 2010, Davidson, Seattle, 2010; Davidson Galleries, Seattle, 1999-2002 & 2004-07; Bellevue Art Mus, 1999, 2000 & 2009; Bumbershoot Visual Arts Exhib, Seattle Ctr, 1999, 2002 & 2005; Boise Art Mus, 2000 & 2009; Laura Russo Gallery, Portland, 2000; Pratt Manhattan Gallery, New York, 2002; San Francisco Int Art Exhib, 2003-05; John Michael Kohler Arts Ctr, 2003, 2004 & 2006; Aqua Art, Miami, 2005 & 2006; SPUR Projects, Portola Valley, Calif, 2006; Whatcom Mus, 2009; Ballenglen Art Ctr, Ballina, County Mayo, Ireland, 2009; Am Acad Arts & Letts Invitational, New York, 2010. *Awards:* Wilard L Metcalf Award in Art, Am Acad Ars & Letts, 2010. *Mailing Add:* c/o Davidson Galleries 313 Occidental Ave South Seattle WA 98104

GRADO, ANGELO JOHN
PAINTER, INSTRUCTOR
b New York, NY, Feb 17, 1922. *Study:* Art Students League, with Robert Brackman; Nat Acad Design, with Robert Philipp & Frank Reilly. *Exhib:* Am Watercolor Soc Exhibs, 58-71; Allied Artists Am Exhibs, 61-78; Nat Acad Design, NY, 63; Am Artists Prof League, NY, 63-2005; Hudson Valley Art Asn, 69-88, 99-2006; Pastel Soc Am; 14 solo exhibs. *Teaching:* Pvt classes, Nat Art League & von Liebig Art Ctr, Naples, Fla. *Awards:* Salmagundi Club Prize, 69; Eighteen Am Artists Prof League Awards, 69-81 & 83-2004; Hudson Valley Art Asn Awards, 69, 70, 72 & 84-95; 78 Nat Awards. *Bibliog:* Billi Boros (auth), New talent, Art Times Mag, 64; Int Artist Magazine, 2004, Pastelagram Magazine, 2006. *Mem:* Am Watercolor Soc; Am Artists Prof League (pres emer, 89-); Hudson Valley Art Asn; Pastel Soc Am; Fine Arts Fedn New York. *Media:* Oil, Pastel. *Collection:* National Academy Design, New York. *Publ:* Auth, Mastering the Craft of Painting, Watson-Guptill Publ; Int Artist Mag, 10/2004-11/2004. *Dealer:* Harbor Gallery 24 W 57th St New York NY 10019; Alterman Art Gallery 2504 Cedar Springs Dallas TX 75201. *Mailing Add:* 641 46th St Brooklyn NY 11220

GRADUS, ARI
PAINTER, PRINTMAKER
b Karkur, Israel, Oct 26, 1943; US citizen. *Study:* New York Univ, 66-70; Art Students League, New York, 71-73. *Work:* Mus Lower East Side, NY; Jerusalem City Hall, Mayor's Off, Israel. *Comn:* Mural, Temple Anshe Emmeth, New Brunswick, NJ, 86; mural, NCZ Corp, NY, 88. *Exhib:* Solo exhibs, Patricia Judith Gallery, Boca Raton, Fla, 84, Sansiano Gallery, Tokyo, 85, Goldman Gallery, Rockville, Md, 88, Short Hills Community Gallery, NJ, 89, Shainberg Mus, Memphis, 90 & Gallery 2000, Coral Springs, Fla, 92 & 93; Images, Israeli-Am Ctr, Tel Aviv, 86; 20th Century Artists, Brownstone Gallery, NY, 94; Bergen Co YMHA, NJ, 99; Art Warehouse Gallery, Boca Raton, Fla, 2000; Landscapes for Landsake, Cambridge, NY, 2011. *Awards:* Award of Excellence, City of Boca Raton, Fla, 93; Best in Show Award, City of Highland Park, Ill, 98; First Place Award, Washington Square Art Exhib, New York, 98; Best in Show, Summer Art Fair, Ann Arbor, Mich, 2008 & 09; Merit Award, Skokie, Ill, 2008. *Bibliog:* Ari Gradus - Artist, Miami Herald, 4/92; A Place Called Yesterday, Channel 2 TV, Israel, 95; Artist in the News, PBS Radio, Wickeford, RI. *Mem:* Mich Art Guild. *Media:* Acrylic; Serigraphs. *Mailing Add:* 423 6th St Brooklyn NY 11215

GRADY, RUBY MCLAIN
PAINTER, SCULPTOR
b Bedford Co, Va, Jan 11, 1944. *Study:* Corcoran Sch Art, Washington, DC, with Richard Lahey; Md Univ, with Pietro Lazzari. *Work:* Am Fine Art Exhibs, Washington, DC; NASA Gemini Collection, Washington, DC; Imprimerie Arte Galerie Maeght, Paris, France; West Collection, St Paul, Minn. *Comn:* Corrections (painting, cover textbk), West Publ Co, Minn, 97. *Exhib:* Va Mus Art, Richmond; Washington Sq Sculpture Exhib, Pub Art Trust, Washington, DC, 84; solo exhibs, Jack Rasmussen Gallery, DC, 79, Roanoke Fine Art Mus, Va, 80 & VVKR Atrium, Int Architect Firm, Alexandria, Va, 84; Chrysler Mus Biennial, 86; West Art and the Law (travel exhib), USA & Can, 88-89; Shared Visions, IBM Gallery Sci & Art, NY, 90; Art in Pub Places Sculpture, Rockville, Md, 92 & 97; Kennedy Galleries, NY, 93; Nat Travel Show, Paine Webber Gallery, NY, 93; Am Art Group Exhib, Minn Mus Am Art, 94; Creative Will Show, Grey Gallery, NY, 95; Art in Pub Places Sculpture Exhib, Rockville, Md, 97. *Pos:* Art illusr, FBI, Washington, DC, 56-59; exhib coord for 3 Washington, DC restaurants, 61-73. *Awards:* Annapolis Fine Arts Exhib Award for Metal Sculpture, 74; Washington Artist Photog Exhib, Corcoran Gallery, Washington, DC, 77; Two Purchase Awards, West Collection, St Paul, Minn, 82-87. *Bibliog:* Frank Getlein (introd), Ruby Grady, booklet, Brooks Johnson, 72; Allen Smith (dir), Solo Exhibit in Washington (film), WTTG-TV, 72; article, Am Bar Asn J, Chicago, 82; Thomas W Sakolowaki (auth), The Creative Will Book (4 pages), travel show, NY, 96. *Media:* Steel, Acrylic. *Publ:* Contribr, Nat Community Arts Prog Publ, Govt Printing Off, 70, & Art and the Law National Exhibition Book, West Publ, 82, 83 & 86; The West Collection (Coffee Table Bk), West Publ Co, St Paul, Minn, 87; Photograph, Senses, inside cover mag, NY, 94; Artist Calendar, Pomegranate Publ, Calif, 97. *Mailing Add:* Potowmack Bay Studio 431 Broadcreek Dr Fort Washington MD 20744

GRAESE, JUDY (JUDITH) ANN
PAINTER, ILLUSTRATOR
b Loveland, Colo, Nov 8, 1940. *Study:* Augustana Col, 58-59; Univ Colo, Boulder, 65-67. *Work:* Nat City Bank, Denver, Colo; Rose Medical Ctr, Denver, Colo; Kent-Denver Day Sch, Colo; Enid Libr, Okla. *Comn:* Ink on stone, comn for Murray Louis, 78 & woodetching, comn for Hanya Holm, 81, by Colo Contemp Dance; ink on stone, Kent-Denver Country Day Sch, Colo, 83; watercolor, Estes Park Music Festival, 85, Children's Hospital, Denver, 89, 90. *Exhib:* Solo exhibs, Two-Twenty Two Gallery, El Paso, Tex, 71-73, Artisan, Princeton, NJ, 72 & 74 & Bishop's Antiques & Gallery, Scottsdale, Ariz, 73-96, pvt studio exhib, 93-2002, 2004, 2009, 2012; Adobe Patio, Mesilla, NMex, 85; Beeches' Gallery, Carmel, Calif, 88, 91; Savageau Gallery, Denver, 89, 90 & 91; Colo Contemp Dance, 92; Kent Denver Alumni Exhib, 95-2003. *Pos:* Designer, display dept, May D&F, 67-69; costume designer, Denver Metrop State Coll, 2004-2010, design & construction of puppets, 2007; dir costuming, Kent Denver Sch, 2006-, artist-in-residence, 2007-. *Teaching:* Instr contemp dance, Kent-Denver Sch, Colo, 68-87 & 92-95, visual & performing arts, 88-2006, costume designer, 89-. *Awards:* The Richard A Drew award for Outstanding Teaching, 1999. *Bibliog:* Robert Downing (auth), Ad Lib, Denver Post Roundup Sect, 2/2/75; Betty Harvey (auth), Judy Graese, Artists of the Rockies, 5/75; Marie Torrisi (auth), Colo Monthly Mag, 85; Susan Dugan (auth), Washington Park Profile, 4/2005. *Mem:* Carson-Brierly Dance Libr; Colo Button Club; Denver Art Mus; Denver Art Mus. *Media:* Watercolor; Wood; Bronze; Stone; Etchings; Silk Screen; Papier Mache. *Interests:* Vintage & antique garments and accessories. *Publ:* Illusr, The Song of Francis, Northland Press, 73; The Treasure is the Rose, Pantheon Press, 73; Art prints, Woodhill Press, 83, Colo Music Festival, 85, Children's Hosp, 89 & 90, Mermaids, Laughing Elephant Bks, 98; illusr, Taming the Dragon, Crown Peak Pub, 2012. *Mailing Add:* 2055 S Franklin Denver CO 80210

GRAFF, FREDERICK C
PAINTER, INSTRUCTOR
b Lodi, OH, Oct 15, 1945. *Study:* Miami Univ, BS, 1968; Pvt instr with Franklin A Bates, 1962-72. *Work:* Zanesville Art Mus, OH; North Canton Libr, OH; Medina Co Court House, OH; Governor's Mansion, Columbus, OH. *Exhib:* Am Watercolor Soc (juried), Galleries of Salmagundi Club, New York City, 1977; Midwest Watercolor Soc (juried), Tweed Mus of Art, Duluth, Minn, 1977; Nat Watercolor Soc (juried), Brand Libr Art Galleries, Glendale, Calif, 1978; retrospective, Zanesville Art Mus, OH, 1995; Nat Watermedia (juried), Canton Mus Art, OH, 2001; Transparent Watercolor Soc of Am (juried), Elmhurst Art Mus, Ill, 2004. *Teaching:* instr art, Berea City Schools, OH, 1968-2001; watercolor workshop instr, 1972-. *Awards:* Emily Goldsmith, Am Watercolor Soc, 1989; Winsor Newton, Midwest Watercolor Soc, 2000; Millard Sheets Mem Medal, Am Watercolor Soc, 2006. *Bibliog:* Marilyn Hughey Phillis (auth), Watermedia Technique for Releasing the Creative Spirit, Watson-Guptill, 1992; Int Artist Editors (auth) International Showcase of Prize Winners, Int Artist Mag, 2/2005 & 3/2005; Mark Mehaffey (auth) Creative Watercolor Workshop, North Light Books, 2005. *Mem:* Am Watercolor Soc; Nat Watercolor Soc; Transparent Watercolor Soc of Am; Ohio Watercolor Soc (treas 1978-80); Whiskey Painters of Am. *Media:* Watercolor. *Mailing Add:* 403 E Liberty St Medina OH 44256

GRAFF, LAURENCE
COLLECTOR
b London, 1938. *Pos:* Founder & chmn, Graff Diamonds Int, London & New York, 1960-. *Awards:* Named one of Top 200 Collectors, ARTnews mag, 2003-13; named one of World's Richest People, Forbes mag. *Mem:* Guggenhiem Mus (int dirs coun exec comt); Tate Mus. *Collection:* Modern and contemporary art. *Mailing Add:* Graff UK 28 Albemarle St London United Kingdom W1S 4JA

GRAFTON, RICK (FREDERICK) WELLINGTON
PAINTER
b Middletown, Conn, May 3, 1952. *Study:* Calif Coll Arts & Crafts, BFA (high distinction), 76. *Work:* Metrop Mus Art, Chase Manhattan Bank, NY; Art Inst Chicago; Arco Ctr Visual Art, Los Angeles; Bank Am, San Francisco, Calif. *Comn:* Meridian Building (watercolor), comn by J Lee, San Francisco, 83. *Exhib:* Solo exhib, Grapestake Gallery, San Francisco, 80 & 83, Galleria del Cavallino, Venice, Italy, 81 & San Jose Mus Art, 82; Light & Heavy Light, Mem Union Art Gallery, Univ Calif, Davis, 85; Discreet Power: Reductive Issues in Contemp Painting, Rockford Art Mus, Rockford, Ill, 88; Waterworks, Sierra Nevada Mus Art, Reno, Nev, 88; Almost Alchemy, Transamerica Pyramid Gallery, San Francisco, Calif, 96; Hidden Treasurers, Sonoma State Univ, Calif, 98. *Teaching:* Instr watercolor, Asn Students Univ Calif, Berkeley. *Awards:* Watercolor Award, Calif State Expo, 78. *Mem:* Emeryville Artists Coop. *Media:* Watercolor on Paper, Acrylic and Oil on Canvas and Panel. *Mailing Add:* 1420 45 St #30 Emeryville CA 94608

GRAHAM, BOB
PAINTER, MURALIST
b Canton, Tex, Jan 1, 1947. *Study:* N Tex State Univ, 66-69; Cape Sch, with Henry Hensche, 71-82. *Work:* New Orleans Mus Art, La. *Comn:* Portrait Alton Oschner, Oschner Found, New Orleans, La, 85; portrait Frank Barker, Nichols State Univ, Thibodaux, La, 86; Life of Moses (mural) Jerry Katz & Jewish Community Ctr, New Orleans, 87; portraits First Parrish Judges (4) Jefferson Parrish, Metairie, La, 90; History of Kenner (mural) Kenner, La City Coun, 91. *Exhib:* Kansas Pastel Society, Wichita, 85; Seldom Seen Figures, New Orleans Hist Soc, 88; Allied Artist, Nation Arts Club, NY, 89; Texas & Neighbors, Irving, 89; Am Realism Competition, Parkersburg Art Ctr, WVa, 90. *Awards:* Best of Show, Salmagundi Open, New York, 87; Best Painting in Any Medium, Am Artist Prof League, New York, 88; Best Printing in Any Medium, Knickerbocker Artists, New York, 90. *Bibliog:* Satoru Fugii (auth), Outstanding American Illustrators- Graphic-Sha Japan, 84; Stephen Doherty (auth) Southern Plantation, Am Artist, 1/89. *Mem:* Master pastellist, Pastel Soc Am; founder Degas Pastel Soc. *Media:* Oil, Pastel

GRAHAM, K M
PAINTER, PRINTMAKER
b Hamilton, Ont, Sept 13, 1913. *Study:* Univ Toronto, BA. *Hon Degrees:* Trinity Col, Toronto, hon fel. *Work:* Art Gallery Ont; Art Bank Can, Ottawa; Edmonton Art Gallery, Alta; MacDonald Stewart Centre, Guelph, Ont; J Barnike Gallery Hart House, Toronto, Ont; Nat Gallery, Can; Art Gallery of Hamilton, Ont; plus others. *Exhib:* Art Gallery of Ont, Toronto, 74; Montreal Mus of Fine Arts, Que, 76; Edmonton Art Gallery, Alta, 77; Galerie Wentzel, Hamburg, WGer, 77; Canada House, London; Cult Ctr, Paris; Am Artists Assoc, NY; David Mirvish Gallery, Toronto; Klonaridis Inc, Toronto; Mem Art Gallery, St Johns Nfld, Beaverbrook, NB; Art Gallery Fredericton, NB; and others. *Awards:* Can Coun Travel Award, 73-74 & 79; Hon Fel, Trinity Col, Univ Toronto, 88. *Bibliog:* Karen Wilkin (auth), The late blooming vitality of Toronto Art, Artnews, 2/80; Ingrid Jenkner, KM Graham 1970-85 (catalogue), Macdonald Stewart Art Ctr, Guelph, Ont; Lora Carney (auth), Brick #39: The Art of KM Graham, 90; Patricia Grattan (auth), KM Graham Eternities of Space (catalog), 94. *Mem:* Royal Can Acad of Arts; Arts & Letters Club, Toronto. *Media:* Acrylic, Canvas; Dry Points, Lithographs. *Specialty:* Canadian art. *Interests:* Painting and drawing. *Dealer:* Douglas Udell Gallery of Edmonton Alberta Vancouver BC Canada; Feheley Fine Arts 14 Hazelton Ave Toronto ON M5R 2E2 Canada; Moore Gallery Toronto 80 Spadima Ave Suite 404 Toronto ON M5V2J3 Canada. *Mailing Add:* 26 Boswell Ave Toronto ON M5R 1M4 Canada

GRAHAM, LANIER
ART HISTORIAN, CURATOR, ARTIST, POET
b Shawnee, Okla, Mar 6, 1940. *Study:* Kenyon Col, 58-60; Am Univ, BA, 63; Columbia Univ, MA, 66; Renaissance & Baroque studies under Rudolf Wittkower & Julius Held, Modern studies under Meyer Schapiro & Theodore Reff, NY Univ Inst Fine Arts, 66-67; studied under Robert Goldwater & AH Mayor. *Work:* Multiple, Mus Mod Art, New York & Mus Arts Decoratifs, Paris; Vitra Mus, Ger; Fine Arts Mus San Francisco. *Exhib:* Mus Mod Art, New York, 67-; Art Info Ctr, 68-94; Calif State Univ, Hayward, 95-2010. *Collection Arranged:* Gods & Goddess: Ancient Greek Coins, 61, Leonardo's Book Illustrations, 61; Botticelli's Illustrations for Dante, 62; Light in the Prints of Durer, 63; Soluna: Sun & Moon in Alchemical Prints, 65; Mies van der Rohe Drawings, 66; Feathered Forms: The Early Books of Max Ernst, 67; Hector Guimard, 70; TE & Tullah Hanley Collection, 71, Armand Hammer Collection, 71, Three Centuries of Am Painting, 71, Three Centuries of Flemish Painting, 71; 19th Century French Painting, 72, Three Centuries of British Painting, 72; Three Centures of French Art: Selections from the Norton Simon Mus, 73; Am Still-life Painting, 74; The Rainbow Show, 75, Luminous Visions: Sacred Art of the East & West, 75; Artists Books & Multiples, 76; Flaming Waters: Books by William Blake, 77; Color Symbolism: Books on Color, 78; The Color of Light: Books by Matisse, 79, The Smile of Light: Books by Duchamp, 79, Brother Sun & Sister Moon, Alchemical Symbols, 79; Leonardo & The Androgyne: Images of Nonduality, 80; I Am Woman I Am Artist Bay Area Printmakers, 81; Mexican-American Murals in San Francisco, 82, Native-American Art Today, 82; Symbols of the Earth Spirit: Taoism, Hinduism, & Buddhism, 83, Symbols of the Sky Spirit: Judaism, Christianity, & Islam, 83; The Spontaneous Gesture: Prints & Books of the Abstract Expressionist Era, 87; Dreaming in Color: The Art of Matisse, 89; Vincent van Gosh: Painter, Printmaker, Collector, 90; Impossible Realities: Marcel Duchamp & the Surrealist Tradition, 2001; Life, Death, & Laughter: Masami Teraoka, 98; The Art of the Book: The Livre d'Artiste, 99; Andy Warhol & Social Consciousness: Another Side of Pop Art, 2000; The Lions Roar: Tibetan Thangkas, 2000; Marcel Duchamp: Artist, Humorist, Philosopher, 2001; Zen & Modern Art: Echoes of Buddhism in Western Paintings & Prints, 2003; Robert Rauschenberg, Artist-Citizen: Posters for a Better World, 2004; Flaming Pages: The Illuminated Books of William Blake, 2006; The Spirit of the Renaissance: A Visitt to the Urbino Studiolo, 2007; Global Vision: A Survey of World Art, Part 1, 2006; Global Vision: A Surgey of World Art, Part II, 2008; The Cost of War from the World Wars to Iraq, 2008; Stones & Bones that Speak: Inscribed Chinese Art, Ancient to Modern, 2009; Nike: Goddess of Victory, 2010; Looking at Leonardo, 2011; The Heritage of Afghanistan, 2012. *Pos:* Assoc cur, Mus Mod Art, New York, 65-70; deputy dir, Collections, Exhib & Publ & chief cur, Fine Arts Museums of San Francisco, 70-76; dir/cur, Cult Resource Mgt Ctr, 76-83 & Australian Nat Gallery, 84-87; cur, Norton Simon Mus Art, Pasadena, 87-91; dir/cur, Art Info Ctr, Antioch, Calif, 91-97, Univ Art Gallery, CSU, East Bay, 98-2010; cur, Univ Libr, CSU East Bay, 2010-2014. *Teaching:* Art hist, religious studies, mus studies, CSU, Arcata, 95-97, CSU East Bay, 98-. *Mem:* Int Coun Mus; Inst Aesthetic Develop; World History Assn; Internat Soc Poets. *Media:* Prints, Objects, Illustrated Books. *Res:* Symbolism: Renaissance, Modern, & Contemporary. *Collection:* Prints, Illustrated Books, & Sacred World Art. *Publ:* The Illustrated Poem-Books of Sun Moon Press, 63; The Sin of 100 Debts, 66; Chess Sets, 68; The Illustrated Poem-Books of Hand Made Press, 70; Hector Guimard, 70; Claude Monet: Paintings from California Collections, 73; The Rainbow Book, 75, 76, & 79; The Illustrated Poem-Books of Sun/Moon Press, 83; The Spontaneous Gesture: Prints & Books of the Abstract Expressionist Era, 87; Giorgione & the Experts, 93; Leonardo's Light in the Last Supper & Christ Among the Doctors, 95; Goddesses in Art, 97, Duchamp & Androgyny: Art, Gender, and Metaphysics, 2003; Portraits of Poets, Objets Poetiques, vol 1, 2004; Personal Poems: Objets Poetiques, vol 2, 2005; Images of Nothingness, Objets Poetiques, vol 3, 2007; Inside of Now, Objets Poetiques, vol 4, 2009; Global Vision: A Survey of World Art, vol 1, 2006; Global Vision: A Survey of World Art, vol 2, 2008; Global Vision: a Survey of World Art, vol 3, 2010. *Mailing Add:* California State University East Bay University Library 258 Carlos Bee Blvd Hayward CA 94542

GRAHAM, PAUL
PHOTOGRAPHER
Work: Mus Mod Art, New York; Guggenheim Mus, New York; Whitney Mus Am Art, New York; Tate Gallery, London; Stedelijk Mus, Amsterdam; Victoria & Albert Mus, London; numerous pvt collections. *Exhib:* Solo exhibs, Ikon Gallery, Birmingham, 1993, Raum Aktueller Kunst, Vienna, 1994, Tate Gallery, London, 1996, Hipploÿte Gallery, Helsinki, 1998, Lawrence Rubin Greenberg Van Doren Fine Art, New York, 2000, Galleria Marabini, Bologna, 2001, PS1 Gallery, New York, 2003, Fundacion Telefonica, Madrid, 2004, Les Filles du Calvaire, Paris, 2006, Mus Mod Art, 2009; EV+A, Limerick City Gallery Art, Ireland, 1996; Pittura Britannica, Mus Contemp Art, Sydney, 1997; Yesterday Begins Tomorrow, Bard Coll Cur Studies, New York, 1998; Some Parts of This World, Finnish Mus Photog, Helsinki, 2000; 49th Venice Biennale, Venice, 2001; Cruel and Tender-Photographs of the 20th Century, Tate Modern, London, 2003; American Pictures, Whitney Mus Am Art, 2004; Les Peintres de la Vie Moderne, Centre Pompidou, Paris, 2006; Summer Exhib, Royal Acad Art, London, 2007. *Dealer:* Greenberg Van Doren Inc 730 Fifth Ave New York NY 10019; Salon 94 12 E 94th St New York, NY 10128

GRAHAM, ROBERT C, JR
ART DEALER
b New York, NY, Sept 6, 1941. *Study:* Middlebury Col, BA, 63. *Pos:* Chmn & pres, James Graham & Sons Inc, New York, 63-2000. *Mem:* Art Dealers Asn Am. *Specialty:* American painting and sculpture. *Mailing Add:* 425 June Rd Stamford CT 06903

GRAHAM, RODNEY
FILMMAKER, PHOTOGRAPHER
b Abbotsford, BC, Can, 1949. *Study:* Univ BC, Vancouver, 1968-71. *Hon Degrees:* Hon Dr, Emily Carr Inst Art & Design, 2002. *Exhib:* Solo exhibs, Fraenkel Gallery, San Francisco, 2000, Art Basel, Switz, 2001, Johnson City Community Coll, Overland Park, Kans, 2002, Madison Arts Ctr, Wis, 2003, 303 Gallery, New York, 2004, Inst for Contemp Art, Philadelphia, 2005, Sprengel Mus, Hanover, Ger, 2006, Lisson Gallery, London, 2007, Centro de Art Contemporaneo De Malaga, Spain, 2008 & Jeu de Paume, Paris, 2009; These Days, Vancouver Art Gallery, Can, 2001; Loop, PS1, New York, 2002; Golden Oldies of Music Video, Mus Mod Art, New York, 2003; Pass the Time of Day, Gasworks Galelry, London, 2004; Superstars, Kunsthalle Vienna & Kunstforum Vienna, Austria, 2005; Altered States, Taipei Fine Arts Mus, 2006; Sympathy for the Devil, Mus Contemp Art, Chicago, 2007; Sydney Biennial, Australia, 2008; Magnetic Landscape, Columbus Mus, Ohio, 2009. *Bibliog:* Mark Godfrey (auth), Video Work, Lisson Gallery, London, Frieze, No 54, 128-29, 9-10/2000; Apollinaire Scherr (auth), Taking a Trip by Bicycle, NY Times, 9/16/2001; Hilarie Sheets (auth), Strange Comfort, Artnews, Vol 101, No 8, 140, 9/2002; Shawn Conner (auth), Ex-punk Rockers Turn up the Volumizer, The Vancouver Courier, 8/13/2003; Christopher Miller (auth), Lost in the Moment, Art in Am, 108-113, 3/2005; Steven Stern (auth), Pop goes the easel, Time Out New York, No 654, 73, 4/10-16/2008. *Publ:* Dir (films), Halcion Sleep, 1994, Vexation Island, 1997, How I Became a Ramblin Man, 1999 & City Self/Country Self, 2001, & The Phonokinetoscope, 2002. *Mailing Add:* 303 Gallery Inc 507 W 24th St New York NY 10011

GRAINGER, NESSA POSNER
PAINTER, COLLAGE ARTIST
b Atlantic City, NJ. *Study:* Philadelphia Mus Sch Art, BA; Tyler Sch Fine Arts;, Pa Acad Fine Arts. *Work:* Zheijiang Mus, Hangzhow, China; Elliot Mus, Stuart, Fla; Mus Mod Art Libr, NY; Artist Libr, Victoria & Albert Mus, London; Nat Mus Am Art Libr, Washington, DC; Penn State Univ, Pa; Philip & Muriel Berman Mus Art; many corporate collections and others. *Exhib:* Solo exhibs, Douglas Coll for Women, NJ, 90; The Interchurch Ctr, NY, 92; Elliot Mus, Stuart, Fla, 93; Somerset Art Asn, NJ, 98; The Baum Sch Art, Allentown, Pa, 2007; Nat Acad Design, NY, 92 & 96; Allied Artists Am, Nat Arts Club, NY, 92; Philip & Muriel Berman Mus Art, 94, 96, 2008; Am Watercolor Soc, 95; Salmagundi Club, New York, 2005, 2006; Rotunda, Bethlehem, Pa, 2012; Banana Factory Art Ctr, Bethlehem, PA, 2014. *Teaching:* Workshops, Sonoma & Livermore, Calif, Palm Beach, Fla, Somerset Art Asn, NJ, NJ Ctr Visual Arts, Lafayette Coll, Easton, Pa, Hudson River Art Workshops, Greenville, NY & Garden State Watercolor Soc, NJ, Banana Factory, Bethlehem, Pa. *Awards:* NJ Watercolor Soc Silver Medal, 85; Audubon Artists of America, Silver Medal, 89; Silver Medal, Knickerbacher Artists, 92; Dale Meyers Medal Honor, Audubon Artists, 96; Mark Freeman Award, Nat Soc of Painters on Acrylic and Casein, 08; NJ Watercolor Soc, 2007, 2008, 2009. *Bibliog:* Dorothy Hall (auth), Parkeast, Art & Artists, 11/87. *Mem:* Am Watercolor Soc; Allied Artists Am; Nat Asn Women Artists; Philadelphia Watercolor Soc; Pa Watercolor Soc; Nat Soc Painters in Casein & Acrylics. *Media:* Mixed Media, Watercolor, Acrylic. *Specialty:* Watercolor, collage, mixed media. *Interests:* Teaching, painting, museums. *Publ:* Splash 3, North Light Books, 94; Collage Techniques (by Gerald Brommer), ed VIII, 96; Best of Watercolor II & The Best of Watercolor Composition, Rockport Publ, 97; Collage in All Dimensions, Nat Coll Soc, Malcom Lewellyn Publ, 2005; Famous Women of Hunterdon Co NJ

GRAND, STANLEY I
DIRECTOR, CURATOR
b Washington, DC, Jan 26, 1945. *Study:* Univ Wis, Madison, BS, 67, MA, 85, PhD, 93. *Collection Arranged:* Tom Bamberger: Photographs 1978-1992 (with catalog), Carlsten Art Gallery, Univ Wisc, Stevens Point, 93; Drawing on the Figure (with catalog), Carlsten Art Gallery, Univ Wisc, Stevens Point, 93; The City Observed: Barry Carlsen, Douglas Safranek, Stuart Shils (with catalog), Sordoni Art Gallery, Wiles Univ, 94; Drum Lithographs: 1960-1963 (with catalog), Sordoni Art Gallery, Wilkes Univ, 94; Paul Georges: Self-Portraits (with catalog), Sordoni Art Gallery, Wilkes Univ, 95; Guy Pene du Bois: The Twenties at Home and Abroad (auth, catalog), Sordoni Art Gallery, Wilkes Univ, 95; Between Heaven and Hell: Union Square in the 1930's (auth, catalog), Sordoni Art Gallery, Wilkes Univ, 96; Robert L Schultz: Drawings: 1980-1995 (auth, catalog), Sordoni Art Gallery, Wilkes Univ, 96; John Sloan: Works on Paper, Sordoni Art Gallery, Wilkes Univ, 96; Eugene Atget: Photographs, Vieux Paris, Sordoni Art Gallery, Wilkes Univ, 96; Philippe Halsman: Celebrity Photographs from the 1940s and 50s, Sordoni Art Gallery, Wilkes Univ, 96; Seymour Lipton: Drawings, Sordoni Art Gallery, Wilkes Univ, 97; The Tuscan

Landscapes of Richard Upton (auth, catalog), Sordoni Art Gallery, Wilkes Univ, 97; Gary Lang: Paintings and Objects 1975-1997, (auth, catalog), Sordoni Art Gallery, Wilkes Univ, 97; Contemporary Realist Art from the Collection of MellonBank (with catalog), Sordoni Art Gallery, Wilkes Univ, 97; Jimmy Ernst: Shadow to Light, Paintings 1942-1982 (auth, catalog), Sordoni Art Gallery, Wilkes Univ, 97; Anthony Sorce: Four Decades (with catalog), Sordoni Art Gallery, Wilkes Univ, 98; Gregory Conniff: Twenty Years in the Field, Sordoni Art Gallery, Wilkes Univ, 99; The Graphic Art of Paul Bacon, Sordoni Art Gallery, Wilkes Univ, 99; The Collector as Bookbinder: The Piscatorial Bindings of SA Neff, Jr, (with catalog) Sordoni Art Gallery, Wilkes Univ, 99; Edward Schmidt: Mythologies, Sordoni Art Gallery, Wilkes Univ, 2000; Hank O'Neal: Portraits (with catalog), Sordoni Art Gallery, Wilkes Univ, 2000; Michael Thomas: Gables, Sordoni Art Gallery, Wilkes Univ, 2001; Audrey Ushenko: Allegories and Myths (with catalog), Univ Mus, Southeast Mo Sate Univ, 2001; A Gift from the Tamara Kerr Art Bank/New York Artists Equity Asn Inc Honoring Placide and George A Schriever (with catalog), Univ Mus, Southeast Mo State Univ, 2002; Violet Baxter: The View From Union Square (with catalog), Univ Mus, Southeast Mo State Univ, 2002; Kenneth A Holder: Discovery: Paintings of the Lewis & Clark Trail, (with catalog), Univ Mus, Southeast Mo State Univ, 2003; Jane Hinton: Bridges (with catalog), Univ Mus, Southeast Mo State Univ, 2003; Kay WalkingStick: Mythic Dances, Paintings from Four Decades (with catalog), Southeast Mo Regional Mus, 2004; Burt Hasen: A Life in Art (with catalog), Southeast Mo Regional Mus, 2005; Cindy Tower: Workplace Series (with Catalog), Crisp Mus, 2008; Gary Lang: Out Standing Time (with catalog), Crisp Mus, 2008. *Pos:* Cur collections, Madison Art Ctr, 86-87; cur, Edna Carlsten Art Gallery, Univ Wis, 91-93; dir, Sordoni Art Gallery, 93-2000; mus dir Southeast Mo State Univ, 2000-2008; exec dir & CEO, Lancaster Mus Art. 2008. *Teaching:* Vis prof art hist, Beloit Col, 91; asst prof art hist, Wilkes Univ, 93-2000; assoc prof Southeast Mo State Univ, 2000-2007; prof, Southeast Mo State Univ, 2007-2008. *Mem:* Asn Am Art Historians; Am Asn Mus; Coll Art Asn; Int Asn Art Critics. *Res:* Twentieth century American figurative art. *Specialty:* Am Art. *Publ:* Auth, Drawing on the Figure (bk), 93; Paul Georges: Self Portraits, Sordoni Art Gallery, 95; coauth, Guy Pene du Bois: The Twenties at Home and Abroad, 95 & Between Heaven & Hell: Union Square in the 1930s, 96, Sordoni Art Gallery; auth, Robert L Schultz: Drawings 1980-1995, Sordoni Art Gallery, 96; and several other exhib catalogs. *Mailing Add:* 135 North Lime St Lancaster PA 17602

GRANDEE, JOE RUIZ
PAINTER, GALLERY DIRECTOR
b Dallas, Tex, Nov 19, 1929. *Study:* Aunspaugh Art Sch, Dallas. *Work:* White House, Washington, DC; Xavier Univ Mus, Cincinnati, Ohio; Mont State Hist Soc Mus, Great Falls; Marine Corps Mus, Quantico, Va; Univ Tex, Arlington; Nat Cowboy & Western Heritage Mus, Okla City, Joe Grandee Mus Frontier West (special wing); Leggett Platt. *Comn:* Twenty Mules of Death Valley, US Borax Co, Hollywood, Calif, 65; Linda Bird & Chuck Robb Off Portrait, comn by Lyndon B Johnson family & friends, 67; portrait of Johnny Carson, comn by Rudy Tellez, Assoc Producer NBC, NY, 67; portrait of Robert Taylor, comn by US Borax Co for Robert Taylor, Hollywood, 68; portrait of Leander H McNelly, Texas Ranger, East Wing of White House, Washington, DC, 72; portrait of Ronald Reagan, comn by US BOrax Co for ROnald Reeagan; total of 11 paintings comn by Nat Cowboy & Western Heritage Mus, Okla City; self-portrait of Grandee comn by and for General Wallace M Green; self-portrait of Grandee comn by and for Paul Harvey. *Exhib:* Solo exhibs, Norton Art Gallery Mus, Shreveport, La, 71, El Paso Mus Fine Arts, Tex, 72 & Tex Ranger Mus Show, Waco, Tex, 72 & US Capitol, 74, High Plain's Heritage Mus, Spearfish, SD; Custer Exhib, Amon Carter Mus Western Art, Ft Worth, Tex, 68; 3 different exhibs, Tex State Capital; US State Dept & Univ Tex Painting & Artifacts Tour, US & Japan. *Pos:* Owner, Joe Grandee Gallery & Mus of Old West, currently. *Awards:* First Official Artist of Texas, Tex Legis & Gov, 71; Grandee painting of Iwojima Ira Hays given from the US Marine Corp for a Medallion to the Indian Code Talkers of World War II; Grandee day, mayor's presentation of document of appreciation showings of art and honors at all banks, Arlington, Tex; Cult Achievement Award, W Tex Chambers of Commerce; Medallions & Silver Plates, Tex Rangers Sesquicentennial Event. *Bibliog:* Wayne Gard (auth), Joe Grandee--painter of the old west, Am Artist Mag, 67; Grandee Paintings (TV film), US Borax Co, 68; Joy Schultz (auth), The West Still Lives: Grandee, Heritage, 70; Western Painting Today, Royal B Hasserick; Garland A Smith (auth), Outstanding Young Texans; Am Artists An Illustrated Survey of Leading Contemp Am; Dorothy Harmsen (auth), Harmsen's Western Americana; Richard C Rattenbury (auth), Hunting the American West; James E Servin (auth), Conquering the Frontiers; John Carroll (auth), The Black Military Experience in the Am West; Bruce Wexler (auth), The Wild Wild West of Louis Lamour. *Mem:* fel, Company of Military Hist. *Media:* Oil, Ink. *Specialty:* Paintings, drawings and sculpture works of Joe Ruiz Grandee and displays of historical artifacts. *Publ:* Illusr, Indian Wars of Texas, 65, Pictorial History of The Texas Rangers, 69, The Grand Duke Alexis in the USA, 72 & The Life of Jim Baker (mountain man), 1818-1898, 72; contribr, Cowboy Series, In: Time-Life Bks, 72; auth, Renaissance of Western Art, Franklin Mint. *Dealer:* Bob Brown Big Horn Galleries 1167 Sheridan Ave Cody Wyoming 82414. *Mailing Add:* 2400 W Pioneer Pkwy Suite 123 Arlington TX 76013

GRANDPRÉ, MARY
ILLUSTRATOR
Study: Minn Coll Art & Design. *Pos:* Conceptual illusr, various local editorial clients, currently; visionary, environ & scenery dept DreamWorks' prod Antz; illusr, Harry Potter Series, 97—. *Media:* Pastels. *Publ:* illusr, Harry Potter & Sorcerer's Stone, 97, Harry Potter & the Chamber of Secrets, 98, Harry Potter & the Prisoner of Azkaban, 99, Harry Potter & Goblet of Fire, 2000, Harry Potter & the Order of the Phoenix, 2003, Harry Potter & the Half-Blood Prince, 2005, children's books, The Snow Storm, 83, The Vegetables Go to Bed, 94, Curtain of Night, 97, Pockets, 98, The House of Wisdom, 99, The Purple Snerd, 2000, Aunt Claire's Yellow Beehive Hair, 2001, The Sea Chest, 2002, Plum, 2003, The Thread of Life, 2003, Henry and Pawl, 2004, Sweep Dreams, 2004, Tales from Shakespeare, 2004

GRANNON, KATY
PHOTOGRAPHER
b Arlington, Mass, 1969. *Study:* Univ Pa, BA, 91; Harvard Univ, MA, 93; Yale Univ, MFA, 99. *Work:* Girls Night Out, Orange Cty Mus Art, LA, 2003, Moving Pictures, Guggenheim Mus, Bibao, Spain, 2003; Open House: working in Brooklyn, Brooklyn Mus Art 2004, Whitney Biennial, Whitney Mus Am Art, 2004, From NY with Love, Covivant Gallery, Tampa, Fla, 2004, Land of the Free, Jack Hanley Gallery, San Francisco, 2004. *Exhib:* Solo exhibs, Dream Am, Kohn Turner Gallery, Los Angeles, 2000, 51 Fine Art, Antewerp Belg, 2001, Morning Call, Salon 94, New York City, 2003, Sugar Camp Rd, Artemis Greenberg Van Doren Gallery, New York City, 2003, Arles Photog Festival, Arles, Frances, 2004, Emily Tsingou Gallery, London, 2005, Jackson Fine Art, Atlanta, Ga, 2005; group exhibs, ArtSpace, New Haven, Conn, 98, Another Girl, Another Planet, Lawrence Rubin Greenberg Van Doren Fine Art, NY, 99, Reflections Through a Glass Eye, Inter Ctr Photog, NY, 2000, Smile, Here, NY, 2001, Boomerang: Collector's Choice II, Exit Art, NY, 2001, Women by Women, Cook fine Art, NY, 2002, True Blue, Jackson Fine Art, Atlanta, 2002, From NY with Love, Covivant Gallery, Tampa, Fla, 2004, Land of the Free, Jack Hanley Gallery, San Francisco, 2004. *Awards:* Rema Hort Mann Found Grant, 99; Bucksbaum Award, 2004. *Mailing Add:* c/o Jan Greenberg 3 Brentmoor Park Saint Louis MO 63105

GRANSTAFF, WILLIAM BOYD
PAINTER, ILLUSTRATOR
b Paducah, Ky, May 17, 1925. *Study:* Kansas City Art Inst, with Ross Braught & Ed Lanning, grad; Am Acad Art, with William Mosby & Bill Fleming. *Comn:* Mural, Cadet Club, Garden City, Kans, 45; Old Homeplace, B J Farless, Princeton, Ky, 70; Vietnam (painting), comn by Nat Am Legion, 75 & Korea (painting), 78; 1st Bank & Trust, Princeton, Ky. *Exhib:* Mid-S, Nashville, Tenn, 53; solo exhib, Planters Bank, Hopkinsville, Ky, 72 & 99. *Pos:* Mem, Art Dirs Club, Nashville, 55-58. *Teaching:* Instr illus, Famous Artist Sch, 59-61. *Awards:* Brackman Blue Ribbon, Nashville, 53; Best of Show, Hopkinsville Discover, 2002. *Bibliog:* Meet your instructors, Famous Artist Mag, 61. *Mem:* Princeton Art Guild. *Media:* Oil, Watercolor. *Interests:* Flying instructor. *Publ:* Illusr, What's in a Word, Abingdon, 65; The Way Out, Moody, 70; Golden Treasury of Bible Stories, Southern, 71; illusr, Man-US & Americas, 72 & Americans All, 72, Benefic. *Dealer:* Heritage Gallery Rosemont Gardens Lexington KY 40503; Bennett Gallery 2104 Crestmoor Rd Nashville TN 37215; Riverwind Gallery 10400 W State Rd 662 Newburg IN 47630. *Mailing Add:* 806 S Jefferson St Princeton KY 42445

GRANT, DANIEL HOWARD
WRITER, CRITIC
b Westport, Conn, Sept 5, 1954. *Study:* Northwestern Univ, BA, 76. *Pos:* Art critic, Newsday, Melville, NY, 80-84, Commercial-Appeal, Memphis, Tenn, 84-86, Boston Herald, Mass, 86-. *Teaching:* Instr artists career skills, Greenfield Community Coll, Mass, 92-95 & Lyme Acad Coll Fine Arts, 2002-. *Mem:* Amherst Cult Coun (chmn, 92-96); Found Community Artists (adv bd mem, 78-84). *Res:* Resources and opportunities for financial support for fine artists. *Publ:* Auth, Business of Being an Artist, 91, How to Start and Succeed as an Artist, 93, Artist's Resource Handbook, 94, Writer's Resource Handbook, 97 & Fine Artist's Career Guide, 98, Allworth Press; Artist's Guide to Making It in New York City, 2001; Selling Art Without Galleries, Allworth Press, 2006. *Mailing Add:* 19 Summer St Amherst MA 01002

GRANT, DEBORAH
PAINTER
b Toronto, Canada, 1968. *Study:* Columbia Coll Chicago, BFA (Painting), 1996; Skowhegan Sch Painting & Sculpture, ME, 1996; Tyler Sch Arts, Elkins Park, Pa, MFA, 1999. *Exhib:* Solo exhibs include The Scene Gallery, New York, 2002, Satellite, New York, 2004, Roebling Hall, New York, 2006, Steve Turner Contemp, Beverly Hills, 2007; Group exhibs include AIM 22 Show, Bronx Mus, New York, 2002; 7 Walls, 8 Views, Arena Gallery, New York, 2003, Seeing Red, 2003; Paper Chase, Raben Gallery, New York, 2004; Bush League, Roebling Hall Gallery, Brooklyn, 2004; Creating Their Own Image, Aronson Galleries, New York, 2004; Greater New York, PS 1 Contemp Art Ctr, New York, 2005; The F Word, Andy Warhol Mus, Pittsburgh, 2006; M*A*S*H* Armory Group Exhib, Momenta Art, Brooklyn, 2007. *Awards:* Tides Lambent Found Grant, 2003; Nimoy Found Grant for HCA Artists, 2004; Joan Mitchell Found Grant, 2007. *Mailing Add:* Steve Turner Contemp 6026 Wilshire Blvd Los Angeles CA 90036

GRASSI, MARCO
CONSERVATOR, RESTORER
b Florence, Italy, July 7, 1934; US citizen. *Study:* Princeton Univ, BA (art hist), 56; apprenticeships at: Gabinetto del Restauro, Uffizi, Florence, 59-60; Istituto Centrale del Restauro, Rome, 60-62; & Schweitzerisches Institut für Kunstwissenschaft, 62. *Pos:* Vis conservator, Thyssen-Bornemisza Collection, Villa Favorita, Lugano, Switz. *Awards:* Ital Legion of Merit. *Mem:* Am Inst Conserv Hist & Artistic Works; Int Inst Conserv Hist & Artistic Works; fel Pierpont Morgan Libr. *Mailing Add:* 158A East 71st St New York NY 10021

GRASSL, ANTON M
PAINTER, PHOTOGRAPHER
b Munich, Ger, Sept 9, 1955. *Study:* Opera of Munich, Ger, apprentice (stage design), 74-76; Bavarian Sch Photog, apprentice, 76-78; Acad der Schonen Kunste, Munich, Ger, BFA, 81; RI Sch Design, MFA(photog), 83. *Work:* Mus Fine Arts, Boston; Rose Art Mus, Brandies Univ, Waltham, Mass; Brockton Art Mus, Mass; Polaroid Collection, Cambridge, Mass; Hypo Bank Art Collection, Munich, Ger; and other private collections. *Exhib:* Solo exhibs, Gallerie Lanz, Bern, Switz, 79, Acad der Schonen Kunste, Munich, Ger, 80, City Hall Mannheim, Ger, 81, Woods Gerry Gallery, Providence, RI, 83, Robert Klein Gallery, Boston, 89 & Cambridge Arts Coun, Mass, 91; Gallerie am Maxwehr, Landshut, Ger, 85; Gallery Laughlin &

Winkler, Boston, 90; 10 Yrs Artist Coop, Fed Reserve Bank, Boston, 93; Am Outdoor Theaters, Univ Calif, Berkeley, 94; Robert Klein Gallery, Boston, 95; Howard Yezerski Gallery, Boston, 99. *Pos:* Freelance Photogr, currently. *Awards:* Fel, Mass Found Arts, 91; Fel, Nat Endowment Arts, 92; Graham Found Advan Studies Fine Arts Grant, 95

GRASTORF, JEAN H
PAINTER, INSTRUCTOR
b Rochester, NY, Oct 24, 1934. *Study:* Rochester Inst of Tech, AAS, 55; Ceramic School at Alfred Univ (paper-making & Lithography), 76, studies with Clara Nelson. *Work:* Neville Public Mus, Green Bay, Wis; State Univ New York at Alfred; Florida Int Univ, Miami; Nat Watercolor Soc, Brea, Calif; Raymond James, St Petersburg, Fla. *Comn:* paintings, Haas Historical Mus, St. Petersburg, Fla, 85; paintings, Bayfront Medical Ctr, St. Petersburg, 85; paintings, St. Anthony's Cancer Care Ctr, St. Petersburg, Fla, 86; paintings, Univ S Fla, St Petersburg, 90. *Exhib:* Am Watercolor Soc, Salmagundi Club, New York, 86, 88, 91, 93-94, 2000-02 & 2005-12; Adirondacks Nat Exhib Am Watercolors, Old Forge Arts Ctr, 93 & 2009; Nat Acad Open, Nat Acad Design, New York, 94; Florida Watercolor Soc, Mus Fine Art, St Petersburg, Fla, 96; Watercolor USA, Springfield Art Mus, Mo, 2002; Fla Watercolor Soc, Leepa-Rattner Mus Art, 2005 & 2010; First Int Invitational Exhib of Contemp Watermedia Masters (catalog), Nanjing, China, 2008, Second Invitational, Nanjing, 2010, Third Invitational, Nanjing, 2012; Shanghai Zhujiajiao Internat Watercolor Biennial Exhib, 2012. *Teaching:* Instr watercolor, The Arts Ctr, St Petersburg, Fla, 82-92; instr watercolor workshops, several state & nat watercolor socs, 85-. *Awards:* First Award, Nat Watercolor Soc, 97; First Award, So Watercolor Soc, 98; Elsie & David Wu Award, Am Watercolor Soc, 2000, Don W Dennis Mem, 2006 & Walser Greathouse Medal, 2007; Susan Lattner Gold Award, Fla Watercolor Soc, 2007, 2009; Skyledge Award, Transparent Watercolor Soc Am, 2008; Hotel des Artistes, Memorial to Mario Cooper, AWS, 2014; AWS Dolphin Fellowship, 2014. *Bibliog:* Stephen Doherty (auth), Easy Solutions-Color Mixing, Quarry Press, 98; Nita Leland (auth), Exploring Color, North Light, 98; Several articles for Watercolor, Watercolor Magic & Int Artist Mag; Christopher Willard, Watercolor-Mixing, Rockport Publ, 2000. *Mem:* Fla Watercolor Soc (2nd vpres, 89 & 1st vpres, 90); Am Watercolor Soc (dir, 2002 & 2003, juror 2002. 2005, & 2014); Nat Watercolor Soc (juror, 2007); Transparent Watercolor Soc Am (juror, 2010); Rocky Mt Nat Watercolor Soc; TWSA Master Status, 2012. *Media:* Watercolor & Acrylics. *Interests:* Travel, art, history, photography. *Publ:* auth, Pouring Light, Layering Transparent Watercolor, North Light Media, 2005; auth, Pouring Transparent Watercolor (video), North Light Media, 2008; auth, Treating Texture in Transparent Watercolor (video), North Light Media, 2008. *Dealer:* Vincent William Gallery Inc 320 Corey Ave Saint Pete Beach FL 33706; Gallery on First 550 First Ave No S Petersburg FL 33701. *Mailing Add:* 6049 4th Ave Saint Petersburg FL 33710

GRAUER, GLADYS BARKER
PAINTER
b Cincinnati, Ohio, Aug 15, 1923. *Study:* Art Inst Chicago, 41-45; Rutgers Univ, 80-84. *Work:* Newark Mus; Montclair Mus; Jane Voorhees Zimmerli Art Mus; Smithsonian Art Book Collection; Noyes Mus; Morris Mus; Morgan State Univ; Artist Libr Victoria & Albert Mus, London; Newark Public Library; NJ State Mus; Nat Mus Am Art Libr. *Comn:* Mural, Art High Sch, Newark, Victoria Foundation & Newark Bd Educ Dedication, 2008; mural, Newark Pub Sch Student Ctr, 2009; mural, Tribute to Newark Jazz Club, City of Newark, 2013. *Exhib:* Emerging & Established, Newark Mus & Jersey City Mus, NJ, 81; solo exhib, The Invincibles, Courtney Gallery, Jersey City, 85; Nat Conference of Artists, Senegal Nat Mus, Dakar, Africa, 85; Tracking the Trends, Pavilion Gallery, Mt Holly, NJ, 86; Celebration, Morristown Mus, NJ, 86; Morristown Atrium, 92-94; 3-woman exhib, Newark Mus, 92; Johnson & Johnson, 92; Retrospective, Rutgers Univ, 2002; Retrospective 1978 Gallery, 2014. *Teaching:* Instr advert design, Essex Co Voc Tech, Newark, NJ, (retired); instr painting, Newark Mus, NJ, currently. *Awards:* First Prize Watercolor, James St Commons, 83; Mixed Media Fel, NJ State Coun Arts, 85; Artist-in-residence, Newark Mus, 91; Innovative Print Fel, Rutgers Univ, 92. *Bibliog:* Edna Bailey (auth), Artists paintings a depiction of blacks, Newark Star Ledger, 1/13/86; Gumbo Ya Ya - Anthology of Contemp African American Women Artists, Art Press, 95; Public Television State of the Arts, Family Focus, 4/96; Art by African Am, In the Collection of NJ State Mus; Transcultural NJ Diverse Artists Shaping Culture & Communities; St James Guide to Black Artists, Schomburg Collection. *Mem:* Newark Arts Coun; Art Inst Chicago Alumni Asn; Black Woman Visual Perspective (pres, 73-75); Newark Mus Nat Educ Asn. *Media:* Mixed Media, Collage. *Dealer:* Bellevue Gallery of Fine Art 209 Bellevue Ave Trenton NJ 08618. *Mailing Add:* 352 Seymour Ave Newark NJ 07112

GRAUER, SHERRARD
PAINTER, SCULPTOR
b Toronto, Ont, Feb 20, 1939. *Study:* Wellesley Col, 56-59; Ecole Louvre, Paris; Calif Sch Fine Art, BFA (hon), 65. *Work:* Vancouver Art Gallery; Mus Art Contemp, Montreal; Ont Heritage Fund; Can Coun Art Bank; Nat Gallery Can, Ottawa. *Comn:* Relief mural, Worldwide Int Travel, Vancouver, 69; ceiling panels (steel & fiberglass), DPW, Fed Bldg, Powell River, BC, 76; banners, City Vancouver, 76; Brave Birdmen (steel mesh ceiling sculpture), Ministry Transport, Cornwall, Ont, 80; relief sculpture, Cygnus, stainless steel mesh & chromed sheet steel, WESGAR Corp, Vancouver, BC, 90; Requeim, North Growth Mgmt, 98; Seals, North Growth Mgmt, 03. *Exhib:* Art From Canada's West Coast, Vancouver Art Gallery, 71; Some Canadian Women Artists, Nat Gallery Can, 75; Current Pursuits, Vancouver Art Gallery, 76; retrospective, Surrey Art Gallery, 80; New Vancouver Art Gallery Inaugural Exhib, 83; Artropolis, Vancouver, 93; Vancouver Art Gallery, Face to Face: Four Centuries of Portraits, 98. *Pos:* Bd mem, hon secy, Van Art Gallery, 76-77; mem found bd, Arts, Sci & Technol Ctr, Vancouver, 80. *Bibliog:* Joan Lowndes (auth), Modalities of West Coast sculpture, Artscanada, Vol XXXI, No 2, 74; Ted Lindberg (auth), article, Sherry Grauer, Vanguard, 11/85; Jill Pollack (auth), monogr, On Certain Paths, 87. *Mem:* Royal Can Acad Art; Canadian Artists Representation. *Media:* Oil, Acrylic; Canvas, Steel Mesh. *Dealer:* Bau-Xi Gallery 3045 Granville St Vancouver V6H 3J9; Bau-Xi Gallery 340 Dundas St W Toronto M5T 1G5. *Mailing Add:* 106-8828 Heather St Vancouver BC V6P 3S8 Canada

GRAUPE-PILLARD, GRACE
PAINTER, PHOTOGRAPHER
Study: City Univ NY, BA, Art Students League, George Bridgman Scholar, with Marshal Glasier and Julien Levi. *Work:* Malcolm Forbes, Forbes Pubs, NY; The New Jersey State Mus, Trenton; City of Orange, Orange, NJ; NJ Transit, Jersey City, Matawan, Aberdeen; Newark Mus, NJ; and many others. *Comn:* Port Authority Bus Terminal, 92; Robert Wood Johnson Med Sch-CAB, New Brunswick, NJ, Porcelain Enamel (9 pcs), 95; City of Orange, NJ, 96; NJ Transit, Garfield Ave Sta, Jersey City (5 sculptures in porcelain enamel, railings, gate), 97-2000; NJ Transit, Matawan Sta, NJ (porcelain enamel sculpture), 98-99; NJ Transit, Hoboken 2d St Sta, Hoboken, NJ (9 sculptures), 2000. *Exhib:* Solo Exhibs: Sally Hawkins Gallery, New York, 90; Port Authority Bus Terminal, New York, 92; NJ State Mus, Trenton, 93; NJ Ctr Visual Arts, Summit, 93; Klarfeld-Perry Gallery, Brookdale Coll, Lincroft, NJ, 99; Donahue-Sosinki Art, 2000; Frist Ctr for Visual Arts, Nashville, Tenn, 2004; The Proposition, New York, 2005; Carl Hammer, Chicago, Ill, 2006; Wooster Arts Space, New York, 2007; Moravian Col, Bethlehem, Pa, 2008; Rupert Ravens Contemp, Newark, NJ, 2008, Rider Univ, NJ, 2010; Art & the Law, Traveling show, 94-95; Noyes Mus, Oceanville, NJ, 96; Donahue-Sosinski Art, 97; 25th Anniversary Benefit Selections, The Drawing Ctr, NY, 2002; The Reflected, Refracted Self, Carl Hammer Gallery, Chicago, Ill, 2004; Group Exhibs: A Knock at the Door, Anthology Film Archives, 2005, Sanctuary, Rupert Ravens Contemp, Newark, NJ, 2007; 183rd Annual Exhib, Nat Acad Mus, 2008; Elizabeth A Sackler Center for Feminist Art, Brooklyn Mus, 2008; New Prints, Int Print Ctr, New York, 2009; Artist as Curator, NJ State Mus, Trenton, NJ, 2009; (Under)Exposed, Carl Hammer Gallery, Chicago, 2009; Art Fem: TV Art & Feminism, 2010; Where There's Smoke, Hampdon Gallery, Amherst, Mass, 2010; Video Festivals, Cologne Off, St. Petersburg, Russia, 2011; NYC Blues, Kunstpakhuset, Denmark, 2012; Gesamt, Lars Von Trier, Copenhagen, Denmark, 2012; Armory Show, Carl Hammer Booth, 2013, Portfolio, 2013; Spectrum of Sexuality, HUC Mus, NY, 2013; Editions/Artist Bookfair, NY, 2013; The Seventh Day, HUC Mus, NY, 2014. *Pos:* dir, Edwin Austen Abbey Mural Found, Nat Acad Mus and Sch Fine Arts, 2003-2010. *Teaching:* Instr painting & drawing, Monmouth Co Parks, 76-; instr mural workshop, Nat Acad Design Mus, NY, 2003-2010. *Awards:* NJ State Coun Grant, 82-83, 92-93, 99-2000; Nat Endowment Arts, 85-86; Ctr Innovative Printmaking, Rutgers Univ, NJ, 91. *Bibliog:* Berta Sichel (auth), Flash Art, 98; Bzdak & Petersen (auths), Public Sculpture in NJ, 99; Nancy Ruhling (auth), Newsday, 6/11/99; Marie Maber (auth), Digital Fine Art, Fall 2000; Review by William Zimmer, NY Times, 4/28/02; Review-Fellowship Show, Dan Bischoff (auth), The Star Ledger, 1/7/01; Review by Alan Artner, Chicago Tribune, 4/7/06; Dan Bischoff (auth), Star Ledger (article), 8/12/07; Marcia Yerman (auth), Relevant Time, 9-10/2007; Marie Marber (auth), Asbury Park Press, 2007; Benjamin Genocchio, NY Times, 7/1/07; Geoff Gettman (auth), Morning Call, 2008; Roger Denson (auth), Political Art Timeline, Parts 4&6, Huffington Post, 5/2012; Yale Univ Radio (interview), 2013; Suzanne Russell (auth), Womens Voices for Change, 2013. *Media:* Video, Oil, Photography. *Collection:* Warehouse Collection. *Dealer:* The Proposition 2 Extra Place New York 10003; Carl Hammer Gallery 740 N Wells Street Chicago Ill 60654. *Mailing Add:* PO Box 213 Keyport NJ 07735

GRAVES, KENNETH ROBERT
PHOTOGRAPHER
b Portland, Ore, June 27, 1942. *Study:* San Francisco Art Inst, with Jerry Burchard & John Collier Jr, BFA, 70, MFA, 71. *Work:* San Francisco Mus Art; Nat Libr, Paris; Ann Bremer Mem Libr, San Francisco Art Inst; Mus Mod Art, NY; George Eastman House, Rochester, NY; Erie Art Mus, Pa. *Exhib:* Three Photographers, San Francisco Mus Art, 71; New Photog in the Bay Area, MH de Young Mus, 73; Exchange DFW-SFO, Ft Worth Art Mus & San Francisco Mus Art, 75; Color as Form, George Eastman House & Corcoran Gallery, 82; solo exhibs, Blue Sky Gallery, Portland, 82 & 85, Portico Gallery, Philadelphia, 83, OK Harris, NY, 89, 91 & 93 & Univ Vt Fleming Mus, 94; Univ Wyo Art Mus, 94; 2 person show with Eva Lipman, Allentown Art Mus, Pa, 95. *Teaching:* Instr photog, San Francisco Art Inst & Photog Film Ctr West, Berkeley; assoc prof photog, Pa State Univ, 77-92, prof, 92-. *Awards:* Nat Endowment Arts Fel, 76; Purchase Award, Alternatives, 83; First Award, Pa Festival Arts, 83-85. *Bibliog:* Joan Murray (auth), interview, Artweek, 1/22/72; Time-Life Photog, 75; Popular Photog Ann, 82. *Publ:* Coauth, American Snapshots, Scrimshaw Press, 77; Ballroom, Milkweed Eds, 89. *Dealer:* Simon Lowinski Gallery 578 Broadway New York NY 10012. *Mailing Add:* 210 Patterson Bldg Penn State Univ Sch Visual Arts University Park PA 16803

GRAVES, MICHAEL
ARCHITECT, EDUCATOR
b Indianapolis, Ind, July 9, 1934. *Study:* Univ Cincinnati, BS (archit), 58; Harvard Univ, March, 59; Am Acad in Rome (fel), Prix de Rome, 60-62. *Hon Degrees:* 11 hon degrees from US cols & univs. *Work:* Mus Mod Art, Metro Mus, Smithsonian Inst, Cooper-Hewitt, Brooklyn Mus, NY; Berlin Mus, Ger; Deutsches Architekturmuseum, Frankfurt, Ger. *Comn:* Walt Disney World Swan & Dolphin Hotels, 87; Hotel NY, Disneyland Park, Paris, 89; Denver Cent Libr, 90; Eng Res Ctr, Univ Cincinnati, 95; Int Finance Corp, 97; US Fed Courthouse Annex, 97; NCAA Headquarters and Hall of Champions, 98; Mus of the Shenandoah Valley, 99; Fed Reserve Bank of Dallas, Houston br, 2000. *Exhib:* Solo exhibs, Johnstown Art Mus, Pa, Syracuse Univ Sch Archit, Syracuse, NY, 90, Marini Marino Mus, Florence, Italy, 91, Mikimoto Hall, Tokyo, Japan, 92 & Cheekwood Fine Arts Ctr, Nashville, Tenn; retrospective, 25 Yrs in Princeton, Princeton Arts Coun, Kirby Art Ctr, Lawrenceville Sch, NJ, 89; Univ Cincinnati, Aronoff Ctr Design & Art, 96; Topeka & Shawnee Co Pub Libr, Topeka,

Kans, 96; New Jersey Inst of Tech Architecture Sch, 80. *Pos:* Dir visual studies prof, Princeton Univ, 70-72; architect-in-residence, Am Acad Rome, Italy, 79. *Teaching:* Lectr archit, Princeton Univ, 62-67, assoc prof, 67-72, prof, 72-2001, emeritus prof, 2001-; vis prof archit, Univ Tex, Austin, 74, Univ Houston, Tex, 78 & Univ NC, Charlotte, 79; prof, Princeton Univ, 72; Robert Schirmer prof of architecture, Univ Calif, Los Angeles, 77. *Awards:* Am Inst Archit Honor Awards, 75, 79, 82, 83, 85, 87, 90, 92 & 98; Progressive Archit Design Awards, 70, 76, 77, 78, 79, 80, 83 & 89; many others including, NJ Soc Archit, Interiors Mag, Progressive Archit Mag, Pa Furniture Design, Inst Bus Design; Nat Medal of Arts, 99; Gold Medal, Am Inst Archit, 01; NJ Gov's Walt Whitman Award for Creative Achievement; Arts Person of the Year, NJ Ctr for Vis Arts; Henry Hering Medal Mem, Nat Sculpture Soc, 86; firm has more than 160 awards and citations including Progressive Archit awards, ten Am Inst Archit Nat Honor awards, and the AIA/Am Libr Asn Award for Denver Cent Libr; Topaz Medallion, Am Inst Archit and the Asn Collegiate Schools Archit, 2010; Michael Graves Lifetime Achievement Award, AIA-NJ; Named to NJ Hall of Fame; and other awards. *Bibliog:* Auth, Kings of Infinite Space: Michael Graves and Frank Lloyd Wright, Academy Eds, 84; Michael Graves Buildings and Projects: 1982-1989, Princeton Archit Press, 90; Michael Graves Buildings & Projects: 1990-1994, Rizzoli, 95; Michael Graves: Design Monograph, Ernst & Sohn, 94; The Master Architect Series III, Michael Graves, Selected and Current Works, Images Pub, 95. *Mem:* Fel Edward MacDowell Colony; Fel Am Inst Archit; Trustee Am Acad Rome; Dir Inst Archit & Urbanism; Am Acad Arts and Letters; Nat Acad. *Media:* Pencil, Colored Pencil; Acrylic Paint. *Collection:* Biedermeier furniture & grand tour. *Publ:* Contribr, Catalogue Venice Biennale, 80; Speaking a New Classicism, Smith Coll Mus Art, 81; auth, Le Corbusier's drawn references, In: Introduction to Le Corbusier Drawings, Acad Ed, London, 81; A Case for Figurative Architecture, Rizzoli, 82; Ritual, The Princeton Journal, 84. *Dealer:* Max Protetch Gallery 37 W 57th St New York NY 10019; John Nichols Printmakers 83 Grand St New York NY 10013. *Mailing Add:* 341 Nassau St Princeton NJ 08540

GRAVING, BRANDON
PRINTMAKER
b New Orleans, 1959. *Study:* Univ Southwestern Lafayette, La, BFA, 1982; Tulane Univ, 1983; Loyola Univ, New Orleans, 1978. *Work:* New Orleans Mus Art; Mass Mus Contemp Art. *Exhib:* Solo exhibs include Dashka Roth Gallery, New Orleans, 1990, Monoprints & Luminokinetics, New Orleans, 1998, Le Mieux Galleries, New Orleans, 2000, 2002 & 2004, Contemp Artists Ctr Gallery, North Adams, Mass, 2002 & 2003, Isaac Delgado Fine Arts Gallery, New Orleans, 2004; group exhibs include Neometix Premier Show, Isaac Delgado Fine Arts Gallery, New Orleans, 1986; Louisiana in Print, Collins C Diboll Art Gallery, New Orleans, 1992, 1994, 1995, 1996, 1999, 2001, 2002, 2003, & 2004; Contemp Arts Ctr, New Orleans, 1992 & 1985; NOPD, Carroll Gallery, Tulane Univ, New Orleans, 1994, 1995, 2002 & 2003; The Gun Show, Positive Space Gallery, New Orleans, 1996; Massive MOCA, Mus Contemp Art, North Adams, Mass, 1999; Ten Printmakers, World Trade Ctr, New Orleans, 2002; Drawing, Contemp Artist Ctr, North Adams, Mass, 2003. *Pos:* Master printmaker & instr experimental monoprinting, Contemp Artist Ctr, North Adams, Mass & Hillary St Studio, New Orleans, 1995-. *Awards:* Pollock-Krasner Found Grant, 2007. *Mailing Add:* 198 Beaver St Ste 305N North Adams MA 01247

GRAY, CAMPBELL BRUCE
MUSEUM DIRECTOR, MUSEOLOGIST
b Australia, Apr 4, 1952. *Study:* Alexander Mackie Coll Adv Educ, 1978; City Art Inst, Sydney Coll Adv Educ, BA (art educ), 1983; Univ Sussex, PhD (art hist, Brit Coun Vice Chancellors & Principals Overseas Res Scholar), 1995. *Exhib:* Reinis Zusters, 1984, Lewers Gallery, Sydney, Australia, The Third Dimension, 1984, Image and Surface, 1984, The Drawn Image, 1985, BIP Selection: A Bi-Polar Situation in Venice, 1986, Self Image-The Immolation Mirage, 1986; Viewers & Audiences: The Mus/Gallery in Context, Reg Galleries Asn NSW Ltd & Wollongong City Gallery, 1995; Western Sites Component of the Australian Perspecta 1991, Art Gallery NSW, Sydney, 1991. *Pos:* Inaugural dir, Lewers Bequest & Penrith Reg Art Gallery, NSW, Australia, 1981-86; cur, Western Sites Component, Sydney, 1990-91; coordr, Postgraduate Studies Unit, Univ Western Sydney, 1995-96; dir, Mus Art, Brigham Young Univ, Provo, Utah, 1996-. *Teaching:* Sr lectr visual arts, Univ Western Sydney, 1986-96, grad chair art hist & criticism, 1994-96; art theory & arts admin, Univ NSW, 1994-96. *Awards:* Nepean Res Grant, Univ Western Sydney, 1995; Exhib Grant, Vis Arts & Craft Bd Australia Coun. *Mem:* Am Asn Mus; Western Mus Asn; Mus Australia Inc. *Res:* The Art Museum: critique, design, function, performance, phenomenology, contextual relevance and value, relationship to recent art and art theory, curatorship, site-specificity in art and the museum. *Publ:* Auth, The Dilemma of Change, Contemp Australian Painting, 90; Context, regionalism & the museum/gallery, 94 & Curatorship: political or critical intervention, 95, Australian Art Monthly; Change in the face of the museum's apparent obduracy, Mus Nat, 95; Looking for the Ground, Angels and the City, 96. *Mailing Add:* Brigham Young Univ Mus Art N Campus Dr Provo UT 84602

GRAY, ELISE NORRIS
SCULPTOR
b Burkesville, Ky, Mar 9, 1936. *Study:* Western Ky Univ, BS, 58; Univ Tenn, MS, 59; Arrowmount Sch Crafts, 59; study with Phyllis Hammond & Barbara Bisgyer, 72-77; Parsons Sch Design, 82. *Work:* IBM Corp, Burlington, Vt; AcQuest Capital Corp, NY; Am Fed Bank, Greenville, SC; AT&T Corp, Somerset, NJ; United Jersey Bank, Woodbury, NJ; Mus Arts & Sciences, Macon, Ga, 97. *Comn:* Clay wall relief, Fla Nat Bank, Jacksonville, 86; wall sculpture, IBM Corp, Gaithersburg, Md, 87; wall sculpture, Fla Educ Dept, Tallahassee, 89; wall relief, GE Capital, 93; sculpture, Mem Garden, Community Church White Plains, 94; wall sculpture, Theatre Macon, Ga Coun Arts, 95. *Exhib:* Solo exhibs, 14 Sculptors Gallery, NY, 79, 82, 84, 86, & 89, Wesleyan Col, Macon, Ga, 92 & Mus Arts & Sci, Macon, Ga, 95; Art of Northeast, Exhib of Painting & Sculpture, Silvermine Guild of Artists, NY, 79, 82 & 83; Works in Clay-Elise Gray, Hudson River Mus, Yonkers, 83; Schick Art Gallery, Skidmore Col, 88; Fired Works (show of Ga ceramics artists), Macon Arts Gallery, Macon, Ga, 4/2007. *Pos:* Co-founder, vpres & pres, Artisans Co-op, Westchester, NY, 73-77; chairperson exhibs publicity, 14 Sculptors Gallery, 78-89. *Teaching:* Field fac adv, archit ceramics, Vt Col Norwich Univ, 86-88; artist-in-residence, Macon Pub Sch, currently. *Awards:* Sculpture Award, Mamaroneck Artist Guild, 78 & 79 Glickenhouse Found Award, 81; Pollock-Krasner Found Grant, 90-91; Individual Artist Grant, Ga Coun Artist, 93-94. *Bibliog:* David Shirey (auth), Art View, New York Times, 6/10/79; Robbie Ehrlic (auth), Elise Gray at 14 Sculptors, Arts Mag, 9/79; Rosalind Schneider (dir), Elise Gray-Fragments and Formations (video), Film Workshop of Westchester, 84. *Mem:* Int Sculpture Ctr; Metrop Mus Art; Nat Mus Women Arts. *Media:* Clay, Cement. *Mailing Add:* 1483 Oglethorpe St Macon GA 31201-1512

GRAY, JIM
PAINTER, SCULPTOR
b Middleton, Tenn, June 4, 1932. *Work:* Carnegie Libr, Regar Mus, Anniston, Ala; Brooklyn Navy Yard; 40 paintings, Loyal Am Life Ins Co, Mobile, Ala; Winsor & Newton, Secaucus, NJ; 16 paintings, Hibernia Nat Bank, New Orleans; 6 paintings, Am Embassy, Oman; Jim Gray Galleries, Knoxville, Tenn, Gatlinburg, Tenn, Pigeon Forge, Tenn; paintings, sculptures, Am Embassy, Tokyo, Japan; painting, Convention Ctr, Knoxville, Tenn; paintings, Am Embassy, Warsaw, Poland; painting, Sen Chamber Office, Washington, DC; and others. *Comn:* Dolly Parton (over lifesize bronze), Sevierville, Tenn; Pres Andrew Johnson (2 bronzes-over life size), Greeneville, Tenn & Capitol grounds, Nashville, 95; Alex Haley (bronze bust), Univ Tenn, Knoxville; Gov John Sevier (bronze bust), Capitol Bldg, Nashville; bronze, Gen John Sevier; oil, Haslam Col, Knoxville, Boyd Col, Knoxville; Senator Howard Baker (bronze bust). *Exhib:* Whiting Mus, Fairhope, Ala, 70, 73, 75 & 92; Watercolor USA, Springfield, Mo, 70; Realist Invitational, Gallery Contemp Art, Winston-Salem, NC, 71; Am Soc Marine Artists Ann, Grand Cent Gallery, NY, 80 & Peabody Mus, Salem, Mass, 81; 400 Yrs of Seafaring, Fine Arts Mus, Mobile, Ala, 82; Mystic Maritime Mus, 86-90; Mariners Mus, Newport News, Va, 87; Md Hist Soc, Baltimore, 89; Retrospective, Arrowmont, Gatlinburg, Tenn, 89; 30th anniv ASMA exhib, 5 mus traveling, 2008-09; Retrospective Tenn Hist Mus, 2011; 15th Nat Exhib, Am Asn Marine Artists, 2011-2013. *Teaching:* Instr painting, Buckhorn Art Workshop Ann, Gatlinburg, Tenn; instr watercolor, Atlanta Artist Club, Ga, 69-; lectr art & humanities, Univ Tenn, Knoxville, 70-71. *Awards:* Best Show & Permanent Trophy, Azalea Trail Arts Festival, 57, 58 & 59; Best Show, Hammel-Adams Glass, Mobile, 62 & 63; Paul VI Award, Paul VI Inst Arts, Washington, 87; Art in Embassies Program, Washington; Distinguished Artist award; Tenn Arts Comn Friend of Art Educ in Tenn, 2003; Lifetime Achievement Award, Arrowmont/Gatlinburg Arts Council. *Bibliog:* Video, PBS, Knoxville. *Mem:* Am Soc Marine Artists (bd dir, 83-, vpres, 88-92); Salmagundi Club; and others. *Media:* Watercolor, Oil; Clay, Bronze. *Publ:* Nat Geographic, 10/68; prints, Painting in Alkyds, Contemp Marine Art, 88; Author Jim Gray, Roads I've Traveled (foreword by Sen Howard Baker); Am Artist Mag 4/77; cover and feature article, Jim Gray's Reason for Being, City View Mag, 12/2004; Carl Sagan (auth), Murmurs of Earth, (photos artist, studio & work on Gold Records aboard Voyager I & II in space). *Dealer:* Greenbriar Inc PO Box 735 Gatlinburg TN 37738

GRAY, LUKE
PAINTER
b NY City, 1961. *Study:* RI Sch Design, Providence; Skowhegan Sch Painting & Sculpture, Maine; Univ Pa, BA, 78-82. *Comn:* Ceiling mural, Transmission, 98; lobby, 1500 Broadway, Times Sq, NYC; mural, Universal Health, Robert Wood Johnson Found, Princeton, NJ; mural, Traveler, Rossrock LLC & Phillip Babb, NY. *Exhib:* Holland Tunnel Art Proj, Brooklyn, NY; Tower Gallery, New York City; Bachelier-Kardonsky Gallery, Kent, Conn; Hamburg Mus Fur Kunst und Gewerbe, Ger; Solo exhib, David Klein Gallery, Birmingham, Mich, Thomas Erben Gallery, New York City, Nicole Klagsbrun Gallery, NY, 89, Galerie Ludwig, Krefeld, Germ, 96, Gary Snyder Fine Art, New York City, 96-2010, Addison-Ripley Fine Art, Washington, DC, 97, 2000; David Richard Contemp, Santa Fe, NMex, 2010; Gary Snyder, Gallery, 2012. *Teaching:* instr, Pentiment Int Acad, Hamberg, Germany, 97, 2011. *Media:* Acrylic, Oil. *Specialty:* Murals. *Dealer:* Gary Snyder Proj Space New York; Addison Ripley Gallery DC; David Richard Contemp Santa Fe NM. *Mailing Add:* 159 Taaffe Pl Brooklyn NY 11205

GRAY, RICHARD
DEALER
b Chicago, Ill, 1928. *Study:* Univ Ill Sch Archit; Northwestern Univ. *Pos:* Managing Partner, director Richard Gray Gallery, 63-; chmn bd governors, Smart Mus Art, Univ Chicago; pres, Art Dealers Asn Am, formerly; art advisory Comt, IRS, formerly; trustee, Art Inst, Chicago, Ill, currently. *Mem:* Chicago Art Dealers Asn (former pres); Coll Art Asn Am; Am Asn Mus; Art Dealers Asn Am; Archives of Am Art. *Specialty:* Paintings, sculpture & drawings by established European and American Modern Masters and the avant garde. *Collection:* Works on Paper: contemporary, classical Modern, 19th Century French & Old Masters. *Dealer:* Richard Gray Gallery 1018 Madison Ave NY 10021. *Mailing Add:* Gallery 875 N Michigan Ave Ste 2503 Chicago IL 60611

GRAY, RICHARD
ADMINISTRATOR, EDUCATOR
Study: Ill State Univ, BS, 76; Rochester Inst Tech, MFA, 82. *Pos:* chair nat bd dirs, Soc Photographic Edn, 2004-2013. *Teaching:* assoc prof photography, Univ Notre Dame, 1982-, dir ctr creative computing, 2004-2012, chair dept art, art history, & design, 2012-. *Mailing Add:* University of Notre Dame Dept Art & Art History 306B Riley Hall Notre Dame IN 46556

GRAY, THOMAS ALEXANDER
COLLECTOR, PATRON
b Winston-Salem, NC, Feb 7, 1948. *Study:* Duke Univ, BA (hist art), 70; Am Cult Winterthur Prog, Univ Del, MA, 74; Summer Inst Arts Admin, Harvard Univ, 74. *Pos:* Dir, Mus early Southern Decorative Arts, Winston-Salem, 76-79; consult, Graylyn Conf Ctr, Wake Forest Univ, 80-84; chmn bd trustees, Old Salem Inc, 94-97;

co-founder, Toy Mus at Old Salem, 2002; donor, Anne and Thomas A Gray Lib and MESDA Rsch Ctr, 2013; Thomas A Gray Rare Book Room. *Awards:* Ruth C Cannon Award, Hist Preserv Found NC, 83; Order of Long Leaf Pine, Gov NC, 2002; Frederick Marshall award, Old Salem Mus & Gardens, 2012. *Mem:* Hist Preservation Soc NC Inc (pres exec comt, 76-78); Hist Preservation Fund NC Inc (bd, 76-, vpres, 79-, pres, 80-82); Stagville Preservation Ctr, Durham, NC (bd, 77-84); Old Salem Inc (develop dir, 74-76, bd, 81-2010, exec comt, 82-2010); Walpole Society (2008-); Am Antiquarian Soc (2012-). *Collection:* Hist Manuscripes, NC, 18th Century, Rare books, NC, 17th/18th Century. *Publ:* auth, Old Salem Toy Mus, Winston-Salem, NC, Old Salem, Inc, 2005. *Mailing Add:* 1080 Saint Joseph St Penthouse1 Carolina Beach NC 28428

GRAYDON, ANDY
VIDEO ARTIST
b Maui, Hawaii, 1971. *Study:* Univ Wash, BA (Comparative History of Ideas), 1994; Northwestern University, MFA (Film& Media Arts), 2000. *Exhib:* Solo exhibs include Williamsburg Arts Nexus, New York, 2003, OfficeOps, New York, 2003, 2004, Remote, New York, 2004, Galeria Galou, New York, 2005, Issue Proj Room, New York, 2005, 2008, Whitney Mus Am Art, New York, 2005, Millennium Film Workshop, New York, 2005, Art In General, New York, 2006, LMAKprojs, Brooklyn, 2006, 2008, Portland Art Ctr, Portland, Ore, 2007,; Group exhibs include Share, The Kitchen, New York, 2003, A Lab is A Lab is A Lab, 2007; VideoBox: MusicBox, White Box Gallery, New York, 2004; m/M, Galeria Galou, Brooklyn, 2005; Darmstadt, Galapagos, New York, 2006; Re-Zoning, Goliath Visual Space, Brooklyn, 2006; Tune Out(side) Sound Festival, Wave Farm, Acra, NY, 2007; Rake, Monkeytown, Brooklyn, 2007; Public Opinion Lab, Brooklyn, 2007; Site Matters, Brooklyn Arts Coun, Brooklyn, 2007; Displacement, Greenbelt, Brooklyn, 2008; Unmonumental: Sound of Things, New Mus Contemp Art, New York, 2008. *Awards:* Best Experimental Film, Locus Solarus, Flicker Film Festival, Chicago, 1997; Princess Grace Found Artist's Grant Award, 1999; Marshall Ctr Media Arts Grant, 2000; Houston Worldfest Gold Award, Life Sentence, 2001; Director's Citation, Farwanderer, Black Maria Film & Video Festival, 2004; Experimental Television Ctr Grant for Monster Manual, 2006. *Mailing Add:* Knaackstrasse 70 Berlin Germany 10435

GRAZDA, EDWARD
PHOTOGRAPHER
b New York, NY, Mar 27, 1947. *Study:* RI Sch Design, BFA, 69. *Work:* Mus Mod Art & Metrop Mus Art, NY; Mus Fine Art, Houston, Tex; New Orleans Mus Fine Art; Corcoran Gallery Art. *Exhib:* solo exhibs, Corcoran Gallery Art, Washington, DC, 93, The Storefront for Art and Archit, New York City, 96-97, Mountain Film at Telluride, 97, The Kent Sch, Conn, 98, Sepia Int, Inc, New York City, 99-2000; group exhibs, Euphrat Gallery, De Anza Col, Cupertino, Calif, 93, Metrop Mus Art, New York City, 94, Queens Coll Cult Ctr, New York City, 95, Nat Arts Club, New York City, 97, The 92nd St Y, NY, 98. *Collection Arranged:* Fogg Mus Art, Cambridge, Mass; San Francisco Mus Modern Art; Metrop Mus Art; Nat Mus Am Art, Washington, DC; Corcoran Gallery Art, Washington, DC; Brooklyn Mus, NY; Ctr for Creative Photog, Tucson, Ariz; Int Ctr Photog, NY; NY Pub Libr; Addison Gallery Am Art, Andover, Mass; Mus Fine Arts, Houston; New Orleans Mus Art. *Pos:* editorial dir, Errata Editions. *Awards:* Nat Endowment Arts Grant, 80, 86; Light Work Residency, 83; NY Found Arts Grant, 86; MacDowell Colony Fel, 94, 96, 99; NY State Coun on the Arts Grant, 96; Metrop Transit Authority Arts for Transit Award, 97. *Bibliog:* Camera, 5/74 & 7/78; Granta, Eng (issue 21), 87, (issue 50), 95; Katalog, spring 2000. *Publ:* auth, Afghanistan 1980-1989, 90; auth, Neighborhoods of Brooklyn, 98; auth, Afghanistan 1992-1998, 99. *Mailing Add:* 17 Bleecker St #73 New York NY 10012

GREAVER, HANNE
PRINTMAKER, PAINTER
b Copenhagen, Denmark, 1933. *Study:* Kunsthaandvaerkerskolen, Copenhagen. *Work:* Beloit Coll, Wis; Univ Ga; Univ Maine, Orono; Mich State Univ; Univ Nebr; Farnsworth Art Mus, Maine; Portland Art Mus, Ore. *Exhib:* Univ Maine, Orono, 70; Five Women Printmakers, Kalamazoo Inst Arts, Mich, 69; Boston Printmakers, 76; Mich Printmakers, 77; Northwest Print Coun Inaugural Exhib, 82; 30 Yr Anniversary, Cannon Beach Gallery, 2008; Two person show: 25 yr Invitational, Cannon Beach Gallery, 2011; Greaver-3 Generations Cannon Beach Gallery, 2013. *Awards:* Purchase Award, Boston Printmakers, 76. *Mem:* Print Arts Northwest (formerly Northwest Print Coun) 82-2003. *Media:* Lithography, Oil. *Dealer:* Greaver Gallery Cannon Beach OR. *Mailing Add:* PO Box 120 Cannon Beach OR 97110

GREAVER, HARRY
PAINTER, PRINTMAKER
b Los Angeles, Calif, Oct 30, 1929. *Study:* Univ Kans, BFA & MFA. *Work:* Amherst Coll, Mass; Univ Maine, Orono; NY Pub Libr; Norfolk Mus Arts & Sci, Va; Univ Utah Mus Fine Arts. *Exhib:* Drawings USA, St Paul, Minn, 63; Drawing & Small Sculpture Show, Ball State Univ, Ind, 68; 2nd Nat Print Show, San Diego, Calif, 71; Drawings by Living Am Artists, Univ Utah Mus Fine Arts, 72-73; 10 Yr Print Retrospective, Cannon Beach Gallery, 89; 30 Yr Anniversary, Cannon Beach Gallery, 2008; 25 Yr Invitational, Cannon Beach Gallery, 2011; Geezer Gallery, Portland, Or, 2012; Greaver-3 Generations Cannon Beach Gallery, 2013. *Collection Arranged:* Paintings by Am Masters, Kalamazoo Inst Arts, Mich, 66, Western Art, 67, The Surrealist, 71 & Reginald Marsh, 74; Harvey Breverman, 76. *Pos:* Dir, Kalamazoo Inst Arts, 66-78; dir, Greaver Gallery, 78-. *Teaching:* Assoc prof art, Univ Maine, Orono, 55-66. *Awards:* Purchase Awards, Norfolk Mus, 63 & 64. *Mem:* Cannon Beach Arts Asn. *Media:* Watercolor; Lithographs. *Mailing Add:* Box 120 Cannon Beach OR 97110

GREAVES, JAMES L
COLLECTOR, CURATOR
b Middletown, Conn, Jan 25, 1943. *Study:* Coll William & Mary, BS; Inst Fine Arts, NY Univ, MA (art hist), 70, dipl (art conserv), 70. *Exhib:* Worlds in Stone, An Introduc Viewing Stones, Pacific Rim Bonsai Collection, Federal Way, Wash, 2007; Am Viewing Stones, Natural Art in An Asian Tradition, Mingei Int Mus, San Diego, 2007-2008; Beyong the Black Mountain, Appreciation of Color, Pattern & Form in Am Viewing Stoens, Nat Bonsai & Penjing Mus, US Nat Aboretum, DC, 2008; Eternal Rhythms, Seasons & Time, Nat Bonsai & Penjing Mus, US Nat Arboretum, DC, 2008-2009; Am Viewing Stones from the James & Alice Greaves Collection, Reynolds Gallery, Westmont Coll, Santa Barbara, Calif, 2010. *Collection Arranged:* A Hidden World of Green, African Malachite/Asian Tradition/Am Vision, Selections from the Ralph Johnson Collection,Huntington Libr, San Marino, Calif, 2009. *Pos:* Conserv intern, Los Angeles Co Mus Art, 68-70, conservator, 70; chief conservator, Detroit Inst Arts, 70-76; conservator, Los Angeles Co Mus Art, 77-, actg head conservator, 79-80, senior paintings conservator, 80-85; consult conservator, Huntington Libr, Art Gallery & Botanical Gardens, 79-; pvt conservator, 85-; dir, Am Viewing Stone Resource Ctr, 2008-. *Teaching:* Instr, Calif State Univ, Fullerton, 80-87; vis lectr, Univ Calif, Los Angeles, 81-85. *Mem:* Fel Int Inst Conserv Hist & Artistic Works; fel Am Inst Conserv; Western Asn Art Conservators (pres, 78-79). *Media:* Natural Stone. *Publ:* Coauth, New findings on Caravaggio's technique in the Detroit Magdalen, Burlington Mag, 74; Am Viewing Stones, Beyond the Black Mountain, Color, Pattern, & Form, 2008. *Mailing Add:* 1018 Pacific St Apt D Santa Monica CA 90405-1442

GREBLEZNIK See Lyons, Carol

GRECO, ANTHONY JOSEPH
PAINTER, ADMINISTRATOR
b Cleveland, Ohio, Apr 24, 1937. *Study:* Cleveland Inst Art, with Louis Bosa, BFA, 60; Kent State Univ, with Joseph O'Sickey, MFA, 66. *Work:* Jimmy Carter Presidential Libr, King & Spalding Attorneys, Atlanta, Ga; Summit Bank Corp, Atlanta, Ga; Kilpatrick & Cody Law Offices, Atlanta, Ga; Chase Manhattan Bank; Nationsbank, Charlotte, NC. *Comn:* Urban Walls Atlanta, one of six inner-city walls. *Exhib:* Butler Inst Am Art Ann; Solo exhibs, Armstrong State Coll, Savannah, Ga, 76 & Javo Gallery, Atlanta, 78; Works on Paper, Kohler Arts Ctr, Sheboygan, Wis, 77; Aug Selection Atlanta Artists, Fay Gold Gallery, Atlanta, Ga, 81 & Unnatural Landscape, 88; Birmingham Biennial, Birmingham Mus Art, Ala, 87; Eighth Ann Auburn Works Paper, Auburn Univ, Ala, 87; Unnatural Landscape, Fay Gold Gallery, Atlanta, 88; Group Show McIntosh Gallery, Atlanta, 91 & 92; and others. *Teaching:* Chmn drawing dept, Atlanta Col Art, 66-75, chmn div advanced studio & asst to pres, 74-76, acad dean, 76-82; vis instr drawing & painting, Univ Wis-Madison, summer 70; prof painting & drawing, currently; prof emeritus, Atlanta Art Col of Art. *Awards:* Purchase Award, Butler Inst Am Art Midyear, 60; Southern Arts Fedn/Nat Endowment Arts Fel, 88; Gallery Affiliation, McIntosh Gallery, Atlanta. *Media:* Miscellaneous Media. *Collection:* Jimmy Carter Presidential Libr, Atlanta; Coca Cola, Atlanta; Nations Bank Headquarters, Charlotte, NC; Chase Manhattan Bank. *Mailing Add:* 825 Clairemont Ave Decatur GA 30030-3502

GREELY, HANNAH
ARTIST
Study: Univ Calif, Los Angeles, BA, 2002. *Exhib:* Sentimental Education, Deitch Projects, NY, 2000; Face Off, The Smell, Los Angeles, Calif, 2001; Spoils, Coleman Gallery, Los Angeles, 2001; Drawing Show, Black Dragon Soc, Vienna, 2001; Something of that Nature, Black Dragon Soc, Los Angeles, 2001; Hannah Greely, Elana Scherr, Tom Grimley, Black Dragon Soc, Los Angeles, 2002; Drawing Show, Julius Hummel Gallery, Vienna, 2002; Sculpture Show, Black Dragon Soc, Los Angeles, 2003; Another Sculpture Show, Angstrom Gallery, Dallas, 2003; Clandestine, 50th Venice Biennale, Venice, Ital, 2003; Grant Selwyn Fine Art, Los Angeles, 2003; Trance Plants, Latch Gallery, Los Angeles, 2003; Black Dragon Soc, apex Art, NY, 2004; solo exhib, Andrea Rosen Gallery, NY, 2004-2005; Waste Material, The Drawing Room, London, 2005; Whitney Biennial, Whitney Mus Am Art, New York, 2006, 2010. *Pos:* res, Bangkok Univ Fine & Applied Arts, Thailand, 2004. *Bibliog:* Jerry Saltz (auth), Sentimental Education, Village Voice, 2000; Charles Ray (auth), Before & After, Frieze, 11/2001; Christopher Miles (auth), The Idolater's Revenge, Flash Art, 5-6/2005, 104-108. *Mailing Add:* Andrea Rosen Gallery 525 W 24th St New York NY 10011

GREEN, ART
PAINTER
b Frankfort, Ind, May 13, 1941; US & Can citizen. *Study:* Art Inst Chicago, BFA, 65. *Work:* Art Inst Chicago; Nat Gallery Can, Ottawa; Pa Acad Fine Arts, Philadelphia; Mus Mod Kunst, Vienna, Austria; Mus Contemp Art, Chicago. *Exhib:* Five-person show, The Hairy Who, Chicago, 66-68; Personal Torment-Human Response, Whitney Mus Am Art, NY, 69 & Extraordinary Realities, 73; three-person show, Darthea Speyer Gallery, Paris, France, 70; two-person show, Pa Acad Fine Arts, Philadelphia, 74; Can Canvas, Time Mag Travel Show, 75-76; Ann, San Francisco Art Inst, 77; Who Chicago Traveling Show, Sunderland Arts Ctr, Eng, 79; solo exhibs, Phyllis Kind Galleries, 74-86, CUE Found Gallery, New York, 2009; The Chicago Imagist Print, Smart Gallery, Univ Chicago, 87; Second Sight, Block Gallery, Northwestern Univ, 96, Corbett vs. Dempsey Gallery, Chicago, Ill, 2011; Group exhibs, Jumpin Back Flash, Chicago Cult Ctr, 2000, Chicago Loop, Whitney Mus Champion, Stamford, Conn, 2000; retrospective, Kitchener-Waterloo Art Gallery & U Waterloo Art Gallery, 2005; Art in Chicago, Pa Acad Fine Arts, Phila, 2006; Chicago Stories: Prints, Art Inst Chicago, 2010; Chicago Imagists, Madison Mus Contemporary Art, Madison, Wisc, 2011; Seeing is a Way of Thinking, A Jim Nutt Companion, Chicago Mus Contemporary Art, Ill, 2011; Certain Subject, Garth Greenan Gallery, NY, 2013. *Teaching:* Asst prof painting, NS Col Art, Halifax, 69-71; asst prof painting, Univ

Waterloo, Ont, 77-84, assoc prof, 84-99, prof, 99-06, chmn fine arts dept, 88-91, 99-02, ret, 2006, distinguished prof emeritis, 2007-. *Awards:* Cassandra Award, Cassandra Found, Chicago, 70; Can Coun Arts Bursary, 71-73 & 76-77; Distinguished Teach Award, Univ Waterloo, 90. *Bibliog:* D Nadel (auth) Article/Interview The Ganzfeld # 3, NY, pg 128-137, 2003; R Enright (auth), Interview Border Crossings # 96, 2005; K Johnson (auth), New York Times, 2009. *Mem:* Royal Canadian Acad Arts. *Media:* Oil. *Dealer:* Corbett Vs Dempsey 1120 N Ashland Ave Chicago IL 60622; Garth Greenan Gallery 529 W 20th St NY New York 10011. *Mailing Add:* 5 Elizabeth St Stratford ON N5A 4Z1 Canada

GREEN, GEORGE D
PAINTER
b Portland, Ore, June 24, 1943. *Study:* Okla State Univ BS, 65, Wash State Univ, MFA, 68. *Work:* Guggenheim Mus, NY; Art Inst Chicago; Denver Art Mus; Detroit Inst Arts; Los Angeles Co Mus Art. *Comn:* AT&T Bldg, NY; Home Box Office Bldg, NY; Bulova Bldg, NY. *Exhib:* Solo exhibs, Triangle Gallery, San Francisco, 77, Louis Mus Am Art, Meisel Gallery, 78, 79, 81-83, 85-88, 90-94 & 95-96, Bernarducci Meisel Gallery, New York, 2010; Abstract Painting Redefined, Danforth Mus, Munson Williams Proctor Inst; Reality of Illusion, Denver Mus, Oakland Mus, Alain Blondel, Paris; Phillip Johnson Art Ctr, Allentown, Pa, 86; Art Now Gallery, Gottenburg, Sweden, 87-88; Art Mus, Univ Ore, Eugene, 87; Bernaducci Meisel, 2004; Louis K Meisel, 2004. *Teaching:* Instr, Univ Tex, Austin, 68-71; assoc prof painting, State Univ NY, Potsdam 71-78; vis artist, Portland Art Mus, Ore, 77. *Bibliog:* Joe Jackobs (auth), The reality of artifice, Arts Mag, 2/83; Robert Atkins (auth), article, Archit Dig, 4/83; Edward Lucie-Smith (auth), American Art Now, 85. *Mailing Add:* c/o Louis K Meisel Gallery 141 Prince St New York NY 10012

GREEN, JESSE ARON
VIDEO ARTIST
b Boston, Mass, 1979. *Study:* Harvard Univ, BA; UCLA Sch Art, MFA. *Work:* Tate Modern, London. *Exhib:* Information for Foreigners, Loeb Experimental Theater, Mass, 2002; Stoneface, Fellows of Contemp Art, 2007; GLAMFA, Calif State Univ, Long Beach, 2008; Bizarre Animals, Harvard Mus Natural Hist, 2010; Whitney Biennial, Whitney Mus Am Art, 2010. *Awards:* UCLA Art Coun Award, 2008; Location One Fel, Trust for Mutual Understanding, 2010; Arthur Levitt Jr Fel, Williams Coll, 2010

GREEN, JONATHAN
PAINTER, PRINTMAKER
b Gardens Corner, SC, Aug 9, 1955. *Study:* Sch Art Inst, Chicago, BFA, 82;. *Hon Degrees:* Univ SC, Columbia, hon DFA, 96; Coastal Carolina Univ, hon DFA, Conway, SC, 2009. *Work:* McKissick Mus Art, Columbia, SC; Morris Mus Art, Augusta, Ga; Norton Mus Art, West Palm Beach, Fla; Gibbes Mus Art, Charleston, SC; Naples Mus Art, Fla; Mus Würth, Kuenzelsau, Ger; Hewitt Collection African-Am Art; Myrtle Beach Collections; Am Embassy, Sierra Leone; Marco Island Mus, Marco Island, Fla; Myrtle Beach Mus Art, SC; Afro-Am Cult Ctr, Charlotte, NC; Schomburg Ctr Res Black Cult, New York; Greenville Mus Art, SC; Nelson-Atkins Mus Art, Kansas City, Mo; Afro-Am Mus Phila, Pa; Univ Va Art Mus, Charlottesville, Va. *Comn:* Oil Painting 40″ x 50″, Seagrams Collection, New York, 80; oil painting 36″ x 48″, Harris Collection, Benicia, Calif, 95; oil painting 48″ x 60″, Hilbert Collection, Hilton Head, SC, 96; oil painting 60″ x 48″, Wroble Collection, Charlotte, NC, 99; lithograph print, NAACP, 2009; lithograph print, Afro-Am Cult Ctr, NC; mural, Sanders Clyde Elementary Sch, SC, 2010; mural, Dock St Theatre, SC, 2010; ceramic mural, Charleston, City Market, Charleston, SC, 2012. *Exhib:* The Black Family, Haggerty Mus Art, Milwaukee, 93; solo exhibs, Greenville Co Mus, SC, 94, Mus Greenwood, SC, 95, Gibbes Mus Art, Charleston, SC, 95, IFCC Cult Ctr, Portland, Ore, 98, Mus African Am Art, Tampa, Fla, 98, Quinlan Art Ctr Mus, Gainesville, Ga, 98, Danville Mus Fine Arts Hist, Va, 98, Southern Images, Franklin G Burrough-Simeon B Chapin Art Mus, Myrtle Beach, SC, 2003, Echoes of the South, Ritz Theatre and LaVilla Mus, Jacksonville, Fla, 2001 & A Sense of Place, Coral Springs Mus Art, Coral Springs, Fla, 2002; Vividly Told, Gibbes Mus Art, Charleston, SC, 94; Von Liebig Art Ctr, Naples, Fla; Greenville Mus Art, SC; H Lawrence McCrorey Gallery Multicultural Art, Univ Vt, Burlington; Rhythms of Life: The Art of Jonathan Green; Myth, Memory and Imagination, Universal Themes in the Life and Culture of the South; Off the Wall & Onto the Stage: Dancing the Art of Jonathan Green; The Evolution of a Ballet; Common Ground: Discovering Community in 150 Years of Art; A History of Color, Diversity Within Unity; Jonathan Green, Soul of the South, Suzanne H Arnold Art Gallery, Lebanon Valley Coll, Annville, Pa, 2006; Landscape of Slavery, Gibbes Mus Art, Charleston, SC, 2008; The Story, Mus Fine Arts, Fla State Univ, Tallahassee, Fla, 2008; Jonathan Green, The Artist & the Collector, Burrough-Chapin Art Mus, Myrtle Beach, SC, 2008; Fla Contemp: Painting & Photographs, Naples Mus Art, Naples, Fla, 2009; A Sense of Time, A Sense of Place, Burroughs-Chapin Art Mus, Myrtle Beach, SC, 2010; Landscapes of Jonathan Green, James E Clyburn Rsch Ctr, Med Univ SC, Charleston, SC, 2011; Fine Art Prints of Jonathan Green, Art Inst Charleston, Charleston, SC, 2011; Preserving a Culture, Univ S, Sewanne, Tenn, 2012. *Pos:* Comt bd mem, Acad Arts, Chicago, 84-86; vpres, United Arts Coun, Naples, Fla, 91-94; trustee, Mus Am Folk Art, New York, 2000-2004; bd visitors, Coll Arts & Scis, Howard Univ, Washington, DC, 2003-2008; bd Int African Am Mus, Charleston, SC, 2010-2012. *Awards:* Alberta G Peacock Award, United Arts Coun, Naples, Fla, 96; Borough of Manhattan Proclamation, New York, 96; Clemente C Pickney Award, SC House Reps, 97; Certificate of Honor, City Portland, Ore, 98; King-Tisdell Cottage Found Award, Savannah, Ga, 2001; History Makers Award in Fine Arts, Hist Makers Nat Arch, Chicago, 2001; Key to the City of Columbia, SC, 2001; Order of the Palmetto Award, Gov SC, 2001; Man of Distinction Award, Educ Found Collier Co, 2003; Century of Achievement in Art Award, Mus Ams, Arlington, VA, 2003; Community Gem, Gem Soc Naples, Fla, 2004; Off Int Ambassador, Arts the State Fla, Fla First Lady, Columba Bush, Sarasota, Fla, 6/2005; Man of the Year, Gulfshore Life Mag, 2005; Eagle Award, SC Asn Community Develop Corps, 2005; Annual Nat Arts Progs Award, Links Inc, Pa, 7/2006; Spirit of the Ctr Award, Afro-Am Cult Ctr, Charlotte, NC, 2008; Key of Life Award, NAACP Image Award, Los Angeles, Calif, 3/2009; Elizabeth O'Neill Verner Award for Life Time Achievement, SC Arts Found, 5/2010; Arts and Educ Advocacy award, SC NAACP, Columbia, SC, 2011. *Bibliog:* Norman E Pendergraft (auth), Gullah Life Reflections, NC Cent Univ Art Mus, 88; Carroll Greene Jr (auth), Green comes home, Am Visions, Vol 5, No 1, 90; Alan Gussow (auth), The Artist as Native, Pomegranate Artsbooks, 92; Walter Edgar (ed), SC Encyclopedia, Univ SC Press, 2006. *Media:* Acrylic, Oil. *Publ:* Illusr, Father & Son, Philomel Bks, 92; contribr, The Artist as Native: Reinventing Regionalism, Pomegranate Art Bk, 93; illusr, Noah, Philomel Bks, 94; Gullah Images: The Art of Jonathan Green, Univ SC Press; illusr, Crosby, Harcourt Brace & co, 96 & Amadeus the Leghorn Rooster, Sandlapper Pub co Inc, Orangeburg, SC, 2004; Gullah Cuisine: By Land & By Sea, Artwork by Jonathan Green, Evening Post Publ Company, Charleston, SC, 2010

GREEN, JONATHAN (WILLIAM)
MUSEUM DIRECTOR, PHOTOGRAPHER, FILMMAKER
b Troy, NY, Sept 26, 1939. *Study:* Mass Inst Technol, 58-60; Brandeis Univ, BA, 63; Harvard Univ, MA, 67. *Work:* Moderna Museet, Stockholm, Sweden; Mus Fine Art, Boston; Mus Art, Houston; Ctr Creative Photog, Tucson, Ariz; Int Ctr Photog, New York. *Comn:* Subway murals MTA, Cambridge Seven Architects, Boston, 66; mural, Cambridge Seven Architects, Rochester, NY, 69; photo projs, Archit Record Mag, 70-75; photo projs, Baumeister, 71-74; Am Images photo proj, Bell System (AT&T), 79. *Exhib:* Four Contemp Photogrs, Fogg Art Mus, Harvard, Cambridge, Mass, 74; solo exhibs, Hayden Gallery, Mass Inst Technol, 76, Carl Seimbad Gallery, Boston, 76 & Art Mus, Ind Univ, Bloomington, 85; Tuseu Och En Bild, Moderna Museet, Stockholm, Sweden, 78; Am Images, Corcoran Gallery, 80; Miami Color, Bass Mus Art, Fla, 86; two-person exhib, Emily Davis, Univ Akron, Ohio, 89; and many other group shows. *Pos:* Ed, assoc, Aperture Quart, New York, 74-76; dir, Univ Gallery & founding dir, Wexner Ctr Arts, Ohio State Univ, Columbus, Ohio, 81-90 & Calif Mus Photog, Univ Calif, Riverside, 90-2007; exec dir, ARTSblock, Univ Calif Riverside, 2007-. *Teaching:* Assoc prof photog, Mass Inst Technol, Cambridge, 68-76; prof photog, Ohio State Univ, Columbus, Ohio, 76-90; prof photog & art hist, Univ Calif, Riverside, 90-. *Awards:* Nat Endowment Arts Photogrs Fel, 78; Bell System (AT&T) Photog Fel, 79. *Bibliog:* Hilton Kramer (auth), Camera work, NY Times Bk Rev, 4/21/74; Joan Murray (auth), American photography, Art Week, 9/84; James Hugunin (auth), American photography, Exposure: 23 1, spring 85. *Publ:* Auth, Camera Work: A Critical Anthology, 73 & The Snapshot, 74, Aperture; contribr, American Images: New Work by 20 Contemporary Photographers, McGraw Hill, 79; A Center for the Visual Arts: The OSU Competition, Rizzoli, 84; auth, American Photography: A Critical History, Abrams, 84 & 92; coauth, with Philip Glass, Kurt Muncasi and Richard Serra, Pink Noise: Three Conversations Concerning a Collaborative Acoustic Installation, 87; auth, Continuous Replay: The Photographs of Arnie Zane, 99; Adam Baer: Displaced Perspectives, 2001. *Mailing Add:* 1984 Bonnie Brae Riverside CA 92506

GREEN, NANCY ELIZABETH
CURATOR, WRITER
b Pittsfield, Mass, Apr 27, 1955. *Study:* Conn Col, BA, 77; Sotheby Parke-Bernet Decorative Arts Prog, 79; Clark Inst Art Inst, Williams Col, MA, 84; Attingham Trust Study, 2002-04. *Collection Arranged:* Six in Bronze (with catalog), 84; The Modern Art of the Print: Selections from the Collection of Lois & Michael Torf (with catalog), 84; Am Modernism: Precisionist Works on Paper (auth, catalog), 86-87; Bryan Hunt: Falls and Figures, (with catalog), 88-89; Arthur Wesley Dow & His Influence (auth, catalog), 90-91; Nature's Changing Legacy: The Photographs of Robert Glenn Ketchum, (auth, brochure), 92-93; Master Prints in Upstate New York (auth, catalog), 95-96; Susan Rothenberg: Drawings and Prints (auth, catalog), 98-99; Arthur Wesley Doward Am Arts and Crafts (auth, catalog), 99-00; Vincent Smith (auth, catalog), 00; Surrealist Drawings from the Drukier Collection (auth, catalog), 2003; Bydcliffe; An Am Arts and crafts colony (auth, ed, catalog), 2004; A Room of Their Own: The Bloomsbury Artists in American Collections (auth, ed, catalog), 2008; Joie de Vivre: Art Nouveau and Art Deco Ceramics from the Shatzman Collection (auth, catalog), 2009. *Pos:* Expert print dept, Christies East, New York, 80-82; curatorial asst, Williams Col Mus Art, 82-85; assoc cur prints, drawings & photographs, HF Johnson, Ithaca, NY, 85-89, cur, 89-, chief cur, 93-2000, sr cur, 2000-. *Teaching:* Cornell Adult Univ, 88-89, 91, 93 & 95-. *Awards:* Moe Prize for scholarly research (Arthur Wesley Dow and his Influence) given by the NY State Hist Asn, 90; Winterthur Fel, 2000, 2005; Getty Curatorial Research Fellowship, 2002; Ragdale Found Residency, 2005-07; Wolfsonian Fel, 2005; Paul Mellon Fel, 2006; Victorian Soc Award, Metrop Chap for Byrdcliffe; Moe Prize for catalogue of distinction (Byrdcliffe), 2007; Harry Ransom Ctr Fellowship, 2007. *Mem:* Olive Press Adv Bd; Print Coun Am; Williamstown Regional Art Conserv Laboratory (trustee); Exhib Alliance (trustee). *Res:* 19th and 20th Century works on paper, Arts and crafts movement. *Interests:* gardening, kayaking, reading, knitting, yoga. *Publ:* Auth, Arthur Wesley Dow and His Influence, 91; Master Prints from upstate NY Museums, 95; Susan Rothenberg: Drawings and Prints, 97; Arthur Wesley Dow and American Arts and Crafts, 99; Surrealist Drawing from the Drukier Collections 2003; Byrdcliffe: An Am Arts and Crafts Colony, 2004; A Room of Their Own: The Bloomsbury Artists in American Collections, 2008; Joie de Vivre: Art Nouveau and Art Deco Ceramics from the Shatzman Collection, 2009. *Mailing Add:* Herbert F Johnson Mus Cornell Univ Ithaca NY 14853

GREEN, ROGER J
CRITIC, HISTORIAN
b New York, NY, Nov 16, 1944. *Study:* Cornell Univ, BA, 67; Tulane Univ, MA, 72; Univ Chicago, PhD, 87. *Pos:* Critic art & archit, Times-Picayune, New Orleans, La, 78-92 & Booth News Service, Ann Arbor, Mich, 92-; corresp, Art News Mag, 78-; New Art Examiner, 92-. *Res:* Art and Architecture in Europe, particularly Berlin, 1920-1940. *Publ:* Auth, Max Papart, Rizzoli, 84; contribr, Berlin/New York, Rizzoli, 91

GREEN, TOM
INSTRUCTOR, SCULPTOR
b Newark, NJ, May 27, 1942. *Study:* Univ Md, BA, 67, MA (painting), 69. *Exhib:* New Sculpture: Baltimore-Washington-Richmond, Corcoran Gallery Art, Washington, DC, 70; Washington Sculpture, Philadelphia Art Alliance, 73; solo exhib, Corcoran Gallery Art, 73; Whitney Biennial, Whitney Mus Art, NY, 75; North, East, West, South & Middle, Traveling Drawing Show, 75. *Pos:* Chair, Fine Arts Dept, Corcoran Sch Art, currently. *Teaching:* Asst prof sculpture & drawing, Corcoran Sch Art, 69-. *Bibliog:* Susan Sollins (auth), Washington report, Arts Mag, 9/73; David Tannous (auth), Tom Green: Words and images, Woodwind Mag, 12/11/73; Ben Forgey (auth), Washington: Pyramid shapes, Grenoble and theatrics, Art News, 1/74. *Mailing Add:* Dept Fine Arts Corcoran Sch Art 500 17th St NW Washington DC 20006-4804

GREENAMYER, GEORGE MOSSMAN
SCULPTOR, EDUCATOR
b Cleveland, Ohio, July 13, 1939. *Study:* Philadelphia Coll Art, BFA; Univ Kans, MFA; Ctr Advan Visual Studies (res fel), Mass Inst Technol, Cambridge. *Work:* Fuller, Brockton Art Mus, Mass; Duxbury Art Complex, Mass; Boston Univ; Laumeier Sculpture Park, St Louis, Mo; Decordova Sculpture Park, Lincoln, Mass. *Comn:* Narrative kinetic sculpture/clock tower, Charlotte, Douglas Intl Airport, NC, 97; narrative kinetic, internally lit, sculpture/wind vane, City of Philadelphia Percent for Art Prog, 98; narrative kinetic clock/sculpture, NJ Dept Labor, Trenton, NH State Coun Arts, 2000; 3 narrative kinetic wind vane/sculptures, Atlantic City Int Airport, Pomona, NJ, South Jersey Trans Auth, NJ State Coun Arts, 99; narrative kinetic, Penn Sta, New York City/NJ Transit, 2002; internally lit, Hoboken Terminal, Hudson-Bergen Light Rail, NJ Transit, 2003; kinetic gateway, Union Station, Union, NJ, NJ Transit, 2005. *Exhib:* Pub Sculpture in Columbus, Univ Gallery Fine Art, 84; Pub Art Process, Miami, Fla, 86; Chesterwood, Stockbridge, Mass, 87; Woodson Art Mus, Wausau, Wis, 98-2000; Decordova Mus, Lincoln, Mass, 2000, 2008. *Teaching:* Prof sculpture, Mass Coll Art, Boston, 81-2004, prof emer, 2005. *Awards:* Artists Fel Grant, Artists Found, Boston, Mass & Tiffany Grant, New York, 77. *Bibliog:* Peter Koenig (auth), article, South Shore Mag, summer 88; John Chandler (auth), article, Sculpture mag, 3-4/88; Nick Capasso (auth), article, Sculpture Mag, May, 99; Doug Norris (auth), rev, Art New England, 2-3/2003; article & photos, Anvil's Ring, Spring, 2004. *Mem:* Artist Blacksmiths N Am; Int Sculpture Ctr. *Media:* Steel, Aluminum. *Mailing Add:* 994 Careswell St Marshfield MA 02050-5637

GREENBAUM, JOANNE
PAINTER
b, New York, NY, 1953. *Study:* Bard Coll, BA, New York, 1975. *Exhib:* Solo exhibs, Small Walls Gallery, New York, 1983, Arena Gallery, Brooklyn, 1996, D'Amelio Terras, New York, 1997-98, Galerie Nicholas Krupp, Switz, 2001, Numark Gallery, Washington DC, 2002, KS Art, New York, 2003, Boom/Shane Campbell, Chicago, 2004, Aurabora Press, San Francisco, 2005; Drawings, Ted Greenwald Gallery, New York, 1986; Well Cultivated Gardens, PS 122, New York, 1990; Vibology, White Columns, New York, 1992; New York Abstract Painting, Salvatore Ala Gallery, 1994; Wacko, The Workspace Gallery, New York, 1995; Un Oeil Americain, Galerie le Carre, Lilles, France, 1996; Painting: Now and Forever, Matthew Marks Gallery, New York, 1998; Exit Art, New York, Examining Pictures, Whitechapel Art Gallery, London, 1999; Examining Pictures, Armand Hammer Mus, Los Angeles, 2000; Accumulations, Kent State Univ Art Gallery, Ohio, 2001; New Prints, Int Print Centre, New York, 2003; Positive, Marella Arte Contemporanea, Milan, 2004. *Awards:* Joan Mitchell Found Grant, 2009. *Media:* Acrylic, Oil. *Mailing Add:* 73 Leonard St New York NY 10012

GREENBAUM, MARTY
PAINTER, SCULPTOR
b New York, NY, Mar 3, 1934. *Study:* Univ Ariz, Tucson, BA, 56; Brooklyn Col, NY, Mass, 91. *Work:* Chicago Art Inst Libr; Art Inst Chicago; Chrysler Mus, Norfolk, Va; The Print Club, Philadelphia, Pa; J Patrick Lannan Found, Santa Fe NMex; The Norman Fisher Collection, Jacksonville Art Mus, Fla; Madison Art Ctr, Wisc; New Paltz Mus, SUNY, New Paltz, NY; Brooklyn Mus Art, NY. *Comn:* Unique Book, J Patrick Lannan Found, Los Angeles, Calif, 68; Sept Calendar (centerfold), Changes Mag, NY, 71; eds of prints, Shenanigan Press at Jones Rd Print Shop, Barneveld, Wis, 74; Cajun Book, James McDonell, NY, 85. *Exhib:* Personal Torment & Human Concern, Whitney Mus Am Art, NY, 69; 4th Ann Contemp Reflections, Aldrich Mus Contemp Art, Ridgefield, Conn, 75; 20th Nat Print Exhib, Brooklyn Mus, NY, 76; The Object as Poet, Renwick Gallery, Smithsonian Inst, Washington, DC, 76-77; New Ways with Paper, Nat Collection of Fine Arts, Smithsonian Inst, 77; solo exhib, Picker Art Gallery, Colgate Univ, 77; Playground PSI, Long Island, NY, 78; Metamorphosis of the Book, Documenta 6, Kassel, Ger; Artists' Books, Georges Pompidou Ctr, Paris, France, 85; Fetishism Contemp & Primitive, Allan Stone Gallery, NY, 92; Talent, Allan Stone Gallery, NY, 97-99; 40th Anniversary, Allan Stone Gallery, NY, 2000; solo exhib, Pacifico Fico Fine Art, NYC, 2001; solo exhib, Artist Books, 5+5 Gallery, Brooklyn, NY, 2002, Safe-T-Gallery, Brooklyn, NY, 2006; Play, Proteus Gowanus, Brooklyn, NY, 2007-; Windsor Whip Works Art Gallery, Windsor, NY, 2007; Safe-T-Gallery Art Now, Miami Beach, Fla, 2007; Things I See: Pastels, Butler Inst Am Art, Youngstown, Ohio, 2008; and others. *Teaching:* Art, PS 63, New York, 88-95. *Awards:* The Inst for Art & Urban Resources Inc, 83; Creative Artists Pub Serv Prog, NY, 72, 75; Nat Endowment Arts Grant; The Inst for Contemp Art, 83. *Bibliog:* Dorothea Baer (producer), Marty & Lulu's Playground, Independent Film, 65; David Bourdon (auth), Marty Greenbaum, Village Voice, 65; Gene Baro (auth), The Object As Poet, Smithsonian Inst Press, 77; Rose Slivka (auth), Paper as Medium Smithsonian Institution Traveling Exhibition Service, 78; Ed McCormack (auth), No Longer Innocent: Book Art in America, 60-80, Betty Bright, 2005. *Media:* Painting, Drawing, Collage, Photography. *Publ:* 30 Years of American Printmaking, The Brooklyn Mus, 77; RE: Pages, An Exhibition of Contemporary American Bookworks, Hera Educational Foundation, 81; Jones Road Printshop & Stable 1971-81: A Catalogue Raisonne, Madison Art Ctr, 83; Marty Greenbaum: Visionary Mojo Man in the Postmodern Age, 2002. *Dealer:* Allan Stone Gallery 113 E 90th New York NY. *Mailing Add:* 505 Court St # 6D Brooklyn NY 11231

GREENBERG, HOWARD
ART DEALER
b Brooklyn, NY, 1949. *Pos:* Photog, Woodstock Times, Woodstock, NY, 1972-77; founder, Ctr Photog at Woodstock, 1977, mem adv bd, currently; founder & owner, Photofind, Woodstock, 1981-86, Howard Greenberg Gallery, New York, 1986-. *Specialty:* 20th Century Photography. *Mailing Add:* Howard Greenberg Gallery Fuller Bldg Ste 1406 41 E 57th St New York NY 10022

GREENBERG, RONALD K
DEALER, COLLECTOR
b St Louis, Mo, July 17, 1937. *Study:* Washington Univ, St Louis, Mo. *Mem:* Art Dealers Asn Am. *Specialty:* Contemporary American art. *Collection:* Works by Lichenstein, Warhol, Stella, Kelly, Motherwell, Frankenthaler, Judd, Serra, Chamberlain and Rauschenberg. *Mailing Add:* 3 Brentmoor Park Saint Louis MO 63105

GREENBLAT, RODNEY ALAN
PAINTER, DESIGNER
b Daly City, Calif, Aug 23, 1960. *Study:* Sch Visual Arts, BFA (hon), 82. *Work:* Groeniger Mus, Amsterdam; Chrysler Mus, Norfolk, Va. *Exhib:* The Threshold, RI Sch Design, Providence, 82; Solo exhib, Gracie Mansion Gallery, NY, 83; Familiar Frontiers, Australian Ctr Contemp Art, Melbourne, 85; Biennial Exhib, Whitney Mus Am Art, NY, 85; Reality and Imagination, Contemp Arts Mus, Houston, 88; Land Ho (with catalog), Chrysler Mus, Norfolk, 92. *Teaching:* Prof computer art, Sch Visual Arts, 92-96. *Bibliog:* Sanfor Shaman (auth), Reality & Imagination, Penn State Univ, 87. *Media:* Multi-media. *Specialty:* Contemporary Art. *Publ:* Auth, Uncle Wizzmo's New Used Car, 90, Aunt Ippys Museum of Junk, 91 Slombo The Gross, 93 & Thunder Bunny, 97, Harper Collins, *Dealer:* Gracie Mansion Fine Arts 101 2nd Ave New York NY 10003. *Mailing Add:* 61 Crosby St New York NY 10012

GREENE, CHRIS (CHRISTINE) E
CARICATURIST, ILLUSTRATOR
b Chelm, Poland, Mar 29, 1945; US citizen. *Study:* Newark Sch Fine & Industrial Arts, cert 62-65; Moore Coll Art, Philadelphia, BFA, 68; Art Students League, 70-71, pvt studio classes with Joe Hing Lowe, 74-75, pvt studio classes with John Howard Sanden, 76-77. *Work:* Northport High Sch, NY; works in numerous pvt collections. *Comn:* Numerous portraits, caricatures & caricature portraits in NY, NJ, Ariz & Fla, 75-92. *Exhib:* Ann Art Show, Nassau Co Mus, Roslyn, NY, 77-78; Huntington Township Art League 25th Ann, Hecksher Mus, NY, 80; Pastel Soc Am Ann Mem Show, Salmagundi Club, NY, 81; Nat Soc Painters in Casein & Acrylic, Nat Arts Club, NY, 83; Kans Pastel Soc 1st Ann Nat Juried Show, Wichita Art Asn, 84. *Pos:* Portrait painter, independent, Hyannis, Mass, 68-69; textile designer, Schwartz & Liebman Textiles, New York, 70-76; Caricatures by Chris Green, independent business, 82-. *Awards:* The Grumbcher Art award, 81; Pastel Soc Am Certificate of Merit, 82; Emily Waxberg Memorial award, Suburban Art League Ann Juried Show, 2015. *Bibliog:* Helen A Harrison (auth), Health building scores, NY Times, 10/4/79; Art around town, Glen Cove Weekender, 11/15/80; Art revs, Sunstorm, 7/15/84; book illustrations, French Fries for Siblings: The Forgotten Children of Autism by Lilli Mayerson, 2009. *Mem:* Independent Art Soc; Suburban Art League; Nat League of American Pen Women. *Media:* Pastels, Markers, Watercolors. *Interests:* Gardening. *Dealer:* Gret Neck Games; Xquisite Flowers and Events New Rochelle NY. *Mailing Add:* 52 Hidden Ridge Dr Syosset NY 11791

GREENE, DANIEL E
PAINTER, INSTRUCTOR
b Cincinnati, OH, 1934. *Study:* Art Student's League, NY. *Work:* Mrs Eleanor Roosevelt; Bryant Gumbel of CBS; Astronaut Walter Schirra; Coca Cola Co; Dave Thomas, Wendy's; Dept Agriculture, Secy Ann Veneman; Cincinnati Mus Fine Arts, OH; Clinton Presidential Libr, Ark; Columbus Mus Art, Ga; Harvard Univ, Mass; Princeton Univ, NJ; Yale Univ, Conn; West Point, NY; Nat Acad Design, NY; Metrop Mus Art, NY; and many others; House Rep, US Capitol. *Exhib:* Loring Gallery, NY, 75; Baker Gallery, Tex, 80; Talisman Gallery, Okla, 80; Miller Gallery, OH, 81, 2004, 2007; Subway Series, Gallery Henoch, NY, 85, 92 & 94, 2007; Hammond Mus, NY, 87; Galerie Gismondi, Paris, 87; Hollis Taggart Gallery, NY, 99; John Pence Gallery, Calif, 2001 & 2003; Loring Gallery, Mass, 2003; Charter Oak Gallery, Conn, 2003; NY Transit Mus, 2004; Elaine Baker Gallery, Fla, 2006. *Teaching:* instr, painting, Nat Acad of Design, formerly; instr, painting, Art Students League, NY, formerly. *Awards:* Am Soc Hall of Fame, 92; Pastel Hall of Fame, 83; Lifetime Achievement Award, Am Artist's Mag; Joseph V Giffuni Award, Pastel Soc Am, 1996, 2001,2003; Artists Fel Benjamin West Clinedinst Medal, 99; Medal Hon, Portrait Soc Am, 2001; Laureate Award, Pastel Soc West Coast, 2003; Herman Margulies Award Excellence, Pastel Soc Am, 2005; Artist in Special Tribute, Hudson Valley Art Asn, 2006; Pres Award, Salmagundi Club, 2003; Gladys E Cook Award Painting, Nat Accad Design, 2007; Great Am Artworks Award, Nat Arts Club, 2007. *Bibliog:* Int Artists Mag, 2006-2008; articles in Am Artist Mag, 85, 93 & 01; article, Int Artist Mag, 2/99; Articles in Artists Mag, 2001 & 2003; Artist's Mag, 2007; Am Art Collector, 2007; and many others. *Mem:* Artists' Fel; Pastel Soc Am; Portrait Soc Am. *Media:* Pastels and Oil. *Publ:* Expressing Yourself in Paintings, 1993; Pastel Interpretations, 1993; Best of Pastel, 96; The Art of Pastel Portraiture, 1996; Pure Color: The Best of Pastel, 98; A Painter's Guide to Design & Composition, 2006; Pure Color, 2006; and many others. *Dealer:* Gallery Henoch NY; Miller Gallery OH; Nedra Matteucci NM. *Mailing Add:* Studio Hill Farm PO Box 4388 North Salem NY 10560

GREENE, LOUISE WEAVER
TAPESTRY ARTIST, LIBRARIAN
b Lancaster, Pa, May 7, 1953. *Study:* Haystack Mountain Sch Crafts, 75; Univ Md, BA (art hist), 92, MLS, 94. *Work:* Gannett Co Inc/USA Today, Washington, DC; Fed Home Loan Mortgage Corp, Washington, DC; Bell Canada, Washington, DC. *Comn:* Woven Tapestry, Gateway Int, Baltimore, Md, 86; Woven Tapestry, Gannett Co Inc/USA Today, Washington, DC, 86; Woven Tapestry, Tyson Corp, Springdale, Ark, 87; Woven Tapestry, Int Point, Washington, DC, 88. *Exhib:* For the Floor, Am Craft Mus, NY, 85; Contemp Crafts, Del Art Mus, Wilmington, Del, 85; Fiber Wall Works, Meredith Gallery, Baltimore, Md, 87; Fiber: State of the Art, Atlanta Financial Ctr, Atlanta, Ga, 88; Light Line & Plane, Scheuer Tapestry Gallery, NY, 88; Peripheral Perspectives, Soc Arts & Crafts, Boston, Mass, 89; Mixed Media Invitational, Miriam Perlman Gallery, Chicago, Ill, 89. *Pos:* Reference Librn, Art Libr, Univ Md, College Park. *Awards:* Judges Choice Award, Wash Craft Show, Renwick Gallery, Smithsonian Inst, Washington, DC, 85. *Bibliog:* Nell Znamierowski (auth), For the Floor, Am Craft Mag, 85; Lisa Hammel (auth), Handmade Rugs at Craft, NY Times, 85; Carol Lawrence (ed), Fiberarts Design Book III, 87. *Mem:* Smithsonian Assoc, Wash, DC; Am Craft Coun, NY; Am Tapestry Alliance; James Renwick Alliance Renwick Gallery; Art Libr Soc NAm. *Media:* Woven Tapestry, Fiber. *Publ:* Contrib, Fiberarts Design Book II, & Fiberarts Design Book III, Lark Books, 83 & 87. *Mailing Add:* 2304 Ashboro Dr Chevy Chase MD 20815

GREENE, THOMAS CHRISTOPHER
ADMINISTRATOR, WRITER
b Worcester, Mass, 1968. *Study:* Hobart Col, BA (English & creative writing); Vt Col, MFA (writing), 1996. *Pos:* Dir pub affairs, Norwich Univ, formerly; founding pres, Vt Col of Fine Arts, 2006-. *Awards:* Milton Haight Turk Scholar. *Publ:* auth, Mirror Lake, 2003, I'll Never Be Long Gone, 2005, Envious Moon, 2007. *Mailing Add:* Vermont College of Fine Arts Office of President 36 College St Montpelier VT 05602

GREENFIELD, AMY
FILMMAKER, VIDEO ARTIST
b Boston, Mass, July 8, 1940. *Study:* Radcliffe Col, with Anne Sexton & William Alfred, BA (hon), 62; New England Conservatory, 63-65; Martha Graham Sch Dance, 66-68. *Work:* Lincoln Ctr Dance Collection, Mus Holography, NY; New York Pub Libr Film Collection; Anthology Film Archives; Williamsburg Art & Hist Soc. *Comn:* Resoled (film), 71 & For God While Sleeping (film), 71, Visual Learning Corp; One-O-One (film), comn by Douglas Dunn, NY, 76; Four Solos for Four Women (videotape), Artists TV Proj, NY, 80; Tribute to Charlotte Morman, Comn by Nam June Paik, 94. *Exhib:* Solo exhibs, Womens Avant-Garde Film Festival, Whitney Mus Am Art, 72, New Videodance, Anthology Film Arch, NY, 77, 80 & 83, The Wave: Film & Holography, Hayward Gallery, London, 79 & Dance-Film-Video, Mus Mod Art, NY, 83, Harvard Film Archive, 90, Anthology Film Archives, New York, 91, Festivals of Arts Without Boarders, 94, Theatres Au Cinema, Paris, 95, Am Mus Moving Image, Queens, NY 96, Am Avant-Garde Film Amy Greenfield, Bologna, Italy, 99, Art Inst Chicago, 2008, Leonard Nimoy Thalia Theater, New York, 2009, CTS Gallery, Brookly,NY, 2009-2010; Two Channel Video, Whitney Mus Am Art, 78; Berlin Int Film Festival, 90; Houston Int Film Festival, 90; Howard Film Archives, 90 & 93; Mus Mod Art, 91; Am Film Inst Independent Film Ser, 91; NY Video Festival, 92; Celebration Arts Without Borders, 94; Am Independent Film, Russia Nat TV, 95; Whitney Mus Am Art, New York, 2000; Berlin Film Festival, Germany, 2003; Boston Int Film Festival, 2006; Lincoln Ctr, New York, 2007; Nat Gallery Art, DC, 2007; Inst Contemp Art, Philadelphia, 2010; Film Forum, The Egyptian Theatre, Los Angeles, Calif, 2012; Art Gallery Ontario, Toronto, Canada, 2012. *Pos:* Freelance filmmaker & writer. *Teaching:* Instr film, Tufts Univ, 72-74; vis asst prof, Univ RI, 77-78 & Montclair State Col, 78-79; guest lectr, Univ Calif Art, San Diego, 93. *Awards:* Nat Endowment Arts Grants, 75, 78, 81 & 84; Rockefeller Found Grant, 80; Ten Best Arts & Entertainment, New York Times, 94; Hon for contrib art, Harvard Univ; Hon for contrib art, Fulbright Found; Nat Endowment Arts, 87; Jerome Found, 94. *Bibliog:* Robert Haller (auth), article, Millennium Film J, 80; Deborah Jowitt (auth), Prisoners of the lens, Village Voice, 80; John Gruen (auth), Dance visions, Dancemag, 83; Valerie Restive (auth), Art of the Camera, Boston Herald Traveler, 72; Carol Zemel (auth), Women & Video, Arts Canada, 73; Ann Sargent Wooster (auth), Amy Greenfield at PS1, Village Voice, 1/18/80; Ernest Leogancle (auth), Crewing the Dance, New York Daily News, 3/21/83; John Gruen (auth), Dance Vision, Dance Mag, 11/83; R Bruce Elder (auth), Body as Knower, The Body in Film, 89; Jennifer Dunning (auth), Best in Arts & Entertainment, New York Times, 12/25/94; Vince Musetto (auth), Weekend Plus, NY Post, 11/14/97; AD Coleman (auth), Crop Rotation, Hamptons Country, July 99; Christine Vellucci (auth), Finding a Muse in Dr Spock, AM New York, 2009; Amy Greenfield: Untitled Nude, CTS Gallery, 2010; Flesh Into Light: The Films of Amy Greenfield, Intellect Books, Univ Chgo Press, 2011. *Mem:* Independent Feature Project. *Media:* Film, Video. *Publ:* Auth, Verticle roll, Film Libr Quart, 78; The Big Apple: First in video, 80 & The case of the vanishing videotape, 81, Am Film; Video and film and video, Video Roma, 82; Filmdance space, time, energy, Film Dance, 83; The tales of Hoffman, Film Comment, 95; We Too Are Alive, Poems After & Before 9/11, Solstice Press, 2002; Curtis Harrington: Cinema on the Edge, Anthology Film Archives, 2005; Field of Visions, Steina's Somersault, 85. *Dealer:* Filmmakers Coop 175 Lexington Ave New York NY 10016; Alive Mind Media (Antigone/Rites of Passion) New York; Canyon Cinema San Francisco; Facets Multimedia Chicago; CJCinema Paris; CTS Gallery Brooklyn NY. *Mailing Add:* 135 St Pauls Ave Staten Island NY 10301

GREENFIELD, JOAN BEATRICE
PAINTER, ENAMELIST
b Bronx, NY, Apr 15, 1931. *Study:* Adelphi Univ, New York, BA, (art hist), 5/78, MA (studio arts), 5/81; Nat Acad Design, Andrew Flack, 90; studied with Miriam Shapiro, Parish Mus, 97. *Work:* Adelphi Univ, New York; Buffalo Children's Hosp, NY; Helentex Inc, New York; Rubin & Kimche law offices, Jerusalem, Israel. *Comn:* Portraits, comn by H Cytryn, Woodmere, NY, 87 & 88 & P Henry, Franklin Square, NY, 84; enamels, comn by M Partem, Jerusalem, Israel, 88; Collage (for article), Biblical Archaeology Review, July/Aug 2008. *Exhib:* Solo exhib, R Harley Gallery, Adelphi Univ, New York, 82; group exhibs, Mus Philos, New York, 82, Figures, Nabisco Brands Gallery, NJ, 86, Salute Women's History Month, Paper Mill Playhouse Renee Foosaner Art Gallery, NJ, 87, Nat Asn Women Artist Fall Collection, Monmouth Mus Fine Arts, NJ, 87, Celebration 89, The Interchurch Ctr, New York, 89, Small works, Marbella Gallery, New York, 89, Roper Gallery, Frostburg State Univ, Md, 90, Hampton Sq Gallery, West Hampton, NY, 91, Galarie des Hampton, 92, Fire House Gallery, Nassau Community Coll, Garden City, NY, 92, Parish Art Mus, Southampton, NY, 95, Art Ctr, Sarasota, Fla, 2000, J Wayne Stark Galleries, Tex A&M Univ, Coll Sta, 2004, Art Explores Jewish Themes, NAWA Gallery, New York, 2004, Meditations on War, New York, 2005, Banana Factory, Bethlehem, Pa, 2005, Port of Call Gallery, Warwick, NY, 2006, Goggle Factory, Reading, Pa, 2006 & Women & Spirituality, Interchurch Ctr Galleries, New York, 2006; Community Fine Arts Ctr, Rock Springs, Wyo, 98; Stocker Ctr Gallery, Elyria, Ohio, 98; Saginaw Arts Mus, Mich, 98. *Pos:* Coordr, spec events 78-81, Alumni Exhib, 80-83, Adelphi Univ, Traveling painting Nat Asn Women Artists, New York, 84-90 & Writings on the Wall Exhib, Nat Asn Women Artists, 97; exec bd & new mem chair, Nat Asn Women Artists, 94-98; cur, 4 Faces of Eve, Downstairs Gallery, Hewlett/Woodmere Libr, 98, Constructing & Destructing Images, Gallery, 2000 & Personal Totems by or about Women of Color, Adelphi Univ, Garden City, NY, 2007; panelist, History of the Nat Asn Women Artists, NAWA Gallery, New York, 2005 & Adelphi Alumni Women in Hist, Adelphi Univ, Garden City, NY, 2007. *Awards:* Greenblatt Mem, Nat Asn Women Artists, Forest Elec-P Rebhum, 4/84; New Concept, Nat Asn Women Artists, anonymous, 4/89; S Kahn Award, Nat Asn Women Artists, 5/96. *Mem:* Kappa Pi; Nat Asn Women Artists (exec bd, 84-92); NY Artist Equity; Women's Caucus for Art; NY Found Community Artists; Am Univ Asn Women. *Media:* Acrylic, Oil. *Publ:* Auth, Upon Thy Doorposts, B Rosenblum. *Mailing Add:* 876 Central Ave Woodmere NY 11598

GREENFIELD-SANDERS, TIMOTHY
PHOTOGRAPHER, FILMMAKER
b Miami Beach, Fla, Feb 16, 1952. *Study:* Columbia Univ, BA (art hist), 74; Am Film Inst, with Slavko Vorkapich, MFA (film fel), 77. *Work:* Mus Mod Art, Metrop Mus Art, Int Ctr Photog, NY; Australian Nat Gallery; Nat Portrait Gallery, Washington, DC; Whitney Mus. *Exhib:* One-man shows, Marcuse Pfeifer Gallery, New York City, 82, 85, 87, Leo Castelli Gallery, NY, 87, Mary Boone Gallery, NY, 88, 99, Zeit-Foto, Tokyo, Japan, 88, Greene Gallery, Fla, 89, Marimura Art Mus, Tokyo, Japan, 90, Mus Mod & Contemp Art, Trento, 91, Mod Art Mus, Ft Worth, Tex, 91, Mus Design, Leipzig, Ger, 96, Kunst-Station Sankt Peter, Koln, Ger, 96, Mus Contemp, Mex City, 97, Los Angeles Theater Ctr, 98, Emilio Mazzoli Gallery, Modena, Italy, 2000, Miami Art Mus, 02; group shows, Mus Mod Art, New York City, 91, 99, Staley-Wise Gallery, New York City, 91, Int Ctr Photog, New York City, 93, Ctr Photog, Woodstock, NY, 93, The Saatchi Collection, London, 94, Lincoln Ctr, New York City, 95, Photog Resource Ctr, Boston, 96, Robert Miller Gallery, New York City, 97, Mus of the City of NY, 01, Paine Webber Art Gallery, New York City, 02. *Awards:* Fine Arts Photogr, Am Photogr Mag, 83. *Bibliog:* Hilton Kramer (auth), NY Artist of 50's in 80's, New York Times, 3/27/81; Robert Schwalberg (auth), Portfolio, Camera Arts Mag, 3/82; Dore Ashton (auth), Avenue, 11/82. *Media:* Black & White, Color Polaroid. *Publ:* Contribr, Barrons, 81-86 & Vogue, 83-86; auth, Downtown in the fifties, 81 & Art of the Real, 83, Horizon; Clarkson Potter, Artnews, 83; The New Irascibles, Arts Mag, 9/85. *Dealer:* Mary Boone Gallery 745 Fifth Ave New York Ny 10021; Steven Kasher Gallery. *Mailing Add:* 135 E 2nd St New York NY 10009

GREENHALGH, PAUL
ADMINISTRATOR, CURATOR
b Bolton, Eng. *Study:* Univ Reading, BA (fine art & art hist), 78; Courtauld Inst Art, MA (art hist, specialty in design), 80. *Exhib:* chief organizer, Art Nouveau exhib, Nat Gallery Art, Washington, DC, 2000. *Collection Arranged:* Art Nouveau: 1890-1914 (traveling exhib; auth, catalog), Victoria and Albert Mus, 2000. *Pos:* Tutor, Royal Coll Art; head art hist, Camberwell Coll Arts, London; head res & dep curator ceramics & glass, Victoria and Albert Mus; pres, Nova Scotia Coll Art and Design, 2001-05; dir & pres, Corcoran Gallery Art & Coll Art and Design, Washington, DC, 2006-2010, adj cur European fine and decorative arts, 2010-; dir, Sainsbury Centre for Visual Arts, Univ East Anglia, 2010-. *Publ:* Auth, Ephemeral Visitas, 88; Modernism in Design, 90; Quotations and Sources on Design and Decorative Arts 1800-1990, 94; The Essential Art Nouveau, 2000; The Persistence of Craft, 2002; The Modern Ideal: The Rise and Collapse of Idealism in the Visual Arts from the Enlightenment to Postmodernism, 2005

GREENLEAF, VIRGINIA
PAINTER
b Chicago, Ill. *Study:* Yale Univ Sch Fine Arts; Am Univ; also with Ivan Olinsky, Robert Brackman & Gene Davis. *Work:* Dept State. *Comn:* Numerous pvt comns. *Exhib:* Solo exhibs, Studio Gallery, Wash, 71-76, Main St Gallery Ann, Nantucket, 71-96, Parsons Dreyfuss Gallery, New York, Gallery 124, New York, 83 & Main St Gallery, Boston; Mus Fine Arts, Brazil; Haller Gallery, New York; Christy Lawrence Gallery, Lyme, Conn; Alva Gallery, New London, Conn; Rittenhouse Fine Arts, Phila, Pa; Cooley Gallery, Old Lyme, Conn, 2003-2006; Diane Birdsall Gallery, 2007, 2008, 2009, 2010, 2011, 2012, 2013, 2014; group exhib, Phillips Collection, Corcoran Gallery, Washington, DC, 2008. *Bibliog:* Revs & articles, Boston Globe, Washington Post, Evening Star, Wash, NY Times, Cape Cod Art, Nantucket Inquirer & Mirror & New London Day, Shoreline News, Wash Star, New London Day, Cape Cod Mag (cover& article), Nantucket Rev. *Mem:* Artists Equity Asn; Old Lyme Hist Asn. *Media:* Acrylic, watercolor, graphite. *Interests:* History & art. *Dealer:* Diane Birdsall Old Lyme. *Mailing Add:* 6336 E Valley Green Rd Flourtown PA 19031

GREENLY, COLIN
ENVIRONMENTAL ARTIST, CONCEPTUAL ARTIST
b London, Eng, Jan 21, 1928; US citizen. *Study:* Harvard Coll, AB, 49; Columbia Univ Sch Painting & Sculpture, 51-53; Grad, Sch Fine Arts, Am Univ, 56. *Work:* Mus Mod Art, NY; Corcoran Gallery Art, Washington, DC; Herbert F Johnson Mus, Ithaca, NY; Philadelphia Mus Art; Albright-Knox Art Gallery, Buffalo; Des Moines Art Ctr; Nat Gallery Art, Washington, DC; and others. *Comn:* 12,000 Feet of Color, Corcoran Sch Art, Washington, DC, 70; Transitional Image, since destroyed, Everson Mus, Syracuse, NY, 71; Participatory murals, NY State Off Bldg, Utica, 73 & Creative Artists Pub Serv Prog, 75; Restoration and Adaptation: The 1878 Hulse Barn, 78-98; aluminum sculpture, Cloudlines, Jeffrey J Sherman Arts Ctr, Langley Sch, McLean, Va, 2009. *Exhib:* Solo exhibs, Royal Marks Gallery, NY, 68 & 70, Corcoran Gallery Art, 68, Andrew Dickson White Mus, Cornell Univ, 72, Finch Coll Mus, 74, Mindy Ross Gallery, SUNY, Newburgh, NY; Group exhibs, De Cordova Mus, Lincoln, Mass, 65; Des Moines Art Ctr, 67; Smithsonian Am Art Mus, Washington, DC, 68; Young Am Printmakers, Mus Mod Art, NY, 53; Contemp Am Painting & Sculpture, Krannert Art Mus, Ill, 69 & 74; Everson Mus, Syracuse, NY, 71; Images, Mus Mod Art, NY, 73; John Weber Gallery, NY, 75; Whitney Mus Am Art, NY, 78; NY State Mus, Albany, 81; World Trade Ctr Site Mem Competition, 2003; Century of the Child: Growing by Design, 1900-2000, Mus Modern Art, NY, 2012; and others. *Pos:* Vis artist, Cent Mich Univ, 72; artist-in-residence, Everson Mus, Syracuse, NY, 72 & Cazenovia Coll, 72; artist-in-residence, Nat Endowment Arts & Humanities, Finch Coll, 74. *Teaching:* Dana prof art, Colgate Univ, 72-73. *Awards:* Nat Endowment Arts & Humanities Grant for Sculpture, 67; Creative Artists Pub Serv Prog Grant for Intangible Sculpture, New York, 72; Creative Artists Pub Serv Fel, 78; Decentralization Grant for Video, NY Coun Arts, 93. *Bibliog:* James Harithas (auth), Colin Greenly, Libr Cong No 68-19952, Corcoran Gallery Art, 1/68; Thomas W Leavitt (auth), Colin Greenly: Intangible Sculpture, Libr Cong No 72-9042, Andrew Dickson Mus Art, Cornell Univ, 72; Dore Ashton (auth), article, In Coloquio Artes, NY, 10/74. *Media:* Multiple Archival Digital Images, Intangible Sculpture. *Res:* Format of most universal image in nature reflecting energy interactions; Incorporated the characteristics of a circle and a square into a single image thereby discovering an effective visual symbol for the concepts of transition and change - 1964. *Interests:* Environ inter-relationships; archit; Art/seeing educ; Change. *Publ:* Auth, A changing image of change, A J for Artists, winter 86; contribr, Images of the Whole, the Artist's Sketchbook (CD-ROM), Leaning Post Productions, 98. *Mailing Add:* 487 Hulsetown Rd Campbell Hall NY 10916

GREENOUGH, SARAH
CURATOR
b Boston, Mass, May 25, 1951. *Study:* Univ Pa, BA; Univ NMex, MA & PhD. *Collection Arranged:* Alfred Stieglitz, 1983; On the Art of Fixing a Shadow: 150 Years of Photography, 1989; Modern Art and America: Alfred Stieglitz and His New York Galleries, 2001; Andre Kertesz, 2005; Irving Penn: Platinum Prints, 2005; The Art of the Am Snapshot, 1888-1978: From the Collection of Robert E Jackson, 2007; Richard Misrach: On the Beach, 2008. *Pos:* Sr cur photographs, Nat Gallery Art, Washington, DC. *Awards:* Int Ctr Photog Publ Award, 1989; George Wittenborn Meml Bk Award, 2002; Alfred H Barr Jr Award for Outstanding Mus Scholar, Coll Art Asn, 2007; Cur & Exhib of Yr Award, Lucie Found, 2009; Infinity Award, Int Ctr Photog, 2010. *Publ:* Auth, Walker Evans: Subways and Streets, 1991; Robert Frank: Moving Out, 1994; Harry Callahan, 1996; Alfred Stieglitz: The Key Set, 2002; coauth (with Malcom Daniel & Gordon Badwin), All the Mighty World: The Photographs of Roger Fenton 1852-1860, 2004. *Mailing Add:* c/o National Gallery of Art Press Office 2000B S Club Dr Landover MD 20785

GREENWALD, ALICE (ALICE MARIAN GREENWALD-WARD)
CONSULTANT, MUSEOLOGIST
b Oceanside, NY, Jan 2, 1952. *Study:* Univ Exeter, Devon, Eng, with Theo Brown, 71-72; Sarah Lawrence Col, Bronxville, NY, BA (anthrop & Lit), 73; Univ Chicago Divinity Sch, Ill, AM (hist relig), 75. *Collection Arranged:* Los Angeles Collects: Works on Paper and Graphic Art from Israel, 78-79; The Five Sense Show, 78; The Custom Cut: Jewish Papercuts, Past & Present, 79; Jewish Marriage Contracts: A Celebration in Art, 79; Bill Aron: Portraits of Life, The Elderly Jews of Venice, Calif, 79-80, The Realm of Torah, 81, Between Holy & Profane: Xerography by Dina Dar, 81, Huc Skirball Mus, Hebrew Union Col, Los Angeles, Calif; The Tallis as a Metaphor of Community: Fiber Sculptures by Laurie Gross, 82 & Odyssey of Freedom: The Canvas Diary of a Soviet Jewish Emigre (paintings & works on paper by Tanya Kornfield), 83, The Am Jewish Experience, 89, Mus Am Jewish Hist, Philadelphia; Daniel's Story, US Holocaust Mem Coun, 91-92. *Pos:* Dir, Mus Am Jewish Hist, Philadelphia, Pa, 81-86; prin, Alice M Greenwald/Mus Serv, 86-2001; tech adv, The Pew Charitable Trusts, Philadelphia, 87; assoc mus dir, US Holocaust Mem Mus, Washington, DC, 2001-06; exec vpres progs & dir, Nat Sept 11 Meml & Mus 2006-. *Teaching:* Mus educator Jewish art, Hebrew Union Col, Los Angeles, Calif, 75-81. *Awards:* Nat Endowment Arts Fel Mus Prof, 81. *Mem:* Am Asn Mus; Int Coun Mus; Coun Am Jewish Mus. *Res:* All areas of Jewish art, emphasis on European ritual art and near eastern archaeology; Holocaust studies. *Publ:* Auth, The Mizrach: Compass of the heart, Hadassah Mag, 10/79; The masonic Mizrach: Jewish ritual art as a reflection of cultural assimilation, J Jewish Art, Vol 10, 83; The American Jewish Experience (exhib catalog), 89. *Mailing Add:* Nat September 11 Mem & Mus World Trade Ctr One Liberty Plz 20th Fl New York NY 10006

GREENWOOD, NORMA
PAINTER
b Brooklyn, NY. *Study:* Hunter Coll, New York, MA, 1968. *Exhib:* Solo exhibs include Washington Arts Club, Washington, 2003, Penn State Coll Gallery, Williamsport, PA, 2004, Foundry, Long Island City, NY, 2007; Group exhibs include Matchbox Show, Art in General, New York, 1997; Offspring, Brooklyn, 2001; Echoes of the New Millennium, Queens Coun Arts, Theater in the Park, New York, 2002; Drawing Show, Artists Space, New York, 2004; Sean Kelly, New York, 2004; NY Spring Exhib, Guild Hall, Easthampton, NY, 2007. *Awards:* Abby Austin Award Mural Fel, Nat Acad Art, New York, 2007; George Sugarman Found Grant, 2007

GREER, JANE RUTH
SCULPTOR
b New York, NY, Jan 28, 1941. *Study:* New York Univ, BFA; Art Students League, with John Hovanes. *Work:* Chrysler Mus, Norfolk, Va; Grey Art Gallery, New York Univ, New York, NY; SE Bank of Fla, Miami; photography, Minneapolis Inst Art. *Comn:* Murals, Holiday Inn, Ft Lee, NJ, 86. *Exhib:* Drawing & Collage, Grey Art Gallery, NY Univ, 77; First Anniversary Exhib, 78 & Works on Paper, 82, Drawing Ctr; photographs, Lyman Allyn Mus, Conn; cut paper, Drawing Ctr. *Media:* Wood, Paper; Photography. *Dealer:* Jane Kahan Gallery 922 Madison Ave New York NY 10021; Gallery Henoch 555 W 25 St New York NY 10001. *Mailing Add:* 81 Wooster St New York NY 10012-4375

GREER, JOHN SYDNEY
SCULPTOR
b Amherst, NS, Can, June 28, 1944. *Study:* NS Coll Art, dipl (bursary), 62-64; Montreal Mus Sch Art & Design, dipl (hon sculpture; scholar), 66; Vancouver Sch Art, dipl, 67. *Work:* Nat Gallery, Ottawa; Art Gallery Ont; Art Gallery NS; Beaverbrook Art Gallery, Fredericton, New Brunswick, Can; MacDonald Stewart Art Ctr Sculpture Garden, Guelph, Ont, Can; plus others. *Comn:* Y D Klein (lithograph), NS Coll Art & Design, 74; The Forks (Winnipeg), Parks, Can, 88; Crow Feather (sculpture), MacDonald Stewart Art Ctr Sculpture Garden, 98; plus others. *Exhib:* Solo exhibs, Sculptured Objective, 68-81, Traveling Exhib, Art Gallery NS, 49th Parallel, NY, Mus d'Art Contemp, Montreal & others, 81-83, Dalhousie Art Gallery, Halifax, 87, Ottawa Sch Art Gallery, 87, Southern Alberta Art Gallery, Lethbridge, 90, St Mary's Univ Art Gallery, Halifax, 90, Black Seeds Glendon Gallery, North York, 97, John Greer Nine Grains of Rice, Nat Gallery of Can, Ottawa, 99, Tantalus, Artsplace, Annapolis Royal, 2000, plus others; Art Contemporain 1990 Savoir-Vivre, Ctr Int Art Contemporain, Montreal, 90; Embodied Viewer, Glenbow Mus, 91; and others. *Teaching:* Assoc prof sculpture, NS Col Art & Design, currently. *Awards:* Can Coun Grant, 85, 88 & 90; Victor Martyn Lynch-Staunton Award, Can Coun, 88. *Bibliog:* Gemey Kelly (auth), review, Vanguard, 82; Ron Shuebrook (auth), review, Vanguard, 9-10/87; Robert Pope (auth), review, Arts Atlantic 29, summer/fall 87. *Mem:* Eye Level Gallery, Halifax (vchmn, 75-); Can Artist Representation, Provincial, Nat. *Media:* Stone, Cast Metal. *Publ:* Auth, Sceptical Spectacles, Dalhousie Art Gallery, 74; Waterrings, Dalhousie Art Gallery, 76; Onion Skin Maker Your Eyes Water, Coach House Press, 81; John Greer Sculptural Objective (exhib catalog), Art Gallery NS, 81; Reconciliation (exhib catalog), 90. *Mailing Add:* PO Box 130 La Have NS B0R 1C0 Canada

GREER, WALTER MARION
PAINTER
b Ware Shoals, SC, Aug 11, 1920. *Study:* The Citadel, BS, 42; Clemson Univ, BS, 47; Atlanta Sch Art, 59 & 60; Nat Acad Design, New York, with Robert Phillipp; also with Ben Shute, Atlanta, 62 & study abroad. *Work:* Telfair Acad Arts & Sci, Savannah, Ga; SC State Collection, Columbia Mus Art; paintings, Sea Pines Plantation Co, Hilton Head Island, SC; Greenville Mus Art, SC; C & S Collection, Atlanta & Greenville, SC; and others. *Comn:* Oil landscape, Gov Mansion, Columbia, 67; three paintings, Phipps Land Co, Hilton Head Island & NY, 70; portrait of pres, Emory Univ, 71; triptych, Simmons Collection, Atlanta, Ga; ltd ed print for Marriott Hotels, 81. *Exhib:* Mead Paper Show, Atlanta, Ga, 60; Hunter Ann, Chattanooga, Tenn, 62; SC Invitational, Columbia, 69; Solo exhibs, Columbia Mus Art, 73 & Telfair Acad Arts & Sci, 74, 76 & 82; Guild SC Artists, 81. *Teaching:* Instr pvt classes, 63-66, 78 & 81; instr spec art classes, USMC, Parris Island, SC, 64-65 & Savannah Art Asn Sch, 66. *Awards:* Savannah Arts Festival Award for Rivers, 66; SC Arts Coun Purchase Award for Pond, 69; SC Archit Award for Pond (Grey Phase), 71. *Bibliog:* Virginia Ball (auth), The man that got away, Atlanta Mag, 65; articles & 28 covers, Islander Mag; Jack Morris & Robert Smeltz (auth), Contemporary artists of South Carolina, 70. *Mem:* Guild SC Artists; hon life mem Beaufort Art Asn. *Media:* Oil, Acrylic. *Publ:* Cover and profile, Southern World Mag, 79 & 80; article, Southern Accents Mag, 82. *Dealer:* Tatler Gallery Hilton Head Island SC 29928. *Mailing Add:* 300 Woodhaven Dr Apt 4104 Hilton Head Island SC 29928-7531

GREER, WESLEY DWAINE
EDUCATOR, CRAFTSMAN
b Weyburn, Sask, Nov 25, 1937; US citizen. *Study:* Univ BC, BEd, MEd; Stanford Univ, PhD. *Comn:* Logo, Chamber Mus Plus Southwest, Tucson, 2006. *Exhib:* Artists Equity Salute to the Bicentennial, Calif Mus Sci & Indust, 80; On the Face of It: 23 Los Angeles Artists, Calif State Univ, Dominguez Hills, 86. *Pos:* Dir, Getty Improving Visual Arts Educ Proj, Los Angeles, 82-92. *Teaching:* Prof art, Univ Ariz, 82-2002, prof emer. *Awards:* Art Educ Year, Nat Art Educ Asn, 88; Purchare Award, Greater Oro Valley Arts Coun, 2006. *Mem:* Distinguished Fel Nat Art Educ Asn. *Media:* Giglee prints. *Res:* Art curriculum and staff develop in pub schs. *Publ:* Auth, Discipline based art education: Approaching art as a subject of study, Studies in Art Educ, 84; Structure for DBAE, Studies in Art Educ, 87; Developments in Discipline Based Art Education (DBAE) Studies in Art Education, 93; Art as a Basic: The Reformation in Art Education, Phi Delta Kappa, 97; Five Ideas From Five Decades, Art Educators On Art Educ, James Madison Univ, 2014. *Mailing Add:* 1240 W San Lucas Dr Tucson AZ 85704

GREEVES, R V (RICHARD VERNON)
SCULPTOR
b St Louis, Mo, Feb 24, 1935. *Work:* Nat Cowboy Hall of Fame, Oklahoma City; Genesee Country Mus, Rochester, NY; Indianapolis Art Mus, Ind; Liberty Hall, Nat Trust Found, Elizabeth, NJ; City of Sheridan, NY. *Comn:* Story Teller (bronze sculpture), Sheridan Publ Libr, Wyo, 77; The Cock (bronze sculpture), Bartlesville

Civic Ctr, Okla, 82; The Unknown (bronze monument), Whitney Gallery of Western Art, Cody, Wyo, 84. *Exhib:* Solo exhibs, Wyo State Art Mus, Cheyenne, 71, Kennedy Galleries, NY, 73, Barclays Int Bank, Chicago, Ill, 76, Wyo State Capitol Bldg, Cheyenne, 82 & Nicolaysen Art Mus, Casper, Wyo, 82-83; Nat Acad Western Art Show, Nat Cowboy Hall of Fame, 75-90; Peking Exhib Am Western Art, Beijing Exhib Palace, China, 81; 3M Western Art Show, Art Ctr Minn, St Paul, 83-84; Masters of the Am West, 96-2005. *Collection Arranged:* Sheepeaters of The Yellowstone, The Autry Mus Western Heritage, Los Angeles; Washakie, Chief of the Shoshone, Buffalo Bill Historical Center, Cody, Wyo, Crazy Horse, Buffalo Historical Center; Bird Woman, Autry Mus Western Heritage. *Pos:* Mem arts ctr adv comt, Cent Wyo Col, Riverton, 85-86. *Teaching:* Instr, Scottsdale Artists School. *Awards:* Gold Medal, 76 & 79 & Prix de West, 77, Nat Acad Western Art, Nat Cowboy Hall of Fame; James Earle Fraser Award Artistic Merit in Sculpture, Nat Cowboy Hall of Fame, 2000; Gold Medal, for sculpture, Autry Mus Los Angeles, Calif, 2004. *Bibliog:* Will Carson (auth), A Genuine Greeves, Western Horseman, 6/71; Dean Krakel II (auth), My Life's Work, Southwest Art, 7-8/75; John Running (auth), The Unknown: A Monument by R V Greeves, 86. *Mem:* Nat Acad Western Art (mem exec comt, 82). *Media:* Bronze. *Publ:* Contribr, Bronzes of the American West by Broder, Abrams, Inc, 74; Contemporary Western Artists, Southwest Art, 82; Sculpture Review, Nat Sculpture Soc, 82 & 86; Art West Mag, 83; Four Centuries of Sporting Art by Schmitt, Genesee Country Mus, 84; Leading the West: 100 Contemporary Artist's Art of the West, 98. *Dealer:* Legacy Galleries Jackson Wyo Scottsdale Ariz; Jackson Wyo; Settlers West Tucson Ariz. *Mailing Add:* PO Box 428 53 N Fork Rd Fort Washakie WY 82514

GREGOR, HAROLD LAURENCE
PAINTER, EDUCATOR
b Detroit, Mich, Sept 10, 1929. *Study:* Wayne State Univ, BSEd, 51; Mich State Univ, MS (ceramics, painting), 53; Detroit Soc Arts & Crafts, 55-57, Ohio State Univ, PhD (painting, art hist), 60; and with Hoyt Sherman. *Work:* Xerox Collection, Stamford, Conn; Springfield Art Mus, Mo; Rose Art Mus, Brandeis Univ; State Ill Bldg, Chicago; Borg-Warner Collection, Chicago; Chicago Bd Trade; Chicago Art Inst; Mus Am West, Los Angeles, Calif; Chemical Bank, London; Hunt Cultural Center, Dallas, Tex; AT&T/Lucent Technologies, Murray Hill, NJ; Cleveland Clinic, Cleveland, Ohio,; SUTX Mus Art, Corpus Christi, Tex; Autry Nat Ctr/Mus Am West, Los Angeles; Ill State Univ, Normal; Lakeview Mus, Peoria, Ill; Daum Mus, Sedalia, Mo; S Ill Medical Ctr, Springfield, Mo; Amoco Corp, NY; Vero Beach Mus, Fla; Ark Medical Ctr, Little Rock, Ark. *Comn:* Two murals, State Ill New Main Libr, Springfield, Ill, 91; Anderson Industries, Rockford, Ill, 94; Mural, McCormick Place-West, Chicago, Ill, 97; Crown Equipment, New Brennan, OH, 2000; Mural, Central Ill Regional Airport, Bloomington, Ill, 2002; Federal Reserve Bank of Chicago, Ill, 2003; Ill Appelate Court Bldg, Springfield, Ill, 2005; A Rotation Coll, The White House's Oval Office Private Dining, 2009-2011; Richard Durbin, Wash DC, 2011-. *Exhib:* Solo exhibs, Nancy Lurie Gallery, 74-83, Tibor De Nagy Gallery, NY, 77-91, Richard Gray Gallery, Chicago, 83-99, traveling, 91 & 93, MB Mod Gallery, NY, 98, 2000 & Katharina Rich Perlow Gallery, NY, 2007; Group exhibs, Land, Sky, Water, Spokane World's Fair, 74 & Gerald Peters Gallery, Santa Fe, NMex, 2001-2008; Contemp Midwest Landscapes, Ind Mus Art, Indianapolis, 86; Retrospective (with catalog), Lakeview Mus Arts & Sci, Peoria, Ill, 87-88, Rockford Art Mus (with catalog), Rockford, Ill, 93-94; Plain Pictures, Univ Iowa Mus Art, 96-97; Rediscovering the Landscape, Gerald Peters Gallery, Santa Fe, NMex, 96-97; From the Road, From the River, From the Sky, Univ galleries, Ill State Univ (with catalog), 2000; Watercolor for Honor Soc, 2000-; Grossmont Coll, El Cajon, Calif, 2001; Gerald Peters Gallery, Santa Fe, NMex, 2001; Art Mus South Tex, Corpus Christi, 2003; Katharina Rich Perlow Gallery, NY, 2003, 2005 & 2007; Loveland Mus Art, Loveland, Colo, 2004; Retrospective: Harold Gregor's Illinois, Mitchell Mus at Cedarhurst, Mt Vernon, Ill, 2006; Tory Folliard Gallery, Milwaukee, Wis, 2006-2011; Radiant Plains, Ill State Univ, Normal, 2009; Land Use/Mis Use: Celebration and Exploitation of the American Landscape, Gerald Peters Gallery, Santa Fe; Watercolor USA, 2011; Tory Folliard Gallery, Milwaukee, Wisc, 2013; McLean County Art Ctr, Bloomington, Ill. *Collection Arranged:* View from Here: Heartland Painters, McLean Co Art Ctr, Bloomington, Ill, 92. *Pos:* juror, Nat Watercolor Soc, San Pedro, Calif, 2011. *Teaching:* Asst prof painting & art hist, San Diego State Univ, 60-63; asst prof painting, Purdue Univ, 63-66; assoc prof painting & art hist, Chapman Col, 66-70; prof painting & art hist, Ill State Univ, Normal, 70-88, distinguished prof, 88-95; distinguished prof emeritus, art, Ill State Univ; master class instr, Springmaid Watermedia Conference, 2007-. *Awards:* Nat Endowment Arts Grant, 73, 86 & 93-94; Lifetime Achievement Award, State of Il, 1992; Watercolor USA Purchase Award, 84, 85, 89, & 2006; Outstanding Teacher & Researcher, Ill State Univ, 85 & 86; Lifetime Achievement Award, Nat Watercolor Hon Soc, 2006. *Bibliog:* Gerald Nordland (auth), Harold Gregor, Rockland, Ill, 93; J Driscoll & A Skolnick (auths), The Artist and the American Landscape, 98; Kevin Sharp (auth), Harold Gregor's Illinois, Cedarhurst, Mt. Vernon, Ill, 2006; and others. *Mem:* Watercolor Honor Soc. *Media:* Watercolor, Acrylic. *Specialty:* Landscape painting. *Interests:* Literature, architecture, museums, travel. *Publ:* Coauth (with K Gregor), Discovering a lost technique, 7/87 & The techniques of a flatscape, 12/86, The Artists Mag. *Dealer:* Richard Gray Gallery 875 N Michigan Suite 2503 Chicago IL 60611; Gerald Peters Gallery 1011 Paseo de Peralta Santa Fe NM 87501; ACA Galleries 529 W 20th St New York NY; Tory Folliard Gallery 221 N Milwaukee Ave Milwaukee Wis. *Mailing Add:* 107 W Market St Bloomington IL 61701

GREGOROPOULOS, JOHN
PAINTER
b Athens, Greece, Dec 16, 1921; US citizen. *Study:* In Athens; Univ Conn, BA. *Work:* Minn Mus Art, St Paul; Ball State Found, Muncie, Ind; Slater Mus, Norwich, Conn; De Cordova Mus, Lincoln, Mass; Berkshire Mus, Pittsfield, Mass. *Exhib:* Whitney Mus Am Art Ann, 54 & Art USA, NY, 58; Pan Helleml Salon, Athens, 57-63; 1st Biennale Christlicher Kunst Gegenwart, Salzburg, 58; Drawings USA, Minn Mus Art, 71; Retrospective, William Benton Mus, 90 & Drawings, Titanium, Athens, Greece, 98. *Teaching:* Prof emer, Univ Conn, 53-84. *Awards:* Small Drawings & Sculpture Purchase Award, Ball State Teachers Col, 55; Grumbacher Award, Chautauqua Art Asn 2nd Nat, 59; Drawings USA, St Paul Art Ctr, 63. *Bibliog:* F Walkey (auth), John Gregoropoulos, Art in Am, 2/55; John Gregoropoulos, Zygos, Athens, 57; Art & the new patron, WEDN-TV, 68. *Publ:* Auth, Change in art, Nea Estia, Athens, 57. *Mailing Add:* 114 Wyassup Lake Rd North Stonington CT 06359-1143

GREGORY, JOAN
EDUCATOR, PAINTER
b Montgomery, Ala, Apr 1, 1930. *Study:* Univ Montevallo, AB, 52; Peabody Col, MA, 53, EdD, 66; Inst Allende, San Miguel Allende, Mex. *Work:* NC Nat Bank; La State Art Comn; Springs Mills, Lancaster, SC; US Park Serv, Gatlinburg, Tenn. *Exhib:* Huntington Galleries, 56-61; Solo exhibs, 63 & 13th Dixie Art Ann, Montgomery Mus Fine Arts; Southeastern Painting Show, Gallery Contemp Art, Winston-Salem, NC, 71 & 79; Ann NC Artists Exhib & Traveling Show, 71-72. *Pos:* Bd dir, Assoc Artists NC, 69-71 & Southeastern Col Art Conf, 74-78; mem state assembly, Nat Art Educ Asn, 71-73. *Teaching:* Instr art, Marshall Univ, 55-61; chmn dept art, Bloomsburg State Col, 63-64; prof art, Univ NC, Greensboro, 64-90, head dept, 74-85; ret. *Awards:* Purchase Awards, Dillard Collection, Weatherspoon Gallery, Univ NC, Greensboro, 66 & Springs Art Show, Lancaster, SC, 72; Merit Award, NC/Va Art Educators, Southeastern Ctr Contemp Art, 75. *Mem:* Nat Art Educ Asn; NC Art Educ Asn (pres, 71-75); Southeastern Coll Art Conf (secy-treas, 81-); Assoc Artists NC. *Media:* Collage. *Mailing Add:* 106 Mansfield Cir Greensboro NC 27455-3400

GREGORY, JOSEPH F
DIRECTOR
Study: State Univ of NY, Binghamton, PhD. *Pos:* dir, Design Arts Gallery. *Teaching:* Asst prof, art hist, dept visual studies Drexel Univ, Philadelphia. *Mailing Add:* Drexel Univ Nesbitt Coll Design Arts 33rd and Market Sts Philadelphia PA 19104

GREGORY-GOODRUM, ELLNA KAY
PAINTER, PRINTMAKER
b Houston, Tex, Oct 3, 1943. *Study:* Univ Okla, BFA, 65; NTex State Univ, MFA, 79. *Work:* Rockwell Int, Brown Found & Consult & Atlantic Richfield, Dallas, Tex; Ford-Renaissance Ctr, Detroit. *Exhib:* 29th Tex Watercolor Soc, McNay Art Inst, San Antonio, 78; Pastel Soc Am, Nat Arts Club, NY, 79; Watercolor Invitational, Birmingham Mus Art, Ala, 79; Nat Watercolor Soc, 85, 87 & 88; Women & Watercolor, Transco Energy Ctr, Houston, 88; Rocky Mountain Nat Water Media, Foothills Art Ctr, 86 & 88; Watercolor USA, Springfield Art Mus, 88; and others. *Teaching:* Instr art, Richland Col, 80-. *Awards:* Best Abstract Award, 79 & Mixed Media Award, Pastel Soc Am, 87; Red Sable Award, Southern Watercolor Soc, 79; Southwestern Watercolor Soc Award, 79, 83, 85 & 88; Nat Watercolor Award, Okla, 88. *Bibliog:* Articles in Park E Publ, New York, 79 & Dallas Morning News, 79. *Mem:* Coll Art Asn; Pastel Soc Am; Tex Watercolor Soc; Southwestern Watercolor Soc; Nat Watercolor Soc. *Media:* Watercolor. *Publ:* Auth, Watercolor '89, Am Artist. *Mailing Add:* 7214 Lane Park Dr Dallas TX 75225-2454

GRELLE, MARTIN GLEN
PAINTER
b Clifton, Tex, Sept 17, 1954. *Study:* Art Instruction Schs, 72; McLennan Community Col, 75. *Comn:* Bosque landscape, Bosque Co Mus, Clifton, Tex, 74; football mural, Cub Stadium, Clifton, Tex, 76; Bosque Autumn (painting), comn by King Olav IV of Norway, 82; mural, Trinity Lutheran Church, Clifton, Tex, 82; Misty Morning Gather (oil mural), Western Savings Asn, Gatesville, Tex, 86. *Exhib:* Am Indian & Cowboy Artists Ann, Sandmas Calif, 77-83; Western Heritage, Houston, Tex, 79, 81 & 84-85; Stamford Art Found, Tex, 79-86; Tex Art Gallery Preview, Dallas, 80-82; First Ann Student Exhib, Cowboy Artists of Am, Kerrville, Tex, 84; Solo exhibs, Tex Art Gallery, Dallas, Tex, 86 & 88, Overland Trail Gallery, Scottsdale, Ariz, 89, 90, 91, 92. *Awards:* Bronze Medal, Am Indian Cowboy Artists Exhib, 77; Gold Medal, Am Indian Cowboy Artists Exhib, 79; Silver Award for oil & Artist's Award, Tex Ranger Hall of Fame Show, 85. *Bibliog:* Article, Art West Mag, 1-2/83, 9-10/90; article, Southwest Art Mag, 3/86; Western Art Digest Mag, 1-2/87. *Media:* Oil, Acrylics. *Dealer:* Overland Trail Fine Art Gallery 7155 Main St Scottsdale AZ 85251

GRESSER, SEYMOUR GERALD
SCULPTOR, WRITER
b Baltimore, Md, May 9, 1926. *Study:* Maryland Univ, BS, 46, MA 72; Inst Contemp Art, 48-50; special study with William Taylor, 49-52. *Work:* St John the Divine Gallery, NY; Fairfield Coll, Hartford, Conn; Pierson Coll (Yale Univ), New Haven, Conn; New Britain Mus Am Art, Conn; Klutznick Nat Jewish Mus, Catholic Univ, Washington, DC. *Exhib:* Religious Art, Sweetbriar Col, Va, 85; Blood Rites/Birth Rites, Duke Univ, Durham, NC, 86; New Sculptures, Montpelier Art Mus, Laurel, Md, 88; Wesley Theology Seminary, Washington, DC, 92; Gomez Gallery, Baltimore, 95; Gallery Ch'i, Brooklyn, NY, 2005; Four Generations: Alex Giampietro, William Taylor, Sy Gresser, Michael Winger, Klutznick Nat Jewish Mus, Wash DC, 1998; Univ Md Art Mus, 2009; Slifka Ctr, Yale Univ, 2009. *Pos:* consult, res. *Teaching:* Instr sculpture, Antioch Coll (Columbia Campus), 79-81; residency, Colgate Univ, Hamilton, NY, 89, Thomas Jefferson Sch, Frederick, Md, 90. *Media:* Stone, wood. *Specialty:* Contemporaries. *Interests:* China/Poetry. *Publ:* auth, Stone, Wood & Words, Kunming Press, Kunming, PRC, 2006. *Dealer:* Gallery Ch'i, Brooklyn, NY. *Mailing Add:* 1015 Ruatan St Silver Spring MD 20903

GRETHER, ESTHER
COLLECTOR
b Switz. *Pos:* Chmn, Doetsch Grether AG, Basel, Switz, 1975-; bd dirs, Swatch Group AG, Biel/Bienne, Switz, 1986-. *Awards:* Named one of Top 200 Collectors, ARTnews mag, 2003-13. *Collection:* Modern and contemporary art. *Publ:* Assoc producer, Yellow Handkerchief (film), 2008. *Mailing Add:* Doetsch Grether AG Steinentorstrasse 23 Basel CH-4002 Switzerland

GREY, ALEX V
PAINTER, SCULPTOR
b Columbus, Ohio, Nov 29, 1953. *Study:* Columbus Coll Art & Design, 71-73; Boston Mus Sch, 74-75. *Work:* Mus Contemp Art-San Diego, La Jolla, Calif; Brooklyn Mus Fine Arts, NY; Krannert Art Mus, Champaign, Ill; Islip Art Mus, NY. *Comn:* Cosmic Christ: Joe Firmage. *Exhib:* Disarming Images, Univ Calif Mus Art, Santa Barbara, 85; Choices, New Mus, NY, 86; Revelations, Aspen Art Mus, Colo, 89; Sacred Mirrors, Univ Colo Mus, Boulder, 90; solo exhib, Univ Galleries, Ill State Univ, Normal, 93; Mus Contemp Art, San Diego, 99; Solway/Jones Gallery, Los Angeles, 2001; Feature Inc, NY, 2002; Tibet House, NY, 2002. *Teaching:* Prof anat of artists, NY Univ, 87-98; prof visionary art, Omega Inst, 94-. *Awards:* Fel in Sculpture, Mass Coun for Arts, 84 & NY Found for Arts, 86. *Bibliog:* Lewis MacAdams (auth), It started out with death, High Performance, spring 82; Carlo McCormick (auth), Through Darkness to Light, Sacred Mirrors/Inner Traditions, 90; John Strausbough (auth), X-ray visions, New York Press, 4/7/92; Alex Grey (auth), Transfigurations, Inner Traditions, 2001. *Mem:* Integral Inst Art. *Media:* Oil, Acrylic; Bronze. *Publ:* Coauth, Art in Transformation: Interview with artist Alex Grey, New Frontier Mag, 89; auth, Sacred Mirrors, Inner Traditions, 90; The Life and Art of Alex and Allyson Grey, Tantra Mag, 92; Visions of Body and Soul, Caduceus Mag, 92; The Mission of Art, Shambhala, 98. *Dealer:* Feature Inc 530 W 25th St New York NY 10001. *Mailing Add:* 725 Union St Brooklyn NY 11215

GRIBBON, DEBORAH
MUSEUM DIRECTOR
b Washington, DC. *Study:* Wellesley Coll, BA (Phi Beta Kappa); Harvard U, PhD (fine arts, Rousseau fel). *Pos:* Cur, Isabella Stewart Gardner Mus, Boston, 1976-1984; asst dir curatorial affairs, J Paul Getty Mus, 1984-1998, dep dir & chief cur, 1998-2000 & dir & vpres, 2000-2004; interim dir, Cleveland Art Mus, 2009-2010. *Publ:* Co-auth (with John Walsh), The J. Paul Getty Museum and its Collections: A Museum for the New Century

GRIBBON, JENNA
PAINTER, VIDEO ARTIST
b Knoxville, Tenn, 1978. *Study:* Univ Ga, BFA (painting & drawing, magna cum laude), 2001. *Comn:* Three portraits for the film Marie Antoinette, Sofia Coppola. *Exhib:* Solo exhibs include Sarah Bowen Gallery, Brooklyn, NY, 2006, Shoshana Wayne Gallery, Santa Monica, Calif, 2008, Priska C Juschka Fine Art Gallery, New York, 2008; two-person show with Sarah Chuldenko, Album Co, New York, 2006; group exhibs include Inaugural Exhib, Athens Inst Contemp Art, Ga, 2002; MoCA Salutes the Young Movers & Shakers, Ga Mus Contemp Art, Atlanta, 2007; With Teeth, Priska C Juschka Fine Art Gallery, New York, 2007; Ann Invitational Exhib, Nat Acad, New York 2008. *Awards:* John Koch Award, Nat Acad, 2008

GRIBIN, LIZ
PAINTER, PRINTMAKER
b London, Eng, Mar 30, 1934; US citizen. *Study:* Art Students League; Mus Mod Art; Boston Univ, BFA, 56; studied with David Aronson, Paul Wood & Patrick Ireland. *Work:* Emily Lowe Gallery, Hofstra Univ; Manhattan Bowery Corp Collection, NY; Boston Univ; Columbia Grammer & Prep Sch; and numerous pvt collections. *Comn:* portrait, commn by Beverly Holmes, 2000. *Exhib:* Solo exhibs, Art Upstairs, East Willison, NY, 89, Gallery Emanuel, Great Neck, NY, 90, 91 & 94, Nassau Co Mus Art, Roslyn, NY, 94, Sholom Gallery, Cherry Hill, NJ, 95, Bridgehampton Cafe, NY, 97 & 98, Port Wash Libr, NY, 97, Newbury Fine Arts, Boston, 2005 & Studio E, Palm Beach Gardens, Fla, 2008; Guild Hall Mus, E Hampton, NY, 88-90 & Elaine Benson Gallery, Bridgehampton, NY, 89; Kirkpatrick Art Ctr, Oklahoma City, Okla, 90; 92nd & 93rd Ann Mem Exhib, Nat Arts Club, 90-91; 35th & 37th Ann Exhib, Heckscher Mus, 90 & 92; 159th Ann Exhib, Nat Acad Design; Nat Arts Club, NY, 90-97; Guild Hall, East Hampton, NY, 95-2003; Arlene Bujese Gallery, East Hampton, NY, 95-97; Ashawagh Hall, East Hampton, NY, 97 & 98; Nan Mulford Gallery, Rockport, Maine, 97-2003; Millennium Gallery, East Hampton, NY, 98; Goat Alley Gallery, Sag Harbor, NY, 98; Artist's Choice, BJ Spoke Gallery, Huntington, NY, 98; Club Colette, Southampton, NY, 2000; Gayle Willson Gallery, Southampton, NY, featured artist, 2002; Newbury Fine Arts, Boston, 2002-2009; Eisenhauer Gallery, Martha's Vineyard, 2005-2009; Edgwater Gallery, Middlebury, Vt, 2011; Newbury Fine Arts, Boston, Mass, 2011; Newbury Fine Art, 2013. *Pos:* Dir, Gallery Emanuel, Great Neck, NY, 90-2000-. *Teaching:* Lectr, Guild Hall, Long Island Art Leagues & Nassau Co Fine Arts Ctr, currently; Studio Classes, Bridgehampton, NY; Guest Lectr, Boston Univ, Col Fine Art; Leventhal-Sidman, JCC Newton, Mass, 2010-; instr figurative painting, 2010-2011. *Awards:* Various Awards, Audubon Artists, 85, 89, 93, 94 & 95; Pall Corp Award, Heckscher Mus Art Ann, 96; Bruce Stevenson Award, Nat Arts Club, 98th Ann Show, 96 & 2000; US Libr Cong Living Legend, 2000; Nat Arts Club Presidents Award, 2003; and others. *Bibliog:* Feature article, Art & Antiques Mag, 1/2001, Emerging Artists Portfolio, 2001, Southampton Press & Bostonia Mag, 2003, Am Style Mag, 6/2006 & Boston Globe Mag Sec, 2/2007; artist spotlight, Originals (TV show). *Mem:* Nat Asn Women Artists; Audubon Artists; Nat Arts Club; Artists Alliance East Hampton. *Media:* Acrylic, Oil; Etching. *Specialty:* 21st century. *Interests:* all 20th century painting. *Publ:* Liz Gribin, Ltd Ed Prints, 2002-2008. *Dealer:* Jonathan Frost Gallery Rockland ME; Newbury Fine Arts Boston MA; Eisenhaurer Gallery Martha's Vineyard MA; Edgewater G Middlebury VT; Walsingham G Newburyport MA; Largaquist Gallery Atlanta Ga. *Mailing Add:* Charles River Landing 300 2nd Ave #3105 Needham MA 02494

GRIEGER, DONALD L
PAINTER
b Niles, Mich, Jan 2, 1934. *Study:* Univ Mich, BS, 57; Air Force Inst Tech, MS, 66. *Work:* US Coast Guard Collection; Nat Warplane Mus, Elmira, NY; Genesee Community Coll, Batavia, NY; Salmagundi Club. *Exhib:* Light on the Landscape, Bryan Mem Gallery, Jeffersonville, Vt, 98-2007; 62nd Grand Nat Exhib, Salmagundi Club, NY, 99; 67th & 68th Grand Nat Exhib, Salmagundi Club, NY, 2004-05; 76th Ann Exhib, Hudson Valley Art Asn, 2007; 95th Ann Exhib, Allied Artists of Am, 2008; World Canal Conference Invitational exhib, Oxford Gallery, Rochester, New York, 2010. *Awards:* Mary Fitch award, Salmagundi Spring Auction, 2004; Salmagundi Club award, 67th Grand Nat Exhib, 2004; Antonio Cirino Mem award, Ann Combined Salmagundi Club, 2005; Martin Hannon Mem Award, Salmagundi Ann Thumb-Box Exhib, 2005; Frank Van Steen Mem Award, Hudson Valley Art Asn 75th Ann Exhib, 2006; Oil Painters Am Award Excellence, 16th Nat Exhib; Gamblin Award, Audubon Artists 66th Ann Exhib; Juror and Merit Awards, GU Plein Air Painters 6th Ann; Merit award, Genesee Valley Plein Air Painters, 2012, 2014; Spring Exhib Jurors' award, Rochester Art Club, 2012; Jurors award, Rochester Art Club, 2012, Merit award, 2014. *Bibliog:* Charles Movalli (auth), A Conversation with Don Grieger, Am Artist, 92. *Mem:* Salmagundi Club, NY; Am Artists Prof League; North Shore Arts Asn; Rochester Art Club; Oil Painters of Am. *Media:* Acrylic, Oil. *Publ:* Louise Grieger (auth), 50 Miles on the Erie Canal, Am Artist, 94. *Dealer:* Union Gallery Lambertville NJ; West End Gallery Corning NY. *Mailing Add:* 5024 Terry Hills Dr Batavia NY 14020

GRIER, MARGOT EDMANDS
LIBRARIAN, ADMINISTRATOR
b Washington, DC, May 15, 1946. *Study:* Old Dominion Univ, with Parker Lesley, BA (magna cum laude), 71; Univ Md, MLS, 72. *Pos:* Serials librn, Nat Gallery Art, Washington, DC, 73-; automation coordr, Nat Gallery Art, Washington, DC, 87-90; adminr, Educ Div Nat Gallery Art, Washington, DC, 90-. *Awards:* Hermitage Found Award, Norfolk, Va, 69 & 70. *Mem:* Art Libraries Soc North Am; Washington Art Libr Resources Comt; Embroiderers' Guild Am. *Res:* Integrated museum online access systems. *Interests:* 20th century Mexican; contemporary; small press art magazines, textile history. *Publ:* Auth, Old St Paul's, Kent Co, Md, St Paul's Episcopal Church, 71; contribr, ARLIS/NA Newsletter, Art Libr Soc, 79-80; co-ed, Art Serials Union List, 81; contribr, Art Doc, 83-; ed, National Gallery of Art Serials, Nat Gallery Art, 83; contribr auth, Gemini GEL Art and Collaboration, Ruth Fine, Nat Gallery Art & New York, Abbeville Press, 84

GRIESEDIECK, ELLEN
MURALIST
b Jan 26, 1948. *Study:* Univ Colo, BFA, 70. *Comn:* Four paintings, Gen Motors, NY, 80; five paintings, Times Mirror Publ, NY, 82; mural, Columbia-Presby Hosp, 96; Wall of America, public art exhib tribute to builders of Am; designer of Newman's Own labels; Wall of Am, Mural in Progress, 99-2005. *Exhib:* Royal Orleans, New Orleans, 78; Spectrum Olympics, Spectrum Gallery, NY, 79; Seagram's Special Exhib, NY, 80; solo exhibs, Gallery Henoch, NY, 85, 89, Tour de France, Galerie de Poche, Paris, 90 & Empire Arts, Grand Forks NDak, 98. *Bibliog:* Richard Martin (auth), Ellen Griesedieck, Arts Mag, 85; Artist's vision of working America, Labors Heritage Quart, 11/96. *Media:* Aluminum, Fiberglass. *Publ:* Illusr, Summer, Addison/Wesley, 90. *Dealer:* Marcel Fleiss Galerie de Poche 3 Rue Bonaparte Paris France 75006; Gallery Henoch New York NY. *Mailing Add:* 173 Low Rd Sharon CT 06069

GRIESGRABER, MICHAEL JOSEPH
PAINTER
b St Paul, Minn, Oct 6, 1940. *Study:* Univ Minn, BFA, 74; Syracuse Univ, MFA, 77; studied with Peter Busa, BFA Studio Arts, 74. *Work:* Souther Nev Mus Fine Art, Las Vegas; Minn Mus Art, St Paul, Minn; Walker Art Ctr, Minneapolis, Minn; Brunz Rosowsky Gallery, Las Vegas, Nev; Andrews Art Mus, Andrews NC. *Exhib:* Watercolor Sketches, Univ Minn West Bank Union Gallery, Minn, 75; Metamorphose/One, Sky Gallery/Dakota Ctr Arts, St Paul, Minn, 76; Fall Foundup, Las Vegas Art Mus, Nev, 2003; Aerial Banners, Aerial Gallery, Las Vegas, Nev, 2003; Andrews Art Mus, NC, 2009; Gaughin in the 21st Century, Southern Nev Mus Fine Art, Las Vegas, 2009; Action Painters, SNMFA, 2010; Neo Action Abstraction, Rain Forest Foundation Gallery, 2011; 14th Ann Int Contemporary Exhib, Upstream People Gallery, Omaha, 2012, 15th Ann Faces Exhib, 2013, 16th Ann Int Contemporary Exhib, 2014; ArtSlant 4th Showcase, ArtSlant ARTshow, Los Angeles, 2012, ArtSlant 3rd Showcase, 2012, ArtSlant 3rd Showcase, 2013, ArtSlant 5th Showcase, 2013, ArtSlant 1st Showcase, 2014, ArtSlant 2nd Showcase, 2014; Art Santa Fe, 2012, 2013; Southern Nevada Mus Fine Art, 2013; Brooklyn Waterfront Artist Coalition (BWAC), Nat Juried Show, 2014; Why Masterworks? Invitational, Historic Fifth St School, Las Vegas, NV, 2014; 16th Annual Contemporary Art Exhib, Upstream People Gallery, Omaha, Nebr, 2014. *Pos:* Assist design cur, Walker Art Ctr, Minneapolis, Min, 64-67. *Awards:* 1st prize, 54th Ann Fine Art Exhib, Minn State Fair, 65; Best of show, Sky Gallery/ Dakota Ctr Arts, St Paul, Minn, 82; 3rd prize, Ann Fall Roundup, Las Vegas Art Mus, 2003; Hon mention, Spring Art Salon Exhib, Fine Arts Dept, Mesquite, Nev, 2004; Winners circle, Celebration Life!, Bridge Gallery, 2006; Special Recognition, 10th Ann Abstraction Int Exhib, Upstream People Gallery, 2008; 3rd Showcase Winner, ArtSlant, 2011; Special Recognition, 8th Ann Color Bold/Subtle Exhib, 2010; Showcase Winner, 3rd ArtSlant Exhib, 2011; Showcase Winner, 4th ArtSlant Exhib, 2011; Special Recognition, 14th Ann Contemporary Art Int Exhib, Upstream People Gallery, 2012; 3rd Showcase Winner, ARTSLANT, 2012; Los Angeles Art Assn, 2012; 15th Annual Faces Exhib, Upstream People Gallery, 2012; Action Abstraction Exhib Winner, Southern Nevada Mus Fine Art, 2012; ArtSlant Showcase Winner, 2013; Special Recognition, 16th Annual Abstraction Exhib, Omaha, Nebr, 2014; 2nd 2014 Showcase Winner, Abstract, ARTslant, Los Angeles, Calif, 2014; 1st 2014 Showcase Winner, Abstract, ARTslant, Los Angeles, Calif, 2014. *Bibliog:* Eric Pratt (auth), M Griesgraber Vents, Rebel Yell/ Univ Nev, Las Vegas, 2003. *Media:* Acrylics, Oil. *Publ:* Las Vegas Mag, 2004; New Art Internat Annual 2008, Book Art Press Ltd, NY, 2008; International Contemporary Masters Vol III, World Wide Books, Santa Barbara, Calif, 2010; International Contemporary Artists Vol II, ICA Publishing, NY, 2011; New Art International Anniversary Edition, Book Art Press, NY, 2012; International Contemporary Artists Vol IV, ICA Publishing, NY, 2012; Art Takes Time Square, See Me Group Inc, Signature Book Printing, 2012; Studio Visit Vol 19, Open Studio Press, 2012; Art Takes Miami, See Me Group Inc, Signature Book Printing,

2012; Creative Contemporary Artists Vol I, Katerina Omeletchuk, Berlin, Ger, 2013; International Contemporary Artists Vol VII, ICA Publishing, NY, 2013; Studio Visit Vol 23, Open Studio Press, 2013; Artist Portfolio Mag Feature: The West vs Midwest Issue, 2014; Colors Square Route, Stephanie Grilli, Mill City Press, 2014. *Dealer:* Self

GRIEVE, MARKUS
INSTALLATION SCULPTOR
Study: Coll Marin, Kentfield, Calif, 1989; San Francisco Art Inst, Calif, 1994. *Work:* Bici Centro, Santa Barbara, Calif; Fleeman Collection, Austin, Tex; and var pvt collections. *Comn:* Temple of Dreams, Burning Man Project, Black Rock City, Nev, 2005; Wheel Arch, San Buenaventura Pub Art Commn, Venutra, Calif, 2008; Pacific Rim, City of San Rafael, Calif, 2009. *Exhib:* A Look Forward, A Look Past, Falkirk Cult Ctr Juried Exhib, 1989; Romance Exhibition, Monterey Peninsula Mus, 1991; solo exhibs, 444 Market St, San Francisco, 1996 & Artworks Downtown, San Rafael, Calif, 2006; Sonoma Creates, Sonoma Valley Mus Art, Calif, 2003; Art League of Northern Calif, Marin Mus Contemp Art, Calif, 2007; Brining Back the Fire: Art & Community, Santa Rosa Junior Coll, Calif, 2008. *Awards:* Artist Grant, Marin Arts Coun, 1996; Pollock-Krasner Found Grant, 2008; Puffin Found Grant, 2009. *Bibliog:* Jennifer Upshaw (auth), San Rafael Artwork Goes Public, Marin Independent J, 1/30/2005; Anthony Haden-Guest (auth), In Defense of Burning Man, Art in Am, 6-7/2006; Carla Roccapriore (auth), Burning Art Highlights Green Issues, Reno Gazette J, 9/2/2007; Kevin Clerici (auth), Artist is assembling sculpture of bike parts, Ventura Star, 4/4/2008

GRIFFIN, ANNE & KENNETH C
COLLECTOR
b Boca Raton, Fla. *Study:* Harvard Univ, BA (econ), 1989. *Pos:* With Glenwood Investment Corp, formerly; founder, pres, and chief exec officer, Citadel Investment Group, 90-. *Awards:* Named to Top 200 Collectors, ARTnews Mag, 2004-13. *Mem:* Chicago Mus Contemp Art (bd trustees, currently); Chicago Pub Educ Fund (bd dir, 2003-); Chicago Pub Libr Found; Art Inst Chicago (bd trustees, currently). *Collection:* Impressionism & post-impressionism. *Mailing Add:* Citadel Investment Group LLC 131 S Dearborn St Chicago IL 60603

GRIFFIN, CHRIS A
SCULPTOR
b Boston, Mass. *Study:* Coll of New Rochelle, NY, BFA, 72; Columbia Univ, MA, 73. *Work:* Pictogram Gallery, New York, NY; ISCIP Mus, NY; Everson Mus, Syracuse, NY; Prudential Insurance, Newark, NJ; Phillip Morris, New York, NY; Mobil; Aramco Everson Mus; Islip Mus; Jersey City Mus. *Exhib:* Lines of Vision, Long Island Univ, NY, 89; Words & Images, Henry Street Settlement, NY, 89; Issues of Identity, Dowling Col, NY, 92; Sculptors Drawings, E Hampton Ctr Contemp Art, NY; Geometric Sculpture, Tribeca 148 Gallery, NY; solo exhib, Jersey City Mus, 97; and others. *Teaching:* Assoc prof sculpture, State Univ NY, Old Westbury, 78-. *Awards:* Sculptor Grant Award, NY State Found for Arts, 85; Artist in Residence Grant, Experimental Glass Workshop, New York, 89. *Bibliog:* Ann Kroncnburg (auth), Chris Griffin, Women Artists News, spring 85; Helen Harrison (auth), article, NY Times, 96; Barry Schwabsky (auth), article, NY Times, 97. *Media:* Mixed Media. *Mailing Add:* 230 W 105th St Apt 3D New York NY 10025

GRIFFIN, RASHAWN
SCULPTOR, PAINTER
b Los Angeles, California, 1980. *Study:* Yale Univ, MFA, 2005; Skowhegan Sch Painting & Sculpture, Skowhegan, MN, 2003, BFA; Maryland Inst Coll Art, Baltimore, 2002. *Work:* Whitney Mus Am Art, New York. *Exhib:* Solo exhibs include l'ours et les deux négociants Galerie Eva Winkeler, Frankfurt/Main, Germany, 2006; two-person exhibs include Moti Hasson Gallery, New York (with Tommy Hartung), 2007; Group exhibs include Frequency Studio Mus Harlem, New York, 2005, Artists in Residence 2005-06, Same difference? 2006; Un-modern Observations, Southfirst, Brooklyn, NY, 2006; Passin' It On, Rush Arts Gallery & Resource Ctr, New York, 2006; M*A*S*H New York, Cottelston Advisors, New York, 2007; Red Badge of Courage, Newark Arts Coun, Newark, NJ, 2007; A Muzzle of Bees, 33 Bond Gallery, New York, 2007; Sonotube Forms: Contemp Art and Transport Santa Barbara Contemp Arts Forum, Santa Barbara, Calif, 2007; I died for beauty, Newman Popiashvili Gallery, New York, 2007. *Awards:* Fannie B Pardee Prize, Yale Univ, 2005; Joan Mitchell Found Grant, 2007. *Dealer:* Galerie Eva Winkeler Bethamnnstr 13 Frankfurt/Main Germany 60311

GRIFFITH, ROBERTA
CERAMIST, PAINTER
b Hillsdale, Mich, May 14, 1937. *Study:* Chouinard Art Inst, BFA, 60; Southern Ill Univ, Carbondale, MFA, 62; Massana Sch, Barcelona, Spain with Llorens Artigas, 62-64; permanent cert in art K-12, NY State Dept Educ. *Work:* Everson Mus Art, Syracuse, NY; Mus Ceramics, Barcelona, Spain; Roberson Ctr Arts & Sci, Binghamton, NY; Gallery State Univ New York, Albany, NY; Inst de Estudios Norte-Americanos & Escuela Massana, Barcelona, Spain; Yager Mus, Hartwick Col, Oneonta, NY; Escuela Massana, Barcelona, Spain; N Am Studies Center, Barcelona, Spain; Munson Williams-Proctor Inst, Mus Art, Utica, NY; pvt collections in the US, Spain, Mex, Ger, Eng & Japan. *Exhib:* Ceramic Invitational, Stockholm, Sweden, 72; solo exhibs, Mus Ceramics, Barcelona, Spain, 81 & 99, Munson-Williams Proctor Inst, Sch Art Gallery, Utica, NY, 82 & 88, Ctr Galleries, Albany, NY, 84, Endicott Coll Gallery, Beverly, Mass, 85, Foreman Gallery, Hartwick Col, Oneonta, NY, 89, Warren Gallery, Yager Mus, Hartwick Col, Oneonta, NY & Winfisky Gallery, Salem State Col, Mass, 92, Ford Gallery, Eastern Mich Univ, 99, Ctr Galleries, Albany, 2001, 50 Yr Retrospective, Yager Mus, 2003, Kauai Mus Mezzinine Gallery, Lihu'e, Hawaii, 2010; Fundacion Miro, Barcelona, Spain, 81, 82 & 84; Channel 13 Television Art Auction, NY, 83 & 84; 41st Ceramic Int, Mus Ceramics, Faenza, Italy, 83; 13th Chunichi Int Exhib Ceramic Arts, Nagoya, Japan, 85; Cooperstown Ann Nat, NY, 1987-1992; Munson-Williams Proctor Inst, Utica, NY, 88; Arlene McDaniel Galleries 7th Nat Invitational Sculpture Show, W Hartford, Conn, 89; Kutani Int Decorative Ceramics, 97; Yager Mus, Hartwick Col, 2000; Univ NC Galleries, 2001; Oceanside Mus Art, Calif, 2001; Shick Gallery, Skidmore Col, 2002; Art Educator Reshaping the Thinking of Our Community, 2005; Essential Art, Cooperstown Art Asn, NY, 2007; The Mansion 2007, Regional Art Exhib, Upper Catskill Community Coun Arts, Oneonta, NY, 2007; 2nd, 3rd & 4th Ann Nat Vasefinder Exhib, 2006, 2007, 2009; Cooperstown 73rd Ann Nat, 2008. *Pos:* Ceramic designer, Design Technics, Stroudsburg, Pa, 65-66; Bd dir, Nat Council on Edu Ceramic Arts (NCECA), 1984-86; N Am correspondent, Ceramic Magazine, Madrid, Spain. *Teaching:* Hartwick College, 1966-2008; Arkell Hall Found Prof Art (Endowed Chair), 1979-2008, ceramics, drawing, painting, Hartwick Col, Oneonta, NY, 1966-, chmn art dept, 1975-1991, chmn Humanities, 1988-1989; prof emeritus of art, Hartwick College, 2008. *Awards:* Fulbright Grantee, Spain, 1962-1964; Nat Merit Award (ceramics) Craftsmen USA, 1966; First Prize (drawing), Hudson-Mohawk Regional, First Albany Corp, 1979; Purchase Prize, Hudson Mohawk Regional, SUNY Albany Univ Art Collection, 1980; First Prize, Norwich Fine Arts Guild, Norwich, NY, 1989; First Prize, category III (ceramic sculpture), 54th Cooperstown, NY Ann Nat, 1989; Nat Endowment Humanities Summer Inst, Ancient Mesoamerican Civilizations, Univ Pittsburgh, 91; Bd Trustees Fac Res Grant, Hartwick Col, 94, 98, 99 & 2005; Teacher/Scholar Award, Hartwick Col, 95-96; Charles B Hunt award for Lifetime Achievements in Arts and Service to Arts Community, UCCCA, NY, 2002. *Bibliog:* Jonathan Fairbanks & Angela Fina (auths), The Best of Pottery, 1996; Edmund De Waal (auth), Design Sourcebook CERAMICS, 2000; Susan Peterson (auth), Contemporary Ceramics, 2000; Tom and Jean Latka (auths), Ceramic Extruding, 2001; Richard Zakin (auth), Mastering the Craft, 1990, 2001; Hua Yilong (ed), Works by Ceramic Artists from Around the World, Shanghai Fine Arts Publ, 2006. *Mem:* Nat Coun Educ Ceramic Arts; Cooperstown Art Asn; Am Crafts Coun; Artist-Craftsmen NY, Inc; Empire State Craft Alliance (bd dir, 2000-03); MOMA; Everson Mus Art; Metrop Mus Art. *Media:* Mixed Media. *Res:* Pre-Columbian Art. *Interests:* travel. *Publ:* Ramey Incised Pottery, Ill Archeology Survey Series, Bull No. 5, 1981; Auth & illusr, Spanish Ceramics, NCECA Newsletter, 1984; NCECA Conference Turns Boston into Clay City, Crafts Report, 1984; Cahokia; Ramey Incised Pottery, NCECA J, 1985; Artigas and Miró, Studio Potter, 1985; The Visual Arts, Up Close and Personal, 3 1/2 Plus Phi Theta Kappa Int Soc, 1996-97 Ann; Regis Brodie, A Vision Defined (retrospective essay), 2007

GRIFFITHS, WILLIAM PERRY
EDUCATOR, JEWELER
b Traverse City, Mich, Sept 20, 1937. *Study:* Western Mich Univ, BS, 61; Univ Wis, MFA, 68. *Work:* Mus Contemp Crafts, NY. *Comn:* Silver pendant, comn by Robert Arneson, Davis, Calif, 68; gold & silver pendants, comn by Don Reitz, Marshall, Wis, 85; silver ring, comn by Jack Youngerman, NY, 86; silver chancellor's chain, Univ Wis Ctr System, Madison, 87. *Exhib:* Objects USA (contribr, catalog), Smithsonian-World, Washington, DC, 69; Wisconsin Directions, 75 & All that Glitters: Personal Ornaments, 86, Milwaukee Art Mus, Wis. *Pos:* working as jeweler, craftsman, commissions by appointment, currently. *Teaching:* Assoc prof art, Univ Wis Ctr, Fond du Lac, 68-2002, retired. *Media:* Silver & Gold, Precious Stones. *Interests:* Zuni Indians, In Zuni NM. *Mailing Add:* 20293 Douglas Rd Interlochen MI 49643-9684

GRIGELY, JOSEPH
INSTALLATION SCULPTOR
b East Longmeadow, Mass, 1956. *Study:* Nat Techn Inst for the Deaf; New England Coll; Oxford Univ. *Work:* Whitney Mus of Am Art; The Tate Mod, London; The Walker Mus, Minneapolis; Louisiana Mus of Mod Art, Humlebaek, Denmark; Wadsworth Atheneum, Hartford; Seattle Art Mus; Univ Calif Mus of Art, Berkeley; Orange County Mus of Art. *Comn:* Neuberger Berman Collection, New York; William and Ruth True, Seattle; Ringier Collection, Zurich; Norton Family Found, Los Angeles; Cisneros Collection, Miami. *Exhib:* Solo exhibs include White Columns, New York, 1994, AC Project Room, New York, 1995, 1996, Revolution Gallery, Detroit, 1997, Masataka Hayakawa Gallery, Tokyo, 1998, Cohan Leslie & Browne, New York, 2000, 2002, 2003, 2006, Whitney Mus of Am Art, New York, 2001, Mus of Art & the Tang Mus, Skidmore College, 2007; Group exhibs include The Natural World, AC Proj Room, New York, 1994; Smells Like Vinyl, Roger Merians Gallery, New York, 1995; Action Station, Santa Monica Mus of Art, Santa Monica, 1995; The Materialization of Life, Printed Matter, New York, 1996; The Power of Suggestion: Narrative &Notation in Contemp Drawing, Mus of Contem Art, Los Angeles, 1996; Sydney Biennial, Sydney, 1998; The Tree-Trimming Party, Matthew Marks Gallery, New York, 1998; The Time of Our Lives, New Mus of Contemp Art, New York, 1999; Whitney Biennial, Whitney Mus Am Art, 2000; Reading: Material, Volume, New York, 2003; Speaking with Hands: Photographs from the Buhl Collection, Guggenheim Mus, New York, 2004; The Early Show, White Columns, New York, 2005; Found Sound, Numark Gallery, Washington, 2005; Centrally Located, Chicago Cultural Ctr, 2005; Home of the Free, Hyde Park Art Ctr, Chicago, 2006; St Ives Int, Tate St Ives, United Kingdom, 2007. *Awards:* Creative Capital Found Grant, 2008. *Mailing Add:* 32 Melwood Ave East Longmeadow MA 01028

GRIGORIADIS, MARY
PAINTER
b Jersey City, NJ, June 23, 1942. *Study:* Barnard Col, BA, 63; Columbia Univ, MA, 65. *Work:* Guild Hall Mus East Hampton, NY; First Nat Bank Chicago; Nat Mus Am Art & Nat Mus Women Arts, Washington, DC; Va Mus Fine Art, Richmond; Allen Mem Art Mus, Oberlin, Ohio; Parrish Art Mus, Southampton, NY; Vorres Mus, Athens, Greece; Chase Manhattan Bank, Greece; Eli and Edythe Broad Art Mus, East Lansing, Mich. *Exhib:* Solo Exhibs: AIR Gallery, NY, 72, 75, 78, 82, 84, 86 & 89; OK Harris Gallery, NY, 76; Gallery K, Washington, DC, 78; Helen Shlien Gallery, Boston, 78, 81 & 83; Barnard Coll, 88; Strokescapes: 70s & 80s, Accola Griefen Gallery, NY,

2013; Biennial Contemp Am Art, Whitney Mus Am Art, 73; Small Works, Albright-Knox Mus Art, 76-77; Pattern Painting, PSI, NY, 77; The Brooklyn Mus, 77; Islamic Allusions, Alternative Mus, NY, 80; Aldrich Mus Contemp Art, Conn, 81; Burning in Hell, Franklin Furnace, NY; Va Mus Fine Art, 90; Establishing the Legacy: Renaissance to Modernism, Nat Mus Women Art, Washington, DC, 95; 25 Yrs of Feminism, 25 Yrs of Women's Art; Rutgers Univ, NJ, 96; Four By Four, 55 Mercer Gallery, NY, 98; Modern Odysseys, Queens Mus Art, NY, 99 & State Mus Contemp Art, Thessaloniki, Greece, 2000; Personal and Political, Guild Hall Mus, East Hampton, NY, 2002; Art in Embassies, US Embassies, Cape Town and Pretoria, 2003; Modern and Contemp Art: Selections Permanent Collection, Nat Mus Women in the Arts, Washington, DC, 2004; Recent Acquisitions: Framing the Collection, Parrish Art Mus, Southampton, NY, 2004; Vistas & Visions, Nat Mus Women in the Arts, Wash, DC 2006; Am Embassy Annex, Athens, Greece, 2007; US Embassy, Belgrade, Serbia, 2008-09; Werkstate Gallery, NY, 2008; The History Show, AIR Gallery, New York, 2008; Recent Acquisitions, 2006-2009; Kresge Art Mus, East Lansing, Mich, 2009; The Other Greece, Kouros Gallery, NY, 2012; Visual Feast: A Pattern and Decoration Exhib, Acola Griefen Gallery, NY, 2012. *Pos:* Founding mem, AIR Gallery, exec comt, 83-86; adv bd AIR Gallery, 2001-. *Awards:* NY Found for Arts, 89. *Bibliog:* Hayden Herrera, reviews, Art in Am, 3-4/77; Joan Marter (auth), Mary Grigoriadis, Arts Mag, 11/84; C Robins (auth), The Pluralist Era, 1968-1981, Harper & Row, New York, 84. *Media:* Oil, Mixed Media. *Publ:* auth, In Her Own Words, Women in the Arts, Nat Mus of Women in the Arts, 2004. *Dealer:* Kat Griefen and Kristen Accola Griefen Gallery 547 W 27th St #634 New York NY 10001. *Mailing Add:* 382 Central Park W, Apt 20P New York NY 10025

GRIGSBY, JEFFERSON EUGENE, JR
EDUCATOR, PAINTER

b Greensboro, NC, Oct 17, 1918. *Study:* Morehouse Col, with Hale Woodruff & Nancy Prophet, BA, 38; Am Artists Sch, with M Hebald, H Harrari & J Groth, 39; Ohio State Univ, with Prof Hopkins & R Fanning, MA, 40; Ecole Beaux Arts, Marseilles, 45; NY Univ, PhD, 63; Philadelphia Coll Art, Hon DFA, 65. *Work:* Tex Southern Univ, Houston; Mint Mus, Charlotte, NC; Nat Mus Ghana, Cape Castle; Richmond Pub Schs, Va; Ariz State Univ; Glendale Community Col; Valley Nat Bank; Bank Am; Milwaukee Art Mus. *Exhib:* Am Negro Expos, Tanner Art Galleries, Chicago, 40; Baltimore Mus, 40; Ariz Ann, Phoenix Mus, 64; Solo exhib, Centennial Celebration, Morehouse Coll, 67; Dimensions in Black, La Jolla Mus, Calif, 70; Dallas City Hall, 81; Ariz State Univ, 86; Benedict Coll, 87; Retrospect Exhib Phoenix Art Mus, 2000-2001; Hub Gallery, Penn State Univ Feb-March, 2005. *Pos:* Head dept art, Carver High Sch, 46-54 & Phoenix Union High Sch, Ariz, 54-66. *Teaching:* Artist-in-residence, Johnson C Smith Univ, 40-41; prof art educ & drawing, Ariz State Univ, 66-88, distinguished res scholar, 82-83, prof emer, 88. *Awards:* Medallion of Merit, Nat Gallery Art, 66; Educator of the Yr, Nat Art Educ Asn, 88 & Retired Educator of the Yr, 98; Ariz Gov Award, 89. *Mem:* Fel Nat Art Educ Asn (vpres, 72-74); Black Orgn Arts; Ariz Artists Guild; Consortium of Black Orgns for the Arts; Nat Conf Artists; Artists of the Black Community, Ariz; Nat Found for the Arts (visual arts panel, 81-84); NAEA Comt on Minority Concerns. *Media:* Acrylic, Serigraph. *Res:* African art, its history, materials used and style. *Publ:* Auth, Ba Kuba art, In: Africa Seen by American Negroes, 58; Encounters (exhib catalog), J C Smith Univ Exhib, 68; Art & Ethnics, William C Brown Co; ed, Sch Arts Mag, 10/79. *Mailing Add:* Dept Art Ariz State Univ 1117 N 9th St Phoenix AZ 85006-2734

GRILLO, ESTHER ANGELA
SCULPTOR, PRINTMAKER

b Rome, Italy, Jan 28, 1954; US citizen. *Study:* Queens Col, NY, study with Tom Doyle, 72-74; Brooklyn Col, BA (cum laude), 77, study with Terris & D'Archangelo & MFA, 81, study with Bontecou, Samuels & Mehlmen. *Work:* Brooklyn Coll Print Collection, NY; Palmer Mus, Pa State Univ. *Comn:* Wall relief (38'), MTA/Creative Stations. *Exhib:* A Gender Show, Group Material, NY, 81; The Wild Art Show, PS 1, NY, 82; Earth Transformed by Fire, Rotunda Gallery, NY, 84; Beginnings & Endings, Mus Borough Brooklyn, NY, 84; Long Island Artists, Islip Art Mus, East Islip, NY, 85; Holocaust Memorial Art Exhib, Queensborough Community Col, NY, 85; Masters of War, Ammo Gallery, Brooklyn, NY, 85; Taking Liberties: Transcendence and Transgression, Pace Univ Art Gallery, Civic Ctr Campus, Pace Plaza, NY, 86; solo exhibs, Narrative Sculpture: Collage and Prints, 14 Sculptors Gallery, NY, 86, Meltdown, Palmer Mus, Pa State Univ, 88 & Esther A Grillo: Installation, Sculpture, Collage, Prints, 14 Sculptors Gallery, Soho, NY, 88; Queens Mus Juried Ann, Queens, NY, 87; and others. *Awards:* Exhibition Award, B J Spoke Gallery, New York, 83. *Bibliog:* Susan Koslow (auth), Esther A Grillo, Arts Mag, 86; David S Martin (auth), Exhib, events meant to raise nuclear awareness, Centre Daily Times, Assoc Press, 1/14/88; Fatal vision, The Palm Beach Post, Meltdown on display, Express-News, Tex & Nuclear art show to feature Meltdown, Cape Coral Press (all from Assoc Press, 1/11/88). *Mem:* Womens Caucus Art; Coll Art Asn. *Media:* Mixed. *Publ:* Contribr, Words-Pictures--Collaborative Work of Women Artists, Women's Caucus Art, 82; Sculpting clay, Nigros H, 92. *Dealer:* 14 Sculptors Gallery 164 Mercer St New York NY 10012. *Mailing Add:* 214 Beach 120th St Far Rockaway NY 11694-1957

GRILLO, JOHN
PAINTER, PRINTMAKER

b Lawrence, Mass, July 7, 1917. *Study:* Hartford Sch Fine Arts, Conn, 35-38; Calif Sch Fine Arts, San Francisco, 46-47; studied with Hans Hoffman, New York & Provincetown, Mass, 48-51. *Work:* Metrop Mus Art, Solomon R Guggenheim Mus Art, Whitney Mus Am Art & Brooklyn Mus, NY; British Mus, London. *Comn:* Brotherhood (painting), Univ Mass Art Dept, Amherst, 87; Emily Dickinson (painting), Jones Libr Inc, Amherst, Mass, 93; Stage settings, CAPE Theater Co, Provincetown, Mass, 97. *Exhib:* The Whitney Ann, Whitney Mus Am Art, NY, 53 & 59; 40 Post War Painters, Guggenheim Mus, NY, 77; The Circus Series, Springfield Mus Fine Arts, Mass, 83 & Univ NH, 97; Selected Paintings 1963-1988, Provincetown Art Asn & Mus, Mass, 88; The Park Series, Museo de Antoquia, Medellin, Columbia, 91; Paper Trails: San Francisco Abstract, Art Mus Santa Cruz, Calif, 93; The San Francisco Sch of Abstract Expressionism, Laguna Art Mus, Calif, 96. *Pos:* Trustee, Provincetown Art Asn & Mus, Mass, 95-96. *Teaching:* Vis artist drawing & painting, Univ Calif, Berkeley, 62-63 & 73; instr, Pratt Inst, New York, 65-66; prof, Univ Mass, Amherst, 67-91. *Awards:* Samuel S Bender Award, San Francisco, 47; Ford Found Grant, Los Angeles, 64; Res Grant, Univ Mass, Amherst, 76. *Bibliog:* John Furbish (dir), John Grillo: World Scale Artist in the Pioneer Valley (film), Pioneer Valley Cable TV, 87; Tony Vevers (auth), John Grillo, Provincetown Mag, summer 88; Susan Landaver (auth), John Grillo, Art Calif Mag, 5/90. *Media:* Oil, Watercolor. *Publ:* Auth, Artist's Statement, John Grillo, It Is Mag, winter 59; Essay: yellow can be black, Scrap Mag, 4/61; Jan Muller: A Remembrance, Provincetown Arts Mag, 90; Essay: George Karen-Zhouf (exhib catalog), Asz Publ, 92. *Mailing Add:* c/o Cove Gallery Commercial St PO Box 482 Wellfleet MA 02667

GRIMES, MARGARET W
PAINTER, EDUCATOR

b New Bern, NC. *Study:* Gov State Univ, BA, 74, MA, 75; Notre Dame Univ, with Alice Neel, 77; Univ Pa, with Neil Welliver, Rudy Burckhaudt, Yvonne Jacquette and Paul Georges, MFA, 80. *Work:* Pittsburgh Plate Glass Co; Conn Insurance Group NAm; Christian Sci Church Ctr, Boston; US Tobacco Co; Bellevue Hosp Ctr, NY; Atlantic Fed Bank, NJ; Nat Acad Sci, Washington; David Hall Gallery, Ma.; Nat Acad Design, NY; Hendrix Coll, Conway, Ark. *Comn:* Print, New York Graphic Soc, 85; Calendar Reproduction, Cairo, Calendar Images, 88. *Exhib:* Pride of Place, Gunn Mus, Washington, Conn, 2000; one-person exhibs, Green Mountain Gallery, NY, 79, Blue Mountain Gallery, NY, biennially 1980-2010, Fischbach Gallery, NY, 86, Weir Farm Heritage Trust, 2004; Group Shows, Columbus Mus Art, Ohio, 87, Newport Art Mus, RI, 88; Fischbach Gallery, NY, 86; Katherina Rich Perlow, NY, 88; Univ Pa, 92; Am Realism & Figurative Painting, Cline Art Gallery, Santa Fe, NMex, 94; Five Aspects of the Am Landscape, John Arthur (cur), Crieger-Dane Gallery, Boston, Mass, 95; A Chaos of Delight, Ctr Contemp Art, Wilmington, Del, 96; Central Conn State Univ, 97; Washington Art Asn, Washington, Conn, 2000; Nat Acad of Design, Juried Invitational, 2004; Nat Acad of Sci, Washington, 2001; Green Woods and Crystal Waters: The Am Landscape Tradition, Philbrook Mus Art, Tulsa, Okla, Ringling Mus Art, Sarasota, Fla, Davenport Mus, Davenport, Iowa, 2000; Salon Show with Henri Matisse, Ober Gallery, Kent, Conn, 2007; 4 Landscape Painters, Chautauqua Inst, 2008; Selected Fac, 25th Ann Chautaugua Sch Visual Arts, Denise Bibro Gallery, New York, 2010; Julie Heller Gallery, 2011; Women's Work, From Protest to Process, Nat Acad Design, NY, 2012; Retrospective, Westrun Conn State Univ, Danbury, Conn. *Pos:* presenter, Conf Liberal Arts & Educ Artist, Sch & Visual Arts, NY, 97; coord, MFA Program, Western Conn State Univ, 2000-2012; presenter, Gunn Mus Pride of Place, Lectr Series, Washington, Conn, 2000; artist-in-residence, American Univ, Corciano, Italy, 2001-2006, Weir Farm Heritage Trust, 2004. *Teaching:* Instr drawing & design, Thornton Community Col, Chicago, 74-79; prof painting & drawing, Western Conn State Univ, 80-; visiting critic, Vt Studio Ctr, Johnson, 95, Vt Col Norwich Univ, Montpelier, 95-96, Tanglewood Inst, Lenox, Mass, 97; guest lectr, Moravian Col, Bethlehem, Pa, 90, Cen Conn State U, New Britain, Conn, 97, Western Conn State Univ, Danbury, Conn, 98 & Weir Farm Hist Site, Wilton, Conn, 98; presenter, Am Univ, Italy, 2001-06; Am Univ, Wash, DC, 2001-2006, presenter & vis artist, Chautauqua Inst, 2003, 2005-2009, 2012; Haverford Coll, Haverford, Pa, 2010; Western Conn State Univ, 2013. *Awards:* Res Grant, Conn State Univ, 85 & 90; Univ Prof, West Conn State Univ, 92; Benjamin Altman Award, landscape painting, Nat Acad Design, 2004. *Bibliog:* Carl Little (auth), Paintings of New England, Down East Press, 96; Jude Schwendenwien (auth), Grimes Paintings Close to Nature, Hartford Courant, 97; John Driscoll (auth), The Artist in the American Landscape, First Glance Press, 98; John Arthur (auth), Greenwoods and Crystal Waters; Paul Smith (auth), Art in America (exhib review), 2004; Ed McCormick (auth), exhib rev, Gallery & Studio, 2007, 2010; Jennifer Sauret (auth), ArtCritical (review), 2013; Kristen Nord (auth), Art in Context (review), 2013. *Mem:* Coll Art Asn; Blue Mountain Gallery; Nat Acad Design. *Media:* Oil. *Publ:* Green Woods and Crystal Waters, John Arthur, Univ Wash Press; John Auther (auth), The Am landscape Tradition, Univ of WA Press, 99; Steve Starger, Art New England, 8/2003; Paul Smith, Art in Am, 2004. *Dealer:* Blue Mountain Gallery 121 Wooster Street New York NY 10012; Ober Gallery PO Box 236 Kent Conn 06757. *Mailing Add:* 27 Wykeham Rd Washington CT 06793

GRIMLEY, OLIVER FETTEROLF
PAINTER, SCULPTOR

b Norristown, Pa, June 30, 1920. *Study:* Pa Acad Fine Arts, William Emlen Clesson traveling scholar, 47, Henry J Scheidt traveling scholar, 50; Univ Pa, BFA & MFA. *Work:* Woodmere Art Galleries, Mus Art, Pa Acad Fine Arts, Philadelphia; Libr Cong, Washington, DC. *Comn:* Murals, Commonwealth Fed Savings & Loan, Norristown, 63, Continental Bank & Trust, 65 & Am Bank, Lafayette Hills, Pa, 72; papier-mache eagle, comn by Leonard Tose, Vet Stadium, Philadelphia, 71. *Exhib:* Whitney Mus Am Art, Libr Cong & Metrop Mus, 52-57; Pa Acad Fine Arts Watercolor Shows, 58-63; Philadelphia Mus Art. *Teaching:* Instr drawing, Hussian Sch Art, 60- & Pa Acad Fine Arts, 65-. *Awards:* Ralph Pallen Coleman Prize for Illus, 73; First Prize for Sculpture, Regional Coun Community Arts Ctr, 74; J W Zimmerman Mem Prize for Work of Distinction, 79. *Bibliog:* Henry Pitz (auth), article, Am Artist, 71. *Mem:* Philadelphia Watercolor Club. *Media:* Pen & Ink, Watercolor; Miscellaneous. *Publ:* Auth, article, Am Artist, 50. *Mailing Add:* 623 Stonybrook Dr Norristown PA 19403-2725

GRINER, NED H
EDUCATOR, CRAFTSMAN

b Tipton, Ind, Dec 14, 1928. *Study:* Ball State Teachers Col, BS; State Univ Iowa, MA; Ind Univ, MFA; Pa State Univ, DEd. *Work:* Evansville Mus Art & Ball State Univ Mus, Muncie, Ind. *Exhib:* Midstates Craft Exhib, 66-67; Jewelry Exhib, Purdue Univ, 67; Indianapolis Mus Art, 75; Ind Univ Mus Art, Bloomington, 76; Ind State Mus, Indianapolis, 77; Ft Wayne Art Mus, Ind, 78; Parade & Events, Ball State Mus Art, 2010. *Teaching:* Asst prof art, Ark State Col, 54-60; asst, Pa State Univ, 60-61; head dept, 70-81; prof, Ball State Univ, 61-94 Ret. *Awards:* Law Head Teaching

Award, Gen Studies, 90; Very Important Volunteer Award, 93; Ball State Univ Pres's Medal Distinction, 2000. *Mem:* Nat & Ind Art Educ Asns; Coll Art Asn Am; Ind Artist Craftsmen (pres, 66-68); Nat Coun Art Adminr. *Media:* Silver, Bronze, Brass. *Publ:* Contrib, Art--search & self discovery, 68; auth, Side by Side with Coarser Plants: The Muncie Art Movement, 1885-1985, Ball State Univ, 85; Boom Gas Society, Minnetrista Cultural Found Inc, 91; J Ottis Adams: A Sense of Place, Minnetrista Cultural Found Inc, 92; Bethel Pike Pottery: The First Thirty Years, Minnetrista Cult Found Inc, 96; The Magnificent benefactors, The history of the Ball State Univ Mus Art, 2002. *Mailing Add:* 4516 N Gishler Dr Muncie IN 47304

GRINNAN, KATIE
PAINTER, SCULPTOR

b Richmond, Va, 1970. *Study:* Studio Arts Ctr Int, Florence, Italy, 91; Carnegie Mellon Univ, BFA (painting), 92; Skowhega Sch Painting & Sculpture, Main, 92; UCLA, MFA in Sculpture, 99. *Exhib:* Katie Grinnan Alice Konitz christie fields, Guggenheim Gallery, Chapman Univ, Calif, 2000; solo exhibs incl Rock Bottom, Acme, Los Angeles, 2001, 2003; Out of the Ground into the Sky Out of the Sky into the Ground, Pond, San Francisco, 2002; Wit Form Rainbow (Part I), The Project, Los Angeles, 2003; Material Faith, Kontainer Gallery, Los Angeles, 2004; Real World: Dissolving Space of Experience, Modern Art Oxford, Eng, 2004; Art on Paper, Weatherspoon Art Mus, Univ NC, 2004. *Mailing Add:* c/o Acme 6150 Wilshire Blvd #1 Los Angeles CA 90048

GRIPPE, FLORENCE (BERG)
PAINTER, INSTRUCTOR

b New York, NY, Jan 6, 1912. *Study:* Educ Alliance, 32-34; Works Proj Admin Art Courses, 34-38; pottery with William Soini, 39-41. *Work:* Rose Art Mus, Brandeis Univ. *Comn:* Portraits comn by Doris Brewer Cohen, Lexington, Mass, 69, Signora Attilio Roveda, Locarno, Switz, 70, Dr Luis Martinez & Julio Farinos Castillo, Valencia, Spain, 70 & Jose Marina Galvao Telles, Lisbon, Portugal, 71. *Exhib:* Brooklyn Mus, 51; Lower East Side Independent Artists 3rd Ann Exhib, 58; Guild Hall, Easthampton, Long Island, 75 & 87; Provincetown Art Asn & Mus, Mass, 78; Himmelfarb Gallery, Long Island, 80-81; Burnside Gallery, Long Island, 81 & 83; and others. *Pos:* Art critic, Art News & Craft Horizons, 61-63. *Teaching:* Instr drawing, painting, sculpture & puppetry, United Art Workshops, Brooklyn Neighborhood Houses, NY, 47-54; instr design & pottery, Brooklyn Mus Art Sch, 51-57. *Bibliog:* S Sheridan (auth), Native handicrafts, New York Times Mag, 7/52; article in Daily Transcript, Boston, 7/19/79; article in Peconic Bay Shopper, Long Island, 10/81; and others. *Mem:* NY Ceramic Soc; Artist Club. *Media:* All. *Res:* Glazing formulas; Art history. *Publ:* Auth, With the brush, Ceramic Age, 3/56; coauth, Art news from Boston, Art News, 61-63. *Dealer:* 1942 Orrefors Gallery; 46 America House. *Mailing Add:* Acme Fine Arts 4th Floor 38 Newbury St Boston MA 02116

GRIPPI, SALVATORE WILLIAM
PAINTER, SCULPTOR

b Buffalo, NY, Sept 30, 1921. *Study:* Mus Mod Art Sch, 44-45; Art Students League, 45-48; Atelier 17, 51-53; Ist Statale d'Arte, Florence, Italy, Fulbright Scholar, 53-55. *Work:* Whitney Mus Am Art & Metrop Mus Art, NY; Joseph Hirshhorn Collection, Washington, DC; St Lawrence Univ; Everson Mus, Syracuse, NY; Herbert F Johnson Mus Art; Allentown Mus Art. *Exhib:* solo exhibs, NY Univ, New York City, 58, Zabriskie Gallery, NYC, 56, 59, Krasner Gallery, New York City, 62, 64, 79, 81, Feingarten Galleries, Los Angeles, Calif, 67, 70, Rex Evans Gallery, Los Angeles, Calif, 65, Everson Mus, Syracuse, NY, 78, Hardwerker Gallery, Ithaca, NY, 78, Wells Coll, Aurora, NY, 72, Hiestand Gallery, Miami Univ, Oxford, Ohio, 84, Herbert Johnson Mus Art, Cornell Univ, 2011, Allentown Mus Art, 2011; Biennials, Corcoran Gallery Art, 59 & 63; Whitney Mus Am Art Ann, 60 & 61; Walker Art Ctr, 60; Recent Painting USA, The Figure, Mus Mod Art, NY & throughout US, 62; Selected Am Painters, Phoenix Art Mus, Ariz, 67; Elvehjem Art Ctr, Univ Wis, 77 & traveling; Brooklyn Mus, NY, 78; Everson Mus, Syracuse, NY, 78; Artists Books, Mus Mod Art, NY, 94; Ital Am Artists, Hunter Col, NY, 94; Work of the Fifties, 2000; Avant Garde of the Fifties and Now, R00d Gallery, Eastport, NY, 2001; Fifties and Sixties Works on Paper, Rood Gallery, 2002; Visually Speaking, Print Herbert Johnson, Mus Art, Cornell Univ; Wellesley Davis Mus and Cult Ctr, 2008. *Teaching:* Instr painting, drawing & 2-D design, Cooper Union Art Sch, 56-59; instr, Sch Visual Arts, 61-62; assoc prof art, Pomona Col & Claremont Grad Sch, 62-68; prof art, Ithaca Col, 68-. *Awards:* Fulbright Scholarship, 53 & Renewal, 54. *Bibliog:* Brian O'Dougherty (auth), Variety of exhibitions, New York Times, 3/22/62; Larry Campbell (auth), article, Art News, 10/64; Henry J Seldis (auth), Art walk: A critical guide to the galleries, Los Angeles Times, 5/29/70; and many others. *Mem:* Life mem Art Students League (treas, 61-62, bd control, 61-64); Coll Art Asn Am. *Media:* Oil, Watercolor; Wood. *Publ:* Auth, Visual impressions of Italy, Inst Int Educ Bull, 56; Turntable kaleidoscope, Mus Mod Art, 56, 57 & 59; contribr, Twenty-one Etchings & Poems, 58; New York School Abstract Expressionists, Artists Choice by Artists, NY Sch Press, 2000. *Mailing Add:* 9 Orchard Hill Rd Ithaca NY 14850

GRISSOM, FREDA GILL
PAINTER, GOLDSMITH

b Groom, Tex. *Study:* WTex State Univ, Canyon, BS; Univ Tex, Austin; also watercolor workshop. *Work:* Montgomery Mus Fine Arts, Ala. *Exhib:* Ann Dixie Exhib, Montgomery Mus Fine Arts, 68; Nat Art Roundup, Las Vegas, Nev, 68; Greater New Orleans Nat, 71; 9th Grand Prix Int, Cannes, France, 73; Galerie Rene Borel, Deauville, France, 73. *Pos:* Co-chmn, Nat Sun Carnival Art Exhib, El Paso, Tex, 65-71. *Awards:* Purchase Award, Montgomery Mus Fine Arts, 68; Second Prize, Greater New Orleans Nat Exhib, 71; Medaille de la Ville de Cannes, First Prize, Watercolor, 9th Grand Prix Int, Cote D'Azur, 73. *Mem:* El Paso Art Asn, Inc (dir, 64-65); El Paso Mus Art; Black Range Art Asn; Tex Watercolor Soc. *Media:* Transparent Watercolor, Acrylic, Oil; Gold, Silver. *Mailing Add:* 399 Vinton Rd Anthony NM 88021-8546

GRISWOLD, WILLIAM M
MUSEUM DIRECTOR, CURATOR

Study: Courtauld Inst Art, London, PhD, 1988. *Pos:* Head dept, drawings & prints Morgan Libr, New York City, 1995-2001, dir, 2008-2014; assoc dir, collections J Paul Getty Mus, LA, 2001-04, acting dir, chief cur, 2004-05; dir, Minneapolis Inst Arts, 2005-07, Cleveland Mus Art, 2014-. *Awards:* Chevalier, Ordre des Arts et des Lettres, France, 2008. *Mailing Add:* Cleveland Museum of Art 11150 East Blvd Cleveland OH 44106

GROAT, HALL PIERCE, SR
PAINTER, MURALIST

b Syracuse, NY, Dec 31, 1932. *Study:* Syracuse Univ, BFA, also Grad Sch Painting; Josef Albers. *Work:* Everson Mus Art, Syracuse, NY; Philatelic Mus, Geneva, Switz; Syracuse Univ, NY; Skaneatelles Savings Bank, NY; Merrill Ctr, Bangor, Maine; Portrait of John Mulroy, Collection, John Mulroy Civic Ctr, Syracuse, NY; Bank of Am, New York. *Comn:* Hist mural, Merrill Trust Co, Bangor, Maine, 75; hist mural (five panels), Bank of Am, 77; hist mural, Skaneateles, NY, 79; mural, Miller Brewing Co, Fulton, NY, 80; mural, Bristol-Myers Squibb, 81; mural, Mutual of New York; North Med Ctr, Syracuse, NY; hist series, Paine Webber, Syracuse, NY, 2000; hist series, Hist of Syracuse, Rudin Mentor, Trivelpiece Law Firm, 2003; Lynn Law Firm, 2007; hist mural, St James Church, Syracuse, NY; hist mural, St John the Evangelist Church, Syracuse, NY; hist mural, St Elizabeth Ann Seton Church, Baldwinsville, NY. *Exhib:* Rochester Finger Lakes Exhib, Rochester Mem Art Gallery, NY, 59 & 63; Springfield Nat, Mass, 62; Everson Mus Regional, Syracuse, 64 & 70; Cooperstown Nat, NY, 67-83; Butler Inst Am Art, Youngstown, Ohio, 68; Western Regional, Albright-Knox Mus Art, Buffalo, NY; Solo exhib, Washington & Jefferson Coll; Well Worth the Struggle, Beard Gallery, SUNY Cortland NY, 2014. *Collection Arranged:* Groat: Two Generations of Am Art, NY Art Collection. *Pos:* self-employed artist, 1966-present. *Teaching:* Instr advan painting, Berkshire Mus. *Awards:* UN Philatelic Award; Int Award for UN Stamp; Berkshire Mus Purchase Award, 62; Purchase Award, Cooperstown Nat, 72; Spec Citation Outstanding Portrait, Albright-Knox Mus Art Western Regional, 94; Jurors Award, Olin Fine Arts Ctr, Washington & Jefferson Coll, Pa, 94; Gordon Steele Mem Medal, Cazenovia Coll, 2000. *Bibliog:* 32nd ann midyear show--Butler, La Rev Mod, 2/68; Rev of selected artist, Art Rev, fall 68; An Artist and His Work (film), WCNY, Syracuse, NY. *Mem:* Sarasota Art Asn; Nat Soc Mural Painters. *Media:* Acrylic, Oil; Watercolor. *Specialty:* impressionist oil paintings landscape, seascape, still life, large portraits. *Interests:* world travel, art & architecture. *Collection:* international including philatelic museum Genva Switzerland- 10 acrylic paintings including Pablo Picasso 90th Birthday First Day of Issue Commemorative Design based on portrait of Maya Picasso. *Publ:* auth story, Peacetime Soldiers During the Cold War. *Dealer:* Hall Groat II PO Box 8781 Endwell NY 13762. *Mailing Add:* 8364 Vassar Dr Manlius NY 13104

GRODSKY, SHEILA TAYLOR
PAINTER, COLLAGE ARTIST

b Newark, NJ, May 7, 1933. *Study:* Douglass Coll, BA (art ed), 54; Md Inst Art, 68-69; also studied with Nicholas Reale, Gerald Brommer, W Carl Burger & Paul St Denis. *Work:* Arch collections, Tate Mus, London; Zhejiang Univ Mus, China. *Exhib:* Salmagundi Club Ann, NY, 92; Catharine Lorillard Wolfe Art Club Centennial Exhib, NY, 96; Garden State Watercolor Soc, 98; NJ Watercolor Soc, 98; NE Watercolor Soc Ann Juried Exhib, 98; Int Soc Experimental Artists Ann Juried Exhib, 98; Nat Acrylic Painters Asn USA Ann Juried Exhib, 98; Int Soc of Experimental Artists Ann Juried Exhib, 99; Nat Acrylic Painters Asn USA Ann Open Exhib, 99; Nat Asn of Women Artists, Women's Expo, Baltimore, 99, Fall Exhib, Art Ctr Sarasota Gallery, Fla, 2000; NJ Water Color Soc Ann Open Juried Exhib, 2000; and others. *Pos:* Bd mem, Sussex Co Arts Coun, 75-80; pres, Gallery 23, 2002-10. *Teaching:* Instr art, Dover High Sch, NJ, 54-56; instr watercolor, Livingston Art Asn, NJ, 90-91; adj prof art, Sussex Co Community Coll, 2007. *Awards:* President's Award, Catharine Lorillard Wolfe Art Club, 93; Avery & Nina Johnson Award, NJ Watercolor Soc, 98; Best in Show, Garden State Watercolor Soc, 98; Best in Show, Int Soc Experimental Artists, 2001; Best in Show, Skylands Ann Juried Show, 2004; Dagmar Tribble Mem Award, Garden State Watercolor Soc Ann Juried Show, Princeton, NJ, 2008. *Mem:* Signature mem NJ Watercolor Soc; Pastel Soc Am; Catharine Lorillard Wolfe Art Club Inc (bd dir, 89, vpres, 97); assoc mem Nat Watercolor Soc; assoc mem Am Watercolor Soc; signature mem Nat Acrylic Painters Asn; Nat Asn of Women Artists; Baltimore Watercolor Soc (signature mem, 99); Int Soc Experimental Artists (signature mem, 2000). *Media:* Watercolor, Acrylic, Mixed Media, Textile, Jewelry. *Interests:* Arts & crafts of Japan. *Publ:* Contribr, Creative Watercolor: A Showcase and Step-by-Step Guide, Best of Watercolor: Painting Color & Floral Inspirations, Rockport Publ, Journeys to Abstraction, North Light Pub; A Walk into Abstracts (dvd), 2010. *Dealer:* Gallery 23 Blairstown NJ 07825. *Mailing Add:* 1 Hillside Dr Apt B212 Mount Arlington NJ 07856

GROFF, BARBARA S
PAINTER

b Hartford, Conn, Apr 10, 1943. *Study:* Hartford Art School, 61; Self taught. *Exhib:* Academic Artist Assoc Annual Nat Exhib, Springfield, Mass, 2001-08, 2010-2015; Allied Artists of Am Ann Exhib, New York, 2003-15; Pastel Soc of Am Ann Open Juried Exhib, New York, 2004-2013, 2015; Hudson Valley Art Asn Nat Juried Exhib, New York, 2004-07, 13; Allied Artists Am Invitational, Bennington Ctr Arts, Vt, 2007, Canton Mus Art, Ohio, 2015; Salmagundi Club Non-Members Nat Exhib, New York, 2008-11; Conn Pastel Soc, Renaissance in Pastels Nat Exhib, Mattatuck Mus, Waterbury, CT, 2010-2012, Slater Mus, Norwich, Conn, 2013, 2014; Am Artists Prof League Nat Exhib, New York, 2008-2012; Catharine Lorillard Wolfe Art Club, NY, 2010-2012; Slater Mus, Norwich, Conn, 2013. *Awards:* Pastel Honor Award (5 time recip), Acad Artists Asn Ann Nat Exhib, 2001, 2004, 2005, 2010, 2014; Gold Medal Award in Pastel, Allied Artists Am 94th Ann Nat Exhib, Dianne Bernhard, 2007, 2014, Am Artists Prof League 85th Grand Nat, 2013; Ruth Richeson Unison Pastels Award, 9th Ann Pastel Journal 100 Competition, Jack Richeson & Co Inc, 2008. *Bibliog:*

Sarah A Strickley (auth), managing ed, Barbara Groff, Pastel Journal, 2008; Tamera Lenz Muente (auth), Barbara S. Groff, Pastel Journal, 2009, Michael Chesley Johnson (auth), Barbara S. Groff, 2011. *Mem:* Pastel Soc of Am Inc; Salmagundi Club, NY; Acad Artists Asn; Conn Acad of Fine Arts; Allied Artists Am. *Media:* Realism, Still life, Graphic Design, Print Media. *Publ:* Kathleen Mellon (auth), Pastels That Slip Life's Hold, Daily Hampshire Gazzette (H.S. Gere & Sons Inc), 2005; Joshua Rose (ed), Challenging Tradition, Am Art Collector, Int Artists Publ Inc, 2008; Anne Hevener (ed, auth), Background Check, Pastel Jour, F & W Pub, 2012; La Redaction, Portfolio Grand Maitres Du Pastel, Practique Des Arts, Diverti Editions, 2012. *Mailing Add:* 60-197 Old Town Rd Vernon CT 06066

GROGAN, KEVIN
MUSEUM DIRECTOR
b Washington, DC, Oct 4, 1948. *Study:* Franklin & Marshall Col, BA; Am Univ, MA; Vanderbilt Univ, MA; Ctr Non-Profit Mgt. *Exhib:* Red Grooms: The Graphic Work, In Pursuit of Serious Fun; Karl Struss: A Retrospective View of His Photog; The Am Scene, 1900-1950; Glamour Defined: The Photog of George Hurrell; Louise Dahl-Wolfe: A Retrospective; Wolf Kahn: Pastels Retrospective; Jim McGuire: Nashville Portraits; Preservation of Place: The Art of Edward Rice; Golden Afternoon: English Watercolors From the Elsely Collection; First Lady Ellen Axon Wilson and Her Circle; Shadows of History: Photographs of the Civil War. *Pos:* Asst cur & asst dir, Phillips Collection, DC, 71-79; dir, Fine Arts Ctr at Cheekwood, Nashville, Tenn, 80-90; dir, Univ Galleries, Fisk Univ, Nashville, Tenn, 92-99; interim exect dir, Knoxville Mus Art, 91; exec dir/pres, Contemp Art Ctr Va, 99-2002; dir, Morris Mus of Art, 2002-; dir, Porter Fleming Literary Competition, 2010-; founder, exec prodr, Southern Soul and Song Concert Series, 2003-. *Teaching:* Adj assoc prof, Dept Fine Arts, Vanderbilt Univ, 82-90 & Art Dept, Fisk Univ, 90-99. *Awards:* Gordon Holl Outstanding Arts Adminr, Tenn, 87; Brotherhood-Sisterhood Award, Nat Conf Christians & Jews, 89; Award of Merit, Tenn Asn Mus, 90; Outstanding Arts, Professional Greater Augusta Arts Coun, 2005. *Mem:* Am Asn Mus; Asn Fundraisings Prof; Art Mus Partnership; Southeast Mus Conf; Int Coun Mus; SE Art Mus Directors Forum; Ga Asn Mus & Galleries; Cosmos Club; Salmagundi Club. *Res:* American art of the late 19th and early 20th centuries; American collectors of the same period; southern art & artists. *Publ:* The Phillips Collection in the Making: 1920-30, Smithsonian Inst; Karl Struss: A Retrospective (exhib catalog); ed & auth foreword, Red Grooms: A Catalogue Raissone of his Graphic Work, rev ed, 85; Art in the Embassy, Paris; Red Grooms: In Pursuit of Serious Fun; Pleasant Journeys & Good Eats Along the Way: Paintings by John Baeder, Univ Press Miss; John Steuart Curry's Hoover & The Flood: Painting History, Univ NC Press; Nashville Portraits: Photographs by Jim McGuire; Preservation of Place: The Art of Edward Rice; Golden Afternoon, English Watercolors from the Elsley Collection, Romantic Spirits: 19th Century Painting in the South from the Johnson Collection, Soldier-Artist: Conrade Wise Chapman, Ellen Axson Wilson and Her Circle, This Happy Land: Paintings by William Entrekin, Oh! Augusta! Photographs by William Greiner; contbr, Encyclopedia of Southern Culture; contbr,Tennessee Encyclopedia of History and Culture; and many others. *Mailing Add:* 709 Somerset Way Augusta GA 30909

GROM, BOGDAN
SCULPTOR, PAINTER
b Devincina, Sgonico-Trieste, Italy, Aug 26, 1918; US citizen. *Study:* Fine Arts Acad, Perugia, Italy, with Gerardo Dottori, Aldo Pascucci, 44; Fine Arts Acad, Venice, Italy, with Guido Cadorin, Armando Pizzinato, Arturo Martini, 44; Fine Arts Acad, Munich, Ger, with Joseph Oberberger, 52. *Work:* Solomon R Guggenheim Mus, NY; Nat Mus Art, Osaka, Japan; Cincinnati Art Mus, Ohio; NJ State Mus, Trenton; Galleria Naz D'Arte Mod, Rome. *Comn:* Sculpture & murals, Winston-Muss Corp, Phoenix, Ariz, 62; glass windows & sculpture, St Vartan Armenian Cathedral, NY, 68; bronze sculpture, New York City Art Comn, Staten Island, 73; stained windows & sculpture, JCC, White Plains, NY, 86; sculpture, Hekemian Co, Hackensack, NJ, 90. *Exhib:* Grom, Opere di Arredo Urbano, 1959-1979, Sala Comunale D'Arte, Trieste, Italy, 79; Art Expo, NY Coliseum, NY, 81; Int Biennial of Graphic Art, Mod Art Mus, Ljubljana, Yugoslavia, 85; Arazzi Mitteleuropei, Palazzo Venezia, Rome, Italy, 87; Int Biennial of Graphic Art, RYU Contemp Art, Kawasaki, Japan, 89; Sefarad 92, Toledo, Spain & Tel Aviv, Israel, 92. *Pos:* Bd mem, North Jersey Art Ctr, Tenafly, 76-78; cur, North Salem Gallery Ltd, New York, 80-84. *Teaching:* Prof art & art hist, PTUJ State Gymnasium, Yugoslavia 45-47; State Teachers Prep Sch & Gymnas, Trieste, Italy, 47-53; vis instr art, Pratt Inst, New York, 60. *Awards:* Am Inst Archit, 85; For Achievement in Art Teaching, Europ Recovery Plan. *Bibliog:* Susan B Hirschfeld (auth), article, Yugoslavia Cult Ctr (catalog), 89; John De Fazio (auth), Grom, 96. *Mem:* Coll Art Asn; Am Medallic Sculpture Asn; Int Sculpture Ctr; Sculptors Asn NJ (pres, 76-78). *Media:* All Media; Tapestry Artist. *Publ:* Illustr, Tom Sawyer, 47 & Huckelberry Finn, 48, Mladinska Knjiga; auth, Slovene Ornaments, pvt publ, 49; Trieste and its Karst, pvt publ, 57; illustr, There is No Such Animal, TB Lippincott, 58. *Mailing Add:* 416 Cumberland St Englewood NJ 07631-4702

GROMALA, DIANE
VIDEO ARTIST, CRITIC
b Menominee, Mich, Feb 24, 1960. *Study:* Univ Mich, BFA, 1982; Yale Univ, MFA, 1990. *Comn:* Dancing with the Virtual Dervish: Virtual Bodies, Meat Book, Pain Distraction, Biomorphic Typography. *Exhib:* Virtual Subjectivities (video), Seattle Art Mus, 1995 & Los Angeles Contemp Exhib, Calif, 1997; Virtual Dervish (video), Meany Theatre, Univ Wash, 1995; Virtual Bodies (video), Western Front Gallery, Vancouver, Can, 1996, Adams Art Gallery, Victoria Univ, Wellington, New Zealand, 1998; Abject Subject (performance), Yale Univ Sch Art, New Haven, Conn, 1997; Excretia, Int Soc for Elec Arts, Paris, 2000, McLuhan Ctr, Univ Toronto, 2001, Univ Catalonia, Barcelona, 2001; Eating Eye (video), Univ Bremen, Germany, 2000; The Meditation Chamber (interactive exhib), SIGGRAPH, Los Angeles, 2001, Univ Ariz, 2002; Immanent Bodies, Univ Santa Cruz, 2001, Univ Calif Los Angeles, 2001; Biomorphic Typography (interactive installation), TechnoPoetry Festival, Atlanta, 2002; Dancing with the Virtual Dervish: Virtual Bodies II, Nat Mus Contemp Art, Athens, Greece, 2002. *Pos:* Chair, UNESCO Art, Sci & Technol initiative, 2002-. *Teaching:* asst prof, Univ Tex, 1990-94 & Univ Wash, Seattle, 1995-2000; assoc prof, Ga Tech, Atlanta, 2000-. *Awards:* Innovative Teaching, Am Inst Graphic Arts, 1992; Foxworth Centennial Fel, Univ Tex, 1994; Fulbright Fel, Fulbright Comn, 1999. *Bibliog:* Liz McQuiston (auth), Suffragetts to She-Devils, Phaidon Press, 1997; Anne Morgan Spalter (auth), The Computer in the Visual Arts, Addison Wesley, 1999; Michael Rock (auth), Design in the Academy, Am Inst Graphic Arts J, Vol 13, 1995. *Mem:* Coll Art Asn; Postmodern Cult (ed bd, 97-2000); Am Inst Graphic Art; Mod Lang Asn. *Media:* Virtual reality, electronic media, biomedical technologies. *Res:* Phenomenology of digital technologies. *Specialty:* Media art. *Interests:* Chronic Pain, biomedical visualizations. *Publ:* Auth, Dancing with the Virtual Dervish, in: Immersed In Technology, MIT Press, 1995, Pain and Subjectivity in VR, in: Clicking In: Hot Links to a Digital Culture, Bay Press, 1996 & Learning the Languages of Babel, Education of an eDesigner, 5/2000,; co-auth, Windows and Mirrors, MIT Press, 2003. *Mailing Add:* Ga Inst Tech 686 Cherry St Atlanta GA 30332-0165

GRON, JACK
SCULPTOR, ADMINISTRATOR, EDUCATOR
b Steubenville, Ohio, 1951. *Study:* Columbus Col of Art & Design, BFA (Sculpture), 1973; Washington Univ, MFA (Sculpture), 1976. *Exhib:* Seven solo and seven group exhibitions. *Pos:* Operated sculpture studio, Chicago, 1976-80; Mem City of Flagstaff Art Advisory Com, 2003-2005, vice chair-elect, 2004-2005. *Teaching:* Taught Sculpture and Ceramics, Univ of Cincinnati, formerly; head of Sculpture, assoc prof of fine art, Col of Fine Arts, Univ Kentucky, Lexington, 1992-2002, chair department of art, 1995-2002; dir, prof of fine art, School of Art, Northern Arizona Univ, Flagstaff, 2002-2005; prof Fine art, chair, department of art, Texas A&M Univ, Corpus Christi, 2005-; taught internationally in Cortona, Italy, Univ Georgia, Ironbridge England and Krakow and Gdansk Poland at the Academies of Fine Arts, vis artist residency, 2007. *Mailing Add:* Texas A&M University-Corpus Christi Center for the Arts 105 6300 Ocean Dr Corpus Christi TX 78412

GRONBORG, ERIK
SCULPTOR, CERAMIST
b Copenhagen, Denmark, Nov 12, 1931; US citizen. *Study:* Univ Calif, Berkeley, BA, 62, MA, 63. *Work:* Oakland Art Mus, Calif; Everson Mus Art, Syracuse, NY; Am Crafts Mus, NY; Univ Art Collections, Ariz State Univ, Tempe; Contemp Crafts Asn, Portland, Ore. *Exhib:* Solo exhibs, 47 exhibs including Musee d'Art Moderne, Paris, Fr, 65, Mus Contemporary Crafts, NY, 69, Mus Contemporary Crafts, Portland, Ore, 67, 72, 77, 80, 2012, Art Mus, Ariz State Univ, Tempe, 72, Art Mus, Univ Ore, Eugene, 73, Craft and Folk Art Mus, Los Angeles, Calif, 73, Univ Santa Clara Mus, Calif, 74, Bonython Gallery, Adelaide, Australia, 76, 78, 83, Grossmont Coll Art Gallery, San Diego, Calif, 75, 90, MiraCosta Coll Gallery, San Diego, Calif, 76, 84, 93, 2001; 250 Group exhibs including, Third Biennale de Paris, Musee d'Art Moderne, Paris, Fr, 63, Creative Casting, Mus Contemporary Crafts, NY, 63, Artists of Ore, Portland Art Mus, Ore, 66, 67, 69, Northwest Artists Annual, Seattle Art Mus, Wash, 66, Ceramic Nat Everson Mus, Syracuse, NY, 66, 68, 23rd Ceramic Invitational, Scripps Coll, Los Angeles, 67, Sculpture NW, Seattle Art Mus, Wash, 67, Ung Dansk Kunst, Charlottenborg, Copenhagen, Denmark, 67, West Coast Now, Portland Art Mus, Seattle Art Mus, de Young Mus, San Francisco, 68, Objects USA Lee Nordness Galleries, NY, 69, Ceramics, 70, Everson Mus Art, Syracuse, NY, 70, Cups Mus Contemporary Crafts, NY, 70, XXIX Int Competition of Artistic Ceramics, Faenza, Italy, 71, 73rd Western Ann Denver Art Mus, Colo, 71, 28th Ceramic Invitational, Scripps Coll, Los Angeles, Calif, 72, International Ceramics Victoria and Albert Mus, London, 72, A Decade of Ceramic Art 1962-72, San Francisco Mus Art, Calif, 72, Int Exhib Ceramics, Nat Mus Gdansk-Oliwa, Poland, 73, Int Cup Exhib, Sea of Japan Exposition, Kanazawa City, Japan, 73, Baroque 74, Mus Contemporary Crafts, NY, 74, World Crafts Council Internat Exhib, Toronto, Can, 74, Allied Craftsmen of San Diego, San Diego Mus Art, Calif, 74, 76, 77, 81, Forms in Metal, Mus Contemporary Crafts, NY, 75, Calif Crafts IX EB Crocker Art Gallery, Sacramento, Calif, 75, Honolulu Acad Arts, Hawaii, 75, Tureen Exhib, Campbell Mus, Camden, NJ, 76, Americana San Francisco Mus Art, Calif, 76, Four Ceramic Artists Univ Calif, Riverside, 77, Phila Crafts Show, Phila Mus Art, Pa, 78, Made from Molds Kohler Art Ctr, Sheboygan, Wisc, 78, New Handmade Furniture Mus Contemporary Crafts, NY, 79, Contemporary Porcelain Renwick Gallery, Smithsonian, Wash DC, 80, Miniature Ceramics Int Acad Ceramics Conferance, Kyoto, Japan, 80, 82, Art in Clay, 1950-80, Municipal Art Gallery, Los Angeles, Calif, 84, Culture Recycled, De Beyard Art Mus, Breda, The Netherlands, 84; Silver/Wood/Clay/Gold, San Diego Mus Art, Calif, 93, A Ceramic Continuum: 50 Years of the Archie Brae Influence, Holter Mus Art, Helena, Montana, 2000, The Diane and Sandy Besser Collection Fine Arts Mus San Francisco, Calif, 2007, Golden State of Craft: Calif 1960-85, Craft and Folk Art Mus, Los Angeles, 2011, San Diego Craft Revolution, Mingei Mus, San Diego, Calif, 2011. *Teaching:* Asst prof ceramics & sculpture, Reed Col, Portland, Ore, 65-69; assoc prof, San Diego State Univ, Calif, 73-75; prof ceramics & sculpture, Mira Costa Col, Oceanside, Calif, 75-. *Awards:* Grand Prix, Mus Mod Art, Paris, 63; Nat Endowment Arts Craftsman Grant, 73; Award, Victoria & Albert Mus, London, 73. *Bibliog:* Kent Hall (auth), Erik Gronborg: the history of the present, Univ Portland Rev, 66; Ida Rigby (auth), Erik Gronborg's accessible art, Artweek, 2/3/79; Judi Nicolaidis (auth), Erik Gronborg: Portrait in Clay (video), Nicolaidis, 79. *Mem:* Am Crafts Coun (state rep, 71-73). *Media:* Wood, Ceramics. *Publ:* Auth, The new generation of ceramic artists, Craft Horizons, 69; Man and art in the urban environment, Nat Park & Conserv Mag, 72; Address to World Crafts Council Conference, Mexico, Ceramic Rev, 77; contribr, Ceramic Art, Comment and Review, 1882-1977, Dutton, 78. *Mailing Add:* 424 Dell Ct Solana Beach CA 92075-1419

GRONK
PAINTER
b Los Angeles, Calif, 1954. *Exhib:* Cult Currents, San Diego Mus Art, Calif, 88; solo exhibs, Gronk, Molly Barnes Gallery, Los Angeles, 84, The Titanic & other Tragedies at Sea, Galeria Ocaso, Los Angeles, 85, The Rescue Party, Saxon-Lee Gallery, 86-89, 50 Drawings, Daniel Saxon Gallery, Los Angeles, 91, Hotel Tormenta, Galerie Claude

Samuel, Paris, France, 92, Fascinating Slippers/Pantunflas, San Jose Mus Art, Calif (originated by Mex Mus), San Francisco, 92 & Fascinating Slippers/Pantunflas Fascinantes, Daniel Saxon Gallery, Los Angeles, 92; Chicano & Latino: Parallels and Divergence (catalog), Daniel Saxon Gallery, Los Angeles, 91, El Paso Mus Art, Tex, 92 & Kimberly Gallery, Washington, DC, 92; Of Nature & the Human Spirit, Part II, Daniel Saxon Gallery, Los Angeles, 91; Myth & Magic in the Americas: The Eighties (catalog), Contemp Art, Monterrey, Mex, 91. *Awards:* Artist of Year, Mex Am Fine Art Asn, 77; Visual Artist Fel, Nat Endowment for Art, 83. *Bibliog:* Susan Kandel (auth), LA in Review, Arts Mag, 12/91; Suvan Geer (auth), Los Angeles Times, Calendar sect, 3/20/91; Leigh Ann Clifton (auth), Gronk at SJMA, Artweek, 4/9/92

GROOMS, RED
PAINTER, SCULPTOR
b Nashville, Tenn, June, 1937. *Study:* Sch Art Inst, Chicago, 55; George Peabody Coll for Teachers, Nashville, 56; New Sch Soc Res, NY, 56; Hans Hoffman Sch Fine Arts, Provincetown, Mass, 57. *Work:* Allen Mem Art Mus, Oberlin, Ohio; Ark Art Ctr, Little Rock; Art Inst, Chicago; Brooklyn Mus, NY; Chrysler Mus, Norfolk, Va; Cleveland Mus Art, Ohio; Del Art Mus, Wilmington; Denver Art Mus, Colo; Everson Mus Art of Syracuse & Onondago Co, NY; Hirshhorn Mus & Sculpture Garden, Washington, DC; Mint Mus, Charlotte, NC. *Comn:* Tut's Fever Movie Palace (environ comn), with Lysiane Luong, Am Mus Moving Image, Astoria, NY, 88; set design for Meilleurs Amis, Nat Dance Inst, 89; set design for The Shooting of Dan McGrew, Nat Dance Inst, 90; set design for The Mysteries & What's So Funny, Serious Fun & Spoleto Festival, 91; set design for Chakra: A Celebration of India, Nat Dance Inst, 91. *Exhib:* Whitney Mus Am Art, 73, 78, 84 (three exhibs), 86-87 & 87-88; Solo exhibs, Brooklyn Mus, 92 & 94-95, Cheekwood Mus Art, Nashville (traveled to Polk Mus Art, Lakeland, Fla, Albany Mus Art, Ga, Michell Art Gallery & St John's Col, Annapolis Md), 95-96, New Brit Mus Am Art, Conn, 96 & Red Grooms, Marlborough & Boca Raton, Fla, 99, 2000, Self Made Men, DC Moore Gallery, NY, 2001, others; Il Cinema Amaggio di Primi 100 Anni del Cinema, Galleria Arte Gabbiano, Rome, 95; Art from the Driver's Seat: Americans & Their Cars (traveling throughout US), incl Hunter Mus Am Art, Tenn, 95-96; Les Champs de la Sculpture II, Champs Elysees Avenue, Paris, France, 98; Outward Bound: Am Art at the Brink of Twenty-First Century, Meridian Int Cen, 99; Deja vu: Reworking the Past, Kotonah Mus Art, NY, 2000; group exhibs incl, Guggenheim Mus New York City, 72, Ruckus Manhattan, New York City, 75-76, 81, State Univ NY, Purchase, 78, Lowe Art Mus Univ, Miami, Fla, 80, The New Gallery, Cleveland, 82, Int Cooperation Admin, Philadelphia, 82, Allen Frumkin Gallery, New York City, 85, Open Air Mus Sculpture, Middelheim, Antwerp, Belg, 85, Sewell Art Gallery Rice Univ, Houston, 85, Artists' Choice Mus, New York City, 86, Mus Art, Ft Lauderdale, Fla, 86, Wilson Art Ctr, Rochester, NY, 86, Allentown, Pa, Art Mus, 86, NY Acad Art, 86, Whitney Mus Am Art at Philip Morris, New York City, 86-87, National Mus Am History Smithsonian Inst, Wash, 86-, Saxon Lee Gallery, Los Angeles, 1988, Baruch Col, New York City, 88, Lockport Gallery, Ill, 88-89, Bucknell Univ, Lewisburg, Pa, 89. *Collection Arranged:* The Brooklyn Mus, NY; Solomon R Guggenheim Mus, HY; The Hudson River Mus Westchester, NY; Nagoya City Art Mus, Japan; The Met Mus Art, NY; Moderna Museet, Stockholm, Sweden; Mus Art, Kochi, Japan; NJ State Mus, Trenton; Philadelphia Mus Art, Pa; Whitney Mus Am Art, NY. *Teaching:* Vis artist, Syracuse Univ, 80, Southern Ill Univ, 80 & Colo State Univ, 81; Albert Dorne Prof, Univ Bridgeport, 82. *Awards:* New York Times Ten Best Illus Children's Bks Award, 86; Gov's Award Arts, State Tenn, 86; Mayor's Award Honor, Art & Cult, NY, 88; Founders Medal, Pa Acad, 90. *Bibliog:* Patrick Pacheco (auth), The art collector as activist: Stewart & Linda Resnick, Art & Antiques, 3/96; Jenifer P Borum (auth), rev, Artforum, 4/96; Terry Sullivan (auth), When influence becomes inspiration, Art Masters, 6/96. *Mem:* Nat Acad. *Publ:* Coauth, Rembrandt Takes a Walk, Potter, New York, 87; auth, Ruckus Rodeo, Abrams, New York, 88; illusr, An artist, present at the Creation, reports (cartoon), NY Times, 7/7/91; cover, New Yorker, 10/19/92

GROOT, CANDICE BETH
CERAMIST
b Berwyn, Ill, Mar 4, 1954. *Study:* Gustavus Adolphus Col, BA, 76; Tex Tech Univ, with Verne Funk, MFA, 80. *Work:* Contemp Mus NMex, Santa Fe. *Exhib:* 9th Marietta Coll Crafts Nat, Ohio, 80; Clay Work/New Work, D W Gallery, Dallas, Tex, 80; Clay Workers Guild, Ill, 81; Small Work Nat, Zaner Gallery, Rochester, NY, 81; Westwood Clay Nat, Calif, 81. *Teaching:* Asst prof ceramics, Gustavus Adolphus Col, St Peter, Minn, 81-. *Awards:* Purchase Prize, Southwest Fine Arts Biennial, Hill Gallery, 78; Juror's Awards, Tex Coll Art Show, 78 & Midland Col, 78. *Mem:* Am Crafts Coun; Nat Coun Educ Ceramic Arts. *Media:* Clay, Paper. *Mailing Add:* 911 Edgemere Ct Evanston IL 60202

GROPPER, CATHY
PAINTER, SCULPTOR
b 1954, Cleveland, Ohio. *Study:* New York Univ, BS, 76; Columbia Univ, MA, 78 under Larry Rivers, Elaine de Kooning, Jane Wilson & Milton Resnick. *Work:* Nathan Cummings Collection & Mrs Harvey Meyerhoff Collection, Baltimore, Md & NY; Lillian Berkman, NY; Nathan Goldman Collection, Palm Beach, Fla & NY; Greek Embassy; George S Kaufman Collection. *Comn:* Nate & Me, 82, Nathan Cummings, NY; sculpture, Schermerhorn Inc, Chicago. *Exhib:* Solo exhibs, Am Merchant Marine Mus, Kings Point, NY, 79, Weintraub Gallery, NY, 86 & 95, Penson Gallery, NY, 89; group shows, Hungers 1990's: Not by Bread Alone, Carson Co Sq House Mus, Panhandle, Old Jail Art Ctr, Abilene, Mus Mod Art, Santa Fe, Amon Carter Mus, Fort Worth, Tex & Denver Art Ctr, Colo 90-92 & Elena Zang Gallery, Woodstock, NY, 95; Helen Drutt Gallery, NY, 92; Galerie Sculptures, Paris, France, 1996-2003; Jonathan Poole Gallery, Oxfordshire, Eng, 93-96; Edinburgh Fringe Festival, 2001. *Pos:* Dir, Artists Exchange, television interviews & documentaries, Conn & NY, 79-; dir, Orgn Independent Artists, NY, 90-94; playwright, 2001-2004. *Teaching:* Exec coun, Teachers Col Columbia Univ, 82-97; guest lectr, Fairfield Co, Conn & Antioch Writers Workshop; adj prof, Broadway League. *Awards:* First Award, Mid-Western States Coll Art Competition, Univ Wis, Madison. *Bibliog:* Lynn Seeney (auth), India theme, Art World, 5-6/85; Amy Penn (auth), Brushing up on young talent, New York Post, 11/8/85; Anita Gates (auth), NY Times, 2/2002; Sara Willcock (auth) The Scotsman, 2/2002. *Mem:* Artists Equity; Visual Artists & Galleries Asn; Dramatists Guild; Conn Soc Sculptors; The Naked Stage; Flashpoint Cult Corp. *Media:* Oil, Welding. *Specialty:* Sculpture. *Collection:* Nathan Cummings. *Publ:* Night Mag, 6/2003. *Dealer:* Jacob Weintraub Galerie Sculptors Paris

GROSCH, LAURA
PAINTER, PRINTMAKER
b Worcester, Mass, Apr 1, 1945. *Study:* Wellesley Coll, Mass, BA (art hist), 67; Univ Pa, Philadelphia, BFA (painting), 68; study with Gertrude Whiting, James Rayen, Sigmund Abeles & Neil Welliver. *Work:* Libr Cong & Smithsonian Inst, Washington, DC; New York Pub Libr, Brooklyn Mus, NY; Boston Mus Fine Arts & Boston Pub Libr, Mass; Calif Palace Legion Honor, San Francisco; Victoria & Albert Mus, British Mus, London, Eng; Kohler Art Ctr, Sheboygan, Wis; Carnegie Mellon Univ, Pittsburgh, Pa; Univ Calif, Los Angeles; Newark Pub Libr, Rutgers Univ, New Brunswick, NJ; Free Libr Philadelphia, Pa; Greenville Co Mus Art, SC; Honolulu Acad Arts, Hawaii; Madison Arts Ctr, Wis; Asheville Art Mus, NC; Western Carolina Univ, Culcowee, NC; Wilmington Art Mus, NC; and numerous others. *Exhib:* Group Exhibs: 30 Yrs of Am Printmaking (with catalog), Brooklyn Mus, NY, 76; Wellesley Coll Alumnae Art Exhib, Jewett Art Center, Wellesley, Mass, 1997; 20th Ann Exhib, Greenhill Ctr NC Ar, Greensboro, 1999; Queen Charlotte's Birds of Paradise, Chairs on Parade, Tryon Ctr for Visual Art, Charlotte, NC, 2001; The Legacy of Romare Bearden, Mint Mus Art, Charlotte, 2002; 15x15, Christa Faut Gallery, Cornelius, NC, 2003; Tribute to Alice Ehrlich, Lee Hansley Gallery, Raleigh, NC, 2003; War Charlotte, The Steeple, Charlotte, 2003; Memories of Kitty, Christa Faut Gallery, 2004; Opening Exhib, Garden Gallery, Raleigh, NC, 2005; Somerhill Gallery, Chapel Hill, NC, 2006; Christa Faut Gallery, Cornelius, NC, 2007-2010; Gentrify, Dialect Gallery, Charlotte, NC, 2009, Eden Now: Hydrangeas & Tiger Swallow Tails, 2012, Duke Cancer Inst, Durham, NC, The Bell Collection, Leland Little Auction Exhib, Hillsbough, NC, 2012, Merrill Jennings Galleries, 2013, Visionary Woman Artis Painting Exhib, Mint Mus of Art Uptown, Charlotte NC, 2015; Solo Exhibs: Eden Now, Davidson Coll Art Gallery, Davidson, NC, 1985; Jerald Melberg Gallery, Charlotte, NC, 87; Hodges Taylor Gallery Charlotte, NC, 89; Christa Faut Gallery, Davidson, NC, 90, 93 & 96; A Prismatic Presence, Milennium Exhib, Rock Sch Arts Found, Valdese, NC, 2000; 250th Ann State of Art, Asn Artists of Winston-Salem, NC, 2004; Goddess/Woman of God, Christa Faut Gallery, Davidson, NC, 97; Solstice Exhib, Les Yeux du Monde, Charlottesville, Va, 97; Garden Gala, Morris Gallery, Columbia, SC, 97. *Collection Arranged:* Works in Alumni Art Collections, The Van Every/Smith Galleries, Davidson Col, NC, 2015. *Teaching:* Community classes, 64-97. *Awards:* Teaching Grant, Mint Mus. *Bibliog:* Larry David Perkins (auth), Collaborative American Printmaking (exhib catalog), Lowe Art Gallery, Syracuse Univ, 87; Lawrence Toppman (auth), Music flows through artist's paintbrush, 5/9/96 & Art of the possible, 10/6/96, The Charlotte Observer. *Mem:* Coll Art Asn. *Media:* Acrylic; Hand-made Litho. *Publ:* The True Essentials of a Feast, Libr Cong, 87; Luminous Impressions (film), Univ NC Pub Television, Grasberg/Littletown, 97. *Dealer:* Merril-Jennings Galleries 463 S Main Davidson NC 28036. *Mailing Add:* 497 S Main St PO Box 10 Davidson NC 28036

GROSS, JENNIFER R
CURATOR, CRITIC
Study: Hunter Coll, New York, MA (art hist); CUNY Grad Ctr, New York, PhD (art hist). *Collection Arranged:* Objective Color, 2001; Claes Oldenburg's Lipstick: Models and Drawings, 2001; Between Language and Form, 2002; The 1948 Directors of teh Societe Anonyme Exhib, 2002; Edgar Degas: Defining the Modernist Edge, 2003; The Societe Anonyme: Modernism for America, 2006. *Pos:* Dir, German van Eck Gallery, New York, 1988-94 & Maine Coll Art Inst Contemp Art, Portland, 1994-97; cur contemp art, Isabella Stewart Gardner Mus, Boston, 1997-2000; Seymour H Knox Jr cur European & contemp art, Yale Univ Art Gallery, New Haven, 2000-2002 & cur mod & contemp art, 2002-; vis critic, Yale Sch Art, New Haven, 2000-. *Teaching:* Adj lectr, Hunter Coll, New York, 1993; vis lectr, Harvard Univ Carpenter Ctr, 1994; asst prof, Maine Coll Art, 1994-96; art hist lectr, Yale Sch Art, 2002-2005. *Awards:* Outstanding Exhib Award, Am Asn Mus Curators, 2006. *Mem:* Am Mus Asn; ArtTable; Coll Art Asn; Contemp Curators Forum; Int Asn Art Critics. *Publ:* Auth, Refracted Sight/Refracted Memory, In: Roger Winter New Paintings, Baxter Gallery, Maine Coll Art, 1996; Illuminating Surfaces, In: Abelardo Morell-Face to Face, 1998; Consider the Object as Evidence, In: The Way Things Are-The Art of David Ireland, Oakland Mus, 2003; ed, The Societe Anonyme-Modernism for America, Yale Univ Press, 2006; auth, Readymade Romantic, In: Kristin Baker-Surge and Shadow, Deitch Projects, 2007. *Mailing Add:* Yale Univ Art Gallery PO Box 208271 New Haven CT 06520-8271

GROSS, JULIE
PAINTER, INSTRUCTOR
b July 24, 1943. *Study:* Pratt Inst, Brooklyn, NY, BFA, 65; Hunter Coll, New York, MA, 74. *Work:* Chase Manhattan Bank; Prudential Life Insurance Co; AT&T Corp; Chait/Chasen, Prepare Inc; Chicago Title; Gulf & Western Corp; Lucent Technol; Suntrust Corp; Pfizer Corp; Bellagio Hotel, Las Vegas; Doubletree Metropolitan Hotel, NY; HSBC Bank, NY; Pfizer Corp; Princess Cruise Lines; UBS Collection; USAA Corp; US Trust Corp. *Comn:* Bronson Fine Art, 99-2000; Soho Myriad, 2007; Bronson Fine Art, 99-2000. *Exhib:* Solo shows, State Univ NY, Rockland Community Col, Suffern, 76, Frank Marino Gallery, NY, 79, Stephen Rosenberg Gallery, NY, 85 & 87, City Univ NY, Kingsborough Community Col, 93 & 55 Mercer St Gallery, 95, Kathryn Markel Gallery, New York City, 2000, Del Valley Arts Alliance, 2003, EO Art Lab, 2008, Julie Mus Space, Boston, 2007; Nahan Contemp Gallery, NY, 90; Jessica Berwind Gallery, Philadelphia, 91; Eastern Mont Col, Billings, 92; Police Bldg, 94; Aldrich Mus Contemp Art, Ridgefield, Conn, 96; Parsons Sch of Design Gallery, New York City, 94, 96, 98; Kathryn Markel Gallery, New York City, 99; Margaret Thatcher

Projects (3 person show), New York City, 2000; Kenise Barnes Gallery (3 person show), Larchmont, NY, 2001; Delaware Ctr for Contemp Art Struct groupshow, 2005; Little Languages/Coded Pictures: Markel Gallery, NY, 2012; Janet Kurnatowski Gallery, Brooklyn, NY, 2012; Synesthia, EO Art Lab, Chester, Conn, 2012; Circular Reasoning, Paris Concret, France, 2012. *Pos:* Fac consult, SADI, Seoul, Korea & KIDI, Kanazawa, Japan, 95 & 96; Ctr for Advan Design, Kuala Lumpur, 97. *Teaching:* Painting, drawing & art hist survey; vis instr, Kutztown State Col, Pa, 75 & Cent Univ NY, Manhattan, 78-79; vis asst prof, Pratt/Manhattan, 75-81 & 86-90; instr, State Univ NY, Rockland Community Col, Suffern, NY, 75-76, Ramapo Col, Wayne, NJ, 76-7, Bloomfield Col, NJ, 77; master teacher painting, State Univ NY, Fredonia, 76-79; instr painting, Metrop Mus Art, 81, RI Sch Design, 81-83; vis instr, Hunter Col, NY, 83-85 & Ctr Advan Design/CENfAD, Malaysia, 97; instr art, Parsons Sch Design, 81- & Fashion Inst Technol, 89-; instr, Parsons Sch, Fashion Inst Tech. *Awards:* New Sch, Fac Develop Fund Grant, 89; Nat Endowment Arts Grant, Painting, 91-92; Caps grant; MacDowell Colony Residence, 92; Grantee The New Sch Faculty Devel Fund, 89, 95; Ucross Found Residency, 96; Nat Acad Mus Mural Painting Fel, 2006; Residency, VCCA, 2007. *Bibliog:* Judith Page (auth), Ground Works (catalog essay), Valencia Community Col, 89; Peggy Cyphers (auth), rev, Arts Mag, 12/90; Meyer R Rubinstein (auth), Isn't It Romantic (catalog essay), 94; Jeff Wright (auth.) Review, Cover Mag., 95; New York Contemporary Art Report, 2000. *Mem:* Barryville Areas Arts Alliance. *Media:* Oil. *Specialty:* painting, sculpture. *Interests:* Travel; Design; Reading; Gardening. *Publ:* Coauth, Women and textiles in five cultures, Heresies, New York, No 4, 78; auth, Sustenance, Appearances, New York, No 3, 79. *Dealer:* Kathryn Markel Fine Arts 529 W 20th St New York NY 1001; Kenise Barnes fine Art, Larchmont, NY; Jules Place Boston. *Mailing Add:* 166 W 22nd St 4F New York NY 10011

GROSS, MARILYN A
PAINTER, PRINTMAKER
b Rolla, Mo, Jan 23, 1937. *Study:* St Louis Univ, BS, 58; Wash Sch Art, Port Washington, NY, 75-78, cert, 78; Sch Art Inst Chicago Oxbow; Saugatuck, Mich, 81; Numerous seminars & workshops with leading teachers around the country, 1978-2013. *Work:* Schiff, Hardin & Waite Corp, Chicago, Ill; Com Nat Bank Corp Collection, Peoria, Ill; Magna Bank Corp Collection, Peoria, Ill. *Exhib:* Ala Watercolor Soc Exhib, Ctr Arts, Fairhope, Ala, 98; Am Watercolor Soc Int Juried Exhib, Salmagundi Club, NY, 98; Watercolor USA, Springfield Mus Art, Mo, 98; Flamingo Exhib, Hilton Leach Studios, Sarasota, Fla, 98; 19th Ann Faber Birren Nat Color Award Exhib, Univ Conn, Stamford, 99; Int Soc Exp Artists, Huntsville Mus Art, Ala, 99; Ariz Aqueous, Tubac Ctr for Arts, Tubac, Ariz, 99; Northern Trust Exhib, Longboat Key, Fla, 2000; Int Soc Exp Artists, Dennos Mus, Traverse City, Mich, 2001; Nat Acrylic Painters Asn Exhib, Segretto Contemp Gallery, Santa Fe, NMex, 2002; Challenge of the Champions, Watermedia, Continental Center, Houston, Tex, 2003; Multimedia Nat Exhib, Lexington, Ky, 2006; Soc of Layerists in Multi-Media Exhib: Illuminations, Sydney & Byrne Davis Art Ctr, Ft Myers, Fla, 2008; The Canvas Project, Atlanta, Ga, 2009; Fine Arts Soc Galleria, Sarasota, Fla, 2010; Solo exhib, Moments in Reality, Womens Resource Ctr, Sarasota, Fla, 2012. *Awards:* Numerous awards from 1975-. *Bibliog:* Kathleen Baxter (auth), Entering Another Dimension, Watercolor Mag, spring 2001; Marsha Fottler (auth), Material Girls, Sarasota Mag, 6-2003. *Mem:* Sarasota Arts Council; Chicago Artists Coalition; Ala Watercolor Soc; assoc mem Am Watercolor Soc; signature mem, Nat Collage Soc; signature mem Nat Asn Acrylic Painters; signature mem Int Soc Exp Artists; and others. *Media:* Watercolor, Mixed Media; Acrylic. *Publ:* The Art of Layering: Making Connections, Society of Layerists in Multi-Media, 2004; The Collected Best of Watercolor, Rockport Art Publs, 2002; Splash 7: The Qualities of Light, North Light Publs, 2002; Am Artist Watercolor Mag, Spring 2001; The Complete Best of Watercolor, Rockport Publs, 2000; Creative Inspirations, Rockport Publs, 1997; Painting Color-Best of Watercolor Series, Rockport Publs, 1997; Painting Composition-Best of Watercolor Series, Rockport Publs, 1997; Watercolor: Abstracts, Rockport Art Publs, 1996; Creative Watercolor, Rockport Art Publs, 1996; Best of Watercolor, Rockport Art Publs, 1995; The Artist's Muse: Unlock the Door to your Creativity, N Light Bks, 2006; The Canvas Project: A Visual Encyclopedia, 2009; Sue St. John (auth) Journeys to Abstraction, North Light Books, 2012; Eyes on Abstracts, Joe Guimera, Blaze Hill Press, 2012. *Mailing Add:* 374 MacEwen Dr Osprey FL 34229

GROSS, RAINER
PAINTER
b Cologne, Ger, Apr 23, 1951. *Study:* Art Acad Col, 71-73. *Work:* Bell Atlantic, Arlington, Va; Chase Manhattan Bank, NY; Hirschhorn Mus, Washington, DC; Kunsthalle, Emden, Ger; Ludwig Collection, Aachen, Ger; Mus Folkwang, Essen, Ger. *Exhib:* NY Now, Kestner Gesellschaft, Hannover, Ger, 82-83; solo exhibs, Musé Cantonal des Beaux Arts, Lausanne, Switz, 84, Kunsthalle Emden (traveling), Ger, Kunstverein Salzburg (traveling), Austria, 89, Mus Gesenkirschen (traveling), Ger, 91, Anderson Gallery, Richmond, Va, 93, Mus SFla, Univ Tampa, 93 & Folkwang Mus, Essen, Ger, 93; Krannert Mus, Champaign, Ill; and various galleries in Ger. *Bibliog:* Gerhard Finch (auth, catalog), Breast Exam, Kunsthalle Emden, 89; Noel Frackman (auth, catalog), Without Words, Ruth Siegel Gallery, NY, 91. *Media:* Oil, Acrylic. *Publ:* Auth, Une Collection s'Anime, Le Musee Cantonal des Beaux-Arts, 84; Ut Poesis Pictura, S D Sauerbier, 86; Without Words, Ruth Siegel Gallery, 91. *Dealer:* Gallery Moos Toronto Can; Gallery Oz Paris France. *Mailing Add:* 108 E 82nd St Apt 9C New York NY 10028

GROSS, SANDRA LERNER See Lerner, Sandra

GROSS BROWN, LINDA J
PAINTER, JUROR
b Akron, Ohio, Mar 6, 1954. *Study:* Kent State Univ, BFA, 76, MA, 84; Studied with Morton Grossman, Joseph O'Sickey. *Work:* Kent State Univ, Ohio; Cleveland Clinic Found; Fed Reserve Bank, Ohio; LDI Corp, Ohio; Fairview Park Hospital. *Exhib:* IAPS Convention Cover, 7th Biennial Convention, Albuquerque, NMex, 2009; Chicago Pastel Painter, Koehncine Mus Art, Des Plains, Ill, 2009; 96 Ann Allied Artists of Am, Nat Arts Club, New York, 2009; 126 Ann Mem Exhib, Salmagundi Club, New York, 2009; Andrews Art Mus, NC, 2010; 11 IACPS Juried Show, Butler Inst Art, Youngstown, Ohio, 2008, 16th, 2010; Richeson 75, Pastel Competition, 2010; Great Lakes Pastel Society, 2010; Salle des Fetes De Giverny, 2010; Int Art Show, 2010; IAPS 1st Master's Circle Exhib, 2010; IAPS 18th Exhib, 2010; 28th Ann Competition, Artists Mag, 2011; Chicago Pastel Painter's 3rd Biennial Nat Exhib, 2011; San Diego Art Inst, 2011. *Awards:* Gold Medal Excellence, 26 Ann mem, Art Spirit Found, 2009; Gold Medal, 96 Allied Artists, Allied Artists Am, 2009; Excellence Award, 7 Biennial Nat Exhib, Roy Lance & Mary Sharp, 2009; PSA Award, 113 Ann Open Exhib, Catharine Lorillard Wolfe, 2009; 2009 Web 4th Place, USPA Web Show, USPA, 2009; 11 Ann Pastel Hon mention, Pstel Journ, 2009; 4th Place, United Society of Pastel Artists (Online Competition), 2009; Anna Hyatt Huntington Bronze Medal, Catherine Lorillard Wolf Art Club, 114th Annual Exhib, 2010; Diane B Bernhard Silver Medal in Pastel, Allied Artists of America, 97th Ann Exhib, 2010; 3 top awards, 1 top merit, Int Art Search, 2010; 2nd Place, Ann Mem Show, Longboat Key Ctr Arts; 2nd Place Non-Oils, Richeson 75 Landscape, Seascape and Architectural, 2011. *Bibliog:* Adam & Renee Kennedy (auth), Best of Am, Pastel II, Kennedy Publ, 2009; James Metcalfe (auth), Love At First Touch, Am Artist, 2009; Adam & Renee Kennedy (auth), Best of World Wide Artists, Kennedy Publ, 2010; Laurent Benoist (auth), Pratique des Arts, June 2010. *Mem:* Salmagundi Art Club; Pastel Soc Am (signature mem); Int Asn Pastel Soc (master circle); Allied Artists Am; Great Lake Pastel Soc; Southwestern Fla Pastel Soc. *Media:* Soft Pastel. *Dealer:* One Artist Rd Santa Fe New Mexico; The Bon Foey Co Cleveland Ohio; River Gallery of the Arts

GROSSE, C(AROLYN) ANN GAWARECKI
PAINTER, INSTRUCTOR
b Rahway, NJ, Oct 30, 1931. *Study:* Douglass Coll, BA, 53; Univ Calif, Berkeley; Univ Colo. *Work:* COMSAT, Washington; Indust Coll Armed Forces, Ft McNair, Washington; James River Corp, Richmond, Va; Georgetown Univ; Texaco; Md Casualty Co; Dunnegan Gallery Mus, Bolivar, Mo; Springfield Art Mus, Springfield, Mo. *Comn:* Pvt comn by Nancy Dickerson, Merrywood, Va; painting, comn by Mr & Mrs Paul Tagliabue. *Exhib:* Solo exhibs, Atlantic Gallery, Georgetown, Washington, 78-81, & 91 & 93, Art League Gallery, Alexandria, Va, 88, McBride Gallery, Annapolis, Md, 91, 20th Century Gallery, Williamsburg, Va, 92, Nat Inst Health, 96, Douglass Coll Alumnae Artist Show, 99, French Embassy, 2000, Byrne Gallery, Middleburg, Va, 2002. *Pos:* Exhibits artist, Mus Nat Hist, Smithsonian Inst, 56-57; partic, Art in Embassies Prog, US State Dept; judge, Nat & Area Watercolor Shows. *Teaching:* Instr art, Highland Park High Sch, NJ, 53-55; instr watercolor, City of Falls Church, 66-; instr watercolor workshops, Del, Md, WVa, Eng, Acapulco, Mex & Ireland, France, Grand Tetons, Wyo, Greece, Italy & Spain; instr watercolor, Art League Sch, 90; Art League Sch, Alexandria, Va, 95-. *Awards:* Va Watercolor Soc State Show, 80-95; Nat Watercolor Soc Award, Brea, Calif, 87, 89 & 95; Rocky Mt Nat, Golden, Colo, 89 & 98; Aqueous 90, Murray, Ky; Allied Artists Am, NY, 90; 22nd La Nat Watercolor, New Orleans, 92; Knickerbocker Artists, NY, 92; WVa Watercolor Soc Award, 94 & Southern Watercolor Soc Award, 94, 2007; 1st Award, Washington Watercolor Soc, 94, 2005; Purchase Award, Watercolor USA, 96 & 98; Mid-Atlantic Regional, 97 & 98; WUSA award, 2003; Va Watercolor Soc, 2004, 2005; Mid Atlantic Show Award, Baltimore Watercolor Soc, 2006; Southern Watercolor Soc Award, Ga, 2007; Strathmore Hall Arts Award, N Bethesda, Md, 2008; Art League Award, Alexandria, Va, 2008; Award & Purchase Award, Springfield Mus Collection, Mo, 2009. *Mem:* Va Watercolor Soc & Art League; Southern Watercolor Soc; Potomac Valley Watercolorists (pres, 74-77); signature mem, Nat Watercolor Soc (Wash, Baltimore, chaps); Watercolor Hon Soc; Wash Watercolor Soc; Miniature Painters, Sculptors, & Gravers Soc of Wash DC; Douglass Soc. *Media:* Watercolor, Casein. *Publ:* Art Voices South, 7-8/80; Cover Hill Rag Cong Guide, 1/85, 1/89, 4/89 & 1/90; Texture Watercolor with Casein, Artist's Mag, 1/91; Best of Watercolor-Places, Artist's Mag, 96; Versatile Vignette, Watercolor Mag, Summer 97; Artistic Touch, Artist's Mag, #3, 98; cover design, A Virginia Village Revisited Inc. *Dealer:* Art League Gallery Alexandria Va; Byrne Gallery Middleburg Va; McBride Gallery Annapolis MD. *Mailing Add:* 7018 Vagabond Dr Falls Church VA 22042

GROSSMAN, BARBARA
PAINTER, EDUCATOR
b New York, NY, Nov 10, 1943. *Study:* Yale Sch Music & Art, 64; Cooper Union, BFA, 65; Fulbright Grant, Academie der Kunst, Munich, Ger, 67-68. *Work:* Corcoran Collection, Washington, DC; Bryn Mawr Coll Lib, Pa; Weatherspoon Art Gallery, Univ NC, Greensboro; Nat Acad Mus, NY; Coll Art Collection, Norwalk Community Col, Conn; Housatonic Mus of Art, Conn; Ark Art Ctr, Little Rock, Ark; Western Carolina Univ, Cullowhee, NC; Hood Mus Art, Dartmouth Col, Hanover, NJ; Portland Community Col, Portland, Oreg; Johnson and Johnson; Hollins Univ, Roanoke, Va; Wright State Univ, Dayton, Ohio; Mattatuck Mus, Waterbury, Conn; The State Mus of Pa, Harrisburg, Pa. *Exhib:* Solo shows incl Bowery Gallery, NY, 73, 77, 81, 85, 88, 92, 95, 98, 2001, 2007, Hollins Univ, Roanoke, Va, 2003, Taft Sch, Watertown, Conn, 2006, Rider Univ, Lawrenceville, NJ, 2009, Dartmouth Coll, 2002, Gross McCleaf Gallery, Phila, Pa, 2010, Univ Tulsa, Okla, 2013, Miss Porter's Sch, Farmington, Conn, 2014; group shows incl Drawing Invitational, Ind Univ, Bloomington, 87, 60th Anniversary Exhib Washington Art Asn, Conn, 2012; Figure Invitational, Coll William & Mary, Williamsburg, Va, 87; Quest, NY Studio Sch, 89; Muscarelle Mus Art, Williamsburg, Va, 94; Western Carolina State Univ, Cullowhee, NC, 98; Mangel Gallery, Philadelphia, Pa, 98; Figurative Painting Now, 55 Mercer, NY, 2000; Wayne Art Ctr, Pa, 2000; Dartmouth Coll, Hanover, NH, 2002, Union Coll, Schenectady, NY, 2003, New Arts Gallery, Litchfield, Conn, 2004, 2006, Wright State Univ, Dayton, Ohio, 2004, Lafayette Coll, Easton, Pa, 2004, Washington & Lee Univ, Lexington, Va, 2005, NY Studio Sch, 2005; Bachelier Cardonsky Gallery, Kent, Conn, 2007, Gross McCleaf, Philadelphia, Pa, 2008; Gross Mccleaf, Philadelphia, Pa, 2010; Reconfiguring the Body, Invitational Acad, NY, 2009; Better than Ever, LIU, La Mar Univ Tex, Rowan Univ, NJ; Chautauqua, A Continuum of Creativity, Deniso Bibro,

New York, 2010; Artists Who Teach, Conn State Univ, Conn, 2010; About the Figure, Marist Coll, NY, 2010; DeCamron, NY Studio School, NY, 2010; C2 Fine Art, Printed, Painted, Pressed, St Petersburg, Fla, 2011; Go Artists, 60 Yrs Washington Art Asn, Washington Depot, Ct, 2012. *Pos:* Applied arts adv comt, Tunxis Community Col, 79-85; vis critic, Yale Univ, 86-2005; chmn exhib comt, Wash Art Asn, 88-; juror, Mattatuck Mus, 2006; bd gov, Nat Acad Design, 2006-, chair nominating, 2009-, secy, 2009-2011; juror, Nat Academy Sch Fine Arts, 2007; juror, Nat Acad Mus, 2008; juror, Carriagg Barn Arts Ctr, New Canaan, Conn; vis critic, Western Conn State Univ, 2011; juror, Union Coll, Schenectady, NY. *Teaching:* Adj prof, drawing, Western Conn State Univ, Danbury, 81-94; resident fac, Chautauqua Inst Art Sch, 87-2007, 2009, 2012; fac, painting & drawing, NY Studio Sch, 88-2001; prof fac, Vt Studio Ctr, 91-95 & 2008; Hartford Art Sch, Univ Hartford, Conn, 92-; Grad Sch Fine Arts, Univ Pa, 93-2000; Univ Conn, 2000; Yale Sch Art, 2003, 2005-2007, 2008-2009; Western Carolina Univ, NC, 2004-06; Nat Acad Sch Fine Art, NY, 2005; Boston Univ, 2005-2010; vis artist, Knox Col, 99-2004, Brandeis Univ, 99-2009, Colby Col, 2000; vis critic, St Anselm Coll, Manchester, NH, 2011, Univ Tulsa, Okla, 2013, Mt Gretna Sch Art, Pa, 2013, Vermont Studio Ctr, Vt, 2013. *Awards:* Ingram Merrill Found Award Painting, 82-83; Nat Acad Design Award for painting, 95; Award, Nat Acad Design, 00; Award, Conn Commn on the Arts, 78, 2002; Fulbright Grant, Munich, Ger, 67-68; Henry Ward Ranger Purchase Award, Nat Acad, 2001. *Bibliog:* Ken Leslie (auth), Oil Pastels, Watson Guptil, 1991; Robert Godfrey (auth), Aspects of Representation: 9 Painters (catalog), 98; interview, Philadelphia Inquirer, 99; Lynn Munson (auth), Exhibitionism, 00; Anna Held Augne (auth), 100 Creative Drawing Ideas, Shambala Press, 2003; Jennifer Bell (auth), Art News, 1/2005; Ken Johnson (auth), NY Times, 10/2001; Andrew Forge & Linda Konheim Kramer (auths), Catalogue, Dartmouth Col, 2002; Barbara Grossman A Survey, (catalogue), 2004-2005; Maureen Mullakey (auth), Artcritical, 6/2005; David Cohen (auth), NY Sun, 1/2007; Tracey O'Shaughnessy (auth), review, Republican Am, Waterbury, Conn, 2008; Jaimie Ferris (auth), review, Litchfield County Times, 2008; Andrew Mangrauite (auth). review, Broad St Renie, Philadelphia, 2008; Harry Ivaar (auth), Forming the Figure (catalogue), Rider Univ, NJ, 2009; Pages, Bowery Gallery, 2010; E Ashley Rooney (auth), 100 Artists of New England, Scheiffer Publ, 2010. *Mem:* Coll Art Asn; Nat Acad (bd dir). *Media:* Oil Paint, Oil Sticks, Charcoal. *Mailing Add:* 2338 Litchfield Rd Watertown CT 06795

GROSSMAN, BONNIE
GALLERY DIRECTOR
b Newark, NJ, 1934. *Study:* Wheelock Coll, BA. *Exhib:* Venice Biennalle, 2013. *Pos:* founder, dir, Ames Gallery, Berkeley, Calif, 70-. *Teaching:* kindergarten teacher, formerly. *Mem:* Calif (formerly Bay Area) Lawyers for the Arts (found mem). *Specialty:* outsider art, folk art. *Publ:* Exec prod, co-dir, prod nine TV programs on Calif artists; contribr articles to prof publ; lectr on antiques

GROSSMAN, MAURICE KENNETH
EDUCATOR, CERAMIC ARTIST
b Detroit, Mich, Sept 16, 1927. *Study:* Wayne State Univ, Detroit, with J Foster, BS (art educ), 50; Alfred Univ, NY, with Dan Rhodes, 51; Ohio State Univ, Columbus, with Paul Bogatay, MFA (ceramics), 53. *Work:* Detroit Mus Art; Phoenix Mus Art; El Paso Mus; Utah State Mus, Salt Lake City; Albuquerque Mus Art, NMex; Tucson Mus of Art, Ariz. *Comn:* commn by Joan Mannheimer, Des Moines, Iowa, Elizabeth Wainstock, NY, Adolph-Berta Wright, Tucson, Ariz, Robert & Mary Wrenm, Tucson, Judity Goldman, Houston. *Exhib:* Ceramic Nat, Everson Mus Art, Syracuse, 50-68; Clay Invitational, Smithsonian Inst, 53 & 59; Westwood Clay Nat, Otis Art Gallery, Los Angeles, 80; Int Invitational, Arabia & Finland, 84; Possessions, Harrison Mus, Logan, Vt, 89; Raku Kansas City Contemp Art, 89; East West Ctr, Honolulu, 90; Int Gallery, San Diego, Calif, 93. *Teaching:* Instr ceramics, Western Wash Col, Bellingham, 53-54; prof ceramics, Univ Ariz, Tucson, 55-88, prof emer, 88-. *Awards:* Alumni Award, Wayne State Univ, 82; Craft Fel, Nat Endowment Arts, 84; Ariz Art Award, 97. *Bibliog:* John Conrad (auth), Contemporary Ceramic Techniques, Prentice Hall, 79; Robert Peipeuburg (auth), Raku Pottery, Pebble Press, 91; Susan Peterson (auth), Craft and Art of Clay, Prentice Hall, 92. *Mem:* Am Crafts Coun (southwest area rep, 63-66), Ariz Designer-Craftsmen (pres, 60); Tucson Art Ctr (bd dir, 68, adv 88); Nat Coun Educ for Ceramic Arts (regional rep, 72); World Crafts Coun. *Media:* Ceramics. *Publ:* Auth, American ceramics, Tanko Mag, Kyoto, Japan, 56; Clay in the Hand, an American in Japan, Inst Int Educ, 56. *Dealer:* Craft Shop Tucson Mus Art 140 N Main Ave Tucson AZ85701. *Mailing Add:* Univ Ariz Dept Art Tucson AZ 85721

GROSSMAN, NANCY
PAINTER, SCULPTOR
b New York, NY, Apr 28, 1940. *Study:* Pratt Inst, BFA, 1962. *Work:* Whitney Mus Am Art, Metrop Mus Art, NY; Princeton Univ Art Mus; Univ Mus, Berkeley, Calif; Dallas Mus Fine Arts; Israel Mus, Jerusalem; Phoenix Art Mus, Ariz; Nat Mus Am Art, Smithsonian Inst, Washington, DC; Va Mus Fine Art, Richmond; Contemp Arts Mus, Honolulu; Greenville Co Art Mus, Greenville, SC; Ark Arts Ctr, Little Rock, Ark; Baltimore Mus Art, Md; Mus Boymans Von Beuningen, Holland; Columbus Mus Art, Ga; Columbus Mus Art, Ohio; Fogg Art Mus, Harvard Univ, Mass; Menil Collection, Houston, Tex; Nat Acad Mus Art, New York; Nat Galleries Scotland, UK; Weatherspoon Art Mus, Univ NC. *Exhib:* Solo exhibs, Krasner Gallery, New York City, 1964-1967, Cordier & Ekstrom, New York, 1968-1971, 1973, 1975, 1976, Church Fine Arts Gallery, Univ Nevada, Reno, 1978, Barbara Gladstone Gallery, New York City, 1980, 1982, Heath Gallery, Atlanta, 1981, 1986, Terry Dintenfass Gallery, 1984, Exit Art, New York, 1991, Sculpture Center, New York City, 1991, Hillwood Art Mus, New York City, 1991, Artemisia, Chicago, 1992, Beacon St Gallery, Chicago, 1992, Ark Art Ctr, Little Rock, 1992, Contemp Mus, Honolulu, 1992, Binghamton Univ Art Gallery, 1992, Hooks-Epstein Galleries, Houston, 1993, 1995, LedisFlam, New York City, 1994, Weatherspoon Art Gallery, Greensboro, NC, 1994, Greenville Cty Mus Art, 2004, Michael Rosenfeld Gallery, New York, 2007, Frances Young Tang Mus, Skidmore Coll, Saratoga Springs, NY, 2012 ; Numerous group exhibs, Whitney Mus Am Art, New York City, 1968-1969, 1973, 1980, 1981, 1993, 1995, 2006; Contemp Arts Mus, Honolulu, 1992; Firefields, Hawaii Ctr, Honolulu, 2000; Gloria: An Exhibit, White Columns, NY, 2002; True Grit: Seven Female Visionaries Before Feminism, Univ Richmond Mus, Va, 2002; In the Eye of the Beholder, George Adams Gallery, New York, 2003; Presence, Chelsea Art Museum, New York, 2004; Collage: signs & surfaces, Pavel Zoubek Gallery, New York, 2005; Lines of Discovery: 225 Years of Am Drawings, The Columbus Mus, Columbus, Ga, 2006; Agents of Change: Women, Art & Intellect, Ceres Gallery, New York, 2007; WACK! Art & the Feminist Revolution, 1965-1980, Los Angeles Mus Contemp Art, 2007; (un)common threads, Michael Rosenfeld Gallery, LLC, New York, 2007; Everywhere: Politics in Art, Ctr Galego Arte Contemp, Spain, 2009; Propose: Works on Paper from the 1970s, Alexander Gray Asn, New York, 2009; Reconfiguring the Body in Am Art, 1820-2009, Nat Acad Mus Art, New York, 2009; Visible Vagina, Francis Naumann Fine Art, New York, 2010. *Teaching:* Instr sculpture, Boston Fine Arts Sch, 85; instr drawing, Cooper Union, 89. *Awards:* Ida C Haskell Award for Foreign Travel, Pratt's Inst, 1962; John Simon Guggenheim Found Fel, 1965-1966; Nat Endowment for the Arts Fel, 1984; NY Found for the Arts Fel, 1991; Joan Mitchell Found Grant, 1996-1997; Pollock Krasner Found Grant, 2001; Lifetime Achievement Award, Women's Caucus for Art, 2008. *Bibliog:* Cindy Nemser (auth), Art Talk, Conversations with 12 Women Artists, Scribners, 75; Charlotte Streifer Rubenstein (auth), American Women Artists, Avon, 82; Arlene Raven (auth), Nancy Grossman, Hillwood Art Mus, 91; Nancy Grossman (auth) Loud Whispers, Four Decades of Assemblage, Collage & Sculpture, Michael Rosenfeld Gallery, Essay by Lowery Stokes Sims; Harriet Gilbert (ed), The Sexual Imagination from Acker to Zola: A Feminist Companion, 93. *Mem:* Nat Acad. *Media:* Sculpture; Drawing; Collage. *Specialty:* Am Abstractionist; Early Abstractionist Expressionist; Underrepresented Am/Modernist Art; Realism; Surrealism; Social Realism. *Dealer:* Michael Rosenfeld Gallery New York NY; Hooks Epstein Galleries Houston TX. *Mailing Add:* Michael Rosenfeld Gallery 24 West 57th Street 7th Floor New York NY 10019

GROSSMAN, SHELDON
MUSEUM CURATOR, HISTORIAN
b New York, NY, Aug 30, 1940. *Study:* Hunter Col, BA, 62; NY Univ Inst Fine Arts, MA, 66. *Collection Arranged:* Cur, Art in the Age of Petrarch, 74, Venetian Drawings from Am Collections, 74, From Caravaggio to Giordano, Painting in Naples 1606-1705 (coauth, catalog), 83 & Caravaggio, The Deposition from the Vatican Collections (auth, catalog), 84, Nat Gallery Art, Washington, DC. *Pos:* Asst cur, Photographic Archives, 71-74 & cur, Northern & Later Italian Paintings, 74-85, Nat Gallery Art, Washington, DC; owner & oper, Grossman Fine Arts Inc, 85-; sr research fel, Corcoran Gallery, Washington, DC, 96. *Teaching:* Rutgers Univ & The State Univ, New Brunswick, NJ, 65 & 66; Manhattanville Col Sacred Heart, Purchase, New York, 66; George Washington Univ, Washington, DC, 74. *Awards:* Fulbright-Hays Travel Grant, 66; Ital Govt Study Grant, 66; Chester Dale Fel, 67-69 & Paul Mellon Vis Sr Fel, 97, Nat Gallery Art, Washington, DC; and others. *Bibliog:* Review, From Rome to Eternity: Catholicism and the Arts in Italy, SF Ostrow, CAA Online Reviews, April 2004. *Res:* Problems in Florentine painting in the late fifteenth and early sixteenth century; analysis of problems of style; archival research; early Baroque art in the context of social, religious and political phenomena; European drawing and the Corcoran Gallery. *Publ:* Auth, National Gallery of Art report and studies in the history of art, 68; Mitteilungen des kunst-historischen institutes in Florenz, 69; Master drawings, 72; National Gallery of Art, Studies in the History of Art, 74; Auth, Ghir landaio's Madonna and Child in Frankfurt and Leonardo's Beginnings as a Painter, Stadel Jahrbuch, Vol 7, 79; Titian and Moroni in Trent, Apollo, Vol 109, 79; The Sovereignty of the Painted Image: Poetry and the Shroud of Turin, in From Rome to Eternity. *Mailing Add:* 2312 Tunlaw Rd NW Washington DC 20007-1816

GROSSMAN, WENDY A
CURATOR, HISTORIAN
Study: Univ Md, BA; Univ Md, College Park, MA & PhD. *Collection Arranged:* Re-Framing Andy Warhol: Constructing American Myths, Heroes, and Cultural Icons (auth, catalog), Art Gallery Univ Md, College Park, 1998. *Pos:* Cur, Int Arts & Artists. *Teaching:* Vis asst prof art & archit hist, Middlebury Coll; instr, George Washington Univ & Univ Md. *Publ:* Auth, Das Faszinosum Afrikas in den Photographien Man Rays, in: Man Ray 1890-1976, Munich, 1996; Perfect Documents: Walker Evans' Photographs of African Art, in: African Arts, summer 2001; (Con)Text and Image: Reframing Man Ray's Noire et Blanche, in: Phototextualities: Photography and Narrative, Albuquerque, 2003; Man Ray's Endgame and Other Modernist Gambits, in: The Art of the Project: Projects and Experiments in Modern French Culture, London, 2005; Portfolio Man Ray: Objects and Images, Tribal Arts, 2005; Modernism between the Enthnographic, the Primitive and the Surreal: Man Ray's Photographs of African Art in the Goldberg/D'Afflitto Collection, in: Man Ray: Luces y Suenos, Madrid, 2006; African art in the Age of Mechanical Reproduction: Photography at the Crossroads, in: Die Schau des Fremden, Stuttgart, 2006; co-auth, Unmasking Man Ray's Noire et Blanche, Smithosian J Am Art, 2006. *Mailing Add:* 9 Hillyer Ct NW Washington DC 20008

GROSVENOR, ROBERT
SCULPTOR
b New York, NY, 1937. *Study:* Ecole des Beaux Arts, Dijon, France, 1956; Ecole Superieure des Arts Decoratifs, Paris, 1957-59; Univ di Perugia, Italy, 1958. *Work:* Whitney Mus Am Art, New York; Storm King Art Ctr, Mountainville, NY; Mus Mod Art, New York; Hirshhorn Mus, Washington, DC; Walker Art Ctr, Minneapolis. *Exhib:* Sculpture for the 60's, Los Angeles Co Mus, 1967; Plus by Minus, Albright-Knox Art Gallery, Buffalo, NY, 1968; Sculpture Ann, Whitney Mus Am Art, NY, 1968, Biennial Exhib Am Painting & Sculpture, 1973 & 200 Yrs Am Sculpture, 1976; 14 Sculptors: the Industrial Edge, Walker Art Ctr, Minneapolis, 1969; Contemp Am Art, Whitney Mus Am Art, 1969, biennial 1973, 200 yrs Am Sculpture, 1976; solo exhibs, Paula

Cooper Gallery, NY, 1970-71, 1974-75, 1978, 1981, 1986, 1988, 1991, 1993, 1996, 1998, 2000, 2003, 2007, 2010, PS1 Inst Art & Urban Resources, Long Island City, NY, 1984, Centre d'Art Contemporair du Domaine de Kerguehennec a Bigan Locmine, France, 1989, Margo Leavin Gallery, Los Angeles, 1990, Galerie Max Hetzler, Cologne, 1992, 1995 & 2005, Kunsthalle, Bern, Switz, 1992 & Lawrence Markey, NY, 1996, Fundacão de Serralvas, Mus Contemp Art, Porto, Portugal, 2005; Art on Paper, Inst Contemp Art, Boston, 1970; Works on Paper, 31st Ann Exhib, Soc Contemp Art, Art Inst Chicago, 1971; Biennial Exhib Am Painting & Sculpting, Whitney Mus Am Art, 1973; 200 Yrs of Am Sculpture, Whitney Mus Am Art, 1976; Private Images: Photographs by Sculptors, Los Angeles Co Mus Art, Contemp Art Galleries, Lytton Halls, 1977-78; Minimal Tradition, 1979 & Postminimalism, 1982, Aldrich Mus Contemp Art; Art on Paper Weatherspoon Art Gallery, 1993; 25 Yrs (Part I), Paula Cooper Gallery, NY, 1993; Country Sculpture, le consort, Dijon, France, 1994; From Minimal to Conceptual Art: Works from the Dorothy & Herbert Vogel Collections Nat Gallery Art, Wash, 1994; Holiday Exhib, Paula Cooper Gallery, 1994; Am Sculptors in the 1960s: Selected Drawings from the Collection, Mus Mod Art, NY, 1995; Forum: Robert Grosvenor, Andreas Gursky, John Wesley, Carnegie Mus Art, Pittsburgh, Pa, 1999; and many others; It Happened Tomorrow, Paula Cooper Gallery, 1999, 2000, 2001, Biennale d'Art Contemo de Lyon, France, 2003; Against the Grain: Contemporary Art from Edward R Broida Collection, Mus Mod Art, NY, 2006; Every Revolution is a Roll of the Dice, Paula Cooper Gallery, New York, 2008; Compass in Hand: Selections from the Judith Rothschild Found Contemp Drawings Collection, Mus Mod Art, New York, 2009; Whitney Biennial, Whitney Mus Am Art, New York, 2010. *Awards:* Guggenheim Fel, 1969; Nat Endowment Arts & Humanities Grant, 1970; Nat Acad Arts & Lett Grant, 1972. *Bibliog:* Jeremy Gilbert Rolfe (auth), Robert Grosvenor: Specific Clarity, Art in Am, 3-4/1976; John Russel (auth), Critics Choice: Galleries, NY Times, 4/21/1978; Deborah Perlberg (auth), Reviews in New York, Artforum, summer 1978; Donald Kupsit (auth), Robert Grosvenor, Artforum, summer 1984; John Russell (auth), Robert Grosvenor, NY Times, 4/18/1986. *Dealer:* Paula Cooper Gallery New York. *Mailing Add:* c/o Paula Cooper Gallery 534 W 21st St New York NY 10011

GROTJAHN, MARK
PAINTER
b Pasadena, Calif, 1968. *Study:* Univ Colo, Boulder, BFA; Univ Calif, Berkeley, MFA. *Exhib:* Solo exhibs include Stephen Friedman Gallery, London; Anton Kern Gallery, NYC; Blum & Poe, Los Angeles; Boom, Chicago; The Saatchi Gallery; Whitney Mus Am Art, NY, 2006; Mus Contemp Art, Los Angeles; UCLA Hammer Muss; London Inst Gallery, 54th Carnegie Internat; Carnegie Mus Art, Pitts, Pa, 2005; Whitney Biennial, Whitney Mus Am Art, NY 2006; Mus Modern Art, NYC; Am Acad Arts & Letts Invitational, New York, 2010. *Mailing Add:* UCLA Hammer Gallery 10899 Wilshire Blvd Los Angeles CA 90024

GROWDON, MARCIA COHN
ADMINISTRATOR, HISTORIAN
b San Francisco, Calif, 1945. *Study:* Stanford Univ, BA, 67, PhD, 76; Univ Mich, BA, 68. *Collection Arranged:* Treasures of the Middle Ages (auth, catalog), 78, The New York School 1940-1960 (ed, catalog), 79, Computers and the Visual Arts: Research & Drawings of H Cohen (auth, catalog), 79, Artists in the Am Desert, Nat Tour (auth, catalog), 80-81 & Sierra Nevada Mus Biennial: The Best of Nevada's Contemporary Art (auth, catalog), 86, Nev Mus Art. *Pos:* Cur, Nev Mus Art, Reno, 78-81, dir, 81-87; vchmn, CITY 2000, Reno Arts Comn, 90-96, chmn, 94-95; chmn, Nev Comn for Cultural Affairs, 91-95; coll comt mem, Nev Mus Art, Reno; mem, Nev Hist Preservation Bd, 85-93, chmn, 89-93; vchmn, Nev State Mus Bd, 93-95. *Teaching:* Lectr art hist, Univ Nev, Reno, 89-; lectr, Nev Mus Art, Reno, 2002-. *Awards:* Samuel Kress Found Fel & Travel Grants, 68-70; Governor's Award for Serv to Arts, Nev, 92. *Mem:* Art Table. *Res:* 19th and 20th century art, particularly in the Far West. *Publ:* Article, Designed by Will Bruder: Nevada Mus Art, 2003; articles & essay, Online Nev Encyl (www.onlinenevada.org), 2007; and many others

GRUBER, J RICHARD
ADMINISTRATOR, HISTORIAN
b Louisville, Ky, Mar 30, 1948. *Study:* Xavier Univ, BA (Eng), 71; Univ Colo, MA (cum laude), 80; Univ Kans, MPH, 82, PhD, 87. *Collection Arranged:* Memphis in Memphis, 83, Sheffield Silver: The Kirby Collection, Australian Art in Our Time & Kentucky Shaker Furniture, 84, Memphis: 1948-1958 (with catalog), 86, Memphis Brooks Mus Art, Tenn; In Plain View: The Collages of Irwin Kremen (catalog), 87; George Wardlaw: Transitions (catalog), 88; We Like Ike, The Eisenhower Presidency & 1950's Am (auth, catalog), 90; Ancient Echos/Silent Messenger: Steve Kestrel, 91; The Dot Man: George Andrews of Madison, Ga (auth, catalog), 94. *Pos:* Cur of collections, Memphis Brooks Mus Art, Tenn, 83-85, interim dir, 84-85, dir, 85-89; dir, Wichita Art Mus, 89-91, Ctr Study Southern Painting, 93-; co-dir, Peter Joseph Gallery, 92; deputy dir, Morris Mus Art, 93-. *Teaching:* Lectr art hist, Univ Colo, Colorado Springs, 79-81; lectr art hist, Augusta Col, 95. *Awards:* Smithsonian Res Fel, Nat Mus Art, 82-83; Kress Found Fel, Kans, 82-83. *Mem:* Am Asn Mus; Am Inst Archit; Coll Art Asn. *Res:* Nineteenth and twentieth century American art and architecture, emphasis on Thomas Hart Benton and regionalism. *Publ:* Memphis: 1948-1958, 86. *Mailing Add:* Morris Mus Art One 10th St Augusta GA 30901-0100

GRUBIN, JOAN
PAINTER
Study: Sarah Lawrence Coll, Bronxville, NY, BA, 1967; Nat Acad Design, New York, 1989-91; Art Students League, New York, 1990-92; Vt Coll, Montpelier, MFA, 2003. *Exhib:* Solo exhibs include Atlantic Gallery, New York, 1988, Columbia Community Gallery, Hudson, NY, 1996, Anthony Nordoff Gallery, Great Barrington, Mass, 1997, Art Design Digression Gallery, Hudson, NY, 2000, 2002, Simon Gallery, Morristown, NJ, 2006; group exhibs include Ceres Gallery, New York, 1985; Craven Gallery, Martha's Vineyard, Mass, 1997, 1998; Subject/Object, OK Harris Gallery, New York, 2003; John Davis Gallery, New York, 2004; Proj Diversity, Corridor Gallery, Brooklyn, NY, 2005; Free Play, Islip Art Mus, East Islip, NY, 2007; Pattern & Concept, Hosfelt Gallery, New York, 2007. *Awards:* New York Found Arts Fel, 2008. *Dealer:* Henry Gregg Gallery 111 Front St Suite 226 Brooklyn NY 11211. *Mailing Add:* 215 West 92 St New York NY 10025

GRUEN, JOHN
CRITIC, WRITER
b Enghien-les-Bains, France, Sept 12, 1926; US citizen. *Study:* City Coll New York; Univ Iowa, BA & MA. *Pos:* Critic of music & art, New York Herald Tribune, 62-68; art critic, New York Mag, 69-73 & Soho Weekly News, 74-; contribr ed, Art News, 76-; sr ed, Dance Mag, 79-. *Teaching:* Lectr, Metrop Mus Art, 79-. *Publ:* Auth, Close-Up Viking Press, 69, The Private World of Leonard Bernstein, 69, The Party's Over Now, 73, The Private World of Ballet, 75 & Erik Bruhn: Danseur Noble, 79; The World's Greatest Ballets, Harry N Abrams, 82; People Who Dance, Princeton Bks, 88; The Artist Observed, A Cappella Bks, 91; Keith Haring, The Authorized Biography, Prentice Hall/Simon & Schuster, 91; and others. *Mailing Add:* 317 W 83rd St New York NY 10024

GRUEN, SHIRLEY SCHANEN
PAINTER
b Port Washington, Wis, Dec 2, 1923. *Study:* Univ Wis, Madison, BS (art educ) 45; Art Ctr Sch, LosAngeles, Calif, 46; Cardinal Stritch Col, Milwaukee, 72-88. *Work:* Mus Wis Art, West Bend, Wis; Milwaukee Art Comn, Wis; Ozaukee Bank, Port Wash, Wis; Heritage Ins, Sheboygan, Wis; Wis Conservatory Music, Milwaukee; Duchy of Luxembourg, Northwestern Inc Co, Milwaukee. *Comn:* three paintings, Port Washington State Bank, 92; two paintings, Marshall & Ilsley Bank, Wis, 93; two paintings, First Financial Savings Bank, 93; Three paintings, Ozaukee Bank, Wis, 94; Heritage Insurance Co, 95. *Exhib:* Solo exhibs, West Bend Gallery Fine Arts, Wis, 81 & Water St Gallery, Moraine Bank, Milwaukee, 84; Salamagundi 11th, 15th, & 18th Ann, NY 88, 92, 95, 2009; Oil Pastel Int Exhib, NY, 89 & 90; WWIA Expressions and Commentary, Neville Mus, Green Bay, Wis, 91; Cedarburg Cult Ctr, Wis, 92; Ariz Aqueous, 93 & 97; Getting There, Neville Mus, Green Bay, Wis 95; Milwaukee Sesquicentennial, 96; Cyberspace, Internet, Virtually the First, WPS, 96; and many others. *Pos:* Owner, Shirley Gruen Studio, Port Wash, Wis, 72-. *Teaching:* Instr watercolor & portrait, Milwaukee Area Tech Col, Wis. *Awards:* Purchase Award, Response 83, Milwaukee Arts Comn, 83; Award, Pa Watercolor Soc, 85; Oil Pastel Award, Salmagundi Club, Oil Pastel Assoc, New York, 88; Citizen of Year, Port Wash Chamber Com, 2003; Citation Historical Art Work of Port Wash, State Leg Wis, 2003; Wall of Fame, Port Wash High Sch, 2010. *Bibliog:* West 80-Art and Law, Am Bar Asn Journal, 7/80; Sally Prince Davis (auth), Selling Your Art, North Light Books, Spring 89; articles in Milwaukee J, Wis, Ozauree Press, 91, 92, 11/2001, 2010. *Mem:* Wis Visual Artists; Wis Watercolor Soc. *Media:* Acrylic, Watercolor. *Specialty:* 20 limited edition prints & various scenes Port Wash. *Interests:* Music, sailing. *Mailing Add:* 303 N Franklin Port Washington WI 53074

GRUNDBERG, ANDY
CRITIC, CURATOR
b Bryn Mawr, Pa, June 25, 1947. *Study:* Cornell Univ, BA, 69; Univ NC, Greensboro, MFA, 71. *Collection Arranged:* Photography and Art: Interactions Since 1946, LA County Mus Art, 87-88; Ansel Adams: A Legacy, Ansel Adams Ctr for Photography, 97-99; In Response to Place: Photographs from the Nature Conservancy's Last Great Places, Corcoran Gallery of Art, 2001-2005. *Pos:* Picture ed, Mod Photog, 74-84; photog critic, Soho Weekly News, 79-81 & New York Times, 81-91; dir, the Friends Photog, San Francisco, 92-97; assoc provost, Corcoran Coll Art and Design, 2011-, dean undergraduate studies, 2011-. *Teaching:* Vis critic, RI Sch Design, Providence, 85; instr art hist, Sch Visual Arts, NY, 86-91 & instr grad photog prog 88-91; vis instr grad photog prog, San Francisco Art Inst, 92; adj prof, Dartmouth Col, 98-99, Univ Hartford, 99-2002, Corcoran Coll Art and Design, 2002-. *Awards:* Reva & David Logan Found Grant, Photog Resource Ctr, 85; Leica Medal of Excellence, 88; Manufacturers Hanover Art/World Award, 89; Infinity Award Int Ctr Photog, 99. *Mem:* Soc Photog Educ (bd dir, 83-88); AAM; Independent Curators Inc; CAA. *Res:* Twentieth century American art and photography, with emphasis on contemporary practice and theory. *Publ:* Contribr, The Camera Viewed, Dutton, 79; contribr, Reading into Photography, Univ NMex Press, 82; auth, Photography and Art: Interactions Since 1989, Abbeville, 87; auth, Grundberg's Goof-Proof Photography Guide, Fireside, 89; auth, Alexey Brodovitch, Abrams, 89; Mike and Doug Starn, Harry N Abrams Inc, 90; Crisis of the Real: Writings on Photography, 1974-1989, Aperture, 90, rev ed, 99; auth, The Land Through a Lens, Smithsonian Am Art Mus, 2003. *Mailing Add:* Corcoran Coll Art and Design 500 17th St NW Washington DC 20006

GRUNWALDT, CARMELA C
PAINTER
b Chicago, Ill. *Study:* Art Inst Chicago. *Work:* Brand Libr Art Gallery, Glendale, Calif; Carville Marine Hosp, La. *Exhib:* Nat Watercolor Soc Traveling Exhibs, 88-89 & 94-95; Fine Arts Fedn, Burbank, Calif, 93; Los Angeles Art Asn, Calif, 93; Foothills Artcenter, Golden, Colo, 94; Muckenthaler Mus, Fullerton, Calif, 94; and others. *Awards:* Experimental Painting Award, Nat Watercolor Soc, 87; Gold Award, 93, Bronze Award, 93, Art of Calif Mag; Alexander Nepote Award, Nat Watercolor Competition, Muckenthaler Mus, Fullerton, Calif, 94; and others. *Bibliog:* Joseph Mugnaini (auth), Expressive Drawing, Davis Publ, 88; Margerita Nieto (auth), Art Scene, Los Angeles, 93; John Adams (auth), Downey Eagle, Downey, Calif, 94. *Mem:* Los Angeles Art Asn; signature mem Nat Watercolor Soc; Calif Collagists Los Angeles; Pasadena Soc Artists. *Media:* Mixed Media

GRUPP, CARL ALF
PAINTER, PRINTMAKER
b Moorhead, Minn, Sept 11, 1939. *Study:* Minneapolis Coll Art & Design, BFA, 64; Vrije Acad, Netherlands, Vanderlip Scholar, 65; Ind Univ, MFA (with hons), 69; and with Rudy Pozzatti, Urban Couch, Marvin Lowe, William Bailey & James McGarrell. *Work:* Minneapolis Inst Art & Univ Minn Gallery, Minneapolis; Am Embassy,

London; Chicago Art Inst; SDak Mem Art Ctr, Brookings. *Comn:* Meditation Mountain, Augustana Coll Libr, Sioux Falls, SDak; Parable Paintings, Gloria Dei Lutheran Church, Sioux Falls, SDak. *Exhib:* Joslyn Art Mus 12th Biennial, Omaha, Nebr, 72; Pratt Graphic Art Exhib, NY, 72-73; Am Printmakers, Ind Univ, US Info Agency Tour Eng, 73; Drawings USA, Minn Mus Art, St Paul, 75; Boston Printmakers, 81; plus many others. *Teaching:* Asst lithography, Minneapolis Coll Art & Design, 64-65; asst intaglio printmaking, Ind Univ, Bloomington, 68-69; asst prof art, Augustana Coll, 69-81, prof art, 88-, emer prof. *Awards:* Mayors Award, Sioux Empire Arts Coun, 2002; Governor's Award, Distinction in Creative Achievement, 2005. *Bibliog:* Spotted talents in America, Frasconi, Grupp, Tendensen, 11/65; Craig Volk (auth), Art of Carl Grupp (video tape), KUSD-TV, Univ SDak, 3/75; Carl Grupp: A Look Back, Northern, State Univ, 91. *Media:* Oil, Printmaking; Watercolor, Photography. *Publ:* The Wonder of Life, A Retrospective Exhib, catalog, Univ SDak, 2004. *Dealer:* Eastbank Art Gallery Sioux Falls. *Mailing Add:* 1614 S Phillips Ave Sioux Falls SD 57105

GRUSS, MARTIN DAVID
PATRON
b New York, NY, Mar 1, 1943. *Study:* Univ Pa, BSE, 64; NY Univ, LLB, 67. *Pos:* Sr partner, Gruss Partners, New York City; bd dir, Mack Cali Realty Corp, NJ; bd trustee, Solomon R Guggenheim Mus, New York City; part-owner, Cleveland Indians MLB team, formerly. *Mem:* NY Bar Asn. *Mailing Add:* Gruss & Co Inc 777 S Flagler Dr West Palm Beach FL 33401

GRUVER, MARY EMMETT
PAINTER, INSTRUCTOR
b Leavenworth, Kans, Nov 9, 1912. *Study:* Univ Calif, Berkeley, BA (fine arts), 34, studied landscape painting with Robert Rishell, portrait with Peter Blos. *Work:* Main Lobby, Martinez Vets Hosp, Calif. *Comn:* Portrait commd by Knights of Columbus/a founder of San Francisco Cath Ch; Portrait Gordan Van Vlek, Calif Sec of Agr, Stockmans Bank in Sacramento. *Exhib:* Calif State Fair-Exhib, Fairgrounds, Sacramento, Calif, 65 & 67; Jack London Sq Art Festival, 14th Ann Outdoor, Oakland, Calif, 68; Santa Cruz Statewide Exhib, Santa Cruz League Bldg, Calif, 70-71; San Francisco 26th Art Festival, Civic Ctr Plaza, 72; Soc Western Artists, 31st Ann Hall of Flowers, San Francisco, 78; and others. *Teaching:* Instr art, State Calif, Adult Educ, 61-75. *Awards:* First & Second Representational Oil, Livermore Art Asn 9th Ann, 65; First Pastel Portrait, Santa Cruz Art Ann, 70-71; First Watercolor & Purchase Award, Placerville Art Ann, 76. *Mem:* signature mem Pastel Soc West Coast, Sacramento, Calif; signature mem Soc Western Artists, San Francisco; PSA, NY. *Media:* All Media. *Publ:* Illusr, Weekend Sect, Mountain Democrat, Placerville, Calif, 9/30/94. *Mailing Add:* 5471 Gold Hill Rd Placerville CA 95667

GRYGUTIS, BARBARA
SCULPTOR, ENVIRONMENTAL ARTIST
b Hartford, Conn, Nov 7, 1946. *Study:* Univ Ariz, BFA, 68, MFA, 71. *Work:* Standing Leaves, Falling Light, Light Sculpture, King Co Public Art Prog, Seattle, Wash, 2002; The Illuminated Page, City of Santa Clara Public Art Collection, Calif, 2004; Journeys Sculptural environment for WMATA, Washington, DC, 2004; Life Lines, Philadelphia PA, Sculptural environment for SEPTA, City Ctr, Philadelphia, Completion date, 2005; The Seasons, Twin Rivers Community Park, Greeley, Colo, 2006; Luminarias, Phoenix, City of Phoenix Public Art Prog, Ariz, 2006; Illuminated Page, Plaza/Entry Gate, Santa Clara Pub Libr, Santa Clara, Calif, 2003; Journeys, Sculptural Environ, WMATA, New York Ave Metro Station, DC, 2004; Life Lines, sculptural environ for SEPTA, City Ctr, Philadelphia, 2006; Universal Signs, Tex Tech Univ, Lubbock, Tex, 2006; Luminarias: Phoenix, Central Ave, Phoenix, Ariz, 2006; Luminarias: The Seasons, Twin Rivers Community Park, Greeley, Colo, 2006; Windswept, Central Light Rail Transit Ctr, Bellevue, Wash, 2006; Imaginary Garden, Walnut St Park, Cary, NC, 2009; Wave, Palm Beach Co Convention Ctr, W Palm Beach, Fla, 2009; Kino Parkway 22nd St, Interchange Bridge, Tucson, Ariz, 2011; Desert Passage, Canopy Dreams, Chandler Gilbert Comm Coll, Gilbert, Ariz, 2009; Signs & Symbols_Symbols & Signs, Gateway to the Humanities, Olympic Coll, Bremerton, Wash, 2009; Imaginary Garden, promenade for Walnut St Park, Cary, NC, 2009; Silver Lining, El Paso Convention Ctr, Tex, 2009. *Comn:* Portal, General Servs Admin, Los Indios, Tex, 93-95; Garden of Constants, Ohio State Univ Percent for the Arts, 94; Never Does Nature Say One Thing & Wisdom Another, West Toledo Branch Libr, OH, 97; Front Row Center, Univ Ariz Coll Fine Arts, Tucson, 99; Railgate, NJ Transit, NJ, 99; Camelback Bridge Over US Interstate I-17, Phoenix Arts Comn, Ariz, 2000; River Run, Ohio Arts Coun, 2002; Common Ground, Gates Family Found, Denver, Colo, 2001; The Color of Snow, Northwest Light Rail Transit Project, Calgary, Can; Bird's Eye View, plaza for Hayes Mansion Conf Ctr, City of San Jose, Calif, 2006; Rookie Card, gateway to ballpark, Jacksonville, Fla, 2005; Flamingo Arroyo Trail, with Buster Simpson & Kevin Berry, Las Vegas, Nev, 2010; Bronx River View, MTA, Whitlock Station, NY, 2010; Drop, Entry Sculpture, Prewett Family Park, Antioch, Calif, 2010; The Green Wall, Palm Beach Co Assembly Plz, W Palm Beach, Fla, 2011; Kuban Park, Phoenix, Ariz, 2011; Seagrass, Ocean Blvd Median Sculptures with Integrate Lighting, Long Beach, Calif, 2011; Garden Under the Bridge, Scott Avenue Plz Transit Station, St Louis, Mo, 2012; Dawn's Silver Lining, South Ninth St Gateway, Sculptural Composition, Salina, Kans, 2012; Echo, Mich State Univ, Brody Amphitheater, East Lansing, Mich, 2012; Sculpture and Plaza, Tysons West Transit Station, Washington Area Metro Transit Authority Silver Line, Dulles Corridor Rail, Extension 2013; Sculptural Railing for the New South Park Bridge Replacement, Seattle, Wash, 2013. *Exhib:* Am Crafts at the White House, Renwick Gallery, Smithsonian Inst, Washington, DC, 76; Mus Contemp Crafts, NY, 76; Everson Mus Art, Syracuse, NY, 76; Landscape, New Views, Herbert Johnson Mus, Cornell Univ, Ithaca, NY, 78; Women Artists: Clay, Fiber, Metal, Bronx Mus, NY, 78; The Parker Collection for the Vice-President's House, Washington, DC, 78; Southwest Sculpture, Scottsdale Ctr Arts, Ariz, 86 (group), 88 (individual); Ceramics in the Urban Setting, 2nd Int Quadriennal Competition, Faenza, Italy, 89; Architectural Clay, Found Archit & Clay Ctr, Philadelphia, Pa, 93; Ala Biennial, Univ Ala, Tuscaloosa, Ala, 93; Socrates Sculpture Park, Long Island City, NY, 94. *Pos:* Artist-in-residence, Tucson Sch Dist 1, 73 & Haystack Mountain Sch Crafts, Deer Isle, Maine, 78. *Teaching:* Master artist workshop, Art in Pub Places, Tucson Mus Art Tucson, Ariz, 86; pub art workshop, Mesa Community Coll, Mesa, Ariz, 93. *Awards:* Nat Endowment Arts, 75 & 87; Governor's Award, Ariz Women's Partnership, 85; Nat Adv Comt: The Pub Art Rev, 93-97; Indiv Artist Fel, Ariz Comm Arts, 97; Ariz Artist Award, Tucson Community Found, 1998; Ariz Alumni Asn Profl Achievement Award, 2002; Best New Pub Art for Common Ground, Denver, by Westword, 2002; Orchid award, with Estrada Land Planning for Robb Field, City of San Diego, Orchids and Onions, 2000; Excellence in Clay Brick in the 10,000 -50,000 sq ft Category, Imaginary Garden, Hardscape, N Am, Cary, NC, 2010; Best in Class, Paving in Landscaping, Imaginary Garden, Nat Brick Industry, Cary, NC, 2010; Masterworks Hon Mention, Bronx River View, NY Municipal Art Soc, NY, 2011. *Bibliog:* John Perreault (auth), Impressions of Arizona, Art in America, 4/81; Wayne King (auth), Tucson: Art, Sand, Mules and Taillights, International Herald Tribune, 85; Fabio Bianchetti (auth), La Cermaica Nell, Arredo Urbano, 89; Charlotte Lowe (auth), A Talk with Barbara Grygutis & Peter Warshall, Public Art Review, 90; Albuquerque Art Project, CNN News, 7/13/91; Tucson's Tiled '54 Chevy Sparks Albuquerque Art Flap, Assoc Press, 7/14/91; Work Ethic was Inspiration for New St Paul Sculpture, Union Advocate, Vol 95, No 10, 10/7/91; Data Book/Int Contemp Art Fair, Int Sculpture Ctr, Yokohama, 3/92; Architecturama, Philadelphia Inquirer, 93; Mary Voelz Chandler (auth), Sculpture Invites Folks Down by the River, Rocky Mountain News, Oct 18, 2002; Robert Neuwirth (auth), Government Issue Art, LIMNW17 Mag Internat Design Issue 3, 1999; Tony Sykes (auth) Marketing to Architects and Designers, Ceramics Art and Perception, No 23, 1996; Ohio State University Sculpture, Lantern, 1994; The Times Union, Jacksonville, FL; Public Art Steps to the Plate, Tanya Perez-Brennan, Jan 18, 2005; The Times Union, Jacksonville, FL; Batter Points the Way to Ballpark, Don Burk, Jan 19, 2005; Washington Post; An Artful Stop Metro, John Kelly, April 11, 2005. *Media:* Public Art. *Mailing Add:* PO Box 3028 Tucson AZ 85702

GRYNSZTEJN, MADELEINE
MUSEUM DIRECTOR
b Lima, Peru, Mar 17, 1962; arrived in US, 1976. *Study:* Tulane Univ, BA (art hist & french), 1983; Columbia Univ, MA (art hist), 1985. *Collection Arranged:* About Place: Recent Art of the Americas, 95; Affinities: Chuck Close and Tom Friedman, 96; The Art of Richard Tuttle, 2005; Take Your Time: Olafur Eliasson, 2007; and others. *Pos:* Intern, Whitney Mus Am Art, New York, 1984-85; assoc cur, San Diego Mus Contemp Art, 1986-92, Art Inst Chicago, 1992-96, acting dept head, 1996; cur, Carnegie Mus Art, Pittsburgh, 1997-2000; Elise S Haas sr cur painting & sculpture, San Francisco Mus Mod Art, 2000-07; Pritzker dir, Mus Contemp Art, Chicago, 2008-. *Awards:* Helena Rubinstein Fel, Whitney Mus Am Art, 1985-86. *Mem:* AAM; Coll Arts Asn; Asn Art Mus Dirs. *Mailing Add:* Mus Contemp Art 220 E Chicago Ave Chicago IL 60611

GUALDONI, ANGELINA
PAINTER
b San Francisco, California, 1975. *Study:* Wash Univ Sch Art, 1995; Md Inst Coll Art, Baltimore, BFA, 1997; Univ Ill Chicago, MFA, 2000. *Work:* Saatchi Gallery, London. *Exhib:* Solo exhibs include Kavi Gupta Gallery, Chicago, 2002, 2004, Finesilver Gallery, San Antonio, 2003, Mus Contemp Art, Chicago, 2005, St Louis Art Mus, 2007; group exhibs include Sunday Dinner, Md Inst Coll Art, Baltimore, 1998; Breathless, Lombard/Fried Fine Arts, New York, 2001; Reality Check, Spike Gallery, New York, 2004; Volta 01, Kavi Gupta Gallery, Basel, Switzerland, 2005; Après moi le déluge, Fa Projs, London, 2006; Poets on Painters, Ulrich Mus Art, Wichita, Kans, 2007; Triumph of Painting Part 6, Saatchi Gallery, London, 2007. *Awards:* Arts Coun Award Art, 2001; New York Found Arts Fel, 2008. *Dealer:* Kavi Gupta Gallery 835 W Washington Chicago IL 60607. *Mailing Add:* 262 Court St Brooklyn NY 11231

GUALTIERI, JOSEPH P
MUSEUM DIRECTOR, PAINTER
b Royalton, Ill, Dec 25, 1916. *Study:* Norwich Art Sch, Conn, dipl; Sch Art Inst Chicago, Ill, dipl. *Work:* Pa Acad Fine Arts, Philadelphia; Wadsworth Atheneum, Hartford, Conn; RI Sch Design Mus Fine Arts, Providence; Lyman Allyn Mus, New London, Conn; Slater Mem Mus, Norwich, Conn. *Comn:* Wall mural, New London Co Mutual Ins Co, Norwich, Conn; portrait, Gov John Dempsey, State of Conn. *Exhib:* Chicago Art Inst, Ill, 41; Pa Acad Fine Arts, Philadelphia, 48 & 51; Whitney Mus Am Art, NY, 52; Corcoran Gallery Art, Washington, DC; Nat Acad Design, NY; Albany Inst Hist & Art, NY; Wadsworth Atheneum, Hartford, Conn; Calif Palace of the Legion of Honor, Lincoln Park, San Francisco. *Collection Arranged:* Retrospective, Converse Art Gallery, Slater Mus, 92. *Pos:* Dir, Slater Mem Mus, Norwich, Conn, 62-. *Teaching:* Instr art, oil painting, figure & portrait, The Norwich Free Acad, Conn, 43-79. *Awards:* First Prize & Logan Medal, Chicago Art Inst, 41; Purchase Prize, Pa Acad of Fine Arts, 48 & 51; Conn Artists Eastern States Expo Award, 51. *Mem:* Conn Acad Fine Arts Asn; Am Asn Mus; New Eng Conf, Am Asn Mus. *Media:* Oil, Mixed. *Mailing Add:* c/o Slater Mem Mus & Converse Art Gallery 108 Crescent St Norwich CT 06360

GUASTELLA, C DENNIS
PAINTER, INSTRUCTOR
b Detroit, Mich, July 8, 1947. *Study:* Macomb Co Community Col, 67; Wayne State Univ, BFA, 72; Eastern Mich Univ, MFA, 75. *Work:* Sheldon Mem Art Galleries, Univ Nebr, Lincoln; NDak Univ, Grand Forks; SDak Mem Art Ctr, Brookings. *Exhib:* Northwest Biennial III, SDak Mem Art Ctr, Brookings, 76; Biennial, Joslyn Art Mus, Omaha, Nebr, 76, 78 & 80; Solo exhibs, Sheldon Mem Art Galleries, Univ Nebr, Lincoln, 76 & Univ Mich, Slusser Gallery, Ann Arbor, 81; Mich Artists 80/81, Detroit Inst Arts & Flint Inst Arts, 81; and others. *Teaching:* Asst prof art, SDak State Univ, Brookings, 75-80; instr visual arts, Washtenaw Community Col, Ann Arbor, Mich, 80-. *Awards:* Purchase Award, Rutgers Univ, Camden, NJ, 75; Best of Show/Purchase

Award, 16th Joslyn Biennial, Joslyn Art Mus, Omaha, Nebr, 80. *Bibliog:* Interview, Detroit Artist Monthly, 11/77; Mike Odom (auth), Exhibit Reflexs 80's Mood, Uno Gateway, Univ Nebr, 1/23/81; Robert Igelhardt (auth), Close examination, distance needed to appreciate works, Ann Arbor News, 8/9/81. *Mem:* Coll Art Asn; Midwest Coll Art Asn. *Media:* Acrylic, String. *Mailing Add:* Dept Visual Arts Washtenaw Community Col 4800 E Huron River Dr Bldg TI 214 Ann Arbor MI 48106

GUBERMAN, SIDNEY
PAINTER, SCULPTOR
b Greenville, SC, Aug 24, 1936. *Study:* Princeton Univ, with Stephen Greene, BA, 58; Univ Pa, with Robert Venturi, MA (archit), 67. *Work:* Nat Mus Am Art, Corcoran Gallery Art, Washington, DC; High Mus Art, Atlanta; Princeton Univ Art Mus; Birmingham Mus Art; and others. *Comn:* Coke USA, 89, McMaster-Carr Atlanta, 90. *Exhib:* One-man show, Greenville Co Mus, SC, 76, Princeton Univ Art Mus, 83, Southeastern Ctr Contemp Art, 84, McKissick Mus, Univ SC, Columbia, 87, Weslyan Col, Ga, 98 & Jacksonville Contemp Art, Fla, 99; William Seitz Mem, Princeton Univ Art Mus, NJ, 77; Artists in Ga, High Mus, Atlanta, 80, 82 & 85; Small Sculpture, Del Mar Col, Corpus Christi, Tex, 81 & 83; Atlanta in France, Paris, & Toulouse, 85; Ten Yrs of Visual Arts at Princeton, 85; Galerie von der Milwe, Aachen, Ger, 90; Susan Conway Carroll Gallery, Washington, DC, 91; Looking South, A Different Dixie, 22 Artists, Four Southern museums; Hodges-Taylor Gallery, Charlotte, NC, 90, 93; Marcia Wood Gallery, 98 & 2000. *Pos:* Exhib dir, Govt Services Savings & Loan, 76-79. *Teaching:* Prof painting, l'Ecole Cantonale Beaux Arts, Lausanne, Switz, 71-73; asst prof drawing, l'Ecole Polytech Fedn Lausanne, Switz, 73-75; vis lectr painting, Princeton Univ, NJ, 81-82; vis prof painting, Univ SC, Columbia, 86-87; vis artist, Atlanta Col Art, 89, 91. *Awards:* Individual Artist's Grant, Nat Endowment Arts, 80-81; Guggenheim Found Fel for Painting, 88-89. *Bibliog:* Benjamin Forgey (auth), An exhilarating abstract painter, Washington Star, 10/78; Mary Swift (auth), Sidney Guberman, Art Voices South, 4/80; Iris Welch (auth), Sidney Guberman, Art Papers, 8/82; Artists New Work Exhibs Maturity & Consistency, Atlanta Constitution, 88. *Mem:* The Ivy Club. *Media:* Acrylic; Steel, Wood. *Publ:* Auth, Frank Stella's polar coordinate series, Art Papers, 2/82; Sensation, Art Papers, 5-6/84; Frank Stella-An Illustrated Biography, Rizzola, 95; Frank Stella through the Eyes of a Fellow Artist, Book Rev, Jan 96; Frank Stella/Imaginary Landscapes, catalog, 2001. *Dealer:* Marcia Wood Gallery Atlanta Ga. *Mailing Add:* 131 NE Montgomery Ferry Dr Atlanta GA 30309

GUERIN, CHARLES
DIRECTOR, PAINTER
b San Francisco, Feb 27, 1949. *Study:* Northern Ill Univ, BFA, 1971, MA (Painting), 1973, MFA (Printmaking), 1974. *Work:* Lloyds of London; Art Inst Chicago; Marriott Hotel, Albany, NY; Ill State Mus; US West Corp; Thresholds, Chicago. *Exhib:* Exhibs include Purdue Univ, 1974, 1976, DePaul Univ, 1976, Colo Springs Fine Arts Ctr, 1977, Mus Fine ARts, Santa Fe, NMex, 1978, Wis State Univ, 1972, Suburban Fine Arts Ctr, Ill, 1974, Colo Woodworking Invitational, Silver Plume, 1977, Colo Craft Invitational, 1981, Leslie Levy Gallery, 1983, Robischon Gallery, 1983, Adam State Coll, Colo, 1984, Univ Wyo Art Mus, 1986-, Elaine Horwitch Gallery, 1990, William Havu Gallery, 1999. *Pos:* Co-dir, Guerin Design Group, Colo Springs, 1972-1977; dir exhibs, Colo Spring Fine Arts Ctr, 1977-1980, cur, fine arts, 1980-1986; dir, Univ Wyo Art Mus, Laramie, 1986-2000. *Mem:* Coll Art Asn Am; Am Asn Mus; Western Mus Conf. *Mailing Add:* University of Arizona Museum of Art POBox 210002 Tucson AZ 85721

GUERRA, KONRADO AVINA
PAINTER, SCULPTOR
b Mexico City, Mex, May 12, 1950. *Study:* Inst Nacional Bellas Artes, La Esmeralda, 71; Univ Nacional Autonoma de Mex, Acad de Sn Carlos, Facuttad de Artes, Lic (artes & plasticas), 71-79. *Work:* Palacio de Bellas Artes, Mex; Rockford Ill-Int Prints, Chicago; OEA, Dept Artes Visuales, Washington; Art Pocket Mus Art Movement, Kobe, Japan; Intergrafik-76 Aites Mus, Berlin, Ger. *Comn:* Dise'n10o-Decoracio'n01, 4 Pedastalos-Salada Go Bernadores, Palacio de Goblerno Chiapas, Chiapas, Tuxtla, 83. *Exhib:* Solo exhibs, Inst Nacional Bellas Artes-Palacio, 88, Mus Art Poket, Art Muvment, 95, B David Gallery, 96, Pan Am Health Orgn, 96, Interamerican Develop Bank, 96; Tokyo Int Art Show, 92; Arte Objeto, Museo de la Cd de Mex, 95; Dalí-Mirí, B David Gallery, 95. *Awards:* 1er Lugar, VNAM, 75; Mension Onorifica, Inst Nacional Bellas Artes, 76. *Bibliog:* Konrado-Work Art, Canal-34, Hollywood, Calif, 80; Kop-Art, Canal-11, IPN, 90; Arte del Surrealismo, Canal-4, Tele-Visa, 91. *Media:* Grabado en metal; oil on canvas, Escttura Bronce. *Publ:* Ed, Inter Grafik, 76, Mus für deutschd, 76; Intergrafik 80-Ausstellungszentrum, am Fernehturm, Berlin, 80; auth, Elgrabado Mexicano en el Siglo XX-1922-81, Hugo Covantes, 81; Diccionario de Escultura Mexicana del Siglio XX, Lily Kassner, 84; coauth, Diccionario de las Artes Plasticas, Francisco del Rio, 94. *Dealer:* Suzuki Minoru 2-13-13 Yamamoto D o10i Chuo-Ku Kobe Japan. *Mailing Add:* Juan Sarabia 153 Mexico DF 02800 Mexico

GUERRERO, RAUL
PAINTER, SCULPTOR
b Brawley, Calif, Oct 9, 1945. *Study:* Chouinard Art Sch, Los Angeles, BFA. *Work:* Phoenix Art Mus, Ariz; Long Beach Mus Art, Calif; La Jolla Mus Contemp Art, Calif; Security Pacific Bank, Los Angeles; Scripps Clinic, La Jolla. *Exhib:* Solo exhibs, Contemp Arts Forum, Santa Barbara & Los Angeles Inst Contemp Art, 82, Barbara Braathen Gallery, NY, 84, Boehm Gallery, Palomar Col, San Marcos, Calif, 86, Saxon-Lee Gallery, Los Angeles, 87 & 88, Linda Moore Gallery, San Diego, 92 & 95; A San Diego Exhib: 42 Emerging Artists, La Jolla Mus Contemp Art, 85; 1987 Phoenix Biennial, Phoenix Art Mus, Ariz, 87; From the Back Room, Saxon Lee Gallery, Los Angeles, 88, 89 & 90; La Frontera/The Border, Centro Cult de la Raza, San Diego, 93; Mus Contemp Art, San Diego, 95; and many other solo & group exhibs. *Pos:* Guest lectr, Univ Calif, San Diego, 92-. *Awards:* Photography Fel, Nat Endowment Arts, 79. *Bibliog:* Melinda Wortz (auth), Psychological manipulations, Artnews, 5/77; Hunter Drohojowska (auth), Raul Guerrero, Los Angeles Inst Contemp Art, Flash Art Int, 3/83; Christopher Knight (auth), Guerrero's art comes close to B-movie mysticism, 6/2/85, Exhibit of works by Raul Guerrero borders on being retrospective, 10/5/86 & Phoenix joins major leagues in art, 8/25/87, Los Angeles Herald Examiner; Judith Spiegel (auth), Nostalgia: The world flattened, Artweek, 4/30/88; and many others. *Mailing Add:* 1610 Myrtle Ave San Diego CA 92103-5121

GUERRIER, ADLER
PHOTOGRAPHER
b Port-au-Prince, Haiti, 1975. *Study:* New World Sch Arts, Miami, BFA, 2000. *Work:* Mus Contemp Art, Miami; Studio Mus in Harlem, New York. *Exhib:* Solo exhibs include Miami Art Mus, 2001, Locust Projects, Miami, 2004, Fredric Snitzer Gallery, Miami, 2005; group exhibs include & Pares Nones, Mus Art Mod, Santo Domingo, Dominican Repub, 2002; Made in Miami, Fredric Snitzer Gallery, Miami, 2003, Lock Stock & Barrell, 2004; Seeds & Roots: Selections from the Permanent Collection, Studio Mus Harlem, New York, 2004; MoCA & Miami, Mus Contemp Art, North Miami, 2005; Metro Pictures, The Moore Space, Miami, 2006; Whitney Biennial, Whitney Mus Am Art, New York, 2008

GUEST, RICHARD G
PAINTER, CONSULTANT
b Pasadena, Calif, Nov 30, 1924. *Study:* Chouinard Art Inst, Los Angeles, Calif, 58-59; Santa Monica City Col, 63; Otis Art Inst, Los Angeles, Calif, 64-65. *Work:* Riverside Art Mus, Calif; Portland Mus Art; Garden Grove Artisans Guild; Kobayaashi Co, Tokyo, Japan; Lindora Med Clin, San Diego, Calif; and many others. *Exhib:* Environmental Exhib, Laguna Beach Mus Art, Calif, 65; Monothon, Riverside Art Mus, Calif, 86; Santa Monica City Col, Calif; Torrance Traditional Artist Group, Calif; Buena Park Open, Calif; Cypress Art League, Calif; Culver City Invitational, Calif; Allied Artists Am, NY; Otis Art Inst, Los Angeles, Calif; Mill House, Garden Grove, Calif; Claystone Studios, Perris, Calif. *Pos:* Dealer, Guest Fine Arts, 68-89; consult & appraiser, Int Soc Appraisers, 88-. *Bibliog:* Art World USA (film), Paramount W Production, 78-79. *Media:* Water Based, Collage. *Dealer:* Randy Holland 420131 Main St Temecula CA 92586. *Mailing Add:* 27289 Capalino Dr Sun City CA 92586

GUIDA, DOMINICK
PAINTER
b New York, NY, June 24, 1946. *Study:* Calif Inst Arts, with Edward Reep & Emerson Woelffer, BFA, 73. *Work:* Chemical Bank & Goldman Sachs & Co, NY; Conn Bank & Trust Co, Norwalk; Continental Corp, Piscataway, NJ; Cologne Life Reinsurance Corp, Stamford, Conn; Hilton SW, Houston, Tex; Nissan Motor Corp, Gardina, Calif. *Comn:* Painting on wood relief structure, Edward Albee Found, NY, 78. *Exhib:* Biennial Exhib, Whitney Mus Am Art, NY, 75; New Spiritual Abstraction of the 1980's, Nora Haime Gallery, NY, 84; Painting & Sculpture Today 1984 (with catalog), Indianapolis Mus Art, Ind, 84; The Gang of 12 from NY in Italy (with catalog), Galleria Centro Mascarella, Bologna & Mus Civico, Siracusa, Italy, 86; Alumni Invitational Exhib, Calif Inst of Arts, Valencia, Calif, 88; Indianapolis Collects, Herron Art Gallery, Indianapolis, Ind, 90; Open Studio 402, Painting Space 122 Asn, PS 122, NY, 95, 97 & 98; Living with Art, Brenda Reinertson Gallery, Oakland, Calif, 98; 7th Ann Exhib, 98 & 63rd Ann Nat, 98, Cooperstown Art Asn. *Bibliog:* Amei Wallach (auth), Artworks of Albee's Barn, Newsday, Long Island, NY, 6/82. *Mem:* Painting Space 122 Inc; PS 122 Comm Ctr, NY (bd dir, 87-); Cooperstown Art Asn. *Media:* Oil, Watercolor. *Mailing Add:* PO Box 1441 New York NY 10009

GUILMAIN, JACQUES
HISTORIAN, PAINTER
b Brussels, Belg, Oct 15, 1926; US citizen. *Study:* Queens Col, City Univ New York, BS, 48; Columbia Univ, MA, 52, univ fel, 57, PhD, 58, and with Meyer Schapiro. *Exhib:* NY Acad Design, 48; Am Watercolors, Drawings and Prints, NY Metrop Mus Art, 52; Univ Calif, Riverside, 59; Queens Col, 61; SUNY, Stony Brook, 69-2003; two-man show, Gallery North, LI, 69; and others. *Teaching:* Vis asst prof hist art, Stanford Univ, 58-59; vis asst prof, Univ Calif, Riverside, 59-60; instr, Queens Col, 60-63; from asst prof to prof emer, State Univ NY, Stony Brook, 63-, chmn art dept, 70-76; vis prof, Columbia Univ, 68 & 70. *Awards:* Am Philosophical Soc Grant, 60; State Univ NY Res Found Grant, 64-79; Nat Endowment Humanities, 81. *Mem:* Medieval Acad Am. *Media:* Collage, Mixed Media, Oil. *Res:* Early Medieval ornaments; Mozarabic manuscript illumination; Carolingian manuscript illumination; early Medieval metalwork. *Publ:* auth, Zoomorphic decoration and the problem of the sources of Mozarabic illumination, XXXV, 60, Illuminations of the Second Bible of Charles the Bald, XLI, 66 & The Geometry of the Cross-Carpet Pages in the Lindisfarne Gospels, LXII, 87, Speculum; Enigmatic beasts of the Lindau Gospels lower cover, Gesta, X, 71; On the chronological development and classification of decorated initials in Latin manuscripts of 10th century Spain, LXIII, 81, Bulletin, John Rylands Univ Libr, Manchester; and others. *Mailing Add:* PO Box 2363 Setauket NY 11733

GUILMET, GLENDA J
PAINTER, PHOTOGRAPHER
b Tacoma, Wash, Mar 28, 1957. *Study:* Univ Puget Sound, Tacoma, Wash, BA (bus admin), 81, BA (art), 89; Clover Park Vocational Tech Inst, Tacoma, Wash, (photog), 82-83. *Work:* Photog collection, Bibliotheque Nat de France; Puyallup Tribe Indians, Wash; Wheelock art collection, Univ Puget Sound, Wash; art collection, Chief Leschi Schs; mixed metaphor-video collection, Seattle Art Mus. *Exhib:* Group exhibs, Gov's Invitational, State Capitol Mus, Olympia, Wash, 90, LA Matiere, L'Ombre, LA Fiction, Bibliotheque Nationale de France, Paris, 95 & Penetrating Image, Univ Ariz Mus Art, Tucson, 97, 43rd Anniversary Art Show, Sacred Circle Gallery, Seattle, 2013, Inner Portraits, Bainbridge Island Mus Art, 2014; Solo exhibs, The Glass People, Daybreak Star Arts Ctr, Seattle, 96-97, Taino Heritage Shadow Dance, Inst Puerto Rican Cult, 94; Retrospective in Paint: 1991-98, Galleria on Broadway, Tacoma, Wash, 98; New Work, Daybreak Star Arts Ctr, Seattle, 99; Womenscapes:

Expressions of Femininity, Daybreak Star Art Gallery, Seattle, 2005; You Know, Odd Art Gallery, Port Angeles, Wash, 2007. *Pos:* Photogr, Univ Puget Sound, Tacoma, Wash, 77-79; chwn, Finance Standing Committee, Tacoma Arts Comn, 90-91; art dir, Tacenda & Willo Trees Press, Eureka, Calif, 2004; owner, Glenda J Guilmet, Visual Artist, 96-. *Teaching:* Instr, Tacoma Arts Comn, 89. *Awards:* First Prize, Shadow Dance, Crosscurrents Arts Contest, 88; Hedgebrook Invitational Residency, Hedgebrook Foun, 2000; 1st place, Warhol's World Community Gallery Art Competition, Ovation TV, 2008. *Bibliog:* Keith Raether (auth), Shadow Stalker, Soundlife, News Tribune, Tacoma, Wash, 98; Mike Dillon (auth), Shadows Dancing on the Wall (what your eyes see is up to you), Queen Anne/Magnolia News, Seattle, Wash, 99; Guilmet's return to Daybreak Star doesn't disappoint, Queen Anne/Magnolia News, 2005. *Mem:* Tacoma Arts Comn, Tacoma, Wash (89-92). *Media:* Painting, Photography, Printmaking & Sculpture. *Publ:* Auth, (statement regarding participation in Fred Wilson's exhib at the Seattle Art Mus), The Museum: Mixed Metaphors, Fred Wilson, by Patterson Sims, Seattle Art Mus, Seattle, Wash, 93; auth, Futurist statement in 27 Wash Artists Look at the Future, Artist Trust J, Seattle, Wash, (summer), 95; coauth with David L Whited, Shadow Dance (nine muses bks), Winston, Ore, 2004. *Mailing Add:* 652 Old Blyn Hwy Sequim WA 98382-9695

GULLY, ANTHONY LACY
HISTORIAN, ADMINISTRATOR
b Orange, Calif, Feb 28, 1938. *Study:* Univ Calif, Riverside, BA; Univ Calif, Berkeley, MA; Stanford Univ, PhD; with Jean Boggs, Jean Bony, Walter Horn, Lorenz Eitner & Albert Elsen. *Teaching:* Instr 17th-18th century art hist, Pomona Col, Claremont, Calif, 65-66; asst prof 19th-20th century art hist, Calif State Univ, Los Angeles, 66-68; assoc prof 18th-19th century art hist, Ariz State Univ, Tempe, 72-83, asst dean col fine arts, 81-, chair grad humanities prog, 83-84; vis prof, Stanford Univ, 81. *Awards:* Nat Defense Educ Act Award, Stanford Univ, 68-71; Mabel McLeod Fel, Rowlandson Study, London, Stanford Univ, 71-72; Nat Endowment Humanities Award, Yale Univ, 76; and others. *Bibliog:* J Hayes (auth), Rowlandson, Phaidon Art Bks, 72; R Paulsen (auth), Rowlandson: New interpretation, Yale Univ, 72; R Wark (auth), Rowlandson drawings in Huntington Libr, 75. *Mem:* Coll Art Asn; Mid-Am Coll Art Asn; Rocky Mountain Conf on Brit Studies (pres, 78-79); Nat Conf Brit Studies; Pacific Conf on Brit Studies. *Res:* Nineteenth century British art; John Sell Cotman, 1782-1842. *Publ:* Auth, Book reviews on eighteenth century art and aesthetics, Current Bibliog: 18th Century, 76; auth, Mr B and the cherubim: William Blake's descriptive catalog, 78, An unpublished sketchbook by Rowlandson, 79 & Milton's unholy trinity, 81, Phoebus; auth, Source of Goya's May 3, 1808, In: Studies in Iconography, 83. *Mailing Add:* 2618 Country Club Way Tempe AZ 85282-2922

GUMMELT, SAMUEL
PAINTER
b Waco, Tex, Aug 28, 1944. *Study:* NTex State Univ, BA, 68; Southern Methodist Univ, MFA, 71. *Work:* Dallas Mus Fine Arts; Am Tel & Tel, Chicago; Ft Worth Art Mus. *Exhib:* Proj South/Southwest, 71 & Focus: Sam Gummelt, 79, Ft Worth Art Mus; Interchange, Dallas Mus Fine Art, 72 & Walker Art Ctr, Minneapolis, 73; Exchange, Ft Worth Art Mus, 75 & San Francisco Mus Mod Art, 76; Recent Works on Paper by Contemp Am Artists, Madison Art Ctr, Wis, 77; Projects: Sam Gummelt, Art Mus STex, Corpus Christi, 78; Am Drawing in Black & White 1970-1980, Brooklyn Mus, NY, 80. *Awards:* Purchase Awards, 4th Ann Prints & Drawing Exhib, Ark Art Ctr, 70, 35th Tarrant Co Ann, Ft Worth Art Ctr, 73 & Tex Invitational, Beaumont Art Mus, 78; Nat Endowment Arts Fel, 82 & 85. *Bibliog:* Jan Butterfield (auth), The young Texans: The phenomenon of interstitial art on America's last frontier, Arts Mag, 73; Jozanne Rabyor (auth), article, Art in Am, 74; Susan Platt (auth), Reviews: Houston, Art Forum, 79. *Media:* Oil, Wax on Canvas. *Dealer:* Janie C Lee Gallery 1209 Berthea Houston TX 77006; Eugene Binder Gallery 2701 Canton Dallas TX 75226. *Mailing Add:* 5909 Palo Pinto Dallas TX 75206-6831

GUMMERSALL, C GREGORY
PAINTER
b Pocatello, Idaho, 1947. *Study:* San Jose State Univ; Vienna Austria Residency, 1992. *Work:* Kanter Family Collection, Thomas McCormick Gallery, Chicago, Ill; Tucson Art Mus; Palm Springs Art Mus; Horwich Family Collection, Chicago, Ill. *Exhib:* Solo exhibs include Graystone Gallery, San Francisco, 1986, Univ of the Pacific, Stockton, Calif, 1988, Posner Fine Art, Los Angeles, 1994, Chac Mool Fine Art, Los Angeles, 1996, Lacy Primitive & Fine Art, Los Angeles, 2001, 2005, Muse Gallery, Jackson, Wyo, 2007, Jean Albano Gallery, Chicago, 2008; group exhibs include San Francisco Mus Mod Art, 1998, Gallery C, Hermosa Beach, Calif, 2006, Riva Yares Gallery, Scottsdale, Ariz, 2006, Cline Fine Art, Scottsdale, Ariz, 2007, Contemp Forum, Phoenix Art Mus, Ariz, 2007, Nat Acad Mus Invitational, New York, 2008, Ellis West Gallery, Durango, Colo, 2008, Cline Fine Art, LA Art Show, 2008; Fordham Univ Mus, Lincoln Ctr, New York, 1990; Telluride Gallery Fine Art, Colo, 1997; Ctr Southwest Studies, 2002; Santa Fe Biennial, 2003; Tucson Mus Art, Ariz, 2004; Artful Sol Gallery, Vail, Colo, 2011; Cumberland Gallery, Nashville, Tenn, 2011; JRB Fine Art, Oklahoma City, 2011-12; The Arts Co, Nashville, Tenn, 2012; Fort Lewis Concert Hall, 2012; Alexander Salazar Fine Art, San Diego, Calif, 2013; Goodwin Gallery, Denver, Colo; Sense Rine Art, Menlo Park, Calif, 2013; TL Norris Gallery, Greenville, SC. *Pos:* West Coast bd pres, New Art Examiner Mag, 1990; adv bd, Int LA/Art Fair, 1992, steering comt, 1993. *Bibliog:* Dave Tourje (auth), Soul Abstractionist, 5/2003; Emily Sachar (auth), Greg Gummersall A Little Country, A Little City, A Lot of Interesting Art, Cowboys & Indians Magazine, 10/2006; Leanne Goebel (auth), On the Road for Art, Durango Herald, 12/8/2006; article, LUXE Mag, vol 4, issue 3, 2008. *Media:* Oil, Acrylic & Collage. *Interests:* sailing, playing on mini ranch. *Dealer:* JRB Fine Art Oklahoma City; Jean Albano Gallery Chicago IL 60610; Sense Fine Art Menlo Park CA; Arthur Soul Vail Co; Alexander Salazar Fine Art San Diego CA; Goodwill Gallery Denver Co; TL Norris Gallery Greenville SC. *Mailing Add:* PO Box 1663 Bayfield CO 81122-1663

GUMPERT, GUNTHER
PAINTER
b Krefeld, Ger, Apr 17, 1919; US citizen. *Study:* Sch Fine Arts Krefeld; Sch Fine Arts, Wuppertal. *Work:* Metrop Mus Art, NY; Denver Art Mus, Colo; Phillips Collection, Washington; Victoria & Albert Mus, London; Albertina, Vienna, Austria; and others. *Comn:* Mural, Inter-Am Develop Bank, Washington, 68; and others. *Exhib:* Kaiser-Wilhelm Mus, 48, 49 & 52; solo exhibs, USA, Latin Am & Eur, 53-2008; Salon Realites Nouvelles, Paris, 58-60 & 62; Int Exhib Abstr Art, Pistoia, 61; Int Exhib Contemp Art, London, 62; Salon Mai, Paris, 62; European Acad Art, Trier, 2000. *Bibliog:* Jean Grenier (auth), Gumpert, Preuves, Paris, 60; Victor Summa (auth), Gumpert & The Evolution of His Art (film), Educ TV Asn, 63; Prof Willy Huppert (auth), Gunther Gumpert, Kunst-und Kunstgewerbe Verein, Pforzheim, 64; Wolfgang Henze (auth), Gunther Gumpert, Bern, 2000; and others. *Media:* All. *Dealer:* Gregory Gallery 41 East 57th St New York NY 10022; Galerie Henze & Ketterer AG Kirchstrasse 26-CH 3114 Wichtrach/Bern Switz. *Mailing Add:* 3752 McKinley St NW Washington DC 20015

GUMPERT, LYNN
MUSEUM DIRECTOR
Study: Ecole du Louvre, Paris, France, 71-72, certificate for completion of first yr, Sorbonne, Paris, France, 71-72; Univ Calif, Berkeley, BA (with honors, art hist), 74; Univ Mich, MA (art hist), 77. *Collection Arranged:* Urban Pulse: The Artist and the City, Pittsburgh Ctr Arts, Pa, 83; East Meets West: Japanese and Italian Art Today (brochure), Third Contemp Art Fair, Los Angeles, Calif, 88; Christian Boltanski: Lessons of Darkness (coauth, catalog), Mus Contemp Art, Chicago, 88, Mus Contemp Art, Los Angeles, 88 & New Mus Contemp Art, 89; FRAMED: From a Troubled Land, Photographs by Paul Graham and I a Woman, The FBI File of Andy Warhol & An Installation by Margia Kramer (brochure), San Francisco Artspace, 89; By Arrangement, Galerie Ghislaine Hussenot, Paris, 92; Reorientations: Looking East (with catalog), Gallery at Takashimaya, new York, 94, Lest We Forget: On Nostalgia (coauth, catalog), 94 & Material Dreams (with catalog), 95. *Pos:* Intern, Nat Mus Am Art, Smithsonian Inst, Washington, DC, Summer, 73; cur asst, Jewish Mus, New York, 78-80; cur, New Mus Contemp Art, 80-84, sr cur, 84-88; independent cur & consult, 88-97; dir, Grey Art Gallery, NY Univ, 97-. *Teaching:* Interim dir mus studies, NY Univ, 99-2000. *Awards:* Chevalier Order Arts & Lett, France; Fel, Univ Mich, 75. *Mem:* Int Asn Art Critics; ArtTable. *Publ:* Auth, Glamour Girls (Yasumasa Morimura), Art Am, Vol 84, No 7, 7/96; Unabashedly Asia, ARTnews, Vol 95, No 10, 11/96; Report From Singapore: A Global City for the Arts? Art Am, Vol 85, No 12, 12/97; Fiber Options & Giving Pleats a Chance, ARTnews, Vol 97, No 11, 12/98; auth, The Art of the Everyday: The Quotidian in Postwar French Culture, 1997. *Mailing Add:* Grey Art Gallery New York Univ 1100 Washington Sq E New York NY 10003

GUNASINGHE, SIRI
EDUCATOR, HISTORIAN
b Ruanwella, Sri Lanka, Feb 20, 1925. *Study:* Univ Ceylon, BA, 48; Univ Paris, PhD, 55; Univ Sri Jayewardene Pura, Sri Lanka, D Litt, 94. *Teaching:* Instr sanskrit, Univ Ceylon, 48-70; prof, Univ Victoria, BC, 70-88, emer 88-. *Awards:* Sr Specialist, Univ Hawaii, 68; Fel, Can Coun Leave, 78; Smithsonian Travel, 87. *Res:* History of Buddhist and Hindu art in India, Sri Lanka and Southeast Asia. *Publ:* Auth, La Technique de la Peinture Indienne, Univ Press France, 56; Masks of Ceylon, Dept Cult Affairs, 63 & Album of Buddhist Paintings from Sri Lanka, Nat Mus, 78, Colombo. *Mailing Add:* 4110 Ebony Terr Victoria BC V8N 3Z3 Canada

GUND, AGNES
COLLECTOR, ADMINISTRATOR, PATRON
b Cleveland, Ohio, Aug 13, 1938. *Study:* Conn Coll, BA (hist); Harvard Univ, MA (hist). *Pos:* Trustee, Cleveland Inst Art, 1968-72, Hirshhorn Mus, Washington, DC, 1987-91, Brown Univ, Providence, RI, 1989-, Andy Warhol Found, NY, 1990-, J Paul Getty Trust, 1994-; bd dirs, Mus Mod Art, New York, 1976-1991, pres bd dirs, 1991-2002, pres emer & chmn int coun, currently; founder & trustee, Studio in a Sch Asn, 1977-1991; bd trustees, Wexner Ctr Found, 1997-; chmn, Mayor's Cult Affairs Adv Comn, New York; bd mem, Barnes Found, Menil Collection, Frick Collection, Found for Contemp Art, PS1 Contemp Art Ctr & Socrates Sculpture Park; hon trustee, Cleveland Mus Art, Indepdenent Curators Int & Mus Contemp Art, Cleveland; bd trustees, Nat Council Arts, 2011-. *Awards:* Gov's Award, Gov Mario Cuomo, 1988; Montblanc de la Culture award, 1997; Nat Medal Arts, 1997; Am Acad Arts & Letts Award, 1998; Arts Educ award, Am for the Arts, 1999; Centennial Medal, Harvard Univ Grad Sch Arts & Sci's, 2003; Evan Burger Donaldson Achievement award, Miss Porter's Sch, 2003; Named one of Top 200 Collectors, ARTnews mag, 2004-13; Women in the Arts award. *Mem:* Fel Am Acad Arts & Sci's; Chess in Schools; Aaron Diamond AIDS Res Ctr; Fund for Pub Schs. *Collection:* Modern and contemporary art. *Publ:* Contribr, Mary Miss Catalogue for Fogg Mus, Harvard, 1980; The New Democracy, Blueprints to Change Washington, Citizens Transition Proj, 1992. *Mailing Add:* Mus Mod Art 11 W 53rd St New York NY 10019

GUNDERSON, BARRY L
SCULPTOR
b Baird, Tex, Feb 9, 1945. *Study:* Augsburg Col, Minneapolis, BA; Univ NDak, Grand Forks; Univ Colo, Boulder, MFA. *Comn:* Large outdoor sculptures, Downtown Plaza, Portsmouth, 79, EOTC, Pendleton, Ore, 86, Porirua, Wellington, New Zealand, 90 & Franklin Park Conservatory, Columbus, Ohio, 92; Ohio State Univ, Marion, 96; Ohio State Fair Grounds, 96. *Exhib:* 5 Ohio Sculptors, Contemp Arts Ctr, Cincinnati, 80; Sculpture Outside in Cleveland, Edgewater Part, Cleveland, 81; Ohio Sculptors II, Taft Mus, Cincinnati, 86; Art for Urban Gardens, Ohio Designer Craftsmen Gallery, Columbus, 89. *Teaching:* Prof sculpture, Kenyon Col, 74-. *Mem:* Coll Art Asn. *Media:* Welded, Painted Aluminum. *Mailing Add:* 205 E Brooklyn St Gambier OH 43022

GUNDERSON, KAREN
PAINTER
b Racine, Wis, Aug 14, 1943. *Study:* Wis State Univ, Whitewater, BEd, 66, Univ Iowa, Iowa City, MA & MFA, 68. *Work:* Wustum Art Mus, Racine & Milwaukee Art; Haggerty Mus, Milwaukee, Wis; Racine Art Mus, Racine, Wis. *Comn:* Paintings, comn by Mr & Mrs Leonard Gordon, NY & Dr & Mrs Clinton Levin, New Bedford, Mass, 88; Our Saviors Lutheran Church, Racine, Wis, 95-96; paintings, comn by David & Blanca Goldman, NY; painting, comn by Ralph Acampora, NY. *Exhib:* Solo exhibs, Wustum Art Mus, Racine, 69 & 85, Wis & Cedar Rapids Art Ctr, Iowa, 69, Minneapolis Inst Art, Minn, 71 & Hopkins Hall Gallery, Ohio State Univ, Columbus, 72, ClampArt, NY, 2007, William Siegal Gallery, Santa Fe, 2009, 2010, Nat Mus Bahrain, Manama, Bahrain, 11/2010; Group exhibs, Hebrew Union Col, NY, 2000; Coll Staten Island, NY, 2000; Holocaust Mus, Houston, 2001; Cornell Coll Art Gallery, MT Vernon, Iowa, 2002; Brattleboro Mus & Art Ctr, VT, 2002; Skilball Mus, Cinn, Ohio, 2002; Gov of the Ministry, Sophia Bulgaria, 2003; Congregation Beth Shalomrodfezedek, Chester, Conn, 2003; Circulo De Bellas Artes, 2004; New Old Masters, Nat Mus, Gdansk, Poland. *Pos:* Bd mem, Sch Arts, Univ Wis, Whitewater, 2005-; Jurist, Hestia Gdanski, Poland, 2009, 2010. *Teaching:* vis artist, Md Inst Coll Art, 85-. *Awards:* Distinguished Alumni Award, Univ Wis, Whitewater, 85; ED Found Grant, 94; Hall of Fame, Washington Park High Sch, Racine, Wis; Lorenzo Magnifico-2nd Place/Painting Florence Biennale, 2001. *Bibliog:* Carter Ratcliff (auth), Karen Gunderson (catalog), Perimeter Press, 85; Linell Smith (auth), Painting pictures in the clouds: Karen Gunderson puts life in cumulus, Baltimore Evening Sun, 87; Donald Kuspit (auth), catalog, 98; Donald Kuspit (auth), Black Paintings, 2004-; Mark Daniel Cohen At the Heart of Light, 2004; Allesandro Riker Interview with, Karen Gunderson, 2004. *Media:* All Media. *Dealer:* Clampart 521-531 West 25th St New York NY 10001; William Siegal Gallery 540 South Guadalupe St Santa Fe NM 87501; Frost & Reed 2-4 King St St James London England. *Mailing Add:* 26 Beaver St No 14 New York NY 10004

GUNN, ELLEN
PAINTER, PRINTMAKER
b Rockville Center, NY, Jan 8, 1951. *Study:* Parsons Sch Design, BFA, 73; Sch Visual Arts, 74; Kala Inst, Berkeley, Calif, 80; Calif Coll Arts & Crafts, studied with Charles Gill, 81-82. *Work:* San Francisco Mus Mod Art, Calif. *Comn:* Paintings, Inn Keeper Asn, San Francisco, 85; paintings & fabric design, Read House Hotel, Chattanooga, Tenn, 86 & Sheraton O'Hare, Chicago, Ill, 90; paintings & monotypes, Kaiser Hosp, Santa Rosa, Calif, 87; paintings & menu design, Phoenix Sheraton, 88, 89. *Exhib:* Art Expo, NY, 90-94. *Awards:* 1st Place, Sr Student Competition, Parsons Sch Design, 73; Dean's Hon List & Grad Cum Laude, Parsons Sch Design. *Media:* All. *Publ:* Auth, Good Housekeeping Mag, 73; Vogue Mag, 74; Fiber Arts Design Book II, Lark Books, 83; The Goodfellows Review of Crafts, 83; California Living, San Francisco Chronicle, 84. *Dealer:* Winn Art Group 6015 Sixth Ave South Seattle WA 98108. *Mailing Add:* 40 Lincoln Ave Piedmont CA 94611

GUNN, PAUL JAMES
PAINTER, EDUCATOR
b Guys Mills, Pa, June 21, 1922. *Study:* Edinboro State Teachers Col, BS, 47; Calif Coll Arts & Crafts, MFA, 48; wood block printing with Hideo Hagiwara, Tokyo, Japan, 61-62. *Work:* Portland Art Mus; Seattle Art Mus; Am Info Serv, Athens, Greece; Bibliot Nat, Paris, France; Victoria & Albert Mus, London, Eng. *Exhib:* Int Bordighera Biennial, Italy; Bay Printmakers Second Ann, Oakland Art Mus, Calif; Ann Northwest Artists, Seattle Art Mus; Western Artists Ann, Denver Art Mus; Ore Artists Ann, Portland Art Mus. *Pos:* Resident dir, Japan Studies Prog, Ore Study Ctr, Waseda Univ, Japan, 72-74 & 83-84. *Teaching:* Prof painting & printmaking, Ore State Univ, 48-88, chmn dept art, 64-72. *Media:* Oil

GUNTER, FRANK ELLIOTT
PAINTER, EDUCATOR
b Jasper, Ala, May 8, 1934. *Study:* Univ Ala, BFA; Fla State Univ, MA. *Work:* Sheldon Swope Gallery, Terre Haute, Ind; Evansville Mus Arts & Sci & Mead Johnson Corp, Evansville, Ind; Ill State Mus, Springfield; Ind State Mus, Indianapolis; Birmingham Mus Art, Ala; Krannert Art Mus, Univ Ill, Champaign; Chase Manhattan Bank, Chicago; Ill Acad Mathematics & Science, Aurora; Turkish Cult Found, Istanbul; New Britain Mus Am Art, Conn; Ind Landmarks, Indiannapolis; Hist Madison Inc, Ind. *Comn:* Painting, Rochester State Bank, Ill, 74; painting of facade, Bank of Ind, Merrillville, 75; Dental Col, Southern Ill Univ, Alton; nat trust property, Filioli, Woodside, Calif. *Exhib:* Cult Ctr for Am Embassy, Paris, 71; Mus Art, Besancon, France, 72; Am Libr, Brussels, Belg, 73; Maison Descartes, Amsterdam, 73; Varieties of Visual Reality, Northern Ariz State Univ, 75; Am Exhib, Krannert Art Mus, Univ Ill, Urbana, 77; Univ Wis, Madison, 84; Hanover Coll, Ind, 92; Rapp Gallery, Louisville, Ky, 2000-2001; Retrospective, Sangatuck Art Center, Mich, 2008. *Teaching:* Instr art, Birmingham Pub Schs, Ala, 56-58; asst prof art, Murray State Univ, 60-62; emer prof art, Univ Ill, Urbana-Champaign, 62-91. *Awards:* Second Award for Painting, Soc Four Arts, 73; Purchase Awards, Wabash Valley Ann, Terre Haute, 74 & Union League Club, Chicago, 74. *Bibliog:* Stephen Spector (auth), Super realists, Archit Dig, 11/12/74; G A Rodetis (auth), Varieties of visual reality, Northern Ariz Univ Art Gallery 1-3/75; Henry Adams (auth), A Tribute, Nelson Gallery, 84; Katherine Manthone (auth), The Other Shore: River Landscapes, 90; Eunice Agar (auth), Am Artists Mag, p 41-45, 8/92. *Mem:* Am Ceramics Circle. *Media:* Acrylic on Canvas. *Dealer:* Rapp Gallery Louisville KY. *Mailing Add:* 211 W Second St Madison IN 47250-3722

GUO-QIANG, CAI
PAINTER, CURATOR
b Quanzhou City, China, Dec 8, 1957. *Study:* attended, Shanghai Theatre Acad, 85. *Comn:* Lion: Feng Shui Project for Mito: Chang Sheng, Art Tower Mito Contemp Art Ctr, Mito Train Station, 94; Eighteen Saints, Tocho-ji Temple, 98; Dragon Boat, Hakata Riverain, Fukuoka, 99; Skylight, Stadtische Galerie Nordhorn, 99; Turtle Fountain, Dentsu, 2002; High Mountain Flowing Water: 3-D Landscape Painting, Mori Arts Ctr, Tokyo, 2003; Lighthouse, City of Niigata, 2003; Ring Stone, Mass Inst Tech Public Art Program, 2010. *Exhib:* Solo exhibs, Sunshine and Solitude, Museo Universitario Arte Contemporaneo, Mexico City, 2010, Platform for Cultural Initiatives, Donetsk, 2011, Move Along, Nothing to See Here, Cohen Gallery, Brown Univ, Providence, 2011, Arab Mus Modern Art, Doha, 2011, Sky Ladder, Mus Contemp Art, Los Angeles, Calif, 2012, Spring, Zhejiang Art Mus, 2012, and many others; Group exhibs, 17th Biennale of Sydney, 2010, Foundation Ctr Contemp Art, 2010, Aichi Triennale, Nagoya, 2010, Koidl Kunsthalle, Berlin, 2010, Asian Art Mus, San Francisco, Calif, 2010, Multimedia Art Mus, Moscow, 2010, Contemp Art Mus Kumamoto, 2011, Ctr Contemp Art Ujazdowski Castle, Warsaw, 2011, Agora Art Project X Space, Taipei, 2011, Kroller-Muller Mus, The Netherlands, 2011, 2012, and many others. *Collection Arranged:* Virgin Garden: Emersion, 51st Venice Biennale, 2005; Everything is Museum, Sackler Ctr Arts Educ, Solomon R Guggenheim Mus, NY, 2008, Nat Art Mus China, 2008; Kiki Smith: Color Still, Mus Contemp Art, 2010. *Pos:* dir visual & special effects, Summer Olympics, Beijing, China, 2008. *Awards:* Japan Cultural Design prize, 95; Golden Lion award, 48th Venice Biennale, 99; New England for Best Installation or Single Work in a Mus, Int Asn Art Critics, 2005; 7th Hiroshima prize, 2007; 20th Fukuoka Asian Culture prize, 2009; Praemium Imperiale (painting), Japan Art Asn, 2012. *Mailing Add:* c/o Cai Studio 40 E 1st St New York NY 10003

GURALNICK, JODY
PAINTER, COLLAGE ARTIST
b Boston, Mass. *Study:* Boston Mus Sch, 1971-72; St Martin's Sch Art, BA in Painting (with honors), 1975; Pratt Inst, Bklyn, MFA in Painting, 1978. *Work:* The Progressive Collection, Cleveland, Ohio; US West Corporate Collection, Denver. *Exhib:* Colorado Biennial (auth, catalog), Mus Contemp Art, Denver, 2000; Aspen Valley Biennial, Aspen Art Mus, Aspen, Colo, 2000. *Teaching:* prof mixed media painting, Colo Mountain Col, 95, 96; prof collage & painting, Anderson Ranch Art Center, 2002, 2004. *Awards:* Visual Arts fellowship, Colo Coun Arts, 1998. *Bibliog:* The collage life, Aspen Mag, 99; Look deep into her work, Aspen Times, 99. *Media:* Oil, Encaustic. *Publ:* Contribr, New American Paintings, The Open Studio Press, 99; contribr, Nine Aspen Artists, The Third Eye Press, 95; contribr, The Progressive Corp, Ann Report, 97; contribr, New Am Paintings, The Open Studio Press, 2001. *Dealer:* David Floria/David Floria Gallery Aspen CO 81611

GURBACS, JOHN JOSEPH
PAINTER, RESTORER
b Budapest, Hungary, Oct 31, 1947; US citizen. *Study:* Miami-Dade Junior Col, AA, 68; Fla State Univ, BFA, 70; Univ SFla, 72-75, with Bruce March & Paul Sarkisian. *Work:* Fla State House of Reps & Fla Senate, Tallahassee; Univ Cent Fla, Orlando; Southern Bell, Jacksonville, Fla; Tampa Elec & Barnett Bank, Tampa. *Exhib:* Am Painting, Soc Four Arts, Palm Beach, Fla, 75; Critic's Choice, 80 & Jim Rosenquist Invitational, 82, Artist Alliance Gallery, Tampa; Mus Choice, Loch Haven Art Ctr, Orlando, 81; New Talent Exhib, Barbara Gillman Gallery, Miami, Fla, 82; Triennial & Gasparilla's Best, Tampa Mus Fla, 85; Four Painters, Fla Ctr Contemp Art, 87; Fantasy Landscapes, Tampa Mus W, 87; Southern Arts Fed/Nat Endowment Arts Regional Fel Awards Exhib, Atlanta Sch Art, 87 & Ruth Eckerd Hall, Clearwater, Fla, 88; Scarfone Gallery, Univ Tampa, 88. *Pos:* Self-employed designer & artist, specializing in wall design & lettering, 77-86; exhib asst, Tampa Mus, 81-82; proj painter, Tampa Theater Restoration Proj, 81-84. *Awards:* Merit Award, Gulf Coast Art Ctr, 78; Individual Artist Fel, Fla Arts Coun, 85; Regional Fel Award, Southern Arts Fedn & Nat Endowment Arts, 86. *Bibliog:* Joanne Rodriquez (auth), Critic's Choice Exhibition, Tampa Tribune, 80; Robert Martin (auth), John Gurbacs exhibition, Tampa Times, 81; Audrey Lawler (auth), Local residents receive state grants, Carrollwood News, 85. *Media:* Acrylic, Oil. *Dealer:* Joan Hodgell Gallery 46 S Palm Ave Sarasota FL 33577. *Mailing Add:* 304 W Kirby St Tampa FL 33604-4048

GUREVICH, GRIGORY
SCULPTOR, PAINTER, GRAPHIC ARTIST, PRINTMAKER, INVENTOR
b Leningrad, St Petersburg, Russia, Dec 26, 1937; US citizen. *Study:* Acad Fine & Indust Arts, Leningrad, St Petersburg, Russia, MFA, 61. *Hon Degrees:* Master Fine Arts. *Work:* New York Pub Libr; Brooklyn Mus Libr; Rare Bks Collection, Newark Libr Mus; Rare Books Libr, St Bonaventure Univ, NY; Mus Russ Contemp Art, Jersey City, NJ; Hermitage Mus prints collection, St Petersburg; Penza Russia Mus; and others. *Comn:* Commuters (7 bronze sculptures), Penn Sta Newark, NJ Transit, 85; Kazuo Hashimoto (bronze bust), NJ Inst Technol, 96; Finn Caspepsen (bronze bust) Banks, NJ, 97; eleven acrylic murals, Union Hill High Sch, NJ, 2001-2006; Community (acrylic mural), Episcopal Church, North Plainfield, NJ, 2005. *Exhib:* Solo exhib, CASE Mus Russ Contemp Art, Jersey City, NJ, 83; Plakat, Plakat Gallery, Copenhagen, 83; Graphicworks, Musee de L'Art Russe Contemporian, France, 85; retrospective, St Bonaventure Univ, NY, 96; Ideas, Morris Mus, Morristown, NJ, 96; Crossroads, Seton Hall Univ, NJ, 97; Pen & Ink Drawing, Jeraldine R Dodge Foundation, 2004. *Pos:* Founder, artistic dir, Arts on Hudson Art Prog, Jersey City, 98-. *Teaching:* Instr sculpture & drawing, Newark Sch Fine & Indust Arts, 82-97; prof sculpture & ceramics, St Johns Univ, Queens, New York, 94-97; Montclair Art Mus, 97-99; Newark Mus, 98-2000. *Awards:* Marian W Reitman Award, Arts Coun Essex Area, 90; Nat Award, Am Artists Prof League, 92; Artist of the Year, Hudson Co Artists, 95; Katherine D Miller Award, 98; Geraldine R Dodge Found, 1998-2004; 1st Place in Watercolor, 1st Place in Painting, Drawing, St Johns Church, 2000. *Bibliog:* Harold Marcus (auth), The Case Mus of Russian Contemporary Art in exile, Arts, 2/88; Amy Kellog (dir), News 12 New Jersey, 8/19/96; Gregory R Gregor (auth), Fine Art Professor is true Renaissance Man, St John's Today, 96; Russia Theater - Russia Unost - Russia, Penzenskaya Pravda, Chelovek trans former, Aug 2008; and articles In: NY Times, Star Ledger, Jersey Journal, Herald Tribune Denmark, Izvestia & others. *Mem:* Am Artists Prof League Inc. *Media:* Pen & ink, watercolor, acrylic,

pencil, bronze, oils, art books. *Specialty:* Paintings, Drawings, Sculptures, Prints, Art Books. *Interests:* Visual Arts, Classical Music, Jazz. *Collection:* Picasso, Utamaro, Chiparus. *Dealer:* Art South Inc 161 Leverington Ave Philadelphia PA 19127; Gen Serv Admin Pub Bldg Serv Washington DC 20405. *Mailing Add:* 282 Barrow St Jersey City NJ 07302

GURLIK, PHILIP JOHN
PAINTER, PRINTMAKER

b Beaver Dam, Wis, Sept 26, 1958. *Study:* Univ Wis, Green Bay, 76-79; Milwaukee Area Coll, 79-80, Excelsior Coll, Albany, NY, BA (music & painting), 99. *Work:* Dwight Merrimon Davidson Collection, Elon Coll, NC; SAP America, Houston; Interchem, Houston; Sheppard Pratt, Baltimore. *Comn:* Painting, SAP Am, 96; painting, Hilton Hotel, Baltimore, 2006. *Exhib:* Watercolor, Miss Mus Art, Jackson, 95; Stamford Mus, 95; Sam Houston Mem Mus, 95; Minot State Univ, 96; and many others. *Teaching:* Artist-in-residence, Md Hall Creative Arts, Annapolis, 2005-2011. *Bibliog:* Best of Painting, North Light Bks, 98. *Media:* Painting. *Interests:* sailing, music, literature. *Publ:* Auth, Selected Works, Tafford Publ, 96. *Mailing Add:* PO Box 4474 Annapolis MD 21403

GURNEY, GEORGE
CURATOR, HISTORIAN

b Sharon, Conn, Nov 26, 1939. *Study:* Brown Univ, BA, 62; Univ Pa, MA, 65; Univ Del, PhD, 78. *Collection Arranged:* Nineteenth Century Sculpture (auth, catalog), Nat Gallery Art, 74; Sculpture and the Federal Triangle, Nat Collection Fine Arts, 79; Elizabeth Catlett, 90; Revisiting The White City: Am Art at the 1893 World's Fair, 93; Man on Fire: Luis Jimenez, 94; Chaim Gross: A Celebration, 96; Lost and Found: Edmmia Lewis's Cleopatra, 96; George Catlin and his Indian Gallery, 2002; Variations in America, 2007; 1934: A New Deal for Artists, 2009; Christo & Jeane-Claude: Remembering the Running Fence, 2010. *Pos:* Guest cur, Nat Mus Am Art, Smithsonian Am Art Mus, Washington, DC, 77-82, assoc cur sculpture, 85-93, cur, 94-99, deputy chief cur, 99-2002, acting chief cur, 2003, deputy chief cur, 2004-2010, acting chief cur, 2010-2011, cur emer, 2011-. *Teaching:* Teaching asst art hist, Univ Pa, Philadelphia, 64-65; instr art hist, Univ Hartford, Conn, 65-66 & Sweet Briar Col, Va, 66-69. *Awards:* Nat Gallery Art Samuel H Kress Fel, 73-74; Nat Mus Am Art Smithsonian Res Fel, 74-75; Herbert Adams Memorial Medal, Nat Sculpture Soc, 87; Sculpture House Award, Nat Sculpture Soc, 2010. *Mem:* Coll Art Asn Am; Soc Archit Historians; Nat Sculpture Soc. *Res:* Nineteenth and twentieth century American sculpture; Archit Sculpture at World's Columbian Exposition, 1893. *Publ:* Contribr, Sculpture of a City: Philadelphia's Treasures in Bronze and Stone, Walker & Co, 74; Sculpture and the Federal Triangle, Nat Sculpture Rev, 79; contribr, Cast and Recast: The Sculpture of Frederic Remington, Smithsonian Press, 81; Sculpture and the Federal Triangle, Smithsonian Press, 85; co-organizer, Revisiting the White City: Am Art at the 1893 World's Fair, Smithsonian, 93; coed, George Catlin & his Indian Gallery, Norton & Co, 2002

GURNEY, JANICE SIGRID
CONCEPTUAL ARTIST, PHOTOGRAPHER

b Winnipeg, Man, Mar 5, 1949. *Study:* Univ Man, BFA, 73. *Work:* Nat Gallery Can; Winnipeg Art Gallery, Man; Robert McLaughlin Gallery, Oshawa, Ont; Can Coun Art Bank, Ottawa, Ont; Labatt's Photog Collection, Toronto, Ont; Art Gallery Ont, Toronto. *Exhib:* For the Audience, Mount St Vincent Univ Art Gallery, Halifax, NS, 86; Name, 49th Parallel, NY, 89; Traveling Theory, Jordan Nat Art Gallery, Amman, 92; Sum over Histories (with catalog), Winnipeg Art Gallery, Man, 92, The Power Plant, Toronto, 93, Mackenzie Art Gallery, Regina, Sask, 93, London Regional Art Gallery, Ont, 94 & Glenbow Mus, Calgary, Alta, 94; McIntosh Gallery, London, Ont, 99. *Pos:* Mem bd dir, YYZ Artists' Outlet, Toronto, 82-89. *Teaching:* Toronto Sch Art, 97-. *Awards:* Can Coun B Grants, 91, 92, 94 & 99. *Bibliog:* Jo-anna Issak (auth), The Mothers of Invention, Hobart & William Smith Col, 89; Mark Cheetham (auth), Remembering Post-Modernism, Oxford Univ Press, 91. *Media:* Mixed Media. *Publ:* Auth, Moveable Wounds (An Essay in Composition), Art Metropole, 84; coauth, The interpretation of architecture, YYZ Toronto, 86; auth, The surface of behaviour, Photo Communique, 88; Mortality, the body, and death, Artviews Visual Arts, 89; The salvage paradigm, YYZ Toronto, 90. *Dealer:* Wynick Tuck Gallery 80 Spadina Ave Toronto Ont M5V 2J3 Canada. *Mailing Add:* 243 Macdonell Ave Unit 2 Toronto ON M6R 2A9 Canada

GURSOY, AHMET
PAINTER

b Turkey, Mar 5, 1929; US citizen. *Study:* Tech Univ Istanbul, Turkey, 47-52; Ill Inst Technol, 54-56; Art Students League, 58-63. *Work:* Chase Manhattan Bank; Cornell Univ; St Lawrence Univ; Grey Gallery, NY Univ; Ulrich Mus, Wichita, Kans. *Exhib:* Wells Col, Aurora, NY, 77; Niagara Arts Ctr, Niagara Falls, NY, 77; Mohawk Valley Community Col, Utica, NY, 77; Nassau Community Col, Garden City, NY, 77; Hyden Collection, Glen Falls, NY, 77; and many others. *Awards:* Painting Prize, 21st Ann New Eng Exhib, Silvermine, Conn, 70. *Bibliog:* Grace Glueck (auth), article, New York Times, 68; C Giuliano (auth), article, 68 & Gordon Brown (auth), article, 70, Arts Mag. *Mem:* Fedn Mod Painters & Sculptors (pres, 75-); Silvermine Guild Artists; Music for People (treas, 71-72). *Media:* Oil. *Publ:* Auth, Convergence of Engineering & Art, 70. *Mailing Add:* 490 Bellwood Ave Tarrytown NY 10591-1426

GUSELLA, ERNEST
VIDEO ARTIST

b Calgary, Alta, Can, Sept 13, 1941. *Work:* Pompidou Ctr, Paris; Lenbachhaus, Munich; Mus Mod Art, NY; Nat Gallery Can; Kawaski Mus Art; and others. *Exhib:* Spiral Gallery, Tokyo, 87; Lewbachhaus, Munich, 90; Jamia Miuia Islamia, New Delhi, 93; Univ SFla, Tampa, 94. *Pos:* Dir, Digital DADA Inc. *Teaching:* Guest prof, State Univ NY, Buffalo, 84-87, Jamia Millia Islamia Uni, New Delhi, Univ Manipur, India; guest artist, Allgemeine Geweres Chule, Basel, 90 & Univ Appl Art, Vienna, 90; prof electronic images, Univ SFla, Tampa. *Awards:* Can Coun Grant, 85-86 & 90; Checkerboard Grant, 87; Fulbright Scholar, India, 93-94. *Bibliog:* The 2nd Link, Banff, 83; Dis/Patches: The Learning Channel, 84; Review, Port Washington News, 85. *Media:* Video, Performance. *Publ:* Contribr, Kunst Und Video Book, Dumont Buchverlag, Koln, 83; Clip, Klapp, Bum, Dumont-Koln, 86. *Dealer:* Scan Gallery Tokyo Japan; The Tape Connection Rome Italy

GUSSOW, SUE FERGUSON
PAINTER, EDUCATOR

b Brooklyn, NY, Aug 2, 1935. *Study:* Cooper Union, with Stefano Cusumano & Bob Gwathmey, dipl, 56; Columbia Univ, BS, 60; Tulane Univ, MFA, 64. *Work:* Dallas Mus Fine Arts; New Orleans Mus Art; Philadelphia Free Libr; The Frick Collection Archives, & The Cooper Hewitt Mus of the Smithsonian; and others. *Exhib:* Print Biennial, Brooklyn Mus, 64; Drawings in St Paul, Minn Mus Art, 71-72; Solo Exhibs: Stanford Univ Mus, Calif, 83; Loyola Marymount Univ, Los Angeles, 83; Benton Gallery, Southampton, NY, 87; Ctr Contemp Art, East Hampton, NY, 88; Marcelle Fine Arts, Southampton, NY, 89 & 90; Palace of Journalists, St Petersburg, Russ, 92; Artists of the Springs Invitational, E Hampton, NY, 93-2014; 40 yr retrospective (with catalog), Houghton Gallery, Cooper Union, NY, 97; On the Books Guild Hall E Hampton NY, 2004; Artist Ann, Guild Hall, E Hampton, NY, 87-2014; Urban Visionaries, 7 World Trade Ctr, 2003-2011; Drawing by Drawing, DAC, Copenhagen Denmark, 2011-2012; Peter Marcelle Gallery, Bridgehampton, NY, 2013. *Teaching:* Prof Emer, Sch of Archit, Cooper Union, 1970-; Vis Prof, The Frick Collection 2002-05; vis prof, Royal Academy Sch Archit, Copenhagen, Denmark, 2011; guest lecturer, Royal Acad Sch Arch, Copenhagen, Denmark, 2012, 2014; guest lectr, Aarhus Sch Architecture, Denmark, 2014. *Awards:* Purchase Prize, Drawings USA, Minn Mus Art, 66; Pamela Djerassi Vis Artist Grant, Stanford Univ, 82-83; and others. *Bibliog:* Ann Glenn Crowe (auth), A French Heritage, Art Week, 7/2/83; Paul Goldberger (auth), The NY Times (review p C11), 4/16/97; Zöe Ingalls (auth), The Chronicle of Higher Education (article p B11), 11/21/97; Joan Baum (auth), The Independent, p B4, 9/21/2008; Lawrence Biemiller (auth), Aligning Hands with Minds, The Chronicle of Higher Education, p A13-15, 2/13/2009. *Mem:* Fel of ARC Soc for Arts & Religion in Contemp Cult. *Media:* Oil, Pastel. *Res:* Recipient of Tides Foundation & Graham Foundation grants, 2004-2008. *Collection:* Dore Ashton, Schuylev B Chapin, Diana & David Rockefeller Jr, Carl Djerassi, George & Mary Schmitt Campbell, Morley Safer, The Estates of Werner Kramarsky, Van Deren Coke, John Hejduk, Jeanette Rockefeller, Werner Muensterberger. *Publ:* Ed, Trees, Cooper Union, 85; auth, Women Artist Newsletter Book Review II, III, IV, V, 94, 95 & 96; auth & illus, DRAW POKER, Cooper Union, NY, 97; Drawing Dimensions, frontispiece & illus, Cynthia Maris Dantzic, Prentis Hall, NJ, 98; cover illus & paintings, 100 New York Painters, Schiffer Books, NJ, 2006; auth, Architects Draw, Princeton Architectural Press, NY, 2008. *Mailing Add:* PO Box 1609 Amagansett NY 11930

GUTIERREZ, YOLANDA
SCULPTOR

b Mexico City, Mex, Feb 10, 1970. *Study:* Univ Nac Autonoma de Mex, licenciatura, 87-92. *Work:* Banco de la Repub Biblioteque Luis Angel Avango, Bogota, Colombia; Mus Univ Contemp de Arte de la Univ Nac Autonoma de Mex, Mexico City. *Comn:* Installation ecologique, Xochitla Res naturel, Tepotzotlan, Mex, 98. *Exhib:* Habana - Sao Paolo, Arte, 95; Fluctuations Fugitives, la ferme de Buisson, Nuisel, France, 96; Tierra Livgen, Alvary Carmen T Carrillo Gil, Mexico City, 97; 5th Ann Biennial d'Estanbul, Turkey, 97; Mex ahova punto de patida, Ohio & PR, 97; La Covriente Installation, Culturgent, Lisbon, Port, 98. *Teaching:* Asst prof dons l'atelier d'experimentation insuelle II, Ecole Nat d'Arts Plastiques & de l'Univ Nac Autonoma de Mex, 92-95. *Mailing Add:* c/o Espace d'Art Yvonamor Palix 13 rue Keller F-75011 Paris France

GUTKIN, PETER
SCULPTOR, DESIGNER

b Brooklyn, NY, 1944. *Study:* Tyler Sch Art, Temple Univ, BFA, 66; San Francisco Art Inst, MFA, 68. *Work:* Sheldon Mem Art Gallery, Lincoln, Nebr; Oakland Mus, Calif; NASA/Ames Res Ctr, Mountain View, Calif; Portland Mus Art, Ore; San Francisco Mus Mod Art; and others. *Comn:* NASA/Ames Res Ctr, 87. *Exhib:* Solo exhibs, San Francisco Mus Art, 72, San Francisco Art Inst, 84, Modernism 90, San Francisco & Jernigan Wicker, San Francisco, 95; Menace, Mus Contemp Art, Chicago, 75; Sculpture in Calif 75-80, San Diego Mus Art, Calif, 80; Am Pop Cult Today, Laforet Mus, Tokyo, Japan, 87; Celebrating Modern Art, The Anderson Collection, San Francisco Mus Mod Art, 2000; 25th Anniversary Exhib, San Francisco, Calif, 2004; and others. *Pos:* Pres, Peter Gutkin Furniture & Design. *Teaching:* Instr, Aspen Sch Contemp Art, Colo, 66, Univ Calif, Berkeley, 72-74, San Francisco Art Inst, 78 & Calif Coll Arts & Crafts, 82, 94, 97 & 99. *Awards:* Nat Endowment Humanities & Art Award, 66; Purchase Prize, San Francisco Art Festival, 72; Nat Endowment Arts Fel, 82 & 84; Product Design Award, Resources Coun, 86. *Bibliog:* Article, Compressed constructions, spiderweb sculptures, Art News, 12/77; Howard Junker (auth), San Francisco, Peter Gutkin at 170 Capp St, Art Am, 5/80; Jerome Tarshis (auth), San Francisco, Peter Gutkin at the San Francisco Art Inst, Art in Am Mag, 10/84; Lois Wagner Green (auth), Site specific, Peter Gutkin takes a furniture commission full circle in residential designs for a San Francisco art patron, Interior Design Mag, 5/86. *Media:* Wood; Miscellaneous. *Interests:* Furniture. *Publ:* Thomas Albright (auth), Art in the San Francisco Bay Area, Chronicle Publ; Denise Domerque (auth), Artists Design Furniture, Abrams Publ. *Mailing Add:* 2248 Jerrold Ave Unit 8 San Francisco CA 94124

GUTMAN, BERTHA STEINHARDT
PAINTER, PROFESSOR

b 1951. *Study:* Queens Col, City Univ NY, BA, 72; State Univ NY, Stony Brook, MFA, 91. *Work:* Artist's Space Slide Registry, Soho, NY; Jewish Fed, Oklahoma City. *Exhib:* 58th Ann Mid Yr Exhib, Butler Inst Am Art, Youngstown, Ohio, 94; Hoyt Nat Art Show, Hoyt Inst Fine Arts, New Castle, Pa, 94; Art Exhibit Celebrating Women

Artists, Hutchins Gallery-Long Island Univ, Brookville, NY, 94; Tabletop Narratives, Bryant Lib Gallery, Roslyn, NY, 94; Art Asn Harrisburg, Pa, 96 & 98; Still Life Show, Islip Art Mus, NY, 96; Armory Art Ctr, West Palm Beach, 96; 42nd Ann Long Island Artists Exhib, Heckscher Mus Art, Huntington, NY, 97; Images 97, Hub Galleries, Pa State Univ, 97; The Time Machine, Anchorage Mus Hist & Art, Alaska, 97; Trial by Jury, City Without Walls Gallery, Newark, NJ, 97; Omni Gallery, Uniondale, NY, 99; Art-trium, Huntington, NY, 2001; The Banana Factory, Bethlehem, Pa, 2002. *Pos:* Mus shop mgr, Jewish Mus, NY, 73-77. *Teaching:* Suffolk Community Col, St Joseph's Col, Adelphi Univ, Empire State Col, Nassau Co Community Col; Delaware Co Community Col, Media, Pa. *Awards:* Special Opportunity Stipend, NY Found Arts, 92-94; Grumbacher Gold Medalion, Art Asn Harrisburg, 95; 12th Ann Nat Women Arts Exhib, Second Place in Art, Women Ctr, Archard Ridge Campus, Oakland Community Col, 98; Grumbacher Gold Medallion, Art Asn Harrisburg, 95. *Bibliog:* Eleanor Martin (auth), A doll's house, Times-Herald Rec 94; Table-Top Narratives at Bryant, Roslyn News, 94; Dina Roberts (auth), Metaphorical Table-Top Narratives, Manhattan Arts Int, 95. *Mem:* Nat Asn Women Artists; Coll Art Asn; Asn Community Coll Profs of Art and Art Hist. *Media:* Oil on Canvas or Linen. *Publ:* Auth, Your Living Art, McGraw Hil Coll Div, 2001. *Dealer:* Gallery 84 Inc 50 W 57th St New York NY 10019. *Mailing Add:* 165 Somerset Dr Blue Bell PA 19422

GUTZEIT, FRED
PAINTER, EDUCATOR

b Cleveland, Ohio. *Study:* Yale Norfolk Summer Sch, 61; Cleveland Inst Art, Mary C Paige Traveling Scholar, 62; Hunter Col, MA, 79. *Work:* Aldrich Mus, Ridgefield, Conn; Alternative Mus, NY; Fashion Moda; Cleveland Art Asn; Chemical Bank, NY; Cleveland State Univ; Mus Modern Art, NY; Cleveland State Univ Art Coll, Cleveland, Oh. *Exhib:* Biennial, Butler Inst Am Art, 65; Contemp Images in Watercolor, Akron Art Inst, 76; solo exhibs, NY State Artist Series, Herbert F Johnson Mus, Cornell Univ, 77 & Distinguished Alumnus, Cleveland Inst Art, 77; Personal Visions, Places/Spaces, Bronx Mus Arts, 78; May Show, Cleveland Mus Art, 82; A Look Back, A Look Forward, Aldrich Mus, 82; Mansfield Art Ctr, Mansfield, Ohio, 2007; Pocket Utopia, Brooklyn, 2008; Next Post, Ruper Ravens Contemp, Newark, 2009; Andre Zarre Gallery, New York, 2010; Sideshow Gallery, Brooklyn, 2012; Conde Nast Lobby, Times Sq, NY, 2011; Rodale Bldg Lobby, NY, 2011; Sideshow Gallery, 2012; Tregoning & Co Gallery, 2013; NY Public Libr, Mulberry St Branch, 2013; Brian Morris Gallery, NY, 2014. *Teaching:* Instr painting, Philadelphia Col Art, 79-82, Brooklyn Mus Art Sch, 81-84 & Cleveland Inst Art, Lacoste France, 84 & 85; vis assoc prof, Pratt Inst, 86-2000; Cleveland Inst Art, 95-97; adj asst prof, City Univ New York, 97-; MFA mentor, Univ Arts, Philadelphia, Pa, 2007-2009. *Awards:* Pollock-Krasner Found Grant, 99-2000, 2006-2007, 2013-2014. *Bibliog:* Patricia Eakins (auth), Fred Gutzeit: An organic approach to images, Am Artist Mag, 10/75 & article, Arts Mag, 4/77; Pete Hamill (auth), Tools As Art, Hechinger Collection, Harry Abrams Publ, 95. *Media:* Acrylic, Watercolor; Inkjet Print. *Specialty:* Fine Arts. *Interests:* Photography, Printmaking. *Dealer:* Joe Amrhein Pierogi Gallery Brooklyn NY; Richard Timperio Sideshow Gallery Brooklyn NY; Rupert Ravens Contemporary Paterson NJ; Yijing Li, Beijing, China; Bill Tregoning Tregoning and Co Cleveland Oh; Brian Morris Gallery NY. *Mailing Add:* 264 Bowery New York NY 10012

GUYER, PAUL
EDUCATOR

b New York, NY, Jan 13, 1948. *Study:* Harvard Univ, PhD. *Pos:* vpres, American Soc for Aesthetics, 2009-2010, pres, 2010-; vpres, Am Philosophical Asn, 2010-2011, pres, 2011-2012. *Teaching:* Teacher, Univ Pa & Univ Ill, Chicago, formerly; Florence RC Murray prof humanities & philosophy, Univ Pa, formerly; Jonathan Nelson prof philosophy, Brown Univ, 2012-. *Awards:* Franklin J Matchette Prize, American Philosophical Asn; Harvard Centennial Medal; John Guggenheim Mem Fellowship; Rsch prize, Alexander von Humboldt Found. *Mem:* Am Philosophical Asn; Am Soc Aesthetics; N Am Kant Soc. *Res:* Kant, History, Philosophy, Aesthetics. *Publ:* Auth, Kant's System of Nature and Freedom, 2005, Values of Beauty: Historical Essays in Aesthetics, 2005, Knowledge, Reason, and Taste: Kant's Response to Hume, 2008; A History of Modern Aesthetics, 2014. *Mailing Add:* Brown University Dept Philosophy Box 1918 Providence RI 02912

GUYTON, TYREE
SCULPTOR, PAINTER

b 1955. *Study:* Ctr Creative Studies, Detroit, 1980-82. *Work:* Detroit Inst Arts; Univ Mich Mus; Studio Mus Harlem; Charles Wright Mus African Am Hist; Del Art Inst. *Exhib:* Solo exhibs include The Heidelberg Proj, Detroit, 1986-, Front Room Gallery, Detroit, 1988, Detroit Inst Arts, 1990, LedisFlam Gallery, New York, 1991, Liberal Arts Gallery, Detoit, 1992, Alexa Lee Gallery, Ann Arbor, Mich, 1994 & 1995, Univ Ind, 1996, C-Pop Gallery, Detroit, 1998, Harvard Univ, 2000, Gallery 4731, Detroit, 2002, Auburn Univ, Ala, 2004, Charles H Wright Mus African Am Hist, Detroit, 2005, Univ Mich Bus Sch, 2006; group exhibs include Visionaries, Urban Inst Contemp Art, Grand Rapids, Mich, 1994; Folk & Outsider Art, Univ Mich Mus Art, Ann Arbor, 1996; Outsider Art in the Midwest, Minn Mus Art, St Paul, 1996; Artists Take on Detroit, Detroit Inst Arts, 2001; D'Troit, GAS Gallery, New York, 2003. *Pos:* Founder, Heidelberg Proj, Mich non-profit community arts org, Detroit, 1986-. *Awards:* David A Harmond Award, City of Detroit, 1989; Spirit of Detroit Award, 1989; Testimonial Resolution Award, Wayne County, Mich, 1990; Michiganian of Yr Award, 1991; Mich Artist of Yr, 1991; Humanity in the Arts Award, Wayne State Univ Ctr Peace & Conflict Studies, 1992; Vol Community Serv Award, Ann Arbor Youth Vol Corps, 1995; Best Known Artist in Metro Detroit, Detroit Free Press, 2001; Wayne County Int Artist Award, 2003; Rudy Bruner Award Urban Excellence, 2005; Pollock-Krasner Found Grant, 2007

GUYTON, WADE
PAINTER

b Hammond, Ind, 1972. *Study:* Univ Tenn, Knoxville, BA, 90-95; Hunter Col, MFA, 96-98. *Work:* Kunsthaus Zurich; Whitney Mus Am Art; Tate Mus, London; San Francisco Mus Modern Art; Princeton Univ Art Mus; Pinakothek der Moderne, Munich; Ctr Georges Pompidou, Paris; MoMA, NY; Mus Ludwig, Cologne; Mus Contemporary Art, Los Angeles, Chgo; Moderna Museet, Stockholm; Museo di Arte Moderna e Contemporanea di Trento e Rovereto; Musee d'art Moderne et Contemporain, Geneva; Knoxville Mus Art; Dallas Mus Art, Tex; Art Inst Chgo. *Exhib:* Solo exhibs, Andrew Kreps Gallery Project Space, NY, 99, Elements of an Incomplete Map, Artists Space, NY, 2003, Objects are Much More Familiar, Power House, Memphis, 2004, Art 36 Statements, Galerie Francesca Pia, Basel, 2005, Color, Power & Style, Kunstverein Hamburg, Germany, 2005, Hard hat Editions, Geneva, 2006, West London Projects, 2006, Haubrokshows, Berlin, 2006, Galerie Gisela Capitain, Cologne, 2007, Friedrich Petzel Gallery, NY, 2007, 2010, 2011, 2012, Galerie Chantal Crousel, Paris, 2008, Gio Marconi, Milan, 2009, Greene Naftall, NY, 2009, Mus Ludwig, Cologne, 2009, Whitney Mus Am Art, NY, 2010, 2012, Baltimore Mus Art, Md, 2010, Mus Ludwig, Cologne, 2010, Gio'Marconi, Milan, 2011, Grafisches Kabinett, Secession, Vienna, 2011, Galerie Francesca Pia, 2011, Kunsthaus Bregenz, 2013, Kunsthalle Zurich, 2013; group exhibs, Against the New Passeism; Understanding this is only the beginning, hope for the end; Build, Destroy, Do Nothing, Andrew Kreps Gallery, NY, 99, After the Diagram, White Box Gallery, 2000-2001, Retrofit, Lombard-Freid Fine Arts, 2001-02, X, Power House, Memphis, 2003, Elements of An Incomplete Map, Artists Space, NY, 2003, Whitney Biennial, Whitney Mus Am Art, 2004, Uncertain States of America, Astrup Fearnley Musset for Moderne Kunst, Olso, Norway, 2005, Delete/How to Make A Perfect Ghost, Anton Kern Gallery, NY, 2006, Imagination Becomes Reality, Sammlung Goetz, Munich, 2006, The Lath Picture Show, Friedrich Petzel Gallery, NY, 2007, Degree Zero, Richard Telles Fine Art, LA, 2007, Someone Else with My Fingerprints, Galerie Chantal Crousel, Paris, 2007, Lyon Biennale, Mus of Contemp Art, Lyon, 2007, Records Played Backwords, curated by Daniel Bimbaum, Modern Inst, Glasgow, 2008, A New High in Getting Low, John Connelly Presents, NY, 2008, Torino Triennale-50 lune di Saturno, curated by Daniel Birnbaum, Torino, 2008, A Wild Night and Another Road, Altman-Siegal Gallery, San Francisco, 2009, Fax, The Drawing Center, NY, 2009, 53rd Int Art Exhib Biennale, Venice, 2009, 55th Int Art Exhib Biennale, 2013, Gavlak Gallery, Palm Beach, 2010, Ribordy Contemporary, 2011, Dallas Mus Art, Tex, 2011, Mus Contemporary Art Chicago, 2012, Almine Reich Gallery, Art Basel, 2012, Palazzo delle Esposizioni, Rome, 2013. *Bibliog:* Klaus Kertess (auth), Painting in the Age of Digital Reproduction, Art in America, pp 74-73, 2013; Achim Hochdorfer (auth), Reviews: Wade Guyton, Artforum, pp 235-237, 2/2013; Christopher Howard (auth), Wade Guyton, Modern Painters, 3/2013; Debra Singer (auth), Wade Guyton, 2004, Artists for Artists: Fifty Years of the Foundation for Contemporary Arts, p 161, 2013; and many others. *Dealer:* Petzel Gallery 456 W 18th St New York NY 10011. *Mailing Add:* c/o Petzel Gallery 456 W 18th St New York NY 10011

GUZAK, KAREN W
PAINTER, PRINTMAKER, PUBLIC ARTIST

b Cambridge, Mass, May 21, 1939. *Study:* Univ Colo, BS (Boettcher Scholar), 61; Cornish Inst Arts, BFA, 76. *Work:* Brooklyn Mus, NY; Portland Art Mus, Ore; Whatcom Co Art Mus, Bellingham, Wash; NY Pub Libr Print Collection, NY; City of Seattle, Wash. *Comn:* design for sculpted elevator enclosure, Sea Tac Airport, Seattle, 94; balcony railing, King Co Coun Chambers, Seattle, Wash, 98; sculpture garden & wall murals, South Seattle Community Coll Libr, 99-2000; landmark sculpture and gateways, Overlake Ctr, Sound Transit, 2002; plaza sculpture, Redmond Town Ctr, 2003; Painted Steel (eight sculptures for city of Bellevue), Wash, 2003-2007. *Exhib:* 22nd Ann Print Show, Brooklyn Mus, NY, 81; Seattle Artists, San Francisco Mus Mod Art, Calif, 83; Laura Russo Gallery, Portland, Ore, 91 & 96; Foster White Gallery, Seattle, Wash, 91, 94, 96, 98 & 2000; Boston Printmakers, 43rd Print Exhib, De Cordova Mus, Mass, 91; Am Print Survey, Baylor Univ, 91; Forum: Art & Sch New Dimensions, Gutersloh, Ger, 94; 9th Nat Computer Art Invitational, Eastern Wash Univ, 96 & 99; Int Print Invitational, Portland Art Mus, 97; Int Exhib Electronic Prints, Arcade II, Univ Broghton, Eng, 97-98; Tacoma Art Mus, Wash, 2002; Ctr Contemp Art, Seattle, Wash, 2000; Edmonds Community Col, 2004. *Pos:* Art comnr, King Co Arts Comn, 81-86, Metro Transit Tunnel Art Comt, 85-91; developer, proj mgr & pres, Sunny Arms Artists' Coop, Seattle, Wash, 88-90; developer & proj mgr, Union Art Cooperative, 93-94; proj mgr, On the Bds Contemp Performance Ctr, 97-98; chair Design Review Bd, city of Snohomish, Wash, 2002-; mayor, City of Snohomish, 2010-. *Teaching:* Instr, Univ Ore Workshop, High Tech/Low Tech, 89. *Awards:* Merit Award, 17th Nat Print Completion, Schenectady Mus, 94. *Bibliog:* Frank Pepper (auth), Art of the Electronic Age, Abrahms Publ, 94; Justin Henderson (auth), The art of co-op living, Interiors Mag, 94; Lois Allan (auth), Contemporary Printmaking in the Northwest, Craftsman House Press, 62-65, 97; Northwest Originals: Washington Women and Their Art, Matria Media Press, 90. *Mem:* Ctr Contemp Art (bd dir, 87); Northwest Print Coun (bd dir, 84-88, hist design rev bd, 2000-); On the Boards (bd dir, 87-90); Artist Trust (bd dir, 94); Artist Trust (pres bd, 96-2000). *Media:* Painting, Prints, Public Art. *Specialty:* Davidson Galleries, Prints & Paintings. *Interests:* Yoga, Teaching Yoga, local politics. *Collection:* Brooklyn Mus, NYC Library, City of Seattle, Tacoma Art Mus, Portland Art Mus, Whation Cty, Art Mus, WA. *Publ:* Auth, Leonardo Between Geometry & Gesture, J Int Soc Arts, Sci & Technol, 19-22, Vol 30, No 1, 97; Chaos, Order and Computers, Contemp Impressions, Vol 7, 99; co-auth, website, www.angelarmsworks.com. *Dealer:* Davidson Galleries 313 Occidental Ave S Seattle WA 98104; Laura Russo Gallery 805 NW 21st Portland OR 97209. *Mailing Add:* 230 Ave B Snohomish WA 98290

GUZEVICH-SOMMERS, KRESZENZ (CYNTHIA)
PAINTER, INSTRUCTOR

b Munich, Ger, May 24, 1923; US citizen. *Study:* Acad Art, Munich; also with Frank Gervasi, Paul Strisik, Louis Krupp, Helen Van Wyk, Ramon Froman & Ken Gore; Acad, Florence, Italy. *Work:* First Nat Bank, Las Cruces, NMex; Truth or Consequences Mus, NMex; Branif Airline Collection. *Exhib:* El Paso Mus Art Exhib, Tex; Grand Nat Exhib, NY; Southwest Intercult Exhib, El Paso; Artists Equity Show, Albuquerque, NMex; Truth or Consequences Hist Mus; NY Overseas Press Club, O'Brians Gallery, Scottsdale, Ariz; int Govt Sponsored shows, starting Venezuela, ending in Mex City; solo exhib, Branigan Cult Ctr, Las Cruces, NMex, 2007.

Collection Arranged: Portfolio in Nat Mus for Woman Artists in Wash, D.C,. *Teaching:* Instr painting, workshops in var states & pvt studio, 65-. *Awards:* Artist of Year & Best in Show Award, Black Range Artists, 68; Best in Show Award, NMex Art League, 69; Largest Exhib in NMex Award. *Mem:* Am Artists Prof League; El Paso Mus Art Asn; Artists Equity Asn; Accademia Italia Delle Arti e Del Lavoro. *Media:* Oil, Acrylic, Egg Tempera. *Interests:* Judging Int dog shows. *Collection:* Branif Airine. *Mailing Add:* 68 Party Time Pl Las Cruces NM 88005

GUZMÁN, DANIEL
DRAFTSMAN
b Mexico City, Mexico, 1964. *Study:* Univ Nat Autónoma de México, Vis Arts, Mexico City, 1989-93. *Work:* West Collection, Oaks, PA; Espacio 1414, Santurce, Puerto Rico. *Exhib:* Solo exhibs include Galería Arena México, Guadalajara, 1994, Vilma Gold Gallery, London, 2002, Annet Gelink Gallery, Ámsterdam, Netherlands, 2004, Kurimanzutto, Mexico City, 2007; two-person exhibs include New Mus, New York, (With Steven Shearer), 2008; group exhibs include In Situ, Licenciado Verdad 13, Mexico City, 1991; Acne, Mus Arte Mod, Mexico City, 1996; Montreal Biennale, Cte Int D'Art, Canada, 2002; Happiness, Mori Art Mus, Tokyo, 2003; September Back Up, Isola Art Ctr, Milan, Italy, 2005; Playback, Mus d'art mod la ville Paris, 2006; Berlin Biennial 5, 2008; Life on Mars, 55th Carnegie Int, Pittsburg, 2008. *Awards:* First Place Installation Prize, X'Teresa Espacio Alternativo, Mexico, 1996. *Dealer:* kurimanzutto mazatlán 5 depto t-6 col condes 06140 Mexico City Mexico; Vilma Gold 6 Minerva St London England E2 9EH UK

GWYN, WOODY
PAINTER
b San Antonio, Tex, 1944. *Study:* Pa Acad Fine Arts. *Exhib:* Solo shows incl Canyon Art Gallery, Tex, 65, Meredith Long & Co, Houston, 68, 69, 70, 71, 72, 73, 74, 75, 77, Elaine Horwitch Gallery, Santa Fe, 78, Allan Stone Gallery, New York, 80, 82, Icons-Iconoclasts, New York, NMex, 81, Laguna Gloria Art Mus, Austin, 81, Modernism Gallery, San Francisco, 84, 86, McAllen Int Mus, Tex, 86, Gerald Peters Gallery, Santa Fe, 88, 2002, 2007, Katharina Rich Perlow Gallery, New York, 89, Louis Newman Galleries, Beverly Hills, 93, Horwitch-LewAllen Gallery, Santa Fe, 95, Cline-LewAllen Gallery, Santa Fe, 97, MB Mod, New York, 2000; group shows incl Norfolk Mus Arts and Scis, Va, 70; Smithsonian Inst, Wash, DC, 71; Mus Fine Arts, Santa Fe, 72, 76, 77; Marion Koogler McNay Art Inst, San Antonio, 73; Contemp Arts Mus, Houston, 74; Elaine Horwitch Gallery, Santa Fe, 79; Western States Art Asn, Wash, DC, 85; Tel Aviv Mus, Israel, 87; Rockwell Mus, Corning, NY, 87; Katharina Rich Perlow Gallery, New York, 88, 92; Gerald Peters Gallery, Santa Fe, 90, 2001, 2003; Hubbard Mus Invitational, 90-91; South Eastern Ctr Contemp Art, 91; Fletcher Gallery, Santa Fe, 94; Horwitch-Newman Gallery, Los Angeles, 96; Phoenix Mus Art, 97; MB Mod, New York, 98; LewAllen Contemp, Santa Fe, 99; Philbrook Mus Art, Tulsa, 99; Van Vechten-Lineberry Libr, 2001; Arnot Mus, Elmira, NY, 2003. *Dealer:* Hacienda de Galisteo Galisteo NM 87401; Gerland Peters Gallery 1011 Paseo de Peralta Santa Fe NM 87501. *Mailing Add:* c/o Gerald Peters Gallery 24 E 78th St New York NY 10021

GXI
PAINTER, WRITER
b Cedar Creek Homestead, Ill. *Study:* Princeton Univ, BA, 69; NY Univ, MA, 92. *Comn:* Mural, State of Ill, 78. *Exhib:* Art Gallery Ont, Toronto, Canada, 74; Bronx Mus Arts, NY, 85; Insul Hombrick, Koln, Ger, 90; Henie Onstad Art Ctr, Oslo, Norway, 95. *Media:* Digital Painting. *Publ:* Artificial Evolution, Mass Inst Technol Press, 97. *Mailing Add:* 361 Canal St New York NY 10013

GYATSO, GONKAR
PRINTMAKER
b Lhasa, Tibet, 1961. *Study:* Central Inst Nationalities, Bejing, China, BA, 1984; Chelsea Coll Art & Design, London, MFA (with distinction), 2000. *Exhib:* Solo exhibs, Modern Tibert Art of Gyatso, The Revolution Exhib Hall of Tibet, Lhasa, Tibet, 1987, The Footprints of Budhha, Int Cultural Centre, New Dehli, India, 1996, Tibetan Word-Art of Commun, The Sweet Tea House-Contemporary Tibetan Art Gallery, London, 2004, Gonkar Gyatso Retrospective, Art Dubai, 2008 and others; The Sweet Tea House, Lassa, Tibet, 1985-1987, Radiant Transmission Contemporary Art & Human Rights, October Gallery, London, 2003, Rethinking Tradition-Contemporary Tibetan Artists in the West, Visual Art Gallery, Emory Univ, Atlanta, 2005, Waves on the Turquoise Lake: Contemporary Expressions of Tibetan Art, Colo Univ Art Mus & The Colo Collection, Boulder, 2006, Terrain, inIVA, London, Terrain, 2007, Tibetan Encounters Contemporary Meets Tradition, Neuhoff Gallery (organized by Anna Maria and Fabio Rossi), NY, 2007, Contemporary Tibetan Art, Art Hong Kong, 2008, Return to Lhasa, Red Gate Gallery, Beijing, China, 2008, Unbound: New Art for a New Century, Newark Mus, NY, 2009, Making Worlds, 53rd Int Art Exhib Biennale, Venice, 2009, Tibet Art Now: on the threshold of a new future, Tibet Art Gallery, Temple, Amsterdam, 2009, and several others. *Collection Arranged:* The Sweet Tea House Contemporary Tibetan Art Gallery, London, 2003; Immigration and Diversity Mus, London, 2004; Pitt Rivers Mus, Univ Oxford, 2005; Rossi & Rossi, London, 2006; Red Gate Gallery, Bejing, China, White Rabbit Gallery, Australia, Burger Collection, Switzerland, Crocker Art Mus, Calif, 2007; White Rabbit Gallery, Australia, Queensland Art Gallery/Gallery of Modern Art, Australia, 2008. *Awards:* Leverhulme Trust Fel, 2003. *Mailing Add:* 264 Globe Rd London United Kingdom E2 0JD

GYERMEK, STEPHEN A
EDUCATOR
b Budapest, Hungary, Nov 9, 1930. *Study:* Rijks Akad voor Beeldende Kunsten, Amsterdam, Holland, with Heinrich Campendonk; Academia de Bellas Artes Madrid, Spain; Univ Okla. *Comn:* Murals, Convent at Madrid, Spain, 55 & US Embassy, Spain, 55; stained glass windows, St Gregory's Abbey, Shawnee, Okla & St Benedict Church, Ada, Okla. *Exhib:* Amsterdam, 52-53; Madrid, 54; Okla Art Ctr, 60. *Collection Arranged:* Archaeology, Europe, Near & Far East, Egypt; Am Indians & Central & South American Ethnology; Paintings from the Italian Renaissance; 19th Century Am Paintings; plus others. *Pos:* Dir, Gerrer Mus & Art Gallery, Shawnee, Okla, 57-62; actg dir, Stovall Mus Sci & Hist, Univ Okla, 62-65; dir, Pioneer Mus & Haggin Art Galleries, Stockton, Calif, 65-70. *Teaching:* Lectr painting methods & religious art; asst prof art hist & art, Univ Okla; instr art hist, San Joaquin Delta Col, 67-. *Awards:* Prizes & Van Alabbe Award, Amsterdam, Holland, 52. *Mailing Add:* San Joaquin Delta College Dept Art 5151 Pacific Ave Stockton CA 95207-6370

GYUNG JIN, SHIN
SCULPTOR, VIDEO ARTIST
b Seoul, South Korea, May 22, 1983. *Study:* Seoul Nat Univ, BFA, 2006; Columbia Univ, MFA, 2010. *Exhib:* Columbia Univ First Year Show, Wallach Gallery, New York, 2009; Columbia Univ MFA Thesis Exhib, Fisher Landau Ctr Art, New York, 2010; B-sides, 6-8 Month Proj Space, New York, 2010; Subtle Anxiety, Doosan Gallery, New York, 2010. *Teaching:* Teaching assist, Columbia univ, 2009-. *Awards:* Prize for Young Artist, Daekyo Found, 2006. *Bibliog:* Tara Kyle (auth), City Life Becomes Art in New Exhib, DNAinfo, 7/31/2010. *Publ:* Subtle Anxiety: This Is How You Feel Now, Doosan Gallery, 2010

H

HA, HYOUNGSUN
PHOTOGRAPHER
b Korea. *Study:* Seoul Inst Arts, Seoul, S Korea, 1993; Sch Visual Arts, BFA, 1996; Pratt Inst, Brooklyn, MFA, 1998. *Work:* Mus Fine Arts, Houston. *Exhib:* Exhibs include Going Through, Sch Visual Art Eastside Gallery, New York, 1995; Mentor Show, One Club Gallery, New York, 1996; Pan Opticon, Swiss Inst Gallery, New York, 1998; Confluence of Cultures, Pratt Manhattan Ctr, 1999; Parsons Benefit Auction, Swan Galleries, New York, 2000; Freedom/Aftermath, Korean Cultural Ctr, Washington, 2001; Illuminance, Buddy Holly Ctr, Lubbcock, Tex, 2002; Moments of Clarity, Sotheby's, NY, 2002; Pass Age Now, Gallery Int, Baltimore, 2003; Green Light, Gallery Korea, New York, 2004. *Awards:* En Foco New Works Photography Award, 2002; Vision Award, First Prize, N Mex, 2003; Clark French Fel, Johnson, Vt, 2003

HAACK, CYNTHIA R
PAINTER, PRINTMAKER
b Eagle Bend, Minn. *Study:* St Cloud State Univ, Minn, AE, 53; Univ Wyo, Laramie, 54; Idaho State Coll, Pocatello, 57-58. *Work:* Wachovia Bank; Glaxo Pharmaceuticals; Burlington Bag & Baggage; Weaver, Bennett & Bland, Matthews, NC; Terry Edwards Assocs, Matthews, NC; Bank of Am, Charlotte, NC; The Schiele Mus, Gastonia, NC. *Exhib:* Invitational, Winston-Salem Arts & Sci Gallery, NC, 79; RSVP Ann Show, Pittsburgh, 86-88; NC Watercolor Soc, 90-2008; Festival In The Park, Charlotte, NC, 92; Charlotte/Mecklenburg Co Sr Games Exhib, 93-2010; A Visual Harvest Show, Gaston Co Artists Guild, Gastonia, NC, 2006; Ann Shows, Matthews Artists Guild, Matthews, NC, 2007, 2008, 2009, 2010; Mint Hill Arts, 1st ann, 2009, 2010; Guild of Charlotte Artists, 2011, 2012, and 2014. *Teaching:* Pvt lessons, 61-66; instr painting, Rawls Mus, Courtland, Va, 72-73. *Awards:* First place Oils & Acrylics, Mooresville Art Guild, Fall Show, 2004; Hon Mention, Stanley Co Artists Guilds, Art Explosion, NC, 2008; 3rd place, Matthews Artist Guild, 2010. *Bibliog:* Staff, Southside scenes, Daily Press Newspaper, 73; Barclay Sheaks (auth), Landscape illusion, 73; Lynn Bonney (auth), Travels inspire art, Emporia Gazette, 81; Becker (auth), Haack donates painting for fundraiser, Independent News Herald, 93. *Mem:* NC Watercolor Soc (sig mem); Guild of Charlotte Artists. *Media:* Acrylic. *Dealer:* Seaside gallery 2716 Virginia Dare trail South Nags Head NC 27959. *Mailing Add:* 9400 Marshbrooke Rd Matthews NC 28105-8499

HAACKE, HANS CHRISTOPH
SCULPTOR, CONCEPTUAL ARTIST
b Cologne, Ger, Aug 12, 1936. *Study:* Staatl Werkakademie, Kassel, Ger, MFA; Atelier 17, Paris, with SW Hayter; Tyler Sch Art, Philadelphia; Hon DFA, Oberlin Col, 1991. *Hon Degrees:* D, Bauhaus Univ, Weimer, Germany, 1999. *Work:* Centre Georges Pompidou, Paris; Tate Gallery, London; Mod Museet, Stockholm; Art Gallery Ont, Toronto; Nat Gallery Can, Ottawa; and many others. *Comn:* courtyard, Reichstag Bldg, Berlin, Ger. *Exhib:* Solo Exhibs: Victoria Micro Gallery, London, 1987, John Weber Gallery, NY, 1988, 1990, 1992 & 1994, Mus Nat d'art Mod, Centre Georges Pompidou, Paris, 1989, Venice Biennial, Ger Pavilion, 1993; Documenta, Kassel, 1972, 1982 & 1987; Venice Biennial, 1976 & 1978; Sydney Biennial, 1984 & 1990; Portikus, Frankfort, 2000; Serpentine Gallery, London, 2001; Generali Found, Fienna, 2002; Walker Art Ctr, 2003; Mus Contemp Art, Los Angeles, 2004; Andrea Rosen Gallery, New York, 2005; Paula Cooper Gallery, New York, 2005, 2008 & 2009; Jim Kempner Fine Art, New York, 2006; PS 1, New York, 2008; Gwang-Ju Biennale, 7th Annual, S Korea, 2008; The Hague Sculpture Ctr, Netherlands, 2008; Armand Bartos, New York, 2009; Kaleidoscope, Fribourg, Switzerland, 2009; Hans Hackle: Weather or not, x Iniative, NY. *Teaching:* Prof art emer, Cooper Union, 1967-2002; guest prof, Hochschule Bildende Kunste, Hamburg, Germany, 1973, 1994, Gesamthochschule Essen, 1979; regents lectr, Univ Calif, Berkeley, 1997. *Awards:* Guggenheim Fel, 1973; Nat Endowment Arts Fel, 1978; Golden Lion, Venice Biennale, 1993; Prize of Helmut-Kraft-Stiftung, 2001; Distinguished Teaching Art Award, Coll Art Asn, 2002. *Bibliog:* Jack Burnham (auth), Hans Haacke's cancelled show at the Guggenheim, Artforum, 5/1971; Douglas Crimp, Yve-Alain Bois, Rosalind Krauss (interview), October, Vol 30, fall 1984; Benjamin Buchlon (auth), Hans Haacke: memory and instrumental reason, Art Am, 2/1988. *Media:* All. *Publ:* Auth, Working conditions, Artforum, summer 1981; Museums, Managers of consciousness, Art in Am, 1984; In the Vice, Art J, fall 1991; coauth, Bodenlos, 1993; Libre-Echange, 1994. *Dealer:* Paula Cooper Gallery 534 W 21st St New York NY. *Mailing Add:* Paula Cooper Gallery 534 W 21st St New York NY 10011

HAAR, TOM
PHOTOGRAPHER, FILMMAKER

b Tokyo, Japan, June 2, 1941; US citizen. *Study:* San Francisco State Col, BA, 64; Univ Hawaii, MFA, 67; Alexei Bradovitch Design Lab, scholar, 68; Int Ctr Photog Advan Workshop, scholar, 75. *Work:* Hawaii State Found Cult & Arts, Contemp Mus. *Exhib:* solo exhibs, Green Collections Gallery, Tokyo, 80, Capen Gallery, State Univ NY, Buffalo, 81, Hamanoya Gallery, Tokyo, 81, Space Art Gallery, Seoul, Korea, 83, Amono Gallery Osaka, Japan, 83, Univ Tsukuba Gallery, Japan, 84 & Nagase Photo Salon, Tokyo, Japan, 86; Three Photographers: Tom Hoor, Lisa Kanemoto and Aaron Dygart, Honolulu Acad Arts, Graphic Gallery, 87; The Second Ann Flora Ho'omaluhia, Ho'omaluhia, Hawaii, 87; Koa Gallery, Kapiolani Community Col, 88; On/Off Paper - An Alumni Exhib, Univ Hawaii Art Gallery, 88; traveling exhibs, Artist of Hawaii, Honolulu Acad Arts, 88, Our Elders, Ourselves: Hawaii 1890-1990, funded by Hawaii Comt Humanities, 90, Budapest Art Gallery, Hungary, 91, Gallery Saka, Tokyo, Japan, 91 & Image XVIII, Amfac Plaza Exhib Rm, 92; and others. *Teaching:* Instr photog, Haystack Mountain Sch Crafts, Maine, 73 & 80 & Univ Hawaii, 74; vis prof photog, Seoul Inst Arts, Korea, 83 & Univ Tsukuba, Japan, 84-86; lectr photog, Kapiolani Community Col, Hawaii, 87-90. *Awards:* Grants, Japan Found & Ishibashi Found, 79, Univ Tsukuba Proj Grant, 84 & Asian Cult Coun Proj Grant, 85. *Publ:* Auth, Color Communication (film), Univ Hawaii, 67; asst dir, Artists of Hawaii (film), Honolulu, 9/75; producer & dir, Festival at Mizumi (film), Japan, 79; dir & camera, PLPL (film), Miami, 82; ed & chief planner, Photo Newsletter (article), Gallery Min, Tokyo, 86-87. *Mailing Add:* 1650 St Louis Dr Honolulu HI 96816-1923

HAAS, RICHARD JOHN
PAINTER, MURALIST

b Spring Green, Wis, Aug 29, 1936. *Study:* Univ Wis, Milwaukee, BA, 59; Univ Minn, MFA, 64. *Work:* Mus Mod Art, Metrop Mus Art & Whitney Mus Am Art, NY; Yale Univ Art Gallery, New Haven, Conn; Walker Art Ctr, Minneapolis; St Louis Mus Art, Mo; Brooklyn Mus Art, NY; Nat Acad Design, NY & Wash, DC; NY Hist Soc; Smithsonian Inst, Wash, DC; Williams Coll Mus Art, Mass; Fort Worth Modern Art Mus; Boston Mus Fine Art; Mus Art Inst Chgo. *Comn:* Huntsville, Tex, 91, 95; Pittsburgh Cult Trust, 93; Fed Courthouse, Kans City, Kans, 94; Gateway to the Waterfront (murals), City of Yonkers, NY, 97; Co Courthouse, Sarasota, Fla, 98; Fed Courthouse, Beckley, W Va, 99; Nashville Pub Libr, Nashville, Tenn, 2003; History of Penn State 1950-2000 (mural), Hub Robeson Ctr, Pa State Univ, Pa, 2005; exterior mural, JD Carlisle Group, NY City, 2005; Lakewood Pub Libr, 2007; NJ Rapid Transit, Bayonne Hub Station Murals, 2010; Homewood, Ill downtown murals, 2011; Homewood Ill Phase 3, 2011, Phase 4, 2012, Phase 5, 2013. *Exhib:* Solo shows incl Michael Ingbar Gallery, NY, 2002, John Szoke Editions, NY, 2003, Elisabeth Michitsch, Vienna, Austria, 2005, David Findlay Jr Gallery, 2006, Boston Coll Archit, 2006, Gerald Peters Gallery, Dallas, 2008, Palmer Mus Art, State Col, Pa, 2008, Villa Terrace Mus, Milwaukee, 2008, The Old Print Shop, 2008, Richard Haas: Huntsville and Other Texas Project, 2009, Gerald Peters Gallery, Dallas, Texas, Permanent Mural Installation, Century Asn, New York, 2009, Harmon Meek Gallery, Naples, Fla, 2012, 2013; Group shows incl Brooke Alexander Gallery, 72, 76, 80, 85 & 89; Galerie Biedermann, Munich, Ger, 78; Museum of the City of NY, 2002, Fabric Workshop & Mus, Philadelphia, Pa, 2003, Mary Ryan Gallery, NY, 2003, Lower Manhattan Cult Coun, NY, 2005, Frederick Baker Gallery, Chicago, Ill, 2005, Hudson River Mus, Yonkers, NY, 2006, Nat Acad Mus, NY, 2006, 2007, Ctr for Contemp Printmaking, Norwalk, Conn, 2007; Drawn by New York, NY Hist Soc, 2008; Recent Acquisitions, Nat Acad Mus, NY, 2008; Town and Country, David Fundlay Jr Gallery, NY, 2008; Prof Painters Exhib, Century Asn, NY, 2009; The Print Club of NY: 17 Years of Commissioned Prints, Nat Arts Club, NY, 2009; 184th Ann Exhib, New York, 2009; Dutch New York, Hudson River Mus, Yonkers, NY, 2009; Collecting for a New Millenium, the Hudson River Mus, Yonkers, 2010; Big Paper Winter, Woodward Gallery, New York, 2010; Hudson River Mus, Yonkers, NY, 2011; David Findlay Jr Gallery, 2012; Printworks, Chgo, Ill, 2012; Century Asn, NY, 2013; Harmon Meek Gallery, 2013. *Pos:* New York City Art Comn, 76-79; bd mem, Pub Art Fund, 80-88 & Preservation League, NY, 83-90, Skowhegan Sch Painting & Sculpture, Hudson River Mus; bd governors, Skowhegan Bd Art, 80-; bd trustees, Hudson River Mus, 1989-2004, 2006-; vpres, Nat Acad Arts, NY, 2000-2008; acting pres, Nat Acad Design, 2008-2009, pres, 2009-2011; chmn, Abbey Mural Fund, 99-2011. *Teaching:* Instr art, Univ Minn, 63-64; asst prof art, Mich State Univ, 64-68; instr printmaking, Bennington Col, 68-80; fac fine arts, Sch Visual Arts, 77-81. *Awards:* Doris C Freedman Award, 89; Alumni of Yr Award, Univ Wis, 91; MacDowel Fel, 2003; Jimmy Ernst Award, Am Acad Arts & Letters, 2005. *Bibliog:* David Dillon (auth), Creating a whole new building solely with paint, Architecture, 11/88; Paul Goldberger (auth), The healing murals of Richard Haas, New York Times, 1/10/89; Amalie R Rothschild (auth), Painting the Town - The Illusionistic Murals of Richard Haas (film), 90. *Mem:* Century Asn; Nat Acad (bd dir, 92-, vpres, pres, 2009-11); Racquet Club on Park Hill. *Media:* Intaglio; Watercolor, oil, mixed media. *Interests:* films, travel, tennis. *Publ:* Auth, An Architecture of Illusion, Rizzoli Publ, New York, 81; The City is my Canvas, Prestel Publs, 2001; Catalogue Raisonne, The Prints of Richard Haas, John Szoke Editions, 2005. *Dealer:* Printworks 311 W Superior St Chicago IL 60610; John Szoke Editions 24 W 57th St Suite 304 New York NY 10019; David Findlay Jr Fine Arts 724 5th Ave 4th Fl New York NY 10019; Harmon Meek Gallery 599 Tamiami Tran N Ste 309 Naples Fl 34102. *Mailing Add:* 361 W 36th St No 5A New York NY 10018

HAASE, CYNTHIA
PAINTER

Study: studied with master pastelist, Deborah Bays. *Exhib:* Louisville Ctr Arts, 2010; Lakewood Arts Coun, 2010; Art Ctr Estes Park, 2010; Own an Original, Littleton Mus, 2010-2011; 6 Squared, 2011; and others. *Pos:* pres, Colored Pencil Soc Am, currently. *Teaching:* instr, painting workshops. *Mem:* Colo Pastel Soc; Daily Paintworks; Daily Painter Originals; Fresh Paint Daily Painters. *Media:* Oil

HAATOUM HAMADY, WALTER SAMUEL
COLLAGE ARTIST, PUBLISHER

b Flint, Mich, Sept 13, 1940. *Study:* Wayne State Univ, BFA, 64; Cranbrook Acad Art, MFA, 66; Wis Alumni Res Found Grants, 68-70, 73, 77-96. *Work:* Libr Cong; Lenin Libr, Moscow; Getty Ctr, Los Angeles, Calif; Whitney Mus Art, NY; Libr Cong; NY Pub Libr. *Exhib:* Am Inst Graphic Art, 67, 69, 76, 80-81, 92, 99-2006; Int Book Design Exhib, Leipzig, Ger, 89; Walter Hamady: 25 Yrs (catalog), Wustum Mus, Racine, 91; The Beauty in Breathing, Marvin Sackner Arch, Miami, 92; Juxtamorphing Space, Wis Acad, 2005; Walter Hamady: Search Engine, Corbett vs. Dempsey, 2011; 50 Yr Retrospective, Corbett vs. Dempsey, 2014. *Pos:* Proprietor, The Perishable Press Limited, 64-. *Teaching:* Prof drawing, bk illus, collage & artists books, Univ Wis-Madison, 66-96, prof emer, 96-. *Awards:* John Simon Guggenheim Fel, 69; Nat Endowment Arts Grant, 76, 78, 80; Howard Found Fel, Brown Univ, Providence, RI, 77. *Bibliog:* Walter Hamady: Handmade Books, Collage and Sculpture (monogr with essays by Toby Olson & Buzz Spector), Wustum Mus Art, Racine, Wis, 91; Mary Lydon (auth), The book as trojan horse of art: Walter Hamady, perishable press limited and gabberjabbs 1-6, Visible Language, Vol 25, No 2/3, 92; The Gift of Gabberjabb, Print Mag, 1/2/97; Wis Acad Review, fall 2005. *Media:* Collage, Books. *Publ:* Auth, Objects in Transition: Contemporary Book Art (exhib catalog), Temari Center, Honolulu, 84; Two Decades of Hamady and The Perishable Press Ltd: An Anecdotally Annotated Check-list for an Exhibition at Gallery 210, Univ of Mo, 84; Designing Literature, printing and the DP of the U, Fine Print, Vol 14 No 3, 7/88; Travelling or Neopostmodrin Premortemism or Dieser Rasen ist Kein Hundeklo II or Interminable Gabberjabb Number Seven, Perishable Press Ltd, 96. *Dealer:* Corbett vs Dempsey Chicago IL. *Mailing Add:* The Perishable Press Ltd 201 N Hay Hollow Mount Horeb WI 53572

HABEL, DOROTHY (DOTTIE) METZGER
EDUCATOR, ADMINISTRATOR

Study: Univ Michigan, MA, PhD (history of art). *Teaching:* Prof, dir Sch of Art, Univ of Tennessee, Knoxville, currently. *Publ:* (auth) The Urban Development of Rome in the Age of Alexander VII, 2002. *Mailing Add:* School of Art University of Tennessee A+A 213 1715 Volunteer Blvd Knoxville TN 37996

HABENICHT, WENDA
SCULPTOR

b Elkhart, Ind, June 7, 1956. *Study:* Beloit Col, Wis, BA, 74-79; NY Studio Sch Drawing, Painting & Sculpture, 79; Columbia Univ, NY, MFA, 81; Phi Beta Kappa. *Work:* Va Ctr Creative Arts, Sweet Briar; Long Island Univ, CW Post Campus, Brookville, NY. *Comn:* Site specific sculpture, Red River Revel Arts, Shreveport, La, 85; site specific sculpture, Oper Greenthumb, NY, 87; site specific sculpture, The Midwest Coast, Art & Agr, Caledonia, Wis, 82. *Exhib:* The Ways of Wood, Queens Col, NY, 84; Sculpture: The Language of Scale, Bruce Mus, Greenwich, Conn, 85; The Chair Fair, Int Design Ctr, Long Island, NY, 86; Outdoor Sculpture, Connemara Conserv Found, Allen Tex, 86; The Engaging Object, The Clocktower, Inst Arts & Urban Resources, NY, 86; 10th Ann Sculpture Exhib, Snug Harbor Cult Ctr, Staten Island, NY, 87; Artists Choose Artists, Socrates Sculpture Park, Long Island, 87; Dream Retreat-City of Tilted Towers, Toronto Sculpture Garden, Can, 89. *Bibliog:* Michael Benson (auth), City as sculpture garden, New York Times, 87; Tiffany Bell (auth), Insight on Site (exhib catalog), Hillwood Art Gallery, Long Island Univ, 88; Connie Hitzeroth (auth), Habenichts inviting retreat, Now, Toronto, 89. *Media:* Wood, Miscellaneous Media. *Mailing Add:* 293 Co Hwy 40 Worcester NY 12197-9735

HABER, IRA JOEL
SCULPTOR, WRITER

b Brooklyn, NY, Feb 24, 1947. *Work:* NY Univ Art Collection; Nueu Gallerie, Ludwig Collection, Aachen, Ger; Guggenheim Mus, NY; Hirshhorn Mus, Washington, DC; Albright-Knox Art Gallery, Buffalo, NY; Whitney Mus Am Art, NY. *Exhib:* Information, Mus Mod Art, NY, 70; Whitney Mus Ann Sculpture Exhib, NY, 70; three one-man shows, Fischbach Gallery, NY, 71-74; Whitney Mus Contemp Art Biennial, 73; retrospective, Kent State Univ Art Gallery, 77, State Univ NY, Stony Brook, 81 & Philadelphia Art Alliance, 84; Tableaux Constructions, Univ Calif, Santa Barbara, 77; Pam Adler Gallery, NY, 78-80 & 82; Eight Sculptors, Albright-Knox Art Gallery; 1979 Street Sights, Inst Contemp Art, Philadelphia, 80; 55 Mercer St Gallery, 91; Bldg References, Rosenwald Wolf Gallery, Phila, PA, 2005. *Teaching:* Instr sculpture, Fordham Univ, 71-74; assoc prof, State Univ NY Stony Brook, 81; vis lectr, Univ Calif, San Diego, 82-84, Ohio State Univ, Columbus, 84; UFT Retiree Program. *Awards:* Creative Artists Pub Serv Grant, 74-75 & 76-77; Nat Endowment Arts Fel, 74-75, 77-78 & 83-84; Pollack-Krasner Fel, 86; Pollock-Krasner Found Grant, 2001; Gottleib Found Grant, 2004. *Bibliog:* Corrinne Robins (auth), Ira Joel Haber, Arts Mag, 11/77; Robert Berlind (auth), Ira Joel Haber at Pam Adler, Art in Am, 12/79; April Kingsley (auth), article, 9/80, Alex Gildzen (auth), article, 5/82 & William Schwedler (auth), article, 4/83, Arts Mag. *Mem:* United Fedn Teachers. *Media:* Mixed. *Publ:* Auth, Radio City Music Hall, 69; Five stories of the Music Hall, St Marks Poetry Proj, 73; Some thoughts on camouflage by John Perreault, Serif-Lit Quart, Kent State Univ, 74; M E Thelen Gallery Piece, Tri-Quarterly, 75; Some reasons why I do what I do, Appearances, Vol 1, 77. *Mailing Add:* 311 85th St Apt 2R Brooklyn NY 11209-4658

HACK, ELIZABETH
PAINTER, EDITOR

b Frankfurt, Germany; US Citizen. *Study:* Univ Miami, BFA, 1976; Univ SC, Master Media Arts, 1979. *Work:* Nelson Gallery, Univ Calif, Davis, Calif; United Self Help, Honolulu, Hawaii; Kala Inst, Berkeley, Calif; L'Ermitage Hotel, Los Angeles, Calif; Montbeliard Mus, France. *Comn:* Paintings for St Regis Resort (8), Soho Myriad Fine Art, Ft Lauderdale, Fla, 2006; Westin Hotel. *Exhib:* Affirmative Abstraction, Sun Gallery, Hayward Forum for the Arts, Hayward, Calif, 2004; Art in Embassies Program, US State Dept, Republic Fiji, 2004; A Multiplicity of Vision, Calif State Univ Gallery, Dominquez Hills, Calif, 2005; Calif Palace of the Legion of Honor,

Wave Series & Other Impressions, Artists in Residence, San Francisco, 2005; Confluence of the Arts, Alameda Mus, Alameda, Calif, 2006; Calif Cooperative Art Project, Calif State Capitol, Sacramento, Calif, 2007; Of Land & Sea, Alameda Mus, 2007; Believe/Achieve, John O'League Galleria, Hayward Arts, Hayward, Calif, 2007; Musee du Chateau de Montbeliard (curated), Montbeliard, France, 2008; Interactions (juried), Elmarie Dyke Gallery, Pacific Grove Art Ctr, Pacific Grove, Calif, 2008; Juror: Andrea Schwartz, Andrea Schwartz Gallery, San Francisco, Calif, 2008; Group exhib, Encore, Robert Roman Gallery, Scottsdale, Ariz, 2008; Artists Embassy Int, Alameda Mus, Calif, 2009; Bay Area Collection, Proscott-Joseph Ctr, Oakland, Calif, 2009; WMSA Gallery, Marin Art & Garden tr, NorCal Juried Exhib, 2009; Occasions by Design Gallery, Scottsdale, Ariz, 2010; Int Harbor Arts Outdoor Galery, Inst Contemp Art, Boston, 2010; Allusions, Alameda Mus, 2012; Believe/Achieve, Nat League Am Pen Women, John O'League Galleria, 2012; Aw Gallery, San Francisco, Calif, 2012. *Awards:* Juror's Award Distinction, 5th Ann Exhib, Berkeley Art Ctr, 1989; Critic's Choice Award, Rhythms, San Francisco Bay Guardian, 1990. *Bibliog:* Masters of Today, Russu Publ, 2007-2008; Trends, 2007; Visual Journeys, Univ NMex Press, 2010. *Mem:* Nat League Am Pen Women, Diablo-Alameda Chap (pres, 1998-2000, secy, 1994-1996, mem chmn, 2008-); Artists Embassy Int (2003-). *Media:* Mixed Media. *Interests:* music, hiking, poetry. *Publ:* Critic's Choice (bk), San Francisco Bay Guardian, 1990; Artist Frees Imagination with Music (bk), W Co Times, 1994; Easing Online (bk), Artist Mag, 2003; California Contemporary (bk), Artweek Mag, 2003; Cover artist for mag (bk), Pen Women, 2004. *Dealer:* Boston Art; Soho Myraid Fine Arts Atlanta GA; Robert Roman Gallery; Fine Art Asn Honolulu HI; Occasions by Design Gallery Scottsdale Ariz. *Mailing Add:* PO Box 8057 Berkeley CA 94707

HACK, PHILLIP S & PATRICIA Y
COLLECTORS
b Ill, Dec 8 (Mr Hack); b Los Angeles, Calif, Dec 21, 26 (Mrs Hack). *Study:* Univ Ariz; Stanford Univ; Oxford Univ; Ariz State Univ; Wabash Col; Purdue Univ. *Collection:* Contemporary paintings, sculpture, prints and drawings. *Mailing Add:* 7370 E Krall St Scottsdale AZ 85250-4518

HACKENBROCH, YVONNE ALIX
CURATOR, WRITER
b Frankfurt, Ger, Apr 27, 1912; US citizen. *Study:* Univ Frankfurt, 32-33; Univ Rome, 33-34; Univ Munich, PhD (summa cum laude), 36. *Pos:* Asst dept Brit & medieval antiq, Brit Mus, London, 36-45; cur, Lee Fareham Collection, Univ Toronto, 45-49, Irwin Untermyer Collection & Western European Arts, Metrop Mus Art, 49-67. *Awards:* Ford Found Grant, 63; Fel Soc Antiquaries, London, 87; Verdienst Kreuz Am Bande, Ger, 88. *Mem:* Siever Soc, London. *Media:* Ren Jewellery. *Res:* Decorative arts. *Publ:* Auth, Renaissance Jewellery, London, 79; Reinhold Vasters Journal, Metrop Mus Art, New York, 86; Smalti E Gioielli dal XV al XIV secolo, Mostra Mus Naz Bargello, Florence, 86; Jewels of Anna Maria Luisa de Medici (exhib catalog), Museo degli Argenti, Florence, 89; Enseignes: Renaissance Hat Jewels, Florence, 96; The Collection of Irwin Untermyer, VII volumes, 1956-63; Renaissance Jewellery, London and Munich, 79; plus others. *Mailing Add:* Flat 4 31 Hyde Park Gardens London United Kingdom W 2ND

HACKETT, DWIGHT VERNON
PUBLISHER, DIRECTOR
b Modesto, Calif, Mar 21, 1945. *Study:* San Francisco Art Inst, Calif. *Pos:* Manager, bronze casting, Nambe Mills Inc, Santa Fe, NMex, 1971-80; dir, Art Foundry Inc (d/b/a/ Art Foundry Editions), Santa Fe, NMex, 1980; founder, Dwight Hackett Projs, Santa Fe, NMex, currently. *Media:* Cast Metal. *Mailing Add:* 2879 All Trades Rd Santa Fe NM 87507

HACKETT, MICKEY
PAINTER, EDUCATOR
b Louisville, Ky. *Study:* Univ Louisville, Univ Tex, 48. *Work:* Brown-Williamson Corp, Brown Forman Distilleries, Univ Louisville, Ky; Philip Morris Corp; Ala Power Co; and others. *Comn:* Convention cover, Ky Bankers Asn, 81, 83 & 85. *Exhib:* Ky W C Soc; Aqueous, Catherine Lorillard-Wolfe, Nat Arts Club, NY, 80-82; Patron's Gala, Okla; J B Speed Mus; Watermedia 83, Mont; Milford Fine Arts Ctr; and many others. *Pos:* Interior designer, George Fetter Co, Louisville, 65-69. *Teaching:* Instr watercolor tech, Jefferson Community Col, Univ Ky, 78-89, col seminars & workshops. *Awards:* Purchase Awards, Kent State Fair, 72-96, Ind Chautauqua Arts, 89, Bank One, Ohio, 90, Mont Miniature Art Soc, 89 & 90, Lincoln Ill Arts Festival, 90-2002 & Golden Armor Exhib, Ft Knox; Del, Ohio Art Fest, Awards, 90-96; Watercolor Award, Akron Arts Expos, 94, Best of Show, 96. *Bibliog:* Featured article, Ky Monthly Mag, 2/2003. *Mem:* Am Soc Artists; Ky Watercolor Soc (founding mem); Mini Art Societies, Fla, NJ & Mont; Nat Soc Painters, Sculptors & Gravers, Washington, DC; Nat Soc Painters in Casein & Acrylic, NY; Miniature Art Soc Fla; Miniature Art Soc NJ; Miniature Art Soc Mont; Whiskey Painters Am; and others. *Media:* Watercolor, Acrylic, 3-D kinetics. *Publ:* Limited Edition Prints & Posters, 92-2002; auth, Canines for Indyesbase, Ky Humane Soc; auth, Guide Dogs for Blind, Ky Humane Soc. *Mailing Add:* 161 Saint Matthews Ave Ste 14 Louisville KY 40207

HACKETT, THERESA
PAINTER, PRINTMAKER
b Los Angeles, Calif. *Study:* Univ Calif, Santa Barbara, BFA; Hunter Coll, New York, MFA. *Work:* Pfizer Corp, New York; Atlantic Records, New York; Emory Univ, Atlanta; Mus Ludwig Koln, Cologne, Ger; PECO Energy, Pa. *Exhib:* Collectors, Provincetown Art Mus, Mass, 1998; Two by Two, Dallas Mus Art, Tex, 2006; 40th Anniversary-Art on Paper, Weatherspoon Art Mus, NC, 2008; Free Arranger, Miami Int Airport, Fla, 2009; solo exhib, Haas Gallery, Bloombsburg Univ, Pa, 2009; Spreading the Influence, Olin Gallery Art, Kenyon Coll, Ohio, 2010. *Pos:* Vis artist & guest lectr, Univ Calif, Santa Barbara, 1996, Univ Conn, Snaford, 1998, Univ Nev, Las Vegas, 1999, Univ Ohio, 2002, Metrop Mus Art, 2003, Kenyon Coll, Ohio, 2003, Ohio State Univ, 2003, Wexner Ctr for the Arts, Ohio, 2003. *Awards:* Pollock-Krasner Found Grant, 1993; NY Found Arts Fel, 2009. *Bibliog:* Mark Curran (auth), Pierogi 2000 Flatfiles, Time Out London, 9/17-24/1997; Marilyn Bauer (auth), Mermaid, Cincinnati Enquirer, 4/12/2002; Paul Smart (auth), Going with the flow, Woodstock Times, 4/13/2006

HACKLIN, ALLAN DAVE
PAINTER, SCULPTOR
b New York, NY, Feb 11, 1943. *Study:* Pratt Inst. *Work:* Whitney Mus Am Art, NY; Dallas Mus Fine Arts; Allen Mus, Oberlin, Ohio; Mus Fine Arts, Houston; NC Mus Art; Aldrich Mus Am Art. *Exhib:* Whitney Mus Am Art, 67; Meredith Long Gallery, 86 & 87; solo exhibs, Meadows Mus 87 & MB Mod, NY, 97. *Collection Arranged:* Many pvt collections. *Pos:* Dir, Glassell Sch Art, Mus Fine Arts, Houston, 82-89; Dir, Leroy Neiman Ctr Print Studios, 96-2002. *Teaching:* Instr painting, Pratt Inst, 69-70; prof, Calif Inst Arts, 70-77, assoc dean, 76; vis prof, Cooper Union, 77-80; prof, RI Sch Design, 79-82, chmn, Painting Dept, 80-82; Meadows prof, Southern Methodist Univ, 87; chmn, Visual Arts Dept, Columbia Univ, 89-97; prof, Leroy Neiman Sch Art, 96. *Awards:* Nat Endowment Arts, 75, 80 & 84. *Publ:* Auth, article, Artforum, 67. *Mailing Add:* 11 Tatashu Farm Ln Jefferson NY 12093

HADDOCK, JON
CARTOONIST
Study: Ariz State Univ, BFA, 1986; Univ Iowa, MA, 1990 & MFA, 1991. *Work:* Whitney Mus Am Art; Ariz State Univ Art Mus, Tempe. *Exhib:* Solo exhibs, Howard House, Seattle, 1999, 2001, 2003, & 2008, Roberts & Tilton Gallery, Los Angeles, 2000, Rhodes Coll, Memphis, 2004, CherrydelosReyes Gallery, Los Angeles, 2004, &Elon Univ, 2005; Bitstream: Art in the Digital Age, Whitney Mus Am Art, New York, 2001; Cyborg Manifesto, or The Joy of Artifice, Laguna Art Mus, 2001; Phoenix Triannial 2001, Phoenix Art Mus; Byte-bi-Byte: Digital Art from Coast to Coast, Howard House, Seattle, 2001; Twelve/Seven, Studio LoDo, Phoenix, 2001; Transit: Survival Skills, Park Paradise Complex, Scottsdale, 2002; Wonderland, Aeroplastics Contemp, Brussels, 2002; Anxious Omniscience: The Aesthetic Politics of the ARts of Surveillance, Princeton Univ, 2002; Without Fear or Reproach, WITTE ZAAL, Ghent, Belgium, 2003; Pulse of America, Aeroplastics Contemp, Brussels, 2004; Band the Machine, Terba Buena Art Ctr, San Francisco, 2004; After the Boom, Two Rivers Gallery, Prince George BC, 2005; Crash, Pause Rewind, Western Bridge, Seattle, 2005; Breaking and Entering, Pace Wildenstein, New York, 2006; Gamecities, Civic Art Gallery of Monza, Italy, 2006; GameWorld, Laboral Centro de Arte y Creacion Industrial, Gijon, Spain, 2007. *Awards:* Ariz Comn on the Arts Grant, 2000; Art Matters Found Grant, 2009. *Bibliog:* Soyon Im (auth), Photographt: Missing in Action, Seattle Weekly, 4/1999; Howard Wen (auth), The Game of Art, Salon.com, 10/2000; Wendy Jackson Hall (auth), Line of Sight, Wired, 4/2001; Chris Chang (auth), Chris Chang Studies Jon Haddock's Screenshots, Film Comment, 1/2002; Regina Hackett (auth), Blunt Messages Delivered with Comic Book Verve, Seattle Post - Intelligencer, 3/2003. *Media:* Acrylic, Oil

HAEG, FRITZ
ARCHITECT
b Saint Cloud, Minn, 1969. *Study:* Carnegie Mellon Univ Sch Archit, BArchit (with honors), 87-92; Inst Univ Archit Venice, with Aldo Rossi, 90-91. *Comn:* designer, Peter Jennings Residence, New York, 99; Testino Townhouse, New York, 2000; Houston's Restaurant, Santa Monica, Calif, 2002; Rialto Residence, Venice, Calif, 2004; Sundown Gardens & Residence, LA, ongoing; Machine Project, LA, 2004; the gardenLAb experiment, Calif Art Center Coll Design, Pasadena, Calif; Edible Estates Regional Prototype Garden #1, Salina Art Center, Kans, 2005, #2, Lakewood, Calif, 2006, #3, Maplewood, NJ, 2007, 2007, #4, Tate Mod, London, 2007, #5, Arthouse, Austin, 2008, #6, Mus Contemp Art Baltimore, 2008. *Exhib:* Solo exhibs include Royal Botanic Gardens, Sydney, 2005, Salina Art Center, Kans, 2005, Southern Exposure, San Francisco, 2006, Millard Sheets Gallery, Pomona, Calif, 2006, Machine Project, LA, 2006, Inst Contemp Art, Philadelphia, 2007, Mass Mus Contemp Art, 2007, Tate Mod, London, 2007, Texas Arthouse, Austin, 2008, Contemp Mus Baltimore, 2008, Indianapolis Mus Art, 2008, San Francisco Mus Mod Art, 2008, Casco Projects, Netherlands, 2008; group exhibs include Hothouse, Parsons Sch Design Gallery, 98; Civic Matters, LA Contemp Exhibs, 2006; From the Fat of the Land, Grand Arts, Kans City, 2007; Edible Cities, Netherlands Archit Inst, Maastricht, 2007; Ecology Video Series, No 9, Toronto Int Art Fair, 2007; Whitney Biennial, Whitney Mus Am Art, New York, 2008. *Collection Arranged:* the gardenLAb experiment, The Wind Tunnel at ARt Center Coll Design, Pasadena, Calif, 2004; Showdown! (Sundown Salon #14), MAK Center, Schindler House, West Hollywood, Calif, 2004; Humans Were Here! (Building in LA), Wattis Inst, Calif Coll Arts, San Francisco, 2006. *Pos:* Founder, Fritz Haeg Studio, New York, 95-99, LA, 99-, Sundown Salon, Los Angeles, 2001-, Sundown Schoolhouse, LA, 2006-, Gardenlab prog, 2001-, Edible Estates initiative, 2005-, Animal Estates, 2008-. *Teaching:* Teaching asst, Carnegie Mellon Univ Sch Archit, Pittsburgh, 91-92; part-time faculty, Product & Furniture Design Dept, Parsons Sch Design, New York, 96-99; adj faculty, Univ Southern Calif, Sch Archit, LA, 2000-04, Roski Sch Art, 2006-07; part-time faculty, Dept Environ Design, Art Center Coll Design, Pasadena, Calif, 1999-2003, prof, 2003-04, co-chair, Art Center Faculty Coun, 2002-03; vis artist, Sch Art, Calif Inst Arts, Valencia, 2005-06. *Awards:* SURG Res Grant, 92; LEF Found Grant, 2001-02; Faculty Enrichment Grant, Art Center Coll Design, 2003; Durfee Found Grant, 2006 & 2007; Macdowell Colony Fel, 2007; MIT Center Advanced Visual Studies Fel, 2008. *Publ:* Auth: Sundown Salon 2001-2006 in words & in pictures, Evil Twin, fall 2008; Edible Estates: Attack on the Front Lawn, DAP/Metropolis Books, spring 2008. *Mailing Add:* Fritz Haeg Studio 2538 Sundown Dr Los Angeles CA 90065

HAFFTKA, MICHAEL D
PAINTER
b New York, Dec 18, 1953. *Work:* Mus Mod Art, Metrop Mus Art, NY; Carnegie Inst, Pittsburgh, Pa; San Francisco Mus Mod Art, Calif. *Bibliog:* Michael Brodsky (auth), Hafftka Selected Drawings, Guignol Books, 81; Sam Unter (auth), Hafftka-Paintings, DiLaurenti Publ, 91. *Media:* Acrylic, Oil. *Mailing Add:* c/o M H Co 32 Tiffany Pl Brooklyn NY 11231

HAFIF, MARCIA
PAINTER, EDUCATOR
b Pomona, Calif, Aug 15, 1929. *Study:* Pomona Col, BA (art), 51; Claremont Grad Sch; Univ Calif, Irvine, MFA, 71. *Work:* Von Der Heydt-Mus, Wuppertal, Ger; Kunsthaus Aarau, Switz; Kunstraum Alexander Buerkle, Freiburg, Ger; Mamco, Geneva, Switz; Albright-Knox Art Gallery, Buffalo; Mus fur KonKrete Kunst, Ingolstadt, Ger; Portland Art Mus, Ore; Mus Modern Art, New York; Mus Contemp Art, Los Angeles, Calif. *Comn:* Ohio Red (clay mural), Wright State Univ, Ohio, 77; 3 paintings, Sheldon Solow, NY, 80. *Exhib:* Abstract Painting: 1960-69, PSI Mus, 83; La Couleur Seule: L'Experience Monochrome, Musee St Pierre, Lyon, France, 88 & Aargauer Kunsthaus, Aarau, Switz, 95; solo exhibs, Inventory PSI Mus, LIC, 90, Von Der Heydt Mus, Wuppertal, Ger, 94, Hans fur Konstruklir & Konkrete Kunst, Zurich (with catalog), 95; Red Colors, Kunsthalle, Winterthur Switz & Wamås, 92; Italian Paintings, Peintures 1962-68, Mus d' Art Moderne et Contemporain, Geneva, 1999; Italian Paintings: 1962-65 FRAC, Bourgogne, Dijon, France, 2000; Italian Paintings: 1961-69, Mus Modern and Contemp Art, Geneva, 2001; Enamel on Wood, Installation, Lenbachhaus, Munich, Ger, 2001; Virtuel/Reel, Escape d'Art Concrete, Mouans-Sartoux France, 2001; Mamco, Geneva, Switz, 2000. *Teaching:* Instr painting & color, Sch Visual Arts, New York, 74-76; instr, Sarah Lawrence Col, 78-80; vis asst prof, Hunter Col, 82 & 85-; vis artist, Univ Calif, Irvine, 83; adj assoc prof & coordr painting & drawing dept, New York Univ, 85-87; lectr, Princeton Univ, 89. *Awards:* Creative Artists Pub Serv Prog Grant, 76; Nat Endowment Arts, 80-81 & 90. *Bibliog:* Lilly Wei (ed), Talking abstract (interview), Art in Am, 7/87; Marcia Hafif: From the Inventory (exhib catalog), Kunsthalle Barmen, 94; Hausfer Konstructiv und Kmkrete Kunst, Zurich, 95; Reinhard Ermin, Eingemalde ist ein Gemalde, zur arbeit von Marcia Hafif, Kunst forum pp 255-265, Jul-Aug 99; Andreas Pinczewski, Bevor Kunst Zur Kunst Wind in Bleistift auf Papier, Marcia Hafif, Galeria Michael Sturm, Stuttgart, 03. *Media:* All Traditional Paint Media. *Publ:* Beginning Again, Art forum, 9/78; Getting on with painting, Art Am, 4/81; Plain painting, Artistes, Paris, 7/84; True Colors, Art in Am, 6/89. *Dealer:* Charlotte Jackson 200 W Marcy St Suite 101 Santa Fe NM 87501; Galerie Mark Muller Gessnerallee 36 CH-8001 Zurich Switz; Larry Becker Contemp Art, 43 N Second St, Phila, US; Galerie Rupert Walser, Fraunhoferstrasse, 19 D-80469 Munich, Ger; Galerie Hubert Winter, Breite Gasse, 17 A-1070 Vienna, Austria. *Mailing Add:* 112 Mercer St New York NY 10012

HAGAN, JAMES GARRISON
SCULPTOR, INSTRUCTOR
b Pittsburgh, Pa, July 11, 1936. *Study:* Carnegie-Mellon Univ, BFA; Iowa State Univ; Univ Pittsburgh, MA. *Work:* Column 5, Nat Gallery Art, Washington, DC; Column 8, Princeton Univ, NJ; Barrier, Newark Mus. *Exhib:* Solo exhib, Zabriskie Gallery, 75; Nine Sculptures, Nassau Co Mus, NY, 76; Wood Works, Wadsworth Atheneum, Hartford, Conn, 77; Wood, Nassau Co Mus, NY, 77. *Teaching:* Prof sculpture, Univ Va, Charlottesville, 63-. *Media:* Wood, Composites. *Dealer:* Zabriskie Gallery New York NY 10019

HAGE, RAYMOND JOSEPH
ART DEALER, LECTURER
b Huntington, WVa, Nov 28, 1943. *Study:* Univ Ky; Marshall Univ, BBA, 66; Darden Grad Sch Bus Admin, Univ Va, TEP, 71. *Pos:* Pres, Raymond J Hage Inc, 84-. *Collection:* American & European prints. *Publ:* Printsource. *Mailing Add:* 2105 Wiltshire Blvd Huntington WV 25701-5344

HAGEMAN, CHARLES LEE
EDUCATOR, JEWELER
b Clay Center, Kans, June 22, 1935. *Study:* Univ Kans, BFA, 57, MFA, 67. *Work:* Ill State Univ, Visual Arts Ctr, Normal, Ill; Univ Mo, Columbia. *Comn:* Univ Mace, Pres Chain of Off & 6 Board of Regent's Medallions, comn by Pres of Northwest Mo State Univ, Maryville, 77. *Exhib:* Juried Craft Exhib, Ark Arts Ctr, Little Rock, 73 & JP Speed Art Mus, Louisville, Ky, 74; Invitational Craft Exhib, Albrecht Mus, St Joseph, Mo, 75; Prof Jewelry Exhib, Univ Mo, Columbia, 76; Mid-Am Metalcrafts, Kansas City Pub Libr, Mo, 77. *Collection Arranged:* Mo Craftsman Exhib, Olive DeLuce Gallery, Maryville, Mo, 73. *Teaching:* Assoc prof jewelry & metals & chmn dept art, Northwest Mo State Univ, Maryville, 67-, emer fac; instr summer jewelry workshop, NMex State Univ, Las Cruces, 74-. *Awards:* Best Metals, Designer-Craftsman Show, Kans, 67; Metals Award, Springfield Art Mus, 69; Best Metals, Mo Craftsman Exhib, 70. *Mem:* Am Craft Coun; Soc NAm Goldsmiths. *Media:* Pewter & Gold. *Mailing Add:* 722 W Second St Maryville MO 64468

HAGER, HELLMUT W
HISTORIAN
b Berlin, Ger, Mar 27, 1926. *Study:* Univ Bonn, PhD, 59. *Collection Arranged:* Architectural Fantasy and Reality, Mus Art, Pa State Univ, 81-82. *Pos:* Asst to dir, Bibliot Hertziana, Rome, 59-63. *Teaching:* Prof art hist, Pa State Univ, 71-, dept head, 72-95. *Awards:* Named Distinguished Prof, 90; Evan Pugh Prof, 96. *Mem:* Coll Art Asn Am; Soc Archit Historians; Am Soc 18th Century Studies; Am Inst Archeol. *Res:* Baroque architecture in Italy and Germany. *Publ:* Auth, Filippo Juvarra e il concorso di modelli del 1715 bandito da Clemente XI per la nuova sacrestia di S Pietro, 70; coauth, Carlo Fontana: The Drawings at Windsor Castle, 77; ed (co-ed, Susan S Munshower), Projects and Monuments in Period of Roman Baroque, Vol I, 84 & Light on the Eternal City- Observations and Discoveries in Art and Architecture of Rome, Vol II, In: Papers in Art History, Pennsylvania State Univ, 84 & 87; Le Accademie di Architetura, Storia dell'Architettura Italiana, Il Settecento (eds, Giovanna Curcio & Elisabeth Kieven), 20-49, I, Milan, 2000; Bernini e l'inizio del Settecento in Italia e oltre, Le Bernini e l'Europe, Du Baroque trioumphant a l'age romantique, 355-374, de l'universite de Paris, Sorbonne, 2002; ed, introd, Carlo Fontana: L'Anfiteatro Flavio, Edizione anastatica del manoscritto del museo di Roma, ix-xxxvii, Rome, 2002; Il modello grande de Filippo Juvarra del 1715 per la Nuova Sacrestia di San Pietro in Vaticano: unal riconsiderazione della genesi progettuale, Palladio, Nuova Serie, Anno XIII, No 26, 39-52, 2000-2001; Carlo Fontana, Storia dell' architettura italiana, il Seicento (ed, Aurora Scotti Tosini), 231-261, I, Milan, 2003. *Mailing Add:* 318 E Prospect Ave State College PA 16801-5449

HAGIN, NANCY
PAINTER
b Elizabeth, NJ, June 19, 1940. *Study:* Carnegie-Mellon Univ; BFA, 62; Yale Univ, MFA, 64. *Work:* Mus Fine Arts, Boston, Mass; Butler Inst Am Art, Youngstown, Ohio; Utah Mus Fine Arts, Salt Lake City; New Britain Mus Am Art, Conn. *Exhib:* Group exhibs, Baltimore Mus Ann Exhib, 65-70, IFA Gallery, Washington, DC, 68-73, Allen Frumkin Gallery, NY, 71, Smithsonian Inst, Washington DC, 74, Indianapolis Mus Art, 76, Butler Inst, Ohio, 77, Lehigh University, Pa, 79, Nassau Co Mus Art, Roslyn, NY, 80, New Britain Mus Am Art, Conn, 82, Rahr-West Mus, Wis, 83, Fitchburg Art Mus, Mass, 84, William Sawyer Gallery, San Francisco, 85, C Grimaldis Gallery, Baltimore, 86, Fay Gold Gallery, Atlanta, 89, Nat Acad Design, NY, 89-90, Rice Univ, Tex, 93, NJ Ctr Visual Arts, 94, Lizan Tops Gallery, NY, 95, Am Acad of Arts & Letters, NY, 2001, Doran Gallery, Tulsa, 2002, 323 West Gallery, NY, 2003, DeCordova Mus & Sculpture Park, Mass, 2003-2004; solo exhibs, Alpha Gallery, Boston, 72, 76, 74, 79, 82, 85, 92, 95, 2000, Univ Md, 73, Terry Dintenfass Gallery, NY, 75, 78, Fischbach Gallery, NY, 81, 82, 85, 87, 89, 91, 93, 95, 98, 99, 2002 & 2004; Contemp Naturalism: Work of the 1970's, Nassau Co Mus, NY, 80; Eight Women-Still Life, New Britain Mus Am Art, Conn, 82; Plimpton Collection of Realistic Art, Rose Art Mus, Brandeis Univ, Mass, 82; Am Realism: 20th Century Drawings & Watercolors, Mus Mod Art, San Francisco, Calif, 85; Four Artists Collaborating, Tatistcheff Gallery, NY, 87. *Teaching:* Prof, Md Inst Col Art, Baltimore, 64-73; prof, Pratt Inst, New York City, 73-74, 85, RI Sch of Design, 74, Fashion Inst Tech, New York City, 74-, Cooper Union, 82-92, State Univ NY Purchase, 94, Univ Arts, Philadelphia, 99. *Awards:* Fulbright Grant, 66; Creative Artists Pub Serv Grant, 75; Nat Endowment Arts Grant, 82 & 91. *Bibliog:* Marjorie Miller (auth), rev, Arts Mag, 82; Elaine King (auth), Celebrations of the Familiar (exhib catalog), Carnegie-Mellon Univ, 82; Gerrit Henry (auth), Hagin (exhib catalog), Lafayette Col, 86; John Arthur (auth), Hagin Exhibition Announcement Essay, 89. *Mem:* MacDowell Art Colony (colonist bd, 85-88); Nat Acad, 92. *Media:* Acrylic, Watercolor. *Dealer:* Fischbach Gallery 24 W 57th St New York NY 10019; Alpha Gallery Boston MA. *Mailing Add:* c/o Fischback Gallery 210 11th Ave #801 New York NY 10001

HAHN, BETTY
PHOTOGRAPHER, EDUCATOR
b Chicago, Ill, Oct 11, 1940. *Study:* Ind Univ, BA, 63, MFA, 66 with Henry Holmes Smith. *Work:* Mus Mod Art, NY; Smithsonian Inst; Nat Gallery Can, Ottawa; Art Inst Chicago; San Francisco Mus Mod Art; and others. *Exhib:* Festival du Photographie, Arles, France, 75; Am Family Portraits 1730-1976, Philadelphia Mus Art, 76; Nat Gallery Can, Ottawa, 80; Smithsonian Inst, 80 & 81; Ctr Creative Photog, 81; Int Mus Photog George Eastman House, 81; San Francisco Mus Mod Art, 81 & 85; Musee d'Art Moderne de la Ville de Paris, France, 81; Houston Ctr Photog, Tex, 82; Hong Kong Arts Ctr, 82; Amerika Haus, Hanover, Berlin, Frankfurt, Heidelburg, Koln & Munich, Ger, 85. *Collection Arranged:* Spanish Photography Today, Univ NMex, 85. *Pos:* Consult, NY Graphics Soc, Boston, Mass, & Visual Arts Referral Serv Creative Pub Serv, NY, 77; guest artist, Tamarind Inst, Albuquerque, NMex, 78; adv, Art Students Asn Gallery & Conceptions Southwest (mag), Univ NMex, 81; consult ed, Univ NMex Press, 84. *Teaching:* Asst prof photog, Rochester Inst of Technol, NY, 69-76; assoc prof photog, Univ NMex, 76-86; lectr, numerous univs; prof photog, Univ NMex, 86-. *Awards:* Creative Artists Pub Serv Prog Grant, New York State Coun, 75; Res Grant, Univ NMex, 77; Nat Endowment Arts Grants, 78 & 83; Polaroid Grant, 79 & 88. *Bibliog:* James N Miho (auth), More than real, Commun Arts, 72; R Sobieszek (auth), Photographer: Betty Hahn, Czech Photo, 74 & Russian Photo Rev, 74. *Mem:* Soc Photog Educ (bd dir, 80). *Publ:* Auth, Speaking with a Genuine Voice: Henry Holmes Smith, IMAGE Eastman House, 73; contribr of chap on Gum Bichromate Printing, In: Darkroom, Lustrum Press, New York, 77; ed, Contemporary Spanish Photography, Univ NMex Press, Albuquerque, 87. *Dealer:* Witkin Gallery 41 E 57th St New York NY 10022; Andrew Smith Gallery 76 E San Francisco Santa Fe NM 87501. *Mailing Add:* Univ NMex 1511 Kit Carson Ave SW Albuquerque NM 87104

HAHN, CHARLES
SCULPTOR
Study: Art Students League, NY; Naguib Sch Sculpture, Ind; Johnson Atelier & Technical Sch Sculpture, NJ. *Exhib:* Allied Artists of Am, NY, 1998-2000; Audubon Artists, Inc, NY, 1998-2000; Cape Cod Art Asn, Cape Cod, Mass, 1998-2000; Am Artists Prof League, NY, 1999-2000; Acad Artist Asn, Springfield, Mass, 1999-2000; Hudson Valley Art Asn, NY, 2000; Springfield Art League, Springfield, Mass, 2000. *Awards:* First Place Award, Sculpture, New Eng Exhib, Cape Cod Art Asn, 1998; Honor Award, Sculpture, Acad Artists Asn, 1999, Dr Robert L Bertolli Award for Traditional Sculpture, 2002; Greg Wyatt Award, Hudson Valley Art Asn, NY, 2000; Richmond Sculpture Award, Salmagundi Club, NY, 2000 ; Jocelyn Edelston Mem Award, Rockport Art Asn, 2003; Richard Reccia Sculpture Mem Award, North Shore Art Asn, 2003; Calvary Baptist Church Award, Am Artists Prof League, 2003 ; The Renee & Chaim Gross Found Award, Audubon Artist, 2003. *Mem:* Salmagundi Club, NY; Rockport Art Asn; North Shore Art Asn; Cape Cod Art Asn; Acad Artists Asn;

Am Artists Prof League; New England Sculptors Asn; Allied Artists of Am, Inc; Audubon Artists, Inc. *Dealer:* McDougall Fine Arts Gloucester MA; Saltbox Gallery Topsfield MA; Sculpture Showcase LTD New Hope PA; Swain Gallery NJ; State of the Arts Gallery Gloucester MA. *Mailing Add:* 122 W Emerson St Melrose MA 02176

HAHN, ROSLYN
DEALER
US citizen. *Study:* Univ Pa, BA, grad studies in art hist; Temple Univ, Tyler Sch of Art. *Collection Arranged:* Benton Spruance, Retrospective, William Penn Mus, Harrisburg, Pa, 77; Benton Spruance Traveling Exhib, (coauth, catalog), with Dr Ricardo Viera, Lehigh Univ, 77-78; Alfred Bendiner, The Philadelphia Years, William Penn Mus, Harrisburg, 78; 17th, 18th and 19th Century Japanese Woodblock Prints, Longwood Gardens, Kennett Square, PA, 82. *Pos:* Dir, Hahn Gallery, Philadelphia. *Mem:* Philadelphia Print Club; Prints in Progress (bd mem, 70-77); Philadelphia Art Dealers Asn; Friends of Artists Equity (bd mem). *Mailing Add:* c/o Hahn Gallery 2401 Pennsylvania Ave Apt 21B27 Philadelphia PA 19130

HAI , WILLOW WEILAN
DIRECTOR, CURATOR
b Wuxi, China. *Study:* Nanjing Univ, BA, 82; Nanjing Univ, MA, 84. *Exhib:* Song of Life (auth, catalog), Naples Mus Art, 2000; Passion for the Mountains: 17th Century Landscape Masterpieces from the Nanjing Mus (cur & auth, catalog), China Institute Gallery, 2003; The Last Emperor's Collection, Masterpieces of painting & calligraphy from the Liaoning Provincial Mus (leading cur & coauth, catalog), China Inst Gallery, 2008; Noble Tombs at Mawangdui=Art and Life in the Changsha Kindom, Third Century BCE to First Century CE (project dir), China Inst Gallery, 2009; Confucious: His Life and Legacy in Art (project dir) China Inst Gallery, 2010; Along the Yangzi River: Regional Culture of the Bronze Age from Hunan (project dir) China Inst Gallery, 2011; Blooming in the Shadows: Unofficial Chinese Art, 1974-1985 (project dir) China Inst Gallery, 2011; Theater, Life, and the Afterlife: Tomb Decor of the Jin Dynasty from Shanxi (project dir) China Inst Gallery, 2012; New China: Porcelain Art from Jingdezhen 1910-2012 (project dir) China Inst Galley, 2013; Dunhuang: Buddhist Art at the Gateway of the Silk Rd (project dir), China Inst Galley, 2013; Inspired by Dunhuang: Re-Creation in Contemporary Chinest Art (leading curator, auth catalog), China Inst Gallery, 2013. *Collection Arranged:* Cur, A Year of Good Fortune, 93, Animals of the Chinese Zodiac, 95 & Calligraphy as Living Art, 96. *Pos:* cur, China Inst Gallery, 95-99, dir, 2000-. *Teaching:* Lectr, The Wharton Sch, Univ Pa, 92. *Awards:* Acclaimed art dir & cur, Carol Kino, 3/21/2010, Holland Cotter, 3/26/2010, NY Times. *Media:* Painting. *Res:* Chinese imperial painting and calligraphy; art in 6 dynasties China. *Specialty:* All media of Chinese art. *Interests:* Chinese art and Impressionism. *Mailing Add:* China Inst Gallery 125 E 65th St New York NY 10065

HALABY, SAMIA A
PAINTER, WRITER
b Jerusalem, Palestine, Dec 12, 1936; US citizen. *Study:* Mich State Univ, with Abraham Rattner & Borris Margo, MA, 60; Ind Univ, with James McGarrell, MFA, 63. *Work:* Art Inst Chicago; Detroit Inst Art; Cincinnati Art Mus; Cleveland Mus Art; Guggenheim Mus; Nat Mus Women in the Arts, Washington, DC; Yale Univ Gallery; British Mus; Indianapolis Mus Art; Inst du Monde Arab, Paris; Sioux City Art Ctr; Alternative Mus, NY; Mead Art Mus, Amherst, Mass; and others. *Comn:* Lithograph, Cleveland Mus Print Club, 74; stage set and costume design, Dance Company Perspective in Motion, Pace Univ, NY, 94. *Exhib:* Solo Exhibs: Phyllis Kind Gallery, Chicago, 71-72; Yale Sch Art Gallery, New Haven, Conn, 72; Marilyn Pearl Gallery, NY, 78; Housatonic Mus, Bridgeport, Conn, 83; Tossan-Tossan Gallery, New York City, 83, 88; Darat Al-Funun, Amman, Jordan, 95; Galerie Atassi, Damascus; Galerie le Pont, Aleppo, 97; Agial Gallery, Beirut, Lebanon, 99, 2004, 2007; Sakakini Art Ctr, Ramallah, Palestine, 2000; Skoto Gallery, NY, 2000; Artim Gallery, Strasbourg, France, 2001; Ayyam Gallery, Damascus, 2008; Ayyam Dubai Gallery, 2009, 2011, Ayyam Beirut Gallery, 2010, Ayyam Gallery, London, 2013; Group Exhibs: Yale Univ Gallery, New Haven, Conn, 73; Guggenheim Mus, New York City, 75; Susan Caldwell Gallery, New York City, 77; Ind Univ Art Mus, 77; Univ Hawaii, 90-91; Sangre de Christo Arts Ctr, Pueblo, Colo, 91; Nat Mus of Women, Washington, DC, 94; Elizabeth Found, UN lobby, NYC, 99; Bradley Univ, Ill, 2001; Musee du Chateau Dufresne, Montreal, 2001; The Station, Houston, 2003; Bridge Gallery, NYC, 2006; Art Paris Abu Dhabi, 2007; Arts and Design, NY, 2008; Scope Basel, 2009; Inst Du Monde Arabe, 2009; Victoria Commonwealth Univ, Qatar, 2010; Abu Dhabi Art, 2011, 2012; Art Dubai, 2011, 2012. *Collection Arranged:* Williamsburg Bridges Palestine, WAH Ctr, Brooklyn, NY; Made in Palestine at the Bridge Gallery, NY, 2003. *Pos:* Artist-in-residence, Tamarind Lithography Workshop, 72; cur, Al Jisser Group, 2001-; guest cur, The Subject of Palestine, at DePaul Univ Mus, 2005; Conult, made in Palestine, Station Mus, Houseton, Tex. *Teaching:* Teaching asst, Ind Univ, Bloomington, 62-63; instr, Univ Hawaii, Honolulu, 63-64; asst prof, Kansas City Art Inst, Mo, 64-66; vis lectr, Univ Hawaii, Honolulu, 66; asst prof, Univ Mich, Ann Arbor, 67-69; assoc prof, Ind Univ, Bloomington, 69-72; vis lectr, Yale Univ Sch Art, New Haven, Conn, 72-73, assoc prof, 73-76, adj assoc prof, 76-82; vis prof, Univ S Fla, 90; adj prof, Cooper Union for the Advancement of Sci and Art, NY, 89-91; vis artist, BeirZeit Univ, Palestine, 97. *Awards:* Creative Artists Pub Serv Prog Grant Painting, 79. *Bibliog:* Art and liberation: Samia Halaby speaks, Aurora, spring 82; Jonathan Goodman (auth), Samia Halaby Arts Mag, 5/88; Kathy Zarur (auth), Looking at the Levant, Art in Am, 9/2006; Inea Bushnaq (auth), Samia Halaby, Fine Arts Pub, Beirut, Lebanon, 2006; Samia (film), by Ammar Al Beik, 2009; Maymanah Farhat (auth), Samia Halaby: Five Decades of Painting and Innovation, Booth Clibborn Editions, London, 2013. *Mem:* Al Jisser Group. *Media:* Oil, Acrylic; Computer. *Res:* Liberation Art of Palestine. *Interests:* Programming moving abstract images. *Collection:* Paintings/drawings done by Palestinian Artists with focus on Libertarian Art. *Publ:* Nature, Reality & Abstract Picturing, Leonardo, 10/87; Pictures in Computer Medium, Proceedings, 9th Symp of Small Computers in the Arts, 89; On Art and Politics, Arab Studies Quart, spring/summer 89; Technology, Abstraction & Kinetic Painting, Papers of the 4th Int Symp Electronic Art, 93; Rhythms, The aesthetics of electronic painting, Papers of the 7th Int Symp Electronic Art, 96; Liberation Art of Palestine, HTTB Publ, 2003. *Dealer:* Ayyam Gallery Dubai UAE. *Mailing Add:* 103 Franklin St New York NY 10013

HALAHMY, ODED
SCULPTOR
b Baghdad, Iraq, Oct 10, 1938; US citizen. *Study:* Bat Yam Sch Fine Art, BA, 65; St Martin's Sch Fine Art, MA, 68. *Work:* Herbert Johnson Mus Art, Ithaca, NY; Soloman R Guggenheim Mus, NY; Hirshhorn Mus and Sculpture Garden, Washington, DC; Chase Manhattan Bank, NJ; Chicago Athenaeum, Chicago, Ill; Jerusalem Mus, Israel. *Comn:* Sukkah (abstract sculpture), Hebrew Union Col, Jerusalem, 79; Family (abstract sculpture), pvt comn, Palm Beach, Fla, 81; Blue Party (abstract sculpture), Aldrich Mus Contemp Art, Ridgefield, Conn, 82. *Exhib:* Montreal Mus Fine Art, 68; Tel Aviv Mus, 70; solo exhibs, Herbert Johnson Mus Art, Ithaca, NY, 74 & Aldrich Mus Contemp Art, Conn, 82-83; Am Int Sculpture Symp, NY, 74; Louis K Meisel Gallery, 88, 90, 91, 93 & 98; Yeshiva Univ Mus, 2003. *Teaching:* Instr art, Ont Col Art, Toronto, 69-70 & Parsons Sch Design, NY, 75-77; vis artist, Cooper Union Art Sch, 71, NY Univ, 71 & New Sch Social Res, 74, NY. *Awards:* Peter Samuel Found Fel, London, 67-68; Am-Israel Cult Found, NY, 75. *Bibliog:* Noel Frackman (auth), article, Arts Mag, 5/74; Gerrit Henry (auth), article, New York Times, 12/79; article, New York Times, 4/3/83. *Mem:* Am Int Sculpture Symp. *Media:* Bronze, Wood. *Publ:* Oded Halahmy in Retrospect: Sculpture from 1962-1997, NY, 97; Homeward: Sculpture of Oded Halahmy, published by Sunrarm Tagore Gallery, 2004; Homelands Baghdad-Jerusalem-NY, published by Yeshiva Univ Mus, 2003; The Common Ground: The Sculpture of Oded Halahmy, published by Sundaram Tagore Gallery, 2002; Oded Halahmy in Retrospect: Sculpture from 62-97, published by Louis K Meisel Gallery, 97. *Dealer:* Louis K Meisel Gallery 141 Prince St NYC 10012; Sundaram Tagore Gallery 137 Greene St NYC 10012; Remy Toledo Gallery 529 W 20th St NYC 10011. *Mailing Add:* c/o Louis K Meisel 141 Prince St New York NY 10012

HALASZ, PIRI
CRITIC, HISTORIAN
b New York, NY, Apr 5, 1935. *Study:* Barnard Coll, BA, 56; Columbia Univ, MA, 76, PhD, 82. *Collection Arranged:* The Expressionist Vision: A Central Theme in NY in the 1940s, Hillwood Art Gallery, C W Post Ctr, Long Island Univ, 83-84; A Year in the Life of Present Modernism, Gathering of the Tribes Gallery, NY, 97-98. *Pos:* Contrib ed, Time Mag, 63-69, writer art sect, 67-69; online columnist, From the Mayor's Doorstep, 96-; contribr, Artcritical.com, 2008-; NY Observer, 2015-. *Teaching:* Adj art hist, C W Post Ctr, Long Island Univ, 76-77, adj prof, 85-86, coordr art, Westchester Campus, 85-86; adj prof, Molloy Coll, 85-86; asst prof, Bethany Coll, WVa, 90-94. *Awards:* Fel, Va Ctr Creative Arts, 86, 89, 97-98, 2001 & 2005; Gold Medal, Independent Publisher Book awards, 2010. *Mem:* Int Asn Art Critics; Nat Coalition of Independent Scholars (bd dirs, 2011-14). *Res:* Twentieth century European and American art, especially in New York in the 1940s. *Interests:* Contemporary art, abstract painting. *Publ:* Online column rev & excerpts, Night, 97-99, NY Arts, 97-2005; David Smith, A Centennial, A Gathering of the Tribes (online), 4/2006; What You Didn't Learn in College, a Gathering of Tribes (online), 1/2011; A Memoir of Creativity: abstract painting, politics & the media, 1956-2008, New York, 2009; A Swinger's Guide to London, NY, 2010; Creativity, Art, and Scholarship, the Independent Scholar Quarterly (online), 2013. *Mailing Add:* 520 E 76th St Apt 3A New York NY 10021

HALBACH, DAVID ALLEN
PAINTER, HISTORIAN
b Santa Barbara, Calif, Jan 12, 1931. *Study:* Chouinard Art Inst, cert grad; with Rex Brandt, Edward Reep & Robert Uecker. *Work:* Permanent Collection, Bank Calif, San Francisco, San Jose & Seattle, Wash, also Buffalo Bill Mus, Cody, Wyo; Favell Mus Western Art, Klamath Falls, Ore; Cowboy Artists Am Mus, Kerrville, Tex. *Exhib:* Cowboy Hall of Fame, Oklahoma City, 75-79 & 81; Western Heritage Show, Houston, Tex, 78-81, 83 & 84, European tour, 83-; Biltmore Celebrity Show, Los Angeles, Calif, 81-84; Governor's Invitational, Cheyenne, Wyo, 81-84; Cowboy Artists of Am, Phoenix Art Mus, Phoenix, Ariz; Solo exhib, Claggett/Rey Gallery, Vail, Colo, 2011. *Pos:* Illusr, US Navy, 52-54; Walt Disney Studio, Burbank, 54-55; illusr & art ed, Cannon Elec Co, Los Angeles, 55-59; art dir, Mowinckle Advert, Los Angeles, 59-63. *Teaching:* Art teacher (adult educ), San Gabriel, Whittier & Covina High Schs, Calif, 65-73. *Awards:* Silver Medalist, Nat Acad-Cowboy Hall of Fame, 75; 7 times Gold Medal & 7 times Silver Medal, Cowboy Artists Am Show, Phoenix, Ariz; First Place, Art Parks Region II, 89; Mus Western Heritage Award, 90. *Mem:* Cowboy Artists Am. *Media:* Watercolor. *Specialty:* Vail, Co. *Interests:* Fishing, Painting. *Publ:* Illusr, Orange Co Illustrated, 75 & Southwest Art, 78 & 98; 1988 Cowboy Artists of America, Art W Mag, 11-12/88; contribr, film proj, Nat Geographic, 97; Am Artist Publ, Watercolor summer issue, 98; Western Art Masterpieces & The West: A Treasury of Arts Literature, Walkins & Walkins. *Dealer:* Claggett/Rey Gallery Vail, CO; Settler's West Tucson AZ. *Mailing Add:* PO Box 1207 Graeagle CA 96103-1207

HALBREICH, KATHY
MUSEUM DIRECTOR
b New York, NY, April 24, 1949. *Study:* Skowhegan Sch Painting and Sculpture, postgrad, Maine, 65; Am Univ, postgrad, Mexico City, 66; Bennington Coll, BA (lit & visual arts), 71. *Collection Arranged:* Cur (with Joan Rothfuss), Craigie Horsfield, 93, (with Neal Benezra), Bruce Nauman Retrospective, 94; Bordering on Fiction: Chantal Akermans DEst, 95. *Pos:* Adminr, spec prog, Bennington Coll, Vt, 75-76; dir comt on visual arts, Hayden Gallery, List Visual Arts Ctr, Mass Inst Technol, Cambridge, Mass, 76-86; dir teaching sem, Asn Collegiate Sch Archit, Wash, 77; vpres prog, trustee, Artist Found, Boston, 79-84; ind cur-consultant, 86-88; consult, St Louis Art Mus, Artists Space, New York City, Capp St Project, San Francisco, Mus Modern Art, New York City, Seattle Arts Comn, Southeastern Ctr for Contemp Art, Louis Comfort

Tiffany Found, Beacon Cos, Frito-Lay Inc, New Eng General Services Admin Art-in-Archit Prog, Nat Endowment for Arts, VA Art-in-Archit Prog; trustee MA Coun on the arts and Humanities; advisor Pub Art Policy Project and Publ, Nat Endowment for Arts, 87; mem nat comt, Pub Art in Am, Conf, Philadelphia, 87; cur contemp art, Mus Fine Arts, Boston, 88-91; dir, Walker Art Ctr, Minneapolis, 91-2007; trustee, Twin Cities Pub TV, 92; comnr, Kwangju Biennale, Korea, 95; assoc dir, Mus Mod Art, New York, 2007-. *Awards:* Curatorial Excellence Award, Bard Coll Ctr Curatorial Studies, 2005; Am Asn Mus Centennial Hon Roll, 2006. *Bibliog:* 50 Most Powerful People in the Art World, ARTnews, 8/95; Americas Most Influential Women, Vanity Fair, 11/98; Power 100, ArtReview Mag, 11/2004. *Mem:* Asn Art Mus Dirs; Andy Warhol Found Visual Arts Inc (bd dirs, 1992); Minneapolis Club. *Mailing Add:* Mus Mod Art 11 W 53 St New York NY 10019

HALBROOK, RITA ROBERTSHAW
PAPERMAKER, PAINTER
b Greenville, Miss, May 22, 1930. *Study:* Miss Art Colony, with Ida Kohlmeyer, 77; Delta State Univ, BFA, 82. *Work:* Northern Electric Co, Laurel, Miss; Deposit Guaranty Nat Bank, Jackson, Miss; The Garnard Collection, Cleveland, Miss; Cottonlandia Mus, Greenwood, Miss; Catfish Capitol Mus, Belzoni, Miss. *Comn:* Vestments, All Saints Cath Church, Belzoni, Miss, 78; cast paper prints, Delta Processors, Indianola, Miss, 85; paper sculptures, Northeast Miss Med Ctr Women's Hosp, 86; cast paper, comn by Am Legislative Exchange Coun for Vpres Dan Quale; cast paper, Catfish Mus, Belzoni, 93; Risen Christ sculpture, St Therese Church, Jackson, 96. *Exhib:* Mid-South Exhib, 66 & 67 & Artist Registry Show, 70, Brooks Mem Mus; Miss Gallery, Miss Mus Art, Jackson, 80-81; Wall Series, Cottanlandia Mus, Greenwood, Miss & Meridian Mus Art, Miss, 83; Regional telecast, Miss Educ TV Studios; Nat League Am Pen Women Biennial, Washington, DC, 88 & Cork Gallery, Belzoni, Miss; Miss Gov Mansion Invitational, 89-90; Miss Craftsmens Guild Invitational, 89; Lincoln Ctr, NY, 94; and others. *Teaching:* Instr workshop, Allison's Wells Sch Arts & Crafts, Canton, Miss. *Awards:* Best in Show, Miss Art Colony, Crosstie Festival, 71 & Cottonlandia Competition, 83 & 90; First & Second Award, Miss Art Colony, 85; Best in Show, Miss Pen Women Statewide Competition, 88 & 95. *Bibliog:* Porioer (auth), Mississippi Artists, Univ Southern Miss Press, 78; Louis Dollahide (auth), Of Arts and Artists, Univ Miss Press, 81. *Mem:* Miss Art Colony (mem bd dir, 80-88); Miss Delta Br, Nat Pen Women; Craftsmen's Guild Miss (bd dir, 92-93). *Media:* Mixed Acrylic; Handmade Paper. *Dealer:* Gulf South Gallery Acton Ave McComb MS 39648. *Mailing Add:* 501 Cohn St Belzoni MS 39038-3703

HALBROOKS, DARRYL WAYNE
PAINTER, PRINTMAKER
b Evansville, Ind, May 3, 1948. *Study:* Univ Evansville, Ind; Murray State Univ, Ky; Southern Ill Univ. *Work:* Brooks Mem Art Gallery, Memphis, Tenn; Huntington Gallery, WVa; Evansville Mus Arts & Sci, Ind; Millikin Univ; Frito-Lay/The Blount Collection; and others. *Exhib:* Dulin Nat Print & Drawing Exhib, Dulin Gallery, Knoxville, Tenn, 76; Exhib 280, 78 & 79; Watercolor USA, 79; solo exhibs, Joy Horwich Gallery, Chicago, Ctr Arts, Kinston, NC & Brooks Mem Gallery, Memphis, Tenn; and others. *Teaching:* Prof painting, Eastern Ky Univ, Richmond, 72-94. *Awards:* Realism Show, Evansville, Ind, 90; Kinston Art Ctr, NC, 92; and others. *Bibliog:* Marion Garmel (auth), Works on Paper, Indianapolis News, 5/74; article, Arts Mag, 5/77; article, New Art Examiner, Chicago, 10/81; and others. *Media:* Acrylic; Encaustic. *Dealer:* Joy Horwich Gallery 226 E Ontario Chicago 60611

HALE, KEITH
PAINTER
Study: San Francisco Art Inst, BFA, 1989, MFA, 1993. *Work:* Berkeley Art Mus, Univ Calif; Tex Pacific Group, San Francisco. *Exhib:* The Italian Motorcycle as Art, Museo Italoamericano, San Francisco, 1992; Corazon Del Barrio, Mission Cult Ctr, San Francisco, 1993; solo exhibs, Belcher Street Gallery, San Francisco, 1993, Space Time Light Gallery, New York, 1994, Bradford Smock Gallery, San Francisco, 1998, Gallery Six Three, Calif, 2004, gallery Paule Anglim, San Francisco, 2006, 2008, 2010; Live Space to Art Space, Bedford Gallery, Walnut Creek, 1995; Confess, Southern Exposure, San Francisco, 1996; Images and Ideas, Berkeley Art Mus, 1999; Mail Art, Sharjah Art Mus, United Arab Emirates, 2000; You Know How I Feel, Ctr for Contemp Art, Santa Fe, 2008. *Teaching:* Vis fac, San Francisco Art Inst, 2001-02 & 2004; vis lectr, Calif Coll Arts & Crafts, 2002, Calif Coll Arts, 2004. *Awards:* Purchase Award, Wallace Gerbode Found, 1998; Pollock-Krasner Found Grant, 2008. *Bibliog:* Roberto Friedman (auth), High Art, Bay Area Reporter, 7/1994; Jeffrey Winters (auth), Spirit of Dildo, Bay Times, 4/1996; Johnny Ray Huston (auth), Space is the Place, Bay Guardian, 3/2006

HALE, NATHAN CABOT
SCULPTOR, WRITER, PAINTER
b Los Angeles, Calif, July 5, 1925. *Study:* Chouinard Art Inst, Los Angeles; Art Students League; Empire State Coll, BS, 73; Union Grad Sch, PhD, 86. *Work:* Bronze madonna, St Anthony of Padua, East Northport, NY; bronze reliefs, Rose Asn Bldg, Bronx, New York; and numerous mus & pvt collections. *Exhib:* Many group & solo exhibs, 47-. *Pos:* Dir, Ages Man Found, 68-; sculptor, Cycle Life Chapel Sculpture Proj, 68-; sr ed, Art/World, 85-89. *Teaching:* Mem fac, Pratt Inst, Brooklyn, 63-64; instr anat & drawing, Art Students League, 66-72, instr & lectr anat, 85-91. *Awards:* Gold Medal, Nat Acad Design; Recipient Purchase Award, sculpture, Los Angeles Co Mus, 55; Silver medal, Audubon Soc Sculpture, 72. *Mem:* Art Students League; Audubon Artists; Nat Acad; hon Fel Nat Sculpture Soc; Century Asn. *Publ:* Auth, Welded Sculpture, 69, Embrace of Life--the Sculpture of Gustav Vigelund, 70 & Abstraction in Art & Nature, 72; Birth of a Family, Doubleday, 79; auth, On the Perception of Human Form in Sculpture, White Whale Press, 2000; contribr, var archit & art mags. *Mailing Add:* 57 Sheffield Rd Amenia NY 12501

HALEGUA, ALFREDO
SCULPTOR
b Montevideo, Uruguay, May 4, 1930; US citizen. *Study:* Sch Bldg Design, Montevideo, Uruguay, 47; Sch Plastic Arts, Montevideo, BFA, 50; MFA 52. *Work:* Nat Gallery Art, Washington, DC; Baltimore Mus Art, Md; Ringling Mus Art, Sarasota, Fla; Denver Art Mus, Colo; Daytona Beach Mus Arts & Sci, Fla; Artist Sculpture Park, Monumental Works, Miami Dade Coll, Fla. *Comn:* Sculpture, 70 & 77, City of Baltimore, Md; obelisk, City of Salisbury, Md, 70; sculpture, Dade Co, Miami, Fla, 82; fountains, City of Charlotte, NC, 89. *Exhib:* Solo exhib, Baltimore Mus, Md, 63 & 68; Int Exhib Contemp Sculpture, Rodin Mus, Paris, France, 66; Halegua-Monumental Sculpture, Baltimore Mus Art, Md, 68; Contemp Am Artists, Baltimore Mus Art, Md, 70; Halegua-Recent Sculpture, Mint Mus Art, Charlotte, NC, 81; Int Biennial Contemp Art, Mus Contemp Art, Montevideo, Uruguay, 81; Five Int Artists in DC, Robert Brown Contemp Art, Washington, DC, 82; Halegua-Pub Sculpture & Proj, Mus Mod Art Latin Am, Washington, DC, 88-89; Washington Int Sculpture Art in Atrium, Washington, DC, 90. *Teaching:* Prof sculpture, Am Univ, Washington, DC, 64-65. *Awards:* Gold & Silver Medal, Nat Salon Fine Arts, Montevideo, Uruguay, 58; Res grant traveling exhib, Govt Uruguay, 59. *Bibliog:* Paul Richard (auth), Mood of elegance in H's, Washington Post, 7/28/68; Doug Davis (auth), Washington Letter, Arts Mag, 12/69 & 1/70. *Mem:* Int Sculpture Ctr. *Media:* Metals. *Publ:* Auth, Style and Content in Modern & Contemporary Art, Fine Arts Soc, 58; The role of art criticism, El Bien Publico, 2/8/59; Current trends in American Art, 9/12/63 & Models for integration of Sculpture & Architecture, 7/15/68, El Dia; The Magic Line-The Drawings of Pedro Figari, Monumental Sculptures, 88

HALEMAN, LAURA RAND
SCULPTOR, ARTIST
b New York, NY, Mar 3, 1946. *Study:* New York Univ, BS (summa cum laude), 68; Sch Visual Arts, Columbia Univ, 83; New Sch Social Res, 83; studio of Minoru Niizuma, 84. *Work:* Citibank Corp, NY; First Long Island Investors Corp, Jericho, NY; Sid Jacobson YMHA & YWHA, Roslyn, NY; Duralee Fabrics Corp, NY; All Co Abstract Corp, Carle Pl, NY; Nubest & Co, Manhasset, NY; Jackie Products Corp, San Juan, PR. *Comn:* Lawrence Jr High Sch Lobby, Cedarhurst, NY, 81; Long Island Hall of Fame: NY Islanders; Gen Aerospace Materials Corp, 88. *Exhib:* Nassau Co Mus Fine Art, Roslyn, 83, 84 & 91; Fine Arts Mus Long Island, 85 & 91; Heckscher Mus, Huntington, NY, 85; CAPA Rotational Arts Exhib, 85-; Lever House, NY, 86-92; Crystal Pavilion, NY, 88 & 92; Blue Hill Cult Ctr, 88 & 92; Elaine Benson, Bridgehampton, NY; Green St Gallery, NY; Strikoff Gallery, NY; LS Singer Gallery, Palm Springs, Calif. *Collection Arranged:* Four Women Artists, 84 & 19 Artists, 85, Great Neck Libr Gallery, Hempstead Harbor Artists Asn, NY. *Pos:* Dir & prin owner, The Sculpture Workshop, Brookville, NY, 80-; artist-in-residence, Lawrence Jr High Sch, 81. *Teaching:* Instr cult arts develop prog, Jericho Pub Sch, 82-83; lectr on the art of stone carving, Sculpture Asn Art Group, currently; instr sculpture seminars, Studio Tours Art Soc & Long Island Pub Sch Syst, currently. *Awards:* First Prize Sculpture, Suburban Art League; Hon Mention, Nassau Co Mus Fine Arts; Sculpture Award, Independent Art League Invitational Open; and others. *Mem:* Stone Sculpture Soc NY; Art Deco Soc NY (bd mem); Hempstead Harbor Artists Asn (bd mem); Independent Art Soc; Huntington Twp Art League; Suburban Art League. *Media:* Sandstone, Marble, Alabaster. *Interests:* interior design; antique collection; archit & landscape design. *Mailing Add:* PO Box 1 Westbury NY 11568

HALEVI, MARCUS
PHOTOGRAPHER
b Croton-on-Hudson, NY, Jan 17, 1942. *Study:* Univ Mich, BArch, 65. *Work:* Peabody Mus, Salem, Mass; Anchorage Fine Arts Mus, Alaska; Photogr Arch, Harvard Univ, Cambridge, Mass; DeCordova Mus, Lincoln, Mass. *Exhib:* As Seen by Both Sides, Boston Univ Art Gallery, Mass, 91; Artists Confront Child Abuse, Howard Yezerski Gallery, Boston, Mass, 92; Pictures of the Year, Nat Press Club, Washington, 92; Living with the Memories, Cambridge Multi-Cult Arts Ctr, Mass, 95; one-person shows, Carpenter Ctr Arts, Harvard Univ, 95, Cambridge Multicultural Art Ctr, 99 & Schlesinger Libr, Radcliffe Col, 2001; DeCordova Mus, Lincoln, Mass, 98; 10 Cambodian Women, Radcliffe Coll Gallery, Cambridge, Mass, 2001. *Awards:* Pulitzer Prize for Gen News, 88; Photog Grant, Nat Endowment for Arts, 92; New Eng Found Arts Grant, 97; Mass Cult Coun Grant, 97; Evelyn Nef Fel (MacDowell residency), 97-98; Leff Found Grant, 99. *Media:* Black & White Photography. *Publ:* Auth, Alaska Crude: Visions of the Last Frontier Photographs by Marcus Halevi, Little, Brown & Co, 77; Building a Tall Ship, Thorndike Press, 85; Bedlum: Romanian Insane Asylums, Palm Press, 2000. *Mailing Add:* 33 Cedar St Somerville MA 02143

HALEY, GAIL E
ILLUSTRATOR, COLLECTOR
b Charlotte, NC, Nov 4, 1939. *Study:* Richmond Prof Inst Va, 59-60. *Work:* Kerlan Collection, Univ Minn, Minneapolis; DeGrummond Collection, Univ Southern Miss, Hattiesburg. *Teaching:* Instr writing & illus for children (artist-in-residence), Appalachian State Univ, 80-. *Awards:* Caldecott Medal Best Illus Children's Book USA, 71; Kate Greenaway Medal Best Illus Children's Book England, 76; Kodai Tosho Award, Japan Best Book, 80; The Kerlan Award, Univ of Minn, 89. *Bibliog:* David Considine (auth), Toys, technology & teaching, Top of the News, summer 85 & An integrated approach to visual literacy and children's books, Sch Libr J, 9/86; Susan Austin (auth), Author illustrator profile, Library Talk, 11-12/89. *Mem:* Puppeteers Am; Int Visual Literacy Asn. *Collection:* Antique and contemporary children's games, toys, books, dolls and puppets from Europe and the US. *Publ:* Of Mermaids, Myths and Meaning: A Sea Tale, The New Advocate, winter 90; Mountain Jack Tales, Dutton, 92; Imagine That Integrating Imagery Intov Instruction, 92; coauth, Dream Peddler, Libraries Unlimited, Dutton, 93; coauth, Visual Messages: Developing Critical Viewing and Thinking Skills Through Childrens Literature, Libraries Unlimited, 94. *Mailing Add:* PO Box 1023 Blowing Rock NC 28605

HALL, CHRISTINE & ANDREW J
COLLECTORS
b Bristol, England, 1951. *Study:* Oxford Univ, grad (chemistry, with honors), 1973; Insead, France, MBA, 1980. *Pos:* With Brit Petroleum, 1973-79 & 1980-82; with Phibro Energy Inc (now Phibro LLC), 1982-, pres, 1987-, chmn & chief exec officer, 1993-. *Awards:* Named one of Top 200 Collectors, ARTnews mag, 2006-13. *Collection:* Contemporary art, especially German. *Mailing Add:* Phibro LLC 500 Nyala Farms Rd Westport CT 06880

HALL, DOUGLAS E
VIDEO ARTIST, PHOTOGRAPHER
b Apr 25, 1944. *Study:* Harvard Univ, BA (Anthropology), 66; Rinehart Sch Sculpture Md Inst Art, Baltimore, MFA, 69. *Work:* Whitney Mus Am Art & Mus Mod Art, NY; San Francisco Mus Mod Art; Mus Contemp Art Chicago; Ctr George Pompidou, Paris; and others. *Exhib:* One-person exhibs, Long Beach Mus Art, 76 & 80, San Francisco Mobius Video Festival, 76, 80 Langton Street, San Francisco, 83, Whitney Mus, NY, 84, Shoshana Wayne Gallery, Santa Monica, Calif, 92, Univ Art Mus, Berkeley, 93, Rena Bransten Gallery, San Francisco, 94, 95, 97, 98 & 2001, Kunstwerke, Berlin, 94, Feigen, New York City, 99, Galerie Micha Kapinos, Berlin, Ger, 99, Rena Bransten Gallery, San Francisco, 01, 03, Bellevue Art Mus, Wash, 01, VOX, Montréal, 02, Feigen Contemp, New York City, 03, and others; Two Channel Video, Whitney Mus Am Art, NY, 78; Space/Time/Sound-1970's: A Decade in the Bay Area (auth, catalog), San Francisco Mus Mod Art, 79; Reading Video, Mus Mod Art, NY, 82; Whitney Mus Biennal, NY, 83 & 85; Video: Recent Acquisitions, Mus Mod Art, NY, 84; Video from Vancouver to San Diego, Mus Mod Art, NY, 85; Bay Area Media & New Acquisitions, San Francisco Mus Mod Art, 90; Video: Two Decades, Mus Mod Art, NY, 92-93; System Aesthetics: Works from the Permanent Collection, San Francisco Mus Mod Art, 96; Dislocations, Philadelphia Mus Art, 96; Vision Ruhr, Zeche Zollern II/IV, Dortmund, Ger, 2000; Photog Now, Contemp Arts Ctr, New Orleans, 2000; Paradise in Search of a Future, CEPA Gallery, Buffalo, NY, 2001; Beyond Boundaries, Ansel Adams Ctr for Photog, San Francisco, 2001; Between Earth and Heaven-New Classical Movements in the Art of Today, Mus of Modern Art, Ostend, Belgium, 2001; Depicting Absence/Implying Presence, San Jose Inst of Contemp Art, Calif, 2001; Sarah Meltzer Gallery, New York City, 02; Vedanta Gallery, Chicago, 02; Henry Art Gallery, Seattle, 02; Elias Fine Art, Boston, 02; Mus Mod Art, 02; and many others. *Collection Arranged:* Mus Mod Kunst, Vienna; Mus Mod Art; Long Beach Mus Art; Mus Contemp Art, Chicago; Brooklyn Mus Art; Kunsthaus Zurich; San Francisco Mus Mod Art; Berkeley Art Mus & Pacific Film Archive, Univ Calif, Berkeley; Ctr George Pompidou, Paris; Berlinsche Galerie, Martin Gropius Bau. *Teaching:* prof, San Francisco Art Inst, New Genres Dept, 81-2006, dept chair, 89-91; vis artist, Va Commonwealth Univ, Richmond, 78, San Francisco Art Inst, 79-80, Minneapolis Col Art & Design, 83, Art Inst Chicago, 87, 94, Univ Sao Paulo, Brazil, 90, Univ Windsor, Can, 94, Univ Ill, Carbondale, 96, Calif Coll Arts, 2006. *Awards:* Governor of Prefecture's Award, Protopia '81, Tokyo, Japan, 81; Award in Video Art, US Film & Video Festival, Park City, Utah, 82; Gilmore D Clarke & Michael Rapuano Rome Prize in Visual Arts, Am Acad, Rome, 95-96; fel, Calif Arts Coun, 92-93; Flintridge Found Award for Vis Artists, 99-00. *Bibliog:* James Scarborough (auth), The Perils of Belief, Art Week, Vol 22 No 11, 3/21/91; Roberta Smith (auth) In Installation Art, A Bit of the Spoiled Brat, NY Times Arts & Leisure Section, p 31, 1/3/93; Mary Hull Webster (auth), In Mr Wizard's Shadow: Doug Hall at UAM Berkeley, Artweek, Vol 24, No 10, p 4-5, 5/20/93. *Mem:* Calif Art Comn (panelist, 92); Nat Endowment for Arts (panelist, 89); Calif Arts Comn (panelist, 87); Bay Area Video Coalition (bd dir, 84-89); San Francisco Art Inst (bd trustees, 80-85, artists comt, 79-85). *Media:* Photography; Video Installation. *Publ:* Sally Jo Fijer (co-ed), Illuminating Video, An Essential Guide to Video Art, Alperture Bks, 90. *Dealer:* Rena Bransten Gallery 77 Geary St San Francisco CA 94108; Feigen Contemporary 535 W 20th St NY 10011. *Mailing Add:* 4131 23rd St San Francisco CA 94114

HALL, MICHAEL DAVID
SCULPTOR, EDUCATOR
b Upland, Calif, May 20, 1941. *Study:* Western Wash State Col, 58-60; Univ NC, BA, 62; Univ Iowa, 62; Univ Wash, MFA (sculpture), 64. *Work:* Princeton Univ Art Mus, NJ; City of Grand Rapids, Mich; Detroit Inst Arts; J B Speed Art Mus, Louisville, Ky; Milwaukee Art Mus; and others. *Comn:* Sculpture, Warren Plaza, Detroit, 80, Galeria Center, Southfield, Mich, 88; Kresge Art Mus, Lansing, Mich, 2009. *Exhib:* Whitney Mus Am Art Ann Sculpture Exhib, NY, 68 & 73; Am Sculpture, Sheldon Mem Art Gallery, Univ Nebr, Lincoln, 70; Hammarskjold Plaza, NY, 72; Sculpture Off the Pedestal, Grand Rapids, Mich, 73; Three Installations, Detroit Inst Arts, 77; Scale & Environment, Walker Art Ctr, Minneapolis, 77; Los Angeles Inst Contemp Art, 80; Nassau Co Mus, Roslyn, NY, 83; Socrates Sculpture Park, Long Island City, NY, 88; Detroit Inst Arts, 2001; Scarab Club, Detroit, 2004; and others. *Collection Arranged:* North by Midwest; The Painting of Charles Burchfield, Columbus Mus of Art Columbus, March-May, 97; Great Lakes Muse; Am Scene Painting in the Upper Midwest 1910-1960, Flint Inst of Art, Flint MI, Nov -Dec 2003. *Pos:* Adj cur Am Folk Art, Columbus Mus Art, Columbus, Ohio, 2007-. *Teaching:* Instr ceramics & sculpture, Univ Colo, Boulder, 65-66; assoc prof sculpture, Univ Ky, 66-70; resident sculptor, Cranbrook Acad Art, 70-90; Miami Univ, Ohio, 91. *Awards:* Guggenheim Found Fel, 73; Nat Endowment Art Fel, 74; Mich Coun for Arts Fel, 85, 88. *Bibliog:* Articles, Arts Mag, 6/79; Sculpture mag, 10/0003; www.thedetroiter.com, 1/2004. *Mem:* Int Sculpture Ctr; Intuit The Ctr for Intuitive and Outsider Art; The Scarab Club of Detroit. *Media:* Steel, Aluminum. *Res:* The paintings of Emerson Burkhart, 1905-1969 (monograph in process). *Collection:* America Folk Art; American Scene Paintings; Inuit Sculpture & Native Am Art. *Publ:* Stereoscopic Perspective, UMI Rsch Press, Ann Arbor, 88; The Artist Outsider, Smithsonian Press, 94; The Paintings of Charles Burchfield: North by Midwest, Abrams, 97; Great Lakes Muse, Flint Inst of Art, Flint MI, 2003; Emerson Burkhaut: An Ohio Painter's Song of Himself, Scala Pub, 2009. *Dealer:* Hill Gallery 407 W Brown St Birmingham MI 48009. *Mailing Add:* 3417 Caniff Ave Hamtramck MI 48212

HALL, ROBERT L
MUSEOLOGIST, PAINTER
b Miami, Fla. *Study:* Fisk Univ, BS (art), 72; George Washington Univ, MAT (mus educ), 75. *Work:* Fisk Univ Mus Art; Carroll Reece Mus, ETenn State Univ. *Comn:* Mural, Miami-Dade Community Col, Cult Arts Ctr, Miami, 73. *Exhib:* Lowe Art Mus, Univ Miami, 70; Zale Mus, Bishop Col, Tex, 78; Black Artists South, Huntsville Mus Art, Ala, 79; Recent Works, Van Vechten Art Gallery, Fisk Univ, 82; Carroll Reece Mus, ETenn State Univ, 84. *Collection Arranged:* Lev Mills Prints (auth, catalog), 78; Betty Blayton (auth, catalog), 79; Recent Acquisitions (auth, catalog), Fisk Univ Mus Art, 80; Portraits by Carl Van Vechten Traveling Show (auth, catalog), 80; Anderson, Hyman and Wood (auth, catalog), 81; Gathered Visions, 92; In the Arms of the Elders, 2002; New Visions, 2003; On their Own, 2005; A Creative Profile, 2007. *Pos:* Cur collections & educ, Fisk Univ Mus Art, 73-84; educ dir, Anacostia Community Mus, Smithsonian Inst. *Teaching:* Instr, Fisk Univ, 76-79. *Bibliog:* 250 Yrs of Afro-American Art: An Annotated Biography, Lynn Moody (auth), TT Bowker, 81. *Mem:* Am Asn Mus; African Am Mus Asn; Commonwealth Asn Mus. *Media:* Acrylic, Oil. *Res:* African American public art in Washington DC. *Publ:* Gathered Visions: Selected Works by African American Women Artists, 92; New Visions, 2003; On Their Own, 2005. *Mailing Add:* Anacostia Community Mus Smithsonian Inst Educ Dept 1901 Fort Pl SE Washington DC 20020

HALL, SUSAN
PAINTER, CERAMIST
b Point Reyes Station, Calif, Mar 19, 1943. *Study:* Calif Coll Arts & Crafts, Oakland, 62-65; Univ Calif, Berkeley, MA, 67. *Work:* Whitney Mus, New York; Brooklyn Mus, New York; Carnegie Inst, Pittsburgh, Pa; San Francisco Mus Art; Nat Mus Women Arts, Washington, DC; Hudson River Mus, Yonkers, NY; New Mus, New York. *Exhib:* San Francisco Mus Art Ann, 66; solo exhibs, San Francisco Mus Art, 67, Whitney Mus, 72, Nancy Hoffman Gallery, New York, 73 & 75, Hamilton Gallery, 78-79 & 81 & Dart Gallery, Chicago, 81; Twenty-six Contemp Women Artists, Aldrich Mus Contemp Art, Ridgefield, Conn, 71; Printmaking-the 70's into the 80's, Mus Fine Arts, Boston; Am Realism, San Francisco Mus Art, 85; Trabia Macafee, New York, 87-89; Milagros, San Antonio, 95; Brendan Walter, Los Angeles, 95; Univ Tex, San Antonio, 96; Jan Holloway Gallery, 97; San Francisco Mus Art Gallery; Gail Harvey Gallery, Los Angeles, 99; Frank Lloyd Wright Civic Ctr, San Rafael, 99; Jernigan Wicker Gallery, San Francisco, 99; Gail Harvey Gallery, 99-2001; Erickson Fine Arts, 2007; Marin Agricultural Land Trust Ranches and Rolling Hills, 2004-2013; Erickson Fine Arts, 2011. *Teaching:* Instr, Univ Calif, Berkeley, 67-70, Sarah Lawrence Coll, Bronxville, NY, 72-75 & Sch Visual Arts, 81-92; vis artist, Univ Tex, Austin, 93, Univ Tex, San Antonio, 95 & San Francisco Art Inst, 96. *Awards:* Nat Endowment Arts Award, 79 & 88; Krasner Pollock Found, 86; Adolph Gottlieb Found Grant, 95; Bd Dirs Award, Marin Arts Coun, 98. *Bibliog:* William Zimmer (auth), article, NY Times-Westchester, 4/84; John R Clarke (auth), Image, technique & spirituality in Susan Hall's new work, Arts Mag, 6/88; Christine Liotta (auth), Review Art News, 3/90; Susan Hall, Finding Her Center, Woman's Art J, spring/summer 2000; Painting Point Reyes, A Book of Susan Hall's Paintings, Green Bridge Press, 2002; John R Clarke (auth), Susan Hall and the discourse of landscape; Independent J, Rick Polito, Point Reyes Perspective; bk of paintings from Home Before Dark Show, Tobys Gallery, Giacomini Gallery, Point Reyes Sta, 2005 & Coll Marin, 9/2008; River Flowing Home, An Artists Life. *Mem:* Marin Arts Coun. *Media:* Oil; Ceramics. *Mailing Add:* Box 1295 Point Reyes Station CA 94956

HALL, WILLIAM A
ARCHITECT
b 1923. *Study:* Univ Okla, BA; Mass Inst Tech, M (city planning). *Mem:* Fel, Am Inst Architects; Nat Acad. *Mailing Add:* William A Hall Partnership 42 E 21 St New York NY 10010

HALLAM, JOHN S
HISTORIAN, ADMINISTRATOR
b Seattle, Wash, Oct 10, 1947. *Study:* Seattle Univ, BA, 70; Univ Wash, MA, 74, PhD, 80. *Pos:* Chmn dept art, Pacific Lutheran Univ, 90-92. *Teaching:* Assoc prof art hist, Pacific Lutheran Univ, 90-92. *Mem:* Coll Art Asn; Am Soc 18th Century Studies. *Res:* 18th & 19th century Europ & Am Art, urban, imagery, still-life, genre painting & sculpture. *Publ:* Auth, Charles Willson Peale and Hogart's Line of Beauty, Mag Antiques, 86; Meaning & Manner in Chardin's La bonne Education, Bulletin Mus Fine Art, Houston, 86; 18th Century American Townscape and the Face of Colonialism, Smithsonian Studies in Am Art, 91. *Mailing Add:* Pacific Lutheran University Dept of Art Ingram Hall Tacoma WA 98447

HALLE, DIANE & BRUCE T
COLLECTORS
b Springfield, Mass, 1930. *Study:* Eastern Mich Univ, BBA, 1950. *Hon Degrees:* Eastern Mich Univ, hon PhD, 1956. *Pos:* Founder & owner, Discount Tire co, Ann Arbor, 1960-. *Awards:* Gold Plate Award, Am Acad Achievement, 1994; Entrepreneurial Fel, Univ Ariz; named one of Top 200 Collectors, ARTnews mag, 2008-13. *Collection:* Latin American art; contemporary sculpture. *Mailing Add:* Discount Tire Co 20225 N Scottsdale Rd Scottsdale AZ 85255

HALLENBECK, POMONA JUANITA
PAINTER, INSTRUCTOR
b Roswell, NMex, Nov 12, 1938. *Study:* Eastern NMex Univ, AA, 65; Sch Visual Arts; Pan Am Sch Art; Arts Students League, MA; Studies with Mario Cooper, John Groth, David Stone Martin, Skip Lawrence, Christopher Schink, Frank Webb, Arne Westerman, Don Andrews, Charles Reid, & Leonard Brooks. *Work:* Eastern NMex Univ, NMex Hist Soc Mus, Roswell, NMex; Union Theological Sem, Levi-Strauss co, New York; Rochester Mus Fine Art, NY; Blue Cross & Blue Shield, Tulsa, Okla; Ghost Ranch Conference Ctr, Santa Fe, NMex; Cotton Inc, New York; Mt Bell Tel & Tel co, NMex; Jack Leib Filmmakers, Chicago; Mus Fine Art, Galveston, Tex; Bitzer

& Johnson, NMex; Piedre Lumbre Mus, NMex; Morgan Nelson, Rosewell, NMex; Cheryl Ellis-Piney Books, Austin, Tex, 2010; Ellis/Ikrais Distributors, Bastrop, Tex; Prof Land Surveyors; Ghost Ranch Libr. *Comn:* Watercolor, Jack Tar Enterprises, Galveston, Tex, 65; banners & posters, UN Action Against Apartheid, New York, 74; fabric designs, Wamsutta, Huckapoo, Burlington & JC Penny, New York, 74; Cotton Inc, 86; Lady J Designs (painting on silk), 88, book covers for Wink Trilogy, Augsburg Fortress', Minneapolis, Minn, 1992, 1996, 2008; Wink, Just Jesus; Southwest Expressions, Chicago; Ghost Ranch & Friends (book cover), Santa Fe, NMex, 92; Rev. Jim Hepler, Pagosa Springs, Colo; Dir Jim & Debra Hepler; Dr Bob Phillips, ENMU, NMex; Dr J Gould, Lovelace, Albuquerque, NMex. *Exhib:* Finishing Touches, Trunk Show, Roswell, MNex, 88; Compadre Conference, Ghost Ranch, NMex; Southwest Expressions, Chicago; St Edwards Univ, Austin, Tex, 94; Bitzer-Johnson Gallery, NMex, 96; Ausburg Press, 2001; Ghost Ranch, NMex, 2005-2006; Roswell Potters Guild, 2006-2007; Piedra Lumbre Ctr, Abiquiu, NMex, 2007; Ghost Ranch Festival, NMex, 2010, 2012; Ghost Ranch Writers, Richard Ralph Prof Land Surveyors, 2011, 2012; Big Brushes. *Collection Arranged:* Majorie Becker, Cindi Ellis, John Gould, Bob Phillips, Rizk Ikhrais. *Pos:* Designer window decor, Highland Mall, Austin, Tex, 77; co-ordination, Ghost Ranch Calendar Project, Santa Fe, NMex, 92; art workshop coordr, Ghost Ranch, Abiquiu, NMex, 94-96, 2000-10; prog selection, Abiquiu, NMex, 2010. *Teaching:* Artist & teacher watercolor & papermaking, Austin Community Coll & Roswell Mus, 85; developer of 3 yr academic course in watercolor for NMex Military Inst, '84, workshops (W/C, Papermaking, Wearable Art) Carrizo Art School Ruidoso, NMex, 86-88; workshops, Ghost Ranch, NMex, 84-2012; instr, Elderhostel Progs, 86-99; artist-in-residence, Ghost Ranch, Santa Fe, 94-2008; instr, Laughing at the Sun Gallery, Austin, Tex, 98, Art After Sch, Bastrop, Tex, 98-2001, Univ Tex, Austin, 98-2008, Bastrop Continuing Educ, 98-2001, Herman Miller Group, 99-2001 & Austin Mus Laguna Art Sch, Tex, 2000-12; instr, Univ Tex, Austin, Tex, 2000-09; instr, Dougherty Art Center, Austin, Tex, 2009-2011. *Awards:* Purchase Award, Am Artist Exhib, 75; Bronze Medallion, Prix d'Paris Exhib, Raymond Duncan Gallery, Paris, France, 81; Hon Mention, NMex Watercolor Soc, 97; Dougherty Arts Ctr, 2008-. *Bibliog:* NMex videos, silk printing & book covers for educational channels; Five Astonishing Women (video), Los Angeles, 96-97; Painting the Pecos, Persimmon Hill Mag, 98; Pomona, Video, 2004; Phillip Newell (auth), Seeing the Song, IONA, 2010; 897 Miles of River, Mother/Daughter Paint the Pecos River; Turkey the Old and New. *Mem:* Women in the Arts, Washington, DC; Tex Watercolor Soc; AWS Asn; Laguna Gloria Mus, Austin, Tex; Florence Hawley Ellis Mus, Abiquiu, NMex; Ghost Ranch Compadre/Comadres; Roswell Potters Guild; Cornerstones, Santa Fe; Sabeel, Palestine; ICPR. *Media:* Watercolor; Fiberart, Silk. *Res:* The sites & colonization of Pecos River; Ellis Island, 2007 & Turkey, Cumbres Toltec Railroad, 2009-2010. *Specialty:* Watercolors on Yupo paper. *Interests:* Jazz musicians. *Publ:* Illusr, Scott Foresman Math, Scott Foresman, 75; Charles Dickens' Anthology, Crown Publ, 76; illusr bk covers, Julian of Norwich, Nachman of Bratslav & Pseudo Dionysius, Paulist Press, 77; Naming the Powers, Unmasking the Powers Engaging the Powers, Augsburg Fortress, 93; The Human Being, 2002; Enigma of the Son of the Man, 2002; My Turkish Sketchbook, 2005; The Human Being, 2009-2010; Just Jesus, 2012. *Dealer:* Bitzere-Johnson Gallery Roswell NM; Trading Post-Abiquiu, NM; Piedra Lumbre Center Albiquiu NM

HALLER, DOUGLAS MARTIN
CURATOR, HISTORIAN

b Detroit, Mich, July 28, 1951. *Study:* Wayne State Univ, BA, 73, MA, 82; Acad Cert Archivists, cert, 89-. *Collection Arranged:* Portals of the Past, Hist Photographs, 83; C Watkins Photographic Murals, Calif Photogr, 83; Seeing Is Believing (auth, catalog), CIGNA Mus, Philadelphia, 89, Univ Pa Mus, 90; Jean Pascal Sebah's Athens, Ottoman Photographs, 93. *Pos:* Co-own & consult, Hermes Antiques, Washington, 74-79; cur photographs, Calif Hist Soc Libr, San Francisco & Los Angeles, 82-86; subject specialist hist photographs, John F Kennedy Univ Ctr for Mus Studies, San Francisco, 83-84; mus archivist, Univ Pa, 86. *Teaching:* Instr Ancient hist, Wayne State Univ,79-82. *Mem:* Soc Am Archivists (pres visual mat sect, 81-, chair, 89-91); Am Asn Mus; Nat Endowment for Humanities; Delaware Valley Archivists Group; Photog Sesquicentennial Proj, Delaware Valley. *Res:* Photographs as historical documents; vintage photographic processes; biography of photographers; portrait and architectural photography. *Publ:* Auth, Watkins photography exhibit, 83, the California Historical Society's Arnold Genthe collection, 84, CHS Courier; coauth, Four pioneer photographers in California, Calif Hist Soc, 86; auth, The William Pepper bust and statue, Univ Pa Mus Newsletter, 87

HALLEY, PETER
PAINTER

b New York, NY, Sept 24, 1953. *Study:* Yale Univ, New Haven, Conn, BA; Univ New Orleans, MFA. *Work:* Guggenheim Mus, NY; Wright State Univ, Dayton; Carnegie Mus Art, Pittsburgh; San Francisco Mus Modern Art, Calif; Addison Gallery Am Art, Andover, Mass; Whitney Mus. *Comn:* Painting for bd rm, Chase Manhattan Bank, NY, 89. *Exhib:* Biennial, Whitney Mus, NY, 87; Viewpoints: Postwar painting & sculpture, Guggenheim Mus, NY, 88; Binational: Am Art of the late 80's, Mus Fine Arts, Boston, 88; Carnegie Int, Carnegie Mus Art, Pittsburgh, 88; Ten plus Ten: Contemp Soviet and Am Painters, Ft Worth Mus, Tex, 89; Abstraction in Question, Ringling Mus Art, Sarasota, Fla, 89; Projects & Portfolios, Brooklyn Mus, NY, 89; Word as Image: Am Art 1960-1990, Milwaukee, Wis, 90; Touring Europ Retrospective, Switz, France, Spain & Amsterdam, 91-92; McClain Gallery, Texas, 2007. *Teaching:* Instr painting & sculpture, Sch Visual Arts, NY, 89-. *Bibliog:* Mark Stevens (auth), Neo-Geo Art's Computer Hum, Newsweek, 11/87; Roberta Smith (auth), Minimalism's Slow Fire, New York Times, 12/89; Jeanne Siegel, Art Talk Da Capo Press, NY, 89. *Media:* Acrylic, Oil. *Publ:* Auth, Collected Essays 1981-1987, Bruno Bischofberger, 88. *Dealer:* Gagosian Gallery 136 Wooster St New York NY 10012

HALLIDAY, NANCY R
ILLUSTRATOR, INSTRUCTOR

b Chicago, Ill, Mar 30, 1936. *Study:* Mich State Univ, East Lansing, 54-56 & 58-61; Art Sch Soc Arts & Crafts, Mich, 56-57; Univ Okla, Norman, BSc, 62; Northeastern Ill Univ, Chicago, MA, 88. *Work:* Fla State Mus, Gainesville; Hunt Inst Botanical Documentation, Pittsburgh, Pa; Visual Arts Gallery, Pensacola Jr Col, Fla. *Comn:* One hundred nine drawings for publs on lichens, Mason Hale, Smithsonian Inst, 67, 69; Watercolor poster, Rare Animal Relief Effort, Inc, NY, 81; nine stamp paintings, Nat Wildlife Fedn, Washington, 82, 83, 85, 89, 92, 93; 12″x18″ illustrated interpretive sign at Morton Grove Prairie, Morton Grove, Ill, 95; eighteen drawings of plants for Winnebago Co Forest Preserve District, Ill, 93; and others; two illustrated interpretive signs, Lincoln Park, Chicago, Il, 2011. *Exhib:* Perfectly Beautiful: Art in Science, Smithsonian Inst, 78; one-person show, Thomas Ctr for the Arts, Gainesville, Fla, 82; two-person show, Macon, Ga, 82; Wildlife in Art, Nat Wildlife Fedn, Vienna, Va, 83; Ann Bird Art Exhib, Leigh Yawkey Woodson Art Mus, Wausau, Wis, 83; Sixth Int Exhib Botanical Art & Illustration, Hunt Inst Botanical Doc, Pittsburgh, 88; Wildlife Art in Am, Bell Mus Natural Hist, Minneapolis, Minn, 94; Art of the Prairie, Chicago Botanic Garden, Glencoe, Ill, 95; Picturing Natural Hist, Smithsonian Inst, 96; Guild of Natural Sci Illusr Ann Mems Exhib, Evora, Portugal, 2000; Mammals Revealed, NY State Mus, Albany, NY, 2005-2006; Soc Animal Artists 50th Anniv Exhib, San Diego Nat History Mus, Calif, 2010; one-person show, Glenview Public Lib, Glenview, Ill, 2012; featured artist, annual Spring exhib of the Nature Artists' Guild of the Morton Arboretum, Lisele, Ill, 2015. *Pos:* Lectr & asst exhib preparator, Mus Mich State Univ, East Lansing, 57-60; asst, Mus Northern Ariz, Flagstaff, summer 63; artist, Nat Mus Natural Hist, Smithsonian Inst, 66-70; illusr, dept natural sci, Fla State Mus, Gainesville, 73-81; artist-naturalist, Forest Preserve Dist Cook Co, Ill, 89-2003. *Teaching:* Instr, animal illus, Univ Fla, Gainesville, 77, 78 & 82, biology illus, Univ Ill, Chicago, 85-86, nature illus, Gov State Univ, University Park, Ill, 93-2000, botanical illus (certified prog), Morton Arboretum, Lisle, Ill, 93-2011; artist-in-education, Ryerson Conserv Area, Deerfield, Ill, 86; artist-in-residence, Rockford Art Mus, Ill, 91; plus many other lectures and workshops; Instr, Guild of Natural Sci Illusr Summer Workshop, (drawing birds, Morton Arboretum, Lisle, Ill, 2002 and drawing mammals, Pierce Cedar Creek Inst, Hastings, Mich, 2008); botanical illusr (certified program), Chicago Botanic Garden, Glencoe, IL, 2010-. *Awards:* First Prize Color Wildlife, Guild Natural Sci Illusr Show, Hunt Inst Botanical Doc, Pa, 79; Second Prize Watercolor, Wildlife Art Exhib, Nat Wildlife Fedn, Vienna, Va, 83; Cur Choice Mammalogy, Guild Nat Sci Illusr Show, Art Inst, Arizona-Sonora Desert Mus, Tucson, AZ, 2005; Special Svc award, Guild of Nat Sci Illustrators, 2013; Honorary membership, Guild of Natural Sci Illustrators, 2015. *Bibliog:* Vera Norwood (auth), Made from this Earth: American Women & Nature, Univ NC Press, 93. *Mem:* Soc Animal Artists; Guild Natural Sci Illusr (historian, 95-); Nature Artists' Guild of Morton Arboretum. *Media:* Watercolor; Pen & Ink, Pastel, Oil. *Res:* History of biological illustration. *Interests:* Bird-watching, bicycling, canoeing & hiking. *Publ:* Illusr, Behavioral ecology of the Yucatan jay, Wilson Bulletin, 76; auth, Bird illustration, In: Guild Handbook of Scientific Illustration (ed, Elaine R S Hodges), second edition, John Wiley & Sons, Inc, 2003; cover illus (2), Natural Areas Jour, 96, 99; illusr, Atlas of Breeding Birds in Pa, Univ Pittsburgh Press, 92; illusr, Mammals of North America, Princeton Univ Press, 2nd ed, 2009; and many other scientific journals. *Mailing Add:* 1156 Pine St Apt 4 Glenview IL 60025

HALLIGAN, ROGER PHILLIP
SCULPTOR, DESIGNER

b Troy, NY, Mar 18, 1948. *Study:* Le Moyne Col, BA, 70; Univ Ga, Athens, MFA, 77. *Work:* Weatherspoon Gallery, Univ NC, Greensboro; NC Ctr Advancement of Teaching, Collowhee, NC; Inst Ecology, Univ Ga, Athens. *Comn:* Sculpture, Shelter Cove/Palmetto Dunes, Hilton Head, SC, 89; sculpture, NC Zoo, Asheboro, 97; sculpture, Triad Regional Farmers Market & State of NC, Greensboro, 98. *Exhib:* Ann Juried Exhib, SECCA, Winston-Salem, NC, 78; Mint Mus Biennial, 79; Zoo Artists, Fayetteville Mus Art, NC, 80; NC in NY, Nat Arts Club, NY, 93; two-person show, Artspace, Raleigh, NC, 96; Art for Arts Sake, Green Hill Ctr NC Art, Greensboro, 97; solo exhibs incl Lee Hansley Gallery, Raleigh, NC, 94, Paisley Pineapple, Greensboro, NC, 99, Hodges-Taylor Gallery and Nations Bank, 2000. *Pos:* Exhib designer, NC Zoological Park, 77-90; guest cur, Green Hill Ctr NC Art, 98; ptnr, Two Oaks Studio, 98-. *Awards:* Best in Show, Sculpture 79, Weatherspoon Gallery, 79; Artist-in-Residence, NC Zoological Park, 97. *Bibliog:* Chuck Twardy (auth), Loading upon art, Raleigh News & Observer, 94; Burton Wasserman (auth), Outdoor Sculpture, Art Matters, Philadelphia; Blue Greenberg (auth), Review, Durham Herald Sun, 96. *Mem:* Tri State Sculptors Educ Asn (pres, 92-97); Int Sculpture Ctr; Green Hill Ctr NC Art (bd dir, 93-98). *Media:* Steel, Concrete. *Specialty:* NC and SE contemp art

HALLMAN, GARY LEE
PHOTOGRAPHER

b St Paul, Minn, Aug 7, 1940. *Study:* Univ Minn, Minneapolis, BA, 66, MFA, 71. *Work:* Mus Mod Art, NY; Int Mus Photog, Rochester; Nat Gallery Can, Toronto; Fogg Art Mus, Harvard Univ; Princeton Univ Art Mus. *Comn:* Photo murals, Dayton-Hudson Corp, Minneapolis, 70. *Exhib:* Gary Hallman and Jeff Murphy, Dept Art Gallery, Univ Northern Iowa, Cedar Falls; Special Collectors' Special Collections, Mus NMex, Santa Fe; solo exhibs, Hudson Valley Inst Art & Photog Resources, Peekskill, NY & Dept Art Hist & Design, Univ Notre Dame, Ind, 96; Trues and Trials Color Photog since 1975, Minneapolis Inst Arts, Minn, 96; Int Photog & Digital Image Exhib, Wellington B Gregg Gallery, ECarolina Univ, Greenville, NC, 97. *Teaching:* Vis artist, Southampton Col, summer 72 & 73; asst prof photog, Univ Minn, Minneapolis, 70-76, assoc prof photog, 76-; vis adj prof photog, RI Sch Design, 77; vis exchange prof, Univ NMex, Albuquerque, 84-85; vis assoc prof, Colo Col, Colorado Springs, 90. *Awards:* Bush Found Fel for Artists, 76; Fel, McKnight Found Photog, 82 & 90; Artist Assistance Fel Grant, Minn State Arts Bd, 96. *Bibliog:* E W Peterson (auth), The photography of Gary Hallman, Image, 9/75. *Mem:* Soc Photog Educ. *Dealer:* Hudson Center For the Arts and Photographic Resource Peekskill NY. *Mailing Add:* 5411 Zenith Ave S Edina MN 55410-2464

HALLMAN, TED, JR
TAPESTRY ARTIST, EDUCATOR
b Bucks Co, Pa, Dec 23, 1933. *Study:* Tyler Sch, Temple Univ, Sen scholar, BFA & BSEd; Fontainebleau Fine Arts, Pew scholar, cert, with Jacques Villon; Cranbrook Acad Art, West scholar, MFA (painting) & MFA (textile design); Bundestextilschule, Austria, cert; Univ Calif, Berkeley, PhD (in educ Psychology). *Work:* Chicago Art Inst; Victoria & Albert Mus, London; Metrop Mus Art, New York; Addison Gallery Am Art, Andover, Mass; Smithsonian Inst, Washington, DC; Mus Applied Arts, Helsinki; Can Mus of Civilization, Ottawa; Royal Ontario Mus, Toronto; Mus Fine Arts, Houston; Musee des beaux arts de Montreal; Brooklyn Mus Art; Philadelphia Mus Art; Capital Art Coll, Santa Fe, NMex; Governor's Gallery, Santa Fe; Mus Arts & Design, New York; Cambridge Gallery, Ontario, Can; Berman Mus Art, Ursinus Coll, Collegeville, Pa; Woodmere Art Gallery Chestnut Hill, Pa; State Mus Pa, Harrisburg, Pa. *Comn:* Translucent tapestry (11'x 21'), Nieman Marcus, Dallas; Reredos (10'x 32'), St John's Church, Allentown, Pa; Garden Divider, Am Chem Soc, Washington; wall hangings, Killenure Castle Co Tipperary, Ireland; woven hangings, Marshal Field, Chicago; Lehigh Valley Hosp Network, Allentown, Pa; Art of Giving, State Mus Pa, Harrisburg, Pa; Claudine Kurtz, A Heart Filled with Gratitude, Interlaced Metal with Precious Stones, Paris, France, 2015. *Exhib:* Solo exhibs, London Regional Art Gallery, Can, Fashion Inst Technol Gallery, NY, 83, Brooklyn Mus Art, 84, Gallery 21, Tokyo, Fuji Gallery, Osaka & Kyoto, Am Ctr, Kyoto, 85, Hamilton Art Gallery, Can, 86, Cambridge Gallery, Ont, 95 & Allentown Art Mus, Pa, 98, 2003, Weavings from the Heart, Mennonite Heritage Ctr, Harleysville, Pa, 2001, Versatile Visionary, Banana Factory, Bethlehem, Pa, 2008, Sunrise Twills with Titles, Arta Gallery, Toronto, 2011Suspended Harmonies, An Installation, Michener Art Mus, Doylestown, Pa, 2012-2013, The Hallman Legacy: Fine Art and Fiber Art, Paintings: H Theodore Hallman, Sr and Textile Sculptures and Hangings: Ted Hallman Jr, the Mennonite Hertitage Ctr, Harleysville, Pa, 2014, Tonal Weavings and Their Word, Fox Optical Gallery, Bethlehem, Pa, 2015, At the Center: Masters of American Craft, Two-Person Show, Phila Mus Art, 2015-2016; group exhibs, Three Centuries of Am Art, Philadelphia Mus Art, 76, Secret Garden, FiberPhiladelphia, Phila Mus Art, 2012, Innovators and Legends: Generations in Textiles and Fiber, Muskegon Mus Art, Mich, Traveled to Seven Venues, 2012-2015, Assemblage: Contemporary Fiber Art, Allentown Art Mus, Pa, 2013-2014, Paul Evans: Crossing Boundaries and Crafting Modernism, Michener Art Mus, Doylestown, Pa and Cranbrook Acad Art Mus, Bloomfield Hills, Mich, 2014; Visionary Women Exhibition 2014, Honoring Helen Drutt English Moore Col Art and Design, Phila, Engage: Color, Ritual, Material Studies, Miller Gallery, Kutztown Univ, Pa, 2014, Gifts from America, The State Heritage Mus St Peterberg, Russia, 2014-2015; The Art Fabric-Mainstream, Am Fedn Arts, Triennale di Milano '69, 1982; Am Wallhangings, Victoria & Albert Mus, London, 62; Fiber Revolution, Milwaukee Art Mus Invitational, 86; Talkative Textiles, Trans-Am Gallery, San Francisco, 93; Focus on Textiles, Chicago Art Inst, 94; Five Decades of Fiber Art, Am Craft Mus, NY, 95; Teachers, Mentors & Makers, Ont Craft Coun, Toronto, 96; Kemerer Mus Decorative Arts, Bethlehem, Pa, 2005; Tokyo Internat Great Quilt Festival, 2010; Crafting Modernism: Mid Century Art and Design, Mus Arts and Design, NY, 2011; Secret Garden, Phila Mus Art, 2012; Memorial Art Gallery, Rochester, NY, 2012; Holding the Eyes and Soul, Berman Mus Art, Ursinus Coll, Pa, 2012; Access-Ability: Deconstructing and Reconstructing Art for Access, Berman Mus Art, Ursinus Coll, 2012; Assumption Univ Chapel, Windsor, Canada, 2012; Innovators and Legends, 2012; Installation, Michener Art Mus, Doylestown, Pa, 2012; representation in mus permanent collections: The State Hermitage Mus, St Petersburg, Russia, 2015; Michener Art Mus, Doylestown, Pa, 2015; American Craft Coun Fellow Panel Participant, Spanning Generations: A Conversation, Craft/NOW, Phila, American Craft Coun symposium, Univ Arts, Phila, 2015 (in conjunction with) At the Center: Masters of American Craft, Phila Mus Art, 2015-2016. *Pos:* Consult, ILO Textiles, Jamaica, summer 68; textile designer, Larsen Inc, NYC, Thaibok Fabrics, NYC; juror, Art of the State, State Mus Pa, Harrisburg, Pa, 2009; juror, Congressional Art Competition, 18th Dist of Pa, 2009. *Teaching:* Instr, Haystack Sch, Maine, Penland Sch Crafts, summers 58-95 & Taos Inst Art, 98-99, 2002, 2003; prof textiles & chmn dept, Moore Col Art, 65-70; assoc prof textile design, San Jose State Univ, 72-75; lectr & workshop leader, US, Can & Eng (incl San Antonio, Vancouver, Ottawa & Mich, 77-78); head textiles, Ont Col Art, Toronto, 79-99; guest lectr, World Craft Conf, Mex, 76, Northern NMex Community Col, summers 92-99, Nancy Block Sch Weaving, Santa Fe, NMex, 92-94, Tyler Sch Fine Art of Temple Univ, 2000-01, Allentown Art Mus, Pa, 2002, Cill Rialaig Project, Co Kerry, Ireland, 2003, Textile Arts Alliance, Wheelwright Mus, Santa Fe, 2004, Georgia O'Keefe Mus, Santa Fe, 2012, Las Tejedoras, Santa Fe, 2012; Lectr: Art Inst Chicago, Carnegie Inst, Pittsburgh, Pa, Fashion Inst Technol, NYC, Nicholas Roerich Mus, NYC, Smithsonian Inst, Washington, DC, World Craft Conference, Mex, Assumption University, Windsor, Ontario, Inst Am Indian Art, Santa Fe NMex, Ga O'Keefe Mus, 2013; workshop teaching, Georgia O' Keefe Mus, Santa Fe, New Mexico, 2014, 2015; keynote spkr, Culture Series, Assumption Univ, Windsor, Ontario, 2012; lectr, Looming Over a Lifetime, Espanola Valley Fiber Art Ctr, New Mex, 2015. *Awards:* Tiffany Found Grant, 62; Textile Prize, Int Kunsthandwerk Expos, Stuttgart, 67; Fel Am Craft Coun, 88; Smithsonian Laitman Archival Amer Artist Proj (selected, first 100 artists). *Bibliog:* Peggy Hobbs (auth), Surface Design J, 41-42, summer 98; Trebbe Johnson (auth), Art: Weaving the Path of the Soul, New Age Mag, 22, 5-6/98; Michael Barnett (auth), Ted Hall - Passionate Weaver of Light, Craft Arts Int, Australia, 98-99; Young, Marcia (auth), Ted Hallman: Moving Beyond Tradition, and Michael Barnett, Embrace Beauty: The Hallman Legacy, Fiber Art Now, 4(1), pp 32-35, fall 2014; Porter, Jenelle (ed), Fiber Sculpture: 1960-Present (p 144), DelMonico Books, Munich, 2014; Smith, Paul J (auth), Masters of Craft: 224 Artists in Fiber, Clay, Glass, Metal, and Wood: Portraits by Paul J Smith, Schiffer Publishing, Atglen, Pa, 2015; Kimmerle, Constance (ed), Paul Evans: Crossing Boundaries and Crafting Modernism (pp 110, 112, 113, 115), Arnoldsche Art Publishers, Stuttgart, Germany, 2014. *Mem:* Philadelphia Coun Prof Craftsmen; Ont Craft Coun; hon mem Zurich, Int Soc Arts & Lett; Nat Soc Lit & Arts. *Media:* Fibers, Wire, Pigment, Installation. *Res:* Woven textile techniques & teaching philosophies. *Interests:* Professional body worker, Rolfer, Alexander Technique teacher. *Collection:* Robert Pfannebecker, Philadelphia, Lloyd Cotson, Los Angeles, Helen Drutt, Philadelphia, Fiber Art Collection, Univ Wis, Madison, Jack Larsen, East Hampton, NY. *Publ:* Textiles: The 1950s and 1960s (exhib catalogue), Innovators and Legends:Generations in Textiles and Fiber, Muskegon, Mich, Muskegon Mus Art, 2012. *Dealer:* Snyderman/Works Gallery Philadelphia PA; Helen Drutt Gallery Philadelphia PA; Okun Gallery Sante Fe NM. *Mailing Add:* PO Box 281 Lederach PA 19450

HALLMARK, DONALD
RETIRED MUSEUM DIRECTOR, LECTURER
b McPherson, Kans, Feb 16, 1945. *Study:* Univ Ill, BFA (art hist), 67; Univ Iowa, MA (art hist), 70; St Louis Univ, PhD, 80. *Collection Arranged:* Richard W Bock Sculpture Collection (with catalog), Greenville Col, 75; 1984 Nat Print Exhib, Springfield Art Asn; Frank Lloyd Wright Decorative Arts Collection, Dana House, 81-88, Post Restoration Reopening of the Collection, 1990-2008. *Pos:* Cur & dir, Richard W Bock Sculpture Collection, Greenville Col, 72-81; supt, hist site, Dana House, Springfield, Ill, 81-2009, retired, 2009-; auth, SITE Brochures, 1981-2007. *Teaching:* Assoc prof art & fine arts, Greenville Col, 70-81, chmn dept art, 75-81, prof, 81-; lectr, Springfield Art Asn, 81-, Sangamon State Univ, 82-90, Art Inst Chicago, High Mus, Atlanta, Ga, Gamble House, Pasadena, Calif, Currier Gallery, Manchester, NH & Oak Park, Frank Lloyd Wright Home & Studio Lecture Series Preserving Historic Interiors Conf, Jefferson City, Mo, Mus Nat Heritage, Lexington, Mass & Nat Bldg Mus, Washington, DC, The Graycliff Conservancy, Buffalo, NY, Wright in Kankakee Annual Meeting. *Awards:* Kress Found Res Grant, Univ Iowa, 69; Shell Found Fac Improv Grant, 72-73; Nat Trust Hon Award for Preservation of Dana House; Frank Lloyd Wright Spirit Award, Frank Lloyd Wright Bldg Conservacy, 2010. *Bibliog:* WR Hasbrouck (auth), Editors note, Prairie Sch Rev, Vol VIII, No 1, 71; H Allen Brooks (auth), Prairie Sch, Univ Toronto, 72; Narcisco Menocal (auth), Taliesin--and Flower in the Crannied Wall, Taliesin Studies, Vol I, 74; D Hoffmann, Frank Lloyd Wright: Architecture & Nature, Dutton, 86; Bob Vila's Guide to Historic Homes, the Dana-Thomas House, TV video appearance, 96; Interview, Frank Lloyd Wright & Prairie Sch, Films for Humanities & Scis, 99. *Mem:* Frank Lloyd Wright Bldg Conservancy; Walter Burley Griffin Soc; Nat Trust Hist Preserv. *Res:* Late 19th and early 20th century painting, sculpture and archit with emphasis on the Chicago School, 1880-1915. *Collection:* Original Frank Lloyd Wright decorative art objects, American Art Pottery, Craftsman Furniture. *Publ:* Auth, Richard W Bock, Sculptor, Prairie Sch Rev, 71; Chicago's prairie sculptor, R W Bock, 82; The Studio Collaborations, Decorative Arts Soc Newslett, 12/88; illusr, Frank Lloyd Wright's Dana-Thomas House, Ill Hist J, summer 89, rev ed 92; Paul Ashbrook (exhib catalog), Springfield Art Asn, 90; auth, Frank Lloyd Wright: The Phoenix Papers-The Natural Pattern of Structure, Vol II, Univ Arizona, 95. *Mailing Add:* 605 W Sheridan Rd Petersburg IL 62675

HALVORSON, JOSEPHINE
PAINTER
b Brewster, Mass, 1981. *Study:* Cooper Union, BFA, 2003; Columbia Univ, MFA, 2007. *Exhib:* Solo exhibs, RKL Gallery, Brooklyn, 2005, Humanities Gallery, Cooper Union, 2005, Fondation des etats-Unis, Paris, 2008, West Gallery, Monya Rowe Gallery, 2009; Special Collection, New York Pub Libr, 2005; Dead Serious, Leroy Neiman Gallery, Columbia Univ, 2006; A Friend Indeed: Contemporary Art and the Academy, Katzen Arts Ctr, Am Univ, Washington, DC, 2008; Breaking into the Human Race, Great Hall Gallery, Cooper Union, New York, 2009. *Pos:* Vis artist, Mason Gross Sch Arts, Rutgers Univ, NJ, 2009, Sch Mus Fine Arts, Boston, 2009, Vassar Coll, NY, 2010. *Teaching:* Adj prof, Columbia Univ, New York, 2007-09. *Awards:* US Fulbright Fel, 2003; Louis Comfort Tiffany Found Grant, 2009; Marie Walsh Sharpe Studio Fel, 2009. *Bibliog:* Litia Perta (auth), rev, Brooklyn Rail, 12/2008; Roberta Smith (auth), Make Room for Video, Performance and Paint, NY TImes, 12/31/2009; Chauncey Zalkin (auth), Artists of the Decade: Women Just in Front of Our Eyes, Huffington Post, 1/3/2010. *Mailing Add:* c/o Sikkema Jenkins & co 530 W 22nd St New York NY 10011

HAMADA, HIROYUKI
SCULPTOR
b Tokyo, Japan, 1968. *Exhib:* Provincetown Art Assn & Mus, Mass, 1998; 33rd Springs Invitational Exhib, Ashawagh Hall, NY, 2000; OK Harris Works of Art, New York, 2001; Halsey Inst COntemp Art, Charleston Coll, SC, 2007; Berkshire Community Coll, Mass, 2009. *Awards:* Pollock-Krasner Found Grant, 1998; Edward F Albee Found Fel, 2003; NY Found Arts Fel, 2009. *Bibliog:* Eric Ernst (auth), Art Invitational's Strength, East Hampton Star, 8/9/2001; RC Baker, Voice Choices, Village Voice, 1/18-24/2006; Jessica Dawson (auth), Just a Tinge of the Color School, Washington Post, 7/7/2007

HAMANN, MARILYN D
EDUCATOR, PAINTER
b Los Angeles, Calif, Nov 24, 1945. *Study:* Univ Calif, Berkeley, BA, 67, with Robert Hudson & Jim Melchert, MA, 70. *Work:* Univ Ky Art Mus, Lexington; Citizen's Fidelity Bank & Trust Co & Liberty Nat Bank, Louisville, Ky; Cincinnati Bell Info Systems; Cent Bank & Trust Co, Lexington; Brown & Williamson Tobacco Corp; Gatton Coll Bus and Econ, Univ Ky. *Exhib:* Whitney Mus Am Art, NY, 73; JB Speed Art Mus, Louisville, Ky, 74, 77, 81, 82 & 89; New Orleans Mus Art, 75; Oakland Mus Art, Calif, 75; Archive Small Press & Communs Space, Antwerp, Belg, 82; Ky Arts & Crafts Fedn, 91 & 92; SC State Mus, 92; Mich Art Train, 93-94; Owensboro Mus Art, 96; Mail Art Shows, Berlin-Zehlendorf Pub Libr, Ger, 2001; Jeju Cult & Art Found, Jeju City, S Korea, 2001; COSLART 03, Concejalia de Cultura, Madrid, Spain; and others. *Teaching:* Assoc prof, Univ Ky, Lexington, 80-. *Awards:* Al Smith Fel, Ky Arts Coun, 86; Ky Found Women Grant, 87; Award of Merit, Huntington Mus Art, 88. *Bibliog:* Jacqueline Rapp (auth), article, New Art Examiner, 78; Guy Mendes (producer), Kentucky Now, Ky Educ Television, 79; New Art Examiner, 2/90. *Mem:* Asn Independent Video & Filmmakers; Ky Woodworkers Asn. *Media:* Mixed Media, Video, Sculpture. *Publ:* Int Soc Copier Artists Quart, Vol 1, No 1 & 3, New York, 82 & 83. *Mailing Add:* Univ Ky Dept Art 207 Fine Arts Bldg Lexington KY 40506-0022

HAMBLEN, KAREN A
EDUCATOR, WRITER
Study: Univ Oregon, BS (art educ), 74, MS, 77, PhD, 81. *Pos:* Co-ed, Green Hills Press Publ, 75-81; ed reviewer, Bull Caucus on Social Theory & Art Educ, 85-86, assoc ed, 87-88; ed bd mem, Studies in Art Educ, 86-88, co-ed, 89-91, sr ed, 91-; contrib ed, Arts Educ Rev of Books, 87-; ed reviewer, J Social Theory & Art Educ, 89 & 90; vis scholar, Getty Educ Inst Arts, 96-97. *Teaching:* Vis asst prof, art educ dept, Univ Ore, 81-82; asst prof, art dept, Calif State Univ-Long Beach, 82-85; assoc prof, Sch Art, La State Univ, Baton Rouge, 85-88, dept curric & instr, 88-90, prof, 90-. *Awards:* Manuel Barkan Mem Award, Scholarly merit of published work, 85; Mary Rouse Mem Award, Women's Caucus of Nat Art Educ Asn, 87; June King McFee Award, 95; Getty Mus Visiting Scholar, 99-2000; Studies in Art Educ Leadership, 2000. *Mem:* Nat Art Educ Asn; Int Soc Educ Through Art; Am Educ Res Asn; Los Angeles Co Art Educ; Coun Policy Studies Art Educ. *Publ:* Auth, Research in art education as a form of educational consumer protection Vol 31, No 1, Studies Art Educ, 89; Local Art Knowledge, Australian Art Education, Vol 14, No 3, 22-29, 90; In the quest for art criticism Equity: A Tentative Model Vol 29, No 1, Visual Arts Res, 91; Neo-DBAE in the 90s Vol 10, No 1, J Arts & Learning Res, 92-93; Beyond the public face of policymaking Vol 92, No 3, Arts Educ Policy Rev, 95. *Mailing Add:* Dept Curric & Instr Peabody Hall La State Univ Baton Rouge LA 70803

HAMBRICK, LYNN C See Lukkas, Lynn C

HAMEL, GARY JAY
PAINTER, ASSEMBLAGE ARTIST
b Ayer, Mass, July 20, 1958. *Study:* Private study (with 22 different admired artists), 1976-1981; Special study with Aidron Duckworth, Larry Howard & Aya Itagaki. *Work:* Davistown Mus, Liberty Village, Maine; Dartmouth Coll, Hanover, NH; Georgia O'Keeffe Mus (Maria Chabot Archives), Santa Fe, NMex; Sabbathday Lake Shaker Mus, New Gloucester, Maine; Enfield Shaker Mus, Enfield, NH; Orange Hist Comn, Orange, NH. *Comn:* Generations (mural), Mascoma High Sch, W Canaan, NH, 1993-1994; The Rochedale (mural), Hanover Consumer Coop, Hanover, NH, 1994; The Evening Star (lobby ceiling), Lebanon Opera House, Lebanon, NH, 2001; Iwami's Garden (multi media installation), Dartmouth Hitchcock Med Ctr, Lebanon, NH, 2010. *Exhib:* Solo Exhibs: Quoneh-ta-cut, St Gaudens Nat Hist Site, Cornish, NH, 1988; Landscapes Without Horizons, Montshire Mus, Norwich, Vt, 1990; Fifteen Years, Dartmouth Coll (collis center), Hanover, NH, 1996; In Solstice Light, Enfield Shaker Mus, Enfield, NH, 1998; In Solstice Light, Sabbathday Lake Shaker Mus, New Gloucester, Maine, 1998; Crow, John Hay Estate, Newbury, NH, 1998; Le Verger de mon pere, Franco Am Centre, Manchester, NH, 2000; A Change of Season, Alumni Cult Arts Center, Haverhill, NH, 2007; Document; the Story of a Mountain & its People, Red Roof Gallery, NH, 2008; Milagro: Aspects of Healing, Norris Cotton Cancer Ctr, Lebanon, NH, 2009. *Collection Arranged:* An Artist Collects (cur 112 works), Newport Libr Arts Center, 1996; Two Artists Collecting (cur 300 works), Hamel Jennings Collection (shown at the hist Tower House), 2005. *Pos:* Archival Framer & art store clerk, 1979-1999; Art columnist (for 2 local newspapers, 1990-1993, 2003-2005; cur, gallery dir, Red Roof Gallery, Enfield, NH, 2005-2007. *Teaching:* Artist in residence, pub, private schs NH, Vt & Mass, 1978-2001; pastel, watercolor, Lebanon Coll, Lebanon, NH, 1986-1989; pastel, Ghost Ranch Conference Center, Abiquiu, NMex, 1990-1997. *Awards:* Nat Window Display 1st Pl, Dartmouth Bookstore, Hanover, NH, 1982. *Bibliog:* Ian McVey (auth, dir & producer), Portrait of a Dairy Farm, Northland Video (short length doc), 1983. *Mem:* Co-founder, Cardigan Mountain Art Asn. *Media:* Pastel, Oil, Assemblage. *Collection:* Art of Northern New Eng (600 plus paintings that include Eliot Porter, Rockwell Kent, Leonard Baskin, Emily Nelligan, Wolf Kahn & Eric Aho and many others). *Publ:* Auth, Small Moments (poems, self pub), 2005; auth, Howling at the Wolf Moon (poems, self pub), 2006; auth, Poems for Maria (poems, self pub), 2007; auth, The First Fifty (poems, self-pub), 2008. *Dealer:* Red Roof Gallery High St Enfield NH 03748; Islesford Artists Little Cranberry Island Islesford Maine 04646. *Mailing Add:* 111 Tuttle Hill Rd Canaan NH 03741

HAMILL, DAVID
PAINTER
Study: State Univ NY Purchase, BFA (Studio Art), 1995; San Francisco Art Inst, MFA (Painting), 2004. *Work:* Microbia, Cambridge, Mass; Savoir Faire, Novato, Calif; Risk Management Solutions, Newark, Calif. *Exhib:* group exhibs include HANG, San Francisco, 2002, 2003; Mapping, Diego Rivera Gallery, San Francisco, 2003; Sprawl, Bank Gallery, Los Angeles, 2006; Moxie, Catherine Clark Gallery, San Francisco, 2006; Art La with Bank Gallery, Los Angeles, 2006; Close Calls, Headlands Ctr Arts, Sausalito, Calif, 2006; Virtual Intervention, 33 Grand, Oakland, Calif, 2006. *Awards:* Kala Board Prize, Kala Inst, Berkeley, Calif, 2005; Pollock-Krasner Found Grant, 2007

HAMILTON, ANN KATHERINE
SCULPTOR
b Lima, Ohio, June 22, 1956. *Study:* St Lawrence Univ, Canton, NY, 1974-76; Univ Kans, BFA (textile design), 1979; Yale Sch Art, MFA (sculpture), 1985. *Hon Degrees:* Honorary Doctorate, RI Sch of Design, 2002, Sch Art Inst Chicago, 2005. *Work:* Albright-Knox Gallery, Buffalo, NY; Brooklyn Mus of Art, NY; Solomon R Guggenheim Mus, NY; Metropolitan Mus of Art, NY; NY Pub Libr, NY; Whitney Mus of Am Art, NY; Oberlin Col, Ohio. *Comn:* Mess Hall, Headlands Ctr Arts, Sausalito, Calif, 1989-90; pub libr, Arts Comn San Francisco, 1990-93; Allegheny Riverfront Park, Pittsburgh Cult Trust, 1994-2001; Pub Art on Campus, Univ of Minn, Molecular and Cellular Biology, 2001; Seattle Central Libr, City of Seattle, 2002-04; Acoustic Tower Proj, Steve Oliver Ranch, Alexander Valley, Calif, 2004-07. *Exhib:* Solo shows incl Stedelijk van Abbemuseum, Eindhoven, Netherlands, 1996, Contemp Arts Mus, Houston, 1997, Musee d'Art Contemporain de Lyon, France, 1997, Musee d'Art Contemporain de Montreal, Canada, 1998, Miami Art Mus, 1998, Aldrich Mus Contemp Art, Conn, 1998, Am Pavilion, Venice, 1999, Irish Mus Modern Art, 2002, Mass Mus Contemp Art, North Adams, 2003, Historiska museet, Stockholm, Sweden, 2004, La Maison Rouge Found Antoine de Galbert, Paris, 2005, Sean Kelly Gallery, New York, 2006; group shows incl The Earth Never Gets Flat, Whitney Mus Am Art, 1987, Dirt & Domesticity: Construction of the Feminine, 1992, Full House: Views of the Whitney's Collection at 75, 2006; Readymade Identities, Mus Mod Art, New York, 1993; Outside the Frame: Performance and the Object, Cleveland Ctr Arts, 1994; Parts, Manoa Art Gallery, Univ Hawaii, 1994; About Place: Recent Art of the Americas, Art Inst Chicago, 1995; Longing and Belonging: From the Faraway Nearby, Site Santa Fe, 1995; Along the Frontier, State Russ Mus, 1996; Jurassic Technologies Reverent, 10th Biennale of Sydney, Australia, 1996; Artist Projects, PS1 Contemp Art Ctr, Long Island City, 1997; Addressing the Century/100 Yrs of Art & Fashion, Hayward Gallery, London, 1998; Art Today, Indianapolis Mus, Ind, 1998; Then and Now and Later, Yale Univ Art Gallery, Conn, 1998; etrenature, Found Cartier pour l'art contemporain, Paris, France, 1998; The Second Look: Poetic Objects and Strategies of Seduction, Apex Art Curatorial Prog, NY, 1999; Venice Bienniale, 1999; The Picture is Still, Akeda Gallery, Japan, 2001; Self and Soul: The Archit of Intimacy, Asheville Art Mus, NC, 2003; Magic Makers, Des Moines Art Ctr, Iowa, 2003; Columbus Mus Art, Ohio, 2004; Robischon Gallery, Denver, 2005; Women Only! In Their Studios, Mus Tex Tech Univ, traveling, 2006; Closed Circuit, Metrop Mus Art, New York, 2007; Invitational Exhib Visual Arts, AAAL, New York, 2008. *Teaching:* Asst prof, Univ Calif, Santa Barbara, 1985-91; prof, Ohio State Univ, 2001-. *Awards:* Guggenheim Mem Fel, 1989; MacArthur Fel, 1993; NEA Visual Arts Fel, 1993; Larry Alrich Award, Larry Alrich Found, 1998; Ohio Women's Hall of Fame, 1999; EDRA/Place Design Award, Allegheny Riverfront Park, Pittsburgh Cult Trust, 2002; Individual Artist, Governor's Awards for Arts in Ohio, 2005; Ohioana Citation for Distinguished Serv, 2006; USA Fel, US Artist, 2007; Merit Award, Am Inst Archits, 2008; Heinz Award for the Arts & Humanities, 2008. *Bibliog:* Wade Saunders (auth), Making art making artists, Art in Am, 1/93; Faye Hirsch (auth), Art at the limit: Ann Hamilton's recent installations, Sculpture, 7/93; Joan Simon (auth), Temporal crossroads: An interview with Ann Hamilton, Kunst & Mus J, Vol 6, No 6, 1995. *Mem:* Nat Acad. *Mailing Add:* 64 Smith Pl Columbus OH 43201

HAMILTON, GEORGE EARL
PAINTER, EDUCATOR
b Pittsfield, Mass, Oct 10, 1934. *Study:* Int Christian Univ, 56-58; with Dr Samine Tuyoda, Japan, 58-60. *Work:* Frye Art Mus, Seattle; Univ Wash; Kaiser Found & First Nat Bank, Portland, Ore; Royal Bank Can; Ore State Univ. *Exhib:* Solo exhibs, Am Watercolor Soc, NY, 75 & 76, North Western Watercolor Soc, Seattle, 75-79, Mus Art, Casper, Wyo, 76, Frye Art Mus, Seattle, 76 & 81, Portland Art Mus, 77 & Univ Mus Art, Eugene, Ore, 77-79. *Teaching:* Instr watercolor, Univ Wash, 76- & Univ Idaho, 79-81. *Awards:* Am Watercolor Soc Award, 76; Ore Agriculture Purchase Award; SE Washington Silver Medal; 1st, 2nd, & 3rd prize, Beverly Hills Affaire in Garoew; Award of Excellence, Saratoga Rotary Show. *Mem:* Ore Watercolor Soc; Northwest Watercolor Soc. *Media:* Watercolor, Collage. *Mailing Add:* 8956 SW 9th Dr Portland OR 97219-4706

HAMILTON, JACQUELINE
CONSULTANT, LECTURER
b Tulsa, Okla, Mar 28, 1942. *Study:* Tex Christian Univ, BA; Stockholm Univ, MA equivalent. *Comn:* Galleria III mural and frieze, Hines, Houston. *Collection Arranged:* Staubach Co, Houston; KPMG, Houston; Four Oaks Place, TIAA-CREF, Houston. *Pos:* Art Consultant. *Teaching:* lectr creativity and cognition class, Univ Houston. *Bibliog:* Lessons in How to be a Corporate Collector, Art Business News, 85; Corporate Art Brings Elevated Perspective to World of Business, Houston Bus Jour, 3/96; Culture Scouts, Houston Press, 8/99. *Mem:* Int Asn of Prof Art Advisors (IAPAA); Tex Women of the Arts. *Publ:* Monthly contributor to KPMG - Houston Corporate Newsletter, 2000-2001; contrib, What is an Art Consultant?, Fr Am Chamber of Commerce, winter 99-2000. *Mailing Add:* Box 1483 Houston TX 77251-1483

HAMILTON, JUAN
SCULPTOR
b Dallas, Tex, Dec 22, 1945. *Study:* City Coll New York; New York Univ; Hastings Col, Nebr, BA (art), 68; Claremont Grad Sch, MFA prog. *Work:* Metrop Mus Art, NY; Art Inst Chicago; Albright-Knox Art Gallery, Buffalo, NY; Mus Fine Arts, Mus NMex, Santa Fe; Jacksonville Art Mus, Fla. *Exhib:* Robert Miller Gallery, NY, 78, 81 & 83; Janie C Lee Gallery, Houston, Tex, 80; Janus Gallery, Los Angeles, Calif, 83; Mus NMex, Santa Fe, 83. *Collection Arranged:* Georgia O'Keeffe: A Portrait by Alfred Stieglitz (coauth, catalog), Metrop Mus Art, NY, 78; Alfred Stieglitz (coauth, catalog), Nat Gallery Art, Washington, DC, 83. *Awards:* Am Bk Award for Alfred Steiglitz: Photographs and Writings. *Bibliog:* Barbara Rose (auth), The Sculpture of Juan Hamilton, Arts Mag, 79; Robert Knafo (auth), Juan Hamilton at Robert Miller, Art in Am, 81; Barnaby Conrad III (auth), Rising stars, Horizon Mag, 82. *Mailing Add:* PO Box 70 Abiquiu NM 87510

HAMILTON, LISA
PAINTER
Study: Acad Minerva, Groningen, Netherlands, 1995; Cooper Union, BFA, 1996; Hochschule der Kunst, Berlin, 2001; Hunter Coll, City Univ NY, MFA, 2003. *Exhib:* Solo exhibs include Saracca Exhib Space, Kyoto, Japan, 1999, Prinz Gallery, Kyoto, 1999, Dodaiji Gallery, Kyoto, 1999; group exhibs include Salad Days, Artists Space, New York, 2004; Faculty Exhib, Hunter Coll, New York, 2005; One of these things is not like the Other, Angela Hanley Gallery, Los Angeles, 2006; FlashPop, NY Found Arts Exhib, 2007; Ann Invitational Exhib Contemp Am Art, Nat Acad Mus, New York, 2008; Freeze Frame, Thrust Projects, New York, 2008. *Awards:* Kyoto Art Action Studio Grant, 1997, 1998; Kyo-Ten Kyoto Munic Mus Art Grant, 1998; Barbara Fishman White Fel, Vt Studio Ctr, 2000; Atlantic Ctr Arts Award, 2005; NY Found Arts Artists Grant, Painting, 2006; Julius Hallgarten Prize, Nat Acad, 2008. *Mailing Add:* c/o Thrust Projects 114 Bowery #301 at Grand St New York NY 10013

HAMILTON, PATRICIA ROSE
DEALER
b Upper Darby, Pa, Oct 21, 1948. *Study:* Temple Univ, BA, 70; Rutgers Univ, MA (art hist), 71. *Hon Degrees:* Harvard Bus Sch, 80. *Collection Arranged:* Ten Am, Masters of Watercolor (with catalogue), 74, Edward Hicks, A Gentle Spirit (with catalogue), 75 & Matta: A Totemic World, 75, Andrew Crispo Gallery; Outdoor Sculpture 1974 (with catalogue), Merriewold West Gallery, Far Hills, NJ, 74; Color and Structure, Hamilton Gallery, 81; Bronze Hamilton Gallery, 82; Contradictions & Complexities: Contemp Art from India, 2008; Western Projects Gallery, Den Gallery, Culver City, Calif; Silver & Gold, Baldwin Gallery, Aspen, 2000-2001. *Pos:* Curatorial asst, Whitney Mus Am Art, NY, 71-73; sr ed, Art in Am, NY, 73-74; cur exhibs, Andrew Crispo Gallery, NY, 74-75; dir, Hamilton Gallery Contemp Art, 77-84, artist agent, 84-90; pvt dealer, 90-. *Awards:* Hon degree, bus, Harvard Univ, 80. *Bibliog:* Laura de Coppet & Alan Janes (auth), The Art Dealers, Clarkson N Potter Bks, 84; David France (auth), Bag of Toys, Warner Bks, 92; Eleanor Munro (auth), Art Table Changing the Equation, Art Table, 2005. *Mem:* ArtTable, New York & Los Angeles (found mem, chap chair, So Calif), 2003-05. *Specialty:* 20th century art. *Interests:* Tennis, music, cooking. *Collection:* Contemp Am art. *Mailing Add:* 6753 Milner Rd Los Angeles CA 90068

HAMILTON, W PAUL C
EDUCATOR, HISTORIAN
b Toronto, Ont, Mar 13, 1938. *Study:* Williams Col, BA, 59; Univ Toronto, MA, 64; Johns Hopkins Univ, PhD (Fel), 73. *Pos:* Coordr educ English, Educ Serv, Nat Gallery Can, Ottawa, 73-76. *Teaching:* Asst prof, Univ Sask, Saskatoon, 70-78, assoc prof, 78-84, head dept, 81-84, prof, 85-. *Awards:* Grant, Italian Govt, 65-66; Can Coun Doctoral Fel, 68-69; Soc Sci & Humanities Res Coun Can Grant, 87-89. *Publ:* Auth, Andrea del Minga's Assunta in S Felicita, Kunsthistorisches Inst, 70; coauth, Grandmaison, Henderson, Kenderdine, Univ Sask, 79; auth, Disegni di Bernardino Poccetti, Olschki, 80; The Palazzo dei Camerlenghi in Venice, J Soc Archit Historians, 83. *Mailing Add:* 1037 13th St East Saskatoon SK S7H0B8 Canada

HAMLIN, LOUISE
PAINTER, PRINTMAKER
b Litchfield, Conn, June 26, 1949. *Study:* Univ Pa, BFA, 72; NY Studio Sch. *Work:* Walker Art Ctr; Univ Iowa; Swarthmore Col; Wellington Mgmt Co; Metro Transit Auth. *Exhib:* Solo exhibs, Blue Mt Gallery, NY, 84, 86, 89 & 92; Carleton Col, 94; Blue Mass Gallery, 95; plus many others. *Teaching:* Assoc prof, Dartmouth Col, 90. *Awards:* Djerassi Found Residency Award, 88; Mellon Found Res Grant, 93; Vt Coun Arts Fel Award, 94. *Bibliog:* Greg Masters (auth), Louise Hamlin, Arts, summer 85; Painting on Location, American Artists, 10/88; Eric Holzman (auth), Louise Hamlin, Cover, 1/90. *Media:* Oil, Pastel; Etching, Monoprint. *Publ:* Auth of art reviews in Arts, 9/82, 3/85, 5/85, cover, 2/87, M/E/A/N/I/N/G, 5/89; Bringing the Baby, 15 Poems by various poets, Coffee House Press, Minneapolis. *Dealer:* Blue Mountain Gallery 121 Worcester St New York NY 10012. *Mailing Add:* Dept Studio Art Dartmouth Col Hinman Box 6081 Hanover NH 03755

HAMMER, ELIZABETH B
PAINTER, ASSEMBLAGE ARTIST
b Washington, DC. *Study:* Univ Kans, Lawrence; Nat Art Sch, Washington, DC; Univ Md, Coll Park, BA (summa cum laude), Academie des Beaux Arts, Kinshasa, Zaire. *Work:* Am Album Vol II, Nat Mus Women Arts, Washington, DC. *Exhib:* Black Mountain Coll, NY, 87; Nat Mus Women Arts, Wash, DC, 91; Montgomery Coll, Rockville, Md, 91; NVCC, Fairfax, Va, 92 & 93; Paris, Deauville & Avignon, France; and others. *Pos:* Illustr & ed, US Govt, formerly; ed, Embassy News, Paris, formerly. *Teaching:* Instr art, Rabat Am Sch, Morocco. *Awards:* Phi Kappa Phi Art Award, 81; Finalist, 34th Grand Prix Int de Deauville, France, 83; Art Citation, Montgomery Co Delegate, 86; Diplome Official, Deauville, Avignon. *Bibliog:* Annuaire National Des Beaux-Arts, 91-92; Les Artistes Independents, L'histoire du Salon des Independants 1884-1984, 1985, Tome I, Tome II; The Contributor, Florence Poor, Melbourn, Fla, 2010-2012. *Mem:* Past Societaire, Salon des Artistes Independents, Paris; Nat Gavel Soc; Nat Hon Soc; Phi Kappa Phi. *Media:* Acrylic. *Res:* Hist of Am Art Schs; Hist of Fr Art. *Interests:* relationships, art history, world genomics. *Mailing Add:* 2238 Rockingham Loop College Station TX 77845-4854

HAMMERBECK, WANDA LEE
PHOTOGRAPHER
b Lincoln, Nebr, Mar 24, 1945. *Study:* Univ NC, Chapel Hill, BA, 67, MA, 71; San Francisco Art Inst, MFA, 77; Yale Univ, post grad. *Work:* Mus Mod Art, NY; Fogg Mus, Harvard Univ, Cambridge, Mass; Houston Mus Fine Arts; San Francisco Mus Mod Art; Oakland Mus; numerous pub & pvt collections; Autry Nat Ctr; Ctr Creative Photography; Spencer Mus; Seattle Art Mus. *Exhib:* Object Illusion & Reality, Calif State Univ, Fullerton, 79; Images Considered, Visual Studies Workshop, Rochester, NY, 80; In Color, Ten California Photographers, Oakland Mus, Calif, 83; Cleveland Inst Art, Ohio, 85; Western Space, Burden Gallery, NY, 85; Pomona Art Mus; Mus fotografi, Norway, 2003; Solo exhibs, San Francisco Mus Mod Art, 78, OK Harris, NY, 79, Schienbaum & Russek Gallery, Santa Fe, 86, Etherton Gallery, Tucson, 86, Fuller Art Mus, 2000; Palm Springs Mus, Calif, 2005; Autry Mus, 2006; Art of an Am Icon: Yosemite, 2006; The Other Side of Paradise, Palm Springs Art Mus, 2006; Post Landscape, Pamona Coll Art Mus, 2001. *Pos:* dir student services, Video Symphony. *Teaching:* Lectr photog & issues in art; guest lectr Mills Col, 1985, Art Ctr, Col Design, Pasadena, 1992 & 1994. *Awards:* Nat Endowment Arts Photogr Fels, 79 & 80 & Serv to Field Award, 80; Guest artist, Ansel Adams Workshops, 86; Tiffany Fel; Haynes Fel, Huntington Libr, 2003. *Bibliog:* Article, Untitled, Friends of Photog; Aperture, Vol 150, Winter 98. *Mem:* Soc for Photog Educ; Friends of Photog. *Media:* Photography. *Res:* Haynes Fel, Huntington Library, Pasadena, CA. *Interests:* Landscape nature & cult. *Publ:* Contribr, Problematic Photography, 80, NFS Press; A River too Far, Univ Nev Press, 91; Arid Waters, Univ Nev Press, 92; Nature through her Eyes: Art & Literature by Women, Nature Co, 94; The Altered Landscape, 99; Aperture, vol 150; Art of An Am Icon: Yosemite, 2006; Fotofest, 2004; Contemp Desert Photography: The Other Side of Paradise, Palm Springs Art Mus, 2006

HAMMERMAN, PAT JO
PAINTER, PRINTMAKER
b New York, NY, Oct 15, 1952. *Study:* Queens Coll, BA, 75; Hunter Coll, MA, 78. *Work:* Grand Rapids Mus, Mich; Brooklyn Mus; Lockhaven Art Ctr, Orlando, Fla; Amarillo Art Ctr, Tex; Firehouse Gallery, Nassau Community Coll, NY; Queens Mus, New York; Guild Hall Mus, East Hampton, NY; Publisher's Clearing House; Pannei Kerr Foster Int; Peachtree Hotel, Atlanta, Ga; Mitsui Bank Los Angeles; Lockhaven Mus, Orlando, Fla; Coldwell Banker, New York. *Comn:* Mural, Queensborough Community Coll, 70; three-panel mural, Panell, Kerr, Foster, New York, 83; Deloitte, Haskins & Sells, Princeton, NJ, 87; Four Seasons Hotel, Newport, Calif, 87; Bankers Trust, New York, 88; Orlando Magic Basketball Team Hq; Hyatt Regency Hotel, Chicago. *Exhib:* Print Biennial, Brooklyn Mus, 81; Handmade Paper Books, Am Craft Mus, NY, 82; Int Impact, Kyoto Munic Mus, Japan, 82; New Am Graphics, Alaska State Mus, Juneau, 83; Queens Mus, Flushing, NY, 85; Am Prints, Cairo Mus, Egypt, 85; Flushing Town Hall, NY; and others. *Pos:* Pres, 10-20 Artspace, pres RealArt currently; pres, Realart Corp, currently. *Teaching:* Asst prof fine art, Queensborough Community Coll, 80-. *Awards:* First Prizes, Firehouse Gallery, Nassau Community Coll, 79 & 26th Ann, Parrish Mus, 79. *Bibliog:* John Fremont (auth), Paperworks, Am Craft Mag, 8/82; Ronnie Cohen (auth), Papermaking, Art News, 10/83; Ronnie Cohen (auth), New editions, Art News, 10/84; Helen Harrison (auth), Paper: medium with a message, NY Times, 3/27/88. *Mem:* Coll Art Asn; Manhattan Graphic Soc; Conn Graphic Art Soc. *Media:* Oil; All Media, etching, printing ink. *Res:* Etching; Acrylic, Oil. *Collection:* African art, German stamps, Zepplin postcards. *Dealer:* John Szoke 164 Mercer St New York NY 10012; Peter Rose Gallery 200 E 57th St New York City NY. *Mailing Add:* 20724 27th Ave Flushing NY 11360

HAMMETT, DAN
CERAMIST, EDUCATOR, ADMINISTRATOR
Study: Northeastern State Univ of Oklahoma, BA (Educ); Univ of Kansas, BFA; State Univ of NY Col of Ceramics at Alfred, MFA (Ceramic Art), 1974. *Exhib:* Exhibitions include Farrell Collection Gallery, Washington, DC, Collectable Crafts, Hardwork Gallery, NY, Ohio Ceramic and Sculpture Show, Butler Inst of Art, Youngstown, Ohio, South Central Regional Exhibition, Denver Art Mus, New Art Forms Exposition, and Navy Pier Chicago. *Pos:* Maintains a private studio, Handcrafted Ceramics; conducted field studies to museums in Italy, Greece, Crete, and The Peoples Republic of China; consultant, project manager, Nat Coun on Educ for the Ceramics Arts award winning PBS style film series. *Teaching:* With, Univ of Dallas, 1974-, department chair, prof graduate and undergraduate ceramics, currently. *Mailing Add:* University of Dallas 1845 E Northgate Dr Irving TX 75062-4736

HAMMETT, POLLY HORTON
PAINTER, INSTRUCTOR
b Oklahoma City, Okla, Jan 31, 1935. *Study:* Univ Okla, 48-50; Union Col, BA, 78; study with Richard V Goetz & Eugene Bavinger. *Work:* Albuquerque Mus Art; Houston Neurosensory Ctr; Women's Hosp-Houston; Houston Power & Lighting; Methodist Hosp, Houston, Tex; Hill Country Arts Found, Tex; Kerr Mus, Okla; II Houston Ctr, Tex; Hutchins Sealy Nat Bank, Galveston, Tex. *Exhib:* Am Watercolor Soc Ann, Nat Acad Galleries, 76, 77, 80 & 82; Watercolor, Southwest Two, Tucson Mus Art, 76 & 82; Nat Watercolor Soc 56th Ann, Laguna Beach Mus Art, Calif, 76; two-artist exhib, Foothills Art Ctr, Colo, 74-76; Western Fed Watercolor Socs, 81; Nat & Am Watercolor Soc Traveling Exhib, 82; Tweed Mus; Frye Mus; Univ Wis; Willamette Univ; Stetson Univ; Foothills Art Ctr, Golden, Colo. *Pos:* Dir educ, Art League Houston, Tex, 86-88; gallery dir, Nine Fine Artisans, 79-82. *Teaching:* Lectr & instr watercolor sem, Okla Arts Coun, 73; instr painting workshops, Colo, Okla, Tex, Calif, Ark, Ariz, SC, NMex, NC, Utah, Va, La, Ga & Wash; Tex Inst Child Psychiatry, Houston, 74 & 75 & Houston Univ, Sch Continuing Educ Drug Abuse Prog, 76-77; instr, Art League Houston 80-90 & Hill Country Arts Found, 83-84. *Awards:* Mus Purchase Award & Merit Award Watercolor, Southwest One, Albuquerque Art Mus, 76; First Award, Southwestern Watercolor Soc, Dallas, Tex, 81; Clara Stroud Mem Award, 127th Int Exhib, Am Watercolor Soc, 94. *Bibliog:* Lynn Haggard (auth), Artist's paintings test limits, Times Record News; Mimi Crossley (auth), Houston Post. *Mem:* Nat Watercolor Soc; Am Art Therapist Asn; Am Watercolor Soc; Art League Houston; Women's Caucus Art. *Media:* Mixed Water Media; Collage, Monoprint. *Publ:* Watercolor, SW Art, 94. *Mailing Add:* 375 N Post Oak Ln Houston TX 77024-5903

HAMMOCK, VIRGIL GENE
CRITIC, PAINTER
b Long Beach, Calif, Aug 5, 1938; Can citizen. *Study:* San Francisco Art Inst, BFA, 65, with James Weeks; Ind Univ, MFA, 67, with James McGarrell. *Work:* Ind Univ, Bloomington; Univ Alta, Edmonton; Art Bank Collection, Can Coun, Ottawa, Ont; Univ Man, Winnipeg; Mt Allison Univ, Sackville; and others. *Exhib:* 84th Ann, San Francisco Mus Art, Calif, 65; Young Alta Painters, Alta Coll Art, Calgary, 68; West-71, Edmonton Art Gallery, 71; Solo exhibs, Owens Art Gallery, Sackville, NB, 73 & Drawings, Dalhousie Art Gallery, Halifax, NS, 77; Olympic Exhib, Montreal, 75; Two solo exhibs, Struts Gallery, Sackville, NB, 85 & 87. *Pos:* Dir exhibs, Univ Alta, 68-70 & Univ Man 70-73; actg dir, Owens Art Gallery, Mt Allison Univ, 88-89; vchmn, NB Arts Bd, 97-. *Teaching:* Instr design & drawing, Univ Alta, Edmonton, 67-68, asst prof drawing & art hist, 68-70; assoc prof art criticism, Univ Man, Winnipeg, 70-75; prof fine art & head, Dept Fine Art, Mt Allison Univ, 75-93 & 93-99, prof fine art, 99-; adjudication comt, Can-US Fulbright Comt, 94-97. *Awards:* Phelan Award, Trustees James D Phelan Awards Lit & Art, 65. *Bibliog:* Cameron (auth), Virgil Hammock, la Nostalgie du Romantisme, Vie des Arts, summer 78; B Sanderson (auth), Virgil Hammock: Studio pictures, Arts Atlantic 31, spring/summer 88. *Media:* Oil, Pencil. *Res:* Contemporary Canadian painting. *Publ:* Contribr, An art critic visits the Soviet Union, Arts Atlantic 37, spring/summer 90; Juan Kiti, Epid Lier, 55-61, 95; Cesar Bailleux, 73-95, 69 & Guy van der Bulcke, 51-61, 97, Roularta Art Bks; Christian Silvain, Lannoo, Tielt, Belg, 223-239, 97; Paul Smolders (ed, Marcel von Jole), pp 50-60, Nu Blonde Sa, Wommelgem, Belg, 94; The 49th parallel: An

opinion, No 28, Artpost, spring 88; Critical word about critical words about art, Arts Atlantic, No 35, fall 89; Take me out to the ballgame: Michael Snow's the audience, Art Post, 35-36, winter/spring 90. *Dealer:* Fog Forrest Gallery Sackville NB Can. *Mailing Add:* Fine Arts Dept Mt Allison Univ 53 York St Sackville NB E4L 1C9 Canada

HAMMOND, GALE THOMAS
PRINTMAKER, EDUCATOR
b Lumberton, NC, Sept 27, 1939. *Study:* Chicago Acad Fine Arts, com art dipl; E Carolina Univ, 62-64, BS & MAEd; Univ NC, Greensboro; Atelier 17, Paris, with S W Hayter, 77. *Work:* Italian Embassy, Washington, DC; NC Mus Art, Raleigh; Del Mar Coll, Corpus Christi; Univ NC Sch Pub Health, Chapel Hill; Frans Masereel Ctr, Belg; Metrop Mus Art. *Exhib:* Colorprint USA, Lubbock, Tex, 71-75; Boston Printmakers, Mass, 72-2006; Budapest Hungary Cartoon Festival, 90; Trento, Italy Humor Exhib, 92; Obra Grafica, Oviedes, Spain, 94 & 96; Int Cartoon Festival, Kyoto, Japan, 2000-05; Print Consortium, Mo, 2005. *Pos:* Mem, SC Governors Award Prog, The Penland Sch; retired prof, Univ Ga. *Teaching:* Drawing & printmaking, Univ Ga, Athens, 70-2001; Western Carolina, Greensboro Coll; prof emer, Univ Ga; instr, Univ Ga Cortona studies abroad & Avignon, France studies abroad. *Awards:* Etching Award, Southeastern Printmakers; Sea Grant, Ossabaw Island Proj. *Media:* Etching, Multimedia, Watercolor. *Mailing Add:* 195 Gibbons Way Athens GA 30605

HAMMOND, LESLIE KING
ART HISTORIAN, WRITER
b Bronx, NY, Aug 4, 1944. *Study:* Queens Col, with Louis Finkelstein, Herb Aach, Paul Frazer, Marvin Belick & Harold Bruder, BA, 1969; Johns Hopkins Univ, MA, 1973, PhD, 1975. *Collection Arranged:* 3400 on State, Baltimore Mus Art, 1973; Baltimore Black Arts Calendar Retrospect, 1973-1978, Morris Mechanic Gallery, 1978; Montage of Dreams Deferred (auth, catalog), Baltimore Mus Art, 1979-1980; Three Episodes in Black Am Art, Harmon Found, Bronx & Queens Mus, 1980; Celebrations: Myth & Ritual in African-Am Art (auth, catalog), Studio Mus Harlem, 1982; Reconstructed Elements, Artscape, 1983, Lyric Theatre, 1983; The Intuitive Eye-The Art of Self Taught Baltimore Artists (auth, catalog), Md Art Place, 1985; 18 Visions/Divisions, Eubie Blake Cult Ctr & Mus, 1988; Art as a Verb-The Evolving Continuum (coauth, catalog), Md Inst Coll Art, 1988; Black Printmakers and the WPA (auth, catalog), Lehman Gallery Art, Lehman College, Bronx, NY, 89; Hale Woodruff Biennial, Studio Mus Harlem, NY, 1989, 1994; Masters, Mentors and Makers, (auth, catalog), Artscape, 1993. *Pos:* Actg dir, Cult Arts, Youth in Action, Bedford, Stuyvesant, NY, 1966; chmn art dept, Performing Art Workshops, Queens, NY, 1967-1969; guest cur & mem bd dir, Morris Mechanic Gallery, formerly; coordr, Philip Morris Scholar for Artists in Visual Arts, 1985-, dean grad studies, 1976-; trustee, Baltimore Mus Art, 1981-1987. *Teaching:* Lectr art hist, Md Inst Col Art, 1973-, dean grad studies, 1976-; doctoral supvr, Dept African Studies & Res, Howard Univ, 1977-1982; instr, Corcoran Sch Art, 1982. *Awards:* New York City SEEK Grant, 1966-1969; Horizon Fel, 1969-1973; Kress Found Fel, 1974; Mellon Grant, 1987; Lifetime Achievement Award, Women's Caucus for Art, 2008, ArtTable, 2011. *Mem:* Nat Conf Artists; Coll Art Asn (secy, 1991-1994). *Res:* Nineteenth and twentieth century Afro-American art; African Art; women artists; self-taught artists. *Publ:* Auth, Art as A Web, Md Inst, Studio Mus Harlem & Met Life Gallery, 1988; May Howard Jackson, Black Women in America, Carlson Pub Co, NY, 1993; Masks and Mirrors-African Art, 1700-Present, Abbeville Press, 1995; Introduction, Gumbo YaYa-A Bibliography of Contemporary African American Women Artists, Midmarch Art Press, 1995; Painting and Sculpture, Encyclopedia of African American History and Culture, Columbia Univ, NY, 1995. *Mailing Add:* Md Inst Col Art 1300 W Mount Royal Ave Baltimore MD 21217-4191

HAMMOND, MARY SAYER
EDUCATOR, PHOTOGRAPHER
b Bellingham, Wash, Oct 1, 1946. *Study:* Univ Ga, BFA (art educ), 69, EDS (art educ), 71, MFA (photo design), 77; Ohio State Univ, PhD (hist photo/art educ), 86. *Work:* Int Mus Photog at George Eastman House, Rochester, NY; Nat Gallery Art, Wash; Nat Mus Women Arts, Wash; Ctr Creative Photog, Tucson, Ariz; Corcoran Gallery Art, Wash. *Exhib:* Pinhole Images, Eleven Photographers, Va Mus Art, 82; Recent Acquisitions, Corcoran Gallery Art, 86 & 89; Through a Pinhole Darkly, Fine Arts Mus Long Island, 88; City on a Hill, Ga Mus Art, 89; Poetics of the Real Am Landscape Photog, Columbus Mus Art, 91; Global Focus: Women in Art, Nat Mus Women Art, Wash, 95; Three Rivers Arts Festival, Carnegie Mus Art, 95. *Pos:* Co dir, Saturday Prog, Univ Ga, 66-76; admin assoc art educ, Ohio State Univ, 78-79; artist-in-residence, Study Abroad Prog, Univ Ga, Cortona, Italy, 81-88; dir, MSH Photog, 88-. *Teaching:* From asst to assoc prof art & Am studies, George Mason Univ, 80-95, prof, 95-98; instr photog, Lyndon House Art Ctr, 2000-04. *Awards:* Photog Fel, Nat Endowment Arts, 82-84; Travel Grant, Samuel H Kress Found, 86. *Bibliog:* Duke T Y Liao (auth), The Charm of Pinhole Photography, Chinese Photography 3, 91; Duke T Y Liao (auth), Light and Shade, Chinese Ann Photog, 93-94. *Mem:* Soc Photog Educ (bd dir, mid Atlantic region); Daguerreian Soc; Coll Art Asn; Nat Art Educ Asn. *Media:* Platinum, Color. *Res:* Photography. *Publ:* Illusr, Pienza: The Creation of a Renaissance City, Cornell Univ, 87; Emphasis Art, Harper Collins, 93; coauth, The Picture Book: Art Source and Resource, Nat Art Educ Asn, 95. *Dealer:* Kathleen Ewing 1609 Connecticut Ave Washington DC 20009. *Mailing Add:* 165 Watson Dr Athens GA 30605-3737

HAMMOND, PHYLLIS BAKER
SCULPTOR
b Elizabeth, NJ, Apr 13, 1930. *Study:* Sch Mus Fine Arts, Boston, Mass, 60; Kyoto City Coll Fine Arts, Japan, 62; Tufts Univ, BS, 64. *Work:* Mem Hall Libr, Andover, Mass; Am Savings Bank, White Plains, NY; Schmeltzer, Aptaker & Shepard, Washington, DC; Conn State Univ, New Haven; Noyes Mus, Oceanville, NJ. *Comn:* Unitarian Fellowship, Mount Kisco, NY, 84; Guest Quarters Hotel, Bethesda, Md, 86; Center point, Fairoaks, Md, 87; William Shakespeare Award, Shakespeare Theater at the Folgers, Washington, DC, 87; Art in Public Places, Hartford, Conn, 90; Pratt Inst, Brooklyn, NY, 2008; Conn Comm for the Arts, Percentage for the Arts Program, Bronze Gateway, 2009. *Exhib:* Clay Sculpture, Hudson River Mus, NY, 76; Art in Transition, Boston Mus, 77; Clay Sculpture, Pinder Gallery, NY, 86; Architectural Ceramics, Franz Badar Gallery, Washington, DC, 87; Clay Transformations, Rockland Ctr Arts Nyack, Flushing, NY, 87; Sculptures as Pub Art, Art Gallery, Washington, DC, 89; Contemp Sculpture, Chesterwood, Stockbridge, Mass, 89; New Bronzes, Elaine Benson Gallery, Bridgehampton, NY, 89; Recent Sculpture, Greene St Gallery, NY, 90; Guild Hall Invit, E Hampton, NY, 2002; Clay Art Ctr, Port Chester, NY, 2007; Surface Gallery, Springs EH, NY, 2008; Mark Borghi Fine Arts Gallery, Bridgehampton, NY, 2009; 23rd Ube Biennale, Tokiwa Mus, Yamaguchi, Japan; V Salon International de Esculturea Contemporanea, Museo Metropolitano de Buenos Aires, 2012; Olhe Brasil: Arte Moderna e Contemporanea, Musea Mube, Sao Paolo, Brazil, 2013. *Collection Arranged:* Renaissance Festival, Westchester Coun Art, NY, 75 & 77. *Teaching:* Adj asst prof, Col New Rochelle Graduate Sch, 81; ceramic sculpture, Mendocino Art Ctr, Calif, 81, 82 & 86. *Awards:* Clarissa Bartlett Traveling Fel, Boston Mus, 60; Second Prize, Mamaroneck Artist Guild, 73; Grant for Apprentice, National Endowment Arts, 76; finalist, Univ Fla at Pensacola, 91; Flowers & Sculptures Prize, 23rd Biennale, Tokiwa Mus, Ube, Japan, 2009. *Bibliog:* Patricia Malarcher (auth), Clay that qualifies as sculpture, New York Times, 4/7/85; Roslyn Tunis (auth), Ancient Inspiration/Contemporary Interpretation (catalog, rev), Robertson Ctr Arts Sci, 85; Lauretta Dimmick & Jonathan Fairbanks (coauths), Contemporary Sculpture at Chesterwood (catalog, rev), 89. *Mem:* Artist-Craftsman New York; Nat Coun Apprenticeship; Int Liaison; Visual Arts Affiliates of Westchester (vpres, 79-81). *Media:* Aluminum. *Dealer:* Borghi Fine Art Englewood NJ; Bibro Fine Arts NY. *Mailing Add:* 1108 Springs Fireplace Rd East Hampton NY 11937

HAMMOND, ROBERT RIGSBY
PAINTER
b San Antonio, 1969. *Exhib:* Solo exhibs include 3 Crosby Street, New York, 1999; group exhibs include Passion, Richard Anderson Fine Arts, New York, 1999; The Metro Show, City Without Walls Gallery, New York, 1999; 4PLY Cooperative Exhib, New York, 2000; Ritz Carlton Collective, Battery Park, New York, 2001. *Pos:* Co-founder, pres, Friends of the High Line, New York, 1999-; early planner, Tribute of Light (WTC Mem Proj), 2001; trustee, Met Mus Art, New York, 2002-. *Awards:* Polsky Rome Prize, Am Acad in Rome, 2008; Named one of Crain's NY Bus 40 Under 40, 2008. *Mailing Add:* Friends of the High Line Ste 8W 529 W 20th St New York NY 10011

HAMMONS, DAVID
SCULPTOR
b Springfield, Ill, 1943. *Study:* Los Angeles Trade Technical City Col, Calif, 1964-65; Chouinard Art Inst, Los Angeles, 1966-68; Otis Art Inst Parson's Sch Design, Los Angeles, 1968-72. *Exhib:* Solo exhibs include The Window, New Mus Contemp Art, 1980, Higher Goals, pub installation, Harlem, 1982, Just Above Midtown, NY, 1986, Exit Art, 1989, Jack Tilton Gallery, 1990 & 1991, Am Acad in Rome, 1992, Hometown, Ill State Mus, 1993, Blues & the Abstract Truth, Kunsthalle Bern, 1998, Museo Reina Maria Sofia, Madrid, 2000, Ace Gallery, NY, 2002 & 2003, Hauser & Wirth, Zurich, 2003; retrospectives include Contemp Art, PS1, Long Island, 1990, Inst Contemp Art, Philadelphia & San Diego Mus Contemp Art, 1991; group exhibs include Heimat, Wewerka & Weiss Galerie, Berlin, 1991; Places with a Past, Spoleto Festival, Charleston, SC, 1991; Dislocations, Mus Mod Art, NY, 1991, MoMA 2000: Open Ends, 1999, Parkett Editions, 2000; Carnegie Int, Carnegie Inst, Pittsburgh, Pa, 1992; Documenta, Kassel, Ger, 1992; Whitney Biennial, Whitney Mus Am Art, NY, 1997; One Planet Under a Groove, Bronx Mus Arts & Walker Art Ctr, Minneapolis, 2001; Stalemate, Mus Contemp Art, Chicago, 2004; Double Consciousness: Black Conceptual Art Since 1970, Contemp Arts Mus, Houston, 2005. *Awards:* Nat Endowment Arts Fel, NY State Coun Arts, 1982; John Simon Guggenheim Mem Found, 1983-84; DAAD, Berlin, 1992; Lifetime Achievement award, Coll Art Asn, 2012. *Bibliog:* Maurice Berger (auth), Interview with David Hammons, Art in Am, 9/90; Michael Brenson (auth), New Curator at Modern Challenges Convention, 12/28/90 & Visual Arts Join Spoleto Festival USA, New York Times, 5/27/91; Dan Cameron (auth), Good-Bye to All That?, Art & Auction, 1/91. *Mem:* Fel Am Acad Arts & Scis. *Mailing Add:* c/o Greenberg Van Doren Gallery 730 5th Ave New York NY 10019

HAMPSON, FERDINAND CHARLES
ART DEALER, CURATOR
b Detroit, Mich, June 26, 1947. *Study:* Wayne State Univ, dipl, 71. *Collection Arranged:* Emergence Art in Glass (auth, catalog), Bowling Green Univ & Kent State Univ, 81-82; Glass: Artist and Influence Traveling Exhib (auth, catalog), 81-82; Kyohe: Fujita Blown Glass (auth, catalog), Leigh Yawkey Woodson Mus & Burgstrom Mus, 81-82; Four Artists Four Views (auth, catalog), Jesse Besser Mus, 82; The Fine Art of Contemporary Am Glass (auth, catalog), Columbus Coll Art & Design, 83; Contemp Czechoslovakian Glass Art (catalog), Boca Raton Mus Art, 85; Bildwerke in Glass 25 Jahre New Glass in Amerika (catalog), Hessisches Landesmuseum Darmstadt, 87; Cristalomancia Arte Contemporaneo en Vidrio (catalog), Museo Rufino Tamayo & Marco Museo de Arte Contemporaneo, Mex, 92; Glass: 1962 to 1992 and Beyond (catalog), Morris Mus, 92. *Pos:* Dir, Habatat Galleries, 71-. *Bibliog:* Mack Talaba (auth), Art craft--glass has come a long way, Artcraft, 8/80; Janet Koplos (auth), Habatat Gallery, Am Craft, 9/80; Maureen Michelson (auth), Inside Habatat, Glass Studio, 4/81. *Mem:* Glass Art Soc; Detroit Art Dealers Asn (vpres, 76, pres, 78-80); Am Craft Coun; Mich Glass Month (chmn, 80-83). *Res:* Written history of contemporary glass. *Specialty:* Contemporary glass art. *Publ:* Auth, article, Glass Art J, 81; auth, article, Nues Glas, Verlagsanstalt Handweek, 81; Glass: State of the Art, 84; Glass: State of the Art II, 87; The Annual Invitational Exhibition 1973-1992: A Tradition in the Evolution of Glass, 92. *Mailing Add:* 3072 Bloomfield Park Dr West Bloomfield MI 48323-3507

HAMPTON, AMBROSE GONZALES, JR
COLLECTOR
b Statesburg, SC, July 24, 1926. *Pos:* Mem, SC State Mus Comn, 73-78; pres, Columbia Mus Art, 75-77 & mem acquisitions comt, 87-; mem collection comt, Gibbes Art Mus, Charleston, SC, 89. *Collection:* Chiefly contemporary oils, graphics and sculpture, with emphasis on South Carolina artists. *Mailing Add:* 937 Sugar Mill Rd Chapin SC 29036

HAMPTON, ANITA
PAINTER, EDUCATOR
Study: Saddleback Col, El Torro, Calif; Laguna Beach Sch Art, Calif; Ventura Col, Calif; Calif Polytechnic State Univ, San Luis Obispo, Calif; Cuesta Col, San Luis Obispo, Calif. *Work:* numerous pvt collections. *Comn:* Numerous pvt comns. *Exhib:* Ann Art Festival, San Juan Capistrano Mission, Calif Art Club, 97, 98, 99 & 2000, Gold Medal Show, 98, 99 & 2000; Oil Painters Am Nat Show, 98; Oil Painters Am Nat Show; San Luis Obispo Art Mus; R Weisman Mus Art, Pepperdine Univ; Carmel Ann Painting Festival. *Pos:* Dir & instr fine art, Cent Coast Studios, Morro Bay, Calif, 94 & 95; juror, Allied Arts Ann Exhib & Cuesta Col Ann Scholarship Show, Calif, 96. *Teaching:* Instr, Cuesta Col, San Luis Obispo, Calif, 94 & 95; instr painting workshops (traveling nat & internat), 95-; art instr, S Bay Community Ctr, Calif, 96-97. *Awards:* Ann Art Festival Award, Calif Art Club, 97 & 98, Gold Medal Show Award, 98; Ann Art Competition Finalist, Artist's Mag, 98. *Mem:* Oil Painters Am; Calif Art Club; Laguna Plein Air Painters Asn; Signature Member of Oil Paints Am;. *Media:* Oil. *Specialty:* California Plein Air, representational impressionist, tonalist in all subject matter. *Interests:* Fine art including portraits, landscapes, seascapes, cityscapes, floral and still-life. *Collection:* Joan Irvine Smith, Roy Rose Plein Air Art Collection 93424. *Publ:* Contribr, Jewel of the Mission Calendar, 98; Best of the West, SW Art Mag, 8/98; The Jewel of the Missions Mag, fall 98; LA Times Newspaper (Metro Sect), Los Angeles, Calif, 8/16/98. *Dealer:* Salisbury Fine Art, 1250 San Luis Bay Dr Avila Valley. *Mailing Add:* 6985 Ontario Rd San Luis Obispo CA 93412

HAMPTON, GRACE
ADMINISTRATOR, CRAFTSMAN
b Courtland, Ala, Oct 23, 1937. *Study:* Art Inst Chicago & Univ Chicago, BAE, 61; Ill State Univ, MSEd, 68; Ariz State Univ, PhD (art educ), 76. *Exhib:* Arizona Women, Tucson Art Mus, 75; Second World Festival of Black and African Arts and Cult, Lagos, Nigeria, 77; Howard Univ, 93; Lockhaven Univ, 97; Cult Diversity Exhib, Pa Coun on the Arts, 99 & 2000. *Collection Arranged:* Dimension and Directions: Black Artists of the South (auth, catalog), Miss Mus Art, Jackson, 80; Africa & the Diaspora: Personal Collections, Penn State, Altoona, 95. *Pos:* Asst dir expansion arts prog, Nat Endowment Arts, Washington, DC, 83-85; mem adv bd, Getty Inst for Educators on Visual Arts, 83-84, fac mem, 85-88; dir, Sch Visual Arts, Penn State Univ, vice provost, 89-95, Exec Asst Develop arts, 96. *Teaching:* Asst prof art educ, Univ Ore, Eugene, 76-78; fac mem art & chairperson dept, Jackson State Univ, 78-83; fac mem, Sch Visual Arts, Pa State Univ, 85-; head dept African and African Am Art, Pa State Univ. *Awards:* Nat Endowment Arts Expansion Arts Prog Fel, 78; Inst Educ Mgt, Harvard, 90. *Bibliog:* Linderman & Herberholz (auths), Developing Artistic and Perceptual Awareness, 74 & Herberholz (auth), Early Childhood Art, 74, W C Brown; Lanier (auth), Studio Potter, 82, The Art We See, 82 & The Visual Arts & The Elementary Child, 83. *Mem:* Nat Art Educ Asn; Nat Conf Artists; Coll Art Asn; Pa Art Educ Soc (bd dir & futures Comt); African Studies Asn. *Media:* Copper. *Publ:* Auth, Hayden House Program: Community involvement in the arts, Sch Arts, 79; auth, book reviews for J Negro Hist & Studies Art Educ; The Arts Education and Popular Culture in West Africa and the United States, Soc Study Educ Through Art, 2003. *Mailing Add:* Pennsylvania State University School of Visual Arts 30B Borland State College PA 16802

HAMPTON, JOHN WADE
SCULPTOR, PAINTER
b Brooklyn, NY, 1918. *Work:* The Cow Punchers, Cowboy Hall Fame, Oklahoma City; Will Rogers, Will Rogers Mem Mus, Claremore, Okla; Race for the Wagon, Ronald Reagan Libr, Calif; CM Russell Mus; Phoenix Art Mus; Cowboy Artists of Am Mus, Kerrville, Tex. *Comn:* mural, Marriott Camelback Inn, Paradise Valley Ariz, 64; mural, Northwestern Univ Libr, Flagstaff, Ariz; portrait, James Coleman, Scottsdale, Ariz. *Exhib:* Cowboy Hall of Fame, Oklahoma City; Mont Hist Soc; Phoenix Art Mus; Will Rogers Mem Mus, Claremore, Okla; Grand Palais, Paris, France; Cowboy Artists of Am Mus, Kerrville, Tex; C M Russell Mus; US Govt Bldgs in Washington, DC; and others. *Collection Arranged:* Cowboy Artists Am Mus, Kerrville, Tex. *Teaching:* Pvt individuals. *Awards:* First Prize, World Telegram Artist Contest, 35; Gold Medal/Sculpture, Cowboy Artist of Am Show, 77, 79, 80, 81 & Silver, 82. *Bibliog:* article in NY Times, 2/77; SH Mcgarry & JH Pontello (coauth), Cowboy Artists of America 25 Yearbook, Southwest Art, vol 20, no 5, 10/90; Jim Jennings (auth), From Corral Dust to Black Tie, Quarter Horse J, vol 43, no 3, 12/90; articles Los Angeles Times, 6/4/90; Art West, vol 11-12, 80, vol 5-6, 81. *Mem:* Founder Cowboy Artists Am. *Media:* Oil, Watercolor; Clay, Bronze. *Publ:* Illusr in Ariz Hwys, The Cowboy in Art, CA His Friends' Cookbook, Cowboy Artists of Am & Western Horseman & other mags & books. *Dealer:* Hampton Studios Ltd HC1 Box 955 Sonoita AZ 85637-9700; Big Horn Galleries 1167 Sheridan Ave Cody WY 82414. *Mailing Add:* Hampton Studios Ltd HC 1 Box 955 Sonoita AZ 85637-9700

HAMPTON, PHILLIP JEWEL
PAINTER, EDUCATOR
b Kansas City, Mo, Apr 23, 1922. *Study:* Citrus Jr Coll, Glendora, Calif; Kans State Univ; Drake Univ; Kansas City Art Inst, BFA, 51, MFA, 52; Univ Mo Kansas City. *Work:* Tuskegee Inst, Ala; Ga Southern Coll, Statesboro, Ga; New Atlanta Life Bldg, Ga; Obata Design, St Louis, Mo; Governor's Mansion, Ill; Southern Ill Univ, Edwardsville; Liberty Nat Bank, Savannah, Ga; St Louis Mus Art, Mo. *Exhib:* Huntsville Mus, Ala, 74; JB Speed Mus, Louisville, Ky, 82; Evansville Mus, Ind, 88; retrospective, King-Tisdell Cottage Found, Savannah, Ga, 95; solo exhibs, KFUO-FM Special, St Louis, Mo, 96, Southern Ill Univ, Edwardsville, 2000, Mayor's off, Complex, St Louis, Mo, 2000, St Louis Mus, Mo, 2000, Sheldon Art Galleries, St Louis, Mo, 2005 & Ethical Soc Gallery, 2006; Looking Back: Art in Savannah 1900-1960, Ga, 96. *Pos:* Co-cur, Collectors' Choices, African Art St Louis Artists Guild, Mo, 98. *Teaching:* Assoc prof art & dir, Savannah State Coll, 52-69; assoc prof painting & design, Southern Ill Univ, Edwardsville, 69-78, prof, 78-92, prof emer, 92-. *Awards:* Dr Scheinfurth Purchase Award, Mitchell Mus, Mt Vernon, Ill, 85; Lida & Jay Herndon Smith Fund Prize, St Louis Artists' Guild, 88; Gov Award, Ill Purchase Award for exec mansion, 90. *Mem:* St Louis Artists Coalition; St Louis Artists Guild. *Media:* Acrylic, Watercolor. *Res:* Investigating synthetic media; water-media techniques; an essence of form. *Publ:* Auth & designer, 3rd World Drawings 1979 (catalog), Soc Ethnic & Spec Studies Exhib, Los Angeles, 79; and others. *Mailing Add:* 832 Holyoake Rd Edwardsville IL 62025

HAMWI, RICHARD ALEXANDER
PAINTER, EDUCATOR
b Brooklyn, NY, June 11, 1947. *Study:* Queens Col, BA (cum laude); Univ NMex, MA; Univ Calif, MFA; Pa State Univ, PhD; also with William Dole, Leonard Lehrer, Harry Nadler, James Brooks, Louis Finkelstein & John Ferren. *Work:* Phillips Mus; Queens Col; Nat Mus Am Art; Vassar Col; Ark Art Ctr; Art Mus, Univ Ky. *Exhib:* Parsons-Dreyfuss Gallery, NY, 79; Staempfli Gallery, 81; Phillips Collection, Washington, 82; solo shows, Queens Col, 82, Mus Art, Pa State Univ, 82, Univ Indianapolis, Ind, 90 & Prince St Gallery, NY, 93; Mus Art, Univ Ky, 90; Art Gallery, Mansfield Univ, 97. *Teaching:* Asst, Univ NMex, 72-73, Univ Calif, 73-74; instr, Pa State Univ, 77-87; assoc prof, Cumberland Col, 87-95 & 95- & Mansfield Univ, 95-. *Awards:* Purchase Award, Ball State Univ, 79; Mem Award, Chautauqua Nat Exhib, 81; Yaddo Fel, 83; Djerassi Found Fel, 87. *Mem:* Coll Art Asn Am; Nat Art Ed Assoc. *Media:* Ink, Watercolor. *Publ:* Thoughtnotes on the Teaching of Art, J Ky Art Educ Asn, 90; Collage with self-prepared colored papers, Arts & Activities Mag, 10/96. *Dealer:* Prince St Gallery 121 Wooster St New York NY 10012. *Mailing Add:* Mansfield Univ Art Dept Mansfield PA 16933

HAN, DEBBIE
PHOTOGRAPHER, PAINTER
b Korea, 1969. *Study:* Univ Calif Los Angeles, BA (Art), 1993; Pratt Inst, New York, MFA, 1999. *Exhib:* Solo exhibs include Steuben East Gallery, Brooklyn, NY, 1999, Gallery 825, Los Angeles, 2002, Brain Factory Gallery, Seoul, Korea, 2004; group exhibs include Indigenous People, T Heritage Gallery, Los Angeles, 1994; Pulp, Gallery 825, Los Angeles, 2001, Transformation, 2002; Hybrid Trends, Hangaram Art Mus, Seoul, Korea, 2006; Society, Trunk Gallery, Seoul, Korea, 2007; In Touch of Present, Wada Fine Arts, Tokyo, 2007; Gegen den Stritch, Kunstlerhaus Bethanien, Berlin, 2007; Wilhelm Hack Mus, Ludwigshafen, Germany, 2007. *Awards:* Korea Arts Found Am Vis Arts Award, Los Angeles, 2000; Pollock-Krasner Found Grant, 2007. *Dealer:* Freddie Fong Gallery 760 Market St Suite 258 San Francisco CA 94102; Gallery SUN contemp 184 Insa-dong Chongno-gu 110-290 Seoul Korea; Galería Punto Avda Barón de Carcer 37 46001 Valencia Spain; LA Contemp 2634 South La Cienega Los Angeles California 90034

HAN, MOO KWON
VIDEO ARTIST
b Kyungju, S Korea. *Study:* Dongguk Univ, S Korea, BFA, 1996, MFA, 1999; Sch Visual Arts, New York, MFA, 2006. *Exhib:* Grand Arts Exhib Korea, Nat Mus Contemp Art, Seoul, 1999; solo exhibs, Kyung In Mus Fine Art, Seoul, 2000, Cue Art Found, New York, 2009, Doosan Gallery, New York, 2009; Asian Contemp Art Week: Fast Futures, Asia Soc Mus, New York, 2006; Counterpoint, Bund18 Creative Ctr, Shanghai, China, 2007; CUE Benefit, CUE Art Found, New York, 2008; Floating World, Lower Manhattan Cult Coun Art Ctr, New York, 2010. *Pos:* Artist-in-residence, Cue At Found, New York, 2008, Lower Manhattan Cult Coun, New York, 2010. *Awards:* John Payson Fel, Skowhegan Sch Painting & Sculpture, 2008; New York Found Arts Fel, 2009; Puffin Found Grant, 2010

HANAN, LAURA MOLEN
PAINTER, GRAPHIC ARTIST
b Ft Monmouth, NJ, Jan 30 1954. *Study:* Univ Calif, BS, 78; Humboldt State Univ, BA, 80; Northwest Coll Art, AOS, 92. *Work:* Bus Internet Svcs Corp Collection, Tacoma, Wash; State Farm Regional vpres off, Columbia Bldg, Tacoma, Wash; pvt collections, Michel Rocchi & John Madden; Pierce Co Libr. *Comn:* pvt comn by Mr & Mrs Ed Knudsen, Gig Harbor, Wash; pvt comn by Kent Halloway, Fox Island, Wash; pvt comn by Ms Betty Anacortes, Wash; Merrill Lynch, Tacoma, Wash. *Exhib:* Emerald City Fine Art Gallery, Seattle, 96-97; Nicholas Joseph Fine Art, New York, 97-98; Hastings Ray Gallery, Southern Pines, NC, 97-2000; The Night Tacoma Danced, Tacoma Art Mus, Juried fundraiser, 99-2001 & 2003; Night Tacoma Danced, Art at Work Studio Tour, Tacoma, Wash, 2008; Harbor Wellness Ctr Comn, Gig Harbor, Wash, 2009; solo exhibs, Brick & Morter Gallery, 2008. *Pos:* Gallery owner, Brick & Mortar Gallery, Tacoma, Wash; creative dir, Pacific Pipeline, 94-95; founder, Rowland Art Workspace. *Awards:* First Place, Peninsula Art League, 95, 2nd Place, 96 & 3rd Place, 97; Peoples Choice Award, Peninsula Art League, 97. *Bibliog:* Irreconcilable Canvases, rev, The Weekly Volcano, Tacoma, Wash, 3/2004; Wildness Controlled, rev, The Weekly Volcano, Tacoma, Wash, 8/2004; Alec Clayton (auth), As If Art Matters, Clayton Works, 2004; Sacred Cows: Portraits from the Brome Scandal, rev, Tacoma News Tribune. *Mem:* Soc Tech Communications. *Media:* Acrylic, Oil. *Specialty:* Contemporary galleries. *Interests:* Writing, camping, fishing, weight lifting, sewing, civic activism; abstract expressionism. *Publ:* Reporter, city ed, photogr, sr tech writer & creative dir, Contra Costa Sun, Contra Costa Times, Canbi Herald, MDS Quartel Bus Computers, Guy F Atkinson co & Pacific Pipeline; tech writer & res, FAA & NAS, 2005-2006

HANCHEY, JANET L
PAINTER, GILDER
b Dry Creek, La, Oct 30, 1956. *Study:* La State Univ, BFA, 78; Parsons Sch of Design, MFA, 81. *Comn:* Recreate 8 paintings (ceiling & murals), New Amsterdam Theatre; reverse gilded glass, Barney's New York; murals, New Amsterdam Theatre, NY, 94-95; Kirtlington Park & Landsdowne Rooms Restoration, Metrop Mus Art, NY, 95; Bradley Mus, Columbus, Ga; IBM Corp, Atlanta, Ga; Marriott Corp, Los Angeles, Calif. *Pos:* Pres/dir Farris Howell Inc (Women's Business Enterprise). *Teaching:* Lectr, Md Inst Col of Art, Baltimore, 88 & Parsons Sch Design, NY, 82-; tech advisor gilding, Studio Sch, NY; guest lectr, Fashion Inst Technol, NY, 89. *Mem:* Nat Artists Club. *Media:* Oil Pigment, Dry Pastel-Goldleaf. *Dealer:* Farris Howell Inc. *Mailing Add:* 35 Wood Rd Sands Point NY 11050

HANCOCK, JORY
ADMINISTRATOR, EDUCATOR
Study: Ind Univ, MS. *Pos:* Mem, Pittsburgh Ballet Theater, formerly; soloist, Houston Ballet, 1978; prin dancer, Northwest Ballet, formerly. *Teaching:* Fac mem dance, Univ Ariz, currently, head Dance Div, Sch Music and Dance, 1990-, chair, Univ Ariz Faculty, 2001-, interim dean Col of Fine Arts, 2009, dean, 2009-. *Mailing Add:* University of Arizona College of Fine Arts PO Box 210004 1017 N Olive Rd Ina Gittings Bldg Rm 121 Tucson AZ 85721-0004

HANCOCK, TRENTON DOYLE
PAINTER, COLLAGE ARTIST
b Okla City, 1974. *Study:* assoc sci, Paris Jr Col,, Tex, 1994; Tex A&M Univ, Commerce, BFA, 1997; Temple Univ Tyler Sch Art, Phila, MFA, 2000. *Exhib:* Solo exhibs include Gerald Peters Gallery, Dallas, 1998, Dunn and Brown Contemp, Dallas, 2000, 2002, 2003, 2005, James Cohan Gallery, NY City, 2001, 2003, 2006, The Life and Death of #1, Contemp Art Mus, Houston, Mod Art Mus Ft Worth, Tex Fine Art Asn at The Jones Ctr for Contemp Art, Austin, 2001, Mus Contemp Art, North Miami, 2003, Cleveland Mus Art, 2003, Paris Junior Col, Tex, 2004, ARCO Internat Art Fair, Madrid, 2005, Fruitmarket Gallery, Edinburgh, Mus Boijmans Van Beuningen, Rotterdam, 2007, FEAR, NY Gallery, 2009, And Then It All Came Back to Me, 2012, Canzani Ctr Art, Columbus Sch Art and Design, Columbus, Oh, 2013; group exhibs include Gerald Peters Gallery, Dallas, 1997, 1998; Blue Star Art Space, San Antonio, 1998; Longwood Arts Gallery, Bronx, 2000; Whitney Biennial, Whitney Mus Am Art, NY City, 2000, 2002, Political Nature, 2004-05; James Cohan Gallery, NY City, 2000, 2006; Contemp Arts Mus, Houston, 2000, 2003, 2004; Glassell Sch Art of Mus Fine Arts, Houston, 2001; New Orleans Triennial, 2001; Studio Mus, Harlem, NY, 2001; Santa Monica Mus Art, 2001; Weatherspoon Art Mus, Univ NC at Greensboro, 2002; Fabric Workshop and Mus, Philadelphia, 2003; Sara Meltzer Gallery, NY City, 2003; Mus Mod Art, NY City, 2006; 181st Ann: An Invitational Exhib of Contemp Am Art, Nat Acad Mus, NY City, 2006; Arcos - Museo D'arte Contemporanea Sannio, Italy, 2006; Jepson Ctr for Arts, Savannah, Ga, 2007; Dallas Mus Art, 2007; Blanton Mus Art, Austin, Tex, 2007; Young Americans, Shanghai Gallery, 2009; Best Laid Plains, The Drawing Room, London, 2010; ZieherSmith, NY, 2011; Radical Presence: Black Performance in Contemporary Art, Contemporary Arts Mus, Houston, Tex, 2012. *Pos:* Core Artist in Residence, Mus Fine Arts Glassell Sch Art, Houston, 2002. *Awards:* Arch and Anne Giles Kimbrough Award, Dallas Mus Art, 1997; Skowhegan Camille Hanks Cosby Fel for African-Am Artists, 1997; Joan Mitchell Found Grant, 1999; Artadia Found Award, 2003; Penny McCall Found Award, 2004; SJ Wallace Truman Fund Prize, 2006; Joyce Alexander Wein Artist Prize, 2007; Greenfield Prize, 2013. *Dealer:* Flatbed Gallery 2830 E MLK Blvd Austin TX 78702; Dunn and Brown Contemp 5020 Tracy St Dallas TX 75205; James Cohan Gallery 533 W 26th St New York NY 10001. *Mailing Add:* c/o James Cohen Gallery 533 W 26th St New York NY 10001

HAND, JOHN OLIVER
HISTORIAN, CURATOR
b New York, NY, Aug 17, 1941. *Study:* Denison Univ, AB, 63; Univ Chicago, MA (art hist), 67; Princeton Univ, MFA (art hist), 71, PhD (art hist), 78. *Pos:* Docent, Nat Gallery Art, 65-69, cur, Northern Europ Painting, 73-84; cur, Northern Renaissance Painting, 84-. *Teaching:* Teacher art & art hist, Denison Univ, 63 & Princeton Univ, 71. *Awards:* Samuel H Kress Found Fel, 71-72; Belg Am Educ Found Fel, 72-73; Nat Gallery Art Cur Fel, 94-95 & 2000-01. *Mem:* Historians Netherlandish Art. *Res:* Northern Renaissance painting; 15th and 16th century Northern Renaissance painting; Joos Van Cleve. *Publ:* Joos Van Cleve: The Early & Mature Paintings, Princeton Univ, 78; co-auth, The Collections of the Nat Gallery of Art Systematic Catalog, Early Netherlandish Painting, Wash, 86; essay, The 16th Century and catalogue entries in The Age of Bruegel, Netherlandish Drawings of the 16th Century (catalog), Nat Gallery Art, Washington; The Pierpoint Morgan Libr, NY, 86-87; German Paintings of the Fifteenth through Seventeenth Centuries (catalog), Nat Gallery Art, Washington, 93; Joos Van Cleve: The Complete Paintings, Yale Univ, 2004; Nat Gallery of Art: Master Paintings from Collection, Wash, 2004; coauth, Prayers and Portraits: Unfolding the Netherlandish Diptych, Nat Gallery Art & Yale Univ Press, 2006. *Mailing Add:* Nat Gallery Art 2000B S Club Drive Landover MD 20785

HANDELL, ALBERT GEORGE
PAINTER
b Brooklyn, NY, Feb 13, 1937. *Study:* Art Students League, New York; La Grande Chaumiere, Paris. *Work:* Bates Col; Brooklyn Mus Art, NY; Schenectady Mus Art, NY; Salt Lake City Mus Fine Arts; Art Students League. *Exhib:* Solo exhib, Schenectady Art Mus NY, Berkshire Mus, Pittsfield, Mass; ACA Gallery, NY, 66 & Eileen Kuhlik Gallery, NY, 72; Harbor Gallery, Cold Spring Harbor, NY; Ventana Gallery, Santa Fe, NMex, 87-94; Two-person exhib, Total Arts Gallery, Taos, NMex, 89; Solo retrospective: Pastel Exhib, Butler Inst Am Art, Youngstown, Oh, 2007. *Teaching:* Instr, Albert Handell Nation-wide Painting Workshops, 84-. *Awards:* Ranger Fund Purchase Prize, Audubon Artist, 68; Elizabeth T Greenshields Mem Found, 72; Master Pastelist, 84, Pastel Hall of Fame, 87, Pastel Soc Am; Cash Award, Am Artist Mag, 94; Silver Medal, 2nd Ann Laguna Plein Air Invitational Painting Competition, Laguna Art Mus, Laguna Beach, Calif, 2000; Numerous Awards in pastels, 2000. *Bibliog:* Heather-Meredith-Owens (auth), The Inner Universe of Albert Handell, Am Artist Mag, 4/71; Joe Singer (auth), Pastel Portraits, Watson-Guptill; Leslie Trainer (auth), Pastel landscapes of Albert Handell, Am Artist Mag, 12/82; and others; Joy Murphy (auth), Albert Handell, Enraptured, Southwest Art Mag, 4/86; and others; Lessons from the Masters: The Right Balance, Albert Handell, Artists Mag, 2004; Salon d'Art, Plein Air Mag, Albert Handell, 2005. *Mem:* Allied Artist Am; Salmagundi Club; Art Students League; Pastel Soc Am (Hall of Fame). *Media:* Pastels, Oil. *Interests:* Swim, dance, hike. *Publ:* Coauth (with Leslie Trainor Handell), Oil Painting Workshop, 80 & Pastel Painting Workshop, 81, Watson-Guptill; (with Leslie Trainor Handell), Intuitive Composition, 89; A Creative Approach to Realistic Painting & Intuitive Light, 95, Watson-Guptill; coauth (with Anita Louise West), Painting the Landscape with Pastel, Watson Guptill Pub, 2000. *Dealer:* Connie Axton, The Ventana Gallery, Santa Fe NM. *Mailing Add:* PO Box 9070 Santa Fe NM 87504

HANDFORTH, MARK
SCULPTOR
b Hong Kong, China, 1969. *Study:* Slade Sch Fine Art, Univ Coll, London, 1988-92; Staatliche Hochschule fur Bildende Kunste, Frankfurt am Main, Germany, 1990-91. *Exhib:* Solo exhibs incl Mus Contemp Art, N Miami, 1996, Gavin Brown's Enterprise, NY, 2002, 2005, Galleria Franco Noero, Italy, 2002, Lamppost, Pub Art Fund, NY, 2003, Mod Inst, Glasgow, 2004, 2006, Roma Roma Roma, Rome, 2004, Stroom, The Hague, 2004, Dallas Mus Art, 2007; group exhibs include Oriental Nights, Gavin Brown's Enterprise, New York, 1998, 20th Anniversary, 2003; Heads-up, Mus Contemp Art, N Miami, 1999, Making Art in Miami, 2000; Lokalzeit, Johanniterbrucke, Basel, 2001; My head is on fire but my heart is full of love, Charlottenborg Exhib Hall, Copenhagen, 2002; It Happened Tomorrow, Lyon Biennale, 2003; Its All An Illusion, A Sculpture Project, Migros Mus fur Gegenwartskunst, Zurich, 2004; Whitney Biennial, Whitney Mus Am Art, 2004; The Uncertainty of Objects & Ideas, Hirshhorn Mus & Sculpture Garden, Washington, 2006; The Freak Show, Musee d'Art Contemporain de Lyon, 2007. *Pos:* Bd mem, Art Basel Miami Beach. *Mailing Add:* c/o Gavin Browns Enterprise 620 Greenwich St New York NY 10014

HANDLER, AUDREY
GLASS BLOWER, SCULPTOR
b Philadelphia, Pa, Dec 9, 1934. *Study:* Tyler Sch Fine Arts, Temple Univ, Philadelphia, 52-54; Art Students League, New York, summer 55; Boston Univ Sch Fine & Appl Arts, BFA, 56, study with David Aronson; Univ Ill, Champaign, 62; sr res fel, Royal Coll Art, London, Eng, 67-68; Univ Wis-Madison, MS, 67, MFA, 70. *Work:* Corning Mus Glass, NY; Lannan Found, Palm Beach, Fla; Royal Coll Art, London, Eng; Lobmeyr Mus, Vienna, Austria; Hastings Coll Glass Collections, Nebr; Ronald Abramson Glass Collection, Washington, DC; Greenville Co Art Mus, SC; Glasmuseum, Frauenau, Ger; Glasmuseum, Ebeltoft, Denmark; Wustum Mus, Racine, Wis; Bergstrom-Mahler Mus, Neenah, Wis; Greenville Co Art Mus, SC; Mus Wisc Art, 2010; Bachman Collection, Madison, Wisc; Racine Art Mus, Wisc; John Michael Kohler Arts Ctr, Sheboygan Wisc. *Exhib:* Nat Collection Fine Art, Renwick Gallery, Smithsonian Inst, Washington, DC, 73; Am Glass Now, San Francisco Mus Art, Calif, 74; Toledo Mus, 79; Renwick Gallery, 80; Metrop Mus Art, 80-81; Calif Palace Legion Honor, 81; Victoria & Albert Mus, London, 81; Musee des Arts Decoratifs, Paris, & Japan, 82; Glasmuseum, Ebeltoft, 86; Hokkaido Mus Modern Art, Sapporo, Japan, 88; Wis Glass Masters, Fairfield Pub Gallery, Sturgeon Bay, 2000; Mint Mus Craft & Design, Charlotte, NC, 2004; Wis Glass Invitational, Zazen Gallery, Paoli, Wis, 2006; Overture Ctr Performing Art, Madison, Wis, 2008; Ctr Visual Arts, Wausau, Wis, 2008-2009; Racine Art Mus, Racine, Wisc, 2010; Grace Chosy Gallery, Madison, Wisc, 2012; Philabaum Glass Gallery, Tucson, Ariz, 2012; Chazen Mus Art, Madison, Wisc, 2012; Bergstrom Mahler Mus, Neehnah, Wisc, 2012; Mus Wisc Art, West Bend, 2013. *Pos:* Wis Gallery Artists Adv Bd, Milwaukee Mus, 80; Nat Glass Adv Council Mem, Mahler Mus, 2012-. *Teaching:* Instr glass, Royal Coll Art, London, 68, Penland Sch Crafts, NC, 71-85, Hunterdon Art Ctr, Clinton, NJ, 72, Haystack Mountain Sch Crafts, Deer Isle, Maine, 73, Archie Bray Found, Helena, Mont, 75, Univ Wis, 84, Os-Box, Saugatuck, Mich, 97; instr commercial art dept, Madison Area Tech Coll, Wis, 73-90. *Awards:* Juror's Awards, 46th & 59th Wis Designer Craftsmen Shows, Milwaukee, 66 & 71 & Madison Artists Exhib, Madison Art Ctr, Wis, 70; Master Craftsmen Apprenticeship Prog Grant, Nat Endowment Arts, 77-78 & 80-81; Wis Visual Arts Lifetime Achievement Award, 2014. *Bibliog:* Paula Orth (auth), Blown Glass, Milwaukee Sentinel, 72; Terri Gabriell (auth), Instructor Makes, Hunterdon Co Dem, Flemington, NJ, 72; S K Oberbeck (auth), Glass menagerie, Newsweek, 4/73. *Mem:* Glass Art Soc Inc (hon life mem & mem bd, 76-78, & 1994); Nat Coun on the Educ of Ceramic Arts; Am Crafts Coun; World Crafts Coun; Wis Designer Craftsmen Coun; Glass Art Soc (History Comt). *Media:* Blown Glass, Wood, Silver & Gold Figures. *Specialty:* Blown glass and wood sculptures. *Interests:* Reading, travel. *Publ:* Women in International Studio Class 1950-1980, New Glass Review #1 & #16, Corning Glass Mus, Glass State of the Art, Ferdinand Hampson Contemporary Class, Susannek Frantz Women Working in Glass, Lucartha Kohler; American Studio Glass 1960-1990, Martha Dexler; Women in International Studio Glass: 1950s-1980s, Debra Ruzinsky, 2012. *Dealer:* Audrey Handler 7560 Marsh View Rd Verona WI 53593. *Mailing Add:* 105 S Rock Rd Madison WI 53705

HANDLER, JANET
SCULPTOR, PAINTER
b New York, NY, July 9, 1940. *Study:* Fairleigh Dickinson Univ, BS (educ); Lehman Col, MA (educ); Art & Life Studio, NY; Art Students League, NY; self taught. *Comn:* Wood & stone sculptures (8), Dr Theodore Sewitch, New York. *Exhib:* Art & Life Studio, 75-80; Central Park Conservatory, 81; Art Students League, League Gallery, 86-; Agora Gallery Group Show, 98; Audubon Artists, 99-2012; Allied Artists, NY, 99-2012. *Collection Arranged:* Ms Esteele Futterman, NY; Mr Steven Mader,

Vancouver, Can; Mr & Mrs Aaron Curler, Larchmont, NY; Mrs. Julia Levine, West Orange, NJ; Mr & Mrs Hal Ritter, Hilton Head, SC. *Pos:* Sculpture Dir, Audubon Artists of Am, 2004-2010. *Teaching:* teacher, currently. *Awards:* Hon Mention, Arts Students League, 95, 2000-04, 2012; Merit Scholarship, Art Students League, 96-97; Group Show Award, Agora Gallery, 98; Cleo Hartwig Award, Audubon Artists Inc. *Mem:* Art Students League; Audubon Artists Inc Allied Artist Am (sculpture dir); Agora Gallery. *Media:* Stone and Wood. *Specialty:* Painting & sculpture. *Interests:* museums. *Collection:* Wood & stone sculpture, Mr & Mrs Stephen Tepperman, NY, Ms Estelle Futterman, NY, Mr & Mrs Stephen Mader, Can, Mr & MRs Mark Ruff, NY, Joan Sheen, NJ, Mr Josh Hartman, NY, Mr Bruce Richardson, NY, Mr & Mrs David Epstein, Mr & Mrs Hal Ritter, Mr & Mrs Bill Chan, Mr & Mrs Aaron Cutler, NY, Mr & Mrs Albert Bernheim, NJ, Mr & Mrs Ray Rivers, NY, Mr & Mrs Danny Mallet, Conn, Dr & Mrs Norman Handelman, NY, Dr & Mrs Theodore Sewitch, NY, Dr Jacek Preibisz & Joanna Prebish, NY, Dr & Mrs Krauser, NY. *Publ:* The Art Students League of New York, Catalog, 2008-2009; Audubon Artist, 2009. *Dealer:* Agora Gallery. *Mailing Add:* 408 W 57th St Apt 10G New York NY 10019

HANES, JAMES (ALBERT)
PAINTER
b Louisville, Ky, Feb 5, 1924. *Study:* Philadelphia Sch Indust Art; US Army Univ, France; Pa Acad Fine Arts; Barnes Found, Pa. *Work:* Pa Acad Fine Arts, Philadelphia; Univ Tampa, Fla; Yale Univ, New Haven, Conn; La Salle Col, Philadelphia; Nat Acad Design, NY. *Exhib:* Palazzo Venezia, Rome, Italy, 52; Palazzo Esposizione, Rome, 53; Nat Inst Arts & Lett, NY, 56; Univ Pittsburgh, 72; Peale House Galleries of Pa Acad Fine Arts, 79; Goldsmith Gallery, Memphis, Tenn, 80. *Pos:* Art ed, Four Quarters, 70-. *Teaching:* Instr painting, Pa Acad Fine Arts, 80-81; asst prof painting & artist-in-residence, La Salle Col, 65-92. *Awards:* Cresson, Thuron & Lambert Awards, Pa Acad Fine Arts, 49; Tiffany First Award, 50; Prix de Rome, Am Acad in Rome, 51-54. *Bibliog:* Valerio Mariani (auth), Un pittore Americano, Idea, 8/16/53. *Mem:* Am Acad in Rome; fel Pa Acad Fine Arts. *Media:* Oil. *Mailing Add:* 415 W Stafford St Philadelphia PA 19144-4407

HANKEY, ROBERT E
EDUCATOR, ADMINISTRATOR
b Fargo, NDak, June 24, 1931. *Study:* Quincy Col, Ill, BA, 57; Cath Theological Union, Chicago, MA, 61; Cath Univ Am, BA (studio art), 61; Loyola Univ Chicago, MEd, 71. *Pos:* Ed & illusr, Troubadour Mag, Franciscan Press, 59-61; dean of students, Minneapolis Col Art & Design, 70-80; freelance designer, 80-84; dir, Minn Indian Consortium Higher Educ, 80-; acad dean, Col Assoc Arts, St Paul, 84-87, pres, 87-93; owner & pres, Rehco, Inc, 93-. *Teaching:* Prof art & design, Col Assoc Arts, 84-93. *Mem:* Nat Asn Schs of Art & Design; Minn Indian Consortium Higher Educ; Am Inst Graphic Arts; Int Coun Design Schs. *Res:* Computer art, electronic media and phenomenology. *Publ:* Auth, Cybernetics, Duns Scotus Philos Rev, 57; Art and Theology, Duns Scotus Theology Rev, 61; Phenomenon of Art, Corcoran Art Gallery, 71

HANKS, DAVID ALLEN
CURATOR, WRITER
b St Louis, Mo, Dec 13, 1940. *Study:* Washington Univ, St Louis, AB & MA. *Collection Arranged:* Am Art of the Colonies and Early Republic (auth, catalog), Art Inst Chicago, 71; The Arts and Crafts Movement in Am, 1876-1916 (contribr, catalog), 73; The Decorative Designs of Frank Lloyd Wright, Renwick Gallery, Smithsonian Inst, 77-78; Innovative Furniture in Am, Smithsonian Inst, 81. *Pos:* Asst cur, Art Inst Chicago, 69-74; cur, Philadelphia Mus Art, 74-77; guest cur, Smithsonian Inst, 77-81; owner & pres, David A Hanks & assocs, 81-; dir, Exhibs Int, 93-2000; curator, Liliane and David M. Stewart Program for Modern Design. *Mem:* Decorative Arts Chap Soc Archit Hist (pres, 74-77); Philadelphia Chap Victorian Soc (pres 75-77). *Res:* American furniture of the 19th and 20th century; International design, 20th century. *Publ:* Auth, Isaac E Scott: Reform Furniture in Chicago, Chicago Sch Archit Found, 74; coauth, Daniel Pabst, Philadelphia Mus Art, 77. *Mailing Add:* Montreal Mus Fine Arts PO Box 3000 Station H Montreal PQ H3G 2T9 Canada

HANKS, STEVE
PAINTER
b San Diego, Calif, Nov 24, 1949. *Study:* Acad Art, San Francisco, 68; Calif Coll Arts & Crafts, BA, 72. *Work:* Gilcrease Mus, Tulsa, Okla; Mus Fine Arts, NMex; Bennington Ctr Arts, Utah. *Exhib:* Solo exhibs, Estevan Gallery/Old Town, Albuquerque, NMex, 81, Hang-Up Shoppe Gallery, 82, Leslie Levy Gallery, Scottsdale, Ariz, 83 & 85-91, Tohn-Atin Gallery, Durango, Colo, 83, Albuquerque Country Club, 86, O'Briens Art Emporium, Scottsdale, Ariz, 92, E S Lawrence Gallery, Aspen, Colo, 92-98 & Gilcrease Mus, Tulsa, Okla, 98; Peppertree Ranch Invitational, Ynez, Calif, 86-98; Artists of Am, Denver Natural Hist, 94-98; Prix de West, Nat Cowboy Hall Fame, Oklahoma City, 94-98; 1998 Rendezvous, Gilcrease Mus, Tulsa, Okla, 98. *Pos:* Bd mem, Albuquerque Arts Coun, 95; coun mem, Norwest Bank Leadership Coun, 97. *Awards:* Gold Medal, Nat Watercolor Soc, 92, Prix de West, 95 & Arts for the Park, 94 & 95. *Bibliog:* Steve Hanks, SW Art, 2/86 & Art of Steve Hanks, 6/98; Featured Artists, American Artist Watercolors 92, fall 92. *Media:* Watercolor. *Publ:* Contribr, Poised Between Heartbeats, Hadley House, 95. *Dealer:* E S Lawrence Gallery Aspen CO. *Mailing Add:* 1290 Calle de Sandias NE Albuquerque NM 87111

HANNA, ANNETTE ADRIAN
PAINTER, INSTRUCTOR
b New York, NY. *Study:* Traphagen Inst Fashion Illus; Art Students League, studied with Greene, Sanden & Passantino, 79-80; pvt study with J H Sanden & Burton Silverman, 82-91; Centenary Coll, BFA, Hackettstown, NJ, 97. *Work:* Am Broadcasting co, NY; US Coast Guard, Washington, DC; Schering Plough Corp, Madison, NJ; Marsh Insurance, Morristown, NJ; Acadia Nat park, Me. *Comn:* Portrait, Hilton Hotels, Parsippany, NJ, 82; portrait, Riker, Danzig, Scherer, Hyland, Morristown, NJ, 84; portrait, State Senator Ret, Convent Station, NJ, 86; portrait, Judge Court of Appeals, Ret, NY, 87; portrait, NJ State CofC, 98. *Exhib:* Grand Nat Am Artists Prof League, 81-2011 & Nat Open Juried Ann, 90-2006, Salmagundi Club, NY; Blackwell St Ctr Arts, members & NJ HS students, 86-2008; Hudson Valley Art Asn, Westchester Co Community Ctr, White Plains, NY, 88-90; Portraits of the Northeast, Creative Workshops, New Haven, Conn, 89; Art Showcase, Schering Plough Corp, Madison, NJ, 89; PSA Nat Arts Club, NY, 91-2008; Conn Pastel Soc, Paul Mellon Arts Ctr, Wallingford, Conn, 96-98; Arts Coun Morris Area, April Arts Biannual, Madison, NJ, 96-2008; Catherine Lorillard Wolfe Art Club, NY, 2000-2012, Nat Arts Club, NY; Morris Mus, Morristown, NJ, 2005; Northwest Pastel Soc, Seattle, Wash, 2005-12; Greenhouse Gallery, Tex, 2007; Pastel Soc, NJ, 2009-12; Allied Artists, NY, 2012-2013; Northwest Pastel Soc, Seattle, Wash, 2005-2013; Schouten Gallery, Greenbank, Wash, 2012, 2013, 2014. *Pos:* Sem admin & adv coun, Nat Portrait Sems, NY, 80-83; bd mem, Morris Co Art Asn, Morristown, NJ, 84-86; bd mem & pres, Blackwell St Ctr Arts, Dover, NJ, 89-2004,vpres, 2004-2013. *Teaching:* Fac mem, portrait, Nat Portrait Home Study, 85-87; painting, portrait, still life, landscape, oil & pastel, Morris Co Art Asn, Morristown, NJ, 89-2012; instr oil, pastel & portrait landscape, Int Workshops, Italy, Panama, 92 & Switzerland, 94 & Coupeville, Wash, 2004; fac mem, Morris Co Art Asn, Ctr Contemp Art, 2008-2012; fac mem, Visual Arts Ctr, Summit, NJ, 2006 & Livingston Art Asn, NJ, 2007-2008; workshops, Langley Wash, 2011-2012, Whidbey Island Fine Art Sch, Langley, Wash, 2011-2013, Morris Mus, 2012-. *Awards:* Portrait & Figure Award, Am Art Prof League, NJ, 81-82, 84-87, Medal of Hon, 2000; Winner, Winsor Newton Nat Painting Competition, 1995; First Place, Am Soc Portrait Art, 98; Gold Medal, Catherine Lorillard Wolfe Club, NY, 2004; Pastel Soc Am, NY, 2002, 2004, 2009; Finalist, Am Artist Mag Nat Portrait Competition, 2006; Finalist, Northwest Pastel Soc, Wash, 2006; Ridgewood Art Inst Award, CLWAC, 2011; Best of 100 Pastel, Pastel Jour, 2006; Finalist, Artists' Mag Nat Portrait Competition. *Bibliog:* Anne Corcoran (auth), Dover gallery, 8/91 & Janet Adamec (auth), Portrait artist, 3/92, Star Ledger, Newark, NJ; Am Artist, 98; Ruth Faulkner (auth), Reflective Moments, Am Artist Mag, 9/99; Portrait Highlights, 2002; Int Artist, 2000. *Mem:* Pastel So Am, NY; Allied Artists of Am; Am Artists Professional League, NY, 81-2013; Arts Coun Morris Area, NJ (visual art chmn, 82 & 92); Morris Co Art Asn, Morristown, NJ (bd, 84-86 & 2004-12); Northwest Pastel Soc, Seattle (2005-12); Catherine Lorillard Wolfe Club, NY, 2000-2012; Portrait Soc Am, Fla, 2000-2012; Pastel Soc NJ, 2009-2012; Northwest Pastel Soc, Seattle Wash, 2005-2013; Catherine Lorillard Wolfe Art Club, NY, 2009-2013. *Media:* Oil, Pastel. *Specialty:* Realism, landscape, still life, portrait. *Interests:* Hiking & reading. *Publ:* Auth, How to Paint Portraits in Oil, Walt Foster Publ, Tustin, Calif, 94; contribr, Best of Pastel 2, Rockport Pub, 98; Best of Am Pastel Artists, 2010. *Dealer:* Blackwell St Ctr Arts PO Box 808 Denville NJ 07834; Revelation Gallery Denville NJ; Design Domaine Gallery Bernardsville NJ; Rob Schouten Gallery Greenbank Wash. *Mailing Add:* 6 Overlook Rd Boonton NJ 07005

HANNA, PAUL DEAN, JR
PAINTER, PRINTMAKER
b Alice, Tex. *Study:* Austin Col, BA; Chouinard Art Inst; Tex Christian Univ, MFA. *Work:* Tex Tech Mus, Lubbock; Pace Collection, San Antonio; Bell Reproduction Collection, Ft Worth; Lubbock Art Asn, Tex; First Nat Bank, Hobbs, NMex. *Comn:* Six glass engraved windows & four stained glass windows, Covenant Presbyterian Church, Lubbock, Tex, 77-. *Exhib:* Two-man show, Witte Mus, San Antonio, 68; Northwest Printmakers' Int, Seattle & Portland, 69; Southwestern Exhib Painting & Sculpture, Dallas, 71; Printmaking Now, Nat Print Exhib, 73; Longview Painting Exhib, 74; Tex Tech Univ, Lubbock, 77, 87 & 88. *Pos:* Paul Hanna Speaker series (ann), Tex Asn Sch Art, 92-. *Teaching:* Emer prof painting & drawing, Tex Tech Univ, 69-. *Awards:* Eight State Painting & Sculpture Award, Okla Art Ctr, 66 & 80; Longview Painting Award, 74; Juror's Award, 23rd Ann, Okla Art Ctr, 80; Grant, Nat Endowment Arts, 82. *Bibliog:* Gene Mittler & James Howze (auths), Creating and Understanding Drawings, Glencoe Publ Co, 89. *Mem:* Tex Watercolor Soc; life mem Tex Asn Schs Art (past pres). *Media:* Acrylic, Oil; Woodcut, Silkscreen. *Mailing Add:* 2831 24th St Lubbock TX 79410-1635

HANNER, JEAN PATRICIA
PAINTER, MURALIST
b Toronto Ont, Can, July 19, 1940. *Study:* Chaffey Jr Coll, RN, AA, 70; Cal Polly Pomona Calif (BA Pub Admin with Hons), BA, 72. *Work:* Pat Hanner Art Gallery, Ontario, Calif; The Innocence Collection (charcoals). *Comn:* Charcoal, pastel portrait, Sugar Ray Leonard, Ontario, Calif, 65; Boston Terrier Portrait, Dr & Mrs S Woolington, Pomona, Calif, 68; Portrait, Mother of Sylvia Rosas, Riverside, Calif, 75; Murals (many large), Lanterman Develop Ctr, Pomona, Calif, 80-83. *Pos:* Owner, Pat Hanner Art Gallery, 95-2007; pres, Hanner Gallery Inc, 2004-2005; bd dirs, Pacific Fed Credit Union; founder, Wakulla Station Christian Community Ctr, Youth Ministry, Wakulla, FL; founder, Here We Grow Child Care Ctr, Pomona, CA; founder, Idea of the Christian Univ Found, Ontario, CA & Wakulla, FL . *Teaching:* Dir, nursing educ, Lanterman Develop Ctr, Pomona, Calif, 92-2003, retired. *Mem:* Bd Registered Nursing. *Media:* Miscellaneous. *Specialty:* Originals in Various Media, Wall Murals Outside. *Interests:* Swim, aerobics, art, gardening. *Collection:* Charcoals, Oils Acrylic, Wall Murals, Spiritual Art. *Publ:* Auth, Ontario City Sewer System, Ontario City Libr, 70; auth, Miracle in the Making, 93. *Dealer:* Pat Hanner Art Gallery 911 W Rosewood Ct Ontario CA 91762; A second Pat Hanner Art Gallery 111 Mt Zion Rd Crawfordville FL (managed by assoc artist, Pastor Greg Jackson). *Mailing Add:* 911 W Rosewood Ct Ontario CA 91762

HANNIBAL, JOSEPH HARRY
EDUCATOR, PAINTER
b Brooklyn, NY, May 4, 1945. *Study:* Austin Peay State Univ, Clarksville, Tenn, BS, 68; Univ Tenn, Knoxville, MFA, 72. *Work:* Austin Peay State Univ; Univ Wis, Stout. *Comn:* various pvt collections. *Exhib:* Solo exhibs, 118 Gallery, Minneapolis, 80, Crossing, Gjethuset Mus, Denmark, 2000, Last Picture Show, Kellogg Gallery, Pomona, 2012; Austin Peay State Univ, 81; Los Angeles City Col, 82; Ontario Mus

Art & History, Calif, 83; Laguna Beach Sch Art, 83; Distinguished Artist Exhib, The Chancellary, Long Beach, Calif, 86; Spacex Gallery, Exeter, Eng, 97; Kellogg Art Gallery, Pomona, Calif, 98; Four Int Artists, Stoberihallen Mus, Denmark, 00; others. *Collection Arranged:* Co-cur, Crossings exhib, Gjethuset Mus, Denmark, 2000. *Pos:* Dir, Art Treasures of Italy, 93 & 98, Art Treasures of Europe, 94; guest cur, UK/LA Festival, 94; cur, The Brewery, Los Angeles, Calif, 94; installation coordr, Memories & Modernity, Venice Biennale, Venice, Italy, 96; Am organizer Ital Summer Fresco Proj, Ital Ministry Cult, Erasmas Europ Educ Agency & Exeter Univ, Eng. *Teaching:* Head, Printmaking Area, Dept Art, Univ Wis-Stout, Menomonie, 72-81; head lithography dept, Cent Col Art & Design, London, Eng, 75-76; chmn art dept, Calif State Polytech Univ, Pomona, 81-85, head painting & photog areas, 85-; Zenobia instr for New Urban Landscape, Venice, Italy, 95; Col Art & Design, Univ Plymouth, Exeter, Eng, 96-97. *Awards:* Gold Medal, Italy, 81; Purchase Award, 12th Nat Drawing Exhib, Minot, NDak, 82; Cash Award, Multicultural Art Inst, San Diego, 82. *Bibliog:* Frederiksvaerk Ugeblad Newspaper, Denmark, 5/3/2000. *Mem:* Coll Art Asn; Los Angeles Printmaking Soc; Los Angeles Art Core. *Media:* Painting; Photography. *Res:* Working on book Grounds. *Publ:* Venice Defocused: An Artist's View, 2008; Venetian Mists, Five Cantos, 2010. *Dealer:* 118 Gallery 1007 Harmon Pl Minneapolis MN 55403. *Mailing Add:* Dept Art Calif State Polytech 3801 W Temple Ave Pomona CA 91768

HANNUM, GILLIAN GREENHILL
EDUCATOR, HISTORIAN

b Jan 16, 1954. *Study:* Principia Coll, BA, 76 (fine arts, highest honors); Pa State Univ, MA (art hist), 81, PhD (art hist), 86. *Collection Arranged:* Photography and Humor (with B & H Henisch & L Greenhill), Pattee Lib, Pa State Univ, 81, Univ Gallery, Calif State Univ, Chico, 81; Shadows and Reflections: Pictorial Photography by Wilbur Porterfield (auth, brochure & checklist), Palmer Mus Art, Pa State Univ, 99, Burchfield-Penney Art Ctr, Buffalo State Col, 2000. *Pos:* Peer reviewer, NEH Preservation and Access Grants, 94-2004; panelist, Ford Found Post-doct Fellowships for Minorities, 98; panelist, Heathcote Award, Cult Devel and Diversity Grants, Westchester Arts Coun, 93-94; bd dirs, Print Club of NY, Inc, 2000-. *Teaching:* Part-time instr, Pa State Univ, 81-86; from asst prof art hist to prof & dept chair, Manhattanville Col, 87-. *Awards:* Mabel Axcy Dominick Award Outstanding Achievement in Art History, Principia Col, 76; Alumni Achievement Award, Coll Arts and Sci, Pa State Univ, 92; Teaching Excellence Award, Ind Coll Fund NY, Inc, 96. *Mem:* Fel Royal Photog Soc Gt Brit; Coll Art Asn; Soc Photog Educators; Phi Kappa Phi; Phi Alpha Eta; Int Ctr Photog; Hist Photog Group; Soc Photog Educators; Print Club of NY, Inc. *Res:* Photographic history; emphasis on pictorialism 1890-1915. *Publ:* contribr, Diane Arbus & Robert Mapplethorpe, Encyl of World Biography, 20th Century Supplement, No 17, 92; contribr, 1902 Stieglitz organizes a group of American photographers as the Photo-Secession, Great Events from History II: Arts and Culture, Salem Press, Inc, 93; Laura Gilpin, Great Lives from History, American Women, Salem Press, Inc, 95; Aubrey Beardsley & Robert Mapplethorpe, Ready Reference: Censorship, Salem Press, Inc, 95; Frances Benjamin Johnston: Promoting Women Photographers, The Ladies Home J, Nineteenth Century, Vol 24, no 2, fall, 2004; In the Mind's Eye: Photographs by Penata Rainer (catalog & essay), Xlibris Press, Philadelphia, Pa, 2005. *Mailing Add:* Manhattanville Col 2900 Purchase St Purchase NY 10577

HANNUM, TERENCE J
CRITIC, DIRECTOR

Study: NYU, projects in painting, 2000; Fla Southern Col, Lakeland, BA in religion/philosophy & Studio Art, 2001; Sch of Art Inst, Chicago, Post-Baccalaureate Cert in Painting & Studio Art, 2002; Sch of Art Inst, Chicago, MFA in painting and drawing, 2004. *Exhib:* Solo exhibs, New Work, Small Gallery, Lakeland, Fla, 2000, New Paintings, Liquid, Naples, Fla, 2001, Valentine's Day Peep Show, Hyde Park Fine Arts, Tampa, Fla, 2000, Sr Thesis Exhib, Melvin Gallery, Fla Southern Col, Lakeland, Fla, 2001, Identities and Autobiographies, VonLiebig Art Ctr, Naples, Fla, 2002, The Pick-Up, 1926, Chicago, Ill, 2002, Fac Biennial, VonLiebig Art Ctr, Naples, Fla, 2002, MFA Post-Baccalaureate Exhib, G2, Chicago, Ill, 2002, Brilliant, Zolla/Lieberman Gallery, 2003, Song Lyrics, So-and-So Gallery, 2003, ArtHotel 2003, Embassy Suites, 2003, Stray Show, Zeek & Neen/Municipal, 2003, Modest Contemp Art Projects. *Pos:* Graphic designer, Steppendwarf Theatre Comp, Lakeland, Fla, 2000; gallery asst, Harmon-Meeks Gallery, Naples, 2001; off asst, painting and drawing dept, 2003; dir, Panel-House.com, Chicago. *Teaching:* painting and drawing instr, The VonLiebig Art Ctr, 2002; teacher asst, for Anatomy II, painting and drawing dept Sch of Art Inst Chicago, 2003. *Mem:* Chicago Art Critics Assoc. *Publ:* Writer (articles) Regulator, F News, Bridge Online, (art reviews) panel-house.com. *Mailing Add:* c/o Panel-House 1046 N Honore St 1F PO Box 220651 Chicago IL 60622

HANSALIK, KONRAD F
PRINTMAKER, PAINTER

b Corona, NY, Dec 11, 1932. *Study:* Hofstra Coll, BS (Educ), 54, MS (Educ), 60; New York Phoenix Sch Design, 57-58; New York Univ, Prof Cert, 66; Hofstra Univ, Admin Cert, 68. *Work:* NYU. *Exhib:* Solo exhibs, Paintings & Woodcuts, 25 Pub Libr & Banks, Nassau & Suffolk Counties, NY, 73-80; Group exhibs, Am Artists Professional League Grand Nat and various other exhibs, 92-2014, Salmagundi Club of NY, non-membership, membership and themed exhibits, 92-2014, Academic Artists Assn 93-96, Am Soc Marine Artists, 92-98, Realism, 93, Parkersburg Art Ctr WV, 93, ASMA NE Region Juried Show, US Merchant Marine Acad Kings Point, NY, 96, Cummer Mus Art & Gardens, Jacksonville, Fla, 97; Realism '93, Parkersburg Art Ctr, WVa, 93; ASMA NE Region Juried Show, US Merchant Marine Acad Mus, Kings Point, NY, 96; ASMA 11th Nat, Frye Art Mus, Seattle, 97; Cummer Mus Art & Gardens, Jacksonville, Fla, 97. *Pos:* district coordinator art & high school dept chair, Massapequa Public Schools, Massapequa, NY, 85-92. *Teaching:* Instr art, William Floyd High Sch, Mastic, NY, 58-59; instr art, Massapequa Pub Sch, NY, 59-93, chmn & coordr, 85-92. *Awards:* Salmagundi 21st Non-Mem Juried, Hudson Valley Art Asn, 98; Salmagundi 22nd Non-Mem Juried, Pen & Brush Inc, 99; Salmagundi 24th Non-Mem Juried, Dick Blick Co, 2001; John B. O'Dwyer Mem, Salmagundi Club Fall Auction, 2002; William D. Zahn Mem, Salmagundi Club Graphics & Sculpture, 2003; Martin Hannon Mem, Salmagundi Club Spring Auction, 2007. *Mem:* Am Artists Prof League, New York (vp, 96-97, 2005-2006, pres, 97-2000 & 2006-09); Salmagundi Club, New York. *Media:* Oil, Woodcut. *Res:* A Comparative Study of the Aesthetic Criteria of De Stijl and Neo-Plasticism and that of Contemporary Art Including Abstract Expressionism; A Comparison of Essential Areas of Agreement and Dissonance Based on Concepts Purported by Principal Protagonists of Two Major Periods in Modern Art

HANSEN, GAYLEN CAPENER
PAINTER, EDUCATOR

b Garland, Utah, Sept 21, 1921. *Study:* Otis Art Inst, 39-40; Art Barn Sch Fine Arts, 40-44; Art Ctr, Sale Lake City, 40-44; Univ Utah, 43-44 & 45-46; Utah State Agricultural Col, BS, 52; Univ Southern Calif, Los Angeles, MFA, 53. *Work:* Wash State Univ, Pullman; Seattle Arts Comn; Utah State Permanent Collection, Salt Lake City. *Comn:* Painting on canvas, Art in Archit Prog, Moscow, Idaho, 80. *Exhib:* Solo exhibs, Monique Knowlton Gallery, NY, 80, 81 & 83, Boise Gallery Art, Idaho, 85, Galerie Redman, Berlin, Ger, 85, 87, 91, 93, Greg Kucera Gallery Art, Seattle, Wash, 87, Whatcom Mus Hist & Art, Bellingham, Calif, 88, Yellowstone Art Ctr, Billings, Mt, 88 & Arts Club Chicago, 90, Koplin Gallery, 92, 94, Linda Hodges Gallery, Seattle, 93, 95, 98, 99, 02, 04, LewAllen Contemp, Santa Fe, 2000, Palo Alto Center, Calif, 2003, AVC Gallery, NY, 2003; retrospectives, Seattle Art Mus, Wash & Univ Art Mus, Pullman, Wash, 85 & Mus Art, Pa State Univ, Portland Ctr Visual Arts, Ore & San Jose Mus Art, Calif, 86; 38th Corcoran Biennial Exhib Am Painting - 2nd Western States Exhib, Washington, DC, traveling, 83; 5 Amerikanische Kunstler, Galerie Redmann, Berlin, Ger, 84; Second Western Biennial, Brooklyn Mus, NY, 85; Beyond the Real, Prichard Art Gallery, Moscow, Idaho, 86; Folk Images: The Animal Kingdome, Hippodrome Gallery, Long Beach, Calif, 87; Masters of the Inland Northwest, Cheney Cowles Mus, Spokane, Wash, 88; Northwest x Southwest Exploring Painted Fictions, Palm Springs Desert Mus, Calif, 90; Northwest Tales: Contemp Narrative Painting, Anchorage Mus Art, Alaska, 91; Drawings II, Koplin Gallery, Santa Monica, Calif, 92; Microsoft Collects, Henry Art Gallery, Seattle, 93; Humor, Frumpkin/Adams Gallery, NY, 94; Interior Idioms, Seafirst Gallery, Seattle, 95; Falling Timber, Tacoma Art Mus, Washington, 96; Outward Bound, American Art at the Brink of the Twenty-First Century, Meridian Int Center, Washington, DC, 1999-2000; Bumerbiennale: Paintings 2000, Bumbershoot, Seattle, Washington, 2000; Seattle Perspective, Washington State Convention Center, Seattle, 2004. *Teaching:* Instr painting & drawing, Univ Tex, Austin, 47-52; prof art, Wash State Univ, Pullman, 57-84. *Awards:* Purchase Prize, Utah State Fair Exhib, 44; First Prize, Fifth Ann Oil Exhib, Woessner Gallery, Seattle, 58; Second Prize, Northwest Watercolor Ann, Seattle Art Mus, 60; Sambuca Romana Prize, The New Mus, NY, 84; Gov's Arts Award, Washington State, 89; Flintridge Found Award for Visual Arts, 2001. *Bibliog:* Lissa August (auth), Western Artists Strut Their Stuff, People Weekly, 3/83; Grace Glueck (auth), Two Biennials: One Looking East & the Other West, NY Times, 3/27/83; Matthew Kangas (auth), Little Romances/Little Fictions, Vanguard, 5/84; Dieterich Kinderman (auth), Don't Mistake Gaylen Hansen's Art for Primitive, Idaho Statesman, 5/85. *Media:* Oil on Canvas. *Mailing Add:* c/o Linda Hodges Gallery 316 First Ave S Seattle WA 98104

HANSEN, HAROLD (HARRY) JOHN
EDUCATOR, PAINTER

b Chicago, Ill, June 18, 1942. *Study:* Univ Ill, BFA, 64; Univ Mich, MFA, 66. *Work:* SC State Art Collection; SC Florence Mus Art; Univ South; Univ Pac; Carroll Reese Mus, E Tenn State Univ. *Comn:* cover, SC, A History, USC Press, 98. *Exhib:* Drawings USA Traveling Show, 73; Potsdam Drawings, Univ NY Potsdam, 79. *Collection Arranged:* SC Collects Watercolors: SC State Mus, 97. *Pos:* Guest cur, SC State Mus, Columbia, 6-8/97. *Teaching:* Instr art, Kendall Sch Design, Grand Rapids, Mich, 66-69; asst prof art, Ferris State Col, Big Rapids, Mich, 69-70; from asst prof art to assoc prof, Univ SC, 70-86, chmn, Div Art Studio, 75-82, assoc head dept art, 75-90 & prof, 86-, assoc head, 95-. *Awards:* First Prize, Caroliniana Watercolor Competition, Columbia, SC, 81; Grand Prize, SC State Fair, Columbia, 87; First Prize, Florence Mus BB&T Art Exhib, Florence, SC, 96. *Mem:* SC Watercolor Soc (bd). *Media:* Encaustic, Watercolor. *Res:* Technical investigation of the encaustic to improve working characteristics and hardness. *Publ:* Auth, A method for modern encaustic painting, Southeastern Coll Art Asn Rev, spring 76; The development of new vehicle recipes for encaustic paints, Leonardo, 77. *Dealer:* City Art, 1224 Lincoln St, Columbia, SC, 29201. *Mailing Add:* Univ SC Dept Art Columbia SC 29208

HANSEN, JAMES LEE
SCULPTOR

b Tacoma, Wash, June 13, 1925. *Study:* Portland Art Mus Sch. *Work:* Seattle Art Mus; Univ Ore Mus Art, Eugene; Civic Transit Mall, Portland, Ore; State Capitol, Salem, Ore, Fresno, Calif. *Comn:* The Shaman, State Capitol Campus, Olympia, Wash, 70; Crescent Probe, Civic Ctr Fountain, Salem, Ore, 78; Stempost, Stadium Plaza Wash State Univ, Pullman, 80; The Oasis, Bur Land Mgt Bldg, Medford, Ore, 80. *Exhib:* 71st Ann Painting & Sculpture exhib, San Francisco Mus Mod Art, 52; Whitney Mus Am Art Ann, 53; NW art Today, Seattle Worlds Fair, Wash, 62; Solo exhibs, Fountain Gallery, Portland, 69, 77, 81 & 84, Univ Ore Mus Art, Eugene, 70, Portland Art Mus, 71, Friedlander Gallery, Seattle, 73 & 77, Hodges/Banks Gallery, Seattle, Wash, 83 & 85 & Abante Fine Arts, Portland, Ore, 86, 88 & 92; Artists of Oregon (paintings & sculpture), Portland Art Mus, Ore, 71; Art of the Pacific Northwest from 1930s to present, Nat Coll Fine Art, Smithsonian Inst, Washington, 74; Mayor's Invit Art Show, Salem Civic Ctr, Ore, 76; Spokane Sculpture Invit, Wash, 77; An Am Tradition: Abstraction, Henry Gallery, Seattle, Wash, 81 & 82. *Pos:* Founder & 1st pres, Alliance of NW Sculptors, 77-80. *Teaching:* Prof sculpture, Portland State Univ, 64-90, emer, 90. *Awards:* Nat Ann, Award for Huntress, 52; Am Trust Co Award, 56 & Award for Ritual, 60, San Francisco Art Mus; Norman Davis Award for Neo Shang, Seattle Art

Mus, 58. *Bibliog:* William Davenport (auth), Art treasures in the West, Lane, 10/66; JA Schinneller (auth), Art/search & self discovery, Int Textbk, 12/67. *Mem:* Portland Art Mus. *Media:* Cast Bronze. *Publ:* New Totems & Old Gods, Surgo Publ, 90. *Dealer:* Bryan Ohno Gallery, 155 S Main St, Seattle, Wa, 98104. *Mailing Add:* Peter Bartlow Gallery 2506 N Clark St Chicago IL 60614

HANSEN, ROBERT
PAINTER, SCULPTOR
b Osceola, Nebr, Jan 1, 1924. *Study:* Univ Nebr, AB, BFA, 48; Escuela Univ Bellas Artes, San Miguel Allende, Mex, MFA, 49; also with Alfredo Zalce, Morelia, Mex, 52-53. *Work:* Mus Mod Art & Whitney Mus Am Art, New York; Los Angeles Co Mus Art; San Diego Gallery Fine Arts; Long Beach Mus Art. *Exhib:* Solo Exhibs: 14 from 57-2006; Carnegie Int, Pittsburgh, Pa, 61 & 63; Painting USA: Figure, Mus Mod Art, New York, 62 & Tamarind: Homage to Lithography, 69; retrospectives, Long Beach Mus Art, Calif, 67 & Los Angeles Munic Gallery, 73; New Vein, organized & mounted in mus of nat capitols in Europe & S Am, Smithsonian Inst, 68-70. *Teaching:* Prof art, Occidental Coll, 56-87, prof emer, 87-. *Awards:* Guggenheim Fel, 61; Fulbright Sr Grant, 61; Tamarind Fel, 65. *Media:* Lacquer, Acrylic. *Specialty:* Modern Gallery. *Publ:* Auth, This curving world: Hyperbolic linear perspective, J Aesthetics & Art Criticism, winter 73; transl, Curvilinear Perspective, Flocon and Barre, Univ Calif Press, 87. *Dealer:* Modern Gallery 6154-6162 Santa Monica Blvd Los Angeles Calif 90025. *Mailing Add:* 1498 Santa Ynez Carpinteria CA 93013

HANSLEY, LEE
ART DEALER, CURATOR
b Roanoke Rapids, NC, Jan 11, 1948. *Study:* Univ NC, Chapel Hill (art hist & journalism). *Collection Arranged:* Awards in the Visual Arts 1-5 (auth, catalogues 1 & 3-5), 81-86; The Art of New Orleans, SECCA, 84; Edith London Retrospective (auth, catalogue), Durham, NC, 92; Silvia Heyden: A Culmination of Tapestry Weaving in NC, 93; E C Langford: A Half-Century of Painting, Sculpture and Collage, 95; The Chapel Hill School: A Shared Aesthetic, 98; New & Hot NC, 2006; Charlotte Robinson: A Retrospective (auth, catalogue), 2007; McDonald Bane Retrospective: 65 Years in Art, 2013; Under the Influence of Gregory Ivy, North Carolina's First Modernist, 2013; Sylvia Hayden and Editor London: Together Again (author, catalogue), 2014. *Pos:* Assoc cur, SECCA, Winston-Salem, NC, 80-86; indep cur, 86-92; proprietor/dir, Lee Hansley Gallery, Raleigh, NC, 93-; art adv and contract cur, The Equitable Life Assurance Soc of the United States, NY, 81-86. *Awards:* Medal of the Arts, City of Raleigh, 2005; Tar Heel of the Week, The News & Observer, NC, 2007. *Specialty:* American contemporary art, the art of North Carolina. *Interests:* Am Art 1945-present, North Carolina's art history. *Publ:* numerous exhib catalogs for solo and group shows. *Mailing Add:* 225 Glenwood Ave Raleigh NC 27603-1404

HANSON, CHRIS
SCULPTOR
b Montreal, Canada, 1964. *Study:* Nova Scotia Coll Art & Design, Halifax, Canada, BFA 1986; Univ Illinois at Chicago, MFA, 1996. *Work:* Mus Mod Art, New York; Mus Contemp Art, Chicago; Art Gallery Ontario, Toronto, Canada; Ernst & Young, London. *Exhib:* Solo exhibs include Vinyl Installation, Gallerie SKOL, Montreal, Canada, 1989, Thomas Blackman Exhib Space, Chicago, 1996, Windows, Brussels, 1998, Los Angeles Contemp Exhib, 1999, White Columns, New York, 2000, Cohan & Leslie, New York, 2001, 2004, 2005, Store, London, 2005, Suburban, Chicago, 2007, Friedrich Petzel Gallery, New York, 2008; group exhibs include Glom, Randolph Street Gallery, Chicago, 1995; Behind Closed Doors, Mus Contemp Art, Chicago, 1998; Greater New York, PS 1 Contemp Art Ctr (with Mus Mod Art), 2000, Building Structures, 2002; Promises, Contemp Art Gallery, Vancouver, Canada, 2001; Back in Black, Cohan & Leslie, New York, 2003; Interstate, Socrates Sculpture Park, New York, 2006; Lath Picture Show, Friedrich Petzel Gallery, 2007; Accident Blackspot, Markus Winter Gallery, Berlin, Germany, 2008; Arena, Art Gallery Nova Scotia, Canada, 2008; Invitational Exhib Visual Arts, AAAL, 2008. *Teaching:* Yale Univ Sch Art, Art & Labor, panel discussion, individual lect, critiques, 2004; Am Univ, Washington, Artist in Resident, lect & individual critiques. *Dealer:* Friedrich Petzel Gallery 535 & 537 W 22nd St New York NY 10011

HANSON, JB
SCULPTOR, WEAVER
b Gadsden, Ala, Oct 23, 1946. *Study:* Md Inst, Coll Art, 72-76. *Work:* Univ Md, College Park; Washington Co Mus Fine Art; Cloisters Children's Mus, Baltimore; Centre Int de la Tapisserie Ancienne et Moderne, Lusanne, Switzerland. *Comn:* 6 banners depicting the History of the Govans Community, City Baltimore, Md, 79, tapestry for Medfield Recreation Ctr, 79; mural, Mallory Ctr, Inst Arts, Inc, 81. *Exhib:* Maryland Ann, Baltimore Mus Art, 72; Maryland Biennial, Baltimore Mus Art, 74; Miniatures, West Tex Mus Art, Lubbock, 76; 11th Int Sculpture Symp, Studio Gallery, Washington, DC, 80; Am Clay 1981, Meredith Contemp Art, Md, 81; Fine Art Auction Exhib, Metrop Mus, Fla, 81; Art of Ceramics, Atheneum Mus, Va, 81. *Awards:* Sculpture Award, Baltimore Mus Art, 74; Sculpture Award, Md Crafts Coun, 78. *Bibliog:* David Tannous (auth), Baltimore art scene, Smithsonian Assoc Mag, 79; Thomas Haulk (auth), reviews, Craft Horizon Mag, 79; Elisabeth Stevens (auth), Pots full of wit: sculptor shows he has a way with animals, Baltimore Sun, 80. *Mem:* Artist Equity Asn (pres, 80-81, nat ECoast vpres, 81-83); Md Crafts Coun (pres, 76). *Media:* Clay; Fibers. *Mailing Add:* 622 Homestead St Baltimore MD 21218-3556

HANSON, JUDY (JUDY COOKE) See Cooke, Judy

HANSON, PHILIP HOLTON
PAINTER
b Chicago, Ill, Jan 8, 1943. *Study:* Univ Chicago, BA, 65; Art Inst Chicago, MFA, 69. *Work:* Mus des 20 Jahrhunderts, Vienna, Austria; Mus Contemp Art, Chicago; Krannert Mus, Champaign, Ill. *Exhib:* Extraordinary Realities, Whitney Mus, 73; Madison Art Ctr, 77; Contemp Chicago Painters, Univ North Iowa Gallery Art, 78; Fabrications, Univ Miami, Lowe Art Mus, 80; Some Recent Art from Chicago, Ackland Art Mus, Univ NC, Chapel Hill, 80; Who Chicago, London, Edinburgh and traveling, 80; Six Chicago Artists, Pace Gallery, NY, 82; Solo exhib, Phyllis Kind Gallery, Chicago, 82, Hyde Park Art Ctr, 85. *Teaching:* Prof, Sch Art Inst Chicago, 72-. *Awards:* Casandra Grant, 73; Nat Endowment Arts Grant, 78 & 83. *Media:* Oil. *Mailing Add:* Sch Art Inst Chicago Columbus Dr & Jackson St Chicago IL 60603

HAOZOUS, BOB
SCULPTOR
b Los Angeles, Calif, Apr 1, 1943. *Study:* Utah State Univ, 61-62; Calif Coll Arts & Crafts, BFA, 71. *Work:* Albuquerque Mus, NMex; Heard Mus, Phoenix, Ariz; Joslyn Mus Art, Omaha, Nebr; Philbrook Art Ctr, Tulsa, Okla; Southwest Mus, Los Angeles; and others. *Comn:* Mahogany relief wall mural, Daybreak Star Art Ctr, Seattle, Wash, 78; ann award bronze, Busn Comt Arts, NY, 83; sculpture for permanent collection, Heard Mus, Phoenix, Ariz, 83; monumental outdoor sculpture, City of Philadelphia, 88; 5 paired monumental sculptures, City of Phoenix, Ariz, 90. *Exhib:* One-man shows, Taylor Mus, Colorado Springs, 87, Wheelwright Mus, Santa Fe, NMex, 88 & Dartmouth Col, Hanover, NH, 89; Muerte/Amor, UNAM, Galeria Aristos, Mexico City, Mex, 90; Recent Major Work, Nev State Mus, Las Vegas, 92; The Vanishing White Man, Scottsdale Ctr Arts, Ariz, 92. *Pos:* Artist-in-residence, Dartmouth Col, Hanover, NH, 89 & Frankfort, Ger. *Bibliog:* Rosalind Constable (auth), Six Artists, Horizon, 82; Lucy Lippard (auth), New Art in Multicultural America, Pantheon Bks, 90; Robin Cembalilst (auth), Pride & prejudice, Artnews, 92. *Media:* Steel. *Mailing Add:* c/o Shidoni Foundry Inc PO Box 250 Tesuque NM 87574

HAPGOOD, SUSAN T
CURATOR, CRITIC
b Riverhead, NY, Oct 18, 1957. *Study:* Univ Rochester, BA, 79; Inst Fine Arts, NY Univ, MA, 85. *Collection Arranged:* Recent Acquisitions, 85, Homage to Louise Nevelson (auth, brochure), 86 & The Early Years: Non-Objective Paintings from the Permanent Collection, (auth, brochure), 88, Guggenheim Mus; Flux Attitudes, Hallwalls, (auth, catalog), 91; New Mus Contemp Art, 92; Neo-Dada: Redefining Art (auth, catalog) 58-62, Equitable Gallery, NY, 95; Video Divertimento, Camera Oscura, Tuscany, Ital, 99. *Pos:* Archivist, Sperone Westwater Gallery, New York, 79-82, asst to dir, formerly; coordr, Art Quest, New Mus Contemp Art, New York, 83-84; cur coordr, Solomon R Guggenheim Mus, New York, 85-89, cur asst, formerly; cur, Woodner Family Collection, New York, 94-97; researcher, ada'web, NY, 97-98; cur exhibs, Am Fedn Arts, New York, 99-2003; dir exhibs, ICI, New York, 2003-. *Teaching:* Instr art hist, Sch Visual Arts, 88. *Awards:* Fel, List Ctr Art & Politics, New Sch, N, 98-. *Mem:* Coll Art Asn. *Res:* Contemporary art. *Publ:* Auth, Remaking Art History, 90 & Whitney Mus: How American Is It?, Art Am, 91; About Art Criticism, Acme Art J, 92; Fonts of Wisdom, Frieze Mag, 96; Doppelhelix: Kunst und Geld, Der Standard, 96

HARA, KEIKO
PAINTER, PRINTMAKER
b Oct 1, 1942; Japanese citizen. *Study:* Gendai Art Sch, (painting), Japan, 64; Oita Junior Art Coll, (painting), Japan, 65; Miss State Univ Women, BFA(painting), 74; Univ Wis, Milwaukee, MA (printmaking), 75; Cranbrook Acad Art, MFA(printmaking), 76. *Work:* Tacoma Art Mus, Wash; Art Inst Chicago; Detroit Inst Art; Milwaukee Art Mus; Libr Cong, Capital Heights, Md; Northwest Art Mus, Wash; MIC Software Co, Wash; Portland Art Mus/Gilkey Ctr Graphic Arts, Ore; Art Inst of Chicago;King Co Art Comn, Wash; Sony Co, Washington, DC; IBM Corp, Chicago; Muskegon Mus Art, Mich; Charles A. Wustum Mus, Wis; The Council House-Johnson Wax Co, Wis; Oita Art Coll Japan; AT & T Co, Chicago; Jundt Art Mus, Gonzaga Univ, Wash; The Wash Art Consortium, Yale New Haven Hospital; Ariz State Univ Art Coll, Temple, Ariz; Hood Mus Art, Dartmouth Coll, Hanover, NH; Worcester Art Mus, Ma. *Comn:* Lithography, Perimeter Gallery, Chicago, 82; Gates - outdoor installation, Whitman Coll, 98; Invitational King Co Pub Art Comn, 2002; painting installation, Wash Public Art Com, 2006; Regional Arts & Cult Coun, Pub Art Comn, 2008. *Exhib:* 30th Am Invitational & 20th Nat Print Show, Brooklyn Art Mus, NY, 76; Gallerie in Den Vierlander, Hamburg, Ger, 81; Charles A Wustum Mus, Rachine, Wis, 81; Tacoma Art Mus, Wash, 94; Mus Art, Univ Ore, Eugene, 95; NW Int Print Art Exhib, Portland Art Mus, Ore, 97; Square Painting/Plane Painting, COCA, Seattle, 97; Topophilia Sumida River, Elizabeth Leach Gallery, Portland, Ore, 97; Japanese/Am: The In Between, Art Gym, Marylhurst Col, Portland, Ore, 98; Perimeter Gallery, Chicago, 98; ColorPrint USA, Nat Invitational Print Portfolio Exhib, 50 US States, 98; P Richard Art Gallery, Univ of Idaho, 99; Perimeter Gallery, Chicago, Ill, 2000, 2003; Foster/White Gallery, Seattle, Wash, 2000; Autzen Gallery, Portland State Univ, Ore, 2001; Lorinda Knight Gallery, Spokane, Wash, 2002; Keiko Hara works on paper 7 Canvas, Perimeter Gallery, NY; Keiko Hara painting & works on paper, 2003; Keiko Hara-Seasons, The Northwest Mus of Arts & Cult, Spokane, Wash, 2004; Keiko Hara, Imbuning in Monet, Perimeter Gallery, Chicago, 2006; Keiko Hara-Verse Imbuing, Walla Walla Foundry Gallery, Walla Walla, Wash, 2006; Keiko Hara-New Painting, Lorinda Knight Gallery, Spokane, Wash, 2007; Topophilia Imbuing, Am Univ Mus at The Katzen, Washington, DC, 2007; Keiko Hara-New Paintings, Lorinda Knight Gallery, Spokane, Wash, 2008; Border Crossings, Three Artists from Brooklyn, New York, Kyoto Int Cult Ctr & Cohju Contemp Art, 2008; Perimeter Gallery, Chicago, Ill, 2009; The Arts: A Celebration Invitational Exhib, Anaortes, Wash, 2009; Verse-Reflected & Reflecting Pub Art (solo exhib), City Archives & Records Ctr, Portland, Ore, 2010; Abstract Art, Perimeter Gallery, Chicago, 2010; Japanese Prints and Works on Paper, Thos Moser Studio, NY, 2010; Someday My Prints Will Come, Wisconsin Printmakers in RAMs Coll, Wustum Art Mus, 2010; Keiko Hara, Works on Canvas and Paper, Perimeter Gallery, Chicago, Ill, 2011; Japanese Print, Jundt Art Mus, Gonzaga Univ, Spokane, Wash, 2012; MI-Lab Artist in Res Preview Exhib, Tokyo, 2012; Work of Keiko Hara, Olympic Ctr, Chicago, Ill, 2012; Keikohara New Work, Perimeter Gallery, 2013; Keiko Hara Prints 1981-2013, Brainbridge Arts and Crafts Gallery, 2013, Pendleton Art Ctr, 2013; Mokuhanga Print, Cullom Gallery, 2013. *Teaching:* Instr printmaking, Carthage Coll, 79-80 & Univ Wis, River Falls,

80-85; prof art, Whitman Coll, 85-2006. *Awards:* Artist Trust Fel, Wash, 94; Purchase Award, Portland Art Mus/Gilkey Ctr Graphic Arts, Ore, 97; The Pollock-Krasner Found Grant, New York, 2005. *Bibliog:* Lois Allen (auth), Contemporary Printmaking in the Northwest, Craftsman House, Australia, 97; Keiko Hara at the Perimeter Gallery, Artnews; Critic's Choice/Chicago Reader, Fred Camper, 2003; Robert C Morgan (auth), Keiko Hara's Springtime, Shreds of Language; Dorothea Dietrich (auth), Keiko Hara: Sense of Place (catalog for the Katzen Art Ctr), Washington, DC; Patricia Grieve Watkinson (auth), The Infinite Surface: Prints and Installations by Keiko Hara, 2013. *Publ:* Distant Rain, Eastern Univ Wash Press; Keiko Hara Prints, 1981-2013. *Dealer:* Perimeter Gallery 750 N Orleans Chicago IL 60610. *Mailing Add:* PO Box 2798 336 N Division Walla Walla WA 99362-0336

HARABASZ, EWA
PAINTER
Study: Med Sch, Czestochowa, Poland, BA; Coll Creative Studies, Detroit, BFA (graphic design); Wayne State Univ, Detroit, MFA (painting/drawing). *Exhib:* Solo exhibs include Synagogue Arts, New Yorke, 2003, Consulate Gen of the Republic of Poland, New York, 2003, John Hartell Gallery, Cornell Univ, 2007, Luxe Gallery, New York, 2007, Le Guern, Warsaw, Poland, 2008; group exhibs include An Imagined Conversation, Brooklyn Jewish Arts, 2003; Second Language, Williams Tower Gallery, Houston, 2004; POZA, Real Art Ways, Hartford, Conn, 2006; Places, Luxe Gallery, New York, 2007; Apex Art, New York, 2007. *Teaching:* Vis asst prof, Coll Archit, Art & Planning, Cornell Univ. *Awards:* Pollock-Krasner Found Grant, 2007

HARBUTT, CHARLES
PHOTOGRAPHER, EDITOR
b Camden, NJ, July 29, 1935. *Study:* Marquette Univ, BS, 56. *Work:* Mus Mod Art, NY; Art Inst Chicago; Smithsonian Inst; Bibliotheque Nat, Paris; George Eastman House, Rochester, NY; Whitney Mus; Ctr Creative Photog, Tucson; and many others. *Exhib:* Solo exhibs include Kalamazoo Art Inst, Kalamazoo, Mich, 76, Ctr Creative Photography, Tucson, Ariz, 97, Visa pour l'Image, Perpignan, France, 2004, Le Moulin Musee, Niort, France, 2005; Group exhibs, Mirrors & Windows, Mus Mod Art, 78; Hoffman Collection, Philadelphia Mus, 2004; Big City, Vienna Mus, Vienna, Austria, 2009; Reality Revisited, Mod Mus, Stockholm, 2009. *Teaching:* Vis artist photog, Art Inst Chicago, 75, RI Sch Design, 76 & Mass Inst Technol, 79; prof Parsons School Design, 93-. *Awards:* Catalog Exposure, NY State Council on the Arts, 73; Best Photog Book, Arles Festival, 74; Grant, Mark Rothko Found, 85. *Bibliog:* Vicki Wilson (auth), The Human Condition, Almost, Am Photog, 7/87; Jean-Claude Lemagny (auth), Reporter des Formes, Le Monde, Paris: 10/30/86. *Media:* Photography. *Specialty:* fine art. *Publ:* ed, America in Crisis: Holt, Rinehart & Winston, NewYork, 69; The Plan for New York, NYC Planning Comn, 70; Travelog, MIT Press, Cambridge, Mass, 73; Progreso: Navarin Editeur, Paris, 86; Departures and Arrivals, Damiani, Bologna, 2012. *Dealer:* Peter Fetterman Gallery 2525 Michigan Ave Gallery A1 Santa Monica CA 90404. *Mailing Add:* One Fifth Ave #16-G New York NY 10003-4312

HARCUS, PORTIA GWEN
DEALER, CONSULTANT
b Brockton, Mass. *Study:* Wheaton Col, BA. *Pos:* Dir, Harcus Krakow Gallery, 64-82; dir & pres, Harcus Gallery, 82-. *Mem:* Art Dealers Asn Am; Asn Int Photog Art Dealers; Art Table Inc; Confederation Int Negociants Oeuvres D'Art. *Specialty:* Contemp painting, sculpture, graphics and major 20th century works. *Mailing Add:* 6 Melrose St Boston MA 02116-5510

HARDEE, RODNEY CHARLES
PAINTER, PATRON
Lakeland, Fl, May, 5, 1954. *Work:* Polk Mus Art, Lakeland, Fla; Mennello Mus, Orlando, Fla; Vassar Coll, Frances Leman Loeb Art Ctr, Poughkeepsie, NY. *Exhib:* Primal Portraits, Adam and Eve Imagery as Seen by Twentieth Century Self Taught Artists, San Francisco Craft and Folk Art Mus, Calif, 90; Mennello Mus, Orlando, Fla, 2000; Outsider vs. Folk, Polk Mus Art, Lakeland, Fla, 2012. *Bibliog:* Betty Carol Sellen, Cynthia J Johnson, Self Taught, Outsider and Folk Art: A Guide to American Artists, Locations and Resources, 99; Gary Monroe (auth), Extraordinary Interpretations, Florida's Self Taught Artists, Fla Univ Press, 2003; Mary Hix (auth), Hardee's Folk Art is Purr-Fection, Lakeland Mag, 2006. *Media:* Acrylic, Oil. *Mailing Add:* 1626 Pinetop Dr Lakeland FL 33809

HARDEN, MARVIN
PAINTER, EDUCATOR
b Austin, Tex. *Study:* Univ Calif, Los Angeles, BA (fine arts) & MA (creative painting); Los Angeles City Coll. *Work:* Whitney Mus Am Art & Mus Mod Art, New York; Smithsonian Inst, Archives Am Art; Hammer Mus, Los Angeles; Los Angeles Co Mus Art; Getty Ctr Arts & Humanities. *Comn:* Lithograph, Neighbors of Watts, 82; lithograph, UCLA Friends Graphic Arts, 86. *Exhib:* Solo exhibs, Rath Mus, Geneva, Switz, 71, Whitney Mus Am Art, 71, Irving Blum Gallery, Los Angeles, 72, Corcoran Gallery, Los Angeles, 78, Newport Harbor Art Mus, 79 & Los Angeles Munic Art Gallery, 82, Ventura Coll Art Gallery, 97, Louis Stern Fine Arts, Los Angeles, 99 ; Amory Ctr Arts, Pasadena, Calif, 92, 94, 97, 2005; Group exhibs, Tel Aviv Mus Art, Israel, 98; Los Angeles Co Mus Art, 65, 68-69, 74, 77, 95 & 96; Schneider Mus Art, Ashland, Ore, 2004; Luckman Fine Arts Complex, Los Angeles, Calif, 2004; Hammer Mus, Los Angeles, 2010. *Pos:* Co-founder, Los Angeles Inst Contemp Art, 73, (exhib comt mem, 73-74); bd dir, Images & Issues, 80-86; mem visual arts panel, Nat Endowment for Arts, 85; chair peer rev bd for visual arts, Los Angeles Cult Affairs Dept, 90. *Teaching:* Instr drawing, Univ Calif, Los Angeles, 64-68 & Los Angeles Harbor Coll, 65-68; prof painting & drawing, Calif State Univ, Northridge, 67-97, prof emer, 97-. *Awards:* Nat Endowment Arts Fel, 72; Awards in Visual Arts fellow, 83; Distinguished Prof Award, Exceptional Merit Serv Award, Calif State Univ, Northridge, 84. *Bibliog:* Karen Anne Mason (auth), African-American Artists of Los Angeles: Marvin Harden, Univ Calif Los Angeles, 95; Marvin Harden Paintings and Drawings 1961-1981, Los Angeles Munic Art Gallery, 82; William Wilson (auth), Soul shapes in an empty field, Los Angeles Times, 3/17/82. *Media:* Painting, Drawing. *Publ:* Marvin Harden (auth), natural selections, Lapis Press, 91. *Dealer:* Cirrus Editions Ltd 542 S Alameda Los Angeles CA 90013 (prints only). *Mailing Add:* Inwardness Ranch PO Box 1793 Cambria CA 93428

HARDER, RODNEY
PAINTER
b OGallala, Nebr, Apr 24, 1950. *Study:* Fresno Pac Col, Calif, BFA, 73; Calif State Univ, Fresno, MA, 75. *Work:* Citibank, NY; IBM, NY; Can Imperial Bank, NY; Baltimore City Health Dept, Md; Fresno Art Mus, Calif; many pvt collections throughout US. *Exhib:* Solo shows, Gallery 25, Fresno, Calif, 82, Fresno Art Mus, Calif, 83 & 89, Farleigh Dickinson Univ, Hackensack, NJ, 87 & Peoples Place Gallery, Intercourse, Pa, 88; Gallery M, Fresno, Calif, 91; Sweet Briar Col, Va, 91; Diverse Visions, Art Ctr Gallery, Del, 92; The Blanket Project, Art in Gen, NY, 93; and others. *Teaching:* Prof art, Fresno Pac Col, Calif, 74-83; art instr, Fresno Art Mus, Calif, 80-83 & Calif State Univ, Fresno, 81-83; art instr/coordr, Col Sch, NY, 84-; adj art instr, NY Sch Visual Arts, 86. *Awards:* Nat Endowment Arts Fel, painting, 90 & 91; Milton Avery Residency Grant, Yaddo, 94; Ragdale Artists Colony Residency, 98; and others

HARDER, ROLF PETER
GRAPHIC DESIGNER, PAINTER
b Hamburg, Ger, July 10, 1929; Can citizen. *Study:* Hamburg Acad Fine Arts, 48-52. *Work:* Libr Cong, Washington, DC; AGI Archives, Poster Mus, Essen, Ger; Nat Archives Can; Univ Reading, Eng; Mus de la Publicite Palais du Louvre, Paris; German Design Coun, Frankfurt; Mus Arts Crafts, Hamburg, Ger; Die Neue Sammlung, State Mus for Applied Arts, Munich; Design Austria, Vienna; Univ NY Coll, Fredonia, NY; Musée du Québec, Can; Université Du Québec Á Montréal, poster collection, Images of Peace, Can; Montreal Mus Fine Arts, Mus Modern Art, New York & San Francisco, Calif; Rochester Inst Tech, NY; Bibliotheque Nationale De France, Paris. *Comn:* 70 postage stamps, Can Post; visual images (symbols), numerous corps and insts; publs, Can Gov Depts. *Exhib:* Design Collaborative Int Traveling Exhib, 70-72; Biennale of Graphic Design, Brno, 70, 74, 78, 80, 82, 84, 92, 94 & 96; Experimental Graphic Design, Venice Biennale, 72; group exhibs, Can, USA, Europe, South Am, Japan, Russia & Korea. *Teaching:* Guest lectr, graphic design. *Awards:* Spec Prize, 4th Biennale Graphic Design, Brno, 70; Spec Prize, Int Poster Competition, Moscow, 87; World Logo Design Award, 98. *Bibliog:* Eberhard Hoelscher (auth), 2/61, Theodore Hilten (auth), Rolf Harder, 9/64 & Hans Kuh (auth), Design Collaborative, 9/70, Gebrauchsgraphic, Munich; Calif Magazine, Calif, 62; Hans Neuberg (auth), Graphis, Switz #143, 69; Peter Bartl (auth), Novum, Munich, 87; Rose Deneve (auth), Print, New York, 90; Gloria Menard (auth), Contemporary Designers, St James Press, London & Chicago. *Mem:* Royal Can Acad Arts; Alliance Graphique Int; fel Soc Graphic Designers Can; Societe des Designers Graphiques du Quebec (hon mem). *Interests:* Music, reading, tennis. *Publ:* Auth, introd, Can Sect, World History of the Poster, Paris; co-publ, Pitseolak: Pictures Out of My Life, 72 & Arts of the Eskimo: Prints, 74; Whos Who in Graphic Art, Switzerland, 83. *Mailing Add:* 43 Lakeshore Rd Beaconfield PQ H9W 4H6 Canada

HARDING, ANN C
PAINTER
b Minneapolis, Minn, Mar 16, 1942. *Study:* Univ Minn, BA, 66; Univ Cincinnati, MFA, 71. *Work:* Lutheran Brotherhood, Minneapolis; Sterling Drug Corp, Philadelphia, Pa; Ochsner Med Found, New Orleans, La; Rhone-Poulenc Rorer Corp, Philadelphia, Pa; Mount Sinai Med Ctr, NY; Random House, NY; and others. *Exhib:* 20th Exhib Southwest Prints & Drawings, Dallas Mus Fine Arts, 75; one-person exhibs, Friends Gallery, Minneapolis Inst Fine Arts, 81, West Baton Rouge Mus, Port Allen, La, 83, Still-Zinsel Contemp Fine Art, New Orleans, La, 91 & Reece Galleries, NY, 2001, 2003 & 2006, Cedar Crest Coll, Allentown, Pa, 2008; Nat Ann Midyear Show, Butler Inst Am Art, 81 & 82; Biennial Piedmont Painting & Sculpture, Mint Mus, 81 & 83; La Women in Contemp Art Traveling Exhib Invitational, 83-84; Hoyt Nat Painting Show, Hoyt Inst Fine Art, 83 & 85; Tampa Triennial, Tampa Mus, Fla, 85; Nat Art Festival, Atlanta, 89; and others; Genova Meets Easton, Satura Asn Cult, Genova, Italy, 2008. *Teaching:* Instr painting & drawing, La State Univ, 73-76, from asst prof to prof, 76-93, emer prof, 93-. *Awards:* Purchase Award, 35th Ann, La State Art Exhib, 80; SECCA Artist Fel, 81; Visual Arts Fel, La State Arts Coun, 85. *Media:* Oil on Canvas, Oil on Paper. *Dealer:* Danette Koke Fine Arts Inc New York NY. *Mailing Add:* 408-410 Northampton St Easton PA 18042-3516

HARDING, NOEL ROBERT
SCULPTOR, VIDEO ARTIST
b London, Eng, Dec 21, 1945. *Work:* Art Gallery Ont, Toronto; Nat Gallery Can, Ottawa, Ont; Mus Mod Art, New York; Windsor Art Gallery, Windsor, Ont; City Amsterdam, The Neth; Mus Sztuki Aktualnej, Krakow, Poland; Hara Mus, Tokyo, Japan; Vancouver Art Gallery, BC. *Comn:* Sculpture, Multnomah Co Bldg, Portland, Ore, 2001; pub art master plan, Hollywood Int Airport Expansion, Broward Co, Fla, 2005. *Exhib:* Minneapolis Coll Art & Design, Minneapolis, Minn, 72; Fleming Mus, Univ Vt, 73; Videoscape, Art Gallery Ont, Toronto, 74; Narrative in Contemp Art, Univ Guelph, Ont, 75; Dundas Valley Sch Art, Dundas, Ont, 76; Winnipeg Art Gallery, Man, 77; Centre Georges Pompidou, Paris, 78; Projects, Mus Mod Art, New York, 79; Canadian Video, PS1, New York, 80; Video Viewpoints, Mus Mod Art, New York, 80; Toronto, Alberta Coll Art, Calgary, 81; Long Beach Mus Art, Los Angeles, Calif, 82; Art Video Retrospective, Palais des Beaux Arts, Charleroi, Belg, 83; Video Art: a Hist, Mus Mod Art, New York, 83; San Francisco Int Video Festival, Calif, 84; Canadian Video Mosaic, Hokkaido Mus Mod Art, Sapporo, Japan, 85; Can House Cult Ctr Gallery, London, Eng, 86; Interference, Seagate Art Gallery, Dundee, Scotland, 87; Physics (Vast Intimacies), de Vleeshal Middleburg, The Neth, 88; Int Sommertheatre Festival, Hamburg, Fed Repub Ger, 89; Mus Sci, Notoro Symposium,

Warsaw, Poland, 90; solo exhibs, Mississauga Civic Ctr Art Gallery, Can, 91, Mus Sztuki Aktualnej, Galeria Potocko, Krakow, Poland, 92, Genereux Grunwald Gallery, Toronto, 93, The Power Plant, Ctr Contemp Art, Toronto, 93, Anti-Heroes (with catalog), Mucsarnok Palace of Exhibs, Budapest, Hungary, 93, Contemp Art Gallery, Vancouver, 93, Anti-Heroes, Nat Gallery Slovakia, Bratislava, 94, Archive Gallery, Toronto, Ont, Can, 97 & Wittmann Lawrence Gallery, Vancouver, BC, Can, 99; Vittu Pane Puu Pallo, Liget Gallery, Budapest, Hungary, 93; Arti et Amicitiae, Amsterdam, The Neth, 93; Kolekcja Artystow, BWA, Bialystok, Poland, 93; Distinguishing Features, MacDonald Stewart Art Ctr, Guelph, Can, 94 & Pleasure Dome, Toronto, 94; Contemp Art Gallery, Vancouver, 95; MacDonald Stewart Art Gallery, Guelph, Ont, 96; Cult Olympiad, Int Sculpture Exhib, Atlanta, 96; Vancouver Art Gallery, BC, 97; John Gibson Gallery, New York, 2001; Scenic Events on a Path of Upheaval, Mus Contemp Can Art, Toronto, 2003; Three Pieces for Circuits, Art Gallery Ont, Toronto, 2004; In Service, Macdonald Strewart Art Ctr, Guelph, Ont, 2005; A Chirp, Nature in the Garage, Harbourfront Ctr, Toronto, Ont, 2006. *Pos:* Lectr, var univs & orgns, US, Europe & Can; cult consult, Rem Koolhaas, off Metrop Archit, Oleson Worland Architects, 2000; art consult, Toronto Zoo, Ont, 2001; design consult, Master Site Plan, Waterfront Village, Marina Park, Thunder Bay, Ont, 2006 & Redevelopment of Eau Claire Plaza, Calgary, 2006. *Teaching:* Instr fine art, Univ Guelph, Ont, 72-79; instr, Dept Photo Electric & Experimental Art, Ont Coll Art, 77-82; fac mem, Akademi voor Beeldende Kunst, AKI, Enschede, The Neth, 84-95 & Durth Art Inst/ArtEZ, Int Post Grad Prog, Enschede, The Neth, 96-2003; adj prof, Univ Windsor, 2004-2007; artist-in-residence, art acads, Eng, Scotland, Norway, Finland, Poland & Holland. *Awards:* Can Coun Arts Grant, 76 & 78-79, Travel Grant, 77 & Proj Grant, 78; Ont Arts Coun Grant, 77 & 79. *Bibliog:* Scott Lauder (auth), The national set-up, The Canadian Forum, 28-30, 12/85; Jane Purdue (auth), Treadmill chickens and solo showdown, Now Mag, 10/9-15/86; Richard Rhodes (auth), Noel Harding, Artforum, 123, 1/87; Carl Loeffler (auth), Noel Harding, Toronto Mag, 22, 3/87; Robin Laurence (auth), Come to dada, Weekend Sun, Vancouver, 1/8/94; Joan Murray (auth), Canadian Art in the Twentieth Century, Dundurn Press, 99; Anne Newlands (auth), Canadian Art: From the Beginning to 2000, Firefly Bks Ltd, 2000; Paul Bennett (auth), Slouching towards Toronto: Elevated wetlands' landscape architecture, Vol 90, No 3, 2, 55, 72-77 & 87, 3/2000; and numerous mus & gallery catalogs. *Mem:* Int Kunstler Gremium, Berlin, Ger; Art Comt for Pub Places, Toronto; Royal Can Acad Arts. *Media:* Diverse Materials. *Publ:* Keith Wallace (ed), Whispered Art History, Twenty Years at the Western Front, Arsenal Pulp Press, Vancouver, BC, 93; Video Art Video, TV Ont, Can, 94; Elevated Wetlands, Detail in Contemporary Landscape, Lawrence King Publ, London, Eng, 2007; Alex Steffen (ed), WorldChanging: A User's Guide for the 21st Century, Harry N Abrams Inc, New York, 2007. *Dealer:* Linda Genereux Gallery 21 Morrow Ave Toronto ON M6R 2H9; Installations/Sculpture: John Gibson Gallery 392 W Broadway New York NY 10012

HARDWICKE OLIVIERI, IRENE
PAINTER
Exhib: Solo exhibs include Matrix Gallery, Austin, Tex, 83, White Room, White Columns, NY, 92, Bridges and Bodell Gallery, NY City, 95, Robert Berman Gallery, Santa Monica, Calif, 96, To Have and to Hold, Margaret Bodell Gallery, NY City, 98, Pleasure Gardens, Robert Berman Gallery, 99, Love Feathers Fur, Finesilver Gallery, San Antonio, Tex, 2000, Bill Maynes Gallery, NY, 2002, New Britain Mus Am Art, Conn, 2004, Light Seeking Eyes, Carl Hammer Gallery, 2005, Climbing the Giant, ACA Galleries, 2006; group exhibs include Neo Persona Gallery, NY City, 98; Bess Cutler Gallery, NY City, 90; Subterranean Devotion, Bachelier-Cardonsky Gallery, 91, Emotional Ties, 93, Their Faces and Their Work, 93, Trees, 94, A Thirty Mile Circle, 96, Tenth Anniversary Exhib, 98, Human Nature, 2000, 2002; Beyond Town and Country, Philippe Staib Gallery, NY, 91; John Post Lee Gallery, NY City, 92; Galeries Fianna Sistu, Paris, France, 92; Update 1993, White Columns, NY, 93; The Symbolic Essence of the Flower, The Culture Ctr, NY, 94; In the Image of Woman, Carl Hammer Gallery, Chicago, 97; Wishful Thinking, James Graham & Sons Gallery, 98; Faces Make Places, Gunn Memorial Mus, Conn, 99; Con-Text, Coll Mainland, Tex City, 2001. *Mailing Add:* c/o ACA Galleries 5th Floor 529 West 20th St New York NY 10011

HARDY, DAVID WHITTAKER, III
PAINTER, INSTRUCTOR
b Dallas, Tex, Oct 5, 1929. *Study:* Austin Coll; Southern Methodist Univ; Univ Colo; Laney Coll; Am Acad; Art Students League; Sch Visual Art; Calif Coll Arts & Crafts; and with Ramon Froman, William Mosby, Joseph Van Der Brock, Robert Beverly Hale & Frank Mason. *Work:* Hall of Justice, Hayward, Calif; Dow Chemical Co, Freeport, Tex. *Comn:* Pvt collections in US & abroad. *Exhib:* Solo exhibs, North Park, Dallas, 64, Pantechnicon Gallery, San Francisco, 70, Arden Van Wijk Gallery, Saratoga, Calif, 84, Alma Gilbert Galleries Inc, Burlingame, Calif, 92 & The Parrish Connection, Venice, Fla, 92; Hemisfair Art, Witte Mem Mus, San Antonio, 68; Soc Western Artists, M H De Young Mus, San Francisco, 70; San Francisco Ann, 71; J J Brookings Gallery, San Francisco, 96; and others. *Pos:* Guest, Wurlitzer Found, Taos, NMex, 65; owner, 13th Street Crafts Garden, Oakland, 73-76; training prog, Fine Arts, Mus San Francisco, 82 & 86. *Teaching:* Pvt art classes, 60-; instr art, Mendocino Art Ctr, Calif, 73-74 & Calif Coll Arts & Crafts, Oakland, 79-86; guest lectr, Univ Calif, Berkeley, 81, 82 & Docent training prog, Fine Arts Mus, San Francisco, 82, 86; founder & dir, Atelier Sch Classical Realism, Oakland, Calif. *Bibliog:* Daniel M Mendelowitz & Duane A Wakeham (coauth), A Guide to Drawing, 5th ed, Holt, Rinehart & Winston Inc; The Best of Oil Painting, Rockport Publ, Mass, 96; The Best of Flower Painting, N Light Bks Cincinnati, Ohio & Cassell Publ, London, 97; Peter Steinhart (auth), The Undressed Art: Why We Draw, Alfred A Knopf, Inc, 2004. *Mem:* Berkeley Art Festival Guild (pres, 72-77); Soc Western Artists; Lillian Paley Ctr Visual Arts (bd trustees, 74-78). *Media:* Oil, Pastel; Charcoal, Chalk. *Res:* Old master Baroque painting techniques. *Specialty:* Still lifes & landscapes. *Publ:* Am Artist Mag; Am Artist Drawing Mag; auth, Taking the Temperature, Am Artist Mag, 8/2002; American Artist Workshop Mag, Spring 2009. *Dealer:* John Pence Gallery 750 Post St San Francisco CA 94109. *Mailing Add:* 4220 Balfour Ave Oakland CA 94610-1750

HARDY, (CLARION) DEWITT
PAINTER, INSTRUCTOR, PRINTMAKERS
b St Louis, Mo, June 25, 1940. *Study:* Syracuse Univ, 58-62. *Hon Degrees:* Heartwood Coll Art, 2005. *Work:* San Francisco Mus; Cleveland Mus Art; British Mus; Joseph Hirshhorn Found; Butler Art Inst Am Art, Youngtown, Ohio; Robert Johnson, San Francisco; Kennebunk Savings Bank. *Exhib:* Solo exhibs, Frank Rehn Gallery, NY, 66-71 & Robert Schoelkopf Gallery, NY, 81-83; Art on Paper, Weatherspoon Art Gallery, Univ NC, Greensboro, 81; Am Realism, San Francisco Mus Mod Art, 86; Portland Mus Biennial, 98; Wentworth Coolidge, Portsmouth, NH, 2000; McCandless-Epstein, Portland, Me, 02; Jane Haslem Gallery, Washington DC, 2006. *Collection Arranged:* Young Am Draughtsmen, Mus Art Ogunquit, 69 & Heartwood Coll Art. *Pos:* Assoc dir, Mus Art Ogunquit, 64-77; Scenic Charge, Ogunquit Playhouse, Ogunquit, Maine. *Teaching:* Instr, Heartwood Col Art & NH Art Inst; instr, Sch at Mus of Fine Arts, Boston. *Awards:* First Prize for Drawing, Summit Art Ctr, NJ, 65; Purchase Award, Butler Inst Am Art, 69; Best in show, Kennebunk Yacht Show, Maine, 98; Best in Show, K'bunk Yacht, 2000; Patron's Prize, K'bunk Yacht, 02. *Bibliog:* The watercolor page: Dewitt Hardy, Am Artists, 11/81; American Realism, San Francisco Mus Mod Art; The Face of America, Arts Ctr Old Forge, NY, 95. *Mem:* Ogunquit Art Asn, Maine. *Media:* Watercolor, Drawing. *Res:* 75 anniversary show & catalogue, Ogunquit Art Asn. *Specialty:* Regional Art Asn. *Interests:* art hist, set design. *Publ:* Am Artist Mag. *Dealer:* Mast Cove Gallery Rte 9 & Mast Cove Lane Kennebunkport ME; Serge Sorokko Gallery San Francisco CA; Jane Haslem Washington DC; June Fitzpatrick Gallery Portland ME. *Mailing Add:* 32 Tibbetts St South Berwick ME 03908

HARDY, JOHN
PAINTER
b Tours, France; US citizen. *Study:* Ga State Univ, BFA, 69. *Work:* Brooklyn Mus, NY; Nat Mus Am Art & Art in Embassies, US State Dept, Washington, DC; Mint Mus, Charlotte, NC; High Mus Art, Atlanta, Ga; Greenville Co Mus, SC; Morris Mus, Augusta, Ga; Mus of Western Va, Roanoke; Hunter Mus of Am Art, Chattanooga, Tenn. *Comn:* Portrait Michael Sovern, pres, Coll Univ NY, 79; portrait Judge Wilfred Feinberg, Coll Univ NY, 88. *Exhib:* Brooklyn Mus, NY, 80; Hunter Mus Am Art, Chattanooga, Tenn, 83; Ratner Gallery, Chicago, 91; Michael Walls Gallery, NY, 93; J Gibson/Hemphill Fine Arts Gallery, Washington, 93; Hurlbutt Gallery, Greenwich, Conn, 94; Brenda Taylor Gallery, NY, 96; Morris Mus Art, Augusta, Ga, 99; Art in General, NY, 01; Lizan Tops Gallery, East Hampton, NY, 01; DFN Gallery, NY, 02, 03, 06; R2 Gallery, NY, 03; Portraits, Lizan Tops Gallery, Easthampton, NY, 02; Its up to you, New York, New York,Susan Coach House Gallery, Atlanta, Ga, 03. *Teaching:* Chmn visual arts, Sch Archit, Ga Tech, 69-75; vis artist painting, Rice Univ, Houston & La State Univ, Baton Rouge, 79; adj fac painting, NY Univ, 80-82; masters workshop, Huntington Mus, WVa; tchr St Ann's Sch, Brooklyn, NY, 94-02. *Awards:* Nat Endowment Arts Grant, Huntington Mus, WVa, 87; Pollock-Krasner Found Grant, 96-97. *Bibliog:* Ann Weinstein (auth), article, Roanoke Times & World News, 10/7/87; Carol Graham Beck (auth), article, Art Papers, 90; Alan G Artner (auth), rev, Chicago Tribune, 91; Robert Long (auth) Rev, East Hampton Star, NY, 01. *Media:* Oil, Watercolor. *Specialty:* Contemporary Realism. *Dealer:* DFN Gallery 176 Franklin St New York NY 10013. *Mailing Add:* DFN Gallery 46 W 85th St #A New York NY 10024

HARDY, SARALYN REECE
MUSEUM DIRECTOR
Study: Univ Kans, BA, 1976; Univ Kans, MA in Am Studies, 1994; Getty Leadership Inst. *Exhib:* James Turrell: Gard Blue, Spencer Mus Art, 2013-2014. *Pos:* Proj coordr, Helen Foresman Spencer Mus Art, Univ Kans, Lawrence, 1977-79, dir, 2005-; dir, Salina Art Ctr, Kans, 1986-2002; dir mus & visual arts, Nat Endowment Arts, Washington, 1999-2002; Marilyn Stokstad Dir, Spencer Mus Art, Univ Kans, 2005-. *Awards:* Recipient Women of Achievement award, Salina YWCA, Kans Gov's Art Award, 1995; Distinguished Svc award, Nat Endowment for the Arts, 2001. *Mem:* Inst Mus & Libr Serv; Mus Trustee Asn; AAM; Asn Arts Mus Dirs. *Mailing Add:* Spencer Mus Art Univ Kans 1301 Mississippi St Lawrence KS 66045-7500

HARDY, THOMAS (AUSTIN)
SCULPTOR
b Redmond, Ore, Nov 30, 1921. *Study:* Ore State Univ, 38-40; Univ Ore, BA, 42, with Archipenko, summer 51, MFA, 52. *Work:* Whitney Mus Am Art, NY; Seattle Art Mus, Wash; San Francisco Mus Art; Neuberger Mus, NY; Portland Art Mus, Ore; Santa Barbara Mus Calif; Springfield, Mo; Univ Ore, Mus Art, Eugene, Ore; Univ Maine Art Mus, Orono, Maine; Univ Wyo Art Mus, Laramie, Wyo. *Comn:* Diving Birds, Fed Bldg, Juneau, Alaska, 64; Duck Fountain, Univ Ore, Eugene, 64; Flight, Dorothy Chandler Music Ctr, Los Angeles, Calif, 65; wall sculpture, State Dept Agr, Salem, Ore, 68; Bear, Univ Calif, Berkeley, 80; Presidential Seal, FD Roosevelt Meml, Washington, DC, 97. *Exhib:* 3rd Biennial, Sao Paulo, Brazil, 55; Am Watercolors, Drawings & Prints, Metrop Mus Art, 56; Mus Mod Art Sculpture Exhib, 63; Whitney Mus Am Art Sculpture Ann, 64; Exhib Cand Grants, Am Inst Arts & Lett, 68. *Pos:* Mem, Portland Art Mus & Friends Mus Art, Univ Ore; comnr, Metrop Arts Comn, 81-85 & Portland Rev Comn, 86. *Teaching:* Lectr, Univ Calif, Berkeley, 56-58; instr, Calif Sch Fine Arts, San Francisco, 56-58; assoc prof sculpture, Tulane Univ, La, 58-59; artist-in-residence, Reed Col, 60-61; vis prof sculpture, Univ Wyo, 75-76. *Awards:* Color Lithography Award, Soc Am Graphic Artists, 52; Seattle Art Mus Northwest Ann Sculpture Award, 55; Distinguished Serv Award, Univ Ore, 64; Ore State Gov Ann Art Award, 86; Webfoot Award, Univ Ore, 87. *Bibliog:* H Wurdemann (auth), Recent art of the West Coast, Art Am, 2/55; Metal sculptures by Tom Hardy, Am Artist, 4/55; L Jones (auth), Tom Hardy: Sculptor-craftsman, Creative Crafts, 7/62. *Media:* Welded Bronze, Aquatint. *Dealer:* Kraushaar Galleries 724 Fifth Ave New York NY 10019. *Mailing Add:* 1300 SW 5th Ave Ste 3000 Portland OR 97201

HARGIS, BARBARA PICASSO
GALLERY DIRECTOR
b Painesville, Ohio, May 28, 1930. *Study:* Citrus Coll, AA, 85. *Pos:* Artist Art Gallery, La Puente, Calif, 84-94; owner, Hargis Chim Gregg Art Gallery, Pomona, Calif, 94. *Awards:* Grantee, Millenn Production, Pomona, Calif, 94-97. *Mem:* Carlsbad Oceanside Art Life, life mem; DA Gallery Non Profit, Pomoma Valley Art, life mem (dir, 88); Corona Art Asn, life mem; Women in Arts Mus, charter mem; Covina Arts & Crafts, Parks & Recreation, life mem; Vallejo Community Arts Found; Ralph Fetterly Fine Arts; Visual & Performing Arts. *Interests:* amateur radio, tennis, swimming, sewing, pool. *Dealer:* BHUA El Cerrito CA 92881

HARI, KENNETH
PAINTER, SCULPTOR, PRINTMAKER
b Perth Amboy, NJ, Mar 31, 1947. *Study:* Newark Sch Fine & Indust Arts, dipl, 66; Md Inst Art, BFA, 68; also with Leon Franks & John Delmonte, Yale Univ, New York Univ. *Hon Degrees:* Beijing UNV, Sorbone, Paris. *Work:* Mus Mod Art, Barcelona, Spain; Nat Portrait Galleries, London, Eng & Washington; Vatican, Rome, Italy; Gore Vidal; Paul Newman. *Comn:* Portraits, W H Auden & M Moore, NY, 69, Pablo Casals, comn by Mrs Pablo Casals, Vt, 70, Salvador Dali, NY, 72, Ernest Hemingway, Hemingway House, Cuba, Michael York, & Aaron Copland, 82; Paul Robeson, for Paul Robeson Ctr, Rutgers Univ, 79; Douglas Fairbanks Jr, Nat Portrait Gallery, London, Eng, 92; Nirvasha, 2006. *Exhib:* Union Col, 69; Monmouth Col, 70; Newark Mus, 71; Trenton State Mus, 72; Va Polytechnic Inst, 74; Solo exhibs: Centenary Col, NJ & Tennessee Williams Portraits, Pargot Gallery, NJ, 91; Atlantic City Art Mus, 2008; Yi Shui Ge Mus, Beijing, China, 2008; Tenn State Mus. *Pos:* Dir, NJ Art Festival, 64-69. *Teaching:* Lectr, various Univs. *Awards:* Pulaski Award, Kosciuszko Found, 63; Felice Found Award, 69; Trenton State Mus Award, 72. *Bibliog:* Art in the Hamptons, 69 & feature story, 73, NY Times; M Lenson (auth), Portrait of Casals, Newark News, 71; D Brown (auth), Poetess an artist, Home News, 72. *Mem:* Atlantic City Art Mus (bd dirs). *Media:* Oil, Graphite, Sculpture, Lithographs. *Interests:* Creating important works of art. *Publ:* Illusr, Vermont, 72, Folk Singer, 72 & Time for Peace, 72, H S Graphics; Abraham, 74, Marcel Marceau, 75, The Prophet, 92 & 94, Beatrice, 92, Moses, 92, Harmony, 92 & Portrait of 5, 92; Portrait of Anna, 96 & Pablo Casals Poster, 96; Paul Robeson Portrait Poster, 2000; Nirvasha, 2006; Billy Mills, 2006. *Dealer:* Xiaoyi Liu Homage 2010 Retrospect Art Show Perth Amboy Mus; John Watson Art Gallery PO Box 243 Keasbey NJ 08822

HARJO, BENJAMIN, JR
PAINTER, PRINTMAKER
b Clovis, NMex, Sept 19, 1945. *Study:* Inst Am Indian Arts, cert, 66; Okla State Univ, BFA, 74. *Work:* Inst Am Indian Arts, Santa Fe; McFarlin Libr Indian Collection, Univ Tulsa & Tulsa City Co Libr; US Embassy, Mogadishu, Somalia; Mus Northern Ariz. *Exhib:* Young Am Indian Artist, Riverside Mus, NY, 65-66; Nat Indian Arts Exhib, Heard Mus, Phoenix, Ariz, 66; Philbrook 30th Ann Am Indian Arts Exhib, Tulsa, 75; Ann Competition, 5 Tribes Mus, Muskogee, Okla, 76 & 80; Southern Plains Indian Mus, Anadarko, Okla, 80; Trail of Tears Ann, Cherokee Mus, Tahlequah, Okla, 81; Native Am Ctr Living Arts, Niagara Falls, NY, 81; solo exhib, Wheelwright Mus, Skylight Gallery, Wichita Art Mus, 91; Franco-Am Inst, Renne, France, 92; Nat Cowboy Hall of Fame, 2000. *Pos:* Cult recreational coordr, Tulsa Indian Youth Coun, 74-76. *Teaching:* Jr gallery instr Indian cult, Philbrook Art Ctr, Tulsa, 76-77. *Awards:* Grand award, 1st place painting & 2nd place graphics awards, Red Earth Festival; Best of division, 1st place painting-miniature, 2nd place painting & 1st place graphics award, 67th ann Indian Market; 1st place painting, Masters Show, Five Tribes Mus, 88; First Place, 69 Ann Indian Market, Santa Fe, 90; Woody Crumbo Mem Award; Second Prize, Red Earth, 90; Best of Class, Fine Art, Ann Heard Mus Guild, Indian Fair, 96; Spirit of Oklahoma Award, Masters Show Five Civilized Tribes, 97; Best of Show Five Civilized Tribes Mus, Muskogee, Okla, 2000; plus others. *Bibliog:* Peggy Ridgeway (auth), Benjamin Harjo Jr, Art Voice S, 81; Rennard Steickland (auth), Indians of Oklahoma, Okla Press, 81; Southwest Art Mag, 3/88; Southern Living Mag, 10/88. *Mem:* Master Artist Five Civilized Tribes, Muskogee, Okla. *Media:* Gouache, Acrylic; Etching, Woodblock. *Mailing Add:* 1516 Northwest 35th Oklahoma City OK 73118-3214

HARKEY, RONALD P See Rophar

HARKINS, DENNIS RICHTER
ADMINISTRATOR, PHOTOGRAPHER
b Nelsonville, Ohio, July 20, 1950. *Study:* Ohio Univ, BFA, 72, MA (int affairs), 73. *Collection Arranged:* African Art (with catalog), Ohio Univ, Alden Libr, 73. *Pos:* Educ chmn, Prof Photogr Guild Fla, 78-79 & bd dir, 79. *Teaching:* Dir photog, Art Inst Ft Lauderdale, 74-81; vpres & dir educ, Art Inst Atlanta, 81-. *Awards:* Cert Prof Photogr, 79; Lecture Award, Fla Prof Photogr Conf. *Mem:* Prof Photogr Am; Kodak Educ Adv Coun, Nat. *Mailing Add:* 2931 Mabry Ln NE Atlanta GA 30319-2603

HARKINS, GEORGE C, JR
PAINTER
b Philadelphia, Pa, June 15, 1934. *Study:* Philadelphia Coll Art, BFA, 56; Univ Ariz, MFA, 69. *Work:* Charleston Mus Fine Art, SC; Montgomery Mus Fine Art, Ala; Arnot Art Mus, Elmira, NY; Tucson Mus Art, Ariz. *Exhib:* Am Realism: 20th Century Watercolors & Drawings, San Francisco Mus Mod Art, 85; Watercolor USA, Monumental Image, Springfield Art Mus, Mo, 86; The Face of the Land, S Alleghenies Mus Art, Loretto, Pa, 88; Realism Today: Am Drawings from the Rita Rich Collection, Nat Acad Design, NY, 88; Watercolor: Contemp Currents, Riverside Art Mus, Calif, 89; Representing Representation II, Arnot Art Mus, Elmira, NY, 95. *Awards:* Walser Greathouse Medal, Am Watercolor Soc, 2010. *Bibliog:* Alvin Martin (auth), American Realism: 20th Century Drawings & Watercolors, H N Abrams, 86; Steven Doherty (auth), George Harkins, Am Artist, 5/89; John Arthur (auth), Spirit of Place, Bullfinch Press, Little Brown Co, 89. *Media:* Watercolor, Oils, Pastels. *Dealer:* Jane Haslem Gallery 2025 Hillyer Pl NW Washington DC 20009. *Mailing Add:* 137 Duane St 5E New York NY 10013

HARKNESS, HILARY
PAINTER
b Detroit, Mich. *Study:* Univ Calif, Berkeley, BA, 1993; Yale Univ, MFA, New Haven, Conn, 1996. *Exhib:* MFA Thesis Show, Yale Sch Arts, 1996; Women in the Arts, Erector Square Gallery, New Haven, Conn, 1996; Southern Exposure Gallery, San Francisco, 1998 & 1999; Lizabeth Oliveria Gallery, San Francisco, 2000; Wonderland, Mass Col Art, Boston, 2001; Pixerina Witcherina, Univ Galleries, Ill State Univ, 2001; Heroine, Dee/Glasoe Gallery, New York, 2001; Best of the Season, Aldrich Mus Contemp Art, Ridgefield, Conn, 2001; View Five: Westworld, Mary Boone Gallery, New York, 2001; solo exhibs, Bill Maynes Gallery, New York, 2001; Daniel Weinberg Gallery, Los Angeles, 2002, Mary Boone Gallery, 2004, 2005 & 2008; Dangerous Beauty, Jewish Cmty Ctr Manhattan, 2002; Into the Woods, Julie Saul Gallery, New York, 2002; Am Acad Arts and Letts Invitational, New York, 2002, 2009; Fusion Cuisine, Deste Found, Athens, 2002; American Art Today: Face and Figures, Art Mus Fla, 2003; OnLine, Feigen Contemp, New York, 2003; Future Nois, Grossman Gallery, Lafayett Col, Easton, Pa, 2003; Unforeseen, Portland Inst Contemp Art, Ore, 2003; Endless Love, DC Moore Gallery, New York, 2004; Men, I-20 Gallery, New York, 2006; Old School, Hauser & Wirth Colnaghi, London, 2007; Pleasures of Collecting, Part II: Contemporary and Cutting Edge, Bruce Mus, Greenwich, Conn, 2007. *Awards:* Rosenthal Family Found Award in Painting, Am Acad Arts and Letts, 2009. *Bibliog:* MCA creates a wonderland, Boston Sunday Herald, 1/28/2001; Mac Adam (auth), On the edge: bruegel of the seaside brothels, Art News, 11/2001; Ichihara Kentaro (auth), Hilary Harkenss: powems of war and industrial fetishism, COMPOSITE, 10/2004; Go figure, NY Times, 4/17/2005; Adam Mac Adam, Old school, Art News, 9/2007; Figurative women we love: the sailors in Hilary Harkness's paintings, Esquire, 11/2008. *Media:* Oil on Linen. *Mailing Add:* Mary Boone Gallery 745 5th Ave New York NY 10151

HARKNESS, JOHN CHEESMAN
ARCHITECT
b NY City, Nov 30, 1916. *Study:* Harvard Univ, BFA (cum laude), 38; Harvard Univ, BArch, MArch, 41; Phi Beta Kappa. *Pos:* Archit, Saarinen & Swanson, Birmingham, Mich, Harrison, Fouilhoux & Abramovitz, New York City, Skidmore, Owings & Merrill, New York City, prior to 45; Mem design fac, Harvard Grad. Sch Design, 46-50, mem vis comt; prin, The Archit Collab, Cambridge, Mass, 45-95, pres, 66-67, 77-84, bd dir, chmn bd, principals, 84-86; mem vis comt, RI Sch Design; mem, capitol area planning bd, Minn State. *Awards:* Recipient various competition & archit design awards incl 6 awards, Am Asn Sch Adminr, 60-67; William Ware Award, Boston Soc Archit honor award, 93. *Mem:* Fel Am Inst of Archit; Nat Acad, Boston Soc Archit (pres, formerly); Mass State Asn Archit (pres, formerly); Archit League NY, Harvard Grad Sch Design Alumni Asn (pres, formerly), Harvard Univ Alumni Asn (dir, formerly, 88). *Publ:* Auth: Encyl of Archit, 89

HARKNESS, MADDEN
PAINTER
b Montclair, NJ, July 21, 1948. *Study:* Calif Coll Arts Crafts, MFA, 85; Boston Mus Sch, Tufts Univ, BS, 72. *Work:* Everson Mus, Syracuse, NY; Fresno Art Mus, Calif. *Exhib:* Solo exhib, Forum 88, Hamburg, Ger, 88; On the Horizon: Emerging in California, Fresno Art Mus, Calif, 87; Figurative Dimensions, Univ Art Gallery, Calif State Univ, Dominquez Hills, Calif, 88; Madden Harkness, Southern Calif Art Inst, Laguna Beach, 89 & Pepperdine Univ (catalog), Malibu, Calif, 90; The Figure, Tatistcheff Gallery, Santa Monica, Calif, 91; Addictions (catalog), Santa Barbara Contemp Arts Forum, Calif, 91; and others. *Awards:* Purchase Award, Everson Mus, 88; Julia Morgan Mem, Riverside Art Mus, 87; vis artist, Am Acad in Rome, Italy, 90; Artist-in-Residence, Ragdale Found, 87. *Bibliog:* Colin Gardener (auth), The Galleries, Los Angeles Times, 12/18/87; Beth Ann Brown & Arlene Raven (auths), Exposures; Women and Their Art, 89; David Pagel (auth), When Reason Dreams-Madden, Harkness, Vol II, No 3, Visions, 88. *Media:* Mixed Media, Oil. *Dealer:* Jan Baum 170 S LaBrea Ave Los Angeles CA. *Mailing Add:* PMB 78-180 827 Union Pacific Blvd Laredo TX 78045-9452

HARLE, MATT
SCULPTOR
Exhib: Derek Eller Gallery, NY City, 98; Painting Pushed to Extremes, Worcester Art Mus, Mass, 2000; 181st Ann: An Invitational Exhib Contemp Art, 2006; Some Lions Do Walk, Some Lions Do Not Walk, Genovese/Sullivan Gallery, Boston, 2006. *Awards:* Guggenheim fellow, 99. *Mailing Add:* c/o Genovese/Sullivan Gallery 94 N Main St Andover MA 01810-3515

HARLEMAN, KATHLEEN TOWE
MUSEUM DIRECTOR
b Boston, Feb 6, 1953. *Study:* Middlebury Coll, Vt, BA (art hist), 1975; Johns Hopkins Univ, MA (art hist), 1977; Univ Ottawa, MBA, 1981. *Pos:* Chief of registration, Nat Gallery Can, Ottawa, 1985-88; registrar, Art Gallery Ontario, Toronto, 1988-89, acting dir art support, 1989-90, mgr collection & exhib projects, 1990-92, dir exhibs & facilities, 1992-94; assoc dir, dir cult & academic programs, Davis Mus & Cult Ctr, Wellesley Coll, Mass, 1994-98; dir, chief exec officer, Mus Art, Ft Lauderdale, Fla, 1998-2001; exec dir, Bellevue Art Mus, 2002-03; consult, Can Ctr Archit, 2003-04; dir, Krannert Art Mus, Univ Ill, 2004-. *Teaching:* Lectr, Wellesley Coll Dept Art, 1996. *Mem:* AAM. *Mailing Add:* Krannert Art Mus 500 E Peabody Dr Champaign IL 61820

HARLESS, CAROL P
SCULPTOR
b Atlanta, Ga. *Study:* Shorter Col, Rome, Ga, BA (biology) (cum laude); studied with Joan Danziger. *Work:* Study in Time, Sundial/Moultrie Mem, Erskine Col, SC; Grief, Inspired by Martha Graham's dance, Lamentation, Martha Graham Sch, NYC; Charles Wadsworth, Father of Am Chamber Music Movement, Wadsworth Hall, Newnan, Ga; Dancers, Entrance to corp off, HPG Inc, Newnan, Ga; Lady of the

House, Greenville Street Park, Newnan, Georgia. *Comn:* Victory, Heritage Sch, Newnan, Ga; On the Wing, Emory Univ, Atlanta, Ga. *Exhib:* Solo exhibs, West Ga Col, Cashen Hall Gallery, 92, Shorter Col, Rome, Ga, 95; Group Exhibs: Christmas Show, Reg Artists, Spruill Ctr Gallery, Atlanta, Ga, 93; Art in Motion, An Exhib Hon Athletic Excellence, Ga Tech, Atlanta, 94; Audubon Artists, 55th Ann Exhib, NY, 97; Sculpture Now-The Figure, Wash Sq, Wash, DC, 98; Southeastern Juried Exhib (12 states), Mobile Mus Art, 99; Eleventh Ann Summer Showcase, Thomasville Cult Ctr, Ga, 2000, Gala 2000, Brenau Univ Invitational, Gainsville, Ga, 2000; Allied Artists Am, 94th Annual Exhib, NY, 2007; Nat Sculpture Society, 75th Annual Awards Exhib, Brookgreen Gardens, 2008; juried exhib: Going for the Gold, National Sculpture Soc, NY, 1996, Nat Sculpture Soc Sports, NY, 2002, Nat Sculpture Soc 70th Annual Awards Exhib, Brookgreen Gardens, SC & NY, 2003, Contemp Realism 2005, Cavalier Galleries, NY, 2005; Bronze, Lamar Dodd Art Ctr, La Grange Coll, Ga, 2003; 2nd Int Salon, Art Renewal Ctr, 2005; 67th Ann Exhib, Audubon Artists Inc, New York, 2009; Red River Valley Exhib, Vernon, Tex, 2011. *Pos:* Comptroller, human res int consult firm, 68-93; owner, sculpting studio, 89-. *Awards:* Jurors Award, Savannah Nat, Ga, 92; Elliot Liskin Mem Award, Audubon Artists, 55th Annual Exhib, NY, 97; second place, Armory Art Ctr, West Palm Beach, Fla, 99; Tallix Foundry, Nat Sculpture Soc, NY, 2003; Medal of Honor, Catharine Lorillard Wolfe Art Club Inc 107th Annual Exhib, NY, 2003; finalist 2nd Int ARC Salon Comp, Art Renewal Ctr, 2005; 101st Ann Exhib, Calvary Baptist Church Award, Catharine Lorillard Wolfe Art Club, 97; Chair Gross Found Award, Autubon Artists Inc, 98; Jurors Choice award, Red River Valley Exhib, Tex, 2011. *Mem:* Audubon Artists Inc.; Catharine Lorillard Wolfe Art Club Inc; Allied Artists of Am Inc; Hall of Fame, Ctr for Performing & Visual Arts, Newnan, Ga. *Media:* Sculptor, Bronze, Terracotta. *Mailing Add:* PO Box 1903 Newnan GA 30264

HARLOW, ANN
MUSEUM DIRECTOR, CURATOR
b Glen Cove, NY, June 15, 1951. *Study:* Stanford Univ, BA, 73; Univ Calif, Berkeley, MA, 77. *Collection Arranged:* William Keith Collection (150 paintings, 1867-1911 & catalog 1988), St Marys Col, 92-94. *Pos:* Cur asst, Oakland Mus, Calif, 77-78; asst dir, Mills Col Art Gallery, Oakland, Calif, 80-82; dir, Hearst Art Gallery, St Mary's Col, Moraga, Calif, 82. *Mem:* Asn Coll & Univ Mus & Galleries (pres 88-90). *Publ:* Co-auth, The Color Woodcut in America, 1895-1945 (exhib catalog), 84; auth, The MA Circle: Budapest and Vienna, 1916-1925 (exhib catalog), 85; Bicoastal artists of the 1870s (exhib catalog), Art Calif, 7/92; William Keith, Am Art Review, 12/94. *Mailing Add:* St Mary's Col of Calif Hearst Art Gallery St Mary's Rd PO Box 5110 Moraga CA 94575

HARMAN, MARYANN WHITTEMORE
PAINTER
b Roanoke, Va, Sept 13, 1935. *Study:* Univ Va, Mary Washington Col, BA; Va Polytech Inst & State Univ, MA. *Work:* Mint Mus, Charlotte, NC; Philip Morris Corp, Richmond, Va; Hunter Mus, Chattanooga, Tenn; Gen Motors, Detroit; Boston Mus Fine Arts; Fed Reserve Bank; General Electric; 3-M; VA Mus; Manufacturers Hanover Trust; NC Am Can Corp; Hines Coll, Boston, Mass; Bank of America; and others. *Exhib:* Solo exhibs, Andre Emmerich Gallery, NY, 76 & 78, Allen Rubiner Gallery, Detroit, 77, 79, 90 & 92, Meredith Long Gallery, NY, 80, Haber-Theodore Gallery, NY, 82, 83 & 85, Osuna Gallery, Washington DC, 82, 83, 85, 90 & 92, Wade Gallery, Los Angeles, Calif, 85, 87, 88, 91, Gallery K, Washington, DC, 94, Anderson Gallery, Richmond, Va, 2004; Sandy Carson Gallery, Denver, 89-2008; Gallery One, Toronto, Can, 90-2006; Schulte Gallery, NJ, 90-2013; Studios in the Square, 2000-2007; Lee Hansley Gallery, Raleigh, 2001-2014; Page Bond Gallery, Richmond, Va, 2008-2012; Lin-dor Gallery, Roanoke, Va, 2010-2014; Shulte Gallery, 2014; School of the Arts, Va Tech, 2014; Fresh Paints, VA Tech Armory Art Gallery, 2014. *Pos:* Artist-in-residence, Emma Lake Workshop, Univ Saskatchewan, Can. *Teaching:* Assoc prof painting & drawing, Va Polytech Inst & State Univ, 64-81, prof, 81-99, prof emeritus, 99-. *Awards:* Purchase Awards, Hunter Mus, 74; Cert of Distinction, Va Mus Fine Arts, 74 & 76; Purchase Award, Mint Mus, 83; Award, High Mus, Atlanta. *Bibliog:* Barclay Sheaks (auth), Painting Natural Environment, 74 & Painting with Oils, 77, Davis; Marsha Miro (auth), rev, Detroit Free Press, 12/78; Edgar Buonagurio (auth), rev, Arts Mag, 5/80, 81, 82 & 84; articles, Los Angeles Times & Hollywood Press, 86. *Mem:* Coll Art Asn Am; Southeastern Coll Art Asn; Va Mus Fine Arts; Am Fedn Arts; Taulman Mus. *Media:* Acrylic, Oil and Watercolor. *Dealer:* Lin Dor Gallery Roanoke Va; Lee Hansley Gallery Raleigh NC; CS Schulte Gallery Orange NJ. *Mailing Add:* 1120 Nellies Cove Rd Blacksburg VA 24060

HARMON, BARBARA SAYRE
PAINTER, BOOK ARTIST
b Yerington, Nev, Aug 8, 1927. *Study:* Bisttram Sch Fine Art, painting & drawing; etching with Lawton Parker; Black Mountain Coll, bookbinding with Johanna Jalowitz. *Work:* Harwood Mus, Univ NMex; Stanford Univ Libr, Univ NMex; Univ NMex Libr; Taos Art Mus; pvt collections, Ernest Blumenschein, Greer Garson, Carl Dentzel, Jan & Paul Johnson, Laurel Varney & Celisa Jane Lucien. *Comn:* Numerous pvt comns for fantasy and portrait paintings; original graphics acquisition fund, Harwood Mus Art, Univ NMex, Taos, 2005; book art display, Black Mountain Coll Mus & Art Ctr, Ashville, NC, 2005. *Exhib:* Continuous exhibs in southwestern galleries, 63-; Univ NMex, 2011-2012; Black Mountain Coll; Harwood Mus Art; Thought Flowers, The Evolution of the Aquagraph, Hulse Warman Gallery, Taos, 2012; Russian Night in Taos, Taos Art Mus and Nicolai Fechin House, 2012; Suspension of Disbelief, The Fantasy Worlds of Barbara Harmon etc, Harwood Must Art, Univ NMEx, 2012; Retrospective exhib, Magic and Mastery, 65 Years Painting in Taos, The Blumenschein Mus of the Taos Historic Museums, Taos, NMex, 2012. *Pos:* Owner & founder, Children's Gallery Press; co-dir, Torreon Gallery. *Awards:* EL Blumenschein award, Taos Historic Mus, 2014. *Bibliog:* Mary Carrol Nelson (auth), Barbara Harmon: magic & mastery, Am Artist Mag, 5/75; Kelly Malore Cribbs (auth), The tumpfee wood world of Barbara Harmon, Santa Fe Mag, 7/79; Tricia Hurst (auth), All things are possible, NMex Mag, 81. *Mem:* Harwood Mus Art Alliance, Univ NMex; Taos Hist Mus; Blumenschein Mus; Taos Art Mus; Nicolai Fechin House. *Media:* Watercolor; Original graphic mediums. *Res:* Extensive research in technology of lithography, monotype and dry point since 1948. *Specialty:* Fantasy, figures & still life. *Interests:* Evolution of unique printmaking methods, floral and still life studies, dancing and song writing. *Publ:* Auth & illusr, Tabbigail's Garden, 67, The Little People's Counting Book, 68, Monday's Mouse, 70, This Little Pixie, 69, The Tumpfee Wood Acorn Book, 77 & Thimbly Hill, 80, The Children's Gallery Press & The Baker co. *Dealer:* The Torreon Gallery Taos NM 87571; Hulse Warman Gallery Taos NM. *Mailing Add:* 234 Las Cruces Rd 6584 NDCBU Taos NM 87571

HARMON, CLIFF FRANKLIN
PAINTER
b Los Angeles, Calif, June 26, 1923. *Study:* Bisttram Sch Fine Art, Los Angeles, Calif & Taos, NMex, with Emil Bisttram, 46-48; Black Mountain Coll, NC, with Joe Fiore, 49-50; Taos Valley Art Sch, with Louis Ribak, 50-52. *Work:* Mus NMex, Santa Fe; Okla Art Ctr, Oklahoma City; Harwood Found, Univ NMex; Taos Art Mus & Fechin House. *Exhib:* NMex & Southwest Biennials, NMex Mus, 66, 70-72 & Watercolor NMex, 74; 11th Midwest Biennial, Joslyn Art Mus, Omaha, Nebr, 70; 1st Four Corners Biennial, Phoenix Art Mus, Ariz, 71; Bertrand Russell Centenary Art Exhib, Rotunda Gallery, London, Eng, 72; Modern Artists, 95; 60 Yrs in Taos Tri-Exhibits: Taos Art Asn, Van Vechtan-Lineberry Mus Taos Art, Total Arts, 96, NMex; Masters of Taos Art, Fall Ars Festival, 2008; Retrospective Exhib, Emil Bistraim & the Taos Sch Art, Student 1946-88, Roswell Mus Art Ctr, NMex, 2010, Blumenschein, 65 Yr Retrospective, Taos Historic Mus, 2011, Hulse Warman, Harwood, Mus Univ NMex, 2011; Black Mountain Coll; Harwood Mus Art; Univ NMex, 2011-2012; Gallery 203 Fine Art; Modern Artists of Taos, 2014. *Awards:* First Premium for Abstract Painting, NMex State Fair, 68; Hon Mention, NMex Mus & Phoenix Art Mus, 71; 1st Place Blue Ribbon, Taos Art Asn, 94; Charles Strong Lifetime Achievement award, Taos Autumn Art Festival, 2013. *Mem:* Taos Art Asn (first vpres, 68-69, pres, 78-79); Taos Asn Artists (hon mem). *Media:* Oil, Acrylic, Watercolor, Collage, Monoprints. *Specialty:* traditional & contemporary art. *Dealer:* The Torreon Gallery Taos NM 87571; Hulse-Warman GalleryTaos NMex 87571. *Mailing Add:* 234 Las Cruces Rd Taos NM 87571

HARMON, DAVID EDWARD
PAINTER, EDUCATOR
b St Louis, Mo, May 30, 1953. *Study:* Webster Univ, St Louis, Mo, BFA, 77; Penn State Univ, MFA, 82. *Work:* Univ Mo, St Louis; Univ Southern Miss, Woods Gallery, Hattiesburg; Liverpool Inst Higher Ed, UK; Univ Scranton, Pa; River Park UMC, South Bend, Ind; Environ Labs, South Bend, Ind. *Comn:* Painting, Crane Sch Music, Potsdam, NY, 86-87. *Exhib:* 30th Ann Nat Draw/Print Show, Univ NDak, Grand Forks, 87; 49th Ann juried exhib, Munson-Williams-Proctor Inst, Utica, NY, 87; Christ Imagery in Contemp Art, Albany Inst Art/Hist, NY, 88; South Bend Reg Mus Art, Inc, 92-93; Solo exhib, US Air Force Acad, 97; Arte Sagrado Exhib, Concordia Univ, Austin, Tex, 98; West Valley Mus Art, Surprise, Ariz, 2001; Nat Landscape Exhib, Annapolis, Md, 2009; Sense of Place, Gertrute Herbert Art Inst, 2010. *Pos:* Art dir, Bethel Col, 90-; ed bd mem, Collegiate Press, Alta Loma, Calif, 92; moderator panel discussion, Nat Coun Art Adminr Conf, Anchorage, Alaska, 96 & Mid Am Col Art Asn Conf, Lexington, Ky, 98, Louisville, Ky, 2000, Nat Conf on Liberal Arts and Educ, 2006, 2007; vis artist, Mont Artist Refuge Basin, 99, Jentel, Wyo, 2003; residency, Byrdcliffe Colony, Woodstock, NY, 2004, Julia-David White Colony, Costa Rica, 2009, Anam Cara, Cork, Ireland, 2010. *Teaching:* vis prof gallery art hist, Univ SMiss, 82-83; vis prof paint draw design, Univ Ariz, Tucson, 84-85; prof art paint draw design, State Univ NY, Potsdam, 85-89; vis prof, Keystone Jr Col, La Plume, Pa, 89-90; art dir & assoc prof art, Bethel Col, Mishawaka, Ind, 90-; prof art, Savannah Col Art and Design, 2005-08; assoc prof art, Sterling Col, Sterling, Kans, 2008-2012; chair, Dept Art, SW Baptist Univ, Bolivar, Mo, 2012-. *Awards:* Purchase Award, Mo Photog, Univ Mo, St Louis, 76 & 5th Miss Annual, Univ Miss, 83; First Place, Sacred Arts Nat Show, Wheaton Col, 90; Purchase Award, Midwest Mus Am Art, Elkhart, Ind, 2000; 3rd place, Nat Landscape exhib, Annapolis, Md, 2009. *Bibliog:* Blair Schiller (auth), Group shows explore reality and dreams, Art Speak, 12/89; Carol Kotlarczyk (auth), Artist brings out intensity in soft colors, Daily Herald, 9/7/91; Julie York Coppens (auth), Picture Perfect, South Bend Tribuen, 11/5/2000. *Mem:* Coll Art Assoc, NY; Southeastern Coll Art Asn; Mid Am Coll Art Asn; Nat Coun Art Adminrs. *Media:* Oil, Acrylic; Pastel. *Interests:* Reading, physical fitness, travel, direct observation sketching, pre-historic petroglyphs and pictographs, world rock art. *Publ:* Contribr, Contemp Southwest Art, Gibson Gallery, 88; illusr, The Insanity of Samuel Beckett's Art, Paint Brush Press, Parker, Colo, 98. *Dealer:* Griffin Gallery South Bend IN

HARMON, PAUL
PAINTER, PRINTMAKER
b Nashville, Tenn, Jan 23, 1939. *Study:* Univ Tenn. *Work:* Principality of Monaco, Monte Carlo; Hotel de Ville, Caen, France; Tenn State Mus, Nashville; George Bush Presidential Libr & Mus; Tampa Mus Art, Fla; Vanderbilt Univ Fine Arts Ctr; Capital Cult Ctr, Tallahassee; Georgetown Univ Libr; Data Concepts Inc; 3M Corp; Nissan, USA; United Cities Gas Co; Fred S James & Co; Stouffer's Hotels; numerous corp collections. *Comn:* Wall mural, Biological Therapy Inst, Franklin, Tenn, 87; three lobby paintings, Vanderbilt Henry Joyce Cancer Ctr, Nashville, 89; glass panels, Bridgestone/Firestone USA, Nashville, 90; An American Mosaic (6x12' painting), Philip Morris USA, NY, 91; 4x6' Painting, Tenn State Mus, Nashville, 94; 9 monumental sculptures, Patriot's Park, Clarksville, Tenn. *Exhib:* Eglise du St Sepulcre, Caen, France; Galerie Art Pub, Paris; Galerie Art-Expo, Paris; Galerie Sabala, Paris; XXIV Prix int d'art contemp de Monte-Carlo; Mus de Lons-le-Saunier, France; 67th salon de la Soc des Artistes Bas-Normands, Caen; Galerie Deprez-Bellorget, Paris; Art Contemp, St Martin du Tertre, Val d'Oise, France; Michel Vockaer Gallery, Brussels; IV Bienal de Arte, Medellin, Columbia; Galerie JPF, Montpellier, France; Folon & Rigsby Gallery, Nashville; Tenn State Mus, Maj Retrospective, 1984; Cavaliero Fine Arts, NY; Carl Van Vechten Gallery, Fisk Univ,

Nashville; Vanderbilt Univ Fine Arts Center, Nashville; Smithsonian Inst Nat Collection Fine Arts, Washington; Southern Lit Festival, Nashville; Madison Art Directions Gallery, NY; Cheekwood Fine Arts Center, Nashville; Windsors Gallery, Miami; Zeitgeist Gallery, Nashville; Parthenon, East Gallery, Nashville; GMB Galerie Int, Royal Oaks, Mich; Laura Pollack Gallery, San Diego; Aronson/Healey Gallery, Atlanta; Phoenix Fine Arts, Md; Studio/L'Atelier, Nashville; Phoenix II Gallery, Washington; Malton Gallery, Cincinnati; South Wharf Gallery, Nantucket; Zantman Art Galleries, Palm Desert; Sande Webster Gallery, Phila; Edith Caldwell Gallery, San Francisco; Nashville Int Airport; Robert Roman Gallery, Scottsdale, Ariz; Zeitgeist Gallery, Nashville, Tenn; LivAspenArt, Aspen, Colo. *Awards:* Prix Ville de Monaco, Monte Carlo, 90; Prix Soc EJA, Monte Carlo, 90; Commemorative Medal, St Martin Tertre, 90. *Bibliog:* Ganne Heinitsh (auth), Paul Harmon (exhib catalog), 88; Monique Vacarisas (auth), L'Oil Mag, Paris; Marilyn Mars, former cur contemp art Tampa Mus Art; Georganne Harmon (auth), poet; Solange Yver de la Vigne-Bernard (critic), Paris; Robert Mcgrath (auth), Art Historian, Emeritus, Dartmouth Coll. *Media:* Oils on Canvas, Paper, Prints. *Publ:* Coauth, La Voyage, the Electronic Coffee Table Art Book (CD-ROM & internet site), Bookpage Inc, 95; Dante's Stones, 2000; Paul Harmon, exhib catalog; Paul Harmon: Crossing Borders, 1961-2009 selected paintings, Essay by Robt McGrath. *Mailing Add:* 1304 Wilson Pike Brentwood TN 37027-6731

HARNETT, LILA
COLLECTOR, CRITIC

b New York, Oct 4, 1926. *Study:* Brooklyn Coll, BA; New Sch Social Res. *Hon Degrees:* Hon Dr Fine Arts, Univ Richmond, Richmond, Va . *Collection Arranged:* Cur, Weeden & Co Art Collection. *Pos:* Publ, Bus Atomics Report, 53-63; cult reporter, NY State newspapers, 64-74; fine arts ed, Cue Mag, 75-80; NY State Coun Arts, 80-88; founder, Phoenix Home & Garden, 80-, assoc publ, 88-, ed, 95-99; publ, Scottsdale Scene, 92-98; founder, ArtTable Inc. *Mem:* Phoenix Art Mus (bd mem); Heard Mus; Joel & Lila Harnett Mus Art, Univ Richmond, Va. *Interests:* Reading, Travel, Learning. *Collection:* Works by Burchfield, Hopper, Marsh, Warhol, Anuszkiewcz, Tooker, Pearlstein, Lamis, Fletcher Benton, Audobon, Catlin, Beal, Birmelin, Allan Houser, Fritz Scholder, and Dennis Numkena. *Mailing Add:* 4523 E Clearwater Pkwy Paradise Valley AZ 85253

HARNICK, SYLVIA
PAINTER

b New York, NY. *Study:* Brooklyn Col, BA, 54; C W Post with Robert Yasuda, 87-89. *Work:* Fine Arts Mus Long Island, Hempstead, NY; Queensborough Community Coll Art Gallery, Bayside, NY; Islip Art Mus, E Islip, NY; Collection of Citibank, 2006; Citibank. *Exhib:* Art of the Northeast USA, Silvermine Guild Arts, New Canaan, Conn, 90; Nat Drawing Asn, SW Tex State Univ, San Marcos, Tex, 94; 12" X 12" (X 12"), Islip Art Mus, East Islip, NY, 94; Drawing, Rathbone Gallery, Sage Jr Col, Albany, NY, 96; Layers: Mining the Unconscious, Western NMex Univ, 96; Photoesque, Anthony Giordano Gallery, Dowling Col, Oakdale, NY, 97; Artas Spectacle, Katonah Mus Art, NY, 98; Long Island Artists: Focus on Materials, Univ Art Gallery, State Univ NY, Stony Brook, 98; A Survey of Contemp Art, NY State Biennial, NY State Mus, Albany, 98; Personal Archeologies, Bryant Libr, Hecksher Mus Art, Roslyn, NY, 98; NJ Ctr for Visual Arts, Summit, 99; Faber Birren Nat, Stanford, Conn, 99; Parrish Art Mus, Southampton, NY, 99; Katonah Mus, Breaking the Rules, 01; Lamar Univ, Dishman Art Gallery, Beaumont, Tex, 2002; Nat Small Work, Scholarie Co, Cobleskill, NY, 2002; Gallery North, Setauket, NY, 2003; Painting Ctr, Solto, New York City, Big Abstract Show, 2003; Poughkeepsie Art Mus Point of View, 2004; Celebrating Color/Alpan Gallery, Huntington, NY, 2003, 2004; Summer Sch Mus, Biennial NLAPW, Washington DC, 2004; The Sixth Borough, Anthony Giordano Gallery, Dowling Coll, Oakdale, NY, 2005, 2006; Solo shows: Shelter Rock Art Gallery, Unitarian Congregation, Manhasset, NY, Art Council, Ft Wash, Lib, 2008, Albuquerque Mus, 2009, Mesquite Fine Art and Gallery, 2010, Ariel Fine Art, Locust Valley, NY, 2010, Alpan Gallery, Huntington, NY, 2010, Exposed Surfaces, Omni Gallery, Uniondale, NY, 2011; and others; LI Biennial, Heckscher Art Mus, Huntington, NY, 2012. *Awards:* Best in Show, Earthly Visions, Nassau Co Mus Art, 92; Finalist, Grumbacher Hall Fame Award, 96; Liquetex Art Award Excellence, Nat League Am Pen Women; Dir's Award-Nat'l Smallwork's Schlorie, Cobleskill, NY, 2002; S Magnet Knapp Award, NAWA, 2002; NAWA Medal of Honor, 2005; 1st Place, Mesquite Fine Art, Nev. *Bibliog:* Helen Harrison (auth), Turning photographs into the metaphorical, New York Times, 11/9/97; D Dominick Lombardi (auth), Not in New York, The Record Rev, 12/5/97; William Zimmer (auth), Innovative use of material, New York Times, 3/1/98; Helen Harrison (auth), Layers of Intention, NY Times, 5/26/02; Helen Harrison (auth), Winter Selections, NY Times, 1/19/03; Helen Harrison-A Celebration of the Outdoors & Its Colors, 1/23/2005. *Mem:* Nat Asn Women Artists (mem jury, 92-97); Nat League Am Pen Women; Long Island Network Women Artists; Soc Layerists Multi-Media; 9 East Contemporary Art, Huntington, NY. *Media:* Acrylic, Mixed Media. *Specialty:* Abstract Work. *Collection:* Islipart Mus, East Islip, NY, (Famil), Hempstead, NY, QCC Art Gallery, Queensborough Community College, Bayside, NY, CitiBank. *Dealer:* Nese Alplan Karakaplan. *Mailing Add:* Four Parkside Dr Great Neck NY 11021

HAROOTUNIAN, CLAIRE M
SCULPTOR, EDUCATOR

b Philadelphia, Pa, Feb 7, 1930. *Study:* Univ Pa, BA, 52; Univ Del, MEd, 64; Syracuse Univ, MFA (sculpture), 79. *Work:* Munson-Williams Proctor Inst, Utica, NY; Cazenovia Col, NY; Va Ctr Creative Arts, Sweetbriar; Everson Mus Art, Syracuse, NY. *Exhib:* Solo exhibs, Everson Mus, Syracuse, NY, 83 & Ben Mangel Gallery, Philadelphia, 84; Ransburg Art Gallery, Indianapolis, Ind, 84; Arco Art Fair, Madrid, 92; Fundacion Centro Civico, Guayaquil, Ecuador, 94; Int Sculpture Exhib, Technikon, Pretoria, S Africa, 96. *Teaching:* Instr sculpture, Everson Mus Art, Syracuse, 79-80; adj prof sculpture, Syracuse Univ, 80-94. *Awards:* Fel, Va Ctr Creative Arts, 83-85 & 88; Yaddo Fel, Saratoga Springs, NY, 83; Fel, Int Workshop, San Pere, Barcelona, Spain, 88. *Media:* Cast Metal, Forged Metal. *Mailing Add:* 602 Jamesville Ave Syracuse NY 13210

HAROUTUNIAN, JOSEPH HALSEY
PAINTER

b Chicago, Ill, Sept 22, 1944. *Study:* Lawrence Univ, BA, 67; Art Inst Chicago, with Paul Wieghardt, 68-69. *Work:* Portland Mus Art, Maine; Univ Maine Art Mus, Orono; Visual Arts Ctr, Mass Inst Technol; Bates Coll Art & Mus, Lewiston, Maine; Univ Maine; and others. *Exhib:* Life Is the Secret, Univ Maine Art Mus, Orono, 74; 59 Faces of Cadillac Mountain, Univ Maine Art Mus, Orono, 79; Effects of Time, Frank Bustamante Gallery, NY, 90; Art in the Embassies, US Embassy, Bogota, Colombia, 94; Coll Atlantic, 96; Univ Maine, Machias, 98; Asian Identities, East & West (traveling show), Hammond Mus, NY & Robert Ferot Ctr, Ga Inst Technol, 98; Frequencies of Nature (traveling show), Fernbank Mus, Atlanta & Tallahassee Mus Hist & Natural Sci, Fla. *Awards:* Purchase Award, Hassam & Speicher Fund Exhib, Am Acad & Inst, 80. *Bibliog:* Robert Taylor (auth), Review, Art Gallery Mag, 2/71; Jill Janows (auth), 2 artists explore fantasy, Boston Globe, 9/14/79; Michael Kimmelman (auth), Review, NY Times, 5/12/89. *Media:* Oil. *Dealer:* Frick Gallery 139 High St Belfast ME 04915; Creiger Dane Gallery 36 Newbury St Boston 02116. *Mailing Add:* Rogers Point Rd Steuben ME 04680

HARPER, GREGORY FRANKLIN
DIRECTOR, CURATOR

b Covington, Ky, May 7, 1954. *Study:* Northern Ky Univ, BA (art hist), 76; Univ Cincinnati, MA (art hist). *Work:* Behringer-Crawford Mus, Covington, Ky; Contemp Arts Ctr, Cincinnati, Ohio; Cincinnati Pub Schs, Ohio; Cape Mus Fine Arts, Dennis, Mass. *Collection Arranged:* Harlan Hubbard: A River Way of Life (auth, catalog), 86; Frank Duveneck; Dreaming Before Nature: Non Objective, 93; Permanent Collection, Cape Mus Art, 93. *Pos:* Exec dir, Behringer-Crawford Mus, Covington, Ky, 79-92; exec dir & cur, Cape Mus Fine Arts, Mass, 93-. *Teaching:* Adj prof art hist, Thomas More Col, Crestview Hills, Ky, 89-91. *Awards:* Citizen of the Year, N Ky CofC, 89; Outstanding Alumnus, N Ky Univ, 92; Service Above Self, Hyannis Rotary, 97. *Res:* American decorative arts; American art; performance art; Red grooms; Franz Kline. *Publ:* Auth, River Heritage Week, Classroom Celebration (exhib catalog), Behringer-Crawford Mus, 87. *Mailing Add:* c/o Cape Museum of Fine Arts 60 Hope Ln PO Box 2034 Dennis MA 02638

HARPER, MICHAELE ANN
PAINTER

b Port Clinton, Ohio, Jan 20, 1943. *Study:* Jefferson Community Col, Ky, AS (com art), 76; Western Ky Univ, Bowling Green, BFA (magna cum laude), 85. *Work:* United Cerebral Palsy Metro Found, Dallas. *Comn:* Paintings, Hotel Lutetia, Paris, France; paintings, Opera Cadet Hotel, Paris, France; painting, comn by pvt parties, Highland Park, Tex. *Exhib:* Selected Students Show, Western Ky Univ, Bowling Green, 81; 8 States Ann: Painting, Speed Art Mus, Ky, 82; The Laurel Art Guild Art Show, Montpelier Art Ctr, Md, 89 & 92; All Media Mem Show, Art League Gallery, Torpedo Factory, 89; Paint the Town Pink, Washington Post, DC, 90; United Cerebral Palsy Metro Dallas, Tex; Laurel Art Guild Mem Show, Slayton House Gallery, Md, 91; Art in the Metroplex, Tex Christian Univ & Templeton Art Ctr, Ft Worth, 93; The Art of Penwomen, Gallery 10, Ft Worth, 95; Landscapes: Real and Imagined, La Salle Gallery, Tex, 95; Women of Worth, Ft Worth, 95, 96 & 97; Southwestern Watercolor Soc Ann Mem Exhib, Dallas, 96, 97 & 2000; Dallas Visual Art Ctr Mem Exhib, Tex, 97, 98, 99, 2000; Four Artists Alumni, Western Ky Univ, Bowling Green, 97; The Art Annex, Coppell, Tex, 2004; Woodbine Furniture Company, Keller, Tex, 2004; The Gardens Restaurant, Ft Worth Botanical Gardens, Ft Worth, Tex, 2004; Creative Arts Studio & Gallery, Colleyville, Tex, Feb, 2005; Langdon Ctr of Tarleton State Univ, Granbury, Tex, June, 2005; Coastal Frame & Gallery, Rehoboth, Del, 2006; Solo Exhibs: This and That, Langdon Center of Tarleton State Univ, Granbury, Tex, June, 2005; Recent Work, Creative Arts Studio & Gallery, Colleyville, Tex, Feb, 2005; Abstraction 3rd, Coastal Frame and Gallery, Rehoboth, Delaware; Three Person Show: Marsha's Gallery, Bowling Green, Ky, 2005; Home and Abroad (with Marsha Heidbrik and Susan Struckert), 2006; Three Rivers Festival, St Tammany Art Asn, Covington, La, 2007; Fresh, Bowling Green Gallery Hop, Memphis Marsha's Gallery, Feb, 2008; Ashes to Ashes, Dust to Dust, St Tammany Art Asn, Spring for Art, 2008; Summer in France, Western Ky Univ, Dowling Green, Ky, 2008; Sizzle, Memphis Marsha's Art Gallery, Bowling Green, Ky, 2008. *Pos:* Pres, Laurel Art Guild, Md, 91-92; dir, owner & cur, Yellow House Gallery, Ft Worth, Tex, 96-2001; juror various art festivals and shows, 82-; juror, 12 County High School Art Comp, UNT Health Science Center, Atrium Gallery, Fort Worth, Tex, 2005. *Teaching:* Instr com art, Jefferson Community Col, Louisville, Ky, 78-80; instr continuing educ, Anne Arundel Col, Md, 92-93; pvt instr The Gallery, 94-; Instructor FW Woman's Club Art Department Fort Worth, 2001-2005, led workshops in England, France, Spain, & Nicaragua. *Awards:* Equal Award, Torpedo Factory Art League, Alexandria, Va, 91, 92; First Place, SWA Nat Juried Show, Ft Worth, Tex, 99; Winsor Newton Award, SWS 37th Ann Mem Juried Show, Dallas, Tex; plus others. *Bibliog:* Panorama Am Published by Estel Arts & Communications Centre, Columbia, Maryland; Interviewed for Art and Culture Article, Spring, 1999; Alumni Published by Western Kentucky Univ, Bowling Green, Kentucky: Interview for Article, Fall 2000; Biographical Encyclopedia of American Painters, Sculptors & Engravers of the US-Colonial to 2002, Published by Dealers Choice Books Inc., Land O' Lakes, FL, 2002. *Mem:* SW Watercolor Soc, Dallas; SWA, Fort Worth; Signature Member. *Media:* Paper & Canvas, Mixed Media. *Specialty:* Original work in a Variety of Mediums by Artists in England, France, Argentina & US. *Interests:* Travel and Art. *Dealer:* Woodbine Furniture Cp Keller TX

HARRELL, MARGARET ANN
PHOTOGRAPHER, WRITER

b Greenville, NC, 1940. *Study:* Duke Univ, BA (hist), (magna cum laude), 62; Columbia Univ, MA (contemp brit & am lit), 64; Univ NC, 76; Carl Jung Inst, Zurich, Switz, 87; Inst Human Devel, Ghent, 92; Studies at Tobias Sch Art, summer 93; LuminEssence energy studies, Belgium, Ibiza, Spain, Ore, 92-. *Work:* Cloud Medley (4 experimental studies in unusual play of light/dark), Het Toreke Mus, Tienen, Belg,

Tienen Skies, Het Toreke. *Exhib:* Solo exhib, The Sun in Profile: So Bright It's Dark, Sibiu, Romania, 2005; Galerie Gora, Montreal, Canada, 2010; Galiara, The Artists Alley; 13th Ann Photographic Processes, Upstream People Gallery; Contemporary Art, Art Time 2; La Galerie des Artistes du Portail des Antiguaires; 2nd Annual Raleigh Artists & Author's Showcase, 2013. *Pos:* Copy ed/assis ed, 65-68, Random House, freelance ed, 68-; asst, to psychologist, dream res, 83-84; co-organizer, US & Indian workshops & lectrs, Belgium, 93-; int editing coordr, Mus Exhib on Life of Jan Mensaert (book), 95-2001. *Teaching:* Instr, dance, 69; guest lectr, Sibiu Univ, 95; pvt teacher, LuminEssence, Awakening Your Light Body, 2002-, Radiance: Self Exciting, 2004-, Light Body Conciousness 2009-. *Awards:* Fel MacDowell Colony, 69-70 & 73. *Bibliog:* Reviewer's Choice, Small Press Bookwatch, Midwest Bookreview, June & July, 2005; A Feast for the Gonzo Soul, HSTBooks, 2011; Memoir Shelf, Midwest Bookreview, 2011; 100 Fine Art Photographers, 2011-2012, 75 Fine Art Photographers, 2013-2014. *Mem:* Kayumari, various wildlife orgns; NC Writers Network; Romanian Sacred Cave Hist & Res Soc (hon mem); Raleigh Outdoor Photography Club. *Media:* Photography. *Res:* Effects of direct & other sunlight in photog. *Interests:* T'ai chi, energy studies, art & computers. *Publ:* Auth, Love in Transition: Vol. I: Voyage of Ulysses: Letters to Penelope, 96, Vol. II: Voyage of Ulysses: Letters to Penelope, 96, Vol. III: The Christ State, 96, Vol. IV: The Bedtime Tales of Jesus, 98, Marking Time with Faulkner: A Study of the Symbolic Importance of the Mark and of Related Actions, 99, Space Encounters I: Chunking Down the 21st Century (Love in Transition Vol. VI), 2002, Space Encounters II: Chunking Down the 21st Century (Love in Transition Vol. VII), 2002, Space Encounters III: Inserting Consciousness into Collisions (Love in Transition Vol. VIII), 2003, Toward a Philosophy of Perception: The Magnitude of Human Potential: Cloud Optics, 2005, Keep This Quiet! memoir, 2011, Keep THIS Quiet Too! memoir, 2012, Keep This Quiet! III: Initiations; Int editing coordr, Life, Page One (museum e-book and 2 music CD-ROMS), 2001; contribr, articles to prof jour; auth, numerous poems; contribr, Cloud images: Love in Transition (photogr book covers), 96-03. *Dealer:* Harrell Communications; Light Angel Image Gallery; Le Portail des Antiquaires. *Mailing Add:* 5048 Amber Clay Ln Raleigh NC 27612

HARRIES, MAGS (MARGARET) L
SCULPTOR, EDUCATOR

b Barry, SWales, Gt Brit, April 6, 1945. *Study:* Leicester Coll Art & Design, England, dipl, 67; Univ Southern Ill, MFA, 70. *Hon Degrees:* Doc Fine Arts, Regis Coll, MA, 98. *Work:* Boston Mus Fine Arts; Univ Southern Ill; Nat Mus Wales; Rose Art Mus, Brandeis Univ, Waltham, Mass; Waterworks, Phoenix, Ariz, 2003; Simmons Coll, Boston, Mass. *Comn:* 19 Sculptures, Wall Cycle to Ocotillo, City of Phoenix, Ariz, 91; floor, City of the Falls, Commonwealth Convention Ctr, Louisville, Ky, 2000; water works, Drawn Water, City of Cambridge, Mass, 2000; installations, Nat Park Svc, Bronx River, NY, 98-99, Regis Coll, Western Mass, 99, Nat Park Svc, Merrimac River, Lawrence, Mass, 99-2000, many others; Connections, Central Conn State Univ; Benefit of Mr Kite, San Diego, Calif, 2004; Park, Terra Fugit, Miramar, Fla, 2005; outside amphitheater, The Big Question, Des Moines Sci Mus, 2007; Concord River Greenway Trail, City of Lowell, Mass & NEFA, 2007; Moontide Garden, Portland, Maine, 2008; 15 sculptures, Sunflowers, An Electric Garden, Austin, Tex, 2009; Zanjero's Lime, Phoenix, Ariz, 2009; Terpsichore for Kans City, Arts District Parking Garage, Kans City, Mo, 2011; Xixi Umbrellas, Xixi Wetlands, Hangzhou, China, West Lake Int Invitational Sculpture Exhib, 2012; Meeting Place, The Downtown Greenway, Greensboro, NC, 2014; Light Gate, Manhattan Beach, Calif, 2015. *Exhib:* Solo shows incl DeCordova Mus, Lincoln, Mass, 82, Lucid Moment, Regis Col, Weston, Mass, 99, Boston Sculptors Gallery, Boston Mass, 2013, Rising Waters, Boston Sculptors Gallery, 2015; group shows incl Border Gardens Installation, San Diego Mus Contemp Art, La Jolla, Calif, 90; Changing Places, Cardiff Bay Art Trust, Wales, 97; Knowing Limits (traveling show), Pratt Inst & Nat Park Svc, 2000; Projections through Glass, NAO Project Gallery, Boston, Mass, 2003; Reaching Water, CAC Gallery, Cambridge, Mass, 2004; Our River, Noble & Greenough Sch, Dedham, Mass, 2007; One Legged Table, Mills Gallery, Boston Ctr for the Arts, 2008; Remediate/Revision: Pub Artists Engagin the Environ, Wave Hill, Bronx, NY, 2010; 2 Person Show, Boston Sculptors Gallery, Boston, Mass, 2011; Ripple Effect: The Art of H2o/Glass Pieces, Peabody Essex Mus, Salem, Mass, 2011-2012; 40 yr Retrospective of Art Park, Art Park, Lewiston, NY, 2013; Sculpture Embraces Horticulture, Blithewold Mansion and Aboretum, Bristol, RI, 2014; Chesterwood, Stockbridge, MA, 2015; 34, curated by Liz Devlin. *Teaching:* Fac sculpture, Sch Mus Fine Arts, Boston, 78-. *Awards:* Govs Design Award, Mass, 86; Artist Educ Award, Boston Mayor's Off, 92; Top Honor Award for design collab, Boston Soc Architects, 93; Individual Artist Grant, Mass Cult Council, 2003; Valley Forward Presidential Award, top award for Water Works, Ariz, 2003, Crescordia Award for Ghost Trees and Arbors, 2005; AICA Award, 2004; Award of Excellence, Waterfront Ctr, 2006 & 07; Livable City Vision Award for Excellence, Austin, Tex; Public Art Network Yr in Review award, A Moontide Garden, Portland, Me, 2008; The Bogliasco Found Fel, Residency, Genoa, Italy, 2010; Livable City Vision award for Esthetics, Sunflowers, An Electric Garden, Austin, TX, 2010; Valley Forward award for Merit for Site Development, The Zanjeros Line, Phoenix, Ariz, 2010; Valley Forward Crescordia award for Site Art in Public Places, The Zanjero's Line, Phoenix, Ariz, 2010; Public Art Year in Review award, Passage, Phoenix, Ariz, 2012; Public Art Network Year in Review award, Terpsichore for Kans City, MO, 2012; Valley Forward Crescordia award for Art in Public Places, Passage, Phoeniz, Ariz, 2012; CoDA awards, Landscape Merit award, Xixi Umbrellas, Hangzhou, China, 2013; CoDA awards, Art and Technology Merit award, Passage, Ariz, 2014. *Bibliog:* Creating a 'there, there', Landscape Architecture, 2002; Drawn Water, Sculpture Mag, 2002; Waterworks Arizona Falls, Sculpture Mag, Feb 2004; Uncovered Landscape, Landscape Architecture, Feb 2005; Sculpture Mag, 10/2005; Landmarks-5 Projects that Left a Mark on the 70's, Architecture Boston, 7/2006; Public Art: Greenways, Sonic Trees & Waterways, Art New England, 2009; High Tides, low Tide, Landscape Archit, 2010; Landscape Architecture Magazine March Sunflowers Sprout on Texas Highway-Marty Carlock, 2011; 100 Boston Artists, Schaefer Press-Chawkey Fren, 2011; Sculpture Magazine September Mags Harries Review Boston Sculptors Gallery-Christine Temin, 2011; Orion Magazine, The Art of Infrastructure, 2013; Clay, Brutal Magazine, Issue 2, 2015. *Mem:* Am for the Arts; Pub Art Network. *Media:* All Media. *Mailing Add:* 34 Porter Rd Cambridge MA 02140

HARRINGTON, CHESTEE MARIE
PAINTER, SCULPTOR, PRINTMAKER

b New Iberia, La, Dec 5, 1941. *Study:* Art Students League, New York, with Sidney Simon & Michael Pelletieri, 84; Woodstock Sch Art, with Richard McDaniel, 85; Shidon, Bronze Foundry, with Marshall Glazier, 84, Tommy Hicks, 86. *Work:* Art Ctr SW La, Lafayette, La; Mc Ilhenny Collection, La State Univ, Baton Rouge; La State Mus, New Orleans; Hist New Orleans Collection, La; Inst Applied Ontology, Atlanta, Ga. *Comn:* Bronze bust, Bouligny Plaza, New Iberia, La, 76; wood Polychromatic bas relief, St Landry Bank, Opelousas, La, 81; Lead Relic Tricentennial, Dept Cult, Baton Rouge La, 83; Woman's Hosp Wood Polychromatic bas relief, Baton Rouge, La, 87; mural, wood polychromatic bas relief, Cameron State Bank, Sulphur, La, 89. *Exhib:* Solo exhibs, Art Ctr SW La, Lafayette, La, 68-75, Masur Mus, Monroe, La, 76, Zigler Mus, Jennings, La, 77 & Meet the Artist, McNeese State Univ, Lake Charles, La, 84, Sans Souci Gallery, Lafayette, La, 97, Mus Gulf Coast, Port Arthur, Tex, 99, Jean Lafitte Nat Historic Park, Lafayette, La, 99, Shadows on the Teche, Nat Trust: L'Esprit de la Louisiane, New Iberia, La, 2003, Corcoran Gallery, DC, 2003, Cigar Factory Red Room, Charleston, SC, 2005; group exhibs, French Louisiana Bicentennial, Fr Radio Network, Paris, Fr, 75 & Legacy in Progress, La State Univ, Alexandria, La, 85; Tricentennial Celebration, La State Mus, New Orleans, La, 84; We're Saving a Place for You, Shadows on the Teche, Nat Trust; 60 Yr Retrospective, La State Univ Rural Life Mus, 2013. *Collection Arranged:* The White House, Washington, DC; Mus Moncton, New Brunswick, Can; Sunrise Ranch, Loveland, Colo; McIlhenny Collection, La State Univ, Baton Rouge; Touro Hosp, New Orleans. *Teaching:* Instr, basic drawing, Iberia Parish Park Serv, 66-68. *Awards:* Grammy Nominee for L'Esprit de la Louisiane (Cajun music CD), 2000. *Bibliog:* Morris Raphael (auth) Battle in the Bayou Country, Harlo Press, 75; Kenneth Nahan (auth) Chestee Harrington Biog, Nahan Galleries, 75; Cristy Viviano (auth), L'Esprit de la Louisiana, & E'Samtele Louisiana, 99, Tree House Press. *Mem:* Nat Artist Equity; Nat Trust. *Media:* Wood, Polychromatic Bas Relief. *Res:* Louisiana Folk Housing, 68-2013, Cajun Music. *Interests:* moments of spiritual expressionism set in the multicultural south Louisiana environment. *Publ:* Illusr, Battle in the Bayou Country, Harlo Press; 75; So you want to invest in art, Baton Rouge Mag, 82; auth, The Advocate, Baton Rouge, 71, 80, 82, 83, 99; auth, The Daily Advertiser, Lafayette, La, 69, 75, 87, 99; auth, Beaumont Enterprise, Tex, 99; auth, Charleston City Paper, SC, 1/12/2005; auth, The Independent, Lafayette, La, 11/5/2003; The Advocate; Art Critic; Robin Miller, 2013. *Dealer:* Chestee Harrington Gallery New Iberia LA 70560. *Mailing Add:* 1065 W Main St New Iberia LA 70560

HARRINGTON, GLENN
PAINTER

b NY, 1959. *Study:* Pratt Inst, BFA, 1981. *Exhib:* Solo exhibs include Wells Gallery, Charleston, SC, 2002, 2006, 2007, Travis Gallery, New Hope, Pa, 2002, 2003, 2004, 2005, 2006, Cassique Club, Kiawah Island, SC, 2003, Eleanor Ettinger Gallery, NY, 2004, 2006, 2007; group exhibs include Museum of American Illustration Exhib, Norman Rockwell Gallery, 1999; 4 NY Painters, Kirin Art Space, Tokyo and Osaka, Japan, 1999; Bianco Gallery, Doylestown, Pa, 1999; Phillips Mill Gallery, New Hope, Pa, 1999; NY Soc Illustrators, 2000; Summer Exhib, Eleanor Ettinger Gallery, NY, 2000, 2001, 2002, 2004, Figure in American Art, 2002, 2004, 2005, 2007; Bucks Fever, Travis Gallery, New Hope, Pa, 2001, 2007; Faces of Bucks County, Aldie Mansion, Doylestown, Pa, 2002; Mus Am Illustration, NY, 2002; Wells Gallery, Charleston, SC, 2002; 30 Paintings, Jack Nicklaus Mus, 2002; World Golf Hall of Fame, St Augustine, Fla, 2002, 2003, 2004, 2006; En Plein Air, Gibbs Art Mus, Charleston, SC, 2002; Murfield Village, Columbus, Ohio, 2003, 2004, 2006; Portrait Soc Am, Washington, DC, 2005; State Mus Pa, Harrisburg, Pa, 2005; Salon d'Arts, Denver, Colo, 2006; Medici Gallery, London, 2007; Art Obsessions Gallery, Tokyo, Japan, 2007. *Dealer:* Travis Gallery 6089 Lower York Rd New Hope PA 18938; Wells Gallery One Sanctuary Beach Dr Kiawah Island SC 29455. *Mailing Add:* c/o Eleanor Ettinger Gallery 24 W 57th St Ste 609 New York NY 10019

HARRINGTON, WILLIAM CHARLES
SCULPTOR

b Chicago, Ill, 1942. *Study:* Univ Ill, Champaign-Urbana, with Roger Majorowicz & Frank & Julio Gallo, BFA; Univ Hartford Art Sch with Ted Behl & Lloyd Glasson, MFA. *Work:* Nat Archives, Washington, DC; NC Zoological Park, Ashboro; Art in Pub Places, Bristol, Tenn. *Comn:* 15 ft concrete & steel, Cabot, Cabot & Forbes, Seattle, Wash, 75; 4 ft wood relief, Amalgamated Spirits & Provisions, Ames, Iowa, 75 & Cedar Rapids, Iowa, 76; carved compos, Cabot, Cabot & Forbes, Bellevue, Wash, 84; Top Walk (mixed media), Arlington, Va. *Exhib:* Fuel for Thought, Attleboro Mus, Mass, 96; Burlington Sculpture Garden Exhib, Pemberton, NJ, 91-97; Environmental Arts Inc, Fuller Mus, Brockton, Mass, 97; Mass: Outdoor Sculpture, Green Hill Ctr NC Arts, Greensboro, 97-99; Red, Cambridge Art Asn, Mass, 2000; Sculpture at New Horizons, Salisbury, Conn, 2000-02; Salmagundi V, Rocky Mount, NC, 2001-02; Lucia and Me, Warwick Mus Art, RI, 2002; Art Inst Boston, 2002; Earthworks, NC Zoological Park, Ashboro, 2002-03; Five Vets, Randolph Art Ctr, Ashboro, NC, 2002; Summer Exhib, Grounds for Sculpture, Hamilton, NJ, 2002; Sculpture Mile, Madison, Conn, 2003-06; Burlington Co Col, Pemberton, NJ, 2003-05; 8th Int Shoebox Sculpture, Hawaii, Taiwan, Guam, mainland US, 2003-05; Salmagundi IX, Rocky Mt, NC, 2005-06; Sculpture Mile, Middletown, CT, 2005-07-; Salmagundi X, Rocky Mt, NC, 2006-07; MicroMonumentals, Lowell, Mass Winston/Salem, NC, 2007; Arts Alliance Mountain Empire, Bristol,Tenn, 2007-; Arts in Public Places, Ashboro, NC, 2007-2009; Art in Public, Bristol, Tenn, Va, 2008-2009; Sculpture in the 21st Cent, Towson Univ, Md, 2010; Unbound Artistry Gallery, Woodstock, Vt, 2011; Gallery 55, Natick, Mass, 2011; 54th Nat Multimedia

Exhib, Imperial Ctr, Rocky Mt, NC, 2011; The Shape Shifter, Gallery 55, Natick, Mass, 2012; Tri State Sculptures, East Carolina Univ, Greenville, NC, 2012; Sculpture Mile, Madison Ct, 2013. *Collection Arranged:* NC Zoological Park, Asheboro, NC; State of Hawaii Found on Cult and the Arts. *Pos:* Workshop asst, George Rickey, East Chatham, NY, 65; mem, Combat Artists Team VII, Vietnam/Hawaii, 68-69. *Teaching:* Asst prof sculpture & drawing, Ind State Univ, Terre Haute, 69-72; asst prof sculpture, Iowa State Univ, 74-78; creative consult, Babson Co, Babson Park, Mass, 96-99. *Mem:* Tri-State Sculptors Guild. *Media:* Carved Wood, Assemblage, Mixed Media, Collage. *Publ:* Contribr, Collage Art, JL Alkinson Quarry Press, 96; Art of War: Eyewitness US Combat from the Revolution through the 20th Century, H Avery Chenoweth Friedman Publishing Group Inc, 2002. *Mailing Add:* 120 Goulding St Holliston MA 01746

HARRIS, CAROLYN
PAINTER
b Wilmington, NC, Jul 16, 1937. *Study:* Univ NC, Greensboro, BFA (painting), 59; New York Univ, MA (art educ), 61. *Work:* Cape Ann Mus, Gloucester, Mass; Erie Art Ctr, Pa; NC State Univ, Raleigh; Scott Mem Study Collection, Bryn Mawr Coll, Pa; State Univ NY, Potsdam; Calif Hist Soc, San Francisco; Western Carolina Univ, Cullowhee, NC; Jackson Libr, Gold Star Collection, Univ NC, Greensboro; San Francisco Pub Libr, Special Collections. *Exhib:* Group exhib, Art from the Fifties, Woman's College of the Univ of NC, 1950-1963, Marita Gilliam Gallery, Raleigh, NC, 94; Women in the Visual Arts, Hollins Coll, Roanoke, Va, 96; Art and Friendship, II: Selections from the Nell Blaine Collection, Tibor de Nagy Gallery, New York, 98; Kinds of Drawings, Western Carolina Univ, Cullowhee, NC, 99; Zeuxis: A Movable Feast, Westbeth Gallery, New York, 2003; Watercolor, Kouros Gallery, New York & Schweinfurth Memorial Art Ctr, Auburn, NY, 2003; Alice Ehrlich & Her Students, Lee Hansley Gallery, Raleigh, NC, 2003; Watercurrents: 12 Artists Working in Watercolor, Kouros Gallery, New York, 2004; Watercurrents, Kouros Gallery, New York, 2005; On Board, Lori Bookstein Fine Art, NY, 2007; Painting in the Park, Lori Bookstein Fine Art, NY, 2008; Women Artists from the Cape Ann Mus Collection, Cape Ann Mus, Gloucester, Mass, 2009; Solo Exhib: Carolyn Harris, Paintings and Works on Paper, Tibor de Nagy Gallery, New York, 2004-05, & 2008; In Plein View, Cape Ann Mus, Gloucester, Mass, 2009. *Pos:* Asst to Alfred H Barr Jr & Dorothy C Miller, Mus Collections, Mus Mod Art, New York, 1961; asst to adminr & asst mgr bookshop, San Francisco Mus Mod Art, 1962-65. *Awards:* grant, Creative Artists Pub Serv Prog, NY, 1974; Benjamin Altman (Landscape) Prize, 159th Ann Exhib, Nat Acad Design, 1984. *Bibliog:* Cape Ann Hist Asn Bull, Vol 13, No 2, 4-6/1993; Blue Greenberg (auth), Women artists show skills, Herald-Sun, Durham, NC, 8/7/1994; Hilton Kramer (auth), Carolyn Harris Solos, Capturing Cape Ann in Inspired Landscape, New York Observer, 1/10/2005; Bill Scott (auth), Carolyn Harris at Tibor de Nagy, Art in Am, 6-7/2005; Molly Hutton (auth), Carolyn Harris: Drawing in Paint, Gettysburg Rev, 2006. *Media:* Oil, Watercolor. *Publ:* Illusr, Parker Hodges, Heart of a Plum/Heart of an Owl, Conahan Press, San Francisco, 1965; John Heath-Stubbs, Four Poems in Measure, Helikon Press, New York, 1973; Natural Selection: A Portfolio of Ten Landscape Prints (including Carolyn Harris), Univ Richmond Mus, Richmond, Va, and Center Street Studio, Milton, Mass, 2006. *Dealer:* Tibor de Nagy Gallery 724 Fifth Ave New York 10019. *Mailing Add:* 210 Riverside Dr Apt 8A New York NY 10025

HARRIS, CHARNEY ANITA
PAINTER, SCULPTOR
b Chicago, Ill. *Study:* Univ Arts, Philadelphia; Philadelphia Mus Art, 64-68; New Sch Social Res, 70-73. *Work:* Philadelphia Mus Art; Allentown Art Mus, Pa; Hobson Pitman Mus House, Bryn Maur, Pa; First Ronald McDonald House; Mus Mod Art. *Comn:* Universal Domain, Hudson River Mus, Yonkers, NY, 85 & Moore Coll Art, Philadelphia, 86; James A Michener Art Mus, Pa, 97; Millicent Roger Mus, Taos, NMex, 96. *Exhib:* AJ Wood Galleries, Philadelphia, 79, 80; Mangel Gallery, Philadelphia, 82, 91; Mangel Gallery, 85, 90, 92-95, 98-2000, 2002-2008; Artists Xmas Show, Cleveland Ctr Contemp Art, 86; Millicent Roger Mus, Taos, NMex, 96; James Michener Art Mus, Doylestown, Pa, 97; Solo exhib: James A Michener Art Mus, 98. *Awards:* Painting Prize, New York Sch Social Res, 70; Painting Prize, Pa Acad Fine Arts. *Bibliog:* Victoria Donohoe (auth), article, Philadelphia Inquirer, 82 & 88; article in the Washington Post, 84; Aimee Young Jackson (auth), article in Kalliope, 89, 93 & 94. *Mem:* Artists Equity Asn Inc; Am Fedn Arts. *Media:* Oil; Wood. *Publ:* Contribr, Bucks County & Country Living, 96, Spring 2009; Art Matter, 98; Time-Off, 2002; Town and Country Living, 2009. *Dealer:* Mangel Gallery 1714 Rittenhouse Sq Philadelphia PA 19103. *Mailing Add:* 2 Sunnyside Ln Yardley PA 19067

HARRIS, CONLEY
PAINTER, PRINTMAKER
b Kans, July 7, 1943. *Study:* Univ Kans, BFA, 65; Univ Wis, MFA, 68. *Work:* Fogg Art Mus, Harvard Univ, Cambridge, Mass; Boston Mus Fine Art; Wichita Art Mus, Kans; Citi-Corp Bank & Rockefeller Financial Serv, NY; Fed Reserve Bank, Chicago; De Cordova & Dana Mus, Lincoln, Mass; Portland Mus Art, Portland, Maine; CitiBank, NY; Fidelity Management & Research, Boston, Mass; Met Life Insurance, NY; Mass Financial Services co, Boston, Mass; Federal Reserve Bank, Chicago, Ill; John Hancock Insurance, Int Div, Boston, Mass; pvt collections, Mary Darmstaetter, Yasuko & Dr. John Bush, Gerard Evers, Fredricka Merck, Rita Fraad, Barbara & Steve Grossman and many others. *Comn:* Oil painting, Chubb Insurance co, 85; Oil painting, Gannett co, 87; pastel drawings, Fidelity Mgt & Res, 94; Harvard Univ, 98; oil paintings, comn by Eaton Vance Mana, Boston, 2000; Gannett co Inc, Rosslyn, Va; State St Bank, Boston, Mass, 2006. *Exhib:* Solo exhibs, Barridoff Galleries, Portland, Maine, 83, Thomas Segal Gallery, Boston, Mass, 85 & DeCordova Mus, Lincoln, 85, Pursuing Beauty & Light, David Findlay Jr Fine Art, NY, 2001, Silas Kenoyn Gallery, Provincetown, Mass, 2001-2002; Am Drawings, Smithsonian tour, 83-85; Figuration on Paper, Boston Mus Fine Arts, 83; Made in Boston, Fogg Art Mus, Harvard Univ, Cambridge, Mass, 80; New Prints, EES Studio, Estampe du Rhin, Strasbourg, France, 90; Barbara Greene Gallery, Miami, Fla, 91; Gallery Viva, Kawasaki, Japan, 94; Andrea Marquit Fine Art, Boston, 95 & 97; David Findlay Jr Fine Art, NY, 98; Bradford Campbell Gallery, San Francisco, 2000; New Landscapes, Art Life Mitsuhashi Gallery, Kyoto, Japan, 2001; The Landscape, Virginia Lynch Gallery, Tiverton, RI, 2002; Intimate Views, Silas-Kenyon Gallery, Provincetown, Mass, 2002 & 2005; Hindu Deities, Haughton Asia Art Fair, Theresa McCullough Ltd, NY, 2003; Hindu Tableaux, Bernard Toale Gallery, Boston, MA, 2003; Paintings, Drawings, Judith Dowling Asian Art, Boston, MA, 2004; Victoria Munroe Fine Are, Boston, Mass, 2007; Danforth Art Mus, Lyric Tableaux, Framingham, Mass, 2008; Twenty Paintings, Univ NH Art Mus, Durham, NH, 2008; New Paintings, Downtown Art Ctr, Univ Tenn, Knoxville, Tenn, 2008; Indar Pasricha Contemp, London, UK, 2008; Mus Fine Arts Boston, Mass, 2009-2010. *Teaching:* Vis artist drawing, Boston Univ, Mass, 69-70; assoc prof drawing & painting, Univ NH, Durham, 70-88; Art New England Workshops, Bennington Col, 84, 85, 87, 88 & 90. *Awards:* Wurlitzer Found Residence Grant, Taos, NMex, 75; Purchase Prize, Am Drawing, Portsmouth, Va, 76; Mass Artist Found Fel, 86; Visual Artist residency, Sanskriti Found, New Delhi, India, 2013. *Bibliog:* Nancy Stapen (auth), rev, Art News Mag, 11/95; John Arthur (auth), New England Landscape Painting, Art New Eng, 6/97; Cate McQuaid (auth), Toying with Reality Rev, Art New Eng, 11/97; Cate McQuaid (auth), New Paintings, Boston Globe, 4/2007. *Mem:* Asian Art Soc New Eng; Collections Comm, Harvard Univ Art Mus; Collections Comm, Mus Fine Arts, Boston. *Media:* Oil, Watercolor; Monotype. *Interests:* Indian/Persian art. *Dealer:* Victoria Munroe Fine Art Boston Mass; Indar Pasricha London UK. *Mailing Add:* 1140 Washington St Boston MA 02118

HARRIS, DAVID JACK
PAINTER, DESIGNER
b San Mateo, Calif, Jan 6, 1948. *Study:* San Francisco State Univ, BA, 72, MA, 75. *Work:* San Francisco State Univ, Bain & Co, Pacific Bell & Int Red Cross, San Francisco; Stanford Univ, Palo Alto, Calif; Litton Industs, Mountain View, Calif; N Cent Wash Mus, Wenatchee, Wash; Maturugo Mus, Ridgecrest, Calif. *Comn:* Lawry's, Beverly Hills, Calif; Sheraton Grande, Los Angeles; Royal Family, Saudia Arabia; Uoysys Corp, Fremont, Calif; Spieker Partners, Pleasanton, Calif; and others. *Exhib:* Fine Arts Mus, San Francisco, 68-70; San Mateo Co Mus, Calif, 70; California Artists, Palace Fine Arts, San Francisco, 75; solo exhib, Hewlett Packard Gallery, Palo Alto, Calif, 86, California Concepts, N Cent Wash Mus, Wash, Coastal Arts League Mus, San Mateo, Calif, 88 & Matur Augo Mus, Ridgecrest, 92. *Collection Arranged:* murals for public and private bldgs, San Francisco, Calif, 2009-. *Pos:* Dir, Galerie de Tours, San Francisco, 71-72; pres, 1870 Gallery & Studio, Belmont, Calif, 86-87; UP Coastal Arts League Mus, 90-. *Teaching:* Instr painting & art hist, Chabot Coll, Hayward, Calif, 76-81. *Awards:* Best of Show, Univ Santa Clara, Calif, 75; First Place, Bay Area Artists Group, San Francisco Co, 78; First Place, San Mateo Co Artist Show, 80. *Bibliog:* Mary Helen McAllister (auth), David Harris, N Co Publ, 84; Mark Stevens (auth), David Harris: A World in Motion, Valley Mag, San Clemente, Calif, 89; Spectacular Houses of California; Finest Designers in California. *Mem:* Int Soc Interior Designers; 1870 Gallery & Studios; Coastal Arts League, San Mateo, Calif; Coll Art Asn. *Media:* Oil, Acrylic. *Specialty:* Abstract Acrylics. *Interests:* hiking, camping, travel. *Publ:* Auth, California Concepts brochure, N Cent Wash Mus Publ. *Dealer:* A Gallery 73-580 El Paseo Palm Desert CA 92260. *Mailing Add:* 1412 Quail Ct Santa Rosa CA 95404-2043

HARRIS, LILY MARJORIE
ART DEALER, ADMINISTRATOR
b Rochester, NY, Nov 12, 1956. *Study:* Syracuse Univ, BFA (textile design), 78; Victoria & Albert Mus, London, 78; Rochester Inst Technol, MS, 81. *Pos:* Restorer, Metrop Mus Art, New York, 78-79; colorist, Thomas Strahan Co, Chelsea, Mass, 79; asst dir, George Frederic Gallery, Rochester, NY, 82-83; admin asst, Thomas Burke Woodworkers, Rochester, NY, 84-85; dir-owner, Galerie Oboussier, Nantucket, Mass, 84-86; asst dir, Main St Gallery, Nantucket, 86-92, decorative painter, 92-. *Teaching:* Instr, Mem Art Gallery, Rochester, 80; workshop instr, Nantucket Island Sch Design & Arts, 81. *Mem:* Am Asn Mus. *Specialty:* Contemporary art, fine crafts, and photography. *Mailing Add:* 7 1/2 Back St Nantucket MA 02554

HARRIS, PAUL
SCULPTOR
b Orlando, Fla, Nov 5, 1925. *Study:* With Joy Winslow, Orlando; Univ NMex; New Sch Social Res, with Johannes Molzahn; Hans Hofmann Sch. *Hon Degrees:* Universidad de Catolica, Chile, 62. *Work:* Los Angeles Co Mus Art; Mus Mod Art, NY; San Francisco Mus Mod Art; Neue Galerie der Stadt Aachen; Univ Art Mus, Berkeley; Cath Univ Chile; and many others. *Exhib:* Sculpture USA, 59 & Hans Hofmann & His Students, 64-65, Mus Mod Art, NY, 58, 63; Sculpture of the Sixties, Los Angeles Co Mus & Sao Paulo Biennial, 67; Crocker Art Gallery Asn, Sacramento, 68; Soft Art, NJ Mus, 69; New Vein Show, Vienna, Cologne, Belgrade, Baden-Baden, Geneva, Brussels & Milan, 69-70; solo exhibs, San Francisco Mus Art, 72, Univ Calif, Santa Barbara, 72, Univ NMex, 73, Ark Art Ctr, Little Rock, 74 & Galerie Redmann, Berlin, 90, 91 & 92; Iannetti-Lanzone, San Francisco, 89; C Grimaldis, Baltimore, 89; Fresno Mus Art, 99 & 2007; The Coll of Marin Gallery, Kentfield, Calif, 2000 & 2007; Wiegand Gallery, Notre Dame de Namur Univ, Belmont, Calif, 2003. *Pos:* founder, Wrongree Press, 73. *Teaching:* Instr art, Univ NMex, Knox Col, BWI, State Univ NY, New Paltz, San Francisco Inst Art, Universidad Catholica de Chile, NY Univ & Univ Calif, Berkeley; prof art, Calif Col Arts & Crafts, retired; vis critic, lectr, USFS Ctrs, Valparaiso and Concepcion, Chile, 62, Rinehart Sch Sculpture, Spring 81, Md Inst Art, (9 times), 63-86, Univ Oreg, Eugene, 68, Newark State Univ, NJ, 70, Mont State Univ, Bozeman, 70, 74, State Univ NMex, Las Cruces, 71, Montclair Col, 77, Phila Col Art, 77, RI Sch Design, 77, Univ Ariz, Tucson, 86. *Awards:* Neallie Sullivan Award, 67; Tamarind Fel, 69-70; Resident MacDowell Colony, 77; Longview Found Grant, 78; Guggenheim Fel, 79; artist-in-residence, Rinehart Sch Sculpture, Md Inst Art, 81; Lebovitz Fund Grant, 78; Fulbright Fel, Univ Catolica de Chile, 61-62. *Bibliog:* Paul Harris (auth), Pas D'Une Bolinas, Ca, Wrongtree Press, 82; Thomas Albright (auth), Art in the San Francisco Bay Area 1945-1980, Univ Calif Press,

Berkeley, 85; Bill Berkson (auth), Paul Harris, Works in Bronze, Iannetti-Lanzone Gallery, 89. *Media:* Bronze. *Publ:* Contribr, Art News & Art in Am; illusr, Dorothy Schmidt's Torso, 74 & Pas d' Une, 79; Phases of The Moon, Wrongtree Press, 95; design of book Motives and Cues, Marguerite Harris (auth), 93; lithographs, Paradise: Variations, 96; drawings, Paul Harris, 98; Paul Harris, Fifty Years, Univ Wash Press, 99

HARRIS, PAUL ROGERS
CURATOR, CONSULTANT
b Dallas, Tex, Jan 2, 1933. *Study:* Univ N Tex, BA, 54, MA, 56; NY Univ, 65-67; Inst Arts Admin, Harvard Univ, cert, 78. *Exhib:* 50 Yrs in Art, Mt View Coll, Dallas, Tex; Shared Visions: Texas Artists Then & Now (with catalog), Arlington Mus Art, 2006. *Collection Arranged:* Emerging Texas Photographers (with catalog), 80; Inaugural Exhibition, Gateway Gallery, Dallas Mus Fine Art, 84; Handmade in Texas, Craft Guild Dallas, 87; City Life: Views of the City, Zoomorphism: Animals in Art & A Decade of Dallas Crafts, 1949-1959, 88; Houses of God: Charles De Bus, 89; Texas Printmakers: 1940-1965, Meadows Mus Southern Methodist Univ, 90; Mystery and Intrigue, Peregrine Gallery, Dallas, 91; Metal and Mettle: Art and Spirit, Ida Green Gallery, Austin Col, Sherman, Tex, 92; Landscape Remembered: Paintings by Mary Vernon, Wichita Falls Mus & Art Ctr, Tex, 93; Point of No Return, 94; A Point of View: Texas Women Painters, 1900-1960, El Paso Mus Art, Tex, 96; Breaking Into the Mainstream: Texas African-Am Artists, Irving Arts Ctr, Tex, 96; Portraits & Self-Portraits: Fact or Fiction, Brazos Gallery, Richland Coll, Dallas, 96. *Pos:* Coordr educ servs, Mus Mod Art, New York, 65-70; dir, Art Ctr, Waco, Tex, 74-86; chmn visual arts & archit adv panel, Tex Comn on Arts, 80-83; bd dir, Tex Arts Alliance, 80-86; exec dir, Craft Guild Dallas, 86-88; mem, Arts Adv Comt, African-Am Mus, Dallas, 90-. *Teaching:* Supvr art, Children's House, Dallas Mus Contemp Arts, Tex, 60-65; head dept art educ, Southern Methodist Univ, Dallas, Tex, 70-74; instr art, El Centro Coll, Dallas, 92-95, Navarro Coll, Corsicana, Tex, 92-95 & Mt View Coll, 95-2005. *Awards:* Alumni Hon, NTex State Univ, 85; Twentieth Anniversary Celebration, Art Ctr, Waco, 92; Legend Award, Prof Dallas Ctr for Contemporary Art, 2002; Scholarship named PRH for Art Student at Univ, 2004-2006; Distinguished Alumnus, N Dallas HS, 2007. *Bibliog:* Janet Kutner (auth), Texas small museums discovering each other, Art News, 2/77; Charlotte Moser (auth), Texas museums: Gambling for big change, Art News, 12/79; Janet Kutner (auth), A celebration of city life, Dallas Morning News. *Mem:* Tex Asn Schs Art; Dallas Visual Arts Ctr; McKinney Ave Contemp; Dallas Mus Art. *Media:* Digital Artist. *Interests:* photography, contemporary art, folk art. *Collection:* Shared Vision: Texas Artists Then & Now. *Publ:* Auth, Gillian Bradshaw-Smith: Soft Sculptures & Drawings, 76, Richard Hunt: Sculpture, Drawings, Prints, 78, Pedro Friedeberg, 78 & many others. *Mailing Add:* 7211 Concord Ave Dallas TX 75235-4414

HARRIS, ROBERT GEORGE
PAINTER, ILLUSTRATOR
b Kansas City, Mo, Sept 9, 1911. *Study:* Kansas City Art Inst, with Monte Crews; Grand Cent Sch Art, with Harvey Dunn; Art Students League, with George Bridgeman. *Work:* Portraits, Phoenix Jr Col, Dept of Justice, Washington, DC, Seabury Western Theol Sem, Chicago, Ill, Wabash Col, Crawfordsville, Ind & Franciscan Renewal Ctr, Scottsdale, Ariz; also in many pvt collections in US. *Exhib:* Soc Illusr; Art Dirs Club, 43-46; New Rochelle Art Asn, 49; Westport Artists, 50; Solo exhib, portraits, Phoenix Art Mus, 62. *Mem:* Soc Illusr; Phoenix Fine Art Asn; Phoenix Art Mus. *Media:* Oil. *Publ:* Illusr, McCall's, 39-60, Sat Eve Post, 39-61, Good Housekeeping, 40-60, Ladies' Home J, 40-61 & other nat mags

HARRIS, RONNA S
PAINTER, EDUCATOR
b Los Angeles, Calif, July 25, 1952. *Study:* San Francisco Art Inst, 73; Calif State Univ, Northridge, BA, 74; Univ Calif, Santa Barbara, MFA, 77. *Work:* Jacksonville Art Mus; White House Visitor Center; New Orleans Art Mus. *Exhib:* Birmingham Biennial, Birmingham Art Mus, Ala, 87; Fla Artists, Jacksonville Art Mus, 87; Magic Realism, Vero Beach Ctr Arts, Fla, 88; Women Artists, Metrop Mus & Art Ctr, Coral Gables, Fla, 88; Still, Zinsel, 90, 92, 94, 96, 99, 2003, 2005; Impostorphobia, Contemp Art Ctr, New Orleans, 92; Contemp Work, Pensacola Art Mus, Fla, 93; Univ Western Ala, 2003; Palma Gallery, New Orleans, 2005; Northwestern State Univ, Natchitoches, La, 2006; Appalachian State Univ, Turchin Ctr for the Arts, Boone, NC, 2006. *Collection Arranged:* Jacksonville Art Mus, Fla; Claiborne Collection, Baton Rouge, La; White House Hist Asoc, Washington DC; Huntsville Art Mus, Ala; Birmingham Art Mus, Ala; Morris Art Mus, Ga. *Pos:* Scenic artist, Universal, Disney, NBC & ABC, Los Angeles, Calif, 79-85. *Teaching:* Instr painting & drawing, Humboldt State Univ, Calif, 77-78; asst prof figure drawing, Univ Miami, Fla, 85-89; assoc prof painting & drawing, Tulane Univ, New Orleans, 89-. *Awards:* Purchase Award, Fla Artists, Jacksonville Art Mus, 87; Max Orovitz Res Grant, Lowe Art Mus, Univ Miami, 88; Fel Grant, Newcomb Col, 90 & 93; LA Division of the Arts. *Bibliog:* Heidi Schiff Tuby (auth), In Sharp Focus, Boca Raton, 88; WCA Miami Chap, The Way of the Woman Artist (film), Dade Co Television, Channel 1, 89; New American Paintings, Southern Edition, Open Studio Press, 95. *Mem:* Coll Art Asn. *Media:* Oil, Pastel. *Mailing Add:* 1134 St Andrew St New Orleans LA 70130

HARRIS, WILLIAM WADSWORTH, II
PAINTER, COLLAGE ARTIST
b New Haven, Conn, 1927. *Study:* Yale Univ, BA; Univ Mich, MA; also with Richard Wilt, Deane Keller & Jerry Farnsworth. *Work:* Galerie Moos, Geneva, Switz; Toledo Mus Fine Arts, Ohio; Yale Univ Collection; Mattatuck Mus Arts & City Nat Bank, Waterbury, Conn; Northwestern Conn Coll, Winsted; Drufva Collection, Denver, Colo; Mary Wade Home Collection, New Haven, Conn; and in pvt collections in Europe, Mid East & US. *Comn:* Paintings, pvt comns by Mr & Mrs Gary Davidson, N Madison, Conn, 2003, Mr & Mrs Richard Drufva, Mt Carmel, Conn, 2004, Mr & Mrs Patrick Mulski, Sandy Hook, Conn, 2004, Mr Bryan Ledyard, Old Saybrook, Conn, 2004 & Dr J P Waller, Paris, France, Mr Michael Dolomont, Killingworth, Conn, 2009, Anne Haines, Jackson, NJ, 2010, Mr Stephen Caneccasio, New York, 2010. *Exhib:* Ringling Mus Art, Sarasota, Fla, 61; Galerie Georges Moos, Geneva, Switz, 64-69; Hub Gallery, Pa State Univ, State Coll, 73; Conn Soc Fine Arts, Wadsworth Atheneum, Hartford, 74; Am Painters in Paris Exhib, France, 75-76; Berkshire Mus Fine Arts, Pittsfield, Mass, 77; Munson Gallery, New Haven, Conn, 80-83; solo exhib, Scranton Mem, Madison, Conn, 97; Wall St Gallery, Madison, Conn, 2001-03. *Pos:* Semi-retired, currently. *Teaching:* Instr, Art Asn Members & pvt lessons, 65-. *Awards:* Top Awards, Waterbury Arts Festival, Conn, 67 & 68; Winsted Award, 75 & Top Purchase Award, 79, Northwest Conn Art Asn; New Brit Mus Am Top Award, 97. *Bibliog:* Prize Winning Art, Bk 7, Allied Publ, 67. *Mem:* New Haven Paint & Clay Club (bd dir, 67-69); New Haven Festival Arts (bd dir, 71-73); Conn Acad Fine Arts. *Media:* Oil on Canvas, Collage in Mixed Media. *Dealer:* Wall St Gallery Madison CT

HARRISON, ALICE
PAINTER, COLLAGE ARTIST
b New York, NY, Nov 17, 1934. *Study:* Art Students League; Cornell Univ; NY Univ. *Work:* Johnson & Johnson Corp, NJ; Noyes Mus, NJ; Int Mus Collage, Mex; Art Colle, France; Turchin Ctr, Boone, NC; Tsank Laurenov, Plovdiv, Bulgaria. *Exhib:* Paterson Mus, NJ, 95; Jersey City Mus, NJ, 96; Bergen Mus, Paramus, NJ, 98; Arts Club of Washington, DC, 98; Pleeiades Gallery, New York, 2000; Lake City Mus, Ill, 2001; Galleries NJ, Pa, Minn, Vt, 2002; Print Spain, England, France, 2003; Graz Austria, 2003; Sergines France, 2003, Northampton Univ Vt, 2004; Lincoln Ctr, New York, 2004; Evergreen Co, Mystic, Conn, Boone, NC, New York, New Zealand, 2005; Hunterdon Mus, 2006; Albuquerque Mus; Belskie Mus; Montclair Art Mus; Broadfoot Gallery, New York, 2007; Albert Schweitzer Inst, Quinipiac Univ, Conn, 2007; Albuquerque Mus, NMex, 2008; Broadfoot Gallery, New York, 2008; NJ Arts Ann Morris Mus, NJ, 2009; NJ Print Counc, NJ, 2009, Johannesburg, S Africa; NJ Arts Ann, NJ State Mus, Belskie Mus, 2010; Solo Pieces for Peace, NJSO Arabian Nights Sketchbook Project, D & R Greenway, Princeton, NJ; Viewpoints, Newark, NJ; Seeing Trees, Blue Hill Plaza, NY; Solo Pine Gallery, 2011; Solo Atrium Gallery, 2012; Belskie Mus, NJ; Painting Ctr, NY; 73 See Gallery, Montclair, NJ, 2013; Arts in Healing, Morristown, NJ, 2013. *Pos:* Co-creator, Art Press Publ, LLD. *Teaching:* Instr, collage, home studio, currently; instr, SCAHC, Art School at OC, ACNNJ, Hunterdon Mus, Newark Mus, CCA, Bedminster, Peters Valley, MCAA. *Awards:* Skylands Select, NJ, 2002; Celebration Landscape, MD, 2003; NAWA Annual, NY, 2004; Mixed Media, Gaelen Gallery, NJ, 2006; Drawing Award, Salutetowa, NJ, 2007; Collage Award, NAWA, 2008. *Mem:* NAWA; SLMM; ISEA; Salute to Women in Arts; Painting, Printmaking, Affiliates, NJ; NY Artists Cir. *Media:* Mixed media, paint & collage. *Publ:* Contribr, Art of Layering: Making Connections, SLMM, 2003; Am Art Collector, Alcove Bks, 2004, 07; auth, Artists Guidebook to a New Creative Life; Masters: Collage. *Mailing Add:* 2 Hamilton Rd Apt 4E Morristown NJ 07960

HARRISON, CAROL LOVE
PHOTOGRAPHER, DESIGNER
b Washington, DC, 1950. *Study:* Georgetown Univ Sch For Serv, BSFS, 73; Univ Md, MFA, 83; Prof studies, Digital Imaging, 2010, St. Petersburg Polytechnical State Univ, 2011. *Hon Degrees:* Georgetown Univ, Hon BSFS, 1973. *Work:* Am Center Polish Cult; Photos of Sam Gilliam, Smithsonian Mus Int Mod & Contemp Art Arch; Ogden Mus Southern Art, US Holocaust Mus; Nat Gallery of Art, Wash DC; Corcoran Gallery of Art, Wash; Va Mus Fine Art, Richmond, Va; US Holocaust Mus Portraits of Jan Karski, Wash; Virginia Power; United Va Bank; Howrey & Simon, Wash DC; Maguire, Woods; Battle & Booth, Richmond, Va; Mississippi Mus Art; David C Diskell Ctr for the Study of Visual Arts and Culture of African Americans & the African Diasporea, Univ Md Coll, College Park, Md; Nat Mus Art, Md; Women in the Arts. *Comn:* Color Photographs, Nat Strategy Info Ctr, Wash, 2002-2004; Georgetown B&W Photographs, Swidler and Berlin, Wash, 85; 350 Yrs of Art and Archit, The Art Gallery, Univ Md, 85. *Exhib:* The Beijing Exchange Exhib, The Cult Palace, Beijing, 86; Snapshot, The Contemp Mus, Baltimore, 99-03; Moca DC's Ann Show, Mus of Contemp Art, Washington, 2000-02; The Pursuit of Excellence, Southeast Exhib at Cen Gallery, NC, 87; Kathleen Ewing Gallery, 2005; Future Studio, Los Angeles, Calif, 2007; O'Melveny & Myers, Washington, DC, 2007; Pass Gallery, Washington, DC, 2007; Masters Quartet, Photoworks, 2010; Life and Mission: Jan Karski, The Polish History Mus, Poland, 2012; Crowell & Moring, Wash DC, 2014. *Pos:* fine art photog; judge, DC Short Film Festival. *Teaching:* teacher artist workshop prog, The Va Mus of Fine Arts, 88-89; advanced portraiture lectr, No Va CC, Alexandria, Va, 90; artist Fairfax Co Coun of the Arts, Mobil Oil Corp, 90, 92; instr, The Bullis Sch, 2005-2008. *Awards:* Excellence in Photography, The Nex Juried Show, Va Mus of fine Arts, 83-85; Honorarium, Calliope, Fla Dept Cultural Affairs, 98. *Bibliog:* C-Dezinformatsia: Active Measures in Soviet Strategy, Pergamon, 84; C-The Photo Review, Nat Photographic Com, Brasseys, 86; C-The Washington Rev, 80-90; C-The Antietam Rev; C-The Washingtonian. *Mem:* Nat Mus of Women in the Arts; Corcoran Gallery of Art; Metropolitan Mus Art. *Specialty:* Fine Art Photog. *Interests:* Films, music & literature, swimming, creating artistic books. *Publ:* Washington Post; Antietam Review; Sam Gilliam and Olivia, Photographs: a Fixed Point in Time From Which a Series of Years is Reckoned, 2010-2011; Mia Mango, 2010-2011; Lillian Turns One, The Revelers; Turkiye, An Adventure, 2012; Rockne Krebs: Photographs & Interpretations; Rockne Krebs: Crystal & Star Illuminations; Los Surrealista Patos de Espana; Jan Karski, Photographs; L'Orphelin de chat Noir; Orphan & Cowboy; Yuriko Yamaguchi Photographs Sirenes Contemporaines; Olivia, Blake, and Harrison. *Dealer:* Reynolds Gallery. *Mailing Add:* 666 Live Oak Dr Mc Lean VA 22101-1569

HARRISON, CAROLE
SCULPTOR
b Chicago, Ill, Oct 30, 1933. *Study:* Cranbrook Acad Art, BFA, 55, MFA, 56; Cent Sch Art, London, with Robert Adams, Fulbright Scholar, 58. *Work:* Springfield Mus Art, Ill; Kalamazoo Inst Art; Cranbrook Mus Art; Fine Arts Complex, Western Mich Univ; Nat Mus Women Arts, Washington, DC. *Comn:* Unity and Growth (brass & copper), City Oak Park, Ill, 66; Seated Figure (cast brass), Kalamazoo Art Inst, 69; Fountain

(welded brass); Three Figures (welded brass), 72 & Motif (welded brass & copper), Western Mich Univ, 82; Friends Meet (welded brass), Cottey Coll, Nevada, Mo, 84. *Exhib:* Second Biennial Am Painting & Sculpture, Detroit Art Inst & Pa Acad Fine Arts, 59; New Horizons in Sculpture, McCormick Pl, Chicago, 61; Painting & Sculpture Today, Herron Mus Art, Indianapolis, 67; solo exhib, Women & Landscape, Kalamazoo Inst Arts, 76; Nat Acad Design Exhib,NY, 82 & 92; Sculpture Ctr, NY, 85. *Teaching:* Assoc prof sculpture, Western Mich Univ, 60-74 & State Univ NY, Fredonia, 75-78. *Awards:* Tiffany Found Fel, 60; First Prize, New Horizons in Sculpture, McCormick Pl, Chicago, 61; 161st Ann Artists Fund Prize, Nat Acad of Design, 86; Fulbright fellow, Eng, 57. *Bibliog:* Cesta Peekstok (producer), Art and Architecture in Kalamazoo (video), Western Mich Univ, 76; Marcia Wood (auth), Sculpture, Carole Harrison, Kalamazoo Col, 77; Cesta Peekstok (producer), Art is All Around Us (video), Western Mich Univ, 80; Fay L. Hendry (auth), Outdoor Sculpture in Kalamazoo, 80; Virginia N Jones (auth), Contemporary American Women Sculptors, Oryx Press, 86. *Mem:* New York Artists Equity; Nat Asn Women Artists; Sculptors Guild. *Media:* Metal, Wood. *Publ:* Auth, Building three figures, Western Mich Univ Press, 73. *Dealer:* Water Street Gallery Saugatuck MI 49453. *Mailing Add:* Box 19555 Kalamazoo MI 49019

HARRISON, HELEN AMY
MUSEUM DIRECTOR, CRITIC

b New York, NY, Dec 4, 1943. *Study:* Adelphi Univ, Garden City, NY, AB (art), 65; Brooklyn Mus Art Sch, Max Beckmann Mem scholar in sculpture, 65-66; Hornsey Coll Art, London, Eng, 66-67; Case Western Reserve Univ, Cleveland, MA (art hist), 75. *Collection Arranged:* Seven Am Women: The Depression Decade (co auth, catalog), 76; David Burliuk: Years of Transition, 1910-1931 (auth, catalog), 78; Dawn of a New Day: the 1939/40 New York World's Fair (auth, catalog), 80; Larry Rivers: Performing for the Family (auth, catalog), 83; Jimmy Ernst: A Survey, 1942-1983, 85; Crosscurrents: East Hampton and Provincetown (coauth, catalog), 86; Ibram Lassaw: A Retrospective Survey, 1929-1988 (auth, catalog), 88; En Plein Air (coauth, catalog), 89; East Hampton Avant-Garde (auth, catalog), 90; Alfonso Ossorio: The Victorias Drawings, 1950, 91; Betty Parsons: Paintings on Paper, 92; The Abstract Spirit: John Ferren, 93; Jackson Pollock: The New-Found Screen Prints, 95; Lee Krasner Drawings, 95; New Possibilities 1947/1997, 97; Photographs by Martha Holmes, 98; NOT Pollock/NOT Krasner, 2000; Pollock at 100, 2011; Memories Arrested in Space, 2012; Men of Fire, 2012; Larry Rivers: Collaborations & Appropriations, 2012. *Pos:* Cur, Parrish Art Mus, Southampton, NY, 77-78 & Guild Hall Mus, East Hampton, NY 82-90; art critic, NY Times, Long Island Weekly, 78-2006; guest cur, Queens Mus, Flushing, NY, 79-81; exec dir, Pub Art Preserv Comt, 80-82; dir, Pollock-Krasner House Study Ctr, East Hampton, NY, 90-. *Teaching:* Instr, Sch Visual Arts, 85 & 86 & State Univ NY, Stony Brook, 92 & 94. *Awards:* Acad of Distinction, Adelphi Univ Alumni Asn, 86; Media Awards, Press Club of Long Island, 86, 87. *Mem:* Int Asn Art Critics, Am Section; Am Studies Asn. *Res:* Federal art patronage projects of the New Deal era, especially mural painting; the 1939/40 New York World's Fair; contemporary American Art. *Publ:* contribr, The Figurative Fifties (exhib catalog), Newport Harbor Art Mus, 88; Remembering the future, Queens Mus, Rizzoli, 89; The American Art Book, Phaidon, 99; Such Desperate Joy: Imagining Jackson Pollock, Thunder's Mouth Press, 00; Hamptons Bohemia (coauth), Chronicle, 2002; The Jackson Pollock Box, Cider Mills Press, 2010; Subject Matter of the Artist, 2013. *Mailing Add:* 760 E Hampton Tpke Sag Harbor NY 11963-4230

HARRISON, HELEN (MAYER) & NEWTON
ENVIRONMENTAL ARTIST, CONCEPTUAL ARTIST

b New York, NY. *Study:* Helen: Queens Coll, BA; Cornell Univ; New York Univ, MA, 53; Newton: Yale, BFA, MFA, 63-65. *Work:* Brooklyn Mus; Mus Mod Art, New York & Chicago; The Pompidou Ctr, Paris; Les Abattoirs, Le Mus D'Art Mod et Contemp, Toulouse, France; The Albertina Mus, Vienna, Austria; Stanford Archives, Stanford, Calif. *Comn:* Baltimore Promenade: Two Lines of Sight and an Unexpected Connection Comprise a Promenade for Baltimore, comn by Md Inst, 81; Calif Wash: A Memorial, comn by Santa Monica Arts Coun, 88-96; Green Heart Vision, comn by Cult Coun S Holland, exhib at Jerusalem Kappel, 94; Kunst Mus, Bonn, Germany, 97; The Endangered Meadows of Europe, comn by Kunst und Austellungshalle, Bonn, Ger, 96-98; Ronald Feldman Fine Arts, 2003; The Santa Fe Drain Basin: Lessons from the Genius of Place, comn by Santa Fe Inst, 2004-; Greenhouse Britain: Losing Ground, Gaining Wisdom, UK Dept Environ, Food, and Rural Affairs, 2006; Santa Fe Watershed: Lessons From the Genius of Place, Santa Fe Art Inst, 2004. *Exhib:* Los Angeles Co Mus, 71; La Jolla Mus Art, 71; Venice Biennale, 76 & 80; Detroit Inst Arts, 76; San Francisco Mus Mod Art, 77; Whitney Mus, Downtown Space, New York, 77; Chicago Mus Art, 80; Los Angeles Inst Contemp Art, 80; Ringling Mus, Sarasota, Fla, 82; Hirshhorn Mus, Washington, DC, 83; San Jose Mus Art, Calif, 83 & 2005; The Johnson Mus, Cornell Univ, 85; Sao Paulo Biennale, 85; Grey Art Gallery, New York Univ, 87; Documenta 8, Kassel, Fed Repub Ger, 87; Maritn Gropius-Bau, Berlin, 88; Mus Mod Art, Ljubljana, Slovenia, 90; Mus Revolution, Zagreb, Croatia, 90; 2nd Int Biennale, Nagoya, Japan, 91; Kunst Mus, Bonn, Ger, 96; San Diego Mus Art, 2001; Los Angeles Mus Contemp Art, 2001; Contemp Art Ctr, Cincinnati, Ohio, 2002; Ludwig Forum Int Art, Aachen, Ger, 2002; Les Abattoirs, Mus Mod & Contemp Art, Toulouse, France, 2002; Kastell Groenevald, Baarn, Holland, 2003; Hudson River Mus, Yonkers, NY, 2004; Santa Fe Art Inst, NMex, 2005; UCLA Fowler Mus, 2006; Georgia Mus Art, Athens, 2007, Schneider Mus, Ashland, Ore, 2005; Boulder Mus Contemp Art, 2007; Greater London Authority, City Hall, London, Traveling, 2008; Kala Art Inst, Berkeley, Calif, Cardwell-Jimmerson Gallery, Culver City, Calif, Ronald Feldman Fine Arts, New York, NY, 2009, 2011; Sonoma State Univ Art Gallery, Rohnert Park, Calif, 2012; Sesnon Gallery, Univ Calif, Santa Cruz, 2013. *Pos:* Consult, Presidential Task Force Educ, Nat Endowment Arts, 79; mem, Pub Art Adv Bd, San Diego, 83-88. *Teaching:* Newton: asst prof, visual arts, Univ NMex, 65-67, Univ Calif, San Diego, La Jolla Campus, 67-93, emer & retired; Helen: Instr, lit, Univ NMex, 65-67, prof visual arts, Univ Calif, San Diego, La Jolla Campus, 80-94, emer & retired; rsch prof, Univ Calif Santa Cruz, 2011-. *Awards:* DAAD Fel, Berlin, 88 & 89; 2nd Prize, Nagoya Biennale, 92; Greenevald Prize, Netherlands, 2001; Dept Environment, Food & Rural Affairs Grant, Greenhouse Britain: Losing Ground Gaining Wisdom, 2006; Awe Inspring award for Arts & the Environment, Chartered Inst Water & Environmental Mgmt in Assn with the Ctr for Contemporary Art and the Natural World, CIWEM Annual Dinner, 2010. *Bibliog:* Lagoon Cycle, Carter Radcliff (auth), catalog essay & Michel de Certeau (auth), catalog essay, 85; Peter Selz (auth), Helen and Newton Harrison: Art as survival instruction, 130, Vol 52, No 6, Arts Mag, 2/85; Arlene Raven (ed), Art in the public interest, Univ Mich Press, 89; Kim Levin (auth), Helen and Newton Harrison: New Grounds for Art, Vol 52, No 6, Arts Mag, 2/92; Craig Adcock (auth), Conversational drift-Helen Mayer Harrison and Newton Harrison, 35-45, Vol 51, No 2, Art J, summer 92; Timothy Murray (auth), Like a Film: Ideological Fantasy on Screen Camera and Canvas (chap), Routledge, London, 94; David Raskin (auth), Jetties and Lagoons (chap), Tracing Cultures-Art Hist, Criticism & Critical Fiction, Whitney Mus Am Art, New York, 95; Charles Green (auth), The Third Hand: Collaboration in Art from Conceptualism to Postmodernism (chap), Univ Minn Press, 2001; Davina Thackera (auth), Nurturing Nature, Peninsula Europe, Pub Art J, 4/2001; Eleanor Heartney (auth), Mapping a better world, Art in Am, 10/2003; Jon Hughes (auth), What if Life Imitated Art? (pages 32-37), Ecologist, 12-1/2008; Erika Yarrow (auth), Wise Words II, Water and Environment Mag 13, No 2, 2008; Jane Ingram Anon (auth), A Marriage Made on Earth: Helen Mayer Harrison and Newton Harrison, II Public Art Jour, 38, 2008; Peter Selz (auth), Mapping a Better World, The Berkeley Daily Planet, 2009; Leah Ollman Art Review: Newton and Helen Mayer Harrison at Carowell-Jimmerson, LA Times, 2009; Lucy Lippard (auth), An Insurmountable Opportunity, Public Art Review 40; Cathy Lebowitz (auth) Newton Harrison and Helon Mayor Harrison, Art in America, Vol 97, No 5, 2009; Dewitt Chen (auth), The Angry Blue Planet, East Bay Express, 2009; Frank Cebulski (auth), Helen Mayer Harrison and Newton Harrison at Kala Art Inst Gallery, Berkeley Examiner, 2010; Megan Bainum, Professor Connects Global Issues and Art, Utah Statesman, 2010; Nathalie Blanc (auth), Ecoplasties, Helen et Newton Harrison: Penser Notre Future Globalment, Paris, 2011; Yates McKee (auth), Helen Mayer-Harrison and Newton Harrison, Ronald Feldman Fine Arts, Artforum XLIX No 8, 2011; Elmar Zorn (auth), Die Kunst in Der Nature: Eine Almanz Fur Unsere Zukunft, Artprofile, 2011; Transdiscourse 1: Mediated Environments, Helen and Newton Harrison in Conversation with Brandon Ballengee, ed Juanita Schlapfer-Miller, 2011; Amanda Boetzkes (auth), West of Center: Art and The Counterculture Experiment in America, 1965-77, Unn Minn Press, 2011; Sacha Kagan (auth), Art and Sustainability, Transcript Verlag, Biffeld Ger, Helen and Newton Harrison, 2011; Leonardo, cover article, MIT Press, 2012; Charles Gargoian, Sustaining Sustainabililty, Jour Article in Studies Art Edn, 2012; Susan Wentraub (auth), To Life, Eco-Art in Pursuit of Sustaible Planet, 2012. *Media:* Mixed Media. *Publ:* Illusr, One full work and part of another, 12/77-1/78 & Great Lakes Meditations, summer 79, New Wilderness Lett, New York; auth, The Book of the Grab, In: Dialogue, Discourse, Research, Santa Barbara Mus Art, 79; The Book of the Seven Lagoons, Limited Eds Artists Bk, 85; A Lattice or a Serpentine, Seattle Arts Lett, 92; cover illusr, Leonardo 26, 93; Jane Ingram Allen (auth), How Big is Here, (pages 49-53), Sculpture Mag, 12/07. *Dealer:* Ronald Feldman Fine Arts 31 Mercer St New York NY 10013. *Mailing Add:* 417 Linden St Santa Cruz CA 95062-1023

HARRISON, JAN
PAINTER, SCULPTOR

b West Palm Beach, Fla, 44. *Study:* Univ Ga, Athens, BFA, 67; Wright State Univ, Ohio, 72; Int Inst Experimental Printmaking, Calif, 74; San Jose State Univ, MA, 76. *Work:* Samuel Dorsky Mus Art, New Paltz, NY; Cincinnati Art Mus; Wexner Ctr for Visual Arts, Ohio State Univ, Columbus; Arco Ctr for Visual Arts, Los Angeles; Women's Studio Workshop, Rosendale, NY. *Comn:* structure, Divining House, Alan Baer (architect), Contemp Arts Ctr, Fed Res Plaza, Cincinnati, 86. *Exhib:* Solo Exhibs: Montalvo Ctr for Arts, Saratoga, Calif, 78; Animal Wishes/Animal Desires, CAGE Gallery, Cincinnati, 1981; Emerging Talent (ten solo exhibs); Wright State Univ, Dayton, Ohio, 82; Chidlaw Gallery, Cincinnati, 88; Nancy Moore Fine Art, New York, 96; Chaosmos, Kleinert/James Arts Ctr, Woodstock, NY, 2001; Sentient Animals, Gallery at R & F, Kingston, NY, 2005; Bestial Beings (retrospective), Cabaret Voltaire Art Ctr, Poughkeepsie, NY, 2007, Divinanimality, Drew Univ, Madison, NJ, 2011, Wired Gallery, Hich Falls, NY, 2013, Piermont Straus Gallery, Piermont, NY, 2014, Visceral Voices, Word & Image Gallery, Bright Hill Literary Ctr, Treadwell, NY, 2015; Group Exhibs: Hudson Valley Artists: Myth, Spirituality, and Culture, College Art Gallery, SUNY New Paltz, NY, 1991; Animal-Anima-Animus (traveling), Mus Voor Moderne Kunst, Arhhem, Holland, 98, Porin Taidemuseo, Pori, Finland, 98, PS1 Contemp Art Center, NY, 99, Winnipeg Art Gallery, Winnipeg, Can, 2000; Making Their Mark, Cincinnati Art Mus, 2003, Aviary: A Group Show Curated by Elizabeth Ennis, Elevator Gallery at the Catskill Art Soc., Livingston Manor, NY, 2015; Ideas Into Objects: Reinterpreting the Notebooks of Leonard da Vinci, Alice F and Harris K Weston Art Gallery, Aronoff Ctr for Arts, Cincinnati, 2005; Encaustic Works: 2005, Samuel Dorsky Mus, New Paltz, NY, 2005; 7+14, Kleinert James Art Ctr, Woodstock, NY, 2006; Beyond Self, Contemp Exploration in Art & Spirit Muroff Kotler Visual Arts Gallery, SUNY Ulster, Stone Ridge, NY, 2007; The Sparky Show, Schroeder Romero/Winkleman Gallery, New York, 2008; Talking Tongues & Other Organs, Soup Kitchen Series Kleinert James Art Ctr, Woodstock, NY, 2009; Body, Line, Motion, Selection from the Permanent Collection, Samuel Dorsky Mus Art, New Paltz, NY, 2010; Marks That Matter, Muroff Kotler Visual Arts Gallery, SUNY Ulster, Stone Ridge, NY, 2010; The Dream of the Red Chamber invitational, White Box, New York, 2007; Mus Mission & Meaning, Selections from the collections Samuel Dorsky Mus Art, New Paltz, NY, 2007; Standing Heat, The Front Gallery, New Orleans, LA, 2010; Peaceable Kingdom, DVAA, Narrowsburg, NY, 2011; Transcendental Freakout, Remote, Barcelona, Spain, 2011; Animals People, A Shared Environment, Pop Gallery, Brisbane, 2011; Animal Exchange, O + Festival, Kingston, NY, 2011; Dear Mother Nature, Samuel Dorsky Mus Art, New Paltz, NY, 2012; Other than Human, Kingston Mus Contemp Art, Kingston, NY, 2012; The Animals Look Back at Us, Kleinert James Art Ctr, Woodstock, NY, 2013; The Animals Look Back at Us, Williamsburg Art & Historical Ctr, Brooklyn, NY, 2013. *Collection Arranged:* Emerging Talent, Wright State Univ, Dayton, Ohio, 82; New Work, First San Jose

Biennial, San Jose Inst Contemp Art, Calif, 86; 1987 Ohio Selection-Graphics, Dayton Art Inst, Ohio, 87; Object, Image, Icon, Cont. Art Ctr, Adelaide, Australia, 88; New Acquisitions, Cincinnati Art Mus, 89, Making Their Mark, 2003; Definitive Am Cont. Quilt, Bernice Steinbaum Gallery, 90; Museum, Mission and Meaning, Samuel Dorsky Mus, 2006. *Pos:* Mem artists adv com, Contemp Arts Ctr, Cincinnati, 87-88; panelist, Ohio Arts Coun, Columbus, 91, Dutchess Co Arts Coun, NY State Coun on Arts, 97-98; membership dir, Women's Studio Workshop, 92-93. *Teaching:* Vis asst prof painting, Antioch Col, Yellow Springs, Ohio, 86-87; adj lectr painting, Marist Coll, Poughkeepsie, NY, 99-2005. *Awards:* Individual Artist Fels, Ohio Arts Coun, 83, 85 & 88; Ohio Arts Coun New Works Grant, 86; Summerfair Aid to Individual Artist Grant, 89. *Bibliog:* Linda Weintraub (auth), In the Making: Creative Options for Contemporary Art, DAP distributed Art Pub, New York, 2003; Paul Smart (auth), Painting In The Language of Animals, Ulster Pub, 11/17/2005; Linda Weintraub and Marketta Seppälä (auths), Animal Anima Animus, Finland, 1998; Singing in Animal Tongues: An Inner Journey; Paj: A Journal of Performance and Art, NY. *Mem:* Women's Studio Workshop. *Media:* Pastel, encaustic, clay, wax. *Res:* Contemp investigation of the animal & human interface. *Interests:* Animals, animal communication, philos, ecology & theology. *Publ:* Betty Collings (auth), Ten Solo Exhibitions (catalog, essay), Wright State Univ, Dayton, Ohio, 1982; The Definitive American Contemporary Quilt, 90; Animal, Anima, Animus, Pori Contem Art Mus, Frame Publ, 98; Arcana Mundi (auth), Jan Harrison: Selected Works, Station Hill, Barrytown, NY, 1979-2000; Encaustic Works, Samuel Dorsky Mus, 2005; The Animals Look Back at Us, Sara Lynn Henry, 2013. *Mailing Add:* 34 Hunter St Kingston NY 12401-6022

HARRISON, JIMMIE
JEWELER, CRAFTSMAN

b Shiprock, NMex, Feb 4, 1952. *Study:* Univ NMex, 71-73; Acad Arts, Paris, France, 76. *Work:* Heard Mus, Phoenix, Ariz; Wheelwright Mus, Santa Fe, NMex; Northern Ariz Mus, Flagstaff; Squash Blossoms, Vail, Colo. *Comn:* Gold buckle, watchband & bolo tie, Toh-Atin Gallery, Durango, Colo, 84. *Exhib:* All Navajo Show, Northern Ariz Mus, Flagstaff, 81, 87 & 88; Santa Fe Indian Market, NMex, 84, 85, 87 & 88; Indian Arts & Crafts Asn, Denver, Colo, 84 & 88; Gallup Ceremonials, Red Rock State Park, Gallup, NMex, 87 & 88; Northern Pueblo Show, San Idelfonso, NMex, 88; Heard Mus, Phoenix, Ariz, 88; Palm Springs Indian Art Show, Palm Springs, Calif, 88; Gallery of Functional Art, Santa Monica, Calif, 88. *Awards:* Best of Show, All Navajo Show, Northern Ariz Mus, 81; Best of Show, Navajo Nation Fair, 81; Best in Class & Design, Northern Pueblo Show. *Bibliog:* Article, Aspen Times, 2/84; Off hours, Farmington Daily Times, Farmington, NMex, 4/86. *Mem:* Indian Arts & Crafts Asn; Am Crafts Coun & Enterprises. *Media:* Gold, Silver. *Dealer:* Christophers Enterprises PO Box 25621 Albuquerque NM 87125; Packards 61 Old Santa Fe Trail Santa Fe NM 87501. *Mailing Add:* Victoria Price Art & Design 1512 Pacheo St Bldg B Suite 102 Santa Fe NM 87505

HARRISON, MYRNA J
PAINTER, INSTRUCTOR

b Hollywood, Calif, Jan 31, 1932. *Study:* Hans Hofmann Sch Fine Art, NYC & Provincetown, Mass, 1953-57; NY Univ, NYC, with Philip Guston, BA, MA, 1959-60; Univ Calif, Berkeley, 1960-64. *Work:* Brandeis Univ Rose Art Mus, Waltham, Mass; Cape Cod Mus Art, Dennis, Mass; Provincetown Art Assoc & Mus, Mass; Phoenix Art Mus, Ariz; and many more throughout the US & Canada. *Comn:* Triptych of Boulder Mountains, Idaho, Elmer Johnson, Chicago Ill, 2003. *Exhib:* Retrospective, Provincetown Art Asn & Mus, 2012; Juried Group Shows, Provincetown Art Assoc & Mus, Mass, 1952-57; Int Watercolor Show, Brooklyn Art Mus, NY, 1953; Juried Group Shows, Cape Cod Mus Art, Dennis, Mass, 1954-56; Juried Group Shows, Staten Island Mus, NY, 1955-57; Raft - A Grand Canyon Landscape Exhib, Scottsdale Mus Contemp Art, Ariz, 1983; Ariz Paintings, Coconino Ctr Arts, Flagstaff, Ariz, 1995; Desertscapes, James Ratliff Gallery, Sedona, Ariz, 2001, Desertscapes 2, 2002, Desertscapes: 2004-2005, 2005, New Works, 2007, Desertscapes: 2008-2010, 2010, From East to West, Fifty Plus Years of Painting, 2012; Ocean & Desert, Gallery Ehva, Provincetown, Mass, 2011, Sixty Years of Drawing, 2012, Recent Work, 2013; Sixty Years of Painting, Beauregard Fine Art, NJ, 2012; North East by South West: The Lively Landscapes of Myrna Harrison, 2012; The Western Work-1960-2013, Desert Caballeros Western Mus, Wickenburg, Ariz, 2013. *Pos:* dean, San Jose City Col, Calif, 76-80; pres, Rio Salado Col, Phoenix, Ariz, 80-85; pres, Gateway Col, Phoenix, Ariz, 85-87; pres, Phoenix Col, Phoenix, Ariz, 87-92; interim dir, Desert Caballeros Western Mus, Wickenburg, Ariz, 1996-97. *Teaching:* vis art painting, Vermont Studio Ctr, Johnson, 2004-2005, lectr/teacher, Provincetown Art Asn and Mus, 2009-2012, Scottsdale Mus Contemp Art, 2004-2009. *Awards:* Hans Hofmann Found, 2012. *Bibliog:* Betsy Dillard Stroud, Abstract Art and the Gleb J Fracks Factor, Int Artist, Oct/Nov 1988; Open Portfolio: Myrna Harrison, Sedona Monthly, 9/2005; 2006 Art/Architecture Tour, Sedona Monthly, 5/2006; Andre Van der Wende (auth), Northeast by Southwest: the Lively Landscape of Myrna Harrison, Cape Cod Time, 6/29/12; Sebastian Smee (auth) Two Provincetown Exhibs that Rise Above, Boston Globe, 6/6/12; Lillian Orlowsky (auth), A Life in Art, Lillian Orlowsky Catalog, 2007. *Mem:* Asian Arts Council Phoenix Art Mus, Ariz (bd mem 2006-09); Desert Caballeros Western Mus, Wickenburg, Ariz (bd mem 1997-2001); Scottsdale Mus Contemp Art, Ariz; Provincetown Art Assoc & Mus, Mass; Nat Mus Women in Arts, Wash, DC. *Media:* All Media. *Publ:* auth, William Freed: A Disciplined Passion for Art, William Freed Catalog, 2003. *Dealer:* Acme Fine Art and Design 38 Newbury St Boston MA 02116; Beauregard Fine Art 109 E River Rd Rumson NJ 07760; James Ratliff Gallery 431 Hwy 179 Sedona, AZ 86336. *Mailing Add:* PO Box 3139 Wickenburg AZ 85358

HARRISON, RACHEL
SCULPTOR, PHOTOGRAPHER

b New York, NY 1966. *Work:* Solomon R Guggenheim Mus, Met Mus Art, Whitney Mus Am Art & Mus Mod Art, New York; Carnegie Mus Art, Pittsburgh; LA Mus Contemp Art. *Exhib:* Solo exhibs, Should Home Windows, Arena Gallery, Brooklyn, 96, Look of Dress-Separates, Greene Naftali Gallery, New York City, 97 & If I Did It, 2007, Brides & Bases, Oakville Galleries, Can, 2002, Posh Floored as Ali G Tackles Beck, Galerie Arndt & Partner, 2004, Car Stereo Parkway, Transmission Gallery, Glasgow, 2005, When Hangover Becomes Form, Contemp Art Gallery, Vancouver & LA Contemp Exhibs, 2006, Voyage of the Beagle, Migros Mus, Zurich, 2007; The Neurotic Art Show, Four Walls Gallery, Bklyn, NY, 91; Open Bar, Flamingo East, New York, 91; Simply Made in America, Aldrich Mus Contemp Art, Ridgefield, Conn, 92; 1920: The Subtlety of Subversion, The Continuity of Intervention, Exit Art, New York, 93, Poverty Pop: The Aesthetics of Necessity, 93; Pre-Existing Condition, The Puffin Room, New York, 94; Looky Loo, Sculpture Center, New York Dark Room, Stark Gallery, New York, 95; Facing the Millennium: The Song Remains the Same, Arlington Mus, Tex, 96; Post Hoc, Stark Gallery, New York, 96; Sculpture Incorporating Photography, Feature Inc, New York, 96; Summer Exhib, Greene Naftali Gallery, New York, 96, Super Freaks: Post Pop & The New Generation, 98, Free Coke, 99, Trailer, 2000, Pictures, 2002, American Idyll, 2004, The Jeweleigha Set, 2005, Motore Immobile, 2006; Space, Mind, Place, Andrea Rosen Gallery, New York, 96, The New God, 97; Paper Trail, Pierogi, 2000, Bklyn, NY, 97; Answer Yes, No, Or Don't Know, Andrew Kreps Gallery, New York, 99, Photography About Photography, 2000; Greater New York, PS1 Contemp Art Center, Long Island City, NY, 2000, Building Structures, 2002; Walker Evans & Co, Mus Mod Art, New York, 2000; Whitney Biennial, Whitney Mus Am Art, New York, 2002, 2008; The Structure of Survival, Venice Bienale, 2003; Of Mice & Men, Berlin Biennale, KW Inst Contemp Art, Berlin, 2006; The Uncertainty of Objects & Ideas, Hirshhorn Mus, Washington, 2006; For the People of Paris, Sutton Lane Gallery, Paris, 2007; 53rd Int Art Exhib Biennale, Venice, 2009. *Media:* Miscellaneous Media. *Mailing Add:* c/o Greene Naftali Gallery 526 W 26th St New York NY 10001

HARRISON, TONY
PAINTER, EDUCATOR

b Eng, Aug 18, 1931; US citizen. *Study:* Northern Polytech Eng; Chelsea Sch Art, London; Cent Sch Arts & Crafts, London. *Work:* Aldrich Mus Contemp Art, Ridgefield, Conn; Achenbach Found, Calif Palace Legion Hon, San Francisco; Arts Coun Gt Brit, London; Royal Collection, Stockholm, Sweden; Nat Gallery S Australia; and many others. *Exhib:* Solo exhibs, San Francisco Mus Art, 64, Bertha Shaefer Gallery, NY, 68-69, 72 & 74 & Soho Ctr Visual Artists, NY, 77; Third Int Biennial Print Exhib, Taiwan, 87; Nat Inst Arts & Lett, NY, 73; Wood, Anita Shapolsky Gallery, NY, 90; and others. *Pos:* Printmaking Workshop, NY, 74-75. *Teaching:* Instr drawing & printmaking, Columbia Univ, 71-94; sr lectr painting, NY Univ, 72. *Awards:* Nat Endowment Arts Grant, 75; Creative Artists Pub Serv Grant, 76; Fel, NJ State Coun Arts, 87. *Bibliog:* Robert Erskine (producer), Artists proof (film), St Georges Gallery, 57; Collectors Choice, produced on ITV, London, 62. *Media:* Acrylic, Mezzotint. *Mailing Add:* 106 Hopkins Ave Jersey City NJ 07306

HARRITY, GAIL M
MUSEUM DIRECTOR

b Rosemont, Pa. *Study:* Boston Univ, BA (Sociology), 1973; Yale Sch Mgt, Masters (Public & Private Mgt), 1982. *Pos:* Spec Asst to President & Asst Treas & Chief of Budget, Planning, Govt Relations, Metrop Mus Art, New York, 1982-1989; deputy dir finance & admin, Guggenheim Mus, 1989-95; proj dir, Guggenheim Mus Bilboa, 1995-96; CEO, Philadelphia Mus Art, 1997-2008, interim CEO, Philadelphia Mus Art, 2008-2009 & pres, 2009-. *Awards:* Eisenhower Fel, 2002. *Mem:* Parkway Coun Found Board Mem; Greater Philadelphia Cult Alliance Board Mem; Philadelphia Conv & Visitors Bur Board Mem; Int House Board Mem; Am Assoc Mus Board Mem; Int Coun Mus Board Mem; Yale Sch Mgt Board of Advs Mem. *Mailing Add:* Philadelphia Mus Art 26th St & Benjamin Franklin Parkway Philadelphia PA 19130

HARROFF, WILLIAM CHARLES BRENT
CONCEPTUAL ARTIST, ILLUSTRATOR

b Elkhart, Ind, Nov 20, 1953. *Study:* Purdue Univ, BA, 78; Ind Univ, MLS, 81; ISBK, Salzburg, Austria, under Luis Murschetz, dipl, 83. *Work:* Franklin Furnace, NY Pub Libr, NY; Victoria & Albert Mus, London, Eng; Artpool, Budapest, Hungary; Lovejoy Libr, Southern Ill Univ, Edwardsville, Ill. *Comn:* Electronic Designs, Ill OCLC Users Group, 2001; Electronic Designs, Lewis & Clark Libr System, 2002. *Exhib:* Group 90, Vasarely Mus, Budapest, Hungary, 91; Artists Book Works, Ill Art Gallery, Chicago, 93; Artists' Books & Art, Pratt Manhattan Gallery, NY, 93; solo exhibs, New Harmony Gallery Contemp Art, Ind, 97, William Harroff: Pictures & Books, Books & Pictures, Arts Iowa City, 2000, Ebooks, McKendree Col, Lebanon, Ill, 2001, Southwestern Ill Coll, 2010; Third Int Artists' Book Exhib, King St Stephen Mus, Oskola,Hungary; Second Int Artists' Book Triennial Vilnius 00, Contemp Art Ctr, Akademija Gallery, Vilnius, Lithuania; Imagining the Book, Bibliotheca Alexandrina, Alexandria, Egypt, 2002; Future of the Book, Cairns Convention Centre, Cairns, Australia, 2003; Exlibris in Chengdu, Sichuan Exlibris Asn, Sichuan, China, 2003; The Spines that Bind, Buddy Holly Mus, Lubbock, Tex, 2003; Sea Words, Wexford Arts Centre, Wexford, Ireland, 2003; Mobilivre, Bookmobile Project, Traveling Exhib, Eastern Can & Northeast US, 2004; Readers Art 5, Susan Hensel Gallery, Minneapolis, Minn, 2005; 1st Int Book Arts Symposium, Cairo, Egypt, 2009; Nat touring exhib, All of Us or None - Responses and Resistance to Militarism (Am Friends Serv Comt), 2014-16. *Pos:* Staff writer & illusr, Art St Louis, 86-91; mem bd dir, Madison Co Arts Coun, Edwardsville, Ill, 86-91, St Louis Volunteer Lawyers & Accountants for Arts, 91-; assoc ed, Int Journal of the Book, 2004-; keynote speaker, Guadalajara, Mex Book Fair, 2008; Keynote speaker, Campus Marketing Expo, Orlando, 2009; art residency, New Pacific Studio at Mount Bruce, New Zealand, 2014. *Teaching:* Librn archit, Okla State Univ, 81-84; artist illus, ISBK, Salzburg, Austria, 84-85; vis artist, Madison Co Arts Coun, Edwardsville, Ill, 85-90 & Fine Arts Inst, Wash Univ, St Louis, 95; librn, McKendree Univ, Lebanon, Ill, 97-. *Awards:* Art Matters Inc Fel, 92; Regional Artists Proj Grant, Nat Endowment Arts, 93; Arts Midwest Nat Endowment Arts Fel, 95; First Prize Postcard Art Competition/Exhib '99, Wauconda, Ill, 99; First Prize Scrolling the Page Competition, Am Print Alliance, Peachtree City, Ga, 99; Ill First Grant, E-T Tech Fund, 2000; Ill First Grant, E-T Tech Fund, 2000 & 2002; Planting the Seed Grant, LCLS/LSTA, 2001; First Prize, P22

Fonts in Use, 2002; Int Artist Travel Award, Ill Arts Coun, 2003; Technos Int Award, Tanaka Ikueikai Educ Trust, Tokyo, Japan, 2006; Japan found Grant, Arts & Cult, 2006. *Bibliog:* USA/USSR Calligraphia, Int Typeface Corp, 91; Bess Liebenson (auth), What is a book, NY Times, 6/5/94; Bess Liebenson (auth), On Beyond the Book, Forum For Contemporary Art, 95; In a snowglobe, Contemporary Impressions, Fall, 2000; Martha Hellion (auth), Artist's Books: Ulises Carrion. D.A.P., 2003. *Mem:* Chicago Artists' Coalition; Ctr Book Arts; Art St Louis; Minn Ctr Book Arts. *Media:* Book Art. *Res:* Electronic bks and literacy. *Interests:* Comic art, book art, digital art, conceptual art. *Publ:* Auth, Ill artists overcoming disabilities, Chicago Artists Coalition, 93; auth & illusr, Artists overcoming disabilities, Chicago Artists' News, 9/92; Artists overcoming disabilities, Art Papers, 3/93; Dealing with disabilities, Art Calendar, 2/94; contribr with Charlotte Johnson, (r)Evolutionary (e) Books Website, McKendree Col, 2000-2003; auth, A Road Less Traveled, Afterimage, 11, 11-12/2001; co-auth with Charlotte Johnson, (r)Evolutionary (e)Books, William Harroff Studios & Shypoke Press, 2002; co-auth, (r)EVOLUTIONARY (b)OOKS Model, Intl Journal of the Book, 2004; The New Art of Making Books, netConnect/Libr Jour, Chicago, 8-12, spring/2006. *Dealer:* Towata Gallery PO Box 675 206 W Third Alton IL 62002. *Mailing Add:* 453 Cass Ave Edwardsville IL 62025

HARROUN, DOROTHY SUMNER
PAINTER, GRAPHIC ARTIST
b El Paso, Tex, Nov 29, 1935. *Study:* With Roderick Mead, 44-53; Univ NMex, BFA; Univ Paris, France (Fulbright Scholar), 57; Univ Colo, MFA, 60; with Peter Hurd, 63. *Work:* Univ Colo Fine Arts Mus, Boulder; Mus Fine Arts, Carlsbad, NMex; Nat Conf Women (albums), Nat Mus Women in Arts, Washington, DC; NMex State Capitol; Nat Mus of Women in the Arts. *Comn:* mural, Sandia Mountains, comn by Jon ver Ploegh, Albuquerque, 77; oil portrait, Barbara Blackwell, 2011; oil portrait, Bill Blackwell, 2012. *Exhib:* Group Exhibs: Gondolier Gallery, Boulder, Colo, 61; Art Mus, Coos Bay, Ore, 80; Church Farm House Mus, London, Eng, 88; Governor's Gallery, State Capitol, Santa Fe, NMex, 88; New Eng Fine Art Asn, Boston, Mass, 93; Masterworks Shows, Albuquerque, NMex, 2000; St Johns Col, Santa Fe, 2008; Solo Exhibs: Macey Fine Arts Center, Socorro, NMex, 83; 12th Ann Int Biog Centres, Int Arts Congress, Budapest, Hungary, 85; Rathaus Kelkheim, Frankfurt, Ger, 87; St John's Coll, Santa Fe, 91; Eleftheira Gallery, Santa Fe, 97; United World Coll, Montezuma, NMex, 2001; Back Street Bistro Gallery, Santa Fe, 2006; El Paso Mus Art, El Paso, Tex, 87; New Eng Fine Art Asn, Nat Juried Show, Boston, Mass, 93; Juried Show, Carlsbad Mus Art, 2004; San Taos Gallery, Santa Fe, 2006; and many others. *Pos:* Art dir, Wood-Reich Advert Agency, Boulder, Colo, 60-61. *Teaching:* Instr, Univ Colo, 61-62, San Francisco State Coll, 63-65, Art Ctr Sch, Albuquerque, 75-79, Sanado Group, Sandia Base, Albuquerque, 78-80 & Univ NMex, 80-81. *Awards:* First Place Painting, Ouray Nat Show, Colo, 78; First Prize Watercolor, Carlsbad Area Art Asn, Carlsbad Fine Arts Mus, 80 & Black Canyon Nat Art Show, Hotchkiss, Colo, 80; Lobo Award of Distinction, Univ NMex, 2000. *Mem:* Nat League Am Penwomen (pres Albuquerque branch, 82-84); Signature mem, NMex Watercolor Soc (pres 85-86); Artists Equity Asn (pres Albuquerque chap & mem nat bd, 77-79); Albuquerque United Artists (mem bd, 78-80); Am Asn Univ Women (State Cult chmn, 80-84); Univ NMex Fine Arts Alumni Bd (pres, 89-91); Santa Fe Concert Asn (bd mem, 2001-12). *Media:* Tempera, Watercolor; Oil, Pen & Ink. *Interests:* Gardening, stamp collecting, languages. *Publ:* Auth & illusr, Take Time to Play and Listen, Chapman Press, 63; Phun-y Physics, Living Vine Press, 75; illusr, Mini Walks on the Mesa, 89. *Mailing Add:* 1365 Thunder Ridge Santa Fe NM 87501

HART, ALLEN M
PAINTER, EDUCATOR
b New York, NY, June 12, 1925. *Study:* Art Students League, with Anne Goldthwaite, Frank Vincent Dumond & Jean Liberte; Brooklyn Mus Art Sch, with Vincent Candell; Morelia, Mex with Alfredo Zalce. *Work:* Butler Inst Am Art, Youngstown, Ohio; Univ Mass, Amherst; Slater Mem Mus, Norwalk, Conn; Children's Aid Soc, New York; Union Am Hebrew Congregations; George Biddle Coll; Harry Ransom Ctr for Arts and Humanities, Austin, Tex, 2008; Rare Book Art Collection; Andrew J Mangravite Chemical Heritage Found, 2012. *Exhib:* Cober Gallery, 66-70; Solo Exhibs: Visual Arts Ctr, 70, Boiborik Gallery, 76, NJ Cult Arts Ctr, 78, Broome Street Gallery, 92; Joseph & Betty Harlem Gallery; Lerner Heller Gallery, 73; Visual Arts Ctr, 74-90; Flat Rockbrook's Wildlife Exhib, 92; Multimedia Arts Gallery, 92; S Presb Church Gallery, 98; Arrowwood Conv Ctr, 98; Art Int, Javits Ctr, 98; Works on Paper Exhib, Park Ave Armory, 98; Westchester Arts Coun Gala, 99-2000; Am Festival Art, Sulmona, Italy, 2000; Collectors Exhib, Rockland Ctr Arts, Nyack, NY, 2000; retrospective Atelier A/E, New York, 2000; Hudson Rivergal Conservators, 2001; Westchester Community Coll, Valhalla, NY, 2002; Rockland Ctr Arts, Nyack, NY, 2003; Nat Arts Club, New York, 2004; Upstream Gallery, New York, 98-2005; Butler Hall Gallery, Fordham Univ, 2005; Upstream Gallery, 2006-2012; Dalet Gallery, Philadelphia, Pa, 2011; Blue Door Gallery, Yonkers, 2012; Dalet, 2012; Upstream, 2014; Scarsdale Art Assn, Book Art, 2014. *Teaching:* Instr painting, Samuel Field YMHA & YWHA, Little Neck, NY, 62-68; dir painting, Visual Arts Ctr, 68-92, adminr, 92-; dean visual arts, Union Am Hebrew Congregations, 70-85, resident artist, 72-; art consult, Bd Coop Educ Serv, 71-; art consult, Children's Aid Soc, New York, painting instr adult dept; dir visual arts Childrens Aid Soc. *Awards:* Merit Scholarship, Brooklyn Mus Art Sch; Hammond Mus Award, Westchester, NY, 2002. *Bibliog:* New York Illustrated, NBC-TV, 70; illusr, Allen M Hart, In Retrospect, 1965-1999, Rattapallax Pubs; video documentary with CD-ROM, Life and Works of Allen M Hart, 2000. *Mem:* Life mem Art Students League; Artists Equity Asn; Katonah Art Mus Asn; Gallery on the Hudson; Rivertown Arts Coun; Westchester Arts Coun. *Media:* Oil, Mixed Media. *Interests:* art, art history, historical research. *Publ:* Auth, articles, Lower Manhattan Twp, 2/20/71 & Herald, 5/1/71; articles, NY Times, Art Digest, Berkshire Fine Arts, CSA Jour, 2009; Philadelphia Inquirer, 2011; Broad St Review, 2012; Carrier Pigeon Mag, 2013. *Dealer:* Atelier Gallery NY. *Mailing Add:* 105 Beacon Hill Dr Dobbs Ferry NY 10522

HART, HEATHER
INSTALLATION SCULPTOR
Exhib: Counterpoint, St Petersburg Art Ctr, Fla, 2005; Boredom: I Learned It By Watching You, Portland Art Ctr, Ore, 2006; The Feminine Mystique, Jersey City Mus, NJ, 2007; Neo-Constructivism: Art, Architecture, Activism, Paul Robeson Galleries, Rutgers Univ, NJ, 2008; The New Numinous Negro, Mus Mod Art PS1 Art Ctr, 2010. *Pos:* Designer asst, StoughIt, Seattle, 1998-2000; artist-in-residence, Seattle Ctr, 1998-99, Santa Fe Art Inst, 2006, Franconia Sculpture Park, Minn, 2010; vis artist, Cornish Coll Arts, 2004; asst to Deborah Willis, 2008 & Martha Rosler, 2009. *Teaching:* Asst instr, Seattle Arts Acad, Wash, 1995-97; fac, Cornish Coll Arts, Seattle, 1999, Brearley Sch, Nwe York, 2005, Rutgers Univ, NJ, 2007-08; vis artist instr, Long Island City High Sch, 2007. *Awards:* Skowhegan Sch Fel, 2006; Joan Mitchell Found Grant, 2006; Emerging Artist Fel, Socrates Sculpture Park, 2006; NY Found Arts Fel, 2009. *Bibliog:* Meieli Sawyer Detoni (auth), Out on a Limb - Treesweaters, Thread, 4/28/2006; Jerry Saltz (auth), Yurts and Stalagmites: Outdoor sculpture as more than decorative object or propaganda tool, Village Voice, 10/11/2006; Holland Cotter (auth), United Black Girls, NY Times, 3/30/2007

HART, KIMBERLEY
SCULPTOR
Study: Univ Calif, Davis, BA, 1992; RI Sch Design, MFA (sculpture), 1996. *Exhib:* She's so crafty...and so is he sometimes, White Columns, New York, 2002; Playground, Inst for Contemp Art, Portland, Maine, 2002; Better Homes and Gardens, Zoller Gallery, Pa State Univ, 2003; Terrarium, Bronx River Art Ctr, NY, 2003. *Pos:* Artist-in-residence, Fine Arts Work Ctr, Provincetown, Mass, 2000-01, McDowell Colony, NH, 2001, McColl Ctr for Visual Art, Charlotte, NC, 2005. *Awards:* Robert Motherwell Endwoed Fel, 2000; Myron Stout Endowed Fel, 2001; NY Found Arts Fel, 2009. *Bibliog:* Hank Hoffman (auth), Home is Where the Art is, New Haven Advocate, 7/20/2000; Chris Thompson (auth), Extended Play, Portland Phoenix, 6//6/2002; Holland Cotter (auth), Sampling Brooklyn, Keeper of Eclectic Flames, NY Times, 1/23/2004

HARTAL, PAUL
PAINTER, WRITER
b Szeged, Hungary, Apr 25, 1936; Can citizen. *Study:* Hebrew Univ Jerusalem, BA, 64, dipl, 66; Concordia Univ, Montreal, MA, 77; Univ Delle Arti, Salsomaggiore, Italy, Hon Dipl, 82; Columbia Pacific Univ, San Rafael, Calif, PhD, 86. *Work:* Mus Fine Arts, Montreal; Nat Gallery, Ottawa; Guggenheim Mus; Israel Mus, Jerusalem; Galleria Naz Arte, Rome; Musee du Quebec; Seoul Int Fine Art Ctr, Korea; Ramezay Mus, Montreal; Hanseo Univ Art Mus, Seoul, Korea. *Comn:* Olympic Project (graphs), Seoul, Korea, 86; Pour Une Pedagogie Interactive by Jean Marc Denomme et Madeleine Roy (bk cover painting); Einstein Mind & Matter (frontis piece), comn by Clifford Pickover, Strange Brains and Genius, Plenum, NY, 98; Danilo Carrer Mus, Milano, Italy, 2000; Dr Patch Adams, MD, Gesundheit Inst, Arlington, 2000. *Exhib:* Musee du Luxembourg, Paris, 1978; Spaceweek Int Art Exhib, Invitational Juried, Houston, Tex, 94; Centro Civico Social, Alcorcon Int Invitational, Madrid, Spain, 94; Galleria Communale d'Arte Mod, Italy, 94; Intercommunication Ctr, Tokyo: CD-Rom, 94; solo exhibs, Tribute to Paul Hartal's Works, Munic Libr, Saint-Laurent, Que, Can, 94, Contemp Art Gallery, Budapest, 2000, Galerie Alef, Montreal, 99; Musee de la Poste, Paris, 94; Art Electrografica, Palazzo Gambacorti, Pisa, 95; Univ Calif, Berkeley, 95; Seoul Int Fine Art Ctr, Icepco Plaza Gallery, 95; Galerie Michel-Ange, Montreal, Can, 97; Dansung Gallery, Seoul, Korea, 98; Lincoln Ctr, New York, 1999; Adell McMillan Gallery, Univ Oreg, Eugene, 2000; Hanseo Univ Art Mus, Seoul, 2004; Chateau Ramezey Mus, Montreal, 2005; Mus Fine Arts, Budapest, 2007. *Collection Arranged:* Natl Gallery of Canada, Ottawa; Hanseo Univ Art Mus, Seoul. *Pos:* Dir, Ctr Art, Sci & Technol, 87-; consult, McGill's Teacher Training Prog. *Teaching:* Lectr, McGill Univ, Montreal, Canada; Lectr, Univ Oregon, Eugene, OR. *Awards:* Selected Olympic Artist, Seoul, Korea, 88; Ed Choice Award, Judith Grant, NY; Poetry Can, Prix de Paris; and others; British Libr Award, 2010. *Bibliog:* Barbara Costa (auth), Dall aeropittura futurista alla Space Art, Epiphaneia, Italy, 38-42, 3/97; Clifford A Pickover (auth), Mazes for the Mind, St Martin's Press, pages 277-279, 1992; Paul Hartal's Exhibition, The Seoul Daily, 5/22/98; Kim Edward (auth), East Meets West in Joint Exhibit, The Korea Herald, Seoul, 5/23/98; and many others; Can Who's Who, Univ Toronto Press. *Mem:* Int Soc Artists; Graphic Soc; Les Surindependants, Paris; founding mem Lyrical Conceptualist Soc (dir, 77-); Orbiting Unification Ring Satellite Project, Switz; Can Fed Poets Writers Union of Can. *Media:* Acrylic & Oil, Watercolor, Collage, Drawings. *Res:* Interdisciplinary aspects of the relationships of art & space exploration; art & mathematics; Lyrical conceptualism: Lyco Art. *Publ:* Auth, To Humanize the World, YLEM, Orinda, Calif, 9/94; Abstract Art is Like Math, Montreal Gazette, 5/19/94 reproductions), Orbiter Mag, 1-2/95; Manifesto on Lyrical Conceptualism, 1995, 1975; Rendering Science More Scientific through Art, Lo Straniero, Italy, 95; auth & illusr, The Kidnapping of the Painter Miro, or the Butterfly Kite, Elore Publ, 97; The Brush and the Compass, Univ Press Am, 88; Homage to a blue planet: aeronautical and astronomical art works, Leonardo, Vol 25, No 2, 92; Love Poems, Montreal: Editions La Galerie Fokus, Seoul: Hanseo Univ, 2004; The Songs of the Double Helix: The Symmetry and Lyrical Conceptualism, I hargittai & T Laurent Eds, Symmetry, London, 2000; Cesarean Section, Poetry Canada, Summer, 2004; Auth, Orange monad Edition, Postmodern Light, Montreal, A collection of Poetry, San Diego, 2006. *Dealer:* Edge Gallery Hong Kong; Ward-Nasse Gallery New York; Seoul Int Fine Arts Ctr. *Mailing Add:* Galerie d'art Michel-Ange Montreal PQ H4M 1N Canada

HARTE, JOHN
PAINTER
b Omaha, Nebr, June 11, 1927. *Study:* Univ Wyo, Laramie, BA, 55; Chicago Art Inst; Univ Calif, Berkeley, study with Glen Wessels; Calif Coll Arts & Crafts, Oakland; Univ Ariz, Tucson. *Work:* Grand Canyon Nat Park, Ariz; Oakland Mus, Calif; Palm Springs Desert Mus, Calif; Chevron Corp, Richmond, Calif; State of Fla Pub Art,

Tallahassee, Fla; Archeol Conserv, Albuquerque, NMex; Pfizer Inc, NYC; Lemoyne Art Tallahassee, Fla; Mus Fine Arts, St Petersburg, Fla. *Comn:* painting, Geraldine C M Livingston Found, Greenville, Fla; Loews Hotels, St Petersburg, Fla. *Exhib:* Univ Calif, Morgan Hall, Berkeley, Calif, 65; Frank Lloyd Wright Marin Co Civic Ctr, San Rafael, Calif, 77; Grand Canyon Nat Park, 84; Mesa Verde Nat Park, Chapin Mesa Mus, Colo, 86; Chevron Corp, San Francisco, Calif & Richmond, Calif, 88; Gov's Gallery, State Capitol, Tallahassee, Fla, 99; Lemoyne Art Found, Hoover Gallery, Tallahassee, Fla, 01; Millennium Arts Center, Washington, DC 01; The Arts Center, St Petersburg, FL 06, 2012, 2013; Studio 620, St Petersburg, Fla; Loews Hotels, Endeavor Catamaran Corp, Clearwater, Fla; Munson Graphics, Santa Fe, NMex. *Awards:* Gold Star, Marin Soc Artists, Ross, Calif, 71; Hon Mention, Renaissance Vinoy Hotel Anniversary, 02; Hon Mention, The Arts Ctr, St Petersburg, Fla, 02; People's Choice, Studio 620, St Petersburg, Fla, 2012. *Bibliog:* California Art Review, 1989, 1991. *Mem:* Mus Fine Arts, St Petersburg, Fla; Studio 620, St Petersburg, Fla; Dali Mus, St Petersburg, Fla. *Media:* Watercolor, Miscellaneous Media. *Interests:* Botanical, Archit subjects, Moths, Butterflies, & Boats. *Publ:* Contrib, Calif Art Rev, 89 & 91; Contrib, The New St Pete News, 02; Who's Who in America; St Petersburg Times, 2006. *Dealer:* Red Cloud Indian Arts 208 Beach Dr St Petersburg FL; Soho Myriad Gallery 1250B Menlo Dr Atlanta Ga; Soho Myriad Gallery 1551 Robertson Blvd Ste G Los Angeles Ca; Studio 620 St Petersburg FL. *Mailing Add:* PO Box 1523 Saint Petersburg FL 33731-1523

HARTFORD, JANE DAVIS
TEXTILE ARTIST, CRAFTSMAN

b Erick, Okla, Aug 21, 1927. *Study:* Univ Okla, Norman, BFA, 49; Univ Louisville, Ky, MA, 60; Parson's Sch Design; Univ Ill, art hist; Univ Hawaii, graphics with Jean Charlot; weaving with Lou Tate, Theo Moorman, Sallie O'Sullivan, Irene Waller, Mary Jane Leland & Jon Eric Riis. *Comn:* Ceremonial basket, Mrs LeRoy W Horne, Tulsa, Okla, 78; tapestry, Mr & Mrs Leonard Good, Chickasha, Okla, 82; Eucharistic Vestments, Zion Lutheran Church, Salt Lake City, Utah, 86 & 89. *Exhib:* Liturgical Weaving Convergence, Toronto, Can, 86; Conference of S Calif Handweavers, Riverside, 91; Fabrics of Faith, Nat Cathedral, Washington, DC, 92; Fiber 7 Textile Exhib, Univ Wis, 95; Fiber Arts Fiesta, Albuquerque, NMex, 97; solo exhib, Univ Okla, 98. *Pos:* Bd dir, Handweavers Guild Am Inc, 80-88, pres, 83-85, chmn bd, 85-88; bd dir, Intermountain Weavers Conf, 79-83. *Teaching:* Utah Handweavers Conf, Logan, 82; Midwest Weavers Conf, Denver, Colo, 86; Conference S Calif Handweavers, Riverside, Calif, 91. *Awards:* Merit Award, Southwest Crafts Biennial, NMex Art Mus, 75; Fiber Award, Utah Arts Coun Exhib, 80; Cash Award, Intermountain Weavers Conf Exhib, 83; First Prize (cash award), Containers, Branigan Cult Ctr, Las Cruces, NMex, 90; HGA Award, Las Tejedoras Guild Exhibit, Fuller Lodge Art Ctr, Los Alamos, NMex, 91. *Mem:* Hon life mem, M M Atwater Weavers Guild (pres, 74-75); Cross Country Weavers; Las Tejedoras de Santa Fe y Los Alamos, NMex (vpres 90-92); Midwest Weavers Conf. *Media:* Handweaving, Surface Design. *Publ:* Auth, Fashion Ballet, winter 74, auth, Sheep to shawl, spring 77, & coauth, Flight into fantasy, fall, 80, Shuttle, Spindle & Dyepot; contribr, Weaving for Worship, Robin & Russ Handweavers Inc, McMinneville, Ore, 98

HARTIGAN, LYNDA ROSCOE
CURATOR, HISTORIAN

b Scranton, Pa, Aug 26, 1950. *Study:* Bucknell Univ, Lewisburg, Pa, BA (art hist, cum laude), 72; George Washington Univ, DC, MA (art hist), 75. *Collection Arranged:* James Hampton: The Throne of the Third Heaven for Naives and Visionaries (contribr, catalog), Walker Art Ctr, 74; Joseph Cornell: An Exploration of Sources, 82 & Sharing Traditions: Five Black Artists in 19th Century Am (auth, catalog), 85, Nat Mus Am Art; Joseph Cornell: Navigating the Imagination, Peabody Essex Museum, 2007. *Pos:* Curatorial asst, 20th Century Painting & Sculpture Dept, Nat Mus Am Art, Smithsonian Inst, Washington, DC, 74-76, asst cur, 76-86, cur, Joseph Cornell Study Ctr, 78; chief cur, Peabody Essex Mus, Salem, Mass, currently. *Teaching:* Vis art critic, Md Inst, Col Art, Baltimore, 85. *Awards:* Grad internship, Nat Collection Fine Arts, Smithsonian Inst, DC, 73-74; Nat Endowment Humanities Res Grant, 76-78; Smithsonian Inst Scholarly Studies & Special Exhib Grants, 86-89. *Bibliog:* Peggy Thomson (auth), Museum People, Prentice-Hall, 77. *Mem:* Coll Art Asn; Art Table; Am Folklore Soc. *Res:* 20th century American art, especially sculpture 1930s to present, with major research conducted on Joseph Cornell; American folk art; Afro-American art. *Publ:* Contribr, Joseph Cornell: A Biography (monograph), Mus Mod Art, New York, 80; Yuri Schwebler: His Art and the Studio (exhib catalog), Hudson River Mus, Yonkers, NY, 81; Sited Toward the Future: Proposals for Public Sculpture (exhib catalog), Arlington Arts Ctr, Va, 84; auth, Made with Passion: Hemphill Folk Art Collection, Smithsonian Inst Press, 90. *Mailing Add:* Chief Curator Peabody Essex Museum East India Square Salem MA 01970

HARTLEY, KATHERINE ANN
PAINTER, INSTRUCTOR

b Chatham, MA Jan 11, 1959. *Study:* Scottsdale Community Col, 1987; Private instr, John Court, 1988-1989; Art Students League, David Leffel, NYC, 1990-1992. *Work:* Cape Cod Mus of Art, Dennis, Mass; Oyster Harbor Country Club, Osterville, Mass. *Comn:* still life painting, comn by Don Shellenberger, Brewster, Mass, 2000; still life paintings (3), comn by Gloria & Victor Leon, Orleans, Mass, 2001-2003; still live painting, comn by John Murphy, Orleans, Mass, 2005; still life painting, comn by Bob & Marion Howard, Orleans, Mass, 2005. *Exhib:* Fanellis Show, OK Harris, NYC, 1998; Women Creating, Cahoon Mus, Dennis, Mass, 1998; Mystic Art Asn, Mystic, Conn, 2003; Of Time & Light, Cape Cod Mus of Art, Dennis, Mass, 2005. *Teaching:* Instr oil painting, Cape Cod Mus of Art, 2006-. *Awards:* Silver Medal of Honor, Allied Artists, 1995; Augie Napoli Award, Salmagundi, 1996; Len G Everett Mem, Allied Artists, 2003. *Bibliog:* Kevin Mullany (auth), Katherine Ann Hartley, Province Town Banner, 2001; Beth Seiser (auth), Katherine Ann Hartley, Cape Arts Review, 2005; Lynne Moss Perricelli (auth), Focus on Painting, Am Artist, 2006. *Mem:* Allied Artists of Am; Oil Painters of Am; Art Students League (lifetime mem); Cape Cod Mus of Art (contrib mem). *Media:* Oil. *Dealer:* David Findlay Galleries 984 Madison Ave NYC 10021; Kiley Court Gallery 445 Commercial St Province Town MA 02657; Hearle Gallery 488 Main St Chatham MA 02633

HARTLEY, PAUL JEROME
PAINTER, EDUCATOR

b Charlotte, NC, Dec 30, 1943. *Study:* NTex State Univ, BA; ECarolina Univ, MFA. *Work:* Glaxo Welcome, Inc; Southeastern Ctr Contemp Art; Rausch Indust Collection; NC Art Soc, Raleigh; Greenville Mus Art. *Teaching:* Prof, ECarolina Univ, 75-. *Media:* All. *Dealer:* Lee Hansley Gallery Raleigh NC. *Mailing Add:* Sch Art E Carolina Univ Greenville NC 27834

HARTMAN, JOANNE A
PAINTER, EDUCATOR

b Brooklyn, NY, Nov 15, 1931. *Study:* Brooklyn Col, City Univ New York, BA, 52; Queens Col, City Univ New York, MFA, 75. *Exhib:* Solo exhibs, Ingber Gallery, NY, 81 & Nassau Co Mus Fine Arts, Roslyn, NY, 88; 55 Mercer, NY, 87; June Kelly Gallery, NY, 87; Fed Hall, NY, 90; Islip Art Mus, NY, 90; Gallery North, Setauket, NY, 91. *Teaching:* Adj assoc prof art, Suffolk Community Col, Selden, NY, 75- & NY Inst Technol, Westbury, NY, 82-. *Awards:* Va Ctr Creative Arts, 87-88 & 90; Ragdale Found, 89. *Bibliog:* Phyllis Braff (auth), Diverse paths at Nassau Museum, NY Times, 1/88; Karin Lipson (auth), Visual and mental images, Newsday, 1/88; Betty Booker (auth), Colony gives artists time for creativity, Richmond Times Dispatch, 7/88. *Mem:* Coll Art Asn; Nat Drawing Asn. *Media:* Acrylic, Mixed Media. *Dealer:* June Kelly 591 Broadway New York NY 10012. *Mailing Add:* 526 W 26th St Rm 612 New York NY 10001

HARTMAN, ROBERT LEROY
PHOTOGRAPHER, EDUCATOR

b Sharon, Pa, Dec 17, 1926. *Study:* Univ Ariz, BFA & MA; Colo Springs Fine Arts Ctr, with Vaclav Vytlacil & Emerson Woelffer; Brooklyn Mus Art Sch. *Work:* Nat Collection Fine Arts, Smithsonian Inst, Washington, DC; Colo Springs Fine Arts Ctr; Oakland Mus Art, Calif; Henry Gallery, Univ Wash; Princeton Art Mus; Photo Mus, Osaka, Japan. *Exhib:* Santa Barbara Mus Art, 73; Whitney Mus Biennial, NY, 73; photog, San Jose Mus Art, 83; Bluxome Gallery, San Francisco, 84 & 86; Univ Art Mus, Berkeley, 86, 90; Triangle Gallery, San Francisco, 92, 93, 95 & 97, 99-2002; Oakland Mus, Solo Flights, 2002; Viewpoint Photog Art Ctr, Sacramento, 2006; Fla Mus Photog Art, Tampa, Fla, 2007; Gallery Paule Anglim, San Fran, 2011; and others. *Teaching:* Instr art, Tex Technol Coll, 55-58; asst prof, Univ Nev, Reno, 58-61; from assoc prof to prof art, Univ Calif, Berkeley, 61-91, prof emer, 91-. *Awards:* Emanuel Walter Fund First Prize, 85th Ann San Francisco Art Inst, 67; Hon mention, 4th Int Young Artists Exhib Am-Japan, 67; Award, Snap! Photography '85, San Francisco Arts Comn Gallery. *Bibliog:* Peter Nabokov (auth), Flight patterns--photographs by Robert Hartman, Camera Arts, 1/83; Philip Morsberger (auth), Solo Flights - The Aerial Photog of Robert Hartman, Oakland Mus Exhib (catalog), 2002. *Media:* Photography, Oil. *Dealer:* Gallery Paule Anglim 14 Geary St San Francisco Calif 94108. *Mailing Add:* 1265 Mountain Blvd Oakland CA 94611

HARTMAN, ROSE
PHOTOGRAPHER, WRITER

Study: City Col, NY, BA. *Work:* Paterson Mus, Paterson, NJ; Newark Mus; Whitney Mus, Experience Music Project. *Exhib:* The Cream of the Crop, Mus City NY, 94; The Warhol Look, Whitney Mus Am Art, New York, 97; DFN Gallery, New York, 2000; Artmosphere Gallery, New York, 2000; Eqizios Project, New York, 2000; Disco: A Decade of Saturday Nights, Experience Music Proj, 2002; Performing Arts, Lincoln Ctr, 2005; Dean Project, 2007; Galerie Belage, 2007. *Collection Arranged:* Peterson Mus, Paterson, NJ. *Pos:* Photogr. *Bibliog:* Ins & Outs, Cosas Mag. *Mem:* Prof Women Photogrs, New York. *Media:* Social Documentary. *Interests:* Int travel, biking, yoga, swimming. *Collection:* Jane Holzer, Paul Wilmont, Bianca Jagger, Jerry Hall, Ralph Rucci. *Publ:* Auth & photogr, Birds of Paradise-An Intimate View of the NY Fashion World, Delacorte Press, 80; contribr, True colors: the real life of the art world (photog), Atlantic Monthly, 96; Basquiat, Viking, 98; Trust No One, St Martin's Press; auth, Anna Wintour, Front Row, St. Martin's Press, 2005. *Dealer:* Dean Project Long Island City NY. *Mailing Add:* 88 Charles St New York NY 10014

HARTSHORN, WILLIS E
DIRECTOR, PHOTOGRAPHER

b Fairfield, Conn, Sept 9, 1950. *Study:* Univ Rochester, NY, BA, 73; Pratt Inst, Brooklyn, NY, 75; Visual Studies Workshop, Rochester, NY, MFA, 81. *Work:* Visual Studies Workshop Arch, Rochester, NY. *Exhib:* Contemp Still Life Photog Traveling Exhib, 82-84; solo exhib, Mass Inst Technol, 83; Washington Projects Arts, Washington, DC, 83; The Bond Gallery, NY, 86; Lieberman & Saul Gallery, NY, 88; White Columns, NY, 88; and others. *Pos:* Assoc dir exhibs, Int Ctr Photog, 82-85, dir, 86-89, deputy dir progs, 90, exec dir, 94-. *Teaching:* Instr photog, Int Ctr Photog, New York, 79-90; teaching asst photog, Sch Visual Arts, New York, 79; instr, Univ Rochester, NY, 73-74. *Awards:* Resource Access Develop Proj, State Univ NY, 79; Materials Grant, Polaroid Corp, 79; Major Fel in Photog, Nat Endowment Arts, 81 & 86. *Mem:* Asn Art Mus; Coll Art Asn. *Media:* Black & White. *Publ:* Auth, Printletter, Zurich, Switz, 80; coauth (with John Esten), Man Ray/Bazaar Years, Rizzoli, NY, 88; auth, Man Ray: Fashion, ICP, New York, 90; coauth, Czech Modernism, Mus Fine Arts, Houston, 90. *Mailing Add:* 98 Luquer St Brooklyn NY 11231

HARTWIG, HEINIE
PAINTER, INSTRUCTOR
b Santa Clara Co, Calif, Feb 3, 1939. *Study:* Self taught. *Work:* Monterey Inst Foreign Studies, Calif; Brigham Young Univ, Provo, Utah; Mills Col, Oakland, Calif; Robert Louis Stevenson Sch, Monterey, Calif. *Pos:* pres, Groveland Art Asn Calif, 2005. *Teaching:* Instr art, pvt studio. *Awards:* First Place, Triton Mus, Santa Clara, Calif, 71; First Place Oil, First Place Popular & Best of Show, Twain Harte Art Show, 81; Best of Show, Grand Nat 2000 Celebration of Western Art, San Francisco Cow Palace, Second place, 2003. *Media:* Oil. *Mailing Add:* PO Box 976 Soulsbyville CA 95372

HARTZ, JILL
MUSEUM DIRECTOR, CURATOR
b Montreal, Quebec, Can, Jul 25, 1950. *Study:* Oberlin Univ, undergrad study, 71; Univ St Andrews, Scotland, MA (Eng Lang & Lit, with honors), 73; Student, Cornell Univ, 94. *Collection Arranged:* Karen Shea: Odyssey, Univ Va Art Mus, 2004; Mi Cuerpo Mi País: Cuban Art Today, Univ Va Art Mus, 2005. *Pos:* Mgr, Tompkins Co Arts Coun, Ithaca, 81-82, Grapevine Graphics, Ithaca, 82-83; co-ed, Grapevine Weekly Mag, 83-84, Living Publ, Ithaca, 84-86; coordr exhib, asst to dir, Herbert F Johnson Mus of Art, Cornell Univ, 76-81, dir, pub relations and publ, 86-93; asst to chair, dept of art Cornell Univ, 93-94; coordr, pub relations and spec programs, Coun for the Arts, Cornell Univ, 93-94; dir commun Arts & Scis Develop Office, Univ Va, Charlottesville, 94-97; interim dir, Univ Va Mus Art, Bayly Art Mus, 97, dir, 97-2008, dir, Jordan Schnitzer Mus Art, Univ Ore, 2008-; Co-cur, Agnes Denes exhib, 91-92, ed monogr; co-found & partner, LunaMedia Pub Relations co, Ithaca, 93-94. *Awards:* Am Asn Mus Peer Reviewer Award, 2005. *Mem:* Am Asn Mus; Art Table; Asn Acad Mus & Galleries; Western Mus Asn. *Res:* Mus Schs; Cuban Contemp Art. *Specialty:* Univ Mus, more than 10,500 works in a range of media, representing world cultures from ancient times to present. *Publ:* Ed, Siting Jefferson: Contemporary Artists Interpret Thomas Jefferson's Legacy, Univ Va Press, 2003; In Pursuit of Art, The Museum: Conditions and Species, Selections from the University of Virginia Art Museum, Univ Va Art Mus, 2004; Infuse Your Museum with Passion, Vision, and a Business Sense, The Business of Museums, A Behind the Scenes Look at Curatorship, Management Strategies and Critical Components for Success, Aspatore Books, 2004. *Mailing Add:* Jordan Schnitzer Museum of Art 1223 University of Oregon Eugene OR 97403

HARVEST, JUDITH R
CONCEPTUAL ARTIST, PAINTER
b Miami, Fla. *Study:* Barry Univ, Miami, Fla, BFA (cum laude), 73; Tyler Sch Art, Temple Univ, Rome, Italy, 73; NY Studio Sch, with Robert Storr, Ross Bleckner & Peter Agostini, .85; Sch Visual Arts, Urbino, Italy, with Enzo Cucchi & Kounellis, MFA, 87. *Work:* Aldrich Mus Contemp Art, Ridgefield, Conn; Art Forum, Galerie Thomas, Munich, Ger. *Comn:* Campbell Soup Painting, comn by Dorrance Family, Paradise Valley, Ariz, 92. *Exhib:* Recent Acquisitions, Aldrich Mus Contemp Art, Ridgefield, Conn, 88; Judith's Harvest, Artforum, Galerie Thomas, Munich, Ger, 88; Il Soffio Di Eolo, Isole Eolie, Salina, Sicily, 90; Small Works, 80 Wash Square East, NY, 91; Art from Italy, Harvest, Pistoietto, Paladino and Baj, Greene Gallery, Bal Harbour, Fla, 91; Modern Times Through the Concerned Eye, Katonah Mus, NY, 92; National Showcase Exhib, Alternative Mus, NY, 92. *Awards:* Honorable Mention, Small Works, NY, Brooke Alexander, 91. *Bibliog:* Andrea Pagnes (auth), Judith Harvest, Veranda del Arsenale, Venice, Flash Art, summer 90; Stuart Morgan (ed), Judith Harvest 1990, Artscribe, 5/90; Isa Vercelloni (ed), The seasons of Judith, Casa Vogue, 10/90. *Media:* Oil on Linen, Motorized Sculptures. *Publ:* Auth, Il Soffo Di Eolo, Mazzotta, Milano, 90; Where have all the suicides gone?, Pig Mag, Erik Oppenhiem, 92; auth & illusr, Safe Art, Spark, Romar & Melamio's Sch Bayonne, 92. *Dealer:* Bugno & Samueli Campo San Fantin 1966/A Venice Italy 30124

HARVEY, ANDRE
SCULPTOR
b Hollywood, Fla, Oct 9, 1941. *Study:* Univ Va, BA; with Michael Anasse, Valauris, France. *Work:* Del Art Mus, Wilmington; Hunter Mus, Chattanooga; Greenville Mus Art, SC; Brandywine River Mus, Chadds Ford, Pa; Crystal Bridges Mus Am Art, Bentonville, Ark. *Comn:* Sculpture, Simon Property Group, Indianapolis, In, 89, 90; Frederik Meijer Gardens, Grand Rapids, Mich, 95; Botanic Garden Ctr & Conserv, Ft Worth, Tex, 98; Winterthur Mus, Winterthur, Del, 2000; Mt Cuba Ctr, Hockessin, Del, 2009. *Exhib:* Hunter Mus, Chattanooga, Tenn, 77; Nat Sculpture Soc, 81-2009; Brandywine River Mus, Chadds Ford, Pa, 91 & 2005; Nat Sculpture Soc, Palazzo Mediceo, Seravezza, Italy, 94; Longwood Gardens, Kennett Sq, Pa, 96; Art in Embassies Prog, Malawi & Zambia, 2009-2012; and others. *Awards:* Joel Meissner Award, 80, Nat Sculpture Soc & Tallix Foundry Award, 89. *Bibliog:* Susan Stiles Dowell (auth), Pure Brandywine, Southern Accents, Mar/Apr, 93; Edgeworth & Zeidner (auth), Brandywine, 3/95; Arthur Williams (auth), Sculpture, 95; Arthur Williams (auth), Beginning Sculpture, 2005, The Sculpture Ref, 2005; Catherine Quillman (auth), Artists of the Brandywine Valley, 2010; Roger Morris (auth), Andre Harvey Turns the Page, The Hunt, Spring 2011; and others. *Mem:* Fel Nat Sculpture Soc; Artists Equity; Int Sculpture Ctr. *Media:* Metal, Stone. *Dealer:* Gerald Peters Gallery 1011 Paseo De Peralta Santa Fe NM 87501. *Mailing Add:* PO Box 8 Rockland DE 19732

HARVEY, BUNNY
PAINTER
b NY, 1946. *Study:* RI Sch Design, BFA, MFA. *Exhib:* Solo shows incl Butler Inst Am Art, Youngstown, Ohio, Mus Art, RI Sch Design, Providence, Fuller Art Mus, Brockton, Mass, Newport Art Mus, RI; group shows incl Chrysler Mus, Va; Soviet Hall Art, Moscow; Mus Fine Arts, Boston; Indianapolis Mus Art; Davis Mus and Cult Ctr, Wellesley. *Teaching:* Harvard Univ & RI Sch Design; chmn studio art dept, Wellesley Coll. *Awards:* Rome Prize in Painting, Am Acad in Rome, 74; Pell Award for Excellence in Arts, 99; Artist Grant, RI Sch Design; Pinanski Tchg Prize, Wellesley Coll, 2004. *Media:* Oil on Canvas. *Mailing Add:* Berry-Hill Galleries 11 E 70th St New York NY 10021

HARVEY, DERMOT
KINETIC ARTIST, SCULPTOR
b Amersham, Eng, June 26, 1941. *Study:* Univ Dublin, Trinity Col, MA; Univ London, MPhil. *Work:* Okla Art Ctr. *Comn:* Muse Aurora (liquid projections exhib operated by viewer), Brooklyn Children's Mus, 70; portable, multi-image aurora, Okla Art Ctr, 73; liquid projection exhib, Arnot Mus, Elmira, NY, 75; portable muse aurora, Continuum Mus, Ft Lauderdale, Fla, 76. *Exhib:* 24 Hour Technicolor Dream, Alexandra Palace, London, 67; Alliance of Light Artists, Fillmore East, NY, 69; Liquid Projections, Montreux Television Festival, Switz, 69; Projected Environments, NY Avant Garde Festival, 72, 74 & 75; Light Works, Intermedia Found, Garnerville, NY, 75. *Pos:* Dir theater of light prog, Intermedia Found, 74-; spec effects lighting for revue, Hot Stuff, Wailea Town Ctr, Maui, Hawaii, 80. *Teaching:* Instr kinetic & light art, Rockland Community Col, Suffern, NY, 75-77. *Awards:* Creative Artists Pub Serv Grant, NY Cult Coun, 71. *Bibliog:* Martha Geacintov (auth), He practices his art in the light side, 3/5/74 & Michael Hitzig (auth), Theater of light, 5/4/75, Journal News; Carol Lawson (auth), Film night with a Gothic twist, NY Times, 6/18/76. *Mailing Add:* 17 Church St Garnerville NY 10923

HARVEY, DONALD
PAINTER, PRINTMAKER
b Walthamstow, Eng, June 14, 1930; Can citizen. *Study:* West Sussex Coll Art, nat dipl painting; Brighton Coll Art Eng, art teachers dipl. *Work:* Montreal Mus Fine Arts; Charlottetown Confedn Gallery, PEI; Seattle Art Mus, Wash; Albright-Knox Mus, Buffalo, NY; Saskatdrewan Arts Bd; and others. *Comn:* Large mural, BC Provincial Govt, Nelson, BC, 75. *Exhib:* Brit Print Biennial, Bradford, Eng, 68; Int Print Exhib, Seattle, 69; Art Gallery Greater Victoria, 79; Kyles Art Gallery, Victoria, 80; Can Nat Exhib, Toronto, 80; and others. *Teaching:* Prof painting, Univ Victoria, 61-94, emer prof, 94-. *Awards:* Sadie & Samuel Bronfmann Purchase Prize, Montreal Mus, 63; First Prize, Vancouver Island Show, Art Gallery Gt Victoria, 64-66 & 69; First Prize, Exhib Can Art, Vancouver Art Gallery, 64. *Bibliog:* Tony Emery (auth), Canadian art today, Artscanada, 65. *Mem:* Royal Can Acad Arts. *Dealer:* Paul Kuhn Fine Arts Gallery Calgary AB Canada; Fran Willis Store St Victoria BC Canada. *Mailing Add:* 1025 Joan Crescent Victoria BC V8S 3L3 Canada

HARVEY, DONALD GENE
SCULPTOR, INSTRUCTOR
b Louisville, Ky, June 25, 1947. *Study:* Dixie Col, 65; Utah State Univ, BFA, 69; Univ Hawaii, MFA, 71. *Work:* Honolulu Acad Arts, Hawaii; State Found Cult & Arts, Honolulu; Utah State Univ; Honolulu Community Col; Honolulu Int Airport; and others. *Exhib:* Hawaii Craftsman, 69-70; Artist of Hawaii, 70; Easter Art Festival, Honolulu, 70-71; Solo exhib, Contemp Art Ctr Pac, 72; Artist Hawaii, Honolulu Acad Arts, 83. *Teaching:* Lectr art, Univ Hawaii, 70-71; instr art, Kamehameha High Sch, 71-. *Awards:* Honolulu Acad Arts Purchase Award, 70; Purchase Award, Contemp Art Ctr, Hawaii, 78; Juror's Award of Excellence, Easter Art Festival, 79. *Bibliog:* Nicholas Roukes (auth), Masters of Wood Sculpture, Watson-Guptill. *Mem:* Hawaii Painters & Sculptors League; Nat Art Educ Asn. *Media:* Mixed Media. *Mailing Add:* 204 W Coshocton St Johnstown OH 43031-1111

HARVEY, ELLEN
ARTIST
b Kent, Eng, 1967. *Study:* Harvard Coll, AB, MA, 89; Hochsch der Kunste, Berlin, 90; Yale Univ Law Sch, JD, 93; Whitney Mus Am Art, New York, Independent Study Prog, 98-99. *Work:* Whitney Mus Am Art, New York; Pa Accad Fine Art, Philadelphia; Princeton Art Mus, NJ; Hammer Mus, LA; Gwangju Art Mus, Korea; New York Beautification Project, various locations, New York, 1999-2001; 100 Free Portraits, various locations, New York, 2001. *Comn:* A New Booth for Tammy, Creative Time, Dreamland Artists' Club, Coney Island, NY, 2004; New is Old (mosaic), MTA Arts for Transit, Queens Plaza Subway Station, Long Island City, NY, 2005; Carpet (mosaic), Chicago Transit Authority, Francisco EL Station, Chicago, 2007. *Exhib:* Solo exhibs include Alexandre de Folin Gallery, New York, 98, Stefan Stux Gallery, New York, 99, De Chiara Gallery, New York, 2000, 2001, Marella Art Contemp, Milan, 2001, Whitney Mus at Phillip Morris, New York, 2003, Mullerdechiara Gallery, Berlin, 2003, Center Contemp Art, Ujazdowski Castle, Warsaw, 2003, Pa Accad Fine Arts, Philadelphia, 2005, Schmidt Gallery, Fla Atlantic Univ, Boca Raton, 2006, Peddie Sch, Hightstown, NJ, 2006, Magnus Muller, Berlin, 2006, Luge Gallery, New York, 2007; group exhibs include Current Undercurrent: Working in Brooklyn, Brooklyn Mus Art, 97; Benefit Art Exhib, New Mus Contemp Art, New York, 2000; Super Duper New York, Pierogi 2000, Brooklyn, 2000; Against the Wall, Inst Contemp Art, Philadelphia, 2001; Berlin Wall Paintings, Art Frankfurt, Ger, 2002; After Matisse/Picasso, PS1 Contemp Art Center, Long Island City, NY, 2003; Stop & Stor, Luxe Gallery, New York, 2004, Simply Drawn, 2004, It's Not About Sex, 2005, Sublime, 2006, What a Great Space You Have, 2006, Places, 2007; Post Notes, Inst Contemp Art, London, 2005; Whitney Biennial, Whitney Mus Am Art, New York, 2008. *Awards:* Adams House Art Prize, Harvard Coll, 89; Independent Project Grant, Artists Space, New York, 2001; Lily Auchincloss Found Fel, 2002; Philadelphia Exhibs Initiative Award, 2004; Rema Hort Mann Found Grant, 2004; Pennies From Heaven Grant, New York Community Trust, 2007

HARVEY, PETER FRANCIS
PAINTER, DESIGNER
b Quiriqua, Guatemala, Jan 2, 1933; US citizen. *Study:* Univ Miami, Fla, BA, 55; studied at Art Students League NY. *Work:* Lincoln Ctr Libr for the Performing Arts, New York, 1956-2004. *Comn:* Original ballet design for Anthony Tudor, Metropolitan Opera Co, NY, 64; 3 act ballet design for George Balanchine's "Jewels", Linc Kirstein & New York City Ballet, 67; full length ballet design for "A Midsummer Night's Dream", George Balanchine & Zurich Opera, Switz, 78; 4 Balanchine ballets for tv, WNET-PBS, NY, 79; oil portrait for libr benefactor, Millis, Mass, 94; Recreated original '67 "Jewels" design for Kirov Ballet, St Petersburg, Russia, 2000; Semperoper Ballet, Dresden, Germany, 2009, 2010; Re-design of Balanchine's

"Jewels," New York City Ballet, 2004; Recreated original "67 Jewels" design for La Scala Ballet, Milan, Italy, 2011. *Exhib:* Tops in NY - 10 Designers, Melvin Gallery, Fla Southern col, Lakeland, 72; solo exhibs, Southern-Newman Gallery, Gaylordsville, Conn, 78, The Unknown Remembered, Nicholas Davies & Co, NY, 96, Text/Eros, Riskpress Gallery, Los Angeles, Calif, 2006; group exhibs, Water Color Today, Creative Arts Workshop, New Haven, Conn, 92; John Martin Gallery, London, Eng, 94; Family Values, White Columns, NY, 97; Art Group Pride, Vincent Louis Gallery, NY, 98; Working for Balanchine, Gotham Book Mart Gallery, NY, 98; Dance for a City, NY Hist Soc, 99; Other Rooms: Paintings of Interiors, Hudson Guild Gallery, NY, 2005; Images from the Triangle, Leslie-Lohman Found Gallery, New York, 2008; Finding Venice Exhib, Emily Harvey Found Gallery, 2012. *Collection Arranged:* Lincoln Ctr Libr Performing Arts, NY; cur, Stagestruck, The Magic of Theatre Design, Leslie-Lohman Found Gallery, New York, 2007. *Pos:* co-curator with Jonathan Katz exhib, Paul Thek and His Circle-The 1950s, Leslie-Lohman Mus, NY, 2013. *Teaching:* Instr theatre design, Pratt Inst, 70-87. *Awards:* Los Angeles Drama Critics Award for Best Set Design of Yr, 69; Excellence in Scenic Design, Soc Educ Television Asn, 78; Residency in Venice, Emily Harvey Found, 2011. *Bibliog:* Lynn Pecktal (auth), Designing & Painting for the Theatre, Holt-Rinehart & Winston, 75; Lynn Pecktal (auth), Drawing for the Theatre, McGraw-Hill, 95; Laurie Fitzpatrick (auth), History at ground zero-paintings by Peter Harvey, Art & Understanding, Vol 5, No 5, 7/96; David Leddick (auth), Male Nude Now, Universe Publ, 2001; David Leddick (auth), The Nude Male, Universe Publishing, 2008. *Mem:* RI Watercolor Soc; Salmagundi Club; United Scenic Artists. *Media:* Oil, Watercolor. *Publ:* Auth, Design journals of Peter Harvey - working for Balanchine, Dance Chronicle, Vol 20, No 2, Mercel Dekker, Inc, New York, 97, Vol 20, No 3, 97 & Vol 21, No 1, 98; David Leddick (auth), Male Nude Now, Universe Publ, 2001; Reed Massengill (auth), Text/Eros (catalog), 2006

HASEGAWA, NORIKO
PAINTER
b Toyama Prefecture, Japan; US citizen. *Study:* Toyama Univ, Japan, BS (pharmacy), 56 & Tokyo Univ, PhD (pharmacy), 71; private intsr Ikebana, MA (design), 65. *Work:* Nat Mus Women Art, Washington, DC; San Francisco Art Comn, Calif; Toyama Med & Pharm Univ, Japan; Nat Asn Women Artist Permanent Collection at Rutgers, J V Zimmerli Mus Art, NJ; State Univ NY, Plattsburgh Art Mus; Calif Palace of Legion of Honor. *Comn:* Painting of Koi, Redwood City Pub Libr, Calif, 88. *Exhib:* Plattsburgh State Art Mus, 84; Nat Exhib, Nat Watercolor Soc, 87, 90, 94-96 & 2002; France Japan Exhib, Grand Palais, Paris, Tokyo Metrop Mus Art & Osaka City Mus Art, Japan, 93-95; Butler Inst Am Arts, Youngstown, Ohio, 99-2004; Around the House, Stanford Fac Club, Calif, 2000; Chatahoochee Valley Art Mus, 2001; Biennial Watercolor Exhib, 2001-2004; Quicksilver Mine Co, 2004; Biennial, Sonoma Valley Art Mus, Calif, 2005; LELA Int, Museo de Arte Contemporaneo, Ensenada, Mex, 2005; Triton Mus Art, Calif, 2007-2008. *Awards:* Gold Medal Audubon Artists Ann Exhib, 98; Purchase Award, Springfield Art Mus, 2000; Merit Award, La Grange Nat Biennial, Ga, 2000. *Bibliog:* John Schwartz (auth), East meets west, Am Artists Mag, Spring, 90; Extended Education Catalog, Sonoma State Univ, fall 94; Ginny Blair (auth), Color Blue, Am Artists Mag, spring 95. *Mem:* Signature mem Nat Watercolor Soc; Allied Artists Am; Rocky Mt Nat Watermedia Soc; Watercolor USA Honor Soc. *Media:* Watercolor. *Publ:* Contribr, The Best of Watercolor, Rockport Publs, 95, 97 & 99,; Less is more, Artists Mag, 12/99. *Dealer:* Ren Brown Collection Gallery 1781 Hwy 1 Bodega Bay CA 94923; Quicksilver Mine co Forestville CA. *Mailing Add:* 3105 Burkhart Ln Sebastopol CA 95472

HASELTINE, JAMES LEWIS
PRINTMAKER, PAINTER, CONSULTANT
b Portland, Ore, Nov 7, 1924. *Study:* Portland Mus Art Sch, Ore, 47 & 49; Art Inst Chicago, 47-48; Brooklyn Mus Sch, 50-51. *Work:* Portland Art Mus, Ore; Oakland Art Mus, Calif; Mus Art, Univ Ore; Fine Art Mus, Univ Utah; Tacoma Art Mus; Hallie Ford Mus Art, Willamette Univ, Salem, Ore. *Exhib:* Libr Cong, Washington, DC, 51; Brooklyn Mus, New York, 51-52; Portland Art Mus, Ore, 51-58; Seattle Art Mus, Wash, 52-53, 57 & 59; San Francisco Mus Art, Calif, 53-54; Phillips Gallery, Salt Lake City, Utah, 79 & 84; Evergreen State Coll, 82; Childhood's End Gallery, Olympia, Wash, 84, 88, 93, 95, 2000 & 2006; White Sturgeon Gallery, Vancouver, Wash, 2002. *Pos:* Dir, Salt Lake Art Ctr, Utah, 61-67; exec dir, Wash State Arts Comn, Olympia, 67-80. *Teaching:* Vis lectr art hist, Univ Utah, 64-65. *Awards:* Purchase Prize, Portland Art Mus, 53; Best Monogr, Mormon Hist Asn, 65. *Mem:* Western Asn Art Mus (pres, 64-66); Brit Am Arts Asn (bd mem, 80-83); Nat Assembly State & Prov Arts Agencies (exec comt, 68-70); Nat Endowment Arts (mus panel, 70-72 & visual arts policy panel, 77-79). *Media:* Oil; Woodcut, Drawing. *Publ:* Auth, 100 Years of Utah Painting, 65; contribr, Mus News, 65; Utah Hist Quart, Dialogue & American West, 66; Don Olsen (monogr), Salt Lake Art Ctr, Utah, 84; Francis Zimbeaux (Monogr), Salt Lake Art Ctr, Utah, 90. *Dealer:* Childhood's End Gallery 222 West 4th Ave Olympia WA 98501. *Mailing Add:* 1000 6th St SW Apt 222 Bandon OR 97411

HASHIMOTO, KELLY ANN
CONCEPTUAL ARTIST, VIDEO ARTIST
b Chicago, Sept 22, 1960. *Study:* Fullerton Col, AA (studio & art hist), 84; Univ Calif, Los Angeles, BA (studio & art hist), 88; Calif Inst Arts, Valencia, MFA (photog & critical theory), 91; Deutscher Akad Austausch Dienst Stipendium, Hochsch Bildende Kunst, Hamburg, independent art/res proj, 91. *Work:* pvt collections in Boston, Los Angeles, NY, Ger & Switz. *Exhib:* SITE/Seeing: Travel & Tourism in Contemp Art (exhib catalog), Whitney Mus Am Art, 91; Joint Ventures, Basilico Fine Arts, NY, 96; Spec/OK, allgirls galerie, Berlin, Ger, 96; Buck Stop: Pro-Vanities in the Bathroom, 71 Spot, NY, 96; Catalogue of Knowledge: Los Angeles Co Mus Art Libr Renovated, Blast/X-Art Found, NY, 96; Babes in Toyland (working title), NY, 97. *Pos:* Staff photogr, Hornet, Fullerton Col, 83; archit photog, Barry Schweiger, 84; corp photog, Cushman-Wakefield, Bunker Hill, 85; admin asst & media & performing arts cur, Mus Contemp Art, Los Angeles, 88; libr asst, Los Angeles Co Mus Art, 90; admin asst, Richard Meier & Partners, Architects, NY, 93; freelance computer, Pat Hearn Gallery, FlashArt Mag & Gale Elston, Esq, 96. *Teaching:* vis artist & lectr, Univ S Fla, Tampa, 96. *Bibliog:* Hair-hanging was research for senior's thesis, Daily Bruin, 5/19/88; David Mori (auth), Act examines personal/political, High Performance, fall 88; Brigitte Werneberg (auth), Entschieden gewitzt: Kunst in Berlin jetzt, die tageszeitung, 7/13-14/96. *Mem:* Coll Art Asn. *Media:* Performance; Photography, Video. *Publ:* Auth, Special/OK, Art Link (website), 96; Art and architecture (in prep), Flash Arts, 97. *Mailing Add:* 501 Silver Canyon Wy Brea CA 92821

HASKELL, BARBARA
CURATOR
b San Diego, Calif, Nov 13, 1946. *Study:* Univ Calif, Los Angeles, BA (philos & art hist), 69. *Exhib:* Retrospective (auth, catalog): Whitney Biennial, 77, 79, 81, 83, & 85; Marsden Hartley, 80; Milton Avery, 82; Ralston Crawford, 85; Charles Demuth, 87; Donald Jud, 88; Burgoyne Diller, 90; Agnes Martin, 93, traveling, 93-94; Joseph Stella, 94; The American Century: Art and Culture 1900-1950, 99; Edward Steichen, 2000; Elie Nadelman: Sculptor of Modern Life, 2003 & Oscar Bluemner: A Passion for Color, 2005, Georgia O'Keefe: Abstraction, 2009. *Pos:* Asst registrar, Pasadena Mus Mod Art, 69, from asst cur to cur painting & sculpture, 70-73, dir exhib & collections, 74; cur, San Francisco Mus Art, 74; cur painting & sculpture, Whitney Mus Am Art, New York, 75-; panel mem, Nat Endowment Arts, Art Comn of City of New York; adv bd, Edith C Blum Art Inst, Bard Col; past adv bd, Int Mus Photog at George Eastman House. *Awards:* Woman of the Year, Mademoiselle Award, 73; Leadership Among Professional Women, Los Angeles Soroptimist, 73. *Publ:* New Masters-Bryan Hunt (exhib), Amerika Haus, Berlin, 83; Bryan Hunt: Sculpturen und Zeichnugen (exhib catalog), Knoedler Gallery, Zurich, 85; Georgia O'Keefe, Works on Paper-A Critical Essay (exhib catalog), Mus Fine Arts, Mus NMex, Santa Fe, Mus NMex Press, 85; Transcendental Realism in the Steiglitz Circle (exhib catalog), The Expressionistic Landscape, Birmingham Mus Art, 87; Yoko Ono: Arias & Objects, Peregrine Smith Books, Salt Lake City, 91; and others. *Mailing Add:* Whitney Mus Am Art 945 Madison Ave New York NY 10021

HASKELL, HEATHER
DIRECTOR
Study: Smith Coll, BA, 1983; Univ Mass, Amherst, MA (Art History), 1987. *Pos:* Assoc prof, Shaanxi Teachers Univ, China, 1987-1988; asst registrar Mus Fine Arts & George Walter Vincent Smith Art Mus, Springfield, Mass, 1988-1990, asst cur collections, 1990-1992, cur collections & exhibs, 1992-1995, cur art, 1995-1998, dir, 1998-; grant reviewer, Nat Endowment for Arts, 1992. *Awards:* Fellow NEA, 1986; Fanny Bullock Workman Fel, 1983. *Mem:* New England Mus Asn; Am Asn Mus. *Mailing Add:* George Walter Vincent Smith Art Museum 21 Edwards St Springfield MA 01103

HASKELL, JANE
ENVIRONMENTAL ARTIST, PAINTER
b Cedarhurst, NY, Nov 24, 1923. *Study:* Skidmore Col, Saratoga Springs, NY, BS, 44; Univ Pittsburgh, Pa, MA, 61. *Work:* Carnegie Mus Art, Pittsburgh; Mead Art Mus, Amherst, Mass; Milwaukee Art Mus, Wis; Mus Neon Art, Los Angeles; Westmoreland Mus Am Art, Greensburg, Pa. *Comn:* Tree of Knowledge (neon 12' x 18'), William Pitt Student Union, Univ Pittsburgh, 87; Windows of Light (neon), Massport, Boston, Mass, 90; Let the Waters Teem with Living Creatures and Let Birds Fly Above the Earth, Genesis (fiberoptic light installation), Ft Lauderdale Airport, Fla, 94; Leaves of Light (stairwell-painted panels with fiberoptics), Pressure Chem Inc, Pittsburgh, 95; Neon installation, Pittsburgh Ctr Arts, 97. *Exhib:* Solo exhibs, Color & Light Environment, Allegheny Col, Meadville, Pa, 85, Drawings & Neon Constructions, Assoc Artists Pittsburgh Ctr Arts, Pa, 87, Construction with Light & Installation with Light, AIR Gallery, NY, 88, 90 & 92, Window Series, Concept Art Gallery, Pittsburgh, 91, Vineyard Studio Gallery, 94 & Westmorland Mus Am Art, 96; St Petersburg Bienniale, Neon Installation, Russ, 96; To the Edge of Time: A Two Decade Retrospective, Jewish Community Ctr Asn, Pittsburgh, 97; Drawings in Light, Asn Artists Pittsburgh Gallery, 98; Light Installation, Pittsburgh Biennial, Ctr for the Arts, 2000; Gestures, An Exhibition of Small Site-Specific Work, Mattress Factory, Pittsburgh, Pa, 2002; The Bells of Amherst, Contemp Women Artists in the Collections of the Mead Art Mus and the Univ Gallery, Univ of Amherst, MA, 2002; Panopticon, an Art Spectacular, Carnegie mus of Art, Pittsburgh, Pa, 2002; Light and Glass, Challange Exhib, Gallery 707, Pittsburgh, Pa, 2005; 2006 Artist of the Year, Pittsburgh Ctr for the Arts, Pittsburgh, Pa; and others. *Pos:* Bd trustees, Pittsburgh Ctr Arts, 91-94; bd trustees, Carnegie Mus of Art, 99-. *Teaching:* Instr art hist, Duquesne Univ, Pittsburgh, Pa, 68-78; Symp on Light, Pittsburgh Ctr for the Arts, Pittsburgh, Pa, 2006. *Awards:* AAP Juror's Award, Assoc Artists Pittsburgh, Susan & Morton Gurrentz, 82; Jury Award, Soc Sculptors, Pittsburgh, Pa, 95; Award of Distinction, Art for AIDS, Persad Ctr, Pittsburgh, 95; Juror's Award, Soc Sculptor's Ann Exhib, 97; Juror's Award, Assoc Artist Pittsburgh, Red Exhib, Red Alert, Pittsburgh, Pa, 2006; Sculpture Award, Pittsburgh Ctr Arts, 2010. *Bibliog:* Vilma Barr (auth), Best of Neon, Allworth Press/Rockport Pubs, 92; Marty Carlock (auth), Guide to Public Art in Greater Boston, revised ed, Harvard Common Press, 93; Abigal Pesta (auth), Electric art, Jane Haskell's neon creations: Changing colors, changing moods, Lighting Dimensions Mag, 4/94. *Mem:* Soc Sculptors; Asn Artists Pittsburgh; Pittsburgh Ctr Arts; Carnegie Mus Art. *Media:* Neon, Fiber Optics, Florescent Light, Black Light, Oil Stick, Paint on Paper, Canvas. *Dealer:* Concept Art Gallery, 10315 Braddock Ave, Pittsburgh, PA 15218; Christine Frechard Gallery Pittsburgh PA. *Mailing Add:* The Park Mansions Apt 6AD 5023 Frew St Pittsburgh PA 15213

HASLEM, JANE N
DEALER
b Knoxville, Tenn, Dec 26, 1934. *Study:* DePauw Univ, BA; Ind State Univ; Grad Studies Art Hist, Univ Md, 90-93. *Work:* Var Nat & Int collections. *Exhib:* Numerous mus exhibs. *Pos:* Dir, Jane Haslem Gallery, Chapel Hill, NC, 60-65, Madison, Wis, 65-71 & Washington, 69-71; Pres & CEO, Haslem Fine Arts Inc, Washington, DC, 71;

creator & owner Artline.com, 95-. *Teaching:* Instr art, Mecklenburg Co, NC, 58-59; resident assoc prog, Smithsonian Inst, 1970. *Mem:* Washington Print Club (bd adv); Art Dealers Asn Greater Washington (found mem & bd dir, 81-93 & 97, treas 84-89, secy, 91-93, pres 97-2001); Int Fine Print Dealers Asn, NY (founding mem); Arttable NY. *Specialty:* Contemporary American paintings, prints and works on paper; publisher of art catalogues and CD presentations; internet exhibs. *Collection:* American self portraits & oversize watercolors by American artists. *Publ:* Selected publ, Jane Haslem Gallery Newsletter, 72-; auth, American Drawings/Realism Idealism, 86; David Hollowell, 86; Larry Day Paintings: 1958-1988, 88; Gabor Peterdi: Pacific and Other Recent Works, 90; and others including those on artline.com. *Mailing Add:* 2025 Hillyer Pl NW Washington DC 20009

HASSANAL BOLKIAH, HIS MAJESTY MU'IZZADDIN WADDAULAH
COLLECTOR
b Darussalam, Brunei, July 15, 1946. *Study:* Student Victoria Inst, Kuala Lumpar, Malaysia, 61-63, Royal Military Acad, Sandhurst, England, 63-67. *Pos:* Appointed crown prince and heir apparent for State of Brunei, 61; Ruler of state, sultan, 67-, prime minister, 84-, minister fin and home affairs, 84-86, minister of defense, 86-. *Awards:* Named One of Top 200 Collectors, ARTnews Magazine, 2004, 2005, 2006. *Collection:* Impressionism and Islamic art. *Mailing Add:* Office of HM The Sultan Bandar Seri Begawan Brunei Darussalam

HASSENFELD, KIRSTEN
SCULPTOR
Study: RI Sch Design, Providence, BFA, 1994; Univ Ariz, Tucson, MFA, 1998. *Exhib:* Solo exhibs, Hudson Walker Gallery, Mass, 2000, Bellwether Gallery, New York, 2004, Rice Gallery, Rice Univ, Tex, 2007, Smack Mellon Gallery, New York, 2009, Bell Gallery, List Art Ctr, Brown Univ, 2009; Open House: Working in Brooklyn, Brooklyn Mus Art, New York, 2004; Greater NY, PS1 Contemp Art Ctr/Mus Mod Art, New York, 2005; Out of Line: Drawings from the Collection of Sherry and Joel Mallin, Herbert F Johnson Mus Art, Cornell Univ, 2006; Material Pursuits, Robert Hull Fleming Mus, Univ Vt, 2007; 475 Kent Lives, Queens Mus, NY, 2008. *Awards:* Space Program, Marie Walsh Sharpe Found, 2004; Pollock-Krasner Found Grant, 2006; NY Found Arts Fel, 2009. *Bibliog:* Jill Conne (auth), Presence of Light, Sculpture mag, 3/2005; Ken Johnson (auth), From Carved Creatures to Disneyland Rugs, Boston Globe, 9/24/2006; Meredith Mendelsohn (auth), Paper Pushers, ARTnews mag, 2007

HASTINGS, JACK BYRON
SCULPTOR, AUTHOR
b Kennett, Mo, Nov 16, 1925. *Study:* La State Univ, 1946-47 & 1949-50; Escuela Pintura & Escultura, Mexico City, 1951. *Comn:* Playground Percussion sculptures (bronze), NY Dept Educ, Harlem Elem Sch, 1960; public seating & plant containers (carved cement), Ariz Sonora Desert Mus, Tucson, 1970; Homage to Calder (painted metal mobile), Tenn Valley Authority Hqrs, Chattanooga, Tenn, 1982; Environmental Garden (carved cement sculptures), Tenn Dept Tourism, 1-75 Welcome Ctr/Tenn Arts Commn, 1984; Dancing on Air (2 painted metal mobiles), Metro Nashville Airport Authority, 2000. *Exhib:* Solo exhibs, Work on Jack Hastings, New Orleans Mus, 1954, Barone Gallery, New York City, 1959 & Art for the Garden, Am Craft Gallery, Cleveland, 1989; Now in New Orleans, Riverside Mus, NY, 1955; Orleans Gallery Founders, NO Historic Collection Gallery, New Orleans, 1982; Sculpture Invitational, Radford Univ, Radford, Va, 1988; Seven Sculptors, Zimmerman Saturn Gallery, Nashville, 1989. *Collection Arranged:* New Orleans Historic Collection; The Children's Mus; Tenn State Mus, Nashville. *Awards:* Purchase Awards, New Orleans Mus of Art, Tenn Crafts Fair & Rutherford Bicentennial Exhib. *Bibliog:* Archit Record; Interiors; ARTNews; Crafts Horizons; Arts and Archit; Sunset; Nashville!. *Media:* Metal, Cast, Welded, Fabricated. *Publ:* Auth, The Illuminated History of Darkness, Cosmic Aye Press, 2000. *Dealer:* Tinney Contemp Nashville Tenn; Sixty One Main Andes NY. *Mailing Add:* 464 Wildwood Lane Sewanee TN 37375

HATCH, CONNIE
PHOTOGRAPHER, EDUCATOR
b Muskogee, Okla, Apr 12, 1951. *Study:* Univ Tex Austin, BFA, 73; San Francisco Art Inst, MFA, 79. *Comn:* Art in the Urban Landscape, Capp St Proj & The Wallace Alexander Gerbode Found, San Francisco, 95. *Exhib:* Who Counts?, Randolph St Gallery, Chicago, Ill, 90; Spectacular Women, Film Cities, St Paul, Minn, 90; After the Fact, Mills Coll Art Gallery, Oakland, Calif, 90; Picture Plane to Object, Brea Cult Ctr, Calif, 91; In and Around: Selections From the Permanent Collection, Univ Art Mus, State Univ NY, Binghamton, 91; Sightlines, Newport Harbor Art Mus, Calif, 91; Navigational Crossroads, Capp St Proj, San Francisco, 95-96; Gallery, NY, 92; (Original Accounts) of the Lone Woman of San Nicolas, 18 Street Complex, Santa Monica, Calif, 98; Fin de Siecle Terrain Gallery, San Francisco, 99. *Teaching:* Fac, Calif Inst Arts, Valencia, 83-2003; vis lectr photog, Univ Calif, Los Angeles, 91-92. *Awards:* Charlene Engelhard Found Award, 88; Visual Artists' Fel, New Genre, Nat Endowment Arts, 91; Comn Award, Wallace Alexander Gerbode Found, 95. *Bibliog:* David Trend (auth), Connie Hatch at Mills Col, Art Am, 5/91; H Pakasaar, Brian Wallis, William Wood (auths), Camera Lucida: What is not Seen, Camera Lucida, Banff Centre, Alta, Can, 91; Daniel Veneciano (auth), Power rips, Artweek, 12/26/91. *Media:* Photography, New Genre. *Publ:* The DeSublimation of Romance: Consider the Difference, Spec Issue Sexuality, Wedge, winter 84; Serving the Status-Quo, Blasted Allegories: An Anthology of Writings by Contemp Artists, 87; Small Miracle, red, New Langton Arts: The First 15 Years, San Francisco, 90; After the Fact, Exposure, Boulder, Colo, 90; The De Sublimation of Romance (excerpts), Reframings: New American Feminist Photographies, Temple Univ Press, 95. *Mailing Add:* c/o Calif Inst Arts 24700 McBean Pkwy Valencia CA 91355

HATCH, (MR & MRS) MARSHALL
COLLECTORS
b Seattle, Wash, Aug 26, 18 (Mr Hatch); b Seattle, Wash, July 7, 18 (Mrs Hatch). *Study:* Mr & Mrs Hatch, Univ Wash. *Pos:* Mr Hatch, pres, Seattle Art Mus, formerly. *Collection:* Morris Graves, Mark Tobey, other Northwest artists, The Eight (Ashcan Group), Mexican paintings and ethnic art

HATCH, MARY
PAINTER
b Saginaw, Mich, Dec 12, 1935. *Study:* Skidmore Col, 51-53; Western Mich Univ, MA (painting), 72; studied with Harvey Breverman, 74-77. *Work:* St Johns Univ, NY; Southwestern Mich Col, Kalamazoo Inst Arts, Mich, Art Ctr Battle Creek, Mich; Upjohn Co; Mich Comn Art in Pub Places. *Exhib:* One-person exhibs, CPL Cult Ctr, Chicago, 82 & Gilman-Gruen Galleries, Chicago, 96, 2000; New Talent--New Visions, Zolla/Lieberman Gallery, Chicago, 83; Kouroi & Korai, Kouros Gallery, NY, 84; Constructing A Modern World, Mich Coun Arts, Detroit, 90; West, Art & the Law, 20th Ann Exhib, Nev Mus Art & Springfield Mus Art, Ohio, 95; Death Matters, Urban Inst Contemp Art, Grand Rapids, Mich. *Awards:* Susan Kahn Prize, 83 & Charles Horman Mem Award, 85, Nat Asn Women Artists; Mich Coun Arts Grant, 85-86 & 88-89. *Bibliog:* Ben Mitchell (auth), To Get Hold of the Invisible, Passages North, Winter 87; Western Michigan Presents, Western Mich Univ, Vol 3, No 3; Effie Mihopoulos (auth), Silent Messages, Reader, Chicago, 92. *Mem:* Chicago Artists Coalition. *Media:* Oil. *Mailing Add:* 6917 Willson Dr Kalamazoo MI 49009

HATCH, W A S
PAINTER, EDUCATOR
b Bridgeport, Conn, Mar 19, 1948. *Study:* Syracuse Univ, BFA, 70; Pratt Inst, MFA, 72. *Work:* City Coll NY; Kemper Collection, Chicago, Ill; US Info Agency Embassy Collection; Univ Leeds; San Diego Mus; Bank of America; Widener Univ, Chester, PA. *Comn:* Spec ed prints, Pratt Graphic Ctr, NY, 73; Large murals in pvt homes, Pa. *Exhib:* Brooklyn Mus 19th Nat Print Exhib, 74-75; 5th Int Drawing Show, Mus Mod Art, Rijeka, Yugoslavia, 76; World Print Competition, 77; Am Printmakers, Venice, 77; Sande Webster Gallery, Philadelphia, Pa, 75, 77 & 84; New Talent in Printmaking Show, Assoc Am Artists, NY, 77; 6th Brit Int Print Biennale, 79; Handmade Paper, Silver Cloud Gallery, Chicago, 81; Delaware Art Mus, 85 & 91; one-person show, Carspecken-Scott Gallery, Wilmington, Del, 99, Station Gallery, Greenville, Del, 92, Blue Streak Gallery, Wilmington, Del, 99, Widener Univ, Chester, Pa, 2005, Carolyn Roberts Gallery, Hockessin, Dela, 2005, Carspecken Scott Gallery, Wilmington, Dela, 2008, Dela Theatre Company, Wilmington, Dela, 2009; and many others. *Pos:* Cur, The Making of Print, DCCA, Del, 90. *Teaching:* Asst prof printmaking, Bradley Univ, 73-79; instr drawing, Columbia Col, 79-80; adj prof, Widener Univ, 82-; instr watercolor, Del Art Mus, 82-. *Awards:* Purchase Award, Los Angeles 2nd Nat Print Exhib, 74; Merit Award, Boston Printmakers 26th Ann Exhib, 74; Purchase Award, Eastern Regional Drawing Exhib, 83; Dela Art Mus, 2009. *Bibliog:* The European Graphic Biennale, Print Rev, 77. *Mem:* Del Ctr Contemp Arts (vpres, 82-83). *Media:* Watercolor, acrylic painting. *Interests:* custom mural painting. *Dealer:* Carspecken-Scott Gallery 1707 N Lincoln St Wilmington DE 19806. *Mailing Add:* 2100 Kentmere Pkwy Wilmington DE 19806-2016

HATCHER, GARY C
EDUCATOR, ADMINISTRATOR, CERAMIST
Study: Univ North Texas, BFA (ceramics); Texas A&M, Commerce, MFA (sculpture). *Exhib:* Participated in over 300 exhibits nationally and internationally, including Baylor Univ, Dallas Mus of Fine Arts, Houston Ctr for Contemporary Crafts, Austin Coll, Tyler Mus of Art and Irving Arts Ctr. *Collection Arranged:* Works are in numerous private and public collections. *Pos:* Apprenticed in ceramic art studios in Devon, England with Michael Leach and David Leach, 1976-79; maintains studio in Texas with wife Daphne Roehr Hatcher; curator for a number of exhibitions for Univ of Tex at Tyler and Tyler Mus of Art. *Teaching:* With Univ of Texas, Sch of Visual and Performing Arts, Tyler, 1992-, Art prof, Art Chair, Ceramics, Small Metals, Dept Art and Art History, currently. *Publ:* Published articles in Ceramics Art and Perception, Ceramics Technical and Ceramics Monthly, The Studio Potter and American Craft. *Dealer:* Goldesberry Gallery, Houston. *Mailing Add:* University of Texas at Tyler Department of Art and Art History 3900 University Blvd Office ARC 120 Tyler TX 75799

HATCHETT, DUAYNE
SCULPTOR, PAINTER
b Shawnee, Okla, May 12, 1925. *Study:* Univ Mo; Univ Okla, BFA & MFA. *Work:* Whitney Mus Am Art; Rochester Mem Mus, NY; Ft Worth Art Mus, Tex; Carnegie Inst, Pittsburgh, Pa; Albright-Knox Gallery, Buffalo, NY; Pittsburgh Univ, Pa; many others. *Comn:* Whitney Mus Am Art, 1967; Nat Endowment Arts, Downtown Riverfront Park, Flint, Mich, 1978-79; GSA Fed Bldg, Rochester, NY, 1978; Ashford Hollow (NY) Sculpture Park, 1986; other pub and private comns. *Exhib:* Solo exhibs, Rockefeller Art Ctr, Fredonia, NY, 82, Kirkpatrick Ctr, Okla City, 87, Chautauqua Art Asn Galleries, NY, 87 & Concept Gallery, Pittsburgh, Pa, 90, Dunkirk Art Center, NY, 1991, Alexandre Hogue Gallery, Tulsa Univ, 1992, Daemen Col, Buffalo, 1993; Pub Works, Smithsonian Gallery, Washington, 80; Sculptors Drawings: 1910-1980, 81 & The Sculptor as Draftman, 83, Whitney Mus Art NY; Outside New York City: From Drawings to Sculpture, Syracuse Univ, NY, 82; The Wayward Muse, 87, & Western NY Invitational, Albright Knox Art Gallery, Buffalo, NY, 89; The Eloquent Object, traveling show, 87-89; Big Orbit Gallery, Buffalo, 1991; Hallwalls Gallery, Buffalo, 1992; Anderson Gallery, Buffalo, 1993, 94. *Pos:* Comt chmn, Coun for Int Exchange of Scholars, Washington. *Teaching:* Assoc prof sculpture, Ohio State Univ, 64-68; prof art, State Univ NY Buffalo, 68-92, ret. *Mem:* Nat Sculpture Soc. *Media:* Sculpture/Metal, Printmaking. *Mailing Add:* 18 Essex St Buffalo NY 14213

HATFIELD, DAVID UNDERHILL
PAINTER
b Plainfield, NJ, July 16, 1940. *Study:* Miami Univ, BFA, 62; Sch Visual Arts, 63; Art Students League, 64. *Work:* Southern Vt Art Ctr; West Point Mil Acad; Fed Court House, White Plains, NY. *Exhib:* Nat Acad Design Ann, NY, 70, 73, 84 & 94; Nat Arts Club Ann, NY, 69-72, 75 & 76; Am Artists Prof League Grand Nat, NY, 71-77; Solo exhibs, Nat Arts Club, 76, Christopher Gallery, NY, 81 & Southern Vt Art Ctr, 86, 91, 93, 96 & 2004. *Awards:* Wm Meyerowitz Award, Rockport Art Asn, 90; Robert Nally Award, Rockport Art Asn, 91 & Portrait Award, 98; W M Meyerowitz Mem Award, North Shore Arts Asn, 96 & Gorton's of Gloucester Award, 98; George D Davies, Silver Medal, Rockport Art Asn, 99; Rockport Art Assoc, Silver Metal, 98, Paul Strisik Gold Metal, 00, Amee B Davis Award, 04, Dr Henry Kaplan Mem Award; Paul Strisik Mem Award, North Shore Arts Assoc, 2007; and others; Marguerite Pearson Gold Medal, Rockport Art Asn, 2011; Newington Award, Hudson Valley Art Asn, 2011. *Bibliog:* C Movalli`(auth), article, Am Artist Mag, 12/81. *Mem:* North Shore Arts Asn; Allied Artists Am; Rockport Art Asn; Southern Vt Artists Inc; and others. *Media:* Oil. *Publ:* Cover painting, Prevention Mag, 1/82. *Dealer:* J R Leigh Gallery PO Box 70116 Tuscaloosa, AL 35407; State of the Art Gallery 4 Wonson St Gloucester MA 01930; Lily Pad Gallery 1 Bay St Watch Hill RI 02891. *Mailing Add:* 9 River St Hoosick Falls NY 12090

HATFIELD, DONALD GENE
PAINTER, EDUCATOR
b Detroit, Mich, May 23, 1932. *Study:* Northwestern Mich Col, AA; Mich State Univ, BA & MA; Univ Wis, MFA; Studied with Abraham Rattner, Warrington Colescott & Robert Grilley. *Work:* Jacksonville State Univ, Ala; Tuskegee Inst, Ala; Brandt Corp, New Orleans; South Cent Bell, Birmingham; Southern Servs, Birmingham; Montgomery Mus Art, Ala; and others. *Exhib:* solo shows, La Crosse State Coll Mus, QI, 63, Birmingham Southern Coll Gallery, Ala, 70; 48th-50th Ann Exhib Wisc Art, Milwaukee Art Ctr, 62-64; 59th Ann Jury Exhib, Birmingham Mus Art, Ala, 67; Ann Mus Gallery Exhib, Mus Arts & Science, Macon, Ga, 68; Ala Watercolor Soc Show, Birmingham Mus Art, Ala, 68; 30th Ann Nat Competition, Ala Watercolor Soc, Birmingham Mus Art, Ala, 69; Ala Art League, Montgomery, 81; Columbia Col, Mo, 83; Del Mar Col, 83; Ala Works on Paper, Auburn, Ala, 83; Competition for Spoleto, Marble Arch Gallery, Charleston, SC, 83; 17th Ann Nat Drawing & Small Sculpture Show, Del Mar Col, Corpus Christi, Tex, 83. *Teaching:* Elem art supvr, Auburndale Elem Sch Syst, Wis; instr jr & sr high art classes, Auburndale High Sch, 62-64; Instr, Auburn Univ, 64-94; asst prof art, Auburn Univ, 64-71, assoc prof art, 71-81, prof art, 81-94, student academic adv, 90-94, prof emer, 94; part time instr hist archit & art, Tuskegee Inst, 68-69. *Awards:* Purchase Award, 49th Ann Exhib Wisc Art, Milwaukee, 62; Purchase Award, Opelika Arts Festival, Opelika Arts Asn, Ala, 71-72; Purchase Award, 5th Ann Miniworks Exhib, Jacksonville State Univ, Jacksonville, Ala, 83; plus many others. *Bibliog:* La Revue Moderne des Art de la Vie, Paris, Francem 64; Ernest Kay (ed)Dictionary of Intl Biography, Vol 6 IX, Melrose Press Ltd, Cambridge, England 72-73; Les Krantz (auth), The New York Art Review, an Illustrated Survey of the City's Mus, Galleries & Leading Artists, Americas References, Inc, Chicago, IL. 88. *Mem:* Ala Art League (first vpres, 69-70, pres, 70-72); Opelika Arts Asn (bd trustees, 71-73). *Media:* Watercolor. *Mailing Add:* 550 Forest Park Cir Auburn AL 36830

HATGIL, PAUL
EDUCATOR, PAINTER
b Manchester, NH, Feb 18, 1921. *Study:* Harvard U, summer 50; Mass Coll Art, BFA, 50; Columbia Univ, MFA, 51. *Work:* Fed Aviation Agency, Balboa, CZ, Panama; Litton Industs; Ft Worth Nat Bank; Mitchell Energy Corp; Tandy Corp; Univ Tex, Performing Arts Ctr, Austin. *Comn:* St Paul's Lutheran Church, Austin, Tex; Univ Tex Bus & Admin Bldg, Austin; Our Saviour's Lutheran Church, Victoria, Tex; Design Assocs Bldg, Dallas, Tex; Rio Bldg, Austin; plus others. *Exhib:* 4th-6th Int Invitational, Smithsonian Inst, Washington, DC; Int Invitational, Gulf-Caribbean Exhib, Houston, Tex; Philbrook Art Ctr Int, Tulsa, Okla; US World's Fair Pavilion, New York; Hemisphere 1969, Tex Pavilion, San Antonio, Tex; US Senate, St Petersburg, Jacksonville & Fla Mus; solo exhibs, Sunset Galleries, Austin, Tex, 91, Univ Tex 54th Ann Art Faculty Exhib, 91, Baylor Univ Mus Fine Arts, Waco, Tex & numerous others. *Teaching:* Instr, Columbia Univ, San Antonio Art Inst & Tex Fine Arts Asn, Austin; prof art, Univ Tex, Austin, 51-86, prof emer, 86. *Awards:* Univ Tex Res Inst Grants, 64 & 65. *Bibliog:* The Artists Bluebook, 2011. *Mem:* Am Craftsmen Coun; Coll Art Asn Am; Nat Educ Found; Nat Maritime Historical Soc; Hellenic Voice. *Media:* Encaustic Painting. *Collection:* naval artifacts. *Publ:* Auth, articles In: Ceramic Monthly, Sch Arts, Tex Trends Art Educ, La Rev Mod, Ceramic Age & Hellenic Chronicle. *Mailing Add:* 2203 Onion Creek Pkwy Unit 7 Austin TX 78747

HATKE, WALTER JOSEPH
PAINTER, EDUCATOR
b Topeka, Kans, Jan 11, 1948. *Study:* Great Lakes Coll Assoc Arts Prog, NY; 1st painting asst to Jack Beal, 69 & 72-73; DePauw Univ, BA, 71; asst to Alexander Calder, 74-76; Univ Iowa, Iowa City, MA, 81, MFA, 82. *Work:* Art Inst Chicago; Metrop Mus Art, NYC; RI Sch Des Mus; Sheldon Mus Art, Lincoln, Nebr; Mulvane Mus Art, Topeka, Kans; Palmer Mus Art, Univ Park, Pa. *Comn:* Mobile sets, Nat Tribute to Alexander Calder, Socrate NY, 77; 3 Bus Pioneers, Wilkes Univ, Wilkes-Barre, Pa, 2000; Oil on Linen Portraits, Union Coll, Pres Hull, 2005, Dean Fac Sorum, 2006, Schenectady, NY. *Exhib:* Solo exhibs, Swarthmore Col, 84, DePauw Univ, 86, Robert Schoelkopf Gallery, NY, 77, 80, 83, 89, Babcock Galleries, NY, 92 & 93, Gerald Peters Gallery, Santa Fe, NMex, 2002, NYC, 2004, Mandeville Gallery, Union Coll, Schenectady, NY, 2000 & 2005; Group exhibs, Am Realism traveling exhib, San Francisco Mus Mod Art, 86-87, Narrative Paintings & Sculpture, Nassau Co Mus Art, NY, 91, Major Works, John Pence Gallery, San Francisco, 92-2000 & The Artist as Native, traveling, 93-94; Am Drawings, Nat Acad of Design, NY, Travel 87-88; Disegno, Nat Acad Design, NY, 2005; 182nd Mem Ann, Contemp Am Art, Nat Acad Design, NYC, 2007. *Collection Arranged:* (juror) 1992 Mohawk, Hudson Art Exhib, Albany Inst Art, Schenectady Mus & Planetarium, Univ Art Mus, State Univ NY-Albany. *Pos:* Asst to dir, Perls Galleries, New York, 73-77; vis artist/critic/lectr, Am Univ, Washington, DC, Dartmouth Col, Hanover, NH, Kansas City Art Inst, Smith Col, Northampton, Mass, Swarthmore Col, Pa; Yale Univ, New Haven, Conn. *Teaching:* Asst prof, Pa State Univ, 82-86; prof Fine Arts, Union Coll, Schenectady, NY, 87-, Baker prof visual arts, endowed chair. *Awards:* Painting Award, Am Acad Arts & Letters, 80; Ingram Merrill Grant, 81; Nat Endowment Arts Fel, 85; Pa State Univ Res Initiation Grant, 85; Union Coll Humanities Develop Grants, 87-2005; Fel, Vt Studio Ctr, 99. *Bibliog:* John Russell (auth), The many faces of naturalism, New York Times, 8/11/80; John Arthur (auth), The Spirit of Place, Little Brown, 89; Alan Gussow (auth), The Artist as Native, Pomegranate, 93; Jordan Smith (auth), Upstate Diary, Gerald Peters Gallery, 2002; Anna Held Audette (ed), 100 Creative Drawing Ideas, Random House, 2003; Caleb Linville (auth), If Walls Could Speak, Watercolor, fall/2005; Rachel Seligman & Jordan Smith (auths), Walter Hatke: Recent Work, Union Coll, Schenectady, NY, 2005. *Mem:* Nat Acad, NYC. *Media:* Oil, Watercolor, Drawing. *Specialty:* Am painting & Sculpture, 19th-21st century. *Interests:* Fishing, hiking, boating. *Dealer:* Gerald Peters Galleries 24 E 78 NYC 10021 & 1011 Paseo de Peralto Santa Fe NM. *Mailing Add:* 1513 Lenox Rd Schenectady NY 12308-2005

HATTEN, THOMAS M See Kocot & Hatton

HATTON AND KOCOT, MARCIA X See Kocot & Hatton

HAUER, ERWIN FRANZ
SCULPTOR, EDUCATOR, DESIGNER
b Vienna, Austria, Jan 18, 1926; citizen: Austria. *Study:* Acad Appl Arts, Vienna, Austria, dipl, 47-54; post grad studies with Marino Marini, Acad di Brera, Milan, Italy; with Gilbert Franklin, RI Sch Design; (US Dept State Fulbright travel grant), 55 & with Josef Albers, Yale Univ, 56-57. *Hon Degrees:* Yale Univ, Hon MFA, 87. *Work:* Chicago Art Inst; Kunsthaus, Basel, Switz; Wadsworth Atheneum, Hartford, Conn; Chase Manhattan Bank, NY; Benson Sculpture Park, Loveland, Colo; Brooklyn Mus Art, NY; Yale Univ Art Gallery, New Haven, Conn; Univ Conn Health Center, Farmington, Conn; Soaring Mus, Elmira, NY; Nat Acad Design Mus, NY; and others. *Comn:* Trellis wall, Nat Race Track, Caracas, Venezuela, 58; room divider, Showroom Knoll Int, Mex, 61; ceiling treatment, Imperial Can Bank Com, Montreal, Que, 63; wall treatment, Coca Cola Bldg, NY Worlds Fair, 64; E Pluribus Unum (sculpture), Super Ct Bldg, New London, Conn, 86; Bas-Reliefs, Centria, Rockefeller Ctr, New York, 2007, World Bank, DC, 2010; Screens, Elie Tahari Studios, New York, 2008, Standard Hotel, New York, 2008, Boston Mus Fine Art, 2010. *Exhib:* Solo exhibs: Old Dominion Col, Norfolk, Va, 64; Am Mex Inst Cult Relations, Mexico City, 63; Yale Univ, 64, 65; Dartmouth Col, Hanover, NH, 76; Sindin Galleries, New York City, 77; Mid Hudson Arts and Sci Ctr, Poughkeepsie, NY, 81; Smithsonian Inst, 81; Univ Conn, Storrs, 81; Hartford Childrens Mus, 82; 1708 E Main St, Richmond, Va, 83; Nat Soaring Mus, Elmira, NY, 84; Group exhibs: Vienna, Rome, Italy, Boston, Cleveland, Ann Arbor, Hartford, Manchester, NH, Yale Univ, Galerie Chalette, New York City, 61, 68; Sculptors Guild, New York City, 83, 84; Silvermine Collection, Westport, Conn, 84; Silo Gallery, New Milford, Conn, 84; Arrowwood, Purchase, NY; Reflections of the Inner Light, Lyman Allyn Mus, New London, Conn, 93; Vital Forms, Brooklyn Mus of Art, NY, 2001; San Diego Mus Art, 2002; Frist Ctr for Visual Arts, Nashville, 2002. *Teaching:* Prof emer, sculptor, Yale Univ, New Haven, Conn, 57-60 & 63-90; artist-in-residence, Dartmouth Col, Hanover, NH, 76; vis critic sculpture, Univ Pa, 79-80. *Awards:* Fulbright Grant, 1955; Ann Award, Indust Designers Inst Chicago, 59; Editor's Award, Int Contemp Furniture Fair, NY, 2006; inducted in Hall of Fame, Interior Design, 2008. *Bibliog:* Horacio Flores Sanchez (auth), La Escultura en la Construccion, Arquitectura, Mex, 9/57; Wilhelm Mrazek (auth), Modernes Mass & Gitterwerk, Alte und Moderne Kunst, Austria, 6/61; Karen O'Brien (auth), A Blurring of boundaries, Yale Scientific, 89. *Mem:* Sculptors Guild, NY; Int Soc Interdisciplinary Study Symmetry, Budapest, Hungary; Nat Acad, NY. *Media:* Plastic, Metal. *Publ:* Contribr, Olgyay and Olgyay: Solar Control & Shading Devices, Princeton Univ Press, 57; George Rickey: Constructivism Origins & Evolution, 68 & Jack Burnham: Beyond Modern Sculpture, 68, George Braziller; Senechal and Fleck: Shaping Space, A Polyhedral Approach, Birkhauser, 86; Zelanski and Fisher: Shaping Space, Harcourt, Brace, 87; auth, Princeton Architectural Press, NY, 2004; auth, Erwin Hauer: Continua Architectural Screens & Walls, 2007. *Dealer:* New Arts Gallery Litchfield CT; Francis Frost Newport RI. *Mailing Add:* 303 Wooding Hill Rd Bethany CT 06524

HAUFT, AMY
SCULPTOR
b Cincinnati, Ohio. *Study:* Univ Calif, Santa Cruz, BA, 80; Skowhegan Sch Painting & Sculpture, 81; Art Inst, Chicago, MFA, 83. *Comn:* Outdoor installation, Art Awareness, Lexington, NY, 87; outdoor installation, Art Park, Lewiston, NY, 88; outdoor installation, Pub Art Fund, Cadman Plaza Park, Brooklyn, NY, 93. *Exhib:* Working in Brooklyn-Installations, Brooklyn Mus, NY, 90; Int Artists' Mus, Lodz, Poland, 93; Disaster Plans: NY, Andrea Rosen Gallery, NY, 93; Counting To Infinity, Lipton & Owens Co, NY, 94; The Unreliable Narrator, Neuberger Mus, Purchase, NY, 95; Drawn & Quartered, Katonah Mus, NY, 96; If This Is True-Version 2, Derek Eller Gallery, NY, 98; Period Room: A Project By Amy Hauft (with catalog), Beaver Coll Art Gallery, Glenside, Pa, 98; Working Knowledge, Am Acad, Rome, Italy, 99; When I say Marco You say Polo, Cooper Union, NY, 99; Spray Skirt in a folding field, Art Container project, NY, 2001, 2003; Biennial Exhib of Pub art, Neuberger Mus, Purchase NY, 2003; Fog Area, Univ NC, Chapel Hill, 2006; Open EVA 2007, Limerick, Ireland, 2007; Counter Re-Formation, Western Mich Univ, Kalamazoo, Mich, 2009, Anderson Gallery, VCU Arts, Richmond, Va, 2009. *Pos:* Leslie Waggoner prof sculpture, Univ Tex Austin. *Teaching:* Vis instr installation sculpture, Cal Arts, Los Angeles, 88; vis lectr sculpture, Princeton Univ, 89; Tyler sch Art, Philadelphia, 89-2004; Chair & prof, VA Commonwealth Univ, Richmond, 2004-2012. *Awards:* Residency, Civitella Ranieri Found Fel, Italy, 95; Grant, NY Found Arts, 95; Philadelphia Exhibs Initiatives/PEW Charitable Trusts, 98; St Gaudens Memorial Fel,

99; NY Found Arts, 2002; and others. *Bibliog:* Charlotta Kotik (ed), Working in Brooklyn- Installations (exhib catalog), Brooklyn Mus, 90; Connie Butler (auth), Terrible Beauty & Enormity Space, Art & Text, 93; Eileen Neff (auth), Amy Hauft at Beaver College Art Gallery, Artforum,98; Richard Torchia (ed), Period Room; Projects by Amy Hauft (exhib catalog), Beaver Gallery, 99; Ashley Kistler (ed), Amy Hauft Counter, Reformation (exhib brochure), Anderson Gallery, VCU arts, 2009; Dinah Ryan (auth), Amy Hauft, Art Papers, 2010. *Mem:* CAA; SECAC; NCAA. *Media:* Installation Sculpture. *Publ:* Relativity 1st ed (exhib catalogue), Richmond, Va, 2005; Candy Coated Poeple, Peanuts, and a Prize: Ann Agee Boxing in the Kitchen, Va Commonwealth Univ, 2007; 1st ed (exhib catalogue), Reynolds Gallery, Richard, Va, 2008; The Sizes of Things in the Mind's Eye, 1st ed, Visual Arts Ctr, Richmond, Va, 2008. *Mailing Add:* 4313 Ramsey Ave Austin TX 78756

HAULENBEEK, NANCY E
CONSULTANT, DEALER
b Neptune, NJ. *Study:* Harcum Coll, Assoc of Business, Bryn Mawr, Pa, 74; Sch Visual Arts, New York, BFA, 83; RI Sch Design, Providence, RI; New Eng Sch Design, Boston, 79; Pratt Phoenix Sch Design, New York, 80; Nat Acad Fine Art, New York, 82; Parson Sch Design, New York, 85; Brookdale Comm Coll, Lincraft, NY, 2008. *Collection Arranged:* Assembled, arr, & cataloged the following exhibs, W Carl Burger, Frederick Galleries, Allenhurst, NJ, 2006; Process of Intention, Frederick Galleries, 2008; Contours of the Figure, Frederick Galleries, 2007; Childrens Art & Music Exhib, Forrestadale Sch, Rumson, NJ, 2006; Breeders Cup Exhib, Frederick Galleries, 2007; Vanishing Beauty of Land & Seg, Frederick Galleries, 2007. *Teaching:* lectr for art gallery representation, Monmouth Mus, Monmouth County Arts Coun, 2008. *Bibliog:* Monmouth Mus, Charish the Mus Exhib, Press Release, Feb 2008; Jane Meggitt, Unbridle- the Artist Inside the Animal, Examiner, Sept 2007. *Mem:* Monmouth Mus (bd mem for emerging artists), Lincroft, NJ; Monmouth Co Arts Coun, Red Banks, NJ; Manasquan River Group of Artist (recording secy), NJ; Audubon Artists (exec bd/pub relations, 2009), New York. *Mailing Add:* 111 Main St Allenhurst NJ 07711

HAUPTMAN, SUSAN
PAINTER
b Detroit, Mich, 1947. *Study:* Carnegie Inst Technol, Pittsburgh, Pa, 65-66; Univ Mich, Ann Arbor, BFA, 67-68; Wayne State Univ, Detroit, Mich, MFA, 69-70. *Work:* Corcoran Gallery Art, Washington, DC; Detroit Inst Art; Minn Mus Art, St Paul; Metrop Mus Art, NY; Oakland Mus, Calif; and others. *Exhib:* Solo exhibs include Jeremy Stone Gallery, San Francisco, 84, 89, Allan Stone Gallery, NY, 84, 88, Corcoran Gallery Art, Washington, DC, 90, Tatistcheff Gallery, Santa Monica, Calif, 92, Norton Gallery Art, West Palm Beach, Fla, 92, Tatistcheff & Co, NY, 93, Campbell-Thiebaud Gallery, San Francisco, 93, Tatistcheff/Rogers Gallery, Santa Monica, Calif, 96, Tatistcheff Gallery, NY, 96, Forum Gallery, NY, 99, 02, Ga Mus Art, Athens, 2000, Huntington Mus Art, WVa, 2000, Forum Gallery, 2006, 2010, Lux Art Inst, Encinatas, Calif, 2009-2010; group exhibs include Drawing USA, Minn Mus Art, St Paul, 71, 73 & 75; 19th Drawing & Sculpture Exhib, Ball State Univ, Muncie, Ind, 73; Under the Influence: Mentors/Teachers/Colleagues, Tatistcheff Gallery, Santa Monica, Calif, 92; (Basically) Black & White, Riverside Art Mus, Calif, 92; The Female Nude in Western Art, Ind Univ Art Mus, Bloomington, 92; Nat Drawing Invitational, Ark Art Ctr, Little Rock, 94; Contemp Still Life, Contemp Art Ctr Va, Va Beach, 99; New Visions by Nine Contemp Women, Forum Gallery, NY, 99; Nude + Narrative, PPOW, New York City, 2000; Drawings, McNeese State Univ, Lake Charles, La, 01; Magic Vision, Ark Arts Ctr, Little Rock, 01-02; Dog Days of Summer, Savannah Coll Art Design, Ga, 02; A Decade of Am Contemp Figurative Drawing, Frye Art Mus, Seattle, 02; New Generation of Magic Realists, Sangre de Cristo Art Ctr, Pueblo, Colo, 03; Transforming the Commonplace, Susquehanna Art Mus, Harrisburg, Pa, 03; Modern and Contemp Portraits curated by Townsend Wolfe, Forum Gallery, NY, 03; Koplin Del Rio Gallery, Los Angeles, 2004; Sheldon Mem Art Gallery, Univ Neb, 2005-2006; Butler Inst Am Art, Ohio, 2007; Long Beach Mus Art, Calif, 2007-2008; Naples Mus Art, Naples, Calif, 2007-2008; Contemp Am Figurative Paintings & Drawings, 2008; Kalamazoo Inst Arts, Mich, 2008; Cleveland State Univ Art Gallery, 2009; St Anselm Coll, NH, 2009; Casa Dell' Art, Istanbul, Turkey, 2010. *Collection Arranged:* Drawing USA, Minn Mus Art, St Paul, 71, 73 & 75; 19th Drawing & Sculpture Exhib, Ball State Univ, Muncie, Ind, 73; solo exhibs, Jeremy Stone Gallery, San Francisco, 84 & 89, Allan Stone Gallery, NY, 84 & 88, Corcoran Gallery Art, Washington, DC, 90, Tatistcheff Gallery, Santa Monica, Calif, 92, Norton Gallery Art, West Palm Beach, Fla, 92, Tatistcheff & Co, NY, 93 & Campbell-Thiebaud Gallery, San Francisco, 93, Tatistcheff/Rogers Gallery, Santa Monica, Calif, 96, Tatistcheff Gallery, NY, 96, Forum Gallery, NY, 99, Ga Mus Art, Athens, 2000, Huntington Mus Art, WVa, 2000; Under the Influence: Mentors/Teachers/Colleagues, Tatistcheff Gallery, Santa Monica, Calif, 92; (Basically) Black & White, Riverside Art Mus, Calif, 92; The Female Nude in Western Art, Ind Univ Art Mus, Bloomington, 92; Nat Drawing Invitational, Ark Art Ctr, Little Rock, 94. *Pos:* vis artist, St Lawrence Univ, Canton, NY, 74, Univ Calif, Davis, 85, Wayne State Univ, Detroit, Mich, 90, San Francisco Art Inst, 90, Anderson Ranch, Aspen, Colo, 95, Univ Calif, Santa Barbara, 96, Oreg Sch Arts and Crafts, 96, Harvard Univ, Cambridge, Mass, 97, 00-02. *Teaching:* instr, Univ Pittsburgh, Pa, 72-74; asst prof, Skidmore Univ, Saratoga Springs, NY, 74-78; Lamar Dodd prof chair, Univ Ga, Athens, 97-00. *Awards:* Nat Endowment Arts Fel Drawing, 85, 91; Art Matters Inc Grant, 89, 95; Visual Artist Fel, Calif Arts Coun, 90; Adolph and Esther Gottlieb Found Grant, 96; Elizabeth Found for the Arts Grant, 96; Pollock-Krasner Found Grant, 2002 & 2008. *Bibliog:* Jan Sjostrom (auth), Inner limits, Palm Beach Daily News, 5/4/92; Gary Schwan (auth), Art review, Palm Beach Post, 5/8/92; Helen L Kohen (auth), Art review, Miami Herald, 5/10/92. *Media:* Mixed Media. *Dealer:* Forum Gallery 745 Fifth Ave New York NY 10151. *Mailing Add:* 262 Mott St #324 New York NY 10012

HAUSMAN, FRED S
SCULPTOR, DESIGNER
b Bingen on Rhine, Ger, Apr 27, 1921; US citizen. *Study:* Pratt Inst; New Sch Social Res, with Stuart Davis. *Work:* Emily Lowe Collection, Univ Miami; Mus Mod Art, Bogota, Colombia; Evansville Mus; Rutgers Univ; Fordham Univ. *Exhib:* NY Univ, 66; Contemp Art USA, Norfolk Mus, 67; Columbia Univ, 68; Black & White Show, Smithsonian Inst, 69-70; 2nd Biennial, Medellin, Colombia, 70. *Media:* Acrylic. *Dealer:* Bodley Gallery 1063 Madison Ave New York NY 10028

HAUSMAN, JEROME JOSEPH
EDUCATOR
b New York, NY, May 4, 1925. *Study:* Pratt Inst, 42-43; Cornell Univ, AB, 46; Columbia Univ, 47-48; Art Students League, 48; NY Univ, MA, 51, EdD, 54. *Pos:* Mem arts & humanities panel, US off Educ, 64-70; ed bd, J Aesthetic Educ, 68-80; consult, John D Rockefeller III Fund, 68-75; pres, Minn Alliance Arts Educ, 77-79; bd dir, Arts, Educ & Ams, 79; bd trustees, Minn Mus Art, 79-82, Ragdale Found, 87-, Evanston Art Ctr, 93-2002, Chicago Artists Coalition, 2004- & Art Encounter, Evanston, Ill, 2005-. *Teaching:* Instr art, Elizabeth Pub Schs, NJ, 49-53; dir & prof, Sch Art, Ohio State Univ, 53-68; vis lectr, Sch Art, Syracuse Univ, 57; vis prof art educ, Pa State Univ, 58; prof div creative arts, New York Univ, 68-75; pres & prof, Minneapolis Coll Art & Design, 75-82; vpres acad affairs, Mass Coll Art, 82-85, prof art, 82-85; dir, Ctr Curric Planning & Evaluation, Urban Gateways, Chicago, 86-95; vis prof, Dept Art, Univ Wis, Milwaukee, Art Inst Chicago & Northern Ill Univ; vis prof, Art Inst Chicago. *Awards:* Art Educator Award, Nat Art Educ Asn, 86, Lifetime Achievement award, 2012. *Mem:* Distinguished fel Nat Art Educ Asn, 84-; Nat Comn Art Educ (chmn); Am Soc Aesthetics; Western Arts Asn; Inst Study Art Educ; Art Student's League (life mem); Critical Visual Arts Educ Club. *Publ:* Ed, Research in Art Education (yearbk), Nat Art Educ Asn, 59; contribr, articles in prof journals; ed, Arts and the Schools, McGraw-Hill, 80; Art Education J Nat Art Educ Asn, 89. *Mailing Add:* 1501 Hinman Apt 7A Evanston IL 60201

HAUSRATH, JOAN W
PRINTMAKER, WEAVER
b Detroit, Mich, May 29, 1942. *Study:* Bowling Green State Univ, Ohio, BS (educ), 64, MFA (printmaking), 66; Ohio State Univ, MA (art hist), 70. *Work:* Teradyne Inc, Nashua, NH; Nat Fire Prevention Agency, Quincy, Mass; Bowling Green State Univ, Ohio; Iceland Air, Reykjavik; Pub Libr, Plymouth, Mass. *Comn:* Fiber panel, Spaulding & Slye, Burlington, Mass; Sheraton Hotel, Tulsa, Okla; Magner-Harris, Atlanta, Ga. *Exhib:* Marietta Coll Craft Nat, GM Hermann Art Ctr, Ohio, 80 & 81; solo exhibs, Signature Gallery, Boston, 82, Bridgewater State Col, 89 & 97; Am Crafts in Iceland, Kjarvalsstadir Mus, Reykjavik, 83. *Collection Arranged:* New Eng Fiber Arts, Newport Mus, RI, 85; Fiber, Atlanta Financial Ctr, 87; Monotype Guild New Eng, Fed Reserve Bank, Boston, 98. *Teaching:* Instr art hist, Ohio State Univ, Columbus, 70-71; prof art, Bridgewater State Col, Mass, 71-; craft instr weaving, Summer Workshops, Eastern Conn State Col, Willimantic, 79-81. *Awards:* Mass Artists Found Fel Crafts, 83; Bridgewater State Coll CART Grant, 95 & 98. *Bibliog:* Roger Dunn (auth), The Ikats of Joan Hausrath, a painterly approach to weaving, Fiberarts Mag, 11-12/81. *Mem:* Monotype Guild New Eng; Boston Weavers' Guild. *Media:* Ikat, Monotypes. *Mailing Add:* Bridgewater State Col Dept Art Bridgewater MA 02325

HAVARD, JAMES
PAINTER
b Galveston, Tex, 1937. *Study:* Sam Houston State Col, Tex, BS, 59; Philadelphia Acad Fine Arts, 65. *Exhib:* Solo exhibs at Marion Locks Gallery, Philadelphia, 70, 73, 74, 77, 82, 88, 91, OK Harris Gallery, NY City, 71, R Gimple & Weitzenhoffer, NY City, 73, Gallerie Lund, Sweden, 74, Gallerie Fabian Carlsson, Goteborg, Sweden, 74, Louis K Meisel Gallery, NY City, 75, 79, 81, Gallerie Krakeslatt, Bromolla, Sweden, 75, Delahunty Gallery, Dallas, Tex, 76, Tolarno Galleries, Victoria, BC, Canada, 80, Hokin Kaufman Gallery, Chicago, 80, 83, 93, Janus Gallery, LA, Calif, 84, Lavignes, Bastille, Paris, France, 86, Allan Stone Gallery, NY, 91, 97, 2006, Elaine Horwich Gallery, Santa Fe, 92, Robert Kidd Gallery, Birmingham, Mich, 93, Allene LaPides Gallery, Santa Fe, 95, 99, The Lowe Gallery, Atlanta, Ga, 2001; groups exhibs at Indianapolis Mus Art, 76; Baltimore Mus Art, Md, 76, 77; Butler Inst Am Art, Youngstown, Ohio, 76; Senans Gallery, Basel, Switzerland, 77; Shore Gallery, Boston, Mass, 77; Solomon R Guggenheim Mus, NY, 77; American Haus, Frankfurt, Ger, 78; Elaine Horwich Gallery, Scottsdale, Ariz, 79; Mus Fine Arts, Springfield, Mass, 79; Phoenix Art Mus, Ariz, 79; Denver Art Mus, Colo, 80; Albright Knox Mus, Buffalo, NY, 80; Mus Southwest Tex, Midland, 81; Moos Gallery, Toronto, Can, 82; Tamarind Inst, Albuquerque, New Mexico, 87; LA Art Fair, Calif, 88; Marion Locks Gallery, 89, 91; Chicago Int Art Expo, 90; Tokyo Art Fair, Japan, 91; Cedar Rapids Mus, Iowa, 98. *Mailing Add:* Allan Stone Projects 535 W 22nd St New York NY 10011

HAVEL, JOSEPH G
SCULPTOR
b Minneapolis, Minn, Aug 20, 1954. *Study:* Univ Minn, BFA, 76; Pa State Univ, MFA, 79. *Work:* Mus Fine Art, Houston; Dallas Mus Art; The Barrett Collection, Dallas. *Exhib:* Solo exhibs, A Century of Texas, Sculpture, Huntington Gallery, Austin, 89, Barry Whistler Gallery, Dallas, Tex, 91, Davis/McClain Gallery, Houston, Tex, 92, Linda Farris Gallery, Seattle, Wash, 92. *Teaching:* Assoc dir, Glassell Sch Art, Houston. *Awards:* Nat Endowment Visual Arts Fel, 86; Otis & Velma Dozier Travel Grant, Dallas Mus Art, 91. *Bibliog:* Joan Davidow (auth), Balancing act, Detour Mag, 3/90; Elizabeth McBride (auth), Multiples, Art News, 5/90; Don Bacigulup (auth), Houston Contemp Mag, 9/89; Susan Chadwick (auth), Sculpting with poetic license, Houston Post, 7/89; Patricia Johnson (auth), Introductions gains strength, Houston Post, 7/89. *Media:* Miscellaneous. *Mailing Add:* 515 W 18th St Houston TX 77008-3607

HAVELOCK, CHRISTINE MITCHELL
HISTORIAN, EDUCATOR
b Cochrane, Ont, June 2, 1924; US citizen. *Study:* Univ Toronto, AB; Radcliffe Col, AM; Harvard Univ, PhD(Charles Eliot Norton Fel, Am Asn Univ Women Fel), 58. *Teaching:* Prof art hist, Vassar Col, 53-90, cur classical collection, formerly. *Awards:* Radcliffe Grad Medal, 87; Fel, Coll Teachers, Nat Endowment Humanities, 86; MC Mellon Chair, Vassar Coll, 75-97. *Res:* Greek sculpture of Hellenistic period. *Publ:* Auth, Hellenistic Art, W W Norton, rev ed 81; The Aphrodite of Knidos and Her Successors: A Historical Review of the Female Nude in Greek Art, 95. *Mailing Add:* 1010 Waltham St Lexington MA 02421

HAVENS, JAN
SCULPTOR, PRINTMAKER
b Norfolk, Va, 1948. *Study:* Atlantic Christian Col, BS, 70; Peabody Col, Vanderbilt Univ, Nashville, Tenn, MA, 73. *Work:* Tenn Botanical Garden & Fine Arts Ctr, Nashville; Dirkson Senate Office Bldg, Washington, DC; Appalachian Cult Ctr, Boone, NC; Radio City Music Hall Golden Jubilee, NY; Hanes Collection, Winston-Salem, NC. *Comn:* Sculpture, Radio City Music Hall, NY, comn by, Governor Alexander, Nashville, Tenn, 81. *Exhib:* Solo exhibs, Cheekwood Botanical Gardens, Nashville, 80, Tenn Botanical Garden & Fine Art Ctr, Nashville, 81, Southeast Ctr Contemp Art, Winston-Salem, NC, 83 & Zimmerman/Saturn Gallery, Nashville, Tenn, 91; The Animal Image: Contemp Objects and the Beast, Renwick Gallery, Smithsonian Inst, Washington, DC, 81; Images of Faith III, Blue Spiral Gallery, Ashville, NC, 93; Printmaking: Image and Technique, AVA Gallery, Chattanooga, Tenn, 98; Best of Tennessee Crafts, TACA Biennial, Nashville, Tenn, 98; Power of Excellence, Southeastern Ctr Contemp Art, NC, 2004. *Bibliog:* Virginia Watson-Jones (auth), Contemporary American Women Sculptors, Oryx Press, 86; The Crafts Report, 1/87; Cecelia Tichi (auth), Electronic Hearth: Creating an American Television Culture, Oxford Univ Press, 91. *Mem:* Kent Guild Artists & Craftsmen; Tenn Artist-Craftsmen's Asn; Southern Highland Guild; Piedmont Craftsmen; Carolina Designer Craftsmen. *Media:* Clay; Etching. *Mailing Add:* 1121 Graybar Ln Nashville TN 37204

HAVENS, SUE
PAINTER
b Rochester, New York, 1972. *Study:* Cooper Union, New York, BFA, 1995; Bard Coll, Annandale-on-Hudson, New York, MFA, 2004. *Exhib:* two-person exhibs include If Then Else End If, Postmasters, New York, (With Kristin Lucas), 2007; group exhibs include Aeronautica, Carpe Diem, Rochester, New York, 1992; Vote With Your Art, OK Harris Gallery, New York, 2004; Blue, Jeff Bailey Gallery, New York, 2005, Its Gouache & Gouache Only, 2008; No Show-Face Off, One Night Stand, Brooklyn, NY, 2006; Before & After, And/Or Gallery, Dallas, 2008; 6x6, Rochester Contemp, Rochester, NY, 2008. *Awards:* New York Found Arts Fel, 2008. *Mailing Add:* 4107 47th Ave Apt 4E Long Island City NY 11104

HAVERTY, GRACE
PAINTER
b Brooklyn, NY. *Study:* Coll Du Page, Glen Ellen, Ill, 70-89. *Exhib:* Catherine Lorillard Art Club 101st Ann Exhib, Nat Watercolor Soc, 2007; Arizona Watercolor Soc, 2000; Ariz Watercolor Asn Mem Exhib, 2002-10; Western Fed Watercolors 27th Ann Exhib, 2002, 2010; Ariz Aqueous XVIII Nat Exhib, 2003-05; Rocky Mt Nat Watermedia Exhib, Golden Colo, 2004; Transparent Watercolor Soc Am, 96, 2003-2009; Watercolor West, 2011; Ariz Watercolor Asn, 2011; Am Watercolor Soc, 2012. *Teaching:* Watercolor, Pastel & Sketching. *Awards:* Pastel Soc Am Award, NY, 88, 93, 95, 96 & 2000; Best of Show, Honorable Mention, Ariz Watercolor Asn, 2004; Nat Watercolor Soc, 2009; Best of Show, AWA, 2012. *Bibliog:* O'Toole & Triner (auths), Profile of an Arts Life, Ill Benedictine Col, 92. *Mem:* Ariz Watercolor Asn; master pastelist and signature mem, Pastel Soc Am; signature mem, Pastel Soc of Am; signature mem, Nat Watercolor Soc, 2007, 2009; signature mem, Transparent Watercolor Soc of Am; signature mem, Ariz Watercolor Asn. *Media:* Pastel, Watercolor, Oil. *Publ:* The Best of Pastel 2, Rockport Publ; The Best of Watercolor, Vol 3, Rockport Publ; Pushing the Limits of Pastels, Artist Mag, 10/2000; Pastel Artists Int Mag, 11/2000; Pushing the Limits of Pastel, Artist's Amg, 10/2000; 100 Ways to Paint Still Life, Artist Publ, 11/2000 & 1/2001; Sketches of LIfe, Artist's Sketchbook, fall 2001; Uninhibited Watercolors, Watercolor Mag, summer 2006; Strokes of Genius: The Best of Drawing, F&W Publ; Stroke of Genius #4; Splash 15. *Mailing Add:* 11795 N 95th St Scottsdale AZ 85260

HAVICE, CHRISTINE
ADMINISTRATOR
Study: Pa State Univ, PhD in Art History, 1974. *Pos:* Assoc Dean, Col of Fine Art, Univ Kentucky, 1998-2003; dir, Sch of Art Facility, Kent State Univ, currently. *Mem:* Nat Assn Schools of Art and Design (mem com on nominations, 2012-2014). *Mailing Add:* 211 Art Building Kent State University PO Box 5190 Kent OH 44242-0001

HAWKINS, MARGARET
CRITIC, EDUCATOR, WRITER
Teaching: Teacher, Sch of the Art Instit, Chicago. *Mem:* Chicago Art Critics Asn. *Publ:* Contribr weekly column in the Chicago Sun Times; Chicago Corr, ARTnews; contribr articles to a number of other nat and local art publ. *Mailing Add:* 1835 Old Briar Rd Highland Park IL 60035

HAWKINS, MYRTLE H
PAINTER, WRITER
b Merritt, BC. *Study:* Harnell Col, AA; San Jose State Univ; Univ Calif; WValley Col; also with Marshall Merritt, Maynard Stewart & Thomas Leighton. *Work:* Nat Easter Seal Soc, Chicago. *Comn:* Portrait, Rev John Foster, First Congregational Church, San Jose, Calif, 70; portrait, Rose Shenson, Triton Mus, Santa Clara, Calif, 71. *Exhib:* De Saisset Gallery, Santa Clara, 68; Hartnell Col, 69; one-man shows, Triton Mus Art, 71 & Rosicrucian Mus Art, San Jose, 73 & 77; Am Artist Prof League Nat Exhib, Lever House, NY, 71. *Pos:* Judge & juror of many art shows. *Teaching:* Instr painting, Calif State Dept Vocational Rehab, San Jose & Palo Alto, 69-71; also pvt painting lessons. *Awards:* First Place, Nat Easter Seal Soc, Chicago, 65; Gold Seal Award, de Saisset Art Gallery, 66; Best of Show, St Mark's Art Ann, Santa Clara, 68. *Bibliog:* Article, Rosicrucian Digest, 11/73; article, Grit, 8/28/77; Directory of American Portrait Artists, 8/85; Little Known Women: Twenty Extraordinary Achievers, 10/87. *Mem:* Encaustics Network Unlimited; Gualala Art Asn; Triton Mus Art. *Media:* Pastel, Oil. *Publ:* Illusr, The Adventures of Mimi, Books I & II, 66; auth, Art as Therapy, Recreation and Rehabilitation for the Handicapped, 74. *Mailing Add:* 646 Bucher Ave Santa Clara CA 95051

HAWKINS, THOMAS WILSON, JR
PAINTER, INSTRUCTOR
b Los Angeles, Calif, 1941. *Study:* Pasadena City Coll, AA, Calif State Univ, Long Beach, BA (design) & MA (drawing, painting); Calif State Univ, Los Angeles, art hist, design & ceramics. *Work:* Overholt & Overholt Law Off, Los Angeles; Home Savings & Loan Art Collection; Dr Clinton Roath, Diana Roath Collection; Roath Collection; DB Hawkins. *Exhib:* Southern Calif Expos, Del Mar, 67-77; Inland Exhibs, 68-77; Butler Inst Am Art, Youngstown, Ohio, 70; DaVinci Open Art Competition, NY, 70; Bertrand Russell Centenary Art Exhib, London & Nottingham, Eng, 73; Rio Hendo Coll; Whittier Asn Summer Show, 2011. *Teaching:* Instr drawing & design & introd to art, painting, Rio Hondo Community Coll, Whittier, Calif, 67-; instr art, drawing & art hist, Long Beach City Coll, 67-72; instr painting, Golden West Coll, Huntington Beach, Calif, 72-78; instr painting (part-time), Tenured, 74, CSC, 79; lab instr ceramic, photo, studio gallery display, Rio Hondo Coll, 2009-. *Awards:* Best Painting, Art in All Media, Southern Calif Expos, 67, Third Prize, 70; Second Award, Inland Exhib, San Bernardino Art Asn, 71 & 73; Purchase Award 25th All City Los Angeles Art, Barnsdall, 77; Whittier Art Asn, 2006. *Mem:* Whittier Art Asn; Nat Educ Asn; Calif Teachers Asn. *Media:* Oil, Clay, Acrylic. *Res:* Florence, Italy, Alaska. *Interests:* Painting backyard, landscape, still-life, ceramics. *Collection:* Dr Clinton Roath Art. *Publ:* Lecture Outline Notes for Art 101, LCC 93, TX3-611-938, edits 2 & 3. *Mailing Add:* 414 Fairview Ave Arcadia CA 91007

HAWKINSON, TIM
SCULPTOR
b San Francisco, Calif, 1960. *Study:* San Jose State Univ; Univ Calif, Los Angeles, MFA, 89. *Work:* Egg, 97; Bird, 97; Shatter, 98; Aerial Mobile, 98; Pentecost, 99; Bear, Univ Calif, San Diego, Stuart Collection, 2005; Uberorgan, Mass Mus Contemp Art. *Exhib:* Solo exhibs includes How Man Is Knit, Pacewildenstein, NY, 2007; group exhibs include Venice Biennale, 99; Mass Mus Contemp Art, 2000; Power Plant, Toronto, Can, 2000; Whitney Biennial, 2002; Corcoran Biennial, Washington, DC, 2003; Akira Ikeda Gallery, Japan; Serpentine Gallery, London; Cartier Found, Paris. *Mailing Add:* c/o Stuart Collection 0010 U Calif San Diego 9500 Gilman Dr La Jolla CA 92093-0010

HAWLEY, ANNE
MUSEUM DIRECTOR
b Iowa City, Iowa, Nov 3, 1943. *Study:* Univ Iowa, BA, 1966; George Washington Univ, MA, 1969; Sr Exec Prog, Kennedy Sch Govt; Lesley Col, DLett, 1987, Babson Col, 1990; Williams Col, LHD, 1989. *Hon Degrees:* Doc Letters, Babson Coll; Doc humane Letters, Williams Coll; Doc humanities, Lesley Coll; Hon D, Emmanuel Coll, Boston, 2012. *Pos:* Exec dir, Cult Educ Collab, 1974-77 & Mass Coun Arts/Humanities, 1977-89; Norma Jean Calderwood dir, Isabella Stewart Gardener Mus, Boston, 1989-. *Awards:* Lyman-Ziegler Award; Polaroid Travel Grant; Fulbright Fel; Aspen Inst Festival of Ideas Fel; Wheaton Coll Distinguished Fel; Reginald Townsend Award, New England Soc City New York; Boston Soc Archit Award, Oustanding Contrib Archit in Boston, 89; Travel grant, Fund for Mutual Understanding, USSR; Travel grant, Women's Travel Club, 82. *Mem:* Am Asn Mod Dirs; Mass Hist Soc; Saturday Club; Save Venice; Inst Contemp Arts (bd overseers). *Publ:* Contribr, Economics of Art Museums, 1991. *Mailing Add:* Isabella Stewart Gardner Mus 280 The Fenway Boston MA 02115-5807

HAXTON, DAVID
PHOTOGRAPHER, FILMMAKER
b Indianapolis, Ind, Jan 6, 1943. *Study:* Univ SFla, BA, 65; Univ Mich, MFA, 67. *Exhib:* Two-person show, Whitney Mus Am Art, NY, 78 & Biennial Exhib, 79; Cineprobe, Mus Mod Art, NY, 78; Photog in the 70's, Art Inst Chicago, 79; solo exhib, Sonnabend Gallery, NY, 79 & 83; Whitney Biennial Exhib, 79, 86; Recent Color, San Francisco Mus Art, 83; This Is Not A Photograph, Ringling Mus, Sarasota, Fla, 88; Siggraph Electronic Theater, Chicago, Ill, 92; Cimematheque Francaise, Un Cabinet D'Amateurs, Paris, France, 95; Ikon Gallery, 2001; Siggraph Art Show, Los Angeles, 2001; True Fictions, Kunstverein Dresden, Ger, 2002; Stadtische Galerie Erlangen, Ger, 2003; Constructed Realitites, Orlando Mus Art, 2003; True Fictions, Stadtmus, Hofheim a, Taunus, Ger, 2004; The Form Itself, Priska C Juschka Gallery, 2008; Color Photographs, 2009. *Collection Arranged:* Whitney Mus Am Art, Mus Mod Art, NY; Denver Mus Art; Albright-Knox Gallery, Buffalo, NY; Univ SFla Art Mus, Tampa. *Teaching:* Instr art, San Diego State Univ, 69-72; computer graphics, William Paterson Col, Wayne, NJ, formerly; prof art, Univ Cent Fla, 95-. *Awards:* Caps grant for filmmaking, NY State Coun for the Arts, 77-78; fel in film, Nat Endowment for the Arts, 78-79; fel in photog, NEA, 79-80. *Bibliog:* David Shapiro (auth), Inner city, Camera Arts, 1-2/82; Gene Markowski (auth), The Art of Photography, Prentice Hall, 84, Art and Photography, David Campany, 2003; Gary Kolb (auth), Photographing in the Studio, Brown & Bengamark, 93; The Polaroid Book,Taschen, 2005. *Media:* Photographs. *Dealer:* Cinedoc Paris 18 Rue Montmartre 75001 Paris France; Lux London; Priska C Juschka. *Mailing Add:* 2036 Sharon Rd Winter Park FL 32789-1517

HAY, A JOHN
HISTORIAN, EDUCATOR
b Penang, Malaysia, May 9, 1938; Brit citizen. *Study:* Exeter Col, Oxford Univ, BA, 61; Princeton Univ, PhD, 78. *Teaching:* Asst prof Asian art hist, Univ Denver, 76-77; from asst prof Chinese art hist to assoc prof, Harvard Univ, 77-84; assoc prof, Inst Fine Arts, NY Univ, 84-. *Res:* Chinese art, especially painting. *Publ:* Auth, The human body as a microcosmic source of macrocosmic values in calligraphy, Bush, Theories of Arts in China, 83; Values and history of Chinese painting I and II, RES 6, 83-84; Surface and the Chinese painter, Archives of Asian Art, 85; Kernels of Energy, Bones of Earth: The Rock in Chinese Art, China Inst, NY, 85. *Mailing Add:* Inst Fine Arts New York Univ One E 78th St New York NY 10021-0178

HAY, (GEORGE) AUSTIN
PAINTER, FILMMAKER
b Johnstown, Pa, Dec 25, 1915. *Study:* Pa Acad Fine Arts; Art Students League; Nat Acad; Univ Rochester; Univ Pittsburgh, BS & MLitt; Columbia Univ, MA; also with Robert Brackman & Dong Kingman. *Work:* Metrop Mus Art, New York; Dept Army; Libr Cong, Washington, DC; NY Pub Libr; numerous pvt collections. *Exhib:* Carnegie Inst, Pittsburgh, 72; Duncan Galleries, New York, 73; Manufacturers Hanover Trust, 73; Bicentennial Exhib of Am Painters in Paris, 76; Watergate Gallery, Washington, DC, 81; Salon des Nations, Paris, 83. *Pos:* Multimedia specialist, US Govt, 1955-2010. *Awards:* Documentary Award, Int Film Festival, Zagreb, Yugoslavia, 75; Academy Gold Medal, Accademia Italia, 80; Pictorial Award, Smithsonian Inst, 82. *Bibliog:* Subject, Speak for Yourself (film), 90; feature article, Living on the Edge of Stardom, Washington Post, 7/2/10. *Mem:* Am Artists Prof League; Allied Artists Am; Nat Soc Arts & Lett; Nat Acad Television Arts & Sci. *Media:* Oil, Miscellaneous Media. *Res:* The life & work of American artists William Merritt Chase & Robert Henri. *Specialty:* American Art. *Interests:* Art and painting depicted in motion pictures. *Collection:* Collection of Yuletide needlepoint, enlarged representations of Christmas US postage stamps by skilled cross-stitching artists. *Publ:* Auth & illusr, Seven Hops to Australia, 45; Life About the Universe (television prog), Nat Coun Churches, 65; The Performing Arts Experience, 69; auth & dir, Visit to the Museum of Modern Art (film), 72; dir, Highways of History (film depicting 100 oil paintings), 76; Motion Picture: An Austin Hay Film Festival. *Dealer:* Arts Club Galleries 2017 Eye St NW Washington DC 20006. *Mailing Add:* 2022 Columbia Rd NW Washington DC 20009-1314

HAY, DICK
SCULPTOR, EDUCATOR
b Cincinnati, Ohio, Nov 19, 1942. *Study:* Ohio Univ, BFA; NY State Coll Ceramics, Alfred Univ, MFA. *Work:* Butler Inst Am Art, Youngstown, Ohio; Latvia Art Mus, Riga; Sea of Japan, Kanazawa-shi, Japan; Pushkin Mus, Moscow; Won-Kwang Univ, Chun-Bok, Korea. *Exhib:* Contemp Ceramic Sculpture, Univ NC, Chapel Hill, 77; Nat Clay, Univ Hartford, Conn, 81; The Art of Ceramics, Paducah Gallery, Ky, 89; Maj Artists, Ctr for Arts, Phoenix, Ariz, 91; Am Exhib, Latvia Art Mus, Riga, 91; Int Invitational Exhib, Seoul, Korea, 95; and over 250 others. *Teaching:* Prof art/ceramics, Ind State Univ, Terre Haute, 66-; guest lectr, Sheridan Col Appl Arts, Toronto, Ont, 74, La State Univ, 76, Univ Miami, 76, Col Santa Fe, 77, Princeton Univ, 79, Ga State Univ, 83, NDak State Univ, 85, Alfred Univ, 86 & Buffalo State Univ, 90, Dzintari Inst Art, Jurmala, Latvia, 91, Muju Int Art Symposium, Korea, 95 and over 230 others. *Awards:* Nat Coun Educ Ceramic Arts Fel; Distinguished Teaching Award, Ind State Univ; Lifetime Achievement Award, Nat Council Educ Ceramic Arts. *Mem:* Nat Coun Educ Ceramic Arts (pres, 78-80). *Media:* Clay. *Dealer:* Martha Schneider Gallery Inc Chicago IL; Signature Gallery Boston MA. *Mailing Add:* 2108 W 340 Brazil IN 47834

HAY, IKE
SCULPTOR, EDUCATOR
b Atlanta, Ga, Apr 28, 1944. *Study:* Univ Ga, BFA & MFA. *Work:* Indianapolis Mus Art; New Orleans Mus Art; Mint Mus Art, Charlotte, NC; Chancellor's off, Pa Univ System, Harrisburg; State Mus Pa, Harrisburg; Millersville Univ, Pa; Mansfield Univ, Pa; Boy Scouts Exec Ctr, Birmingham, Ala; Smithsonian Mus Natural History. *Comn:* Gerald Hines Corp, Tulsa, Okla, 82; City of Phila, Pepsi Co, 82; Hines Industrial Develop Corp, Tulsa, 83; Reading Redevelopment Authority Ctr Park Place, Reading, Pa, 86; Harrisburg/Dauphin Co, 86; Rouse & Assoc, Univ Place, Tampa, Fla, 88; Environ Compliance Servs Corp, Exton, Pa, 92; Phoenix Contact, Harrisburg, Pa, 87; Rose & Associates, Tampa, Fla, 88; City of Lancaster, Pa, 89; Environmental Compliance Office, Exton, Pa, 93. *Exhib:* High Mus Art, 69; Solo exhibs, New Orleans Mus Art, 69 & Franklin & Marshall Coll, 81; Nat Sculpture 73 traveling show, 73; Pa State Mus, Harrisburg, Pa, 79; PSEA, State Mus Pa, 84; Invitational, Messah Col, Grantham, Pa, currently. *Pos:* Nat Endowment artist-in-residence, Decatur, 74-75. *Teaching:* Asst prof sculpture, Purdue Univ, West Lafayette, 69-74; asst prof sculpture, Millersville Univ, Pa, 75-81, assoc prof, 81-95, prof, 95-. *Awards:* Rosenblatt Scholarship, Univ Ga, 68; Grant in Aid, Arts Festival Atlanta, 68; Fac Grant, Purdue Univ, 70. *Bibliog:* John Spofforth (auth), The Ike Hay workshop, Ala-Arts, Ala State Arts Coun, 74. *Mem:* Am Asn Univ Prof; Napoleonic Soc Am (bd mem, currently); fel Int Napoleonic Soc. *Media:* Steel, Bronze. *Mailing Add:* 3200 Blue Rock Rd Lancaster PA 17603-9451

HAYES, CAROLYN HENDRICK
PAINTER, SCULPTOR
b Green Valley, Ill, Nov 25, 1925. *Study:* MacMurray Col, Jacksonville, Ill, AB (painting), 47; Univ Iowa, 48; Colo Springs Sch Fine Arts, 48; Univ Colo, studied with James Guy, Ricardo Martinez, James Pinto, Clifford Still, Richard Diebenkorn & Joan Brown, 56, 60 & 64; Univ Ill, 56; Cranbrook Acad Art, 60; Instituto Allende, San Miguel Allende, Mex, MFA (painting), 68. *Work:* Ill State Mus, Springfield; Yugoslavian Mus Solidarity, Montenegro; Peruvian Mus Collection, Lima; Instituto Mexicanonorteamericano, Mex; Galeria Libertad, Quertaro, Mex. *Comn:* Sagrado Corazon de Jesus (drawing), Munic Govt, San Miguel, Mex, 92. *Exhib:* Six States Exhibit, Joselyn Mem Art Mus, Omaha, Nebr, 48; Northen Miss Arts Exhibit, Ill State Mus, Springfield, 60, 61, 81; Northern Mirrijoyi Exhib, Springfield, IN, 60,61,66,68,71; Peoria Area Art Show, Peoria Art Mus, Ill, 66; Mac Allen Art Mus, 81; Havana Gallery, Cuba, 96; solo exhibs, IL State Mus, 74-75; Una Danza de Colores Geom, Museo de Universidad de Puebla, Mex, 83-84; Fiesta de Colores Geometrico, Diego Rivera Mus, Gto, Mex, 83; Humanidad del Arte Moderno, Casa de La Cultura, San Luis Potosi, Mex, 97; Technica Mixta, Instituto Nat Bellas Artes, San Miguel Allende, Mex, 99; Casa Diana Exhib, San Miguel Allende, Mex 2003; Kunsthaus Exhib, 2005; Ra Luz Sala de Arte, Mex, 2006; El Centro Cultural Ramirez (Bellas Artes), Mexico City, 2007. *Pos:* head art dept, Ill State Lib, Springfield, 56-60; head art, music & drama, Flint Pub Libr, Mich, 61-63. *Teaching:* instr art, Peoria Pub Schs, Ill, 51-52. *Awards:* Instituto Allende Award for contribution to art, 2001. *Bibliog:* Robert Evans (auth), Carolyn Hayes, State IL, 74: Robert Somerlott (auth), Art of Carolyn Hayes, Inst Allende, 97; Ana Quiroz (auth), Carolyn Hayes-Culturas Cruzadas, Kuns thaus Publ Mex, 2000. *Media:* Acrylic, Sand; Wood, Plastic. *Interests:* write poetry, Travel, photogr, ballet, film, theater, latin music. *Publ:* Picasso and the library, 58; Experiment with art, 59, IL Librs; Ink Drawings, 94, Illustrations of my original paintings, 98 & illustration of my original painting and poem, 2000, O'Zone. *Dealer:* San Francisco 11 Apartado 552 San Miguel Allende Guanajuato Mex 37700. *Mailing Add:* Apartado 678 San Miguel Allende Guanajuato Mexico 37700

HAYES, CHERYL
ADMINISTRATOR, EDUCATOR
Study: Univ New Orleans, MFA. *Pos:* assoc prof, chair dept fine arts, Univ New Orleans, currently. *Mailing Add:* University of New Orleans Department of Art 2000 Lakeshore Dr New Orleans LA 70148

HAYES, GERALD
PAINTER, PHOTOGRAPHER
b Los Angeles, Calif, Apr 9, 1940. *Study:* Auburn Univ, BVA, 62; Univ Ill, MFA, 66. *Work:* Art Ctr Am, Englishtown, NJ; AT&T, Liberty Corner, NJ; Huntsville Mus Art, Ala; Mobile Mus Art, Ala; Stockton State Col, Pomona, NJ; Addison Gallery of Art, Phillips Acad, Andover, MA. *Exhib:* Elements of Art, Mus Fine Art, Boston, 71; Tondos & Squares; Newcastle Salutes NY, Polytech Art Gallery, Eng, 83; Small Scale Abstraction, Grace Borgenicht Gallery, 86; Impact, Fine Arts Mus S Mobile, Ala, 95; Photographism in Painting, Pratt Manhattan Gallery, NY, 96; solo exhibs, Harm Bouckaert Gallery, NY, 82, Calkins Gallery, Hofstra Univ, NY, 90, Stockton State Col, Pomona, NJ, 90, Drawings after the Arcade, Southern Cross Univ Art Mus, Lismore, NSW, Australia, 96 & Southern Queensland Mus, 97, Abstraction INDEX, Condesco/Lawler Gallery, NY, 97, Signature Painting, Gallery Korea, NY, 98, Reconstructing Abstraction, Mitchell Algus Gallery, NY, 2000. *Teaching:* Prof grad art, Pratt Inst, 71-83, chmn painting & drawing, 83-85, asst chmn fine arts, 92-; vis prof painting, Parsons Sch Design, 81-83; prof, asst chmn fine arts, Pratt Inst, 92-. *Awards:* Pollock-Krasner Found Grant, 2002. *Bibliog:* Virginia Gunter (auth), Gerald Hayes: The Creativity of the Psychological Eye, Artforum, 5/73; Robert Pincus-Witten (auth), Entries: Styles of Artists and Critics, Arts Mag, 11/79; Mario Naves (auth), Studio View, New Art Examiner, summer 93; Saul Ostrow (auth), Gerald Hayes, Tema Celeste Art Review, 6/93. *Mem:* Coll Art Asn, NY. *Dealer:* Mitchell Algus Gallery

HAYES, LAURA M
CONSERVER, ART APPRAISER
b Birmingham, Ala, Nov 28, 1927. *Study:* Univ Wyo. *Collection Arranged:* Nick Eggenhofer, Roy Kerswill, Conrad Schwiering, Hans Kleiber; Northern Natural Gas, Peggy and Herald Samules, Winold Reiss, Harry Jackson, Tony Gomez; Many Western Artists... *Pos:* Head photog section, Wyo State Art Gallery, 65-74, art registrar, 67-71 & cur art, 71-79; owner, Wild Goose Gallery, Cheyenne, Wyo; retired. *Mem:* Wyo Press Women; Nat Fedn Press Women; and others. *Media:* Watercolor, oil. *Res:* Wyoming artist. *Specialty:* Original works of art & limited edition prints, work for collectors. *Publ:* contribr, The Illustrated Biographical Encyclopedia of Artists of the American West

HAYES, RANDY (RANDOLPH) ALAN
PAINTER
b Jackson, Miss, June 11, 1944. *Study:* Rhodes Col, Memphis, Tenn, 62-65; Memphis Coll Arts Acad Arts, BFA (Ford Found Grant), 68; Univ Ore, Eugene, 68. *Work:* Laguna Beach Mus Art, Calif; Seattle Art Mus; City Seattle One Percent for Art; Wash State One Percent for Art, Olympia; Mississippi Mus Arts; Microsoft Corp, Redmond, Wash. *Comn:* Murals, Seattle Ctr, 83 & State of Wash, Monroe, 83; Port Seattle Hqs, Wash, 92. *Exhib:* Outside NY: Seattle, The New Mus, NY, 83 & Seattle Art Mus, 83; solo exhib, Linda Farris Gallery, Seattle, 84; Setting the Stage, Los Angeles Co Mus Art; Scapes, Univ Calif Art Mus, Santa Barbara; Linda Farris Gallery, Seattle, Wash, 86; Cheney Cowles Mus, Spokane, Wash, 92; G Gibson Gallery, Seattle, 94; Comus Gallery, Portland, 94. *Awards:* WGBH New TV Workshop Grant, Boston, 75; Visual Arts Award, Mississippi Inst Arts & Letters, Jackson, 90. *Bibliog:* Regina Hackett (auth), Seattle artists come home in New York show, Seattle Post-Intelligencer, 10/20/83; Lynn Smallwood (auth), Seattle art from New York City, The Weekly, 10/26/83; Bruce Guenther (auth), 50 Northwest Artists, Chronicle Bks, 83; Lynn Smallwood (auth), Randy Hayes, Art News, 5/1/86; Bill Berkson (auth), Report From Seattle, Art in Am, 86. *Media:* Pastels, Oils. *Mailing Add:* 2014 9th Ave Seattle WA 98121

HAYES, SHARON
INSTALLATION SCULPTOR
b 1970. *Study:* Bowdoin Coll, BA, 1992; Whitney Mus Am Art, Independent Study Prog, New York, 1999-2000; Univ Calif, Los Angeles, MFA, 2003. *Exhib:* Solo exhibs, PS1 Mus Contemp Art, New York, 2001, Parlour Proj, Williamsburg, NY, 2002, Andrew Kreps Gallery, New York, 2003, Art in General, New York, 2005, Room Gallery, Univ Calif, Irvine, 2005, New Mus Contemp Art, New York, 2007, Tate Modern, 2008, Tanya Leighton Gallery, 2008, Warsaw Mus Modern Art, Poland,

REDCAT, Los Angeles, 2008, 2009, Context Gallery, Ireland, 2009, Objectif Exhibs, Antwerp, Belgium, 2009, Goteborgs Konsthall, Sweden, 2010, MoMA, NY, 2011, 2012, Performing Garage, NY, 2011, Vancouver Contemporary Art Gallery, 2011, Art Inst Chgo, 2011, Frances Young Tang Teaching Mus and Art Gallery, Saratoga Springs, NY, 2012, Museo Nacional Centre de Arte Reina Sofia, Madrid, Spain, 2012; Group exhibs, Democracy When, Los Angeles Contemp, 2002; Secondary Sources, Front Room Gallery, Williamsburg, NY, 2002; Sandwiched, Public Art Fund, New York, 2003; Republican Like Me, Parlour Proj, New York, 2004; Imagine, Deitch Proj, New York, 2004; When Artists Say We, Artists Space, New York, 2006, In the Poem About Love You Don't Write the Word Love, 2006; Altered, Stitched & Gathered, PS 1, Queens, NY, 2006; Two or Three Things I Know About Her, Carpenter Ctr for the Visual Arts, Cambridge, Mass, 2008; Whitney Biennial, Whitney Mus Am Art, 2010; Kunstwerk, Berlin, 2010; 54th Int Art Exhib Biennale, Venice, 2011, 55th Int Art Exhib Biennale, 2013; Deutsche Guggenheim, Berlin, 2012; Cooper Gallery, NY, 2012; Ackland Art Mus, Chapel Hill, NC, 2013; Oakville Galleries, Oakville, Ontario, 2013. *Awards:* D'Arcy Hayman Award, UCLA, 2000; Jacob K Javits Fel, US Dept Educ, 2001; Louis Comfort Tiffany Found Grant, 2008. *Bibliog:* Bea Espejo (auth), Sharon Hayes Eschuchar es un acto tan politico como habler, El Cultural, 6/2012; Joseph R Wolin (auth), Time Out Says, Time Out, 2012; Lance Esplund (auth), Protest Artist Creates Big Noise at New York's Whitney, Bloomberg, 7/2012; Brady Welch (auth), From New York: There's So Much I Want to Say to You, Artpractical, 7/2012; Kyle Chayka (auth), Sharon Hayes Occupies the Whitney with her Personal and Passionate Spin on the Politics of Identity, Artinfo, 2012; and many others. *Dealer:* Tanya Leighton Kurfurstenstrabe 156 10785 Berlin Germany

HAYES, STEPHEN L
EDUCATOR
b Memphis, Tenn, Mar 28, 1950. *Study:* Univ Ark, BA, Bpine Bluff, Ark, 68-73. *Exhib:* dir & musical conductor, Madison Square Garden, 92, East Room of the White House, 97, Carnegie Hall, 99, Kennedy Ctr for Performing Arts, 2009, Inaugural Anthem, 52nd Inauguration of the Pres of the US. *Pos:* artistic dir, CA Tindley Sch Music, San Francisco, Calif, 2002-2003. *Teaching:* Instr music, Philander Smith Coll, Little Rock, Ark, 74-75, Ark Arts Ctr, Little Rock, Ark, 79-82; assistant prof & dir music, Philander Smith Coll, Little Rock, Ark, 85-93; dir univ choirs, Tuskegee Univ, Tuskegee, Ala, 93-99; prof music, LeMoyne-Owen Coll, Memphis, Tenn, 99-2002; vis Lectr & dir music, Wiley Coll, Marshall, Tex, 2004-. *Awards:* First place trophy, Am Negro Spiritual Festival, 92, 97. *Mem:* Marshall Symphony Orchestra, Marshall, Tex, 2004-2006; Marshall Arts Coun, Marshall, Tex, 2009; Glenn E Burleigh Found, Fort Worth, 2009. *Mailing Add:* Wiley College 711 Wiley Ave Marshall TX 75672

HAYES, TUA
PAINTER
b Anniston, Ala. *Study:* Converse Col, BA; Columbia Univ Teacher's Col; also with Henry Lee McFee. *Work:* Del Art Mus, Wilmington; Wilmington Trust Co; Univ Del; Blount Collection; Converse Col, Spartanburg, SC; and others. *Exhib:* Philadelphia Pro-Show, Pa, 67; Nat Acad Design, NY, 70; Baltimore Mus Regional Show, Md; Am Drawings 1976, Portsmouth, Va; Distinguished Mid-Atlantic Artists, Univ Del, 80; Del Ctr Contmep Art, 83; and other group and one-man shows. *Awards:* First Prize for Drawing, Del Art Mus, 67; Second Prize, Asn Community Art Ctrs, Philadelphia, 82; First Prize, Hercules Expo, 82. *Mem:* Philadelphia Art Alliance; Studio Group, Inc (pres, 54-56); Del Art Mus (bd dir, 62-80); Hilton Head Art League; Delaware Ctr Contemp Arts. *Media:* Oil, Watercolor. *Dealer:* Red Piano Art Gallery 220 Cordillo Pkwy Hilton Head Island SC 29928. *Mailing Add:* c/o Carspecken-Scott Gallery 1707 N Lincoln St Wilmington DE 19806-2390

HAYNES, DAVID
HISTORIAN, CONSULTANT
b Washington, DC, Jan 13, 1942. *Study:* Univ Tex Austin, BJ, 63, BA, 64 & MA, 69. *Res:* 19th century Texas photography and photographers. *Publ:* Auth, Descriptive catalog of filmic items in Gernsheim Collection, Performing Arts Res, 75; Conservation of historic photographs, Proc Mt Plains Mus, 79; Where did you find that one?, Photogrs, 91; Catching Shadows: Directory of 19th Century Texas Photography, Tex State Hist Asn, 93; Photography, New Handbk Tex, 96. *Mailing Add:* 1810 W Mulberry San Antonio TX 78201

HAYNES, DOUGLAS H
PAINTER, EDUCATOR
b Regina, Sask, Jan 1, 1936. *Study:* Provincial Inst Technol & Art, Calgary, Alta, with R Spickett; Royal Acad Fine & Appl Arts, The Hague, Holland. *Work:* Edmonton Art Gallery, Alta; Confederation Art Gallery, Charlottetown, PEI; London Pub Mus & Art Gallery, Ont; Univ Calgary, Alta. *Comn:* Edmonton City Hall. *Exhib:* Fifth Biennial Exhib Can Art, London, Eng & Ottawa, Can, 63 & Sixth Biennial Exhib, Ottawa, 65; All Alberta '70, Edmonton, 70; West '71 Exhib, Edmonton, 71; Royal Can Acad Arts 91st Ann, Montreal, 71; Nat Can Touring Exhib, 91-92. *Pos:* Art adv, Govt Alta, 67-70. *Teaching:* From assoc prof to prof art & design & chair dept, Univ Alta, 70-. *Awards:* Govt of Neth Scholar, 60; All Alta First Prize, Jacox Gallery, 65; Can Coun Sr Award, Can Govt, 67. *Bibliog:* N Yates (auth), Three from Edmonton, Arts Can, 10/69; K Wilkin (auth), Western Canada, a survey, Art in Am, 5-6/72. *Mem:* Assoc Royal Can Acad Arts; Univ Art Asn Can. *Media:* Acrylic, Mixed. *Dealer:* Kathleen Laverty Gallery Edmonton AB Canada. *Mailing Add:* 14312 Ravine Dr Edmonton AB T5M 3M3 Canada

HAYNES, R (RICHARD) THOMAS
PAINTER, ILLUSTRATOR
b Rome, Ga, Feb 17, 1934. *Study:* Auburn Univ, BS, 56; painting with James Harmon, 60; watercolor with Zoltan Szabo, 75. *Work:* Univ Pac, Stockton, Calif; Colby Col, Waterville, Maine; Mo Hist Soc Print Collection, St Louis. *Exhib:* NMex Int, Portales, 76; St Louis Artists Guild, Webster Groves, 77; Southern Watercolor Soc, Columbus Art Mus, Ga, 78; Pittsburgh Aqueous 78, Pa; Ark Wildlife Fedn, Pine Bluff, 78 & 79; and others. *Awards:* First Place, St Louis Co Div Parks, 75; Second Place, NMex Int, 76. *Bibliog:* Member of the issue, North Light Mag, 81. *Mem:* Southern Watercolor Soc; Acad Professional Artists. *Media:* Egg Tempera, Watercolor. *Dealer:* Aldridge Fine Arts I & II 104 Romero NW Albuquerque NM 87104. *Mailing Add:* 206 Thiebes Rd Labadie MO 63055

HAZLEHURST, FRANKLIN HAMILTON
HISTORIAN, EDUCATOR
b Spartanburg, SC, Nov 6, 1925. *Study:* Princeton Univ, BA, 49, MFA, 52, PhD, 56. *Teaching:* Instr art hist, Princeton Univ, 54-56; lectr art hist, Frick Collection, New York, 56-57; from asst to assoc prof, Univ Ga, 57-63; prof & chmn dept fine arts, Vanderbilt Univ, 67-91; prof fine arts, emeritus, 1995. *Awards:* Fulbright Fel, 53-54; Am Coun Learned Soc Grant in Aid, 67; Madison Sarratt Prize, Vanderbilt Univ, 70; Officier-de l'ordre des arts et des leffres, Paris, 2006. *Mem:* Am Archaeol Soc; Coll Art Asn Am; Southeastern Coll Art Asn (pres, 73-74); Soc Archit Historians. *Res:* Seventeenth and 18th century French art, especially landscape architecture. *Publ:* Auth, Artistic origins of David's oath of the Horatii, Art Bulletin, 60; auth, Jacques Boyceau and the French Formal Garden, 66; auth, Additional sources for the Medici Cycle, Bulletin Musees Royal Beaux Arts Belg, 67; ed, French Formal Garden, Third Colloquium Landscape Archit, Dumbarton Oaks, 74; auth, Gardens of Illusion: The Genius of Andre Le Nostre, 80; and others; Le jardins d'illusion, Le genie d'Andre Le Nostre, 2005. *Mailing Add:* 2104 Golf Club Ln Nashville TN 37215

HAZLEWOOD, CARL E
CURATOR, PAINTER
b Georgetown, Guyana, SAm, Apr 28, 1950; US citizen. *Study:* Brooklyn Mus Sch (scholarship), 71 & 73-74; Skowhegan Sch Painting & Sculpture (scholarship), 73; Pratt Inst, New York, BFA(with honors), 75; Hunter Coll City Univ New York, MA, 77. *Work:* Dept of the Treasury, State NJ, Trenton; Nat Collection Fine Arts, Georgetown, Guyana; Booker Brothers & McConnel & Co Ltd, London, Eng; State Legislative Bldgs, Albany, NY; Borough Manhattan Community Col, City Univ NY. *Comn:* Many portraits in Am & abroad, 67-72. *Exhib:* Vital Abstractions, William Carlos Williams Ctr Arts, Rutherford, NJ, 87; Four Artists, Newark Mus, NJ, 90; Monochrome, Inst Contemp Art, Clocktower Gallery, NY, 90; Generated Realities, Middleton-McMillan Gallery, Charlotte, NC, 91; Drawings from Beginning to End, Ben Shahn Galleries, William Paterson Col, Wayne, NJ, 92; Curators as Artists/Artists as Curators, Bergen Mus Art, NJ, 95; Nat Gallery Art, Smithsonian Inst, Washington, DC, 96-97; Castellani Art Mus, Niagara Univ, NY, 96-97; Recent Acquisitions, Georgetown, Guyana, 96-97. *Collection Arranged:* Revelations (paintings; auth, catalog), Hallwalls, NY, 87; Nexus, Transformation/Transfiguration (auth, catalog), PS 122, 3 Artists of Diverse Cultures, 89; Environmental Explorations (auth, catalog), Three Part Ser, 90-91; Selections (auth, catalog), NY & NJ Artists, Multi Media Work, 90; Essential Structures (auth, catalog), 3 Installations, NJ, 92; Current Identities: Recent Painting in the United States (auth, catalog), IV Int Bienal de Pintura, Cuenca, Ecuador, 94; Required Nuance (sculpture; auth), Studio Mus, Harlem, 95. *Pos:* Cur, Hazlewood Fine Art, Brooklyn, NY, 77-; co-founder & artistic dir, Aljira, Ctr Contemp Art, Newark, NJ, 84-; auth & ed, Nka J Contemp African Art, Cornell Univ, 94-. *Teaching:* Instr painting, Newark Mus Art, NJ, 91; adj prof art hist, Jersey City State Col, NJ, 91-. *Awards:* Edward Arthur Mellinger Found Scholar; Max Beckmann Int Award for Advanced Study; Anco-wood Found Award/Rosalie Retrash Schmidt Mem Award Exhib Grants-Artist Space. *Bibliog:* Joseph E Young (coauth with Barbara Cortright), Phoenix letter, Artspace Mag, 8/86; Vivian Raynor (auth), Art: Drawing from beginning to end, NY Sunday Times, 4/92; Who's Who in the East, Silver Anniversary 25th ed, Marquis Who's Who in Am, 95-96. *Mem:* Newark Arts Coun; Nat Asn Artists Orgn; NY State Arts Coun Visual Arts Panel. *Media:* Multi Media. *Publ:* Auth, Newark Boasts Long History of Public Art, Newark Arts Coun, 88; illusr (cover), The Signal Network Int Lit, Art Ideas, Signal, 89; auth, In Marble Hill: Peter Spaans, The Art of Peter Spaans, Under Construction Art Proj Ltd, Amsterdam, Neth, 93; Interior life contests, conservatism, Flash Art Int, Rome, 11-12/97; Art by African Americans in the Collection of the New Jersey State Museum (catalog), NJ State Mus, 98

HEAD, ROBERT WILLIAM
PAINTER, EDUCATOR
b Springfield, Ill, Aug 6, 1941. *Study:* MacMurray Coll, BA (art educ), 63, with Sidman & Foresterling; Kent State Univ, MFA, 65, with Shock, Morrow & Petersham, Colo Outward Bound Sch, 71. *Hon Degrees:* DHL, MacMurray Coll, 95. *Work:* JB Speed Art Mus, Louisville, Ky; Mint Mus, Charlotte, NC; Del Mar Coll, Corpus Christi, Tex; MacMurray Coll, Jacksonville, Ill; Massillon Mus, Ohio. *Exhib:* Ball State Univ Nat Drawing Show, Muncie, Ind; Bucknell Nat Drawing Exhib, Lewisburg, Pa; Mainstreams Int Painting Exhib, Marietta, Ohio; Brooks Mem Gallery Show, Memphis, Tenn; Weatherspoon Ann Drawing Exhib, Univ NC; solo exhibs, JB Speed Mus, Louisville, Ky, Univ Mass, Amhurst, Yeiser Art Ctr, Paducah, Ky, Capitol Arts Ctr,& Western Ky Univ, Bowling Green, Ky, Sangamon State Univ, Springfield, Ill, Concord Coll, Athens, WVa, Doane Coll, Crete, Nebr, Cocino Arts Ctr, Flagstaff, Ariz; The Parthenon, Bd Parks & Recreation, Nashville, Tenn; Louisville Vis Arts Asn, Ky. *Teaching:* Prof emer drawing & painting, Murray State Univ, 65-; assoc prof drawing & introd art, World Campus Afloat, Chapman Coll, spring 70 & 72; vis prof, Univ Alaska, Fairbanks, fall 86. *Awards:* Merit Award for Excellence in Teaching, Murray State Univ, 70; Purchase Award, Mid-States Exhib, Evansville Mus; Distinguished Prof, Murray State Univ. *Mem:* Wilderness Soc; Ky Ornith Soc. *Media:* Paint. *Mailing Add:* 2438 Univ Station Murray KY 42071

HEADLEY, DAVID ALLEN
PAINTER
b Washington, Pa, Dec 11, 1946. *Study:* Washington & Jefferson Col, BA, 68. *Work:* Corcoran Gallery Am Art, Washington, DC. *Exhib:* Eastern Mich Univ, Ypsilanti, Mich, 67; Butler Inst Art, Youngstown, Ohio, 67 & 68; Detroit Inst Art, 72; Corcoran Gallery, Washington, DC, 76 & 77; Health, Educ & Welfare Bldg, Washington, DC,

79-80; Manhattan Ctr Gallery, NY, 83; Pratt Inst Gallery, NY, 83; and others. *Awards:* First Prizes, Washington & Jefferson Arts Festival, 65 & 66 & Morgantown Art Asn, WVa, 66 & 67. *Bibliog:* John Deckert (auth), David Headley, Arts Mag, 9/81. *Mailing Add:* c/o Tepper Takayama Fine Arts 20 Park Plaza Suite 600 Boston MA 02116

HEALY, ANNE LAURA
SCULPTOR, EDUCATOR

b New York, NY, Oct 1, 1939. *Study:* Queens Col, New York, BA, 62. *Work:* Chemical Bank, NY; NY Cult Ctr; Allen Art Mus, Oberlin, Ohio; City Univ Grad Ctr, NY; Mich State Univ, East Lansing; and others. *Comn:* Washington State, 85; City of Oakland, 85; Stanford Univ, 90-91; Art Inst Southern Calif, 89; State Wash, 85 & 95; Grace Cathedral, San Francisco, Calif; Cities of Kitsap & Spokane, Wash State. *Exhib:* Individual exhibs, AIR Gallery, NY, 72, 74, 78, 81 & 83, Matrix Gallery, Sacramento, Calif, 82, Pub Art Fund, NY, 83, Douglas Col, Rutgers Univ, New Brunswick, NJ, 84, Festival Lake, Oakland, Calif, 85 & San Francisco Mus Mod Art Artists Gallery, 88; Mus Contemp Crafts, NY, 72; Sculpture Outdoors, Nassau Co Mus Fine Arts, Roslyn, NY, 75; Int Women's Yr, Bronx Mus, NY, 75; South East Tex Mus, Corpus Christi, 77, Baruch Col, NY, 78, Candidates for Grants, Am Acad & Inst of Arts & Lett, 79 & Hofstra Univ, Hempstead, NY, 80; New Directions in Drawing, 1950-80; A Women's Place, Kingsborough Community Col, Brooklyn, NY, 82; KQED Art Auction Invitational, Fuller-Golden Gallery, San Francisco, Calif, 85; Am Heart, San Francisco Art Inst, Calif, 86; Terrain Gallery, San Francisco, 98; AIR Gallery, NY, 2006 & 2008; Heritage Bank, San Jose, Calif, 2007, Werkstate Gallery, NY, 2008. *Pos:* Bd mem, bd dir & head curatorial comt, San Francisco Arts Comm Gallery, Calif, 85-89; bd trustees, San Francisco Art Inst, Calif, 85-88; art comnr for Sculpture City of San Francisco, head, visual art comt, mem, civil design comt, 89-; pres, San Francisco Art Comn, 92-96. *Teaching:* Instr sculpture, St Ann's Sch, Brooklyn; vis artist, Mich State Univ, East Lansing, 73 & Broward Col, Ft Lauderdale, Fla, 76; vis artist-in-residence, Univ Cincinnati, 76; adj asst prof, Baruch Col, City Univ New York, 1976-81; guest lectr, Sch Visual Arts, New York, 77, Bard Col & Univ Iowa, 78 & Univ Northern Iowa, 79; vis prof sculpture, Univ Iowa, Iowa City, 79; asst prof, Univ Calif, Berkeley, 81-85, assoc prof, 85-93, chair art dept, 90-94, prof, 93-2003. *Awards:* Award for Sculpture, Asn Am Univ Women, 76-77; Am Acad & Inst Arts & Lett, 79-80; MacDowell Colony, 80. *Bibliog:* Ellen Lubbell (auth), Healy's double header, Soho Weekly News, 10/18/78; Corinne Robins (auth), Anne Healy: Ten years of temporal sculpture, Arts, 10/78; The great goddess, Heresies 5th Issue, spring 78. *Mem:* Coll Art Asn; Women's Caucus Art Asn. *Media:* Sculpture, Drawing. *Res:* public art, sculpture. *Specialty:* contemporary art. *Interests:* film, photography, popular culture, feminist theory, theatre

HEALY, DEBORAH ANN
ILLUSTRATOR, EDUCATOR

b Newark, NJ. *Study:* Coll New Rochelle, BA; Montclair State Univ, MA, 76; Syracuse Univ, with Isadore Selzer, James McMullen, Doug Johnson & others, MFA, 79. *Work:* Danish Pub Television; Swedish Pub Television; Italian Pub Television; Vanderbilt Univ; Forbes Mag; Johnson & Johnson. *Comn:* Films, animated Women, 80, Owl & Pussycat, Little Birds, 81 & Three Love Poems; paintings & illus for Harper & Row, Doubleday, Glazen Advert, Douglas Group, Monsanto, Donald Sacks, Inc, United Nations, Yankee, New Eng, Living, Simon & Schuster, Bantam, New Am Libr, Philadelphia Mag, Enquirer & others. *Exhib:* Film Festival, Morris Mus Arts & Sci, Morristown, NJ, 76; Artist in Am Series, Fairleigh Dickenson Col, Madison, NJ, 76; Annecy Int Film Festival, Paris, France, 77; Zagreb Int Animation Festival, Yugoslavia, 78; Sinking Creek Winners' Invitational, Chicago Art Inst, 78; Invitational, Montclair Art Mus, NJ, 79; Painting Exhib, Soc Illus, 85 & 95; paintings of Turkey in Pentagon, Airforce Artist, 89; Earth Island proj, UN, 90. *Teaching:* Prof visual communications, Moore Col Art, Philadelphia, Pa, 86-; lectr, Parsons Sch Design, 82- & Kean Col, 85; hist illusr, Rochester Inst Technol & Second Ann Graphic Design Symposium. *Awards:* First Prize-Best in Show, Stockton State Spring Film Festival, NJ, 78; Nat Mag Nomination, Philadelphia Mag, 88; Film Grant, NJ State Coun Arts, 81-82 & 85-86; and others. *Bibliog:* Interview, Edison Black Maria Film Fest, NJ Independent Filmmakers, NJ Cablevision, 5/29 & 6/15/85. *Mem:* Art Dirs Club NJ; Coll Art Asn; Graphic Artists Guild; Soc Illustrators; Soc Childrens Book Writers & Illus. *Media:* Oil & Watercolor. *Publ:* Illusr, Elizabeth and The Water Troll, The Little Old Man and His Dream, Waiting For You, Desserts, Harper & Row, 87-89; Branta, Simon Schuster, 94; The Gift of the Fawn, 95. *Dealer:* Clapp & Tuttle Gallery CT

HEALY, JULIA SCHMITT
PAINTER, EDUCATOR

b Elmhurst, Ill, Mar 28, 1947. *Study:* Univ Chicago, 66-70; Yale Univ Summer Sch, 69, with Mel Bochner, Bob Mangold & Bob Moskowitz; Art Inst Chicago, BFA, 70, MFA, 72. *Work:* Can Coun Art Bank, Ottawa, Ont; NS Art Bank, Halifax; Confederation Art Gallery, Charlottetown, PEI; Mount St Vincent Univ Art Gallery, Halifax; Dept Educ, Prov of NS, Halifax; Staten Island Mus; Roger Brown Collection; pvt collections of Don Baum, John Perreault, Jeff Weinstein, Dennis Adrian, Charles Riley and others. *Comn:* Halifax Diary (print), Dept Pub Works, NS, 75; Staten Island Children's Mus, 89-91; Cowparade, 2000; Dolphin Sitings, 2005. *Exhib:* Intercourse (co-cur with Ray Johnson), Wabash Transit Gallery, Chicago, 71; Art Inst Chicago, 72 & 76; Grassroots-Nova Scotian Folk Art, Eye Level Gallery, Halifax, 75; solo exhibs, Owens Art Gallery, Mt Allison Univ, Sackville, NB, 77 & Susan Whitney Gallery, Regina, Sask, 81 & 83; Atlantic J (traveling exhib), Nat Gallery Can, 76-77; Artists Space, 89, 90 & 91; Guggenheim Soho, 94; Soho 20, 96; ArtLab, 96; Soho 20 Chelsea, Phyllis Kind Gallery; Chrystie Street Studios, 2003-2006; Sch Art Inst Chicago, 2005; Pleiades Gallery, NY, 2006; Oxbow, Saugatuck, Mich, 2006; Pleiades Gallery, NY, 2007. *Pos:* Dir, Eye Level Gallery, 75-76; dir related arts, West Hempstead Schs, NY, 2005-. *Teaching:* Instr painting & drawing, Sch Art Inst Chicago, 71-72; instr visual art, Ocean Co Col, Toms River, NJ, 79-82; asst prof, Pratt Inst, Brooklyn, NY, 91-94, dir, Saturday Sch, 92-94; Howell Road Sch, Valley Stream, NY, 94-2005; CUNY, 98-. *Awards:* Can Coun Arts grant, 76-77 & 77-78; Staten Island Coun Arts Grant, 87 & 91; Distinguished Alumni, SAIC; Fel, San Gallo Studio, Florence, Italy, 2007. *Bibliog:* Ron Shuebrook (auth), The Atlantic Provinces: Letter, Artscanada, 3/75; Marilyn Smith (auth), Some Nova Scotian Women Artists, 12/75 & Ron Shuebrook (auth), Some Major Nova Scotian Painters, 10-11/76, Art Mag; Vivian Raynor (auth), Eccentric vision, Humorous touches, NY Times, 8/27/89; John Perreault (auth), Dispatches from the Front, 89, Artmakers Staten Island Advance, 90-. *Mem:* Coll Art Asn; Chancellors Art Adv Bd, 91-95; Nat Art Educ Asn. *Media:* Mixed Media. *Res:* Motivation in Art Education. *Specialty:* Canadian Art, folk art, contemporary art. *Interests:* Opera. *Publ:* Ed, Recent Work: Julia Schmitt Healy, Dalhousie Art Gallery, 76; illusr, What Kids Like to Do, 94; Artmakers Activity Book, 95; doodlelines, 95. *Dealer:* Susan Whitney Gallery 2220 Lorne St Regina SK Can

HEARN, M F (MILLARD FILLMORE), JR
ADMINISTRATOR, HISTORIAN

b Lincoln, Ala, Aug 18, 1938. *Study:* Auburn Univ, Ala, BA, 60; Ind Univ, MA (hist), 64, MA (art hist), 66, PhD, 69; Univ Calif, Berkeley, study with Jean Bony, 65-66; Courtauld Inst Art, 66-67. *Pos:* bd dir, Int Center Medieval Art, 85-88; academic dean, Semester at Sea, 98, 2001 & 2006; bd dir, Pittsburgh Chamber Music Soc, 2001-06. *Teaching:* From instr to prof medieval & mod archit, Univ Pittsburgh, 67-2006, actg chmn fine arts dept, 73-74, chmn, 74-78, dir archit studies prog, 81-2006; vis prof, Carnegie Mellon Univ, 79. *Awards:* Grant, Nat Endowment Humanities Summer Inst, 84; Grant, Nat Endowment Humanities Summer Stipend, 90; Grant, CASVA, Paul Mellon Vis Senior Fel, 92. *Mem:* Soc Archit Historians; Int Ctr Medieval Art; Brit Archeol Asn. *Res:* Twelfth-century architecture of England and Northern France; Romanesque sculpture; theory of architecture. *Publ:* Auth, The Rectangular Ambulatory in English Medieval Architecture, J Soc Archit Historians, Vol 30, 71; Romanesque Sculpture: The Revival of Monumental Stone Sculpture in the Eleventh and Twelfth Centuries, Ithaca and Oxford, 81; Ripon Minster: The Beginning of the Gothic Style in Northern England, Philadelphia, 83; The Architectural Theory of Viollet-le-Duc: Readings and commentary, Cambridge, Mass, 90; Canterbury Cathedral and the Cult of Becket, Art Bull, Vol 76, 94; Ideas that Shaped Buildings, Cambridge, Mass, 03, Spanish & Chinese transl, 2006, Russian Travel, 2013

HEARTNEY, ELEANOR
CRITIC, CURATOR

b Des Moines, Iowa, Aug 5, 1954. *Study:* Univ Chicago, BA (humanities) 1976, MA (art hist), 1980. *Collection Arranged:* Public Interventions, Inst Contemp Arts, Boston, 1994. *Pos:* Ind art critic, New York City, 1982-; contribg ed, Art Am, New Art Examiner, Artpress, 1986-, Art in Am, 1989-; ed assoc, Art News, 1986-93; vis cur, Inst Contemp Art, Boston, 1994; critic in residence, Sculpture Mag, Washington, 1989-90; panelist, vis critic, lectr for various nat and int organizations. *Teaching:* Vis lectr, Univ New Mex, Albuquerque, 1995-96. *Awards:* Frank Jewitt Mather Award for Disting Art Criticism, Coll Art Asn, 1992; NY Found Arts Grant, 1993; Am Crafts Coun Grant, 1995; Asian Cult Coun Grant, 1995; Chevalier, Ordre des Arts et des Lettres, 2008. *Mem:* AICA (co-pres AICA USA, 2006); Etant Donnes (adv bd, 1994-97); Coll Art Asn. *Publ:* Auth, A necessary transgression: pornography & postmodernism, New Art Examiner, 11/88; The whole earth show part II, Art Am, 7/89; Social Responsibility in Censorship, In: Culture Wars, Richard Bolton, ed, New Press, 1992; New World Order, In: Beyond PC: Toward a Politics of Understanding, Pat Aufterheide, ed, Graywolf Press, 1992; Eco-poetry, Eco-politics, Inc: But is it Art?, Nina Felshin, ed, Bay Press, Seattle, 1994; Critical Condition: American Art at the Crossroads, Cambridge Univ Press, 1997, Tate Gallery Pubs, 2001; Postmodern Heretics: The Catholic Imagination in Contemp Art, Midmarch Arts Press, 2004; Defending Complexity: Art Politics & the New World Order, Hard Press Eds, 2005; Art & Today, Phaidon Press, 2008

HEATH, DAVE (DAVID) MARTIN
PHOTOGRAPHER

b Philadelphia, Pa, June 27, 1931. *Study:* Philadelphia Coll Art, 54-55; New Sch, with W Eugene Smith, 59 & 61. *Work:* Nat Gallery Can, Ottawa; CMCP, Ottawa; Mus Mod Art, NY; Int Mus Photog, George Eastman House, Rochester, NY; Minneapolis Inst Art; Hallmark Collection, Kansas City, MO; and others. *Comn:* Collab with Robert Frank, Robert Heinecken & John Wood, William Johnson & Susan Cohen (dir), 83-85. *Exhib:* Solo exhibs, A Dialogue with Solitude, Eastman House, Rochester & Art Inst Chicago, 64 & Minneapolis Art Inst, 94, Le plaisir de voir, la passion du regard, Light Impressions Spectrum Gallery, Rochester, 88, Photofind Gallery, NY, 88, Lesley Walker, a collaborative portrayal, Artscourt, Ottawa, 89, ADWS (master set & layout maquette), Simon Lowinsky, NY, 97, Barry Singer Gallery, Petaluma, Calif, 99, Howard Greenberg, NY, 2001, Hereford Photography Festival, Hereford, England, 2002; Group exhibs, Nat Gallery Can, 67, 74 & 81; Photog in Am, Whitney Mus Art, New York, 74; Mirrors & Windows: Am Photog since 1960, Mus Mod Art, New York, 78; Songs of Innocence, Harbourfront Gallery, Toronto, 81; The Street, Can Mus Contemp Photog, 2006; plus others; Heritage of Meaning, Ottawa Art Gallery, 2013. *Pos:* Artist in residence, Univ Minn, Minneapolis, 65 & Int Ctr Photog, NY, 78. *Teaching:* Instr photog, Sch Dayton Art Inst, 65-67; asst prof photog, Moore Coll Art, Philadelphia, 67-70; prof photog, Ryerson Polytech Univ 70-96; adj fac, Visual Studies Workshop, 76-77. *Awards:* Guggenheim Found Fel, 63 & 64. *Bibliog:* Charles Hagen (auth), Le grand ALBUM ordinaire, Afterimage Visual Studies Workshop, 2/74; James Borcoman (auth), David Heath: a dialogue with solitude, J 34, Nat Gallery of Can, 10/79; Michael Torosian (auth & ed), David Heath, Extempore, Reflections on Art & Personal History, Lumiere Press, Toronto, 88 & 2004; Michael Torosian (auth & ed), Korea, Photographs 1953-1954, Fiftieth Anniversary Portfolio, Lumiere Press, Toronto, 2004. *Media:* Chromogenic Print, Journals, Digital Color. *Publ:* Auth, A Dialogue with Solitude, Community Press, 1965, 2nd edit, Lumiere Press, 2000; contribr, Photography in the 20th Century, 67; Photography in America, 75; Mirrors and Windows, 78; Magicians of Light, 80; Wonderland, 99; Dave Heath's

Art Show, Anonymous Press, Toronto, 2007; Eros and the Wounded Self, 2010; Dave Heath, Heritage of Meaning, Michael Schreier, 2014. *Dealer:* Steven Bulger Gallery 700 Queen St East Toronto Ontario Canada M6J; Howard Greenberg 4 E 57th Ste 1406 New York NY 10022. *Mailing Add:* 120 Wolfrey Ave Toronto ON M4K 1L3 Canada

HEATH, DAVID C
DEALER
b Atlanta, Ga, June 6, 1940. *Study:* Vanderbilt Univ; Univ Vienna; Columbia Univ. *Pos:* Pres, Heath Gallery, DC Heath & Assoc & Adv on Int Sculpture Inc, currently. *Specialty:* 20th century American & large scale sculpture. *Mailing Add:* c/o Gallery Revel 416 E Paces Ferry Rd NE Atlanta GA 30305

HEATH, SAMUEL K
MUSEUM DIRECTOR
b Exeter, NH, Sept 10, 1954. *Study:* Yale Univ, BA (art hist), 76; Columbia Univ, Dept Art Hist, MA, 83, MPhilos, 84. *Pos:* Staff lectr, Nat Gallery Art, Washington, DC, 76-78; curatorial intern, Boston Mus Fine Arts, 80-81; proj dir inventory & catalog colonial paintings, Cuzco, Peru, Int Found Art Res, NY, 83-85; lectr spec exhibs, Dept Pub Progs, Metrop Mus Art, 83-90; prog specialist Spain & Latin Am, World Monument Fund, NY, 88-90; cur Span art, Meadows Mus, Southern Methodist Univ, Dallas, Tex, 90-92, dir, 92-; dir, Lamont Gallery, Phillips Exeter Acad, 97-. *Teaching:* Instr art hist, Phillips Exeter Acad, NH, summers 76-79, Sch Visual Arts, NY, 85 & Southern Methodist Univ, Dallas, Tex, 90-. *Awards:* Columbia Univ Pres Fel, 79-80 & Univ Fel, 80-81; Samuel H Cress Found Res Fel, 85; Chester Dale Fel, Metrop Mus Art, 86-87. *Mem:* Int Coun Mus; Am Asn Mus; Coll Art Asn; Art Mus Asn; Asn Art Mus Dirs; and others. *Publ:* Auth, Spanish Polychrome Sculpture 1500-1800 in United States Collections (catalog), Spanish Inst New York, 92

HECHT, IRENE
PAINTER
b New York, NY, Dec, 1, 1949. *Study:* Case Western Reserve Univ, BA, 71; Art Student League with Everett Raymond Kinstler, Burt Silverman & Aaron Shikler & David Levine. *Work:* Portraits of Isaac Stern, Martin Bookspan & Zubin Mehta, Nat Arts Club, Prof Eugene P Wigner, Princeton Univ; Lotos Club: Kathleen Battle, Bill Bradley; Nat Arts Club, Itzak Perlman, Emanuel AX, and Lorin Maazel; Robert Morganthau, David Rockefeller, Sandra Day O'Conner; The Players Club, Julie Harris; Thorton Wilder; Rosemary Harris; Judith Malina. *Comn:* Portraits, Louis Nizer, 82, Arthur Krim, 83 & Charles Scribner IV, 86, NY; portrait, Nobel Laureate Nuclear Physicist Prof Eugene P Wigner; portrait, Marjorie Wynn, Beinecke Rare Books & Manuscript Libr, Yale Univ. *Exhib:* First Street Gallery; Audubon Artists; Am Acad Eguine Art; Nat Portrait Gallery. *Pos:* Portrait Painter. *Teaching:* Instr portrait painting, Delaware Art Mus, 84-87; instr, Figure Painting Workshop, Nat Acad Design; instr, Art Students League, 93-2010. *Awards:* Betty Salzmann Award, 80; Bruce Stevenson Mem Award, 91 & 92; Exhi Comt Award, Nat Arts Club, 93; President's Award, 2000. *Mem:* Artists Fel; Lotos Club; Players Club. *Media:* Oil. *Interests:* animals, ballroom dance. *Collection:* New York Univ; Princeton Univ; Univ Pa; National Arts Club; Lotos Club; David Rockefeller; Aaron Shikler, etc... *Publ:* painting in Allure Mag, 93; Am Artist Mag 2008; Portraits of a Lady (documentary). *Dealer:* Portraits Inc Birmingham Ala; Sewell Fine Portraiture LLC 1365 York Ave 10021. *Mailing Add:* 1 Grove Mews Chappaqua NY 10514

HEDBERG, GREGORY SCOTT
ART DEALER, GALLERY DIRECTOR
b Minneapolis, Minn, May 2, 1946. *Study:* Princeton Univ, BA, 68; Inst Fine Arts, NY Univ, MA, 71, PhD, 80. *Collection Arranged:* Picasso, Braque, Leger (coauth, catalog), 75; Charles Biederman: A Retrospective (auth, catalog), 76; Millet's Gleaners (auth, catalog), 78; Victorian High Renaissance (auth, catalog), Manchester City Art Galleries, Minneapolis Inst Arts & Brooklyn Mus, 78-79; Leger's Le Grand Dejeuner (auth, catalog), 80; German Realism of the Twenties: The Artist as Social Critic (auth, catalog), Minneapolis & Chicago, 80; The Tremaine Collection (auth, catalog), Hartford, 84; J Pierpont Morgan, Collector (coauth, catalog), travelling exhib, 87; Soviet Art from the Academy, NY Acad Art, 88. *Pos:* Lectr, Frick Collection, NY, 71-74; cur paintings, Minneapolis Inst Arts, 74-81; chief cur, 81-86, asst dir, 86-87, Wadsworth Atheneum, Hartford, Conn; dir, NY Acad Art, 87-92; dir European Art, Hirschl & Adler Gallery, NY. *Res:* Fifteenth century painting in Rome. *Publ:* Auth, The Farnese Courtyard Windows and the Porta Pia: Michelangelo's creative process, Marsyas, 71; auth, The Jerome Hill bequest: Delacroix's Fanatics of Tangiers and Corot's Silenus, 76 & In favor of Nicola di Maestro Antonio d'Ancona, 77, Minneapolis Inst Arts Bulletin. *Mailing Add:* 336 E 69th St New York NY 10021

HEDDEN, CLAIRE
SCULPTOR
b Huntsville, Pa, 1977. *Study:* New York State Coll Ceramics, Alfred Univ, BFA, 2000, MFA, 2007. *Exhib:* Archie Bray Residents Show, Clay Studio Missoula, Mont, 2004; Commune, Robert Turner Gallery, Alfred, NY, 2006; Fosdick-Nelson Gallery, Alfred, NY, 2007; Wonderland, Cazenovia Coll Art Gallery, 2009; 66th Ceramic Annual, Scripps Coll, Calif, 2010. *Pos:* Asst registrar, Schein-Joseph Int Mus Ceramic Art, 1997-98; production potter, Front Pond Pottery, NC, 1998; furniture designer, Jeffry Mann Woodworking Studio, Basalt, Co, 2000-02; ceramic sculptor, Creekside Pottery, Mont, 2002-04; studio asst, Rebecca Hutchinson Studios, Mass, 2005, Phillippe Barde, 2007. *Teaching:* Adj instr, New York Sch Ceramics, Alfred Univ, 2007-09, Coll Fine Arts, Ill State Univ, 2009. *Awards:* NY Found Arts Fel, 2009

HEDMAN, TERI JO
PRINTMAKER, PAINTER
b St Paul, Minn, Oct 10, 1944. *Study:* Univ Minn, BS (design); also with Paul Hapke, Toshi Yoshido, Pat Austin & Marge Horton. *Exhib:* All Alaska Exhib, 72, 74, 75 & 78; Solo exhibs, Univ Minn, 67 & Artique Ltd, 73-80. *Pos:* Designer-draftsman, Minneapolis Housing Authority, 68-70; interior designer, Tiptons Interiors, Anchorage, 70-71. *Teaching:* Traveling instr printmaking, Naknek, Bethel & Nome, Alaska, 73. *Awards:* Print Award, All Alaska Juried Exhib, 78; Purchase Award, State Art Bank, State Print Competition, 79. *Mem:* Alaska Artists Guild (prof chmn, 72, funding chmn, 73, vpres, 74, pres, 75, mem bd, 76, vpres, 80); Anchorage Arts Coun (visual arts adv comt, 75). *Mailing Add:* 2219 St Elias Dr Anchorage AK 99501

HEDREEN, BETTY
COLLECTOR
Pos: Bd trustees, Seattle Art Mus. *Awards:* Named to Top 200 Collectors, ARTnews Mag, 2006, 2007, 2008. *Collection:* Modern and contemporary art. *Mailing Add:* 836 36th Ave E Apt 19I Seattle WA 98112

HEDREEN, ELIZABETH & RICHARD
COLLECTOR
Study: Univ Wash, Seattle, BA (civil eng), 1957. *Pos:* Chief exec officer, pres, and founder, RC Hedreen co, 1965-; bd dirs, Terabeam Corp, formerly, Benaroya Music Ctr Hall, currently. *Awards:* Named one of Top 200 Collectors, ARTnews Mag, 2006-13. *Collection:* Modern and contemporary art. *Mailing Add:* 836 36th Ave E Apt 19I Seattle WA 98112

HEDRICK (FKA DIETRICH), LINNEA S
ART HISTORIAN, EDUCATOR
b Lebanon, Pa, July 26, 1944. *Study:* Am Univ, AB, 66, Univ Del, MA 67, PhD, 73. *Teaching:* From asst prof to prof art hist and women's studies affiliate, Univ S Fla, 68-89, 2007 (Retired); prof, Miami Univ, Oxford, Ohio, 89-. *Awards:* Hampton Int Travel Grant to Egypt-Effective Educ, Nat Sci Found, 89. *Mem:* Coll Art Asn; Women's Caucus Art; Historians 19th Century Art; Mid-west Art Hist Asn; American Research Center in Egypt. *Res:* 19th and 20th century art history and theory; pedagogy and critical thinking; Women in art; Islamic art. *Publ:* Auth, On Audrey Flack, Arts Mag, 81; Form & Content, In: Death of Art, Arthur Danto, 84; Gauguins' Notebook for Aline, Art Criticism, 91; 6 books on art history, Reinderr Co, 96; Aging & Contemporary Art, J Aging & Identity; auth, Arab & Persian Women Artists, Woman's Art J. *Mailing Add:* 4080 Shollenbarger Rd Oxford OH 45056

HEEKS, WILLY
PAINTER
b Providence, RI, Apr 28, 1951. *Study:* Univ RI, BFA, 73; Whitney Mus Am Art Independent Study Prog, 73; Tyler Sch Art Grad Prog, 76; RI Col, Hon Dr Fine Arts, 95. *Work:* Brooklyn Mus Art; Corcoran Gallery Art, Washington; Mus Fine Arts, Boston, Mass; Mus Mod Art, NY; Mus Mod Art, San Francisco; and others. *Exhib:* Solo exhibs, David Beitzel Gallery, NY, 87-90, 92, 94 & 96, Nielsen Gallery, Boston, 92 & 96, Larry Becker Contemp Art, Philadelphia, 92 & 97, Soma Gallery, LaJolla, Calif, 93, 95, 97 & 2000, Nancy Drysdale Gallery, Washington, 94, Mark Moore Gallery, 95 & 97 & Stephen Wirtz Gallery, San Francisco, 97, David Beitzel Gallery, NY, 99 & 2000, Salve Regina Univ, Newport, RI, 01; The Unique Print, Boston Mus Fine Arts, 90; 42nd Biennial Contemp Am Painting, Corcoran Gallery Art, Washington, 91; Vital Forces: Nature in Contemp Abstr, Hecksher Mus, Huntington, NY, 91; Organic Abstr, Nelson Atkins Mus Art, Kansas City, Mo, 91; Smith Coll Mus Art, 94; New Acquisition, Mus Art, RI Sch Design, Providence, 95; Newance, Stephen Wirtz Gallery, San Francisco, 96; The Forty-Fifth Biennial: The Corcoran Collects, 1907-1998 (with catalog), Corcoran Gallery Art, Washington, DC, 98; Cleveland Collects Contemp Art (with catalog), Cleveland Mus Art, Ohio, 99; Six Painters, Sonoma State Univ Art Gallery, Rohnert Park, Calif, 2000; Layering, Elizabeth Leach Gallery, Portland, Ore, 01. *Teaching:* Grad Prog, Vermont Col, 96. *Awards:* Artists Fel, Nat Endowment Arts, 78, 87 & 89; Painting Award, Am Acad & Inst Arts & Letts, 89; Pollock-Krasner Found Grant, 97. *Bibliog:* Edith Newhall (auth), Fall preview-galleries, NY Mag, Sept 20, 99; Mario Naves (auth), Beauty is back? Willy Heeks' tender, sensuous pictures, The NY Observer, Sept 27, 99; Ann Landi (auth), New York: Reviews, Willy Heeks at David Beitzel Gallery, ARTnews, 12/99. *Dealer:* David Beitzel Gallery 102 Prince St New York NY 10012; Nielsen Gallery 179 Newberry St Boston MA 02116

HEFFERNAN, JULIE
PAINTER
b Peoria, Ill, 1956. *Study:* Univ Calif, Santa Cruz, BFA (high hons, painting & printmaking), 81; Yale Sch Art, New Haven, Conn, MFA (painting), 85; Goethe Inst, Regensburg, Ger, 86; Alliance Française, 87. *Work:* The Palmer Mus Art, Pa; Columbia Mus Art, SC; Norton Mus Art, West Palm Beach, Fla; Knoxville Mus Art, Tenn; The Prudential Corp, NJ; Wake Forest Univ, NC; The Progressive Corp, Ohio; Weatherspoon Art Mus, NC. *Exhib:* The Enduring Figure in Contemp Art, Norton Mus Art, West Palm Beach, Fla, 2000; Am Art Today: Fantasies and Curiosities, The Art Mus at Fla Int Univ, Miami, 2000; Littlejohn Contemp, NY, 2000; Pixeria Witcheria, Univ Galleries Ill State Univ, Normal, 01; Herter Art Gallery, Univ Mass, 2003. *Teaching:* Instr drawing, Santa Cruz Art Ctr, Calif, 81; grad asst, Yale Col, New Haven, Conn, fall 84; vis asst prof fine arts, Univ Ind, Bloomington, 92 & dir Florence Italy & Abroad Drawing Prog, 92; vis asst prof fine arts, Univ NC, Greensboro, 92-93; asst prof fine arts, Pa State Univ, University Park, 94-98; vis artist, Univ Ariz, Tempe, fall 96 & Boston Mus Sch, fall 96; asst prof fine arts, Montclair Univ, NJ, 98-. *Awards:* Inst Res Grant & Coll Fac Res Grant, Pa State Univ, 95; Individual Artist's Grant, Nat Endowment Arts, 95 & NY Found Arts, 96; Lila Acheson Wallace Reader's Digest, Artists at Giverny Prog, individual artists grant & residency, France, 97. *Bibliog:* Grace Glueck (auth) rev, Rich Mix of Styles and Stimulations Under One Roof, The New York Times, 2/2000; Edward Gomez (auth), Florida: Where Exuberant Dreams Often Sink Out of Sight, The New York Times, 4/01; Joel Silverstein (auth), Conversation with Julie Heffernan, NY Arts, 4/01. *Publ:* James Elkins (auth), Strange Stories, and The Balm (exhib catalog essay), 01; Mario Naves (auth) rev, Even the Intricacies are Self-conscious, The New York Observer, 4/01

HEFLIN, TOM PAT
PAINTER, DESIGNER
b Monticello, Ark, July 18, 1935. *Study:* Northeast La State Coll; Chicago Art Inst. *Work:* Ill State Libr, Springfield; Blue Cross & Blue Shield Hq, Chicago; Sundstrand Corp, Rockford, Ill; Clarcor Co, Rockford, Ill; Rockford Art Mus; Maietta Oil, Chicago, Ill; pvt collection, Harry Stonecipher, CEO Boeing Aircraft; and many others. *Comn:* Winter Fields (painting), State Ill, Ill State Libr; Clarcor Corp, 97; Alpine Bank, 98; St Anthony Hosp, 92. *Exhib:* Butler Inst Am Art, Youngstown, Ohio, 73; New Horizons in Art, Chicago, 75; Am Watercolor Soc, NY, 75; Arts for the Parks, Jackson Hole, Wyo; Allied Artist Am, NY. *Teaching:* Instr painting, Burpee Art Mus, 69-71 & Rock Valley Coll, 70-. *Awards:* First Prize Medal, Nat Soc Painters Casein & Acrylic; First Prize, Ark Nationwide Bicentennial Medal Design, Franklin Mint; First Prize in Painting, Mainstreams 72, Ohio; Historical Medal Award, Arts for the Parks, Jackson Hole, WY, 2003. *Bibliog:* Articles in Famous Artists Mag, 70 & Contemp Western Artists, Southwest Art Publ, 82. *Mem:* Nat Soc Painters in Casein & Acrylic; Rockford Art Asn; Fishy Whale Litho Workshop, Milwaukee. *Media:* Oil, Acrylic. *Publ:* Auth, Quiet Places, 77; The Art of Heflin (video), 89; illusr, The First Forest, 90; Roots & Wings, The Art of Tom Heflin, 97. *Dealer:* Heflin Gallery Rockford IL. *Mailing Add:* 1162 S Weldon Rd Rockford IL 61102

HEFUNA, SUSAN
VIDEO ARTIST, PHOTOGRAPHER
b Cairo, Egypt, 1962. *Work:* Victoria and Albert Mus, London; Institut du Monde Arabe, Paris; Univ Colo Art Mus; Sharjah Art Mus, United Arab Emirates; Neue Galerie am Joanneum, Graz, Austria. *Exhib:* Solo exhibs, Kunstverein Ludwigsburg, 1994, Galerie Brigitte March, Stuttgart, Ger, 1998, National Gallery, Cape Town, South Africa, 2000, Bluecoat Arts Centre, Liverpool, UK, 2004, Townhouse Gallery, Cairo, 2007, Third Line Gallery, Dubai, 2008, Kemper Mus Contemp Art, Mo, 2010; Regards des Photographes Arabes Contemporains, Institut Du Monde Arabe, Paris, 2005; Lasting Foundations, Charles H Wright Mus African Am Hist, Detroit, 2006; Museum as Hub: Antikhana, New Mus, New York, 2008; 53rd Int Art Exhib Biennale, Venice, 2009; On Line: Drawing Through the Twentieth Century, Mus Mod Art, New York, 2010. *Mailing Add:* c/o Townhouse Gallery 10 Nabrawy St Cairo Egypt

HEGARTY, VALERIE
SCULPTOR
Study: Middlebury Coll, Vt, BA, 1989; Acad Art Coll, San Francisco, BFA, 1995; Sch Art Inst Chicago, MFA, 2002. *Exhib:* Solo exhibs, Mus Contemp Art, Chicago, 2003, Mus 52, London, 2007, Kohler Arts Ctr, Wis, 2008, Highline Pub Art Project, NY, 2009; Play Pen, The Drawing Ctr, New York, 2004; Odd Lots, White Columns, NY, 2005; Among the Trees, Visual Arts Ctr NJ, Summit, 2006; Baroque-Ademia, Nassau County Mus Art, NY, 2007; 21: Selections of Contemporary Art from the Brooklyn Museum, Brooklyn Mus, 2008. *Awards:* Louis Comfort Tiffany Found Grant, 2003; Rema Hort Mann Found Grant, 2004; NY Found Arts Fel, 2009. *Bibliog:* Jenna Comita (auth), Louisville Sluggers, W Mag, 7/2006; Roberta Smith (auth), In These Shows, The Material is the Message, NY Times, 8/10/2007; Jaleh Mansoor (auth), On Being an Exhibition, ArtForum, 2/2008

HEGINBOTHAM, JAN STURZA
SCULPTOR
b New York, NY, Dec 8, 1954. *Study:* Univ Md, BA, 75; pvt study with Boris Blai, Philadelphia, 76-78; Am Univ, Washington, DC, with Mark Oxman & Stanley Lewis, MFA (sculpture, fel), 92. *Comn:* Spirit (bronze sculpture), Montgomery Co Pub Sch, Burtonsville, Md, 88. *Exhib:* Solo exhibs, Cannon Rotunda, US Cong, Washington, DC, 85; Holy Family Col, Pa, 85; Glenview Mansion Gallery, Rockville Civic Ctr, Md, 2004; two-person show, Staunton Fine Arts Mus, Va, 89; The Nude, Loudon House Gallery, Ky & Perry House Gallery, Va, 97; Raab Gallery, Philadelphia, Pa, 99; Art Inst & Gallery, Salisbury, Md, 99; Group exhibs, Allied Artists of Am, New York, 82, 86, 88, 89; Nat Small Sculpture Exhib, Hattiesburg, Miss, 2000; Washington Square, DC, 2000; Craig Flinner Contemporary Gallery, Baltimore Md, 2001-2004; Nathen D Rosen Mus, Boca Raton, Fla, 2002, 2004 & 2006; Wash County Mus Fine Arts, Hagerstown, Md, 2003, 2004; Glenview Mansion Gallery, Rockville Civic Ctr, Md, 2004; Palm Springs Desert Mus, Calif, 2005; Attleboro Mus, Mass, 2005; Owensboro Mus, Ky, 2005. *Pos:* Sculptor's asst, Barry Johnston, Washington, DC, 81 & Raymond Kaskey, Md, 92; drawing group coordr, Arlington Arts Ctr, Va, 86-90. *Teaching:* Asst sculpture, Am Univ, Washington, DC, 90-92. *Awards:* Mayor Marion Barry Cert Award, City Hall, 81; Orion Nova, Mem & Assocs Award, Allied Artists Am, NY, 82 & 86; Award, Washington Co Mus Fine Art, Hagerstown, MD, 2003 & 2004. *Bibliog:* David Scott (auth), The Daily Times, Salisbury, Md, 3/99; Alice Ross (auth), Elan Magazine, Great Falls, Va 11/01; Great Falls Connection, 10/15/2009, 10/14/2010. *Mem:* Washington Sculptors Group, Washington, DC; Wash Proj Arts, DC; Great Falls Studios, Va. *Media:* Plasticine Clay, Bronze

HEIDEL, THERESA TROISE
PAINTER, INSTRUCTOR
b Teaneck, NJ, Aug 16 1950. *Study:* St Peter's Col, BA; Acad delle Belli Arti (post grad work), Florence, Italy; Ridgewood Art Inst, NJ. *Work:* Series of paintings of Casino Complex, Convention Hall & Mayfair Theatre, Asbury Park, NJ; Salvation Army, Asbury Park, NJ; Ridgewood Art Inst, Ridgewood, NJ; Hamilton House Mus, Clifton, NJ. *Comn:* Homeland, Barbara Havenick, Bolton Landing, NY; Elberon Beach Club, Long Branch, NJ; Robin and Ivor Braka, Deal, NJ; Chateau Hotel, Spring Lake, NJ. *Exhib:* Solo exhibs, St Peter's Col, Jersey City, NJ, Fort Lee Libr, Fort Lee, NJ, Oceanside Gallery, Belmar, NJ, Lakeshore Gallery, Bolton Landing, NY; group exhibs, Talent, Allan Stone Gallery, NY; Audubon Artists Ann Nat Juried & Ann Non Mems Juried Art exhib, Salmagundi Club, NY; Watercolors of the Garden State, Monmouth Mus, Lincroft, NJ, Ridgewood Art Inst, NJ, New American Gallery, Princeton, NJ; NJ ann juried watercolor exhib, NJ Watercolor Soc, 2005, 06. *Collection Arranged:* Latham & Watkins Law Int Law Firm, Newark, NJ; Holy Name Hos, Teaneck, NJ; Jersey Shore Med Ctr, Neptune, NJ; Salvation Army, Asbury Park, NJ; Ocean Grove Hist Soc, Ocean Grove, NJ. *Teaching:* pvt instr; instr, Troise Heidel Studio, Ridgefield, NJ; artist-in-residence (instr), Cunard Lines, Queen Mary II. *Awards:* Catharine Lorillard Wolfe Art Club Award, Ridgewood Art Inst 17th Regional Open Juried Show, Ridgewood, NJ; Pennell Memorial Award, Kent Art Asn, Kent, Conn; Marie La Greca Award, Hudson Valley Art Asn. Ann, 2005. *Bibliog:* Beatrice Goodrich (auth), Happy Hollow Books I, II & III, Windswept House, Mt Desert, Maine, 1987; Marie Maber (auth), The Many Faces of Asbury Park, Asbury Park Press, 2004; Louise Hafesh (auth), Splashes of Color, 201 Mag, N Jersey Media Group Inc, W Paterson, NJ, 2005. *Mem:* Catharine Lorillard Wolfe Art Club; NJ Watercolor Soc; Kent Art Asn. *Media:* Watercolor. *Res:* Archit details of Casino Complex, Conv Hall & Mayfair Theatre, Asbury Park, NJ. *Interests:* Painting, piano, travel. *Publ:* Integrating Studio Work & Outdoor Painting, Am Artist Mag, 1989; Ad Book J, Monmouth Co Cancer Soc, 1994; Jersey Shore Guide Book, Jersey Shore Vacation Guide, Jersey Shore Home & Garden, Jersey Shore Publs, Bay Head, NJ, 1995-; contrib (fifty paintings), To the Jersey Shore Once More, Vols I, II. *Dealer:* Lakestore Gallery of Bolton Landing 4985 Lakeshore Dr (Rte 9 & Sagamore Rd) Bolton Landing, NY 12814; New Am Gallery Princeton Junction NJ. *Mailing Add:* 333 Main St Ridgefield Park NJ 07660

HEIFERMAN, MARVIN
CURATOR, WRITER, PUBLISHER
b New York, NY, 1948. *Study:* Brooklyn Coll, BA, 68; Columbia Univ: Sch Arts, Film Div; Sch Visual Arts, New York; Brooklyn Mus Art Sch. *Collection Arranged:* The Family of Man 1955-84, PS 1 Mus; Color Photographs, 77, Pictures: Photographs, Castelli Graphics, 79, Whitney Mus Am Art, 83; To the Rescue: Eight Artists in Am Archive Int Ctr of Photog, The Real Big Picture, Queens Mus, 86; Image World: Art and Media Culture, Whitney Mus Am Art, 89; The Indomitable Spirit, 90, Talking Pictures, Int Center Philosophy, 94; Fame After Photography, Mus Modern Art, NY, 99; Paradise Now: Picturing the Genetic Revolution, Exit Art, Tang Teaching Mus & Art Gallery, 2000-; Genomic Issue(s): Art & Sci, Art Gallery of the Grad Ctr, City Univ NY, 2003; John Waters' Change of Life, New Mus, NY, 2004; Orange Co Mus Art, Calif, 2004; City Art: NY's Percent for Art Prog, Ctr for Archit, New York, 2005; Now vs Then: Snapshots from the Maresca Collection, Newark Mus, 2007; Bill Wood's Business, Int Ctr Photog, 2008; Click! Photography Chages Everything, Smithsonian Photography Initiaive, 2010. *Pos:* Asst dir, Light Gallery, NY, 72-74; dir photog, Castelli Graphics, NY, 75-82; founder, ptnr, Lookout, NY, 91-2003; creative cons, Smithsonian Photog Initiative, Smithsonian Inst, 2005-2011. *Teaching:* MFA prog photog and related media, Sch Visual Arts, 91-; instr, ICP & BARD Coll Prog in advan photog studies, 2004-. *Publ:* Still Life, Callway Editions, 83; Image World: Art and Media Culture (catalog), 89; The Indomitable Spirit (catalog), 89; Im so Happy, Vintage Books, 90; Talking Pictures (catalog), Chronicle Books, 94; Love is Blind, Power House, 96; Coauth, Growing Up with Dick and Jane: Learning and Living the American Dream, Collins, 96; To the Rescue: Eight Artists in An Archive, 99; Paradise Now: Picturing the Genetic Revolution, Tang/DAP, 2002; John Waters: Change of Life (catalog), Abrams, 2004; City Art: New York City's Percent for Art Program, Merrell, 2005; Now is Then: Snapshots from the Maresca Collection, Princeton Archit Press, 2008; Bill Wood's Business, ICP/Steidl, 2008; auth, Photography Changes Everything, Aperture Found, 2012

HEIN, JOHN
CRAFTSMAN
b Albany, NY, July 21, 1955. *Study:* Temple Univ, Philadelphia, AB, 77. *Work:* Zimmerli Art Mus, New Brunswick, NJ; Mt Holyoke Coll, South Hadley, Mass; Newark Mus, NJ; Keuka Coll, Keuka Park, NY. *Exhib:* NJ Arts Ann: Crafts, NJ State Mus, Trenton, 86, 92 & 96, Noyes Mus Art, Oceanville, NJ, 88, 90 & 98 & Morris Mus, 91 & 97; Am Craft at the Armory, Seventh Regiment Armory, NY, 90; Contemp Furniture Makers of the Am Northeast, Gallery at Bristol-Myers Squibb, Princeton, NJ, 91; Meredith Gallery, Baltimore, Md, 91, 92, 93, 95-97; solo exhibs, Newark Mus, NJ, 92, Meredith Gallery, Baltimore, Md, 93 & The Finer Side, Salisbury, Md, 93; and others. *Collection Arranged:* Out of the Woodwork, Holman Hall Gallery, Coll of NJ, Trenton, NJ. *Pos:* Advisor, The Forest Refined, Trenton City Mus, NJ; grant rev panelist & on-site arts evaluator, NJ State Coun Arts, 98. *Teaching:* Lectr, Works in Wood, NJ Designer Craftsmen Gallery, New Brunswick, 89, Cent Jersey Woodworker's Asn, 97. *Awards:* NJ State Coun Arts Individual Fel, 88; Nat Endowment Arts Visual Artists Fel, 90; NICHE Award Winner, wood, functional category, NICHE Mag, Baltimore, Md, 92, Wood one-of-a kind, 93 & 96 & Wood traditionally joined, 99 & 2000. *Bibliog:* Am Style, Baltimore, Md, summer 95 & 9/99; Art & Antiques, Studio Session, 4/2000; NY Times, 10/1/2000; The Artful Home, Larks Books, Asheville, NC, 2007; many others. *Mem:* Am Craft Coun; Am Soc Furniture Artists; The Furniture Soc; Arts Wire; Nat Asn Independent Artists. *Media:* Wood. *Mailing Add:* 105 Featherbed Ln Hopewell NJ 08525

HEIN, MAX
GRAPHIC ARTIST, EDUCATOR
b Lincoln, Nebr, Dec 27, 1943. *Study:* San Diego State Univ, AB, 66; Univ Calif, Los Angeles, MA, 68, MFA, 69. *Work:* Int Mus Photog, George Eastman House, Rochester, NY; Frederick S Wight Galleries, Univ Calif, Los Angeles; Newport Harbor Mus Art, Calif; Bradford City Art Gallery, Yorkshire, Eng; DeAnza Coll Art Gallery, Calif; plus others. *Exhib:* Four Printmakers: Benson, Foote, Hein & Quandt, San Francisco Mus Art, 71; 3rd Brit Int Print Bienniale, Bradford City Art Gallery, Yorkshire, Eng, 72; Recent Photog, NS Coll Art & Design, Halifax, 72; San Francisco Bay Area Printmakers, Cincinnati Art Mus, Ohio, 73; 8th Nat Print & Drawing Competition, Dulin Gallery Art, Knoxville, Tenn, 74-75; Smithsonian Traveling Exhib, Nat Collection Fine Art, Washington DC. *Teaching:* Instr silkscreen printmaking, Univ Calif, Los Angeles Exten, 68-69; instr art, Santa Rosa Jr Col, Calif, 69-; vis artist silkscreen printmaking, Visual Studies Workshop, Rochester, NY, summer 75. *Awards:* Guest Ed Award, 6th Ann Los Angeles Printmaking Soc Exhib, 69; Purchase Award, 3rd Brit Int Print Biennale, 72 & Bay Area Print Exhib, DeAnza

Coll Gallery, 75. *Bibliog:* Alfred Frankenstein (auth), Photo image in printmaking, San Francisco Chronicle, 11/71; Carole Schuck (auth), Max Hein prints, 9/72 & Gerry Payne (auth), Geometric dynamics, 11/75, Art Week. *Media:* Painting, Mixed Media. *Publ:* Illusr, Half a Century, Nat Football League, 70. *Mailing Add:* Dept Art Santa Rosa Jr Col 1501 Mendocino Ave Santa Rosa CA 95401

HEINEMANN, PETER
PAINTER, INSTRUCTOR
b Denver, Colo, Apr 22, 1931. *Study:* Black Mountain Col, 1 yr, with Joseph Albers, 48-49. *Comn:* Multi-figure oil mural, NY Coun Arts, 71-72. *Exhib:* Nat Inst Arts & Lett, NY, 60, 61 & biennially 70, 71 & 72; Heckscher Mus, Huntington, NY, 79; Nat Acad Design, 81 & 82; Gallery 120, NY, 83; Visual Arts Mus, 83; Schlesinger Boisante Gallery, NY, 85, 87, 89, 92 & 94. *Teaching:* Instr painting & drawing, Sch Visual Arts, NY, 60-, Studio Sch, NY, 83-84. *Awards:* Creative Artists Pub Serv Grants, 71-72, 74-75 & 77-78; Childe Hassam Purchase Award, 72; Nat Endowment Arts, 83-84; NY Found Arts Grant, 86. *Mem:* Nat Acad. *Media:* Oil. *Mailing Add:* Sch Visual Arts 209 E 23rd St New York NY 10010-3994

HEINICKE, JANET L HART
PAINTER, EDUCATOR
b Richmond, Ind. *Study:* Wittenberg Univ, BS (art educ, cum laude), 52; Univ Wis-Madison, MS (art educ), 56, study with Colescott & Meeker; Northern Ill Univ, EdD, 76, MFA (painting), 77 & Syracuse Univ, 92. *Work:* Richmond Art Asn, Ind; Kankakee Community Coll, Ill; Simpson Coll, Indianola, Iowa; Wausau Medical Group, Wis; Iowa Lakes Community Coll, Estherville, Iowa; We-toast Corp, Chicago, Ill; Artists of Iowa Collection, Nat Bank Waterloo; Hy Vee Corp, Des Moines, Iowa; Caterpillar Corp, Peoria, Ill; Farm Services Corp, Blooming, Ill; EMC Insurance, Des Moines, Iowa; Dickenson, Tyler, Hagen, & Hachawa, Des Moines, Ia. *Comn:* Painting, Caterpillar Corp, Peoria, Ill, 80; Leadership Coll, Tanzania, East Africa. *Exhib:* Solo exhibs, Western Ill Univ, Macomb, 83 & Cedar Rapids Mus Art, Iowa, 84, Small Surprises, Kirkwood Community Coll, 2005 & Roots in Richmond, Richmond Art Mus, Ind, 2008; Stavropol City Mus, Stavropol Krai, Russia, 92; State Mus, Cherkassy Oblast, Ukraine, 98; Woodland Scenes, Kirkwood Community Coll, 2000; Ariz Aquons, Tubac Ctr for the Arts, 2003; Ia Watercolor Traveling Exhib 2004-2005; Nat Exhib of Sacred Art, First Methodist Church, Evanston, Ill, 2004; Watercolor Nat Show, Norris Ctr, St Charles, Ill, 2005; Reima Gardens, Iowa State Univ, 2006-2007; DM Metro Arts Expo, 2006-2007; In Her Own Voice, Ankeny Arts Ctr, Ankeny, Iowa, 2008; Rooted in Richmond, Richmond Art Mus, 2008; 3rd Ann Horizontal Grandeur Show, Stevens Co Mus, Morris Minn, 2009; Centrl Iowa Art Asn Fisher Community Ctr, Marshalltown, Iowa, 2009; The Light of God, Significant Visionary Works, Emerald Gallery, 2009; Marschalltown Community Coll, 2010; Heritage Gallery, Des Moines, Iowa, 2010; Ariz Aqueous Competition, Tubac Ctr Arst, 2010; Iowa Watercolor Soc, 2010; 20x20x20, Nat Compact Exhib, La State Univ, 2010; Nat All Media Show, Octagon Gallery, Iowa, 2011; Transitions, Ann Curry Art Ctr, 2012. *Collection Arranged:* Iowa Grasses, Yamanashi Prefecture, Japan, 2011; Gov. Terry Branstad, Iowa. *Pos:* Art dept prog coordr, Kankakee Community Coll, Ill, 77-81; guest lectr, Univ Dar es Salaam Tanzania, E Africa. *Teaching:* Asst prof art, Judson Coll, Elgin, Ill, 69-74; chmn art dept, Simpson Coll, Indianola, Iowa, 81-2001, prof & chmn fine arts div, prof emer, 2001-; educ consult, Univ Latvia, Riga, 93; vis scholar, Fukuoka Jo Gakin, Japan, 93; vis lectr, Univ Phillipines, Cebu, 95, Univ Cantho, Cantho Province, Vietnam, 95 & Cherkassy, Ukraine, 98; teacher, relief printmaking, Japanese paper, Malaysian silk batik, Des Moines Art Center, educ progr; pres & instr art history, Pappajohn Ctr Higher Educ; Wetworks, experimental work with water color, DM Art Ctr, 2008-; In Our Own Background, Regional Artists of Midwest, Senior Coll, Des Moines. *Awards:* Best in Show, Landscape Painters Midwest, Tower Park Gallery, Peoria, Ill, 79; Research Award, Simpson Coll, 94, Governors Award, 95 & Fac Serv Award, 94; Merit Award, Iowa State Fair, 97; Merit Award, Bismarck Art Asn, 2001; Alumni Award, Wittenberg Univ, 2002; Fourth Place Prize, Iowa Watercolor Asn Ann Show; Robert Ray Award, Iowa Sister States, 2007; Grand prize, Community Art Competition, City of Des Moines & Greater Des Moines, Pub Art Found, 2009; Best of Show, Iowa Exhibited, Heritage Gallery, Des Moines, Iowa, 2012. *Mem:* Iowa Arts Coun; Ill Arts Coun; Coll Art Asn; Chicago Artists Coalition; Christians in Visual Art; Women Graduates USA; Int Fed Univ Women. *Media:* Acrylic, Watercolor, Mixed Media, Monoprint, Collagraph. *Publ:* Iowa Women Artists, Oral Hist Project, 2000; reviewer, Choice, Am Libr Asn. *Mailing Add:* 813 Robin Glen Indianola IA 50125

HEINRICH, CHRISTOPH
MUSEUM DIRECTOR
b Frankfurt, Germany, 1960. *Study:* Ludwig-Maximillian Univ, Munich, PhD. *Collection Arranged:* Andy Warhol: Photography, 1999; Mona Hatoum, 2004; Storytellers, 2005; Francis Bacon: The Portraits, 2005; Return to Space, 2005; Mahjong: Contemporary Chinese Art from the Sigg Collection, 2006; Daniel Richter: A Major Survey, 2007; Fuse Box: Bjorn Melhus, 2008; Focus, The Figure, 2008; Embrace, 2009. *Pos:* Chief cur contemp art, collection & exhibs, Hamburger Kunsthalle, Hamburg, Germany, 1994-2007, co-founder, Young Friends of the Kunsthalle; Polly & Mark Addison cur mod & contemp art, Denver Art Mus, 2007-2009, dep dir, 2009-2010, Frederick and Jan Mayer dir, 2010-. *Teaching:* Vis lectr, Inst Art Hist, Hamburg Univ, 2000-2007. *Mem:* Andy Warhol Authentication Bd (bd dirs); Asn German Art Historians. *Publ:* Auth, Andy Warhol, Photography, catolog, Andy Warhol Mus, Ed Stemmle, 99; Monets Legacy Series - Order & Obsession, catalog, Hamburg Kunsthalle, 2001; Mona Hatoum, catalog, Hamburg Kunsthalle, 2004; Daniel Richter-Die Palette, catalog, Hamburg Kunsthalle, 2007; coauth (with Uwe M Schneede), Weltempfanger - Bestandskatalog der Galerie der Gegenwart, Hamburg Kunsthalle, 2007; (with Dan Jacobs & Cydney Peyton), Jonas Burgert - Enigmatic Narrative, Univ Denver, 2008. *Mailing Add:* Denver Art Mus 100 W 14th Ave Pkwy Denver CO 80204

HEINTZ, FLORENT
APPRAISER
Study: Harvard Univ, ThM, 93, PhD, 99. *Pos:* Keeper of Coins, Harvard Univ Art Mus; cur asst, Worcester Art Mus, Mass; head antiquities dept, Sotheby's, New York, 2001-. *Awards:* Named Dunbarton Oaks Junior Fel, Harvard Univ, 98-99. *Publ:* Auth, Agnostic Magic in the Late Antique Circus, 99. *Mailing Add:* Sotheby's NY 1334 York Ave New York NY 10021

HEINZ, SUSAN
ADMINISTRATOR
b RI. *Study:* Brown Univ, BA; Harvard Univ, MA; Univ Calif, Los Angeles, MA (film hist & criticism); Phi Beta Kappa. *Pos:* Educ coordr, Jr Arts Ctr, Los Angeles Munic Arts Dept, 68-73; mem, Los Angeles Munic Arts Comn, 73-78; exec dir, Palos Verdes Art Ctr & Mus, Rancho Palos Verdes, 74-78; mem, Mayor's Citizen's Adv Comt Arts, Los Angeles; dir, Corp Progs, Asia Soc, New York, 78-, vpres, 95-97; consultant on Asian affairs and arts educ, 97-00, retired. *Awards:* Am Film Inst Scholar, 72-73; Smithsonian Inst Grant (res in India), 74. *Mem:* Cosmopolitan Club, NY. *Interests:* Travel, reading, theater, performing arts, visual arts. *Mailing Add:* 315 E 68th St New York NY 10065-5692

HEINZEN, MARYANN
PAINTER, ASSEMBLAGE ARTIST
b Bronx, NY, July 30, 1952. *Study:* Art Students League, 86, with Mario Cooper & Joseph Rossi; Nat Art League, Douglaston, NY, with Ed Whitney; Pvt instr, 6 yrs with Yukio Tashiro. *Work:* DuPont Pharmaceuticals, Endo Bldg, Garden City, NY. *Exhib:* Salmagundi Club Exhib, NY, 83, 88 & 91; Nat Arts Club Exhib, NY, 88; Nassau Co Mus Art, Vaali, 88 & Artists at Work, 91; The Expert Eye, Wunsch Gallery, Coun Arts, Long Island, 90; solo shows, James Beard House, Greenhouse Gallery, NY, 93-94 & 97-98 & Natural Eclectic, Nyack, NY, 98. *Pos:* Pres, Nat Art League, Douglaston, NY, 90-92, vpres, 92-; demonstr, Nat Art League, Floral Park, Flushing Art League, NY & Tri Co Artists. *Teaching:* Teacher watercolor, formerly; artist-in-residence, Freeport Coun Arts, Chelsea Ctr, E Norwich, 93-94; instr watercolor, Nat Art League, Douglaston, 91-92. *Awards:* Award of Excellence, Tri Co Exhib, Tri Co Art League, 90 & 94; First Prize, Rockville Ctr Guild Arts, 90; Award of Excellence, Indep Art Soc, Long Island, 90; Best in Show, North by South Exhib, Nassau Co Mus Art, 93; Gene Alden Walker Award, Nat Asn Women Artist, NY, 74; and others. *Mem:* Nat Asn Women Artists; Coast Guard Artists (mem chmn 88-90, pres 90-92 & vpres, 92-); Nat Art League. *Media:* Watercolor. *Publ:* Contribr, The Artists Guide to Showing & Selling Your Work, North Lights Books, 89; summer & fall issues of continuing educ, Queensboro Community Coll Catalog; Queens Borough Community Col, 92. *Dealer:* Chandler-Edwards Gallery Port Washington NY; Owl 57 Gallery Woodmere NY. *Mailing Add:* 208 Waters Edge Valley Cottage NY 10989

HEISS, ALANNA
MUSEUM DIRECTOR
b Louisville. *Study:* Lawrence Univ, Appleton, Wis, BA (music). *Hon Degrees:* San Francisco Art Inst, Hon Doctor, 2001. *Pos:* Founder, Inst Art & Urban Resources (now Inst Contemp Art), New York, 1971; dir, Clocktower Gallery, 1972-2008; dir, PS1 Contemp Art Ctr, Long Island City, NY, 1976-2008; dep dir, Mus Mod Art, New York, 2000-08; founder, exec prodr, WPS1 online radio station, 2004-2008. *Awards:* Award given by New York Mayor Koch, 1980; Knighted by Swedish Govt, 1984; Chevalier Arts & Letters, France, 1987; Skowhegan Award, 1989. *Publ:* Coauth (with John Wesley), Paintings: 1961-2000, 2001; coauth (with Janet Cardiff), A Survey of Works, Including Collaborations with George Bures Miller (foreword), 2002. *Mailing Add:* PS1 Contemp Art Ctr 22-25 Jackson Ave Long Island City NY 11101

HEIZER, MICHAEL
ENVIRONMENTAL ARTIST, SCULPTOR
b Berkeley, Calif, Nov 4, 1944. *Study:* San Francisco Art Inst, 63-64. *Work:* Mus Contemp Art, Los Angeles; Metrop Mus, NY; Detroit Inst Arts, Mich; Rijksmuseum Krôller-Mûller, Otterlo, Holland; Kunsthalle, Berne, Switz. *Comn:* This Equals That (outdoor sculpture), Capital Plaza, Lansing, Mich, 77-80; Platform, Oakland Mus, Calif, 80; Levitated Mass, IBM Corp, NY, 82; North, East, South, West, Rockefeller Develop Corp, Los Angeles, Calif, 82; Effigy Tumuli (sculpture), Ottawa Silica Found, 85. *Exhib:* Currents 7, St Louis Art Mus, Mo, 80; The Americans: The Landscape, Contemp Arts Mus, Houston, Tex, 81; 20 Am Artists: Sculpture 1982, San Francisco Mus Mod Art, Calif, 82; Geometric Extraction, Mus Contemp Art, Los Angeles, Calif, 84; Dragged Mass Geometric, Whitney Mus Am Art, NY, 85; Art Before Life, Ace Gallery, 94; Works: 1972-76, Galerie Frank + Schulte, Berlin, Germany; Negative - Positive +, Fondazione Prada, Milan, Italy, 96; Hard Edge Ejecta, Knoedler & Co, NY, 98; PaceWildenstein, NY, 2006. *Bibliog:* Ellen Joosten & Feliz Zdenek (coauths), Michael Heizer Mus Folkwang & Rijksmuseum Keoller-Muller, 79; Julia Brown (ed), Michael Heizer sculpture in reverse, Mus Contemp Art, Los Angeles, 84; David Bourdon (auth), Working with earth Michael Heizer makes art big as all outdoors, Smithsonian, Vol 17, No 1 pg 68-74 & 76-77, 4/86. *Media:* Earthworks

HELD, (JOHN) JONATHAN, JR
MAIL ARTIST, WRITER
b New York, NY, Apr 2, 1947. *Study:* Utica Coll, Syracuse Univ, BA, 69, Sch Info Sci, MLS, 71; Studied with Prof Emer Antje Lemke; Soc Independent Artists, 99. *Hon Degrees:* Doctorate, Soc Independent Artists, San Francisco, Calif, 2013. *Work:* Jean Brown Collection, Getty Ctr Humanities, Santa Monica, Calif; Mus Mod Art Libr, NY; papers, Arch Am Art, Smithsonian Inst; Musee de la Poste, Paris, France, Mayakovsky Mus, Moscow Russia. *Comn:* Am Philatelic Soc, 2002. *Exhib:* Stampworks, Stempelplaats Gallery, Amsterdam, The Neth, 76; Timbres d'Artistes, Mus de la Poste, Paris, France, 93; 1st Int Post-Futurist Exhib, Mayakovsky Mus, 2003; My Spiritual Life, Haricom Gallery, Jeju, S Korea, 2006; Parastamps: Four Decades of Artist Stamps from Fluxus to the Internet, Nat Must Fine Arts, Budapest,

2007; Dallas SITES, Dallas Mus Art, Tex, 2013; The Walls of Venice: Photographs and Postage Stamps, artspace Edition Shimizu, Shimizu, Japan, 2015. *Collection Arranged:* Faux Post, Various Venues, Visual Arts Resources, Portland, Ore, 95-98; Bay Area Dada, San Francisco Pub Libr, San Francisco, Calif, 98; Printed Matter, NY, 99; Peace Island, Jeju Island, South Korea, 2001; Correspon-Dance: Mail Art from the Collection of John Held Jr, Linc Art, San Francisco, 2005; Fluxus, Mail Art, Rubber Stamps, Stendhal Gallery, New York, 2010; Beat by the Bay, Ever Gold Gallery, 2012; Gutai, San Francisco Art Inst, San Francisco, Calif, 2013; mail/art/back, San Francisco Ctr for the Back, 2014. *Pos:* Video librn, Mid-York Libr System, Utica, NY, 76-81; art librn, Dallas Pub Libr, 81-95; Stamp Art Gallery, San Francisco, Calif, 95-97; dir, Modern Realism Gallery, San Francisco, 97-; staff writer, San Francisco Arts Quarterly, 2011-. *Awards:* Tartu Artists Soc, Estonia, 90; Jeju Island Cult & Art Found, S Korea, 2001. *Bibliog:* Vittore Baroni (auth), Arte Postale; Guida al Network della Corrispondenza Creativa, AAA Edizioni, Bertiolo, Italy, 98; Saper, Craig, Networkd Art, Univ of Minn, Press, 2001; Amy Spencer (auth), DIY: The Rise of Lo-Fi Culture, 2005; Reiko Tomii (auth), Mail Art Central, Shin Bijutsu Shinbun, Tokyo, Japan, 2013. *Mem:* Int Union of Mail Artists. *Media:* Mail Art, Rubber Stamps, Artist Postage Stamps. *Res:* History of 20th century avant-gardes; Russian modernism, dada, fluxus, mail art; Gutai; interviews with John Cage, Ray Johnson, Allan Kaprow, Shozo Shimamoto, Anna Halprin, Lawrence Ferlinghett. *Specialty:* Relics and Documents of the 20th Century Avant-Garde. *Interests:* Mail art, artistamps, rubber stamps. *Collection:* Mail Art Primary & Secondary Sources, Aspects acquired by Getty, Mus Mod Art. *Publ:* Contribr, Dictionary of Art, Grove, 96: (auth) Mail Art; An Annotated Bibliog, Scarecrow Press, 91; Rubber Stamp Art, AAA Edizioni, Betiolo, Italy, 99; A Living Thing In Flight; Collection and Preparing Contemporary Avant-Garde Materials for an Archive, Archives Am Art Jour, 2000; At a Distance, MIT Press, 2005; We'll Chop His Suey...Ray Johnson, Red Fox Press, Ireland, 2007; Where the Secret is Hidden, Pts 1 & 2, 2011; Small Scale subversion: Mail Art and Artistamps, TAM Publications, The Netherlands, 2015. *Dealer:* Mod Realism Gallery 263 8th Ave San Francisco CA 94118. *Mailing Add:* PO Box 410837 San Francisco CA 94141

HELDER, DAVID ERNEST
PAINTER, SCULPTOR
b Seattle, Wash, Feb 4, 1947. *Study:* Calif Coll Arts & Crafts, BA, 69, MFA, 71; Stanford Univ, MA, 75. *Work:* Oakland Mus, Calif. *Exhib:* Galex 23 Nat Juried Exhib, Galesburg Civic Art Ctr, Ill, 89; The Surrealist Salon, RayKo Ctr, San Francisco, 91; The Summer Salon, Helio Gallery, NY, 91; Macro/micro Int Exhib, Helio Gallery, NY, 91; and others. *Pos:* Aesthetic ed consult, Isaacson Inst, Berkeley, Calif, 72-74 & Univ Minneapolis, 88-; Aesthetic Ed Consult, Univ of Minneapolis,88-. *Awards:* Westmorland Award, 88; Cert of Excellence Int Art Comp, Westmorland Art and Heritage Festival, 88. *Bibliog:* Charles Shere (auth), Mind in the matter, Oakland Tribune, 5/74; Bob Harrison (auth), Artist makes it easy to see, San Francisco Visitors News, 2/81; Diane L Saiget (auth), David Helder's magic doors, City Arts, 2/81. *Media:* Acrylic, Oil; All Media. *Dealer:* Michael Bell 140 Page St No 1 San Francisco CA 94102. *Mailing Add:* 636 Stanyan St San Francisco CA 94117-1807

HELDT, CARL RANDALL
EDUCATOR, PAINTER
b Stanford, Ill, Sept 8, 1925. *Study:* Wittenburg Coll, Springfield, Ohio, 43-44; Univ Ill, Urbana, BFA, 53; Ariz State Univ, Tempe, 60-61. *Work:* Fennemore Craig Law Firm, Phoenix; Hallmark Cards, Kansas City; Phoenix Coll, Phoenix; Tucson Art Mus, Univ Ariz; Univ Ariz Art Mus; State Farm Insurance Bloomington Ill. *Comn:* Designed highlights for Children Mag, Honesdale, Pa, 60; Murals, Kahler Hotel, Rochester, Minn, 54; watercolors, Ford Motor co, Dearborn, Mich, 63; cards, toys & crafts, Hallmark Cards, Kansas City, 68-73; Baptismal Font, Fountain of Life Lutheran Church, Tucson; stained glass, Ascension Lutheran Church, Tucson; and many illustrated books, greeting cards, stained glass windows, church alters and baptismal fonts. *Exhib:* Southwestern Invitational, Yuma Art Ctr, Ariz, 67-75; Cedar City Invitational, Utah, 67-76; 4 Corners Biennial, Phoenix Mus, Ariz, 71; 22nd Ann NY Soc Illustrators; solo exhib, Univ Ill, Urbana; plus others. *Pos:* Med illusr, Univ Ill, Urbana, 49-53; art dir, Our Wonderful Encyl, Champaign, Ill, 53-55; artist-in-residence, Hallmark Cards, Kansas City, 68; bd dir, Waste Management Symp, Tucson, 93. *Teaching:* Instr graphic design, Univ Ill, Urbana, 55-60; prof graphic design, Univ Ariz, 61-90. *Awards:* Phoenix Art Dirs Club, 68; Purchase Award, Cedar City Invitational; Coll Southwestern Utah, 75. *Bibliog:* Elma Delic (auth), Abstract Marvels, Ariz Daily Star, 2009. *Mem:* Tubac Ctr Arts, Ariz. *Media:* Oil, Acrylic, found-wood. *Res:* cast bronze sculptures, Noah's Ark. *Interests:* Pylons of desert, steel sculptures, found-wood sculptures, bronze sculptures. *Publ:* Illusr, NY Times, 62 & Ford Times Mag, 63; contribr, Arizona Alumnus Mag, Univ Ariz, 79; Arizona Review Mag, 80; Arizona Highways, 85; Nuclear Tech, 90; Tucson Lifestyle Mag, 2008. *Dealer:* Details Art & Design 3001 Skyline Dr Tucson AZ 85718. *Mailing Add:* 4560 N Via Sinuosa Tucson AZ 85745-9764

HELFAND, FERN M
PHOTOGRAPHER, DIGITAL ARTIST
b Toronto, Ont. *Study:* York Univ, Toronto, BA (studio art, honors), 74; Univ Fla, with Jerry Uelsmann, MFA, 80; Sheridan Coll, cert (computer graphics), 94. *Work:* Can Coun Art Bank, Can Mus Contemp Photog & Dept External Affaires Can, Ottawa, Ont; McIntosh Gallery, Univ Western Ont, London, Ont; Nat Gallery Malaysia, Kuala Lumpur; London Life Insurance; London Regional Art & Hist Mus; Kelowna Art Gallery. *Exhib:* Work of Art & Scholar (with catalog), Fac Show, Univ Western Ont, 85; London/Havana Exchange, Casa de las Americas, Cuba, 88; Beyond the Document, Forest City Gallery, London, Ont, 89; Arts & The Social Context, Nat Gallery Malaysia, Kuala Lumpur, 91; Women & Creativity, Nat Gallery Malaysia, Kuala Lumpur, 92; Bengawan Solo Sekali Sekala (Penang artists), Maybank Gallery & Univ Kebangsaan, Kuala Lumpur, 92; solo exhib, London Regional Art Gallery & Mus, London, Ont, 94-95 & McIntosh Gallery, Univ Western Ontario, London, Ont, 99; Niagara, Art Gallery Windsor, Ont, 2000; Valley 2000, Kelowna Art Gallery & Kelowna Mus, 2002; Photo Gallery, Harbourfront, Toronto, 2003; Kelowna Art Gallery & Kelowna Mus, 2005 & 2007; Kaunas Photo Days '06, Kaunas, Lithuania, 2006. *Pos:* Bd mem, Forest City Gallery, Sunfest Int Music & Arts Festival; pub art com, City Kelowna; pres, Alternator Gallery, Kelowna, Can. *Teaching:* Asst prof photog, Univ Western Ont, 82-89; vis prof, Univ Sci Malaysia, 89-92; vis lectr, Ont Coll Art, 94-95; assoc prof, Okanagan Univ, 98-2005 & Univ BC, Okanagan, 2005-. *Awards:* Can Coun B Grant, 83; First Place, Nat Gallery Malaysia, 91; Millennium grant, Govt Can, 2000. *Bibliog:* Rodney Gilchrist (auth), The transcendental tourist, Photo Life, 7/89; James Patton (auth), Fern Helfand, Another Time, Another Place, London Regional Art Gallery Mus, 12/94; Catherine Elliot Shaw (auth, ed), Fabricated Communities, McKintosh Gallery, 2000; Dr Robert Belton (auth), Sites of Resistance, Can Visual Cult, 2001; Artspots CBS Television & Website, 2002. *Mem:* Int Vis Sociology Asn. *Media:* Digital Imaging, Photography. *Res:* Visual sociology; tourism; fabricated communities. *Mailing Add:* University British Columbia Okanagan 3333 University Way Kelowna BC V1V 7766 Canada

HELFENSTEIN, JOSEF
MUSEUM DIRECTOR
b Lucerne, Switzerland, 1958. *Study:* Univ Geneva, MA; Univ Bern, PhD. *Pos:* Dir, Kunstmuseum, Bern, 1983-2000, assoc dir, 1995-2000; chief cur prints & drawings dept, Paul Klee Found, 1988-2000, project head, 9-vol catalogue raisonné of the artist's work, 1990-; dir, Krannert Art Mus, Univ Ill, Urbana Champaign, 2000-04; dir, Menil Collection, Houston, 2004-. *Teaching:* Prof, Sch Art & Design, Univ Ill, Urbana-Champaign, 2000-04. *Publ:* Co-auth, Maria Lassnig: Zeichnungen & Aquarelle, 1946-1995, 1995, Deep Blues: Bill Traylor 1854-1949, 1999, Lichitz & the Avant-Garde, 2002, Drawings of Choice from a New York Collection, 2003; auth, Louise Bourgeois, 2002. *Mailing Add:* Menil Collection 1511 Branard St Houston TX 77006

HELGESON, PHILLIP LAWRENCE
PAINTER, ILLUSTRATOR, GRAPHIC ARTIST
b Albuquerque, NMex, June 11, 1960. *Study:* Cincinnati Art Acad, BFA, 60, studied with Stuart Goldman, Anne Miotke, Constance McClure, Cole Corathers, Michael Scott & Robert Fabe. *Work:* Clossons Art Gallery, Cincinnati Art Club & Lexington Art Works Expo, Cincinnati, Ohio; Janet Gamin, 97; Tina Montano, 97; Jennie Heine, 97; Cincinnati Pub Libr. *Comn:* Marathon mural, comn by Mark Mandefield, Helgeson, Cincinnati, 83; portrait, comn by Vicky Elsbrock, Cincinnati, 87; Indian painting, comn by Donald Helgeson, Ocean Springs, Miss, 89; Garden portrait, Clossons Art Gallery, Cincinnati, 98. *Exhib:* Art Acad Show, Cincinnati Art Mus, 84; Art Acad Sr Show, Art Acad Cincinnati, 84; Members Show, Cincinnati Art Club, 97; Clossons Art Gallery, Cincinnati, 97 & 99; Clossons Say It With Flowers Exhib, Cincinnati, 97-98; Viewpoint Exhib, 98; Cinergy Art Exhib, 98; Montgomery Art Show. *Collection Arranged:* Collections of: Paul Sawish; James Wilson; Brad Kendom; Marianne Chappell; Ali Asad; Scott Tachetl (has several); M Chappelle; and many others. *Awards:* Scholarship painting, Acad Cincinnati, 83. *Bibliog:* Art exhibitions, City Beat, 97; Gallery News, Clossons, 97; City Beat, 2/16/2005. *Mem:* Art Acad Alumni Asn; Taos Art Asn; Cape Ann Art Asn; Ohio Watercolor Soc; Cincinnati Art Club; Am Impressionists Soc; Alumni Asn. *Media:* Oil, Watercolor; Gouache. *Specialty:* Impressionism. *Interests:* Music, art collecting. *Collection:* Artists from Golden Age of Cincinnati including Constance McClure, Charles Kaelin, Carl and Carolyn Zimmerman, Robert Fabe and John Weis; Reginald Grooms; Julie Papaditz collection (8 paintings); Mr Rhein collection; Peter Setalle; Kathryn Kranbulle; M Bardes; Dr S Woodruff; and many others. *Dealer:* Clossons-Marie Rigney 10100 Montgomery Rd Cincinnati OH 45242-5324. *Mailing Add:* 12009 Stillwood Dr Cincinnati OH 45249

HELLER, REINHOLD AUGUST
HISTORIAN
b Fulda, Ger, July 22, 1940; US citizen. *Study:* St Joseph's Col, Philadelphia, BS, 63; Ind Univ, Bloomington, MA, 66, PhD, 68, with Albert Elsen, John Jacobus & Sven Loevgren. *Pos:* Guest cur, Nat Gallery, Washington, DC, 78-79. *Teaching:* Prof art hist, Univ Pittsburgh, 68-78 & Univ Chicago, 78-. *Awards:* Foreign Area Prog Fel, 66-68; Guggenheim Found Fel, 73-74; d'Harnoncourt Fel, Mus Mod Art, New York, 70. *Mem:* Coll Art Asn; Ger Studies Asn; Historians of Ger & Cent Europ Art. *Res:* Art criticism; Symbolism; Expressionism; German Romanticism; German art of the 1920's. *Publ:* Auth, Art of Wilhelm Lehmbruck, Nat Gallery, Washington, DC, 72; Hildegard Auer: A Yearning for Art, Belserverlag, 87; Brücke: German Expressionist prints in the Granvil and Marcia Specks Collection, Block Gallery, Northwestern Univ, Evanston, Ill, 88; Art in Germany 1909-1936: From Expressionism to Resistance, The Marvin and Janet Fishman Collection, Prestel-Verlag, 90; Toulouse-Lautrec: The Soul of Montmartre, Prestel-Lerlag, 97 & Gabriele Munter: The Years of Expressionism, 97. *Mailing Add:* 1325 Linden Rd Homewood IL 60430

HELLER, SUSANNA
PAINTER, INSTRUCTOR
b New York, NY, 1956. *Study:* Nova Scotia Coll Art & Design, BFA, 74-77. *Work:* Art Gallery of Ontario; Concordia Univ, Montreal; Canadian Art Bank, Ottawa; TD Waterhouse Corp; Air Canada Corp. *Exhib:* Mus London, Can, Concordia Univ Gallery, Mocca-Contemp Art, Toronto, Shangha Art Mus, China, Nova Scotia Mus Art; Olga Korper Gallery, Toronto, Luise Ross Gallery, NY, Galerie Paul Andresse, Amsterdam, AIR Gallery, NY, Tibor de Nagy Gallery, NY. *Teaching:* lectr, painting & drawing, Purchase Col, The New Sch, Bennington Col, Yale Univ, Nova Scotia Col Art. *Awards:* The Nat Endowment for the Canada Council; John Simon Guggenheim Mem Found Fel, 88. *Bibliog:* John Clark (auth), No Apologies, Vanguard, Vancouver, 2-3/89; Robert Berlind (auth), review, Art in Am, 2/89; Ken Johnson (auth), The New York Times, review, 1998; March Gregoroff (auth), Flash Art, review, 2002; Gary Michael Dault (auth), The Globe & Mail, Toronto, review, 2002. *Mem:* Coll Art Asn. *Media:* Acrylic, Oil. Mixed Media. *Specialty:* Fine Arts. *Publ:* auth, From Here, catalogue, Mus London, color & 3 essays, 2002

HELM, ALISON
EDUCATOR, ADMINISTRATOR
Study: Cleveland Inst of Art, BFA; Syracuse Univ, MFA. *Comn:* Splendor of the Seas for deck of Cruise Ship by Caribbean Cruise Lines. *Exhib:* Exhibited work extensively at many galleries, museums and sculpture parks throughout the US, Japan, Taiwan, and Mexico, including the Cultural Center, Charleston, West Virginia, National Mus of Women in the Arts, Washington, DC, Carnegie Mus, Pa, and the Huntington Mus, Charleston, West Virginia. *Collection Arranged:* Work represented in numerous private and public collections. *Teaching:* Coordinator of sculpture in the division of art, 1983-, West Virginia Univ, dir Sch of Art & Design, prof sculpture, graduate advisor, currently. *Awards:* NEA Grants for Underserved area artists from the Cultural Center, Charleston, WVa. *Mailing Add:* Division of Art and Design West Virginia University College of Creative Arts Center 2251A PO Box 6111 Morgantown WV 26506-6111

HELSELL, CHARLES PAUL
CURATOR
b Ft Dodge, Iowa, Nov 13, 1940. *Study:* Mont State Univ, BS, 63. *Collection Arranged:* Hylton A Thomas Collection (paintings, drawings & prints; auth, catalog), Univ Minn Art Mus, 70; Mr Possum and Friends: Prints by Malcolm Myers (auth, catalog), 82; Women in Print: Prints from 3M by Contemporary Women Printmakers (auth, catalog), 3M, 95 & Made in Minnesota I: Art at 3M by Artists Born Before 1930, 97; Country Life, City Life: Prints from the Harold D Peterson Collection (auth, catalog), 96. *Pos:* Asst cur, Dept Prints, Minneapolis Inst Arts, 66-69; cur, Weisman Art Mus (formerly Univ Art Mus), Minneapolis, 69-84; cur art collection, 3M, 84-99; dir Blanden Mem Art Mus, Fort Dodge, Iowa, 2000. *Mem:* Coll Art Asn; Print Coun Am

HELZER, RICHARD BRIAN
METALSMITH, SCULPTOR
b Hastings, Nebr, Aug 27, 1943. *Study:* Kearney State Col, Nebr, BA, 65; Univ Kans, MFA, 69. *Work:* C M Russell Mus, Great Falls, Mont; Rocky Mountain Coll Libr, Billings, Mont. *Comn:* Altar serv, St Elizabeth's Episcopal Church, Nebr, 69 & Hope Lutheran Church, Kans, 70; alter cross, Univ Kans Chapel, Lawrence, 70 & Sacred Heart Cath Church, Butte, Mont, 86. *Exhib:* Hist of Gold & Silversmithing in Am, Lowe Art Mus, Univ Miami, Coral Gables, Fla, 75; NW Invitational Silversmiths, Seattle Art Mus, Wash, 76; US Off Info Goldsmiths Exhib, Melbourne, Australia, 76; 3rd Profile of US Jewelry, Tex Tech Univ, Lubbock, 77; Metal-non Metal, Synopsis Gallery, Chicago, 80; North Am Goldsmiths European Exhib (traveling); San Francisco Mus Mod Art, 89; Art Equinox Exhib, Paris Gibson Mus Art, Great Falls Mont, 92; Ana 22, Holter Mus, Helena, Mont, 93; and others. *Pos:* Guest cur, Metalsmithing Invitational, Yellowstone Art Ctr, Billings, Mont, 81; vis artist, E Carolina Univ, 89, Arrowmont Sch, Tenn, 88, Penland Sch, NC, 92. *Teaching:* Teaching asst, Univ Kans, Lawrence, 68-69; asst prof art, Mont State Univ, Bozeman, 70-74, assoc prof, 75-80, prof, 80-, dir sch art, 95-. *Awards:* Nat Endowment Arts Fel, 76 & 78; Best of Show, Art Equinox Exhib, Paris Gibson Mus Art, 92; Best of Show, Ana 22, Holter Mus, 93; Western States Fel, 79. *Bibliog:* Jewelry Making, Bovin Publ, 80; Oppi Untracht (auth), Jewelry Concepts & Technology, Doubleday & Co; Alice Sprintzen (auth), Jewelry: Basic Techniques & Design, Chilton. *Mem:* Soc NAm Goldsmiths; Am Crafts Coun. *Media:* Multi-Metals, Wood. *Dealer:* Gallatin River Gallery Big Sky Mont; Wood Street Gallery Chicago Ill. *Mailing Add:* 52 Hitching Post Rd Bozeman MT 59715

HEMBREY, SHEA
PAINTER, SCULPTOR
b Newport, Ark, Aug 21, 1974. *Study:* Lyon Col, BA, 96; Univ Canterbury, COP, 98; Ark State Univ, MA, 99; Cornell Univ, MFA, 2007. *Work:* Ark State Capitol, Little Rock; Lyon Col, Batesville, Ark; Ark State Univ, Jonesboro; Cornell Univ, Ithaca, NY. *Exhib:* Guaranteed Fresh: Still Life Today, Invitational, Davidson Galleries, Seattle, Wash, 2003; Summer in the City, J Cacciola Gallery, NY, 2003; Ark Arts Coun Fellows Exhib, Criswell, Hembrey, McCann & Musgnug, Univ Ark Gallery, Little Rock, 2003; Offerings: Shea Hembrey Paintings, David Lusk Gallery, Memphis, Tenn, 2003; Ark State Senate Chambers, Little Rock, 2003; US Artists Am Fine Art Show, Philadelphia, Pa, 2003; Holiday, David Lusk Gallery, Memphis, Tenn, 2004; Wallflowers, Bradbury Gallery, Ark State Univ, 2004; Celebrating Art, The Anderson Ctr, Red Wing, Minn, 2004; Art at Steepletop, Millay Colony for the Arts, Austerlitz, NY, 2004; Bound-Paintings by Shea Hembrey, Helen Day Art Ctr, Stowe, Vt, 2005; New Works, The Anderson Ctr, Red Wing, Minn, 2005; Gags, Tjaden Gallery, Cornell Univ, Ithaca Univ, NY, 2005; Mind the Gap, Tjaden Gallery, Cornell Univ, Ithaca, NY, 2006; Four Walls, Hartell Gallery, Cornell Univ, Ithaca, NY, 2006; Ark Artists, Cox Gallery, Little Rock Public Libr, 2006; Mirror Nests, Correll Lab of Ornithology, Ithaca, NY; Nothing is Lost, Newspace Center for Photog, Portland, Ore, 2007; New American Paintings, Vol 70 (an exhib in print curated by Charlotte Kotik, Brooklyn Mus Art, contemp cur), 2007. *Awards:* Artist Fel Grant, Ark Arts Coun, 2003; Ucross Found Residency, 2004; Caldera Residency, 2005; Weir Farm Residency, 2005; Patterson Decade Award, Lyon Col, 2006; Artist in Residence, Fundacion Valparaiso, Mojacar, Spain, 2007. *Mem:* CAA (Coll Art Asn). *Media:* Acrylic on Board. *Interests:* Anthropology, folk wisdom, ornithology. *Collection:* Mus quality mezzotint collection with prints by 40 int artists. *Dealer:* David Lusk Gallery, 4540 Poplar Ave, Memphis, TN, 38117. *Mailing Add:* 610 Jackson 63 Newport AR 72112

HEMMERDINGER, WILLIAM JOHN, III
PAINTER, CRITIC
b Burbank, Calif, July 7, 1951. *Study:* Coll Desert, Calif, AA, 72; Univ Calif, Riverside, BA, 73; Claremont Grad Sch, MFA, 75, PhD, 79. *Work:* Smithsonian Inst; Barbara Hepworth Mus, Cornwall, Eng; Fed Reserve Bank, San Francisco; Mus Contemp Art, Los Angeles; Mobil Oil Corp, NY; Nat Lib Canada, Ottawa, Long Beach Mus Art. *Comn:* Biblioteca Laurenziana, pvt residence, Indian Wells, Calif, 87; Bronze Fountain, pvt residence, Indian Wells, Calif, 88; Bronze Fountain, pvt residence, Rancho Mirage, Calif, 94; California Stories, Indian Wells, Calif, 97; Plaza Hotel Murals, NY; Shelburne Hotel murals, NY, 2004; Affina Fitzpatrick, Chicago, 2007; Bronze Sculpture, Cotvit Tide Ball, Pvt Residence, NY, 2014; and others. *Exhib:* Cirrus Eds, Ltd, Los Angeles, 82, 84, Brand Libr Art Ctr, Glendale, Calif, 90; Olympic Arts Festivals, Los Angeles, Calif & Seoul, Korea; Los Angeles Co Mus Art; Scripps Coll, Claremont, Calif; Boyusan Citizen's Hall, Pusan, Korea; Lalit Kala Acad, Nat Gallery Art, New Delhi; Cahoon Mus Am Art; Pyong-Taek Municipal Mus, Pyong-Taek, Korea; Nat Acad Design, NY; Am Watercolor Soc, NY; Int Contemp Art Fairs, London, NY, Chicago, Basel, Paris, Frankfurt, Miami, 72-2000; Los Angeles Co Mus Art, 77; Mus Mod Art, Seoul, Korea; Fukuoka Prefecture Mus, Japan; Otto Galerie, Munich, Ger; Kitakyushu Mus of Art, Kyushu, Japan; Double Vision Gallery, Los Angeles, 2002; Thomas Moser, Cabinetmakers, Boston, Mass, 2006; Brickbottom Gallery, Boston, 2006; Cotuit Ctr Arts, Cotuit, Mass, 2006; The Studio on Slough Rd, Brewster, Mass, 2011; Addison Gallery Art, Orleans, Mass; Miller White Fine Arts, Provincetown, Mass, 2013; Lela Terakoya, Los Angeles, 2013; Rela Internat, Los Angeles, 2014. *Teaching:* Boston Archit Coll, Mass, 2002-2014, emeritus senior freehand drawing master, 2014-; faculty, Fine Arts Work Center, Provincetown, Mass, 2011. *Awards:* Award for Drawing, Nat Watercolor Soc, 74; Nat Watercolor Soc, 79; Artists Fel & Residency, Julia & David White Artist Colony, Costa Rica, 99. *Bibliog:* Michael Zakian, PhD (auth), William Hemmerdinger: Paintings, Old Selectmen's Bldg Gallery; Katherine Holland (auth), The Art Collection, Fed Reserve Bank, San Francisco; Robert Perine (auth), The California Romantics, Artras Press; Kathleen Sidwell (auth), William Hemmerdinger at the Studio on Slough Road, Studio on Slough Road. *Media:* Mixed Media Painting & Sculpture. *Res:* William Hemmerdinger Papers, Getty Rsch Inst, Los Angeles, Calif. *Publ:* Auth, Lowell Nesbitt (exhib catalog), Louis Newman Galleries, Los Angeles, 87; Matsumi Kanemitsu (exhib catalog), Japanese Am Community Cult Ctr, Los Angeles, 88; Katherine Chang-Liu (exhib catalog), Louis Newman Galleries, Beverly Hills, 88; Chinese Artists (exhib catalog), Macao Mus, 93; Bong Tae Kim: Thirty Years of Printmaking, Song Bong Ku Press, Seoul, Korea, 94. *Mailing Add:* 299 Mariner Circle Cotuit MA 02635

HEMPEL, WES
ARTIST
b El Monte, Calif, 1953. *Study:* Calif State Univ, Northridge, BA, 85; Univ Colo, Boulder, MA, 88. *Exhib:* Solo exhibs, Robischon Gallery, Denver, 97-98, 2001, 2003, 2005, Wes Hempel, Paintings - The Frist Seven Years, Univ Wyo Art Mus, 98, The Canceled Field Trip, Claire Oliver Fine Art, Philadelphia, 2000, Injury and Desire, Jenkins Johnson Gallery, NYC, 2006; Group exhibs, Boxes/Books, River Art Works, Denver, 87; Objects and Place, Sibell-Wolle Gallery, Univ Colo, 88; Small Sculpture, Robischon Gallery, Denver, 90-91; Holy Wars, Arte Vitale Gallery, Denver, 93; You Call That Art?, One West Art Center, Fort Collins, Colo, 94; 11th Ann Invitational Exhib, Microsoft Corp, Redmond, Wash, 95; Private Worlds: 200 Years of American Still Life Painting, Aspen Art Mus, 97; New Acquisitions, Columbus Mus, Ga,98; Re-presenting Representation IV, Arnot Art Mus, Elmira, NY, 99; Art Miami, Claire Oliver Fine Art, 1999-2001; The Male Form in Contemp Art, Hollywood Art Center, Fla, 2000; The Dream Mill, Lakewood Cultural Center, Colo, 2001; Winter Group Show, Davidson Gallery, Seattle, 2002; Summer Group Exhib, Tatischeff Gallery, NY, 2003; Allure, Leslie Lohman Found, NYC, 2004; A Tribute to JB Harter, Contemp Arts Center, New Orleans, 2005; Decades of Influence, Mus Contemp Art, Center for Visual Arts, Denver, 2006. *Collection Arranged:* Denver Art Mus, Colo; Columbus Mus, Ga; Microsoft Corp, Seattle; Styskal, Wiese & Melchione, Los Angeles; Hyatt Regency Hotel, Borgen Investment Group Inc, First Western Trust Bank, Denver, Colo; Leslie Lohman Found, NYC. *Awards:* Creative fel in Lit, Colo Coun on Arts, 92; creative fel in Painting, Colo Coun on Arts, 2002. *Publ:* Contribr, New American Paintings #12, The Open Studio Press, 97; contribr, Naked Men Too, 2000 & Male Nude Now, 2001, David Leddick, Universe Publishing/Rizzoli; contribr, Great American Writers of the Twentieth Century, Vol VII, Marshall Cavendish Publishers, 2002; No Worry is Necessary on Your Part: Paintings by Wes Hempel, XY Magazine, San Diego, 2003; Pleides Literary Journal, Vol XXV, 2005. *Mailing Add:* c/o Robischon Gallery 1740 Wazee St Denver CO 80202

HENDELES, YDESSA
GALLERY OWNER, COLLECTOR
b Germany, 1948. *Study:* Univ Toronto, grad; New Sch Art, Toronto. *Hon Degrees:* Nova Scotia Coll Art & Design, Doctorate, 1996; Univ Toronto, Doctorate, 2000. *Pos:* Owner & dir, Ydessa Gallery, Toronto, 1980-88; founder, Ydessa Hendeles Art Found, Toronto, 1988-; grand founder, Art Gallery Ontario. *Teaching:* Instr art hist, New Sch Art, Toronto. *Awards:* Outstanding Achievement Award, Ontario Asn Art Galleries, 1998; Fel, Ontario Coll Art & Design, 1998; named one of Art World's 50 Most Powerful People; named one of Top 200 Collectors, ARTnews mag, 2006-13. *Mem:* Ontario Asn Art Galleries; Order of Ontario; Tate Gallery, London (int coun); Mus Mod Art, New York. *Collection:* Contemporary art; photography. *Mailing Add:* Ydessa Hendeles Art Found 778 King St W Toronto ON M5V1N6 Canada

HENDERSHOT, J L
PRINTMAKER, EDUCATOR
b Cleveland, Ohio, Nov 3, 1941. *Study:* Cleveland Inst Art, with H C Cassill, Louis Bosa & Julian Stanczak; Syracuse Univ, NY, with George Vander Sluis & Donald Cortesse. *Work:* Rochester Mus Art, NY; Pennell Fund, Libr Cong. *Comn:* Drawing, Alumni Asn, St John's Univ, Collegeville, Minn, 73; drawing for gift, Spira Dance Co, Portland, Ore, 74; print, St Cloud State Col, 75; 50th Anniversary lithographs (50 ed), Minn Mus; lithographs ed, Asn Am Artist. *Exhib:* Solo exhibs, RI Sch Design, Providence, 75, Assoc Am Artists Gallery, NY, 76, Red River Art Ctr Mus, Moorehead, Minn, 76 & Uptown Gallery, NY, 77; 7th Nat Biennial Drawing US Show, St Paul, Minn, 75; and others. *Pos:* Art gallery dir, St John's Univ, 75-. *Teaching:* Asst instr drawing & printmaking, Syracuse Univ, 68-70; asst prof drawing & printmaking, St John's Univ, 71-. *Awards:* Philadelphia Print Club Purchase Award,

Philadelphia Mus Art, 68; Univ NDak Purchase Award, 15th Nat Print & Drawing Exhib, 72; Minn Mus Art Purchase Award, 7th Nat Biennial Drawing US Show, 75. *Mem:* Graphic Soc, Hollis, NH; Boston Printmakers; Pratt Graphics Print Club, NY. *Media:* Intaglio, Lithography. *Mailing Add:* 169 Riverside Dr NE Saint Cloud MN 56304-0437

HENDERSHOT, RAY
PAINTER
b Bangor, Pa, May 26, 1931. *Study:* Self taught. *Exhib:* Arts for the Parks Top 100, Nat Parks Acad of the Arts, Jackson Hole, 93; Nat Watercolor Soc, Brea Civic & Cult Ctr, Calif, 99; Pa Watercolor Soc, Berman Gallery, Ursinus, Collegeville, Pa, 2003; Philadelphia Watercolor Soc, Berman Gallery, Ursinus, Collegeville, Pa, 2006; Am Watercolor Soc, Salmagundi Club, New York, 2006. *Awards:* Barse Miller Mem, Am Watercolor Soc, Barse Miller Estate, 2000; Anne Williams Glushien, Am Watercolor Soc, 2006. *Bibliog:* Stephen Doherty (auth), Textures to Simulate Memories, Am Artist, 2001; Guan Weixing (auth), Ray Hendershot, Chinese Watercolor, 2003; Tom Zeit (auth), Artist's, Recycling For, Artist's Sketchbook, 2004. *Mem:* Signature mem, Am Watercolor Soc & Nat Watercolor Soc; signature mem & Sylvan Grouse Recipient, Pa Watercolor Soc; signature mem & Crest Medal Recipient, Phila Watercolor Soc; Int Soc of Acrylic Painters. *Publ:* Auth, Blizzard of '93, Palette Talk/Grumbacher, 94, Texture Techniques for Winning Watercolors, North Light, 99, Growing Old, Artist's Mag/North Light, 2003 & My World, The Paintings of Ray Hendershot. *Mailing Add:* 1007 Lakeview Terr Pennsburg PA 18073

HENDERSON, LINDA DALRYMPLE
HISTORIAN, EDUCATOR
Study: Dickinson Col, BA, 69; Yale Univ, MA, 72, PhD, 75. *Pos:* assoc cur mod art, Mus Fine Arts, Houston, 74-76, cur, 76-77. *Teaching:* asst prof, Univ Tex, Austin, 78-84, assoc prof, 84-91, prof, 91-, centennial prof art hist. *Awards:* Vasari Award, Dallas Mus Art, 85; Guggenheim Fel, 88-89; Regents Outstanding Teaching award, 2009; Senior Fel, IKKM Inst, Weimar, 2010, 2011; Berlin prize, Am Acad Berlin, 2014. *Mem:* Coll Art Asn; Soc for Sci, Lit & the Arts; Int Soc for Arts, Sci and Technol. *Res:* Twentieth century European and American art, including its interaction with geometry, science and technology, and mysticism/occultism. *Publ:* The Fourth Dimension and Non-Euclidean Geometry in Mod Art, Princeton Univ Press, 83; auth, Mysticism as 'the Tie that Binds': The Case of Edward Carpenter and Modernism, Art J, 87; X-rays and the Quest for Invisible Reality in the Art of Kupka, Duchamp and the Cubists, Art J, 88; Duchamp in Context: Science and Technology in the Large Glass and Related Works, Princeton Univ Press, 98; The Large Glass Seen Anew: Reflections of Contemp Science and Tech in Marcel Duchamp's Hilarious Picture, Leonardo, 99; co ed, From Energy to Information: Representation in Science and Technology, Art and Literature, Stanford Univ Press, 2002; Ed's Introd: Writing Modern Art & Sci-An Overview; Cubism, Futurism & Ether Physics in the Early 20th Century, Sci in Context, 2004; Four Dimensional Space or Space Time: The Emergence of the Cubism Relativity Myth in NY in the 1940's, in The Visual Mind II, ed Michele Emmer, MIT Press, 2005; auth, Einstein & 20th Century Art: A Romance of Many Dimensions in Einstein for the 21st Century (ed, Peter Galison et al), 2007; auth, Park Place Gallery Group in 1960s, New York, Blanton Mus Art, 2008; Augmented, The Fourth Dimension and Non-Euclidean Geometry in Modern Art, MIT, 2013. *Mailing Add:* Univ Tex Dept Art & Art Hist Austin TX 78712

HENDERSON, MIKE
PAINTER, FILMMAKER
b 1943. *Study:* San Francisco Art Inst, BFA, 69, MFA, 70. *Work:* Crocker Art Mus, Sacramento; Honolulu Acad Arts; Oakland Mus; San Francisco Mus Mod Art. *Exhib:* San Francisco Mus Mod Art, 74 & 78; Whitney Mus, NY, 70 & 71; Honolulu Acad Arts, 78; solo exhibs, Walter/McBean Gallery, San Francisco, Calif, 90, Haines Gallery, San Francisco, Calif, 91, 92, 94, 99, 2002, Calif Mus Art Luther Burbank Ctr, Santa Rosa, Calif, 96 & San Marco Gallery Dominican Col, San Rafael, Calif, 96, Triton Mus, Calif, 2003; Oakland Artists '90, Oakland Mus, Calif, 90; From the Studio: Recent Paintings & Sculpture by 20 California Artists, Oakland Art Mus, Calif, 92; Selections from the Rene & Veronica di Rosa Collection, Oakland Mus, Calif, 94; Triton Mus Art, Santa Clara, Calif, 97; Beyond Color, CN Gorman Mus, Univ Calif, Davis, 97; The Painters Craft, Reese Bullen Gallery, Humbolt State Univ, Arcata, Calif, 97; What Is Art For?, Oakland Mus Calif, 99; Music in My Soul, Portsmouth Mus, Virginia, 01; and others. *Teaching:* Instr art, Univ Calif, Davis, 70-. *Awards:* Guggenheim Fel, 73; Nat Endowment Arts, 78 & 89; Adeline Kent Award, 90; Distinguished Alumni Award, San Francisco Art Inst, 90. *Bibliog:* Peter Frank (auth), Four & Four, Prism-Arts of Pacific, 6/95; Gretchen Giles (auth), Paint it Black, Sonoma Co Independent, 5/96; Kenneth Baker (auth), Substance with Style, 8/96, Celebrating Art's Generations, 9/96, Painter with Open Heart, 7/99, San Francisco Chronicle; and others; Painting that Power the Imagination, 1/2010. *Dealer:* Haines Gallery. *Mailing Add:* c/o Haines Gallery 49 Geary St San Francisco CA 94108

HENDERSON, ROBBIN LEGERE
PAINTER, CURATOR
b Stockton, Calif, April 19, 1942. *Study:* Reed Col, 59-61; Univ Calif, Berkeley, BA, 63; San Francisco Art Inst, 68-70. *Exhib:* Solo exhibs, Mills Coll Gallery, 76, Floating Mus, 77, Southern Exposure Gallery, San Francisco, 78 & 85, Intersection Gallery, San Francisco, 82 & Berkeley Store Gallery, 94; Art for Giving & Collecting, 78, San Francisco Mus Mod Art; San Francisco Exchange Show, Fashion Moda, NY, 82; San Francisco Art Inst Ann, 84; Alternative Mus, 84; Mission Cult Ctr, 85; Southern Exposure, 94; Intersection Gallery, 95. *Collection Arranged:* Alice Neel, Paintings from 1920-1974, Am Can Gallery, 74; Ethnic Notions: Black Images in the White Mind, 82 & Mothers Gifts to their Children, 84, (with catalogs), Berkeley Art Ctr; Beyond 1992, 92; 10x10: Ten Women Ten Prints, 95; Bodies & Souls, 94. *Pos:* Dir, Southern Exposure Gallery, San Francisco, 74-77; cur, Intersection Gallery, San Francisco, 77-79; cur & exec dir, Berkeley Art Ctr, 79-85 & 91-; artist-in-residence, Calif Arts Coun, 83-86. *Bibliog:* Robert MacDonald (auth), Images of women, Artweek, 4/79; Charles Shere (auth), article, Oakland Tribune, 8/30/82; Artweek, 7/94. *Mem:* Non-Profit Gallery Asn (pres); AFA. *Media:* Oil on Canvas, Mixed Media. *Mailing Add:* Berkeley Art Ctr 1275 Walnut St Berkeley CA 94709-1406

HENDERSON, VICTOR
PAINTER, MURALIST
b Cuyahoga Falls, Ohio, Nov 30, 1939. *Study:* San Francisco State Col, BA, 63. *Work:* Newport Harbor Mus, Newport Beach, Calif; Chicago Art Inst; M H De Young Mem Mus, San Francisco; Los Angeles Co Mus. *Comn:* Beverly Hills Sidhartha, Michael Huit, Los Angeles, 69-70; Venice in the Snow, Jerry Rosen, Los Angeles, 70; Isle of Calif, Jordy Hormel, Los Angeles, 70-72; Hippy Knowhow, French Govt, Paris, 71; Ghost Town, Ed Janss, Thousand Oaks, Calif, 72-73 (all the above murals were executed under the name Los Angeles Fine Arts Squad); Breakers Mural, comn by Arco Co, Santa Barbara, Calif, 78-79; City of Los Angeles, Calif, 95; City of Montebello, 98; City of Santa Fe Springs, 99. *Exhib:* LA Eight, Los Angeles Co Mus Art, Calif, 76; 100-plus, Los Angeles Inst Contemp Art, 77; Illusion & Reality, Australian Nat Gallery, Canbera, and six other Australian galleries & mus, 77; Victor Henderson Takes a Walk, Newport Harbour Art Mus, 78; one-person shows, Ulrike Cantor Gallery, Los Angeles, 81 & 83 & Los Angeles Co Mus, Calif, 83; Artists Space, NY, 83; and others. *Pos:* Co-founder, Los Angeles Fine Art Squad, Calif, 69-73. *Teaching:* Lectr drawing, Univ Calif, Los Angeles, 75-77; Otis Art Inst, Los Angeles, 80-83 & Univ Calif, Irvine, 84-85. *Awards:* Nat Endowment Arts Painting Fel, 83-84. *Bibliog:* T H Garver (auth), Artforum, Vol 9, 71; Peter Plagens (auth), Sunshine Muse, Praeger, NY, 73; Eva Cookcroft (auth), Towards a People Art, E P Dutton & Co, NY, 76; Volger Barthelmeh (auth), Street Murals, Alfred A Knopt, 82; Edward Lucie-Smith (auth), American Art Now, William Marrow, 85. *Publ:* Auth, Mega Murals & Big Art, Running Press, Philadelphia, 77. *Mailing Add:* 474 Lewis St Los Angeles CA 90042

HENDON, CHAM
PAINTER
b Birmingham, Ala, Sept 14, 1936. *Study:* Art Inst Chicago, BFA, 63; Univ NMex, MA, 65; Univ Wis, MFA, 77. *Work:* Metrop Mus Art, NY; Mus of City NY; Neuberger Mus Art, Purchase, NY; New Mus Contemp Art, NY; Birmingham Mus Art, Ala. *Exhib:* Bad Painting, New Mus, NY; Painting & Sculpture Today, Indianapolis Mus, Ind; Dialoghi Nell Arti, Palazzo Ducale, Gubio, Italy, 85; Nueva Pintura Narrativa, El Museo Rufino Tamayo, Mexico City, 85; Painting: The 1980's, Ringling Mus Art, Sarasota, Fla, 91. *Pos:* dir, Madison Art Center, Wis, 67-76. *Media:* All Media

HENDRICKS, BARKLEY LEONNARD
PAINTER, PHOTOGRAPHER
b Philadelphia, Pa. *Study:* Pa Acad Fine Arts, 1963-67; William Cresson European Traveling scholar, 1966; Yale Univ Sch Fine Art, BFA, MFA, 1972. *Work:* Philadelphia Mus Art; Pa Acad Fine Arts, Philadelphia; Cornell Univ; Wichita State Univ, Kans; Nat Gallery, Washington, DC; Nasher Mus Contemp Art, Duke Univ; Tate Modern, Mus Va. *Comn:* Brodsky Ctr for Innovative Eds, Rutgers Univ, NJ. *Exhib:* Fel Exhib, Pa Acad Fine Arts, 1967-72; Nat Acad Design Ann, NY, 1970-71 & 1974-75; Contemp Black Artists, Whitney Mus Am Art, NY, 1971; Childe Hassam Fund Exhib, Am Acad Arts & Lett, 1971 & 1975; Nat Inst Arts & Lett Ann, 1971-72; Birth of Cool, Nasher Mus Contemp Art, Duke Univ, 2008, Studio Mus in Harlem, NY, 2009, Santa Monica Mus Art, 2009; 30 Americans, Miami, Fla, Raleigh, NC; Barkley L Hendricks: Some Like it Hot, William Benton Mus Art, Univ Conn, Storrs, Conn. *Teaching:* instr painting & drawing, Pa Acad Fine Arts, 1971-72; asst in painting, Yale Univ, 1971-72; asst prof painting & drawing, Conn Coll, 1972-81, prof, 1981-2010. *Awards:* Julius Hallgarten Second Prize, Nat Acad Design, 1971; Richard & Hilda Rosenthal Award, Nat Inst Arts & Lett, 1972; Fel, Visual Arts, US Artists, 2008; Joan Mitchell Found Award, 2009; Disting Body of Work Artist award, Coll Art Asn, 2010. *Bibliog:* Barkley L. Hendricks: Birth of the Cool (exhib catalog), 2008. *Media:* Oil, Acrylic. *Dealer:* Jack Shainman Gallery. *Mailing Add:* 22 Addison St New London CT 06320-5309

HENDRICKS, DAVID CHARLES
PAINTER, VISUAL ARTIST
b Hammond, Ind, Mar 25, 1948. *Study:* Skowhegan Summer Sch Painting & Sculpture, Maine, 69, Univ Ill, BFA, 70; Ox-Bow Summer Sch Painting, Saugatuck, Mich, 70. *Work:* Brooklyn Mus, NYNEX & Reader's Digest, NY; Hirshhorn Mus & Sculpture Garden, Washington, DC; NC Nat Bank; AT&T; Haynes & Boone, Dallas, Tex; Nat Health Insurance Underwriters, Dallas, Tex; and others. *Exhib:* Solo exhibs, Monique Knowlton Gallery, 77, Fischbach Gallery, NY, 84, 87, 88 & 90, Keene State Col, NH, 89; Davidson Nat Print and Drawing Show, Davidson Col, NC, 76; Childe Hassam Foundation Show, Am Acad & Lett, NY, 76; Queensboro Community Col, Bayside, NY, 77; Wave Hill Ctr for Environ Studies, Riverdale, NY, 79; Portsmouth Community Arts Ctr, Va, 82; Greenville Co Mus Art, SC, 85; William Sawyer Gallery, San Francisco, Calif, 85; traveling exhib, San Francisco Mus Mod Art, De Cordova & Dana Mus & Park, Lincoln, Mass, Archer M Huntington Art Gallery, Austin Tex, Mary & Leigh Block Gallery, Evanston, Ill, Arkon Art Mus, Ohio, Madison Art Ctr, Wis; 50th Nat Midyear exhib, Butler Inst Am Art, Ohio, 86; Face of the Land, Southern Alleghenies Mus Art, Loretto, Pa, 88; Art on Paper 1988, Weatherspoon Art Gallery, 88; Drawn from Life: Contemp Interpretive Landscape, Sewall Art Gallery, Tex, 88; Utopian Visions, Art Adv Serv Mus Mod Art, NY, 88; Water, Pfizer Inc, Art Adv Service Mus of Mod Art, 89. *Awards:* Mary C McLellan Scholar, 70; MacDowell Colony Fel, Peterborough, NH, 71, 72, 74, 75, 79, 80, 83, 85 & 86; Fel, Ossabow Island Proj Found, Ga, 76; Davidson Nat Print & Drawing Show Purchase Award, Davidson Col, NC, 76; Fel, Yaddo Corp, Saratoga Springs, NY, 77, 81 & 82; Nat Endowment for the Arts, Visual Arts Fel, 77 & 80. *Bibliog:* John Russell (auth), Invigorating breezes of the fall season, NY Times, Arts & Leisure, 10/2/76; Lenore Malen (auth), David Henricks, Arts Mag, 2/77. *Media:* Pencil, Graphite; Oil. *Dealer:* Fischbach Gallery 24 W 57th St New York NY 10019. *Mailing Add:* 652 Broadway No 7F New York NY 10012-2316

HENDRICKS, EDWARD LEE
SCULPTOR, KINETIC ARTIST
b Charleston, WVa, Nov 9, 1952. *Study:* Birmingham Southern Col, BFA, 74; Univ NC, Chapel Hill, MFA, 76. *Work:* Hunter Mus Art, Chattanooga, Tenn; Mint Mus Art, Charlotte, NC; New Orleans Mus Art; Phoenix Art Mus, Ariz; Birmingham Mus Art, Ala. *Comn:* Sculpture, Birmingham Bd Educ, 76; sculpture, Birmingham Realty Co, 85; sculpture, Birmingham Mus Art, 86; sculpture, Am Republic Insurance, Des Moines, 86; sculpture, Datran Ctr, Coral Gables, Fla; sculpture, Turco Develop Co, St Louis, 89. *Exhib:* Solo exhibs, Southeastern Ctr Contemp Art, 80, 84, Alexander F Milliken Inc, NY, 80, 82, 84 & 89, Montgomery Mus Fine Arts, Ala, 81, Osuma Gallery, Washington, DC, 81 & 83, O K Harris West, Scottsdale, Ariz, 81, 83 & 84, Birmingham Mus Art, 81 &84, Hunter Mus Art, 82, Eric Makler Gallery, Philadelphia, 82 & 83 & Davis McClain Gallery, Houston, 85, 87 & Ardew Gallery, Boston, 87; Elaine Horwitch, Palm Spring, Calif, 88 & 90. *Awards:* Second Award, Nat Sculpture, 75; Juror's Award, Birmingham Art Asn, 79; Southeast Artists Fel, Southeastern Ctr Contemp Art, 83. *Bibliog:* Bob Yoskowitz (auth), articles, Arts Mag, 80 & 81; Carol Donnel-Kotrozo (auth), article, Art Express, 82; Vivien Raynor (rev), article, NY Times, 10/5/84. *Media:* Metal. *Dealer:* Alexander F Milliken Inc 98 Prince St New York NY 10012. *Mailing Add:* c/o McClain Gallery 2242 Richmond Houston TX 77098

HENDRICKS, GEOFFREY
PAINTER, ENVIRONMENTAL ARTIST
b Littleton, NH, July 30, 1931. *Study:* Amherst Col, BA, 53; Norfolk Art Sch, Yale Univ, scholar, summer 53; Cooper Union Art Sch, 53-56; Columbia Univ, MA, 62. *Work:* Mus Mod Kunst, Vienna, Austria; Wilhelm Lehbruck Mus, Duisburg, Ger; Mus Mod Art, NY; Staatsgalerie, Stuttgart, Ger; Nordjyllands Kunstmuseum, Aalborg, Denmark; and many others. *Exhib:* Silverman Collection, Cranbrook Art Mus, Bloomfield Hills, Mich, 81; Fluxus (catalog, ed by Jon Hendricks & Clive Phillpot), Mus Mod Art, NY, 88; In the Spirit of Fluxus, Walker Art Ctr, Minneapolis, Minn, 93 & Whitney Mus Am Art, NY, 93; The Living Art Mus, Reykjavik, Iceland, 84; Galerie Baecker, Cologne, Ger, 86; Himmels Aquarelle, Rupertinum, Salzburg, Austria, 92; Day into Night, Kunsthallen Brandts Kloedelfabrick, Odense, Denmark, 93, Kjarvalsstadir, Munic Art Mus, Reykjavik, Iceland, 94, Porin Taidemuseo, Pori, finland, 94, Henie-Onstad Kunstsenter, Hovikodden, Oslo, Norway, 94; Solo exhibs, Ctr Contemp Art, Ujazdowski Castle, Warsaw, Poland, 94, Unimedia Modern Genoa, Italy, 97, 2000, 2008, Confederation Art Ctr, Charlottetown, Can 2003, Winnipeg Art Gallery, Can, 2004, Parel Zoubok Gallery, 2006, Egon Schiele Art Centrum, Cesky Krumlov, Czeck Rep, 2006, Art Gallery of Winsor, Ontario, 2006, Galerie Etage, Münster, Germany, 2008; Fluxus EAST, Berlin, Krakow, Budapest, 2007-2010; and many other group & solo exhibs. *Teaching:* Asst instr, Art Dept, State Univ NJ, Rutgers, Douglass Col, 56-58, instr, 58-61, asst prof, 61-67, assoc prof, Visual Arts Dept, Mason Gross Sch Arts, 67-80, prof, 80-94, Prof, 94-2002, prof emeritus, 2002-; instr art, New York Fine Arts Winter Term Prog of Earlham Col, Richmond, Ind, 65-69; prof, Skowhegan Sch, Maine, 2002; prof, Salzburg Int Summer Acad, Austria, 89, 92, 2002, 2004, 2006, 2009. *Awards:* Fel, Nat Endowment Arts, 76 & 77; Deutscher Akad Austauschdienst, Berlin Artist Prog, 83; Barkenhoff Stiftung, Found Fel, Worpswede, Ger, 85-86; Kunstlerstatte Schloss Bleckede Residency, 93. *Bibliog:* Marianne Beck & Robert Rosenblum (auths), Night into Day (catalog), interview with Cars Movin for traveling retrospective exhib, 93 & 94; Jill Johnston (auth), Secret Lives in Art, 94; Henry Martin (auth), Anatomy of the Sky (catalog), 95; Shauna McCabe, Between Earth & Sky (in knowing one, one will know the other), 2003. *Mem:* Coll Art Asn Am; Am Asn Univ Prof; Fluxus; Bd dir, pres, Visual ACDS. *Media:* Acrylic, Intermedia, Watercolor. *Publ:* Auth, Between Two Points/Fra Due Poli, Edizioni Pari & Dispari, Reggio Emila, Italy, 75; La Capra, Edizioni Morra, Napoli, 79; Sky Anatomy, Rainer Verlag, Berlin, 84; 100 skies, Barkenhoff Found, Worpswede, Ger, 87; 100 Skies, Money for Food Press, New York, 93; Critical Mass Happenings, Fluxus, Performance Intermedia & Rutgers Univ, 1958-1972, Rutgers Univ Press, 2003; From Sea to Sky, Recasting the Riace Bronzes, F Conzeditions, Verona, 2005. *Dealer:* Galerie Etage Prinzipal Markt 37 D-48143 Münster Germany; Unimedia Modern Palazzo Squariafico Piazza Invrea 5/6 I 16121 Genova Italy. *Mailing Add:* 486 Greenwich St New York NY 10013-1313

HENDRICKS, JAMES (POWELL)
SCULPTOR, PAINTER
b Little Rock, Ark, Aug 7, 1938. *Study:* Univ Ark, Fayetteville, BA, 63; Univ Iowa, MFA, 64. *Work:* Mus Fine Arts, Springfield, Mass; Smithsonian Inst, Washington; Ark Arts Ctr, Little Rock; Hudson River Mus, Yonkers, NY; Mus Fine Arts, Boston; Seoul Inst Arts, Korea. *Comn:* Painting, Apollo 14 Launch, Nat Gallery Art & NASA, 71; painting (cover), Time Mag, 8/9/71. *Exhib:* Solo exhibs, Smithsonian Inst Nat Air & Space Mus, 69, Hudson River Mus, Yonkers, 70, Westwood Gallery, NY, 2007; Group exhibs, Helen Shlien Gallery, Boston, 80, 82 & 84; IV Int Bien de Arte Medellin, Colombia, SAm, 81; Tyler Art Gallery, 83; Portland Sch Art & Baxter Gallery, 85; Mus Fine Arts, Springfield, Mass, 86; Space Art Gallery, Seoul, Korea, 86; Slater-Price Fine Arts, NY, 89 & 90; Works on Paper (traveling exhib), Umetnicka Galerija, Prilep, Daut Pastin Aman, Skopje, Bitola & Repub Macedonia; Westwood Gallery, NY, 96, 2001-2002 & 2007. *Collection Arranged:* Assemblage/Collage: Works by 24 Artists & Poets, Seoul Inst of the Arts, Korea, 88. *Pos:* Vis artist, Portland Sch Art, ME, 85 & Seoul Inst Arts, Korea, 86. *Teaching:* Grad instr drawing, State Univ Iowa, 63-64; instr art, Mt Holyoke Col, 64-65; from asst prof to assoc prof painting & drawing, Univ Mass, Amherst, 72-79, dir grad progs in art, 72-, prof art, 79-2004, prof emeritus, currently. *Awards:* Painting Awards, Soc Four Arts, 68 & Silvermine Guild Artists, 69; Ark Traveler Award, 71. *Bibliog:* Robert Ackermann (auth), article, Arts Mag, 9-10/74 & Art in Am, 3-4/76; Nancy Stapen (auth), article, Artforum, 1/83; and others. *Media:* Acrylic, Wood; Bronze, Mixed Media. *Publ:* Illusr cover, Time, 71. *Dealer:* Westwood Gallery New York NY. *Mailing Add:* Univ Mass Dept Art Amherst MA 01003

HENES, DONNA
CEREMONIAL ARTIST, SCULPTOR, WRITER, PHOTOGRAPHER
b Cleveland, Ohio, Sept 19, 1945. *Study:* Ohio State Univ; City Coll New York, BS, 70, MS, 72. *Work:* Mus Modern Art; Islip Art Mus; Libr of Cong. *Comn:* Pub participatory event, Bicentennial Comn, NY, 76; Vernal Equinox Celebration, Port Authority NY & NJ, 80-90; web installation, Indianapolis Mus, 83; installation, Maine Monument, New York Cult Affairs Dept, 83; seasonal pub celebrations, Lower Manhattan Cult Coun, 83; Olympic Ticker Tape Parade, New York City Mayor's Off, 84; Holiday Lighting Installation, Rosendale, NY, 86 & 87, Bay Shore, NY, 88; Vernal Equinox Celebration, Battery Park City Authority, 91-94; Blessing of the Kleet, NY State Gov, 2010. *Exhib:* Women in Am Archit, Brooklyn Mus & traveling, 77; Hilosphia, Spain, 82; Sculpture Tricentennial, Philadelphia Arts Alliance, 82; solo exhibs, Wash Proj Arts, 82 & Indianapolis Mus Art, 83; At Home, Newport Harbor Mus, Calif, 83; Artist Books Biennial, Ctr Arte & Communicacion, Buenos Aires, 83; Latitudes of Time, New York City Gallery, 85; Streets, Gardens & Altars, Cent Hall Gallery, 86; Public Visions-Public Monuments, Soho 20 Gallery, 86; Ritual in the 20 Century, Islip Mus Art, 87; The Meeting of the Holy Pictures, Panstwowe Mus Ethograficzne, Warsaw, Poland, 91; Completing the Circle, Minn Ctr Bk Art & Nat Tour, 92-93; Images of 9/11, The Prints and Photographs, Div of Libr Cong, Washington, 2003; Salute to the Sun, Socrates Sculpture Park, NY, 2004; Vlepo Gallery, Staten Island, NY, 2004; WACK! Art & the Feminist Revolution (traveling), Mus Contemp Art, Los Angeles, Calif, 2006-2007; Biennial, Incheon, Korea; 40 Yrs of Women Artists, Rutgers Univ, E Brunswick, NJ, 2009; History of Disappearance, Arhus Kunstbyghing, Arhus, Denmark, 2010; Desire, OiFurturo Gallery, Rio, Brazil, 2012; You, Me, We, She, Fleisher Ollman Gallery, Phila, Pa, 2012; Desire, Futuro Gallery, Rio, Brazil, 2012; Artists Rutgers Univ, New Brunswick, NJ. *Pos:* Writer, nationally syndicated column, currently; columnist, The Huffington Post, Beliefnet and United Press Int Religion & Spirituality Forum. *Teaching:* Minneapolis Coll Art & Design, 87 & 89; Pratt Inst, 91; Cooper Union, 92; Parsons, 99. *Awards:* Fel, Nat Endowment Arts, 83 & 84; NY Found Arts Fel, 86 & 90. *Bibliog:* Lucy Lippard (auth), Overlay, Pantheon Books, 82; Eggs on end, New Yorker, 83; Moira Roth (auth), The Amazing Decade, Astro Art, 83; Artists' Books: A Critical Anthology, Visual Studies Workshop, 85; Annie Gottlieb (auth), Do You Believe in Magic?, 87; Encyclopedia of Women & World Religion, 98; Kay Turner (auth), Beautiful Necessity, 99; Brigitta, Johnsdattir (ed), The World Healing Book, 2002; Oberon & Morning Glory Zell, Raven leant(ed), Creating circles & Ceremonies, 2006; Cristina Biaggi (ed), The Rule of Mors, 2006; Barbara Love (ed), Feminists who changed Am, 1963-1975 & 2006; Sayne work (auth), Radical gestures, 2006; Nature's Gifts, Trudeau Ed, 2010; Spirit of a Woman, Gopadze, 2010; She is Everywhere, 2012; Anthologies: Saracinot Moser; Mob Wives Television, VH1; What is Laughter, 2012; Live from the Couch TV, CBS, Million Dollar Listing TV, Bravo, Peace, Love & Misunderstanding, Hollywood Film. *Mem:* Founding mem Ctr Celebration (bd dir, 80-); Soc Women Geographers; Women's Wellness Soc; Author's Guild. *Media:* Ritual Celebration, Environmental Transformation. *Res:* Ongoing Independent Studies in Astronomy, Anthropology, Folklore, Mythology, Travel. *Interests:* Research, reading, spiritual pursuits, travel. *Publ:* Contribr, The Politics of Women's Spirituality, Doubleday, 81; auth, Dressing Our Wounds in Warm Clothes, Astro Artz, 82; ed, Celebration News, 86; auth, Celestially Auspicious Occasions, Putnam-Berkley, 96; Reverence to Her, Part I, Mythology, Matriarchy & Me (CD), 10 Productions, 98; auth, Moon Watcher's Companion, Galison Press, 2002; ed, Serenity Young; The Moon Watchers Companion, Marlowe & Co Pub, 2004; The Queen of My Self, Monarch Press, 2005; United press int, weekly columnist gov, The Huffington Post, Beliefnet, and UPI, Religion & Spirituality forum; ed, Serenity Young. *Mailing Add:* PO Box 380403 Brooklyn NY 11238-0403

HENKLE, JAMES LEE
SCULPTOR, DESIGNER
b Cedar Rapids, Iowa, Mar 13, 1927. *Study:* Univ Nebr, BA; Pratt Inst, cert (indust design). *Work:* Univ Okla Art Mus, Norman; Okla State Art Collection, Okla Arts & Humanities Coun, Okalahoma City; Ark Art Ctr, Little Rock; Springfield Art Mus, Mo. *Comn:* Sculpture mural, Numerical Anal Res Ctr, Norman, 63 & Tulsa Pub Libr, Tulsa Hist Soc, Okla, 65; sculpture, Norman Pub Libr, 75th Anniversary Comt, 66; wall sculpture, Dale Hall, Univ Okla; communion table, First Presby Church, Norman, 88; Furniture Designs, Mabee-Gerrer Mus Art, Shawnee Okla, 90. *Exhib:* Eight State Art Exhib, Oklahoma City Art Ctr, 61; Solo sculpture exhib, Univ Okla Mus Art, 68 & Philbrook Art Ctr, Tulsa, 70; Okla State Univ, 79; Okla Designer Craftsman Exhibs, 76-81; Vision Makers, Kilpatrick Ctr, Oklahoma City, 88; Philbrook Art Ctr, Tulsa, Okla, 88. *Pos:* Designer, Dave Chapman Design Firm, 52-53. *Teaching:* Prof art, Univ Okla, 53-; prof art, emer, 90. *Awards:* Purchase Prize Sculpture, Okla Art Ctr, 65; Purchase Prize Painting, Springfield Art Mus; Purchase Award Crafts, Eighth Ann Print, Drawing & Crafts Exhib, Ark Arts Ctr, 75. *Mem:* Okla City Art Mus; Firehouse Art Ctr; Univ Okla Art Mus. *Media:* Wood; Acrylic Paint. *Publ:* Contribr, Fine Woodworking Biennial Design Book, Vols 1-4, Taunton Press. *Mailing Add:* 2719 Hollywood Ave Norman OK 73072

HENNE, CAROLYN
SCULPTOR, ADMINISTRATOR
Study: Col of William and Mary, B in Economics and Fine Arts, 1983; attended Lacoste Sch of the Arts, studied fine and studio arts, 1985-1986; Va Commonwealth Univ, MFA (Sculpture), 1990. *Teaching:* Asst dean, student affairs, Va Commonwealth Univ, Sch of Arts, 2005-2010; prof, chair, Dept of Art, assoc dean Col of Visual Arts, Fla State Univ, 2010-. *Mailing Add:* Department of Art Florida State University PO Box 3061150 220 Fine Arts Building Tallahassee FL 32306-1150

HENNESSEY, WILLIAM JOHN
MUSEUM DIRECTOR
b Summit, NJ, July 15, 1948. *Study:* Wesleyan Univ, BA, 1970; Ford Found fel, Worcester Art Mus, 1971-73; Columbia Univ, PhD, 1978. *Collection Arranged:* The Am Portrait: From Stuart to Sargent (auth, catalog), Worcester Art Mus, 1973; Artists Look at Art (auth, catalog), 1978 & Permanent Collection, 1978, Spencer Art Mus,

Univ Kans; Hudson Valley People, Vassar Coll Art Gallery, 1982; Russel Wright: Am Designer, Gallery Asn NY State & MIT Press, 1983; Thomas S Noble, Univ Ky Art Mus, 1988; Havemeyer Tiffany Collection, Univ Mich, 1992; From Ansel Adams to Andy Warhol, Univ Mich, 1994. *Pos:* Res assoc, Solomon R Guggenheim Mus, 1973-74; cur, Spencer Art Mus, Univ Kans, 1975-79; dir, Vassar Col Art Gallery, 1979-82, Univ Ky Art Mus, 1982-90, Univ Mich Mus Art, 1990-97; dir, Chrysler Mus Art, Norfolk, Va, 1997-. *Teaching:* Instr, Brooklyn Col & Sch Visual Arts, 1973-75; asst prof, Univ Kans, 1975-79 & Vassar Col, 1979-82; adj prof art, Univ Ky, 1982-90; assoc prof, Univ Mich, 1990-97. *Mem:* Coll Art Asn; Soc Archit Historians; Asn Art Mus Dirs. *Res:* 19th & 20th Century architecture & design. *Publ:* Auth, A Handbook of the Worcester Art Museum, 73; Friedrich Overbeck's Drawing of Elijah, Regist Spencer Mus, spring 77; Frank Lloyd Wright and the design of the Guggenheim Museum, Arts Mag, 4/78; series of 24 articles for the World Book Encyclopedia; Michelangelo & the Art of Automobile Design, 93. *Mailing Add:* Chrysler Mus Art 245 W Olney Rd Norfolk VA 23510

HENNESSY, RICHARD
PAINTER
b Rochester, NY, 1941. *Study:* Columbia Coll, BA, 1963; Inst Fine Arts, New York Univ, 1963-66. *Work:* Albright Knox Gallery; Brooklyn Mus; Metrop Mus Art, New York; Mus Mod Art, New York; Philadelphia Mus Art; San Francisco Mus Mod Art; Whitney Mus Am Art; Wadsworth Atheneum, Conn; and many more. *Exhib:* Solo exhibs, Grey Art Gallery, New York Univ, 1976 & Ball State Univ, Muncie, Ind, 1989; American Painting: The Eighties, Grey Art Gallery, New York Univ, 1980; Points of View, Univ Okla, Norman, 1982; Critical Perspectives, PS1 Contemp Art Ctr, New York, 1982; New American Painting, Univ Tex, Austin, 1984; Contemporary Art, Samuel P Harn Mus, Univ Fla, Gainesville, 1991; The Artist, The Writer and the Book Design, Columbia Univ, 1992; Aaron Copland's America, Heckscher Mus Art, Huntington, NY, 2000; Abstarct Landscapes, Snug Harbor Cult Ctr, 2006. *Awards:* Pollock-Krasner Found Grant, 1988 & 2008. *Bibliog:* Grace Glueck (auth), Various artists discuss Picasso, NY Times, 6/22/1980; Douglas Crimp (auth), On the Museume's Ruins, MIT Press, 1993; Brooks Adams (auth), Hodgkin's Subtext, Art in Am, 5/1996; Patrick Maynard (auth), Thinking Through Photography: The Engine of Visualization, Cornell Univ Press, 1997; Michael Duncan (auth), New worlds of Color, Modern Painters, 2000. *Media:* Oil

HENNESSY, TRICIA
EDUCATOR, DIRECTOR, GRAPHIC ARTIST
Study: Ohio Univ, BFA; Basel Sch of Design, Switzerland, MFA (internat equivalent in graphic design), 1982. *Collection Arranged:* Permanent Collection: Zurich Mus of Design, Switzerland. *Pos:* Partner, Adleta and Hennessy Designers, Providence, formerly; presenter for AIGA and CAA. *Teaching:* Tchr, Rhode Island Sch of Design, formerly; dir. Design Center for Education and Research, graphic design program head, Gwen Frostic Sch of Art, Western Michigan Univ, 1988-2011, prof art-design educator, currently, dir Gwen Frostic Sch of Art, 2011-. *Dealer:* Sointu Gallery, NYC. *Mailing Add:* Gwen Frostic School of Art Western Michigan University 1903 W Michigan Ave R3108 Richmond Ctr Kalamazoo MI 49008-5213

HENNESY, GERALD CRAFT
PAINTER
b Washington, DC, June 11, 1921. *Study:* Corcoran Sch Art; George Washington Univ; Am Univ; Univ Md; also with C Gordon Harris. *Work:* Nat Hq Am Legion & Nat Hq Daughters Am Revolution, Wash; Md State Exec Mansion, Annapolis; US House Rep Off Bldg, Wash; Hq FDIC, Washington, DC. *Comn:* Paintings, Gibson Bldg, Fairfax, Va, 74, United Va Bank, Richmond, 75, Hq Blue Cross & Blue Shield Asn, 82 & Nat Hq Fed Deposit Insurance Corp, 83, Washington. *Exhib:* Baltimore Mus Art Regional, 63; NY World's Fair, 65; Solo exhib, Pla Gallery, McClean, Va, 67; Allied Artists of Am, NY, 75 & 76; Venable Nestage Galleries, Wash, 93; Marin-Price Galleries, Chevy Chase, MD, 95-96, 2000, 02, 04, 06, 2009-12; Prince Royal Gallery, Alexandria, Va, 99, 2003, 05, 09; Byrne Gallery, Middleburg, Va, 2008-12. *Pos:* Advert artist, Washington Times Herald, Washington, 41-42. *Awards:* First Prize, Gilham Show, 66; Lorbmer Award, Salmagundi Club, 94; Wright Award, Hudson Valley Art Asn, 2004; Loughlin Award, 2005. *Mem:* Wash Soc Landscape Painters (treas, 73-77, 87-89); Hudson Valley Art Asn, 2005-. *Media:* Oil, Watercolor. *Publ:* auth, Exagerate A Little to Improve Your Paintings, Int Artist Mag, 2-3/2010. *Dealer:* Marin-Price Gallery, 7022 Wisconsin Ave, Chevy Chase, Md, 20815. *Mailing Add:* 6811 White Rock Rd Clifton VA 20124

HENRICH, SARAH E
MUSEUM DIRECTOR
Study: Muhlenberg Coll, BA (Art History); Syracuse Univ, MFA (Museology), 1982. *Pos:* Acting dir, Rockwood Mus, Wilmington, Del, 1979-1980; collections/educ cur, Hist Speedwell, Morristown, NJ 1982-1984, dir, 1986-1996; collections cur, Fort Dix Mus, 1984-1986; Mus cert inspector Ctr for Mil History, US Dept Def, 1984-; exec dir, Hist Soc of Rockland County, New City, NY, 1996-2001; exec dir, Mus of Am Quilter's Soc, Paducah, Ky, 2001-2003; Consult, HH Culural Resources & Consortium, 2003-; dir, Murray State Univ Galleries, 2004-2005; exec dir, Headley-Whitney Mus of Decorative Art, Lexington, 2005-. *Teaching:* asst prof art, Murray State, Univ, 2004-2005. *Mem:* Trustee Hist, Morris Visitors Ctr, 1990-1995, pres, 1994-1995; NJ Asn Mus, 1987-1990; co found, Northern NJ Mus Roundtable, 1986; NJ Hist Comn, pub prog adv, 1993-1996, grant reviewer, 1994-1999; Ky hist Consortium, 2002; Paducah Rotary; Lexington Rotary Club; Vpres, Ky Mus Heritage Asn, 2010. *Publ:* Philip Johnson, An Analysis of Mus Archit, 82. *Mailing Add:* Headley-Whitney Museum 4435 Old Frankfort Pike Lexington KY 40510

HENRY, DALE
PAINTER
b Anniston, AL, Feb 8, 1931. *Work:* Legion of Honor Mus, San Francisco; Mills Coll Art Gallery, Oakland, Calif; Albert A List Found; Vera List collection, NY; Brutten-Herrick Collection, Philadelphia; Elise Haas Found, San Francisco; Marconi, Milan. *Comn:* The Clocktower, Inst for Art and Urban Resources, NY, 75; Room Installation, Inst Art and Urban Resources, Long Island City, NY, 76; Ben Shahn Gallery, William Paterson Coll, Wayne, NJ, 80; Works and Projects of the 70s, USIA World Traveling Exhib, Washington, 77-80; Builtworks, Sarah Lawrence Coll, Yonkers, NY, 85. *Exhib:* Solo exhibs, Gallery Nine, Berkeley, Calif, 61, Legion of Honor, San Francisco, 61, Esther Robles Gallery, Los Angeles, 65, Mills Coll Art Gallery, Oakland, Calif, 68, Fischbach Gallery, NY, 71, John Weber Gallery, NY, 72-73, 76-77, 79, Galleria Toselli, Milan, 72, Hal Bromm Gallery, NY, 78, William Paterson Col, Ben Shahn Gallery, Wayne, NJ, 80 & Sarah Lawrence Col, Yonkers, NY, 85; Calif Palace Legion of Honor, San Francisco, 60-64, Esther Robles Gallery, 65, Inst for Art & Urban Resources, Long Island City, NY, 76; Moore Coll Art, Philadelphia, 77; Grommet Gallery, NY, 82; and others. *Teaching:* Instr fine arts, Sch of Visual Arts, NY, 70-86. *Awards:* Award Nat Endowment Arts, 82; award, CAPS, NY, 81. *Bibliog:* (auth) John H.I. Baur, The New Landscape, Art in Am, Summer 63; (auth) Nancy Foote, Apotheosis of the Crummy Space, ArtForum, Oct 76; (auth) Marcia Hafif, Beginning Again, ArtForum, Sept 78; (auth) Marcia Hafif, Getting on with Painting, Art in America, 4/1981; (auth) Peter Bellamy, The Artist Project, 91. *Res:* Fraught perception of art. *Interests:* Lost looking in Western painting history. *Publ:* photo, Primer Sets of a Revealingly Graphic Personal History of Western Painting Using the Complete and Basic Iambus Throughout, Flash Art, 1/1973; and others

HENRY, DAVID EUGENE
PAINTER, SCULPTOR
b Rome, Ga, Dec 10, 1946. *Study:* Ga Tech, BA (archit), 69; Ga State Univ, MVA (visual arts), 72; Art Students' League NY; studied under Philip Pearlstein, 96, George Beattie, Julian Hoke Harris, Albert Christ-Janer. *Work:* Albany Mus Art, Ga; Olgethorpe Univ Mus, Atlanta; Morris Mus Art, Augusta, Ga; Ga Mus Art, Athens; La State Mus, New Orleans; Edisto island Mus, Edisto Island, SC; Indianapolis Mus Art; MC Carlos Mus, Atlanta; Marietta-Cobb Mus Art, Ga. *Comn:* Murals, Ga Tech Univ, 72; mural, Atlanta Area Tech Sch, 72; mural, Bayfront Mcpl Civic Ctr, St Petersburg, Fla. *Exhib:* 23rd Southeastern Exhib, High Mus Art, Atlanta, Ga, 69; drawing exhib, Montgomery Mus Art, Ala; Ga Artists Exhib II, High Mus Art, 72; Ninth Piedmont Graphics Exhib, Mint Mus Art; Third Greater New Orleans Nat Exhib; 54th Nat Painting Exhib, Ogunquit Art Ctr, Ogunquit, Maine; 3rd Biennial Tweed Mus Exhib; 16th All Am Exhib, Barnegat Light; Heroes to Dudes, Ga Mus Art, 2003; Travelers in Foreign Land, MC Carlos Mus, 2003. *Teaching:* Instr painting, Eckerd Coll, St Petersburg, Fla, 76-77; instr drawing, Am Coll Applied Arts, Atlanta, Ga, 96-; Am Intercontinental Univ, 98; instr painting, Gov's Honor Program, Wesleyan Coll, 74. *Awards:* Purchase Award, Piedmont Exhib, NC Nat Bank, 72; First Prize in Painting, Arts Festival Atlanta, 75; Mural Design Competition, Nat Endowment Arts, St Petersburg, Fla, 77. *Bibliog:* Robert Creps (auth), Biographical Encyclopedia Am Painters, Sculptors & Engravers of the US, 2002. *Mem:* Salmagundi Club; Allied Artists Am; Nat Soc Artist; Am Soc Classical Realism; Am Artists Prof League; and others. *Media:* Paint, Charcoal, Bronze. *Mailing Add:* 1484 E Gem Circle Palm Springs CA 92262

HENRY, FREDRICK B
PATRON
Pos: Pres Bohen Found, 84-; bd mem, Am Ctr, Paris, 91; bd trustee, Solomon R Guggenheim Mus, 2002-; bd dir, Georges Pompidou Art & Cult Found, Paris & Houston, Aspen Valley Community Found, Aspen, Colo, Brooklyn Acad Music, Des Moines Art Ctr, Iowa, Dia Ctr for Arts, New York City, Pub Agenda Found, New York City, Whitney Mus Am Art, New York City; chmn, Am Ctr Found. *Mailing Add:* Bohen Found PO Box 8712 New York NY 10116-8712

HENRY, JAMES PEPPER
MUSEUM DIRECTOR
Study: Univ Ore, Grad. *Pos:* Visual arts coordinator, Inst Alaska Native Arts, Fairbanks, Alaska, 1990-1992; visual arts mgr, Interstate Firehouse Cultural Ctr, Portland, Ore; interim cur, Am Indian Art Portland Art Mus; dir, Kanza Mus of Kaw Nation, Okla, 1994-1998; assoc dir community & constituent serv, Nat Mus Am Indian, Smithsonian Inst, Washington, 1998-2007; dir, chief exec officer, Anchorage Mus of History & Art, Alaska, 2007-. *Mem:* Kaw Nation, Okla; Founder, Nat Pow Wow. *Mailing Add:* Anchorage Museum at Rasmuson Center 121 W 7th Ave Anchorage AK 99501

HENRY, JEAN
PAINTER, INSTRUCTOR
b San Francisco, Calif. *Study:* Art Acad, Amsterdam, Holland; Am Univ Berlin; Md Inst, Baltimore; Western Reserve Univ. *Exhib:* Soc Western Artists, De Young Mus, 68; De Saisset Gallery, Santa Clara, Calif, 69; solo exhib, Triton Mus Art, 70; Marin Art & Garden Show, 71; Rosicrucian Mus Invitational Show, 71; impressionist painting at semi-ann exhibs, Vel Oyana Gallery, Tokyo, Japan & Nihon Gallery, Nagoya, Japan; and others. *Pos:* Jean Henry Sch Art, San Francisco, currently. *Teaching:* Instr portrait painting, Md Inst, Johns Hopkins Univ, 58-60; owner & instr painting, Jean Henry Sch Art, San Francisco, 69-. *Awards:* First Award, De Young Mus, 68; First Award, Antioch Outdoor Festival, 69; First Award for Portrait, De Saisset Gallery Ann, 70. *Mem:* Soc Western Artists. *Media:* Oil, Acrylic. *Specialty:* impressionism. *Dealer:* Galleria Luna Half Moon Bay CA. *Mailing Add:* Jean Henry Sch Arts 2640 Ocean Ave San Francisco CA 94132-1616

HENRY, JOHN B, III
MUSEUM DIRECTOR
b Colorado Springs, Jul 7, 1949. *Study:* Univ SC, BFA (Sculpture); Univ Miss, MFA (Art Hist). *Pos:* cur fine arts, Columbus Mus Arts, Columbus, Ga, 1973-77; vpres, Southeastern Sculptors Asn, Columbus, Ga, 1973-78; dir collections & exhibs, Miss Mus Art, Jackson, Miss, 1977-85; exec dir, Vero Beach Mus Art, Fla, 1985-96; exec dir, Flint Inst Arts, Flint, Mich, 1996-; mem adv bd, Ctr Grad Studies, Baker Coll, Flint, Mich, 1997-99; dirs adv coun, Nat Trustee Asn, 1999-2002; mem bd trustees, Marshall Fredericks Sculpture Mus, 2005-2010; mem, Flint Master Plan Steering Comt, 2011-. *Awards:* Man of Yr, Am Arab Asn, 2002; Pres Award, Flint CofC, 2005; Henry Libr Dedication, 2006. *Mem:* AAM; Asn Art Mus Dirs. *Publ:* Artist: The Game; American Art at the Flint Institute of Arts (Hudson Hills Press); To Be Or Not To Be: 400 Years of Vanitas Painting; Edmund Lewdowski: Precisionism and Beyond; Magnificence and Awe: Renaissance and Baroque Art in the Viola E Bray Gallery at the Flint Inst Arts. *Mailing Add:* Flint Inst Art 1120 E Kearsley St Flint MI 48503

HENRY, JOHN RAYMOND
SCULPTOR
b Lexington, Ky, Aug 11, 1943. *Study:* Univ Ky; Univ Wash; Univ Chicago; Art Inst Chicago, BFA; Edward L Reyerson fel, 69; Univ Ky, Hon Dr Art, 96. *Hon Degrees:* D Arts, Univ Ky, 96. *Work:* British Mus; Smithsonian Inst, Washington, DC; Dade Co Art in Pub Places, Miami, Fla; Dallas Mus Art, Tex; Hunter Mus Art, Chattanooga, Tenn. *Comn:* Illinois Landscape (sculpture), Nat Endowment Arts, Works of Art Pub Places, Nathan Manilow Sculpture Park, Govs State Univ, Univ Park, Ill, 74; Bridgeport (sculpture), State Ill, 82; Anchorage (sculpture), Anchorage Int Airport, Alaska, 85; Alachua (sculpture), Fla Art State Bldgs, Fla Arts Coun, Univ Fla, Gainesville; Dance of the Sun (sculpture), Sonje Mus Contemp Art, Kyongju City, Korea, 91. *Exhib:* Art Inst Chicago, 68; solo exhibs, Ill State Mus, Springfield, 73, Riverside Park, NY, 75; Retrospectives, Evolution in Scale, 88-89, Art Mus STex, Corpus Christi, Mus Art, Ft Lauderdale, Mus Fine Arts, St Petersburg, Fla, Hunter Mus Art, Chattanooga, Tenn & Ctr for the Arts, Vero Beach, Fla, 91; FIAC, Paris, France, 93; Seo Hwa Gallery, Seoul, Korea, 93; MANIF-Seoul, Korea, 96; Art in Chicago 1945-1995, Mus Contemp Art, Chicago, 96; and many others. *Pos:* Bd trustees, Nat Found Advancement Arts, 91-, Int Sculpture Ctr, 96-, chmn bd trustees. *Teaching:* Vis prof, Univ Iowa, 69; artist-in-residence, Univ Wis-Green Bay, 69-70; vis prof, Univ Chicago, 70-71; vis lectr, Art Inst Chicago, 78. *Awards:* Edward L Ryerson Fel, Art Inst Chicago, 69; Individual Artists Grant, Nat Endowment Arts, 75. *Bibliog:* James L Reidy (auth), Chicago Sculpture, Univ Ill Press, Urbana, Chicago, London, 81; Claudia Sabin & Philip Yenawine (auths), Evolution in scale: The Sculpture of John Henry 1967-1988, Design Found, Chicago, Ill, 88; Victoria Lightman (auth), John Henry: Defying Gravity, Seoul, 93. *Mem:* Int Sculpture Ctr, Hamilton, NJ; Chicago Artists Coalition; Nat Found Advancement Arts, Miami, Fla; hon life mem Southeast Sculpture Asn. *Media:* Metal, Stone. *Dealer:* T Curtsnoc Fine Art 1100 E 16th St, Chattanooga, Tenn, 37408. *Mailing Add:* 7809 Joyce Dr Louisville KY 40219-4131

HENRY, ROBERT
PAINTER, EDUCATOR
b Brooklyn, NY, Aug 3, 1933. *Study:* Hans Hofmann Sch Fine Art, New York & Provincetown, Mass; Brooklyn Col, with Ad Reinhardt & Kurt Seligmann, BA. *Work:* Neuberger Mus, Purchase, NY; Tucson Mus, Ariz; Provincetown Art Asn, Mass; Columbia Univ, NY; Cape Code Mus, Dennis, Mass; Kressge Mus, E Lansing, Mich; State Univ NY, Albany; Miss Mus Art, Jackson; Univ Colo Boulder; New Britain Mus Am Art. *Exhib:* Solo exhibs, Green Mountain Gallery & Ingber Gallery, NY; PAAM, Provincetown, Ma, 2008; Hudson River Mus, Yonkers, NY, 71; Berta Walker Gallery, Provincetown, Mass, 91-2013; Laurel Tracey Gallery, Red Bank, NJ, 2005-07; Highline Loft, NY, 2013. *Teaching:* From asst prof to emer prof, Brooklyn Col, 60-. *Awards:* Hans Renata and Maria Hofman Trust Grant, 2008; Lifetime Achievement Award, Cape Cod Found Arts, 2009. *Bibliog:* L Campbell (auth), Stop, look & look & look, Art News, 2/72; April Kingsley (auth), The interiorized image, Soho Weekly News, 2/5/76; Susan Koslow (auth), Robert Henry, Arts, 80; Andre van Der Wende (auth), Stop, Look, Listen, 2008; April Kingsley (auth), From the Beginning, 2005. *Mem:* Provincetown Art Asn & Mus; Truro Center for the Arts. *Media:* Oil, Watercolor. *Interests:* Jazz Guitar. *Publ:* Auth, Horizontally oriented rotating kinetic painting, Leonardo, 69; contbr Hofmann, Farnham Emily, 67-75. *Dealer:* Berta Walker Gallery 208 Bradford St Provincetown MA 02657; Laura Tracey Gallery Red Bank NJ; New Hope Side Tracks Gallery, New Hope, Pa

HENRY, SARA CORRINGTON
HISTORIAN, CRITIC
b Teaneck, NJ, Sept 24, 1942. *Study:* Denison Univ, BFA; NY Univ, with Robert Goldwater, BA (art hist); Univ Calif, Berkeley, with Peter Selz & Herschel B Chipp, PhD. *Teaching:* Lectr art hist, Goucher Col, Towson, Md, 70-71; vis instr, Ohio State Univ, Columbus, 71-72; instr, Carnegie-Mellon Univ, Pittsburgh, 73-76; assoc prof, Drew Univ, 76-. *Mem:* Coll Art Asn; Women's Caucus for Art. *Res:* Paul Klee; abstract expressionism; contemporary art. *Publ:* Contribr, New Catholic Encyclopedia, McGraw-Hill, 66; Selection 1968, Univ Art Mus, Univ Calif, Berkeley, 68-69; coauth, The Political Art of Duncan MacPherson, Can Dimension, 3-4/70; auth, Form-creating energies: Paul Klee & physics, Arts Mag, 9/77; Klee's Kleinwelt & creation, Print Rev, fall 77. *Mailing Add:* BC Drew Univ Dept Art 36 Madison Ave Madison NJ 07940

HENRY, STEVEN P.
GALLERY DIRECTOR
Study: Northwestern Univ, BA (art history and political sci); Southern Methodist Univ, MBA & MA (admin). *Pos:* With, Dallas Mus Art, Dallas, Mus Contemporary Art, NY, formerly; assoc dir, Margo Leavin Gallery, LA, formerly; dir, Paula Cooper Gallery, NY, 1997-; bd advisors, Little Opera Theatre of NY & Inner City Found of NY; volunteer, Robert Wilson Byrd-Hoffman Found; bd dirs, Harlem Sch of the Arts, currently. *Mailing Add:* Paula Cooper Gallery 534 W 21st St New York NY 10011

HENSELMANN, CASPAR
SCULPTOR, ILLUSTRATOR
b Mannheim, Ger; US citizen. *Study:* Univ Ill Coll Med, dipl Med-Art, 1955; Art Inst Chicago, BFA, 1956; Northwestern Univ, 1950-52; Columbia Univ, 1961-62. *Work:* Lehmbruck Mus, Duisburg, Ger; Kunsthalle Bremen, Ger; Ritterhaus Mus, Offenburg, Ger; Technicon Corp, Tarrytown, NY; Lindenau Mus, Altenburg; Villa Haiss Mus, Zell AH, Ger. *Comn:* Glass lobby piece (oil, air), Marshall-Ilsley Bank, Milwaukee, 71; Technical Core Sci Ctr, Tarrytown, NY, 69; Union Bank Switzerland, NY, 83; SMS Eng, Pittsburg, Pa, 89; Deutsche Bank, NY, 90; Bank Julius Bear, NY, 92; Swiss Paraplegic Ctr, Nottwil, Switzerland, 2000; Deutsche Bank, NY; SMS Engineering, Pittsburgh; F Scheidt Collection, Essen Kettwig, Ger; Mannesman Int, Dusseldorf, Ger; Police Dists, Denver, Colo, 2006. *Exhib:* solo exhib Wilhelm Lehmbruck Mus, Duisburg, Ger, 1982, Dorothea Van Der Koelen, Mainz, Ger, 1989, Sandra Gering Gallery, 1989, Kunstverein Bielefeld Mus, Waldhof, Ger, 1991, Stadt Gallery, Lahr, Ger, 1993, Bill Bace Gallery, NY, 1992, 1995, Offenburg Mus, Ger, 1994, Walter Bischoff Gallery, Berlin, Stuttgart, 1986, 1990, 1994, 1997, Lindenau Mus, Altenburg, Ger, 1997, Kingsborough Community Col, Brooklyn, 1997, Robert Pardo Gallery, NY, 1999, Neuberger Mus, Purchase, NY, 1999, others; Nanjing Art Col, China, 1997; Robert Pardo Gallery, NY, 1999, 2002 & 2004; Pardo-Lattuada Gallery, Milan, 2001; Chelsea Studio Gallery, NY, 2002; Wooster Arts Space, 2003-2005, 2007; Riverton Arts (2 man show), 2007; Ger Consulate, NY, 2008; Fafa, NY, 2009-2011. *Pos:* freelance pharmaceutical/surgical illustrator, 3-D models, 1968-; art dir, Aron & Falcone Advert, Chatham, NJ, 1972-73; ptnr, Johnson Med Illustration Studio, New York, 1962-68; fel, WB Saunders Publ Co, Phila, 1956. *Teaching:* Instr, St Cloud State Col, 75; prof, C W Post Ctr, Long Island Univ, 1976-77, Univ NC, Chapel Hill, 1983, Hofstra Univ, Hempstead, NY, 1987-88; lectr, critic, Columbia Univ Grad Sch Architecture, 1994; prof, LI Univ, Brooklyn, 1996-2011; vis artist, Memphis Acad Arts, 2002. *Awards:* Ford Found Artist in Residence, Am Fedn Arts, 1965; Nat Endowment Arts Award, 79, Grant, 1984; Gottlieb Award, 2003. *Bibliog:* Articles in: The Village Voice, 74 & 79 & The Soho News, 76, 77, 78 & 79. *Specialty:* Contemporary Art, Robert Prado Artefact, NY. *Publ:* Ambulatory Surgery of the Hernia, E Trabucco, Piccoli Press, Padua, Italy; Anatomy, Gardner, Gray O'Rahilly, WB Saunders Co, Phila; Atlas of Biliary Tract Surgery, F Glenn, Macmillan Publ Co; Atlas of Hernia Surgery, G Wantz, Raven Press; Knee Arthroplasty, ed: Paul A Lotke, Raven Press; Master Techniques in Orthopedic Surgery; Office Hernioplasty & the Trabucco Repair, Trabucco Ann Ital Chir, 1994; Atlas of Operative Strategy in General Surgery, Jameson Chassen, Springer-Verlag, NY. *Mailing Add:* 21 Bond St New York NY 10012

HENSLEY, JACKSON MOREY
PAINTER
b Portales, NMex, Sept 6, 1940. *Study:* Nat Acad Design, 59-61. *Work:* Arabian Horse Trust Mus, Denver, Colo; Los Angeles Natural Hist Mus, Calif; Leanin Tree Mus, Boulder, Colo; Taos Art Mus, NMex; Madewood Plantation House Mus, New Orleans; Southside Bank Collection, Tyler, Tex; Highlands Univ Collection & Fire House Collection, Taos, NMex; and others. *Exhib:* Nat Acad Fine Arts, New York; Nat Arts Club; Salmagundi Club, New York; solo exhibs, Knickerbocker Artist Exhib, Stamford Mus, Conn, Jones Gallery, La Jolla, Calif, Farleigh Dickerson Traveling Exhib & Burr Galleries, Denver; and over 200 other exhibs. *Awards:* Dr Ralph Weiler Award, Nat Acad, 60; Arthur T Hill Mem, Salmagundi Club, New York, 63; Mary Hingman Carter Award, Nat Arts Club, 63. *Bibliog:* Peggy & Harold Samuels (auth), Contemporary Western Artist, 82. *Media:* Watercolor, Oil. *Publ:* Illusr, Rockies Mag & Landscape Printers Am. *Dealer:* Reflection Gallery 201 Canyon Rd Santa Fe NM; Thompson Gallery New York NY

HEPLER, ANNA
SCULPTOR, ASSEMBLAGE ARTIST
b Boston, Mass, 1969. *Study:* Oberlin Coll, BA, 1992; Univ Wis, Madison, MFA, 1994. *Work:* Nat Gallery Art, Washington DC; Tate Gallery, London; DeCordova Mus & Sculpture Park, Mass; Libr Congress; Wellesley Coll, Mass. *Exhib:* Solo exhibs, Univ Dayton, Ohio, 1998, Mus Contemp Art, Tokyo, Japan, 2000, Hollins Univ Gallery, Va, 2002, Ctr for Maine Contemp Art, Rockport, 2006, Montserrate Coll Art, Mass, 2009, Portland Mus Art, 2010; Singular Visions, Tamarind Inst, NMex, 2002; Exquisite Corpse Today, Walker Art Mus, Bowdoin Coll, 2004; Maine Printmakers: 1980-2005, Ctr for Maine Contemp Art, Rockport, 2006; Collaborations, Portland Mus Art, Maine, 2008; Am Acad Arts & Letts Invitational, New York, 2010. *Pos:* Founder, BEO Press, 1989-. *Teaching:* Vis asst prof, Bowdoin Coll, Maine, 2003-09. *Awards:* Henry Luce Found Fel, 1999; Good Idea Grant, Maine Arts Comn, 2007; Fel for Emerging Artists, St Boltoph Found, 2009. *Bibliog:* Cate McQuaid (auth), Controlled Chaos, Boston Globe, 5/6/2006; Ken Greenleaf (auth), A Print Apart, Portland Phoenix, 11/28/2008; Bob Keyes (auth), Garbage on a Grand Scale, Maine Sunday Telegram, 2/15/2009

HEPPER, CAROL
SCULPTOR
b McLaughlin, SDak, 1953. *Study:* SDak State Univ, Brookings, BS, 75. *Work:* Mus Mod Art, Metrop Mus, Solomon R Guggenheim Mus & Dannheisser Found, NY; Portland Art Mus, Ore; Walker Art Ctr, Minneapolis, Minn; Newark Mus, NJ; Detroit Inst Arts, Mich; and many others. *Exhib:* Material Matters, Permanent Collection Sculpture, Walker Art Ctr, Minneapolis, Minn, 80; New Perspectives in Am Art (with catalog), Guggenheim Mus, 83; Am: Art and the West (with catalog), Art Gallery of Western Australia, Perth, 86 & Art Gallery of New South Wales, Sidney, 87; solo exhibs, Worchester Art Mus (catalog), Mass, 92, Orlando Mus Art (catalog), Fla, 94; Innovations in Sculpture, 1985-1988, Aldrich Mus Art, Ridgefield, Conn, 88; 100 Drawings by Women, Hillwood Art Gallery, Long Island Univ, 89; Material Identity: Sculpture between Nature & Cult, Portland Art Mus, 93; Fabricated Nature, Boise Art Mus, Idaho, 94. *Collection Arranged:* Portland Art Mus, Portland, OR. *Pos:* Lectr, Princeton Univ. *Teaching:* Instr drawing, Standing Rock Sioux Indian Community Col, Ft Yates, NDak, 80-82 & Sch Visual Arts, NY, 84; vis fac sculpture, Md Art Inst,

Baltimore, & RI Sch Design, 88, State Univ NY, Purchase, 89 & Princeton Univ, NJ, 90; Harvard Univ, 2000. *Awards:* Louis Comfort tiffany, 84; NY Found, 89; Nat Endowment Arts, 90; and others. *Bibliog:* Cynthia Nadelman (auth), New American sculpture, 1/84 & Gabo's Progeny, 12/87, Art News; Michael Brenson (auth), Sculpture breaks the mold of minimalism, NY Times, 11/23/86; Diane Waldman (auth), Emerging artists 1978-86: Selections from the Exxon Series & Deborah Pearlburg (auth), New York: Day by day, 9/88, Art News. *Media:* All Media. *Mailing Add:* 250 W 16th St 3-A New York NY 10011

HERA
SCULPTOR, ENVIRONMENTAL ARTIST
b New Orleans, La, Sept 28, 1940. *Study:* Mt Holyoke Col; Sch Art Inst Chicago; Univ Dallas, Tex, BA, 70; Southern Methodist Univ, MFA, 74. *Work:* In Collections of: Okla Arts Ctr, Oklahoma City; Longview Mus, Tex; Rose Art Mus, Brandeis Univ, Waltham, Mass; Mount Holyoke Coll Art Mus; Tampa Mus Art; Texas Instruments, New Orleans Mus. *Comn:* Snail Shell Maze, Boxford MA, 1979, Storm Flower Univ New Orleans, 1980, Floribunda, Queen, NY, 1980 Spirit House, Laumeier Sculpture Park, St Louis, Mo, 86; Singing Rock Sitting Place, Arboretum, Fairmont Park, Philadelphia, 88; Orbital Connector, Gov Smith Houses, Manhattan, 89; Tower as Inland Lighthouse, Marion St Transit Pkwy, Tampa, Fla, 90; Community Based Design Pilot, Philadelphia Art Comn, 91-92; Dream House, Hera's Farm, 2007. *Exhib:* Solo exhibs, Lifeways, Inst Contemp Art, Boston, 76, Butcher Shop, Brooks Jackson Gallery Iolas, NY, 79; Family Room, Contemp Art Ctr, New Orleans, La & Nexus Gallery, Philadelphia, 81; Dream Feast, Alternative Mus, NY, 81; Niagara-Knossos-Carranza Connector, Artpark, 82. *Pos:* Procession designer, First Night, Inc, Boston, 77-78; consult, Women's Slide Arch, Schlesinger Libr Hist Women Am, Radcliffe Col, 77-80; vis artist, Sch Mus Fine Arts, Boston, 78; artist-in-residence, Palisades Interstate Park Com, Bear Mountain, NY, 81; major proj artist, Artpark, 82; vis artist, Gerrit Rietveld Acad, Amsterdam, 85; design team, Marion St Transit Pkwy, Tampa, Fla, 88. *Teaching:* Artist-in-residence painting, drawing & sculpture, Fed Correctional Inst, Nat Endowment Arts Pilot Prog, Tallahassee, Fla, 75-76; instr, Framingham State Col, Mass, 77-78, & Cooper Union, 91-92; lectr, State Univ NY, New Paltz, 96. *Awards:* America the Beautiful Fund, 82, Glickenhaus Found 82, NY State Council on the Arts, 83, Committee for Visual Arts, 83, Dept Cult Affairs NY Award, 83 & 87; NY State Coun Arts Award, 83; Unity Day Citation from David Dinkins, NY, 88; Thanks to be to Grandmother Winifred Found, 95. *Bibliog:* Lucy Lippard (auth), Overlay, Pantheon, 83; Placemakers II, Fleming & Von TsCharmer, Hastings House, 87; George McCue (auth), Sculpture St. Louis Hudson Hills Press, NY 88; Marinna Harrison & Lucy Rosenfeld (auths), Artwalks in New York, Michael Kesend Publ, NY, 94; Artonsite Harrison & Rosefeld Kensend Pub 94; In the Footsteps of the Goddess Biaggi: Kit, 2000; Detours Peonides: 10LKOS, Athens GR, 2000. *Mem:* Coll Art Asn; Women's Caucus Art; Woodstock Guild. *Media:* Steel, Wood; Plants, Fabric, Fiberglass. *Interests:* Sailing, X-C Skiing, Hiking, Travel, Languages, Poetry. *Publ:* The Tent Book, Hatton Houchton Mifflin, 79; Overlay, Lucy Lippard, Pantheon, 83; Sculpture City: St Louis, McCue, Finn & Binder Hills Press, NY, 88; Art Walks Harrison & Rosenfeld Pub, 94; Sculpture Parks & Gardens, Mc Carthy & Epstein; Kensend Pub, 96. *Mailing Add:* 145 Cold Brook Rd Bearsville NY 12409

HERARD, MARVIN T
SCULPTOR, EDUCATOR
b Puyallup, Wash, July 4, 1929. *Study:* Burnley Sch Art, Seattle; Seattle Univ; Univ Wash, BA; Cranbrook Acad Art, MFA; Acad Fine Arts, Florence, Italy; Fonderia Artistica Florentina, Italy. *Comn:* Sculpture, Renton Pub Libr; Lemieux Libr, Seattle Univ. *Exhib:* Palazzo Venezia, Rome, 62; Seattle Art Mus, 65-67; Gov Exhib, State Capitol Mus, 67-69; Henry Gallery, Univ Wash, 68; Cheney Cowles Mus, Spokane, Wash, 69; and others. *Teaching:* Instr, Seattle Pub Schs, 56-58; teaching fel sculpture, Cranbrook Acad Arts, 59-60; from assoc prof to prof art & chmn fine arts dept, Seattle Univ, 60-94; instr painting, Pius XII Inst Art, Florence, Italy, 62. *Awards:* Am Craftsmen Award, Henry Gallery, 61 & 65; Spokane Pac Northwest Exhib, 63, 64 & 66; Seattle Art Mus, 65; and others. *Mem:* Nat Art Educ Asn; Am Asn Univ Prof. *Mailing Add:* 1131 23rd Ave E Seattle WA 98112

HERBERT, ANNICK & ANTON
COLLECTORS
Awards: Named one of Top 200 Collectors, ARTnews, 2009-13. *Collection:* Contemporary art, especially Conceptual, Minimalism, arte povera, and 1980s

HERBERT, FRANK LEONARD
PAINTER, EDUCATOR
b New Orleans, La, Apr 27, 1956. *Study:* La Tech Univ, BFA (Rome Studies Fel), 78; Colo State Univ, MFA, 82. *Work:* Peat, Marwick, Mitchell & Co, Denver; Rapid Transit of Denver, Colo; East Carolina Univ, Greenville; Poudre Valley Reg Hosp, Ft Collins, Colo; Colo State Univ, Ft Collins. *Exhib:* New Am Talent, Laguna Gloria Art Mus, Austin, 93; Miss Gallery, Bay St Louis, Mo, 95; 39th Ann Invitational, Longview Mus Fine Arts, 98; The Song of Images, Acad Fine Arts, Hoshiarpur, India; Indian Acad of Fine Arts, Amritsar, India, 99; A Backward Glance, Tower Gallery, Shreveport Regional Arts Coun, Shreveport, La, 99; The Secret Garden, Fine Arts Ctr, Kingwood Coll, Kingwood, Tex, 99; East Tex Regional Exhib, Longview Mus Fine Arts, 2004; Paris Junior Coll, Paris, Tex, 2005; Temple Coll, Temple, Tex, 2006; Northeast Tex Community Coll, 2007. *Pos:* Bd dir, Tex Asn Sch Arts, 89-92. *Teaching:* Instr art, Kilgore Coll, Tex, 84-86, lead instr, 86-93, chmn visual arts, 93-97, coord visual arts, theater, commun, 97-2000, adj instr, 2007-. *Awards:* Visual Arts Fel, Mid-Am Arts Alliance, Nat Endowment Arts, 90; Nat Endowment Arts Fels Elec Database, Nat Mus Am Art, Washington, 96. *Mem:* Tex Asn Sch Arts (pres elect, 92-94, pres, 94-96); Coll Art Asn; Nat Asn Sch Art & Design. *Media:* All Media. *Publ:* Contribr, Poudre Mag, 82-83. *Dealer:* Art Dept Kilgore Coll 1100 Broadway Kilgore TX 75662. *Mailing Add:* 608 E Melton Longview TX 75602-1806

HERBERT, JAMES ARTHUR
PAINTER, FILMMAKER
b Boston, Mass, Feb 13, 1938. *Study:* Dartmouth Col, AB (art hist, magna cum laude); Univ Colo, MFA; also with Clyfford Still, Kenzo Okada & Stan Brakhage. *Work:* Whitney Mus Am Art, NY; Mus Mod Art, NY; Walker Art Ctr; Royal Film Arch Belgium; Centre Pompidou, Paris, France; Archive Acad of Motion Picture Arts & Sci; and others. *Comn:* Film, Libr Congress, 83; Kennedy Ctr, 84. *Exhib:* Hradiste Film Festival, Czech Repub, 94; 100 Yrs Cinema, Paris, 95; Mus Mod Art, Barcelona, 98; New Harvest Film Festival, Leuveen, Bel, 98; Oberhausen Film Festival, 99; Retrospective, Atlanta Contemp Art Ctr, 2000; Premiers, Mus of Modern Art, 2005; London Film Festival, British Film Inst, 2005; Rotterdam Int Film Festival, 2007. *Teaching:* Resident artist, Yale Summer Sch Art & Music, Norfolk, Conn, 65; prof painting, Univ Ga, 62-2006, Res prof, 92-2006; Distinguished Res Prof Emeritus, Univ Ga, 2006. *Awards:* Guggenheim Mem Found Fel, 71 (film) & 89 (paintings); Nat Endowment Arts Grant, 75, 78, 81 & 82; Louis Comfort Tiffany Found Award, 80; Awards in the Visual Arts 7, Rockefeller Found, 88; Adolph & Esther Gottlieb Found, 92; Rockefeller Found, 93. *Bibliog:* Roger Greenspun (auth), Quick-who are David Rimmer & James Herbert?, NY Times Sunday Ed, 10/8/72; Larry Kardish (auth), Of Light and Texture, Andrew Noren/James Herbert, Mus Mod Art, 81; Larry Kardish (auth), Afterimages, Ga Rev, spring 89; Stephen Holden (auth), Taking Liberties with the World, NY Times, 10/5/92; Donald Kuspit (auth), James Herbert, Demonic Painter, Atlanta Contemp Art Ctr, 2000. *Publ:* Stills, Photographs by James Herbert, Twelvetrees Press, Santa Fe, NMex, 92. *Dealer:* Sandler Hudson Gallery 1831 Peachtree Rd Atlanta GA 30309. *Mailing Add:* 243 Dearing St Athens GA 30605

HERBERT, ROBERT L
HISTORIAN, EDUCATOR
b Worcester, Mass, Apr 21, 1929. *Study:* Wesleyan Univ, Middletown, Conn, BA, 1951; Inst Art & Archeol & Ecole du Louvre, Paris, Fulbright Scholar, 1951-52; Yale Univ, MA, 1954, PhD, 1957; Am Coun Learned Soc Grant, 1960; Morse fel, London, 1960-61; sr fac fel, Paris, 1968-69; Guggenheim fel, Paris & New Haven, Conn, 1971-72. *Collection Arranged:* Barbizon Revisited, Mus Fine Arts, Boston, Toledo Mus Art, Cleveland Mus Art & Calif Palace of the Legion of Honor (auth, catalog), 1962-63; Neo-Impressionism (auth, catalog), Guggenheim Mus, New York, 1968; JF Millet (auth, catalog), Reunion des musees nationaux, Paris & Arts Coun, London, 1975-76; Millet's Gleaners (auth, catalog), Minneapolis Inst Arts, 1978; Leger's Le Grand Dejeuner (auth, catalog) Minneapolis Inst Arts & Detroit Inst Arts, 1980; Seurat (auth, catalog), Reunion des musees nationaux, Paris & Metrop Mus, New York, 1991; Peasants and Primitivism, French Prints from Millet to Gauguin (auth, catalog), Mount Holyoke Art Mus, RI Sch Design Mus Art, Smart Mus Art Univ Chicago, 1995-96; Seurat and the Making of La Grande Jatte (auth, catalog), Art Inst Chicago, 2004; Amherst Women of Art and Science, Orra White Hitchcock (co-cur), Mead Art Mus, Amherst, 2011. *Pos:* Cur, var exhibs, 1962-2004; chmn, Sessions Mod Art, Coll Art Asn, 1965, 1971, 1981 & 1985. *Teaching:* Asst instr hist of art, Yale Univ, 1954-55, actg instr, 1955-56, instr & mem comt hist, arts & lett, 1956-60, from asst prof to prof hist art, 1960-74, Robert Lehman prof hist of art, 1974-90, dir undergrad studies, 1962-64, actg chmn, 1965-66, chmn, 1966-68; Slade prof, Oxford Univ, 1978; prof art, Mount Holyoke Coll, 1990-97, prof emer humanities, 1997-. *Awards:* Distinguished Teaching of Art Hist Award, Coll Art Asn, 1982, Lifetime Achievement in Art Writing Award, 2007; Rockefeller Found Humanities Fel, 1986; elected mem, Am Philos Soc, 1993. *Bibliog:* Impressionism, originality, and laissez-faire, Radical Hist Rev 38, spring 1987. *Mem:* Ordre Arts Lettres (chevalier, 1976, off, 1990); Fel of Am Acad Arts & Sci, 78. *Res:* 19th and 20th century French art. *Publ:* Contrib, French Cities in the Nineteenth Century, Hutchinson, London, 1982; auth, Impressionism: Art, and Partisan Soc, New Haven and London, Yale Univ Press, 1988; Léger, the Renaissance, and "Primitivism", Mélanges Michel Laclotte, Paris, 1994; Monet on the Normandy Coast, Tourism and Painting 1867-1886, 1994, Nature's Workshop: Renoir's Writings on the Decorative Arts, 2000, Seurat: Drawings and Paintings, 2001 & From Miller to Leger, Essays in Soc Art History, 2002, New Haven & London, Yale Univ Press; 46 essays on art hist, In: Artforum, Art Bull, Art Am, Burlington Mag, Mus Studies, NY Bk Rev, Oxford Art Rev, Radical History Rev, Revue de l'art, Revue du Louvre, Social Research, Van Gogh Studies and more, 1958-2007; ed & introduction, A Woman of Amherst: The Travel Diaries of Orra White Hitchcock, 2008; ed & introduction, The Correspondence of Edward Hitchcock and Benjamin Silliman, 1817-1841, Amherst Coll, 2012. *Mailing Add:* 26 Ashfield Ln South Hadley MA 01075-1341

HERDLICK, CATHERINE
GAME DESIGNER, CONSULTANT
Study: Wesleyan Univ, Middletown, Conn, BA, 2000; Parsons New Sch Design, New York, MFA, 2003. *Pos:* Community outreach coordr, Boston Childrens Mus, 2000-2001, community educator, 2002; programming intern, GameLab LLC, New York, 2003, producer, 2003-2006, dir production, 2006-2008; project & community mgr, MaMaMedia Inc, New York, 2005-2006; game designer, writer & community mgr, WDDG, New York, 2007 & Lawn Games for Life, 2008; community & product mgr, Lime Wire LLC, New York, 2008; game design consult, Iwin Inc, San Francisco, 2008-2009; creator & founder, Cowgirl Way Soc, 2008-. *Teaching:* Adj fac, Electronic Design & Multimedia Arts Prog, City Coll, New York, 2008. *Awards:* Grant for Emerging Fields, Creative Capital Found, 2009. *Bibliog:* Jill Duffy (auth), For the Love of All Games: How Catherine Herdlick Broke Into the Industry, Game Career Guide, 9/4/2007; Justin McElroy (auth), Quick change: How Jojo swtiched outfits and became a star, Gamezebo, 1/22/2008. *Publ:* Coauth (with Eric Zimmerman), Redesigning Shopmania: A Design Process Case Study, IGDA Casual Games Quarterly, Vol 2, Issue 1, fall 2006

HERFIELD, PHYLLIS
PAINTER
b Dec 6, 1947. *Study:* Art Students League, 65; Tyler Sch Art, Rome, 67-68; Temple Univ, BFA, 69; Nat Acad Design, 79-80. *Work:* Brooklyn Acad Music; Metrop Mus Art; Ft Lauderdale Mus; Cincinnatti Mus; Nat Portrait Gallery; Hunter Col; Univ of Indianapolis; Montefiore Medical Ctr; Mount Union Col; Portland Art Mus; Yale Univ Art Gallery; Forbes Collection, New York; Ft Lauderdale Mus Art, Fla; Century Club, New York. *Comn:* Prints: Orion Gallery; portraits: Salander O'Reilly Galleries, Portraits Inc. *Exhib:* Mus Mod Art, Paris, 75; Butler Inst, Youngstown, Ohio, 85; Solander O' Reilly, NY, 85; OK Harris Works of Art, NY, 90; Helander Gallery, Palm Beach, 91; Vered Gallery, East Hampton, NY, 93; Gallery Henoch, NY, 94; Foster Goldstrom, NY, 94; Steibel Modern, NY, 94; Nat Portrait Gallery, Washington, 96; Lizan-Tops, East Hampton, NY, 96; Marymount Manhattan Coll Gallery, NY, 99; Portland Art Mus, 2002; Armory Art Ctr, W Palm Beach, 2005; Papermag.com, 2005; Philoctetes Ctr, New Yori, 2008; Pharmaka, Los Angeles, 2008; Sideshaw, Brookyln, New York, 2010. *Awards:* Julius Hallgarten Prize, Nat Acad Design, 81. *Bibliog:* Reviews, Print Collectors Newslett, 5-6/77 & 5-6/78; Hilton Kramer (auth), rev, NY Times, 3/5/81; article, Christian Sci Monitor, 3/81; Valentin Tatransky (auth), article, Arts Mag, 10/85; Diversions, 2/89 & Femme Mag, 1/89. *Mem:* Nat Acad Mus; Cooper-Hewitt Mus; Metrop Mus. *Media:* Oil. *Publ:* Illusr, NY Times, Esquire, Psychology Today; Criticism, New York Reviews of Art; and many others. *Dealer:* Portrait Inc 7 West 51st St 10019. *Mailing Add:* 172 E 90th St New York NY 10128-2619

HERHUSKY, ROBERT
SCULPTOR, ADMINISTRATOR
Study: Studied at Calif State Univ, Chico, 1979-1981, Penland School, 1981, and Pilchuck Art Ctr, 1984; Calif Col Arts and Crafts, MFA, 1985. *Teaching:* With Calif State Univ, Chico, 1989-, dept chair, currently. *Mailing Add:* Department of Art and Art History California State University Chico Ayres Hall Room 107B Chico CA 95929

HERIC, JOHN F
SCULPTOR
b Reno, Nev, Feb 28, 1942. *Study:* Ariz State Univ, with Ben Goo, BFA, 63; Southern Ill Univ, Carbondale, with Milt Sullivan, MFA, 65. *Work:* Scottsdale Ctr Arts; Northern Ill Univ; Ariz State Univ Mus Art; Tucson Mus Art; Univ Ariz Mus Art. *Comn:* Steel sculpture, Ridgewood High Sch, 64; courtyard, Sopori Sch, Sahaurita Sch Dist, Ariz, 71; Downtown Develop Corp, Tucson, Ariz; The Bohm Co, Tucson, Ariz; City of Phoenix; City of Tucson. *Exhib:* St Paul Mus Art, Minn, 65; Solo exhibs, Univ Wis-Milwaukee, 66, Grossmont Coll, 69 & Elaine Horwitch Gallery, Scottsdale, 74; Southwestern Invitational, Yuma, Ariz, 69-74; Romanek Sculpture Park, Chicago, Ill; Sculpture at the Crossroads, Indianapolis, Ind; Construct Gallery, Chicago, Ill; Univ NDak, Grand Forks; Ariz State Univ, Tempe; Tucson Mus Art, Ariz; Grossmont Coll, El Cajon, Calif; Pac Lutheran Univ, Tacoma, Wash. *Pos:* Vis artist, Grossmont Col, 74-75. *Teaching:* Instr sculpture, Wis State Univ-Platteville, 65-67; vis lectr sculpture, Ariz State Univ, 67-69; from lectr sculpture to assoc prof art, Univ Ariz, 69-; Southern Ill Univ, Carbondale. *Awards:* Best of Show, Ariz Designer Craftsmen, 68; First Award Sculpture, Ariz Ann, 68; Purchase Award, Southwestern Invitational, 71, 72 & 74. *Media:* Stone, Plastics. *Dealer:* Elaine Horwitch Gallery 4200 N Marshall Way Scottsdale AZ 85251. *Mailing Add:* Univ Ariz Dept Art Tucson AZ 85721

HERMAN, ALAN DAVID
DESIGNER, GRAPHIC ARTIST
b Kew Gardens, NY, Mar 8, 1947. *Study:* Pratt Inst Sch Art & Design, Ida D Haskell scholarship & BFA (cum laude), 69. *Comn:* Consumer advert promotion, Carrier Air Conditioning Co, Southern Calif, 73-; med insurance commun & marketing prog, Johnson & Higgins, Los Angeles, 76-; international design programs, Xerox Corp, 80-; product launches int corps, Dupont, Mitsubishi, Kinemetrics & Nat Peripherals; exterior bus graphics system, City of Los Angeles. *Exhib:* 1972 Exhib of Best Advertising & Editorial Art in the West, 72; IAM Graphics Exhib, NY, 74; Indust Graphics Int, San Jose, Calif, 77; AIGA Packaging Exhib, Chicago, 80; Creativity 80 Show, NY. *Pos:* Pres & creative dir, Alan Herman & Assoc, Inc, Los Angeles, 70-. *Awards:* Top Package of the Yr, Print Mag, 76; IGI Distinctive Merit, 77; AIGA Graphic Design USA Award, 79. *Mem:* Art Dir Club Los Angeles; Los Angeles Co Mus Art. *Mailing Add:* c/o Alan Herman & Assoc 146 E Walnut Ave Monrovia CA 91016-3431

HERMAN, BERNARD J
DIRECTOR
Pos: chief exec, various hospitals, formerly; exec dir & CEO, Bakersfield Mus Art, Calif, currently. *Mailing Add:* Bakersfield Museum of Art 1930 R St Bakersfield CA 93301

HERMAN, DAVID H
PAINTER
b Brooklyn, NY, Apr 28, 1940. *Study:* NY Univ, BS, 61; Art Students League NY, with Rudolf Baranik, Brooklyn Col, MA, 70. *Work:* Sch for Strings, New York City; East Meadow Jewish Center, NY. *Comn:* Mural, Elmont Mem High Sch, NY, 94. *Exhib:* Int Small Works Exhib, Amos Eno Gallery, New York, 98; Denise Bibro Gallery, New York, 99 & 2003; Am Drawing Biennial, Muscarelle Mus Art, Williamsburgh, Va, 2000; Albright-Knox Gallery, Buffalo, NY, 2000-2001 & 2002-2003; Exposed, Fairleigh Dickinson Univ, Fair Lawn, NJ, 2001; Denis Bibro Gallery, New York, Champions of Modernism III, 2004; Mills Pond House, St James NY, 2004; Denise Bibro Fine Art, New York, 2006; solo exhib, Fractures, Denise Bibro Fine Art, New York, 2008, People/Places, July 2010; Mills Pond House, St James, NY, 2009; Denise Bibro Fine Art, NY, People/Places II, 2013. *Teaching:* dir orchestral music, Elmont Mem High Sch, NY, 64-94; founding mem, Rudolf Baranik Ongoing Art Sem, 96-98. *Awards:* First Place, Jewish Arts Festival, 99; Honorary Award, Am Drawing Biennial 7, 2000; Expo XX, BJ Spoke Gallery, Huntington, NY, 2001. *Bibliog:* Using Recent Events as a Theme for Social Commentary, NY Times, 6/10/94; Turning Photographs into the Metaphorical, NY Times, 11/9/97; Donald Kuspit (auth), Exposed, Denise Bibro, 2000; Divided by Beliefs, but United in Abstraction, 3/18/2001; Helen Harrison (auth), Photographs that Comment on the Subject, NY Times, 2/2004. *Mem:* Appraisers Asn Am; NY Artists Equity. *Media:* Acrylic. *Interests:* Contemporary Art. *Dealer:* Denise Bibro Fine Art New York NY; Nexus Gallery New York NY. *Mailing Add:* 1511 Dieman Ln East Meadow NY 11554

HERMAN, LLOYD ELDRED
MUSEUM DIRECTOR
b Corvallis, Ore, Mar 19, 1936. *Study:* Ore State Univ, 54-56; Univ Ore, 58-59; Am Univ, Washington, DC, BA (lib arts), 59-60. *Pos:* Prog mgr, off dir-gen mus, Smithsonian Inst, 66-71; dir, Renwick Gallery, 71-86; cur, mus consult & auth, Am craft & design topics, 86-; consult dir, Cartwright Gallery, Vancouver, BC, Can, 88-90, curatorial consult, 90-92; act cur, Can Craft Mus, Vancouver, BC, 92-; actg sr cur, Mus Glass, Tacoma, Wash, 98-99. *Awards:* Potomac Chap Am Soc Interior Designers Award, 79; Decoration, Order of Leopold II King of Belgians, 79; Decoration, Order of Danebrog, Chevalier, Queen of Denmark, 82; founders circle award, Mint Mus Craft and Design, 2007; One of a Kind, James Renwick Alliance, 2009. *Mem:* Hon fel Am Craft Coun; Bellingham Munic Arts Comn (chmn, 95); Normandy Park Arts Comn, Wash, 2008; Highline Hist Soc (bd mem, 2008-). *Interests:* Twentieth century crafts and industrial design, musical theater, travel. *Publ:* Auth, Brilliant Stories: American Narrative Jewelry, US Info Agency, 92; Clearly Art: Pilchucks Glass Legacy, Whatcom Mus Hist & Art, Bellingham, Wash, 92; coauth (with Matthew Kangas), Tales & Traditions: Storytelling in Twentieth Century American Craft, Craft Alliance, St Louis, 93; The collectors Eye, Koffler Gallery, Toronto, 94; Trashformations: Recycled Materials in Contemporary American Art & Design, Whatcom Mus His & Art, Bellingham, Wash, 98; co-auth (with Andre Codrescu), Thomas Mann, Metal Artist, Guild Publs, Madison, Wis, 2001; Trashformations East, Fuller Craft Mus, Brockton, Mass, 2005; Pulp Function, Fuller Craft Mus, Brockton, Mass, 2007. *Mailing Add:* 17816 2nd Ave SW Normandy Park WA 98166

HERMAN, ROGER
PAINTER, PRINTMAKER
b Saarbruchen, Saarland, Nov 21, 1947; Ger citizen. *Study:* Kunstakademie Karlsruhe, MFA, 79. *Work:* Walker Art Ctr, Minneapolis; Los Angeles Co Mus, Calif; San Francisco Mus Art; Denver Art Mus; Newport Harbor Art Mus. *Exhib:* Solo exhib, La Jolla Mus, 83; III Bienale, San Francisco Mus, 84; Painters Who Print, Walker Art Ctr, Minneapolis, 84; Inst for Contemp Art, Philadelphia, 84; Larry Gagosian Gallery, Los Angeles, 85, 86. *Awards:* New Talent Award, Los Angeles Co Mus, 83; Nat Endowment Art, 83 & 89. *Media:* All; Woodcuts. *Dealer:* Ace Gallery 5514 Wilshire Blvd Los Angeles CA. *Mailing Add:* 729 Academy Rd Los Angeles CA 90012-1004

HERMUS, LANCE JAY
ART APPRAISER, ART DEALER
b. Bklyn., Mar. 2, 1954. *Study:* BA in Art with highest honors, Coll. S.I., 1992; Cert. in Art Appraising, NYU, 1996. *Comn:* Various exhib murals for Snug Harbor Cultural Ctr, Staten Island, NY, Photo History Exhib of Snug Harbor, 91, Murals for Vistors Ctr, 91, Post Cards from Snug Harbor, 92. *Pos:* Registered art appraiser Appraiser Assn. of Am. Freelance photographer, artist, SI, 1972-92; video prodn. art dir. Master Prodns., SI, 1988-90; conservator, curator, appraiser Santo Bruno Fine Art, SI, 1992-96; conservator, curator William Myers Collection, NYC, 1993-94; appraiser, dealer, art cons. Hermus Fine Arts, SI, 1996-. Asst. lectr., edn. dept. Met. Mus. of Art, N.Y.C., 1990-93; artist, photo restoration Snug Harbor Cultural Ctr., S.I., 1990-93. *Mem:* Dem. County Com., S.I., 1974, poll watcher, 1975; Appraiser Assn. of Am. (assoc.); Am. Inst. for Conservation of Hist. and Artistic Works. *Res:* museum and collections. *Interests:* writing, coaching basketball, art collecting, reading. *Collection:* Alexander Archi Panko, Irving Amen, Jacob Agam, Leonard Baskin, Cecil Bell, Santo Bruno, Mortimor Borne, Alexander Calder, Timothy Colo, Gaston Chaissac, Salvador Dali, Noah Elam, George Grosz, George Wain Wright Harvey, Louis Icourt, Marlette Lydis, John Marin, John Noble, Max Pauhstein, George Rovault, Jean Pierre Pozzella, Roger Selchon, Emile Schuffenecker, Raphael Soyer, Henry Van Notte; various pastels, watercolors, etchings, lithographs, drawings, woodcuts. *Mailing Add:* 20 Woodrow Rd Staten Island NY 10312

HERNANDEZ, ANTHONY LOUIS
PHOTOGRAPHER
b Los Angeles, Calif, July 7, 1947. *Study:* E Los Angeles Coll, 66-70; Ctr Eye, Aspen, Colo, 69; Studied with Lee Friedlander. *Work:* Univ Calif, Davis; Mus Mod Art, NY; Bibliot Nat, Paris, France; Int Mus Photog, George Eastman House, Rochester, NY; Corcoran Gallery Art, Washington, DC. *Comn:* Photographs, Corcoran Gallery Art, Washington, DC, 76. *Exhib:* Solo exhibs, Corcoran Gallery Art, Washington, DC, 76, Orange Coast Col, Costa Mesa, Calif, 78, Univ Calif, Santa Barbara, 79, Calif Mus Photog, Riverside, 82, Susan Spiritus Gallery, Newport Beach, Calif, 84, Northlight Gallery, Ariz State Univ, 85, Opsis Found, NY, 90, Turner/Krull Gallery, Los Angeles, 91 & 93, Sprengel Mus, Hanover, Ger, 95, Mus l'Elysee, Switz, 96, Centre Nat Photog, Paris, France, 97, Galerie POLARIS, Paris, France, 97, 99 & 2001, Calif Coll Arts and Crafts, Oakland, 2001, Pictures for Los Angeles, Grant Selwyn Fine Art, 2003; Photog and the City, Seattle Art Mus, 1980; Facets of the Collection: Urban Am, San Francisco Mus Modern Art, Calif, 82; Slices of Times: Calif Landscapes, 1860-1880, 1960-1980, Oakland Mus, Calif, 82; Exposed and Developed: Am Photog in the 1970's, Nat Mus Am Art, Washington, DC, 84; Recent Acquisitions, Oakland Mus, Calif, 87; Landscape Photographs from the Permanent Collection, Corcoran Gallery Art; Washington, DC, 88; Picturing California, Oakland Mus, Calif, 89; Between Home and Heaven: Contemp Am Landscape Photog, New Orleans Mus Art, La, 92; Wasteland: Landscape Form Now On, Fotografie Biennale III, Rotterdam, The

Netherlands, 93; Crossing the Frontiers: Photographs of the Developing West, 1849 to the Present, San Francisco Mus Modern Art, Calif, 96; TRASH: When Waste Materials Become Art, Mus d'Arte Mod Contemporania Trento e Rovereto, Italy, 97; Hasselblad Center, Goteberg, Sweden, 99; Identification of a Landscape, Venezie-Marghera, Venice, Italy, 2000; Documents and Beyond, Reina Sofia Mus, Madrid, Spain, 2001; Made in Calif, 1900-2000, Los Angeles Co Mus Art, Calif, 2001; Calif Invitational, Ansel Adams Ctr Photog, San Francisco, Calif, 2001. *Awards:* Ferguston Grant, Friends Photog, Carmel, Calif, 72; Nat Endowment Arts Photog Fel, 75 & 78; Rome Prize, Am Acad, Rome, 98-99; US Artists Hillcrest Fel, 2009. *Bibliog:* Photography view: between home and heaven, contemporary American photography, NY Times, 6/4/92; A Gueze (auth), Wasteland, Blauwe Kamer, 9/92; Peter Kosenko (auth), No one home: Anthony Hernandez at Turner/Krull Gallery, 4/22/93; Ann Walters (auth), Fotografie Biennale Rotterdam III, Art Press, 11/94; K McKenna (auth), A career begins to click, LA Times, Calendar, 10/29/95; David Pagel (auth), Nature's beauty, LA Times, 11/9/96; David Pagel (auth), LA Times, Calendar, 6/20/97; Claudine Ise (auth), Photos from a very unpleasant decade, 9/18/98; Ralph Rugoff (auth), Familiar haunts: the photography of Anthony Hernandez, Artforum, 11/2000. *Dealer:* Grant Selwyn Fine Arts Los Angeles CA. *Mailing Add:* 255 1/2 S Carrondelet Ave Los Angeles CA 90057-2065

HERNANDEZ, ESTER
MURALIST, PRINTMAKER

b Dinuba, Calif, 1944. *Study:* UC Berkeley. *Exhib:* Numerous solo and group shows throughout US and worldwide; represented in permanent collections Nat Mus Am Art - Smithsonian, San Francisco Mus Mod Art, Mex Mus, San Francisco, Frida Kahlo Studio Mus, Mex City. *Teaching:* Creativity Explored visual art ctr, San Francisco. *Media:* Serigraphy, Silkscreen. *Mailing Add:* PO Box 410413 San Francisco CA 94141-0413

HERNANDEZ, JO FARB
MUSEUM DIRECTOR, CURATOR

b Chicago, Ill, Nov 20, 1952. *Study:* Univ Wis-Madison, BA, 74; Univ Calif, Los Angeles, MA, 75; Univ Calif, Berkeley; Mus Mgt Inst, cert, 81. *Collection Arranged:* Jewish Marriage Contracts, 83; Harriete Estel Berman: A Family of Appliances You Can Believe In (auth, catalog), 83; New Work/New Looks, 83; Day of the Dead: Tradition and Change in Contemporary Mexico (coauth, catalog), 81; Crime and Punishment: Reflections of Violence in Contemporary Art (auth, catalog), 84; Henrietta Shore: Retrospective (ed, catalog), 85; The Monterey Photog tradition: The Weston Years (ed, catalog), 85; Adat: Tribal Imagery/Ancestral Law, 86; The Artist and Myth (auth, brochure), 87; The Art of Eating, 88; Colors & Impressions: The Early Work of E Charlton Fortune (ed, catalog), 89; Lorser Feitelson: Exploration of the Figure, 1919-1929 (auth, brochure), 90; Chipping Away at the Layers: The Puzzle of Tramp Art, 91; The Quiet Eye: Pottery of Shoji Hamada & Bernard Leach (ed, catalog), 91; Painted Tintypes, 92; Julius Hatofsky: Against the Grain, 93; Jeannette Maxfield Lewis: A Centennial Celebration (auth catalog), 94; Sam Colburn: Creating a Style/The Early Years, (co-auth, catalog), 94; Jeremy Anderson: The Critical Link/A Quiet Revolution (auth catalog), 95; AG Rizzoli: Architect of Magnificent Visions (auth, bk), 97; Misch Kohn: Six Decades/Beyond the Tradition, (auth, bk), 98; Paul Pratchenko: Metarealistic Paintings, 2001; Diana Bates: Sculpture, 2002; Irvin Tepper: When Cups Speak (coauth, bk), 2002; Sam Richardson: Shaping Space (coauth, catalog), 2002; Jennifer & Kevin McCoy: Stardust, 2003; Marc D'Estout: Domestic Objects (auth, catalog), 2003; Contmp Cuban Art and the Art of Survival, 2003; James Surls: From the Garden, 2003; Misch Kohn: A Life in Prints, 2004; Machiko Agano/Masako Takahashi, 2004; Peter Shire, Go Beyond the Ordinary (coauth, catalog), 2004; Nunca Mas/Never Again, 2004; Forms of Tradition in Contemporary Spain (auth, book), 2005; Ron Nagle, 2005; Nic Nicosia: Making Pictures, 2006; Oliver Jackson: Drawing/the Incised Line, 2006; Marko Peljhan: Spectral System, 2006; Charles Krafft, Ceramic Sabotage, 2006; Points of View: Experiences in the Industrial Design Profession, 2006; Robert Hirsh: World in a Jan War and Trauma, 2007; Gerald Walburg: Looking, Thinking, Making (auth, bk), 2007; Gabriel Wiese: Cork Art, 2007; Gottfried Helnwein, I Walk Alone, 2008; Don Reitz: Out of the Ashes, 2008; William Brice: A Memorial Exhib, 2009; Collaboration: Robert Hudson & Richard Shaw with William Wiley, 2009; Pre-Postmodern Swiss Posters, 2009; Nathan Oliveira: Site-Specific/Content & Context, 2010; Italo Scanga: Metaphysicals, 2010; Richard Barnes: Animal Logic, 2010; Miguel Palma: In Process, 2010; Chicago Imagisms, 2010; Connor Everts, 2011; Dread Scott: Revolutionary Archive, 2012; Bean Finneran: Polka Dot Plateau, 2012; Nancy Nowacek: In Space, 2012; Michele Pred, 2012; Gordon Cook: Everyday Scenes/Ethereal Visions, 2012; Jon Serl (coauth, bk), 2013; The Mutability of Being; Singular Spaces: Spanish Art Environments (auth, bk), 2013; SJSU Centennial Exhibs (coauth, bk), 2013; Andy Paiko: Indefinite Sum, 2014; Ted Fullwood: Imaginary Confidants, 2015. *Pos:* Curatorial asst, Mus Cult Hist, Los Angeles, 74-75; guest cur, lectr, and juror various mus & univs, 75-; cur/educ asst, Dallas Mus Fine Arts, 76-77; dir & chief cur, Triton Mus Art, Santa Clara, Calif, 77-85 & Monterey Peninsula Mus Art, 85-93; consulting cur, Monterey Peninsula Mus Art, Calif, 93-2000; prin, Curatorial & Mgt Serv, 93-; dir, San Jose State Univ Gallery, Calif, 2000-; Dir, Spaces (Saving and Preserving Arts and Cultural Environment), 2006-; resident dir, Calif State Univ Int Programs, Madrid and Granada, Spain, 2015-2016. *Teaching:* Adj prof, ETex State Univ, 77, John F Kennedy Univ, 78, Univ Calif, Santa Cruz, 99-2000, prof & gallery dir, San Jose State Univ, 2000-. *Awards:* Ralph C Altman Award, UCLA, Calif, 75; Rockefeller Fel, Dallas Mus Fine Arts, 76-77; Leader of the Decade-Arts, Leadership Monterey Peninsula, 92; Golden Eagle Award, Cinematographic, 92; Tech Asst Grant, Alliance Calif Traditional Arts, 2002; Chicago Folklore Prize, Univ Chicago & Am Folklore Soc, 2006; CSU Research Grants, Lottery Awards & Dean's Awards, San Jose State Univ, 2000-2015; Fulbright Senior Research Award, 2008; Am Alliance of Mus, Publ Design Award, 2014; San Jose State Univ, President's Scholar, 2014. *Mem:* Calif Asn Mus (bd dir, 85-, vpres, 87-91, pres, 91-92); Western Mus Conf (bd dir, 89-91, exec comt, 89-91, prog chmn, 90); Am Folklore Soc; Am Alliance Mus; Alliance Calif Traditional Arts (exec bd); Friends of Fred Smith (nat adv bd); (int ed bd) Raw Vision mag; Bd Dirs, Spaces (Saving & Preserving Arts & Cultural Environments) (pres, 2006-); Vollis Simpson Whirligig Park (nat adv bd); (int ed bd); Elsewhere: Int Jour of Self-Taught and Outsider Art. *Res:* art environments, outsider arts, Spanish traditional/folk arts, contemporary art. *Publ:* auth, Jeremy Anderson: The Critical Link/A Quiet Revolution, 95; AG Rizzoli: Architect of Magnificent Visions, 97; auth, Misch Kohn: Beyond the Tradition, 98; Mel Ramos: The Galatea Series, 2000; coauth, Fire & Flux: The Art of Charles Strong; Irvin Tepper: When Cups Speak: Life with the Cup, 2002; Sam Richardson: Color of Space, 2002; Marc D'Estout Domestic Objects, 2003; Peter Shire: Go Beyond the Ordinary, 2004; auth, Forms of Tradition in Contemp Spain, 2005; auth, Gerald Walburg: Looking, Thinking, Making, 2007; coauth, Jon Serl: The Mutability of Being, 2013; coauth, ed, Creativity, Change, Commitment: A Celebration of 100 Years of the Deaprtment of Art, 2013; auth, Singular Spaces: From the Eccentric to the Extraordinary in Spanish Art Environments, 2013; chap auth, Sabato Rodia's Towers in Watts: Art, Migrations, Developments, 2014; intro, Where the Heaven Flowers Grow: The Life and Art of Leonard Knight, 2015; articles, Western Folklore, 2006, 2008, 2009; articles, Folk Art Messenger, 2006, 2008, 2013, 2014; articles, Folk Art, 97, 2007; articles, Keramieki Techni, Greece, 2004; articles, Am Art Rev, 93, 98; articles, Raw Vision, 96-; Encyclopedia of Am Folklife, 2006; Follies Jour, 2011; Encyclopedia of Outsider Art, 2012; Elsewhere: Int Jour of Self-Taught and Outsider Art, 2013; Follies Jour, 2013; Environment, Space and Place, 2014; Osservatorio Outside Art, 2014; Out of Art, 2015; Forecast Public Art - Public Art Review, 2015. *Mailing Add:* 345 White Rd Watsonville CA 95076

HERNANDEZ, SAM
SCULPTOR, EDUCATOR

b Hayward, Calif, Jan 23, 1948. *Study:* Calif State Univ, Hayward, BA, 70; Ariz State Univ, 73; Univ Wis-Madison, MFA, 74. *Hon Degrees:* Univ Sonora, Hermosillo, Mex, diploma. *Work:* Yale Univ Art Gallery; Smithsonian Am Art Mus, Washington, DC; Stanford Univ Cantor Arts Mus; Oakland Mus, Calif; Arco Collection, Los Angeles, Calif; City of San Jose Publ Art Prog; Contemp Mus, Honolulu; Mex Mus, San Francisco; Mus of Contemp Art Skopje, Macedonia; New Orleans Mus of Art; Santa Lucia Preserve, Rancho San Carlos; San José Mus of Art, Calif; Monterey Co Agricultural Comm; Crocker Art Mus, Sacramento, Calif. *Comn:* Monterey Co Agricultural Commission, 95; Santa Lucia Preserve, Carmel Valley, Calif, 96; Pvt residences, Calif, 2004. *Exhib:* San Francisco Mus Mod Art, 79-80; Elvehjem Mus Art, Madison, Wis, 80; Crocker Art Mus, Sacramento, Calif, 84 & 2002; San Jose Mus Art, 84, 86 & 94; Monterey Penisula Mus Art, Calif, 85; Contemp Art Ctr, Cinn, 86; Mex Mus, 86; Am Craft Mus, NY, 86; Philbrook Mus Art, Tulsa, 87; College Arts & Crafts, Oakland, Calif, 89, Univ Calif, Davis, 90, Oakland Mus, 92, Palm Springs Desert Mus, 93, Honolulu Acad Arts, 94, Redding Mus, 95, Univ Ore Mus, 95 & Calif Mus Art, 95; Calif State Univ, Sacramento, 99; Southwest Sch Art & Craft, San Antonio, Tex, 2000; Magdalena Baxeras Gallery, Barcelona, 2001; Univ Paris, Sorbonne, 2003; Wiegand Gallery, Notre Dame de Namur Univ, 2005; de Saisset Museum, Santa Clara, Ca, 1981, 1988, 1997, 2007; Washtenaw Community Col, Ann Arbor, Mich, 2006; San Francisco Mus Craft and Design, 2007; de Saisset Mus, Wiegand Gallery, Notre Dame de Namur Univ, 2007; William Siegal Gallery, Santa Fe, NM, 2009; Haystack Mountain Sch, Deer Isle, Maine, 2009; Euphrat Mus Art, 2009; Nat Acad Mus, New York, 2010; Galeria d'Art Horizon, Spain, 2010; Cantor Arts Ctr, Stanford Univ, 2011-2012; Triton Mus Art, 2011-2012; Castello d'Empuries, Spain, 2012; San José Mus of Art, 2014; Cabrillo Coll Art Gallery, Calif, 2014; Alex Bult Gallery, Sacramento, Calif, 2015. *Collection Arranged:* The Day of the Dead: Tradition and Change in Contemporary Mexico (coauth, catalog), Triton Mus Art, 79; Columbus: The Good, The Bad & The Ugly, Univ Santa Clara, 92; Cartoneria, Santa Clara Univ, 2005. *Pos:* Mem adv bd, Triton Mus Art, 81-85; adv bd, Djerassi Found, 95-96; artists' residency adv bd, Montalvo Ctr for Arts, 98-99; Art in Publ Places Commissioner, City of San Jose, 90-93. *Teaching:* Instr sculpture, E Tex State Univ, Commerce, 74-77; asst prof, Santa Clara Univ, Calif, 77-83, chmn art dept, 80-86, assoc prof sculpture, 83-96, prof, 96-2013; vis prof sculpture, Univ Wis-Madison, summer 80, Honolulu Acad Arts, 92, Anderson Ranch, 94, 95, 2001, 2005 & Haystack Mountain Sch, 94, 2009; vis artist Calif State Univ, Sacramento, 99. *Awards:* San Francisco Found Phelan Award, 79; Fel, Cult Coun Santa Clara Co, 83; Nat Endowment Arts Fel, 84; Sr Fulbright Scholar, 86; Individual Artist Grant, Nat Endowment Arts, 89; Award for Sustaned Excellence in Scholarship, 2009; Artist Laureate, Arts Council, Silicon Valley, 2013. *Bibliog:* Henry Hopkins (auth), Sam Hernandez, 88; L Price Amerson (auth), Sam Hernandez, 89; Bruce Guenther (auth), Sam Hernandez: Abstract Imagist, 93; Elizabeth Adan (auth), 100 Meditations, 2002; Frank Cebulski (auth), Sam Hernandez, 2005. *Mem:* Coll Art Asn; Int Sculpture Asn; Nat Coun Educ Ceramic Arts. *Media:* Wood, Bronze, Steel, found objects, mixed media, oil painting. *Res:* Spanish Traditional Arts, Performance events, art environments. *Publ:* Co-Auth, Day of the Dead: Tradition and Change in Contemporary Mexico, Triton Mus Art, 79; co-auth, Mexican Indian Dance Masks, Triton Mus Art, 82; A Conversation with Dr Jake (video), 94; videographer, Forms of Tradition in Contemporary Spain, 2006; Art Environments & Outsider Art, entries for Encyclopedia of Am Folklife, 2006; Sublime Spaces & Visionary Worlds, JM Kohler Arts, 2007; co-auth, Timeless of Form, Humberto Hermosillo, Sculptor, 2008; The Incredible Power of One, Japan, 2008, Korea, 2009; Singular Spaces: From the Eccentric to the Extraordinary in Spanish Art Environments, Raw Vision, 2013. *Mailing Add:* 345 White Rd Watsonville CA 95076

HERRERA, CARMEN
PAINTER

b Havana, Cuba, May 31, 1915; US citizen. *Study:* Studio Federico Edelman, Havana; Marymount Col; Paris, France; Sch Archit, Havana; Art Students League. *Work:* Havana Mus; Cintas Collection; Jersey City Mus, NJ; Mus Del Barrio, NY; Housatonic Mus Art, Conn; Mus Modern Art, NY; Tate Modern, London; Hirshhorn Mus, Wash DC. *Exhib:* Art Cubain Contemporain, Mus Mod Art, Paris, 51; Ctr Interam Rels, 68 & 75; Inst Int Educ, 80-81; Buecker & Harpsichords, 81; Solo Exhibs: Rastovski Gallery, NY, 87 & 88, Lisson Gallery, London, Eng, 2012; Outside

Cuba, Jane Vorheeszimerli Art Mus, Rutgers, State Univ NJ, 87; Duo Geo; Two Geometric Artists, Carmen Herrera & Ernesto Briel, Jadite Galleries, NY, 92; Latin Collector, NY, 2003, 05 & 08; Mus Modern Recent Acquisitions, NY, 2008; Ikon Gallery, Birmingham, Eng, 2009. *Collection Arranged:* Rusk Inst; Cintas Found Collection; Ella Cisneros; Carnen Ana Unaue; Viola McCausland; Mus Modern Art, NYC; Tatemodern, London; Mus Minneapolis. *Awards:* Creative Artists Pub Serv, 77-78. *Bibliog:* Don Bacigalupi (auth), Contemporanea, 6/89; Holland Cotter (auth), NY Times, 7/24/98 & 2004; Edward J Sullivan (auth, catalog), Concrete Realities, 4/14/04; Grace Glueck (auth), NY Times, 2005. *Dealer:* Lisson Gallery 51-54 Bell St London NWI5DA. *Mailing Add:* 37 E 19th St New York NY 10003

HERRIDGE, ELIZABETH
ART HISTORIAN
Study: Wellesley Col, BA (French); Christie's Educ, NY, MA (Connoisseurship and the Art and Auction Market), 1998-99. *Pos:* Retail equity sales support, internal audit positions, NY and Montreal, EF Hutton & Co, Inc, 1981-86; manager internal audit and institutional equity sales compliance positions, Kidder Peabody, 1986-90; branch audit manager, Fidelity Investments, FMR Corp, operations audit and analysis division, Boston and NY, 1990-93; vpres and compliance dir, BEA Associates, Credit Suisse, 1993-96; assoc dir fixed income compliance-high yield and emerging markets, Bear Stearns, 1996-97; Managing dir, Guggenheim Hermitage Mus at The Venetian, Las Vegas, 2003-2008; interim dir Las Vegas Philharmonic, 2008; managing dir, The Springs Preserve, 2009-10; principal, Elizabeth B Herridge Fine Arts, LLC, 2010-; researcher, archivist and educator at a number of museums including The Las Vegas Art Mus, Montclair Art Mus, NJ, and the Mus of Arts and Design (formerly the American Craft Mus), NY. *Teaching:* Adjunct faculty mem art dept, Col of Fine Arts, Univ of Nevade, Las Vegas. *Mem:* Western Mus Asn

HERRING, JAN (JANET) MANTEL
PAINTER, WRITER
b Havre, Mont, May 17, 1923. *Study:* Northern State Teachers Col; also painting with Frederic Taubes. *Work:* Grumbacher Collection, NY; Lubbock Art Ctr, Tex; Univ Idaho, Pocatello; Roswell Mus, NMex. *Exhib:* Solo exhibs, El Paso Mus Art, Santa Fe Mus Art, Tulsa Art Ctr, Roswell Mus & Brigham Young Univ. *Teaching:* Pvt instr. *Bibliog:* F Taubes (auth), article, Am Artist Mag, 55; articles, La Rev Mod, 61 & House Beautiful, 64. *Publ:* Auth, The Painters Composition Handbook, 71 & The Painter's Complete Portrait and Figure Handbook, 77, Poor-Henry Publ Co. *Mailing Add:* 3701 Mystic Cir Montgomery TX 77356-5328

HERRING, WILLIAM ARTHUR
PAINTER
b El Paso, Tex, Feb 18, 1948. *Study:* Tex A&M Univ, BA, 71; spec studies with Jan Herring, 72-82 & Charles Reid, 80-83. *Work:* San Angelo Mus Fine Art, Tex; El Paso Mus Fine Art, Tex; Tex A&M Univ, College Station; Eastern NMex Univ, Portales; US Air Defense Mus, Fort Bliss, Tex; Univ Science & Arts Oklahoma, Tulsa; US Dept Interior Nat Park Serv, Chamizal Nat Mem, El Paso, Tex; pvt collections, former President Ronald Reagan, Peter Coors & Goldie Hawn. *Comn:* Watercolor, horse racing, Ruidoso Racetrack Jockey Club, NMex, 87; watercolor, dancer, Viva El Paso Production Co, 90; rodeo drawing, Coors World Finals Rodeo, El Paso, Tex, 90; watercolor, prints of three cultures, El Paso Legislative Days, 90; pastel landscape, El Paso Symphony Orchestra, 91. *Exhib:* Solo exhib, Centenial Mus, El Paso, Tex, 86, When Fun Takes Over, Chamizal Nat Mem, El Paso, Tex, 2002; 75th Allied Artists of Am, Nat Arts Club, NY, 88; Borderlands Exhib, Americana Mus, El Paso, Tex, 89; 1992 Knickerbocker Artists, Salmagundi Club, NY, 92; Sierra Med Ctr 25th Exhib, El Paso Mus Art, 92; and others. *Pos:* Founder, The Master Class, Cloudcroft, NMex, 91-2006. *Teaching:* Guest artist, fashion illustration, Parsons Sch Design, NY, 91. *Awards:* William Hollingsworth Award, Miss Watercolor Soc Exhib, 87; Gold Medal for Watercolor, El Paso Mus Art, Melvin Simon & Assocs, 88; Bd Dirs Award, Pastel Soc Am, NY, 90. *Bibliog:* William Herring, artist, Santa Fean Mag, 5/87; Museum shows off top paintings, Accent Mag, El Paso Herald Post, 6/87; Cover artist, Southwest Guide Mag, 4/88; Herring of Many Colors, Wash Times, 4/9/94. *Mem:* Knickerbocker Artists, NY (pres, emeritus); Pastel Soc Am, NY; Am Artists Prof League, NY; Acad Artists Am, Mass; Blackhat Soc. *Media:* Pastel, Watercolor, Acrylic. *Res:* Pvt studies, Mex, 87, Eng, 88, France, 95-96, Ital, 96, Peru, 99, Russia, 2004, Austria, 2005 & Czech Rep, 2005. *Specialty:* landscapes of Southwest with animals, figurative works in a ballet of line and color. *Interests:* Karate, Gongoristic Aphorisms. *Collection:* Esoteric decorative works that draw on symbolism and synthesis, the collection aspires to express the noble spirit, beauty, and poetry. *Publ:* Auth, The Wonderful Madness of Becoming a Horse of a Different Color, Red Tree Publ Co; features in SW Art Mag, 4/94 & Am Artist Mag, 3/97; featured in Lambs Among Wolves, Bob Briner (auth), 1996. *Dealer:* Home Studio. *Mailing Add:* 3342 Le Blanc San Antonio TX 78247

HERRITT, LINDA S
SCULPTOR
b Columbus, Ohio, June 20, 1950. *Study:* Ohio State Univ, BFA, 78; Univ Mont, MFA, 80. *Work:* Univ Mont; Boulder Mus Contemp Art. *Exhib:* Decor/Decorum, Art Inst, San Francisco, Calif, 90; Washington Proj Art, Washington, Dc, 91; Return of the Cadavre Exquis, The Drawing Ctr, NY, 93; Barcelona Proj FAD, Spain, 93; Mexico City, Mex 95; solo show, Pierogi 2000, Brooklyn, NY, 98 & Galeria Nina Menocal, Mex City, 98. *Teaching:* Instr, Univ Maine, 80-82; assoc prof art, Univ Colo, 82-. *Awards:* Sculpture Fel, Nat Endowment Arts, 90; Colo Coun Fel, 93 & 96; Rockefeller/Forica US Mex Fund Cult, 98. *Bibliog:* Glen Helfand (auth), rev, Artweek, 8/16/90; Kathleen Mendus Dlugos (auth), New Art Examiner, 5/93; Ruth Noak (auth), Before Information, Vienna, Austria, 96. *Mem:* Coll Art Asn; Women's Caucus Art

HERRMANN, JOHN J, JR
CURATOR
b Chicago, Ill, Mar 16, 1937. *Study:* Yale Col, BA, 59; Inst Fine Arts, NY Univ, MA, 64, PhD, 73. *Collection Arranged:* coauth, catalog, Pompeii AD 79; auth, Roman and Classical and Hellenistic Greek Galleries, 1979; auth, The Excavations of Assos Revisited, 1979; coauth, catalog, The Search for Alexander, 1981; auth, catalog, The Gods Delight, 1988; auth, Human Figure in Early Greek Art, 1988; auth, Bronze Age Gallery, 1994; auth, catalog, In the Shadow of the Acropolis: Popular and Private Art from 4th Century Athens, 1984; auth, Ancient Gold, Wealth of the Thracians, 1998; coauth, catalog, Light From the Age of Augustine, 2002; coauth, catalog, Games for the Gods, 2004. *Pos:* Fel, Comt Rescue of Italian Art, 69-70; asst cur, Mus Fine Arts, Boston, 76-85, assoc cur, 85-96, John F Cogan Jr and Mary L Cornille cur, 96-2004, cur Classical Art, emer, 2005-. *Teaching:* instr, Am Univ, Rome, Italy, 74-75, Ctr Materials Res Archeol, Mass Inst Technol, 97-2003. *Mem:* Archeol Inst Am; Asn Study Marble & other Stones In Antiquity (vice pres, 2009-); Inst Nautical Archeol; bd of dir, Dedham Hist Soc, 2005-2012. *Interests:* Marble in ancient Greece & Rome; Roman North Africa. *Publ:* Auth, Ionic Capital in Late Antique Rome, Rome, 88; Rearranged Hair, J Mus Fine Arts, Boston, 91; Carrieres et Sculpture en Marbre a L'epogue Romaine et Tardive, Dossiers d'archeologie, 92; A Passion for Antiquities, J Paul Getty Mus, 94; Exportation of Dolomitic Marble from Thasos, 95 & Further research on Boston three-sided relief, 96, Study of Marble and Other Stones; Egyptian Demeter, Jahrbuch German Archeol Inst, 99; editor, auth, Asmosia 5: Interdisciplinary Studies on Ancient Stone, 2002; auth, Asmosia 6, Interdisciplinary Studies on Ancient Stone, 2002; auth, The Sphinx as A Theological Symbol, The Wisdom of Egypt, 2005; auth, Games for the Gods, 2004; auth, Celsus' Competing Heroes: Jonah, Daniel, and their Rivals, Poussieres dechristianisme et judaïsme antiques, 2007; auth, Apocalyptic Thought in Early Christianity, 2009; auth, Asmosia 7: Interdisciplinary Studies on Ancient Stone, 2009; auth, Asmosia 8: Interdisciplinary Studies on Ancient Stone, 2009; auth, Deconstructing & Reconstructing the Harvard Vatican Boy in Teaching with Objects, 2010; auth, Multimethod Analyses of Roman Sarcophagi in the Musco Nazionale Romano, Life Death, and Representation, 2011; auth, A Marble Maenad from the Holy Land, Cantor Art Ctr Jour, 2011; auth, Asmosia 9, 2012; auth, Africa Romana 19, 2012; auth, Dolomitic Marble from the Louvre, 38th Internat Symposium on Archaeometry, 2013

HERSCH, GLORIA GOLDSMITH
PAINTER, LECTURER
b New York, NY, Jan 5, 1928. *Study:* Community Coll Allegheny Co; Westmoreland Co Community Coll; Pa State Univ. *Work:* Hoyt Inst Fine Arts, New Castle, Pa; Monroeville Pa Pub Libr; Export Volunteer Fire Hall, Export, Pa; HJ Heinz Co, World Hq, Pittsburgh, Pa; Greater Latrobe, Pa School District Art Coll, over 200 Works Started, 1936. *Comn:* Portrait, John Minadeo Public Sch, Pittsburgh, Pa, 92; painting, comn by Dr & Mrs Charles Einolf, Mitchellville, Md, 98; portrait, comn by Dr & Mrs Bruce Malen, Monroe, NY, 99, 2001, & 2011; portrait, comn by Mr & Mrs Dennis Malen, Jericho, NY, 99 & 2003; portrait, comn by Mr & Mrs Paul Wursch, Erie, Pa, 99; portrait, comn by Ms Kathy Rogers, 2005. *Exhib:* Solo exhibs, Gallery Space, Monroeville, Pa, 97 & 2005, Hoyt Inst Fine Arts, New Castle, Pa, 2001 & 2011, Pa State Univ, New Kensington, Pa, 2002 & Maggie L Gallery, Murrysville, Pa, 2003, Murrysville Pa Municipal Bldg, 2008, Palace Theatre, Greensburg, Pa, 2007,2008; Group exhibs, Southern Alleghenies Mus Art, Loretto, Pa, 96, 2004, 2007, 2009; Westmoreland Art Nat, Youngwood, Pa, Greensburg, Pa, 1996-98, 2001-2003 & 2005-2010, 2011, 2013; SW Pa Art Exhib, Westmoreland Mus Am Art, Greensburg, Pa, 96, 2001, 2006, 2007, 2008, 2010; SW Pa Coun Arts, 96-2002, 2004 & 2006-2007; 62nd Nat Midyear, Butler Inst Am Art, Youngstown, Ohio, 1998; Southern Alleghenies Mus Art, Ligonier, Pa, 1998, 2001 & 2005-2010; Southwestern Pa Regional, Saint Vincent Gallery, Latrobe, Pa, 1999; PSA's First Biannual, Butler Inst Am Art, Salem, Ohio, 1999; Cent Pa Robeson Art Gallery, State Coll, Pa, 2000-2005 & 2007-2008; Harlan Gallery, Seton Hill, Greensburg, Pa, 2001, 2005, 2009, 2010; Hudson Valley Asn 73rd Ann, Hastings-on-Hudson, NY, 2004; SPC Arts Hist through Art, 2004-2005; Five Co Arts Asn, 2005-2007; Art in Bloom, Fundraiser, Westmoreland Mus Am Art, Greensburg, Pa, 2006-2008, 2010; C Rohns & Colitis Benefit, Southside Works, PGH, Pa; Westmoreland County Pa Courthouse, Greensburg, Pa, 2008; Fein Art Gallery, Pittsburgh, Pa, 2008-2010; Carnegie Mus Art, Pittsburgh, Pa, 2009; Penn Art Assn, 2013. *Pos:* Senior advert & marketing specialist, Pittsburgh-Corning Corp, Pa, 75-91. *Teaching:* Instr, pvt workshops & presentations. *Awards:* Merit, Hoyt Inst Fine Arts, 2001; Best of Show, Somerset Co Ann, 2002; Best of Show, Westmoreland Co Arts & Heritage Festival, 2003, People's Choice, 2010; Best of Show, Cranberry Township Festival, 2003; Best of Show, McKeesport, Pa, 2005-2006; Memorial award for Artistic Expression, Penn Art Assn, 2006, 2007, 2009, 2013; over 247 awards. *Bibliog:* An Artist's Life, Pittsburgh Post-Gazette, 7/21/96 & 6/29/2005; Artist Paint Realism, Tribune-Review, 6/27/1997, 9/22/2001, 5/12/2008 & 6/16/2008; Monroeville, PA TV Station, 97 & 2004; The Write Side, Penn State Univ, spring 98-99; Pittsburgh Area Gateway Press, 1/10/2001, 8/27/2003, 8/30/2006, 3/14/2007 & 5/21/2008; Mckeesport Daily News, 5/21/2001; Jewish Chronicle, 2/27/2003; Pittsburgh City Paper, 1/1/2003; Penn Franklin News, 1/13/2003 & 2011; Murrysville, Pa Star, 1/16/2008 & 2011; Unique Vision of Art, catalog of special collection of greater Latrobe, Pa Sch Distric, 2008; Valley News Dispatch, 2013; Plum Advance Leader, 2013. *Mem:* Pittsburgh Soc Artists (prog chair, 2002-2009); East Suburban Artists League; Penn Art Asn; Assoc Artists Pitt; Hoyt Artists Asn. *Media:* Acrylic, Pastel, Ink. *Mailing Add:* 309 Grandview Dr Verona PA 15147

HERSCH, JEFF
PHOTOGRAPHER
b Gary, IN, Sept 25, 1947. *Study:* Art Inst of Chicago, 63; Ind Univ, BA, 70. *Comn:* Calendar, Mountain Inst, Franklin, W Va, 99. *Exhib:* Portrait of Nepal, Foothills Art Center, Colo, 94; Gallery Soap, Japan, 99; Christmas Show, Arvada Ctr for Arts, Colo, 99; Colo Coun Expo, Republic Plaza, 02. *Collection Arranged:* Smithsonian Inst, Washington DC; Mus of Art, Denver. *Awards:* Anderson Ranch Fel, Anderson Ranch, 98, 00; Colo Coun of Arts Fel, State of Colo, 02. *Publ:* Photographers Forum, Serbin, 96; Travelers Tales Nepal, O'Reilly, 98

HERSCHLER, DAVID ELIJAH
SCULPTOR, PAINTER
b Brooklyn, NY, Mar 1, 1940. *Study:* Acad Belli Arte, Perugia, Italy, 60; Univ Rome, 60; Cornell Univ, BArch, 62; Claremont Grad Sch, MFA, 67. *Work:* Joseph H Hirshhorn Found, Washington; La Jolla Mus Art, Calif; Storm King Art Ctr, Mountainville, NY; Palm Springs Mus, Calif; Israel Mus, Jerusalem; Hartford Life Insurance; Daimler-Benz Corp; General Motors; Mercedes-Benz; NASA; Allegheny Teledyne. *Comn:* Sculptures, comn by Mr & Mrs NS Walbridge, La Jolla, 70, Sigmund Edelstone, Chicago, 71, Mr & Mrs JW Constance, Santa Barbara, 72, Mr & Mrs Marvin Smalley, Beverly Hills, 72 & Storm King Art Ctr, 72. *Exhib:* Solo exhibs, La Jolla Mus, 72, Santa Barbara Mus, 74, Palm Springs Mus, 77, Aspen Inst, 85, NASA-Kennedy Space Ctr, 86 & Westment Coll, 90, Pac Asian Art Mus, 97. *Awards:* United States Info Serv Golden Eagle Award; Kurt Diebus Trophy Award; Setp Trophy Award. *Media:* Stainless Steel, Gold. *Mailing Add:* c/o New Horizon Gallery PO Box 5859 Santa Barbara CA 93150-5859

HERSHEY, NONA
PRINTMAKER, PAINTER
b New York, NY, 1946. *Study:* Tyler Sch Art in Rome, BFA, 67, MFA, 69; Instituto Statale d'Arte di Urbino, dipl, 79; Yoshida Hanga Acad, Tokyo, 91. *Work:* Libr Congress, Washington, DC; Metrop Mus Art, NY; Minn Mus Am Art, St Paul; Pa Acad Fine Arts, Philadelphia; Fogg Art Mus, Harvard Univ, Cambridge. *Exhib:* group exhibs incl, Smithsonian Inst, Wash, 73, Honolulu Acad Arts, 73, USIS, Rome, 73, Jane Haslem Gallery, 74, 75, Mus Fine Arts, Boston, 75, Garden Gallery Modern Art, Raleigh, NC, 75, Metrop Mus, Fla, 77, USIS, Bucharest, Hungary, 78, Am Acad, Rome, 78, Laboratorio Artivisive, 81, 92, Rassegna di Grafica Contemporanea, Casalpusterlungo, Italy, 82; Clark Gallery, Lincoln, Mass, 83, Mary Ryan Gallery, 83-86, 88, 91, 92, Noyes Mus, NJ, 84, Galleria Il Ponte, 84, Dolan/Maxwell Gallery, 85, Calcografia Nazionale, Rome, 86, Palazzo Ducale, Pesaro, Italy, 86, Brooklyn Mus, 86, Walker Art Center, Minneapolis, 86, Garton & Cooke Gallery, London, 87, Istituto per la Grafica, Latina, Italy, 87, Premio Sassoferrato, Italy, 87, Premio Int Biella per l'Incisione, Italy, 87, Pa Acad Fine Arts, Philadelphia, 87, Premio Internazionale d'Arte Contemporanea, Campobello di Mazara, Italy, 88, Greenville Mus Fine Arts, NC, Taipei Fine Art Mus, 88, Dedalos Gallery, San Severo, Italy, 90, Gallery Kabutoya, Tokyo, 91, Art Multiple, Dusseldorf, Ger, 92, GW Einstein Gallery, NY City, 93; New Talent in Printmaking, Asn Am Artists, NY, 75; solo exhibs, Galleria Il Ponte, Rome, 82, 85 & 90, Mary Ryan Gallery, NY, 83 & 87, Miller Block Gallery, Boston, 95, 99, 2002, 2004; Great Am Prints, Dolan-Maxwell Gallery, Philadelphia, 85; 24th Nat Exhib, Brooklyn Mus, NY, 86; 12th Int Print Biennial, Krakow, Yugoslavia, 88. *Pos:* over 35 int pub & corp collections. *Teaching:* Asst prof printmaking, Temple Abroad, Rome, Italy, 79-90; assoc prof, Temple Univ Japan, Tokyo, 90-91; prof, Mass Col Art, Boston, Mass, 93-. *Awards:* Award, MacDowell Colony, Peterborough, NH, 89 & 93; Award, Ballinglen Arts Found, Ireland, 2001; grant, Mass Cult Council, 2004; and others. *Bibliog:* Marisa Volpi Orlandini (auth), Nona Hershey, Artisti Contemporanei, Interviste, 85; Ellen Lask (auth), Nona Hershey (exhib catalogue), Palazzo-Sormani, Milan, Italy, 92; New Am Paintings, Open Studio Press, 2004. *Mem:* Boston Printmakers; Printmaking Coun NJ; Nat Acad; Soc Am Graphic Artists. *Media:* All Media. *Dealer:* Miller Block Gallery 14 Newbury St Boston MA 02116; Dolan/Maxwell Inc 2046 Rittenhouse Sq, Philadelphia, PA, 19103

HERTZ, RICHARD A
EDUCATOR, CRITIC
b La Crosse, Wis, Aug 19, 1940. *Study:* Univ Calif, Los Angeles, BA, 62; Univ Calif, Santa Barbara, MA, 64; Univ Pittsburgh, PhD, 67. *Teaching:* Asst prof philos, Calif Inst Technol, 68-74; instr art theory, Calif Inst Arts, 74-79; chmn acad studies & grad prog, Art Ctr Col Design, 79-. *Mem:* Coll Art Asn, Mus Contemp Art, Los Angeles. *Res:* Twentieth century art theory and criticism. *Publ:* Auth, Philosophical foundations of modern art, Brit J Aesthet, summer 78; ed, J Los Angeles Inst Contemp Art, summer 82; auth, A critique of authoritarian rhetoric, Real Life Mag, summer 82; ed, Theories of Contemporary Art, Prentice-Hall, 85, 2nd ed, 93-; ed, with Norman Klein, Twentieth Century Art Theory: Urbanism, Politics and Mass Culture, Prentice-Hall, 90. *Mailing Add:* Art Ctr Col Design 1700 Lida St PO Box 7197 Pasadena CA 91103-1999

HERZBERG, THOMAS
ILLUSTRATOR, EDUCATOR
b Chicago, Ill. *Study:* Northeastern Ill Univ, BA, 75; Art Inst Chicago, 76-77; Northern Ill Univ, MFA, 79. *Work:* Van Straaten Gallery, Chicago; De Cordova Mus, Lincoln, Mass; Terrance Gallery, Palenville, NY; Metrop Mus & Art Ctr, Coral Gables, Fla; Silvermine Guild Artists; USAF. *Exhib:* Chicago and Vicinity Show, Art Inst Chicago, 78 & 84; Boston Printmakers, De Cordova Mus, Lincoln, Mass, 78, 79 & 82; 13th Nat Print Exhib, Silvermine Guild Artists, New Canaan, Conn, 80; Mus Publs Competition, Am Asn Mus, 90; Ann Awards Competition, Soc Newspaper Design, 91; Excellence in Graphics, Am Soc Bus Press Eds, 92; Creativity 1993, Art Direction Mag, 93; Print's Regional Design Ann, 94, 96 & 97; 28th, 39th & 41st Ann Exhib, Soc Illusrs, NY; 141st Am Watercolor Soc Show, NY, 2008, 142nd, 146th; 24th Annual Ill Watercolor Soc Show, 2008; USAF Art Pres Show, 2000, 2002, 2004, 2006, 2008, 2010, 2012. *Pos:* Illusr, Chicago Mag, Advertising Age, Playboy Mag, World Bk, Am Bar Asn, Chicago Tribune, Washington Post, Lincoln Park Zoo, Art Inst Chicago, Goodman Theater, Am Med Asn. *Teaching:* instr, Am Acad Art, Chicago, Ill, 2000-, chair fine art dept, 2005-2013, illustration dept chair, 2013; Instr photog, Oak Park River Forest High Sch, 76-77; asst printmaking, Northern Ill Univ, 78-79, instr, 81-82. *Awards:* 3 Certs Distinction, Creativity Show, Art Direction Mag, 93; Cert Design Excellence, Print's Regional Design Ann, Print Mag, 94 & 96; Honorable Mention, Ill Watercolor Society Show. *Bibliog:* Best of Newspaper Design, 7th, 10th, 12th & 13th eds; Illusr, No 28, 39, 41; Watercolor Artist, 2010; Drawing, Winter, 2013. *Mem:* Air Force Art Prog; Am Watercolor Soc (signature mem); Ill Watercolor Soc (signature mem). *Media:* Pen & Ink; Watercolor, Acrylic. *Mailing Add:* 4128 W Eddy St Chicago IL 60641

HERZOG, ELANA
SCULPTOR
Study: Bennington Coll, BA, VT; State Univ New York, Alfred, MFA. *Exhib:* Solo exhibs include Momenta Art, Brooklyn, 1997, Florence Lynch Gallery, New York, 1998, GAGA, New York, 2000, Richard L Nelson Gallery, Univ Calif Davis, Calif, 2001, Diverse Works, Houston, 2002, Herbert F Johnson Mus, Ithaca, NY, 2005, Gahlberg Gallery, Coll Dupage, IL, 2006, Smack Mellon, Brooklyn, New York, 2007; Group exhibs include Archipelago, Mus Contemp Art, Denvor, 2002; Decade, Schroeder Romero Gallery, Brooklyn, 2003; Open House, Working in Brooklyn, Brooklyn Mus Art, 2004; Entropy Interrupted, 115 Front St, Brooklyn, 2005; In Practice, the Sculpture Ctr, Long Island City, New York, 2005; Regeneration Room, Lmak Productions, Brooklyn, 2006; Thread Bare, Kleinert/James Art Ctr, Woodstock, NY, 2006; Intelligent Design, Momenta Art, Brooklyn, 2007; Radical Lace & Subversive Knitting, Mus Art & Design, New York, 2007. *Awards:* Lambent Fel in the Arts of the Tides Found, 2003; Lillian Elliot Award, 2004; Individual Artists Fel, NY Found Arts, 2007; Louis Comfort Tiffany Found Grants, 2008

HESIDENCE, DANIEL
PAINTER
b Akron, Oh, 1975. *Study:* Univ Tampa, BFA, 98; Hunter Coll, MFA, 2001. *Work:* Charles Saatchi; Mus Contemporary Art Chgo. *Exhib:* Solo exhibs, Feature Inc, NY, 2002, 2003, 2008, M du B, F, H, & g, Montreal, 2002, 2003, Kantor Feuer Gallery, Los Angeles, 2005, Shaheen Modern & Contemporary Art, Cleveland, Oh, 2006, Kevin Bruk Gallery, Miami, 2007, Greener Pastures Contemporary Art, Toronto, 2008, Andrea Rosen Gallery, Gallery 2, NY, 2009; Group exhibs, Feature Inc, NY, 2001, 2003, 2005, 2008, Marc Foxx, Los Angeles, 2002, 2005, Derek Eller Gallery, 2002, Michael Steinberg Fine Art, NY, 2003, Tracy Williams Ltd, NY, 2005, 2009, PS 1 Contemporary Art Ctr, Long Island City, NY, 2005, Artspace, New Haven, Conn, 2005, Bortolami Dayan, NY, 2006, Mus Boijmans Van Beuningen, Rotterdam, 2006, Mitchell Algus Gallery, NY, 2006, Sandroni Rey, Los Angeles, 2006, Royal Acad Arts, London, 2006, Univ Tampa, Fla, 2006, Bravin Lee Productions, NY, 2006, D'Amelio Terras, NY, 2007, Kantor/Feuer, Los Angeles, 2007, Kevin Bruk Gallery, 2007, Samson Projects, Boston, 2008, White Columns, NY, 2008, Philip Slein Gallery, St Louis, 2009, Kumukumu Gallery, NY, 2009, 55th Int Art Exhib Biennale, Venice, 2013. *Bibliog:* Piper Marshall (auth), Cave Painting: A Conversation with Bob Nichas, Art in America, 6/22/2009; Bob Nickas (auth), Painting Abstraction: New Elements in Abstract Painting, Phaidon Press, NY, 2009; and others. *Mailing Add:* D'Amelio Gallery 525 W 22nd St New York NY 10014

HESS, DONALD MARC
CONTEMPORARY ART COLLECTOR
b Bern, Switz, Aug 3, 1936. *Study:* Ecole Superieure De Commerce, Neuchatel Univ; Brewmaster, Doemens, Munich, 1957. *Pos:* chmn, Hess Holding, 1968-, CH, Hess Ltd, Bern; co-founder, Kunst Heute Found, Bern, 1982, 2005; pres & mem exec comt, Int Green Cross Switz, 1994-96; chmn Hess Art Collection Ltd, Bern, CH, 1998-; founder, Contemp Art Mus, Napa, Calif, 1989-, Hess Art Coll, Glen Winery in Paarl, South Africa; The James Turrell Mus at Bodega Colomé, Mohhos, Province Salta, Argentina, The Hess Collection Winery, Napa, Calif, includes Contemporary Art Mus, Glen Carlou Winery, Paarl, South Africa, with a Contemporary Art Mus, Bodega Colomé, Mohhos, Prov Salta, Argentina, includes James Turrell mus with works from the 1960s-2005. *Awards:* named one of Top 200 Collectors, ARTnews mag, 2004-2013. *Collection:* International contemporary art. *Publ:* Ed, Hess Collection, 1989 (named one of best books in Switz, 1989), Hess Collection New Works, 1998, Franz Gertsch, Hess Collection, 1999, Georg Baselitz, Works from the Hess Collection, 2003, Hess Art Collection, 2009. *Mailing Add:* Hess Art Collection Hohle Gasse 4 Liebefeld CH-3097 Switzerland

HESS, F SCOTT
PAINTER, INSTRUCTOR
b Baltimore, Md, 1955. *Study:* Univ Wis, Madison, BSA, 77; Acad Fine Arts, Vienna, Austria, 79-83. *Work:* Oakland Mus, Calif; Smithsonian Inst, Washington, DC; Univ Wis, Madison; Los Angeles Co Mus Art, Orange Co Mus, Calif; Prudential Insurance Co Am, Newark, NJ; Norton Family Found, Santa Monica, Calif; Kinsey Inst of Sex Res, Bloomington, Ind; Oesterreiches Tabakmuseum, Vienna, Australia. *Exhib:* One-person exhibs, Ovsey Gallery, Los Angeles, 94, Art Inst Southern Calif, 96, Mount San Antonio Col, Walnut, Calif, 97, Hackett-Freedman Gallery, San Francisco, Calif, 99, 2002, Orange Co Mus Art, Calif, 01; Figures, Frye Art Mus, Seattle, Wash, 2000; Pvt to Pub: Gift to the Boise Art Mus from Eileen and Peter Norton, Boise Art Mus, Idaho, 2000; Representing Los Angeles: Pictorial Currents in Contemp Southern Calif Art, Frye Art Mus, Seattle, Wash, 2000-01; The Importance of Being Earnest, Occidental Col, Los Angeles, Calif, 2001; Storytellers: The Figure in Time and Place, Fine Arts Gallery, San Francisco State Univ, Calif, 2001; and others. *Teaching:* Instr, Art Ctr Col Design, Pasadena, 95-; instr, Univ Southern Calif, Los Angeles, 95-96. *Awards:* Getty Fel Award, 91; Nat Endowment Arts Award, 91; Faculty Enrichment Grant, Art Ctr Coll of Design, Pasadena, Calif, 99. *Bibliog:* Michael Duncan (auth), F. Scott Hess: The Passing Hours, Hackett-Freedman Gallery (exhib catalog), San Francisco, 99; Color Reproduction, Harper's Mag, 4/2000; Gordon L Fuglie (auth), Realism Today: Representing L.A., Southwest Art, 1/01. *Mem:* The Drawing Group. *Dealer:* Hackett/Freedman Gallery 250 Sutter St San Francisco CA 94108

HESS, STANLEY WILLIAM
CURATOR, MUSEOLOGIST
b Bremerton, Wash, 1939. *Study:* Olympic Community Col, 58-60; Univ Wash, BA, 64 & grad work, 67-71; Case Western Reserve Univ, MSLS, 76. *Exhib:* Aurora Valentinetti, Holiday Exhibit, 2003-2004; Gift of Puppets: Bridging Oceans and Borders to Bring Understanding and Knowledge of the History and Cult of China, Through Art of Puppets to Young People, WA, 2004 & 2005; The World of Childhood, Books and Puppetry, 2005; All Creatures Great & Small, 2005; Nutcrackers & Pop-up Books, 2005; Punch & Judy, 2006; Everyman & Friends, 2006; Special Exhib featuring Aurora Valentinetti Puppet Mus & Evergreen Children's Theatre, Lt Gov's Office, Olympia, Wash, 2005; German Nutcracker, Tony White Mem, 2007; Happy New Year 2008 (Yr of the Rat), 2008; All Hands on Stage, Puget Sound Comminity Coll, Olympia, Wash, 2009. *Collection Arranged:* Catalogued, Valentenetti Puppet Mus, Bremerton, Aurora Valentinetti collection, Seattle Marshall Campbell Collection, Palm Springs, Calif; Journey to the West, Chiense Puppets, World Kite Mus, Long Beach, Wash, 2009; Bremerton Sister City Kure, Japan gift, 2010. *Pos:* Supvr, Photog & Slide Libr, Seattle Art Mus, Wash, 64-73; assoc librn photographs & slides, Cleveland Mus Art, 73-80; head librn, Spencer Art Reference Libr, Nelson-Atkins Mus Art, Kansas City, 80-91; consult & librn, 92-; bd dir, Evergreen Children's Theater, 97-, cur puppet mus, 98-. *Awards:* Best Thesbian, CKHS, 58; Pi Beta Mus, 76; Mayor's Citizen Recognition Award, 2011. *Mem:* Art Libr Soc NAm, (Central Plains, secy-treas, 86-87, vchmn-chmn, 90-91 & Northwest Chap, 92-94); Spec Libr Asn (picture div, pres elect & pres, 78-79); Kansas City Metrop Libr Network (mem, 80-91, secy, 85-86); Kitsap Hist Soc (bd dir, 96-97); Evergreen Children's Theatre (bd 97-present). *Res:* American arts & crafts silver; life & work of Clara Barck Welles; production of the Kalo shop of Chicago and New York; Am & int puppet collections of Aurora Valentinetti Puppet Mus, Bremerton, Wash, & Collection, Seattle, Wash; and Marshall Campbell Collection, Palm Springs, Calif. *Specialty:* Museum Puppetry-International, Asian, and American. *Interests:* Publishing, lecturing and teaching about the visual resources in the fine arts, information resources, history of puppetry. *Collection:* Pop-up books, 1988-. *Publ:* Auth, Annotated Bibliography of Slide Library Literature, Sch Info Studies, Syracuse Univ, 2/78; coauth, with A Hoffberg, et al, Directory of Art Libraries, Neal-Schuman Publ, 5/78; contribr, Picture Librarianship, Libr Asn, London, 81; and others. *Mailing Add:* PO Box 925 Bremerton WA 98337

HESSEL, MARIELUISE
COLLECTOR
b Germany. *Awards:* Named one of 200 Top Collectors, ARTnews mag, 2003-11. *Collection:* Contemporary art. *Mailing Add:* 65 Avalanche Canyon Dr Jackson WY 83001-9009

HESTER, NATHANIEL CHRISTOPHER
PAINTER
b Durham, NC, 1976. *Study:* Rice Univ, BA (art hist), 1999; Boston Univ, MFA (painting), 2005; New York Studio School, with Graham Nickson, Drawing Marathon, 2001. *Work:* Agnes Mongan Ctr, Cambridge, MA; Fogg Art Mus, Cambridge, MA; NY Pub Libr, New York; Allen Mem Art Mus, Oberlin, OH; Newark Pub Libr, Newark, NJ; Univ Miami, Miami, FL. *Exhib:* Heart & Hands, Nat Book Art Ctr, Lincoln, NE, 2004; The Ship of Fools Paintings, Olin Gallery, Roanoke Col, Salem, VA, 2007; Paintings & Prints, West Art Gallery, Pfeiffer Univ, Salisbury, NC, 2008; New Prints Spring 2008, Int Print Ctr, NYC, NY, 2008; Recent Paintings, Gallery at Penn Col, Williamsport, PA, 2009. *Teaching:* Adj instr art & art hist, Piedmont Com Col, Roxboro, NC, 2008; Art instr, Governor's School, Winston-Salem, NC, 2008. *Awards:* Clyde Ferguson Bull Traveling Fel, 2000; Constantin Alajalov Merit Fel, 2003-2005; George Sugarman Found Grant, 2008. *Bibliog:* Ben Wattenberg (auth), Art Under the Radar, Think Tank Special, BPS, 2002; Black & White Imagery Captures the Eye at Dangenart, Tennessean, Nashville, Tenn, 2007; Artist Embraces Nature, News & Observer, Raleigh, NC, 2008. *Media:* Oil Painting. *Publ:* Coauth (with S. Noecker), cover design The New Delta Review, Louisiana State Univ Press, winter 2007; coauth (with C. Thompson), The Harvard Review, Harvard Univ Press, winter 2007; coauth (with R. Viana), Remembering 9/11: Through the Eyes of a Printmaker, 2007; coauth (with R. Taylor), Kakalak 2008 Anthology of Carolina Poets, Main Street Rag, Spring 2008. *Dealer:* Adam Cave Fine Art 115 1/2 E Hargett St 2nd Flr Raleigh NC 27601; Chroma Gallery 31 Barnard St Savannah GA 31401; The Print Center 1614 Latimer St Philadelphia PA 19103. *Mailing Add:* PO Box 261 Hurdle Mills NC 27541

HESTON, JOAN
PAINTER, INSTRUCTOR
b Hartford, Conn. *Study:* Pratt Inst, three yr cert; Art Students League, with Robert Brackman; Stamford Mus, 73; Silvermine Guild Art, 73-74; Studio II, 75-76; with Charles Reid, 76-78. *Exhib:* Nat Acad Design, NY; Am Watercolor Soc Traveling Exhib; Nat Acad Arts & Lett, NY; Wadsworth Atheneum, Hartford, Conn; Frye Mus, Seattle, Wash; Tweed Mus, Duluth, Minn; Salmagundi Club, NY; Loveland Mus, Colo; Stamford Mus, Conn; Grants Pass Mus, Ore; Fairfield Univ Art Gallery, Conn; and others. *Teaching:* Instr oils & watercolor, Silvermine Guild of Arts, 86-; Int workshops, The Oil Painters Solution Bk, 90. *Awards:* Gold Medal, Catharine Lorillard Wolfe Art Club, 81 & 83; Silver Medal, Allied Artists Am, 85 & Knickerbocker Artists, 86; and many others; B Stevenson Portrait award, Nat Arts Club. *Bibliog:* Jolene Goldenthal (auth), Show at Atheneum, The Hartford Courant, 6/29/75; Muriel Brooks (auth), Art scene, New York Sunday News, 12/26/76; Public interest, Channel 13, 12/81 & 12/82; Letter from the editor, Artist's Mag, 9/85. *Mem:* Allied Artists Am (pres, 84 & hon lifetime pres); Silvermine Guild; Audubon Artists; Nat Arts Club; Catharine Lorillard Wolfe Art Club (mem, bd dir,82); Conn Acad Fine Arts. *Media:* Oil, Watercolor. *Publ:* Contribr, Painting Flowers in Watercolor, 80, Light: How to See It, How to Paint It, 88, The Watercolor Painter Solution Book, 88 & Tonal Values, 88, North Light Bks; auth, Concept and design in oil painting, Artist Mag, 9/85; The Oil Painters Solution Book. *Mailing Add:* 29 Hemlock Dr Stamford CT 06902

HETHOM, JANET
DESIGNER, EDUCATOR, ADMINISTRATOR, WRITER
Study: Central Washington Univ, BAEd, 1980, BA, 1980; Univ of Minnesota, PhD, 1987. *Teaching:* Head, Design Inst, Univ Delaware, currently, prof, chair, currently. *Awards:* Best Sustainable Design award, International Textiles and Apparel Design Exhibition, 2006, 2008; Director's award, Nat Textiles Ctr, Research Excellence, Masculine Style(s) team, 2007. *Publ:* (auth) Sustainable Fashion, Why Now, 2008. *Mailing Add:* University of Delaware Department of Art 104B Recitation Hall Newark DE 19716

HETTMANSPERGER, SUE
PAINTER
b Akron, Ohio, 1948. *Study:* Yale Univ Summer Sch Music & Art, 1971; Univ New Mexico, BFA, 1972, MA, 1974. *Work:* Des Moines Art Ctr, San Francisco Mus Mod Art; Art Inst Chicago, Metrop Mus Art, New York; Metrop Mus Art, New York. *Exhib:* Solo exhibs include Frumkin & Struve Gallery, Chicago, 1981, A.I.R. Gallery, New York, 1990, 1994, 1999, 2003, 2007, 2011, 2014, CSPS Alternative Space, Cedar Rapids, Iowa, 1992, Artemisia Gallery, Chicago, 1995; group exhibs include Mus Art Inst Chicago, 2012; Evanston Art Ctr, 1986, Hyde Park Art Ctr, Chgo, 1992; Des Moines Art Ctr, Iowa, 1996; Kathryn Sermas Gallery, New York, 1992; Univ Texas Art Gallery, San Antonio, 2002; Grinnell Col, 2003; Art Saint Louis, Missouri, 2004; Bowling Green State Univ Mus, 2005; Northern Arizona Univ Mus Art, 2005; represented in the book New Paintings-Midwest, 2005, 2010; Cedar Rapids Mus Art, 2006, 2012, 2015; Figge Mus, 2010, 2015. *Collection Arranged:* Mus of the Art Inst of Chgo, Des Moines Art Ctr, Metropolitan Mus of Art. *Pos:* Artist residencies: MacDowel Colony, 1977, Roswell Art Mus, 1990, UCROSS Found, 1992, Corporation of Yaddo, 2011. *Teaching:* Prof Art, Univ Iowa, 1977-Present. *Awards:* Fel, Nat Endowment Arts, 1983; Univ Iowa Faculty Scholar, 1996-97; Mem Found Fel in Painting, John Simon Guggenheim, 2008; IA Arts Council, (Public Art), 2009; Univ Iowa Arts Humanities awards 2006, 2009, 2011, 2013. *Mailing Add:* Faulconer Gallery Sixth Avenue and Park Street Grinnell IA 50112

HEUSSER, ELEANORE ELIZABETH HEUSSER FERHOLT
PAINTER
b North Haledon, NJ. *Study:* Cooper Union, dipl; Columbia Univ Sch Painting & Sculpture, fel, 45-46; Innsbruck Univ, Fulbright Fel, 52-55; Montclair State Univ (fine arts, printmaking), 91-2003. *Work:* Newark Mus; Lending Libr Mus Mod Art, NYk. *Exhib:* Kunsthistorisches Inst, Innsbruck, Austria, 54; Konzerthaus Gallery, Vienna, Austria, 54; Fulbright Grantees Show, Duveen-Graham Gallery & mus throughout US, 57-58; Pa Acad Fine Arts Ann, Philadelphia, 59 & 65; NJ Artists Biennial, NJ State Mus, Trenton, 72 & 79. *Pos:* Juror, Fulbright Painting Fel, 85-87; juror, Fulbright Collaborative Res Grant, 87. *Teaching:* Instr fundamentals art, Columbia Univ Sch Painting & Sculpture, 46-52; instr drawing, City Col New York, 60-62; pvt instr painting, New York, 60-72 & North Haledon, NJ, 72-. *Awards:* Pvt Grant Study in Mex, provided by George Grebe, 43. *Bibliog:* M Finkelstein (auth), Artist in the Alps, Inst Int Educ News Bull, 6/55; article, Revue Mod, 10/72. *Media:* Ink, Oil, Etching

HEWITT, DUNCAN ADAMS
SCULPTOR, EDUCATOR
b New York, NY, April 5, 1949. *Study:* Colby Col, BA, 71; Univ Pa, MFA, 75. *Comn:* Bronze, stone & earthwork installation, Univ Maine, Augusta; installation, Bonney Eagle Middle Sch, Standish, Maine. *Exhib:* Philadelphia Mus Art, 72; Inst Contemp Art, Philadelphia, 73-75; Payson Gallery Art, Portland, Maine, 81; Maine Artists Invitational, Bowdoin Coll Mus Art, 83; one-person exhib, Baxter Gallery, Portland Sch Art, Maine, 85; Perspectives, three-person show, Portland Mus Art, 89; Contemp Sculpture at Chesterwood, Stockbridge, Mass, 91; Barrows Rotunda, Dartmouth Col, 94. *Teaching:* Asst prof art, Univ Southern Maine, 76-92, assoc prof, 82-, chairperson dept, 82-; vis artist, Colby Col, fall 82 & Portland Sch Art, spring 83, chairperson, spring 92. *Mem:* Visual Arts Panel; Maine State Comn Arts & Humanities. *Media:* Steel, Wood. *Mailing Add:* Pleasant Hill Rd Hollis Center ME 04042

HEWITT, LESLIE
PHOTOGRAPHER, SCULPTOR
b New York, NY, 1977. *Study:* Cooper Union Advan Sci & Art, New York, BFA, 2000; NY Univ (Africana Studies), 2001-2003; Yale Univ, MFA, 2004. *Work:* Whitney Mus Am Art, New York; High Mus Art, Atlanta; Studio Mus Harlem, New York. *Exhib:* Solo exhibs include It's Just A Feeling..., D'Amelio Terras, New York, 2007; two-person exhibs include I Wish it Were True, Proj Row House, Houston, (with William Cordova), 2005, I Wish it Were True, Jamaica Art Ctr, Queens, NY, (with William Cordova), 2006; group exhibs include Sunrise Sunset, Smack Mellon Gallery, Brooklyn, NY, 2004; AIM 25, Bronx Mus Arts, Bronx, NY, 2005; Make It Now: New Sculpture in New York, Sculpture Ctr, Long Island, NY, 2005; Happenstance, Harris Lieberman, New York, 2005; Frequency, Studio Mus Harlem, New York, 2005; Emerge 7, Aljira, Ctr Contemp Art, Newark, NJ, 2006; Civil Restitutions, Thomas Dane Gallery, London, 2006; black alphabet: conTEXTS Contemp African-Am Art, Zacheta, Nat Gallery Art, Warsaw, Poland, 2006; Passin' It On, Rush Arts Gallery & Resource Center, New York, 2006; Leslie Hewitt: Replica of a Lost Original, Artists Space, New York, 2007; Alabama, Office Baroque Gallery, Antwerp, Belgium, 2007; Nexus Texas, Contemp Arts Mus, Houston, 2007. *Awards:* Clark Found Fel, 2001-2003; Art Matters Found Grant, 2008; Found for Contemp Arts Grant, 2010

HEYMAN, DANIEL
PRINTMAKER, EDUCATOR
Study: Dartmouth Coll, BA (visual studies, cum laude), 1985; Univ Pa, MFA (painting), 1991. *Work:* NY Pub Libr; Baltimore Mus Art; Minneapolis Inst Arts; Univ Iowa Mus Art; Hood Mus Art; Spencer Mus Art; Davis Art Mus; NDak Mus Ar. *Pos:* Exhib comt, William Way Ctr, Philadelphia, 1997-98; chmn selection comt, 55 Mercer

Gallery, New York, 1999-2000, treas, 2000-; treas & bd mem, Philagrafika Biennial Comt, 2003-06. *Teaching:* Adj prof, Philadelphia Univ, 1997- & Princeton Univ, 2010-; prof 2D foundation principles, Tyler Sch Art, Pa, 2004-; prof relief printmaking, RI Sch Design, 2004-; prof printmaking, Swarthmore Coll, 2006-. *Awards:* Forest Fel, Edna St Vincent Millay Colony for the Arts, NY, 1995; Develop Grant, RI Sch Design, 2005; MacDowell Fel, NH, 2007; Yaddo Fel, Saratoga, NY, 2008; Pew Ctr Arts Fel, 2009; Guggenheim Found Fel, 2010. *Bibliog:* Robin Rice (auth), Taking it Personally, City Paper, Philadlephia, 10/24-30/1997; Edward Sozanski (auth), Green Thoughts, Philadelphia Inquirer, 10/29/1999; Anna Fiorentino (auth), Salt, The Exhibit, Hartford Courant, 5/2-8/2002; Roberta Fallon (auth), Young at Art, Philadelphia Weekly, 7/6/2004; Kristian Vieru (auth), RISD Prof Uses Art to Bear Witness to the Abu Ghraib Victims, Providence Phoenix, 1/20/2006. *Mem:* Coll Art Assn Gay & Lesbian Caucus (treas, 1995-2000)

HEYMAN, IRA MICHAEL
ADMINISTRATOR, EDUCATOR
b New York, NY, May 30, 1930. *Study:* Dartmouth Col, AB (govt), 51; Yale Law Sch, JD, 56. *Pos:* Secy, Smithsonian Inst, 1994-2000. *Teaching:* Prof law, Univ Calif, Berkeley, 61-96

HEYMAN, LAWRENCE MURRAY
PAINTER, PRINTMAKER
b Washington, DC, 1932. *Study:* Tyler Sch Fine Arts, Temple Univ, BFA, 54, BS (educ), 55; Atelier 17, Paris, experimental printmaking with SW Hayter, 60-63, 69-70; Am Univ, MFA, 72. *Work:* Brooklyn Mus; Biblio Nat, Paris, France; Brooks Mem Mus, Memphis, Tenn; Portland Art Mus, Ore; Free Libr Philadelphia; Mus City NY. *Comn:* Print eds, Asn Am Artists, NY, 64, 68 & 69 & Antares Eds d'Art, Paris, France, 70, 71 & 72; cover painting for History of American West, US Info Agency, for Vent d'Ouest Book Collection, Paris, France, 65; prints, Judith Selkowitz Fine Arts, NY, 78; oil painting, Providence Art Club, 97. *Exhib:* Northwest Printmakers Int, Seattle Mus Fine Arts, 62-65; Audubon Artists Ann, Nat Acad Design, NY, 76; Realites Nouvelles, Parc Floral, Paris, 76 & 78; Le Trait, Cite des Arts, Paris, 77; World Print Competition '77, San Francisco Art Mus, 77; Atelier 17 Retrospective, Brooklyn Art Mus, 77-78 & Elvehjem Art Ctr, Minn, 77-78; L'Estampe Aujourd hui 73/78, Biblio Nat, Paris, 79; solo exhibs, Mus City NY, 84, Nat Inst Health, Bethesda, Maryland, 89-90; The Capital Image Today, Plum Gallery, Kensington, Md, 85 & 89; New Eng Artists, Newport Art Mus, Newport, RI, 88; Galerie Foret-Verte, Paris, 2004; Art Festival, LaGarde Freinet, France, 2010. *Pos:* Critic/evaluator printmaking books, Choice Mag, Middletown, Conn, 77-79. *Teaching:* Instr printmaking, RI Sch Design, 67-69, asst prof, 72-79 & dir print prog, 76-79; lectr printmaking, Am Univ, Washington, DC, 71-72. *Awards:* Purchase Award, Le Trait, Biblio Nat, Paris, 77; Nominated & Finalist Nat Art Medal, Nat Endowment Arts, 87; Finalist, Nat Portrait Painting Competition, Artists Mag, 89. *Bibliog:* Dale Jacquette (auth), Lawrence Heyman's paintings of street life, RI Rev, 1/81; Jo Ann Lewis (auth), Heyman paintings at Plum, Wash Post, 10/86; Les Krantz (auth), Artist Profile: Lawrence Heyman, NY Art Rev, 3rd ed, 88. *Media:* Oils, Watercolor; Intaglio. *Publ:* Auth, Painting the Town City Scapes of New York, Yale Univ Press, 2000; Painting and Essay, Times Square Feature; auth, Painting the Town, Cityscapes of New York, Paintings from the Mus of the City of New York, Yale Univ Press, 2000; Providence Art Club 1880-2005, Providence Art Club 2007, Presidential Portrait Painting. *Dealer:* Whitegate Representation. *Mailing Add:* 71 Faunce Dr Providence RI 02906

HEYMAN, RONNIE FEUERSTEIN
COLLECTOR
b New York, NY, 1948. *Study:* Harvard Univ, BA, 1969; Yale Univ, JD, 1973. *Pos:* Estab, The Heyman Chair in Legal Ethics Yale Law Sch; The Samuel and Ronnie Heyman Ctr for Ethics, Pub. Policy and the Prof Duke Univ; The Samuel & Ronnie Heyman Ctr on Corp Governance Yeshiva Univ, bd trustees, bd dir Benjamin N Cardozo Sch Law; trustee Barnard Col; exec comt int dirs' coun Guggenheim Mus; collectors' comt Nat Gallery, Wash, currently; Atty & principal, Heyman Properties, Westport, Conn, currently. *Awards:* Named one of Top 200 Collectors, ARTnews mag, 2000-2009. *Mem:* Bar: Conn 1973. *Collection:* Modern & Contemporary art, especially Miro, Meger, Gorky, Giacometti & Dubuffet. *Mailing Add:* Heyman Properties 333 Post Rd W Westport CT 06880

HIBBS, BARBARA J E
PAINTER, INSTRUCTOR
b New York, NY. *Study:* With A Haff; Art Student's League, with Sydney Dickinson, Dan Greene & Mario Cooper. *Work:* Wall Street Transcript & Ackerman Realty Co, NY. *Exhib:* Allied Artists Am, Nat Acad/Nat Arts Club, NY; Salmagundi Club Ann, NY; Knickerbocker Artists, Nat Arts Club/Salmagundi, NY; Hermitage Found Mus, Norfolk, Va, 83; Hammond Mus, 95; Lever House; Xian Acad Fine Arts, Nanking, China; Butler Mus & John Brown Univ, 2005-2006. *Teaching:* Pastel painting, Pastel Soc Am, Nat Arts Club, 82-83. *Awards:* Gold Medal Hon, Wall Street Transcript; Purchase Award, Pastel Soc Am, 96 & MH Hurliman-Armstrong Award, 97, 98; Pastel Soc Award for Pastel, Allied Artists, 97; Pastel Soc Purchase Award, 2003; Audubon Artist Silver Medal, 2004; Allied Artists Silver Medal, 2005. *Mem:* Pastel Soc Am (recording secy, 81-); Allied Artists Am (dir watercolor 91-); Knickerbocker Artists; C L Wolfe Art Asn; life mem Art Student's League NY. *Media:* Pastel, Watercolor. *Publ:* Bets of Pastels II, Rockport Publ. *Mailing Add:* 23 E 81st St New York NY 10028

HIBEL, EDNA
PAINTER, PRINTMAKER
b Boston, Mass, Jan 13, 1917. *Study:* With Gregory Michaels, 30-34; Boston Mus Sch Fine Arts, with Alexandr Yakovlev & Karl Zerbe, Cert, 35-39; with Elliott O'Hara Watercolor Sch, 36-37. *Hon Degrees:* United Nats Univ for Peace, Hon Dr Art, 88; Mt St Mary's Col, LHD, 88; Eureka Col, LHD, 95; Providence Col, 96; Northwood Univ, 97; Simmons Col, 2005. *Work:* Mus Fine Arts, Boston; Detroit Art Inst; Milwaukee Art Mus; Phoenix Art Mus; Russian Acad Art, St Petersburg; Lomonosov Porcelain Mus, Russ Acad Art, St Petersburg, Russ; Harvard Univ; UN Hq, NY; Palais des Nations, Geneve, CH; Norton Mus Art, West Palm Beach, Fla; and others. *Comn:* Hello Dolly, comn by Ginger Rogers, Palm Springs, Calif, 67; Prince of Peace, 85, Holy Family, 86, Soc Little Flower, Darien, Ill; Our Mother Before Us, Found US Nat Archs, Washington, 95; The Most Reverend Robert F Mulvee, Catholic Charities, Providence, RI, 96. *Exhib:* Solo Exhibs: Nat Mus Fine Arts, Rio de Janeiro, Brazil, 76; Hebrew Univ Mus, Jerusalem, 83; China Nat Art Gallery, Beijing, 86; Celebration of Life, Nat Mus Costa Rica, 88; Peace Through Wisdom, Dubrovnik Mus, Yugoslavia, 88; A Golden Bridge, Nat Mus Women Arts, Washington, 89, Soviet Union Acad Art Mus, Leningrad, 90; Grenchen Mus Art, Switz, 92; Lyme Acad Fine Arts, Conn, 94; Mitsukoshi Fine Art Gallery, Tokyo, 95; Klutznick Nat Jewish Mus, Wash, DC, 1987; Nat Libr Mus, Philadelphia, Pa, 1998. *Pos:* Founder, Boston Art Festival, 54; Art Dir, Edna Hibel Gallery, Boston & Palm Beach, Fla, 60-; cur, Hibel Mus Art, 77-. *Teaching:* Watercolor, Elliott O'Hara Watercolor Sch, 37; pvt lessons, oil painting, 57-58. *Awards:* Medal Hon, The late Belgian King Baudouin, Brussels, 83; Medal Hon & Citation, Pope John Paul II, Vatican, 85; Leonardo da Vinci World Award of Arts, World Cultural Council, Utrecht, 2001; Lifetime Achievement Award, Women in Visual Arts, 2001; Honoree, U.S. Nat Women's History Month, 2008. *Bibliog:* Kay Pedrik (auth), Edna Hibel: An Album and Biography, Tradition Inks, 85; Hibel's Russian Palette (film), Hibel Mus Art, 91; Olga Cossi (auth), Edna Hibel: Her Life and Art, Discovery Enterprises, 94; Shawn McAllister (auth), The Life & Art of Edna Hibel, Star Group International, West Palm Beach, Fla; Millie Brown (auth), Edna Hibel: An Artist's Story of Love & Compassion, Pelican Publ Co, New Orleans, LA. *Mem:* Edna Hibel Soc; World Acad Art & Sci; Royal Soc Art; Women in Visual Arts; Nat League Am Penwomen. *Media:* Oil; Stone Lithography, Serigraphy, Etching. *Specialty:* Paintings, stone lithographs, porcelain art & giclées of Edna Hibel art. *Interests:* Tennis, gardening, reading. *Publ:* Auth, Paintings of Edna Hibel, JAR Publ, 74, Progressions of a Lithograph, 77, coauth, The Sundial Ticking, 78, Fay Burg's Lake Kezar Cookbook with a Gallery of Paintings by Edna Hibel; auth, Hibel Mus Art Datebook, Hibel Mus Art, 81; auth, Stories that Warm the Heart, Hibel Mus Art, 96; artwork for, Andy Plotkin (auth), Black Block Legend, Publish America, Baltimore, MD. *Dealer:* Edna Hibel Corp 1910 7th Ave N Lake Worth FL 33461; Ednas Fine Art 5505 S Dixie Hwy West Palm Beach Fl; Hibel Mus Art MacArthur Campus of Florida Atlantic Univ 5353 Parkside Dr Jupter Fl 33458

HICKMAN, PAUL ADDISON
EDUCATOR, SLIDE CURATOR
b Iowa City, Iowa, May 24, 1950. *Study:* Coll Liberal Arts, 71-72; Univ Ill, Urbana-Champaign, BA, 73; Columbia Coll, Chicago, BA, 75; Princeton Univ, 77; Ariz State Univ, Tempe, MA (art hist), 79; Univ NMex, Albuquerque, with Beaumont Newhall, Thomas F Barrow & Bill Jay, PhD (art hist), 87. *Work:* Mus Contemp Photog, Chicago, Ill; Chicago Hist & Archit Landmarks, Ill. *Exhib:* Group exhibs, Mus Contemp Photog, Chicago, 74-75, Mont State Univ, Boseman, 76, Phoenix Art Mus, Ariz, 76, Northlight Gallery, Tempe, 76; solo exhibs, Ark State Univ, 90, Books & Books, Coral Gables, Fla, 91. *Collection Arranged:* William J Lucas: documentary photographs taken alongside Route 66, 86; Early Photographs of the Southwest, 76; West of Eden: Conceived, organized, prepared & installed, 89; Solicit, select, publicize & install seven exhibs per year in univ res libr, 89-92. *Pos:* Slide cur, Ark State Univ, 92-96 & slide librn, 96-. *Teaching:* Asst, Art Hist Survey, Ariz State Univ, 75-76; assoc photog hist, Univ NMex, Albuquerque, 78-81; instr, Coll Santa Fe, NMex, 88; asst prof art hist, Ark State Univ, 89-. *Awards:* Nat Stereoscopic Asn Award, Best Stereo World, articles on Historical Stereoscopy, John James Reilly, 2008. *Mem:* Coll Art Asn; Visual Resources Asn; Soc Photog Educ; Friends Photog; Nat Stereoscopic Asn. *Media:* Photography. *Collection:* Niagara Falls, Trans-Mississippi West, California, Yosemite, Big Trees & Sierra Nevada, Carleton E Watkins, John James Reilly, Martin Mason Hazeltine, George Fiske, Charles Bierstadt, Thomas Houseworth, C.L. Pond, John P. Soule. *Publ:* Coauth, George Fiske, Yosemite Photographer, Northland Press, 80; auth, Art, Information and Evidence: Early Landscape Photographs of the Yosemite Region, Exposure, 84; John James Reilly, 1838-1894, Univ Microfilms Int, 88; Martin Mason Hazeltine, 1827-1903: A Chronology, Stereo World, 94; Carleton E Watkins in Yosemite Valley, 1861-1866, Hist Photog, 96; Genesis and Revelation: Geologic Theory and Photographic Practice in Yosemite Valley, 1859-1900, Architecture of Chicago Gold Coast, 1880-1920; John James Reilly: catalog, two articles, Old Series (1867-75) & Views (1865-70), New Series (1879-86) & Views (1870-86), Additions to Chronology (1864-76) & Old & New Series Titles & Views (1865-86), Stereo World, 2008; John James Reilly: New Publ of Reilly's Stereographs, New Bibliography, & New Old & New Series Views, Stereo World, 2010; Buffalo Photographer of Western Expeditions, Charles Lyman Pond, Stereo World, 2010; Charles Bierstadt's Trip to the Western United States in 1870, Stereo World, 2012; Mount Lyell in the High Sierra and Controversy in Yosemite: Whether the Rock on Union Point Trail is Called Agassiz Column, the Magic Tower or Ten Pin Rock, Stereo World. *Mailing Add:* 1306 Warner Ave Jonesboro AR 72401-3827

HICKS, SHEILA
SCULPTOR
b Hastings, Nebr, July 24, 1934. *Study:* Yale Univ, BFA, 1957, MFA, 1959; RI Sch Design, Hon Dr, 1985. *Work:* Mus Mod Art & Metrop Mus, NY; Stedelijk Mus, Amsterdam; Mus des Arts Decoratifs, Paris; Victoria & Albert Mus, London; Mus Mod Art, Tokyo & Kyoto, Japan; Mus des Arts Deco, Prague; Cooper Hewitt, NY; Boston Mus; Centre Pompidou, Paris. *Comn:* 7 wall panels, Mecca, Saudia Arabia, 1971; stage curtain, Fiat Tour, Paris, 1974; auditorium tapestry, Dresdner Bank, Frankfurt, 1979; textile sculpture, Embarcadero Ctr, San Francisco, 1981; Bas-Relief, Fuji City Cul Ctr, Japan, 1992. *Exhib:* Solo shows incl Art Inst Chicago, 1962, Stedelijk Mus, 1974, Belfast Festival, 1988, Matsuya-Ginza, Tokyo, Japan, 1990, Seoul Art Ctr & Sonje, Korea & Mus Decorative Arts, Prague, 1993, Bard Grad Ctr, 2006; Grand Palais, Paris, 1978, 1979 & 1984; Milwaukee Art Mus, 1986; Am Crafts Mus, 1986, 1987 & 1988; Addison Gallery of Am Art, ICA, Philadelphia, 2011; Mint

Mus, Charlotte, NC, 2011; Sekima Jenkins, NY, 2011. *Pos:* Chief ed, Am Fabrics & Fashions, 1980-83; trustee, Textile Mus, Washington, DC, currently; trustee, Int Sculpture Ctr, Washington, DC. *Teaching:* Instr, The Hague, 1978, Middlebury Coll, Vt, 1979 & Fontainbleau, 1981-88; Madesa, Unesco, Capetown, 2008; RISD, 2009. *Awards:* Gold Medal for Craftsmanship, Am Inst Architects, 1974; Hon fel Royal Acad Art, Hague, 1975; Fel, Am Crafts Coun, 1983; Silver Medal, Academie de Architecture, Paris, 1986; Smithsonian Archives of Am Art Medal. *Bibliog:* M Levi-Strauss, Sheila Hicks Studio Vista, London, 1974; B Diamondstein (auth), Handmade in America, Abrams, NY, 1983; article, Cimaise, Paris, No 158; B Freudeheim (auth), article, NY times, 4/1986. *Mem:* Yale Club, NY; Centre Int d'Estudes des Textiles Anciens, France; Art Table, NY. *Media:* Textiles. *Dealer:* The Merrin Gallery 724 Fifth Ave New York NY; Cora de Vries Kaizergracht 516 1017 Amsterdam The Netherlands. *Mailing Add:* 3 Cour de Rohan Paris 75006 France

HIDE, PETER NICHOLAS
SCULPTOR, EDUCATOR

b Carshalton, Surrey, Eng, Dec 15, 1944. *Study:* Croydon Coll Art, 61-64; St Martin's Sch Art, 64-67. *Work:* Tate Gallery, London, Eng; Mus Fine Art, Boston; Univ Calif; Arts Coun Gt Brit, London; Can Coun Art Bank, Ottawa; City of Barcelona; Univ Alta; Sculpture at Goodwood, Sculpture Park, Sussex, UK, 2000. *Comn:* Sculpture for traveling show, Arts Coun Gt Brit, 69; Sculpture, cast iron & concrete, Peter Stuyvesant Found, Southampton, Eng, 72; Steel sculptures, Commonwealth Games Comt, Edmonton, Alta, 78 & City of Red Deer, Alta, 81; Stainless steel sculpture, Campeaux Corp, Edmonton, 84; The Winspear Centre for Performing Arts, Edmo, 97. *Exhib:* The Condition of Sculpture, Hayward Gallery, London, Eng, 75; Silver Jubilee Exhib, Battersea Park, London, 76; solo exhibs, Serpentine Gallery, London, 76, Sculpture Made in USA, Clayworks Gallery, NY, 84, Peter Hide in Canada, Edmonton Art Gallery, Alta, 86, Recent Sculptures, Mira Godard Gallery, Toronto, 88 & Andre Emmerich Gallery, NY, 90; Peter Hide in Context, 25 yr Retrospective, Edmonton Art Gallery, 98; Poussin Gallery, London, 2007; Scott Gallery, Edmonton, 2011. *Pos:* Artist/advisor, Triangle Workshop, NY & Hardingham Sculpture Works; President Edmonton Cont Art Soc. *Teaching:* Lectr sculpture, Norwich Sch Art, Norfolk, Eng, 68-74; lectr, St Martins Sch Art, London, 71-78; prof, Univ Alta, Edmonton, 77-. *Awards:* Canada Coun A Grant, 92; McCalla Professorship, 97. *Bibliog:* Terry Fenton (auth), Peter Hide & the monolith, Vanguard Mag & Peter Hide in Canada (catalog), Edmonton Art Gallery, 86; Peter Hide in Context (Catalog) Edmonton Art Gallery; The Life & Works of Peter Hide, Univ Ariz Press. *Mem:* Edmonton Contemp Art Soc (ECAS). *Media:* Steel. *Interests:* Edgar Degas sculpture. *Dealer:* Scott Gallery 12323 104 Ave, Edmonton; Andre Emmerich Gallery 41 E 57th St New York NY 10022; Poussin Gallery Block K 175 Bermondsey St London SEI 3UW. *Mailing Add:* Dept Art & Design Univ Alberta Edmonton AB T6G 2C9 Canada

HIGBY, (DONALD) WAYNE
PAINTER, SCULPTOR

b Colorado Springs, Colo, May 12, 1943. *Study:* Univ Colo, BFA, 66; Univ Mich, MFA, 68. *Work:* Philadelphia Mus Art; Am Craft Mus, Brooklyn Mus, Metrop Mus Art, Mus Contemp Crafts, NY; Minneapolis Mus Art, Wis; Everson Mus Art, Syracuse; Mus Fine Arts, Boston; Nat Mus Art, Tokyo; Renwick Gallery, Smithsonian, Washington, DC; Los Angeles Co Mus Art; and others. *Comn:* Arrow Int, Reading, Pa, 95; Miller Performing Arts Bldg, Alfred, 2006; Miller Performing Arts Ctr, Reading, Pa, 2009, Miller Theatre, Alfred, NY, 2012. *Exhib:* Solo exhibs, Joslyn Art Mus, 69, Mus Contemp Crafts, 73, Helen Drutt Gallery, NY, 88 & 90 China, 85; The Eloquent Object, Philbrook Mus Art, Tulsa, Okla, 87; Power over the City: Am Studio Potters, Detroit Inst Arts, Mich, 88; East-West Contemp Ceramics Exhib, Seoul Olympic Arts Festival, South Korea, 88; Power Over the Clay: Am Studio Potters, Detroit Inst Arts, Mich, 88; Everson Mus Art, Syracuse, NY, 89; Am Craft Mus, NY, 90; Kanazawa Ishikawa Pref, Japan, 91; Mus Mod Art, Tokyo, Japan, 93; Ark Art Ctr, Little Rock, 94; Krannert Art Mus, Champaign, Ill, 94; Clay into Art, MET Mus Art, NY, 98 & Los Angeles Co Mus Art, 2000; Retrospective, Smithsonian Am Art Mus, 2013. *Pos:* Chmn, Div Ceramic Art, NY State Coll Ceramics, Alfred Univ, 84-91; adv, Task Force Individual Artist, NY State Coun Arts, 80-82; bd dir, Haystack Mountain Sch Crafts, Deer Isle, Maine, 83-; adv, Nat Endowment Arts, 89-91; coun of dir, Int Acad of Ceramics, 99-. *Teaching:* Asst prof ceramic art, RI Sch Design, 70-73; prof ceramic art, NY State Coll Ceramics, Alfred Univ, 73-; hon prof art, Jingdezhen Ceramic Inst, Repub China, 94-, Shanghai Univ, 2000-. *Awards:* Nat Endowment Arts Fels, 73-74, 77-78 & 88-89; Individual Artist Grant, NY Found Arts, 85 & 89; Coll Fels, Am Craft Coun, 95; Am Craft Visionary Award, Am Craft Mus, 95; Honorary Prof Jingdezhen Ceramics Inst; Honorary Prof Shanghai Univ; Dist Edu Award, Bd of the Renwick, Smithsonian Inst, 2002; Master of the Media Bd of the Renwick Smithsonian Inst, Nat Gallery of Am Art; Honorary Citizen of Jingdezhen, PR China May, 2004; Honor of the council, NCECA (Nat Coun of Educ in Ceramic Art), 2005; Robert C Turner Chair, Ceramic Art, Alfred Univ, 2005; Kruson Distinguished Prof Award, Alfred Univ, 2007. *Bibliog:* The Eloquent Object, Philbrook Mus Art, Univ Wash Press, 87; Ceramics Monthly, 12/87; Robert Tuner (auth), feature article, Ceramic Art & Perception, 91; Kenneth Trapp (auth), Skilled Work, Renwick Gallery, Smithsonian, 98; Timothy Burgard (auth), Art of Craft, Fine Arts Mus of San Francisco, 99; Infinite Place: The Ceramic Art of Wayne Higby, 2013. *Mem:* Fel Am Crafts Coun; Empire State Craftsmen; NCECA; Haystack Mont Sch of Crafts, (hon bd mem), Bd Mem Art Gallery, Rochester, NY; Int Acad Ceramics (vpres). *Media:* Clay, Glaze, Fire. *Publ:* Contribr, Craft Horizons, ed by Rose Slivka, Am Crafts Coun, 70; Creative Landscape Containers, by Jane Holtz Kay, Christian Sci Monitor, 73; High Crafts (collecting boom), by Monica Meenan, Town & Country, 77; Ceramic Art, Comment and Review, 78 & Century of Ceramics in The United States, 79, by Garth Clark, E P Dutton; Handmade In America, B Dramousteir, 86 & 95; The New Ceramics, P Dormer, Thames & Itedson, 86 & 94; Earth Cloud, Wayne Higby, Annddrcte Arnoldsche, Stuttgart, Ger, 2007. *Dealer:* Helen Drutt Gallery Philadelphia PA 19106. *Mailing Add:* 1842 Route 244 Alfred Station NY 14803

HIGGINS, BRIAN ALTON
PAINTER, GALLERY DIRECTOR

b Brookline, Mass. *Study:* Motion Picture Sch, Fort Monmouth, NJ; Emerson Coll; Mus Fine Arts, Boston, Mass. *Work:* Va Mus Art; Boyle Co Sch Sys; Constitution Sq, Danville, Ky; Univ Mass Health Ctr, Worcester; Int Mus Art, El Paso, Tex; numerous pvt collections; Merriam Libr, W Brookfield, Mass. *Exhib:* Nat Art Club, New York City; Salmagundi Club, New York City; Pastel Soc Am, New York City; Lyme Art Ctr, Conn; San Diego Art Inst; Red River Valley Mus, Tex; Mass Gen Hosp, Mass; Danforth Mus Art, Mass; Slater Mus Art, Norwich, Conn; Mystic Art Ctr, Conn; Providence Art Club, RI; Butler Mus Am Art, Ohio, 2007, 2009, 2010, 2014. *Pos:* Chmn bd, Mass Symphony Orch. *Awards:* Perkins-Elmer award, Silvermine Art Guild, Conn, 99; Purchase award, Gallery Constitution Sq, Danville, Ky, 2000; Grumbacher Gold Medal, Cooperstown, NY Art Ctr, 2003; Createx award, Mystic Art Ctr, 2006; San Diego Art Inst, 2007; Purchase award, 2008, Int Mus Art, El Paso, Tex, 2009. *Bibliog:* Robt Moler, Ky Sunday Advocate, 2001; N Basbanes, Among the Gently Mad, Henry Holt Pub, 2002; Nancy Sheehan (auth), Arts Watch, Sunday Telegram, Worcester, Mass. *Mem:* Degas Pastel Soc; United Pastelists of Am; Conn Acad Fine Arts; Pastel Soc Am; Acad Artists Asn; Allied Artists Am; Pastels Painters Soc Cape Cod; Lyme Art Asn; Arts Worcester. *Media:* Pastels. *Publ:* William Zimmer, Art of the Week, NY Sunday Times, 99; Nancy Chapman, Featured Artist, Pastelink Monthly, 2001; Davenport's Art Guide, 2009-10; art book revs, Worcester Sunday Telegram, Mass. *Dealer:* The Edgington Collection of American Art Ridge Rd West Brookfield MA 01585; Caladan Gallery Peabody MA 01915. *Mailing Add:* PO Box 1011 West Brookfield MA 01585

HIGGINS, EDWARD FERDINAND III See Doo Da Post, Edward Ferdinand Higgins III

HIGGINS, EDWARD KOELLING
CERAMIST, JEWELER

b Milwaukee, Wis, Apr 30, 1926. *Study:* Univ Wis, Milwaukee, BS (art educ), MS (ceramics); Univ Wis-La Crosse; Northwestern Univ. *Work:* Mus of Contemp Crafts, NY; Theo Portney Gallery, NY; many pvt collections. *Exhib:* Mississippi River Art Festival, Jackson, Miss, 67-; Southern Tier Art & Craft Exhib, Corning Mus, NY, 69-; Crafts-1970, Inst of Contemp Art, Boston, 70; Appalachian Corridors Exhib, Charleston Art Gallery, WVa, 70-; Harrisburg Festival of the Arts, Harrisburg Art Gallery, Pa, 70; Cooperstown NY Festival of the Arts, 70. *Collection Arranged:* Fantasy in Silver, Akron Art Inst, Ohio; Jewelers, USA, Calif State Coll at Fullerton; Am Evolution in Art, Chambers Gallery, Pa State Univ; Box Exhib, Kohler Art Ctr; Celebration 20, Mus of Contemp Crafts, NY; Forms in Metal, Montgomery Mus of Fine Arts, Fine Arts Mus at Mobile, Ala, Philbrook Art Ctr, Tulsa, Okla, Va Mus of Fine Arts, Richmond & Huntsville Mus of Art, Ala; 100 Artists Celebrate 200 Yrs, Fairtree Gallery, NY; Xerox-Fun & Fantasy Exhib, Xerox Hall, Rochester, NY. *Teaching:* Asst prof jewelry, Mansfield State Col, Pa, 69-70; assoc prof jewelry, ceramics & photog, Mercyhurst Col, 71-82. *Awards:* Sculpture Award & Merit Award for Metal, Mississippi River Art Festival, Jackson Art Gallery; Silver Award, Appalachian Corridors Exhib, Charlestown Art Gallery. *Bibliog:* Dona Meilach (auth), Box Art Assemblages, Crown, 76; Jewelry: The Fine Art of Adornment Fabrication Method & Jewelry: The Fine Art of Adornment Casting Method (filmstrips), Warner Educ Productions; Casting, Bovin Publ. *Media:* Silver, Clay, Wood. *Interests:* Wood Sculpture. *Publ:* Contribr, Body Jewelry, Regnery, 73; contribr, Box Art Assemblages, 76 & Career Opportunities in Crafts, 77, Crown. *Dealer:* Somerhill Gallery, Chapel Hill, NC

HIGGINS, LARKIN MAUREEN
INTERDISCIPLINARY ARTIST, EDUCATOR

b Santa Monica, Calif. *Study:* Calif State Univ, Long Beach, BA, 76; Calif State Univ, Fullerton, MA, 83; Otis Coll Art & Design, MFA, 95. *Work:* Grunwald Col, Armand Hammer Mus, Los Angeles; Erie Art Mus, Erie, Pa; Calif Mus Photography, Riverside; Laguna Beach Mus Art, Calif; Univ Nebr Art Galleries, Lincoln; Charles E Young Res Libr, Univ Calif, Los Angeles; Univ S Fla Contemp Art Mus; Avant Writing Collection, Ohio State Univ Libraries. *Comn:* Wall installation, Nicki Huggins/Scott Sternberg, Topanga, Calif, 97; Artist Book, Los Angeles Poetry Festival, Calif, 99. *Exhib:* Contacts, Western Heritage Mus, Omaha, Nebr, 80; Photonational, traveling exhib, Erie Art Mus, Pa, 84; Bare Facts, Sly Humor, Irvine Fine Arts Ctr, Calif, 88; Words & Windows, Sam Francis Gallery, Santa Monica, Calif, 94; Before/Now, Artworks/Bookarts, Santa Monica, Calif, 98; Artists & Writers Simpatico, dA Ctr for the Arts, Pomona, Calif, 2000; Pillow Talk: Small Comforts in Hard Times, Ruth Bachofner Gallery, Bergamot Station, Santa Monica, Calif, 2007; Visual Poetry Mail Art Exhib, Skylab Gallery, Columbus, Oh, 2010; Spin/S: A Fluxus Festival, Cade Ctr Fine Arts Gallery, Md, 2013; Solo exhib, Couples, Harvard Univ, Visual & Environ, Cambridge, Mass, 85, Book /Object, Dickson Art Ctr, Art Libr, Univ Calif, Los Angeles, 89, Image & Text: Inside, Outside, Kwan Fong Gallery Art & Cult, Thousand Oaks, Calif, 2006, Vis-Po, Pearson Libr, Calif Lutheran Univ, 2009, Logographic Drawings, Counterpath, Denver, Colo, 2014. *Pos:* bd dir, Westwood Ctr of Arts, 79-81; chmn, lectr comt, Los Angeles Ctr for Photographic Studies, 83; Artist in Residence, Dorland Mountain Arts Colony, Temecula, Calif, 2000, 2001, 2002; chmn, art dept, Calif Lutheran Univ, 2004-2005. *Teaching:* Assoc Prof Art, painting & drawing, Calif Lutheran Univ, 94-2001, prof art, painting, drawing, interdisciplinary art, 2001-. *Awards:* Cash Award, ASA Southwest Reg Show, ASA Gallery, Univ NMex, 82; Purchase Award, Photonational, Erie Art Mus, 84; Fac Develop Grant, Hewlett Found, 1987, 1999, 2004, 2006, 2013-14. *Bibliog:* Betty Marks (auth), Assembled Photographs, Antiques & The Arts Weekly, 1982; Lucy Lippard (auth), (introduction to exhib catalog), From History to Action, The Woman's Building, 1984; Peter Frank, Stick-To-It-Iveness, LA Weekly, 88; Leah Ollman, A Wry Look at Life, Artweek, 88; Neal Menzies (auth), Artweek, 3 & 12/80; Jessica Bethoney, A Primer in Colorful Expressions, The Boston Globe, 81; Los Angeles Times, 10/28/1993, pp H1 & H10, (Inland Valley Ed), 6/15/2000, p A2; Nicole D'Amore (auth), Discarded Books inspire professor/artist, Ventura Co Star, 2/11/2009. *Mem:* Coll Art Asn;

Beyond Baroque Found; Dusie Kollektiv. *Media:* Inter-Disciplinary. *Res:* shared intersection of text and visual. *Interests:* Visual Poetry, text-based art & performance. *Collection:* Artists' books. *Publ:* Real Couples, U-Turn Art Mag, 85; Once Upon a Moment, Women's Graphic Center, 89; A Bibliophile's Rebellion: A Mixed Media Essay, Genre 14: Flux, 92; Matchbook, Red Wind Bks, 99; The Architect's Ruminations, DIAGRAM, issue 7.6, 2008; Discernible, Visio-Textual Selectricity, Runaway Spoon Press, 2008; Eleven Eleven, Issue 11, 2011; Of Materials, Implements, Dusie Kollektiv (paper edition), 2012; LA Telephone Book, Vol 1, 2011-2012 and Vol 2, 2012-2013; Of Traverse and Template, Mindmade Books, 2013; Comb-ing Mine-ings, Dusie, 2015. *Dealer:* Independent Artist. *Mailing Add:* PO Box 341751 Los Angeles CA 90034-8751

HIGGINS, MARYLOU
CERAMIST, PAINTER
b Milwaukee, Wis, June 27, 1926. *Study:* Univ Wis-Milwaukee, BS (art educ), MS (weaving). *Work:* Mint Mus, Charlotte, NC; Newark Mus, NJ; Northern Telecom Res, Glaxco Res, Triangle Park, NC; High Mus, Atlanta, Ga; Fayetteville Mus Art, Fayettville, NC; and others. *Comn:* 10 stoneware goblets, comn by Ctr Women Policy Studies to be given to recipients of Wise Women Awards, Washington, DC. *Exhib:* Solo exhibs, Sol Del Rio, San Antonio, Tex, 77-80, Shelia Nussbaum Gallery, NJ, 85, 88, 93 & 95, Somerhill Gallery, Chapel Hill, NC, 91, 94, 97, 2000 & 2004 & NC Pottery Ctr, Seagrove, 2005-06; Northern Telecom Juried Sculpture, Ceramic, NC, 85-88; Biennial '88 Ceramics, Mint Mus, Charlotte, NC; Auction Benefit, Bewitched by Craft, Am Craft Mus, New York, 88-89; North Carolina Clay, invitational, Visual Arts Ctr, NC State Univ, Raleigh, 92; Feats of Clay VII, Lincoln, Calif, 94; Fanciful & Functional: Art Furniture, Hickory Mus, Hickory, NC; Interiors Invitational, Blue Spiral 1, Asheville, NC, 2000 & 2004; plus others. *Teaching:* Instr art educ & fiber & fabrics, Mansfield State Coll, 69-71; asst prof ceramics, fiber & fabrics & art educ, Mercyhurst Coll, 71-74. *Awards:* Purchase Award, 4th Ann Exhib NC Sculpture, Northern Telecom, 85; Mint Mus Biennial Purchase Award, Sculptural Vessel, Charlotte, NC, 88; Merit Award, Feats of Clay VII, Lincoln, Calif, 94; and others. *Bibliog:* Nancy Tilly (auth), Carolina original, NC Homes & Gardens, 12/90; Harriet Gamble (auth), Mary Lou Higgins, Arts & Activities, 92. *Mem:* Am Craft Coun. *Media:* Clay, Graphite. *Publ:* Contribr, Basketry, 44, A New Look at Crochet, 75 & Wearable Crafts, 76, Crown; Inventive Fiber Crafts, Prentice-Hall, 77; Career Opportunities in Crafts, Crown, 77; The Jeweler's Art - A Multimedia Approach, Davis, 94; Handbuilt Ceramics, 97, The Clay Lover's Guide to Making Molds, 98, The Ceramic Design Book, 98, Surface Decoration, 99 & 500 Figures in Clay, 2004, Lark Bks; auth, A Show Story, Pottery Making Illustrated, Winter 98. *Dealer:* Somerhill Gallery 303 S RoxBoro St Durham NC 27701. *Mailing Add:* 166 Fearrington Post Pittsboro NC 27312

HIGH, KATHRYN
PAINTER, WRITER
Study: Colgate Univ, BA, 77; State Univ NY, Buffalo, MA (arts & humanities), 81. *Exhib:* Not So Ancient Hist, Women & Medicine/Voices in My Head, Mus Mod Art, NY, 90; Underexposed: Temple of the Fetus, Women & Medicine/Voices in My Head (video), Mus Mod Art, NY, 93; Art in General, NY, 95; Images Film/Video Festival, Toronto, 95; L'Oggetto/Arte e Video Negli Stati Uniti, Mus Laboratorio Di Arte Contemporanea, Rome, Italy, 95 & Mus Mod Art, NY, 96; Topographies, Vancouver Art Gallery, BC, 95. *Pos:* Panelist & juror, Media Bur, 87, NY Found Arts, 88, Boston Film & Video Festival, 91, Nat Endowment Arts/Media Arts, 91, Conn Arts Coun, 92, UFVA Student Festival, 93-94, Pew Fel, 94 & Black Maria Film/Video Festival, 96; ed & publ, FELIX, J Media Arts & Communications, 89-; co-cur, Landscapes Prog, Robert Flaherty Film Seminar, Int Film Seminars, NY, summer 96; cur, Reel New York, series of independent film/video, WNET & PBS, NY, 96-97. *Teaching:* Lectr, Film/Video Dept, Sch Visual Arts, NY, 88-92, Dept Computer Graphics, Pratt Inst, Brooklyn, spring 93, video production/theory classes, Vis Arts Prog, Princeton Univ, NJ, spring 95, 96 & 97 & NY Univ, fall 96. *Awards:* Fels Nat Endowment Arts, 89 & 95; Fel, Art Matters Inc, 95; Award for The 23 Songs of the Chromosomes, Jerome Found, 95; Guggenheim Found Fel, 2010. *Mem:* NY Found Arts; Lyn Blumenthal Found; Int Film Seminars; Standby Prog Inc. *Publ:* Auth, Finding One's Voice: Releasing the Other Into American Media (exhib catalog), Nat Ctr Video & New Media Art, London, 91; Wide Angle, Robert Flaherty Seminar issue, 95; Hallwalls Twenty Years, Hallwalls Gallery Publ, 95; 23 Questions, in Gender and Technology, Routledge, 96; (A few) statistics on the (possible) meaning of an encounter with (some) (middle-class) academic women, In: Mixed genres issue, Chains, spring 96. *Mailing Add:* 69 Lakeshore Dr Averill Park NY 12018

HIGH, STEVEN S
MUSEUM DIRECTOR, CURATOR
b Twin Falls, Idaho, June 17, 1956. *Study:* Univ Utah, Salt Lake City, 1974-76; Antioch Coll, Yellow Springs, Ohio, BA, 1979; Williams Coll, Williamstown, Mass, MA, 1985; Va Commonwealth Univ, Richmond, MBA, 1995. *Collection Arranged:* Young German Painters, 1986; Antoni Tapies: Graphic Work, 1988; Abstraction Contemporary Photography, 1989; Nightmare Works: Tibor Hajas (auth, catalog), Anderson Gallery, 1990; Alfredo Jaar: Geography-War, 1991; Anonymity & Identity (auth, catalog), 1993; Repicturing Abstraction (auth, catalog), 1994; The Rites of Science (auth, catalog), 1997. *Pos:* Researcher, San Francisco Mus Mod Art, Calif, 1979-80; preparator/asst cur, MIT Mus, Cambridge, Mass, 1980-82; dir, Baxter Gallery, Portland Sch Art, Maine, 1985-88, Anderson Gallery, Va Commonwealth Univ, Richmond 1988-96, Telfair Mus Art, Savannah, Ga, 2007-; dir/CEO, Telfair Mus Art, Savannah, Ga, 2007-. *Teaching:* Instr art hist, Portland Sch Art, Maine, 1985-88; asst prof art, Va Commonwealth Univ, Richmond, 1988-94, assoc prof, 1995-96. *Mem:* Am Asn Mus (bd, 2006-2009); Nev Mus Asn (pres, 2002-2004); Western Mus Asn (bd, 2004-2007); Richmond Arts Coun (bd mem, 1989-96). *Publ:* Auth, Antoni Tapies: Graphic Work 1947-1987, Baxter Gallery, Portland, Maine, 1988; Young German painters, Art Criticism, spring, 1988; contribr, Clemens Weiss: Towards Knowledge, Neurer Achener Kunstverein, 1990; Alfredo Jaar: Geography equals War, Va Mus & Anderson Gallery, 1991; New Art from an Ancient Land, 1996. *Mailing Add:* Telfair Mus Art PO Box 10081 Savannah GA 31412

HIGH, TIMOTHY GRIFFIN
PRINTMAKER, SCULPTOR
b Memphis, Tenn, Mar 10, 1949. *Study:* Tex Tech Univ, BFA (printmaking & drawing), 73; Univ Wis-Madison, MA(printmaking), 75, MFA (printmaking & art hist), 76. *Work:* Chicago Art Inst; Grunwald Ctr Graphic Arts, Univ Calif, Los Angeles; Brooklyn Mus Fine Art, NY; Jack S Blanton Art Mus, Univ Tex, Austin; Milwaukee Art Mus, Wis; Boston Mus Fine Art; Fogg Mus, Harvard Univ; Metrop Mus Fine Art, NY; 21C, Mus Louisville, Ky; Mus Fine Art, Houston, Tex. *Comn:* Point of Departure (portfolio), Univ Wis, 84; Colorprint USA (portfolio), Tex Tech Univ, 98; Tex Comn for the Arts, 2000; Tex Prints, 2001. *Exhib:* Seventh & Eighth Brit Biennale, 79 & 82; Metrop Ctr Visual Arts, Denver, Colo, 91; Creative Spirit I & II, Austin, Tex, 92 & 93; solo exhibs, Amarillo Art Mus, Tex, 93 & Flatbed Press & Gallery, Austin, Tex, 96; Veiled Images, Art Mus S Tex, Corpus Christi, Tex, 94; Nat Screenprinters Invitational, Mus Sch, Boston, Mass, 94; and others; Contemp Am Serigraph, 2004-2007; Semegraphics I & II, 2006, 2010; Atelier, 2007; JS Branton Mus, Austin, Tex; The Now-Contemp Prints, Hist Perspective, Katherine E Nash Gallery, Minneapolis, Minn, 2010; Survey of Contemporary Printmaking, East Carolina State Univ, 2011. *Collection Arranged:* Metropolitan Mus of Art, NY; Chicago Art Inst; Library of Congress; Fogg; Art Mus, Cambridge, MA; Boston Mus of Art; Houston Mus of Art; State of the State, The Seriagraph Portfolio, Venice Biennale, Venice, 2011. *Pos:* Studio Art, Univ Tex, Austin, 76-. *Teaching:* Assoc prof serigraphy-printmaking, papermaking, drawing & design, 82-; Found, Serigraphy Prog, Dept Art & Art Hist. *Awards:* Juror's Purchase Awards, 5th Int Nat Media Exhib, Dickerson, NDak, 75, Boston Print, De Cordova Mus; Longview Art Mus Best of Show, 35th Ann Invitational Art Exhib, 94. *Bibliog:* EC Cunningham (auth), Printmaking: A Primary Form of Expression, 92; EC Cunningham (auth), Printmaking: A Primary Form of Art, 92; Glenn R Brown (auth), rev, Art Papers, 93 & 94; Steven T Zevitas (auth), New American Painting, Open Studio Press, 97; Roni Henning (auth), Water Based Screen Printing Today, 2008. *Mem:* Boston Printmakers; Tex Fine Arts Asn; Austin Christian Arts Fel (pres, 94-96); Christians in Visual Arts; Southern Graphics Coun Int. *Media:* Prismacolor, Enamel Drawing; Serigraphy, Papermaking, Waterbased Ink. *Interests:* Travel, Art Collecting, Guitar Playing, Collecting. *Publ:* Contribr, New American Graphics--1975, Univ Wis-Madison, 75; Terrence Greider (auth), Artist & Audience, 90. *Dealer:* Adair Margo Gallery 415 E Yandell El Paso TX 79902. *Mailing Add:* Univ Tex Dept Art & Art History Austin TX 78712

HIGHSTEIN, JENE
SCULPTOR
b Baltimore, Md, 1942. *Study:* Univ Md, BA, 63; Univ Chicago, 63-65; New York Studio Sch, 66; Royal Acad Sch, London, dipl, 70. *Work:* Victoria & Albert Mus, London; Mus Contemp Art, Chicago; Los Angeles Co Mus Art; Rose Art Mus, Brandeis Univ, Mass; Guggenheim Mus, Mus Mod Art, NY; Balt Mus Art; Walker Arts Center; and many others; Nations Gallery, Wash DC. *Comn:* Granite carvings, General Mills Corp, 89; granite carvings, Walker Arts Ctr, 89; concrete sculptures and Park, Rutgers Univ, 90; concrete sculpture, Laumier Sculpture Park, St Louis, Mo, 91; granite carving, Carnegie Bank, Stockholm, 98; Tower, Fountain and Park, Stone, Houston, Tex, 2005; Jene Highstein, New Sculpture, Danese Gallery, 2011. *Exhib:* Solo exhibs, Univ Art Mus, Berkeley, Calif, 79, Renaissance Soc, Univ Chicago, 80, Ugo Ferranti Gallery, Rome, Italy, 81, Oscarsson Hood Gallery, NY, 82, Miami-Dade Community Coll, 83, Anders Tornberg Gallery, Lund, Sweden, 84, Mattress Factory, Pittsburgh, 85 & Flow Ace Gallery, Los Angeles, 86; An Int Survey of Recent Painting and Sculpture, Mus Mod Art, New York, 84; Ace Gallery, NY, 96; Art Space Seoul, 96; Stark Gallery, NY, 97; Anders Tornberg Gallery, Lund, Sweden, 98; Todd Gallery, London, 98; Grant Selwyn Gallery, Los Angeles, Calif, 2000; Bilboa Guggenheim, Bilboa, 2000; Grant Selwyn, NY, 2001; Art Mus Memphis, Tenn, 2001; Tex Gallery, Houston, 2002; Anthony Grant Fine Art, NY, 2004; Jene Highstein Madison Sq Art, Madison Sq Park, NY, 2005; Baum Gartner Gallery, NY, 2006; Drawings for Flatland, Bjorn Ressle Gallery, NY, 2007; A Survey of Drawings & Prints, Andrews Hall, William & Mary Coll, Williamsburg, Va, 2008; Lighter than Air, Texas Gallery, Houston, Tex, 2008; The Body as Thought, Ilju Seonhwa Gallery, Seoul, Korea, 2010. *Teaching:* Instr, Sch Visual Arts, 73, Parsons Sch Design, 83 & New York Univ, 84-85, NY; vis artist, Yale Univ, 74-75, C W Post Coll, Old Westbury, NY, 75 & 79, Emily Carr Coll, Vancouver, BC, 80, Rutgers Univ, Camden, NJ, 82, Miami-Dade Community Coll, Fla, 83, William & Mary Coll, Williamsburg, Va, 2008; artist-in-residence, Sarah Lawrence Coll, Bronxville, NY, 76; vis lectr, Harvard Univ, 96; vis distinguished prof, Southern Methodist Univ, Dallas, 98. *Awards:* Sculpture Awards, Creative Artists Pub Serv Prog, 79 & Nat Endowment Arts, 84 & 94; Guggenheim Fel, 85; St Gauden's Mem Prize, 92; IASPUS Residency, Stockholm, Sweden, 1998. *Bibliog:* Linda Forshey (auth), Jene Highstein, La Jolla Mus, Calif, 87; Jean Feinberg (auth), Jene Highstein at Wave Hill, Wave Hill, 89; Thomas McEvilley (auth), New Sculpture, Anthony Grant Inc, 2004; Lily Wei (auth), Madison Square Art, 2006, Jene Highstein, 2006; Laura Matlioli Rossi (ed), Lines in Space, Caarta Ed, 2008. *Media:* All Media. *Publ:* auth, Gallery/Landscape Santa Barbara, Contemp Arts Forum, 91; auth, A Survey of Sculpture & Drawing, Skape Gallery, Seoul, Korea, 2008; New Sculpture, Danse Gallery, 2011. *Dealer:* Texas Gallery Houston TX; Hill Gallery Birmingham MI; Danese Gallery NY. *Mailing Add:* 515 W 36th St New York NY 10018

HIJAR, ALBERTO SERANO
CRITIC, EDUCATOR
b DF Mex, Dec 7, 1935. *Study:* Univ Nac Autonoma de Mex de Filosofia, Maestro, 74; Diplomados Ministeris de Cultura, Nicaragua Univ, 82 & 98; Acad de Cienciar de Cuba, Medalla 30 aniversaio. *Work:* Mus estudeo Diego Rivera, Mex; Mus de Arte Mod, Mex; Fundacion Maria y Pablo O'Higgins, Mex; Inst Colimeuse de Cultra,

Colima, Mex; Secretaria de Relacionale Exterior, Mex; Univ de Guerrero, Mex; Univ de Morelos, Mex; Univ Nacional Autonoma, Mex; Inst Nacional de Bellas Artes. *Collection Arranged:* Diego Rivera Centenial, Cuba, 89; Influencias Mutuar, San Antonio, Tex, 92; Alfredo Zulce Homenaje, Mex, 93; Adolfo Mexiac, Libertad de expresiorio, Dist Fed, Mex, 98 & 2009; Centro Cultural El Juglar; Casa Benemerito de las Americas, Coyoacan, Mex; Museo de Arte de Oaxaca. *Pos:* Vincular, articular, fusionar, Taller de Arte e Ideologia, Mex-Italia, 74-98; Arte y luchar populars, Diplomador en Aguascalientes y el Dist Fed, Mus de Arte Contemp, Centro Nac Artes, 96-2009. *Teaching:* Estetica contemp, Univ Nac Mex, Fac Filusofia, Dist Fed, Mex, 61-90; teoria de la ideologia contemp, Esc Nac Antropologia, Dist Fed, Mex, 68-97; Arte mod America, Esc de Restauracion y Causervacion, Dist Fed, 70-80. *Bibliog:* Esther Civret (auth), Teoria y muralismo, Univ Aut Metrop, 84; Alicia Azuela (auth), Diego Rivera en Detroit, Inst Inv Esteticas, Univ Nac Autonoma Mex, 85; Raquel Bolauos (auth), Armar la nacion, Taller de Arte Ideologia, 98. *Mem:* Comt Mexicano de Hist de Art; Found Maria y Pablo O'Higgins; Taller de Arte e Ideologia; Proyecto Archiopielago, Baja, Calif. *Publ:* Coauth, Alfonso Michel, Inst Colimeuse de Cult, 97; Siqueiros Iconografia, Inst Nac de Bellas Artes, 97; Auth, Introducion al Neoliberalismo, Taller Art e Ideologia, 98; Adolfo Mexiac, libertad de expresior, Inst Nac de Bellas Artes, 98; coauth, Armar la nacion, Taller Art e Ideologia, 98. *Mailing Add:* Tezoquiqa 46 14090 DF Distrito Federal Mexico

HILD, NANCY
PAINTER
b Cincinnati, Ohio, Apr 7, 1948. *Study:* Ind Univ, BFA, 70, MFA, 76. *Work:* Ind Standard Oil, Chicago; Sandoz Corp, Des Plaines, Ill; Tri-Star Med Serv, Houston; Ind Univ Fine Arts Dept, Bloomington. *Exhib:* Artists of Chicago & Vicinity, Art Inst Chicago, 77 & 81; John Yau Selects Portraits, Urban Inst Contemp Art, Grand Rapids, Mich, 89; Face to Face, Chicago Cult Ctr, Ill, 92; Latina/Americana: Fertile Ground, La Sala De Exposiciones, Cali, Columbia, 93; Pets: Artists & An Am Obsession, Charles A Wustum Mus Fine Arts, Racine, Wis, 93; Artemisia at Transmission, Transmission Gallery, Glasgow, Scotland, 94; Nancy Hild with Silvia Malagrino (with catalog), Catalyst Gallery, Belfast, Northern Ireland, 96; Sesquicentennial Celebration Faculty Exhib, Elvehjem Mus Art, Madison, Wisc, 98; The Nat Mus Women in the Arts, Ill Women Artists: The New Millennium, Washington and The Ill State Mus, Springfield, 2000; The Chicago Cult Ctr, 2001; Shanghai in the Eyes of World Artists, China, 2002; Casa de la Cultura Oaxaquena, Mexico, 2003; Gescheidle Gallery, 2005; Lidxi Guendabiaani Casa De La Cultura, Juchitán, Mex, 2005; Womanmade Gallery, Chicago, 2006. *Collection Arranged:* Mothers & Daughters, Julius Tobias, Artemisia Gallery, Chicago, 91-92; Jack and Jill, Womanmade Gallery, Chicago, 94. *Pos:* Vpres & grant dir, Artemisia Gallery, Chicago, 90-92. *Teaching:* Lectr & prof painting, Univ Wis, Madison, 98. *Awards:* Munic Art League Prize, Artists Chicago & Vicinity, Art Inst Chicago, 81; Arts Midwest General Support Award, Nat Endowment Arts, 91; Chicago Arts Int Award, Catalyst Art Belfast, 96. *Bibliog:* M Therese Southgate MD (auth), Nancy Hild, the cover, Jour Am Med Asn, 9/26/90; Janina Ciezadlo (auth), Nancy Hild: New signs of the feminine, Chicago Reader, 10/9/94; Ken Indermark (auth), Nancy Hild, Home Brew Video, Harold Washington Libr, 96; Ivy Sundell (auth), Living Artists, 2005; Gedardo Valdivieso Parada (auth), Nancy Hild Y Manuel Cabrera Aquí y Allá, Tiempo del Istmo, 5/20/2005. *Mem:* Nat Women's Caucus Arts; Chicago Artists' Coalition. *Media:* Acrylic. *Dealer:* Gescheidle Gallery 300 W Superior, Chicago, IL 60610

HILDEBRAND, JUNE MARIANNE
PRINTMAKER, ILLUSTRATOR
b Eureka, Calif, Nov 2, 1930. *Study:* Calif Coll Arts & Crafts; Art Students League, scholar; Queens Col, BFA; Hochschule Bildende Künste Berlin, scholar; Hunter Col, MA; Pratt Graphic Ctr. *Work:* Philadelphia Mus Art, Pa; Univ Wis-Madison; NY Pub Libr; Everson Mus Art; Univ Minn; Hunt Inst, Carnegie Mellon Univ. *Exhib:* Pratt Int Miniature Print Exhib, 66 & 68; Oneonta State Univ, 67; Montclair State Col, 68; Gotham Bk Mart, NY, 69; St John's Univ., Staten Island, NY, 86; and others. *Mem:* Alumni, DAAD, NY; Hunter Coll, NY; Ctr for Book Arts, NY. *Media:* Linoleum, Silkscreen. *Interests:* Book arts, neighborhood Hist Preservation. *Publ:* Illusr, Eight Poems by Michael Benedikt, Assoc Am Artists, 65; contribr, articles, Artists Proof Mag, 66 & 67; Wild Fruits and Flowers, 80 & A Book of Flowers, 81, Claremount Press; Four Poems by Kirby Congdon, Claremount Press, 2007. *Mailing Add:* 229 E 12th St Apt 2 New York NY 10003

HILDEBRAND, PETER L
PAINTER
Study: Univ Wash, Seattle, BFA (graphic design), 1987; San Francisco Art Inst, 1990; Slade School, London, 1992; Hunter Coll, New York, MFA (painting), 1993. *Exhib:* Solo exhibs include Pierogi, Brooklyn, 2000 & 2006; group exhibs include Aljira 1, Aljira Ctr Contemp Art, Newark, NJ, 1995, Diverse Dialogues, 1998; Wild, Exit Art/The First World, New York, 1998, Tis the Season, 1999, Winter Wonderland, 2001, The Print Show, 2004, I Love Exit Art, 2006, The Building Show, 2007; Outer Boroughs, White Columns, New York, 1999; Superduper New York, Pierogi, Brooklyn, 2000 Vacation Nation, 2004, Reconfigure, 2005. *Awards:* Luetz/Riedel Endowment Fund, 1991; Aljira Nat Award, 1995; Pollock-Krasner Found Grant, 1998, 2007. *Dealer:* Pierogi 177 N 9th St Brooklyn NY 11211. *Mailing Add:* 258 Van Brunt St #3 Brooklyn NY 11231

HILDRETH, JOSEPH ALAN
PRINTMAKER, PAINTER
b Bowling Green, Ky, Sept 2, 1947. *Study:* Western Ky Univ, BFA, 69; Pratt Inst, with Walter Rogalski, MFA, 71. *Work:* Mint Mus, Charlotte, NC; Erie Fine Arts Ctr, Pa; State Univ NY Col, Potsdam. *Exhib:* Eight Upstate, Artists' Space Gallery, NY, 74; Nat Print Exhib, Second St Gallery, Charlottesville, Va, 76; 16th Bradley Nat Print Exhib, Bradley Univ, Peoria, Ill, 77; NY Landscape, Plaza Gallery, Albany, 81; 11th Nat Print & Drawing Exhib, Minot State Col, NDak, 82; and many others. *Pos:* Chmn art dept, State Univ NY, Potsdam, 86-94, prof printmaking, 94-. *Teaching:* Assoc prof printmaking, State Univ NY Col Potsdam, 71-. *Awards:* Carnegie Found Grant, 81; NY State Coun Arts Grant, 82. *Media:* Mixed. *Res:* Intaglio printmaking. *Publ:* Auth, Contemporary Realism (catalog essay), 82. *Mailing Add:* Pierpoint Ave Dept Art State Univ Potsdam Potsdam NY 13676

HILER, SETH RUGGLES
PAINTER
b Morristown, NJ, May 31, 1980. *Study:* Syracuse Univ, BFA, 2002; New york Acad Art, MFA, 2005. *Work:* Monmouth Mus Art, Lincroft, NJ; Syracuse Univ; Salmagundi Club, New York. *Exhib:* Solo exhibs, Monmouth Mus Art, Lincroft, NJ, 2010; Groups exhibs, NJ Fine Arts Ann, Morris Mus, NJ, 2009; Timeless, Art of Drawing, Morris Mus, NJ, 2008. *Teaching:* Instr art & writing, Discovery Charter Sch, Newark, NJ, 2009-; instr, art & writing, Emily Fisher Charter Sch, Trenton, NJ, 2010-. *Awards:* Syracuse Univ Remebrance Scholar, 2002; 1stplace, All Island Art Show, Martha's Vineyard, Mass, 2003; Pres Award, Scholarship & Junior Mem Exhib, Salmagundi Club, 2009; Hon Mention, Portrait Exhib, Salmagundi Club, New York, 2009; Frank Dumond Award, New Works Exhib, Salmadundi Club, New York, 2010. *Bibliog:* Philip Clark (auth), Seth Ruggles Hiler: Finding the Portrait Inside, The Art Point Blog, 2009; Bryan Borland (auth), Life of Adam, Sibling Rivalry Press, 2010; Ramon Johnson, Harlem Kicks off with Coming Out Art Show, About.com, 2010; Bryan Borland (auth), Portfolio: 20 Something, Gany Mede Mag, 2010; Ashley E Rooney, 100 Mid Atlantic Artists, Schiffer Publ, 2010. *Mem:* Alumni Asn New York Acad (dir of mem, 2010); Scholarship & Junior Mem Committee, Salmagundi Club, 2008-2010. *Dealer:* BIO's New Hope PA; Casa Frela Gallery New York; Speak-Easy Art Gallery Boonton NJ

HILL, CHARLES CHRISTOPHER
COLLAGE ARTIST, PAINTER
b Greensburg, Pa, Mar 4, 1948. *Study:* E Los Angeles Col, AA (art), 68; Univ Calif, Irvine, BA, 70, MFA 73. *Work:* Guggenheim Mus, NY,; Metrop Mus Art, NY; Mus Nat d'Art Moderne, Ctr George Pompidou, Paris; Los Angeles Co Mus Art, Calif; Honolulu Acad Art, Hawaii. *Comn:* Painting, Northrup, El Segundo, Calif, 80; Drawings, Hilton Hotels, Narita, Japan 87. *Exhib:* Market St Prog, Oakland Mus Art, Calif 73; Los Angeles Artists, Mus Mod Art, NY, 76; Eighth Int Painting Festival, Cagnessur Mer, France, 77; Matter-Meaning-Memory, Honolulu Acad Art, Hawaii, 80; One-person exhibs, Cirrus Gallery, Los Angeles, 80, 82-84 & 87-88, Simon Lowinsky Gallery, San Francisco, 81, Galerie Maurer, Zurich, 81 & 82, Baudoin Lebon, Paris, 82 & 85, Van Straaten Gallery, Chicago, 83, DBR Gallery, Cleveland, 84, Galleria del Cavallino, Venice, 85 & Ctr d'Action Culturelle de St-Brieuc, France, 87. *Teaching:* Vis instr, Art Ctr Col Design, 78-79; Univ Calif, Los Angeles, 80-81. *Awards:* Young Talent Award, Los Angeles Co Mus Art, 76; Grant, Slides, Nat Endowment Arts, 76; Special Mention, Modern Trends, City of Cagnes sur Mer, France, 76. *Bibliog:* Deborah Irmas (auth), Charles Hill, Carte d'Arte, Messina, Italy, 11/87; Gilbert Lascault (auth), Le Bamboo, Bambouserie de Prafrance, 8/88; Constance Glenn (auth), New Venice vernacular, Angeles Mag, 11/88. *Media:* Watercolor & Paper. *Dealer:* Cirrus Gallery 520 S Alameda Los Angeles CA 90291

HILL, CHRISTINE
CONCEPTUAL ARTIST
b Binghamton, NY, 1968. *Study:* Md Inst, Coll Art, BFA, 1991. *Exhib:* Solo exhibs include Galerie Eigen+Art, Berlin, 1995, 2000, 2003, 2006, 2008, Deitch Projects, New York, 1999, Ronald Feldman Fine Arts, New York, 2000, 2003, 2008, Mus Contemp Art, Leipzig, Germany, 2002, Mus Contemp Art, Cleveland, 2003, Times Square Alliance, New York, 2005; group exhibs include A Day Without Art, Mus Contemp Art, Baltimore, 1991, Snapshot, 2000; Water Bar, David Zwirner Gallery, New York, 1993; Venice Biennial, 1995, 2007; Trailer, Art Cologne, 1995; Berlin Biennale, 1998; Wish You Luck, PS1 Contemp Art Ctr, New York, 1998, Children of Berlin, 1999; Moving/In, Kunsthalle Hamburg, Germany, 2000; Tele (Visions), Kunsthalle Vienna, 2001; Ad-Hoc, Weatherspoon Art Mus, Chapel Hill, SC, 2004; Open House: Working in Brooklyn, Brooklyn Mus Art, 2004; Trade Show, Mass Mus Contemp Art, 2005; Cottage Industry, Contemp Mus, Baltimore, 2008. *Teaching:* Prof, chair of media, trend & pub appearance, Bauhaus Univ, Weimar, Germany. *Awards:* Berlin Pool Fel, 1996; Pub Art Fund of New York Project Award, 1999; Bickford Teaching Award, 2002. *Dealer:* Galerie Eigen+Art Auguststrasse 26 D-10117 Berlin Germany. *Mailing Add:* c/o Ronald Feldman Fine Arts 31 Mercer St New York NY 10013

HILL, DANIEL G
PAINTER
b Providence, RI, Apr 6, 1956. *Study:* Brown Univ, Providence, RI, BA, 79; Hunter Col, City Univ New York, MFA, 85. *Work:* Prudential Insurance Co Am; Parasol Press, Ltd; Ark Art Ctr, Little Rock; Mem Sloan-Kettering Cancer Ctr, New York. *Exhib:* Solo exhibs, Thomas Hunter Gallery, NY, 84 & Koussevitzky Gallery, Berkshire Community Coll, Pittsfield, Mass, 88, Wilmer Jennings Gallery, Kenkeleba, New York, 97, Sq One Gallery, New York, 2004; 1: One, Herter Art Gallery, Univ Mass, 97; Condeso-Lawler Gallery, 97; Katharina Rich Perlow Gallery, 98; Hillwood Art Mus, Long Island Univ, 2000; Yellow Bird Gallery, 2005; St Peter's Coll Art Gallery, 2007. *Teaching:* Asst prof art, Col Holy Cross, Worcester, Mass, 85-87; lectr visual arts, Princeton Univ, 90; adj lectr, Hunter Coll, New York, 87-91, adj asst prof, 91-2000; adj fac, Parsons Sch Design, 95-2001, asst prof, 2005-. *Awards:* Batchelor (Ford) Summer Fac Fel, Coll Holy Cross, Worcester, Mass, 86; Artist Grant, Artists Space, New York, 90; Fel, Nat Endowment Arts, 93-94. *Mem:* Am Abstract Artists (97-); Coll Art Asn (2000-). *Mailing Add:* 219 E Second St No 2D New York NY 10009

HILL, DRAPER
EDITORIAL CARTOONIST, HISTORIAN
b Boston, Mass, July 1, 1935. *Study:* Harvard Col, BA (magna cum laude), 57; Slade Sch Fine Arts, London, Eng, 60-63. *Work:* Wiggin Gallery, Boston Pub Libr; Univ Va; Lyndon B Johnson Libr, Austin; Nat Gallery Can, Ottawa; Detroit Inst Arts. *Exhib:* Int Salon de Caricature, Montreal, PQ, 66-86; Image of Am in Caricature and Cartoon, Amon Carter Mus, Ft Worth, 75; Am Presidency in Political Cartoons, Univ Art Mus, Berkeley, 75-76; retrospective, Political Asylum, Art Gallery of Windsor, Ontario, Can, 85-86; A Brush with Satire, Detroit Hist Mus, 96; and others. *Collection Arranged:* Cartoon and Caricature from Hogarth to Hoffnung, 62 & James Gillray 1756-1815, 67, Arts Coun Gt Brit; exhib on hist caricature, Boston Pub Libr, 64, 66 & 70. *Pos:* Ed cartoonist, Worcester Telegram, Mass, 64-71, Com Appeal, Memphis, Tenn, 71-76 & Detroit News, 76-; contrib ed, Eighteenth Century Life, Williamsburg, Va, 80-88; ed bd mem, Inks Cartoon & Comic Art Studios, Columbus, Ohio, 93-. *Teaching:* Instr life drawing, Sch Worcester Art Mus, 67-71; lectr, Amon Carter Mus, Ft Worth, Tex, 75 & Yale Ctr for British Art, New Haven, Conn, 84. *Awards:* Guggenheim Fel, 83-84; Thomas Nast Prize, Landau, Ger, 90. *Bibliog:* Lydel Sims (auth), article, Cartoonist Profiles, 3/75; Guy Northrop (auth), The Editorial Art of Draper Hill, Brooks Gallery, Memphis, 75; Alan Westin (auth), Getting Angry Six Times a Week, Beacon Press, Boston, 79. *Mem:* Asn Am Ed Cartoonists (vpres & dir, 70-75, pres, 75-76). *Collection:* Caricature and cartooning, with particular emphasis on eighteenth and nineteenth century English satire. *Publ:* Illingworth on Target, 70; co-illusr, The Decline and Fall of the Gibbon, 74; auth, The Satirical Etchings of James Gillray, 76; three collections of cartoons about Detroit's Mayor Coleman Young, 77, 82 & 86; auth, Cartoons and Caricatures, Vol III, Time-Life Encycl of Collectibles, 78; and others. *Mailing Add:* c/o Detroit News 615 W Lafayette Blvd Detroit MI 48226

HILL, ED(WARD) J See Manual, Ed Hill & Suzanne Bloom

HILL, GARY
VIDEO ARTIST
b Santa Monica, Calif, Apr 4, 1951. *Study:* Art Students League, Woodstock, 69. *Comn:* Video installation, Musee Nat d' Art Moderne, Centre Georges Pompidou, Paris, 88. *Exhib:* Solo exhibs, Mus Mod Art, NY, 80 & 90, Whitney Mus Am Art, NY, 83, Galerie des Archives, Paris, 90 & 91, Watari Mus Contemp Art, Tokyo, Japan, 92, Mus Mod Art, Oxford, Eng, 93, Mus Contemp Art, Los Angeles, 94, Mus Contemp Art, Chicago, 94, Inst Contemp Art, Philadelphia, 96, Whitney Mus Art, NY, 98-99, Language Willing, Boise Art Mus, Ariz State Univ Art Mus, Northwest Mus of Art and Cult, Art Gallery of Nova scotia, Can, Salt Lake Art Ctr, 2002, Kunstmuseum Wolfsburg, Germ, 2002 & 03, Barbara Gladstone Gallery, NY, 2007; retrospectives include Am Ctr, Paris, 83, Whitney Mus Am Art, NY, 86, St Gervais, Geneva, 2nd Seminar on Int Video, 87, ELAC Art Contemporain, Lyon, France, 88; Group exhibs, Biennial Exhibition, Whitney Mus Am Art, 91 & 93; Light Into Art, Contemp Arts Ctr, Cincinnati, Ohio, 94; Facts and Figures, Lannan Found, Los Angeles, 94; Multiplas Dimensoes, Centro Cultural de Belem, Lisbon, Portugal, 94; Beeld, Mus van Hedendaagse Kunst, Ghent, Belg, 94; Video Spaces, Mus Mod Art, NY, 95; Being and Time: The Emergence of Video Projection, Albright-Knox Art Gallery, Buffalo, 96; MOMA 2000, Mus of Modern Art, NY, 99-2000; Seeing Time: Selections from the Pamela and Richard Kramlich Collection of Media Art, San Francisco Mus of Art, 99-2000; The Am Century: Art & Cult Part II 1950-2000, Whitney Mus of Am Art, NY, 99-2000; Between Cinema and a Hard Place, Tate Modern, London, 2000; 46th Biennial Exhib: Media/Metaphor, The Corcoran Gallery of Art, Washington, 2000-01; and many others. *Pos:* Founder & dir, Open Studio Video, Tarrytown, NY, 77-79; artist-in-residence, Experimental Television Ctr, Binghamton, NY, 75-77, Portable Channel, Rochester, NY, 78, Sony Corp, Hon Atsugi, Japan, 85, Chicago Art Inst, 86, Calif Inst Arts, Valencia, 87 & Hopital Ephemere, Paris, 91, Capp St Project, San Francisco, 98. *Teaching:* Vis assoc prof, Ctr Media, State Univ NY, Buffalo, 79-80; vis prof art, Bard Col, Annandale-on-Hudson, NY, 83; art fac, Cornish Col Arts, Seattle, Wash, 85-92. *Awards:* First Prize, Int Asn Art Critics (AICA), 95; Artist Award for Distinguished Body of Work, Coll Art Asn, NY, 96; MacArthur Found Fel, 98; Joseph H Hazen Rome Prize Fel, Am Acad in Rome, 2000-01; Kurt Schwitters Award, 2000; Joseph H Hazen Rome Prize Fel, Am Acad, Rome, 2000 & 01, Skowhegan Medal for Video Installation, 2003, Artist Trust, wash State Art Comn Fel, 2003. *Bibliog:* Ruth Barter (auth), Doubletake, Art Monthly, 4/92; Bruce Barcott (auth), Gary Hill, New Art Examiner, 5/93; Deloris Tarzan Ament, Artist uses videos to tease viewers, Seattle Times, 2/22/93. *Publ:* Auth, Primarily Speaking, 1981-83, Whitney Mus Am Art, 83; Primarily Speaking, Communications, 88; And if the Right Hand did not Know What the Left Hand is Doing, Illuminating Video, 90; Unspeakable Images, Camera Obscura, 91. *Mailing Add:* Donald Young Gallery 224 S Michigan Ave Suite 266 Chicago IL 60604

HILL, JAMES BERRY
DEALER
b New York, NY, June 24, 1945. *Study:* Cornell Univ, AB, 67. *Collection Arranged:* Coggins Collection, Selections from the Robert P Coggins Collection of Am Painting, 76. *Pos:* Co-dir, Berry-Hill Galleries, Inc, 67-. *Awards:* Presidential Appointment (2 terms), Cult Property Adv Comt, Washington, DC. *Mem:* Nat Arts Club; Appraisers Asn Am; Artists Fel; Art Dealers Asn Am. *Specialty:* American art of the nineteenth and early twentieth century; China trade paintings. *Mailing Add:* Berry-Hill Galleries 11 E 70th St New York NY 10021

HILL, J(AMES) TOMILSON
COLLECTOR
b Westbury, New York, May 24, 1948. *Study:* Harvard College, BA, 1970; Harvard Bus Sch, MBA, 1973. *Pos:* Vpres, mergers and acquisitions, 1st Boston Corp, New York, 1973-79; sr vpres, Smith Barney, Harris Upham & co Inc, 1979-82; managing dir, dir mergers and acquisitions & co-head investment banking div, Shearson Lehman Brothers Inc, 1982-90; vchmn, co-chief exec officer, Lehman Brothers, 1990-93; bd dirs, Shearson Lehman Brothers Holdings, Inc, co-pres, co-chief operating officer, 1993; co-chief exec officer, Lehman Brothers, 1993, Shearson Lehman Brothers, 1993, SLB Asset Mgt, 1993; vchmn, mem investment and mgt comt, Blackstone Group, New York, 1993-; pres, chief exec officer, Blackstone Alternative Asset Mgt, 1995-; bd dirs, Allied Waste & Milton Acad Nightingale-Bamford Sch. *Awards:* Named one of 200 Top Collectors, ARTnews mag, 2003-13. *Mem:* Coun Foreign Relations (chmn investment subcom); Piping Rock Club; Meadow Brook Club; Links Club; River Club; Knickerbocker Club; Hirshhorn Mus and Sculpture Garden (chmn bd dirs); Lincoln Ctr Theater (vice chmn). *Collection:* Postwar American and European art; Renaissance bronzes. *Mailing Add:* Blackstone Group 345 Park Ave Ste New York NY 10154-0004

HILL, JANINE
COLLECTOR
Pos: Assoc Sullivan & Cromwell; vpres corp financial dept, Salomon Brothers; asst treas, Time Inc; deputy dir studies admin, Coun For Relations, New York City; bd advs, Duke Univ Nasher Mus Art; mem bd Am friends, Louvre. *Awards:* Named one of Top 200 Collectors, ARTnews mag, 2003-08. *Collection:* Postwar American and European art. *Mailing Add:* Coun For Relations Harold Pratt House 58 E 68th St New York NY 10021

HILL, JOHN CONNER
ART DEALER, DESIGNER
b Philadelphia, Pa, Feb 17, 1945. *Study:* Pratt Inst, BID, 68; Cosanti Found, Paradise Valley, Ariz, with Paolo Soleri, 72-76. *Exhib:* Ariz Photog Biennial, Phoenix Art Mus, 69; Southwest Biennial, Int Folk Art Mus, Santa Fe, NMex, 70, NMex Biennial, 71; Tucson Festival Crafts Exhib, Tucson Mus, Ariz, 77; Ariz Textile Exhib, Matthews Ctr, Ariz State Univ, Tempe, 77. *Pos:* Bronze sculpture casting, Cosanti Found, 72-76; publ-owner, Kokopelli Press, Phoenix, 76-90; Owner Antique Indian Art Gallery, Scottsdale, Ariz, 89-; adv bd mem, Ariz State Univ Art Mus, 2000-2006. *Teaching:* Instr art, Rough Rock Demonstration Sch, Navajo Nation, Ariz, 68-70. *Awards:* Third Award, Ariz Textile Exhib, Scottsdale Ctr for the Arts, 76. *Mem:* Charter mem Antique Tribal Art Dealers Asn. *Specialty:* Early American Indian art, American folk art. *Dealer:* John C Hill Antique Indian Art Gallery 6962 First Ave Scottsdale AZ 85251. *Mailing Add:* 6962 E First Ave Scottsdale AZ 85251

HILL, MEGAN LLOYD See Romero, Megan H

HILL, PATRICK
SCULPTOR
b Royal Oak, Michigan, 1972. *Study:* Otis Coll Art & Design, Los Angeles, MFA, 2000. *Work:* Whitney Mus Am Art, New York. *Exhib:* Solo exhibs include David Kordansky Gallery, Los Angeles, 2004, Shane Campbell Gallery, Chicago, 2005, Golden Syrup Reliance, London, 2006, Bortolami, New York, 2007; group exhibs include Tapestry From An Asteroid, David Kordansky Gallery, Los Angeles, 2004; LA, Lucas Schoormans Gallery, New York, 2005; Alpha Flight II, John Connelly Presents (JCP), New York, 2005; Split, The Approach, London, 2005; Ask the Dust, D'Amelio Terras, New York, 2005; Symmetry, MAK Ctr Art & Archit, W Hollywood, 2006; Symmetry, Museum für angewandte Kunst (MAK), Vienna, 2006; H/Q/S, Galerie Michael Hall, Vienna, 2006; Cloudbreak, Hiromi Yoshii Gallery, Tokyo, 2006; Exit Music (for a Film), ANDREAS GRIMM - München, Munich, 2007. *Dealer:* Bortolami 510 W 25th St New York NY 10001; Shane Campbell Gallery 1431 W Chicago Ave Chicago IL 60622; David Kordansky Gallery 510 Bernard St Los Angeles CA 90012; The Approach Approach Rd London England E2 9LY; Galerie Michael Hall Diehlgasse 51 1 Stock 1050 Vienna Austria

HILL, PETER
PAINTER, EDUCATOR
b Detroit, Mich, Nov 29, 1933. *Study:* Albion Col, AB, 56; Cranbrook Acad Art, Bloomfield Hills, Mich, MFA, 58. *Work:* Joslyn Art Mus, Omaha, Nebr; Sheldon Mem Gallery, Lincoln, Nebr; Springfield Art Mus, Mo; Sioux City Art Ctr, Iowa; Spiva Art Gallery, Joplin, Mo. *Exhib:* Springfield Art Mus Ann, Mo, 70 & 74; Midwest Biennial, Joslyn Art Mus, 72, 74, 78, 82 & 84; Colo-Nebr Exchange Exhib, Denver, 73; Solo exhib, Sheldon Mem Art Gallery, Lincoln, Nebr, 78; Am Art, Pillsbury Co, Minneapolis, 81; Watercolor Now, Springfield Art Mus, Mo, 87; and others. *Teaching:* From instr to chmn dept, Univ Nebr, Omaha, 58-99. *Awards:* Ann Exhib Purchase Awards, Springfield Art Mus, 63 & 74; Best Painting, Joslyn Mus, 78 & 82; Purchase Award, Nat Competitive Exhib, Peru State Col, Nebr, 89. *Mem:* Watercolor USA Honor Soc. *Media:* Acrylic, Oil, Watercolor. *Dealer:* Adam Whitney Gallery Omaha NE 68102; Haydon Art Gallery Lincoln NE 68508. *Mailing Add:* 11734 Shirley St Omaha NE 68144-2914

HILL, ROBYN LESLEY
PAINTER, DESIGNER
b Sydney, New South Wales, Australia, Apr 28, 1942. *Study:* Nat Art Sch, Sydney, Australia, ASTC, 62; studied with Edward Betts, Nita Engle & Fred Leach in USA. *Work:* Key West Mus, Fla; Springfield Mus Art, Utah; Palm Springs Desert Mus, Calif; Nat Arts Club, New York; Canton Art Inst, Ohio; Massillon Mus Invitational, Ohio. *Exhib:* Am Watercolor Soc Traveling Exhib, Salmagundi Club, New York; Nat Watercolor Soc Traveling Exhib, Palm Springs Desert Mus, Calif; Catherine Lorillard Wolfe Nat Exhib, Nat Arts Club, New York; Watercolor USA, Springfield Art Mus, Mo; solo exhib, Moments in Nature, Wagner Gallery, Sydney, Australia; Massilon Mus Invitational, Ohio, 87; Adirondacks Nat Show, New York. *Pos:* Art dir, Am Greetings, (1st woman in marketing) Cleveland; sr prog dir, Those Characters from Cleveland, Ohio. *Teaching:* Art mistress, Sydney Church of Eng Girls Grammar Sch, Redlands, Sydney, Australia, 62-65. *Awards:* Humana Award, Blue Grass Biennial, Humana Inc; Southern Ohio Bank Award, Ohio Watercolor Soc; Springfield Art Mus

Award, Watercolor USA. *Mem:* Watercolor USA; Nat Watercolor Soc; Ohio Watercolor Soc; N Coast Collage Soc; Watercolor Hon Soc; Am Watercolor Soc. *Media:* Watercolor, Watermedia. *Publ:* Contribr, The Best of Flower Painting, N Light Bks; article, Palette Talk, No 75, Grumbacher; Artists directory, Portfolio 83, Cleveland, Ohio

HILLER, BETTY R
CONSULTANT, APPRAISER
b El Paso, Tex, Sept 25, 1925. *Study:* Univ Tex, El Paso; Univ NMex; Univ Southern Calif, BFA, 46; Univ Nebr, Omaha; Creighton Univ. *Collection Arranged:* Arthur Andersen Co, Omaha, Nebr; Brody Coll African Art, Univ Nebr, Omaha, 73; Robert Nelson Prints; Warrington Colescott Prints, 70's; and others. *Pos:* Ed arts, Spectrum Page, Sun Newspaper, 68-69; gallery dir, Creighton Univ, Omaha, 68-70; original developer, Children's Mus of Omaha, 75, first mus pres, 77-78; gallery dir, Univ Nebr, Omaha, 76, dir & mgr gallery, 76-78. *Awards:* Special Achievement Award, Am Soc Appraisers, 93. *Bibliog:* Beth Weiver (auth), Rancho Bernardo J; Jimmy Thornton (auth), San Diego Union; Bernardo News, 93. *Mem:* Am Soc Appraisers (retired). *Interests:* 19th, 20th Century Am and European Art; Art travel and art appraising. *Collection:* Pre Columbian, Contemp and Mod Am and European

HILLER, SUSAN
CONCEPTUAL ARTIST
b Tallahassee, FL, Mar 7, 1940. *Study:* Smith Coll, BA, 1961; Tulane Univ, MA, 1965; Dartington Coll Arts, Eng, Hon Fel, 1998. *Exhib:* Solo exhibs incl Gallery House, London, 1973, Royal Coll Art Gallery, London, 1974, Gardner Ctr for Arts, Univ Sussex, 1975, Serpentine Gallery, London, 1976, Mus Mod Art, Oxford, 1978, Spacex, Exeter, 1980, Gimpel Fils, London, 1980, 1982, 1983, 1984, 1994, 1995, Ikon Gallery, Birmingham, 1981, Eye Level Gallery, Halifax, Nova Scotia, 1982, Orchard Gallery, Londonderry, Northern Ireland, 1984, Tate Gallery, London, 1985, Inst Contemp Art, London, 1986, Pat Hearn Gallery, New York, 1987, 1989, 1991, Univ Art Mus, Calif State Univ, 1988, Third Eye Ctr, Glasgow, Scotland, 1990, Matt's Gallery, London, 1991, Tom Solomon's Garage Gallery, Los Angeles, 1992, Sigmund Freud Mus, London, 1994, Dia Ctr for Arts, NY, 1996, Foksal Gallery, Warsaw, 1997, Ctr Contemp Photog, Melbourne, Australia, 1998, Inst Contemp Art, Philadelphia, 1998, Tensta Konshalle, Stockholm, 1999, Gagosian Gallery, NY, 2001, Galerie Volker Diehl, Berlin, 2002, Baltic Ctr Contemp Art, Gateshead, England, 2004, Kunsthalle Basel, 2005, Castello di Rivoli, Turin, 2006, Moderan Museet, Stockholm, 2007; group exhibs incl Gallery House, London, 1973; Artists Meeting Place Gallery, London, 1974; British Coun, London, 1975; Univ Gallery, Leeds, Eng, 1976; Mus Mod Art, New York, 1977, 1999; Hayward Gallery, London, 1978, 1980; Nat Gallery Can, Ottawa, 1981; Sydney Biennal, 1982, 1996, 2002; Winchester Gallery, Eng, 1983; Gimpel Fils, 1984, 2003; Irish Biannual Exhib of Living Art, Hopstore, Dublin, 1985; Tate Gallery, London, 1985, 1989, 1990, 1995, 1997, 2001, 2002, 2004; Victoria Miro Gallery, London, 1986; Pyramids Art Ctr, New York, 1987; Leeds City Mus and Art Gallery, Eng, 1988; Pat Hearn Gallery, New York, 1989; Harris Mus & Art Gallery, Preston, Eng, 1989; Mus Mod Art, Oxford, 1990, 1994; Tokyo Met Mus Photog, 1991; Musee de la Ferme Buisson, Paris, 1993; Anthony d'Offay Gallery, London, 1996; Mus Contemp Art, Los Angeles, 1998, 2007; Bienale de Habana, Cuba, 2000; Tokyo Int Forum, 2003; Andrea Rosen Gallery, New York, 2005; Basle Art Fair, 2006; Givon Gallery, Tel Aviv, 2007. *Teaching:* Slade Sch Art, London, 1982-90; prof fine art, Sch Art & Design, Univ Ulster, Belfast, 1991-97; vis prof, Univ Calif, Los Angeles, currently; prof contemp art, Univ Newcastle, 1998-2004. *Awards:* Gulbenkenian Found Visual Artist's Award, 1976 & 1977; Nat Endowment Arts, 1982; Guggenheim Fel, 1998. *Mailing Add:* 83 Loudon Rd London United Kingdom NW8 ODL

HILLIS, RICHARD K
PAINTER, PRINTMAKER
b Cincinnati, Ohio, Oct 3, 1936. *Study:* Ohio Univ, BFA, 60, MFA, 62, Carnegie Mellon Univ, DA (Dr Arts), 73, San Francisco Art Inst, 81-83; Burne Hogart Anat Workshop, 93; Burt Silverman Master Class, 94; Portrait Inst Am, New York, 96; David Leffel Master Class, 99; Raymond Kinstler Master Class, 2002. *Work:* Muscarelle Mus Art, Coll William & Mary, Williamsburg, Va; Hoyt Inst Fine Arts, New Castle, Pa; Ark Art Ctr, Little Rock; Glendale Publ Libr, Ariz; Southwest Airlines; Gammage & Burnham Law Firm, Phoenix, Ariz. *Comn:* Comn numerous portraits. *Exhib:* 49th Ann Midyear Exhib, Butler Inst Am Art, Youngstown, Ohio, 84; Art USA Exhib, Western Colo Ctr Arts, Grand Junction, 86; 64th April Salon, Springville Art Mus, Utah, 88; Am Drawing Biennial, Muscarelle Mus Art, Va, 88; Los Angeles Nat Watercolor Exhib, 91; 35th Chataqua Nat, 92; West Valley Art Mus, Sun City, Ariz, 99; Phoenix Coll, 2000; and others. *Pos:* Founder, chair Peoria Arts Comn, 90. *Teaching:* Asst prof art, Kent State Univ, Ohio, 69-73; assoc prof, Tex Tech Univ, Lubbock, 73-74; prof, Glendale Coll, Ariz, 82-2003, prof emer, 2003-. *Awards:* Cash Award 11th Ann Nat Realist Exhib, 99; Best of Show 37th Ann Glendale Art Exhib, 2000; First Prize Best of Show, Ariz State Fair Art Exhib, 2002; Best of Show, Ariz State Fair, 2003; Best of Show, Peoria Art Exhib, 2005. *Mem:* Coll Art Asn Am; Am Asn Univ Professors. *Media:* Oil. *Interests:* etching & tennis. *Publ:* Auth, Line Shape & Contrast, Sch Arts Mag, 88; Hooked on Colored Pencils, Sch Arts, 91; Drawing on Gray Toned Paper, Sch Arts, 95; Shape Self Esteem & the Self Portrait, Sch Arts, 96; Accountability in Art, Sch Arts, 98; Best of Sketching & Drawing, 98; A Simple Motif for Exploration of Line, Weight & Value, Sch Arts, 2001. *Mailing Add:* 6741 W Cholla Peoria AZ 85345

HILLMAN, ARTHUR STANLEY
GRAPHIC ARTIST, EDUCATOR
b Brooklyn, NY, Feb 21, 1945. *Study:* Philadelphia Coll Art, with Jerome Kaplan & Benton Spruance, BFA; Univ Mass, Amherst, MFA. *Work:* Libr Congress, Washington, DC; Northern Ill Univ. *Exhib:* Prize Winning Am Prints, 69 & 4th Int Miniature Print Exhib, 71, Pratt Graphics Ctr, NY; Solo exhibs, Philadelphia Art Alliance, 70, Alfred Univ, Suny, 77, Simon's Rock Coll, 83-84, 90, 93, 95, 97, 2000, 2002 & 2005; Williams Coll Mus Art, 76; 29th Nat Print Exhib, Hunterdon Art Ctr, NJ, 85; 16th Nat Works on Paper, Minot State Col, NDak, 86; Northern Nat, Nicolet Col, 89; Group exhibs, Welles Gallery, 94, Spazi Contemp Art, 94 & 96, Berkshire Community Col, 97, Albany Ctr Galleries, 99, The Berkshire Mus, 2005. *Teaching:* Instr & asst prof printmaking & chmn dept, Mass Col Art, Boston, 68-74; prof printmaking, design & photog, Simon's Rock Col, Great Barrington, Mass, 74-, chmn arts div, 81-84 & 89-92, chmn visual arts prog, 87-89. *Awards:* Univ Mass Fel, 67; Pennell Fund Purchase Award, Libr Cong, 69; Northern Ill Univ Purchase Award, 70. *Mem:* Coll Art Asn Am; Philadelphia Print Club; Photog Resource Ctr, Boston Univ. *Media:* Digital photography. *Collection:* Work in collections of library of congress; Northern Illinois Univ; Philadelphia Coll Art; Simmons Col, Boston Mass; Stanislaus State Col, Turlock, Calif

HILLS, PATRICIA
HISTORIAN, CURATOR
b Baraboo, Wis, Jan 31, 1936. *Study:* Stanford Univ, BA, 57; Hunter Col, City Univ New York, MA, 68; NY Univ Inst Fine Arts, PhD, 73. *Collection Arranged:* Eastman Johnson (auth, catalog), Clarkson-Potter, 72; The Am Frontier: Images and Myths (auth, catalog), 73; The Painter's Am: Rural and Urban Life, 1810-1910 (auth, catalog), Praeger, 74; Turn-of-the-Century Am: Paintings, Graphics, Photographs (auth, catalog), 77 & The Figurative Tradition and the Whitney Mus (coauth, catalog), 80, Whitney Mus Art; John Singer Sargent (cur, auth, catalog), Abrams, 86; Social Concern and Urban Realism: Am Painting of the 1930s (auth, catalog), Boston Univ Art Gallery, 83; Eastman Johnson: Painting Am (co-auth, catalog), Rizzoli, 99; Sycopated Rhythms: 20th Centruy African Am Art from the George & Joyce Wein Collection (coauth, catalog), Boston Univ Art Gallery, 2005. *Pos:* Assoc cur, Whitney Mus Am Art, 72-74, adj cur, 74-87; Dir, Boston Univ Art Gallery, 80-89. *Teaching:* Assoc prof, York Col, City Univ New York, 74-78; assoc prof Am painting, Boston Univ, 78-88, prof, 88-. *Awards:* Fel, Guggenheim, 82 & Nat Endowment Humanities, 95; Mid-Career Award, Women's Caucus for Art, 87; W E B DuBois Inst, Harvard Univ, 91-92 & 2006-07; Fel, Gilder Lehrman Inst of Am Hist, 2005; Fel, Smithsonian Am Art Mus, 2005-06; Fel, Georgia O'Keeffe Mus Research Ctr, 2006; Award for Distinguished Teaching in Art History, Coll Art Asn, 2011. *Mem:* Coll Art Asn; Women's Caucus for Art; Am Studies Asn; AAM. *Res:* American painting from Civil War to present, particularly figurative painting; art & politics; African-American art. *Publ:* Alice Neel, Abrams, 83; Stuart Davis, Abrams, 95; Modern Art in the USA: Issues and Controversies of the 20th Century, Prentice Hall, 2001; May Stevens, Pomegranate, 2005; Painting Harlem Modern: The Art of Jacob Lawrence, Univ Calif Press, 2009. *Mailing Add:* Dept Art Hist Boston Univ 725 Commonwealth Ave Boston MA 02215

HILSON, DOUGLAS
PAINTER, EDUCATOR
b Flint, Mich, Dec 7, 1941. *Study:* Cranbrook Acad Art, Bloomfield Hills, Mich, BFA; Univ Wash, MFA. *Work:* Indianapolis Mus Art; Ill Art Mus, Springfield, DeWaters Art Inst, Flint, Mich; Decatur Art Mus, Ill; Western Mich Univ Art Mus, Kalamazoo. *Comn:* 5 works reproduced for 298 rooms for Charles Hotel, Cambridge, Mass, 2006. *Exhib:* Solo exhibs, Bernice Steinbaum Gallery, NY, 83 & 85, Donahue/Sosinski Gallery, NY, 99, 206 drawings, Del Art Ctr, NY, 2005; New Still Life, Borgenicht Gallery, NY, 90; Artist's Space, New York City, 92-; Rosenberg Gallery, Hempstead, NY, 96; 10 Yr Retrospective, Bradford Coll, Mass, 97-98; Broadway Suites, New York, 2010. *Pos:* Chair, Dept Fine Arts, Art Hist, & Grad Humanities, Hofstra Univ, Hempstead, NY; advisory bd, Look & Listen Festival, New York, 2002- & Hofstra Univ Mus. *Teaching:* Prof painting & dir grad painting prog, Univ Ill, Champaign, 65-; vis prof, Pratt Inst, 81-; prof art, Hofstra Univ, 86-. *Awards:* Ctr Advanced Study, 73-74; First Prize, Nat Works Art on Paper, 76; Purchase Award, 29th Ill Invitational, Ill Art Mus Permanent Collection, 76. *Bibliog:* Peter Plagens (auth), catalog essay. *Media:* Oil, Acrylic. *Specialty:* paintings, drawings. *Dealer:* Stephen Rosenberg Fine Arts. *Mailing Add:* 161 Anawanda Lake Rd Callicoon Center NY 12724

HILTY, THOMAS R
GRAPHIC ARTIST, PAINTER
b Gary, Ind, May 29, 1943. *Study:* Ind Univ; Western State Col, Colo, BFA, 65; Univ NMex; Bowling Green State Univ, MFA, 68. *Work:* Dayton Art Inst, Ohio; Toledo Mus Art, Ohio; Omni Marketing Inc, Chicago; IBM Corp; Toledo Trust Corp. *Comn:* Frames of Reference, Boston New TV Workshop, 79-80; Musical Arts Ctr, Bowling Green State Univ, 80; J Barrett Galleries, Toledo, 82; R Valicenti Design, Chicago, 83; Riverside Hosp, Toledo, 86. *Exhib:* Ankrum Gallery, Los Angeles, 83; US Nat Fine Arts Competition & Int Exhib, 84; 20th Cent Am Drawing, Chicago, 84; Rosenthal Gallery, Chicago, 84 & 86; and others. *Pos:* Dir, Sch Art, Bowling Green State Univ, 86-94; bd dir, Nat Asn Schs Art & Design, 93-95 & Studio Art Ctrs Int, 93-. *Teaching:* Prof art, drawing & painting, Bowling Green State Univ, 68-. *Awards:* Purchase Awards, All Ohio Exhib, Ohio Arts Coun, 72, All Ohio Exhib, Dayton Art Inst, 76, 80 & 81 & Toledo Area Artists Exhib, Toledo Mus, 80, 81, 82, 84 & 85. *Bibliog:* Louise Bruner (auth), Thomas Hilty, Am Artist, 80. *Mem:* Nat Asn Schs Art & Design. *Media:* Graphite, Charcoal; Pastels, Conte. *Publ:* Auth, article, Art News, 6/83. *Dealer:* Miller Gallery 2715 Erie Ave Cincinnati OH; Robert L Kidd Assoc Inc 107 Townsend St Birmingham MI 48011. *Mailing Add:* 21 Parkwood Dr Bowling Green OH 43402-3644

HIMMELFARB, JOHN DAVID
PAINTER, SCULPTOR
b Chicago, Ill, June 3, 1946. *Study:* Harvard Univ, BA, 68, MAT, 70. *Work:* Art Inst Chicago; Nat Mus Am Art, Smithsonian Inst, Washington, DC; Musee Nat d'Art Moderne Centre George Pompidou, Paris, France; The British Mus, London; Mus Mod Art, New York. *Comn:* Ceramic tile mural, Omaha Pub Schs, Nebr, 92 & Univ of Nebr, Lincoln, 2003; ceramic tile mural, Chicago Transit, Author, 2004; painting, Delta Airlines Terminal Logan Boston, 2005; Bucktown Wicker Park Libr, Chicago, 2007. *Exhib:* Works on Paper, 78, Prizewinners Revisited, 79, Prints and Multiples, 81

& 81st Chicago and Vicinity Show, 85, Art Inst Chicago; Am Drawings in Black and White: 1970-1980, 80 & Monumental Drawings: 20 Contemp Americans, 86, Brooklyn Mus, New York; solo exhibs, Kalamazoo Inst Arts, 89, Huntington Mus Art, WVa, 90, Chicago Cult Ctr, Ill, 96 & Ctr Contemp Art (COLA), 2001; Large Drawings & Objects, Ark Art Ctr, 96; Jean Albano Gallery, Chicago, 96, 98, 2000, 2002 & 2005; Second Sight: Printmaking in Chicago 1935-95, Block Gallery, Northwestern Univ, Evanston, Ill, 96; Cultured Pearl, Metrop Mus Seoul, Korea, 96; Chgo Cultural Ctr, 2011; and others. *Pos:* Artist. *Teaching:* Vis artist, New Master Workshop, Huntington, Mus Art, WVa, 90, Miami Univ, Oxford, Ohio, 90, Kalamazoo Inst Art, 90, Ind Univ, Northwest, Gary, 92, & Herron Sch of Art, 2012. *Awards:* Nat Endowment Arts, 82 & 85; Chicago Artist Abroad, 89; Ill Arts Coun, 86 & 2003; Pollock, Krasner, 86 & 2002. *Bibliog:* Alan Artner (auth), Galleries, Chicago Tribune, 1/25/96; Barbara Buchholz (auth), Gallery Scene, Chicago Tribune, 1/23/96 & 9/27/96; John Brunetti (auth), John Himmelfarb at Jean Albano Gallery (rev), New Art Examiner, 1/97; Alan Artner (auth) Galleries, Chicago Tribune 2/25/2005; Lisa Stein (auth), Art Galleries Art Scene John Himmelfarb, One Man renaissance, Chicago Tribune, 3/11/2005; Janet Farber (auth), Keep on Truckin, The Reader, Omaha, Nebr, 2012; Edward M Gomez (auth), Still Abstract After All These Years, Arts and Antiques, 2013. *Mem:* Chicago Artist Coalition; Arts Club Chicago. *Media:* Acrylic. *Publ:* The Prints of John Himmelfarb, Hudson Hills Press, 2006. *Dealer:* Luise Ross Gallery 511 W 25th St #307 New York NY 10001. *Mailing Add:* 2400 S Oakley 2R Chicago IL 60608

HINDES, CHUCK (CHARLES) AUSTIN
CERAMIST, EDUCATOR

b Muskegon, Mich, May 30, 1942. *Study:* Univ Ill, Urbana-Champaign, BFA (crafts), 66; RI Sch Design, MFA (ceramics), 68. *Work:* St Louis Mus Art; Everson Mus Art. *Exhib:* Teapots, De Pauw Univ, Greencastle, Ind, 91; Redefining Clay, St Louis, Mo, 91; Contemp Views: Teapots, Pro-Art Gallery, St Louis, Mo, 92; Teapot Exhibition, Octagon Art Ctr, Ames, 92; One on One, group exhib, Northwest Craft Ctr, Seattle, Wash, 92; and others. *Teaching:* Instr ceramics, Univ Fla, Gainesville, 69-72; adj prof, RI Sch Design, 72-73; from asst prof to prof, Univ Iowa, Iowa City, from 1973, prof emeritus, currently. *Awards:* Purchase Award, Nat Exhib Ceramic Sculpture & Jewelry, Brigham Young Univ, 76; First Prize Ceramics, 32nd Ann Iowa Artists Exhib, Des Moines Art Ctr, 80; Hon Mention Int Ceramics Festival, Mino, Japan; Hon Mention, The Dripless Spout: Innovative Teapots, Arrowmont Sch, 88. *Mem:* Nat Coun Educ Ceramic Arts. *Publ:* Auth, Saggar firing, Studio Potter, 79. *Mailing Add:* PO Box 564 Coupeville WA 98239

HINES, JESSICA
PHOTOGRAPHER

b St Louis, Mo, Nov 4, 1958. *Study:* Washington Univ, St Louis, BFA (photog), 82; Univ Ill, Champaign-Urbana, MFA (photog), 84. *Work:* Erie Art Mus, Pa; State of Ga; numerous pvt collections. *Exhib:* Solo exhib, Women's Studio Workshop-Ctr Visual Arts, NY, 86, Ark State Univ Gallery, Jonesboro, 88, Exhib A Gallery, Savannah Sch Art & Design, Ga, 89, Ga Coun Arts, Carriage Works Gallery, Atlanta, 93, Hollins Col, Roanoke, Va, 95, Lamar Dodd Gallery, Univ Ga, Athens, 96 & Sch Art & Archit, La Tech Univ, Rustin, 97; Artists in Georgia, Nexus Contemp Art Ctr, Winston-Salem, NC, 88; National Exposures '90: A National Exhibition of Photog, Winston-Salem, NC, 90; Photonominal '91 (auth catalog), Forum Gallery, Jamestown Community Col, NY, 91; Women Viewing Women, Rockford Col, Ill, 91; New Visions Gallery Contemp Art, Atlanta, Ga, 92; Crealde Sch Art Invitational, Winter Park, Fla, 94; Georgia State Capitol: Selections from the State Art Collections, Governor's Off, Atlanta, 94; At Issue: Our Environment, An Exhib of Contemp Landscapes, San Giuseppe Art Gallery, Coll Mount St Joseph, Cincinnati, 95; SE Art Exhib, Savannah, Ga, 95; Toledo Friends Photog Nat Photo Exhib, Ctr Visual Arts, Univ Toledo, 95; One Light, Three Visions, Rocky Mt Ctr Arts, Wilson, NC, 96; Art & Science: A National Exhibition of Artworks Inspired by the Sciences, Mariobe Gallery, NJ, 97; Derivatives of the Landscape, Athena Gallery, Savannah, Ga, 98; Photog, A Multi Vision Art, Assoc Artists, Sawtooth Ctr, Winston-Salem, NC, 99; Photon Rangers, Eight Southeastern Photographers, Art Coun Wilson, NC, 99. *Teaching:* Instr photog, Univ Ill, Champaign-Urbana, 83-84; prof art, Ga Southern Univ, 84-. *Awards:* Alternative Media Excellence Award, Nat Exposures '90, Sawtooth Galleries, Asn Artists, Winston-Salem, NC, 90; Individual Artist's Grant, Spirit of Place, Ga Coun Arts, 92; Am Coun Grant, Universidade Federal de Pernambuco, Brazil, 97. *Mem:* Soc Photog Educ; Coll Art Asn. *Mailing Add:* 108 Nottingham Tr Statesboro GA 30458-4265

HINMAN, CHARLES B
PAINTER, EDUCATOR

b Syracuse, NY, Dec 29, 1932. *Study:* Syracuse Univ, BFA, 1955; Art Students League, with Morris Kantor. *Work:* Mus Mod Art, NY; Whitney Mus Am Art, NY; Los Angeles Co Mus; Hirshhorn Mus, Smithsonian Inst, Washington; Mus Mod Art, Nagaoka, Japan; Louisiana Mus, Humlebaek, Denmark; Musee' des Beaux Arts de l'Ontario, Toronto, Ontario, Can; Detroit Inst Art, Mich; Chase Manhattan Bank, NY; The Rockefeller Collection, NY; Tel Aviv Mus, Israel; Shearson Co, NY; Denver Mus, Co; Blanton Mus, Austin, Tex; and others. *Comn:* Red Vista, 3-D painting, Continental Group, Stamford, Conn, 1981; Excelsior, 3-D painting, Southeast Bank, Miami, Fla, 1983; Adretto, 3-D painting, Europ Am Bank, Huntington, NY, 1985; Aviary, suspended 3-D painting, Greenway Plaza, Hempstead, NY, 1986; Zephyr, stainless steel sculpture, Burton Resnick, NY, 1987; pvt collections include Harry Abrams, Larry Aldrich, Armand & Celest Bartos, Selig Burrows, Elaine Dannheiser, Max & Marjorie Fisher, Constantine& Heidi Goulandris, Peter & Mary Kalikow, Sydney & Frances Lewis, SI Newhouse, John & Kimiko Powers, Meshulam Riklis, Nelson & Happy Rockefeller, Eugene Schwartz, Burton, Emily Tremaine, Frank Stella & Robert Indiana. *Exhib:* Smithsonian Inst, Washington, 1968; Solo exhibs, Richard Feigen Gallery, NY, 1964, 1966, Chicago, 1966, Irving Galleries, Milwaukee, 1977, Palm Beach, 1977-1987, Donald Morris Gallery, Birmingham, Mich, 1979, Douglas Drake Gallery, NY, 1990, 1994; Honolulu Acad Arts, Hawaii, 1968; Mus Mod Art, NY, 1969; Whitney Mus Am Art, NY, 1969; Aldrich Mus Contemp Art, Ridgefield, Conn, 1971, 1975, 1977; Mus Art, Ft Lauderdale, Fla, 1980-1981; Hickory Mus, NC, 1990-1992; Douglas Drake Gallery, NY, 1990-1994; Ga Mus Art, 1994; Bergen Co Mus, NJ, 1997; Boca Raton Mus Art, Fla, 2001; Butler Inst Am Art, Youngstown, OH, 2006-2008, 2011-2012; David Richard Gallery, Santa Fe, NMex, 2011, 2012; Marc Straus Gallery, NY, 2012-; Untitled, Miami-Basel, 2012; Marc Straus, aPulse, NY, 2013. *Pos:* Artist-in-residence, Aspen Inst, Colo, 1966. *Teaching:* Instr painting, Cornell Univ, New York, 1967-1968, Syracuse Univ, 1971, Pratt Inst, Brooklyn, 1975, Sch Visual Arts, New York, 1976, Cooper Union, New York, currently; vis prof, Princeton Univ, NJ, 1994, 1996; Lamar Dodd Distinguished prof art, Univ Ga, Athens, Ga, 1991-1994; Art Students League, NY, 1995-. *Awards:* Int Prize Exhib, Torcuato di Tella, Buenos Aires, 1957; First Prize, Mus Contemp Art, Nagoaka, Japan, 1965; Grant, Nat Endowment Arts, 1980; Adolph & Esther Gottlieb Found Grant, 1996; Lee Krasner Award, 2007; Pollock-Krasner Found Grant, 2007-09; Guggenheim Fel, 2012. *Bibliog:* Richard Pincus-Whitten (auth), Exhibition at Feigen, Art Forum, 3/1996; Henry Geldzahler (auth), Charles Hinman, Metrop Mus Art Mag, 1970; Donald Kuspit (auth), The Cunning of Unreason: Charles Hinman's Absurdist Constructions, Idiosyncratic Identities, Cambridge Univ Press, 1996; Carter Ratcliff (auth), Robert Morgan (auth), Meteorshowers, Boca Raton Mus Catalog, 2001; Claudine Humblet (auth), La Nouvelle Abstraction Americaine (in French), 2005; La Nouvelle Abstraction Americaine (in English), 2007; Michael Amy (auth), Charles Hinman at Wooster Arts Space, Art in Am, 12/2005; Robert Morgan (auth), New Work, Brooklyn Rail, 2012. *Mem:* Coll Art Asn; Am Abstr Artists. *Media:* Acrylic, Pigment on Fabric; Wood. *Res:* Three Dimensional Painting. *Dealer:* Studio 231A Bowery #5 New York NY 10002; Marc Strauss 109 Grand St New York NY 10002. *Mailing Add:* 231A Bowery #5 New York NY 10002

HINSON, TOM EVERETT
CURATOR, HISTORIAN

b Henderson, Tex, Oct 25, 1944. *Study:* Univ Tex, Austin, BA (art hist), BS (archit studies); Case Western Reserve Univ, Cleveland, Ohio, MA (art hist). *Pos:* Mus fel, Toledo Mus Art, Ohio, 70-71; asst cur, Dept Mod Art, Cleveland Mus Art, Ohio, 73-77, assoc cur, 78-81, cur contemp art, 82- & cur contemp art & photog, 96-. *Mem:* Am Asn Mus. *Res:* Contemporary and modern art; 19th and 20th century photography; 20th century architecture. *Publ:* Contribr exhib catalogs, Cleveland Mus Art, 91-98. *Mailing Add:* c/o Cleveland Mus of Art 11150 E Blvd Cleveland OH 44106

HIRSCH, GILAH YELIN
PAINTER, WRITER

b Montreal, Que, Aug 24, 1944. *Study:* McGill Univ; Hebrew Univ; Sir George Williams Univ; Boston Univ; San Francisco State Univ; Univ Calif, Berkeley, BA, 67; Univ Calif, Los Angeles, MFA, 70. *Work:* Calif State Univ & Greenberg & Glusken, Los Angeles; City of Santa Monica Art Bank, Calif; Nat Endowment Arts, Washington; Charles Wustum Mus Fine Arts, Racine, Wis; Tyrone Guthrie Ctr, Annamagkerrig, Ireland; Bank of America, UCLA; Cedar Silver Medical Arts collection. *Exhib:* Whitney Mus Am Art, NY, 72; Santa Monica Libr, 94; Walton Art Ctr, Fayetteville, Ark, 94; Univ Judaism, La, 95; Barnsdall Munic Gallery, Los Angeles, 95; Irvine Fine Arts Ctr, 96; Claremont Sch Theology, Kresge Chapel, 97. *Collection Arranged:* Metamagic (auth, catalog), Calif State Univ, Dominguez Hills, 78. *Pos:* chair art dept, Calif State Univ, Dominguez Hills. *Teaching:* Prof art, Calif State Univ, Dominguez Hills, 73-; fac tutors, Int Col, 80-. *Awards:* Award, Banff Ctr for the Arts, 85; Nat Endowment Arts Fel, 85; Rockefeller Bellagio Grant, Italy, 92; and others. *Bibliog:* Articles in over 100 international newspapers, journals & magazines. *Mem:* Artists Equity. *Media:* Oil, Acrylic. *Publ:* Auth, Joan of art seminars, Artweek, 72; Emily Carr, Feminist Art J, 76; The Pararational, Visionary and Mystical Perspective, Calif State Univ, Dominguez Hills, 77; Emily Carr, Women's Studies, 78; Persistence of time and memory: The art of Ruth Weisberg, Woman's Art J, winter 85; The illusion of potential: The delusion of the creative person in relationships, The Quest, autumn 92; Bringing the Himalayas Home, Salimar Mag, 99; Art & Healing, 99. *Mailing Add:* Dept Art Calif State Univ Dominguez Hills 1000 E Victoria Ave Carson CA 90747

HIRSCHEL, ANTHONY G
MUSEUM DIRECTOR

Study: Univ Mich, BA (European Hist & Art, summa cum laude); Yale Univ, MA (Art Hist) & MPhil (Art Hist); Mus Mgt Inst/Getty Leadership Inst, grad. *Pos:* Asst to dir, Yale Univ Art Gallery, 1987-91, asst dir, 1991; dir, Bayly Art Mus, Univ Va, 1991-97, Michael C Carlos Mus, Emory Univ, 1997-2001; dir & CEO, Indianapolis Mus Art, 2001-04; Dana Feitler dir, David & Alfred Smart Mus Art, Univ Chicago, 2005-. *Mem:* Asn Art Mus Dirs (bd trustees, 2002-04); Am Fedn Arts (bd trustees, 1999-). *Mailing Add:* Smart Mus Art Univ Chicago 5550 S Greenwood Ave Chicago IL 60637

HIRSCHHORN, THOMAS
SCULPTOR

b Bern, Switzerland, 1957. *Study:* Schule fur Gestaltung, Zurich, 1978-83. *Exhib:* Solo exhibs include Mus de Arte Contemp de Castilla y Leon, Spain, 2006, Alexanderplatz Station, Berlin, 2006, Stephen Friedman, London, 2007, Arndt & Partner, Berlin, 2007, Galerie Chantal Crousel, Paris, 2007; Group exhibs include Art Inst Chicago, Chicago, 2000; Cavemanman, Barbara Gladstone Gallery, New York, 2002, Superficial Engagement, 2006; Anschool II, Mus Serralves, Portugal, 2005; Surprise, Surprise, Inst Contemp Art, London, 2006; Into Me/Out of Me, PS 1 Mus Mod Art, New York, 2006; Collage: The Unmonumental Picture, New Mus, New York, 2007; Stand-Alone, Mus Tamayo, Mex, 2008. *Awards:* Prix Marcel Duchamp, Paris, 2000; Rolandpreis für Kunst im öffentlichen Raum, 2003; Joseph Beuys-Preis, 2004. *Mailing Add:* Gladstone Gallery 515 W 24th St New York NY 10011

HIRSH, ANNETTE MARIE
SILVERSMITH, GOLDSMITH
b Milwaukee, Wis, Oct 20, 1921. *Study:* Milwaukee State Teachers Coll, 39-41; Milwaukee Area Tech Coll, 53-57;. *Work:* Milwaukee Art Mus, Baron Mus Judaica, Milwaukee, Wis; Madagascar Nat Mus; Israeli Embassy, Washington, DC; synagogues in Wis, Ill, Ariz, Mich, Conn, and others; Mizel Mus Judaica, Denver, Col. *Comn:* Silver spice-box, North Shore Congregation Israel, Glencoe, Ill, 70; silver kiddush cup, Shalom Temple, Sun City, Ariz, 76; silver rimonim & torah pointer, Congregation Emanuel, Chicago, Ill, 81; breast-plate (silver & semi-precious stones), Sinai Temple, Champaign, Ill, 85; Holocaust Mem (brass & wood), Milwaukee Jewish Home, 90. *Exhib:* Biennial Painting & Sculpture, Walker Art Inst, Minneapolis, Minn, 47; Small Sculpture, Ball State Coll, Muncie, Ind, 65, 67 & 68; Religious Art, Cranbrook Acad, Bloomfield Hills, Mich, 66; Mississippi River Craft Show, Brooks Mem Art Gallery, Memphis, Tenn, 69; Chicago and Vicinity Biennial, Chicago Art Inst, 77; Chicago Area Jewish Artists, Spertus Mus, Chicago, 85; Contemp Artifacts, Nat Mus Am Jewish Hist, 87-93; Marquette Milwaukee Haggerty Mus 2007; Judaic Exhibit, Chas Allis Mus, Milwaukee, 2000. *Collection Arranged:* Old Testament, 72 & Exodus, 74, Milwaukee Jewish Community Ctr; Jewish Scriptures, Congregation EmanuEl, Milwaukee, 94. *Pos:* Illusr, Boston Store, Milwaukee, Wis, 42-44 & Goldblatt's Dept Store, Chicago, Ill, 44-46; mus chmn & cur, Baron Judaica Mus, Milwaukee, 70-. *Teaching:* Instr drawing & watercolor, Milwaukee Area Tech Coll, Wis, 68-2001. *Awards:* Purchase Award, Wis Designer Crafts Exhib, Milwaukee Art Mus, 64; Sculpture Award, Wright Art Ctr, Beloit, Wis, 66; Purchase Award, Mizel Mus Judaica, Denver, Colo, 86; First Prize, Judaica, Dallas, 2006; and others. *Bibliog:* Bob Orvis (auth), Point of view, Milwaukee Mag, 2/78; James Auer (auth), Hebrew imagery, an updating, Milwaukee J, 4/5/81; Rachel Heimovics (auth), The Chicago Jewish Source Book, 81; James Auer (auth), Dual Show, Milwaukee J, 11/19/89; James Auer (auth), Judaica, 3/15/00. *Mem:* Wis Designer Crafts Coun (treas, 60-66, historian, 90-2008); Soc N Am Goldsmiths. *Media:* Metal Jewelry; Small Sculpture, Judaica Objects. *Publ:* A Guide to Jewish Wisconsin, 2007. *Mailing Add:* 4124 N Ardmore Ave Milwaukee WI 53211

HIRSHFIELD, PEARL
PAINTER, SCULPTOR
Study: Sch of Art Inst, Chicago, BA, 79; Northwestern Univ, Columbia Coll. *Work:* Peace Mus, Chicago, Ill; Joan Flasch Artists Bk Collection, Flaxman Libr, Sch Art Inst, Chicago; Fla Holocaust Mus, St Petersburg, Fla; Exhib Hall, Budapest, Hungary, 85; Klein Gallery, Chgo, 85; Mary & Leigh Block Mus Art Libr, Evanston, Ill; and many pvt collections. *Exhib:* Holocaust Memorial Project Int, Union, NJ, 81; Metropolitan Mus & Art Ctr, Coral Gables, Fla, 86; Evansville Mus Arts & Sci, Ind, 86; Krasl Art Ctr, St Joseph, Mich, 86; The Clocktower, NY, 86, 89; Am Inst Architects, San Francisco, Calif, 87; Holocaust Meml Found Mus, Skokie, Ill, 88; Ground Zero Int Conf Ctr, Hiroshima, Japan, 89; Franklin Furnace Mus, NY, 91; Los Angeles Contemporary Exhib, Gallery, Calif, 92; Arthur Woods Gallery, Embach, Switz, 92; Palais de Congres, Montreax, Switz, 92; Artemisia Gallery, Chgo, 94; Aurora Univ, Ill, 94; Minn Mus Am Art, 95; solo exhib, Univ Wis, River Falls, 95; Columbus Mus Art, Ohio, 95; Finegood Art Gallery, Los Angeles, 96; Nat Mus Women in Arts, Washington, DC, 96; Orange Co Ctr Contemp Arts, Santa Ana, Calif, 96; Finegood Art Gallery, West Hills, Calif, 96; Blaffer Gallery, Houston, Tex, 97; Aurora Pub Art Comn, Ill, 97; Found Auschwitz, Brussels, Belgium, 97; Knoxville Mus Art, Tenn, 98; Northern Ill Art Mus, Chicago, 98; Tampa Bay Holocaust Mus, St Petersburg, Fla, 98; NJ State Mus, Trenton, 99; Okla City Art Mus, 99; Nat Mus of Women in the Arts, Washington, DC, 99; Telfair Mus, Savannah, Ga, 99; DeCordova Art Mus, Boston, 2000; Huntsville Mus Art, Ala, 2000; Tucson Art Mus, Ariz, 2000; Frye Mus, Seattle, Wash, 2001; Holocaust Mus, St Petersburg, Fla, 2002; Int Biennale, Lodz, Poland, 2004; Woman Made Gallery, Chicago, 2007-2008. *Pos:* Film coordr, Peace Productions, Inc, 83; art adv & consult, Gallery Workshop, Evanston, Ill. *Awards:* Visual Arts Award, Ill Arts Coun, 83 & 84 & 93, fellowship 86; Citizens Alert Bill of Rights Award for Visual Arts, 91; Visual Arts Award, Task Force Against Police Brutality Orgn, 93; Puffin Found Grant, 96; Best Three-Dimensional Art Award, 22nd Annual Baer Competition, 98; Award for excellence in arts, Chicago Women's Caucus Art, 2010. *Bibliog:* Matthew Baigell (pub), Jewish American Artists and the Holocaust, Rutgers Univ Press, 56, 90-91, fig 27, 97; Pub, Art After Auschwitz: The other side of memory, Response, A Contemporary Jewish Review (article), 30th Anniv Issue, 167, fig 172, 97; Kennan Heise (pub), Chaos Creativity and culture: A Sampling of Chicago in the 20th Century, Gibbs Smith/Peregrine Smith, 168-170, 98; Daniel Weyssow & Yannis Thanassekos, The Memory of Auschwitz in Contemporary Art, Foundation Auschwitz Publ, Brussels, Belgium, 98; Stephen C. Feinstein, Reclaiming Memory; American Representations of the Holocaust, Memory and Re-memory: American Installation Artand Holocaust Imagery, Pirjo Ahokas & Maxine Chard-Hutchinson, Univ Turku (publ), Finland, 98; Hedwig Brenner, Judische Frauen in der bildenden Kunst 11, German Text, Konstanz, Germany, 2004. *Mem:* Nat Women's Caucus Art; Chicago Artists Coalition; Nat Mus Women Arts, Washington, DC; Woman Made Gallery, Chgo, Ill. *Media:* All Media. *Interests:* social-political issues, literature, theater, opera. *Publ:* Auth, Limited Edition Portfolio of 13 Major Artists, Ctr Constitutional Rights, New York, 72; Conspiracy, The Artist as Witness, Godine Press; Sculptural Constructions Involving Water Dynamics, Leonardo, Pergamon Press, Vol 18, Issue 3. *Mailing Add:* 1333 Ridge Ave Evanston IL 60201

HIRST, DAMIEN
CONCEPTUAL ARTIST, COLLECTOR
b Bristol, England, June 7, 1965. *Study:* Goldsmiths Coll, London, grad, 1989. *Exhib:* Solo exhibs, When Logics Die, Emmanuel Perrotin, Paris, 1991, Where's God Now, Jay & Donatella Chiat, New York, 1992, Visual Candy, Regen Projects, LA, 1993, Currents 23, Milwaukee Art Mus, 1994, Still, Jay Jopling/White Cube, London, 1995, No Sense of Absolute Corruption, Gagosian Gallery, New York, 1996, The Beautiful Afterlife, Bruno Bischofberger, Zurich, Switz, 1997; Southampton City Art Gallery, 1998, Pharmacy, Tate Gallery, London, 1999, Sadler's Wells, London, 2000, Damien Hirst's Art Education, The Reliance, Leeds, 2002, Romance in the Ave of Uncertainty, White Cube, London, 2003, The Agony & the Ecstasy: Selected Works from 1989-2004, Archaeol Mus, Naples, 2004, Works on Paper, Andipa Gallery, London, 2005, The Elusive Truth!, 2005, The Death of God, Galeria Hilario Galguera, Mex, 2006, Corpus: Drawings 1981-2006, 2006, Beyond Belief, 2007, Superstition, Gagosian Gallery, LA, 2007, New Religion, Palazzo Pesaro Papafava, Venice, 2007, Nothing Matters 2009, No Love Lost, Wallace Collection, 2009, For the Love of God, Palazzo Vecchio, 2010, Medicine Cabinets, L & M Arts, NY, 2010, Stolpher Gallery, London, 2010, Cornucopia, 2010, Dark Trees, Galeria Hilario Galguera, Leipzig, Mex, 2010, Theology, Philosophy, Medicine, Justice, Galerie Andrea Caratsch, Zurich, 2010, End of an Era, Gagosian Gallery, 2010, Poisons, Remedies, 2010, Forgotten Promises, 2011, The Complete Spot Painting, 2012, 25 Year Retrospective, Tate Modern, 2012, and others; On the Edge of the Western World, Yerba Buena Ctr Arts, San Francisco, 2000; Hyper Mental, Kunsthaus Zurich/Hamburger Kunsthalle, 2000; Art-Tube 01, Café de Paris, London, 2001; Artist's London: Holbein to Hirst, Mus London, 2001; From Twilight to Dawn, Frist Ctr Visual Arts, Nashville, 2002; Love Over Gold, Gallery Mod Art, Glasgow, 2003; Is One Thing Better Than Another, Aurel Scheibler, Cologne, 2004; Vertigo, Meadow Gallery, Sudeley Castle, Winchcombe, Eng, 2005; Extreme Abstraction, Albright Knox Gallery, Buffalo, 2005; Revelation, Laing Art Gallery, Newcastle-upon-Tyne, 2005; Picture This, Bargehouse, London, 2006; Sculpture, Gagosian Gallery, Beverly Hills, 2006; How to Improve the World, Hayward Gallery, London, 2006; Aftershock, Capital Mus, Beijing, 2007; The Turner Prize: A Retrospective, Tate Britain, London, 2007; You Dig the Tunnel, I'll Hide the Soil, White Cube, London, 2008; and others. *Awards:* Turner Prize, 1995; named one of Top 200 Collectors, ARTnews mag, 2008-13; named one of 10 Most Important Artists of Today, Newsweek mag, 2011. *Collection:* Modern and contemporary art. *Mailing Add:* c/o White Cube Gallery 48 Hoxton Sq London United Kingdom N1 6PB

HITCH, JEAN LEASON
PAINTER
b Sydney, Australia, Oct 18, 1918; US citizen. *Study:* Melbourne Tech Art Training Sch, Australia; Leason Sch Painting; Wayman Adams Sch Painting, Adirondacks, NY. *Hon Degrees:* Fel Am Artist Professional League. *Work:* Dr Hall, Cape Cod Community Col; Co Sheriff Gerry Bowes, Barnstable Co Ct House, Cape Cod; Dr Irving Bartlett, Cape Cod Community Col, 92; Mass Maritime Acad. *Comn:* Buccaneer, Mass Maritime Acad, 82. *Exhib:* One-man show: Cape Cod Cultural Ctr, 2008; Allied Artists Am, Am Artist Prof League & Catharine Lorillard Wolfe Art Club, NY; Newton Galleries; Salmagundi Club; Nat Arts Club; Richmond Co Country Club; Burr Galleries. *Pos:* Art cur, Staten Island Inst Arts & Sci, 45-51; former dir & owner, Dennis Common Fine Art Gallery. *Teaching:* instr, gallery, Yarmouth Port, Mass. *Awards:* Anna Hyatt Huntington Horse-Head Award, 72; Am Arts Coun Award; Margaret Dole Portrait Award, 91; 1st prize, Creative Arts Ctr, Chatham, Mass, Cultural Ctr Cape Cod, Yarmouth, Mass, Cape Cod Art Assn. *Mem:* Cape Cod Art Asn (instr painting, formerly); Allied Artists Am (hon mem); Catharine Lorillard Wolfe Art Club; Am Artist Prof League (hon mem); Copley Arts Soc, Boston. *Media:* Oil. *Mailing Add:* 51 Gordon Ln Yarmouth Port MA 02675

HITCHCOCK, HOWARD GILBERT
EDUCATOR, SCULPTOR
b Ava, Mo, Aug 20, 1927. *Study:* Coll Puget Sound, BA, 50; Univ Wash, with Glen Alps, Everett DuPen & Alexander Archipenko, MFA, 53; Brooklyn Mus Art Sch, fall 62; Teachers Col, Columbia Univ, EdD, 63. *Work:* JB Speed Mus, Louisville, Ky; Mus de la Acuarela Mus, Coyoacan, Mex; First Repub Bank Ore, Portland, Ore; Casa Museo Vladimir Cora, Acaponeta, Nayarit, Mex. *Comn:* Altar cross & candelabra, Los Altos United Methodist Church, Long Beach, Calif, 65; sculpture, Am Cancer Soc, Long Beach, Calif, 86; sculpture, comn by Jack Dameron family, Long Beach, Calif, 93; relief sculpture comn by Richard and Karen Clements, Long Beach, Calif, 98. *Exhib:* Solo exhibs, Gallery West, Portland, Ore, 77-83, Allied Arts Gallery, Huntington Beach, Calif, 83, Civic Ctr, Anjo, Japan, 89, Heaton House Gallery, Edmonds, Wash, Magnolia Fine Arts Gallery, Seattle, Wash, 94 & Anderson Gallery, Sunset Beach, Calif, 96, 96-2012, Sandstone Gallery, Laguna Beach, Calif, 2008-2012; Five Calif Artists, Mus de la Acuarela Mexicana, Coyoacan, Mex, 93; Sculpture '93, City Brea Gallery, Brea, Calif, 93; First Int Watercolor Biennial, Mus dela Acuarela Mexicana, Coyoacan, Mex, 94; All Calif: All Media, Downey Mus of Art, Calif, 96; So Calif Open Juried Exhbn, Laguna Art Mus, Laguna Beach, Calif, 97. *Pos:* Chmn, Dept Art, Calif State Univ, Long Beach, 76-82; mem, Comn Accreditation, Nat Asn Sch Art & Design, Reston, Va, 81-83. *Teaching:* Instr art, Sue Bennett Col, London, Ky, 53-54; asst prof, Union Col, Barbourville, Ky, 54-57; from assoc prof to prof art educ & sculpture, Calif State Univ, Long Beach, Calif, 58-90. *Awards:* First Prize, Automobile in Art, Long Beach Arts, 96. *Bibliog:* Shirle Gottlieb (auth), Beauty in bronze: The evolution of a sculptor's technique, Long Beach Press-Telegram, 11/1/83; Anastacia Grenda (auth), Searching for Consensus, Orange Coast, Dec 2009; Rick Manly (auth), A Life cast in bronze, Emerities/CSULB, vol 16 no 1 spring 2010. *Media:* Cast Metal; All Painting Media. *Publ:* Auth, Out of the Fiery Furnace: Casting Sculpture from Ceramic Shell Molds, William Kaufmann, Inc, 85. *Dealer:* Anderson Gallery 16812 Pacific Coast Hwy Sunset Beach CA 90742; Sandstone Laguna Gallery 384A N Coast Hwy Laguna Beach CA 92651; Lanning Gallery 431 Hwy 179 Sedona AZ 86336; Bridge Gallery Ventana Plz 5425 N Kolb Rd Ste 113 Tucson Az 85750; Just Art Contemporary Art Gallery 60 Valley St Ste 107B Providence RI 02909. *Mailing Add:* 17161 Friml Ln Huntington Beach CA 92649-4510

HITE, JESSIE OTTO
MUSEUM DIRECTOR
b Apr 4, 1947; US citizen. *Study:* Univ Tex, Austin, BS, 1969, MA, 1981. *Pos:* Asst cur, Archer M Huntington Art Gallery, Univ Tex, Austin, asst dir pub affairs, 1984-91, acting dir, 1991-93, dir, 1993-2007. *Mem:* Am Asn Mus; Asn Art Mus Dirs. *Mailing Add:* c/o Univ Tex at Austin Archer M Huntington Art Gallery Austin TX 78712

HITNER, CHUCK
PAINTER, EDUCATOR

b Nashville, Tenn, Sept 10, 1943. *Study:* Mid Tenn State Univ, with David LeDoux, BS (art), 67; Southern Ill Univ, Carbondale, MFA (painting & drawing), 68. *Work:* Chrysler Mus, Norfolk, Va; Southern Ill Univ, Carbondale; Allersmaborg, Ezinge, Neth; Tucson Mus Art, Ariz. *Exhib:* Calif State Poly-Tech Univ, Pomona, Calif, 81; Triton Mus Art, Santa Clara, Calif, 84; Mus Art, Univ Ariz, Tucson, 87; Univ Ctr Gallery, Univ Mont, Missoula, 88; Traditions 3 Thousand Gallery, NY, 88; Pentonville Gallery, London, Eng, 88; Allersmaborg, Ezinge (Gr), The Neth, 88; Roland Gibson Gallery, State Univ NY, Potsdam, 88; Selections 45, Drawing Ctr, NY, 89. *Teaching:* Asst prof painting & drawing, Eastern Ky Univ, 69-72; assoc prof painting & drawing, Univ Ariz, 72-82, prof, 82-; prof, Univ Ariz, Tucson, 82-. *Bibliog:* Donald Kuspit, Chuck Hitner: Recent Work (catalog), Mus Art, Univ Ariz, Tucson, Ariz, 87; Robert Quinn, Frantic images from a calm hand, Artspace Mag, 85; Marcia Tucker, 20 Arizona artists (catalog), Phoenix Art Mus, 78. *Media:* Drawing, Painting. *Mailing Add:* 3839 E Calle Ensenada Tucson AZ 85716-5127

HIXON, KAREN J
PATRON

Pos: Supporter of numerous environ orgn's; bd trustees, Amon Carter Mus, Ft Worth. *Awards:* Named a Texas Legend of Conserv, Nat Fish & Wildlife Found, 2004

HLAVINA, RASTISLAV
SCULPTOR, WRITER

b Topolcany, Slovakia, June 5, 1943; Can citizen. *Study:* Art Col, Bratislava, with A Drexler & L Korkos, dipl (sculpture), 62; Nat Conserv & Restoration Inst, Pelhrimov, with Vaclav Vanek, 66. *Hon Degrees:* Cult DFA, W Univ Ariz, 88. *Work:* Hakone Open-Air Mus; Utsukushi-Ga-Hara Open-Air Mus; Slovak Nat Gallery; City of Fukuoka; pvt collections in Can, Czech Repu, France, Russia, Slovak Rep & US. *Comn:* Restorations: Altarpiece Dobra Voda, 64-65, Loreta, Royal Summer Palace, Prague, 65 & Monastery Libr Cistercian Abbey, Vyssi Brod, 65-66, Nat Heritage Inst, Prague; sculpture, Melody, Prov Gov, Japan, 88. *Exhib:* Look, Pub Art Gallery Sarnia, Ont, 82; Synthesis: Idea and Form, Multicult Mus & Gallery, Toronto, 82; New Artists, NY, 82; Artists of Czechoslovak Origin, Univ Pittsburgh, 82; CKOC Arts Hamilton, Art Gallery Hamilton, 82-83; Int Juried Art Competition/Exhib, by IJAC, NY, 85; First & Second Rodin Grand Prize Exhib, Hakone Open-Air Mus, 86-88; A Praise of Small Format in Contemp Art, Paris, 2000, 2001; Solo exhibs, Intro to Multiple Sculpture Stage I, Nepean Point Park, in coop with Nat Capital Comn, 72, Intro to Multiple Sculpture Stage II, Legacy of Vinland, Nat Libr Canada, sponsorship of Czecho-Slovak Soc of Arts & Sci, Canada, 81. *Collection Arranged:* From the Origin of the Multiple/Multilateral Sculpture to Conclusion in the Multiple/Multilateral Thought and Understanding, Hlavina Family Trust. *Pos:* Conservator & restorer fine arts, Nat Conserv & Restoration Inst Fine Arts, Pelhrimov, Czech, 64-66; art dir, MIER Nat Enterprise, Topolcany, Slovakia, 67-68. *Awards:* Merit Distinction, Expo Brno, 67; Award, Outstanding Achievement in Sculpture, IJAC, New York, 85; Superior Prize, 1st Rodin Grand Prize Exhib, Hakone Open-Air Mus, 86; Superior Prize, 2nd Rodin Grand Prize Exhib, Hakone Open-Air Mus, 88. *Bibliog:* Jenny Bergin (auth), Sculptor takes your all, Ottawa Citizen, 10/28/72; Nancy Baele (auth), Perseverance pays off, Citizen, 11/26/81; Margarat Virany (auth), Aylmer sculptor starts art movement, Aylmer Bulletin, 12/17/81; Celina Bell (auth), Area artists to exhibit with best in New York, Citizen, 8/23/85; Utsukushi-ga-hara, Sora to, Against the Sky, 30th Anniversary Book, Open Air Mus, 2011. *Mem:* Independent. *Media:* All. *Res:* From multiple sculpture (1969) to multiple thought & understanding; art & the emergence of a new comprehension of reality; global interpretation; art as an introductory element & an educational tool in the process of development of our society. *Interests:* music, philosophy. *Collection:* Hlavina family trust; Betakova-Hlavina Art Coll-The Pearls of N Am. *Publ:* Auth, Legacy of Vinland: The Multiple Sculpture, pvt publ, 81; Introduction, Multiple Sculpture and the Multiple Art, ABIRA Digest, Spring, 88; Collection of postal cards Les Artistes et Matres du XXe siecle (Artists & Masters of XXth Century), Inclusion in The Golden Book for Art Collectors and Art Lovers, Arts et Images du Monde, Paris, France; Le Grand Livre d'Art des Salons et Biennales De France et de leurs Exposants, Editions Pergame, Geneve, 94; Europ'ART, Genève, 2005; Digital Publication: Multiple Sculpture 1983-2013; Deposit with Nat Library & Archives, 2014. *Dealer:* independent. *Mailing Add:* 1769 Rte 148 Luskville PQ J0X 2G0 Canada

HO, FRANCIS T
PHOTOGRAPHER, EDUCATOR

b Honolulu, Hawaii, Aug 29, 1938. *Study:* Yale Univ, BFA, 61; Rochester Inst Technol, MFA, 67. *Work:* Nikon Camera Co, NY; Canon Photo Gallery, Amsterdam; Photo Gallery Int, Tokyo; Silver Image Gallery, Seattle. *Comn:* Photograph, Seattle Arts Comn, 83. *Exhib:* Focus Gallery, San Francisco, 73; A Temporary Possession: The Human Image in 20th Century Photog, Wash State Univ Mus Art, 76; solo exhibs, Canon Photo Gallery, Amsterdam, 77 & Photo Gallery Int, Tokyo, 80; Fantastic Photog in the USA, Mus Fundacio Miro, Barcelona, 78, Hall Palais Beaux Arts, Brussels, 78 & Mus Mod Art, Mexico City, 79. *Teaching:* Prof photog & graphic design, Wash State Univ, 67-; exchange prof graphic design, Nihon Univ, Tokyo, 79-80. *Awards:* Cert Excellence, Exhib Communication Graphics, Am Inst Graphic Arts, 74-75; Merit Award, The One Show, New York Art Dirs Club, 75; Award Excellence, 16th Ann Exhib, Communication Arts Mag, 75. *Bibliog:* Drukkerij Rosbeek (auth), Hose Valley, Hoensbroek, Neth, 76; Attilio Columbo (auth), Fantastic Photographs, Random House & Gordon Frazer, 79; Yaomi Yoshikawa (auth), article, Commercial Photo, Japan, 80; Tokumi Sawamoto (auth), article, Camera Mainichi, Tokyo, 2/80. *Mem:* Friends Photog. *Mailing Add:* 7103 NE 136th St Kirkland WA 98034-5009

HO, KONG
MURALIST, EDUCATOR

b Hong Kong. *Study:* Chinese Univ, Hong Kong, BFA, 1985; Tex Tech Univ, MFA (painting & drawing), 1994. *Work:* United Nations HQ, New York; Clymer Mus & Gallery, Washington, DC; Amarillo Mus Art, Tex; Fine Art Mus, NMex; Joseph D Carrier Art Gallery, Can; Hong Kong Mus Art. *Comn:* Mural, McKean County Arts Coun, Pa, 2004; mural, Bradford Office Economic & Community Develop, Pa, 2007; mural, Blaisdell Hall, Univ Pitts, Bradford, 2008. *Teaching:* Assoc prof & dir, Divsn Comm & Arts, Univ Pitts, Bradford; prof, Hong Kong Baptist Univ, Western Tex Coll & Univ Hong Kong, formerly. *Awards:* Sasakawa Fel, Am Asn State Colls & Univs, 2005; Acad Visual Arts Fel, Hong Kong Baptist Univ, 2006; Teaching Artist Fel, VSA, 2009; Fulbright Grant, 2010. *Bibliog:* Jean Ann Bowman Cantore (auth), The Science of Art, Texas Techsan, Vol 57, No 2, 24-29, 3-4/2004; Glen Brown (auth), Toward Complexity, Asian Art News, Vol 14, No 4, 54-57, 7-8/2004; Roger Newton (auth), The Mural of Hope, Bradford Era, 9/23/2004. *Mem:* Hong Kong Mural Soc (founder & chmn). *Mailing Add:* 110 Blaisdell Hall Bradford PA 16701

HOARE, TYLER JAMES
SCULPTOR, PRINTMAKER

b Joplin, Mo, June 5, 1940. *Study:* Univ Colo, 59; Sculpture Ctr, New York, 60; Univ Kans, BFA, 63; Calif Coll Arts & Crafts, Oakland, 66;. *Work:* US Info Agency, Washington, DC; State Univ NY Albany; Oakland Mus, Calif; Calif Coll Arts & Crafts; and many pvt collections. *Exhib:* Solo exhibs, John Bolles Gallery, San Francisco, Calif, 69, 71, 74, Camberwell Sch Art, London, 71, Cent Sch Art & Design, London, 74, Purdue Univ, Gallery 1, West Lafayette, Ind, 76, Geotrope Gallery, Berkeley, Calif, 81, Studio Nine, Benicia, Calif, 82, Oakland Art Asn Gallery, Calif, 86, Costal Art League Mus, Half Moon Bay, Calif, 89, George A Spiva Art Ctr, Joplin, Mo, 97, Epperson Gallery, Crockett, Calif, 98, Epperson 1998, 2002, Peninsula Mus Art, 2009; Group exhibs include 22nd Nat Print Exhib, Libr Cong, Washington, DC, 71; Xerographic Art, Xerox Corp, NY; Int Mail Art, Guanajuato, Mex, 81; The Centre Documentazione Organizzazione, Parma, Italy, 82; Works by California Cookbook Artists, San Francisco Mus Mod Art, 82 & Artists, in the Spotlight, 84; Whitney Mus Am Art Libr, 83; Gracie Mansion Gallery, NY, 83; Contemp Surrealism Slide Lect, San Francisco Art Inst, Calif, 84; San Francisco Mus Mod Art, Rental Gallery, 85; San Francisco Arts Comn Festival, 86; Calif Mus Photog, Riverside, Calif, 84, 86, 87, 88, 89, 90; Cleveland Inst Art, 89; Ore State Univ, Corvallis, 90; Gallery One, Point Reyes, Calif, 90; Contemp Art Gallery, Aono, Japan, 91; Univ Tex, Dallas, 93; Gallery Without Walls, Australia, 94; Mus Mod Art, 96; Epperson Gallery, Crockett, Calif, 98, 99, 00, 01, 02, 06; Calabi Gallery, Petaluma, Calif, 2010-2011; Art of the Automobile, Artworks, San Rafael, Calif, 2010-2011; South Bank Center, Royal Festival Hall, England, 2010-2011; Nelsen Arts Gallery, Berkeley, Calif, 2010-2011; Preseon Center, Oakland, Calif, 2010-2011; Maconga Casquelourd Center for the Arts, Oakland, Calif, 2010-2011; Lake Wales Art Center, Lake Wales, Fla, 2010-2011. *Collection Arranged:* US Info Agency, Washington, DC; SUNY at Albany; Oakland Mus, Calif; Harvard Univ, Cambridge, Mass; Achen Bach Collection Legion of hon, SPOP; Bancroft Lib, Univ Calif Berkeley. *Pos:* guest cur, Magic Machine, Ctr Gallery, Univ Calif, San Francisco, 73, The Trading Company, 74, 88, Ctr Visual Arts Catalog, Oakland, 82. *Teaching:* guest lectr, San Francisco Art Inst, 72, San Francisco State Univ, 72-75, Oakland Mus, Calif, 74, Calif State Univ, Hayward, 74 & 79, Col of San Mateo, 75, Mo Southern State Col, 79, Univ Wyo, Laramie, 79, Colo State Univ, 79, Solano Community, Suisun City, Calif, 83, Calif Col Arts & Crafts, 84; instr, Univ Calif, Berkeley, 73-74. *Awards:* Master of Painting Honoris Causa, Accademia Italia. *Bibliog:* Thelma Newman (auth), Innovative Printmaking, Crown Publ, Inc, NY; article, Spotlight on Sculpture, Tyler James Hoare, Ctr Visual Arts, 82; Nicholas Roukes (auth), Art Synectics, Juniro Arts Publ, Calgary, 84; Bob Colin (auth), Mud Flat Sculpture by Tyler Hoare (40 pg book); and many others. *Mem:* Richmond Art Ctr, Calif; LA Print Soc; Oakland Mus Asn; San Francisco Art Inst; San Francisco Mus Art; Ctr for Vis Arts, Oakland, Calif. *Media:* Wood, Metal. *Interests:* custom cars. *Publ:* Megan Greenwell (auth), Albany Sculptor Brings Art Back to East Bay Shoreline, Berkeley Daily Planet, 7/18/2003; Matthew Artz (auth), Art at Sea: Berkeley artist still building relics along East Bay coast, Berkeley Daily, 10/9/2006. *Dealer:* Nielson Arts 1537 Solano Ave Berkeley CA 94707. *Mailing Add:* 30 Menlo Pl Berkeley CA 94707

HOBBS, FRANK I, JR
PAINTER, INSTRUCTOR

b Lynchburg, Va, Dec 3, 1957. *Study:* Art Inst Pittsburgh, 75; Va Polytech Inst/State Univ, BA, 80; Am Univ MFA (painting), 84. *Work:* Univ Va Hosp, Charlottesville; Med Coll of Va, Richmond; Lynchburg Col, Va; Va Polytech Inst & State Univ, Blacksburg; Mary Baldwin Coll, Staunton, Va. *Exhib:* Contemp Realism, Gallery Alexy, Philadelphia, 96; Small Figurative Works, Armory Art Ctr, Palm Beach, Fla, 96; The Virginia Landscape: A Cult History, Va Hist Soc, Richmond, 2000, Mus Western Va, 2000; Transitions: Narratives of Change, Danville Mus Art, Va, 2000; Commerce Sch Gallery, Lexington, Va, 2001; College of William and Mary, Andrews Art Gallery, Williamsburg, Va, 2002. *Pos:* Founder, pres, isntr Beverly Street Studio Sch, Staunton, Va, 92-. *Teaching:* Asst prof painting/drawing, Mary Baldwin Col, Staunton, Va, 87-91; asst prof printmaking/drawing, Randolph Macon Womans Col, Lynchburg, Va, 92-94; asst prof drawing, Washington & Lee Univ, Lexington, Va, 97; adj asst prof art, Va Military Inst, Lexington, Va, 96-. *Awards:* Va Mus Fine Art Fel, 82; Fel Works on Paper, NEA/Mid Atlantic Arts Found, 96; Fel in Painting, Va Comn for the Arts, 2000. *Bibliog:* Mearne Pardee (auth), Virginia Realism, Second Street Gallery,94; James Kelly-William Rasmussen (co-auths) The Virginia Landscape: A Cultural History, 2000. *Mem:* Coll Art Asn. *Media:* Painting, Drawing, Printmaking. *Dealer:* Reynolds Gallery 1514 W Main St Richmond VA 23220

HOBBS, GERALD S
DEALER, PUBLISHER
b New York, NY, Nov 5, 1941. *Pos:* Publ, Am Artist Mag, 73, The Artist Mag, 76, Art & Antiques: The Am Mag for Connoisseurs & Collectors, 78-, Interiors Mag, 78, Residential Interiors Mag, 78 & Int Soc Artists. *Mem:* Nat Arts Club; Salmagundi Club; Nat Art Material Trade Asn; Artists' Fel. *Specialty:* Publisher of The American Artist Collection (unlimited edition prints). *Mailing Add:* 29 E 64th St Apt 8D New York NY 10021

HOBBS, JACK ARTHUR
EDUCATOR, WRITER
b Lincoln, Nebr, Dec 26, 1930. *Study:* Univ Iowa, BA, 52, MA, 56, PhD, 71. *Work:* Sioux City Art Ctr, Iowa. *Exhib:* 14th & 17th Nat Exhibs Prints, Libr Cong, Washington, 56 & 59 & Invitational Traveling Show, 59-61; Art in the Embassies Prog, Dept State, Washington, 69. *Pos:* Publ ed, Studies in Art Educ, 85-87; Ed Bd, Studies in Art Educ, 89-93. *Teaching:* Emer prof art appreciation & art educ, Ill State Univ, 70-94. *Bibliog:* Robert Hiedemann (auth), bk rev, Art Educ J, Vol 29, 1/76; Howard Conant (auth), bk rev, Leonardo, spring 77; Georgia C Collins (auth), bk rev, Studies in Art Educ, Vol 27, 3/86. *Mem:* Nat Art Educ Asn. *Publ:* Auth, Art in Context, Harcourt Brace Jovanovich, 75, 2nd ed, 80, 3rd ed, 85 & 4th ed, 91; Arts, Civilization and Ideas, Prentice-Hall, 89, 2nd ed, 92; The Visual Experience, Davis Publ, Inc, 90, 2nd ed, 95 & 3rd ed, 2005; Arts in Civilization: Prehistoric culture to the twentieth century, Bloomsbury Bks, London, 92; Teaching Children Art, Prentice-Hall, 97; (reissue) Waveland Press Inc, 2006. *Mailing Add:* 601 Lutz Rd #4207 Bloomington IL 61704

HOBBS, ROBERT
HISTORIAN, CURARTOR
b Brookings, SDak, Dec 6, 1946. *Study:* Univ Tenn, Knoxville, BA, 69; Univ NC, Chapel Hill, MA, PhD, 75, Music Mgt, Univ Calif, Berkeley, 81. *Comn:* comn by US Comissioner, Venice, Biennale, 82; comn by US Comissioner, Sao Paulo Bienal, 2002. *Exhib:* Abstract Expressionism: the Formative Years, 78; Robert Smithson Sculpture, 81; Art of the Red Earth People, the Mesquakie of Iowa, 89; Richard Pousette-Dart, 90; Earl Cunningham, Painting an American Eden, 94; Mark Lindquist, Revolutions in Wood, 95; Lee Krasner, 99; Milton Avery, the Late Paintings, 2001; Kara Walker: Slavery! Slavery, 2002; Mark Lombardi: Global Networks, 2003. *Pos:* Cur, Mint Mus Art, 69-71; adj cur, Cornell Univ, Herbert F Johnson Mus, 76-; sr cur & chmn curatorial div, Tehran Mus Contemp Art, 78; dir, Univ Iowa Mus Art, 83-87; mem ed bd, Grove Ency Art, Oxford Univ; Thalhimer Endowed chair, VCU, 91-. *Teaching:* Lectr mod art, Yale Univ, 75; asst and assoc prof mod art, Cornell Univ, Ithaca, NY, 76-83; vis prof, Yale Univ, 2004-. *Mem:* Coll Art Asn; Independent Cur Int. *Res:* Peter Galley and Joseph Kosuth. *Publ:* coauth, Abstract Expressionism: The Formative Years, Whitney Mus & Cornell Univ Press, 78; Auth, Robert Smithson: Sculpture, Cornell Univ Press, 81; auth, Lee Krasner, Abrams, 99; auth, Malk Hombardi: Global Networks, D.A.R., 2003; auth, Alica Aycock: Sculpture and Projects, MIT Univ, 2003. *Mailing Add:* 2221 Grove Ave Richmond VA 23220-4438

HOBGOOD, E WADE
ADMINISTRATOR, EDUCATOR
b Wilson, NC, June 28, 1953. *Study:* ECarolina Univ, Greenville, NC, BFA, 1975, MFA, 1977; Am Inst Philanthropic Studies, Cert Planned Giving, 1995; Inst Educ Mgt, 1997. *Work:* RJ Reynolds, Winston-Salem, NC; Orthopedic Hosp, Charlotte, NC; Gov's Off, Little Rock, Ark; ECarolina Univ, Greenville, NC; Winthrop Univ, Rock Hill, NC. *Exhib:* NCarolina Photogrs Invitational, High Point Mus Art, NC, 1980; Western Carolina Univ Invitational, Black Mountain, NC, 1981; solo exhib, Limestone Col, Gaffney, SC, 1985; Southern Vision's, traveling exhib, 1987; Art Fac Exhib, Stephen F Austin State Univ, Nacogdoches, Tex, 1992; and others. *Pos:* Chmn dept art & design, Winthrop Univ, Rock Hill, SC, 1984-89; bd dir, Graphic Design Educ Asn Inc, 1986-90; proj dir, Arts in Basic Curriculum, Nat Endowment Arts, 1987-92; sr evaluator, Nat Asn Schs Art & Design, 1987-; assoc dean, Col Visual & Performing Arts, Winthrop Univ, 1988-92; dean, Col Fine Arts, Stephen F Austin State Univ, Nacogdoches, Tex, 1992-93; field reader, US Dept Educ, 1992-; dean, Col Arts, Calif State Univ, Long Beach, 1993-2000; chancellor, NC Sch Arts, 2000-2005. *Teaching:* Asst prof design & photog, Ark State Univ, Jonesboro, 1977-78; asst to assoc prof, Western Carolina Univ, 1978-84; prof, mass commun, Univ NC, Asheville, 2006-. *Awards:* Higher Educ Art Educator of Yr, SC Art Educ Asn, 89; Art Educator of Yr, SC Art Educ Asn, 90; Fel Japanese Studies, Grants Sashakawa/Nippan Found, 1998. *Mem:* Bd dirs, Int Coun Fine Arts Deans, 1998-; Fine Arts Affil. *Mailing Add:* Univ NC One Univ Heights 306 Karpen Hall CPO# 2120 Asheville NC 28804-8509

HOCHFIELD, SYLVIA
EDITOR
Pos: Assoc Ed, ARTnews Mag, NYC. *Publ:* Auth, Beautiful Loot: Soviet Pluder of Europe's Art Treasures, 95; auth, Stolen Treasure: The Hunt for the World's Lost Masterpieces, 95. *Mailing Add:* ARTnews Magazine 48 W 38th St New York NY 10018

HOCHHAUSER, MARILYN HELSENROTT
PAINTER, EDUCATOR
b Chicago, Ill, April 18, 1928. *Study:* C W Post Ctr, Long Island Univ, BA (art educ; magna cum laude), 73, MA (painting; scholar), 75; New York Univ, Mus Studies, 86-88. *Work:* Language Plus, Alma, Que; Ore Art Inst, Portland; Elings Park, Santa Barbara, Calif. *Exhib:* Muscarelle Mus Art, 88; Coll William & Mary, Williamsburg, VA, 88; Sculpture & Abstract, San Francisco State Univ, 90; Columbia Col, Mo, 91; Perth Galleries, Australia, 92; The Hall of AWA Int Paper Art, Japan, 93; Contemp Art Forum, 94, Korean Cult Ctr, Los Angeles, 96; Westmount Col, Calif, 97, Univ Minn, 98; Santa Barbara City Col, 99, West Coast Paper Co, 99; Maryland Fed Art, 2000; Fresno Mus, Fresno, Calif, 2004; Westmount Col, Montecito, Calif, 2005; Elings Park Found, Santa Barbara, Calif, 2006; and others. *Collection Arranged:* Oregon Art Inst. *Pos:* Prof Art, Trenton State Col, 80-85. *Teaching:* Art Lectr, Adult Educ, Roslyn & Merrick, NY, 71-79; prof, Trenton State Col, 80-85; instr, Santa Barbara Mus Art, 89-90 & City Col Art, 90. *Bibliog:* Lelac-Jean Papier (auth), article, Alma, PQ Canada, 2/82; C Laforge (auth), New York Daily News, 9/83; Joan Shepard (auth), article New York Post, 9/83. *Mem:* Women in Arts. *Res:* Japanese Paper Making. *Mailing Add:* 5041 Via Lara Ln Santa Barbara CA 93111

HOCHSTETLER, T MAX
PAINTER, EDUCATOR
b Terre Haute, Ind, May 13, 1941. *Study:* Univ Evansville, BA, 64; Southern Ill Univ, MFA, 67. *Work:* Owensboro Art Mus; Tenn State Mus & Cheekwood Fine Arts Ctr, Nashville; Evansville Mus Arts & Sci; Tenn Valley Authority. *Comn:* Nashville murals, 76-77 & Centennial murals, 80-81, Opryland Hotel, Nashville; Cheatham Co Paintings, Dominion Bank of Ashland City, Tenn, 82; Public Square Clarksville (mural); First Am Bank, Clarksville, Tenn, 83; Hist Broadcasting mural, the Nashville Network (TNN), Nashville, 85; decade mural, TNN, Nashville, 94. *Exhib:* Ind Artists Exhib, Evansville Mus, 75; Tenn Bicentennial Exhib, State Mus, Nashville, 76; Mid-Am Art Exhib, Owensboro Mus Art, Ky, 79; Tenn Artists, Doyle Fine Arts Ctr, Western Ky Univ, Bowling Green, 79; Choice Painting Invitational, Ctr Contemp Art, Univ Ky, 82; Ten in Tennessee, Dulin Gallery Art, Knoxville, 86. *Teaching:* Prof painting & drawing, Austin Peay State Univ, 67-99, emer prof art and artist-in-residence, 99-. *Awards:* Second Place Award, City of Owensboro, 74; Patrons Purchase Award, Evansville Mus, 75; Mus Purchase Award, Owensboro Mus, 79. *Mem:* Tenn Watercolor Soc; Coll Art Asn; Southeastern Coll Art Asn. *Media:* Acrylic, Watercolor. *Mailing Add:* Dept Art Austin Peay State Univ 601 College St Clarksville TN 37044

HODES, BARNEY
SCULPTOR
b Mar 11, 1943. *Study:* Columbia Coll, AB, 64; Brooklyn Mus Art Sch, 64-66; Univ NC, MFA, 68. *Work:* Art Students League; Univ Richmond. *Exhib:* NC Mus Art; Brooklyn Mus, Brooklyn Mus Art Sch; Artists & Friends, First St Gallery, 81; Numeroff Gallery; The Human Presence, First Street Gallery, 95; Denise Bibro Gallery, 99; solo exhib, Weatherspoon Gallery, Suffolk Co Community Coll, 2000. *Pos:* Co-dir & co-founder, NY Acad Art & New Brooklyn Sch, formerly. *Teaching:* Lectr, Fairleigh Dickinson Univ, Teaneck, NJ, 70-72; instr, Brooklyn Mus Sch Art, 70-81, Brooklyn Coll, 73-76; assoc prof, St John's Univ, 77-83, NY Acad Art, 83-86, New Brooklyn Sch Life Drawing, Painting & Sculpture, 80-83 & Art Students League, 86-; instr sculpture, Nat Acad Design, 2000-. *Awards:* Art Students League Award. *Media:* Cement, Clay. *Interests:* Portraits & nudes, monumental portraits & torsos. *Publ:* Auth, Linea, 98-2000, 2008. *Mailing Add:* Art Students League 215 W 57th St New York NY 10019

HODES, SUZANNE
PAINTER, PRINTMAKER
b New York, NY. *Study:* Radcliffe Col, Brandeis Univ, BA (fine arts, magna cum laude), 60; Columbia Univ, MFA, 62; studied with Oskar Kokoschka, Salzburg, Austria, & George Grosz, Maine. *Work:* Fogg Art Mus, Cambridge, Mass; De Cordova Mus, Lincoln, Mass; Print & Drawing Collection, Boston Pub Libr, Mass; Rockefeller Univ, NY; Casali Inst, Jerusalem; Esec Lending Company, Boston & London; and many others; Mus Mod Art Libr Collection, NY. *Comn:* Lithograph, Physicians Social Responsibility, Cambridge, Mass, 84; landscape painting, New Eng Life Co, Burlington, Mass, 85; Portrait of Judge Doyle, Middlesex Bar Asn, Waltham, Mass, 93. *Exhib:* Figure & Landscape, De Cordova Mus, Lincoln, Mass, 88; Tenth Sept Competition, Alexandria Mus Art, La, 91; Solo Exhibs: City Reflections, (with catalog) Bunting Inst Radcliffe Col, Cambridge, Mass, 1996; NY Reflections, Joan Whalen Gallery, NY, 2002-2003; People and Places, paintings, drawings & monotypes, Schlesinger Libr at Radcliffe, 2002-2003; Pine Manor Coll, Newton Mass, 2006; Artana Gallery, Brookline, Mass, 2006; "One of a kind" Monotype Exhib, Sigma Gallery, NY, 91; solo show, paintings, Reflections, Artana Gallery, Brookline, Mass, 04; 4 person show, Rotenberg Gallery, 04; Reflections: Paintings of City and Landscape, Artana Gallery, 4/2008; City Rhythms: Paintings, Regis Coll, Weston, Mass, 2011. *Pos:* Co-founder, Artists for Survival, 82-92; pres, Artists West Studios, 85-89; teacher, mem, Mayor's Cult Comn, Waltham, Mass, 87-90. *Teaching:* painting, Cambridge Ctr Adult Educ, 72-74 & Sr Citizen Prog, Waltham, Mass, 90-93; painting, Lesley Univ Seminars. *Awards:* Grumbacher Award, Audubon Artists Exhib, 63; Fulbright Fel, Fulbright Comn, 63-64; Bunting Inst Fel, 70-72; Phi Beta Kappa, hon membership award, 2010. *Bibliog:* W Zimmer (auth), Review of one of a kind monotypes, New York Times, 7/29/90; Suzanne Hodes '60: Something of the spirit, Brandeis Review, spring 91; C Temin (auth), Review of creativity & spirituality, Boston Globe, 1/5/94. *Mem:* Boston Printmakers (artist mem, 86-94); Monotype Guild New Eng; Copley Soc & Copley Master; Soc Bunting Inst Fel; Women's Caucus for Art; Nat Asn Women Artists, New York. *Media:* Acrylic, Oil, All Media. *Collection:* Fidelity Investment, Wempe Jewelers, Yawkey Ctr, Cabot Corp, Bank of Am. *Publ:* Contribr (with Julia Ayres), Monotype Techniques, Watson Guptill, 91; Printmaking Techniques, Watson Guptill, 93; New American Paintings, Open Studios Press, 93; Suzanne Hodes' New York: Expressionism Redefined, exhib catalog, 1999; contrib, Boston Modern, Judith Bookbinder (auth), 2005; article and interview, Am Art Collector, 5/2008. *Dealer:* Artana Gallery; ART 3 Gallery, Manchester, NH; Boston Art Drydock Ave Boston MA. *Mailing Add:* 35 Riverside Dr Waltham MA 02154

HODGE, R GAREY
PAINTER
1937. *Study:* Eastern Ill Univ, BS, 61, MA (painting), 73. *Exhib:* Tri-State Exhib, Evansville Mus, Ind, 59; Miss Valley Exhib, Ill State Mus, Springfield, 64; Ill Bell Tel Exhib, Chicago, 67; River Roads Exhib, St Louis, 69, 70 & 72; 5th Int Biennial Sport Fine Arts, La Pinacoteca, Barcelona, Spain, 75; Western Ill Univ, 78. *Teaching:* Instr painting, graphics & design, Springfield High Sch, formerly. *Mem:* Ill State Mus Soc. *Media:* Acrylic, Watercolor. *Mailing Add:* 2413 Raleigh Rd Springfield IL 62704-6111

HODGES, JIM
PAINTER
b Spokane, Wash, 1957. *Study:* Ft Wright Col, Wash, BFA, 80; Pratt Inst, MFA, 86. *Exhib:* Solo exhibs, A Diary of Flowers, CR Gallery, NY, 94, States, Fabric Workshop & Mus, Philadelphia, 96, yes, Marc Foxx, Santa Monica, Ca, 96, Every Way, Mus Contemp Art, Chicago, 99, This and This, CR Gallery, NY, 2002, Colorsound, Addison Gallery Am Art, Phillips Acad, Mass, 2003, Returning, Art Pace, San Antonio, 2003, Don't be Afraid, Worcester Art Mus, Mass, 2004, Heaven & Earth, Centro Galego de Arte Contemporanea, Santiago de Compostello, Spain, 2005; group exhibs at Selections From The Artists File, Artists Space, NY, 88, Partnership for the Homeless with AIDS, Christie's, NY, 90, Our Perfect World, Grey Art Gallery, NY, 93, Ethereal Materialism, Apex Art, NY, 94, It's How You Play the Game, Exit Art/The First World, NY, 94, New Works, Feigen Gallery, Chicago, 95, Poetics of Obsession, Linda Kirkland Gallery, NY, 97, Age of Influence: Reflections in the Mirror of Am Cult, Mus Contemp Art, Chicago, 2000, Gardens of Pleasure, John Michael Kohler Arts Ctr, Sheboygan, Wis, 2000; CAMERA WORKS: The Photog Impulse in Contemp Art, Boesky Gallery, NY, 2001, Life Death Love Hate Pleasure Pain, Mus Contemp Art, Chicago, 2002, In Full View, Andrea Rosen Gallery, NY, 2003, Treble, Sculpture Ctr, Long Island City, NY, 2004, Whitney Biennial, Whitney Mus Am Art, 2004, Visual Music: 1905-2005, Mus Contemp Art, Los Angeles, 2005, Landscape Confection, Wexner Ctr Arts, Columbus, Ohio, 2005. *Awards:* Recipient, Mid Atlantic Arts Found, Nat Educ Asn, 92, Albert Ucross Prize, 2001; Reg Fel, Paper & Works on Paper, 92; grantee Louis Comfort Tiffany Found, 95; Alpert Award in Visual Arts, Calif Inst Arts, Valencia, 2006. *Mailing Add:* c/o CR Gallery 535 W 22nd St 3rd fl New York NY 10011

HODGKIN, CARTER
PAINTER, PRINTMAKER
b Warrenton, Va. *Study:* Va Commonwealth Univ, Richmond, BFA (painting & printmaking), 1976. *Work:* NYNEX Corp, NY; Pfizer Corp; Goldman Sachs; Zimmerli Art Mus, NJ; Libr Congress, Washington, DC; and many more. *Comn:* Percent for Art Program, Remsen Hall, Queens Coll, New York, 2009. *Exhib:* Solo exhibs, Nature Mortre Gallery, New York, 1983, White Columns, New York, 1986, Berland/Hall Gallery, New York, 1991-92, Ctr for Art Media, Karlsruhe, Ger, 1997, Cheryl Pelavin Fine Art, New York, 2004; Biennale, Bronx Mus, New York, 1987; Strange Attractions - Signs of Chaos, New Mus, New York, 1989; Excess in the Technomediacratic Society, Musee Dole, France, 1992; The Exquisite Corpse, Drawing Ctr, New York, 1993; Book Porjects from Dieu Donne, Berkshire Mus, Mass, 1994; Liminal, Univ Mass, Amherst, 2003; Midnight Full of Stars, NJ Ctr for the Arts, Summit, 2008. *Awards:* Printmaking Fel, Avocet Portfolios, New York, 1987; New York Found Arts Fel, 1988, 2009; Workspace Fel, Dieu Donne Papermill, New York, 1991; WTC Recovery Grant, Pollock-Krasner Found, 2002; Gottlieb Found Fel, 2004

HODGKINS, ROSALIND SELMA
PAINTER
b Farmington, Maine, May 25, 1942. *Study:* Univ SFla; Pratt Inst, BFA; Art Students League. *Work:* Southern Ill Univ, Carbondale; Bronx Mus Fine Arts, NY; Hewitt Sch, NY; Prudential Insurance Co. *Exhib:* Solo exhibs, Warren Benedek Gallery, NY 72 & 73 & James Yu Gallery, NY, 76; Kensington Arts Asn, Toronto, Ont, 75; PS 1 Pattern Painting Show, NY, 77; O1A Art in Pub Places Show, NY, 77; Soho Ctr Visual Arts Show, NY, 81; 55 Mercer Gallery, NY, 86. *Awards:* MacDowell Colony Fel, 77-78. *Media:* Oil

HODLEY, JANE See Dixon, Jenny (Jane) Hoadley

HOEBER, JULIAN
VIDEO ARTIST
b Philadelphia, 1974. *Study:* Tufts Univ, BA (Art History); Karel deGrote Hogeschool, Antwerp, Belgium; Sch Mus Fine Arts, Boston, BFA ; Art Ctr Coll Design, Pasadena, Calif, MFA. *Exhib:* Solo exhibs include Blum & Poe, Santa Monica, Calif, 2002, 2005, Essor Gallery, London, 2003, Galleria Francesca Kaufmann, Milan, 2007, Armory Show, New York, 2007; Group exhibs include Intro, Jenn Joy Gallery, San Francisco, 1998; Face to Face, The Stage Gallery, Merrick, NY, 1999 ; Morbid Curiosity, Los Angeles, 2001; I See a Darkness, Blum & Poe, Santa Monica, Calif, 2003; Premiere, A Gavlak Projs Prod, New York, 2003; Very Early Pictures, Luckman Gallery, Calif State Univ, Los Angeles, 2004; The Wonder & Horror of the Human Head, 4F, Los Angeles, 2006; Jim Shaw's Army, Rental Gallery, Los Angeles, 2006; A Selected State, Emily Tsingou Gallery, London, 2006; Trudi: No Jerks, Rental Gallery, New York, 2007; Against the Grain, Los Angeles Contemp Exhibs, Los Angeles, 2008. *Dealer:* Blum & Poe Gallery 2754 S La Cienega Blvd Los Angeles CA 90034

HOFER, INGRID (INGEBORG)
PAINTER, INSTRUCTOR
b New York, NY. *Study:* Meisterschule Fuer Mode, Hamburg, Ger, BA, 48; Univ Hamburg; Traphagen Sch Design, New York, 51; with A Odefey, Goettingen, Ger, Albert Bross, Jr, John R Grabach, Adolf Konrad & Nicholas Reale; Kathrine Chang Liu, master classes with Prof Glenn Bradshaw, 98. *Work:* Fairleigh Dickinson Univ, NJ; Good Shepherd Hosp, Ill; Lumus Co, NJ; Dana Corp, Ohio; Piedmont Tech Coll, SC. *Comn:* Many pvt comns in Ger, Switz, Sweden, England, Australia & US, 56-. *Exhib:* Tweed Mus; Union League, Chicago, 81; Women Alive, Toledo, Ohio, 86, 87 & 89; Winter Sojourn, Edison Plaza, Toledo, 87; Collectors Corner, Toledo Mus, 89-93 & 98-; Women on Paper, Anderson, SC, 96; Arnold Gallery, Aiken, SC, 97-98; Aiken Ctr for the Arts, SC, 2009; solo exhibs, Channing Gallery, Toledo, Ohio, Covenant Club Gallery, Chicago, Ill, Coach House Gallery, Detroit, Arnold Gallery, Aiken, SC; USAA Etherredge Art Gallery, 2002-2010; Gertrude Herbert Inst Art, Georgia, SC. *Teaching:* Instr mixed media, Acad Artists, Trailside Mus, Mountainside, NJ, 68-70; instr, Grosse Pointe War Mem, Mich, 74-78, Country Side Art Ctr, Arlington Heights, Ill, 81-83, Toledo Arts Club 81-93, Lourdes Coll, Sylvania, Ohio, 90,McCormack Arts Council, 94-2006; art instr (retired). *Awards:* Am Watercolor Soc Traveling Show Award, 73; Purchase Award, Union League, Ill, 81; Nat Award, Ga Watercolor Soc, 94, 96; Best of Show, Etheridge Ctr, 2008. *Mem:* Fel Am Artists Prof League; Catharine Lorillard Wolfe Art Club; SC Watercolor Soc; NJ Watercolor Soc; assoc Am Watercolor Soc; Ga Watercolor Soc. *Media:* Watercolor, Mixed Media, Acrylic. *Interests:* Watercolor, pastel, acrylic, mixed media, abstract, traditional painting. *Dealer:* Aiken Ctr for the Arts Aiken SC 29801; Art on Board, Augusta GA; Am Gallery Sylvania OH; Toledo Mus OH. *Mailing Add:* 209 Old Ferry Rd McCormick SC 29835

HOFERER, MARIETTA
ARTIST
Study: Hunter Coll, New York, BFA, 1993; Hochschule der Kunste, Berlin, Ger, MFA, 1995. *Work:* Columbus Mus, Ga; Ark Arts Ctr; Acad Art Mus, Easton, Md; Bellagio, Las Vegas; Saks Fifth Avenue. *Comn:* Zurich Capital Markets, One Chase Manhattan Plaza, New York, 2001. *Exhib:* Solo exhibs, Galerie im Kunsthaus Erfurt, Ger, 2002, Sandler Hudson Gallery, Atlanta, 2003, Dust Gallery, Las Vegas, 2005, Kentler Int Drawing Space, Brooklyn, 2006, Acad Art Mus, Easton, Md, 2008, NY Pub Libr, 2009, Hosfelt Gallery, San Francisco, 2010; Post-Systemic Art, Hunterdon Mus Art, Clinton, NJ, 2002; Frequencies, Marist Art Coll Gallery, Poughkeepsie, NY, 2003; Nat Drawing Invitational, Ark Arts Ctr, Little Rock, 2005; Art on Paper, Weatherspoon Art Mus, Univ NC, Greensboro, 2006; Variations in Black and White, BAM Brooklyn Acad Music, 2007; Reinventing Silverpoint, Connecticut Coll, Cummings Art Ctr, New London, 2009; Stuck Up, Islip Art Mus, East Islip, NY, 2010. *Awards:* Edward Albee Found Award, 1997, 2002, 2006; Pollock-Krasner Found Grant, 2004; NY Found Arts Fel, 2009. *Bibliog:* Holland Cotter (auth), A Flock of Fledglings, Testing Their Wings, NY Times, 1997; Jerry Cullum (auth), Lots of variations within Repetition, Atlanta Journal-Constitution, 2001; Cate mcQuaid (auth), Transporting their art past the merely lovely, Boston Globe, 2004; Chuck Twardy (auth), The Ideal and the Possible, Las Vegas Weekly, 2006. *Mailing Add:* EFA Studio Ctr 323 W 39 St Studio 813 New York NY 10018

HOFF, MARGO
PAINTER, COLLAGE ARTIST
b Tulsa, Okla. *Study:* Tulsa Univ; Art Inst Chicago; Pratt Graphics Ctr; St Marys Col, Notre Dame, hon DFA, 69; Drew Univ, hon DFA, 86. *Work:* Whitney Mus Am Art, NY; Brooklyn Mus, NY; Art Inst Chicago; Krannert Mus, Univ Ill; Rosenwald Found Collection; Metrop Mus, NY, 82-86. *Comn:* Wall design, Home Fed Bank, Chicago, 66; Mirror to Man (mural), Mayo Clinic, Rochester, Minn, 68; stage set & costumes for Murray Louis Dance Co, 69; portrait of S Madeleva, St Marys Col, Notre Dame, 70; two murals, New Govt Bldg, Plattsburgh, NY, 77-79; Wall Hanging: Peat, Marwick, Mitchel, Washington, DC. *Exhib:* Solo exhibs, Banfer Gallery, NY, 64, 66 & 68, Fairweather Hardin Gallery, 64-79, 81, 83, 86, Bednarz Gallery, Los Angeles, 67 & Babcock Gallery, NY, 74; Hadler Rodriguez Galleries, 78 & 79; Betty Parsons Gallery, NY, 81-82. *Teaching:* Teaching Grant, Duke Foun, Am Univ, Beirut, 56-57; artist-in-residence, Univ Southern Ill, 66-67; artist-in-residence, St Marys Col, Notre Dame, 69-70, 78, 82, & 84; teaching grant, Goretti Sch, Fort Portal, Uganda, E Africa, 71; Col St Maria, Sao Paulo, Brasil; AIR, Rhode Island Sch Design, 80. *Publ:* Illusr, Christmas House, Coachhouse, 65; illusr, 4 Seasons & 5 Senses, 66 & Christmas Cupboard, 67, Funk & Wagnall. *Mailing Add:* 114 W 14th St New York NY 10011-7304

HOFFMAN, ERIC
PAINTER, PRINTMAKER
b Santa Cruz, Calif, July 16, 1952. *Study:* Cabrillo Col, Aptos, Calif, AA, 72; San Jose State Univ, BA, (painting), 75, & MFA (painting), 78. *Work:* Am Express; Monterey Peninsula Mus Art, Calif; San Jose Mus Art; E F Hutton, NY; Bumper Develop Corp, Ltd, Calgary; Price-Waterhouse; Merril, Skidmore, Owens, NY. *Comn:* Large scale 2-part panel painting, Bumper Develop Corp Ltd, Calgary, Alta, 81; 2-part panel painting, Juan Montoya Design, NY, 83; 3-part enviro piece, Emerald Fund, San Francisco, Calif, 84; 3-part panel, Battenberg, Fillhardt & Wright, San Jose, Calif, 84; series of 28 monogotypes, Arts Coun, Santa Clara Co, 86. *Exhib:* Oakland Mus, Calif, 81; Chain Reaction, San Francisco Arts Comt, Calif, 85; Scratching the Surface, San Jose Mus Art, Calif, 85; San Jose Inst Contemp Art, Calif, 86; Metrop Mus Art, Miami, Fla, 86; Miller-Brown Gallery, San Francisco, 86; Expressive Surfaces, Beverly Gordon Gallery, Dallas, Tex, 88; Twining Gallery, NY, 88; Maison du Cult, Grenoble, France, 88. *Pos:* Asst preparator, San Jose Mus Art, Calif, 76-79. *Teaching:* Guest lectr expressive drawing, Calif Polytech Univ; grad seminar ceramics & pictorial arts, San Jose State Univ, 85; instr, color-design, Cabrillo Col. *Awards:* Du Credit Commercial de France Award, 85; Du Ministere de al Culture, Paris, France, 85; De la Villa de Granonle, France, 85. *Bibliog:* Article, Arts Mag, 82; Sally Robertson (auth), Art in San Jose, Art Week, 76; Catalog, E F Hutton Collection, 86. *Mem:* San Jose Inst Contemp Art. *Media:* Miscellaneous. *Dealer:* Twining Gallery 568 Broadway Suite 107 New York NY 10012; Katia LaCoste Gallery 227 N First St San Jose CA 95062

HOFFMAN, HELEN BACON
PAINTER
b San Antonio, Tex, July 14, 1930. *Study:* Ogontz Coll, Philadelphia; Parsons Sch Design. *Work:* NAm-Mex Inst Cult Relations, Mexico City; Corcoran Gallery Art, Washington, DC; Chicago Art Inst; Nelson-Atkins Art Gallery, Kansas City, Mo. *Exhib:* Solo exhibs, NAm-Mex Inst Cult Relations, Mexico City, 62, Veerhoff Galleries, Washington, DC, 65, 67, 72, 77, 81, 87 & 97, North Star Gallery, San Antonio, Tex, 66, 70, 72 & 77, Grand Cent Art Galleries, New York, 66, 71, 73-74, 76, 85 & 89, Pritchard Galleries, San Antonio, Tex, 78 & 80, Musselman Gallery, San Antonio, Tex, 82 & 86, Nan Ette Richardson Fine Art, San Antonio, Tex, 96 & 2006. *Awards:* Pastel Soc of Am, New York, 76, 78, 85, Designated master Pastelist, Pastel

Soc Am, 85; Pa Acad Fine Arts, Philadelaphia, 69; First Place Painting, Salmagundi Club, New York, 74; and many others. *Mem:* Artists Equity Asn; Soc Washington Artists; Pastel Soc Am; Nat Arts Club; Catharine Lorillard Wolfe Art Club; Am Art League, New York; Nat Soc Arts & Letters, Washington, DC; Salmagundi Club; and others. *Media:* Oil, Pastel. *Res:* Realism, action of light on everyday subjects. *Interests:* Avocation, growing orchids. *Dealer:* Nan Ette Richardson Fine Art 555 E Basse Rd Ste 105 San Antonio TX 78209; Lagerquist Gallery 3235 Pace's Ferry Pl NW Atlanta GA 30305. *Mailing Add:* 8320 Woodgrove Rd Jacksonville FL 32256

HOFFMAN, MARGUERITE STEED
COLLECTOR
Study: Univ Okla, BA (classics); Univ Va, MA (art hist). *Pos:* Dir, Gerald Peters Gallery, formerly; dir mktg & pub rels, Dallas Mus Art, formerly, bd dirs, currently; bd dirs, Dignitas Int, Hockaday Sch, Bard Coll Ctr for Curatorial Studies, Tex Freedom Network & Pub Radio Int. *Awards:* Named one of Top 200 Collectors, ARTnews mag, 2003-11. *Collection:* Postwar American and European Art; Chinese monochromes. *Mailing Add:* Dallas Mus Art 1717 N Harwood Dallas TX 75201

HOFFMAN, MARILYN FRIEDMAN
DIRECTOR
b Jan 27, 1946. *Study:* Brown Univ, Providence, RI, BA (art hist), 67, MA (art hist), 71. *Hon Degrees:* Montserrat Coll Art, Beverly, Mass, Hon Dr Fine Arts, 96. *Pos:* Cur asst, Educ Dept, Mus Art, RI Sch Design, 67-68; gallery asst, Adelson Galleries, Inc, Boston, 68-69 & 70-71; grad asst, Educ Dept, Metrop Mus Art, New York, 69; adj lectr, Dept Pub Educ, Mus Fine Arts, Boston, 70-71; cur, Brockton Art Mus-Fuller Mem, Mass, 71-73, actg dir, 73-74, dir, 74-84; cur, Currier Gallery Art, Manchester, NH, 84-88, dir, 88-95; prinicpal Mus Search & Reference, Exec Search for Mus, 2003-. *Mem:* Am Asn Mus; Coll Art Asn Am; New Eng Mus Asn (treas); Arts 1000; Federated Arts Manchester (trustee, 91-92); NH Coun on the Humanities (adv bd, 99-); NH Charitable Found Manchester Regional Community Found (bd mem, 2001). *Publ:* Auth, Pssst, Airbrush Painting (catalog), 72, The Good Things in Life/19th Century American Still Life (catalog), 73 & Unstretched Paintings (catalog), 73, Brockton Art Ctr-Fuller Mem; Museum Loans at Brockton, Art J, Vol 32, 73; contribr, The Rise of Landscape Painting in France: Corot to Monet, Currier Gallery Art, 91. *Mailing Add:* 45 Hardy Rd Londonderry NH 03053-2872

HOFFMAN, MARTIN
PAINTER, ILLUSTRATOR
b St Augustine, Fla, Nov 1, 1935. *Study:* Univ Miami, 55; Fla State Univ, 56. *Work:* Miami Mus Mod Art; Va Mus Fine Arts, Richmond; Indianapolis Mus Art; JB Speed Mus, Louisville, Ky; Norton Gallery of Art, West Palm Beach, Fla; Flint Inst Arts (the epic series); Witchita State Mus; Maine Mus Mod Art, Miami; Mus Mod Art, New York. *Comn:* numerous paintings & illus, Playboy Mag, 66-05; Basile, Milan, 80-82; NASA Space Shuttle Program, 82-92; Hakehodo Agency, Tokyo, 85; Toyo Cinema, Japan, 86. *Exhib:* Air & Space Mus, Smithsonian Inst, 82-83; Johnson Space Ctr, Univ Houston, 83; The Educated Eye, State Mus, Albany, NY, 84; The Epic New York Paintings, Stetson Univ, 90; Intimate Works, R Thames Fine Art, Ormond, Fla, 91; The Realist Painting, Ormond Mem Mus, 91; Ok Harris Works of Art, New York City, 72-75. *Collection Arranged:* Joan & Roland Des Combes, Windermere, Fla; Mary T & James Zaengle, Cooperstown, NY. *Pos:* Art dir, numerous Miami advert agencies, 57-70; designer-illusr, Graphic Arts, Inc, 60-70. *Teaching:* Instr grad painting & drawing, Univ Miami, 69-71 & Casements Cult Ctr, 91-92. *Awards:* Art Dir Awards, Miami Art Dirs Club, 59-70; Illus Awards, Chicago Advert Club, 71-79; Elegance for the Eighties, Best Serv Illusr, Playboy, 79; and others. *Bibliog:* Griffin Smith (auth), article, Tropic Mag, 9/71; article, Illus Japan, No 18, 10/82; Diane Copelon (auth), article, Ormond Beach Observer, 8/26/90; John Wirt (auth), article, Daytona Beach News-J, 5/26/91; Chuck Twardy (auth), article, Orlando Sentinel, 6/2/91; Ellen Fischer (auth), Vero Beach Mag (10 page article), Feb 2007, April 2009. *Media:* Acrylic, Oil, Watercolor. *Res:* Classical painting methods, Pompeii, Herculaneum, Autobiographies. *Interests:* Asian and Western philosophy; Modern music. *Collection:* Numerous private collections. *Publ:* Illusr, Playboy, 67-2005, Italian, Spanish, Japanese edits Playboy, 67-2000; Art Direction, 4/72; NY Times & Artforum, 74; Fortune, 74; illustr Rolling Stone, 73, Record World Cover, 80; Vero Beach Mag, 2007. *Mailing Add:* 1840 Waterford Dr #2 Vero Beach FL 32966-8039

HOFFMAN, NANCY
DEALER
b New York, NY, Feb 23, 1944. *Study:* Wellesley Col, 62-64; Barnard Col, Columbia Univ, BA (art hist), 66. *Pos:* Asst registrar, Asia House Gallery, New York, 64-69; dir, French & Co Contemp Gallery, New York, 69-72 & Nancy Hoffman Gallery, New York, 72-. *Mem:* Art Dealers Asn Am. *Specialty:* Contemporary art: paintings, drawings, sculpture and graphics. *Mailing Add:* c/c Nancy Hoffman Gallery 520 W 27th St Ste 301 New York NY 10001-5548

HOFFMAN, NEIL JAMES
ADMINISTRATOR, EDUCATOR
b Buffalo, NY, Sept 2, 1938. *Study:* State Univ NY Buffalo, BS, 60, MS, 67. *Pos:* Dir, Prog Artisanry, Boston Univ, 74-79; dean & chief admin officer, Otis Art Inst Parsons Sch Design, 79-83; pres, Sch Art Inst Chicago, 83-85, Calif Col Arts & Crafts, 85-93 & Otis Col Art & Design, 93-. *Teaching:* Art & chmn unified art dept, Grand Island Pub Schs, NY, 61-68; assoc prof design & art educ & assoc dean col fine & appl arts, Rochester Inst Technol, 68-74. *Mailing Add:* 9045 Lincoln Blvd Los Angeles CA 90045

HOFFMAN, WILLIAM MCKINLEY, JR
PAINTER, EDUCATOR
b Blairsville, Pa, Jan 25, 1934. *Study:* Pa Acad Fine Arts & Univ Pa, BFA, 62; Tyler Sch Art, Temple Univ, MFA, 67. *Work:* NJ State Mus, Trenton; Stedman Art Gallery, Rutgers Univ, Camden, NJ; Camden Co Cult & Heritage, NJ; Thomas Jefferson Univ, Philadelphia; City Camden, NJ; Woodmere Art Mus, Philadelphia. *Comn:* Portrait paintings, Sch of Law, Rutgers, Camden, 86 & 88; landscape painting, Marriott Corp, 87; cityscape, Copper Hosp Univ Med Ctr, 92; Latrobe Trinity Lutheran Church, 2002. *Exhib:* Eastern Regional Drawing Soc Show, Philadelphia Mus Art, 65; 55th Ann, Allied Artists Am, Nat Acad Design, NY, 68; 164th Ann, Pa Acad Fine Arts, Philadelphia, 69; 34th & 35th Ann, Butler Institute Am Art, Youngstown, Ohio, 69 & 70; Earth Art 1 & 2, Philadelphia Civic Ctr Mus, 73 & 79; Art from NJ IX & X, 74 & 75 & Visual Arts Fel Winners Exhib, 80, NJ State Mus, Trenton; Peale House Gallery, Pa Acad Fine Arts, Philadelphia, 83; retrospective (with catalog), Stedman Gallery, Rutgers Univ, Camden, 91; St Martin-in-the-Fields Gallery, London, Eng, 94; St Vincent Coll, Latrobe, Pa, 2001; Laurel Arts, Somerset, Pa, 2007. *Teaching:* Instr to prof, Rutgers Univ, Camden Coll Arts & Sci, NJ, 67-, chmn, Dept Art, 67-76, 79-82 & 92-95, prof emer, 2000; adj prof, St Vincent College. *Awards:* Purchase Award, Earth Art 3, Touche, Ross & Co, Philadelphia, 79; Artists Fel, NJ State Coun Arts, 80 & 84; Purchase Award, City of Camden, NJ, 88; and others. *Bibliog:* Piri Halasz (auth), State artists display skills, New York Times, 7/6/75; Robert Baxter (auth), Romantic realist, Courier Post, NJ, 10/30/81; Judy Baeher (auth), Preserving Camden's history on canvas, Philadelphia Inquirer, 4/7/91; Marjorie Wertz (auth), Pa has a Friend in Uruguay, Greenburg Tribune-Review, 6/2/2002. *Mem:* Artists Equity Asn; fel Pa Acad Fine Arts; Coll Art Asn. *Media:* Oil, Casein. *Mailing Add:* 110 Beech Dr Ligonier PA 15658

HOFFMANN, ERIKA
COLLECTOR, PATRON
b Germany. *Pos:* Founder, Lady van Laack, Berlin, 1968; co-founder, Collection Hoffmann/Sammlung Hoffmann, Berlin, 1997. *Awards:* Named one of Top 200 Collectors, ARTnews mag, 2006-13. *Collection:* Contemporary art. *Mailing Add:* Collection Hoffmann Sophie-Gips Hofe Aufgang C Sophienstrasse 21 Berlin 10178 Germany

HOFMANN, DOUGLAS WILLIAM
PAINTER, PRINTMAKER
b Baltimore, Md, Feb 13, 1945. *Study:* Md Inst Coll Art, BFA (cum laude), studied with Joseph Sheppard, 64-68. *Work:* Del Art Mus, Wilmington; Joslyn Art Mus, Omaha; Marquette Univ Fine Art Collection, Milwaukee; Nat Mem Mus & Archives, Washington, DC; Nassau Co Mus, NY. *Comn:* Painted stained glass panels, Baltimore City Schs, Md, 70. *Exhib:* Peale Mus, Baltimore, 70; Md Biennial, Baltimore Mus Art, 71 & 73; Realism in Maryland, Washington Co Mus, Hagerstown, Md, 72; Allied Artists Am, 74 & Audubon Artists Ann, 76, Nat Acad, NY; Ann Mid-Yr Exhib, Butler Inst, Youngstown, Ohio, 74-75; Cherry Creek Gallery, Denver, 78; solo exhib, Jack Gallery, NY, 79, 81, 84 & 89; 30th Nat Print Exhib, Hunterdon Art Ctr, Clinton, NJ, 86; Nat Acad Design, NY, 87; Halcyon Gallery, London, 94. *Teaching:* Instr painting, Md Inst, Baltimore, 74-75. *Awards:* Best Traditional Painting, Md Biennial, Baltimore Mus, 71; Award, Soc Am Graphic Artists, New York, 87; Award, Salmagundi Club, New York, 88. *Bibliog:* Jack Solomon (auth), Douglas Hofmann, Circle Fine Art Corp, 81; Will Grant (auth), Old and established, Artspeak, 6/2/81; Jerry Tallmer (auth), Mr Vermeer say hello to this here Mr Hofmann, New York Post, 10/31/81. *Media:* Oil; Lithography. *Publ:* Auth, A Retrospective Exhibition 1978-1989, Circle Fine Art Corp, New York, 89; Tales of Hofmann, Dance Pages Mag, 94. *Dealer:* Washington Green 59/60 The Pallasades B24XJ Birmingham England; Halcyon Gallery London. *Mailing Add:* 15 W Mt Vernon Pl Baltimore MD 21201-5108

HOFMANN, KAY
SCULPTOR
b Green Bay, Wis, Dec 3, 1932. *Study:* Art Inst Chicago (Ryerson Fel), grad, 55; studied at Acad de Grande Chaumiere, Paris, with Ossip Zadkine, 55-56. *Work:* Borg Warner, Chicago. *Comn:* Marble sculpture, Continental Plaza Hotel, Chicago, 70; two wood carvings, comn by Hugh Hefner, Los Angeles, 77; marble portrait, Gonstead Med Ctr, Mt Horeb, Wis, 81; alabaster sculpture, Arthur Anderson Assocs, Chicago, 84-90. *Exhib:* Solo exhibs, Art Inst Chicago, 78 & Rahr-West Mus, Manitowoc, Ill, 85; 30th Illinois Invitational, Ill State Mus, Springfield, 78; 37th & 40th Indiana Salon Shows, Northern Ind Arts Assoc, Munster, Ind, 79 & 83; Lakeview Mus, Peoria, Ill, 79; Foothills Art Ctr, Golden, Colo, 83. *Teaching:* Instr sculpture, N Shore Art League, Winnetka, Ill, 58-83; instr stone carving, Suburban Fine Arts Ctr, Highland Park, Ill, 59-90 & Blackhawk Mountain Sch Art, Colo, summers 83-90. *Awards:* Best of Show, 29th Ann Open Spectrum, Libertyville Art Ctr, 83 & Arthur Baer Competition, 85. *Bibliog:* Elaine Snyderman (producer), Viewpoints/Kay Hofmann, Cable TV, 86; Michael Bonesteel (auth), Caught in the Coils, Pioneer Press, 86; Arthur Williams (auth), Sculpture: Technique, Form, Content, 89. *Mem:* N Shore Art League; Suburban Fine Arts Ctr; Nat Wildlife Fedn; World Wildlife Fund; Sierra Club. *Media:* Stone, Wood. *Interests:* Collectible dolls and toys; wildlife. *Mailing Add:* 3140 N 77th Ave Elmwood Park IL 60707

HOGAN, FELICITY
MUSEUM DIRECTOR
b England. *Work:* Mus Contemp Art, 1997-. *Exhib:* Clark & Hogan; Paintings & Collab, Barry Gallery, 2002—03; Clark in Context: Day of the Revolutionary, 2003. *Pos:* Co-Dir, Mus Contemp Art, Wash, 96-. *Mailing Add:* Museum of Contemporary Art 1054 31st St Washington DC 20007

HOGBIN, STEPHEN
SCULPTOR
b Tolworth Surrey, United Kingdom. *Study:* Kingston Coll Art, United Kingdom, NDD; Royal Coll Art, United Kingdom, Des RCA. *Work:* Art Bank Can Coun, Ottawa, Ont; Australia Coun, Sydney; Ariz State Univ Art Mus; Can Mus Civilization, Ottawa; Yale Univ Gallery; Tom Thomson Mem Art Gallery, Ont; Los Angeles Co Mus; and others. *Comn:* Sculpture, Melbourne State Col, Australia; entrance & screen, Metrop Toronto Libr Can, 77 & 89; murals, Queens Park, 80 & CIL Inc, Toronto, 81; installation, Cambridge Gallery, Ont; City of Owensound, Ont. *Exhib:* Chairs, Art Gallery Ont, Toronto, 75; Art of Woodturning, Am Craft Mus, NY, 83; Painted Reliefs

Traveling Exhib (catalog), 89; Re; Turning (catalog), 90, John B Aird Gallery, Toronto; McMaster Univ, Hamilton, 92; Progress of Walking: The Body in Pub Art, Can Ctr Arts at Owen Sound, 92; Two Chairs, Jamieson Gallery, BC, Travel-Winnipeg Gallery, BC, Nelson Gallery, BC & Mary Black Gallery, Halifax, 07; Unity and Diversity, Cheongsu Int Craft Biennale, 09. *Collection Arranged:* Political Landscapes: Sacred and Secular Sites, Tom Thomson Gallery, 91; Curators Focus: Turning in Context, W Turning Ctr, 97; Wood: An Aesthetic and Social Ecology, Tom Thomson Gallery, 98; Fragments, Cafe Gallery Projects, London, Tom Thomson Gallery. *Pos:* Artist-in-residence, Melbourne State Col, Australia Coun, 75-76, Haystack Mountain Sch Crafts, 96, Australian Nat Univ, 02, Univ of the Arts, Philadelphia, 02. *Teaching:* Col Educ, Univ Toronto, 71-72; instr sculpture, Georgian Col, Barrie, Ont, 85-87; lectures & workshops, Royal Col Art, UK, RI Sch Design, USA, Melbourne State Col, Australia, Forestech Australia, 99; and others. *Awards:* Award, Ontario Arts Coun, 99, Can Coun, 02, Royal Coll Art; Queen Elizabeth II, Diamond Jubilee medal. *Bibliog:* D L McKinley (auth), The forms of Stephen Hogbin, Craft Horizons, 4/74; Jeanne Parkin (auth), Art in Architecture, 82; Edward Cooke (auth), The makers hand, Wood Turning in NAm, 03; Mark Sfirri (auth) Hogbin Reflections Woodwork, 08. *Mem:* Royal Can Acad. *Media:* Wood. *Res:* investigation of fragmentation. *Publ:* Auth, Turning full circle, Fine Woodworking, 79; Wood Turning, Van Nostrand Reinhold, 80; Curator's Focus, Wood Turning Ctr, 97; Wood: An Aesthetic and Social Ecology, Tom Thomson Gallery, 98; Appearance & Reality, Cambium Press, 00; Evaluating: The Critque in the Studio Workshop, Ginger Press Inc, 08. *Dealer:* David Kaye Gallery, 1092 Queen St W, Toronto M6J 1H9 Canada. *Mailing Add:* 462528 Con 24 Georgian Bluffs ON Canada NOH2TO

HOGE, ROBERT WILSON
CURATOR, EDUCATOR
b Wilmington, Del, Apr 5, 1947. *Study:* Univ Colo, BA (anthrop), 69; Univ Chicago, 69-70; Univ Colo, Teacher cert, 73. *Collection Arranged:* Thematic Exhibitions in Art & Sci, Sanford Mus & Planetarium, 76-81; Exhibits of Coins, Paper Money, Tokens & Medals, Mus Am Numismatic Asn, 81-98; Two Bits: the Quarter Dollar in Am History; ANA Mus: Recent Acquisitions; Money of Vermont; ANA Hall of Fame, Mus Am Numismatic Asn, 99; A Salute to the Dollar, Mus Am Numismatic Asn, 99; The 1943 Copper Cent, Mus Am Numismatic Asn, 99; Balkan Bonanza, Roman Provincial Coins in the ANA Mus, Mus Am Numismatic Asn, 99; Holiday Numismatics, Mus Am Numismatic Asn, 99; Let Us Show You the Money?, Mus Am Numismatic Asn, 2000; The Wonderful World of Money: Coming to 'Terms' with Numismatics, Mus Am Numismatic Asn, 2000; Coinage of the Romans: Selected Themes, Mus Am Numismatic Asn, 2000; Numismatic Technology, Mus Am Numismatic Asn, 2000; Platinum: a Metal with a Message, Mus Am Numismatic Asn, 2000. *Pos:* dir, Sanford Mus and Planetarium, 76-81; cur, Mus Am Numismatic Asn, 81-; mgr, Am Numismatic Asn Authentication Bur, 90-; prog partic, Int Partnerships among Mus, Am Asn Mus & Int Coun Mus, 90; cons, Native Am Rights Fund/Pawnee Indians repatriation Mus Nebr Hist, Nebr Hist Soc, Lincoln, 90, Joslyn Art Mus, Omaha, Nebr, 91 & Art and Architecture Thesaurus, Getty Art Hist Info Prog, Williamstown, Mass, 91. *Teaching:* tchr, Boulder Valley Sch Sys, Colo, 73-75; instr anthrop, Buena Vista Col, Storm Lake, Iowa, 76; sem instr, Colo Col, Colorado Springs, 83-. *Awards:* Outstanding Young Men of Am, 81. *Mem:* Am Numismatic Soc; Int Coun Mus; Colo-Wyo Asn Mus; Am Asn Mus; Mountain Plains Mus Asn; Royal Numismatic Soc. *Res:* American archaeology, historical studies; Old World archaeology; numismatics. *Publ:* Ed, Northwest Chapter Newsletter, Iowa Archaeol Soc, Sanford Mus; Museum, Column, The Numismatist, 83-; auth, Crack-up! Notes on a Vietnamese Issue, Asia Numismatics, No 1, 2000; Chinese numismatics in American museums, ICOMON: Int Com Money and Banking Mus, 2000; ed, contribr, reviewer, Oxford English Dictionary, New Am edit, 2001. *Mailing Add:* Am Numismatic Asn 818 N Cascade Ave Colorado Springs CO 80903

HOGLE, ANN MEILSTRUP
PAINTER
b San Francisco, Calif, Sept 23, 1927. *Study:* Univ Ore; Portland Mus Sch; Calif Coll Arts & Crafts, BFA, MFA, 79. *Work:* Neuberger Collection, NY; Kemper Group, Long Grove, Ill; St Francis Mem Hosp & Security Pac Bank, San Francisco; Int Bus Machines; Merrill Lynch; Portland Art Mus, Portland, Ore; Fresno Art Mus, Fresno, Calif; de Saisset Mus, Santa Clara, Calif; Bolinas Mus, Bolinas, Calif; and others. *Comn:* Triptych, Menlo Park Pub Libr, Calif. *Exhib:* Artists of Oregon, Portland Mus, 63 & 70; Phelan Awards, Calif Palace Legion Hon, San Francisco, 65; solo exhibs, William Sawy Gallery, San Francisco, 88, 90 & 93, Butters Gallery, Portland, Ore, 93, Bolinas Mus, Calif, 98, Smith Andersen Gallery, Palo Alto, Calif, 98, Fresno Art Mus, Calif, 98, de Saisset Mus, Santa Clara Univ, Calif, 98 & Commonweal, Bolinas, 99; Syntex, Palo Alto, 89; group exhib, Monterey Mus, Calif, 93, Bolinas Mus, Calif, 94; Spur Projs, Portola Valley, Calif; Natsoulas Gallery, Davis, Calif. *Bibliog:* Peninsula painter brings Bay Area's terrain to life, San Jose Mercury News, 5/31/98; Ann Hogle at the De Saisset Museum, Artweek, 7-8/98; Artist paints her life's story one brushstroke at a time, San Jose Mercury News, 9/20/98. *Media:* Oil. *Dealer:* Paragone Gallery Los Angeles CA; John Natsoulas Gallery Davis CA. *Mailing Add:* 45 Upper Lake Rd Woodside CA 94062-2634

HOI, SAMUEL CHUEN-TSUNG
EDUCATOR, ADMINISTRATOR
b Hong Kong, Mar 25, 1958; US citizen. *Study:* Columbia Col, NY, AB, 80; Columbia Sch Law, NY, JD, 83; Parsons Sch Design, NY, AAS, 86. *Pos:* Dir, AAS degree prog, Parsons Sch Design, NY 87-88; dir, Parsons Sch Design, Paris, 88-91; dean, Corcoran Sch Art, Wash, DC 91-2000; pres, Otis Coll Art & design, LA, 2000-2014; pres, Md Inst Coll Art, Baltimore, Md, 2014-. *Mem:* Asn Independent Sch Art & Design; Nat Asn Sch Art & Design; Partnership Community Health. *Mailing Add:* Maryland Institute College of Art 1300 W Mount Royal Ave Baltimore MD 21217

HOIE, CLAUS
PAINTER
b Stavanger, Norway, Nov 3, 1911; US citizen. *Study:* Pratt Inst; Art Students League; Ecole Beaux Arts, Paris. *Work:* Brooklyn Mus, NY; Norfolk Mus, Va; Butler Inst Am Art, Youngstown, Ohio; Okla Mus Art; Guild Hall Mus, East Hampton, NY; South St Seaport Mus, NY. *Exhib:* Am Watercolor Soc Ann, NY, 60-94; Brooklyn Mus Watercolor Biennial, 63; Mus Watercolor Painting, Mexico City, Mex, 68 & 89; Pa Acad Fine Arts Ann, 69; Childe Hassam Award Exhib, Nat Inst Arts & Lett, 73; solo exhibs, Akershus Castle Mus, Oslo, Norway, 82, South St Seaport Mus, NY, 92, Mystic Seaport Mus, 94 & 98, Nordic Heritage Mus, Seattle, 98; Retrospective, Watercolors, and Drawings, 43-2003; Guild Hall Mus, East Hampton, NY, Nov 13, 2004- Jan 9, 2005; and many others. *Awards:* Award for Painting, Am Acad Arts & Lett, 75; Award of Merit, Nat Acad Design, 81 & Obrig Prize, 85; Marine Environmental Wildlife Award, Mystic Seaport Mus Int, 98, 2002. *Mem:* Nat Acad (coun mem); Am Watercolor Soc (vpres, 60-62); Nat Arts Club, Audubon Soc. *Media:* Watercolor, Graphics. *Publ:* Auth, Technique of watercolor, Am Artist Mag, 57; My views on watercolor painting, North Light Mag, 70; The Log of the Whaler Helena, Two Bytes Publ Ltd, 94. *Mailing Add:* Hook Pond Ln PO Box 1323 East Hampton NY 11937

HOLABIRD, JEAN
PAINTER, PRINTMAKER
b Boston, Mass, 1946. *Study:* Art Students League, New York, 65-69; Inst Allende, Mexico, summers 65-69; Bennington Coll, Vt, BA, 69. *Work:* Prudential Life Insurance Co, Newark, NJ; First Nat City Bank, Chicago; Staatmuseum, West Berlin, Ger; Ragdale Found, Lake Forest, Ill; Metrop Mus Art, New York. *Comn:* Drawings, Bennington Rev, Vt, 69-70; cover illus, World Mag, New York, 80; cover, Hanging Loose Mag, New York, 81; and others. *Exhib:* Camden Coun Arts, London, Eng, 73; Two Painters, Saray Y Rentschler Gallery, New York, 78; solo exhib, Nathan A Bernstein Ltd, New York, 80; Hand-colored Etchings, Sarah Y Rentschler Gallery, New York, 82; Usdan Gallery, Vt, 84; Neo Persona, New York, 88, 90 & 91; Keyes Gallery, Sag Harbor, NY, 99 & 2000; Camos Gallery, Sag Harbor, 2001 & 2005-2006. *Teaching:* Instr painting, Inst Allende, San Miguel Allende, Mexico, summer 68; guest lectr, Parsons Sch Design, Pratt Inst, Cooper Union, New York, 75 & Sch Visual Arts, 79; artist-in-residence, Ragdale Found, 81. *Awards:* and others. *Bibliog:* Palmer Hasty (auth), A collaboration, Villager, 3/82; Bob Mahoney (auth), Arts Mag, 5/88; Greg Masters (auth), Interview Cover Mag, 5/91. *Media:* Watercolor, Oil. *Interests:* Literature, gardening. *Publ:* Auth, Out of the Runs - A New York Record, Gingko Press, 2002; Vladimir Nabokov's Alphabet in Color, Gingko Press, 2005. *Mailing Add:* 81 Warren St New York NY 10007

HOLBROOK, PETER GREENE
PAINTER, PRINTMAKER
b New York, NY, Apr 13, 1940. *Study:* Dartmouth Coll, BA (Marcus Heiman Award), 61; Brooklyn Mus, with Reuben Tam, cert (Beckman Fel), 63. *Work:* Nat Collection Fine Arts, Washington, DC; Brooklyn Mus, NY; Art Inst Chicago; Springfield Art Mus, Mo; Tucson Mus Art, Ariz; Oakland Mus Art, Calif; Mus of the Southwest, Midland, Tex. *Comn:* Gen Serv Admin (painting), Fed Courhouse, Sacramento, Calif, 98. *Exhib:* Chicago and Vicinity, Art Inst Chicago, 65 & 67-69; Solo Exhibs: Indianapolis Mus Art, 70, Peter Holbrook: Paintings (with catalog), Mesa SW Mus, Ariz, 96, N Ill Univ Art Mus, DeKalb, 97 & Springfield Art Mus, 97; Koffler Fund Collection, Smithsonian Inst, 79; Davidson Collection, Pa Acad Fine Arts, Philadelphia, 82; Green Woods and Crystal Waters, Phil Brook Mus Art, Tulsa, 99; Ten Painters, Morris Graves Mus Art, Eureka, Calif, 2000; Images of Water, Eureka City Hall, 2000; Magnifying the Mark, Morris Graves Mus Art, 2002; Landscape Interpretations, Grace Hudson Mus, Ukiah, Calif, 2005; The Grand Canyon from Dream to Icon, Tucson Mus of Art, Tucson, 2006; Masters of Illusion, Tempe Center for the Arts, Tempe, Ariz, 2008; A View from the Edge, Leslie Levy Fine Art, Scottsdale, Ariz, 2009; Rock of Ages, Peterson Cody Gallery, Santa Fe, NMex, 2009; Canyons, Scottsdale Fine Art, Ariz, 2012; Colo Plateau, Morris Graves Mus Art, Eureka, Calif, 2012; High Sierras, Sewell Gallery, Eureka, Calif, 2013. *Teaching:* Lectr painting, Univ Ill, Chicago Circle, 68-70 & Calif State Univ, Hayward, 70-71. *Awards:* Wild, Bartels & Clark Prizes, Chicago and Vicinity, Art Inst Chicago, 65, 67 & 68; Walter H Stevens Award, Watercolor USA, Springfield Art Mus, 81; Raffael Prize for Watercolor, Humboldt Cult Ctr, Eureka, Calif, 81. *Bibliog:* William Struve (auth), An American Landscape Collection, Zurick Kemper Dist Inc, Chicago, Ill, 97; Joni Louise Kinsey (auth), Majesty of the Grand Canyon: 150 Years in Art, First Glance Books, Cobb, Calif, 98; Katharine Kia Tehranian (auth), The Aesthetics of Presence: The Landscape Paintings of Peter Holbrook & Prospects: An Ann Am Cult Studies, Cambridge Univ Press, Mass, 99; Donald Haggerty (auth), Leading the West, Northland Publ, 97; Mary Anderson (auth), Close to the Land, Eureka Times tandard, Eureka, Calif, 9/16/2008; Peter Holbrook, Am Art Collector Mag, April 2006 & Feb 2009; Rosemary Carstens (auth), Getting Real Southwest Art Mag, 1/2011; Art of the National Park, Stern and McGarry, Fresco Fine Art Press, Santa Fe, NMex, 2013. *Media:* Oil. *Publ:* Auth, article, 11/67 & The Chicago saga of Carolee Schneemann, 3/68, Art Scene Mag; auth, Peter Holbrook Canyon Paintings, 2007; auth & publ, Peter Holbrook: Paintings A Catalog of the Touring Exhib, 96-97, 96. *Dealer:* Scottsdale Fine Art AZ; Sewell Gallery Eureka CA. *Mailing Add:* 5719 Briceland-Thorn Rd Redway CA 95560

HOLCOMB, GRANT
MUSEUM DIRECTOR, EDUCATOR
b San Bernardino, Calif, Sept 30, 1944. *Study:* Univ Calif, Los Angeles, AB, 67; Univ Del, MA, PhD, 72. *Pos:* dir, Memorial Art Gallery of Rochester, present . *Awards:* Kress fel, Nat Gallery Art, 71; Am Coun 7 Learned societies, 79; NEA, 99; NY State Coun of the Arts, 00. *Mem:* Asn Art Mus Dirs; Asn Art Mus; Coll Art Asn. *Publ:* Auth, The Forgotton Legacy of Jerome Myers, Am Art J, 5/77; John Sloan in Santa

Fe, Am Art J, 5/78; John Sloan, The Gloucester Years, Mus Fine Arts, Springfield, 80; John Sloan, The Wake of the Ferry, Timken Art Gallery, 84; Joyce Treiman, Friends & Strangers, Univ Southern Calif, 88. *Mailing Add:* Memorial Art Gallery University of Rochester 500 University Ave Rochester NY 14607

HOLDEMAN, JOSHUA
COLLECTOR, APPRAISER
Study: Bates Col, ME, BA & MA. *Pos:* Dept head, Photography Dept, Phillips de Pury & Luxembourg; photograph expert, Robert Miller Art Gallery. *Mailing Add:* Christie 20 Rockefeller Plz New York NY 10020

HOLDEN, DONALD
PAINTER, WRITER
b Los Angeles, Calif, Apr 22, 1931. *Study:* Parsons Sch Design, New York, 46-47; Art Students League, 48; Columbia Univ, BA, 51; Ohio State Univ, MA, 52; Maine Coll Art, LLD, 86. *Hon Degrees:* Maine Coll Art, hon LLD, 86. *Work:* Corcoran Gallery; Fine Arts Mus San Francisco; Metrop Mus Art; Victoria & Albert Mus; Nat Gallery Art; Philadelphia Mus Art; British Mus; New Britain Mus Am Art; Phillips collection; Nat Acad; Yale Univ Art Gallery; Smithsonian Am Art Mus; and others. *Exhib:* Solo exhibs, Manhattanville Coll, 83, Century Asn, 84, 2002, Susan Conway Gallery, 90, 92, 99, Campbell-Thiebaud Gallery, 93, Hudson River Gallery, 98, 2000, Curwen Gallery, 99 & Butler Inst Am Art, 99; Portland Mus of Art, Maine, 2004; Springfield Art Mus, MO, 2004; Round Top Arts Ctr, 2004; White Gallery, 2004; Davidson Galleries, 2007; numerous other group & solo exhibs. *Pos:* Dir, pr & personnel, Henry Dreyfuss Assocs, NY, 56-60; assoc mgr pr, Metrop Mus Art, NY, 60-61; art consult, Fortune Mag, 62; ed dir, Watson-Guptill Publ, 63-79, ed consult, 79-88; ed dir, Am Artist Mag, 71-75. *Teaching:* Instr painting & drawing, Scottsdale Artists Sch, Ariz, 85-92. *Awards:* Florsheim Art Fund Grant, 99; Adolph and Clara Obrig Prize, Nat Acad Design, 2001; Century Medal, 2005; Jo Ann Leiser Mem Award, Salmagundi Club, 2005. *Bibliog:* M Stephen Doherty (auth), Donald Holden, Am Artist Mag, 4/89; Richard J Boyle (auth), Donald Holden Watercolors, 2004; Daniel Brown (auth), Rivers and Mountains, Artist's Mag, 9/2008. *Mem:* Nat Art Educ Asn; New York Artists Equity Asn; Nat Acad; Century Asn; Salmagundi Club. *Media:* Aquamedia, Drawing. *Publ:* Auth, Creative Color for the Oil Painter, 83; The Complete Acrylic Painting Book, 89, Oil Painting Book, 89, Watercolor Book, 89; Painting from Nature in the Studio, Watercolor 93, Fall 93; Donald Holden Watercolors, Butler Inst Am Art (exhib catalog), 99; Artist to ArtistL Donald Holden, Watercolor Mag, Summer/2007. *Dealer:* Pucker Gallery 171 Newbury St Boston MA 02116; Stremmel Gallery 1400 S Virginia St Reno NV 89502; Davidson Galleries 313 Occidental Ave S Seattle WA 98104; White Gallery 342 Main St Lakeville CT 06039; and others

HOLDEN, MICHAEL B
PAINTER, SCULPTOR
b San Francisco, Calif, Dec 30, 1969. *Study:* Univ Calif, Santa Cruz, BA, 93; Boston Univ, MFA, 96; Santa Rosa Jr Col, AA (lib arts), 91. *Exhib:* Small Works Show, Sonoma Mus Visual Art, Santa Rosa, Calif, 94; solo show, Cobra Valley Ctr for the Arts, Globe, Ariz, 2001, Agilent Technols, Palo Alto, Calif & Sherman Gallery, Boston Univ, Boston, 2002. *Teaching:* adj drawing prof, Santa Rosa Jr Col; teaching asst beginning non-major drawing & advanced drawing, 95-96; adj drawing instr, Santa Rosa Jr Col, 2002; guest lectr, Santa Rosa Campus, Santa Rosa Jr Col, Boston Univ, Grad Art Dept, 2002. *Awards:* Fel, Vt Studio Ctr, 96 & grant, 2000; Fel, John Simon Guggenheim Mem Found, 2000; Fel, Vermont Studo Center, 96; Grant, Vermont Studio Center, 2000; Painting Fel, John Simon Guggenheim Mem Found, 2000. *Bibliog:* Tanya Schevitz (auth), Guggenheim felllowships awarded to 14 in Bay Area, San Francisco Chronicle, 4/12/2000; Taylor McNeil (auth), Abstract in Arizona, Bostonia, Number 2, summer 2001. *Mem:* Coll Art Asn. *Media:* Oil. *Res:* petroglyphs, pottery chards & archit vestiges of two unchartered Hohokam cities in Ariz wilderness. *Interests:* Painting in Johnson, Vermont, Italy, France, Switz & Eng. *Dealer:* Ebert Gallery 49 Geary St San Francisco CA 94108

HOLDER, KENNETH ALLEN
PAINTER, EDUCATOR
b Heald, Tex, Sept 11, 1936. *Study:* Tex Christian Univ, BFA (com art), 59; Art Inst Chicago, MFA (painting), 65. *Work:* Ill State Mus, Springfield; Cultural Activities Ctr, Temple, Tex; Ratir/West Mus, Manitowoc, Wis; Mazur Mus, Monroe, La; Univ Chicago, Ill. *Comn:* Fresno City Col, Calif, 73; Va Commonwealth Univ, 73; Cent Mich Univ, 75; all in collab with Harold Gregor. *Exhib:* Watercolor USA, Springfield, Mo, 77, 80-82, 85 & 87-88; Chicago Vicinity Show, Art Inst Chicago, 73; The Chicago Connection, Crocker Gallery, Sacramento, Calif; Solo exhibs, Nancy Lurie Gallery, Chicago, 75 & Zolla/Lieberman Gallery, Chicago, 82 & Conduit Gallery, Dallas, 90, 2003, 2008, Ill State Mus, 2002, Anderson Art Mus, Ind, 2004, Eiteljorg Mus, Ind, 2004, Irving Art Mus, Tex, 2005, Two person exhib, Heartlands & Western Vistas Corpus Christi Art Mus, 2003. *Teaching:* Asst prof drawing & painting, Western Ill Univ, 65-69; prof drawing & painting, Ill State Univ, 69-. *Awards:* NEA Artist Fel, 81-82. *Bibliog:* Henry Glover (auth), Artist (video), Ill State Univ, 72; "Ken Holder's Autobiographical Art," American Artist, 9/86. *Mem:* Charter mem, Watercolor USA Honor Soc. *Media:* Acrylic; Mixed Media; Watercolor. *Publ:* Ken Holder (auth, catalog for one-man, travelling show), 84-85; Show catalogs include Retrospective at Irving Art Mus, 2005, Lewis & Clark Trail Proj, SW Mo State Univ, 2003. *Dealer:* Conduit Gallery Dallas

HOLDER, TOM
PAINTER
b Kansas City, Mo, Jan 21, 1940. *Study:* San Diego State Univ, BA; Univ Wash, MFA. *Work:* Metromedia Collection, Los Angeles; ITT, Los Angeles, Calif; San Diego Fine Arts Gallery, Calif; Valley Bank, Las Vegas & Reno, Nev; Las Vegas Art Mus, Nev. *Comn:* Mural, Seattle-Tacoma Int Airport, 73; exterior wall mural, Seattle Steam Corp Plant, Seattle Arts Comn, 75; exterior wall mural, CETA Bldg, Las Vegas, Nev, 79; painting, State Capitol Bldg, Nev, 81. *Exhib:* Univ Mass, Amherst, 91; Pensacola Art Mus, Fla, 91; Brenau Col, Gainesville, Ga, 91; Brendan Walter Gallery, Santa Monica, Calif, 92; Northern Ariz Univ Art Mus, Flagstaff, 92. *Pos:* Founding dir, Nev Inst Contemp Art, 85-91. *Teaching:* Instr painting, Univ Wash, 67-69; prof painting, Univ Nev, Las Vegas, 71-. *Awards:* Charles Vanda Award for Creative Excellence, 92; Visual Arts Fel, Nev State Coun of the Arts, 92-93. *Bibliog:* James P Rupp (auth), Art in Seattle's public places, Univ of Wash Press, Seattle, 92. *Dealer:* William Traver Gallery 110 Union St Seattle WA 98101; Brendan Walter Gallery 1001 Colorado Ave Santa Monica CA 90401. *Mailing Add:* 740 N Magic Way Henderson NV 89015-4709

HOLEN, NORMAN DEAN
SCULPTOR, EDUCATOR
b Cavalier, NDak, Sept 16, 1937. *Study:* Concordia Coll, BA, 59; State Univ Iowa, MFA, 62; Univ Minn, Minneapolis, 72. *Work:* 3M co, Minneapolis, Minn; Univ Lutheran Church of Hope, Minneapolis; Augsburg Coll, Minneapolis; Civic Plaza, Richfield, Minn; and others. *Comn:* 36' brazed steel bas relief, Luther Theological Seminary, St Paul, Minn, 77; half life size terra cotta figures, Vinge Lutheran Church, Wilmar, Minn, 80; brazed steel sculpture & baptismal font, St Paul, Minn, 86; 12' stainless steel abstract piece, Augsburg Col, Minneapolis, Minn, 89; 12' stainless steel sculpture, Kirchbak Gardens, Richfield, Minn, 2000. *Exhib:* Solo exhib, Minneapolis Inst Art, 68; Nat Gallery, Washington, DC, 69; Nat Sculpture Soc, 77, 80-86; Allied Artists Am, NY, 80, 82, 83 & 85; Port of Hist Mus, Philadelphia, Penn, 87. *Teaching:* Prof art, drawing, sculpture & ceramics, Augsburg Coll, 64-2002. *Awards:* Rachel Leah Armour Award, 80 & 82 & In Memorium Award, 83, Allied Artists Am; Bronze Medal, 80 & Joel Meisner Award, 83, Nat Sculpture Soc; Alumni Achievement Award, Concordia Coll, Moorhead, Minn, 85. *Bibliog:* Sculptor likes 'em ample, Chicago Sun-Times, 6/25/89; Paul Levy (auth), Extending the left foot: Augsburg College's Norman Holen makes devices to help his students produce art, Star Tribune Mag First Sunday, 10/7/90; Sheldon Green (ed), Instinctive ingenuity, NDak Horizons, spring 93. *Mem:* Allied Artists Am; Nat Sculpture Soc; Minn Sculptors Soc. *Media:* Stoneware Clay, Cast Bronze, Welded Steel. *Interests:* Making tools and sprints for physically challenged art students; playing classical guitar music. *Publ:* Auth, Setting up a studio, Int Sculpture Mag, 9/85; Expressing the human form in terra cotta, 11/86 & Drawing nature close up, 5/95, Am Artist; Sculpting made simple, Artist's Mag, 9/96; Ceramic figures made from molds, Clay times, 3/2003. *Mailing Add:* 7332 12th Ave S Minneapolis MN 55423

HOLL, STEVEN MYRON
ARCHITECT
b Bremerton, Washington, Dec 9, 1947. *Study:* Univ Washington, BA, 71; postgrad in Rome and London. *Comn:* Loisium Visitors' Ctr, Langenlois, Austria, 2003 (NY Am Inst Architects Project Award); Simmons Hall, Mass Inst Technology (Award for Design Excellence, Am Inst Architects, 2003). *Exhib:* Whitney Mus Am Art, 84, 85; Facade Gallery, 84; Architecture in Transition, Berlin, Ger, 84; VII Triennale Milan, 87; John Nicols Gallery, NY City, 87; GA Gallery, Toyko, 87, 82, 97, 99; Mus Modern Art, NY City, 87, 99, 200; Aedes Gallery, Berlin, 89; Venice Biennial, Italy, 91, 2002; Walker Art Ctr, 91; Henry Art Gallery, Seattle, 91; Canadian Ctr Architecture, Montreal, 92; Ctr de Cultura Contemporania de Barcelona, 96; Mus Contemp Art, Los Angeles, 98; Mus Modern Art, San Francisco, 99; Cooper Hewitt Mus, NY, 2000; Max Protetch Gallery, Parallax, NY, 2000, 2002; Van Allen Inst, NY, 2001; Am Acad Rome, 2001; Nat Bldg Mus, Washington, DC, 2002; Basilica Palladiana di Vicenza, Italy, 2002; Arkiteckturmuseet, Stockholm, 2003; Nat Acad Mus, NYC, 2006. *Pos:* Individual practice architecture, San Francisco, 74-76, NY City, 77-. *Teaching:* Architect, tchr archit design, Univ Washington, Seattle, 79; prof grad sch architecture, Columbia Univ, 81-. *Awards:* Nat Endowment Arts Award, 82; Progressive Archit Award, 78, 82, 84, 86-87, 90; Am Inst Architects Award, 85-86, 89-90; Arnold W Brunner Prize in Archit, Am Acad and Inst Arts and Letters, 90; Cooper Hewitt Nat Design Award in Archit, Smithsonian Inst, 2002; Frontiers of Knowledge Award, BBVA Found, 2008; named America's Best Architect, Time Magazine, 2001; Fellow in Archit, NY State Coun Arts, 79; Nat Endowment Arts Grant. *Mem:* NCARB; Am Inst Architects; Am Asn Mus; Hon Whitney Cir; Alvar Aalto Found; Nat Acad. *Publ:* Auth, The Alphabetical City, 80; auth, Urban and Rural House Types in North America, 83; auth, Within the City, 88; auth, Anchoring, 89. *Mailing Add:* Steven Holl Architects 11th Floor 450 W 31st St New York NY 10001

HOLLADAY, HARLAN H
HISTORIAN, PAINTER
b Greenville, Mo, Dec 10, 1925. *Study:* SE Mo State Coll, BS (educ); Wash Univ, St Louis Mo; State Univ Iowa, MA; Cornell Univ, PhD; NEH, Venice, summer 79 & Rome, summer 84. *Work:* Munson-Williams Proctor Inst, Utica, NY; St Lawrence Univ Collection, Canton, NY; Des Moines Art Ctr, Iowa; SE Mo State Univ Collection; Springfield Art Mus, Mo. *Exhib:* Corcoran Gallery Art Biennial, Washington, DC, 51; Whitney Mus Am Art, New York, 52; Pa Acad Fine Arts, Philadelphia, 52, 53 & 59; 61st Nat Watercolor Ann, Washington, DC, 58; and others. *Teaching:* Art instr, Poplar Bluff Pub Schs, Mo, 51-53 & Des Moines, Iowa, 53-55; from instr to asst prof drawing & painting, Univ Nev, Reno, 55-58; asst prof to prof fine arts, St Lawrence Univ, 61-91, head dept, 65-71, LM&GL Flint prof, 67-91, prof emer, 91; prof art & artist-in-residence, Am Coll Switz, 68-69. *Awards:* Hon Mention, 61st Nat Watercolor Ann, Washington, 58; First Prize Painting, NY State Fair, Syracuse, 74; plus others. *Mem:* Coll Art Asn Am; St Lawrence Co Hist Asn. *Media:* Oil, Acrylic. *Res:* 15th century art, especially Italian painters; mosaics & studies related to Venice. *Publ:* Auth, Art in the liberal arts curriculum, 64 & The value of a teaching collection, 70, St Lawrence Bull; Catalogue for the McGinnis Collection, St Lawrence Univ, 70. *Mailing Add:* Saxony Village Duplex 62 2825 Bloomfield Rd Cape Girardeau MO 63703-6335

HOLLADAY, WILHELMINA COLE
COLLECTOR, PATRON
b Elmira, NY. *Study:* Elmira Col, BA, 44; Univ Paris; Univ Va; Dr Humanities Moore Coll Art, Dr, 88. *Hon Degrees:* (hon) DHL, Mount Vernon Coll, 88, Elmira Coll, 89, (hon) DFA, Univ Findlay, 94, (hon) DHL, John Cabot Univ, 2013. *Pos:* Dir, Holladay Corp, Interior Design, Washington DC, 72-84; pres, The Holladay Found, Washington

DC, 80-84; chmn bd, Nat Mus Women in the Arts, 81-. *Awards:* Induction, Nat Women's Hall Fame, 96; Gold Medal Honor Award, Nat Inst Social Scis, 2000; Nat Women in Arts Award, Phoenix Art Mus League, 2003; Visionary Woman award, Moore Coll. Art & Design, 2005; Nat Medal of Arts, Nat Endowment Arts, 2006. *Mem:* Corcoran Gallery; Am Asn Mus; Am Federation Art; Mus Mod Art; Women's Caucus Art; Nat Women's Economic Alliance (bd); Am Asn Univ Women; Am Friends of the Louvre; Am New Women's Club; Archives of Am Art; Art Libraries of N Am; Art Table; Am Civil Liberties Union; Capital Speakers Club; Chesapeake Bay Found; Coll Art Asn; Crystal Bridges Mus Am Art; Folger Shakespeare Libr (founders soc); Golden Circle of the Kennedy Ctr; Internat Women's Forum; Nat Gallery of Art (collector's comt, circle mem); Nat Org for Women; Nat Mus Women in the Arts; Nat Mus Women in the Arts; Dirs Cir; Nat Portrait Gallery (presidents circle); Nat Trust for Historic Preservation; Smithsonian James Smithson Soc; Wash Nat Opera (artists circle). *Interests:* Contribution of women to history through art from Renaissance to present. *Collection:* Women's art from the Renaissance to contemporary period. *Mailing Add:* 3215 NW R St Washington DC 20007

HOLLAND, HILLMAN RANDALL
ART DEALER
b Athens, Ala, Apr 17, 1950. *Study:* Auburn Univ, BA, 73; Ga State Univ, BS, 75; Atlanta Law Sch, JD, 76; Parsons in Paris, cert, 80; Attingham Summer Sch, Eng, cert, 82; Winterthur Summer Inst, Del, cert, 83. *Pos:* Dir, Hillman Holland Gallery, 83-; Trustee, Atlanta Col Art; Trustee Nexus Contemp Arts Ctr; & Trustee Decorative Arts, High Mus Art, Atlanta. *Specialty:* International avant-garde art, Arnulf Rainer, Milan Kunc, Tishan Hsu, Barbara Kruger, Tim Head, Pat Courtney, Thomas Nozowski, Francesco Clemente & Mimmo Paladino

HOLLAND, JULIET
PAINTER
b Buffalo, NY. *Study:* NY Univ; Harvard Univ, Cambridge, Mass; New Eng Sch Art, Boston, Mass. *Work:* Reading Pub Mus, Pa; Univ Iowa Mus Art, Iowa City; Housatonic Mus Art, Bridgeport, Conn; San Antonio Mus Mod Art, Tex; Stamford Mus, Conn; Sakai City Municipal Coll, Japan. *Comn:* Fragmented Tablets, MBIA, Armonk, NY; Twelve Fragments, General Electric, Stamford, Conn; Blue Elements, Loctite Corp, Hartford, Conn; Ancient Sources, comn by Dr Michael Albom, NY; Elements, R R Donnelley & Sons, NY. *Exhib:* Mixed Media, Albright-Knox Mus Gallery, Buffalo, NY, 85; Cortland Jessup Gallery, Provincetown, Mass, 91-2001; The Nature of Our Collection, Stamford Mus, Conn, 92; Earth, Matter & Spirit, Gallery Poem, Tokyo, Japan, 92-97; Recent Work, Reece Gallery, NY, 95; Earth, Man & Spirit, Sun Cities Art Mus, Ariz, 95; Bridge, Sakai City Mus, Japan, 98; Elusive Traces, Univ RI Art Gallery, Kingston, 98; Matter of Abstraction, Cortland Jessup Gallery, NY, 98; Housatonic Mus Art, 2000; Sakai City Mus, Japan, 2001, 02; CJG Projects Int, Gallery Poem, Tokyo, 2002; CJG Projects Int, Gallery 141, Nagoya, Japan, 2003; Gallery Marya, Osaka, Japan, 2004; Gallery LL, Kobe, Japan, 2004; Cella Surland, Fairfield, CT, 2004; Hammond Mus, North Salem, NY, 2004; Lamia Ink! ArtBridge, Jarfo, Kyoto, 2005; Cursive, Hong Kong Arts Develop Exhib, 2007; Silvermine Gallery, New Canaan, Conn, 2008; Confluences, Osaka and Kobe, Japan & NY, 2011; The ArtBridge Project - 20th Anniversary Exhib, Lamia Ink!, Kyoto & NYC, 2013. *Collection Arranged:* Sakai City Municpal Art Collection, Sakai City, Japan; Pepsico Corp, Purchase, NY; IBM Corp, Atlanta GA; Citibank, NY City. *Pos:* co-founder, assoc Dir, cur, Lamia Ink! Art Bridge Project, 1991-. *Teaching:* Instr painting, Stamford Mus. *Bibliog:* Dr Robert P Metzger (auth), Juliet Holland, Provincetown Arts, 95; Anthony Crisafulli (auth), Juliet Holland Rev, Cover-Arts NY, 95; Mark Daniel Cohen (auth), Juliet Holland-Matter of Abstraction, Rev NY, 97; Nobuhiro Matsumoto (auth) Elements & Structure of Expression in Art (book) (Juliet Holland's), Tokyo, Japan; John Gimour, Author & Professor of Philosophy, 2005; Dr. Thalia Vrachopoulos, Cursive, 2007; Suzanne Gerber (auth) The Matter of Art, 2007. *Mem:* Artist Equity; Int Friends Transformative Art; Silvermine Artist Guild; Women's Caucus Arts. *Media:* Acrylic, Mixed Media. *Specialty:* Contemporary American and Japanese Fine Art. *Dealer:* CJG Projects Cortland Jessup 640 Broadway 4B New York NY 10012; AM Gallery East Village NY; CJG Projects. *Mailing Add:* 640 Broadway No 4RW New York NY 10012

HOLLAND, TOM
PAINTER
b Seattle, Wash, 1936. *Study:* Willamette Univ, 54-56; Univ Calif, Santa Barbara & Berkeley, 57-59. *Work:* Whitney Mus Am Art, Mus Mod Art & Guggenheim Mus, NY; St Louis City Mus; San Francisco Mus Art; Los Angeles Co Mus, Calif; Art Inst Chicago; plus many others. *Exhib:* Kid Stuff, Albright-Knox Art Gallery, Buffalo, NY, 71, Working in Calif, 72; New Options in Painting, Walker Art Ctr, Minneapolis, 72; California Prints, Mus Mod Art, NY, 72; Calif Printmakers, Whitney Mus Am Art, 73, New Aquisitions, 78; Corcoran Biennial, Washington, DC, 75; solo exhibs, San Francisco Art Inst, 79, Blum-Helman Gallery, NY, 79 & Watson-De Nagy, Houston, 79; Felicity Samuel Gallery, London, 80; James Corcoran Gallery, Los Angeles, Calif, 80, 82 & 84-88; Charles Cowles Gallery, NY, 81-86, 88-90 & 93-2000; Berggruen Gallery, San Francisco, 87-89, 91-93 & 96-98; Group Exhibs: Celebrating Modern Art: The Anderson Collection, San Francisco Mus Mod Art, 2000; An American Focus: The Anderson Graphic Arts Collection, Palace of the Legion of Honor, San Francisco, Calif, 2000; San Francisco Int Art Exposition, 2003; Invitational Exhib Contemp Am Art, 179th Ann, Nat Acad, NY, 2004; Paint on Metal; Tucson Mus Art, Tucson, Ariz, 2005; Breaking Out! Sculptural Explorations in Metal & Wood, Palm Springs Art Mus, 2006; An Architeck Collects: Robert D Kleinschmidt, Krannert Art Mus, Univ Ill, 2007 and others. *Teaching:* Instr art, San Francisco Art Inst, 61-68 & 72-80, Univ Calif, Los Angeles, 68-69, Berkeley, 78-79 & Cornish Inst, Seattle, 78. *Awards:* Fulbright Grant, Santiago, Chile, 59-60; Nat Endowment Arts Sculpture Grant, 75-76; Guggenheim Fel, 79. *Bibliog:* John Gruen (auth), Controlled Frenzy, Art News, 3/1987; William Wilson (auth), Art Walk, Los Angeles Times, 10/1987; Roberta Smith (auth) Art in Review, NY Times, 2/2000. *Media:* All. *Dealer:* John Berggruen Gallery 228 Grant Ave San Francisco CA 94108; Charles Cowles Gallery 420 W Broadway New York NY 10012; Imago Gallery 45-450 Highway 74 Palm Desert CA 92260. *Mailing Add:* 28 Roble Rd Berkeley CA 94705

HOLLEN-BOLMGREN, DONNA
PAINTER, PAPERMAKER
b Willmar, Minn, May 28, 1935. *Study:* Univ Minn, BS (art educ), 57; Univ Pittsburgh, 58; Carnegie-Mellon Univ, 59. *Work:* Blount Inc; Westinghouse; Alcoa; McDonalds; Zanesville Art Ctr, Ohio; many corp & pvt collections. *Comn:* Vista Int Hotel, Pittsburgh. *Exhib:* Gallery Upstairs, Pittsburgh Ctr for Arts, 70, 76 & 82; William Penn Mus, Harrisburg, Pa, 71-73; Ogleby Mus, Wheeling, WVa, 72; Butler Inst Am Art Mid-Year Nat, Ohio, 73 & 81; 10 year retrospective, Allegheny Co Courthouse Gallerie, 85; Chataugua Nat Painting, Gallery 6, 89; and others. *Teaching:* Instr design, Pittsburgh Ctr for Arts, 70-, instr painting & papermaking, 73-. *Awards:* Excellence in Contemp Art, William Penn Mus; Assoc Artist, Pittsburgh, Carnegie Mus Art, 87; Frank Ross Award, Pittsburgh Craftsmen's Guild, 91-92; and others. *Mem:* Assoc Artists of Pittsburgh (pres, 74-); Craftsmen's Guild; Artists Equity; Int Asn Papermakers & Artists; Friends of Dard Hunter Mus. *Media:* Pure Pigment; Handmade Paper Pulp. *Dealer:* Gallery G 211 Ninth St Pittsburgh PA 15222; Artsouth Philadelphia PA

HOLLERBACH, SERGE
PAINTER, INSTRUCTOR
b Pushkin, Russia, Nov 1, 1923; US citizen. *Study:* Acad Fine Arts, Munich, Ger, 46-49; Art Students League, with Ernst Fiene, 50; Am Art Sch, with Gordon Samstag, 51. *Work:* St Paul Gallery Art, Minn; Bridgeport Mus Art, Sci & Indust, Conn; Ga Mus Art, Athens; Seton Hall Univ Art Gallery; Russian Mus, St Petersburg, Russia. *Exhib:* Am Watercolor Soc Ann Exhib; Nat Acad Design Ann Exhib; Drawings USA, St Paul, Minn; 200 Yrs of Watercolor Painting in Am, Metrop Mus Art, NY; Am Acad Arts & Lett, NY. *Teaching:* Various painting workshops across America. *Awards:* Gold Medal, Allied Artists Am, 85, 87; Gold Medal, Am Watercolor Soc, 83; Silver Medal, Am Watercolor Soc, 89, 90, 95. *Bibliog:* Aleksis Rannit (auth), Arts Mag, 1/81; Scott Elliot (auth), Portrait of an artist, Artists' Mag, 6/86. *Mem:* Am Watercolor Soc (vpres, 79); Audubon Artists; Allied Artists; Nat Acad. *Media:* Acrylic, Watercolor. *Publ:* Auth, Composing in Acrylics, Watson-Guptill Publ, 88; sketches in pen & ink & watercolor, The Beach (exhib catalog), Newman & Saunders Galleries, Albatross Publ, Paris. *Dealer:* Newman & Saunders Galleries Wayne PA. *Mailing Add:* 304 W 75th St New York NY 10023

HOLLINGER, MORTON
PAINTER
b Port Chester, NY. *Study:* Syracuse Univ, BA, 49; studied with Louis Di Valentin, 1950; Studied oboe with Wm Arrowsmith, princ oboeist with Metropolitan Opera. *Exhib:* Regional Competition, West Chester Co Ctr, White Plains, NY, 58, won first prize oils (475 entries); Award Winners Show, Stamford Mus, Conn, 68; Group Show, Stamford Mus, Conn, 91-95; Soto Gallery, Boston, Mass, 2004. *Awards:* Cash Award, Westchester Co Ctr Regional Competition, 58; first prize, (475 entries) Westchester Arts Crafts Guild, Westchester Co Ctr, White Plains, NY, 58; Stamford Mus, Conn, 68; Windsor & Newton Award, Stamford Mus, Conn, 91. *Bibliog:* William Zimmer (auth), A show that's refined and raucous, NY Times, 4/93; Vivien Raynor (auth), Familiar names at the Conn art show, NY Times, 4/94; Among a judge's choices, NY Times, 4/95. *Mem:* Stamford Art Asn, Conn. *Media:* Oil. *Interests:* music. *Publ:* Illusr, Paintings of Morton Hollinger, S H Pierce & Co, Cambridge, Mass, 98. *Mailing Add:* 11 Ledge Ter Stamford CT 06905

HOLLINGSWORTH, ALVIN CARL
PAINTER, INSTRUCTOR
b New York, NY, Feb 25, 1930. *Study:* City Univ New York, BA, 56, MA, 59; Art Students League, with Kunioshi, Ralph Fabri & Dr Bernard Myers, 50-52. *Work:* Chase Manhattan Bank, NY; Brooklyn Mus Permanent Collection, NY; IBM Collection, White Plains, NY; Williams Coll Art Collection; Johnson Publ Permanent Art Collection, Chicago; plus others. *Comn:* Don Quixote limited ed lithographs, Orig Lithographs Inc, 67; Don Quixote murals, Don Quixote Apts, Bronx, NY, 69; mural, Rutgers Univ, New Brunswick, NJ, 70. *Exhib:* Emily Lowe Award Exhib, 63; Traveling Exhib Black Painters Am, Univ Calif, Los Angeles, 66; 15 New Voices, Hallmark Gallery, NY & traveling, 69; Am Black Painters, Whitney Mus Am Art, NY, 71; One-person shows, The Women, Interfaith Coun of Churches, 78, Reflections of the Prophet, Pa State Univ, 78 & others. *Pos:* Consult art & art coordr, Harlem Freedom Sch, Off Econ Opportunity, 66-67; dir, Lincoln Inst Gallery, Lincoln Inst Psycho-Ther, 66-68; supvr art, Proj Turn-On, New York, 68-69. *Teaching:* Instr graphics, High Sch Art & Design, 61-70; instr painting, Art Students League, 69-75; asst prof painting, Hostos Community Col, 71-77, assoc prof, 77-, prof visual & performing arts, currently. *Awards:* Emily Lowe Art Competition Award, 63; Whitney Found Award, 64; Award of Distinction, Smith Mason Gallery, 71. *Bibliog:* Cedric Dover (auth), American Negro Art, 61; Samella Lewis (auth), Black Artist on Art, pvt publ, 71. *Media:* Acrylic, Collage. *Res:* Aesthetic use of fluorescent materials in the fine arts. *Publ:* Auth & illusr, I'd like the Goo-gen-heim, Regnery, 69; coauth, Art of Acrylic Painting, Grumbacher, 69; illusr, The Sniper, McGraw, 69; illusr, Black Out Loud, Macmillan, 70; illusr, Journey, Scholastic, 70. *Dealer:* Lee Nordness Gallery 252 W 38th St New York NY 10021; Harbor Gallery 43 Main St Cold Spring Harbor NY 11724. *Mailing Add:* 12 Edgewood Ave Hastings On Hudson NY 10706-2024

HOLLISTER, VALERIE (DUTTON)
PAINTER
b Oakland, Calif, Dec 29, 1939. *Study:* Stanford Univ, AB, 61 & MA, 64 San Francisco Art Inst, 63; Coll Art Study Abroad, Paris, 64-65. *Work:* Madison Art Ctr, Wis; Williams Col; Woodrow Wilson Sch-Princeton Univ; Russell Sage Found, NY. *Comn:* Winter Light (outdoor mural), Swarthmore Col, 88. *Exhib:* Biennial Contemp

Am Painting & Area Show, Corcoran Gallery Art, Washington, DC, 67; Whitney Mus Ann Contemp Am Painting, 67-68; solo exhibs, Jefferson Place Gallery, Washington, 66, 68, 69, 72, Madison Art Ctr, Wis, 68, Swarthmore Col, Pa, 72, 77, 82 & 90, 2004; Westbroadway Gallery, NY, 73 & Selected Paintings Since 1965, Washington Proj for the Arts, Wash, DC, 78; Widener Univ Art Mus, Chester, Pa, 93; and other solo & group exhibs; Painting 75-76-77, Sarah Lawrence Coll, NY, 77; Am Fed Art, Miami Fla, 77; Contemp Art Ctr, Cincinatti, Ohio, 77; The Computer & the Book, Victoria & Albert Mus, London, 95; Digital Art in Philadelphia, Art in City Hall, 2003; Outside/In, Philadelphia Art Alliance, 2006. *Awards:* Artist residency Yaddo Corp, 2000. *Media:* Painting. *Publ:* Coauth, Toward A History of Women's Traditional Arts, Heresies, winter 78; Auth, Seven Computer Landscapes, Occasional Works, Woodside, Calif, 93. *Mailing Add:* P O Box 25 Swarthmore PA 19081

HOLLOWAY, EVAN
SCULPTOR
b La Mirada, Calif, 1967. *Study:* Univ Calif, Santa Cruz, BA, 89; Univ Calif, LA, MFA, 97. *Work:* Broadcast Moment, LA X-Ray, KPFK, 98; Three Musical Lengths; As I Love You, You Become More Pretty, Karin Gulbran's Garden Exhib, 2000. *Exhib:* Solo exhibs, Arts Comn Gallery, Tacoma, Washington, 94; ROOM 702, Los Angeles, 97; Marc Foxx Gallery, LA, 97, 99, 2001, 2003, 2004; The Approach, London, 2001, 2003, 2005; Raucci/Santamaria Gallery, Naples, Italy, 2002; Xavier Hufkens, Brussels, Belgium, 2002, 2005; Art Now, San Francisco Mus Modern Art, 2004; Social Epistemology, Harris Lieberman, NY, 2006; Group exhibs, About Face, Tacoma Art Mus, 93; Einstein's Birthday, Duff Gallery, Tacoma, 94; Lexicanus Linguisticus, 504 Gallery, Tacoma, 96; Wish You Were Here, Univ Calif, LA, 97; Brighten the Corners, Marianne Boesky, NY, 98; Obviously 5 Believers, Action: Space, Los Angeles, 98; Standing Still & Walking in Los Angeles, Gagosian Gallery, 99; I Can Live With That, The Approach, London, 2000; The Fact Show, Pittsburgh Ctr for Arts, 2001; California Biennial, Orange County Mus Art, 2002; A Show That Will Show..., The Project, 2002; Whitney Biennial, Whitney Mus Am Art, NY, 2002; Younstars, Krinzinger Projekto, Vienna, Austria, 2003; Guided by Heroes, Z33, Hasselt, Belgium, 2003; for nobody know himself, Marc Foxx, LA, 2004; Painting on Sculpture, Tanya Bonakdar Gallery, NY, 2004; We Disagree, Andrew Kreps Gallery, NY, 2005; Think Blue, Blum & Poe, LA, 2005; Drunk vs Stoned II, Gavin Brown's Enterprise, NY, 2005; Gone Formalism, Inst Contemp Art, Philadelphia, 2006; The Uncertainty of Objects and Ideas: Recent Sculpture, Hirshhorn Mus, Washington, DC, 2006. *Pos:* Resident Jentel Artists Residency Program, Banner, Wy, 2003. *Awards:* Louis Comfort Tiffany Found Award, 2002; Penny McCall Found Award, 2004; FOCA Grant, 2005. *Media:* miscellaneous media

HOLM, BILL
HISTORIAN, PAINTER
b Roundup, Mont, 1925. *Study:* Univ Wash, BA, 49, MFA, 51. *Work:* Alaska State Mus; Can Mus Civilization. *Exhib:* Burke Mus, 92. *Collection Arranged:* Arts of the Raven (with Doris Shadbolt, Bill Reid & Wilson Duff), Vancouver Art Gallery, 67; Crooked Beak of Heaven, Henry Art Gallery, Univ Wash, Seattle; Smoky-Top (auth, catalog), Pac Sci Ctr, 83; The Box of Daylight (auth, catalog), Seattle Art Mus, 83; Crossroads of Continents, Smithsonian Inst, 88. *Pos:* Cur, Northwest Coast Indian art, Thomas Burke Mem Wash State Mus, Univ Wash, Seattle, 68-85, cur emer, 85-. *Teaching:* Prof Northwest Coast Indian art, Univ Wash, Seattle, 68-85, Prof emer, 85-. *Awards:* Governor's Art Award, 76; Governor's Writers Award, 66, 77 & 81; Honor Award, Native Am Art Studies Asn, 91. *Bibliog:* Sun Dogs and Eagle Down: The Indian Paintings of Bill Holm, Univ Wash Press, 2000. *Mem:* Native Am Art Studies Asn. *Media:* Acrylic. *Res:* All aspects of Northwest Coast Indian art, with concentration on form and style and relation to ceremonialism. *Publ:* Auth, Northwest Coast Indian Art: An Analysis of Form, 65; auth, Crooked Beak of Heaven, 72, Univ Wash Press; coauth (with Bill Reid), Indian Art of the Northwest Coast, Univ Wash Press, 76; The Art and Times of Willie Seaweed, Univ Wash Press, 83; auth, Spirit and Ancestor, Univ Wash Press, 87. *Mailing Add:* 1027 NW 190th St Shoreline WA 98177

HOLMAN, ARTHUR (STEARNS)
PAINTER
b Bartlesville, Okla, Oct 25, 1926. *Study:* Univ NMex, BFA, 51; Hans Hofmann Sch Art, Provincetown, Mass, 51; Calif Sch Fine Arts, San Francisco, 53. *Work:* San Francisco Mus Art; Oakland Mus, Calif; Achenbach Collection, Fine Arts Mus San Francisco; Stanford Univ; Mills Coll; Eureka Coll, Ill; Di Rosa Art Preserve, Napa, Calif. *Comn:* Mrs Paul Matzger, Berkeley, Calif, Dr Richard Viehweg, San Rafael, Calif, Mr Alfred Desantz-Newell, Munich, Germany, Mr & Mrs Robert Berryman, San Mateo, Calif, Mrs Barbara Siddall, Bushey, England. *Exhib:* Solo exhibs, Esther Robles Gallery, Los Angeles, 60, M H De Young Mem Mus, San Francisco, 63, San Francisco Mus Mod Art, 63, Gumps Gallery, San Francisco, 64-66, 69 & 87, Marin Civic Ctr Gallery, 70 & 95, William Sawyer Gallery, San Francisco, 71, 73-74 & 76, David Cole Gallery, Inverness, Calif, 80, Braunstein/Quay Gallery, San Francisco, 92 & Art Foundry Gallery, Sacramento, Calif, 2003; Bay Area Regionalists, Hall of Flowers, San Francisco, 85 & 86; 20th Century Landscape Drawings, De Young Mus, San Francisco, 89; Jan Holloway Gallery, San Francisco, 89; Bolinas Mus, 97; San Francisco Art Inst, 2001; Marin Civic Ctr, 2005; San Geronimo Art Ctr, Calif, 2006-2012; Celebrating Color, 8 Different Ways, San Geronimo Art Ctr, 2013. *Awards:* Purchase Award, Invitational Show, Stanford Univ, 62; Pub Vote Prize, Bay Area Art, First Savings Bank of San Francisco, 64. *Media:* Oil. *Mailing Add:* Box 72 Lagunitas CA 94938

HOLMES, DAVID VALENTINE
SCULPTOR, PAINTER
b Newark, NY, Nov 27, 1945. *Study:* Temple Abroad Tyler Sch, Rome, Italy, 66-67; Tyler Sch Art, Temple Univ, Philadelphia, Pa, BFA (cum laude), 68; Univ Wis, Madison, MFA, 72. *Work:* Milwaukee Art Mus, Wis; Kohler Arts Ctr, Sheboygan, Wis; Madison Art Ctr, Wis; Kent State Univ. *Comn:* Murals, Racine, Kenosha & Madison Pub Schs, Wis. *Exhib:* Chicago & Vicinity, Chicago Art Inst, Ill, 75; Solo exhibs, Madison Art Ctr, Kohler Arts Ctr, Wis, 72 & 77 & Ringling Sch Art, 91; Harmonious Craft, Am Craft Mus, NY & Renwick Gallery, Smithsonian Inst, Washington, DC, 79; Two-person exhib, Milwaukee Art Mus, Wis, 80; Animal Images, Renwick Gallery, Smithsonian, Washington, DC, 81; Renwick Souvenir Show, Smithsonian Inst, 82; Solo exhib (traveling), Ind State Univ, Kent State Univ & Northwestern Univ, 83; Midwest Int Exhib, Cent Mo State & Maastricht, The Neth, 87; Alchemic Emporium (traveling exhib), Swope Art Mus, Terre Haute, Ind; MacNider Mus, Mason City, Iowa; Fed Reserve Bank, Kansas City, Mo; Southeast Ark Arts Ctr, Pine Bluff, Ark, Edison Community Col, Ft Meyers, Fla, Bergstrom-Mahler Mus, Neenph, Wis, Muscatine Art Ctr, Muscatine, Iowa, 91-93; Coll Lake Co, Grays Lake, Ill, 96. *Teaching:* Resident artist, Madison Pub Schools, Wis, 72-74; asst prof drawing & design, Univ Wis, Milwaukee, 74-76; prof drawing & design, Univ Wis-Parkside, Kenosha, 77-. *Awards:* Nat Endowment Arts Fel, US Government, 76-77. *Media:* Wood; Acrylic. *Mailing Add:* 2915 Washington Ave Racine WI 53405-5004

HOLMES, LARRY W
PAINTER, EDUCATOR
b Kansas City, Kans, Nov 12, 1942. *Study:* Pittsburg State Univ, Kans, BFA, 64, MS, 65; Cranbrook Acad Art, with George Ortman, MFA, 73. *Work:* Cranbrook Acad Art, Bloomfield Hills, Mich; Pittsburg State Univ, Kans; City of Newark, Del; City of Parsons, Kans; St Lawrence Univ, Canton, NY; Hoyt Inst Fine Arts, New Castle, PA. *Exhib:* Solo exhibs, Del Art Mus, Wilmington, 84, Greenville Mus Art, NC, 87, Littlejohn-Smith Gallery, NY, 88, Littlejohn-Sternau Gallery, NY, 94, Hoyt Inst Fine Arts, New Castle, Pa, 96, Jack Meier Gallery, Houston, Tex, 96 & 98, Del Ctr for the Contemp Art, Wilmington, Del, 2005; Dog Days of August, Littlejohn-Smith Gallery, NY, 86; The Nature of the Beast, Hudson River Mus, NY, 89; A XX Century Bestiary, Renee Fotouhi Fine Art, NY, 90; Pastels: Big and Otherwise, Asheville Mus Art, NC, 92; 40 Yr Retrospective at the Univ of Del, Newark, Del, 2004. *Teaching:* Prof painting, Univ Del, Newark, 73, chmn dept art, 82-92, retired, prof emer, currently. *Awards:* Yaddo Fel, Yaddo Corp, Saratoga Springs, NY, 80; Outstanding Teacher Award, Coll of Arts and Sci, 2003. *Bibliog:* Ann Jarmusch (auth), Larry Holmes at Arch St Gallery, Art News, summer 79; Carrie de Santis Tull (auth), Larry Holmes at Delaware Art Mus, New Art Examiner, 1/85; Victoria Donohue (auth), Larry Holmes at Rosenfeld, Philadelphia Inquirer, 6/21/86; Frank Thomson (auth), Catalogue for Pastels: Big and Otherwise, Asheville Mus Art; Janis Tomlinson (auth), Catalogue for 40 Yr Retrospective at the Univ of Delaware. *Mem:* Coll Art Asn. *Media:* Pastel, Oil. *Mailing Add:* 141Rocky Glen Rd Oxford PA 19363

HOLMES, WILLARD
MUSEUM DIRECTOR
b Saskatoon, Saskatchewan, Can, 1949. *Study:* Univ British Columiba, Grad in art hist, 1972. *Pos:* With Fine Arts Gallery, Univ British Columbia; head of exhib Nat Gallery of Can; cur Vancouver Art Gallery; dir, Pender St Gallery, from 1975; chief cur, dir, Charles Scott Gallery, head cur studies prog Emily Carr Col, 1976-87; chief cur, interim dir, then dir, Vancouver Art Gallery, 1987-93; deputy dir, Chief Exec Officer, Whitney Mus Am Art, New York City, 1994-2003; dir Wadsworth Atheneum Mus Art, Hartford, Conn, 2003-07; assoc dir admin, Mus Fine Art, Houston, 2007-. *Mailing Add:* Mus Fine Arts 1001 Bissonet St PO Box 6826 Houston TX 77265-6826

HOLO, SELMA R
MUSEOLOGIST, MUSEUM DIRECTOR
b Chicago, Ill, May 21, 1943. *Study:* Northwestern Univ, BA, 65; Hunter Col, City Univ NY, MA, 72; Univ Calif, Santa Barbara, PhD, 80. *Work:* Norton Simon Mus, Pasadena, Calif; Getty Mus, Malibu, Calif; Fisher Gallery, Univ Southern Calif, Los Angeles; Milwaukee Art Mus. *Pos:* Cur acquisitions, Norton Simon Mus, 77-81; dir, Fisher Gallery, Univ Southern Calif, 81-. *Teaching:* Instr art hist, Art Ctr Col Design, Pasadena, 73-77. *Awards:* La Napoule Distinguished Scholar Fel, 88; Tokyo Fuji Mus Fine Arts Award, 90. *Bibliog:* Eric Young (auth), Los Disparates, Burlington Mag, 2/77; various reviews in Los Angeles newspapers. *Mem:* Am Asn Mus; Coll Art Asn; Int Coun Mus. *Res:* Goya. *Publ:* Auth, Despreciar los Insultos: A New Goya Acquisition, 83 & An Unsuspected Poseur in a Goya Drawing, 85, J Paul Getty Mus J; Joseph Alsop's The rare art traditions, Art News, 83; Training Future Curators to buy Art, Mus Studies J, 85; Interns Ins & Outs, Mus News, 89. *Mailing Add:* c/o Fischer Gallery Univ S Calif Univ Park 823 Exposition Blvd Los Angeles CA 90089-0292

HOLOUN, HAROLD DEAN
PAINTER, SCULPTOR
b Ord, Nebr, Oct 16, 1939. *Study:* Hastings Col, Nebr, BA, 61; Univ Wyo, Laramie, MA, 62. *Work:* Sheldon Mem Gallery, Univ Nebr, Lincoln; Nebr Art, Kearney; Nebr Wesleyan Univ, Lincoln. *Comn:* Portrait, Baker Univ, Baldwin, Kans, 75; two portraits, Liberty Glass Corp, Sapulpa, Okla, 79; painting-sculpture, City of Grand Island, Nebr, 81. *Exhib:* Painting-Sculpture Today, Indianapolis Mus Art, Ind, 78; Visions 81, Mid-Am Arts Alliance Touring Exhib, Kansas City, 80-81; Sheldon Mem Gallery, Lincoln, Nebr, 81; Art and Artists in Nebraska, Sheldon Mem Gallery, Lincoln, Nebr, 82; Twelve Midwest Realists, Sioux City Art Ctr, Iowa, 82; Reflectons Exhib, Elder Gallery, Lincoln, Nebr, 83; MJF Gallenigi, Kansas City, Mo, 85. *Awards:* Juror's Award, Reflections Exhib, Elder Gallery, 83. *Media:* Oil, Alkyd; Bronze, Photography. *Dealer:* Pickaro Galleries Inc 7108 N Western Oklahoma City OK 73116. *Mailing Add:* 812 Moore Dr Bellevue NE 68005-4436

HOLOWNIA, THADDEUS J
PHOTOGRAPHER, EDUCATOR
b Bury St Edmunds, Eng; Can citizen. *Study:* Univ Windsor, BA. *Work:* Nat Gallery Can; Mus Fine Arts Houston; Can Mus Contemp Photog, Ottawa; Can Coun Art Bank, Ottawa; Am Inst Graphic Arts, NY. *Comn:* Large Aeolian Piano (sound sculpture), with Gordon Monahan, Sound Symp, St John's, Nfld, 88; on-site photog, Can Mus Contemp Photog, Ottawa, 90; Landscapes in Times; Twelve Artists Reflects

on the Nature of Canada (landscape photographers) The Nature Conservancy of Canada, Ottawa, 2005. *Exhib:* Dykelands, Art Gallery Hamilton, Ont, 86; Beau, Can Mus Contemp Photog, Ottawa, 92; The Landscape: Eight Canadian Photographers (with catalog), McMichael Gallery, Kleinberg, Ont, 92; 150 Yrs of Children in Photog, Winnipeg Art Gallery, Manitoba, 92; Sable Island: An Elemental Landscape (with catalog), Art Gallery NS, Halifax, 96; Extended Vision; The Photog of Thaddeus Holowina, 75-97; (with catalogue) The Canadian Mus of Contemp Photog, Ottawa, 98; Owens Art Gallery, Sackville, 99, Saint Mary's Univ Art Gallery, Halifax; Beaverbrook Art Gallery, Frederiction, 2000; Mc Michael Gallery, Kleinberg; Centro de la Imagen, Mexico City, 2002; Monet's Legacy; Series-Order and Obsession, Hamburger Kunsthalle, Hamburg, 2001; Anatomy of a pipeline, Owens Art Gallery, Sackville, 2003; 24 Studies for Henry David Thoreau, Tsongas Gallery at Walden Pond, Concord; Broken Ground; Canadian photographs from the New World, Martin-Gropius-Bau, Berlin; Exhib A Newfoundland and Labrador Project, The Rooms, The Art Gallery of Newfoundlands and Labrador, St, John's 2006. *Pos:* Prof Head of Dept, of Fine Arts, Mount Allison Univ, Sackville, NB. *Teaching:* Prof fine arts, Mt Allison Univ, 77-. *Awards:* AIGA Book Show, 50 Best Books 89 Graphic Design USA, Am Inst of Graphic Arts Book Show NY, Award of Excellence for Dykelands, 89; AIGA Book Show 50 Best Books, 99 Graphic Design USA, Am Inst of Graphic Art Books Show NY, Award of Excellence for extended Vision, 99; Fulbright Fel, Fulbright Found, 2001; Strathbutler Award, the Shelia Hugh McKay Found, 2003. *Bibliog:* Robert Tombs, The Newfoundland Project, Thaddeus Holownia's Coney Island of the Mind, Art Atlantic, Summer 2002, vol #72; Robert Enright, The Landscape of Thaddeus Holownia, Border Crossing # 84, 2002; Sarah Milroy, Tangled up with Walden, The Globe and Mail, Nov, 22, 2004. *Mem:* Royal Canadian Acad; N Am Nature Photography Asn. *Media:* Photography. *Publ:* Ironworks, Anchorage Press, 96; Extended Vision; The Photography of Thaddeus Holownia, 75-97, The Canadian Mus of Contemporary Photography, 98, Ova Aves, Anchorage Press, 2003; Arborealis, Ancorage Press, 2005. *Dealer:* Jane Corkin Gallery 179 John St Toronto Ont Can; Corkin Shopland Gallery 55 Mill St Bldg 61 Toronto Ontario M5A 3C4 Canada 416-979-1980; Hollinger Collins Contemporary Art 4928 Sherbrooke Ouest Montreal Quebec H3Z 1H3 Canada. *Mailing Add:* 440 Jolicure Rd Jolicure NB E4L 2S4 Canada

HOLSINGER, JAYNE
PAINTER
b Mishawaka, Indiana. *Study:* Ringling Sch Art Sarasota, Fla, BFA, 1977; Ind Univ, Bloomington, 1977; NY Studio School, New York, 1981-84. *Exhib:* Solo exhibs include Margaret Thatcher Projs, New York, 2001, 2007; group exhibs include Landscape of the Mind, Mt San Jacinto College Art Gallery, San Jacinto, Calif, 1998; Artist in the Marketplace, Bronx Mus Arts, Bronx, NY, 1999; 11 Bulls, Proj Green, Brooklyn, NY, 2002; Study, Pierogi, Brooklyn, NY, 2004; True Colors, Ormeau Baths Gallery, Belfast, Ireland, 2004; ArtHouse, Margaret Thatcher Projs, New York, 2004; I Love the Burbs, Katonah Mus Art, Katonah, NY, 2006; MFA Thesis Show, OK Ctr Contemp Art, Linz, Austria, 2007. *Awards:* Pollock-Krasner Found Award, 1999; New York Found Arts Fel, 2008. *Dealer:* Kenise Barnes Fine Arts 1955 Palmer Ave Larchmont NY 10538

HOLSTAD, CHRISTIAN
ARTIST
b Anaheim, Calif, 1972. *Study:* Kans City Art Inst, BFA, 94. *Exhib:* Solo exhibs, Sand Day: A Show of Artifacts, Absentia Art Gallery, Williamsburg, NY, 2002, Chris Verene The Self-Esteem Salon: The Baptism Series, Deitch Projects, NY, 2003, Life is a Gift, Daniel Reich Gallery, 2002, Sonnenaufgang, Aurel Scheibler Gallery, Ger, 2003, Sonnenuntergang, Daniel Schmidt Gallery, Ger, 2003, The Birth of Princess Middlefinger, Prague Biennial, 2003, The Housekeepers, Daniel Reich Gallery, NY, 2003, Am Express, Galeria Massimo de Carlo, Milan, Italy, 2004, Moving toward the Light, Daniel Reich Gallery, 2004, Innocent Killers, P S 1 Contemp Art Ctr, Queens, NY, 2004, Gaity; Discovering the Lost Art, Kunsthalle, Zurich, Switz, 2004; Group exhibs, Midwest Bound, Chorus Gallery, Minneapolis, 95, Sauna Hut Available, 96, Cult of Claude, Here Arts Gallery, NY, 97, Fleshy Juggler, Brownies, NY, 98, Car Show, Reported Injuries Art Space, Brooklyn, 99, Slide Show, John Michael Kohler Art Ctr, Sheboygan, Wis, 2000, Zeek Sheck Collaboration, Knitting Factory, NY, 2001, Bathroom Group Show, Daniel Reich Gallery, NY, 2002, Now Playing, D'amelio Terras, NY, 2003, Calif Earthquakes, Daniel Reich Gallery, NY, 2004, Whitney Biennial, Whitney Mus Am Art, 2004

HOLSTE, THOMAS JAMES
PAINTER, EDUCATOR
b Evanston, Ill, Jan 12, 1943. *Study:* Calif State Univ, Fullerton, study with Vic Smith, BA, 67, MA, 68; Claremont Grad Sch, study with Guy Williams & Mowry Baden, MFA, 70. *Work:* La Jolla Mus Contemp Art, Calif; Chase Manhattan Bank, NY; Solomon R Guggenheim Mus, NY; Security Pac Nat Bank; Int Tel & Tel, NY. *Exhib:* The Market St Prog, Los Angeles Co Mus Art, Los Angeles, 72; Solo exhibs, Newspace Gallery, Los Angeles, 73-88; Aber, Buchanan, Holste, Newport Harbor Art Mus, Newport Beach, Calif, 76; Mind Set: An Ongoing Involvement with the Rational Tradition, John Weber Gallery, NY, 79; Four Artists, Otis Art Inst Parsons Sch Design, Los Angeles, 79; Emergent Americans, Guggenheim Mus, NY, 81; Alice Aycock, Tom Holste, Michael Singer, Fort Worth Art Mus, Tex, 81; Concepts in Construction: 1910-1980 Traveling Exhib, 83-; and others. *Teaching:* Prof painting, Calif State Univ, Fullerton, 69-. *Awards:* Individual Artists Fel Grant, Nat Endowment Arts, 80. *Bibliog:* Peter Frank (auth), Review-Tom Holste, Artforum, 2/78 & Unslick in LA, Art Am, 9-10/78. *Media:* Mixed. *Mailing Add:* 8708 Central Valley Rd NE Bremerton WA 98311-9150

HOLT, DAVID JOHN
PAINTER, EDUCATOR
b Salt Lake City, Utah, July 16, 1954. *Study:* Academia delle Belle Arti, Florence, Italy, dipl in painting, 78; Univ Utah, BFA, 80; Am Univ, MFA, 84. *Work:* Watkins Mem Collection, Am Univ, Washington, DC; Montgomery Co Collection Contemp Art, Bethesda, Md. *Exhib:* Approaching the Figure, Georgetown Univ, Washington, DC, 90; 72nd National Exhibition, GWV Smith Art Mus, Springfield, Mass, 91; Small Immeusities, The Paintings Ctr, NY, 03; Bowery Gallery, NY, 95, 03-05; Ceres Gallery, NY, 96; Solo exhibs, Albertus Magnus Coll, New Haven, Conn, 87, Erector Sq Gallery, New Haven, Conn, 87, Butler Gallery, Marymount Coll, Tarrytown, NY, 88, 2002, Dudley House, Harvard Univ, Cambridge, Mass, 91, Atlantic Gallery, NY, 92, John Lyman Center, Southern Conn State Univ, New Haven, 93 & Courtyard Gallery, Wash Studio Sch, DC, 86, 86, 89, 90, 94 & 98, Bowery Gallery, 04; District Visions, Diverse Pursuits, Coll of William and Mary, Williamsburg, Va, 2001. *Pos:* chmn dept art, Marymount Col of Fordham Univ, Tarrytown, NY, 94-. *Teaching:* assoc prof art, Marymount Col of Fordham Univ, Tarrytown, NY, 93-98, prof art, 98-. *Awards:* Painting Grant, Ludwig Vogelstein Found, 87. *Bibliog:* Anne Behrens (auth), The eyes have it, The Washington Post, Virginia Weekly, 4/26/84; Mark St John Erickson (auth), Visual orchestration, The Virginia Gazette, 3/20/85; Mary Jane Pagan (auth), Approaching the figure, Georgetown Univ, 90. *Mem:* Coll Art Asn; Founds in Art: Theory & Educ. *Media:* Oil. *Dealer:* Bowery Gallery 530 W 25th St 4th Fl NY NY 10011. *Mailing Add:* Marymount College Department of Art 100 Marymount Ave Tarrytown NY 10591

HOLTZ, ITSHAK JACK
PAINTER, PRINTMAKER
b Skernewiz, Poland, Dec 14, 1925; US citizen. *Study:* Bezalel Acad Art, Jerusalem; Art Students League; Nat Acad Design, NY. *Exhib:* Karlebach Gallery, Fair Lawn, NJ, 65-85; Audubon Artists of NY, 66; Tyringham Galleries, Mass, 66-86; Allied Artists Am, NY, 72; Nat Acad Design, 77; Yeshiva Univ Mus, NY, 83 & 92; Jewish Community Ctr on the Palisades, 90; YMWA, Washington Township, NJ, 91. *Awards:* Gold Medal, Academia Italia, 83; Bd Dir Award, NY Arts Interaction, 89-90. *Bibliog:* Articles in Art Rev Mag, 5/66 & La Rev Mod, 6/66. *Mem:* Art Students League; Academia Italia delle Arti; Artists Equity Asn NY. *Media:* Oil, Felt Pen & Ink; Lithography

HOLTZMAN, CHUCK
GRAPHIC ARTIST
b, Boston, Mass. *Study:* Sch Mus Fine Arts, Boston, 1974. *Work:* Addison Gallery Am Art; Fogg Art Mus; Mus Fine Arts Boston; Rose Art Mus; Univ Mass Art Gallery; Whitney Mus Am Art. *Exhib:* Solo exhibs, Barbara Krakow Gallery, Boston, 1987, 1990, 1993, 1995, Victoria Munroe Gallery, New York, 1988, Cherry Stone Gallery, Wellfleet, 1991, Ctr St Studios, Boston, 1995, 234 Gallery, Wellfleet, 1996, Elias Fine Art, Allston, 2001, Victoria Munroe Fine Art, Boston, 2006, 2008, Dartmouth Coll Hopkins Ctr, 2008; Boston Now: Works on Paper, Inst Contemp Art, Boston, 1988; Architectonic Art, Boston Architectural Ctr, 1989; Metaphor as Reality, Danforth Mus Art Art, Framingham, 1993; New England Today, Chinese Cult Inst, Boston, 1995; Contemporary Sculpture and Sculptor's Drawings, Brandeis Univ Rose Art Mus, Waltham, 1998; Print show, Attleboro Mus, 1999; Barnet Rubenstein and His Legacy, Sch Mus Fine Arts, Boston, 2002; Fenway Studios Centennial Exhib, St Botolph Club, Boston, 2005; Uncommon Denominator, Trustman Gallery, Simmons Coll, 2007; Naples Mus Art, Fla, 2008. *Awards:* Nat Endowment for the Arts Grant, 1984; Pollock-Krasner Found Grant, 1995; Nat Acad Prize for Graphics, Nat Acad Invitational Exhib Contemp Art Awards, 2010

HOLVERSON, JOHN
CURATOR, MUSEUM DIRECTOR, ART DEALER
b Marshfield, Wis, June 14, 1946. *Study:* Univ Iowa, 65-66; MacMurray Col, Jacksonville, Ill, BA, 67; Univ Iowa, Iowa City, MA, 71; Attingham Summer Sch, 82. *Exhib:* The Century Assn, 1986. *Collection Arranged:* Images of Women Photog Exhib (auth, catalog), 77; The Revolutionary McLellans, 77; Miss Mary Cassatt: Impressionist from Pennsylvania, 79; James Brooks: Paintings and Works on Paper 1946-1982, 83; Winslow Homer: The Charles Shipman Payson Collection, 83; Maine Light: Temperas by Andrew Wyeth, 83; Gaston Lachaise: Sculpture & Drawings (auth, catalog), 84; Jamie Wyeth: An Am View, 84; 1985 Maine Biennial; John Marin in Maine, 85; Carlo Pittore, Erotic Drawings, 2000; The Paperweights of Charles Zaziun, 2002; The Jockers Paperweight Collections, 2003; A Survey of American Paperweights, 2010. *Pos:* Summer intern, Art Inst Chicago, 68-69; grad asst, Mus Art, Univ Iowa, 68-69, head grad asst, 69-70; cur, Portland Mus Art, Maine, 70-73, cur collections, 73-81, actg dir, 73-75, dir, 75-87; consult; founder, J H Holverson Co, Portland, 87-; dir, Jones Mus of Glass & Ceramics, Sebago, Maine, 99-2002; dir, Mus Glass & Ceramics, 2002-2005; mus consult dir, Concho Belt Indian Arts & Crafts, Albuquerque, NMex, 2005-. *Teaching:* Asst dept art, MacMurray Col, Jacksonville, Ill, 63-67; grad asst, Univ Iowa Mus Art, 68-69, head grad asst, 69-70; Mus Collab Mgt Inst Cult Inst, Arden House Columbia Univ Grad Sch Bus, 82, vis fac mem, 83; sponsored & collaborated with Maine Hist Preserv Comn on The Portland Glass Company: Background Research & Survey Plan, 86; scholar, Paul Getty Trust & Art Mus Asn, Mus Mgt Inst, 87; instr community progs, Univ Southern Maine, 90-91; invited participant New Art Mus Construction in the 1980's, Nat Gallery Art, Inst Advan Studies; adj lecturer, Univ NMex. *Awards:* Excellence Award, Am Inst Architects, 85. *Mem:* Am Asn Mus; Asn Art Mus Dirs; Archives Am Art; Coll Art Asn. *Media:* Oil. *Res:* Iridescent glass, paperweight techniques. *Specialty:* fine arts, sculpture, works on paper, antiques, decorative arts, Native American rugs, pottery, jewelry. *Publ:* Auth, Rene Dubois and the cathedrals of the future, Greater Portland Landmarks Observer, fall 73; Fire buckets and bags in Portland, 1783, Antiques, 3/74. *Mailing Add:* 292 Spring St Portland ME 04102

HOLVEY, SAMUEL BOYER
SCULPTOR, DESIGNER
b Wilkes Barre, Pa, July 20, 1935. *Study:* Syracuse Univ, BFA, 57; Am Univ, MA, 69. *Comn:* Bas-relief mural, Wyo Valley Country Club, Wilkes Barre, 62. *Exhib:* Corcoran Gallery Area Show, Washington, 68; Greater Wash Area Show, 72; 2nd Ann Wash Area Sculpture Show, 74; The Am Genius, Corcoran Gallery, 76. *Pos:* Designer, William Fertig Interiors, Kingston, Pa, 57-58, 63-64; art dir, WFM-TV, Eatontown, NJ, 60-61; designer display exhibs, The Displayers Inc, NY World's Fair Pavilions,

61-63; designer, Robert Kayton Assocs, NY, 62; pres, Holvey Assoc Inc, 87-97. *Teaching:* asst prof design, Univ Md, College Park, 67-78; Assoc prof graphic design, Corcoran Sch Art, Washington, 78-93. *Mem:* Art Dirs Club Metrop Washington; Graphic Design Educators Asn. *Media:* Metal Direct Construction, Lumia

HOLZER, JENNY
CONCEPTUAL ARTIST
b Gallipolis, Ohio, July 29, 1950. *Study:* Ohio Univ, BFA, 72; RI Sch Design, MFA, 77; Whitney Mus Independent Study Prog, fel, 77. *Work:* Van Abbe Mus, Eindhoven, Neth; Mus Contemp Art, Chicago; Tate Gallery, London; Mus Mod Art Lending Serv, NY. *Comn:* Project Grand Central, Remy Martin, NY, 80; posters, Nouveau Mus, Lyon, France, 82; sign, City Amsterdam, 82; spectacolor board, Pub Art Fund, NY, 82; Urban Art Works Proj, City Seattle, 83; Green Table (granite table with benches, 20 x 6 feet), Univ Calif, San Diego, 93. *Exhib:* Solo exhibs, Seattle Art Mus, 84, Cranbrook Mus, 84, Dallas Mus Art, 84-93, Brooklyn Mus, 88, Solomon R Guggenheim Mus, 89, Walker Art Gallery, 91, Albright-Knox Art Gallery, 91, Kukje Gallery, Seoul, 2005; Groups exhibs, 74th Am Show, Art Inst Chicago, 82; 1983 Biennial Exhib (catalog), Whitney Mus Am Art, NY, 83; The Human Condition Biennial III (catalog), San Francisco Mus Art, 84; Mus d'Art Mod, Paris, 84; 1985 Biennial Exhib (catalog), Whitney Mus Am Art, NY, 85; Currents 7: Words in Action, Milwaukee Art Ctr, 85; Dissent: The Issue of Modern Art in Boston, The Expressionist Challenge (catalog), Inst Contemp Art, Boston, 85; Musee d'Art Contemporain de Montreal, 85; In Other Words (catalog), Corcoran Gallery Art, Washington, DC, 86; Committed to Print: An Exhib of Recent Am Printed Art with Social and Political Themes (catalog) Mus Mod Art, NY, 88; 1988: The World of Art Today, Milwaukee Art Mus, 88; Modes of Address: Language in Art Since 1960, Whitney Mus Am Art Downtown Fed Plaza, NY, 88; Image World-Art & Media Cult (catalog), Whitney Mus Am Art, 89; Affinities-The Gerald S Elliot Collection (catalog), Art Inst Chicago, 90; Language in Art, Aldrich Mus Contemp Art; High & Low: Modern Art & Popular Cult, Mus Mod Art, NY, 90; Am Art in the 20th Century Traveling Show (catalog), Royal Acad Arts, London, 93; The Language of Art, Kunsthalle, Vienna, 93; Don't Ask, Don't Tell, Don't Pursue, Fairfield Univ, Conn, 93; Virtual Reality: An Emerging Medium, Guggenheim Mus, 93; Translucent Writings, Neuberger Mus Art, NY, 94. *Awards:* Blair Award, 79th Americans Show, Art Inst Chicago, 82; Gold Medal Award for title & edition design, Art Dir Club, Ger, 93; Kaiserring, Goslar, Ger, 2002; Pub Art Network Ann Award, Am for Arts, 2004; Medal Order of Arts and Letters, French Ministry Culture, 2006; Distinguished Women in the Arts Award, Mus Contemp Art, Los Angeles, 2010. *Bibliog:* Time Span (portfolio), Fundacio Caixa de Pensions, Barcelona, 90; Hiroko Tanaka (auth), Art is Beautiful: Interviews with New York Artists, Kawade Shobo Shinsha, Tokyo, 90, 98-115; Susan R Suleiman (auth), Subversive Intent: Sender, Politics and the Avant-Garde, Howard Univ Press, Cambridge, 90. *Mem:* Collaborative Proj, NY. *Media:* Multi-Media. *Publ:* Coauth, Position papers, Art Forum, 80; contribr, Hotel, 80 & coauth, Eating Through Living, 81, Tanam Press; coauth, Eating Friends, Top Stories, 81; auth, Truisms and Essays, Press NS Coll Art & Design, 83. *Mailing Add:* 80 Hewitt Rd Hoosick Falls NY 12090

HOM, MEI-LING
SCULPTOR
b New Haven, Conn, 1951. *Study:* Kirkland Col, BA, 73; NY State Coll Ceramics Alfred Univ, MFA, 87. *Work:* Phila Mus Art. *Comn:* ChinaWedge, Philadelphia Conv Ctr, 94; Moss Ghosts, pvt comn by Marsha & Jim Moss, 2000; Cloudsphere, Philadelphia Int Airport, 2010; Cloudscape, Raleigh Durham Int Airport, 2010. *Exhib:* Challenge Exhib, Fleischer Art Mem, Philadelphia, 91; Thai Space, Silpakorn Univ Gallery, Bangkok, Thailand, 93; Offering, Alternative Mus, NY, 96; 20 Philadelphia Artists, Philadelphia Mus Art, 98; Biennial Exhib of Pub Art, Neuberger Mus of Art, Purchase, NY, 2001; solo exhib, Fleisher-Olman Gallery, Philadelphia, PA, 2004, 2010; Matchmaking at Suzhou Creek, East Link Gallery, Shanghai, China, 2004; Chinatown Influx, Asian Arts Initiative, Philadelphia, Pa, 2005; solo exhib, Mercer Gallery, Rochester, NY, 2005; Mid Career Show, Asian Am Arts Ctr, NY, 2005; solo exhib, Koppelman Gallery, Tufts Univ, Boston, Mass, 2005; Perpectives at the Sacker Pavillion, Smithsonian Inst, Washington, DC, 2005; Art in Embassy, Seoul, S Korea, 2009; Solo exhib, Fleisher Ollman Gallery, Phila, Pa, 2010, Abington Art Ctr, Sculpture Park, Pa, 2011; Green Acres, Rosenthal Ctr Contemp Art, Cincinnati, Oh, 2012; In the Clouds, Duke Gallery, Wallingford, Pa, 2013; East and West Clayworks, Hunterdon Art Mus, Clinton, NJ, 2013. *Teaching:* prof art (Emerita), Community Col Philadelphia, 83-2006. *Awards:* Creative Artists Exchange Fel, US, Japan, 96; Pew Fel Arts Grant, 98; Pa Council on the Arts, Special Opportunity Stipend, 2002; Independence Found Arts Fel, 2003; Joan Mitchell Found, Visual Arts Grant, 2005; Pew Fel Prof Develop Grant, 2009; Fulbright Senior Rsch Fel, South Korea, 2007-2008 ; Joan Mitchell Arts Ctr, New Orleans, Artist Residency, 2013. *Media:* All Media. *Dealer:* Fleisher-Ollman Gallery 12th & Arch Walnut St Philadelphia PA. *Mailing Add:* 2306 Fitzwater St Philadelphia PA 19146

HOMER, WILLIAM INNES
HISTORIAN, EDUCATOR
b Merion, Pa, Nov 8, 1929. *Study:* Princeton Univ, BA; Harvard Univ, MA & PhD. *Pos:* Cur, Mus Am Art, Ogunquit, Maine, 55-58; actg asst dir, Princeton Univ Art Mus, 56-57. *Teaching:* Asst prof art & archeol, Princeton Univ, 61-64; assoc prof art hist, Cornell Univ, 64-66; prof art hist, Univ Del, 66-99, chmn art hist dept, 66-81, 86-93. *Awards:* Am Coun Learned Soc Fel, 64-65; Guggenheim Fel, 72-73; Nat Endowment Humanities Fel, 80-81. *Mem:* Coll Art Asn; Royal Photog Soc; Royal Soc Arts; Nat Arts Club; Cosmos Club. *Res:* Thomas Eakins, art and theory. *Publ:* Alfred Stieglitz & the American Avant-Garde, 77; Alfred Stieglitz & the Photo-Secession, 83; coauth, Albert Pinkham Ryder: Painter of Dreams, 89; auth, Thomas Eakins: His Life and Art, 92; The Language of Contemporary Criticism Clarified, 99; Stieglitz and the Photo-Sccession, 1902, 2002; ed, The Paris Letters of Thomas Eakins, 2010. *Mailing Add:* PO Box 4195 Wilmington DE 19807-0195

HOMITZKY, PETER
PAINTER
b Berlin, Ger, Dec 7, 1942; US citizen. *Study:* Art Students League, with F Reilly, J Leberte, J Hirsh, 59-63; San Francisco Art Inst, 65-66. *Work:* Wichita Mus Art, Kans; San Francisco Mus Art; Prudential Ins Co, Newark, NJ; Newark Mus, NJ; NJ State Mus, Trenton, NJ; Rutgers Univ; Jane Voorhees Zimmerli Mus. *Exhib:* Solo exhibs, Roko Gallery, NY, 74 & State Mus, Trenton, NJ, 77; Alonzo Galleries, NY, 76-77; Educ Testing Serv, Princeton, NJ, 82; Jersey City Mus, 84 & 2002; Robeson Gallery, Rutgers Univ, Newark, 84; Frank Caro Gallery, NY, 89; Art Awareness, Lexington, NY, 89; Morris Mus, Morristown, NJ, 90; Aljira Ctr Contemp Art, Newark, NJ, 98; Del Valley Ctr, 2000; Freedman Gallery, Reading, Pa, 2006. *Teaching:* Instr painting, Art Students League, New York, currently. *Awards:* Purchase Awards, First NJ Biannual, Newark Mus, 77 & NJ State Mus; Aidekman Found, Newark Mus, 78; Distinguished Artist, NJ State Coun Arts, 81 & 82, NJSCA Fel, 82. *Bibliog:* Diane Cochrane (auth), Industrial American landscapes of Peter Homitzky, Am Artist, 5/74; Susan Myer (ed), 20 Landscape Painters, Watson-Guptill, 77; Hilton Kramer (auth), article, New York Times, 12/9/77; Peter Frank (auth), essay, exhib catalogue, Coro Gallery, 89; Wm Zimmer (auth), Alejandro Anreus PhD, interview for retrospective catalogue, NC Mus, 2007; and others. *Media:* Oil, Pastel. *Dealer:* Frank Caro Gallery 41 E 57th St New York NY. *Mailing Add:* 15 3rd St Athens NY 12015-1315

HOMMA, KAZUFUMI
PAINTER
b Matudo-City, Japan, Apr 21, 1943. *Study:* Tokyo Contemp Art Sch, 66-68; Brooklyn Mus Art Sch, 68-71. *Work:* Chase Bank Int & Home Insurance, New York, NY. *Comn:* Acrylic on canvas, Repub Bank, Houston, Tex. *Exhib:* Surugadi Gallery, Tokyo, Japan, 68; Brooklyn Mus Community Gallery, NY, 75; Brooklyn '81, Brooklyn Mus, 81; Solo exhibs, Limbo Lounge, 84 & Hal Bromm Gallery, 84 & 88, NY. *Collection Arranged:* Mixed Bag (auth, catalog), Alternative Mus, 82. *Media:* Acrylic. *Dealer:* Hal Bromm Gallery 90 W Broadway New York NY 10007. *Mailing Add:* 437 16th St No 4L Brooklyn NY 11215-5822

HONIG, ETHELYN
SCULPTOR, VIDEO ARTIST
Study: Studied with Alice Adams and Tom Doyle; Sch Visual Arts, Video Editing, NY; Sarah Lawrence Coll, BA, Bronxville, NY; Bennington Coll, Vt. *Work:* Smith Coll Mus Art, Northampton, Mass; Patrick Lannon Found; Mus Modern Art, NY; Gillman Found; Lisson Gallery, London, Eng. *Exhib:* Solo exhibs, Things that Do Not Work, Katonah Gallery, 81, One Hundred Yrs of Solitude, 55 Mercer Gallery, 83, Making Magic, 84, Dream Spaces, 85, Carnival Again, 86, Trouble in Paradise, 87, It Feels Like the Fifties Again, 89, Patent, 91, Love, Loss, and Atlantic City, 94, Pilgrimage to Coney Island and Other Places, 96, Between Us, 98, Vocabulary, 2003, Coney Island, Jan Van Der Donk Gallery, Chelsea, NY, 99, Small Murders Under the Sea, Ceres Gallery, NY, 2010, and many more; Group exhibs, 128 Rivington Gallery, NY, 98, 2001, Open Studios, Brooklyn, NY, 2000, Whitney Biennial, Whitney Mus Am Art, 2006, New Mus Archive, 2008, Ceres Gallery, NY, 2009, Mus Modern Art, 2009, and many others. *Pos:* pres, 55 Mercer Gallery, 97, cur, 2003. *Awards:* Artists Res, Yosemite Nat Park, 99; Artists Res, Vermont Studio Ctr, 2003, 2004. *Bibliog:* Frank Merling (auth), Somerstown: Rooms with A View, Vol 3, Issue 4, The News-Times Extra, 1/88; Irving Petlin (auth), Whitney Biennale, Art Forum, 2006. *Publ:* Review of Six Artists, The Weekend Trader, Gannett Press, 1/88; Bowery Artist Tribute Update, Vol 4, p.9, New Mus Paper, 2008. *Mailing Add:* 137 E 95th St New York NY 10128

HONJO, MASAKO
PAINTER
b Gi Fu Pref, Japan, May 3, 1948. *Study:* Art Student League, 82. *Exhib:* Nat Asn Women Artists Traveling Painting Exhib USA, Monmouth Mus, NJ, 87, Hiddenite Art Mus, NC, 88 & Nicolaysen Art Mus, Casper, Wyo, 88; 100 Yrs/100 Works, Nat Asn Women Artists, Islip Mus, East Islip, NY, 89, Fine Art Mus of the S, Mobile, Ala, 89, Chattanooga Regional Hist Mus, Tenn, 89, Longview Mus Art, Tex, 89 & Kirkpatrick Art Ctr, Oklahoma City, 90. *Awards:* Zluta & Joseph Akston Found Award, 88. *Bibliog:* David Howard (auth), David Howard art seen, Visual Studies, 90. *Mem:* Nat Asn Women Artists (oil juror, 88-89); Hudson River Contemp Artists; Am Soc Contemp Artists. *Media:* Oil. *Dealer:* 55 Mercer Gallery 55 Mercer St New York NY 10013

HONJO, NAOKI
PHOTOGRAPHER
b Tokyo, Japan, Jan 28, 1978. *Study:* Tokyo Polytechnic Univ, BA, 2002, MA, 2004. *Work:* Metrop Mus Art, New York. *Exhib:* Reality Check: Truth & Illusion in Contemp Photography, Metrop Mus Art, New York, 2008. *Awards:* Kimura Ihei Photography Award, the Asahi Shimbun Company, 2006. *Publ:* Small Planet, Little More, 2006. *Dealer:* Tai Gallery 1601 B Paseo de Peralta Santa Fe NM 87501. *Mailing Add:* Naoki Honjo Superstore Inc #310 2-2-8 Kudan Minami Tokyo 102-0074 Chiyoda-Ku Japan

HOOD, GRAHAM STANLEY
MUSEUM DIRECTOR, WRITER
b Stratford-on-Avon, Eng, Nov 6, 1936; US citizen. *Study:* Keble Col, Oxford Univ, MA (mod hist); Courtauld Inst Art, London Univ. *Work:* Detroit Inst Art; Colonial Williamsburg Found, Va. *Pos:* Cur Europ decorative arts, Wadsworth Atheneum, Hartford, Conn, 61-64; assoc cur, Garvan Collection, Yale Univ Art Gallery, New Haven, 64-68; cur Am art, Detroit Inst Art, 68-71; vpres, Carlisle H Humelsine & cur, Colonial Williamsburg Found, 71. *Teaching:* Adj prof hist art, Wayne State Univ; lectr hist art, Col William & Mary, Williamsburg, Va, 74-. *Mem:* Asn Art Mus Dirs; Am Antiquarian Soc. *Publ:* Auth, American Silver, a History of Style, 1650-1900, Praeger Publ, 71; coauth, The Garvan Collection of American Silver at Yale, Yale Univ Art Gallery, 71; auth, Bonnin and Morris of Philadelphia: The First American Porcelain

Factory, Univ NC Press, 72; co-auth, The Williamsburg Collection of Antique Furnishings, 73 & auth, Charles Bridges and William Dering: Two Virginia Painters, 1735-1750, 78, Colonial Williamsburg Found; The Governor's Palace in Williamsburg: A Cultural Study, Colonial Williamsburg Found & Univ NC Press, 91

HOOD, MARY BRYAN
MUSEUM DIRECTOR, PAINTER
b Central City, Ky. *Study:* Ky Wesleyan Col, dipl (theatre), 60, dipl (art & art hist), 74. *Collection Arranged:* The Am Artist Looks at the Am Soldier: 1915-1975, 80; The Kentucky Tradition in Am Landscape Painting (coauth, catalog), 83; Kentucky Expatriates: In Major Am Mus Collections (ed, catalog), 84; The Art of the Native Am: The Southwest 19th Century to the Present (auth, catalog), 85; Christianity and the Visual Arts: Kentucky Collections (ed, catalog), 86; The Kentuckians (ed, catalog), 87; The Experienced Eye (auth, catalog), 88; Contemplating the Am Watercolor: The Transco Collection (auth, catalog), 89; Kentucky Spirit: The Naive Tradition (auth, catalog), 91; Art of Africa: Before it was Art it was Life, 95; Dreamtime: Art of the First Australians, 96; The Legacy of Spanish Colonial Am, 98; Glorious Glass: Late 20th Century Studio Art Glass, 97; Navajo Folk Art: The Rosenak Collection, 99; Kentucky Womens artists: 1850-00, co-curator; Crossroads: Spirituality in American Folk Traditions (cur), 2007. *Pos:* Exec dir, Owensboro Arts Comn, Ky, 73-77; founding dir, Owensboro Mus Fine Art, Ky, 77-; pres Owensboro Mus Fine Art Found, Inc, 95-. *Mem:* Ky Arts Comn (mem bd, 77-78); Am Asn Mus; Ky Citizens for the Arts (exec bd, 84-); Ky Bicentennial Steering Comt (mem, 90-92); Year of American Craft (Ky comt, 91-93); Ky Asn Mus (pres 83); Owenboro Pub Art Comn chmn, 2003-. *Res:* Am art with emphasis on art and artists with Ky connections & Southeastern Folk Art. *Mailing Add:* 432 Maple Ave Owensboro KY 42301

HOOD, WALTER KELLY
HISTORIAN, PAINTER
b Catawba Co, NC, 1928. *Study:* Antioch Coll, 48-49; Pa Acad Fine Arts, 49-53; Am Acad Rome, 53-55; Univ Pa, BFA, 57; Univ Hawaii, MFA, 61; Northwestern Univ, PhD (art hist), 66; mural studies with George Harding & Jean Charlot. *Work:* Pa Acad Fine Arts, Philadelphia; Fred T Foard Sch, Vale, NC; Corriher-Linn-Black Libr, Salisbury, NC. *Comn:* Six egg tempera murals, Christ's Life, Death & Resurrection, St Peter's Episcopal Church, Glenside, Pa, 57-58; three frescoes, Bd Regist for Engrs, Architects & Land Surveyors, Honolulu, 61; egg tempera mural, Hist Rowan Co, Salisbury Mall, NC, 90. *Exhib:* III Mostra de Pittura Americana, Bordighera, Italy, 55; solo exhib, Archit League NY, 56; 152nd Ann Exhib, Pa Acad Fine Arts, 57; 1974 Grand Nat Exhib, Am Artists Prof League, Lever House, NY, 74. *Teaching:* Prof art & chmn art dept, Catawba Coll, Salisbury, NC, 71-90, prof emer, currently. *Awards:* Cresson European Traveling Award, Pa Acad Fine Arts, 52 & Schiedt Foreign Traveling Award, 53; Abbey Mural Fel, Am Acad Rome, 53-54. *Bibliog:* Frederick Williams (auth), To the Glory of God: Glimpse of a Man (biog film), 70. *Mem:* Nat Soc Mural Painters; fel Am Acad Rome. *Media:* Fresco, Egg Tempera. *Res:* Definitive study of the art life of George Harding. *Publ:* Auth, Fire and Autumn Frost, 92; Flake and Petal White, 93; Dust and Drops of Dew, 94; Petals On a Rainy Path, 95; Clouds Beyond a Valley, 96 & Fall Diminuendo, 97, pvt publ; Days of Powdered Vapor, 98; Cold and Springtide Sun, 99; Winter in Declension, 2000; Leaves of Weathered Gold, 2001; Snow and Days of Lent, 2002. *Mailing Add:* 195 Indian Trail Salisbury NC 28144

HOOKS, EARL J
EDUCATOR, SCULPTOR
b Baltimore, Md, Aug 2, 1927. *Study:* Howard Univ, BAE; Cath Univ; Rochester Inst of Technol, NY, cert. *Work:* DePauw Univ, Greencastle, Ind; Harmon Found, NY; City of Gary, Ind; State of Tenn Arts Comn. *Comn:* Ceramic sculpture, State Gift to Gov Ray Blanton, Tanzania, 77. *Exhib:* Howard Univ Invitational, 61; 21st Syracuse Biennial Traveling Exhib, Smithsonian Inst, 61-62; Int Minerals & Chemicals, Skokie, Ill, 66; three-man show, Art Inst Chicago, 67; Ball State Mus, Muncie, Ind, 69; Two Centuries of Black Am Art, Los Angeles Co Mus Art, 76; Dallas Mus Fine Arts, 77; High Mus, Atlanta, 77; Brooklyn Mus, 77. *Teaching:* Instr ceramics & drawing, Shaw Univ, Raleigh, NC, 53-54; instr & art consult, Gary Pub Schs, Ind, 59-68; instr ceramics & drawing, Ind Univ, Gary, 64-67; assoc prof sculpture & ceramics & chmn dept art, Fisk Univ, 68-. *Awards:* Second Prize, Arts & Crafts, John Herron Art Sch, 59; Purchase Prize, Dedication of Art Bldg, Howard Univ, 60; Cert of Honor, Int Festival of Lagos, Nigerian Govt, 77. *Bibliog:* Cedric Dover (auth), American Negro Art, 60; Elton Fax (auth), Seventeen Black Artists, Dodd-Mead, 71; The Rites of Color and Form, Fisk Univ, 74. *Media:* Ceramics. *Publ:* Coauth, Extended Services in Museum Science Training, 72 & Ben Jones (catalog), 77, Fisk Univ

HOOKS, GERI
DEALER, COLLECTOR
b Houston, Tex, Apr 24, 1935. *Study:* Stephens Col, AA, 53; Tex Univ, 53-54. *Pos:* Pres/dir, Hooks-Epstein Galleries Inc, currently. *Mem:* Houston Art Dealers Asn (founder). *Specialty:* Late 19th century, 20th & 21st century representational American, European and Latin paintings, sculpture and works on paper; Fine arts glass. *Collection:* Sculpture and works on paper of 20th century American and European Masters. *Mailing Add:* 2631 Colquitt Houston TX 77098

HOOPER, JACK MEREDITH
PAINTER, PRINTMAKER
b Los Angeles, Calif, Aug 26, 1928. *Study:* Los Angeles City Col, AA (art), 51; Coll Am, Mexico City, asst to Siqueiros, BA (art; cum laude), 52; Acad Julian, Paris, with Chaplin Midi & Pierre Jerome, 54; Univ Calif, Los Angeles, MA (art), 56. *Work:* Lannan Found, Fla; Stanford Univ Mus; Long Beach Mus; Univ Calif, Los Angeles & Santa Cruz. *Exhib:* The Artist's Environment--The West Coast, Oakland Art Mus, Amon Carter Mus, Ft Worth & Univ Calif, Los Angeles Galleries, 62; Fifty Calif Artists, Whitney Mus Am Art, Albright Art Gallery & Walker Art Ctr, 62-63; Art Across Am, San Francisco Mus Mod Art & Knoedlers Galleries, NY, 65-66; retrospective, Smith & Cowell Gallery, Santa Cruz & Univ Santa Cruz, 75; Sixth Hawaii Nat Print Exhib, Honolulu Acad Art, 82. *Pos:* Dir, Sculptural Walls, Los Angeles, 62-66. *Teaching:* Asst prof art, Univ Calif, Los Angeles, 57-62; vis prof, Univ Colo, Boulder, 62; prof, chmn dept & dir art galleries, Mt St Marys Col, 63-69; prof, Univ Calif, Santa Cruz, 76. *Awards:* New Talent in America--Top 100 in Nation, Art in Am, 57; Los Angeles Ann Award Painting, 59; Purchase Award, Long Beach Mus Art, 65. *Bibliog:* Jack Hooper, Univ Calif, Santa Cruz, 75. *Mem:* World Print Coun. *Mailing Add:* c/o LaGuna De Sta Maria Oro Nayarit 63830 Mexico

HOOVER, GEORGE SCHWEKE
ARCHITECT
b Chicago, Jul 1, 1935. *Study:* Cornell Univ, BArch, 58. *Collection Arranged:* Principal works incl: Douglas Co Admin Bldg, Light of the World Catholic Church, Univ Colo Bldg, Denver, Denver Diagnostic & Reception Ctr, Labs for Atmospheric & Space Physics, Univ Colo, Boulder, Colorado Academy Master Plan, Univ Ariz Engineering Complex Master Plan, Multipurpose Arena, Nat Western Stockshow, Nat Wild Animal Research Center, Colo State Univ Conference Ctr, Storage Tech. Corp, Aerospace & Mechanical Engineering Bldg Univ Ariz, Environ & Natural Resources Building Univ Ariz, Master Plan Cummins Power Generation Group Hdqs., Fridley, Minn, Master Plan Fleetguard and Manufacturing Plant, Cookeville, Tenn; finalist Denver Cen. Libr. Competition, 91; exhib Gund Hall Gallery, Grad. Sch Design, Harvard Univ, 86; mem ed bd Avant Garde. *Pos:* Draftsman, Holabird Root and Burgee, Chicago, 57; Designer, James Sudler Assoc, Denver, 61-62; archit, Ream, Quinn Assoc, 62-65, Muchow Assoc, Denver, 65-76; principal, Hoover Berg Desmond, 76—. *Teaching:* Tenured prof, archit Univ Colo Col Archit & Planning, chmn dept archit, 97-; vis lectr Univ NMex, Okla State Univ, Harvard Univ, Miami Univ, currently. *Awards:* named Outstanding Young Archit, Archit Record, 74; Honor award Interfaith Forum on Religion, Art, and Archit, 86; Tau Sigma Delta medal, 91. *Mem:* Fel Am Inst of Archit (steering comt, Pittsburgh Corning award 89, Nat Honor award 75, 83, 90, Firm of Yr award Colo chap 91, Regional Firm of Yr award 92, Archit of Yr award Colo chap 95); Nat Acad; Nat Comt Design (steering comt, chmn awards task group, 89-92); Nat Comt Archit Educ (steering comt 90-92)

HOPKINS, B(ERNICE) ELIZABETH
PAINTER
b Marinette, Wis, Mar 7, 1926. *Study:* Maryville Col, Tenn. *Work:* Edna Carston Gallery, Univ Wis, Stevens Point; Visual Arts Ctr NW Fla, Panama City; City of Tallahassee, Fla. *Exhib:* Pastel Soc Am, Nat Arts Club, NY, 84 & 87, Hermitage Mus, Norfolk, Va 84, Monmouth Mus, Lincraft, NJ, 85 & Harmon Meek Gallery, Naples, Fla, 91-92; Degas Pastel Soc, World Trade Bldg Gallery, New Orleans, La, 87; Societe des Pastellists de France, Lille, France, 88; Pastel Soc West Coast, Sacramento Fine Arts Ctr, Carmichael, Calif, 88. *Awards:* Still Life, Pastel Soc Am, Philip M Lahn, 84; Still Life, Pastel Soc Am, David Rosenthal, 87; Still Life, Pastel Soc Am, Morilla-Conson-Talens, 89; Master Pastelist Status, Pastel Soc Am, NY, 88; Best of Show, Bay Ann Exhib, Visual Arts Ctr, 99. *Bibliog:* Best of Pastel, Rockport Publ, 93. *Mem:* Pastel Soc Am; signature mem Pastel Soc N Fla; Visual Arts Ctr NW Fla (secy, 86-88). *Media:* Pastel. *Publ:* Auth, The Best of Pastel, Quarry Books. *Dealer:* The Gallery of Art 36 Beach Dr W Panama City FL 32401; LeMoyne Art Found Inc 125 N Gadsden St Tallahassee FL 32301. *Mailing Add:* 3270 Hillside Dr Apt 215 Delafield WI 53018-2183

HOPKINS, BRYAN
CERAMIST, SCULPTOR
Study: West Chester Univ Pa, BS, 1990; State Univ NY, New Paltz, MFA (ceramics), 1995. *Teaching:* Instr, Niagra County Community Coll, 1997-; coord & instr, Ceramic Studio, Buffalo Arts Studio, 2000-. *Awards:* NY Found Arts Fel, 2009. *Mailing Add:* 2495 Main St Ste 500 Buffalo NY 14214

HOPKINS, JULIE
PAINTER
Study: studied with Daniel James Keys, Albert Handell, Doug Dawson, Bob Rohm, Richard McKinley, Gene Cadore, and Clayton Beck. *Exhib:* Conn Pastel Soc Mem Exhib, Hartford Conn, 2011; Am Artists Profl League, Salmagundi Club, NY, 2011; Rockport Art Asn, Mass, 2011; Audobon Artists Online Ann Exhib, 2012; and many others. *Awards:* Marquis Who's Who in Am Art Reference award in Pastels, Audubon Artists, New York, 2012. *Mem:* Audubon Artists. *Media:* Pastels. *Mailing Add:* 41 Mulberry St Ridgefield CT 06877

HOPKINS, SETH M
MUSEUM DIRECTOR
b Dexter, Maine, March 18, 1967. *Study:* Syracuse Univ, BS (Broadcast Journalism), 1989; Univ Okla, MA (Mus Studies), 2005. *Collection Arranged:* cur, Selling the Sizzle: The Art of Movie Posters. *Pos:* Exec dir, Booth Western Art Mus, Catersville, Ga, 2000-; found, Bartow Christmas Coalition, Cartesville, Ga, 1993-2002. *Mem:* Etowah Rotary (Lee Aerondale Award, 2004). *Mailing Add:* Booth Western Art Museum 501 Museum Drive PO Box 3070 Cartersville GA 30120

HOPKINS, TERRI
CURATOR, ADMINISTRATOR
Study: Oberlin Col, BA (art hist), 71; Univ Chicago, MA (art hist), 72. *Collection Arranged:* Approximately 300 exhibs, 80-. *Pos:* Dir art gym, Marylhurst Univ, 80-. *Teaching:* Marylhurst Univ. *Awards:* Governor's Arts Award, 2004-2005. *Mem:* Art Table. *Res:* Contemp Northwest Art. *Specialty:* Contemp Northwest Art. *Collection:* Tad Savinar, 1999 ; Stephen Hayes, 2000; M J Anderson, 2001; Marilyn Lanfear, 2003; Laura Ross-Paul, 2006. *Publ:* Auth, Paul Sutinen: Five Works 1982-1987, 87, Barbara Thomas: Paintings, 89, Fernanda D'Agostino: Offering, 89, Barbara Fealy's Gardens, 90 & Unabandoned Abstraction, 91, Marylhurst Col; Sally Haley: A Lifetime of Painting, 93; Representing the object, 94; Album-Artist portraits of Artists, 2010; JoeMacca: Two Man Show, 2011. *Mailing Add:* Art Gym Marylhurst Univ 17600 Pacific Hwy Marylhurst OR 97036

HOPPER, DENNIS
PHOTOGRAPHER
b Dodge City, Kans, 1936. *Exhib:* Primus/Stuart Gallery, Los Angeles, 63; Calif Now, Robert Fraser Gallery, London, Eng, 65; Pasadena Art Mus, Calif, 67; Corcoran Gallery Art, Washington, DC, 71; AIACE Torino, Italy, 88; Kunsthalle Basel, Switz, 88; Hoffman Borman Gallery, Santa Monica, Calif, 87; Graham Parson Gallery, London, Eng, 84; LA Louver, Venice, Calif, 89; Davis/McClain, Houston, Tex, 90; Kiyomuizu Temple, Kyoto, Japan, 90 & 94; Parco Gallery, Tokyo, Japan, 90 & 94; Proof: Los Angeles Art and the Photog 1960-1980 (with catalog), Laguna Mus Art, Calif, 92; Photographs and Paintings, 1961-1993, Galerie Thaddeus Ropac, Paris, France, 92 & Speilraum fur Kunst, Furth, Ger, 92; New Work, Sena Galleries, Santa Fe, NMex, 92; Dennis Hopper: Fotos und Gemalde, Aktionsforum City-Ctr Furth, Ger, 92; James Corcoran Gallery, Santa Monica, Calif, 92; Dennis Hopper and Ed Ruscha, Tony Shafrazi Gallery, NY, 92; Bad Heat: Photographs and Paintings, 1961-1993 (with catalog), Fronto Colom, Univ Pompeu Fabra, Barcelona, Spain, 93; Photog Resource Ctr, Boston, Mass, 94; Photographs 1961-1967, Karolinum, Prague, Czech Repub, 95; Beat Cult and the New Am: 1950-1965 (with catalog), Whitney Mus Am Art, NY, 95; George Herm, From There and Then to Here and Now, with a little Help From His Friends, Wallace Berman, Bruce Connor & Dennis Hopper, Tony Shafrazi Gallery, NY, 95; Whitney Mus Am Art Biennial, NY, 95; Halls of Mirrors: Art and Film Since 1945, Mus Contemp Art, Los Angeles, Calif, 96; Tony Shafrazi Gallery, NY, 96; Ochi Gallery, Kethum, Idaho, 96. *Bibliog:* Dennis Hopper lit sur les murs, La Liberation, 9/23/92; Dennis Hopper: James Dean m'a pousse a faire de la photo, Le Figaro, 9/24/92; Ann Hindry (auth), Cinema and art, Galeries Mag, 10-11/92. *Publ:* Coauth, Hopper, Dennis: A Tourist, File Inc, Kyoto, Japan, 94

HOPTMAN, LAURA
CURATOR
Collection Arranged: Love Forever; Yayoi Kusama (auth, catalog), 1998; Drawing Now; Eight Propositions, 2002; Tomma Abts, (auth, catalog), 2007; Elizabeth Peyton (auth, catalog), 2008. *Pos:* Cur drawing, Mus Mod Art, New York 1995-2001; cur contemp art, Carnegie Mus Art, New York, 2001-2006; Kraus Family sr cur, New Mus, New York, 2006-. *Publ:* Co-ed (with Tomas Pospiszyl), Primary Documents: A Sourcebook for Eastern and Central European Art since the 1950s, The MIT Press, 2002. *Mailing Add:* 235 Bowery New York NY 10002

HORMUTH, JO
SCULPTOR, PRINTMAKER
b Grand Rapids, Mich, 1955. *Study:* Slade Sch Art, London, 78; Grand Valley State Col, Allendale, Mich, BFA, 81; Art Inst Chicago, MFA, 83. *Work:* Art Inst Chicago; Cranbrook Acad Art; MacArthur Found. *Exhib:* Group Show, Sch Gallery, Art Inst Chicago, 85; What Price Beauty; Looking at Labor, Randolph St Gallery, Chicago, 91; Home Sweet Home, Columbia Coll Art Gallery, Chicago, 92; Buy/Low, Prairie Ave Gallery, Chicago, 91; Valentine's Day Auction, NAME Gallery, Chicago, 92; Forecast, Zolla/Lieberman Gallery, Chicago, 92. *Bibliog:* Carol Vogel (auth), Visions of Home Sweet Home, NY Times, 2/14/91; Alan Artner (auth), Installations: Things to Catch the Eye and Ear, Chicago Tribune, 7/24/92; Mandy Morrison (auth), The Harder They Drum, The Reader, 8/14/92. *Media:* Mixed. *Mailing Add:* 1742 W Haddon Chicago IL 60622-3222

HORN, ALAN F
COLLECTOR
Study: Harvard Univ, MBA with distinction. *Pos:* With Proctor & Gamble, Tandem Productions, TAT Commun, Embassy Commun, 1973-86; pres, Chief Operating Officer, 20th Century Fox Film Corp, 1986-87; co-founder, chmn, Chief Exec Officer, Castle Rock Entertainment, Beverly Hills, 1987-99; pres, Chief Operating Officer, Warner Brothers Entertainment, Burbank, Calif, 1999-; bd dirs, Univision Commun, Natural Resources Defense Coun; vice chmn, bd trustees, Autry Mus Western Heritage; mem bd assocs, Harvard Bus Sch; founding mem, bd dirs, Environ Media Asn. *Awards:* Named one of 50 Most Powerful People in Hollywood, Premiere mag, 2004-06, Top 200 Collectors, ARTnews mag, 2006-08; Milestone Award, Producers Guild Am, 2008. *Mem:* Hollywood Radio and TV Soc; Am Film Inst; Acad TV Arts and Scis; Acad Motion Picture Arts and Scis

HORN, BRUCE
PAINTER, EDUCATOR
b Circleville, Ohio, June 30, 1946. *Study:* Miami Univ, BFA, 68; Ohio State Univ, MFA, 70; Arnot Mus, New York with Clyde Aspevig; Fechin Inst, NMex with Gregg Kreutz. *Work:* Trenton State Col, NJ; Tyler Sch Art, Philadelphia; Nat Gallery Art, Washington; Honolulu Acad Arts, Hawaii; and others. *Exhib:* Sixteenth Nat Exhib, New Orleans Art Asn, La, 95 & 97; Grand Exhib, Akron Soc Artists, Ohio, 95; solo exhib, Prescott Fine Art Asn Gallery, Ariz, 96, Paris & Normandy, Hudgens Gallery Fine Art, Flagstaff, Ariz, 2006, Silent Music, Tanglewood Fine Art, Flagstaff, Ariz, 2007; Nat Realism Exhib, Parkersburg, WVa, 98; Art Colo Plateau, Aspen Fine Arts Gallery, Flagstaff, Ariz, 99 & 2000; retrospective, Northern Ariz Univ, 2001; Oil Painters of Am, Western Region Exhib; Waterhouse Gallery, Santa Barbara, Calif, 2003; Nat Fine Art Exhib; Morro Bay Art Asn, Calif, 2005; Ariz Plein Air Painters, Phippen, Mus Western Art, Precott, Ariz, 2008, W Valley Art Mus, Surprise, Ariz, 2009; Am Artists Prof League, Nat Exhib, Salmagundi Club, New York, 2008; Non Mem Nat Exhib, Salmagundi Club, New York, 2009. *Pos:* Package designer, Diamond Nat Paper Co, Middletown, Ohio, 68; art dir, Eighth Ann Flagstaff Summer Festival, Ariz, 74. *Teaching:* Prof painting, Blackburn Col, Carlinville, Ill, 70-72 & Northern Ariz Univ, 72-99, prof emeritus. *Awards:* Purchase Award, Int Exhib Prints, Wesleyan Col, Macon, 83; Gold Medallion Award, Nat Printing Exhib, NMex Art League, 95; Bronze Award, Int Film Festival, Houston, 99. *Mem:* assoc Oil Painters Am; Calif Art Club; Artists' Coalition Flagstaff; Am Artists Prof League; Plein-Air Artists Northern Ariz; Ariz Plein Air Painters. *Media:* Oil, Miscellaneous Media. *Interests:* etching, art hist, mus study. *Publ:* No Ariz Mountain Living Mag. *Dealer:* Artists Gallery 17 N San Francisco St Flagstaff AZ 86001; Elk Run Studio 2197 N Twisted Limb Way Flagstaff AZ 86004. *Mailing Add:* 2197 Twisted Limb Way Flagstaff AZ 86004

HORN, CINDY HARRELL
COLLECTOR
b Durham, NC. *Pos:* Model, actress, 1975-88; mem, Nat Educ Adv Coun, 1991; founding trustee, Heal the Bay, Archer Sch Girls; bd mem, Coalition for Clean Air, Tree People, Natural Step, Bay Keeper, Center Environ Educ, Univ Calif Los Angeles Sch Pub Health; mem painting conservatory coun, J Paul Getty Mus. *Awards:* Named one of Top 200 Collectors, ARTnews mag, 2006-08; Legislative Woman of Yr, State of Calif. *Mem:* Environ Media Asn (co-founder, bd mem). *Collection:* Western art. *Mailing Add:* Environmental Media Association 8909 W Olympic Blvd Ste 200 Beverly Hills CA 90211

HORN, REBECCA
INSTALLATION SCULPTOR
b Michelstadt, Germany, 1944. *Study:* Hochschule fur Bildende Kunste, Hamburg, Germany, 1963; St Martins Coll Art, London, 1971. *Exhib:* Solo exhibs include Marian Goodman Gallery, New York, 1991, 1994,1998, Biennale di Venezia, Venice, 1997, Galerie de France, 2001, Sean Kelly Gallery, New York, 2002, 2005, 2008, K20 Kumtsammlung, Düsseldort, 2004, Hayward Gallery, London, 2005, Artin Gropius Baum, Germany, 2006, Mus Wiesbaden, Germany, 2007, Fondazione Bevilacqua, Venice, 2009; Tempo, Mus Mod Art, Queens, New York, 2002; Live Culture, Tate Modern, London, 2003; A Short History of Performance IV, Whitechapel Art Gallery, London, 2006; Lights, Camera, Action: Artists' Films for the Cinema, Whitney Mus Am Art, New York, 2007; WACK! Art and the Feminist Revolution, PS 1 Long Island City, New York, 2008. *Awards:* Carnegie Prize, Carnegie Intl, Pittsburgh, 1988; Barnett and Annalee Newman Award, New York; Hessian Cultural Prize, Ger, 2010; Praemium Imperioals Award, Japan, 2010. *Mailing Add:* Sean Kelly Gallery 528 W 29th St New York NY 10001

HORN, RONI
SCULPTOR
b New York, NY, 1955. *Study:* RI Sch Design, BFA, 75; Yale Univ Sch Art, MFA, 78. *Work:* Toledo Mus Art, Toledo, Ohio; Harfa, Chinati Found, Presidio Co, Tex. *Comn:* Collection of Eric Mosel, comn by Doln Mühle. *Exhib:* Solo exhibs incl Fotomuseum Winterthur, Switz, 97, Patrick Painter Gallery, Los Angeles, 98, Gallery Xavier Hufkens, Brussels, 98, Jabloonka Galerie, Cologne, 98 & 99, Mus fur Gegenwartskunst, Basel, 98 & De Pont Found Contemp Art, Tilburg, The Neth, 98, Matthew Marks Gallery, NY, 99, 2002, Musee d' Art Moderne de la Ville de Paris, 99, CAPC Musee d' Art Contemporain, Bordeaux, 99, Whitney Mus of Am Art, NY, 2000, Timothy Taylor Gallery, London, 2000 & Gastello di Rivoli, Torino, 2000, Dia Ctr for the Arts, NY, 2002, Reykjavik, Iceland, 2003, 2007, PS1 Contemp Art Ctr, 2005; group exhibs incl Kunstforum Lenbachaus State Mus, Munich, Ger, 83; Glyptothek Mus, Munich, Ger 83; Neuberger Mus, State Univ NY, Purchase, 86; Similia/Dissimilia, Castelli Gallery, NY & Kunstalle, Dusseldorf, Ger, 87; Detroit Inst Arts, Mich, 88; Whitney Biennial, Whitney Mus Am Art, 91, 2004; Sleight of Mind/The Angle of a Landscape, Ctr Curatorial Studies Mus, Bard Col, Annandale-On-Hudson, NY, 97; Galerie Nacht St Stephan, Vienna, 97; Density of the Unimaginable Mus, Centre d'Art Contemporain du Domaine de Kerguehennec, Bignan, France, 97; Maverick, Matthew Marks Gallery, NY, 98; Pi, Sydney Biennale, 98; Travel & Leisure, Paula Cooper Gallery, NY, 98; Surrogate: The Figure in Contemp Sculpture and Photog, Henry Art Gallery, Univ Wash, Seattle, 98; View 2, Mary Boone Gallery, NY, 98; 00, Barbara Gladstone Gallery, NY, 2001; Xavier Hufkens, Brussels, 2001; The Photographers' Gallery, London, 2001; Silent Poetry, Timothy Taylor Gallery, London, 2002; Matthew Marks Gallery, New York, 2002; Andrea Rosen Gallery, New York, 2005; Helga de Alvear, Belém, 2006; Mus Mod Art, New York, 2006; Kunstmuseum Bonn, 2007; Cagosian, 2008. *Awards:* Nat Endowment Arts Fel, 84, 86 & 90; Guggenheim Fel, 90; Alpert Award in the Arts, 98. *Bibliog:* Sue Scott (auth), The Edward R Broida Collection, Orlando Mus Art, Fla, 98; Monique Beudert (auth), Contemporary Art: The Janet Wolfson de Botton Gift, Taft Gallery Publ, London, 98; Jill Connor (auth), Roni Horn: Earth's grow thick, Art Papers, 5-6/98. *Dealer:* Galería Helga de Alvear Doctor Fourquet 12 28012 Madrid Spain; Hauser & Wirth London 196A Piccadilly London W1J 9DY United Kingdom; Xavier Hufkens Sint-Jorisstraat 6-8 Rue Saint-Georges B-1050 Brussels Belgium; i8 gallery Klapparstig 33 101 Reykjavik Iceland; Jablonka Galerie Hahnenstrasse 37 D-50667 Cologne Germany; Margo Leavin Gallery 812 N Robertson Blvd Los Angeles CA 90069; Runyon Fine Arts 10010 Gaywood Rd Dallas TX 75229. *Mailing Add:* c/o Matthew Marks Gallery 523 W 24th St New York NY 10011

HORNE, RALPH ALBERT
PAINTER, WRITER
b Haverhill, Mass, 1929. *Study:* Sch Mus Fine Arts, Boston, cert; San Francisco Art Inst; Univ Ariz, Florence, Italy; MIT, Cambridge, Mass, BS; Boston Univ, MA; Univ Vt, MS; Columbia Univ, PhD; Law Sch, Suffolk Univ, JD. *Work:* John D Merriam Collection, Boston Pub Libr. *Exhib:* Boston Pub Libr; San Francisco Art Inst; Currier Gallery, Manchester, NH. *Mem:* Boston Mus Fine Arts. *Media:* Mixed Watercolor & Poster Paint on Masonite Panels. *Res:* 19th century American art; antiques and architecture. *Interests:* restoration & furnishing of 18th and 19th century houses. *Collection:* 19th century Am Houses, art, antiques. *Publ:* Articles in Victorian Homes, 91 & 94

HOROWITZ, DIANA
PAINTER
b New York, NY, 1958. *Study:* Rome prog, State Univ NY, Purchase, BFA, 80; Tyler Sch Art, Philadelphia, MFA, 84; Brooklyn Col, MFA, 87. *Work:* Hunter Mus Am Art; Sheldon Swope Art Mus, Terre Haute, Ind; Bellevue Hosp, NY; Brooklyn Union Gas Co, NY. *Exhib:* 25 Yrs of Visual Arts, Neuberger Mus, Purchase, NY; Work by Newly Elected Mems, Am Acad Arts & Letters, NY; Artists Select Artists, Trenton City Mus, NJ; Landscape Painting 1960-1990, Gibbes Mus Art, Charleston, SC; NY Acad Art, NY. *Awards:* Ingram Meml Found Grant, 88; Pollock-Krasner Grant, 89 & 93; Rosenthal Found Award, Am Acad Arts & Letters, NY, 96. *Bibliog:* John Hollander

(auth), Italian Tradition in American Art (exhib catalog), Gibbes Mus Art, Charleston, SC, 90; Lois Martin (auth), Classical landscapes, Am Artist, 94; Laurie S Hurwitz (auth), Oil highlights: Landscapes, Am Artist, 95. *Mem:* Nat Acad. *Media:* Oil, Canvas. *Mailing Add:* 2319 12th ave San Francisco CA 94116-1907

HORRELL, JEFFREY L
LIBRARIAN
b Carbondale, Ill, Sept 19, 1952. *Study:* Miami Univ, Oxford, Ohio, BA, 75; Univ Mich, AMLS, 76, MA (art hist), 78; Syracuse Univ, MPhil, 95, PhD, 95. *Pos:* Archivist, Mus Art, Univ Mich, 76-78; libr internship, Nat Gallery Art, Wash, DC, 77; asst art librn, Art & Arch, Libr, Univ Mich, 78-80; art librn, Sherman Art Libr, Dartmouth Col, 80-86; asst librn, Personnel, Budget & Planning, Syracuse Univ Libr, NY, 86-92; librn, Fine Arts Libr, Harvard Univ, 92-97; assoc libr, Harvard Col for Collections, 98-2005; dean libr, Dartmouth Col, 2005. *Awards:* Coun Libr Resources Acad Libr Mgt Intern, 86-87. *Mem:* Art Libr Soc NAm (treas, 82-84, vpres & pres elect, 86-88); Coll Art Asn; Am Libr Asn; The Grolier Club. *Res:* Development of automated database on art works produced in Florence and Siena in the 13th and 14th centuries. *Interests:* Art documentation and access. *Publ:* Auth, The picturesque: Literature of the English landscape garden, Dartmouth Coll Libr Bull, 83; contribr, Treasures of the Hood Museum of Art, Hudson Hills Press, 85; Second international conference on automatic processing of art history and data documents, Art Doc, 85; Seneca Ray Stoddard: Transforming The Adirondack Wilderness in Text and Image, Syracuse Univ Press, 99. *Mailing Add:* 5 Hathoin's Hell Woodstock VT 05091

HORT, MICHAEL & SUSAN
COLLECTORS
Pos: Founder, Rema Hort Mann Found, New York, 1995-. *Awards:* Named one of Top 200 Collectors, ARTnews mag, 2003-13. *Collection:* Contemporary art. *Mailing Add:* Rema Hort Mann Found 153 Hudson St New York NY 10013

HORVAT, OLGA
PAINTER, WRITER
b Yugoslavia. *Study:* Studied with Cambridge & Ely Brass Rubbing Ctr, England, Cert, 78; Faculty Arts, Zagreb Univ, Croatia, BA, 87; Fashion Inst Tech, NYC, MA, 91. *Work:* San Francisco Folk Art Mus, Calif; Los Angeles Folk Art Mus, Calif; Renwick Gallery of Nat Mus Am Art, Washington, DC; CASE Mus, Jersey City, NJ; The Mus New Art, Detroit, Mich; AKC Museum of the Dog, St Louis, Mo. *Comn:* fabric constructions, Walt Disney World Co, Orlando, Fla, 95; wall hanging, Mr & Mrs Walters, Los Angeles, Calif, 96; fabric constructions, D & D Building, NY, 97; mixed media (silk & paper), Gemelli at the World Trade Ctr, NY, 99; custom portraits, Mr & Mrs Tomson, Chicago, Ill, 2000. *Exhib:* Cooks Third Voyage, Acquario Di Genova Area, Genova, Italy, 90; Magies, Gallerie Vanuxem, Paris, France, 92; Artist Friends of Ceres, Ceres Gallery, NY, 98; Plan for Peace, Times Square Gallery, NY, 99; Novoye, CASE Mus, Jersey City, NJ, 99; A Salute to Hispanic Herigage, Borough Presidents Gallery, NY, 2000; Colored Artworks, Queens Mus Art, NY, 2000; Expressions, Khan Mus, Ashkelon, Israel, 2000. *Pos:* curator asst, The Met Mus Art, 90-91; rsch asst, AD Lederman Fine Art Gallery, 91-92; art dir, Absolute Image, Inc, 94-98; Asst to Pres Basically Kids, 98-2001; Dir, Olga Horvat Art, 2001-present; pres, Royal Dogs Gallery, 2007-; host, Pet Friendly Living, MN Network, 2013-. *Awards:* cert excellence Plan for Peace, NY Times, 99; Twentieth Century Achievement Award, Am Biographical Inst, 99; Accademia Internazionale Greci-Marino, Italy, 2000. *Bibliog:* videocassette, Olga Horvat Collection, Absolute Image, Inc, New York, 96; Jeremy Sedley (auth), Newart International, Art Press, Woodstock, NY, 98; Marilyn Wachtel (auth), Olga Horvat's Post-Pop Celebrity Puzzles, Gallery & Studio, 99; Roberto Puviani (auth), Dizionario Enciclopedico Internazionale D'Arte Contemporane, Case Editrice Alba, Ferrara, Italy, 99; Renee Phillips (auth), A Salute to Ashekelon, Manhattan Arts Internat, 2000. *Mem:* Nat Mus Women in Arts; NY Artists Equity Asn; Queens Mus Art; Nurture Art; Dog Writers Asn Am. *Media:* Mixed Media, Oil, Digital Art. *Interests:* Tennis, Aerobics, Travel. *Publ:* auth, Paranormal Pooch: A True Story of the Dog Who Healed One Family, Omega Publs, 2011. *Mailing Add:* 1465 Royce St Ste 1H Brooklyn NY 11234-5902

HORVAT, VLATKA
PHOTOGRAPHER, SCULPTOR
b Croatia, 1974. *Study:* Columbia Coll, Chicago, BA (Theater), 1996; Northwestern Univ, Evanston, Ill, MA (Performance Studies), 1997. *Exhib:* Solo exhibs include STUK Kunstencentrum Leuven, Belgium, 2003, Galerija Nova Zagreb, Croatia, 2005, Waygood Gallery, Newcastle Upon Tyne, UK, 2007; Group exhibs include Directed Dialogues Parsons Sch Design Galleries, New York, 2002; Based on a True Story, Artists' Space, New York, 2004, Ten People Smiling, 2005; Codependent, The Living Room, Miami Beach, 2005; AIM 25, Bronx Mus Arts, New York, 2005; Body City Doors Art Found, MK Gallery, New York, 2006; Slow Revolution, Rotunda Gallery, Brooklyn, 2006; The Beat, Haswellediger & Co Gallery, New York, 2006; Wild Girls, Exit Art, New York, 2006; Am Dream Sequence, Jerry Riggs, Miami, 2007; Cut Away, Anna Kustera Gallery, New York, 2008; White Columns, New York, 2008. *Awards:* Filip Trade Art Award Finalist, Zagreb, Croatia, 2005

HORVATH, SHARON
PAINTER
Study: Cooper Union, NY City, BFA, 1980; Tyler Sch Art, Philadelphia, Pa, MFA, 1985. *Exhib:* Solo exhibs include Zoe Gallery, Boston, 1987, 1990, Victoria Munroe Gallery, NY City, 1989, 1991, 1993, 2004, 2005, 2007, Jessica Berwind Gallery, Philadelphia, 1993, Am Acad Rome, 1997, Tibor de Nagy Gallery, Ny City, 1998, 1999, 2001, 2005, Anderson Gallery, Va Commonwealth Univ, 1999, Gallery 817, Univ of Arts, Philadelphia, 2001, The Drawing Room, East Hampton, NY, 2006; group exhibs include Cleve Mus Art, 1985; Victoria Munroe Gallery, NY City, 1987, 1990, 1993; Zoe Gallery, Boston, 1987, 1989, 1990; ACA Gallery, NY City, 1988; Levy Gallery, Philadelphia, 1989; Philadelphia Mus Art, 1990; Bridgewater State Coll, Mass, 1991; Ark Arts Ctr, 1992; Am Acad Arts and Letters, NY City, 1993, 1999, 2002; Maier Mus Art, Lynchburg, Va, 1994; Tibor de Nagy Gallery, NY City, 1996, 2001; Elizabeth Harris Gallery, NY City, 1997; DNA Gallery, Provincetown, Mass, 1998, 2002, 2003; Gallery Campo and Campo, Antwerp, 1999; Mass Coll Art, 2000; Geoffrey Young Gallery, Mass, 2000, 2001, 2002, 2003, 2004; Bernard Toale Gallery, Boston, 2001; Fine Arts Workcenter, Provincetown, Mass, 2002; Gallery Joe, Philadelphia, 2003; Rice Pollock Gallery, Boston, 2005; Drawing Room, East Hampton, NY, 2006; Proteus Gowanus, Brooklyn, NY, 2007; EFA Gallery, NY City, 2007. *Teaching:* assoc prof, Purchase Coll, SUNY. *Awards:* Provincetown Fine Arts Work Ctr Fel, 1986; John Simon Guggenheim Mem Fel for Painting, 1992; Richard and Hinda Rosenthal Found Award, Am Acad Arts and Letters, 1993; Pollock-Krasner found Grant for Painting, 1994, 1997; Elizabeth Found for Arts Grant for Painting, 1994; Rome Prize, Am Acad Rome, 1996-997; Hassam, Speicher, Betts and Symons Purchase Award, 1999; NY City Edwin Palmer Mem Prize in Painting, Nat Acad Mus, 2004; Richard C von Hess Fac Prize for Outstanding Commitment as a Tchr and Mentor, Univ Arts, 2004; Anonymous was a Woman Award for Painting, 2005; Cert of Hon, Tyler Sch Art Alumni Asn, 2007. *Media:* Dispersed Pigment, Oil, Acrylic. *Dealer:* Tibor de Nagy Gallery 724 Fifth Ave NY City NY 10019; Adam Baumgold Gallery 74 E 79th St NY City NY 10021

HORVAY, MARTHA J
PAINTER, ENVIRONMENTAL ARTIST
b Schenectady, NY, Jan 7, 1949. *Study:* Univ Mich, Ann Arbor, BS (design), 71, Univ Louisville, MA, 74, Temple Univ, Tyler Sch Art, MFA, 80. *Work:* Sheldon Mem Gallery Art & Sculpture Garden, Lincoln, Nebr; Hastings Coll, Nebr; Del Mar Coll, Corpus Christi, Tex; Mus Nebr Art, Kearney. *Comn:* 2 paintings, Bessey Hall, Univ Nebr, Lincoln; one percent-for-Art, Nebr, pub outdoor sculpture, Univ Nebr-Lincoln. *Exhib:* 34th Small Drawing & Sculpture, Ball State Univ, Muncie, Ind, 88; two-person exhib, Quincy Coll Art Gallery, Ill, 89; 33rd Chautauqua Nat, Chautauqua Art Asn Gallery, NY, 90; Midlands Invitational 1990, Joslyn Art Mus, Omaha, Nebr, 90; New Am Talent, Laguna Gloria Art Mus, Austin, Tex; Solo Exhibs: A Personal Geometry, Sheldon Mem Gallery Art, Lincoln, Nebr, 92; Haydon Gallery, Lincoln, Nebr, 95; Mod Arts Midwest Gallery, Lincoln, Nebr, 2007; Morehead State Univ, Ky, 98. *Collection Arranged:* Bemis Center for Contemporary Art, 2004; AIR Gallery, 2004. *Teaching:* Vis asst prof drawing found, Univ Tex San Antonio, 81-82; temporary instr drawing design, Kans State Univ, Manhattan, Kans, 82-83; prof visual literacy, Univ Nebr, Lincoln, 83-2007, sr lectr (part time); Sr Lectr, Dept Textiles, Clothing, and Design, Univ Nebr, Lincoln. *Awards:* Juror's Award, 49th Ann Competition, Sioux City Art Ctr, Iowa, 90; Artist's Fel Award, Nebr Arts Coun, 91 & 98; Individual Artist's Fel Award, Mid-Am Arts Alliance, 92. *Bibliog:* Kyle MacMillan (auth), Unusual work explores space, volume, time, Omaha World-Herald, 7/24/91; Daphne Anderson Deeds (auth), A Personal Geometry, Sheldon Memorial Gallery Art, 92; Joel Geyer (producer), Is It Art? (film), Nebr Educ TV, fall 92; Kent Wolgart, Art Papers, Jan. 2004. *Mem:* FATE (Foundations in Art: Theory and Education). *Media:* Acrylic. *Specialty:* Regional Contemporary Art. *Interests:* Pattern, isometric drawing, abstractions. *Publ:* New American Paintings, 10/98. *Dealer:* Modern Arts Midwest, 800 P St, Lincoln, NE 68508. *Mailing Add:* 4433 Pawnee St Lincoln NE 68506

HORVITZ, SUZANNE REESE
PAINTER, SCULPTOR
b Philadelphia, Pa. *Study:* Philadelphia Coll Art, BFA, MA, 72; Columbia Univ, doctorate, 77. *Work:* Corning Mus Glass, Corning, NY; Musee d'Art Contemporain, Chamaliéres, France; Fyns Kunstmuseum, Odense, Denmark; Mus Am Glass, Millville, NJ; Glasmuseum, Ebeltoft, Denmark. *Comn:* Wallwork, Legent Corp, 94. *Exhib:* Solo exhibs, Harbiye Sanat Galerisi, Istanbul, Turkey, 85, Utah Mus Fine Arts, Salt Lake City, 87, Mus Greater Victoria, BC, Can, 90, Musee d'Art, Contemporain, Chamaliéres, France, 91, Centro de Arte Moderna, Portugal, 91, Fyns Kunst Mus, Odense, Denmark, 91, Centre d'Art Contemporain, Niort, France, 91, Mangel Gallery, Philadelphia, Pa, 93 & Kunstzaal Marktzeventien, Enschede, The Neth, 94. *Pos:* Exec Dir, Found Today's Art/Nexus, Philadelphia, 75-. *Teaching:* instr, Pa Acad Fine Arts, 80-81. *Awards:* Masterworks Fel, Creative Glass Ctr Am, 90; Visual Arts Fel, Mid Atlantic States, 92; Grant, Pa Coun Arts, 93. *Bibliog:* E F Sanguinetti & Thomas V Southam (auths), Suzanne Reese Horvitz, Utah Museum of Arts, 87; Corrine Robbins (auth), Arts Mag, 11/88; Otis Larren (auth), Suzanne Horvitz, Glass Mag, 90. *Mem:* Philadelphia Art Alliance (vpres, 79-); Artists Equity Asn; Women's Caucus Arts. *Media:* Acrylic, Oil; Metal, Glass. *Publ:* Auth, Rope Trick, 80; Thou Hast Ravished My Heart, 81; Sick of Love, Synapse Press, 81; coauth, Vampyr, Synapse Press, 85; Tender Tearful Places, VSW Press, 92. *Dealer:* Mangel Gallery 1714 Rittenhouse Sq Philadelphia PA 19103; Galerie Tower 33 rue du Fauburg Poissonniére 75009 Paris France. *Mailing Add:* 2310 Perot St Philadelphia PA 19130-2526

HORWITZ, CHANNA
CONCEPTUAL ARTIST, PAINTER
b Los Angeles, Calif, May 21, 1932. *Study:* Art Ctr Sch Design, 50-52; Calif State Univ, Northridge, 60-63; Calif Inst Arts, BFA, 72. *Work:* Nat Gallery Art, Washington; Los Angeles Co Mus Art, Grunwald Ctr Graphic Arts, Univ Calif & Armand Hammer Mus Art, Los Angeles; Hartford Atheneum, Conn; Neuberg Mus, State Univ New York, Purchase; Pardo Lattuada Gallery, 00. *Comn:* Volt Industs, Orange Co, Calif; Ramada Renaissance Hotel, Long Beach, Calif; Grand Champion Hotel, Indian Well, Calif. *Exhib:* Los Angeles Co Mus Art, 73; Musical Drawings, PSI, Brooklyn, NY, 79; Los Angeles Munic Art Gallery, 88; Drawing in Southern Calif, 93; Armand Hammer Mus Art, Univ Calif Los Angeles, 94; Sonakinatography: Sound & Motion Notations (with catalog), Los Angeles Munic Art Gallery, 96; Beyond Geometry 1940-1970, Los Angeles County Mus Art, 2004; Language Series (with catalogue), Solway Jones Gallery, Los Angeles, 2005. *Awards:* James D Phelan Award, 63; Winner's Circle, Los Angeles, Calif, 65; Artist Fel, Nat Endowment Arts, 78. *Mem:* Los Angeles Artists Equity Asn. *Media:* Acrylic, Oil. *Publ:* Auth, My statement, 76; auth, Sun & Moon-A Quarterly Statement by Artist, Howard Fox, 76; auth, Channa Horwitz, Full Circle 1964-2005 (catalogue). *Dealer:* Solway Jones Gallery 5377 Wilshire Blvd Los Angeles CA 90036. *Mailing Add:* 1742 S Barrington #4 Los Angeles CA 90025

HOSTETLER, DAVID L
SCULPTOR
b Massillon, Ohio, Dec 27, 1926. *Study:* Indiana Univ, BA; Ohio Univ, MA. *Work:* Mus Fine Arts, Boston; Columbus Mus Fine Arts, Ohio; Speed Mus, Louisville, Ky; Butler Art Inst, Youngstown, Ohio; Trump Int Hotel & Tower, NY. *Comn:* Semaphore Woman, Philharmonic Ctr Arts, Naples, Fla, 94; Standing Woman, Ohio Univ, 95; Cape Lady, comn by Tom Kershaw, Beacon Hill, Boston, 97; The Duo, Trump Int, NY, 97; Summertime, Grounds for Sculpture, Hamilton, NJ, 98; DeCordava Mus and Sculpture Park, Lincoln, Mass. *Exhib:* Columbus Collects, Columbus Mus Art, Ohio, 93; Hostetler Major Woods, Parkersburg Art Ctr, WVa, 97; 7 World Trade Ctr, NY, 2000; Univ Hartford, Conn, 2003; City of Stamford, 2003; DeCordava Mus, 2003; Grounds for Sculpture, 2005; Sculpture Ctr, 2005. *Teaching:* Prof art sculpture, Ohio Univ, 48-85. *Awards:* Prof Year, 79 & 80; Ohioanna Career Medal Lifetime Achievement, 89. *Bibliog:* Roulker (auth), Masters of Wood Sculpture, 80; Hostetler, Four Decades (film), PBS TV, 88; Dick Wooten (auth), Hostetler the Carver, Ohio Univ Press, 92. *Media:* Wood. *Mailing Add:* PO Box 989 Athens OH 45701

HOSTVEDT, ANNA
PAINTER
b New York City, Jan 12, 1971. *Study:* Cooper Union, New York, BFA (Painting), 1993. *Exhib:* Solo exhibs include Tibor de Nagy Gallery, New York City, 2004, 2007; group exhibs include Dumbo Arts Ctr Gallery, Brooklyn, NY, 2002; Realism, Plum Gallery, Williamstown, Mass, 2002; Paying Attention, Creative Arts Workshop, New Haven, Conn, 2003; Blueprint, Silo, New York, 2004; Invitational Exhib Visual Arts, Am Acad Arts & Letters, New York, 2008. *Teaching:* Tech asst, painting/drawing, Cooper Union Sch Art, 2007. *Awards:* Purchase Award, Excellence in Art Student Grant Prog, 1990; Barbara White Fel, Vt Studio Ctr, 1997; Purchase Award, Am Acad Arts & Letters, 2008. *Mem:* Triangle Arts Asn. *Media:* Oil. *Mailing Add:* c/o Tibor de Nagy Gallery 724 Fifth Ave New York NY 10019

HOTARD, SUSAN F
PAINTER
b Oct 14, 1953. *Study:* New Orleans Acad Fine Arts, studied with Auseklis Ozols, Carol Pebbles, & M Dell Weller; La Tech Univ, BFA. *Exhib:* Solo exhibs, Galerie Eclat, New Orleans, 2003, 2005; Group exhibs, New Orleans Sch of Glassworks, 2000, 2001, Degas Pastel Soc, 2000, 2001, 2004, New Orleans Art Asn, 2002, Galerie Eclat, 2003, 2004, World Trade Ctr, New Orleans, 2006, St. Tammany Art Asn, 2006, River Oaks Square Art Ctr, 2008, Academy Gallery, 2009, Audubon Artists Online Ann Exhib, 2012, and many others. *Pos:* lectr, Design and Composition, New Orleans Mus Art, 2006. *Teaching:* instr, Delgado Comm Coll, Jewish Comm Ctr, & many other workshops. *Awards:* Marquis Who's Who in Am Art References award in Oil & Acrylics, Audubon Artists, New York, 2012. *Bibliog:* New Orleans Homes & Lifestyles, 2002; The Advocate Mag (review), 11/2004, 12/2005; Gulf Coast Arts & Entertainment Review, 2004; How Did You Paint That? 100 Ways to Paint Still Life & Florals, Int Artist Pub, 1/2004; The Artist's Mag, 2005; Am Artist mag (cover story), 7/2005, 8/2005; Times-Picayune: Artistic Expression, 2006. *Mem:* Audubon Artists; New Orleans Art Asn; La Watercolor Soc; Degas Pastel Soc; Portrait Soc Am; Pone Aliquid Contra Faciem Meam Carbone Delineabo; La Nouvelle Salon; The Woodlands Art League; Oil Painters of America; Am Women Artists. *Media:* Oil, Pastel. *Dealer:* The Garden District Gallery New Orleans La

HOTCHNER, HOLLY
MUSEUM DIRECTOR, CONSERVATOR, CURATOR
b New York, NY. *Study:* Trinity Coll, Hartford, Conn, BA (art hist & studio art, Phi Beta Kappa), 1973; Inst Fine Arts, NY Univ, MA (art hist), 1982; Mus Mgmt Inst, Univ Calif, Berkeley, 1992, exec leadership Harvard Univ, 2012. *Pos:* Collections & exhib cataloguer, Mus Mod Art, NY, 1973-76; intern, paintings conserv, Hirshorn Mus, Washington, DC, 1980, Tate Gallery, London, Eng, 1980-81; chief conserv, NY Hist Soc, 1984-88, founding mus dir, 1984-95; pres, Holly Hotchner Fine Arts Mgmt, 1995-96; founding dir, Mus Arts & Design (formerly Am Craft Mus), NY, 1996-2013, built new mus at Two Columbus Cir. *Awards:* Conserv Internship Grant, Nat Mus Arts, 1982-83; Samuel H Kress Found Grant, 1983-84; Visionary award, Mus Arts and Design, 2008. *Mem:* Elected mem Art Table; NY Landmarks Conserv (bd trustees, 1996-present); Fel, Am Inst Conserv; Fel, Int Inst Conserv; Assn Art Mus Dirs (elected mem, 99). *Publ:* Auth, John James Audubon: The Watercolors for the Birds of America, Random House, New York, 1993; Forty Years, Anniversary Issue, Am Craft Mus, NY, 1996, Beatrice Wood: A Centennial Tribute, 1997 & Four Acts in Glass: Installations by Chihuly, Morris, Powers, ad Vallien, 1998; contribr, Institutional Trauma: Major Change in Museums and Its Effect on staff, Am Asn Mus, Washington, DC, 1997, dir exhibitions highlights; Radical Lace and Subversive Knitting, 2007; Second Lives: Remixing the Ordinary, 2008; Slash: Paper Under the Knife, 2009; The Global Africa Project, 2010; Crafting Modernism: Midcentury American Art & Design, 2011; Otherworldly: Optical Delusions and Small Realities, 2011, Changing Hands: Art Without Reservation, 2002, 2005, 2012; Against the Grain: Wood in Contemporary Art, Craft, and Design, 2013; Tripled and Digitalized the Permanent Collection

HOUGH, JENNINE
PAINTER, INSTRUCTOR
b Charlotte, NC. *Study:* Univ NC, Chapel Hill, BA, 70; Univ NC, Greensboro, MFA with cert, 73; Skowhegan Sch Painting & Sculpture, Maine, summer 74. *Work:* High Mus Art & Ga Arts Coun, Atlanta; Columbus Mus Art, Ga; Miss Mus Art, Jackson; Gibbes Art Mus, Charleston, SC; State of Ga; Bradley Mus, Columbus, Ga; Mobile Mus Art, Alabama; Arts Coun, Gainsville, Ga; DeKalb Pub Libr, Atlanta, Ga; Fidelity Investments; Bridgestone Corp; Southern Progress Corp. *Comn:* Dekalb Co Libr Syst, Dunwooday, Ga, 91; Ducks Unlimited, 96; IAHI, 96. *Exhib:* Solo exhibs, Columbus Mus Fine Arts, Ga, 77, Monique Knowlton, NY, 82, Trinity Gallery, Atlanta, 90-92, Jane Haslem Gallery, Washington, 91 & 93, Marita Gilliam Gallery, Raleigh, 91; Fernbank Mus Natural Hist, Atlanta, 94; Ghost Ranch Mus, Abiquiu, NMex, 94; Contemp Southwest Galleries, Santa Fe, 98; Vectr in Aspen, 2001; Aspen Chapel Gallery, 2002-2010; Aspen Art Mus Ann, 2001, 2003, 2005, 2007, 2009; Moca-Ga Atlanta, 2004; Red Brick Ctr Arts, 2008, 2009, 2010, 2011; Asherville Gallery of Art, 2012, 2013; Atelier Gallery, 2012, 2013; Biltmore Hilton, 2014. *Pos:* docent, Asheville Art Mus. *Teaching:* Eve prog, Emory Univ, 79-84; Atlanta Col Art, 86-87; Colo Mountain Coll, Aspen, 2010, 2011; Red Brick Ctr Arts, 2009-2010, 2011; continuing workshops, Aspen, Asheville, Black Mountain, Asherville, Blue Ridge Community Coll, Super Saturdays UNC-A, 2012, 2013, Reuters Ctr, 2013; Montreal Coll, 2013-14. *Awards:* Nat Endowment Arts & Southeastern Ctr Contemp Arts Fel Grant, 80; Archives Nat Mus Women Arts, 90; Art in Embassy Prog, US State Dept, Barbados, 94-96. *Bibliog:* Southern Realism, Art in Am, 12/80; Articles in Am Artist, 85, 91 & 95; Southern Accents, Honoring American Artists, 87, 95. *Mem:* Nat Asn Women Artists, NY; Nat Portrait Soc; Nat Mus Women Arts (charter mem); Am Asn Univ Women. *Media:* Oil; Watercolor. *Interests:* painting, teaching, piano, gardening, reading, running and my animals. *Mailing Add:* PO Box 5402 Asheville NC 28813

HOUGH, MELISSA ELLEN
MUSEUM DIRECTOR, CURATOR
b Philadelphia, July 24, 1951. *Study:* Beaver Coll, BA, 1973; Univ Pa, MA, 1980. *Pos:* Asst cur, INA Copr Mus, Philadelphia, 1980-1982; cur, CIGNA Mus & Art Collection, 1982-1984, chief cur, dir, 1984-. *Mem:* mem, Am Assn Nat Assn Copr Art Mgr (adv bd), 1990-1997; prog chair, Mus Coun Greater Dela Valley, 1987-1991; exec bd mem, vp, Fireman's Hall Mus, 1994-1999; collection comt chair, Slate Belt Heritage Ctr, 1999-. *Mailing Add:* CIGNA Mus & Art Collection 1601 Chestnut St Philadelphia PA 19192

HOUGH, WINSTON
PAINTER, DRAFTSMAN
b Hartford, Mich, July 12, 1928. *Study:* Art Inst Chicago, BFA, 53; Northeastern Ill Univ, MA, 71. *Comn:* 14 Watercolors Midwest Stock Exchange Serv Corp, 67. *Exhib:* Exhib Momentum Midcontinental, Chicago, 53; Chicago Artist, Art Inst Chicago, 55; Richmond Artist, Valentine Mus, Va, 57-59; Virginia Artist, Chrysler Mus, Norfolk, 57-60 & Va Mus Art, 58; Winston-Salem Gallery Fine Art Semiannual, NC, 57-68; Seven Arts Ann, Palm Beach, Fla, 65 & 73; Solo exhibs, Paul Theobald Book Store Gallery, 78, Gruen Gallery, Chicago, 84, Concordia Coll Fergeson Gallery, River Forest, Ill, 87, Beverly Arts Ctr Pillsbury Concourse Gallery, Chicago, 88 & Artreach Gallery, Columbus, Ohio, 90. *Teaching:* Asst prof, Va Commonwealth Univ, Richmond, 56-62; lectr art, Univ Ill, Chicago, 64-65. *Awards:* Best Painting, Birmingham Mus, 58; Cert of Award, Rockport Publ, 98. *Bibliog:* Leslie Judd Ahlander (auth), New Painter, Washington Post, 61. *Media:* Oil, Watercolor. *Publ:* Illusr, Best of Oils, Best of Acrylics & Portrait Inspirations, Rockport Publ, 97-98; Watercolor Expressions Selected by B L Schlemm, 2000. *Mailing Add:* 937 Echo Ln Glenview IL 60025

HOUGHTON, BARBARA JEAN
PHOTOGRAPHER, VIDEO ARTIST
b Chicago, Ill, Nov 2, 1947. *Study:* Univ Ill, Chicago, BA (art), 71; Sch Art Inst Chicago, MFA (photog), 73, also grad study with Shigeko Kubota. *Work:* Art Inst Chicago; Atlantic Richfield Corp, Denver & Houston; Chase Manhattan Bank, NY; Am Oil Co, Denver; Ctr Creative Photog, Univ Ariz, Tucson. *Exhib:* 74th Chicago & Vicinity Show, Art Inst Chicago, 73; Lensless Photog, Franklin Inst, Philadelphia, 82; Colo; State of the Arts, Denver Art Mus, 82; New Epiphanies, Ohio Found Arts & traveling, 83; Unsportsmanlike Conduct, Sebastian-Moore Gallery, Denver & Univ Conn, 83 & 84; Photograms, John Michael Kohler Art Ctr, Sheboygan, Wis, 85; The Art of Tattoo, City of Denver, 85; I Always Cheat at Croquet, Ctr Idea Art, Denver, 86. *Teaching:* Prof art & photog, Metrop State Col, Denver, 74-92 & Northern Ky Univ, 92-. *Awards:* Nat Endowment Arts Photog Grant, 78; Grant, Mayor's Comn Cult Affairs, City of Denver, 85; Interdisciplinary Grant, Nat Endowment Arts/Rockefeller Found, 86. *Bibliog:* Andy Grundberg (auth), From this land, Mod Photog, 6/79; William Peterson (auth), 4/81 & Jane Fudge (auth), summer 84, Photography Notes, Artspace. *Mem:* Coll Art Asn; Soc Photog Educ. *Mailing Add:* Fine Arts Dept Rm 312 Northern Ky Univ Highland Heights KY 41099

HOUK, PAMELA P
CURATOR
b Dayton, Ohio, Jan 8, 1935. *Study:* Skowhegan Sch Painting & Sculpture, Maine, 54; Sch Dayton Art Inst, Ohio, 55-65; Cincinnati Art Acad, Ohio, 61-63; Wright State Univ, Dayton, Ohio, BS, 71, MA, 81. *Work:* Bradford Col, Haverhill, Mass; Cincinnati Mus Art, Ohio. *Collection Arranged:* Bookforms (auth, catalog), Artists' Books, 78; Patterns Plus (auth, catalog), Patterns and Systems, 79; Japanese House (auth, catalog), Household Objects of Edo Period, 79; Woodworks II: Folk Traditions in Ohio and Kentucky (auth, catalog), 81; Cloth Forms (auth, catalog), Fabric Constructions, 82; Inside Self, Someone Else (auth, catalog), The Alter Ego as Self Portrait, 83; Lines of Art Nouveau (auth, catalog), Aspects and Sources of International Art Nouveau Movement, 83-84; Ink Under Pressure (auth, catalog), 84; Clay (auth, catalog), 85; Thomas Macaulay: Sculptural Views on Perceptual Ambiguity, 1968-1986 (coauth, catalog), Dayton Art Inst, Ohio, 86; Art for the Public: New Collaborations (coauth, catalogue), 88; Art that Flies (book, coauth), Sky Art, 90; Fit to Print, Basic Printmaking Processes in 500 years of Master Prints, 92; Inside Japanese Space, Japanese Aesthetic Concepts Related to Space, 93; Making Faces, 93-94; Starting with Art (introd to looking at art), 94-95; Stories in Art (introd for families to the exhib, Botticelli to Tiepolo), 95-96; Art Zoo, 97-98; Color Connections, 99-. *Pos:* Dir, Living Arts Ctr Gallery, Dayton, Ohio, 72-76; cur, Experiencenter Gallery, Dayton Art Inst, Ohio, 76-. *Awards:* Governors Award for Excellence in Art Educ, Ohio, 93. *Mem:* Am Asn Mus. *Mailing Add:* Dayton Art Inst 456 Belmonte Park N Dayton OH 45405-4700

HOULE, ROBERT JAMES
PAINTER, CONSULTANT
b St Boniface, Man, Mar 28, 1947. *Study:* Univ Man, Winnipeg, BA (art hist), 72; Int Summer Acad Fine Arts, Salzburg, Austria, 72; McGill Univ, Montreal, BEd (art), 75. *Work:* Art Gallery of Ontario, Toronto; Heard Mus, Phoenix; Mus Contemp Art, Sydney; Nat Gallery Can, Ottawa. *Comn:* Mural, McGill Univ, Montreal, 73; poster, Assembly First Nations, Ottawa, 81; Gambling Sticks, Sculpture, The Forks, Winnipeg Art Gallery, 99. *Exhib:* Works on Paper, Galerie Sarah McCutcheon, Montreal, 81; New Work by a New Generation, Norman Mackenzie Art Gallery, Regina, Sask, 82; New Growth from Ancestral Roots, Koffler Gallery, Toronto, 83; Contemp Native Am Art, Okla State Univ, Stillwater, 83; Innovations: New Expressions in Native Am Painting, Heard Mus, Phoenix, 83. *Collection Arranged:* New Work by a New Generation, 82. *Pos:* Cur contemp Indian art, Nat Mus Man, Ottawa, 77-80; art consult, Indian & Northern Affairs, Ottawa, 80-81 & Assembly First Nations, Regina, Sask, 82; Cons Contemp First Nations art holding: McMichael Can Collection, 85. *Teaching:* Specialist art, James Lyng High Sch, Montreal, 74 & Verdun Cath High Sch, Montreal, 75-76; Ontario Col Art & Design, 90-03. *Bibliog:* Carol Phillips (auth), New Work by a New Generation, Artscanada, 11/82; Nancy Baele (auth), Indian adds to Mondrian, Ottawa Citizen, 6/4/83. *Mem:* Royal Can Acad. *Media:* Acrylic, Watercolour. *Res:* Contemporary native art in Canada. *Publ:* Auth, Search for identity, Tawow, Vol 1, No 3, 70; auth, Alex Janvier: 20th century native symbols and images, 78 & Odjig: An artist's transition, 78, Native Perspective; auth, A firm statement on the demoralization of Indian people, Gazette, 79; Dibaajimowin/Storytelling, The Art of Bonnie Devine, Algoma Gallery, Sault Ste Marie, 03. *Dealer:* Goodwater Gallery, 800 Dundas St W, Toronto. *Mailing Add:* 387 Ontario St Toronto ON M5A 2V8 Canada

HOURIAN, MOHAMMAD
PAINTER, ART DEALER
b Hamedan, Iran, 1955. *Study:* Apprentice with Haj Hosen-Esalmiyan, 67-77; Univ Tehran, BA (art), 77. *Work:* Swanson Fine Arts Gallery, Tate Gallery, San Francisco, Calif; Galerie Rivolta, Lausanne, Switz; Roma Gallery, Rome, Italy; Sweden Helsingborg, Lajos Flesser Gallery, 98. *Comn:* 3 paintings, comn by Charlotte Tilton, Beverly Hills, Calif, 85; painting, comn by Geoffrey Watson, Oakland, Calif, 89. *Exhib:* Persian Art, Fine Arts Mus, Tehran, 75; Persian Art, Mus Fine Arts, Brussels, 76; Persian Art, Fine Arts Mus, Tokyo, Japan, 85; Persian Art, Antiques Gallery, San Francisco, 92, Tresidder Union, Stanford Univ, Palo Alto, 97, Vorpal Gallery, San Francisco, 2000, Int Artexpo, NY, 2006. *Collection Arranged:* Persian Art, Noori Gallery, 90; Persian Art, Swanson Fine Arts, 92. *Teaching:* Prof art, Univ Tehran, Iran, 78 & Univ Calif, Berkeley, 87. *Awards:* Gold Medal, Int Tehran Exhib, 75; First Prize, Tehran Painters Exhib, 76. *Media:* Watercolor, Gold Base Acrylic. *Collection:* Persian miniature art. *Publ:* Auth,Dreams of Realty in Perian Art, 90. *Dealer:* Nat Art Gallery Tokyo Japan

HOURIHAN, DOROTHY DIERKS
PAINTER, EDUCATOR, WRITER
b Columbus, Ga, Aug, 19, 1935. *Study:* Gulf Park Coll, Miss, AA, 55, Univ Colo, with Mark Rothko, BFA, 57; Columbia Univ, Teachers Coll, MA, 60 Ed D, 84. *Work:* Montclair Art Mus, NJ; Columbus Mus, Ga; Hebrew Home for the Aged, Riverdale, NJ; NJ City Univ; Noyes Mus, Oceanville, NJ; NJ Ctr Visual Arts; Albrecht Art Mus, St. Joseph, Mo; Springfield Art Mus, Mo; 9/11 Mem Found Slide Collection; Mus City NY Slide Collection. *Comn:* Comn by Mr & Mrs Leonard Block, New York. *Exhib:* 1st Ann Opening Show, Birmingham Mus, 59; St Louis Art Mus, Mo, 61; solo exhibs, Viridian Gallery, New York, 87, 89, 92, 95, 2011 Montclair Mus, NJ, 89, Courtney Gallery, NJ City Univ, 98, Pen & Brush Club, New York, 98, 2000 & 2006 & New Fine Arts Bldg Gallery, City Univ, NJ, 2003; Mussavi, NY, 88; Nabisco Gallery, 88; Columbus Mus (group), Ga, 90; Korean Cult Ctr, New York, 90 & 96; KL Fine Arts, Chicago, 99; 50 Yr Retrospective, Pen & Brush Inc, 2009; Viridian Gallery, Chelsea, NY, 2011. *Pos:* Bd dir, Nat Asn Schs Art & Design, 86-92; cur, Lever House Group Show, New York, 92; adv coun, Hudson Repertory Dance Theatre; bd trustees, Thomas A Edison Film Consortium. *Teaching:* Prof painting, NJ City Univ, 62-94, chmn dept art, 82-91, chmn media arts dept, prof emer, fine arts, 95-; dean, Sch Arts & Scis, 91-94; retired, 94. *Awards:* Second Prize Watercolor, 12th Ann Juried Exhib, Summit Art Ctr, NJ, 76; Cert Appreciation, Jersey City Cult Arts Comn, 85. *Mem:* Hudson Co Cult & Heritage Coun (adv coun, 84-85); Nat Asn Sch Art & Design (bd dir, 85-); Hudson Repertory Dance Theatre (adv bd, 85-); Pen & Brush Club; Veridian Gallery, New York. *Media:* Oil, Mixed Media. *Interests:* Writing, Golf, Traveling. *Publ:* auth, 1919: A Kansas Tale, 2012; auth, A Fatal Gift, 2012. *Dealer:* Pen & Brush Inc New York NY; Viridian Artists Inc 530 W 25th St Chelsea New York NY. *Mailing Add:* 257 Kerrs Corner Rd Blairstown NJ 07825

HOUSE, JOHN C
EDUCATOR, ADMINISTRATOR
Study: Auburn Univ, BFA; Univ Tennessee, MFA (communications). *Teaching:* Prof Graphic Design, program coordinator Graphic Design, Univ of Southern Mississippi, currently, chair Dept Art and Design, currently. *Mailing Add:* Department of Art and Design Fine Arts Building 108 118 College Dr Box #5033 Hattiesburg MS 39406-0001

HOUSE, SUDA KAY
PHOTOGRAPHER, VIDEO ARTIST
b Du Quoin, Ill, Jan 31, 1951. *Study:* Univ Southern Calif, BFA, 73; Calif State Univ, Fullerton, MA, 76. *Work:* Polaroid Corp, Boston; Los Angeles Co Mus Art; Mus Photog Arts, San Diego; Creative Ctr Photog, Univ Ariz; Minneapolis Inst Arts. *Exhib:* Attitudes: Photog in the 1970s, Santa Barbara Mus Art, 79; Uniquely Photog, Honolulu Acad Art, 79; Electro Works, George Eastman House, Rochester, NY, 81; Photographer as Printmaker, Arts Coun Gt Brit, London, 82; Eight from San Diego, San Diego Mus Art, 82; Polaroid: The Big Picture, Mus Photog Arts, San Diego, 83. *Teaching:* Guest instr photog, Univ Calif, Los Angeles Exten, 77; instr, East Los Angeles Col, 78-79; prof, Grossmont Col, 79-. *Awards:* Nat Endowment Arts Emerging Photogr Fel, 80. *Mem:* Los Angeles Ctr Photog Studies (trustee, 74-81, pres, 75-78); Soc Photog Educ (chmn western region, 81-82). *Publ:* Auth, Artistic photographic processes, Amphoto, 81. *Mailing Add:* Dept Commun Arts & Sci Grossmont Col 8800 Grossmont College Dr El Cajon CA 92020-1798

HOUSEAGO, THOMAS
SCULPTOR
b Leeds, UK, 1972. *Work:* Rubell Family Collection, Miami; Saatchi Gallery, London; Stedelijk Mus, Amsterdam; SMAK Stedelijk Mus voor Actuele Kunst, Belgium. *Exhib:* Transformers, Donna Beam Fine Art Gallery, Univ Nev, 2006; Strange things permit themselves the luxury of occurring, Camden Arts Ctr, London, 2007; Academia: Qui es-tu?, la Chapelle de l'Ecole des Beaux-Arts, France, 2008; The Craft of Collecting, Mus Contemp Art, Chicago, 2009; Whitney Biennial, Whitney Mus Am Art, 2010; All Together Now, L&M Arts, Los Angeles, 2011. *Mailing Add:* Michael Werner 4 East 77th St New York NY 10075

HOUSER, JIM (JAMES C)
PAINTER, EDUCATOR
b Dade City, Fla, Nov 12, 1928. *Study:* Ringling Sch Art, BS, 49; Fla Southern Col, BFA, 51; Art Inst Chicago, postgraduate, 52; Univ Fla, MFA, 53. *Work:* Univ Notre Dame; Cornell Univ; NY Univ; Soc Four Arts Collection, Palm Beach, Fla; Syracuse Univ Art Collection; Boca Raton Mus Art, Fla; and others. *Exhib:* Solo exhibs, Grand Cent Mod, NY, 66-, Lehigh Univ, Bethlehem, 68, Gallery Camino Real, Boca Raton, Fla, 72-89, 99, 2003 & 2005, 2007, Brevard Community Coll, Cocoa, Fla, 73, Valencia Community Coll, Orlando, Fla, 74, David Findlay Galleries, New York City, 76, 78, 81, 83, Northwood Inst, 86, Palm Beach Community Coll, 88 and others; Group shows, Dept State Spec Exhib, Wash, 67, Major Fla Artist Invitational Exhib, Sarasota, Fla, 81-92, North Miami Mus and Art Center, North Miami, Fla, 85, Men's Art Northwood Univ, West Palm Beach, Fla, 94, Festival Int Peinture, Cagnes-sur-Mer, France, 2001; Mainstreams USA, Ohio, 68; David Findlay Galleries, NY, 76-84; Yellow Banks 50th Art Exhib, Owensboro, Ky, 89; Ft Lauderdale Mus Art Invitational Exhib, 91; Martin County Cult Ctr, 2008. *Pos:* painter, judge local and nat art competitions; lectr in field. *Teaching:* Sr instr art, Ky Wesleyan Coll, Owensboro, 54-60, fine arts chm, 58-60, art chmn, 64-70, dir art gallery, 74-91; prof art & painting, Palm Beach Coll, 60-92, gallery dir, 74-90. *Awards:* Merit Award, 16th Hortt Competition, Ft Lauderdale Mus Arts, 74; Akston Award, Soc Four Arts, 77; Atwater/Kent Award, Soc of the Four Arts, 77-89, 91; Philip Hulitar Award, 82; Four Arts Award, Soc of the Four Arts, West Palm Beach, 92, 93, 95; Established Connie and Jim Houser Award for the Contemp Exhib Soc of the Four Arts, 96-. *Bibliog:* Articles, Arts Mags, 81-85; numerous magazine articles, 1964-2007; Connie Houser (auth) The Letters, Portrait of an Artist: Jim Houser, 2007. *Mem:* Soc of the Four Arts (Certificate of Appreciation 1996, 18 other awards). *Media:* Acrylic. *Interests:* painting, camera, watching the world go by. *Publ:* Auth, Color for the Artist, Palm Beach Jr Coll, 75; Perspective, video, Palm Beach Jr Coll, 86; Perspective Drawing, video, Palm Beach Jr Coll, 90; Anatomy of a Painting, co-auth with Connie Houser, 2009. *Dealer:* Gallery Camino Real; David Findlay

HOUSEWRIGHT, ARTEMIS SKEVAKIS JEGART
PAINTER, SCULPTOR
b Tampa, Fla, 1927. *Study:* Fla State Univ, Tallahassee, BA, 49, MA, 52; study with Edmund Lewandowski & Karl Zerbe. *Work:* Tallahassee Democrat Bldg, Fla; Gulf Life Insurance Bldg, Jacksonville, Fla; Washington Federal Bldg, Hollywood, Fla; Tallahassee Community Col, Admin Bldg, Fla; Student Union Bldg, La State Univ, Baton Rouge; Mus Art, Greenville, SC; MD Artists, Univ MD; Fla State Univ, Tallahassee, Fla. *Comn:* Cement & Shell Mosaics, Phipps family mansion, Old Westbury Gardens, Old Westbury, Long Island, NY, 1969; Shell mosaic wall sculpture & 3 rug hangings, Wash Fed Bank, Hollywood, Fla, 77; oil painted murals done in private residences throughout the US, 85, 88, 89, 95 & 96; cement/shell mosaic panels, 2nd Nat Bank, Washington, 88; mural & archit decor, Ceresville Mansion, Md, 90; oil mural, Fla State Univ, Tallahassee, 2000; 13x13 oil mural, Fla State Univ, 2003. *Exhib:* One-person shows, 30 exhibs in galleries in Fla, Va, Ga & NY, 53-72, Cosmos Club, Washington, DC, 81, 97, Points of the Compass, Fla State Univ, Fine Arts Mus, 98, Retrospective Painting exhib, Vero Beach Mus Art, 2003, Painting exhib, Claude Pepper Foundation Gallery, Tallahassee, Fla, 2003; 21st Ann Mid-Year Show, Butler Inst Am Art, Youngstown, Ohio, 56, 57 & 60; two-person exhib, Jacksonville Mus Art, Fla, 58, Fla State Art Gallery, Tallahassee, 59; Invitational Paul Miller exhib, Jacksonville Art Mus, 61; 66 Artists of the Southeast, Delgado Mus, New Orleans, La, 66; Watergate Gallery, Washington, DC, 72; OMS, Cosmos Club, Wash DC, 97; group exhibit, Lew Allen Gallery, Santa Fe, NMex, 2006; 50 Yr Retrospective, Vero Beach Mus Art, Fla, 2003. *Collection Arranged:* 85 Pigs. *Awards:* 1st Prize, Purchase Award, Soc Four-Arts, Palm Beach, Fla, 55, 56 & 57; 1st Prize, James Johnson Sweeney, Dir Whitney Mus, 55; 1st Prize, Dorothy C Miller, Modern Mus, NY, 56; 1st Prize, Purchase Award, Tampa Art Inst, 57; 1st Prize, Edgar Schenck, Brooklyn Mus Art, NY, 57; 1st Prize, Purchase Award, Mississippi Art Asn, 57. *Mem:* Artists Equity. *Media:* Oil, Sand, Cement, Shell. *Interests:* design; architecture. *Publ:* Contrib, Washington Star (newspaper mag), 76, Baltimore Sun (newspaper mag), 77, Golden Eye (bk), 83, Interior Design (trade mag), Washington Home & Garden (mag), 90, House & Garden (mag), 92, The Grove (bk), 98, Coast to Coast (bk), 99 & Frederick Mag, 7 & 10/99; Cover art (book) Voices, 150 Yr Informal History of Florida State University, 2002; Hugh Sidey's Color prints of Greenwood, Iowa, paintings for historic preservation, 2003. *Mailing Add:* 9 Vista Estrella S Lamy NM 87540-9621

HOUSMAN, RUSSELL F
PAINTER, EDUCATOR
b Buffalo, NY, Jan 13, 1928. *Study:* Albright Art Sch, Buffalo, dipl; State Univ NY Coll Buffalo, BS; NY Univ, MA & PhD; also with Hale Woodruff & Revington Arthur. *Work:* Anderson Col, SC; Butler Inst Am Art; Chautauqua Ctr Visual Arts, NY; Dayton Art Inst, Ohio; Sivermine Guild Arts Ctr, Conn; and others. *Comn:* Mural,

USA, Kans Munic Auditorium, 52; painting, L Goodyear Collection, 57; Discovery Ctr, Human Resources Ctr, 72. *Exhib:* Solo exhib, Wellons Gallery, NY, McFall Gallery, NY, Silvermine Guild Arts Ctr, New Canaan, Conn, Albany Inst Hist & Art, Country Art Gallery, Locust Valley, NY, Nassau Community Col, NY, Southern Vt Art Ctr, Chaffee Art Ctr; retrospective, Albany Inst Hist & Arts, Nassau Co Mus & Nassau Community Col; Willard Gallery; Nordness Gallery; Kornblee Gallery; Arms & Armor, Civil War Cent, Decatur City Art Ctr; Images & Industry Exhib & Conf, Milliken Univ. *Pos:* Dir, Decatur City Art Ctr, 59-61 & Art Sch Adventure, Long Trail Sch, Dorset, Vt, 94-; art consult, Human Resources Ctr, Albertson, NY, Aging in Am & Nat Ctr Disability Serv Others; founder & dir, Firehouse Gallery, Nassau Community Col, 63-70. *Teaching:* chair art, Adelphi Univ, 56-59, Millikin niv, 59-61, Nassau Community Coll, 63-, Prof Emeritus, Hofstra Univ, 53-56. *Awards:* Purchase Award, State Univ NY, 68; Prizes, Silvermine Art Guild & Chautauqua Art Ctr; Nat Endowment Arts; NY State Coun Arts; Grand Concourse, Albany, NY. *Bibliog:* Viscardi (auth), The School, Eriksson, 64; 21 Paint in Hyplar, Grumbacher, 68; Watson (auth), The Senseous Carrot-The Artist as a Cook, Country Art Gallery, 72. *Mem:* Am Fedn Art; Silvermine Art Guild; NY State Art Teachers (ed, 69); Long Island Art Teachers; Phi Delta Kappa. *Media:* Oil. *Res:* Design of the art room, Hofstra Univ; Psych/Warfare capilities & vulnerabilities found in contemp Soviet Art, New York Univ; An Arts Core, Curriculum for severely disabled students, Human Resources Sch. *Interests:* Sch & community issues, chair sch bd, Clerk supermsory union, justice & peace, town auditor. *Publ:* Auth, Psychological Warfare Capabilities & Vulnerabilities as Found in Soviet Art, 54; The Design of an Art Room, 55; Utilization of Artist Personnel in Psychological Warfare, 63; Telephone Assisted Teaching Devices, 69; Core Humanities Curriculum for Disabled Children, 70; illustr, Penn's Stocking, A Childs Christmas Tale. *Dealer:* Country Art Gallery Locust Valley NY; Beside Myself Gallery Manchester VT. *Mailing Add:* 38 McKee Rd Arlington VT 05250

HOUSTON, BRUCE
SCULPTOR, ASSEMBLAGE ARTIST

b Iowa City, Iowa, Jan 23, 1937. *Study:* Univ Nebr, Lincoln, BA, 59; Art Ctr Coll Design, Los Angeles, 61-62; Univ Calif Los Angeles, MA (graphic design), 65; Univ Iowa, MFA (painting), 74. *Work:* Univ Art Mus, Albuquerque; Palm Spring Art Mus. *Comn:* Outdoor sculpture, Progressive Corp, Cleveland, Ohio. *Exhib:* solo exhibs, Chrysler Mus, Norfolk, Va, 91, Palm Springs Desert Mus, Calif, 92 & Lamont Gallery Phillips Exeter Acad, NH, Jan Baum Gallery, 95, 98, Molly Barnes Gallery, Santa Monica, Calif, 2000, Imago Galleries, Palm Desert, Calif, 2001; Lost & Found in Calif Four Decades of Assemblage Art, James Corcoran Gallery, Santa Monica, Calif, 88; Forty Yrs of Calif Assemblage, Frederick Wight Gallery, UCLA, Los Angeles, San Jose Mus Art, Fresno Art Mus & Joslyn Art Mus, Omaha, Nebr, 89; Calif Surrealism, Bronx River Art Gallery, Bronx, New York, 89; Des Moines Art Ctr, 87; Egyptian Mus, Berlin, Germany, 99; Palm Springs Art Mus, 2009; Lora Schlesinger Gallery, Los Angeles, Calif, 2008, 2011. *Teaching:* Slide lectr in many colls & univs throughout Calif, 79-. *Awards:* Best in Show, Davenport Art Mus, 72. *Bibliog:* Suzanne Muchnic (auth), Bruce Houston assemblages, Art Voices S, 1/80; Nicholas Roukes (auth), Humor in Art: A Celebration of Visual Wit, Davis Publ, Worchester, Mass; Reed Johnson, Orlando, Los Angeles Times, 11/19/99; Von Gisela Blanki, Offnet, Schauplatz Mus, 4/16/99; The High Point, Variations on Queen Nefertete, Berliner, 4/23/99; Peter Frank, ARTPICK of the Week, LA Weekly, 10/20/2000; and many more. *Mem:* Smithsonian Mag; Palm Springs Art Mus, Calif. *Media:* assemblage, drawing. *Interests:* jazz, drawing, concert live. *Dealer:* Allan Stone Galleries; Imago Galleries 45-450 Hwy 74 Palm Desert CA 92260; Lora Schlesinger Gallery Bergemot Station 2525 Michigan Ave T3 Santa Monica CA 90404. *Mailing Add:* PO Box 580016 North Palm Springs CA 92258-0016

HOUSTON, JOHN STEWART See Stewart, John Stewart Houston

HOVSEPIAN, LEON
PAINTER, DESIGNER

b Bloomsburg, Pa, Nov 20, 1911. *Study:* Worcester Art Mus Sch, cert; Yale Univ, Alice Kimball traveling fel, BFA, 42; Fogg Mus. *Work:* Worcester Art Mus, Mass; Fitchburg Art Mus, Mass; Fine Arts Collection, Washington; Springfield Mus, Mass; Mus Mod Art, Yerevan, Armenia, USSR. *Comn:* Mosaics, Oblate Fathers Retreat House, Willimantic, 61; stained glass, Holy Cross Col, Worcester, 65; portraits, Leiceister Jr Col, Mass, 68-69; fresco mural, Church of the Annunciation, Washington, 74; portrait, Judge Morris N Gould, Worcester, Mass; design of Archeveque Chapel, Papeet, Tahiti, 83; resurrection mural, St Joseph's Cemetery, Chelmsford, Mass, 84; portrait, Dr Vincent Mara, Pres, Fitchburg State Coll, 87; portraits, "Spag" & Olive Borgatti, 90. *Exhib:* Art Inst Chicago, 41; Albright Art Gallery, 46; Nat Gallery Art, 47; RI Sch Design, 48; Worcester Art Mus Am Biennial, 48; By the People For the People--New Eng, De Cordova Mus, Lincoln, Mass, 77; Solo exhib, Armenian Libr & Mus Am Inc, Watertown, Mass, 91; Looking past the painting--Underlying Structure (traveling), Fitchburg Art Mus, Mass, 92-93. *Collection Arranged:* ARTSworcester, Aurora Gallery, Worcester, Mass; Worcester Pub Lib; AGBU Gallery, New York. *Pos:* Dir, Boylston Summer Art Sch, Mass, 41-; fac, Clark Univ Sch Worcester Art Mus, formerly. *Teaching:* Instr art, Bancroft Sch, 36-38; prof, Woman's Col, New Haven, 38-40; instr, Worcester Art Mus Sch, 40-, instr, Pub Educ Div, 41-56. *Awards:* St Wulstan Soc Art Award, 38-40; Painting Prize, Fitchburg Art Mus; Ford Found Grant to exhib in Armenia, USSR. *Bibliog:* Adlow (auth), Stuart Gallery, Christian Sci Monitor, 46; Sandrof (auth), Artist in his studio, Feature Parade, 53; Browne (auth), Leon Hovsepian, Art News, 11/66. *Mem:* Bohemians Inc; elected mem Pi Alpha, Yale Univ. *Media:* Oil, Acrylic; Watercolor, Tempera. *Publ:* Illusr, Worcester Federal, Past--Present--Future, 52; illusr, Androck, 58. *Dealer:* Triart Studios 96 Squantum St Worcester MA 01606. *Mailing Add:* 96 Squantum St Worcester MA 01606

HOWARD, DAN F
PAINTER, EDUCATOR

b Iowa City, Iowa, 1931. *Study:* Univ Iowa, BA, 53, MFA, 58. *Work:* Joe & Emily Lowe Art Mus, Miami, Fla; Chautauqua Inst, NY; Sheldon Mus Art, Univ Nebr, Lincoln; Smithsonian Nat Mus Am Art, Washington, DC; Joslyn Art Mus, Omaha, Nebr; Hallmark Coll, Kansas City, Mo; Mus Nebraska Art, Kearny, NE; and many others. *Exhib:* Contemp Am Painting Exhib, Soc Fine Arts, Palm Beach, Fla, 79, 83, 84, 85, 86, 89, 96; Butler Midyear Show, Butler Inst Am Art, Youngstown, Ohio, 66, 83, 84, 89, 93; traveling retrospective, 83-84; Solo Exhibs, Wichita Art Asn Galleries, Kans, 88, New Gallery, Houston, Tex, 89 & 93; Joy Horwich Gallery, Chicago, Ill, 90 & Vorpal Gallery, NY, 91; The Artist in his 75th Year, Eisentrager-Howard Gallery, Univ Nebraska Lincoln, 2007; West/Art & Law Touring Exhib, 93-94; group exhibs, 90, 92, 93 & 94; Univ Northern Iowa, Cedar Falls, 94; Soliloquium, Mus Nebr Art, Kearney, 2004-05; Dan Howard Drawings, 1990-2010, Sheldon Mus Art, Lincoln, 2011; 80th Birthday Celebration: New Paintings, Kiechel Fine Arts, Lincoln, Neb, 2011; Kiechel Fine Arts, Lincoln, Nebr, 2013. *Teaching:* From instr to assoc prof painting & drawing, Ark State Univ, 58-71, chmn div art, 65-71, dir art gallery, 67-71; prof painting & drawing & head dept art, Kans State Univ, 71-74; prof art, Univ Nebr, Lincoln, 74-96, chmn dept, 74-83, prof emer, 96-. *Awards:* Butler Institute Top Award, Nat Midyear Show, Youngstown, Ohio, 84; Hulitar Prize, Contemporary Am Painting Exhib, Palm Beach, Fla, 97; artist fel, Nebr Arts Coun, 95; and over 100 other prizes, awards and honors. *Bibliog:* In View of the Law, West Publishing Co, St Paul, Minn, 79; Dan Howard: A Retrospective: A Selection of Paintings from 1968-1982, Blanden Mem Art Mus/Sioux City Art Ctr; Christin J. Mamiya (auth), Valedictory Exhib Tribute, 97; Cristin J. Mamiya (auth), Decisive Line: Drawings by Dan Howard (monograph), 2011; All New! Commentory by Marissa Vioneault (gallery guide), 2013. *Mem:* Coll Art Asn Am; Mid-Am Coll Art Asn (vpres, 75, pres, 76, bd dir, 75-79); Nebr Art Asn (bd trustees, 74-83). *Media:* Oil Painting, Drawing. *Specialty:* American Art, Regional 1930s & 40s, Contemporary. *Collection:* Dan & Barbara Howard Collection Am Popular Art; Sheldon Mus Art, Lincoln, Nebr; 125 original works of comic strip & comic book art. *Dealer:* Kiechel Fine Art 1208 O Street Lincoln NE 68516

HOWARD, DAVID
PHOTOGRAPHER, PAINTER

b Brooklyn, NY, Jan 25, 1952. *Study:* Ohio Univ, 69-71; San Francisco Art Inst, MFA, 74; addn study with Ansel Adams, Jerry Uelsmann, Ralph Gibson, Robert Heineken, Arron Siskin & Robert Frank. *Work:* Mus Mod Art, 75; San Francisco Mus Modern Art, 75; Whitney Mus Am Art, 85; Hirshorn/Smithsonian, DC, 85; Oakland Mus, Calif, 73; San Francisco Art Inst, 85; City of San Francisco, 73; De Saisset Mus, Santa Clara, 72; Art Ctr, Waco Tex, 86; Memphis Brooks Mus, Tenn, 87; Akron Art Mus, Ohio, 88; Houston Mus Fine Art, 89; Black Star Publ, New York, 97; Metropolitan Mus Art; Arts of Africa, Oceania and the Americas Photo Collection, 2011; The Field Mus, Anthropology Photography Collections, Chicago, Ill, 2013. *Exhib:* Solo exhibs, Horshorn/Smithsonian East Village, DC, 85, Fourth St Gallery Photographs, New York, 76, Fourth St Gallery, Photographs, New York, 85, San Francisco Art Inst East Village, 85, G Ray Hawkins Gallery Photographs, Los Angeles, 88, Hosftra Univ, NY, 85, Univ Calif San Francisco, 75, Images Gallery Photographs, New York, 77, 544 Natoma Performance Gallery, San Francisco, 83, Madison Art Ctr, Wis, 76, Lehigh Univ Art Galleries, Pa, 85, John Bolles Gallery Photographs, San Francisco, 74, Ohio Univ, 71, Oakland Univ, Mich, 85, Artist's Workshop & Gallery, Brooklyn, 70, Intersection Gallery, San Francisco, 72, Marc Richards Gallery, Los Angeles, 86, EZTV Keith Karing, Los Angeles, 87, Philadelphia Mus Art, 90, Martin Weber Gallery, San Francisco, 86, Thomas Crow Gallery, Los Angeles, 73, Caskey Lees Tribal Show, San Francisco, Calif, 2012; Group exhibs, Hansen Fuller Gallery, San Francisco, 73, Whiteney Mus Am Art, 85, De Young Mus, San Francisco, 75, Oakland Mus, 74, Camera Works Photography & Language, 76, 78, Multiple Media Travel to 8 US Inst, 74, Ohio Silver Gallery, Nat Exhib, Los Angeles, 75, Calif Mus Photography, 84, Palace of Fnie Arts, San Francisco, 72, Guggenheim Gallery Photography, Calif, 78, Neary Gallery Contemp Photography, Calif, 79, De Saisset Art Gallery & Mus, Calif, 72, San Francisco Art Inst, 72, 86, 74, 73, 78, Erie Art Ctr, Pa, 74, Images Gallery, Horizons, NY, 76, Vorpal Gallery, East Village, San Francisco, 85, Calif State Univ, 88, San Francisco Pub Libr, 87, Squiggles Gallery, San Francisco, 86, Hadley Martin Gallery, San Francisco, 87, Fine Arts Mus Long Island Art, 89, Chandler Gallery, Wash, 91, The Universe of Keith Haring, 2008. *Collection Arranged:* 19th Century Landscapes; The Last Filipino; Head Hunters; The Figure; 64 Video Tapes about Art; The 60's; Nepal: Everest to the Sacred Hindu Shrines; Photographic Abstraction; Filipino Tribal Artifacts; English Engravings From 1877; Palawan: The Final Filipino Frontier; The Renaissance; Land Sea and Sky; The Yoruba: An Africa's Tribe's Bead Work; Antique Cameras and Photographs; Mexico: The Noble Nation; Monastery and Tribal Buddhism; African Art; Catholic Icons and Art; Relics of the Reborn: Sacred Skulls; Pop Art and Beyond; Photographic Sculpture; Rural Am; European Architecture; Theme Variations; Naga Artifacts and Historical Photographs; Sacred Journey: The Ganges to the Himalayas. *Pos:* Vis artist art hist, San Francisco City Col, 73; dir photog, San Francisco Ctr Visual Studies, 74-, photog instr, 73-78; dir, Art Seen (wkly cable series), San Francisco, 87-; Art Seen, New York, 89-. *Teaching:* Vis instr, City Col San Francisco; grad instr, San Francisco Art Inst. *Awards:* Black Star Syndicated Photogr, Photog Agency, NY; Purchase Award, 27th San Francisco Art Festival, City of San Francisco, 73. *Bibliog:* Flashart, 12/89; Soma Mag, No 18, 92; Art Calendar Mag, 2/95; Janos Gereben (auth), Global Microcosm of Art at Fort Mason, San Francisco Examiner, Calif, 2012. *Media:* Photography, Video, Painting. *Interests:* Tribal art collections, pop art collections, book publ. *Publ:* The World of Tribal Art, 4/98; Filipinas Mag, 4/98; Broadcast, KMTP-32, San Francisco, 3/94; numerous TV broadcasts & weekly TV series, Art Seen; produced & directed numerous videos & films; auth, The Last Filipino, Head Hunters, 2001; Sacred Journey, The Ganges to the Himalayas, 2004; Ten Southeast Asian Tribes From Five Countries, 2008; The Hidden World of Naga, 2003, The World of Tattoo, 2005; Perspectives with Ansel Adams, Jerry Uelsmann, Ralph Gibson & Robert Heinecken, 78, Realities, 76; Last Filipino Head Hunters

Photography, French Television Broadcast, 2011; Arts & Entertainment, San Francisco Examiner, Global Microcosm Art, Fort Mason, San Francisco, 2012; Tapping Ink: Tattooing Identities, Tradition and Modernity in Contemporary Kalinga Society, 2013; Vietnam Odyssey in Southeast Asian Stream, 2013. *Dealer:* Scott Nichols Gallery San Francisco CA. *Mailing Add:* c/o Visual Studies 49 Rivoli St San Francisco CA 94117

HOWARD, LINDA
SCULPTOR
b Evanston, Ill, Oct, 22, 1934. *Study:* Chicago Art Inst, 53-54; Northwestern Univ, 54-55; Univ Denver, BA, 57; Art Students League, NY, 63-64; Hunter Coll, NY, MA, 65-71; City Coll, Sch Archit, NY, 82. *Work:* K & B Plaza, Virlane Found, New Orleans, La; Allstate Insurance Corp, Bush Corporate Ctr, Columbus, Ohio; Zig-Zag, Coll City Tampa, Fla Council, Spain, 82; Space Wave (8' x 3' x 3' aluminum), Kotterman Collection, Univ Cent Fla, Orlando, 2004; New Orleans Mus Art, 2003; Wings of Protection (12' x 9' x 4' aluminum), Ormond Beach, Fla, 2006; Kuan (19' x 9' x 9' aluminum), Univ Miami, Coral Gables, Fla, 2007. *Comn:* Space Wave (aluminum), Barclays Bank, Miami, 90; Up/Over Around (5' x 15' x 8' aluminum), Tropicana Corp, Bradenton, Fla, 90; Wall Wave (12' x 6' x 6' aluminum), Gen Servs, Miami, Fla, 91; Archway (12' x 18' x 9' aluminum), Fla Int Univ, Miami, 91; Centerpeace (aluminum), Bradley Univ, Peoria, Ill, 91; 6'4 x 11'W x 8'D moved-refurbished, aluminum painted white, Double Speral Arch, New Coll, Univ S Fla. *Exhib:* Solo exhibs, Sculpture Now Gallery, NY, 75 & 78, Northwestern Univ, Ill, 78, Construct Gallery, Chicago, 80, Max Hutchinson Gallery, NY, 80, Heath Gallery, Atlanta, 88, Mus Art, Ft Lauderdale, 93, Harn Mus, Univ Fla, Gainesville, 94, Gulf Coast Mus, Largo, Fla, 2005-06; New Reflections, Aldrich Mus, Ridgefield, Conn, 73; Penthouse Show, Mus Mod Art, NY; 100 Yrs, 100 Artists, Chicago Art Inst, 80; Sculpture, The Language of Scale, Bruce Mus, Greenwich, Conn, 85; Am Women, Am Art, Stamford Mus, Conn, 85; Park Sculpture, Whitney Mus, 86 & Stamford Mus, Conn, 86 & 87; Contemp Sculpture, Univ Fla, Gainesville, 87; Artpark, Art Mus, Fla Int Univ, Miami; Paris Art Int, France, 82; Sculpture, The Language of Scale, Bruce Mus, Greenwich, Conn, 85; Am Women, Am Art, Stamford Mus & Nature Ctr, Stamford, Conn, 85; Continuity and Change, The Gallery, Ringling Art Sch, Sarasota, Fla; Sculpture Fields, Kenosa Lake, NY; Contemp Sculpture from Fla Collections, Univ Gallery, Univ Fla, Gainesville, 87. *Pos:* Vis artist, Alfred Univ, NY, Bennett Coll, Milbrook, NY & Colgate Univ, Hamilton, NY, 73, Potsdam State Univ, NY, 75, San Jose State Univ, Calif & Northwestern Univ, Evanston, Ill, 78; designer-model studio, Skidmore, Owings & Merrill Archits, NY, 84-85; vis artist master print prog & sculpture, Bradley Univ, Peoria, Ill, 91. *Teaching:* Asst prof sculpture, Hunter Col, NY, 69-72 & Lehman Col, NY, 73-76; assoc prof, NY Univ, 76-77 & Hunter Col, 77-82; adj assoc prof, Univ S Fla, Tampa, 85; adj prof, Manatee Community Col, Bradenton, Fla, 89; Fla Coll Natural Health, Bradenton, 2006-07. *Awards:* NJ Cult Coun; City Univ New York Fac Res Grant, 74 & 75; Creative Artists Pub Serv Grant, NY State, 75. *Bibliog:* Doc films, Linda Howard, Sculpture, 76, Constructions Sculpture, 76 & 500 Mile Sculpture Garden, 76, Nebr Educ TV; and others; Shaping Space The Dynamics of Three-Dimensional Design, Holt, Rinehart & Winston, 87 & 90; The Art of Seeing, Prentice Hall, 3rd Ed, 94; Larson Algebra 2, McDougal Littel/Houghton Mifflin Co, 2001 & 04. *Publ:* and others. *Dealer:* Barbara Gilman Miami FL. *Mailing Add:* 330 60th St W Bradenton FL 34209

HOWAT, JOHN KEITH
HISTORIAN
b Denver, Colo, Apr 12, 1937. *Study:* Harvard Univ, BA, 59, MA, 62. *Collection Arranged:* David Smith, Hyde Collection, 64; John F Kensett (with catalog), Am Fedn Art, 68; 19th Century America: Paintings & Sculpture (with catalog), 70, Am Paintings & Sculpture, 71, Heritage of Am Art: Paintings from the Collection, 75 & A Bicentennial Treasury: Am Masterpieces from the Metropolitan, 76, Am Wing, Metrop Mus Art, 80; John Frederick Kensett (with catalog), 85; Am Paradise: The World of the Hudson River School (with catalog), 87; Art and The Empire City: New York, 1825-1861 (with catalog), 2000. *Pos:* Cur, Hyde Collection, 62-64; asst cur Am painting, Metrop Mus Art, 67-68, assoc cur, 68-70, cur Am painting & sculpture, 70-81, chmn, Dept Am Art, 81. *Awards:* Ford Found Fel, 65; Chester Dale Fel, Metrop Mus Art, 65-67; Lawrence A Fleischman Award for scholarly excellence in the field Am art hist, Archives Am Art, Smithsonian Inst, 2000. *Mem:* Arch Am Art. *Res:* American paintings of 18th and 19th centuries, especially the Hudson River School. *Publ:* Auth, Hudson River & Its Painters, 72; Frederic Church, 2005

HOWE, NANCY
PAINTER
b Summit, NJ, Nov 17, 1950. *Study:* Middlebury Col, Vt, AB, 1973. *Work:* Nat Mus Wildlife Art, Jackson Hole, Wyo; Leigh Yawkey Woodson Art Mus, Wausau, Wis; Ella Carothers Dunnegan Gal of Art, Bolivar, Mo; R W Norton Art Gal, Shreveport, La; Bennington Ctr Arts, Vt. *Exhib:* Birds in Art, Woodson Art Mus, Wausau, Wis, 1991-2012; Art and the Animal, Soc of Animal Artists, varied venues, 1993-2006, 2010, & 2011; Artists of Am, Colo Hist Mus, Denver, Colo, 1994-2000; Great Am Artists, Cin, Ohio, 1996-2003; Wildlife Art for a New Century, Nat Mus Wildlife, Jackson, Wyo, 2000 & 2005; Int Masters of Fine Art, Int Mus of Contemp, San Antonio, Tex, 2001-12; Oil Painters of Am Nat Juried Exhib, varied venues and locations, 2002-05, 2009-2012. *Awards:* Int Masters Award, Int Mus Contemporary Masters of Fine Art, 2001; Gold medal, Best in Show, Eastern Regional Oil Painters of Am, 2009; Award of Recognition, Am Women Artists Show, 2010. *Bibliog:* Gussy Fauntleroy (auth), Renaissance Woman, Southwest Art Mag, 6/2003; Ken Stroud (ed), The Art of Nancy Howe, Wildscape: A Journal of Wildlife Art & Conserv, 6/2003; Kim Kiser (auth), The Sky's The Limit, Wildlife Art Mag, Jan-Feb, 2004. *Mem:* Soc Animal Artists. *Media:* Oil. *Publ:* Ill, Working with Your Woodland, Beattie Thompson Levine, 1983; contribr, The Best of Wildlife Art (1&2), 1997 & 1999 & Art from the Parks, 2000, North Light Books; contribr, Wildlife Art, Rockport Publ, 1999; contribr, Wildlife Art: Sixty Contemp Masters and their Work, Portfolio Press, 2001. *Mailing Add:* 3916 Mad Tom Rd East Dorset VT 05253

HOWE, NELSON S
DESIGNER, ASSEMBLAGE ARTIST
b Lansing, Mich, Nov 5, 1935. *Study:* Univ Mich, BA, 57, MA, 61. *Work:* New Orleans Mus Fine Arts, La; Libr Collections, Mus Mod Art, NYC Pub Libr, Finch Coll Mus Art & Chase Manhattan Bank Collection, NY; Univ Calif, Berkeley; and others. *Comn:* Wall I (fabric wall), comn by Mr & Mrs Keith Waldrop, Providence, RI, 68; Fur Music (installation unit), Mus Contemp Crafts, NY, 71; Fur Score (fur wall), New Orleans Mus Fine Arts, 72. *Exhib:* Solo exhib, Little Gallery, Minneapolis Inst Art, Minn, 67; Fur & Feathers Show, Mus Contemp Crafts, 71; Experimental Sound, ICES Festival, London, Eng, 72; Mus Mod Art, NY; and other solo & group exhibs. *Pos:* Pres & founding artist mem, bd dir, Participation Proj Found, 73-. *Teaching:* Adj instr, Parsons Sch Design, NY, 67-68; instr, NJIT, Newark, NJ, 67-74. *Awards:* 50 Best Books of the Yr Award, Am Inst Graphic Arts, 69; Intermedia Found Grant for Lab Serv, 72. *Bibliog:* Rose De Neve (auth), Art - notation - art, Print Mag, Vol 25, No 1; Source: Music Avant Garde, No 9, 72; and others. *Mem:* Nat Expressive Therapy Asoc; Nat Inst Expressive Therapy. *Publ:* Illusr, To the Sincere Reader, 68 & Body Image, 70 & co-auth, Job Art, 71, Wittenborn; illusr & auth, Daily translating systems, Circle Press (London), 71; contribr, Harpers' Mag Wraparound Sect, 5/73; and others. *Mailing Add:* 637 Carlton Ave Brooklyn NY 11238-3809

HOWELL, JAMES
PAINTER
b Kansas City, Mo, Nov 17, 1935. *Study:* Univ Washington, Seattle, 58; Stanford Univ, BA, 57, BArch, 61; Nelson Art Inst, Kansas City, 47. *Work:* Albright-Knox Art Mus, Buffalo, NY; Davis Mus & Cult Ctr, Wellesley Coll, Mass; Werner H Kramarsky Collection, New York,; von Bartha Collections, Basel, Switzerland; Museo de arte Contemporáneo Esteban Vicente, Segovia, Spain; Miriam & Ira D Wallach Art Gallery, Columbia Univ, New York. *Exhib:* Univ Washington, 93, Charlotte Jackson Fine Art, 95, 2000, 2004, Sharon Traux Fine Art, 95; New Works, Henry Art Gallery, Univ Wash, Seattle, 93; Bartha Contemp, London, 2004, 2008; Albright-Knox Art Gallery, Buffalo, NY, 2008; Santa Monica Art Mus, Calif, 1999-2009; Museo des Artes Contemporáneo, Spain, 2009; Mies van der Rohehaus, Berlin, 2013, 2014. *Awards:* Art Prize, Hill Sch, 53; Humanities Prize for the Arts, Stanford Univ, 61. *Bibliog:* Richard Campbell (auth), Jim Howells Good Cheer, Seattle Post Intelligencer, 10/6/74; Regina Hackett (auth), James Howell Paints on the Outer Edge of Abstraction, Seattle Post Intelligencer, 6/9/92; Lis Bensly (auth), Subtle Spaces Midway between Light, Dark, Santa Fe New Mexican, 11/10/95. *Media:* Painting, acrylic. *Publ:* Auth, James Howell Series, Sharon Truax, 95; James Howell Gradient Intervals, Gerngrosse Co, 95. *Dealer:* Bartha Contemporary Art 25 Margaret St London W1W 8RX; Conny Dietzschold Gallery Cologne & Sydney, Australia; von Bartha Collections, Basel, Switzerland; Charlotte Jackson Fine Art 554 S Guadelupe Santa Fe NM 87801. *Mailing Add:* 140 Perry St 2nd Fl No 5 New York NY 10014-2364

HOWELL-COON, ELIZABETH (MITCH)
PAINTER, ILLUSTRATOR
b Hartselle, Ala, Feb 27, 1932. *Study:* Birmingham Southern Coll, BA; also with Edgar Whitney, Zoltan Szabo & Charles Reid; NALL, Vence, France. *Work:* Birmingham Mus Art, Ala; Montclaire Gallery, Birmingham; Firt Nat Bank, Decatur, Ala; Southtrust Bank of Hartselle, Ala; Parkway Med Ctr, Decatur, Ala. *Comn:* Illus & cover for cook bk, Decatur Jr Serv League, Inc, 72; portraits of vpres Dan Quayle & Gov Guy Hunt by USX; Crew of Challenger, NASA Astronauts. *Exhib:* Williamsburg Art Exhib, Va, 70; Charleston Art Exhib, SC, 70; Int Platform Asn Art Exhib, Washington, 71; Ala Watercolor Soc Nat Exhib, 80; solo Exhib, Kennedy Douglas Ctr Arts, Florence, Ala, 98. *Pos:* Dept head, Hubert Mitchell Industs, Inc, Hartselle, 49-55; owner, Howell-Baxter Gallery, Hartselle, Ala, 83- & Mitch Howell Studio, 96-. *Teaching:* Head dept fine art, Morgan Co High Sch, 64-66. *Awards:* Hannah Elliott Award, Lovemans, Birmingham, 69; Medwise Best of Show, Univ Ala, Birmingham, 98. *Bibliog:* France-Amerique, Courrier Etats-Unis, New York, 69; Huida G Lawrence (auth), article, Park East News, New York, 69; article, Aufbau, New York, 69. *Mem:* Life mem Kappa Pi (pres Coll chap, 53-54); founding mem Decatur Arts Coun; Decatur Art Guild (founder, actg pres, publ chmn & vpres, 67-); Ala Watercolor Soc; Carnegie Visual Arts Ctr. *Media:* Watercolor. *Specialty:* Watercolor portraits. *Interests:* travel, music, cooking. *Publ:* Illusr, Emmanuel-God With Us, 67 & Cotton Country Cooking, 72; When the Knead Rises, 93; auth & illusr, Paint a Prayer; Southern Scrumptious, 97; Southern Scrumptious Entertains, 2002. *Dealer:* Mitch Howell Studio 805 Barkley St SW St Hartselle AL 35640; Slate Framing & Gallery 333 Main St West Hartselle AL 35640. *Mailing Add:* 805 Barkley St SW Hartselle AL 35640

HOWES, ROYCE BUCKNAM
PAINTER
b Mt Clemens, Mich, Sep 20, 1950. *Study:* RI Sch of Design, BFA, 73; Skowhegan Sch of Painting & Sculpture, 74; Tyler Sch Art, MFA, 77. *Work:* Metrop Mus Art, NY; Univ Tenn, Knoxville; Kans State Univ, Manhattan. *Bibliog:* Wayne Toepp (auth), The Image Combines of Royce Howes, Arts Mag, 1/88. *Media:* Oil. *Dealer:* Grace Borgenicht Gallery 724 Fifth Ave New York NY. *Mailing Add:* 5 Fourth St Apt 10 Brooklyn NY 11231-4558

HOWLETT, D(ONALD) ROGER
ART DEALER, HISTORIAN
b Syracuse, NY, 1945. *Study:* Hamilton Col, NY, BA, 66; State Univ NY, Cooperstown, grad prog, MA, 67; Yale Univ, PhD prog, art hist. *Exhib:* D Roger Howlett: Watercolors, Monotypes, Oil Paintings, St Botolph Club, Boston, 3/27/2006-5/8/2006. *Collection Arranged:* George Luks (auth, catalog), 73-74 & Molly Luce: Eight Decades of the Am Scene (auth, catalog), 83, Childs Gallery, Boston. *Pos:* Vpres, Childs Gallery, Boston, 73-83, pres, 83-2008, Senior Research Fel, 2008-. *Mem:* Antiquarian Booksellers Asn Am; Internat Fine Print Dealers Asn; Emerson Gallery, Hamilton Col, NY (bd adv, currently); Lyme Acad Fine Arts

(trustee, 93-2002); New England String Ensemble (dir, vpres, 2004-05, pres, 2005-2009); Boston Athenaeum (proprietor); Harvard Musical Asn; St Botolph Club. *Media:* Watercolor. *Res:* 19th and 20th century American artists, including Molly Luce, I M Gaugengigl, Laura Hills, Donald De Lue and George Luks. *Specialty:* American and European paintings, prints and drawings, 16th to mid 20th centuries; 19th and 20th century realist sculpture; Japanese prints and China Trade paintings. *Publ:* The Sculpture of Donald De Lue: Gods, Prophets, and Heroes, David R Godine, 90; American Figurative Sculpture of the Thirties: A Rebirth in Bronze, The Journal of Decorative and Propaganda Arts, No 16, 90; William Partridge Burpee: American Marine Impressionist, Northeastern Univ Press, 91; The Lynn Beach Painters, Lynn Hist Soc, 98; Gertrude Beals Bourne: Artist in Brahmin Boston, Northeastern Univ Press, 2004. *Mailing Add:* Childs Gallery 169 Newbury St Boston MA 02116-2895

HOWLETT, RAY
SCULPTOR
b Lincoln, Nebr, Aug 6, 1940. *Study:* Univ of Nebr, BFA, 1963. *Work:* Frederick R Weisman Art Found, Los Angeles, Calif; Mus of Science, Boston, Mass; Mus of Neon Art, Los Angeles, Calif; Midwest Mus of Am Art, Elkhart, Indiana; West Valley Art Mus, Surprise, Ariz. *Comn:* Electric Light & Glass, Zerox Corp, Webster, NY, 2005; Electric Light & Glass, UDS Uniphase, Santa Rosa, Calif, 1980. *Exhib:* Dichroism in Light, Midwest Mus of Am Art, Elkhart, Ind, 2001; Ray Howlett, Light, Masur Art Mus, Dothan, Ala, 2002; Dichroic Color, Electric Light, Blanden Mem Art Mus, Ft Dodge IA, 2003; Glass Sculpture, Nat Liberty Mus, Philadelphia, Pa, 2004; Solo Exhibs: Lakeview Mus Arts & Sci, Peoria, Ill, Mus Neon Art, Los Angeles, Calif, La Art & Sci Mus, Baton Rouge, La, Western Ill Univ Art Gallery, Macomb, Ill, West Valley Art Mus, Surprise, Ariz, 2000; Midwest Mus Am Art, Elkhart Ind, 2001; Mansur Art Mus, Dothan, Ala, 2002; Blanden Mem Art Mus, Fort Dodge, Iowa, 2003; Nat Liberty Mus, Philadelphia, Pa, 2004; SDak Art Mus, Brookings, SDak, 2005; Butler Inst Am Art, Youngstown, Ohio, 2006; Erie Art Mus, Erie, Pa, Loveland Mus, Loveland Colo, 2007; Amarillo Mus Art, Amarillo, Tex, 2008. *Bibliog:* Space-Age Artwork, Lincoln J Star, 8/23/1996; Light as a Plaything, NY Times, 2/14/1999; Inner Light, So Bend Tribune, 8/1/2001. *Media:* Misc Media, Dichroic Glass, Fluorescent Light. *Mailing Add:* 4230 W St Lincoln NE 68503

HOWZE, JAMES DEAN
DRAFTSMAN, WRITER
b Lubbock, Tex, Apr 8, 1930. *Study:* Austin Coll, BA; Art Ctr Coll Design; Univ Mich, MS. *Work:* Del Mar Coll, Corpus Christi; Hobbs Pub Schs, NMex; San Antonio Coll; San Diego State Univ, Calif; Trenton State Coll, NJ; Texas Tech Univ Mus, Lubbeck, Tex. *Exhib:* Two Smithsonian Inst Traveling Exhibs, US & Can, 79-82; Am Drawing II & III, Portsmouth, Va, 79 & 81; Nat Small Works Exhib, Schoharie Co, NY, 83; Toys Designed by Artists, 12th Ann Exhib, Ark Arts Ctr, Little Rock, 84; Nat Drawing Asn, Hermitage Found Mus, Norfolk, 88, CW Post Ctr, Long Island Univ, NY, 89 & Md Inst Coll Art, Baltimore, 92; Nat Drawing Asn (various venues), Trenton State Coll; et al, Fine Arts Festival Gallery, Lubbock Arts Alliance, 2003-2004 & 2006-2007. *Pos:* Prof emer, Coll Fine Arts, Tex Tech Univ, currently. *Teaching:* Assoc prof, Dept Archit & Allied Arts, Tex Tech Univ, 58-68, prof studio art, Dept Art, 68-92, dir core curric, 79-87, assoc chmn, 88-91. *Awards:* Cash Awards, Nat Drawing & Small Sculpture Exhib, Del Mar Coll, 70, 74, 78 & 81; Best in Exhib, Nat Mensa Mem Exhib, 71; Nat Digital Art Exhib, E Tenn State Univ, 97; and others. *Mem:* Hon mem Dallas-Ft Worth Soc Visual Commun; Lubbock Arts Alliance Asn; Tex Asn Schs Art. *Media:* Charcoal Pencil, Digital Images; Mixed Media, Assemblage. *Interests:* Choral music, poetry writing, antique; Firearms (post 1873). *Publ:* Contribr, cartoons & humorous verse, Sports Car Graphic, 65-66; poet & illusr, Images from the High Plains, Staked Plains Press, Canyon, Tex, 79; drawing, Cheatham, Cheatham & Haler, Design Concepts and Applications, Prentice Hall, p 86, 83; drawing, Frank M Young, Visual Studies, Prentice-Hall, p 86, 85; auth & illusr, Creating and Understanding Drawings, Mittler & Howze, Glencoe, 89, 94, 2001, 2005, & 2010; Creating & Understanding Drawings. *Mailing Add:* 2503 45th St Lubbock TX 79413-3629

HOY, ANNA SEW
SCULPTOR
b Auckland, New Zealand, 1976. *Study:* Sch Visual Arts, BFA, 1998; Hunter Coll, New York, MFA, 2001. *Work:* Altoids Collection, New York, 2004. *Exhib:* Solo Exhibs include Storefront Project #1, A-Z House by Andrea Zittel, New York, 2001, Massimo Audiello Gallery, New York, 2002, Peres Projs, Los Angeles, 2003, Karyn Lovegrove Gallery, Los Angeles, 2007, LAX Art, Los Angeles, 2008; Group exhibs include Lost & Found, Massimo Audiello Gallery, New York, 1999; Talleres: Collection of the Guadalajara Workshops, Mex Cultural Inst, New York, 2000; Meat Market Art Fair, Momenta Art, New York, 2000; Perfunctory, Team Gallery, New York, 2001; Artists on Artists, Ace Gallery, New York, 2002; Unknown Pleasures, Daniel Reich Gallery, New York, 2002; The Rules Everyone Will Follow From This Day Forth, Peres Projs, Los Angeles, 2003; Drunk vs Stoned, Gavin Brown's Enterprise, New York, 2004; And I And I And I And I, Locust Projs, Miami, 2004; Phiiliip: Divided by Lightning, Deitch Projs/John Connelly Presents, New York, 2004; Kicking Rocks, Champion Fine Art, Los Angeles, 2005; Sugartown, Elizabeth Dee Gallery, New York, 2005; Astro Focus Disco Room, Mus Contemp Art, Los Angeles, 2005; Nevermind the Bollocks, Here's Amanda Lear, Envoy Enterprises, New York, 2006; Rebecca Morris, Karen Lovegrove Gallery, Los Angeles, 2006; Too Much Love, Angles Gallery, Los Angeles, 2006; Eden's Edge, Hammer Mus, Los Angeles, 2007; Against the Grain, Los Angeles Contemp Exhibs, Los Angeles, 2008. *Awards:* Marie Walsh Sharpe Art Found, 2002; United States Artists Fellow, 2006

HOY, HAROLD H
SCULPTOR
b Spokane, Wash, May 16, 1941. *Study:* Central Wash Univ, BA, 65; Univ Oregon, MFA (painting), 67, MFA (sculpture), 69. *Exhib:* Solo exhibs: Univ Oregon Art Mus, Eugene, 79, William Sawyer Gallery, San Francisco, Calif, 79, Blackfish Gallery, Portland, Ore, 81 & Univ Northern Iowa, Cedar-Falls, 89; The Animal Image, Smithsonian Mus, Washington, DC, 81; Animals, Celebration, Communion, San Jose Mus, Calif, 81; Oregon Biennial Exhib, Portland Art Mus, Ore, 81; Quartersaw Gallery, Portland, Ore, 91, 93 & 95. *Pos:* Gallery Dir, Lane Community Col, 70-. *Teaching:* Instr art, Lane Community Col, 70-. *Awards:* Fel Oregon Arts Comn, 71 & 77. *Bibliog:* Jean Cutler (auth), Sculpture of the Pacific Northwest: A Photographic Essay, Univ Ore Press; Thelma R Newman (auth), Encyclopedia of Woodworking, Crown Publ; 2nd Biennial Book, Fine Woodworking Mag. *Mem:* Coll Art Asn. *Media:* Sculptor. *Dealer:* Quartersaw Gallery 528 NW 12th Ave Portland OR; Linda Cannon Gallery 520 Second Ave Seattle WA. *Mailing Add:* Lane Community College Art Gallery 4000 E 30th Ave Eugene OR 97405

HOYT, ELLEN
ASSEMBLAGE ARTIST, LECTURER, JUROR
b Brooklyn, NY, Nov 8, 1933. *Study:* Pratt Inst, 53; Brooklyn Mus & Mus Nat Hist, 65-75 & 83; with Ed Whitney, Frank Webb, Jankowski DeStefano & Ernest Chrichlow. *Work:* Gateway Nat Recreation Area, NY; Austrian Lender Bank; Stuhr Mus Prarie, NB; Griplock Corp; Health Hosp Corp, NY. *Comn:* Painting, Sierra Club for Gateway Nat Park, NY, 82; British Consulate Gen, 92. *Exhib:* Lever House, NY, 85; Fed Bldg NY, 89; Pam Am Bldg, NY, 91; Metrotech, Brooklyn, 92; Cornell Med Ctr Libr, NY, 97; Dag Hammer Kjold Tower Condo Gallery, 98; Adlephi Univ Gallery, 98; Riverside Lib, Lincoln Ctr, NY, 2012; Grace Bldg, NY; Solo exhib, Brooklyn Public Libr; Group show, Riverside Gallery, Lincoln Ctr, Brooklyn Watercolor Soc; Coney Island Hospital Gallery; Brooklyn Working Artists Collection Gallery; Brooklyn Public Libr, Rings Hwy Branch. *Collection Arranged:* Coney Island Hospital, Sierra Club, New York. *Pos:* Instr, consult auth & juror, Nat Contemp Expos Artists Achievement, Fed Bldg, NYC, 87; Dir, art, Salt Marsh Nature Ctr, currently. *Teaching:* Instr art, Kingsway Acad, 70-75, Studio Dragonette, 77-80 & Unger Studios, 83-90; Hemlock Farms Art Soc, 88-92; Brand Studio, 91-93; Sierra Art Club Inst, 93-98; Watercolor Art Soc, 94-; Ellen Hoyt Acad, Rockaway Artist Alliance; Brooklyn Mus. *Awards:* Best in Show, Brooklyn Mus, 80; Travel Award, Washington Sq Outdoor Art Exhib, 81; Pilots Club Award, 83, 4th prize 87 & Landscape Award, 90; 2nd Prize, Byram River Arts Festival, 2004; Plainfield Festival of Arts, 2006. *Bibliog:* Emanuel Stromm (auth), Profile of an artist, Courier, 82; Eve Wilen (auth), New Exciting Approach, NY Artists Equity, 82. *Mem:* Artists Equity, NY; Visual Individualist; Brooklyn Watercolor Soc (secy, 79-86); Am Artist Prof League; Assoc Am Watercolor Soc; Nat Assoc Prof Women. *Media:* Watercolor. *Specialty:* White Silo Gallery; Metropolitan Transit Authority Gallery, NY; Snug Harbor Gallery, Staten Island, NY, 2007; Monmouth Beach Cult Ctr, NJ, 2009, 2010-2011; Honesdale Gallery, Honesdale, Pa. *Interests:* Hiking, reading & people. *Collection:* Many pvt collections nationally and internationally. *Publ:* Auth, Flare Printing, 75; Mariner, Flare Printing, 75; Never on Sunday Cookbook, Peerless Press, 70; NY Art Review, 88, 89; Sierra Club Periodical, 88-92. *Dealer:* Daphne Arts Brooklyn Gallery. *Mailing Add:* 1551 E 29th St Brooklyn NY 11229

HRICKO, RICHARD
PRINTMAKER
Study: Rochester Inst Technol, BFA, 1974; Tyler Sch Arts, Temple Univ, MFA, 1979. *Work:* Philadelphia Mus Art; LaSalle Univ Art Mus; Woodmere Art Mus, Philadelphia. *Exhib:* Solo exhibs include Print Ctr, Philadelphia, 1996 & Dennison Univ, Ohio, 1996; group exhibs include Silvermine Prints Int Exhib, New Canaan, Conn, 1996; Philadelphia Printmakers, Art in City Hall, Philadelphia, 1998; Paradise Endangered, Am Print Alliance, Washington, 1998; 183rd Ann: Invitational Exhib Contemp Am Art, Nat Acad Mus, New York, 2008. *Pos:* Co-founder, Crane Arts, LLC, Philadelphia. *Teaching:* Assoc prof art, Tyler Sch Art, Temple Univ, Philadelphia; asst dean students, Ctr Emerging Visual Artists, Philadelphia. *Media:* Lithography

HSIAO, CHIN
PAINTER, SCULPTOR
b Shanghai, China, 1935. *Study:* Taipei Normal Coll, BA; with Li Chun-Sen, Taipei, Taiwan. *Hon Degrees:* Knight of Italian Solidarity, 2005. *Work:* Mus Mod Art & Metrop Mus Art, New York; Nat Gallery Mod Art, Rome, Italy; Philadelphia Mus Art; Detroit Inst Art; Mus de Arte Mod, Barcelona; Art Gallery Ont; Taiwan Mus Art, Taichung. *Comn:* Mural, Mr S Marchetta, Messina, Sicily, 71. *Exhib:* Carnegie Inst, Pittsburgh, 61; Int Malerei 1960-1961, W Eschenbach, 61; Art Contemporain, Grand Palais, Paris, 63; 7th Biennial, Sao Paulo, Brazil, 63; 4th Salon Galeries-Pilotes, Lausanne, Switz & Paris, 70; Quadriennale Naz di Roma, 77. *Collection Arranged:* Mus Mod Art, New York; Galleria Nazionale d'Arte Moderna, Rome, Italy. *Teaching:* Instr art, Southampton Coll, Long Island Univ, 69; prof visual commun, Inst Europ Design, Milan, Italy, 71-72; vis artist, La State Univ, Baton Rouge, 72-; prof decoration, Turin Fine Arts Acad, Italy, 84-85; prof printmaking, Milan Fine Arts Acad, Italy, 85-96; Prof artistic anat, Urbino Fine Arts Acad, Italy, 83-84; prof creative art, Nat Taiwan Arts Coll, 96-2005. *Awards:* City of Capo d'Orlando, Italy Prize, 70; Gold Medal, Norwey Print Biennial, 84; First achievement Award Contemp Painting, Li Chun-Shen Found, Taipei, 89; Award for Nat Vis Prize, Taiwan Nat Art, 2002; Order of Knight of Italian Solidarity Star, Decorated by Italian Presidency, 2005. *Bibliog:* W Schonenberger (auth), Hsiao, Prearo, 72; La Via Di Hsiao, Nuova Foglio, 78 & Hsiao, Vanessa, 79; Hsiao Chin, Monography, Mazzotta ed, Milan, 88; and others. *Media:* Acrylic, Ink; Ceramic. *Res:* Spirituality in art. *Interests:* art, music, extraterrestrial lines. *Publ:* Retrospective, print portfolio, Milan, 63; Oh Che Vertigine, poems & prints, Milan, 66; Un processo di penetrazione, lithograph collection, Milan, 72; Ch'an, prints portfolio, Milan, 77. *Dealer:* Giorgio Marconi 15 Via Tadino Milan Italy; Lin/Keng Gallery Taipei Beijing. *Mailing Add:* Via G Modena 35 Milan 20129 Italy

HSIAO, GILBERT L
PAINTER
b Pennsylvania, 1956. *Study:* Columbia Univ, New York, 1974-77; Pratt Inst, Brooklyn, NY 1978-80. *Exhib:* Solo exhibs include White Columns, New York, 1986, Tomoko Liguori Gallery, New York, 1989, Tower 49, New York, 2004; group exhibs include Catherine Street Gallery, New York, 1985; Soho Ctr Vis Arts, New York, 1987; 25th Anniv Show, Drawing Ctr, New York, 2002; Movement, Hudson Guild, New York, 2005; War is Over, Sideshow Gallery, Brooklyn, NY, 2006; Minimalisms, Gallery W 52, New York, 2006; Presentational Painting III, Hunter Coll Grad Gallery, New York, 2006; Brooklyn, Westport Arts Ctr, Westport, Conn, 2006. *Awards:* New York Found Arts Fel, 2008. *Dealer:* Ober Gallery 14 Old Barn Rd PO Box 236 Kent CT 06757

HSIEH, TEHCHING
PERFORMANCE ARTIST
b Nan-Chou, Taiwan. *Exhib:* Solo exhibs, Am News Bureau, Mus Modern Art, 2009; solo performances, Taiwan, One Year Performance, 1978-79, 1980-81, 1981-82, 1985-86, Art/Life One Year Performance, 1983-84, one-man show, 1986-99; The Third Mind: American Artists Contemplate Asia, 1860-1989, Guggenheim, 2009. *Awards:* Fel, Visual Arts, US Artists, 2008. *Publ:* auth, One Year Performance Art Documents 1978-1999 (DVD-ROM), 2000 & One Year Performance 1980-1981 (film), 2006; Coauth (with Adrian Heathfield), Out of Now, MIT Press, 2009

HSU, PANG-CHIEH
EDUCATOR, PRINTMAKER
Study: Sch Visual Arts, New York, BFA, 2000; Univ Mass, Amherst, MFA, 2003. *Exhib:* Isolated Moments, Westside Gallery, New York, 2000; Views and Visions, South Gallery, Univ Mass, 2002; solo exhibs, Herter Gallery, Univ Mass, 2003, Valdosta State Univ, Ga, 2006, Thomasville Cult Ctr, Ga, 2007, Taipei Fine Arts Mus, Taiwan, 2008, Rosewell Mus, NMex, 2010; Joan Mitchell Fels Exhib, CUE Gallery, New York, 2004; Within State Line, Mus Contemp Art, Ga, 2006; The Art of Politics, Hooks-Epstein Gallery, Houston, 2008. *Teaching:* Assoc prof drawing & painting, Armstrong Atlantic State Univ, Savannah, Ga. *Awards:* McDowell Colony Fel, Peterborough, NH, 2003; Joan Mitchell Fel Grant, 2003; MacArthur Found Travel Grant, 2004; Yaddo Resident Artists Program Fel, 2006; Pollock-Krasner Found Grant, 2008. *Bibliog:* Amy Petersen (auth), The Neglected Existence, Houston Press, 9/23/2006; Jen Reis (auth), House of Pang, South Mag, 4-5/2007; Ian Bartholomew (auth), Ancient Maps and Modern Conveniences, Taipei Times, 7/30/2008. *Mailing Add:* Armstrong Atlantic State University Dept Art 11935 Abercorn St Rm 125 Savannah GA 31419

HU, MARY LEE
GOLDSMITH, EDUCATOR
b Lakewood, Ohio, Apr 13, 1943. *Study:* Miami Univ, Oxford, Ohio, 61-63; Sch for Am Craftsmen, Rochester Inst Technol, with Hans Christensen; Cranbrook Acad Art, Bloomfield Hills, Mich, BFA, 65, with Richard Thomas; Southern Ill Univ, MFA, 67, with Brent Kington. *Work:* Mus Contemp Crafts, NY; Renwick Gallery, Washington; Yale Univ Art Gallery, New Haven, Conn; Art Inst Chicago; Victoria & Albert Mus, London; Mus Fine Arts, Boston; Tacoma Art Mus, Wash; Metrop Mus, NY; Mus Fine Arts, Houston. *Exhib:* 4th Int Jewelry Art Exhib, Mikimoto, Tokyo, 79; Goldsmith '78, Schmuck Mus, Pfortzheim, Ger & touring 8 Europ countries, 79-80; Silver in Am Life, Carnegie Inst, Pittsburgh & touring US, 79-81; Good as Gold, Renwick Gallery & touring US & S Am, 81-84; Jewelry USA, Am Craft Mus, NY & touring US, 84-85; Am Jewelry Now, Am Craft Mus & touring Asia, 85-87; Craft Today: Poetry of the Physical, touring US, 86-88; Korean Am Contemp Metalwork Exhib, Seoul, Korea, 88; Craft Today USA, Touring Europe, 89-92; 6 NW Jewelers, Seattle Art Mus, 93; Retrospective exhib, Knitted, Knotted, Twisted & Twined, The Jewelry of Mary Lee Hu, Bellevue Arts Mus, Wash, 2012. *Teaching:* Vis artist metalsmithing, Univ Iowa, Iowa City, fall 75; lectr, Univ Wis, Madison, 76-77; asst prof, Mich State Univ, East Lansing, 77-80; assoc prof metal design, Univ Wash, Seattle, 80-85, prof, 85-2006. *Awards:* Nat Endowment Arts Craftmen's Fel, 76, 84 & 92; Alumni Achievement Award, Southern Ill Univ, Carbondale, 88; Master of the Medium Award, James Renwick Alliance, Washington, DC, 98; Flintridge Found Award for Vis Arts, 2001-02; Peterson Fel, Wash State, 2002; Artist Trust Twining Humber Award, Lifetime Artistic Achievement, 2008. *Bibliog:* Carolyn Benesh (auth), Mary Lee Hu, Ornament, spring 83; Karen Du Priest (auth), Craft into art: Mary Lee Hu takes gold & silver jewelry in a new direction, Connoisseur, 10/86; Annette Mahler (auth), Mary Lee Hu: The purpose and persistence of wire, Metalsmith, winter 89; Carolyn Benesh (auth), Mary Lee Hu, Working with Wire, Ornament, Vol 35, No 3, 2012; Jeanne Falino, Janet Koplos, and Stefano Catalani (auths, essays), Knitted, Knotted, Twisted, & Twined: The Jewelry of Mary Lee Hu (exhib catalogue), Bellevue Arts Mus, 2012. *Mem:* Soc North Am Goldsmiths (vpres, 76-77, pres, 77-80); Fel Am Crafts Coun (craftsman trustee, 80-84); Northwest Designer Craftsmen; Seattle Metals Guild. *Media:* Silver, Gold Wire. *Res:* history of body adornment. *Publ:* Contribr, Body Jewelry--International Perspectives, Henry Regnery, 73; Wire Art, Crown, 75; Jewelry Concepts & Technology, Doubleday, 82; Artists at Work, Alaska NW Bks, 90; Contemporary American Jewelry Design, Van Nostrand Reinhold, 91; Textile Techniques in Metal, Altahont Press, rev ed, 96. *Dealer:* Facere Jewelry Art Seattle WA; Mobilia Gallery, Cambridge MA,. *Mailing Add:* PO Box 16508 Seattle WA 98116-0508

HUANG, FRANK C
COLLECTOR
b Nov, 1949. *Study:* Nat Taiwan Univ, BA (physics), 1971; Mount Sinai Sch Med, New York, PhD, 1978. *Pos:* Founder, UMAX Data Systs Inc, 1987-, chmn, currently; founder, Powerchip Semiconductor Corp (PSC), 1994-, chmn, currently; chmn, Taiwan Semiconductor Industry Asn; pres, Taipei Computer Asn. *Awards:* Named one of Top 200 Collectors, ARTnews mag, 2004-13. *Collection:* Chinese porcelain, Impressionist and modern paintings. *Mailing Add:* UMAX Data Systems Inc 8F 68 Sec 3 Nanking E Rd Taipei Taiwan

HUBBARD, JOHN
PAINTER
b Ridgefield, Conn, Feb 26, 1931. *Study:* Harvard Univ, Cambridge, Mass, AB, 53; Art Students League, New York, study with Morris Kantor, 56-58; study painting with Hans Hofmann, Provincetown, Mass. *Work:* Tate Gallery, London, England; Scottish Nat Gallery Mod Art, Edinburgh; Arts Coun Great Brit, London; Arts Coun Northern Ireland, Belfast; Australian Nat Gallery, Melbourne; Penna Acad Fine Arts; Phila Mus Art. *Comn:* Midsummer, 83 & Sylvia, 85, Royal Opera House, Covent Garden, London; Waddesdon Manor, UK, 99 & 2000; Said Business Sch, Oxford, 2005; Kew Gardens, United Kingdom, 2006. *Exhib:* Brit Colour (SAm tour), Brit Coun, 78-79; Solo exhibs, Fischer Fine Art, London, 79, 81, 88, 91 & Warwick Arts Trust, London, 81; Mus Mod Art, Oxford, 85; Yale Ctr Brit Art, 86; Purdy Hicks Gallery, London, 94 & 96; Scottish Paintings, UK Tour, 96; Marlborough Fine Art, 2000, 2004, 2008. *Pos:* Mem, Coun Mgt, SPACE/AIR, London, 71-75; collabr, Mark Rothko Mem Portfolio, London, 73; chmn, Art Panel, Southwest Arts, Exeter, Devon, 73-75; mem, Arts Panel, Arts Coun Great Brit, London, 73-78; consult, J Sainsbury Ltd, 79-81; adv, Tate Gallery, St Ives, 93-98. *Teaching:* Vis painting instr, Camberwell Sch Art, London, 63-65. *Awards:* Jerwood Prize, 96. *Bibliog:* Hubbard's Search, Art Int, 78-79; article, Times, London, 2/81; Jeff Dunlop (dir), film, London Weekend Television, 3/81; Journey of John Hubburd, Douglas Hall, 96. *Publ:* Second Nature, 84; Portrait of New Harmony, 89; Spirit of Trees, 2006. *Dealer:* Marlborough Fine Art 6 Albemarle St London WIX. *Mailing Add:* Chilcombe Chilcombe NR Bridport Dorset United Kingdom DT6 4PN

HUBBARD, TERESA
FILMMAKER
b Dublin, Ireland, 1965. *Study:* Univ Tex, Austin, BFA; attended, Skowhegan Sch Painting & Sculpture, 87; Yale Univ, MFA (sculpture), 88; Nova Scotia Coll Art & Design, Halifax, MFA, 92. *Work:* Columbus Mus Art, OH; Neues Mus, Nuremberg, Ger; Ulrich Mus Art, Wichita, Kans; Yokohama Mus Art, Japan; and numerous other works. *Exhib:* solo shows, Slow Place, Mus Fur Gegenwartskunst Basel, 97; Stripping, Kunstlerhaus Bethanien, Berlin, 98; Gregor's Room, Gallery Bob van Orsouw, Zurich, 99; Motion Pictures, Gallery Barbara Thumm, Berlin, 99; County Line Road, 2003; Arsenal, Bonakdar Jancou Gallery, NY, 2000; Tanya Bonakdar Gallery, NY, 2002; ArtPace Found Contemp Art, San Antonio, Tex, 2002; Single Wide, Whitney Mus Am Art, NY, 2004; Editing the Dark, Kemper Mus Contemp Art, Kansas City, 2005; Little Pictures at Mrs Owens House, Centro Galego de Artr Contemporanea, Santiago de Compostela, 2005; House with Pool, Miami Art Mus, 2006; Galerie Barbara Thumm, Berlin, 2006; group shows, Nonchalance Revisited, Akademie der Kunste, Berlin, 98; Solitude in Budapest, Kunsthalle, Budapest, 99; Every Time, La Biennale de Montreal, 2000; New Work, Tanya Bonakdar Gallery, NY, 2001; Out of Place: Contemp Art & The Architectural Uncanny, Mus Contemp Art, Chicago, 2002; Adolescence, Reina Sofia Mus, Madrid, 2003; Eight, Centre Culturel Suisse, Paris, 2004; Swiss Experimental Film, Image Forum, Tokyo, 2005; Roaming Memories, Ludwig Forum, Aachen, 2005; Melancholy, Nationalgalerie, Berlin, 2006; Picture Ballot, Kunsthaus, Zurich, 2006; Raised by Wolves, Art Gallery Western Australia, Perth, 2006. *Teaching:* lectr various univs & insts, 92-; prof, dept Art & Art History, Univ Tex, Austin, 2000-; core fac mem, Milton Avery Grad Sch Arts, Bard Col, NY, 2004-. *Bibliog:* Dora Imhof (auth), Teresa Hubbard & Alexander Birchler, House with Pool, Kunstforum, Vol 161, 3-4/2004, 504-505; Amoreen Armetta (auth), Teresa Hubbard/Alexander Birchler, Flash Art, 1/2005, 69; Rene Morales (auth), Teresa Hubbard & Alexander Birchler, MAM Portrait: Miami Art Mus, Miami, 7-9/2006, 6; and many others. *Mailing Add:* c/o Tanya Bonakdar Gallery 521 W 21st St New York NY 10011

HUBERMAN, ANTHONY
CURATOR
Pos: Cur & educ dir, PS1 Contemp Art Ctr, New York, formerly; cur, Sculpture Ctr, New York & Palais de Tokyo, Paris, formerly; chief cur, St Louis Contemp Art Mus, 2007-. *Mailing Add:* 3750 Washington Blvd Saint Louis MO 63108

HUBERT, ANNE M
CURATOR, COLLECTOR
Study: Boston Mus Fine Art, spec studies, with Claude Croney & King Coffin. *Exhib:* James Fitzgerald 1898-1971, Hopkins Ctr, Dartmouth Col, Hanover, NJ, 75, Mead Gallery, Amherst Col, Mass, 76, Ctr Visual Arts, Antioch Col, Columbia, Md, 77, Danforth Mus, Framingham, Mass, 77, Monterey Peninsula Mus Art, Calif, 79 & 85, Mass Coll Art, Boston, 80, Farnsworth Mus, Rockland, Maine, 84, DeCordova Mus, Lincoln, Mass, 85, Portland Mus Art, Maine, 92 & Plattsburgh Art Mus, NY, 92; Mass Coll Art, Boston, 97; St Botolph Club, Boston, Mass, 97; Susquehanna Univ, Selens Grove, Pa, 97. *Pos:* Cur, James Fitzgerald Collection, James Fitzgerald Mem Studio, Monhegan, Maine, 71-. *Mem:* Hon charter mem Steinbeck Ctr Found; Portland Mus Art; Boston Mus Fine Arts; Farnsworth Libr & Art Mus. *Collection:* Twentieth century watercolors, oils and prints. *Publ:* Auth, Legacy of beauty, Kent Collector, 76; auth, Recollections of the Artist, Fitzgerald Mem Studio, 77. *Mailing Add:* PO Box 1813 Windermere FL 34786-1813

HUBSCHMITT, WILLIAM E
EDUCATOR, ADMINISTRATOR
b NJ, May 23, 1949. *Study:* Sate Univ NY, Binghamton, PhD, 84. *Exhib:* Nat Computer Art Invitational, Univ Wash, Spokane, 90; William Hubschmitt Recent Work, Canovassio, Rome, Italy, 94; Figure Painting - Digital Works, Mus Hartwick, Oneonta, NY, 95; S Ill Nat, Mitchell Art Mus, Mt Vernon, 97. *Teaching:* State Univ NY, Oneonta, 82-96; chmn & asst prof art hist & computer art, E Ill Univ, Charleston, 96-. *Awards:* Best in Media, S Ill Nat, Mitchell Art Mus, 95. *Media:* Computer art. *Res:* Dutcy Baroque - genre and artist in studio images. *Publ:* Auth, Distorted View of Delft, Apocrypha, Binghamton Univ Press, fall 80; Intro to Andrea Modica (exhib catalog), Miami-Dade Community Coll Art Mus, 89; Art History and the Computer in Liberal Arts Environment, Univ Vt, 92; Figure Painting Works by Bill Hubschmitt (CD Rom), Hartwick Col, 95. *Mailing Add:* 819 Jackson Charleston IL 61920

HUCHTHAUSEN, DAVID RICHARD
SCULPTOR, EDUCATOR
b Wisconsin Rapids, Wis, 1951. *Study:* Univ Wis, BS, study with Harvey K Littleton; Ill State Univ, MFA, study with Joel Philip Myers; Vienna Univ Applied Arts (Fulbright scholar). *Work:* Hokkaido Mus Art, Saporro, Japan; Smithsonian Inst; Metrop Mus Art, New York; Musee du Verre, Liege, Belg; Art Mus, Dusseldorf, Ger; Mus Fine Arts, Lausanne, Switz; Corning Mus Glass, New York; High Mus Art, Atlanta; Los Angeles Co Mus Art; and many others. *Comn:* Sculpture, Hospital Corp Am, 85. *Exhib:* Solo exhibs, Habatat Galleries, 75-94, St Louis Art Mus, Missouri, 85 & Mus Contemp Photogr, Chicago, 85; Lake Superior Int Crafts Exhib, Tweed Mus Art, Duluth, Minn, 75-77; New Glass, Corning Mus Traveling Exhib, 79-81; Huntsville Mus, Ala, 81; Corning Mus, New York, 90; Naples Mus Art, Fla, 93; Tamayo Mus Art, Monteray, Mex, 93; Mus S, Ala, 93; Toledo Mus Art, Ohio, 93; Birmingham Mus Art, Ala, 94; and others. *Pos:* Consult, Woodson Art Mus, Wausau, Wis, 77-; vis artist, J & L Lobmeyr, Vienna, 77-78; design dir, Milropa Studios, New York, 79-80. *Teaching:* Instr glass, Ill State Univ, Normal, 76-77; lectr glass, Royal Coll Art, London, 78; assoc prof, Tenn Tech Univ, 80-90. *Awards:* Newberry Award, Univ Wis, 73; Elizabeth Stein Fel, Ill State Univ, 76; Nat Endowment Arts Grant, 82. *Bibliog:* Cover article, Neues Glas, Eng/Ger ed, 9/83; Sidney Goldstein (auth), Huchthausen, solo exhib catalog, St Louis Mus Art, 84; Robert Silverman (auth), cover article, Am Craft, 9/87; Int Art Glass Quart, cover article, Vol 3, 2007; Sidney Goldstein (auth), American Craft, cover article; World ArtGlass Quarterly, cover article, Vol 3, 2007; Tina Oldknow (auth), Voices of Contemporary Glass, Corning Mus, 2009; Hutchthausen, A Retrospective (exhib catalog), Dow Mus, Midland, Mich, 2012. *Mem:* Am Craft Coun; Glass Art Soc; Classic Yacht Asn; MFG Industrial Coun. *Media:* Glass, Light. *Interests:* Historic Preservation. *Publ:* Auth, Americans in Glass, Marathon Press, 78, 81 & 84. *Dealer:* Scott Jacobson Gallery New York NY 90021. *Mailing Add:* 3911 Airport Way S Seattle WA 98108

HUCKABY, SEDRICK ERVIN
PAINTER
b 1975. *Study:* Boston Univ, BFA, 1997; Yale Univ, MFA, 1999; Skowhegan Sch Painting & Sculpture, Maine, 2004. *Exhib:* Solo exhibs include Miracle of Life & Venice Again, Wendell Street Gallery, Boston, 1997, Fragments from Life, Evelyn Siegel Gallery, Fort Worth, Texas, 2001, A Love Supreme, African Am Mus, Dallas, Texas, 2003, Portraits & Quilts, Valley House Gallery, Dallas, 2005, Nat Black Fine Art Fair, New York, 2006, Masur Mus Art, Monroe, Louisiana, 2006, San Angelo Mus Fine Arts, Texas, 2006, Galveston Arts Ctr, Texas, 2006, Greenville County Mus, South Carolina, 2006, Quilts & Portraits, Nielsen Gallery, Boston, 2006; two-person exhibs include Wendell Street Gallery, Boston, (with Marian Parry), 1999; group exhibs include First Expressions, Boston, 1996; Grad Thesis Exhib, Yale Univ, 1999; Nat Black Fine Arts Show, Soho, New York, 1999; Naked-in-Waiting, Rush Arts Gallery, New York, 2004; 2006 McNay Print Fair, McNay Art Mus, San Antonio, Texas, 2006; Works on Paper, Art Fair, New York, 2006; Art Int, Barker Hangar, Santa Monica, California, 2006; Parallel Vision, Nielsen Gallery, Boston, 2007; Art Show, Art Dealer's Assoc Am, Park Ave Armory, New York, 2007; Contemp Art Dealers Dallas Inaugural Art Fair, 333 1st Ave, Texas, 2007. *Awards:* John Simon Guggenheim Mem Found Fel, 2008. *Dealer:* Valley House Gallery 6616 Spring Valley Rd Dallas TX 75254-8635

HUDDY, MARGARET TERESA
PAINTER, PHOTOGRAPHER, ILLUSTRATOR, WRITER
b Philadelphia, Pa, July 4, 1939. *Study:* Moore Coll Art, Philadelphia, Pa, 57-59; Monterey Peninsula Coll, Monterey, Calif, 64-66. *Work:* Supreme Court US, Washington, DC; US Dept State, US Embassy, Botswana, Africa; Texaco Inc, Harrison, NY; Am Dental Asn, Washington, DC; Marriott Corp, Washington, DC; Nat Park Serv; Carnegie Mus Art; Nat Cathedral, Washington, DC; JW Marriott Hotel, Wash DC; Glacier Nat Park, Montana; Sleeping Bear Dunes Nat, Lakeshore, Mich; Supreme Court of the United States; Bank of America, Wash DC; Texaco Inc, Harrison, NY; Nat Cathedral, Wash DC; Marsh USA, Wash DC. *Comn:* The Evening Parade (painting), USMC, 83; paintings-5 DC monuments, Am Security Bank, Washington, DC, 88; Farragut Square (painting), Palmer Nat Bank, Washington, DC, 89; The Supreme Court (painting), Supreme Court Hist Soc, Washington, DC, 92; The Capitol (painting), Allied Capital Corp, Washington, DC, 93. *Exhib:* Nat Midyear Exhib, Butler Inst Am Art, Youngstown, Ohio, 85; Nat Watercolor Soc, Brea Cult Ctr, Calif, 93; Irene Leach Mem Exhib, Chrysler Mus, Norfolk, Va, 94; Am Watercolor Soc, Salmagundi Club, New York, 94; Okla Watercolor Soc, Kirkpatrick Ctr Mus, Oklahoma City, Okla, 94; solo-exhibs, Carnegie Mus Art, Oxnard, Calif, 96, Walter Wickiser Gallery, New York, 96 & Ellen Noel Mus, Odessa, Tex, 97; Butler Inst Am Art, Youngstown Ohio, 99 & 2000; Watercolor USA, Springfield Art Mus, Mo, 2000; Foxhall Gallery, 2002-2003; Butler Inst Am Art, Youngstown, Ohio, 2001 & 2006. *Collection Arranged:* Supreme Court US; Baker Botts, LLC. *Pos:* Residency, Glacier Nat Park, 2002, Dinan, France, 2006, Sleeping Bear Nat Park, Mich, 2007. *Teaching:* Elem art teacher, Marymount Jr Sch, Arlington, Va, 69-76; art teacher adult educ, Coastal Carolina Community Coll, 78-80, Fairfax Co Pub Sch, 80-85 & Art League Sch, Alexandria, Va, 92-; prof watercolor, Corcoran Coll Art and Design, Washington, DC, 98-. *Awards:* Award of Excellence, La Watercolor Soc, 89; Aaron Bros-Strathmore Excellence Award, Nat Watercolor Soc, 91; CFS Medal, Am Watercolor Soc, 94; Open Exhib Award, Annandale, Va, 98; Southern Watercolor Soc Award, 99; Va Watercolor Soc, 2002; Watercolor USA, 2003; Nat Watercolor Soc, 2004; Am Artist Abroad, Paraguay, 2005. *Bibliog:* Ginny Baier (auth), The Color Red, Watercolor/94, Am Artist, 94; Best of Watercolor, Rockport Publ, 95; Ginny Baier (auth), The Color White, Watercolor/95, Am Artist, fall, 95. *Mem:* signature mem Nat Watercolor Soc; signature mem Am Watercolor Soc; signature mem Pa Watercolor Soc; Watercolor USA Hon Soc. *Media:* Watercolor. *Interests:* Plein air painting, travel. *Publ:* Auth, The Color of Light, Watercolor Magic/Artist's Mag, winter, 97; Sharing the Joy, Watercolor Magic, 2002; Ship to Shore, Artist's Sketchbook, 2002; Exaggerate Reality, Artists Mag, 2003; Secrets to Plein Air Painting, Artists Mag, 9/2006; An American Artist in Brittany, Artist Mag, 7/2007. *Dealer:* Foxhall Gallery Washington, DC. *Mailing Add:* 105 N Union St No 203 Alexandria VA 22314

HUDSON, EDWARD RANDALL
PATRON
b Ft Worth, Tex, July 24, 1934. *Study:* Univ Tex, BA, 1955; Harvard Univ, JD, 1958; Phi Beta Kappa. *Pos:* Owner, oil producer, Hudson Oil, Ft Worth; bd dir, Kimbell Art Found, Aspen Ctr Physics; sect bd dir, Burnett Found; chmn, bd dir, Modern Art Mus Ft Worth, formerly; nat comt, founding co-chmn bd dir, Aspen Art Mus; formerly Mus Panel, NEA; cult property comt, US State Dept; chmn, Tex comns, Arts & Humanities. *Mem:* Kimbell Mus; Modern Mus, Fort Worth; MoMA; Whitney Mus; Metropolitan Mus. *Collection:* Contemp Art, Mex Folk Art. *Mailing Add:* 55 Westover Terrace Fort Worth TX 76107-3106

HUDSON, JON BARLOW
SCULPTOR, ENVIRONMENTAL ARTIST
b Billings, Mont, Dec 17, 1945. *Study:* Calif Inst Arts, with Allen Kaprow, Paul Brach, Lloyd Hamroll & Judy Chicago, BFA, 71, MFA, 72; Stuttgart State Art Acad, West Germany, with Rudolph Hoflehner, 69; Dayton Art Inst, with Charles Ginnever, Bob Koepnick, Ann Tabatchnick & Kimber Smith, BFA, 75. *Work:* Eupopos Parkas; Vilniaus, Lithuania; City of Brisbane, Australia; Benburb Heritage Park, Co Armagh, Northern, Ireland; Sculpture Park, Dunaujvaros, Hungary; Green Co Pub Libr, Yellow Springs, Ohio; Granite Mus Stanstead, Quebec, Canada; Nat Mus, Manamah, Bahrain; Ichinomiya Hist Mus, Japan; Wu Zi Xiong Glass Art Gallery, Taizhou City, Zhejiang Prov, China; Cedarville Univ, Ohio; Beijin Olympic Park, China. *Comn:* Sublime Portal: Pi (sculpture), Mulia Tower, Jakarta, Indonesia, 91; Rivers of Time Sculpture, Royal Abjar Hotel, Dunbai, United Arib Emerites, 92; Oh, Peace Wall & Gate, Lion & Lamb Peace Arts Ctr, Bluffton Col, Ohio, 97; Ts'ung Tube XXVII, Lapidea Naturstein, Mayen, Ger, 97; Caduceus Fountain, Med Col, Ohio, Toledo, 98; and many others. *Exhib:* Group show, Univ Dayton, 94; Westward Ho, Nat Sculpture Soc, NY, 95; Herndon Gallery, Antioch Univ, 95 & 96; NAm Sculpture, Foothills Art Ctr, Colo, 96; Gremillion & Co Gallery Artists Furniture, Houston, Tex, 96. *Teaching:* Vis sculptor, Stephens Col, Columbia, Mo, 75-76; adj instr sculpture, Wright State Univ, Dayton, Ohio, 75-77; asst prof sculpture, Antioch Univ, Yellow Springs, Ohio, 80. *Awards:* Projs Grant, 78 & Prof Develop Award, 85 & 94, Ohio Arts Coun; Lusk Mem Fel, IIE, Italy, 82-83; Ludwig Vogelstein Found Grant, 96. *Bibliog:* Johan DeRoey (auth), Geometry of mysticism, KNACK, Brussels, Belgium, 2/80; B Lealman & E Robinson (auths), Exploration into Experience, Knowing and Unknowing, Manchester Col, 81; Baile Oakes (auth), Sculpture expo in Australia, Sculpture, 5-6/89. *Mem:* Int Sculpture Ctr, Washington, DC; Royal Brit Soc Sculptors Int; Visual Artists Ireland. *Media:* All. *Publ:* Auth, Pluralistic Vocabulary of Spiritual Unity, Studia Mystica, Calif State Univ, Sacramento, 80. *Dealer:* Art Exchange 17 Brickel St # A Columbus OH 43215; XYZ Gallery, Beijing, China; Levant Gallery, Shanghai, China. *Mailing Add:* 325 N Walnut PO Box 710 Yellow Springs OH 45387

HUDSON, ROBERT H
PAINTER, SCULPTOR
b Salt Lake City, Utah, Sept 8, 1938. *Study:* San Francisco Art Inst, BFA, 62, MFA, 63. *Work:* Los Angeles Co Mus; San Francisco Mus Art; Mus Mod Art Boston & Whitney Mus, NY; Mus Fine Arts, Boston; Chicago Art Inst; and others. *Comn:* Fed Bldg, Anchorage, Alaska. *Exhib:* Five Whitney Mus Am Art Ann, NY, 64-72; Los Angeles Co Mus Art, 67; Philadelphia Mus Art, 67; Art Inst Chicago, 67; Walker Art Ctr, Minneapolis, 69; Retrospective, Moore Coll of Art, 77; solo exhibs, Allan Frumkin Gallery, NY, 78, 81, 84 & 86, Hansen Fuller Gallery, San Francisco, Calif, 79 & 82, Morgan Gallery, Shawnee Mission, Kans, 83 & 96, A Survey, San Francisco Mus Mod Art, Albright Knox Art Gallery, Buffalo, NY, Art Mus Fla Int Univ, Miami, Laguna Beach Mus Art (with catalog), Calif, 85-86, Dorothy Goldeen Gallery, Santa Monica, Calif, 87 & 89, Fresno Art Mus, Calif, 89-90, John Berggruen Gallery, San Francisco, Calif, 91 & 94, Struve Gallery, Chicago, Ill, 95 & Nancy Margolis Gallery, NY, 98; Collaborations: William Allan, Robert Hudson, William Wiley, Palm Spring Desert Mus, Palm Springs, Calif, Art Mus Fla Int Univ, Miami, 98, Wash State Univ Mus Art, Pullman & Scottsdale Mus Art, Ariz, 99; Wild Things: Artists' Views of the Animal World, John Berggruen Gallery, San Francisco, Calif, 98. *Teaching:* Instr, San Francisco Art Inst, 64-65, chmn, Sculpture & Ceramic Dept, 65-66 & asst prof art, 76-78; asst prof art, Univ Calif, Berkeley, 66-73. *Awards:* Purchase Prize, San Jose State Col, 64; Nealie Sullivan Award, San Francisco, 65; Guggenheim Found Fel, 76; plus others. *Bibliog:* Peter Selz (auth), Funk, Univ Calif, 67; Maurice Tuchman (auth), American Sculpture of the Sixties, Los Angeles Co Mus Art, 67; Graham Beal (auth), Robert Hudson, A Survey, San Francisco Mus Mod Art, 85. *Dealer:* John Berggruen Gallery 228 Grant Ave San Francisco CA; Dorothy Golldeen Gallery Santa Monica CA. *Mailing Add:* 392 Eucalyptus Cotati CA 94931

HUEMER, CHRISTINA GERTRUDE
LIBRARIAN
b Orange, NJ, May 24, 1947. *Study:* Mt Holyoke Col, BA, 69; Columbia Univ, MS, 70; Cornell Univ, MA, 75. *Pos:* Asst art librn, Cornell Univ, Ithaca, NY, 70-75; indexer, Art Index, H W Wilson Co, Bronx, NY, 75-76; art librn, Oberlin Col, 76-80; deputy librn, Avery Library, Columbia Univ, 80-85; librn, ICCROM, 85-87 & Am Acad Rome, 92-; ed, RILA/BHA, 88-92. *Teaching:* Instr, Sch Libr Serv, Columbia Univ, New York, 83. *Mailing Add:* 9920 Diamond Reef Way Las Vegas NV 89117-0906

HUERTA, BENITO
PAINTER, CURATOR
b Corpus Christi, Tex, Apr 30, 1952. *Study:* Univ Houston, BFA, 75; NMex State Univ, MA, 78. *Work:* Mus Fine Arts, Houston; Menil Collection, Houston; El Paso Mus; Ariz State Univ Art Mus; Weatherspoon Art Gallery Univ NC. *Comn:* design (with Ray de la Reza), Metro Transit Authority, Houston, 95-; sculpture, San Antonio, Tex, 97-; design, Dallas Area Rapid Transit, 98-. *Exhib:* Attempted, Not Known, Nez Son-Atkins Mus, Ky, San Jose (Calif) Mus Art, Univ North Tex, Denton, Contemp Arts Mus, Houston, 91-93; Out Of This World, Contemp Arts Mus, Houston, 94; To Transcend, Tonegate and To Preserve, Ariz State Univ Art Mus, Tempe, 94; The

Figure In The New Millenium, Art Mus South Tex, Corpus Christi, 94; Highlights from Permanent Collection, El Paso Mus Art, 2000; Fire and Earth, San Antonio Mus Art, 2000. *Collection Arranged:* Working Class Heroes, 97-2000; Inescapable Histories, 97-99; Cultura de Southern Tex, 98; Stories Your Mother Never Told You, 2000-. *Teaching:* vis artist, East Carolina Univ, Greenville, NC, 90-91; vis artist, Univ NC, Greensboro, 95; asst prof, Univ Tex, Arlington, 97-. *Bibliog:* Charles Dee Mitchen (auth), Art In America, 10/97; Janey Tyson (auth), 10 Artists on the Brink of Big Time, 98; J Claire Van Ryzin (auth), Patterned Out of Order-Chaos, Austin Am State, 3/2000. *Mem:* Ft Worth Art Dealers Asn. *Publ:* coauth, American Images: The SBL Collection, Abrams, 96; auth, A Place for All People, MFAH, 96; coauth, 5000 Artist Return To Artist Space: 25 yrs., Artist Space, 98; auth, Texas: 150 Works From Museum of Fine Arts, Hoolton Abrams, 2000; coauth, Comtemporary Chicana & Chicano Art, Bilingual Press, 2000. *Dealer:* Berman Gallery-Austin; Parchman-Stremmer Gallery, San Antonio

HUETER, JAMES WARREN
SCULPTOR, PAINTER
b San Francisco, Calif, 1925. *Study:* Pomona Col, BA; Claremont Grad Sch, MFA, with Henry Lee McFee, Albert Stewart & Millard Sheets. *Work:* Scripps Col, Claremont, Calif; Univ Calif, Davis, Calif; Long Beach State Col; Pomona Col, Claremont, Calif; Security Pacific Nat Bank, Los Angeles, Calif; Carnation Co, Calif; Sam & Alfreda Maloof Found Mus, Alta Loma, Calif; Claremont Mus Art, Calif. *Exhib:* Artists Los Angeles & Vicinity, Los Angeles Co Mus, 52 & 54-59; Denver Mus Art Ann, 54 & 59; Solo exhibs, Pasadena Art Mus, 55 & Mt San Antonio Coll, Walnut, Calif, 77; Butler Inst Am Art Midyear Ann, 55, 57-59 & 62; Long Beach Mus Art Drawing Exhib, 60; Southern Calif 100, Laguna Beach Mus, 77; 38th Corcoran Biennial Am Painting, Washington, DC, 83; Univ Calif, Davis, Calif, 86; Univ Calif, Santa Cruz, Calif, 95; Cuttress Gallery, Pomona, Calif, 2002; Orange Co Ctr Contemp Art, Santa Ana, Calif, 2004; Claremont Grad Univ, Calif, 2006; James Hueter: A Retrospective, Claremont Mus Art, Calif, 2009. *Teaching:* Instr sculpture, Pomona Col, 59-60; instr drawing, Claremont Grad Sch, summer 63; lectr art, Pitzer Col, 72. *Awards:* First Prize for Sculpture, Los Angeles Co Mus, 55; First Prize for Painting, Frye Mus, Seattle, 57; Nat Design Award Drawing, Boulder Ctr Visual Arts, Colo, 82. *Bibliog:* A Segunda (auth), Reviews, Vol 1, No 8 & Delores Yonker (auth), James Hueter, Vol 2, No 2, Artforum; Fidel Danieli (auth), Rev, Artscene, 86. *Media:* Wood, Oil. *Dealer:* Tobey C Moss Gallery 7321 Beverly Blvd Los Angeles CA 90036. *Mailing Add:* 190 E Radcliffe Dr Claremont CA 91711

HUEY, MICHAEL CM
CONCEPTUAL ARTIST, PHOTOGRAPHER
b Sept 21, 1964. *Study:* Amherst Coll, BA (German), 87; Univ Vienna, MA (art hist), 99. *Work:* Mus der Moderne, Salzburg, Austria; Mead Art Mus; Amherst Coll, Mass; Sigmund Freud Mus, Vienna; Cleveland Mus Art. *Exhib:* Solo exhibs, Full Death, Galerie Lisa Ruyter, Vienna, 2005, Betsy & I Killed the Bear, Charim Galerie, Vienna, 2007, Ruined Album, Blumen, Vienna, 2007, Keep in Safe Place, Newman Popiashvili Gallery, New York, 2007, ASH inc, Song Song, Vienna, 2009, Story Problems, Josh Lilley Gallery, London, 2010, Houseguests, Galerie Schloss Damtschach, 2010, China Cupboard, Newman Popiashvili Gallery, NY, 2011, The Darling of Decay, Agnes Reinthaler Galerie, Vienna, 2014; Don't Say Things, Kunsthalle Wien, Vienna, Austria, 2009; Archivaria, Sigmund Freud Mus, Vienna, 2012; The Last Days of Pompeii, Cleveland Mus Art, 2013. *Bibliog:* JS Marcus (auth), Latent Images, Betsy & I Killed the Bear, 2007; Abraham Orden (auth), Back into Life, ASH inc, Schlebrügge, 2008; Monika Faber (auth), Nachrichten, die uns noch erreichen, Eikon 64, 2008; Gabriel Coxhead (auth), Michael Huey, Time Out, London, 2/4/2010; Ossian Ward (auth), Out of the Past, Art in Am, June/July 2010; Jennie Hirsh (auth), Cabinets of Curiosity: Domestic Archives in Recent Work by Michael Huey, China Cupboard, Schlebrugge, 2011; Philipp Blom (auth), Landscapes of Desire, China Cupboard, Schlebrugge, 2011; Emily Hall (auth), Michael Huey/Newman Popiashvili Gallery, Artforum, 2011; Vince Aletti (auth), Goings on About Town, New Yorker, 2011; Jasper Sharp (auth), A Matter of Undoing, ASH, inc, Schlebrigge, Vienna, pp 14-15, 2008; Catharina Kahane (auth), Das Familiare der Dinge, The Family of Things, Archivaria, Schlebrigge, Vienna, pp 11-21 (23-33), 2012; Jon L Seydl (auth), The Last Days of Pompeii: Decadence, Apocalypse, Resurrection, pp 26, 238-239, J Paul Getty Mus, Los Angeles, 2012. *Mem:* Secession, Vienna. *Media:* Photography, Assemblage, Installation, Video. *Publ:* ed, The Place of Beginning, 2001; ed, Viennese Silver, Modern Design 1780-1918, Hatje Cantz, 2003; auth, Betsy & I Killed the Bear, Schlebrügge, 2007; auth, ASH, inc, Schlebrügge, 2008; auth, Houseguests/China Cupboards, Schlebrugge, 2011; auth, Dearie-Louis Betts Portrait of Harriet King Huey, Schlebrugge, 2011; Archivaria, Schlebrugge, 2012; Straight as the Pine, Sturdy as the Oak, Skipper & Cora Beals and Major & Helen Huey in the Early Years of Camp Leelanu for Boys, the Leelanau Schools, and the Homestead in Glen Arbor, Vol 1: 1921-1963, Schlebrugge, 2013. *Dealer:* Newman Popiashvili Gallery 504 W 22nd St New York NY 10011; Josh Lilley Gallery 44-46 Riding House St London England W1W7EX

HUFF, LAURA WEAVER
PRINTMAKER, INSTRUCTOR
b Mt Vernon, NY, Dec 24, 1930. *Study:* Syracuse Univ, NY; Univ Del, Newark, BA, 64; painting with James Twitty, Corcoran Sch Art, 65-67; George Wash Univ, Washington, MFA, 68. *Work:* Libr Cong Collection of Fine Prints; Am Embassy, Jakarta, Indonesia; Corcoran Gallery Art, Washington; Nat Mus, Women in Arts, Washington; Nat Mus Am Hist, Graphic Arts, Smithsonian Inst, Washington. *Comn:* 200 silkscreen posters, Amelia Earhart's Lockheed Vega, 85, comn by Carol Heiderman; 200 posters, The Tin Goose, Nostalgic Aviator, Alexandria, Va, 87. *Exhib:* One-person shows: Wash Printmakers Gallery, 86 & 89; Am Asn Advan Sci, Washington, 86 & 89; Pacat Branch Unifarcan Universalist Church, Adelphi, Md, 2005, 18th Ann Strathmore Artist Mem Exhib, Bethesda, Md, 2009, Retrospective, Paint Branch Unitarian Universalist, Church of Rockville, MD, 2011; Wash Area Printmakers, Nat Mus Women Arts, Washington, 96; Spring Open, Rock Creek Gallery, Washington, DC, 98; Hand Pulled: Contemp Print (juried show), Target Gallery, Alexandria, Va, 02; Annual Int Exhib of Fine Art in Miniature, Strathmore Art Center, Bethesda, MD, 2005-2010; Blackrock Art Center, Germantown, MD, 2007; Glenview Mansion, Rockville, Md, 2007; The Five Senses (juried show), Target Gallery, Alexandria, Va, 2008; Best in Show, Art League Gallery, 2009; Imprint, Target Gallery, Alexandria, Va, 2010; Plus many others. *Teaching:* Lectr painting, Howard Community Col, Columbia, Md, 70-71; instr screen printing, Graphics Workshop, Glen Echo Park, Md, 74-76, Chautaqua artist/instr, 91-92; lectr screen printing, NVa Community Col, Alexandria, 76; drawing & painting for sr adults continuing educ, Montgomery Col, Germantown, Md, 89-91, instr drawing 1, 93-95, art appreciation, 94 & 95, color, 96 & 97; Visual art and art history, Arts for the Aging, Bethesda, Md, 89-2010 & D C Coalition for Homeless, 98-2005; Am art slide/lectures for three senior cens through Arts Coun Montgomery Co grants, 95, 96 & 98. *Awards:* Best in Show, Art League Gallery, Alexandria, Va, 2009. *Bibliog:* Colleen Caprara, (auth), Laura Huff-Designing with Nature's Beauty, World & I 6/86; JoAnn Goslin (auth), Making a Mark in Silkscreens, Potomac Life, 9/90. *Mem:* Art League, Alexandria, Va; Md Printmakers; Senior Arts Alliance; Torpedo Factory Art Center, Alexandria, Va. *Media:* Screenprinting, Miscellaneous Media. *Interests:* Writing, music, gardening. *Publ:* Illusr, Copycat Sam, Human Sci Press, New York, 82; Where You Can Make a Difference: Teaching Art to Homeless Men, Women Art Educators V: Conversations Across Time (ed by Kit Grauer, Rita L. Irwin, and Erid Zimmerman), Nat Art Educ Asn, 2003. *Mailing Add:* 11636 Brandy Hall Ln Gaithersburg MD 20878

HUFF, ROBERT
SCULPTOR, PAINTER
b Kalamazoo, Mich, Jan 4, 1945. *Study:* Univ SFla, BA, 66, MFA, 68. *Work:* Ringling Mus Art, Sarasota, Fla; Mus Art, Ft Lauderdale, Fla; Erie Art Ctr, Pa; Nat Acad Sci, Washington, DC; Miami Dade Co Art in Pub Places Trust, Miami; Valencia Community Coll, Orlando; Fed Reserve Bank, Atlanta; Dade Co Pub Lib, Miami, Fla; Gulf Coast Mus Art, Largo, Fla; Health South, Birmingham, Ala. *Comn:* Sculptures, Dade Co Art in Pub Places, Miami, 77, 81 & 95; paintings, Broward Co Art in Pub Places, 91; paintings, Palm Beach Art in PubPlaces, 92; painting, Art in State Buildings, Univ Fla, 95; ceramic tile, Miami Dade Co Art in Pub Places, 92, 95, 2002; painting, Art in State Buildings, Fla Atlantic Univ, 2008. *Exhib:* Chicago Int Art Expos, Lakeside Gallery, Ill, 91 & 92; SFla Invitational: George Bolge Selects, Mus Art, Ft Lauderdale, 91; Chicago Int New Art Forms Expos, Lakeside Gallery, Ill, 91; 41st Ann All Fla Juried Exhib, Boca Mus, Boca Raton, 92; Sculpture for Sculptors, New Gallery, Univ Miami, Fla, 92; Gulf Coast Mus Art, Largo, Fla, 2000; Cross Fire, Bernice Steinbaum Gallery, Miami, Fla, 2001; Crossroads, Edge Zones, Miami, Fla, 2006; Robert Huff, Va Piedmont Community Coll, Charlottesville, Va, 2007; and many more. *Teaching:* Prof sculpture, Miami Dade Community Col, 68-2005, chmn dept, 78-2005; vis artist, Soviet Artists Union & Lakeside Studios, USSR, 89; vis artist sculpture, Univ Miami, 90. *Awards:* Fla Fine Arts Fel, Fla Arts Coun, 78, 80 & 98-2006; Hon Mention, Fla Nat, Fla State Univ, 88. *Bibliog:* Robert Sindelir (auth), Art corner, Ideas, 78; Elisa Turner (auth), Artists the critics are watching, Art News, 86; Leslie Judd Ahlander (auth), Miami art scene, Miami News, 87. *Mem:* Int Sculpture Ctr. *Media:* Miscellaneous Media. *Dealer:* Carol Jazzar Contemporary Art 158 NW 91st St Miami Fl 33150. *Mailing Add:* 7231 SW 61st St Miami FL 33143

HUGGINS, VICTOR, JR
PAINTER, PRINTMAKER
b Durham, NC, July 23, 1936. *Study:* Univ NC, Chapel Hill, AB & MA. *Work:* Ackland Art Ctr, Univ NC, Chapel Hill; B Carroll Reece Mus, ETenn State Univ; Brooks Mem Gallery Art, Memphis, Tenn; Vanderbilt Univ; Weatherspoon Art Gallery, Univ NC, Greensboro. *Comn:* Mural, Colonial Williamsburg Found, Durham, NC, 84. *Exhib:* Solo exhibs, Jane Haslem Gallery, Washington, DC, 71, 20th Century Gallery, Williamsburg, Va, 71, B Carroll Reece Mus, Johnson City, Tenn, 72 & Somerhill Gallery, Durham, NC, 85; Group exhib, Nat Mus Am Art, Washington, DC, 81. *Teaching:* Asst prof art, Vanderbilt Univ, 68-69; prof, Va Polytech Inst & State Univ, currently. *Awards:* First Purchase Awards, NC Nat Bank, 67, Springs Art Contest, Springs Mills, 67 & Ann Southern Contemp Painting Exhib, 68. *Media:* Acrylic

HUGHES, BEVERLY
DESIGNER, WEAVER
b Belcrossing, NC, Feb 24, 1949. *Study:* Barn Studio, Millville, NJ, studied with Pat Witt, 71-74; Acad Fine Arts, studied with Morris Blackburn, 74; Moore Coll Art, Philadelphia, Pa, BFA, 76, Moore Coll Art, Art Ed Cert, 90. *Work:* Fidelity Bank, Philadelphia, Pa; Afro-Am Cult Mus, woven mask, permanent collection, 89; Arco Chemical Corp, raffia mask, permanent collection, 91; United Bank, Philadelphia, Pa; Franklinia postcard, Bartram Garden Tencentennial Celebration, 99. *Comn:* rose illus, comn by West Philadelphia Cult Alliance for Paul Robeson House; Blue Delphiniums illus, pvt comn in Paris, 99. *Exhib:* botanical postcards, Philadelphia Flower Show, 98. *Pos:* Owner-designer, Winterwood Designs, Philadelphia, Pa, 85-; team mem, West Philadelphia High Sch Coun, 95-96; mem adv comt, Community Col Philadelphia, Western Region, 95-97; invited artist, mask making workshop, Children's Inaugural Salute, State Mus, Harrisburg, Pa for Gov Tom Ridge, 95. *Teaching:* Instr art textiles, Moore Col Art, Philadelphia, Pa, 76; art teacher, Philadelphia Sch Dist, 86-91; Moore Col Art Saturday classes, Philadelphia, Pa, 90; botanical illus teacher, Univ City Arts League, 2000. *Awards:* First Prize, Expressions 80, Afro Am Cult Mus, 80; Outstanding Achievement Award, Fabric Workshop at Long Beach Island Found Arts & Scis, Loveladies, NJ, 94. *Bibliog:* Edward J Sozanski, rev masks, Philadelphia Inquirer, 9/9/91; appeared in Int Hair, 3/95. *Mem:* Philadelphia Soc Botanical Illusrs. *Media:* Colored Pencil, Ink. *Publ:* creator, off t-shirt for 2001 Philadelphia Flower Show, Pa Horticultural Soc

HUGHES, EDWARD JOHN
PAINTER
b North Vancouver, BC, Feb 17, 1913. *Study:* Vancouver Sch Art. *Hon Degrees:* Emily Carr Inst, DLitt, Vancouver, BC, 97; Malaspina Coll Univ, DLitt, Nanaimo, BC, 2000. *Work:* Nat Gallery Can, Ottawa; Art Gallery Ont, Toronto; Vancouver Art Gallery; Montreal Mus Fine Art; Gtr Victoria Art Gallery; Nat War Mus, Ottawa. *Comn:* murals, San Francisco Golden Gate Exposition, 39; murals, Can Pacific RR Dome, 54. *Exhib:* Retrospective, Vancouver Art Gallery, 67 & Surrey Art Gallery, 83; Art Gallery of Greater Victoria, 83; Edmonton Art Gallery, 83; Nat Gallery Can, 83; Glenbow Mus Calgary, 83; and others. *Pos:* War artist, Can Army, 40-42, off war artist, 42-46. *Teaching:* prof fine art, Univ Victoria, 95-. *Awards:* Emily Carr Scholar, Lawren Harris, 47; Can Coun Fels & Awards, 58, 63 & 67, Short Term Grant, 70. *Bibliog:* Doris Shadbolt (auth), E J Hughes, Can Art Mag, spring 53; Anthony Robertson (auth), E J Hughes, Vanguard Mag, 12/81; Patricia Salmon & Leslie Black (auths), E J Hughes, Raincoast Chronicles Mag, 10/83. *Mem:* Royal Can Acad Art. *Media:* Acrylic, Oil. *Dealer:* Mr Michel Moreault Gallery 709-1545 Dr Fenfield Montreal PQ H3G 1C7. *Mailing Add:* 2449 Heather St Duncan BC V9L 2Z6 Canada

HUGHES, PAUL LUCIEN
DEALER, CONSULTANT
b New York, NY, Apr 8, 1938. *Study:* NY Univ, BA, 67; Sch Visual Art, 68-69. *Exhib:* State Wyo Fel, 88. *Collection Arranged:* Harry Bertoia Retrospective (guest cur), Colorado Springs Fine Arts Mus, 80; Vance Kirkland retrospective, 28-81; George Rickey, 84, 87 & 90. *Pos:* Dir, Inkfish Gallery, Denver. *Mem:* Alliance for Contemp Art; DADA. *Specialty:* Contemporary abstract art. *Collection:* Bertoia, Anuszkiewicz, Henry Moore, Herbert Bayer, Vance Kirkland, Dave Yust, George Rickey, Philip Tsiaras, Italo Scanga, Werner Drewes and many others. *Mailing Add:* c/o Inkfish Gallery 1672 S Lansing St Aurora CO 80012

HUGHES, SÍOCHÁIN I
SCULPTOR, PHOTOGRAPHER
b Dublin, Ireland, Mar 1, 1961; US citizen. *Study:* Parsons Sch Design, New York, BFA, 83; Hunter Coll MFA (sculpture, William Graf Travel Grant, 89), 92. *Work:* Musee Carnavalet, Paris, France; and var pvt collections. *Exhib:* Solo exhibs, Sandford Gallery, Clarion Univ, Pa, 1987, Galerie Lambert, Paris, 1997, Westminster Art Gallery, Bloomfield Coll, 1998, Galerie Am Scheunenviertel, Berlin, Ger, 1999, Koran Gallery, Drew Univ, 2000, Thomas Hunter Project Room, Hunter Coll, 2010, Suffolk Co Community Coll, NY, 2010; May Show, Cleveland Mus Art, Ohio, 1987; Fac Exhib, Rockland ctr for Arts, NY, 1991; Casual Ceremony, White Columns, NY, 1992; Three Rivers Arts Festival, Carnegie Mus Art, Pittsburgh, 1993; America is On Your Side, Amerika Haus, Berlin, Ger, 1994; Fac Exhib, Times Sq Gallery, Hunter Coll, 1996; Paris en 3d, Musee carnavalet, Paris, 2000; First Ann Great Falls Exhib, Paterson Mus, 2008. *Pos:* Dir, Korn Gallery Art, Drew Univ, 1998-2000; art dir, Christine Valmy, Inc, Pine Brook, NJ, 2001-; asst to the mus registar, Jersey City Mus, 2006-08; cons designer, The Mosatche Group, 2008, Ask Dr. M, 2009. *Teaching:* Instr art, St Gabriel Elem Sch, Riverdale, NY, 1982-83; instr language, St Nicholas Elem Sch, Williamsburg, NY, 1983-84; instr ceramics, Rockland Ctr for the Arts, NY, 1990-93; adj asst prof, Union Co Coll, Cranford, NJ, 1995-96, Bloomfield Coll, NJ, 1995-99, Hunter Coll, New York, 1995-99; adj lectr, Drew Univ, Madison, NJ, 1996-99 & 2003-05; vis artist prof, Hunter Coll, New York, 2001-. *Awards:* Madeline Sadin Award, Greewich House Pottery, 81; Fulbright Fel, 1993-95; Selection Award, Leo Castelli Gallery, 95; Fac Technol Grant, Hunter Coll, 2010. *Bibliog:* Roberta Smith (auth), Art in Review, Casual Ceremony, NY Times, 1/3/1992; Gretchen Faust (auth), New York in Review, Arts Mag, 79, 3/92; Anja Oberhardt (auth), Kunst aus dem Waggon ein Wunder auf Schienen, Die Welt, B3, 1/20/94; Mitchell Seidel (auth), Photographer sahres her views of Germany before and after war, Sunday Star Ledger, Style, 12, 4/12/98. *Mem:* Coll Art Asn; Am Asn Mus (curs comt); Fulbright Alumni Asn, New York. *Media:* Photography, Digital Art; Sculpture, All Media. *Publ:* Auth, Paris in 3D: From stereoscopy to virtual reality 1850-2000 (exhib catalog), Musee Carnavalet, Paris, France, 2001; Layout (exhib catalog), SUNY Suffolk Co Community Coll, 2009

HUGHTO, MARGIE A
CERAMIST, CURATOR
b Endicott, NY, March 29, 1944. *Study:* State Univ NY, Buffalo, BS (art educ), 65; Cranbrook Acad Art, Bloomfield Hills, Mich, MFA (ceramics), 71; with Richard DeVore. *Work:* Boston Mus Fine Arts, Mass; Albright-Knox Art Gallery, Buffalo, NY; Everson Mus Art, Syracuse, NY; Cranbrook Acad Art Mus, Bloomfield Hills, Mich. *Comn:* Ceramic wall pieces, Marina Casino, NJ, 80; ceramic wall pieces, United Energy Resources, Houston, Tex, 81; ceramic wall pieces, Presbyterian Hospital, Philadelphia, Pa, 81. *Exhib:* Language of Clay, Birchfield Ctr, Buffalo, NY, 79-80; Century of Ceramics US, Everson Mus Art, Syracuse, NY, 79-81; Women Artists, Suzanne Brown Gallery, Scottsdale, Ariz, 80; Scripps Invitational, Scripps Coll Mus, Claremont, Calif, 81. *Collection Arranged:* New Works in Clay by Contemp Painters & Sculptors (auth, catalog), Am Ceramics, 76, 78 & 81; A Century of Ceramics in the US 1878-1978 (auth, catalog), Am Ceramics, 78. *Pos:* Cur of Ceramics, Everson Mus Art, Syracuse, NY, 73-81; dir, Syracuse Clay Institute, NY, 75-81. *Teaching:* Prof ceramics, Syracuse Univ Sch Art, NY, 71-81. *Bibliog:* Sherry Chayat (auth), The Ceramic Fans of Margie Hughto, Ceramics Monthly, 5/80; Earth, Fire & Water (film), Philip Morris Corporation, 78. *Mem:* Inst Ceramic History. *Media:* Ceramic, Handmade Cotton Paper Pulp. *Res:* Contemporary American ceramics. *Mailing Add:* 6970 Henderson Rd Jamesville NY 13078

HUGUNIN, JAMES RICHARD
CRITIC
b Milwaukee, Wis, June 20, 1947. *Study:* Art Ctr Coll Design, Los Angeles, 71; Calif State Univ, Northridge, BA, 73; Univ Calif, Los Angeles, MFA, 75. *Work:* Santa Barbara Mus Art; Grunewald Print collection, Univ Calif, Los Angeles; Shaker Seed House, Tyringham, Mass. *Exhib:* Language & Image, Santa Barbara Mus Art, 77; Narrative Art: 1967-1976, Contemp Arts Mus, Houston, 77; Book Exhib, Art Ctr, Sonja Henie--Neils Onstand Found, Hovikodden, Norway, 78; Los Angeles Invitational, Fisher Gallery, Univ Southern Calif, 79; Object, Illusion & Reality, Muckenthaler Gallery, Calif State Univ, Fullerton, 79; Kunstenaarsboeken, Stedelijk Mus, Schiedam, The Neth, 81. *Pos:* Founder, ed & publ, Dumb Ox & U-Turn Art Mags, 76-80 & 82-; contrib ed, Obscura Mag, 79-82; Midwest ed, New Art Examiner, 89-90. *Teaching:* Prof art, Calif Lutheran Col, 77-85; lectr, Chaffey Col, 82, Art Ctr Col Design, 83, Calif Inst Arts, 85 & Sch Art Inst Chicago, 85-86; vis prof, Art Inst Chicago, 85-; sr lectr, Roosevelt Univ, Chicago, 89-. *Awards:* First Place, Calif Coll Photog Exhib, Calif State Univ, Northridge, 74; Purchase Award, Light II, Calif State Univ, Humbolt, 76; David & Reva Logan Grant New Critical Writing, 83. *Bibliog:* Howardina Pindell (auth), article, Print Collectors Newsletter, 9-10/77; Marcia Corbino (auth), Contemporary art criticism, Am Art, 10/83. *Mem:* Int Art Critics Asn. *Publ:* Auth, Apocryphal conversations, Afterimage, 6/81; Photography: A bourgeois success story, J Los Angeles Inst Contemp Art, 5-6/82; Joe Deal's Optical Democracy, Reading into Photography, Univ NMex, 82; Meditations on an Uranian Easter egg, Vies, Photog Resource Ctr, 83. *Mailing Add:* 454 Iowa St Oak Park IL 60302-2268

HUI, PAT
PAINTER
b Hong Kong, Aug 25, 1943; US citizen. *Study:* Study of Chinese ink painting with Lui Shou-Kwan, 61-64; Univ Hong Kong, BA, 67; Univ Minn, 67-71. *Work:* McDonald Corp, Hong Kong Landmark Ctr. *Exhib:* Shadow of Poetry, Honeywell Corp Gallery, Minneapolis, Minn, 85; Poetic Vision, Alisan Fine Arts, Hong Kong, 87; Lesch Gallery, Minneapolis, 88; Asian Fine Arts, Minneapolis, 89; Alisan Fine Arts, Hong Kong, 93, 2005; Chung Chi Coll, Chines Univ Hong Kong, 2007; Traffic Zone Gallery, Minneapolis, 2009, 2010. *Collection Arranged:* Lui Shou-Kwan, 1919-1975, Gallery 80's, Toronto, 80; Nine Chinese Artists, Honeywell Corp Gallery, Minneapolis, Minn, 82; New Visions in Chinese Painting, 84 & Painting, Poetry & Calligraphy, 85, Hui Arts, Minneapolis, Minn. *Pos:* Cur, Gallery 80's, Toronto, 80; dir, Hui Arts, Minneapolis, 82-; steering comt, Asian Art Coun, Minneapolis Inst Arts, 83-2005. *Bibliog:* Laura Weber (auth), Hui Arts, Minnesota Design, 5/83; Mark Stanley (producer), Pat Hui, Video, 5/85; Wilma Wenick (auth), Shadow of poetry, Artnews, Minneapolis, 5/85. *Mem:* Art Dealers Asn Twin Cities (vpres, 83-85, treas, 85); Minneapolis Inst Arts; Am Art Coun; Walker Art Ctr. *Media:* Watercolor, Ink on Paper and Silk. *Specialty:* Contemporary Chinese artists in all media. *Publ:* Auth, Alisan Fine Art Ltd, Hong Kong, 93; auth, The Poetic Visions, 2005. *Dealer:* Alisan Fine Arts Hong Kong. *Mailing Add:* Hui Gallery 1225 LaSalle Ave Minneapolis MN 55403

HULDISCH, HENRIETTE
CURATOR
Collection Arranged: Small: The Object in Film, Video & Slide Installation, Whitney Mus Am Art, 2005; 2007 Nat Juried Exhib Winners, Phoenix Gallery, New York; co-cur: Whitney Biennial, 2008. *Pos:* Asst cur Whitney Mus Am Art, New York

HULEN, JEANNIE
CERAMIST, ADMINISTRATOR
Study: Kansas City Art Inst, BFA, 1995; Louisiana State Univ, Baton Rouge, MFA, 2000. *Exhib:* Solo Exhibitions include Gardening the Human Form, Dirt Gallery, Kansas City, Missouri, 1996, s/he, Foster Gallery, Baton Rouge, 2000, trans mutations, Ritter Art Gallery, Boca Raton, Fla, 2001, by bi, buy products, Fine Arts Ctr Gallery Univ Arkansas, Fayetteville, 2003, gender rendering: bi products, Central Gallery, Houston Community Col Central Campus, 2004, Sculpture Installation, Pratt at Munson Williams Protor Art Inst, Utica, NY, 2005, bi products Race Street Gallery, Urban Inst for Contemporary Arts, Grand Rapids, Michigan, 2005, Zone Gallery, Kansas City, Missouri, 2005, Innocent Play, Fine Arts Gallery, Moberly Community Col, 2008, Made in Taiwan, Tainan Nat Univ of The Arts, Taiwan, 2009, Taipei, Taiwan, 2011, Made in USA, Arkansas, 2011, Walton Art Ctr, 2012; group exhibitions including Nine-Fold, Group Show, Houston Community Col Central, 2000, Summer Artist Series, Market Street Gallery, Lockport, NY, 2003, Clay Mechanics, Charlie Cumming Clay Studio, Fort Wayne, 2007, Material Transcendence: Clay As Commentary, NCECA, Pittsburg, 2008, Jingdezhen Contemporary International Ceramics Exhibition, Jingdezhen Ceramic Mus, The China Jingdezhen International Ceramic Fair, China, 2009, shows in conjunction with the Nat Council for the Educ of Ceramics Arts, 2007-2011. *Pos:* Resident visiting artist, Graduate Inst of Applied Arts, Tainan Nat Univ of the Arts in Tainan, Taiwan, 2009; juror, Student Juried Show, Anne Kittrell Gallery, Univ of Arkansas Union, 2004; Guest lecture/critic, Lawrence Lee, Art Prof of Univ Arkansas, Fort Smith, 2006, Stateline Wood-Tuners, Jones Ctr in Springdale, Arkansas, 2007; Juror of awards, Fayetteville Fine Arts Festival, 2008, Juror, Students First Diversity Art, Univ of Arkansas, 2009, Juror, Bentonville Fine Arts Walk, 2010. *Teaching:* Chair Department of Art, 2010-, assoc prof ceramics, Univ Arkansas, currently. *Mailing Add:* Department of Art Fine Arts Center FNAR 116 University of Arkansas Fayetteville AR 72701

HULICK, DIANA EMERY
SCULPTOR, PHOTOGRAPHER
b Boston, Mass, 1950. *Study:* Bryn Mawr, AB, 71; Ohio Univ, MFA, 73; Princeton Univ, MFA, 78, PhD (McCormick Fel), 84. *Work:* Carleton Coll; Photoworks, Boston; Graphic Arts Collection, Princeton Univ; Smithsonian Inst; Cathedral Ctr Arts, Phoenix, Ariz; Stephens Coll, Mo. *Comn:* Advent Wreath, 2000, Stations of Cross, 2004 & Grail Fountain, 2005, Trinity Cath, Phoenix, 2005; metal sculpture, Burning Bush, St Barnabas in the Desert; Jerusaleum Cross, All Saints, Phoenix, Ariz, 2004; Cathedral Ctr Arts; Brazier Baptismal font, Trinity Catherdral, Phoenix, 2007. *Exhib:* Smithsonian Inst, Washington, DC, 73; Kansas City Art Inst, 76; New Photogs, 76; RI Sch Design, 79; Cathedral Ctr Arts, Phoenix, Ariz, 2004. *Collection Arranged:* Waldo Pierce: A New Assessment (auth, catalog), 84; Sabbathday Lake Shakers, Exhib Time & Eternity (with catalog), 85; Through Their Own Eyes, The Personal Portfolios of

Edward Weston and Ansel Adams (with catalog); Romanian Glass Icons, Cathedral Ctr Arts, Phoenix, Ariz, 2006, 2012. *Pos:* Modernist & gallery dir, Univ Denver, 82-83; dir & cur, Univ Maine, Orono, 83-86; adjudicator, Nat Found Advan Arts, Fla, 83-87; int adv bd, Hist Photog (an int quart). *Teaching:* Asst prof art hist, Univ Maine, 83-86 & Univ NMex, 85; asst prof photo hist, theory & criticism, Ohio State Univ, 86-88; asst prof art, Ariz State Univ, 88-95. *Awards:* Dayton Hudson Distinguished Vis Artists Carleton Coll, 80. *Mem:* Artist-Blacksmith Asn N Am. *Media:* Photography, Mild steel. *Res:* Shaker photography; Diane Arbus, minority and women photographers; Romanian folk art. *Publ:* Co-ed, Photography as Document: Shaker Spirituality and the Modern Age, Vol 11, NMex Studies Fine Arts, 87; The Transcendental Machine? A Comparison of Digital Photography and Nineteenth Century Theories of Photographic Representation Leonardo, a refereed int quart, Vol 23, No 3, 419-425, summer, 90; Continuity and Revolution: The Work of Ansel Adams and Edward Weston, Through Their Own Eyes: The Personal Portfolios of Edward Weston and Ansel Adams, 22-23, Univ Wash, Seattle, 91; From Prohibition to Acceptance: Shakers and Photography in the Nineteenth and Twentieth Centuries, Visual Resources, vol VIII, 81-103, fall, 91; George Platt Lynes: The Portrait Series of Thomas Mann, History of Photography, an int quart, Vol 15, No 2, 211-221, fall, 91; coauth, Photography, 1900 to the Present (with J Marshall), Prentice Hall, 98. *Mailing Add:* 805 N Robson Mesa AZ 85201

HULL, CATHY
ILLUSTRATOR, CONCEPTUAL ARTIST
b New York, Nov 4, 1946. *Study:* Conn Coll, New London, BA, 68; Sch Visual Arts, New York, cert, 70. *Work:* Fourth World Cartoon Gallery, Skopje, Yugoslavia; Collection of Caricatures and Cartoons, Basel, Switz; The Sixth World Cartoon Gallery, Skopje, Int Cartoon Exhib, Istanbul, Mus of Caricatures of Cartoons, Basel, Switz. *Exhib:* Solo exhib, 6th World Cartoon Gallery, Skopje, Yugoslavia, 74; Group exhibs, Seventeenth Nat Print Exhib, Brooklyn Mus, 70; Soc Illusrs Ann, NY Times Show, 73; Pompidou Ctr, Paris, 77; Women in Design, Pac Design Ctr, Los Angeles, 80; Women in Design Int Ariz, Scottsdale Ctr Arts, 81; Contemp Graphics, Design & Illus, The Md Inst, Baltimore, 81; Collection of Caricatures & Cartoons Show, Basel, Switz, 80, 82, 90; Contemp Design & Illus Show, Butler Inst Am Art, Youngstown, Ohio, 83; Quebec City Exhib, 85; Bienniale of Humor, Fredikstad, Norway, 87; 6th Int Cartoon Competition, Istanbul, Turkey, 88, Soc Illusrs Ann, 93, Smithtown Twp Arts Counc, 95; The Ripple Effect, Mus Am Illus Exhib, NYC, 2006; Artists Against the War, Mus Am Illus Exhib, NYC, 2008; Pen & Brush Galleries, 2009; 47th Ann Wired Fine Arts Exhib, Putnam Arts Coun, 2009. *Pos:* Freelance illusr, 71-; Designer, Publ, Distribr to Mus Shops (Bridge) Playing Cards in Europe, Asia & US. *Teaching:* Instr, illus & portfolio, Sch Visual Arts, NY, 83-94 & Parsons Sch Design, 94-97. *Awards:* Certificate of Excellence, Am Inst Graphic Arts Inside Show, 71; Silver Award & 2 Certificates of Merit, Soc Publ Designers, 74; Fifty Best Books of the Year Award, 74; Award of Excellence, Soc Newspaper Design, 84-85. *Mem:* Exec Bd of (the friends of Art & Design) FAD 2002-2006. *Media:* Computer. *Collection:* Karikatur & Cartoon Mus Basel, Switz. *Publ:* Contribr & illusr, Graphis #164, 72-73; Print, 5-6/77; Art Direction, 5/77; Nebelspalter, 75-83; U & LC, 86; illus, Artists Against the War, 2006; illus, Mus of Am, 2008; illus, All the Art that's Fit to Print (and Some That Wasn't): Inside the NY Times Op-Ed Page, 2008; Celebrating Women's Work, The Pen & Brush Inc, 3/8/12

HULL, GREGORY STEWART
PAINTER
b Okmulgee, Okla, Sept 2, 1950. *Study:* Univ Utah, BFA, 73, MFA, 77, studied with Alvin Gittins. *Work:* State Utah Inst Fine Arts, Salt Lake City; Butler Inst Am Art, Youngstown, Ohio; Utah State Art Collection, Salt Lake City. *Comn:* Westin Kierland Resort and Spa, Scottsdale, Ariz; Montage Resort & Spa, Laguna Beach, Calif; Patricia Hearst (portrait), John Mellencamp (portrait), Indiana Co, Pa Judges (portrait), 74-. *Exhib:* Group exhibs, 7th Intermountain Biennial, Salt Lake Art Ctr, 75; 52nd Ann, Springville Mus Art, Utah, 76; Utah Mus Fine Arts, Salt Lake City, 76; Munic Art Gallery, Los Angeles, 78; Butler Inst Am Art, Youngstown, Ohio, 81; 64th Ann, Springville Mus Art, Utah, 88; East Coast Ideals, West Coast Concepts, Carnegie Art Mus, Oxnard, Calif, 98; PAPA Plein Air Show 99 & 2000; Ann Juried Exhib, Calif Art Club, Pasadena Mus Calif Art, 2003, 2005 & 2008; Modern Masters Invitational, Grand Canyon Nat Park, 2009; The Residue of my Investigation, Yavapai Coll Art Gallery, Ariz, 2010; Grand Canyon Celebration of Art, Grand Canyon Nat Art, 2010, 2011. *Teaching:* Asst, Univ Utah, 75-77; Sedona Art Ctr, 2000. *Awards:* Best Show-Purchase, Utah Painting & Sculpture, 76; 1st Prize, Davis Co Art Ctr, Utah, 76; Am Artists' Golden Anniv Nat Art Competition Winner, 87; Best of Show, Members Exhibit, Sedona Arts Ctr, 99; 1st Place, Members Art Exhibit, 2000; 2nd Place, Crystal Cove Alliance, 2004 & 2008; Honorarium, Tucson Plein Air, 2005. *Bibliog:* M Stephen Doherty (auth), Closing in on a Strong Painting, Am Artist, 7/98; Lynn Pyne (auth), An Eclectic Approach, Southwest Art, 5/99; Kathleen Bryant (auth), Into the Heart of the Grand Canyon, Am Artist, 12/2000; The Grand Adventure, Art of the West, 11-12/2000; Lynn Pyne Davis (auth), Arizona Regionalists, Southwest Art, 9/2002; Amy Abrams (auth), Plein and Simple, Arizona Highways, 8/2009. *Mem:* Calif Art Club; Metro Opera Guild; Ariz Plein Air Painters. *Media:* Oil. *Publ:* Enchanted Isle by Sapap, 2003; From Sea to Shining Sea: A Reflection of America, Haggin Mus; San Diego Flora, Lightner, 2007; California Light, A Century of Landscapes, 2011. *Dealer:* John Pence Gallery 750 Post St San Francisco CA 94109; Medicine Man Gallery 7000 Tanque Verde Rd Tucson AZ 85715; Redfern Gallery 1540 S Coast Hwy Laguna Beach CA 92651. *Mailing Add:* 3665 Zia Dr Sedona AZ 86336

HULL, JOHN
PAINTER
b New Haven, Conn, Feb 14, 1952. *Study:* Yale Univ, BA, 77; Univ Ill, MFA, 81. *Work:* Metrop Mus Art; Yale Univ Art Gallery; New Mus Contemp Art; Israel Mus, Jerusalem; Greenville Co Art Mus, SC; Yellowstone Art Mus, Billings, Mont; Denver Art Mus, Colo; Ulrich Mus, Wichita, Kans; Wichita Art Mus, Wichita, Kans; Missoula Mus Art, Missoula, Mont. *Exhib:* Metrop Mus Art, NY, 88; Nat Gallery, NZ, Wellington & Art Gallery Western Australia, Perth, 89; Solo exhib, (auth, catalog), JB Speed Art Mus, 90, Yellowstone Art Ctr, Billings, Mont, 92, Grace Borgenicht Gallery, New York, 92 & 94, Jonson Gallery, Univ NMex, Albuquerque, 93, Kohn Turner Gallery, Los Angeles, 95 & Tatistcheff & Co Inc, NY, 96 & 99; Butler Mus Am Art, 92; Richard Bosman and John Hull, ART Resources, NY, 98; Selections from permanent collection, Yellowstone Mus, billings, Mont, 98; Art of the Am West, Denver Art Mus, Colo, 99; Ron Judisg Fine Arts, Denver, Colo, 99 & 2002; Tatistcheff & Company, Inc, NY, 99 & 2001; Arvada Ctr Arts and Humanities, Nevada, 99; The Figure: Another Side of Modernism (auth, catalog), New House Ctr Contemp Art, Snug Harbor, NY, 2000; Crowded Prairie, Nicolaysen Art Mus, Casper, Wyo, 2000; (auth, catalog), Roseberg Gallery, Goucher Col, Baltimore, Md, 2001; Edwin A Ulrich Mus, Wichita State Univ, Kans, 2001; Ctr Contemp Art, Univ Colo, Colorado Springs, Colo, 2002; Mus Contemp Art Boulder, Boulder, Colo, 2003; E J Bellocq Gallery, La tech Univ, Ruston, La, 2004; Nicolaysen Art Mus, Casper, Wyo, 2005; Univ Wyo Art Mus, 2005; Alpha Gallery, 2007; Redux Contemp Art, 2010; Corrigan Gallery, 2010; Moberg Gallery, 2010. *Teaching:* Assoc prof painting, Yale Univ Sch Art, New Haven, Conn, 88-97; prof painting, Univ Colo, 98-2007; prof, Coll of Charleston, 2007-. *Awards:* Fel, Nat Endowment Arts, 82-86 & 87; Achievement Award for Acrylic, Am Artist, 95; Thomas Benedict Clark Prize, Nat Acad Design, 2004. *Bibliog:* Pictures from Sonny's place (catalog for exhib) by Annie Proulx, Ucross Found & Univ Wyo Art Gallery; Marcia Tucker (auth), Outpost of Progress: The Paintings of John Hull (catalog for exhib), New Mus Contemp Art, NY, 85; Lance Esplund (auth), John Hull at Tatistcheff, Art in America, 12/99; Alexi Worth (auth), The New Yorker, 4/20/2001; Ann Dailey & Michael Paglia (auth), Landscape of Colo, 2006. *Publ:* The 179th Annual: An Invitational Exhib of Contemp Am Art, Nat Acad Design, NY, 2004; Auth, A Creative Legacy, A History of the National Endowment for the Arts Visual Artists Fel Program, Harry N. Abrams, NY, 2002; auth, Baseball: The National Pastime in Art and Literature, edited by David Colbert, Time Life Books, NY, 2000; Epoch, Vol 58, Cornell Univ, 2009. *Dealer:* Plus Gallery 2350 Lawrence St Denver CO 80205; Alpha Gallery 14 Newbury St Boston MA 02116. *Mailing Add:* 839 Burnett Dr Charleston SC 29412-5015

HULL, STEVEN
PAINTER, ILLUSTRATOR
b Lakewood, Calif, 1967. *Study:* Calif Inst Arts, Valencia, BFA, 1995, MFA, 1997. *Exhib:* Some Young Fun, Richard Heller Gallery, Santa Monica, 1997; solo exhibs, Rosamund Felsen Gallery, Santa Monica, 1998, 2000, 2002, 2004-06, Galerie Rolf Ricke, Koln, 2002, Angstrom Gallery, Dallas, 2002, Steven Turner Gallery, Los Angeles, 2007; Shimmer, Los Angeles Munic Art Gallery, 2000; Wallpower, Dallas Ctr Contemp Art, 2002; Chocolate, What Else, Galerie Rolf Ricke, Koln, Ger, 2003; Human Presence: The Geometry of Color/The Singular Body, San Diego Mus Art, 2004. *Pos:* Lectr, Univ Southern Calif, Los Angeles, 2001, San Franciso Art Inst, 2002, Calif Inst Arts, Valencia, 2003, Otis Coll Art & Design, Los Angeles, 2003, Univ Tenn, 2007; vis artist, Cooper Union, New York, 2001, Loyola Marymount Univ, Los Angeles, 2001. *Awards:* Louis Comfort Tiffany Award, 2001; Joan Mitchell Found Grant, 2010. *Bibliog:* Jan Tumlir (auth), Color Me Mine, LA Weekly, 4/3/1998; Christopher Knight (auth), Unsteady Glow, Los Angeles Times, 3/17/2000; Brent McCabe (auth), California Dreaming, Dallas Observer, 9/6-12/2001. *Publ:* Illusr, Landscape Memories II, 2009 & The Runnaway Cutters, 2009

HUMMEL, CHARLES FREDERICK
ADMINISTRATOR
b Brooklyn, NY, Sept 16, 1932. *Study:* City Coll New York, BA (magna cum laude), 53; Univ Del, MA, 55, (hon) DFA, 2013; Mus Mgmt Inst, Univ Calif, 85. *Hon Degrees:* hon doctorate, Univ Del, 2013. *Exhib:* Tiffany Glass: Painting with Color and Light, Winterthur Galleries, 2014-2015. *Collection Arranged:* Philadelphia Reviewed, 61; Rugs from the Orient, 64; The Pennsylania Germans, 82-84; North Am Wood Turning Since 1930, 2001-02. *Pos:* Curatorial asst, H F du Pont Winterthur Mus, Del, 55-56, asst cur, 58-60, assoc cur, 60-67, cur, 67-79, deputy dir for collections, 79-89, deputy dir mus & libr dept, 89-91 (retired). *Teaching:* Adj assoc prof art hist, Univ Del, 64-93, adj prof, 93-2002. *Awards:* Winterthur Fel, 53-55; Katherine Coffey Award, Mid-Atlantic Asn Mus, 89; Winterthur Cur Emer, 91; Charles F Hummel internship, The Chipstone Found; AAM, 2012; Distinguished Service to Mus, AIC, 2012; Distinguished Service to Mus award, Am Asn Museums, 2012; Disting Allied Professional award, Am Inst for Cons of Historic and Artistic Works, 2012. *Mem:* Int Rug Soc (dir, 71); Am Asn Mus (secy, 88-90); Chipstone Found (trustee, 1991-); Philadelphia Soc for Preservation of Landmarks (trustee, 1993-1999); Wood Turning Center Philadelphia (trustee, 1993-1999, 2001-2006); Strawbery Banke Mus (advisory committee, 1997-2002, 2004-2009, hon mem Nat Coun, 2010-); Am Inst Conserv Hist & Artistic Objects; Nat Inst Conserv Cult Property; Nat Coun (collections & nominations comt, 2006). *Res:* Pocket watch ownership, L.I. and Conn., 1762-1827. *Publ:* Auth, With Hammer in Hand, Univ Press Va, 68, 73, 77 & 83; contribr, Furniture to 1790, Britannica Encycl of Am Art, Encycl Brit Inc, 73; auth, A Winterthur Guide to American Chippendale Furniture: Middle Atlantic & Southern Colonies, Crown/Rutledge, 76; Floor coverings in 18th century America, Irene Emery Textile Roundtable 1975, Textile Mus, 77; coauth, The Pennsylvania Germans: A Celebration of Their Arts, Philadelphia Mus Art, 82. *Mailing Add:* Berkshire 1112 Braken Ave Wilmington DE 19808

HUMPHREY, JUDY LUCILLE
GRAPHIC ARTIST, PRINTMAKER
b Columbia, SC, April 6, 1949. *Study:* Univ Ga, BFA (art educ), 71, MFA (printmaking), 73. *Work:* Tenn Valley Authority Art-in-Archit, Shiloh, & Knoxville, Tenn; E Tenn State Univ, Johnson City; McDonalds Corp Hqs, Chicago, Ill; Williams House Collection, Winston-Salem, NC; Contemp Drawing Collection, Trenton State Collection, Queens Coll Gallery, Bayside, NY. *Exhib:* Hoyt National New Castle, PA, 92; Northern Nat, Nicolet Gallery, Rhinelter, WI, 93,94; Print Club Int, Philadelphia, PA, 93; Boston Printmakers 44th Print Exhib, Boston, MA, 93; Paper in Porticulor,

Columbia, MI, America's 2000 Int, Minot, ND, 93; Art on Paper Gallery on Circle, MD, 93; Prints and Paper, San Diego Art Inst Mus, San Diego, Calif, 93; 6th Print Ann, New World Sch Gallery, Miami, Fla, 94; All Am Print Comp Mory Moody Gallery, Canyon Tex, 94; 5th Ark Biennial Art & Sci Ctr, Pine Bluff, Ark, 94; Priva Gross Int, Qcc Gallery, Bayside NY, 94; 44th Ann Exhib of Contemp Realism; Church Gallery, Springfield, MA, 94; All Am Print Comp Univ Gallery, Canyon, Tex, 94; 18th Art on Paper; Gallery on Circle Innopolis, MD, 94; Printmakers Renaissance II Rolling Stone Press, Atlanta GA, 95; Stockton National VIII, Haggin Mus, Stockton CA, 95; Artistic Impression of the Environment Dept of Interior Mus, Washington, DC, 96; Stockton National IX Haggin Mus, Stockton, Calif, 96; Border Biennal, Mus of York, Rock Hill, SC, 98; 18th Nat Print Ex Artistic Gallery, Fort Loayne, in 98; On/Off Paper EX, Green Hall Gallery, Murfresboro, NC, 99; Celebrating Legacy of Romare Bearden, McColl Center, Charlotte, NC, 2002; Southern Printmaking Biennal, Holg Gallery, Dattonega, GA, 2002. *Teaching:* Prof 2D design, printmaking & photog, Appalachian State Univ, 73-. *Awards:* Purchase Award, 9th Ann Henley Southeastern Spectrum, NC, 90; Merit Award, 72nd Nat Exhib, 91; Purchase Award, 33rd NDak Print & Drawing Ann, 91; Regional Artist Project Grant From NC Art Council, 2000; URC Grant, Crotis Williams Graduate Sch and Univ Research Council, ASU, Boone NC, 2000; Univ of NC of Governor's Excellence in Teaching Award, 2002. *Mem:* Southern Graphics Coun; NC Print & Drawing Soc; Coll Art Assoc, Southeastern Coll Art Assoc. *Media:* Pencil, Gouache; Etching, Mixed Media Collage, Relief, MonoType, Polaroid Transfers, PineHole Photography. *Mailing Add:* Appalachian State Univ Dept Art Boone NC 28608

HUMPHREY, NENE
SCULPTOR, INSTRUCTOR

b Portage, Wis, Mar 18, 1947. *Study:* St Mary's Col, Notre Dame, Ind, BFA, 69; Goddard Col, Boston, MA, 72; York Univ, Toronto, Can, MFA, 78. *Work:* York Univ, Toronto, Ont; Hofstra Univ; Best Products, Va; High Mus Art, Atlanta, Ga; Smithsonian, Washington, DC. *Comn:* Enclosed Garden-Landscape (sculpture), Artpark, Lewiston, NY, 80; Meadow Passage-Forest House (sculpture), Morris Mus, Morristown, NJ, 81; Roadrise-Resting Space, Creative Time, NY, 83; Atlanta Road, Atlanta Arts Festival; Passages (sculpture), St Mary's Col, Notre Dame, Ind. *Exhib:* Lines of Vision: Drawings by Contemp Women, Hillwood Gallery & Blum Helman Warehouse, NY; Threadwaxing Space, NY; Boise Art Mus, Idaho; High Mus, Atlanta, Ga; Sculpture 94, SC State Mus, Columbia; Sandler Hudson Gallery, Atlanta, Ga; Univ Colo; Katonah Mus, 99; Hecksler Mus, 99. *Pos:* Consult, Art in Pub Places, Seattle Arts Commission, 81-; adv panel, Recontres Choregraphiques Int/Danspace, NY, 97. *Teaching:* Vis artist, Nova Scotia Col Art & Design, 82, Parsons Sch Art, NY & Princeton Univ, 98, RI Sch Design. *Awards:* Macdowell Fel, Macdowell Colony, 78; Nat Endowment Arts Grant, 83; Rockefeller Artist Fel, Bellagio, Italy, 87; Anonymous Was A Woman Award, 98. *Bibliog:* Cynthia Nadelman (auth), Recent Drawings by Sculptors: A Common Language, Drawing, 7/94 & 8/94; Susan Hapgood (auth), Feminine Strategies, Object Lessons, Feminine dialogues with the surreal, Mass Coll Art, 95; Susan Krane (auth), Nene Humphrey, A Wild Patience, Univ Colo, 98. *Mem:* Coll Art Asn; fel mem MacDowell Colony. *Publ:* Illusr & contribr, Three stories, Criss-Cross Communications Mag, Colo, 81; Lines of Vision: Drawings by Contemporaves Women, Hudson Hills Press, NY, 89

HUNDLEY, ELLIOTT
SCULPTOR

b 1975. *Study:* RI Sch Design, BFA (Printmaking), 1997; Skowhegan Sch Painting & Sculpture, Maine, 2005; Univ Calif Los Angeles, MFA, 2005. *Exhib:* Solo exhibs include Hammer Mus, Univ Calif Los Angeles, 2006, Andrea Rosen Gallery, New York, 2007; Group exhibs include Art on Paper, Weatherspoon Art Mus, Greensboro, NC, 2002; Group Show: Retreat Peres Projs, Los Angeles, 2003; Threedimetrical, The Happy Lion, Los Angeles, 2003; Calif Earthquakes, Daniel Reich Gallery, New York, 2004; Old News, Los Angeles Contemp Exhib, 2004; Paper Beats Rock, Cherry & Martin Gallery, Los Angeles, 2005; From Close To Home, Mus Contemp Art Grand Ave, Los Angeles, 2007; The Shapes of Space, Solomon R Guggenheim Mus, 2007; Unmonumental: The Object In The 21st Century, New Mus Contemp Art, New York, 2007. *Mailing Add:* Andrea Rosen Gallery 525 W 24th New York NY 10011

HUNG, CHIN-CHENG
CALLIGRAPHER, PAINTER

Study: Nat Military Inst; Fu Hsing Kang Col; Savannah Coll Art & Design, MFA, 77. *Comn:* Many pvt collections. *Exhib:* numerous group and solo exhib's. *Pos:* Off, Rep China Army, Taiwan, formerly. *Teaching:* instr, Found Studies, 99-. *Awards:* numerous juried awards. *Media:* Paints, Oils and Pastels

HUNGERFORD, CONSTANCE CAIN
EDUCATOR, HISTORIAN

b Chicago, Ill, Apr 26, 1948. *Study:* Wellesley Col, BA, 70; Univ Calif, Berkeley, MA, 72, PhD, 77. *Teaching:* From instr to prof hist art, Swarthmore Col, Pa, 75-, chmn dept art, 81-87. *Awards:* Am Coun Learned Soc, 78; Am Philos Soc, 80; Am Asn Univ Women, 82-83; NEH, 92-93. *Mem:* Coll Art Asn. *Res:* Nineteenth century French painting, specifically Ernest Meissonier (1815-1891). *Publ:* Auth, Meissonier's Souvenir de Guerre Civile, Art Bulletin, 79; Meissonier's first military paintings, Parts I & II, Arts Mag, 80; Meissonier and the founding of the Societe Nationale des Beaux Arts, Art Journal, 89; Meissonier's Siege de Paris & Ruines des Tuileries, Gazette des Beaux-Arts, 90; Ernest Meissonier Rétrospective, Musée des Beaux Arts, Lyons, 93. *Mailing Add:* Swarthmore Col Dept Art Swarthmore PA 19081

HUNKLER, DENNIS
PAINTER, DRAFTSMAN

b Oakland, Calif, Mar 3, 1943. *Study:* New Sch Art, Toronto, 65-69; studio asst to Jack Bush, Toronto, 69-70; San Francisco Art Inst, BFA, 72. *Work:* Oakland Mus, Calif; Mus de Arte Contemp Int, Salvador, Bahia, Brazil; Franklin Furnace Archives, Mus Modern Art, New York, NY. *Comn:* Walks, US of A (set design), Jane Brown & co. *Exhib:* Origins - Past and Future, Art Dialogue Gallery, Toronto, 90; Bohmische Dorfer, Mus Osdeutsche Galerie, Regensburg, 91; Okresni Vlastivedne Mus, Krumau, CSFR, 92; Adalbert Stifter Verin, Munich, 92; Blind Mirror, Newman Gallery, Toronto, 96; Abstract Reality, Simcoe Gallery, 99; Five Painters Invitational, Gallery NA, Seoul, Korea, Nov 3-9, 2004; Korean-Canadian Exchange Exhib of Contemp Art, Gallery of Korean Consulate Gen, Toronto, June 3-10, 2005; Venice Two: A Multimedia Installation with Betty Ferguson, Mackenzie Hall Cultural Centre, Windsor, Ontario, 4/30-5/11, 2008; Venice Two, A Photographic Exhib in Collboration with Betty Ferguson, Joseph D Carrier Gallery, Toronto, 2009; DE (SKS) ET, A photographic installation on large drawings, Artcite Inc, Windsor, Ontario, 2010; Imposters, A Sculptural Installation in Collaboration with Betty Ferguson, Franklin Carmichael Art Gallery, Toronto, 2011. *Pos:* Asst dir, Artists Resource Ctr, Oakland, Calif, 73; mem adv comt, Jane Brown Found Dance & Related Studies, Oakland, 79-83; vice pres bd dirs, Artcite Inc, Windsor, Ont, 2013-. *Teaching:* Instr figure drawing, Cent Tech Sch, Toronto, 88-89. *Bibliog:* Alexander Fried (auth), The fantasy of three artists, San Francisco Examiner, 12/6/74; Thomas Albright (auth), Unique visions of nature, San Francisco Chronicle, 12/11/74; RF Stepan (auth), Dennis Hunkler's private world, Artweek, Vol 6, No 26. *Media:* Acrylic on Canvas; Pen and Ink. *Publ:* IXTUS: Poesia La Visibilidad de Lo Invisible, 2004; illus, Numero 44, Mex. *Mailing Add:* 380 Pelissier St #302 Windsor ON N9A6V7 Canada

HUNT, COURTENAY
PAINTER, INSTRUCTOR

b Jacksonville, Fla, Sept 17, 1917. *Study:* Ringling Sch Art, Studies with Jerry Farnsworth. *Work:* Univ Fla; Independent Life Insurance; Circuit Court, Jacksonville, Fla; Jacksonville Univ; Shrine Mus, Washington, DC. *Exhib:* Allied Artists Am; Sarasota Art Asn, Fla; Audubon Artists Am; Soc Four Arts, Palm Beach, Fla; Fla Artist Group Inc, Norton Gallery, Palm Beach; St Augustine Art Asn; Cummer Gallery, Jacksonville, Fla. *Teaching:* Instr, Jacksonville Art Mus & Jacksonville Jr Col & Cummer Art, Jacksonville, Fla, currently. *Awards:* St Augustine Awards, SFla Univ. *Mem:* St Augustine Art Asn. *Media:* Oil, Pastel. *Interests:* Piloting aircraft. *Publ:* Artist of Fla, 90; American Art Review. *Mailing Add:* 2248 Carnes St Orange Park FL 32073-5418

HUNT, DAVID CURTIS
MUSEUM DIRECTOR, CURATOR

b Oswego, Kans, Dec 7, 1935. *Study:* Univ Tulsa, BA (com design), 58, with Alexandre Hogue, MA (art hist), 68;. *Exhib:* Okla Artists Ann, Philbrook Art Ctr, Tulsa, 62-65; Legacy of the West, Joslyn Art Mus, Omaha, Nebr, 82. *Collection Arranged:* Currier & Ives' Am: The Conagra Collection, Permanent installation for Conagra Inc, Omaha, Nebr, 91; Views of a Vanishing Frontier, Bodmer Exhib, InterNorth Art Found, Omaha, Nebr, 95; Paintings of Native America, Stark Mus Art, Mus Fine Arts Houston, Tex, 2001; Taos Modern: Works by W.H. Dunton, Mus Fine Arts Houston, 2004; Bierstadt to O'Keefe: Highlights from the Stark Mus Art, Mus Fine Arts Houston, Tex, 2006. *Pos:* Ed, Am Scene Quart, Gilcrease Mus, 65-72, cur art, Gilcrease Inst, Tulsa, Okla, 67-72; cur collections, Stark Mus, Orange, Tex, 72-76, chief cur, 96 & 97-, dir, 98-2006; dir, Missoula Mus of the Arts, Mont, 77-80; cur art, Ctr Western Studies, Joslyn Art Mus, Omaha, 80-95. *Teaching:* Instr mus practices, Univ Tulsa, 70-72. *Awards:* Wrangler Award, Nat Cowboy Hall of Fame & Western Hertiage Ctr, 72; George Wittenborn Mem Award, Art Libr NAm, 85; Silver Medal, Int Bk Exhib, Leipzig, Ger, 89; Okla Bk Award, Okla Libr Asn, 89. *Mem:* Am Asn Mus. *Res:* 19th & 20th century American western artists and works. *Publ:* Art of the Old West, Alfred A. Knoff, 71; The Missoula Co Courthouse Murals, Missoula Mus Arts, 80; Coauth, The West as Romantic Horizon, Joslyn Art Mus & Univ Nebr Press, 81; auth, Guide to Oklahoma Mus, Univ Okla Press, 81; Legacy of the West, Joslyn Art Mus and Univ Nebr Press, 82; coauth, Karl Bodmer's America, Univ Nebr Press, 84; Views of A Vanishing Frontier, Univ Nebraska Press, 84; auth, The Lithographs of Charles Banks Wilson, Univ Okla Press, 89; Bodmer's America: The Aquatint Atlas, Alecto Hist Ed, London, 91; coauth, Tribes of the Buffalo: A Swiss Artist on the American Frontier, Cleveland Mus Natural Hist, 94; others; coauth, Fifty Favorites, Joslyn Art Mus, 95; coauth, Karl Bodmer's Studio Art, Univ Illinois Press, 2002; coauth, Artists of the American West: 1830-1940, St. Petersburg, State Russian Mus, 2003. *Mailing Add:* 6780 E 51 Pl Tulsa OK 74145

HUNT, MICHAEL
DIRECTOR

Study: Wash Univ, PhD (music composition), 1974. *Pos:* prog adminr, Mo Arts Coun & OASIS Inst, formerly; exec dir, Fine Arts Society of Indianapolis, formerly, St Louis Artists' Guild & Galleries. *Teaching:* Composer in residence, Fontbonne Univ, formerly. *Mailing Add:* St Louis Artists' Guild Two Oak Knoll Park Saint Louis MO 63105

HUNT, RICHARD HOWARD
SCULPTOR

b Chicago, Ill, Sept 12, 1935. *Study:* Art Inst Chicago, BAE, 1957. *Hon Degrees:* Lake Forest Coll, 1972; Dayton Inst Art Sch, 1973; Univ Mich, Ann Arbor, 1976; Ill State Univ, Normal, 1977; Colo State Univ, 1979; Sch Art Inst Chicago, 1982; Northwestern Univ, 1984; Monmouth Coll, 1986; Roosevelt Univ, 1987; Tufts Univ, 1991; Columbia Coll, 1996; Governors State Univ, 1997; NC A&T Univ, 2004; Univ Notre Dam, 2007. *Work:* Mus Mod Art, Metrop Mus Art & Whitney Mus Am Art, NY; Cleveland Mus Art, Ohio; Art Inst Chicago; Hirshhorn Mus; Mus 20th Century, Vienna, Austria; Nat Mus Art, Wash; Albright-Knox Gallery, Buffalo, NY; Mus Contemporary Art Chicago; Nat Gallery, Smithsonian Am Art Mus; Nat Mus American Art, Wash DC; Los Angeles Co Mus, Calif. *Comn:* A Bridge Across and Beyond (welded bronze), Howard Univ, 1978; Build-Grow (welded stainless steel), York Col, Queens, NY, 1986; Freedman's Column (welded bronze), Howard Univ, Wash, 1989; Spatial Interactions (welded bronze), Hunter Mus Art, Chattanooga, Tenn, 1991; Build-Grow, Growth Columns, Branching Column and Crane Column (welded bronze), Edward Bennett Williams Bldg, Wash, 1992; Nature's Palette (welded bronze), Kalamazoo Coll, Mich, 1993; Sculptural Improvisations (welded bronze), Ravinia Festival Park, Ill, 1994; Victory Reconstruction (corten steel), Potter Ctr, Jackson Community Coll, Mich, 1995; Chi-Town Totem (welded bronze & stainless steel), McCormick Place, Chicago, 1997; Celestial Conversation (welded bronze) Mount Mary Coll, Milwaukee, 2000; Memorial Cross (welded bronze), Immanuel Lutheran Church, Valparaiso, Ind, 2002; Victory Victory (welded stainless steel), Fort Des Moines Memorial Park, 2004; We Will (welded stainless steel), Heritage Bldg, Chicago, 2005; Quest for Peace (welded stainless steel), Adlai Stevenson HS, Lincolnshire, Ill, 2006; Quest for Peace, Adlaistevenson High Sch, Ill, 2006; Muskegon Rising, Muskegon, Mich, 2008; Sculptural Improvisations, Mich State Univ, 2008; Silverlinings, Lakeland Hospital, St Joseph, Mich, 2008; Sea & Sails, Chicago, 2009; Of the Rivermounds & Bridges, East St Louis, Ill, 2010; Build a Dream, Newport News, Va, 2011; Columnar Construction, Ruth Mott Found, Flint, Mich, 2011; Beyond the Frame and Bench, Joan Ravinia Festival Park, Highland Park, Ill, 2012; Building and Growing, Chicago State Univ, Ill, 2012; Valpo Variations, Valparaiso Univ, Ind, 2012. *Exhib:* BC Holland Gallery, Chicago, 1963, 1966, 1968, 1970 & 1976; Retrospective, Milwaukee Art Ctr, 1967; Dorsky Galleries, NY, 1969, 1970, 1971, 1973, 1975, 1976, 1977, 1979, 1987 & 1989; Retrospective, Mus Mod Art, NY, 1971; Retrospective, Art Inst Chicago, 1971; Okla Art Ctr, 1973; Century City, Los Angeles, 1987; Touring Exhim, Mus African Am Art, 1987-88; Kalamazoo Inst Art, Mich, 1990; Gwenda Jay Gallery, Chicago, 1991; Louis Newman Gallery, Los Angeles, 1991; Shiduni Gallery, Santa Fe, NMex, 1992; Woodlot Gallery, Sheboygan, Wis, 1994; Worthington Gallery, Chicago, 1995, 1996, 1998 & 2006; Studio Mus in Harlem, NY, 1997; Mus African-Am History, Detroit, 1998; Laumeier Sculpture Park, St Louis, 1999; Frederik Meijer Sculpture Garden, Grand Rapids, Mich, 2000; Foundry Gallery, Sacramento, Calif, 2000; Noel Gallery, Charlotte, NC, 2001; Lubeznik Art Ctr, Mich City, Ind, 2007; Elmhurst Coll, Ill, 2007; The Sculpture Ctr, Cleveland, 2008; Scad Mus Art, Savannah, Ga, 2009; David Weinberg Gallery, Chicago, 2009; GRN'Namdi Gallery, Chicago, 2009; Willis Tower, Chicago, 2010; 515 N State, Chicago, 2010; Belian Art Ctr, Troy, Mich, 2010; David Findlay Jr Gallery, NY, 2011; Thomas McCormick Gallery, Ill, 2012; Brauer Mus Art, Valparaiso, Ind, 2012; Galesburg Civic Art Ctr, Ill, 2013. *Pos:* Mem, bd gov, Sch Art Inst, Chicago, 1985-91, nat chmn Alumni Coun, 1983-87; with Nat Coun Arts, 1968-74; bd trustees, Ravinia Festival, 1974-81, 1983-92, 1994, 1996-2001, life trustee, 2002; bd trustees, Mus Contemp Art, Chicago, 1975-79; bd govs, Skowhegan Sch Painting & Sculpture, 1979-84; comnr, Nat Mus Am Art, Smithsonian Inst, 1980-88; bd trustees, Am Acad in Rome, 1980-82; pres & founder, Chicago Sculpture Soc, 1982-88; dir, Internat Sculpture Ctr, 1984-96; nat bd dirs, Smithsonian Inst, 1994-97; Am Acad Arts & Letters, 98. *Teaching:* Asst prof, Sch Art Inst Chicago, 1960-62, Univ Ill, 1961-63; vis artist, Yale Univ, 1964, Northwestern Univ, 1968-69 & Washington Univ, 1977-78; artist-in-residence, Eastern Mich Univ, Ypsilanti, 1988 & Harvard Univ, 1989-90. *Awards:* Guggenheim Fel, 62-63; Tamarind Artist Fel, Ford Found, 65; Am Acad Arts & Letts Award, 98; Lifetime Achievement Award, Int Sculpture Ctr, 2009; Legacy Award, United Negro Coll FUnd, 2010. *Bibliog:* Dore Ashton (auth), American Sculpture, New York, 68; Cedric Dover, Am Negro Art, New York Graphic Soc, Greenwich, Conn, 60; Elsa Honig Fine, Afro-American Artist: A Search for Identity, New York, 82; Sharon F Patton, African-American Art, Oxford Univ Press, 98; Richard Hunt: Extending Form, Charles R Loving and Sharon F Patton (essays), Snite Mus Art, Univ Notre Dame, Ind, 2012; Richard Hunt: Mutable Currency Past & Present, Daniel Schulman (essay), Thomas McCormick Gallery, Chgo, Ill, 2012; exhibs catalogues include Mus Mod Art, 71, NJ State Mus, 6 Black Americans, Trenton, 80, Bronx Mus Art, Traditions & Tranformations, Contemp Afro-Am Sculpture, Bronx, 89, Nev Mus Art, Reno 93, Snite Mus Art, Notre Dame, Ind, 96, Int Arts & Artists, DC, 98. *Mem:* Am Coun Arts (bd dir, 1974-97) test; Coll Art Asn Am (bd dir, 1972-76); Am Acad Rome (bd trustees, 1980-82); Nat Acad Design. *Media:* Welded Metal, Cast Metal. *Dealer:* Printworks Gallery 311 W Superior St Ste 105 Chicago IL 60610; David Findlay Jr Fine Art 724 Fifth Ave New York NY 10019; Thomas McCormick Gallery 835 W Washington Blvd Chicago Il 60607. *Mailing Add:* Richard Hunt Studio 1017 W Lill Ave Chicago IL 60614

HUNTER, DEBORA
PHOTOGRAPHER, EDUCATOR
b Chicago, Ill, June 16, 1950. *Study:* Northwestern Univ, BA, 72; RI Sch Design, MFA (photog), 76. *Work:* Yale Univ Art Mus; Wesleyan Univ Art Mus; Dallas Mus Art; RI Sch Design, Providence; Amon Carter Mus Art; Houston Mus Fine Art. *Exhib:* Dallas Mus Fine Arts, 79; The New Season, Witkin Gallery, NY; Second Sight, Carpenter Ctr Arts, Harvard, 81; Invisible Light Traveling Exhib, Smithsonian Inst, 80; one-person shows, Delahunty Gallery, Dallas, 80, The Light Factory, Charlotte, NC, 81, Int Mus Photog, 80, Meadows Mus, Southern Methodist Univ, 89 & Emporia State Univ, 89; Directions 1981, Hirshhorn Mus, 81; Mus Contemp Photog, Chicago, 85; Trains & Boats & Planes, Witkin Gallery, NY, 88; Portrayal, Bridge Ctr Contemp Art, El Paso, Tex, 89; two person show, Sitting Pretty, Art Inst Chicago, 92. *Teaching:* Instr, Swain Sch Design, New Bedford, Mass, 75-76; assoc prof photog, Southern Methodist Univ, Dallas, 76-; vis assoc prof Sch Art Inst Chicago, 84-85. *Awards:* Boston Ctr for the Arts Award, Photovisions, 75; First Prize in Photog, Tarrant Co Ann, Ft Worth Art Mus, 76; Mid Am Arts Alliance, NEA, 87. *Bibliog:* Lucy Lippard (auth), From the Center: Feminist Essays on Women's Art, Dutton, 76; David Dillon (auth), From the lighthouse, D Mag, Dallas, 78; article, Artforum, 4/81; article, Chicago Tribune, 12/6/85; article, Dallas Life Mag, Dallas Morning News, 11/5/89; article, Photo J Asahi Camera (Japanese), 8/90. *Media:* Black & White, Color. *Publ:* Contribr, Camera, 8-9/75; Women See Women, Crowell, 76; A Ten Year Salute, Addison House, 79; Popular Photog, 8/80. *Dealer:* Witkin Gallery 41 E 57th St New York NY 10022. *Mailing Add:* Dept Art Southern Methodist Univ Dallas TX 75275

HUNTER, ELIZABETH IVES-VALSAM
MUSEUM DIRECTOR
b Boston, Sept 26, 1945. *Study:* McGill Univ, Montreal, Canada, BA (Econ, Political Sci), 1967. *Pos:* Asst libr dir, Emerson Coll, 1971-1973; asst examiner, Fed Reserve Bank, 1974-1976, sr analyst, 1976-1979; asst treas State St Bank, 1979-1982; foreign exchange cons, 1982-1989; Fashion cons, Needham, Mass, 1989-1995; cur advisor, RH Ives Gammell Studios Trust, 1994-2000; guest cur, Maryhill Mus Art, Goldendale, Wash, 2000-2003; exec dir, Cape Cod Mus Art, Dennis, Mass, 2003-; advisor, Gimmell Studio Trust, Boston, 1981-2000. *Teaching:* Acad for Life Long Learning, Barnstable, Mass; Warry Center, Cape Cod, Mus Art. *Mem:* bd overseers, Boston Opera Assn, 1985-1993, bd advisors, 1985-1992; trustee, Chestnut Hill Sch, 1989-1997, vice chmn, 1991-1992, treas, 1992-1995; sec, Fairbanks Family in Am, 1998-1992, treas, 1992-1995, bd dir, 1998-2003; leadership com Sch to Careers Partnership, 2003-; bd advisors, Cape Cod Art Asn, 2007. *Publ:* ed, Boston Painters 1900-1930, Parnassus Imprints, Mass, 86; coauth, Transcending Vision, RH Ives Gammell Studies Trust, Boston, Mass, 2001. *Mailing Add:* Cape Cod Mus Art PO Box 2034 Route 6A Dennis MA 02638

HUNTER, LEONARD LEGRANDE, III
SCULPTOR, EDUCATOR
b Washington, DC, July 3, 1940. *Study:* Univ Miami, BA; Grad Sch Archit, Univ Pa; Univ Calif, Berkeley, MFA. *Work:* Hopkins Ctr, Dartmouth Col; The City of San Francisco; Headland Ctr Arts; The City of Busan, Korea. *Comn:* Environmental outdoor hydraulic-kinetic sculpture, Crossroads Plaza, Lexington, Ky, 74. *Exhib:* Solo exhib, Univ Art Mus, Berkeley, 72; Biennial, New Orleans Mus Art, 73; Annual, Whitney Mus Am Art, 75; Film Festival of the Americas, Virgin Islands, 77; Busan Biennale, Korea; Asan, S Korea; Qiradao, China, and others. *Pos:* Asst dir, Visual Arts Prog, Nat Endowment Arts, 80-83, acting dir, 81-82. *Teaching:* Assoc prof art, Univ Ky, 72-80, chmn dept art, 78-80; prof art, San Francisco State Univ, 83-2010. *Awards:* Teaching Fel, Univ Ky, 73-74; Golden Venus Medallion, Film Festival of the Americas, 77; and others. *Media:* Stainless Steel. *Res:* Public art & community research. *Interests:* Public art & architecturally-scaled sculpture. *Mailing Add:* San Francisco State Univ Dept Art 1600 Holloway Ave San Francisco CA 94132

HUNTER, PAUL
PAINTER, SCULPTOR
b Paris, France; US citizen, Canadian citizen. *Study:* Laval Univ, Quebec City, BA (vis arts), 77; Concordia Univ, Montreal, MFA, 79. *Work:* Coca-Cola Co, Atlanta, Ga; Quebec Mus; Refco Group Ltd, Chicago, Ill; Lighting Asn Inc; March & McClennan, Boston, Mass; Bessemer Trust Co, Los Angeles, Calif; Nationsbank, bd rm, Miami, Fla; Alston & Bird LLP, lobby & conf room, NY; Reliance Int, NY; Art Mus Princeton, NJ; Arthur Anderson & Co, NY; Butler Inst Am Art, Youngstown, Ohio; Montreal Mus Fine Art; and others. *Comn:* Mural, St Francis Hosp, Quebec City, 1988; murals, Madeleine Islands Hosp, PQ, 1992; McKinsey and Co, Miami, Fla, 1998. *Exhib:* Solo Exhibs, Chants-contre-Champs, Galerie Motivation V, Montreal, 81, White Noise, The Grey Art Gallery, New York, 87, Reflected Landscapes, Tibor de Nagy Gallery, New York, 92, Luminous Landscape, Central Fine Arts Gallery, New York, 2000, Liquid Landscapes, Sugar Hill Art Ctr, New York, 2002, Recent Work, Contor Galleries, Toronto, 2004, Selected Paintings, Byron Roche Gallery, Chicago, 2005, Gotik, Matermushaus XX, World Youth Day, Cologne, 2005, Nucturnes Series, Byron Roche Gallery, 2005, Variations on a Theme, Pan Am Gallery, DAllas, 2005, Life Paintings, 150 E 4nd St, New York City, 2006, Works on Paper, Andrea Horstmann-Osterich, Cologne, 2006, Spirit of Ecstasy, Hammer Rolls-Royce, Cologne, Ger, 2007, Andrea Horstmann-Osterloh Gallery, Cologne, Germany, 2008, Shain Gallery, Charlotte, NC, 2009, Panorama Studies-Halle-Hamburg-Rome-London, AHO Fine Arts, Cologne, Ger, 2009, Halleluja! Handel Project, Rex Theater, Wuppertal, Ger, 2009, and many others; Les Temps Chauds, Montreal Mus Contemp Art, traveled, France & Belg, 88; Tribute to Tibor de Nagy, Butler Inst Am Art, Youngstown, Ohio, 89; Miniature Environments, Whitney Mus Art at Philip Morris, NY, 89; Harmond & Discord: Am Landscape Painting Today, Va Mus Fine Arts, Richmond, 90; Paul Hunter in Perspective, Musee du Que, Can; All Than Glitters, Islip Art Mus, NY, 2003; Small Treasures, A&C Fine Art, East Greenwich, RI, 2003; Chicago Art Fair, 2004; Landscape Abstracts, Allen Sheppard Gallery, New York City, 2004; Works on Paper, Andrea Horstmann-Osterich, Cologne, 2006; Absolute Vision 12, Chicago Art Dealer's Assoc, 2007; Aho Gallery, Cologne, Germ, 2008; Utstallinssalongen, Stockholm, Sweden, 2009; Shain Gallery, Charlotte, NC, 2009; Prague Contemporary Art Fair, Czech Republic, 2010; Natura Sublime, Addington Gallery, Chicago, Ill, 2010; Inaugural Exhib, Lumen Gallery, NY, 2010; Art Toronto 2010, The 11th Toronto International Art Fair, 2010; Rhythm & Movement, Galerie NuEdge, Montreal, 2011; any many others. *Collection Arranged:* The Art Mus of Princeton Univ, Princeton, NJ; The Butler Inst, of American Art, Youngtown, OH; Montreal Mus of Fine Art, Montreal, QC; Quebec Mus, Quebec, QC. *Teaching:* instr, Lower East Side Printshop, NY. *Awards:* Can Coun grant, 1986-1988, 1991; Pollock-Krasner Found Award, 87; Quebec Govt artists fel, 1984, 1988, 1991; Nat Studio Program, Inst Art & Urban Resources, 1985, 1986. *Bibliog:* Jurgen Kisters, J Deutsch-Kanadischen Gesellschaft, 3/2005 & Kolner Stadt-Anzeiger, 8/23/2005; Michel Bois (auth), Le Soleil, 10/23/2005; and others. *Media:* Mixed Media on Gold on Canvas. *Specialty:* painting. *Publ:* Auth, Les Temps Chauds (exhib catalog), Montreal Mus Contemp Art, 88; Drawn from Life: Contemporary Interpretive Landscape (exhib catalog), Sewell Art Gallery, Rice Univ, Houston, Tex, 88; Paul Hunter in Perspective (exhib, catalog), Musee du Que, Can, 90; All That Glitters, Karen Shaw, Islip Art Mus, Islip, NY, 2004. *Dealer:* Byron Roche Gallery, Chicago IL. *Mailing Add:* 3280 Broadway Rm 313 New York NY 10027

HUNTER, ROBERT DOUGLAS
PAINTER, INSTRUCTOR
b Boston, Mass, Mar 17, 1928. *Study:* Cape Sch Art, Provincetown, Mass, with Henry Hensche; Vesper George Sch Art, Boston; also with R H Ives Gammell, Boston. *Work:* Northeastern Univ, Boston; Tufts Univ; Boston Univ Med Ctr; Mass Inst Technol; Harvard Univ; BMFA, 2010; New Britain Mus Am Art, 2010; Boston Mus Fine Arts, 2011. *Comn:* Epiphany mural, Church St Mary of the Harbor, Provincetown, 56; altar frontal, Emmanuel Church, West Roxbury, Mass, 62. *Exhib:* Acad Artists Show, Springfield, Mass, 61; Am Artist Prof League Show, NY, 66, 67 & 70; New Eng Artists Exhib, Boston, 70 & 74. *Teaching:* Instr fine arts, Vesper George Sch Art,

55-83 & Worchester Art Mus, 70-79. *Awards:* 15 Richard Mitton Gold Medals, New Eng Artists Exhib, 54-70; Newington Prize, 66 & 67, Am Artists Prof League; Frederick Thompson Found Award, 76. *Bibliog:* Richard Goetz (auth), Sight sized method, Am Artist, 70; Edward Fett (auth), Robert Douglas Hunter The Boston School Tradition, Am Artist, 90. *Mem:* Am Artists Prof League (dir, 60-70); Guild Boston Artists (vpres, 68-73, pres, 73-78); Acad Artists Asn; Copley Soc Boston. *Media:* Oil. *Dealer:* Tree's Place Gallery Orleans Mass; J Todd Gallery Wellesley Mass; The Guild of Boston Artists. *Mailing Add:* 492 Lincoln Rd Walpole MA 02081

HUNTER, ROBERT HOWARD
PAINTER
b Auburn, Wash, May 17, 1929. *Study:* Ore State Univ, 47-49; Univ Ore, BS & MFA, 49-53; Univ SC, 55-56. *Work:* Greenville Co Mus Art, SC; SC State Mus; Pepsico Corp, Purchase, NY; IBM Charlotte, NC; MCI Corp, Rye, NY; Springs Mills, Inc, NY; Wachovia Bank, Charlotte, NC; N Cascades Nat Bank, Charlotte, NC. *Exhib:* 159th Ann Painters & Sculptors, Philadelphia, 64; 7th Nat Show Art, Brockton, Mass, 64; Art on Paper, Weatherspoon Art Gallery, NC, 65; Solo exhib, Ackland Art Ctr, Univ NC, Chapel Hill, 68; 16th Ann Drawing & Small Sculpture Show, Ball State Univ, 70; Solo retrospective (with catalog), SC State Mus, Columbia, 92. *Pos:* Gallery dir, Rudolph Lee Gallery, Clemson Univ, 58-68; Ford Found fel, Univ NC, Chapel Hill, 66-67. *Teaching:* Instr figure drawing, Univ Ore, 52-53; prof printmaking, painting & basic design, Clemson Univ, 56-92, head dept visual arts 67-71, prof art, 68-92; prof emer, visual arts, 1992. *Awards:* Guild of SC Artists Awards, 56-63; Springs Art Contest, SC, 61 & 77; 8th Ann Painting of Yr, Atlanta Art Asn, 62. *Media:* Painting, Watercolor. *Publ:* Auth, Twenty Lithographs by Robert Hunter, 61; The Shape of R Hunter, 66; illusr, The Binnacle, R Peterson, 67; contribr, Contemporary Artists of South Carolina, 70; auth Robert Hunter, SC TV, 92; Hunter, Alaska, 2000; Robert Hunter (promotional video), Hunter Art Studio, 2001; Hunter, 2003. *Dealer:* Hunter Art Studio 9B Front St Coopperville WA 98239

HUNTER-STIEBEL, PENELOPE
CURATOR
b Washington, DC. *Study:* Barnard Col, BA; Inst Fine Art, NY Univ, MA. *Collection Arranged:* Twentieth Century Decorative Arts Gallery, 71-74 & 78-83; The Grand Gallery Int Exhib (ed, catalog), 74; New Glass Exhib, Metrop Mus Art, 80; The Fine Art of the Furniture Maker (coauth, catalog), Mem Art Gallery, Rochester, 81; Elements of Style: The Art of the Bronze Mount in the 18th and 19th Century France (auth, catalog), 84, A Bronze Bestiary (auth, catalog), 85 & Menuiserie, the Carved Wood Furniture of 18th Century France, 86, Chez Elle, Chez Lui, At Home in 18th Century France (auth, catalog), 87, Rosenberg & Stiebel Inc; Louis XV & Madame De Pompadour: A Love Affair with Style (auth, catalog), Dixon Gallery, Memphis, Rosenberg & Stiebel; William Beckman: Dossier of a Classical Woman (auth, catalog), Stiebel Mod, Ind Univ Art Mus, 91; Stroganoff the Palace & Collections of a Russian Noble Family (ed, catalog), Portland Art Mus, Oreg, 2000. *Pos:* Asst cur, Metrop Mus Art, 75-80, assoc cur, 80-83; contrib cur, Philbrook Art Ctr, Tulsa, 82-87; guest cur, Detroit Inst Arts, 83-85; principal, Rosenberg & Steibel Inc, 86-2000; adv coun, Grad Prog, Fashion Inst Technol, currently; consult cur European art, Portland Art Mus, 2000-. *Res:* Sixteenth through twentieth century decorative arts. *Publ:* Auth, Gustav Serrurier-Bovy, a forgotten master of Art Nouveau, Connoisseur, 11/82; The transcendent materialism of Albert Paley, Mus Fine Arts, Springfield, Mass, 85; Four masters of art deco, Antiques, 8/85; French Furniture of the Eighteenth Century by Pierre Verlet, Univ Press Va, 91; Art collecting, Encyclopedia Americana, 96; and others

HUNTINGTON, JIM
SCULPTOR
b Elkhart, Ind, Jan 13, 1941. *Study:* Ind Univ, Bloomington, 58-59; El Camino Col, 59-60. *Work:* Addison Gallery Am Art, Andover, Mass; Oakland Mus, Calif; Whitney Mus Am Art, Chase Manhattan Bank, Madison Square Garden Corp & Storm King Art Ctr, NY; Aerobay Off Ctr, Burlingame, Calif; and others. *Comn:* Taubman Co, Stoneridge Ctr, Pleasanton, Calif, 80; Henry Segerstrom, South Coast Plaza, Costa Mesa, Calif, 81; Hahn Co, Santa Rosa, Calif, 82; Insurance Co NAm, Wilmington, Del, 82; IBM, San Jose, 84. *Exhib:* Selections 1964, Inst Contemp Art, Boston, 64; Art Across Am, Inst Contemp Art, Boston, 65; Biennial, Corcoran Gallery, Washington, 65 & 67; Art for Embassies, Inst Contemp Art, Boston, 66; Ann, Whitney Mus Am Art, NY, 68 & 69; Solo exhibs, Hayden Gallery, Mass Inst Technol, 68, David McKee Gallery, NY, 75, 76 & 80, Leah Levy Gallery, San Francisco, 82, Gallery Paule Anglim, San Francisco, 85, RC Erpt Gallery, NY, Stephen Wirtz Gallery, San Francisco, 88, 89, 91 & 92 & Putter/Pence Gallery, Los Angeles, 88; Bay Area Sculpture: Metal, Stone and Wood, Palo Alto Cult Ctr, Calif, 88; Traveling Exhib, Sightings: Drawing with Color, NY, Spain & Portugal, 88; Wood, Metal Stone, Andre Zarre Gallery, NY, 89; Sculptural Intimacies: Recent Small-Scale Work (with catalog) Security Pac Gallery, Los Angeles, 89; and others. *Teaching:* Instr art, Cooper Union, NY, 68, Hunter Col, NY, 70-72, Lehman Col, NY, 70-76 & Princeton Univ, NJ, 78. *Awards:* Grand Prize Award, Sheraton-Boston Competition & Blanche Colman Award, Boston, 65; Nat Endowment Arts Fel, 80-81 & 84-85; Pollock-Krasner Found Grant, 86; Adolph & Esther Gottlieb Found Grant, 86. *Bibliog:* Kenneth Baker (auth), San Francisco Chronicle, 72, 88, 91 & 92; Steven Appleton (auth), A Visual Conspiracy, Artweek, 12/28/89; Susan Geer, Los Angeles Times, 11/25/88. *Media:* Stone, Cast Iron. *Mailing Add:* c/o Stephen Wirtz Gallery 49 Geary St San Francisco CA 94108

HUNTOON, ABBY E
SCULPTOR, CRAFTSMAN
b Providence, RI, Sept 8, 1951. *Study:* Boston Univ, MFA (ceramics), 83. *Work:* Index Group Inc & Putnam, Hayes, Bartlett Inc Cambridge, Mass; Standish, Ayer & Wood, Boston, Mass. *Comn:* Wallhanging, Mast Landing Elem Sch, Freeport, Maine, 92; wall hanging, Woodside Elem Sch, Topsham, Maine, 93; Wall Hanging, Pitston Elem Sch, Pitston, Maine, 94. *Exhib:* Everson Mus, Syracuse, NY, 87-89; Tenth Ann Exhib, Maine Coast Artist, Rockport, 89; 46th Ceramics Ann, Lang Art Scripts Col, Claremont, Calif, 90; one-woman show, Frick Gallery, Belfast, Maine, 90; Frick Gallery, Belfast, Maine, 92; Lakes Gallery, Casco, Maine, 94; and others. *Awards:* Merit Award, Biennial Exhib Maine Crafts, 86; Nat Endowment Arts Visual Artists Grant, 88. *Bibliog:* articles in various mags incl Ceramics Monthly, Am Craft, Portland Mag, Greater Portland Mag, 86-90. *Mem:* Maine Art Comn. *Publ:* Auth, The Best of Pottery, 96

HUOT, ROBERT
PAINTER, FILMMAKER
b Staten Island, NY, Sept 16, 1935. *Study:* Wagner Col, Staten Island, 53-57, BSc, 57; Hunter Col, grad art, New York, 61-62. *Work:* Frank Stella, NY; Paula Cooper, NY; William Rubin Collection, NY; Doberman Collection, Munster, Ger; Mus of Mod Art, NY; Mus Contemp Art, Los Angeles. *Exhib:* Systematic Painting, Guggenheim Mus, NY, 66; The Art of the Real Traveling Exhib, 68 & Recent Acquisitions, 78, Mus Mod Art, NY; Whitney Painting Ann, Whitney Mus, NY, 67 & 69; New Art USA, Mod Mus of Art, Minchem, WGer, 68; Seattle Art Mus, Wash, 69; Modular Painting, Albright-Knox Gallery, Buffalo, NY, 70; Solo exhibs, Paula Cooper Gallery, NY, 69-74, Millennium, NY, 75 & 79 & State Univ of NY, Albany, 76; Utica Coll, 79-80; Hetzler Galerie, WGer, 80-81; Hunter Col, 98; Mus Contemp Art, Los Angeles, 2004; Galerie Arnaud Lefebvre, Paris, 2006, 2008. *Pos:* Pigment chemist, Sun Chemical Co, Staten Island, 57-58 & 60-62; plant mgr, Neti Art Color, New York, 62-63. *Teaching:* prof, drawing & filmmaking, Hunter Col, New York, 63-91. *Awards:* Nat Coun Arts Grant, New York, 66 & with Twyla Tharp Dance Co, 77. *Bibliog:* S MacDonald (auth), article, 4/79 & An interview with Robert Huot, 2/80, Afterimage. *Media:* Unstretched Canvas; Film. *Dealer:* Canyon Cinema San Francisco CA; Arnaud Lefebvre Paris France. *Mailing Add:* 339 Spurr St New Berlin NY 13411

HUPP, FREDERICK DUIS
PAINTER, EDUCATOR
b Streator, Ill, Dec 21, 1938. *Study:* Univ Ariz, BFA, 62, MFA, 66. *Work:* Tucson Mus Art, Ariz. *Exhib:* Univ Man, Winnipeg, 76; SW Biennial, Mus NMex, Santa Fe, 76; Eight State West Biennial, Grand Junction, Colo, 76; Four Corners Biennial, Phoenix, Ariz, 77; Univ Ariz Art Mus, Tucson, 79; and others. *Pos:* Cur, Univ Ariz Art Mus, 60-61 & Mus Fine Arts, Santa Fe, 62; instr, Fenster Ranch Sch, Tucson, 64-65. *Teaching:* Instr design, Univ Ariz, 68-79; asst prof drawing & painting, Tucson Mus Sch, 68-80, dir educ, 68-70; instr design & drawing, Pima Col, Tucson, 77-. *Awards:* Eight West State Biennial Cash Award, Grand Junction, Colo, 74; Four Corners Biennial Cash Award, Phoenix, Ariz, 75; Cash Award, Cedar City Nat, Utah, 76. *Media:* Acrylic, Mixed. *Mailing Add:* PO Box 174 Morro Bay CA 93443-0174

HUREWITZ, FLORENCE K
PAINTER, EDUCATOR
b Passaic, NJ. *Study:* Cooper Union Sch Art & Archit, BFA, 76; Art Students League; Am Art Sch. *Work:* Bergen Community Mus, Paramus, NJ. *Exhib:* Biannual Show, NJ State Mus, Trenton, NJ; Invitational for Prize Winners, Jersey City Mus, NJ; Am Drawing Biennial, Norfolk Mus Art, Va; Nat Asn Women Artists Travel Oil Show, Pallazzo Vechio, Florence, Italy; Audubon Artists, Nat Acad, NY. *Pos:* Designer stained glass, Rambusch & Co, NY; asst exhib cur, Cooper Union Mus. *Teaching:* Inst fine art painting, Bergen Community Col, Paramus, NJ, 73-85; Art Ctr of N NJ, New Milford, 85-. *Awards:* Medal of Honor, Nat Asn Women Artists, 75; Medal of Honor, Nat Asn Women Artists, 86; Jersey City Mus Medal; Painters & Sculptors Soc. *Bibliog:* David Spengler (auth), Woman as an Artist, Bergen Record, 74; Kathy Damecker (auth), Studio Visit--F Hurewitz, Cablevision, NJ, 82; Eileen Watkins (auth), Woman on the Verge, Star Ledger, Newark, 89. *Mem:* Coll Art Asn; Nat Asn Women Artists; Womans Caucus for Arts; Artist's Equity of New York. *Media:* Oil. *Dealer:* Kornbluth Gallery Fairlawn Ave Fairlawn NJ 07410. *Mailing Add:* 17 Darling Rd Waldwick NJ 07463

HURLSTONE, ROBERT WILLIAM
GLASS ARTIST, EDUCATOR
b Chicago, Ill, June 3, 1952. *Study:* Ill State Univ, BS, 74; Southern Ill Univ, MFA, 78. *Work:* Corning Mus Glass, NY; Am Crafts Mus, NY; Rahr-West Mus & Civic Ctr, Manitowoc, Wis; Ind Univ Art Mus, Bloomington. *Exhib:* New Glass Traveling Exhib, 78-; Art for Use, Olympics Exhib, Lake Placid & Am Crafts Mus, NY, 80; Small group, Sales Gallery Show, Smithsonian Inst, Washington DC, 80; Ohio Glass Artists, Massillon Mus, Ohio, 80; Solo exhib, New Works, Habatat Gallery, Mich, 81; Am Glass Now, III, touring Japan, 81-. *Teaching:* Asst prof glass, 3-D design, Bowling Green State Univ, 78-. *Awards:* Mus Dirs Award, Evansville Mus, 77; Third Place Award, Toledo Mus, 81. *Bibliog:* Terri Sharp (auth), Artist profile, Art Craft Mag; Portfolio Section, Am Craft Mag; Photograph of work, Village Voice. *Mem:* Glass Art Soc; Ohio Designer Craftman. *Media:* Glass. *Mailing Add:* 1771 Kettle Run Ct Perrysburg OH 43551-5414

HURST, ROBERT JAY
PATRON
b New York, NY, Nov 5, 1945. *Study:* Clark Univ, BA, 66; Admin, Univ Pa, Master in govt, 68; Univ Pa, Pub Fin fel, 69. *Pos:* Fac, investment banking div Merrill Lynch, Pierce, Fenner & Smith, Inc, New York City, 69-74; vpres, 74, Goldman, Sachs & Co, New York City, 74-80, general partner, 80-2000, mem mgt comt, 90-2000, co-head investment banking div, 90-96, head investment banking div, 96-99, mem exec comt, 95-2000, vchmn, 99-2000; chmn, Jewish Mus, 97-2002; trustee, Whitney Mus Am Art, 98-, pres, 2002-; Chief Exec Officer, 9/11 United Servs Group, 2001-; trustee coun, Nat Found for Teaching Entrepreneurship, bd dir, currently; mem bd overseers, Wharton Sch, Univ Pa, coun on foreign relations, comt for economic develop; bd trustees, Manhattan Inst; trustee coun Nat, Gallery Art; trustee Committee Economic Develop, Central Park Conservancy; bd dir, Air Clic Inc, New York City 2012, IDB Holding Ltd, Constellation Energy Group, VF Corp. *Awards:* Recipient Louis Marshall Award, Jewish Theological Soc, 2000. *Mem:* Maroon Creek Club (Aspen), Atlantic Golf Club (Bridgehampton), Univ Club. *Mailing Add:* 500 Jalanda Ln Aspen CO 81611

HURTIG, MARTIN RUSSELL
PAINTER, SCULPTOR
b Chicago, Ill, Aug 11, 1929. *Study:* Inst Design Chicago, BS, 52, MS, 57; Atelier 17, Paris, 55. *Work:* Bibliot Nat, Paris; Philadelphia Free Libr; Carroll Reese Mus, Johnson City, Tenn; Honolulu Acad Art; Mus Contemp Art, Chicago. *Comn:* Stained glass windows & mural wall, Union Church, Lake Bluff, Ill, 63; outdoor court sculpture, Waukegan Pub Libr, Ill, 64; lobby relief sculpture, Midwest Iron Works, Chicago, 67. *Exhib:* Nat Print Exhib, Brooklyn Mus, 58 & 68; Solo exhibs, Flint Inst Arts, 61 & 68, Alonzo Gallery, 66 & 67 & Ecole Spec Archit, Paris, 69; 6th Am Artists Traveling Show, Paris & 12 French cities, 69-70; Jan Cicero Gallery, Chicago, 80, 81 & 83; Mus Mod Art, Paris, 85; Osaka Triennale, Japan, 90; Chicago/Paris Abstract Affinities, Ukranian Mus Mod Art, Chicago, 95; Koehline Gallery, Desplaines, Ill, 2000; Bradley Univ, Peoria, Ill, 2001. *Teaching:* Asst prof drawing & design, Mich State Univ, 57-62; prof painting, Univ Ill, Chicago, 62-; dir, Sch Art & Design, Univ Ill, Chicago, 82-88, prof painting, 88-91, ret, 91. *Awards:* Purchase Awards, Carroll Reese Mus, 67 & Honolulu Acad Arts, 71. *Bibliog:* F Schulze (auth), Art news in Chicago, Art News, 11/71; A Goldin (auth), Vitality vs greasy kids stuff, Art Gallery Mag, 4/72; D Guthrie & J Allen (auth), Waging polemical warfare, Chicago Tribune, 4/30/72; Charles Fambro (auth), exhib rev, New Art Examiner, 5/90. *Dealer:* Corbett vs Dempsey 1120 N Ashland Ave Chicago IL 60622. *Mailing Add:* 1727 Wesley St Evanston IL 60201

HURTUBISE, JACQUES
PAINTER
b Montreal, Que, Feb 28, 1939. *Study:* Beaux Art Sch, Montreal, BFA, 60. *Work:* Mass Inst Technol; Peter Stuyvesant Art Found, Amsterdam; Galerie Nat Can, Ont; Art Gallery Ont, Toronto; Vancouver Art Gallery; and others. *Comn:* Murals, Ottawa Univ, 69, Place Radio Can, Montreal, 72 & Ministry of Defense, Ottawa, 72. *Exhib:* 300 Yrs of Canadian Art, Nat Gallery Can, Ottawa, 67; Art d'Aujourd'Hui, Paris, Rome, Lausanne, Brussels, 68; Seven Montreal Artists, Mass Inst Technol, Cambridge, Gallery Mod Art, Washington & Stratford Festival, Ont, 68; Grand Formats, Musée d'Art Contemporain, Montreal, 70; Birmingham Festival of the Arts, Ala, 79; Mem Univ Art Gallery, St John's, Nfld, 85; Art Gallery, Acadia Univ, Wolfville, NS, 86; Art Gallery NS, Halifax, 86; Beaverbrook Art Gallery, Fredericton, NB, 86; Galerie Restigouche, Campbelton, NB, 87; Confederation Ctr Art Gallery & Mus, Charlottetown, Pei, 87; plus many other solo & group exhibs. *Pos:* Artist-in-residence, Dartmouth Col, 67. *Awards:* Max Beckmann Scholar, 60; First Prize, Concours Artistique Que, Que Govt, 65; Prize, Expos Hadassah, 68; and others. *Bibliog:* Laurent Lamy (auth), Hurtubise, Lidec, 71. *Mem:* Royal Can Acad Art. *Media:* All. *Mailing Add:* RR 1 Marjaree Harbor Cape Breton NS B0E 2B0 Canada

HURWITZ, ADAM
ART DIRECTOR
Study: Boston Univ, BFA, 89; Yale Sch Art, MFA, 94. *Exhib:* Solo shows at Debs and Co, NY, 2002, Michael Steinberg Fine Art, NY, 2004; group shows at Domestic Bliss/Cloning, DNA Gallery, Provincetown, Mass, 97; Diverse Works/Urban Configuration, Starwoos Urban, Washington, DC, 98; Exit Art, NY, 99; The Road Show, DFN Gallery, NY, 99; Distilled Life, Bard Col, Annadale-on-Hudson, NY, 99; Outer Boroughs, White Columns, NY, 99; Night Vision, 2003; Flat File, Bellwether Gallery, Brooklyn, NY, 2000; Violent Beauty, Debs and Co, NY, 2001. *Pos:* Art dir, designer, Fence Magazine, formerly. *Awards:* Joan Mitchell Found Award, 99

HURWITZ, MICHAEL H
CRAFTSMAN, MOSAIC ARTIST
b Miami, Fla, Feb 26, 1955. *Study:* Mass Coll Art, 74-75; Boston Univ, BFA, 79; studied with Kenkichi Kuroda, Kyoto, Japan, 90-91. *Work:* Gallery Am Art Renwick Smithsonian, Washington, DC; Mus Fine Arts, Boston, Mass; Mus RI Sch Design, Providence; Art Gallery Yale Univ, New Haven, Conn; Altos De Chavon Found, NY. *Exhib:* New Am Furniture, Mus Fine Arts, Boston, 89 & Oakland Mus Art, Calif, 90; solo exhibs, Pritam & Eames Gallery, East Hampton, NY, 89 & Peter Joseph Gallery, NY, 92; Child's Play, Mem Art Gallery, Rochester, NY, 94; Living, Peter Joseph Gallery, NY, 94; A Good Cup of Coffee & other Antidotes for Modern Day Living, Peter Joseph Gallery, NY, 94; Peter Joseph Gallery, 96; John Elder Gallery, NY, 98; and others. *Teaching:* Slide lectr, various univs, schs & mus, 83-94; assoc prof & prog head furniture, Univ Arts, Philadelphia, 85-90; instr, Haystack Mountain Sch Crafts, Deer Isle, Maine, 94. *Awards:* Nat Endowment Arts, 88, 90, & 92; Visual Arts Fel, 90 & 92; Grand Prize, Am Craft Awards, Krauss Sikes Publ Co, 90; Japan Found Fel, 96; Pew Fel for Arts, 99; Louis Comfort Tiffany Found Grant, 2009. *Bibliog:* B Steinbaum (auth), The Rocker, An American Design Tradition, New York, 92; Now That's Rockin, Am Woodworker, 11-12/93; Peter Joseph & Emma Cobb (auths), Masterworks Two, Peter Joseph Gallery, New York, 94. *Media:* Furniture Maker, Wood and Other Natural Materials. *Mailing Add:* 16 S 3rd St Philadelphia PA 19156

HURWITZ, SIDNEY J
PAINTER, PRINTMAKER
b Worcester, Mass, Aug 22, 1932. *Study:* Sch Worcester Art Mus; Brandeis Univ, BA; Boston Univ, MFA; Stuttgart Acad Art, Ger; Skohegan Sch, Maine. *Work:* Libr Cong, Washington, DC; Mus Mod Art, NY; Mus Fine Arts, Boston; Minneapolis Mus, Minn; Victoria & Albert Mus, London; Worcester Art Mus. *Comn:* Mosaic mural, Skowhegan Sch Art, Maine, 64; ed of woodcuts, Wellesley Col, Mass, 67; six paintings of London, Japan Int Bank, London, 73; ten etchings, Bldg Design & Construction Mag, Chicago. *Exhib:* Am Drawing, Mus Mod Art, NY, 56; Print Biennial, Libr Cong, Wash, DC, 62; Pa Acad, Philadelphia, 64; New Eng Artists, Boston, 71; Martin Sumers Gallery, NY; Mary Ryan Gallery, NY; British Int Print Biennale; Old Print Shop, New York. *Teaching:* Prof art, Boston Univ, 62-99, prof emer, currently; prof, Wellesley Col, Brandeis Univ, Amherst Col. *Awards:* Louis Comfort Tiffany Award, 66; Artist Award, Am Inst Arts & Lett, 69; Mass Found Arts Fel, 76. *Mem:* Coll Art Asn Am; Boston Printmakers Soc; Nat Acad; Soc Am Graphic Artists. *Media:* Painting, Printmaking. *Publ:* Auth, Etchings of Sigmund Abeles, 66 & My woodcut technique, 67, Am Artist; Etchings, Scarecrow Press, 85. *Dealer:* Audrey Pepper Gallery 38 Newbury St Boston MA 02216; Old Print Shop New York NY; Davidson Gallery Seattle WA. *Mailing Add:* 175 Parker St Newton MA 02459

HUSHLAK, GERALD
COMPUTER ARTIST, PAINTER
b Edmonton, Alta, Feb 15, 1945. *Study:* Univ Alta; Univ Calgary, Alta; Univ Calif; Royal Coll Art, London, Eng, MARCA. *Work:* Can Coun Art Bank, Ottawa, Ont; San Francisco Mus Mod Art, Calif; Vancouver Art Gallery, BC; Smithsonian Inst, Washington, DC; Alta Art Found. *Exhib:* Glenbow Mus, Calgary; Mendel Mus, Sask; Art Gallery Greater Victoria, BC; York Univ Art Gallery, Toronto; Mus Art Mod, Paris; and others. *Teaching:* Assoc prof painting, Univ Calgary, Alta, 75-. *Awards:* Purchase Award, World Print Competition, San Francisco Mus Mod Art, 77. *Bibliog:* Articles, Vanguard Mag, 80, Arts Can, 80, Art Mag & Artweek, 80. *Mem:* Royal Can Acad; Royal Can Acad Art. *Media:* Computers; Acrylic. *Mailing Add:* Dept of Art Univ Calgary 2500 University Dr NW Calgary AB T2N 1N4 Canada

HUSSONG, RANDY
SCULPTOR, PRINTMAKER
b Redwood City, Calif, 1955. *Study:* Univ Calif, Berkeley, BA, MFA, 76-80; studied with Jim Melchert. *Work:* Mus Modern Art, San Francisco, Calif; Di Rosa Art Preserve, Napa, Calif; Oakland Mus, Calif; CA Progressive Insurance, Chicago, Ill. *Exhib:* Los Angeles Co Mus of Art, 2000; Mus Art & Hist, Santa Cruz, Calif; Milwaukee Art Mus; traveling exhib, Japan, 98-2000; Solo exhib, Gallery Paule Anglim, San Francisco, Calif, Mincher/Wilcox Gallery, San Francisco, Calif, Inst Contemp Art, San Jose, New Langton Arts. *Teaching:* instr, sculpture, printmaking, Univ Calif, Berkeley, 94-2001. *Mem:* San Francisco Art Inst, Calif. *Media:* Metal, auto parts, woodcuts, blown glass. *Specialty:* Political themes, abstract sculptures, wall constructions

HUSTON, PERRY CLARK
CONSERVATOR
b Mo, Jan 4, 1933. *Study:* Univ Mo, AB, 55, Medical Sch, 55-57; Nelson Art Gallery, with James Roth, 63-70; special study with Sheldon & Caroline Keck, 68. *Pos:* Assoc conservator, Nelson Art Gallery, 66-70; chief conservator, Kimbell Art Mus, 71-. *Teaching:* Supervisor internships, Conserv Grad Progs, Cooperstown & Oberlin Grad Conserv Progs, 72-, teaching consult, 75-77. *Mem:* Fel Am Inst for Conserv Hist & Artistic Works (vpres, 78-79, pres, 80-). *Mailing Add:* 324 N Bailey Ave Fort Worth TX 76107-1003

HUSTON, STEVE
ILLUSTRATOR
b Anchorage, Alaska, 1959. *Study:* Art Ctr Coll Design, BFA, 1983. *Exhib:* Solo exhibs include Mendenhall Gallery, Pasadena Calif, 1999, Eleanor Ettinger Gallery, NY, 2000, 2005, DNFA Gallery, Pasadena, Calif, 2001, Blue Color, Sullivan Goss: An American Gallery, Santa Barbara, Calif, 2004, 2006; group exhibs include Acad Art Col, San Francisco, Calif, 1998-99; Carnegie Art Mus, Oxnard, Calif, 1996; Mendenhall Gallery, Pasadena, Calif, 1966; Eleanor Ettinger Gallery, NY, 1998-99, Figure in American Art, 2001, 2002, 2003, 2005, 2006, 2007, Summer Salon, 2001, 2003, 2004, 2006, Int Winter Salon, 2004, Autumn Salon, 2005; Am Figurative Painting, Albemarle Gallery, London, 1999; Diane Nelson Gallery, Laguna Beach, Calif, 1999; Pasadena Mus Contemp Art, 2003. *Pos:* Illustrator, Paramont Pictures, formerly, MGM, formerly, Warner Brothers, formerly. *Teaching:* Teacher, Art Ctr Col Design, 1985-96. *Dealer:* Timothy Yarger Fine Arts 329 N Beverly Dr Beverly Hills CA 90210. *Mailing Add:* c/o Eleanor Ettinger Gallery 24 W 57th St Ste 609 New York NY 10019

HUTCHENS, JAMES WILLIAM
ADMINISTRATOR, EDUCATOR
b High Point, NC, Oct 3, 1947. *Study:* Western Carolina Univ, BA, 70; Ga State Univ, MVA, 75; Fla State Univ, PhD, 79. *Teaching:* Prof art educ, Ohio State Univ, Columbus, 79-88, assoc dean, Col Arts, 88-92; prof & chair, Dept Art, Appalachian State Univ, Boone, NC, 92-. *Mem:* Coun Policy Studies Art Educ (exec secy); Nat Coun Art Adminrs; Nat Art Educ Asn. *Res:* Art education; art administration. *Publ:* Coauth, Disciplinary & institutional bases for arts research, Design Arts Educ, 88; Preparing arts administrators of the future, Design Arts Educ, 89; auth, Civilization and arts education, J Aesthetic Educ, 89; contribr, Future of the Arts: Public Policy & Arts Research, Praeger, 90

HUTCHINS, ROBIN
ART DEALER, GALLERY DIRECTOR
b Newark, NJ, May 26, 1938. *Study:* Nat Art Acad, Washington, DC, BFA, 59; Kean Col, Union, NJ, MA, 73. *Teaching:* Lectr, Montclair Hist Soc, NJ, 91; lectr computer art, Fedn, Artists, NJ, 91. *Awards:* ASID Presidential Citation, 90; Daily Point of Lite Presidential Award, AIDS Resource Found, White House, 91. *Mem:* Burgdorf Cult Comn (bd mem, 90-); Maplewood Cult Comn (co-chmn, 88-); Fed Artists NJ; Newark Mus Ballentine House Restoration Comt. *Specialty:* Contemporary American Art. *Mailing Add:* 2719 Bright Star Pl Las Cruces NM 88011

HUTCHINS-MALKMUS, JESSICA JACKSON
SCULPTOR, COLLAGE ARTIST
b Chicago, Ill, 1971. *Study:* Oberlin Coll, BA, 94; Sch Art Inst Chicago, MFA, 99. *Work:* Brooklyn Mus, NY; Eli and Edythe Broad Art Mus, East Lansing, Mich; The Hammer Mus, Los Angeles; Mus Modern Art, NY; Portland Art Mus, Ore; Tang Mus, Saratoga Springs, NY; Seattle Art Mus, Wash; Whitney Mus American Art, NY. *Exhib:* Read Gallery, Kent Inst Art & Design, Canterbury, UK, 2004; Gone Formalism, Inst Contemp Art, Univ Pa, 2006; Home/Office Landscapes, Chapman Univ, Calif, 2007; Begin Again Right Back There, White Columns, New York, 2008;

Whitney Biennial, Whitney Mus Am Art, New York, 2010; Jessica Jackson Hutchins: The Important Thing About a Chair, Atlanta Ctr Contemporary Art, Ga, 2011; Inst Contemporary Art, Boston, Mass, 2011; Hepworth Wakefield Mus, West Yorkshire, UK, 2013; Art Basel Statements with Laurel Gitlen, Basel, 2013; The Genres: Still Life Featuring Jessica Jackson Hutchins, Eli and Edythe Broad Art Mus, Mich State Univ, East Lansing, Mich, 2013; 55th Int Art Biennale, Venice, 2013. *Bibliog:* Aofie Rosenmeyer (auth), Art Basel, Art Agenda, 6/13/2013; Chris Sharp (auth), Basel Round Up, Art Agenda, 6/15/2013; Linda Yablonsky (auth), Way Out West, Artforum, 6/17/2013; Mark Brown (auth), Saatchi Gallery Hosts Display of Dictators in their Youth, The Guardian, 6/17/2013; Ben Luke (auth), Paper, Saatchi Gallery (review), London Evening Standard, 6/18/2013; and others. *Dealer:* Laurel Gitlen 122 Norfolk St New York NY 10002. *Mailing Add:* Laurel Gitlen Gallery 122 Norfolk St New York NY 10002

HUTCHINSON, PETER ARTHUR
CONCEPTUAL ARTIST, ENVIRONMENTAL ARTIST
b London, Eng, Mar 4, 1932. *Study:* Univ Ill, BFA, 60. *Work:* Mus Mod Art, NY; Mus Pompidou, Paris, France; Frac Limousin, France, 2006; ARP Mus; MOMCA Mus, Geneva; Ludwig Mus, Ger; Loulouse Mus, Fr; Dorothy and Herb Vogel; Paam Mus, Provincetown; Mus Art, Boston; Rice Mus, Tex; New Mus, NY; Krefeld Mus, Ger; Bank of Spain, Hartford Mus; Whitney Mus Am Art; Mus Fine Art, Boston; FRAC, France. *Comn:* Only in America, Sculpture, Philadelphia, 87; sculpture Basel Art Fair, Switzerland, 2000; thrown rope sculpture, Arp Mus, Ger, 2001. *Exhib:* Images: 2 Ocean Projects, 69 & Information, 70, Mus Mod Art; Nature & Art, Krefeld Mus, Haus Lange, Ger, 72; Stedelijk Mus, Amsterdam, 74; Venice Biennale, Am Pavilion, 79; James Mayor Gallery, London,Eng, 93; Holly Solomon Gallery, 91 & 94; Galerie Gaillard, Paris, 99; Galerie Bugdahn und Kaimer, 2000, 2005; Galerie Blancpain, Geneva, 2001, 2004; Frac Limousin, France, 2006; Behind the Facts, Mus Banco de Bogota, 2008; Freight & Volume, New York, 2008; 50 year retrospective, Arp Mus, Germany, 2009-2010; DNA Gallery, Mass, 2010, 2011; Liidwig Mus, Land Art, 2011 ; P420 Gallery, Bologna, Italy, 2011; Ends of the Earth, Moca, La, 2012; and others. *Teaching:* Instr, Sch Visual Arts, New York, NY, 77. *Awards:* A & E Gottlieb Found, 87; Nat Endowment Arts Individual Artist Award, 74; Krasner-Pollack Grant, 89. *Bibliog:* Scheldahl (auth), Breadworks as earth works, NY Times, 69; Back to nature, Time, 6/70; Carter Ratcliff, Peter Hutchinson, Art in Am, 12/2002. *Mem:* Am Rock Garden Soc. *Media:* Mixed Media; Photograph collage; Thrown Rope land sculptures. *Specialty:* Art. *Interests:* Hist, botany, horticulture, chess and bridge. *Publ:* Auth, Earth in upheaval, Arts, 68; Science fiction: an aesthetic for science, Art Int, 68; Is there life on earth, 68 & Foraging: being an account of a hike through the snow-mass wilderness as a work of art, 72, Art Am; Alphabet Cottage Book, OONA Press, Ger, 80; Dissolving Clouds, Provincetown Arts Press, 94; Undersea Sculpture, 2d edit, 2002; auth, Thrown Rope, Blind Spot Mag & Princeton Archit Press, 2006; auth, Night Journ, Nick Lawrence; Gallery A, Amsterdam, 2011; Journal, Galerie A, Amsterdam (book). *Dealer:* Galerie Bugdahn, Kaimer Germany; Blancpain/Stepczynski Geneva; Freight & Volume Gallery New York NY; Mayor Gallery London. *Mailing Add:* 10 Holway Ave Provincetown MA 02657

HUTCHISON, JANE CAMPBELL
EDUCATOR, HISTORIAN
b Washington, DC, July 20, 1932. *Study:* Western Md Col, BA (cum laude), 54; Oberlin Col, With Wolfgang Stechow, MA, 58; Kunsthist Inst, Utrecht, with J G van Gelder, 60-61; Univ Wis, with James S Watrous, PhD, 64. *Work:* Pennell Collection, Libr Cong, Washington, DC. *Exhib:* US Nat Printmakers, Libr Cong, 56. *Collection Arranged:* Dutch & Flemish Paintings from Private Collections, 74 & Graphic Art in the Age of Martin Luther, 83, Elvehjem Mus, Univ Wis, Madison. *Pos:* Libr asst, Toledo Mus Art, Ohio, 58-59; consult to Rijksprentenkabinet, Amsterdam & Stadelsches Kunstinstitut, Frankfurt, 85; consult, Cincinnati Art Mus, 91-92; consult, US Nat Gallery; consult, Federal Ct, Southern District of NY, 2001. *Teaching:* Instr art hist, Univ Wis, Madison, 63-64, from asst prof to assoc prof, 64-75, prof, 75-2011, emerita, 2012-, & dept chmn, 77-80 & 92; vis asst prof, Tyler Sch Art, Temple Univ, summer 67. *Awards:* Fulbright Fel, 60-61; Nat Endowment Humanities Grant, 83; Am Coun Learned Soc Grant, 84; Alumni award, Western Maryland Coll, (now Macdaniel Coll), 85; Deutscher Akademischer Austauschdienst (DAAD), 89. *Mem:* Coll Art Asn; Medieval Acad Am; Midwest Art Hist Soc (secy-treas 81-83, pres 83-); Historians Netherlandish Art (treas, 94-98); Am Asn Mus; Print Coun Am; St Andrew's Soc Madison (pres 2009-); Univ Club (bd dirs, past pres, 78). *Media:* Intaglio. *Res:* Late fifteenth and early sixteenth century Dutch and German engravings. *Interests:* Opera, German Lieder. *Publ:* Ed, Early German Artists: The Illustrated Bartsch, Plate, Vols 8 & 9, Commentary, Vol 9, Part II & Vol 8, Part I, Abaris, 80, 81, 91 & 96; auth, Albrecht Durer: A Biography, Princeton Univ Press, 90; Six Centuries of Master Prints: Treasures of the Herbert Greer French Collection, Cincinnati Art Mus, 93; Schongauer Copies and Forgeries, In: Colloque Internationale Schongauer, Mus d'Unterlinden, Colmar, France, 94; Campas Verlag, Ger ed, Frankfurt Am Main, 94; auth, Albrecht Durer: A Guide to Research, Taylor & Francis, NY/London, 2000; Oxford Univ Press Online, Art History: Albrecht Durer. *Mailing Add:* 8101 Connecticut Ave #N503 Chevy Chase MD 20815

HUTT, LEE
SCULPTOR, PHOTOGRAPHER
b New York, NY. *Study:* Columbia Univ, MS; New Sch; Univ Lourain, Belg, Art Cert. *Exhib:* Ann Exhib, Nat Sculpture Soc, NY, 1996-2002, 2005; Contemp Sculpture, Chesterwood Nat Trust, Lennox, Mass, 1997, 2000; Ann Exhib, Allied Artists of Am, NY, 1998-2006; Ann Exhib, Pen & Brush, NY, 1999-2005; Ann Exhib, Brookgreen Gardens, SC, 2000-2002; Changing the Am Landscape thru Sculpture, Ind Univ, South Bend, Ind, 2003. *Pos:* Sculpture chair, Allied Artists of Am, NY, 2005-. *Awards:* Ann Award Show, Nat Sculpture Soc, 1996, 2000; Pen & Brush, Ann Exhib, Pen & Brush, 1999, 2000, 2001; Medal of Honor, Ann Exhib, Catharine Lorillard Wolfe, 2000. *Mem:* Nat Sculptor Soc; Catharine Lorillard Wolfe Club; Allied Artist Am (sculpture chair), 2005-; Pen & Brush Inc; Acad Artists Asn; Audubon Artists Inc. *Media:* Clay, Bronze and Plaster. *Mailing Add:* 106 Woodbridge St South Hadley MA 01075

HUTTER, JEAN M
PAINTER, JEWELER
b Scranton, Pa June 25, 1948. *Study:* Self taught. *Exhib:* Sole Exhib, Ocean Co Artists Guild, Island Heights, NJ, 2003; La Watercolor Soc 34th Int Exhib, New Orleans, La, 2004; Biennial Juried Show, Noyes Mus Art, Oceanville, NJ; NJ Watercolor Soc 65th Ann Opened Juried Exhib, 2007; 15th Ann Open Juried Show, Monmouth Mus, Lincroft, NJ 2007. *Awards:* Holbein Merit Award, La Watercolor Soc, 2004; Sylvox Scientific Award, NJ Watercolor Soc, 2004; Nicholas Reale Mem Award, NJ Watercolor Soc, 2007; Abstract Award, Guild Creative Arts, 2007. *Mem:* Noyes Mus Art (Signature Mem),; Ocean Co Artists Guild; Guild Creative Arts. *Media:* Acrylic, Mixed Media. *Mailing Add:* 1662 Hidden Ln Lakewood NJ 08701

HWANG, KAY
SCULPTOR, PRINTMAKER
Study: Southern Ill Univ, Carbondale, BFA, 1994; Univ Ga, Athens, MFA, 2000. *Work:* Fidelity Investment, Pa; Ga Mus Fine Arts; Atlanta Hartsfield Airport; Alton & Bird, Atlanta; King & Spalding, Atlanta. *Exhib:* Solo exhibs, Dalton Gallery, Agnes Scott Coll, Ga, 2000, Cheekwod Mus Art, Nashville, 2001, Montgomery Coll Gallery, Md, 2003, Md Art Place, Balitmore, 2004; Do It, Atlanta Coll Art Gallery, Ga, 2000; Fifth Biennial, AIR Gallery, New York, 2003; CLAY, Mus Contemp Art, Atlanta, Ga, 2003; Works on Paper, Park Ave Armory, New York, 2005; Multiplicity, Contemporary Ceramic Sculpture, Portland Art Ctr, Ore, 2006-07. *Awards:* Individual Artist Grant, Md State Art Coun, Balitmore, 2006; Pollock-Krasner Found Grant, 2008. *Bibliog:* Pamela Blume Leonard (auth), Ceramics a Welcome Break from Commerce, Altanta Jour Constitution, 7/14/2000; Stephanie Bowman (auth), The Truth About Beauty, Sculpture Mag, 3/2001; Sarah Schaffer (auth), Disparate Styles, Techniques, and Subject Matter, Baltimore Sun, 7/17/2003; Amy Grimm (auth), Multiplicity: Contemporary Ceramic Sculpture, Artlies, No 51, 2006. *Dealer:* Goya Contemporary 3000 Chestnut Ave Baltimore MD 21211; Pentimenti Gallery 145 N Second St Philadelphia PA 19106

HYAMS, HARRIET
STAINED GLASS ARTIST, SCULPTOR
b Jersey City, NJ, 1929. *Study:* Rutgers Univ, BA, 50; Columbia Univ, MA, 72; with Zorach, J Hovannes, Marshall Glasier, Lorrie Goulet. *Work:* Delta Dental Health Plan of NJ; Columbia Univ. *Comn:* SW Ohio Senior Citizens Inc, Springdale, Ohio, 77; stained glass windows, New Dorp High Sch, Staten Island, NY, 82; stained glass windows, St Vartanantz Church, Ridgefield, NJ, 83; stained glass wall, Harcourt Brace Jovanovich, Orlando, Fla, 84; stained glass skylight for sailing yacht, pvt comn, 91; stained glass windows for Jewish Cadet Chapel, West Point, NY, 98; stained glass windows, Dominican Congregation of Our Lady of the Rosary, Sparkill, NY, 2001; etched folding doors for Trinity Luthern Church, Tenafly, NJ, 2003; stained glass windows for Jersey City Med Ctr (Wilzig Hosp), 2004; Two stained glass windows, Palisades Free Libr, Palisades, NY, 2008; Stained glass, Temple Beth Shalom, Cayman Brac, Cayman Islands, 2010; 12 stained glass windows, Blauvelt Libr, Blauvelt, NY, 2011. *Exhib:* Stained Glass Int, NY, 82; Glass Am, NY, 84; Solo Exhib: Harriet Hyams: Stained Glass and Sculpture, Rockland Ctr Arts, Nyack, NY, 88; Montclair Art Mus; Newark Art Mus; welded sculpture & stained glass, Blue Hill Cult Ctr, Pearl River, NY, 2005-06; Then and Now, St Thomas Aquinas Col, Sparkill, NY, 2008; Hist Soc Rockland County, 2010. *Pos:* Co-cur, Catherine Konner Sculpture Park Rockland Ctr for the Arts, Nyack, NY, 2005-06. *Teaching:* Instr stained glass, Columbia Univ, 72-74. *Awards:* Purchase Award, Columbia Univ, Arthur Wesley Dow Award, 72; Compendium 1976, Corning Mus, 76; Bene Awards, Ministry & Liturgy Mag, 2002; Keep Rockland Beautiful (Public Arts Award), NY, 2007; Nominee, County Executive Award (Visual arts), 2008. *Bibliog:* Yehuda Yaniv (auth), Film on Stained Glass, Ed Devel Corp, 72; Richard Avidon (auth), Harriet Hyams, Bergdorf Goodman, Glass Arts Mag, 76; Richard Hoover (auth), Dancing on the ceiling, Stained Glass Quart, fall 92; Lucartha Kohler (auth), Women working in glass, 2003; Stained Glass, Fall, 2006; Robert Sowers (auth), The Language of Stained Glass. *Mem:* Stained Glass Asn Am; UAHC Accredited List of Synagogue Artists & Craftsmen; Interfaith Forum on Relig, Art and Archit, Affiliate of AIA; American Glass Guild. *Media:* Stained Glass. *Publ:* Art in Architecture, Glass Mag, 1/78; auth, A sculptor turns to stained glass, Stained Glass, 82; The Chairman's Office, 85-86; From Gallery to Gallery, Stained Glass Quart, summer 89; front cover, Extending the Shade (by Betty S Flowers), 90; Stained Glass Quar, fall, 92, winter, 93, spring, 2003, fall, 2006; front cover, Blue Lioness (by Betty S Flowers), 2002; Michele Cohen (auth), Public Art for Public Schools, full page colored image, 2009; Hook, March/April, 2011. *Mailing Add:* PO Box 178 Palisades NY 10964

HYDE, JAMES
PAINTER
b Philadelphia, Pennsylvania, 1958. *Study:* Univ Rochester, 1975-77. *Work:* Mus Mod Art, NY; Guggenheim Mus Art, New York. *Exhib:* Solo exhibs include St Peter's Church at Citicorp, New York, 1982, John Good Gallery, New York, 1988, 1989, 1991, 1993, Queens Mus, NY, 1997, Zwemmer Gallery, London, 2001, In The Future We Will Know More, Reynolds Gallery, Richmond, VA, 2005, Glass Box Paintings, 2007, Contemp Links 4, San Diego Mus Art, 2006, Painting Then for Now, David Krut Projs, New York, 2007; two-person exhibs include Zurich, Switzerland, (with Barney Kulok), 2008; group exhibs include Photocollect, New York, 1981; Gray Matter, Barbara Guggenheim, New York, 1983; Possible Things, Bardamu Gallery, New York, 1994; Baumgartner Galleries, Washington, 1995; Farbe, Galerie Art In, Nuremberg, Germany, 1995; Painting Outside Painting, Corcoran Gallery Art,

Washington, 1995, Corcoran Collects, 1998; Works on Paper, Gallery MC, New York, 2005; Archicule, Makor Gallery, New York, 2006; Citadel 1 Front Room/Killing Room, David Risley Gallery, London, 2007; Photograph as Canvas, Aldrich Contemp Art Mus, Ridgefield, CT, 2007; Building Spills & Spins Past Midnight, Galerie Les Filles Du Calvaire, Brussels, 2007. *Awards:* Joan Mitchell Found Fel, 2000; Greenwich House Pottery Artist Fel, 2002; Fallk Vis Artist Fel, 2004; John Simon Guggenheim Mem Found Fel, 2008. *Dealer:* Artware Editions 327 W 11th St New York NY 10014 . *Mailing Add:* Gallery MC 549 West 52nd Street New York NY 10019

HYDE, SCOTT
PHOTOGRAPHER, PRINTMAKER
b Montevideo, Minn, Oct 10, 1926. *Study:* Art Ctr Sch, Los Angeles; Columbia Univ, with Ralph Mayer; Art Students League. *Work:* Mus Mod Art, Metrop Mus Art, Int Ctr Photog, NY; Int Mus Photog, Rochester, NY; Bibliot Nat, Paris. *Exhib:* Synthetic Color, Southern Ill Univ, Carbondale, 74; Mirrors & Windows: Am Photog Since 1960, 78; Master Photogrs Focus Gallery, San Francisco, 81; Off the Press, Coll Art Gallery, State Univ NY, New Paltz, 84; City Light, Int Ctr Photog, 86; The Sense of Abstraction, Mus Mod Art, 60; Photog in the 20th Century, Nat Gallery, Canada, 67; Silver and Silk Photog Silk Screen Prints, Smithsonian Inst, 75; plus others. *Teaching:* Adj prof photog, Cooper Union, 68-70, New York Univ Exten, 71-72 & Manhattanville Col, 72-75. *Awards:* Guggenheim Fel, 65; Creative Artists Pub Serv Prog Grants, 72 & 75. *Bibliog:* Syl Labrot (auth), Scott Hyde photographs, Aperture, 70; Thomas Dugan (auth), Photography between covers, Light Impressions, 75; Naomi Rosenblum (auth), A World History of Photography, 84. *Mem:* Soc Photographic Edn. *Media:* Offset Lithography. *Publ:* CAPS Book, 75; Auth, Dust Map, 79; auth, The Real Great Society Album, 79. *Mailing Add:* 7411 Dreyfuss Dr Amarillo TX 79121-1411

HYDE, TIM
PHOTOGRAPHER
Study: Vassar Coll, New York, BA (History), 1992; Columbia Sch Arts, MFA, 2005. *Exhib:* Exhibits include Fuzzy Logic, Southern Exposure Gallery, San Francisco, 2001; Mediated Images, Nieman Gallery, New York, 2003; Video Wall Installation, Rudin Foundation, New York, 2004; Video Art, Outpost for Contemp Art, Los Angeles, 2005; Max Protetch Gallery, New York, 2007; Philadelphia Museum of Art, Live Cinema, 2008. *Awards:* Louis Comfort Tiffany Found Grants, 2008

HYLAND, DOUGLAS K S
MUSEUM DIRECTOR
b Salem, Mass, Oct 7, 1949. *Study:* Univ Pa, BA, 70; Univ Del, MA, 76, PhD, 80. *Pos:* Cur painting & sculpture, Spencer Mus Art, Univ Kans, 79-82; dir, Memphis Brooks Mus Art, 82-84, Birmingham Mus Art, 84-91, San Antonio Mus Art, 92-98, Fuller Mus Art, 98-99, New Britain Mus Am Art, 99-2009. *Teaching:* Asst prof art hist, Univ Kans, 79-82; vis prof, Southwestern Univ, Memphis, 83-84 & Univ Ala, 84-. *Awards:* Fels, Kress Found, 78 & Smithsonian Inst, 78-79 & 92; Chevalier Des Arts Et Lettres, 90. *Mem:* Coll Art Asn; Asn Art Mus; Am Asn Mus Dirs. *Res:* American and European painting and sculpture of the 19th and 20th centuries. *Publ:* Lorenzo Bartolint & American Sculptors, 86; Birmingham Photography Proj, 88; Anders Zorn, 89; Kelley Collection of African American Art, 94; 500 Years of French Art, 95; and others. *Mailing Add:* 56 Lexington St New Britain CT 06052

HYMAN, ISABELLE
HISTORIAN, EDUCATOR
b New York, NY, Apr 19, 1930. *Study:* Vassar Coll, BA, 51; Columbia Univ, MA, 55; Inst Fine Arts, NY Univ, MA, 66, PhD, 68. *Teaching:* From instr to assoc prof, NY Univ, 63-79, prof hist art, 79-, prof emer. *Awards:* Fel, Villa I Tatti, Florence, 72-73; John Simon Guggenheim Mem Found Fel, 88-89; Fel, Graham Found Advanced Studies Fine Arts, 88-89. *Mem:* Coll Art Asn (bd dir, 82-86); Soc Archit Historians (bd dir, 93-); Renaissance Soc Am. *Res:* Art and architecture in Renaissance Florence; archit of Marcel Breuer. *Publ:* Ed, Brunelleschi in Perspective, Prentice-Hall, 74; auth, Fifteenth Century Florentine Studies, Garland, 77; articles relating to Italian Renaissance art and the architecture of Marcel Breuer in scholarly journals; coauth, Architecture: From Pre-History to Post Modernism, Harry N Abrams Inc, 86. *Mailing Add:* New York University Fine Arts Dept 303 Main Bldg New York NY 10003

HYNES, FRANCES M
PAINTER
b New York, NY, Feb 20, 1945. *Study:* St Johns Univ, BA, Queens, NY, 66; NY Univ, MA, New York, 68; Acad Fine Arts, cert, Florence, Italy, 70; Art Students League, Studied with Robert Angeloch, Woodstock, NY, 72-73. *Work:* Brooklyn Mus, NY; Portland Mus Art, Portland, Maine; New Britain Mus Am Art, New Britain, Conn; Telfair Mus Art, Savannah, Ga; Nat Mus Women in the Arts, DC; Farn Sworth Art Mus, Maine; Newark Mus, NJ; Bates Coll, Mus Art, Maine; Kirkland Fine Arts Ctr, Milliken Univ, Ill. *Comn:* 30 foot long mural, Mary Dugans Restaurant, Litchfield, Conn, 88; series of watercolors for childrens wing, Bellevue Hospital, New York, 84. *Exhib:* Solo exhibs, Paintings, Inst Contemp Art, PS 1 Long Island City, NY, 80, Conversations: Recent Paintings, Springfield Mus Art, Ohio, 93, New Now, New Britain Mus Am Art, New Britain, Conn, 97, Dawn Chasing Night, Jacksonville Mus Contem Art, Fla, 98, Images of Events, 1989-1999, Ogunquit Mus Am Art, Maine, 99, Thought Charts, Visual Diaries, Suraci Gallery, Visual Arts Ctr, Marywood Univ, Scranton, Pa, 2003, Present Past, Past Present, Foreman Gallery, Anderson Ctr Arts, Yager Mus, Hartwick Coll, Oneonta, NY, 2003 ; Am Acad Arts & Letter, New York, 94, 2008; Nat Acad Design, New York, 2004, 2008. *Collection Arranged:* Romare Beardon; Ruben Nakian; Bob Blackburn's Print Making Workshop; Hanukkah Lamps, Jewish Mus, NY; Hughie Lee Smith; photographs, James Van der Zee. *Pos:* Visual Arts dir, Flushing Art Coun, Flushing, NY, 85-95; Visual Arts Consult, Queens Coun on the Arts, Queens, NY, 94-98; dir, Lucaks Gallery, Fairfield Univ, Fairfield, Conn, 99-2001. *Teaching:* assoc prof for painting & drawing, LaGuardia Community Coll, New York, 80, 98-; visiting artist prof for painting, Lahti Polytec Inst Fine Arts, Lahti, Finland, 2000; prof for painting, Savannah Coll Art & Design, 96-97; vis artist prof, Barren Coll Art, Ireland, Central Mich Univ, Ill State Univ. *Awards:* Nat Workspace Prog, PS 1 Contemp Art Ctr, NY, 76-78; Artist's Residency, Tyrone Gutherie Ctr, Newbliss, Co Monaghan, Ireland, 95; Artist's fel, Nat Endowment for the Arts, 80; artist's residency, the Cill Rialaig Proj, Ballinaskelligs Co Kerry, Ireland, 96; Edwin Palmer Mem Prize (painting), 183rd Ann: An Invitational Exhib of Contemp Am Art, Nat Acad Design, NY, 2008. *Bibliog:* Robert Kurtz (auth), 56 Nat Midyear Exhib, Butler Mus Am Art, Ohio, 92; Mark Chepp (auth), Conversations Recent Paintings, Springfield Mus Art, 93; Robert Henry Flood (auth), Dawn Chasing Night, Jacksonville Mus Contemp ARt, 98; Michael Culver (auth), Images & Events, Ogunquit Mus Art, 99; Mario Naves (auth), North Light, June Kelly Gallery, 2009; Edward Leffingwell (auth), Frances Hynes, June Kelly Gallery, Art in Am, 2009; Hearne Pardee, Frances Hynes: North Light Recent Painting, 2009. *Mem:* Prof Staff Congress, City Univ New York. *Media:* Oil paint, watercolor. *Dealer:* June Kelly Gallery 591 Bradway New York NY 10012

HYSON, JEAN
PAINTER
b Alvarado, Tex, Mar 4, 1931. *Study:* NY Univ with William Baziotes, 52; Art Students League with Yasuo Kuniyoshi, George Grosz & Harry Sternberg, 52-56. *Work:* Walter Barriese Collection, Metromedia, NY; Oakland Art Mus, Calif; Int Banking Ctr, Sutro, Madison, Pillsbury, Levi-Strauss, City of San Francisco, Bill Graham & Pac Bell, San Francisco, Calif; Santa Barbara Mus, Calif; Container Corp Am, Chicago. *Exhib:* One-person shows, San Francisco Mus Art, 67, Calif Palace of the Legion of Honor, 69, William Sawyer Gallery, San Francisco, 72, Richmond Art Mus, Calif, 77, Calif Med Asn, 87 & Nat Small Painting Exhib, Boise State Univ, Idaho, 91; Fine Arts Contemp Exhib, Northern Ill Univ, 69; California Artists, Western Art Mus Asn, 70 & 92; Mus Mod Art Rental & Sales Gallery, NY, 71; Collectors Gallery, Oakland Mus, 86. *Teaching:* Instr & Artist in Res, Mex Exten, Calif Col Arts & Crafts, Critiques & Painting, Oakland, 70-74. *Awards:* Adolph & Esther Gottlieb Found Grant, 91; Pollock-Krasner Found Grant, 96. *Mem:* Artists Equity Asn, Washington, DC; Mechanics Inst San Francisco; San Francisco Women Artists. *Media:* Oil, Acrylic, Watercolor. *Specialty:* To provide juried shows. Non-profit gallery. *Interests:* Chess, volunteering, special events, San Francisco Symphony. *Dealer:* SFWA Gallery San Francisco CA

I

IANNETTI, PASQUALE FRANCESCO PAOLO
ART DEALER, COLLECTOR
b Florence, Italy, Apr 10, 1940; US citizen. *Study:* Univ Florence; Acad di Belle Arti, Florence; Univ Minn, Minneapolis. *Pos:* Pres, Pasquale Iannetti Inc Galleries, San Francisco. *Teaching:* Lectr fine prints, Col Marin, Kentfield & Univ Calif, Davis. *Mem:* Int Soc Appraisers; Graphic Art Coun, Los Angeles Co Mus & Achenbach Found, San Francisco; Museo Italo Americano, San Francisco. *Specialty:* Fine original prints, drawings and other unique works form the sixteenth century through the twentieth century. *Collection:* Contemporary prints, drawings and paintings; Pre-Columbian and African art; antiquities

IANNONE, DOROTHY
PAINTER, WRITER
b Boston, Mass, Aug 9, 1933. *Study:* Boston Univ BA (phi beta kappa), 57; Brandeis Univ, studied literature & criticism with J V Cunningham, Phillip Rahv & Irving Howe, 58. *Work:* Nat Mus Women Arts, Washington; Mus Drawings & Prints (Kupferstichkabinet), Berlin, Ger; Ludwig Mus Collection, Aachen, Ger; Mus Mod Art, Saint-Etienne, France; Kunst Mus, Basel, Switz. *Exhib:* Boxes (Boites), Mus Mod Art, Paris, France, 76; Daily Bul, Foundation Maeght-St Paul De Vence, Mus Mod Art, Paris, France, 76; Dorothy Iannone, Ludwig Mus (Neue Galerie Stadt Aachen), Ger, 80; Listening with the Eyes, Mus Mod Art, Paris, France, 80; Artists' Books, Centre Pompidou (Beaubourg), Paris, France, 85; The Caravan Passes And, Mus Mod & Contemp Art, Nice, France, 91; one-woman show, New Soc Fine Arts (NGBK), Berlin, 97 & Mus Mod Art, Arnhem, The Neth, 98; Sprengel Mus (w Dieter Roth), Hanover, Ger, 2005; Whitney Biennial, Whitney Mus Art, NYC, 2006. *Pos:* guest artist, Rijs Acad, Amsterdam, 82 & 84, Jan Van Eyck Acad, Maastricht, Holland, 82 & 83 & Enschede Acad, Holland, 83. *Teaching:* instr open workshop, Col Art, West Berlin, 77 & 79. *Awards:* Berlin Artists' Prog (Deutscher Akademischer Austauschdienst), 76; Art Found Bonn Grant, 88; Women Artists Prog, Berlin Senate, Ger, 94. *Bibliog:* Barbara Wien (auth), John Lennon & Cleopatra, Tip, Berlin, 6/89; Ulrike Abel (auth), Love is Forever Isn't it, Berlin, 97; Annette Tietenberg (auth), Can Painting Really be a Sin?, Frankfurter Allgemeine, 6/97; Dieter Roth & Dorothy Iannone, Spengel Museum, Hanover, 2005. *Mem:* Phi Beta Kappa. *Media:* Acrylic, Gouache. *Publ:* auth, Story of Bern, Dieter Rot, Dusseldorf, 70; The Berlin Beauties, Mary Dorothy Verlag, Berlin, 78; The Whip, Rainer Verlag, Berlin, 80; Censorship & the Impressible Drive toward Love and Divinity, Ars Viva, Berlin, 82; 720 Courting Ajaxander, Haus am Lutzow Platz, Berlin 93; Dieter & Dorothy, Bilger Verlag, Zurich, 2001. *Dealer:* Andy Jullien Gallery Rami Strasse 18 8001 Zurich Switzerland. *Mailing Add:* Olivaer Platz 16 Berlin 10707 Germany

ICE, JOYCE
MUSEUM DIRECTOR
Study: Univ Texas, Austin, PhD (Anthropology & Folklore). *Pos:* Mgr, develop of prog, Milner Plaza, Santa Fe Int Folk Art Market; panelist, Nat Endowments; folklorist, Fel County Hist Asn, Delhi, NY; asst dir, Mus Int Folk Art, Santa Fe, 1990, dir, 1999-. *Mem:* State Art Coun, NMex, Colo, NY; bd mem, Fund for Folk Culture. *Mailing Add:* Museum of International Folk Art PO Box 2087 Santa Fe NM 87504

ICHIKAWA, ETSUKO
GLASS BLOWER
b Tokyo, Japan. *Study:* Tokyo Zokei Univ, Japan, BFA (painting), 1987. *Work:* Sumitomo Corp Am; Microsoft Corp . *Comn:* Hinode Indusl Arts, Hokkaido, Japan; Four Seasons Hotel, Hong Kong; Convington Middle Sch, Wash State Arts Comn; Gallia Hotel, Milan, Italy. *Exhib:* Apex in LA, Angels Gate Cult Ctr Gallery, San Pedro, Calif, 2002; LELA, Mod Art Gallery, Los Angeles, 2003; solo exhibs, Kirkland Arts Ctr Gallery, Wash, 2003 & Bellevue Arts Mus, 2008; She Stole the Show, Capitol Hill Arts Ctr, Seattle, 2004; Impressed, Arts Coun Snohomish Co, Everett, Wash, 2006; The East and the East, Ueno Royal Mus, Tokyo, Japan, 2008; Elusive Elements, Mus Northwest Art, La Conner, Wash, 2009. *Awards:* CityArtist Projets Grant, Seattle Office Arts & Cult Affairs, 2006; Spl Projects Grant, Bellevue Arts Comn, Wash, 2008; Pollock-Krasner Found Grant, 2008. *Bibliog:* Matthew Kangas (auth), A delightful show of team spirit at SOIL, Seattle Times, 1/20/2006; Adriana Grant (auth), Not Pyromaniacl Art, Seattle Weekly, 4/4/2007; Kristen Peterson (auth), Marking moments in time in two styles, Las Vegas Sun, 7/24/2008; Victoria Josslin (auth), Afterburn, Glass Quart, 2009. *Dealer:* Davidson Galleries 313 Occidental Ave S Seattle WA 98104

IDA, SHOICHI
PAINTER, PRINTMAKER
b Kyoto, Japan, Sept 13, 1941. *Study:* Kyoto Munic Univ Art, BFA (oil painting), 65. *Work:* Nat Mus Mod Art Tokyo, Japan; Mus Mod Art, NY; Mus Cincinnati, Ohio; Mus Mod Art, Chicago; Mus Mod Art, San Francisco. *Exhib:* Ten Selected Artists, Mus Mod Art, Chicago, 80; Japanese Prints of the 20th Century, Portland Mus Art & St Louis Mus, Ore, 83; 25th Anniversary Show for Crown Point Press, Mus Mod Art, NY, 87; Contemp Art Fair, Los Angeles, 88; retrospective exhibs, Mus Portland, Ore, 89 & Art Mus Cincinnati, Ohio, 90. *Media:* Multi Media. *Mailing Add:* c/o Irene Drori 138 N Orange Dr Los Angeles CA 90036-3015

IGLESIAS, LISA
PRINTMAKER, BOOK ARTIST
b New York, NY, 1979. *Study:* Harpur Coll, SUNY, Binghamton, BA (summa cum laude), 2001; Coll Fine Arts, Univ Fla, MFA, 2006. *Exhib:* Deconstruction and Reconstruction: The Family Experience, Fla State Univ Mus, 2006; Heads and Shoulders, Spin Gallery, New York, 2007; Art All-State Group Exhib, Worcester Art Mus, Mass, 2008; solo exhibs, Pratt at MWP Inst, Utica, NY, 2008, CIte Int des Art, Paris, France, 2009, Atrium Gallery, Jersey City Mus, 2010, Gallery Art & Design, Univ Ctrl Mo, 2010; Queens Int 4, Queens Mus Art, 2009; Pages, Paragraph Gallery, Kans City, Mo, 2010. *Awards:* Joan Mitchell Found Grant, 2006-07; Brundage Found FEl, Vt Studio Ctr, 2007; NY Found Arts Fel, 2009. *Bibliog:* Kevin Murphy (auth), Green Road to Sumter: Charleston artists take part in the Green Revival, Charleston City Paper, 10/17/2007; Kim Levin (auth), Young Curatores, New Ideas II, ARTnews, 4/9/2009; John Hansen (auth), Off-Easel, The Sedalia Democrat, 3/10/2010

IGO, PETER ALEXANDER
PRINTMAKER, PAINTER
b Riverhead, NY, Jan 9, 1956. *Study:* Colo Rocky Mountain Sch, Carbondale, 71-74; apprentice to Thomas Benton, printmaker, Aspen, Colo, 74; Univ Calif Los Angeles, 75; Univ NMex, 76-78; Univ Calif, Berkeley, 79; Belles Artes Nat Fine Arts Sch Mex, lithography with Ralph Bishop, 86; studied non-silver photog with Debra Flynn, 88; Indian Arts Mus NMex, Japanese rice paper making with Suki Hughes, 89. *Work:* Mus NMex, Sch Am Res & Sen Jeff Bingaman, Santa Fe, NMex; Maxwell Mus Anthrop, Univ NMex, Mountain States Insurance Co & Prudential Bache, Albuquerque, NMex; Sen Jeff Bingamann & World Bank, Washington; Verde Valley Sch, Sedona, Ariz; First Nat Bank & Mission Insurance, Phoenix, Ariz. *Comn:* Paper cast petroglyph, E F Hutton, Santa Fe, NMex, 85; paper cast petroglyph, Hilton Hotel, 85 & Quail Run Develop, Santa Fe, 88. *Exhib:* Solo exhibs, Primitive i gallery, Chicago, 79, Sch Am Res, Santa Fe, 84, Bank Santa Fe, 84, St Johns Col, 86; Govs Gallery, NMex, 89; Best of the Southwest, Dallas, 91; Am Wildlands: An Artistic Inspiration, Santa Fe, 94; El Dorado Arts Show, Santuario de Guadalupe, Santa Fe, 95. *Pos:* Master serigraph printer, ltd eds, 87-96. *Teaching:* Part time instr, screen printing, Verde Valley Sch, Sedona, Ariz, 80-82 & 84. *Media:* Acrylic on Paper & Canvas, Serigraphy

IHARA, MICHIO
SCULPTOR
b Paris, France, Nov 17, 1928; US citizen. *Study:* Tokyo Univ Fine Arts, BFA, 53; Mass Inst Technol, Fulbright Fel; also with Gyorgy Kepes, 61. *Work:* Wind, Wind, Wind, Kanagawa Mus Mod Art, Kamakura, Japan. *Comn:* Metal screen, Rockefeller Ctr, 78; suspended sculpture, Neiman-Marcus, Beverly Hills, 79; Pavilion Hotel, Singapore, 82, AT&T Long Lines, Atlanta, 82 & Marriott Hotel, NY, 85; plaza sculpture, New World Ctr, Hong Kong, 82; wall sculpture, Harvard Univ, Mass, 86; Tokyo City Hall, 91; and others. *Exhib:* Selection 64, Inst Contemp Art, Boston, 64 & Boston Celebrations, 75; Trends Contemp Art, Kyoto Mus Mod Art, 68; Ann Exhib, Nat Inst Arts & Lett & Am Acad Arts & Lett, 73; Japanese Artists in Am, Tokyo Mus Mod Art & Kyoto Mus Mod Art, 73-74; Solo exhibs, Staempfli Gallery, NY, 77, 80 & 84. *Pos:* Fel, Ctr Advan Visual Studies, Mass Inst Technol, 70-75. *Teaching:* Instr basic design, Musashino Fine Arts Univ, Tokyo, 66-68. *Awards:* Graham Found Fel, 64; Ann Award, Am Acad Arts & Lett & Nat Inst Arts & Lett, 73; First Prize, Fitchburg Libr Art Competition, Mass Coun Arts & Humanities, 74; others. *Mem:* Japanese Artists Asn. *Media:* Stainless Steel, Brass, Copper, Gold. *Mailing Add:* 63 Wood St Concord MA 01742

IIMURA, TAKAHIKO
FILMMAKER, VIDEO ARTIST
b Tokyo, Japan, Feb 20, 1937. *Study:* Keio Univ, Tokyo, BA (political sci), 59. *Work:* Anthology Film Arch, Metrop Mus Art & Whitney Mus Art, NY; Centre Beaubourg des Art Plastiques, Paris; Royal Film Arch, Brussels, Belg; Neuer Berliner Kunstverein, Berlin. *Comn:* Film/video, Metrop Mus Prog for Art on Film, NY, 89. *Exhib:* Japanese Experimental Films, Mus Mod Art, NY, 66; Solo exhibs, Mus Mod Art, NY, 75, Whitney Mus Am Art, 79, Millennium, NY, 92, Mus Sound & Image, Sao Paulo, Ariz State Univ, 92, Electronic Cafe, Santa Monica, 93, Mint Mus Art, Charlotte, NC, 94, Tokyo Metrop Mus Photog, 95, Japan Cult Ctr, Rome, 97, Lux Ctr, London, 98 & Filmmuseum, Munich, 98; Pandemonium Festival, ICA, London, 96; New Zealand Film Festivals, Auckland, 98; Int Kurzfilmtage, Oberhausen, 98; Videonale, Bonn, 98. *Teaching:* Vis tutor film, Schiller Col, Berlin, 73, Univ Minn 75-76; vis asst prof film, Kent State Univ, 76; State Univ NY, Binghampton, 78; vis prof, Osaka Univ Arts, Osaka, 85-92; prof, Nagoya Zokei Univ Arts & Design, 92-2000 & Tokyo Poly Univ, 2000-. *Awards:* Japan Found Fel, Tokyo, 82, 85, 89, 90 & 92; Gt Brit-Sasakawa Found Fel, Tokyo, 98; Japan Art Funds Fel, Tokyo, 94, 97 & 98. *Bibliog:* Carl Eugene Loeffler (auth), Media World of Takahiko Iimura II, Kirin Plaza Osaka, 93; Bruno Di Marino (auth), From Time to See You, Takahiko Iimura, Istituto Giapponese di Cultura, Diagonale, 97; Makolm Le Graice (auth), Takahiko Iimura at the Lux, 98. *Mem:* Filmmakers Coop, NY; Japan Soc Image Sci, Tokyo; London Film Makers Coop. *Media:* Film, video. *Publ:* Auth, Eizo Jikken No Tameni (For Visual Experimentation), Seido Sha, Tokyo, 86; Film and Video of Takahiko Iimura, Anthology Film Arch, New York, 90; CD-ROM: Eizo Jikken No Temeni (For Visual Experimentation), Euphonic, 97; CD-ROM: Observer/Observed, Banff Art Ctr & Euphonic, 98. *Mailing Add:* 115 E 9th St No 18H New York NY 10003

IKEDA, YOSHIRO
CERAMIST, EDUCATOR
b Kushikino-City, Kagoshima, Japan, Apr 10, 1947; US citizen. *Study:* Portland State Univ, Ore, BS (painting & drawing), 70; Kyoto City Univ Fine Art, Japan, cert, 73; Univ Calif, Santa Barbara, MFA, 77. *Work:* Japanese Govt Ministry Educ, Tokyo; Kyoto City Univ Fine Art, Japan; Utah State Univ, Logan; Calif Polytech State Univ, San Luis Obispo; Topeka Pub Libr, Kans; & others. *Exhib:* El Paso Mus, Tex, 79; Foothills Art Ctr, Denver, 79; Cooperstown Art Asn, NY, 81; Purdue Univ Gallery, West Lafayette, Ind, 81; War Mem Mus, Aukland, NZ, 81; Wichita Mus, Kans, 81; Jinro Int Ceramics Art, Korea; The Fletcher Brown Build Int Pottery Show, 87, 88, 92 & 95. *Teaching:* Instr ceramics, Utah State Univ, 73-74 & Ventura Col, 77-78; asst prof ceramics, Kans State Univ, 78-, area head, 81-, prof ceramics, 89. *Awards:* First Place Award, Austin Art Asn, 78; Juror's Award, Calif Polytech State Univ, 78; Merit Award, Fletcher Brownbuilt Pottery Guild, 81. *Mem:* Nat Coun Educ Ceramic Arts; Kans Artist Craftsman Asn; Kans Designer Craftsman Asn. *Media:* Clay. *Publ:* Auth, Asymmetrical thrown form, Ceramic Monthly, 6/78. *Dealer:* Marcia Rodell Gallery 11714 San Vicente Blvd Los Angeles CA 90049

ILES, CHRISSIE
CURATOR
Study: Bristol Univ, BA; City Univ, London, grad studies. *Collection Arranged:* Co-cur, Whitney Biennial, 2004 & 2006; co-cur (with Eric de Bruyn), Flashing into the Shadows - The Artist's Film after Pop and Minimalism 1966-1976; cur, Scream and Scream Again: Film in Art; Signs of the Times: Film, Video and Slide Installations in Britain in the 1980s; Into the Light: The Projected Image in Am Art 1964-1977, NY, 2002 (best exhib in NY City, Int Asn Art Critics); Jack Goldstein - Films and Performance; The Origin of the Night (Lothar Baumgarten); 31 (Lorna Simpson); Blind Side (Liisa Roberts); Ana Mendieta: Earth Body; War! Protest in Am 1965-2004; James Lee Byars: The Perfect Silence. *Pos:* Head of exhibs, Mus Modern Art, Oxford, Eng, 1988-97; cur, Whitney Mus Am Art, NY, 1997-; mem adv comt, NY State Council on Arts. *Teaching:* Adj prof, Columbia Univ; faculty mem, Ctr for Curatorial Studies, Bard Col; external examiner, Goldsmith's Col, London. *Mailing Add:* Whitney Museum of American Art 945 Madison Ave New York NY 10021

IMANA, JORGE GARRON
PAINTER, MURALIST
b Sucre, Bolivia, Sept 20, 1930; US citizen. *Study:* Univ San Francisco Xavier, Sucre, MA; Academia de Bellas Artes. *Work:* Nat Mus, La Paz, Bolivia; Univ San Francisco Xavier Mus, Sucre; Nat Mus, Bogota, Colombia; Casa de la Cult, Quito, Ecuador; Bolivian Embassy, Moscow & Washington DC. *Comn:* Hist mural, Bolivian Govt, Junin Col, Sucre, 58; History of Education in Bolivia (mural), comn by Bolivian Govt, Padilla Col, Sucre, 59; Social History in Peru (mural), Constructors Union, Lima, Peru, 61; Ciudad de Dios Sch (mural), comn by students' parents, Lima, 62. *Exhib:* Nat Salon, La Paz, 62; Latin Am Show, Fine Arts Gallery, San Diego, 64; Bolivian Paintings, Mus of Mod Art, Paris, France, 73 & Nat Gallery, Warsaw, Poland, 75; House of Friendship of the Peoples, Moscow, 75; Gallery IDB, Washington, DC, 76; plus 102 solo exhibs. *Teaching:* Prof drawing, Univ San Francisco Xavier, Sucre, 54-60; prof drawing & watercolor, Nat Acad, La Paz, 60-62; dir art dept, Inst Normal Superior, La Paz, 60-62. *Awards:* Nat Award, Nat Show, La Paz, Bolivian Govt, 62; Watercolor Award, Nat Watercolor Show, Lima, Peru, Watercolor Soc, 62; Purchase Awards Oil & Watercolor, Ann Show, San Diego Art Inst, 64. *Bibliog:* Bits of Sucre Bollivia, Order of Gram Mariscal de Apacucho, 1.910. *Mem:* La Jolla Art Asn; San Diego Art Inst; Accademia Italia delle Artie del Lavoro. *Mailing Add:* 2510 Torrey Pine Rd Apt 212 La Jolla CA 92037-3450

IMLAH, RACHEL CRAWFORD
PAINTER, PHOTOGRAPHER
b Asheville, NC, Dec 7, 1940. *Study:* Univ Tex scholar, El Paso, 57-58; Acad Fine Arts scholar, Naples, Italy, 58-59; Furman Univ, Greenville, SC, BA, 62. *Work:* Acad Fine Arts, Naples, Italy; Columbia Mus Art, SC; Thompson Gallery Permanent Collection, Furman Univ, Greenville, SC; and others. *Comn:* Nat advert poster, World Book Encyl, El Paso, Tex, 57; socio-political cartoonist, Univ Tex, El Paso, 57-58, Furman Univ, Greenville, SC, 60-62, World Bank, Washington, DC, 74-78. *Exhib:* Carolina's Fourth Coll Art Ann, Columbia Mus Art, SC, 62; Jeddah Fine Arts Soc Third Ann Int Exhib, Jeddah Dome, Saudi Arabia, 79; solo exhibs, Buttonwood Tree, Middletown, Conn, 93, Brownsboro Gallery, Louisville, 96, Galleria Palacio, El Paso, 97 Art Int Asheville, NC, 97; and other group shows. *Collection Arranged:* First Ann

Saudi Arabian Beaux Arts Exhib, Kings Pavilion, Yanbu, Saudi Arabia, 82. *Pos:* Cartoon ed, Univ Tex, El Paso, 57-58, Furman Univ, Greenville, SC, 60-62; tech illusr, WR Grace & Co, Greenville, SC, 62-63; ed consultant, Washington, DC, 71-78. *Teaching:* Instr oil painting, US Army, Ft Bliss, Tex, 57 & pvt individuals, New Orleans, Washington & Saudi Arabia, 64-82. *Bibliog:* Anonymous (auth), Maturity in Exhibit at Furman, Greenville Piedmont, 5/8/62; Jim Landers (auth), Pristine pictures at an exhibition, Arab News, 4/9/79 & 4/11/79; Julie Lynch (auth), Artist helps out, Middletown Press, 6/18/93. *Media:* Oil on linen. *Publ:* Auth, Guide to Research, Washington Sch Secys, 72; ed, The Design of Rural Development, World Bank, 75; Turkey: Prospects & Problems of an Expanding Economy, World Bank, 75; Korea: Problems & Issues in a Rapidly Growing Economy, World Bank, 76; Mexico: Tourism, World Bank, 78; Best of Floral Painting, North Sight Books, 1999. *Mailing Add:* 199 Markham St Middletown CT 06457

IMMONEN, GERALD
PAINTER

b Detroit, Mich, 1936. *Study:* Cooper Union Art Sch, cert, 58; Yale Univ, New Haven, BFA, 60, MFA, 62. *Work:* Memphis Brooks Mus Art; Metrop Mus Art, New York; Herbert F Johnson Mus Art, Cornell Univ, Ithaca, NY; Mus Art, RI Sch Design, Providence; Suomi Coll, Hancock, Mich; Mus Art, Univ Maine. *Exhib:* Prelude to Discoveries and Disclosures, George Ciscle Gallery, Baltimore, Md, 85; RI Sch Design: Selected Faculty, George Ciscle Gallery, 86; Gerald Immonen: Paintings, Acme Art, San Francisco, 87; New Works by Gallery Artists, Charles Cowles Gallery, 87-88; solo exhibs, Sixth Ann Suomi Coll Contemp Finnish-Am Artist's Exhib, Finnish-Am Heritage Ctr, Hancock, Mich, 96, Taichung Municipal Cult Ctr, Taichung, Taiwan, 8/98, G Watson Gallery, Stonington, Maine, 2005; and others; Burnt Cove Watercolors of Maine, Mus Art, 2010. *Teaching:* Prof, RI Sch Design, Providence, currently. *Awards:* Alice Kimball English Fel, Yale Univ, 60; John F Frazier Award for Excellence in Teaching, RI Sch Design, 90. *Bibliog:* Kenneth Baker (auth), Art in America, 3/85 & Chronicle, 10/28/87. *Dealer:* Gwatson Gallery Stonington ME; Turtle Gallery Deer Isle ME. *Mailing Add:* 19 Creighton St Providence RI 02906

IMPIGLIA, GIANCARLO
PAINTER, SCULPTOR

b Rome, Italy, Mar 9, 1940; US citizen. *Study:* Tech Sch Photog, Rome; Artistic Lyceum, Rome; Acad Fine Arts, Rome. *Work:* Jane Voorhees Zimmerli Art Mus, New Brunswick, NJ; Snite Mus Art, Notre Dame, Ind; Mus City New York. *Comn:* Five panel mural, Am Insurance Bldg, NY, 75-76; mural, 57th Street Playhouse, NY; two panel mural, Fortunoff Co, NY, 79; five panel mural, Cafe Soc, NY, 87; three murals, Queen Elizabeth 2, 94. *Exhib:* Solo exhibs, Rizzoli Gallery, NY & Chicago, 81 & 82, Alex Rosenberg Gallery, NY, 84, Carolyn Hill Gallery, NY, 85, Long Island Focus on Art Show, Old Westbury, NY, 89, RVS Fine Art, Southampton, 89, 9th Ann Philadelphia Art Show, Philadelphia, 89, Uptown Gallery, NY, 90, Robert Mondavi Winery, Oakville, Calif, 90, Hansen Galleries, NY, 91 & 92, Ministero per i Beni Culturali e Ambientali, Rome, 92, Deco Gallery, Wash, DC, 92, Gallery 13, Palm Beach, Fla, 93 & Laura Paul Gallery, Cincinnati, Ohio, 94; Elaine Benson Gallery, Bridgehampton, NY, 94 & 95; Artexpo, Jacob Javitz Conv Ctr, NY, 94; Wilfredo Lam Ctr, Havana, Cuba, 95; Bruce R Lewin Gallery, NY, 95. *Teaching:* Instr, studio seminars. *Awards:* Philadelphia Bowl, 86; Black Tie Award, Am Formal Wear, Inc, 86. *Bibliog:* Ronnie Cohen (auth), Giancarlo Impiglia, Art News, 9/84; Laurel Graeber (auth), The Patron Saint of the Formal Wear Industry, Daily News Record, 9/86; The Art of Giancarlo Impiglia, Rizzoli Int Publ Inc. *Media:* Oil, Acrylic; Wood. *Dealer:* Elaine Benson Gallery Bridgehampton NY; Claudia Carr Gallery New York NY

INCANDELA, GERALD JEAN-MARIE
PHOTOGRAPHER, MURALIST

b Tunis, Tunisia, Feb 19, 1952; French citizen. *Study:* Univ Paris, Nanterre, France, 70-72. *Work:* Getty Mus, Malibu, Calif; Metrop Mus Art & Mus Mod Art, New York; Albright-Knox Mus, Buffalo, NY; Mus Fine Arts, Houston, Tex; Philadelphia Mus Art, Pa. *Comn:* Bronx Zoo Animals, comn by Robert Wooley, New York, 78; View of Central Park, Mus of Mod Art, New York, 79; murals of puppies & penguins, Thermo Electric Co, NJ, 80; paintings, Archer Daniel Midland Co, 83. *Exhib:* Solo exhib, The Kitchen, New York, 81; Corcoran Gallery, Washington, DC, 78; Photo Start, Bronx Mus, New York, 82; Counterpart, Metrop Mus Art, New York & traveling, 82; How to Draw What to Draw, Parrish Art Mus, Southampton, NY, 82; Still Modern After All These Years, Chrysler Mus, Norfolk, Va, 82; Drawing Ctr, New York & traveling, 82; Mus Modern Art, NY, 83; Mus Modern Art, Oxford, Eng, 86; J Paul Getty Mus, Santa Monica, 98 & Malibu, Calif; Gallerie Beyeler, Basel, Switz, 2002; Metrop Mus Art, New York; Albright-Knox Mus, Buffalo, NY; Philadelphia Mus; Mus Fine Arts, Houston, Tex; Chase Manhattan Bank, New York; Johnson Wax, Racine, Wis; First Bank, Minn; Che Mondo Lamab, 2013. *Bibliog:* Deborah C Phillips (auth), Gerald Incandela photo images, Print Collector's Newslett, 79; Klaus Kertess (auth), Developing an image, Artforum Mag, 81; Pepe Karmel (auth), Photography: Urban disjunctions, Art in Am, 82. *Collection:* Estee Lauder Corp, New York. *Publ:* Coauth with Brad Gooch, Pictures-Story, Oakhurst, 81; coauth with Derek Jarman, Caravaggio, Thames & Hudson, 87

INDICK, JANET
SCULPTOR

b Bronx, NY, Mar 3, 1932. *Study:* Hunter Coll, with Robert Motherwell & Dong Kingman, BA (art), 53; The New Sch, with Gregorio Prestopino & Richard Pousette-Dart, 61. *Work:* Jane Voorhees Zimmerli Art Mus, Rutgers Univ & Rutgers State Libr, New Brunswick, NJ; Bergen Mus Art, Paramus, NJ; Amp Corp, Lancaster, Pa; Myron Manufacturing Corp, Maywood, NJ; Yeshiva Univ Mus, New York, NY; Nat Mus Women Art, Washington, DC; Millennium Collection, Nat Asn Women Artists, New York, NY; CUNY Coll, NY; Ithica Coll, NY. *Comn:* Steel sculpture, The Jewish Ctr, Teaneck, NJ, 74; steel menorah, Franklin Lakes Pub Sch, NJ, 80; bronze wall sculpture, 81 & sanctuary, wall & wood menorah, 83, Temple Beth Rishon, Wycoff, NJ; sculpture, Temple Sharey Tefilo Israel, South Orange, NJ, 93; outdoor Holocaust steel sculpture, North Shore Synagogue, Syosset, NY, 93; Logo award sculpture, Diabetes Found Ridgewood, NJ. *Exhib:* Morris Mus, NJ, 84; Interplay, Summit Art Ctr Invitational, NJ, 86; Solo exhibs, Edward Williams Gallery, Fairleigh Dickinson Univ, NJ, 86, Bergen Mus, Paramus, NJ, 94, Kerygma Gallery, Ridgewood, NJ, 99, Interchurch Ctr Gallery, NY, 99 & Boathouse Gallery, NY, 99, Broadfoot & Broadfoot, Boonton, NJ, 2000-01, Atrium Gallery, JCC, Washington Township, NJ, 2002, Johnson & Johnson Corp, New Brunswick, NJ, 2003, Yeshiva Univ Mus, NY, 2004, Teaneck Public Lib, NJ, 2010, Fidem Medallic Exhib, Glasgow, Scotland, 2011; Traveling exhibs, US mus organized by Nat Asn Women Artists, 100 Yrs/100 Works, USA, 89-90, Sculpture Show, India, 89-90 & Art Exhib, Athens, Greece, 96, traveling painting show, US, 98-99; Virtual exhib, 40 Years of Women Artists, Douglass Lib, 2012. *Collection Arranged:* Art Explores Jewish Themes, N.A.W.A. Gallery, NY City, 2004. *Awards:* Nat Endowment Arts Fel Grant, 81; Manhattan Arts Int Award, 2000; Catherine Lorrilard Wolfe Art Club Annual, 2001; Medallic Art Award, Pen & Brush Club, 2001; Nat Asn Women Artists Award (sculpture), 2001; Medal of Honor (sculpture), 2001; Inducted into Hall of Fame, Hunter Coll, NY, 2011. *Bibliog:* Articles in The NY Art Rev, 88, Sculpture Fundamentals, 88 & Women Artists in America, Appolo Bks, 88; Biographical Ency of Am; Painters Sculptors and Engravers of US; New York Art Review, Am Reference Publ Corp, 88; The Architect's Source of Artists & Artisans, Kraus Sikes, Inc, 93; International Artist Magazine, 2-3/2002, 14; Gallery & Studio 4-5/2002; Best of American Sculpture Artists Volume III, Kennedy Publishing, 2012. *Mem:* Nat Asn Women Artists (vpres, 94-96, pres, 97-99, bd dirs, 2006); Sculptors League NY; NY Soc Women Artists (sculptor chair, 96-99); Nat Asn Women Artists; Catherine Lorrilard Wolfe Art Club; Artists Equity NY. *Media:* Metal, Welded. *Specialty:* Am Artists- Contemp. *Interests:* Music & theatre. *Publ:* Dictionary of American Painters and Sculptors, Appolo Bks, 88; Women Artists in America, Appolo Books, 98; Contemporary Women Artists, St James Press, 99. *Mailing Add:* 428 Sagamore Ave Teaneck NJ 07666

INDIVIGLIA, SALVATORE JOSEPH
PAINTER, INSTRUCTOR

b New York, NY, Nov 16, 1919. *Study:* Leonardo da Vinci Art Sch; Sch Indust Arts; Pratt Inst, BA; fresco & mural painting with Alfred D Crimi; also with Buck Ulrick, Nicholas Volpe, Earl Winslow & George Harrington, Jr. *Hon Degrees:* The Honor Chair at the Brigade Activities Center, US Naval Acad Section QQ Seat No 5, 1994. *Work:* USN Combat Art Collection, Washington, DC; Grumbacher & Sons Collection, NY; Mutual Benefit Life Insurance Co, NJ; Annin Flag Co & Morris Davis Collection, Emily Lowe Found, NY; Nassau County Veterans Service Agency, NY. *Comn:* Assisted Alfred D Crimi with hist mural for Northampton, Mass, 40, Gen Anthony Wayne Mural for Wayne, Pa, 41 & Bowery Mission Mural for Bowery Mission, NY, 42. *Exhib:* Allied Artists Am, 48-98 & 1999-2000; Am Watercolor Soc Ann, NY, 53-83 & 1999-2004, 2007; Audubon Artists Ann, NY, 53-2004, 2007; Joe & Emily Lowe Found Show, 55 & 60; Operations Palette, USN Combat Art, Smithsonian Inst, Wash, DC, 65; Nat Acad Design, NY, 65-75. *Collection Arranged:* Salvatore J Indiviglia Collection, McClean Libr, Hofstra Univ, NY; Vets Still Out in the Cold, Nassau Co Service Agency Collection, NY. *Pos:* Art dir, acct exec & vpres, formerly; off comdr, USN combat artist, 61-79. *Teaching:* Asst & instr, City Col New York, 46-69; private classes, 46-72; instr watercolor, East Williston Libr, New York, 60-72; instr fine & appl arts, Mechanics Inst, New York, 62-66. *Awards:* Pauline Law Award in Oil, Knickerbocker Artists, 74; Gold Medal Watercolor, 75; Liquitex Watercolor Award, Allied Artists Am, 97; Vets Still Out in the Cold, Nassau Co Citation, NY, 2008; Beatrice Vackson Award in oil, Audubon Artists, 2009; Hon Chair, Midshipmen Activities Ctr, US Naval Acad, 5/19/74. *Mem:* Artists Fel (pres, 60-63); Am Watercolor Soc (dir, chmn, 53-72); Allied Artists Am (secy, 59-62); Knickerbocker Artists (vpres, 57-59); US Naval Acad Allemni Asn (assoc mem, 65-05). *Media:* Watercolor, Oil. *Collection:* McLean Lib Coll, Hofstra Univ, Salvatore J Indiviglia Collection. *Publ:* auth, 8 Watercolors of Franklin Sq, Franklin Sq Hist Soc, circa, 51-53; Watch, USNR, 67; Naval Aviation News, 68; All Hands, Bur Naval Personnel, 69; auth, Watercolor page, Am Artist Mag, 71. *Mailing Add:* 974 Lorraine Dr Franklin Square NY 11010

INGALLS, EVE
SCULPTOR, PAINTER

b Cleveland, Ohio, Sept 29, 1936. *Study:* Skowhegan Sch Art; Smith Col, BA, 58; Yale Univ Sch Art, BFA, 60, MFA, 62. *Work:* G D Searle Com Collection; Zimmerli Mus, New Brunswick, NJ; NJ State Mus, Trenton, NJ; Jersey City Mus, Jersey City, NJ; New Jersey State Coun on the Arts, Trenton, NJ; Schokland Mus, The Neth. *Exhib:* Butler Inst Am Art, 66; Art & Archit Gallery, Yale Univ, 77; Contemp Reflections, Aldrich Mus, 77 & 87; Cleveland Mus, 77, 80 & 86; Conn Painting, Sculpture and Drawing Traveling Exhib, 78; SoHo 20 Gallery, NY, 80, 81, 84, 86, 90, 92, 97, 99, 2004, 2006, 2008, 2009, 2010; Conn Comm on the Arts, Hartford, 85; Columbus Mus Art, Columbus, Ga, 85; Paula Allen Gallery, NY, 87 & 88; New Brit Mus Am Art, 89 & 96; Kulturforum Monchengladbach, WGer; Conn Biennial, Bruce Mus, Greenwich, 91; Lyman Allyn Mus, New London, 92; Virginia Miller Gallery, Coral Gables, 93; Transmission, de Zaaijer, Amsterdam, The Neth, 98; Chesterwood Mus, Stockbridge, Mass, 2000; Sculpture Now, Berkshire Botanical Gardens, Stockbridge, Mass, 2002, Unmoored, Phillips Mus Art, Franklin & Marshall Col, Lancaster, Pa, 2002, 100 NJ Artists Make Prints, traveling show, 2002, Schokland Mus, The Neth, 2003; Art Forum Jarfo-Kyoto, Kyoto, Japan, 2005 & 2007; Holland Paper Biennial, Coda Mus & Rijswijk Mus, 2006; In-Site, Sculptors Guild on Governors Island, NY, 2008; Surfactant, Rupert Ravens Contemp, Newark, NJ, 2008; Sketch to Suspension, Mitchell Gallery, St Johns Coll, Annapolis, Md, 2009; Churches de Mar, Nat Gallery Art, San Jose, Costa Rica, 2010; Encounters, Sculptor Guild, Gov Island, New York, 2010. *Teaching:* Instr painting & drawing, Silvermine Guild Sch Arts, 72-; vis lectr, Yale Univ, 79; lectr, State Univ NY, Col at Purchase, 85; vis asst prof, Trinity Col, Hartford, 91; instr, Pyramid Atlantic, Silver Springs, Md. *Awards:* Artist of the Year, Art/Place Gallery, Southport, Conn, 98; NJ Printmaking Fel, Rutgers Ctr for Innovative Print & Paper, Mason Gross Sch Arts, New Brunswick, NJ; Visiting Artist Fellowship, Awagami Factory/Fuji Papermills Cooperative, Tokushima,

Japan, 2007. *Bibliog:* William Zimmer (auth), rev, New York Times, 89, 91, 92 & 98; Pado Van De Velde (auth), Warm Onthal Voor, De Courant, Amsterdam, 98; Michael Rush (auth), rev, Art New England, 97; Jill Conner (auth), rev, Sculpture, 3/2005; Edward S. Casey (auth), Earth Mapping, Chap 5, 2005; Pat Summers (auth), rev, Sculpture, 2006; Elspeth Lamb (auth), Papermaking for Printmakers, A & C Black, London, 111-112 & 123-124; and others; KM Zomer, 2006; Holland Paper Biennale, page 9, 2006; La Nacion, San Jose, Costa Rica, page 20, 1/16/2008. *Mem:* Sculptors' Guild, Int Sculpture Ctr. *Media:* Mixed. *Dealer:* SoHo 20/ Chelsea Gallery 511 West 25st New York NY 10001. *Mailing Add:* 9 Veblen Cir Princeton NJ 08540

INGBER, BARBARA
DEALER, CURATOR
b New York, NY, Apr 18, 1932. *Study:* New York, Univ. *Pos:* Dir, Barbara Ingber Assocs, 72-89; founder, dir & cur, The Artists Mus, New York, 89-. *Mem:* Mus Mod Art; Whitney Mus Am Art; Guggenheim Mus; Metrop Mus. *Specialty:* 20th century American art. *Collection:* Paintings, drawings, sculpture and photographs by contemporary American artists. *Mailing Add:* 32 Indian Trail N Greenwood Lake NY 10925

INGHAM, TOM (EDGAR)
SCULPTOR
b Puyallup, Wash, Feb 23, 1942. *Study:* Self Taught. *Work:* Ball State Univ, Muncie, Ind; Univ Puget Sound, Tacoma, Wash. *Comn:* 14 Illus, Playboy Mag, Chicago, Ill, 74-88; poster, British Railways, London, Eng, 85; poster, Seattle Chamber Music Festival. *Exhib:* 8th Ann Exhib, Calif Mag, Palo Alto, 83; Physicians for Social Responsibility: Peace Forum & Art Exhib, Calif Polytech, San Luis Obispo, Calif, 86; 14th Ann Int Competition, Watcom Art Mus, Bellingham, Wash, 94; Biennial Competition, Tacoma Art Mus, Wash, 95; The Art of Paper, W Coast Paper Co, Kent, Wash, 96. *Awards:* Gold Medal, 23rd Ann, Soc Illusr, 80; Award of Excellence, 8th Calif Mag Exhib, 83; Third Prize, Puget Sound Area Exhib, Frye Art Mus, 90. *Media:* Handmade Asian Paper, Recycled Styrofoam. *Publ:* Contribr, Illusr 23 & 25, Soc Illusr, 82 & 84; Graphics Annual, Graphic Press Corp, Switz, 83; California Art Annual, Calif Mag, 83; Outstanding American Illustrators Today, Graphic-sha, Tokyo, 85

INGRAM, MICHAEL STEVEN
PAINTER
b Ft Campbell, Ky, Feb 13, 1973. *Exhib:* Represented in collections of World Grotto Gallery, Knoxville, Tenn, Knoxville Mus Art. *Collection Arranged:* Sir Real, The Art of Steve Ingram, World Grotto Gallery, 2006. *Bibliog:* Pluto Sports, Southern Comfort Skate Video, Thrasher magazine, 95. *Media:* Oil, Mixed Media. *Publ:* New Millennium Literary Magazine cover art, vol 1, ed 1 & 2, 97. *Dealer:* Brian C Irwin, 512 Post Oak Lane, Knoxville, Tenn, 37920

INJEYAN, SETA L
PAINTER
b Aleppo, Syria, May 3, 1946; US citizen. *Study:* Beirut Univ Col, Lebanon, 69; Art Ctr Coll Design, Pasadena, Calif, with Richard Diebenkorn, Lorser Feitelson, Llyn Foulkes, Ann McKoy & Peter Alexander, BFA, 76. *Work:* Kaloust Gulbenkian Found, Lisbon, Portugal; Wells Fargo Bank, Los Angeles; Eastern State Hosp, Medical Lake, Wash. *Exhib:* Art Rental Gallery, Los Angeles Co Mus Art, 80 & 92-93; one & two-person exhibs, Merging One Gallery, Santa Monica, Calif, 87, Parker-Blake Gallery, Denver, Colo, 89, Photo Art Gallery, Burbank, Calif, 91, El Camino Col, Torrance, Calif, 92, Brand Libr Art Galleries, Burbank, Calif, 92, Burbank Municipal Art Gallery, Calif, 93 & Brendan Walter Gallery, Santa Monica, Calif, 94 & 95; Art Coun Auction/Exhib, Butterfield & Butterfield, Los Angeles, 91; Unnatural Landscapes, Century Gallery, Sylmar, Calif, 94; Brendan Walter Gallery, Santa Monica, Calif, 94; Artists and Architecture, Artspace Gallery, Woodland Hills, Calif, 94; and others. *Awards:* First Place, Armenian Allied Arts Coun, 75; Best Show, Soc Art Ctr Alumni, Art Ctr Coll Design, 76; Three Purchases Prizes, Wash State Arts Comn, 83. *Bibliog:* Nancy Kapitanoff (auth), Marks on the Earth, Los Angeles Times, 4/29/94; Nancy Kapitanoff (auth), Building an impression, Los Angeles Times, 5/13/94; Joe Futtner (auth), City of Dreams, NOHO Mag, 6/94. *Mem:* Artists Equity Asn; Los Angeles Inst Contemp Art; LALMA. *Media:* Miscellaneous Media. *Mailing Add:* 5610 Pinecone Rd La Crescenta CA 91214-1418

INOUE, KOZO See Kozo

IPCAR, DAHLOV
PAINTER, ILLUSTRATOR
b Windsor, Vt, Nov 12, 1917. *Study:* Oberlin Coll, 33-34. *Hon Degrees:* Univ Maine, LHD, 78; Colby Coll, DFA, 80; Bates Coll, DFA, 91. *Work:* Brooklyn Mus, Metrop Mus Art & Whitney Mus Am Art, NY; Portland Mus Art, Maine; Colby Coll Mus Art, Waterville, Maine; Bates Coll, Lewistown, Maine. *Comn:* mural, Shriner's Hosp for Crippled Children, Springfield, Mass, 79; mural, Kingfield Elementary Sch, Maine, 80; mural, Narragansett Elementary Sch, Gorham, 81; mural, Crescent Park Elementary Sch, Bethel, Maine, 94; mural, Mid Coast Hosp Brunswick, Maine, 2000. *Exhib:* Solo exhibs, Mus Mod Art, NY, 39, Portland Mus Art, Maine, 59, 63, 70 & 2000, Del Art Mus Libr, 76, Frost Gully Gallery, Portland, 77, 85 & 96, Hobe Sound Galleries, Fla, 79, Colby Coll Mus Art, Waterville, 80, Mus Art, Olin Arts Ctr, Bates Coll, Lewiston, Maine, 90, Frost Gully Gallery, Freeport, Maine, 2001, 2003, 2005, 2007, 2009, 2011, Univ New Hampshire Art Mus, 2011, Univ New England Art Mus, 2011; group exhibs incl, PA & Detroit Ann, 40; Colby Coll Mus Art, 74; Maine State Mus, 76; Joan Whitney Payson Art Mus, Westbrook Coll, 82-85. *Awards:* Deborah Morton Award, Westbrook Coll, 78; Kerlan Award, Univ Minn, 98; Maryann Hartman Award, Univ Maine, 2003. *Bibliog:* Anne Commire (ed), Something About the Author Vol 49, Gale Research, 87; Maine Masters Proj, Dahlov Ipcar, Pcov, Video, 2001; Carl Little (auth), The Art of Dahlov Ipcar, Down East Books, Maine, 2010. *Media:* Oil, Watercolor. *Publ:* Auth & illusr, One Horse Farm, Island Port Press, 2011; Calico Jungle, Island Port Press, 2011; The Land of Flowers, Viking, 74; Lobsterman, Down East Bks, 80; Brown Cow Farm, Down East Bks, 2004; and others. *Dealer:* Thomas R Crotty Frost Gully Gallery 1159 US Rt 1 PO Box 202 Freeport ME 04032

IPSEN, KENT FORREST
GLASSWORKER, CRAFTSMAN
b Milwaukee, Wis, Jan 4, 1933. *Study:* Univ Wis-Milwaukee, BS; Univ Wis-Madison, MS & MFA; also with Harvey K Littleton. *Work:* Milwaukee Art Ctr, Wis; Toledo Mus Art, Ohio; Corning Glass Mus, NY; Chrysler Mus, Norfolk, Va; Chicago Art Inst; and others. *Comn:* First Gov Awards for the Arts, State of Va, 79. *Exhib:* Vidrios, Estudio Actual, Caracas, Venezuela, 74; Wis Directions, Milwaukee Art Ctr, 75; Looking Forward, Fairtree Gallery, NY, 75; Relig & Art, Vatican Mus, 78; New Glass, Int Competition Corning Mus, 79; and others. *Teaching:* Asst prof glassworking, Mankato State Col, Minn, 65-68; assoc prof glassworking, Chicago Art Inst, 68-72; assoc prof glassworking & chmn dept crafts, Va Commonwealth Univ, 73-76, prof, 76-. *Awards:* Nat Endowment Arts, US Govt, 72 & 75. *Bibliog:* Lee Nordness (auth), Objects USA, Viking, 71; Ray Grover (auth), Contemporary Art Glass, Crown, 75. *Mem:* Am Craft Coun; Ill Craft Coun (pres, 70-72); Nat Coun Educ in Ceramic Arts; Nat Coun Art Adminr. *Media:* Glass. *Dealer:* Habatat Galleries 28235 Southfield Rd Lathrup Village MI 48076; Heller Gallery 965 Madison Ave New York NY 10021. *Mailing Add:* 715 Bowe St Richmond VA 23220-3011

IQBAL, MALA
PAINTER
b 1973. *Study:* Columbia Univ, New York, BA (Vis Art & Eng), 1995; RI Sch Design, Providence, MFA (Painting), 1998. *Work:* Queens Mus Art, NY. *Exhib:* Solo exhibs include Artist Access Gallery, Snug Harbor Cult Ctr, Staten Island, NY, 2001, Richard Heller Gallery, Los Angeles, 2002, Bellwether Gallery, Brooklyn, NY, 2003, PPOW, New York, 2007; group exhibs include Untouchables, Maxwell Freeman Contemp Pictures, Houston, 2001; Escape from New York, NJ Ctr Vis Arts, Summit, 2003; Open House, Brooklyn Mus Art, NY, 2004; 6th Ann Altoids Curiously Strong Collection, New Mus Contemp Art, New York, 2004; Fatal Love, Queens Mus Art, NY, 2005; PULSE Art Fair, PPOW Gallery, New York, 2006, Art Chicago, 2008; Fire Walkers, Stux Gallery, New York, 2008. *Awards:* New York Found Arts Fel, 2008

IRELAND, PATRICK
CONCEPTUAL ARTIST
b Ireland, 34. *Study:* Univ Col, Dublin, Ireland; Cambridge Univ; Harvard Sch Pub Health, Cambridge, Mass, MA. *Work:* Chase Manhattan Bank Collection, Metrop Mus Art, Mus Mod Art, NY; Butler Inst Am Art, Youngstown, Ohio; Nat Mus Am Art, Washington, DC; Kilkenny Gallery Mod Art, Hugh Lane Gallery Mod Art, Ireland; Nat Gallery Australia; Hirshhorn Mus & Sculpture Garden, Smithsonian Inst, Washington; Metrop Mus Art, NY; Mus Modern Art, NY. *Exhib:* Cranbrook Acad, Bloomfield Hills, Mich, 81; Neuberger Mus, Purchase, NY, 82; Brooklyn Mus, NY, 83; Poetry and the Visual Arts, Univ NC, Charlottesville, 84; Univ Va, Charlottesville, 84; The Minimal Line, Bard Col, Annandale-on-Hudson, NY, 85; Galerie Hoffman, Friedberg, W Ger, 86; Summer Exhib, Charles Cowles Gallery, NY, 87; Detroit Inst Arts, Mich, 87; Art on Paper, Weatherspoon Art Gallery, Univ NC, Greensboro, 88; Pvt Works for Pub Spaces, RC Erpf Gallery, 88; Fuller-Gross Gallery, San Francisco, Calif, 89; solo shows, Elvehjem Mus Art, Univ Wis, Madison, 92, Butler Inst Am Art, 94, Brigham Young Univ Mus Art, 95, Crawford Munic Art Gallery, Cork, Ireland, 95, Old Yacht Club, Cobh, Ireland, 96, Orchard Gallery, Derry, N Ireland, 98 & Charles Cowles Gallery, NY, 98 & 99; New Talent - New Ideas, Charles Cowles Gallery, NY, 96; Art and the Am Experience, Kalamazoo Art Inst, Mich, 98; Works on Paper, A to Z, Charles Cowles Gallery, NY, 98; Gotham Group, Charles Cowles Gallery, NY, 98; Primarily Structural, PS I Contemp Art Ctr, Long Island City, NY, 99; Toward a Society for All Ages: World Artists at the Millenium, UN Visitors' Lobby, NY, 99. *Teaching:* Vis prof, Univ Calif, Berkeley, 67; adj prof, Barnard Col, Columbia Univ, 70; prof fine arts & media, Southampton Col & Long Island Univ, 97-. *Awards:* Mather Award Art Criticism, Coll Art Asn, 65; Franklin Murphy Lectr, Spencer Mus, Univ Kans, 80. *Bibliog:* Ken Johnson (auth), article, NY Times, 10/23/98; Caoimhin Mac Giolla Leith, article, Artforum, 11/98; Thomas McEvilley (auth), An artist & his aliases, Art in Am, 05/99

IRISH, JANE
PAINTER, ADMINISTRATOR
Study: Md Inst Coll Art, Baltimore, BFA, 1977; CUNY Queens Coll, MFA, 1980. *Work:* Bryn Mawr Coll, Pa; Pa Acad Fine Arts; Philadelphia Mus Art; Women's Hall Fame, Seneca Falls, NY. *Exhib:* Solo exhibs, Fells Point Gallery, Baltimore, 1981, Univ City Sci Ctr, Philadelphia, 1982, Kling Gallery, Philadelphia, 1984, Sharpe Gallery, New York, 1985, 1987, 1989, Rosenwald-Walf Gallery, Univ Arts Philadelphia, 2000, Pa Acad Fine Arts, 2002; Made in Philadelphia 6, Inst Contemp Art, Philadelphia, 1984; An Inside Place, Noyes Mus, Oceanville, NY, 1985; NYC, New York, Del Art Mus, Wilmington, 1986; Romanticism and Cynicism in Contemporary Art, Haggerty Mus Art, Marquette Univ, 1986; Diamonds are Forever, Artists and Writers on the National Pastime, New York State Mus, Albany, 1987; Painting for Walls, Cheltenham Ctr Arts, Pa, 1997; Snapshot, Arcadia Univ Art Gallery, Glenside, Pa, 2001; Philadelphia Selections 6, Moore Coll Art, 2006; The Gun Show, Shore Inst Contemp Art, Long Branch, 2007; Dirt on Delight: Impulses That Form Clay, Univ Pa Inst Contemp Art, 2009. *Pos:* MFA prog coordr, Univ Pa, currently. *Awards:* Artist Fel, Creative Artists Program Svc, 1981; Pa Coun Arts Fel, 1982 & 1984; NEA Painting Fel, 1982; Joan Mitchell Found Grant, 2010. *Bibliog:* Suasn Hagen (auth), History Repeating, Philadelphia City Paper, 1/2/2003; Roberta Fallon (auth), Irish Rebellion, Philadelphia Weekly, 8/31/2005; Roberta Smith (auth), Crucible of Creativity, Stoking Earth Into Art, NY Times, 3/20/2009. *Dealer:* Locks Gallery 600 Washington Sq S Philadelphia PA 19106. *Mailing Add:* Univ Penn Morgan Bldg 205 S 34th St Rm 100 Philadelphia PA 19104-6312

IRMAS, AUDREY MENEIN
COLLECTOR
Pos: Co-founding trustee, Audrey & Sydney Irmas Charitable Found, 83-, projects incl Audrey & Sydney Irmas Campus of the Wilshire Blvd Temple, Audrey & Sydney Irmas Los Angeles Youth Ctr; bd trustees, Mus Contemp Art, Los Angeles, 92-, pres, chmn, formerly, Hirshhorn Mus. *Awards:* Named one of Top 200 Collectors, ARTnews Mag, 2004, 2007. *Interests:* Photography. *Collection:* Contemporary art. *Mailing Add:* 5045 Rubio Ave Van Nuys CA 91436-1139

IRVIN, MARIANNE FANELLI
PAINTER, COLLAGE ARTIST
b Philadelphia, Pa, Sept 9, 1947. *Study:* Philadelphia Coll Art, with Karl Sherman, BFA (painting), 69; Md Inst Coll Art, with Al Hurwitz, 85; Rudolph Steiner Coll, Calif State Univ, Sacramento, with David Elkind, 89. *Comn:* Infant portrait studies, comn by Dr Norman J Santora, Upper Darby, Pa, 70; portrait of Marie, comn by Clarence Carroll, Upper Darby, Pa, 81; vestments to honor the Holy Spirit, comn by Rev Patrick C Stephenson, American Canyon, Calif, 94; floral photog, cover art cd, Bouquet, Francesca & Leonardo, 2000 & A Christmas Rose, Francesca & Leonardo, 2003; floral photog, Commemorative Poster, Purple Passion, Benefit Concert, Am Canyon, Calif, 2003. *Exhib:* California Small Works, Calif Mus Art, Santa Rosa, 89-90; Napa Co Spring Fair, Calif, 89; Fairfield Regional Juried Art Show, Calif, 92; State of the Art 93 Int Invitational, New Eng Fine Arts Inst, Boston, Mass, 93; Festa Artisanos Juried, Am Canyon, Calif, 93; Postcard Art Competition & Exhib, Teich Archives, Lake Co Discovery Mus, Wauconda, Ill, 2007, 2009; 33rd Ann Miniworks on Paper Exhib, Jacksonville State Univ, Dept Art, Jacksonville Ala, 2012. *Pos:* Art dept head fine arts, Rosemont Sch Holy Child, Pa, 82-84; founding artist bd mem, Am Canyon Arts Found, Calif, 92-; art educ consult creative & mental growth, Butterfly Hope Nature Ctr, Denver, Colo, 93; artist-in-residence, Bransford Elem Sch, Fairfield, Calif, 94. *Teaching:* Adj art instr, Delaware Co Community Coll, Media, Pa, 87 & 88 & Napa Valley Coll, Calif, 89-92; vis art instr Making Arts Grow in the Community, Fairfield Calif Civic Arts, 94-97. *Awards:* Anna Jones Mem Award, Main Line Ctr Arts Mem Group Exhib, 82; Best of Show, Festa Artisanos, City Am Canyon, 93. *Bibliog:* Mary Wallis (auth), Napa Valley artists to open studios, Napa Valley Register, 9/92; Felix A Bedolla (auth), Local artist wins award, Artscan, Napa Valley Arts Coun, 5-6/94; Dan German (auth), Canyon artist puts her mark on festival, Napa Valley Register, 7/94. *Mem:* Nat Mus Women Arts. *Media:* Oil Paint on Silk, Pantone Letrafilm Matt Colors. *Publ:* Contribr, Contemporary Women Artist Desk Calendar, Bo Tree Publ, 89; Todays Great Poems, Famous Poets Soc, 94; Reflections of Light, Nat Libr Poetry, 95. *Dealer:* Muzzys Secret Garden Gallery American Canyon CA 94503. *Mailing Add:* 202 Manor Court American Canyon CA 94503

IRVINE, BETTY JO
LIBRARIAN, INSTRUCTOR
b Indianapolis, Ind, July 13, 1943. *Study:* Ind Univ, AB, 66, MLS, 69, PhD, 82. *Pos:* Fine arts slide librn, Sch of Fine Arts, Ind Univ, Bloomington, 66-68, asst fine arts libr, 68-69, fine arts librn, 69-2007, retired, currently. *Teaching:* Instr art bibliog, Sch of Fine Arts, Ind Univ, Bloomington, 69- & instr art librarianship, & Info Sci, 86-. *Awards:* Officer's Grant, Coun of Libr Resources, Washington, DC, 71; Teaching Excellence Recognition Award, Ind Univ, 2000. *Mem:* Am Libr Asn (vchmn-chmn-elect art sect, 78-79); Midwest Art Hist Soc (session chmn, 76); Art Libr Soc NAm (chmn, Standards Comt, 83-, vpres, 91 & pres, 91). *Res:* Organization and management of slide libraries; art library planning and design; women in libraries. *Publ:* Organization and management of art slide collections, Libr Trends, 1/75; coauth (with L Korenic), Survey of periodical use in an academic art library, In: Art Documentation, Bulletin Art Libr Soc NAm, 10/82; auth, Sex Segregation in Librarianship, Greenwood Press, 86; ed, Facilities Standards for Art Libraries and Visual Resources Collections, Art Libr Soc NA & Colo Libr Unltd, 91; auth, Chinese art libraries: developments and trends, Parts I-II, Art Libr J, 2000, 01. *Mailing Add:* c/o Fine Arts Libr Ind Univ Bloomington IN 47401

IRVING, DONALD J
ADMINISTRATOR, WRITER
b Arlington, Mass, May 3, 1933. *Study:* Mass Coll Art, BA, 55; Columbia Univ Teachers Col, MA, 56, EdD, 63. *Pos:* Chmn dept art & dir, Peabody Mus Art, George Peabody Col Teachers, Nashville, Tenn, 67-69; dir sch, Sch of the Art Inst Chicago, 69-83; dean, fac fine arts, Univ Ariz, Tucson, 83-90, prof art, 90-91, adj prof, 91-. *Teaching:* Teacher art, White Plains High Sch, NY, 58-60; instr art, State Univ NY Col Oneonta, 58-60; prof art & dean, Moore Col Art, Philadelphia, 63-67. *Mem:* Nat Asn Schs Art (treas & mem bd dir, 72-75); Union Independent Cols Art (bd dir, 72-, chmn bd, 79-); Nat Coun Art Adminr (bd dir, 73-); Fedn Independent Ill Cols & Univs (bd dir, 74-). *Res:* Application of industrial materials and techniques to contemporary sculpture. *Publ:* Auth Sculpture: Material and Process, Van Nostrand Reinhold, 70. *Mailing Add:* PO Box 974 Sonoita AZ 85637-0974

IRWIN, GEORGE M
PATRON, COLLECTOR
b Quincy, Ill, May 2, 1921. *Study:* Univ Mich, BA, 43. *Hon Degrees:* Culver-Stockton Col, DFA, 73; Western Ill Univ, DHL, 90; Quincy Univ, Ill, DHL, 2000. *Pos:* Chmn bd, Am for Arts, Washington, DC, 62-72 & Ill Arts Coun, 63-71; mem bd, Mus Contemp Art, Chicago, formerly; mem bd, Ill State Mus & Mus Contemp Art, Chicago; pres, Quincy Soc Fine Arts, 47-77. *Awards:* Lifetime Award, Ill Arts Alliance Found, 90; Studs Terkel Lifetime Arts Award, Ill Humanities Coun, 99; R Driehaus Fedn Award, Landmarks Preservation Coun Ill, 99. *Mem:* Life mem Art Inst Chicago; Nat Trust Hist Preserv; and others. *Collection:* Twentieth century American artists. *Publ:* producer, Historic Quincy Architecture, 96. *Mailing Add:* 1636 Hampshire St Quincy IL 62301

IRWIN, LANI HELENA
PAINTER
b Annapolis, Md, Oct 27, 1947. *Study:* Am Univ, Washington, BFA, 69, MFA, 74. *Work:* Nat Mus Am Art, Washington; Bayly Mus, Charlottesville, Va; Hirschorn Mus, Washington, DC; Huntington Mus, WVa; Corcoran Gallery Art, Washington, DC. *Exhib:* Md Biennial, Baltimore Mus, 74; 19th Area Exhib, Corcoran Gallery Art, Washington, 74; Graham Gallery, NY, 77; Huntington Mus, W Va, 2001; solo exhibs, Gallery K, 81, 83, 86, 94 & 98; Katharina Rich Perlow Gallery, NY, 96-97, 2000, 2003 & 2007; 179th Ann Art Invitational, Nat Acad Design, NY, 2004; The Figure in American Painting and Drawing 1985-2005, Ogunquit Mus Am Art, Ogunquit, Maine; What is Realism, Albemarle Gallery, London, 2005; Boulder Mus Contemp Art, Colo, 2007. *Teaching:* Md Inst Coll Art, Baltimore, 2007. *Awards:* Pollock-Krasner Found Grant, 95. *Bibliog:* Jill Wechsler (auth), Lani Irwin, Am Artist, 6/83; James Mann (auth), The metaphysical art of Lani Irwin, Am Arts Quart, spring 94; Jeff Wright (auth), Lani Irwin, Cover, summer 96; Gail Leggio (auth), The Interior Theater of Lani Irwin, Am Arts Quart, 2001. *Media:* Oil. *Dealer:* Katharina Rich Perlow Gallery 41 E 57th New York NY 10022. *Mailing Add:* Porziano 68 Assisi 06081 Italy

IRWIN, ROBERT
ENVIRONMENTAL ARTIST
b Long Beach, Calif, Sept 12, 1928. *Study:* Otis Art Inst, 48-50; Jepson Art Inst, Los Angeles, 51; Chouinard's Art Inst, Los Angeles, 52-54; San Francisco Inst Art, Hon Dr, 79, Otis-Parson's Art Inst, Hon Dr, 92. *Hon Degrees:* Hon dr art, San Francisco Art Inst, 79, Otis-Parson's Art Inst, Los Angeles, 92. *Work:* Art Inst Chicago; Walker Art Ctr, Minneapolis, Minn; San Francisco Mus Mod Art, Calif; Mus Contemp Art, Lannen Found, Los Angeles; Mus Mod Art, Whitney Mus Am Art, NY; Mus Contemp Art, San Diego. *Comn:* 9 Spaces 9 Trees, Seattle, Wash, 83; 56 Shadow Planes, Old Post Off, Gen Servs Admin, Washington, DC, 83; Arts Enrichment Master Plan, Miami Int Airport, 86-88; Central Garden, J Paul Getty Mus, Los Angeles, 92-97; 1-2-3-4, Mus Contemp Art, San Diego; Light and Space III, Indianapolis Mus Art, 2008. *Exhib:* Solo exhibs, Pace Gallery, NY, 92, Pace Wildenstein Gallery, Los Angeles, 98, 2006, Musee d'Art Contemporain de Lyon, France, 98, Dia Ctr Arts, NY, 98-99, Pace Gallery, 2010; retrospective, Whitney Mus Am Art, NY, 77, Mus Contemp Art, Los Angeles, Kunstverein, Cologne, Ger, Mus d'Art Moderne de la Ville, Paris & Reina Sofia, Madrid, Spain, 93-95, Mus of Contemp Art, Los Angeles (traveling), 93-95; group exhibs include Pace Wildenstein Gallery, 94, 98 & 99; Contemp Art in Transition-from the Collection of the Ho-Am Art Mus, Ho-Am Art Gallery, Seoul, Korea, 97; California Scheming Mus Contemp Art, Chicago, 98; Material Perfection: Minimal Art & its Aftermath Selected from the Kerry Stokes Collection, Lawrence Wilson Art Gallery, Univ Western Australia, Perth, 98; and others. *Teaching:* John J Hill lect prof, Univ Minn, 81; Cullinan lect prof, Rice Univ, 87-88. *Awards:* MacArthur Found Award, 84; Guggenheim fel, 76; MacArthur fel, 84-89; Thomas Jefferson Found medal in archit, Univ Va Sch of Archit, 2009. *Bibliog:* Calvin Tompkins (auth), Knowing in Action, The New Yorker, 85; Rosalind Krauss (auth), Overcoming the Limits of Matter, Studies in Mod Art, Mus Mod Art, 91; Roberta Smith (auth), Matter Turned into Light & Space, New York Times, 92; Lawrence Weschler (auth), Seeing Is Forgetting the Name of the Thing One Sees, 2009; and others. *Mem:* Am Acad Arts and Letters; Nat Acad. *Media:* All. *Publ:* Auth, Notes Toward A Model (catalog), Whitney Mus, 77; Set of Questions, American Artists on Art from 1940-1980, 80; Being and Circumstance: Notes Towards A Conditional Art, 85; The Hidden Structures of Art (Robert Irwin catalog), Mus Contemp Art, Los Angeles, 93; Robert Irwin: Getty Garden, Los Angeles: The J Paul Getty Mus, 2002. *Dealer:* PaceWildenstein 32 E 57th St New York NY 10022. *Mailing Add:* PaceWildenstein Gallery 32 E 57th St 2nd Fl New York NY 10022

ISAACS, RON
PAINTER, SCULPTOR
b Cincinnati, Ohio, Oct 14, 1941. *Study:* Berea Col, BA, 63; Ind Univ, MFA, 65. *Work:* Huntsville Mus Art; McDonalds Corp, Oakbrook, Ill; Am Express, AT&T & Chase Manhattan Bank, NY. *Comn:* Three painted sculptures, Univ Hosp, Cleveland, Ohio, 94; painted sculpture, Menorah Park Foundation, Beachwood, Ohio, 02. *Exhib:* One-person exhib, Monique Knowlton Gallery, NY, 80, 82 & 85, Robert L Kidd Galleries, Birmingham, Mich, 85, Pittsburgh Ctr for the Arts, 86 & Sazama Gallery, Chicago, 92; More Than Land or Sky: Art from Appalachia, Nat Mus Am Art, Animal Image, Renwick Gallery, Smithsonian Inst, Washington, DC, 81; Realism Invitational, Southeastern Ctr for Contemp Art, Winston-Salem, NC, 82-83; Illusions, Greenville Co Mus Art, SC, 84; More Than Meets The Eye: The Art of Trompe L'Oeil, Columbus Mus Art, 85-86; The Medium as Illusion, Calif State Univ, Fullerton, 86; and others. *Teaching:* Instr fine arts, Sue Bennett Col, London, KY, 65-69; prof painting & drawing, Eastern Ky Univ, Richmond, 69-01; professor emeritus, 01-. *Awards:* First Purchase Awards, Preview 73, Coll of Mount St Joseph, Cincinnati, Ohio, 72, Fifth Berea Drawing Biennial, Berea Col, Ky, 83. *Bibliog:* Madeleine Burnside (auth), Ron Isaacs (rev), Art News, 11/78; Dona Z Meilach (auth), Woodworking: The New Wave, Crown Publ, New York, 81; Phyllis George (auth), Kentucky Crafts, Handmade & Heartfelt, Crown Pubol, NY, 89. *Mem:* Am Crafts Coun; Nat Art Educ Asn. *Media:* Acrylic, Birch Plywood. *Publ:* True Lies (art/essay), Nouvei Object VI, Design House Publ, Seoul, Korea, 01. *Dealer:* Schneider Gallery 230 W Superior St Chicago IL 60610; Toni Birckhead Gallery 342 W 4th St Cincinnati OH 45202; Snyderman Gallery 303 Cherry St Philadelphia PA 19106. *Mailing Add:* 420 Adams Ln Richmond KY 40475-8764

ISAACSON, LYNN JUDITH
PAINTER, SCULPTOR
b New York, NY, Nov 8, 1948. *Study:* Queens Col, with Herb Aach & Louis Finkelstein, MS (art educ), 74; Lehman Col, MFA (painting), 81. *Comn:* Relief construction, Oppenheimer & Co Inc, NY, 81; styrofoam & wood construction, Saratoga Construction Inc, Montreal, Que, 84. *Exhib:* Liberty and the Pursuit of Liberty, Nat Women's Caucus Arts, 86; Lehman Coll Alumni Show, Lehman Coll Art Gallery, Bronx, NY, 86; solo show, Soho Gallery, NY, 86 & 89; Vangarde Gallery,

New London, Conn, 68, Soho Gallery, 90; Educ Alliance, NY, 92. *Pos:* Membership secy, Bd Dir, Women's Caucus Arts, 80-86. *Teaching:* Teacher fine arts & ceramist, Jr High Sch 117, Bronx, NY, 71-. *Awards:* Queens Youth Ctr Arts Award, Queens Col, 74. *Bibliog:* Ellen Lee Klein (auth), article, Arts Mag, 9/83. *Media:* Mixed Media on paper based on quilt design. *Publ:* Illusr, Working Big: A Teacher's Guide to Environmental Sculpture (coauths, John Lidstone & Clarence Bunch), Van Nostrand Reinhold Co, 75. *Dealer:* Soho Gallery 168 Mercer St New York NY 10012; Vangarde Gallery 331 Captains Walk New London CT 06320. *Mailing Add:* 229 E 21st St No 4 New York NY 10010-6433

ISAACSON, MARCIA JEAN
ARTIST, EDUCATOR
b Atlanta, Ga, Sept 25, 1945. *Study:* Univ Ga, Athens, BFA & MFA. *Work:* Minn Mus Art, St Paul; High Mus Art, Atlanta, Ga; Greenville Coun Mus of Art, Greenville, SC; Fla House Rep, Tallahassee; Ala Powers Co; Duke Univ Mus Art, Durham, NC; Eastman Pharmaceuticals, Melvern Pa; Ark Art Ctr. *Exhib:* Drawings USA, Minn Mus Art, St Paul, 71 & 73; 35 Artists in the SE Traveling Exhib, High Mus Art; Southeastern Graphics Invitational: Drawing, Mint Mus Art, Charlotte, 79; West 79 & 84: Art and the Law, Minn Mus Art, St Paul; Drawing Show, Southeastern Ctr Contemp Arts, Winston-Salem, NC, 82; Kipnis Gallery, Atlanta, 81 & 82; Nat Drawing Invitational, Ark Art Ctr, Little Rock, 86; Ten Yrs Southeastern Seven, Southeastern Crt Contemp Arts, Winston-Salem, NC, 87; Duke Univ Mus of Art, Durham, NC, Nat Drawing Invitational Emporia State Univ, Emporia, KS. *Pos:* Selection panels, SECCA Grants, Southeastern Ctr Contemp Art, 77, Nat Endowment Arts Fel Grants, 80-81, Ill Art Coun Grants, 85 & Fla Art Coun Grants, 85. *Teaching:* Instr printmaking & drawing, Wesleyan Col, Macon, Ga, 70-73; asst prof drawing, Univ Fla, Gainesville, 73-80, assoc prof, 80-. *Awards:* Teacher of the Year, Coll Fine Arts, Univ Fla, 77-78; Nat Endowment Arts-Southeastern Ctr Contemp Art Fels, 77; Fla Fine Arts Coun Fel, 79 & 89; Purchase Award, Davidson Col, NC, 73 & State Univ Col, NY, 75. *Media:* Pencil, Charcoal. *Mailing Add:* 1803 NW Tenth Ave Gainesville FL 32605-5311

ISAACSON, PHILIP MARSHAL
CRITIC, WRITER
b Lewiston, Maine, June 16, 1924. *Study:* Bates Col, BA, 47; Harvard Law Sch, LLB, 50. *Hon Degrees:* Bowdoin Col, DFA, 83 & 84; Bates Col, DHL, 97. *Work:* Portland Mus Art, Maine. *Exhib:* Maine 2000, Maine Coast Artists, Rockport, Maine, 2000. *Pos:* Adv mem, Maine Lawyers & Accountants for the Arts, 94-; mem, Exec Adv Comt, Bates Col Mus Art, 96-; mem, Maine Hist Pres Comn, 98-. *Awards:* Boston Globe-Horn Book Awards, Honor Bk, 89; Cult Recognition Award, Maine Community Cult Alliance, 92. *Mem:* Maine State Comn Arts & Humanities (chmn, 75-). *Res:* The American eagle as a decorative device; architecture of Maine since 1920; esthetics of architecture. *Publ:* Auth, The American Eagle, NY Graphic Soc, 75; contrib, Marine Forms of American Architecture, Colby Col, 76; auth, Round Buildings, Square Buildings & Buildings that Wiggle Like a Fish, Knopf, 89; A Short Walk Around the Pyramids & Through the World of Art, Knopf, 93. *Dealer:* June Fitzpatrick Gallery 112 High St Portland ME 04101. *Mailing Add:* 75 Park St Lewiston ME 04240

ISHAQ, ASHFAQ
ADMINISTRATOR
Study: Govt Col, Lahore, Pakistan, BA; Univ, MPA, Punjab; Econ, George Washington Univ, PhD. *Pos:* chairman, Int Child Art Found, George Washington Univ, 84-90. *Awards:* Grantee Hesselbein Community Fel, Peter Drucker Found, 2001; World Culture Open award for Humanitarian Svc, 2004; Zeigteld award for Outstanding Int Leadership in Arts Edu, 2011; Dist Svc award, US Sports Acad 2011. *Bibliog:* (auth) Success in Small & Medium Scale Enterprises, 87; founder, editor ChildArt magazine, 98—. *Mem:* Int Acad Digital Arts and Scis (adv bd mem), World Psychiatry Asn. *Res:* Children's creative & empathic develop. *Interests:* neuroscience. *Publ:* Child Art Quarterly Mag. *Mailing Add:* International Child Art Foundation PO Box 58133 Washington DC 20037

ITALIANO, JOAN
SCULPTOR, LITURGICAL ARTIST
b Worcester, Mass, 1928. *Study:* Siena Heights Univ, PhB, Studio Angelico, MFA; Barry Univ Miami, Fla; Nino Caruso, Rome, Italy, Beani & Cacia Foundry; Pietrasanta, Italy. *Comn:* Tree of Life Fountain, Mary Manning Walsh Carmelite Home, NY, 71; Shrine to the American Saints (ceramic on wood), Our Lady of Good Counsel Church, W Boylston, Mass, 86; memorial panel (ceramic on wood), Mercy Ctr, Worcester, Mass, 90; Little Flower, Shrine to St Theresa (stoneware & granite), Boylston, Mass, 96; Processional Cross (enamel on copper & wood), Wellesley Coll, Mass, 98. *Exhib:* Norton Gallery, West Palm Beach, Fla; Cantor Gallery, Holy Cross Col, Worcester, Mass; Pindar Gallery, NY; Women Exhibiting in Boston, Prudential Ctr; Wolfe Gallery, W Palm Beach, 96; and others. *Collection Arranged:* Mount Holyoke Coll Mus; Norstar Security Trust, Rochester, NY; Bingham, Dana & Gould, Boston; Int Ctr for Ceramics, Rome, Italy; Brown, Rudnick, Freed & Gesmer, Boston. *Pos:* Dir, Art Gallery, Barry Col, 56-58; consult liturgical art, Dick Bros Archit Interiors, 62-72; dir, Studio Beato Angelico N, West Boylston, Mass, 59- & Studio Beato Angelico S, West Palm Beach, Fla, 91-; consult, Reader's Digest Art Trade Books, 93-96. *Teaching:* Instr sculpture, Barry Col, Miami, Fla, 56-58; assoc prof sculpture & ceramics, Col of the Holy Cross, 69-89, chmn fine arts dept, 77-80. *Awards:* First Prize in Sculpture, Palm Beach Art League 37th & 38th Ann; Bachelor Ford Fel, 76; Prize, Northeast Sculptors Assoc, Boston, 83 & 86; Fac Fel, Coll Holly Cross, 88. *Bibliog:* Vivian Raynor (auth), review, Pindar Show, New York Times, 7/6/84; James Reil (auth), article, Worcester Mag, 5/20/81; George French (auth), Sculptor Joan Italiano's New Direction Is Right On Course, Evening Gazette, Worcester, Mass, 10/22/82; and many others. *Mem:* New Eng Sculptors, Asn; Int Sculpture Ctr; Lay Dominican. *Media:* All Media. *Res:* fired clay sculpture. *Dealer:* Art South 4401 Cresson St Philadelphia PA; Pindar Gallery 127 Greene St New York NY

ITCHKAWICH, DAVID MICHAEL
PRINTMAKER, ILLUSTRATOR
b Westerly, RI, Aug 18, 1937. *Study:* RI Sch Design, BFA. *Work:* John Sloane Study Collection, Univ Del; Charles Dana Mus, Colgate Univ; NY Pub Libr; Munson-Williams-Proctor Inst, Utica, NY; Metrop Mus Art, NY. *Exhib:* Nat Print Exhib, Brooklyn Mus, NY, 70 & 72; Davidson Nat Print Show, Davidson Univ, 73-75; Solo exhibs, Munson-Proctor-Williams Inst, Utica, NY, 76, Newport Art Asn, RI, 78; Martin Sumers Graphics, 76; Nat Exhib, NY Soc Illusr, 78; and others. *Bibliog:* The visions of David Itchkawich, Intellectual Dig, 2/72; John Mattingly (auth), When Men Were Animals and Animals Were Men: A Study of the Graphic Work of David Itchkawich, Angelica Press, NY, 76; Suzanne Boorsch (auth), The pleasure of creation: The work of David Itchkawich, Print Collector's Newslett, 9-10/78. *Dealer:* Horizon Gallery 45 Christopher St New York NY 10014. *Mailing Add:* c/o FDR Gallery 670 Broadway New York NY 10012

IVERS, CHRISTINE D
PAINTER, INSTRUCTOR
b New York, NY, Jan 23, 1951. *Study:* Hartford Art Sch, Univ Hartford, BFA, 73; Studied with Margaret Carter Baumgaertner, Richard McKinley, Rudolph Zallinger, Doug Dawson, Susan Ogilvie, Alan Flattmann, Frank Federico, Lorenzo Chavez, Max Ginsburg. *Work:* John Dempsey Hosp, Univ Conn, Farmington, Conn; Salmagundi Club, NY. *Comn:* Paul Danylik, Pastel, Handel's Ice Cream; Chief Court Justice Donald Pogue, Oil, Portrait. *Exhib:* New Britain Mus Am Art, New Britain, Conn, 2008, 2009, 2010; Salmagundi Club, New York, 2007-2009, 2010, 2011, 2012, 2013, 2014; Nat Arts Club, New York, 2008, 2009,, 2011, 2012, 2013; Lyme Art Asn, Old Lyme Conn, Conn, 2006-2009, 2010, 2011, 2012, 2013, 2014; Slater Mus, Norwich, Conn, 2007, 2008, 2010, 2012, 2013, 2014; Mattatuck Mus, Waterbury, Conn, 2009, 2010. *Pos:* past pres, Conn Pastel Soc. *Teaching:* pastel painting, Gallery 53, ACAM, Meriden, Conn, 2007-2008, Christine Ivers Studios, Meriden, Conn, 2009-; digital photo & photoshop elements, Salmagundi Club, New York, 2008; various workshops, 2007-. *Awards:* Richard Poink Mem, Audubon Artist, Inc, 2009-2011, 2013; Top 100 Paint Am, US Parks, Pastel Journ, 2010; Art Spirit Found Silver Medal for Excellence in Pastel, 2010; Rasalie Nadeau Award, Pastel Painters of Cape Cod, 2010; best in show, Conn Women Artits, 2010; best in show, New Britain Mus Am Art, 2010; best in show, Art Guild Middletown, Conn, 2011; best in show, SACA, Conn, 2011; Joseph Hartley Award, Salmagundi Club, 2011. *Mem:* Elected Artist, Lyme Art Assoc (bd mem), Conn; master, Pastel Soc Am; signature mem, bd govs, Audubon Artist; signature mem, Allied Artists Am; master mem, Int Assoc Pastel Soc; signature mem, Academic Artists Am; elected artist, West Hartford Art League, Conn; full artist mem, Salmagundi Club, NY. *Media:* Pastel, oil. *Publ:* Articles in Pastel Journ, Am Artist Mag, Studio Mag, New York Times. *Mailing Add:* 207 Broad St Meriden CT 06450

IVERS, LOUISE H
HISTORIAN
b May 30, 1943. *Study:* Boston Univ, BFA, 64; Univ NMex, MA, 67, PhD, 75. *Teaching:* Prof art, Calif State Univ, Dominguez Hills, 71-2008 (Emeritus). *Awards:* Sunbird Grant, Getty Ctr Educ Arts, 89; Women's Archit League Award, 94; Calif Coun for Humanities Grant, 2000; Evalyn M Bauer Found grant, 2002 & 2004; Grant, Long Beach Naval Memorial Heritage Asn, 2008. *Mem:* Soc Achit Historians. *Media:* Photography. *Res:* 1920s and 1930s Architecture in California. *Publ:* Auth, Montezuma Hotel at Las Vegas Hot Springs New Mexico, J Soc Archit Historians, 74; Cecil Schilling, Jazz Age Architect, Carson: Calif State Univ, Dominguez Hills, 94; Cecil Schilling, Long Beach Architect, Southern Calif Quart, summer 97; Evolution of modernistic architecture in Long Beach, Southern Calif Quarterly, 86; Hugh Davies, Architect & Innovator, CSU Dominguez Hills, 2002; An Architectural Stylist, W. Horace Austin & Eclecticism in California, Calif St Univ, Dominguez Hills, 2005; Swiss Chalets in Long Beach, Southern Calif Quart, fall 2006. *Mailing Add:* Calif State Univ Dominguez Hills 1000 E Victoria St Carson CA 90747

IVERSEN, EARL HARVEY
PHOTOGRAPHER, EDUCATOR
b Chicago, Ill, Jan 26, 1943. *Study:* Univ Ill, Chicago Circle, BA, 70; RI Sch Design, MFA, 73. *Work:* Mus Mod Art, NY; Univ Colo Art Mus, Boulder; Sheldon Gallery, Univ Nebr, Lincoln; Spencer Art Mus, Univ Kans, Lawrence; Sioux City Art Ctr, Iowa. *Exhib:* The Great West, Denver Art Mus, 77; solo exhib, Mass Coll Art, 78, Metropolitan Col, Denver, 78, Kresge Gallery, Mich State Univ, Ann Arbor, 80 & Sioux City Art Ctr, 82; An Open Land, Chicago Art Inst, 83; two-person exhib, Spencer Art Mus, Lawrence, Kans, 83. *Teaching:* Instr photog, Mass Col Art, 73-74; assoc prof design & photog, Univ Kans, Lawrence, 74-, photogr, Univ Theater, 81-. *Awards:* Excellence Award Photog, Univ & Coll Designers Asn, 76; grant, 76 & fel, 83, Nat Endowment Arts. *Publ:* Illusr, Photo Art Mag, #12 & #14, 81; illusr, Erotic Photography, Demarais Press, 81; illusr, Kansas in Color, Regents Press Kans, 82. *Mailing Add:* Univ Kans Dept Design Lawrence KS 66045

IVES, COLTA FELLER
CURATOR, EDUCATOR
b San Diego, Calif, Apr 5, 1943. *Study:* Mills Col, BA, 1964; Columbia Univ, MA, 1966, MS 2008. *Collection Arranged:* The Great Wave (auth, catalog), Metrop Mus Art, NY, 75; Felix Nadar Photog, Metrop Mus Art, NY, 77; The Painterly Print (coauth, catalog), Metrop Mus Art, NY, 80; Albrecht Durer & Holy Family, Metrop Mus Art, NY, 82; Eugene Delacroix: Drawings & Prints, Metrop Mus Art, NY, 84; Pierre Bonnard: The Graphic Art (coauth, catalog), Metrop Mus Art, NY, 89; Daumier Drawings (coauth, catalog), Metrop Mus Art, NY, 93; Goya in the Metrop Mus Art, NY, 95; Toulouse-Lautrec in the Metrop Mus Art (auth, catalog), NY, 96; The Private Collection of Edgar Degas (coauth catalog), Metrop Mus Art, NY, 1997; Romanticism & the School of Nature (author, catalog), Metrop Mus Art, NY, 2000; The Lure of the Exotic: Gauguin in NY collections (coauth catalog), Metrop Mus Art, NY, 2002; Vincent van Gogh: The Drawings (coauth catalog), Metrop Mus Art, NY, 2005. *Pos:* Mem staff, Metrop Mus Art, New York, 66-, cur-in-charge, dept prints & illus bks,

75-93, sr cur, Dept Drawings & Prints, 93-2009, cur emerita, 2009-. *Teaching:* Adj prof art hist, Columbia Univ, 70-87. *Awards:* First Place Award Exhib Catalog, Art Libr Asn New York, 75; Best Mus Exhib in Eastern US, Asn Art Mus Curators, 2005; Best Historical Show, 2005-2006. *Mem:* Assoc Hist Nineteenth Cent Art, Print Coun Am (exec bd, 76-78, 84-86, vpres, 89-91); Assoc Art Mus Cur (exec bd 2004-2005). *Res:* Nineteenth century French drawings, prints and illustrated books; landscape design. *Interests:* Landscape Design. *Publ:* The Great Wave, Metropolitan Mus Art, NY, 75; Photos in & out City Limits, New York, ULAE, 1981; French Prints in the Era of Impressionism & Symbolism, Metrop Mus Art, New York, 89; Pierre Bonnard: The Graphic Art, Metropolitan Mus Art, NY, 89; coauth, The Wrightsman Pictures, Metrop Mus Art, NY, 2007; Daumier Drawings, Metropolitan Mus Art, NY, 93; Toulouse-Lautree in the Metropolitan Mus Art, NY, 96; The Private Collection of Edgar Degas, Metropolitan Mus Art, NY, 97; Romanticism and the School of Nature, Metropolitican Mus Art, NY, 2000; The Lure of the Exotic, Gauguin in NY Collections, Metropolitan Mus Art, Ny, 2002; Van Gogh: The Drawings Metropolitan Mus Art, NY, 2005. *Mailing Add:* Dept of Prints & Photographs Metrop Mus Art New York NY 10028

IVEY-WEAVER, JACQUELYN KUNKEL
PAINTER, SCULPTOR

b Richmond, Ky, Mar 14, 1931. *Study:* Wesleyan Coll, BFA, 1987; Workshops with numerous artists. *Work:* Monroe County Hospital, Forsyth, Ga; Mus Arts & Sci, Macon, Ga. *Comn:* M/M David Attaway (portraits & sculptures), Mrs Sheryl Byrd (oil portraits), Mr & Mrs Brutus Bankston (sculptures), M/M Ed Jones (portaits), and more. *Exhib:* Mid Ga Art Asn Gallery, Macon, 1980-2010; Stofko-Dixon Fine Arts, Bolingbroke, Ga, 1996-2001; Self Family Art Ctr, Hilton Head Island, SC, 2001; Mus Arts & Scis, Macon, 2002, 2005, 2007; Brazier Art Gallery, Richmond, Va, 2002; Gallery 51, Forsyth, Ga, 2003-05; Roundtree Gallery, Seaside, Fla, 2003-04; Monroe County Arts Alliance, Forsyth, 2004-10; Richard Schmid Fine Art Auction, Bellvue, Colo, 2004, 2005, 2006-10; Macon Arts Alliance Gallery, 2005-10; Attaway Cottage, Macon, Ga. *Pos:* Owner JK Ivey Fine Art, Macon, Ga, 1974-91, JK Ivey Art Studio, 1991-; bd dirs & treas, Mid-Ga Art Asn, Macon, 1981-84, publicity chmn, 1988-1989, chmn nominating comt, 1997, finance comt, 1998-99, audit comt, 1998. *Teaching:* JK Ivey-Weaver Art Studio, 1991-2009. *Awards:* many nat, regional, & local awards. *Mem:* Monroe County Arts Alliance; Oil Painters Am, Inc; Mid Ga Art Asn; Catherine Lorillard Wolf Art Club; Mus Arts & Scis; Nat Mus Women in Arts; charter mem, Monroe County Arts Alliance. *Media:* Oil on Linen or Canvas. *Interests:* Walking, reading, ballroom dancing. *Publ:* Towards Creativity, Monroe County Arts Alliance, Middle Ga Art Asn, Macon, Ga. *Dealer:* Richard Schmid Fine Art Auction, Bellvue, Colo; Attaway Cottage; MCAA Forsyth GA; MGAA Macon GA; Macon Arts Alliance GA. *Mailing Add:* PO Box 816 Macon GA 31202

IWAMASA, KEN
EDUCATOR, PRINTMAKER

b Manzanar, Calif, Apr 28, 1943. *Study:* Calif State Univ, Long Beach, BA, 66, MA, 72. *Work:* El Camino Col; City of Los Angeles; Rio Hondo Col. *Exhib:* Solo exhibs, Rio Hondo Coll, 76 & Old Dominion Univ, 77; World Print Competition, San Francisco Mus Mod Art, Calif, 77; Detroit Nat Print Symposium, Cranbrook Acad Art, 80; Fantastic Art, Castle San Giorgo, Italy, 81; Works on Paper, Cheney-Cowles Mem Mus, Spokane, 81; Artist as Social Critic, Mich State Univ, Ann Arbor, 81; and others. *Teaching:* Asst prof drawing & printmaking, Univ Colo, Boulder, 72-. *Awards:* Grants & Purchase Awards from Scott Found, Japan Found & Univ Colo. *Media:* Screen, Lithography. *Dealer:* Miriam Perlman Gallery 505 N Lake Shore Dr Chicago IL 60611; Sebastian Moore Gallery 1411 Market St Denver CO. *Mailing Add:* 64 Huron Court Boulder CO 80303-4414

IWAMOTO, RALPH SHIGETO
PAINTER

b Honolulu, Hawaii, Sept 13, 1927. *Study:* Art Students League, with John Von Wicht, Vaclav Vytlacil & Byron Browne, 48-49 & 51-53. *Work:* Butler Inst Am Art, Youngstown, Ohio; Herbert F Johnson Art Mus, Cornell Univ; State Found on Cult & Arts, Honolulu; Wadsworth Atheneum, Hartford, Conn; Zimmerli Mus Art Rutgers Univ, New Brunswick, NJ. *Exhib:* Solo exhibs, Columbia Mus Art, SC, 59, Elmira Coll, NY, 68, St Mary's Coll, Md, 89, Gallery Onetwentyeight, NY, 2001 & David Findlay Jr, Gallery, New York, 2004; Bergen Co Mus, NJ, 83; Contemp Mus, Honolulu, 90; New Britain Mus, Conn, 2003; Wellesley Coll, Davis Mus, Mass 2004; Real Art Ways Ctr, Hartford, Conn, 2004; First Hawaiian Ctr, Contemp Mus, Hawaii, 2005; Nat Acad Mus, New York, 2005; The Gallery at 6th & 6th, Tucson, Ariz, 2008. *Awards:* Purchase Prize, Butler Inst Am Art, 57; Fel, John Hay Whitney Found, 58; Grant, Adolph & Esther Gottlieb Found, 87; Pollock-Krasner Found Grant, 2002. *Bibliog:* K Ichida (auth), article, Ichimai Art Mag, Tokyo, 12/80; Helen A Harrison (auth), article, NY Times, 12/29/85; Fred Camper (auth), rev, Chicago Reader, 10/17/97; Jeffrey Wechsler (auth), Preface to catalog, Findlay Gallery Show, 2004; Elisa Decker (auth), Review, Art in Am, 1/2005. *Mem:* New York Artists Equity. *Media:* Acrylic, Oil. *Publ:* Auth, Octagon Concepts. *Mailing Add:* 463 W St A-1110 New York NY 10014

J

JACHNA, JOSEPH DAVID
PHOTOGRAPHER, EDUCATOR

b Chicago, Ill, Sept 12, 1935. *Study:* Univ Mo Photo-J Workshop, 57; Ill Inst Technol Inst Design, with Aaron Siskind, Harry Callahan & Frederick Sommer, BS (art educ), 58, MS (photog), 61. *Work:* George Eastman House, Int Mus Photog, Rochester, NY; Art Inst Chicago; Photog Collection, Exchange Nat Bank of Chicago; Mass Inst Technol; Mus Mod Art, NY. *Exhib:* Solo exhibs, Art Inst Chicago, 61, Nikon Salon, Tokyo, 74, Visual Studies Workshop Gallery, Rochester, NY, 79, Chicago Ctr Contemp Photog, 80, Focus Gallery, San Francisco, 81 & Tweed Mus, Duluth, Minn, 86; City Gallery Photog, Hist Water Tower, Chicago, 2007, Gahlberg Gallery, Coll Dupage, Glen Ellyn IL, 2011, Stephen Daiter Gallery, 2012, Univ North Fla, Mus Contemporary Art, Jacksonville, MOCA, 50-60 prints, 2013; Photog: Midwest Invitational, Walker Art Ctr, Minneapolis, 73; Photographers and the City, Mus Contemp Art, Chicago, 77; Second Sight, Carpenter Ctr Visual Arts, Harvard Univ, 81; Josephson, Jachna & Siegel: Chicago Experimentalists, San Francisco Mus Mod Art, 88; Vanishing Presence, Walker Art Ctr, Minneapolis, 89; Passing the Torch, The Chicago Students of Callahan & Siskind, Stephen Daiter Gallery, Chicago, 2010. *Collection Arranged:* Richard Nickel, Photographs, fall, 72 & Harold Allen, Photographs, spring, 75, Ward Gallery, Univ Ill, Chicago; Co-cur Robert Stiegler, Photographs, Gallery 400, Univ Ill, Chicago, fall, 86. *Teaching:* From instr to asst prof photog, Inst Design, Ill Inst Technol, 61-69; from asst prof to prof photog, Univ Ill, Chicago Campus, 69-2001, prof emer, currently; workshops, Peninsula Sch Art, Door Co, Wis, summers 69-71. *Awards:* Fac Grant Color Photog, Univ Ill, Chicago Circle Campus, 72; Ferguson Grant, Friends of Photog, Carmel, Calif, 73; Nat Endowment Arts, 76; John Simon Guggenheim Mem Found Fel, 80. *Bibliog:* Landscape illusions, In: Photography Year 1974, Time-Life Bks, 74; John B Turner (auth), Joseph D Jachna, Photo-Forum, Auckland, NZ, 75; Light Touching Silver (monogr), Chicago Mus Photog, 80. *Publ:* Art in Am, New Talent Issue, 62; Camera Mainichi '74-9, 74; Photog & Art-Interactions since 1946, 87; Landscape As Photograph, Yale Univ Press, 85; Vanishing Presence, Walker Art Ctr & Rizzoli, 89. *Dealer:* Stephen Daiter Gallery 230 W Superior St. *Mailing Add:* 5707 W 89th Pl Oak Lawn IL 60453

JACIR, EMILY
PHOTOGRAPHER

b Palestine, 1970. *Study:* Univ Dallas, BA (art), 1992; Memphis Coll Art, MFA, 1994; Whitney Ind Study Program, NY City, 1998-99. *Work:* Mus Modern Art, Arnhem, Netherlands, 2003, Herbert F Johnson Mus, Cornell Univ, NY, 2001, Queens Inter, Queens Mus Art, 2002, Made in Palestine, Art Car Mus, Houston, 2003, Whitney Biennial, Whitney Mus Am Art, 2004, Cheekwood Mus Art, Nashville, 2004. *Exhib:* Solo exhibs, Anderson Ranch Arts Ctr, Snowmass Village, Colo, 1997, Eastfield Coll Gallery, Mesquite, Tex, 1997, Everywhere/Nowhere, SPACES, Cleveland, 1999, From Paris to Riyadh (Drawings For My Mother), Univ Gallery, US, Sewanee, Tenn, 2000, New Photog: Bethlehem to Ramallah, Debs & Co Project Room, NY, 2002, Where We Come From, 2003, Belongings, O-K Ctr Contemp Art, Linz, Austria, 2003, The Neth, 2003, Los Angeles Inter Art Biennial, Frumkin Duval Gallery, Santa Monica, Calif, 2003, Artspace Annex II, New Haven, Conn, 2003, Woher wir kommen, Künstlerhaus, Bremen, 2004, Den I: a på Moderna: Emily Jacir: Where We Come From, Moderna Museet, Stockholm, 2004, The Khalil Sakakini Cult Ctr, Ramallah, 2004, Nuova Icona, Venice, 2004, Kunstraum Innsbruck, Innsbruck, 2004, Accumulations, Alexander & Bonin, NY, 2005; group exhibs, 7th Ann McNeese Nat Works on Paper, McNeese State, Lake Charles, La, 1994; Women in Art: 12 Texas Women, Contemp Art Ctr, Houston, 1997; Xmas, Kent Gallery, NY, 1999; Free for All, Temporary Art Services, Chicago, 2000; Carnival in the Eye of the Storm; War/Art/New Technol, Pacific Northwest Coll Art, Portland, Ore, 2000; Greater NY, PS 1 Contemp Art Ctr, Long Island City, 2000; Strangers/Estrangers, PS 1 Clocktower Gallery, NY, 2001, 2001; Made in Transit, Vacancy Gallery, NY, 2001; Unjustified, Apex Art, NY, 2002; Submerged, Nuremberg, 2002; Right2Fight, Sarah Lawrence Col, Bronxville, NY, 2002; Settlement, Gallery 400, Chicago, 2002; Global Priority, Hester Art Gallery, Univ Mass, 2003; Shatat, Colo Univ Art Galleries, Boulder, 2003; VEIL, Inst Int Arts, London, 2003; 8th Istanbul Biennial, 2003; 100 Cuts, Gallery 312, Chicago, 2004; Empire: Videos for a New World, Md Inst Coll Art, Baltimore, 2004; Cover Girl: The Female Body & Islam in Contemp Art, Ise Cult Found, NY, 2004; Neither Here Nor There: Video Artists Navigate Cult Displacement, Election, Am Fine Arts, NY, 2004; Sometime: Six Works for Film & Video, Anthony Reynolds Gallery, London, 2004; Desenhos: A-Z, Porta 33, Funchal, Ilha da Madeira, 2005; Venice Biennale, 2007. *Awards:* Hugo Boss Prize, 2008; Alpert award, Calif Inst of the Arts, 2011. *Dealer:* Alexander & Bonin 132 Tenth Ave New York NY 10011

JACKLIN, BILL (WILLIAM)
PAINTER, PRINTMAKER

b Hampstead, London, Eng, Jan 1, 1943. *Study:* Walthamstow Sch Art, Essex, BA (painting), 64; Royal Coll Art, London, MA (painting), 67. *Hon Degrees:* Tate Gallery, London. *Work:* Victoria & Albert Mus & Brit Mus, London; Metrop Mus, NY; Mus Mod Art, NY; Yale Ctr British Art, New Haven, Conn; Tampa Mus Mod Art; The Libr of Congress, Anglo American; Morgan Library & Museum, New York. *Comn:* Mural, Cesar Pelli & Assoc, Washington Nat Airport, DC; painting futures market, Bank of England, London, 88; tapestry, DeBeers, London, 94. *Exhib:* Mus Mod Art, NY, 72; British Painting Today, Mus Mod Art, Paris, 73; British Painting 1952-77, Royal Acad Art, London, 77; Directors Choice, Tampa Mus Art, Fla, 87; Metrop Mus, NY, 90; Britain & Sao Paulo Biennale 1951-91, Brit Coun, London, 92; Urban Portraits NY 1986-92 (with catalog), Mus Mod Art, Oxford, Eng, 92-93; Urban Portraits Hong Kong, Brit Coun Hong Kong, 93-95; New Acquisitions, 20th Century Wing, Metrop Mus Art, NY, 96-97; L'ecole Londres, de bacon a Bevan, Found Vierny, musee Maillol, Paris, 98; People and Places, Marlborough Gallery, 90, 97, 99, 2002, 2007, 2008, 2009, 2012. *Pos:* Artist-in-residence, Hong Kong. *Teaching:* Instr painting, Numerous Art Cols Gt Brit, 67-75. *Awards:* Bursary Award, Arts Coun London, 75. *Bibliog:* John Russell Taylor (auth), Bill Jacklin Recent Work, Marlborough Gallery, 87 & Bill Jacklin (monograph), Phaidon Press, 97; Robert Rosenblum (auth), Urban Portraits, Marlborough Fine Art Catalogue, 88; Tina Eden Productions (dir), Bill Jacklin in New York (film), 92; Phoebe Hoban (auth) The Connected Image, Marlborough Catalogue, New York, 99; Jill Llyod (auth) Sihouettes & Shadows New York City, Marlborough Catalogue, London, 2000; Sandler Irving (auth), Art Transplant: British Artists in NY, 2001; British Consulate General, NY, 2004; Mary Rose Beaumont (auth), A Venetian Affair, Marlborough Catalogue, 2007; Lloyd, Jill (auth), People and Places, Marlborough Catalogue, 2007; Michael Peppiatt (auth), People & Places II, Marlborough Catalogue, 2008, London/Monaco, 2009; Margaret

Priest (auth), A Stranger in NY (catalogue introduction), Marlborough Gallery, NY, 2012; Dr Ihor Holubizky (auth), Bill Jacklin, The Art of Being There, Time Out, Marlborough Gallery, London, 2013. *Mem:* Elected mem Royal Acad, 90; Royal Acad London; Royal Soc Painters; Printmakers of London. *Media:* Oil; All Media. *Specialty:* Contemporary Artists. *Dealer:* Marlborough Gallery Inc 40 W 57th St New York NY 10019

JACKOBOICE, SANDRA KAY
ARTIST
b Detroit, Mich, Jul 22, 1936. *Study:* Mich State Univ, East Lansing, 56; Aquinas Col, Grand Rapids, Mich, BA, 89; post grad study with prominent Am artists. *Work:* City Hall, Bielsko Biala, Poland; Downtown Mgt bd, Grand Rapids, Mich; Corp Off, Monarch Hydraulics, Grand Rapid, Mich; Aquinas Coll, Grand Rapids, Mich; Florida State Capital, Tallahassee, Fla; Lee Mem Hosp, Fort Myers, Fla. *Comn:* West Mich Iris Soc, New Hybird Iris, Grand Rapids, Mich; St. Roberts Church, Ada, Mich; plus mant pvt comn. *Exhib:* Great Lakes Pastel Soc, Juried Exhib, Midland, Mich, 99 & 2003; Girl Scouts of Am Invitational Exhib, Grand Rapids, Mich, 2002; Int Assoc of Pastel Soc, Demonstrator's Exhib, Albuquerque, NMex, 2003 & 2007; Artist in Residence, Franciscan Life Process Ctr, Lowell, Mich, 2003; Pastel Soc of Am, Invitational Exhib, Dunedin, Fla, 2004; plus many other solo & group exhibs. *Pos:* Co-found, pres, adv to bd dir, Great Lakes Pastel Soc, 1997-, bd adv & satellite coord, 2001-; exhib coordnr, Peninsular Club, Grand Rapids, Mich, 1997-2001; lifetime mem, Southwest Fla Pastel Soc, 2001-; found, Pastel Group of Southwest Fla, 2001; mem ch, Int Asn Pastel Soc, 2001-2007, vpres, 2005-2007. *Teaching:* Coordnr, instr, pastel classes, Grand Rapids Art Mus, 2000-01; pastel instr, Von Liebig Art Ctr, Naples, Fla, 2001-; workshop instr, Marco Island Art Ctr, Marco Island, Fla, 2002-; pastel instr, Aquinas Coll Emer Prog, Grand Rapids, Mich, 2004-; instr pastel, Philharmonic Ctr for the Arts, Naples, Fla; demonstr, Int Assoc Pastel Soc Conv, 2007. *Awards:* West Mich Iris Soc, 1994; Botanical Images award, 1995, 96; Great Lakes Pastel Soc, 2003. *Mem:* United Arts Coun, Collier Co, Fla (bd mem); Pastel Soc Am (signature mem); Artist Alliance; Great Lakes Pastel Soc; Southwest Fla Pastel Soc (life mem); Int Assoc Pastel Soc (membership chair, 2001-2007, vp, 2005-2007). *Media:* Pastel, Acrylic. *Interests:* Painting, photography, golf, travel. *Publ:* Artists Photo Reference Flowers, North Light Books, 2002; Pastel Artists Int Mag, 3rd edition; Getting to Know Pastel, brochure IAPS Convention, 2003; Original Pastel Under Sail, The Artist Mag, 2003; Pastel on Canvas, Pastel Jour, 2004; The Ultimate Guide to Painting from Photographs, North Light Books, 2005. *Dealer:* Sweet Art Gallery Naples FL 34109

JACKSON, CHARLOTTE
PAINTER, INSTRUCTOR
b New York, NY, Nov 21, 1926. *Study:* Traphagen Art Inst, 43-45. *Work:* White House, Washington, DC; NYC Courthouse, Mayor's Mansion, NY; Royall Cornwall Gallery & Mus, Minneapolis; Joe Franklin TV Show (exhib), NY; and many mus & corp collections throughout the world. *Comn:* Hester St, comn by Phil Coffaro (of Art Expo) NY, 75; Cesars Palace, comn by decorator, Las Vegas, Nev, 79; Cover of Plate Collector Magazine (self portrait), Kermit, Tex, 80; Lynn's Rose, Dover Financial Corp & NBSR, NY, 81; Sands Hotel, comn by decorator, Las Vegas, Nev, 82. *Exhib:* Brooklyn Mus, Brooklyn, NY, 75; Whitney Mus, NYC, 77; R Johnson Gallery, Fla. *Collection Arranged:* Pictures on Exhibition, 78-79, 81; Somerset Mus, 90-91. *Pos:* Art dir, Southwest Art, NYC, 94-96. *Teaching:* instr oil painting, Pearl Paint, Fla, 2004-; AC Moore, Fla, 2007; Coral Ridge Country Club, Fla. *Media:* Oil. *Interests:* Oil painting, sketching. *Publ:* Henry Youngman (auth), Art That I Like, Dalton Publishing, 84; Ray Johnson (auth), Realism Art, Dalton Publishing, 85; Ray Johnson (auth), The Art of Flowers, Ray Johnson, 85

JACKSON, HERB
PAINTER, PRINTMAKER
b Raleigh, NC, Aug 16, 1945. *Study:* Davidson Col, BA, 67; Philips Univ, Marburg, WGer; Univ NC, MFA, 70. *Work:* Brit Mus, London; Libr Cong, Washington; Victoria & Albert Mus, London; Brooklyn Mus Art, NY; Baltimore Mus Art, Md; Whitney Mus Am Art, NY; Minneapolis Inst Arts; Mint Mus, Charlotte, NC. *Comn:* Mural, Vail Commons, Davidson Col, 84; First Union Nat Bank, 88. *Exhib:* Solo Exhibs: Mint Mus Art, Charlotte, NC; Springfield Art Mus, Mo; Fundacao Calouste Gulbenkian, Lisbon, Portugal; Ashville Mus Art, NC; Greenville Mus Art, Greenville NC, 2000; Fayetteville Mus Art, Fayetteville, NC, 2003; Small Paintings, Art Preserve, Charlotte, NC, 2004; Paintings, Christa Faut Gallery, Cornelius, NC, 2005; Small Paintings, Stetson Univ, Deland, Fla, 2006; Small Oil Paintings, Univ of the South, Sewanee, Tenn, 2006; Drawings from the Adriatic, Davidson Coll, Davidson, NC, 2006; New Paintings, Somerhill Gallery Chapel Hill, NC, 2006; Veronica's Veils-A Retrospective, McColl Center for Visual Art, Charlotte, NC, 2007; Veronica's Veil Drawings, Christa Faut Gallery, Cornelius, NC, 2007, Firestorm in the Teahouse, Claire Oliver Gallery, NY, 2011, Pure Abstraction, Lee Hansley Gallery, Raleigh, NC, 2012, Veils, Claire Oliver Gallery, NY, 2013; Group Exhibs: Mint Mus Art, Charlotte NC, 68, 70-71, 79 & 81; Am Accad & Inst Arts & Letters, NY 81 & 87; Brooklyn Mus Art, 81; Knoxville World's Fair, Tenn, 82; Contemp Arts Center, New Orleans, La, 88; Kunstammlungen der Veste Coburg, Ger, 88; Lorenzelli FIne Art, Milan, Italy, 89; Exhib Hall of Union Moscow Artists, Moscow, USSR, 89; Samuel P Harn Mus, Gainesville, Fla, 90; Utah Mus Art, Salt Lake City, 98; Thomas McCormick Gallery, Chicago, 2002; Peace Tower, Whitney Mus Art, MYC, 2006; Stetson Univ, Deland, Fla, 2006; Claire Oliver Gallery, New York, 2010; Southern Abstraction, Mobile Mus Art, Ala, 2012; Beyond Bling, Claire Oliver Gallery, NY, 2013. *Teaching:* Prof fine art, (Douglas C Houchens Professorship) Davidson Col, 69-. *Awards:* NC Award, 1999; Boswell Fel, 2007; ASC Lifetime Achievement award, 2009. *Bibliog:* Dr Roger Lipsey (auth), Herb Jackson Drawings at the Mint Museum, Arts, 6/83; Dr Donald Kuspit (auth), Herb Jackson: The Archeological Surface, 11/88; Frank Getlein (auth), Herb Jackson: Vitreographs, 8/90; Richard Sniff (auth), Thinking by Hand, 9/2007; Brad Thomas and Roger Manley (auths), Excavations, 2011. *Media:* Acrylic, Graphics. *Dealer:* Claire Oliver Gallery 513 West 26th St New york NY 10001. *Mailing Add:* PO Box 10 Davidson NC 28036

JACKSON, JEANINE CARERI
PAINTER, INSTRUCTOR
b Hoboken, NJ, Oct 10, 1954. *Study:* Acad Holy Angels, NJ, Coll Prep/Art, 1972; Fairleigh Dickinson Univ, Philos, 1976; Univ of Florence, Italy (studied med), 1985; Marvin Mattelson, Sch Visual Arts, 2002; Portrait Soc Am, Conn-Ambassador, 2004. *Comn:* Portrait, comn by Giorgio Family, Greenwich, Conn, 2003; Portrait, comn by Rose Anne Hoffman, Darien, Conn, 2005; Portrait, comn by Howard Pierce, Westport, Conn, 2006; Tarpon Bus (mural), Grosse Pointe Develop, Cape Coral, Fla, 2007; House Portrait, Hilderbrand 's Hyatt-Byard House, Silvermine, Conn, 2007. *Exhib:* Jackson Watercolors, Contact Art, Paris, France, 2000; Visual Poetry, Flinn Gallery, Greenwich, Conn, 2002; Jeanine Jackson PeopleScapes, Gertrude White Gallery, Greenwich, Conn 2003; Faces of Winter 04, Bendheim Gallery, Greenwich, Conn, 2004; Faces of Newtown 05, Newtown Libr, Newtown, Conn, 2005; Faces of Spring 05, Lyme Art Asn, Old Lyme, Conn, 2005; Faces of Winter 06, Bendheim Gallery, 2006; Faces of Spring 07, Lyme Art Asn, 2007. *Pos:* Founder Pres Emer, Conn Soc Portrait Artists, 2002-; Conn Ambassador, Portrait Soc Am, Tallahassee, Fla, 2004-; Main teacher, Yeorge Passantino, Silvermine Sch Art, New Canaan, Conn, 1999-2001. *Teaching:* Instr portraits, Jackson Studios, Cape Coral, Fla, 2005-; Cape Coral Art League, 2006-. *Awards:* Honorable Mention, Juried Show, Art Society of Old Greenwich (ASOG), 2002; 1st Prize Oils, Spring Show, ASOG, 2002, 2003, 2004; Honorable Mention, Faces of Winter 03, Conn Soc Portrait Artists, 2003; Merit Award, Faces of Winter 06, Conn Soc Portrait Artists, 2006. *Bibliog:* Lisa Pierce Breunig (auth), Portrait of an Artist, Living in Stamford Mag, Feb-Mar 2001; (staff), Insite Business, The Advocate, Stamford Conn, 9/3/2001; New YWCA Exhibit, Greenwich Time, 3/26/2003; Betty Coughlin (auth), The Art of the Portrait, 3/31/2002; Artistic Avenues, Greenwich Time, 5/19/2002. *Mem:* Conn Soc Portrait Artists (found, 2002; pres & co-chair, 2002-2006; pres emer, 2006-); Art Soc Old Greenwich (bd dirs, 2003-2005); Portrait Soc Am, (conn ambassador, 2004-); Cape Coral Art League (fac, 2005-); Catherine Lorillard Wolf Art Soc (mem). *Media:* Oil on Canvas. *Publ:* Auth, A New Chapter for Connecticut, The Portrait Signature, 2002; auth, The Language of Flowers and Art, Westport News, 2003; auth, The Role of Contemporary Portraiture, NY Arts Mag, 2004

JACKSON, MARION ELIZABETH
HISTORIAN, EDUCATOR
b Saginaw, Mich, July 7, 1941. *Study:* Univ Mich, PhD (art hist), 85, with Rudolf Arnheim, Evan Maurer, Marvin Eisenberg & Roy Rappaport. *Collection Arranged:* Inuit Sculpture (auth, catalog), Univ Mich Mus Art, 79; The Vital Vision: Drawings by Ruth Tulurialik (auth, catalog), Art Gallery Windsor, Ont, 86; Contemporary Inuit Drawings, Macdonald Stewart Art Ctr, Univ Guelph, 87; Ruth Weisberg - Paintings, Drawings, Prints 1986-1988, Univ Mich Sch Art, 87; Parr: Drawings, Mt St Vincent Univ, 88. *Pos:* Assoc dean, Univ Mich Sch Art, 86-91. *Teaching:* Lectr, art hist, Eastern Mich Univ, Ypsilanti, 83-84; assoc prof, Univ Mich Sch Art, 86-91, Carleton Univ, Ottawa, Can, 91-95; prof & chair, Art & Art His, Wayne State Univ, Detroit, Mich. *Mem:* Coll Art Asn; Native Am Art Studies Asn; Nat Asn Humanities Educ; African Studies Asn; Brazilian Studies Asn. *Res:* Native arts, particularly North American Inuit art; folk arts; outsider arts; & art criticism; African American art. *Publ:* Contemp Print Drawings, Macdonald Stewart Art Ctr, 87; Ruth Weisberg: Paintings, Drawings, Prints, 1968-1988, Univ Mich Sch Art, 88; Tyree Guyton: Listen to His Art, Detroit Inst Arts, 90; auth, Pudlo: Thirty Years of Drawing, Nat Gallery of Can, 90; Inuit Women Artists: Voices from Cape Dorset, 94. *Mailing Add:* 1336 Nicolet Pl Detroit MI 48207

JACKSON, MATTHEW DAY
INSTALLATION SCULPTOR, ASSEMBLAGE ARTIST
b Panorama City, Calif, 1974. *Study:* Univ Wash, Seattle, BFA, 1997; Rutgers Univ, Mason-Gross Sch Arts, New Brunswick, NJ, MFA, 2001. *Exhib:* Solo exhibs include By No Means Necessary, Chinati Gound, Marfa, Tex, 2004; Perry Rubenstein Gallery, 2005; Paradise Now, Port Inst Contemp Art, 2006; Jack S Blanton Mus Art, Austin, 2007; two-person exhib with Huma Bhabha, Peter Blum Gallery, New York, 2007; group exhibs include San Titre, Boulder Mus Contemp Art, Colo, 1999; Rabbett Gallery, New Brunswick, NJ, 2001; Drift, Manasquan, NJ, 2002; Portland Mus Art Biennial, Maine, 2003; White, Black, Yellow, Red, Storefront 1838, New York, 2003; Spiritual Hunger, Daniel Silverstein Gallery, New York, 2003; Relentless Proselytizers, Feigen Contemp, New York, 2004; Mommy! I! Am! Not! An! Animal!, Capsule Gallery, New York, 2004; The Greater New York Show, PS1 Contemp Art Ctr, 2005; Bridge Freezes Before Road, Barbara Gladstone Gallery, New York, 2005; Sticks & Stones, Perry Rubenstein Gallery, New York, 2005; Day for Night, Whitney Biennial, Whitney Mus Am Art, New York, 2006; USA Today, Saatchi Gallery, London, 2007; The Martian Museum of Terrestrial Art, Barbican Ctr, London, 2008; The Violet Hour, Henry Art Gallery, Seattle, 2008. *Awards:* Scholar Skowhegan Sch Painting & Sculpture, Skowhegan, Maine, 2002; vis scholar Chinati Found, Marfa, Tex, 2004; Named One of 10 Artists on the Verge of a Breakthrough, NY Mag, 2005. *Mailing Add:* c/o Peter Blum Gallery 20 W 57th St New York NY 10019

JACKSON, OLIVER LEE
PAINTER, SCULPTOR
b St Louis, Mo, 1935. *Study:* Ill Wesleyan Univ, BFA, 58; Univ Iowa, MFA, 63. *Work:* San Francisco Mus Mod Art & Fine Arts Mus San Francisco; Oakland Mus; Seattle Art Mus; New Orleans Mus Art; Mus Mod Art & Metrop Mus, NY; Portland Art Mus, Ore; Mus Contemp Art, Chicago & San Diego; many others; Nat Gallery of Art, DC. *Comn:* Painting for state off bldg, San Francisco, Calif Arts Coun, 87; marble sculpture for Gen Servs Admin Bldg, Oakland, Calif, 88, 96. *Exhib:* Solo exhib, Seattle Art Mus, 82, St Louis Art Mus, 90 & Crocker Art Mus, Sacramento, Calif, 93, Newport Harbor Art Mus, Newport Beach, Calif, 93 & Fresno Art Mus, 2000, Sert Gallery, Harvard Univ, 2002-2003; Biennial Exhib, Whitney Mus, 83; An Int Survey of Recent Painting and Sculpture, Mus Mod Art, NY, 84; States of War, Seattle Art Mus, Wash, 85; California Figurative Sculpture, Palm Springs Desert Mus, 87; The Appropriate Object, Albright-Knox Gallery, Buffalo, NY, 89. *Pos:* Vis artist, Art Inst

Chicago, 69; artist in res, Wake Forest Univ, SE Ctr Contemp Art, 80 & NC Sch Arts, Winston-Salem, 80; vis artist, Univ Calif, Santa Barbara, 85, Univ Wash, Seattle, 85, Univ Ill, Champaign, 88, Univ Calif, Berkeley, 89, Univ Hawaii, Hilo, 93 & 2001, San Francisco Art Inst, 93, Calif Col Arts & Crafts Summer Invitational, Paris, 2000 & Harvard Univ, 2000. *Teaching:* Instr, Southern Ill Univ, East St Louis, 67-69, Oberlin Col, 69-70; prof art, Calif State Univ, Sacramento, 71-2002. *Awards:* Award in Painting, Nat Endowment Arts, 80; Eureka Fel, Fleishhacker Found, 93; Awards for the Visual Arts, Flintridge Foundation, 2004. *Bibliog:* Regina Hackett (auth), Oliver Lee Jackson (catalog), SE Ctr Contemp Art, 80; Thomas Albright & Jan Butterfield (co-auth), Oliver Jackson, Seattle Art Mus, 82; Robert Pincus (auth), Oliver Jackson, Iannetti-Lanzone Gallery, San Francisco, 88; Oliver Jackson, Fresno Art Mus, 2000. *Media:* Oil; Marble; Intaglio prints. *Dealer:* Artists Forum. *Mailing Add:* c/o Anne Kohs & Assoc 115 Stonegate Rd Portola Valley CA 94028

JACKSON, PAUL C
PAINTER

b Lawrence, KS, Mar 25, 1968. *Study:* Mississippi State Univ, BFA, 1989; Univ of MO, MFA, 1992. *Work:* MO State Capitol, (gov's portrait), Jefferson City, MO; Mo Gov's Mansion, Jefferson City, MO; MO Supreme Court, Jefferson City, MO; Margaret Harwell Mus, Poplar Bluff, MO; Univ of MO, Columbia, MO. *Comn:* Tiber Spot Mosaic, Univ of MO, Columbia, MO, 2001; Mo Commem State Quarter, US Mint, Washington, DC, 2003. *Exhib:* Rocky Mtn Watermedia, Foot Hills Art Ctr, Golden, Colo, 1996; Kans Watercolor So, Wichita Art Mus, Wichita, Kans, 1996; Am Watercolor Soc, Salmagundi Club, New York City, 2006; MO Watercolor Nat, Christian Memorial, Fulton, MO, 2006; La Watercolor, St Charles Place, New Orleans, La, 2006. *Collection Arranged:* First Glimpse Back, Pensacola Mus, 2000. *Pos:* judge, Alaska Watercolor Soc, 2003; judge, La Watercolor Soc, 2005. *Awards:* Hardie Gramatky Award, 1992; Distinguished Alumni, Univ of MO, 2001; Dong Kingman Award, Am Watercolor Soc, 2006. *Mem:* signature mem, Am Watercolor Soc, 1998. *Media:* Watercolor. *Publ:* Auth, Painting Spectacular Light Effects, North Light, 2000; illus, The Physicians Guide to Investing, 2005. *Mailing Add:* 2918 Bluegrass Columbia MO 65201

JACKSON, ROBERT COLEMAN
PAINTER

b Kinston, NC, Oct 17, 1964. *Exhib:* Solo exhibs, Nat Inst Health, Bethesda, 97, Zenith Gallery, Washington, DC, 97-98, 2001 & 2004, SomervilleManning Gallery, Greenville, Del, 97, 2000 & 2003, Somerhill Gallery, Chapel Hill, NC, 2000, 2002, 2005, Arden Gallery, Boston, 2001 & 2004-2005; Realism, Parkersburg Art Ctr, WVa, 98; Off the Wall Humor, Zenith Gallery, Washington, DC, 99Food Glorious Food, 2005; Still, Kougeas Gallery, Boston, 99; Still Life Invitational, Somerhill Gallery, NC, 99; Still Life, Bennett Galleries, Knoxvillle, Tenn, 2000; Realistic Vision, Cudahy's Gallery, Richmond, Va, 2000; Realism Today, John Pence Gallery, San Francisco, 2000; Butler Art Inst, Youngstown, Ohio, 2001; Del Ctr Contemp Arts, Wilmington, 2001; Feathers and Sticks, Bennett Galleries, Knoxville, 2001; Emerging Artists, Jenkins Johnson Gallery, San Francisco, 2001, Annual Realism Invitational, 2001; Contemp Realism II, Carol Henderson Gallery, Ft Worth, Tex, 2001; Jackson 4, Del Art Mus Sales Gallery, 2004. *Mailing Add:* 284 Longview Lane Kennett Square PA 19348

JACKSON, SUZANNE
PAINTER, PRINTMAKER

b St Louis, Mo, Jan 30, 1944. *Study:* San Francisco State Col, BA, 66; Sch of Drama, Design, Yale Univ, MFA, 90; Otis Art Inst, Los Angeles, with Charles White & Noel Quinn, 1968. *Work:* Adam Clayton Powell Jr, State Office Bldg, Harlem; Palm Springs Desert Mus; California African-Am Mus; Daniel, Mann, Johnson & Mendenhall, Co, Los Angeles; Indianapolis Mus Art; Jen Libr, Savannah Coll of Art & Design, Ga; Carnegie Art Mus, Oxnard, Calif; Art in Embassies Program, Belgrade, Serbia. *Comn:* Peace Bird, Secy State Edmund G Brown, Jr, Sacramento, 72; Stephen Chase, Arthur Elrod & Assoc, Palm Springs, 74; Artful Living, William Chidester Co, Pac Design Ctr, Los Angeles, 75; mural, New Health Ctr, Los Angeles, 79; and many others. *Exhib:* Solo exhibs, Ankrum Gallery, 68-84, Calif State Off Bldg, Los Angeles, 81-82, Multi-Cult Art Inst, San Diego, 83, Fashion Moda, New York, 84, Ingber Gallery, NY, 84, Ankrum Gallery, Los Angeles, 84, Sargent Johnson Gallery, San Francisco, 85, Black Like Me Gallery & San Francisco, 86, Suzanne Jackson: Paintings & Monoprints, Pinnacle Gallery, Savanna, GA, 2005 & Marshall House Galleries, 2005-2006, Carnegie Art Mus, Oxnard, Calif, 2008, Albany Mus Art, Albany Ga, 2008, Peninsula Fine Arts Ctr, Newport News, Va, 2008, Parkersburg Fine Arts Ctr, 2009, Robert Ferst Fine Arts Ctr, Richard & Westbrook Galleries, 2009,Danville Mus Fine Arts & Hist, 2010; African Am Artists in Los Angeles, A survey exhib: Pathways, 66-89; Calif African Am Mus & Los Angeles Munic Art gallery; Forever Free, Works by African-Am Women Artists Traveling Exhib, Ctr Visual Arts, Univ Ill, Normal, 80-82; 19-Sixties, Calif Mus African-Am Hist & Cult, Los Angeles, 81-89; Mus African-Am Art, Los Angeles, 85; Libr for the Performing Arts at Lincoln Ctr, New York City, 95; Savannah Int Airport, 96; John Slade Fly House, New Haven, Conn; York W Bailey, Penn Ctr, St Helena Island; World Festival of Art on Paper, Ljubjliana, Slovenia, 02; Int Biennale fur Bildende Kunst-Austria, 02; Thurgood Marshall Postal Stamp exhib, RED Gallery, Savannah, Ga, 03; Nine, Painting Faculty, Pinnacle gallery, 2003; Ars Femina, Stockholm, Sweden, 2002-2006; Recent Am Watercolors, Peninsula Fine Arts Ctr, 2007, We Too, Make Books, Minn Center Bk Arts, 2007 & 30 Year Retrospective, Normal Editions Workshop, Ill, 2007; Why Go Anywhere Else? Serbia & Montenegro touring exhib, Lancaster Mus Art, Pa, 2010; Pacific Standard Time: Art in LA 1945-1980 - Now Dig This: Art & Black, Los Angels, 1960-1980, 2011-2012; Hammer Mus & MOMA PS 1, Long Island, NY, 2012-2013. *Pos:* Vchairperson, Calif Arts Coun, 75-78; artist-coordr, Brockman Gallery Productions CETA Pub Art Prog, 77-78; Century City Cult Comn, 78-79; dir, Int Women's Writing Guild, 79-; proj dir, Cult Exchange Prog, Lagos, Nigeria/Wajumbe Cult Inst, San Francisco, 85-86. *Teaching:* Lectr, Calif Inst Women, 74; Idyllwild Sch Music & Arts, 81-82; chairperson, Fine Arts, painting, drawing & dance, Elliott Pope Prep Sch, 82-85; vis lectr, San Francisco State Univ, 87; asst prof/scenographer, St Mary's Col, Md, 94; prof painting, Savannah Col Art & Design, Ga, 96; retired, 96- 2009; adj prof grad painting, SCAD eLearning, 2009-. *Awards:* Cave Canem Poetry Fel, 96-99; Scad Painting fac artist-in-residence, artlink at Elizabeth Found Studios, New York City, 2002; Presidential fel fac develop in printmaking, & painting, Savannah Coll of Art & Design, 2003-2007; SECAC Outstanding Achievement Creative Arts, 2007; Ossabaw Island Found visiting artist residency, 2010. *Bibliog:* Four Plus One (catalog), Nat Urban League Conf, San Francisco, 86; Gumbo Ya Ya, 95; St James Guide to Black Artists, St James Press/Schomberg Ctr for Res in Black Cult, 97; The Int Biennale Fur Bildende Kunst (catalogue), Austria, 2002; William Zimmer, NY Times Art Critic (catalogue), 2005; African Am Visual Arts Database (www.aavad.com), 2006; Why Go Anywhere Else? (catalogue), 2011; Marks from the Matrix, Normal Editions Workshop; Lynn Kienholz (auth), LA Rising: Social Artists before 1980; LA Object and David Hammons Body Prints, Tilton Gallery, NY; Kelli Jones (auth), Art and Black Los Angeles 1960-1980. *Mem:* Int Women's Writing Guild; United Scenic Artists, Local 829; Costume Soc Am; Ctr Study Beadwork; St Mary's Women's Writing Group; Telfair Mus, Art Telfair com Mem, 2002-2006; Southeastern Coll Art; Coll Art Asn, 2004-2010; Telfair Mus FAAA, 2009; Womens Caucus for Art, 2011. *Media:* Acrylic, Watercolor, Graphite Drawing. *Res:* Gallery 32, Risk Innovation, Survival, Ending the Sixties, Inherent Retention of African Cult by Blacks in the Americas, 1972 . *Publ:* Auth, What I Love (paintings & poetry), Contemp Crafts, 72; Animal (paintings & poetry), continuity transcripts and features, 78. *Mailing Add:* 15 W 41st St Savannah GA 31401-8984

JACOB, NED
PAINTER, LECTURER

b Elizabethton, Tenn, Nov 15, 38. *Study:* Pvt studies with Robert Gilbert, Robert Lougheed & Bettina Steinke. *Work:* Denver Art Mus; Indianapolis Mus Art; Whitney Gallery Western Art, Cody, Wyo; Albrecht Art Mus, St Joseph, Mo; Washburn Univ, Topeka, Kans. *Exhib:* Solo exhibs, Univ Sask, Saskatoon, Can, 59, Nat Cowboy Hall Fame & Western Heritage Ctr, Oklahoma City, 72, Birger Sandzen Mem Gallery, Lindsborg, Kans, 76, Whitney Gallery Western Art, 76, Frye Gallery, Seattle, 79, Coe Kerr Gallery, NY, 82, Wichita Art Mus, 83 & El Paso Mus Art, 83; Twenty-fifth Anniversary Exhib, James Fisher Gallery, Denver, 84; Mus of SW, Midland, Tex, 97. *Pos:* Independent painter, lecturer. *Teaching:* Guest lectr, painting & figure drawing, Fechin Inst, Taos, NMex, 88-92, Art Students League, Denver, 89-94, Scottsdale Artists Sch, Ariz, 90-94 & Sun Valley Ctr Arts & Humanities, Idaho, 92; Lyme Art Asn, Old Lyme Conn, 2007. *Awards:* John F & Anna Lee Stacy Fel, 74. *Bibliog:* Sandra Dallas (auth), Ned Jacob, Fenn Galleries Publ Inc, 79; W Bradley (auth), Twenty-five Years--Ned Jacob, Artists of Rockies, 85; DW LaCour (auth), Artists in Quotation, McFarland & Co Inc, Jefferson, NC, 89. *Mem:* Salmagundi Club, NY; Chelsea Arts Club, London; Nat Arts Club, NY. *Media:* Oil, Charcoal; All. *Specialty:* Fine drawing. *Interests:* history and craft of traditional painting. *Dealer:* Independent

JACOB, WENDY
EDUCATOR

Study: Williams Col, BA, 80; Sch of Art Inst Chicago, MFA, 89. *Work:* Centre Georges Pompidou, Paris Mus Contemp Art, San Diego, Calif; David & Alfred Smart Mus Art, Univ Chicago, Ill. *Exhib:* Galerie Walcheturm, Zurich, Emmanuel Perrotin, Paris, Galerie Karin Schorm, Vienna, Milwaukee Inst Art & Design, Schipper and Krome, Cologne, Ger, Centre Nat d'Art Contemporain, Grenoble, France, Temple Gallery, Tyler Sch Art, Philadelphia, Mass Inst of Technol List Visual Arts Ctr, Cambridge, Chicago Project Room, Centre Georges-Pompidou, Paris, Forum for Contemp Art, St Louis, Kunsthaus Graz, Austria, Whitney Mus Am Art, NYC. *Pos:* Mem, Haha artists collaborative, 89. *Teaching:* asst prof, visual arts Mass Inst of Technol, Cambridge, 99; asst prof, dept sculpture Col Fine Arts Ill State Univ. *Awards:* Creative Capital Found Grant, 1999; Ill Arts Coun Artist's Fel Award, 1999; Bunting Inst Fel, Radcliffe Inst Advanced Study, Harvard Univ, 2004—05. *Mailing Add:* Mass Inst of Technol Visual Arts Prog 265 Mass Ave N51-317 Cambridge MA 02139

JACOBOWITZ, ELLEN SUE
CURATOR, DIRECTOR

b Detroit, Mich, Feb 21, 1948. *Study:* Univ Mich, BA, 69, MA, 70; Courtauld Inst Art, 70-71; Bryn Mawr Col, 89. *Collection Arranged:* AmGraphics: 1860-1940 (auth, catalog), Rijkmuseum & Philadelphia Mus Art, 82; The Prints of Lucas van Leyden and His Contemporaries (auth, catalog), Nat Gallery Art & Boston Mus Fine Arts, 83; From Mantegna to Goya: Old Master prints from the Berman collection, Philadelphia Mus Art, 85; New Art on Paper, Philadelphia Mus Art, 88. *Pos:* Cur, Philadelphia Mus Art, 72-90; asst/acting dir, Cranbrook Inst Sci, 91-94; vol archives, Temple Beth, 94-2014; acting dir, Temple Emanuel, 95-96; vol bookstock literary program, 2009-2014. *Awards:* Smithsonian Grant, 77-78; Gold Medal, Netherlands Soc Philadelphia, 83; Fel, Nat Endowment Arts, 87. *Mem:* Print Coun Am (bd mem, 74-90, 80-83); Print Club Philadelphia (bd mem, 78-84); Illustrated Bartsch (ed & bd mem); Neth-Am Amity Trust (bd mem, 81-90); Nat Jewish Women; Bookstock, 2009-2014; Detroit Inst Arts (90-2014); AARP (95-2014). *Res:* Early 16th century Netherlandish printmaking; Am printmaking since the late 19th century; contemporary printmaking. *Interests:* The arts, sports, cooking, walking; Knitting. *Publ:* Auth, Three Centuries of Chiaroscuro Woodcuts, Pa Acad Fine Arts, 73; contribr, Philadelphia: Three Centuries of American Art, Philadelphia Mus Art, 76; coauth, The Illustrated Bartsch--Lucas van Leyden, Abaris, 81; auth, American Graphics, 1860-1940, Rijks Mus, Phila Mus, 82; New Art on Paper, Philadelphia Mus Art, 88

JACOBS, DAVID (THEODORE)
SCULPTOR, KINETIC ARTIST

b Niagara Falls, NY, Mar 1, 1932. *Study:* Orange Coast Coll, AA; Los Angeles State Coll, AB & MA. *Work:* Guggenheim Mus, NY; Mus Art, Richmond, Va; Otterbein Coll, Ohio; Valley Mall, Hagerstown, Md; Hofstra Mus, Hempstead, NY; Otterbein Col, Ohio; Ohio State Univ; Virgina Mus. *Comn:* Cloud Fountain (sculptured fountain), Valley Mall Assoc, Hagerstown, Md, 74; Paul Radin Mem (bronze relief), Hofstra Univ Libr, 74; Ventura High, Deer Park High Sch, NY, 76; Rainframe (sculptured screen), Dawn-Joy Corp, NY, 76. *Exhib:* The Art of Assemblage, Mus Mod Art, NY, 61; Numerous solo exhibs, 61-95; 68th Am Exhib, Art Inst Chicago, 66; Sound, Light, Silence, Art That Performs, W R Nelson Gallery, Atkins Mus, Kansas City, 66; Inflatable Sculpture, Jewish Mus, NY, 69; Sound Sculpture, Vancouver Art Gallery, 73; Adelphi univ Outdoor Sculpture Biennial, 2010-2012. *Pos:* Sculpture cur consult, Hofstra Mus, formerly. *Teaching:* Prof sculpture, Hofstra Univ, 62-95, chmn dept fine arts, 82-89; vis critic sculpture, Cornell Univ, New York Prog, 69 & 70, Baruch Coll, City Coll, New York, 77-79. *Awards:* Res grant, Hofstra Univ, 68; Creative Artists Pub Serv Grant, 73 & 76; Artist-in-Sch Grant, Nat Endowment Arts & NYFA, Central HS, Valley Stream, 79. *Bibliog:* D J Irving (auth), Sculpture: Materials & Processes, Van Nostrand Reinhold, 68; Wayne Craven (auth), Sculpture in America, Crowell, 68; Chichura & Stevens (auths), Super Sculpture: Using Science, Technology and Natural Phenomena in Sculpture, Van Nostrand Reinhold, 74. *Media:* Aluminum, Rubber. *Mailing Add:* 51 Eighth Ave Sea Cliff NY 11579

JACOBS, HAROLD
PAINTER, SCULPTOR
b New York, NY, Oct 29, 1932. *Study:* Cooper Union, 53; NY Univ; New Sch Social Res; Sorbonne, Fulbright scholar, 61. *Work:* Whitney Mus Am Art, NY; Portland Art Mus, Ore; Kalamazoo Art Ctr; Philadelphia Mus Art; Pa Acad Fine Arts; Woodmere Art Mus, Pa. *Comn:* Performance sculpture, Group Motion Dance Co; ltd ed, Akiba Acad, Merion, Pa; outdoor mural, Meridian Books, Philadelphia; sculpture, ARA lobby, Philadelphia; entrance mural, Le Bon Marche Dept Store, Paris, 98, 2000. *Exhib:* Solo exhibs, Pa Acad Fine Arts, 78 & Portland Ctr Visual Arts, Ore, 81; retrospective, Selected Works 1966-1985, Moore Coll Art, 85; VIA Paris, 91; Asphalte, Paris, 92; Snyderman Gallery, Philadelphia, 96, 99; 3 Part Retrospective, France, 2001; Retrospective, Am Years, France, 2010; Un Art Autie Galerie 1900-2000, Paris, 2013; Travail Sur Papier Galerie Convergence, Paris, Galerie Inviti, Paris, 2014. *Teaching:* Prof painting, Moore Col Art, 66-89 & emer prof, 89-; prof emeritus, Moore College of Art; full time studio artist, currently. *Awards:* Nat Endowment Arts Collaboration Grant Visual & Performing Arts, 75; Distinguished Artist Award, Moore Coll Art, 83. *Media:* Mixed. *Publ:* Harold Jacobs Selected Works 1966-1985 (exhib catalog & video tape), Moore Coll Art, 85; Harold Jacobs Createur, L'espace Asphate, Paris, 92; Catalog of 3 part Retrospective, 2001; Catalog of Retrospective, the American Years, 2010; Harold Jacobs: Travail Sur Papier, Catalog, 2014. *Dealer:* Gallerie 1900-2000 Paris; Galerie Convergences Paris; Galerie Inviti Paris. *Mailing Add:* Le Grand Logis Ligre Par Chinon 37500 France

JACOBS, JIM
PAINTER, PRINTMAKER
b New York, NY, May 26, 1945. *Study:* Boston Univ, BA; Bryn Mawr Col, study with Richmond Lattimore; Harvard Univ; Boston Mus of Fine Arts. *Work:* Rose Art Mus, Brandeis Univ, Waltham, Mass; Chase Manhattan Bank; Arman; Smith Mus. *Exhib:* Expressions of the Seventies, NY, 77; Elizabeth Weiner Gallery, NY, 79 & 80; Danforth Mus, Framingham, Mass, 81; Smith Mus, Springfield, Mass, 81; Gallery Yves Arman, 81 & 82; Oscarsson Siegeltuch & Co, NY, 86; and others. *Pos:* Archivist, Leo Castelli Gallery, 67-68. *Teaching:* Instr vase painting, Boston Univ, 65, Harvard Univ, 66, Bryn Mawr Col, 67; lectr, Boston Mus Fine Arts, Mus Sch, Boston, Harvard Univ; instr vase painting, Bryn Mawr Col, 67. *Awards:* Creative Artists Pub Serv Prog Grant, 81-82. *Bibliog:* Article, Art News, 6/80; article, Arts Mag, 5/81; article, Art Am, 2/83; Michael Komanecky & Virginia Fabbri Butera (coauth), The Folding Image: Screens by Western Artists of the nineteenth & twentieth centuries, (exhib catalog), Yale Univ Art Gallery & Nat Gallery Art, 84. *Media:* Lacquer, Board. *Dealer:* Oscarson Siegeltuch & Co 568 Broadway New York NY 10012

JACOBS, PETER ALAN
SCULPTOR, EDUCATOR
b New York, NY, Jan 31, 1939. *Study:* State Univ NY Coll New Paltz, with Ilya Bolotowsky, BS (art educ), 60, MA(art), 62; Vanderbilt Univ-George Peabody Col, EdD (fine arts), 65. *Work:* Bloomsburg State Col, Pa; Coll Mainland, Texas City, Tex; Muskingum Col, New Concord, Ohio; George Peabody Mus, Nashville, Tenn; Mus Satire & Humor, Bulgaria; Whitney West Mus, Buffalo Bill Hist Ctr, Cody, Wyo. *Exhib:* New Directions in Art, Beloit Mus, Wis; Wis Designer-Craftsman, Milwaukee Art Ctr & Wis Painters & Sculptors, 68 & 69; Southwest Invitational, Yuma, Ariz, 73 & 74; 65 solo exhibs incl, Work on Tour by Ariz Arts & Humanities Comn, Ariz, Tex, Ohio & Wis, 74-75 & Univ Ohio, Univ Colo, Grand Canyon Art Ctr & Univ Wyo Art Mus; Banares Hindu Univ, Varanasa, India, 80; Mostra di Grafica, Soc Delle Belle Arti, Firenze, Italy, 83; 6th Int Biennial, Gabrova, Bulgaria, 83; Int Salon of Jazz Posters, Bydgoszcz, Poland, 85; 28th Ann Art Zone, Denver, 88; Mondak Art Ctr, Foothills Art Ctr, 2000-01; Retrospective Exhib, Curfman Gallery, 2007. *Collection Arranged:* Ilya Bolotowsky Retrospective, Crossman Gallery, Univ Wis-Whitewater, 68 & Northern Ariz Univ Mus, 73; Christo & Jeanne Claude, 80, Andy Warhol, 81, Robert Rauschenberg, 81, Roy Lichtenstein, 82, James Rosenquist, 82, Sam Francis, 83 & Willem de Kooning, 84, Colo State Univ. *Teaching:* Chmn art dept, Univ Wis-Whitewater, 65-70; head dept art, Northern Ariz Univ, 70-74; dept chair & prof, Cent Mich Univ, 74-76 & Colo State Univ, 76-86, prof (emeritus), 88, & 2008; fac, Semester at Sea, Univ Pittsburgh, fall semester, 98; Univ Mediation Officer; vis prof, Native Am Studies, Guanxi Normal Univ, Guilin, China, 2001. *Awards:* Higher Educ Art Educator of the Year, Colorado Art Educ Asn, 2007; Higher Art Educator of the Year, pacific region, Nat Ed Asn, 2008; Alumnus of the Year, State Univ NY, New Paltz, 2009. *Mem:* Hon life mem Nat Coun Art Adminr (founder & chmn bd dir, 72-77); Coll Art Asn Am; Mich Soc Arts, Lett & Sci (chmn fine arts div, 75); Nat Art Educ Asn; Native Am Art Study Asn. *Media:* Wood, Natural Materials. *Res:* American Indian arts. *Interests:* Canoing, Camping, Fishing, Northwest Coast Native Arts. *Publ:* Auth, Visual Arts in the Ninth Decade, Nat Coun Art Adminr, 80; The Native Am Collction, Bradford Brinton Mus, Am Indian Art, 2006. *Dealer:* Philip Bareiss Contemporary Exhibitions PO Box 2739 150 Ski Valley Road Taos NM 87571. *Mailing Add:* 1727 Rangeview Fort Collins CO 80524

JACOBS, RALPH, JR
PAINTER
b El Centro, Calif, May 22, 1940. *Study:* With Evelyn Nadeau, Frederic Taubes & Abel G Warshawsky. *Work:* Beirut Art Mus, Lebanon; Continental Telephone Co, Ga; Frost Art Mus, Fla Int Univ, Miami, Fla. *Comn:* Many pvt collections in Can, Japan, Australia & SAm. *Exhib:* Rosicrucian Mus, San Jose, Calif, 63, 67 & 71; Coun Am Artists Soc Nat Exhib, NY, 64; Nat Exhib, Springville Mus Art, Utah, 65; Soc Western Artists Ann Exhibs, de Young Mus, San Francisco, 65 & 69; Armenian Allied Arts Ann, Los Angeles, 66; Monterey Co Exhib, Monterey Mus Art, 96. *Awards:* Klumpkey Mem Award for Classic Nude, de Young Mus, San Francisco, 65; Second Place Award & Spec Peoples Choice Award, Monterey Co Fair, 95. *Mem:* Monterey Peninsula Mus Art. *Media:* Oil. *Specialty:* Oil paintings of various subject matter in traditional Realism and Impressionism. *Collection:* Antique furniture and Oriental ceramics. *Publ:* Award Winning Paintings, 1964, Prize Winning Paintings, 1965, 1966, Allied Publs, Inc; Exhibit 26, Mag Art, spring & summer 68. *Mailing Add:* PO Box 5906 Carmel CA 93921

JACOBS, SCOTT E
PAINTER, ILLUSTRATOR
b Westfield, NJ, Oct 24, 1958. *Study:* Ducret Sch Design, NJ, 92; Parsons Sch Design, NY, 92; Airbrush Illus Getaway, 94-95. *Work:* Engineered Fasteners, St Louis; San Diego Chargers, Calif. *Comn:* 85 paintings, Harley Davidson, Milwaukee, 93-2000; painting, Sorrento Cheese, Hamburg, NY, 96; 8 paintings, Chevrolet Corp, Detroit, 96-98; painting, Mattel Corp, El Segundo, Calif, 97; painting, Porsche USA, Phoenix, 98. *Exhib:* Motorcycles as Art, Peterson Mus, Los Angeles, 96; Harleys 95th Anniversary, Milwaukee Pub, 98; Behes & Black Leather, St Louis Guild, 99. *Awards:* Varga Lifetime Achievement Award, Airbrush Action, 98; Rookie of Yr Award, Chevrolet Corp, 98. *Bibliog:* Neil Evans (auth), Biker Dreams, Epicenter Films, 97. *Mem:* Rancho Santa Fe Art Guild. *Media:* Acrylic. *Publ:* auth, Big Twin, Filapashy, 96, VQ Mag, Paisano Publ, 96, US Art Mag, MSP Commun, 96, American Iron, Tam Commun, 96, Art of Scott Jacobs, Airbrush Action, 2000, Easyriders, The Motorcycle Art of Scott Jacobs. *Dealer:* Segal Fine Art 594 S Arthur Ave Louisville CO 80027. *Mailing Add:* PO Box 2677 Rancho Santa Fe CA 92067

JACOBSEN, COLTER
PAINTER, DRAFTSMAN
b Ramona, Calif, 1975. *Study:* San Francisco Art Inst, BFA, 2001. *Exhib:* Strictly Ballroom, Stanford Univ, Calif, 2002; Plates, San Francisco Arts Comn, 2003; Felix Variations, Calif Coll Arts, 2004; Open Walls, White Columns, New York, 2005; Elusive Material, New Langton Arts, San Francisco, 2006; Moby Dick, CCA Wattis Inst Contemp Art, 2009. *Awards:* Louis Comfort Tiffany Found Grant, 2009. *Bibliog:* Roberta Smith (auth), Even a Little Space Can Hold an Abundance of Ideas, NY Times, 11/25/2005; Johnny Ray-Huston (auth), Your Future, San Francisco Bay Guardian, 7/11/2006; Julian Meyers (auth), rev, Frieze, 9/2007

JACOBSEN, HUGH NEWELL
ARCHITECT
b Grand Rapids, Mich, Mar 11, 1929. *Study:* Univ Md, BA, 51; Archit Asso Sch Archit, London, Eng, 54; BArch, MArch, Yale, 55. *Hon Degrees:* Gettysburg Col, LHD (hon), 74; Bradford Col, LHD (hon), 90; Univ Md, DFA (hon), 93. *Comn:* principal works incl; US Embassy, Paris, addition to US Capitol, two Smithsonian Mus (renovations), Southern Vt Art Ctr. *Exhib:* Fundação Armando Alvares Penteado in São Paolo, Brazil, 98; Nat Bldg Mus Retrospective in Washington DC, 99; Va Ctr for Archit, 2005. *Pos:* Archit, with Philip Johnson, New Canaan, Conn, 55; archit, Keyes, Lethbridge & Condon, Wash, 57-58; principal, Hugh Newell Jacobsen, FAIA, 58. *Teaching:* Lectr, univs; vis prof, Univ Cairo, Egypt, 70. *Awards:* Nat Am Inst of Archit honor awards 69, 74, 78, 80, 85, & 88; AIA Centennial Award; AD Deans Design, 2005. *Mem:* Fel Am Inst of Archit; Nat Acad of Design (elected); Century Asn; Yale Club (New York City). *Collection:* Homage to the Square; Oil on Bd 48' x 48' Joseph Albers 1961. *Publ:* Ed: A Guide to the Archit of Wash DC, 65; Hugh Newell Jacobsen Architect, (monogr), 88; Hugh Jacobsen Architect, Recent Work, (monogr), 94. *Mailing Add:* 2529 P St NW Washington DC 20007-3024

JACOBSEN, MICHAEL A
HISTORIAN, EDUCATOR, PAINTER
b Pasadena, Calif, June 4, 1942. *Study:* Univ Calif, Santa Barbara, BA, 65, MA, 70; Columbia Univ, PhD, 76. *Work:* Calif Polytechnic Univ, Pomona; Western Found Vertebrate Biology. *Comn:* watercolors of N Am birds, various pvt collectors. *Exhib:* Craig Ellwood Archit Drawings, Cal Poly Gallery, 94; Jupiter & His Children, Ga Mus Art, 97. *Teaching:* Asst prof Renaissance art, Cleveland State Univ, Ohio, 73-77, Univ Ore, 77-79; assoc prof art, Univ Ga, 79-87; vis assoc prof art, Stanford Univ, 87, Univ Calif, Riverside, 88-89; lectr, Calif Polytechnic Univ, Ponoma, 89-99, assoc prof, 99; retired, 2005. *Awards:* Kress Fel, 72-73. *Mem:* Coll Art Asn; Southern Calif Art Hist Soc; Soc Automotive Historians. *Media:* Watercolor. *Res:* Automotive history, Italian 15th century. *Publ:* Mantegna's battle of sea monsters, Art Bull, 12/82; Perspective in Mantegna's early panels, Arte Venenta, 83; Dolphins in Renaissance art, Studies in Iconography, fall 83; Durer's Johannes Kleberger Source, 91; Agostino diDuccio's Virtues, pages 13-18, Antichita Viva, 95; co-ed, Jupiter's Loves and His Children, Univ Georgia Press, 97; Back and Forth: The Renaissance and Mythology, 51-66, Archeologia Transatlantica, XVI, 98; The Marque MG and Road Racing, Classic MG, XVI, 12-15, 2004; The Role of MG in the History of Automotive Styling, Classic MG, XXXVII, 16-19, 2009; epublication, monthly column, thechicaneblog.com; Peddle Beach 1953, Vintage Racecar-Journal, vol. XIV, 6, pgs 52-57, 2011

JACOBSHAGEN, N KEITH, II
PAINTER, PHOTOGRAPHER
b Wichita, Kans, Sept 8, 1941. *Study:* Kansas City Art Inst, Mo, BFA; Art Ctr Coll Design, Los Angeles; Univ Kans, MFA. *Work:* Sheldon Mem Gallery, Lincoln, Nebr; Univ Kans Mus Art, Lawrence; Mus Art Okla Univ; Oakland Mus, Calif; Pasadena Art Mus, Calif. *Exhib:* A Sense of Place: The Artist & the Am Land, Sheldon Mem

Art Gallery, Lincoln, Nebr, 74; Southern Ark Univ, Magnolia & Westark Community Col, Ft Smith, Ark, 78; In Respect of Space, Swan River Mus, Paola, Kans, 79; Group, Volga-Consalvo Gallery, Boston, Mass, 79; Corp Exhib, auspices of Minneapolis Art Inst, 79 & NAm Casualty Exhib, 79; and others. *Teaching:* Assoc prof art, Univ Nebr-Lincoln, 68-80. *Awards:* Owen H Kenan Award, 34th Ann Contemp Am Painting, 72; Frank Woods Fel, Univ Nebr, 75. *Bibliog:* Alan Gussow (auth), A Sense of Place: the Artist and the American Land (film), Nebr Educ TV, 74. *Media:* Oil. *Publ:* Contribr, Twelve Photographers: A Contemporary Mid-America Document, Mid-Am Arts Alliance, 78; Special report: Midwest art, Art in Am, 7-8/79; Artists work range through human emotions, Kansas City Star, 8/12/79; Cottonwood Rev, fall 79; In respect of space, Forum/Kansas City Artists Coalition, 12/79; and others. *Dealer:* Dorry Gates PO Box 7264 Kansas City MO 64113; Charles Campbell Gallery 647 Chestnut St San Francisco CA 94133. *Mailing Add:* c/o Kiechel Fine Art 5733 S 34th St Lincoln NE 68516

JACOBSON, FRANK
ADMINISTRATOR
b Philadelphia, Pa, Sept 14, 1948. *Study:* Univ Wis, BA, 70; Boston Univ Sch Fine Arts, MFA, 73. *Pos:* Exec dir, Arvada Ctr Arts & Humanities, 79-85; mgr, Theaters & arenas, Denver, 85-87; pres & chief exec off, Scottsdale Cult Coun, 87-. *Teaching:* Asst prof theater, Univ Mont, 73-75. *Mem:* Metrop Denver Arts Alliance (pres, 81-83); Asn Performing Arts Presenters (bd, 84-87). *Publ:* Auth, Performing Art Centers - Market the Arts, FEDAPT, 83; Municipal Connections, ACUCAA Bulletin, Vol 29, No 7, 86. *Mailing Add:* Scottdale Cultural Council 7380 E Second St Scottsdale AZ 85251

JACOBSON, HEIDI ZUCKERMAN
CURATOR
Study: Hunter Coll, MA. *Pos:* Asst cur, 20th Century Art Jewish Mus, New York, formerly; Phyllis Wattis cur, Matrix Prog, Berkeley Art Mus, Univ Calif, 1999-2005; dir & chief cur, Aspen Art Mus, Aspen, Colo, 2005-. *Mailing Add:* Aspen Art Museum 590 North Mill St Aspen CO 81611

JACOBUS, JOHN M
EDUCATOR, HISTORIAN
b Poughkeepsie, NY, Sept 15, 1927. *Study:* Hamilton Col, AB, 52; Yale Univ, MA, 54, PhD, 56. *Teaching:* From instr to asst prof, Princeton Univ, 56-60; from asst prof to assoc prof, Univ Calif, Berkeley, 60-63; assoc prof to prof, Ind Univ, Bloomington, 63-69; prof, Dartmouth Col, 69-. *Res:* Nineteenth & twentieth century art, both architecture & painting. *Collection:* Prints & graphic arts from 18th century to present. *Publ:* Auth, Philip Johnson, Braziller, 62; auth, Twentieth Century Architecture: The Middle Years, Praeger, 66; auth, Matisse, Abrams, 73. *Mailing Add:* 5 Hilltop Dr Hanover NH 03755-2317

JACQUARD, JERALD (WAYNE)
SCULPTOR
b Lansing, Mich, Feb 1, 1937. *Study:* Mich State Univ, BA, 60 & MA, 62. *Work:* Kresge Mus, Mich State Univ, East Lansing; Kalamazoo Inst Art, Mich; Laumeier Sculpture Park, St Louis; Chicago Inst Art; Ind Univ Art Mus, Bloomington; Hamilton Corp I; Ind Mus of Art. *Comn:* Sculpture, Chicago Transit Authority, 74; Sculpture, Mich Manufacturing, Lansing, Mich, 94. *Exhib:* Solo exhibs, Detroit Inst Art, 65, Ill Inst Technol, 69, Univ Chicago, 70, Indianapolis Mus, 75, Kalamazoo, 89, South Bend Regional Mus Art, 93 & Grand Rapids Mus Art, 93; Bicentennial Sculpture for a New Era, Chicago, 75; Restrospective, Kalamazoo Inst Art, 92, Ind Mus Art, 94 & 2002. *Teaching:* Assoc prof sculpture, Univ Ill, Chicago Circle Campus, 66-75; prof sculpture, Ind Univ, Bloomington, 75-2000, prof emeritus, 2000-. *Awards:* Fulbright Award, 63; Guggenheim Fel, 73; Nat Endowment Arts, 80; Eli Lilly Fel, 84. *Mem:* Int Sculpture Asn. *Media:* Steel, Bronze. *Publ:* Major Color Catalogue of Jacquard & His Art (from 75-94) to Accompany Traveling Mus Exhibitions, 92, 94, INd Hist Mus, & Ind Mus Art. *Mailing Add:* Ind Univ Dept Art Bloomington IN 47405

JACQUEMON, PIERRE
PAINTER
b Lyon, France, Aug 6, 1935; US citizen. *Study:* Self-taught. *Work:* Goteborg Mus, Sweden; Magdalene Col, Cambridge, Eng; Mus d'Art Mod, Paris, France; St Paul Sch, NH; Ika-Shika Nat Univ, Tokyo, Japan. *Exhib:* Solo exhibs, Temple Gallery, London, 62, Bianchini Gallery, NY, 63, Weeden Gallery, Boston, 68, Berkshire Mus, Mass, 69 & Atrium Gallery, Geneva, Switz, 74, Weeden Gallery, Boston, Mass, 71, Temple Gallery, London, Eng, 72, Bernard Letu, Geneva, Switz, 80 Galerie Philadelphia, Paris, France, 81, Suzanne de Coninck, Paris, France, 82, Phoenix Gallery, NY, 85 & Gallery Juno, NY, 93 & 95; Inst Contemp Art, Boston, 70; Bertha Schaeffer Gallery, NY, 78; Abreu Gallery, NY, 83; Summer Show, Gallery Juno, NY, 95 & 97 & Small, 95. *Bibliog:* Pierre Jacquemon, Gallerie de Bellecour, Lyon, France. *Media:* Oil. *Dealer:* Gallery Jund 568 Broadway Suite 604B New York NY 10012

JACQUES, RUSSELL KENNETH
SCULPTOR, PAINTER
b Springfield, Mass, Feb 19, 1943. *Study:* Boston Univ, BFA, 66. *Work:* DeCordova Mus, Lincoln, Mass; Abilene Fine Arts Mus, Tex; Mead Mus, Amherst, Mass; Nat Gallery Nova Scotia, Halifax; Boston Univ; and others. *Comn:* Kinetic wood sculpture, Nat Ballet Can, Toronto, 81; stainless steel sculpture, Boston Univ, 82; bronze & stainless steel sculpture, Tex Commerce Bank, Dallas, 82; bronze & stainless steel floor sculpture, First Bank Boston, 83; stainless steel sculpture, Hammerson Can Inc, Toronto, 83; Boston Ballet Co, 79-83. *Exhib:* Counterpoint at the Quadrangle, Springfield Fine Arts, Mass, 82; Boston Mus Fine Arts, 83; Interim I,II & III Chesterwood Outdoor Invitational, Stockbridge, Mass, 83; Abilene Christian Univ, Tex, 83; Brea Mus, Brea, Calif, 93; Whitney Mus Am Art, NY, 94; Bowers Mus, Santa Ana, Calif, 94; and many others. *Collection Arranged:* GTE Boston; Muskegon Art Mus; La Quinta Arts Found. *Teaching:* Instr basic drawing, Holyoke Community Col, 75, instr advan design & compos, 76. *Awards:* Second Place, Best in Show, 71 & Award of Excellence, 78, Springfield Art League, George Walter Vincent Smith Mus. *Bibliog:* Nancy Norcross (dir), The Emerging Artist (film), Mass Arts & Humanities Coun, 80; Outdoor Sculpture in the Berkshires II, Nat Trust Hist Preservation, Libr Congress, 7-9/80; Nancy Goebel (auth), article, Art Voices, 8/81; Claudia Elferdink (dir), Art in Common: Russell Jacques--Sculptor (film), Continental Cablevision Channel 57, Springfield, 83. *Media:* All. *Specialty:* stainless & bronze sculpture

JACQUETTE, JULIA L
PAINTER
b New York, NY, Dec 17, 1964. *Study:* Skowhegan Sch, 85; Skidmore Col, BS, 86; Hunter Col, MFA, 92. *Work:* Sheldon Mem Gallery & Sculpture Garden, Lincoln, Nebr; Mus Modern Art, New York City; Univ Ariz Mus Art, Tucson. *Exhib:* The Next Word, Neuberger Mus, Purchase, NY, 98; Mus Contemp Art, Sydney, Australia, 98; Mus Modern Art, New York City; Virtues and Vices, Judy Ann Goldman Fine Art, Boston, 2001; White Paintings, Michael Steinberg Fine Art, NY, 2004; I Dreamt, Tang Mus, Saratoga Springs, NY, 2004; My Houses, Michael Steinberg Fine Art, NY, 2006; Complicit!, Univ Va Art Mus, Charlottesville, Va, 2006. *Teaching:* RI Sch Design, 2005, 06; Princeton Univ, 2005, 06. *Awards:* Pollocl/Krasner Award, 94. *Bibliog:* Bon Bon of the Vanities, (style and entertaining supplement), NY Times Mag,. *Publ:* Julia Jacquette (auth), I Dreamt, publ by Tang Mus, 2004. *Dealer:* Michael Steinberg Fine Art NY. *Mailing Add:* 110 E 1st St New York NY 10009

JACQUETTE, YVONNE HELENE
PAINTER, PRINTMAKER
b Pittsburgh, Pa, Dec 15, 1934. *Study:* RI Sch Design, 1952-56, with John Frazier & Robert Hamilton; also with Herman Cherry & Robert Roche. *Work:* Staatliche Mus, Berlin; Colby Coll Mus, Waterville, Maine; Stanford Mus, Stanford, Calif; Utah Mus, Salt Lake City; Hudson River Mus, Yonkers, NY. *Comn:* Five panel painting in oil, NCent Bronx Hosp, NY, 1973; five color lithograph, Horace Mann Sch, Riverdale, NY, 1974; mural installation for Fed Bldg & Post Off, Gen Serv Admin, Bangor, Maine, 1979-82; Night View Wash DC, Jefferson Mem, 1984; Triptych of Minneapolis (mural), First Bank, 1985; prints, Provincetown Fine Arts Work Ctr, 1992, Zimmerli Mus Rutgers Univ, 1993, Bus Com for the Arts, 1994, Cleveland Print Club, 1999, Sch. Hardknocks Dance Theatre Workshop, New York City. *Exhib:* Solo Exhibs: Currents 22, St Louis Art Mus, 1983-84; Recent Paintings and Works on Paper, Berggruen Gallery, San Francisco, 1984 & 1991; Yurakucho Seibu-Takanawa Art, Tokyo, Japan, 1985; Tokyo Nightviews, Brooke Alexnder Inc, NY & Bowdoin Coll Mus Art, Maine, 1986; Mary Ryan Gallery, 1997; Huntington Mus, 1997; DC Moore Gallery, 1997, 2000, 2003, 2006, 2008; Mus of the City of NY 2008; group shows incl New Image in Painting, Int Biennial, Tokyo, Japan, 1974; Brook Alexander Inc, NY, 1982, 1985, 1988, 1989, 1992 & 1995; Survival of the Fittest II, Ingber Gallery, NY, 1985-86; 19th Ann Acad-Inst Purchase Exhib, Am Acad & Inst Arts & Letters, NY, 1987; Univ S Maine, Gorham, 1998; Cantor Arts Ctr, Stanford Univ, 2002; Paula Brown Gallery, Toledo, Ohio, 2004; Ctr Contemp Printmaking, Norwalk, Conn, 2006; Lemberg Gallery, Ferndale, Mich, 2007; Mus of City of New York, NY, 2007. *Teaching:* Instr, Moore Coll Art, Philadelphia, 1972; Vis artist & instr painting, Univ Pa, 1972-76 & 1979-82; vis artist, Nova Scotia Coll Art, 1974; instr, Parsons Sch of Design, 1975-78; instr, Grad Sch Fine Arts, Univ Pa, Philadelphia, 1979-84, Pa Acad Fine Arts Grad Sch Philadelphia, vis critic, 1991-2006. *Awards:* Am Acad Arts & Letts, 1990; John Simon Guggenheim Mem Found, 1997-98; Nat Acad Painters Award, 1998; Nat Acad Print Award, 1999; and others. *Bibliog:* Carolyn Eyler (auth), Yvonne Jacquette, Maine Aerials, Univ S Maine, 1998; Paul Mattick (auth), Art in America, Yuonne Jacquette at DC Moore, 12/2000; Robert Berlind (auth), Eye in the Sky, Art in America, March 2002; Bill Berkson (auth), Cat Mus of City of NY, 2008; John Yau (auth), Catalog, DC Moore Gallery. *Mem:* Artists Equity Asn; Nat Acad, Mem; Showhegan Sch Painting & Sculpture (gov); Am Accad Arts & Letters (mem, 1994-). *Media:* Oil, Pastel; Miscellaneous. *Specialty:* Contemporary Painting and Sculpture. *Interests:* Tibetan Buddhism. *Publ:* Illusr, Country Rush, Adventures in Poetry, 1972; illusr, Aerial, Eyelight Press, 1981; Jeff Wright and drawings, Toothpaste Press, 1982; Jayne Anne Philips, 1984; collabr, (with Rudy Burckhardt, film), Night Fantasies; coauth (with Maureen Owen), Erosion's Pull, 2004. *Dealer:* DC Moore 724 Fifth Ave New York NY 10019; Mary Ryan Gallery 24 W 57 St New York NY 10019; Crown Point Press Gallery 20 Hawthorne St San Francisco CA 94105; Gallery Karl Oskar 3008 W 71 Prairie Village KS 66208; Lemberg Gallery 23241 Woodward Ave Ferndale MI 48220. *Mailing Add:* 50 W 29th St New York NY 10001

JAEGER, BRENDA KAY
PAINTER
b Ladd Field, Alaska, July 20, 1950. *Study:* Eastern Wash Univ, Spokane, Wash, BA, 72; Whitworth Col, Spokane, Wash, MAT, 76; research with Kohei Fukuda, Japan, 83, 84 & 89; Lower Columbia Col, Longview, Wash, cert Pulp & Paper Technol, 85; Wash State Univ, Vancouver, Master in Teaching, 96, K-8 cert, endorsements K-12 art, 4-12 English, Japanese. *Work:* Alaskan State Coun Contemp Art Bank, Alyeska Pipeline Serv Co, Anchorage Mus at Rasmuson Ctr; Dean Witter Reynolds; Ketchikan Pioneers Home, Alaska; Standard Production Co; Corporate Office Copper River Seafoods. *Exhib:* The Cheney Cowles Mem Mus, Spokane, Wash; Handmade Paper Works, Anchorage Mus History & Art, Alaska, 79; Int Hand Papermakers Conf, Boston Sch Artisanry, Mass, 80; 8th Nevada Ann: Contemp Works of Paper, Sierra Nevada Mus Art, Reno, 81; 30th & 32nd Ann Southwest Washington Exhib, 83 & 85, State Capitol Mus, Olympia, Wash; Second Ann Patrons Watercolor Gala, Gallery of the Kresge Fine Art Ctr, Oklahoma City, 84; 45th Ann Exhib Northwest Watercolors, Bellevue Art Mus, Wash, 85; Ann Alaska Juried Watercolor Exhib, 90 & Winter Landscapes, 86, Anchorage Mus Hist & Art; Stonington Gallery, 86-92; Front and Center, 2 Friends Gallery, 2009; 33rd All Alaska Exhib, Anchorage Mus at Rasmuson Center, 2010; Cordova Fish Follies, Cordova Historical Mus, 2011, 2013; 38th Ann, Alaska Watercolor Soc, 2012; Solo exhibs, Rustic Fire Island Bake Shop, Anchorage, Ak, 2012; Alaska Pacific Univ, Anchorage, 2013. *Pos:* Artist with studio, Brenda K

Jaeger Art Studio, 78-. *Teaching:* Instr art, Whitworth Col, 74-75, Spokane Art Sch, 74-75, Art Arouse Prog, ESD 101, 74-75, Columbia Basin Col, 76-77 & Walla Walla Community Col, 76-77; vis artist, Wash State Cult Enrichment Prog, 75-76, 77-78; instr art, Univ Alaska, Anchorage, 78; pvt instr, 78-; artist-in-educ programs, Alaska, 85-, Utah, 88-92, Iowa, 88-90, Ore, 90-96, Auburn, Wash, 90-92; Lower Columbia Col, spring 87 & 88; Lower Kuskokwim Community Col, 88; Univ Alaska Southeast Islands Col, Petersburg, 90; head Art Dept, Pac Northern Acad, 96-; Southcentral Alaska Suzuki Camp, 2010. *Awards:* Best of Show, All Alaska Juried Watercolor exhib, 79, 81, 84 & 85; Best of Show, 32nd Ann Southwest Washington Exhib, 85; Allied Arts Juried Painting Show, 87; Eastern Wash Watercolor Soc Juried Competition, 83. *Bibliog:* Schiller (auth), The revolution in paper, Am Artist, 77; Beverly Plummer (auth), How does your garden grow, Fiberarts, 79. *Mem:* assoc Midwest Watercolor Soc; assoc Am Watercolor Soc; NW WC Soc Signature Lifetime Member; assoc Nat Watercolor Soc; assoc Alaska Watercolor Society. *Media:* Watercolor. *Publ:* Contribr, Flying Blind: Sunstruck at Merrill Field, & Breakfast, Vol VII, No 3, Calyx, summer 83; Shishaldinskaya, Northward J, Can, 83; illusr, Lake County Diamond, Tim Hunt (auth), Pope in Space, Barbara Blatner (auth) & 17 Toutle River Haiku, James Hanlen (auth), Intertext, 89; auth, Karasuyama Poems, Intertext, Anchorage, Alaska, 95; illusr, Lynx, 89 & 90; Cirque Mag, Vol 3, No 1. *Dealer:* Blue Hollomon Gallery; Georgia Blue & Gina Hollmon Anchorage AK. *Mailing Add:* Box 141361 Anchorage AK 99514

JAFFE, IRA S
EDUCATOR, CRITIC
b New York, NY, Aug 19, 1943. *Study:* Columbia Univ, New York, AB, 64, MFA (cinema), 67; Univ SC, PhD (cinema), 75. *Pos:* Presidential lectr, Univ NMex, 84-86; dir, Int Cinema Lect Series & vpres Southwest Film Str, 88; head, Media Arts Prog, Univ NMex, 89-. *Teaching:* Lectr cinema, Univ Southern Calif, Los Angeles, 70-72; assoc prof, Univ NMex, Albuquerque, 72-88, prof, 88-, chair dept media arts, retired, 2003, assoc dean Col Fine Arts, 2001-02. *Res:* Study of Charles Chaplin, Orson Welles, Errol Morris; women filmmakers in Third World cinemas; hybrid films; slow movies. *Publ:* Auth, Film as the narration of space: Citizen Kane in Perspectives on Citizen Kane, GK Hall, NY, 96; Fool for love: the shifting frontier, Artspace, 86-87; co-ed, Women filmmakers and the politics of gender in third cinema, Univ Colo Press (for Frontiers: J Women Studies), 94; Fighting Words: City Lights, Modern Times, The Great Dictator, Hollywood as Historian: Am Film in a Cultural Context, Univ Press, Ky, 97; Redirecting the Gaze: Gender, Theory and Cinema in the Third World, State Univ NY Press, 99; Hollywood Hybrids: Mixing Genres in Contemporary Films, Rowman & Littlefield, 2008; Errol Morris's Forms of Control, in Three Documentary Filmmakers, State Univ NY Press, 2009; Envoi, in Gus Blaisdell Collected, Univ NMex Press, 2012; Slow Movies, Wallflower Press & Columbia Univ Press. *Mailing Add:* HC 66 Box 118 Mountainair NM 87036

JAFFE, IRMA B
HISTORIAN, EDUCATOR
b New Orleans, La. *Study:* Columbia Univ, BS, MA, PhD. *Exhib:* Whitney Ann, Whitney Mus Am Art, 64-65; Conditional Commitment, Long Island Univ, 66. *Pos:* Res cur, Whitney Mus Am Art, New York, 64-65; ed bd, Am Art J, currently; contrib ed, Art News. *Teaching:* Chmn dept art hist, Fordham Univ, 66-77, prof, 66-; prof art hist Fordham Univ, 66-87. *Awards:* Nat Endowment Humanities Fel, 73-74; Am Coun Learned Soc, 73 & 82; Award of Merit, Am Asn Mus, 84; Distinguished Serv Award, Fordham Univ, 86; Virgiliana Medal, Italian Encyclopedia Inst, 86; Knight in the Order of Merit of the Italian Republic; Ausonian Soc Cornaro Award. *Mem:* Coll Art Asn Am; Am Studies Asn; Am-Italian Soc of Legions of Merit. *Res:* American art; Italian art and literature. *Interests:* Poetry, Italian Lit. *Publ:* The Italian Presence in American Art 1760-1860, 89 & The Italian American Presence in American Art 1860-1920, Fordham Univ Press, 91; Imagining the New World: Columbian Iconography, IEI Press, 91; Joseph Stella's Symbolism, Pomegranate Art Bks, Chamelon Bk, 94; Italian-American Art, The Italian-American Experience, An Encyclopedia, Garland, 99; Shining Eyes, Cruel Fortune: The Lives and Loves of Italian Renaissance Women Poets, Fordhamn Univ Press, 2002; Eleanora Falletti and Giuseppe Betussi: The Poems and Dialogue, Gradiva Int J of Italian Poetry, 2006; Zelotti's Epic Frescoes at Cataio: The Obizzi Saga, Fordham Univ Press, 2008; more than 25 major articles in int scholarly jours. *Mailing Add:* 880 Fifth Ave New York NY 10021

JAFFE, SHIRLEY
PAINTER
b NJ, 1923. *Study:* Cooper Union Sch Art, NY, 1945; Phillips Art Sch, Wash, DC, 1949. *Exhib.:* Solo exhibs include Galerie Nathalie Obadia Paris, 1999, Musée d'Art Moderne de Céret, 1999, Palais des Congrès Perpignan, 1999, Galerie Brigitte Weiss, Zuruch, 2000, Galerie Nathalie Obadie, Paris, 1999, 2001, 2008, Tibor de Nagy Gallery, NY City, 2002, 2005, 2010, Maison d'Art Contemporain Chaillioux, Fresnes, 2004, Galerie Fernand Léger, 2004, Domaine de Kerguéhennec, 2008; group exhibs: Galerie Kornfeld et Klipstein, Berne, 1959; Galerie Hanschin, Bale, 1961; Galerie Jean Fournier Paris, 1969; Calif State Univ, Northridge, 1977; Fondation du Chateau de Jau, Cases de Pène, 1977, 1989; Centre d'Art de Flaine, Haute Savoie, 1981; Zwanzig Jahr Kunst in Frankreich, Mainz, Allemagne, 1983; Vent'Anni d'Arte in Francia, Bologne, Italy, 1984; Found Cartier pour l'Art Contemporain Jouy-en-Josas, 1987; Holly Solomon Gallery, NY City, 1988, 1991, 1992; Artists Space, NY City, 1989; Centre Georges Pomidou, Paris, 1993; Galerie Therése Roussel, Perpignan, 1994; Livres d'Artistes, Ecole des Beaux Arts Perpignan, 1995; Galerie Brigitte Weiss Zuruch, Switzerland, 1996; Apex Art, NY City, 1997; Centre Culturel de Bourges, 1998; Espace de l'Art Concret, 1999; Ateliers au Féminin, Fondation COPRIM, 2000; Fondation Florence et Daniel Guerlain, Les Mesnuis, 2001; Tibor de Nagy Gallery, 2007; Raymond Handler and Artists from his 'avant garde' Circle (1950's-1970's), Katharina Rich Perlow Gallery, NY, 2008; Exploring Art A to Z, The Dayton Art Inst, Dayton, Ohio, 2008. *Mem:* Nat Acad. *Media:* Oil. *Dealer:* Galerie Nathalie Obadia 3 rue du Cloître Saint-Merri 75004 Paris France; Tibor de Nagy Gallery Geta Meert Brussells. *Mailing Add:* c/o Tibor de Nagy Gallery 724 Fifth Ave New York NY 10019

JAGGER, GILLIAN
PAINTER, SCULPTOR
b London, Eng, Oct 27, 1930. *Study:* Carnegie Inst Technol, BFA, 1953; Univ Buffalo, 1951; Colorado Springs Fine Arts Ctr, with Vytlacil, scholar, 1952; Columbia Univ, 1955; NY Univ, MA, 1960. *Work:* Finch Coll Mus, NY; Brompton's, Montreal, Can; Carnegie Inst, Pittsburgh; Aldrich Mus Contemp Art, Conn. *Comn:* Portrait comns, 1947-51. *Exhib:* Solo exhibs, Ruth White Gallery, NY, 1961, 1963 & 1964, Newhouse Gallery, Snug Harbor Cult Ctr, Staten Island, NY, 1987, Snita Shapolsky Gallery, New York, 1991, Trans Hudson Gallery, Jersey City, NJ, 1995 & 1997, Katona Mus Art, NY, 1995, Phyllis Kind Gallery, New York, 1998, 1999 & 2002, Davis & Hall Gallery, Hudson, NY, 2001, Elvehjem Mus Art, Univ Wis, Madison, 2003; Group exhibs, Loft Gallery, 1955-57; Finch Coll Mus, 1964; Lerner-Heller Gallery, 1971, 1973, 1975 & 1977; The Exceptions & the Exceptionals: Women Artists at Pratt, Pratt Manhattan Gallery, New York, 1987; Benefit Auction, Sculpture Ctr, New York, 1990, 1991, 1992, 1995; Wood: The Eternal Medium, Anita Shapolsky Gallery, New York, 1991, Women of the '60s, 1992, In the Tradition, 1992, Continuing the Tradition, 1993, Fantasy & Myth, 1994; Bosch's Garden of Delights, Exit Art, New York, 1994; Out of Wood, Recent Sculpture, Lowe Art Mus, Univ Miami, 1994; Body as Metaphor, Proctor Art Ctr, Bard Coll, NY, 1995; Presence, Absence, Trans Hudson Gallery, Jersey City, NJ, 1995; Outdoor Sculpture Show, Elena Zang Gallery, Woodstock, NY, 1996; From the Ground Up, Socrates Sculpture Park, Long Island City, NY, 1997; Aedicules, Art Omni, Ghent, NY, 1997; Symbols of Survival: Images of Animal & Recent Sculpture, Dorskey Gallery, New York, 2000; Invitational Exhib Visual Arts, Am Acad Arts & Letters, New York, 2008. *Pos:* Textile designer, Wamsutta Mills, Fruit of the Loom, 1955-57. *Teaching:* Lectr art, Radio Free Europe, cols & prof art schs; instr painting, NY Univ, Post Col & New Rochelle Acad, formerly. *Awards:* Creative Artists Pub Serv Grant, 1980; Guggenheim Fel, 1983; NY Found Arts Grant, 1985; Distinguished Prof Award, Pratt Inst, 1986; Louis Comfort Tiffany Found Grant, 1993; Adolf & Esther Gottlieb Found Grant, 1994; Anonymous Was a Woman Grant, 2003. *Dealer:* Phyllis Kind Gallery 236 W 26th St Ste 503 New York NY 10001-6736. *Mailing Add:* 48 Boice Mill Rd Kerhonkson NY 12446-2705

JAIDINGER, JUDITH CLARANN SZESKO
PRINTMAKER, PAINTER
b Chicago, Ill, Apr 10, 1941. *Study:* Art Inst Chicago, BFA. *Work:* State Found Cult & Arts, Honolulu, Hawaii; Portland Art Mus, Ore; Ill State Mus, Springfield; Ashmolean Mus, Oxford, Eng; Kemper Group, Long Grove, Ill; Ukrainian Independent Contemp Art, USSR. *Comn:* Wood engraving, Face to Face, Ltd Ed, Penmaen/Busyhaus Publ, 85; wood engraving illustrations, comn by David R Godine, 2006. *Exhib:* West '79 The Law Exhib, Minn Mus Art; 3rd Int Biennial Print Exhib, Taipei Fine Arts Mus, Taiwan ROC, 87; Interprint '90, Int Print Exhib, LUIV Mus Hist of Religion & Atheism, Ukraine, USSR, 90; 23rd Bradley Univ Print & Drawing Exhib, Ill, 91; Wood Engraving Here & Now, Ashmolean Mus, Oxford, Eng, 95; San Diego Art Inst, Calif, 92; Beyond Boundaries N Am Printmaking Exhib, Calif Soc Printmakers, Richmond, 97; Prints USA 2001, Springfield Art Mus, Mo, 2001; Nat Printmaking 2001, Coll of NJ, Ewing, 2003; Solo exhib, How Well I Knew Her Not, Wood Engravings Muskegon Mus Art, 2005-06. *Teaching:* Instr wood engraving, Office Field & Continuing Educ, Northeastern Ill Univ, 80-. *Awards:* Smithsonian Traveling Exhib Award, Contemp Am Drawings V, Norfolk Mus Arts & Sci, 71-74; Purchase Awards, Minot State Coll, NDak, 70 & 77; Graphic Award, Int Competition Printmakers, Clary-Miner Gallery, Buffalo, NY. *Mem:* Soc Am Graphic Artists, New York; Soc Wood Engravers, Eng; fel, Royal Soc Painter Printmakers Eng; Boston Printmakers Mass. *Media:* Wood Engraving; Opaque Watercolor, Mixed Media. *Publ:* Engravers Two, Silent Bks, Cambridge, Eng, 92; Endgrain: Contemporary Wood Engraving in North America, 94; An Engraver's Globe, 02; Lancelot and the Lord of the Distant Isles & The Tale of Galehaut Retold, David R Godine Publ, 2006. *Dealer:* Bankside Gallery London. *Mailing Add:* 6110 N Newburg Ave Chicago IL 60631

JAKOB , BRUNO
PAINTER
b Switzerland, 1954. *Exhib:* Galerie Peter Kilchmann, Zurich, 2006, Drawing, Thinking, Von Lintel Gallery, NY, 2007, Positionen09, Das Seewerk, Moers, Germany, 2009, Golden Agers & Silver Servers, Switzerland, 2009, Greater NY PS1, Contemporarty Art Ctr, NY, 2010, The Evryali Score, David Zwirner, NY, 2010, Die Nase des Michelangelo, Galerie Peter Klichmann, Marktgasse, Zurich, 2010, 54th Int Art Exhib Biennale, Venice, 2011. *Media:* Acrylic, Oil. *Mailing Add:* c/o David Zwirner 525 W 19th St New York NY 10011

JAKUB, JEFFREY ANDREW
PAINTER, ILLUSTRATOR
b Rahway, NJ, Mar 29, 1943. *Study:* Newark Sch Fine & Indust Art, AA, 1963. *Work:* Newark Mus of Art, Newark, NJ; Greenville Mus of Art, Greenville, NC; Mary Kay Cosmetics Corp Hq, Dallas, Tex; The Palm Beach Co, NY; First South Bank Collection, 9 cities, NC. *Comn:* Peach Floral Painting, Rosalynn Carter, Whitehouse, Washington, DC, 1980; Grant: Sculpture/painting, NC State Beaufort Col, Washington, NC, 1996; Rural Churches Eastern NC, NC Coun for the Arts, Raleigh, NC, 1997; Paintings for Capitol Bldg, state Sen Marc Basnight, Raleigh, NC, 2003; Hackney Corp, Hodges Hackney, Washington, NC, 2006. *Exhib:* Dimensions Nat Exhib, Sawtooth Galleries, Winston Salem, NC, 2001-2004; Watercolor Soc NC, Artsspace Bank of Arts, Salem Coll Raleigh, Winston Salem, NC, 2001-2005; Adirondack Int Exhib, Old Forge Arts Center, Old Forge, NY, 2004; Raleigh Soc Arts - Int, Meredith Col, Raleigh, NC, 2004; Am Watercolor Soc 139th Int, Salmagundi Club, NY, 2006. *Pos:* Pres & CEO, Jeff Jakub Design Hillsborough, NJ, 1973-; Exec Art & Advert Dir, Roots of Summit, NJ, 1963-1973; Creative Dir, WT Quinn Advert Agency, Somerset, NJ, 1983-1986. *Teaching:* Instr, advert, illus, life drawing, Spectrum Inst of Advert Arts, NJ, 1982-1984; instr, workshops, Boca Raton, Fla, Elizabeth City, NC, Balto, Md, 1984-2006; instr, oil, watercolor, Beaufort /Pittsburg Community Cols, 1986-1999. *Awards:* 57th Juried Edhib, Watercolor Soc NC, 2003; Second place, 59th Juried Exhibition, Watercolor Soc, NC, 2005; Nell Storer, 139th

Int Awards, Am Watercolor Soc, 2006. *Bibliog:* Jakub Wins Triple Crown, Raleigh News & Observer, 1997; John Underwood (auth), He Paints Like a Native, Washington Daily News, 1997; Al Critcher (auth), Immortalized Artist Capture, Williamston Enterprise, 1999. *Mem:* Beaufort Co Arts Coun (pres), Washington, NC, 1994-1996; Watercolor Soc NC (signature mem, E Regional Chair), 2005-; Greenville Brushstrokes (nom pres), Greenville, NC, 2006-; Am Watercolor Soc; Assoc Artists Winston Salem, NC; Nat Watercolor Soc; Allied Artists Am; Southern Watercolor Soc. *Media:* Watercolor, Oil, Pen/Ink, Pastel, Charcoal. *Interests:* Interior Design, Fashion Design, Opera. *Dealer:* Riverwalk Gallery 139 W Main St Washington NC 27889; River Street Gallery 207 E River St Savannah GA 31401. *Mailing Add:* 104 Forecastle Ct Washington NC 27889

JAMES, A EVERETTE, JR
PATRON, WRITER
b Oxford, NC, Aug 22, 1938. *Study:* Univ NC, AB, 59; Duke Univ Sch Medicine, MD, 63; Harvard Medical Sch; 66-69; Johns Hopkins, ScD, 71; Harvard Business Sch, 79; Royal Soc Med, London, 74. *Work:* Asheville Art Mus; US Embassies; Greenville Art Mus; Kenan Inst; John Hope Franklin Ctr, Duke Univ; Ctr for Honors, UNC; Boston Anthaneum; Cosmos Club; Mint Mus; Duke Univ; John Hopkins, Hickory Mus; Chickwood, Ctr for Study of the Am South, Greensboro Col; Martin Co Courthouse; Morris Mus; and others. *Exhib:* Southern Folk Art, 94-95; Antique Decoys, 94-95; NC Pottery, 94-95; NC Quilts, 97-98; Southern Women Artists (1840-1940), 98; NC Painters (1850-1950), 98; Southern Painters (1840-1940), 98-99; Southern Art, Huntsville Art, Mobile, Ala, 2003; African American Images, Nat Civil Rights Inst. *Collection Arranged:* The Ahls: An Am Art Family (auth, catalog), 80-83; Spectrum of Portraiture, 82; James Collection, 83 & The Am Scene, 83, University Club, Nashville; Eugene Healon Thomason Retrospective (catalog), 85; Royster Collection (catalog), 86; Pattie Royster James Collection, 87; Indiana Impressionism (catalog), 89; Collection Antique Waterfowl Decoys (with catalog), Tenn State Mus, 90; Tonalism and Nocturnes (catalog), 91; James Collection, 92 & Works on Paper, Cosmos Club, 93; The South (1840-1940), Knoxville Mus Art, Tenn, 92; Radiography & Art, NY, Washington, DC, London, Paris, Atlanta & Boston, 88-96; Southern Folk Art, Sawtooth Ctr, Winston-Salem, NC; Folk Art, Fine Arts Mus South, Mobile, Ala; Folk Art, Fisk Univ, Fayetteville State Univ, Elizabeth City State Univ & Nat Civil Rights Mus, Memphis, 94-98; Quilts, Ward Mus & Chapel Hill Mus, 98-99; Women Art of South, SC; Wesleyan, Merith, Asheville Art Mus; The South (1840-1940) Huntsville Art Mus, 2004; Hickory Art Mus, 2005; African Am Quilts, NC Farm Mus, Lucy Craft Ctr, 2005; and others. *Pos:* Ed, J Art Med; treas, bd mem, Int Soc Art Med; art comt, Cosmos Club; bd Am Visionary Art Mus; guest cur, Chapel Hill Mus Art,1999-2000, NC Pottery Mus, 2005-06. *Teaching:* Lectr Am Impressionism, Woman's Club, Centennial Club & Dixon Gallery, Memphis, Tenn, 81; instr, Philadelphia Antiques Show & Ark Art Coun, 86; African-Am Folk Tradition, Fisk Univ, 92; Elizabeth City State Univ, Women Artists (1840-1940), Chapel Hill, 98; Women's Studies UHC, 2003; John Hope Franklin Ctr, 2004; Morris Mus Art, 2005; AM Soc Ceramics, New York City, 2005; Miss Univ, 2005. *Awards:* Distinguished Med Alumnus, Duke Univ, 92; Carraway Award, Preservation NC, 94; Humanitarian Award, Duke Univ, 2003; Gold Medal, Am Roentgen Ray Soc, 03. *Bibliog:* Collections of Paintings in Hospitals, Int J Art in Med, 94; James Collection of Southern Folk Art, Ala Arts Coun, 94; Paintings in Hospitals, Royal Soc Medicine; Monograph African Am Quilts, 2004. *Mem:* Nat Trust Historic Preserv; Soc Preservation Tenn Antiquities; Explorer's Club; Cosmos Club; Alpha Omega Alpha. *Res:* Use of imaging techniques to evaluate paintings; visual physiology and art. *Interests:* Am Art, 1865-1940. *Collection:* American impressionism; American landscape; Antique Decoys, NC Pottery, Southern Folk Art; The South 1840-1940; NC Quilts; African-Am Quilts. *Publ:* Coauth, Digital Radiography; A Focus on Clinical Unity, 82; Certain radiographic techniques to evaluate paintings, Am J Roentgenology, 83; Digital radiography in the analysis of paintings, a new and promising technique, J Am Inst Consev, 83; auth, An introduction to Eugene Healan Thomason: The 'Ashcan Artist' who came to the mountains, Appalachian J, 83; Investing in American Impressionism, MD Mag, 83; Not every canvas is down for the count, Med Econ, 84; A physician's opportunity to contribute to the arts, The Pharos of Alpha Omega Alpha, summer 85; American Art: Thoughts of a Collector, 94; Essays in Folk Art, 01; North Carolina Art Pottery (1900-1960), 2003; Collecting Am Paintings, 2005. *Dealer:* Vose Gallery Newbury St Boston MA; Knoke Galleries Atlanta Ga; Foothills Gallery, Tryon NC

JAMES, BILL (WILLIAM) FREDERICK
PAINTER, ILLUSTRATOR
b Manchester, Conn, Oct 7, 1943. *Study:* Syracuse Univ, BFA, 65. *Work:* Dept Commerce, Montgomery, Ala; Panasonic, Japan; Business Weekly, NY; McGraw-Hill Pubs, NY. *Comn:* Mag illus, Tennis Mag, 91; mag & poster illus, Alfa Romeo, 91; mag illus, Golf Illus, 92; video illus, Rabbit Ears Productions, 92; card illus, NBA, 92; calendar, Panasonic, 95; 2 paintings, Fox News, 2005. *Exhib:* Cornucopia Ballerinas, Natl Watercolor Soc, 2004; Cornucopia Ballerinas, Am Watercolor Soc, 2006; Been There-Done That, Pastel Soc Am, 2006; Cuban Grandmother, Nat Watercolor Soc, 2007; 27th Va Pastel Soc Am, 2007. *Awards:* Silver Metal Award, Pastel Soc, Am, 93; Silver Metal Award, Am Watercolor Soc, 2001; Borse Miller Mem Award, Am Watercolor Soc, 2006; Best in Show, Southern Watercolor Soc, 2007. *Bibliog:* Watercolor Magic Mag Nov, 2003; Maureen Bloomfield, The Pastel Journal, Oct 2004; Int Artist Mag, Feb/Mar, 2007 . *Mem:* Pastel Soc Am; Am Watercolor Soc; Nat Watercolor Soc; Knickerbocker Artists. *Media:* Pastel, Watercolor; Oil. *Publ:* Int Artist Mag, 12-01/01; Watercolor Magic Mag, 11/2003; Pastel Jour, 10/2004. *Dealer:* Telluride Gallery of Fine Art 130 E Colorado Box 1900 Telluride CO; Broden Gallery Ltd 218 N Henry St Madison WI; Art 4 Business, 161 Leverington Ave, Philadelphia, PA; Coconut Grove Gallery 2790 Bird Ave Coconut Grove FL. *Mailing Add:* 509 NW 35th St Ocala FL 34475

JAMES, CHRISTOPHER P
PHOTOGRAPHER, PAINTER
b Boston, Mass, May 8, 1947. *Study:* Cummington Community Arts, 68; Mass Coll Art, BFA, 69; RI Sch of Design, MAT, 71. *Work:* Mus Mod Art, NY; Int Mus Photog, George Eastman House, Rochester, NY; Metrop Mus Art, NY; Boston Mus Fine Arts, Mass; Minneapolis Inst Arts Mus; and others. *Comn:* Subway steel enamel panels, Cambridge Arts Coun, 80. *Exhib:* Solo exhibs, Minneapolis Inst Arts, 77, Int Mus Photog, George Eastman House, 77, Centre d'Art Contemporain, Geneva, 79, Univ Ore Mus Art, 80, Witkin Gallery, NY, 81, 83, 85, 87 & 90; Weston Gallery, Carmel, Calif, 84, 86, 89 & 91, & Lizardi Harp Gallery, Pasadena, Calif, 87-88 & 90 and others; Mirrors and Windows, Mus Mod Art, NY, 78; Counterparts, Metrop Mus Art, NY, 82. *Teaching:* Asst prof photog & design, Greenfield Community Col, 71-78; artist-in-residence, Keene State Col, 77-78; lectr, Mass Inst Technol, Philadelphia Col Art, Univ Ore, Parsons Sch Design & RI Sch Design; instr, Chulalongkorn Univ, Bangkok, Thailand & Rencontres Internationales De La Photographie, Arles; prof, Harvard Univ, 78-91, Art Inst Boston, 91-. *Awards:* Daguerre, Niepce Medal, Phot-Univers USA/USSR, Minister of Foreign Affairs, Paris, 76; Mass Arts Found Fel, 78. *Bibliog:* Hilton Kramer (auth), New York Review, Esman, New York Times, 9/23/77; David Bourdon (auth), New York Review, Esman, Village Voice, 10/10/77; John Russell (auth), New York Review, Witkin, New York Times, 10/21/83. *Mem:* Soc Photog Educ. *Media:* Photo; Watercolor. *Publ:* Contribr, Alternative Photographic Process, Morgan & Morgan, 78; portfolio, Popular Photography, NY, 79; portfolio, American Photographer, NY, 79; cover & portfolio, Camera, Suisse, 4/79. *Dealer:* Witkin Gallery New York NY; Lizardi/Harp Los Angeles CA. *Mailing Add:* c/o Art Inst of Boston 700 Beacon St Boston MA 02215-2598

JAMIE, CAMERON
FILMMAKER
b Los Angeles, California, 1969. *Work:* Ellipse Found, Alcoitão, Portugal; Ctr Pompidou, Paris. *Exhib:* Solo exhibs include B-1 Gallery, Santa Monica, Calif, 1991, Spencer Brownstone Gallery, New York, 1998, Galerie Praz-Delavallade, Paris, 1999, Ctr Nat L'estampe et L'art Imprimé, Chatou, France, 2001, Galerie Christine König, Vienna, 2003, JO, Neue Galerie Graz am Landsmuseum Joanneum, Graz, Austria, 2004, Studies for Three Films, Bernier/Eliades Gallery, Athens, 2005, Walker Art Ctr, Minneapolis, 2006, Ink Carvings, Galerie Nathalie Obadia, Paris, 2007, MIT List Vis Arts Ctr, Cambridge, Mass, 2007; group exhibs include Best of the West, Zero One Gallery, Los Angeles, 1988; Cronologias, Temistocles 44, Mexico City, 1994; Casino 2001, SMAK Stedelijk Mus, Gent, Belgium, 2001; Adolescents, Reina Sofia, Madrid, 2003; Audio Lab 2, Ctr Georges Pompidou, Paris, 2003; Contrepoint, Mus du Louvre, Paris, 2004; Biennial Exhib, Whitney Mus Am Art, New York, 2006; Edit!, Cascais, Portugal, 2007; When things cast no shadow, Berlin Biennial, 2008; Amateurs, Ctr Contemp Arts Wattis Inst, San Francisco, 2008. *Awards:* Found Contemp Arts Grant, 2008; Yanghyun Prize, South Korea, 2008. *Dealer:* Bernier/Eliades Gallery 11 Eptachalkou GR-11851 Athens Greece; Galerie Nathalie Obadia 3 rue du Cloitre Saint-Merri Paris France 75004; Galerie de multiples 17 rue Saint-Gilles Paris France 75003; Christine König Galerie Schleifmühlgasse 1a 1040 Vienna Austria. *Mailing Add:* Gladstone Gallery 515 West 24th Street New York NY 10011

JAMISON, PHILIP
PAINTER
b Philadelphia, Pa, July 3, 1925. *Study:* Philadelphia Mus Sch Art, 50. *Work:* Pa Acad Fine Arts, Philadelphia; Wilmington Soc Fine Arts, Del; Nat Acad Design, New York; Flint Inst Art, Mich; Frye Art Mus, Seattle, Wash; Nat Air & Space Mus, Washington, DC; Brandywine River Mus, Pa; Boston Mus Art; The Fine Arts Mus San Francisco. *Comn:* NASA Artist for Apollo-Soyuz Space Launch, 75 & Space Shuttle Mission 51-G, 85. *Exhib:* Solo exhibs, Hirschl & Adler Galleries, New York, 59-80, Delaware Art Mus, 73, Janet Fleisher Gallery, Philadelphia, 77, Newman Galleries, Philadelphia, 82, 84, 86, 90 & 93, Ruthven Gallery, Lancaster, Ohio, 86, Patricia Carega Gallery, Washington, DC, 85 & 87 & Hahn Gallery, Philadelphia, 93, 98 & 2002; 200 Yrs of Watercolor Painting in Am, Metrop Mus Art, New York, 67; Chester Co Hist Soc, 99; Chester Co Art Assn, 2011; Philip Jamison and His Collection, Woodmere Art Mus, Phila, Pa, 2013. *Pos:* Artist, Apollo Soyuz Space Launch, Kennedy Space Ctr, Fla, Nat Aeronautics & Space Admin, 75. *Teaching:* Instr watercolor, Philadelphia Coll Art, 61-63. *Awards:* First Prize, Wilmington Soc Fine Arts, 57, 59 & 61; Bainbridge award Allied Artists Am, 58 & 60; Recipient Dawson medal, Pa Acad Fine Arts, 59 & 77; Dana Medal, Pa Acad Fine Arts, 61; Medal of Honor, Knickerbocker Artists, New York, 61; William Church Osborn prize Am Watercolor Soc, 61 & 79; First Award, Nat Arts Club, New York, 61; Lena A Mason prize Nat Acad Design, 62; Ranger Fund purchase prize, Nat Acad Design, 62 & prize, 67; MW Zimmerman Mem prize Philadelphia Watercolor Club, 63; Gold Medal Honor, Allied Artists Am, 64; Gold medal honor, Allied Artists Am, 64; Childe Hassam Fund purchase prize, Am Acad Arts & Lett, 65; CFS award, 66; Nat Acad Design Prize, 67; Thornton Oakley Mem prize, Philadelphia Watercolor Club, 67; Samuel Finley Breese Morse medal Nat Acad Design, 69; Edgar A Whitney award, 71; High Winds award, 72; Whitney award, 73; Ted Kautzky Memorial award, 74; Adolph and Clara Obrig award, 74; Gold medal, Franklin Mint Gallery Am Art, 74; Merit award, Nat Watercolor Exhib, Springfield Art Asn, Ill, 79; Walter Biggs Mem award Nat Acad Design, 82; Alfred Easton Poor award, 99; Zella W Pine award, 2003; Pike prize, 2003. *Mem:* Am Watercolor Soc; Philadelphia Watercolor Club; Nat Acad Design. *Media:* Watercolor, Oil. *Publ:* Contribr, Am Artist Mag, 62; auth, Capturing Nature in Watercolor, 80; Making Your Paintings Work, Watson-Guptill, 84; A Painting Without Spirit is Like Flat Beer, pvt publ, 88; I Hate People Who Refer to Works of Art As Pieces, 95. *Dealer:* Newman and Saunders Galleries 120 Bloomingdale Ave Wayne PA 19087

JANIS, CONRAD
DEALER, COLLECTOR
b New York, NY, Feb 11, 1928. *Collection Arranged:* Participated in arranging all exhibitions at Sidney Janis Gallery from New Realism, 62 through Sharp Focus Realism, 72; and others. *Pos:* Co-owner, Sidney Janis Gallery. *Specialty:* All historic movements in 20th century art to the present. *Collection:* Contemporary American art

JANJIGIAN, LUCY ELIZABETH
PAINTER, MURALIST
b Jerusalem, Palestine, Dec 14, 1932; US citizen. *Study:* Heidelberg Col, Tiffin, Ohio, BA, 55; Emory Univ, Atlanta, Ga, MS, 56; Art Students League, with Robert Hale, 70, Fogerty, 71 & Glasier, 72; study with Victor D'Amico, 72-74; Stacy Wkshp Studio, New York, NY, 74-. *Work:* Am Cyanamid Hq, Wayne, NJ; Berliner Handels & Frankfurter Bank, NY; Mekhitarist Mus, Vienna, Austria; Gallery Phillip, Toronto; Arab Bank, NY. *Comn:* Two acrylic murals, St Leon's Church, Fairlawn, NJ, 81; acrylic mural, Armenian Evangelical Union of NAm, Los Angeles, Calif, 85; acrylic mural, Armenian Missionary Asn, Paramus, NJ, 87; Christmas cards & Christmas stamps-American Evangelical Church, NY, 87 & 89. *Exhib:* Passaic Co Community Col, NJ, 88; Convention Hall Philadelphia PA, 89; Capital Place Gallery, Trenton NJ; Heidelberg Col, Tiffin, Ohio, 90; Am Libr Mus Am Inc, Watertown, Mass, 92; one-person show, Presby Publ Corp, Louisville, Ky, 94; and others. *Pos:* Mem art comt, Armenian Gen Benevolent Union, Saddle Brook, NJ, 79-; bd trustees, Bergen Mus Arts & Sci, Paramus NJ, 84-90 & Artists for Mental Health, Paterson, NJ, currently. *Awards:* Hon Mention, Bergen Co Artists, 70; Hon Mention, Franklin Lakes Art Show, 72; First Place Acrylic Abstract, Gregg Galleries-Nat Arts Club, 81. *Bibliog:* Hope Noah (auth), article, Weekend Times, NJ, 8/88; Sean Siman (auth), The painterly conscience of Lucy Janjigian, Artspeak, 12/1/88; Nancy Kleinhenz (ed), Portraits of Inhumanity - The Advertizer Tribune, Tiffin OH, 10/2/90. *Mem:* Cath Artists of the 80's; Composers, Authors & Artists of Am; Burr Artists; Nat League Pen Women; Westside Arts Coalition & NY Artists Equity Asn Inc, NY. *Media:* Acrylic. *Mailing Add:* 268 Edgewood Rd Franklin Lakes NJ 97417-2007

JANKOWSKI, THEODORE ANDREW
PAINTER, MURALIST
b New Brunswick, NJ, Dec 14, 1946. *Study:* Rhode Island Sch Design, 71; Cape Sch Art, 71-73, 80-86. *Work:* State Mus Reserve of Palace of Peter the Great, Leningrad, USSR; Hiroshima Peace Mem Mus, Hiroshima, Japan; Cigna Mus Art Collection, Philadelphia, Pa; Johns Hopkins Evergreen House Perm Collection, Baltimore, Md; Provincetown Art Asn Mus, Mass; Yad Vashem Holocaust Mus, Jerusalem. *Exhib:* Hensche & Friends, Michael Ingbar Gallery, NY, 88; Provincetown Mus, Mass, 93; State of the Art, Boston, Mass, 93. *Media:* Oil. *Dealer:* Green Flash Gallery Kawaehae HI. *Mailing Add:* PO Box 791 Kapaau HI 96755

JANNETTI, TONY
GRAPHIC ARTIST, FINE ARTIST
b Yonkers, NY, May 27, 1947. *Study:* Pratt Inst, BFA, 69. *Work:* Mus Mod Art, NY; Yale Univ Art Gallery, New Haven; Althea Corp, NY; IBM Collection, New York, Dallas, Hartford; Chase Manhattan Bank, NY; Zimmerli Mus, New Brunswick, NJ; and others. *Comn:* Rahini II, Edward Durrell Stone Asn, NY, 80. *Exhib:* Resurrection Show, 55 Mercer St Gallery, NY; Nimbus Gallery, Dallas, Tex, 83-85; Relief Painting in the 80s, Zimmerli Mus, 88; Marcus-Gordon Gallery, 89; invitational, Artists Space, 94; Enderlin Gallery, 2004; Williams Ctr Arts (with Ping Chong), Easton, Pa, 2006; Window Gallery, Pine Hill, NY, 2009-2011; Shandaken Studio Tour, 2012. *Pos:* mulitmedia & graphic designer, consultant, Fiji Co, 72-81, Ping Chong & Co, 72-. *Teaching:* Instr, Fordham Univ, 83-84. *Awards:* Hon Mention, Rx Award, 2003, 2004; Blurb Book Design Award, 2009. *Media:* Natural Materials, Computer Design. *Publ:* Auth, articles in Artforum, 9/81 & 9/86, New York Art Review, 88 & J of the Printworld, annually. *Mailing Add:* Media Wall Design 261 Bowery New York NY 10002-1201

JANNEY, CHRISTOPHER DRAPER
ENVIRONMENTAL ARTIST, DESIGNER
b Washington, DC, Mar 14, 1950. *Study:* Princeton Univ, with Michael Graves & James Seawright, BA (archit, visual arts), 73; Mass Inst Technol, with O Piene, MS (environ art), 78. *Work:* Smithsonian Inst; Miami Art in Pub Places Trust; NationsBank Collection, Sacramento Metrop Art Comn; San Antonio Arts Comn; NY Metrop Transit Auth. *Comn:* REACH-NY, 96; Rainbow Pass, Coral Gables, Fla; Harmonic Runway, Miami Airport, 95; and others. *Exhib:* Soundstair, Boston Mus Fine Arts, 79, Walker Art Ctr, 80, Nat Gallery Art, 80, Corcoran Gallery Art, 80, Second Int Electronic Music Conf, Brussels, Belg, 81 & Santa Barbara Mus Art, Calif, 82; Sonic Pass, Miss Mus Art, Jackson, 81; Wall-to-Wall John Cage, Symphony Space, NY, 82; Inside Rhythms, Inst Contemp Art, Boston, 83; Steamshuffle (with catalog), Pub Art in Am, Philadelphia, Pa, 87; Heartbeat:mb, with M Baryshnikov, City Ctr, NY, 98. *Pos:* Res fel, Ctr Advan Visual Studies, Mass Inst Technol, 1978-92; chmn, Inst for Performance Sculpture Inc, 1987; coun mem, CEIS, Fulbright Found, 1995-. *Teaching:* Instr, Mass Col Art, 1984-85 & State Univ NY, Purchase, 1987; vis prof, Cooper Union Sch Archit, New York, RI Sch Design, 1995. *Awards:* Nat Endowment Arts Grant, 91; Mass Coun Grant, 91; New England Found Grant, 92. *Bibliog:* Daria Sommers (auth), The Elephant on the Hill (film), Smithsonian World, PBS, 6/86; Andy Scheleucan (auth), Studio 7 (film), WNEV-TV; Martha Teishner (auth), An Ear for Art, CBS This Morning, WCBS-TV, 95. *Media:* Sound, Electronics. *Publ:* Articles in The New York Times, 10/84 & 9/86 and People Mag, 10/79; Sand and communication, 4/94; Light Waves, Cover/Feature, Archit Record, 11/95. *Mailing Add:* 75 Kendall Rd Lexington MA 02173

JANNICELLI, MATTEO
PAINTER, PHOTOGRAPHER
b Newark, NJ, Aug 26, 1935. *Study:* Montclair Art Mus, 61; study with Michael Lenson, 61-62; Kean Univ, BA (fine art), 76; pvt lessons with Vincent Nardone. *Work:* Hoffman LaRoche Pharmaceutical Corp, Nutley-Clifton, NJ; Munic Bloomfield, NJ; Newark Pub Libr, NJ; Atlantic City Art Ctr, NJ; Micro Industrial Corp, Bayville, NJ; Kean Univ Mus Permanent Collection; Temple Sha'arey Shalom, Springfield, NJ; Ocean Co Coll, NJ; pvt collections, Louis Ricco, Carl Burger, Dick LaBonte, Rhoda Yanow & Bill Nagengast. *Comn:* Roman Antiquities (mural), Three Brothers Italian Restaurant, Old Bridge, NJ, 83-84. *Exhib:* NJ 28th Water Color Show, Morris Mus Arts & Sci, Morristown, NJ, 70; Am Art at Mid Century, Northfield YMHA, West Orange, NJ, 74; Jersey Five, Ocean Co Coll, Toms River, NJ, 98; Jersey Five, Bay Head, NJ, 99; Brick 2000 Cult Arts Ctr, 2000; solo exhib, Anchor & Palette Gallery, Bay Head, NJ, 2004; Display Yarn Paintings, Georgian Court Univ, Lakewood, NJ, 2001; juried exhibs, Audubon Artist Art Soc, 2000-2006 & TV Art Auction, Rosehill Auction Gallery, Englewood, NJ, 2006; Fabrick Show, Beyond the Stitch II, Artist Guild, Ocean Co, NJ, 2006. *Pos:* Pres, Bloomfield Art League, 70-73; vpres, Federated Art Asn NJ, 71-72; pres, Manasquan River Art Group, 88-91. *Teaching:* Instr watercolor, Newark Sch Fine & Indust Art, 70-75; instr painting, Artist & Craftsman Guild, Cranford, NJ, 72-73; instr graphics & printmaking, Annex Sch Art, Montclair, NJ, 72-73. *Awards:* Mixed Media Award, 24th Annual Sr Citizens State Show, 2000; Award, Ocean Co Senior's Art Show, 2002; Diane B Bernhard Award for Merit, Audubon Artists 62nd Annual Nat Art Spirit Found, 2004. *Bibliog:* Ruth Ann Williams (auth), Graven images-featured artist, NJ Music & Arts Mag, 74; Esther Forman Singer (auth), The art part, Worrel Publ Suburban News, 76; The Ocean Star Newspaper, 10/1/99; Encyl Am Painters, Sculptors & Engravers of the US Colonial, 2002. *Mem:* Ocean Co Camera Club; Ocean Co Artist Guild; Manasquan River Group Artists (pres, 88-91); Audubon Artists; Allied Artists; Atlantic City Art Ctr. *Media:* Mixed Media, Graphic Arts, Fabric Collage. *Publ:* Illusr, Jersey Five, 99. *Dealer:* Ann LaBonte Neff 45 Mount St Bayhead NJ 08742; Anchor & Palette Gallery; Tycoon Art Gallery Manasquan NJ

JANOWICH, RONALD
PAINTER
b Baltimore, Md, 1948. *Study:* Coll Art Md Inst, BFA, 70, MFA, 72. *Work:* Metrop Mus Art, NY; Aldrich Mus Contemp Art, Ridgefield, Conn; Bank of Boston; Cleveland Mus Art, Ohio; Tate Gallery, London, Eng; and others. *Exhib:* The 1980's: A New Generation, Metrop Mus Art, NY, 88; solo exhibs, Galerie Malmgran, Goteburg, Sweden, 90, Galleri JMS, Oslo, Norway, 90, Monotypes 1989-90 (with catalog), Gallery Kuranuki, Osaka, Japan, 90, Compasse Rose Gallery, Chicago, Ill, 91, Galerie Lelong (with catalog), Paris, France, 91 & Pamela Auchincloss Gallery, NY, 92 & 94; Painting, 91 & Transcendence & Immanence, 92, Galerie Lelong, NY; Collaborations in Monotype from the Garner Tullis Workshop, Sert Gallery, Carpenter Ctr Visual Arts, 92; Inaugural Exhib, Tennisport Arts, Long Island City, NY, 92; Lillian Heidenberg Gallery, NY, 93; Shape, Pamela Auchincloss Gallery, NY, 94; After the Fall, Aspects of Abstract Painting 1970-Present, Newhouse Ctr Contemp Art & Snug Harbor Cult Ctr, NY, 97; and many others. *Collection Arranged:* Metrop Mus Art; Tate Gallery, London; Cleveland Mus Art; numerous pvt collections. *Teaching:* Assoc prof painting, drawing, 2 & 3-D design, printmaking & independent study, Lafayette Col, Pa, 80-85; drawing, Parsons Sch Design, NY, 84; vis artist, Prog Painting, Kent State Univ, Ohio, 92 & 96, Cleveland Inst, Ohio, 93 & 96, undergrad, grad painting & advanced drawing, Grad Seminar, Ohio State Univ, 96, undergrad & grad painting, Photo Seminar, Univ Fla, 96-98; vis asst prof, painting and drawing, Fla State Univ, 98-. *Awards:* Nat Endowment Arts Fel, 76, 89. *Bibliog:* Margaret Moorman (auth), Painting, ARTnews, 134, 11/91; David Carrier (auth), rev, Tema Celeste, 87-89, spring, 93; Vivian Raynor, Geometry now, NY Times, 10/24/97; and others. *Media:* Oil. *Publ:* Auth, On Horizontality: A Structural Approach, 82; Brice Marden at Pace, Art Gallery Rev, Fall 82; Contemp Abstract Painting (exhib catalog), Muhlenberg Col, Allentown, Pa, 83; Small Works: New Abstract Painting (exhib catalog), Lafayette & Muhlenberg Cols, 84; Black Oil: Aspects of Dimensionality, J Artists, No 6, spring 86; and others. *Dealer:* Pamela Auchincloss Gallery 601 W 26th St 12th Floor New York NY 10001. *Mailing Add:* 302 FAC PO Box 115801 Gainesville FL 32611-5801

JANOWITZ, JOEL
PAINTER
b Newark, NJ, Nov 29, 1945. *Study:* Brandeis Univ, BA, 67; Univ Calif, Santa Barbara, MFA, 69. *Work:* Mus Fine Arts, Boston; Fogg Mus; Harvard Univ; Rose Art Mus; Brandeis Univ, Waltham, Mass; Whitney Mus, Metrop Mus, Brooklyn Mus, Minneapolis Inst of Arts; MIT, Cambridge, Mass; Yale Univ Art Gallery; NY Public Library; Boston Public Library. *Comn:* Mural, Alewife Subway Sta, Mass Bay Transportation Authority, Cambridge, 85. *Exhib:* Whitney Biennial, Whitney Mus Am Art, NY, 73; Boston Watercolor Today, 76, A Private Vision: Contemp Art from the Graham Gund Collection, 83 & Recent Paintings and Sculpture 1944-1984, 85, Mus Fine Arts, Boston, Mass; Hassam Fund Purchase Exhib, Am Acad & Inst Arts & Lett, NY, 80 & 87; solo shows, Munroe, NY, 83, 86, 88 & 92, Bernard Toale Gallery, Boston, 87 & 98, Clark Gallery, Lincoln, Mass, 2002; Herbert W Plimpton Collection of Realist Art, Rose Art Mus, Brandeis Univ, Waltham, MA, 95; Painting Ctr, NY, 96; Contemp Works on Paper: 1990-2000, Minneapolis Inst Arts, 1; Visions & Revisions, Mus of Fine Arts, Boston, 2003; solo: High Point Ctr for Printmaking, Minneapolis, MN, 2005; Victoria Munroe Fine Art, Boston, 2005, 2007, 2009, 2011; Changing Soil Contemporary Landscape, Nagoya, Japan, 2010. *Teaching:* Asst prof, painting & drawing, Brown Univ, Providence, RI, 73-75 & 77; instr painting, Harvard Univ Summer Sch, 80, 81, 94-98 Mus Fine Arts Sch, 85, 94-2000, Princeton Univ, 1997, Fine Art Work Ctr, Provincetown, Mass, 99-present, Wellesley Col, 2003-2010, Mass Art Fine Arts Work Ctr, Low Res, MFA Prog, 2006-2010. *Awards:* Artists Fel, Mass State Grants Artists, 75 & 79 & Nat Endowment Arts, 76 & 82; Hassam & Speicher Fund Purchase Award, Am Acad & Inst Arts & Lett, 80 & 87; Artists Fel, New York Found for Arts, 88; Artists Fel, Mass Cultural Council, 2008. *Bibliog:* Greg Masters (auth), Joel Janowitz, Arts Mag, 12/84; Robert C Morgan (auth), New York in Review, Arts Mag, 9/88; Robert C Morgan (auth), Tactility & contrast: The Italian sojourn of Joel Janowitz, In: Between Modernism & Conceptual Art, McFarland Press, 97; Gerry Bergstein (auth), Art Feature Joel Janowitz, Agni 53, Boston Univ, 2001; Francine Koslow Miller (auth), Joel Janowitz's Greenhouses, Art New England, 6-7/2002; Cate McQuaid (auth), Seeing Life's Lushness Through Blurred Lines, Boston Globe, 2005;

David Mickenberg (auth), Joel Janowitz: Recent Work 2000-2005 (catalog), 2005; Louis Postel (auth), Rhythms of Life, New England Home, p. 110, 2008; Cate McQuaid (auth), At Victoria Munroe, Final Show Spotlights Six Artists, Boston Globe, 2012. *Media:* Oil, Watercolor. *Mailing Add:* 158 Vassal Lane Cambridge MA 02138

JANS, CANDACE
PAINTER, PRINTMAKER
b Rockville Centre, NY, Oct 22, 1952. *Study:* Wheaton Col, Norton, studied with Vaino Kola, BA, 74; Villa Schifanoia Grad Sch Fine Arts, Florence, Italy, MA, 75; RI Sch Design, studied with Wolf Kahn & Irving Petlin, MFA, 79. *Work:* Hunter Mus, Chattanooga, Tenn; Am Express Co, NY; Wheaton Col, Norton, Mass; Cabot Corp, Wellington Mgt Corp, Mass Financial Servs, Boston, Mass; TRW, Inc, Cleveland; Commerce Bancshares, Kansas City, Mo. *Exhib:* The Mood of New Eng, Boston Jubilee 350, Copley Soc, Mass, 80; Boston Now, Brockton Mus Triennial, Mass, 80; Contemp Boston Portraits, Boston Univ Gallery, Mass, 80; Collector's Gallery XVIII, Marion Koogler McNay Art Inst, San Antonio, Tex, 84; Group exhib, Bayly Art Mus, Univ Va, Charlottesville, 87; solo exhibs, Fischbach Gallery, NY, 84, 86, 89 & 95 & Wheaton Col, Mass, 92, 2000; Fischbach Gallery, One Woman Show, 2005; and others. *Collection Arranged:* Springfield Art Mus, Springfield, MO. *Mem:* Boston Visual Artists Union; Women's Caucus Arts (Boston chap); Boston Athenaeum. *Media:* Oil, Lithography. *Dealer:* Larry DiCarlo Fischbach Gallery 210 Eleventh Ave 8th Fl New York New York 10001. *Mailing Add:* 291 Adams St Milton MA 02186

JANSCHKA, FRITZ
PAINTER, GRAPHIC ARTIST
b Vienna, Austria, Apr 21, 1919. *Study:* Acad Fine Arts, Vienna, with A Paris Guetersloh. *Hon Degrees:* Title Prof, Pres Austria, 75. *Work:* Albertina, Vienna; Mus XXth Century, Vienna; Philadelphia Mus Art, Pa; Grafische Sammlung, Zurich, Switz; Hist Mus, Vienna; Art Inst Chicago; Wien Mus, Vienna, Austria; Fort Worth Mus, Tex; Chicago Inst Art, Chicago; Weatherspoon Mus, Greensboro, NC; and many more pvt & pub collections; Phantasten Mus, Wien, Austria. *Comn:* One Hundred Etchings to World Literature Edition, Harenberg, Dortmund, Ger; 36 Watercolors to 36 Poems by J Joyce, comn by Clyde Joyce, Vienna, 89; Richard Levy, Greensboro, NC; Anderson/Henderson, Greensboro, NC; Hans Prankl, Vienna, Austria. *Exhib:* Pa Acad Fine Arts, Philadelphia, 51-54; Graphische Sammlungen, Zurich, 72; Fantastic Realists, Wiener Schule, Near East & Far East Countries, 72-74; Die Wiener Schule de Phantastischen Realismus, Mus Am Ostwall, Dortmund, Ger, 79; XXth Century, Art Club, Oesterreich Mus, Vienna, 81; Solo exhibs, Orangerie Palais Auersperg, Vienna, 82, Rupertinum Salzburg, Austria, 87 & Illustration's To Sonne & Mond, Gallery at Oper, 89, My Choice: Joyce!, Cantor Fitzgerald, Gallery, Haverford Coll, Haverford, PA, 2000; Graphic 24, Albertina, Wien, Austria, 96; Albertina, Wien, Austria, 2002; Wake Tarot, Weatherspoon Art Mus, Art on Paper, Bianuel, NC, 2004; Belveder, Wien, Austria, 2007-2008; Weatherspoon Mus, Greensboro, NC; Woodmere Gallery, Phila, Pa, 2012. *Collection Arranged:* Finnegan's Re-turns, Weatherspoon Mus, 2008-2009. *Pos:* Vis artist, UNCG, 92. *Teaching:* Prof emer fine arts, Bryn Mawr Coll, Pa, Fairbanks prof in Humanities emer. *Awards:* M Slaughter Teaching Award, 85; Gold Medal of Merit, City of Vienna, Austria, 89. *Bibliog:* J Norton-Smith (auth), A Tribute to James Joyce's Ulysses, Reading Univ, Eng, 73; Johann Muschik (auth), Janschka Monograph & Vienna school of fantastic realism, Jugend & Volk, Vienna/Munich, 74; Robert Waissenberge (auth), Die Wiener Schule Kat, Bozen, Univ Wien, 80; E Halton (auth), An unlikely meeting of the Vienna school and the New York school, NY, 80; Otto Breicha (auth), Der Art Club, Oesterreichs, J & V, Vienna, 81; The Larger Austria, Edition Tusch, Sotrifer, Vienna, 82; Aichele K Porter (auth), Self Confrontation in the early works of the Vienna School, NJ, 88; Gerhard Habarta (auth), Kunst in Wien Nach 1945, Wien, 96 & Das Neue Osterreich, Belvedere, Wien, 2007; Joe Scott (auth), FJ Photographer of the Subconscious, News & Record, Greensboro, NC, 2000; Phantastische Realismus Belveder, Wien, Austria, 2008; Loring Mortensen: Fritz Janschka Homages to the Masters, Paperback, Lulu Press. *Mem:* Art Club, 46-51. *Media:* Oil, water, ink, pencil. *Res:* Translation: Apollinaire, Bestiary into German. *Specialty:* Newman Contemporary, Phila, Pa. *Interests:* Poetry, music. *Collection:* Dr. Fred Lopp, Greensboro, NC, Joan Tobias, Gladwynne, Pa, Mr and Mrs Richard Levy, Greensboro, NC, Mr and Mrs Semsh, Media, Pa, Dustin Spear, Pound Ridge, NY, Anderson-Henerson Coll, Greensboro. *Publ:* Auth, 26 etchings to James Joyce's Ulysses, Rizet, 72; Vom Denken der Dichter, Bibliophile Taschenbuecher, Dortmund, WGer; contribr, After Surrealism, 72, auth, Ulysses Alphabet, 73 & contribr, After Classicism, 73, PropyLaen, Berlin, Germany; Dr Erika Patka (auth), Zeichnungen Zum Roman, Sonne Und Mond, Von A P Gutersloh, Fur Angewandte Kunst, Wien, 2002. *Dealer:* Newman Galleries 1625 Walnut St Philadelphia PA 19103; Galerie Habarta A2824 Seebenstein Austria

JANSEN, ANGELA BING
PAINTER, PRINTMAKER
b New York, NY, Aug 17, 1929. *Study:* Brooklyn Col, BA; NY Univ, MA; Atelier 17, New York, with S W Hayter; Brooklyn Mus Art Sch. *Work:* Metrop Mus Art, Mus Mod Art & NY Pub Libr, NY; Philadelphia Mus Art; Art Inst Chicago; Tate Gallery, Victoria & Albert Mus, London, Eng; Brooklyn Mus; Bibliothequé Nat, Paris; And others. *Exhib:* Brooklyn Mus Nat Print Exhib, 50, 70 & 76; Nat Exhib of Prints, Libr of Cong, Washington, DC, 69 & 71; Biennial de Venice, Italy, 72; Biennial of Graphic Art, Wein, 72 & 77; Lang of Print, Pratt Ctr, NY, 73; Solo Exhib, Gimpel & Weitzenhoffer Gallery, NY, 74, 78 & 80; Five Printmakers, Martha Jackson Gallery, NY, 75; Nat Print Exhib, NY, 76; Madison Art Ctr, Wis, 77; Now Drawing Is, Int Exhib, Imbashi Gallery, Kyoto, 78; Int Exhib original drawings, Rijeka, 80; Images, Printing, 81, Int Exhib, Bruxelles, 81. *Teaching:* high school music & art. *Awards:* First Prize, Asn Am Artists, Int Miniature Print Exhib, 71; George Roth Prize, Philadelphia Print Club, 71 & 74; Grant for Printmaking, Nat Endowment Arts, 74-75; and others. *Bibliog:* Article, The Print Collector's Newsletter, 7-8/73; Judith Goldman (auth), The language of print, Review #I, Art Forum, summer 79; Francine Tyler (auth), Angela Jansen, Printmaker, ARTFORUM, Summer 79. *Media:* Etching, Painting. *Mailing Add:* 1646 First Ave New York NY 10028

JANSEN, CATHERINE SANDRA
PHOTOGRAPHER, ENVIRONMENTAL ARTIST
b New York, NY, Dec 14, 1950. *Study:* Cranbrook Acad Art, Bloomfield Hills, Mich, BFA, 71; Acad di Belle Arti, cert, 72; Temple Univ, MFA, 76. *Work:* Philadelphia Mus Art; Ctr Creative Photogr; Fine Arts Mus Honolulu; Frans, Kline & French; Bell of Pa; ARA Co. *Exhib:* Unique Photographs: Multiple Sculpture, Mus Mod Art, NY, 73; Three Centuries of Am Art, Philadelphia Mus Art, Pa, 76; Am Family Portraits, Philadelphia Mus Art, 76; solo exhibs, Ctr Creative Photog, Tucson, Ariz, 83, Hicks Gallery, Bucks Co Community Col, Newtown, Pa, 84, Univ Va, Charlottesville, 85, Photog Resource Ctr, Boston, 87, Spaces Gallery, Cleveland, 88, Owen Patrick Gallery, Philadelphia, 89 & Moore Coll Art, Philadelphia, 91; The Camera Rediscovered, Woodmere Art Mus, Philadelphia, 95; Complexity & Contradiction, Paley Design Ctr, Philadelphia, 96; and others. *Teaching:* Instr photog, Bucks Co Community Col, Newtown, Pa, 73-. *Awards:* Individual Artist Grant, Pa Coun Arts, 81, 88 & Nat Endowment Arts, 83; Cult Insertive Grant, 82 & 95. *Mem:* Pa State Coun Arts. *Publ:* Introduction to Visual Literacy, Curtis, Prentice Hall Publ, 88; Nancy Howell-Koehler, The Creative Camera, Davis Publ, 88; Photo Art Process, Davis Publ Inc, 91; Philadelphia Mag, Manayonic Art Festival, 95; Mildred Constantine & Laurel Reuter, Whole Cloth, Monticello Press, 98. *Mailing Add:* c/o Dept Art/Bucks Co Community Col Swamp Rd Newtown PA 18940

JANSEN, MARCUS ANTONIUS
PAINTER
b Manhattan, NYC June 28, 1968. *Study:* Berufsfachschule for Design, Moenchengladbach, Ger, 85-86; Berufsfachschule for Painters, Moenchengladbach, Ger, 3 yr Journeyman Cert, 86-89; US Army. *Work:* Nat Taiwan Mus Fine Art, Taiwan; Ford Motor Co Hq, Dearborn, Mich; Smithsonian Anacostia Mus, Washington, DC; Southwest Fla Mus Hist, Ft Myers, Fla; Moscow Mus Mod Art, Russia. *Comn:* Mural (school), Berufsfachschule, Moenchengladbach, Ger, 87; 4 Hist works of Art, Ford Motor Co, Dearborn, Mich, 2003; 11 Hist works of Art, Southwest Fla Mus Hist, 2006; Oasis Towers Permanent Collection, Jorge Perez (The Related Group of Florida), Miami, Fla, 2006; and others. *Exhib:* Solo exhibs, Am Art Gallery, Deauville, France, 2002-2004, Gallery One, Nashville, Tenn, 2005, Damien B Contemp Art Ctr, Miami, 2007; Group exhibs, Ford Motor Co Paintings, Charles H Wright Mus, Dearborn, Mich, 2003; Bob Rauschenberg Gallery, Fort Myers, Fla, 2004; Tampa Mus Art, Fla, 2006; Nat Taiwan Mus Fine Art, Taiwan, 2006; Kuandu Mus Fine Art, Taiwan, 2006-2007; Exhib Hall Manege, Russia; Société des Beaux Arts de Garches, France; Nat Kaohsiung Normal Univ, Taiwan, 2007; Angel Art Gallery, ROC, Taiwan, 2007; Lawrence Asher Gallery, Los Angeles, 2007; Oi Futuro Inst, Rio de Janeiro, 2007. *Awards:* Best in Show Award, Gallery 27, Reflect Arts Inc, New York, 2006; Diploma Award for Mod Urban Expressionism, 8th Int Biennale Mod Art "Dialogues", St Petersburg, Russia, 2007; Who's Who in Visual Art; Who's Who in International Art. *Bibliog:* Jerome A Donson (auth), Modern Urban Expressionism, the Art of Marcus A Jansen; Alba di Roberto Puviani (auth), Int Encyclopedic Dictionary Modern & Contemporary Art, Casa Editrice, Ferera, Italy; Famous 120 Contemporary Artists, World of Art Books, London; William & Mary Review. *Mem:* Artist Rights Soc, NY. *Media:* Acrylic, Oil, Mixed Media-Painting. *Publ:* Auth, Modern Urban Expressionism, Am Art Gallery, Paris, France, 2006. *Dealer:* Museum Works Gallery 525 E Cooper Ave Aspen CO 81611

JAQUE, LOUIS
PAINTER
b Montreal, PQ, May 1, 1919. *Study:* Inst Appl Arts, Montreal. *Work:* Nat Gallery Can, Ottawa; Montreal Mus Fine Arts; Mus Quebec; Mus d'Art Contemporain, Montreal; Societe Publicite Editoriale Collection, Milan, Italy; Mus Sherbrooke; Mus Joliette. *Comn:* Mural, Quebec Pavilion, Expo 70, Osaka, Japan, 70; mural, Maison de Radio-Canada, Montreal, 72; mural, Place de la Bourse, Montreal, 74. *Exhib:* Europa 72, 3rd Int Exhib Painting, Milan, 72; Salon Int d'Art Contemp, Paris, 74 & 75; retrospective, Montreal Mus Fine Arts, 77; solo exhib, Can Cult Ctr, Paris, France, 78; Arte Universal a Traves de los Tempos, Mus Palacio Bellas Artes, Mex. *Collection Arranged:* Retrospective, 25 Years of Painting, Montreal Mus Fin Arts. *Teaching:* Instr design & design hist, Inst Applied Arts, Montreal, 59- 83. *Awards:* Jessie Dow Award, Montreal Mus Fine Arts, 60; Can Art Coun Grant to Artist, 64 & 72; Europa 72 Bronze Medal, City of Milan, 72. *Mem:* Founder Soc Prof Artists Que (pres, 64-65); Royal Can Acad. *Media:* Oil, Tempera. *Publ:* Art in New York, Time Mag, 10/31/69; Considerations over a concept, D'ars Mag, Italy, Nos 53 & 54; 16 Quebec painters in their milieu, La Vie Des Arts, 78; Monique Brunet-Weinmann (auth), Louis Jaque: le point de vue d'icare, La Vie Des Arts, spring 85; Monique Brunet-Weinmann (auth), Louis Jaque, 89. *Dealer:* Han Art Gallery 4209 Ste Catherine W Westmount PQ Can H3Z 1P6

JAQUET, LOUIS
CONCEPTUAL ARTIST, PAINTER
b Paris, France, Mar 27, 1944. *Study:* Acad De La Grande Chaumiere, Paris, 65; Acad Julian, Paris, 66; Ecole Nat Superieure, Des Beaux Arts, Paris, 72. *Work:* Palais Des Expositions, Zurich, Switz; Mus Modern Art, Tel Aviv, Isreal; Mus Modern Art, Bologna, Italy; Palazzo Pitti Mus, Florence, Italy; Vatican Mus, Vatican City, Italy. *Comn:* Fresco 11x 13 painting, Swiss Govt, zurich, 85; painting, City Scape, Am Embassy, Paris, 96; painting, Vatican City, Pope John Paul II, Vatican City, 2004. *Exhib:* Int Biennial Exhib Contemp Art, Salsomaggiore, Terne, Italy, 82; Int Biennial Exhib, Graphic Arts, Tokyo, Japan, 83; Int Biennial Exhib, Contemp Art, Los Angeles, Calif, 84; Royal Acad, London, 84; Biennial Contemp Art, Palazzo Corsini, Rome, Italy, 84; Int Biennial Exhib, Zurich, Switz, 85; Int Biennial Exhib, Tsukuba, Japan, 86. *Awards:* First Prize, Tokyo Japan, Int Graphic Art Exhib, 85; Special Distinction Award, Tsubuka, Japan Int Biennial Exhib, 86; First prize, painting, Nat Exhib, Italy, 87. *Mem:* Maison Des Artistes, France; Routhschild Found, Paris, France. *Media:* Oil

on canvas, all media. *Publ:* Auth, The Israel J, J Aoilion, 83; auth, Gazzetta de Reggio, Annusca Campani, 84; auth, Il Popolo, Ivanna Arnaldi, Rome, Italy, 85; auth, E Benezit Dictionnaire, Librairie Grund, 98; auth, Giorgio Ruggeri, Louis Jaquet, Edision d'Arte Ghelfi, 2001. *Dealer:* Gallerie 454 15105 Kercheval Ave Grosse Pointe MI 48230

JARAMILLO, VIRGINIA
PAINTER
b El Paso, Tex, Mar 21, 1939. *Study:* Otis Art Inst, 58-61. *Work:* Long Beach Mus Art, Calif; Pasadena Art Mus, Calif; Aldrich Mus Contemp Art, Ridgefield, Conn; Schenectady Mus, NY. *Exhib:* Whitney Mus Am Art Ann, NY, 72; Contemp Reflections 1971-72, Aldrich Mus Contemp Art, Ridgefield, 72; group exhib, Douglas Drake Gallery, Kansas City, Kans, 75 & one-man show, 76; plus others. *Pos:* Assoc dir & aesthet adv, Hybrid Inc, 72-74. *Awards:* Ford Found Grant, 62; Nat Endowment Arts, 72-73; Creative Artists Pub Serv Prog Grant, 75. *Bibliog:* F Bowling (auth), Outside the galleries: Four artists, Arts Mag, 11/70; Deluxe show, Houston Chronicle, 8/71; C Ratcliff (auth), The Whitney Annual, Part I, Artforum, 4/72. *Mem:* Nat Soc Lit & Arts. *Media:* Acrylic, Oil. *Res:* Religious architecture throughout Europe. *Publ:* Auth, Post-minimal artists, Arts Mag, 9/75

JARVIS, JOHN BRENT
PAINTER
b American Fork, Utah, Nov 28, 1946. *Study:* Snow Col, AS, 65; Utah State Univ, BS, 71; Brigham Young Univ. *Work:* Brigham City Mus, Utah; Latter Day Saints Church Mus; Springville Mus Art, Springville, Utah. *Comn:* Painting, Latter Day Saints Church, 84. *Exhib:* Salt Lake Art Ctr Regional Show, 76; Am Watercolor Soc, NY, 76; Solo exhibs, Brigham Young Univ, Provo, Brigham City Mus, Bertha Eacles Gallery, Ogden, & Trivoli Gallery, Salt Lake City, Utah; Northwest Rendezvous Show, Helena, Mont, 89-90. *Awards:* Merit Award, Utah Painting & Sculpture, Utah Inst Fine Arts, 74; Ann Noye Watercolor, Salt Lake Art Ctr Intermountain, 76; Merit Award, Mormon Art Show, Brigham Young Univ, 77. *Media:* Multimedia, Watercolor. *Dealer:* Lido Gallery Park City Utah. *Mailing Add:* 1355 E 250 N Pleasant Grove UT 84062-3054

JASHINSKY, JUDY
PAINTER, CURATOR
b Oconto Falls, Wis, Dec 27, 1947. *Study:* Univ Wis, Stevens Point, BS, 70; Mich State Univ, MFA, 73. *Work:* Nat Gallery Art, Washington, DC; Springfield Art Mus, Mo; Univ Mich Sch Med, Ann Arbor; Smith-Barney, NY; Muskegon Mus Art, Mich. *Comn:* Portrait, comn by Mrs Gilbert Hart Kinney, Washington, DC, 91; 6 portraits, comn by Mary Hynes Berry, Chicago, 91-93; 50th Anniversary Screen, Meyer Found, Washington, DC, 94. *Exhib:* Contemp Am Indian Art, Smithsonian Mus Nat Hist, 84; Deutsch-Amerikanisches, Stadtische Galerie, Regensburg, Ger, 89; one-man shows, Washington Proj for the Arts, Washington, DC, 89, Susquehanna Art Mus, Harrisburg, Pa, 92-93 & Rosenberg Gallery, Goucher Col, Baltimore Md, 94; The Return of the Cadavre Exquis, The Drawing Ctr, NY, 93 & Corcoran Gallery Art, Washington, DC, 94; Artists Select, Artists Space, NY, 94; solo exhib, Roman Fever, Artemifia Gallery, Chicago, Ill, 98, Artists Mus, Washington, DC, 98, Academy Celebration 1616, Gibson Creatives, 98; Past, Present, Future, Clare Spitler, Ann Arbor, Mich, 98; Jolt, Baum Garther Gallery, Washington, DC, 99. *Collection Arranged:* Primal Painting, Marlboro Gallery PGCC, Largo, Md, 85; Memento Mori, Fondo del Sol Visual Arts Ctr, 90; Boudoir and Luparar (catalog), Washington Proj for the Arts, Washington, DC, 95. *Pos:* Chair, Community Outreach Comt, Washington Proj Arts, 91-93. *Teaching:* Instr painting & drawing, Prince Georges Community Col, Largo, Md, 80-86, Trinity Col, Washington, DC, 84-87 & Westshore Community Col, Scottville, Mich, 90-93. *Awards:* American-Russian Cult Found, Sponsorship, Roman Fever Exhib, Artist Mus, Washington, DC, 89; New Forms Regional Grant, Painted Bride, Philadelphia, Pa, 93; Mayors Award Excellence, Service to the Arts, 92. *Bibliog:* Robert Bersson (auth), Beyond Painting & Sculpture, Worlds of Art, Mayfield Publ, 91; Mary McCoy (auth), Reviews, New Art Examiner, 1/93; Shenandoah, Wash & Lee Univ Review, 10/98. *Mem:* Washington Proj for the Arts; Coalition of Washington Arts. *Media:* Acrylic, Oil. *Publ:* Lost Work of Judy Jashinsky (catalog), 96. *Dealer:* Clare Spitler 2007 Pauline Court Ann Arbor MI 48103. *Mailing Add:* 225 N Columbus Dr, Unit 6106 Chicago IL 60601

JASUD, LAWRENCE EDWARD
PHOTOGRAPHER, EDUCATOR
b Chicago, Ill, Oct 26, 1942. *Study:* Southern Ill Univ, BS (photog), 69; Ohio State Univ, MA (photog), 80. *Work:* J Paul Getty Mus; Univ Tenn, Knoxville; Schearing Plow Corp Coll, Memphis; Malone & Hyde Corp Coll, Memphis; Tokyo Coll Photog. *Exhib:* Naked, Univ Colo, Boulder, 85; Magic Silver, Univ Northern Iowa, Cedar Falls, 91; Photog Book Arts in US, Univ Tex, San Antonio, 91; Brooks Biennial Invitational, Memphis Brooks Mus Art, 92; Windows on Tennessee, Cheekwood, Nashville, 94. *Teaching:* Assoc prof photog, Univ Memphis, 81-. *Awards:* Media Fel, Tenn Eastman Co, 87; Individual Artist's Fel, Tenn Arts Comn, 87; Dean's Creative Achievement Award, 96. *Bibliog:* Robert McGowen (auth), Memphis Brooks Biennial Catalog (essay), Memphis Brooks Mus, 92. *Mem:* Coll Art Asn; Soc Photog Educ (reg secy, 83-86). *Publ:* Auth, Words, Sounds & Power, Logan Elm Press, 91; auth & illusr, A Portfolio of My "Myths & Rituals" Photographs, History of Photography, 92; auth, Memphis Brooks biennial catalog (essay), Memphis Brooks Mus, 94; Through a pinhole brightly, View Camera Mag, 95; Wisdom of the forest, Number: 30, 96. *Dealer:* Jay Etkin Gallery Memphis Tenn. *Mailing Add:* 244 S Greer St Memphis TN 38111-3434

JAUDON, VALERIE
PAINTER
b Greenville, Miss, Aug 6, 1945. *Study:* Miss State Coll Women, Columbus, 63-65; Memphis Acad Art, Tenn, 65; Univ Am, Mexico City, 66-67; St Martin's Sch Art, London, Eng, 68-69. *Work:* Hirshhorn Mus & Sculpture Garden, Nat Mus Women Arts, Washington, DC; Mus Mod Art, NY; Fogg Mus, Cambridge, Mass; Albright-Knox Art Gallery, Buffalo, NY; Birmingham Mus Art, Ala; Whitney Mus Am Art, New York, NY. *Comn:* Pilot (oil on canvas), Atlanta City Hall, Ga, 89; Freestyle (ceramic tile wall mural), Equitable Bldg, NY, 89; Reunion (3 acre paving plan, brick and granite), Municipal Bldg, NY, 89; Refraction (ceramic mural), Lab Sci Bldg, Staten Island, NY, 94; and others; Filippine Garden (grass & gravel garden) Thomas F Eagleton Courthouse, St Louis, MO, 2004. *Exhib:* Solo shows incl Pa Acad Fine Arts, 77, Corcoran Gallery, Los Angeles, 81, Dart Gallery, Chicago, 83, Amerika Haus, Berlin, Ger, 83, Sidney Janis Gallery, NY, 83, 85, 86, 88, 90, 93 & 96, McIntosh/Drysdale Gallery, Washington, 85 & Miss Mus Art (with catalog), Jackson, 96, Stadel Mus, Frankfurt, Ger, 99; Von Lintel Gallery, NY, 2003, 2005, Von Lintel Gallery, 2008, 2010; group shows incl Mus Mod Art, NY, 75; Hirshhorn Mus & Sculpture Garden, Washington, DC, 77; Nat Gallery, Washington, DC, 80; Mus Fine Arts, Boston, Mass, 82; Generations of Geometry, Whitney Mus Am Art at Equitable Ctr, NY, 87; Making Their Mark, Cincinnati Art Mus & traveling, 89; Holly Solomon Gallery, New York, 77-79, 81; Galerie Bischofberger, Zurich, 79. *Teaching:* Instr, Sch Visual Arts, New York, 83-84; assoc prof, Hunter Col, New York, 85, prof, 92. *Awards:* Vis Arts Fel Grant, Nat Endowment for the Arts, 88; Art Award, Excellence in Design, Art Comn, New York, 88; NY State Fel Painting, 92; Merit Award, Am Soc Landscape Archits, Ala Chap, 94; Art award, Miss Inst Art and Letters, 97. *Bibliog:* John Perreault (auth), Allusive depths: Valerie Jaudon, Art in Am, 10/83; Barry Schwabsky (auth), Degrees of symmetry, Art in Am, 10/96; Anna Chave (auth), Disorderly Order: The Art of Valerie Jaudon (with catalog), Valerie Jaudon, Mississippi Mus Art, Jackson. *Media:* Acrylic, Oil. *Dealer:* Sidney Janis Gallery 100 W 57th St New York NY 10019; Von Lintel Gallery 520 W 23th St New York NY 10011. *Mailing Add:* 44 King St New York NY 10014

JAWORSKA, TAMARA
FIBER ARTIST, TAPESTRY ARTIST
b Archangelsk, Russia, 1928; Can Citizen. *Study:* State Acad Fine Arts, Poland, BFA, Fac Design Art Weaving, MFA; Royal Can Acad Arts, fel academician, Acad Italia Delle Arti e del Lavoro Fel Acad, Fel, York Univ, Toronto. *Work:* Nat Mus, Warsaw, Poland; Molson Can, Toronto; York-Hanover Corp, Toronto; JDS Investment Corp, Toronto; Nat Mus A Puschkin, Moscow, Russia; Can Embassy, Ryiadh, Saudi Arabia; Dept External Affairs, Can; Nat Mus Textile Art, Warsaw, Nat Mus Home Army, Krakóv, Poland; Nat Mus of Civilization, Ottawa, Canada; and many pvt collections. *Comn:* Tapestries-Gobelin, Olympia & York co, Place Bell Can, Ottawa, 71 & Bank Montreal, Toronto, 75, Metrop Life Ins co, Ottawa, 77, JDS Finch 1000, Toronto, 76 & var pvt collections in US, Can, Switz, Eng, Sweden & France. *Exhib:* Solo exhib, 7 Mus, Art Galleries, Spain, 80-91; retrospectives, Ctr Nat de la Tapisserie D'Aubusson, Galerie Inard, Paris, traveling abroad, 81-82, 84, 86, 89 & 91 & Royal Acad Arts, John B Aird Gallery, Toronto, 92; Centennial Exhib RCA, Toronto; Mus Appl Arts, Budapest, Hungary, 95; Mus Fine Arts/Dresden Design Zentrum, Ger, 96; Manifesto 96, Int Festival of Archit & Design, 96; Mayor Retrospective, Peak Gallery, Toronto, Can, 97, Gallery Solo, King City, Toronto, 2003-2005; Mayor Exhib, Weavers Art Gallery, Toronto, 2006; Mayor Exhib, Design Walk, Toronto, 2007; Index, Int Exhib Design & Art, Dubai, UAE, 2007; Prime Gallery, Toronto, 2008; Samuel J Zacks Art Gallery, York Univ Int Art Show, Toronto, 2009. *Pos:* Dir pvt design-weaving art studio, Toronto, currently. *Teaching:* Instr post grad workshop design & weaving, Ont Coll Arts, Can. *Awards:* Master Painter Honoris Causa, Acad Ital delle Arti; Gold Medal & First Prize, Int Art Competition, New York, 85; Gov Gen, 125th Anniversary Medal, 93; Order of Canada (CM), by HRH Queen Elizabeth II, Outstanding Achievements in Creative Arts, 94; Golden Jubilee Medal - by HRH Queen Elizabeth II; Fel, York Univ; Polish Medal Gloria Artis, 2009. *Bibliog:* Tapestries by Tamara Jaworska (film), CBS Toronto, 70 & Tamara's Tapestry World, CBS Arts & Sci Prog in Film, Toronto, 75; film, Tapestries by Tamara, New Collection, CBC Arts Film, Toronto, 80; film (mini-series), A Modern Country, Tamara's Tapestry World, Textures & Canadian Reflections, Can Broadcasting Co; film, Portrait of the Artist, CHCH TV & CHEX TV; film, Tamara-The Art of Weaving, Bravo, 2008; and articles in American & European variety mag, art mag, art books & daily newspapers. *Mem:* Royal Can Acad Arts; Acad Italia del Arti a del Lavoro. *Media:* Wool, Artificial Yarns. *Publ:* Tamara-The Art of Weaving, Bernardinum Art Book, 2009. *Dealer:* Poles Ltd Art. *Mailing Add:* 49 Don River Blvd Toronto ON M2N 2M8 Canada

JAY, BILL
PHOTOGRAPHIC HISTORIAN, CRITIC
b Maidenhead, Berkshire, Eng, Aug 12, 1940. *Study:* Berkshire Coll Art, dipl; Univ NMex, MA & MFA; spec study with prof Van Deren Coke & prof Beaumont Newhall. *Work:* Int Mus Photog, Rochester, NY; Bibliotheque Nat, Paris, France; Art Mus, Univ NMex, Albuquerque; plus many pvt collections. *Exhib:* Mod Art, var locations in Brit & Europe, 67; Art Mus, Univ NMex, 76; Solo exhibs, Micro-Gallery, Phoenix, Ariz & Northlight Gallery, Tempe, Ariz, 77. *Collection Arranged:* Brit Documentary Photog 1850-1970, Brit Coun, 71; The English Scene, Tony Ray-Jones & Sir Benjamin Stone 1864-1914, 71, Inst Contemp Arts, London; plus others. *Pos:* Ed/dir, Album Mag, London, Eng, 69-71; dir photog, Inst Contemp Arts, London, Eng, 69-71. *Teaching:* from asst prof to assoc prof art hist, 19th century & 20th century photog, Ariz State Univ, Tempe, Ariz, 74-. *Mem:* Soc for Photog Educ (mem bd dir, 74-78); Royal Photog Soc Gt Brit (mem Royal comn, 72). *Res:* Photography of the 19th and 20th centuries, especially British topographical work of the wet-plate era. *Publ:* Auth, Robert Demachy: Photographs and Essays, 74, Acad Ed; auth, Victorian Cameraman: Francis Frith 1822-1898, 73 & Victorian Candid Camera: Paul Martin 1864-1944, 73, David & Charles; Negative/Positive: A Philosophy of Photography, Kendall-Hunt, 79; Addison House and Photography: Current Perspectives, Light Impressions, 79. *Mailing Add:* c/o Sch of Art Ariz State Univ Tempe AZ 85287

JAY, NORMA JOYCE
PAINTER
b Wichita, Kans. *Study:* Wichita State Univ; Art Inst Chicago; Calif State Univ, Long Beach. *Work:* Irvine Found; Edwin Morris Collection; Deloitte, Haskins & Sells; Niguel Art Asn, Laguna Niguel, Calif; MJ Brock & Sons, N Hollywood, Calif. *Exhib:* Peabody Mus of Salem, Mass, 81; Mystic Maritime Gallery, Mystic Seaport Mus, Mystic, Conn, 82-83, 85, 90, 92 & 95; Las Vegas Art Mus, 84; Palm Springs Desert Mus, Calif, 84; Coos Bay Art Mus, Ore, 94, 96, 98 & 2003; Frye Mus, Seattle, Wash, 97; Cummer Mus Art, Jacksonville, Fla, 97-98; Newport Harbor Nautical Mus, Newport Beach, Calif, 98-99 & 2003; Maine Maritime Mus, 2003; Conn River Mus, Essex, 2004; Vero Beach Mus Art, Fla, 2004; Maritime Mus San Diego, 2007; Nat Gallery Art, Washington, DC, 2007; Chase Riverfront Ctr for the Arts, Wilmington, Del, 2008; Chesapeake Bay Maritime Mus, St Michaels, Md, 2008; Nayers Mus, Oceanville, NJ, 2009; Spartanburg Art Mus, Spartanburg, S Carolina; New Bedford Art Mus, Mass, 2009; Cornell Mus Ash and Am Culture, Delray Beach, Fla, 2011; Mobile Mus Art, 2012; Ash Mus Southeast Tex, Beaumont, 2012; Coos Art Mus, Coos Bay, Ore, 2012; Haggin Mus, Stockton, Calif, 2013; Coos Art Ark Mus, 2013; Minn Marine Art Mus, 2013. *Awards:* Best Show, Ford Nat Competition, 61; Artists Award, Chriswood Galleries, 73; First Place, Traditional Artists 10th Ann, 76; Best of Show Award, Newport Harbor Nautical Mus, Newport Beach, Calif, 99 & 2003. *Bibliog:* Peter Rogers (auth), review, Sea Hist, winter 80-81; Contemporary Marine Art, Nimrod Press, 81; article, Antiques & Arts Weekly, 12/82; Rebecca Smith (auth), Norma Jay, West Coast Impressions, Nautical Quart, autumn 84; Yacht Portraits, Sheridan House. *Mem:* Am Soc Marine Artists (fellow emeritus). *Media:* Oil. *Specialty:* marine paintings. *Interests:* marine paintings. *Publ:* Norma Jay's Life 2015 in the Arts. *Mailing Add:* 24903 Moulton Pkwy Apt 142 Laguna Beach CA 92653

JEAN, BEVERLY STRONG
PAINTER, ART DEALER
b Eugene, Ore, Oct 1, 1927. *Work:* Atlanta Bowe Co, Ga. *Pos:* Owner, Tiqua Gallery, Santa Fe, NMex, currently. *Media:* Oil Painting, Monoprints. *Specialty:* Contemporary paintings; antique folk art; American Indian art; colonial Mexican art. *Mailing Add:* PO Box 4741 Santa Fe NM 87502

JEAN, JAMES
ILLUSTRATOR
b 1979. *Study:* Sch Visual Arts, New York, grad, 2001. *Comn:* Comic book cover artist, Batgirl, 2000, Green Arrow, 2001, Fables, 2002-, Fables: The Last Castle, 2003, Amazing Fantasy, 2004, Monolith, 2004, Machine Teen, 2005, Runaways, 2005, Escapists, 2006, Fables: 1001 Nights of Snowfall, 2006, Jack of Fables, 2006-, The Umbrella Academy, 2007; cover artist, Freaks: Alive on the Inside (novel), 2006; album artist, The Black Parade, My Chemical Romance, 2006. *Awards:* Eisner Award, Best Cover Artist, 2004-07; Harvey Award, Best Cover Artist, 2005 & 2007; Eagle Award, Best Comic Book Cover, 2007; Bronze Lion, Cannes Lions Int Advert Festival, 2008. *Publ:* Process Recess vol 1: The Art of James Jean, AdHouse Books & Process Recess vol 2: Portfolio

JEFFERS, WENDY
CURATOR, ARTIST
b Providence, RI, Sept 5, 1948. *Study:* Univ Mass, BFA, 71; Pratt Inst, MFA (painting), 74; also attended NY Inst Fine Arts, Art Students League, Tyler Sch Art, Am Univ, New Sch Social Res, Mass Coll Art, Columbia Univ, Corcoran Mus Sch, NY Acad Art & Nat Acad Design. *Work:* Port Authority NY & NJ; Chase Manhattan Bank, New York; Continental Group, Stamford, Conn; Miller, Tabak & Hirsch, New York; pvt collections, Dr & Mrs Jack Aslanian, Mr & Mrs George Demeter, Mr & Mrs William Hayden; and many others. *Exhib:* The Icarus Odyssey, Guadalajara & Mexico City, 79; Wash Square East Galleries, NY Univ, 80; Paperworks 80, Hudson River Mus, Yonkers, NY, 80; AIR Gallery Invitational, New York, 82-85; solo exhib, Bristol Art Mus, RI, 84; Fairleigh Dickinson Univ, NJ, 84; Sculptures-Drawings, Berkshire Artisans Art Ctr, Pittsfield, Mass, 84. *Collection Arranged:* First Nat City Bank Art Collection, New York, 73-74; Seven Decades at the Colony (auth, catalog), New York, 76; A Curators Choice: A Tribute to Dorothy C Miller, Rosa Esman Gallery, New York, 82; Niles Spencer A Portrait in Words and Images, Archives Am Art, New York, 90; Niles Spencer Exhib, Whitney Mus Am Art, Equitable Ctr, spring 90; Holger Cahill and Dorothy C Miller: An Exhib of Paintings, Sculpture and Documents from the Decade 1929-1939, Archives of Am Art, 93. *Pos:* Independent cur. *Awards:* Max Beckmann Fel, Brooklyn Mus, 71-72; Grad Fel, Pratt Inst, 73-74; MacDowell Colony Fel, 77. *Bibliog:* Kay Larson (auth), article, NY Mag, 3/1/82; Michael Kimmelman (auth), Review of Niles Spencer exhib, NY Times, 6/15/90; Michael Kimmelman (auth), Review of Archives Exhib, NY Times, 5/14/93. *Mem:* Arch Am Art, Smithsonian Inst (bd mem). *Media:* Oil, Graphite. *Res:* Working on Catalogue Raisonne of Niles Spencer's painting and sculpture; Working on biography of Dorothy C Miller retired senior curator of the Museum of Modern Art. *Specialty:* Early 20th Century Am Modernism. *Publ:* Niles Spencer, Whitney Mus Am Art, 90; Dorothy C Miller: A Profile, New Eng Antiques J, 5/90; Holger Cahill & Am Art J Arch Am Art, fall 92 & Holger Cahill & Am Folk Art, Antiques Mag, 9/95; auth, Abby Alderich Rockefeller: patron of the modern, Antiques Magazine, 11/2004. *Mailing Add:* 61-63 Crosby St New York NY 10012

JELLICO, NANCY R
PAINTER, SCULPTOR
b LaGrange, Ga, Sept 22, 1939. *Study:* Colo Inst Art, Denver, with John Jellico & Charlie Dye, diploma, 60; Univ Denver, with John Witaschek, 81; CA-10 Wkshp, Cowboy Artists of Am Mus, Kerrville, Tex, 86, Marble/Marble V, Marble, Colo by Art Students Leage of Denver, Colo, 93. *Work:* Four 4'x8' murals, Chadron State Coll, Nebr, 2002. *Comn:* The Good Things Don't Change (four paintings), 82, sculptures: Bunch Quitter, 83, He Ain't Heavy, 84, Head to Head, 88 & Lendin' a Hand, 90, The Upjohn Co, TUCO Div, Kalmazooo, Mich; Flag design, ProRodeo Hall of Champions & Mus of the Am Cowboy, Colo Springs, 83; archit sculpture (to scale), St Thomas Sem, Denver, Colo, 85, 88 &90. *Exhib:* Mountain Oyster Club's Ann Contemp Western Art Show, Tucson, Ariz, 1984-2000; Classic-Am Ann Western Art Show & Sale, Beverly Hills, Calif, 87-90 & 94; solo exhib, Nat Cowgirl Hall Fame, Hereford, Tex, 90; Women Artists & the West, Tucson Mus Art, Ariz, 91-94; Happy Canyon Western Art Invitational, Pendleton, Ore, 91-97; Wyoming Western Images, Murisaki Gallery, Tokyo, Japan, 92; Spirit of the Great Plains, Mus Nebr Art, Kearney, 98, 2000. *Pos:* Registrar, Colo Inst Art, Denver, 61-65. *Teaching:* Instr figure drawing & anatomy, Colo Inst Art, 64-65. *Awards:* Artist of the Year & Best Show/Oil-base Medium, Rushmore Prof Fine Artists Show, Rapid City, SD, 85; Inducted into Colo Inst Art Hall of Fame, Denver, Colo, 91. *Bibliog:* Deborah S Borg (auth), article, Equine Images, fall 89; Shirley Behrens (auth), article, Art of the West, 3-4/90; Ann Thompson (auth), article, Wild West, 2/95; included in An Encyclopedia of Women Artists of the West, Univ Tex Press, 98, Directory of American Portrait Artists, Premiere Issue, Am Portrait Soc, 85. *Media:* All Media. *Publ:* Illusr of five art textbooks, Int Correspondence Schs, 60-65; Portrait of Franklin Booth for feature article, Am Artist Mag, 66; Portrait of Pawel Kontny for feature article, Artists Rockies & Golden West Mag, 81; auth & illusr, feature article in: Int Cowboy Mag, Surrey, Eng, 12/87-1/88; illustr, Leaning into the Wind, Anthology/Western Lit, Houghton Mifflin Co, 97. *Mailing Add:* 85558 479th Ave Amelia NE 68711-3233

JENCKS, PENELOPE
SCULPTOR
b Baltimore, MD, Mar 23, 1936. *Study:* Hans Hoffmann Sch, 55; Swarthmore Col, student, 56; Skowhegan Art Sch, 57; Boston Univ, BFA, 58; Stuttgart (Ger) Kunstakademie, 59. *Work:* Decordova Mus & Sculpture Park, Lincoln, Mass; Provincetown Art Asn & Mus, Provincetown, Mass; The White House, DC; Nat Acad Design, New York; Boston Pub Libr; Cape Mus Fine Arts, Dennis, Mass; Roosevelt Univ, Chicago; Memphis Botanic Garden; Bibliotheca di Pietrasanta, Italy. *Comn:* Samuel Eliot Morison Commonwealth Ave, Boston; Family Portside Festival Park, Ohio; Farber Libr, Brandeis Univ; Danbury Family Art in Pub Spaces, Conn; Family Group Readers Digest Corp, NY; Eleanor Roosevelt Mem, New York; Robert Frost Amherst Coll, Mass, 2007. *Exhib:* Solo exhibs, Fitchburg (Mass) Art Mus, 76, Landmark Gallery, New York City, 77 & 81, Art Inst Boston, 78, Helen Shlein Gallery, Boston, 81 & 85, Berta Walker Gallery, Provincetown, Mass, 2006, 2008, List Gallery, Swarthmore Coll, Pa, 2006, Provincetown Art Asn & Mus, Provincetown, Mass, 2006, Boston Univ, 2006; group exhibs, at USIS, Amerika Haus, Freiburg, Ger, 60, Nat Inst Arts & Letters, New York City, 66, Mass Coun Arts & Humanities, Boston, 66, Thayer Acad, Braintree, 71, Boston Visual Artists Union, 74, Pa State Univ Mus Art, 74, Kennedy Galleries, New York City, 77, GVW Smith Art Mus, Springfield, Mass, 77, Clark Univ Mus Worcester, Mass, 78, Mass Artists Found Fed Reserve Bank, Boston, 80, Danforth Mus, Framingham, Mass, 80 & 84, Rose Art Mus Brandeis Univ, 82, MacDowell Colony Benefit, Cambridge, Mass, 83, Brockton Mass Art Mus, 83, Currier Gallery Art, Manchester, NH, 84, Fitchburg Art Mus, 84, Newton Arts Ctr, 85, Boston Univ, 86, Alchemy Gallery, Boston, 87, Helen Bumpus Gallery, Duxbury, Mass, 89, Rising Tide Gallery, Provincetown, Mass, 89, Contemp Sculpture, Chesterwood, Stockbridge, Mass, 89. *Pos:* Instr, Braintree (Mass) Art Asn, 71-72, Art Inst Boston, 75-79, Boston Col, Newton, Mass, 78. *Teaching:* Resident, MacDowell Colony, 75, 76, 78, & 87; prof, Saltzman vis artist Brandeis Univ, Waltham, 81-83; guest lectr, in field, currently. *Awards:* Commendation for Design Excellence, Nat Educ Asn, 81; grantee Brandeis Univ, 83; Henry Hering Mem Medal, Nat Sculpture Soc, 88; Distinguished Alumni Award, Sch Vitual Arts, Boston Univ, 91; Fel, Bogliasco Found, Centro Studi Ligure, 98; Agop Agopoff Prize sculpture, Nat Acad Design, 2005; New England Award, 5th Ann, Int Asn Art Crititcs, 2007. *Bibliog:* Blair Birmelin (auth), Penelope Jencks, Sculpture, Mass Rev, 83; Philip Hamburger (auth), Mrs Roosevelt, Eight Feet Tall, New Yorker, 94; Joyce Johnson (auth), Wellfleet Sculptor Distills Essence of Eleanor Roosevelt, 95; Eleanor Munroe (auth), Penelope Jenck's Eleanor Roosevelt, Princetown Arts Mag, 96; Jonathan Shahn, Penelope Jencks' Eleanor Roosevelt, Scultpure Rev, 97; Beach Series II, Disrobing Woman, Xilografia in SMENS, Torino, Italy, 2001; Gianfranco Schialvino (auth), Ritratti d'artista: Penelope Jencks, UTZ, 2001; Ann Cook (auth), Penelpe Jencks, Banne, Provincetown, Mass, 2006; Ellen Lebow (auth), Penelope Jencks, Cape Cod Voice, Orleans, Mass, 2006; Cate McQuaid, Sculptures that stand up to scrutiny, Jencks examines human vulnerability in her large terra cotta and plaster works, Boston Globe, 2006. *Mem:* Nat Acad of Design; Royal British Soc Sculptors; Nat Sculpture Soc. *Dealer:* Berta Walker Gallery Provincetown MA; Big Town Gallery Rochester VT. *Mailing Add:* c/o Nat Acad Design 1083 Fifth Ave New York NY 10128

JENDRZEJEWSKI, ANDREW JOHN
SCULPTOR, ADMINISTRATOR
b Fremont, Mich, July 1, 1946. *Study:* Tyler Sch Art, Rome & Philadelphia, BFA, 68; Wash Univ, St Louis, MFA, 73. *Exhib:* Show Case Show, Water Tower, Louisville, Ky, 85; Omnibus '88 Invitational, Herron Gallery, Indianapolis, Ind, 88; 40th Ann Four State Ilmoian, Quincy Art Ctr, Ill, 90; Midwest Sculpture, South Bend Regional Mus Art, Ind, 90; Indian Sculpture Invitational, Munster Art Ctr, Ind, 94. *Pos:* Mus technician, Univ Mich Mus Art, 73-75. *Teaching:* Prof art & sculpture & art dept chmn, Vincennes Univ Jr Col, 77-. *Bibliog:* Steve Mannheimer (auth), The Vincennes group, Indianapolis Star, 10/31/82; Marion Garmel (auth), Strong entries in Omnibus Exhib, Indianapolis News, 7/14/84; Hollis Sigler (auth), Jurer's Statement, 20th Ind Artists Catalog, 85. *Mem:* Nat Asn Sch Art & Design; Mid Am Coll Art Asn. *Media:* Miscellaneous. *Mailing Add:* 404 N Fifth St Vincennes IN 47591-2106

JENKENS, A LAWRENCE
ADMINISTRATOR
Study: Harvard Col, AB; NY Univ, Inst Fine Arts, MA, PhD. *Pos:* Founding dir, UNO-St Claude Gallery, New Orleans; frequent participant at national and international conferences having delivered papers at the Col Art Asn, 1993, session chair, 1998, the Renaissance Soc of America, 1997, 2000, 2003, and the Soc of Architectural Historians, 2001. *Teaching:* Prof, chair Dept Fine Arts, Univ New Orleans, formerly; head, prof art history, Univ of North Carolina, Greensboro, 2010-.

Awards: HEH Fellowship of Col Teachers, 1997-98; Residential Fellowship, Harvard Univ Ctr for Italian Renaissance Studies, Florence, Italy, 2001-02. *Publ:* Co-editor of a volume of papers in honor of Prof Richard Krautheimer's 100th Birthday, 1997; (auth) Constructing a Dynasty: The Buildings of Pius II and his Family in Siena, 1459-1510, 2003. *Mailing Add:* University of North Carolina Greensboro Art Department 527 Highland Ave 138 Gatewood Studio Arts Building Greensboro NC 27412

JENKENS, GARLAN F
CURATOR, PAINTER
b Stamford, Tex, Aug 26, 1949. *Study:* N Tex State Univ, Denton, BFA, 74, MFA, 76; Univ Ore, Eugene, PhD, 82. *Work:* N Tex State Univ Collection, Denton; Koger Corp, Exec Ctr, Little Rock, Ark; Corvallis Art Ctr Collection, Ore; Mountain View Community Col, Dallas, Tex; Worthen Banking Corp, Pine Bluff, Ark. *Exhib:* Amarillo Competition, Amarillo Art Ctr, Tex, 75; Watermark, Issac Hathaway Fine Art Ctr, Pine Bluff, Ark, 88; Stockton Nat IV, Haggin Mus Art, Calif, 88; Ark Art 91, Henderson State Univ, Arkadelphia, 91; The Arkansas Collection, Univ Ark, Little Rock, 91; The Inaugural Exhib: Selected Ark Artists, Collector Gallery, Washington, DC, 92; Dramas Recent Works by David Bailin, Arts & Sci Ctr, SE Ark, Pine Bluff, 93 & Artists of the Am West, 93; David Bailin, Works on Paper, Hathaway Howard Arts Ctr, Univ Ark, Pine Bluff, 94, Signs, Sentences and Symbols, 95, Environmental Surfaces; Speaking Through Textures, 95 & Surreal Journeys, 95; New Works, Baum Gallery Fine Art, Univ Cent Ark, Conway, 96, Impressions of Arkansas, 96, An Anthology, 96; and others. *Collection Arranged:* Mark Chagall: Illustrations for the Old Testament (auth, catalog), 88; Frederick Remmington: Illustrator of the Old West (auth, catalog), 89; Drawing: A Survey of the 20th Century (auth, catalog), 90; A Treasury of Am Prints (auth, catalog), 91; Dali: The Divine Comedy (50 woodcuts; auth, catalog), 92; Recent Paintings: Frits van Eeden, Artist-in-Residence (auth, catalog), Brevard Mus Art, Melbourne, Fla, 93; John M Howard Retrospective: 1947-1977, 94. *Pos:* Dir & chief cur, Baum Gallery, Univ Cent Ark, currently. *Teaching:* Instr, Art Dept, Univ Cent Ark, Comway, currently; instr, Univ N Tex, Denton. *Awards:* Purchase Award, Tex A&I Invitational, 76; Purchase Award, 2nd Ann Juried Exhib, 81; Purchase Award, 5th Nat Biennial, 87. *Mem:* Am Asn Mus; Southeastern Mus Asn; Coll Art Asn; Nat Art Educ Asn. *Media:* All

JENKINS, MARY ANNE KEEL
PAINTER
b Pitt Co, NC, Nov 20, 1929. *Study:* Ferree Sch Art, Raleigh, NC; E Carolina Univ, Greenville; NC State Univ Sch Design, Raleigh; San Carlos Art Sch, Mexico City. *Work:* Weatherspoon Art Mus; NC State Univ Gallery Design; Greenville Art Mus; Wilson Collection, Univ NC, Chapel Hill; NC Mus Hist, Raleigh; HC Taylor Art Gallery, A&T State Univ, Greensboro, NC; NC Mus Art, Raleigh; Minn Mus Art, Minneapolis. *Comn:* Interior mural, Radio Station WPTF, Raleigh, 71; Philip Morris, 82; mural, First Union Nat Bank, Raleigh, 91, Chamber Commerce, Raleigh, 91. *Exhib:* NC Mus Art, Raleigh; Danville Art Mus, Va, 82; Raleigh Munic Bldg Exhib, 88 & 93; Duke Univ Law Sch, 98; 50-yr retrospective, Greenville Art Mus, 99-2000; Women Artists, Greenville Mus Art, 04; Four Decades, Gallery C, Raleigh, NC, 05; The Best in NC, Gallery C, Raleigh, 2004-2012. *Awards:* Drawings USA Purchase Award, Minn Mus Art, St Paul, 71; Purchase Award & Hon Mention, Piedmont Exhib, Mint Mus, Charlotte, NC, 77; Raleigh Art Achievement Award, 87; Raleigh Medal of Art, 94; 12th Nat Jury Show, Paul Lindsay Sample Mem Award, Chautauqua Exhib of Am Art, 1969. *Bibliog:* Rubel Romero (auth), Ten Best (All That Was Great in 88) Our Critic's Choices - Deep Perspective, Spectator Mag, 1/89; Blue Greenberg (auth), Jenkins Exhibit: A Whole & It's Parts, The Durham Morning Herald, 4/29/90; Dick Bell (auth), A lifetime devoted to art, Spectator, 5/26/94; Mary Anne Keel Jenkins, A retrospective, Greenville Mus Art, 2000. *Mem:* NC Mus Art (life). *Media:* All Painting Media. *Mailing Add:* 740 Smallwood Dr Apt 42 Raleigh NC 27605-1363

JENKINS, ULYSSES SAMUEL, JR
VIDEO ARTIST, MURALIST
b Los Angeles, Calif, Sept 19, 1946. *Study:* Southern Univ, BA, 69; Otis Art Inst, MFA, 79. *Work:* Calif Inst Arts, Santa Clarita; Long Beach Mus Art; Am Mus Moving Image, Astoria, NY; Electronic Arts Intermix, NY. *Comn:* Mural hist of motor vehicles, Calif Dept Motor Vehicles, Los Angeles, 76; Cake Walk (vid doc), Houston Conwill, NY, 83; Being Witness: The Haids Proj (doc), Headlands Ctr Arts, Sausalito, Calif, 91. *Exhib:* James D Phelan Awards, San Francisco Mus Art, 93; Int Festival Electronic Arts, San Paulo & Rio de Janerio, Brazil, 94; When Worlds Collide, Mus Mod Art, NY, 94; New Media Research/The Art & Virtual Environments Proj, Baniff Ctr for Art, Alta, Can, 94; Governor's Conf on Art & Technology VI, Calif Arts Coun, Santa Claria, 95; and others internationally. *Pos:* Artistic dir, Othervisions Studio, 83-. *Teaching:* Vis lectr video art, Univ Calif, San Diego, 79-81, Otis Parsons Art Inst, Los Angeles, 85; asst prof, Univ Calif Irvine, 93-. *Awards:* NEA Grant, 80, 82 & 95; Calif Arts Coun Fel, 86-97; Black Filmmakers Hall of Fame, 90 & 92. *Bibliog:* Judith Wilson (auth), Black Artist 87-88, Garland Press, 89; Lorraine O'Gady (auth), Interview of Maren Hassinger, Hatch Billops Collections Inc, 93. *Mem:* Bay Area Video Coalition, San Francisco (bd mem, 90-96). *Media:* Video & Performance Art, Telecommunications Art. *Publ:* Auth, Video visions, electronic dreams, Oakland Mus & Mus Calif, 90; Doggerel Period: California Arts Council Multi-cultural Grant, pvt publ, 91; What are you going to do after you drink up the ocean?, Video Networks, 92; Scratching the belly of the beast, Film Forum Catalog, 94; Headlands virtual ritual, Headlands J, 94. *Dealer:* The Electronic Arts Intermix 536 Broadway 9th floor New York NY 10012

JENNERJAHN, W P
EDUCATOR, PAINTER
b Milwaukee, Wis, June 15, 1922. *Study:* Univ Wis, Milwaukee, BS, 46; Univ Wis, Madison, MS, 47; Black Mt Coll, with Josef Albers, 48-50; Acad Grande Chaumiere, Paris, 50; Acad Julian, Paris, 50-51; also with Gerard Wagner, Dornach, Switz, 78 & 81. *Work:* Josef Albers Found; Black Mt Coll Art Mus; AT&T; AVIS; Asheville Art Mus, NC; Johnson Collection, SC; Sedona Ariz Public Lib . *Comn:* Stained glass panel, Long Island Jewish Hosp, New York; stained glass mural, comn by Dr Fredrick Lane, Great Neck, NY; stained glass mural (with John Urbain), JFK Airport Int Hotel; murals for eight ships (with Elizabeth Jennerjahn), Mil Sea Transport Serv; painting, Avis World Hq, Garden City, NY. *Exhib:* Exhib Momentum, Chicago; Milwaukee Ann, Univ Wis; Birmingham Ann, Ala; Dulin Ann, Tenn; Black Mt Coll Invitational, Johnson City, Tenn. *Teaching:* Art instr, Black Mt Coll, NC, 49-50, Cooper Union, 52-54, Hunter Coll, 53 & Elderhostel Prog, N Ariz Univ, Sedona; prof art, Adelphi Univ, 54-87; retired. *Awards:* Tiffany Found Grant, 52; Adelphi Univ Humanities Grants, 62, 68 & 84. *Mem:* Sedona Arts Ctr; Sedona Visual Artists Coalition. *Media:* Oil, Watercolor, Acrylic. *Interests:* Playing woodwinds, writing music. *Publ:* Illusr, Respect for Life, 74; contribr (with Geo K Russell), Laboratory Investigations in Human Physiology, MacMillan, 78; contribr, The Structurist, Univ Saskatewan, Saskatoon, Sask. *Dealer:* Art in Living Spaces Cornville Ariz; Yvette Torres Fine Art PO Box 163 South Bristol ME 04568. *Mailing Add:* 106 Claredon Dr Valley Stream NY 11580

JENNINGS, JAN NOREUS
WRITER
b Chicago, Ill, Apr 4, 1943. *Study:* Northwestern Univ, Evanston, BSJ; Univ Mo-Columbia, grad studies journalism & art. *Pos:* Art writer, San Diego Tribune, Calif, 71-88; asst dir mus, Mingei Int Mus World Folk Art, San Diego, 90-91; writer, publicist art & humanities, Univ Calif, 95-2009; art dir, writer, The Frederic Whitaker and Eileen Monaghan Whitaker Found, San Diego, Calif, 2001-. *Mem:* San Diego Mus Art; San Diego Mus Contemp Art; Mingei Int Mus World Folk Art; Calif Center for the Arts, Escondido; charter mem, Nat Women's Hist Mus. *Res:* Artists Frederic Whitaker and Eileen Monaghan Whitaker. *Collection:* Various collections from representational works to abstract, op, pop & animation. *Publ:* Free-lance writer with contributing features to Southwest Art Mag, Am Artist, Western Art Digest, Art of California, Ranch & Coast; Contrasts That Complement: Eileen Monaghan Whitaker - Frederic Whitaker (auth), Marguand Books Inc, Seattle, 04. *Mailing Add:* 1750 Galveston St San Diego CA 92110

JENRETTE, PAMELA ANNE
PAINTER, COSTUME DESIGNER
b Ft Bragg, NC, Aug 24, 1947. *Study:* Univ Tex, BFA, 69. *Exhib:* Clean, Well-lighted Place (two-artist show), Austin, Tex, 71; Whitney Biennial, NY, 75; Cologne Art Festival, Ger, 75; one-artist show, Artists Space, New York, NY, 75. *Pos:* Studio asst, Lawrence Poons, New York, 71-75. *Awards:* Competition Award, Conde Nast, 69. *Bibliog:* Martha Utterback (auth), Texas, Artforum, 1/71. *Media:* Acrylic, Watercolor

JENSEN, CLAY EASTON
SCULPTOR, EDUCATOR
b Salt Lake City, Utah, Mar 14, 1952. *Study:* Univ Utah, Salt Lake City, BFA, 75; Univ Calif, Berkeley, MA, 78, MFA, 79. *Work:* Oakland Mus, Calif; Crocker Art Mus, Sacramento, Calif; San Jose Mus Art; Reynolds Gallery, Westmont Coll; Southern Calif Edison, Los Angeles. *Comn:* Sculpture, Fed Reserve Bank, San Francisco, Calif, 83; sculpture, Syntex Corp, Palo Alto, Calif, 84; sculpture, AT&T, Pleasanton, Calif, 84; sculpture, William Wilson & Assocs, San Mateo, Calif, 86; sculpture, Dealy, Renton & Assocs, Oakland, Calif, 86. *Exhib:* Solo exhibs, San Francisco Mus Mod Art (with catalog), Calif, 83, Fuller Cross Gallery, San Francisco, 85 & 88, Christopher Grimes Gallery, Santa Monica, Calif, 90, Erickson & Elins Gallery, San Francisco, 92; Utah Mus Fine Arts, Salt Lake City, 75; New Affirmations, Oakland Mus, Calif, 80; MFA Exhib, Univ Art Mus, Univ Calif, Berkeley. *Pos:* affiliated assoc prof, sculpture, Calif Coll Arts. *Teaching:* Assoc instr, Univ Utah, Salt Lake City, 75-76; vis fac, Calif Col Arts & Craft, 80-82, asst prof, 87-; guest lectr sculpture, Univ Calif, Berkeley, 84-85; asst prof, San Jose State Univ, 84-85 & 89-90. *Awards:* Fel, Nat Endowment Asn, 78; Soc Encouragement Contemp Art Award, San Francisco Mus Mod Art, 83. *Bibliog:* Alfred Jan (auth), article, in: Images and Issues, 1/84; Suzaan Boettger (auth), rev, in: Art Forum, 4/84; Robert McDonald (auth), Rural Urban Dichotomies, Vol XIIII, No 39, Art Week, 11/19/83; James Scarborough (auth), Galactic Perspective Clay Jensen at Christopher Grimes Gallery, Vol 21, No 35, Artweek, 10/90. *Media:* Painted Steel, Cast Bronze. *Dealer:* Morgan Gallery Kansas City MO. *Mailing Add:* 951 62nd St Emeryville CA 94608

JENSEN, DEAN N
DEALER, CRITIC
Study: Univ Wis, BA; Roosevelt Univ, Chicago; Univ Chicago. *Collection Arranged:* Center Ring: The Artist (auth, catalog), Milwaukee Art Mus, Columbus Mus Art, NY State Mus, Albany & Corcoran Gallery Art, 81; Material Obsessions: Folk and Outside, Art from Wisconsin Collections (auth, catalog), Milwaukee Inst Art & Design, 89. *Pos:* Art ed & critic, Milwaukee Sentinel, Wis, 67-87; owner, Dean Jensen Gallery, Milwaukee, 87-. *Teaching:* Milwaukee Inst Art & Design, 91-. *Awards:* Res & Study Fel, Univ Mich, 85-86. *Res:* Contemporary art; Circus as a theme in art. *Publ:* Auth, The Biggest, The Smallest, The Longest, The Shortest, Wis House, 75; Reunion in Hell: The Drawings of Paul Caster, Perimeter Press, 82; contribr, Art News, Arts, Midwest-Art & others. *Mailing Add:* c/o Dan Jenson Gallery 759 N Water St Milwaukee WI 53202

JENSEN, ELISA
PAINTER
Study: Smith Coll; NY Studio Sch. *Exhib:* Morso Kunstforening, Denmark; Bond Market Asn, NY; Wash Art Asn, Conn; Danish Consulate, New York; Bickett Gallery, Raleigh; Gallery 100, Sarasota Spings; Icehouse Gallery, Greenport, NY; 6 Danish Artists in New York, Trygvie Lie Gallery, New York; Visions of the Figure, Repetti Gallery, Long Island City, 2008; Am Acad Arts and Letts Invitational, New York, 2009. *Teaching:* Painter, teacher, NY Studio Sch, 1993-. *Awards:* John Koch Award, Am Acad Arts & Letts, 2009; Nat Acad Prize for Painting, Nat Acad Invitational Exhib Contemp Art Awards, 2010 . *Media:* Oil. *Mailing Add:* NY Studio Sch 8 W 8th St New York NY 10011

JENSEN, LEO
SCULPTOR, PAINTER
b Montevideo, Minn, July 10, 1926. *Study:* Walker Art Ctr, scholar, 46-48. *Work:* US Info Agency, Washington, DC; Brown Univ; Walker Art Ctr, Minneapolis, Minn; Mattatuck Mus, Waterbury, Conn; Achenbach Coll, San Francisco; bronze & concrete Spool-Frog sculpture, Windham, Conn, 2000; Mark Twain Libr, Redding, Conn; Acad Educ Develop, Washington, DC; bronze fountain, Vinnie's Restaurant, Old Saybrooke, Conn, 2000. *Comn:* Construction, Macmillan Publ co, New York, 68; polychrome relief, Med World News, New York, 70; Wood Model for Spool-Frog Bridge sculpture, Windham, Conn, 95; four 3000 lb bronze frogs for bridge, Willimantic, Conn, 2001. *Exhib:* solo exhibs, Amel Gallery, New York, 64-65, Sakovitz Gallery, Houston, 64, New Britain Mus Am Art, Far Gallery, NY, 73, Arras Gallery, New York, 76, A Book Gallery, San Francisco, 78, Frank Fedele Gallery, New York, 81, Vorpal Gallery, New York, 87, Mattatuck Mus, Waterbury, Conn, 90 & Childers Gallery, Ft Lauderdale, Fla, 91, Amarillo Mus Art, Tex, 2010-2011; Group exhibs, Butler Inst Am Art, Ohio, 53 & Mattatuck Mus, Conn, 90; Mus Mod Art, 64-65 & Am Mus Nat Hist, 82, New York; Milwaukee Art Ctr, 65; Chicago Hist Soc, 81; Baseball Hall Fame, 83; Castle Gallery Coll, New Rochelle, NY, 87; Hollycroft Int, 96; and other mus in 64 countries. *Pos:* Founder, Wildcat Fine Art Trust, New Haven, Conn, 88. *Awards:* US Fed Hwy Comn Award, 2003; Special award, AIA. *Bibliog:* M B Scott (auth), The Artist & the Sportsman, Renaissance, 68; D Z Meiloch (auth), Contemporary Art With Wood, Crown, 68; H N Abrams Publ, Champions of Am Sport, Smithsonian Inst, 81; Ronald Lee Fleming (auth), The Art of Placemaking, Merrel, London & New York; Lucy R Lippard (auth), Pop Art, Thames & Hudson, 85. *Media:* Bronze, Wood, Acrylic, Watercolor, Tin Cans. *Dealer:* Cooley Gallery 25 Lyme St Old Lyme Conn; Pop Int Soho NY. *Mailing Add:* PO Box 264 Ivoryton CT 06442

JENSEN, ROBERT
EDUCATOR, ADMINISTRATOR
Study: Univ of Berkeley, PhD. *Pos:* Principal reader on a numner of M.A. thesis paper projects. *Teaching:* With Univ Kentucky, 1994-, assoc prof art history, dir Sch of Art & Visual Studies, currently. *Publ:* (auth) Marketing Modernism in Fin-de-siecle, 1994. *Mailing Add:* School of Art & Visual Studies Room 203A Fine Arts Building University of Kentucky Lexington KY 40506-0022

JERDON, WILLIAM HARLAN
PAINTER, INSTRUCTOR
b Hamilton, Ohio, May 30, 1944. *Study:* Bowling Green State Univ, 66, MA, 72, MFA, 73. *Work:* Western Reserve Hist Soc, Cleveland, Ohio. *Comn:* mural, Standard Oil Ohio, Cleveland, Ohio, 84; mural, Good Year Aerospace, Akron, Ohio, 84; mural, Chase Brass & Copper Co, Inc, Cleveland, Ohio, 85; mural, Deloitte, Haskins, Sells Accounting, Cleveland, Ohio, 85. *Exhib:* 55th Ann Exhib, Toledo Mus Art, Toledo, Ohio, 73; 36th Ohio Artist and Craftsmen show, The Massillon Mus, Massillon, Ohio, 74; invitational painting exhib, Southern Alleghenies Mus Art, Loretto, Pa, 78; Butler Inst Am Art, Youngstown, Ohio; A Celebration of the Nude, Digital Three Gallery, Sarasota, Fla; Alla Prima Gallery, Modern Masters, St Petersberg, Fla; Grass Roots Gallery, Englewood, Fla; Fla Southern Col, Lakeland, Fla; Int Alumni Exhib, Bowling Green State Univ, Ohio; Venice Art Ctr, Venice, Fla; Sarasota Art Ctr, Sarasota, Fla. *Pos:* educ testing adv, Educ Testing Serv, Princeton, NJ, 86-87; continuing researcher, Nat Arts Educ Research Ctr, NY Univ, NY, 87-88; test writer, Educ Testing Serv, Princeton, NJ, 88-89. *Teaching:* teacher, Art & Photog, Cleveland Heights High Sch, Cleveland Heights, Ohio, 66-97; instr, Drawing, Cleveland Inst Art, Cleveland, Ohio, 78-80; instr, Drawing & Painting, Ringling Coll Art and Design, Sarasota, Fla, 2001-2003; master class (painting & drawing), 2003-. *Awards:* US Presidential Distinguished Teacher Award, White House Comn on Presidential Scholars, 85; Fel for Teachers of the Arts, John F Kennedy Ctr for the Performing Arts, Washington DC, 86; Honors Fel, RI Sch Design, Providence, RI, 87. *Bibliog:* Timothy Dvin (auth), Heights teacher sees honors, The Plain Dealer, 6/10/86; Helen Cullinan (auth), Fitting tribute to gallery head, Cleveland Plain Dealer, 7/31/91; Susan Chapman (auth), Englewood's Bill Jerdon, Sarasota Herald Tribune, 6/3/2004. *Mem:* Sarasota Portrait Artists Asn. *Media:* Oil, Charcoal, Graphite. *Res:* Perception and psychology in Representational art. *Specialty:* Contemporary art. *Interests:* 19th century European figurative art, American figurative art. *Publ:* auth, A Course of Study for Art History, Cleveland Heights, Univ Heights BOE, 74; auth, A Course of Study for Photography, Cleveland Heights, Univ Heights BOE, 75; auth, A Course of Study for Advanced Photography, Cleveland Heights, Univ Heights BOE, 75; auth, A Course of Study for Studio Problems, Cleveland Heights, Univ Heights BOE, 76; auth, A Course of Study for Advanced Studio Problems, Cleveland Heights, Univ Heights BOE, 76. *Dealer:* Dabbert Gallery 76 S Palm Ave Sarasota FL 84236. *Mailing Add:* 5854 Welcome Rd Bradenton FL 34207

JERGENS, ROBERT JOSEPH
PAINTER, EDUCATOR
b Cleveland, Ohio, Mar 18, 1938. *Study:* Cleveland Inst Art; Skowhegan Sch Painting & Sculpture; Yale Univ, BFA & MFA; Am Acad in Rome. *Work:* Cleveland Mus Art; NAm Col, Rome, Italy; Skowhegan Sch Painting & Sculpture; Brooklyn Art Mus; and others. *Comn:* Cleveland Pub Libr, 60 & 89. *Exhib:* Cleveland Mus Art, 57-64; Exhib by US Info Agency; Mus Mod Art, NY; Corcoran Gallery Art, Washington, DC; Mostra Univ, Rome; and others. *Teaching:* Instr design, Cooper Union, formerly; instr drawing, Sch Art & Archit, Yale Univ, formerly; instr design, Cleveland Inst Art, currently. *Awards:* Prix de Rome, 60 & 61; Mary C Page Grant, 61; Prize, Cleveland Mus Art, 61; and others. *Mailing Add:* 5356 Regency Dr Cleveland OH 44129-5961

JERINS, EDGAR
PAINTER
b Lincoln, Neb, June 12, 1958. *Study:* Pa Acad Fine Arts (4 yr cert), 76-80. *Work:* Ark Art Ctr, Little Rock; Mus of Nebr Art, Kearney, Nebr; Moravian Coll, Bethlehem, Pa. *Exhib:* My Friend, My Brothers, Payne Gallery, Moravian Col, PA, 2004; solo exhib, Tatistchett Gallery, NY; Traditions and Departures, Mentors and Protoges, Vose Gallery, Boston, MA; collectors exhib, Ark Art Ctr, Ark, 2004; Re-Presenting Representation VI, Arnot Art Mus, Elmira, NY; Sacred & Profare, Portsmouth Mus Fine Art, NH, 2010; On the Edge, ACA Galleries, New York, 2008. *Pos:* Adj fac, New York Acad Art. *Awards:* Elizabeth Greenshilds Found Grant, 80; The Pollock-Krasner Found Grant, 2004; The Elizabeth Found for the Arts Grant, 2003; George Sugarman Found Grant, 2002, 2006; ED Found Grant, 2001; Fel in printmaking/drawing/artists books, New York Found Arts, 2005. *Bibliog:* Helen A Harrison (auth), 76 Artworks review 86 & 87, Islip Mus Show, 89, NY Times. *Mem:* Fel, Pa Acad Fine Arts. *Media:* Oil, Pastel, Drawing, Charcoal. *Dealer:* ACA Galleries 529 W 20th St NYC 10011. *Mailing Add:* 326 E 84th St No 4C New York NY 10028

JERRY, MICHAEL JOHN
EDUCATOR, CRAFTSMAN
b Grand Rapids, Mich, Aug 18, 1937. *Study:* Sch Am Craftsman, Rochester Inst Technol, AAS & BFA, 60, MFA, 63; Cranbrook Acad Art, 60-62. *Work:* Wustum Mus Fine Art, Racine, Wis; Mus Contemp Crafts, NY; Metrop Mus of Art, NY; Brooklyn Mus Art, NY. *Exhib:* Int Trade Fair Jewelry Exhib, Munich, Ger, 71; The 6th Goldsmiths Expos, Kersnikova, Yugoslavia, 72; Goldsmiths, Renwick Gallery, Washington, DC, 74; Contemp Metals US, Downey Mus Art, Calif, 85; Am Pewter Guild Design Competition, James Michener Mus, Pa, 94. *Teaching:* Assoc prof metalsmithing, Wis State Univ, Menomonie, 63-70; prof metalsmithing, Syracuse Univ, 70-. *Mem:* Am Crafts Coun; Soc NAm Goldsmiths. *Media:* Metal. *Publ:* Contribr, American jewelry, Design Quart, 59; Philip Morton, Contemporary Jewelry, Holt, 69; Objects: USA, Viking, 70; The Craftsman in America, Nat Geog Soc, 75; Metalsmith, Vol 8, fall 88 & Vol 1, Winter 92. *Mailing Add:* Syracuse Univ Dept Art Syracuse NY 13244-1010

JERVISS, JOY
PRINTMAKER
b Palmerton, Pa, Feb 14, 1941. *Study:* Apprentice to Andre Girard; Empire State Col, SUNY, BS. *Work:* Colgate Univ Libr & Syracuse Univ Art Collection, NY; Bibliot Nat, Paris; Miami Mus Mod Art, Fla; Ariz State Univ, Tempe; Princeton Univ Art Mus, NJ; Lehigh Univ Art Galleries, Pa; Art Inst Zanesville, Ohio. *Pos:* Art exhib dir, N K Winston Corp, New York, 66-73; pres, United Press & Pallet, Northport, NY, 68-; founder, Northport Art League, 71-; CEO, Joy J. Industries, Inc, 68-. *Teaching:* Asst instr printmaking, North Shore Community Arts Ctr, Great Neck, NY, 66-68; instr printmaking, Union Free Sch Dist 4, Northport, NY, 70-72; instr, BOCES III, 82-86. *Media:* Etching. *Mailing Add:* 84 Ocean Ave Northport NY 11768

JESSEN, SHIRLEY AGNES
PAINTER
b Brooklyn, NY, Jan 23, 1921. *Study:* New York Sch Applied Design Women, scholar, cert, 39; Fashion Art Inst, Rockefeller Ctr, 40; also with Lou Eisele, Frederick Lehman, Paul Wood & Norman Nodell, 60-99; Huntington Town Art League, 1992-2003; Long Island Coun Arts, 91-99. *Work:* Sotheby Art Auctions; Channels 13: Art & Auctions, 79-87; Channel 21 Art Auctions, 79-87. *Exhib:* Solo exhibs, Shelter Rock Libr, Roslyn, NY, 96, Garden City Libr, 96, Art League Long Island, 98, 99 & 04, Huntington Art Coun, 99, Unitarian Universalist Church, Garden City, 2000, Farmingdale Libr, 2000, Township Oyster Bay, 2000-03, Adelphi Univ, 2005 & others; Winthrop Univ Hosp, 50-2003; St Pauls Cult Arts Exhib, Garden City, 96; Directors Invitational, Chelsea Art Ctr Cult Arts, Muttontown, 96-2003; Gold Coast Art Show, AHRC, Brookville, 96; Planting Fields Art Show, Coe Estates Hist Park, 96; Island Landmark Exhib, Mill Mus, 97; and others. *Pos:* Illusr, Wantagh Parent Teachers Asn, 50-65; illusr, United Cerebral Palsy, 59-75; illusr, Nassau Co Med Soc Auxiliary, 59-95; illusr, Georgia O'Keeffe, Community Club, 88 & 93-. *Teaching:* Expo Films 70-71; On the Casino, Community Club of Hempstead and Garden City, 2003. *Awards:* Cash Award, Suburban Art League, 81; Finalist, Lincoln Ctr, 81 & 82; Am Artists Mag; Award of Excellence in Oil, Town of Oyster Bay, 2004. *Bibliog:* David L Shirey (auth), Critical Rev, NY Times, 3/9/80; Book review, NY Art, 87-91; Robert Clarke (auth), Critical Rev, Garden City Life, 4/25/96. *Mem:* Freeport Arts Coun; Long Island Arts Coun Freeport; Knickerbocker Artists, NY; Art League Long Island; Allied Artists Am; Nassau Co Med Soc Alliance (hon life mem, bd dir & pres); Cerebral Palsey (pres). *Media:* Oils, Acrylics; Watercolor, pen and ink. *Interests:* Flying airplanes & dancing. *Publ:* Newsday, New York Times, Garden City Life, Garden City News, 96-2007

JESSUP, ROBERT
PAINTER
b Moscow, Idaho, July 18, 1952. *Study:* Univ Wash, Seattle, BA (art hist), BFA (painting), 75; Univ Iowa, Iowa City, MA (painting), 77, MFA (painting), 78. *Work:* Metrop Mus Art, NY; High Mus Art, Atlanta, Ga; Huntington Art Gallery, Univ Tex, Austin; Roswell Mus & Art Ctr, NMex. *Comn:* Relief painting, comn by Donald B Anderson, Roswell, NMex, 81; painting, comn by Robert Dornbush, Atlanta, Ga, 85. *Exhib:* Solo exhibs, Roswell Mus, NMex, 81, Nicola Jacobs Gallery, London, Eng, 84, Jan Turner Gallery, Los Angeles, 86, Zola-Lieberman Gallery, Chicago, 86 & Ruth Siegel, Ltd, NY, 86, 87, 88, 89, Va Mus Fine Arts, 89, Zolla Lieberman Gallery, Chicago, 90, Fay Gold Gallery, Atlanta, 91, 93, 95, 98, 2001, 2003, 2005, 2007, Conduit Gallery, Dallas, 93, 94, 95, 97, 2000, 2002, 2005, 2007, Joseph Rickards Gallery, NY, 2000, Mus East Tex, 2000, McMurtrey Gallery, Houston, 2001, 2003, Amarillo Mus Art, 2003, Berman Gallery, Austin, 2003, Schomburg Gallery, Santa Monica, 2005; group exhibs, New Figurative Painting, Asheville Art Mus, NC, 85; Painting & Sculpture Today, Indianapolis Mus Art, Ind, 86; Landscape, Seascape, Cityscape, Contemp Arts Ctr, New Orleans, La, 86; Three NY Painters, Conduit Gallery, NY, 87, 92, Art Texas, 93, Dallas Fine Art Exposition, 94, Summer Exhib, 94, Works on Paper, 98, Santa Fe Art Fair, 99, Twentieth Anniversary Exhib, 2004; Unnatural Landscape, Fay Gold Gallery, Atlanta, 88, Int Contemp Art Exhib, 93, Summer Exhib, 96, 99, San Francisco Int Art Fair, 2001, Palm Beach Int Art Fair, 2001, 2002, Chicago Art Fair, 2002, Gallery Artists, 2004; Review/Preview, Ruth Siegel Gallery, NY, 87; Classical Myth and Imagery in Contemp Art, The Queens

Mus, NY, 88; New Work - New York, Helander Gallery, Palm Beach, 89; Collector's Choice, Ctr for Arts, Vero Beach, Fla, 89; Landscape/Mindscape, Carlo Lamagna Gallery, NY, 90; Summer Show, Little John-Sternau, NY, 92; Looking West/Glancing East: New Texas Art, Amarillo Mus Art, 94; Envisioned and Re-envisioned, Robischon Gallery, Denver, 95, Summer Show, 96; Moddy Gardens Aquarium Celebration, Galveston Art Ctr, 99; Six Ways of Seeing, Univ Art Gallery, Midwestern State Univ, Tex, 99; Forbidden, McMurtrey Gallery, Houston, 2000. *Teaching:* Artist-in-residence, Roswell Mus and Art Ctr, NMex, 80-81; lectr & vis artist painting, Ohio State Univ, Columbus, Ohio, 81-82; asst prof painting, Ga State Univ, Atlanta, 82-83 & Cornell Univ, Ithaca, NY, 83-86; vis adj prof, Univ Hartford, Conn, 89-90, asst prof, 90-91; asst prof, Univ North Tex, Denton, 91-96, assoc prof, 97-. *Bibliog:* John Russell (auth), Aspects of the figure, New York Times, 7/2/82; Theodore F Wolff (auth), How artists improve, Christian Sci Monitor, 7/2/86. *Media:* Oil on Canvas & Linen; Charcoal on Paper. *Dealer:* Ruth Siegel Ltd 24 W 57th St New York NY 10019

JESSUP, WESLEY
MUSEUM DIRECTOR
Study: Calif State Univ in Fullerton, BA; City Univ New York, MA (Art History, Museum Studies). *Pos:* Mgr Budgeting & Planning for Int Progs, Solomon R Guggenheim Mus, New York, 1994-1998; asst dir, Spencer Mus Art, Univ Kans, 1998-2000; exec dir, Pasadena Mus Calif Art, 2000-2007; exec dir, Boise Art Mus, 2007-. *Mailing Add:* Boise Art Museum 670 Julia Davis Drive Boise ID 83702

JEVBRATT, LISA
DIGITAL ARTIST, EDUCATOR
b 1967. *Study:* Cadre Inst, San Jose State Univ, MFA. *Exhib:* Walker Art Ctr, Minneapolis; Banff Ctr for the Arts, Can; New Mus, New York; Swedish Nat Pub Art Coun, Stockholm; Biennial, Whitney Mus Am Art, New York. *Pos:* Bd mem, New Langton Arts Gallery, San Francisco. *Teaching:* Assoc prof, Art Dept & Media Art Technol Prog, Univ Calif, Santa Barbara. *Awards:* Grant for Emerging Fields, Creative Capital Found, 2009. *Bibliog:* Christiane Paul (auth), Digital Art, Thames & Hudson, 2003; Rachel Greene (auth), Internet Art, Thames & Hudson, 2004. *Publ:* Contribr (ed, Tom Corby), Network Art-Practices and Positions, Routledge, 2006. *Mailing Add:* Media Arts and Technology Univ Calif 309 Phelps Hall 2228-B Art Studio Santa Barbara CA 93106-6065

JEWELL, JOYCE
PAINTER, PRINTMAKER
b Washington, DC, Oct 11, 1945. *Study:* Montgomery Col, Md, AA, 65; Am Univ, Washington, DC, BA, 67; George Washington Univ, MFA, 72; Tamarind Inst Lithography, NMex, 74. *Work:* Montgomery Co Contemp Print Collection, Md; Owensboro Federal Savings & Loan Asn, Ky. *Exhib:* 19th Area Exhib, Corcoran Gallery Art, Washington, DC, 74; Irene Leache Mem Art Exhib, Chrysler Mus, Va, 78, 80; Va Printmakers, 1979, Va Mus Fine Arts, 79; 17th Bradley Nat Print & Drawing Exhib, Lakeview Mus, 79; Mid-Am Nat Art Exhib, Owensboro Mus Fine Art, Ky, 80; 22nd Area Exhib: Works on Paper, Corcoran Gallery Art, 80; Collage & Assemblage: A Nat Invitational Traveling Exhib, Miss Mus Art, Jackson, Miss, 81-83; Maryland Biennial: Works on Paper, Baltimore Mus Art, 83-84. *Pos:* Graphic designer, John Hoskins & Assocs, Arlington, Va, 67-71. *Teaching:* Prof design, drawing, etching & lithography, Montgomery Col, Md, 71-. *Awards:* Printmaking Award, Montgomery Co Juried Art Show, 78; Mid-Am Volunteers Purchase Award, Owensboro Mus Fine Art, 80; Owensboro Federal Savings & Loan Purchase Award, Mid-Am Nat Art Exhib, 80. *Bibliog:* Article, Gargoyle Mag, No 17/18, 81; Collage & Assemblage, Miss Mus Art, 81. *Media:* Collage. *Mailing Add:* c/o Montgomery Col 7600 Takoma Ave Takoma Park MD 20912-4197

JEYNES, PAUL
SCULPTOR, PAINTER
b Millburn, NJ, 1927. *Study:* Yale Univ, BA, 49; with Frank Eliscu, 74. *Comn:* Tiger, US Filter Corp, NY, 76; Cougar & 2 Cubs, Rye Country Day Sch, NY, 90; Dog & Cat, Bide-A-Wee, NY, 99. *Exhib:* Allied Artists, NY, 84-93; St Hubert's Giralda, 88-90; Nat Acad Design, 90; Central Park Zoo, NY, 90; Marymount Manhattan Col, NY, 2008-2009. *Pos:* Dir, Art Founders Guild Am Inc, 79-88; Ed, The Artist's Foundry 79-99. *Awards:* First Prize for Wondrous Wildlife, Cincinnati Zoo, 83; Gold Medal, Allied Artists, 85; St Hubert's Giralda Award of Distinction, 89; and others. *Mem:* Soc Animal Artists Inc; Allied Artists Am Inc. *Media:* Acrylic, Cast Bronze. *Mailing Add:* 305 E 70th St New York NY 10021

JILG, MICHAEL FLORIAN
PAINTER, PRINTMAKER
b Albert, Kans, June 28, 1947. *Study:* Fort Hays State Univ, BA, 69 & MA, 70; Kent State Blossom Festival, with Jack Tworkov, Alex Katz & James Melchert, 70; Wichita State Univ, with John Fincher, MFA, 72. *Work:* Joslyn Art Mus, Omaha, Nebr; Wichita Art Mus, Kans Arts Commission; Purdue Univ Galleries; Alice and Hamilton Fish Libr, Garrison, NY. *Comn:* George Washington Mural Project, Ellis Bicentennial Comt, Kans, 76; St Ann (painting), St Ann Parish, Olmitz, Kans, 81; mural proj, Sherridan Coliseum. *Exhib:* Mid-Am V, Nelson Gallery Art, Kansas City, Mo, 74; Mainstreams 74, Herman Fine Art Ctr, Marietta, Ohio, 74; Selected Kansas Artists, Kans State Capital, Topeka, 77; Allied Artists Am, Nat Acad Galleries, NY, 77-78; 1st Kans Artists Competition, Judicial Bldg, Topeka, 81; Kans Watercolor Soc Five State Exhib, Wichita Art Mus; 11th Ann Paper in Particular Nat Exhib, Columbia Col, Md; The Intaglio Process: Print Consortium Traveling Exhib; Images Women Prints, Embassy of US, Bonn, Ger, 88; Artists: A Kansas Collection, 89. *Teaching:* Prof painting, Ft Hays State Univ, 81-. *Awards:* Junior League Omaha Purchase, 70; Purchase Award, Kans Arts Commission, 80; Cash Award, Kans Arts Commission, 81; Kans Govs Artist, 91; FHSU Disting Scholar, 2001. *Bibliog:* The Best Kansas Arts & Crafts, 88; Erotic Art by Living Artists, 89; A Kansas Collection, 89. *Mem:* Kansas City Artists' Coalition; High Plains Printmakers; Hays Arts Coun (mem bd dir, currently); Boston Printmakers; Kans Watercolor Soc; Gabinetto Disegni E Stampe Degli Uffizi, Florence, Italy (scholar mem). *Media:* Drawing, Acrylic; Intaglio. *Specialty:* Contemporary art. *Dealer:* Strecker-Nelson Gallery Manhattan KS. *Mailing Add:* Dept Art Ft Hays State Univ 600 Park St Hays KS 67601

JIMENEZ, IVELISSE
PAINTER, INSTALLATION SCULPTOR
Study: Univ Puerto Rico, BFA, 1993; NYU, New York, MFA, 1999. *Exhib:* Festival de la Juventud, Casa Las Americas, Havana, Cuba, 1996; solo exhibs, Instituto de Cultura Puertorriquena, San Juan, 1996, Sin Titulo Gallery, San Juan, 1999, Taller Boricua, New York, 2001, Box Gallery, Turin, Italy, 2004, Jacob Karpio Gallery, Miami, 2005; Kimball Hall, NYU, 1997; Int Group Show, Gallery 605, New York, 1998; 22nd Ann Small Works, 80 Washington Sq Gallery, NYU, 1999; U/Topistas, Mus Contemp Art, San Juan, 2000; More or Less Painting, Univ Conn Art Gallery, 2001; Art Chicago, Jacob Karpio Gallery, Miami, 2003; Island Nations, RI Sch Design Mus, 2004; none of the above, Museo de Arte De Puerto Rico, 2005; Diversidades Formales, Centro de Arte Caja de Burgos, Burgos, Spain, 2006. *Awards:* Joan Mitchell Found Grant, 2010

JIMERSON, ANNETTE PRINCESS
PAINTER, SCULPTOR
b Chgo, Ill, Oct 12, 1966. *Study:* studied with Jessie Lee Phillips Jimerson. *Work:* Weems Art Gallery, Albuquerque, NMex; San Diego City Coll Archives, San Diego, Calif; Contemporary Art Gallery, Jacksonville, Fla; Art Price Gallery, Paris, France. *Comn:* still life drawing, Doug Dailard, San Diego, Calif, 1989; portrait, Herbert Broadway, Little Rock, Ark, 1997, Arthur Broadway, North Little Rock, 1997; eve, Benjamin Phillips, Albuquerque, NMex, 2006; pretty red flower, Jessica Jimerson, San Jacinto, Calif, 2011. *Exhib:* Peppertree Art Gallery, Cedar Rapids, Ia, 1992; Meet the Artist, Berisford Art Gallery, Jacksonville, Fla, 1992; Eyes of a Tiger, The Wildlife Gallery, Orlando, Fla, 1993; Fine Art in America, NY, 2012; Art Price, Paris, France, 2012; Laguna Beach Fine Art Gallery, 2013. *Pos:* art dir, Adept Films, Los Angeles, Calif, 2009-2013. *Awards:* Best in Show, Memphis State U, 1975. *Bibliog:* Albuquerque Art Review (feature), 2010; 75 Artists of All Time, Interweave Mag, 2010; Neeraj Kamdar (auth), Extra Imaginary (interview), 2012. *Mem:* Art Professionals World Wide; Black Art in America; DeviantArt. *Media:* Acrylic, Pen and Ink, Oils. *Publ:* Art Through Their Eyes, Forbes Mag, 1993; Annette Jimerson, Picture of An Artist, Issue 2, Vol 5, Perspective Newspaper, 2006; Dick Blick Art Supply, 2013; Blick Studio Winter Sale Magazine, 2013; Annette Jimerson Art Book, 2013; State of the Art Book Internat, 2013. *Dealer:* Weems Art Gallery 7200 Montgomery NE Blvd Albuquerque NMex 87109; Ancient Traditions 400 San Felipe St Albuquerque NMex 87104; Contemperena Art Gallery 333 N Laura St Jacksonville Fla 32202. *Mailing Add:* 527 Offering Way San Jacinto CA 92583

JOANNOU, DAKIS
COLLECTOR
Study: Cornell Univ, BCE; Columbia Univ, MCE; Univ Rome, DArch. *Pos:* Chmn, J&P-Avax SA, Athens, 2000-, Athenaeum Hotel & Touristic Enterprises SA, Athens, YES Hotels & Restaurants, Athens; pres & exec bd dirs, J&P Group, Cyprus; chmn bd & dir, DESTE Found Contemp Art, Athens; bd trustees, New Mus Contemp Art, New York; int bd dirs, Coun Solomon R Guggenheim, New York, Mus Contemp Art, Los Angeles, Tate Gallery, London. *Awards:* Named one of Top 200 Collectors, ARTnews mag, 2003-13. *Mem:* Tate Modern Coun. *Collection:* Contemporary art. *Mailing Add:* Fragoklissias 9 Athens 15125 Greece

JOELSON, SUZANNE
PAINTER
b Paterson, NJ, Jan 12, 1952. *Study:* Bennington Col, BA, 69. *Work:* Eli Broad Collection, Los Angeles; New Sch, Chase Manhattan Bank & CW Post Col, NY. *Exhib:* Solo exhibs, Wolff Gallery, NY, 88, Fernando Alcolea Gallery, Bacelonea, 90, White Columns, NY, 90 & Lipton/Owens Co, NY, 94; McNeil Gallery, Philadelphia; Lipton/Owens Co, NY, 95; Debs & Co, NY, 98; 177th Annual: An Invitational Exhib, Nat Acad Design, 2002; Seismic Disturbance, Lohin-Geduld Gallery, New York, 2004; Am Acad Arts & Letts Invitational, New York, 2010. *Teaching:* Instr painting & color, Sch Visual Arts, 89-; instr painting, Columbia Univ, 91-97, Chautagua Inst, 94-95; instr masters painting prog, Bard Col, NY, 99; instr masters fine arts, NY Univ. *Awards:* Nat Endowment Arts Fel, 87. *Bibliog:* Robert Mahoney (auth), Suzanne Joelson at Debs & Co, Time Out/NY, 12/10/98; Ken Johnson (auth), Suzanne Joelson at Debs & Co, NY Times, 12/11/98; Alexi Worth (auth), Suzanne Joelson at Debs & Co, New Yorker, 12/21/98. *Media:* Painting. *Specialty:* Contemporary art. *Publ:* Auth, In Her Own Voice, Bomb, fall 87. *Dealer:* Debs & Co New York City. *Mailing Add:* 530 Canal St New York NY 10013

JOHANNINGMEIER, ROBERT ALAN
PAINTER, WRITER
b St Louis, Mo, Aug 29, 1946. *Study:* Kansas City Art Inst, BFA, 68. *Work:* Concordia Seminary, St Louis, Mo; Wis Lutheran Seminary; Bethany Lutheran Theological Seminary, Minn; Concordia Theological Seminary, Ft Wayne, Ind; Mich Lutheran Seminary. *Comn:* Faith in God's Mercy, or Self-righteousness, pvt collection, 2007. *Exhib:* Sun Carnival, Mus Fine Art, El Paso, Tex, 67; Allied Artists Am, NY, 80; Audubon Artists Ann Exhib, NY, 80; Grand Nat Exhib, NY, 80 & 81. *Teaching:* Instr, Old Masters Painting Techniques Workshop. *Awards:* First Place, Tri-State Art Exhib, Carlsbad Area Art Asn, NMex, 68. *Bibliog:* Flo Wilks (auth), Radiating harmony, SW Art, 82; Arejas Vitkauskas (auth), American scene, Worldwide News Bur, 83; Trish Garrigus (auth), Art of investing/collecting, Ctr Econ Revitalization, 83. *Media:* Oil. *Res:* Artistic styles and painting techniques from 1400 to the present; topics of special interest to collectors. *Publ:* Auth, The protection of works of art, Art & Commun, 79, Art as investment, 79; auth & illusr, The Art of Investing While Collecting, Art & Commun, 83, Our Culture Crisis, 87 & How to Inspire Our Family and Appreciate Our Heritage, 92. *Dealer:* Galerie Kornye 2530 Fairmount St Dallas TX 75201. *Mailing Add:* 812 N Edwards Carlsbad NM 88220

JOHANSEN, JOHN MACLANE
ARCHITECT
b NY City, June 29, 1916. *Study:* Harvard Univ, BS, 39; Harvard Grad Sch Design, MArch, 42. *Pos:* Principal, Johansen-Bhavnani, New York City, 73-89; pvt practice, 89—. *Mem:* Fel Am Inst of Archit (honor award 72, medal of honor NY, 76); Am Acad in Rome, Nat Acad of Design, Am Acad Arts and Letters (Brunner award 68), Architectural League (NY pres, 68-70); Nat Acad. *Publ:* auth, A life in the Continuing Modern Archit

JOHANSON, GEORGE E
PAINTER, PRINTMAKER
b Seattle, Wash, Nov 1, 1928. *Study:* Portland Mus Sch, Ore; Atelier 17, NY. *Work:* Nat Collection, Washington, DC; Chicago Art Inst; NY Pub Libr; Victoria & Albert Mus, London, Eng; Oldham Co Coun, Eng; and many others. *Comn:* Civic Auditorium, Portland, 69; Portland Bldg, 88; Bremerton High Sch, Wa, 89; Ore State Univ, Corvallis, 92; Peninsula Park, Portland, 98. *Exhib:* Calif Palace Legion Hon, San Francisco; Am Embassy, London, Eng; Seattle Art Mus; Portland Art Mus, Ore; Univ Ariz, Tucson; Univ Ill; Western NMex Univ; Palm Springs Desert Mus, Calif; Univ Houston, Tex. *Pos:* Pres, Northwest Print Coun, 81-83. *Teaching:* Instr painting & printmaking, Portland Mus Art Sch, 55-80; lectr, Reed Col, Portland, Ore, 77; instr printmaking, La State Univ, Baton Rouge, 92. *Awards:* First Ed Award, Ore Arts Comn, 76; Award, Ore State Fair, Salem, 77; Governors Award for the Arts, 92; and others. *Bibliog:* Bruce Guenther (auth), 50 Northwest Artists, Chronicle Bks, 83; Lois Allen (auth), Contemporary Art in the Northwest, Craftsman House, 95 & Northwest Printmakers, 97; Equivalents, Portland Art Mus, 2001. *Mem:* Portland Art Asn; Northwest Print Coun (pres, 83). *Media:* Oil, Etching. *Publ:* Creator, Etching and Color Intaglio (film), 73 & Printmaker (film), 76; Drawings Retrospective, Univ of Oreg, 89; Image and Idea, Retrospective, Hallie Ford Mus Art, Salem, Ore. *Dealer:* Augen Gallery 716 NW Davis Portalnd OR 97209. *Mailing Add:* 2237 SW Market St Dr Portland OR 97201

JOHANSON, PATRICIA
SCULPTOR, ENVIRONMENTAL ARTIST
b New York, NY, Sept 8, 1940. *Study:* Brooklyn Mus Art Sch; Art Students League; Bennington Coll, BA, 62; Hunter Coll, MA, 64; City Coll Sch Archit, BS & BArch, 77. *Hon Degrees:* Mass Coll Art, Hon DFA, 95. *Work:* Mus Mod Art, New York; Storm King Art Ctr, Mountainville, NY; Dallas Art Mus, Tex; Metrop Mus Art, New York; Nat Mus Women Arts, Washington, DC. *Comn:* Fair Park Lagoon, Dallas, Texas, 81-86; Endangered Garden, Candlestick Cove, San Francisco Arts Comn, 87-97; Ulsan Dragon Park, Yukong Ltd, South Korea, 96-; Ellis Creek Water Recycling Facility, Petaluma, Calif, 2000-2007; The Draw at Sugar House, Salt Lake City, Utah, 2003-2011. *Exhib:* Art of the Real, Mus Mod Art, New York, Grand Palais, Paris, Kunsthaus, Zurich & Tate Gallery, London, 68-69; Women in Am Archit, Brooklyn Mus, New York, 77; Recent Acquisitions, Mus Mod Art, New York, 79; Am Drawings in Black & White, Brooklyn Mus, 80; Recent Acquisitions, Metrop Mus Art, 82; Fragile Ecologies, Queens Mus, New York, 92; Creative Solutions to Ecological Issues, Dallas Mus Natural Hist, 93; Differentes Natures, La Defense, Paris & La Virreina, Barcelona, 93-94; Tres Cantos Da Terra, Nat Mus Fine Arts, Rio de Janeiro, 93; Cosmic-Maternal, Gallery Nikko, Tokyo, 94; Chalk Circle, Michael Fuchs Galerie, Berlin, 97; Jardin 2000, Villa Medici, Rome, 2000; Ecovention, Contemp Arts Ctr, Cincinnati, 2002; A Minimal Future, Mus Contemp Art, Los Angeles, 2004; Green Acres, Contemp Art Ctr, Cincinnati; Ends of the Earth (Land Art to 1974), Mus Contemp Art, Los Angeles and Haus Der Kunst Munich, 2012, Johanson Retrospective, Contemp Mus, Baltimore, 2012; Mus Het Domein Sittard, Netherlands, 2013. *Pos:* Design consult, Consolidated Edison Corp, New York, 72, Yale Univ, 72, Bartholomew Consolidated Sch Corp, Columbus, Ind, 73, Int Yr Child Comn, 79, Corning Park, Albany, 82, Fair Park, Dallas, 82, Pelham Bay Park, NY, 84 & Cathedral Sq, Sacramento, 84; San Francisco Clean Water Prog, 88; Pub Art Master Plan, Rockland Co, NY, 90; mem, Omame Proj, Earth Summit, Brazil, 92 & Global Forum, Kyoto, Japan, 93; Sanart, Ankara, Turkey, 97; City Plan, Brockton, Mass, 97 & Petaluma, Calif, 98; consult, Oikos, Yukong Ltd & Seoul Develop Inst, South Korea, 96-99 & City Salina, Kans, Carollo Engrs, 2001-05; grants selection comt, Nat Endowment Arts, Washington, DC, 2000; designer, French Embassy Cult Srvs, New York, 2000, Salt Lake City Planning & Design, 2003, Duluth, Minn Planning & Design, 2004-2006 & Zhang Jia Jie, Nat Forest Park, China, 2004, Marywood Univ, Scranton, Pa, 2008; City of Santa Fe, Planning & Design, 2010. *Teaching:* Vis prof art, State Univ NY, Albany, 69; vis artist, Mass Inst Technol, 74, Oberlin Coll, 74 & Alfred Univ, 74; lectr, Colby Coll, Maine, 81; W Tex State Univ, Canyon, 88 & Mass Coll Art, 94; sem, Yale Univ, 89, Olesen Fel, Bennington Coll, 91-92; Calif State Univ, Monterey Bay, 97,99 & 2006; Westminister Coll, Salt Lake City, Distinguished Resident, 2007, Wentworth Inst Technol, Boston, 2006-2009; vis artist, Univ Wisc, 2011; Seminar Univ Gothenburg, Sweden, 2013. *Awards:* Guggenheim Fel, 70 & 80; Gold Medal, Academia Italia Delle Arti, 79; Governor's Grand Achievement Award, Envision Utah, 2004. *Bibliog:* Caffyn Kelley (auth), Art and Survival: Patricia Johanson's Environmental Projects, Islands Institute, 2006; Xin Wu (auth), Patricia Johanson's House and Garden Commission: Reconstruction of Modernity, Dumbarton Oaks, 2008, Patricia Johanson and the Re-Invention of Public Environmental Art, Ashgate, 2013. *Mem:* Global Forum Arts Group, New York. *Publ:* Architecture as Landscape, Princeton J, Vol 2, 85; Art and Survival: Creative Solutions to Environmental Problems, Gallerie Monogr, Vancouver, BC, 92; La Ville Comme Forme D'Art Ecologique: La Trace de Rocky Marciano, Les Annales de la Recherche Urbaine, Paris, No 85, 99; Beyond Choreography: Shifting Experiences in Uncivilized Gardens, Landscape Design and the Experience of Motion, Dumbarton Oaks, 2003; Fecund Landscapes: Art and Process in Public Parks, Landscape and Art, London, Number 29, 2003. *Mailing Add:* 179 Nickmush Rd Buskirk NY 12028

JOHNS, CHRISTOPHER K(ALMAN)
PAINTER, EDUCATOR
b Racine, Wis, Dec 2, 1952. *Study:* Univ Wis, Milwaukee, 71-73; San Francisco Art Inst, BFA, 75; Stanford Univ, MFA, 77. *Work:* Continental Bank, Chicago, Ill; Best Products Co, Richmond, Va; Univ Wis, Platteville; Stanford Univ, Calif; Charles Wustum Mus Fine Art, Racine, Wis; La State Univ Mus of Art, Baton Rouge, La. *Exhib:* West-the Law, Minn Mus Art, St Paul, 79 & 80; Hassam Fund Purchase Exhib, Am Acad & Inst Arts, NY, 80; Abstraction in Louisiana, 80 & Festival of New Work, 84, Contemp Art Ctr, New Orleans, La; View from Southeast Wis, Charles Wustum Mus, Racine, Wis, 81; Southern Abstraction, City Gallery, Raleigh, NC, 87; solo exhibs, Union Gallery, La State Univ, Baton Rouge, 83, Univ Ala, Huntsville, 91 & Art at Koll, New Orleans, 97, Sylvia Schmidt, 2001, Albert Blue Gallery, Baton Rouge, La, 2000; Perimeter Gallery, Chicago, 98, 02; Abstraction, Sylvia Schmidt Gallery, New Orleans, 99, Images of Water, 02; Return of the Men, Peltz Gallery, Milwaukee, 02; New Artists Show, Baton Rouge Gallery, La; group exhib: Baton Rouge Gallery, 2006; 2nd Line, Ad Hoc Gallery, Brooklyn, NY, 2007. *Pos:* vis artist, David & Julia White Artists Colony, Costa Rica. *Teaching:* Instr painting, Charles Wustum Mus, 77-78; prof painting & drawing, La State Univ, Baton Rouge, 79-2011. *Awards:* Southern Arts Fedn Artists Fel, 88; Visual Arts Grant, State of Louisiana Arts Div, 86. *Bibliog:* Juliana Harris-Livingston (auth), Abstraction still not convinced, Figaro, New Orleans, La, 8/80; Christopher Fischer (auth), Three Abstractionists. New Orleans Art Rev, La, 99. *Media:* Oil, Acrylic. *Dealer:* Perimeter Gallery, Chicago, Ill; Peltz Gallery Milwaukee WI. *Mailing Add:* 3300 Michigan Blvd Racine WI 53402

JOHNS, JASPER
PAINTER
b Augusta, Ga, May 15, 1930. *Study:* Univ SC. *Work:* Victoria & Albert Mus, London; Mus Mod Art & Whitney Mus Am Art, NY; Albright-Knox Art Gallery, Buffalo, NY; Wadsworth Atheneum, Hartford, Conn; Mus Mod Art, Paris; San Francisco Mus Mod Art, Calif; Stedelijk Mus, Amsterdam, Neth; Hirshhorn Mus & Sculpture Garden, Washington, DC; Tate Gallery, London; Moderna Museet, Stockholm; Kunst Mus, Basel; White Flag, 55; Flag, 55; False State, 59; Study for Skin, 62; Seasons, 86. *Exhib:* Solo exhibs incl Leo Castelli Gallery, New York, 58, 60, 61, 63, 66, 68, 76, 81, 84, Galerie Rive Droite, Paris, 59, 61, Galleria D'Arte Del Naviglio, Milan, 59, Ileana Sonnabend, Paris, 63, Jewish Mus, New York, 64, White-chapel Gallery, London, 64, Pasadena Mus, Calif, 65, Minami Gallery, Tokyo, 65, 75, Smithsonian Inst Nat Collection Fine Arts, 66, Mus Mod Art, 68, 70, 86, 92, Whitney Mus Am Art, 77, Kunsthalle, Cologne, 78, Centre Pompidou, Paris, 78, Hayward Gallery, London, 78, Seibu Mus, Tokyo, 78, San Francisco Mus Mod Art, 78, Kunstmuseum, Basel, 79, Des Moines Art Ctr, 83, St Louis Art Mus, 85, Kunsthalle, 86, Wight Art Gallery UCLA, 87, Galerie Daniel Templon, Paris, 87, Mus Contemp Art, Los Angeles, 87, Philadelphia Mus Art, 88, Walker Art Ctr, 90, Mus Fine Arts, Houston, 90, Fine Arts Mus, San Francisco, 90, Montreal Mus Fine Arts, 90, Nat Gallery Art, Wash, 90, Kunstmus Basel, 90, Hayward Gallery, London, 90, Cana Art Gallery, Seoul, Korea, 91, Gagosian Gallery, NY, 92, Prints & Drawings from the Castelli Collection, Palaus de Luppe, La Fondation Vincent Van Gogh, Arles, France, 92, Milwaukee Art Mus, Wis, 92, Galeria Weber Alexander Cobo, Madrid, Spain, 92, Usuyuki, Craig F Starr Assocs, NY, 2006, Leanne Hull Fine Art, 2006, Spanierman Mod, New York, 2006, Nat Gallery Art, Wash, DC, 2007, Leo Castelli, New York, 2010; group exhibs include Mus Contemp Art, Chicago, 71-72; Art Inst Chicago, 74; Walker Art Ctr, Minneapolis, 74; Saidye Bronfman Ctr, Montreal, 80; Pace Gallery, NY, 80; Whitney Mus Am Art, NY, 80; Hirshhorn Mus, Washington, DC, 80; Stedelijk Mus, The Neth, 80; Margo Leavin Gallery, Los Angeles, 81; Leo Castelli Gallery, NY, 81; Hotel des Arts, Paris, France, 92; Mus Mod & Contemp Art, 92; Kunst Mus, Basel, 2007. *Pos:* Dir, Found Contemp Performance Artists, 63-. *Awards:* Recipient 1st prize Print Biennale Ljubljana, Yugoslavia, prize IX Sao Paulo (Brazil) Biennale; Skowhegan medal for painting Skowhegan Sch of Painting and Sculpture; Skowhegan medal for graphics; Mayors award of Hon for Arts and Culture City of NY; Wolf prize for painting, Wolf Found; Int prize Venice Biennale, 88; Nat Medal of Arts, 90; named to SC Hall of Fame, 89; Presidential Medal of Freedom, The White House, 2010. *Bibliog:* C Kelder (auth), Prints: Jasper Johns at Hofstra, Art in Am, 3/73; D Ward (auth), Jasper Johns drawings, Arts Rev, 9/74; J Reichardt (auth), The rendering is the content, Archit Design, 12/74. *Mem:* Am Acad Arts and Letters (Gold medal for graphic art); Royal Acad Arts; Nat Inst Arts and Letters; Am Acad Arts and Scis. *Mailing Add:* PO Box 642 Sharon CT 06069-0642

JOHNSON, ANITA LOUISE
PAINTER, GRAPHIC ARTIST
b Silver Creek, NY, Oct 22, 1931. *Study:* Albright Art Sch, Buffalo, NY, BFA, 1952; Grad Courses (art), Univ Buffalo, 1963-1968. *Work:* City Hall, Buffalo, NY; Buffalo Gen Hosp; Inland Div Ford Motor Co, Dayton, Ohio; Women & Childrens Hosp, Buffalo, NY; Blue Cross Western NY, Buffalo, NY. *Exhib:* Director's Choice, Albright Art Gallery, Buffalo, NY, 1990; Invitational Studio Exhib, Burchfield-Penny Center, Buffalo, NY, 1994; Solo Exhibs, Garrett Club, Buffalo, NY, 1994, Studio Arena Theatre, Buffalo, NY, 1995, Upstairs at Sutherlands Gallery, Buffalo, NY, 1996, 1995, Arts Coun Buffalo Erie Co, Buffalo, NY, 2001, Art Dialogue Gallery, Buffalo, NY, 2012, and numerous others; Nat League Pen Women, Center for Tomorrow, State Univ Buffalo, NY, 1995; Carnegie Cult Center, Nat League Pen Women, Tonawanda, NY, 1997; Somarts Gallery Invitational, San Francisco, Calif, 1999; Buffalo Soc Artists, Castellani Mus Art, Niagara Falls, NY, 2005 & 2009; Niagara Frontier Exhib, Kenan Center, Lockport, NY, 2006; Carnegie Art Gallery, Tonawanda, NY, 2010. *Pos:* Asst art Dir, Buffalo Courier Express, Buffalo, NY, 1952-1981; art dir, Buffalo News, Buffalo, NY, 1981-1991. *Awards:* Merit Award, Theodore Roosevelt Hist Mansion, Buffalo Soc Artists, 1987; 2nd Prize Oil, Kenan Center, Lockport Savings Bank, 1993; Award, Nat League Am Pen Women, Kenan Center, 2000; Millicent Heller Award, Burchfield Penney Art Ctr, Buffalo, NY 2004; Bronze Medal, Buffalo Soc Artists, 2008; ESpirit De Corps Aw, Burchfield Penney Art Ctr, Buffalo, NY, 2009; and

numerous others. *Mem:* Buffalo Soc Artists (bd dirs, 1980-1985 & 1987-1992, pres, 1989-1990); Nat League Am Pen Women of W NY; Hallwalls Contemp Art Center. *Media:* Acrylic, Oil, All Media. *Dealer:* Art Dialogue Gallery Buffalo NY. *Mailing Add:* S 5677 Sterling Rd Hamburg NY 14075

JOHNSON, AUDEAN See Audean

JOHNSON, BARBARA LOUISE
PAINTER, PRINTMAKER
b Worcester, Mass, Nov 10, 1927. *Study:* Univ Miami, Fla, 46-48; Smith Col, Mass, AB, 50; Univ Calif-Berkeley, 51; Univ Mich, BS, 57, MFA, 59. *Work:* Zimmerli Mus, Rutgers Univ; Contemp Art Mus, Chamalieres, France; Monterey Peninsula Mus Art; Am Express Int, Tokyo; Banco Int, Lima, Peru; others. *Comn:* 17 mixed media pieces, Lodge at Pebble Beach, Calif, 94; 180 mixed media works on paper, Inn at Spanish Bay, Pebble Beach, Calif, 96. *Exhib:* Los Angeles Printmakers Ann, 88-94; Contemp Am Prints, Barbican Ctr, London, 89; Norske Grafikere, Oslo, Norway, 93; Spencer Mus Art, Univ Kans, 95; Univ Wis, 95; Los Angeles Print Making Soc, Exchange Exhib, Belfast, Ireland, 2006; Hunterdon Mus Art, NY, 2007; Univ Calif, Santa Cruz, 2007; Boston Printmakers N Am Print Biennial, 2007; Nat Small Print Exhib, Univ Wisc, Parkside, 2007; Visual Telephone & Current Voyages, Monterey Peninsula Coll & Holualoa Hawaii Exchange Exhib, Kona, HI, 2007; Visual Arts Soc, Denton, Tex, 2007. *Collection Arranged:* A. Expres Int; Tolman Collection- Tokyo, Japan; Baer & Assoc, Att, Palo Alto, CA; Bank of Boston, MA; Life Scan Corp, Pebble Beach Corp, Seagete Corp, Scotts Valley, Ca; PES Environmental Inc, Novato; Read-Rite Corp, Milpitas, CA; Mus of Contemporary Art, ChamaLieres, France; Sp.-Bay resort, Pebble Beach, CA; Pan-Pacific Corp, Guatemala; Tolber Int Design, J. Knutsen Int Design-San Francisco, Ca; The Spa at Pabble Beach, CA; Univ of Calif, Santa Cruz, Calif, 2007. *Teaching:* Jr High School, Mclean, Va; Senior Citizens, Carmel, CA. *Awards:* Leila Sawyer Mem Award, 87, Shelley Sterling Mem Award, 89 & Medal Honor & Jack Key Cotton Mem Award, 91 Nat Asn Women Artists, NY; Dorothy Tabak Mem Award; Nat Asn Women Artists, Collage, 2006. *Bibliog:* Jeanne Davidson (auth), Barbara Johnson/artist & printmaker, Print World, spring 87. *Mem:* Calif Soc Printmakers; Los Angeles Printmaking Soc; Nat Asn Women Artist, NY; Carmel Art Asn, Calif. *Media:* All. *Specialty:* Paintings; sculpture. *Interests:* Travel & Reading. *Publ:* Journal of the Print World. *Dealer:* Winfield Gallery PO Box 7393 Carmel CA 93921; Carmel Art Asn PO Box 227 Carmel CA 93921; The Gallery 329 Primrose Rd Burlingame CA 94010; RFA 200 Kansas St San Francisco CA 94103; Jeanne Davidson: Fine Prints New York NY; 33 Hilltop Rd San Mateo Calif. *Mailing Add:* 3548 Greenfield Pl Carmel CA 93923-9441

JOHNSON, BARBARA PIASECKA
COLLECTOR, PATRON
b Staniewicze, Poland, Feb 25, 1937. *Study:* Univ Wroclaw, Poland, MA (art hist), 65. *Collection Arranged:* Opus Sacrum, (auth, catalog), Royal Castle, Warsaw, Poland, 90 & Liechtensteinische Staatliche Kunstsammlung, Vaduz, Liechtenstein, 91, Musee de la Chapelle de la Visitation, Monaco, 95-; Cultural Heritage in Europe, Jan Vermeer, St Praxedis, Wawel Royal Castle, Krakow, Poland, 91-92; The Flight into Egypt, Musee de la Chapelle de la Visitation, Monaco, 97; Saint Praxedis, Musee de la Chapelle de la Visitation, Monaco, 98. *Pos:* Trustee, dir, chairperson, The Barbara Piasecka Johnson Found, currently; trustee, chairperson, The Paderewski Ctr, currently; pres, Centrum Ignacego Paderewskiego, currently; mem, Chmns Counc Metrop Mus Art, New York, 86; mem, Collectors Comt Nat Gallery Art, Washington, DC, 80-91; mem, US Dept State Fine Arts Coun, 78-85; mem, Coun Found Univ Wroclaw, 91-92; trustee & dir, Atlantic Found & Harbor Branch Found, 72-85; bd mgrs, Wistar Inst Philadelphia, 89-91. *Awards:* Polish Am Congress Heritage Award, 89; Living Legacy Award, 94; Order of St Charles Officer decoration (for serv to Principality of Monaco), conferred by HSH, Prince Rainer III, 95. *Bibliog:* Antoni Dzieduszycki (auth), Love is Greater Barbara Piasecka Johnson & Eleven Arts Inc (prods, film), 90; Roger M Williams (auth), Wealth in the Service of Poland, Found News, 1-2/91. *Collection:* Paintings 13th-19th Century (emphasis on old masters); Furniture & Decorative Arts 16th-19th Century (emphasis on French Furniture); Sculpture 15th-19th Century. *Mailing Add:* 4519 Province Line Rd Princeton NJ 08540

JOHNSON, BRENT
PAINTER
b Tyler, Tex, Aug 25, 1941. *Study:* Cent State Univ, BFA, 67; Univ Okla; Univ Md. *Comn:* Okla Dept Wildlife Conservation, 2006. *Exhib:* Watercolor USA, Springfield Art Mus, Mo, 75; Am Watercolor Soc, Nat Acad Design, NY, 75-81; La Ann, La Mus Art, Shreveport, 76; Delta Art Asn, Ark Art Ctr, Little Rock, 76; San Diego Nat Watercolor Exhib, Cent Fed Tower, 77; Rocky Mountain Nat Watermedia Exhib, Foothills Art Ctr, Golden, Colo, 77; Arts for the Parks, 2002; and others. *Pos:* Bd dir, Oklahoma City Arts Coun, 79-80. *Teaching:* various workshops. *Awards:* Mercantile Bank Award, Watercolor USA, 75; Bus Community Award, Rocky Mountain Nat Watermedia Exhib, 77; John Young Hunter Mem Award, Am Watercolor Soc, 81. *Bibliog:* Lynn Martin (auth), Today's art, Syndicate Mag Inc, 74; Dean G Graham (auth), Outdoor Oklahoma, Okla Dept Wildlife, 1/76; Marcia Lionberger (auth), Oklahoma Art Gallery, Wall & Wall Publ Co Inc, fall 81. *Mem:* Prof Artist Asn Okla (pres, 77-78); Whiskey Painters Am. *Media:* Watercolor, Oils. *Dealer:* Griffith Gallery of Art 229 N Main St Salado TX. *Mailing Add:* 513 Sweetgum Oklahoma City OK 73127

JOHNSON, BRUCE (JAMES)
PAINTER
b Riverside, Calif, May 6, 1944. *Study:* Univ Hawaii, Honolulu, BFA, 66; El Camino Col, Gardena, Calif; Calif Coll Arts & Crafts, Oakland, MFA, 70. *Exhib:* James D Phelen Awards Exhib, Calif Palace of Legion of Honor, San Francisco, 69; Western Wash State Nat Drawing & Small Sculpture Exhib, Western Wash State Univ, Bellingham, 70; San Francisco Art Inst Centennial Exhib, 71 & Work on Paper, 73, San Francisco Mus Mod Art; Grids, Inst Contemp Art, Univ Pa, Philadelphia, 72; Eighteen Bay Area Artists, Los Angeles Inst Contemp Art, 76 & Univ Calif, Berkeley Art Mus, 77; Art Hawaii Ann, Honolulu Acad Arts, 78, 79 & 83; Artists Hawaii Cult Exchange Exhib, Ohio & Manila, 80-81. *Teaching:* Instr art, Santa Rosa Jr Col, Calif, 72-76; lectr drawing, Univ Hawaii, Honolulu, 78-79; instr, Honolulu Acad Arts, 81. *Awards:* MacDowell Colony Fel, 71; Young Artist Award, Contemp Art Comt of Oakland Mus Art Guild, 73. *Bibliog:* Judith L Dunham (auth), Johnson and Linhares, Artweek, 3/73; Alfred Frankenstein (auth), She's somebody to watch, San Francisco Chronicle, 4/3/73. *Media:* All Media. *Mailing Add:* 3318 Woodlawn Dr Honolulu HI 96822

JOHNSON, CAROL M
CURATOR
b Weymouth, Mass. *Study:* Mass Coll Art, BFA, 80; Univ Md, Coll Park, MLS, 88. *Collection Arranged:* Carl Van Vechten & Miguel Covarrubias, About Face, 94; Am Daguerreotypes, 1842-1862, (online exhib); Ansel Adam's Photogs of Japanese-Am Internment at Manzanar, 2002; Civil War Photogs, Stereograph Cards, 2005; The Last Full Measure: Civil War Photographs from the Liljenquist Family Coll, 2011; Down to Earth: Herblock and Photographers Observe the Environment, 2012. *Pos:* Cur photog, Libr Cong, Prints & Photog Div, Washington, DC, 99-. *Awards:* Daguerrean Soc Fel award, 2011. *Mem:* Am Asn Mus; Daguerreian Soc. *Publ:* Auth, Panoramas of Duluth, Minn, History of Photography, 92; Faces of Freedom: Portraits from the American Colonization Society Collection, Daguerreian Ann, 96; coauth, Eyes of the Nation: A Visual History of the US, 97; Gathering History: The Marion S Carson Collection of Americana, 99; coauth, Framing the West: The Survey Photographs of Timothy H O'Sullivan, Yale Univ Press, 2010. *Mailing Add:* 405 Windover Ct NW Vienna VA 22180

JOHNSON, CECILE RYDEN
PAINTER, PUBLISHER
b Jamestown, NY. *Study:* Augustana Col, AB; Pa Acad Fine Arts; Art Inst Chicago; Am Acad Fine Arts; Univ Colo; Univ Wis. *Work:* Chicago Mus Sci & Indust; Davenport Munic Mus; Macalester Col; General Mills; Minn Mining; Augustana Col; Wagner Col; American Express; New England Ski Mus; Vermont Ski Mus; National Sking Hall Fame. *Comn:* Trans World Airlines; Rockefeller Resorts; Jamaican Govt; CBS/World Tennis; Official artist (lithographs), 1980 US Lake Placid Olympics & 1990 Winter Olympics, Albertville, France; and many others. *Exhib:* Am Watercolor Soc; Washington Watercolor Soc; US Info Agency & State Dept Traveling Exhib to Europe, Asia, Africa & South Am; Solo exhibs, Davenport Munic Mus & Hudson River Mus; US Tennis Open, Nat Stadium, 83; Grand Cent Gallery; and others. *Teaching:* Instr workshops, Ghost Ranch, Abiquiu, 82, Bermuda, 83. *Awards:* Catharine Lorillard Wolfe Art Club Gold Medal; Prizes, Am Watercolor Soc, Knickerbocker Artists & others. *Bibliog:* Feature article, Am Artist, 1/83; Kent (auth), 100 Watercolorists, Watson Guptill; Creating in Watercolor (film), Crystal Productions; Feature Article, Am Artist, 5/86. *Mem:* Am Watercolor Soc; Hon mem Nat Arts Club; Soc Illusr; hon mem Nat League Pen Women; Allied Artists, Audubon Soc; US Skit Journalists Assoc. *Media:* Watercolor, Acrylic. *Res:* World travel. *Specialty:* Am Swedish Inst-Scandinavian Artists in USA. *Interests:* Winter Sports, Landscapes/Water. *Publ:* Contribr, illus, 42 issues Skiing Mag & Ski Impact Mag; Contribr, Snow Country, American Artist. *Dealer:* Columbine Gallery Frisco CO; Lake Placid Market Lake Placid NY; Pablo's Gallery Tahoe City CA; New England Ski Mus Franconia Notch NH; Vermont Ski Mus Stowe VT. *Mailing Add:* Des Artistes One W 67th St New York NY 10023-6200

JOHNSON, CHARLES W
EDUCATOR, HISTORIAN
b New York, NY, Apr 7, 1938. *Study:* Westminster Col, BMEd, 60; Union Theol Seminary, MSM, 62; Ohio Univ, PhD, 70. *Exhib:* Curator: Renaissance Prints in Social Context, 1999; The Art of Stephen Della, Univ Richmond Va, 2001. *Teaching:* Asst prof, State Univ NY Col New Paltz, summer 66; From asst prof art hist to assoc prof, 67-81, Univ Richmond, prof, 82-, chmn dept fine arts, 67-; Pro Art Hist, Chmn, Dept of Art & Art History, 67-2003; Senior Scholar, Jepson Sch Leadership, Univ Richmond, Va. *Awards:* Pres Citation, Westminster Col, 95; Distinguished Educ Award, 1993; State Council of Higher Educ for Va (SCHEV), Outstanding Faculty Award, 96; Golden Key Intl Hon Soc, (hon mem), 2002; The Charles Johnson Lectureship in Art Hist, Univ Richmond, 2005. *Mem:* Coll Art Asn Am; Popular Culture Asn of South; Prog Enhancing Teaching Effectiveness, (ch); Univ Richmond Trustee Committee. *Interests:* Italian & Northern Renaissance art, Mannerism & the Baroque; Survey of art: Early Renaissance through Modernism; 18th Century Studies. *Publ:* The Renaissance Print in Social Context, Exhib Catalogue, Univ of Richmond, 99; The World of Stefano della Bella(1610-1664), Italian Printmaker, Univ of Richmond & The Virginia Mus of Fine Arts, 2001; Eighteenth Century Prints Catalogue, UR, 2005; Exhib Catalogue, Univ of Richmond, 2001; intro, Prints and the Courtly World of Mozart, Univ of Richmond, 2006. *Mailing Add:* Dept Art and Art History Univ of Richmond Richmond VA 23173

JOHNSON, D'ELAINE A HERARD See D'Elaine

JOHNSON, DIANA L
GALLERY DIRECTOR, CURATOR
b New York, NY, July 13, 1940. *Study:* Radcliffe Col, Harvard Univ, BA, 62; Brown Univ, MA, 71. *Pos:* Assoc cur prints & drawings, Mus Art, RI Sch Design, 69-76, actg chief cur, 74-76, cur prints, drawings & photogs & chief cur, 76-79, actg dir, 78-79; dir, Brown Univ, David Winton Bell Gallery, 90-. *Mem:* Print Coun Am (treas, 82-89); Asn Coll & Univ Mus & Galleries (RI rep, 90-); Am Fed Arts (exhib comt). *Publ:* Auth, Spaces (exhib catalog), 78 & Fantastic Illustration and Design in Britain 1860-1930, 79, Mus Art RI Sch Design; Reprise: The Vera G List Collection, 91 & coauth, The Collections of Brown Univer, 92, Brown Univ. *Mailing Add:* David Winton Bell Gallery List Art Center Brown Univ 64 College St Providence RI 02912-9021

JOHNSON, DIANE CHALMERS
HISTORIAN, EDUCATOR
b Dubuque, Iowa, Jan 3, 1943. *Study:* Harvard Univ, Radcliffe Col, BA (fine arts), 65; Univ Kans, MA (art hist), 67, PhD (art hist), 70. *Teaching:* prof modern European Am art history, Col Charleston, dept chair, 70-78 & 91-2001. *Awards:* Nat Endowment Humanities Res Fel, 81-82; Addlestone Chair Am Art, Coll Charleston, 89-94. *Mem:* Coll Art Asn Am; Historians Am Art Asn; SECAC. *Res:* Nineteenth and twentieth-century European and American art; Art Nouveau and Symbolist art; Picasso's late work. *Publ:* Auth, Odilon Redon's apocalypse de Saint-Jean, Arts Va, 72; American Art Nouveau, Harry N Abrams Publ, 79; Picasso's Papiers Colles, In: XXVI Int Congress for the History of Art, Univ Pa Press, 89; Albert P Ryderts Siegfried and the rhine maidens, Am Art, 94; contribr, American Symbolist Art: Nineteenth Century, 2004. *Mailing Add:* 59 Smith St Charleston SC 29401

JOHNSON, DOUGLAS WALTER
PAINTER, CERAMIST, PUBLISHER
b Portland, Ore, July 8, 1946. *Study:* Self-taught. *Work:* Permanent Collection, Mus NMex, Santa Fe; Am Nat Collection, Am Nat Ins Co, Galveston, Tex; NMex State Capitol Bldg, Santa Fe; De Vries Insurance Agency, St Joseph, Mich; Hotel Eldorado, Santa Fe, NMex. *Comn:* Rio Grande (mural), El Dorado Hotel, Santa Fe, NMex. *Exhib:* Inner Sanctums, Gerald Peters Gallery, Santa Fe, NMex, 88; Contemp miniatures, J N Bartfield Gallery, NY, 89; Birds of Magic, Gerald Peters Gallery, Santa Fe, NMex, 90; 35 Yr Retrospective Exhib, NMex State Capitol, Governors Gallery, Santa Fe, 93; Flowers, Pots & Trains, Parks Gallery, Taos, NMex, 96; Hist Windows, Nedra Mattrucci Gallery, Santa Fe, NMex, 01. *Teaching:* Prime-Time sch proj drawing & painting, Espanola Sch District, 93-94. *Awards:* Jurors Award, NMex Biennial, Mus NMex, 73; Second Prize Award, Watercolor NMex, NMex Watercolor Soc, 74; Santa Fe Opera Poster, NMex, 81; Cert of Achievement, US Dept Agr Nat Forest. *Bibliog:* Douglas Johnson (auth), Cliff-Dweller, NMex Mag, 4/94; Robert Ewing (auth), Birds of Magic, Douglas Johnson, 90; Robert Ewing (auth), Painters Odessey, Clear Light Publ, Santa Fe, NMex, 97. *Media:* Casein on Paper, Clay. *Specialty:* Contemporary and work of Dead American Masters; Spanish Colonial period, New Mexico; Archeology of above. *Interests:* History, Southwestern Pre-history (1050-1450 AD Pueblo Indians). *Collection:* Southwest Indian. *Publ:* NMex Mag Calendar, 06; Spanish Colonial Churches of NMex, Obsidian Mountain, 03; and numerous others. *Dealer:* JN Bartfield NY NY; Fenn Galleries Santa Fe NM; Parks Gallery Taos NMex; Nedra Matteucci Gallery Santa Fe NMex. *Mailing Add:* PO Box 9 Coyote NM 87012

JOHNSON, DUNCAN
PAINTER
Study: Pratt Inst, BFA, Brooklyn, 1987. *Exhib:* Solo exhibs, Univ Mass, Lowell, 1995, 55 Mercer Gallery, New York, 1996 & 1997, Litchenstein Ctr Arts, Pittsfield, Mass, 1997, Nations Bank, Atlanta, 1997, Rosewood Art Ctr, Kettering, Ohio, 1997, JJ Brookings Gallery, San Francisco, 1999, 2000 & 2001, Marcia Wood Gallery, Atlanta, 2003, Rotunda Gallery, Dartmouth Col, Hanover, NH, 2004 & MOCA Jacksonville, 2007; Manhattanville Coll, Purchase, NY, 1995; Marcia Wood Gallery, Choices, Atlanta, 1996; Woodward Gallery, Estival, New York, 1996; Newport Ctr Mall, Jersey City, 1996; Pelham Arts Ctr, NY, 1996; Rotunda Gallery, Brooklyn, 1997; 55 Mercer Gallery, New York, 1997; Soho Downtown Arts Festival, New York, 1997; Target Gallery, Alexandria, Va, 1999; Austing State Univ, Nacogdoches, Tex, 1999; Cinque Gallery, New York, 1999; Sam Houston Mem Mus, Huntsville, Tex, 1999; Barrett Art Ctr, Poughkeepsie, NY, 1999; Soc Contemp Crafts, Pittsburgh, 1999; Nese Aplan Gallery, Roslyn, NY, 1999 & 2003; Foreman Gallery, Oneonta, NY, 1999; Lee County Alliance for Arts, Fort Meyers, 1999; Matrix Gallery, Sacremento, 1999; Metaphor Contemp Art, Brooklyn, 2002; Art in Embassies Prog, Wash, DC, 2003; AVA Gallery, Lebanon, NH, 2004; Oxbow Gallery, Northhampton, Mass, 2005; Univ NH, Durham, 2005; Newton Art Ctr, Mass, 2006; Am Acad Arts & Letts Invitational, New York, 2009. *Awards:* Sculpture fel, NY Found for Arts, 2001; Individual Artist Grant, Vt Arts Coun, 2005; Acad Award in Art, Am Acad Arts and Letts, 2009. *Media:* Mixed Media. *Mailing Add:* David Findlay Jr Fine Art 724 5th Ave New York NY 10019

JOHNSON, EDWARD C, III
COLLECTOR
b Boston, Mass, June 29, 1930. *Study:* Harvard Univ, AB, 1954. *Pos:* Analyst, Fidelity Investments, Boston, 1957, mgr Trend Fund, 1960, mgr Fidelity Int Fund (renamed Magellan), 1963-72; pres, FMR Corp, Boston, 1972-77, chmn bd & chief exec officer, 1977-; hon trustee, Mus Fine Arts, Boston; bd dirs, Ctr Neurologic Diseases. *Awards:* Named one of Forbes Richest Americans, 1999-; named one of World's Richest People, Forbes Mag, 2000-; named one of Top 200 Collectors, ARTnews mag, 2009-10. *Mem:* Am Acad Arts & Scis (fel); Mass Hist Soc. *Collection:* 19th & 20th century paintings and furniture. *Mailing Add:* Fidelity Investments 82 Devonshire St Boston MA 02109

JOHNSON, ERIN (STUKEY)
PAINTER, SCULPTOR
b New York, NY. *Study:* Studied with Jacque Lipchitz, Italy, Wattana Wattanapan, Sherri Hunter & Anton Weiss; Rhodes Col, BA, 73. *Work:* Highland Terrace Med Ctr; Jane Voorhees, Zimmerli Mus, Rutgers, NJ; Childrens Discovery Ctr, Murfreesboro, Tenn. *Exhib:* Cheekwood, Nashville Artist Guild, Tenn; Ann Nat Asn Women Artists, NY; Tenn All State, Parthenon Mus, Nashville; Tenn Watercolor Soc, Hunter Mus, Chattanooga; ASCA Ann, NY; Central South Exhib, Nashville. *Pos:* Docent, Masterworks & Jacksonian Exhib, Tenn State Mus, Nashville; gallery supv, pres, Nashville Artists Guild. *Teaching:* Instr art, elem & high sch. *Awards:* 1st & 2nd Place & Best Show, Murfreesboro Art League; League 3, Juror Award, Tenn Watercolor Soc; Am Soc Contemp Artists; Nat Asn Women Artist; Central South. *Bibliog:* Clinton Confehr (auth), Acquisition of art, Daily News J, 92; Arlyn Ende (auth), Visual impressions, Daily News J, 93; Susan Knowles (auth), Art in recovery, Nashville Scene, 93; NY Times, Art Review, 2002; Daily News J, 2004-2005. *Mem:* Nashville Artist Guild (pres, 94-95); Nat Asn Women Artists; Am Soc Contemp Artists; Tenn Asn Craft Artists; Tenn Watercolor Soc. *Media:* Mixed Media, Sculpture. *Dealer:* Midtown Gallery Nashville TN. *Mailing Add:* 2211 Shannon Dr Murfreesboro TN 37129

JOHNSON, EUGENE JOSEPH
HISTORIAN
b Memphis, Tenn, May 22, 1937. *Study:* Williams Col, BA, 59; NY Univ, MA, 63, PhD, 70. *Teaching:* Prof art, Williams Col, Williamstown, Mass, 65-, chmn art dept, 78-80, 90-91. *Mem:* Soc Archit Hist; Renaissance Soc Am. *Publ:* Auth, S Andrea in Mantua, the Building History, 75; Charles Moore, Building & Prog, 86; coauth, Memphis: Archit Guide, 90; coauth, Drawn from the Source, The Travel Sketches of Louis I Kahn, 96. *Mailing Add:* Williams Coll Dept Art 15 Lawrence Hall Dr Williamstown MA 01267-2607

JOHNSON, GUY
PAINTER
b Fort Wayne, Ind, 1927. *Study:* Fla State Univ, MA, 52. *Exhib:* Solo exhibs include Hundred Acres Gallery, NY, 71 & 72, Gallerie Fabian Carlsson, Gothenberg, Sweden, 74, Stefanatti Gallery, NY, 74, Basel Int Art Exhib, Switz, 78, Galerie d'endt, Amsterdam, The Neth, 78 & Galerie Arenthon, Paris, 89, Louis K Meisel Gallery, 79, 83, 85, 87, 88, 89, 90, and 2007; group exhibs include Tomasulo Gallery, Union Col, Cranford, NJ, 85; Art in the Armory, NY, 88; Trains and Planes: The Influence of Locomotion in Am Painting, traveling exhib, 89-90; 79th Ann Exhib, Maier Mus Art, Randolph-Macon Women's Col, Lynchburg, Va, 90. *Teaching:* Murray State Univ, Ky, 53-56, Lee Col, Tex, 56-63, Univ Bridgeport, Conn, 64-68. *Bibliog:* Jose Pierre (auth), Guy Johnson, Editions Pilipacchi, 88; John L Ward (auth), American Realist Paintings 1945-1980, UMI Res Press, 89; Chiong Yiao Chen (auth), A small bite of the Big Apple - Small-scale works of art from New York galleries, Maier Mus Art, Randolph-Macon Women's Col, 90. *Publ:* Les Hyperrealistes Am, Eds Filipacchi, Paris, France, 73; Superrealism, E P Dutton, Co, New York, 75; Superrealist Painting and Sculpture, William Morrow Co, New York, 80; Cover illus, Harper's 5/87; American Realist Painting 1945-1980, UMI Res, Inc, Chicago, 88. *Mailing Add:* c/o Louis K Meisel 141 Prince St New York NY 10012

JOHNSON, HOMER
EDUCATOR, PAINTER
b Buffalo, NY, Dec 24, 1925. *Study:* Pa Acad Fine Arts with Julius Bloch & Hobson Pittman, 46-52; Studies at Balkan Bridges to Peace, Kragujevac, Serbia, 2002. *Work:* Butler Inst Am Art, Youngstown, Ohio; Smith, Kline & French Labs, Philadelphia; Pa Acad Fine Arts. *Exhib:* Pa Acad Fine Arts Regional; W Village Meeting House, Brattleboro, VT, 88; Artists House, Philadelphia, 93 & 95; Atlantic Community Col, 96; Southern Vt Art Ctr, 96; Main Line Unitarian Church, Devon, Pa, 99; The Hill Sch, Pottstown, Pa, 2000; Exhibs, S Vt Art Gallery, Windham Art Gallery, Brattleboro, Vt & Philadelphia Sketch Club, 2000-2005. *Teaching:* Instr, Pa Acad Fine Arts & Fleisher Art Mem. *Awards:* Purchase Prize, Am Watercolor Soc, 72; First Prize Aqueous Media, Philadelphia Watercolor Club, 79; Percy Owens Award, Distinguished Pa Artist, 93; Dene M Louchheim Fac Fel, Fleisher Art Mem, 95; Crest Award, Philadelphia Watercolor Club, 97. *Mem:* Am Watercolor Soc. *Media:* Watercolor, Acrylic. *Dealer:* Artists House Gallery Philadelphia PA 19106

JOHNSON, J STEWART
CURATOR, CONSULTANT
b Baltimore, Md, Aug 31, 1925. *Study:* Swarthmore Col, BA; Univ Del, Winterthur Prog in Early Am Cult, MA; Harvard Univ, Loeb Fel. *Pos:* Cur decorative arts, Newark Mus, 64-68; cur decorative arts, Brooklyn Mus, 68-73, vice dir collections, 70-72; consult contemp glass, Corning Mus Glass, 73-74; cur decorative arts, Cooper-Hewitt Mus Design, 75-76; cur design, Mus Mod Art, New York, 76-86; Consult design & archit, Dept 20th Century Art, Metrop Mus Art, 90-. *Teaching:* Boston Univ, 86-87; FIT, 88-90. *Mem:* Victorian Soc Am (pres, 66-69); Am Friends of Attingham Park (pres, 80-83). *Publ:* Auth, Eileen Gray: Designer, 79; The Modern American Poster, 83. *Mailing Add:* Dept Twentieth Century Art Metrop Mus Art 1000 5th Ave New York NY 10028-0198

JOHNSON, JAMES ALAN
GRAPHIC ARTIST, EDUCATOR
b Malden, Mass, Apr 2, 1945. *Study:* Mass Coll Art, Boston, BFA, 67; Wash State Univ, Pullman, MFA, 70. *Work:* Denver Art Mus, Colo; Minneapolis Mus Fine Arts; Mus Mod Art, New York; Chicago Art Inst; San Francisco Art Inst. *Exhib:* Artist Book Works, Chicago, 90; Multiples, Nexus Gallery, Atlanta, 90; CAGE Gallery, Cincinnati, 91; Walker's Point Ctr Arts, Milwaukee, 93; First Sightings Recent Mod & Contemp Acquisitions, Denver Art Mus, 93; 34d Ann NY Digital Salon (with catalog), Sch Vis Arts, 95; Options 1, Denver Art Mus, 96; The View from Denver (with catalog), Mus Moderner Kunststiftung, Ludwig Wien, Vienna, Austria, 97; Strong Words: Art, Text and Lang, Arvada Ctr Arts & Humanities, Arvada, Colo, 98; Denver Art Mus, 98-2000 & 2004; Dairy Ctr Arts, Boulder, Colo, 2001; Boulder Mus Continental Art, Colo, 2003; CU Art Mus, Boulder, Colo, 2006; Mus Continental Art, Denver, 2006. *Teaching:* Instr graphics, dept archit, Wash State Univ, Pullman, 70; asst prof painting & drawing, Univ Colo, Boulder, 70-78, assoc prof, 78-95, assoc chmn, 88-91, prof, 95-, chmn, dept fine arts, 2002-, dir, Ctr Arts, Media, Performance, Atlas Inst, 2005-2007. *Bibliog:* The View From Denver, Mus Moderner Kunst Stiftung, Ludwig, Vienna, 97; Preble, Preble & Frank, Art Forms, Prentice Hall, 2001; Peter Lang (auth), Elizabeth Menon, Images & Imagery, Web Installation Art, New York, 2005. *Media:* All Media. *Publ:* Auth, A Thousand Words, Boulder, 91; Words on Works, Leonardo, Vol 25, No 1, 92; Loose Watch, Invisible Bks, London, 98; Aurora A-Z, Denver, 2005; Magic Squares 1-9, Denver, 2007. *Dealer:* Printed Matter Inc 535 W 22nd St New York NY 10011. *Mailing Add:* Fine Arts Dept Univ Colo Campus Box 318 Boulder CO 80309

JOHNSON, JOYCE
WRITER, SCULPTOR
b Newton, Mass, July 12, 1929. *Study:* Escuela de Artes Oficios y Tecnicos, Madrid, Spain, with Don Ramon Mateu, cert; Sch of Mus Fine Arts, Boston, with Harold Tovish & Oscar Jespers, cert, grad fel. *Work:* Cushing Acad, Ashburnham, Mass; Cape Cod Conserv, Barnstable, Mass; Provincetown Art Asn & Mus; Habitat, Belmont, Mass; de Cordova Mus, Lincoln, MA; Cape Mus of Fine Arts, Dennis, MA. *Comn:* Sculpture, Botanical Gardens, Cornwall, Eng, 85; High Head, Commemorative Plaque, 89. *Exhib:* Solo exhibs, Annhurst Col, South Woodstock, Conn, 74 & Cape Cod Conserv, 83, 85 & 86; 20-Year Retrospective, Wellfleet Art Gallery, Mass, 77; Art in Transition--A Century of the Mus Sch, Mus Fine Arts, Boston, 77; Cape Mus, 88, 91 & 92; Chandler Gallery, 88-91; Addison Art Gallery, 96-; Central Conn State Univ, 97; Forest Hills Cemetery 150th ann, sculpture show, 98-; Forest Lawn Cemetery, 100th ann, Buffalo, NY, 99-; Retrospective: Cape Cod Mus of Art Dennis MA, 2005; Prinvincetown Art Asn & Mus, 2008. *Pos:* Asst dir, Beaupre Arts Ctr, Stockbridge, Mass, 59-62; dir-founder, Nauset Sch Sculpture, North Eastham, Mass, 68-71; dir & founder, Truro Ctr for the Arts, Mass, 72-94; trustee, Lower Cape Arts Coun, 84-88; writer, Cape Codder Newspaper, retired, 2000; founder-Mem, Peaked Hill Trust to Save Dune Shacks, 85; founder, Outer Cape Artists Residency Consortium, 95; Exhib Comt, Provincetown Art Asn & Mus, 95-00; Steering Comt, Campus Provincetown and Highland Ctr, Cape Cod Nat Seashore, 99-; Oral Hist Prog on Pub Radio WOMR-FM, Sands of Time, 85-. *Teaching:* Instr sculpture from life, Cape Cod Conserv, Barnstable, Mass, 73-87, Truro Ctr for the Arts, Truro, Mass, 74- & Provincetown Mus Sch, 83-89. *Awards:* First Prize Pictorial Photograph, New Eng Press Assoc, 85; First Prize Sculpture, New Eng Ann, Cape Cod Art Asn, 91; Living Treasure Award, Cape Cod Women Creating, 97; voted, Truro Treasure, Town of Truro, 2008. *Bibliog:* Articles in Cape Arts, Cape Codder, Cape Cod Times & Boston Globe, 72-94. *Mem:* Provincetown Art Asn (trustee, 76-78); Castle Hill; Cape Cod Mus, Dennis. *Media:* Wood Carving, Clay. *Specialty:* Fine Arts. *Interests:* History, Photography. *Publ:* Joyce Johnson Cape Cod Arts, 2001; Truro Center for the Arts-30th Anniversary The Cape Codders, July 11, 2001; Listed in Who's Who in American Art and Who's Who in Women since 1978; and many others. *Dealer:* Addison Gallery 45 S Orleans Rd Orleans MA 02653. *Mailing Add:* PO Box 201 Truro MA 02666

JOHNSON, K CARLTON
PAINTER, PRINTMAKER
b Laurium, Mich, Feb 14, 1948. *Study:* Coll of William & Mary, BA (fine arts), 70; Corcoran Sch of Art, 70; Evenston Artists League, Evanston, Ill, 77. *Work:* Mich Tech Univ Dept of Humanities, Houghton, Mich; Bay Coll, Escanaba, Mich; Dept of Educ, Ctrl Mich Univ, Mt Pleasant, Mich; Am Acad of Rome, Italy; Anderson Ctr, Red Wing, Minn; Saginaw Art Mus, Saginaw, Mich. *Exhib:* Solo exhibs, New Work on Paper, Omphale Gallery, 2004; Group exhib, 50th Ann Show, Neveille Pub Mus, 92; Art Gallery, Acadia Univ, Nova Scotia, Can, 2001; Int Invitational, Anderson Ctr, Red Wing Minn, 2005; Artists in the UP, DeVos Art Mus, Northern Mich Univ, 2006; 2007 Mich Fine Arts Competition, Birmingham Bloomfield Art Ctr, 2007; Clara M Eagle Gallery, Murray State Univ, Murray, Ky, 2008; 12th Ann Open Competition, Alfred Berkowitz Gallery, Univ Mich Dearborn, 2008; 2nd Ann Upper Midwest Juried Art Exhib, DeVos Mus, Northern Mich Univ, 2009. *Teaching:* drawing, Lake Linden Schools, 80-2000; drawing, Ojibway Community Coll, 2005-2006; instr, Drawing, Calumet Art Ctr. *Awards:* Mich Coun for the Arts Grant, Mich, 99. *Mem:* MAPC. *Media:* Painting on Canvas, Works on Paper. *Res:* Local Artists of the Keweenaw. *Publ:* Keweenaw Artist Peder Gordon Kitt (1918-2004), Superwi Signal, Aug 2009; Alice Mann Renolds (1908-1999), Preserved the Keweenaw Art, Superwi Signal, Aug 2007; Copper Country Assoc Artists, 1959-2009, Rockland House Press, 2010. *Dealer:* Michigamme Moonshine Art Gallery 136 East Main Michigamme MI 49861; Ed Gray Gallery Calumet MI

JOHNSON, KAYTIE
CURATOR
b San Francisco, July 26, 1964. *Study:* Ariz State Univ, BA, 87; Ariz State Univ, MA, 01. *Exhib:* Leaving Aztlan, 2005; DePauw Biennial, 2005, 2007; Borderabilia & Mus Globalized Other, 2005; Sally Heller: Material Minutiae, 2005; Skirting the Line: Conceptual Drawing, 2006; Chuck Ramirez, Deeply Superficial, 2006; Diana Al-Hadid, Pangaea's Blanket, 2006; The Logic of Place, Yuki Nakamura, 2007; Kevin McCarty, I'm Not Like You, 2007; David Herel, Babes in the Woods, 2007; Jen Liu, An innocent Revolution, 2007; Zoe Straus, Work in Progress, 2008; Andy Warhol, Faces & Names, 2008; Felipe Dylzaides, Nothing Happens, Twke, 2008; White Noise, 2009; Chris Gentile, Always in the Sun, 2009; Terence Hannum, New Rites, 2010. *Pos:* Dir & cur, Univ Galleries, Mus, Collections, DePauw Univ, 2002-. *Mem:* Asn Latin Am Art; Am Asn Mus. *Res:* Contemp art. *Publ:* Contemporary Chicana and Chicano Art: Artists, Works, Culture and Education, Bilingual Rev/Press, 02; St. James Guide to Hispanic Artists: Profiles of Latino and Latin American Artists, Bilingual Rev/Press, 02. *Mailing Add:* DePauw Univ Richard E Peeler Art Center 10 W Hanna St Greencastle IN 46135

JOHNSON, LEE
PAINTER, EDUCATOR
b Albion, Nebr, Nov 9, 1935. *Study:* Minneapolis Coll Art & Design, BFA; Skowhegan Sch Painting & Sculpture, with Alex Katz; Univ NMex, MA. *Work:* Denver Art Mus, Colo; Roswell Mus & Art Ctr, Roswell, NMex; Mus of NMex, Fine Arts, Santa Fe; Jonson Gallery, Univ NMex, Albuquerque, NMex; and others. *Exhib:* 1st Ann Painting Invitational, Mus NMex, 68; Masterpieces from the Mus of NMex, McNay Art Inst, San Antonio, Tex, 70; Five Artists from Colo Traveling Exhib, Rocky Mountain Coun Arts, 71-72; Rocky Mountain Coun Arts Traveling Exhib, Eight Western States, 72; 8 West Biennial, Grand Junction, Colo, 72-74; solo exhib, Western Ctr Arts, Grand Junction, Colo, 96; ARSC Traveling Exhib, Sic Univs & Colls, 1999-2001. *Pos:* Asst dir-cur, Roswell Mus & Art Ctr, NMex, 62-68; dir, Gunnison Coun on Arts & Humanities, Colo, 73-75. *Teaching:* Instr drawing & painting, Eastern NMex Univ, Roswell, 62-67; asst prof drawing & painting, Western State Col, Gunnison, Colo, 68-81, prof art, 84. *Awards:* First Prize Painting, 8 West Biennial, W Co Art Ctr, 74; Artist-in-Residence Grant, Roswell Mus & Art Ctr, 75. *Mem:* Mid-Am Coll Art Asn; Coll Art Asn. *Media:* Acrylic, Watercolor. *Mailing Add:* Dept Art Quigley Hall 101 Western State Coll Colorado Gunnison CO 81231

JOHNSON, LESTER L
PAINTER, EDUCATOR
b Detroit, Mich, Sept 28, 1937. *Study:* Univ Mich, BFA, 73, MFA, 74. *Work:* Detroit Inst Arts; Osaka Univ Arts, Japan; St Paul Co, Minn; The Tougaloo Coll Art Collections, Miss; Univ Mich Mus Art; Fed Res Bank Chicago-Detroit Br; Univ Mich, Cardiovascular Center, Ann Arbor; DANA-FARBER Cancer Inst, Boston, Mass. *Comn:* Martin Luther King Community Ctr, Holtzman and Silverman Companies, Farmington Hills, 82; Bishop Int Airport, Flint, 94. *Exhib:* Art for Technology: A Reunion of Mural Artists, Martin Luther King Neighborhood Network, Detroit, 2000; Appreciation and Insight, Nicolet Area Technical Coll, Rhinelander, Wis, 2001; A Cult Heritage: Selected Works of African Am Art From the DIA's Collection, Detroit Inst of Arts, 2001; Intercambio 2001, Centro de Memoria e Cult dos Correios, Salvador, Brazil; Jordan Road Gallery, Sedona, Ariz, 2003; Reverberations, Contemp Art by African-Amerian Artists of Southeastern Mich, Klemm Gallery, Siena Heights Univ, Adrian, 2004; Pluperfect Plural, Buckham Gallery, Flint, 2005. *Pos:* Participant dept, art and art hist 3d Annual African Am Lecture Series, Wayne State Univ, 2000, int conference on African Influences in the Visual Arts of the Ams, 2001. *Teaching:* Prof drawing & painting, Coll for Creative Studies, Coll Art & Design, 75-. *Awards:* Andrew W Mellon Found Proj Res/Travel Grant, 82 & 84; Mus African-Am Hist, 83; Recognition Award, African-Am Music Festival,90

JOHNSON, LINDA K
ART EDUCATOR, ADMINISTRATOR, WRITER
Study: Univ Houston, BFA (Graphic Communication), 1980; Va Commonwealth Univ, MFA (Visual Communications), 1984. *Exhib:* International exhibitions include: Turning the Page International Books Arts Exhibition, Honolulu Printmakers, 1996, Nexus Press Atlanta Book Prize, Atlanta, Georgia, 2000, Transactions, Eastern Edge Gallery, Saint Johns, Canada, 2001, Art of the Book '03, Canadian Bookbinders and Book Artist Guild, Canada, 2003-2005, Works with Paper: Artists' Books, Univ Art Gallery, Univ of the South, Tennessee, 2006-2007, The Story is The Thing, ACT Writers Centre, Gorman House Arts Centre, Australia, 2010, Canadian Book Arts and Bookbinding, Canada, 2013-2014 and many others; National juried exhibitions include: Collection of Artist Books, Cambridge Artist Cooperative, 1997, Storytelling, Minn Ctr for Book Arts, 1998-1999, Small Sanctuaries, Oregon Book Arts Guild, Sixth Book Biennial Show, 2000, Artist Made Books, Buddy Holly Ctr, Texas, 2003, An Open Book Art Exhibit, Cuyahoga Community Col, Ohio, 2004, Imagine That, La Jolla Fiber Arts, 2004 and several others; Solo exhibitions include: Women's Studio Workshop, Rosendale, NY, 1997; Regional juried exhibitions include: Florida Artists' Book Prize, Bienes Ctr for the Literary Arts, Fort Lauderdale, 1998, 1999, 2001-2009, 2012; Invitational exhibitions include: Van Goghs Ear and Other Art Stories, Faculty Exhibition, Purdue Univ, 1996, Pyramid Atlantic Sixth Book Arts Fair, The Corcoran Gallery of Art, Washington, DC, 1999, Art Basel: Florida Atlantic Univ Faculty Exhibition, The Living Room Gallery, Design District, Miami, 2003, Women Outside Design 2, Second Avenue Studio Gallery, Fort Lauderdale, 2009, The SMART Ride Art Exhibit, 2011, Book Arts as Art Forum, Univ Mary Washington, Virginia, 2013 and many others. *Collection Arranged:* Resides in public and private collections including Tate Britain, Nat Mus of Women in the Arts, Harvard Univ, Yale Univ, UCLA, Sackner Archives of Concrete and Visual Poetry, Art on Paper, Art Inst of Chgo, Reed Col, NY Public Library, and many others. *Pos:* Invited speaker in the field. *Teaching:* Adj prof, communications arts & design dept, Va Commonwealth Univ, 1993-95, asst prof, visual and performing arts dept, Purdue Univ, 1995-97, asst prof, graphic design, dept of visual arts and art history, Dorothy F Schmidt Col of Arts and Letters, Fort Lauderdale, Fla, Fla Atlantic Univ, 1997-2000, assoc prof, 2000-2007, prof, 2007, dept chair, prof, 2008-2012, interim assoc dean, 2012-. *Awards:* Nat Mus for Women in the Arts Book Artist Fellowship; Fla Artists' Book prize. *Mem:* The Ctr for the Book, Col Book Arts Asn, Canadian Bookbinders and Book Artist Guild, Guild of Bookworkers. *Publ:* Work is included in several publications and catalogs. *Mailing Add:* 111 E Las Olas AT 317 Fort Lauderdale FL 33301

JOHNSON, LOIS MARLENE
PRINTMAKER, EDUCATOR
b Grand Forks, NDak, Nov 17, 1942. *Study:* Univ NDak, BS, 64; Univ Wis-Madison, MFA, 66. *Work:* Philadelphia Mus Art; Elvehjem Art Ctr, Madison; McCray Gallery, Univ NMex, Albuquerque; Univ NDak, Grand Forks; Adolph Behn Mem Collection, NY. *Comn:* Poster, Philadelphia Mus Art, 72. *Exhib:* Soc Am Graphic Artists, NY, 65-67, 70 & 71; Northwest Printmakers Int, Seattle, 68; Am Color Print Soc, 68-72; Silk Screen, Philadelphia Mus Art, 72; 18th Biennial Exhib, Brooklyn Mus, NY, 72; and others. *Teaching:* From asst prof to assoc prof printmaking & chmn dept, Philadelphia Col Art, 67-. *Awards:* Abraham Hankins Award, Am Color Print Soc, 68; Award, Prints in Pa, 69; Eyre Medal, Philadelphia Watercolor Club, 71. *Mem:* Print Club; Am Color Print Soc (coun, 68-72); Philadelphia Watercolor Club (bd dir, 72); Soc Am Graphic Artists; Philadelphia Art Alliance. *Media:* Intaglio, Silkscreen. *Publ:* Contribr, Artist proof, Pratt Graphic Ctr, 67. *Dealer:* The Print Club 1614 Latimer St Philadelphia PA 19102

JOHNSON, MARK M
MUSEUM DIRECTOR
b Rochester, Minn, Dec 10, 1950. *Study:* Univ Wis, Whitewater, BA (art hist), 1974; Univ Ill, Urbana-Champaign, MA (art hist) & cert arts mus studies, 1976. *Collection Arranged:* Idea to Image: Preparatory Studies from the Renaissance to Impressionism (auth, catalog), Cleveland Mus Art, 1980; Japanese Woodblock Prints: Themes &

Techniques, Cleveland Mus Art, 1980; Photographs by Yousuf Karsh, traveling, 1987-98; Am Drawing Biennial, Muscarelle Mus Art, Va, 1988, 1990, 1992 & 1994; King William's Praise: Romeyn de Hooghe's Etchings of William III (auth, catalog), Muscarelle Mus Art, Va, 1989; Literacy through Art (auth, catalog), Muscarelle Mus Art, 1990; Contemp Abstract Painting: Resnick, Reed, Laufer & Moore, Muscarelle Mus Art, 1991; Contemp Inuit Drawings, Muscarelle Mus Art, Va, 1993; Nissan Engel: Nouvelles Dimensions (auth, catalog), Muscarelle Mus Art, Va, 1994; Hans Grohs: An Ecstatic Vision (auth, catalog), Montgomery Mus Fine Arts, 1996; After History: The Paintings of David Bierk (auth, catalog), Montgomery Mus Fine Arts, 2000; Ginny Ruffner (auth, catalog), Montgomery Mus Fine Arts (traveling), 2003-05; Am Painting Collection (auth, catalog), Montgomery Mus Fine Arts, 2006; Sonja Blomdahl (auth, catalog), Montgomery Mus Fine Arts, traveling exhib, 2007-2008; Ala Quits, Montgomery Mus Fine Arts, 2009; Edgar Soberon, Montgomery Mus Fine Arts, 2010; Stephen Rolfe Powell, Montgomery Mus Fine Arts, 2012. *Pos:* Lectr mus ed, Art Inst Chicago, 1976-77; cur art hist, Cleveland Mus Art, 1977-81; asst dir & cur Europe painting, Krannert Art Mus, Ill, 1981-85; dir, Muscarelle Mus Art, Va, 1985-94, Montgomery Mus Fine Arts, Ala, 1994-. *Teaching:* Instr art hist, Cuyahoga Coll, Cleveland, 1977-81; instr mus studies, Univ Ill, Urbana-Champaign, 1981-85 & Auburn Univ, Montgomery, 1995-2005; instr art hist & mus studies, Coll William & Mary, 1985-94. *Awards:* Numerous grants for mus opers, conserv, exhibs, res, educ & mus studies. *Mem:* Am Asn Mus; Coll Art Asn; Nat Art Educ Asn; Asn Art Mus Dirs; Int Coun Mus. *Mailing Add:* Montgomery Mus Fine Arts PO Box 230819 Montgomery AL 36123-0819

JOHNSON, MARTIN BRIAN
ASSEMBLAGE ARTIST, PAINTER
b Elmer, NJ, 1951. *Study:* Va Tech, B Arch, 74, Univ NC, Chapel Hill, MFA, 77. *Work:* Ball State Univ, Muncie, Ind; The Vogel Collection, Nat Gallery Art, Washington, DC; Chrysler Mus, Norfolk, Va; Nat Gallery Art, DC; Birmington Mus Art, Ala; Ark Art Ctr, Little Rock, Ark; Yellowstone Art Mus, Montana; Montclair Art Mus, NJ; Pa Acad Fine Arts; Dallas Mus Fine Art; Va Mus Fine Art; Miami Art Mus, Fla; Yale Univ Art Gallery, Conn; and many more. *Exhib:* Pleady Entreaty, Va Mus Fine Arts, Richmond, 90; Hesheunisallforone (44 4 x 4S 30 part), Southeastern Ctr Contemp Art, Winston Salem, NC, 92; Forty-Four Four by Fours, Art Mus Western Va, Roanoke, Va, 94; New Works Fellowships (with catalog), City Gallery Contemp Art, Raleigh, NC & Arlington Mus Art, Tex, 94; Cheekwood Mus Art, Nashville, Tenn, 95; Nexus Contemp Art Ctr, Atlanta, Ga; Forinstance Gallery, Richmond, Va, 2005-2009; Forward, Visual Arts Ctr, Richmond, Va, 2011; For Insance: The Art of Martin Johnson, Tauban Mus, Roanoke, Va, 2014. *Pos:* Owner, Forinstance Gallery, Richmond, Va. *Awards:* Northern Telecom Fel, City Gallery Contemp Art, Raleigh, NC, 93. *Bibliog:* Allan Schwartzman (auth), article, Arts Mag, 1/80; Donald B Kuspit (auth), articles, Art Am, 9/83, Artforum, 5/85; Linda McGreevy (auth), article, Arts Mag, 5/88. *Media:* Gesture, Oeuvre. *Specialty:* The Lifetime Oeuvre Evolution of Martin Johnson's Process. *Interests:* Jazz, food, eternity. *Publ:* Herb & Dorothy 50x50. *Dealer:* Forinstance Gallery 107 E Cary St Richmond VA 23219. *Mailing Add:* 424 N 25th St Richmond VA 23223

JOHNSON, MIANI
DEALER, CONSULTANT
b New York, NY, July 14, 1948. *Study:* Barnard Col, BA. *Pos:* Dir, Willard Gallery, currently. *Media:* All. *Specialty:* Contemp painting & sculpture. *Interests:* Chinese contemp calligraphy, ink painting. *Mailing Add:* c/o Willard Gallery 12 E 12 St New York NY 10003

JOHNSON, RASHID
PHOTOGRAHER
b Chicago, 1977. *Study:* Columbia Col, BA, 2000. *Exhib:* Solo exhibs, The Dead Lecturer: Laboratory, Dojo, and Performance Space, Power House Memphis, 2009, Smoke and Mirrors, Sculpture Center, Long Island City, NY, 2009, Other Aspects, David Kordansky Gallery, Los Angeles, 2000, Our Kind of People, Salon 94, NY, 2010, There are Stronger Villages, Galerie Guido W Baudach, Berlin, 2010, Between Nothingness and Eternity, Carlson/Massimo De Carlo, London, 2010, 25 days after October, Massimo De Carlo, Milan, 2010, Mus Contemporary Art, Chicago, 2011, Miami Mus Art, 2012, High Mus Art, Atlanta, 2012, Kemper Art Mus, St. Louis, 2012; group exhibs, Lush Life, Lehmann Maupin, NY, 2010, 30 Americans, The Rubell Family Collection, NC Mus of Art, Raleigh, 2011, Corcoran Gallery Art, Washington, DC, 2011, Becoming: Photography from the Wedge Collection, The Nasher Mus Art, Duke Univ, 2011, With one color, Van de Weghe Fine Art, NY, 2011, American Exuberance, Rubell Family Collection, Miami, 2011, 54th Int Art Exhib Biennale, Venice, 2011. *Awards:* David C. Driskell prize, High Mus Art, Atlanta, Ga, 2012. *Mailing Add:* c/o Richard Gray Gallery 4th Floor 1018 Madison Ave New York NY 10075

JOHNSON, RICHARD WALTER
PAINTER, SCULPTOR
b Glen Cove, NY, Aug 11, 1946. *Study:* State Univ NY, Oneonta, BA, 72; State Univ NY, Albany, MA, 76. *Work:* Fla Atlantic Univ; State Univ NY, Albany; Woodbull Arts, Milford, NY. *Comn:* Contemp Fine Arts, Mus Oronta, NY. *Exhib:* Sculpture Now, Gallery 151, Palm Beach, Fla, 86; Steel & Iron, John Lavine Gallery, Palm Beach, 87; New Sculpture, Eugenia Palacios Gallery, Palm Beach, 94; Steel Forms, Florence Gallery, Palm Beach, 95; Steel in Focus, Woodbull Art Ctr, Milford, NY; Bobby Sharp Gallery, Oneonta, NY, 09; Christina Varga Gallery, Woodstock, NY, 09; Tread Well Mus Fine Arts, Tread Well, NY; Fine Art Ranch, Markland, NY. *Collection Arranged:* Art Inc, Palm Beach, Fla; Ivan Karp Collection, NYC; Blackwood Sculpture Space, Maryland, NY. *Pos:* Founder, Bear Trap School, Fla, 80-; sculptor in residence, Ground Zero Sculpture Park, 93-. *Teaching:* Vis prof, sculpture, Vero Beach Ctr Arts, Fla, 2000; vis instr, Glimmer Glass Creative Learning Ctr, Cooperstown, NY, 2006. *Awards:* Key Bank Award, 84; Sculpture Award, NY State Fair, 93; Sculptor in Residence, Blackwood Sculpture Space, Maryland, NY, 2005. *Bibliog:* Les Krantz (auth), American artists, Am References, 90, NY Art rev, 91. *Mem:* Cooperstown Art Asn; Upper Catskill Art Asn; Int Sculpture Ctr. *Dealer:* Jillian Bos Cooperstown NY. *Mailing Add:* 217 Leonard Rd Maryland NY 12116-2307

JOHNSON, ROBERT FLYNN
CURATOR, HISTORIAN
b Jersey City, NJ, Mar 20, 1948. *Pos:* Cur asst, Worcester Art Mus, Mass, summer 72; asst cur prints & drawings, Baltimore Mus Art, 73-75; cur in chg, Achenbach Found Graphic Arts, Fine Arts Mus San Francisco, 75-. *Teaching:* San Francisco Art Inst, 81. *Awards:* Nat Endowment Arts Fel, 75. *Mem:* Print Coun Am; Print & Drawing Soc of Baltimore Mus Art (vpres, 74-75); Bay Area Graphic Arts Coun (adv). *Res:* American prints of the 19th and 20th century; 19th century French drawings. *Publ:* Auth, American Prints, 1870-1950, Univ Chicago Press, 76; Lucian Freud Works on Paper, Thames & Hudson, 89. *Mailing Add:* 126 20th Ave San Francisco CA 94121-1308

JOHNSON, RONALD W
HISTORIAN, EDUCATOR
b Rockford, Ill, July, 29, 1937. *Study:* Calif State Univ, San Diego, BA, 59 & MA, 63; Univ Calif, Berkeley, MA (hist art), 65 & PhD (hist art), 71. *Teaching:* Asst prof hist art, Univ Iowa, Iowa City, 70-73; prof hist art, Humboldt State Univ, Arcata, Calif, 73; vis instr hist art, Univ Calif, San Diego, 76; vis instr hist art, Univ Calif, Berkeley, 81. *Mem:* Coll Art Asn Am. *Res:* Picasso's and late 19th century art; emphasizing conceptual relationships between art and poetry. *Publ:* Auth, Picasso's old guitarist and the symbolist sensibility, Artforum, 12/74; Dante Rossetti's Beata Beatrix and the new life, Art Bulletin, 12/75; Poetic pathways to Dada: Marcel Duchamp & Jules Laforgue, 5/76, Vincent van Gogh and the vernacular: His southern accent, 6/78 & Picasso's Demoiselles d'Avignon and the theatre of the absurd, 10/80, Arts. *Mailing Add:* Humboldt State Univ Dept Art Arcata CA 95521

JOHNSON, TILLIAN
PAINTER, EDUCATOR
b. New York, NY, 50. *Study:* Sch Visual Arts, BFA, 72, MFA, 76. *Work:* Mus Mod Art, NY; Whitney Art Mus, NY; Atlantic City Art Ctr, Atlantic City, NJ; Garden State Discovery Mus, Cherry Hill, NJ. *Exhib:* Solo exhibs, Rider Univ, NJ State Mus, Temple Univ, Mary Mac Gallery, Stockton Univ, Montclair State Univ, Monmouth Univ; Port Hist Mus; Pa State Univ; Lancaster Art Mus; Lora Lifeland Mus; Smithsonian Art Mus; Morris Mus. *Pos:* artist on campus, Pa State Univ; artist-at-large, NJ State Asn; founder, Meriks Art Ctr, 2000-2012, Meriks Gallery, 2013-. *Teaching:* instr painting, Rutgers Univ, 2000-2012, prof emer, 2012-; adj prof, Univ Ariz; workshop instr, Allaet High Sch Dist. *Awards:* Best in Show, Meriks Art Ctr, 2013. *Res:* African American Art. *Interests:* Taxidermy, Salmon fishing, Travel, Gardening. *Collection:* Andy Warhol, Vincent Van Gogh. *Publ:* Auth, Painting Your Way to Love, UP Press, 2000; auth, What Color Are You?, Ariz Gazette, 6/24/2001; auth, He vs She: The Paintoff, 2005; auth, Your True Colors, 2009, vol 2, 2016; coauth, Let Your Visions Shine Through the Canvas, 2015

JOHNSTON, BARRY WOODS
SCULPTOR
b Florence, Ala. *Study:* Ga Inst Technol, B (arch), 69; Art Students League, with Joseph De Creeft; Pa Acad Fine Arts, with Walker Hancock, Harry Rosen & Tony Greenwood; Nat Acad Fine Arts, with Michael Lantz; also studied in Italy, with Enzo Cardini & Madame Simi. *Work:* The Vatican Mus, Rome; Martin Luther King Libr, Georgetown Univ & Lutheran Church Reformation, Washington, DC; CBN Univ, Va. *Comn:* Medal, Ann Letelier Moffitt Award, Inst Policy Studies, Washington, DC; Journey to Jerusalem, US Citizens Cong, Washington, DC; lobby centerpiece, Fentress Cancer Ctr, Hillside Methodist Hosp, Waco, Tex; Sen Sparkman bust, C of C, Hartsell, Ala; Wedlock (sculpture), Lafayette Ctr, Washington, DC; Mariner, Hampton, Va; Mother & Child, Evanston, Ill. *Exhib:* Solo exhibs, St John's Church, 75, George Washington Univ Libr, 76, Folger Shakespeare Libr, 79, Washington, DC & City Hall, Hampton, Va, 86, Columbia Art Ctr, 93, Md Fedn of Art Gallery on the Circle, Annapolis, 95, Mulligan Gallery, Virginia Beach, Va, 95, Worldwide Gallery, Atlanta, 95, James A Michener Art Mus, Doylestown, Pa, 99; Four Realists, Foundry, Georgetown, 76; Nat Sculpture Soc Ann Group Show, NY, 80-86; Martin Luther King Libr, 83; Allied Artists Am Exhib, NY, 86; Centre Int D'Arte Contemporian, Paris, France, 86; Arts Festival, Castello di Besozzo, Italy, 86; Bucca di Magra, Massa, Italy, 87. *Awards:* Second Prize for Figurative Sculpture, Ga Marble Fest, 83; Pres Award Nat Arts Club Ann, 94; Cassidy Meml Award, Salmagundi Club, 98. *Mem:* Nat Sculpture Soc; Founder, Art For Humanity Found (pres, 78-81); Am Medallic Sculpture Asn. *Media:* Clay, Bronze. *Publ:* Auth, articles in Sculpture Rev, winter 85-86 & spring 86, Sculptor's Int, vol 3, 84 & spring 86. *Mailing Add:* 2423 Pickwick Rd Gwynn Oak MD 21207-6635

JOHNSTON, RANDY JAMES
CERAMIST, SCULPTOR
b Austin, Tex, 1950. *Study:* Univ Minn, Minneapolis, BFA (studio art), 72; studied with Tatsuzo Shimaoka Mashiko, Japan, 75; Southern Ill Univ, Edwardsville, MFA, 90. *Work:* Dustin & Lisa Hoffman, Los Angeles; Univ Art Mus, Ariz State Univ, Tempe; Univ Art Mus, Univ Minn, Minneapolis; Burke Found, NY; Banff Sch Art, Alberta, Can; Minneapolis Inst Arts, Minn; Los Angeles Co Mus, Calif. *Exhib:* Solo shows, Viterbo Col, LaCrosse, Wis, 83, Wis Acad Sci, Arts & Lett, Madison, 87, Pro Art, St Louis, Mo, 87 & 90; Manchester Inst Arts & Sci, NH, 92; Babcock Gallery, NY, 95; Seibu, Tokyo, Japan, 98; DAI Icki Arts, NY, 99; Lacoste Gallery, Concord, Mass, 2000. *Pos:* Studio, River Falls, Wis, 72-; guest cur, Col St Catherine Gallery, St Paul, Minn, 77; consult, Minneapolis Sch Art & Design, Minn, 77, St Cloud State Col, Minn, 78 & adv bd, Northern Clay Ctr, St Paul, Minn, 91. *Teaching:* Guest lectr, var univ & col, 74-2000; teacher, Rochester Art Ctr, 73-74 & 76, Univ Minn, Quadna Summer Art Ctr, 76, 78 & 79, Univ Minn Studio Arts, 78-79 & Bergen Sch Art, Norway, 81; assoc prof art, Univ Wis, River Falls, 92-98; workshop, Univ Wis-Stout,

87; Emily Carr Sch Art, Vancouver, BC, 88; Southern Ill Univ, Edwardsville, 89; spec asst prof, Kansas City Art Inst, Mo, 92; Huara Huara Studio, Santiago, Chile. *Awards:* Craftsmen's Apprenticeship, 78-79, Craftsmen's Fel, 78-79 & Visual Arts Fel, 90-91, Nat Endowment Arts; Individual Artist Fel, Proj Grant, Wis Art Bd, 83; Bush Artists Fel, 98. *Bibliog:* Am Craft, 12/90-1/91; Fragile Blossoms Enduring Earth, 89; Warren MacKenzie, An Am Potter, 91; Coil Minoque/Sanderson (auth), Wood Fired Ceramics. *Publ:* Wood firing, Vol II, No 1, 83 & article, winter 89, Studio Potter; Between two fires, essay, Am Wood Fired Catalog, Univ Iowa, 91; Portfolio, Ceramics Monthly, 10/91; Ceramic Art & Perception, No 16, 94; Color and Fire, Rizolli Publ Lauria. *Dealer:* Trax Gallery Berkeley CA; Babcock Gallery New York NY. *Mailing Add:* N 8336 690th St River Falls WI 54022

JOHNSTON, RICHARD M
SCULPTOR, EDUCATOR
b Kankakee, Ill, Sept 22, 1942. *Study:* El Camino Jr Col; Calif State Col, Long Beach, BA; Cranbrook Acad Art, MFA. *Work:* Weber State Col; Salt Lake Co Bar Asn; Cranbrook Acad of Art. *Comn:* Steel wall sculpture, Western Airlines, Los Angeles, 69; bronze wall sculpture, Telemation Inc, Salt Lake City, Utah, 71; gold leaf/steel sculpture, Sun Valley Ski Corp, Idaho, 71; Temple Kol Ami, Salt Lake Int Ctr. *Exhib:* Craftsman USA, Los Angeles Co Mus Art, 66; Nat Crafts Exhib, Univ NMex, 68; Inter-Mountain Biennial, Salt Lake Art Ctr, 70; 73rd Western Ann, Denver Art Mus, 71; Nat Small Sculpture & Drawing Show, San Diego State Col, 72; Solo exhib, Salt Lake Art Ctr, 80. *Teaching:* Prof, Univ Utah, 68-90, Calif State Univ, San Bernadino, 90. *Awards:* First Prize, Sterling Silversmiths, 68; Purchase Award, Utah Mus Fine Art, 69; Purchase Award, Salt Lake Art Ctr, 70. *Media:* Metal. *Mailing Add:* 528 Amigos Dr Ste A Redlands CA 92373-6258

JOHNSTON, ROY
PAINTER, HISTORIAN
b Tyrone, N Ireland, June 12, 1936. *Study:* Belfast Coll Art, BA & NDD, 66; Cardiff Coll Art & Univ S Wales, DAE, 69; Trinity Col, Univ Dublin, PhD, 92. *Work:* Irish Mus Mod Art, Dublin, Ireland; Ulster Mus, Belfast, N Ireland; Hugh Lane Munic Gallery Mod Art, Dublin, Ireland; Arts Coun Great Britain, London, Eng; Munson-Williams Proctor Inst, Utica, NY. *Comn:* Posters for the environment, 70, wall relief, 76 & suite of six drawings, 82, Arts Coun N Ireland, Belfast; tapestry mural, Univ Coll Galway, 73. *Exhib:* Irish Imagination, Corcoran Gallery, Washington, 72; Aos Og, Mus d'Art Moderne, Paris, France, 73; retrospective, Hugh Lane Munic Gallery Mod Art, Dublin, 85; Artists of Central NY, Munson-Williams Proctor Inst, Utica, NY, 89; The Abstract Irish, Right Bank Gallery, Brooklyn, NY, 92; Ateliers D'Artistes De Pont-Aven, Mus De Pont-Aven, France, 93; Albany Ctr Gallery, NY, 94; A Land of Heart's Desire-300 Years of Irish Art, Ulster Mus, Belfast, 1999; Irish Art of the 70's, Irish Mus Mod Art, Dublin, Ireland, 2006; Dayton Art Inst, Dayton, Ohio, 2007; and others; Object, National Craft, Kilrenny, Ire, 2009; Weston Art Gallery, Cincinnati, 2010; Binding Connections. *Collection Arranged:* Roderic O'Conor Vision & Expression (exhib catalog), Hugh Lane Munic Gallery Mod Art, Dublin; Roderic O'Conor (1860-1940), Retrospective (exhib catalog), Mus de Pont-Aven, France, 84 & Ulster Mus, Belfast & Barbican Art Gallery, London, 85; The Prints of Roderic O'Conor, Nat Gallery Ireland, Dublin, 2001. *Pos:* Artist/Art Historian. *Teaching:* Sr Lectr, fine art, Univ Ulster, Belfast, 69-87; prof, drawing & painting, Skidmore Col, Saratoga Springs, NY, 87-94; Eastern Mich Univ, 94, 2004. *Awards:* Key Bank Prize, Cooperstown Nat, Key Bank, 88 & 89. *Bibliog:* Dorothy Walker (auth), The Intelligent Eye, Hibernia Review, 72; Dr Brian Kennedy (auth), Roy Johnston 1965-1985, Arts Coun N Ireland, 85; Cyril Barrett (auth), Roy Johnston, Art Monthly, 85; Aidan Dunne (auth), Roy Johnston, Art News, 12/1992; Liam Kelly (auth), Thinking Long. *Media:* Acrylic, Oil. *Res:* School of Pont-Aven and the life and work of Roderic O'Conor 1860-1940. *Publ:* Auth, Systems and Art, Introspect, 75; Sean Scully, Circa Mag, 82; Roderic O'Conor in Brittany, 84 & Roderic O'Conor: The Elusive Personality, 85, Irish Arts Review; O'Conor Gravures, Arts de L'Ouest, Rennes, 86; Roderic O'Conor in Grove Dictionary of Art, 96; Roderic O'Conor in Art & Architecture of Ireland, 2014. *Dealer:* Oliver Dowling Gallery 19 Kildare St Dublin Ireland 2; Fenderesky Gallery Belfast N Ireland. *Mailing Add:* 1136 Signature Dr Sun City Center FL 33573

JOHNSTON, THOMAS ALIX
PAINTER, PRINTMAKER
b Oklahoma City, Okla, June 4, 1941. *Study:* San Diego State Col, BA, 65; Univ Calif, Santa Barbara, MFA, 67; Atelier 17, Paris & Atelier Lacouriere et Frelaut, Paris, 80. *Work:* Henry Art Gallery, Univ Wash & Seattle Art Mus, Seattle; Portland Art Mus; Mod Art Mus, Kobe, Japan; Royal Collection, Riyadh, Saudi Arabia; and others. *Comn:* Du Regard a la Vision, Lacouriere et Frelaut, Paris, 1994. *Exhib:* 52nd Biennial, Libr Cong, Washington, DC & Blackfish Gallery, Portland, 84; NW Ann, Seattle Art Mus, 72, Evergreen State Col, 80, Wash; Black and White Drawings by 150 Americans 1970-1980, Brooklyn Mus, 80; Davidson Gallery, Seattle, 82 & 91; Francine Seders Gallery, Seattle, 84, 86 & 87; Galerie Jean Claude Riedel, Paris, 89; Johnston/Schier, PONCHO Exhib, Seattle Art Mus, 1992; McIntosh Gallery, Atlanta, Ga, 93; IXL Gallery, San Francisco, 94; Second Int Graphic Art, Prague, Czech Rep, 99; Evergreen State Col, Olympia, Wash, 2001; Northlight Gallery, Everett, Wash, 2002. *Collection Arranged:* 25 Am Print Artists, La Jeune Gravure Contemporaine, Paris, 95. *Pos:* Dir, Western Gallery, Western Washington Univ, 83-87; auth & ed, Western Gallery News, Western Wash Univ, 83-88. *Teaching:* Prof art, Western Wash Univ, prof emeritus. *Awards:* First Place/Graphics, 14th Northern Calif Ann, Calif State Univ, Chico, 70; Purchase Award, 57th NW Ann, Seattle Art Mus, Wash, 72; Artist in Residence, Chateau Suduiraut, Sauternes, France, 93. *Bibliog:* Nicholson, Baker (auth), Discards, The New Yorker, 94; Fred Moody (auth), It's in the Cards, Seattle Weekly, 98; Simeona Hoskova (ed), Labyrinth, The Ministry of Culture of the Czech Republic, 98. *Media:* Intaglio, Acrylic, Oil. *Publ:* Illusr Concerning Poetry, Western Wash Univ, 73-80; The Ventriloquist, R Huff, Univ Press Va, 77; Beyond the veil: The etching of Helen Loggie, Whatcom Mus, 79; Anthropomorphic Consciousness, Joe's Garage (artists bk), Olympia, Wash, 2005. *Mailing Add:* PO Box 12593 Olympia WA 98508-2593

JOHNSTON, WILLIAM RALPH
ADMINISTRATOR, CURATOR
b Toronto, Ont, Feb 15, 1936. *Study:* Univ Toronto Trinity Col, Hon BA, 59; NY Univ Inst Fine Arts, MA, 66. *Collection Arranged:* Anatomy of a Chair: Regional Variations in 18th Century Furniture Styles, Metrop Mus, NY, 62; J W Morrice (with catalog), Montreal Mus Fine Arts, Nat Gallery Can, 68. *Pos:* Cur, Robert Lehman Collection, New York, 62-63; gen cur, Montreal Mus Fine Arts, 64-66; asst dir, Walters Art Gallery, 66-83, assoc dir, 83-, sr cur emer, 2009-. *Awards:* Fel, Am Wing, Metrop Mus Art, 63-64. *Mem:* Am Ceramic Circle; Victorian Soc Am. *Res:* 18th & 19th century painting & decorative arts. *Publ:* Coauth, Japonisme, Cleveland Mus; auth, The Nineteenth Century Paintings in The Walters Art Gallery, Baltimore, 82; coauth, Alfred Jacob Miller, Artist on the Oregon Trail, Ft Worth, 82; Masterpieces of Ivory from the Walters Art Gallery, 85; Alfred Sisley, London, 92; William and Henry Walters, The Reticent Collectors, J.H.U. Press, Baltimore, MD, 99; The Triumph of French Painting (coauth), London, 2000; The Faberge Menagerie, (coauth), Baltimore, 2003; coauth, The Essence of Line, French Drawings from Ingres to Degas, Baltimore, 2005; coauth, Untamed: The Art of Antoine-Louis Barye, Baltimore, 2006. *Mailing Add:* Walters Art Mus 600 N Charles St Baltimore MD 21201

JOHNSTON, YNEZ
PAINTER, PRINTMAKER
b Berkeley, Calif, May 12, 1920. *Study:* Univ Calif, Berkeley, MFA, 46. *Work:* Mus Mod Art, Whitney Mus Am Art & Metrop Mus Art, NY; Hirshhorn Mus & Sculpture Garden, Washington, DC; Milwaukee Art Ctr, Wis; plus others. *Comn:* Etchings, Int Graphic Arts Soc, NY; drawings, Washington Gallery Mod Art, Washington, DC, 65; etchings, Roten Galleries, Baltimore, Md, 66-67; etching, Los Angeles Co Mus, 81. *Exhib:* Solo retrospective, San Francisco Mus Art, 67, Kennedy Mus Am Art, Athens, Ohio, 97; Mekler Gallery, Los Angeles, 72, 74, 77, 82, 84 & 88; Mitsukoshi Galleries, Tokyo, Japan, 77; Worthington Gallery, Chicago, 83, 86 & 88; Retrospective Exhib Paintings, Sculptures, Prints 1950-1992, Fresno Art Mus, Calif, 92; Schmidt-Bingham Gallery, NY, 98; The Norton Simon Mus of Art, Exhib of 30 Works owned by the Mus, 2004. *Teaching:* Instr etching, Colorado Springs Fine Arts Ctr, 54-56 & Univ Judaism, 67; instr painting, Calif State Univ, Los Angeles, 66-67, 69 & 72-73; instr, Otis Art Inst of Parsons Sch of Design, Los Angeles, 78-81; artist-in-residence, Fullerton Col, 82. *Awards:* Guggenheim, 52; Tamarind Fel, 66; Nat Endowment Arts, 82 & 86. *Bibliog:* Theodore F Wolff (auth), Christian Sci Monitor, 86; John Berry (auth), View from the wind palace, Mankind Mag, 75; Gerald Nordland (auth), Ynez Johnston, Grassfield Press (in coop with Univ Ohio), 96. *Media:* Mixed Media, Acrylic. *Interests:* literature, fiction, poetry. *Dealer:* Tom d'Alessandro Tomlyn Gallery Tequesta FL; Tobey Moss Gallery Los Angeles CA. *Mailing Add:* 579 Crane Blvd Los Angeles CA 90065

JOHNSTONE, MARK
CONCEPTUAL ARTIST, CURATOR
b St Louis, Mo, 1953. *Study:* Colo Col, BA, 75; Univ Southern Calif, MFA, 82. *Work:* Calif Mus Photog, Univ Calif, Riverside; Nestle, North Am, Glendale, Calif; Centro Documentazioni Arti Visive E Archivo/Rosamilia, San Giorgio, Italy; Biblioteque Nat, Paris, France; Ctr Creative Photog, Tucson, Ariz. *Comn:* Many multimedia productions, comn in Colo, Calif, Missouri, Ky, Washington, Idaho, Italy, England, France, and Japan, 97-. *Exhib:* Solo exhib, Vista: Some Landscape Observations, Calif Mus Photog, Riverside, 81; Ten Yr Selection, Martin Schweig Gallery, St Louis, Mo, 87; Recent Work, Min Gallery, Tokyo, Japan, 88; and others. *Collection Arranged:* Joe Deal: Southern California Photographs, 1976-86, Los Angeles Munic Art Gallery, 77-89 & 92; Eileen Cowin & John Divola, Recent Work, No Fancy Titles, La Jolla Mus Contemp Art, Calif traveling, 85; Robert Mapplethorpe & Edward Weston, The Garden of Earthly Delights (traveling), Calif Mus Photog, Riverside, 95. *Pos:* Contrib ed, Artweek, 77-89; series content adv, The Photographic Vision, KOCE-TV PBS, Huntington Beach, Calif, 83-84; vpres, cur exhibs, Security Pac Corp, Los Angeles, 88-92; adminr, Pub Arts Div, Cult Affairs Dept, City of Los Angeles, 95-2001; bd advisors, Public Art Review, Forecast, Minneapolis, MN, 99-; photog, ed, Int Doc mag, 2004-2006; consult pub art, City of Ketchum, Idaho, 2006-2008; arts comnr, City of Hailey, Idaho, 2006-2012; consult, Sun Valley Ctr Arts, 2006-2008; regional pub art advisor, Idaho Comn on the Arts, 2005-2006, 2008-2011; consult, Idaho Comn for Humanities, 2007-2008; public art advisor, State of Id, Id Comn Arts, 2012-2013; Arts Comn, City of Couer d'Alene, 2015-present; exec producer, Media Arts Advocates, LLC, producing and writing documentary films, 2014-present. *Teaching:* Vis prof photog, Colo Coll, Colorado Springs, summers 79-83; instr, Art Ctr Coll Design, Pasadena, 82-83, 94; lectr hist photog, Calif State Univ, Fullerton, 81-88. *Bibliog:* Colin Gardner (auth), Calendar-Galleries, 9/6/85 & Suzanne Muchnic (auth), A focus on creativity, 3/1/87, Los Angeles Times; Chuck Nicholson (auth), Exploring Culture & Photography, Artweek, 4/29/89; plus others. *Media:* Miscellaneous Media. *Res:* Contemporary photography & art. *Interests:* researching archives. *Publ:* Auth, The photographs of Larry Burrows, In: Observations: Essays on Documentary Photography, Friends of Photog, 84; Melting the Material World, Fotokritik, 6/86; Contemporary Art in Southern California, Craftsman House, 99; Epicenter-San Francisco Bay Area Art Now, Chronicle Bks, 2002. *Mailing Add:* 114 E Foster Coeur D Alene ID 83814

JOLLEY, DONAL CLARK
PAINTER
b Zion Nat Park, Utah, Oct 20, 1933. *Study:* Brigham Young Univ, BS, 59; with Glen Turner, J Roman Andrus. *Work:* First Nat Bank Nev, Reno; San Bernardino Co Mus, Redlands, Calif; Aerospace Corp, El Segundo, Calif; Church of Jesus Christ of Latter-Day Saints, Salt Lake City, Utah; Brigham Young Univ, Provo, Utah; Smithsonian Inst; Mayo Clinic; St George Art Mus, Utah; Art Mus, Ont & Calif. *Comn:* McDonald's, Lake Arrowhead, Blue Jay, Calif. *Exhib:* Solo exhibs, Brigham Young Univ, Utah, 75 & 81 & Univ Nev, Reno, 78; Traditional Artists, San Bernardino Co Mus, Redlands, 76-79 & Fine Arts Inst, 78-79 & 91; Kimball Art Ctr, Park City, Utah, 86; Peppertree Ranch, 88-2006; Mid Am Indian Ctr, Wichita, Kans,

90; Autry Mus, Los Angeles, 96; Segil Gallery, Monrovia, Calif, 2006; Art for Heaven's Sake, Redlands, Calif, 2006. *Pos:* Jr illusr, Space Technol Lab, Redondo, Calif, 60-61; sr illusr, Aerospace Corp, El Segundo, Calif, 61-71. *Teaching:* Instr painting, San Bernardino Valley Col, 73-81. *Awards:* Brand XII Award, 83; Riverside Centennial Award, 83; Gold Medal, Am Indian & Cowboy Artists, 90 & 94, Bronze, 92; Best of Show, San Dimas, Calif, 2004; and others. *Bibliog:* Fred Kiemel (auth), Making a presentation brochure self-promotion, Camera Life Mag, 5/80; Peggy & Harold Samuels (coauths), Contemporary Western Artists, 82; Patricia Dunsmore (auth), Elan Mag, 11/88; Gerald F Brommer (auth), Understanding Watercolor, 93; The Best of Watercolor, Schlemm & Nicholas, 95; Donna L Poulton & Vern G Swanson, Painters of Utah's Canyons and Deserts; A Century of Sanctuary, Zion Natural Hist Asn. *Mem:* Nat Watercolor Soc (vpres, 91); Watercolor West (vpres, 78-79 & 97-98). *Media:* Watercolor, Acrylic. *Interests:* Five string banjo, classic hot rods. *Dealer:* Studio Gallery 26375 Apache Trail Rimforest CA 92378

JOLLY, ERIC J
MUSEUM ADMINISTRATOR
Study: Univ RI, BA (psychology), 1979; Univ Okla, MS (psychology and psychometrics), 1983, PhD (psychology), 1984. *Pos:* vpres, sr scientist, Educ Develop Ctr, Newton, Mass; pres, CEO, Science Mus of Minn, St Paul, 2004-2015; mem math sciences educ bd, NAS; cochmn, Nat Task Force in Tech & Disability, 2001-02; founder, Nat Inst Affirmative Action, 1994; bd trustees, The Minneapolis Found; pres., CEO, Minn Philantrophy Partners, 2015-. *Mem:* AAAS (chair comn on opportunities in science, 2001-03); Nat Science Teachers Asn; Nat Coun for Teachers in Math; Nat Action Coun for Minorities in Eng; Soc for Advancement of Chicanos & Native Americans in Science (life). *Publ:* auth, Engagement, Capacity and Continuity: A Trilogy for Student Success, Bridging Homes and Schools, Beyond Blame: Reacting to the Terrorist Attack; contribr articles to prof jours. *Mailing Add:* Minnesota Philanthropy Partners 101 Fifth St East Ste 2400 Saint Paul MN 55101-1800

JONAITIS, ALDONA
HISTORIAN, ADMINISTRATOR
b New York, NY, Nov 27, 1948. *Study:* State Univ NY, Stony Brook, BA, 69; Columbia Univ, with Douglas Fraser, MA, 72, PhD, 77. *Exhib:* Chiefly Feasts: The Enduring Kwakiutl Potlatch, Am Mus Nat Hist, 91. *Pos:* Vpres pub progrs, Am Mus Nat Hist, 89-93; dir, Univ Alaska Mus of the North, 93-2010, interim dir, 2013-. *Teaching:* Lecturer to prof art, 73-89, State Univ NY, Stony Brook, chair art dept, 83-85, assoc. provost, 85-86, vice provost undergraduate studies, 86-89; prof anthrop, Univ Alaska, Fairbanks, 93-; adj prof art history and archeology Columbia Univ, 90-93; vis distinguished prof American art history, Stanford Univ, 2002. *Awards:* Chiefly Feasts, Winner, Am Asn Mus Curs Comt Award for Excellence in Exhib, 91. *Mem:* Native Am Art Studies Asn; Am Asn Mus; AAM/ICOM. *Res:* Northwest Coast Indian art. *Publ:* Auth, Tlingit Halibut Hooks: An Analysis of the Visual Symbols of a Rite of Passage, 1981; Robert Davidson; Eagle of the Dawn, 1993; Art of the Northern Tlingit, Univ Wash Press, 86; From the Land of Totem Poles: The Northwest Coast Indian Art Collection at the American Museum of Natural History, Univ Wash Press, 88; A Wealth of Thought: Franz Boas on Native American Art, Univ Wash Press, 93; Chiefly Feasts: The Enduring Kwakiutl Potlatch, Univ Wash Press, 91; A Wealth of Thought: Franz Boas on Native American Art, 95; Looking North: Art From the Univ of Alaska Mus, 98; The Yuguot Whalers' Shrine, 99; Art of the Northwest Coast, 2006; The Totem Pole: An Intercultural History, 2010. *Mailing Add:* Univ Alaska Mus PO Box 756960 Fairbanks AK 99775

JONAS, JOAN
VIDEO ARTIST, CONCEPTUAL ARTIST
b New York, NY, July 13, 1936. *Study:* Mount Holyoke Coll, BA (art hist), Mass; Boston Mus Sch, Mass; Columbia Univ, New York, MFA, 65; Sch Mus Fine Arts, Boston. *Work:* Mus Mod Art, New York; Organic Honey's Visual Telepathy, 1972; The Juniper Tree, 1976; Volcano Saga, 1985; Revolted by the Thought of Known Places..., 1992; Woman in the Well, 1996-2000; My new Theater series, 1997-99; Lines in the Sand, 2002; The Shape, The Scent, The Feel of Things, 2004. *Exhib:* Solo exhibs, Anthology Film Archives, NY, 1975, Inst Contemp Arts, Los Angeles, 1975, Stedelijk Mus, Amsterdam, Kunstmuseum, Bern, Van Abbemuseum, Eindhoven, Holland, San Francisco Mus Art & Univ Art Mus, Berkeley, Infinito Botanica, ArtPace, San Antonio, 1996, Tableau Vivant, The Alamo, San Antonio, 1998, New Painting y Mas, Galeria Ortiz, San Antonio, 1999, Infinito Botanica: NY, Ctr Curatorial Studies, Bard Col, 1999, Mexique, El Museo del Barrio, New York City, 2000, Untitled Grid No 7, Infinito Botanico: St Louis, Des Lee Gallery, Wash Univ 2001, SHOP, Jessica Murray Projects, Brooklyn, 2001, Dust in the Wind, NY Pub Art Fund, 2002, Market Squared, Galeria Ortiz, San Antonio, 2002, Nacho de Paz (and Other TexMex Miracles), Frederieke Taylor Gallery, New York City, 2002, Pan in the Park, Laumeier Sculpture Park, St Louis, 2003, Rosamund Felson, Los Angeles, 2003, Pat Hearn Gallery, NY City, 2003; Artists Mus, Lodz, Poland, 91-92; San Antonio Sculpture Symposium, 1989; Planta de Arte Nuclear, San Antonio, 1990; Tex Dialogues, Shrines, Milagros Contemp Art Gallery, San Antonio, 1992; El Impacto de Dos Mundos, Art Space Gallery, New Haven, Conn, 1992; Closets: Queer Experience, Esperanza Peace and Justice Ctr, San Antonio, 1993; Hispanic Artists of 1993, Guadalupe Cult Arts Ctr, San Antonio, 1993; The Illusive Object, Diverse Works, Houston, 1993; Blue Star VIII, Blue Star Art Space, San Antonio, 1994; Synthesis and Subversion: A Latino Direction in San Antonio Art, Art Gallery Univ Tex San Antonio, 1995; Double Trouble: Mirrors/Pairs/Twins/Lovers, Blue Star Art Space, San Antonio, 1995; Tres Proyectos Latinos, The Business of Art, Instituto Cult de Mexico, San Antonio, 1998; Trade, Salon 300, Brooklyn, 1998; The Ecstatic, Trans-Hudson Gallery, New York, 1999; Yard Sale, Downtown Arts Project, New York, 2000; Texans in the Whitney, Arthur Roger Gallery, New Orleans, 2000; Infinito Botanico, Downtown Arts Project, New York, 2000; City Lights: Art Walk, Comite Colbert, New York, 2000; Ultrabaroque: Aspects of Post-Latin Am Art (traveling exhib), 2000-03; Hopscotch, Gallery Art, Kean Univ, NJ, 2001; Lost in Space, Gary Tatinsian Gallery, New York, 2001; Caribbean Biennial, Santo Domingo, Dominican Republic, 2001; ARS01-KIASMA, Infinito Botanica: Spain, ARCO, Madrid, 2002; Parklife, MetroTech Ctr, Brooklyn, 2002-03; Dreamspaces/Entresuenos, Deutsche Bank, New York, 2003; Ballroom Marfa, Tex, 2004; 53rd Int Art Exhib Biennale, Venice, 2009. *Pos:* Guest lectr, Yale Univ, New Haven, Conn, 74, Princeton Univ, 74 & Minneapolis Coll Art, Minn; vis artist, Otis Art Inst, Los Angeles, Calif, 75, Minneapolis Coll Art & Design, 79, Wright State Univ, Dayton, Ohio, 80 & Long Beach State Coll, Calif, 80. *Teaching:* Assoc prof, Hunter Coll, 85-88; tutor, Rijksakademie, Amsterdam; fac, Mass Inst of Technol, Cambridge, Mass, 2000; prof vis arts, Mass Inst Tech. *Awards:* Creative Artists Pub Serv Prog, 72, 73 & 75; Nat Endowment Arts Grant, 73 & 75; Maya Dern Award in Video, Am Film Int, 88; Rockefeller Award, 90; Hiroshima Art Prize, 1998; Kepes Art Prize, Cou Arts, Mass Inst of Technol, 2004; Artist Award for Distinguished Body of Work, Coll Art Asn, 2004; Found for Contemp Arts Grants to Artists Award, 1995; US Artists Friends Fel, 2009. *Bibliog:* Wulf Herzgenrath (auth), Video Ein Neue Medium in der Bildenden Kunst, Mag Kunst, Mainz, 7/74; Marcus Guterich (auth), Art Presented According to the Evolution Principle, Kunst Kunst Kunst, Cologne, Ger, 74; Howard Junker (auth), Joan Jonas: The mirror staged, Art Am, 2/81. *Mem:* Nat Acad. *Media:* Mirrors; Videotape. *Publ:* Auth, Organic Honey's visual telepathy, Drama Rev, New York, 72; coauth, Show Me Your Dance, Art & Artists, London, 10/73. *Dealer:* Electronic Arts Intermix 536 Broadway New York NY. *Mailing Add:* Mass inst of Tech Visual arts Program 265 Mass Ave Cambridge MA 02139

JONES, ALLEN CHRISTOPHER
PAINTER, PRINTMAKER, SCULPTOR
b Southampton, Eng, Sept 1, 1937. *Study:* Royal Coll Art, London, 59-60; Hornsey Coll Art, London, NDD & ATD, 59-61. *Hon Degrees:* Hon PhD, Southampton Solent Univ, 2007. *Work:* Chicago Mus Art; Hirshhorn Mus & Sculpture Garden, Washington DC; Mus Modern Art, New York; Nagoaka Mus, Japan; Nat Portrait Gallery, London; Sunderland Art Gallery, Sunderland; Tate Gallery, London; Walker Art Gallery, Liverpool. *Comn:* O Calcutta, 70; Eric Satie's Cinema, 87; Signed in Red, Royal Ballet, 95-96. *Exhib:* Solo exhib, Southampton Univ, 66, Hamilton Gallery, London, 67, Marlborough Graphics, London, 71, 2008, 2010, Oriel Gallery, Cardiff, 75, Arnolfini, Bristol, 75, Fruit Market Gallery, Edinburgh, 75, Serpentine Gallery, London, 79, Barbican Art Gallery, London, 95, Thomas Gibson Fine Art, 97 & Alan Cristea Gallery, 2003; retrospective, Inst Contemp Art, London, 78 & Walker Art Gallery, Liverpool, 79; The Folding Image, Nat Gallery Art, Washington, DC, 84; Pop Art, Royal Acad, London, 91-92 & Musee Des Beaux-Arts, Montreal, 92-93; The Portrait Now, Nat Portrait Gallery, London, 94; Allen Jones Prints Retrospective, Barbican Art Gallery, London, 95; Kunsthalle Darmstadt, 96; Trussardi, Milan, 98; SmithKline Beecham, London, 2000; Galleria d'Arte Maggiore, Bologna, 2002; Palazzo dei Seite, Orvieto, 2002; Gallery Levy, Hamburg, 2001, 2003; Royal Acad Arts, London, 2002, 07. *Pos:* Trustee, British Mus, 90-99, Wetterling Gallery, Stockholm & Gothenburg, 2011. *Teaching:* Guest prof painting, Univ S Fla, 68-69, Univ Calif, Los Angeles, 77 & Hochschule de Kunste, Berlin, 82-83; lithography, painting & drawing, Eoyda Coll Art, 61-63, Chelsea Sch Art, 64, Hohchule fur Lbildeden Kunst, Hamburg, 68-70, Univ Los Angeles, Irvine, 73 . *Awards:* Prix Des Jeunes Artists, Paris Biennale, 63; Art & Work Award (sculpture, London Bridge City), Wapping Arts Trust, London, 89; Heitland Found Award, Ger, 95. *Bibliog:* Marco Livingstone (auth), Allen Jones: Sheer Magic, Thames & Hudson, 79; Charles Jencks (auth), Allen Jones, Acad Ed, 93; Marco Livingstone (auth), Allen Jones Prints, Prestel, 95; Andrew Lambirth: Allen Jones, Brookhadpta Press, 1997, Allen Jones Works, The Royal Acad, 2005; and others. *Mem:* Royal Acad Arts. *Media:* Paint; Prints; Sculpture. *Specialty:* Contemporary Art (in all cases). *Publ:* Illusr, Allen Jones Figures, Galerie Mikro, Berlin, 69; Allen Jones Projects, 71 & Waitress, 72, Mathews Miller Dunbar, London. *Dealer:* Thomas Levy Galerie Osterfeld Strasse 6 22529 Hamburg; Galerie Ernst Hilger Dorotheerstrasse 5/1 A-1010 Vienna Austria Milan 20124 Italy; Lorenzelli Arte 2 Corso Bueno Aires; Galerie Trigand Paris. *Mailing Add:* 41 Charterhouse Sq London United Kingdom EC1M 6EA

JONES, ARTHUR F
EDUCATOR, ADMINISTRATOR
Study: State Univ of NY, New Paltz, BA; Case Western Reserve Univ, MA, PhD (art history). *Work:* Works include themes of Medusa as a Non-Wearable Pendant and Bone of Contention with Barking Squirrel. *Pos:* Scholar in Residence, Pollock/Krasner House and Study Ctr, East Hampton, NY; curator of art exhibitions producing numerous catalog essays for museums and art galleries as well as ither published articles and books. *Teaching:* Instructor, Univ Kentucky, formerly; art dept chair, Radford Univ, Va, formerly; prof, art dept chair, Univ North Dakota, 2003-. *Mailing Add:* Hughes Fine Arts Center Dept of Art & Design University of North Dakota 3350 Campus Rd, Stop 7099 Grand Forks ND 58202

JONES, BEN
PAINTER, SCULPTOR
b Paterson, NJ, May 26, 1942. *Study:* Sch Visual Arts; NY Univ, MA; Pratt Inst, MFA; Univ Sci & Technol, Kumasi, Ghana, New Sch Social Research. *Work:* Newark Mus, NJ; Howard Univ; Studio Mus, NY; Johnson Publ, Chicago. *Exhib:* Mus Mod Art; Studio Mus in Harlem; Black World Arts Festival, Lagos, Nigeria; Newark Mus, 77; Fisk Univ, 77; Bishop Col, Dallas, Tex, 78; solo shows, Newark Mus, 84, NJ State Mus, 84 & 96, Jersey City Mus, NJ, 94 & Jadite Gallery, 96, 97 & 98; Gallery 62, NY, 83 & Dallas Conv Ctr, 85; Mus Am Life & Cult, Dallas, Tex, 86; Pa Acad Art, Philadelphia, 86; Montclair Mus, NJ, 87 & 92; Dallas Mus Art, Tex, 89; High Mus Art, Atlanta, Ga, 90; Milwaukee Art Mus, 90; Newark Mus, NJ, 91; Md Inst, Coll Art, Baltimore, 97; Southshore Art Ctr, Chicago, Ill, 98; and others. *Pos:* Art dir, Urban League Essex Co Exhib, 72. *Teaching:* Prof art, Jersey City State Univ, NJ, currently; adminr, Alumni Faculty, currently; coordr Fine Art, BFA Comt & adv bd, Afro Studies Ctr. *Awards:* Nat Endowment Arts, 74-75; NJ Arts Coun Grant, 77-78 & 83-84; Delta Sigma Theta-Excellence in the Arts, 85; and others. *Bibliog:* Articles, Art Am, 71; articles, New York Times, 72 & 82-85. *Mem:* World Print Coun; Nat Conf Artists. *Res:* African art and culture in WAfrica and Paris, France. *Mailing Add:* 117 Kensington Ave Apt 206 Jersey City NJ 07304

JONES, CARTER R, JR
SCULPTOR
b Mount Kisco, NY, Mar 6, 1945. *Study:* Sch Visual Arts, with Edward Giobbi, 64-65; Boston Mus Sch, dipl, 69; pvt study in Paris, 69-71. *Work:* First fish, Brookgreen Gardens, Pawleys Island, SC, 2008; Numismatic Mus, NY; pvt collections of William Maxwell, NY, Beauford Delaney, Paris, Vera Newman, Croton on Hudson, NY, Herman Schneider, Martha's Vineyard Mass, Humfer Noyse, Portland, Ore; British Mus, London, Eng; Smithsonian Inst, Washington, DC; Nat Sculpture Soc, Slide Libr. *Comn:* 25 portraits (sculpted), comn in Boston, NY & Paris; Walt Disney Prodns, 81-; Henson Assocs, 86-; Warner Bros, 94-; Nickelodeon, 95-; over thirty-five medallions and coins executed for var mints incl Medallic Art Corp, The Lincoln Mint, Judaic Heritage Soc and Art Medals Inc; Lion, Horace Mann Sch, Riverdale, NY, 2003; Brookgreon medal, Brookgreon Gardens, Pawleys Island, SC, 2005; Lt Petrusino Bas Relief Petrosino Sq, NY, 2013. *Exhib:* Boston Mus Sch, 69; Lever House, NY, 81, 83, 90; Numismatic Mus, NY, 83, 84; Nat Sculpture Soc, NY, 91, 2000; Am Towers, NY, 96-97, 2000; Atelier 14, NY, 98; 515 Greenwich Studio Complex, NY, 99; Nat Sculpture Exhib, 2000, 2001, 2004, 2011; Brookgreen Gardens, 2006, 2007, 2011; Sculpture in the Performing Arts, Tampa, Fla, 2011-. *Teaching:* Instr human & animal anatomy, Sch Visual Arts, New York, 80-82; The Compleat Sculptor; instr The Compleat Sculptor, 2000-; Brookgreen Gardens, Pawleys Island, SC, 2010. *Awards:* Art Dirs Award, Art Dirs Am, 79; Youth Award, Nat Sculpture Soc, 80; Nat Sculpture Soc Award, 81; Art Dir's Award, New York, 84; Nat Sculpture Soc Fel, 85-. *Bibliog:* Arthur Williams (auth), The Sculpture Reference. *Mem:* Fel Nat Sculpture Soc; Soc Artists Anatomists; Am Medallic Sculpture Asn (pres 83-85); Am Anatomy Asn. *Media:* Clay, Bronze, Stone. *Interests:* The human and animal figure. *Publ:* The Sculpture Reference Illustrated. *Mailing Add:* 39 Bond St Apt 2 New York NY 10012-2427

JONES, CHARLOTT ANN
EDUCATOR, MUSEUM DIRECTOR
b Jonesboro, Ark, May 27, 1927. *Study:* Coll St Scholastica, BA, 62; NTex State Univ, MS, 70; Pa State Univ, PhD, 78. *Collection Arranged:* Anuskiewicz Silkscreen Prints, 83, Rauschenberg Purina Chow Prints, 83 & Anuskiewicz, Judd, Marisol Prints, 83, Stephens Collection; The Figure and Other Paintings, 83; Paintings and Ceramics, 83; Arkansas Treasures: Twenty Outstanding Black Arkansans (auth, catalog), 87; Delta Genius: Clementine Hunter; A Personal Statement: Arkansas Women Artists (auth, catalog), Arkansas Arts Ctr, Little Rock & Nat Mus Women Arts, Washington, 92. *Pos:* Dir emer, Mus Ark State Univ 83-98; cur Nat Mus Women Arts, Ark. *Teaching:* Dir children's art, Charlott Jones Sch Art, Jonesboro, Ark, 72-; asn prof art, Ark State Univ, Jonesboro, 75-90. *Bibliog:* Alumni Profiles, Coll St Scholastica Times, spring 89. *Mem:* Nat Art Educ Asn; Ark Art Educ; Am Asn Mus; Ark Women in Higher Education; Ark Mus Asn. *Media:* Mag articles. *Res:* Free will in art making. *Publ:* Auth, The wellspring of Dylan, English J, 66; Women and art, Delta Kappa Gamma Bulletin, 82; contribr, Gifted and Talented in Art Education (monogr), Nat Art Educ Asn, 83; Eugene B Wittlake, Ark Biographies, 99

JONES, CYNTHIA CLARKE
COLLAGE ARTIST, GRAPHIC ARTIST
b Brooklyn, NY, Aug 12, 1938. *Study:* Brooklyn Mus, 53-57; Art Students League Art Career Sch, 57-58; Hunter Coll, with L Kimmel, 63-65. *Work:* Nat Mus Women Artists, Washington, DC. *Exhib:* Solo exhibs, Queens Pub Libr, Jamaica, NY, 86 & Int Art Gallery, Jamaica, NY, 93; Works on Paper, Gallery Ten, Rockford, Ill, 94; Works On/Off Paper, Queens Community Coll Art Gallery, Bayside, NY, 94; Concept to Depiction, Cork Gallery Lincoln Ctr, NY, 94; Violence in the Media, St Johns Univ Gallery, Jamaica, NY, 94; Colo Coalition for Abstinence, traveling art show, Boulder, 94-95; Collection 94 traveling show, Towson State Univ, Baltimore, Md, 94-95; Juried Show, Upsteam People Gallery, 2005; Liturgical Arts & Sacred, Riverside Interchurch juried show, 2006; Invitational Summer, Upsteam People Gallery, 2006. *Awards:* Fine Arts & Painting Award, Queensboro Soc, 73; France Lieber Mem Award, Nat Asn Women Artists Ann, Nat Asn Women Artists, 92 & Kreindler Mem Award, Nat Asn Women Artists, 95; Lill Award, Int Art Gallery, 93. *Bibliog:* Lisa A Rue (auth), Art for Awareness, Friends First, 94. *Mem:* Nat Asn Women Artists; Artists Equity New York; Coll Art Asn; Womens Caucus for Art; Guild Am Papercutters. *Media:* Kiri-e. *Publ:* Illusr, Scholastic Mag, 57; Statistics Department Baruch Coll, 73; Employers Local 384 Newsletter; logo designer, Int Art Gallery, 92; Kiri-e method featured, North Light Mag, 95; Christians In, In the Visual Arts Directory, 2000; Cutpaper, featured in Daniel Smith (catalog) summer 2005-2006; Cut paper, Velt Shenere Gallery (permanent collection), Calif. *Mailing Add:* 113-32 Mayville St Saint Albans NY 11412

JONES, DENNIS
SCULPTOR, EDUCATOR, ADMINISTRATOR
Exhib: Exhibited work nationally. *Collection Arranged:* Completed many large-scale sculpture commissions for public and private collections. *Teaching:* Dir sculpture area, 1983-87, prof sculpture, Univ Arizona, currently, dir Sch of Art, 2002-. *Mailing Add:* Arizona University School of Art PO Box 210002 1031 N Olive Rd J Gross Gallery Rm 101D Tucson AZ 85721-0007

JONES, DONALD GLYNN
PAINTER, ILLUSTRATOR
b Lyons, Kans, Jan 20, 1935. *Study:* Univ Okla, BFA, 58; Bongart Sch Art, with Sergei Bongart, Rexburg, Idaho, 83. *Exhib:* 29th Ann, Soc Illusrs, New York, 87; Nat Soc Painters Casein & Acrylic, 87, 90, 92, 95-2013; Lotus Club, New York, Award Exhib, 92; Allied Artists Am, Nat Arts Club, New York, 87, 96, 2007, & 2013; 55th Midyear Exhib, Butler Inst, Youngstown, Ohio, 91 & 66th Midyear Exhib, 91 & 2002; Audubon Artists, Nat Arts Club, New York, 92-94, 98-2001 & 2005-2006 & 2008-13; Rocky Mt Nat, Foothills Art Ctr, Golden, Colo, 95, 98-99, 2002 & 2008; Watercolor USA, Springfield Art Mus Mo, 2001 & 2004-2005; 10th Invitational Exhib, 2008, 11th Invitational Exhib, 2012; Great 8 Exhib, Kansas Watercolor Soc, Wichita, Kans, 2008; Kans Watercolor Soc Nat Exhib, 2009. *Awards:* Juror's Award, 42nd Ann Nat, Colo Springs Art Guild, 86, Merit Award, 86; Dr David Soloway Mem Award, 39th Ann, Nat Soc Painters Casein & Acrylic, 92, John J. Newman Medal, 2003 & Winsor Newton Award, 52nd Ann, 2005; Madonna Aldredge Mem Award, 25th Ann, Rocky Mt Nat, 98; Jane Gottleib-Brown Award, Assoc Artists Southport, NC, 86; Juror's Award, Watercolor USA, 2004. *Mem:* Nat Soc Painters Casein & Acrylic, New York; Audubon Artists, New York; Rocky Mt Nat Watermedia Soc; Watercolor USA Honor Soc. *Media:* Acrylic. *Publ:* Contribr, Illustrators 29, Soc Illusrs, 88; The best of acrylic painting, Rockport Publs, 96. *Mailing Add:* 6812 Sandlewood Dr Oklahoma City OK 73132-3911

JONES, DOUG DOUGLAS MCKEE
PAINTER, SCULPTOR
b Sewell, Chile, Oct 16, 1929; US citizen. *Study:* San Diego Fine Arts & Crafts; San Diego State Col; Los Angeles Art Ctr Coll Design, grad; also with Lorser Feitelson, Audubon Tyler, Leon Franks, Sergei Bongart, Dan Greene & Harley Brown. *Work:* Hall of Champions, Univ San Diego, Calif Western Sch Law, Aerospace Mus, San Diego, Calif. *Comn:* Portraits, Mayor Charles Dail, San Diego & Mayor Kiyoshi Nakarai, Yokahama, San Diego Chap, Am Inst Architects, 63; 43 portraits, Int Aerospace Hall Fame, San Diego, 64-72; portrait, Gen Claire Chenault, Flying Tigers Asn, 71; portrait, Marie Winzer, Scripps Hosp; and others. *Pos:* Owner & dir, The Jones Gallery, 64-; art appraiser, currently. *Awards:* Merit Award, New York Portrait Club, 79. *Mem:* Sr mem Am Soc Appraisers; Am Portrait Soc. *Media:* Oil, Pastel. *Specialty:* Paintings and sculpture by distinguished 19th and 20th century American artists. *Publ:* Auth, article, Southland Artist Mag & illusr cover. *Mailing Add:* 3525 Werbert St San Diego CA 92103

JONES, FAY
PRINTMAKER, PAINTER
b Boston, Mass, 1936. *Study:* RI Sch Design, BFA, 1958. *Comn:* poster, Bumbershoot Festival, Seattle; poster, Earshot Jazz Festival; Seafirst Bank, Seattle; Seattle Arts Comn; Seattle Walls Project; poster, lithograph, US West New Vector Group, Bellevue, Wash; mural, Westlake Metro Station, Seattle, Wash, 1983. *Exhib:* Solo exhibs incl Francine Seders Gallery, Seattle, 1970, 1973, 1976, 1978, 1980, 1981, 1983, 1985, 1987, 1990, 1993, Tacoma Art Mus, 1974, Western Wash Univ, 1979, Brunswick Union Gallery, 1983, Wentz Gallery, Portland, Ore, 1984, Potland Ctr for Visual Arts, 1985, Seattle Art Mus, 1985, Shoshona Wayne Gallery, Los Angeles, 1986, 1989, 1991, The Laura Russo Gallery, Portland, Ore, 1988, 1992, 1994, 1997, 1999, 2002, 2004, Whatcom County Mus, Bellingham, Wash, 1990, Sarah Spurgeon Gallery, Ellensburg, Wash, 1992, 20 yr retrospective, Boise Mus Art, 1997, Grover/Thurston Gallery, Seattle, 1996, 1997, 1998, 2000, 2004, Kimura Art Gallery, 1997, Mus Northwest Art, LaConner, Wash, 1998, Robischon Gallery, Denver, Colo, 1999, Salt Lake City Art Ctr, 1999,; group exhibs incl Ellensburg Community Gallery, Wash, 1972; Henry Art Gallery, Seattle, 1972, 1981, 1982, 1984, 1986, 1993; Seattle Art Mus, 1978, 1979, 1980, 1990; Open Space Gallery, Seattle, 1981; William Sawyer Gallery, San Francisco, 1982; New Mus, New York, 1983; Bellevue Art Mus, Wash, 1983, 1986, 1987, 1988, 1995; Ann Acad and Inst Arts and Letters Purchase Exhib, New York, 1984; Fountain Gallery, Portland, Ore, 1985; Laura Russo Gallery, 1986, 1998, 2001, 2002, 2003; San Jose Mus Art, Calif, 1987; Cheney Cowles Mus, Spokane, Wash, 1989; Francine Seders Gallery II, Seattle, 1993; Tacoma Art Mus, Wash, 1993, 1994; Whatcom Mus, Bellingham, Wash, 1995; Holter Mus Art, Helena, Mont, 1997; Mus Northwest Art, La Conner, Wash, 1998; Archer Gallery, Vancouver, Wash, 2001, 2005; Seattle Arts Comn, 2002. *Teaching:* Fac, Factory Visual Arts, Seattle, 1976-78, Cornish Coll of Arts, Seattle, 1985-87. *Awards:* Nat Endowment for Arts visual arts Fel, 1983, 1990; Wash State Arts Comn visual arts Fel, 1984; Twining Humber Award, Artist Trust, 2005. *Bibliog:* Regina Hackett (auth), Sondra Shulman (auth), Sandy Harthorn (auth), Fay Jones: A Twenty Year Retrospective (exhib catalog), 1997 & Sheila Farr (auth), Fay Jones, 2000, Univ Wash Press. *Media:* Acrylic, Oil, Etching, Lithograph. *Dealer:* Laura Russo Gallery 805 NW 21st Ave Portland OR 97209. *Mailing Add:* c/o Grover Thurston Gallery 319 Ave S Seattle WA 98104

JONES, FREDERICK
PRINTMAKER
b Llanymymech, Wales, Mar 6, 1940. *Study:* Cardiff Coll Art, Wales; Univ Pittsburgh; Univ Wis-Madison; print workshop, London & Atelier 17, Paris. *Work:* Lakeview Ctr for Arts, Peoria, Ill; Brit Mus, London; Victoria & Albert Mus, London; Krannert Mus, Univ Ill; Southern Ill Univ, Carbondale; Ill State Mus, Springfield, Ill; plus others. *Comn:* Large three part drawing, Ill State Libr, 92. *Exhib:* Int Print Biennial, Seoul, Korea, 71; Mid-Am Exhib, Montreal, Can, 71; Nat Image on Paper Show, Springfield, Ill, 72; Nat Print & Drawing Show, Macomb, 75; Heartland Painters Exhib, Bloomington Art Ctr, Ill, 92. *Teaching:* Lectr design drawing, Chester Col Art, Eng, 66-68; prof printmaking, Western Ill Univ, 68-, gallery dir, 69-71. *Awards:* First Prize for Drawing, Ill State Fair, 94; Grants,The Ill Landscape Portfolio, 97; Stipend Award, Western Ill Univ, Art in Pub Places, 97, Ill Humanities Coun Award, 2000; Landscape Workshop Award, Arrowmont Sch Arts and Crafts, Tenn, 2000; plus others. *Bibliog:* Mack Stegmaier (auth), Fred Jones, Am Artist, 2/88. *Media:* Pastel, Charcoal, Watercolor. *Dealer:* J Rosenthal Fine Arts 230 W Superior Chicago IL 60610; Peoria Art Guild 1831 N Knoxville Peoria IL 61603. *Mailing Add:* c/o Dept Art Western Ill Univ Macomb IL 61455

JONES, JAMES EDWARD
PAINTER, PRINTMAKER
b Paducah, Ky, Jan 27, 1937. *Study:* Philadelphia Coll Art, with Henry Pitz, Benton Spruance & Jerome Kaplan, dipl (illus), 60, fel, 56-61, BFA, 61; Univ Pa, with Barnett Newman, Angelo Seville, David Smith, Richard Stankiewicz & James Van Dyke, MFA, 62. *Work:* McDonogh Sch, Md; Dennison Univ; Smith Mason Gallery; 23 pieces, The Studio Mus in Harlem, NY; Soc Art & Culture, Columbia, Md; Columbia, MD Print Consortim Col; 23 pieces, Morgan State Univ, MD; Princess,

Anne MD; 45 prints, Newark Pub Libr, Newark NJ; Newark Public Lib, NJ; Morgan State Univ, Md. *Comn:* Prints, Heritage Mus, Baltimore, Md, 93; paintings, Great Blacks in Wax Mus. *Exhib:* Morgan State Univ, 62-80; juried shows, Baltimore Mus 63-67; Corcoran, Wash, DC, 68; Del Fine Arts Mus, 68; Baltimore Co Campus, Univ Md, 79; Smith Mason Gallery, Washington, DC, 79, 80 & 82; Huntsville, Ala, 80; Burkett Gallery, Md, 88; Senoje Gallery & Collection, 89-2007; Senoje Gallery, Baltimore, 90; Morgan State Univ Ann Fac Show, 90, 91, 92 & 94; Eulipion Gallery, Baltimore MD, 2000; Newark Pub Lib, 2002; Morgan St Univ, Convergence, 2003; James E Lewis Mus, 2009-2010. *Collection Arranged:* The Senoje Collection, Balt, 89-2002; The Great Blacks in Wax, Nat Mus, Baltimore, Md, 2005; Encaustics and Gouaches & Prints. *Pos:* Dir, The Senoje Collection, Balt, 90-91, exec dir, 91-92, 96 & 98-2005. *Teaching:* From assoc prof to prof art educ, painting & printmaking, drawing & visual arts, Morgan State Univ, 62-93; instr, Dundalk Community Coll, 77-78, Baltimore City Community Coll, 94-98 & Sojourner Douglass Coll, 94-98. *Awards:* Stewart Art Award, NJ State, 56; Univ Pa Fel & Thorton Oakley Creative Achievement Award, 62; Morgan State Univ Grant, 63-68; Huntsville Mus Art, Huntsville Ala Invitational, 80. *Bibliog:* Afro Am Slide Registry, Univ S Alabama, 74,75, 76; Convergence, the James E Lewis Mus, Md, Morgan St Univ, 2002; Southern Born Afro Artists USA, Huntsville Mus Art, Ala, 80. *Mem:* Print Consortium (Kansas City); The Senoje consortium, Founder in 1989: Dir. *Media:* Miscellaneous Media. *Specialty:* The Senoje Collection, Representing 8 artists, New York, Baltimore, MD. *Interests:* Writing, photog & gardening. *Collection:* 10 works by artist friends and colleagues, American and foreign prints, paintings, and drawings. *Publ:* Dr. Weaver Cur Convergence Catalogue, 2003; Morgan State Univ; coauth (with E Tillman), Nez-Noir Photos and Text; coauth (with E Tillman), Centering & Portrait of the Artist, Senoje Collection, Baltimore, Md (in press); auth (brochures), How to Understand Modern Jazz, 2004 & How to Invest in the Fine Arts, 2007, Senoje Collection, Baltimore, Md; library books co-authored by Elva Elizabeth Tillman; coauth, Conformity & Non-Conformity, Centering, Ner-Noir, Happyness Is. *Dealer:* The Senoje Collection. *Mailing Add:* 2930 Silver Hill Ave Baltimore MD 21207

JONES, JANE
PAINTER
b Denver, Colo, Apr 3, 1953. *Study:* Metrop State Coll, BS, 76; Regis Univ, MLS, 2005. *Work:* St Louis Univ Mus, Mo; Marriott Corp, Bethesda, Md. *Exhib:* Oil Painters Am Exhib, Chicago, 92; Realism, Packersburg Art Ctr, WVa, 94, 95; Lekae Gallery, Scottsdale, Ariz, 96, 98, 99, 2003 & 05; Turner Art Gallery, Denver, Colo, 98; Am Art in Miniature, Gilcrease Mus, Tulsa, Okla, 2000-2002, 2004, 2006-2009; Horizon Fine Art, Jackson, Wyo, 2001; Horizon Fine Art, 2001; Nat Mus Wildlife Art, 2001-2010; Realism Invitational, Santa Fe, NMex, 2001 & 02; West Valley Art Mus,Phoenix, Ariz, 2003; Colo Hist Mus, 2004; Peterson Cody Gallery, Santa Fe, NMex, 2007, 2009, 2011; The New Reality: The Frontier of Realism in the 21st Century, Wichita Art Mus, Kans, The Springfield Mus, Miss & RW Horton Gallery, Shreveport, La, 2008-; Masters of Illusion: Unveiling the Mystery of Trompe L'oeil, Tempe Ctr for the Arts, Ariz, 2008; Bonner David Gallery, Scottsdale, Ariz, 2010, 2013; Sugarman-Peterson Gallery, Santa Fe, NMex, 2013; American Still Lifes, The RW Horton Gallery, 2014. *Collection Arranged:* Marriott Corp, Bethesda, Md; St. Louis Univ Mus, St. Louis, Mo. *Teaching:* Inst art hist, art appreciation, painting & drawing, Red Rocks Community Coll, 90-2007; Metrop State Coll, 2005-2007; Art Students League of Denver, 2004-present. *Awards:* Juror's Choice Award, County Lines, Arvada Ctr Arts, 91; Floral Award, Am Artists Prof League, NY, 92, 94, 99; Juror's Choice Award, Colo Artist Asn, 97; Florence and Ernst Thorne Thompson Mem Award, Allied Artists Am, 2002; Vera C Rosenhaft Award; Am Artists Prof League, 2004; Award of Excellence, Blossom II: Art of Flowers, Naples Art Mus, 2011; Floral award, International Guild of Realism, Tempe, Ariz, 2013. *Mem:* Am Artists Prof League (assoc); Allied Artists Am; Int Guild of Realism. *Media:* Oil. *Specialty:* Contemp Realism. *Collection:* St Louis Univ Mus; Marriott Corp. *Publ:* Auth, Classical Still Life Painting, Watson-Guptill Publs, 2004. *Dealer:* The Peterson Cody Gallery 130 W Palace Ave Santa Fe NM 87501; Dean Day Gallery 2639 Colquitt Houston Tx 77098; Horizon Fine Art 165 North Center St Jackson Wy 83001; Bonner David Gallery 7040 E Main St Scottsdale AZ 85251. *Mailing Add:* 9141 W 75th Pl Arvada CO 80005

JONES, JENNIE C
MULTIMEDIUM ARTIST
Study: Sch of Art Inst Chicago, BFA, 1991; Rutgers Univ, Mason Gross Sch of Arts, MFA, 1996. *Work:* Deutsche Bank; Weil, Gotshal & Manges. *Exhib:* Exhibs include Los Angeles Juried Exhib, William Grant Still Arts Ctr, 1993; San Diego Art Walk, Artist Choose Artist, 1994; Don't try this at Home, Factory Video Lounge, New York, 1997; Current Undercurrents, Artist Living & Working in Brooklyn, Brooklyn Mus of Art, 1997; Generations, AIR Gallery, 1997; Pavement, Martinez Gallery, New York, 1999 ; Snap Shot, Contemp Mus, Md, 2000 ; Bounce: An Evening of New Media Art & Music, Bronx Mus of Arts, 2002 ; Drawing, G Fine Art, Washington, 2003 ; Sunrise / Sunset, Smack Mellon, New York, 2004 ; Double Consciousness: Black Conceptual Art Since 1970, Houston Contemp Art Mus, 2005; Simply Because You're Near Me, Artists Space, New York, 2006; Same Old / Same New, Monya Rowe Gallery, New York, 2008; Absorb/Diffuse, The Kitchen, 2011; Harmonic Distortion-ARRATIA, Beer Gallery, Germany, 2012; Higher Resonance, Hirshhorn Mus, 2013. *Awards:* Wheeler Found, 1999; Pollock-Krasner Grant, 2000; NY Community Trust-Pennies from Heaven Fund, 2006; Rema Hort Mann Found, 2006; Creative Capital Found, 2008; Joyce Alexander Wein Artist Prize, Studio Mus Harlem, 2013

JONES, KIM
CONCEPTUAL ARTIST
b San Bernardino, Calif, 1944. *Work:* Mus Contemp Art, Los Angeles; Mus Mod Art, New York; Metrop Mus Art, New York. *Exhib:* Performances include Mudman, Los Angeles, 1974, Telephone Pole, Los Angeles, 1978, Window Dummy, Artworks, Venice, Calif, 1979, Ash Line, Lincoln Ctr Out-of-Doors, New York, 1990; solo retrospectives: Univ Buffalo Art Gallery, NY, 2006, Luckman Fine Arts Complex, Calif State Univ, Los Angeles, 2007 & Henry Art Gallery, Seattle, 2008; solo exhibs include PS1 Contemp Art Ctr, New York, 1983, Lorence Monk Gallery, New York, 1988, 1990, 1991, John Weber Gallery, New York, 1997, 1999, Pierogi, Brooklyn, NY, 2002, 2004, 2005, 2008, ArtPace, San Antonio, 2003, Zeno X Gallery, Antwerp, 2004, 2006, Pierogi, Leipzig, Germany, 2007; group exhibs include LACE, Los Angeles, 1980; The Year of the Rat, PS1 Contemp Arts Ctr, New York, 1984, Salvaged, 1984, Out of Site, 1990; Biennale de Paris, 1985; Am Acad Arts & Letters, New York, 1985; Burning in Hell, Franklin Furnace, New York, 1991; The Return of the Cadavre Exquis, Drawing Ctr, New York, Corcoran Gallery Art, Washington, Santa Monica Mus Art & Forum Contemp Art, St Louis, 1993; Mapping, Mus Mod Art, New York, 1994, Drawing on Chance, 1995, A Decade of Collection, 1997; Temporarily Possessed, New Mus, New York, 1995, Artists' Performance, 1997, Collage: The Unmonumental Picture, 2008; Face a l'histoire, 1933-1996, Ctr Georges Pompidou, Paris, 1996; Out of Actions: Between Performance & the Object 1949-1979, Mus Contemp Art, Los Angeles, Austria Mus Applied Arts, Vienna, Mus d'Art Contemp, Barcelona & Mus Contemp Art, Tokyo, 1998; Drawn from Artists' Collections, Drawing Ctr, New York & Hammer Mus Art, Los Angeles, 1999; Online, Feigen Contemp, New York, 2003; Disparities & Deformations: Our Grotesque, SITE Santa Fe Int Biennial, 2004; The Photograph as Canvas, Aldrich Contemp Art Mus, Ridgefield, Conn, 2007; Venice Biennale, 2007; The Third Mind: American Artists Contemplating Asia, 1860-1989, Guggenheim Mus, New York, 2009; Sydney Biennale, 2010. *Awards:* US Artists Rockefeller Fel, 2009. *Mailing Add:* c/o Zeno X Gallery Leopold De Waelplaats 16 Antwerp 2000 Belgium

JONES, KRISTIN See Jones & Ginzel

JONES, LIAL A
MUSEUM DIRECTOR
Study: Univ Del, BA, 1979; Mus Mgt Inst, Univ Calif, Berkeley, 1996. *Pos:* Assist dir, Del Art Mus, Wilmington, 1979, deputy dir, Chief Exec Officer; dir, Crocker Art Mus, Sacramento, 1999-. *Awards:* Recipient Art Educator of Year, Art Educators of Del, 1993, Paul Getty Trust Scholarship, 1996. *Mailing Add:* Crocker Art Mus 216 O St Sacramento Sacramento CA 95814

JONES, LOIS SWAN
WRITER, HISTORIAN
b Dallas, Tex, July 3, 1927. *Study:* Univ Chicago, PhB, 47, BS, 48, MS, 54; NTex State Univ, PhD, 72; Ctr Univ d'Ete des Pyrenees, Univ Toulouse, summer 75. *Pos:* Conductor, Le Petite Cercle d'Art, Dallas, 60-79; auth, narrator & photogr, Five Nights in Europe, Dallas Country Club, 63-75; co-owner, Swan Jones Prodns, 92-. *Teaching:* Lectr art hist, Univ Tex, Arlington, 69-70; from asst prof to prof art hist, Univ NTex, Denton, 72-92, emer prof, 92-. *Awards:* Commendation, Catholic Audio Visual Educ, 93 & 95; Distinguished Serv Award, Art Libr Soc NAm, 97; Worldwide Books Publ Award, 2000. *Mem:* Art Libr Soc NAm; Coll Art Asn; Visual Resources Asn. *Res:* Art bibliography and research methodology; Christian iconography; art & the Internet. *Publ:* Auth, Art Libraries & Information Services, Acad Press, 86; Art Information: Research Methods & Resources, Kendall/Hunt, 78, 84 & 90; The Development of Christian Symbolism Video Series: Madonna & Child, 92, Crucifixion & Resurrection, 94, Heaven or Hell: The Last Judgment, 94, Virgin Mary in Art, Swan/Jones prod, 96; Art Information and the Internet: How to Find It, How to Use It, Oryx Press, 98. *Mailing Add:* 8362 San Cristobal Dr Dallas TX 75218-4336

JONES, LOU MARY LOUISE HUMPTON
PAINTER, SCULPTOR
b West Chester, Pa. *Study:* Pa State Univ, BA (Eng lit), 49; with Gene Davis, 68-72; George Mason Univ, Fairfax, Va, BA (art hist), 77; Corcoran Sch Abroad, Leeds Univ, Eng. *Work:* Phillips Collection, Washington, DC; Northern Va Community Col, Alexandria; Am Embassies, Damascus, Syria, Bern, Switz & Bamako, Mali; Univ DC, Washington. *Comn:* Nat Mus Women Arts, Washington. *Exhib:* 19th Area Show, Corcoran Mus, Washington, DC, 74; Va Artists, Va Mus, Richmond, 77 & 79; Coastal Exchange Show, Richmond, 88; New Ways to Collage, George Mason Univ, Fairfax, Va; New Work on Paper, Susan Conway Gallery, 90; Arlington Showcase III, 94; Global Focus, NMWA, Washington; UN Conf on Women, Bejing, China; Gallery K, Washington DC, 94 & 96; Marymount Univ, Arlington, Va, 1999-2000; Gallery 10, Washington, DC, 2000. *Pos:* Panelist, Women Visual Arts, Women's Ctr, Washington, DC, 75, Artists Survival, Univ Md, 78, Am Univ, 79 & Corcoran Sch Art, Washington, DC, Md Inst Art, Baltimore; art consult, Am Corrections, DC, 77-80; dir educ, Athenaeum Mus, Alexandria, Va, 85-; docent, Phillips Collection, Washington, DC, 90. *Teaching:* Instr drawing-mixed media children, Corcoran Gallery, Washington, DC, 75-80; vis prof, Univ Md, 81; adj prof, Marymount Univ, Arlington, Va, 85-94 & Geo Mason Univ, Fairfax, Va, 89-. *Awards:* Purchase Award, Northern Va Community Col, 75; Fel, Va Ctr Creative Arts, Sweet Briar, 81; Artist Equity Award, Form & Substance. *Bibliog:* Jan Allen (auth), article, Washington Times, 10/83; Pam Kesseler (auth), Yellow and gold, Washington Post, 7/88; Michael Welzenbach (auth), Lou Jones at Conway Carroll, Washington Post, 7/89; Mary McCoy (auth), Ellipse in Arlington, Washington Post, 8/94. *Media:* Paper, Collage. *Mailing Add:* 329 Maple Ave Falls Church VA 22046

JONES, MICHAEL BUTLER
SCULPTOR, FREELANCE CURATOR
b Chicago, Ill, Oct 7, 1946. *Study:* Ohio State Univ, BFA, 68, MFA, 78. *Comn:* Ten outdoor murals, Nat Endowment Arts, Dayton, Ohio, 73; 18 outdoor murals in Ohio & Chicago; ten ceramic landscapes, State of Ohio, Columbus, 74; sixteen commemorative bas relief terra cotta panels, Univ Minn, Minneapolis, 85. *Exhib:* Dayton Art Inst, Ohio, 85; Massillon Mus, Ohio, 87; Cleveland Ctr for Contemp Art, Ohio, 88; Cleveland Inst Art, 89; Ohio Univ, 89; Ohio Craft Mus, 95. *Collection Arranged:* Film Installations: Works by Paul Sharits, Bill Lundberg, Anthony McCall & Al Wong, 87; Craft As Content: Nat Metals Invitational, 87; Takaaki Matsumoto: Installation Proj & Design Works, 88; Dan Friedman: Installation Proj & Design

Works, 91; Printed Matter, 92. *Pos:* Dir, Univ Gallery, Wright State Univ, Dayton, Ohio, 78-82 & Univ Akron, 85-91. *Awards:* Ohio Arts Coun Fel, 80. *Bibliog:* Pam Houk (auth), Gary Bower & Michael Jones, Am Ceramics, 86. *Mem:* Artists' Orgn Cols Ohio; Coll Art Asn; Am Craft Asn. *Media:* Clay, Steel. *Publ:* Ed, Athena Tacha: Tape Sculptures, 78 & Regional Fel Recipients Traveling Exhib Cat, Wright State Univ, 79; Pyramidal Influence in Art, 79, Triad, Sculpture Projects, 81 & Ten Solo Exhibitions, 82, Wright State Univ, Dayton, Ohio; Aspects of Perception, Bard Coll & Va Commonwealth Univ, Richmond, 82; coauth, Film Installation Works, Univ Akron, Ohio, 86; Harold Kitner, Univ Akron, 88. *Mailing Add:* 790 Wright St Yellow Springs OH 45387

JONES, NORMA L
PAINTER
b Morrisonville, Ill. *Study:* Univ Houston, Clear Lake City, 75-76; Univ NMex; Univ Mo; Tex Univ; Washington Univ, St Louis; also studied with Rex Brandt, George Post & Edward Betts. *Work:* Banco de Brazilia, Pondereille Oil Co; Tex Instruments Co, Tenneco; AMACO, Houston; Bank Am, NMex. *Comn:* D Regan, Manhatten, NY; Susan Davis, Las Cruces, NMex; Mr & Mrs Ron Biagi, Balboa Island, Calif; Mr & Mrs Randy Luck, Rochester Hills, Mich. *Exhib:* Am Watercolor Soc, Nat Acad, NY; Watercolor USA, Springfield Mus, Mo; Western Fedn, Albuquerque Mus, San Diego & Houston; Magnifico 94; Western Fedn, San Antonio & traveling, 96; Rocky Mountain Nat, 97; Nat Collage Soc, 97; Watercolor USA, 98; Arts Crawl, Albuquerque, NMex, 2000. *Teaching:* Instr, Pickwickian Schools, Houston, Texas & various workshops in Houston & Albuquerque. *Awards:* Merit Award, Western Fedn, San Antonio (traveling), 96; Rocky Mountain Nat Award, 97; Purchase Award, Watercolor USA, 98; Masterworks of NMex Award, 2000. *Bibliog:* Article in NMex Mag, 5/92; Gerald Brommer, Collage Techniques (bk), 97; article in Albuquerque Arts Mag, 3/98. *Mem:* NMex Watercolor Soc Signature Group; Soc Layerists Multi-Media; Southwestern Fedn Watercolorists; North Coast Collage Soc; Am Univ Asn. *Media:* Acrylic, Mixed Media. *Publ:* Contribr, Twelve New Mexico Landscape Painters. *Dealer:* Dartmouth St Gallery Albuquerque NM; Weyrich Gallery Albuquerque NM; Patrician Design Albuquerque NM; The Johnsons Madrid NM; Vladimir Fine Arts Kalamazoo Mich

JONES, PATTY SUE
PAINTER, CURATOR
b New Orleans, La, Aug 18, 1949. *Study:* Auburn Univ, 67-69 & 74; Univ Calif, Los Angeles, photog with Robert Heinecken, BA, 72, MA, 74; Univ Wash, with Jack Lenor Larsen, summer 75. *Work:* Yuma Fine Arts Ctr, Ariz. *Comn:* Paintings, Regent Hotels Int, Beverly Hills, Calif, 74; tapestry, Fluor Corp, Irvine, Calif, 78; tapestry, Security Pac Bank, Topanga Canyon, Calif, 79. *Exhib:* Tucson Mus Art, Ariz, 75; Ariz State Univ, Tempe, 79; Security Pac Hq, Los Angeles, 81; Occidental Col, Los Angeles, 81; Los Angeles Inst Contemp Art, 81; and many others. *Collection Arranged:* Robert Delgado, Mural Making: The Process, 80, The Mask: Object and Image, 80, Paper: Cast/Torn/Formed, 80 & California Dada, 80, Old Venice Jail Gallery, Venice, Calif. *Pos:* Dir's coun mem, Yuma Fine Art Ctr, Ariz, 76-77; cur exhibs, Old Venice Jail Gallery, Venice, Calif, 79-81. *Teaching:* Teaching asst, Univ Calif, Los Angeles, 73-74; instr, Ariz Western Col, Yuma, 74-77, Ariz State Univ, Tempe, 75-76 & St Mary's Col, Los Angeles, 82. *Awards:* Purchase Award, 10th Ann Southwestern, 75. *Bibliog:* Laurel Meinig (auth), Artists-in-residence (catalog), Yuma Art Ctr, Ariz, 76; William Wilson (auth), Lint drawings (review), Los Angeles Times, 80. *Media:* Oil. *Publ:* Contribr, Spectrum: New directions in color photography, Univ Hawaii, 79. *Mailing Add:* 311 N Ave 66 Los Angeles CA 90042

JONES, PIRKLE
PHOTOGRAPHER
b Shreveport, La, Jan 2, 1914. *Study:* Calif Sch Fine Arts, cert, 49. *Hon Degrees:* Grant in photography, NEA, 77; Cert of Recognition, Nat Urban League, 61; Doct Fine Arts, San Francisco Art Inst, 04. *Work:* San Francisco Mus Mod Art; Art Inst Chicago; Ctr Creative Photog, Univ Ariz; Yokohama Mus, Japan; Mus Mod Art, NY; Metropolitan Mus Art, NY; Nat Mus Modern Art, Koyoto, Japan; Santa Barbara Mus Art. *Comn:* Commemorative UN Portfolio, Bank Am, San Francisco, 55; The Story of a Winery, Paul Masson, John Bolles, San Francisco, 59; Courthouses, Bicentennial Proj, Joseph E Seagram Inc, NY, 75. *Exhib:* Photog in the Twentieth Century, Nat Gallery Can, 67; A Photog Essay on the Black Panthers, De Young Mus Art, 68, Studio Mus Harlem, 70, Hopkins Ctr, Dartmouth Col, 70 & Univ Calif, Santa Cruz, 70; Courthouse, Photographs from the Segrams' Collection, Mus Mod Art, NY, 78; Messages From West Coast, Photo Gallery Int, Tokyo, 79; Curator's Choice: By John Humphery, San Francisco Mus Mod Art, 80; Awards of Honor, A Documentary Exhibition, San Francisco Arts Commission, Gallery, Bank Am, World Hq, San Francisco, 83; Photog in California: Pushing the Boundaries 1945-1980, San Francisco Mus Mod Art, 84; Made in Calif: Art, Image & Identity, 1900-2000, Los Angeles (Calif) Co Mus Art, 2000-01; Pirkle Jones, 60 yrs in Photog, Santa Barbara Mus Art, 2001-2002; Black Panthers 1968, Berkeley Art Mus, Berkeley, Calif, 2003; Pirkle Jones & the Changing California Landscape, San Francisco Mus Modern Art, 2003-2004; Black Panther Rank & File, Yerba Buena Ctr for the Arts, San Francisco, 2006; A Sense of Place Photographs by Pirkle Jones, The Marin Community Found, Novato, Calif, 2006-07. *Teaching:* Instr photog, Calif Sch Fine Arts, 52-58, Ansel Adams Workshops, Yosemite Nat Park, 66-74 & San Francisco Art Inst, 70-97; master class, Univ Calif, Santa Cruz, 84, 88. *Awards:* Award Hon Photog, A Documentary Exhib, San Francisco Arts Comn, 83. *Bibliog:* Ansel Adams (auth), article, US Camera Mag, 10/52; Nancy Newhall (auth), article, Aperture Mag, 56; Robert Holmes (auth), article, Brit J Photog, 10/80. *Publ:* Auth, Portfolio One, Commemoration Signing United Nations Charter, private publ, 55; coauth, Death of a valley, Aperture Mag, 60; The Vanguard, A Photographic Essay on the Black Panthers, Beacon Press, 70; auth, Berryessa Valley The Last Year, Vacaville Mus, 94; auth, Pirkle Jones California Photographs, Aperture, 2001; co-auth, Black Panthers 1968, Greyball Press, 2002. *Dealer:* Shapiro Gallery, 49 Geary Ste 208, San Francisco, CA, 94108; Lumiere, 425 Peachtree Hills Ave 29B, Atlanta, Ga, 30305

JONES, RONALD LEE, JR
ADMINISTRATOR, WRITER
b Beckley, WVa, Dec 4, 1942. *Study:* Shepherd Univ, BA (art and English); Ariz State Univ, MA; Univ Md, PhD (aesthetics educ). *Pos:* Contrib ed, Art Voices, S Palm Beach, Fla, 78-; chmn, WVa Arts & Humanities Comn, Capitol Complex, Charleston, 78-; secy, Int Coun Fine Arts Deans; pres, Fla Arts Deans Network. *Teaching:* Prof art & chmn dept, Shepherd Col, Shepherdstown, WVa, 69-, chmn, Div Creative Arts, formerly & dean, Sch Arts, formerly; dean, Col of The Arts, Univ S Fla, formerly; pres, Memphis Col Art, 2011-. *Mem:* Nat Art Educ Asn; Nat Coun Policy Study Art Educ; Coll Art Asn, WVa (pres, 71, 72 & 75); Nat Asn Arts Adminr; Nat Asn State Art Agencies; Tampa Mus Art (bd trustees). *Res:* Aesthetic response; writing art criticism for art journals. *Publ:* Auth, A re-examination of Mittler's efforts toward modern art attitude, Studies in Art Educ, 75; contribr, Artists in Schools: Analysis and Criticism, Univ Ill Bur Educ Res, 78; auth, Phenomenological analysis effects on aspective perception: a review, Rev Res in Visual Arts, 78; Critical reviews of artists, Art Voices/S 78-80; Phenomenological balance and the aesthetic response, J Aesthetic Educ, 79. *Mailing Add:* Memphis College of Art Office of President 1930 Popular Ave Memphis TN 38104

JONES, RONALD WARREN
ARTIST, CRITIC
b Ft Belvoir, Va, July 8, 1952. *Study:* Huntington Col, BA, 74; Univ SC, MFA, 76; Ohio Univ, PhD (art hist), 81. *Work:* Baltimore Mus Art; Moderna Museet, Stockholm, Sweden; Whitney Mus Am Art, Moca, La; Mus Mod Art, NY. *Comn:* Pritzker Park, City of Chicago; and others. *Exhib:* High Mus Art, Atlanta, 86; Metro Pictures, NY, 87-90; Metro Pictures, NY, 87 & 88; Sebui Mus, Tokyo, 90; Mind Over Matter Whitney Mus Am Art, NY, 90; Galerie Lehman, Switz, 92 & 94; Sonnabend Gallery, NY, 93; Metro Pictures, 97. *Teaching:* RI Sch Design, 88-90; Yale Univ, 89-98; Sch Visual Arts, 89-90; chmn, Visual Arts Div & dir, Digital Media Ctr, Sch Arts, Columbia Univ, 98; provost, Art Ctr Col of Design, 2000-. *Awards:* Mellon Found Stipend, 83; Fel, Nat Endowment Visual Artist, 84. *Bibliog:* Peter Halley (auth), Ronald Jones, Marcel Duchamp, and the New South (catalog essay), San Jose Mus Art; Richard Flood (auth), Ronald Jones (catalog essay), Isabella Kacprzak, Koln; Roberta Smith (auth), The New York Times, 88-90; Eleanor Heartney (auth), Ronald Jones at Metro Pictures, Art in Am, 1/88. *Mem:* Coll Art Asn. *Publ:* Auth, various articles, essays & reviews, in: Artforum, Parkett Arts Mag, C Mag, Art in Am, Artscribe & Flash Art. *Dealer:* Metro Pictures 150 Greene St New York NY; Sonnabend Gallery New York NY. *Mailing Add:* Art Center 1700 Lida St Pasadena CA 91103

JONES, RUTHE BLALOCK
PAINTER, EDUCATOR
b Claremore, Okla, June 8, 1939. *Study:* Bacone Col, with Dick West, AA; Univ Tulsa, with Carl Coker, BFA; Northeastern State Univ, Tablequah, Okla, MS. *Work:* Mus Am Indian, Heye Found, NY; Indian Arts & Crafts Bd, US Dept Interior, Washington, DC; Heard Mus, Phoenix; Philbrook Art Ctr, Tulsa; Williams Performing Arts Ctr, Tulsa, Okla. *Comn:* Minnetrista Cult Ctr, Muncie, Ind, 93. *Exhib:* Contemp North Am Indian Painting, Mus Natural Hist, Smithsonian Inst, Washington, DC, 82; Am Indian Community House, NY, 82; Southeastern Indian Artists, Fine Arts Ctr, Atlanta, Ga, 88; 9th Symposium, Int Soc Polyaesthetic Educ, Schloss Mittersill, Austria, 90; Moving the Fire, Official Okla State Event 1993 Pres Inauguration, Washington, DC, 93; Watchfall Eyes Invitational, Heard Mus, Phoenix, Ariz, 94; From the Earth X, Am Indian Contemp Arts, San Francisco, Calif; Symbols of Faith and Belief Gil Crease Mus, Tulsa, Okla 2000-; Visions and Veeces Millbrook Mus, Tulsa, 1998-. *Teaching:* Instr art, Bacone Col, Muskogee, Okla, 79-85, 87-. *Awards:* First Painting Award, Red Earth Art Competition, Oklahoma City, 90; Gov Award, State Capitol, Oklahoma City, 93; Crumbo Mem Award, SWAIA Indian Market, Santa Fe, NMex, 94. *Bibliog:* J Snodgrass (auth), Handbook American Indian Artists, Mus Am Indian, 67; H Meredith (auth), The Bacone School of Art, Chronicles Okla, LVIII, No 1, spring 80; article, Okla Today, Vol 35, No 4, 7-8/85. *Mem:* Southwestern Indian Art Asn, Santa Fe, NMex; Indian Arts & Crafts Asn, Albuquerque, NMex; Jacobson Found, Norman, Okla. *Media:* Watercolor, Acrylic, Graphics. *Res:* Ceremony of Delaware and Shawnee tribes of Indians; traditional American Indian painting. *Specialty:* Native Am Art. *Publ:* Mini Myths and Legends of Oklahoma Indians, Wise, Lu Celia, 78; State of Oklahoma Indian Education Curriculum Guides, 78; Bacone Indian University: A History, Williams & Meredith, 80; Auth, Keepers of Culture, (exhib catalog), Anniston Mus of Natural Hist, Ala, 88; Legends of Tree Delaware Indians (cover art), 99. *Dealer:* Native American Art 323 S Main Mall Tulsa OK 74172 74145; Indian Images Box 3621 Evansville IN 47735. *Mailing Add:* 517 S Woodlawn Ave Okmulgee OK 74447-5347

JONES, THEODORE JOSEPH
SCULPTOR, PRINTMAKER
b New Orleans, La, Sept 14, 1938. *Study:* Xavier Univ, BA; Mich State Univ, MA; Univ Mont, MFA; Fla A&M Univ, cert; Fisk Univ, cert. *Work:* Johnson Publ Co, Chicago; Mus African Art, Washington, DC; First Am Nat Bank, Nashville. *Exhib:* Solo exhibs, Ala A&M Univ, Normal, 75, Tenn State Mus, 75 & Creatadrama Art Gallery, Bloomington, Ind, 75; 17th Tenn All-State Artists Exhib, Centennial Park Galleries, Nashville, 77; From These Roots Exhib, Tenn State Mus, Nashville, 77; Smith-Mason Galleries, Washington, DC, 77; and many others. *Pos:* Touring artist, Tenn Arts Comn, 70-; art consult, Claiborne Ave Design Team Symp, New Orleans, La, 74-. *Teaching:* Instr art, Fla A&M Univ, 65-68; from assoc prof to prof art, Tenn State Univ, 68-. *Awards:* Tenn State Univ Grant, 70; Third Place Sculpture, Tenn Art League, 74; Lyzon Galleries Award Graphics, Cent South Exhib, 75. *Bibliog:* Clara Hieronymus (auth), Ted Jones Exhibition, Tennessean Newspaper, 75; Kenneth Weedman (auth), article, Sculpture Quart, 75. *Mem:* Tenn Lit Arts Asn; Southern Independent Artists Asn; Southern Asn Sculptors; Southeastern Graphics Coun; Tennessee Art League. *Publ:* Contribr, Galaxy III Communication Arts Seminar Basic

Holography, 74; ed, Faculty exhibition catalogs & brochures, Tenn State Univ, 74-75; auth, Thoughts and Verses (poetry and prints), 75 & Masonite-Printing: A New Approach in Relief Printing, 77, New Dimension Studio, Nashville. *Mailing Add:* 1003 Cross Bow Dr Hendersonville TN 37075-9403

JONES, THOMAS WILLIAM
PAINTER
b Lakewood, Ohio, Aug 13, 1942. *Study:* Cleveland Inst Art, dipl, 64. *Work:* City of Seattle Selects II (For Pub Collection of Seattle City Light, Wash); Rainier Bank Collection, Pac Northwest Bell Collection, Seattle; Pac Car & Foundry & Eddie Bauer, Inc, Seattle. *Comn:* 25 landscape paintings, Gen Tel Co of the Northwest, Everett, Wash, 68; paintings of Old Holland, Western Int Design Serv, St Francis Hotel, San Francisco, 72; paintings for bd dirs, Seattle First Nat Bank, 74; four seasonal landscapes & 60th anniversary catalog cover, Eddie Bauer Inc, Seattle, 75, 80 & 82; Presidential Christmas Card, comn by White House, 85, 86, 87, 88; Vice Presidential Christmas Card, 2002-2003. *Exhib:* Solo exhib, Frye Art Mus, Seattle, 73 & 99; 154th Nat Acad Design, NY, 79; Northwest Art Today, 75, Works on Paper, 75 & Wash Open, 79, Seattle Art Mus; Artists of Am, Denver, 81-98; Nat Acad of Western Art & Prix de West, Oklahoma City, 81-2006; Celebration of Northwest Art, Gov's Mansion, Olympia, Wash, 84. *Awards:* Ted Kautzky Mem Award, Am Watercolor Soc, 75 & Bronze Medal of Honor, 79; First Place, Water Media, Rocky Mountain Nat, 76; Silver Medal, Nat Acad Western Art, 84 & Gold Medal, 87. *Bibliog:* Auth, Watercolor page, Am Artist, 9/79; Southwest Art feature article, Southwest Art Inc, (9/85 & 12/96); Patricia Black Bailey (auth), article, US Art, 1/90; Art in the White House-A Nations Pride-White House Hist Asn, 92; Myrna Zanetell (auth), Art of the West, Duerr & Tierney, 2004; Mary Evans Seeley, Season's Greetings from the White House, Presidential Christmas Corp, 2005. *Mem:* Hon mem Fed Can Artists. *Media:* Watercolor. *Dealer:* AJ Kollar Fine Paintings LLC 1421 E Aloha St Seattle WA 98112. *Mailing Add:* 18226 Dubuque Rd Snohomish WA 98290-8534

JONES & GINZEL
SCULPTORS, VISUAL ARTISTS, EDUCATORS
b Washington, Aug 1, 1956 (Jones); b Chicago, Ill, July 14, 1954 (Ginzel). *Study:* Jones: St Martin's, London, 78-79, RI Sch Design, BFA, 79, Yale Univ, MFA, 83; Ginzel: self-taught. *Work:* Mus d'Arte Contemporanea, Prato, Italy; Wadsworth Atheneum, Hartford, Conn; Brooklyn Mus, New York; Kunsthalle, Basel, Switz; Targetti Art Light Collection, Florence, Italy. *Comn:* Mnemonics, Battery Park City Authority, 92 & Occulus, Metrop Transit Authority, New York, 99; Principia, Ore Convention Ctr, Portland, 90; Plethora, Arts Am Prog, New Delhi, India, 91; Diaxiom, Com Sq One, IM Pei & Partners, Philadelphia, Pa, 91; Apostasy, 1996 Olympic Arts Festival, Woodruff Park, Atlanta, 96; Metronome, One Union Sq, New York, 99; Tevereterino, Rome, Italy, Polarities, Kans City Airport, 2004; Spiraculum, Tampa Int Airport, 2005; Panopia, Chicago, 2005; Metro, St Louis, Mo, 2008; Ohio State Physics, Columbus, Ohio, 2009; Snow Coll, Utah, 2010; Univ Colo, Boulder, Colo, 2010, 2012; Fluent, Hoboken Ferry Terminal, 2011. *Exhib:* Ad Infinitum, Whitney Mus Am Art at Philip Morris, New York, 85 & 88; solo exhibs, Va Mus Fine Arts, (catalog), 86, New Mus Contemp Art, New York, 86, Wadsworth Atheneum, 88 & List Visual Arts Ctr, Mass Inst Technol, Cambridge, 88; Interaction, 88 & Metathesis, Aldrich Mus Contemp Art, Ridgefield, Conn; Antithesis (with catalog), Kunsthalle, Basel, Switz, 89; Axis, Mechanika, Contemp Arts Ctr, Cincinnati, Ohio, 90-92; Synchysis, Chicago Cult Ctr, Ill, 93; Apotheosis (with catalog), Pub Art Fund Inc, New York, 94; Ellipsis, Aquario Romano, Rome, 95; Enigmas, Frederieke Taylor, New York, 96. *Teaching:* Ginzel: Instr Sculpture, Sch Visual Arts, New York, 85-; Jones: instr sculpture, Philadelphia Coll Art, 86; Both: lectr, Tyler Sch Art, Philadelphia, 87 & 94; vis artists, Yale Univ, New Haven, Conn, 88 & 96, Cornish Sch Art, Seattle, Wash, 88, RI Sch Design, Providence, 89, 96, 2006, 2012 & Harvard Univ, Cambridge, Mass, 89. *Awards:* Fel, Nat Endowment Arts, sculpture, 86 & 94; Visual Arts Fel, Nat Endowment Arts, 86; Louis Comfort Tiffany Found, 91; Pollock-Krasner Found, 94; Rome Prize, Am Acad Rome, Italy, 94-95. *Bibliog:* Edith Newhall (auth), Happening Time and Again, NY Mag, 10/25/99; David Masello (auth), New York's 50 Best Works of Art in Public Places, City & Co, 99; Tom Finkelpearl (auth), Dialogues in Public Art, MIT Press, 2000. *Mem:* Int Sculpture Ctr; fel, Am Acad Rome. *Media:* Mixed Media. *Dealer:* Frederieke Taylor 535 W 22nd St New York NY 10001. *Mailing Add:* 289 Bleecker St New York NY 10014

JONSSON, TED (WILBUR)
SCULPTOR
b Berkeley, Calif, Oct 2, 1933. *Study:* Univ Calif Davis, BFA (philos fine art), 52-57; Univ Wash, MFA (sculpture), 62-64. *Work:* City of Seattle, Permanent Works Collection, Wash; Seattle Art Mus, Wash; Manoogian Collection, Detroit, Mich; Fed Reserve Bank San Francisco, Seattle, Wash; Wash State Art Collection; Alaska Coun on the Arts; Seattle Pub Art Collection. *Comn:* Seattle Water Dept (fountain), City of Seattle, Wash, 75; Seattle Int Airport (sculpture), Port of Seattle, Wash, 72; Univ Alaska (sculpture), Alaska Coun Arts, Anchorage, 76; Olympia Tech Coll (sculpture), Wash State Art Comn, 79; Fed Reserve, New Plaza (sculpture), Fed Reserve Bank San Francisco, Seattle, Wash, 91; Fountain, SAP Labs Inc, Palo Alto, Calif, 98; Kennelly Commons (sculpture fountain), Green River Col, auburn, Wash, 2005. *Exhib:* West Coast Now, Current Art from Western Seaboard, Traveling West Coast Mus Show, 68; Gov's Invitational Int, Olympia, Wash, 69, 72, 73, 75 & 76; Art in Pub Places, Henry Gallery, Univ Wash, 72; Northwest 77, Seattle Art Mus Pavillion, Wash, 77; Northwest Invitational, Artists Today: Part II, Seattle Mod Art Pavillion, 77; Seattle Sculpture 27-87, Bumberbiennial, 87; Northwest Ann, Seattle, 90; Barcelona/Seattle exhib, Seattle, 90, Barcelona, Spain, 91; Holland Meets the USA, Galerie Daneel, Amsterdam, 92; Hungary/USA Exchange, Galeria Vizual Art, Galeria Ava Gera, Budapest, Hungary, 93. *Pos:* Cur, Wash State Capitol Mus, 62-63; art curator, Washington State Capitol Mus, Olympia, 62. *Teaching:* Art instr sculpture, Highline Community Col, Midway, Wash, 68-79; sculpture instr, Calif State Univ, Humbolt, 88-89; sculpture tech instr Humbolt State Univ, 89-90. *Awards:* First Prize, Pacific Northwest Ann, Spokane Mus Art, 67; Sculpture Award, Ann Exhib Northwest Painting & Sculpture, Seattle Art Mus, 73; Visual Arts Honors Award Outstanding Visual Artist, Wash State Art Comn, 87; and others. *Bibliog:* Louis G Redstone (auth), Art and Architecture & Public Art New Directions, McGraw-Hill, 79; John Beardsley (auth), Art in Public Places (pg 135), 1981; Charlie B Tomlins (auth), Water Sculpture USA, Univ Tex Press, 86; CB Tomlins (auth), Water Sculpture USA, Univ Tex Press, 1986. *Mem:* Artist Equity Wash State Chap Nat Affil (vpres 86-92); Int Sculpture Ctr; Artist Trust; The Artist Group (charter mem, bd dir 71, bd dir 72, 73, vice chair bd dir 74, 75, pres 77). *Media:* Stainless Steel, Granite, Water. *Interests:* Sailing, flying, skiing. *Dealer:* OK Harris Gallery 383 W Broadway New York NY 10012; Davidson Galleries 313 Occidental S Seattle WA 98104. *Mailing Add:* 805 NE Northlake Way Seattle WA 98105

JOO, EUNGIE
CURATOR
Study: Vassar Coll, BA (Africana studies), 1991; Univ Calif, Berkeley, PhD (ethnic studies), 2002. *Collection Arranged:* Regards, Barry McGee, Walker Art Ctr, Minneapolis, 1998; Widely Unknown, Deitch Projects, New York, 2001; Abstruction, Artists Space, New York, 2003; Time After Time: Asia & Our Moment, Yerba Buena Ctr Arts, San Francisco, 2003; Museum as Hub: Six Degrees, New Mus Contemp Art, New York, 2008, The Ungovernables, 2012. *Pos:* Curatorial asst, Walker Art Ctr, Minneapolis, formerly; independent cur & writer, New York & Oakland, Calif, formerly; artistic com, Etant Donnés, currently; bd dirs, William H Johnson Found, currently; adv bd, Yerba Buena Ctr Arts, San Francisco & Side Street Projects, currently; edit bd, Afterall, currently; founding dir & cur, Roy & Edna Disney/CalArts Theater (REDCAT) Gallery, Los Angeles, 2003-07; Keith Haring dir & cur edn & pub programs, New Mus Contemp Art, New York, 2007-2012; adv com, Carnegie Int, Carnegie Mus Art, Pittsburgh, 2008; nat commissioner, Korean Pavilion, Venice Biennale, 2009; dir. art & cultural programs Instituto Inhotim, Minas Gerais, Brazil, 2012-. *Teaching:* Instr & vis artist, Calif Inst Arts, formerly. *Awards:* Walter Hopps Award for Curatorial Achievement, 2006. *Publ:* Prodr, Recollection (film), Lorna Simpson, 1998, Duets, Thirty-One. *Mailing Add:* Instituto Inhotim Rua B, 20 Brumadinho 35460 Brazil

JOOST-GAUGIER, CHRISTIANE L
ADMINISTRATOR, HISTORIAN
b Ste Maxime, France; US citizen. *Study:* Radcliffe Coll, BA (hon); Harvard Univ, MA, PhD; Univ Munich, postgrad; Endowed Postdoc Fel AAUW. *Hon Degrees:* Harvard Univ, Phi Beta Kappa (hon), 2005. *Teaching:* Asst prof Renaissance art, Tufts Univ, 69-75; prof Renaissance art, NMex State Univ, 75-85, head art dept, 75-81; prof Renaissance art, Univ NMex, 85-2000, chair art dept, 85-87; lectr, Smithsonian Inst & Univ Maryland; prof & chair, dept of art & history, Wayne State Univ, 2008-. *Awards:* Am Coun Learned Socs Grant; Kress Found Grant for Publ; Kress Found Grants for Libr Enrichment; NEH Travel Grants; Am Philos Soc Res Grants; Delmas Found Grant; Fulbright Fel; and others. *Mem:* Coll Art Asn (bd dir, 80-86); Nat Coun Arts Administrators; Renaissance Soc Am (coun); Women's Caucus Art (adv bd); 16th Century Soc; Intellectual Hist; and others. *Res:* Venetian drawings, series of famous men and women; Quattrocento art in Florence and Venice; Lombard architecture; Raphael and Rome; Michelangelo; intellectual history; Greek and Roman lit history, The Pantheon; Pythagoreanism in the renaissance; early history of wine in antiquity. *Interests:* Art history as intellectual history. *Publ:* Auth of var articles in Gazette des Beaux-Arts, Art Bull, Zeitschrift fuer Kunstgeschichte, Commentari, Antichita Viva, Acta Historiae Artium, Artibus et Historiae, Arte Lombarda, Arte Veneta, Storia dell'Arte, Studi Veneziani; auth, The Selected Drawings of Jacopo Bellini, auth, Raphael's Stanza della Segnatura: Meaning and Invention; Measuring Heaven: Pythagoras and His Influence on Thought and Art in Antiquity and the Middle Ages; Pythagoras & Renaissance Europe: Finding Heaven; Pitagora e il Suo Iflusso Sull 'Arte e Cultura nel antichita. *Mailing Add:* Dept Art & Art Hist Art Bldg Wayne State Univ Detroit MI 48202

JORDAN, BETH MCANINCH
PAINTER
b Corn, Okla, Nov 23, 1918. *Study:* Southwestern State Univ, grad; Taber Col, Hillsboro, Kans; also with Jack Vallee, Millard Sheets & others. *Work:* Okla Art Ctr, Southwest Christian Col, State of Okla Collection of Okla Art & Humanities Coun; Oklahoma City Arts Coun; Kerr Conv Ctr; and over 50 corp collections. *Exhib:* Okla Nat Printmakers & Watercolor Show, 61; Southwestern Watercolor Soc Regional & Open, Dallas, Tex, 67, 69 & 71; 8 State Exhib Painting & Sculpture Ann, Okla Art Ctr, 71; Watercolor USA, Springfield, Mo, 73 & 79; Okla Artists Ann, Philbrook, Tulsa, 61-72; Butler Inst Am Art, Youngstown, Ohio, 78; Ann solo exhib for the past 32 yrs; Audubon artists, NY; Nat Womens Show, NY. *Pos:* Art bd, Omiplex, Kirkpatrick Gallery, formerly. *Teaching:* Instr painting & drawing, pvt classes, 60-70; instr painting & drawing, Okla Sci & Art Found, 62-66. *Bibliog:* Oklahoma City Key & Oklahoma City Down Towner, 85. *Mem:* Southwestern Watercolor Soc. *Media:* Watercolor, Pencil, Collage. *Dealer:* Linda Howell & Assocs Inc 6432 N Western Ave Oklahoma City OK 73116. *Mailing Add:* 1606 Drakestone Ave Oklahoma City OK 73120-1207

JORDAN, GEORGE EDWIN
HISTORIAN, CONSULTANT
Study: Univ Ky; Ringling Sch Art, Sarasota, Fla, BFA; ETenn State Univ. *Pos:* Cur, Reece Mus, Johnson City, Tenn, 66-69; cur Am art & registrar, New Orleans Mus Art, La, 69-72; art critic, New Orleans Times-Picayune, La, 74-77, ed, World of Art column, 77-79; freelance art writer, lectr, appraiser & consult, 79-; contrib ed, Art & Auction, 81-84; co-ed, New Orleans Art Rev, 82-; auth, Critics Choice monthly column, Go Mag, 83-88; guest cur, Seldom Seen Figures, Arts Coun New Orleans, 86. *Teaching:* Guest instr hist contemp painting, Adult Educ, Tulane Univ, 76-79; instr painting & art hist, New Orleans Acad Fine Arts, 84-85; vis scholar, Hist New Orleans

Collection, 2001-02; Advisor, John Burton Harter Charitable Trust. *Res:* Artists who worked in New Orleans and the Southeast, late 18th, 19th and early 20th centuries. *Interests:* advisor, JB Harter Trust for gay related art & hist. *Publ:* auth, Louisiana Artists 19th Century, WYES-Educ Television, New Orleans, 72-73; contribr, Encyclopedia of New Orleans Artists, 1718-1918, Historic New Orleans Collection, 87; auth, Josephine Crawford, In: Eight Southern Women Artists (catalog), Greenville County Mus of Art; coauth, Complementary Visions of Louisiana Art, Hist New Orleans Collection, 96; contribr (film), Brothers in Art, Ellsworth & William Woodward & their Art in the South, Hist New Orleans Collection, 97; auth, George L Viavant, Artist of the Hunt, Hist New Orleans Collection, 2003. *Mailing Add:* 745 Lakeside Dr Bridgeport CT 06606

JORDAN, JOHN L
SCULPTOR, VIDEO ARTIST
b Houston, Tex, Dec 21, 1944. *Study:* Art League Houston, with Jack Birch, 66; studied with John Howley, St Kilda, Australia, 83 & Rick Conti, Ceramics, Woodstock Guild, Byrdcliffe, 2007. *Work:* Catskill Alliance for Peace, Woodstock, NY, 91-98; Woodstock Mus, NY. *Comn:* Billboard mural, US Air Force, Ellington AFB, Tex, 66. *Exhib:* Larimer Sq, Denver, Colo, 80-81; House of Emeralds, Waikiki, Hi, 83; Homage to Dali with Fried Eggs, Manhattan Pub TV, NY, 91; Jonathan Oliver Straus, Nemesis II Gallery, Soho, NY, 88-92; Clouds Gallery, Robert Ohnigian, curator, Woodstock, 92-98; Intimate Views, Woodstock Artists Asn, 94; Hiroshima on the Hudson, with congressman Maurice Hinchey, Town Hall, Woodstock, NY, 2000; Woodstock Guild 5x7 Show, 2001; Group show, Standing Earth Mother, 2009-2012; Little Dancer, 2010-2012; Deus Ex Makina, 2013; Lion Ring, 2013. *Pos:* Artist & designer, Jerusalem Jewels, Denver & Hawaii, 77-85; art dir, Gaudeamus Jordan, Woodstock, Bethlehem & Allentown, 86-87, NY, 88-; art rep, Whitney Morse Art Group, New York, 88-91; producer & host, Ramble On, WATV, Woodstock, NY, 90-2006; exec producer, Woodstock Winter Video Festival, 94; producer, Woodstock Music Asn, 2002-05. *Teaching:* Art teacher wax prep, Onteora Sch Dist, Woodstock, NY, 88 & 91. *Awards:* Spec Award, Am Fedn Gem & Mineralogical Soc Nat Show, Astrohall, Tex, 82; Exhib Award, Montgomery Co Fair, Conroe, Tex, 85; Exhib Award, Allentown Art Mus, Pa, 88. *Bibliog:* Ron Ronck (auth), Arts scene, Honolulu Advertiser, 84; Kevin O'Brian (auth), Woodstock Times, NY, 12/29/88; Sharon Cherven (auth), Woodstocks' Jordan Romances the Stones, Daily Freeman, Kingston, NY, 11/27/89; Artist Creates Dali tribute triptych, Art Bus News, 3/90. *Mem:* Woodstock Artists Asn, NY; Woodstock Guild Artists, NY, 89-; Catskill Alliance for Peace, 91-98; Mid Hudson Valley Gem & Mineral Soc, 92-; Woodstock UFO Network, 94-. *Media:* All Media. *Res:* Reassignment recycling. *Specialty:* eclectic things that matter. *Interests:* artists such as musicians, writers, poets, songwriters, actors, magicians, jugglers, singers, painters, sculptors, DJs, producers, cross genre art history. *Collection:* over 700 artists in the colony of the arts, interviews or examples, video format. *Publ:* Homage to Dali with Fried Eggs (video), 92; auth, Color Me-No Bikini Atoll, 92; Earl Bennett-Jack of Diamonds (video), 93; Roxy Dawn's Benefits with Billy Mitchell (video), 92-94; painter, Hong Nian Zhang (video), 91 & 96; Peter Max in Woodstock (video), 94; Pete Seeger on Solar (video), 97; Mudstock at Max Yasgur's Farm (video); The Dharma Bums in Woodstock (video), 1999-2005; Alf Evers-Historian, Artist, Writer, (video, interview), Woodstock, 98; When in Rome (woodstock) Video for TV Festival, Rome, NY, 99; The Sand Painters of Tashi Lhunpo (video), 2002; Woodstock Dam Restoration Project, 06-09; co-prod, On the Road with the Dalai Lama (WATV), Woodstock/Dharmsala, 2008; Chris Zaloom, local musician, plays everwhere (interview), 93; Steve Knight-Keyboardist, Mississippi Queen by Mountain, with Papalordi, Felix interview, 93; Joe Fig Artist, Video, 94; Phil Void and his Band, The Dharma Bums, Musical Productions Worldwide (videos), 2002-2006; Standing Earth Mother, with Little Dancer, 2010; prod, Goodnight Irene, Woodstock Cable TV & Internet, 2011-2013; prod, In Orbit Around the Sun, Woodstock Cable TV & Internet, 2012-2013. *Dealer:* Woodstock-Byrdcliffe Guild. *Mailing Add:* c/o John Jordan PO Box 932 Woodstock NY 12498

JORDAN, MARY ANNE
EDUCATOR, ADMINISTRATOR
Study: Univ Mich, BFA; Cranbrook Acad of Art, MFA. *Exhib:* Work exhibited nationally across the US and internationally in Japan, Poland, South America, France and Canada. *Teaching:* Taught workshops at Arrowmont, Haystack, Penland, Splitrock, and the Quilt and Surface Design Symposium; Prof textiles, Sch of Fine Arts, chair, Univ Kansas, currently. *Awards:* Research Fellow, Internat Quilt Study Ctr, Univ Nebraska, 2005-06. *Publ:* Work has been published in various exhibition catalogs, magazines, and journals such as Fiberarts, Surface Design Journal, and American Craft. *Mailing Add:* Department of Visual Art Art & Design Buliding 1467 Jayhawk Blvd Room 300 Lawrence KS 66045-7531

JORDAN, WILLIAM B
HISTORIAN, CONSULTANT
b Nashville, Tenn, May 8, 1940. *Study:* Washington & Lee Univ, BA, 62; NY Univ, MA, 64, PhD, 67. *Hon Degrees:* So Methodist Univ, LHD, 95. *Pos:* Chmn div fine arts, Meadows Sch of the Arts, Southern Methodist Univ, 67-73, dir, Meadows Mus, 67-81; deputy dir, Kimbell Art Mus, 81-90; bd trustees, Chinati Found, Marfa, Tex, 2001- & Nasher Found, Dallas, 2001-. *Teaching:* Assoc prof Span art hist, Southern Methodist Univ, 68-75, prof Span art hist, 75-81. *Awards:* Spanish Knight Awards, Order of Isabel la Catolica, 86; Vassari Award, Dallas Mus, 86; Order of Civil Merit, 88. *Mem:* Am Soc of Hispanic Art Hist Studies (gen secy, 76-78); Hispanic Soc of Am. *Publ:* Auth, Juan van der Hamen y Leon, Univ Microfilms, 67; The Meadows Museum: A Visitor's Guide to the Collection, Meadows Mus, 74; El Greco of Toledo (catalog), Toledo Mus Art, 82; Spanish Still Life in the Golden Age: 1600-1650 (catalog), Kimbell Art Mus, 85; Still Lifes of Juan Sanchez Cotan, Museo del Prado, 92; Spanish Still Life from Velazquez to Goya (catalog), Nat Gallery, London, 1995; Juan van der Hamer y Leon & the Court of Madrid, Yale Univ Press, 2005

JORGENSEN, AURORA DIAS See Dias-Jorgensen, Aurora Abdias

JORGENSEN, BOB (ROBERT A)
PAINTER, INSTRUCTOR
b Long Island, NY Dec 1, 1928. *Study:* Pratt Inst, Brooklyn, NY, 45-46; SUNY, Farmingdale, Assoc (art), 48; Fitchburg State Col, teaching cert, 77. *Work:* Bennington Ctr Arts, Bennington, Vt; Ashland Pub Libr, Ashland, Mass; Ashland High Sch, Ashland, Maass. *Exhib:* Arts for the Parks, 95, 98 & 2006; Am Watercolor Soc, Salmagundi Club, NY, 96; Birds in Art, Leigh Yawkey Woodson Art Mus, Wausau, Wis, 96, 98, & 08; Allied Artists of Am; Nat Arts Club, NY, 96-2000; Nat Acad Design, NY, 2000; Butler Inst Am Art, 2001; New England Watercolor Society, 1996-2011; Bennington Center for the Arts, 1998-2011. *Teaching:* Com art, Joseph P Keefe Tech Sch, Framingham, Mass, 1977-1990. *Awards:* Air Float Systems Award, Hudson Valley Art Asn, 99; Past Pres's Award, RI Watercolor Soc Nat, 2000; Silver Medal of Honor, Allied Artists of America, 2001; First Place, Soc Watercolor Artists, Tex, 2007; Audubon Artists, NY. *Bibliog:* Final Touch, WIldlife Arts Mag, 11/99. *Mem:* Allied Artists Am; sig mem, New Eng Watercolor Soc (bd dir); Hudson Valley Art Asn; sig mem, RI Watercolor Soc (bd dir, 1st vp, 96-99, pres, 99-2001, instr watercolor, 96-99); American Artists Prof League, (fel); sig mem, Pa Watercolor Society; sig mem, North East Watercolor Society. *Media:* Watercolor. *Dealer:* Premier Image Gallery Ashland MA; Artica Gallery Duxbury MA; Sharon Arts Center Peterboro NH. *Mailing Add:* 20 Woodland Rd Ashland MA 01721

JORGENSON, DALE ALFRED
EDUCATOR, ADMINISTRATOR
b Litchfield, Nebr, Mar 20, 1926. *Study:* Harding Coll, Ark, philos with J D Bales, BMus, 48; George Peabody Coll, Tenn, MA, 50; Ind Univ, aesthetics with John Mueller, PhD, 57; Harvard Univ, cert arts admin, 72. *Teaching:* Prof aesthetics, Bethany Coll WVa, 59-62; dir fine arts, Milligan Coll, Tenn, 62-63; head fine arts div & teacher aesthetics, Northeast Mo State Univ, 63-87; retired. *Mem:* Am Soc Aesthetics; Midwest Coll Art Asn. *Res:* Aesthetics and elementary aesthetics for contemporary students. *Publ:* Auth, The campus and the arts, Proceedings of the Nat Asn Sch Music, 70; Preparing the educator for related arts, Music Educr J, 5/70; The French lieutenant's woman, or to forego manipulation, Christianity Today, 5/11/73; Theological-Aesthetic Roots in the Stone-Campbell Movement, Thomas Jefferson Univ Press, 1/89; The Life & Legacy of Franz Hauser, Southern Ill Univ Press, 95. *Mailing Add:* 1512 S Cottage Grove Kirksville MO 63501

JOSEPH, STEFANI A
PAINTER, EDUCATOR
b Newport, Gwent, Eng. *Study:* Ruskin Sch Drawing & Fine Art, Oxford Univ, BA, 75; Royal Acad Sch, London; Savannah Coll Art & Design, Ga, MFA, 2001, MA (art hist), 2009. *Work:* St Hilda's Coll, Oxford Univ, Eng; Templeton Coll, Oxford, Eng; Sr Common Room, Westminster Coll, Oxford, Eng; Isle of Wight Area Health Authority, Newport, Eng; St Bartholomew's Hosp, London; Spring Into Art, Annette Howell Gallery, Turner Ctr Arts, 2013. *Comn:* Portraits of profs, St Hilda's Coll Oxford Univ, Eng. *Exhib:* Ibizagrafic, Mus Contemp Art, Ibiza, Spain, 86; Seoul Print Biennial, Mus Contemp Art, Korea, 88; Group Exhibs: Mus Mod Art, Oxford, 88 & The Gallery Cork St, London, 97; Perpignan Biennial, Mus Contemp Art, France, 90; Selections, Broome St Gallery, New York, 98; 98 China Art Expo, China Int Exhib Ctr, Beijing, 98; Warren-Britt Galleries, Ala State Univ, 2000; juried exhib, The Hite Art Inst, Univ Louisville; State Capitol Gallery, Atlanta, Ga, 2001; Franklin Sq Gallery, Southport, NC, 2001-2002; Faces of Woman, Las Vegas Arts Coun, 2003; Red Gallery, Savannah, 2003; Art with a Southern Drawl, Univ Mobile, Ala, 2003; Trinidad Nat Fine Art Exhib, AR Mitchell Mus, Colo, 2003 & Galerie Gora, Montreal, 2003; Art Now Galeria Zero, Barcelona, 2004; Miami Art Fair, The Chattahoochee Valley Art Mus, 2004; The Babcock Sch Bus Mgt and Sch Law, Wake Forest Univ, NC, 2004; Fine Art Exhib, Mt Valley Arts Coun, 2005; Franklin Square Gallery, 2006-2007; Jan & Gary Dario Gallery, 2006-2007; Palm Beach Community Coll, Lake Worth, Fla, 2006; Solo Exhibs: Mt Valley Arts Coun, Guntersville, Ala & Annette Howell Ctr Arts, Valdosta, Ga, 2006; The Roush Family Gallery, Carrollton Cult Center, Carrollton; Arts Center Manatee, Bradenton, Fla; 42nd Ann Cent S Art Exhib, Tenn Art League, 2007; Mt Valley Arts Coun Juried Show, Bevill Ctr, Snead State Community Coll, Boaz, Ala, 2007; Tex Artists Mus, 2009; 64 Arts Nat Juried Exhib, Buchanan Ctr Arts, Monmouth, Ill, 2010; The Moot Gallery, Hong Kong, 2011; Baker Arts Ctr, Liberal, Kans, 2012; Spring into Art, Annette Howell Gallery, Turner Ctr Arts, Valdosta, Ga, 2012; Annette Howell Gallery, Valdosta, 2013. *Teaching:* Prof found studies, Savannah Coll Art & Design, 93-. *Awards:* Prize winner, Ann July Nat Exhib, Franklin Sq Gallery, 2002; Prize Winner, Winterfest Fine Art Exhibit, 2005; Presidential Fel, Savannah Coll Art & Design, 2005. *Bibliog:* Zoe Randall (auth), Duplicity and Intrigue, Connect Savannah, 99; Daniel Smith (auth), Meeting With Mystery, The Ga Guardian, 99. *Mem:* Southeastern Coll Art Asn. *Media:* Oil on Canvas. *Dealer:* Off The Wall Gallery Savannah GA; Bender Fine Art Marietta GA; Galerie Gora, Montreal. *Mailing Add:* 24 E Liberty St Apt 22 Savannah GA 31401

JOSEPH, TOMMY
SCULPTOR, CRAFTSMAN
Comn: Numerous totem poles for private collections; 20-foot totem pole, Veterans Admin, Anchorage, Alaska, 1994; 35-foot Haa leelk'u Kaa sta heeni deiyi (Indian River) pole, Sitka Clans, Alaska, 1996; shaman reburial bentwood box, Sitka, 1996; 10-foot Strongman pole, Alaska Indian Cult Ctr, Sitka, 1997; 4-foot model canoe, Moore House, Skagway, Alaska, 1997; 15-foot reproduction Chief Saanheit house post, Nat Park Serv, Sitka, 1998; 35-foot traditional Tlingit canoe, 1999; 35-foot Kiks adi K'alyaan Memorial Pole, Kiks adi Clan, Sitka, 1999; 35-foot Haa Kuteeya (Eagle), Petersburg, Alaska, 2000, 17-foot crest pole, 2001 & 35-foot Haa Kuteeya

(Raven), 2001; 20-foot totem pole, Sitka Community Schools, 2004; 20-foot totem pole, Shee Atika Inc, Sitka, 2005. *Pos:* Artist in residence, Southeast Alaska Indian Cult Ctr, Sitka, Alaska, currently. *Awards:* US Artists Kippy Stroud Fel, Crafts & Traditional Arts, 2007. *Mem:* Alaskan Native Artists. *Media:* Wood. *Mailing Add:* 620 Merrill St Sitka AK 99835-7436

JOSEPH, WENDY EVANS
ARCHITECT
Study: Univ Pa, B in Design of Environ (summa cum laude), 77; Harvard Univ, MArch (with hons.), 81. *Pos:* with, Archit Resources Cambridge Inc, Boston, 78, Pei Cobb Freed, 85-93; mem archit team, US Holocaust Meml Mus, Wash; founder, Wendy Evans Joseph Archit (now Cooper Joseph Studio), 96-2011, co-partner, Cooper Joseph Studio, 2011-. *Awards:* Rome prize, Am Acad in Rome, 84. *Mem:* Nat Acad; Archit League (vpres archit); AIA (chair). *Mailing Add:* Cooper Joseph Studio 500 Park Ave New York NY 10022

JOSKOWICZ, CLAUDIA
VIDEO ARTIST, EDUCATOR
b Santa Cruz de la Sierra, Bolivia. *Study:* Univ Houston, BArch; NYU, MFA. *Work:* El Museo del Barrio; Bronx Mus Arts; Galerie Chez Valentin, Paris; Soap Factory, Minneapolis; Dallas Contemp, Tex. *Exhib:* Solo exhibs, Momenta Art Gallery, New York, Lawndale Art Ctr, Tex, Sara Meltzer Gallery, Kinz, Tillou & Feigen Gallery, LMAK Projects, Ctr for Bk Arts, Socrates Sculpture Park, Artists Space, Exit Art, New York, McDonough Mus Art, Ohio & Dukwon Gallery, Seoul, South Korea. *Pos:* Artist-in-residence, Lower Manhattan Cult Coun & Bronx Mus Arts. *Teaching:* Adj fac, Steinhardt Sch Cult, Educ & Human Develop, New York. *Awards:* Vt Studio Ctr Fel; Digital Photog Salon grand prize, Fundacion Patino, Cochambamba, Bolivia; Urban Artists Initiative Fel, 2008; East Harlem Arts Grant, 2009; Fulbright Grant, 2010

JOSTEN, KATHERINE ANN
CONCEPTUAL ARTIST, DIRECTOR
b Dayton, Ohio, Feb 27, 1949. *Study:* Ohio Univ, BS, 71; Atlanta Coll Art, BFA, 81; Univ Wis, Madison, MFA, 86. *Work:* Tucson Mus Art; Ariz State Univ Mus Art, Tempe. *Exhib:* Origins, Univ Ariz Mus Art, 87; 23rd Southwestern Traveling Exhib, Northern Ariz Univ, Flagstaff, 90; Ariz Artist Mus Collection, Ariz State Univ Art Mus, 93; Ariz Biennial, Tucson Mus Art, 93 & 99, Wide Open Spaces, 94; Earth, Man & Spirit, Sun Cities Art Mus, Ariz, 95; Global Art Proj Exhib, Nat Inst Arts, Taipei, Taiwan, 98, Tucson Mus Art, Ariz, 99; Women Artists in the Mus Collection, Tucson Mus Art, 99; Dirs Choice, Tucson Mus Art, Ariz, 2000; Int Tsai MS Art Exhib, Taichung City, Taiwan, 2011; Tuscon Mus Art, 2012. *Pos:* Founder & dir, Global Art Proj, Tucson, Ariz, 93-. *Teaching:* Instr color & design, Univ Ariz, 90-91; adj fac basic design, color & design, painting, Pima Col, Tucson, 87-2000. *Awards:* Pollack-Krasner Found Grant, 94; Rockefeller Found Flow Fund Grant, 98; 2002, UNESCO Peace Prize Nominee; and many others. *Bibliog:* Carrie Rothburd (auth), Serendipity in Action: A Conversation with Katherine Josten on the Global Art Project, The Cath Found, Vol XIV, No 2, Seeds Unfolding, 97; Timothy Gassen (auth), Art connects the world: Tucson woman rides herd on Global Art Project, Ariz Daily Star, 2/19/98; Kristen Coughlin (auth), Artist organizes third biennial worldwide art exchange, Crafts Report, 4/98; and others. *Mem:* Tucson Mus Art; Ariz State Univ Art Mus; Int Neworking Mus Peace (advisory bd). *Publ:* Auth, Visions of Global Unity: Inspired Images from the Global Art Project, Artifact Press, 96. *Mailing Add:* 4061 E 4th St Tucson AZ 85711

JOW, PAT See Kagemoto, Patricia Jow

JOYAUX, ALAIN GEORGES
MUSEUM DIRECTOR
b Lansing, Mich, Oct 28, 1950. *Study:* Mich State Univ, BFA (studio), 75, MFA, 77, MA (art hist), 78. *Collection Arranged:* European Tools From the 17th Century to the 19th Century (auth, catalog), 81; Am Naive Painting: The Edgar William and Bernice Chrysler Garbish Collection (auth, catalog), Flint Inst Arts, 82; The Elisabeth Ball Collection of Paintings, Drawings and Watercolors: The George and Frances Ball Foundation (auth, catalog), 83; Childe Hassam in Indian (auth, catalog), 85; Europ & Am Paintings & Sculpture: Selected Works (auth, catalog), 94. *Pos:* Asst dir, Flint Inst Arts, Mich, 78-83; dir, Ball State Univ Mus of Art, 83-2003 Retired. *Mem:* Am Asn Mus; Intermuseum Conserv Asn. *Res:* Late 19th century European art; Degas. *Mailing Add:* Antiques & Plunder 22 N Sycamore St Petersburg VA 23803

JOYNER, JOHN BROOKS
HISTORIAN, MUSEUM DIRECTOR
b Baltimore, Md, Nov 24, 1944. *Study:* Univ Md, BA, 1966, MA, 1969. *Collection Arranged:* Asian & African Art, Towson State Univ, 1972-73; Permanent Collections, Univ Calgary, 1975-76; George Rickey Sculpture, South Bend Art Ctr, 1982; Patronage in Southern Art Mus, The Grand Tour, 1988; Art of the Eighties: Selections from the Whitney Mus, 1990. *Pos:* Dir, Nickle Arts Mus, Univ Calgary, 1975-81, South Bend Art Ctr, Ind, 1983-87, Montgomery Mus Fine Arts, formerly, Gilcrease Mus, 1996-2001 & Joslyn Art Mus, Omaha, 2001-2010. *Teaching:* Lectr art hist, Towson State Univ, Baltimore, 1972-74, Univ Calgary, Can, 1972-80 & Univ Alta, Edmonton, Can, 1980-83. *Mem:* Asn Art Mus Dirs; Am Asn Mus; Int Coun Mus. *Res:* 19th-20th century Europe & American painting & sculpture; Arshile Gorky's drawings & Canadian art. *Publ:* Auth, The Drawings of Arshile Gorky (monogr), Univ Md, 69; auth, Stephen Andrews-Banff, Art Mag, 10/77; auth, Printmaking in Alberta, Art Mag, 2/77; ed, the Sculpture of George Rickey (exhib catalog), South Bend Art Ctr, 85; auth, Marion Nicoll RCA, Masters Gallery Ltd, 80. *Mailing Add:* Joslyn Art Mus 2200 Dodge St Omaha NE 68102-1292

JUAREZ, BENJAMIN
EDUCATOR
Study: Calif Inst of the Arts, MFA, 1973. *Pos:* Head music and dance, Nat Univ of Mexico, 1978-79; prin guest conductor, asst conductor, State of Mexico Symphony Orchestra, 1979-81; assoc conductor, Mexico City Philharmonic Orchestra, 1983-87; music dir, Gran Festival de la Ciudad de Mexico, 1989, 1990; dir cultural activities, Univ Anahuac del Sur, formerly; dir, Centro Nacional de las Artes, 2007-09; dean, Col of Fine Arts, Boston Univ, 2010-. *Mailing Add:* Boston University College of Fine Arts 855 Commonwealth Ave Boston MA 02215

JUAREZ, ROBERTO
PAINTER
b Chicago, Ill, 1952. *Study:* San Francisco Art Inst, BFA; Univ Calif, Los Angeles, 78-79. *Work:* Newark Mus, NJ; Atlantic Richfield Co, Los Angeles; Gulf & Western, NY; Goldman & Sachs, NY; Rutgers Univ, New Brunswick, NJ; Metrop Mus Art, NY; General Mills Corp, Minneapolis, Minn. *Comn:* 25' X 9 1/2' mural painting, Tri Am, Coral Gables, Fla, 90; Miami Beach Police Station, 93; NY Pub Sch, 94. *Exhib:* Solo exhibs, San Francisco Art Inst, Calif, 77, Robert Miller Gallery, NY, 77, 81, 84, 86 & 87, Staller Ctr Arts, State Univ NY, 91, Charles Cowles Gallery, NY, 2006, 2008; Group exhibs, New Wave, NY, Inst Art & Urban Resources, PS1, NY, 81; New Visions, Aldrich Mus, 81; Back to the USA, Kunstmuseum, Luzern, Theinisches Landesmuseum, Bonn & Wurttembergischer Kunstverein, Stuttgart, 83 & 84; Am Artist as Printmaker, Brooklyn Mus, 83-84; An Int Survey of Recent Painting and Sculpture (with catalog), Mus Mod Art, NY, 84; New Am Painting: A Tribute to James & Mari Michener, Archer M Huntington Art Gallery, Univ Tex, Austin, 84; Blast, 84 & Double Vision, 85, B-Side Gallery, NY; Innovative Still Life, Holly Solomon Gallery, NY, 85; This Way-This Way, Thorpe Intermedia Gallery, Sparkhill, NY, 85; Midtown Payson Galleries, NY, 92; Betsy Rosenfield Gallery, Chicago, Ill, 92; Neuberger Mus, State Univ NY, 92-93; A Field of Wild Flowers, Comn for Grand Cent Terminal, New York, 97; A Sense of Place, Mus Contemp Art, North Miami, Fla, 2003; New Paintings, Charles Cowles Gallery, 2006. *Pos:* Artist-in-residence, Gulf & Western Co, Altos de Chavon, Dominican Republic, 84; painting workshops, Anderson Ranch, Aspen, 88, 89 & 90. *Teaching:* Vis artist, Pilchuck Glass Ctr, Stanwood, Wash, 91; vis artist, Yale Univ, Norfolk, Conn, 91; vis artist, Anderson Ranch, Snow Mass, Colo, 92; vis prof, Williams Coll, Williamstown, Mass, 2005-2006. *Bibliog:* Roberta Smith (auth), article, Village Voice, 12/81; Grace Glueck (auth), article, New York Times, 1/28/83; Susan Hapgood (auth), article, Flash Art, 3/83. *Media:* Oil, Acrylic. *Dealer:* Robert Miller Gallery 41 E 5th St New York NY 10022; Charles Cowles Gallery 537 W 24th St New York NY 10011. *Mailing Add:* PO Box 478 Canaan NY 12029-0478

JUDD, DE FORREST HALE
PAINTER, EDUCATOR
b Hartsgrove, Ohio, Apr 4, 1916. *Study:* Cleveland Inst Art, grad, 38, post grad scholar, 39; Colorado Springs Fine Arts Ctr, with Boardman Robinson, 39-42. *Work:* Cleveland Mus Art, Ohio; Dallas Mus Fine Arts, Tex; Beaumont Mus Art, Tex; Univ Tex, Austin; Southern Methodist Univ. *Exhib:* Am Painting Today, Metrop Mus Art, 50; Tex Contemp Artists, Knoedler Gallery, NY, 52; New Accessions, USA, Colorado Springs Fine Arts Ctr, 52; Ten Texas Painters, Frank Perls Gallery, Beverly Hills, Calif, 53; Texas Painting & Sculpture, 20th Century, Southern Methodist Univ, 71. *Teaching:* Prof painting, Southern Methodist Univ, 46-82, prof emer, 82. *Awards:* First Prize, Cleveland Mus Art, 41; E M Dealey Purchase Award, Tex Painters & Sculptors Exhib, 50; First Prize, 2nd Ann Exhib, Beaumont Mus Art, 53. *Media:* Oil, Acrylic. *Mailing Add:* 1604 Concord Pl Carrollton TX 75007-2925

JUDGE, MARY FRANCES
PAINTER, GRAPHOLOGIST
b Minneapolis, Minn, July 31, 1935. *Study:* Coll New Rochelle, NY, BA (art), 61; Univ Notre Dame, Ind, MFA (painting), 71. *Work:* Carnegie Mus, Pittsburgh, Pa; Springfield Coll Gallery, Ill; Nobles Co Art Ctr, Worthington, Minn; Oak Ridge Mus, Tenn; and other pvt and pub collections; Fla Atlantic Univ Galleries. *Comn:* Interpretive Family Portraits, New York City, Stockholm; Pvt Residence Frescoes, Ceyras, France, 1992. *Exhib:* Midwest Biennial, Joslyn Mus, Omaha, Nebr, 72; Ann Mid-States Exhib, Evansville Mus, Ind, 71; Brooks Mus Art, Memphis, Tenn, 70 & 71; solo exhibs, Moody Gallery, Austin, Tex, 72, Contemp Gallery, Dallas, 73, Reflections Gallery, St Louis, Mo, 73, Hansen Galleries, NY, 77-78, Dolly Fiterman Gallery, Minneapolis, Minn, 80, Ross Gallery, Scottsdale, Ariz, 81, Rosenberg Libr, Harris Gallery, Galveston, Tex, 83, Max Gallery, NY, 85, Leonarda Di Mauro Gallery, NY, 88, Univ Tex, Dallas, 84-90, Lee Co Alliance Arts Cult Ctr, Ft Myers, Fla, 92 & Oak Ridge Art Mus, Tenn, 94, Monogramma Galleria, Rome, Italy, 2001, Digital Sandbox Gallery, New York City, 2003; Beverly Gordon Gallery, Dallas, Tex, 87; Leonarda Di Mauro Gallery, NY, 88; All Out, Long Island Univ, Brooklyn, NY, 94; Recycling with Imagination, Portland, Ore, Phoenix, Ariz, NY & Pittsburgh, Pa, 94-2011; Minneapolis Inst Arts, 2000-01. *Pos:* Mem bd, Dallas Mus Fine Arts, Tex, 76-77. *Teaching:* instr, Col of New Rochelle, New York City. *Awards:* Strathmore Nat Art Award, Scholastic Art Awards, Strathmore Papers, 50; Bixby Portrait Award, St Louis Artists Guild, 71. *Bibliog:* Articles in Arts Mag, 3/77 & 10/78; Terry Trucco (auth), Artnews, 5/79; Marian Courtney (auth), article, New York Times, 6/26/83; Dennis Wepman (auth, article), Manhattan Arts, 90; Knoxville News Sentinel, 5/15/94; David Howard (dir), Mary Frances Judge (film); Il Giornale D'Italia, 6/22/2001. *Mem:* St Louis Women Artists (bd mem, 72-74); Artist Equity (NY & bd mem Dallas, 74-78); Nat Asn Female Execs; Nat Soc Graphologists. *Media:* Mixed media painting. *Specialty:* Contemporary abstracts. *Interests:* graphology, ann painting trip to Italy, European countries. *Collection:* Giovanni Morabito, Rome. *Publ:* Bovarchè, II editzone, Italy. *Dealer:* Galleria Monogramma Rome Italy

JUDGE, VAUGHAN
EDUCATOR, ADMINISTRATOR, PHOTOGRAPHER
Study: Derby Univ, MA. *Exhib:* Solo shows in NY, Glasgow, and Edinburgh. *Teaching:* Prof, dir, Sch of Art, Montana State Univ, currently. *Bibliog:* cited in two history of photography books light from the darkroom; Scottish photography: A history by Doctor Tom Normand of St Andrews Univ. *Mailing Add:* School of Art 213 Haynes Hall PO Box 173680 Montana State University Bozeman MT 59717-3680

JUGO DE VEGETALES See Thompson, Jack

JULIO, PAT T
EDUCATOR, CRAFTSMAN
b Youngstown, Ohio, Mar 1, 1923. *Study:* Wittenberg Col, BFA, with Ralston Thompson; Univ NMex, MA, with Raymond Jonson & Lex Haas; Univ Colo, with Robert Lister; Ohio State Univ, with Edgar Littlefield; Tex Western Col, with Wiltz Harrison. *Comn:* Stained glass windows, Episcopal Good Samaritan Church, Community Church & pvt collections. *Exhib:* Denver Art Mus, 50 & 63; Pueblo Art Mus, 60; Pueblo Coll, 60 & 69; Solo exhibs, Pueblo Art Mus, 64 & Western State Art Gallery, 69. *Teaching:* Prof art, Western State Col, from 1971, prof emeritus, currently. *Mem:* Coll Art Asn Am; Western Art Asn; Am Ceramic Soc; Am Crafts Coun; Inst Indian Studies; and others. *Mailing Add:* PO Box 1507 Gunnison CO 81230

JULY, MIRANDA
FILMMAKER, WRITER
Work: Mus Mod Art, New York; Guggenheim Mus; Whitney Mus Am Art. *Exhib:* 53rd Int Art Exhib Biennale, Venice, 2009. *Awards:* Spl Jury Prize, Sundance Film Festival; Camera d'Or, Cannes Film Festival; Frank O'Conner Int Short Story Award, 2007. *Bibliog:* Johnny Ray Houston (auth), The Marvelous World of Miranda July, San Francisco Bay Guardian, 6/1998; Alison Maclean (auth), 99 Channels and Nothing ON, filmmaker Mag, spring 1999; Chris Chang (auth), Renaissance Riot Grrl Rising, Film Comment, 7/2000; Julia Bryan-Wilson (auth), Some Kind of Grace, Camera Obscura, 55, 2004; Karen Durbin (auth), Hollywood Can Wait, NY Times, 6/19/2005. *Publ:* Dir, Me and you and Everyone We Know, 2005; auth, No One Belongs Here More Than You, 2007; Learning to Love You More, Prestel, 2007. *Mailing Add:* PO Box 26596 Los Angeles CA 90026

JUNG, HUGO & INGRID
COLLECTORS
Awards: Named one of Top 200 Collectors, ARTnews mag, 2009-12. *Collection:* Postwar and contemporary art

JUNG, KWAN YEE
PAINTER
b Toysun, China, Nov 25, 1932; US citizen. *Study:* Chinese Univ Hong Kong New Asia Col, BA (painting), 61; San Diego State Univ, postgrad studies, 68. *Work:* Springville Mus Art, Utah; San Diego Chinese Hist Mus, Calif; Nat Acad Mus, NY; Hickory Mus Fine Art, NC; San Bernadino Art Asn, Calif; IBM; Gen Atomics; Holiday Inn, Calif. *Comn:* Holiday Inn, Rancho Bernardo, Calif. *Exhib:* Calif Nat Watercolor Soc Ann, 72-79; Watercolor USA, 72 & 75; Am Watercolor Soc Ann Exhib, 73-78; Nat Acad Design Ann, 74, 82, 86 & 92; solo exhibs, Univ Hong Kong, 75, Edward Dean Mus, Calif, 77 & US Int Univ, San Diego, 83; group exhibs, Water to Women Margaret Cross Gallery, Old Pasadena, Calif, 95, May Snow Kim's Art Gallery, Rowland Heights, Calif, 95, Co-art Int Gallery, Vancouver, British Columbia, Can, 96, Kruglak Gallery, Mira Costa Col, Oceanside, Calif, 97, San Diego Chinese Hist Mus, 97, The Earl & Birdie Taylor Libr, San Diego, 98, 174th Ann Exhib Nat Acad of Design, 99. *Pos:* Commercial artist advertising dept Hong Kong Soy Bean Products co, 61-63; owner Jung's Gallery, La Jolla, California, 76-78; freelance artist, instructor, demonstrator San Diego, 78-. *Awards:* Am Watercolor Soc Award, 76, 78, 87 & 98; Best of Show, Sumi-E Soc Am, 79; Merit Award, Nat Acad Design, 92. *Bibliog:* Interview, Artist-TV 51, San Diego, 83; article in SW Art Mag, 1/83; article in Western Arts Digest, 5-6/86; article in Watercolor Mag, 98. *Mem:* Nat Watercolor Soc; Am Watercolor Soc; Nat Acad Design. *Media:* Watercolor, Oil; Acrylic on rice paper. *Publ:* Special Focus on California, Art Voices, 2/83; Splash 1 & 2, America's Best Contemporary Watercolor, North Light, 91 & 92; Kwan Y Jung & Yeewah Jung, Art of Calif, 11/92; Chinese Brush Painting Step by Step, North Light Bks, 2003; Splash 10; and others

JUNG, YEE WAH
PAINTER
b Canton, China, Sept 4, 1936; US citizen. *Study:* Chung Man Art Sch, WuHun, China, 54-58; Chinese Univ Hong Kong New Asia Col, 58-62. *Comn:* The Tours of Confucius (mosaic painting), Facade of Ambassador Hotel (with Chiu Fung Poon), 59. *Exhib:* Watercolor USA, 73-75 & 88; Nat Acad Design, 74; Butler Inst Am Art, 74; Mira Costa Col, Kruglak Gallery, Calif, 97; San Diego Hist Chinese Mus, Calif, 98; Taiwanese Am Ctr, Calif, 2000; Celebrating Tradition, San Francisco State Univ Invitational, 2-7/2008; Watercolor Now! Springfield Art Mus, 4-6/2008. *Awards:* First Place, Southern Calif Expo Art, Del Mar, 71; Calif Nat Watercolor Soc Award, Watercolor USA, 73-78; Watercolor USA Award, Calif Nat Watercolor Soc, 77; First Prize, 25th Art Festival Exhib, 88; Seventh Ann King's Award, Advent Fine Arts Exhib, 89. *Bibliog:* Interview, Spectrum-TV 10, San Diego, 82; article, SW Art Mag, 1/83; Betty Lou Schlemn & Tom Nicholas (auths), The Best of Watercolor, Rockport Publ Inc, 96. *Mem:* Nat Watercolor Soc; Watercolor USA Hon Soc. *Media:* Oil, Watercolor. *Publ:* Auth, Environmental Escape, Southwest Art, 1/83; Splash 1, America's Best Contemporary Watercolor, North Light, 91; Kwan Jung & Yeewah Jung, Art of Calif, 11/92; Abstract in Watercolor, 96. *Mailing Add:* 5468 Bloch St San Diego CA 92122

JUNGEN, BRIAN
SCULPTOR
b Fort St John, BC, Can, 1970. *Work:* Art Gallery Ontario; Mus Contemp Art, Chicago; Nat Gallery Can, Ottawa; Tate Mod, London; Vancouver Art Gallery. *Exhib:* Solo exhibs include Contemp Art Gallery, Vancouver, 2001, Catriona Jeffries Gallery, Vancouver, 2002, 2007, Henry Art Gallery, Seattle, 2003, Wattis Inst Contemp Arts, San Francisco, 2004, New Mus, New York, 2005, Vancouver Art Gallery, 2006, Casey Kaplan Gallery, New York, 2006, 2008 Tate Mod, London, 2006, Witte de With, Rotterdam, 2007; group exhibs include Long Time, Vancouver Art Gallery, 2001, This Place, 2002; The Beachcombers, Gasworks, London, 2002; Watery, Domestic, Renaissance Soc, Chicago, 2002; The West Coast in Contemp Art, Seattle Art Mus, 2003; Baja to Vancouver: The West Coast in Contemp Art, Wattis Inst Contemp Arts, San Francisco, Vancouver Art Gallery & Mus Contemp Art San Diego, 2004; Noah's Art, Nat Gallery Can, 2004; Short Stories: Contemp Selections, Henry Art Gallery, Seattle, 2005; Holy Land: Diaspora in the Desert, Heard Mus, Phoenix, 2006; Shapeshifters, Time Travelers & Storytellers, Royal Ontario Mus, Toronto, 2007; The Martian Museum of Terrestrial Art, Barbican Art Gallery, London, 2008. *Dealer:* Casey Kaplan Gallery 525 W 21st St New York NY 10011. *Mailing Add:* Catriona Jeffries Gallery 274 E 1st Ave Vancouver BC V5T146 Canada

JURNEY, DONALD (BENSON)
PAINTER
b Rye, NY, Jan 7, 1945. *Study:* Pratt Inst, NY, 71-72; Art Students League, 79. *Work:* Mus City of New York; Hudson River Mus, Yonkers, NY; Bank Am, San Francisco, Calif; Oakland Mus, CA. *Comn:* Lobby Paintings, Clorox Co, Oakland, Calif. *Exhib:* Berkshire Art Asn, Berkshire Mus, Pittsfield, Mass, 80; Silvermine Guild, New Canaan, Conn, 80; 45th Ann Mid-Year Exhib, Butler Inst, Youngstown, Ohio, 81; Parrish Art Mus, Southampton, NY, 81; 159th Ann Exhib, Nat Acad, NY, 84; 163rd Ann Exhib, Nat Acad, 88. *Awards:* C R Gibson Award, 31st New Eng Exhib, 80; Award of Merit, 62nd Nat Exhib, Springfield Art League, 81; Special Award, 19th Ann Exhib, Putnam Arts Coun, 81. *Bibliog:* Eric Widing (auth), Donald Jurney, 11/82 & M Stephen Doherty (auth), Motifs for landscape painting, 2/84, Am Artist; film, Reflections on the Hudson, CBS-TV, 9/84. *Mem:* Century Asn. *Media:* Oil, Watercolor. *Dealer:* Hoorn-Ashby Gallery 766 Madison Ave New York NY 10021. *Mailing Add:* 110 Hitch Pond Cir Seaford DE 19973-6221

JUROVICS, TOBY
CURATOR
Study: Univ NC, BA (art hist and english), 1988; Univ Del, MA (art hist), 1992. *Collection Arranged:* Emmet Gowin: Aerial Photographs, 1998; Photographs by Barbara Bosworth, 2000; Robert Adams: From the Missouri West, 2004. *Pos:* With Princeton Univ Art Mus, NJ, 1991-2006, assoc cur photog, cur photogr; cur photogr, Smithsonian Am Art Mus, Washington, DC, 2006-. *Mailing Add:* Smithsonian American Art Museum Victor Bldg 750 Nineth St NW Washington DC 20001

JURY, SAM
PHOTOGRAPHER, VIDEO ARTIST
b Hertfordshire, England, Mar 12, 1969. *Study:* Loughborough Coll Art & Design, BA, England, 96; Cornell Univ, MFA (painting), 98. *Work:* Rose Art Mus, Waltham, Mass; Herbert F Johnson Mus, Ithaca, NY; Mus Palacio Consistorial, Cartagena, Spain; Univ Hertforshire, Hatfield, United Kingdom. *Exhib:* Solo exhibs, Royal Acad Sch, London, 2002; Group exhibs, Invisible Rays- The Surrealism Legacy, Rose Art Mus, Waltham, Mass, 2009; Light Divided, louise Blouin Inst, London, 2008; Explum 10, Ctr Sociocultural, Puerto Lumbreras, Spain, 2009; Context, Pingyao Int Photography Festival, Pinyao, China, 2009; One Hour Photo, Am Univ Mus, Wash DC, 2010; Sill & Still Moving, Irish Mus Mod Art, Dublin, Ireland, 2010; Forever is Never, Herbert F Johnson Mus, Ithaca, NY, 2010. *Pos:* Artist in Residence, Irish Mus Mod Art, Dublin, 2009-2010; Fel in Print & Digital Media, RA Sch, Royal Acad Art, London, UK, 2000-2002. *Awards:* Grant, We Are Just Watching, Elephant Trust, London, 2007; Res Grant, Social Sci, Arts & Humanities Res Inst, 2007, 2009; Grant for the Arts, Art Coun, Eng, 2007, 2008, 2009. *Bibliog:* Malcolm Ferris (auth), All the Things Between, Art Map Mag, China; Michael Rush (auth), Sam Jury- Who Are You Looking At?, Art on Paper, 2008; Matthew Reis (auth), Artistic Video Blurs Reality, The Ithacan, 2010; Michael Rush (auth), Michael Rush Speaks with Sam Jury, Art on Air, 2010. *Mem:* Contemp Art Soc, London. *Media:* Constructed Photography, Video. *Dealer:* Stephen Haller Gallery 542 W 26th St New York NY 10001

JUSTIS, GARY
SCULPTOR, KINETIC ARTIST
b Wichita, Kans, Apr 4, 1953. *Study:* Wichita State Univ, BFA, 77; Sch Art Inst Chicago, MFA, 79. *Work:* Mus Contemp Art, Borg-Warner Corp, Chicago; Ill State Mus, Springfield; Krannert Mus Art, Champaign, Ill; Alexandria Mus Art, La; US Equities Corp, Chicago, Ill; Durindol Inc, Chicago, Ill. *Comn:* Wall sculpture, Carson's Int, O'Hare Int Airport, Chicago, 87; sculpture, Carson's Int, O'Hare Int Airport, 90; Garden Park Comn, Gary Justis & LJ Douglas, Evanston, Ill, 92. *Exhib:* solo exhibs, Compass Rose Gallery, Chicago, Mus SE Tex, Klein Art Works, Chicago, Tough Gallery, Chicago, Mus Sci & Indust, Chicago, 82, Chicago Cult Ctr, 85 & Alexandria Mus Art, La, 86, The Causal Garden, Compassrose Gallery, Chicago, 88, Quiet Works 1989-91, Compassrose Gallery, 91, Functionality, Kinetic Sculpture, Midland Ctr Arts, Mich, 98-99, This is the thing, Klein Art Works, Chicago, 2000, Head on Horizon, Tarble Art Ctr, Eastern Ill Univ, 2001; Painting & Sculpture Today, Indianapolis Mus, 84; Art Inst Chicago, 84; Ten Yrs of Collecting, Mus Contemp Art, Chicago, 84; PULSE Nat Exhib, Edwin A Ulrich Mus Art, Wichita, Kans, 92; Nature of the Machine, Chicago Cult Ctr, 93; Art in Chicago, 1945-1995, Mus Contemp Art, 96; Incrementum: Selected Works 1979-1996, Klein Artworks & Tough Gallery, Chicago, Ill, 96; Sound & Vision, Rockford Art Mus, Rockford, Ill, 98; Chicago Abstraction, Klein Art Works, Chicago, 99; Contemp Figurative Sculpture, Tweed Mus Art, Duluth, Minn, 2000. *Teaching:* Instr sculpture, Sch Art Inst Chicago, 86-; adj asst prof, Univ Ill, Chicago, 88-89; guest lectr, Northwestern Univ, Chicago, 91-98;

asst prof, Ill State Univ, 98-. *Awards:* Edward L Ryerson Fel Award, 79; Nat Endowment Arts Grant, 84 & 90; Ill Arts Coun Fel, 84. *Bibliog:* Judith Russi Kirshner (auth), Gary Justis--MSI, Art Forum, 12/82; Dan Cameron (auth), New generation of Chicago artists, Art News, 10/84; Michael Bonesteel (auth), article, Art in Am, 6/85; James Yood (auth), article, Artforum, 12/88; Lauri Dahlberg (auth), article, Dialogue Mag, 90. *Media:* Miscellaneous Media. *Publ:* Auth, Speakeasy, New Art Examiner, Summer 90. *Mailing Add:* Ill State Univ School of Art Campus Box 5620 Normal IL 61790

K

KABAKOV, EMILIA
CURATOR, ART DEALER
b USSR, Dec 3, 1945; arrived in Israel, 1973; arrived in US, 1975. *Study:* Moscow Sch Music, 1952-59; Coll Music, Irkutsk, 1962-66; Univ Moscow, 1969-72. *Hon Degrees:* Hon diploma, Venice Biennale, 1993; hon PhD, Univ Bern, 2000. *Exhib:* Solo and two-person exhibs with Ilya Kabakov include Inst Contemp Arts, London, 1989, Inst Contemp Art, Philadelphia, 1989, Ronald Feldman Fine Arts, New York, 1990, 1992, Mus Contemp Art, Chicago, 1993, Ctr Georges Pompidou, 1995, Palais Beaux-Arts, Brussels, 1996, Barbara Gladstone Gallery, 1997, Irish Mus Mod Art, 1998, Galleria Lia Rumma, Naples, 2000, Univ Calif Santa Barbara, 2001, Cleveland Mus Contemp Art, 2004, Sculpture Ctr, New York, 2004, State Hermitage Mus, St Petersburg, Russia, 2004, 2005, Opera National de Paris, 2006, Reykjavik Art Mus, Iceland, 2006, Tufts Univ Art Gallery, 2007; group exhibs include Dislocations, Mus Mod Art, New York, 1990, Take Two, 2005; Carnegie Int, Carnegie Mus Art, Pittsburgh, 1991; Venice Biennale, 1993, Plateau of Humanity, 2001, Utopia Station, 2003, Think with the Senses-Feel with the Mind, 2007; Whitney Biennial, Whitney Mus Am Art, 1997; Examining Pictures: Exhibiting Art, Whitechapel Art Gallery, London, 1999; Between Cinema & a Hard Place, Tate Mod, London, 2000, Open Systems: Rethinking Art c 1970, 2005; Moscow-Berlin, Hist Mus, Moscow, 2003, The Man Who Flew Into Space from His Apartment, 2004; Artists' Favorites, Inst Contemp Art, London, 2004, Surprise, Surprise, 2006; Universal Experience: Art, Life & the Tourist's Eye, Mus Contemp Art, Chicago, 2005; Russia!, Solomon R Guggenheim Mus, New York, 2005. *Pos:* Cur & art dealer, New York, 1975-. *Awards:* DAAD Fel, 1989; Kunstpreis Aachen, 1990; Arthur Kopcke Award, 1992; Max Beckmann Prize, 1993; Joseph Beuys Prize, 1993; Chevalier, Ordre des Arts et des Lettres, France, 1995; AICA Best Show Award, 1997; Kaiserering der Stadt Goslar, 1998; Oskar Kokoschka Preis, 2002; Praemium Imperiale, 2008. *Mailing Add:* c/o Barbara Gladstone Gallery 515 W 24th St New York NY 10011

KADLEC, KRISTINE
COLLAGE ARTIST, WRITER
b Green Bay, Wis, 1953. *Study:* Pasadena City Coll, AS, 98. *Work:* Leaving Los Angeles (paper-weave collage), Maura Harrington, Pasadena, Calif. *Exhib:* Weave Collage, Borders Bookstore, Glendale, Calif, 2002; Reuse/Recycle w/Paper Weave Collage, Los Angeles Fine Arts Bldg, Los Angeles, Calif, 2003; Czech into Paper Weave Collage, Consulate of Czech Republic, Westwood, Calif, 2004; New Member Slide Registry Group Exhibit, Los Angeles Munic Art Gallery, Barnsdall Art Park, Calif, 2008. *Awards:* Project Grant, Artistic Recycling, Yellow Fox Found, 2002; Project Grant, Reuse/Recycle w/Paper Weave Collage, Puffin Found, 2003; 3rd Place, Casa Verdugo Libr Juried Exhib, Glendale Art Asn, 2003. *Bibliog:* Shannon Wilkinson (auth), Take Charge of your Marketing, Art Calendar Mag, 2003; Michelle Taute (auth), Collage your way to Creativity, Artist's Sketchbook, 2003; Dian Page (auth), That's Life, Green Bay Press Gazetter, 2004; Scrap & Stamp Arts Magazine, Scott Publ, 2005; Artist's Sketchbook Magazine, F & W Publ, 2005. *Media:* Paper-Weave Collage, Representational. *Publ:* Notions (art), American Sewing Guild, 2000; Artists' Magazine (Art) F & W Publ, 2002; Fiberarts Magazine (Art), Interweave Press, 2005; auth, Getting Creative with Basic Collage Techniques, Scott Publ, 2005; Paper Fabric Collage Picture Frame, House of White Birches, 2007; What's Your Musical Sewing Personality?, Threads Mag, Taunton Press, 2007

KAERICHER, JOHN CONRAD
PRINTMAKER, EDUCATOR
b Springfield, Ill, June 6, 1936. *Study:* Millikin Univ with David Driesbach, BFA, 59; Univ Iowa, with Mauricio Lasansky, Stuart Edie, James Lechay & Robert Knipschild, MFA, 63. *Work:* Univ Iowa; Dordt Col; Northwestern Coll Iowa; plus pvt collections. *Comn:* Medal, Northwestern Coll, 66. *Exhib:* Kottler Galleries, NY; Va Polytech Inst Ann; Benjamin Galleries, Chicago; Iowa Printmakers Invitational, Iowa Arts Coun, Des Moines; Maastricht Int Printmaking Bienale, The Neth; selected prints Private Collection of Masters 20th Printmaking, Arkansas State Univ; 32 solo exhibs; 115 group exhibs. *Pos:* Founder and gallery dir, Northwestern Coll, 63-79 & 81-97; founder, major in art, Northwestern Coll; founder and devel, Fine Arts Permanent Collection, Northwestern Coll. *Teaching:* Prof printmaking & drawing, 63-2005, chmn art dept, 63-84, rotation chmn art dept, 89-2005 & emeritus prof (art) 8/2005-, Northwestern Coll, Iowa; creator of numerous art dept facilities and courses plus pre-professional programs. *Awards:* Creative Prod Grants Northwestern Coll Iowa, 66, 68, 75, 77, 81, 84 & 94 for sabbatical leaves; named Most Influential Printmaker in the Northwestern quadrant of Iowa, Des Moines Print Club. *Bibliog:* Rev of NY exhib in Park East Periodical; Kaericher and His Art (video), television, newspaper articles. *Mem:* Mid-Am Coll Art Asn; Iowa Print Group; Northwestern Printmakers. *Media:* Drawing, Intaglio Printmaking. *Publ:* Survey of Iowa Printmakers; numerous other artist publ. *Mailing Add:* 202 Arizona NW Orange City IA 51041

KAGAN, ANDREW AARON
HISTORIAN, CONSULTANT
b St Louis, Mo, Sept 22, 1947. *Study:* Wash Univ, AB, 69; Harvard Univ, MA, 71, PhD, 77. *Collection Arranged:* Samuels Collection. *Pos:* Contributing ed, Arts Mag, NY; critic art & architecture, St Louis Globe-Democrat, Mo; consultant, principal, Andrew Kagan, PhD & Assocs. *Teaching:* Critic-in-residence, Bennington Col, Vt, 72-73; vis prof art hist, Wash Univ, St Louis, Mo, 80-81. *Awards:* Ford Found Res Grant. *Bibliog:* Musikforschung, 39, 86; Publ Weekly, 9/20/93; Chronicle of Higher Education, 8/95. *Mem:* Wed Night Soc. *Res:* Paul Klee studies; theory of absolute art; 18th & 20th century art hist, theory, criticism; 19th & 20th century architectural history & criticism. *Interests:* restoring historic bldgs; golf. *Publ:* Marc Chagall, Abbeville, 89; Paul Klee at the Guggenheim Mus, 93; contribr, Dictionary of Art, Grove's/McMillan; Absolute Art, Gottingen, 93, Grenart/Green, 95; and others; Improvisations: Notes on Pollock and Jazz, Avalon, 2000; Paul Klee - Art & Music, 83, 87. *Mailing Add:* 15021 Claymoor Ct Suite 8 Chesterfield MO 63017

KAGANOVICH, YEVGENIYA
ADMINISTRATOR, EDUCATOR, METALSMITH
Study: Univ Ill-Urbanan-Champaign, BFA, 98; State Univ NY-New Paltz, MFA, 2002. *Work:* Riga Porcelain Mus, Latvia; Mus Internat Ceramics Studio, Kecskemet, Hungary; Samuel Dorski Mus Art, New Paltz, NY. *Exhib:* The Vault Project, Quirk Gallery, Richmond, Va, 2007; One from Wisconsin, West Bend Art Mus, Ill, 2008; Body Politic, Richmond Ctr Visual Arts, Western Mich Univ, Kalamazoo, 2009; 20201 NURTUREart Benefit, ZieherSmith Gallery, NY, 2010; Equilibirum, Landmark Arts, Tex Tech Univ, 2011; and others. *Pos:* designer, goldsmith, Peggie Robinson Designs, Studio of Handcrafted Jewelry, Evanston, Ill, 1992-2000; jewelry & metalsmithing adjunct faculty, Chgo State Univ, Ill 1998-2000; metals instr, Lill St Studios, Chgo, Ill, 2001; studio asst, Myra Mimlitsch-Gray, Stoneridge, NY, 2002; asst prof, Univ Wisc-Milwaukee, 2002-2008, assoc prof, dept chair, 2008-. *Bibliog:* Frank Lewis (auth), Women of Metal, Metalsmith Mag, p 61, 3/29, 2009; Lena Vigna and Wiggers, Namita Gupta (auths), Mining History: Ornamentalism Revisited, Metalsmith Mag, p 46-57, 3/29/2009; Kathrin Fiedler (auth), Lincoln Village's Most Interesting People, Bringing a Passion to Lincoln Village, Lincoln Village Voice, p 1-2, 11/2009; Phil Renato (auth), Body/Image, Metalsmith Mag, p 56, 3/30/2010; Lena Vigna (auth), Adornment and Excess: Jewelry in the 21st Century, Oxford, Miami Univ Art Mus, p 11, 13, 2010; Talya Baharal (auth), 500 Silver Jewelry Designs, Lark Books, 2011; and others. *Mailing Add:* University of Wisconsin at Milwaukee Peck School of the Arts 2400 E Kenwood Blvd Milwaukee WI 53211

KAGEMOTO, HARO
FILMMAKER, PHOTOGRAPHER
b Tokyo, Japan, Jan 9, 1952; US citizen. *Study:* Sch Mod Photog, NJ, cert, 72; Univ Hawaii, Manoa, BFA, 77; State Univ NY, New Paltz, MFA, 79. *Work:* Everson Mus Fine Art, Syracuse, NY; Erie Art Mus, Mich; Libr of Cong, Washington, DC; Calif Mus Photog, Santa Barbara; Guggenheim Mus, NY; Univ Hawaii; NY Pub Libr. *Exhib:* 53rd Ann Nat Acad Design, NY, 78; Selected Works, Woodstock Artists Asn, NY, 79; Prints & Drawing Invitational, Mariam Graves-Mugar Gallery, New London, NH, 81; Leisure Am, Tampa Mus Art, Fla, 83; Classical Photographs, Boston Mus Art, 83; Dada Duchamp Exhib, Colby-Sawyer Coll, New London, NH, 83; Alaskan Mail Art Exhib, Ketchikan Arts Coun, 83 & 84; Games 92, St Cloud, Minn, 92; Contained Art, Central Mich Univ, Mt Pleasant, 97; Small Works, Finley Community Ctr, Santa Rosa, Calif, 97; and others. *Pos:* Production mgr & asst dir, Wonderland Productions, San Francisco, 83-88, dir, 89-99; contract off, San Francisco State Univ, 2000-2008, asst dir, 2008-. *Teaching:* Instr etching-intaglio, Communications Village Ltd, Kingston, NY, 77-79; vis artist photo-silkscreen, Univ Calif, Berkeley, 80-83; vis lectr printmaking, San Francisco State Univ, 83. *Awards:* Charles Eugene Banks Award, Honolulu, Hawaii, 77. *Mem:* Am Film Inst; Am MENSA; San Francisco Mus Mod Art; Int MENSA. *Media:* Video Art, Documentary. *Mailing Add:* 2806 Truman Ave Oakland CA 94605-4847

KAGEMOTO, PATRICIA JOW
PHOTOGRAPHER, PAINTER
b New York, NY. *Study:* Syracuse Univ Sch Art, NY, 70-71; Hunter Coll, New York, 71-72; State Univ NY, New Paltz, BFA (magna cum laude), 75; Printmaking Workshop, New York, studied with Robert Blackburn, 84. *Work:* Collection of Bellevue Hosp, NY; Printmaking Workshop, NY; Calif Mus Photog, Riverside, Calif; The Robert Blackburn Printmaking Workshop Collection, Libr of Cong, Washington, DC; and other pub, corp & pvt collections. *Comn:* Intaglio print eds, Communications Village Ltd, Kingston, NY, 75. *Exhib:* Mohawk-Hudson Regional, Univ Art Gallery, State Univ NY, Albany, 76; Schenectady Mus, 77; Albany Inst Hist & Art, NY, 78; Invitational Art Exhib, Ctr Galleries, Albany, NY, 83; Affirmations of Life, Kenkeleba House, NY, 84; In a Stream of Ink, Coll Art Gallery, State Univ NY, & Alumni Printmakers' Invitational, New Paltz, NY, 84; All Media I, Woodstock Artists' Asn, NY, 85 & 91; Games '92, St Cloud, Minn; Contained Art, Cent Mich Univ Art Gallery, Mt Pleasant, 97; Small Works, Finley Comm Ctr, Santa Rosa, Calif, 97; and others. *Pos:* Consult printer, Printmaking Workshop, NY, 84; exhib auditor, NY State Coun Arts, NY, 84-87; gallery asst, Watermark/Cargo Gallery, Kingston, NY, 88-91. *Teaching:* Instr etching & color viscosity, Commun Village Ltd, Kingston, NY, 75-80; vis artist color viscosity printing, State Univ Coll, Fredonia, NY 78; dir children's print workshop linocuts, Woodstock Libr, NY, 89. *Awards:* Am the Beautiful Award, Printmaking, Am the Beautiful Fund, 76; First & Second Place Graphics, Sullivan Cult Ctr, Catskill Art Soc, 83; Ulster Co Decentralization Grant, Intaglio Prints, NY State Coun Arts, 89. *Bibliog:* Graphic Arts, Educ Audio Visual Inc, 77; Liam Nelson (auth), Harris and Jow merit High Watermarks, The Daily Freeman, 89; Steven Kolpan (auth), Intaglio dragons, Woodstock Times, 89. *Mem:* Ansel Adams Ctr Photog; Nat Mus Women in Arts; San Francisco Mus Modern Art; Metrop Mus Art. *Media:* Acrylic Paintings, Photographs, Watercolors, Intaglio Prints. *Mailing Add:* 2806 Truman Ave Oakland CA 94605-4847

KAGLE, JOSEPH L, JR
PAINTER, MUSEUM DIRECTOR, ART HISTORIAN
b Pittsburgh, Pa, May 2, 1932. *Study:* Carnegie Mus Sch Art, 38-51; Dartmouth Coll, AB, 55; Univ Colo, MFA, 58, UALR, MEd, 84. *Hon Degrees:* Tbilisi Fine Arts Acad, Tbilisi, GA, Hon Prof Art, 2002; Mongolia Univ Art & Culture, Hon Prof Art, 2004. *Work:* Southeast Ark Arts & Sci Ctr, Pine Bluff; Alcoa Collection, Pittsburgh; Nat Mus

Taiwan, Taipei; Kimon Friar Collection, Athens, Greece; Sanford Besser Collection, Little Rock, Ark; Am Embassy, Tbilisi, Ga. *Comn:* Concrete mural, Hafa Adai Theatre, Agana, Guam, 72-73; mosaic mural, State Arts Coun, Univ Guam, 74; concrete mural, Nat Endowment for Arts, Agana, Guam, 75; acrylic painting, Bank of Guam, Agana, 75; sculptures, comn by lawyer in Guam, 75. *Exhib:* Solo exhibs, US Info Serv Lincoln Ctr, Taipei, Taiwan, 75, Tyler Mus & Art Ctr, Waco, 98; Image of the South Pacific, Nat Mus Taiwan, Taipei, 76; NY State Ann, Arnot Mus, 77; Lakeview Series, Southeast Ark Arts & Sci Ctr, Pine Bluff, 79; retrospective, Hopkins Ctr, Dartmouth Coll, Hanover, NH, 80; Prague Tex Exhib, Czech Repub, 94; Arts Ctr of Waco, Tex, 99-2000; Chicago Int Art Exhib, Lincoln Park, 2001; Nat Gal, Tbilisi, GA, 2002 & 03; Red Car Gal, Ulaan-Baatar, Mongolia, 2004; Retrospective: Collecting and Creating, Kingwood Galleries, 2008; Upstream People Gallery, 2007-; Open the Door, French/American Exhib, French Consolate of Houston, 2013. *Collection Arranged:* Buddhist Hell Scrolls (auth, catalog), travel exhib throughout South, 80; John Howard and Friends, group show of minority art, 80; Southeast Ark Arts & Sci Ctr Permanent Collection, 80; Wildlife Collection Ann Exhib, 80; Arkansas Annual, 80; Texas Artists Exhib, 94. *Pos:* Exec dir, Southeast Ark Arts & Sci Ctr, 78-84, Brockton Art Mus, 84-87, Art Ctr Waco, 87-; Freelance, Waco Herald-Tribune, 88-. *Teaching:* Assoc prof art & chmn dept, Keuka Coll, Keuka Park, NY, 64-68; assoc prof & artist-in-residence, Wash State Univ, 65-66; assoc prof art, World Campus Afloat, 68-69; prof art & chmn dept, Univ Guam, 70-76, McLennan Community Coll, Waco, Tex, 90-2005, Tbilisi State Acad Art, 2001-2002; staff, inst of Art and Culture, Ulaan Baatar, Mongolia, 2004, Kingwood Coll, Tex, 2006. *Awards:* First Award in Painting, Cheney Cowles Mus, 66; Pac Artist of Yr, Am Inst Architects, Pac Chap, 77; Grant, Found Proj Scholar, 83 & 84; Fulbright Scholar, 2001, Fulbright Specialist, 2003-; Hon Rubait, Georgian Artist Union, Tbilisi; Hon Faculty, State Acad Art, Tbilisi. *Bibliog:* State Council on the Arts Artists of Guam, Nat Endowment for Arts, 74; Getting better all the time, PB Com (Paul Greenberg), 78; Work by J Kagle, Dartmouth Coll, 80. *Mem:* Coll Art Asn; Am Mus Asn; Southeast Mus Asn; Mid-Southern Watercolorists; Tex Asn Mus; Rotary Club Southwest, 2006-; Rotary Global History Fellowship, Peace Historian, 2006-, pres, 2010-2011; Rotary E-Club of the Southwest, pres, 2010-2011. *Media:* Acrylic, Watercolor, Collage, Pen, Ink, Art Consultant. *Res:* Oceanic Art, Georgian Artists and American Architecture and Painting. *Specialty:* Contemporary Art. *Interests:* Painting, Writing, Museum Consulting, Architecture. *Collection:* Oriental and Modern American Art. *Publ:* Auth, The Twenty-Four Hour Day, China Press, 75; Osiik is Dead, Glimpses, Guam, 76; contribr, The Future is Now, Com Press, 80; auth, Long walks at twilight and dawn, Islands Mag, 80; The good old boy of art, Art Consortium, 80; An American Supra, 2003. *Dealer:* Lone Star College Kingwood Gallery. *Mailing Add:* 3758 Glade Forest Dr Kingwood TX 77339

KAHAN, ALEXANDER
DEALER, CONSULTANT
Study: State Univ NY. *Pos:* Owner, Alexander Kahan Fine Arts Ltd, New York, currently. *Mem:* Appraisers Asn Am. *Specialty:* Paintings and graphics of 19th and 20th century. *Collection:* Appel, Matta, Dubuffet, De Chirico, Riopelle, Calder, Dufy, Miro, Francis, Chagall, Picasso, Renoir, Marini & Utrillo, Vlaminck, Metzinger & Valtat. *Mailing Add:* 565 W End Ave New York NY 10024

KAHAN, LEONARD
DEALER, PAINTER, ART APPRAISER, CONSULTANT
b Bronx, NY, Jan 21, 1935. *Study:* Pratt Inst, BFA, 57; Brooklyn Col, MFA, 64; studied Brooklyn Mus Art Sch, 48, Art Students League, NY, 51-52. *Exhib:* Grand Central Art Gallery, New York City, 55, CCC Gallery, Brooklyn, 55, 58, Pratt Inst, 57, Walt Whitman Gallery, NY, 62, Copland Gallery, Woodstock, NY, 66, 67, Satori Gallery, NYC, 67, Ashby Gallery, New York City, 70, 81, 82, Varsovie Gallery, NYC, 82, 83, Lee Witkin Gallery, New York City, 83, Ledel Gallery, New York City, 83; NJ Ann Photog Contest, 85; Mus Mod Arts, Buenos Aires, Argentina, 90, 91; Otterbein Coll Art Gallery, Cleveland, 92; Frederick Clement Gallery, Montclair, NY, 97; Univ Colo Art Gallery, 99; Watermark/Cargo Gallery, Kingston, NY, 2000, 02; Woodlands Gallery, West Orange, NJ, 2002; Angel Orensanz Found Ctr for Arts, New York City, 2002, Printmaking Coun NJ, 2003, Washington Square East Galleries, 2003. *Pos:* retired owner, L Kahan Gallery, Inc; curator, Queensborough Community Col Art Gallery, Queens, NY, 2003-05. *Teaching:* art lectr, Queens Col, 68-70; art lectr, Brooklyn Col, 63-68; art instr, Brooklyn YMCA, 61-63; asst dir, art instr, Community Cult Ctr, Brooklyn, 56-58. *Mem:* Appraisers Asn Am. *Media:* Acrylic, Collage. *Specialty:* African art. *Mailing Add:* 16 Moran Rd West Orange NJ 07052-2252

KAHAN, MITCHELL DOUGLAS
MUSEUM DIRECTOR, HISTORIAN
b Richmond, Va. *Study:* Univ Va, BA, 1973; Columbia Univ, univ fel, 1973, MA, 1975; City Univ NY Grad Sch, univ fel, 1975-76, MPhil, 1979, PhD, 1983. *Collection Arranged:* Art Inc: Am Paintings from Corporate Collections (coauth & ed, catalog), Montgomery Mus & Brandywine Press, 1979; Am Paintings of the Sixties and Seventies: Selections from the Whitney Mus of Am Art (auth, catalog), Montgomery Mus, 80 & Roger Brown (coauth, catalog), 1980; Nicholas Africano (auth, catalog), 1983 & Heavenly Visions: Art of Minnie Evans (auth, catalog), 1986, NC Mus. *Pos:* Cur painting & sculpture, Montgomery Mus Fine Arts, Ala, 1978-82; cur Am & contemp art, NC Mus Art, 1982-86; dir, Akron Art Mus, 1986-; vpres, Intermus Conserv Asn, 1988-90, pres 1990-92 & 1994-95. *Awards:* Helena Rubinstein fel, Whitney Mus Art, 76; Smithsonian fel, Nat Collection Fine Arts & Hirshhorn Mus, 76-78; Nat Endowment fel, 87; Distinguished Mus Prof Award, Ohio Mus Asn, 2003; Cleveland Art Prize, 2008; Mandel Leadership Award, Case Western Reserve Univ, 2008. *Mem:* Intermus Conserv Assoc (trustee 86-95, pres 90-92, 95); Akron Roundtable (pres, 2001); Asn Art Mus Dirs (trustee, 2004-2006), Akron Area Arts Alliance (pres 2003-04). *Res:* American art, contemporary art. *Publ:* Contribr, Robert Colescott: Pride & Prejudice in a Retrospective, San Jose Mus, 1987; coauth, Akron Art Museum: Art Since 1850, An Introduction to the Collection, 2001. *Mailing Add:* Akron Art Mus 1 South High Akron OH 44308

KAHN, KATIE (KATHRYN) ANNA
PAINTER
b Chicago, Ill, Oct 21, 1949. *Study:* Univ Chicago, 67-68, Calif Coll Arts & Crafts, BFA, 74; Yale Univ Sch Art, MFA, 76. *Exhib:* solo exhibs, Field Gallery, Martha's Vineyard, Mass, 72, 79, 83, Studio I, Oakland, Calif, 73, Leedy-Voulkos Gallery, Kansas City, Mo, 89, Transco Gallery, Houston, 93, Merwin Gallery, Ill Wesleyan Univ, Bloominton, 99, Univ Tex of the Permian Basin, Odessa, 99, Roswell Mus & Art Ctr, NMex, 00, Concordia Gallery, Bronxville, NY, 01, Artemisia Gallery, Chicago, Ill, 03, Gallery 1756, Chicago, 97, 99, 02, Atlantic Gallery, NY, 03; selected group exhibs, Swarthmore Coll Art Gallery, 76, Fairweather Hardin Gallery, Chicago, 80, 85, 86, Katherine Lincoln Press, San Francisco, 82, Berkeley Art Ctr, Calif, 83, 84, World Print Coun, San Francisco, 83, Euphrat Gallery, De Anza Col, Cupertino, Calif, 83, 84, 59th & 60th Ann Crocker-Kingsley Exhibs, 84, 85, San Francisco Arts Comn Gallery, 84, Arts Coun of San Mateo, Belmont, Calif, 85, Walnut Creek Civic Art Gallery, Calif, 85, 87, Chabot Coll Gallery, Hayward, Calif, 85, Pro Arts, Oakland, Calif, 85, 86, Atlantic Gallery, NY, 86, Coll of Lake Co, Grayslake, Ill, Kohler Art Ctr, Sheboygan, Wis, Sonnenshein Gallery, Lake Forest Col, Ill, Adler Cult Ctr, Libertyville, Ill, 86, Alternative Space, Kansas City, Mo, 88, The Watson-Ess Gallery, Kansas City, Mo, 88, Clara Hatton Gallery, Colo State Univ, Ft Collins, 88, Leedy-Voulkos Gallery, Kansas City, Mo, 88, Mark Four Gallery, Lincoln, Nebr, 88, New Gallery Bemis Found, Omaha, 88; Esther Saks Gallery, Chicago, 89, 90, Evanston Art Ctr, Ill, 90, Lawndale Art and Performance Ctr, Houston, 90, 93, Sewall Art Gallery, Rice Univ, Houston, 91, 93, Transco Gallery, Houston, 91, Dolphin Gallery, Kansas City, Mo, 92, Barnes-Blackman Galleries, Houston, 93, Coll of Santa Fe Arts Gallery, NMex, 96, Jack Olson Gallery, Northern Ill Univ, DeKalb, 96, West End Gallery, Houston, 96, 97, 98, New Bedford Art Mus, Mass, 97, Northern Ill Univ Art Gallery, Chicago, 98, Beverly Art Ctr, Chicago, 98, Carlson Tower Gallery, N Park Univ, Chicago, 00, Artemisia Gallery, Chicago, 01, Kingsbury St/Stable Studios, Chicago, 02, Atlantic Gallery, NY, 02, 03. *Pos:* juror Ragdale Found, Lake Forest, Ill, 88-91, Kansas City, Art Coalition, Mo, 89, Roswell Mus & Art Ctr, NMex, 00, Artist-in-Residency Program, 96; lectr, workshops, studio visits, panels, critiques, Calif Col Arts & Crafts, Oakland, 85, 86, Univ Calif, Berkeley, 86, Vassar Col, Poughkeepsie, NY, 86, Kansas City Art Inst, Mo, 87, Univ Houston, 91, Rice Univ, Houston, 93, 94, Randolph Macon Women's Col, Lynchburg, Va, 94, Jack Olson Gallery, Northern Ill Univ, DeKalb, 96, 03, Gallery 1756, Chicago, 97, 99, SAIC, Chicago, 97, Ill Wesleyan Univ, Bloomington, 99, Albuquerque Arts Soc, NMex, N Park Univ, Chicago, 00, Concordia Col, Bronxville, NY, 01. *Teaching:* teaching asst, printmaking dept, Calif Col Arts & Crafts, Oakland, 73; instr, Educ Ctr Arts, New Haven, Conn, 75, Blackhawk Mountain Sch Art, Colo, 81, ASUC Studios, Univ Calif, Berkeley, 84-85, San Francisco State Univ, 84 & 85, and Walnut Creek Civic Arts, Calif, 85-87; vis lectr, Rice Univ, 91, 94-95; asst prof, Kansas City Art Inst, Mo, 87-89, spec asst prof, 91-92; assoc prof, Northern Ill Univ, DeKalb, currently. *Awards:* res fel, Ragdale Found, Lake Forest, Ill, 84, Roswell Mus & Art Ctr, NMex, 99-00, Ucross Found, Clearmont, Wyo, 02; fel Yale Summer Sch Music & Art, Norfolk, Conn, 73; nat visual artist grant, Nat Endowment Arts, 93-94. *Bibliog:* WFMT Fine Arts Radio, Chicago, 80; New Art Examiner, 80, 89; Oakland Tribune, 86; Omaha World Tribune, 88; KKFI Radio, Kansas City, Mo, 89; Kansas City Star, 89; Where two realities meet, Southern Accents, 91; Creative partners, Houston Post, 91; The Standard Times, New Bedford, Mass, 97; Gulf Coast, 97; Faces are startling revelations, Chicago Sun Times, 99; Vision Mag, Roswell Daily Record, 99; Abstract paintings that cross barriers of time and place, NY Times, Westchester ed, 01. *Dealer:* Gallery 1756 1756 Sedgewick Chicago IL; Atlantic Gallery, New York. *Mailing Add:* 1759 N Cleveland Ave Chicago IL 60614

KAHN, TOBI AARON
PAINTER, SCULPTOR
b New York, NY, May 8, 1952. *Study:* Hunter Coll, New York, BA (summa cum laude), 76; Pratt Inst, New York, MFA, 78. *Hon Degrees:* Jewish Theological Sem, Hon Dr, New York, 2007. *Work:* Solomon R Guggenheim Mus, Jewish Mus & Swiss Bank Corp, New York; Ft Wayne Mus, Ind; Nat Gallery Art, Washington, DC; Houston Mus Art; Minneapolis Inst Art, Minn; Mus Art, Fort Lauderdale, Fla; Neuberger Mus Art, New York; Weatherspoon Art Gallery, NC. *Comn:* Paintings, Mitchell & Co, Boston, 85; painting, First City Corp, New York, 86; sculptures for set designs, Solomons Dance Co, 88, Muna Iseng Dance Proj & Elizabeth Swados, 90; sculpture, Robert Lee Blaffer Trust For New Harmony, Ind, 93; Holocaust Mem Garden, La Jolla, Calif, 2000; Healthcare Chaplaincy Meditative Room, 2002; Meditative Space/Chapel, Zicklin Hospice Residence, 2005; Lobby installation, UJA Fedn, New York, 2006; Meditative Chapel, Congregation Emanu-El B'ne Jeshurun, Wisconsim, 2009 . *Exhib:* A View of Nature, Aldrich Mus, Ridgefield, Conn, 86; The New Romantic Landscape, Whitney Mus Am Art, Stamford, Conn, 87; Art on Paper, Weatherspoon Art Gallery, Greensboro, NC, 88; Eco-92, Mus Mod Art, Rio de Janeiro, Brazil, 92; solo exhibs, Mary Ryan Gallery, New York, 93, Allene Lapides Gallery, Santa Fe, NMex, 94, Edwin A Ulrich Mus Art, Wichita, Kans, 2000, Neuberger Mus, Purchase, NY, 2003, Cape Mus Fine Arts, Dennis, Mass, 2003, Mus Craft & Folk Art, San Francisco, 2005 & Works on Paper, Philadelphia, Pa, 2006; Metamorphoses, Houston Mus Fine Art, Tex, 97-99; Landscape at the Millennium, Albright-Knox Art, Buffalo, NY, 2000; plus others; Tobi Kahn, Sacred Spaces for the 21st century, Mobia, NY, 2009. *Teaching:* Lectr, Sch Visual Arts, New York, 86-. *Bibliog:* Douglas Dreishpoon (auth), Tobi Kahn, the essence of vision, Arts Mag, 1/85; Michael Brenson (auth), article, NY Times, 11/6/87; Susan Kandel & Elizabeth Hayt-Adkins (coauths), article, Art News, 1/88; Holland Cotter (auth), Tobi Kahn, NY Times, 11/26/93; Susan Kleinman (auth), Blending modern art with objects of the spirit, New York Times, 4/26/2000; Jeff Daniel (auth), Kahn's works reflect the sea and the sky, but they're not landscapes, Saint Louis Dispatch, 3/29/98; Tobi Kahn: Correspondence, Edwin A Ulrich Mus of Art, 2000; Margaret Moorman (auth), Spaces for the Spirit, Art News, summer 2001; Ted Prescott (auth), image, Tobi Kahn: A Profile, J Arts & Religion, spring 2002; Victoria Donohoe (auth), Landscapes with glamour, Philadelphia Inquirer, 4/9/2002; Benjamin Genocchio (auth), Nature's

majesty, NY Times, 8/3/2003. *Mem:* Coll Art Asn. *Media:* Acrylic; Wood, Bronze. *Dealer:* Harmon-Meek Gallery 601 5th Ave South Naples, FL 34102; Hooks-Epstein Galleries 2631 Colquitty Houston Texas 77098; Works on Paper Philadelphia PA. *Mailing Add:* 1223 Jackson Ave Long Island City NY 11101-5501

KAHN, WOLF
PAINTER, LECTURER

b Stuttgart, Ger, Oct 4, 1927. *Study:* New Sch Social Res, with Stuart Davis; Hans Hofmann Sch; Univ Chicago, BA, 51. *Hon Degrees:* Wheaton Coll, 2002; Union Coll, Schenectady, NY, 2004. *Work:* Whitney Mus Am Art, Mus Mod Art & Metrop Mus Art, New York; Houston Mus Fine Arts; Los Angeles Co Mus Art, Calif; Brooklyn Mus, New York; Asheville Art Mus, Asheville, NC; Nat Bank Tulsa, Tulsa, Okla; Port Authority NY & NJ; Summit Art Ctr, Summit, NJ; Transamerica Corp, Charlotte, NC. *Comn:* Portraits, Jewish Theological Sem, New York, 67 & 68; landscape, comn by Young Smith, Litchfield Plantation, SC, 70; The Four Seasons, AT&T Hq, New York, 85; 2000 K Street, Washington, DC, 87; Designed First Day of Issue for UN Philatelic Collection, 92; The Atlantic Golf Club, Bridgehampton, NY, 95; Color etching comn by the Am Acad & Inst Arts & Lett for their 100th Anniversary. *Exhib:* group exhibs, Whitney Mus Am Art, 57, 58, 60-61 & 77 & Invited! Works on Paper, First St Gallery, New York, 2001; Albright-Knox Art Gallery, 58; Pa Acad Fine Arts, 61 & 65; Dallas Mus Art, 62; Students of Hans Hoffmann, Mus Mod Art, New York, 63; Am Places, Corcoran Gallery Art, 79; Recent Acquisitions, Metrop Mus Art, New York, 79-80; Jerald Melberg Gallery Inc, Charlotte, NC, 84-96 & 2005; The Janss Collection, San Francisco Mus Mod Art, 85; Inaugural Exhib, DC Moore Gallery, 95; solo exhibs, Stremmel Gallery, Reno, Nev, 95, Grace Borgenicht Gallery, New York, 95, Color, Brattleboro Mus, Vt, 95-2006, Boca Raton Mus Art, Fla (traveling to Butler Inst Am Art), 96, Vered Gallery, East Hampton, New York, 96, D C Moore Gallery, New York, 96 & Ameringer Yohe Fine Art, Boca Raton, Fla, 2002-2003 & New York, 2003-2009; Pastels by Ten Contemp Artists, DC Moore Gallery, New York, 96; Contemp Directions, Abstraction & Realism, Jacqueline Holmes & Assoc Inc, Jacksonville, Fla, 96; Mus fur Kunst und Gewerbe, Hamburg, Ger, 2001; Holiday Group Exhib; Westport Arts Ctr, Westport, Conn, 2004; Kunsthaus Bühler, Stuttgart, Ger, 2004-2007, 2011; Hans Hofmann: The Legacy, The Painting Ctr, New York, 2005; Ogden Mus Southern Art, New Orleans, 2006; Provincetown Art Asn & Mus, 2006; American Masters, Recent Acquisitions, Marianne Friedland Gallery, Naples, Fla, 2006; Amerigner, Yohe Fine Art, NY, 2011; Reynolds Gallery, Richmond, Va, 2011. *Collection Arranged:* Ameringer/McEnery/Yohe, New York. *Pos:* Trustee, Brattleboro Mus, Vt Studio Ctr, Marlboro Coll, Vt; cur, Nat Acad, New York, 2005. *Teaching:* Vis assoc prof painting, Univ Calif, Berkeley, 60-61 & Cooper Union, New York, 60-77; artist-in-residence, Dartmouth Coll, 84; instr, Vt Studio Ctr, Johnson, Vt, 89-2005. *Awards:* Guggenheim Fel, 67-68; Hassam Fund Purchase Award, Am Acad & Inst Arts & Lett, 79; Ranger Fund Purchase, Nat Acad Design, 79; Prize, Nat Acad Design, 87; Am Artist Achievement Award, 93; Lifetime Achievement Award, Vt Coun on the Arts, 98; Hon Degree Dr Fine Arts, Wheaton College, 2000. *Bibliog:* Justin Spring (auth), Wolf Kahn, Abrams Publ, New York, 96, 2nd ed, 2011; Autumn's artist, CBS Sunday Morning, 10/20/96. *Mem:* Nat Acad Design; Am Acad Arts & Lett (treas, 2004-2007). *Media:* Oil, Pastel Monotype. *Interests:* Writing, lecturing. *Publ:* Connecting incongruities, Art Am, 11/92; gently down the stream, Art New Eng, 10-11/93; Wolf Kahn Paints the South, Morris Mus, Augusta, Ga, 99; Mus Fuer Kunst und Gewerbe, Hamburg, Ger, 00; Wolf Kahn Pastels, Abrams Publ, New York, 1998; Wolf Kahn's America, Abrams Publ, New York City, 2002; auth, Stout Shines at BMAC Show, Brattleboro Reformer, 9/21/2000; auth, Artist's Notebook: Belgium, Travel & Leisure, 9/2000; auth, A Reader's Response to Life at the Vermont Studio School, The Brooklyn Rail, 12/2003-1/2004; auth, Allan Kaprow (1927-2006), The Brooklyn Rail, 5/2006. *Dealer:* Reynolds Gallery Richmond Va; Thomas Segal Gallery Baltimore MD; Jerald Melberg Gallery Charlotte NC; Marianne Friedland Gallery Naples Fla; Addison Ripley Fine Art Washington DC; Stremmel Gallery Reno Nev; Ameringer/McEnery/Yohe Gallery W 22nd St New York NY; Kunsthaus Buhler Stuttgart Germany. *Mailing Add:* 217 W 21st St New York NY 10011

KAIDA, TAMARRA
PHOTOGRAPHER

b Lienz, Austria, 1946. *Study:* Goddard Col, Plainfield, Vt, BA, 74; State Univ NY, Buffalo, MFA, 79. *Work:* Ctr Creative Photog, Tucson, Ariz; Int Mus Photog, George Eastman House, Rochester, NY; Santa Fe Mus Fine Arts, NMex; Mus Mod Art, NY; Polaroid Corp, Cambridge, Mass; and others. *Exhib:* Curator's Choice, Lieberman and Saul Gallery, NY, 89; Current Works, Gallery Kansas City Artists Coalition, Mo, 89; group show, Anderson Ranch Arts Ctr, Aspen, Colo, 89; solo exhib, Fine Arts Gallery, Rhode Island Sch Design, 89 & OPSIS Found Gallery, NY, 90; Arizona Photographs: The Snell and Wilmer Collection, Ctr Creative Photog, 90; Photog Book US, 91. *Collection Arranged:* Contemporary European Portraiture, Northlight Gallery, Ariz State Univ, Tempe, 83; Mixed Signals: Photographs with Text (co-cur Rod Slemmons), Northlight Gallery, Ariz State Univ, Tempe, 88. *Pos:* Asst dir educ dept, Int Mus Photog at George Eastman House, Rochester, NY, 76-79. *Teaching:* Vis lectr, Ariz State Univ, 79-80, asst prof, 80-85, assoc prof, 85-; prof, Sch Art, Katherine K Herberge Col Fine Arts, Tempe, Ariz. *Awards:* Fel, Nat Endowment Arts, 86; Photography Fel, Ariz Comn Arts. *Publ:* Coauth (with Rita Dove), The Other Side of the House, Pyracantha Press, Ariz State Univ Sch Art, 88; auth, Tremors from the Faultline, Visual Studies Workshop Press, 89. *Dealer:* Califia Books San Francisco CA. *Mailing Add:* PO Box 139 UBUD Gianyar Bali Indonesia 80571

KAINO, GLENN
SCULPTOR

Exhib: Group exhibs, Whitney Biennial, Whitney Mus Am Art, 2004; The Bronx Mus Art; Studio Mus, Harlem; Walker Arts Ctr; Int Film Festival Rotterdam. *Pos:* Co-founder, Deep River Gallery, LA; head programming and creative dir, Universal Music Group and Sony Music Entertainment joint venture; chief creative officer, Napster, formerly; exec vpres creative and online, IMF: The International Music Feed, 2006-. *Teaching:* Prof, UCLA and Univ Southern Calif, formerly

KAISER, BENJAMIN
SCULPTOR, DESIGNER

b Tel Aviv, Israel, July 2, 1943; US citizen. *Study:* San Jose State Univ, BA, 77, MFA, 79. *Work:* Mus Contemp Art in Glass, Valencia, Spain; City Palo Alto, City San Jose, Calif. *Comn:* Fountain, Villa Monterey Country Club, Phoenix, 82; glass panels, Rolm Corp, San Jose, Calif, 83. *Exhib:* New Glass Int Exhib, Corning Mus Art, 79; Contemp Glass: Australia, Canada, USA and Japan, Nat Mus Mod Art, Kyoto & Tokyo, Japan, 81; Int Directions in Glass Art, Art Gallery Western Australia, Perth, 82; Sculptural Glass, Tucson Mus Art, 83; Vicointer 83, Mus Contemp Art in Glass, Valencia, Spain, 83. *Teaching:* Instr glass-blowing, Bezalel Acad Art & Design, Jerusalem, 72-74. *Media:* Glass, Stainless Steel

KAISER, DIANE
COLLAGE ARTIST, PHOTOGRAPHER

b Brooklyn, NY, May 27, 1946. *Study:* Brandeis Univ, BA; Columbia Univ, MFA; additional study with Peter Grippe & Sahl Swarz. *Hon Degrees:* Brandeis Univ, Hon Scholar. *Work:* Columbia Univ; Inst for Advanced Study. *Comn:* Amherst Arts Lottery, 90 & 92; Westwood Arts Lottery, 95; Westwood Educ Found, 96 & 98. *Exhib:* Rose Art Mus, 74; Contemp Reflections, Aldrich Mus Contemp Art, Ridgefield, Conn, 75; solo exhibs, Douglas Coll, 75 Drawings & prints, Comt Visual Arts Inc, 77 & Mus Fine Arts, Springfield, Mass, 89; Mus Fine Arts, Springfield, Mass, 81; 14 Sculptors Gallery, New York, 85 & The Living Room, 86; Outdoor Sculpture of Chesterwood, Mass, 86-87; Outdoor Sculpture of Stamford Mus & Nature Ctr, Conn, 88; Outdoor Sculpture at Bradley Palmer State Park, Mass, 92; Douglas Coll, 96, 2009; Outdoor Sculpture installation, Duxbury Art Complex, 97; Belmont Hill Sch, Mass, 98; NH Inst Art, 2009; Target Gallery, Torpedo Art Ctr, Alexandria, Va, 2010; Hebrew Coll, Newton, Mass, 2010; Photoplace Gallery, Vt, 2010; Danforth Mus, Framingham, Mass, 2011; Int Print Ctr, NY, 2011; Springfield Art Mus, Springfield Mo, 2011; New Bedford Art Mus, Mass, 2013; Danforth Art Mus, Framingham, Mass, 2013; Zullo Gallery, Medfield, Mass, 2013; Danforth Art Mus, Framingham, Mass, 2014. *Collection Arranged:* Drawings & prints, independent exhib prog, Comt Visual Arts Inc, NY, 77; The Living Room: sculpture and furniture, 14 Sculptors Gallery, NY, 86. *Pos:* art dir, Westwood Pub Schs, Westwood, Mass, 94-2013; independent lectr, 2012-. *Teaching:* Chmn & instr art dept, Chapin Sch, New York, 70-79, St Hilda's & St Hugh's Sch, New York, 90-; vis artist, Dwight-Englewood Sch, NJ, 76; instr, Northfield-Mount Hermon Sch, Northfield, Mass, 79-80; lectr art dept, Smith Coll, Northampton, Mass, 80-83; asst prof art, Elms Coll, Chicopee, Mass, 90-94; dir art, Westwood Pub Schs, Mass, 94-2013; instr advanced placement art, Fitchburg State Univ Prof Develop Ctr, 99-; Mass Master Teacher, 2001-2009. *Awards:* MacDowell Colony Fel, 73; Teachers Fel, Skidmore Coll, 97. *Mem:* Coll Art Asn; Mass Dirs Art Educ; Nat Art Educ Asn; Boston Printmakers; Monotype Guild of New England. *Publ:* Contribr, Children, Clay & Sculpture. *Mailing Add:* 15 Fairview Rd Canton MA 02021

KAISER, PAUL
DIGITAL ARTIST

b Munich, Germany, Feb 24, 1956. *Study:* Wesleyan Univ, BA (film & art hist, summa cum laude, Phi Beta Kappa), 1978; Am Univ, MEd (with honors), 1984. *Exhib:* Solo exhibs include Brooklyn Acad Music, NY, 2001; group exhibs include BIPED, CalPerformances, Berkeley, Calif & Ctr Performing Arts, New York, 1999 ; How long does the subject linger on the edge of the volume, Lincoln Ctr Rose Theater, 2005, Monaco Dance Forum, Monaco, France, 2005; Enlightenment, Lincoln Ctr Performing Arts, New York, 2006; Recovered Light, York Minster, York, England, 2007; Breath, Lincoln Ctr Performing Arts, New York, 2007; Moves, Ctr Contemp Art, Glasgow, Scotland, 2007-08. *Teaching:* Instr film & art hist, Wesleyan Univ, 1997-98, instr film studies, 1999-2003; multimedia studies lectr, San Francisco State Multimeda Studies Prog, 1996-99; lectr, Harvard Univ, Grad Sch Design, 2002; instr computer music, studio art & film, Columbia Univ, 2003. *Awards:* Computer World/Smithsonian Award, 1992; Found Contemp Arts Grant, 1996 & John Cage Award, 2008; John Simon Guggenheim Mem Found Fel, 1996; Outstanding Publ Award, Cong Res Dance, 2000; Arts in Multimedia Award, Lucent/Brooklyn Acad Mus, 2000; Bessie Award, 2000; Osher Fel, 2000; NY Found Arts Fel, Computer Arts, 2002; Ars Electronica Award of Distinction, 2005; Media Arts Fel, Rockefeller Found, 2006. *Mailing Add:* 501 W 122 E 3E4 New York NY 10027

KAISER, S(HARON) BURKETT
PAINTER

b 1946. *Study:* Calif State Univ, Northridge, 64-65, San Diego, BA, 69; Brandes Art Inst, 82-83; Calif Art Inst, 84-88, study with Russ Sergei Bongart, 82-85; studies with Charles Movalli, 93-98. *Work:* Princess Cruise Lines. *Exhib:* Art Expo, Los Angeles, Calif, 91; Tokyo Inst Art Show, Japan, 92; California Art Club-85 Yrs of Art, Carnegie Art Mus, Oxnard, Calif, 94; Calif Heritage Gallery, San Francisco, 96; one woman show, Premier Gallery, Fredricksberg, Va, 96; and many other one-person & group shows. *Bibliog:* Molly Siple (auth), article, Calif Art Club Newslett, 1/95; M Stephen Doherty (auth), Creative Oil Painting, Rockport Publ; Oil highlights, Am Artist, 96. *Mem:* Signature mem Calif Art Club. *Media:* Oil. *Dealer:* Colville Publishing 2909 Oregon Court Torrance CA 90503

KAISER, VITUS J
PAINTER

b Erie, Pa, May 3, 1929. *Study:* NC State Coll; Veterans Sch, Erie, with Joseph Plavcan; Univ Pittsburgh. *Work:* Erie Pub Libr. *Exhib:* Am Drawing Biennial, Norfolk Mus, Va, 71; Albright-Knox Art Gallery, Mem Gallery, Buffalo, 72; Butler Inst Am Art, 73; Am Drawings III, Portsmouth, Va, 80; Am Drawings, Smithsonian Inst traveling exhib, 81; and others. *Teaching:* Retired. *Mem:* Erie Art Mus; Soc Watercolor Painters Pa; NPAA; and others. *Media:* Watercolor, Multimedia. *Interests:* Painting & Drawing. *Mailing Add:* 551 W 26th St Erie PA 16508

KAISH, LUISE
SCULPTOR, PAINTER
b Atlanta, Ga. *Study:* Syracuse Univ, with Ivan Mestrovic, BFA & MFA; Escuela de Pintura y Escultura, Mexico City, Mex; Taller Grafico. *Work:* Whitney Mus Am Art, NY; Jewish Mus, NY; Rochester Mem Art Gallery, NY; Smithsonian Inst; Metrop Mus Art, NY; Nat Mus Am Art, Washington. *Comn:* Ark of Revelations (bronze), Temple B'rith Kodesh, Rochester; Great Ideas of Western Man & Walter Paepke Award Sculpture, Container Corp Am; Christ in Glory (bronze), Holy Trinity Mission Sem, Silver Spring, Md; ark doors, menorahs, eternal light (bronze), Temple Beth Shalom, Wilmington, Del; Continental Grain Co, NY; The Saltine Warrior, Syracuse Univ. *Exhib:* Sculpture USA, Metrop Mus Art, NY; Recent Sculpture USA, Mus Mod Art, NY; Albright-Knox Mus, Buffalo; Hopkins Ctr, Dartmouth Col, Hanover, NH; Whitney Biennials, Whitney Mus Am Art, NY; Solo exhibs, Minn Mus Art, Staempfli Gallery, NY, Rochester Mem Art Gallery & Jewish Mus, NY; plus others; USIS Rome, Italy; Century Asn, NY; Univ Ark. *Pos:* Artist-in-residence, Hopkins Ctr, Dartmouth Col; vis artist, Univ Wash, Seattle & Univ Haifa, Israel. *Teaching:* Prof sculpture, Columbia Univ, NY, 80-93, chmn div painting & sculpture, 80-86, emer prof, 93-. *Awards:* Guggenheim Fel Creative Sculpture; Louis Comfort Tiffany Grant Creative Sculpture; Rome Prize Fel in Sculpture, Am Acad, Rome; Arents Pioneer Medal, Syracuse Univ. *Bibliog:* Roger Lipsey (auth), An Art of Our Own, the Spiritual in Twentieth Century Art, Shambhala, 88; Gerrit Henry (auth), Luise Kaish: A Lyrical Essay Vol 62 No 7, Arts Mag, 3/88; Charlotte Streifer Rubinstein (auth), American Women Sculptors: a history of women working in three dimensions, GK Hall, 90. *Mem:* Century Asn; Am Acad in Rome (emer trustee, currently); Nat Acad Design. *Media:* All. *Dealer:* Kaish Studios 610 W End Ave Apt 9A New York NY 10024. *Mailing Add:* 610 W End Ave Apt 9A New York NY 10024

KAISH, MORTON
PAINTER, EDUCATOR
b Newark, NJ, Jan 8, 1927. *Study:* Syracuse Univ, BFA; Acad de la Grande Chaumiere, Paris; Ist d'Arte, Florence; Acad delle Belle Arti, Rome. *Work:* Brooklyn Mus, NY; British Mus, London; Whitney Mus Am Art; Metrop Mus, NY; Nat Mus Arts, Smithsonian Inst, Washington, DC. *Exhib:* Young Am Printmakers, Mus Mod Art, NY, 53; Solo exhibs, Staempfli Gallery, NY, 64-89, New Sch Social Res, 74 & Hollis Taggart Galleries, NY, 93-96; Art Inst Chicago, 64; Whitney Mus Ann Am Painting, 66; Am Inst Arts & Lett, 66, 73 & 74; US Info Serv, Italy, 72; Minn Mus Art, 75; Springfield Mus Art, 75; Taft Mus, 82; USIA Jerusalem, Israel, 85; Irving Galleries, Fla, 96-2011. *Teaching:* Prof painting & drawing, Fashion Inst Technol, State Univ NY, 73-; instr, New Sch, 74-77 & Art Students League, 74-82; artist-in-residence, Dartmouth Col, 74 & Univ Haifa, Israel, 85; vis prof, Queens Col, 79, Univ Wash, Seattle, 79 & Boston Univ, 87; vis artist, Columbia Univ, 86; FIT, Univ Florence, 90-. *Awards:* Benjamin Altman Landscape Prize, Nat Acad Design, 89; Andrew Carnegie Prize, Nat Acad Design, 92; Benjamin West Clinedinst Medal (Achievement in the Arts), Artists' Fellowship, 2006; Lifetime Achievement award, Nat Acad Mus, 2011. *Bibliog:* R Bass (auth), article, Art News 11/83; R Martin (auth), article, Arts Mag, 11/86; S Doherty (auth), article, Am Artist, 12/93; W Caporale (auth), International Artist (article), 1/2012. *Mem:* Academician Nat Acad Design; Artists Fel; Century Asn. *Media:* Oil, Acrylic. *Dealer:* Irving Gallery Palm Beach FL. *Mailing Add:* 610 W End Ave New York NY 10024

KAKAS, CHRISTOPHER A
PRINTMAKER, PAINTER
b Dayton, Ohio, Dec 11, 1941. *Study:* Miami Univ, Ohio, BFA, 66; Univ Iowa, MA, 68, MFA, 69. *Work:* Minneapolis Inst Art; Sheldon Mem Art Gallery, Univ Nebr, Lincoln; Mus Art & Archit, Univ Mo, Columbia; Cleveland Mus Art, Ohio; Rockford Col, Ill; and others. *Exhib:* Metrop Mus, Coral Gables, Fla, 80; Univ SDak, Vermillion, 80; Solo exhibs, Hiestand Art Gallery, Miami Univ, Oxford, Ohio, 80, Montgomery Mus Fine Arts, Ala, 82 & Sarratt Gallery, Vanderbilt Univ, Nashville, Tenn, 86; Rockford Int, Rockford Col, 83; 40th NAm Print Exhib, Brockton, Mass, 88; Biennial Exhib Contemp Southern Art, Huntsville, Ala, 88; Artists Proof, 89; Greenville Mus Art, NC, 89. *Teaching:* Asst prof, Syracuse Univ, NY, 75-76; asst prof art, Western Ky Univ, Bowling Green, 76-78; assoc prof, printmaking, Univ Ala, Tuscaloosa, 78-. *Awards:* Purchase Awards, 1st Ann Nat Print Exhib, San Diego State Univ, 68, 2nd Ann Nat Print Exhib, Ga Comn Arts, 71 & 4th Annual Nat Print Exhib, Moravian Col, 85; Award, Rockford Int, 83; Award, 6th Alabama Works on Paper, 85. *Mem:* Coll Art Asn; Los Angeles Printmaking Soc; Southern Graphics Coun. *Media:* Intaglio, Lithograph; Gouache, Acrylic. *Dealer:* Miriam Perlman Inc Lake Point Tower Suite 1902 505 N Lake Shore Dr Chicago IL 60611; Maralyn Wilson Gallery 2010 Cahaba Rd Birmingham AL 35223. *Mailing Add:* Univ Ala Dept of Art PO Box 870270 Tuscaloosa AL 35487-0270

KALB, MARTY JOEL
PAINTER, EDUCATOR
b Brooklyn, NY, Apr 13, 1941. *Study:* Mich State Univ, BA, 63; Yale Univ, BFA, 64; Univ Calif, Berkeley, MA, 66. *Work:* Klutnick Nat Jewish Mus, Washington; Metrop Mus Art, NY; Cleveland Mus Art, Ohio; Libr Cong, Washington; JB Speed Art Mus, Louisville; and many others. *Exhib:* Nat Drawing Competition Gallery, 84, NY, 95; Witness & Legacy, Contemp Art about the Holocaust, Columbus Mus Art, Ohio, 95; Invitational Survey Painting, Columbus, Ohio, 95; 171st Ann Exhib, Nat Acad Design, NY, 96; Nat Mid Yr Exhib, Butler Inst Am Art, 97 & 2002; Ind Univ, 98; Mus Art South Bend, Ind, 99; Fla Holocaust Mus, St Petersburg, 2000; Sinclair Col, Dayton, Ohio, 2003. *Teaching:* Instr, Univ Ky, 66-67; assoc prof painting, Ohio Wesleyan Univ, 67-81, prof, 81-2007, prof emeritus, 2007-; lectr at numerous coll & univ in US & Great Britain; consult, Holocaust educ proj. *Awards:* Chess Award for Drawing, Columbus Art League, 91; Steidel Award for Visual Arts, Columbus Art League, 96; Fabri Prize for Graphic Work, Nat Acad Design, 96; Anderson Award, Ohio Wesleyan Univ, 2005; Welch Award, Ohio Wesleyan Univ, 2007. *Bibliog:* Numerous articles in NY Times, Dialogue & Columbus Dispatch; M Baigell (auth), Jewish American Artists and the Holocaust; The Holocaust's Ghost: Writings on Art Politics, Law and Education. *Mem:* Asn Holocaust Org; Ohio Art League; Ohio Council on Holocaust Educ. *Media:* Acrylic, Pastel. *Res:* Graphic & abstract artwork inspired by the Holocaust. *Collection:* numerous private and corporate collections. *Publ:* feature story, Art of Our Time, Dayton Art Inst, 87; review, The Photographs of Joseph Albers, Allen Mem Art Mus, 1/3/88; rev, Art in Europe and America, Wexner Ctr, Ohio State Univ, 5/90; auth, New Currents, Recent Art in Spain, Riffe Gallery Col, Ohio; Labyrinth of the Spirit, Smithson, Fox, Viola, Serrano, Lancaster, Ohio; Thoughts on the Creation of the Artwork "Holocaust Portraits," Dossier: L'Antifascismerevisite Revue Pluridiscplinair De La Fondation Auschwitz, Belgium, 7-9/2009; The Holocaust in History and Memory, Vol 3, 2010, Vol 4, 2011, Univ Essex, UK. *Dealer:* Art Access 540 S Drexel Ave Columbus OH 43209; Ayer Delano LLC 404 Asbury Ave Asbury Park NJ 07712; artservicesabsolutearts.com. *Mailing Add:* 165 Griswold St Delaware OH 43015

KALINA, RICHARD
PAINTER, PRINTMAKER
b New York, NY, May 21, 1946. *Study:* Univ Pa, BA, 66. *Work:* Indianapolis Mus Art; Norton Gallery Art, Palm Beach, Fla; Lehman Brothers Kuhn Loeb, Inc & NY Univ, NY; Amstar Corp; Pa Acad Fine Arts; and others. *Exhib:* Solo exhibs, O K Harris Gallery, NY & Jack Glenn Gallery, Los Angeles, 70, Tibor de Nagy Gallery, NY, 79, 80, 82 & 84, Piezo Electric (with catalog), NY, 86 & 87, Elizabeth McDonald Gallery, NY, 88-89, Diane Brown Gallery & Ledis Flam Gallery, 92 & Lennon, Weinberg Gallery, NY, 93, 95, 98, 2001, 2003 & 2006, Lennon Weinberg Gallery, NY, 2007; Group exhibs, Sidney Janis Gallery, NY, 90; Lennon Weinberg Gallery, NY, 92, 2009, 2010, 2012; Pamela Auchincloss Gallery, NY, 92; Diane Brown Gallery, NY, 92; and others. *Pos:* sr critic, Yale Univ; vpres & bd dir, Int Asn Art Critics, USA sect; contrib ed, Art in Am. *Teaching:* Lectr, Art New York City Prog, State Univ NY, 77, Montclair State Col, 91 & Yale Univ, Norfolk, Conn, 91; painting panel discussion, NY, 79 & Morton G Neumann Family Found, NY, 80; panel discussion, Sch Visual Arts, NY, 81, New Sch, 88, Hunter Col, 89 & Inst Contemp Art, PS1, 90; sem, Aspen Inst Humanistic Studies, Baca, Colo, 82; studio lectr, Bates Col, 89 & Drew Univ, 90; art hist fac, Bennington Col, Vt, 89-90, panel discussion, 91; artist-in-residence, Fordham Univ, Col Lincoln Ctr, NY, 90, chmn dept theatre and visual arts, prof studio art & art hist, 90-; vis artist, Glassel Sch Art, Houston Mus Art, Tex, 91 & New York Univ, Grad Sch Art, 91; prof, Fordham Univ, NY. *Awards:* Visual Arts Fel, Nat Endowment Arts, 92. *Bibliog:* Robert C Morgan (auth), The new end game, 1-3/92 & Alain Kirili (auth), Interview with Richard Kalina, 4-5/92; Steven Henry Madoff (auth), A new lost generation, Art News, 4/92; Richard Kalina, Bomb, winter 92. *Media:* Oil on Canvas. *Publ:* Imagining the Present: Context, Content & the Role of the Critic, Routledge Press, London & NY, 2006; contribr ed, Art in America. *Dealer:* Lennon Weinberg Inc 514 W 25th St New York NY 10001. *Mailing Add:* 44 King St New York NY 10014-4960

KALISH, HOWARD
SCULPTOR
Study: Cooper Union Art Sch; NY Studio Sch. *Exhib:* Solo exhibs, Bowery Gallery, NY, 73, 75, Armstrong Gallery, NY, 87, Denise Bibro Fine Art, NY, 2001; Group exhibs, Bowery Gallery, NY, 70, 94; State Univ NY, Albany, 70; First Street Gallery, NY, 73; Green Mountain Gallery, NY, 77; Prince Street Gallery, NY, 77; Pratt Manhattan Ctr, NY, 80; Kent State Univ Art Gallery, 81; Gallery 120, NY, 81; 55 Mercer Street Gallery, NY, 81; Nat Acad Design, NY, 82; Sculpture Ctr, NY, 82; Queens Mus, NY, 83; Sutton Gallery, NY, 83; Artists Choice Mus, NY, 84; Henry Street Settlement House, NY, 88; Sculptors Guild, NY, 90; 110 Green Street, NY, 91; Cast Iron Gallery, NY, 91, 93, 95; Kyoto Art Gallery, Japan, 93; Chesterwood Mus, Stockbridge, Mass, 94, 98, 99, 2000; Lever House, NY, 94; Union League Gallery, NY, 95; Lycoming Col, Williamsport, Pa, 95; FFS Gallery, NY, 95; Stamford Mus, Conn, 96; Williamsburg Art and Historical Ctr, Brooklyn, 97; Fordham Univ, Lincoln Ctr, NY, 97; Calif State Univ, Art Gallery, Fullerton, 97; Vedanta Gallery, Chicago, 99, 2000; Long Beach Island Found for Arts, Loveladies, NJ, 99; Waterside Gallery, W Stockbridge, Mass, 2000; Art Ctr of the Capitol Region, Troy, NY, 200; Wyndy Morehead Fine Arts, New Orleans, La, 2001. *Pos:* Exec bd mem Sculptors Guild, NY; bd dirs Artists Choice Mus, NY. *Teaching:* Prof, Nat Acad, NY, NYU, Nassau County Mus Art Sch, Roslyn, NY, Brooklyn Mus Art Sch; vis artist Kent State Univ, Ohio. *Awards:* Nat Endowment for Arts Sculpture Grant. *Mem:* Nat Acad (acad, 2004). *Media:* pigmented cement, steel, bronze. *Mailing Add:* PO Box 220088 Brooklyn NY 11222

KALISHER, SIMPSON
PHOTOGRAPHER
b New York, NY, July 27, 1926. *Study:* Ind Univ, BA, 48. *Work:* Milwaukee Mus Mod Art, Milwaukee, Wis; Jewish Mus, NY; Nelson-Atkins Mus, Kansas City, Mo; Mus Modern Art, NY; San Francisco Mus Modern Art; Mus Fine Arts Houston; Everson Mus Art. *Comn:* Photo essay, refugee camp in Lavrion, Greece, Intergovernmental Commission for Europ Migration (ICEM), 56; one yr grant for photog essay Syracuse (renewed 3 times), NY, NY Coun on the Arts, 68-72; various corp including PepsiCo, Phillip Morris, IBM, IT&T, and others. *Exhib:* Group exhib: Young Photogs, Mus Mod Art, NY, 1951; Family of Man, Mus Mod Art, NY, 1955; Four Directions in Photog, Albright-Knox Art Gallery, 64; Hist of Picture Story, Mus Mod Art, NY, 67; Harlem on My Mind, Metrop Mus Art, NY, 68; Photog in Am, Whitney Mus, 75; Mirrors and Windows, Mus Mod Art, NY; Discovering Am, Art Inst Chicago, 78; Am Children, Mus Mod Art, 81; Poses & Gestures, Mus Mod Art, 94; Am Photog 1890-1965, Musee Nat d'Art Mod, Paris, 96; Propaganda and other Photographs, Keith de Lellis Gallery, NY, 98; solo exhibs: Geo Eastman House, 62 and Art Instit of Chicago, 1963; The City Seen, Everson Mus Art, Syracuse, NY 01; solo exhib Propaganda and other Photographs, The Alienated Photographer, Mus of Fine Arts Houston, 2011; and others. *Teaching:* Instr photog, Sch Visual Arts, NY, 80-83. *Bibliog:* Thomas H Garver (auth), 12 Photographers of the American Social Landscape, 67; Robert Doty (ed), article, Photogr in America, 74; Ian Jeffrey (auth),

Time Frames. *Media:* Photography. *Publ:* Auth, Railroad Men: Photographs and Collected Stories, Clarke & Way, 61; Propaganda and Other Photographs, Addison House, 76; illusr, Clinical Sociology, 79; The Alienated Photographer, Two Penny Press, NY, 2011. *Dealer:* Keith de Lellis Gallery 47 East 68 St New York NY 10128. *Mailing Add:* 1115 SW 22nd Ave #316 Delray Beach FL 33445

KALLENBERGER, KREG
SCULPTOR
b Austin, Tex, 1950. *Study:* Univ Tulsa, Okla, BFA, 72, MA, 74. *Work:* Mus Fine Arts, Boston; Detroit Inst Arts; Los Angeles Co Contemp Art; Hokkaido Mus Art, Sapporo, Japan; High Mus Art, Atlanta. *Comn:* Glass & marble 5 x 5 x 5, SW Res Inst, San Antonio, 96; glass & marble, City of Tulsa Water Treatment, Okla, 98. *Exhib:* Collecting Am Decorative Arts & Sculpture, Mus Fine Art, Boston, 91; Glass from Ancient Craft to Contemp Art, Morris Mus, Morristown, NY, 92; Form & Light, Am Craft Mus, NY, 94; Glass Today by Am Studio Artist (with catalog), Mus Fine Art, Boston, 97; Glass, Owensboro Mus Fine Art, Ky, 97; Glass Today, Cleveland Mus Art, 97; Masters of Contemp Glass (with catalog), Indianapolis Mus Art, 97; Glass, Los Angeles Co Mus Art, 98. *Pos:* Technician, Pilchuck Glass Ctr, Stanwood, Wash, 83; juror, Mid-Am Arts Alliance Fel Awards, Kansas City, Mo, 87; artist-in-residence, Rocky Mountain Nat Park, 95; juror & speaker, Okla Scholastic Art Awards, Tulsa, 95. *Teaching:* Adj prof art, Univ Tulsa, 79-84. *Awards:* Bronze Medal, Int Art Competition, Olympics, Los Angeles, 84; Nat Endowment Arts Fel Grant, 84; Silver Prize, Int Exhib Glass Kanazawa, Japan, 95. *Bibliog:* Many articles in var bks and mags, 81-97; Dan Klein (auth), Glass a Contemporary Art, Rizzoli Int, 89; Tsuneo Yoshimizu (auth), Survey of Glass in the World, Kyoryudo Publ Ltd, Tokyo, 92; Patrick Frank (auth), Artforms, Rev 7th Ed, pages 218-19, Prentice Hall, 2004. *Media:* Glass. *Dealer:* Leo Kaplan Modern 965-A Madison Ave New York NY 10021; Habatat Galleries MI & FL; MA Doran Gallery Tulsa OK

KALLIR, JANE KATHERINE
ART DEALER, WRITER
b New York, NY, July 30, 1954. *Study:* Brown Univ, Providence, RI, AB, 76. *Exhib:* NY State Mus, Albany, 83; Austrian Nat Gallery, 90, 2011; San Diego Mus Art, 94 & 2001; Nat Gallery, Wash, 94; Orlando Mus Art, 2001; Museo del Vittoriano, Rome, 2001; Hangaram Mus, Seoul, 2009; Belvedere, Vienna, 2011. *Pos:* Dir, Galerie St Etienne, New York, 79-. *Teaching:* Guest lectr, Mus Am Folk Art, New York, 82-85, NYU, 82-85, Nat Gallery Art, 94, Ft Lauderdale Mus Art, 96, Mus Mod Art, 97, Int Found for Art Res, 98, Wexner Ctr, Columbus, Ohio, 99, San Diego Mus Art, 2001, Columbus Mus Art, 2002 & Clark Art Inst, 2002, Van Gogh Mus, 2005, Belvedere, 2011, S Methodist Univ, 2013. *Awards:* Silver Medal for Service to the Austrian Nation; Elie Faure Literary Award, France. *Mem:* Art Dealers Asn Am (bd dir, 94-97, vice pres, 2003-2006); Art Table. *Res:* Austrian & German expressionism; international naive art, especially in its relationship to modernism. *Specialty:* Klimt, Schiele, Kokoschka, Kubin, Kollwitz, Grandma Moses, Modersohn-Becker, Corinth, Sue Coe, Leonard Baskin. *Publ:* Auth, Austria's Expressionism, 81; Viennese Design and the Wiener Werkstaette, Braziller, 86; Gustav Klimt: 25 Masterworks, 89; Egon Schiele: The Complete Works, 90 & 98; Richard Gerstl/Oskar Kokoschka, 92; Egon Schiele, 94; Egon Schiele: 27 Masterworks, 96; Grandma Moses in the 21st Century, 2001; Egon Schiele: Watercolors and Drawings, 2003; Eyon Schiele: Love and Death, 2005; Gustov Klint: In Search of the Total Artwork, 2009; Egon Schiele: Self-Portraits and Portraits, 2011; Egon Schiele's Women, 2012; and others. *Mailing Add:* c/o Galerie St Etienne 24 W 57th St New York NY 10019

KALTENBACH, STEPHEN
SCULPTOR
b Battle Creek, Mich, 1940. *Study:* Santa Rosa Jr Coll, Calif, 58-63; Univ Calif, Davis, BA, 66, MA, 67. *Work:* Crocker Art Mus, Sacramento; San Francisco Mus Mod Art; Evanston Mus Art, Ill; Univ Calif, Davis; Mus Mod Art, New York. *Comn:* Natomas Sta, Folsom, Calif, 93; Esquire Plaza Project, Sacramento, Calif, 99. *Exhib:* Solo exhibs include San Francisco Mus Art, 67, Whitney Mus Am Art, New York, 69, Reese Palley Gallery, San Francisco, 69 & 70, Crocker Art Mus, Sacramento, 79, Oakland Art Mus, 80, Newport Harbor Mus, Calif, 80, Emmanuel Gallery, Colo State Univ, 82, Matrix Gallery, Sacramento, 85, Natsoulas Novaloso Gallery, Davis, Calif, 87, 88 & 90, Biola Univ, La Miranda, Calif, 87, Else Gallery, Calif State Univ, Sacramento, 88, Los Angeles County Mus Art, 96, Mus Contemp Art, Los Angeles, 96, Lawrence Markey Gallery, New York, 2000, Konrad Fischer, Dusseldorf, Ger, Another Year in LA, Los Angeles, 2005; group exhibs include New Modes in Calif Sculpture, La Jolla Mus Art, Calif, 66; Nine at Leo Castelli, Castelli Warehouse, New York 68-69; Earthworks, Dwan Gallery, New York, 68, Dwan Word Show, 69, Language III, 69; Attitudes, Brooklyn Mus Art, 70; Information, Mus Mod Art, New York, 70; San Francisco Art Inst, 70-71; Evanston Art Mus, Ill, 72; Univ Art Mus, Berkeley, Calif, 74-75; Additions & Arrangements, Acme Gallery, Sacramento, 76; Stone Maple, Crocker Art Mus, Sacramento, 76, Oakland Mus Art, 77, San Jose Mus Art, 78; Disarming Art, Matrix Gallery, Sacramento, Calif, 84, Matrix Show, 90; 4 Ceramic Sculptors, Natsoulas Novaloso Gallery, Davis, Calif, 87, Local Artists for Global Thought, 87, Clay Sculptors, 87, Faculty-Alumni Show, 88, Ann 30 Ceramic Sculptors, 88-91, Artists for Amnesty, 88 & 89, Arneson Tribute, 91; Calif A to Z, Butler Inst Am Art, 90; Crocker Kingsley Artists, Crocker Mus, Sacramento, 90; 30 Ceramic Sculptors, John Natsoulas Gallery, Davis, Calif, 92, 97 & 98, New Art Forms, 93, The Figure, 95, History of Figurative Ceramic Art Sculpture, 96; Gift Shop, Another Year in LA, Los Angeles, 2006. *Teaching:* Teaching asst, Ceramics Exten, Bob Arneson, 65-66; Univ Calif, Davis, 66 & 68; Sch Visual Arts, New York, 68-69; Calif State Univ, Sacramento, 1970-2005. *Awards:* Regents Scholar, Univ Calif, Davis, 63, Regents Fel, 66; Nat Endowment Arts Award, 77-78; Guggenheim Fel, 79-80. *Mem:* Phi Kappa Phi. *Publ:* Auth: The End, Xulon Press, 2004. *Dealer:* Another Year in LA 2121 N San Fernando Rd #13 Los Angeles CA 90065; Lawrence Markey Gallery 311 Sixth St San Antonio TX 78215. *Mailing Add:* 327 I St Davis CA 95616-4214

KAM, MEI K
PAINTER, INSTRUCTOR
b Chungshan, Guangdong, China, Aug 7, 1938; US citizen. *Study:* New York Univ, Cert Interior Decor, 67; Art Students League, New York, 77-78; Edgar Whitney Workshop, New York, 79-82. *Work:* Pastel Soc Am, Nat Art Club, NY. *Comn:* Watercolor paintings, US Coast Guard, Washington, DC, 84-85. *Exhib:* Three Contemp Artists, NY Univ Prog Bd, 86; 121st Exhib, Am Watercolor Soc, NY, 88; Hudson Valley Art Asn Ann, Westchester Co Ctr, 82-88; Audubon Artists Ann, Nat Art Club, NY, 80 & 88; Nat Acad Design, 92. *Teaching:* Instr watercolor, Salmagundi Club, NY, 82-85 & Jackson Heights Art Club, Queens, NY, 85-86; instr pastel, Pastel Soc Am, NY, 87. *Awards:* Award of Excellence, Charles Davis Mem Fund, 85; Artist Fel Award, Elizabeth K Ellis, 86 & 87; Morilla Canson Talent Award, Pastel Soc Am, 87. *Bibliog:* Dorothy Hall (auth), Art and Artists, Park East, 1/82; Palmer Poroner (auth), The Problem of Conservative Art, ArtSpeak, 4/16/84. *Mem:* Salmagundi Club; Pastel Soc Am; Hudson Valley Art Asn; Knickerbocker Artists; US Coast Guard Artists; Audubon Artists Inc. *Media:* Watercolor, Pastel. *Publ:* Contribr, Readers' pictures exhibited, The Artist (Eng), 8/81; Drawing with Pastels by Ron Lister, Prentice-Hall, 82. *Mailing Add:* 45-23 Union St Flushing NY 11355

KAMEN, REBECCA
SCULPTOR, EDUCATOR
b Philadelphia, Pa, July 8, 1950. *Study:* Pa State Univ, BS, 72; Univ Ill, MA, 73; RI Sch Design, MFA, 78. *Work:* Uniweave co Showroom, Chicago; IBM, Baltimore, Md & Raleigh, NC; Tower Construction, Bethesda, Md; Gannett Corp, Roselyn, Va; Advisors Financial, Vienna, Va; Capital One; KPMG Peat Martwick Corp; Inst Def Analysis; Arlington Co, Va. *Comn:* Welded steel sculpture, Lynhaven Career & Vocational Ctr, Columbia, SC, 75; welded steel sculpture, Lancaster High Sch, Lancaster, SC, 75; laminated wood wall relief, Pa State Univ, 76. *Exhib:* Works on Paper, 80 & Collage on Paper, 81, Corcoran Gallery Art; Collage and Assemblage, Miss Mus Art, Jackson, 81; Joe Guy/Rebecca Kamen, Leslie Cecil Gallery, New York, 87; Primitivism, Artscape 1987, Baltimore, MD, 87; Rebecca Kamen: Recent Painting & Sculpture, Winston Gallery, Washington, DC, 88; Jones Troyer Fitzpatrick Gallery, Washington, 90 & 92; Abstract Icons, Roanoke Mus Arts, Va, 92; Cortland Jessup Gallery, Provincetown, Mass, 93-94; Across Borders/Sin Fronteras, Art Mus Ams, Washington, DC, 94; Traces: Connecting Drawing & Sculpture, Md Art Place, Baltimore, 95; Portsmouth Mus, Va, 96; Am Ctr Physics, 2005; McLean Proj Arts, 2005; plus many others. *Pos:* Artist-in-residence, SC Arts Comn, 74. *Teaching:* Prof sculpture, Northern Va Community Coll, Alexandria, 78-. *Awards:* Award, Alexandria Sculpture Fest, Alexandria, Va, 83; Sculpture Award '84, Washington, 84; Pub Art Trust, 84; Va Mus Art Fel, 2000; Pollack Krasner Grant, 2006; and others. *Bibliog:* Eric Gibson (auth), Garden blends indoors, outside, Washington Times, 92; Mary McCoy (auth), Sowing the seeds of two cultures, Washington Post, 94; Mary McCoy (auth), On common ground, art takes root, Washington Post, 95; Sarah Tanguy (auth), Sculpture Mag, 2006; and others. *Mem:* Int Sculpture Ctr; Washington Sculptors Group. *Media:* Wood, Mylar, Wire. *Dealer:* Carla Massoni Gallery, 203 High St, Chestertown, Md, 21620. *Mailing Add:* 1554 Great Falls St Mc Lean VA 22101

KAMI, Y Z
PAINTER
b Tehran, Iran, 1956. *Study:* Univ Calif, Berkeley, 1974-75; Sorbonne, Paris. *Exhib:* Solo exhibs include Deitch Projects, New York, 1998, 1999 & 2001, Gagosian Gallery, Beverly Hills, Calif, 2008, John Berggruen Gallery, San Francisco, 2008; group exhibs include Istanbul Biennial, 2005; Without Boundary: Seventeen Ways of Looking, Mus Mod Art, New York, 2006; All the More Real: Portrayals of Intimacy & Empathy, Parrish Art Mus, Southampton, NY, 2007; Venice Biennale, 2007. *Mailing Add:* c/o Gagosian Gallery 456 N Camden Dr Beverly Hills CA 90210

KAMINSKY, JACK ALLAN
PHOTOGRAPHER, PRINTMAKER
b New Brunswick, NJ, Sept 8, 1949. *Study:* Brooklyn Col, BS, 72, MFA (fel), 75. *Work:* LaGrange Col, Ga; Arch Am Art, Smithsonian Inst, Washington, DC. *Comn:* Graphic designs, Off of Neighborhood Govt & New York Mass Transit Authority for Eastern Pkway Subway Sta, 74. *Exhib:* Brooklyn Scenes by Brooklyn Artists, Brooklyn Mus Community Gallery, 79; Summer Exhib, Salmagundi Club, NY, 79; Doors & Chairs & Windows, Snug Harbor Cult Ctr, Staten Island, NY, 79; Never Fail Imagery Show, Sch Mus Fine Arts, Boston, 80; Invitational, Henry Hicks Gallery Ltd, Brooklyn, NY, 81; Rotunda Gallery, Brooklyn Borough Hall, Brooklyn, 82; Queens Mus Commercial Gallery, Queens, NY, 83; Brooklyn Mus, Brooklyn, NY, 84; Gallery 72, Omaha, Nebr, 85; Wiesner Gallery, Brooklyn, NY, 87; Soho Photo Gallery, NY, 88; Lever House, NY, 88; Stuhr Mus, Grand Island, Nebr, 90; Gov's Mansion, Lincoln, Nebr, 90. *Pos:* Photogr, Aunt Len's Doll & Toy Mus, 74-; gallery asst, Ann Kendall Richards Inc, NY, 81-88; photogr, PEN, NY, 84-; asst dir photo dept, Baby Togs, NY, 88-. *Teaching:* Head graphics & photog dept, Brooklyn Mus Art Sch, 73-85; instr photog, Pratt Inst Continuing Educ, Brooklyn Botanic Gardens, 85; Long Island Univ, Continuing Educ, Brooklyn, NY & The Educ Alliance, NY, 85-. *Mem:* US Coast Guard Artists; Salmagundi Club. *Publ:* NY Woman Mag, 88. *Mailing Add:* 1760 Marine Pkwy Brooklyn NY 11234

KAMM, DAVID ROBERT
PRINTMAKER, EDUCATOR
b West Union, Iowa, Jan 22, 1952. *Study:* Wartburg Coll, BA, 74; Univ Iowa, with Mauricio Lasansky, MA, 86, MFA, 88. *Work:* Vatican Collection Mod Art, Rome, Italy; Fine Art Asn, Ho Chi Minh City, Vietnam; Elon Coll Fine Arts Collection, Elon Coll, NC; Univ Iowa; Int Mus Collage, Assemblage & Construction, Cuernavaca, Mex; Art Colle, Sergines, France. *Comn:* original print, for The Prairie Suite: A Study of Place, Grinnell Col, Iowa, 2001; CIVA Codex VII, Portfolio Print ed, 2010. *Exhib:* Bradley Nat Print & Drawing Exhib, Peoria, Ill, 89; Pac States Nat Biennial Print Exhib, Hilo, Hawaii, 90; Points of Reference, CSPS Arts Ctr, Cedar Rapids, Iowa, 92; Harper Nat Print & Drawing Exhib, Palatine, Ill, 94; Pages from a Small World,

Charles H MacNider, Mason City, Iowa, 96; Schoharie Co Nat Small Works Exhib, Cobleskill, NY, 97; The Print & the Process, Albrecht-Kemper Mus Art, St Joseph, Mo, 2000; Sanctuary, Concordia Col, Moorhead, Minn, 2003; Nat Drawing & Small Sculpture Show, Corpus Christi, Tex, 2005; Speaking Volumes: Transforming Hate, Holter Mus Art, Helena, MT, 2008; SE Minn Regional, Winona, Minn, 2010; The Art of Digital and Hand Built Collage/Assemblage, Dorat Coll, Sidux Cener, Iowa, 2010; Drawing Connections, Siena Art Inst, Italy, 2011; Is This Freedom? Wiseman Gall, Rogue Comm Col, Grant's Pass, Oregon, 2013; Lines Drawn, Charles Krause/Reporting Fine Art Gall, Washington, DC, 2014; Transformation, Pyramid Atlantic Art Ctr, Silver Springs, Md, 2015. *Pos:* Residency artist, Iowa Arts Coun, 78-88; gallery coordr & preparator, Luther Coll, 89-; residency artist, Henry Luce III Ctr for the Arts & Relig, Wesley Theological Soc, Washington, DC, 2007; Luthern Acad Scholars, Harvard Univ, Mass, 2008. *Teaching:* Asst prof art printmaking & drawing, art found, Luther Coll, Decorah, Iowa, 90-; Instr art appreciation & drawing, NE Iowa Community Coll, Calmar, 92-2001. *Awards:* Fulbright Study in Russia, Iowa State Univ, 92. *Mem:* Found Art Theory & Educ; Print Consortium, Kansas City, Mo. *Media:* Collage, Printmaking. *Publ:* Auth, Art within the Liberal Arts, National Conference Proceedings, Sch Visual Arts, NY, 93; Etchings of Roi Patridge, Print World, 94; I Know What I Like, Fate in Review, Univ Hawaii, 94-95; Coauth, From Aasland to Zorn, Agora, Luther Coll, 95; auth, Resurrecting Content, Fate in Review, Univ Hawaii, 97-98; Touching the Aesthetic Elephant, Fate in Review, NE Tex Community Coll, 02-03; illus, Marguerite Wildenhain: A Diary to Franz, South Bear Press, Decorah, IA, 2005; Riding the Light: Visual Thinking and Constructive Mind, Fast Forward #2, Manifestos and Manifestations, Integrative Teaching Int, Univ GA, Atlanta, 2011. *Mailing Add:* 607 John St Decorah IA 52101

KAMM, DOROTHY LILA
PAINTER, WRITER
b Chicago, Ill, Apr 6, 1957. *Study:* Northern Ill Univ, BFA, 79; Sch Art Inst Chicago, MFA, 84. *Comn:* 9-piece dresser set, comn by Dr & Mrs Michael Dennis, Ft Pierce, Fla, 89; set of 33 name stands, comn by Mr & Mrs Tommy Bruhn, Ft Pierce, Fla, 90; Urn, 92 & Framed painting on porcelain canvas, comn by Richard Rendall, Cincinnati, 93; Framed painting on porcelain canvas, comn by Dr Shirley Dunbar, Naples, Maine, 96; Nativity set, comn by Linda Geary, Stuart Fla, 11/97. *Exhib:* Art-i-ture: Furniture by Artists, Ctr Arts, Stuart, Fla, 90 & 91; Lighthouse Gallery, 90; Porcelain Fine Art Gallery, Denver, 94; A E Bean, Backus Gallery, Ft Pierce, Fla, 97; Hand Painted Porcelain, Hist Soc Martin Co, Elliot Mus, Stuart, Fla, 97. *Teaching:* Instr basic design & advance interior design, MacCormac Jr Coll, Chicago, Ill, 81-84; instr color light & sound, Dayton Art Inst, Ohio, 85; instr china painting, Art Gallery, Smithfield Coll, Stuart, Fla, 88-94, Martin Co Coun Arts, Stuart, Fla, 94-2000 & St Lucie West, 2000-04. *Awards:* Purchase Award, 26th Ann Lighthouse Gallery Art & Craft Festival, 89; Merit Award, Art Assoc Martin Co, 93. *Bibliog:* For Mother with Love, Traditional Home Mag, 4/91; Dorothy Kamm, China Decorator, 94 Porcelain Sets from Interior Finishes, 5-6/91; Ingrid Nordemar (auth), Artists Medium Is China Syndrome, Tribune, 10/17/97; Ike Crumpler (auth), Opening up to china an expert guides others on painting porcelain, The News, 10/15/2000; Sharon Wernlund (auth), Painted porcelain a passion for Port St Lucie Woman, The Palm Beach Post, 7/17/2000; Susan S Frackelton (auth) Woman of Fire, Sinsinawa Dominicans, 2004. *Mem:* Int Porcelain Artists & Teachers Inc; Nat League Am Pen Women, (vpres, 90-96); Am Asn Univ Women; Fla State Asn Porcelain Artists (corr sec 99-). *Media:* Porcelain. *Publ:* Ed, Dorothy Kamm's Porcelain Collector's Companion, 92-2002; Painting Dresden Flowers, Brit Porcelain Artist & China Decorator, 94; Creating depth & shadow using warm & cool tones, China Decorator, 1/95; Garnering Design Inspiration from old Porcelains, British Porcelain Artists, 1-2/97; auth, Victorian Inspiration, 2/97, Garden Triptych, 6/97 & Winter Landscape in Lavender Light, 11/97, China Decorator; American Painted Porcelain: Collector's Identification & Value Guide, Collector Bks, 97, reprinted, 99; Comprehensive Guide of American Painted Porcelain, Antique Trader Bks, 99; Judy Knight (auth), Decorating with Hand Painted Porcelain, Country Collectibles, summer 2000; Painted Porcelain Jewelry & Buttons, Collector Bks. *Mailing Add:* 10786 Grey Heron Ct Fort Pierce FL 34986

KAMPF, AVRAM S
EDUCATOR, CURATOR
b Jan 1, 1920. *Study:* New York Univ, BA, 51; New Sch Social Res, MA, 53; PhD, 62; Columbia Univ, with Meyer Schapiro, Rudolph Wittkower & Julius Held. *Collection Arranged:* Avraham Ofek, Paintings (auth, catalog), Catherine Noren, The Camera of My Family (auth, catalog), Luise Kaish, Sculpture (auth, catalog), 73 & Jewish Experience in the Art of the 20th Century, 75-76 (auth, catalog), Jewish Mus, NY. *Pos:* Chief cur, Jewish Mus, New York, 71-76; dir & founder, Haifa Univ Art Gallery, Israel, 78-85. *Teaching:* Prof art hist, Montclair State Col, 57-; assoc mem art hist, Columbia Univ, 61-65; vis prof art hist, Hebrew Univ, Haifa Univ, Jerusalem, 76-. *Awards:* Fulbright lectr, Hebrew Univ, 66; Kenneth B Smilen Literary Award, Jewish Mus, 84; Mus Award Original Res, Israel Mus, 85. *Mem:* Coll Art Asn; Interfaith Forum on Religion & Archit; Hebrew Union Congregation-Comn Art & Archit. *Res:* Jewish motifs in Twentieth Century art. *Publ:* Auth, Contemporary Synagogue Art, Jewish Publ Soc, 65; The Jewish Mus, An institution adrift, Judaism, 68; Aspects of the relationship to architecture, painting and sculpture, Scripta Hierosolymitana, 72; Jewish Experience in the Art of the Twentieth Century, Bergin & Garvey, 84; Ardon, the Bauhaus and the search for transcendence, Tel Aviv Mus, 85. *Mailing Add:* 372 Central Park W New York NY 10025

KAMYS, WALTER
PAINTER, EDUCATOR
b Chicago, Ill, June 8, 1917. *Study:* Art Inst Chicago, 43, with Hubert Ropp, Louis Ritman & Boris Anisfeld; also with Gordon Onslow-Ford, Mex, 44. *Work:* Regional Contemp Art Collection, Fargo, ND; Boston Pub Libr; Albion Coll, Ohio; Thorne-Sagendorph Art Gallery, Keene, NH; Wright State Univ Art Gallery; Westfield State Coll; Univ Mass Fine Arts Ctr; NY Univ; Univ Vt, Burlington Art Mus; Smith Coll; Mt Holyoke Coll; Soc Anonyme Coll, Yale Univ; Harvard Univ; and others; Art Inst Chicago. *Exhib:* Solo exhibs, Bertha Schaefer Gallery, New York, 55, 57 & 60, New Vision Ctr Gallery, London, Eng, 60 & East Hampton Gallery, New York, 70; Recent Drawings, USA, Mus Mod Art, 56; 22nd Int Watercolor Biennial, Brooklyn Mus, 63; Inst Contemp Art, Boston, 66; Smithsonian Inst, 68; retrospective, Herter Art Gallery, Univ Mass, 86; Works on Paper, Nada-Mason Gallery, Mount Herman Sch, Northfield, Mass, 90; Overview - Thorne - Sagendorph Art Gallery, Keene, NH. *Teaching:* Instr art, Putney Sch, Vt, 45; G W V Smith Art Mus, Springfield, Mass, 47-60; prof painting & drawing, Univ Mass, 60-87, dir, Art Acquisition Prog, 62-74, emer prof, 87-. *Awards:* Prix de Rome, 42; Boston Art Festival Award, 55; Award, Drawing & Small Sculpture Shows, Ball State Teachers' Coll, Art Gallery, Muncie, Ind, 61-62; Westfield State Coll Purchase Prize, 68. *Bibliog:* Harriet Janis & Rudi Blesh (auth), Collage: Personalities, Concepts, Techniques, Chilton, 62; Morris Risenhoover & Robert T Blackburn (auths), Artists as Professors, Conversations with Musicians, Painters, Sculptors, Univ Ill Press, 76; The Societe Anonyme & The Dreier Bequest, Yale Univ. *Mailing Add:* N Main St Sunderland MA 01375

KAN, KIT-KEUNG
PAINTER
b Quangdong Province, China, Dec 7, 1943. *Study:* Studied Chinese painting with Leung Pak-Yu, Chou Yat-Fung and Kan Maytin, 58-62; Univ Md, PhD, 75. *Work:* Hong Kong Mus Art; Am Asn for Advancement of Sci, Washington, DC; Chinese Univ Hong Kong; Am Embassy, Moscow; Art Bank, US Dept of States, Washington, DC; Internat Monetary Fund; Anhui Mus, Shenzen Fine Arts; Xiamen Art Mus; Zhongshen Inst Painting & Calligraphy. *Comn:* Cathay Bank, El Monte, Calif, 2010. *Exhib:* one-man shows, Robert Brown Contemp Art, Wash, DC, 86, 87, 89, 91, 92 & 94, Hsiung Shih Gallery, Taipei, 88 & 91, Roberts Gallery, Tawson State Univ, Baltimore, 89 & 92, Alisan Fine Art, Hong Kong, 90 & 96 & Taipai Fine Arts Mus, 95; Lung Men Gallery, Taipei, 97; Del Ctr for Contemp Art, Wilmington, 2002; Kwang Hwa Information & Cult Ctr, Hong Kong, 2002; Hood Col, Frederick, Md, 2003; Harmony Hall Reg Ctr, Ft Wash, MD, 2004; Grotto's Fine Art, Hong Kong, 2005, 2008; Red Door Gallery, Richmond, Va, 2011. *Teaching:* Vis artist, Chinese Univ Hong Kong, 2007. *Awards:* First Prize, Watercolor, Open Art Competition, Chatham Gallery, Hong Kong, 64; First Prize, Ann Fine Art Exhib, Greater Reston Art Ctr, Va, 82; Distinguished Alumni, Chung Chi Coll, Chinese Univ Hong Kong, 2002. *Bibliog:* Washington Post, 12/26/87, 9/17/93, 9/25/93 & 10/7/2004; Asian Art News, 3/95 & 7/95; Kit-Keung Kan's Paintings: 1965-1995, Hsiung Shih Art Books Co Ltd, Taipei, 95; tradition & Modernism: Kan Kit-Keung's Painting, Calligraphy & Installations, 1996-2007, Chung Chi Coll, Chinese Univ hong Kong, 2009. *Mem:* Artist Equity; Coalition Washington Artists. *Media:* Chinese Ink, Watercolor on Rice Paper, Chinese Calligraphy. *Dealer:* Grotto's Fine Art 2F 31C-D Wyndham St Hong Kong; Lung Men Art Gallery 218-1 Chunghsiao East Rd Sec 4 Taipei Taiwan; Robert Brown Gallery 2030 R St NW Washington DC 20009; B Deemer Gallery 2650 Frankfort Ave Louisville KY 40206; Red Door Gallery Richmond Va. *Mailing Add:* 6809 Tammy Ct Bethesda MD 20817

KAN, MICHAEL
HISTORIAN, ADMINISTRATOR
b Shanghai, China, July 17, 1933; US citizen. *Study:* Columbia Col, BA (art hist & archeol), 53; State Univ NY Agr & Tech Coll Alfred, MFA (ceramics & sculpture), 57; Columbia Univ, MA (art hist), 69, MPhil, 74. *Collection Arranged:* African Art & Simpson Collection, Brooklyn Mus, 70; guest cur, Ancient Art of West Mexico, Los Angeles Co Mus Art, 70; curatorial consult, African Art Tribal Art from West Africa, Portland Mus, 71; curatorial consult, Pre-Columbian Art in the Collection of Jay C Leff, Allentown Mus, 72; Detroit Collects African Art, 77; Treasures of Ancient Nigeria: Legacy of 2000 Years, 79. *Pos:* Assoc cur primitive art, Brooklyn Mus, 68-70, cur, 70-73, chief cur, 73-76; cur African, Oceanic & New World cult, Detroit Inst of the Arts, 77-. *Teaching:* Lectr art hist, Univ Calif, Berkeley, 64-66; lectr art Eastern Asia, Finch Col, 66-67; lectr African art, NY Univ, 70-. *Mem:* Mus Collaborative Inc (trustee, 75); Am Asn Mus. *Res:* The art of early cultures of pre-Columbian Peru and pre-Columbian Mexico; African art education. *Publ:* Contribr, Early Chinese Art and the Pacific Basin, 68; auth, African Sculpture, 70; coauth, Ancient Art of West Mexico, 70. *Mailing Add:* 10 Shore Rd Danbury CT 06811

KANATSIZ, SUZANNE L
SCULPTOR, EDUCATOR
Study: San Diego State Univ, BA (painting), 1982; San Jose State Univ, MFA (sculpture), 1988. *Work:* Weber State Univ, Utah; Fullerton Art Mus, Calif; Nev Mus Art, Reno; San Diego State Univ; Island Inst, Sitka, Alaska; and many pvt collections. *Exhib:* Figure in Drawing, Am Ctr, Paris, 1984; New Painting of Northern California, Hayward Forum Arts, 1986; solo exhibs, San Jose State Univ Gallery, 1986, 1988, Sun Gallery, Hayward, Calif, 1987, The Lab Gallery, San Francisco, 1989, Capp Strett Project, San Francisco, 1992, 1078 Gallery, Chico, 1994, Site Gallery, Los Angeles, 1995, Southern Nev Community Coll, Las Vegas, 1996, Southern Ore State Univ, Ashland, 1997, San Jose City Coll Gallery, 1998, Boise State Univ, 1999, Nev Mus Art, 2000, Nicolaysen Art Mus, Casper, Wyo, 2002, Bush Barn Art Mus, Salem, Ore, 2003, Sabanci Univ Fass Gallery, Istanbul, 2006; Xchange, San Jose Inst Contemp Art, 1987; Small Works, Calif Must Art, Santa Rosa, 1992; Sctrictly Sculpture, Orange County Ctr Contemp Art, 1995; Visual Faculties, Nev Mus Art, Reno, 1997; Art Equinox, Paris Gibson Sq Mus Art, Mont, 1999; Mirror of the Invisible, Fullerton Art Mus, 2000; Outdoor Sculpture Invitational, Maryhill Mus Art, Goldendale, Wash, 2003; Earthworks Now, Hi-Desert Mus & Copper Mountain Coll, 2005; High Stairway, Korean Cult Ctr, Los Angeles, 2007; Open House, Baer Art Ctr, Iceland, 2008. *Collection Arranged:* Hand, Mind, and Spirit (auth, catalog), 1997, Mr X-Acto (auth, catalog), 1998, Renowind, 1998, Paintings, 1998, Animal Nature, 1999, Univ Nev, Reno. *Pos:* Lectr, San Jose Univ, Calif, 1986-88, Creativity Unlimited, San Jose, 1987-89, William James Asn, Santa Cruz, 1990-95, Deuel Vocational Inst, Tracy, Calif, 1993-95; assoc dir, The Eye Gallery, San Franciso, 1989-91; artist-in-residence,

Creativity Explored, San Francisco, 1989-95. *Teaching:* Asst prof & gallery dir, Univ Nev, Reno, 1995-99; prof sculpture, Weber State Univ, Ogden, Utah, 1999-; vis prof, Sabanci Univ, Istanbul, 2006 & UAE Univ, Al Ayn, 2009-. *Awards:* Individual Artist Grant, Sierra Arts Found, 1996 & 1999; various grants & fels, Nev Arts Coun, Utah Arts Coun & Weber State Univ, 1997-2007; Artist Residency Grant, Helen Wurlitzer Found, 2000; Earthworks Now Honor Award, Copper Mountain Coll, Calif, 2005; Fulbright Grant, 2010. *Bibliog:* Michael Oliver (auth), Artistic Freedom in Confinement, The Orion, 4/19/1994; Kathy Curtis (auth), Strictly Contemporary, Sculpture as an Artistic Antidote, Los Angeles Times, 10/10/1995; Amy Paris (auth), Can An Artist Make it Big in Reno, Reno News & Rev, 7/1/1998; Chuck Twardy (auth), A Separate Peace, Las Vegas Weekly, 6/19/2002; Kim Fink (auth), Appropriation as Expression in the Ear of Open Content, Contemp Impressions, J Am Print Alliance, 5/2005. *Dealer:* A Gallery 1321 S 2100 E Salt Lake City UT 84108; C Gallery 708 Canyon Rd Santa Fe NM 87501. *Mailing Add:* Weber State Univ 2001 University Cir Ogden UT 84408

KANE, BILL
PHOTOGRAPHER
b Holden, Mass, Feb 18, 1951. *Study:* Univ Mass, BA, 73; San Francisco State Univ, MA, 78; NY Univ, cert (multimedia design & prod), 97. *Work:* Mus fur Moderne Kunst, Frankfort, Ger; San Francisco Mus Mod Art; Carnegie Mellon Inst, Pittsburgh, Pa; The Oakland Mus, Calif; Stanford Univ, Calif; DeYoung Mus, San Francisco; Worcester Art Mus, Mass. *Comn:* Neon installation, Washington Project Arts, Washington, DC, 81; photo/neon mixed media, Southland Corp, Dallas, Tex, 82; mixed media, sculpture, Heathman Hotel, Portland, Ore, 84; photo/neon mixed media, Cognata & Assocs, San Francisco, 84; photo/neon mixed media, NW Ayer Advert, New York, 89. *Exhib:* Contemp Glass, Nat Mus Tokyo & Kyoto, 81; Int Directions in Glass Art, Nat Gallery Victoria, Melbourne, Australia, 83; Examining the Perimeters of 20th Century Photog, San Francisco Mus Mod Art, 85; dalla Pop Art Americana, alla Nuoua Figurazuove, Padiglione d'Art Cont, Milano, Italy, 87; Explorations, extending the boundaries of cont photog, Mus Contemp Photog, Chicago, 87; Am Art Today, Fla Int Univ Art Mus, Miami, 92; Modernism, San Francisco, Calif, 2004 & 2007. *Awards:* Photog Award, Eyes & Ears Found, 79 & 84; Nat Endowment Arts, Photog, Fel, 80; Nat Endowment Arts, Painting, Fel, 91. *Bibliog:* Bill Kane-Photo/Neon Works, Boca Raton Ctr Arts, 82 & Foster Goldstrom Inc, 83; Carl Little (auth), Bill Kane at Foster Goldstrom, Art Am, 12/89; Rudy Stern (auth), Contemporary Neon, Retail Reporting Corp, 90. *Media:* Neon, Paint, Wood, Miscellaneous Media. *Publ:* Auth, Bill Kane, Selected Photography and Neon Works, Foster Goldstrom Inc, 83; Extending the Perimeters of Twentieth Century Photography, San Francisco Mus Mod Art, 85; Dalla Pop Art Americana, alla Nuova Figurazione, opere del Museo d' Arte, Moderna di Francorforte, Padiglione d'Arte Contemporanea, Milano, 87; Modernism - 25 Years, 79-2004. *Dealer:* Modernism 685 Market St San Francisco CA 94105

KANEGIS, SIDNEY S
DEALER
b Winthrop, Mass, Sept 6, 1922. *Study:* Boston Mus Fine Art Sch. *Pos:* Owner & dir, Kanegis Gallery, Boston, 50-. *Specialty:* Modern master graphics

KANG, IK-JOONG
PAINTER, SCULPTOR
b Cheong Ju, Korea, July 21, 1960; US citizen. *Study:* Pratt Art Inst, New York, MFA, 84; Hong IK Univ, Seoul, Korea, BFA, 86. *Work:* Whitney Mus Am Art; Mus Contemp Art, Los Angeles; Bronx Mus Art, NY; Sam Sung Cult Found, Seoul, Korea. *Comn:* Queens Main St Subway Sta, Metrop Transit Authority, NY, 91; Occupational Training Ctr, Dept Cult Affairs, NY, 92; San Francisco Int Airport, San Francisco Art Comn, Calif, 94. *Exhib:* Solo exhib, Queens Mus Art, NY, 92; Multiple Dialogue, Whitney Mus Am Art, 94, & Eight Thousand Four Hundred Ninety Days of Memory, 96; Throw Everything Together and Add, Capp St Proj, San Francisco, 94 & Korean Pavillion, Venice, Italy, 97; Habana Int Biennial, Centro Wifredo Lam, Cuba, 96; Three Hundred Sixty Five Days Eng, Contemp Arts Forum, Santa Barbara, Calif, 96; The Year of the Tiger, Ludwig Mus, Aachen, Ger, 98. *Awards:* Joan Mitchell Found Fel, 96; Special Merit Award, 47th Venice Biennale, 97; Louis Comfort Tiffany Found Fel, 98. *Bibliog:* Arlene Raven (auth), Throw Everything Together and Add (rev), Village Voice, 12/9/90; Grace Glueck (auth), 8,490 Days of Memory (rev), NY Times, 8/2/96; Carol Lutfy (auth), Artist profile: Ik-Joong Kang, Art News, 3/97. *Media:* All Media

KANGAS, GENE
SCULPTOR, AUTHOR
b Concord, Ohio, May 22, 1944. *Study:* Miami Univ, BFA; Bowling Green Univ, MFA; Univ Ky. *Work:* Butler Inst Am Art, Ohio; City Miami, Fla; City Upper Arlington, Ohio; Case Western Reserve Univ & Cleveland Pub Libr, Cleveland. *Comn:* Sculptures, Cuyahoga Co Justice Ctr, Cleveland, Ohio, 77, Frank J Lausche State Off Bldg, Cleveland, 80, Case Western Reserve Univ, Cleveland, 81, Dade Co, Miami, Fla, 83, Coral Springs, Fla, 84, Boynton Beach, Fla, 85. *Exhib:* Sculpture Invitational, Art Acad Cincinnati, 80; City of Upper Arlington Sculpture Invitational, Columbus, Ohio, 82; Art Assemblage, Columbus, Ohio, 82; Invitational Sculptor Exhibs; and numerous solo & group exhibs. *Teaching:* Instr sculpture, Univ NC, 68-71; asst prof sculpture, Cleveland State Univ, 71-75, assoc prof, 75-84, prof, 84-. *Awards:* Univ Res Grant, Univ NC, 68-70; First Prize in Sculpture, Cleveland Mus Art, 75; RCAC Res Grant, Cleveland State Univ, 91-93; and others. *Bibliog:* Hollander (auth), Plastics for Artists and Craftsmen; Campen (auth), Outdoor sculpture in Ohio; McCelland (dir), Public Sculpture of Cleveland (film), 82. *Media:* Metal, Wood. *Publ:* Coauth, Decoys; A North American Survey, Hillcrest Publ, 83; Decoys, Collector Bks, 91; Collectors Guide to Decoys, Wallace-Homestead Publ, 92; New World Folk Art, Cleveland State Univ Publ, 92

KANIDINC, SALAHATTIN
CALLIGRAPHER, DESIGN CONSULTANT
b Istanbul, Turkey, Aug 12, 1927. *Study:* Defenbaugh Sch Lettering, under Roger I Defenbaugh; Zanerian Coll Penmanship, text lettering under John P Turner; State Univ Iowa, cert lettering, under Prof Meyer; Univ Minn, cert lettering; Univ Calif, cert advert. *Work:* The White House, Washington, DC; Independence Hall, Philadelphia; Franklin Mint Mus Medallic Art, Franklin Ctr, Pa; Peabody Inst Libr, Baltimore, Md. *Comn:* Presidential designs, Tiffany & Co, NY, 70; Genius of Michelangelo Medals, Franklin Mint, 71; medal design, Fedr Turkish-Am Socs, NY, 73; Christmas Card Design, UNICEF, NY, 73 & 91; postage stamp designs, United Nations, 78, 82 & 86; and others. *Exhib:* 1000 Yrs of Calligraphy & Illumination, Baltimore, 59; Bertrand Russell Centenary Int Art Exhib, London, 72-73. *Pos:* Chief calligrapher, Deniz Basimevi MD, Istanbul, Turkey, 50-61; lettering artist, Buzza-Cardozo, Anaheim, Calif, 62-64; asst art dir, Rust Craft Publ, Dedham, Mass, 64; lettering specialist-designer, Tiffany & Co, New York, 64-72; owner-creative dir, Kanidinc Int, New York, 72-82; graphic design eng, NBC-TV, 82-91; corp design cons, 92-. *Awards:* First Prize, Ann McKay Christmas Card Contest, 74. *Mem:* Int Asn Master Penmen & Teachers Handwriting; Int Ctr Typographic Arts; Queens Coun Arts; Soc Scribes & Illuminators; Int Graphological Soc; Handwriting Analysts Int. *Media:* Ink, Gouache. *Publ:* Contribr, Alphabet Thesaurus, Vol II, III, 65-71; contribr, Turkish-Am Encycl Dig. *Mailing Add:* 3344 93th St Apt 5P Jackson Heights NY 11372

KANJO, KATHRYN
MUSEUM DIRECTOR
Study: Univ Redlands, BA (history and English literature); Univ Southern Calif, MA (art history and museum studies). *Pos:* Branch manager, Equitable Center, Whitney Mus Am Art, NY, formerly; cur contemp art, Portland Art Mus, 1996-2000; exec dir, ArtPace, San Antonio, Tex, 2000-07; dir, Univ Art Mus, Univ Calif, Santa Barbara, 2007-2010; assoc cur, Mus Contemp Art, San Diego, formerly, chief cur, 2010-. *Mailing Add:* Univ Art Museum Univ Calif Santa Barbara Santa Barbara CA 93106

KANTER, LORNA J
PAINTER, PRINTMAKER
b Passaic, NJ, Apr 10, 1931. *Study:* Am Art Sch, AAS (4 yr merit cert completion), 62; Pratt Graphics Art Ctr (scholar), 63; Art Students League (scholar), 77-80. *Work:* White House, Washington; Ronald W Reagan Libr, Simi Valley, Calif; Intrepid Sea/Air/Space Mus, NY; Douglas MacArthur USO, NY; Colonial Williamsburg Found, Va,. *Comn:* Portrait of Gen Douglas MacArthur & George Washington, comn by Military Order of Purple Heart, Intrepid Mus, NY, 85; Two Portraits of Pres Ronald Reagan, comn by Military Order of Purple Heart, White House Washington & Intrepid Mus, NY, 86. *Exhib:* Traveling Exhib, Fairleigh Dickinson Univ, Teaneck, NJ, 64; 30th Ann Painters & Sculptors Soc NJ, Jersey City Mus, 71; Libby Girl Among the Flowers, Cartier Inc, NY, 86; Realism Today, Am Artist Mag Nat Competition, Carol Siple Gallery, Denver, Colo, 88-89; Sundance Gallery, Bridgehampton, NY, 96. *Teaching:* Portraiture & Drawing, Am Art Sch, New York, 65-66. *Awards:* Green Ribbon, Nat Arts Club, Knickerbocker Artists, 64; Artist Yr Award, Salmagundi Club, Beaux Arts, Inc, 84; Nat Competition, Award, Am Artist Mag, 88-89. *Bibliog:* Mermelstein (auth), Dreams of gold & ancient queens, Herald-News, 85; A portrait of courage, NY Post, 85; Daryln Brewer (auth), Er-satz masterpieces for your home, NY Times, 90. *Mem:* New York Artists Equity; Beaux Arts Inc; life mem, Art Students League. *Media:* Oil, Drawing Mediums. *Publ:* Auth, Pain & TMJ: The Experience & Survival of a Patient, Mod Nutrition News, 87; Coll Craig House Garden, (lithographs world-wide), ART Inc, 89. *Mailing Add:* 24 Janice Terr Clifton NJ 07013-4214

KAPHEIM, THOM
PRINTMAKER, PAINTER
Study: Northern Ill Univ, BFA (sculpture), 67, MFA (prints & drawing), 71. *Work:* Ill State Mus, Springfield. *Pos:* Chmn art dept, Wauconda High Sch

KAPLAN, BETSY HESS
EDUCATOR
b Bridgeton, NJ. *Study:* AB, Wesleyan Coll, 1947; BFA, Wesleyan Conservatory, 1948. *Pos:* admin assist, Ethel K Beckham, Miami-Dade Co Sch Bd, 1980-82; mem sch bd, 1988-2004, chair, 1993-95, ret, 2004. *Teaching:* Miami-Dade Co Pub Sch, Fla, 1950-53; educ & cult arts adv, 1961-88; instr, Miami Dade Co Coll, 1979-81. *Awards:* Named Woman Worth Knowing, Miami Beach Comn on Status of Women, 1994; Woman of the Yr, King of Clubs, 2000; Miami-Dade Co Women's Park Wall of Hon, 2005; Alumnae Disting Achievement award, Wesleyan Coll, 1987; French Acad Palms award, French Min of Educ of Youth & Sports, 1991; Ruth Wolkowsky Greenfield award, Am Jewish Congress, 1993; Trailblazer award, Women's Com of 100, 1993; Woman of Impact award, Comty Coalition for Women's Hist, 1995; Co of Women Pioneer award, Miami-Dade Co Pks Dept, 1997; Red Cross Spectrum award, Women in Educ, 1997; Lifetime Serv to Mus Educ in Fla & US, Fla Mus Educ Asn, 2000; Branches of Learning award, Women's Div Greater Miami State of Israel Bonds Org, 2001; Hearts of Arts award, New World Sch Arts, 2004; Pillar award, Black Heritage Planning Com, Miami-Dade Co, 2004; Joseph R Narot award, Temple Israel of Miami, 2004; Cervantes award, Nova Univ, 2004; Serving the Arts, Arts& Educ award, Children's Cult Coalition & Arts & Bus Coun, 2004; Coll Assistance Prog honoree, Dade Comty Found, 2005; Serv award, M Athalie Range Cult Found, 2007; Breaking the Glass Ceiling award, Jewish Mus Fla, 2013. *Mem:* local, state nat PTA'S, 1960-; chair fed rels network Fla Sch Bds, Tallahassee, 1996-98; bd dirs, New World Sch Arts, Miami, 1996-2005, found bd, 2004-, bd dirs, arts learning, 2002-; Performing Arts Ctr Trust, Miami, 1993-2004, student mentor, 1997-2007; Human Servs Coalition, 1995-; AAUW, Phoenix award, 1999; LWV, Margery Rankin award, 2004; Art South, Homestead, exec bd, 2007-; Women's Hist Coalition, bd mem 2002-, pres, 2006-2008; M Athalie Range Cult Found, bd dir, 1995-2002, exec com, 2002-; Jewish Mus Fla, bd dir, 1999-2003, exec bd, 2003-2004, adv bd, 2004-2009; Alliance

for Aging, mem adv bd, 1996-2004 ; Fla Sch Bds Assn, bd dirs, 1990-1999, Pres's award, 2001; Phi Kappa Phi; Delta Kappa Gamma; Phi Delta Kappa; Miami Dade Co Educators; Miami Dade Co Music Educators. *Interests:* lectures; visiting museums and galleries worldwide. *Mailing Add:* 2 Grove Isle Dr #1603 Miami FL 33133

KAPLAN, FLORA EDOUWAYE S
EDUCATOR, CURATOR
b New York. *Study:* Hunter Coll, BA (cum laude); Columbia Univ, MA; Grad Ctr, City Univ New York, PhD, 76. *Hon Degrees:* Chieftancy Equiv, Honorary Edo, Benin, Nigeria. *Collection Arranged:* Time Landscape, Greenwich Village, NY, 74; Images of Power: Art of the Royal Court of Benin, Grey Gallery & Study Ctr, NY Univ, 81; Women in Mus, Citibank, NY, 82; In Splendor & Seclusion: Royal Women & Art of the Court of Benin, Nigeria (photographs), 82, 84-85 & 86-90; Art of the Royal Court of Benin, Benin Nat Mus, Benin City, Nigeria, 85; Fragile Legacy: The Photographs of S O Alonge, As Cultural & Political History, Nigeria, Benin Cult Ctr, Nigeria, 97. *Pos:* Cur, Dept Primitive Art & New World Cult, Brooklyn Mus, NY, formerly; consult, Dahesh Mus, NY, 88-2006 & interim dir, 2006-; ed adv bd, Encycl Cult Anthrop, 93-95; ed bd, NY Univ Electronic J Sci & Arts, NY Univ Ctr Digital Media, 95-; co-ed, Mus Meanings (bk series), Routledge Ltd, London, 97-; exhib comt, Nat Parks Serv: Statue of Liberty, Ellis island, 98-; ed bd, Mus and Soc, Leicester Univ Press, United Kingdom, 2003-; ed & adv bd, Mem Revista de Museos de Mexico y del Mundo, 2003-; reviewer, Fulbright Awards, 2003-2004. *Teaching:* Adj lectr, Herbert H Lehman Coll, City Univ NY, 70-73, lectr, 73-74, grad fel, 74-76; adj asst prof, Dept Anthrop, NY Univ, 76-77, asst prof, 77-84, assoc prof & founding dir, GSAS Prog Mus Studies, 84-90, prof & dir, Cert Prog Mus Studies, Grad Sch Art & Sci, 90-99, prof anthrop & mus studies, 99-2004, prof emeritus, 2004-. *Awards:* Fulbright fel, Univ Benin, Nigeria, 83-85; NY Univ Humanities Coun Challenge Fund Grant, 88; Ford Found Grant & Samuel H Kress Found Grant, Intl Conference, Guardians of Monuments and Memory: Case Studies in Urban Conservation and Mus in the Middle East, 97-99. *Mem:* African Studies Asn; fel Am Anthrop Asn; fel NY Acad Sci; Am Asn Mus; Soc Visual Anthrop; Inter Coun Mus Explorers Club; Coll Art Asn. *Res:* Art and culture of the Benin Empire (Nigeria); Gender & museum theory. *Publ:* ed & contribr, Images of Power: Art of the Royal Court of Benin, Nigeria, New York Univ, 81; auth, Iyoba, The Queen Mother of Benin: Images and Ambiguity in Gender and Sex Roles in Court Art, Vol 16, No 3, 386-407, Art Hist, 9/93; A Mexican Folk Pottery Tradition: Cognition and Style in Material Culture in the Valley of Puebla, Carbondale, Southern Illinois Univ Press, 94; Exhibitions as communicative media, In: Museum, Media, Message, Routledge Press, London, 95; Museum Anthropology, and Museum Studies, Museology, Museography, In: Encyclopedia of Cultural Anthropology, Vol 3, Yale Univ, New Haven, 96; ed & contribr, Queens, Queen Mothers, Priestesses and Power: Case Studies in African Gender and Power, Annals of the New York Academy of Sciences, Vol 810, 97; Museums and the Making of "Ourselves:" The Role of Objects in National Identity, Univ Leicester Press, Pinter Publ, London, 3d edit, 98; auth, Some Thoughts on Ideology, Beliefs, and Sacred Kingship Among the Edo People of Nigeria, In: African Spirtuality, Crossroads Press, New York, 2000; Understanding Sacrifice and Sanctity in Benin Indigenous Religion, In: Beyond Primitivism, Routledge, London, 2003; Twice Told Tales, In: Orisha Devotion as World Religion, Univ Wis Press, Madison, 2006; Benin Women in Society and Art, and The Queen Mother-Iyoba, In: Bening Kings and Rituals, Snoeck, Vienna, 2007; Politics in an African Royal Harem, In: Servants of the Dynasty, Univ Calif, Los Angeles, 2008; The Ancient City Walls of Great Benin, In: Patrimony and Identity, Routledge, London, 2008; Seeing Women in Oral Tradition, In: The Tragic Heroine as Modern Woman, Ctr for Gender Equality, Delphi, Greece, 2009. *Mailing Add:* New York Univ Museum Studies Program 240 Greene St Ste 400 New York NY 10003-6675

KAPLAN, JACQUES
COLLECTOR, DEALER
b Paris, France, Oct 22, 24. *Study:* Sorbonne Univ, France, PhD. *Awards:* Croix de Guerre. *Bibliog:* Articles in New York Times, 66, Life Mag, 68, Time & Newsweek. *Collection:* Contemporary American art, 19th century European art and the Old Masters. *Mailing Add:* 15 Jennings Rd South Kent CT 06785

KAPLAN, JULIUS DAVID
HISTORIAN
b Nashville, Tenn, July 22, 1941. *Study:* Wesleyan Univ, Middletown, Conn, BA; Columbia Univ, MA & PhD. *Collection Arranged:* Symbolism, Europe and Am at the End of the 19th Century, 80, Gaston Lachaise, Sculpture and Drawings, 80, Kate Steinitz, Art and Collection, Avant-Garde Art in Germany in the 1920's and 1930's, 82 & Selections from The Edward-Dean Mus of Decorative Arts, 84, Art Gallery, Calif State Univ, San Bernardino; The Evans Collection of Oriental Ceramics, 88; The Dechter Collection of Greek Vases, 89. *Teaching:* Lectr, Colby Col, Waterville, Maine, 66; asst prof, Univ Calif, Los Angeles, 69-77; assoc prof art hist, Calif State Col, San Bernardino, 77-, chmn dept, 78-82, prof, 82-, assoc dean grad prog, 86-, dean grad studies, 89-, res & fac develop, 91-99. *Awards:* Grant-in-aid, Am Coun Learned Socs, 77; Nat Endowment Arts Grant, 81; Calif Art Coun Grant, 81, 82 & 83; Fine Arts Comt, City of San Bernardino, Calif, 88. *Mem:* Coll Art Asn. *Res:* Academic and official art in France, 1850-1900. *Publ:* Auth, The religious subjects of James Ensor 1877-1900, Revue Belge d'Archaeol d'Hist l'Art, 66; Gustave Moreau, Los Angeles Co Mus Art, 74; Gustave Moreau, UMI Res Press, 82. *Mailing Add:* Dept Art Calif State Univ 5500 University Pkwy San Bernardino CA 92407

KAPLAN, MURIEL S
SCULPTOR, COLLECTOR
b Philadelphia, Pa, Aug 15, 1924. *Study:* Cornell Univ, BA, 46; Sarah Lawrence Coll, Grad Work, 58-60; Oxford Univ, Eng, cert, 71; Art Student's League, New York, 75-88. *Work:* Columbia Univ Law Libr, New York; Brandeis Univ, Waltham, Mass; Lyndon Johnson Libr, Univ Tex, Austin; John F Kennedy Sch, Jerusalem, Israel; Johnson Mus, Cornell Univ, 98. *Comn:* portrait bust, Vera List, 75; portrait bust, Charles E Smith, 90; portrait bust, Bel Kaufman, 93; portrait bust, Morris Levinson, 97; portrait bust, Frank Rhodes, Cornell Univ pres, 98. *Exhib:* Allied Artists Am Ann, Nat Acad Art, New York, 58-73; Nat Asn Women Artists Ann, Fed Bldg, New York, 66-85; Artists and Engineers in Technology, Brooklyn Mus, New York, 68; Artist's Guild, Norton Mus Art, Palm Beach, Fla, 81-90; Folk Art Exhib, Barrington Mus, Delray Beach, Fla, 84; Art in Pub Places, Govt Ctr, West Palm Beach, Fla, 85-86 & 88 & Northwood Inst, West Palm Beach, Fla, 93; Armory Art Ctr, 2000; Nat Sculpture Soc, New York, 2000; Nat Asn Women Artists, 2006; 68 Yr Retrospective, Armory Art Ctr, West Palm Beach, Fla, 2010. *Pos:* Secy, Comt to Estab Art Mus, Westchester, NY, 56-58; co-chair, First Televised Art Auction, WNET, NY, 64; mem, Comt Art in Pub Places, Palm Beach, Fla, 83-84; art adv bd, Boca Raton Mus Art, Fla, 88-90; bd dir, Palm Beach Co, Coun Arts, 92-94, Armory Art Ctr, West Palm Beach, Fla, 93-2008. *Teaching:* Instr portrait sculpture, pvt studio, 66-70; instr, Armory Sch, 87-92. *Awards:* Sculpture Prize, Nat Asn Women Artists Ann, 66; Robert Kennedy Humanitarian Award, Settlement House, New York, 68; Portrait Award, Allied Artists Am Ann, 69; First Prize Sculpture, Barrington Mus Art, 84; Sculpture Prize, Norton Art Mus, 88; Best in Show, Nat Asn Women Artists, 2006. *Bibliog:* Dorothy Ann Flor (auth), Casted characters, Ft Lauderdale Sun Sentinel, 5/17/84; Muriel Kaplan Keeps Ahead in the Sculpture Business, Arts Mag, 7/92; Jan Sjostrom (auth), Kaplan: Through A sculptors eyes, Palm Beach Daily News, 1/23/94. *Mem:* Art Students League; Nat Asn Women Artists; Nat Sculpture Soc; Norton Gallery & Sch Arts, Lect Sponsor; Soc of 4 Arts, Palm Beach, Fla; Int Sculpture Ctr; Palm Beach Cultural Council. *Media:* Clay, Bronze. *Specialty:* portraits. *Collection:* Works of Wayne Thlebaud, Ernest Trova, Janet Fish, Larry Rivers, Viola Frey & Patti Warahina. *Dealer:* Portraits Inc 7 W 51st St New York NY 10019. *Mailing Add:* 1106 Devonshire Way Palm Beach Gardens FL 33418

KAPLAN, PHYLLIS
PAINTER, COMPUTER ARTIST
b Brooklyn, NY, 1950. *Study:* Cooper Union, BFA, 72; Domus Acad, post grad studies, 85. *Work:* Nat Mus Women Arts, Washington, DC; Mitsubishi pvt collection, Japan; Sharjah Arts Mus, United Arab Emirates; Coll Univ S Fla, Coll Marine Sci; Coll City of Balatonfured, Hungary. *Exhib:* Bershire Art Asn, Berkshire Mus, Pittsfield, Mass, 70; Three Rivers Arts Festival, Carnegie Mus Art, Pittsburgh, Pa, 95-96 (catalogs); Global Focus, Nat Mus Women Arts, Beijing, China, 95; Heat Exhaustion, Fine Arts Mus Long Island, Hempstead, NY, 96; 14th & 15th Juried Exhib, Fine Arts Mus Long Island, NY, 96 & 97; Halpert Biennial, Appalachian State Univ, Boone, NC, 97 (catalog); World Artists for Tibet, Blue Mountain Gallery, NY, 98; 1st Int Biennial, Trevi-Flash Art Mus, Trevi-Perugia, Italy, 98 (catalog); solo exhibs, Kings Gallery, Brooklyn, NY, 74, Long Island Univ, Brooklyn, 75, Tribeca Gallery, NY, 97, Verge, Manhattan Mini Storage, NY, 99; Mayfair, Open Space Gallery (catalog), Allentown, Pa, 2000; Sharjah Arts Mus, United Arab Emirates, 2000; 4th Ann Juried Exhib, Canajoharie Libr & Art Gallery, Canajoharie, NY, 2000 & 2002; Snapshot, Contemp Mus, Baltimore, 2000; Virtue, Visual Art Gallery, St Paul, MN, 2000; 35th Int Exhib, San Bernardono Co Mus, Calif, 2000-01; Sharjah Int Arts Biennial, Sharjah, United Arab Emerites, 2001; Univ S Fla, Coll of Marine Sci, St Petersburg, 2001; Cambridge Art Asn, Nat Prize Show, MA, 2001; New Symbols, Montgomery Coll, Rockville, Md, 2002; Viziraros Gallery, Budapest, Hungary, 2004; Central EU Gallery, selections from HMC Residency Collection, Budapest, Hungary, 2006. *Collection Arranged:* LandShapes, Orgn Independent Artists, 96; Flights of Fantasy, Broadway Mall, 97. *Pos:* Artist-in-residence, F J Music Sch, Balatonfured, Hungary, 2002. *Teaching:* Instr oil painting, Monroe Co Arts Coun, 2001. *Awards:* Hon Mention, Orgn Ind Artists Salon Show, 94; Hon Mention, 1st Int Biennial Female Artists, Art Addiction Gallery, 94; Artists Space/Independent Project Grant, 99; Hon Mention, Mayfair, 2000; Univ S Fla, Award Best in Show, 2001, Hon Mention, Canajoharie Libr & Art Gallery, 2003. *Bibliog:* Carey Lovelace (auth), Dreamlike visions, Newsday, 8/2/96; Jane Shapiro (auth), Heats on over at FAMLI, The Herald, 8/22/96; Chris Geiger (auth), Fantasy flies in West Side Arts Coalition Group Show, Artspeak, 1/98. *Media:* Acrylic, Oil, Computer Artist. *Publ:* Contribr, Artist Exhibits, Kings Courier, 74; 1st Annual Organization of Independent Artists Calendar, Orgn Ind Artists, 94; Reality, Villager, 94; Pierrepont Place Brooklyn Heights, Brooklyn J Arts, 94; Looking out on artistic landscapes, Courier Lifestyles, 96. *Mailing Add:* 213 W Sarah St Milford PA 18337

KAPLAN, SANDRA
PAINTER, PRINTMAKER
b Cincinnati, Ohio, May 23, 1943. *Study:* Art Acad Cincinnati, with Julian Stanczak, 60-61; Pratt Inst, with Richard Lindner & Lennart Anderson, BFA (with hons), 65; City Univ New York, 68-70. *Work:* ALCOA Pittsburgh, Pa; Am Express Co, Inverness Park, Colo; Hyatt Regency Hotel, Dubai, United Arab Emirates; Blue Cross, Blue Shield, Denver; Neiman Marcus Corp Hqs, Los Angeles; Kaiser Permanente & Qwest; Weisman Art Mus, Univ Minnesota. *Comn:* Vail Athletic Club, 79; Saudi Arabia, 5-panel watercolor; Standard Textile Corp, Cincinnati; monotypes, Fairmont Hotels, San Jose & Chicago, 87; watercolors, Marriot Hotel, Hong Kong; Art in Public Places, watercolor, Colo Coun Arts, 89; mural, Univ Colo Sch Pharmacy, 94; 4 paintings, Platte Valley Medical Ctr, 2007. *Exhib:* Dubins Gallery, Los Angeles, 88 & 90; Eva Cohon Galleries Ltd, Chicago & Highland Park, 89; Olson Larsen Gallery, Des Moines, Iowa, 90; Arvada Ctr Arts, 91; Nicolaysen Art Mus, Casper, Wyo, 92; Wave Hill Gallery, Riverdale, NY, 95; Boulder Mus Contemp Art, Boulder, Colo, 97; Laura Paul Gallery, Cincinnati, 98; Cline Fine Art, Santa Fe, 99 & 2000; Mizel Ctr for the Arts, Denver, 03; Above & Below, William Havu Fine Art, 2003; Recent Paintings, Post Modern Co, Denver, Colo, 20072008; Shaver-Ramsey Gallery, Denver, 2009; Fulginiti Ctr Bioethics, Univ Colo, 2014. *Teaching:* Instr painting & design, Arapahoe Community Col, 74-75; art instr, Metrop State Col, 77-78; guest art instr, Denver Univ, 78-79; instr painting, Art Students League Denver, 01-; instr, Abbondanza Toscana, Lucca, Italy, 2006, 2008, 2011; numberous pleinair workshops around country including Draguignon, France and Lucca, Italy. *Awards:* First Place, Rocky Mountain Regional Print Show, 82; Best of Show, Colo Art Expo; Covisions Grant, Colo Coun on the Arts, 86. *Bibliog:* Roberta McIntyre (auth), summer's

garden, Focus, Santa Fe, 10/87; Carole Katchen (auth), Watercolor, the very large picture, Artists Mag, 9/88; Lynn Kari Petrich (auth), Painting floral objects, Am Artist/Watercolor, 89; Christian Science Monitor, 12/2/91; The New York Times, 8/13/95; The Rocky Mountain News, 5/30/03; The Denver Post, 5/2/03; interview with Suzanne McCarroll, KCNC TV News 4, 6/17/03. *Mem:* Trustee (2002-2008), Mus of Contemporary Art/ Den. *Media:* Watercolor; Oil, Acrylic; Collage. *Interests:* Movie buff, dogs, gardens, science. *Publ:* Illusr, Rationale, 65; contrib, Art Work, No Commercial Value, Grossman, 71; Landscapes (catalog), Arvada Ctr Show, 91; Human and/or Nature (brochure), Nicolaysen Mus, 92. *Dealer:* Sharks Inc 2020 9th St Boulder CO 80302; Sandra Phillips Gallery 420 W 12th Ave Denver CO 80204. *Mailing Add:* 2939 S Lafayette Dr Englewood CO 80113

KAPLAN, STANLEY
PRINTMAKER, MURALIST

b Brooklyn, NY, Sept 4, 1925. *Study:* Cooper Union Sch Art, cert fine arts, 49; NY Univ, BS, 52; Pratt Inst, New York, MS, 68. *Work:* Metrop Mus Art, NY; Brooklyn Mus, NY Pub Libr; Columbia Univ; Philadelphia Mus Art; Newark Mus Art; Challahoochee Valley Art Mus; Portland Art Mus; Hunterdon Mus Art, NJ. *Comn:* Murals, AT & T Community Develop Corp, NY & Fla, 73, 74 & 75; mural, Manuche's Restaurant, NY, 62; Illustrations of Poetry, 94. *Exhib:* 45 solo exhibs incl ACA Gallery, New York, 54 to Stone Metal Press Gallery, 2004; 236 group exhibs incl Libr of Cong, Washington, DC, 51 to Allied Artist of Am, 2004; Old Print Shop Gallery, New York, 2007. *Pos:* Mgr, Tortoise Press, 78-. *Teaching:* Art teacher, Levittown Pub Schs, NY, 54-59; prof art, Nassau Community Coll, Garden City, 65-95. *Awards:* Sixth Ann Competition Award, Port Washington Pub Libr, 71; Purchase Award, Soc Am Graphic Artists 55th Nat Print Exhib, 77; Philadelphia Watercolor Soc, 2004; Academic Artists Asn, 2004; Puffin Found, 2004; Allied Artists of Am, 2004; Purchase Award, Farmington Mus, NMex, 2008; Life Achievement Awardm SAGA, 2008; Best of Show, Red River Valleym 2009; Purchase Award, Minot Stae Univ; 55 awards all together. *Mem:* Soc Am Graphic Artists (vpres, 72-74, pres, 76-78); Southern Graphic Coun; Mid Am Print Coun; Albany Print Club. *Media:* Woodcut, Etching, Book Art. *Specialty:* Prints, maps, books. *Interests:* Music, Films, Travel. *Publ:* Nassau Review, Jewish Currents, Wordsmith, KAVR Pub, Tortoise Press; and many others. *Dealer:* The Old Print Shop NYC. *Mailing Add:* 47 Trapper Ln Levittown NY 11756

KAPLAN, THEODORE N
CONSULTANT

Study: Reed Coll, BA, 63; Univ Hawaii, MA, 65; NYU Law Sch, JD, 68. *Pos:* Gen coun, Sotheby's; partner, Kaplan Fox, 80-; bd mem, Heckscher Mus; chmn planning bd, Village Northport, Long Island. *Teaching:* Adj prof, Fashion Inst Tech. *Mem:* Asn Bar of City of NY; Century Asn; NY Committee for Young Audiences (pres, formerly, bd mem, formerly); Int Found Art Rsch; Ballet Found (secy); Nat Acad (coun). *Mailing Add:* Kaplan Fox & Kilsheimer LLP 850 3rd Ave 14th Fl New York NY 10022

KAPLINSKI, BUFFALO
PAINTER, WATERCOLORIST

b Chicago, Ill, May 25, 1943. *Study:* Art Inst Chicago; Am Acad Art. *Work:* Denver Pub Libr-Western Art Collection; Johns-Manville, Denver, Colo; Denver Art Mus; Dallas Power and Light, Tex; United Bank, Denver, Colo; Petro-Lewis, Denver, Colo; Eastman-Kodak, Windsor, Colo; and others. *Comn:* Fredrick Ross Co, Denver; Prudential Bache Securities, Denver; painting, Red Rocks Visitor Ctr, 03. *Exhib:* Grand Junction Group Art Show, Western Colo Ctr for the Arts, 03; Taos Art Fest, Total Art Gallery, 03; solo exhib, The Art Center, Grand junction, Colo, 04, Pinon Gallery, Littleton, Colo, 2006; Rist Canyon Art Exhib, Belvue, Colo, 04; and many others; Art Student Art Show, Denver, 2013; Art Ctr, Grand Junction, Colo, 2013. *Pos:* recognized mem, Denver 7. *Teaching:* Instr, Colo Inst Art, Univ Denver; instr watercolor, Art Students' League, Denver, 88-94. *Awards:* Southwestern Biennial Hon Mention, NMex Arts Mus, Santa Fe; Nat Cowboy Hall of Fame, Oklahoma City, Okla, 93; Artist of the West, Pioneer Mus, Colorado Springs, 93; Best of Category Award, Mitchell Mus, Trinidad, Colo; Plum Creek Wine Label, Los Angeles Co Fair Wine Competition, 01; Award of Excellence, Thomas Moran Invitational, Plein Air Paintings, Zion Nat Park, 2012, Poster Artists, 2013. *Bibliog:* Article in Am Artist Mag, 8/72; article, Artists Rock; Harold & Peggy Samuels, Contemp Western Artists, 11/82; articles in Am Artist, 6/84 & Art West Mag, 9-10/84; Harmon S Graves (auth), Passionate Landscape/Painting Journeys of Buffalo Kaplinski, Sunstone Press, Santa Fe, NMex, 2006; Invitational Plein-Air, In Footsteps of Thomas Moran, St George Utah Zion Nat Park, 2009; Zion Centennial, St George, Utah, 2008; Direct, Efficient, Confident, Watermedia Painting by Steve Doherty Travels and Adventures with Clarissa Pinkola Estes, Xulon Press, 5/2013. *Mem:* AWS. *Media:* Acrylic, Watercolor. *Res:* traveling around the world. *Specialty:* Fine Art Landscape. *Interests:* Christian evangelism & tool collecting. *Dealer:* West Southwest Gallery 257 Fillmore St Denver CO 80206; Tracy Miller Fine Art 16 Ruxton Manitou Springs CO 80829; Evergreen Fine Art 3042 Evergeen Parkway Evergreen CO 80439. *Mailing Add:* PO Box 44 Elizabeth CO 80107

KAPOOR, ANISH
SCULPTOR

b Bombay, 1954. *Work:* Albright-Knox Mus, Buffalo, NY; Carnegie Mus Art, Pittsburgh; Hirshhorn Mus & Sculpture Garden, Washington; Mus Mod Art, New York; Walker Art Mus & Sculpture Garden, Minneapolis. *Exhib:* Solo exhibs include Lisson Gallery, London, 1983, 1986, 1988, 1989, 1993, 1995, 1996, 1998, 2000, 2003, Barbara Gladstone Gallery, New York, 1984, 1986, 1989, 1990, 1993, 2001, 2001, 2003, 2007, 2008, Inst Contemp Art, Boston, 1986, 2008, Albright-Knox Gallery, Buffalo, 1986, Venice Biennale, 1990, Stuart Regen Gallery, Los Angeles, 1992, 1994, Mus Contemp Art, San Diego, 1992, Tel Aviv Mus Art, 1993, Angles Gallery, Santa Monica, Calif, 1996, Hayward Gallery, London, 1998, Regen Projects, Los Angeles, 2000, 2006, Rockefeller Ctr, New York, 2006, Royal Acad of Arts, London, 2009; group exhibs include Affinities & Institutions, Art Inst Chicago, 1990; Masterworks from the Guggenheim Collection, Ctr Arte Reina Sofia, Madrid, 1991; 1991 Turner Prize Exhib, Tate Gallery, London, 1991; Documenta 9, Kassel, Germany, 1992; Venice Biennale, 1993, 1994; Sculpture, Leo Castelli Gallery, New York, 1993; Dissonant Wounds: Zones of Display/Metaphors of Atrophy, Ctr Curatorial Studies, Bard Coll, NY, 1996; Belladonna, Inst Contemp Arts, London, 1997, Surprise Surprise, 2006; Beauty-25th Anniversary, Hirshhorn Mus & Sculpture Garden, Washington, 1999; Around 1984: a Look at the 80's, PS1 Contemp Art Ctr, New York, 2000; The Inward Eye, Contemp Arts Mus, Houston, 2001; Retrospective: 25 Yrs of Collection, Denver Art Mus, 2002; Marsyas, Turbine Hall of Tate Modern, London, 2002; Inaugural Exhib, Regen Projects, Los Angeles, 2003; Simply Red, Fabric Workshop & Mus, Philadelphia, 2007; Traces du Sacre, Ctr Pompidou, Paris, 2007; Counterpoint III, Louvre, Paris, 2007; Leviathan, MONUMENTA 2011, Grand Palais, Paris, 2011; Orbit for 2012 Olympic Games, London. *Awards:* Premio Duemila, Venice Biennale, 1990, 1992; Turner Prize, 1991; London Inst Hon Fel, 1997; Royal Inst Brit Arch Hon Fel, 2001; Commander, Order Brit Empire, 2003; Praemium Imperiale award (Sculpture category), Japan Soc, 2011. *Dealer:* Regen Projects 633 N Altmont Dr Los Angeles CA 90069; Lisson Gallery 52-54 Bell St London NW1 5DA UK. *Mailing Add:* c/o Barbara Gladstone Gallery 515 W 24th St New York NY 10011

KAPP, E JEANNE
PAINTER, PHOTOGRAPHER

b Hagerstown, Md. *Study:* Studies in Los Angeles Valley Col, 60-63, Univ Utah, 76-82; cert interior design, Los Angeles Interior Design Sch, 67-69; Joseph Raphael Workshop, 76; Univ Utah, 76-82; Earl Pierce Civic Arts, 85-90. *Comn:* McLaren Lodge (painting), comn by Mrs James Cooney, San Francisco, Calif, 95. *Exhib:* Festival 83, Mus Natural Hist, Salt Lake City, 83; Utah 84, Mus Fine Art, Salt Lake City, 84; Five Star Art, Salt Lake Art Ctr, 84; Salon Des Nations, Centre Int D'Art, Paris, France, 84; Painting Eden, Calif Heritage Gallery, San Francisco, 96; Valley Landscape, Danville Fine Arts Gallery, Calif, 97; Inspirations from the Earth, Gallery Concord, Calif, 98; Fall Exhib, Valley Art Gallery, Walnut Creek, Calif, 98; Invitational Exhibs: Mt Diablo, Robert Butler Gallery, Vineyards, Jessel Gallery, Napa, Calif, 2005-06; Studio 7 Gallery, Pleasanton, Calif, 2002-06; Pioneer Art Gallery, Danville, Calif, 2008-09; Artists and their Work, San Ramon Valley Mus, 2009; Hayward Arts Council, Hayward, Calif, 2009. *Pos:* Cur fine arts, Contra Costa Co Libr, Pleasant Hill, Calif, 95-98. *Awards:* Alamo Danvill Artists Award, 90-95; Lamorinda Arts Alliance Award, 95-97; 2nd Place Oil, Las Juntas Artists, 97, 1st Pl, 98; 1st Place, Contra Costa Co Fair (yearly awards), 98-2008; 2nd Place, Discover Art League, 2000. *Bibliog:* Utah 81, Utah Travel Coun, 1981; Various articles in Contra Costa Times, 89-97. *Mem:* Alamo-Danville Artists Soc (circuit leader, 90); Las Juntas Artists (juror's asst, 92); Oil Painters Am, 1997-2004; Benicia Fine Arts; Lamorinda Arts Alliance. *Media:* Oil. *Publ:* auth, The Am Connection, Pub Creative Art Enterprises, 1985; Focus on the Pros, Minolta Press, 84; Guide Book of Western Aritists, Art of the West Mag, 2001. *Dealer:* Valley Fine Art Gallery 1661 Botelho Dr Walnut Creek CA 94549; St Germain Gallery Tiburon CA 94920. *Mailing Add:* 411 Donegal Way Lafayette CA 94549

KAPROV, SUSAN
PAINTER, MURALIST

b New York, NY, Aug 11, 46. *Study:* City Coll New York, BA, 67; Dartmouth Col, Hanover, NH, MA, 68. *Work:* Mus Mod Art & Metrop Mus Art, NY; Corcoran Gallery Art, Washington, DC; Nat Mus Am Art, Washington, DC; Brooklyn Mus; Rose Art Mus; Gernsheim Col, Waltham, Mass. *Comn:* Austin Co, Atlanta, Ga; Reeves Communication Corp, NY, 81; NASA, Washington, DC, 81 & 92; Prudential Insurance Co, 82; Hexcel Corp, 83; City of NY; Port Authority, NJ, 90; Liberty Sci Ctr, 92. *Exhib:* Prints: Acquisitions 1973-76, Mus Mod Art, NY, 77; solo exhibs, Hayden Planetarium, NY, 78 & Brooklyn Mus, 81; Recent Acquisitions, Nat Mus Am Art, Washington, DC, 78; Art-Technol, Philadelphia Print Club, 79 & 92; Alternative Imaging Systems, Everson Mus, Syracuse, NY, 79; installation, Granite Gallery, Nat Mus Am Art, 83-84; Fay Gold Gallery, Atlanta, 90; Neikrug Gallery, NY, 92; Midtown Y Gallery, 92; Women Artist of the NASA Art Program, National Mus of Women in the Arts, Washington DC, 2001; NY Visions, Merrick Gallery, St Petersburg, Fla, 2002; Digital 2004, NY Hall of Science; Convergence, Fort Collins CO Mus of contemp Art, 2005; Project Diversity; Rotunda Gallery, 2005. *Teaching:* Sch Visual Arts, NY, 92. *Awards:* MacDowell Colony Fel, 71 & 73; Ossabaw Island Proj Fel, 73; Creative Artists Pub Serv fel, NY State Coun on Arts, 79-80; Palenville Interarts Ctr, Palenville, NY, 96; Brandywine Workshop, Philadelphia, PA, 96. *Bibliog:* Donald Saff (auth), History of American Printmaking, Holt, Rinehart, Winston, 77; Ellen Lubell (auth), article, Art in Am, 81; V Butera (auth), article, Arts Mag, 81. *Mem:* Am Inst Architects, NY Chap. *Media:* Fired Enamel on Glass, Glass Mosaic, Mixed Media Prints, Photography, Drawing. *Interests:* Architecture, archaeology, science. *Publ:* New York Arts/Berliner Kunst: Susan Kaprov; Capturing the Public Sphere, feature article by John Perreault; The Public Review, 5/2003; NY Times 3/2003. *Mailing Add:* 149 Willow St No 5C Brooklyn NY 11201-2259

KARAMETOU, MARIA
ASSEMBLAGE ARTIST, EDUCATOR

Study: Univ Md, BA (cum laude); Md Inst Art, with Grace Hartigan, MFA. *Work:* Vorres Mus Contemp Art, Athens, Greece; Baltimore Mus Art. *Pos:* Bd dirs, Arlington Arts Ctr. *Teaching:* Asst prof art, George Mason Univ, Fairfax, Va; instr, George Washington Univ, Univ Md, Univ La Verne & Montgomery Coll, formerly. *Awards:* Artist grant, Md State Arts Coun; Fulbright Grant, 2010. *Mailing Add:* George Mason Univ Art & Design Bldg 4400 University Dr Rm 2030 Fairfax VA 22030

KARDON, CAROL
PAINTER, INSTRUCTOR

b Mt Vernon, NY. *Study:* Art Students League, New York, 55-56; Bennington Col, Vt, BA, 56; Univ Pa, Grad Sch Fine Arts, spec student, 70; also studied with Wolf Kahn, Dan Greene & Albert Handell, Barnes Found, Merion, Pa. *Work:* Shell Oil; Bon Secours Mem Reg Med Ctr, Mechanicsville, Va; RJ Reynolds Industs; Shearson

Lehman Brothers; Smith, Barney, Harris & Upham Co; and others. *Comn:* William Penn House, Philadelphia; Chester Valley Country Club, Malvem, Pa. *Exhib:* Cheltenham Award Show, Mus Philadelphia Civic Ctr, Pa, 80 & Cheltenham Art Ctr, Pa; one-woman shows, Gross McCleaf Gallery, Philadelphia, Pa, 80-82 & 84 & Gallery Ave Kobe, Nishinomiya Hyogo, Japan, 87; Great Swamp XXV Exhib, Nabisco Brands Corp, East Hanover, NJ, 85; Ann Exhib, Pastel Soc Am, NY, 86, 87, 89 & 92; group show, Neville-Sargent Gallery, Chicago, Ill, 89-92; Cooper Gallery, Lewisburg, WVa; Carspecken-Scott Gallery, Wilmington, Pa. *Teaching:* Pastel & color, Main Line Ctr Arts, Wayne Art Ctr, Wayne, Pa; landscape workshop in Santa Fe, NMex, Pa Acad Fine Arts, Philadelphia, 91. *Awards:* Pastel Soc Am Plaque Award, Salmagundi Club, New York, 96; Marion Strueken-Bachmann Award for Landscape, Pastel Soc Am, New York, 96; Pastel Soc W Coast Award, 96; over 30 total awards. *Mem:* Pastel Soc Am; W Coast Pastel Soc; Salmagundi Club, NY. *Media:* Pastel, Oil. *Publ:* Contribr, Best of Pastel, Rockport Publ, 96. *Dealer:* Carspecken-Scott Gallery Wilmington DE; Summa Gallery New York NY. *Mailing Add:* 248 Beech Hill Rd Wynnewood PA 19096

KARDON, JANET
MUSEUM DIRECTOR, CURATOR

b Philadelphia, Pa. *Study:* Temple Univ, BS (educ), 55; Univ Pa, MA (art hist), 66; Am Mgt Asn, 86. *Hon Degrees:* Moore Coll Art, Hon Dr Humanities, 84. *Collection Arranged:* Seventies Painting (auth, catalog), Univ Arts, 78, Siah Armajani (auth, catalog), 78, Alice Avcock (auth, catalog), 78 & Point (auth, catalog), 78; David Salle (auth, catalog), Inst Contemp Art, 86, traveling, 86-87; Robert Kushner (auth, catalog), Inst Contemp Art, 87, traveling 87-89; Robert Mapplethorpe: The Perfect Moment, Inst Contemp Art, 87, traveling, 87-89; Building a Permanent Collection: A Perspective on the 1980's Explorations: The Aesthetic of Excess (auth, catalog) & Costumes by Pat Oleszko, Am Craft Mus, 90; History of Twentieth Century Craft Three Volumes - The Ideal Home, Craft in the Machine Age, Revivals, Diverse Traditions, 93-96. *Pos:* Dir exhibs, Univ Arts, 75-78; consult & panelist, Nat Endowment Arts, 75-, mem overview panel mus prog, 84, 85 & 89; dir, Inst Contemp Art, Univ Pa, 79-89 & Am Craft Mus, 89-96; visual arts panel mem, Pa Coun Arts, 78-83, vchmn, 82-83 & 88; US Comnr, Venice Biennale, 80; spec proj panel mem, Pa Coun Arts, 78-83, panel mem, Art in Pub Spaces, Vet Admin, 80, Nat Endowment Arts Mus Seminar, Baltimore Mus Art, 81, Inter-Arts Prog, Nat Endowment Arts, 84, oversight panel, Visual Arts Prog, 89 & 90; consult, Artists Spaces Site Visitations, Visual Arts Prog, Nat Endowment Arts, 80, Inter-Arts Site Visitations, 83-84; session leader, Am Kunsthalle, Col Art Asn, 83; chair, Frank Jewitt Mather Award in criticism, Col Art Asn, 84; bd advs, Awards in Visual Arts, Southeastern Ctr Contemp Art, 84-; chair selection panel Int exhibs, US Info Agency, 87. *Teaching:* Lectr, Gwynedd Mercy Col, 67, Univ Arts, 68-75; vis assoc prof, Fashion Inst Technol & Pratt Inst, 97-99. *Awards:* Helena Rubenstein Fel, Whitney Mus Am Art, 75; Nat Endowment Arts Res Grant, 78. *Bibliog:* Ron Javers (auth), Art breaking, Philadelphia Mag, 2/91; Patricia Malarcher (auth), American Craft Museum launches centenary project, Crafts Report, 2/91; Leslie Ferrin (auth), Controversy breeds confrontation at American Ceramics Annual Art of Collecting Symposium, Crafts Report, 5/91; and others. *Mem:* Coll Art Asn; Pa Coun Arts; Am Asn Mus; Asn Art Mus Dirs. *Res:* Twentieth century; post-World War II; earthworks performance sculpture. *Publ:* Auth, Lenore Tawney: A Retrospective (exhib catalog), Am Craft Mus, 90; The History of Twentieth-Century American Craft: a centenary project - 3 Vol 1900-1945 Am Craft Mus. *Mailing Add:* 150 E 69th St Apt 12J New York NY 10021-5704

KARIMI, REZA
PAINTER

b Isfahan, Iran, Aug 23, 1946; US citizen. *Study:* Sch Fine Arts, Isfahan, 66; Queens Col, Univ NY, BA, 76 & Brooklyn Col, MFA, 78. *Comn:* Pvt collection in London, NY, NJ, Ind, Vt & Ga. *Exhib:* Memories of Iran, Borghi & Co, NY, 90, Mina Renton Gallery, London, 92 & Hammer Galleries, NY, 93; Harrison Celebrates Art (A Tricentennial Tribute), Neuberger Mus Art, Purchase, NY, 96; New York City in 1997, Hammer Galleries, NY, 97; World of Drawing and Watercolor, The Dorchester, London, 98. *Awards:* Grant, Ancient Persepolis, Fine Arts Ministry, Iran, 66; 1st Prize, Prof Show, Putnam Arts Coun, 87. *Bibliog:* Portrait of an Artist (film), 92 & Exhibition Review at Hammer (film), 93, Aftab Productions, WNYC TV Network; Honar Dastan, Isfahan TV. *Mem:* Am Inst for Conservation; Putnam Arts Coun. *Media:* Watercolor, Oil on Canvas. *Publ:* Contribr, Technology in the service of art, Armon Mag, 9/91; Interview with Reza Karimi (painter), Ispand Mag, Summer 93; Exceptional images, Golchin Publ, 7/94; He views simplicity & creates the sublime, Persian Heritage, Fall 96; Hunter of light & memories, Golchin Publ, 5/98; Clientele, Preserving the Light, March/April 2008. *Dealer:* Art Restoration Inc PO Box 29 School St Mahopac Falls NY 10542. *Mailing Add:* 126 School St PO Box 29 Mahopac Falls NY 10542

KARIYA, HIROSHI
CONCEPTUAL ARTIST

b Kamaishi, Iwate Pref, Japan, Apr 14, 1948. *Work:* New Mus Lib, NY; Inst Contemp Art, Univ Pa, Philadelphia; McCarthy Arts Ctr, St Michaels Col, Winooski, Vt; Kubo Mus, Mooka, Japan. *Exhib:* Sign of the Times 1993, Art Tower Mito, Ibaraki, Japan, 94; Sutra; One thing in everything; Everything in one thing, Inst Contemp Art, Univ Pa, Philadelphia, 90; Sutra, Exit Art, NY, 89; Sound Show, PS 1 Mus, NY, 79; Int Drawing Biennale, Camden Arts Ctr, London, 79; World Print Competition, San Francisco Mus Art, 77. *Bibliog:* Kay Larson (auth), Sound Show, Village Voice, 10/29/79; Edward J Sozanski (auth), Contemplating creation, rebirth, Philadelphia Inquirer, 3/18/90; Miki Miyatake (auth), Signs of hope, Japan Times, 4/17/94. *Media:* Multi Media. *Mailing Add:* 143 S Eighth St No 3B Brooklyn NY 11211-6167

KARLEN, PETER H
EDUCATOR, WRITER

Study: Univ Calif, Berkeley, BA (hist), 71; Univ Calif, Hastings Coll Law, JD, 74; Univ Denver Coll Law, MS (law & society), 76. *Pos:* Art attorney, self-employed, 78-86, owner, Peter H Karlen, A Prof Law Corp, 86-; writer, Artlaw column, 79-96; contrib ed & columnist, Artweek, 79-95, Art Calendar, 89-96; Art Cellar Exchange, 89-92; Equine Images, 92-95; pres, Neonym Naming & Trademark Svc, 2008-; pres, Neonym Corp, 2008-. *Teaching:* Lectr law & the arts, Univ Warwick Sch Law, 76-78; adj prof, Univ San Diego Sch Law, 79-84; adj prof, Western State Univ Col Law, 76, 79, 80, 88 & 92. *Mem:* Am Soc Aesthetics; Brit Soc Aesthetics. *Res:* Property rights in aesthetic creations; expert opinions, fakes & forgeries; artist's moral rights. *Publ:* Auth, What is art? A sketch for a legal definition, Law Quart Rev, 78; Legal aesthetics, Brit J Aesthetics, 79; Moral rights in California, Univ San Diego Law Rev, 82; Aesthetic quality & art preservation, J Aesthetics & Art Criticism, 83; Fakes, Forgeries & Expert Opinions, J Arts Mgt & Law, 86; Worldmaking: Property Rights in Aesthetic Creations, Jour Aesthetics & Art Criticism, 86; Appraiser's Responsibility for Determining Fair Market Value, Columbia - VLA, J Law & Acts, 89; The Aesthetics of Trademarks, Contemp Aesthetics, 2008. *Mailing Add:* 1205 Prospect Ste 400 La Jolla CA 92037

KARLSTROM, PAUL JOHNSON
HISTORIAN, WRITER

b Seattle, Wash, Jan 22, 1941. *Study:* Stanford Univ, BA (Eng lit), 64; Univ Calif, Los Angeles, MA (art), PhD, 73. *Collection Arranged:* Venice Panorama (auth, catalog), Grunwald Ctr Graphic Arts, Univ Calif, Los Angeles, 69; Louis M Eilshemius in the Hirshhorn Mus Traveling Exhib (auth, catalog), 78; Claude Buck (auth, catalog), Glastonbury Gallery, San Francisco, 83. *Pos:* Asst cur, Grunwald Ctr Graphic Arts, Univ Calif, Los Angeles, 67-70; guest cur, Smithsonian Inst Traveling Exhib Serv, Washington, DC, 77; dir, West Coast Regional Ctr, Arch Am Art, Smithsonian Inst, San Francisco, 73-91 & San Marino, 91-2003; self-employed, Writer & Historian, 2003-; mem adv bd, Humanities West; bd dir, Bay Area Video Coalition & Southwest Art Hist Coun, formerly; secy, Va Steele Scott Found; vpres, Noah Purifoy Found; bd dirs, Meridian Gallery, San Francisco, Calif; ed consult, California History (jour Calif Hist Soc). *Teaching:* Instr, Renaissance to mod art, Calif State Univ, Northridge, 72-73; vis instr mus practices, Calif Coll Arts & Crafts, Oakland, 76. *Awards:* Samuel H Kress Fel, Nat Gallery Art, Washington, 70-71; Acad Distinction, Coll Fine Arts, Univ Calif, Los Angeles, 74. *Mem:* Calif Hist Soc (edit bd); Oral Hist Asn; Am Studies Asn (former). *Res:* American art and culture, 19th and 20th century, modernism. *Publ:* Louis Michel Eilshemius, Harry N Abrams, Inc, 78; The Spirit in the Stone: Visionary Art of James W Washington, Jr, Univ Wash Press, 89; Turning the Tide: Early Los Angeles Modernists 1920-1956, Santa Barbara Mus Art, 90; Fletcher Benton, Harry N Abrams, 90; ed, On the Edge of America: California Modernist Art, 1900-1950, Univ Calif Press, 97; contribr, Diego Rivera: Art and Revolution, INBA, 99, The Complete Jacob Lawrence, Univ Wash Press, 2000 & Reading California, Univ Calif Press, 2000; auth, Raimonds Staprans, Art of Tranquility and Turbulence, Univ Wash Press, 2005; ed, Leo Holub: A lifetime of photography (exhib catalog), Himmelberger Gallery, 2007; co-ed, Asian American Art: A History, 1850-1970, Stanford Univ Press, 2008; auth, Peter Selz: Sketches of a Life in Art, Univ Calif Press, 2011; contbr, Hassel Smith: Paintings 1937-97, Prestel, 2012. *Mailing Add:* 73 Carmelita St San Francisco CA 94117

KARMEL, PEPE
EDUCATOR

Study: Harvard Coll, BA, 1977; NYU, PhD, 1993. *Teaching:* Assoc prof art hist, NYU. *Res:* Picasso, Pollock, Cubism, Minimalism, Contemporary Art, Critical Theory, Art and Perception. *Publ:* Auth, Report from Milan-The '30s: Art and Culture in Italy, Art in Am, 43-47, 10/1982; Beyond the Guitar: Painting, Drawing, and Construction, 1912-14, in: Picasso: Sculptor/Painter, London, The Tate Gallery, 189-197, 1994; A Sum of Destructions, in: Jackson Pollock: New Approaches, Mus Mod Art, 71-100, 1999; Jean Dubuffet: The Would-Be Barbarian, Apollo, Vol CLVI, No 489, 12-20, 20/2002; The Year of Living Minimally, Art in Am, 90-101, 12/2004. *Mailing Add:* New York University Silver 303 100 Washington Sq E New York NY 10003

KARN, GLORIA STOLL
PAINTER, PRINTMAKER

b New York, NY, Nov 13, 1923. *Study:* Art Students League; also with Eliot O'Hara & Samuel Rosenberg. *Work:* Yale Univ; Brooklyn Mus; Pittsburgh Pub Schs; Carnegie Inst Mus Art; Westinghouse Collection. *Exhib:* Assoc Artists Pittsburgh Ann, 49-; Butler Inst Am Art Ann, 61; solo exhibs, Pittsburgh Plan for Art, 65, Carnegie Inst Mus, 66 & NHAC, 78, 83, 91 & 98; Sacred Arts Show, St Stephens, Pittsburgh, 66; PWS Aqueous Open Int, 95, 98, 2000, 2002-06, 2009-2010; work exhibs, several Pittsburgh Art Shows, currently. *Pos:* Illusr, cover artist, Pulp Mags, 41-49. *Teaching:* Instr painting & collage, North Hills Art Ctr, 65-; instr, Community Coll Allegheny Co, 73-79. *Awards:* Carnegie Inst Purchase Prize, 60; Westinghouse Purchase Prize, 66; Aqueous Open Award of Merit, Pittsburgh Watercolor Soc, 98 & 2006; Third Prize, PWS Aqueous Open Int, 98; Third Prize, Pittsburgh Watercolor Soc; Second Prize, NHAC, 2000-2003, 2008, 2009, First Prize, 2002, Hon Mention, 2007, 4th Prize, 2010; Hon Mention, Waterworks, Pittsburgh Watercolor Soc, 2002 & Waterworks Award, 2007. *Bibliog:* Rusty Hevelin (auth), Pulpcon 30 Guest of Honor, the Pulpster #11, 2001; John Wooley (auth), Pulp Adventures (interview by auth), 2001; David Saunders (auth), feature article: Gloria Stoll Karn (interview by auth), Illustration Mag #25, 2009. *Mem:* Assoc Artists Pittsburgh; Group A, Pittsburgh (pres, 66-70); Pittsburgh Ctr Arts (bd mem, 69-72); North Hills Art Ctr (bd mem, 70-72 & 78-80, pres, 80-81); Pittsburgh Watercolor Soc (bd mem, 2000-2006). *Media:* Oil, Watercolor; Etching, Lithography; Acrylic. *Interests:* Gardening. *Mailing Add:* 151 Louise Rd Pittsburgh PA 15237

KARNES, MARK
EDUCATOR, PAINTER

Study: Philadelphia Coll Art, BFA; Yale Univ, MFA, 1972. *Exhib:* Am Acad Arts & Letts Invitational, New York, 2009. *Teaching:* Prof, drawing and painting, Md Inst Coll Art, 1974. *Awards:* Nat Endowment of the Arts Grant; Md State Arts Coun Grant; Fulbright-Hayes Grant; Purchase Prize, Am Acad Arts and Letts, 2009. *Media:* Oil. *Mailing Add:* Maryland Inst Col Art 1300 Mount Royal Ave Baltimore MD 21217

KARP, AARON S
PAINTER
b Altoona, Pa, Dec 7, 1947. *Study:* State Univ NY Coll Buffalo, BA, 69; Ind Univ, MFA, 73. *Work:* Guggenheim Mus, NY; Albuquerque Mus, Albuquerque Airport & Univ NMex Art Mus, Albuquerque; Ackland Art Ctr, Chapel Hill, NC; Roswell Mus, NMex; American Airlines Corp & ITT Corp, Dallas, Tex; and many others. *Exhib:* Solo Exhibs: Janus Gallery, Santa Fe, NMex, 88 & 90; Watson Gallery, Houston, Tex, 89; Katherina Rich Perlow Gallery, NY, 89 & 91; State Univ NY, Albany, NY, 90; Barclay Simpson Gallery, Lafayette, Calif, 90; Robischon Gallery, Denver, Colo, 91; Amarillo Art Ctr, Tex, 92; Helander Gallery, Palm Beach, Fla, 92; Barclay Simpson Fine Art, Lafayette, Calif, 92; Eva Cohon Gallery, Chicago, 93 & 95; Erikson & Elins Fine Art, 94; Sandy Carson Gallery, Denver, 97; Craighead-Green Gallery, Dallas, 97, 2000 & 02; Elliot Smith Contemp Art, St Louis, 98; Lee Hansley Gallery, Raleigh, NC, 99; Duke Univ Fine Art Gallery, Durham, NC, 2000; R Duane Reed Gallery, St Louis, 2001 & 05; Tercera Gallery, San Francisco, 2002; Carson-Masuoka Gallery, Denver, 2002; William Havu Gallery, Denver, 2004; Bemis Grids, Albuquerque Mus, Albany, NMex, 2007; School of the U, Fine Art Mus, Univ NMex, Albuquerque, 2000; Man and Nature, Adair Margo Gallery, El Paso, Tex, 2001, Finca Las Culebras, 2003; Colored By Process, Contemp Art Gallery, Colo State Univ, Colorado Springs, 2002; Systems, Duke Univ, Durham, NC, 2006; For Lack of Focal Point, Albuquerque Mus, NM, 2006; and others. *Pos:* Oper supervisor, Guggenheim Mus, 74-75; dir, E Carolina Univ Gallery, Greenville, NC, 77-79. *Teaching:* Asst prof, Univ NMex, Albuquerque, 79-84. *Awards:* Artist-in-Residence Grant, Roswell Mus & Art Ctr, NMex, 81 & 85, Anderson Ranch Art Ctr, Snowmass, Colo, 98, Djerassi, Woodside, Calif, 2000, MacNamara Found, Westport Island, Maine, 2004 & Fundacion Valparaiso Mojacar, Spain, 2006; Research Allocation Grants, Univ NMex, Albuquerque, 82; Exxon Corp Purchase Award, Guggenheim Mus, New York, 84; Grants MacDowell Colony, Peterborough, NH, 2000, Pollock-Krasner Found, 2001, John Anson Kittredge Found, 2002 & Julia and David White Artists' Colony, Ciudad Colon, Costa Rica, 2003; Visiting Artist, Bemis Center for Contemporary Art, Omaha, Nebr, 2007. *Bibliog:* Diane Waldman (auth), Emerging Artists 1978 to 1986: Selections from the Exxon Series (catalog), Solomon R Guggenheim Mus, 87; Louise Krasniewicz (auth), review, The Times Union, Albany, NY, 3/17/90; Sandy Ballatore (auth), Aaron Karp, Artspace, 9-10/90. *Media:* Acrylic. *Dealer:* Erickson & Elins Gallery 345 Sutters St San Francisco CA; Duane Reed Gallery 7513 Forsyth Blvd St Louis Miss 61305. *Mailing Add:* 7811 Guadalupe Trail NW Albuquerque NM 87107-6507

KARP, RICHARD GORDON
PAINTER, LECTURER
b Brooklyn, NY, May 17, 1933. *Study:* City Coll New York, BBA (advert) & MA (fine art); Brooklyn Mus Art Sch, with John Bageris. *Work:* Aankoop Gemete, Stedlijk Mus, Amsterdam, Neth; Northern Ill Univ, DeKalb. *Exhib:* Stedlijk Mus, Amsterdam, 70; RAI Exhib, Amsterdam, 70; Heckscher Mus, Huntington, NY, 74; Viridian Gallery, NY, 77; Parrish Mus, South Hampton, NY, 78. *Bibliog:* Julie Attkiss (auth), Karp, riding his intuition, Holland Herald, 3/69. *Mem:* Visual Artist & Gallery Asn; Artists Equity. *Media:* Oil & Mixed Media. *Dealer:* Ronald Hunnings Inc 139 Spring St New York NY 10012; Kunsthandel K 276 Keizersgracht 276 Amsterdam Netherlands. *Mailing Add:* 1201 Queen Anne Rd Teaneck NJ 07666

KARPOV, DARINA
PAINTER
Study: Moscow Inst Technol, 1991; Md Inst Coll Art, Baltimore, BFA, 1998; Yale Sch Art, MFA, 2001 (Carl Purlington Rollins Fel, Bradbury Thompson Mem Prize). *Exhib:* Solo exhibs include Pierogi, Brooklyn, NY, 2007 & 2008; group exhibs include into_the_far_nature, AG Gallery, Brooklyn, 2005; Coupling, Rosenberg Gallery, NY Univ, 2006; Inaugural Exhib, Pierogi, Leipzig, Germany, 2006, The Whole Sea is Storming, 2007, Group Show, 2008; Summer Group Show, Pierogi, Brooklyn, 2006, (Un)Natural Selection, 2007; Block Party II, Daniel Weinberg Gallery, Los Angeles, 2007, Pierogi & Friends, 2008; Art Forum Berlin, 2007; Future Tense: Reshaping the Landscape, Neuberger Mus, State Univ NY, Purchase, 2008; 183rd Ann: Invitational Exhib Contemp Art, Nat Acad, New York, 2008; Drawn to Detail, DeCordova Mus & Sculpture Park, Lincoln, Mass, 2008; Next Wave Visual Arts Prog, Brooklyn Acad Music, 2008. *Awards:* William A Paton Prize, Nat Acad, 2008; Pollock-Krasner Found Grant, 2008. *Dealer:* Pierogi 177 N 9th St Brooklyn NY 11211

KARTEN, NOWELL J
GALLERY DIRECTOR
Pos: Dir, Angles Gallery, Los Angeles, Calif, currently. *Specialty:* contemporary art, emphasizing conceptual work. *Mailing Add:* Angles Gallery 2754 S La Cienega Blvd Los Angeles CA 90034

KASH, MARIE (MARIE KASH WELTZHEIMER)
PAINTER
b Akron, Ohio, May 5, 1960. *Study:* Univ Cent Okla, Edmond, Okla, BA (com art), 82; studies with Alan Flattman, Sally Strand, Lorenzo Chavez, Rick McClure. *Work:* Goddard Art Ctr, Ardmore, Okla; Corp: Laureate Psychiatric Clinic & Hosp, Tulsa, Okla; Coca Cola, Moscow; Am Bank & Trust, Edmond, Okla; Lawyers Title Oklahoma City Inc. *Comn:* Pvt portrait, comn by Mr & Mrs Sherwood Taylor, Norman, Okla, 89, 90, 93 & 97; pvt portrait, Mr & Mrs David Rainbolt, 89, 97, 2003; pvt portrait, Mr & Mrs John Baumert, 99, 2000, 2001, 2005; pvt portrait, Mr. and Mrs. Greg Lindsey, 2002, 2009, 2010; Accounting Firm Off of Tullius Taylor Sartain & Sartain. *Exhib:* 19th, 21st & 25th Ann Open Exhib, Pastel Soc Am, NY, 91, 93 & 97; solo exhibs, Goddard Art Ctr, Ardmore, Okla, 93, 2005, 2008 & Kirkpatrick Gallery Okla Artists, Oklahoma City, 95; Telluride Pastel Invitational, Telluride Gallery, Colo, 95; Person to Person, W Valley Art Mus, Ariz, 97; Paseo Art Space Gallery, 2009; Okla Art Guild, 2009, 2011; and others. *Pos:* Graphic media artist, Okla Water Resources Bd, Oklahoma City, 84-88. *Awards:* Stephen Leitner, Esq Award, 19th Ann Open Exhib, Pastel Soc Am, 91; Best Show, Okla Art Workshop 11th Ann Juried Exhib, Tulsa, 94; Best of Show, Okla Pastel Soc, 2008. *Bibliog:* John Brandenburg (auth), Paintings Capture Music for the Eyes, The Daily Oklahoman, 9/8/95; The Best of Pastels, Rockport Publ, 96; The Pastel Journal, Taking the Temperature of Color for Strong Complementary Contrasts, by, Ruth Summer, May/June, 2000. *Mem:* Pastel Soc Am (sig mem); Okla Pastel Soc; Edmond Art Asn. *Media:* Pastel, Oil. *Mailing Add:* 2513 Woodruff Rd Edmond OK 73013

KASHDIN, GLADYS SHAFRAN
PAINTER, EDUCATOR
b Pittsburgh, Pa, Dec 15, 1921. *Study:* Art Students League, with Stefan Hirsch; Univ Miami, BA (magna cum laude), 60; Fla State Univ, with Karl Zerbe, MA, 62, PhD (humanities), 65. *Work:* Tex Tech Mus, Lubbock; Futan Univ, Shanghai, China; Columbus Mus Arts, Ga; Mus Sci and Industry, Tampa; Jan Phatt Libr,Tampa. *Comn:* Silkscreen eds, LeMoyne Art Found, Tallahassee, Fla, 70, 71 & 73; City of Tampa Publ Art Prog, Oil, Acrylic Large Paintings, 2004-05. *Exhib:* 28th Ann Brooklyn Mus, 44; Solo exhibs, Palm Beach Art, LeMoyne Art Found, Tallahassee, 66-74, Columbus Mus Arts, Ga, 73, 76 & 83, Univ SFla, 75, 81 & 2002, Tex Tech Mus, 78, Fla Dept of State, Tallahassee 85 & 86, Kresge Mus Art, E Lansing, Mich, 87, Ferris State Univ, Mich, 89, Fla A&M, Tallahassee, 91 & Tampa Mus Art, 96-97; Fla State Univ, Appleton Mus Art, 99, 2001-2002; Mus Sci and Industry, Tampa, 2003. *Collection Arranged:* Dr & Ms Cecil Mackey, pvt collection, Mich; Univ So Fla, Colleges of Bus, Social Studies, Special Collections Libr; Mus Sci and Indust; Wheeler, Herman, Hopkins & Lagor, Pa; Dr & Ms William Dalton, pvt collection. *Pos:* Photogr, Shafran Co, NY & Fla, 38-60. *Teaching:* Instr & dir oil painting, Adult Educ, Palm Beach Co, Fla, 56-60; instr watercolor, Thomasville Art Guild, Ga, 61-62; prof humanities, Univ SFla, Tampa, 65-87, Humanities Visual Arts Workshops, 66-71, prof emer humanities, 87-. *Awards:* Gold Medal, Univ Miami, 60; Citizens Award, Mus Adv Bd, Hillsborough Co, 84; Phi Kappa Phi Artist-Scholar Award, 87; Award of Merit, Norton Mus Art, 1957, 60, 63. *Bibliog:* Dr Hans Juergensen (auth), Kashdin's Everglades series, 73 & Herb Allen (auth), Local rivers series theme, 75, Tampa Tribune; Pam Renner (auth), Gladys Kashdin: An artist in her sun-lit years, Bay Life, 79; Gladys Shafran Kashdin: The Creative Spirit, 1999; Gladys Shafran Kashdin: Gaia's Daughter, 2001, rev ed, 2003; Gladys Shafran Kashdin: In Retrospect, 95-96. *Mem:* Tampa Mus Art; Metrop Mus Art; Nat Mus Women in Art. *Media:* Watercolor, Acrylic. *Publ:* Auth, A new approach to a humanities-visual arts workshop, Humanities J, fall 70; Life long education for women--general & liberal studies from their point of view, Perspectives, winter 74; Women artists and the institution of feminism in America, SEASA, 79; auth, In Retrospect, Tampa Mus Art, 96

KASKEY, RAYMOND JOHN
SCULPTOR, ARCHITECT
b Pittsburgh, Pa, Feb 22, 1943. *Study:* Carnegie Mellon Univ, BA (archit), 67; Yale Univ, Sch Art & Archit, also sculpture with Erwin Haver, 69. *Work:* Mus Mod Art, NY; First Interstate Bank, Ore; Kaiser Permanente, Portland, Ore. *Comn:* sculpture, Portland Bldg, Ore, 85; sculpture, Harold Washington Library Ctr, Chicago, 90; sculpture, Nat Law Enforcement Officers Memorial, Washington, DC. *Exhib:* Nat Sculpture Soc Ann, Equitable Gallery, NY, 80 & 81; Barbara Fendrick Gallery, Washington, DC; John Nichols Gallery, NY, 86; Barbara Fendrick Space, NY, 88. *Teaching:* Asst prof arch & design, Univ Md, College Park, 69-76; vis critic, Yale Univ, New Haven, Conn, spring 77 & Kans State Univ, Manhattan, spring 78. *Awards:* Mrs Louis Bennett Prize, 82 & Henry Hering Mem Medal, 86, Nat Sculpture Soc; Creative & Performing Arts Award, Univ Md, 70 & 72. *Bibliog:* video, Portlandia, Rogers Cable Network, Ore; Hail, Portlandia, Art News, 12/85; article, Archit Mag, 12/85; article, Newsweek, 7/86; article, Mus & Arts, 10/88. *Mem:* Nat Sculpture Soc; Am Inst Archit. *Media:* Bronze, Stone. *Dealer:* Barbara Fendrick Gallery 3059 M St NW Washington DC 20007. *Mailing Add:* 2221 Hall Pl NW Washington DC 20007-1837

KASNOWSKI, CHESTER N
PAINTER, INSTRUCTOR
b Perth Amboy, NJ, Jan 23, 1944. *Study:* Dayton Art Inst, Ohio, BFA, 71; Tulane Univ, New Orleans, La, MFA, 73. *Work:* Brooklyn Mus, NY; Guggenheim Mus; Stedelijk Mus, Amsterdam; Mus Mod Art, NY; Cleveland Mus, Ohio. *Exhib:* One-person exhibs, Ball State Univ, Muncie, Ind, 74 & McKissick Mus, Columbia, SC, 78; Contemp Arts Ctr, New Orleans, La, 78; Dartmouth Coll Galleries, Hanover, NH, 79; Class Portrait, Robert Hull Fleming Mus, Burlington, Vt, 81; Invitational, Franklin Furnace, NY, 82. *Teaching:* instr, watercolor, acrylic painting, currently. *Awards:* Nat Endowment Arts Grant, 74; Drawing Grant, 78 & Spec Mention, Illuminated Thoughts Exhib, 79, Vt Coun Arts. *Media:* Acrylic. *Dealer:* Bertha Urdang Gallery 23 E 74th St New York NY 10021; Depot Gallery Ludlow Vt. *Mailing Add:* PO Box 1 Weston VT 05161

KASS, EMILY
MUSEUM DIRECTOR
Study: Skidmore Coll, BA (Art Hist); Univ Minn, MA (Art Hist); NY Univ & Harvard Univ Design Sch, Mus Planning & Design studies, 2001; Getty Leadership Inst, Calif, Cert Mus Mgmt. *Pos:* Asst dir to acting dir, Univ NMex Art Mus, Albuquerque, 1981-84; exec dir, Ft Wayne Mus Art, Ind, 1985-96; exec dir, Tampa Mus Art, Fla, 1996-2006; dir, Ackland Art Mus, Univ NC, Chapel Hill, 2006-. *Awards:* Mus Prof Fel, Nat Endowment Arts. *Mailing Add:* University of North Carolina at Chapel Hill Ackland Art Museum Campus Box 3400 Chapel Hill NC 27599-3400

KASS, RAY
PAINTER
b Rockville Centre, NY, Jan 25, 1944. *Study:* Univ NC, BA, 67, MFA (painting), 69; also painting with Keith Crown, 67 & John Cage, 83-90. *Work:* Addison Gallery Am Art, Andover, Mass; Boston Pub Libr; Univ Mass, Amherst; Montgomery Mus Art, Ala; Norton Mus Art, W Palm Beach, 02; Taubman Mus Art, Roanoke, Va; Neuada

Mus Art, Reno, Nev. *Comn:* Ethyl Corp, Richmond, Va; Grayco Corp, Richmond, Va. *Exhib:* Allan Stone Gallery, NY, 72, 75, 77, 81 & 86, Addison Gallery Am Art, 74, Osuna Gallery, Washington, DC, 79, 84 & 88 & Southeastern Ctr Contemp Art, NC, 80; Reynolds Gallery, Richmond, Va, 91, 95, 96, 2001, 2003, 2007; Franz Bader Gallery, Washington, DC, 93 & 95; Art Mus Western Va, Roanoke, 93; AVC Contemp Arts, NY, 2000-2002; Zone: Chelsea Ctr Arts, New York, 2006; Baumgartner Gallery, New York, 2007; 77 Contemp Art, New York, 2010. *Collection Arranged:* John Cage: New River Watercolors (auth, catalog), Va Mus, Richmond, 88; Morris Graves: Vision of the Inner Eye, Braziller, NY, 83; John Cage, Zen Oxherding Pictures, Univ Richmond, 2009. *Pos:* Guest cur, Phillips Collection, Washington, DC, 80-83; Dir, Mountian Lake Workshop, Va Tech Found, 85-. *Teaching:* Asst prof painting, Va Polytechnic Inst Sch Visual Arts, Blacksburg, Va, 76-81, assoc prof, 81-84, prof, 84-, prof emeritus, 2003-. *Awards:* Individual Artists Grant, Nat Endowment Arts, 81; Va Mus Artists Fel, 84; and others. *Bibliog:* Donald B Kuspit (auth), Painting in the South: 1564-1980, Va Mus, Richmond, 80; Theodore F Wolff (auth), How Nature Engages Artists, Christian Sci Monitor, 6/29/90; Donald B Kuspit (auth), Images of the Winged Earth: The Painting of Ray Kass, Art Mus Western Va, Roanoke, 93; John Yan (auth), Ray & Jacob Kass, Allan Stone Gallery, Art in Am, 98; Jonathan Goodman (auth), Ray Kass at Zone Chelsea, Art in Am, Feb 2006. *Mem:* Coll Art Asn Am; Folk Art Soc Am; Jargon Soc. *Media:* Watercolor, Oil. *Res:* On-going collaborative art projects of the Mountain Lake Workshop of the Virginia Tech Found. *Interests:* Folk & outsider art, collaborative & contemp art. *Publ:* Auth, Morris Graves: Vision of the Inner-Eye (book), Braziller, NY, 83; auth, Sounds of the Inner-Eye: Mark Tobey, John Cage, Morris Grave, Univ of Wash Press, Seattle, 2002; John Cage: Zen Oxherring Pictures, Braziller, New York, 2009. *Dealer:* Reynolds Gallery 1514 W Main St Richmond VA 23220. *Mailing Add:* 1360 N Fork Rd Christiansburg VA 24073

KASSNER, LILY
HISTORIAN, CRITIC

b Mexico City, Mex, Nov 16, 1940. *Study:* Universidad Nacional Autonoma de Mexico, Mexico City, Mex, BA (hist), 65, MA (art hist), 76 & PhD (art hist), 97. *Collection Arranged:* Transicion y Ruptura, Europalia 93, Noortman Gallery, Maastricht, Holland, 93; La Escultura Mexicana al fin del Milenio, Europalia 93, Park Leopold Vindictive Laan, Oostende, Belgium, 93; Actualidad Plastica en Mexico, Europalia, 93, Provincaal Mus Voor Moderne Kunst, Oostende, Belgium, 93; Francisco Zuñiga: Homenaje, 94 & Ricardo Martinez Homenaje, 94, Museo del Palacio de Bellas Artes, Instituto Nacional de Bellas Artes, Mexio City, Mexico; Cur on EDS Collection, 96-97; Collab, Catalogue, Mexico Eterno Exhibition, Palacio de Bellas Artes, Mexico Petit Palais, France, Museo Marco, Monterrey, Mexico, 99; Catalog, Helen Escobedo Exhibition, Estar y No Estar, Muca UNAM, Mexico; Catalogue Expression del Nuevo Milenio Presencia de Mexico, Museo de Arte Contemporaneo, Puerto Rico, 2001; Catalogue Santiago Calatrava, UNAM, Mexico; Collab, Aztecs Catalogue Royal Acad Arts Exhibition, UK, 2002; Collab, Catalogue, La Estetica de Jesus Reyes, Ferreira Exhib, Mexico, 2002; Research Cur, Article, Tiempo, Piedra Y Barro, Exhibition, UNam Mexico, Centro Cultural Santo Domingo, Oaxaca, Macay, Youcatan, 2002-2003; Collab, Acqua-Wasser, Catalogue, UNAM, Goethe Inst, Mexico, 2003. *Pos:* Coordr (second state of El Espacio Escultorico), Universidad Nacional Autonoma de Mexico, Mexico City, 80-83, dir, Urban Art Laboratory of Experimentation, Coordinacion de Humanidades, 80-83, dir genl artes plasticas Universidad Nacional Autonoma de Mexico, 2000-2004; adv plastic arts, Instituto Nacional de Bellas Artes, Mexico City, Mex, 92-95; researcher, Coordinacion de Difusión Cultural, UNAM. *Teaching:* Instr mod & contemp sculpture, Universidad Iberoamericana, Mexico City, Mex, 78-80, instr hist Mex sculpture, 78-80; Studies Ctr for Culture & Arts, Casa Lamm, Mexico, 2004-2008. *Awards:* From Nat Research Syst Nat Researcher, 2001-04; Cult Inst for Mex-Israel, 99; Recognition from the State Secy, PR, 2001; Diploma Colegio de San Ildefenso, AC, UNAM, Mex, 2003. *Mem:* Vocalia de Arte Urbano, Instituto Mexicano de Administracion Urbana, Mexico, City; Departamento de Artes Plasticas de la Universidad Metropolitana, Mex (mem-adv, 97-98); Directors Council Music Acad, Palacio de Mineria, AC UNAM, Mex; plus others. *Media:* Contemporary sculpture and comparative analysis of sculptoric tendencies. *Res:* Influence of pre-Hispanic on modern and contemporary Mexican sculpture. *Interests:* new tendencies on Mexican Contemporary Art, 60-present. *Publ:* Auth, Jesus Reyes Ferreira: Su Universo Pictorico, Coleccion de Arte NC 34, Universidad Nacional Autonoma de Mexico, 78; La Figura en la escultura Mexicana, Bancreser, Mex, 86; Armando Morales, Americo Arte Editores, 95; Diccionario de Escultores Mexicanos del Siglo XX, 97 & Mathias Goeritz: Vida y Obra, Consejo Nacional para la Cultura y Artes, 97; La Geometria Sensual de Sebastian, Circulo de Arte, Dir, GRAL de Publicaciones CNCA, Mexico, 2000-2002; Chucho Reyes, Editorial RM First & Second Edition, Mexico, 2000-2002; Augusto Escobedo Circulo de Arte, Dir GRAL de publicaciones, CNCA, Mexico, 2004; Vicente Ganduia, Grupozurich, Mexico, 2004; Diccionario de Escultores Mexicanos del Siglo XX, Third Ed, Digital Library, CNCA, 2005; Yolanda Gutierrez, Circulo de Arte, CNCA, Mex, 2006; auth, et al Homenage Luis Ortiz Monasterio Academia de Artes, Mex, 2006; Mathias Goeritz, Una Biografia y Obra II Edicion, INBA, Mex, 2007; and others. *Mailing Add:* Sierra Guadarrama 33-4 Mexico DF 11000 Mexico

KASSOY, HORTENSE
SCULPTOR, PRINTMAKER

b Brooklyn, NY, Feb 14, 1917. *Study:* Pratt Inst, grad; Columbia Univ Teachers Coll, with Oronzo Maldarelli & Charles J Martin, BS & MA; Am Artists Sch, with Chaim Gross; Studied sculpture with Sabl Swarz, Oronzio Maldarelli & Chaim Gross; Studied advanced printmaking at Lehman Coll with Arun Bose. *Work:* Slater Mem Mus, Norwich, Conn; Bocour Artists Colors Inc; Amalgamated Houses; Bronx Inst; Va Ctr Creative Arts; and many pvt collections; Lehman Coll. *Comn:* Maternal Force (marble sculpture), Amalgamated Housing Coop Towers, Bronx, NY, 71. *Exhib:* Sculpture Today, Toledo Mus & Toronto Mus, 47; Nat Acad Design, New York, 71; Inaugural exhib, 28 Contemporaries, Bronx Mus Art, 71, Ann, 72, Yr of the Woman, 75; Brooklyn Mus, Contemp Artists Guild, 74; 150th Ann, Nat Acad Design, 75; solo exhibs, Caravan House Gallery, New York, 75, Women in the Arts Gallery, 78, Vladeck Gallery, 81, 85 & 97, Lehman Coll Birthday Exhib, 83-2005 & 2007, Ward-Nasse Gallery, 86 & Pioneer Gallery, Cooperstown, NY, 87, 91, 97 & 2002; Int Sculpture Exhib, Forte dei Marmi, 76, Pietrasanta, 76, Italy; Am Soc Contemp Artists Ann, 79-2006; Palisades Gallery Inaugural Exhib, Hudson River Mus, 82; Between the Wars, Bronx Mus, NY, 85-86; retrospective, Vladeck Gallery, 2002; Mini-retrospective, Smithy Pioneer Gallery, Cooperstown, NY, 2002 & 4 group exhibs ann; 2 group exhibs, Hilton Bloom Gallery, Gilbertsville, NY. *Pos:* Chmn visual arts, Bronx Coun Arts, 73-76; corresp secy, US Comt, Int Asn Art (UNESCO), 79-89. *Teaching:* Instr sculpture, painting & 3D design, Evander Childs High Sch, Bronx, 61-72; instr sculpture, Harriet FeBland Advan Workshop, 75-80; instr art appreciation, Madison High Sch, Brooklyn, 47-49. *Awards:* Grumbachers First Prize in Watercolor, Painters Day at World's Fair, 40; Erlanger Award in Sculpture, 80; Rizzoli Award in Sculpture, 83; Am Soc Contemp Artists, 90, 92, 94, 96 & 2000, 2002; Fel, Va Ctr Creative Arts, 86, 88-89, 92, 94 & 96; Jeane Pierce Walker Prize for Sculpture, 2002. *Bibliog:* David Howard (dir), Hortense Kassoy (film). *Mem:* Artists Equity Asn, New York (bd dir, 71-75 & 79-83, vpres, 75-79 & adv bd, 89-91); Contemp Artists Guild; Am Soc Contemp Artists (assoc pres, 87-89 & vpres, 90-94, 99-2000 & 2003); Fedn Modern Painters & Sculptors. *Media:* Sculpture, All Media; Serigraphy. *Dealer:* Smithy-Pioneer Gallery Cooperstown NY

KASTNER, BARBARA H
PAINTER

b Perryton, Tex, Dec 2, 1936. *Study:* San Antonio Art Inst, 75-78; Tex Tech Univ, BS, 59, MS, 64. *Work:* Nebr Wesleyan Univ, Lincoln; Omaha Airport Authority, Nebr; Pillsbury Int Hq, Minneapolis; AT&T, Northwestern Bell Tel Co, Omaha, Nebr; CONAGRA, Omaha, Nebr; Norwest Corp, Omaha, Nebr. *Exhib:* Am Watercolor Soc Exhib, New York, 77, 82-83, 85, 90-91 & 94; Rocky Mt Nat Watermedia Exhib, Foothills Art Ctr, Golden, Colo, 79, 82-83 & 92; Nat Watercolor Soc Exhib, Brea Civic & Cult Ctr, Los Angeles, 81-82 & 89; Watercolor USA, Springfield Art Mus, Mo, 83 & 94; Ann Exhibs, Nat Acad Design, New York, 84, 90 & 92; two-person exhibs, Joslyn Mus Art, Omaha, Nebr, 85 & 87; Allied Artists Am Exhib, Nat Arts Club, New York, 86. *Pos:* Bd dir, Tex Watercolor Soc, 78-79, San Antonio Watercolor Soc, 77-79; juror of awards, Am Watercolor Soc, 91; appointed mem, Evergreen Area Coun for the Arts, Evergreen, Colo, 92-95; chairperson, Rocky Mt Nat Watermedia Exhib, Golden, Colo, 95. *Awards:* Ogden M Pleissner Mem Award, Nat Acad Design, 90; Walter Greathouse Medal, Am Watercolor Soc, 90, Elsie & David Wu Ject-Key Mem Award, 94; Pike's Peak Watercolor Soc award, Watermedia VII, Colo Springs Fine Art Ctr, Colo Springs, Colo, 95. *Bibliog:* Roger Catlin (auth), Flatness of summer landscape transformed into art, Omaha World Herald, 7/25/82; Stephen Doherty (auth), Five ways to strengthen your landscapes, Watercolor '91, Am Artist's Mag, spring; Maureen Bloom (auth), Night visions, Watercolor Magic, 11/2000; Katherine Mesch (auth), Against the Night, The Artists' Mag, 8/2005; Kathleen H Sutton (auth), Barbara Kastner: Capturing the Mystery Just Outside Your Door, Elevated Living Mag, 11-12/2005. *Mem:* Am Watercolor Soc (juror awards, 91); Nat Watercolor Soc. *Media:* Casein, Acrylic. *Interests:* Writing, Travel. *Publ:* Impact, the art of Nebraska Women, Dora Hagge (ed), pub by Impact & Nebraska Arts Coun, 88; auth, Making night scenes sparkle, Artists Mag, 4/91; contribr, Dramatize Your Paintings with Tonal Value, Carole Katchen (auth), Northlight Publ, 93; Color & Light for the Watercolor Painter, Christopher Schink (auth), Watson Guptill, 95; Have Watercolor Crayons, Will Travel, Watercolor Magic Mag, summer, 2001; Landscape Lessons, Watercolor Magic Handbook, 7/2002; Watercolor Yearbook, publ Watercolor & Magic, 2003; The Artists Mag, 8/2005. *Mailing Add:* 30012 Troutdale Ridge Rd Evergreen CO 80439

KATANO, MARC
PAINTER

b Tokyo, Japan, July 17, 1952. *Study:* Calif Coll Arts & Crafts, Oakland, BFA (with distinction), 75. *Work:* RT Metro Coll Greens Sta Comn, Sacramento, 87; San Francisco Arts Comn at San Francisco Int Airport, 88. *Exhib:* Solo exhibs, Stephen Wirtz Gallery, San Francisco, 80, 83, 86, 87, 91, 94 & 95, Sharon Traux Fine Art, Venice, Calif, 93, Gallery Fresca, Tokyo, Japan, 94, Thomas Babeor & Co, La Jolla, 95, Bently Gallery, Scottsdale, Ariz, 95, La Art Core Ctr, Calif, 97 & Stremmel Gallery, Nev, 97; Traditions Transformed, Oakland Mus, 84; GH2 Gallery, 92; Contemp Japanese-Am Artists in Calif, PacTel Corp, Walnut Creek, Calif, 92; "Drawings from LA", Galleria Finarte, Na Goya, Japan, 92; Gallery IV, Los Angeles, 93; Galleria Finarte, Nagoya, Japan, 93; Organized Nature, Korean Cult Ctr, Los Angeles, 94; Inaugural Exhib, LA Artcore, Los Angeles, 94; SF to BC, Elizabeth Leach Gallery, Portland, 94; Equinox: An Autumn Group Exhib, Thomas Babeor & Co, La Jolla, 95; All Things Great but Small V, Stremmel Gallery, Reno, 95; Newance, Stephen Wirtz Gallery, San Francisco, 96; California Painting Sampler, Bank Am Art Collection, San Francisco, 97; Works on Paper, Stephen Wirtz Gallery, San Francisco, 98. *Awards:* KQED Award, Crown Zellerbach Inc, 80; award, Soc Encouragement Contemp Art, 81. *Bibliog:* Dorothy Burkhart (auth), Generations of abstractions, San Jose Mercury News, 1/20/89; Dare Michos (auth), A legacy of abstraction, Artweek, 2/25/89; Betsy Oberthier (auth), Visions Art Quart, fall 93. *Media:* Oil, Acrylic. *Mailing Add:* c/o Stephen Wirtz Gallery 49 Geary St San Francisco CA 94108

KATAYAMA, TOSHIHIRO
PAINTER, DESIGNER

b Osaka, Japan, July 17, 1928. *Study:* Self-taught. *Work:* Fogg Art Mus, Harvard Univ, Cambridge, Mass; De Cordova Mus, Lincoln, Mass; Ohara Mus Art, Kurashiki, Japan; Toyama Mus Mod Art, Japan; Setagaya Art Mus, Tokyo; and others. *Comn:* Granite wall sculpture (26' x 100'), Ohara Mus Art, Kurashiki, 91; grand floor landscape design, incl steel sculpture & water fall (33' x 15' x 35'), Pasonic Hdq Off, Tokyo, 92; stone sculpture (granite 150 tons) & wall relief (wood & plaster 12' x 120'), Mitsui Fire & Marine Insurance, Hq, Chiba, 94; theater foyer-wall mural (copper 10' x 40') & corridor-wall mural (9' x 115'), JT Hq Bldg, Kobe, 98; monumental sculpture (titanium & stainless steel), World Health Orgn Hq, Kobe, 98; and others. *Exhib:* Graphic Image, Cent Mus Mod Art, Tokyo & Kyoto Nat Mus, Japan, 73 & 74; Solo exhibs, Am Inst of Graphic Arts, NY, 68, Rose Art Mus, Brandeis Univ, 71, Kunstler

Haus, Wine, Austria, 77 & Nantenshi Gallery, Tokyo, 78, 80, 83, 86, 89 & 96; and others. *Pos:* Art dir, Nippon Design Ctr, Tokyo, 60-63; graphic designer, Geigy, Basel, Switz, 63-66; dir, Carpenter Ctr Visual Arts, Harvard Univ, 90-93. *Teaching:* Prof graphic design, visual & environ studies, Harvard Univ, Cambridge, Mass, 66-95; prof emeritas, Harvard Univ. *Awards:* Artist (in Architectural space work) of the Year, 98. *Bibliog:* The Work of Toshi Katayama, Kajima Inst Publ Co, 81. *Mem:* Alliance Graphique Int (head official, Zurich, 75). *Media:* Mixed. *Publ:* Coauth, Three Notations, Rotations with Mr Octavio Paz, Harvard Univ, 74; Toshi Katayama's class work at Harvard Univ, Musashino Art Univ, Tokyo, 93. *Dealer:* Nantenshi Gallery 3-6-5 Kyobashi Chuo-Ku Tokyo Japan. *Mailing Add:* c/o Carpenter Ctr Harvard Univ 24 Quincy St Cambridge MA 02138

KATCHEN, CAROLE LEE
PAINTER, WRITER

b Denver, Colo, 1944. *Study:* Ripon Coll, Wis; Univ Colo, Boulder, BA (cum laude), 65. *Work:* Northwest Community Hosp, Arlington Heights, Ill; AGIP, Houston, Tex; Cherry Creek Nat Bank, Denver Symphony Orchestra, Denver, Colo; Mus Outdoor Art, Englewood, Colo; Penrose Community Hosp, Colorado Springs; Baptist Methodist Ctr, Little Rock, Ark; Gene Codes Corp, Ann Arbor, Mich; Children's Hosp, Little Rock, Ark; St Joseph's Hosp, Hot Springs, Ark; Ping Tung Nat Univ Educ, Taiwan; Mus Indigenous People's Cult Ctr, Ping Tung, Taiwan; Heifer Found, Little Rock, Ark; Winthrop Rockefeller Cancer Inst, Little Rock, Ark. *Exhib:* Solo exhibs, Centro Colombo-Americano, Bogota, Colombia, 74, Mus Southwest, Midland, Tex, 82, River Market Artspace, Little Rock, Ark, 99, Legacy Fine arts Gallery, Hot Springs, Ark, 2000, Telluride Gallery of Fine Art, Telluride, Colo, 2002, Bryant Gallery, New Orleans, 2002, Alpha Gallery, Little Rock, 2002, Gallery Cent, Hot Springs, 2003, Gore Creek Gallery, Vail, Colo, 2004, Legacy Gallery, Hot Springs, 2005, Angel Gallery, Taipei, 2007, Tainan Co Cult Ctr, Shin Ying, Taiwan, 2007 & At the Gallery, Oak Park, Ill, 2007 ; 8 State Exhib Painting & Sculpture, Okla Art Ctr, Oklahoma City, 78; Midwestern Printmaking & Drawing, Tulsa Libr, Okla, 78; Rocky Mt Nat Watermedia, Foothills Art Ctr, Golden, Colo, 80; Alliance Contemp Art, Denver Art Mus, 82; Pastel Soc Am Ann, Nat Arts Club, New York, 90; Pastels USA, Sacramento Fine Arts Ctr, 94; Pastel Soc Southwest, Longview Art Mus & Irving Art Ctr, Tex, 95; Reynolds Gallery, Univ Pac, Stockton, Calif, 96; Am Inaugural Art Exhib, Washington, DC, 97; Ark Governor's off, Little Rock, 97; IAPS Pastel Comp, Colo State Hist Mus, Denver, 98; Sen Blanch Lincoln off, Washington, DC, 2000; Ark Capitol Bldg, Little Rock, 2003; Mus Contemporary Art, Hot Springs, Ar, 2012. *Pos:* Contrib ed, Today's Art & Graphics, New York, 80-81 & The Artist's Mag, Cincinnati, 86-; chmn, arts adv comn City Hot Springs; producer, Children's TV show, Symphony Sam; columnist, Pastel J, 2007-2008. *Teaching:* Lectr, Rocky Mt Coll Art & Design, Denver, 83-85, Univ Calif Artsreach, Los Angeles, 88-89 & Shanghai Univ, China, 2005; artist-in-residence, Ping Tung Nat Univ Educ, Taiwan, 2006. *Bibliog:* John Jellico (auth), Drawing from life, Am Artist Mag, 9/75; Betty Harvey (auth), Carole Katchen, Artists Rockies, 76; Barbara Moss (auth), Profile, Design Notes, 92; Ellis Widner (auth), Artist-in-residence, AR Democrat-Gazette, Little Rock; Susan Pierce (auth), Hot Springs Artist has a story to tell, Active Yrs, 99; Chuck Dodson (auth), Bon Voyeur, Number Mag, 2000; Living in the present: The masterpieces of Carole Katchen, Active Yrs, 7/2006; Pastel Journeys, The Pastel J, 2/2007. *Media:* Pastel, Oil, Bronze sculpture. *Publ:* Promoting and Selling Your Art, Watson-Guptill, 76; Figure Drawing Workshop, Watson Guptill, 85; Painting Faces and Figures, Watson Guptil, 86; Auth, Dramatize Your Paintings with Tonal Value, 93; Painting With Passion, North Light Bks, 94; Make Your Watercolors Look Professional, 95, How to Get Started Selling Your Art, 96 & 200 Great Painting Ideas for Artists, 98, North Light Bks, Ohio; illusr, That Sweet Diamond, Atheneum, 98; Express Yourself with Pastels, Int Artists Bks, 2000; Planning Your Paintings Step by Step, Watson Guptill, 88. *Dealer:* Telluride Gallery Fine Art 130 E Colo Ave Telluride CO 81435; Angel Gallery 1F No 41 Sec 3 Xin-Yi Rd Taipei Taiwan; Carole Katchen Art Gallery 618 W Grand Ave Hot Springs AR 71901; Legacy Fine Art 804 Central Ave Hot Springs AR 71901; Gallery Orange 819 Royal St New Orleans La 70116. *Mailing Add:* 624 Prospect Ave Hot Springs AR 71901

KATHERINE, TURCZAN M
PHOTOGRAPHER, EDUCATOR

b Montclair, NJ, 1965. *Study:* Cooper Union Sch Art & Sci, BFA (photog), 1987; Yale Univ Grad Sch Art, MFA (photog), 1990. *Work:* Metrop Mus Art, New York; Brooklyn Mus Art; Mus Mod Art, New York; Chicago Inst Art; Getty Mus, Los Angeles; Mus Fine Arts Houston; Milwaukee Mus Art; New Orleans Mus Art. *Exhib:* Solo exhibs, Cooper Union, New York, 1987, Underground Gallery, New Haven, 1990, Savannah Coll Art & Design, Ga, 1992, Maine Coll Art & Design, Portland, 1994, Univ Minn, 1996, Yancey Richardson Gallery, 1997, Minneapolis Inst Art, 1998, Univ Northern Iowa Art Gallery, Cedar Falls, 2000, Yossi Milo Gallery, New York, 2001, Mus Contemp Art, Budapest, 2002, Franklin Art Works, Minn, 2006; New Southern Photography, New Orleans Mus Art, 1992; Zoller Gallery, Pa State Univ, 1993; Anderson Ranch Gallery, Snowmass Village, Colo, 1994; Lower Columbia Coll Fine Arts Gallery, Longview, Wash, 1995; Ctr Wash Univ, Ellensburg, 1996; Eye of the Beholder, Internat Ctr Photog, 1997; Future-Present, Aldrich Mus, Ridgefield, Conn, 1998; Two Women, Weinstein Gallery, Minneapolis, 2001; Recent Acquisitions, Chicago Inst Art, 2003; Tehran Mus Contemp Art, Iran, 2004; Weisman Art Mus, Univ Minn, 2007. *Teaching:* Assoc prof & Media Arts chmn, Minneapolis Coll Art & Design, 1995-. *Awards:* Bush Found Artist Fel, 1995; McKnight Photog Fel, 1996 & 2003; Fulbright Grant, 2010. *Bibliog:* Elizabeth Pearce (auth), Documenting History, Ga Guardian, 1/1992; Mary Abbe, Circling Home, Minneapolis Star Tribune, 12/7/1997; Kira Obolensky (auth), From Where My Parents Come, Arts Mag, 1/1998; Grace Glueck (auth), Female, NY Times, 9/17/1999; Vince Aletti (auth), Children of a Higher God, Village Voice, 7/10/2001

KATLAN, ALEXANDER W
CONSERVATOR

b New York, NY, Sept 29, 1948. *Study:* Lake Forest Coll, BA, 70; Rosary Coll Villa Schifanoia, MFA (painting conserv), Italy, 79; Queens Coll, City Univ of NY, MA (art hist), 87; special study, conservation & pigment microscopy with Dr Walter McCrone, McCrone Inst, 82-83. *Exhib:* The Palette Reveals the Artist, Long Island Mus, Stony Brook, NY, 2004-2005, Butler Mus, Youngstown, Ohio, 2005. *Collection Arranged:* cur, Conservation storage & collection prioritization, the Long Island Mus, Godwin-Ternbach Mus, Heckscher Mus, Ossining Hist Soc. *Teaching:* seminar lectr, Gilding Conserv Symposium, Philadelphia Mus Art, 88, Albert Bierstadt, Art & Enterprise Symposium, Nat Gallery of Art, DC, 92; adj prof examination of Artwork, CW Post Univ Appraisal, 81-85; adj prof, examination of Artwork, Appraisal Studies, New York Univ, 87-99. *Awards:* fel, Smithsonian Nat Mus Art, 77-79; Samuel H Kress, Microscopy course fel, 83; Medal of Hon & Merit, Salmagundi Club President's Award, 2008; Funded Katlan Family Seascape Award (non mem), Salmagundi Club, 2000-2012, Katlan Family Seascape Award, Allied Artists of Am, 2004-2009, A Katlan Family City Scape Award, Audubon Artists, 2009-2012. *Bibliog:* Conservation in Aid of Authentication, IFAR Joun, 98; American Artist's Tools & Materials for On-Site Sketching, JAIC Vol 38, 99; William S Mount's Palette & Pigments, The Microscope, 2001; Early Wood-Fiber Panels: Masonite Hardboards & Lower Density Boards, Joun of AIC, Vol 33, 94. *Mem:* Am Inst for Conserv of Hist & Artistic Works, 77-; Int Inst Conserv, 75-; Heritage Perservation; Salmagundi Club, 82-; Audubon Artists, 2008-. *Res:* 19th Century Am artist materials. *Specialty:* Hist exhib records Salmagundi Club. *Publ:* auth, American Artist Materials Suppliers Directory Noyes Press, 87; auth, American Artist Materials, Vol II, Sound View Press, 92; Black & White Exhib, Salmagundi Sketch Club 1878-1887, A Katlan Inc, 2007; Salmagundi Club Painting Exhib Records 1889-1939, A Katlan Inc, 2008; Salmagundi Club Painting Exhib Records, A. Katlan Inc, 1940-1951; Watercolor Exhib Records 1900-1951, A. Katlan Inc, 2009; Artists Letters, Notes and Sketches: A Guide to Letters, Ephemera, Watercolors, Drawings, Etchings, and Ink Washes in the Katlan Collection, A Katlan Inc, 2012

KATO, KAY
CARTOONIST, ILLUSTRATOR

Study: Pa Acad Fine Arts; Am Acad Dramatic Arts. *Work:* NJ Gov Brendan Byrne; Newark Pub Libr Spec Collections, 57 cartoon originals from weekly column, depicting libr programs & events, 92; NJ Gov Thomas Kean; Bob Hope. *Comn:* Cover, Am Tel & Tel Mag, 54; book jacket for The Television-Radio Audience and Religion, Harper & Bros, 55; cover, Today's Living, NY Herald-Tribune, 57; also covers for Christian Sci Monitor, Sat Eve Post & others. *Exhib:* Solo exhibs, RC Vose Galleries, Boston, 45, Boston Pub Libr, 45, Newark Pub Libr, 92, Newark Mus, 80 & 93, Montclair State Coll, 87 & Belleville Pub Libr, 89; Montclair Art Mus, 53, 56 & 57; At Man and His World, Int Salon of Cartoons, Montreal, Que, 75-88; Traveling exhibs, West Caldwell Pub Libr, Livingston Pub Libr & Passaic Pub Libr, 92; and others. *Pos:* Columnist, "On location in Jersey", weekly cartoon column, Sunday Star Ledger, 64-95. *Teaching:* Instr, Cambridge Ctr Adult Educ, Mass, 44-47; instr, South Orange & Maplewood Adult Sch, 63. *Awards:* First Prize Award for Cartoons, NJ State Fedn Women's Clubs, 77 & 78; Plaque Award, Newark Mus Paleontology Prog, 79 & Livingston Hist Soc, 90; Special Reception, Gov Kean & Secy of State Jane Burgio, State House, 89. *Bibliog:* Foremost Women in Communication, Foremost Am Publ Corp, 70; Essex Co Libr Prog, Channel 3, Cablevision TV, 79. *Publ:* Contribr, This Week, Nation's Bus, NY Times Mag, Parade, Am Weekly & others; Staten Island Advance, 77; Marriage and Family Reality, Harper & Row, 89; auth, Park Art, Sunday Star Ledger Collection Columns, Donning Co Publ, 4/99; and others

KATSELAS, MILTON GEORGE
PAINTER, ART DEALER

b Pittsburgh, Feb 22, 1933. *Study:* Carnegie-Mellon Inst, BFA, 54. *Work:* Beverly Hills Playhouse & Klein, Gardner & Assoc, Calif; also pvt collection of Tasso Katselas, Pittsburgh. *Exhib:* Emily Lowe Painting Competition, NY, 65; solo exhibs, Gallery PS 962, Los Angeles, 86, 275 La Cienega, Los Angeles, 89 & Green Gallery, Santa Monica, Calif, 93; Four, Gallery 258, Beverly Hills, Calif, 95. *Media:* Acrylic, Mixed Media. *Specialty:* Contemp American Art. *Publ:* Auth, Dreams into Action, Dove Press, 96. *Dealer:* Gallery 258 258 S Robertson Blvd Beverly Hills CA 90211. *Mailing Add:* 254 S Robertson Blvd Beverly Hills CA 90211

KATSIFF, BRUCE
PHOTOGRAPHER, MUSEUM DIRECTOR

b Philadelphia, Pa, Dec 10, 1945. *Study:* Philadelphia Coll Art, 64-65; Rochester Inst Technol, BFA, 68; Pratt Inst, MFA, 73; Oxford Univ, 85-87. *Work:* George Eastman House, Rochester, NY; Am Arts Doc Ctr, Exeter, England; Allentown Art Mus, Pa; Erie Art Mus, Pa. *Exhib:* Photog as Printmaking, Mus Mod Art, NY, 68; Vision & Expression, Int Mus Photog, 69; Philadelphia Mus Art, 70; Underground Gallery, NY, 70; Pa Acad of Fine Arts, 73; Pa Photogrs, Allentown Art Mus, 87; Am Photogrs; Taingin, China, 87; Pa Acad Fine Arts, 90; Santa Fe Photo Ctr, 88; Woodmore Art Mus, 02; Legacy Gallery, 97; Krasdale Gallery, 99; River Run Gallery, 2005. *Pos:* Eastman Kodak, 67-69; dir, James A Michener Art Mus, 90-. *Teaching:* Prof art, Bucks Co Community Col, 69-, chmn art & music, 75-89 & Thomas Edison Col, 76-78. *Awards:* PA Art Fel, 89. *Bibliog:* Gene Thorton (auth), Photography Review, NY Times, 70; A D Coleman (auth), article, Village Voice, 71. *Mem:* Am Asn Mus; Soc Photographic Educators. *Mailing Add:* James A Michener Museum 138 S Pine St Doylestown PA 18901

KATZ, CIMA
PRINTMAKER

b NY. *Study:* Carnegie Mellon Univ, BFA, 71; Ind Univ, MFA, 74. *Exhib:* Solo shows incl Leedy Voulkos Gallery, Kans City, Mo, 97, Hastings Coll Gallery, Nebr, 2001; group shows incl Cent Lakes Gallery, Minn, 97; Print Gallery/CPC, Chicago, 97; Spencer Mus Art, Lawrence, Kans, 98; Kennedy Mus, Athens, Ohio, 98; Aberdeen Art

Gallery, Scotland, 98; Warren M Lee Gallery, SDak, 2000; Tower Fine Arts Gallery, Brockport, NY, 2000; Fine Arts Gallery, Georgetown, Tex, 2001; Gallery Ujpesti Gyermekes Ifjusagi Haz, 2002; Sungkok Art Mus, Seoul, 2002; Alexandre Hogue Gallery, Tulsa, 2003; Mod Arts Midwest, Nebr, 2004; Mus Contemp Art, Fort Collins, Colo, 2004; Kolboth Art Asn, Norway, 2004; Grandview Coll, Des Moines, Iowa, 2005; Regina Miller Gallery, Pittsburgh, 2006; Charlotte Price Gallery, Louisville, Ky, 2006. *Pos:* Bd mem, Mid-Am Print Coun, 94-96, 2002-04. *Teaching:* Prof art, Sch Fine Arts, Univ Kans. *Mem:* Print Coun Philadelphia; Boston Printmakers; Am Print Alliance; Southern Graphic Coun. *Media:* Digital Collage, Mixed Media. *Mailing Add:* Univ Kans Art and Design Bldg 1467 Jayhawk Blvd Lawrence KS 66045-7531

KATZ, DON
SCULPTOR, STAINED GLASS ARTIST
b Chicago, Ill, Feb 14, 1925. *Study:* Art Inst Chicago, 46-47; Art Students League, NY, 48-49; Ctr D'Art Sacre, Paris, 50-51. *Comn:* door carvings, Temp Beth Esmeth, Brooklyn, NY, 55; door carvings, Temp Anch Chesed, Youngstown, Ohio, 57; Ark (carving), comn by Vassar J Cerrill, Poughkeepsie, NY, 58; stained glass, Richmond J Ctr, Va, 59; stained glass, Bayside JC, Queens, NY, 68. *Mem:* NY Artist Equity; Audubon Artists. *Media:* Wood, Glass. *Mailing Add:* 59-15 47th Ave Woodside NY 11377

KATZ, JONATHAN G
ADMINISTRATOR
Pos: Exec dir, Kans Arts Comn; CEO, Nat Assembly of State Arts Agencies, 1985-; US Nat Comn on UNESCO. *Teaching:* Prof pub policy & admin & dir grad program in arts admin, Univ Ill, Springfield, 1978-85, founder Sangamon Inst in Arts Admin. *Publ:* co-auth, Advancing America's Creativity: An Agenda for Leadership in Support of the Arts & Cultural Activities; co-auth, State Arts Agency Strategic Planning Toolkit; co-auth, Facing Controversy: Arts Issues & Crisis Communications; auth, Report of the Task Force on Cultural Pluralism; ed, Arts & Education Handbook: A Guide to Productive Collaborations; co-ed, Serving the Arts in Rural Areas: Successful Programs & Potential New Strategies. *Mailing Add:* Nat Assembly of State Arts Agencies 2nd Fl 1029 Vermont Ave Washington DC 20005

KATZ, LEANDRO
CONCEPTUAL ARTIST, FILMMAKER
b Buenos Aires, Arg, June 6, 1938; US citizen. *Study:* Univ Nac Buenos Aires, BA, 61; Pratt Graphic Arts Ctr, 65-67. *Work:* Rare Book Collection, Houghton Libr, Harvard Univ; Ruth & Marvin Sackner Arch, Fla; Brooklyn Mus Collection; Museo de Barrio, NY; Museo de Arte Moderno, Argentina; Sterling Meml Libr, Yale Univ; Mus Mod Art, New York; Reina Sofia Mus, Spain. *Exhib:* Cineprobe, Mus Mod Art, NY, 79; The Lunar Alphabet, Clocktower, NY, 80; Metropotamia, PS1, Long Island City, 81; The Judas Window, Whitney Mus Am Art, 82; Orpheus Beheaded, RI Sch Design Mus, 83; 1987 Whitney Biennial Exhib, Whitney Mus Am Art; The Decade Show, New Mus Cont Art, 90; El Museo Del Barrio, 96; Art Inst Chicago, 98; Gwkngju Bienal, 2010, Mus Reina Sofia, 2009; and others. *Collection Arranged:* Mus Modern Art; Reina Sofia Mus, Spain. *Teaching:* Fac mem pre-Columbian art, Sch Visual Arts, NY, 71-; fac mem semiotics & cinema, Brown Univ, 81-; fac mem, Film Dept, New Sch Social Res, NY, 86-; fac mem, Dept Commun, Film Prog, William Paterson Univ, retired. *Awards:* Fel, Nat Endowment Arts, 79 & 94; Fel, Guggenheim Mem Found, 80; Fel, Rockefeller Found, 93; New York State Coun on the Arts Grant, 98. *Bibliog:* Lucy Lippard (auth), Overlay, Pantheon Books, 83; Dore Ashton (auth), American Art Since 1945, Oxford Univ Press; Susana Torruella Leval (auth), Recapturing History, Coll Art Asn, 92; Jacqueline Barnitz (auth), Twentieth Century Latin American Art, Univ of Tex Press. *Media:* Photography, Language Assemblages, Film, Digital Imaging. *Res:* Latin Am subjects; Photographic installations and prints. *Publ:* Self Hypnosis, TVRT Press, 75; Auth, The Milk of Amnesia, CEPA & The Visual Studies Workshop Press, 85; 27 Windmills, Viper's Tongue Books; Burnt Book/Libro Qvemado, Nexus Press, 95; Che/Loro, Viper's Tongue Press, 98; Chegueuara in Bolivia: A Chronology, Viper's Tongue Books, 2001; The Ghosts of Nanca Huazu, Viper's Tongue Books

KATZ, MORRIS
PAINTER
b Poland. *Study:* Ulm, Ger & Gunsburg; with Hans Facler; Art Students League, NY, 50-56. *Work:* Evansville Mus Arts & Sci, Ind; Jr Coll Albany, NY; Butler Inst Am Art, Youngstown, Ohio; St Lawrence Univ Giffiths Art Ctr, Canton, NY; Univ Art Gallery, State Univ NY Binghamton. *Comn:* Pope Paul VI painting, comn by Thomas A Dexter, 65; pictures, Smithsonian Inst; mural, City of NY, comn by Detective Endowment Assn, NY; mural, Synagogue, Brooklyn, NY. *Exhib:* Instant live art shows, more than 10,000 throughout the world; 6000 oil paintings, JA Olson Co, Winona, Miss, 60-63; Morris Katz Int Art Studio, NY. *Pos:* art cons, Bd Edn, New York City, 88-68. *Teaching:* Instr, Learning Annex, NY. *Awards:* World's Most Prolific and Speedy Artist, The Guinness Book of World Records, 1980-. *Bibliog:* Howard Jacobson (auth), Root Schmoots, Penguin; Bob Garfield (auth), Waking up Screaming, Scribner; Sondra Farrel (auth), One Minute Super Stars; Jane & Michael Stern (auth), The Encyclopedia of Bad Taste, Harper Collins; William E. Geist (auth), City Slickers, New York Times. *Mem:* Am Guild of Variety Artists; Int Platform Asn; Artists Equity Asn; Int Arts Guild Monaco; Am Fedn Television & Radio Artists; Am TV Arts & Sci. *Media:* Oil, Pencil. *Publ:* Auth, Paint Good and Fast, Sterling Publ, NY, 1985; The Presidents of America, Jerusalem-Simonim; auth, Up Late with Joe Franklin, Scribner

KATZ, TED
PAINTER, EDUCATOR
b Philadelphia, Pa, July 29, 1937. *Study:* Franklin & Marshall Col, AB, 59; Art Students League, 61-65; Acad Grande Chaumiere, Paris, 64-65; Harvard Univ, Grad Sch Educ, 68-72, EdM, 69, EdD, 72. *Exhib:* John F Kennedy Ctr; Demuth Found; Philadelphia Coll Art; Moore Coll Art; Millersville Univ. *Pos:* Fel, Grad Sch Educ, Harvard Univ, 68-72; dir Aesthetic Education Proj, Northwest Regional Educ Lab, Portland, Ore, 71-72; dir, Ford Found Proj, Inst Am Indian Arts, Santa Fe, NMex, 72-75; dir, Appalachia Regional Arts Prog, NC Arts Coun, Raleigh, NC; chief educ div, Philadelphia Mus Art, Pa, 77-84; dep dir, Ore Art Inst, Portland, 84-86. *Teaching:* lectr, Philadelphia Col Art, 78-84. *Awards:* Grant, Carnegie Corp; Grant, Ford Fund; Grant, Nat Endowment Arts. *Bibliog:* Howard Taubman (auth), Awakening the defeated, New York Times, 11/12/66; Museums as Schools, Newsweek, 10/15/79; Museums for a New Century, a Report of the Commission on Museums for a New Century, Am Asn Mus, Washington, 84. *Media:* Aquamedia. *Publ:* Auth, Art as a Reflection of Human Concerns and Other Common Denominators, In: Museums, Adults & the Humanities: A Guide for Educational Programming, Am Asn Mus, Washington, 81; Museums & Schools: Partners in Teaching, Pa Dept Educ, Harrisburg, 84; The Philadelphia Museum of Art Institute as research and development, Arts & Learning Spec Interest Group Proceedings J, Am Educ Res Asn, 84; coauth, Understanding & Creating Art (with Golstein, Kowalchuk & Saunders), MCgraw Hill Pub Co, 91; auth, The Studio Within, Portland State Univ, 2010. *Dealer:* Butters Gallery Ltd 520 NW Davis Portland OR 97209. *Mailing Add:* 8096 SW Woody End St Portland OR 97224

KATZEN, HAL ZACHERY
DEALER
b Baltimore, Md, July 16, 1954. *Study:* San Francisco Coll Art; Johns Hopkins Univ; Md Inst Coll Art, BFA, 76. *Pos:* Asst dir, B R Kornblatt Gallery, Baltimore, Md, 76-78; assoc dir, Transworld Art, Alex Rosenberg Gallery, formerly; owner & dir, Katzen/Brown, Hal Katzen Gallery. *Mem:* Appraisers Asn Am. *Specialty:* Contemporary art, American painting and sculpture. *Mailing Add:* 305 E 40th St New York NY 10016-2189

KATZIVE, DAVID H
ADMINISTRATOR
b San Francisco, Calif, Mar 23, 1942. *Study:* Brown Univ, BA; Univ Chicago, MA. *Pos:* Chief educ div, Philadelphia Mus of Art, 70-76; consult, Art Park, Lewiston, NY, 74-; asst dir, Brooklyn Mus, 76-81; dir, DeCordova Mus, 81-. *Teaching:* Instr art hist, Univ Chicago Exten, 66-68 & Ill Inst Technol, Chicago, 68-70. *Mem:* Am Asn Mus; Coll Art Asn; Art Mus Asn; Asn Art Mus Dirs. *Mailing Add:* 57 Hicks St No 2 Brooklyn NY 11201-1356

KATZMAN, LAWRENCE (KAZ)
DESIGNER, CARTOONIST
b Ogdensburg, NY, June 14, 1922. *Study:* Univ Pa, BS; Art Students League, with Reginald Marsh. *Pos:* Vpres & chmn bd, Kaz Inc, 47-56, chmn & Chief Exec Officer, 56-98; pres & chmn bd, Kaz Int, 98-2000; dir, World Bus Coun, World Pres Orgn, Metrop Pres Orgn & Princeton Rev, 70-95; treas, Nat Cartoonists Soc, Milt Gross Fund, 90-2006; chmn emer, Kaz Inc, 2000-2011. *Awards:* Silver Cup of City of Bordighera, Italy, 59; Palma d'Oro, Salon of Humor, Bordighera, Italy, 66; Gold Key Award, Nat Cartoonists Soc, 2005. *Mem:* Art Students League; Nat Cartoonists Soc (dir); Authors Guild. *Media:* Pen & Ink. *Publ:* Auth & illusr, numerous Dell books, 58-70; Auth & illusr, For Doctors Only, Eng, 60; Prima y Dopo i Pasti, Italy, 60; illusr, greeting cards & bks, Gibson-Buzza; Headlines(TM) Acrostic Type Puzzles (2 vols), Random House, 93; many other bks & cartoon collections in many languages

KAUFMAN, HENRY
PATRON
b Wenings, Ger, Oct 20, 1927. *Study:* NYU, BA, 48; Columbia Univ, MS 49; NYU, PhD, 58. *Hon Degrees:* NYU, LLD, 92; Yeshiva Univ, LHD, 86. *Pos:* Asst chief, econ res dept Fed Reserve Bank NY, 57-61; with Salomon Brothers, Inc, New York City, 62-88, gen partner, 67-88, mem exec comt, 72-88, managing dir, 81-88, chief econ, charge bond market res, industry & stock res & bond portfolio analysis res & corp bond res depts, also vchmn; Pres, Money Marketeers, NY Univ, 64-65; founder, Henry Kaufman & Co, 88-; bd dir, Lehman Brothers Holdings Inc, 95-. *Mem:* Am Econ Asn; UN Asn (bd dir, co-chmn econ policy coun, currently); Coun Foreign Relations; Econ Club New York City (dir, currently); Whitney Mus Art (trustee, currently)

KAUFMAN, IRVING
PAINTER, EDUCATOR
b New York, NY, Oct 4, 1920. *Study:* Art Students League; NY Univ, BA & MA. *Work:* Univ Mich Mus Art; Saginaw Mus Art; Ohio State Univ; Parke-Davis Co; Columbia Univ Law Libr. *Exhib:* Various solo & group exhibs. *Teaching:* Assoc prof art, Univ Mich, Ann Arbor, 56-64; prof art, City Coll New York, 64-86, emer prof, 86-; vis prof art educ, Teachers Coll, Columbia Univ, New York, 86-90. *Awards:* Manual Barkan Award, Nat Art Educ Asn, 81; Lowenfeld Mem Lectr, Nat Art Educ Asn, 88. *Mem:* Inst Study Art in Educ (pres, 72); Coll Art Asn Am; Univ Coun Art Educ. *Media:* Oil. *Publ:* Auth, Art & Education in Contemporary Culture, 66; contribr, Concepts in Art Education, 70; New Ideas in Art Education, 72; ed, Arts Issue, Curriculum Theory, Network, 74; contribr, Arts in Society, 75; auth, Studies In Art Educ, 88; and others. *Dealer:* Rehn Gallery 655 Madison Ave New York NY 10021. *Mailing Add:* 525 E 86th St #4G New York NY 10028

KAUFMAN, JANE
PAINTER, SCULPTOR
b New York, NY, May 26, 1938. *Study:* Cornell Univ, 56-58; NY Univ, BA, 60; Hunter Col, MFA, 65. *Work:* Whitney Mus Am Art, NY; Wooster Mus Fine Arts, Mass; Mus Mod Art S Australia, Canberra; Brooklyn Mus, NY; Aldrich Mus Contemp Art, Ridgefield, Conn; and others. *Exhib:* One Man's Choice, Dallas Mus Fine Arts, Tex, 69; Highlights of 1970 Season, Aldrich Mus Contemp Art, Ridgefield, Conn, 70; solo exhibs, Whitney Mus Am Art, 71 & 73, Droll/Kulbert Gallery, NY, 78 7 80, PM & Stein Gallery, NY, 82, Bernice Steinbaum Gallery, NY, 85 & 88, Art in General, NY, 98; Corcoran Gallery Art, 72 & 73; Critic's Choice, Lowe Art Gallery, Syracuse Univ, NY & Munson-Williams-Proctor Inst Mus Art, Utica, 77; Decorative Art:

Recent Works, Douglas Coll Gallery, New Brunswick, NJ, 78; Intricate Struct-Repeated Images, Tyler Sch Art, Philadelphia; Contemp Screens, Mus through United States, 86; Absolute Henri, Henri Gallery, Washington, DC, 91; Bellas Artes Gallery, NY, 92; Labor of Love, New Mus Am Art, NY, 96; and many others. *Teaching:* Instr fine arts, New York Pub High Schs, 60-69; Lehman Col, Bronx, NY, 69-70, Bard Col, Annandale-on-Hudson, NY, 71-73 & Brooklyn Mus Art Sch, 72-73; lectr, Queens Col, 73-74; vis artist, workshops & lect, var cols & univs, US & Can, 74-; instr fine arts, Cooper Union Sch Art, New York, 81-92; instr, State Univ NY Westchester Community Col, Valhalla, 96-97. *Awards:* Guggenheim Fel, 74; Nat Endowment for Arts Fels, 79 & 89; Creative Artists Pub Serv Prog Grant for sculpture, 81. *Mailing Add:* 151 W 18th St New York NY 10011

KAUFMAN, LORETTA ANA
SCULPTOR, PAINTER, INSTRUCTOR
b New York, NY, 1946. *Study:* Palm Beach Jr Coll, AA. *Work:* Westpoint Stevens, New York; Arcadia Ctr, Pretoria, S Africa; Bank Am, London, Eng; Environ Res Found, Wash; Oconee Co Sch Dist, SC; Nashville Jazz Workshop, Tenn; San Angelo Mus Fine Arts, Tex. *Exhib:* Solo exhibs, Exhibit A Gallery, Savannah Coll Art & Design, Ga, 87 & New Work, Piedmont Craftsmen Ctr, Winston-Salem, NC, 90; NCECA Clay Nat, Ariz State Univ Art Mus, Tempe, Touring, 91-92; SC State Mus, Columbia, 94; From the Ground Up, Austin Mus Art, Tex, 98; Appalachian Ctr Crafts, Tenn, 2002; Power of Excellence, Southeastern Ctr, Contemp Art, Winston, Salem, NC, 2004; TACA Biennial Tenn State Mus, Nashville, Tenn, 2004; The Definitive Era, Rhodes Ctr Arts, Winston Salem, NC, 2013. *Pos:* Cur, Tri State Sculptors Exhib, Spartanburg Co Arts Ctr, SC, 91. *Teaching:* Instr, sculpture, Greenville Co Mus Art, SC, 88-90, SC Arts Comn, 88-94; vis artist ceramics, Greenville Co Sch Dist, 89-90, Univ SC, Columbia, 93; artists-in-residence sculpture, Shriner's Hosp Crippled Children, Greenville, SC, 90-91; artist-in-residence ceramics, Spartanburg Co Sch Dist, SC, 96. *Awards:* First Place, 3rd Ann Monarch Tile Nat Ceramics Competition, 88. *Bibliog:* Ann Spencer (auth), Exhibit to feature noted sculpture, Charlotte Observer, NC, 12/29/89; Olivia Fowler (auth), Interview with a Sculptor, Montgomery, Ala Lakeside Living Mag, 90; Dr Kathryn Bennett (auth), Tri State Sculptors, Atlanta Art Papers, 5-6/91; and others. *Mem:* Piedmont Craftsmen; TACA. *Media:* Acrylic Paint, Mixed Media. *Publ:* Contribr, Monarch tile national, Ceramics Monthly, 11/1/88. *Dealer:* Carlisle Consulting PO Box 140781 Nashville TN 37214. *Mailing Add:* 5221 Whispering Valley Dr Nashville TN 37211

KAUFMAN, MICO
SCULPTOR
b Romania, Jan 3, 1924; US citizen. *Study:* Acad Fine Arts, Rome & Florence, Italy, 47-51; Univ Mass Lowell, DHL, 2011. *Hon Degrees:* Univ Mass Lowell, LHD, 2011. *Work:* Bronze sculpture, Rouses Mem, Lowell, Mass, 80; Homage to Women (bronze sculpture), Hist Nat Park, Lowell, Mass, 84; Ann Sullivan & Helen Keller "Water", Tewkesbury, Mass, 85 & Agawam, Mass, 92; Claude Debussy (bronze sculpture), Univ Mass, Lowell Campus, Mass, 87 & St Germain en Laye, France; Italia (bronze sculpture), Town Hall, Lowell, Mass, 87; bronze sculpture, Muster Park Fountain, Tewksbury, Mass, 92; St Germain, Laye, France, 98; Touching Souls, United Methodist Church, Tewkesbury, Mass, 93 & Tewkesbury Abbey, Tewkesbury, Eng, 99; James McNiel Whistler, Whistler Mus, Lowell, Mass, 2002; The Spirit of the Marathon, Bronze, Marathon, Greece, 2004; Spirit of Marthon, Bronze Hopkinton, Mass, 2006; Maestro Arthur Fiedler, Smithsonian:Portrait Gallery, Symphony Hall, Boston, Mass. *Comn:* Off Ford VPres Commemorative Medal, 73; Off Ford Pres Commemorative Medal, 74; 200 Bicentennial Medals, Danbury Mint; Off Pres Reagan/VPres Bush Medal, 85; Off Pres Bush Commemorative Medal, 89; 38th Pres Ford, 40th Pres Reagan, 41st Pres, George Bush medals. *Exhib:* Prudential Art Festival, New Eng Sculpture Soc, 69; Int Fedn Medal Producers, Lisbon & Port, 79, Florence, Italy, 83, Stockholm, Swed, 85, Commemorative Medal, Colo, 87 & Freedom British Mus, London, Eng, 92; Helsinki, Finland, 90; retrospective, Am Numismatic Soc, 92; Budapest, Hungary, 94. *Teaching:* Instr sculpture, Boston Ctr Adult Educ, 59-62, New Eng Sch Art, Boston, 69-70 & Nashua Arts & Sci, 70-71. *Awards:* Alma & Ulysses Ricci Award for Best Conservative Painting or Sculpture, Rockport Art Asn, 67; Sculptor of Year, Houston, Tex, 78 & J Sanford Saltus Award for Signal Achievement in Art of the Medal, Am Numismatic Soc, 92; Nat Medal of Technol, Washington, DC, 84; James McNeill Whistler Award, Distinguished Artist Award, 2010. *Bibliog:* Ann Schecter (auth), Vivid sculptural works, 11/19/67 & Perlinax (auth), Maggie Walker Medal, 11/11/71, Lowell Sun, Mass; Brenda Badolato (auth), The sculpture of Mico Kaufman, Lawrence Eagle Tribune, Mass, 6/18/68. *Mem:* Life fel Nat Sculpture Soc; New Eng Sculpture Asn; Cambridge Art Asn; Rockport Artists Asn; Nat Soc Lit and Arts; Fel Am Numismatic Soc; Am Medallic Sculpture Asn; Fedn Internationale de la Medaille. *Media:* Bronze, Stainless Steel. *Publ:* Auth, The Making of Mold Block and Case, 60; Your most penetrating portrait ever, Nat Sculpture Rev, 72. *Mailing Add:* 23 Marion Dr Tewksbury MA 01876-1224

KAUFMAN, NANCY
ART ADVISOR, WRITER
b Woonsocket, RI. *Study:* Boston Univ, AB (art hist), 60; Univ Calif, Berkeley, art & archit hist. *Comn:* Matt Mullican (wall relief), Zeckendorf Co, 89; Harry Roseman, bronze (wall relief), J P Morgan & Co, 90; Andrew Leicester Maya Linn, LIRR, 94. *Exhib:* Studio to Site: Pub Art NY, 93. *Collection Arranged:* NY City Transit Authority, Livingston Plaza Facility, 92; Haight Gardner Poor & Havens, 87; St Luke's/Roosevelt Hosp, 93-. *Pos:* Dir visual arts referral serv, Creative Artists Pub Serv prog, 74-79; bd dir, Ctr for Arts Info, 78-83; partner, Kaufman Randolph Tate, Fine Art Services, 79-83; pres, Nancy Kaufman Fine Art Servs, 83-; search cons, Opportunity Resources, Inc, 96-. *Teaching:* Mem fac, New Sch Social Res, 84-86. *Bibliog:* At Home with Art (column), House Beautiful, 83-86. *Mem:* Arttable (bd dir, 90-93 & 2007-); Asn Prof Art Adv (bd dir 83-88). *Mailing Add:* 305 W 86th St New York NY 10024

KAUFMANN, ROBERT CARL
ART LIBRARIAN
b Birmingham, Ala, Apr 27, 1937. *Study:* Birmingham Southern Col, Ala, BS (Fr & hist), 61; Sch Libr Serv, Columbia Univ, New York, MSLS, 65, MA candidate in art hist, 65-69. *Pos:* Asst librn, Fine Arts Libr, Columbia Univ, New York, 64-68, fine arts librn, 68-69; librn, Cooper-Hewitt Mus, Smithsonian Inst, New York, 65-; art libr, Div Art, Donnell Br, New York Pub Libr, 69; art & archit librn, Yale Univ, New Haven, Conn, 71-74. *Awards:* Joe Delmore Langston Award, Ala Libr Asn, 63; Comt to Rescue Italian Art Res Fel, Bibliot Naz Centrale, Florence, Italy, 69-71. *Mem:* Victorian Soc Am; Art Libr Soc NAm. *Res:* Nineteenth century furniture and decorative arts; subject headings for twentieth century decorative arts

KAULITZ, GARRY CHARLES
PRINTMAKER, PAINTER
b Rapid City, SDak, Oct 6, 1942. *Study:* Rochester Inst Technol, BFA & MFA. *Work:* Anchorage Mus Hist & Art; Art Inst Chicago; Humana Inc; Am Life Insurance; Art Acad China. *Comn:* Steeltect Industs, Louisville; Norton Hosp, Louisville. *Exhib:* Solo exhibs, JB Speed Art Mus, Louisville, 71, Bellarmine Coll, Ky, 76 & 90, Brookhaven Coll, Tex, 79, 2001, Bear Gallery, Fairbanks, Alaska, 2000, Ind Univ Southeast, New Albany, 2000 & Alaska Pacific Univ, 2000; Int Miniature Print Exhib, NY, 78; Print Club of Philadelphia, 79-80; Freichen Int Print Exhib, 80; Crackow Biannual, 80; Decker Morris, AK, 95 & 98; Univ Alaska, 97; Colorprint USA, 98; Prints Across the Pacific, 98; and others. *Teaching:* Prof printmaking, Louisville Sch Art, 68-82; vis artist, Brookhaven Col, Tex, 79, 83 & 88 & Southern Ill Univ, 79; guest speaker, Detroit Print Symposium, 80; instr, Univ Louisville, 87-93; prof printmaking, Univ Alaska, 93-. *Awards:* Evansville Mus Ann Exhib Award, 68; Arthur D Allen Mem Award, Regional Fine Arts Biennial, 71; Alsmith Fel, 92; and others. *Bibliog:* Sarah Lansdell (auth), Review of work, 2/71 & Linda Bousch (auth), A printmaker's excursion into fact & fantasy, 2/75, Courier-J & Times; Mike Dunham (auth), Anchorage Daily News, 11/97; Julie Decker (auth), Kebreakers, Alaska's Most Innovative Artists, 99. *Mem:* Southern Print Coun; NW Print Coun; Mid-Am Print Coun. *Media:* Oil; Mixed Media. *Publ:* Auth, A Portfolio of Prints & Poems, pvt publ, 73. *Dealer:* Decker Morris Gallery Anchorage AK. *Mailing Add:* c/o Univ Alaska 3211 Providence Dr Anchorage AK 99508-4614

KAVANAGH, CORNELIA KUBLER
SCULPTOR, DESIGNER
b April 8, 1940. *Study:* Barnard Coll, BA (art hist), 62; Teacher's Coll, Columbia Univ, MA, 72. *Hon Degrees:* Pine Manor Coll, Honoris Causa, Doctor of Arts, Chestnut Hill, Mass, 2010. *Work:* Dwight-Englewood Sch, NJ, 2007; Smilow Cancer Hospital at Yale, New Haven Hospital, 2010; Yale-New Haven Hospital, 2010; Univ Medical Ctr, Princeton, Plainsboro, NJ, 2012. *Comn:* Stone sculptures, comn by Merinoff Family, Lake Success, NY, 96; bronze sculpture, Kirshenbaum & Bond, Partners, NY, 97; Bronze Lion (sculpture), Lancaster Vineyards, Napa, Calif, 2000; bronze sculpture, comn by Leventhal Family, Tenafly, NJ, 2000; Long Wharf Theater, New Haven, Conn; Marnier-Lapostolle, Paris, France, 2005; and many more. *Exhib:* Art Asia, Hong Kong Convention Ctr, 91; 22nd Ann Competition, Stamford Mus & Nature Ctr Conn, 92; Five from Conn, Norwalk Community Coll Conn, 95; Five Winners, Discovery Mus, Bridgeport, Conn, 97; Qualita Fine Art Gallery, Las Vegas, 2000; Connecticut Women Artist Inc, Univ Hartford, 2000; Art of Northeast, Silvermine Guild Arts Ctr, New Canaan, Conn, 2000; Bronze, Plaster, Stone, Tucker Robbins Gallery, New York, 2001 & 2004; The Shape of Time, Kirshenbaum Bond & Ptnrs, New York, 2002; Art Place, Yale Physicians Building, New Haven, 2002; Garden Art Pequot Libr, Southport, Conn, 2002; Sculpture Invitational Mill Brook Gallery, Concord, NH, 2004; Improvisation on a Square, Blue Mt Gallery, New York, 2004; Openasia, Venice, Italy, 2004; Art Place, Yale Univ Med Sch, New Haven, Conn, 2005; Hargate Art Gallery, St Pauls Sch, Concord, NH, 2005; La Biennale de Venice, Venice, Italy, 2005; solo exhib, The Tsunami Project, Blue Mt Gallery, New York, 2006; Zane Bennett Contemp Art, Santa Fe, NMex; Sofa Chicago, Chicago, Ill; The Elements - Water, Gallery Contemp Art, Sacred Heart Univ, Fairfield, Conn, 2006; CWA Member's Juried Exhib, Meriden, Conn, 2007; Open Sculpture Exhib, Venice, Italy, 2007; JalanJalan, collab with Tucker Robbins, Miami, Fla; Arctic Ice Melt, Am Mus Nat Hist, New York, Int Polar Weekend, Blue Mountain Gallery, New York, 2009; The Reshaped World, Wash Art Asn, Wash Depot, Conn, 2009; Cornelia Kubler Kavanagh Retrospective, Hess Gallery, Chestnut Hill, Mass, 2010; Ripple Effect: The Art of H20, Peabody Essex Mus, Salem, Mass; The Pteropod Project: Charismatic Microfauma, Blue Mountain Gallery, NY, 2012; Colors, Heather Gaudio Fine Art, New Canaan, Ct, 2012, Patterns and Forms, 2012, Waterways, 2012; OPEN, Venice, Italy, 2012; Fragile Beauty: The Art and Science of Sea Butterflies, Smithsonian's Nat Mus Natural History, Sant Ocean Hall, 2013; Waterways II, Heather Gaudio Fine Art, New Canaan, Conn, 2013. *Collection Arranged:* Cornelia Kubler Kavanagh Retrospective, Hess Gallery, Chestnut Hill, Mass, 2010. *Awards:* Discovery Mus Best Sculpture, Bridgeport, Conn, 97; Amidor Mem Award for Stone Sculpture, New Canaan, Conn, 2000; Jurors Choice, Conn Women Artists Inc, 2003. *Bibliog:* Vivien Raynor (auth), Local Show of the Northeast, Wider Themes, NY Times, 95; Betty Tyler (auth), Art 2000, The Norwalk Hour, 2000; Martha S Scott (auth), Cornelia Kubler Kavanagh, 2001; Robert Mahoney, Cornelia Kubler Kavanagh Sculpture; Mark Treatise, The Shape of Time, New York, 2001; Victor M Cassidy (auth), Cornelia Kubler Kavanagh, New York, Sculpture Mag, 5/2003; De grandes Paolo, A Bridge Between E & W at Openasia, New York Arts, 11-12/2004; Paolo DeGrandis & Victor Cassidy (coauths), Venice Biennale show catalog, 2005; William Zimmer (auth), Tsunami Project rev, Sculpture Mag, 12/2006; Elena M Dixon (auth), New England Home's Conn, Spring/Summer, 2010; Artscope, May/June, Brian Goslow, Capsule Preview of Hess Gallery retrospective, May 2010; Water Works (review), The Boston Globe, 8/2010; Artist's Space, At Home A-List Winners, 2011; Exhibit Spotlights Sea Butterflies, Oceanus, 2012; The Pteropod Project, Cornelia Kavanagh Featured Member, Art & Science Collaborations, Inc, ASCI, 2012; President Obama and the Giant Pteropods, A Sea Change Blog, 2012; Ari Daniel Shapiro (auth), Sea Butterflies (podcast), EOL, 2012. *Mem:* NSS; Conn Women

Artists Inc; Nat Asn Women Artists; Nat Sculpture Soc. *Media:* Bronze, Plaster, Stone, Acrylic-covered Foam. *Specialty:* contemporary art. *Interests:* Modernist sculpture & architecture. *Publ:* Cornelia Kubler Kavanagh Shape of Time Sculpture, Paolo De Grandis, 51st Venice Biennale, 2005; OPEN 10, Paolo De Grandis, Arte Communications, 2007; Best of American Sculpture Artists, Adam P and Renee Kennedy, 2009; American Art Collector-Juried Competition of New Work, Howard Eige, 2010; The Pteropod Project: Charismatic Microfauna, BLURB, Inc, 2012; ArtNet monograph, 2013. *Dealer:* Heather Gaudio Fine Art 21 South Ave New Canaan Ct. *Mailing Add:* 24 Point Rd South Norwalk CT 06854

KAVANAUGH, WADE
SCULPTOR
b Portland, Maine, 1979. *Study:* Bowdoin Coll, BA (econ), 2001. *Exhib:* Exquisite Corpse, Bowdoin Coll Mus Art, 2004; AIM 25, Bronx Mus Arts, New York, 2005; Carriage House, Islip Art Mus, NY, 2005; You Were Never Here, Soap Factory, Minneapolis, Minn, 2006; solo exhibs, Lower Manhttan Cult Coun, New York, 2006, Art Gallery Greater Victoria, Victoria, BC, 2006, Coleman Burke Gallery, Maine, 2007 & Suyama Space, Seattle, 2008; Biennial, Portland Mus Art, 2009. *Teaching:* Instr sculpture, Bowdoin Coll, 2007-. *Awards:* Jerome Found Fel, Franconia Sculpture Park, 2005; Sculpture Fel, New York Found for Arts, 2007; Pollock-Krasner Found Grant, 2008. *Bibliog:* Leah Oates (auth), Responding to Location in DUMBO, New York Arts Mag, 6-7/2006; Regina Hackett (auth), Artists Meld Surface and Space to Conjure the Best and Worst of the Environment, Seattle Post Intelligencer, 10/2/2008

KAVLESKI, CHARLEEN VERENA
CONCEPTUAL ARTIST, SCULPTOR
b Ellenville, NY, Nov 19, 1942. *Study:* Orange Co Community Coll, AA, 63, AAS, 64; John Herron Sch Art, 64; State Univ NY, New Paltz, BS, graduate studies fine arts, 65-72. *Work:* Crosscurrents; Franklin Sq Gallery, Southport, NC; Shimizu Am Corp, Durham, NC; Nat Asn Women Artists, New York; pvt individual collections; and others. *Comn:* Installation of painted constructions, comn by Dr Gustav Gavis, Monticello, NY, 94 & comn by Dr Goddard Lainjo, Middletown, NY, 95, Christopher Coleman interior designs, NY, 2013. *Exhib:* Solo exhibs, Westbroadway Gallery, NY, 82 & 83, Amos Eno Gallery, NY, 86, 87, 90, 91, 94, 97, 98, 99, 2001, 2003, 2005, 2007, 2010, 2012, 2014, 2016; Stockton Nat, Haggin Mus, Calif, 85; Three Rivers Arts Festival, Pittsburgh, Pa, 86, 87 & 89; 51st Ann Nat, Butler Inst Am Art, Youngstown, Ohio, 87; Mohawk-Hudson Regional, Schenectady Mus, NY, 89; Measure for Measure, NY Acad Sci, 92; Nat Asn Women Artists Millenium Collection (touring), NY, 92-2005; Shimizu Am Corp, Durham, NC; Nat Asn Women Artists ann exhibs, 92-2016; Beck Gallery, Hurleyville, NY, 2003; Sullivan Co Mus & Cult Ctr, Hurleyville, NY, 2003; Plotkin Gallery, Dobbs Ferry, NY, 2006; Albany Ctr Gallery, 2008, 2009, 2010, 2011, 2012; Catskills Artists Gallery, Liberty, NY, 2007-2011. *Pos:* Antiques and art dealer, Brockmann's, Milford, NY, 83-2009; treas & bd mem, Amos Enos Gallery, 91-94, 2014-2016; Albatross Antiques and Art Dealer, South Fallsburg, NY, 2009-. *Teaching:* Art teacher, Monticello Central, NY, 68-99; art adv ed, lit & art mag, Monticello Middle Sch, NY, 89-99. *Awards:* First Place-Installation, Nepenth Mundi Emerald City Classic, 87; Miriam E Halpern Mem Award, 105th Ann Exhib, Nat Asn Women Artists, 94 & Clara Shainess Mem Award, 107th Ann Exhib, 96, Nat Asn Women Artists Catalog, 2013-2014, 125th Nat Asn Women Artists exhib, Time Warner NY news video; Catskills Artists Gallery, Liberty, NY, 2011; Elizabeth Horman Mem award for Digital Art, Nat Assn Women Artists 125th Ann Exhib, 2015. *Bibliog:* Les Krantz (auth), The New York Art Review, Am References, 88, Times Herald Record, 97, Temple Emanuel of Great Neck and Great Neck Record, 97, Sullivan County Dem, 97, 2001, 2003, 2005, 2007; Bau Gallery, Beacon Arts Community Asn, 2011. *Mem:* Nat Asn Women Artists; NY State Art Teachers Asn; Ret Teachers Asn NY; Catskill Art Soc; Nat Mus Women in the Arts, Albany Center Gallery. *Media:* Miscellaneous Media. *Specialty:* Visual Art. *Interests:* Art history; contemporary art; antiques; collectibles. *Dealer:* Amos Eno Gallery 594 Broadway New York NY 10012; Amos Eno Gallery III Front St Dumbo Brooklyn NY 11201; Amos Eno Gallery 1087 Flushing Ave Brooklyn NY 11237; Albatross So Fallsburg NY 12779

KAWASHIMA, SHIGEO
BAMBOO ARTIST
b Tokyo, Japan, Jan 31, 1958. *Study:* Oita Prefectural Indus Res Inst, Beppu (2 yr cert), Japan, 79. *Work:* Franklin Park Conservatory & Chihuly Collection, Columbus, Ohio; Am Univ, DC; Asian Art Mus, San Francisco, Calif. *Comn:* Site Specific Sculpture, Villa Montalvo, Saratoga, Calif, 2002; Installation, Visual Arts Ctr of Richmond, Va, 2006; Outdoor Installation, the Kennedy Ctr, DC, 2008; Indoor Installation, Franklin Park Conservatory & Chihuly Collection, Columbus, Ohio, 2008; Installation, Oita Prefectual Art Hall, Oita, Japan, 2009. *Exhib:* Nan-O-Tube, Toklyo Int Forum, Tokyo, Japan, 1999; The Next Generation, Univ of Ark, Little Rock, Ark, 2002; HIN: Quiet Beauty of Japanese Art, Chicago Cult Ctr, Chicago, Ill, 2006, Grinel, Ill, 2006; Beyond Basketry: Japanese Basket Art, Mus Fine Arts, Boston, Mass, 2006-2007; Masters of Bamboo, Asian Art Mus, San Francisco, Calif, 2007; New Bamboo Contemp Japanese Masters, The Japan Soc, New York, 2008. *Awards:* Beppu City Art Exhib Prize, Beppu City New Art Exhib, Oita Prefecture, 82. *Publ:* HIN: The Quiet Beauty of Japanese Bamboo Art, Art Media Resources, 2006; Masters of Bamboo, Asian Art Mus, 2007; New Bamboo Contemporary Masters, Japan Soc Inc, 2008. *Dealer:* Tai Gallery 1571 Canyon Rd Santa Fe NM 87501. *Mailing Add:* 1601 B Paseo de Peralta Santa Fe NM 87501

KAWASHIMA, TAKESHI
PAINTER, SCULPTOR
b Takamatsu City, Japan, Jan 13, 1930. *Study:* Musashino Univ Art, 55-56; Art Students League New York, 65-67; Daniel Schnakenberg Scholar, 65-66; Board of Control Scholar, 66-69. *Work:* Mus Mod Art, NY; Ohara Mus Art, Kurashiki; Tokyo Metrop Mus Art; Hiroshima City Mus Contemp Art, 99; Okazaki City Mus, 2000; State Univ, Pottsdam, NY; Frederick R Weisman Art Found; Chrysler Art Mus, Mass; Nat Mus Mod Art, Tokyo & Kyoto; Housatonic Community Coll Mus Art, Conn; Takamatsu City Mus Art; The Kagawa Mus, Takamatsu. *Exhib:* Mus Modern Art, New York, NY 1965-66 & 67; Wadell Gallery, New York, NY, 67, 69 & 72; Aldrich Mus Contemp Art, Ridgefield, Conn, 67; Nat Mus Art, Osaka, Japan, 77; Tradition & Today, Bergen Mus Art Sci, NJ, 83; Japan: Dynasty '83, Sante Webster Gallery, Philadelphia, 83; Japanese Contemp Painting, 1960-80; solo retrospectives, Takamatsu City Mus Art, Takamatsu City, 89, Kagawa Mus, Takamatsu, 2002, Mirua Mus Art, Matsuyama, 2007; solo exhibs, Haenah-Kent Gallery, NY, 95, Walter Wickiser Gallery, 98, State Univ, Potsdam, 2004 & Mitchell Algus Gallery, NY, 2006; and others. *Collection Arranged:* Hosetsu Ohtsuka Calligraphy (auth, catalog), 82. *Awards:* Silvermine Prize, 18th Ann New Eng Exhib, New Canaan, Conn, 67. *Bibliog:* Udo Kulterman (auth), The new painting, Frederick A Praeger, 69; Joseph Love (auth), Art Int, 71; Holland Cotter (auth), NY Times, 04/21/2006; Edward Leffingwell (auth), Art in Am, 141 & 143, 1/2007. *Media:* Acrylic, Oil, Watercolor; Stone, Metal. *Publ:* Contribr, Decoration art, 72 & The base of sculpture, 78, Shincho-Sha; Chronicle of Art, Vol 6 1976-1989, Mainichi News Paper, 74-75, 91; New York for twelve years, Shikoku Shinbun, 76; contribr, Exclusive, Soho, Seikatsu-no-tome-sha, 54, 89; auth, I Love New York, essay, US Japan Publ New York, Inc, 104, 92. *Dealer:* Mitchell Algus Gallery 511 W 25th St New York NY 10001; Artspace Company 135 W 29th St Ste 401 New York NY 10001. *Mailing Add:* 11 Mercer St 2A New York NY 10013-2079

KAWECKI, JEAN MARY
SCULPTOR, GALLERY DIRECTOR
b Liverpool, Eng; US citizen, June 24, 1926. *Study:* Liverpool Coll Art, Eng; Art Career Sch, New York; also with Douglas Prizer. *Work:* Hoffman LaRoche Pharmaceutical Co; First Montclair Housing, NJ; The Carrier Found, Belle Mead, NJ; Noyes Mus Art. *Comn:* Wall sculpture, First Montclair Housing Corp, 83; Site-Specific Works for Temple Anshe Emeth, New Brunswick, 87; Eight Sculptures, Ctr Women Policy Studies, Washington, DC. *Exhib:* Nat Miniature Soc, Nutley, NJ, 75; Audubon Artists, Nat Acad Design, NY, 78; Newark Mus, 78; Nabisco World Hq, 79; solo show, NJ Inst Technol, 80-; Bergen Mus, 81; Montclair State Col, 90; NJ Arts Ann, 1998 & 2001. *Pos:* Free lance illusr mag, London, Eng, 46-51, Sol Vogel & Am-Mitchell Publ, New York, 51-53, Tobias Meyer & Nebenzahl, New York, 58-66; co-founder & dir, Doubletree Coop Art Gallery, Upper Montclair, 74-88; vpres, co-founder, exhib chair, Studio Montclair Inc, An Asn of Prof Visual Artists, 1997-. *Awards:* Patrons Award, Hudson Artists at the Bergen Mus, 76; Sculpture Award, Audubon Artists at Nat Acad Galleries, New York, 78; First Prize, St John's Ann Juried Show, Newark, 79, 86. *Bibliog:* Anne Betty Weinshenker (auth), M & A on Art, NJ Music & Arts, 12/76; Eileen Watkins (auth), article in Star Ledger, 87; Betty Freudenheim (auth), article in Sunday NY Times, 89. *Mem:* Artists Equity Asn NY; Doubletree Coop Gallery (dir & chmn hanging comt & spec shows, 74-88); Women Artists Montclair. *Media:* Found Stone, Metal & Epoxy. *Publ:* Work on Cover of Geraldine R Dodge Found Ann Report. *Dealer:* Scott Broadfoot Broadfoot & Broadfoot Gallery Boonton NJ. *Mailing Add:* c/o Studio Montclair Inc 108 Orange Rd Montclair NJ 07042

KAY, REED
PAINTER, WRITER
b Boston, Mass, Mar 29, 1925. *Study:* Sch Mus Fine Arts, Boston, dipl, 49, with Karl Zerbe. *Work:* Cape Ann Mus, Gloucester, Mass; De Cordova Mus, Lincoln, Mass; Rose Art Mus, Brandeis Univ, Waltham, Mass; Wiggin Collection, Boston Pub Libr; Nat Acad Mus, New York; Danforth Mus, Framingham, Mass. *Exhib:* Kanegis Gallery, Boston, 56; Boris Mirski Gallery, Boston, 64-65; Amherst Coll, 73 & 94; A Selection of Am Art, Inst Contemp Art, Boston, 76; Art in Transition, Mus Fine Arts, Boston, 77; solo exhib, Alpha Gallery, Boston, 78, 83, 90, 96, 2000, 2002 & 2005; Circle Gallery, Washington, DC, 86; Danforth Mus Art, Framingham, Mass, 95 & 2007; Boston Athenaeum, 96; Nat Acad Mus, New York, 98, 2004-2005 & 2007; Univ NH, 2000; Cape Ann Mus, Gloucester, Mass, 2002, 2010; Boston Univ Art Gallery, 2002; Painting Retrospective, 1953-2004, Danforth Art Mus, Framingham, Mass, 2013; Reed Kay: Mark of Truth, Eli Marsh Gallery, Amherst Coll, 2013. *Teaching:* Instr painting, Sch Mus Fine Arts, Boston, 49-50 & 51-56; instr painting techniques, Skowhegan Sch Painting, Maine, 52-60; instr painting, Boston Univ, 56, prof painting, 68-90. *Awards:* James William Paige Traveling Fel, 50-51; Artist Fel Grant for Painting, Nat Endowment Arts, 81-82. *Bibliog:* Articles: Joanna Fink, Alpha Gallery, 3/96; Judith Bookbinder, Boston Modern Univ New Hampshire Press, 2005; Sinclair Hitchings and Stephanie Mayer, The Visionary Decade, Boston Univ Art Gallery, Boston Public Libr, 2002; Katherine French, Reed Kay, Mark of Truth, Danforth Mus, 2013. *Mem:* Nat Acad (acad, 2003). *Media:* Oil, Gouache. *Res:* Effects of painter's materials and media on aesthetic qualities of pictures and the way they change with age. *Publ:* Auth, The Painter's Companion, Webb Bks, 61; contribr, World Bk Encycl, 72-88; The Painter's Guide to Studio Methods & Materials, Doubleday, 72 & rev ed, Prentice-Hall, 83. *Dealer:* Alpha Gallery 37 Newbury St Boston MA 02116. *Mailing Add:* 109 Rawson Rd Brookline MA 02445-4509

KAYE, DAVID HAIGH
TEXTILE ARTIST, ART DEALER
b Kingston, Ont, 1947. *Study:* Ont Coll Art, Toronto, AOCA; Univ Guelph, BA; Cranbrook Acad Art, Bloomfield Hills, Mich, MFA. *Work:* Jean A Chalmers Collection Contemp Can Crafts, Ont Crafts Coun, Toronto; Can Coun Art Bank, Ottawa; Nat Mus Mod Art, Kyoto, Japan; Massey Found Collection, Ottawa; Prudential Insurance co Am, Toronto. *Comn:* Linen & Jute (tapestry), comn by P Farlinger, Glouchester News, Toronto, 74; Relief Illusion (tapestry), comn by L Gladstone, Videogenic Corp, Toronto, 81; Relief Illusion Number Two (tapestry), comn by Helena Hernmarck & Niels Diffrient, Ridgefield, Conn, 82. *Exhib:* 100 Yrs: Evolution of the Ontario College of Art, Art Gallery Ont, Toronto, 76; Fiberworks, Cleveland Mus Art, Ohio, 77; Fiber Works: Americas & Japan, Nat Mus Mod Art, Kyoto & Tokyo, Japan, 77-78; Engaged Reliefs, Macdonald Stewart Art Ctr, Guelph and traveling, 82-83; Canada Mikrokosma, Barbican Ctr, London, Eng, 82 &

Textilmuseum, Krefeld, Fed Repub Ger, 83; Tapices Canadienses Contemporaneos, Palacio de Cristal, Madrid, Spain, 83; Here and Now-Canadian Fibre Art, Cambridge Arts Ctr, Cambridge, Ont, 86; and others. *Awards:* Lt-Gov's Medal, Grad Medal, Ont Coll Art, 72; Can Coun Short-Term Grant, Ottawa, 75 & 78; F Javier Sauza Arts Award, 80; Craftsmen Grant, Ont Arts Coun, Toronto. *Bibliog:* M E Bevlin (auth), Design Through Discovery, Holt, Rinehart & Winston, 77; S W Keene (auth), Toronto artist seeks integrity of idea, materials, technique, Weaving & Fiber News, Homer, NY, 80; J Parkin (auth), Art in Architecture, Visual Arts, Ont, 82. *Media:* Natural Fibers, Mixed Media. *Mailing Add:* 128 Dovercourt Rd Toronto ON M6J 3C4 Canada

KAYE, MILDRED ELAINE
INSTRUCTOR, PRINTMAKER

b New York, NY, Sept 24, 1929. *Study:* Ind Univ, Ind, 51; Montclair State Col, MA, 77. *Work:* Works to 95: Serigraph: After 95, Primarily Digital Art, also various traditional media. *Comn:* Logos and corporate images; illustration of filmstrips for Troll Assoc; Portraits, Graphic Designer. *Exhib:* Solo Shows; Kurth Cottage Gallery; Hamilton House Mus, Montclair, NJ; Norman Alexander Art Gallery, Scarsdale, NY; Talli's Gallery, NY; Gallery North, Paramus, NJ; Gallery One, Montclair State Univ; Vineyard Gallery, NY; Group shows; Art Inst of Calif, San Francisco; Missouri Western State Col; Williamsburg Art and Historic Ctr; Cleveland Mus of Art; Silicone Valley Mus of Art; Salmagundi Club NY; Audubon Artists; Salmagundi Club; Mus of the City of NY; United Nations Bldg (Millennium Collection); Times Sq Lobby Gallery. *Collection Arranged:* Nabisco Brands; John Herron Institute, Indianapolis; Am Cultural Center, Taipei; NJ Board of Education, Trenton; Cisco Systems; Leonard Boucour Co; Passaic Community Coll; Indiana Univ, Bloomington IN; Montclair State Univ, NJ;. *Pos:* Art ed, Am Book Co, 52-56; Illus, Film Strips, 60-65; graphic designer, Guy-Mar Printing, 65-72; cur, Summerfun Theater, 93- & NJ State Bd of Educ Bldg, 98-. *Teaching:* Graphic design, Bergen Co Vocational Schs, 72-99; art, Art Ctr Northern NJ, 90-95. *Awards:* Director's Choice; Mo Western State Col; Showcase Award; Manhattan Arts Int; Int Mac World Digital Gallery, Int Small Works Show; Bergen Mus, Best in Show; Fair Lawn Art Asn First Prize; Image used for poster, MacWorld Expo, San Francisco; Atrium Gallery, First Prize Experimental; First Prize, Cork Gallery (Lincoln Ctr); Pen and Brush Invitational, HM. *Bibliog:* Segment on exhibit (film), NJ Nightly News, 11/81; Henry Doren (auth), The face of the coin, NJ Artform, 12/81; Art in Orange County, 83; The New York Art Review. *Mem:* Charter Member of Salute to Women in the Arts; Nat Asn Women Artists (vpres); Nat Print Consortium, Pen & Brush; Studio Montclair; Steering Committee Art Educators of NJ. *Media:* Serigraph, Computer. *Specialty:* Fine Arts. *Interests:* Art History, especially Surrealism; the web. *Publ:* Auth, The Want Ad, 10/80, The Other Side of the Coin, 12/80, The Layout and Paste-Up, Self Taught, 8/81, Introduction to Typography, 10/81 & Introduction to Copyfitting, 2/82, NJ Artforms; dir, The Carousel, an Idyl (animated film), 86; Life Cycles: 2 Flatworms (scientific animated film), 86; Gallery Guide, 2000. *Dealer:* Nathans Gallery 1205 McBride Ave West Paterson NJ 07026; Talli's Fine Arts 132 E 82nd St New York NY 10028; Ward-Nasse Gallery, New York City. *Mailing Add:* 208 Greenleaf Ct Pompton Plains NJ 07444-1534

KAZOR, VIRGINIA ERNST
CURATOR

b Detroit, Mich, Sept 28, 1940. *Study:* Univ Southern Calif, BA, MA. *Collection Arranged:* Separate Realities (catalog), 73; 24 From Los Angeles (with catalog), 74; Dreams for Sale: The Great Work of Hollywood Still Photographers 1927-1949, 76; Greene and Greene: Architecture and Related Design of Charles Sumner Greene and Henry Mather Greene, 1894-1934 (with catalog), 77; The Barnsdall Projects: Drawings by Frank Lloyd Wright, 80; Frank Lloyd Wright: Designs for Hollyhock House, 86; Frank Lloyd Wright in Los Angeles 1919-1926: An Architecture for the Southwest (with catalog), 88. *Pos:* Curatorial asst mod art, Los Angeles Co Mus Art, 65-68; cur, Los Angeles Munic Art Gallery, 70-78 & Frank Lloyd Wright's Hollyhock House, 78-. *Mem:* Los Angeles Bicentennial Orgn (chmn mus comt, 74-); Soc Archit Hist, Southern Calif Chap (pres, 81-83, exec bd, 83-86). *Mailing Add:* Hollyhock House Barnsdall Park 4800 Hollywood Blvd Los Angeles CA 90027

KEARNEY, JOHN (W)
SCULPTOR

b Omaha, Nebr, Aug 31, 1924. *Study:* Cranbrook Acad Art, Bloomfield Hills, Mich, 45-48; Univ Stranieri, Perugia, Fulbright Grant Italy & Ital Govt Grant Sculpture, 63-64. *Work:* Mus Contemp Art, Chicago Ill, Standard Oil Bldg & Mus Sci & Indust, Chicago; Detroit Children's Mus; Mitchell Mus, Mt Vernon, Ill; Edwin A Ulrich Mus of Art, Wichita, Kans; New Sch Social Res, NY; Milwaukee Mus, Milwaukee, Wis; Children's Mus, Detroit; and others. *Comn:* Large outdoor sculptures, Wichita State Univ, Chicago, Chicago Park Dist, Wichita Coliseum & Lincoln Park Zoo, Chicago, 1982; King Ranch, Tex; Interfirst Plaza, Dallas; large outdoor bronze, Oz Park, Chicago, Ill; Mitchell Mus, Mt Vernon, Ill; 4 large outdoor works, Staley Transportation, Munster, Ind, 2000; bronze, Goudy Sch, Chicago, Ill, 2003 & 2008; Tin Man, Cowardly Lion, Scare Crow, Dorothy & Toto, Oz Park, Chicago, 2007. *Exhib:* Am Fulbright Artists, Palazzo Venezia, Rome, 64; Solo exhibs, ACA Galleries, NY, 65, 69, 72, 74, 76 & 79, 2003-2004: Ill Inst of Technol, 76 & 98, Ulrich Mus of Art, Wichita, 76 & Contemp Art Workshop, Chicago, 81 & 84; Two-person exhib, Art Inst Chicago, 77; Cherrystone Gallery, Wellfleet, Mass, 80 & 92; Goldman-Kraft Gallery, Chicago, 85; Group Gallery, 87, Berta Walker Gallery, Provincetown, Mass, 92-95, 97 & 2005; Retrospective, Mitchell Mus, Mt Vernon, Ill, 94. *Pos:* Dir, Contemp Art Workshop, Chicago, 49-90, pres, 92-2009; mem adv bd, Art Inst Art Rental & Sales Gallery, Art Inst of Chicago; juror, Sch Art Inst Chicago, 96. *Teaching:* Instr sculpture, Contemp Art Workshop, Chicago, 50-70 & Mundelein Col, 70-71; instr, Fine Arts Work Ctr, Provincetown, Mass, 96. *Awards:* Man of Year, Adult Educ Coun Chicago, 62; Fulbright Award, Italy, 63 & 64; Ital Govt Grant, 63 & 64; vis artist, Am Acad in Rome, 85, 92, 98, 03; commendation 2002 park sculpture, City Coun Chicago, 2008; and others. *Bibliog:* Articles, People Mag, 10/16/89, Chicago Mag, 6/89, Chicago Sunday Tribune, 5/10/92; Nickelodeon - TV, With Linda Ellerbee, 10/5/97, KDFN-TV, Fox News Time for Kids, Dallas, 10/2/98 & 10/12/98, KERA-TV, On the Record, 10/4/98; Archives of Am Art (Interview); Archives of Am Art, Oral History Program, 2009. *Mem:* Provincetown Art Asn & Mus (vpres, 62-70); Fine Arts Work Ctr, Provincetown (adv bd). *Media:* Bronze, Welded Steel Bumpers. *Interests:* Italian Renaissance Art, Egypt, Southeast Asia. *Collection:* Mus of Contemporary Art, Chicago Field Mus, Chicago; Mitchell Mus at Mt Vernon, IL: Ulrich Mus, Wichita, Provincetown Art Assoc. & Mus City of Chicago; State of IL Mus, Springfield; Detroit Childrens Mus; Cranbrook Mus; New School for Social Research, NYC; AON Building, Chicago; Oakton Comm College, Desplaines, IL; Mundelein College, of Loyola Univ, Chicago; Northwestern Univ, Evanston; Peace Mus, Chicago; Francis Parker School-Chicago; Plus Dozen of other Public and private Collection, Fayetteville Arkansas Youth Ctr; Oz Park, City of Chicago, 4 sculptures of Tin Man, Cowardly Lion, Dorothy, Toto & Scare Crow; Milwaukee Art Mus, Wis. *Publ:* Provincetown Arts Mag, 2005. *Dealer:* ACA Gallery 529 W 20th St New York NY 10011; Berta Walker Gallery 208 Bradford St Provincetown MA 02657. *Mailing Add:* 830 Castlewood Terr Chicago IL 60640

KEARNEY, LYNN HAIGH
CURATOR

b Chicago, Ill, Nov. 16, 1927. *Study:* Northwestern Univ, BA, 49; Harvard Univ/Harvard Bus Sch, cert arts admin,78. *Exhib:* Weaving Art Inst of Chicago, 54. *Collection Arranged:* exhibs, Contemp Art Workshops. *Pos:* dir, Contemp Art Workshop, Chicago, 1951-80, co-dir, 1980-91, dir, 1992-2009; Mid-North Assoc, Board, 81-84; Oriana Singers, Advisory Board, 85-present; trustee, Francis Parker Sch, Chicago, 1981-84, Provincetown Art Asn & Mus, 1980-84, Dedalus Found, Trustee, (Robert Motherwell Found), 1991-2005; panelist, Chicago Off Fine Arts, Sch Art Inst Chicago, 1994; dir, Contemp Art Workshop, 92-2009. *Teaching:* Visiting Artist Am Acad in Rome, 92-98, 2003. *Bibliog:* Beverly Price (auth), Off the Record with Rob Weller, ABC/TV documentary, 5/81; Barbara Varro (auth), Man who turns bumpers into beasts, Chicago Sun Times, 3/22/81. *Mem:* Provincetown Arts Asn & Mus (trustee 80-84); Chicago Artists Coalition; Nat Asn Artists Org; Field Mus. *Media:* Exhib Curated of Emerging Art, All Media. *Specialty:* Young emerging artists, contemp art, all media. *Interests:* Italian renaissance; early cults; egyptology; Tibetan, Buddhism, Southeast Asian Art. *Publ:* Auth, Bumper Art, Body Engineering J, 10/76. *Mailing Add:* 830 Castlewood Terr Chicago IL 60640

KEARNS, JAMES JOSEPH
SCULPTOR, PAINTER

b Scranton, Pa, Aug 7, 1924. *Study:* Art Inst Chicago, BFA, 51. *Work:* Mus Mod Art & Whitney Mus Am Art, New York; Newark Mus Art; NJ State Mus, Trenton; Nat Collection Fine Arts, Smithsonian Inst & Hirshhorn Mus, Washington, DC; Hirshhorn Mus, Washington, DC. *Exhib:* Nat Inst Arts & Lett, 59; Whitney Mus Am Art Ann, 59-61; Johnson Wax Collection, World Tour, 62-67; Pa Acad Fine Arts, Philadelphia, 64-65; The Figurative Tradition, Whitney Mus Am Art, 80; solo exhibs, Rider Coll, NJ, 87, Dir Choice, Hunterdon Art Ctr, 87 & Trenton State Mus, 88; Continuities, Rider Univ, 2006. *Pos:* Mem bd gov, Skowhegan Sch Painting & Sculpture, 64-70. *Teaching:* Instr drawing, painting & sculpture, Sch Visual Arts, 60-90; instr sculpture, Fairleigh-Dickinson Univ, 62-63; instr painting & sculpture, Skowhegan Sch Painting & Sculpture, summers 62-65. *Awards:* Nat Inst Arts & Lett Grant, 59. *Bibliog:* Selden Rodman (auth), Conversations With Artists, Devin Adair, 57 & The Insiders, La State Univ, 60; Lee Nordness (auth), Art USA Now, Viking, 63. *Media:* Bronze, Fiberglass. *Publ:* Illusr, Can these bones live, New Directions, 60; illusr, The Heart of Beethoven, Shorewood Press, 62. *Dealer:* Grippi Gallery 315 E 62nd St New York NY 10021. *Mailing Add:* 452 Rockaway Rd Dover NJ 07801

KEARY, GERI
PAINTER

b Salt Lake City, Utah, Feb 22, 1935. *Study:* Diablo Valley Jr Coll, 77-88; Workshops with Charles Movalli. *Comn:* Kaiser Permante; City of Clayton; Alameda Fair Bd; San Mateo Fair Bd. *Exhib:* Am Watercolor Int Exhib, Salmagundi Club, NY, 93-95; Sixth Ann Oil Painters of Am, Quast Galleries, Taos, NMex, 97; Calif State Capital, Off of Gray Davis, San Francisco, Calif, 99; Seventh Int Exhib, Cornel Mus, Delray Beach, Fla, 2003; Nat Watercolor Exhib, Muckenthaler Cult Ctr, Fullerton, Calif, 2004; Trition Mus Art; Coos Bay Mus Art; Oxnard Maritime Mus. *Teaching:* Instr, Martinez Adult Sch, 70-71. *Awards:* Purchase Award, Triton Mus, 92; Donor's Award, Nat Watercolor Soc, 95; Best Landscape, Calif State Fair, 95; Third place, Calif Watercolor Asn Nat, 97; Painters of Am Award, 2006. *Bibliog:* Greenville Killeen, Acrylic Technics, Northlight Books, 94; Al Barnes, Paint the Wonders of Water, Artist's Mag, 99; Loraine Crouch, Acrylic Essentials, Artist's Mag, 2002; and many others. *Mem:* Am Watercolor Soc (signature mem); Nat Watercolor Soc (signature mem); Calif Watercolor Asn (signature mem); Int Soc of Marine Painters (signature mem); Northwest Watercolor Soc (signature mem); Calif Art Club; Acrylic & Cassein Painters; Nat Acrylic Painters Asn. *Media:* Acrylic, Casein & Oils. *Dealer:* Marin Soc of Artists PO Box 203 Ross CA 94957; Art Concepts N Calif Blvd Walnut Creek CA 94596. *Mailing Add:* 3870 Canyon Way Martinez CA 94553-3716

KEAVENEY, SYDNEY STARR See Starr, Sydney

KECK, JEANNE GENTRY
PAINTER

b Goochland Co, Va, Nov 29, 1938. *Study:* William & Mary Col, 58-59; Dayton Art Inst, 74-75; Berkshire Sch Contemp Art, 91; Vt Studio Ctr, 92; special study with Don Dennis, Fred Leach, Nita Engle, Glen Bradshaw, Al Brouillette, Robert Lassig, Ed Betts, Frank Webb, Maxine Masterfield & Marilyn Phillis; independent studio prog, Assisi, Italy, 93. *Work:* Green Brokers, Englewood, Colo; Ford Aerospace & Communication Corp, Hanover, Md; Fed Reserve Bank, Baltimore, Md; Anne Arundel Hosp, Annapolis, Md; Nation's Bank, Charlotte, NC; and others. *Exhib:* One-person show, Springfield Art Mus, Ohio, 78-79, Twentieth Century Gallery, Williamsburg, Va, 86, Md Fed Arts, Annapolis, 84 & 87, C Grimaldis Gallery,

Baltimore, Md, 89 & Md Hall Creative Arts, Annapolis, 89 & 94; Southern Watercolor Soc, Oklahoma City, 86; Ruby Blakeney Gallery, Savage Md, 91; Virginia Lynch Gallery, Tiverton, RI, 92; Brenda Taylor Gallery, Boston, Mass, 94; Taylor Gallery, Lynchburg, Va, 94; and others. *Teaching:* Instr painting, Fairborn Art Asn, Ohio, 77-81; instr watercolor, brush & palette, Wright-Patterson AFB, Ohio, 80. *Awards:* Bronze Medal, Ohio Watercolor Soc, 84; Silver Award, Mid Atlantic Regional, 84; Second Award, Southern Watercolor Soc, 86. *Bibliog:* Jeanne Dobie (auth), Making Color Sing, Watson-Guptill, 86; Mark St John Erickson (auth), Economy & expression, Williamsburg Gazette, Va, 86; Jeanne Dobie & Marilyn Phillis (auth), Watercolor Techniques for Releasing the Creative Spirit, 92. *Mem:* Md Fedn Art (mem bd dir, 82-86); Ohio Watercolor Soc; Baltimore Watercolor Soc (juror, 84); Ga Watercolor Soc; Pa Soc Watercolor Painters; Annapolis Watercolor Club (pres, 83-84, vpres, 84-86). *Media:* Acrylic, Oil. *Publ:* Auth, Making Color Sing, Watson-Guptill, 86. *Dealer:* Brenda Taylor Gallery New York NY; Virginia Lynch Gallery Tiverton RI. *Mailing Add:* 1117 Kalmia Ct Crownsville MD 21032-2126

KEECH, JOHN H
PAINTER
b Winston-Salem, NC, May 28, 1943. *Study:* Washington Univ, BFA, 65; Univ Iowa, MFA, 68. *Work:* Masur Mus Art, Monroe, La; The Stephens Collection & Ark Art Ctr, Little Rock; Muhlenberg Col, Allentown, Pa; United Parcel Serv, Greenwich, Conn. *Exhib:* Third Ann Fla Nat, Fla State Univ, Tallahassee, 88; In Search of Am Experience, Fed Plaza, NY, 89; New Am Talent, Laguna Gloria Art Mus, Austin, Tex, 89; St Mary's Col, Notre Dame, Ind, 93; Sam Houston State Univ, Huntsville, Tex; Acme Art Co, Columbus, Ohio, 98; Kansas City Artist Coalition, Kansas City, Mo, 98. *Teaching:* Asst prof painting & drawing, Ark State Univ, 68-78, assoc prof, 78-89, prof, 89-. *Awards:* Best of Show, 10th Monroe Nat Ann Exhib, Masur Mus Art, La, 73; Merit Awards, Multiple Media Exhib, Erie Art Ctr, 74 & Spar Nat Art Exhib, 83; Third Ann Fla Nat, Fla State Univ, Tallahassee; New Am Talent, Austin, Tex, 89; 22nd Bradley Nat Print & Drawing Exhib, Peoria, Ill; Nat Endowment for Arts Fel Award, Mid-Am Art Alliance, 92. *Media:* Oil, Plexiglass. *Publ:* Auth, Jazz-Eye, private publ; contrib, Two Untitled Works, River City Review, 85

KEEGAN, DANIEL T
MUSEUM DIRECTOR
Study: Univ Wis, Green Bay, BA; Southern Ill Univ, MFA. *Pos:* Dir, Kemper Mus Contemp Art, Kans City, Mo, 97-2000, San Jose Mus Art, 2000-2008, Milwaukee Art Mus, 2008-; bd mem, Zero One San Jose, 2006-2008. *Teaching:* Assoc prof & coordr Dept Art, Avila Coll, Kansas City, Mo; chmn Dept Art, WVa Weslyean Coll, 97-97. *Mailing Add:* Milwaukee Art Mus 700 N Art Museum Dr Milwaukee WI 53202

KEEGAN, KIM E
ADMINISTRATOR, SCULPTOR
b Mt Kisco, NY, Apr 18, 1955. *Study:* Univ NH, BA (studio art), 84; Plymouth State Col, MEd, 98. *Pos:* Dir admis, Columbus Col Art & Design, 86-87; vpres prog, NH Inst Art, 87-96; dean fac, Monserrat Col Art, Beverly, Mass, 97-. *Mem:* NH Art Educators Asn (pres, 94-95); Nat Art Educators Asn; Am Asn High Educ; Asn Supv & Curric Develop. *Publ:* Auth, Customer Satisfaction, Course Trends, 12/92. *Mailing Add:* 190 Brook St Manchester NH 03104

KEELER, DAVID BOUGHTON
PAINTER
b Cleveland, Ohio, Feb 11, 1931. *Study:* Cleveland Inst Art, dipl; Case Western Reserve Univ, Cleveland. *Work:* Cleveland Inst Art, Ohio; Cleveland Art Asn; Nat Mus Am Art, Washington, DC; Hirshhorn Mus & Sculpture Gallery, DC; Cameron Art mus, Wilmington, NC. *Exhib:* Cleveland Mus Art Regional, 60-63, 65, 67, 74 & 76; Butler Inst Am Art Nat, Youngstown, Ohio, 60 & 62; Corcoran Gallery of Art, Washington, DC, 65 & 69; solo exhibs, 323 Gallery, Alexandria, Va, 65; Studio Gallery, Alexandria, Va, 66; Barbara Fielder Gallery, Washington, DC, 76; Wolfe St Gallery, Alexandria, 77; Studio Gallery, Washington, DC, 83; Curzon Gallery, Boca Raton, Fla, 89 & 91; Soc Four Arts Nat, Palm Beach, Fla, 91; Boca Raton Mus All Fla Show, 99. *Pos:* Preparator & exhib designer, Cleveland Mus Art, 61-64; tech asst to cur, Nat Collection Fine Arts, Washington, DC, 66-71 & chief exhib & design, 72-85. *Bibliog:* Andrew Hudson (auth), article, Washington Post, 10/65 & 10/66; Ben Forgey (auth), article, Washington Evening Star, 4/76; Absorb Art Mag, 2010. *Mem:* Boca Raton Mus Artist Guild. *Media:* All Media. *Dealer:* Lazzaro Signature Gallery Fine Art 184 W Main Gtonghton WI 53589. *Mailing Add:* 399 NE 20th St Boca Raton FL 33431-8136

KEELEY, SHELAGH
HISTORIAN, PAINTER
b Oakville, Ont. *Study:* York Univ, Toronto, BA (art hist), 77. *Work:* Mus Mod Art, NY; Art Metropole, Toronto; Art Gallery Ontario, Toronto; Walker Art Ctr, Minneapolis; Nat Gallery Can, Ottawa. *Exhib:* Works from the Permanent Collection, Nat Gallery, Can, 91; Drawn in the Nineties, Independent Inc, NY Traveling Exhib, 92-94; X Mostra da Gravura, Musea da Gavura Cidada de Curitiba, Brazil, 92; Natural Sci, John Gibson Gallery, NY, 92; La Fabbrica di Seta Arezzo, Italy, 92; From the Intimacy of the Page, The Power Plant, Toronto, 92; solo-exhibs, Art Metropole, Toronto, 90, De Fabriek, Eindhoven, 91, Granary Books, NY, 91 Nexus Contemp Art Ctr, Atlanta, 91, Axe Né-7, Hull Quebec, 92, Contemp Mus, Honolulu, 92, Exit Art, NY, 93; and many others. *Pos:* Asst cur, Art Gallery York Univ, 79-81; artist-in-residence, Imadate Paper Workshop, Japan, 89; De Fabriek, Eindhoven, Holland, 91; Banff Centre, Alberta, 91; PS 1 Studio, NY, 91-92. *Teaching:* Painting instr, Emily Carr Col Art, Vancouver, 86. *Awards:* Lower East Side Printshop, NY, 90; Pyramid Atlantic, Washington, 91; Nexus Press Book Residency, Atlanta, 93. *Mailing Add:* c/o Pelavin Editions 13 Jay St New York NY 10013-2848

KEENA, JANET L
PAINTER, DESIGNER
b St Joseph, Mo, Sept 11, 1928. *Study:* Univ Kans; Univ Calif, Los Angeles; Am Acad Art, Chicago. *Work:* Albrecht Mus, St Joseph, Mo; Arthur Andersen & Co, Washington; NY Marriot Hotel; AARP Hq, Washington DC. *Comn:* AARP Hq, Washington; Oliver Carr Co. *Exhib:* Albrecht Art Mus, 72; Ark Art Ctr, Little Rock, 72; Richmond Mus, Va, 72; Henoch Gallery, NY; Nat Arts Club Ann, NY; South Bend Regional Mus Art, 94; Nelson Atkins Mus Art, Kansas City, Mo. *Teaching:* Artist-in-residence, William Jewell Col, 73. *Awards:* First Publ Award, Fine Arts Discovery Mag, 70; First Prize, Renwick Mus Award, Nat Arts Club Ann, Mo State Fair, 71 & 72 & Northern Va Community Col. *Bibliog:* Donald Hoffmann (auth), Art in Mid-America, Kansas City Star, 5/69 & 5/74; Jean Trusty (auth), Art, Kansas City Squire Mag, 4/71; R C Seine (ed), Contemporary American Artists, La Rev Mod, Paris, 11/71. *Mem:* Nat Arts Club, NY; Washington Women's Art Asn. *Media:* Oil, Watercolor. *Dealer:* Foxhall Gallery 3301 New Mexico Ave NW Washington DC 20016

KEENER, POLLY LEONARD
ILLUSTRATOR, CARTOONIST
b Akron, Ohio, July 14, 1946. *Study:* Conn Coll, New London, BA, 68; Kent State Univ, 67; Princeton Univ, NJ, Medieval Art with Kurt Weitzman, 68. *Work:* Stan Hywet Hall Found & West Point Market, Akron, Ohio; Acme Grocery Stores, Akron, Ohio; Heidleberg Univ, Tiffin, Ohio. *Comn:* Mural (20 ft), Acme Store, Hudson, Ohio; mural, Heidleberg Univ Honors Dept, Tiffin, Ohio, 98; numerous pvt & corp illus comns, 78-; mural (45 ft) Acme Store, Tallmadge, Ohio, 2010. *Exhib:* 13th Ann Baycrafters Show, Baycrafters Gallery, Bay Village, Ohio, 75; Group Christmas Show, Mus Nat Hist, Cleveland, Ohio, 79; Our Own Show, Soc Illus Mus Am Illus, New York, 91; Univ Akron Fac Traveling China Exhib, 92-93; Traveling Cartoon Show, Ohio/Mich Chap Nat Cartoonists Soc, 96-98, Funny Papers, Cartoon Art Show, Thurber Center Gallery, Columbus, Ohio, 2001-2002. *Pos:* Pres, Keener Corp, Akron, Ohio, 77-2007; mem, hon bd trustees, Stan Hywet Hall Found, Akron, 79-; part-time graphic designer, freelance, 79-; mem bd trustees, Womens Hist Proj, Akron, 93-96; mem bd dir, Nat Cartoonists Soc, 97-2001; founding mem, Toonseum, Children's Mus, Pittsburgh, Pa, 2006-, bd dirs mem, 2006-2009; chmn, Great Lakes Chapter, NCS, 96-2000, 2010-; mem, bd dirs, Cuyahoga Portage DAR, 2008-; bd advs, Toonfest Art Competition, 2011, 2012, 2013. *Teaching:* Instr soft sculpture, Univ Akron, 79-84, cartooning, 79-2004; cartooning, Northeastern Ohio Univ Coll Med, 92-95. *Awards:* Unsung Hero Award, Jr League of Akron, 88; Woman of the Year in Creative Arts, Women's Hist Proj, 89; Artist of the Year, Heidleberg Coll, 98; Tim Rosenthal Award, Nat Cartoonists Soc Chap, 2006. *Bibliog:* Suzanne Severin (auth), Tooned in, Northern Ohio Living Mag, 7/93; Erica Barkemeyer (auth), Cashmakers: artful entrepreneur, Cash Saver Mag, 2/94; Becky Snyder (auth), Polly Keeners labor of love: Cartooning, Focus Newspaper, 11/94; Cartoon Art Puts Message on Wall at 'Berg', Tribune Newspaper, Tiffin, Ohio, 98. *Mem:* Soc Illusrs, New York; Nat Cartoonists Soc, NCS, Great Lakes Chap & DAR. *Media:* Pen & Ink, Watercolor. *Res:* History, techniques and psychology of cartooning. *Interests:* History, Miniature Furniture, Theoretical Physics, Architecture. *Collection:* many private collections. *Publ:* Illusr, Eat Dessert First, Fairlawn Press, 87; auth, Interview with Mischa Richter, Cartoonists Profiles Mag, 88; illusr, It's Our Serve, Jr League, Long Island, 89; auth, Cartooning, Prentice Hall, 92; illusr, 80 + Great Ideas for Making Money At Home, Walker & Co, New York, 92; Writers Little Instruction Book, Writers World Press, Aurora, Ohio, 97; Hamster Alley (cartoon strip) DBR Media, 3/2000- & Hamster Alley: The Early Strips bk, Comics Libr Int Publ, 2001; Fox: Lost and Found, Creoximius Publ, 2007; syndicated puzzle features, Sudoku Happi & Mystery Mosaic, georgetoon.com; Hamster Alley, syndicated comic strip. *Mailing Add:* 400 W Fairlawn Blvd Akron OH 44313

KEEVER, KIM
PHOTOGRAPHER, PAINTER
b New York, NY, May 13, 1955. *Study:* Old Dominion Univ, Norfolk, Va, BS, 76. *Work:* Microsoft, Seattle; Mus Mod Art & Metrop Mus, NY; Chrysler Mus, Norfolk, Va; Brooklyn Mus, NY; Hirshhorn Mus, Washington; George Washington Univ, DC; Va Mus of Fine Art, Richmond, Va; Nassau County Mus Fine Art, Roslyn, NY; New England Mus Fine Arts, Brooklyn, Conn; Patterson Mus, Patterson, NJ. *Exhib:* Irene Leach Exhib, Chrysler Mus, Norfolk, Va, 86; Recent Acquisitions, Mus Mod Art, NY, 86; M-13 Gallery, NY, 86; Brody's Gallery, Washington, 88; Queens Mus, NY, 92; Art Space, Raleigh, NC, 96; De Chiara/Stewart Gallery, NY, 98, 2000; Fotogalerie Wein, Vienna, Austria; Fassbender Stevens, Chicago, Ill; Cornell Dewitt, NY; David Floria Gallery, Aspen, Colo, 2004; Feigen Contemp Gallery, NY, 2005; Carrie Secrist Gallery, Chicago, 2006; Feigen Contemp, NY, 2007; Carrie Secrist Gallery, Chicago, Ill, 2008; Kinz & Tillou Fine Art, New York. *Awards:* NY Found for Artists Award, NYFA Grant, 2008. *Bibliog:* Everett Potter (auth), Kim Keever & Promises, Promises, Arts Mag, 86; Klaus Ottman (auth), Supermannerism, Flash Art, 86; Garett Holg (auth), rev, Art News, 2002; Ed Leffingwell (auth), rev, Art in Am, 2005; Joseph Jacobs (auth), Art & Antiques (rev), 2007; Roger Pickney (auth), Orion (rev), 2007; Leah Oates (auth), the Altered Landscape: An Interview with Kim Keever, New York Arts Mag, May 2007 (photo); Jeffrey Cyphers Wright (auth), Chelsea Now (rev), 2008; Teresa Annas (auth), Art, Virginian Pilot, 2009; Mark St John Erickson (auth), Luminous Landscapes, Metro Mix Hampton Roads, 2009; Michael Wilson (rev), Art Forum, 2009 (photo). *Media:* Cibachrome, Video; Oil, C-Print. *Publ:* Auth-illusr, Yes & No, Prints & Poetry, Kaldewey Press, 82; illusr, Twenty Love Poems and a Song of Desperation (Pablo Naruda, auth), Kaldewey Press, 89. *Dealer:* Kinz Tillou & Feigen Gallery 529 W 20th St New York NY 10011; Carrie Secrist Gallery 835 W Washington Blvd Chicago IL 60607; Adamson Gallery 1515 14th St NW Washington DC 20005

KEHLMANN, ROBERT
CRITIC, ARTIST, PRESERVATIONIST
b Brooklyn, NY, 1942. *Study:* Antioch Coll, Ohio, BA, 63; Univ Calif, Berkeley, MA, 66. *Work:* Corning Mus Glass, NY; Leigh Yawkey Woodson Art Mus, Wausau, Wis; Hessisches Landes Mus, Ger; Mus Art Decoratifs, Lausanne, Switz; Hokkaido Mus Mod Art, Japan; Mus Für Zeitgewoössische Glasmalerei, Langen, Ger; Toledo Mus Art, Ohio; Oakland Mus, Calif; Mus Arts & Design, NY. *Comn:* Lincoln Sq Res Lobby, NY; Four Seasons Hotel, San Francisco. *Exhib:* New Stained Glass, Mus Contemp Crafts, NY, 78; New Glass, Corning Mus Glass, NY, 79; Int Directions in Glass Art, Art Gallery Western Australia, Perth, 82; Oakland Mus, Calif, 86; Craft Today USA, Am Craft Mus, NY, 89-90; Hist Am Glass, Corning Mus, Glass, NY, 89; World Glass Now, Hokkaido Mus Art, Sapporo, Japan, 91; Glass Now 93, Yamaha Corp, Japan, 93; 25 yr retrospective, Hearst Art Gallery, St Mary's Col, Moraga, Calif, 96. *Collection Arranged:* Current Trends in Glass (auth, catalog), Walnut Creek Civic Art Gallery, Calif, 80; Emerging Artists in Glass (auth, catalog), Calif Crafts Mus, Palo Alto, 81; Glass Art Nat, Downie Mus Art, Calif, 86; Inaugural exhib, Mus Glass, Tacoma, Wash, 2002. *Pos:* Contributing ed, Glass Art Mag, Oakland, Calif, 75-76; ed, Glass Art Soc J, Seattle, Wash, 81-84; contrib ed, New Glass Work Mag, 87-88; chmn/founder, Berkeley Historical Plaque Project, 97-2012. *Teaching:* Instr Glass Design, Calif Col Arts & Crafts, Oakland, Calif, 78-80, 90 & Pilchuck Glass Ctr, Stanwood, Wash, 78-80; instr design, Miasa Bunka Ctr, Miasa, Japan, 85. *Awards:* Craftsman's Fel Grant, Nat Endowment Arts, 77; Art Critic's Fel Grant, Nat Endowment Arts, 78. *Bibliog:* Grace Glueck (auth), Art People, The New York Times, 2/10/78; Johannes Schreiter (auth), Die Glasbilder von Robert Kehlmann, Neues Glas, 3/81; Interview: Robert Kehlmann, Stained Glass Art, Japan, fall 85; Paul Smith (auth), Poetry of the Physical, Craft Today, 86; Susanne K Frantz (auth), Contemp Glass, H N Abrams, 89; Janet Koplos (auth), Robert Kehlmann at the Hearst Art Gallery, Art in Am, 9/96. *Mem:* hon life mem Glass Art Soc (bd dir, 80-84 & 89-92). *Media:* Glass; Drawing. *Specialty:* www.robertkehlmann.com. *Interests:* historic preservation. *Publ:* Auth, 20th Century Stained Glass: A New Definition, Kyoto Shoin Co Ltd, Kyoto, Japan, 92; The Inner Light: Sculpture of Stanislau Libensky and Jaroslava Brychtova, Univ Wash Press, 2002. *Dealer:* Heller Gallery New York NY. *Mailing Add:* 2207 Rose St Berkeley CA 94709

KEISTER, STEVE (STEPHEN) LEE
SCULPTOR
b Lancaster, Pa, Aug 22, 1949. *Study:* Tyler Sch Art, Philadelphia & Rome, BFA, 1971, MFA, 1973. *Work:* Whitney Mus Am Art; Mus Contemp Art, Chicago; Dallas Mus Fine Arts; Lannan Found, West Palm Beach, Fla; Mus Contemp Art, Los Angeles; High Mus Art, Atlanta; Milwaukee Art Mus; Castellani Art Mus, Niagara Univ, NY; New Mus Contemp Art, NY. *Exhib:* Solo exhibs include Nancy Lurie Gallery, Chicago, 1977, 1979 & 1991, Pam Adler Gallery, NY, 1978, Options, Mus Contemp Art, Chicago, 1980, BlumHelman Warehouse, NY, 1981, 1982, 1986 & 1988, Larry Gagosian Gallery, Los Angeles, 1983, Galerie Rudolf Zwirner, Cologne, 1984, Carol Taylor Gallery, Dallas, 1984, Solo Gallery, NY, 1989, Nina Freudenheim Gallery, Buffalo, NY, 1990, Inst Archaeology, Bill Maynes Contemp Art, 1996, Rosenberg Gallery, Hofstra Univ, NY, 1998, Bill Maynes Gallery, NY, 1999 & 2002; group exhibs include New Work-NY, New Mus, 1978, Language, Drama, Source & Vision, 1983; Eight Sculptors, Albright-Knox Gallery, Buffalo, 1979; Biennial, Whitney Mus Am Art, NY, 1981, Selected Painting & Sculpture Acquired Since 1978, 1982, Minimalism to Expressionism, 1983, Painted Metal Sculpture, 1990, Altered & Irrational: Selections from the Permanent Collection, 1995; Beelden-Sculpture 1983, Rotterdam Arts Coun, The Neth, 1983; The Barry Lowen Collection, Mus Contemp Art, Los Angeles, 1986; From Object to Image, High Mus Art, Atlanta, 1987; Skulpturen Rebublik, Kunstraum Wien, Vienna, 1988; A Drawing Show, Cable Gallery, NY, 1988; Newer Sculpture, Charles Cowles Gallery, NY, 1990; Fabricators, Grace Borgenicht Gallery, NY, 1991; A Marked Difference, Maatschappij Arti et Amicitiae, Amsterdam, 1992; Nine Sculptors and their Printer, Bernard Toale Gallery, Boston, 1993; In Context, NY Univ, 1994; NY Univ Faculty Exhib, Apex Art, NY, 1995; The Flying Saucer Project, Pat Hearn Gallery, NY, 1996; 30th Ann Temple Rome Exhib, Italy, 1996; Art Resources Transfer, Inc, NY, 1997; Glyphriff 2, NY Art Exchange, 1998; Snapshot, Contemp Mus, Baltimore, 2001; Rosenwald-Wolf Gallery, Univ of the Arts, Philadelphia, 2001; Travelers Islip Art Mus, Long Island, NY, 2003. *Teaching:* Instr, Sch Visual Arts & New York Univ. *Awards:* Pollock Krasner Found Scholar, 1987; Nat Endowment Arts Fel, 1988; Adolph & Esther Gottlieb Found Grant, 1999; Guggenheim Mem Fel, 2000. *Bibliog:* Peggy Kutzen (auth), article in Arts Mag, 5/81; Prudence Carlson (auth), Otherworldly geometrics, Art in Am, 10/81; Jeanne Silverthorne (auth), article in Artforum, 1/83. *Media:* Plywood, Miscellaneous Media. *Publ:* Steve Keister: Recent Work (exhib catalog), 88; Steve Keister: Sculpture (exhib catalog), Nina Freudenheim Gallery, Buffalo, 90

KELBAUGH, ROSS J
COLLECTOR, HISTORIAN
b Baltimore, Md, June 13, 1949. *Study:* Univ Md, BA, 71; Johns Hopkins Univ, MLA, 77. *Exhib:* Baltimore Collects, Baltimore Mus Art, 82; Solomon Nunes Carvalho, Jewish Hist Soc, Baltimore, Md, 89; Threads of Life, Jewish Hist Soc, 91; A House Divided, Md Hist Soc, 91; Southern Shadows, Atlanta Hist Ctr, 96. *Mem:* Daguerreian Soc; Am Photog Hist Soc; Regional Photog Group. *Res:* Photographic history of 19th and early 20th century Maryland and other Mid-Atlantic states. *Collection:* Nineteenth century photographic portraiture of the Victorian era. *Publ:* Auth, Directory of Maryland Photographers, 1839-1900, 89, Directory of Civil War Photographers, Vol 1-3, 90-93, Hist Graphics; Introduction to Civil War Photography, Thomas Publ, 91; Monumental Daguerreotypes of Baltimore, Daguerreian Soc, 94. *Mailing Add:* 7023 Deerfield Rd Baltimore MD 21208-6008

KELLAR, JEFF
SCULPTOR
b Washington, DC, Sept 25, 1949. *Study:* Univ Pa, BA, 71, film with Rudy Burkhardt. *Work:* Univ S Maine, Gorham, Maine; Portland Mus Art, Maine; Mus Am Art, Philadelphia, Pa; Portalnd Mus Art, Maine; Farnsworth Mus, Rockland, Maine. *Comn:* Arc Temple Bet Ha-Am, Portland, Maine, 87; exterior sculpture for the Percent for Art Prog, Kennebunk Sch System, Kennebunk, Maine, 90; interior sculpture, Sanford Sch System, Sanford, Maine, 90; interior sculpture, Freeport Sch System, Maine, 92; interior sculpture, Belfast Sch System, Maine, 92. *Exhib:* Artist Designed Furniture, Norton Gallery Art, W Palm Beach, Fla, 86; Ten, Portland Mus Art, Portland, Maine, 88; Interstices, Farnsworth Mus, Rockland, Maine, invitational, 89; Art That Works, traveling exhib, 14 mus across the country, 90-93; solo exhibs, Gallery Camino Real, Boca Raton, Fla, 91, Portland Mus Art, Maine, 95, Univ Southern Maine, Gorham, 95, Dean Velentgas Gallery, Portland, Maine, 96 & Gallery Joe, Philadelphia, 97; Retrospective, Univ Maine, Farmington, 94; The Unbroken Line, Mus Am Art, Philadelphia, 97. *Pos:* Adv panel, Maine Arts Comn, 88-91; Gov's Adv Bd, Maine Aspirations Compact, 88. *Teaching:* Artist-in-residence, Sculpture, Univ S Maine, Gorham, 87; instr, Haystack Mountain Sch Crafts, 87. *Awards:* Design Award, Maine Times Design, Maine Times, 87; Individual Artist fel, State of Maine, 96; Penna Acad Fine Art Fel Purchase Award, 97. *Bibliog:* Sherry Miller (auth), Ten, Portland Mus Art, Art New Eng, 6/88; Shirley Jacks (auth), rev, Art New Eng, 7-8/90; Martha Severins (auth) essay, Portland Mus Art Bull, 11/90; and others. *Mem:* Int Sculpture Ctr. *Media:* Miscellaneous Media. *Publ:* Contrib, Designing Furniture, Taunton Press, 89; Maine Art Now, Dog Ear Press, 90. *Mailing Add:* 7 Wolcott Ave Falmouth ME 04105

KELLAR, MARTHA ROBBINS
PAINTER, INSTRUCTOR
b Alamogordo, NMex, 1949. *Study:* Murray State Univ, Ky, 67-69; NMex State Univ, Alamogordo, 79-81, spec study with Ramon Froman, Albert Handell, David Leffel, Sherrie McGraw. *Comn:* Oil portraits, Coll Bus Admin & Econ, NMex State Univ, Las Cruces, 92; postar image and benefit auction, Rotary Tularosa Basin Wine Festival, 2011. *Exhib:* Pastel Soc Am Nat Open, Nat Arts Club, NY, 85-86 & 87; Salmagundi Club Non-Member Exhib, NY, 86, 87 & 93; Catherine Lorillard Wolfe Art Club Ann Exhib, Nat Arts Club, NY, 87; Carlsbad NMex Reg Art Mus, 98; Audubon Artist Ann Nat Exhib, Salmagundi Club, NY, 2000; Am Women Artists Ann Nat Exhib, Contemp Southwest Galleries, Santa Fe, N Mex; Nita Stewart Haley Mem Libr, 27th Ann Art Show, Midland, Tex, 2005; Oil Painters of Am Nat Exhib, 2008; Solo exhib: Enchanted Art Benefit, 1st Nat Bank, Alamagordo, NMex, 2010. *Teaching:* Instr pastel, oil painting, Kellar Art Studio, La Luz, NMex, 86-; instr figure drawing, Eastern NMex Univ/Ruidoso, NMex, 91-. *Awards:* Andrews/Nelson/Whitehead, Pastel Soc Am Nat Open, 85; J B McReynolds Mem, Salmagundi Club Non-Members Exhib, 87; Degas Award, Pastel Soc West Coast Nat Open, 89. *Bibliog:* Steve Wall (auth), Unity, harmony & clarity: the life and work of Martha Kellar, Mountain Passages Mag, winter/spring 92; T Nicholas & JC Terelak (eds), The Best of Oil Painting, Rockport Publ; Western Art Collector, Dec 2008. *Mem:* Pastel Soc Am; Pastel Soc West Coast; Asn Oil Painters Am. *Media:* Oils, Pastels. *Interests:* Asian antiquities. *Dealer:* Longcoat Fine Art 2825 Suddeth Plaza Ruidoso NMex 88345; Santa Fe Art Collector 221 W San Francisco Santa Fe N Mex 87501. *Mailing Add:* Three Robin Ln La Luz NM 88337

KELLER, FRANK S
PAINTER
b Minneapolis, Minn, Aug 31, 1951. *Study:* Creighton Univ, Nebr, 69-70; Univ Minn, Minneapolis, BA, BFA, 74; Pratt Inst, MFA, 77. *Work:* Phillips Collection; Mus Art, Carnegie Inst, Pittsburgh; Mus Fine Arts, Houston; Edwin A Ulrich Mus Art, Wichita, Kans; Philips Collection, Washington, DC; and others. *Exhib:* Minnesota Artists, Rochester Art Ctr, 72 & 74; Baltimore Mus Art, 75; solo exhibs, 57th St Galleries, New York; Ariz Nat Painting Exhib, Scottsdale Ctr Arts, 78; Art in Embassies, Dept State, Am Embassy, Bonn, Fed Repub Ger, 79-; Am Works on Paper: 100 Yrs of Am Art History Traveling Exhib, 83-85. *Awards:* Purchase Award, Baltimore Mus Art, 75. *Bibliog:* Ann Sargent Wooster (auth), article, Art News, 5/77; Peter Frank (auth), article, Village Voice, 1/2/78; Christa Lancaster (auth), Frank Keller: Tending the formal tradition, Arts Mag, 11/81. *Mem:* Visual Artists & Galleries Asn. *Media:* Drawing, Painting. *Publ:* Auth, Frank Keller-Paintings 1975-1981 (exhib catalog), 81. *Mailing Add:* 57 Thompson St 6A New York NY 10012

KELLER, RHODA
SCULPTOR, ASSEMBLAGE ARTIST
b Mar 31,1932, New York. *Study:* Southern Conn State Coll, BA, 63; Hofstra Univ, MA, 71. *Exhib:* Group exhibs include More Than Meets the Eye, Pace Univ Gallery, New York, 1997; Postcards from the Edge, Visual AIDS Benefit, Galerie Lelong, New York, 2003; 183rd Ann: Invitational Exhib Contemp Am Art, Nat Acad Mus, New York, 2008; Joint Assemblage/Sculpture exhib, Paris, New York, Kent Gallery, Conn, 2005; Group Painting & Sculpture, Bachalier & Cardonsky Gallery, Conn, 2005; Small Works Exhib NYU Grey Gallery, New York, 2008; Koma Terra Cotta Sculptures & Pygmy Bark Paintings, LaGuardia Community Coll, NY, 2009. *Mem:* Art Dept Coun, LaGuardia Community Coll, NY. *Media:* Mixed Media, Terra Cotta. *Publ:* Exhib Brochure essays, Koma Terra Cotta African Sculptures and Pygmy Bark Paintings, LaGuardia Community College, Long Island City, NY, 2009. *Mailing Add:* 440 E 62nd St Apt 14F New York NY 10065

KELLER, SAMUEL
MUSEUM DIRECTOR
b Basel, Switz, 1966. *Pos:* Dir, Art Basel, Switz & Art Basel Miami Beach, Fla, 2000-2007; dir, Fondation Beyeler, 2008-; chmn, Art Kunstmesse AG. *Awards:* Poder-BCG Bus Award, 2003; Medal of Honor, City of Miami Beach, 2007. *Mailing Add:* Fondation Beyeler Baselstrasse 101 Riehen Switzerland CH-4125

KELLEY, CHAPMAN
PAINTER, DEALER

b San Antonio, Tex, Aug 26, 1932. *Study:* Hugo D Pohl Art Sch, San Antonio; Trinity Univ; Pa Acad Fine Arts, with Franklin Watkins, Hobson Pittman, Walter Steumpfig, Abraham Rattner, Morris Blackburn, Julius Bloch, Harry Rosin, Francis Speight, Roswell Weidner, John McCoy, & Dr. Adah Robinson. *Work:* Mulvane Art Ctr, Topeka, Kans; Witte Mem Mus, San Antonio; Dallas Mus Fine Arts; Tex Instruments, Inc, Dallas; Colorado Springs Fine Arts Ctr; Oklahoma City Mus; Pepsi co; Frito Lay. *Exhib:* Southwestern Art Exhib, Dallas Mus Fine Arts, circulated nationally by Am Fedn Art, 57; 157th Ann Am Painting & Sculpture, Pa Acad Fine Arts, Philadelphia, 62; Childe Hassam Fund Exhib, Am Acad Arts & Lett, New York, 63; Butler Inst Am Art Midyear Shows, 64 & 66-67; 11th Midwest Biennial, Joslyn Mus, Omaha, Nebr, 70; Artists Southeast & Tex Biennial, Delgado Mus, New Orleans, 71; and many other solo & group exhibs. *Collection Arranged:* Mr. and Mrs. Joseph Hirshhorn; Elaine and WM DeKooning. *Teaching:* Pvt instr, Dallas, 57-68 & 71-83; instr painting & drawing, Dallas Mus Fine Arts, 59-67; sem instr, Northern Ill Univ, 71. *Awards:* Amer Acad Arts and Letters, 63; SJ Wallace Truman, 63; 1st Prize, Longview Mus Art, Tex, 63; Tex Ann, 60, 64; Top Purchase Award, Okla Art Ctr, 65; El Paso Mus Art Purchase Prize, Sun Carnival Nat, 69; Eight State Exhib, Okla City Mus Art. *Bibliog:* Sold out art, Life Mag, 9/20/63; article, Burlington Mag, 64. *Media:* Oil, Pastel, Watercolor. *Specialty:* Contemporary, major twentieth century and impressionist works. *Interests:* music, literature, art history. *Collection:* Twentieth century and contemporary works. *Mailing Add:* 1811 Greenville Ave #3140 Dallas TX 75206

KELLEY, DONALD CASTELL
GALLERY DIRECTOR

b Boston, Mass. *Study:* Sch of Mus Fine Arts, Boston, dipl; Yale Univ, BFA & MFA. *Work:* numerous pvt collections; Boston Public Lib; Boston Mus Fine Arts; Boston Athenaeum. *Pos:* Gallery dir, Boston Atheneum, 68-90; juror, North End, Boston, 2012; retired. *Media:* oil painting, drawing. *Specialty:* Contemporary New England Artists. *Interests:* Work of 20th century American contemporary artists and photographers. *Dealer:* D.C. Kelley; Soprafina Gallery 450 Harrison Ave Ste 55 Boston MA 02118. *Mailing Add:* 22 Oak St Charlestown MA 02129-1811

KELLEY, DONALD WILLIAM
PRINTMAKER, SCULPTOR

b Tulsa, Okla, July 20, 1939. *Study:* Univ Tulsa, with Alexandre Hogue & Duayne Hatchett, BA, 62; Claremont Grad Sch, MFA, 66; Univ NMex with Garo Antreasian, 66; Tamarind Lithography Workshop, Los Angeles, 66-69. *Work:* Los Angeles Co Mus Art, Los Angeles; Mus Mod Art, NY; Norton Simon Mus Art, Pasadena, Calif; Nat Gallery Art, Washington, DC; Univ NMex Art Mus, Albuquerque, NMex; Pub Libr Cincinnati; and others. *Exhib:* Solo exhibs, Not in NY Gallery, Cincinnati, 74, Antioch Coll, 75, Cincinnati Invitational Awards Exhib, Cincinnati Art Mus, 75, Clay Street Press Gallery, Cincinnati, 2005; Alternative Landscape, Contemp Art Ctr, Cincinnati, 72; Environ Sculpture--Proposals for Sawyer Point Park, Contemp Arts Ctr, Cincinnati, Ohio, 77; Persistent Vision, Claremont Grad Sch, 85; Six Contemp Printmakers, Suzanna Terrill Gallery, Cincinnati; 18th Korean Int Contemp Prints, Seoul, Korea, 2003; Earth: Adoration/Rarishment, Flat File Galleries, Chicago, 2004. *Collection Arranged:* Exhib cur, Pushing Boundaries: Lithographs from Nine Am Fine Art Presses. *Teaching:* Prof art, Univ Cincinnati, 69-75, currently; vis artist lithography, Antioch Col, 75; prof art, Sch Art Univ Cincinnati. *Awards:* Ohio Arts Coun Artists Project Grant, 97; Excellence Award, Ohio Arts Coun, 2008. *Bibliog:* Jules Engel & Ivan Dryer (auth), Look of a lithographer (film), Tamarind Lithography Workshop, 69; Kristin L Spangenberg (auth), Cincinnati Invitational Awards Exhibition: Drawings and Prints, Midwest Art, 3/75. *Media:* Lithography, Sculpture. *Publ:* Auth, Pushing Boundaries: Lithographs from Nine American Fine Art Presses (exhib catalog), DAAP Galleries, Univ Cincinnati, 98. *Mailing Add:* c/o Fine Arts Dept Univ Cincinnati 6335 Dept Art & Archit Cincinnati OH 45221

KELLEY, HEATHER RYAN
PAINTER, DRAFTSMAN

b New Haven, Conn, Jan 19, 1954. *Study:* Southern Methodist Univ, BFA, 75; Northwestern State Univ, MA, 84. *Work:* Univ NDak; Austin Peay State Univ, Clarksville, Tenn; Southern Methodist Univ, Dallas; Univ Maine, Presque Isle; James Joyce Ctr, Dublin, Ireland; Univ Kans, Fort Hayes; Harry Ransom Humanities Rsch Ctr, Austin, Tex; Appalachian State Univ, Boone, NC. *Comn:* Mural-scaled painting, St Patrick Hosp, Lake Charles, La, 92; devotional paintings (series), Our Lady of Lourdes Hosp, Lafayette, La. *Exhib:* solo exhib, Sum of the Parts, Hooks-Epstein Galleries, Houston, Tex, 98, James Joyce Ctr, Dublin, Ireland, 97; Mixed Media, Slidell Cult Ctr, La, 98; What is Drawing Now?, Weber State Univ, Ogden, Utah, 2000; In Celebration of James Joyce, Am Irish Historical Soc, NY, 2001; Round One, Hooks Epstein Galleries, Houston, 2002; TABOO X Portfolio - Print Gumbo, Southern Graphics Conference, 2002, Ulane Univ, 2002, Fine Arts Academy, Poznan, Poland, 2002; Nat Small Painting Exhib, Wichita Ctr for Arts, 2002; Recent Drawings, Prints and Photographs, La State Univ, Baton Rouge, 2002; 36th Nat Drawing and Small Sculpture Show, Delmar Col, Corpus Christi, Tex, 2002. *Teaching:* vis lectr art, McNeese State Univ, 82-84, asst prof, 84-90, assoc prof, 90-96, prof, 96-; Endowed prof, Col Lib Arts, 93-94, 95, 96; Jack V Noland Endowed Professorship Chair, Col Lib Arts, 2001-04. *Awards:* Distinguished Fac Award, McNeese State Univ, 87; Best of Show, 21st Ann Juried Exhib, Masur Mus, 94; Artist of the Year, Arts & Humanities Coun SW La, 97; Ind Artist Grant, La Divsn of Arts, 95; Shearman Rsch Fel, 88, 89, 91, 2000. *Mem:* Coll Art Asn; Phi Kappa Phi (South Central Artist award 2001-04). *Media:* Oil, Collage. *Res:* James Joyce's Finnegans Wake. *Specialty:* paintings, prints, mixed media works. *Dealer:* Hooks-Epstein Galleries Houston. *Mailing Add:* 821 S Division St Lake Charles LA 70601

KELLEY, LAUREN
FILMMAKER

b Baltimore, Md, 1972. *Study:* Md Inst Coll Art, BFA, 1997; Sch Art Inst Chicago, MFA, 1999. *Exhib:* group exhibs include Wig Works, DiversWorks, Houston, 2001; Burnt Fried Pulled & Curled, Hyde Park Art Ctr, Chicago, 2002; Telling our Story, Prairie State Coll, Chicago Heights, Ill, 2003; Proj Row Houses Round 21 1/2, Proj Row Houses, Houston, 2004. *Teaching:* Lectr Southwest Tex State Univ, 2000, Glassell Sch, Mus Fine Arts Houston, 2005; Art Prof, Prairie View A&M Univ, Present. *Awards:* Interdisciplinary Fel, Illinois Art Coun, Chicago, 2002; Outstanding Art Fac Mem Award, Prairie View A&M Univ, Prairie View, Tex, 2004; Altoids Award, Altoids & New Mus, 2008

KELLEY, RAMON
PAINTER

b Cheyenne, Wyo, Feb 12, 1939. *Study:* Colo Inst Art. *Work:* Santa Fe Art Mus, NMex; Marietta Col, Ohio; Mus Native Am Cult, Spokane, Wash; Tex Tech Univ Mus, Lubbock; Charles & Emma Frye Mus Fine Art. *Exhib:* Ann Exhib, Am Watercolor Soc, 71-77; Mainstreams, Marietta, Ohio, 72, 75 & 76; Allied Artists Am, 72, 73 & 74; Nat Arts Club Pastel Exhib, 74; Pastel Soc Am, 75-79; and others. *Awards:* Artists & Dealers Award, Mus Native Am Cult, 79; Mem Award Portrait, Pastel Soc Am, 79; Best of Show Medal, Kalispell Art Show & Auction, 79; and others. *Mem:* Pastel Soc Am (juror, 78), Nat Arts Club; Am Watercolor Soc (nat juror); Allied Artists Am; Pastel Soc Am. *Media:* Oil, Watercolor. *Publ:* Contribr, Am Artist Mag, 3/69 & 12/72 & Southwest Art Mag, 11/73; contribr, Joe Singer's How to Paint Figures in Pastel, Watson-Guptill, 76; coauth, Ramon Kelley Paints Portraits & Figures, Watson-Guptill, 77. *Dealer:* Canyon Rd Art Gallery 710 Canyon Rd Santa Fe NM 87501. *Mailing Add:* c/o Ventana Fine Art 400 Canyon Rd Santa Fe NM 87501-2718

KELLNER, TATANA
VISUAL ARTIST, INSTALLATION ARTIST, PHOTOGRAPHER, PRINTMAKER

b Prague, Czech, Nov 21, 1950; US Citizen. *Study:* Univ Toledo, BA, 72; Rochester Inst Technol, MFA, 74. *Work:* US Holocaust Mus, Washington, DC; Nat Mus Women Art, Washington, DC; Toledo Mus Art, Ohio; Metrop Mus Mod Art, NY; Pepsico Co, Purchase, NY; Tate Libr Collection, London; New York Pub Libr; Md Inst Art Libr; Rochester Inst Technol; Vassar College; Columbia Univ Lib, NY. *Exhib:* Retrospective, Queens Mus Bulova Ctr, NY, 91, Hartwick Col, Oneonta, NY, 94, Bloomsburg Univ, Pa, 95, Soc Contemp Photog, Kansas City, Mo, 95 & Univ Toledo, Ohio, 97; Photo Nominal 95, Forman Gallery, Jamestown, NY, 95; Between Spectacle & Silence, Photog Resource Ctr, Boston, 95; Solo Exhibs: Floating Gallery, Winnipeg, Man, Can, 96, Univ Arts, Philadelphia, 97, Marist Col, Poughkeepsie, 97 & Ft Lewis Col, Durango, Colo, 97; A Woman's Place (with catalog), Monmouth Mus, NJ, 96; Goldstrom Gallery, NY, 98; Eye Witness, Ctr for Photog, Woodstock, NY, 2000; CEPA Gallery, Buffalo, NY, 2002; Ulster Community Coll, Stone Ridge, NY, 2003; Bennington Mus, Vt, 2008; Samuel Dorsky Mus, New Paltz, NY, 2008; Albany Center Galleries, Albany, NY, 2008; Kunstler Hause Ziepelhutle, Darnstadt, Germany, 2009; Guerson Mus, 2010; Kean Univ, Union, NJ, 2009; Webster Univ, St. Louis, Mo, 2011; Samuel Dorsky Mus, New Paltz, NY; Everson Mus, 2012; Univ Mus, State Univ Coll, Albany, NY, 2012. *Pos:* Artistic dir, Women's Studio Workshop, Rosendale, NY, 74-; vis artist, Univ Southern Maine, 97. *Teaching:* Women's Studio Workshop. *Awards:* Individual Artist Fel, NY Found Arts, 92 & 96; Banff Ctr Arts, 95; Pollock-Krasner Found Grant, 2005; Puffin Found Grant, 2008. *Bibliog:* Johanna Drucker (auth), Century of Artists Books, Granary Books, 95; Nancy Miller and Jason Tougan (authors), Extremities: Trauma, Testimony, and Community, Univ Ill Press, 2002; Norah Hardin Lind (auth), In Memory: An Examination of Tatana Keller's Paired Artist Books, Fifty Years of Silence, J of Artists Books, Vol 23, Spring, 2008 ; Mary Stewart (auth), Launching the Imagination, McGraw-Hill Pub, 2010; Jean-Marc Dreyfus and Daniel Loangton (editors), The Body, in Writing the Holocaust, Bloomsbury, London, 2011. *Media:* Miscellaneous Media. *Specialty:* Monique Goldstrom. *Mailing Add:* 552 Binnewater Rd Kingston NY 12401

KELLY, ARLEEN P See Schloss, Arleen P

KELLY, ELLSWORTH
PAINTER, SCULPTOR

b Newburgh, NY, May 31, 1923. *Study:* Pratt Inst, 41-42, Hon DFA, 93; Boston Mus Sch, 46-48; Ecole Des Beaux-Arts, Paris, 48-49; Bard Col, DFA (hon); Royal Coll Art, London, Hon Dr, 97, Harvard U, 2003, Williams Coll, 2005, Brandeis U, 2013. *Work:* Metrop Mus Art, Whitney Mus Am Art, Guggenheim Mus & Mus Mod Art, NY; Art Inst of Chicago, Ill; Mus Contemp Art, Los Angeles; Stedelijk Mus, Amsterdam, Holland; Nat Gallery of Art, Washington, DC; Tate Gallery, London; Philadelphia Mus Art; St Louis Art Mus, Mo; and others. *Comn:* sculpture, Ryda & Robert H Levi Sculpture Garden, 88; painting, IM Pei, Morton H Meyerson Symphony Ctr, Dallas, Tex, 89; sculpture, Carre d'Art, Musee d'Art Contemporain, Nimes, France, 93; Tokyo Int Forum, Japan, 96; Boston Fed Courthouse, Boston, 98; and others. *Exhib:* Solo exhibs, Inst Contemp Art, Boston, 63-64, Albright-Knox Gallery, 72 & 80, Mus Mod Art, NY, 78, 90, 99, Whitney Mus Am Art, 82, 2003, Art Inst Chicago, 89, Margo Geavin Gallery, LA, 91, John Berggruen Gallery, San Francisco, 91, Paula Cooper Gallery, NY, 91, Galerie Nationale du Jeu De Paume, Paris, 92, Westfalisches Landesmuseum, Munster, Ger, 92, Matthew Marks Gallery, NY, 92, 94, 96, 98, 99 & 2001, Tate Gallery, London, 93, Metrop Mus of Art, NY, 98, Boston Univ Art Gallery, 98, New Britain Mus of Am Art, Conn, 98, Newcomb Gallery of Art, Tulane Univ, La, 98, Bemis Ctr for Contemp Art, Omaha, Nebr, 98, Fogg Art Mus, Cambridge, Mass, 99, High Mus of Art, Atlanta, 99, Art Inst Chicago, 99, Kunstmuseum Winterthur, Switz, 99 Stadtische Galerie im Lenbachhaus, Munich, Ger, 99, Mittchell-Innes & Nash Gallery, NY, 99, Dela Art Mus, Wilmington, 99, The Drawing Ctr, 2002, Mus of Contemp Art, San Diego, Calif, 2003, Matthew Marks Gallery, 2007, Middlesbrough Inst Modern Art, UK, 2010, Mus Wiesbaden, 2012;

group exhibs, Geometric Abstraction & Minimalism in Am, Solomon R Guggenheim Mus, 89; Biennial Exhib, Whitney Mus Am Art, 91; The Art of this Century, Guggenheim Mus, 92; Haus der Kunst, Munich, 96; Metrop Mus Art, NY, 98; William Hayes Fogg Art Mus, Harvard Univ, Cambridge, Mass, 98; Newcomb Gallery Art, 98; High Mus Art, 99; Art Inst Chgo, 99; Kunstmus Winterthur, 99; Stadtische Gallery, 99; Kunstmuseum Bonn, 99; Del Art Mus, 99; Smithsonian, 2000; Whitney Mus Am Art Philip Morris, 2000; San Francisco Mus Art, 2002; Phila Mus Art, 2007; MoMA, NY, 2007; Musee d'Orsay, 2008; Haus der Kunst, 2012; Mus Wiesbaden, 2012; Nat Gallery of Art, Wash DC, 2013. *Collection Arranged:* cur, Clark Art Inst, Williamstown, Mass, 2015. *Awards:* Smithsonian Inst Award, Smithsonian Inst, 99; Edward MacDowell Medal, MacDowell Colony, 99; Praemium Imperiale, Japan Art Asn, 2000; Nat Medal of Arts, Nat Endowment for the Arts, 2012; James Smithson Bicentennial Medal, 2015. *Bibliog:* Francesco Bonami (auth), Spotlight: Ellsworth Kelly, Flash Art, 3-4/93; Louis Inturrisi (auth), Tales of the Palazzo Cenci, Archit Digest, 4/93; Daniel Shapiro (auth), African Art Life, ArtNews, 5/94; and others. *Mem:* Nat Inst Arts & Lett; Fel Acad Arts and Scis; Nat Acad of Design (acad, 1994-). *Publ:* Auth, Fragmentation and the single form, Artists Choice, Mus Mod Art, NY, 90; and others. *Mailing Add:* c/o Matthew Marks Gallery 523 W 24th St New York NY 10011

KELLY, FRANKLIN WOOD
CURATOR, HISTORIAN
b Richmond, Va, June 1, 1953. *Study:* Univ NC, Chapel Hill, BA (art hist), 1974; Williams Col, Mass, Kress Fel, MA (art hist), 1979, Univ Del, Newark, PhD (art hist-outstanding dissertation), 1985. *Collection Arranged:* Problems in Connoisseurship and Conservation, Minneapolis Inst Arts, 1985; The Early Landscapes of Frederic Edwin Church (with catalog), Amon Carter Mus, 1984; Frederic Edwin Church (with catalog), Nat Gallery Art, 1989-90; Winslow Homer (with catalog), Nat Gallery Art, 1995-96. *Pos:* Cur asst, Va Mus, Richmond, 1975-77; assoc cur paintings, Minneapolis Inst Arts, 1983-85; asst cur Am art, Nat Gallery Art, Washington, DC, 1985-87, cur Am painting, 1987-88, cur Am & Brit painting, 1990-2002, sr cur Am & Brit painting, 2002-08, chief cur & dep dir, 2008-; cur collections, Corcoran Gallery of Art, Washington, DC, 1988-90. *Teaching:* Univ Md, 1990, Princeton Univ, 1991 & Univ Del, 1995; adj assoc prof, Univ Md, 1991. *Awards:* Kress Fel, Ctr Advan Study, Nat Gallery Art, Washington, 1981-83. *Mem:* Coll Art Asn. *Res:* American art, specializing on 19th century landscape painting, especially that of Frederic Edwin Church and Thomas Cole; Winslow Homer, George Bellows. *Publ:* auth, Portraits of John Durand, Antiques Mag, 82; Thomas Cole's paintings of Mount Etna, Arts in Va, 83; The Early Landscapes of Frederic Edwin Church, 87; Frederic Edwin Church & The National Landscape, 88; Frederic Edwin Church, 89. *Mailing Add:* Nat Gallery Art 2000 B S Club Dr Landover MD 20785

KELLY, JOE RAY
PAINTER
b June 11, 1934. *Comn:* 9 LaBoca Street Scenes (acrylic & oil), Piropos Restaurant, Kansas City, Mo, 2006. *Exhib:* Group exhibs, Internat Spiritual, Period Gallery, Omaha, 1999, All Media, 2000, Realism IV, 2002; Cult & Agriculture Show, New Visions Gallery, Marshfield, Wis, 2000; Best of America, Nat Oil & Acrylic Painters' Soc, 2000-2001 & 2004-2009; Perspectives on Life, Agora Gallery, New York, 2001; Juried Spring Art Show, Okla Art Guild, Oklahoma City, 2002; Nat Juried Show, Nat Society Artists, League City, Tex, 2002, Alvin, Tex, 2003; Ann Nat Juried Art Show, Texas City Festival, 2002; Mo State Fair, Sedalia, Mo, 2002; Int Art Biennale, Florence, 2003; Christ Glorified, Studio Gallery, Hays, Kans, 2003; River Market Regional Exhib, Kansas City Artists Coalition, Kansas City, Mo, 2003, Re:Members, 2003; Louisville Art Festival, Louisville, Colo, 2003; Art from the Heartland, Eldorado, Kans, 2003 & 2004; Ann Exhib, Nat Soc Painters in Casein & Acrylic, Inc, Bethlehem, Pa, 2003 & 2006; Ann Fall Exhib, Artists of Northwest Ark, Fayetteville, Ark, 2003; Visual Arts Alliance, Houston, Tex, 2004; Int Soc Acrylic Painters, Seattle, 2005, Del Ray Beach, 2006 & Santa Cruz, 2009; Girardot Nat Exhib, Arts Coun of Southeast Mo, Cape Girardeau, Mo, 2005; Nat Oil & Acrylic Painters Soc Signature Artists, Rozier Gallery, Jefferson City, Mo, 2005; Divine Feminine, Bohemian Gallery, Kansas City, Mo, 2005; NOAPS Signature Artist Invitational, Lyssa Morgan Gallery, Tampa, Fla, 2006; NSPCA Ann, Salmagundi Club, 2006-2007. *Awards:* Dir's Award, 2nd Internat Spiritual '99, Period Gallery, Omaha, 2003; People's Choice Award, Studio Gallery, Hays, Kans, 2003; 2nd Place, River Market Regional, Kansas City, 2003; 3rd Place, Mid Winter Art Fair, Kansas City, 2007. *Mem:* Int Soc Acrylic Painters (signature artist); Nat Soc Artists (signature artist); life mem Nat Oil & Acrylic Painters' Soc (signature artist, chmn bd govs); Visual Arts Alliance; Kansas City Artist Coalition; Nat Soc Painters in Casein & Acrylic, Inc. *Media:* Acrylic, Oil. *Dealer:* Northland Exposure Artists' Gallery 110 Main St Parkville MO 64152; Images Art Gallery 1520 Walnut St Kansas City MO 64108; Gallery on the Green 73 Plum St Beavercreek OH 45440. *Mailing Add:* Joes Fine Art 6 Beaconsfield Ln Bella Vista AR 72714

KELLY, KEVIN T
PAINTER
b Covington, Ky, Sept 6, 1960. *Study:* Art Acad Cincinnati, BFA (magna cum laude), 87. *Exhib:* Solo exhibs, Bruce R Lewin Gallery, New York City, NY, 95, 96, Marta Hewett Gallery, Cincinnati, Ohio, 96 & Suzanna Terrill Gallery, Cincinnati, Ohio, 99, Sex, Flames and Tracers, C-Pop Gallery, Detroit, 2001, End Games, Linda Schwartz Gallery, 2002, Mr Bad Example, Kidder-Smith Gallery, Boston, 2003, Beyond the Pale, Carnegie Arts Center, Covington, Ky, 2004, Drawings, Manifest Creative Res Gallery and Drawing Center, 2005, Stasis Quo, Dayton Art Inst, 2005; group exhibs include C Stands For..., C-Pop Gallery, Detroit, Mich, 99; Pop and Circumstance, Media Bridges, 2004; The Director Selects, Trinity Gallery, Atlanta, Ga, 2004; Skin Deep, 708 Walnut St, 2004; Carnivale d'Expose, Carnegie Visual and Performing Arts Center, 2005; Welcome Back: Alumni Invitational, Ruthe G Pearlman Gallery, Art Acad Cincinnati, 2006; Cincinnati Timeline, Phyllis Weston-Annie Bolling Galleries, 2006. *Pos:* Studio asst to Tom Wessellmann, 89-94. *Teaching:* Guest lectr, Artists Reaching Classrooms, Artworks Inc, Cincinnati, 99-2000; instr, Baker Hunt Found, Ky, 2002-; adj instr, Art Acad Cincinnati, 1998-. *Awards:* Al Smith Fel, Ky Arts Council, 2000. *Bibliog:* Lee Horvitz (auth), Kelly at Marta Hewett Gallery, Antenna Arts Mag, 8/96; William Livingstone (auth), The Current Revival of Pop Art, www.Texaco.com, 11/99; Diane Heilenman (auth), View Points: Cover Art, Louisville Courier Jour, 7/2000; Vick Prichard (auth), Postmodern Provocative: Kevin Kelly's Pop Art More Than Skin Deep, The Sunday Challenger, 2004; Sara Pearce (auth), Pop in to these must-see shows, Cincinnati Enquirer, 2005, Artist takes off on American pop culture, 2005; Ron Rollins (auth), Let's talk about sex (or not), Dayton Daily News, 2005; Jud Yalkut (auth), Sexplosion: The provocation super-graphics of Kevin T Kelly, Dayton City Paper, 2005. *Media:* Acrylic. *Publ:* contribr, Business as Usual (exhib catalog), Marta Hewitt Gallery, 92, The Big Pig Gig (exhib catalog), Cincinnati Art Mus, 2000 & New American Paintings, Vol 28, 2000; New American Paintings Vol 28, Open Studios Press, Wellesley, Ma, 2000; New American Paintings Vol 46, Open Studios Press, 2003; Stasis Quo, Dayton Art Inst, Ohio, 2005. *Dealer:* Bruce R Lewin Fine Art 136 Prince St New York NY 10012; Kidder-Smith Gallery, Boston, Mass; Trinity Gallery, Atlanta, Ga; Phyllis Weston/Annie Bolling Gallery, Cincinnati, Ohio

KELLY, MARY
CONCEPTUAL ARTIST, SCULPTOR
b Ft Dodge, Iowa, June 7, 1941. *Study:* Coll St Teresa, Minn, BA, 63; Pius XII Inst, Florence, Italy, MA, 65; St Martins Sch Art, London, 68-70. *Work:* Zurich Mus, Switz; Australian Nat Gallery, Canberra; Arts Coun Gr Brit; Tate Gallery, London, Eng; Art Gallery of Ont, Can, Vancouver Art Gallery, New Mus, NY. *Comn:* New Hall, Cambridge Univ, New Mus, NY. *Exhib:* Solo exhibs, Postmasters Gallery, NY, 89 & 93, New Mus Contemp Art, NY, 90, Vancouver Art Gallery, Can, 90, Knoll Gallery, Vienna & Budapest, 91, Mackenzie Art Gallery, Can, 92, Herbert Johnson Mus Art, Cornell Univ, 92, C Zilkha Gallery, Wesleyan Univ, 92; Barbara Toll Fine Art, NY, 90, The Decade Show, New Mus, 90; Whitney Mus Am Art, 91; Carnegie Mus Art, 92; PostMasters Gallery, NY, 93; Galleri F15, Norway; Uppsala Konst Mus, Sweden, 94; Helsingfors Stads Konst Mus, Finland, 94; and others. *Pos:* Dir studio, independent study program, Whitney Mus Am Art; dir, studios Ind Study Prog Whitney Mus Am Art, New York City, 1989-1996. *Teaching:* Vis artist & fel, New Hall Col, Cambridge Univ, England, 1985-1986; Regents lectr, Univ Calif, Los Angeles, 94-95; prof-interdisciplinary study UCLA. *Awards:* Visual Arts Fel, Nat Endowment Arts, 1987. *Bibliog:* Parveen Adams (auth), The Art of Analysis, Fall, No 58, 10/91; Emily Apter (auth), Fetishism and Visual Seduction in Mary Kelly's Interim, Fall, No 58, 10/91; Laura Mulvey (auth), Impending Time: Mary Kelly's Corpus, Lapis, 92. *Mem:* New Mus Contemp Art (adv bd); X Art Found. *Media:* Miscellaneous Media. *Publ:* Auth, Interim, New Mus Contemp Art, New York, 90; Pecunia Olet, Top Top Stories, City Lights Books, San Francisco, 91; Magiciens de la Mer(d), Art Forum, New York, 91; Gloria Patri, Wesleyan Univ, Pvt Pub, 92; Mary Kelly, Selected Writings, The MIT Press, 95. *Mailing Add:* Postmasters Gallery 54 Franklin St Ground Fl New York NY 10013

KELLY, ROBERT JAMES
PAINTER, GRAPHIC ARTIST
b Billings, Mont, 1958. *Study:* Minnesota State Univ, Moorhead, BA, 80; Sch Commun Arts, 91. *Work:* Southern Plains Indian Art Mus, Anadarko, Okla; Northern Wolf Mus, Sci Mus Minn & Smithsonian Inst, Ely. *Comn:* Wolf dance costume (with Wolf Feather Artist Cooperative), Sci Mus Minn, Ely, 83; mixed media sculpture, (with Wolf Feather Artist Cooperative), First Bank, Duluth, 84; GBW O/C painting, pvt collector, Minneapolis, 89; mapping servs O/C, pvt collector, Minneapolis, 90; three paintings, Arusa Inc, Minneapolis, 91. *Exhib:* 7th Ann Art From the Earth, Galleria, Norman, Okla, 83; Heart of the North, Raven Gallery, Edina, Minn, 84; Invitational Exhibit, Southern Plains Indian Art Mus, Anadarko, Okla, 85; Artist Soc Int Exhib, Juried, San Francisco, 87; Transmutations, Red Gallery, Minneapolis, 90. *Pos:* Mktg Communication Mgr, Emerson Control Techniques, Ellen Prairie, MN; artist-in-residence, White Earth Indian Reservation Sch, summer 1987. *Mem:* Minn Artists Asn; HTML Writers Guild; Graphic Artists Guild. *Media:* Oil on Canvas, Pastel on Paper. *Mailing Add:* 18097 Liv Ln Eden Prairie MN 55346-4108

KELM, BONNIE G
MUSEOLOGIST, ASSEMBLAGE ARTIST
b Brooklyn, NY, Mar 29, 1947. *Study:* Buffalo State Univ Coll, BS (art educ), 68; Bowling Green State Univ, MA (art hist), 75; Ohio State Univ, PhD (arts admin), 87; NY Univ, USPAP Cert, 2004. *Exhib:* Buddha Abides, Caruso Woods Gallery, Santa Barbara, Calif, 2010; Birds Feathers and Flight, The C Gallery, Los Alamos, Calif, 2011; One Foot at a Time, C Gallery, Los Alamos, Calif, 2011; Faces, Carpinterial Valley Art Coun Gallery, 2012; Black and White, Carpinteria Vallery Arts Coun Art Gallery; Oncology on Canvas, Nat Traveling Exhib Series, 2012; Cell Photography Exhib, The C Gallery, Los Alamos, Calif, 2013. *Collection Arranged:* Art in Columbus-50 Years, Columbus Mus Art, 80; Three Views from Columbus (with catalog), Arts Consortium, Cincinnati, 81; Artworks: A Tribute to Women Artists (with catalog), Columbus Cult Arts Ctr, 83; Connections: An International Exhibition of Visual Arts & Cultural Artifacts, (with catalog), Ohio State Univ Galleries, 85; Into the Mainstream: Contemporary Am Folk, Naive and Outsider Art, (with catalog), Miami Univ Art Mus, 90; Traditions, Transitions & Transformations, Yearlong Exhib Prog, 92; Collecting by Design: The Allen Collection, 94; Barbara Hershey: A Retrospective, 96; Completion of Miami Univ 3-acre sculpture park works, Nancy Holt, Richard Hunt, Mark DiSuvero & Others; Facing the Past: Portraits from the Permanent Collection, 99; Georgia O'Keeffe in Williamsburg, The Coll William & Mary (with catalog), 2001; Out of Site: Selections fron the Glazer Collection (with catalog), 2005; Roger-Brown, La Conchita: Reclaiming its Past, 2010; Barbara Chavous Memorial Retrospective, 2010; Barbara Chavous Catalogue Raisonne, 2012. *Pos:* Pres bd trustees, Columbus Inst Contemp Arts, Ohio, 77-81; founding dir, Bunte Gallery, Franklin Univ, Columbus, Ohio, 78-88; dir, Miami Univ Art Mus, Oxford, Ohio, 88-96, Muscarelle Mus Art, Coll Wm & Mary, Williamsburg, Va, 96-2002 &

Univ Art Mus, Santa Barbara, 2002-06; chair, Art in Pub Places Grant Panel, Ohio Arts Coun, 91-94; bd trustees, Ohio Mus Asn, 93-96 & US Nat Comt, Int Coun Mus, 97-2004; bd dirs, Asn Univ & Coll Mus & Galleries, 98-2006, Int Com Univ Mus, AAM Accreditation Visiting Com, 99-, & Women Beyond Borders, 2007-; advisor & appraiser, Anna C Sime Assoc, 2007-; bd dir, Maya Forest Alliance, 2007-. *Teaching:* Prof art hist, Franklin Univ, Columbus, Ohio, 76-88; vis prof art ed/admin, Ohio State Univ, Columbus, 80-83; assoc prof arts admin, Miami Univ, Oxford, Ohio, 88-96; assoc prof art & art hist, Coll William & Mary, Williamsburg, Va, 96-2002, adj prof art hist, Univ Calif, Santa Barbara; distinguished lectr, VISTAS Program, The Issues & Dilemnas of Holocaust Era Art, Mariners Mus Auditorium, 2013. *Awards:* Ohio Art League Distinguished Serv Award, 84; Outstanding Teaching award, Franklin Univ, 86; Eleanor E Gelpe Award for Arts & Cult Affairs, YWCA, 87; Fulbright Award, USIA & Neth Am Comn for Educ Exch, 88; NEH Summer Sem Fel, 92; Southeast Mus Conf Cur Award, 99; Marantz Art Education award, Ohio State Univ, 2000; Presidents Research grant, Miami Univ, 2001. *Bibliog:* Mark St. John Crickson (auth), The Daily Press, Va, 5/2002; Charles Donlan (auth), ArtScene, Santa Barbara News Press, 2/2004; Lorraine Wilson (auth), Glazer Exhibit is Out of Site, Santa Barbara News Press, 1/2005; Barney Brantingham (auth), Pride without Prejudice, Santa Barbara Independent, Calif, 2011; Evan Sherwood (auth), The Little Utopia, Ventura Star, Calif, 2011. *Mem:* Am Asn Mus; Int Coun Mus; Int Com of Modern Art; Int Found Art Rsch; Fulbright Asn; East-West Found Asn. *Media:* Jewelry, Mixed Media. *Res:* Modernist women artists; feminist art history; art & ritual; folk art. *Interests:* history of jewelry and feminine decoration in art and fashion; history of art and design. *Publ:* Contribr, Into the Mainstream: Contemporary American Folk, Naive & Outsider, Miami Univ Art Mus, 90; Aminah Robinson, Kunstforum Int, 91; Traditions, Transitions & Transitions, Visual Arts Res, 92; Museums as interpreters of culture, Arts Management, Law & Society, 93; Madge Tennent: Contested Images from Paradise (bk chap), Modernism, Gender & Culture, Garland Publ Inc, 97; Hottest Ticket in Town, Va Gazette, 2001; auth & ed, Georgia O'Keeffe in Williamsburg, 2001; Contributor, Lot:EK-MDU, 2001, Professional Procedures for Matters Related to Holocaust Era Art Museums, AAM, 2002; coauth (bk) Greater Carpinteria, Summerland & La Conchita, 2009. *Mailing Add:* PO Box 1104 Carpinteria CA 93014

KELMENSON, LITA
SCULPTOR, EDUCATOR

b Buffalo, NY, June 30, 1932. *Study:* Albright Art Sch, Cert, 53; State Univ NY, Buffalo, BS, 54; Queens Col, NY, MS, 64. *Work:* Mari Galleries of Westchester Ltd, Mamaroneck, NY; Nat Asn Women Artists Collection, Jane Voorhees Zimmerli Art Mus, Rutgers, State Univ NJ. *Exhib:* Nat Asn Women Artists Exhib, Bergen Community Mus, NJ, 83 & Monmouth Mus Fine Arts, NJ, 87; Nassau Co Mus Fine Arts, Roslyn, NY, 88; Invitational, In the Best Tradition, Heckscher Mus; Fine Arts Mus Long Island, Hempstead, NY, 91; Social Stigmas, Tribeca 148 Gallery, NY, 92; A View of One's Own, Zimmerli Art Mus, Rutgers Univ, 94; Derived from Wood, Ormond Mem Art Mus, Ormond Beach, Fla, 2003; 3Deluxe, Mason Murer Fine Art, Atlanta, 2005; Parrish Art Mus, Southampton, NY, 2005. *Pos:* Adv bd, Islip Art Mus, 76-79. *Teaching:* Vis lectr plastic sculpture, Adelphi Univ, Garden City, NY, 74; assoc prof, Hofstra Univ, Hempstead, NY, 75-76; adj prof, Nassau Community Col, Garden City, NY, assoc prof. *Awards:* Spec Award, Nassau Co Mus Fine Art, 88; Chase Manhattan Award for Works on Paper, 89; Medal Honor & Amelia Peabody Mem, Nat Asn Women Art, Amelia Peabody Estate, 90. *Bibliog:* Malcolm Preston (auth), Social commentaries, Newsday, 1/12/82; Phyllis Braff (auth), Inner concepts, outer forms, NY Times, 1/15/89; Helen Harrison (auth), Grace and intrigue highlight sculpture, NY Times, 7/9/95, Interactive Elements, 4/14/02. *Mem:* Nat Asn Women Artists; Artist-Craftsmen New York; Orgn Independent Artists. *Media:* Wood, Polyester Resin. *Publ:* Auth, A wholesome commitment, The Graphic, 82; A sense of Mexico, Spanish Today, 85, Nat Art Educ Asn J, 85; An historical perspective, NY State Art Teachers Asn J, 88; The Sculpture Ref by Arthur Williams. *Mailing Add:* 199 N Marginal Rd Jericho NY 11753

KELSEY, JOHN
DIRECTOR, WRITER

Study: Comparative Lit, student, Columbia, Univ; Film Production student, NYU. *Exhib:* Group exhibs at Whitney Biennial, Whitney Mus Am Art, 2006, 2012. *Pos:* Writing consult (films), Synthetic Pleasures, 1996; writer Artforum Mag, 2004; Co-dir, Reena Spaulings Fine Art Gallery, NYC; Permanent mem, Bernadette Corp, NYC. *Mailing Add:* Reena Spaulings Fine Art 165 E Broadway 2nd Fl New York NY 10002

KELSEY, ROBIN E
EDUCATOR

Study: Harvard Univ, PhD, 2000. *Teaching:* Asst prof, hist of art and archit Harvard Univ. *Awards:* Recipient Arthur Kingsley Porter Prize, Coll Art Assoc for essay "Viewing the Archive; Timothy Sullivan's Photogs for the Wheeler Survey, 1871-74", 2004; fel, Sterling & Francine Clark Art Inst, Williamstown, Mass, 2004. *Mailing Add:* Harvard Univ Dept Hist Art Archit Sackler Mus 485 Broadway Cambridge MA 02138

KELSO, DAVID WILLIAM
PRINTMAKER, ART DEALER

b Van Nuys, Calif, Jan 29, 1948. *Study:* Univ Calif, Riverside, BA, 69; Univ Calif, Berkeley Extension with Kathan Brown, 71. *Work:* Rutgers Arch, Zimmerli Mus, New Brunswick, NJ; US Dept of State, Washington, DC; Fine Arts Mus San Francisco; Gilkey Ctr Graphic Arts, Portland Art Mus, Ore; McNay Art Mus, San Antonio, Tex; Achenbach Found, San Francisco; Citibank, NYC; Fairmont Hotel, Chicago; Hewlett Packard, Palo Alto, Calif; Palm Inc, Sunnyvale, Calif; Adobe Systems, San Jose, Calif; Heidrick & Struggles, Singapore; Charles Schwab, Boston. *Exhib:* Folio 73, San Francisco Mus Mod Art, Calif, 73; Prints Calif, Oakland Mus, Calif, 75; Third and Sixth Hawaii Nat Print Exhib, Honolulu Acad Arts, 75 & 83; Art in Pub Places, Cheney Cowles Mem Mus, Spokane, Wash, 77; Bay Area Fine Art Presses, Walnut Creek Civic Arts Gallery, Walnut Creek, Calif, 78; Six Printmakers, San Francisco Mus Mod Art, Calif, 78; Selections from the Rutgers Arch, Grolier Club, New York, 85; Process Prints, Richmond Art Ctr, Calif, 86; Intaglio Printing in the 1980's (catalog), Zimmerli Mus, Rutgers Univ; Directions in Bay Area Printmaking: Three Decades (catalog), Palo Alto Cult Ctr, 92; Bay Area Fine Art Presses, Off of Mayor Frank Jordan, San Francisco, 93; Bay Area Prints, Amerika Haus, Stuttgart, Ger, 93; A Fifteen Yr Survey, Mulligan - Shanoski Gallery, San Francisco, 95. *Collection Arranged:* Achenbach Found, San Francisco, Calif; Citibank, New York; Fairmont Hotel, Chicago, Ill; Portland Art Mus, Oreg; Hewlett Packard, Calif; McNay Mus, Tex; US Dept State, Washington, DC. *Pos:* Founder, dir, Made in California Intaglio Press, Oakland, 80-. *Awards:* Int Print Exhib, Purchase award, Portland Art Mus, Ore, 96; Janet Turner Nat Print Competition, Hon mem, Nat Print Competition, Calif State Univ, Chico, 97; 14th Nat Exhib, Purchase Award, Los Angeles Printmaking Soc, 97. *Bibliog:* Abrams (auth), Printmaking in America: Collaborative Prints and Presses 1960-90, Northwestern Univ Press, 95. *Mem:* Graphic Arts Coun; Los Angeles Printmaking Soc. *Media:* Intaglio Printmaking. *Specialty:* Contemp intaglio prints (primarily Calif Artists). *Interests:* Bicycling; social dancing. *Publ:* Auth, Frank Lobdell: Proofing for Prints, Print Collector's Newsletter, 88; Printing Gertrude (catalog), San Francisco Mus Mod Art Rental Gallery, 96; August Francois Gay (catalog), Monterey Mus Art, 97; S Solscheck Walters (auth), The California Printmaker, 96; auth, Consuming Art, ZYZZYVA, 99; My Monterey in the etching of August Francois Gay, Noticias Monterey, Monterey Hist & Art Asn, Vol VIV, No 3, 20-50, summer 2005. *Dealer:* SFMOMA Artists Gallery Bldg A Ft Mason San Francisco CA 94123; Printworks Ltd; Dolby Chadwick San Franciso & Chicago; Dolan Maxwell Gallery. *Mailing Add:* 3246 Ettie St No 16 Oakland CA 94608

KELTNER, STEPHEN (LEE)
SCULPTOR, EDUCATOR

b Eugene, Ore, Apr 1, 1949. *Study:* Roanoke Col, Va, BFA, 72; Pratt Inst, New York, MFA, 76. *Comn:* Wall Work, Belevue Hosp, NY, 83. *Exhib:* Solo exhibs, Piedmont Gallery, Martinsville, Va, 72, Va Mus, Roanoke, 73, Dorsey Gallery, Roanoke, 74, Coll New Rochelle, NY, 94; AIR Gallery, NY, 86-87; Mus Discovery & Sci, NY, 93; Downey Mus Art, Calif, 93; Trenton City Mus, NJ, 94; Silicon Gallery, 95; Convergence IX, Providence, RI, 96; Greene Gallery, Ridgefield, Conn, 97; Anita Shapolsky Gallery, NY, 96; Fordham Univ, Ridgefield, Conn, 97; Montclair Art Mus, NJ, 97. *Teaching:* Adj prof sculpture, State Univ NY, Purchase, 86, Brooklyn Col, City Univ NY, 93- & Col New Rochelle, 94-96. *Awards:* Biennial Cert of Distinction, Va Mus, Richmond, 73; Grants, Nat Endowment Arts, Va Arts & Humanities and others, 73-80; Artist in Residence, NY State Coun Arts, 78-79. *Mem:* Sculptors Guild (vpres, 93-95, pres, 93-95); Int Sculptors Ctr. *Media:* Steel. *Mailing Add:* 109 Sterling Pl Brooklyn NY 11217

KEMENYFFY, STEVEN
CERAMIST, EDUCATOR

b Budapest, Hungary, Aug 18, 1943; US citizen. *Study:* Augustana Col, Rock Island, Ill, BA, 65; Univ Iowa, Iowa City, MA, 66, MFA, 67. *Work:* Everson Mus, Syracuse, NY; State Univ NY, Geneseo; Butler Inst Am Art, Youngstown, Ohio; Smithsonian Inst, Washington, DC; Cincinnati Art Mus, Ohio; Erie Art Mus, Pa. *Comn:* Ceramic wall murals (with Susan Kemenyffy), Rohm & Haas Pharmaceutical, Philadelphia, Pa; Kaiser Permanente Med Ctr, Irvine, Calif; Int Fur Co, Montgomery, Ala; Scott Enterprises, Erie, Pa; Penn Bank, McBrier Properties Group, Erie, Pa; and numerous pvt commissions. *Exhib:* Ceramics '70 Plus Wovenforms, Everson Mus, Syracuse; Ceramic Sculpture Invitational, Univ of NC, Chapel Hill, 77; Soup Soup, Beautiful Soup, Campbell Mus, Camden, NJ, 83; 75 Yrs of Pittsburgh Art, Its Influences, Carnegie-Mellon Univ, Pa, 85; Pattern & Decoration Contemp Approaches, Craftsman Potters Asn, London, Eng, 88; A Festival of Ceramics, Rufford Craft Ctr, Nottinghamshire, Eng, 88; Nat Ceramics 88, New Zealand Soc Potters Inc, Wellington, NZ, 88; Raku-Arts, Kansas City Contemp Art Ctr, Kansas City, Mo, 89; Exhib 280: Works OffWalls, Huntington Mus Art, WVa, 89; J M Kohler Art Ctr, Sheboygan, Wis, 90; Celebrating Clay, Miller Gallery, Cincinnati, Ohio, 90; Cent Pa Festival of the Arts Crafts Nat 24, Zoller Gallery, State Col, Pa, 90; Traveling Craft Exhib, Pittsburgh, Pa, 90; Miller Gallery, Cincinnati, Ohio, 92; Ceramics Invitational Exhib, Kipp Gallery, Ind Univ Pa, 92; Am Crafts, Cleveland, Ohio, 92; Figurative Clay, Claytrade, Portland, Ore, 92. *Teaching:* Prof Ceramics, Edinboro State Col, Pa, 69-, Edinburgh Art Col, Edinburgh, Scotland, 85, Miami Univ, Oxford Ohio, 86, San Diego Potters Guild, Calif, 87, Nat Ceramics 88, Wellington, NZ, 88, Ringling Sch Art & Design, Sarasota, Fla, 88; Int Experimental Ceramic Studio, Kecskemet, Hungary, 87, Congresso Nacional De Technicas Para Arte Ceramica, San Paulo, Brazil, 89, Phoenix Col, Ariz, 90, Bussum, Holland, 90, Fla Community Col Jacksonville S Campus, Fla, 90; Kingston, RI, 91, Walnut Creek, Calif, 91, Toronto, Ont, Can, 91, Renwick Gallery Nat Mus Am Art, Smithsonian Inst, Washington, DC, 91, Eastern Ky Univ, Lexington, 92. *Awards:* Cash Ceramic Award, Cleveland May Show, Cleveland Mus Art, 72; Nat Endowment Arts Grant, 77; Assoc Artists of Pittsburgh Ann Award, Carnegie Mus, 83. *Bibliog:* John Gibson (auth), Contemporary Pottery Decoration, Chilton Bk Co, Radnor, Pa, 87; Steve Branfman (auth), Raku, A Practical Approach, Chilton Bk, Randnor, Pa, 91; Susan Peterson (auth), The Craft & Art of Clay, Prentice Hall, Englewood Cliffs, NJ, 92. *Mem:* Nat Coun Educ Ceramic Arts; Pittsburgh Craftsman Guild; Pa Guild Craftsmen; Assoc Artists Pittsburgh. *Media:* Clay. *Dealer:* Sybil Robins Craftsman Gallery Scarsdale NY; Fenton Moore Buffalo NY. *Mailing Add:* c/o Edinboro Univ Dept Art Edinboro PA 16444

KEMENYFFY, SUSAN B HALE
ARTIST

b Springfield, Mass, Oct 4, 1941. *Study:* Syracuse Univ, New York, BFA, 63, Robert Marks; Art Students League, Arnold Blanch, Woodstock, NY; Univ Iowa, Iowa City, IA, 66, Mauricio Lasansky, MFA (with hons), 67. *Work:* Erie Art Mus, Erie, Pa; Philadelphia Mus of Art, PA; The Internat'l Cermic Mus, Kecskemet, Hungary; Everson Mus, Syracuse, NY; Smithsonian Inst, Renwick Gallery, Washington, DC;

Cincinnati Art Mus; Canton Art Inst, Ohio; Carnegie Inst Mus Art, Pittsburgh, Penn; Am Mus Ceramic Art, Pomona, Calif; Manchesters Craftmans Guild, Pittsburgh, Pa; Butler Inst Am Art, Youngstown, Oh. *Comn:* Kaiser Permanente Med Ctr, Irvine, Calif; The Tom Ridge Ctr at Presque Isle, Erie, PA; The School Dist of the City of Erie, PA; Rohm & Haas, Philadelphia, Pa; Ubukata Indust Co, Inc, Nagoya, Japan; St Vincents Hosp, Erie, Pa; Pa Governors Residence Gardens, Harrisburgh, Pa, 2005; PAWSitively Ogunquit, Pub Art Traveler, Mass, 2007; Hands, St Joseph's Chapel, Erie, Pa, 2007; Fowler Gardens, Slippery Rock, Pa, 2007-12; Garden Design Comn (restoration Victor Manor House), Lake Erie Col, Painesville, Ohio, 2008; The Carrie T Watson Linear Park Garden, Erie, Pa, 2012. *Exhib:* Ann Exhib, Assoc Artists Pittsburgh, Carnegie Mus Art, Pittsburgh, Pa, 78-82, 83-87, 88 & 90-92; Keramia Fesztival, Vigado Galeria, 97 & Nemzetkozi Szimpozium, 97, Tolgyfa Galeria, Budapest, Hungary; The Scottish Gallery Edinburgh Scotland; Rufford Craft Center, Eng; Lerchenborg Slot Kalundborg, Denmark; Hungarian Cult Inst Stuttgart, Ger; Raku-Investigations into Fire, Scottish Gallery, Edinburgh, Scotland, 2002; Tracey Contemporary Drawing Issues, Sketchbooks, Loughborough Univ Sch Art & Design, Loughborough, Leicestershire, UK, 2002, 2007, 2010; Square Root of Drawing, Temple Bar Gallery, Dublin, Ireland, 2006; 15th Mini Print Int Exhib, Roberson Mus, Binghamton, NY, 2006; Preparations: Artists' Sketchbooks & Joun, State Univ NY Brockport & Univ Tenn, 2009-2010; Botanica, Garden Club of Am Photography Exhib, Chicago, Ill, 2011; Mercyhurst Univ, Erie, Pa, 2012, 2012; 102 Associated Artists of Pittsburgh, Carnegie Mus, Henry & Elsie Hellman award, 2013. *Pos:* Chairwoman Emer, Pa Council on the Arts; chair Advisory Coun, Erie Community Found, Erie, Pa, 2005-2007; trustee, Erie Community Found, Erie, Pa, 2007-2012; Zone V Rep, Garden Club Am, Garden History & Design, Zone V Rep, 2011-2012; judge, Nat Soc Arts & Letts, Nat Print Competition, Warhol Mus, Pittsburgh, Pa, 2013. *Teaching:* Escuela Madrilena de Ceramica de la Moncloa; Edinburgh Col Arts Edinburgh, Scotland, 85; Miami Univ, Oxford, Ohio, 86; Ringling Sch Art & Des, Sarasota, Fla, 88; lectr at numerous univs and art asns, 78-98; instr Master Drawing Class, Loughborough Univ Sch Art & Design, Leicestershire, UK, 2007; Potters' Coun Symposiums (keynote speaker), Drawing is not Decoration, Indianapolis, Ind, 2008; Chautauqua Inst, Chautauqua, NY, 2010; Jefferson Educational Soc, Erie, Pa, 2010 & 2012; Masters Gardeners of Erie Co, Erie Art Mus, Erie, Pa, 2011; Artist Image Resource, Pittsburgh, Pa, 2013. *Awards:* Nat Endowment Arts Grant, 73 & 77; Assoc Artist's Pittsburgh Award, Carnegie-Mellon Mus, 81, 83 & 87; Pa Honor Roll of Women, 96; Distinguished Pennsylvanian, Gannon Univ, Erie, 01; Women Making History, Erie, PA, 2005; Award of Distinction: Kemenyffy Drawings, 13th Ann Communicator Awards, Ashand, Ky, 2007; Harriet de Wade Puckett Creativity award, 2009, 2012, Garden Club of Am, Watson Flower Show, Carrie T Trec, Erie, Pa; Pa Govs award for the Art, Artist of the Year, 2012. *Bibliog:* Susan Peterson (auth), The Craft & Art of Clay, Prentice Hall, 92, 96 & 99; Shawn Irwin Sims (auth), American Ceramics: The Female Body in Clay Form, 94; Robert Piepenburg (auth), The Spirit of Clay, A Classic Guide to Ceramics, Pebble Press, 96; Marriage of true minds, Donald Miller Premier, Pittsburgh Post-Gazette, 97; Artist of the Year, Pa Gov Award for the Arts, 2012. *Mem:* Assoc Artists Pittsburgh; Pittsburgh Craftsman Asn; Am Soc Landscape Architects (2008); Royal Horticultural Soc; The Garden Club of AM/Carrie T Watson Garden Club; Garden Conservancy; Hardy Plant Soc/Mid-Atlantic Group; Garden History Soc; Am Rose Soc; Cleveland Mus Art Print Group, Design Network, Cleveland, Oh. *Media:* Printmaking, Graphics, Landscaping. *Res:* Garden Hist of Erie Co Pa, 1910-2010. *Interests:* Landscape Design. *Publ:* Illusr, Write tough, Poems by Peggy Godfrey, Behrend Quart, Pa State Univ, 95; The Making of a Garden, Logan House, Pa, 97; Surface design, J Surface Design Mag, Vol 22, No 4, 98; The Heritage Mag; The Making of the East High Tile Mural, 2001; contrib, Painted Clay, Graphic Arts & the Ceramic Surface (by Paul Scott), A&C Black, Eng, Watson Guptill, NY, 2001; auth, Kemenyffy, A Drawing Life, Gohr Printers, Erie, Pa, 2006; Drawing-The Purpose (co-eds Leo Duff & Phil Sawdon), Essay: Landscape Drawing/Drawing Landscape, Intellect Ltd, Bristol, UK, 2007; drawing, The Purpose, Leo Duff & Phil Sawdon (co-ed), Landscape Drawing/Drawing Landscape, Intellect Ltd, Bristol, UK, 2008, Univ Chicago Press, Chicago, Ill, 2008; Too Brief Moments, Japanese Sketchbook, Swift Creek Press, Mekean, Pa, 2011; Am Soc Landscape Architects, LAND on Line Profile, 2010; Jour Print World, 2013; Jour American Theater Organ Society, 2013. *Mailing Add:* Raku Place 4570 Old State Rd McKean PA 16426

KEMP, ARNOLD JOSEPH
PAINTER
Study: Tufts Univ, Medford, Mass and Sch Mus Fine Arts, Boston BA/BFA (Eng Lit/Studio Art); Stanford Univ, MFA. *Work:* The Studio Mus Harlem; Met Mus Art, New York. *Exhib:* Solo exhibs, San Francisco African AM Hist Soc, 1991, Gallery ESP, San Francisco, 1998, Luggage Store, San Francisco, 2000, Debs & Co, New York, 2001, Quotidian Gallery, San Francisco, 2002, CCSRE, Stanford, 2004, Stephen Wirtz Gallery, San Francisco, 2006 & Portland Inst Contemp Art, Portland, 2007; Pop Life, New Langton Arts, San Francisco, 1993; Bong, Kiki, San Francisco & Alleged, New York, 1994; Obsession, Souther Exposure, 1995, San Francisco & Luscious, 1996; Stirred Not Shaken, Refusalon, San Francisco, 1997; Bottoms Up, The Lab, San Francisco, 1998; SF Drawing Show, New Image Art, Los Angeles, 2000; Freestyle, Studio Mus Harlem, New York, 2001 & Collection in Context, 2006; Rendered, Works on Paper, Sara Meltzer Gallery, New York, 2003; Un/Familiar Territory, San Jose Mus Art, 2004; I Love Music, Creative Growth Art Ctr, Oakland, 2004; Poets Theater, Calif Coll of Arts, San Francisco, 2005; Crooked Mirror, envoy, New York, 2007; A Dead Serious Group Show, Sister, Los Angeles, 2008; Hyères 2008 Festival, France. *Pos:* Assoc visual arts cur, Yerba Buena Ctr for the Arts, San Francisco, 1003-2003; chair, Master in Fine Arts in Visual Studies Program, Pacific Northwest Coll Art. *Awards:* Acad Am Poets Prize, 1989; Tufts Univ Poetry Prize, 1991; Pen Writers Grant, 1993; The ArtCoun Grant, 2001; Fel, Joan Mitchell Found, 2001; Pollock Krasner Found Grant, 2003; Art Matters Found Grant, 2009. *Bibliog:* David Bonetti (auth), Kemp: An artist unmasks the past, San Francisco Examiner, 3/1997; Amy Berk (auth), Arnold Kemp at ESP, Art in Am, 6/1998; David Horton (auth), Color Theory at the Luggage Store, Artweek, 9/2000; Jason Schmidt (auth), The New Masters, Vibe, 5/2001; holland Cotter (auth), Arnold J Kemp, NY Times, 11/2001; Jesse Hamlin (auth), A necessary labor of art, San Francisco Chronicle, 9/2002. *Media:* Acrylic, Oil, Watercolor. *Mailing Add:* c/o PDX Contemp Art 925 NW Flanders Portland OR 97206

KEMP, FLO
PRINTMAKING
b Oct 21, 1941. *Study:* Montclair State Coll, NJ, BA, 63; Hofstra Univ, NY, MA, 73. *Work:* Securities Exchange Comn, Manhattan Savings Bank, NY; United Jersey Bank, NJ; Mikasa, Tokyo; Art in Embassy Program, US State Dept, Taipei; Stony Brook Sch Med, NY. *Comn:* Seiskeya Ballet Prog Cover, Seiskeya Ballet Studios, St James, NY; Gurneys Resorts Etching, Gurney's Inc, Montauk, NY; holiday cover, Herald, 95. *Exhib:* Marbella Art Gallery Exhib, NY, 91; Local Color, Northport Galleries, Northport, NY, 95; The Environment, Elaine Benson Gallery, Bridgehampton, NY, 95, 96; print travel show, Nat Asn Women Artists, 98; Catharine Lorillard Wolfe Ann Exhib, 2000 & 2008; CW Post Traveling Exhib, Gallery North, Setauket, NY, 2000-2008. *Pos:* chmn, Neighborhood Artists, 82-2006; Vpres, Northport Galleries, NY, 88-90; chmn, Nat Travel Print Exhib, Nat Asn Women Artists, 90-92, asst chmn, 95-96; bd dirs, Catharine Lorillard Wolfe Art Club, 2008. *Awards:* Landscape Award, Wash Sq, New York, 98; Nat Asn Women Artists Graphics Award, Los Olas Mus, Fla, 97; 1st in Graphics Award, Mystic Art Festival, 2000; Best in Show, Ann Arbor, 2000; First in Graphics, Rittenhouse Sq Art Festival, Philadelphia, 2003; Best of Category, Duneiden Festival Art, Fla, 2003-04; Graphics award, Festival of Masters, Disney, Fla, 2009; 1st in Graphics, Artigrass, Jupiter, Fla, 2013; Woman of Yr in Arts, Village Times Beacon, 2012. *Bibliog:* Village Tunes, 96; Improper North Shoran, 2008. *Mem:* Nat Asn Women Artists; Art League of Long Island; Nat Asn Independent Artists; Catharine Lorillard Wolfe Art Club; Smithsonian Arts Council. *Media:* Etching. *Collection:* Mikasa, Japan. *Publ:* Three Village Herald, 92; Cover, J Forestry, 2/2001. *Mailing Add:* Box 2202 Setauket NY 11733

KEMP, JANE
LIBRARIAN, EDUCATOR
b Davenport, Iowa, Apr 10, 1944. *Study:* Univ Iowa, BA, 66; Univ Pittsburgh, MLS, 71. *Collection Arranged:* Coll Fine Arts Collection Ann Exhib; Gerhard Marcks Centenary (auth, catalog), 89; Marguerite Wildenhain: Her Life & Works (auth, catalog), 96; Pond Farm Collection (auth, catalog), 2003. *Pos:* Supervisor, Fine Arts Collection, Luther Col, 81-2010, spec collections librn, 97-2010, libr dir, 2004-2010. *Teaching:* Prof bibliog instr, Luther Col, 81-, prof art collections care, 90-; prof, Paideia Prog (interdisciplinary Eng/Hist), 2004-2011. *Mem:* Am Libr Asn, Arts Section; Asn Coll & Res Libr; Asn Coll & Univ Mus & Galleries; Iowa Mus Asn. *Res:* Academic art collection management; research on artists represented in college fine arts collections. *Interests:* Art collection registration methods; art conservation techniques; art collection promotion ideas. *Publ:* Auth, Bibliography in Kath, Ruth, The Letters of Gerhard Marcks & Marquerite Wildenhain, Iowa State Univ Press, 91; Art in the Library, J Acad Librarianship, 94; coauth, Displays & Exhibits in College Libraries, Am Libr Asn, 97; principal auth, Fine Arts Collection website, http://finearts.luther.edu

KEMP, PAUL ZANE
EDUCATOR, SCULPTOR
b Apache Creek, NMex, Nov 6, 1928. *Study:* NMex Highlands Univ, BA, 50, MA, 54; Cranbrook Acad Art, MFA, 60. *Comn:* Oil portrait, Murray Watson, 2002; sheet copper sculpture, Christ with Dove, 1st Presbyterian Church, Waco, Tex, 2005. *Exhib:* Tex Fine Arts Asn Ann Citation Show, Austin, 69 & 70; 8th Baytown Ann, Tex, 74; Metals Invitational Show, 81 & Blue Bonnets and Other Flora, 86, Cult Activities Ctr, Temple, Tex; The Art Ctr Cent Tex Biennial, Waco, Tex, 89; retrospective, Baylor Univ, Waco, Tex, 93; and others. *Teaching:* Asst prof art, Baylor Univ, 61-64, assoc prof, 64-69, prof, 69-96 (retired). *Awards:* Jurors Choice, Tex Fine Arts Asn Citation Show, 69 & 70; Purchase Entry, Ark Art Ctr, 69; Cash Award, 8th Baytown Ann, 74. *Media:* Sheet Metal, Miscellaneous Media. *Publ:* Contribr & illusr, Tex Trends Art Educ, spring 69. *Mailing Add:* 14200 Wagner Dr Waco TX 76712-9645

KEMP, SUE
PAINTER, INSTRUCTOR
b Dallas, Tex, May 21, 1946. *Study:* Univ N Tex, BS (educ), 67, M Educ, 72; studied with M Douglas Walton, La Tech Univ, 86-87. *Work:* Seton Hospital, Austin, Tex. *Exhib:* Tex Watercolor Soc, Rockport Ctr Arts, Rockport, Tex, 2001; Southwestern Watercolor Soc, Northpark Ctr, Dallas, Tex, 2003, Plano Art Ctr, Plano Tex, 2009; Louisiana Watercolor Soc, New Orleans, 2011-2012; Tex Watercolor Soc, 2012; San Antonio Art League; Western Federation of Watercolor Societies, Ariz, 2014. *Pos:* pres, Tex Watercolor Soc, 2011-2013. *Teaching:* faculty, Contemporary Austin/Art Sch, Austin, Tex. *Awards:* First place in watercolor, 7th Annual Wildlife Exhib, 2008; Merit Award, Waterloo Watercolor Group, 2008; 1st place, Tex Watercolor Soc Mem Show, 2011; 2nd place, Waterloo Watercolor Show, 2011; Phillips Memorial award, Waterloo Watercolor Show, 2012. *Bibliog:* Mark Mitchell (auth), A Teacher's Journey, Watercolor Mag, summer 2003. *Mem:* Waterloo Watercolor Group (pres, 97); Soc Children's Books Writers & Illustrators, 2008-09; Captiol Art Soc (secy, 2008); Southwestern Watercolor Soc (signature mem); Tex Watercolor Soc (signature mem). *Media:* Watercolor. *Publ:* contribr, Encyclopedia of Watercolor Landscape Techniques, Quarto Publ, London, 97; illustr, Sick Bay, Astoria Productions, 98; contribr, Painting Great Pictures from Photographs, Quarto Publ, 99; contribr, Splash: A Celebration of Light, North Light Books, 2002; illustr, A Night in Old San Antonio posters, San Antonio Conserv Soc, 2001, 2007; Wildflower Days (poster), Lady Bird Johnson Wildflower Ctr, Austin, Tex, 2007

KEMPE, RICHARD JOSEPH
COLLECTOR, CURATOR
b New York, NY, Oct 28, 1922. *Study:* New York Univ, BS, 47; PhD, 53; Univ Oslo, cert, 48. *Collection Arranged:* Metrop Young Artists Show, Nat Arts Club, 58 & 59; Sch Paris Exhib, Nat Arts Club, 63; Books and Graphics of the Cobra Artists, City Gallery, NY City Dept Cult Affairs, 86. *Pos:* UN Delegate to World Conf on Intellectual Property (WIPO), Stockholm, 67. *Mem:* Centro De Artes Creativas, De Cuernava, Calif. *Interests:* Modern and contemporary art, collection also contains extensive group of artists' books, currently emphasizing artwork of young Mexican artists. *Publ:* Ed, Cobra Prints Cobra Books, Franklin Furnace Arch Inc, 86; contribr, Hendrik Glintenkamp: un debujante norteamericano en Mexico, 1917-1920, Inst Nac de Bellas Artes, Mexico, 87. *Mailing Add:* Rio Lerma 156-502 Mexico 06500 Mexico

KEMPER, RUFUS CROSBY & MARY BARTON STRIPP
COLLECTOR
b Rufus: Kansas City, Mo, Feb 22, 1927. *Study:* Phillips Acad, Andover, Mass, 42; Univ Mo; Beta Theta Pi. *Hon Degrees:* LLD (hon), William Jewel Col, 1976; DFA (hon), Westminster Col, 1983. *Pos:* Joined, City Nat Bank & Trust Co (now UMB Financial Corp), Kansas City, 50; exec vpres, UMB Financial Corp, 57-59, pres, 59-71, chmn & Chief Exec Officer, 71-2000; sr chmn, UMB Financial Corp & UMB Bank, 2000-2004; retired, 2004; hon trustee, Thomas Jefferson Found; mem nat comt Whitney Mus Am Art, New York City; comnr Nat Mus Am Art, Wash; founder, chmn bd trustees, The Kemper Mus Contemp Art, Kansas City, 94-; trustee, Kemper family found; founder, mem bd dir, The Agriculture Future of Am, 96-. *Awards:* Recipient Key Man Kansas City Jr CofC, 52; Distinguished Serv, 64; Man of Yr Award, Kansas City Press Club, 74; Outstanding Kans Citian Award Native Sons Kansas City, 75, 82; 1st Advocacy Award Mid-Continent Small Bus Asn, 80; Banker Adv of Yr Award, Small Bus Admin, 81; Lester Milgram Humanitarian Award, 82, Man of Yr Award Downtown, Inc, 82, Pirouette Award Kansas City Ballet Guild and Kansas City Tomorrow Alumni Asn, 83; fac Alumni Award Univ Mo Columbia Alumni Asn, 82; Mo Arts Coun Award, 84; Kansas City Chancellor's Medal Univ Mo, 84; Distinguished Serv Award St Paul Sch Theology, 87; Advocacy Award Mo Citizens for the Arts, 87; Outstanding Patron of Excellence in the Arts & Archit Am Inst Archit - Kansas City, 94; VIP Leadership Award Centurions Leadership Prog Greater Kansas City CofC, 95; Kans Citian of Yr, 97; named one of Top 200 Collectors ARTnews Mag, 2004. *Mem:* Am Royal Asn (vpres, bd dir, currently); Clubs: River, Carriage, Kansas City Country, Kansas City, 1021, Mo, Chatham, Mass, Garden of the Gods, Cheyenne Mountain Country (Colorado Springs, Colo). *Interests:* Sailing, tennis, horseback riding & raising cattle. *Collection:* Old Masters, Modern & Contemporary Art

KEMPINAS, ZILVINAS
INSTALLATION SCULPTOR
b Plunge, Lithuania, 1969. *Study:* Vilnius Art Acad, BFA (Painting), 1993; Hunter Coll, City Univ NY, MFA (Combined Media), 2002. *Exhib:* Solo exhibs include Contemp Art Ctr, Vilnius, Lithuania, 1994, 2007, Jutempus Gallery, Vilnius, 1996, The New Year of King Nebuchadnezzar, Vilnius, 1996, PS1 Contemp Art Ctr, Long Island City, NY, 2004, Spencer Brownstone Gallery, New York, 2004, 2006, 2007, Palais de Tokyo, Paris, 2006, Kunsthalle Vienna, 2008; group exhibs include Advent Bunch, Contemp Art Ctr, Vilnius, 1992, Good Evils, 1992, For Beauty, 1994, Art in Lithuania, 1994, After Painting, 1998, Lithuanian Art 1989-1999, 1999; Whale's Stomach installation, Vilnius, 1995; Holy Lie press proj, Vilnius, 1996; Footnotes, Reykjavik Munic Art Mus, Iceland, 1997; Prague Quadrennial, Czech Republic, 1999; Drawings/Works with Paper, Spencer Brownstone Gallery, New York, 2005, Red, White, Blue, 2005; The Last Seduction: A Welcome Surrender to Beauty, Carrie Secrist Gallery, Chicago, 2007; New Work, San Francisco Mus Mod Art, 2008. *Dealer:* Spencer Brownstone Gallery 39 Wooster St New York NY 10013

KEMPNER, HELEN HILL
COLLECTOR, PATRON
b Houston, Tex, Jan 30, 1938. *Pos:* Bd trustees, Contemp Arts Mus, Houston, 77-, vpres, 77-78, secy, 78-79, pres, 79-. *Collection:* Contemporary paintings and sculpture; primitive, mostly African art

KENDALL, THOMAS LYLE
CERAMIST, ADMINISTRATOR
b St Louis, Mo, 1949. *Study:* Ill State Univ, BS, 71, MS, 73. *Work:* Ill State Univ, Normal; Kalamazoo Inst Arts, Mich; Mich Arts Coun, Lansing; Cooper Hewitt, NY. *Comn:* Large scale out door sculptures, Battle Creek, Mich, 89; Large scale sundial sculpture, Kalamazoo, Mich, 2000. *Exhib:* Columbus Mus Art, Ohio, 75 & 79; Marietta Col, Ohio, 78; Raku V-Nat, Peters Valley, NJ, 79; solo exhib, Craft Alliance Gallery, St Louis, Mo, 81; Mich Ceramics, 83; Functional Ceramics Invitational, St Louis, 85; Wooster Col, 86; Karen Kendall Gallery, 89; Kalamazoo Inst Arts, 94; Carnagy Ctr Art, 94; Diversity in Clay, Muskegon, Mich, 2000. *Collection Arranged:* Contemporary Ceramics: The Artist's Viewpoint (auth, catalog), 77. *Pos:* Dir, Sch Kalamazoo Inst Arts, 83-96, fac, 73-96; exec dir, Hand Workshop Art Ctr, 96. *Teaching:* Chmn, Dept Ceramics, Kalamazoo Inst Arts, Mich, 73-96; vis fac ceramics, Kalamazoo Col, 84-86, 94-96 & 98-99; vis artist, Penland Sch Crafts, 81 & 84 & ceramics, Truro Art Ctr, 83 & 84; instr ceramics, SIAS Western Mich Univ, 87-96. *Awards:* First Place, Battle Creek Craft Biennial, 79; Purchase Award, Kalamazoo Art Competition, 83; Cash Award, Mich Ceramics, 83, Kalamazoo Arts Festival, 99; Functional Ceramics Nat Exhib award. *Mem:* Nat Conf Educ Ceramic Arts; Am Crafts Coun. *Media:* Clay. *Publ:* Auth, Computerized glass calculation, Ceramics Monthly, 12/83. *Dealer:* Synchronicity Glen Arbor MI. *Mailing Add:* 10936 Three Mile Rd Plainwell MI 49080

KENNA, MICHAEL
PHOTOGRAPHER
b Widnes, Cheshire, Eng, Nov, 20, 1953. *Study:* Upholland Col, Lancashire, Eng, 65-72; Banbury Sch Art, Oxfordshire, 72-73; Coll Printing, London, HND Distinction, 73-76. *Work:* Australian Nat Gallery, Canberra; Bibliotheque Nationale, Paris, France; San Francisco Mus Mod Art; Fox Talbot Mus, Lacock, Eng; Milwaukee Art Mus; Victoria & Albert Mus, London. *Exhib:* Arbres, Georges Pompidou Ctr, Paris, France, 82; solo exhibs, Fox Talbot Mus, Lacock, Wiltshire, Eng, 83 & Bampton Arts Ctr, Oxfordshire, 84; 20th Century Photographs, Honolulu Acad Arts, Hawaii, 84; Madison Art Ctr, Wis, 85; Chateau d'Eau Mus, Toulouse, France, 86; Nicephore Niepce Mus, Chalon-Sur-Saone, France, 86; Gallery Min, Tokyo, Japan; Photographers Gallery, London, 87; Mus Ludwig, Cologne & Kunstverein Gottingen, Fed Repub Ger, 87. *Teaching:* Friends of Photography, San Francisco, Calif. *Awards:* Friends of Imogene Cunningham Award, San Francisco, Calif, 81; KQED/Zellerbach Award, San Francisco, Calif, 81. *Bibliog:* Jean Francois Chevrier (auth), Michael Kenna: Photographs, Stephen Wirtz Gallery & Weston Gallery, 84. *Publ:* Michael Kenna 1975-1987 (exhib catalog), Gallery Min, Tokyo, Japan; Michael Kenna - Night Walk, San Francisco Friends of Photography. *Mailing Add:* c/o Weston Gallery PO Box 655 Carmel CA 93921

KENNEDY, BRIAN P
MUSEUM DIRECTOR
b Dublin, Ireland, Nov 5, 1961. *Study:* Univ Coll, Dublin, Ireland, BA (history of art), 1982, MA, 1985, PhD, 1989. *Pos:* Irish Dept Educ, 1982; European Comn, Brussels, 1983; Chester Beatty Libr, Ireland, 1983-85; Gov Publ Office, Ireland, 1985-86; Dept Finance, Ireland, 1986-89; asst dir, Nat Gallery Ireland, 1989-1997; dir, Nat Gallery Australia, Canberra, Australia, 1997-2004, Hood Mus Art, Dartmouth Coll, Hanover, NH, 2005-10, Toledo Mus Art, Ohio, 2010-. *Teaching:* Adj Prof, art hist, Dartmouth Coll, Hamilton, NH, 2007. *Awards:* Australian Century of Federation Medal (serv to Australian Soc & its art). *Mem:* Irish Asn Art Historians, 1996-97; Coun Australian Art Mus Dirs (chair, 2001-03); Asn Art Mus Dirs; Am Asn Mus; Int Asn Art Critics. *Publ:* Auth, editor, Alfred Chester Beatty and Ireland 1950-1968: A Study in Cultural Politics, Glendale Press, 1988; Auth, editor, Dreams and Responsibilities: The State and Arts in Independent Ireland, Arts Coun of Ireland, 1990; Auth, editor, Jack B Yeats: Jack Butler Yeats, 1871-1957 (Lives of Irish Artists), Unipub, 10/1991; The Anatomy Lesson: Art and Medicine, Nat Gallery of Ireland, 1/1992; Irish Painting, Robert Rinehart Publs, 1994; Sean Scully: The Art of the Stripe, Hood Mus Art, 10/2008. *Mailing Add:* Toledo Museum of Art 2445 Monroe St Toledo OH 43620

KENNEDY, GENE (EUGENE) MURRAY
PHOTOGRAPHER, EDUCATOR
b San Diego, Calif, Mar 13, 1946. *Study:* San Diego State Univ, BA, 69, MA, 76. *Work:* Mus Mod Art, NY; Cent Wash Univ; San Diego Natural Hist Mus & San Diego State Univ, San Diego; Hallmark Contemp Collection, Kansas City; Calif State Libr. *Exhib:* Solo exhibs, Moore Coll Art, 83 & 89, San Diego Nat Hist Mus, 83, Lightwork Gallery, Sacramento, 86, 87 & 89, Northern Ill Univ, 87, Univ Calif Exten, 88, Univ the Pacific, 88; Group exhibs, San Francisco Camerawork, 83, Purdue Univ, W Lafayette, 85, Mus Contemp Photog, 85; View Point Gallery, Sacramento, 94; Univ Pacific, Stockton, 94; and others. *Collection Arranged:* Robert Bechtle: Reference and Realism in Four Modes, 78, Fletcher Benton Sculpture, 79 & Helen Levitt: Color Photographs, 80, Tom Holland: Works from 1969-1979, 80, Manuel Neri: Twenty Years, 81 & Helen Shirk: Metalwork, 81, Grossmont Coll Gallery, El Cajon, Calif. *Pos:* Dir, Art Gallery Grossmont Col, 73-81; The Darkroom, Sacramento, 86-. *Teaching:* Instr photog, San Diego State Univ, 70-73, Grossmont Col, El Cajon, Calif, 72-81, Univ Calif, San Diego, 82-83, Maine Photographic Workshops, 82; Univ The Pacific, 87-88; Univ Calif, Davis, 89; Sierra Col, Rocklin, Calif, 89-91; Cosumnes River Col, Sacramento, 90-91. *Awards:* Spec Award of Excellence, Moore Coll Art, 83; Nat Endowment Arts Grant, 84. *Bibliog:* Portfolio: Photographs by Gene Kennedy, J Am Photog, 3/85; Jan Haag (auth), Gene Kennedy: Ravaged Landscapes, View Camera Mag, 3/89; Gary F Kurutz (auth), Violations of the Landscape: The California Photography of Gene Kennedy, Calif State Libr Found Bull, 7/90. *Mem:* Soc Photographic Educ; Friends of Photog. *Media:* Photography. *Publ:* Ed, Garry Winogrand, 76, ed & illusr, Carol Shaw-Sutton: Crossing Over, 78, Viewpoint: Ceramics 78 & 79, 78 & 79 & ed, Helen Levitt: Color Photographs, 80, Grossmont Coll Publ. *Dealer:* The Darkroom 708 57th St Sacramento CA 95819

KENNEDY, JAMES EDWARD
PAINTER, SCULPTOR
b Jackson, Miss, Sept 30, 1933. *Study:* Ala State Univ, BS; Ind Univ, MAT (painting); Spring Hill Col. *Work:* Johnson Publ Co Collection, Chicago. *Exhib:* Atlanta Univ Nat Exhib, 60-64; Eastern Shore Art Gallery, 67; Birmingham, Ala Festival Arts Centennial Exhib, 72; Ala State Univ, 72; Univ WFla, 73. *Teaching:* Prof art hist & painting, Univ S Ala, Mobile, 68-, chmn dept art, currently; guest instr Afro-Am art, Morehead State Univ, Minn, summer 72. *Awards:* Afro-Am Art Slide Grant, 69 & Ethnic-Am Minority Art Slide Libr Grant, 71, Samuel H Kress Found. *Bibliog:* Afro-American Artists, Boston Pub Libr, 73. *Mem:* Nat Conf Artists; Coll Art Asn Am. *Publ:* Coauth, An Afro-American Slide Project, Art J, 70-71 & An Afro-American Art and Artist's Finders Index, Am Revolution Bicentennial Comn, Washington, DC, 73. *Mailing Add:* 5408 Gaillard Dr Mobile AL 36608-2532

KENNEDY, MARLA HAMBURG
ART DEALER, CURATOR
b Newark, NJ, Jan 3, 1961. *Study:* Art Students League, 1978; Barnard Col, Columbia Univ, BA (summa cum laude), 1983. *Collection Arranged:* Terrae Motus, Naples, Italy, 1986; A Decade of Contemporary Painting, Tokyo, 1993; A History of Landscape Photography, Los Angeles, 1994; Kissing, 1995; Wedding Days, 1996. *Pos:* Dir's assoc, PSI Inst Art & Urban Resources, New York, 1985-86; assoc dir, Galerie Lucio Amelio, Naples, Italy, 1985-89; dir, Richard Green Gallery, Los Angeles, 1989-92, Angles Gallery, Los Angeles, 1992-94, G Ray Hawkins Gallery,

Los Angeles, 1993-96, Howard Greenberg Gallery, New York, 1996; vpres, Onview.com; partner, Kennedy Boesky Photographs, Chelsea, NY; owner, Hamburg Kennedy Photographs, NY City, 2002, Picture This Publ. *Specialty:* Photography, vintage and contemporary. *Publ:* Coauth, Terrae Motus, Motta, 1985; The Nude and Nobuyoshi Araki, H2O Ltd, 1994; Kissing, H2O Ltd/Graystone, 1995; Wedding Days, H2O Ltd, 1996. *Mailing Add:* 54 Stone St Apt 2 New York NY 10004

KENNEDY, ROBYN L
GALLERY DIRECTOR
Collection Arranged: Designer, Star-Spangled Presidents: Portraits by Liza Lou, Renwick Gallery, 2000, The Furniture of Sam Maloof, 2001, George Catlin and His Indian Gallery, 2002, Light Screens: The Leaded Glass of Frank Lloyd Wright, 2003, Right at Home: American Studio Furniture, 2004, High Fiber, 2005, Ruth Duckwork: Modernist Sculptor, 2006 & Going West! Quilts and Community, 2007. *Pos:* With Smithsonian Am Art Mus, Washington, 1980-, designer, formerly, interim chief, Renwick Gallery, 2003-04, chief, Renwick Gallery, 2004-. *Mailing Add:* Renwick Gallery Smithsonian Am Art Mus MRC 510 PO Box 37012 Washington DC 20013-7012

KENNEY, DOUGLAS
CERAMIST, CLAY SCULPTOR
b San Diego, Calif, 1962. *Study:* San Diego Mesa Col, AA, 83; San Diego State Univ, BFA, 85; Rochester Inst Technol, Scholar, 87, MFA (ceramics), 89. *Comn:* Three custom relief tile disks on plywood, comn by Carole Kraus, 92. *Exhib:* solo exhibs, Creative Arts Gallery, San Antonio, 92, Gallery Authentique, Roslyn, 93, Santa Fe Connection, Tex, 95, Artables Gallery, Houston, 95, Cube Gallery, Shigaraki, Japan, 96, Funaoka Gallery, Otsu, Japan, 96 & Gallery Tao, Tokyo, Japan, 96; US Artists 93, Native to Neon, Philadelphia, 93; Galveston Arts Ctr, Tex, 94; Clay for the Wall, Salt Lake City Art Ctr, 95; RIT Alumni Exhib, NCECA, Rochester, 96; Exhib of Works Born at the Park, Shigaraki Ceramic Cult Park Mus, 96; Six Shigaraki Artists, Shiga Ikeda Cult Ctr Hall, Otsu City, Japan, 96; Five Int Ceramic Artists, La Galerie Art Present, Paris, France, 96; To Art Space, Seoul, Korea, 97; Gallery 500, Elkons Park, Pa, 97; Mind's Eye Gallery, Scottsdale, Ariz, 99; Art Inc Gallery, San Antonio, Tex, 99. *Teaching:* Instr ceramics, San Antonio Col, 89-95; guest lectr, Univ Calif-Davis, 90; guest lectr/workshop, Univ Tex, San Antonio, 91, Jingdezhen Porcelain Sculpture Factory, China, 93, Jewish Community Ctr, San Antonio, 93, SW Tex State Univ & Galveston Col, 94; Artist-in-residence, Shigaraki Ceramic Cult Park, Japan, 95-96. *Awards:* Patron Purchase Award, Wichita Nat, 88; Wallace Mem Libr Purchase Award, 89. *Bibliog:* Karen Robin (auth), Douglas Kenney-Geometric Perspectives, Ceramics & Art Perception No 18, 94; Joy Onozuka (auth), Just spinning his wheels, Tokyo Daily Yomuri English Newspaper, 2/16/96; review, Asahi Daily Newspaper, 2/16/96; Karen Robin (auth), Geometric Perspectives, feature art, Ceramics: Art & Perception, No 18, pgs 51-53, 12/94. *Mem:* Coll Art Asn; Am Craft Coun; Nat Coun Educ Ceramic Arts. *Media:* Clay; Enamel on Metal. *Publ:* Am Craft, Gallery Sect, B/W photo, 12/89, 1/90 & 8-9/92; Art Calendar Mag, B/W cover photo & statement, 12/90; Raku: A Practical Approach, B/W photo & statement, Chilton Bk Co, 91; Raku Integrations, Ceramics Mo, 6-8/91; color photog, Deco Deco, Japanese Interior Design Mag, 2/92; Airbrush Action, article (6 pages w/color photos), 98. *Mailing Add:* 700 Bond Ave Santa Barbara CA 93103

KENNEY, ESTELLE KOVAL
ART THERAPIST, PAINTER
b Chicago, Ill, Feb 15, 1928. *Study:* Sch Art Inst Chicago, with Joshua Kind, BFA, 76, MFA, 78; registered art therapist, ATR; Chicago Inst Psychoanalysis, TEP grad, 78; Loyola Univ Chicago, 82-. *Work:* Ill State Mus, Springfield; Union League Club Chicago. *Exhib:* The Chicago Connection, traveling, 76-77; Contemp Issues--Works on Paper by Women, Woman's Bldg, Los Angeles, plus others, 77-78; solo show, Renaissance Soc, Bergman Gallery, Univ Chicago, 80; Navy Pier, Chicago, 80; Artists Urban Gateways, 81; and others. *Pos:* Art therapist, Grove Sch Handicapped, Lake Forest, Ill, 72-77, New Triar E & C, Spec Educ, Winnetka, Ill, 77-78, Cove Sch Learning Disabled, Evanston, Ill, 79-81 & North Shore Inst Therapy through Arts, Winnetka, Ill, 79-81; contrib ed, Format Mag, 78-. *Teaching:* Art therapy lectr, Univ Ill Circle Campus, Chicago, 77 & Nat Col Educ, Evanston, Ill, 77; dir art therapy prog, Loyola Univ Chicago, 81-. *Awards:* First Purchase Prize, Union League Club of Chicago, 74 & Ill State Mus, Springfield, 75. *Mem:* Ill Art Educ Asn; Nat Art Educ Asn; Am Art Therapy Asn; Ill Art Therapy Asn (pres). *Media:* Enamel, Watercolor. *Publ:* Auth, Joshua Kind: Naive painting in Illinois, Format Mag. *Dealer:* Sonia Zaks Gallery 620 North Michigan Ave Chicago IL 60611. *Mailing Add:* 3830 N Clark St Chicago IL 60613

KENNINGTON, DALE
PAINTER
b Savannah, Ga, Jan 24, 1935. *Study:* Huntington Coll, Montgomery, Ala, BA; Univ Ala, BA (art), 57; Auburn Univ, post-grad. *Work:* Butler Inst Am Art, Youngstown, Ohio; Columbus Mus Art, Ga; Cheekwood Mus Art, Nashville, Tenn; Mobile Mus Art, Ala; Maitland Art Ctr, Fla; Chattahoochee Valley Art Mus, LaGrange, Ga; Huntsville Mus Art, Ala; Jule Collins Smith Mus Fine Art, Auburn Univ, Ala; Montgomery Mus Fine Arts, Ala; Belk Visual Arts Ctr, Davidson Coll, NC; Wiregrass Mus Art, Dothan, Ala; Paul & Lulu Hilliard Univ Art Mus, Univ La, Lafayette, La; Mennello Mus, Orlando, Fla; Birmingham Mus Art, Birmingham, Ala; Smithsonian Am Art Mus, Washington, DC; Mason Scharfenstein Mus Art, Piedmont Coll, Demorest, Ga. *Exhib:* Huntsville Mus Art, Ala, 98; Hunter Mus Am Art, Chattanooga, Tenn, 99; Columbus Mus, Ga, 99; Nat Mus Women Arts, Washington, DC, 2000; Butler Inst Am Art, Youngstown, Ohio, 2001; Birmingham Mus Art, Ala, 2002; Montgomery Mus Fine Arts, Ala, 2004; Wiregrass Mus Art, Dothan, Ala, 2004 & 2008; Mobile Mus Art, Ala, 2005; Jule Collins Smith Mus Fine Art, Auburn Univ, Ala, 2009; Paul & Lulu Hilliard Univ Art Mus, Univ La, 2010; Mason Scharfenstein Mus Art, Demorest, Ga, 2013; Vero Beach Mus Art, Vero Beach, Fla, 2014. *Awards:* Art in Embassies Prog, US State Dept, 2000; Ambassador for the Arts Award, Year Ala Arts, State of Ala, 2007; Governor's Arts Award, Ala State Coun on the Arts, 2011. *Bibliog:* Dr Dorothy Joiner (auth), Dale Kennington: Contemporary Mythologies, Montgomery Mus Fine Arts, 2004; Georgine Clark (auth), Alabama Masters, Alabama State Coun Arts, 2008; Dr Dorothy Joiner (auth), Dale Kennington: Subjective Mythologies, The SECAC Rev, Vol XV, No 3, 2008; Lee Gray (auth), Dale Kennington: Subjective Mythologies, Wiregrass Mus Art, 2009; Jerry Siegel (photog), Facing South, Portraits of Southern Artists, 2012; Frank Holt (auth) Style and Grace, Masterworks of American Art from the Collection of Michael and Marilyn Mennello; E Ashley Rooney (auth), 100 Southern Artists, 2012. *Media:* Oil on Canvas

KENNON, ARTHUR BRUCE
EDUCATOR, EDITOR
b Mine la Motte, Mo, Feb 18, 1927. *Study:* Southeast Mo State Univ, BS, 58, Southern Ill Univ, MFA, 67, Univ Mo, Specialist Art Educ, 74. *Hon Degrees:* PhD Art Ed-Kappa Pi. *Pos:* Coord first ABC Art Program, St Louis Art Mus, Ferguson-Florissant Sch Dist, 91-92; Evaluator Fine Arts Survey, State La Dept Educ, Arts/Humanities Div, 91. *Teaching:* Dir Art Educ, Desloge Mo Pub Schs, 59-64; coordr art, Ferguson & Florissant Mo Schs, 64-; adj fac art & educ, Webster Univ, Webster Groves, Mo, 70. *Awards:* Art Educator of the Year, Mo Art Educ Asn, 78; Outstanding Contributions to Art Educ, Nat Arts Educ Asn, 79; Host Comt, NAEA Conv, Kansas City, 90. *Bibliog:* Jean Dean (auth), Art Leaders, Northwest Journal, 10-10-88; Clarissa Start (auth), Creative Way, St Louis Post Dispatch, 7-15-88; Garnet Leader (auth), Our New President, The Sketch Book, Spring 88; John Archibald (auth), Art Kennon, St Louis Post-Dispatch, 11/89. *Mem:* Royal Soc Encouragement Arts (Fel); life mem Kappa Pi Int Hon Art Fraternity (pres); Mo Art Educ Asn (pres, 76-78); St Louis Art Supervisors Asn (pres, 65-67); Berkeley Community Teachers Asn (pres 66-67 & 72-73); St Louis Suburban Retired Teachers Asn, 2006-. *Media:* Oil, Watercolor, Printmaking, Acrylic. *Res:* new trends in art education. *Specialty:* oil. *Interests:* singing, piano, dancing, design, dancing. *Publ:* Auth, Art is Basic, Kappa Pi, 87; Andy Warhol, Kappa Pi Sketch Book, Spring 87; ed, The Sketch Book of Kappa Pi (mag) Kappa Pi, 76-; auth, Arts Integration in the Elementary Curriculum, La Dept Educ, 92. *Dealer:* Burgees Galleries; Ellie Studios. *Mailing Add:* 9321 Paul Adrian Dr Saint Louis MO 63126-2607

KENNON, BRIAN
PAINTER
b 1972. *Study:* Calif State Univ Fullerton, BA, 1995, MA (Fine Art), 2000 ; Art Ctr Coll Design, MFA (Art), 2005. *Work:* Mus Mod Art, New York; Mus Contemp Art, Los Angeles; Midway Contemp Art, Minneapolis. *Exhib:* Solo exhibs include Art Ctr Coll, Pasadena, Calif, 2005, Trudi, Los Angeles, 2006, 2007, Daniel Hug Gallery, Los Angeles, 2007; Group exhibs include New Wight Biennial, Univ Calif Los Angeles Wight Gallery, Los Angeles, 2003; Supersonic, Los Angeles Design Ctr, Los Angeles, 2005; Deitch Paper Store, Art Basel Miami Beach, 2006; Trudi: No Jerks, Rental Gallery, New York, 2007; Don't Torture the Rotten Ducklings, Inst Visual Arts, Milwaukee, 2007; Beyond Kiosk, Inst Contemp Art, Philadelphia, 2008; Gaping Hole Found In Universe, Danial Hug Gallery, Los Angeles, 2008; You, Who's Beauty Was Famous In Rome, Mandarin Gallery, Los Angeles, 2008; A Dead Serious Group Show, Sister, Los Angeles, 2008; Machine for Living Color, Mus Mod Art, New York, 2008; Against the Grain, Los Angeles Contemp Exhibs, Los Angeles, 2008. *Dealer:* Daniel Hug Gallery 510 Bernard St Los Angeles CA 90012

KENNON, ROBERT BRIAN
PRINTMAKER, HISTORIAN
b St Louis, Mo, Oct 5, 1965. *Study:* Webster Univ, St Louis, Mo, BFA (printmaking), 87; Univ Iowa, MA (art), 89, MFA, 90, MA (art hist), 93. *Work:* Slovenija Int Art Club, Slovenia, Europe; The Print Club, Albany, NY; The Md Printmakers Inc, Baltimore; The Print Consortium, Kansas City, Mo; The Print Club, Philadelphia. *Exhib:* Spiritual Visions, Webster Univ Regent's Col, London, Eng, 91; Md Print Exhib, Univ Brasilia, Brazil, 93; Calif Print Soc Exhib, Mission Cult Museo, San Francisco, 93; 17th Nat Open Competition, Schenectady Mus, 93; Diversity & Vision, Triton Mus Art, Santa Clara, Calif, 94; Spiritual Visions, ND State Univ, Fargo, ND, 98; Soc of Am Graphic Artists, 68th Nat Members Exhib, NY, 2000; Triton Mus Art, Santa Clara, Calif, 2001; Spiritual Visions, Med Coast Fine Arts Gallery, Quad-City Airport, Moline, Ill, 2002. *Pos:* Co-owner & dir, Albion Print Studio, Marion, Iowa, 90-. *Teaching:* Asst prof, Mt St Clare Col, Clinton, Ia, 96- & Franciscan Univ, Clinton, Ia, 96-; assoc prof, Culver-Stockton Coll, Canton, Mo, 2006-. *Awards:* Gabor Peterdi Award for Printmaking, Soc Am Graphic Artists. *Bibliog:* Hope Greer (auth), Earth rock & sky, Levenworth Times, 93; Ralph Slatton (auth), Landscapes, Greenville Sun, 93; Liz Greenbaum (auth), Metamorphic Insights, Bloomington Arts Ctr, 93; Ralph Slatton (auth), Featured Artist Robert Kennon, In Print, 98. *Mem:* Calif Soc Printmakers; Print Club Albany Inc; Md Printmakers Inc; Fla Printmakers Soc; Soc Am Graphic Artists; LA Printmakers Soc. *Media:* Printmaking

KENNY, STEVEN
PAINTER
b Peekskill, NY, 1962. *Study:* RI Sch Design, BFA, 80-84, European Honors Program, Rome, Italy, 83-84. *Exhib:* Solo exhibs, Works in Oil, Glassworks Gallery, Sperryville, Va, 97, Commissions of Fantasy, 98, Portraits and Effigies, Middles Street Gallery, Washington, Va, 98, Arcadia No 32, 99, Paintings, 2001, Paintings, Gallery K, Washington, DC, 2001, Recent Paintings, Fraser Gallery, Washington, DC, 2001, Lights and Darks, 2002, New Work, van de Griff/Marr Gallery, Santa Fe, New Mexico, 2002, Dust to Dust: Paintings 1999-2003, Sleeth Gallery, West Va Wesleyan Coll, 2003, Noble Savages, Klaudia Marr Gallery, Santa Fe, 2003, 2006, Anthropics, 2004, Flying Lessons, 2006, Paintings, Trinity Gallery, Atlanta, Ga, 2006; group exhibs include 1Annual Small Works Show, Washington Square East Galleries, NY Univ, 88, 89; Sense of Place, Middle Street Gallery, Washington, Va, 98, As Big As It Gets, 99, Artists Speak, 2003; Annual Georgetown Int Art Exhib, Fraser Gallery, Washington, DC, 2000, 2003, Figurative Painting, 2004; Summer Show, Gallery K, Washington, DC, 2000-2002, Small is Beautiful, 2000-2002; Faces on Places, St

Louis Artists Guild, 2000; Dreamscapes/Landscapes, Gallery 214, Montclair, NJ, 2000; Annual Realism Invitational, van de Griff/Marr Gallery, Santa Fe, 2001, 2002; Annual Realism Invitational, Klaudia Marr Gallery, Santa Fe, 2003-2005, Winter Guests, 2004, Gallery Artists Portfolio, 2005-2006; The Director Selects, Trinity Gallery, Atlanta, Ga, 2004; Birds&B(ees), Gescheidle Gallery, Chicago, 2004; Voergaard Slot, Denmark, 2005; The Resurrection Show, Packing Shed Gallery, Washington, Va, 2005, A Measure of Beauty, 2005; Flora and Fauna, Courthouse Galleries, Portsmouth, Va, 2005; Contemporary Imaginings: The Howard A and Judy Tullman Collection, Mobile Mus Art, Ala, 2006; Inaugural Exhib, Galerie Brusen, Saeby and Copenhagen, Denmark, 2006. *Awards:* Nancy Freund Prize, St Louis Artists' Guild, 2000; Individual Artists Fellowship, Va Comn Arts, 2001; Visual Arts Fellowship, Va Ctr Creative Arts, 2003; Visual Arts Grant, Franz and Virginia Bader Fund, Washington, DC, 2004

KENT, H LATHAM
PAINTER
b Mass, June 20, 1930. *Study:* Vesper George Sch Art, 51, Boston, Mass; apprentice with Artie McKenzie, Fla. *Exhib:* Coral Gables Art Gallery, Coral Gables, Fla; Int Boat Show Art Exhibs, Miami Beach, Fla; Gingerbread Sq Gallery, Key West, Fla; The Wilson Gallery, Dennis, Mass; Aries East Gallery, Brewster, Mass; Dodge House Gallery, Chatham, Mass; Lyman Eyer Gallery, Provincetown, Mass; Charles-Baltivik Gallery, Provincetown, Mass; Provincetown Art Mus & Gallery; Salong, pvt showings at studio. *Pos:* Artist, Steve Hannagan, NY 51-54 & Bronzini of NY, 54-57; com artist, Coco-Cola, Union Pacific Railroad, Libbey Glassware & Admiral, currently; pres & off, Southern Chap, Am Arist Prof League, formerly. *Mem:* Copley Soc, Boston, Mass; Int Soc Marine Painters, Fla; Am Artists Prof League, SFla (pres, 78-83); Provincetown Art Asn & Mus. *Media:* Oil. *Specialty:* Traditional Am Art, impressionistic

KENTON, MARY JEAN
PAINTER, ENVIRONMENTAL ARTIST
b Fayette Co, Pa, 1946. *Study:* Pomona Col, Claremont, Calif, BA, 68; San Francisco Art Inst, MFA, 74. *Work:* Mattress Factory, Pittsburgh, Pa; Laughlin House Property, Grindstone, Pa; Mus Contemp Art, Los Angeles, Calif. *Comn:* Painting, The Floating Rectangles, comn by John Cage, 90; design & lighting for Merce Cunningham's Breakers, comn jointly by Merce Cunningham Dance Co & Boston Ballet, 94. *Exhib:* Geometry of Color, Laughlin House Property, Grindstone, Pa, 89; Mary Jean Kenton: A Survey, 1973-1990, Allegheny Coll Art Galleries, Meadville, Pa, 90; Carnegie Int 1991, John Cage Proj, Carnegie Mus Art & Mattress Factory, 91-92; Roly Wholyover A Circus, Los Angeles Mus Contemp Art, 93, Menil Collection, Houston, Guggenheim Mus, Soho, Mito Art Towers, Japan, Philadelphia Mus Art, Pa, 94-95; Botanica, Tweed Mus Art, Duluth, Minn, 99; New Paintings & Garden Commission, Seton Hill Univ, Greensburg, Pa, 99; Westmoreland Mus Am Art Biennial, Greensburg, Pa, 2006; You are Here, SPACE Gallery, Pittsburgh, Pa, 2008; The Pen and Brush, New York, NY, 2010-2013; Lacquered Landscape Screen, Westmoreland Co Community Coll, Youngwood, Pa, 2011; Southern Vermont Arts Center, 2012. *Pos:* Ed (for Pittsburgh), New Art Examiner, 86-94; contribr, Sculpture, 96-2001. *Teaching:* adj fac, Westmoreland Co Community Col, Youngwood, Pa, 2002-2007; adj prof, Waynesburg Col, Pa, 2003-2008. *Awards:* Pa Coun Arts Fels in Art Criticism, 87-88, 90-91, 93-94. *Bibliog:* Sheena Wagstaff (auth), Earth Colors, Pittsburgh Mag, Pa, 22-23, 8/92; Kathleen M Dlugos (auth), Mary Jean Kenton: Mattress Factory, exhib rev, New Art Examiner, 12/98-1/99; Robert Raczka (auth), Mary Jean Kenton's Freedom (with limits), Pa State Jour Contemp Criticism, #3, pp34-38; Anna Kisselgoff (auth), Painterly Contemplation in Cunningham's "Breakers", NY Times, 3/11/94, pC3. *Media:* Oil, Watercolor; Horticultural Material. *Interests:* interaction between artmaking and the natural world, and the way in which theory colors perception. *Publ:* Auth, Mary Jean Kenton: The Geometry of Color, pvt publ, 89; Points of View IV: Artist's Choice (catalog, essay), Westminster Coll Art Gallery, New Wilmington, Pa, 92; The Geometry of Color, Its First Twenty Years (photographs by Jim Rosenberg). *Mailing Add:* Box 42 Merrittstown PA 15463

KENTRIDGE, WILLIAM
FILMMAKER, SCULPTOR
b Johannesburg, South Africa, 1955. *Study:* Univ Witwatersrand, Johannesburg, South Africa, 73-6; Johannesburg Art Found, Johannesburg, South Africa, 76-8; Ecole Jacques LeCog, Paris, France, 81-82. *Hon Degrees:* Hon DFA, Royal Coll Art, London, 2010; Hon DFA, Rhodes Univ, South Africa. *Work:* Mus Modern Art, New York, NY; Mus Contemp Art, Los Angeles, Calif; Hirshhorn Mus, Wash DC; San Fran Mus Modern Art, Calif; Nat Gallery of Canada, Ottawa, Ontario. *Comn:* 59 min video art of the Times Sq astrovision, Creative Time and Panasonic, NY, 2001; firewalker, comn by Gerhard Marx, Johannesburg, South Africa, 2009. *Exhib:* Norton Mus Art, West Palm Beach, Fla, 2009; Mus Modern Art, Fort Worth, Tex, 2009; Jeu de Paume, Paris, 2010; Albertina Mus, Vienna, 2010; Mus Modern Art, NY, 2010; Israel Mus, Jerusalem, 2011. *Teaching:* mentor, Rolex Mentor and Protege Arts Initiative. *Awards:* Hugo Boss Prize, Soho Guggenheim, 98; Carnegie Prize, Carnegie Mus Art, 2000; Shaijah Biennial 6 Prize, United Arab Emirates, 2003; Kaisemine Prize, Mus fur Modern Kunst, 2003; Oskar Kokoschka Prize, 2008; Kyoto Prize, 2010. *Bibliog:* Bronwyn Law-Vilijoen (auth), William Kentridge, Phaidon, 99, Flute, David Krut Publishing, 2007; Mark Rosenthal (auth), William Kentridge Five Themes, San Fran Mus Mod Art, 2009; Kyle Bentley (auth), Trace, Mus Modern Art, 2010. *Media:* Animation, Printmaking. *Dealer:* Marian Goodman Gallery 24 West 57th St New York NY 10019; Goodman Gallery 163 Jan Smuts Ave Parkwood Johannesburg South Africa 2193

KENYON, COLLEEN FRANCES
PHOTOGRAPHER, ADMINISTRATOR
b Dunkirk, NY, Aug 6, 1951. *Study:* Skidmore Col, Saratoga Springs, NY, BS, 73; Ind Univ, Bloomington, with Henry Holmes Smith in photog, MFA, 76. *Work:* Mus Mod Art, NY; Int Mus Photog, George Eastman House, Rochester, NY; Akin, Gump, Strauss, Hauer & Feld Corp Collection, NY; Metrop Mus Art, NY; Avon Collection, NY. *Exhib:* Mirrors & Windows: Am Photog Since 1960, Mus Mod Art, NY, 78; one-person show, Foto Gallery, NY, 80, Camerawork Gallery, San Francisco, 80, Sacred Children, ARCO Ctr Visual Art, Los Angeles, Calif, 80, Color & Hand-Colored Photographs, Silver Image Gallery, 81, Catskill Ctr Photog, Spring 82, Shadai Gallery, Tokyo, 93 & Gallery 292, NY, 97; 15 yrs retrospective, Kleinert Gallery, Woodstock, NY, 86; Pleasures & Terrors of Domestic Comfort, Mus Mod Art, NY; Pleasures and Terrors of Domestic Comfort, Mus Mod Art, NY (traveling, Baltimore Mus Art, Los Angeles Co Mus Art), 91-93; Artists Who Work, Kleinert-James Arts Ctr, Woodstock, NY, 95; Double Feature, Syracuse Stage, NY, 95; fac exhib, Woodstock Sch Art, NY, 96; Eye of the Beholder, ICP, NY, 97; The Passion, Kingston, NY, 98. *Pos:* exec dir, Ctr for Photog, Woodstock, NY. *Teaching:* Instr photog, Slippery Rock State Col, Pa, Jan-May, 77; instr photog, Bard Col, Annandale, NY, winter 79; residency Va Ctr for Arts, 98, Nantucket Sch Art & Design, 96, 99. *Awards:* Photog Fel, NY Found Arts, 89; Agfa Corp Award, 94; Mats Grant, Yaddo Artists Colony, Saratoga Springs, NY, 95. *Bibliog:* Catherine Marx (ed), Right Brain Left Brain Photography, Amphoto, Watson-Guptill, New York, 94; Grace & George Schaub (auths & eds), Marshall's Hand Coloring Guide & Gallery, G&G Schaub, 95; Fine Art Photography, Graphis Press, Switz, 96. *Mem:* Soc for Photog Educ; Women's Caucus for Art; Nat Asn Artists Orgn; Am Fedn Arts. *Media:* Photography; Painting. *Dealer:* Sarah Morthland Gallery New York NY. *Mailing Add:* 3 Beckley St Saugerties NY 12477-1807

KEOUGH, JEFFREY
DIRECTOR
b Concord, Mass, Oct 30, 1953. *Study:* Sch of the Mus Fine Arts, Boston, Mass. *Pos:* Dir of Exhibs, Mass Col Art, currently. *Mailing Add:* Mass Col Art Baklar & Huntington Gallery 621 Huntington Ave Boston MA 02115

KEPALAS
SCULPTOR, PAINTER
b Vilnius, Lithuania; US citizen. *Study:* Ont Coll Art, Toronto; Brooklyn Mus Sch Art. *Work:* Pa Acad Fine Arts, Philadelphia; Univ Mass Art Gallery, Amherst; Libr & Mus Performing Arts, Lincoln Ctr, NY; Lithuanian Mus, Adelaide, Australia; Mus Mod Art Lending Serv, NY. *Comn:* Bronze bust, Mr Louis Horst, NY, 62; bronze bust, Mrs Gunilla Kessler, NY, 71; bronze bust, Mr Robert Spring, 87; bronze reliefs of 4 American Saints: Frances Cabrini, John Neumann, Elizabeth Ann Seton & Isaac Jogues, 92. *Exhib:* Pa Acad Fine Arts, Philadelphia, 68; Silvermine Guild Artists Ann, New Canaan, Conn, 69; Jersey City Mus, NJ, 69-71; Phoenix Gallery, NY, 70, 72, 74, 76, 78-81 & 84. *Awards:* First Prize, Coun Advan Lithuanian Cult, Chicago, Ill, 78; Accademico d'Italia con Medaglia d'Oro, Salsomaggiore, Italia, 80; Doris Kreindler Mem Award, Am Soc Contemp Artists, 83. *Bibliog:* Edgar Buonagurio (auth), Elena Kepalas, Art Mag, 6/79; Elena Kepalas Bronze Sculptor, New York Arts J, 79; Palmer Poroner (auth), Discoveries in Arts, Art Speak, 11/81. *Mem:* Am Soc Contemp Artists; Metrop Painters & Sculptors. *Media:* Bronze; Acrylic, Oil. *Mailing Add:* 1047 2nd St Apt 10 Santa Monica CA 90403-3612

KEPETS, HUGH MICHAEL
PAINTER, PRINTMAKER
b Cleveland, Ohio, Feb 6, 1946. *Study:* Carnegie-Mellon Univ, BFA, 68; Ohio Univ, MFA, 72. *Work:* Metrop Mus Art, NY; Philadelphia Mus Fine Arts; Cleveland Mus Art; Libr Cong, Washington, DC; Yale Univ Art Gallery; and others. *Comn:* Cover, Paris Rev 65, spring 76; City Walls Inc, NY, 76; Outdoor three dimensional wall painting, Three Rivers Arts Festival, Pittsburgh, 82. *Exhib:* Cleveland Mus Art, 68-93; Brooklyn Mus, NY, 72 & 76; 35th Midyear Show, Butler Inst Am Art, 72; Works on Paper, Va Mus Fine Arts, Richmond, 74; solo exhibs, Fischbach Gallery, NY, 74, 76 & 78, Marcus/Gordon Assoc, Pittsburgh, 81, Roger Ramsay Gallery, Chicago, 84 & 88, David Adamson Gallery, Washington, 86 & 92, Randall Beck Gallery, Boston, 76, 79, 86 & 89 & Brenda Kroos Gallery, Cleveland, 93 & 96; Boston Printmakers 27th Ann, Boston Mus Fine Arts, 75; West '79/The Law, Minn Mus Art, St Paul, 79; Am Acad Arts & Lett, NY, 78 & 80; plus many others group and solo exhibs. *Awards:* Nat Endowment Arts Grant, 76; Cleveland Arts Prize, 79; Creative Artists Pub Serv Grant, 80. *Dealer:* Brenda Kroos 1300 W 9th St Cleveland OH 44113. *Mailing Add:* 13 Chinmoy Ln New Milford CT 06776

KEPNER, RITA
SCULPTOR, WRITER
b Binghamton, NY, Nov 15, 1944. *Study:* Elmira Col, NY, 62-63, Harpur Col, State Univ NY, BA, 66, Okla Univ, 88; Seattle Pac Univ, 90; Western Wash Univ, 91-92; City Univ Seattle, MA, 98; Edward R. Murrow Coll, Wash State Univ, PhD, 2010. *Hon Degrees:* Acad Bedriacehse Calvatore, Italy, hon MFA, 84. *Work:* Warsaw Mus, Poland; Seattle City Collection, Wash; Kenmore Libr; Wash Mutual, Seattle; Children's Hosp, Seattle; Cowlitz Indian Tribe, Wash; Womens' Ctr, Wash State Univ; Binghamton Univ Mus, NY; The Kinsey Inst, Indiana Univ, Womens' Ctr, Wash State Univ. *Comn:* wood Sculpture, City of Znin, Poland, 76; wood sculpture, City of Zalaegerszeg, Hungary, 77; bronze sculpture, Develop Authority, Seattle, 78; granite sculpture, Seattle Publ Libr, 78; cast stone sculpture, US Army Corps of Engineers, Savannah, Ga, 94 & 96; bicentennial portrait bronze sculpture, Soren Kierkegaard, 2013. *Exhib:* Wood Sculpture, Portland Art Mus, Ore, 76; Artist in the City, 75, Seattle Art Mus, Wash, 77; Int Sculptors, Znin, Poland, 76 & Hajnowka, 77; Zalaegerszeg, Hungary, 77; Am Artist in Poland, Zoliborz Mus, Warsaw, 81; Am Artist in Wiesbaden, Die Roemer, Ger, 88; Quimper Arts, Port Townsend, Wash, 93, 94, & 2013; Univ Art Mus, State Univ NY, Binghamton, 96; Ichikawa, Japan, 97; Bruskin Gallery, Port Townsend, Wash, 98; Arts Alliance Gallery, Port Townsend, Wash, 2002, 03 & 04; Gallery 9, Port Townsend, 2004; Northwind Arts Ctr, 2013. *Pos:* artist-in-residence, Seattle, 75, 77-78. *Teaching:* Instr Sculpture Experimental Col, Univ Wash, 72-74; master sculptor, Evergreen Col Internship Prog, Olympia, Wash, 74-78. *Awards:* Appointed Visual Arts Ambassador-informal-between USA & Poland, 76-81; Kosciuszko Found Travel Grant Award Winner, 75, 76, 79, 81. *Bibliog:* Something Happened in Seattle, NEA Newslett, 76; David Miller (dir, video), Rita

Kepner Sculptor, 81; Stephanie Irving (auth), In support of the arts, Peninsula Mag, fall 91; Symon Bojko, Polish American Artists, Warsaw, Poland, Women Artists of Am, Vol 2. *Mem:* Bainbridge Island Arts & Humanities Coun (founder, 86); Int Artists Asn UNESCO, Paris; Artists Equity Asn; Int Artists Coop, Edelvecht, Ger; Quimper Arts, Port Townsend, Wash; Northwind Arts Ctr, Port Townsend, Wash. *Media:* Sculpture, stone, wood, ceramic, bronze and drawing. *Res:* Polyester Resin and Bone Sculpture, Leonardo Mag. *Specialty:* local artists. *Interests:* Art, educ, reading, gardening, writing, editing. *Collection:* other works are found in collection of Lisa T. Painter; Dana and Lindsey Hofman; Amanda and Emmett Doerr; Karen and Harvey Putterman; Dr & Mrs Kenneth Lindsay; Stewart Matthiesen; John Matthiesen; retrospective and current works collection of hundreds of Rita Kepner pieces donated to City Univ Seattle Headquarters by Lisa T. Painter, 2014. *Publ:* Contribr, Northwest Art, The Arts, Leonardo Mag, Poland Mag, Polska Panorama, Seattle Post Intelligencer. *Dealer:* Northwind Arts Ctr Port Townsend Wa

KERESZI, LISA R
PHOTOGRAPHER, LECTURER
b Pa, 1973. *Study:* Bard Coll, Annandale-on-Hudson, NY, BA, 1995, studied with Stephen Shore; Yale Univ Sch Art, MFA (Ward Cheney Mem Award), 2000. *Work:* Altoids Curiously Strong Collection, New Mus Contemp Art, New York; Am Mus Natural Hist; Brooklyn Mus Art; Whitney Mus Am Art; Yale Univ Art Gallery, Univ Libr, Sch Art. *Exhib:* Solo exhibs include Pierogi, Brooklyn, 2002 & 2003, Yale Summer Sch Art, Norfolk, Conn, 2003, Gov's Island, Urban Ctr Gallery, New York, 2005, Yancey Richardson Gallery, New York, 2005 & 2007, Moore Coll Art, Philadelphia, 2005, Univ Calif, Berkeley Art Mus, 2005, Alcott Gallery, Univ NC, Chapel Hill, 2006; group exhibs include Current Undercurrent: Working in Brooklyn, Brooklyn Mus, 1998, Open House: Working in Brooklyn, 2004, Looking Back from Ground Zero, 2006; New Photographs, Baumgartner Gallery, New York, 2000; Here is New York, traveling, 2001; Life of the City, Part II, Mus Mod Art, New York, 2002; Ways & Means, Faculty Show, Sch Int Ctr Photog, New York, 2002; Next Next Wave Art, Brooklyn Acad Music, 2002; A River Halg Empty, Aldrich Mus Art, Conn, 2003; Artist in the Marketplace, Bronx Mus Art, New York, 2003; Pictures from Within, Whitney Mus Am Art, New York, 2003; Subway Series: The NY Yankees & the Am Dream, Bronx Mus Art, New York, 2004; Subway Series: The NY Mets & Our Nat Pastime, Queens Mus Art, New York, 2004; On View: Photographing the Museum, Yancey Richardson Gallery, New York, 2005, Storefront Stories, 2006, Easy Rider, 2007; World Trade Ctr Mem Found Touring Exhib, 2007. *Pos:* Asst to Nan Goldin, New York, formerly. *Teaching:* Int Ctr Photog, New York, 2002-; lectr, Undergrad Photog Detp, Yale Univ, 2003 & 2005, lectr & acting dir undergrad studies in photog, 2006-. *Awards:* Distinctive Merit Awards, Art Dir's Club NY, 2002; Baum Award Emerging Am Photogs, Berkeley Art Mus & Pacific Film Archive, 2005; Conn State Arts Coun Grant, 2008. *Specialty:* Photography. *Publ:* Governors Island, 2004; Fantasies, 2008; Fun and Games, 2009; Joes Junk Yard, 2012. *Dealer:* Yancey Richardson Gallery. *Mailing Add:* Yancey Richardson Gallery 3rd Fl 535 W 22nd St New York NY 10011

KERMES, CONSTANTINE JOHN
PAINTER, PRINTMAKER
b Pittsburgh, Pa, Dec 6, 1923. *Study:* Carnegie-Mellon Univ, BFA; also with Victor Candell, Leo Manso, Glenn Bradshaw, Catherine Liu & Frank Lloyd Wright. *Work:* Lancaster Mus Art, Pa; Notre Dame Art Mus, South Bend, Ind; Stockmanshove Mus, Damme, Belg; Pa State Univ, Univ Park; Lebanon Valley Coll, Pa; Pa State Univ, Pa; Elizabethtown Coll, Pa; Kutztown Univ, Kutztown, Pa; Lancaster Mus Art, Lancaster, Pa. *Comn:* Murals, Pa Hist & Mus Comn, Cornwall Mus, 68; Fontrier Found, Paris; assemblage murals, Ford New Holland, Pa & Brussels, Belg; Farm & Indust Equip Inst, Wrigley Bldg, Chicago. *Exhib:* Design Rev, Smithsonian Inst, Washington, DC, 69; solo exhibs, Grimaldis Gallery, Baltimore, 79, Reading Mus, 80; ten solo exhibs at Seligmann Gallery, New York & Demuth Found Gallery, Lancaster Mus Art, 93 & Pfenninger Gallery, Lancaster Pa, 2007; Pa Watercolor Soc, 79-80 & 84-85; Hancock Shaker Mus, Pittsfield, Mass, 89; Art of the State, William Penn Mus, 2000; Dumuth Mus, Lancaster, Pa, 2000-2003; Westmoreland Mus Am Art, Greensburg, Pa, 2003-2004; and many others. *Awards:* Traveling Exhib Painting Prize, Petrol Industs, 71; Award Oxford, Md Ann Exhib, 91-92; Best Show, Lancaster Mus Art Summer Show, 96; Top Award, Berks Art Alliance, Hazelton, Pa, 2000; Mid-Atlantic States Exhibit, 2001; Philadelphia Watercolor Soc Award, 2003-05. *Bibliog:* Morse (auth), Shakers & Worlds People, Dodd Mead, 80; Horgan (auth), Shaker Holy Land, Harvard Press, 82; S Stein (auth), Shaker Experience in America, Yale Univ Press, 92. *Mem:* signature mem, Pa Watercolor Soc & AWS; signature mem, Baltimore Watercolor Soc; signature mem, Philadelphia Watercolor Soc. *Media:* Oil, Acrylic, Watercolor; Woodcut, Lithography. *Publ:* Auth, Shaker Architecture, 70; auth & illusr, American Icons, 75; Folk images of rural Pennsylvania, Pa Folklife, 6/75 & 6/81; Symbols of Love in Folk Art, 87. *Dealer:* Jacques Seligmann Gallery 5 E 57th St New York NY 10022

KERN, ARTHUR (EDWARD)
EDUCATOR, SCULPTOR
b New Orleans, La, Oct 27, 1931. *Study:* Tulane Univ La, BA, 53, MFA, 55. *Exhib:* Solo exhibs, Ariz State Univ, 74 & Int Sculpture Conf, Tulane Univ, 76; South Houston Gallery, NY, 75. *Teaching:* Asst prof drawing, Univ Southwestern La, 67-69; assoc prof painting & sculpture, Tulane Univ La, 69-, assoc chmn dept art, 72-. *Media:* Apoxy. *Mailing Add:* 500 State St New Orleans LA 70118

KERN, KAREN R
PAINTING
b March 1952. *Exhib:* Artisan Gallery, Northport, NY; Isis Gallery, Port Wash, NY; Environ Sculpture Exhib, Schure Plaza, Old Westbury, NY; Nassau Co Celebration of Arts, Nassau Co Mus, Roslyn, NY; Women in Visual Arts Exhib, Univ Okla; Long Island Artists, Heckscher Mus, Huntington, NY; Amsterdam, Whitney Int Fine Art, Chelsea, New York City. *Collection Arranged:* Sessions Data Placement, Glen Cove, NY; Morton Commun, Great Neck, NY; Apollo Co, NY; Admiral Commun Co, NY; Deloitte, Haskins & Sells, Inc, One World Trade Ctr, NY. *Pos:* asst, photo realism, Audrey Flack, formerly

KERN, STEVEN
MUSEUM DIRECTOR
Study: Univ Mass, Grad; Johns Hopkins Univ, MA (art hist). *Pos:* Cur European art & exhibs, George Walter Vincent Smith Art Mus, Springfield, Mass, formerly; cur paintings, Sterling & Francine Clark Art Inst, Williamstown, Mass, formerly; cur European Arts, San Diego Mus Art, 97-2006; dir, William Benton Mus Art, Univ Conn, 2006-2008, exec dir, Everson Mus Art, Syracuse, NY, 2008-2013, Newark Mus, 2014-. *Teaching:* Lectr, Williams Coll, formerly. *Mailing Add:* Newark Museum 49 Washington St Newark NJ 07102

KERNS, ED (JOHNSON), JR
PAINTER
b Richmond, Va, Feb 22, 1945. *Study:* Va Commonwealth Univ, BFA; Md Inst Coll Art, Baltimore, with Grace Hartigan, MFA. *Work:* Aldrich Mus Art, Ridgefield, Conn; Chase Manhattan Bank, NY; Edward Albee Found, NY; Citicorp, NY; Corcoran Gallery, Washington, DC. *Exhib:* Albright-Knox Art Gallery, Buffalo, NY, 71 & 72; San Francisco Mus Mod Art, 78; Pa Acad Fine Arts, 82; Ben Shahn Gallery, NJ, 89; Muhlenberg Coll Ctr Arts, Allentown, Pa, 91; Williams Ctr Arts Gallery, Easton, Pa, 92 & 93; Open Space Gallery, Allentown, Pa, 92; Solo exhibs, M-13 Gallery, NY, 95 & 97; State Theatre Gallery, Easton, Pa, 98; Ruffino de Tamayo Print Mus, Mex, 98. *Pos:* Head art dept, Lafayette Col, Easton, Pa. *Teaching:* Eugene H Clapp, Prof humanities & art, Lafayette Col, Easton, Pa, 80-. *Awards:* Art Achievement Key, Va Commonwealth Univ, 67; Artist of the Year, Larry Aldrich Assoc, New York, 71. *Bibliog:* Articles, Arts Mag, 1/79 & Artforum, 1/80, Art News, 12/84, Morning Call, 1/90, The Express, 2/90 & Philadelphia Inquirer, 6/91. *Mem:* Coll Art Asn. *Media:* Acrylic, Collage. *Publ:* Coauth (with Loder), Tracks in the Straw, 85, Eavesdropping on the Echoes, 87 & Wrestling the Light, Luriamedia Press, 91. *Dealer:* Howard Scott 520 W 20th St New York NY 10012. *Mailing Add:* Lafayette Col Dep Art Easton PA 18042

KERRIGAN, MAURIE
SCULPTOR, PAINTER
b Jersey City, NJ, Apr 28, 1951. *Study:* Moore Coll Art, Philadelphia, Pa, BFA, 73; Art Inst Chicago, MFA, 77; Whitney Mus Am Art, 77; Salus Univ, MS (visual impairment), Philadelphia, 99. *Work:* Philadelphia Mus Art & Please Touch Mus, Philadelphia, Pa; Lanon Found, Palm Beach, Fla; Phillips Collection, Smithsonian Inst, Washington, DC; Nat Women's Mus, Washington, DC; Best Corp Collection, NC. *Comn:* Mural, Candy Corns Visit Chicago, Pippers Alley, Chicago, Ill, 76; exterior sculpture, Three Boats, Reading Mus, Reading, Pa; sculpture, The Muse 34th Vessel, Am Express Col, NY. *Exhib:* Chicago & Vicinity, Art Inst Chicago, Ill, 77; Contemp Drawings, Philadelphia Mus Art, Pa, 79; Projects IV, Inst Contemp Art, Philadelphia, Pa, 80; Awards in the Visual Arts I, Nat Mus Am Art, Washington, DC, 82-83; De Moines Art Ctr, 82-83; Denver Art Mus, 82-83; one women show, Rockin, Philadelphia Mus Art, 87, Walkin, Pennsylvania Acad Fine Art, 89. *Pos:* Pres, Kerrigan Painting Co. *Awards:* Artist Fel, Pa Coun Art, 82; MacDowell Colony Fel, 86 & 87; Penny McCall Found Award, 87. *Bibliog:* Jean Silverthorne (auth), Maurie Kerrigan, Arts, 12/79; Ann-Sargent Wooster (auth), Maurie Kerrigan at Touchstone, Art in Am, 12/81; Wendy Slatkin (auth), Maurie Kerrigan, Arts, 5/83. *Mem:* Women's Caucus Art; Int Sculpture Ctr. *Media:* Handmade Paper, Wood; Oil Pastels. *Publ:* auth, Rockin, 84 & Walkin, 89. *Dealer:* Max Hutchinson Gallery 131 Green St New York NY 10012. *Mailing Add:* 1714 North St Philadelphia PA 19130-3307

KERSELS, MARTIN
CONCEPTUAL ARTIST
b LA, 1960. *Study:* Univ Calif, Los Angeles, BA (art), 1984, MFA (art), 1995. *Work:* Mus Contemp Art, San Diego; LA County Mus Art, Mus Contemp Art, LA; Mus Contemp Art, Miami; Madison Mus Contemp Art, Wis; Ctr Georges Pompidou, Paris. *Exhib:* Solo performances, Sweaters, UCLA Fine Arts Prodns, 1984, Sweaters (part B), Backlot Theatre, Hollywood, 1987, The Shape of Pools Today, Wallenboyd Theatre, LA, 1987, Pools, Kid Aileck Gallery, Tokyo, 1989, Breath, Odyssey Theatre & Powerhouse Theatre, LA, 1989, Measured Tale, LACE, 1990 & Weight, 1992; solo exhibs, Madison Art Ctr, Wis, 1997, Dan Bernier Gallery, LA, 1998, 1999, Kunsthalle Bern, Switzerland, 2000, Galerie Georges-Phillippe & Nathalie Vallois, Paris, 1999, 2002, 2005, ACME, LA, 2001, 2002, 2003, 2006, 2008, Tang Mus Art, Saratoga Springs, NY, 2007, Santa Monica Mus Art, 2008; group exhibs, Ten LA Artists, Stephen Wirtz Gallery, San Francisco, 1997; Whitney Biennial, Whitney Mus Am Art, New York, 1997; W-139, Amsterdam, 1998; EXTRAetORDINAIRE, Le Printemps de Cahors, Paris, 1999; Made in California, LA County Mus Art, 2000; Majestic Sprawl: Some LA Photography, Pasadena Mus Calif Art, 2002; 100 Artists See God, Independent Curators Int, New York, 2004; Dionysiac, Pompidou Ctr, Paris, 2005; Disorderly Conduct: Art in Tumultuous Times, Orange County Mus Art, Calif, 2008; Whitney Biennial, Whitney Mus Am Art, 2010. *Pos:* Founding mem, SHRIMPS performance collaborative. *Teaching:* Co-dir, Program in Art, Calif Inst Arts, Valencia, currently. *Awards:* Individual Artist Grant, City of LA Cult Affairs Dept, 1996; Found Contemp Performance Arts Fel, 1999; Guggenheim Fel, 2008. *Publ:* David Schafer

(auth), rev, Art Papers, 5-6/98; William Wilson (auth), Commotion pulls viewer into artist's wacky life, LA Times, 10/21/98; Michael Darling (auth), The fat man sings, LA Weekly, 10/30/98-11/4/98. *Dealer:* ACME 6150 Wilshire Blvd Spaces 1 & 2 Los Angeles CA 90048. *Mailing Add:* Calif Inst Arts Program in Art 24700 McBean Pkwy Santa Clarita CA 91355

KERSTETTER, BARBARA
PAINTER
b Pa. *Study:* Pa State Univ, BA; Sch Mus Fine Arts, Boston; Am Univ, Washington; Corcoran Sch Art, Washington; Georgetown Univ Sch Medicine. *Work:* NY Piano Acad; Saks Fifth Ave, New York & Columbia, Md; Beethoven Piano Co, New York; NY Mercantile Exchange; City Univ NY Grad Ctr. *Exhib:* Solo Exhibs include Foreign Press Ctr, Washington, 1982, Catholic Univ Gallery, Washington, 1982, Saks Fifth Ave, New York, 1985, Vorpal Gallery, New York, 1985-96 & 1998, Galerie Auberge la Fontaine, Venasque, France, 1999, 2000 & 2001, Marian Alexander Gallery, London, 2004 & 2005, DS Cohen Fine Arts, New York, 2007; group exhibs include US Senate Leadership Circle, Arthur Cowles Gallery, Washington, 1982; Staet St Gallery, Sarasota, Fla, 1998 & 1999; Malca Fine Arts, New York, 2000; Studio Gallery of John Allen Holt, New York, 2003; Benefit Auction for New Orleans, TV NY 1 & NY Found Arts, 2006; 183rd Ann: Invitational Exhib Contemp Art, Nat Acad Mus, New York, 2008. *Teaching:* Guest speaker, Am Univ Dept Fine Arts, 1980, 1981-82; instr life drawing, Georgetown Univ Hosp, 1981-82, Georgetown Univ Sch Medicine, 1982-83, Columbia Univ Coll Physicians & Surgeons, 1985-2006, Archit Thierry Despont & Staff, New York, 1996-98, NY Univ Med Coll, 2004-06; instr watercolor & life drawing, Mt Vernon Coll, Washington, 1981-82; instr mixed media painting, Marymount Coll, NY, 1991-92. *Awards:* Benjamin Altman Prize, Nat Acad Design, 2008. *Mailing Add:* 4 Washington Sq Village Apt 9B New York NY 10012

KERTESS, KLAUS
CURATOR, WRITER
Collection Arranged: Whitney Mus Am Art Biennial, 1995; Willem de Kooning: Drawing Seeing/Seeing Drawing, Drawing Ctr, New York, 1988; Mediations in Emergency, Mus Contemp Art, Detroit, 2007; Image Matter, Mary Boone Gallery, Chelsea, New York, 2009. *Pos:* Co-founder & dir, Bykert Gallery, New York, 1966-1975; adj cur drawing, Whitney Mus Am Art, 1989-. *Awards:* Lawrence A Fleischman Award for Scholarly Excellence in Am Art Hist, Smithsonian Inst Archives Am Art, 2009

KERTESZ, SHOSHANA
PAINTER
b July 24, 1979, Budapest, Hungary. *Study:* Montazs Art Sch, Hungary, 1994-1998. *Exhib:* Solo exhibs, Jerusalem Theater, Israe, 2009, Home Galeria, Budapest, Hungary, 2010, Hanna Studio Gallery, Ringwood, NJ, 2011; Group exhibs,Mus Fine Arts, 2001, 2001; David Citadel Hotel, Jerusalem, 2004; Home Gallery, Budapest, Hungary, 1993, 1997, 2002, 2004, 2006, 2008; Cartel Coffee/Art Gallery, Ariz, 2009; Conspire Art Gallery, Phoenix, 2009; bigail Gallery, Auction, Budapest, Hungary, 2010; Avenue A Gallery, G2 Lounge, New York, 2010; Townhouse Art Gallery, Brooklyn, 2010; ArtPrize, Grand Rapids, Mich, 2010; Eszterhazy Palace, Hungary, 2010; Hanna Studio Gallery, Ringwood, NJ, 2010; Redeemer Church, New York, 2010; Greenpoint Gallery, Brooklyn, 2011; Gelabert Studio Gallery, New York, 2011. *Awards:* Showcase winner, Art Slant, 2010; May-June Showcase Winner, Artslant, 2010. *Media:* Oil, Pencil, Pastel. *Publ:* Janos Kobanyai: To the Paintings of Shoshana Kertesz, Mult es Jovo, Mag, Hungary; Exodus, Catalog of Paintings

KERZIE, TED L
PAINTER, EDUCATOR
b Tacoma, Wash, May 10, 1943. *Study:* Wash State Univ, Pullman, BA, 65; Claremont Grad Sch, Calif, MFA, 72; Calif State Univ, Bakersfield, MAH. *Work:* Power Mus, Sydney, Australia; Wayne Anderson Collection, Boston; Luigiani Rossi Collection, Milan, Italy; Arco Collection Visual Arts, Los Angeles; Reader's Digest Collection, NY; Stouffers, Capital Group, Los Angeles; Merv Griffin, Palm Desert. *Comn:* Stouffers, Dion-Ross. *Exhib:* Solo show, Cirrus Gallery, Los Angeles, 80, Sherry Frumkin Gallery, Santa Monica, Calif, 91; Tengin Salon Gallery, Fukuoka, Japan, 81; Ten Calif Colorist Traveling Exhib; Valerie Miller Gallery, Palm Desert, Directors Guild, Hollywood, Calif, 92; Adamar Fine Arts, Miami, Fla, 94; West Coast Process Art, Bakersfield Mus Art, Calif, 97; and others. *Collection Arranged:* Los Angeles Abstract Painting (catalog), Univ Calif, Riverside, 80. *Pos:* Vpres, TRT Enterprises Casting Agency, Bakersfield, Calif; captain, photograph eng, USAF, 66-71, Motion Picture Off, 70-75. *Teaching:* Asst prof fine arts, Scripps Col & Claremont Grad Sch, Calif, 73-76; prof fine arts, Calif State Col, Bakersfield, 76-, summer arts, 86-. *Awards:* Bautzer Award for Univ Advance Planning, 98-99. *Bibliog:* William Wilson (auth), article, 80 & Suzanne Munchnic (auth), article, 8/81, Los Angeles Times; Melinda Wortz (auth), article, Art News, 80 & 83; Pick of the week, LA Weekly, 11/91. *Mem:* Aircraft Owners & Pilot Asn; Angel Flight Pilots. *Media:* Acrylic, Mixed Media. *Dealer:* Adamar Fine Arts 177 NE 39th St Miami FL 33137. *Mailing Add:* Dept Art California State Col 9001 Stockdale Hwy Bakersfield CA 93309

KESSLER, ALAN
PAINTER, SCULPTOR
b Philadelphia, Pa, Oct 15, 1945. *Study:* Philadelphia Coll Art, BFA; Yale Univ Summer Sch, Norfolk, Conn, Yale fel, 66; Md Inst Coll Art, Baltimore, Hoffberger fel painting, MFA, 69. *Work:* Am Fedn Arts, NY; NY Univ Collection; Brockton Art Mus, Mass; Rose Art Mus, Brandeis Univ; State Univ NY Coll Cortland. *Exhib:* Solo exhibs, Brown Univ, 77, O K Harris Gallery, NY, 77, 79, 80, 83, 85 & 89, Everson Mus Arts, Syracuse, NY, 78 & Morgan Gallery, Kansas City, Mo, 78; Directions, Hirshhorn Mus, Washington, DC, 79; Real, Really Real, Super Real, Directions in Contemp Am Realism, 81 & 82; and others. *Teaching:* Instr painting & drawing, Md Inst Col Art, 68-69; instr, Hudson River Mus, 74; asst prof art, Brown Univ, 77-. *Awards:* First Prize in Painting, Acad Arts, Easton, Md, 68; Elizabeth T Greenshields Mem Found Grant in Painting, Montreal, 74; Artist in Residence Grant, Nat Endowment Arts, Del State Arts Coun, 75-76. *Bibliog:* Gregory Battcock (auth), Super Realism a Critical Anthology, Dutton, 75; Vivian Radnor (auth), Art: While waiting for tomorrow, New York Times, 10/23/77; Kim Levin (auth), Preview exhibition wood sculpture, O K Harris Gallery, Arts Mag, 10/77. *Mem:* Antique Tribal Art Dealers Asn. *Media:* Polychrome, Wood. *Specialty:* contemporary art; antique Native American. *Publ:* Collecting Kachina Dolls: 1880-1940, Alan Kessler Publisher, 1988 & 96. *Dealer:* Alan Kessler Gallery 836 Canyon Rd Sante Fe NM 87501. *Mailing Add:* 305 Camino Cerrito Santa Fe NM 87501

KESSLER, HERBERT LEON
EDUCATOR
b Chicago, Ill, July 20, 1941. *Study:* Univ Chicago, BA, 61; Princeton Univ, MFA, 63, PhD, 65. *Teaching:* From asst prof to prof hist art, Univ Chicago, 65-76; prof, Johns Hopkins Univ, 76-, chmn dept, 76-90 & 95-98, Dean, Sch Arts & Sci, 98-99; Richard Krautheimer guest prof, Bibl Hertziana, 96-97; Croghan prof, Williams Col, 2006; MacDonald prof, Emory Univ, 2007. *Mem:* Fel Medieval Acad Am; Fel Am Acad Arts & Sci. *Res:* Medieval art. *Publ:* Frescoes of the Dura Synagogue & Christian Art, Dumbarton Oaks, 90; Studies in Pictorial Narrative, Pindar, 94; The Poetry and Paintings of the First Bible of Charles the Bald, Mich, 97; Rome 1300: On the Path of the Pilgrim, 2000; Spiritual Seeing: Picturing God's Invisibility in Medieval Art, 2000; Old St. Peter's and Church Decoration in Medieval Italy, 2002; Seeing Medieval Art, 2004; Neither God nor Man, 2007; Judaism and Christian Art, 2011. *Mailing Add:* Dept Hist Art Johns Hopkins Univ Baltimore MD 21218

KESSLER, JANE Q
CURATOR, WRITER
b Charlotte, NC, June 14, 1946. *Study:* ECarolina Univ, BS, 69; Yale Univ Printroom, 82; Boston Pub Libr Printroom, 83. *Collection Arranged:* Harvey Littleton: Glass, 78; Southeastern Graphics Invitational (auth, catalog), 79-82; Southeastern Contemporary Metalsmiths (auth, catalog), 80 & 81; Contemporary Am Prints from the Permanent Collection of the Mint Mus (auth, catalog), 83; Ida Kohlmeyer: Thirty Years (auth, catalog), 83; Southern Comfort/Discomfort, 87, Made in Am, 88, Va Beach Arts Ctr; Counterbalance: LeWitt, Tinguely, Peart, Bechtler Gallery, 91; RSV: 6 Artists Respond, Bechtler Gallery, 92; Chiaroscuro, Montgomery Mus Biennial, Ala, 94; I Found Context, installations, 96; North Carolina Pottery Mus, permanent installation, 96-97. *Pos:* Cur exhibs, 78-84, cur contemp art, Mint Mus, 84-88; principal partner, Curs' Forum, 88-94, Artcentral Inc, 94; bd dir, Penland Schs; Chmn & founder, Context Visual Arts Ctr; consult & cur, Carillon Gallery, Shorenstein Co, 95-. *Awards:* Prof Fel Grant, Nat Endowment Art Mus. *Bibliog:* Interview, New Arts Examiner, 86 & Fiber Arts, 94. *Mem:* NC Print & Drawing Soc (pres bd, 83); Southeastern Coll Arts Conf (bd dirs, 82-85); Southern Graphics Coun; World Print Coun; Am Crafts Coun Southeastern Assembly; Southeastern Mus Coun. *Res:* Regional exhibitions of prints, drawings and crafts; history of American prints; southern art; American crafts; crafts of the Southern Appalachians. *Publ:* auth, Un-making it, Art Papers, 85; Rude Osonik, Am Craft, 90; Randy Schull, NC State Univ; auth, From Mission to Market, Appalachian Crafts (catalogue essay), Am Craft Mus, New York, 94; Southern Arts & Crafts (catalogue essay), Mint Mus, 96

KESSLER, LEONARD H
ILLUSTRATOR OF CHILDREN'S BOOKS
b Akron, Ohio, Oct 28, 1921. *Study:* Carnegie Inst of Tech, BFA (painting & design), 49. *Work:* De Grummond Collection, Univ Southern Miss; Kerlan Collection, Univ Minn. *Awards:* New York Times 10 Best Illus Children's Books, 54, 55 & 57. *Mem:* Soc Illusr; Graphic Artists Guild; Author's League; Author's Guild; Soc Children's Books Writers. *Media:* Pen & Ink, Pencil, Watercolor, Markers, Acrylic. *Publ:* Auth & illusr, Old Turtles, 90 Knock-Knock, 91 Greenwillow; Here Comes Strikeout rev ed, Harper Collins, 92; illusr, Is There a Penguin at Your Party?, Simon & Schuster, 94; Is There a Gorilla in the Band?, Simon & Schuster, 94; Kick Pass & Run, New illus ed, 96; Last One is a Rotten Egg, rev ed, Harper Collins, 99; auth, Mr Pine's Purple House, 2002, Mr Pine's Mixed-up Signs, 2003, Mrs. Pine Takes a Trip, 2005, Republished by Purple House Press. *Mailing Add:* 1624 Treehouse Cir Sarasota FL 34231

KESSLER, LINDA
PAINTER, PHOTOGRAPHER
b Brooklyn, NY, Aug 20, 1954. *Study:* Brooklyn Coll, BA, 75; Northeastern Univ, M Ed, 78; Atelier apprentice to Anton P Russev, New York, 81-85; Art Students League, with David Leffel, Frank Mason & Thomas Fogarty, New York, 81-88; Pratt Inst, MFA, 97. *Work:* Hosp for Joint Diseases/Orthopaedic Inst, NY; La Posada de Las Monjas, San Miguel de Allende, Mex; Mt Sinai Hosp, NY; and others. *Comn:* Portrait, Colin Gary, NY, 90; portrait, Paulo De Castro, Sao Paulo, Brazil, 92; portrait, Esther & Dennis Rodriguez, Sao Paulo, Brazil, 92; landscape, Julia Newton, Venice, Calif, 94. *Exhib:* Westbeth Gallery, NY, 93; Womens Show, Pratt Inst, Brooklyn, NY, 94; Nat Asn Women Artists, 395 W Broadway Gallery, NY, 94; Recycling with Imagination, AIA Gallery, Pittsburgh, Pa, 96; Brazilian Contemp Art, Boston City Hall Gallery, Mass, 97; Offspring, Brooklyn, NY, Feminist Expo, Baltimore, Md, 2000; 112th Ann Exhib Nat Asn Women Artists, NY, 2001; Cork Gallery, Lincoln Square, NY, 2002; Images Against War, Gallery Lichtblick, Cologne, Ger, 2003; Real Brooklyn - A Day in Our Life, Borough Hall, Brooklyn, NY, 2003; Peaceworks, Times Square Lobby Gallery, NY, 2003; Benefit Show, Muskegon Pregnancy Services, Mich, 2004; The Studiospale & Gallery, Silver City, NMes, 2006-2008; Americana, MLT Gallery, New York, 2010; Subjects of Affection, Calumet Gallery, New York, 2010; Manhattan Borough Presidents Offices, Small Works Exhib, NY, 2011; Calumet Gallery, NY, 2011; Soho Photo Gallery, Krappy Kamera Exhib, NY, 2012; TCC Photo Gallery, Holga out of the Box, Longview, TX, 2012; Powerhouse Arena, Abadonment, Brooklyn, NY, 2012; The Sylvia Walk & Po Kim Art Gallery, Nat Assn Women Artists Annual Mem Exhib, NY, 2013; Brooklyn Fire Proof Gallery, We, Au Naturel, Brooklyn, NY, 2014. *Pos:* Coordr, Art & Play Therapy, Hosp for Joint

Diseases/Orthopaedic Inst, New York, 82-86; photogr, owner, Focus Pocus, A Fine Art Photography Studio, New York, 97-; Linda Kessler Fine Art & Photography, 2014. *Teaching:* Pvt painting lessons in Sao Paulo, Brazil, 91-92; fine art tchr, Early Coll High Sch, Brooklyn, NY, 2000-. *Awards:* Best Show Award, Micro/Macro Exhib, Helio Gallery, New York, 89. *Bibliog:* Will Grant (auth), Varied generations, varied dimensions, Artspeak, New York, 12/90; Audrey Bernard (auth), For art's sake, Daily Challenge, New York, 11/90; Liam Nelson (auth), Drawn to sculpture, Kingston Daily Freeman, NY 9/90; Best of Acrylic Painting, Rockport Publ, 96; Landscape Inspirations, Rockport Publ, 97; plus others. *Mem:* Nat Asn Women Artists; Professional Women Photographers. *Media:* Acrylic, Mixed Media. *Interests:* Fgn travel, cross-country skiing. *Publ:* Auth, The Rainbows End, The Int Libr Photography, 2000. *Dealer:* Focus Pocus Photo 140 Cadman Plaza W Brooklyn NY 11201. *Mailing Add:* Linda Kessler 140 Cadman Plaza W Brooklyn NY 11201-1877

KESSLER, MARGARET JENNINGS
PAINTER
b Auburn, Ind, Aug 15, 1944. *Exhib:* Top 100, Nat Arts for the Parks Show, traveling, 89. *Teaching:* Instr painting workshops internationally. *Awards:* Silver, 82, Bronze, 83, Gold Medal, 89 & 94, Grumbacher Art Awards; Hon Mention, Am Artist's Prof League, Salmagundi Club, NY, 84; Gold Medal, Oil Painters Am Regional, San Antonio, 94; and others. *Bibliog:* Article, Southwest Art Mag, 12/84; article, Watercolor Mag, fall 93. *Mem:* Signature mem Artists & Craftsmen Asn (pres, 85-86). *Media:* Oil. *Publ:* North Light Mag, 4/85 & The Artists' Mag, 1/85, 2/85 & 1/88; contribr, cover, The Artist's Mag, 2/85; Painting Better Landscapes, Watson-Guptill Publ, New York, 87; Everything You Ever Wanted to Know About Oil Painting, Watson-Guptill Publ, New York, 93

KESSMANN, DEAN
EDUCATOR, ADMINISTRATOR
Study: Southern Ill Univ, Carbondale, MFA. *Exhib:* solo exhibitions include Orlando Mus Art, Conner Contemporary Art, Washington, DC, Calif State Univ, Chico, White Flag Projects, St Louis, and Carnegie Mellon Univ, Pitts., Pa.; two and three person exhibitions include Ellen Curlee Gallery, St Louis, School 33 Art Ctr, Baltimore, and 1708 Gallery, Richmond; group exhibitions include Cerasoli Gallery, Los Angeles, Mus of Contemporary Religious Art, St Louis, Photographic Resource Ctr, Boston, Project Row Houses, Houston, and ARC Gallery, Chicago. *Teaching:* chair, assoc prof photography, George Washington Univ, currently. *Mailing Add:* George Washington Univ Smith Hall of Art Room A-101-A or 2A01 801 22nd St NW Washington DC 20052

KESTER, GRANT
EDUCATOR, HISTORIAN
Study: Md Inst, Col of Art, BFA (photography), 1986; Univ Rochester, MA (art history), 1995, PhD (visual and cultural studies), 1997. *Pos:* Washington, DC/Mid-Atlantic editor, New Art Examiner, formerly; editor, Afterimage, 1990-96. *Teaching:* Scholar-in-residence, coord critical studies prog, Cranbrook Acad Art, Bloomfield, Mich, formerly; asst prof modern art history and theory, Wash State Univ, 1997-99, asst prof contemporary art and theory, Ariz State Univ, 1999-2000; assoc prof art history, Univ Calif San Diego, La Jolla, 2000-, dir grad studies, Dept Visual Arts, 2003-09, chair, formerly, dir Univ Art Gallery, currently. *Awards:* Fellow, Whitney Mus Am Art Independent Study Program, 1986-87. *Mailing Add:* University of California, San Diego Visual Arts Department 9500 Gilman Dr La Jolla CA 92093-0084

KETCHUM, ROBERT GLENN
PHOTOGRAPHER, CURATOR
b Los Angeles, Calif, Dec 1, 1947. *Study:* Univ Calif, Los Angeles, with Heinecken & Teske in photog, BA (design, cum laude), 70; Brooks Inst, 71; Calif Inst Arts, MFA (photog), 74. *Work:* Mus Mod Art & Metrop Mus Art, NY; Los Angeles Co Mus Art, Los Angeles; Nat Mus Am Art & Corcoran Gallery, Washington, DC. *Comn:* Seafarm (book), comn by Harry N Abrams, Int Ocean Inst, NY, 77; portfolio, traveling exhibit, Lila Acheson Wallace Fund, NY, 82-84; color portfolio of Alaska, The Wallace Ford Fund, NY, 82-84; Chattahoochee Suite, Cousins Properties, Atlanta, Ga, 85-87; color portfolio, Cleveland Found, Gund Found, Akron Art Mus, Ohio, 86-. *Exhib:* White House, Washington, DC, 79; Smithsonian Traveling Exhib Service, 80-84; Am Photogr and Nat Parks Traveling Exhib, 81-83; Solo exhib, Sheldon Mem Art Gallery, Lincoln, Nebr, 84; Lyndon Johnson Libr, Austin, Tex, 84; Nat Mus Am Art, 85; and others. *Pos:* Cur, Nat Park Found, DC, 78-; bd trustees, Los Angeles Ctr Photog Studies, 75-81, pres & exec dir, 79. *Teaching:* Founder & teacher photog workshop, Sun Valley Ctr Arts & Humanities, 71-73; instr photog, Calif Inst Arts, 75; instr & adv bd, Appalachian Arts Ctr, Highlands, NC, 82-. *Awards:* Nat Park Found Award, 78 & 79; Mat Res Award, Ciba-Geigy, 79; NY State Coun on the Arts Grant, 85. *Bibliog:* Suzanne Muchnic (auth), Ketchum, Evert at Municipal, Los Angeles Times, 6/14/83; Gene Thorton (auth), Critics choice/photography, New York Times, 12/29/85; Margaret Moorman (auth), New York Reviews/Robert Glenn Ketchum, Art News, 3/86. *Mem:* Friends Photog. *Media:* Cibachrome Color Prints, Books. *Publ:* Coauth, Outerbridge, Los Angeles Ctr Photog Studies, 76; auth, Photographic Directions: Los Angeles 1979, Security Pac Bank, 79; Landscape Photographers and America's National Parks, Nat Park Found, 79; The Hudson River and the Highlands, Aperture, 85

KETNER, JOSEPH DALE
EDUCATOR, ADMINISTRATOR
b Anderson, Ind, Oct 30, 1955. *Study:* Ind Univ, BA, 77, MA, 80. *Collection Arranged:* Grace Hartigan, 81 (with catalog), 81; Beautiful, Sublime & Picturesque (with catalog), 84; Carl F Wimar (with catalog), 91; Robert S Duncanson (with catalog), 93; A Gallery of Modern Art (with catalog), 94; Art & Science: Investigating Matter, Catherine Wagner (with catalog), 97. *Pos:* Cur-registr, Ft Wayne Mus Art, Ind, 79-82; cur, Washington Univ Gallery Art, 82 & dir, 89-98; cur, Ros Art Mus at Brandeis Univ, Waltham, Mass, 98-2005; chief cur, Milwaukee Art Mus, 2005-2008. *Teaching:* Lois & Henry Foster Chmn contempt art theory & practice, Emerson Coll, Boston, 2008-. *Mem:* Midwest Art Hist Soc, Univ Mus Comt (co-chair, 92); incorporating mem, St Louis Area Mus Collaborative. *Publ:* Auth, Continuing Search of Grace Hartigan, Artnews, 81; Robert S Duncanson: Late Literary Landscapes, Am Art J, 83; coauth, Beautiful, Sublime, & Picturesque, Washington Univ, 84; Carl F Wimar: Chronicler of the Missouri, R Amon Carter/Abrams, 91; auth, Emergence of the African-American Artist, Univ Mo, 93

KETTLEWOOD, BEA CARD
PAINTER, STAINED GLASS ARTIST
b Pompton Plains, NJ, Jun 7, 1929. *Study:* Kean Univ, BS, 51; New York Univ, MA, 55, EDD (creative art), 72. *Work:* Arnot Mus, Elmira, NY; Rutgers Univ, New Brunswick, NJ; City Hall, Jersey City, NJ; Nairn Old Parish, Scotland; Paterson Libr, NJ; Pa State Univ; Pequannock Twp Public Lib; Cod Cove Inn, Me. *Comn:* Stained glass window designs, Chilton Mem Hosp, Pompton Plains, NJ, 90, Morristown Mem Hosp, NJ, 94, Rehabilitation Inst, Morristown, NJ, 95, Hackettstown Community Hosp, NJ, 2000; 3 stained glass windows, 1st Reformed Church, Pompton Plains, NJ, 86; oil painting Nairn Church, comn by Choir of 1st Reformed, Nairn Scotland, 97. *Exhib:* State Show, Montclair Mus, NJ, 62; Burr Artists Show, Jersey City Mus, NJ, 68; Juried Open Show, Farnsworth Art Mus, Rockland, ME, 69-77; Juried Open Show, New Eng Fine Arts Inst, Boston, 93; Ellasue Open, Trenton City Mus, NJ, 96; Juried Open Show, Monmouth Mus, Lincroft, NJ, 98; Art From The Start, SUNY Orange, Middletown, NY, 2004; Juried Open Show, Butler Inst of Am Art, Youngstown, Ohio, 2005; 53rd Solo Show, 2012; Pa State Univ, 2012. *Pos:* Retired art educator 33 yrs; lecturer, art & art hist; gallery dir, FRC Church House Art Gallery. *Teaching:* Educator & dept chmn, New Milford High, New Milford, NJ, 51-84; lectr art & art hist, freelance, 84-. *Awards:* Ringwood Golden Jubilee, 68; First Award, Jersey City Bicentennial, 76; Award of Merit, Bergen Mus, 83; and many others. *Mem:* Maine Art Gallery (62-2004); Women's Caucus for Art NJ, NY chap (80-95); Arts Coun Orange Co, NY Gallery Comt (85-95); Ringwood Manor Asn Arts (91-). *Media:* Oil, Watercolor. *Res:* Visual Space in Painting: 49-69; Hist Am Archit. *Interests:* Am Archit; Writing Children's Books. *Publ:* Ourselves and Others. *Mailing Add:* 45 Wilrue Pkwy Pompton Plains NJ 07444-1717

KETTNER, DAVID ALLEN
ARTIST, EDUCATOR
b Sunman, Ind, Oct 19, 1943. *Study:* Skowhegan Sch Painting and Sculpture, 64; Cleveland Inst Art, BFA, 66; Ind Univ, MFA, 68. *Work:* Pa Acad Fine Arts; Philadelphia Mus Art, Pa; Rutgers Univ, Coll Arts & Sci, Camden, NJ. *Exhib:* Six Self-Portraits 1975 Series, Whitney Mus Am Art, NY, 76; 41st Int Eucharistic Congress Liturgical Arts Exhib, Civic Ctr, Philadelphia, 76; Philadelphia Houston Exchange, Inst Contemp Art, Philadelphia, 76; Recent Acquisitions, Philadelphia Mus Art, 77; Am Drawing Show, Fine Arts Gallery, San Diego, Calif, 77; Contemp Drawing, 78 & A Bach Transcription, 81, Pa Acad Fine Arts. *Teaching:* Assoc prof painting & drawing, Philadelphia Col Art, 68-. *Bibliog:* Victoria Donohue (auth), article, Philadelphia Inquirer, 10/9/81. *Mailing Add:* Dept Painting Broad & Pine Sts Univ of the Arts 320 S Broad St Philadelphia PA 19102-4994

KEVESON, FLORENCE
PAINTER, ILLUSTRATOR
b New York, NY. *Study:* The Cooper Union Art Degree; Art Students League, Ford Found Scholar; with Sidney Grosz & Leo Manso. *Work:* CD Morris; E Gruenberg Collection; La Boetie Gallery, NY. *Comn:* Woodstock Hist Soc. *Exhib:* Albany Inst Hist Art; solo exhibs, Silvermine Guild Artists, Marist Coll; Wadsworth Atheneum Mus; Berkshire Mus, Pittsfield, Mass; Painters & Sculptors, Bergen Mus, Paramus, NJ; Butler Inst; Nat Arts Club; Acad Art & Letters; Silvermine Gallery, Marist College; Many others. *Pos:* Illusr, Conde Nast Publ, 49-52; free-lance illusr, 53-; pvt classes in studio. *Awards:* Shandoff Award, Berkshire; G Paley Award, Nat Asn Women Artists; Michael M Engel Award, Am Soc Contemp Artists; Pen & Brush Inc, 95-2005; and numerous others. *Mem:* Audubon Artists; Am Soc Contemp Artists; Nat Asn Women Artists; Silvermine Guild; Pen & Brush Inc. *Media:* Oil. *Specialty:* Semi-abstract paintings, Contemporary Paintings. *Collection:* CD Morris; Rudolf Collectors; S. Anster; R. Ricci; A. Rein. *Publ:* Illus in Vogue, McCalls, Good Housekeeping, Glamour, Harpers Bazaar, Seventeen; and others. *Dealer:* La Boite Gallery New York NY; Karl Mann Gallery; Rudolph Gallery. *Mailing Add:* 314 E 201 St Bronx NY 10458

KEVORKIAN, RICHARD
PAINTER
b Dearborn, Mich, Aug 24, 1937. *Study:* Pa Acad of Fine Arts, Philadelphia, 58; Richmond Prof Inst, BFA (painting), 61; Calif Coll of Arts & Crafts, Oakland, MFA (painting), 62. *Work:* Mus Genocide, Yerevan, Armenia; Fed Reserve, Richmond, Va; Southeastern Ctr for Contemp Art, Winston-Salem, NC; IBM, Washington; PBS KAMU, Coll Sta, Tex; Va Commonwealth Univ, Richmond, Va; Banco Nat, Lima, Peru. *Exhib:* Painting in the South, 1564-1980, traveling exhib, Va Mus Fine Arts, Birmingham Mus Art, Nat Acad Design, NY JB Speed Art Mus, & New Orleans Mus Art; Southern Abstraction: Five Painters, Traveling Exhib, Univ Tenn, Clemson Univ, NC State Univ & Cheekwood Fine Arts Ctr, Nashville, Tenn; Contemp Art Acquisitions, Equitable Gallery, NY; 35 Southeastern Artists, High Mus, 76; Southeast 7, Southeastern Ctr Contemp Art, Winston-Salem, 77; Leicester Polytech, Eng; Marita Gilliam Gallery, Raleigh, NC; Eric Schindler Gallery, Richmond, Va; Univ Guam; Muggleton Gallery, Auburn, NY; plus others. *Pos:* vis artist, Nat Col Art & Design, Dublin Ireland; Central School Art and Design, London, Eng; Loughborough Col Art, Leicester, Eng; Winchester, Col Art, Eng; Ulster Col, Belfast, Northern Ireland. *Teaching:* Instr painting, Richard Bland Col, Petersburg, Va, 61-64; prof & chmn dept of painting & printmaking, Va Commonwealth Univ, Richmond, 64-, prof emer, 92. *Awards:* Individual Sr Artists Grant (painting), Nat Endowment Arts, 72; Southeastern

Ctr Contemp Arts Grant (painting), 76; Guggenheim Fel Painting, 78; Traveling Fel Va Mus Fine Arts, 61-62. *Mem:* Nat Coun of Art Adminr. *Media:* Oil, acrylic. *Specialty:* Visual Arts. *Interests:* Fishing, Hunting, Cooking. *Dealer:* Aaron Gallery 1717 Connecticut Ave NW Washington DC 20009; Lee Hansley Gallery 225 Glenwood Ave Raleigh NC 27603. *Mailing Add:* 7909 Rock Creek Rd Richmond VA 23229

KEYSER, ROSY
SCULPTOR
b Baltimore, Md, 1974. *Study:* Cornell Univ, Ithaca, BFA; Sch Art Inst Chicago, MFA. *Exhib:* Olive Tjaden Gallery, Cornell Univ, Ithaca, 1995; Honest Lies, 27 Walker Space, New York, 1999; Postcards From the Edge, Andrew Kreps Gallery, New York, 2000; Out of Nowhere, Sch Art Inst Chicago, 2002; Gallery 400, Univ Ill, Chicago, 2003; Jessica Murray Projects, Brooklyn, 2004; solo exhib, Peter Blum Gallery, New York, 2008; New Work, Reynolds Gallery, Richmond, Va, 2009. *Bibliog:* Holland Cotter (auth), Sampling Brooklyn, Keeper of Electric Flames, NY Times, 1/23/2004; Suzanne Hudson (auth), Stubborn Materials, Artforum, 11/2007. *Mailing Add:* c/o Peter Blum Gallery 20 W 57th St New York NY 10019

KEYSER, WILLIAM ALPHONSE, JR
PAINTER, SCULPTOR
b Pittsburgh, Pa, July 30, 1936. *Study:* Carnegie-Mellon Univ, Pittsburgh, BS, 58; Sch Am Crafts, Rochester Inst of Tech, MFA (furniture design), 61; Sch Art, Rochester Inst Tech, MFA (painting), 2006. *Work:* Mus Art & Design, New York; Artpark, Lewiston, NY; Eastman Kodak Co, Rochester, NY; Mem Art Gallery, Rochester, NY; Sheldon Mus of Fine art, Univ Neb, Lincoln. *Comn:* Subway Benches, Sculptures, Mass Bay Transportation Auth, 84; bench, sculpture, Art Park, Lewiston, NY, 1986; complete sanctuary furnishings, St Mary's Church, Rochester, NY, 87; Rochester Top 100, annual award sculpture, Peat Marwick & Rochester CofC, 1987-2012; chapel furnishings, Diocesan Ctr, Roman Catholic Diocese, Rochester, NY, 2003; Rainbow Moment, wall sculpture, St Catherine of Sienna Church, Mendon, NY, 2007. *Exhib:* Nat Invitational Furniture Show, Mendocino Calif, 90; Craft Art Western NY, Burchfield-Penny Art Ctr, Buffalo, NY, 1990, 1994 & 2006; Kanazawa Arts & Crafts Competition, Kanazawa, Japan, 91; Contemp Crafts NY, NY Mus, Albany, NY, 97; NY State Biennial, NY State Mus, Albany; Studio Furniture: Fine Art Invitational, Memphis Coll of Art, 2000; The Maker's Hand: Am Studio Furniture, 1940-1990, Mus Fine Arts, Boston, Mass, 2003; Pulp Function, Fuller Craft Mus, Brocton, Mass, 2007; Painting & Sculpture, NTID Dyer Art Ctr, 2009; Extraordinary Forms II, Kenan Ctr, Lockport, NY, 2010; Continuation: Painting & Sculpture, Ock Hee's Gallery, Honcoye Falls, NY; Oxford Gallery, Rochester, NY, 2010, 2011, 2012; Made in NY, Schweinfurth Art Ctr, Auburn, NY, 2014; Rochester Finger Lakes Exhibition, Mem Art Gallery, Rochester, NY, 2015; Art in Craft Media, Burchfield Penney Art Ctr, Buffalo, NY, 2015. *Teaching:* Prof Emeritus furniture design, Sch Am Crafts, Rochester Inst of Technol, 62-97-, chmn crafts, 81-89. *Awards:* Young Americans Award, Am Crafts Coun, 62; Craftsmen's Fel, Nat Endowment for the Arts, 75; Distinguished Alumnus, Rochester Inst Tech, 1987; Fel Am Craft Coun, 97; Merit Award, Carnegie Mellon Univ, 1998; Award of Distinction, The Furniture Soc, 03; Coll of Fellows, Am Craft Coun, 97. *Bibliog:* Jonathan Fairbanks (auth), American Furniture 1620 to the Present, 81; Dona Z Meilach (auth), Woodworking: The New Wave, Crown Publ, 81; William Keyser and the MBTA Bench Project (video), Rochester Inst Technol, producer, 84; Edward S. Cooke Jr, Gerald W R Ward & Kelly H L'ecuyer (auths), The Maker's Hand-Am Studio Furniture 1940 to 1990, 2003; Barbara Lovenheim (ed), Breaking Ground, A Century of Craft Art in Western NY, 2010; Vanrt Koplos & Bruce Metcalf, Makers: A History of American Studio Craft, 2010; and others. *Mem:* Am Crafts Coun; The Furniture Soc; Art & Cult Coun Greater Rochester. *Media:* All Media. *Publ:* Auth, Steam Bending--Heat and Moisture Plasticize Wood, 77 & Portfolio: W A Keyser, The Challenge of Churches, 79, Fine Woodworking, Taunton Press; Where Designs Are Born, Home Furniture, Taunton Press, 95. *Dealer:* Pritam & Eames East Hampton NY; Och Hee Gallery 2 Lehigh St Honeoye Falls, NY; Oxford Gallery 267 Oxford St Rochester NY 14607. *Mailing Add:* 8008 Taylor Rd Victor NY 14564

KHACHIAN, ELISA A
PAINTER
b Worcester, Mass, May 6, 1935. *Study:* RI Sch Design, BS, 57; Fairfield Univ, graphic art, 82; Silvermine Coll Art. *Work:* Pvt collection, Town of Fairfield, Conn. *Comn:* Contemp Graphic Center. *Exhib:* Southern Vt Art Ctr; Juried Exhib, Javitts Ctr, Nat Asn Women Artists, NY, 88; Conn Watercolor Soc, New Brit Mus Am Art, 90; First Show Mus, Katonah Mus, NY, 92; Conn Women Artists, New Brit Mus Am Art, 92; Art of the Northeast, 97; Discovery Mus, 98; and others. *Pos:* Art asst, RI Sch Design, Spec Talents, 56-57; art educ, W Concord Sch System, 57-58. *Teaching:* Problem solving, Darien Art Soc, 87-91. *Awards:* Conn Women Artists Award, Merchants Bank & Trust, 89; Seven Awards, 50th Ann Conn Watercolor Soc, 90; Best Drawing/Painting, Discovery Mus, 98; Women's Caucus for Art; Art Place Coop Gallery; New Haven Paint and Clay Merit Award; New Haven Paint and Clay Purchase Award; New Haven Brush Palette Charles Fisher Prize; Conn Watercolor Soc, Ester Fay Memorial award, 2013. *Mem:* Nat Asn Women Artists; Silvermine Guild Ctr for the Arts; Conn Women Artists; Conn Watercolor Soc. *Media:* Watercolor, Collage, Printmaking. *Interests:* writing. *Publ:* Auth, Watercolor, 96; auth, Splash, National Asn Women Artists, Zimmerli Mus, Rutgers Univ, 8/2005 & 9/2006; auth, Splash (8, 9, 10), North Light Publ, 8/2007; auth, Strokes of Genius (int drawing bk), 8/2007; auth, Passionate Brushstrokes, 8/2008; New Directions 2009; Best of Drawing, 2010. *Mailing Add:* 213 Hollydale Rd Fairfield CT 06430

KHALIL, CLAIRE ANNE
PAINTER
b Boston, Mass, Feb 20, 1944. *Study:* Emmanuel Col, BA, 65; Acad di Belle Arte, Florence, Italy, 65-66. *Work:* Am Stock Exch, NY; Janss Found, Sun Valley, Idaho; Venus--the Bittkers-New Haven, Conn, 75. *Comn:* Red Brick House, comn by Gloria Garfinkel, NY, 81; Sweet Briar, comn by Stephanie Axinn, NY, 82; The House of the Three Gables, comn by Carol Butz, NY, 82; Sun Valley and the Janss Collection with Dove, comn by Glenn Janss, Idaho, 84. *Exhib:* Focus on Realism: Selections from the Collection of Glenn C Janss, traveling exhib throughout US, 85; Fireworks: Am Artists Celebrate the Eighth Art, Butler Inst Am Art, Youngstown, Ohio, 85. *Bibliog:* Alvin Martin (auth), American Realism--Twentieth Century Drawings and Watercolors, San Francisco Mus Mod Art & Harry N Abrams, 86. *Dealer:* Nancy Hoffman 429 W Broadway New York NY 10012. *Mailing Add:* c/o Nancy Hoffman Gallery 520 W 27th St Ste 301 New York NY 10001-5548

KHALIL, MOHAMMAD O
GRAPHIC ARTIST, PRINTMAKER
b Burri, Khartoum, Sudan, Jan 8, 1936; US citizen. *Study:* Khartoum Tech Sch, dipl, 60; Acad di Belle Arte di Firenze, dipl, 66. *Work:* Metrop Mus Art, NY; Smithsonian Inst; Libr Congress; Mus Mod Art, Osaka, Japan; Mus Grenoble, France. *Exhib:* 17th Print Biennial, Brooklyn Mus, 70; solo exhibs, Bronx Mus, 87, Inst du Mon de Arab, 87, Nat Mus Am Art, Washington, 95; group exhib, Herbert F Johnson, Ithaca, NY, 93. *Teaching:* Instr printmaking, New Sch Social Res, 70-, Pratt Inst, Brooklyn, 71-83, Parson Sch Design, 88-, NY Univ, 91-. *Awards:* Grant, Bronx Coun on Arts, 87; Bronze Prize, Osaka Triennial, 91; First Prize, Int Biennial Cairo, 93. *Mem:* Nat Acad. *Mailing Add:* c/o Mary Ryan Gallery 527 W 26th St New York NY 10001-5503

KHALILI, NASSER DAVID
COLLECTOR
b Isfahan, Iran, 1945. *Study:* Univ London, PhD, 1988. *Hon Degrees:* Boston Univ, LHD, 2003; Univ Arts London, PhD, 2005. *Pos:* Owner, The Khalili Collections, 1970- & Favermead Property co; int bd overseers, Tufts Univ, Mass, 1997-; bd trustees, Boston Univ, 2003-; co-founder & chmn, Maimonides Found, London; co-founder & bd dirs, Iran Heritage Found, 1995-. *Teaching:* Assoc res prof & Nasser D Khalili Chmn of Islamic Art, Sch Oriental and African StudiesUniv London. *Awards:* Decorated Knight Commander of the Royal Order of Francis I (KCFO), Medaglia Pontifica Pope John Paul II, Knight of the Equestrian Order of Pope St Sylvester (KSS); named Trustee of the City of Jerusalem, 1996; named one of Top 200 Collectors, ARTnews mag, 2004-13. *Collection:* Islamic art, Swedish textiles, Spanish metalwork, Japanese art of the Meiji period & enamels. *Mailing Add:* The Nour Found Nour House 2 Old Burlington St London WIS3AD United Kingdom

KHEDOORI, RACHEL
SCULPTOR, FILMMAKER
b Sydney, Australia, 1964. *Study:* San Francisco Art Inst, BFA, 1988; UCLA, MFA, 1994. *Exhib:* Solo exhibs, Asn Mus van Hendendaagse Kunst, Ghent, Belgium, Rum, Malmo, Sweden, 1995, Hauser & Wirth, Switzerland, 1997, 2002, 2007, David Zwirner Gallery, NY, 1999, Galerie Gisela Capitain, Cologne, Germany, 2000, Villa Arson, Nice, France, 2004, The Box, Los Angeles, 2009.; David Zwirner (with Toba Khedoori), 1994, Wanas Found, Wanas 1996, Knislinge, Sweden, 1996, Holderbank AG, Kunstausstellung Holderback, Switzerland, 1997, Philomene Magers, LA, Munich, Germany, 1999, Mus Contemporary Art, Flight Patterns, Los Angeles, 2000, David Zwirner, I Love New York, 2001, Galerie Michel Rein, Solituded, Paris, 2002, Hauser & Wirth, Ten Years Galerie, Zurich, Switzerland, 2002, Kunsthaus Graz, Imagination-Perception in Art, Einbildung Das Wahrnehem in der Kunst, Austria, 2003, Hamburger Bahnhof, Flick Collection, Berlin, Germany, 2004, San Francisco Art Inst, Work Zones, 2006, David Zwirner, A Point in Space is a Place for an Argument, NY, 2007, Kunsthalle Wien, Western Motel, Vienna, Austria, 2008 Kunsthaus Graz, Austria, Venice Biennale, Making Worlds, 2009, 53rd Int Art Exhib Biennale, Venice, 2009. *Mailing Add:* c/o David Zwirner Gallery 525 West 19th St New York NY 10011

KHEDOORI, TOBA
PAINTER
b Sydney, Australia, 1964. *Study:* San Francisco Art Inst, BFA, 1988; UCLA, MFA, 1994. *Exhib:* Solo exhibs, Regan Projects, Los Angeles, 1995, 2006, 2009, David Zwirner Gallery, NY, 1996, 1999, 2002, 2007, Directions, Hirshhorn Mus, Smithsonian Inst, Washington, DC, 1997-98, Mus of Contemporary Art, Los Angeles, 1997, Walker Art Ctr, Minn, 1997, St. Louis Art Mus, Whitechapel Art Gallery, London, 2001, Royal Hibernian Art Gallery, Dublin, Ireland, 2002, St. Louis Art Mus, 2003, and others; Invitational 93, Regan Projects, Los Angeles, 1993, Whitney Biennial, Whitney Mus American Art, NY, 1995, Some Recent Acquisitions, Mus Modern Art, NY, 1996, Elusive Paradise: Los Angeles Art from the Permanent Collection, Mus Contemporary Art, 1997, 1999, Five Years, David Zwirner Gallery, NY, 1998, Examining Pictures, White Chapel Art Gallery, London, 1999, Mus Contemporary Art, Chicago, 1999, Armand Hammer Mus/UCLA, 2000, Recent Acquisitions, Hirshhorn Mus, 2002, Drawing Now: Eight Propositions, Mus Modern Art, Queens, NY, 2003, Reinstallation of the Collection, Mus Modern Art, NY, 2004, Drawings from the Modern 1975-2005, 2006, The Third Mind, Palais de Tokyo, Paris, France, 2007-08, 53rd Int Art Exhib Biennale, Venice, 2009. *Collection Arranged:* Mus Modern Art, NY; Whitney Mus Am Art, NY; Mus Contemporary Art, Los Angeles; Los Angeles County Mus Art; Walker Art Ctr, Minn; Hirshhorn Mus, Washington, DC; Collection Dakis Joannou, Athens, Greece; others. *Awards:* Louis Comfort Tiffany Found Grant, 1995; John D and Catherine MacArthur Found Award, 2002. *Media:* Miscellaneous Media

KHORRAMIAN, LALEH
PAINTER
b Tehran, Iran, 1974. *Study:* Rhode Island Sch Design, 1995; Sch Art Inst Chicago, BFA, 1997; Columbia Univ, Sch Visual Arts, MFA, 2004. *Exhib:* Solo exhibs include Salon 94, New York, 2005 & 2008, Thirdline, Dubai, United Arab Emirates, 2006, Mills Coll Art Mus, Oakland, Calif, 2007; group exhibs include Artists Books, Leroy Neiman Gallery, Columbia Univ, New York 2002, Turning Points, 2004, After Goya, 2004; E-Flux Video Rental Project, E-Flux, New York, 2004; Greater NY 2005, PS 1 Mus, New York, 2005; Night of 1000 Drawings, Artists Space, New York, 2005;

Edun, Salon 94, New York, Hello I'm Crashing, 2007; Land Mine, Aldrich Contemp Art Mus, Conn, 2006; Palette, Greenberg Van Doren, New York, 2006; Cosmologies, James Cohan Gallery, New York, 2007; East/West Dialogue, LMTH Gallery, New York, 2008. *Awards:* Frances Hook Scholar; Evolving Perceptions Scholar; Agnes Martin Award; Artist Fel Award; Pat Heam & Colin Deland Found Grant; Pollock-Krasner Found Grant, 2007; Gottlieb Found Grant. *Mailing Add:* c/o Salon 94 12 E 94th St New York NY 10128

KIDD, REBECCA MONTGOMERY
PAINTER
b Muncie, Ind, Nov 29, 1942. *Comn:* Double portrait, comn by Delegate & Mrs Robert Bloxom, Mapsville, Va, 73; film illus, Effective Educ Systems, Essexville, Mich, 75; children's portrait, comn by Mr & Mrs Stephen B Tankard, Exmore, Va, 84; Civil War era portrait, comn by Mr & Mrs Louis Floyd, Exmore, Va, 86; double portrait, comn by Mrs Joanne Vankesteren Smith, Onancock, Va, 88. *Exhib:* The Pentagon, Arlington, Va, 74; Int Cong on Arts & Commun Exhib, Queen's Col, Univ Cambridge, Eng, 82; Int Platform Asn Conv Art Exhib, Hyatt Regency, Washington, DC, 84; solo exhib, Eastern Shore Chap Va Mus, Eastern Shore Community Col, Melfa, Va, 87. *Awards:* Popular Choice Award, & Merit Award, IPA Conv Exhib, 84. *Bibliog:* Art by Rebecca Kidd shown, Daily Times, Salisbury, Md, 1/17/82; Artist Rebecca Kidd receives IPA Awards, Eastern Shore News, Va, 8/23/84. *Mem:* Visual Artists & Galleries Asn. *Media:* Oils, Pastels. *Dealer:* Roadside Gallery Main St Melfa VA. *Mailing Add:* 9 Lake St Onancock VA 23417

KIDWELL, MICHELE FALIK
ART HISTORIAN, WRITER
b New York, NY, June 1, 1944. *Study:* Hunter Coll, New York, BA (cum laude), MA. *Pos:* Art tour guide, various mus & galleries, 78-99; sales & appraisals for courts, attorneys, charities & pvt clients, 85-; judge, Cong Arts Caucus, 91; cur, Fedn Protestant Welfare Agencies, 93; exec comt, Hunter Coll Art Gallery; bd, Bacchanalia; chair, Archeology Comt, Nat Arts Club, 2007-. *Teaching:* Fac, New Sch Univ, 78-2002, NY Univ, 84-90 & Coll New Rochelle, 91; lectr in field 78-. *Mem:* Nat Arts Club; Jewish Community Relations Coun; Ladies Village Improvement Soc Landmark Comn; Foreign Press Asn. *Res:* Italian illuminated manuscripts, ancient art & Renaissance women, Egyptian arts, Jewish items. *Interests:* Presentation and landmarks. *Publ:* Auth, Manet, ARTS Mag, 11/83; Avi Adler, To Live Again, 12/85; Bard College pvt collection, Greek objects (exhib catalog), summer, 90; Picasso: His Life and Art, Bridgewater Press, 97; Mary Frances Judge (exhib catalog), Oak Ridge Museum, Tenn, spring 94, (monogr), Roma, 2001,; Metrop Mus, Elder Gazette, 2010; Aprodisiao Scroll, 2011. *Mailing Add:* 495 West End Ave Apt 1K New York NY 10024

KIEFERNDORF, FREDERICK GEORGE
PAINTER, EDUCATOR
b Milwaukee, Wis, May 12, 1921. *Study:* Univ Wis, BA & MS. *Work:* Springfield Art Mus, Mo; Mo State Hist Soc Permanent Collection (painting requested 75); Wis Salon Art, Madison; Sch Ozarks, Point Lookout, Mo; Pittsburgh State Col, Kans. *Exhib:* Ann Delta Show, Little Rock, 67 & 74; Ten Painters of Missouri, Traveling Exhib, Mo State Coun Arts, 68; Springfield Art Mus Midwest Exhib, 72; Retrospective exhib, Park Central Gallery, 81; Two-person exhib, Jordan Creek Gallery, 85; Exhib of drawings & paintings, Springfield Art Mus, 88; Emer Fac Exhib, Southwest Mo State Univ Design Gallery, 96. *Teaching:* Prof art, Southwest Mo State Univ, 53-81. *Awards:* Purchase Award, Springfield Art Mus, 56 & 65 & Award of Merit, 67; Purchase Award, Sch Ozarks, 70 & Award of Merit, 81. *Bibliog:* Edgar A Albin (auth), article in Art Voices/South, 7-8/78; Edgar A Albin (auth), article in Springfield Mag, 1/87; Gregory Thielen (auth), Journeys Near & Far, Springfield Art Mus, 88. *Media:* Polymer, Vinyl Cement

KIEFFER, MARY JANE
PAINTER
b Chicago, Ill. *Study:* Am Acad Art, 37-38; Maholy-Nagi Sch Design; Art Inst Chicago. *Comn:* Numerous pvt comns. *Exhib:* Pasadena Soc Artists Ann, Riverside Art Mus, 68; Invitational, Nat Acad Design, NY, 68; Utah State Univ, Logan, 74-80; Brand XII, Brand Libr, Glendale, Calif; Nat Watercolor Soc Ann, Palm Springs Mus, Calif; Rocky Mountain Nat, Colo Art Mus; Downey Mus, 90; Los Angeles Co Century Gallery. *Awards:* First Award & Purchase Award, Laguna Art Mus, 74, Bruggen Ann Award, 76 & Del Mar Coll Ann Award, 79, Nat Watercolor Soc, 55-85; Purchase Award, Utah State Univ Gallery, Logan. *Mem:* Nat Watercolor Soc (pres, 77-78); Pasadena Soc Artists (pres, 81-82). *Media:* Watercolor. *Publ:* Contribr, Expressive Watercolor Techniques, Davis, 82

KIELKOPF, JAMES ROBERT
PAINTER
b St Paul, Minn, July 13, 1939. *Study:* Minneapolis Sch Art, BFA, 65; Grand Marias Art Colony, summer 63; Skowhegan Sch Painting, summer 64. *Work:* Walker Art Ctr, Minneapolis Inst Art. *Comn:* First Bank Minneapolis, Minn, 82; Republic Bank, Houston, Tex, 83; 3M Corp, St Paul, Minn, 90. *Exhib:* Walker Art Ctr Biennial, 64 & 66; Minneapolis Inst Art Biennial, 67; Interchange, Dallas Mus Fine Arts, Tex, 72; Landmark Ctr, St Paul, 79; Minneapolis Inst of Art, Minn, 86; SDak Art Mus, Brookings, 90. *Media:* Acrylic, Oil. *Dealer:* Thomas Barry Fine Arts 900 6th Ave SE Minneapolis MN 55414. *Mailing Add:* 1963 Ashland Ave Saint Paul MN 55104-5831

KIENHOLZ, LYN
PATRON, ADMINISTRATOR
b Chicago, Ill. *Study:* Sullins Coll; Md Coll Women. *Exhib:* Cowin-Divola (catalog), La Jolla Mus Contemp Art & nat & Europ tour, 85-87; Off the Beaten Track (brochure), Wight Gallery, Univ Calif, Los Angeles, 88; Chinese Influence on West Coast Artists (catalog), Taiwan Mus Art, 88; Lee Miller Photographer (book), Corcoran Gallery Art, nat & int mus tour, 89-93; Individual Realities (catalog), Sezon Mus Art, Tokyo & Japan tour, 91; 12 Artists for Havana, Cuba Biennale, 94; Architecture for the New Millenium (catalog), MOCA Taipei, Taiwan, Macau, and China, 2002-2004; LA 1955-1985 (catalog), Centre Pompidou, Paris, 2006. *Pos:* Asst to artist Edward Kienholz, 66-74; exec dir, Beaubourg Found, Ctr Pompidou, Paris, 77-81; founder & chmn, Calif-Int Arts Found, Los Angeles, 81-. *Bibliog:* Hunter Drohojowska (auth), Carrying a torch for Olympic artists, Los Angeles Herald Examiner, 7/31/83; Suzanne Muchnic (auth), Lyn Kienholz puts sculpture on a pedestal, Los Angeles Times, 6/2/84; Carolyn Mitchell (auth), It Takes ability and connections to establish an arts Foundation, Chattanooga Times, 12/24/85; Jody Leader (auth), C/IAF on a roll, Los Angeles Reader, 7/11/86; Suzanne Muchnic (auth), Museum leaders to get eyeful of Los Angeles, Los Angeles Times, 9/18/90; Charles Koppelman (auth), The Matchmaker, LA Times, 2/26/06, Life, Times, KCET-TV, 4/18/2006; Carol Kino (auth), Southern California Art? Look It Up, NY Times, 12/16/2007; Richard Hertz (auth), The Beat and the Buzz: Inside the LA Art World, 2009. *Mem:* Comite Int Musees d'Art Moderne. *Interests:* All forms of contemporary art. *Publ:* Memoria: Cuban Art of the 20th Century, 2003; LA Rising, Art & Artists Before 1980, 2010. *Mailing Add:* 2737 Outpost Dr Los Angeles CA 90068

KIHLSTEDT, MAJA
PAINTER
b Stockholm, Sweden, 1952. *Study:* The Royal Danish Art Academy, MA, 73-77; Yale School of Art, Norfolk Summer Scholarship Program, 79. *Work:* Nokia, Stockholm, Sweden; Se Banken, Stockholm, Sweden; Nordbanken, Stockholm, Sweden; Virginia Ctr for the Arts, Sweet Briar, VA; Ohrling, Reveco, Lybrant, Stockholm, Sweden. *Comn:* VM Data, Sweden, User Interface Design, Sweden, Diana Krull, US. *Exhib:* Stockholm Int Art Fair, Jan Eric Lowenadler Gallery, Stockholm, Sweden, 97; Painting Object, Gallery Bergman, Stockholm, Sweden, 2000; Anima-Numina, Cortland Jessup Gallery, NY, 2001; Biennale Int Dell'Arte, Florence, Italy, 2001; Transformations, The Sakai City Mus, Sakai Japan, 2001; Beauties, Beasts, and Mystical Beings, SUNY Westchester, Valhalla, NY, 2002; Encaustic Works Biennale, Marist Coll Art Gallery, Poughkeepsie, NY, 2003; AAF Contemp Art Fair, Gallery Galou, NY, 2004, 2005; Encaustic Biennale, Coll New Rochelle, NY, 2009; Marks that Matter, Suny Ulster, 2010; Apocalypse Now, Sideshow Gallery, Bklyn, NY, 2011; Embrace, Vaxjo, Smalands Mus, 2011; Ljungby Kousthall, 2011; Eva Solvang Gallery, Stockholm, Sweden, 2013. *Awards:* Fel, Yaddo Corp, 82; Fel, The McDowell Colony, 82; Fel, VCCA, 82. *Bibliog:* Joel Silverstein (auth), Trace, Essay in Exhibition Catalog, 97; Ricki Neuman (auth), Maja Kihlstedt Far Pris, Svenska Dagbladet, 4/3/2002; Susan Hamburger (auth), Painting and the Self After Postmodernism, Waterfront Weekly, 97; Catarina Åström (auth), TV-2, Rapport from NY (from exhib Embrace), Konstràrlden och Desajn, 05/2005, Sweden. *Mem:* Artist's Circle, NY. *Media:* Painting, Drawing. *Dealer:* Mats Bergman, Gallery Bergman Storgatan 28, Stockholm, Sweden; Eva Solrang Galleri Stockholm Sweden. *Mailing Add:* 27 E 3rd St Apt 6A New York NY 10003

KIKUCHI-YNGOJO, ALAN
PHOTOGRAPHER, COLLAGE ARTIST
b San Francisco, Calif, Feb 6, 1949. *Study:* Diablo Valley Col, 67-69; Univ Calif, Davis, BA, 71, MFA, 75. *Work:* Metrop Mus Art, Alternative Mus, NY; Clarence Kennedy Gallery, Polaroid Corp, Cambridge, Mass; Cleveland Mus Art; Erie Art Ctr, Pa. *Exhib:* Contemp Icons, San Francisco Mus Mod Art, 75; Beyond Photog, Alternative Mus, NY, 80; US Art Now, Gotesborgs Konstforening, Sweden, 81; Painting and Sculpture Today, Indianapolis Mus Art, 82; Counterparts, Metrop Mus Art, NY, 82; solo exhib, Triton Mus Art, Santa Clara, Calif, 82; Recent Acquisitions, Clarence Kennedy Gallery, Polaroid Corp, Cambridge, Mass, 83; Seven Am Artists, Cleveland Mus Art, 83. *Awards:* Nat Endowment Arts Fel, 81. *Bibliog:* Grace Glueck (auth), article in New York Times, 1/15/82; Lynn Zelevansky (auth), article in Art News, 4/82; Christopher French (auth), Redefining figures, Art Week, 7/3/82. *Dealer:* Hal Bromm Gallery 90 W Broadway New York NY 10013. *Mailing Add:* 1615 18th St Apt 24L San Francisco CA 94107-2378

KILAND, LANCE EDWARD
PAINTER, PRINTMAKER
b Fargo, NDak, Nov 27, 1947. *Study:* Moorhead State Univ, BA, 1969; Southern Ill Univ, MFA, 1971. *Work:* Walker Art Ctr, Minneapolis; Art Inst Chicago; Milwaukee Art Mus; Minneapolis Inst Arts; Weisman Art Mus, Minneapolis; Minn Mus Am Art, St Paul. *Exhib:* Mid-States Art Exhib, Evansville Mus Art, Ind, 1970; New Chicago Painting, New Mus, NY, 1982; Biennial Exhib, Whitney Mus Am Art, NY, 1983; Rooted in NDak, NDak Mus Art, Grand Forks, 1984, Landmark Editions, 1991; 39th Biennial Am Painting, Corcoran Gallery Art, Washington, 1985; Viewpoints, Walker Art Ctr, Minneapolis, 1985, Recent Acquisitions: Emerging Artists, 1986; Print & Drawing Exhib, Minneapolis Inst Arts, 1988, Bewildered Image 2, 1995; New Acquisitions, Art Inst Chicago, 1991 & Contemp Prints and Portfolios, 1992; Abstract Painting in Minn, Minn Mus Am Art, 2005; Crate One, Minn Mus Am Art, 2008. *Pos:* Dir art, Prairie Pub TV, Fargo, NDak, 1969-70; graphic designer, Univ Minn, St Paul, 1971-72. *Teaching:* instr, North Hennepin Community Col, Brooklyn Park, Minn, 1972-2011. *Awards:* Fellowship for Artists Grant, The Bush Found, 1984; Visual Arts Fel, McKnight Found, 1985; Artist Fel, Nat Endowment Arts, 1985; Artist Assistance Grant, Minn State Arts Bd, 1988. *Bibliog:* Eleanor Heartney (auth), Lance Kiland, 1/84 & Mason Riddle (auth), Lance Kiland, 10/85, Arts Mag; Chris Waddington (auth), Lance Kiland at Thomson, Art in Am, 6/89. *Mem:* Am Inst Graphic Arts. *Media:* Oil; Lithograph & Woodcut. *Publ:* Landfall Press, Chicago; Landmark Edits, Minneapolis

KILB, JENNY
PAINTER, MURALIST
b Cincinnati, Ohio, Mar 3, 1952. *Study:* Cincinnati Art Mus, 60-70; Dept Painting & Sculpture, Carnegie-Mellon Univ, 70-72. *Work:* NASA Art Collection, Washington, DC; Casa Grande Art Mus, Casa Grande, Ariz; Deming (New Mex) Airport Collection. *Comn:* Award Objects, Excell in Environment (sculptures), City of

Tucson, Ariz, 92; exterior mural (16 X 60 Ft), Tucson Arts Dist Partnership, Ariz, 93; exterior mural, Southwestern Paints, Tucson, Ariz, 94; exterior mural, Oracle Pub Libr, Ariz, 94. *Exhib:* Ten Yrs of Feminist Art Invitational, Murray State Univ, Ky, 95; 26th Ann Exhib, Palm Springs Desert Mus, 95; Showcasing the Woman's Voice Invitational, Louisville Visual Art Asn, Ky, 95; Paper Trail West 1996, Snowgrass Inst Art, Cashmere, Wash, 96; solo exhib, Barn Gallery, Rancho Linda Vista, Oracle, Ariz, Edge of the Cedars Mus, Utah, 97, Ready, Set, D'Art, Benefit for Tucson Mus Art, 1998/2000. *Pos:* Artist in residence, Cincinnati Planetarium, Ohio, 78-79; founder & chair, Oracle Festival Fine Art, Oracle, Ariz, 92-96. *Awards:* 1st & 3rd Place, Landscapes of My Mind, Casa Grande Art Mus, 94; Prof Develop Grant, Ariz Comn Arts, 96; Grant, Four Corners Sch Outdoor Educ, 96; Writing Award, Southwest Writers' Workshop, 1998. *Bibliog:* M Wilson (auth), Ribbons of Color, Ariz Arts & Travel, 1 & 2/84; M Wilson (auth), Jenny Kilb, Kalei Colorscapes, Southwest Art, 12/84. *Mem:* Women's Caucus Art; Earth Angels Artists. *Media:* Color Pencil, Acrylic. *Publ:* Auth, Border Beat Arts J, 97; auth, Dispatch: Oracle (arts commentary), 97; auth, Pilgrim, A Sarah Farling Mystery (novel), Painted Lady Publ, 2002. *Mailing Add:* 474 N Broad St Globe AZ 85501

KILEY, KATIE
PRINTMAKER, PAINTER
b Decatur, Ill, 1951. *Study:* Attended Clarke Col, Dubuque, Iowa; St Ambrose Univ, BA (art), 74; Univ Iowa, MA, 87; Iowa State Univ, MFA, 89. *Exhib:* Drawings, Prints and Paintings, Muchnic Gallery, Atchison, Kansas, 98; Whiskey Gods and Cold Black Beads: Drawings, Paintings and Prints, Alfons Gallery, Milwaukee, 95; Girls! Girls! Girls! Jacqueline Ross Gallery, Chicago, 98; Paintings, Drawings and Prints, Dartmouth Col, 98; Gossamer Veils, Figge-Moss, Stoney Brook Sch, NY, 2000; Conversations, Quigley Gallery, Clark Col, Dubuque, Iowa, 2003; Constructing the Figure, Augustana Col, Rock Island, Ill, 2003; Printmaker's Traveling Show: The Prairie, Grinell, Iowa, 2003; Kiley and Koiso, Midcoast Gallery, LeClaire, Iowa, 2004; Venus Envy, Midcoast Bucktown Gallery, Davenport, Iowa, 2005; Nat Acad Mus, NY, 2006. *Pos:* Mem advertising dept Deere & Co, 72-73. *Teaching:* Prof art St Ambrose Univ

KILGUSS, ELSIE SCHAICH
PAINTER, INSTRUCTOR
b Manhattan, NY, Aug 4. *Study:* RI Sch Design, cert botanical and sci illus, MAT course, BS (advert); Cape Cod Sch Art; studies with Henry Hensche, Lois Griffel, Charles Sovek and others. *Work:* Alfred Butler Inc, New York; Phipps Realty, RI; and numerous pvt & corp collections worldwide. *Comn:* Landscapes, Caribbean Villas, St John, Virgin Islands, 92; portraits, comn by N Barker, Newport, RI, 99; portrait, comn by Laurell C Tripp, RI. *Exhib:* Two-person exhib, B&H Gallery, 86; solo exhibs, Cross Mills Gallery, 86, Wickford Art Festival, 88-2003, Artists Gallery, 89-90, Newport Mus Art, 90-95, The Gallery at Chatham, Mass, 90-99, Sudio Zwei Gallery, 91-2006, RI State House, 93, AS220, 95, Cafe Gallery, 98-99, Dodge House Gallery, Providence, 99, 2001, 2003 & 2007 Warwick Mus Art, 2000 & Sheldon Fine Art 2000-2005, Moitie Gallery, Providence, RI, 2010; Warwick Art Mus, RI Open, 87, 89-91, 95, 97 & 99; Newport Art Mus, RI, 90, 95 & 98; Helme House, Kingston, RI, 90-91, 95, 97-99, 2003-2009; Art Ocean State, Wickford, 90-91 & 94-98; group exhibs, WAA Gallery, 90, 92, 95, 98, 2001 & 2004, Maxwell Mays Gallery, 91, 93, 95 & 97, Woods Gerry Gallery, RI Sch Design, 91, RI Watercolor Soc, 93, 95, 97, 2000 & 2003, Newport Art Mus, 93, 99 & 2002-2003 & Wet Paint, Newport Art Mus, 97, 99 & 2001; Providence Art Club Gallery, 91, 93, 95, 97, 2001, 2003, 2007, 2008, 2009; Spring Bull Gallery, Newport, RI, 93, 99 & 2000. *Pos:* Instr & painter art, Studio ZWEI, 88-. *Teaching:* Instr & demonstr, var art asn, mus, and privately, 80-. *Bibliog:* Video by WJAR, Providence, RI. *Mem:* Providence Art Club; Wickford Art Asn (pres, 90, 91); RI Watercolor Soc; Newport Artists Guild; South Co Art; Oil Painters Am (asst mem, currently); ASMA. *Media:* Oil, Watercolor. *Interests:* gardening, art related activities. *Publ:* Illustr cover, RI Sch Design Catalog, 92 & N Kingstown Villager; var articles In: RI Monthly Mag, Providence Mag, Cape Cod Mag, Providence J Bull, The Standard Times, IRS News Service, Bryant Business & Warwick Beacon; art doc & teaching video, Channel 10. *Mailing Add:* Studio Zwei 14 Pojac Point Rd North Kingstown RI 02852

KILIAN, AUSTIN FARLAND
PAINTER, EDUCATOR
b Lyons, SDak, Sept 19, 1920. *Study:* Augustana Col, SDak, BA, 42; Univ Iowa, MFA, 49; Acad Montmartre, Paris, with Fernand Leger, 51; Mexico City Col, 52; Ohio State Univ, 55; Univ Calif, Los Angeles, 66. *Work:* D D Feldman Collection, Dallas; Univ Iowa Galleries, Iowa City. *Exhib:* Laguna Gloria Mus Citation Regional, Austin, Tex, 58; Art Asn New Orleans, Delgado Mus, 59; Made in Tex by Texans, Dallas Mus Contemp Arts, 59; San Diego Art Instr Show, Art Ctr La Jolla, Calif, 61; Inland Empire Country Club Fac Exhib, San Bernardino, 81; Living Desert, Palm Desert, Calif, 85; and others. *Collection Arranged:* Waco Art Forum Mus Regional Shows, 59; San Diego Art Guild Shows, Fine Arts Gallery, 61; Art In All Media, Southern Calif Expos, Del Mar, 63-70; Coll of the Desert Shows, 70-. *Pos:* Chief Exec Officer, Kilian Studios, 88-; PDN Photog. *Teaching:* Instr photog, Univ Idaho, 49-50; head dept art, Dillard Univ, 50-53; asst prof, Baylor Univ, 53-59; chmn dept art, Calif Western Univ, 59-64; assoc prof, Col Desert, Calif, 70-86, head dept art, 86-87 & prof emer, 87-. *Awards:* Art Asn New Orleans Third Award, Delgado Mus, 52; Sons of Herman Award, San Antonio, Tex, 55; Purchase Award, D D Feldman Exhib, 68. *Bibliog:* Henry Burnett & Orville Voigt, Today Painting (Video Series), Coll Desert, 80-85; William Hemmerdinger (auth), Collectors, Palm Springs Life Mag, 12/81. *Mem:* Art Hist Southern Calif; Palm Springs Desert Mus; Coll Art Asn Am; Am Fedn of Arts. *Media:* Collage, Oil. *Specialty:* wide format color prints. *Publ:* Auth, Catalog loan exhibition of notable works from the Metropolitan, 52, Culture makes a face, KABC-TV, Hollywood, 62, The Two Californias (catalog), 63, Southern California Exposition, Art in All Media (catalogs), 63-70 & article, San Diego Eve Tribune, 6/14/64. *Mailing Add:* 73286 Juniper St Palm Desert CA 92260-4702

KILIMNIK, KAREN
INSTALLATION ARTIST, PAINTER, PHOTOGRAPHER
b Philadelphia, Pa, 1955. *Study:* Temple Univ, Philadelphia. *Exhib:* Videography includes Bananarama Guilty, 1988-91, Nice...introducing Tabitha, 1991, Movie Credits, 1991, Emma Peel, 1991, Avengers (The House That Jack Built), 1992-93, Heathers, 1992-93, Edie and Ciao Manhattan I, 1993, II, 1993, Kate Moss, 1994, Remington Street, 1995; solo exhibs include Galerie Ghislaine Hussenot, Paris, 1998, 1999, Emily Tsingou Gallery, London, 1998, 2000, H & R Projs, Brussels, 1998, 303 Gallery, New York City, 1999, 2001, 2002, 2006, Gallery Side 2, Tokyo, 1999, Galerie Hauser & Writh & Presenhuber, Zurich, 2000, 2002, South London Gallery, 2000, Galerie Sprüth Magers, Munich, 2000, 2003, 2004, Il Capricorno, Venice, 2002, Fairy Battle, Irish Mus Mod Art, Dublin, 2002, Galerie Eva Presenhuber AG, Zurich, 2004, Kirschgarten Basel Historisches Mus, 2005, Fondazione Bevilacqua La Masa, Venice, 2005, Musée d'Art Moderne de la Ville de Paris, 2006, Aspen Art Mus, 2007, Mus Contemp Art, Chicago, 2007, Inst Contemp Art, Philadelphia, 2007, Serpentine Gallery, London, 2007, Le Consortium, Dijon, 2007; group exhibs include Super Freaks, Green Naftali Gallery, New York City, 1998; Heaven, Kunsthalle Dusseldorf, Germany, 1999; Mus Contemp Art, Chicago, 2000; Drawings 2000, Barbara Gladstone Gallery, New York City, 2000; Mus Mod Art, New York City, 2001; The Mystery of Painting, Sammlung Goetz, Munich, 2001; Go Figure, Luxe Gallery, New York City, 2002; Within Hours We Would be in the Middle of Nowhere, 303 Gallery, New York City, 2003; girls don't cry, Parco Mus, Japan, 2003; The Big Nothing, Inst Contemp Art, Philadelphia, 2004; Now is a good time, Andrean Rosem Gallery, New York City, 2004; Ideal Worlds: New Romanticism in Contemp Art, Schirn Kunsthalle, Frankfurt, 2005; Singapore Art Mus, 2006; Whitney Biennial, Whitney Mus Am Art, New York, 2008. *Bibliog:* Patrick Frey (auth), Drawings by Karen Kilimnik, Zurich, 2000; Karen Kilimnik Fairy Battle, Irish Mus Mod Art, Dublin, 2002; Angela Vetesse (auth) and Caoimhin Mac Giolla Léith (auth), Karen Kilimnik, Fondazione Bevilacqua La Masa, Venice, 2005. *Mailing Add:* c/o 303 Gallery 525 W 22nd St New York NY 10011

KILLEEN, MELISSA HELEN
DEALER, GALLERY DIRECTOR
b Binghamton, NY, Oct 28, 1955. *Study:* Syracuse Univ, NY, BFA (cum laude), 76; Johnson Atelier Tech Sch Sculpture, NJ, cert, 78. *Collection Arranged:* Wood Biennial (twelve wood designer-craftsmen; auth, catalog), 78, 80 & 82; Monumental Sculpture Traveling Exhib, 79 & 82; Monumental Weaving, 83; Com Bank, Hq & Br, NJ; Traveler's Mortgage Serv Hq, Cherry Hill, NJ; Jefferson Bank, Philadelphia, Pa. *Pos:* Craft coordr, By Hand Crafts Gallery, NJ, 76-77; mgr, Richard Kagan Gallery, Pa, 78-79; dir & owner, The Gallery at 401, Magnolia, NJ, 79-; owner & dir, Landsman Gallery, 82-; vpres, ArtMarkit Inc, 82-; appraiser, Am Soc Appraisals, 88; art fair/fund raising event planner, 82-. *Teaching:* Asst dept chairperson ceramic shell & plastics, Johnson Atelier, NJ, 76-79. *Mem:* Sr mem Am Soc Appraisers; Am Craft Coun. *Specialty:* Contemp fine art, monumental sculpture and graphic art, corporate art consultation, appraisals. *Mailing Add:* c/o Landsman Gallery 600 S White Horse Pike Somerdale NJ 08083

KILLMASTER, JOHN H
ENAMELIST, PAINTER
b Allegan, Mich, Dec 2, 1934. *Study:* Soc Arts & Crafts, Detroit, Mich; Hope Coll, BA; Univ Guanajuato, Mex, Cranbrook Acad Art, MFA. *Work:* Boise Gallery Art & Boise Cascade World Hq Collection, Boise, Idaho; FMC Corp, Chicago, Ill; Albertsons Inc, Boise, Idaho; Enamel Mus, Coldsprings, KY; Idaho First Nat Bank; Sunshine Mining; The Herret Ctr for Arts at the Coll of Southern Idaho, Twin Falls, ID; and others; Mus Contemp Craft, Portland. *Comn:* Sculpture, Portland Arts Comn, 78-79; murals, Wash State Art Comn, 79, Ore Arts Comn, 80. *Exhib:* San Francisco Mus Mod Art, Calif, 79-80; Nat Mus Am Art, Smithsonian Inst, 79-80; Denver Art Mus, 80; Int Enamel Exhib, Sumida Gallery, Tokyo, Japan, 93; The Cutting Edge, Exhibs, Frey Art Mus, Seattle, Wash, 94; St Petersburg & Moscow Int Enamel Exhib, Russia, 94; Contemp Int Enamelist Exhib, Canadian Clay & Glass Mus, Can, 94; Crossing Boundaries-Enamel Int, Waterloo, Ont, Can, 99; Am Enamels, Tacoma, Wash, 2000; 9th Int Juried Enamel Exhib, Evergreen State Coll Gallery, Olympia, Wash, 2003; Looking Forward-Glancing Back, Northwest Designer Craftsmen at 50 Exhib, Whatcom Mus Art, Bellingham, Wash, 2005; Drawing Power, Nat Automotive Hist Collection, Detroit Pub Libr, Mich, 2005-2006; Paint America Top 100, St George Mus, St George, Utah, 2007; solo exhib, Herret Ctr Arts, Twin Falls, Idaho, 2007, Promethean Images, Figureworks Gallery, Brooklyn, NY, 2009, Surfacing-Enameling in the 21st Century, Oakland, Calif, 2009; Era Messages, Mus Contemp Craft, Portland, 2010; NWDC Confluence, Chase Gallery, Spokane, Wash, 2011; Beyond Borders 11th Int Enamel Exhib, Richmond Art Ctr, Calif, 2012. *Pos:* Illusr & designer, Allied Artists, 55-56 & Ladriere Art Studio, Detroit, 58-61; Blythe, Ambrose & Noyes, 56-58. *Teaching:* Asst prof painting, Ferris State Coll, 69-70; prof art, Boise State Univ, 70-; instr art, Grand Marais Art Colony, Minn, 85; Instr, John C. Campbell Folk Sch, 2003. *Awards:* Governor's Award for Excellence in the Arts, Idaho, 78; Scholar Boise State Univ Found, 95; Woodrow W Carpenter Award, Int Enamelist Soc, 2001. *Bibliog:* The Calif Art Review, Krantz, 89; Art Masters (video), BSU, 89; The Dictionary of Enameling-History Technique, 97; Enameling with Professionals, L Bachrack Pub, 2000; Contemp Enameling Art & Techniques, Schiffer Publishing Ltd, Atglen, Pa, 2006; Bill Patron (auth), When Cars Sat for Portraits, NY Times, 3/13/2006; 500 Enameled Objects, Lark Books Publ, 2009. *Mem:* NW Designer Craftsman Asn; Nat Enamelist Guild, Washington, DC; Enamelists Guild West, San Diego; Enamelist Soc; Intl Enamelist Soc. *Media:* Acrylic, Enamel. *Res:* Innovative approaches/techniques and styles in contemporary architectural large scale enameling. *Publ:* Glass on metal, Int J, 83, 89-91, 95, 2000, 2004, 2009, 2012. *Dealer:* Random Modern Gallery, Tacoma, Wash; Image Maker Artist Consortium Boise ID; Basement Gallery, Boise, ID. *Mailing Add:* 9180 JR Way Middleton ID 83644

KIM, KWANG-WU
ADMINISTRATOR, EDUCATOR
Study: Yale Univ, BA (philosophy); Johns Hopkins Univ, PhD (musical arts). *Pos:* Pres, Longy Sch Music, Cambridge, Mass, formerly; dean, Katherine K Herberger Col of Arts, Ariz State Univ, 2006-09, dean, dir, Herberger Inst for Design and the Arts, 2009-2013; pres, CEO Columbia Col Chicago, 2013-; guest speaker, Harvard Univ Grad Sch Edn, currently; invited panelist for the Nat Asn of Schools of Music; juror, New England Conservatory, Boston Conservatory, and the Boston Arts Academy. *Teaching:* Tchr, Univ Tex, El Paso, Peabody Inst, Dickinson Col, formerly; guest faculty mem, St Lawrence String Quartet Chamber Music Seminar at Stanford U, Rotterdam Conservatory of Music, Royal Conservancy in the Hague, and at the Bannff Centre for the Arts; prof music, Ariz State Univ, formerly; prof music dept, Columbia Col Chicago, 2013-. *Mailing Add:* Columbia College Chicago 600 S Michigan Ave Chicago IL 60605

KIM, PO (HYUN)
PAINTER
b Korea; US citizen. *Study:* Univ Ill, MFA (fel), 57. *Hon Degrees:* LHD. *Work:* Chicago Art Inst, Ill; Solomon R Guggenheim Mus, NY; Seoul Art Ctr, Korea; Kwangju City Art Mus, Korea; NJ Power & Lighting Co; Seoul Nat Mus Contemp Arts, Korea. *Exhib:* Solo exhibs, Kornblee Gallery, NY, 61, Squibb Gallery, Princeton, NJ, 79, Gallery Mod Art, Munich, West Ger, 80, Art Alliance, Philadelphia, Pa, 80; Kwangjn City Mus Art, Korea, 96; Painting & Sculpture Today, Indianapolis Mus Art, Ind, 78; Korean Drawing Now, Brooklyn Mus, NY, 81; Solo Retrospective: Seoul Arts Ctr, Korea, 95; Park Ryu Sook Gallery, Seoul, Korea, 1996; Nahi Gallery, Long Island, NY, 98; Gallery Korea, NY, 2000; Nat Mus Contemp Art, Seoul, Korea, 2000; Gary Snyder Gallery, NY, 2002; Po Kim and Sylvia Wald Gallery, Kwangju, Korea, 2002-; Int Gallery, Smithsonian Inst, Washington, 2003; Tenry Gallery, NY, 2004-2005; Chosun Univ Mus Arts, 2005; 2x13 Gallery, NY, 2006; korea Gallery, NY, 2006; 60 Years Retrospective: Nat Mus Contemp Art, Seoul, Korea, 2007; Silvia Wald and Po Kim Art Gallery, New York, 2009; many others; The Chosun Univ Art Mus, Gwangju, Koera, 2010. *Pos:* pres, Sylvia Wald and Po Kim Art Gallery (non-profit). *Teaching:* Instr, New York Univ, 61-62; prof, Chosum Univ Korea, 46-55. *Media:* Oil, Acrylic. *Mailing Add:* 417 Lafayette St New York NY 10003

KIM, SOO
PAINTER, ILLUSTRATOR
b Seoul, Korea, Sept 29, 1979. *Study:* Fashion Inst Tech, BFA, New York, 2003; Parsons Sch Design, BFA, New York, 2008. *Exhib:* Tiger Translate, Monbijoustr.1, Berlin, Germany, 2007; 100 Postcards from World New Creators, Sunshine Studio, Tokyo, Japan, 2008. *Awards:* RYU Family Found, 2002, 2007. *Bibliog:* Graphic Does Graphic, Graphic Mag, Magma Books, UK, 2003; Artist interview, We Are All Koreans, Singles Mag, Korea, 2004; Gwang Chul Kim (auth), Graphic Mag, Korea, 2007; artist interview, Rise-Asian Kinetic Artists, Tiger Translate Book, IDN Mag, 2007. *Publ:* Contribr, Vogue Girl Mag, Doosan, Korea, 2005

KIMBALL, WILFORD WAYNE, JR
LITHOGRAPHER, DRAFTSMAN
b Salt Lake City, Utah, July 15, 1943. *Study:* Southern Utah State Col, BA, 68; Univ Ariz, MFA, 70; Tamarind Inst, Albuquerque, NMex, fel printing, 70-71, Master Printer, 71. *Work:* Tamarind Collection, Albuquerque, NMex; Brooklyn Mus; Libr Cong, Washington, DC; Lessing J Rosenwald Collection, The Philadelphia Mus of Art & Nat Gallery Fine Arts, Washington, DC. *Exhib:* Brooklyn Mus Biennial Print Exhib, NY, 78; 56th Ann Philadelphia Competition, The Print Club, 80; Colorprint USA, Texas Tech Univ, Lubbock, Tex, 80; Tenth Anniversary Exhib, Tyler Mus Art, Tex, 81; Solo exhibs, Phoenix Art Mus, Ariz, 81, Art Mus STex, 81 & Thirty Am Printmakers Invitational, Univ Gallery Fine Art, Ohio State Univ, 82; Seventh British Int Print Biennale, Cartwright Hall, Bradford, W Yorkshire, Eng, 82; and others. *Pos:* Artist-in-residence, Roswell Mus & Art Ctr, NMex, 72. *Teaching:* Lectr lithography, Univ NMex, 71; vis lectr lithography, Univ Wis, Madison, 72-73 & summers 73 & 74; asst prof lithography & drawing, San Diego State Univ, 73-74; asst prof lithography, Calif State Univ, Long Beach, 74-75; asst prof lithography & drawing, Univ Tex San Antonio, 75-77; lectr lithography, San Diego State Univ, 77-78; prof lithography, Ariz State Univ, Tempe, 78-84 & Brigham Young Univ, Provo, Utah, 84-; prof lithography, Brigham Young Univ, 84-. *Awards:* William H Walker Purchase Award, 55th Philadelphia Ann, 79; Purchase Awards, 17th Bradley Nat Print & Drawing Exhib, 79 & Vermillion '79 Nat Print & Drawing Competition, 79. *Media:* Lithography

KIMES, DON
PAINTER, EDUCATOR
b Oil City, Pa, Nov 18, 1950. *Study:* Westminster Col, BA, 75; Univ Pittsburgh, grad studies, 75-77; Brooklyn Col, City Univ NY, MFA, 80; NY Studio Sch, cert, 78; studied with Agostini, Bell, Campbell, McNeil, Vicente, Heliker, Matter & Carone. *Work:* Chautauqua Inst, NY; Mass Inst Technol, Cambridge, Mass; Mus dell'Acad Belle Arti Pietro Vannucci, Italy; Univ Chicago; Conn State Univ; Watkins Collection, Am Univ, Washington. *Exhib:* Paperworks, Brooklyn Mus, NY, 82; Nat Acad Design, NY, 86; Baltimore Mus, Md, 86; solo exhibs, Madison Mus, Wyo, 93, Cy Katzen Gallery, Washington, 93, Nat Acad Sci, Washington, 93, Casa de Cult, Villahermosa, Mex, 93, Galleria Isa, Italy, 95, Amerika Haus, Munich, 96 & Rocca Paolina, Perugia, Italy, 96; Corcoran Gallery Art, 94 & 96; Galleria di Arti Vivre, Milan, 95; Piazza Broletto, Perugia, Italy, 95; Anton Gallery, Washington, 96. *Pos:* Co-founder & sr critic, Inst Int dell'Arte é Architettura. *Teaching:* Instr painting, State Univ NY, Stonybrook, 79; instr painting, NY Studio Sch, NY, 80- & chmn bd govs, 83-85; artistic dir, Chautauqua Inst Sch Arts, 85-; artist-in-residence, Conn State Univ, 87-88; assoc prof art, dept chmn, Am Univ, Washington, 88-. *Awards:* Yellowstone Nat Park, US Dept Interior Award for Artist Residency, 93; Artist Residency, Camerata di Todi, Italy, 94-95; Mellon Award, Munich, Ger, 96. *Bibliog:* Rossella Vasta (auth), Il Corriere dell'Umbria, Italy; Cynthia Kraman (auth), Don Kimes, The artist as philosopher, Sunstorm Mag, 88; Barbara Rose (auth), Heavy Metal, Don Kimes' New Work (exhib catalog), Acad Belle Arti Pietro Vannucci, Italy, 96. *Media:* Miscellaneous Media, Prints. *Publ:* Auth, In Praise of Space: 19th Century American Landscape, Westminster Press, 76; From Landscape to Collage, Ecker Press, 86; coauth, Chadakoin Review, An Interview with Agostini & Portfolio Reproduction. *Dealer:* Marie Tapparo 15 S Montague Arlington VA 22204. *Mailing Add:* Chautauqua Sch Art PO Box 1098 Chautauqua NY 14722-1098

KIMMEL-COHN, ROBERTA
DEALER, WRITER
b Milwaukee, Wis, Feb 1, 1937. *Study:* Sophie Newcomb Col, with George Rickey; Univ Wis; Boston Univ Sch Fine & Appl Arts, BFA. *Pos:* Art dir, McGraw-Hill Publ Co, New York, 61-62, Macmillan & Co, 64-65 & Walker & Co, 65-67; pres, Roberta Kimmel Advert, New York, 67-; partner, Kimmel/Cohn Photog Arts, New York, 74-. *Bibliog:* Surrealism in advertising, Art Dir Mag, 70; article in Art Dir Ann, 72; People in the news, New York Times, 74. *Specialty:* Photography; Man Ray; nineteenth and twentieth century art. *Publ:* Auth, Erste Landung, portfolio of photographs by George Grosz, 77; Man Ray: Vintage Photographs, Rayographs and Solarizations, 77; In Artist's Homes, Clarkson Potter Inc. *Mailing Add:* 41 Central Park W New York NY 10023

KIMMELMAN, HAROLD
SCULPTOR
b Philadelphia, Pa, Feb 20, 1923. *Study:* Cape Sch Art, Provincetown, Mass; Pa Acad Fine Art, Philadelphia. *Comn:* Burst of Joy, The Gallery, Philadelphia, 77; Marino Monument, Casa Enrico Fermi Corp, Philadelphia, Pa, 77; Man Helping Man, Am Coll Cardiology, Bethesda, Md, 79; Hol; Hand in Hand, Merck Sharp & Doehme, West Point, Pa, 88; Volume III, Drexel Univ, 89. *Exhib:* Pa Acad Fine Arts, 68; Philadelphia Civic Ctr Show, 71; Woodmere Art Mus, 98. *Awards:* Braverman Karp Prize for sculpting, 68; May Audubon Prize for sculpting, 69. *Bibliog:* Sculpture of a City, Walker Publ Co, 74. *Mem:* Artists Equity Asn (pres, Philadelphia Chap, 72); fel Pa Acad Fine Arts. *Media:* Stainless Steel, Bronze

KIMMELMAN, MICHAEL
CRITIC
b New York, NY, May 8, 1958. *Study:* Yale Univ, BA (summa cum laude), 80; Harvard Univ, MA (art hist), 82. *Pos:* Music critic, Atlanta J Constitution, 84, Philadelphia Inquirer, 85-87; culture ed, US News & World Report, Wash, DC, 87; art critic, New York Times, 88-90, chief art critic, 90-. *Teaching:* Lectr in field; sr fel, Nat Arts Journalism Program Columbia Univ, 2000. *Awards:* Named a finalist in criticism for the Pulitzer Prize, 2000. *Publ:* Auth: Portraits: Talking With Artists at the Met, the Modern, the Louvre and Elsewhere, 1999 (named Notable Book of Yr, Wash Post and The Times, named Best Book of Yr, Publs Weekly); contribr to the NY Review of Books, articles to other mags

KIMPTON, LAURA
PAINTER
Study: Univ Iowa, BA (art educ), 86; San Francisco Art Inst, BFA (photog), 90; Univ San Francisco, MA (coun psychology), 96. *Exhib:* Solo exhibs, Still Lights Gallery, San Francisco, 88, Felix Kopala Gallery, Santa Cruz, Calif, 2005, Who's the Judge, supperclub, 2006, Mynd Too, Schomburg Gallery, Los Angeles, 2006; Eye Gallery Photog Auction, San Francisco, 89; San Francisco Art Inst, 89; South of Market Cult Ctr, San Francisco, 89; Artist Television Access, 89; Diego Rivera Gallery, San Francisco, 89; Arts Guild of Sonoma, 2002; The Color of Woman, 2003; La Haye Art Ctr, Sonoma, 2003; Mus Contemp Art, Santa Rosa, Calif, 2004; di Rosa Preserve, Napa, 2005-06; Donna Seager Gallery, San Rafael, Calif, 2006; installations, Arts Guild of Sonoma, 2002, 2004, Pigman Gallery, San Francisco, 2005, NY Studio Gallery, 2007. *Media:* Miscellaneous Media. *Mailing Add:* c/o FabryHess Fine Art Representation 4001 San Leandro St Suite 10 Oakland CA 94601

KIMURA, RIISABURO
PAINTER, PRINTMAKER
b Yokosuka, Japan, Oct 13, 1924. *Study:* Yokohama Univ, 47; Hosei Univ, Tokyo, 54. *Work:* Mus Mod Art & Brooklyn Mus, NY; Nat Mus Mod Art, Kyoto, Japan; US Info Agency; City of Hamburg, WGer; Libr Cong; Los Angeles Co Mus Art; and many others. *Comn:* Print ed, Brooklyn Mus, 75. *Exhib:* Solo exhibs, JICC, Washington, DC, 91, Gallery Aunkan, Osaka, Japan, 91, Artra Gallery, NY, 92 & Tokyo Kyoto Osaka Yokohama Sendai, Art Mus Ginza, Tokyo, 95, Sendai City Mus, 99, Williamsburg Art & Hist Ctr, NY, 2000 & Ono City Off, Fukui, Japan, 2001, trav exhib, Tokyo, Yokohama, Osaka & Kyoto, Japan, 2005-08; USA Pavillion Expo 70, Osaka, Japan, 74; Japanese Artists in the Americas, Nat Mus Mod Art, Kyoto, Japan, 74; Boston Printmakers Exhib, Brockton Art Ctr, Mass, 74; Nora Gallery, NY, 85; Jewish Community Ctr, Minneapolis, Minn, 85; Coll Women's Asn Print Show, Am Club, Tokyo, 86-2001; Pratt Inst, NY, 88; Machida City Mus Graphic Arts, Japan, 92; Brooklyn Mus, NY, 95; New Am Art Show, Mayor's Off, NY, 98; 48th CWAJ Print Show, Am Club, Tokyo, Japan, 2003; Resounding Print Show The Gibson Gallery Col, Univ MD, 2004; Los Angeles Co Mus Art, 2005; Art Mus of SUNY, 2005; Libr Congress, Washington, DC, 2006; Resounding Spirit, The Gibson Gallery, New York, 2007; 53th EWAJ Show, Am Club, Tokoyo, Kobe, Japan; Libr of Congress, Washington, DC, 2008. *Awards:* Int Biennial Print Award, Tokyo, 70. *Bibliog:* Art News, 10/79; Interior Design, 1/79; Art Am, 3/80. *Mailing Add:* 463 W St No G-361 New York NY 10014

KIND, JOSHUA B
EDUCATOR, CRITIC
b Philadelphia, Pa, Nov 5, 1933. *Study:* Univ Pa, Philadelphia, BA, 55; Columbia Univ, PhD, 67. *Pos:* Chicago ed, Art News, New York, 64-70; dir, Oxbow Summer Sch Art, Saugatuck, Mich, 67-68; contrib ed, New Art Examiner, Chicago, 75-85. *Teaching:* Instr art hist, Northwestern Univ, Evanston, Ill, 59-62; instr humanities,

Univ Chicago, 62-65; vis prof art hist, Sch of Art Inst Chicago, 64-76; asst prof art hist & humanities, Ill Inst Technol, Chicago, 65-69; prof art hist, Northern Ill Univ, DeKalb, 69-. *Awards:* Nat Endowment for the Arts Critics Fel, 77. *Mem:* Coll Art Asn; Soc Architectural Historians. *Res:* Modernism; creativity and the avant-garde; Renaissance iconography; modern architecture. *Publ:* Auth, Rouault, 69; Art and the corps of women, 3/78 & The corruption of Norman Rockwell, 1/79, New Art Examiner; contribr, World Bk Year Book & Encyclopedia Britannica Yr Bk, 70-; contrib, Contemp Artists, 1st, 2nd & 3rd ed; contrib, Int Dict of Art and Artists, vol 2, 90. *Mailing Add:* 5619 Dunham Rd Downers Grove IL 60516-1247

KINDAHL, CONNIE
WEAVER, CRAFTSMAN

b Decatur, Ill. *Study:* Univ Ill. *Comn:* Prudential Insurance Co, Washington, DC, 84; Med W Community Health Plan, Chicopee, Mass, 84; Alpha Chi Omega Sorority, Amherst, Mass, 84; Harvard Community Health Fac, W Roxbury, Mass, 86; Dow Chemical Co, Chicago, Ill, 86. *Exhib:* 2-man show, Western New Engl Col, Springfield, Mass, 83; Wichita Nat Decorative Arts Exhib, Wichita, Kans, 85; 8th Ann Vahki Exhib, Mesa, Ariz, 86; Fiber/Fiber, Convergence 86, Toronto, 86; Rugs: Contemp Handwoven Floorcoverings, Mus Am Textile Hist, North Andover, Mass, 86. *Teaching:* Instr rug weaving, Weavers Guild Boston, 84-86 & Augusta Heritage Ctr, Davis & Elkins Col, 88. *Awards:* Chairmans Choice in Fiber, Wesleyan Potters, 82, Special Recognition Award, Nassau Co NY Fiber Arts Forum & Exhib, 85 & First Prize in Rugs, New Eng Weavers Seminar, 85. *Bibliog:* Elizabeth French (auth), Connie Kindahl, Shuttle Spindle & Dyepot Handweavers Guild Am, 86. *Mem:* Am Craft Coun; Handweavers Guild Am; Worcester Craft Ctr; Leverett Craftsmen & Artists. *Media:* Fiber. *Publ:* All White Overshot Rug, spring, 82, Rugs on a Three-End Block Draft, Weavers J, spring 84; Boundweave Rug on an Overshot Threading, Shuttle Spindle & Dyepot, 86. *Mailing Add:* RR 2 364 Daniel Shays Hwy Pelham MA 01002

KINDERMANN, HELMMO
PHOTOGRAPHER, PAINTER

b Lancaster, Pa, Oct 11, 1947. *Study:* Tyler Sch Fine Art, Temple Univ, BFA, 69; study of photog, Visual Studies Workshop, Rochester, NY, 71-73; State Univ NY Buffalo, MFA, 73. *Work:* Miss Art Asn, Jackson; Visual Studies Workshop, Rochester, NY; St Lawrence Univ, Canton, NY; Alternative Mus, NY. *Exhib:* Images, Dimensional, Movable, Transferable, Akron Art Inst, Ohio, 73; New Approaches, Ctr for Exploratory and Perceptual Arts, Buffalo, NY, 75; New Photog/76, Cent Wash State Col, Ellensburgh, 76; Photo/Synthesis, Herbert F Johnson Mus of Art, Ithaca, NY, 76; Auto as Icon, Int Mus Photog, George Eastman House, Rochester, NY, 79; and others. *Pos:* Cur, US Eye Photo Exhib, Nat Fine Arts Comt, XIII Olympic Winter Games, Lake Placid, NY, 78-. *Teaching:* Asst prof photog, Lake Placid Sch Art, Ctr for Music, Drama & Art, NY, 73-81. *Awards:* Purchase Prize, Images on Paper, Miss Art Asn, 71. *Mem:* Soc for Photog Educ; Coll Art Asn Am; Photog Instr Asn; Friends of Photog. *Publ:* New Photographics/76, Cent Wash Col, 76; contribr, Works and Process, CMDA Publ Co, 76; contribr, Photo/Synthesis, Herbert F Johnson Mus Art, 76; contribr, The Photograph Collectors Guide, Lee Witkin & Barbara London, NY Graphic Soc; contribr, Uniquely Photographic, Quiver No 5, Honolulu Acad Arts; and others. *Mailing Add:* 1830 Rose Tree Ln Havertown PA 19083-2728

KING, BRIAN JEFFREY
PAINTER, PHOTOGRAPHER

b Des Moines, Iowa, Oct 22, 1952. *Study:* studied with Ronald Mallory, 90-93; studied with Gustav Likan, 94-96; studied with Armand G Winfield 2002-05. *Work:* Zilker Botanical Gardens, Austin; Austin History Ctr; Oregon Gov Collection; Google Images Collection. *Comn:* World's largest single canvas painting, comn by Robert Cox, Tex. *Exhib:* Ballinthejack Studios, 93-2009; Death of the Unknown Artist, 99; 11-11 Art Show, 95; Prof Fine Art & Photography exhib, NMex Expo, 2009. *Pos:* Artist; art dir, Picture Paper Mag, 94; cofounder, 11-11 Art Show, 95; dir, Ballinthejack Gallery and Design. *Teaching:* Freelance teacher, digital art techniques. *Awards:* First art mag on the net, The Picture Paper-Priceless, 94; Am Legion Nat Medal of Hon. *Bibliog:* Michael Barnes (auth), World art party, Austin Am Statesman, 11/95; The Picture Paper, Excel Mag, Austin Am Statesman, 8/95. *Mem:* World Art Party; NMex Film Commission; NMex Culture Net. *Media:* All Media, Stainless Steel Sculpture, Acrylic, Video. *Res:* Culture, politics, videography, writing. *Specialty:* Acrylic Painting, Decor, Photography. *Interests:* Culture, politics, education. *Publ:* coauth, Mankind's Millennium Manual, 99; coauth, Secrets of the Cavemen, 2000; ed, The Picture Paper Art Mag, Victoria Vranich, 94-97, publ, 95-97; various Prentice Hall Tech Manuals; auth & illus, Moon Freckles, 2007. *Dealer:* Ballinthejack Gallery of Interior Design

KING, CLIVE
PAINTER, DRAFTSMAN

b Feb 11, 1944; Brit citizen. *Study:* Exeter Coll Art, dipl AD, 66; Goldsmiths Coll Art, Univ London, dipl, 67. *Work:* Found Today's Art, Nexus Gallery, Philadelphia; Oxford Brookes Univ, Eng; Cyfarthfa Castle Mus, Wales, Eng; Dartmouth Col, Conn; Carol Damian Col, Fla Internat Univ, Mus Mod Art, Wales. *Exhib:* Solo exhibs include Glynn Vivian Art Gallery, Swansea, Eng, 90, Barbican Ctr, London, 91, Art Mus, Fla Int Univ, Miami, 96, 1708 Gallery, Richmond, Va, 97, Raymond Lawrence Gallery, Atlanta, 98 & Mus Mod Art, Wales, Eng, 99, Raymond Lawrence Gallery, Atlanta, Ga, 2000, Miliken Gallery, Converse Col, SC, 2000, Miami-Dade Cultural Resource Ctr, 2001, Anderson Gallery, Drake Univ, Des Moines, 2002, Omniart, Miami, 2004, Jacksonville Mus Contemp Art, 2006, MIA Gallery, Miami, 2007; group exhibs include Blackheath Gallery, London, 1981; Paperpoint Gallery, London, 1985; Camden Open, London, 1987; GroundLevel Gallery, Miami Beach, 1993; Dunedin Fine Art Ctr, Fla, 1993; Barbara Gillman Gallery, Miami Beach, 1995, 1996, 1999; Ctr for Contemp Art, Salem Winston, NC, 1997; Raymond Lawrence Gallery, Atlanta, Ga, 1999; Nat Mus Wales, 2000; Drost Gallery, Miami, 2000; Lowe Art Mus, Univ Miami, 2000; Gulf Coast Art Ctr, Largo, Fl, 2000; MIA Gallery, Miami, 2001; Rhonda Heritage Park Gallery, Wales, 2001; Lincoln Road Gallery, Miami, 2003; Mexican Cultural Ctr, Miami, 2005; Design District, Miami, 2006. *Pos:* Chair, Art Dept, Fla Int Univ, Miami, 92-98, prof fine art, currently. *Teaching:* Sr lectr visual art, Salisbury Col Art, Eng, 74-79, Oxford Brookes Univ, Eng, 79-92; grad dir MFA program, Fla Internat Univ, Wales, 2000. *Awards:* Southern Arts Fedn Fel, Southeastern Ctr Contemp Art, Nat Endowment Art, 96; Ann Artists Award, 1708 Gallery, Southeastern Coll Art Conf, 97; Individual Artist Fla Fel, Traveling Exhib Prog, Fla Div Cult Arts, 98; Southeastern Coll Art Conference Artist Fel, 2004. *Bibliog:* Bernadine Heller-Greenman (auth), Clive King, Art Papers, 95; Carol Damian (auth), Clive King, Southern Arts Fedn Rev, 97; Nona Hieman (auth), Interview with Clive King, Southeastern Coll Art Conf Rev, 97. *Mem:* Coll Art Asn; Southeastern Coll Art Asn. *Media:* Acrylic. *Res:* SW Native Am ancient sites. *Specialty:* drawing. *Publ:* auth, Painting the Drawing. *Dealer:* Raymond Lawrence Gallery, Atlanta; Barbara Gullman Gallery, Miami

KING, DOUGLAS R
MUSEUM DIRECTOR

Study: Stanford Univ, BS; Univ Wash, MBA. *Pos:* vpres, Am Electronics Asn; pres, Asn Tech Bus Coun; pres, Challenger Ctr for Space Sci Educ, 90-95; pres, CEO, St Louis Sci Ctr, 95-2010; pres, CEO, Mus of Flight, Seattle, 2011-; Founding bd mem, Tech Gateway, bd mem, Acad Sci of St Louis, Forest Park Forever, Asn of Sci/Technology Centers, chair Forest Park South Neighborhood Group, mem, Forest Park Adv, Bd, chmn, NASA Educ Adv Com, mem, NASA Adv Coun. *Mem:* Asn Sci Mus Dirs (past pres); Giant Screen Cinema Asn (bd mem); Missouri Biotechnology Asn (bd mem). *Mailing Add:* Museum of Flight 9404 E Marginal Way S Seattle WA 98108

KING, ELAINE A
CURATOR, HISTORIAN

b Oak Park, Ill, Apr 12, 1947. *Study:* Northern Ill Univ, BS, 68, MA, 74; Ill Inst Design Chicago, photog hist with Arthur Siegel; intern, George Eastman House, summer 77; Northwestern Univ, PhD, 86, with Howard Becker, Leland Roloff, Charles Kleinhaus & Donald Kuspit & Jim Brekenridge; Cert Art Appraisal, New York Univ, NY, 2002. *Collection Arranged:* Exhibs cur include David Humphrey, Emily Cheng, Magdalena Jetelova, Barry Le Va, Martin Puryear, Elizabeth Murray, Mel Bochner, Nancy Spero, Robert Wilson; guest cur, Mari Mater O'Neill retrospective, Mus Art, San Juan, Puerto Rico; guest cur, Mattress Factory, Pittsburgh, Hungarian Master of Graphic Arts & Drawing Biennial, Gyor, Hungary, Prague Triennial, Venice Biennale; Charting Sacred Terrritories, Emily Chang; Likeness: Portrayal After Warhol. *Pos:* Cur, Dittmar Mem Gallery, Northwestern Univ, 77-81; dir, Hewlett Art Gallery, Carnegie-Mellon Univ, 81-89; corresp ed, Dialogue Mag, 84-89; dir, Carnegie-Mellon Univ Art Gallery, 85-91; independent cur, freelance, 91-; art critic in residence, Del Ctr Contemp Art, Wilmington, 92; exec dir & chief cur, Contemp Arts Ctr, Cincinnati, 93-95; guest cur, III Master Graphics Biennial, Gyor, Hungary, 95 & 97, 99, 2001, 03, 05; guest cur, Mus Art, Puerto Rico (Maria Mater Survey), 2/2007; MMM Art, Medana, Slovenia, 2009; Likeness: Transformation of Portrayal After Warhol, Mattress Factory, 2010; invited speaker, Chautaugua Inst, 2007-2011. *Teaching:* Lectr art dept, Northwestern Univ, 77-81; prof art hist & critical theory, Carnegie-Mellon Univ, 81-; sr research fellow, Smithsonian Am Art Mus, 2002; short-term research fellow, Nat Portrait Gallery, 2001; disting art historian in residence, Am Univ, Int Prog, Italy, 2006; inst, The Unknown Unworldly in a Soc of Now, 2010, SACI, Florence, Italy, 2012. *Awards:* The Trust for Mutual Understanding Grant, 94; Art Critic Fel, Pa Arts Coun Grant, 89, 95, 99, 2000; Fac Develop Grant, Carnegie Mellon Univ, 89, 96, 99, 2002; Irex Grant, 2001; Research Fel, Ctrl European Cult Inst, 2002; Fac Research Grant, Dean's Off, Carnegie Mellon, 2006; Research Grant, Ctr for Arts & Soc, 2008; Best of 2009 Art Exhib, Pittsburgh Post-Gazette, Likeness as Mattress Factory; Travel grant, Carnegie Mellon, CFA, 2009-2010; Travel Grant to Cuba, Carnegie Mellon, 2012; Berkman Fellowship, 2013. *Bibliog:* John Russell (auth), Art View: The Best and Biggest in Pittsburgh, NY Times, 11/85; Joanna Hamer (auth), King to Talk Celebrity, Women, Art, and Gaga in VACI Lecture, The Chautauquan Daily, 7/2012. *Mem:* Coll Art Asn (midwestern bd dir, 97-2003); Art Table & Am Asn Mus, Mountain Lake Criticism Symp (bd dir, 81-91); Asn Int Art Critics (bd mem, 2009-2010); Am Asn Historians Am Art; Am Asn Mus; Am & Popular Culture Asn; Coll Art Asn; Nat Press Club. *Media:* Installation, Sculpture, Portraits, Contemporary. *Res:* Portraits in USA, 1960-, Nat Endowment for the Arts & Letters, Impact on Post Modernism, Changing Face, Nature in Contemporary Art. *Interests:* sailing, gardening, reading, cooking, travel, cats. *Publ:* Art in a Kaleidoscope Era, In: After the Fall Aspects of Abstract Painting since 1970 (exhib catalog), Newhouse Ctr Contemp Art, 97; Fictional Theatricality in Cyber Space (exhib catalog), Jersey City Mus, 98; Mel Bochner, CMU Press, 85; Global Tranaesthetics within a Post-Modern Enlightenment Project, Grapheion, 1/2000; Enigmatic Sculpture, Magdalena Jetelova, Sculpture, 5/2000; Barry LeVa, 68-88; Elizabeth Murray, 89; New Generations: Chicago, 90; New Generations: New York, 91; auth, Ethics in Vis Arts, Allworth Press, 2006; Ethics and the Visual Arts, 2006; Artist Interrupted: Selected Works by Maria de Mater O'Neill From Post to After, 1983-2006, 2007; Black & White: Two Portraits, J Am Cult, Blackwell Publ, 2007; A union of the fantastic & proverbial: Joan Danziger's Trees (catalog), Joan Danziger Mythic Headscapes, 4/2008; ADA Bobonis: Anthropomorhic Amalgams, Sculpture, 1/2008; Justin Randolph Thompson, Sculptures, Sculpture, fall, 2008; Euphoric Sculpture: A Conversation with Franz West, Sculpture mag, 6/2009; DC Art Critic Correspondent for Artcritical.com; monthly art rev, Sculpture, 2009-2010; critic, Artes & Art US; Strange Bedfellows: The Relationship of Post-Modern Art and The Arts Endowment, 2012; Abstraction in America 1970-1980, Shifting Realm of Abstraction, Works from Albright Knox Gallery, Chautauqua Inst, 2012; Havana Biennial, 2013. *Dealer:* From the 60s to Now- 3 DC exhib, Ginsburg, Christo & Klein, Artes Mag, 2010; A Conversation with Allord and Calzadilla, Art as Monster, Sculpture Mag, 2011. *Mailing Add:* 5013 W Cedar Ln Bethesda MD 20814

KING, LYNDEL IRENE SAUNDERS
MUSEUM DIRECTOR
b Enid, Okla, June 10, 1943. *Study:* Univ Kans, BA, 65; Univ Minn, MA, 71, PhD, 82. *Pos:* Asst dir, Art Mus, Univ Minn, 1976-78, dir, 1978-; dir, Exhibs & Mus Relations, Control Data Corp, 1979, 1980-81; exhib coordr, Nat Gallery Art, 1980; dir, Art Mus, Univ Minn, 81-, Weisman Art Mus, 1993-. *Teaching:* Art hist, Mus Studies, Univ Minn, 1979-. *Awards:* Recipient Cult Contrib of Yr award, Minneapolis CofC, 1978; Honor award, Minn Soc Archit, 1979. *Mem:* Am An Mus, Int Coun Mus, Upper Midwest Conservation Asn (pres bd dir, 1980-); Minn Asn Mus (steering comt, 1982); Art Mus Asn Am (vpres bd dir, 1984-89); Asn Coll and Univ Mus and Galleries (vpres, 1989-92); Asn Art Mus Dir (bd trustees, 1998-, chmn art issues comt, 1998-2000, chmn tech commun comt, 2000); Am Fedn Arts Bd, currently. *Res:* Nineteenth century England, especially interaction of arts and society. *Publ:* Auth, Exhibition diplomacy, Mus News, 1979; Museums and special exhibitions, Art J, 1980; The industrialization of taste: The Artunian of London, UMI Research Press, 1985. *Mailing Add:* Weisman Art Mus 333 E River Rd Minneapolis MN 55455

KING, MARCIA GYGLI
PAINTER
b Cleveland, Ohio. *Study:* Smith Coll, BA (english); Corcoron Sch Art, Washington, DC, 1978; Univ Tex San Antonio, MFA, 1980. *Work:* MTA Comn for Creative Solutions, Jay St/Borough Hall Station, Brooklyn, NY, 95; Arkansas Art Ctr, Little Rock; Brooklyn Mus, NY; Cleveland Mus Art; Guggenheim Mus; Herbert F Johnson Mus Art, Cornell Univ; McNay Art Mus, San Antonio; Nat Mus women in Arts, Washington, DC; Newark Mus, NJ; San Antonio Mus Art, Tex; Guild Hall, E Hampton, NY. *Exhib:* Solo exhibs, Camden House Gallery, San Antonio, Tex, 70, Faulkner's Gallery, Washington, DC, 73, Spectrum 16 Gallery, San Antonio, 74, McNamara O'Connor Mus, Victoria, Tex, 75, Charlton Gallery, San Antonio, 80, Rutgers Univ, Douglas Coll, New Brunswick, NJ, 81, Mattingly Baker Gallery, Dallas, 84, McNay Art Mus, San Antonio, 84, White Columns Gallery, New York, 85, Manhattan Marymount Coll, New York, 86, Parker Smalley Gallery, New York, 86, Fervor Gallery, New York, 87, Wallace Wentworth Gallery, Washington, DC, 88, Haines Gallery, San Francisco, 88, Katzen Brown Gallery, New York, 88, 90, Valerie Miller Gallery, Palm Desert, Calif, 89, Univ NC, 89, Cleveland Ctr Contemp Art, 89-90, Hal Katzen Gallery, New York, 92, 94, Renee Fotouhi Fine Art, East Hampton, NY, 95, Guild Hall Mus, East Hampton, NY, 95, Arts Acad Eastern Md, 96, Kouros Gallery, New York, 99, Parchman Stremmel Galleries, San Antonio, 2000, San Antonio Art League Mus, 2000, Brooklyn Botanic Garden, 2001, Gallery Camino Real, Boca Raton, Fla, 2002, Gallery 668, Greenwich, NY, 2003, Blue Star Contemp Art Ctr, San Antonio, 2005, San Antonio Mus Art, Tex, 2009, Univ Tex San Antonio, 2009, Southwest Sch Art & Craft, San Antonio, 2009; group exhibs incl Okla Art Ctr, 75, 77; Ark Art Ctr, Little Rock, 76; Ericson Gallery, New York, 83; Charancahau Gallery, Corpus Christi, Tex, 84; Cleveland Ctr Contemp Art, 85, 86; Littlejohn Smith Gallery, New York, 86; Nat Portrait Gallery, Wash, DC, 87; Renee Fotouhi Gallery, New York, 89; Security Pacific Corp Gallery, Los Angeles, 89; Fine Arts Ctr, Kingston, RI, 91; Gathering of the Tribes, New York, 96; MD Mod, Houston, 97; MB Mod, New York, 97; Met Life Gallery, New York, 99; Opelousas Mus Art, La, 2004; Gallery 668, Greenwich, NY, 2005; Charles Cowles Gallery, NY, 2008. *Awards:* Brewer's Digest Award, Lone Star Brewery, 63; Ann Z T Scott Award & Circuit, Tex Fine Arts Asn, 70; Ethel T Drought Mem Award, San Antonio Art League, 71, Artist of Yr, 2000; Best of Show, Tex Watercolor Soc, 71, First Purchase Prize, 72, James Kirby Nat Mem Award, 76; Outstanding Women in San Antonio, Women's Political Caucus, 79; Artist of the Year, San Antonio Art League, Tex, 2000. *Bibliog:* Arthur Danto, Marcia King & the Symbolic Language of Frames, Hall Mus, E Hampton, NY, 95; Henry Sayre, A World of Art 2nd Ed, Prentice Hall, Upper Saddle River, 97, 5th ed, 2008; Eleanor Munro, Am Women Artists, Da Capo Press, New York, 97; John Digby, Collage, Thames & Hudson, London, 85; First Light (video interview), Roy S Teicher, LTV Pub Access, E Hampton, NY, 95; Signals (video interview), Channel 4, London, Eng, 90; Visions: Four New York Artists, Veronica Herman (producer), 87. *Media:* Oil. *Publ:* Visual Arts Critic, Express News Publ Co, San Antonio, Tex, 76-77; Art Critic, Scenein San Antonio, Tex, 2010

KING, MYRON LYZON
DEALER
b Hampton Bays, NY, Oct 22, 1921. *Study:* David Lipscomb Col, Peabody Col, BA. *Pos:* Lyzon Pictures & Frames, Inc, Nashville. *Bibliog:* George Minzel (auth), Portrait of a Flying Lady, Turner Publ. *Specialty:* Contemporary American art; Sterling Strauser, Paul Lancaster, Malva and David Burlink. *Mailing Add:* 932 Evans Rd Nashville TN 32704-4034

KING, RAY
SCULPTOR, LIGHT ARTIST
b Philadelphia, Pa, July 4, 1950. *Study:* Burleighfield House, Loudwater, Bucks, Eng, 75-76. *Work:* Nat Mus Am Art, Washington; Victoria & Albert Mus, London, Eng; Corning Mus Glass, Corning, NY; Best Products, Richmond, Va; Chasco Co, Jericho, NY; E I Dupont de Nemours & Co, Wilmington, Del. *Comn:* Philadelphia Beacons, (four illuminated 42 feet high glass, stainless steel, granite base, light column torches), Avenue of the Arts, Philadelphia, Pa, 94; Light Wave, Rowan Col, Glassboro, NJ, 94; Bristol Beacon, Market Street Wharf, Pa, 95; Sky Garden, Davee Libr, Univ Wisc-River Falls, 96; Double Helical Projections, Iowa State Univ, Ames, 96. *Exhib:* Pa Acad Fine Arts, Philadelphia, 79; Denver Art Mus, Colo, 87; J B Speed Art Mus, Louisville, Ky, 88; Va Mus Fine Art, Richmond, 88; Huntsville Mus Art, Ala, 89; Oklahoma City Art Mus, 89; Contemp Philadelphia Artists, Philadelphia Mus Art, 90; Lane Gallery, San Diego, 93; Galleria, St Petersburg, Fla, 93; Nat Mus Jewish Hist, Philadelphia, 94; Gallery Am Craft, Wheaton Village, Millville, NJ, 95; Urban Glass, Brooklyn, NY, 96. *Pos:* Panelist, fel grants, Nat Endowment Arts, 81; mem bd dir, NY Experimental Glass Workshop, 81-88. *Awards:* Nat Endowment Arts Fel, 84; Pa Coun Arts Fel, 86; Edwin Guth Mem Award, Illuminating Eng Soc, 88. *Bibliog:* Vilma Barr (auth), The Best of Neon, 92; Robert Kehlman and Kyoto Shoin, (coauths), 20th Century Stained Glass: A New Definition, 92; Penny Balkin Back (auth), Public Art in Philadelphia, 92. *Mem:* Int Sculpture Soc; Am Craft Coun. *Media:* Glass, Metal; Light. *Publ:* Contribr, Public Art in Philadelphia, 92; 20th Century Stained Glass: A New Definition, 92; The Best of Neon, 92; The Best of Stained Glass, 91; numerous articles & photograph periodicals. *Mailing Add:* 835 N 3rd St Philadelphia PA 19123

KING, VIKKI KILLOUGH VRANICH
PUBLISHER, PAINTER
b Lubbock, Tex, Feb 15, 1956. *Study:* studied with Gustav Likan, 94-96; studied with Armand Winfield, 2003-05. *Work:* State of Oreg Gov's Collection, Salem; Zilker Botanical Gardens, Austin, Tex; Austin History Ctr. *Comn:* The Party Homage, Gustav Likan. *Exhib:* Global Art Show, Austin, 94; 11.11 Art Show, Austin, 95; Mojo Art Show, Austin, 99; Death of the Unknown Artist, Austin, 99; Ballinthejack Gallery, 2003-2013. *Collection Arranged:* The Kings Things, 2011-2014. *Pos:* Publ, The Picture Paper Mag, 94-97; co-founder, World Art Party-Austin Tea Party, 95. *Teaching:* instr, Art in the Park, Austin, Tex. *Awards:* First art mag on the internet, The Picture Paper-Priceless, 94-97. *Bibliog:* Michael Barnes (auth), World Art Party, Austin Am Statesman, 11/95; The Picture Paper, XL Mag, Austin Am Statesman, 8/95. *Mem:* World Art Party; NMex Film Commission; NMex Culture Net. *Media:* Acrylic. *Specialty:* jewelry, metal, clay. *Publ:* Coauth, Mankind's Millennium Manual, 99 & Secrets of the Cavemen, 2000; Goggle Glass. *Dealer:* The Kings Things. *Mailing Add:* PO Box 21392 Albuquerque NM 87154

KING, WILLIAM
SCULPTOR
b Jacksonville, Fla, Feb 25, 1925. *Study:* Univ Fla, 42-44; Cooper Union Art Sch, 45-48; Brooklyn Mus Art Sch, 49; Academia de Belle Arti, Rome, 49-50; Cent Sch, London, 52. *Hon Degrees:* Hon PhD Art, Univ Fla, Gainesvilla, Fla. *Work:* Univ Calif; Cornell Univ, Ithaca, NY; Hunter Mus, TN; Syracuse Univ, NY; Los Angeles Co Mus, Calif; Brandeis Univ, Waltham, Mass; Metrop Mus Art, Whitney Mus & Solomon R Guggenheim Mus, NY; and many pvt collections; Mus Modern Art. *Comn:* Mural, SS United States, 52; mural, Bankers' Trust, NY, 60; sculpture, Miami-Dade Jr Col, Fla, 72; sculpture, State Univ NY, Potsdam, 73-74; sculpture, Detroit Med Ctr, 79; sculpture, Madison Art & Civic Ctr, Wis, 79; sculpture, Lincoln Libr, Ft Wayne, Ind, 80; sculpture, Palo Alto, Calif, 86; sculpture, Fla State Coun Arts, Lakeland, 87; sculpture, Broward Co Fla, 90; sculpture, City of Philadelphia, 95. *Exhib:* Whitney Mus Am Art, Mus Mod Art & Guggenheim Mus, NY; Philadelphia Mus Art; Los Angeles Co Mus Art; retrospective, San Francisco Mus Art, Calif, 70 & 74; solo exhibs, San Francisco Mus Art, 70, Wadsworth Atheneum, Hartford, 72, Hunter Mus, Chattanooga, Tenn, 87, Peconic Gallery, NY, Brunnier Gallery & Mus, Iowa, 90, Extension Gallery Inc, NJ & Hokin Gallery Inc, Fla, 91; Nat Acad Design, NY, 89; Brenau Univ, Gainesville, Ga, 91; Coming of Age of Am Sculpture, Lehigh, Pa, 91-92; Mus Art, Ft Lauderdale, Fla, 92; 40 Yrs of Works in Wood, Sheridan Past Gallery, 94; Lizan-Tops Gallery, E Hampton, NY, 98; Alexandre Gallery, NY. *Pos:* sculptor. *Teaching:* Instr sculpture, Brooklyn Mus Sch Art, 52-55; lectr sculpture, Univ Calif, Berkeley, 65-66; instr sculpture, Art Students League, 68-69, Univ Pa, 72-73 & State Univ NY, 74-75. *Awards:* Fulbright Fel, 49-50; St Gaudens Medal, Cooper Union, 64; Creative Artists Pub Serv Proj Grant, 74; Gold Medal, Nat Acad Design, New York, 86; lifetime achievement award, Int Sculpture Ctr, 2007. *Bibliog:* S Schwartz (auth), New York letter: William King, Art Int, 11/72; John Sanders (auth), Photography Year Book 1973, London, 72; Hilton Kramer (auth), The Age of the Avant-Garde, London, 74. *Mem:* Nat Arts Club NY; Nat Acad Design (pres, 93-); Am Acad Arts & Letts. *Media:* Wood, Fabric, Metal, Ceramic

KINGSLEY, APRIL
CURATOR, CRITIC, LECTURER
b New York, NY, 1941. *Study:* Inst Fine Arts, NY Univ, BA (art hist) & MA; City Univ NY Grad Ctr, 86, MPhil, PhD, 2000. *Exhib:* Art in the 'toon Age, 2002, traveling 2003-2005. *Collection Arranged:* Paintings That Paint Themselves Or So It Seems, 2005; Blast From the Past: Art of the 1960's (catalogue), 2006. *Pos:* Cur, Kresge Art Mus, MSU, 98-2011, retired 2011. *Teaching:* Sch of Visual Arts, 1973-1990. *Bibliog:* Judy K Collischan van Wagner (auth), Women Shaping Art, 84-. *Mem:* Int Art Critics Asn; CAA; MAHA. *Media:* Art writing. *Res:* Conceptual art; Abstract Expressionism; Ashcan realism; Figurative Expressionism; Art in the Toon Age. *Publ:* The Turning Point: The Abstract Expressionists & the Transformation of American Art, 92; Fiber: Five Decades from the Permanent Collection of the American Craft Museum (exhib catalog), 95; John Clem Clarke, The Am Way, Allentown Art Mus, 98; Abstract Expressions in Context in 300 Years American of Painting: The Montclair Art Mus Collection, 99; Jean Miotle, Abstract Expressionist, 2000; The Paintings of Alice Dalton Brown, 2002; Art in the Toon Age, 2004; Suitcase Paintings: Small Scale Abstract Expressionism, 2007; Emotional Impact: American Figurative Expressionism, MSU Press, 2012. *Mailing Add:* 2449 Wild Blossom Ct East Lansing MI 48823-7203

KINGTON, LOUIS BRENT
SCULPTOR
b Topeka, Kans, July 26, 1934. *Study:* Univ Kans, BFA, 57; Cranbrook Acad Art, MFA, 61. *Work:* Mus Art & Design, NY; Mint Mus of Craft and Design; Renwick Gallery, Smithsonian Inst, Washington, DC; Ill State Mus, Springfield; Phil Mus Art; Cranbrook Mus, Bloomfield Hills, Mich; and others. *Comn:* Memphis Botanical Garden, Tenn; Friendship Hall, Nakajo, Japan; Rend Lake Col, Ina, Ill; Southern Ill Univ Sch Med, Springfield, Ill. *Exhib:* North Am Goldsmiths, Renwick Gallery, Smithsonian, Washington, DC, 74; Am Crafts for the Vatican Mus, Rome, 78; Towards a New Iron Age, Victoria & Albert Mus, London, 82; Craft Today, Poetry of the Physical, Am Craft Mus, NY, 86; The Eloquent Object, Philbrook Art Ctr, Tulsa, Okla, 87; City on a Hill: 20 Yrs of Artists at Cortona, Italy, 89; Artists from Ill, Kunstlerhas Palas, Bregenz, Austria, 91; Retrospective exhibs, 1962-2007; L. Brent Kingston: Mythic Metalsmith, Ill State Mus, Chic, Ill; and others. *Teaching:* Prof metal smithing, Southern Ill Univ, Carbondale, 61-96; retired. *Awards:* Craftsman Fel,

Nat Endowment Arts, 75 & 82; Am Craft Coun, Gold Medal for Excellence; Artist Fel, Ill Arts Coun, 85; L Brent Kington chair at Southern Ill Univ Carbondale created in his honor, 2006. *Bibliog:* L. Brent Kington Mythic Metalsmith, Ill State Mus Soc, 2008. *Mem:* Soc NAm Goldsmiths (pres, 70-74); Am Crafts Coun (trustee, 76-80); Artists-Blacksmiths Asn NAm (dir, 75-79). *Media:* Metals. *Res:* Symbolic objects denoting authority, social distinction and ritual. *Specialty:* Fine Crafts, Painting, Sculpture. *Interests:* 20th Century Painting, Sculpture, Ethnic Arts. *Collection:* African Haitan Early Iron Objects; Folk Paintings. *Dealer:* David Lusk Gallery Memphis TN. *Mailing Add:* 88 Whippoorwill Ln Makanda IL 62958

KINIGSTEIN, JONAH
PAINTER, DESIGNER
b 1923. *Study:* Cooper Union Art Sch, 41-43; Grande Chaumiere, Paris, 47-51; Belle Arte, Rome, Fulbright Fel, 53-54. *Work:* Mus Mod Art, NY; Albright-Knox Art Gallery, Buffalo, NY; Nelson Gallery Art; Washington Mus; Ain Herod Mus, Tel-Aviv, Israel; also in pvt collections. *Exhib:* Butler Inst Am Art, Youngstown, Ohio, 56; Young Americans, Whitney Mus Am Art, NY, 57; Nat Acad Arts & Lett, 68; Solo exhibs, ACA Gallery, 68 & Rittenhouse Gallery, Philadelphia, 75; Washington Irving Gallery, NY, 82; Art & the Law, Landmark Ctr, St Paul, Minn, 82; Rittenhouse Gallery, Philadelphia, 82; Pindar Gallery, NY, 88-89 & 92; Student Univ Art Gallery, Univ Mass, 90; Broom St Gallery, 2007; and others. *Teaching:* Brooklyn Mus Art Sch, 70. *Awards:* Fulbright to Italy, 53; Louis Comfort Tiffany Found Award, 62; Perkins-Elmer Prize, 62; and others. *Mem:* Nat Acad NY. *Publ:* Lee Nordness (auth), Art USA Now, Viking Press, 62; Laurence Shmeckabier (auth), Syracuse Univ Collection, 64; Barry Schwartz, The New Humanism, 74; Catalogue of the Collection of American Art at Randolph-Macon Womens College, Univ Va, 77. *Mailing Add:* 738 Westminster Rd Brooklyn NY 11230

KINKADE, CATHERINE
PAINTER, PRINTMAKER
b Westfield, MA, Apr 3, 1940. *Study:* Boston Univ, BA, 1962; Montclair Mus Sch Art. *Work:* Pastel Soc Am Permanent Collection, NY; Nat Asn of Women Artists UN Millennium Collection, NY; Nature Conservancy Collection, Shelter Island, NY; Grand Cen Galleries Permanent Collection, NY; Exxon-Mobil Hq Permanent Collection, NJ; Environmental Ctr Collection, NJ. *Comn:* Morristown Wetlands (10' 4 panel oil), Tiffany & Co; Change Water (20' oil Triptych), AT&T; Near Chatsworth (oil), BASF; Third River (6 panel monotype), Am Savings Bank; Wisteria (8' oil), Dai Kitchi Japanese Restaurant (Tatami Rm); Champagne (oil & wine bottle label), Angelbecks & Gruet Vineyards, Bethon, France; Verizon NJ (pastels); Yoga & Meditation Ctr, NJ (oil & pastels). *Exhib:* Solo exhibs, La Normandie, Park Ave Club; Van Vleck Gardens en Plein Air, NJ; Reflections, Pen & Brush, NY; La Champagne, Frederick Clement Gallery, Montclair, NJ & NY; Expos Int: Salons des Artists Contemporains, Honfleur, Giverny, Yvetot, France; American Master Pastelists, Pastel Soc Am Traveling Exhibs X'iang, Bejing, Nanchang, China, Lille, France; Connections, Kunstlerbund, Graz, Austria; Expos Ntl: Pastel Masters; Traveling Expos: Butler Inst; Lincoln Cntr, NY; Palette Chisel, Chicago; Hermtg Mus; Naples Mus, Fla; Centennial Nat CLWAC Traveling Exhib, US, 1990-1991; Montclair Colony Past & Present, Montclair Art Mus, Montclair, NJ, 1997; ARTEXPO, NYC & Las Vegas. *Pos:* Instr (pastel painting/color/plein air landscape & mstr class), Montclair Art Mus Sch of Art, 1981; Artist in Residence (landscape en plein air), Van Vleck House & Gardens, 1996. *Awards:* National Best in Show Awards: Nat Arts Club, Pastel Soc Am Nat Ann, 1982; Gold Medal of Honor, Catharine Lorillard Wolfe Art Club Nat Ann, 1989 (pastel), 1993 (oil); Best in Show, Pen & Brush Ann, 1989. *Bibliog:* Kristina Feliciano, ed (auth), Best of Pastels, Rockport, 1996; Kristen Park (auth), In the Taoist Tradition: An Interview with Landscape Painter, Catherine Kinkade, TCM World Newspaper, 2002; The Art of Pastel (l'Art de Pastel en France), 2006. *Mem:* Pastel Soc Am (signature mem 1981-, master pastelist 1985); Catharine Lorillard Wolfe Art Club (vpres exhibs & painting 1984-1987); Viridian Print Studio (exec dir 1996-); Art du Pastel en France (2003); Nat Asn Women Artists (1999); Am Artists Prof League; SMI (Bd Trustee 1998-). *Media:* Oil, Pastel, Montype. *Publ:* Contribr, Meditative Approach to Plein Air Painting, Pastelogram, publ of the Pastel Soc Am, 2003. *Dealer:* Avila Fine Arts (art consult) 1850C Burnt Mills Rd Bedminster NJ; Jaclyn Kling Fine Art 106 Walnut St Montclair NJ 07042; Gallery on the Hudson 91 Broad St Saratoga Schuylerville NY

KINNAIRD, RICHARD WILLIAM
PAINTER, EDUCATOR
b Buenos Aires, Arg, Nov 19, 1931; US citizen. *Study:* Univ Mich, Ann Arbor, 49-51; Carleton Col, Northfield, Minn, BA, 53; Art Inst Chicago, 52; Univ Ill, with Lee Chesney, MFA, 58. *Work:* Seattle Mus of Art; NC Mus of Art, Raleigh; Hanes Knitting Corp & R J Reynolds Corp, Winston-Salem, NC. *Comn:* Thomas Wolfe Mem Sculpture, class gift to Univ NC-Chapel Hill, 66; pediment sculpture, Mint Mus of Art, Charlotte, NC, 72. *Exhib:* Award Winners Exhib of Chicago No-Jury Show, Art Inst of Chicago, 57; Southeastern Ann Painting & Sculpture, High Mus, Atlanta, Ga, 66; Experimental Media, Corcoran Gallery of Contemp Art, Washington, DC, 70; Painting & Sculpture Exhib, Mint Mus of Art, 71; Third Ann Contemp Reflections, Aldrich Mus of Contemp Art, 73; solo exhibs, Sandhurst Art Coun, Aberdeen, NC, 78 & Rowan Art Ctr, Salisbury, NC, 79; Selections from the Collection, Aldrich Mus Contemp Art, Ridgefield, Conn, 78; Patron Art Patron, Southeastern Ctr Contemp Art, 79; Exhib of Works by Tenn Valley States Artists, Tenn Valley Auth Washington Visitors Ctr, DC, 79. *Collection Arranged:* Univ Evansville Fine Arts Exhib, Ind, 73. *Teaching:* Instr printmaking & etching, Auburn Univ, Ala, 60-64; from instr to assoc prof painting, Univ NC, 64-76, prof painting, 76-. *Awards:* Purchase Award, Third Ann Contemp Reflections, Aldrich Mus of Contemp Art, 74; First Painting Award, Spring Mill Ann Art Exhib, Spring Mills Corp, Lancaster, SC, 76; First Award, 40th Ann NC Artists, NC Mus of Fine Art, Raleigh, 77. *Media:* Acrylic, Oil. *Mailing Add:* c/o Dept Art Univ NC Hanes Art Ctr CB 3405 Chapel Hill NC 27599

KINNEE, SANDY
PAINTER, PAPERMAKER
b Port Huron, Mich, Mar 30, 1947. *Study:* Univ Mich, Ann Arbor, BFA (printmaking), 69, grad study, 70; Wayne State Univ, Detroit, MFA (printmaking), 76; Atelier 17, Paris, France, 79. *Work:* Metrop Mus Art, NY; Mus NMex, Santa Fe; Evergreen State Col; Portland Art Mus; Allen Art Mus, Oberlin, Ohio; Madison Art Ctr, Wis; Brooklyn Mus Art; and others. *Exhib:* Works on Handmade Paper, Mus Mod Art, NY, 76; Paper as Medium, Smithsonian, traveling, 78-80; Fans, Philadelphia Mus Art, Pa, 79; Solo exhibs, Coburn Gallery, Colo Col, 92, 1/1 Gallery, Denver, Colo, 92, Art Selection, Zurich, Switz, 94 & TAK Gallery, Schann, Liechtenstein; Art Multiple, Dusseldorf, Ger, 95; SAGA/FICA Edition, Paris, France, 95; 1/1 Gallery, Denver, Colo, 95; Art Selection, Zurich, Switz, 97. *Awards:* Purchase Award, Southwest Biennial, Mus NMex, Santa Fe, 78; Printmakers Fel, Western States Art Found, 79; Pollack Krasner Found Grant, 87. *Bibliog:* Jules Heller (auth), Papermaking, Watson-Guptill, 78; Virginia Butera (auth), Sandy Kinnee, Arts Mag, 6/81; Suzanne M Singletary (auth), Sandy Kinnee, fans and kimonos, Artspace, 1/82. *Media:* Handcolored Intaglio on Handmade Paper; Watercolor. *Publ:* Papermaking (film), Crystal Productions, Aspen, Colo, 80; An Introduction to Printmaking (slide ser) & Printmaking with Basic Equipment (slide ser) Crystal Production, Aspen, Colo, 83; auth, Fans, bridges, kimonos and the role paper plays in my work, Print Club, Philadelphia, 81; Printmaking (film), Crystal Prod, Aspen, Colo, 83; Combat Paper - Hand Papermaking Mag. *Dealer:* Art Selection Zurich Switz. *Mailing Add:* 1202 N Institute Colorado Springs CO 80903

KINNEY, GILBERT HART
COLLECTOR, ADMINISTRATOR
b New York, NY, May 11, 1931. *Study:* Yale Univ, BA, 53 & MA, 54; John F Kennedy Sch, MPA, 73. *Pos:* Trustee, Corcoran Gallery Art, Washington, DC, 74-77, 78-94, chief exec off, 77-78; trustee, Archs Am Art, 74-88, 89-91, 2009, pres, 78-82; trustee, Am Fed Arts, 78-, pres 2000; dir, Am Arts Alliance, 85-91; trustee, Yale Art Gallery, 91-. *Collection:* Major emphasis on post-war American painting and sculpture, also European 20th century painting and sculpture, South and Southeast Asian sculpture especially bronzes. *Mailing Add:* 19 E 72nd St Apt 9A New York NY 10021

KINOSHITA, GENE
ARCHITECT
b Vancouver, BC, Jan 18, 1935. *Study:* Univ BC, BArch (honors), 59; Yale Univ, MArch, 62. *Comn:* McMaster Univ Art Gallery & Libr, Hamilton, Ont, 89-93; Scis Complex, Univ Western Ont, London, 89-91; Whitby Mental Health Ctr, Ont, 91-97; Fenbrook Inst, Gravenhurst, Ont, 94-98, YMCA, Sarnia-Lambton, 95-98; Art Gallery Windsor, Ont, 2000; Univ Toronto Pharmacy Bldg, 2002. *Exhib:* Traveling Exhib Can Art Mus, Royal Can Acad Arts, 67; Can Unit Masonry Awards Prog Traveling Exhib Can, 72; Ont Masons Rels Coun, Traveling Prov Exhib, 73; Am Inst Arch & Am Correctional Asn Traveling Show, 80; Royal Can Acad Gallery, 87; 3rd Int Conf on Justice Archit, 98; over 35 awards for the design of Richmond Olympic oval as a design principa while with common design, 2010-2011. *Pos:* Principal, Moffat Kinoshita Architects Inc, 65-2005; Principal, Cannon Design, 2005-2012; retired, 2013. *Teaching:* Univ Toronto Sch Archit, 69-71 & 80-84. *Awards:* Ont Asn Archit Award of Excellence for Royal Ont Mus & NY Aquatic Ctr, 87 & 89; Gov Gens Award in Archit, for Queen Elizabeth Terraced Galleries of the Royal Ontario Mus, Toronto, 1986; Merit Award for Alumni Ctr, Univ Guelph, Ont, 89; Award of Excellence, Ont Asn Archit, 89; Order of da Vinci Medal, Ont Asn Archit, 2004; and 45 others. *Mem:* Ont Asn Archit; academician Royal Can Acad Arts (pres, 84-88); Ont Coll Art (hon trustee); Art Found Greater Toronto (pres, 93-95); fel Royal Archit Inst Can; and others. *Collection:* Can Art of Royal Can Acad Art Academicians of abstr minimalist paintings & abstr landscape paintings & prints of Candadian artists. Also, American abstract paintings and prints and of Japanese prints of 18th & 19th century artists. *Publ:* Auth, The ROM: A new lease on life, Canadian Collector, 7-8/82; Museums are for people, the evolution of a design concept, Rotunda Mag, Vol 15, No 2, 82

KINSTLER, EVERETT RAYMOND
PAINTER, INSTRUCTOR
b New York, NY, 1926. *Study:* Nat Acad Design, New York; Art Students League, with DuMond; also, John Johansen & Jas Montgomery Flagg; Rollins Col, Hon DFA, 83. *Hon Degrees:* Hon DFA, Rollins Col, 1983; Hon DFA, Lyme Acad Coll Art, 2002; Hon DFA: Acad of Art Univ, San Francisco. *Work:* Metrop Mus Art, NY; Carnegie Inst, Pittsburgh; Brooklyn Mus; Smithsonian Inst, Washington; Mus City NY; Butler Inst Am Art; and others; Nat Portrait Gallery, Washington, DC (71 works). *Comn:* 2500 works:; Portraits of Pres George Bush; Secy State James Baker; off White House Portrait of Pres Gerald R Ford, Pres Ronald Reagan, Pres George W Bush, Pres Bill Clinton, Pres Jimmy Carter, Pres Richard Nixon, 5 US Secs of State; portraits of John Wayne, Katharine Hepburn, Tom Wolfe, Gene Hackman, Peter O'Toole, Paul Newman, Tony Bennett, Donald Trump, official NYC mayoral portrait of Rudolph Giuliani, & Mary Tyler Moore; portraits of presidents of following universities: Yale, Harvard, Princeton, Chicago, Oklahoma, Brown, Pa & Boston; and others. *Exhib:* Solo exhibs, Grand Cent Art Galleries, 83, Lotos Club, NY, 72, Lluisa Gallery, Mich, 81, Artists of Am, Denver, 81-90, Rollins Col, Fla, 83 & Hollis Taggart Gallery, 94, Boston Univ, 2000, Butler Inst Am Art, 2000, Nat Arts Club, 2000, New York Creative, Mus City of NY, 2006; Ann exhibs, Am Watercolor Soc, Nat Acad Arts, Nat Acad Design and others; Retrospective: Norman Rockwell Mus, 2012; Bellarmine Mus, Fairfield Univ, Conn, 2012; Century Club, NY, 2013. *Teaching:* Instr painting & drawing, Art Students League, 70-; instr Nat Acad Design Sch. *Awards:* Nat Arts Club, 1959-1967; Silver Medal, Audubon Artists, 1988; Gold Medal, Allied Artists, 1996; Copley Medal, Nat Portrait Gallery, 2000; Medal, Nat Acad Design, 2003; Gold Medal, Salmagundi Club, NYC, 2005; Copley Soc, 2006. *Bibliog:* Articles, Am Artist, 1/72 & 7/84, People, 7/14/76, Saturday Evening Post, 82, Southwest Art, 3/82, Artists of Rockies, summer 83 & Art Times, 4/88, NY Times, 12/89. *Mem:* Nat Arts Club;

Nat Acad Design; Am Watercolor Soc; Life mem, Players Club; Life mem Lotos Club; Yale Club; Audubon Artists; Allied Artist of Am; Copley Soc (Boston); Pastel Soc of Am (Hall of Fame); Lambs Club (life); Players Club (life); Century Club. *Publ:* Painting Faces, Figures & Landscapes, Watson-Guptill, 81, rev, 95; Everett Raymond Kinstler...An Artist's Journey, PBS Documentary, 2002; auth, My Brush With History, 2005; auth, The Artists Journey Through the Popular Culture, 2005; auth, Paints Ahead, TV documentary, 2006. *Dealer:* Vose Galler, Boston; Matteucci Gallery, Santa Fe; Richland Fine Art, Tennessee. *Mailing Add:* 15 Gramercy Park New York NY 10003

KINZER, ROY
PAINTER
Study: Univ Pa, 78; Pa Acad Fine Arts, cert, 79; Norwich Univ, Vt, MFA, 95. *Exhib:* Solo exhibs include Unicorn Gallery, Hoboken, NJ, 82, Hoboken Cultural Ctr, 82, J Rosenthal Gallery, Chicago, 83, 84, 86, Ill Ctr Tower Two, 84, Slater Memorial Mus, 86, McFall Ctr Gallery, Bowling Green State Univ, 87, Coup de Grace, Hoboken, 88, Julian A McPhee Gallery, Calif Polytechnic State Univ, 90, Montclair Art Mus, NJ, 91, The Sculpture Ctr, NY, 94, Vt Col, 95, domoGallery, Summit, NJ, 2004, Denise Bibro Fine Art, NY, 2007; group exhibs include Bertone Gallery, Montclair, 2001; Montclair Art Mus, Montclair, 2003-04; Metaphor Contemp Art, Brooklyn, 2004; Pierro Gallery, S Orange, NJ, 2005; Tribeca Open Artist Studio Tour, NY, 2005; Denise Bibro Fine Art, NY, 2006, 2007. *Awards:* Fellowship, NY State Council Arts, 86; Artist of Month, Liquitex Artist Acrylic, 2004; Artist Grant, Pollock-Krasner Found, 2003-04

KIOUSIS, LINDA WEBER
PAINTER, ILLUSTRATOR
b Cleveland, Ohio. *Study:* Cleveland Inst Art, dipl; Case Western Reserve Univ, BS, MA. *Work:* Univ Mo Hosp & Clinic, Columbia; Ohio Watercolor Soc; Salem Pub Libr, Ohio; Arches Paper co; Binney & Smith Inc, Pa; Butler Inst Am Art, Youngstown, Ohio; and others. *Comn:* Soc Corp, Cleveland, Ohio, 93; Paintings, Children's Oncology Serv Northeastern Ohio, Inc, 94. *Exhib:* Mainstream America: Collection of Phil Desind, Butler Inst Am Art, Youngstown, Ohio, 87; Am Realism, Parkersburg, WVa, 89; Choices and Decisions, Chelsea Galleries, Beachwood, Ohio, 90; Watercolor Now, Springfield Art Mus, Mo, 91; Watercolor USA, Mo, 91; 34th Ann Chautauqua Nat Exhib Am Art; Woman's Touch, Glass Growers Gallery, Erie, Pa, 91; Art Inspired by Architecture, Great Northern Corp Ctr, Ohio, 92; Graphic Watercolors, Sandusky Cult Ctr, Ohio, 92; Northwest Watercolor Soc, Wash; Cleveland Clinic SW, Ohio; Daniel Smith Artists' Materials, Wash; Farmington Mus, NMex. *Teaching:* Instr, Ohio Watercolor Soc, 97. *Awards:* Best of Show, Santa Fe Trail Days, Colo, 99; Best of Show, Baycrafters, Ohio, 2000; 1st Prize, Western Colo Watercolor Soc, 2000; Best of Show, Ohio Watercolor Soc, Nat Canton Art Mus, Ohio; Best of Show, Winterfest 2002, Guntersville, AL. *Bibliog:* Marilyn Phillis (auth), Watermedia Techniques for Releasing the Creative Spirit; Watercolor Magic, F&W Publ, spring 2001. *Mem:* Ohio Watercolor Soc; Pa Watercolor Soc; Watercolor USA Hon Soc; Nat Asn Women Artists; Midwest Watercolor Soc; Sylvan Grouse Guild; Tex Watercolor Soc; Ala Watercolor Soc; Western Colo Watercolor Soc. *Media:* Transparent Watercolor. *Dealer:* Glass Growers Gallery Erie PA; The Bonfoey Co 1710 Euclid Ave Cleveland OH 44115. *Mailing Add:* 8968 Snow Rd Parma OH 44130-2117

KIPERVASER, ANNA
PAINTER
b L'vov, Ukraine. *Study:* Art Acad Cincinnati, BFA. *Exhib:* Solo exhibs include Highland's, Cincinnati, 2002, Washington Platform, Cincinnati, 2002, Art Acad Cincinnati, 2003, Southgate House, Newport, KY, 2004, D/VISION, Chicago, 2005, Fish & Fowl, Chicago, 2006, Aquarius Star, Cincinnati, 2007; Group exhibs include Assured Environments, NYSP, New York, 2001; Group This!, Milton's, Cincinnati, 2002; 12 X 12 X 12 Artists, SS Nova, Cincinnati, 2003; Semantics Benefit, Semantics, Cincinnati, 2003; Manual Productions: Manifold Abetment, the Mockbee, Cincinnati, 2004; Terrestrial Domains, Manifest Creative Research Gallery, Cincinnati, 2005; Paper Tigers, Three Seasons Gallery, Chicago, 2006; Heartache, Fish and Fowl, Chicago, 2006; Birdhouse Benefit Auction, Mus Contemp Art, Chicago, 2006; Where the Buffalo Roam, Foursided Gallery, Chicago, 2008. *Awards:* Bertha Langhorst Werner Award, 2000, 2001; Womens Art Club Award, 2001, 2002; Three Arts Club Award, 2001, 2002; B Langhorst Werner Award, 2002; Gamblin Paint Award, 2002; Krehbiel Calendar Top Prize, 2003; Wilder Traveling Scholar, 2003; Travel Team Young Artists Traveling Award, 2005; George Sugarman Found Grant, 2007. *Mailing Add:* 408 Dogwood Terr Buffalo Grove IL 60089

KIPNISS, ROBERT
PAINTER, PRINTMAKER
b New York, NY, Feb 1, 1931. *Study:* Art Students League; Wittenberg Coll; Univ Iowa, BA, 52, MFA, 54. *Hon Degrees:* Wittenberg Univ, hon PhD, 79; Ill Coll, LHD, 89. *Work:* Whitney Mus Am Art, New York; The British Mus, Eng; Metrop Mus, New York; Biblioteque Nationale de France, Paris; Pinakothek Moderne, Munich, Ger; Morgan Libr & Mus, New York. *Exhib:* Group exhibs, Recent Acquisitions, Whitney Mus Am Art, 72, Works on Paper from the Permanent Collection, Metrop Mus Art, New York, 2010; solo exhibs, Asn Am Artists, New York, 77, Mus de Arte Moderno, Cali, Colombia, 75 & 80, Enatsu Gallery, Tokyo, 88 & 90, Wichita Falls Mus, Tex, 97, Weinstein Gallery, Calif, 99-2002, 2004 & 2007, Beadleston Gallery, New York, 2001 & 2003, New Orleans Mus Art, 2006, Millenia Gallery, Orlando, Fla, 2006-2007, Hartnett Mus, Richmond, Va, 2006 & McNay Mus, San Antonio, 2007, Franklin Riehlma Fine Art, NY, 2012; III Bienal Americana de Artes Graficas, Museo La Tertulia, Cali, Colombia, 76; Redfern Gallery, London; Am Acad Arts & Lett invitation, 88; Butler Inst Am Art, Ohio, 99; Fitzwilliam Mus, Cambridge, Eng, Recent Acquisitions, 99; Ashmolean Mus, Oxford, Eng, No Day Without a Line, Diploma Prints, Royal Soc Painter-Printmakers, 99; Papertrail: Works on Paper From the Collection, Nat Acad Design, New York, 2000; The British Mus, London, Recent Acquisitions, 2000; Royal Acad Summer Show, London, 2001; many others. *Awards:* Ralph Fabri Prize, Nat Acad Design, 76, Leo Meissner Prize, 80-81, Cert Merit, 97 & Cannon Prize, 99; Printmaking Prize, 76 & 78, Audubon Artists, Silver Medal, 80, Medal of Honor, 83, Louis Lozowick Award, 97 & Daniel Serra-Badue Mem Award, 98; Charles M Lea Prize, Print Club Philadelphia, 78; Purchase Award, Charlotte Printmakers Soc, 79; Printmaking Award, Soc Am Graphic Artists, 79; Speicher-Hassam Purchase Award, Am Acad Arts & Letts, 88; Purchase Award, Albany Print Club, 95; Juror's Commendation, 97, Boston Printmakers & Rembrandt Graphics Award, 99; Lifetime Achievement Award, Soc Am Graphic Artists, 2007; Benjamin West Clinedinst Gold Medal for Lifetime Achievement for the Artists' Fel, New York, 2010. *Bibliog:* Robert Kipniss, The Graphic Works, Abaris Books, 80; Robert Kipniss, Intaglios, 1982-2004, Hudson Hills Press, New York & Manchester, 2004; Seen in Solitude: The Prints of Robert Kipniss from the James F White Collection, The New Orleans Mus Art, Publ, 2006; Robert Kipniss: Paintings 1950-2005, Hudson Hill Press, NY & Manchester, Vt, 2007. *Mem:* Nat Acad Design; Boston Printmakers; Soc Am Graphic Artists; Century Asn, NY; Royal Soc Painter-Printmakers, London, 98. *Media:* Oil; Mezzotint. *Publ:* Illusr, Poems of Emily Dickinson, Thomas Y Crowell, 64; Collected Poems of Robert Graves, Anchor Doubleday, 66; Poems of Rilke, Limited Ed Club, 81; Printmaking Today, London, 96; auth, Robert Kipniss: A Working Artists Life (memoir), Univ Press of New England; Robert Kipness: A Working Artists Life (memoir), The Univ Press New England, 2011. *Dealer:* Redfern Gallery London; Weinstein Gallery San Francisco CA; Acme Fine Art Boson MA; The Old Printshop New York NY; Franklin Riehlman Fine Art NY. *Mailing Add:* Hudson House PO Box 112 Ardsley On Hudson NY 10503

KIPP, LYMAN
SCULPTOR
b Dobbs Ferry, NY, Dec 24, 1929. *Study:* Pratt Inst, 50-52; Cranbrook Acad Art, 52-54. *Work:* Whitney Mus Am Art, NY; Albright-Knox Art Gallery, Buffalo; High Mus of Art, Atlanta, Ga; Univ Ala, Huntsville; State NY Albany Mall. *Comn:* Sculpture for Post Off & Fed Off Bldg, Van Nuys, Calif; sculpture, Village Lake Placid, NY; Grosse Pointe Libr, Mich. *Exhib:* Four Whitney Mus Am Art Sculpture Ann, 64-70; Sculpture in Environ, NY, 67; Cool Art, 68 & Highlights of the Season, 68, Larry Aldrich Mus, Conn; Art of the Real, Mus Mod Art, NY & London, 68, & Paris & Berlin, 69; Change of View, Larry Aldrich Mus, 75; Sculpture in the Constructivist Tradition, Hamilton Gallery, NY, 77; Urban Structures-Monumental Sculpture, Nat Endowment Arts Traveling Exhib originated in Akron, Ohio, 77-79; Art in Pub Places, Ferris State Col, Mich, 79. *Teaching:* Instr sculpture, Bennington Col, 60-63; asst prof sculpture, Hunter Col, 63-66, prof & chmn dept, 75-; prof sculpture & chmn dept, Lehman Col, 66-75. *Awards:* Guggenheim Fel, 66; Fulbright Grant, 66; City Univ Fac Res Awards, 70 & 75. *Mailing Add:* c/o Ianuzzi Gallery 7070 N 59th Pl Paradise Valley AZ 85253

KIRAC, INAN & SUNA
COLLECTOR
Pos: founder, Istanbul Res Inst; founder, Pera Mus, Istanbul, Turkey; founders, Suna & Inan Kirac Found. *Awards:* Name one of Top 200 collectors, ARTnews mag, 2011, 2012. *Mem:* Suna and Inan Kirac Found. *Collection:* orientalist painting; anatolian weights and measures; kutahya tiles and ceramics. *Mailing Add:* Pera Museum Mesrutiyet Caddesi No 65 Istanbul Turkey

KIRK, JEROME
SCULPTOR, KINETIC ARTIST
b Detroit, Mich, 1923. *Study:* Mass Inst Technol, BS. *Work:* San Francisco Mus Mod Art; Sheldon Art Gallery, Univ Nebr; Phoenix Art Mus, Ariz; Storm King Art Ctr, Mountainville, NY; and others. *Comn:* Thirty maj sculpture comn in pub places; Standing Waves, Univ Calif, Berkeley, 80; Torsive Undulations in Space, TRW Hq, 85; Avion, Koll Ctr, Irvine, Calif, 86; Lunaire, Bayside Bus Park, Fremont, Calif, 91; Optimus, Matrix Essentials Inc, Cleveland, 94; and others. *Exhib:* Sculpture, Potsdam, NY, 77; 28 solo and 57 group exhibs; Louis K Meisel Gallery, New York, 76 & 87-88; Artluminium La Gallery d'Art Lavalin, Montreal, 89; Erickson/Elins Gallery, San Francisco, 92, 95, & 98; Erickson Gallery, Healdsburg, Calif, 2002, 2005, & 2012; and others, 2002-2006. *Teaching:* Invited lectr, Univ Mont, 96. *Bibliog:* Exploring Visual Design, Selleck, Worcester, Mass, 87; Environmental Art, Shoichiro, Tokyo, 91; La Sculpture En Acier, Clerin, Paris, 93; and others. *Media:* Aluminum, Stainless Steel. *Res:* Designs for vertical axis wind energy turbines. *Dealer:* Louis K Meisel Gallery 141 Prince St New York NY 10012; Erickson Gallery 324 Healdsburg Ave Headsburg CA 95448. *Mailing Add:* 5648 Bacon Rd Oakland CA 94619

KIRKPATRICK, DIANE
HISTORIAN
b Grand Rapids, Mich, June 28, 1933. *Study:* Vassar Col, BA, 55; Cranbrook Acad Art, MFA, 57; Univ Mich, Ann Arbor, MA, 65, PhD, 69. *Collection Arranged:* Chicago: The City and Its Artists, Univ Mich Art Mus, Ann Arbor, 78; The Fair View: Representations of the World's Columbian, Exposition of 1893, Terra Mus Am Art, Chicago & Univ Mich Art Mus, 93. *Pos:* Manuscript & layout ed, Fideler Publ Co, Grand Rapids, Mich, 57-58; dir children's educ, Grand Rapids Art Mus, Mich, 60-62; dir film & video studies, Univ Mich, 77-78. *Teaching:* asst prof to assoc prof, Univ Mich, 72-82, prof, 82-. *Mem:* Coll Art Asn Am; ACM SIGGRAPH; Soc Photog Ed. *Res:* Contemporary art, including photography, film, video and computers. *Publ:* Religous photography in the Victorian age, 83 & Science, Art, and the human image, 85, Mich Quart Rev; Holography and the art-technology scene, Holography Redefined, 84; The Artists of the 16: Backgrounds and Continuities, 90; La Fotografia ala Nuova Techologia, 92. *Mailing Add:* Hist of Art Dept Univ Mich 110 Tappan Hall Ann Arbor MI 48109-1357

KIRSHNER, JUDITH RUSSI
CURATOR, CRITIC
b St Louis, Mo, Nov 24, 1942. *Study:* Barnard Col, BA, 64; Bryn Mawr, MA, 69. *Collection Arranged:* Claes Oldenburg, The Mouse Mus, 77; June Leaf-Retrospective, 78; Gordon Matta-Clark, Circus-Caribbean Orange, 78; Vito Acconci-Retrospective: 1969-80, 80; Contemporary Chicago Painters-Two Decades, 86. *Pos:* Chief cur, Mus Contemp Art, Chicago, 76-81; cur, Terra Mus Am Art, 85-86. *Teaching:* Asst prof art criticism & contemp art, Sch of the Art Inst Chicago, 81; dir Sch Art and Design, Univ Ill, Chicago, prof art history, dean Col Architecture and teh Arts, currently. *Mem:* Coll Art Asn; Int Art Critics. *Publ:* Auth, Tom Otterness' frieze, 83 & Non-u-ment: Gordon Matta-Clark, 85, Artforum; The possibility of an avant-garde, Formations, 85; numerous reviews in Artforum and numerous mus catalog essays. *Mailing Add:* Univ Ill Dept Art 303 Jefferson Hall 935 W Harrison Chicago IL 60607-7039

KIRSTEIN, JANIS ADRIAN
PAINTER, INSTRUCTOR
b Louisville, Ky, Jul 7, 1955. *Study:* Ind Univ, Bloomington, 73-75; Univ Louisville, BA, 77; Univ Mass, MFA, 81. *Work:* Pub Radio Partnerships, Louisville, Ky; Coldwell Financial, Louisville, Ky; Capital Plaza Hotel, Frankfurt, Ky; Tenn Valley Authority; ICH Corp, Louisville, Ky; Brown, Todd & Ikyburn Law Firm, Louisville, Ky; Sigfried, Fessel & Moller Advertising, Louisville, Ky; Old Nat Bankcorp, Louisville, Ky; Wyatt, Tarrant & Combs Law Firm, Louisville Ky; Tachau, Maddox & Hovious Law Firm, Louisville, Ky. *Comn:* painting, Don Rigazzio, 2000. *Exhib:* Solo exhibs, Floyd County Art Mus, Floyd County, Ind, 78, Artswatch, Louisville, Ky, 88, Swanson Cralle Gallery, Louisville, Ky, 89, McGrath Gallery, Bellarmine Univ, Louisville, Ky, 94, Ann Wright Wilson Art Gallery, Georgetown Coll, Georgetown, Ky, 97, John Harriman Gallery, Pervuian British Cult Ctr, Lima, Peru, 2002, Zephyr Gallery, Louisville, Ky, 2000, 2002, 2004, 2008, 2010; Int Juried Art Competition, Mussavi Art Ctr, NY, 89; Mid Am Biennial Nat Art Exhib, Solomon Guggenheim Mus, NY, 89; La Association Cult Peruano Británica, Lima, Peru, 2002; Alternate Views: Approaches to Abstraction, Univ Louisville Hite Art Gallery, 2004; Int Photog Competitive Exhib, Greeley Sq Gallery, NY, 2004; Hasselblad Int Photo Competition, Linz, Austria, 2004; Through A Lens-Urban Landscape, Nat Juried Photo Competition, Coastal Arts League, Half Moon Bay, Calif, 2004; Int Artist Invitational Exhib, Kaza Gallery, Tokyo, Japan, 2006; First Int Festival Nano Art (competition winner), Kotka Photog Ctr, Kotka, Finland, 2007. *Pos:* Art critic, Courier-Journal Newspaper, 77-78. *Teaching:* Instr beginning drawing, Univ Mass, Amherst, Mass, 79-81, Ind Univ, New Albany, Ind, 84-85; instr fine arts, Western Hills High Sch, Ky, 89-, Governor's Scholars Prog, Ky, 95-98, Ky State Univ, 2004-2005; instr 2D Design, Univ Louisville, Ky, 2000-2001; instr photoshop & advan drawing, Ky State Univ, 2002-2003. *Awards:* Al Smith Fel Ky Nat Found for the Arts, 83 & 2000; Fel Ky Found for Women, 87; Purchase Award, Digital Art Competitive Exhib, Ky State Univ, 2002. *Bibliog:* Julian Munoz (auth), El Arte Que Alento La Esperanza, Tras El 5, Arte Y Naturaleza, Madrid, Spain, 5/18/2004; Paula Ahrens (auth), Interview: Three Artists, A Discussion of the Visual Arts in Their Lives and in Louisville, Louisville Dining, Shopping & Entertainment, 10, 9/2004; Sara Gividen (auth), Art and Science Up Close and Personal, The State Journal, 1, 4/27/2007; Karen S Peterson (auth), Relationship Respite, USA Today, 7/19/2000; Barnaby J Feder, The Art of Nanotech, NY Times, 1/25/2008. *Mem:* Nat Art Educ Asn; Louisville Visual Art Ctr Asn. *Media:* Acrylic, Pastel & Digital Art. *Publ:* Illustr, Am Voice Literary J, Ky Found for Women, 86. *Dealer:* Zephyr Gallery 610E Market Louisville KY 40205

KIRSTEN-DAIENSAI, RICHARD CHARLES
PAINTER, PRINTMAKER
b Chicago, Ill, Apr 16, 1920. *Study:* Art Inst Chicago; Univ Wash; also study in Japan, 58-2004. *Work:* Seattle Art Mus; Bell Tel Co; Libr of Cong, Washington, DC; Metrop Mus Art, NY; Tokyo Mus Mod Art, Japan; De Young Mus, San Francisco; Mus Mod Art, New York. *Exhib:* Seattle Art Mus, numerous shows, 45-69; Frye Mus, Seattle, 60-65 & 69; Gov Invitational, 67; Collector's Gallery, Bellevue, Wash, 67; Richard White Gallery, Seattle, 68; Kirsten Gallery, Seattle, 75-2010; plus many others. *Teaching:* pvt teaching. *Awards:* Purchase Prize, Univ Ore, 68; Purchase Prize, Seattle First Nat Bank, 69; plus others. *Bibliog:* Article, Arts Asia Mag, 1-2/79. *Mem:* Northwest Watercolor Soc (pres, 68 & 69); Artists Equity (pres, Seattle Chap, 52-56), Seattle Chap mem, 89. *Media:* Watercolor, Acrylic; Mixed Media, Bronze. *Publ:* Smile, 365 Happy Meditations, 2010; Love, 365 Happy Meditation, 9/15/2010. *Mailing Add:* c/o Kirsten Gallery 5320 Roosevelt Way NE Seattle WA 98105-3629

KIRTON, JENNIFER MYERS
GRAPHIC ARTIST, JUROR
b Berwick, Pa, Sept 16, 1949. *Study:* Orange Memorial Sch Nursing, Registered Nurse, 1970; Studied under Charles Turzak (WAP artist), 1976-1988. *Work:* Apopka City Hall, Apopka, Fla; Mount Dora Ctr Arts, Mount Dora, Fla; Eustis Lake Mus Art. *Comn:* Mural (65' x 15'), Booster Club, Apopka, Fla, 1999. *Exhib:* Emerging Artists, Serious Studios Gallery, Miami, Fla, 2004; Biennial Juried State Show, Deland Mus Art Cult Art Ctr, Deland, Fla, 2004; First Thursday (juried Shows), Orlando Mus Art, Orlando, Fla, 2004-2008; Juried Competition of New Artwork, Am Art Collector (book of winners), Berkley, Calif, 2005-2008; Best of Fla Artist Registry, City Arts Factory, Peabody Auditorium, Avalon Gallery, Orlando, Fla, 2007-2008; Juried Drawing Show, Osceola Ctr Arts, Kissimmee, Fla, 2007-2008; 100 Contemporary Artists, Artrotque, London, Eng, 2008 ; Work of New Year Winners, Guest Gallery, Lilburn, Ga, 2008; Juried Citrus Show, Comma Gallery, Orlando, Fla; Amory Art Ctr, 59th Exhib Flag, State Art Registry Show, 2009; Solo exhibs: Deltona Art & Hist Ctr, 5th Studio, Mount Dora Art Ctr, 2009, Artisan Gallery, Nat Mus Women in the Arts, 2009, DeBarry Hall, 2009, High Springs Artist Co Op, 2012, Univ Club Winter Park, 2012; Deltona Art & History Ctr; Two Woman show, Lake Eustis Mus, 2014. *Collection Arranged:* Celebration of Women, Art in the Square (assembled, arranged), 2005; Feminine Tribute to Women, Art in the Square (arranged), 2006; Solo Exhib, Minneola City Hall (assembled, arranged), 2008; Visual Illusion, Debary Hall; Deltona Art & History Ctr. *Pos:* Workshop, demos, Leagues, asns & guest, 1986-2009; drawing & gen art, Mount Dora Ctr Arts, pvt art schs, 1990-1995; judge, Apopka Art & Foliage Art Festival (others), 1995-2004, 2009; judge & juror, Webber Gallery Visual Arts Asn; cur, Deltona Arts and Historical Ctr, currently. *Teaching:* Instr, all media, Adult Educ Orange Co Pub Schs, 1988-1993; instr, children, Leesburg for the Arts Hands on Children Mus, 2004; instr, creative drawing, Mount Dora Ctr Arts, Mount Dora Fla, 2006-. *Awards:* Hon Mention, 11 County Juried Art Show, Mount Dora Ctr Arts, 1994, 2004; Best of Show, Spring Shows, Leesburg Art Asn, 2004, 2007; Best of Am Artists & Artisan, 2008, Special Recognition Merit Award (9), Larry Bradshaw, Upstream People Gallery, 2006-2008. *Bibliog:* Debra Kaplan (auth), Local Artist's Work Goes to Europe, Apopka Chief, 1990; Karen Landry (auth), On Location In Orlando, Indie Arts DVD, 2007; Lake Mag, Pretty in Ink, English Communs, 2007; Jacquelin Horkan (auth), Artist Spotlight/State of the Arts, Fla Comt Nat Mus Women in the Arts; Artist of month (interview), Gallery Direct, June 2008; Nat League of Am Penwomen-Nat Mag; Dictionary of Int Artists; Contemp Int Artists; Remington Registry; Art in Vogue; Am Art Collector, 2006-2013; Important Artists of World. *Mem:* Nat League Am Pen Women (2005-2008); Women's Comt Fine Arts (scholar chmn, 2006-2008); Fla Art Group (founding mem, bd dirs); Deltona Art and History Ctr (bd). *Media:* Ink, Ink & Colored Pencils (visionary illusions). *Collection:* Multiple Private Collections. *Publ:* Contribr, Start Your Own Art Collection (syndicated short for TV), Smart Women Ivanhoe Production, 2006; Indie Art, 2008; Nat League Am Pen Women Mag, Summer 2009. *Dealer:* Tony Wynn Serious Studios Berlin 407 Second & Market St Galveston TX 77550; Gallery Direct Can; Art Exchange.com AR; Collectibles Etc. *Mailing Add:* 4703 Meadowland Dr Mount Dora FL 32757

KISCH, GLORIA
SCULPTOR
b New York, NY, Nov 14, 1941. *Study:* Sarah Lawrence Col, BA, 63; Otis Art Inst, Los Angeles, BFA & MFA, 69. *Work:* Los Angeles County Art Mus; Milwaukee Art Mus; Newberger Mus; Va Mus Fine Art; Denver Art Mus; Boca Raton Mus Art; Guild Hall, Newport Harbor Art Mus; Gallery of New South Wales, Sydney, Australia. *Comn:* Aesiona, Harmon Meadow Plaza, Secaucus, NJ, 1984; Apollo (painted steel, Stainless, 24'x8'x6'), Harmon Meadow Plaza, 1986-1988; Dawn, Holyoke Community Bank, Holyoke, Mass, 1989; Three Bells Banner, Estrella Hosp, Phoenix, Ariz, 2004; Deerfield Gates, Dorfman Projects, 2004. *Exhib:* Solo exhibs, Newport Harbor Art Mus, 74, Los Angeles Inst Contemporary Art, 78, PS One, Long Island City, NY, 80, Milwaukee Art Mus, 81, Queens Mus, 83, Bergen Mus Art, 97, Las Vegas Art Mus, 2000, Long Horse Reserve, 2001, San Angelo Mus Fine Arts, Tex, 2008, Guild Hall, 2010. *Bibliog:* Christopher Chambers, A private garden of the mid, Dart int 2006; Arlene Raven, Upright the height & depth of sculpture by Gloria Kisch, Sculpture Mag, 98; Contemporary Artists at work, Film, 1978. *Media:* Metals, Mostly Stainless. *Publ:* The Rocker, Bernice Steinbaum (auth), Rizzoli Publs; International Furniture Design for the 90's, Libr Applied Design; Product Design 4, Libr Applied Design; a Fusion of Opposites, Am Image, 2009; Lyn Kienholz, SoCal Artists Before 1980. *Dealer:* Rosenbaum Contemporary Boca Raton FL

KITAO, T KAORI
HISTORIAN, EDUCATOR
b Jan 30, 1933; US citizen. *Study:* Univ Calif, Berkeley, AB (archit), 58, MA (art hist), 61; Harvard Univ, PhD (art hist), 66. *Pos:* Chmn, Swarthmore Coll, 75-81; vpres, Int Soc Comparative Study Civilizations, 80-83. *Teaching:* Asst prof hist archit, RI Sch Design, 63-66; asst prof art hist, Swarthmore Coll, 66-68, assoc prof, 68-75, prof, 75-2001, William R Kenan prof, 93-2001; adj prof, Long Island Univ, Am Ballet Theatre, 2005-2006; life long learning, Swarthmore Coll, 2010. *Mem:* Soc Archit Historians; Coll Art Asn; Soc Cinema Studies; Semiotic Soc Am; Int Soc Comparative Study of Civilizations. *Res:* Philadelphia architecture; comparative semiotics, east and west; Bernini and Baroque Rome; streets. *Publ:* Auth, Circle and Oval in the Square of St Peter's, NY Univ Press, 74; contribr, La prospettiva rinascimentale, Centro Di, Florence, 80. *Mailing Add:* 418 E 77th St Apt 3C New York NY 10075-2370

KITCHIN, CAMERON
MUSEUM DIRECTOR
b Norfolk, Va, 1969. *Study:* Harvard Univ, BA (fine arts); Coll William & Mary, MBA. *Pos:* Mgr strategic planning, head of political campaign for funding, AAM, formerly; sr assoc, Econ Res Associates, Washington, 1998-2002; exec dir, Contemp Art Ctr Va, 2002-08; dir, Memphis Brooks Mus Art, 2008-. *Mem:* AAM. *Mailing Add:* Memphis Brooks Mus Art 1934 Poplar Ave Memphis TN 38104

KITTREDGE, NANCY (ELIZABETH)
PAINTER
b Ellsworth, Maine, 1938. *Study:* Vesper George Sch Art, Boston, 56-57; Univ NH, Durham, 57-59; Univ Maine, Orono, BA, 61; Univ Miami, Coral Gables, Fla, MA, 63. *Comn:* Portrait, Univ Maine Theatre Dept, Orono, 76; 24' x 36' Backdrop, World Premier, Broad Waters, Malashock Dance & Company, Old Globe Theatre, San Diego, 95. *Exhib:* Solo exhibs, San Diego Mus Art, 81 & 90 & David Zapf Gallery, San Diego, 90, 93, 96, 98, 2001 & 2005 & Karpeles Mus Art, Santa Barbara, Calif, 2006; Contemp Artists' Artists, Sylvia White Contemp Art, Los Angeles, 91; Local Productions: Painters of San Diego Co, Calif Ctr for the Arts, Escondido, Calif, 92; Elements, Los Angeles Munic Art Gallery, Los Angeles, 98; Lindenberg Gallery, New York, 2000; Oceanside Mus of Art, Oceanside, Calif, 2000; San Diego Mus Art, 2002; Oceanside Mus Art, Calif, 2004; Anniversary Exhibition, Sylvia White Gallery, Ventura, Calif, 2009. *Collection Arranged:* Household Corp, Chicago; Women's Clinic & Family Health Care Ctr, Los Angeles; Indust Metals South Inc, New Orleans; Dow Theory Lett Inc, La Jolla, Calif; Luce, Forward, Hamilton & Scripps, San Diego; Univ Maine, Orono; San Diego Mus Art; Laguna Mus Art, Calif. *Teaching:* Instr Tulane Univ, New Orleans, 68-69; Lectr, Salk Inst Art & Sci Forum, 2007. *Mem:* Nat Mus Women in Arts. *Media:* Oil, Mixed Media. *Specialty:* Fine Art; Oils. *Interests:* poetry; philosophy. *Publ:* American Artists: An Illustrated Survey of Leading Contemporary Americans, Krantz Publ Co, Chicago, 85; San Diego Artists, Artra Publ Inc, Encinitas, Calif, 88; The California Art Review, 2nd ed, Am References Publ Corp, Chicago, 89. *Mailing Add:* 13646 Mira Montana Dr Del Mar CA 92014

KJOK, SOL
PAINTER
b Lillehammer, Norway, Mar 16, 1968. *Study:* Univ Vienna, Austria, BA, 1991; Univ Paris, Master in French Lit, 1992; Univ Cincinnati, MA, 1993-96; Parsons Sch Design, New York City, MFA, 1998. *Work:* Cincinnati Art Mus, Ohio; Teckningsmuseet Nat Mus of Drawing, Laholm, Sweden; Kinsey Inst, Ind; Barockrummet, Laholms Teater, Sweden; works in pub and pvt collections, USA, Austria, Belgium, Colombia, Eng, France, Ger, Norway, Sweden. *Exhib:* Solo exhibs incl: Allegro Non Troppo, Brodie Gallery; Cincinnati, Ohio, 1996, Swirling-Sviv Tegnerforbundets Gallery, Oslo, Norway, 2001; Skeins and Veins, Samuel ST Chen Fine Arts Ctr, Conn, 2005; Strings of Beads, Perlestrenger, Galleri 27, Oslo, Norway, 2005; Swift & Slow, Nordic Heritage Mus, Seattle, Strings of Beads, Manifest Gallery, Cincinnati, 2006, Book of Swells, Nordic Mus Drawing, Sweden, 2008, Entre Sol et Ciel, Kunsthaus Tacheles, Berlin, Germany, 2009; Group exhibs incl: Current Trends, Galleri Steen, Oslo, Norway, 2001; Night of 1000 Drawings, Artists Space, NY, 2002; 69th Juried Show, Arnot Art Mus, NY, 2003; Festival Mira! Lubolo, Casa de Am, Madrid, Spain, 2004; Working Artists in Brooklyn, Romo Gallery, Atlanta, Ga, 2005, One Year Later, Romo Gallery, Atlanta, Ga, 2006, Erotica 2006, K Space Art Studios, Austin, Tex, 2006, Her-Humanity: Transformative Agency, Casa Frela, New York, 2007, Facing the Figure, Karin Sanders Fine Art, New York, 2007, Remembering Ruth, Noho Gallery, Chealsea, New York, 2007, Art Out: Stop the War, Morrison Gallery, Kent, Conn, 2008, Represent Brooklyn, The Rising Art Gallery, New York, 2008, Paper Design, the Artcomplex Ctr of Tokyo, Japan, 2009, Darkness Descends II: Norwegian Art Now, Grossman Gallery, Easton, Pa, 2009, Exquisite Corpse, Paul Robeson Galleries, 2009. *Pos:* Graphic designer, Agence Karen, Paris, formerly; dir, ind studies of Norwegian lang/cult, 1993-96; co-producer, Documentary Odd Nerdrum: Savor of Painting, 2002-; lectr (recent work), Center Conn State Univ, 2/2005; lectr (string series), Manifest Gallery, Cincinnati, 1/2006; artist residency, Temple Bar Gallery & Studios, Dublin, 2008. *Teaching:* Teaching asst, art hist Univ Cincinnati, 1995-96; resident, Larroque Artists' Colony, Urt, France, 1997-98; teaching asst, painting Parsons Sch Design, New York City, 1997-98. *Awards:* Robert Rauschenberg's Found, 2001; Honorable mention in Exhib Am Art, RIC Inst, Chicago, 2004; Pub Project Grant Am-Scandinavian Found, New York City, 2005; Cult Heritage Grant, Sons of Norway Found, Minn, 2006; Best in Show, Int Drawing Triennial, Tallinn, 2009. *Bibliog:* Ellen M Rosenholtz (auth), Hopscotch: Associative Leaps in the Construction of Narrative, Painted Bride Art Center, Philadelphia, Pa, 2002; Balansekunstnaren Sol Kjok, Valdres, June 18, Pgs 12-13, 2005; Scandinavian in New York, Nordic Reach, No 15, Vol 18, 28-34, 2006; The World's Greatest Erotic Artists, Signature Press, Fla, 2007; String of Beads, Mod Rev, Can, Spring 2007; Artist presentation in Deborah Rockman: Drawing Essentials: A Guide to Drawing from Observation, Oxford Univ Press, 2008; Ida Svingen Mo, Analog Amour, SNITT Mag, Vol 5-6, 2009. *Mem:* Coll Art Asn; NBK, Norwegian Visual Artists; Tegnerforbundet (Nor Drawing Art Asn). *Media:* Visual Artist (drawing & Painting). *Dealer:* Romo Gallery Atlanta; Manifest Gallery Cincinnati; Galleri 27 Oslo; Tegnerforbundet, Drawing Art Asn Norway. *Mailing Add:* 252 Green St Brooklyn NY 11222

KLAMEN, DAVID
PAINTER
b Dixon, Ill, Jan 20, 1961. *Study:* Univ Ill, Urbana-Champaign, BFA, 83; Sch Art Inst, Chicago, MFA (painting), 85. *Work:* Mus Contemp Art, Chicago; Krannert Mus Art, Champaign, Ill; Ill State Mus, Springfield; Metrop Mus Art, NY; Nat Mus Contemp Art, Seoul, Korea. *Comn:* Large painting, Bartlit Beck, Chicago, Ill, 94. *Exhib:* Chicago & Vicintity Show, Art Inst Chicago, 85; Art and the Law, Rose Art Mus, Waltham, Mass, 88-89; Aids Found Exhib, Mus Contemp Art, Chicago, 89; solo show, Cedar Rapids Art Mus, Iowa, 91; Spirited Visions, Ill State Mus, Springfield, 92; Drawing New Conclusions, Art Inst Chicago, Ill, 92; Mind & Beast, Leigh Yawkey Woodson Art Mus, Wasau, Wis, 92-93; New Acquisitions, Metrop Mus Art, NY, 95; Art in Chicago, Mus Contemp Art, Chicago, 96; Embracing Beauty, Huntsville Mus Art, Ala, 97. *Teaching:* Instr art, Valpraiso Univ, Ind, 85; asst prof, Ind Univ, Gary, 85-91, assoc prof, 91-97, prof, 97-. *Awards:* Top Forty, Forty Under 40, Crains Chicago Bus, 94. *Bibliog:* Garrett Holg (auth), David Klamen, ArtNews, 10/93; Jeff Borden (auth), Forty under 40, Crains Chicago Bus, 9/26/94; Garrett Hold (auth), David Klamen, Art News, 4/97; and others. *Media:* Oil Paint. *Mailing Add:* c/o Richard Gray Gallery 875 N Michigan Ave Chicago IL 60611

KLARIN, KARLA S
PAINTER
b Los Angeles, Calif, Mar, 17, 1953. *Study:* San Francisco Art Inst, BFA, 74; Otis Art Inst, Los Angeles, MFA, 78. *Work:* Los Angeles Co Mus Art; US Consulate, Berlin, Ger; Frederick R Weisman Collection; Loyola Law Sch; Atlantic Richfield Corp, Los Angeles. *Exhib:* Solo shows, Univ Redlands, 83, Claremont Grad Sch, Calif, 83, Karl Bornstein Gallery, Santa Monica, Calif, 84 & 86, Koplin Gallery, Los Angeles, 89, Tortue Gallery, Santa Monica, Calif, 92 & 95; Young Talent Awards: 1963-1983 (with catalog), Los Angeles Co Mus Art, 83; Landscape/Common Ground, Jan Turner Gallery, Los Angeles, 88; California Landscape Art Motif: Plein Air to Present, Downey Mus Art, 88; Natural Selection: The Terrain of Southern California, Riverside Art Mus, 88; California Artists from the Frederick Weisman Collections, Frederick R Weisman Mus Art, Pepperdine Univ, 96. *Awards:* Young Talent Award, Los Angeles Co Mus Art, 82. *Bibliog:* Suzanne Muchnic (auth), Karla Klarin, Los Angeles Times, 86; Suvan Geer (auth), Karla Klarin, Los Angeles Times, 10/20/89; Suzanne Muchnic (auth), Karla Klarin, Artnews, 12/92. *Dealer:* Tortue Gallery 2917 Santa Monica Blvd Santa Monica CA 90404. *Mailing Add:* 500 Ashland Ave Santa Monica CA 90405

KLAUBER, RICK
PAINTER
b July 7, 1950. *Study:* Bard Col, with Murray Reich, BA, 72; apprentice to Helen Frankenthaler, residence apprenticeship with Robert Motherwell, 70-73. *Exhib:* Solo exhibs, Artists Space, NY, 75, Long Point Gallery, Provinctown, Mass, 77, 79 & 81, Oscarsson-Hood Gallery, NY, 80 & Universal Fine Objects, Provincetown, Mass, 91 & 92, Brenda Taylor Gallery, NY, 98; Group exhibs, Albright-Knox, Buffalo, NY, 81; The Drawing Room, AFR Fine Arts, Washington, DC, 88; Crosscurrents, Fine Arts Work Ctr, Provincetown, Mass, 90; In Full Effect, White Columns, NY, 90; Behind Bars, Threadwaxing Space, NY, 92; Drop Dead Painting, 103 Reade Street, NY, 94; Int Biennial, Janos Xantus Mus, Gyor, Hungary, 95; Galerie Ardrea & Wolfram Cornelissen, Georgenbon, Ger, 96; X-section, MMC Gallery, NY, 97; Brenda Taylor Gallery, NY, 1998-2000; KCC Gallery, CUNY, NY, 1996-2000. *Teaching:* Guest teacher drawing & painting, Bard Col, 84-90; School Visual Arts, 85-96; teacher drawing, watercolor painting, Parsons Sch Design, 1989-2000; teacher drawing & painting, Pratt Inst, 1996-2003; teacher art hist & drawing, Kingsborough Comm Col, 1996-2003. *Bibliog:* Tom Breidenbach (auth), Review in Art Forum, 11/98; John Yau (auth), article, Art in Am, 81; B H Friedman & Chris Busa (auth), Crosscurrents: the New Generation, East Hampton Ctr Contemp Art, 90. *Media:* Oil. *Publ:* Contribr, A bird is more (catalog on Robert Motherwell), Im Irker Gallery, St Gal, Switz, 71; auth, article on Fritz Bultman, Provincetown Arts, 86; contribr, Rosebud, Mudfish, 88. *Mailing Add:* 57 Prince St New York NY 10012

KLAUSNER, BETTY
WRITER, CURATOR
b New York, NY, Aug 18, 1928. *Study:* Wells Col, BA, 50. *Collection Arranged:* Masami Teraoka Erotica, 1968-1984, 84; Llyn Foulkes: Portraits, 86; Terry Allen, Big Witness (Living in Wishes), 87; Michael Singer, 87; Joan Snyder Collects Joan Snyder, 88; Home Show, 88. *Pos:* Dir, Contemp Graphics Ctr, Santa Barbara Mus Art, 78-81, Santa Barbara Contemp Arts Forum, 84-92. *Mailing Add:* 2100 Pacific Ave San Francisco CA 94115

KLAVEN, MARVIN L
PAINTER, EDUCATOR
b Alton, Ill, Apr 8, 1931. *Study:* State Univ Iowa, BA & MFA. *Work:* Univ Iowa; Millikin Univ; Mayer Collection, Gilman Collection & Ill Bell, Chicago. *Exhib:* 24 Illinois Artists, 67; Chicago Sun Times Exhib, 68; 21st NMiss Valley Art Exhib, 68; Artists Who Teach, 69; Contemp Am Painting & Sculpture, 69. *Pos:* Dir, Decatur Art Ctr, Ill, 61-69 & Kirkland Art Gallery, 69-. *Teaching:* Asst prof drawing, Northern Ill Univ, 59-61; prof art dept, Millikin Univ, 61-. *Awards:* Tiffany Found Grant, 64. *Media:* Acrylic, Silk Screen. *Mailing Add:* Art Dept Millikin Univ 1184 W Main St Decatur IL 62522-2084

KLECKNER, SUSAN
PHOTOGRAPHER, FILMMAKER
b New York, NY, July 5, 1941. *Study:* Art Students League, with Landes Lewitin; City Univ New York; Pratt Inst. *Comn:* Birth Film, Women's Interart Ctr & NY State Coun Arts, NY, 72; Another Look, Teleprompter & Women's Video Service, NY, 72; Desert Piece, Women Artist Filmakers, 82; media, Feast or Famine, Interart Theatre, 83. *Exhib:* Brooklyn Mus, NY, 72; film Festival, Whitney Mus Am Art, NY, 73 & Mod Mus, Paris, France, 74; Wild Art Show, Project Studio One, NY, 82; AIR Gallery, 82; Moonmade Space, 83; West 22nd St Show, 83. *Pos:* Dir photog workshop, Community Resource Ctr, NY, 68-70; co-dir, Women's Liberation Cinema, 70-71; founding coordr, Women's Interart Ctr, NY, 70-71; video ed, Women's Video News Service, 72-73; artist-in-residence, Cummington Sch Arts, 74 & Women's Interart Ctr, 82; co-dir, Workshops for Women, 80-83. *Teaching:* Asst chmn photog, Pratt Inst, NY, 70-74; consult writing, City Univ NY, 72-73; dir, Fresh Film Ctr Photog, NY Univ Undergrad Film Sch, NY, 73-74; instr, NY Inst Photog, 78-80, Int Ctr Photog, 82-, NY Univ/Int Ctr Photog grad prog, 83 & NY Univ performance studies, 83. *Awards:* Grant, Whitney Mus, NY State Coun Arts, 72. *Bibliog:* Gazzette, Ms Mag, 73; Rochelle Ratner (auth), Beyond the limits, Soho Weekly News, 80; Carrie Rickey (auth), Third wave, Village Voice, 81. *Mem:* Women Artists in Revolution; Feminists in the Arts; Womens Caucus Art; Peacock Brigade; Professional Women Photogr. *Media:* Video, Xerography; Pastel, Watercolor. *Publ:* Auth, A personal decade, Heresies, No 16, 83. *Dealer:* New Yorker Films 43 West 61st St New York NY 10011

KLEEBLATT, NORMAN L
CURATOR, CRITIC
b Bridgeton, NJ, 1948. *Study:* Rutgers Univ, New Brunswick, NJ, AB (art hist), 71; Conserv Ctr, Inst Fine Arts, NY Univ, dip (conserv) & MA, 75. *Exhib:* John Singer Sargent: Portraits of the Wentheimer Family, 1999-2000; Mirroring Evil: Nazi Representations/Contemp Art and Popular Cult, 2001. *Collection Arranged:* Painting a Place in Am: Jewish Artists in New York 1900-1945, Jewish Mus, NY, 91 & Collecting for the Twenty-First Century: Recent Acquisitions and Promised Gifts, 93; Too Jewish? Challenging Traditional Identities Traveling Exhib, Jewish Mus, San Francisco, Univ Calif, Los Angeles, Armand Hammer Mus Art & Cult Ctr, The Contemp, Baltimore & Nat Mus Am Jewish Hist, Philadelphia, 96; An Expressionist in Paris: The Paintings of Chaim Soutine, Los Angeles Co Mus Art & Cincinnati Art Mus, 98; The Dreyfus Affair, 87; and many others. *Pos:* Susan & Elihu Rose Cur Fine Arts, Jewish Mus, NY, 95-2005, curator, 2005-; planning cons Nat Found for Jewish Cult, 95-98, 2000. *Awards:* Post-Grad Fel, Nat Mus Fel Act, 75-76; Presidence d'Honneur, Comite Scientifique, Societe Internationale d'histoire de l'Affaire Dreyfus, 94-; Mus Prof Fel, Nat Endowment Arts, 96. *Mem:* Coll Art Asn; Am Asn Mus; Int Asn Art Critics; Coun Am Jewish Mus. *Publ:* Auth, Merdel The caricatural attack against Emile Zola, No 52, 54-58, Art J, fall 93; Identity politics: multivalent voices, No 83, 29-31 & 35, Art Am, 12/95; The other edge: Representing ethnicity, gender and sexuality in New York, No 5, 22-36, Issues Archit Art & Design, 97; Autour du Corps d'Alfred Dreyfus, No 2, 37-42, Lee Cahiers du Judaisme, summer 98; Master Narratives/Minority Artists, No 57/3, 29-35, Art J, fall 98; Persistence of memory, Art in Am, 6/2000; Faith: The Impact of Judeo-Christian Religion on Art at the Millennium (catalog), The Aldrich Mus of Contemporary Art, 2000; plus many others. *Mailing Add:* 330 E 63rd St New York NY 10021

KLEEMANN, RON
PAINTER
b Bay City, Mich, July 1937. *Study:* Univ Mich, BS (design), 61. *Work:* Guggenheim Mus, Mus Mod Art, New York; Hirshhorn Mus, Washington, DC; Indianapolis Mus Art; Univ Va Art Mus; Air & Space Mus, Washington, DC; Mus Mod Art, Mexico City; and others. *Comn:* Painting for reproduction, Corvette catalog, 86. *Exhib:* Mus Contemp Art, Chicago, 71; Wichita Mus, Wichita State Univ, Kans, 75; New Acquisitions, Mus Mod Art, New York, 77; Flint Inst Fine Arts, 78; Louis K Meisel Gallery, New York, 79, 83, 92 & 94; Rich Perlow Gallery, New York, 87; RH Love Galleries, Chicago, 87; Cheekwood Fine Arts Ctr, Nashville, Tenn, 92. *Pos:* Off artist, Indianapolis 500, 77-79 & Super Bowl XVII, Pasadena, Calif, 83. *Bibliog:* Andrea Mikotajok (auth), American Realists at Louis K Meisel, Arts Mag, 1/75; articles, Indianapolis News, 4/77 & Chicago Tribune, 10/77. *Media:* Acrylic, Oil, Watercolor. *Dealer:* Louis K Meisel Gallery 141 Prince St New York NY 10012. *Mailing Add:* c/o Louis K Meisel Gallery 141 Prince St New York NY 10012

KLEIDON, DENNIS ARTHUR
EDUCATOR, DESIGNER
b Chicago, Ill, Sept 20, 1942. *Study:* Bradley Univ, Peoria, Ill, 60-61; Univ Ill, Champaign, 61-64; Ill Wesleyan Univ, Bloomington, BFA (com art), 66; Ill State Univ, Normal, MS (sculpture), 67. *Work:* Massillon Mus, Ohio; Northern Ill Univ, DeKalb; Ill State Univ; Numa Ltd, Akron. *Comn:* Commemorative sculpture wall piece (wood, assemblage), Akron Nat Bank & Trust, Tuchman, Canute, Ryan & Wyatt, Architects, Rolling Acres Shopping Ctr, 76; promotional design, Scheeser & Buckley, Inc, Akron, 76; illustration, Hesselbart & Mitten Advert, Akron, 75 & Alsides, Inc, Akron, 75. *Exhib:* All-Ohio Exhib, Canton Art Inst, 71 & 72; Images, Nat Drawing Competition, Baldwin Wallace Col, Berea, Ohio, 72; Cleveland Invitational Exhib, Cooper Sch of Art, 72 & Lake Erie Col, 73; Solo exhib, Akron Art Inst, 76; and others. *Pos:* Designer/delineator, Wight & Assoc, Downers Grove, Ill, 65-66 & Richard R Cramer, Architects, Hinsdale, Ill, 67; pres, Kleidon & Assoc, 75-. *Teaching:* Instr drawing, Univ Ill, Champaign, 67-69; From assoc prof to prof graphic design, Univ Akron, 69-. *Awards:* Res grants, Univ Akron, 70 & 77; First Place/Painting, All-Ohio Exhib, Canton Art Inst, 71; Merit Award/Design, Nat Univ & Coll Designers Asn Design Competition, 75. *Bibliog:* Tex Tech Univ, Color Print USA (filmstrip), 71; Packaging education: The case for cooperation, Boxboard Container Mag, 11/79. *Media:* Acrylic, Vinyl. *Dealer:* Gallery 200 200 W Mound Columbus OH 43223. *Mailing Add:* 4670 Granger Rd Akron OH 44333-1312

KLEIMAN, ALAN
PAINTER, SCULPTOR
b Brooklyn, NY, Feb 20, 1938. *Study:* Richmond Prof Inst, BFA; Cranbrook Acad Art, MFA; study with Oscar Kokoschka, Salzburg, Austria. *Work:* Mus Mod Art, Whitney Mus Am Art, Metrop Mus Art, NY; Carnegie Mus, Pittsburgh, Pa; Boston Mus Fine Art, Mass. *Comn:* Abstract fresco, Richmond City Fathers, Va, 57; rubber paint pool mural, comn by Mr & Mrs Pechenik, York, Pa, 60; abstract painted wall, Detroit Archit League, Mich, 65; abstract painted wall, City Walls, NY, 72. *Exhib:* Biennale, Sao Paulo, Brazil, 68; Silvermine, Conn, 70; Carnegie Inst Int, Pittsburgh, 71; In The Realm of the Monocramatic, Chicago & NY, 79; Painting About Painting, Paterson Col, NJ, 81; Beging, NY, 90; Elisabeth Harris Gallery, New York, NY, 94; O'Hara Gallery, New York, NY, 96; Robert Steel Gallery, New York, NY, 97; and others. *Pos:* Asst publicity dir, Artist Tenents Asn, 60-67; vpres, Grand St Artist Group, 70-75; chmn, Soho Artifacts, 71-75. *Awards:* Creative Artists Pub Serv fel & CETA grant, 78; Creative Artists Pub Serv Grant, 83; Nat Found Arts Grant, 90. *Bibliog:* Hans Van Deljen (auth), Alan Kleiman paints Europe, Frie Folkes, Amsterdam, 56; Arts Mag, 97; Review Mag, 97. *Media:* Watercolor, Oil. *Publ:* Auth, Painting Provincetown water, The Beacon, 61; Investigations into the light of red color, Arts, 76; Light dazzle and glow, The Soho Artist. *Dealer:* Area Code Gallery 31 Wooster St New York NY 10013. *Mailing Add:* 70 Grand St No 2 New York NY 10013

KLEIN, BEATRICE (T)
PAINTER, PRINTMAKER
b Lynchburg, Va, Feb 7, 1920. *Study:* Md Inst Coll Art, cert, 42; Art Students League, with Yasvo Kuniyoshi, 42-43; Va Commonwealth Univ, 71-74; study with Hans Hofmann, Provincetown, Mass, 44; Md Inst Coll Art, Hon BFA, 95; MD Inst Coll Art, BFA, 95. *Work:* Va Mus Fine Arts, Fed Reserve Bank, Nations Bank, Phillip Morris Co, Richmond, Va; Rocky Mount Art Ctr, NC; Frances & Sydney Lewis Collection and other pvt collections. *Comn:* Dr Porter Vinson Prof of Medicine (portrait), 70, Dr George Oliver Pres (portrait), 75, Va Commonwealth Univ, Richmond; Mr Harry Schwarzchild Pres (portrait), Cent Nat Bank, Richmond, Va, 78; Rabbi Ariel Goldburg (portrait), Beth Ahabah Synagogue, Richmond, Va, 78. *Exhib:* Six-State Painting Exhib, Anderson Gallery, Va Commonwealth Univ, Richmond, 73; Nat Drawing & Photog Show, 2nd St Gallery, Charlottesville, Va, 75-76; Va Printmakers, Va Mus Fine Arts, Richmond, 76; Va Craftsmen, Va Mus Fine Arts, Richmond, Va, 80; Va Prints & Drawing, Va Mus Fine Arts, Richmond, 81; solo retrospective, Artspace Gallery, Richmond, Va, 94; group exhib, The Figure Pastel Drawings, Artspace Gallery, Richmond, Va, 2003. *Awards:* Cert of Distinction, Va Mus Biennial, Va Mus Fine Arts, 55-59; Irene Leach Mem Prize, Chrysler Mus, Norfolk, Va, 58; 3rd Prize for Painting, State Painting Show, Anderson Gallery, Va Commonwealth Univ, 73. *Mem:* Richmond Artists Asn (pres, 60-64). *Media:* Oil, Watercolor; Silkscreen, Pastel. *Dealer:* Artspace Gallery 6 E Broad St Richmond VA 23226; Artifacts 1608 Harborough Rd Richmond VA 23233. *Mailing Add:* 2304 Cedarfield Pkwy #3827 Richmond VA 23233-1936

KLEIN, CECELIA F
HISTORIAN, EDUCATOR
b Pittsburgh, Pa, June 5, 1938. *Study:* Oberlin Col, BA, 60, MA, 67; Columbia Univ, PhD with Douglas Fraser, 72. *Exhib:* Art of Pre-Columbian Am, Meadow Brook Art Gallery, Oakland Univ, Rochester, Mich, 76.; Mother, Worker, Ruler, Witch: Cross-Cultural Images of Women, Mus Cult Hist, Univ Calif, Los Angeles, 80. *Teaching:* Asst prof art hist, Oakland Univ, Rochester, 72-76; assoc prof art hist, Univ Calif, Los Angeles, 76-88, prof, 88-2011, prof emer, 2011-. *Awards:* Distinguished Teaching of Art History Award, Coll Art Asn, 2000. *Mem:* Coll Art Asn; Asn Latin Am Art. *Res:* Pre-Columbian art history, with emphasis on Aztec art/iconography. *Interests:* Relation Aztec art to social, historical & political context. *Publ:* Auth, The Devil and the Skirt: an Iconographic Inquiry into Prehispanic Nature of the Tzitzimime, In: Ancient Mesoamerica, 2000, In: Estudios de Cultural Nahuatl, 2000; None or All of the Above: Gender Ambiguity in Hahua Ideology, In: Gender in Prehispanic America: A Symposium at Dumbarton Oaks 12 and 13 October 1996, 2001; coauth (with Eulogio Guzman, Elisa C. Mandell, Maya Stanfield-Mazzi, and Josephine Volpe), Shamanitis: A Pre-Columbian Art Historical Disease, In: The Concept of Shamanism: Uses and Abuses, 2001; A New Interpretation of the Aztec Statue Known as Coatlicue, Snakes-Her-Skirt, Ethnohisotry 55, 2008; The Aztec Sacrifice of Tezcatlipoca & its Implications for Christ Crucified, Power, Gender, & Ritual in Europe & the Am: Essays in Memory of Richard C Trexler, 2008; with Naoli Victoria Lona, Sex in the City: The Relationship of Aztec Ceramic Figurines to Aztec Figurines Made of Copal, Mesoamerican Figurines: Small-Scale Indices of Large-Scale Social Phenomena, 2009; Human Sacrafice as Symbolic Capital: Images of the Violated Aztec Body for a Changing World, Crossing Cultures: Conflict, Migration & Convergence, 2009; In the Belly of the Beast, review of Jose Pardos installation of Pre-Columbian Art, Los Angeles Co Mus Art, Artforum, Los Angeles, 1/2009; How Did Mesoamericans Envision the Cosmos: Mexicolore, 8/2010. *Mailing Add:* c/o Dept Art Hist Dodd 100 Univ Calif 405 Hilgard Ave Los Angeles CA 90095

KLEIN, CYNTHIA
APPRAISER
Study: Univ Mass, Amherst, BA(art hist), BS (bus admin); Rutgers Univ, grad studies in Art Hist; Phi Beta Kappa. *Pos:* Specialist, paintings dept to dir, prints dept CG Sloan & Co Auctioneers, N Bethesda, Md, 91-2000; vpres, dir, prints dept Doyle NY, 2000-; Prints appraiser, Antiques Roadshow, WGBH-PBS, currently. *Mem:* Am Hist Prints Collectors Soc; Soc for Japanese Arts. *Mailing Add:* Doyle NY 175 E 87th St New York NY 10128

KLEIN, ELLEN LEE
PAINTER, EDUCATOR
b New York, NY. *Study:* City Coll New York, BA; Pratt Inst, MFA. *Work:* Thirteen Collection, NY; Hofstra Mus, Long Island, NY. *Exhib:* Solo exhibs, Green Mountain Gallery, NY, & Maples Gallery, Fairleigh Dickinson Univ, Sotheby's, NY; 15th Ann Art Show, Fairleigh Dickinson Univ; Cornell Med Ctr, NY; Eubie Blake Mus, Baltimore, Md; City Col, NY. *Pos:* Dir, Art Alumni Asn, City Col, NY & Settlement Arts Consortium, United Neighborhood Housing, NY; adminr, Sch Fine Arts, Nat Acad Design, NY, 80-94; critic & writer, ARTS Mag, NY, 82-88; dir humanities, Educ Alliance, NY, 95-98. *Teaching:* Adv, Robeson Ctr Gallery, Rutgers Univ, Newark, NJ; instr drawing & art hist, High Sch Music & Art, NY; adj prof contemp art, Jersey City State Col; instr painting, Usdan Ctr Creative & Performing Arts, Wyandanch, NY; adj prof, City Col NY. *Bibliog:* Lawrence Campbell (auth), article, Art News, 9/73; Klein at Phoenix, Park East, 3/76; Nina Ffrench-Frazier (auth), Gallery guide, Westsider, 4/27/78. *Mem:* Coll Art Asn Am; Artists Equity; Am Asn Mus; City Coll Art Alumni Asn; Int Council Mus; Nat Asn Female Execs. *Media:* Oil, Paper Collage. *Publ:* Auth, Toby Buonagario: More optical bounce to the ounce, 86, Beneath the surface of Terence La Noue, 86, All kinds of rational questions: An interview with Michael Goldberg, 86 & Debra Weier - in all Dimensions, 88, ARTs Mag; Manhattan Spotlight on Furman J Finck, Manhattan Spotlight, 4/88; auth, Bill Traylor: Observing Life, American Art Review, 99. *Mailing Add:* 139-12 84th Dr No 1F Briarwood NY 11435

KLEIN, JEANNE
COLLECTOR
Study: Univ Tex, BS (educ). *Pos:* Pres, Artpace, San Antonio; adv bd, Blanton Mus Art & Univ Tex Coll Educ; develop bd, Univ Tex; bd dirs, Artlies & Juvenile Diabetes Found; sponsor & founder, Menil Contemporaries, Houston. *Awards:* Named one of Top 200 Collectors, ARTnews mag, 2009-12. *Collection:* Postwar and contemporary art. *Mailing Add:* Artpace 445 North Main Ave San Antonio TX 78205

KLEIN, LYNN (ELLEN)
PAINTER, PHOTOGRAPHER
b San Francisco, Calif, Apr 14, 1950. *Study:* Univ Minn, BA, 74, MFA, 76; Cite Internationale des Arts, Paris, 84-86, 98, and 2008. *Work:* Philadelphia Mus Art; Oakland Mus, Calif; Walker Art Ctr, Minneapolis; Nat Libr Prints & Photographs, Paris, France; San Jose Mus Art, Calif; Crocker Art Mus, Calif; Minneapolis Inst Arts; New York Pub Libr; Toledo Mus, Ohio; San Diego Mus; Libr Cong, Washington, DC; Achenbach Prints, Fine Arts Mus San Francisco; Rutgers Univ Ctr Innovative Prints; Kaiser Permanent, Santa Clara, Calif; AT&T, NY; Atlantic Richfield Co, Los Angeles, Calif; Saks Fifth Ave, Chicago, Ill, Minneapolis, Minn, Denver Colo, Troy, Mich; Chemical Bank, NY; St Marys Hosp, Rochester, Mn; and many others. *Comn:* Mitsukoshi Manno Golf Club, Tokyo, 96; Renaissance Hotel, Hong Kong, 97; Miami Int Airport, Fla, 2000; public art program, Ritz Carlton, Wash DC, 2000; Fairmont Mayakoba, Cancun, Mex, 2004; Ritz Carlton, Palm Beach, Fla, 2005; and others; public mural, Atlantis Dubai, Abu Dubai, 2008. *Exhib:* West 81, Art & Law, 81 & Lighter Shade of Pale, 90, Minn Mus Am Art, St Paul; Solo Exhibs: Coffman Gallery, Univ, Minn, Minneapolis, 82, Print Club, Philadelphia, Pa, 85, Foster White Gallery, Seattle, 89, Carolyn Ruff Gallery, 94 & Robert Green Fine Arts, Mill Valley, Calif, 2000, Diaphanous Muse, Sakata Garo, Sacramento, Calif, 2008; Photog Invitational, Tweed Mus Art, 83; Textile Arts Int: Rauschenberg, Samaras & Klein, 90; San Francisco Bay Area Women Artists Mentors, San Francisco Art Comn Gallery, 96; US Art, San Francisco Int Art Expo, 96; The Painterly Print, Mill Valley, Calif, 96; Craftsman Guild & Calif Heritage Gallery, 98; Calif Artists at Achenbach, Palace Legion Hon, San Francisco, Calif, 2001; Visible Rhythm, San Jose Mus Art, 2003; NeoMod, Recent CA Abstraction, Crocker Art Mus, Sacramento, Calif, 2005; Vermillion Eds LTD: Prints, Minneapolis Inst Art, 2006; Barry Sagata Gallery,

Sacramento, Calif, 2012. *Pos:* Graphic artist, Piper Jaffrey Minneapolis, 72-73; arts coordr, Pillsbury Waite Cult Arts Ctr, Minneapolis, 73-77; asst, Midwest Conserv, Minneapolis, 79-83; vis artist, Iowa State Univ, 84 & Textile Ctr Minn, 2003. *Teaching:* Lectr, design dept, color & 2D design, Univ Minn, Minneapolis, 74-84, instr art educ, 76-78; vis fac, Quadna Mountain Lodge, Hill City, Minn, 78. *Awards:* Minn State Arts Bd Grantee, 78; JD Phelan Award, World Print Coun, 83; Photog Fel, St Paul, Minn, 84; Rockefeller Found Fel, 84-86; Cite Int des Arts Residency, Paris, France, 84-86 & 98; Jerome Found Printmaking Fel, Kala Inst, 89; others. *Bibliog:* Textilforum, Zeitgeossische, 3/93; Peter Selz (monogr), solo exhib, 2000; Yoshiko Wada (auth), Memory on Cloth, 2002; CAT Raisonne, Vermillion Eds, Minneapolis Inst Arts, 2006. *Mem:* Achenbach Graphic Arts Coun. *Media:* Oil; Miscellaneous Media. *Publ:* Double/Absent, Ed 15, Vermillion Eds, Diptych, 83; Wild Women, ed 20, 2002 & Brave New World, ed 20, 2004, Blue Sky Press. *Dealer:* Ira Wolk St Helena CA; Barry Sakata Gallery, Sacramento, Calif

KLEIN, MICHAEL EUGENE
HISTORIAN, WRITER
b Philadelphia, Pa, July 30, 1940. *Study:* Rutgers Col, New Brunswick, NJ, BA, 62; Columbia Univ, New York, MA, 65, PhD, 71. *Collection Arranged:* John Covert, 1882-1960 (auth, bk), Smithsonian Inst Press, 76. *Pos:* Vis cur, Hirshhorn Mus, 76. *Teaching:* Asst prof art hist, State Univ NY, Brockport, 71-73; asst prof, Univ SC, 73-77; asst prof, Western Ky Univ, 77-80, assoc prof, 81-2006, semi-retired prof, 2006-. *Mem:* Coll Art Asn Am. *Res:* American art of early 20th century, especially John Covert; Arnold Friedman; Meyer Schapiro; Willem de Kooning. *Publ:* Auth, John Covert's time: Cubism, Duchamp, Einstein, a quasi scientific fantasy, summer 74 & John Covert's studios in 1916 and 1923, fall 79, Art J; Scotese collection at the Columbia Museum of Art, Southeastern Coll Art Conf J, fall 74; auth, John Covert and the Arensberg circle, Arts Mag, 5/77. *Mailing Add:* Dept Art Western Ky Univ Bowling Green KY 42101

KLEIN, MICHAEL L
COLLECTOR
Study: Univ Tex, Austin, BS (petroleum engineering), 1958, LLB, 1963. *Pos:* Develop bd, Univ Tex, Austin; press adv coun, Univ Tex; bd dirs, Site Santa Fe, Humanities Tex, 2007-; trustee, Hirshhorn Mus & Sculpture Garden, Washington, DC. *Awards:* Named one of Top 200 Collectors, ARTnews mag, 2003-13. *Collection:* Postwar and contemporary art. *Mailing Add:* Ste 1230 500 W Texas Midland TX 79701

KLEIN, RICHARD
DIRECTOR, CURATOR
Pos: Exhibs dir, Aldrich Contemp Art Mus. *Mailing Add:* 258 Main St Ridgefield CT 06877

KLEIN, SABINA
PRINTMAKER
b Brooklyn, NY, 1949. *Study:* Hunter Coll, New York, BA, 1971, MA, 1972; Printmaking Workshop, New York, 1972; Atelier 17, Paris, 1973, 1974; Ecole Beaux-Arts, Paris, 1973, 1974. *Exhib:* Solo exhibs include Found Etats-Unis, Paris, 1974, 1973, New Sch Social Research, New York, 1986, Gallerie Michitsch, Vienna, 2005; group shows include Brit Int Print Biennial, England, 1981; Norwegian Int Print Biennial, 1980, 1982 & 1984; Taiwan Int Print Biennial, 1984 & 1986; Soc Am Graphic Asn, New York, 1986; SE Feinman Fine Arts, New York, 1995-2000; 183rd Ann: Invitational Exhib Contemp Art, Nat Acad Mus, New York, 2008. *Pos:* Owner & dir, SK Fine Arts, NYC. *Teaching:* Instr, Parsons Sch Art & Design, New York, 1984-90. *Awards:* Philip Morris Visual Artist Fel, 1988. *Dealer:* John Szoke Editions 591 Broadway 3rd Fl New York NY 10012

KLEINBAUER, W EUGENE
HISTORIAN, WRITER
b Los Angeles, Calif, June 15, 1937. *Study:* Univ Calif, Berkeley, BA & MA, 62; Princeton Univ, PhD, 67. *Pos:* Pres, Internat Ctr Medieval Art, 87-90. *Teaching:* Asst prof hist art, Univ Calif, Los Angeles, 65-72; chmn, Dept Fine Arts, Ind Univ, 73-76, chmn arts admin prog, 73-75 & fall 78, prof hist art, 77-, prof Near Eastern languages & cultures, 85- & chmn dept hist art, 92-95; Sam & Ayala Zacks vis prof hist art, Hebrew Univ, Jerusalem, 78; assoc dir, Henry Hope Sch Fine Arts, Ind Univ, 88-92; F L Morgan vis prof, Univ Louisville, 96, 2006; prof emer Art Hist, 2006. *Awards:* Nat Endowment Humanities Fel, 76-77; Pres Award Distinguished Teaching, Ind Univ, 99. *Mem:* Coll Art Asn Am; Int Ctr Medieval Art (mem bd dir, 70-73, 74-77 & 81-83, ed, GESTA, 80-83, pres, 87-90); Medieval Acad Am; US Nat Comt Byzantine Studies; Speculum (ed bd, 90-93). *Res:* Specialist in medieval art and architecture; historiography of Western art. *Publ:* E Kitzinger, Art of Byzantium & Medieval West, Ind Univ, 76; auth, Research Guide to the History of Western Art, Am Libr Asn, 82; Early Christian and Byzantine Architecture, GK Hall, 92; Hagia Sophia, 2004; Modern Perspectives in Western Art History, 71 (reprinted in 88); numerous scholarly articles & reviews. *Mailing Add:* Dept Art History Indiana Univ Bloomington IN 47405

KLEINBERG, SUSAN
ARTIST
b Phoenix, Ariz. *Study:* Hunter Coll with Bob Morris & Tony Smith, MA, 72; Pomona Col, BA; Univ Guadalajara, Univ Madrid, grad work. *Work:* Los Angeles Co Mus, Calif; Cincinnati Mus, Ohio; La Jolla Mus, Calif; Am Ctr Paris, France; IBM, NY & Paris, France; Venice Biennale Archive, Italy; White House Collection, Washington, DC; and others. *Comn:* Park-slides, Pomona, Calif, 75; Triptich paintings, Liebman, Adolph, Cherne, NY, 87, Rainen Corp, San Francisco, 88 & Media Ctr for Human Rights, NY, 90; 2 paintings, comn by Mrs L Levin, Los Angeles, Calif, 87; painting, Colo Open Lands, Land Trust, 89; painting, Univ Calif, San Diego, 91. *Exhib:* Los Angeles Co Mus, Calif, 79; Mass Inst Technol, Boston, 82; Mus Mod Art, NY, 82; Light/Walls, Am Ctr Paris/Beauborg, France, 87; Orton Collection, Cincinnati Mus, Ohio, 88; Sarabhai Collection, Ahmedabad, India; Arte Laguna, Milan, Italy, 95; Venice Biennale, Italy, 95; Studio D'Arte Barnabo, Venice, Italy, 96; Wilshire Blvd Temple, Los Angeles, 97; PSI, NY, 99; Venice Biennale, 01; Neuhof Gallery, NY, 02; Spec Projects, Chicago Inst Art Fair, 02; Tasende Gallery, La Jolla, Calif, 02; PSI/Mus Modern Art, 02; Mus Fine Arts, Buenos Aires, 02; Furture Democracy, Istanbul Biennale 2003, Akbank Headquarter, Istanbul, Turkey; Total Mus, Seoul Korea, 2004; Istituto Veneto, 2005, Venice Italy; Chiostio del Brammanta, Rome, 2009; Certosa di Padula, Saperno, 2009; Espaso, Los Angeles, 2009; Venice Biennale, Isle Com Italia, 2009; Citiostio di San Salvador, Parc Foundation, New York, 2008; Visiting Artist Am Acad in Rome, 2009. *Awards:* Nat Endowment Arts, 77; Max Beckman Award, Brooklyn Mus, 80; Am Acad Rome, 95 & 96; City of Venice Grant, 95; Ziegler Found grant, 95, award, 01, 02; Samsung Corp grant, 01-03. *Mem:* Soc Fels; Am Acad Rome; Nat Arts Club. *Media:* Paint, Drawing, Video. *Mailing Add:* 250 W 85th St 14-H New York NY 10024

KLEINMAN, KENT
ARCHITECT, ADMINISTRATOR
Study: Univ Calif Berkeley, BA in Architecture, 1979, Master of Architecture, 1983. *Pos:* mem Architectual Adv Com, bd trustee building and property com, NYC Tech Campus Executive Com, Johnson Mus Adv Coun and Exec Com, Governing Bd Cornell Inst for Public Affairs, Cornell Univ, 2008-; Gale and Ira Drukier Dean Coll Architecture, Art, and Planning, Cornell Univ; academic reviewer, 1996-2009; invited juror 1995-2009; many design projects and several exhibitions for design/studio work. *Teaching:* vis prof, Institute für Wohnbau, Technical Univ, Vienna, 1992, vis prof Meisterschule Prof Gustav Peichi, Akademie der bildenden Künste, Vienna, 1993, vis prof Institute 3D, Danish Royal Acad, Copenhagen, 1995, vis prof, Fakultat für Architektur, Hochschule der Künste, Berlin, 1995, vis critic Col of Art and Architecture, Cornell Univ, 1995-2011, studio critic for many universities; asst prof, Col of Architecture and Urban Planning, Univ of Mich, Ann Arbor, 1991-97, assoc prof, 1997-99; prof, chair dept of architecture, Sch of Architecture and Planning, State Univ of NY, Buffalo, 1999-2005; prof, dean, Sch of Constructed Environment: Parsons The New Sch for Design, NY, chair dept of architecture, interior design, lighting design, 2006-2008; prof, Gale and Ira Drukier Dean of Architecture, Art, and Planning, Cornell Univ, 2008-. *Awards:* Muschenheim Fellow, Col of Architecture and Urban Planning, Univ Mich, 1989-91; Senior Public Goods Fellow, Mellon Found, Univ Mich, 2002-2003; vis scholar, Canadian Ctr for Architecture, 2005; Bordin/Gillette Research Fellow, Univ Mich, 2003, 2008, Faculty Fellow, Atkinson Ctr for a Sustainable Future, Cornell Univ, 2010; Graham Found grants 1991, 2004, 2008; nat Bruner prize; NY Coun on the Arts grant; First alternate award for the Burnham Prize, 1995, American Inst of Architects NY Chapter Educator award, 2011; co-recipient Arnold W Brunner award, 1996, Progressive Architecture Design award, 2001. *Res:* 20th Century European Modernism. *Publ:* Villa Müller: A Work of Adolf Loos, 1997 (named Top Ten Book of the Yr, The Architect's Journal, 1994); Rudolf Arnheim: Revealing Vision, 1998; Mies van der Rohe: The Krefeld Villas, 2005 (named Top Ten Book of the Yr, The Architect's Journal, 2005); The Poetics if a Projecting Wall, 2009, AfterTaste, 2011; articles and reviews in nat and internat publications including Bauwelt, Progressive Architecture, A+U, Bauart, Archis, and the Architects' Journal. *Mailing Add:* Cornell University College of Architecture Art & Planning 129 Sibley Dome Ithaca NY 14850

KLEINSMITH, BRUCE JOHN See Nutzle, Futzie (Bruce) John Kleinsmith

KLEMENT, VERA
PAINTER, WRITER, GRAPHIC ARTIST, PHOTOGRAPHER
b Danzig, Ger, Dec 14, 1929; US citizen. *Study:* Cooper Union Sch Art & Archit, grad, 50. *Work:* Mus Mod Art, Jewish Mus, NY; Philadelphia Mus Art; Northern Trust Bank, First Nat Bank, Chicago; Smart Mus, Chicago; Mus Contemp Art, Chicago; Ariz Mus Art, Tucson; Art Inst of Chicago; Block Mus, Evanston Ill; Ill Art Mus, Springfield; Miami Univ Art Mus, Oxford; Daum Mus of Contemp Art, Sedalia, Mo; Davis Mus, Wellesley, Mass; Mus Contemp Photography, Columbia Coll, Chicago; Rockford Art Mus, Rockford, Ill; Ill Holocaust Mus, Skokie; Spertus Mus, Chicago. *Comn:* Ed of etchings, NY Hilton/Rockefeller Ctr, 61; 27 1/2 ft & 2 ft painting, Kemper Ins Co, Long Grove, Ill, 75; painting, McCormick Place, Chicago. *Exhib:* Walker Art Ctr Invitational, Minneapolis, Minn, 77; Jewish Mus, NY, 82; one-woman show, Spertus Mus, 87; group show, Ill State Mus, Springfield, 90; Corcoran Gallery Art, Washington, DC, 94; Retrospective, Cult Ctr, Chicago, 99; one-person show, Ft Wayne Mus of Art, In, 02, Mary & Leigh Block Mus Art, 02, Univ Ariz Mus Art, Tucson, 01, Tarble Art Ctr, Ea Ill Univ, Charleston, 02; Daum Mus, Sedalia, MO, 2004; Univ Art Gallery, Ind State Univ, 2007; Poetry as Painting, Terre Haute Inst, 2007; Rockford Mus Art, Rockford, Ill, 2008; Printworks Gallery, Chicago, 2009, 2011; Constellations, Mus Contemp Art, Chicago, 2009; Printworks Gallery, Chgo, 2011; travelling exhib, Luminous Ground, Ill State Mus Gallery, 2011; Zolla Lieberman Gallery, 2012, 2013. *Teaching:* Instr painting, Univ Ill, 68-69; asst prof art, Univ Chicago, 69-78, assoc prof, 78-86, prof, 87-95, prof art emeritus, 95-. *Awards:* Louis Comfort Tiffany Found Grant, 54; Guggenheim fel, 81-82; Nat Endowment Arts, 87; Pollock/Krasner Found Grant, 98-99; Ill Arts Coun Grant; Camargo Found Residence, Cassis, France, 2006; and others. *Bibliog:* William S Lieberman (auth), Printmaking & the American woodcut today, Perspectives USA, 53; Amy Goldin (auth), Vitality vs greasy kid stuff, Art Gallery Mag 4/72; article in Artists' Writings, publ by NAME, 77; Dore Ashton (auth), Two Part Connection: Vera Klement's Painting, Arts Mag, 3/84, retrospective catalog, A Question of Drawing, 89; James Yood (auth), Vera Klement, Artforum, 89; Donald Kuspit (auth), Vera Klenent's Poem-Paintings; Sue Taylor (auth) Vera Klement: Things Made Mythic; Lynne Warren (auth), Unnamable; James Yood (auth), Icon Into Image; Vera Klement: An Appreciation. *Mem:* Union League Club of Chicago (Hon Lifetime mem). *Media:* Oil. *Publ:* Vera Klement: Blunt Edge (documentary film), 2011. *Dealer:* Zolla/Lieberman Gallery, Chicago. *Mailing Add:* 727 S Dearborn Chicago IL 60605

KLESH-BUTKOVSKY, JANE
GRAPHIC ARTIST, PAINTER
b Hazelton, PA, Feb 14, 1957. *Study:* Madison Art Sch, with Robert Brackman & Bill Schultz; Cape Sch, with Henry Hensche; Annapolis Art Inst, with Cedric & Jonette Egli; Pocono Pines, Pa, with William Herring, Charles Sovek, Charles Ried & Charles Movalli; Nat Acad Design, with Everette Raymond Kinstler & Sam Adouqui. *Work:* Hazelton Art League, Pa; Penn State, Hazelton, Pa. *Comn:* Penn State Hazelton Campus, 2009. *Exhib:* 171st Ann Exhib, Nat Acad Design, NY, 95; 75th Ann Exhib, Am Artists Prof League, NY, 2003; 5th Ann Exhib, Am Impressionist Soc, Vero Beach, Fla, 2003; 90th Ann Exhib, Allied Artist Am, NY, 2003; 63rd Ann Exhib, Audubon Artists, NY, 2005; Audobon Artists, New York, 2006-08; Am Impressionism Soc, Nashville, 2010; Yellow Springs Art Show, Chester Springs, Pa, 2010; Yellow Springs Art Show, Pa, 2011; 69 Ann Exhib, Audubon Artists, NY, 2011; Allied Artists Am, NY, 2011; Am Impressionist Soc Ann Exhib, Nashville, Tenn, 2011; Am Impressionist Soc, Ann Exhib, Indianapolis, Ind, 2012; Audubon Artists, 70th Ann Online Exhib, NY, 2012; Audubon Artists 71st Annual Exhib, Allied Artists of Am, 100th Ann Exhib. *Teaching:* Instr, drawing, Luzerne Co Community Coll, 1995-; Hazelton Art League, 2007-; instr painting, Luzerne Community Coll; instr drawing & painting, Studio 303. *Awards:* Am Artists Fund Award, Am Artists Prof League 75th, Am Artists Fund, 2003; Butler Inst of Am Allied Artists 90th, Butler Inst, 2003; Best of Show, Hazelton Art League 48th, Evelyn Graham, 2006; Theodore R Laputka Jr Mem Art Award, Hazelton Art League, 2007; PNC Bank Award, 80th Art Exhib, Hazelton Art League, 2008; Silver Medal of Honor in Oils, Allied Artists of America 100th Annual Exhib, 2013. *Mem:* Audubon Artists; Pa Plein Air Soc (signature mem); Portrait Soc of Am; Am Impressionist Soc; Hazelton Art League; Allied Artists of America (elected mem). *Media:* Charcoal, Oil, Watercolor. *Mailing Add:* 216 W Chapel St Hazleton PA 18201

KLETT, MARK
PHOTOGRAPHER
b Albany, NY, Sept 9, 1952. *Study:* St Lawrence Univ, BS, 74; State Univ NY, MFA, 77. *Hon Degrees:* Hon Dr, St Lawrence Univ, 2004. *Work:* Mus Mod Art & Whitney Mus, NY; Los Angeles Co Mus Mod Art & Los Angeles Co Mus Art, Calif; Art Inst Chicago, Ill; High Mus Art, Atlanta; J B Speed Art Mus, Louisville. *Exhib:* Solo exhibs, Los Angeles Co Mus Art, 84, Art Inst Chicago, 84, Kathleen Ewing Gallery, Washington, 94, Addison Gallery Am Art, Andover, Mass, 94, Scottsdale Ctr Arts, Ariz, 94, Nat Mus Am Art Smithsonian Inst, Washington, 94 & Pace Wildenstein McGill, NY, 95, Huntington Art Galleries, 99, Cleveland Art Mus, 98, The Huntington, San Marino, 99, Ariz State Univ, 2004, Nev Mus Art, Reno, 04, Neuberger Mus Art, Purchase, NY, 04, Frost Art Mus, Miami, 05; Photographs from the Last Decade, San Francisco Mus Mod Art, 88; Recent/Ancient Artifacts of the Southwest, Anderson Ranch Arts Ctr, Aspen, Colo, 88; Min Gallery, Tokyo, 88; Three Photographers, Harnett Gallery, Univ Rochester, NY, 88; L'Oeil de la Lettre Evidence of Man, Amon Carter Mus, Ft Worth, 89; On the Art of Fixing a Shadow, One Hundred and Fifty Yrs of Photog, Nat Gallery Art, Washington, 89; Panorama of California, Oakland Mus, Calif, 92; Hidden Faces, Paul Kopeikin Gallery, Los Angeles, 94. *Teaching:* Acad prof, Ariz State Univ, 82-; Regents prof art, Ariz State Univ, Tempe. *Awards:* Art Fel, Nat Endowment Arts, 79, 82, 84 & 93; Visual Arts Fel, AVA, 85; Creative Arts Award, Brandeis Univ, 90; Japan US Friendship Comn 95, Buhl Found, 99; fel, Guggenheim Found, 04. *Bibliog:* William L Fox (auth), View Finder: Mark Klett, Photography and the Reinvention of Landscape, Univ NMex Press, 2001. *Mem:* Soc Photog Educ. *Publ:* Coauth, Second View: The Rephotographic Survey Project, Univ NMex Press, 84; Headlands: The Marin Coast at the Golden Gate, Univ NMex Press, 89; One City/Two Visions, Chronicle Books, 90; Revealing Territory, Univ NMex Press, 92; Desert Legends, Henry Holt, 94; Third Views, Second Sights, Mus NMex Press, 2004; The Black Rock Desert, Univ Ariz Press, 2002. *Dealer:* Pace/MacGill New York. *Mailing Add:* 1136 S Ash Ave Tempe AZ 85281

KLINDT, STEVEN
ADMINISTRATOR
b Davenport, Iowa, Dec 18, 1947. *Study:* Sch of Art, Univ Iowa, BA (studio art), 70, MA (photog), 74. *Collection Arranged:* Photograph Invitational, Galesburg Civic Art Ctr, Ill, 76; Proposals for Lake Sculpture, Evanston Art Ctr, Ill, 77; New Am Photography (auth, catalog), Columbia Col, 82. *Pos:* Dir, Galesburg Civic Art Ctr, 74-76, Evanston Art Ctr, 76-79, Chicago Ctr Contemp Photog, Columbia Col Galleries, 79-83, Mus Contemp Photog, Columbia Col, 83-84, Tweed Mus Art, Duluth, Minn, 84-89; exec dir, Queens Mus Art, New York, 89-93, Morris Mus, Morristown, NJ, 93-. *Teaching:* Mus studies MA program, Columbia Col, Chicago, 79-84; Visual Arts Admin, New York Univ, 92-. *Mem:* Coll Art Asn; Am Asn Mus; Asn Art Mus Dirs; Park Ave Club. *Publ:* Ed, Jerry N Uelsmann, Photographs from 1975-1979, Columbia Col, Chicago, 80; Light Touching Silver-Photographs, Columbia Col, Chicago, 80; and others. *Mailing Add:* Morris Mus 6 Normandy Heights Rd Morristown NJ 07960

KLINE, MARTIN
PAINTER
b Norwalk, Ohio, 1961. *Study:* Ohio Univ, BFA, 83. *Exhib:* Solo exhibs include Line Drawings, Small Space Gallery, Ohio, 83; Egyptian Themes, Sumus Gallery, Portland, 84; Drawings, Oregon Info Technology Inst, 85; Recent Drawings, Stephen Mazoh, NY, 92, Yuccas, 94; 17 Drawings, ACP Gallerie, Zurich, 93 Large Watercolors, 95; Grids, 65 Thompson Street, NY, 96; Allez les Fille Gallery, Ohio, 96; New Works, Marlborough Gallery, NY, 2000, Painting Sculpture, 2002; Copenhagen Suite New Oilstick Paintings, Jason McCoy Inc, Cogenhagen, 2005; Truth Awakens as Fiction, Jason McCoy Inc, NY, 2006, Made in Japan, 2006; group exhibs include Purely Painting, Elizabeth Harris Gallery, NY Univ, 97; Drawings, James Graham & Sons, NY, 98; Summer Exhib, Marlborough Gallery, NY, 1999, 2000, 2001, Sculpture, 2002, 2003; Waxing Poetic: Encaustic Art in America, Montclair Art Mus, 1999-2000; Art 2000, Gagosian Gallery, NY City, 2000; Watercolor: In the Abstract, Sarah Moody Gallery Art, 2001; Rock and Art, Nature Found and Made, Chambers Fine Art, NY, 2001; Inaugural Exhib, Flatfile Contemp, Chicago, 2003; The Western Tradition: Art since the Renaissance, Fogg Art Mus, Harvard Univ, 2004; Los Monocromos, Mus Nacional Centro de Arte Reina Sofia, Madrid, 2004; Summer Exbib, Jason McCoy Inc, NY, 2005; Encaustic Works, Samuel Dorsky Mus Art, State Univ NY, New Platz, 2005; Cornice - Venice Art Fair, 2007

KLINE, PHIL
MUSEUM DIRECTOR
Study: Mich State Univ, BA (Business Admin). *Pos:* Royal & Sun Alliance, 1971-1998; Chief Operating Officer, Mecklenburg Aquatic Club. *Mailing Add:* Mint Museum of Art 2730 Randolph Rd Charlotte NC 28207

KLIPPER, STUART DAVID
PHOTOGRAPHER
b Bronx, NY, Aug 27, 1941. *Study:* Univ Mich, Coll Lit, Sci & Arts, BA, 62, Coll Archit & Design, 62-63. *Work:* Walker Art Ctr, Minneapolis; Art Inst Chicago; Mus Fine Arts, Boston; Mus Mod Art, NY; San Francisco Mus Mod Art; and many others. *Comn:* Anasazi Plates, Univ Mich; Cray I Computer, Cray Res Inc; The World in a Few States, First Bank Systems, Minneapolis. *Exhib:* 20th Century Am Photogr, Atkins Mus Fine Art, Kansas City, 74; Multiple Strip Images, Walker Art Ctr, Minneapolis, 78; Am Photog in the 70's, Art Inst Chicago, 79; Recent Work, Minn Mus Art, St Paul, 80; Art Inst Chicago, 80; Duluth Photogrs, Tweed Mus Art, Minn, 82; Minn Mus Art, 82; Portents in the North: Radiation in Lapland, Minn Mus Art, St Paul, 88; Solo exhibs, Jewish Mus, NY, 88, Czechoslovakia Photog Festival, 91, Minneapolis Inst Art, 92, Thompson Gallery, Minneapolis, 92, Twentieth Century Photog Gallery, NY, 93, Fernbank Mus Natural Hist, Atlanta, 93 & McDougall Gallery Art, Christchurch, NZ, 94; Arctic and Antarctic Photogs, San Francisco Mus Mod Art, 89; On Antarctica 1989 (selections from), Mus Mod Art, NY, 91; Between Heaven and Home, Nat Mus Am Art, 92; Images from a Frozen Land, Arlington Ohio Art Ctr, Byrd Polar Inst, 92; Art from the Rain Forest, Fernbank Mus, Atlanta, 92; Our Town, Burdin Gallery, Aperture Found, NY, 93; Automotive Minn, pArts Gallery, Minneapolis, 93; plus many others. *Collection Arranged:* Seven Photogr (guest-cur), Art Gallery, Macalester Col, St Paul, Minn, 78. *Teaching:* Instr photog, Minneapolis Col Art & Design, 70-71, vis prof, 74-75 & 78; vis prof photog, Colo Col, Colorado Springs, 78, 79, 80, 89. *Awards:* J S Guggenheim Mem Found Photogr Fel, 79-80, 89-90; Antarctic Serv Medal, US Navy, 89; Selectee, Artist in Antarctica Prog, Nat Sci Found, 89, 91 & 93; and others. *Mem:* Minn Artists' Exhib Prog. *Publ:* Auth, The Art of the Twin Cities, Portfolio Mag, summer 80; Bearing South, The Press, Colo Col, 91; numerous photogs in Between Heaven and Home exhib catalog, Aperture Mag, Harper's Newsweek, ArtForum & Art News, 91 & 92; American in a Few States, In: The Creating of the North American Landscape, John Hopkins Univ Press, 93; High Latitudes, Aperture Press, 93. *Mailing Add:* 5044 Xerxes Ave S Minneapolis MN 55410-2226

KLITZKE, THEODORE ELMER
EDUCATOR, HISTORIAN
b Chicago, Ill, Nov 4, 1915. *Study:* Art Inst Chicago, BFA, 40; Univ Chicago, BA, 41, PhD, 53; Kansas City Art Inst, Hon DFA, 80. *Teaching:* Instr art hist, Univ Chicago, 46-47; asst prof art hist, State Univ NY Col Ceramics, Alfred Univ, 53-59; prof art hist & chmn dept art, Univ Ala, Tuscaloosa, 59-68. *Mem:* Am Studies Asn; Coll Art Asn Am; Soc Archit Historians; fel Nat Asn Sch Art. *Res:* Social history of American art; 19th century French art; German expressionism; history of prints and drawings. *Publ:* Contribr, reviews in Coll Art J & Art Bull, 59-; contribr, Alexis de Tocqueville and the Arts in America, Festschrift Ulrich Middeldorf, 68; auth, Melville Price Retrospective: 1920-1970, Frame House Gallery, 70; contribr, Hermann Wilhelm (catalog), 72. *Mailing Add:* 35 Brown Ave Seekonk MA 02771-4401

KLOBE, TOM
GALLERY DIRECTOR, EDUCATOR
b Minneapolis, Minn, Nov 26, 1940. *Study:* Univ Hawaii, BFA, 64, MFA, 68; Univ Calif, Los Angeles, 72-73. *Work:* State Found Cult & Arts, Contemp Mus & Honolulu Acad Arts, Honolulu, Hawaii; City of La Mirada, Calif; Nat Orange Show Collection, San Bernardino, Calif; Downey Mus Art, Calif. *Comn:* Onizuka Ctr Int Astronomy, Hawaii; and others. *Exhib:* Artists of Hawaii, Honolulu Acad Art, 67 & 68; 9th Ann Southern California Exhib, Long Beach Mus Art, 71; Calif-Hawaii Regional, Fine Arts Gallery, San Diego, 71, 72 & 76; Ann Purchase Prize Competition, Riverside Art Mus, Calif, 72-74 & 76; solo exhib, Downey Mus Art, Calif, 74. *Collection Arranged:* Hawaii State Art Mus, 02; Honolulu Acad Art, 1998-2005; Philippine Gallery, 03; Crossings 03: Korea/Hawaii; Labor & Leisure, 05; Treasures Hamilton Libr, 05; Crossings '97: France/Hawaii. *Pos:* Actg dir, Downey Mus Art, Calif, 76; dir, Univ Hawaii Art Gallery, Honolulu, 77-2006. *Teaching:* Prof design & Islamic & Medieval art hist, Univ Hawaii, Honolulu, 77-2006. *Awards:* Print Casebooks, Best in Exhib Design, Koa Furniture of Hawaii, 81, Greek and Russian Icons, 84, 2nd Int Shoebox Sculpture Exhib, 85, The Art of Micronesia, 86 & The Art of Polish Posters, 87; Chevalier de l'Ordre des Artes et des Letters, Rep of France, 2000; Clopton Award, Distinguished Community Serv, Univ Hawaii, 03; Living Treasure of Hawaii Award, 05. *Mem:* Hawaii Mus Asn. *Res:* Exhib design & interpretation. *Publ:* Ed, Int Shoebox Sculpture Exhib, Univ Hawaii Art Gallery, 82, 85, 88, 91, 94, 97, 2000, & 03. *Mailing Add:* Univ Hawaii Art Gallery Honolulu HI 96822

KLOPFENSTEIN, PHILIP ARTHUR
CONSULTANT, PAINTER
b Lake Odessa, Mich, Apr 28, 1937. *Study:* Mich State Univ, with Abraham Ratner & Linsey Decker, BFA; Western Mich Univ, with Harry Hefner, MFA; Harvard Univ, arts admin cert. *Exhib:* State Ark Educ Dept Traveling Exhib, 76-; Mid Southern Watercolor Soc Ann, 72-74. *Collection Arranged:* John Henry Byrd (1840-1880), Southeast Ark Arts & Sci Ctr, Pine Bluff, 70; Ernest Trova One-Man Exhib, 71; Art Inc II (Am paintings from Am corp collections), 80. *Pos:* TV writer & teacher, Ark

Educ TV, Conway, 68-69; dir, Southeast Ark Arts & Sci Ctr, 70-76; exec dir, Augusta Richmond Co Mus, Ga, 77-79; dir, Montgomery Mus Fine Arts, Ala, 79-82; vpres, Res and Reclamation, 83-88. *Teaching:* Instr, Paw Paw Pub Sch, Mich, 63-65; instr painting, watercolor & art educ, Little Rock Univ, 65-68; instr art hist, Auburn Univ, Montgomery, 84-85, Glenwood Pub Sch, 89-97; fed prog coord, Ctr Point Sch Dist, 97-98. *Mem:* Ark Retired Teachers Asn; Southeastern Mus Conf (regional rep, 74-75); Three Rivers Art Guild Inc. *Media:* Watercolor, Oil. *Res:* John Henry Byrd. *Publ:* Auth, John Henry Byrd (1840-1880), 71. *Mailing Add:* PO Box 890 Glenwood AR 71943

KLOSS, WILLIAM
HISTORIAN, WRITER
b Cleveland, Ohio, Dec 23, 1937. *Study:* Oberlin Coll, BA, 62, MA, 68; Univ Mich, 72. *Collection Arranged:* More than Meets the Eye: the Art of Trompe l'Oeil (with catalog), Columbus Mus Art, Ohio, 85. *Pos:* Exhib coordr, Smithsonian Inst Traveling Exhib Ser, 74-78; founder & dir tours, Washington Art Asn Inc, 78-2008; bd dir, Pyramid Atlantic Art Ctr, 95-97; adv bd, George Caleb Bingham catalogue raisonné, 2005-. *Teaching:* Asst prof art hist, Univ Va, Charlottesville, 69-72; lectr art hist, Smithsonian Study Tours, 78- & Sotheby's Inst, 88-; prof great artists Italian Renaissance, Teaching co, 2004, prof History European art, 2005, prof Dutch Masters, 2006, prof Masterworks Am Art, 2008 & prof World's Greatest Paintings, 2010. *Awards:* Fulbright Scholar Study Art Hist in Rome, US Govt, 67-69; Presidential Appt, Comt for Preserv of White House, 90, 93, 97, 2002 & 2006; Winner, Art Category, Nat Indie, 2009; Excellence Awards, Art in the White House: A Nation's Pride, 2nd ed, rev, White House Hist Asn, 2008. *Mem:* Coll Art Asn of Am; Am Asn Mus. *Res:* Preparation of Senate Collection. *Publ:* Auth, Treasures from the National Museum of American Art, Smithsonian, 85; Samuel F B Morse, Harry N Abrams, 88; coauth, Treasures of State, 91; auth, Art in the White House: A Nation's Pride, Harry N Abrams, 92 & 2nd ed, rev, White House Hist Asn, 2007; coauth, US Senate Catalogue of Fine Art, 2003. *Mailing Add:* 1824 Wyoming Ave NW Washington DC 20009

KLUEG, JIM
EDUCATOR, ADMINISTRATOR, CERAMIST
Study: Indiana Univ of Pa, BA (metalry), 1979, MA (ceramics), 1981; Indiana State Univ, MFA (ceramics), 1984. *Exhib:* Hughes Fine Arts Center, Univ North Dakota, 1999; Prevailing Winds: Current Trends in Contemporary Ceramics, Young & Constantin Gallery, Wilmington, Vt, 2000; It's Only Clay, Bemidji Community Arts Center, Minn, 2003; The Narrative Vessel, AKAR Gallery, Sioux City, Iowa, 2005; Plates and Platters: Salon Style, The Clay Studio, Philadelphia. 2007; Mendenhall Center, East Carolina Univ, Greenville, NC, 2007; Texting: Print and Clay, Pewabic Pottery, Detroit, Michigan, 2008; James Klueg, Weapons of Mass Seducation: Ceramic Work 2001-2010, MacRostie Art Center, Grand Rapids, 2010. *Teaching:* Prof art, ceramics area head, Univ of Minnesota, Duluth, 1986-, head art & design, 2008-09. *Awards:* 13th Annual Greater Midwest International Juror's Merit award, 1998; Purchase award, LaGrange National XX Biennial, 1998; First Place, Ceramics: Viewpoints 2000, 2000; Juror's Merit award, LaGrange National XXI Biennial, 2000; 16th Annual Greater Midwest International Juror's Merit award, 2001; Tile Heritage Foundation prize, 2003

KNECHT, JOHN
FILMMAKER, VIDEO ARTIST
b Iron Ridge, Wis, Mar 5, 1947. *Study:* Univ Wis, Oshkosh, BS, 72; Idaho State Univ, MFA, 74. *Work:* Queens Mus, NY. *Exhib:* Solo shows, Collective for Living Cinema, 80, Mus Mod Art, NY, 85, Alternative Mus, NY, 92 & 94, Millennium, 95, Calif Inst Arts, Valencia, Arsenal Kino, Berlin, Ger, London Film Coop, London, Eng, Davidson Col, 95; Edinburgh Film Fest, Edinburgh, Scotland, 81 & 84; 2nd Video Biennial, Mus Mod Art, Columbia, 88; Am Film Inst Videofest, 94; Black Mariafest, 94; Bard Coll, 2007; Dallas Video Festival, 2008; Munson Williams Proctov Arts Inst, 2008; Davidson Coll, 2008; Black Maria Film Festival, 2009; Albany Arts Mus, 2009; Ohio Univ, 2009; and others. *Pos:* Chair, art & art hist, Colgate Univ, 91-99; mem bd govs, Nat Conf Undergrad Res, 93-. *Teaching:* Asst prof, Univ Okla Sch Art, 74-78; assoc prof, Colgate Univ Dept Art & Art Hist, 81-93, prof, 93-; vis lectr, Brown Univ, spring 81; prof of art, art hist, film and media studies, Russell Colgate Univ, 2002-. *Awards:* Lightworks Grant, 83; New York Found for the Arts Video Fel, 89; New Forms Fel Rockefeller & Nat Endowment Arts, 90. *Bibliog:* Mick Eaton (auth), Continuing the adventures of Adrian Block, Film Bulletin, London, 2/83; Lucy R Lippard (auth), A Different War, Real Comet Press; Robert Doyle (auth), Artists of Conscience, John Knecht: Iron. *Mem:* Sculpture Space, Utica, NY (bd dir, 92-95 & 2009); NY Found Arts (artists adv bd, 97); Nat Conf on Undergrad Res Bd, 93-99. *Media:* Film, Video. *Publ:* Friction/non-friction cinematograph, winter 91; Muses & fuses: Trama in the Technosphere, artists space catalogue on the work of Les LeVeque; Motion Catalogue, M.W.P.A.I., 2001; Video Rama Catalogue, Clifford Gallery, 2005. *Mailing Add:* PO Box 83 Hamilton NY 13346

KNECHT, ULI
COLLECTOR, DESIGNER
Awards: Named one of Top 200 Collectors, ARTnews mag, 2009-13. *Collection:* Contemporary Pop and German art

KNEDLER, CORY
PRINTMAKER, EDUCATOR, ADMINISTRATOR
Study: Fort Hays State Univ, BFA, 1994; Univ of South Dakota, Vermillion, MFA, 1998. *Exhib:* Work exhibited in over 100 shows, including exhibits at the Mid America Print Conference and the Brussels National Mus, Belgium. *Teaching:* assoc prof art, chair Col of Fine Arts, Univ of South Dakota, 2002-. *Publ:* (auth) Collaborationism, Morningside Col, pg 21, 2010; (auth) A Collaboration in Mixed Media, Sioux City Art Center, pg 12, 2010. *Mailing Add:* University of South Dakota UFA Warren M Lee Ctr for the Fine Arts 179 414 E Clark St Vermillion SD 57069

KNEPPER-DOYLE, VIRGINIA
PAINTER, ENVIRONMENTAL ARTIST
b San Francisco, Calif, Apr 6, 1932. *Study:* Univ Calif, Berkeley, BA, 55; studied oil painting & drawing with Mex, Dominican & Uruguayan artists, 58-71; De Cordova Mus Art Sch, 71-72; Univ Geneva, Switz, printmaking, 75-78. *Work:* Marin Civic Ctr Frank Lloyd Wright Gallery, San Rafael, Calif; WACE USA, San Francisco, Calif; Strathmore Paper Corp. *Comn:* Painting of Washington, DC pres, Bendix Corp, Detroit, Mich, 80; painting of Washington, DC, Rause & Assoc, Philadelphia, Pa, 80; paintings of San Francisco, US Ambassador, Luxembourg, 90; painting of White House, Milk Lobby, Washington, DC. *Exhib:* Bay Arts, Cult Arts Gallery, Belmont, Calif, 89 & 91; Allied Artists Am Ann Exhib, Nat Arts Club, NY, 90; Biennale des Femmes, Le Grand Palais, Paris, France, 90; 4th Int Exhib, Mus Mougins, Mougins, France, 92; Fourth World's Conference on Women, Beijing, China, Sydney, Australia & Washington, DC, 95; and others. *Pos:* Art consult, Hanson Galleries, San Francisco, 83-85; mem, Arts & Open Space Comn, Belvedere, Calif. *Awards:* First Place for Watercolors, Dept State, Washington, 77, Second Place for Drawing, 78. *Mem:* Nat Mus Women Arts; Alliance Women Artists; Allied Artists Am; San Francisco Women Artists; Womens Caucus for Art. *Media:* Oil, Acrylic. *Dealer:* John Doyle 333 Fremont St San Francisco CA 94105. *Mailing Add:* 10 Tamalpais Cir Belvedere CA 94920

KNERR, ERIKA TILDE
PAINTER, MURALIST
b Lancaster, Pa, Oct 2, 1962. *Study:* Tyler/Temple Univ Abroad, Rome Italy, 83; Tyler Sch Art, Philadelphia, BFA, 85; Sch Visual Art, New York, MFA, 88. *Hon Degrees:* Cum Laude. *Comn:* Mural, Cent Park Zoo, Larson Co Environ & Exhibs, NY, 87; mural, Childrens Mus Manhattan, Sam Kornhauser Archit, NY, 90; mural, NY Hall Sci, Sam Kornhauser Archit, NY, 90. *Exhib:* Solo exhibs: Absorption, Lance Fung Gallery, NYC, 1998; Marking Time, Lance Fung Gallery, NYC, Paintings, Dietz Gallery NYC, 2000; The Biological Clock & The Blue Paintings, Old Church Cultural Ctr, Demarest, NJ, 2001; The Mourning After, Lance Fung Gallery, NYC, 2003; FIVE, Lance Fung Gallery, NYC, 1997; A Collection of Actions, Lance Fung Gallery, NYC, 1998; Lost & Found, Ridge Street Gallery at the Cutting Room, NY, 2000; Smell of Fear (group show), Lance Fung Gallery, NY, 2001; Painting is Dead, or is it, Lance Fung Gallery, NY, 2002; Cambio Constante V Arte en Orbita, Paco Simon, Zaragoza, Spain, The Peekskill Project, Lance Fung, Peekskill, NY, 2004. *Pos:* Art dir, New Observations Mag, 90-96; Art Dir, Gen Ed, New Observations Mag, NYC, 8/1989-10/2000; Designer, Fortune Mag, 2000-2006. *Awards:* The Paula Rhodes Mem Award, Sch of Visual Arts, 1988; Artists Grant, Greenpoint Manufacturing & Design Ctr, 2000. *Bibliog:* Ken Johnson (auth), Marking Time, NY Times, 7/7/2000; Joshua Selman (auth), Marking Time, NY Arts Mag, 7/2000; Garza Aguerri (auth), Un laboratorio de arte independiente, el Periodico, Spain, 5/22/2004. *Media:* Painting, Sculpture. *Res:* Contemporary

KNIGHT, DAVID J
GALLERY DIRECTOR, EDUCATOR
b Tulsa, Okla, Apr 12, 1966. *Study:* Ohio Wesleyan Univ, BFA, 88. *Pos:* Cur, Maritain Gallery, Loveland, Ohio, 89-93; gallery dir collections, Northern Ky Univ, 89-; gallery internship, senior exhib. *Teaching:* Instr, Northern Ky Univ, 90-. *Mailing Add:* Northern Ky Univ Dept Art Nunn Dr Highland Heights KY 41099

KNIGHT, ROBERT
DIRECTOR
b Lincoln, Nebr. *Study:* Wesleyan Univ, BA (Art His & Anthropology); Columbia Univ, MA (Studio Art & Art Hist), PhD (Fine Arts & Educ); Harvard Univ, Master. *Pos:* Gallery asst, Charles Cowles Gallery, New York; Cur Art Mus of South Tex, Corpus Christi; sr cur to mus dir, Scottsdale Ctr for Arts, 1986-1999; founding dir, Scottsdale Mus Contemp Art, 1999-2001; exec dir, Yellowstone Art Mus, Billings Mont, 2001-2005; exec dir, Tucson Mus Art, 2005-. *Teaching:* Painting Instr, NYU; drawing instr, Columbia Univ. *Mem:* vpres, Scottsdale Cultural Coun

KNIGHT, WILLIAM
SCULPTOR, PAINTER
b Miami, July 28, 1942. *Study:* NY Studio Sch Painting, Drawing, and Sculpture, 1989-92; Pa Acad Fine Arts, 1990-91; Fleisher Art Meml, Philadelphia, 1992-95; Studies with Mel Leipzig, NJ, Joy Turner & Sylvia Hamers, Washington, DC. *Work:* pvt collections of J Seward, John Johnson, Dr Steven Gecha, Dr June Laval, Elizabeth Snow; Isabel and Glenn Faix, Grace, David Gardellin, Margaret Knott Snow. *Comn:* Wild Youth Resolved, comn by Isobel Faix, New Lisbon, NJ, 2011. *Exhib:* solo exhibs incl Princeton Univ, 1993, Johnson Arts Ctr, Litchfield, Conn, 1994, 1997, 2001, Widener Univ, West Chester, Pa, 1999, The Gallery at Schering-Plough, Madison, NJ, 2001, Ctr Experimental Psychotherapy, NY, 2002, 03, Vt Studio Ctr, Johnson, Vt, 2002, 2005, 2007, R & F Encaustics Gallery, Kingston, NY, 2005, Educational Testing Serv, Princeton, NJ, 2006, Byrdcliffe Art Colony, Woodstock, NY, 2006-11, Knapp Gallery, Philadelphia, Pa, 2011; group exhibs incl Blue Mountain Gallery, NY, 1993, NY Inst Technol, 1994, Johnson Atelier, Hamilton, NJ, 1994, Ann Metro Show, City Without Walls, 1994, 96, 2001, & 2002, Johnson & Johnson Int Hq, 1995, Breaking the Rules, Katonah Mus, Katonah, NY, 2001, Charles Cowles Gallery, NY, 2002, Nat 2002, Cooperstown Art Asn, Cooperstown, NY, 2002, DCCA Open, Del Ctr Contemp Arts, Wilmington, Del, 2002, Perkins Ctr for Arts, Collingswood, NJ, 2009, NY Studio Show, 2009; oil paintings, Delaware Art Mus, 2002-2004; Am Acad Arts & Letters Ann Exhib, 2003; Perkins Ctr for Arts, Moorestown, NJ, 2003; Ellarslie Mus, Trenton, NJ, 2004-2010; Ceres Gallery, NY, 2004; Brodsky Gallery, Princeton, NJ, 2004; Textile Mus, DC, 2011; Mercer Coll, NJ, 2011; Out of Context, Mus Grounds for Sculpure, Hamilton, NJ, 2013. *Pos:* Sculptor & painting full time. *Awards:* Nat Acad Design Fel, 95; Exceptional Merit (top award), City Without Walls, 2000; Dodge Found Fel, Vt Studio Ctr Dodge Fund, 2002 & 2005; Byrdcliffe Arts Colony, 2006, 2008 & 2011; Ellarslie Mus Open Award, 2010. *Mem:* City Without Walls; TAWA; Int Sculpture Ctr. *Media:* Rubber, Aluminum Wire, Encaustic, Oil, Stainless Steel, Paint, Wood. *Mailing Add:* Grant House 309 Wood St Burlington NJ 08016

KNIGIN, MICHAEL JAY
PAINTER, PRINTMAKER
b Brooklyn, NY, Dec 9, 1942. *Study:* Tyler Sch Art, BFA. *Work:* Whitney Mus Art, Cooper Hewitt Mus, Japan Soc, NY; Nat Collection Fine Arts, US Dept State, Washington; Portland Mus Fine Arts, Ore; Mus Modern Art, Mexico City; Taiwan Mus. *Exhib:* Smithsonian Inst, Washington, 69; Albright-Knox Art Gallery, 70; Mus Mod Art Lending Serv, NY, 71; Recent Acquisitions, Whitney Mus Am Art, NY, 71; Sch Worcester Art Mus, Mass, 72; Israel Mus, Jerusalem, 76; Taiwan Mus, 77; Mus Mod Art, NY, 78; Nat Soc Illusr Show, 78-79; US Dept of State, Washington, 79; Foreign Corresp Club, Tokyo, 79; Brooklyn Mus, 83; Guild Hall Mus, EHampton, NY, 90; NASA Gallery, Cape Kennedy, Fla; and many exhibs both US & abroad. *Teaching:* Prof, Pratt Inst, currently. *Awards:* Ford Found Grant, Tamarind Lithography Workshop, 64; Clio Award, Art Direction, 79; NASA Art Team, 89-92. *Bibliog:* Suzanne Boorsch (auth), article, 78, Ann Jarmusch (auth), article, 79, Art News; Judy Goldman (auth), Art in America, 79; Irene Klotz (auth), article, Fla Today, 89. *Mem:* Soc Am Graphic Artists; Jimmy Ernst Artists Alliance. *Media:* All; Painting, Printmaking. *Publ:* Coauth, The Technique of Fine Art Lithography, 70; auth, Local Choice, Pratt Graphics Ctr, 72; The Contemporary Lithographic Workshop Around the World, Van Nostrand, Mexico City News, 85

KNIPPERS, EDWARD
PAINTER, PRINTMAKER
b Oklahoma City, Okla, Sept 7, 1946. *Study:* Pa Acad Fine Arts, 67; Sorbonne, Paris, 68; Asbury Col, Wilmore, Ky, BA, 69; Int Summer Acad Fine Arts, Salzburg, Austria, with Zao Wou-ki, 70, with Otto Elgau & Wolfgang Zeiszner, 76; Univ Tenn, Knoxville, MFA, 73; S W Hayter's Atelier 17, Paris, fel, 80. *Work:* Int Summer Acad Fine Arts, Salzburg, Austria; Tenn Fine Arts Ctr, Cheekwood, Nashville; Vanderbilt Univ, Nashville; Billy Graham Mus, Wheaton, Ill; Univ Okla Mus Art, Norman; The Vatican, Rome, Italy; Cincinnati Art Mus, Cincinnati, Ohio; The Grunewald Print Coll at the Armand Hammer Art Mus, LA. *Exhib:* Solo exhibs, Tenn Fine Arts Ctr, Cheekwood, Nashville, 74, Foxhall Gallery, Washington, DC, 82, 86 & 94, Wheaton Coll, Ill, 83 & 86, Va Mus Fine Arts, 86-87, Univ Okla, Norman, Okla, 90, Roanoke Mus Fine Arts, Va, 90, Touchstone Gallery, Washington, 95, The Cath Univ Am, Washington, DC, 2002, Brehm Ctr, Fuller Seminary, Pasadena, Calif, 2004, Palazzo dei Sette, Orvieto, Italy, 2007, Wash Theological Union, 2007, White Stone Gallery, Philadelphia, 2008 & Concordia Coll, Seward, Nebr, 2009; group exhibs, Los Angeles Co Mus, 85-86, New Expressionism, SE Ctr Contemp Art, Winston-Salem, NC, 87, Greenbelt Invitational, Castle Ashby, Northhampton, Eng, 92, Gallery Sotos, Thessaloniki, Greece, 94, Hope in the City, Union Station, DC, 99; Urban Art Inst, Chattanooga, Tenn, 2000; Like a Prayer: A Jewish and Christian Presence in Contemp Art, (a group invitational), Tyron Ctr for Visual Art, Charlotte, NC, 2001; Narrative in Contemp Art, Foxhole Gallery, Washington, DC, 2005; The Next Generation: Contemp Expressions of Faith, Mus Biblical Art (MOBIA), NYC, 2005; A Broken Beauty: Figuration Narrative & The Transcendent in North Am Art, Laguna Beach Mus Art, 2005. *Awards:* Salzburg Prize, Int Summer Acad Fine Arts, Austria, 76; Va Prize for painting, Va Comn Arts, hon mention, 89 & 90; Arts Am Prog Award, Int Symp, Nea Fokea, Greece, 93; Knippers Award, Christians in Visual Arts, 2005. *Bibliog:* Howard N Fox (auth), Setting the stage, Los Angeles Co Mus Art catalog; Timothy Verdon (auth), Violence & Faith in Art of Edward Knippers, Univ Okla Mus Art; Theodore Prescott (auth), Edward Knippers: A Profile, Image, J Arts & Relig, 93; James Romaine, Objects of Grace, Conversations on Creativity and Faith, Square Halo Books, 2002. *Mem:* Christians in Visual Arts. *Media:* Oil; Intaglio, Block Prints. *Publ:* Reproduction, Life Mag, 12/94; Reproduction, In: Who Do You Say That I Am, MacMillian, NY, 96; auth, New American Paintings, The Open Studio Press, Mass, 96; contribr, It was Good, Making Art to the Glory of God, chapter, The Old Old Story, Sq Halo Books, Md, 2000, revised ed 2007; Rich Copley (auth) The Body of Christ, Lexington HeraldLeader, 3/14/04 (illusr); A Broken Beauty: Figuration, Narrative & Transcendent in North American Art, Eerdmans, 2005. *Mailing Add:* 2408 Washington Blvd Arlington VA 22201-1116

KNOBLER, LOIS JEAN
SCULPTOR, PAINTER
b New York, NY, Feb 2, 1929. *Study:* Syracuse Univ Coll Fine Arts, BFA; Fla State Univ, MA. *Work:* Worcester Mus, Mass; Fla State Univ Mus; St Lawrence Univ, NY. *Exhib:* two-person show, Hillyer Gallery, Smith Col, Northampton, Mass, 76; solo exhib, Atrium Gallery, Univ Conn, Storrs, 83; Am Traditions in Watercolor, Worcester Art Mus, 87; Installation Vigil, Sesnon Art Gallery, Univ Calif, Santa Cruz, 94; Philadelphia Artists Artwork, City Hall, Philadelphia, Pa, 2000; Philadelphia Artists, Moore Coll of Art, Philadelphia, Pa, 01; Philadelphia Int Airport, 2004-05. *Awards:* Greater Hartford Civic Arts Festival Award, 72. *Bibliog:* American Traditions in Watercolor: The Worcester Art Mus Collection, Abbeville Press, 87; Nouvel Object, Design House Publ, Korea, 98; International Survey of Fine Arts and Crafts, 98. *Media:* Miscellaneous Media. *Collection:* Worcester Art Museum, Mass

KNOCK, SARAH
PAINTER
Study: Boston Univ, BFA. *Work:* MBNA; LL Bean; TD Banknorth. *Exhib:* Colby Coll; Penobscot Marine Mus, 2002; Portland Mus Art Biennial, 2003; Farnsworth Mus; Ctr for Maine Contemp Art. *Awards:* Fel, Maine Arts Commn; Artist-in-residence, Carina House, Monhegan Island. *Publ:* Contribr, Paintings of Maine, The Art of Monhegan Island & The Art of Maine in Winter. *Dealer:* Greenhut Galleries 146 Middle St Portland ME 04101. *Mailing Add:* 84 Maquoit Dr Freeport ME 04032

KNODE, MARILU
CURATOR, ADMINISTRATOR
b Calgary, Alta, Can, Aug 4, 1959; US citizen. *Study:* Univ Grenoble, France, 81-82; Univ Kans, Lawrence, BA (art hist), 81; City Coll New York, MA (contemp art), 84. *Collection Arranged:* Tony Cragg Sculpture (mid-career retrospective; with Paul Schimmel), 90; Different Stories (selections from permanent collection), 91; Mapping Histories (group show with Anne Ayres, auth, catalog), 91-92; Personal Inventory, Ellen Birrell & Nick Vaughn (auth, catalog); In Excess (group show), 94; Llyn Foulkes: Between a Rock and a Hard Place, 95. *Pos:* Sr cataloger, Mus Mod Art, New York, 84-88; Assoc cur, Newport Harbor Art Mus, Calif, 89-91, assoc cur, 91-92; independent cur, 91-94; cur, Huntington Beach Art Ctr, 94-96; sr cur, Univ Wis Inst Visual Arts, 97-2003 & Scottsdale Mus Contemp Art, 2003-2007; assoc dir, Ariz State Univ Future Arts Res, 2007-2009; exec dir, Laumeier Sculpture Park, 2009-. *Teaching:* Aronson prof mod & contemp art, Univ Mo, St Louis, 2009-. *Mem:* Am Asn Mus; Coll Art Asn. *Publ:* Contrib, Tony Cragg Sculpture: 1975-1990, 90, auth, Third Newport Biennial: Mapping Histories, 91, Sarah Seager, 93, Newport; auth, Interview with Nayland Blake, Connie Hatch & Kim Dingle, J Contemp Art, Newport, 92; and others. *Mailing Add:* 12580 Rott Rd Saint Louis MO 63127

KNOEBEL, DAVID J
WRITER, INSTALLATION SCULPTURE
b Elysburg, Pa, July 19, 1949. *Study:* Yale Univ, with William Bailey, BA, 72; Skowhegan Sch, with William Stankiewicz, 72; also with George Sugarman, 79-82. *Work:* Indianapolis Mus Art. *Exhib:* Pool Proj, Artist's Space, NY, 80; Painting & Sculpture Today, Indianapolis Mus Art, 80; solo exhib, Baruch Col, State Univ NY, 82; Gold Show, Mus Mod Art, NY, 82; Smart Art, Harvard Univ, 85; Primo Piano, Rome, Italy, 86; Pa Acad Fine Arts, Philadelphia, 96; Infos 2000, Ljubljana, Slovenia, 2000; Festival Int de Linguagem Electronica, Sao Paulo, Brazil, 2000; Web3D/VRML 2000 Conf, Monterey, Calif, 2000; Carmen Conde Anthology, Cartagena, Spain, 2006; Postmeaning, Facebook, 2011. *Teaching:* Vis artist, Marymount Int Sch, Rome, Italy, 85. *Awards:* Semi Finalist, Joyland Screenplay, Am Zoetrope Screenplay Competition, 2008; Quarter Finalist, ASA Screenplay Competition, 2009; Quarter Finalist, The Road to Success, Bluecat Screenplay Competition, 2009. *Bibliog:* Lisa Russ Spaar (auth), Lines Online: Poetry Journals on the Web, Chronicles of Higher Education, 11/6/2003; Roberto Simanowski (auth), Concrete Poetry in Digital Media, Dichtung-Digital, 3/2004; Rita Raley (auth), Reading Spaces, Iowa Web Rev, 9/2006; Lori Emerson (auth), A Hyperspace Poetics, or, Words in SPace: Digital Poetry Through Ezra Poudn's Vorticism, Confituration, 2009; Arielle Saiber, Henry S Turner (auths), Mathematics & the Imagination: A Brief Introduction, Configurations; Roberto Simanowski (auth), Digital Art and Meaning, Univ Minn Press, 2011; Leonard Floret (auth), Postmeaning by David Knoebel, ilovepoetry.com, 2013. *Media:* Misc Media. *Publ:* auth catalog statement, Light, Islip Art Mus, 82; Words in Space, Ylem, 5-6/99; Euclid: Composing with Words in Space, Web Art & Poetry, 7/2000. *Mailing Add:* PO Box 312 Elysburg PA 17824

KNOLL, ISABEL A GIAMPIETRO See Giampietro, Isabel Antonia

KNOWLES, ALISON
PERFORMANCE ARTIST, PRINTMAKER
b New York, NY, Apr 29, 1933. *Study:* Middlebury Coll, Vt, 52-54; Pratt Inst, BFA, 56, Manhattan Sch Printing, 62; studied with Josef Albers, Rihard Lindner & Adolph Gottlieb. *Hon Degrees:* Hon Doctorate Fine Arts, 2003; hon doctorate Columbia Coll, Chicago, Ill. *Work:* Mus of Mod Art Bk Collection, NY; Oakland Mus, Calif; Jean Brown Archives, Tyringham, Mass. *Comn:* The Identical Lunch (two self-portraits), comn by Alberto Zopellari, 77; Leone D'oro (silkscreen ed), comn by Francesco Conz, 78. *Exhib:* Coeurs Volants, with Marcel Duchamp, 67; The Big Book, Mus Contemp Art, Chicago, 67; Crazy Publishers, Guggenheim Mus, 69; A House of Dust, Cal Arts Campus; SumTime, Everson Mus, Syracuse, NY, 74; 03 23 03, Montreal Mus Fine Arts, Can, 77; Walker Art Ctr, Minneapolis, Minn, 80; solo exhibs, Ruth & Marvin Sackner Archive, Miami Beach, Fla, 86, Unique Cloth & Paper Works, Nordyllands Kunstmuseum, Aalborg, Denmark, Finger Book 2 & Palimpsest Prints, 87-88, Seven Indian Moons, 90, Emily Harvey Gallery, NY, Indigo Island, Stadt Galerie, Saarbrucken, Ger, 94 & Basta Fagioli, Unimedia Galerie, Genova, Italy, 94, Sea Change and Footnotes, Emily Harvey Gallery, NY, 2000, Gallery 400, Chicago, Sound and Vision, Odense Performance Festival, Denmark, 2001, Time Samples, Emily Harvey Found, Venice, Italy, 2006, plus others; Women on the Verge, Wimmer Gallery, NY, 95; Retrospective, Indigo Island (with catalog), Stadtgalerie Saarbrucken, Ger, Ctr Contemp Art, Warsaw, Poland & Museet for Samtidskunst, Roskilde, Denmark, 95; Full of Beans, Bremen, Ger, 96; Queensland Art Gallery, Brisbane, Australia, 97; Out of Actions, Mus Contemp Art, Los Angeles, Calif, 98; Fraven Mus, Bonn, Ger, 98; Caterina Gualco Gallery, Genova, Italy, 98; Two person exhib with Ann Noel, In & Out the Window, Performance Lentil Throw, Fluxust Mus, Poland, 2002; Contemp Selection with performances of The Identical Lunch, Mus Mod Art, 2011. *Pos:* full residency, Int Fellow, Radcliff Univ. *Teaching:* Dir graphics lab, Calif Inst of the Arts, Valencia, 70-72; Fachhochschule, Hamburg, Ger, 94-. *Awards:* Guggenheim Fel, 68; Nat Endowment Arts, 81 & 85; Travel Grant, Deutscher Acad, Ger, 83; Teaching Residency, Sommerakademie für Bildende Kunst, Salzburg; Distinguished Artist Award for Lifetime Achievement, Coll Art Asn, 2003. *Bibliog:* Tom Johnson (auth), Shoes, shoestrings & Gertrude Stein, Village Voice, 78; Kristine Stiles (auth), Something Fishy, 93; Robert C Morgan (auth), Ather the Deluge, 93. *Mem:* Printed Ed; The Performance Workshop. *Media:* Serigraphy, Silkscreen, Cyanotype. *Publ:* Auth, spoken Text, Left Hand Bks; Natural Assemblages and the True Crow, Visual Studies Workshop Press, Rochester, NY, 80; A Bean Concordance, Printed Eds, 83; coauth (with George Brecht), The Red, The Green, The Yellow, The Black and The White, Brussels Ed, Lebeer-Hossman, 83; Bread & Water, Left Hand Books, 94; Book Footnotes, Granary Books, NY, 2000; auth, Time Samples, Granary Books, 2006; Plah Plah Pli Plah, Sara Ranchouse Publ, 2009. *Mailing Add:* 122 Spring St New York NY 10012

KNOWLES, RICHARD H
PAINTER, EDUCATOR
b Evanston, Ill, June 29, 1934. *Study:* Grinnell Col; Northwestern Univ, Evanston, BA, 56; Ind Univ, MA, 61, studied with James McGarrell, Leon Golub & Albert Elson. *Work:* Ind Univ, Bloomington; Ark State Univ; State of Tenn Collection, Reece Mus, Nashville; Brooks Mem Mus Art, Memphis, Tenn. *Comn:* Tuquois Inn, Turcs &

Cacos, 80; Harrah's Inn & Casino, E Chicago, IN, 2001. *Exhib:* Ten in Tennessee, Cheekwood Mus, Nashville, 86-87; Solo shows, Loyola Univ, New Orleans, 87 & Forest Project, W Tenn Regional Art Ctr, Humbolt, 98; Six Americans, Ark Art Ctr, Little Rock, 64; 50 States Exhib & Tour, Rockford Art Asn & Am Fedn Arts, 65-67; Am Painters & Sculptors, Colgate Univ, 75; Edinburgh Arts Festival, Scotland, 80; Two-person show, Memphis Ctr Contemp Art, 88; Arts in the Park, Memphis Brooks Mus Art, Fla, 98. *Pos:* Pres, Mid-Am Col Art Assoc, 86, 88; Publ, Untitled (art jour), currently. *Teaching:* Asst prof art, Univ Ark, 61-65; prof art, Memphis State Univ, 66-99, emer, 99-. *Awards:* Best Entry for Ark Artist, Delta Ann, 61 & 62; Painting Prize, Mid-South Exhib, 72. *Mem:* Sierra Club; Mid Am Coll Art Asn. *Media:* Acrylic, Oil. *Specialty:* Jay Etkin Gallery: painting, drawing, photog. *Interests:* Geology, Paleontology; Hiking; Writing. *Collection:* State Collections often & AR, Harrah's, Memphis Brooks Mus; Many corporate collections. *Dealer:* Jay Etkins Gallery Memphis. *Mailing Add:* 1400 NW Marshall St Unit 631 Portland OR 97203

KNOWLES, SUSAN WILLIAMS
CURATOR, CRITIC

b Washington, DC, Sept 1, 1952. *Study:* Vanderbilt Univ, BA, 74, MA, 86; Peabody Coll, MLS, 75; Middle Tenn State Univ, PhD, 2011. *Exhib:* An Enduring Legacy; ET Wickham: A Dream unguarded; Two paths to progress: WEB DuBois, Charles S Johnson and the New Negro Arts movement, 2001; Red Grooms: Selections from the Graphic Work, traveling show, 2001-05; Traveling shows, The River Inside: Photographs by John Guider, 2008-2012, Tranquil Power: The Art of Perle Fine, 2009. *Collection Arranged:* A C Webb: The Skyscraper Drawings Architectural Perspectives (auth, catalog), 86; Spirit & Form: William Edmondson & Puryear Mims, 88. *Pos:* Registrar & art librn, Cheekwood Mus Art, Tenn, 81-85, cur collections, 85-87; visual arts coordr, Metrop Nashville Arts Comn, Tenn, 87-92; cur, Tenn Exhib, Nat Mus Women Arts, 92-94 & Arts at the Airport, Nashville Int Airport, 94-2005; acting gallery dir, Mid Tenn State Univ, Murfreesboro; producer, Art Feature, Nashville Pub Radio, 2003-; rsch fel, Ctr Historical Preservation, Mid Tenn State Univ. *Teaching:* Instr, 20th century art hist, O'More Coll Design, 92; gallery practices, Mid Tenn State Univ. *Awards:* Fel: US Capitol Historical Soc & Ctr for Historic preserv; Middle Tenn State Univ; grant: Tenn Arts Comn. *Bibliog:* contrib ed, Art Papers 84-2007. *Mem:* Coll Art Asn; Am Asn Mus; Am Hist Asn; Nat Coun Pub Hist. *Res:* Tennessee art & architecture; contemporary artists. *Publ:* Tenn Ed, Art papers, 84-; revs, New Art Examiner, 85-92; auth, Signatures Section: Center Stage Mag, 87-88; Living Artists: Four Installations, Knoxville Mus Art, 90; Pinkney Herbert (exhib catalog), Univ Little Rock, Ark; monthly art column, Nashville Scene, 91-94; An Enduring Legacy, 2001 & Art of Tenn, 2003, Frist Ctr Visual Arts; Two Hundred Years of the Arts in Tenn, 2004; auth, Tennessee Encyclopedia History & Culture; auth, Encyclopedia of Southern Culture; auth, Encyclopedia of Appalachia. *Mailing Add:* S W Knowles & Assocs 4225 Harding Pike Suite 507 Nashville TN 37205

KNOWLTON, DANIEL GIBSON
RESTORER, CONSERVATOR

b Washington, DC, 1922. *Study:* With Marian U M Lane, Washington; Boston Arts & Crafts, grad. *Work:* Univ Chicago Libr; Brown Univ Libr, Providence, RI; Dumbarton Oaks Libr, Washington; Harvard Univ Libr; Cornell Univ Libr; John Carter Brown Libr, Providence, RI; John Hay Libr, Providence, RI. *Comn:* Epistle (gold & leather binding), Grace Church, Providence, 56; The Anguish of the Jews (gold & leather binding), comn by Ciro Scotti, Vatican Libr, 68; Comn to rebind 7 leather book shelves, Fall River Soc, 2000. *Exhib:* Hand bookbinding exhibs, Corcoran Gallery Art, 58; solo exhibs, Bristol Hist Soc RI, 69, RI Sch Design, 71 & 75 & Ctr Bk Arts, NY, 75; Rockefeller Libr, Brown Univ, 81 & 91; Providence Hist Soc, 81 & 91; and others. *Pos:* Bookbinder, Brown Univ, 56-92; owner & bookbinder, Daniel G Knowlton Co, Longfield Studio, Bristol, RI, 74-98 & 2001-2007, 2012, & 2013. *Teaching:* Instr bookbinding, Daniel G Knowlton Co Longfield Studio Home Bindery, 74-96 & 98-2007, 2011. *Bibliog:* Yankee Damon (auth), article in Yankee Mag, 62; Ann Banks (auth), article in Brown Alumni Monthly, 71; Interview, Educ TV 36, Providence, RI, 74 & TV News WJAR-TV, 90; Owen Hartford (auth), A Visit with Dan Knowlton (DVD), Bookbinder, 9/2004. *Mem:* Miniature Painters, Sculptors & Gravers Soc, Washington. *Media:* Bookbinding. *Publ:* Guild of Bk Workers Newsletter (mem profile), No 172, 8, June 2007. *Mailing Add:* 1202 Hope St Bristol RI 02809

KNOWLTON, GRACE FARRAR
SCULPTOR, PHOTOGRAPHER

b Buffalo, NY, Mar 15, 1932. *Study:* Smith Col, BA (art), 54; Columbia Univ Teachers Col, MA (art educ), 81. *Work:* Metrop Mus Art, NY; Newark Mus, NJ; Corcoran Gallery Art; Houston Mus Fine Arts; Victoria & Albert Mus, London, Eng; Brooklyn Mus, NY. *Exhib:* Solo exhibs, Henri Gallery, Washington, DC, 73, Razor Gallery, NY, 74, Parsons-Dreyfuss Gallery, NY, 79, Aaron Berman Gallery, 81, Susan Harder Gallery, 83, Twining Gallery, 85-86 & 87, Witkin Gallery, 86 & 87, Bill Bace Gallery, 89, Smith Coll Mus Art, Mass, 92; Aldrich Art Mus, Ridgefield, Conn, 86; M-13, NY, 92 & 94; Katonah Mus, 93; Hirschl & Adler Mod, 95 & 97; Bates Coll Mus, 2002; Neuberger Mus, 2002; Collaborative Concepts Gallery, NY, 2003; John Davis Gallery, 2004; Van Brunt Gallery, Beacon, NY, 2006; Whirlwind Gallery, NY, 2006; Lesley Heller Gallery, NY, 2008; Ward Pound Ridge Reserve, 2009. *Pos:* Asst to cur graphic arts dept, Nat Gallery Art, Washington, 54-57. *Teaching:* Instr art, Arlington Co Pub Schs, 57-60; Pratt, 2000; Art Students League, 98-2005; William Patterson univ, 2003; Natl Acad Art, 2001; instr, Mixed Media, Art Students League, NY, 2006-2010. *Awards:* Pub Art Fund Inc, 87; Outdoor Installation Proj Grant, EHampton Ctr Contemp Art, 89; Grant: Nadine Russel Endowed Chr, Louisiana State Univ, 2003. *Bibliog:* Three Spheres by Grace Knowlton (video), Mus Outdoor Arts, Denver, Colo, 89; Christine Liotta (auth), Sculpture: A Natural Order, Hudson River Mus, Yonkers, 9-10/91; Roberta Smith (auth), NY Times, 4/24/92. *Mem:* Century Asn. *Media:* Steel, Copper, Concrete. *Publ:* Auth, Grace Knowlton, Layers and Traces (exhib catalog), Smith Coll Mus Art, 4-8/92; Sawhorses, Mixed Media, 2010. *Dealer:* Lesley Heller, New York, NY. *Mailing Add:* 67 Ludlow Ln Palisades NY 10964

KNOWLTON, JONATHAN
PAINTER, EDUCATOR

b New York, NY, Feb 22, 1937. *Study:* Yale Univ, BA; Univ Calif, Berkeley, MA. *Work:* Mus Mod Art, NY; Victoria & Albert Mus, London; Univ Calif Art Mus, Berkeley; La Jolla Mus Fine Art, Calif; Oakland Mus, Calif; Montreal Mus Fine Arts, Ont. *Exhib:* Survey '68, Montreal Mus Fine Arts, 68; 17th Nat Print Exhib, Brooklyn Mus, 70; Edmonton Art Gallery, 72; John Bolles Gallery, San Francisco, 73; Latitude 53, Edmonton, 75; Front Gallery, Edmonton, Alta; Vik Gallery, Edmonton, 89; Edmonton Art Gallery, 93; Fran Willis Gallery, Victoria, BC, 93. *Teaching:* Assoc prof drawing & painting, Univ Alta, 66-90. *Awards:* Purchase Award, Los Angeles Co Mus Art, 61; Fulbright Grant, 64-65; Can Coun Grant, 68-69. *Bibliog:* Phylis Matousek (auth), Knowlton travels many roads, Edmonton J, 11/14/84; The Nuclear Glare Has Its Own Beauty in A-Bomb, Soc, 89; Elizabeth Beauchamp (auth), Knowlton retrospective sheds light on local talent, Edmonton J, 6/1/90. *Media:* Acrylic, Oil, Watercolor. *Publ:* Auth, Riding the mainstream of modern imperatives, Interface, Vol 2, No 9, 11/79. *Dealer:* Fran Willis Gallery, Victoria BC

KNOX, ELIZABETH
PAINTER

b June 13, 1944. *Study:* Parsons Sch Design; New Sch Social Res; Art Students League scholar, with Robert Beverly Hale, 74. *Comn:* Athletic mural, Unity Col, Maine, 94. *Exhib:* Biennial Contmp Am Painting & Sculpture, Whitney Mus Am Art, NY, 75; Maine Maritime Flatworks Exhib, Reed Gallery, Univ Maine, Presque Isle, 95; Summer in Maine, Francesca Anderson Fine Art, Lexington, Mass, 95; December Show, O'Farrell Gallery, Brunswick, Maine, 95; Five Artists, Five Points of View, Round Top Ctr Arts, Damariscotta, Maine, 96; Contemp Master Drawings, Atrium Gallery, Campus Lewiston-Auburn Col, Maine, 96; Solo exhib, More than Meets the Eye, O'Farrell Gallery, Brunswick, Maine, 97; Tenth Anniversary Exhib, Round Top Ctr Arts, 98. *Teaching:* Instr painting & drawing, Round Top Ctr Arts, Damariscotta Maine, 91-. *Bibliog:* Philip Isaacson (auth), In Lewiston, a search for technique in the service of meaning, Maine Sunday Telegram 10/96; Jane Falla (auth), Elizabeth Knox, Digging for deeper meaning, Times Record, 11/96; Words and images, Lit Publ, Univ Southern Maine, 98. *Mem:* Golden Key Nat Hon Soc. *Media:* Oil, Graphite

KNOX, GEORGE
HISTORIAN, WRITER

b London, Eng, 1922. *Study:* Courtauld Inst Art, Univ London, BA, MA & PhD. *Hon Degrees:* Univ Victoria, DLitt, 96. *Collection Arranged:* Tiepolo Bicentenary Exhib, Fogg Art Mus, Cambridge, Mass, 70; Tiepolo Drawings, Staatsgalerie, Stuttgart, 70; Tiepolo: Tecnica e Immaginazione, Palazzo Ducale, Venice, 79; Piazzetta: Disegni, Incisioni, Libri, Manoscritti, Fondazione Giorgio Cini, Venice, 83; Piazzetta, A Tercentenary Exhibition, Nat Gallery Art, Washington, DC, 83; 18th Century Venetian Art in Canadian Collections, Vancouver Art Gallery, 89; Giandomenico Tiepolo: Disegni Del Mondo, Udine, Castello & Bloomington, Ind Univ Art Mus, 96-97. *Teaching:* Instr, Slade Sch Art, Univ London, 50-52, King's Coll, Newcastle, Univ Durham, 52-58 & Queen's Univ, Ont, 69-70; prof fine arts & head dept, Univ BC, 70-87, prof emer. *Awards:* Guggenheim Fel, 2000. *Mem:* Can Comn Hist Art; Comite Int d'Histoire de l'Art; Ateneo Veneto. *Interests:* Venetian 18th century art, particularly the drawings of the Tiepolo family, Piazzetta & Pellegrini. *Publ:* Domenico Tiepolo: Raccolta di Teste, Udine, 70; Giambattista & Domenico Tiepolo, The Chalk Drawings, Oxford, 80; Robert Lehman Collection VI: Italian 18th Century Drawings, New York, 87; Piazzetta, Oxford, 92; Pellegrini, Oxford, 95. *Mailing Add:* 3495 W 11th Ave Vancouver BC V6R 2K1 Canada

KNOX, GORDON
MUSEUM DIRECTOR

Pos: Founding dir, Civitella Ranieri Found, Italy; artistic dir, Montalvo Arts Ctr, Saratoga, Calif & founding dir Lucas Artists Program; dir, Ariz State Univ Art Mus, 2010-. *Mailing Add:* ASU Art Museum 10th St & Mill Ave PO Box 872911 Tempe AZ 85287-2911

KNUDSEN, CHRISTIAN
PAINTER, PHOTOGRAPHER

b June 3, 1945; Danish citizen. *Study:* Sir George Williams Univ, BFA, 69. *Work:* Mus Fine Arts & Musee D'Art Contemporain, Montreal; Art Gallery Ont, Toronto; Vancouver Art Gallery, BC; Can Coun Art Bank, Ottawa. *Comn:* Painting, Govt Can Post Off, Que, 78. *Exhib:* Concordia Univ, Montreal, 74; Vancouver Art Gallery, 78; Montreal Mus, Que, 79; Glenbow Mus, Calgary, 80; Agnes Etherington Art Ctr, Kingston, Ont, 81. *Bibliog:* David Burnett (auth), Knudsen at Godard, Art Am, 1/78; David Burnett (auth), Christian Knudsen, Parachute No 11, summer 78; Robert Swain (auth), Christian Knudsen, Agnes Etherington Art Ctr, Kingston, Ont, 81. *Media:* Mixed Media; Silkscreen. *Dealer:* Paul Kuhn Fine Arts 722 11th Ave SW Calagary Alberta T2R 0E4 Canada. *Mailing Add:* 3827 Drolet St Montreal PQ H2W 2L3 Canada

KNUTSON, MICHAEL
PAINTER, EDUCATOR

b Evertt, Wash, May 1, 1951. *Study:* Univ Wash, BFA (magna cum laude), 1972; Yale Univ Sch Art, MFA, 1975. *Work:* Portland Art Mus, Ore; Everett Pub Libr, Wash; Southwest Was Med Ctr, Vancouver; Ore Health Sciences Univ, Portland; Microsoft Corp. *Exhib:* Solo exhibs, Florence Wilcox Gallery, Swarthmore Coll, 1976, Vollum Gallery, Reed Coll, Portland, 1982, 1985, 1989, 2004, Ronna B hoffman Gallery, Lewis & Clark Coll, Portland, 2006; Oregon Biennial, Portland Art Mus, Ore, 1998; Breaking Down the Barries, Orange County Ctr for Contemp Art, Santa Monica, 1999; Unexpected Watercolors, Lee Ctr Gallery, Seattle Univ, 2007; Pacifist Potential, Carnegie Art Ctr, Walla Walla, Wash, 2008; Am Acad Arts & Letts Invitational, New York, 2010. *Teaching:* Instr & asst prof, Swarthmore Coll, 1975-82; prof art, Reed Coll, 1982-. *Awards:* Individual Artist Grant, Nat Endowment for the Arts, 1982; Juror's Award, Ore Biennial, Portland Art Mus, 1985, 1999; Betty Bowen Meml Spl

Recognition Award, Seattle Art Mus, 1995. *Bibliog:* Delores Tarzan (auth), Exhibit features painted sculpture, Seattle Times, 7/12/1985; Randy Gragg (auth), Cornering variations on an abstract theme, The Oregonian, 1/4/2001; Holland Cotter (auth), GeoMetrics, NY Times, 12/7/2007. *Dealer:* Blackfish Gallery Portland OR; Greg Kucera Gallery Seattle WA. *Mailing Add:* Reed College 3203 SE Woodstock Blvd Portland OR 97202-8199

KNUTSSON, ANDERS
PAINTER, CURATOR
b Malmo, Sweden, May 8, 1937; US citizen. *Study:* Malmo Tech Col, Sweden, BSME, 67; Cincinnati Art Acad, 69. *Work:* Albright-Knox Art Gallery; Arkivmuseet, Lund, Sweden; Fleming Mus, Univ Vt, Burlington; Moderna Museet, Stockholm, Sweden; Univ Maine Mus Art, Orono; Williams Coll Mus Art, Williamstown, Mass; and many other pub & pvt collections. *Exhib:* Solo exhibs, Helen Day Art Ctr, Stowe, Vt, 87, Keith Green Gallery, NY, 87, Gates of Light, Williams Coll Mus Art, Williamstown, (catalog) Mass, 88, Bennett Siegel Gallery, NY, 90, edition Hylteberga, Skurup, Sweden, 90, Lightscapes, Univ Maine Mus Art, Orono, (catalog) 90, Stephen Solovy Gallery, Chicago, & Ami Gallery, Seoul, Korea, (catalog), 93; retrospective (catalog), Gray Art Gallery East Carolina Univ, Greenville, NC, 95; Roger Smith Gallery, NY, 95; Samuel Zacks Gallery, York Univ, Toronto, Can, 96; Manif (catalog), Art Fair, Seoul, Korea, 96; Hishult Konsthalle, Sweden, 98; Ystad Art Mus, Sweden, 99; Karlshamn Konshall, Sweden, 2000; Gallery AMI, Seoul, 2001; Merce Cunningham Studio, NY, 2002; Gallery 718, Brooklyn, NY, 2003; St Thomas Aquinas Col, NY, 2004; Art Downtown, Deutsche Bank, NY, 2004; Gallery U, Cleveland, OH, 2005; Rosewood Gallery, Kettering, OH, 2005; Cool New York Dance Festival, NY, 2005; Keutler Int Drawing Center, Brooklyn, NY, 2006. *Collection Arranged:* res cur, Yolélé Art Gallery, Brooklyn, NY, 2004; Clinton Hill Art Festival, Brooklyn, NY, 2004-2005; chief cur, Magnolia Tree Earth Center, Brooklyn, NY, 2005-2006. *Awards:* Liquitex Artist of the Month, 2003. *Bibliog:* Carlo McCormick (auth), Anders Knutsson and the Promise of Light, Anders Knutsson Lightscapes/Ljusskap, Univ Maine Mus Art, 90; Barnaby Ruhe (auth), Another Conceptual Category, Anders Knutsson: Lightscapes/Ljusskap, Univ Maine Mus Art, 90; Michael Duffy (auth), Anders Knutsson: The Experience of Light, E Carolina Univ, 95; and many others. *Media:* Oil, Wax, Acrylic, Pencil. *Mailing Add:* 93 Lexington Ave Brooklyn NY 11238

KOBASLIJA, AMER
PAINTER
b Luka, Bosnia, 1975. *Study:* Ringling Sch Art & Design, Fla, BFA, 2003; Montclair Sch Arts, NJ, MFA, 2005. *Exhib:* Solo exhibs include Cummer Mus Arts & Gardens, Jacksonville, Fla, 1999, Pecci Gallery, Jacksonville, 2001, Mussallem Gallery, Jacksonville, 2002, Crossley Gallery, Sarasota, Fla, 2003, Haskell Gallery, Jacksonville, 2003, Finlea Gallery, Montclair, NJ, 2004, Jaxon House, Venice, Calif, 2006, George Adams Gallery, New York, 2006, Galerie RX, Paris, 2007; group exhibs include George Adams Gallery, 2006, Inside/Outside, 2007; Joan Mitchell Grant Recipients, Cue Art Found, New York, 2006; Private Viewing, Leroy Neiman Ctr Gallery, Columbia Univ, New York, 2007. *Awards:* Paul Shields Award, 2004; Joan Mitchell Found Grant, 2005; Pollock-Krasner Found Grant, 2007. *Dealer:* George Adams Gallery 525 W 26th St New York NY 10001. *Mailing Add:* 1407 Silver St Jacksonville FL 32206-2490

KOBAYASHI, HISAKO
PAINTER
b Tokyo, Japan, Jan 23, 1946. *Study:* Univ Hawaii, BFA, 78; Pratt Inst, MFA, 80. *Exhib:* Brooklyn Artists, Brooklyn Mus, NY, 79, Walsh Gallery, Chicago, Ill, 97, Alex Gallery, Washington, DC, 97 & 98, Ise Art Found, NY, 98; one-person exhibs, DTW Gallery, NY, 94, Walter Wickiser Gallery, NY, 94 & 95, Cercles Des Collectioneurs D'Art Contemporain, Paris, France, 94, Galerie Ovadia, Nancy, France, 95, Walsh Gallery, Chicago, 96 & Masur Mus Art Monroe, La, 96; Southeby's Auction, Minn, 94; Ise Art Found, NY, 95; Roger Smith Gallery, NY, 95; James Michener Mus, Pa, 97; Hammond Mus, Salem, NY, 98; State Mus Munhen, Ger, 99. *Teaching:* Asst, Pratt Inst, 80. *Awards:* Semi finalist, CAPS Grants Awards, New York State, 81, 82. *Bibliog:* Robert Hicks (auth), Shape provides first idea, Villager, 3/94; Yoshiki Yamamoto (auth), Abstraction and the Contemporary World, Chugai Nippo, 10/94; New York art scene, Asahi Art News, 12/95. *Media:* Oil, All Media. *Mailing Add:* 55 Great Jones St New York NY 10012

KOBER, ALFRED JOHN
EDUCATOR, SCULPTOR
b Great Bend, Kans, June 3, 1937. *Study:* Dodge City Coll, AA, 58; Ft Hays State Coll, BS (art), 60 & MS (art), 66. *Work:* Boise Gallery Art, Idaho; Ft Hays State Col. *Comn:* Two outdoor sculptures, Boise State Univ, 71 & 72; stainless steel sculpture, Bank of Idaho, Boise, 72; welded steel sculpture, Boise Cascade World Hq, Boise, 74; sculpture for Veterans Park, Boise, comn by Idaho Veterans, 76; stainless steel sculpture, Atlantic Richfield, Denver, 78; altar pieces, Central Lutheran Church, Yakima, Wash; restored two historic sculptures, City Payette, Idaho. *Exhib:* Ann Exhib Northwest Artists, Seattle, Wash, 69-74; Mainstreams, 72 & 77; LaGrange Nat Competition II, Ga, 75; 21st Ann Drawing & Small Sculpture Show, Ball State Univ, 75. *Teaching:* Instr art, Hutchinson Community Jr Coll, Kans, 66-68; assoc prof sculpture, Boise State Univ, 68-78, assoc prof, 78, prof, 79 & 99, retired. *Awards:* Purchase Award, Grover M Hermann Fine Arts Ctr, Marietta, 72; Award of Excellence, Marietta Coll, 72; Award, Ball State Univ, 75. *Mem:* Boise Art Asn. *Media:* Mixed. *Res:* Experimental sculpture techniques & materials; Emphasis metal casting. *Interests:* Metal engraving; custom jewelry. *Publ:* Art in Public Places. *Mailing Add:* 2024 Crystal Way Boise ID 83706-4346

KOCAR, GEORGE FREDERICK
PAINTER, ILLUSTRATOR
b Cleveland, Ohio, Sept 28, 1948. *Study:* Cuyahoga Community Coll, Cleveland, Ohio, AA, 75; Cleveland State Univ, Cleveland, Ohio; BA, 77; Syracuse Univ, NY, MFA, 83. *Work:* Cleveland State Univ; Cent Mo State Univ, Warrensburg; Metro Gen Hosp, Cleveland, Ohio; Butler Inst Am Art, Youngstown, Ohio; Ashland Univ, Ohio; Rock and Roll Hall of Fame Mus, Cleveland, Ohio; Billy Ireland Cartoon Mus, Ohio State Univ, Columbus, Oh. *Comn:* Am Greetings Corp. *Exhib:* Butler Mid-Year Exhib, Butler Inst Art, Youngstown, Ohio, 81-85, 87, 94, 96, 98-99 & 2001-2002, 2011, 2012; solo exhibs, Central Mo State Univ, Warrensburg, 87, Lake Erie Coll, Painesville, Ohio, 92, Studio Gallery, Cleveland, Ohio, 95, Lakeland Community Coll, Kirtland, Ohio, 98, Case Western Reserve Univ, Cleveland, Ohio, 99, Ohio State Univ, Newark, 2004 & Mount Vernon Nazarene Univ, Ohio, 2004; Double Take, Firelands Asn Visual Arts, Oberlin, Ohio, 92; Creative Perception, Agora Gallery, New York, 94; Nat Juried Exhib, Phoenix Gallery, New York, 96; Illustrators Only, Visual Club, New York, 96; Art Space, Lima, Ohio, 2000; Montserrat, New York, 2000; Ashtabula Arts Ctr, Ohio, 2001; Kocar/Benvenuto, Roy G BV, Columbus, Ohio, 2003; Ohio State Univ, Newark, 2004; Mt Vernon Nazerene Univ, Vernon, Ohio, 2004; Fitton Ctr for Arts, Hamilton, Ohio, 2005; Astabula Arts Ctr, Ohio, 2006; Beck Ctr, Lakewood, Ohio; Gallery 5400, Cleveland, 2007; KoCarlson, The Art Gallery, Willoughby, Ohio, 2008; The Art Gallery, Willoughby, 2009; Watercolor USA, Springfield, Mo, 2009; West Liberty Univ, W Va, 2011; Arts Collinwood, Cleveland, Oh, 2012; Cuyanoga Comm Coll E, Beachwood, Oh, 2012. *Pos:* Pres, Flying Banana Studio, Bay Village, Ohio; master designer, Am Greeting Corp, 84-2003. *Teaching:* Part-time fac, Akron Univ, Ohio, Cleveland Inst Art, Ashland Univ, Ohio & Cuyahoga Community Coll, Cleveland. *Awards:* Jurors Award, Butler Mid-Year Exhib, Youngstown, Ohio, 85 & 99; Best of Show, Ohio State Expo Ctr, Columbus, 99; Award, Soc Graphic Artists, New York, 2002; 1st in Category, Boston Mills Artfest, Peninsula, Ohio, 2009; Award of excellence in painting, Syracuse Art Festival, NY, 2008. *Bibliog:* Cecily Firestein (auth), George Kocar High Energy Paintings, Manhattan Arts Int, 9-10/93; Jorge Santiago (auth), Creative perception, Artspeak, 9/94; Cindy Barber (auth), article, Cleveland Plain Dealer, 12/14/98; New Art Int, Book Art Press, New York, Vol VII, 2001-2002; Jerelle Kraus (auth), All the Art That's Fit to Print (And Some That Wasn't), Columbia Press, 2008; Studio Visit, vol 6, Open Studio Press, 2009; Splash 12, Northlight Pub, 2011. *Mem:* Saving & Preserving Arts & Cult Environ, Cleveland, Ohio; Northeast Ohio Illustration Soc (pres); Artist Archives of Western Reserve; Cleveland Art Found; Mus Contemp Art, Cleveland. *Media:* Acrylic, Watercolor. *Publ:* Illusr, Us against them, NY Times, 83; Is That You Laughing Comrade?, Citadel Press, 86; auth-illusr, Vacationing with a bunch of Maine-iacs, Cleveland Plain Dealer, 86; auth, Painting the world at large & Fine Art & Illustration-Bridging the Gap, 86, Artist's Mag; illusr, Cooking with Humor, 90. *Dealer:* Tregoning & Co Cleveland Ohio; Fuego 718 Brooklyn New York. *Mailing Add:* 24213 Lake Rd Bay Village OH 44140

KOCH, ARTHUR ROBERT
PAINTER, EDUCATOR
b Meriden, Conn, Feb 26, 1934. *Study:* Wesleyan Univ; RI Sch Design, with John Frazier, BFA, 57; Univ Wash, MFA, 61. *Exhib:* Art: USA: 59, NY; US Info Agency Painting Show, Europe, 62-66; Tex Painting & Sculpture of the 20th Century, 70-71. *Teaching:* Instr studio, Univ NH, 57-59; instr studio, El Centro Col, Dallas, 66-70; head dept studio art, Meadows Sch Arts, Southern Methodist Univ, 70-, assoc prof design & painting, 78-. *Awards:* Ft Worth Art Ctr Award, 70. *Mem:* Dallas Area Artists Equity Asn (pres, 70-71); Artists Equity Asn (vpres, 71); Blue Bonnets Anonymous (chmn, 71-72); Tex Asn Schs Art. *Dealer:* Contemp Fine Arts Gallery 2425 Cedar Springs Dallas TX 75201. *Mailing Add:* 11149 Lanewood Cir Dallas TX 75218-1906

KOCH, EDWIN E
SCULPTOR, PAINTER
b New York, NY, Feb 21, 1915. *Study:* Mus Mod Art Sch; also with E Kramer. *Work:* Butler Inst of Am Art, Youngstown, Ohio. *Exhib:* Am Watercolors, Drawings & Prints, Metrop Mus Art, 52; Int Exhib Watercolors, Prints, Drawing, Pa Acad Design, 52; Int Watercolor Exhib, Brooklyn Mus, 53; Nat Acad Design, 58-75; var solo exhibs. *Awards:* Framemakers Award, Silvermine Guild Artists, 62; Medals of Honor for Watercolor, 70 & Oils, 72, Painters & Sculpture Soc NJ; Grumbacher Award, Audubon Artists, 79. *Bibliog:* Brian O'Doherty (auth), One-man show, 62 & John Canady (auth), One-man show, 66, New York Times. *Mem:* Audubon Artists; Nat Soc Painters in Casein & Acrylic (bd dir, 75-); Knickerbocker Artists (vpres, 77-78); Painters & Sculptors Soc NJ (vpres, 74-); Am Vet Soc Artists (treas, 70-75). *Media:* Oil, Casein. *Interests:* Hiking. *Mailing Add:* 109 Old Hoagerburgh Rd Wallkill NY 12589

KOCH, GERD HERMAN
PAINTER, EDUCATOR
b Detroit, Mich, Jan 30, 1929. *Study:* Wayne State Univ, BFA, 1951; Univ Calif, Los Angeles; Univ Calif, Santa Barbara, MFA, 1967. *Work:* Santa Barbara Art Mus; Los Angeles Co Mus Art; Univ Mont; Va State Mus Fine Art; Calif State Univ Long Beach; Long Beach Art Mus; Univ NC; Carnegie Art Mus, Oxnard, Calif; Ventura City Munic Collection. *Comn:* Design of Ash Grove (folk music cabaret), 58; 6 large paintings, Los Angeles Dance Theater, 59; 20 large painting exhibited, Wilshire Theater, Los Angeles, 59-. *Exhib:* Ferus Gallery, Los Angeles Landmark Gallery, 57; Los Angeles Co Mus Art Ann, 59; solo exhibs, Esther Robles Art Gallery, Los Angeles, 59, 61, 63 & 65, Esther Bear Art Gallery, 65 & 67, Carnegie Art Mus, 88, Momentum City Art Gallery, 91, La Jolla Art Mus, Santa Barbara Co Art Mus, Long Beach Art Mus, Calif & others; Univ NC, 66; Butler Inst Am Art, Youngstown, Ohio, 66; Calif Palace of Legion of Honor, San Francisco, 67; Calif Arts Festival, 68; 57 Yr Retrospective, Studio Channel Islands Art Ctr, 98-; 60 Year Retrospective & 80th Birthday exhib Studio Channel Islands Art Ctr, 2009; 4 Masters, 4 Legends (catalog), Mus Ventura Co, 2011; Gene Koch & Carle Milton, Together, Ventura Art Asn, Ventura, Calif, 2012; Chanel Islands Art Ctr, 2013; Our Journey Together, Artist of

Distinction Exhib, Ventura, Calif, 2013; 13 Invitationals, 2008. *Collection Arranged:* Curated exhib, Ventura Coll, 70-96; Studio Channel Islands Art Ctr, John Nava tapestry Project, Cathedral of our Lady of the Angels, LA, 2003; 135 10' Figures, Gerd Koch Portrait Used for Saint Nicholas Tapestry, Ten Yr Painting Survey, Bel Arts Factory, Ventura, Calif, 97-2007; curated 4th invitational (major artists & catalog) for 10th Anniversary of Studio Channel Islands Art Ctr, CSUCI, 98. *Pos:* Ojai Beautiful, 57-63; Founding mem bd dir, Studio Channel Islands Art Ctr & Gallery on Campus Calif State Univ Channel Islands, 98-, selection comt; mem acquisition comt, Ventura City Art Collection, 2000, 2001, 2003-2005; comnr, Pub Art Comn, Ventura, 2002-; mem task force, Ventura Cult Ctr, 2003-; founder, Ventura Beautiful; bd mem, Focus on the Masters, 98-2012. *Teaching:* Painting workshops, 54-; prof painting & drawing, Ventura Coll, 60-61 & 67-98; instr, Univ Calif Exten, 66-72; teaching asst to Kurt Kranz, Univ Calif, Santa Barbara, 67; German prof, Bauhaus Art Sch, Germany. *Awards:* M Grumbacher Inc Purchase Award, Nat Watercolor Soc, 56 & 65 & 1st Purchase Award, 76; Calif State Fair First Purchase Award, 63; Special Cert Recognition, Ventura Co Bd Supvrs, 2004, 2009; Art Gallery named in his honor, Studio Channel Islands Art Ctr, 2005; La Jolla Art Mus, 65; Morrison Medal, Oakland Art Mus, 61; 1st Purchase Award, Los Angeles Co Mus Art, 59. *Bibliog:* Los Angeles & Vacinity Exhib, Los Angeles Co Art Mus, 59; Prize Winning Oil Paintings, Allied Publ, 61; California Watercolors 1870-1970, 2002. *Mem:* Nat Watercolor Soc; Ventura Art Asn; co-founder, Studio Channel Islands Art Ctr (hon bd mem). *Media:* Oil, Acrylic. *Res:* Art history lectures on Van Gogh 98-2000, Rembrandt 400th birthday, 2006; Portraits of Jesus and the Disciples; Gallery Talk, Gattery Mus Rembrandt Exhib, 2008; abstract art. *Interests:* Photog; travel; hist. *Publ:* 80th Birthday & 60 Year Retrospective, catalog, Studio Channel Islands Art Ctr, 2009; 10th Anniversary Invitational Exhib Catalog, Gerd Koch, cur; Gerd Koch and Carole Milton, Our Journey Together (book), 1973-2013. *Dealer:* Studio Channel Islands Art Ctr Camarillo CA. *Mailing Add:* 444 Aliso St Ventura CA 93001

KOCH, PHILIP
PAINTER, DRAFTSMAN
b Rochester, NY, Mar 30, 1948. *Study:* Oberlin Coll, BA, 70; Ind Univ, MFA, 72; residency in Edward Hopper's Studio, 83, 86, 92, 94, 96, 98, 2000, 2002, 2004, 2006, 2008, 2010, & 2012. *Work:* Butler Inst Am Art; Ind Univ Fine Arts Mus; Minn Mus Am Art; Sheldon Swope Art Mus, Terre Haute, Ind; Washington Co Mus Fine Art, Hagerstown, Md; Saginaw Art Mus, MI; Cod Cod Mus Art, Mass; Mem Art Gallery, Rochester, NY. *Exhib:* Sheldon Swope Art Mus, 95; Butler Inst Am Art, 95; Midwest Mus Am Art, 95, 2010, 2011; Washington Co Mus Fine Arts, 95; Saginaw Art Mus, 96; Blanden Mem Art Mus, 98; Rahr-West Art Mus, 99; Cape Mus Fine Arts, 2003; Univ of Maryland Coll, 2004; Cape Cod Mus Art, 2009; Md Inst Col Art, 2009; George Billis Gallery, NY, 2009, 2012; Clymer Mus Art, 2010; Saginaw Art Mus, 2012; George Billis Gallery, NY, 2012; Meredith Lought Co, Houston, 2013; Isglos Fine Art, Stoninston, ME, 2013; William Baczek Fin Art, Northamption, Mass, 2013. *Teaching:* Instr painting, Cent Wash Univ Coll, 72-73; prof, Md Inst Coll Art, 73-. *Awards:* Ford Found Grant, 79; Mellon Grant, 84; Brenner Grant, 2010. *Bibliog:* Fine Art Connoisseur Mag, 4/2008 & 2009; Am Art Collector Mag, 1/2009; Southwest Art Mag, 1/2009; Fine Art Connoisseur Mag, 2012; Sunday Telegram, Portland, ME, 8/11/2013. *Media:* Oil, Pastel, Vine Charcoal. *Publ:* Auth, Direct painting outdoors, Am Artist, 4/82; Edward Hopper and the American Imagination, Whitney Mus Am Art, 95; On Visiting Edward Hopper's Studio, Oberlin Mag, spring 95; A Vision of Nature: The Landscape of Philip Kody, Univ of Maryland Coll, 2004; Unbroken Thread: The Art of Philip Koch, Univ Md Coll, 2008; A Landscapist Reconnects with His Forerunners, Fine Art Connoisseur Mag, 2012; Unbroken Thread, American Art Collector Mag, 2012. *Dealer:* Jane Haslem Gallery 2025 Hillyer Place NW Washington DC 20009; Isalos Fine Art Stonington ME; George Billis Gallery New York NY; Nichols Gallery Barboursville VA; Meredith Long & Co Houston Tx. *Mailing Add:* 71 Penny Ln Baltimore MD 21209

KOCH, VIRGINIA See Greenleaf, Virginia

KOCHER, ROBERT LEE
PAINTER, EDUCATOR
b Jefferson City, Mo, Dec 19, 1929. *Study:* Univ Mo-Columbia, AB & MA; also with Fred Shane & Paul Brach, Post Grad; Univ Iowa, Iowa City with Jean DeMarko & Robert Knipschild. *Comn:* Religious Feasts, Culver-Stockton Coll Dining Hall, 57; outdoor sculpture, Duane Arnold Residence, Cedar Rapids, Iowa; inaugural comn, Coe Coll pres, 96. *Exhib:* Mid-Am Ann, Kansas City, Mo, 60; All Iowa Artists, Des Moines Art Ctr Ann, 63-75; Miss Corridor Competition, Renwick Gallery, Washington, DC, 80; 32 Solo exhibs, Nat Surface Design Competition; Solo retrospective, Cedar Rapids Mus Art, 97; Retrospective, Paul Engle Center, 2006; Small Show Large Paintings, Kirkwood Coll, Cedar Rapids, Iowa, 2007; Guarantee Bank Gallery, 12 Works, 2011. *Pos:* Dir, New York Term Coe Col, 78-80; curator, Coe Col Art Collections, 96-2010; co-dir, Coe Col Sesquicentennial, 2001. *Teaching:* Prof art, Coe Col, 59-; Marvin D Cone prof, 87-95, emer, 95-. *Awards:* First Prize Painting, All Iowa Artists, Des Moines Art Ctr, 69; Younkers Award; co-recipient, Eliza Hickok Kesler Service Award, Coe Coll, 2006, Heritage award, 2012. *Bibliog:* Andrew Dolkart (auth), The Old Executive Building: A Victorian Masterpiece, Govt Publ Review, 85. *Mem:* Cedar Rapids Art Ctr (bd dir, 61-81), Iowa; Cedar Rapids Marion Coun Arts, Iowa; Friends Adv Bd, Univ Iowa Mus Art, 86-90; Tuesday Club, CRCC; Heritage Club, Coe Coll, 1995 (distinguished serv award, 2011). *Media:* Acrylic, Watercolor, Collage. *Interests:* gardening. *Mailing Add:* 1309 Brendel Hill Dr NW Cedar Rapids IA 52405

KOCHKA, AL
MUSEUM DIRECTOR, ADMINISTRATOR
b Paterson, NJ, June 28, 1928. *Study:* Newark State Teachers Col, NJ, BS, 49; William Paterson Coll NJ, MA, 68. *Pos:* Dir, NJ Coun Arts, Trenton, 76-78, Sangre de Cristo Arts & Conf Ctr, Pueblo, Colo, 79-84, Amarillo, Tex, 84-87 & Muskegon Mus Art, Muskegon, Mich, 88-93; fine art appraiser, 93-; emeritus, Mukegon Mus of Art, 2004; dir, Geissbuhler Project, Cape Cod Mus Art, 2003; guest lectr, French Impressionism, River Seine Cruise, France, 2007; guest lectr, Village Life in Tuscany: Lectures on Futurism, Speed, & Audio Design, Italy, 2008. *Teaching:* Art teacher, Kinnelon High Sch, NJ, 63-68; art educ consult, NJ State Dept Educ, Trenton, 68-74, dir arts & humanities, 74-76; adj, Hope Col, Holland, Mich, 96-97. *Awards:* Art Educator of Yr, Art Educators NJ, 73; NJ Gov Award Excellence, 1975; Mitchell A Wilder Award, Tex Asn Mus, 87. *Bibliog:* Frances Traher (auth), Sangre de Cristo Art Center hits its stride, Art West, Vol 6, 83. *Mem:* Mich Asn Mus; Midwest Mus Conf; Tex Asn Mus (bd trustees, 83-84); Mich Mus Asn (bd trustees, 91-94); Appraisers Asn Am, certified Am Art. *Publ:* Contribr, Dan Coen: The Lamar Series, Colorado Springs Fine Arts Ctr, 84; ed & contribr, Georgia O'Keeffe and Her Contemporaries, 85, Eight Modern Masters, 85 & Holy Family through the Ages, 86, Amarillo Art Ctr; contribr, Georgia O'Keeffe: Raissone Res Catalog, 2001; auth, AskArt.com-Biog of Arnold Geissbuhler, 2003; Prod (art), Public Access TV, Ch 17, Cape Cod, Mass; auth, Arnold Geissbuhler Sculptor Shaped by the 20th Century, Cape Cod Mus Art, Mass, 2009; Pictures of the Best Kind, Muskegon Mus Art, 100th Anniv, 2012. *Mailing Add:* 317 N Peterson Muskegon MI 49445

KOCHMAN, ALEXANDRA D
SCULPTOR, PAINTER
b Poltava, Ukraine, 1936. *Study:* Fashion Inst Technol, New York, AAS, 62; Northeastern Ill State Univ, Chicago, BA, 72; Univ Ill, Chicago, MFA, 78. *Work:* Ill State Mus, Springfield, Ill; State Ill Ctr Governor's Off, Chicago, Ill; John G Shedd Aquarium, Chicago; Milwaukee Pub Mus, Wis; Amoco Corp, Chicago, Ill; Harris Bank, Geneva, Ill; Siemens, Schaumburg, Ill; Saks Fifth Ave, Oakbrook, Ill; Ill Benectine Col, Lisle, Ill; Am Nat Bank, Trust & Rockford, Ill; Cirque Group, Chicago. *Comn:* Sculptural vessels, Swiss Bank, Chicago, Ill, 84; mural, Lincoln Properties Corp, Oakbrook, Ill, 86; ceramic wall sculpture, Barack, Forrazzano & Kirschbaum, Chicago, Ill, 87; Siemens Medical Systems (mural), Schaumburg, Ill, 87; wall sculpture, St Volodymyr & Olha Ukrainian Cath Church, Chicago, Ill, 88. *Exhib:* Women in Visual Arts, 89, Outstanding Am Craftsmen, 90, Judith Racht Gallery, Harbert, Mich; New Horizons in Art, North Shore Art League, Skokie, Ill, 90; Chicago Street Gallery, Lincoln, Ill; Biennale, Ukranian Fine Arts, Lviv, Ukraine, 91; Fine Art of Craft, Scottsdale Ctr Arts, Scottsdale, Ariz, 93; Port Royal Post Off, Port Royal, SC, 2002; Ukrainian Inst Mod Art, Chicago, 97; Dominican Univ, River Forest, 2001; plus many others. *Pos:* consult, Milwaukee Pub Mus, Wis, 80; Cur, The Permanent Collection, Ukrainian Inst of Mod Art, Chicago; juror, Ill Dept Nat Resources, Artisan Prog, 2001. *Teaching:* adj asst prof art & sculpture, Dominican Univ, River Forest, Ill, 83-. *Awards:* First Award, Oakbrook Invitational, Oakbrook C of C, 82; Governor's Purchase Award, Ill State Prof Exhib, State Ill, 86; First Award, Ill State Exhib, Springfield, 89. *Bibliog:* Yuri Myskiv (auth), Alexandra D Kochman and the world in balance, Ukrainian Weekly Rev; Patricia Weismental (auth), feature, Univ Ill Chicagoan, 90; Svito-Vyd, Literary Rev Mag, KyiV, Ukraine, 93; Carol Bradley (auth), Ceramics Monthly, 9/97. *Mem:* Chicago Artists' Coalition (bd mem, 82-82); Ukrainian Inst Mod Art (art juror, 79-). *Media:* Clay, Oil. *Mailing Add:* 5453 N Virginia Ave Chicago IL 60625

KOCOT & HATTON
PAINTERS, CONCEPTUAL ARTISTS
b Northampton, Mass (Kocot); b Kingston, Pa (Hatton). *Study:* Kocot: Pa Acad Fine Arts, CFA, 67; Univ Pa, BFA (magna cum laude), 87; Hatton: Pa Acad Fine Arts, CFA, 68. *Work:* Hunt Manufacturing Co Inc Collection & Julius Bloch Collection, Philadelphia Mus Art, Pa; New Arts Prog, Kutztown, Pa; Fukuya Gallery, Hiroshima, Japan. *Comn:* Photographs, Andy Warhol Mus, Pittsburgh, Pa, 99; video, Del Mus Art, Wilmington, 2000. *Exhib:* Inst Contemp Art, Philadelphia, 99; Del Art Mus, Wilmington, 2000, 2012; Sharjah Arts Mus, United Arab Emirates, 2000; Hunterdon Mus Art, Clinton, NJ, 2002; Del Ctr Contemp Art, Wilmington, 2003; Tufts Univ Art Gallery, Medford, Mass, 2004; Atwater Kent Mus, Philadelphia, Pa, 2004; Bjorn Ressle Gallery, New York, 2008-09; Georg Kargl Fine Arts, Vienna, Austria, 2010; Agency of Unrealized Projects, Basel, Switzerland, 2011. *Pos:* Panel mem, Moore Coll Art, Philadelphia, Pa, 89 & Artists in Collaboration, Inst Contemp Art, Philadelphia, Pa, 96; guest cur, Nexus Gallery Found, Today's Art, Philadelphia, Pa, 97; Panel Mem, New Mus New York, 2009. *Teaching:* Instr, Univ Arts, Philadelphia, Pa, 2000 & 2002; vis artist, Pa Acad Fine Arts, Philadelphia, Pa, 98. *Awards:* Nat Endowment Arts Grant, 79; Fel, Pa Coun, 86 & grant, 89; Franz and Virginia Bader Fund Grant, 2015. *Bibliog:* Eileen Neff (auth), Scale/Ratio-review, ARTFORUM, 4/89; Anne Percy (auth), New Work on Paper-Hunt Collection, Philadelphia Mus, 96; Miriam Seidel (auth) Biennial 2000, Del Art Mus, 2000; Edith Newhall (auth), article, Philadelphia Inquirer, 4/14/2006; Steve Aimone (auth), Expressive Drawings, Lark Bks, 2009; Personal Structures, Time-Space-Existence, Dumont Bks, Cologne, Ger, 2009. *Mem:* Inst Contemp Art; New Arts Prog; Philadelphia Mus Art; Pa Acad Fine Arts. *Media:* Painting, Video, Photography. *Publ:* Axis Paintings, 2012-2014; Lilly Wei (essay), Self Published, 2014. *Dealer:* Larry Becker Contemp Art 43 N Second St Philadelphia PA 19106. *Mailing Add:* PO Box 2148 Philadelphia PA 19103

KOCSIS, JAMES PAUL
PAINTER, MUSEUM DIRECTOR
b Buffalo, NY, Apr 27, 1936. *Study:* Philadelphia Coll of Art, Univ of the Arts, dipl, 58. *Work:* Lessing J Rosenwald Collection, Nat Gallery Art, Libr Cong, Washington, DC; Albright-Knox Art Gallery, Buffalo, NY; Victoria & Albert Mus, London; pvt collections of HM Elizabeth, Queen of Eng, His Royal Highness Charles, Prince of Wales, The Right Hon Lord Kenneth Clark, Nancy & Ronald Reagan, Presidential Collection, The White House; Kendal Mus, Eng; Bodleian Libr, Oxford Univ, Eng; and others. *Exhib:* Solo exhibs, Crucifixion Exhib, Memory of Philadelphia Scourge Period, 72, Columbia Mus Art, SC, 74, Harvard Univ, Mass, 76, Univ Arts, Philadelphia, 76, Sydney Opera House, Australia, 79, Dhahran Central Libr, Saudi Arabia, 82, Jilin U Changchun, China, 82, United World Coll Adriatic, Trieste, Italy & Southern Africa, Mbabane, 84-85, Italsider Steel, Genoa & Alessandria, Ital, 85, US Int Univ-Europe, London, 85, Univ Glasgow, Scotland, 85, James Joyce Mus, Dublin,

Ireland, 85, Int Mus & Art Festival, Glamorgan, Wales, 85, Kendal Mus, Eng, 86; Oxford Univ, Eng, 88; Imo State Libr, Owerri, Nigeria, 89, Nat Arts Theater, Lagos, Nigeria, 89, Progress Bank Nigeria Ltd, Lagos, 89; Freedom Hall, Martin Luther King Jr Ctr & Atlanta-Fulton Public Libr, Atlanta, Ga, 90; US Mission to the UN, New York, 91; United Nations, New York, 91; Sopot and Gdansk, Poland, 91; Zentral-Bibliothek, Cologne, Ger, 92; Ger Am Inst: Saarbrucken, 92; Goethe Inst Am House, Frankfurt, Ger, 92; Freie Univ, Berlin, Ger, 94; Igneous Man Exhib, Missionaries of Charity, Mother Teresa, Calcutta, India, 95; Gandhi Peace Found, New Delhi, 95; Int, India Ctr, New Delhi, 95; Benjamin Franklin Libr, Mexico City, 98; Nat Mus & Libr, Casa de la Cultura Ecuatoriana Benjamin Carrion, Quito, Ecuador, SA, 98; Inst de Investigaciones Esteticias, Univ Nacional de Mexico, Mexico City, 98; Galaria Guillermo Kahlo, la casa de cultura, Jesus Reyes Heroles, Coyoacan, Mexico, 99; Elefterios Venizelos, Int Airport, Athens, Greece, 2003; Vikelaia Libr, Crete, 2003; Acad Athens Univ, Athens, Greece, 2003; Nat Academy Athens Libr, Athens, Greece, 2003; The Hermitage Mus, St Petersburg, Russia, 2005; Dostoevsky Mus, St Petersburg, Russia, 2005; Russian Acad Arts, St Petersburg, Russia, 2005; Georgetown Univ, Intercult Ctr & Pople John Paul II Cult Ctr, DC, 2008; Igneous Man Exhib, The Ch Louvre, Eglise St, Germain l'Auxerrois, Paris, 2008. *Pos:* Illusr, children's books, 61-68; illusr & designer for Random House Publ & 20th Century Fox, 67; publ of catalogues, books, color prints & posters for nat & int distribution. *Teaching:* Instr drawing & pictoral compos, Philadelphia Col of Art Univ of the Arts, 65-67; lectr, Philadelphia Coll of Art Univ of the Arts & Kutztown State Teachers Coll, civic & social groups; dir, James Paul Kocsis Int Independent Mus, established 2012. *Awards:* Am Inst Graphic Arts Biannual Award, 68. *Bibliog:* Portia A Scott (auth), World Renown Artist to Bring Works to Martin Luther King Center, Atlanta Daily World, 3/9/90; Paul Willistein (auth), Art Takes Flight, Morning Call, 5/7/95; Dr Albert Nekimken (auth), Kocsis Scourged, Surviving the Art World, Paragon Press, 99; and others. *Media:* Oil on Linen. *Mailing Add:* PO Box 905 Allentown PA 18105

KOEHLER, HENRY
PAINTER

b Louisville, Ky, Feb 2, 1927. *Study:* Yale Univ, BA, 50. *Work:* Calif Palace Legion Honor, San Francisco; Speed Mus Art, Louisville, Ky; Parrish Art Mus, Southampton, NY; Thomasville Cult Ctr, Ga. *Comn:* Baseball murals, NY Mets, Shea Stadium, 64. *Exhib:* Solo Exhibs: Calif Palace Legion Honor, 66, Speed Art Mus, 67 & Parrish Mus, 70; Wildenstein, London, 71, 73, 76 & 78; Aiken Racing Hall Fame, 78; Galerie La Cymaise, Paris, 82, 84, 87, 91, 95, 97, 2005, & 2008; Spink & Son, London, 90, 92 & 94; Ky Derby Mus, 93; Newhouse Galleries, NY, 94 & 96; Rafael Valls Ltd, London, 98, 2000, 2002, 2004, 2006, 2008 & 2010; Nat Mus of Racing, Saratoga, NY, 2003; Century Asoc, NY, 2005. *Pos:* Hon Trustee, Parrish Mus of Art, Southampton, NY. *Mem:* The Brook, NY; Whites, The Beefsteak, London; Century Asn, NY; Saratoga Reading Rms, NY; Southampton Club, NY; Pratt's, London; Beefsteak Club, London. *Media:* Oil, Drawing. *Dealer:* Rafael Valls Ltd London England; Galerie La Cymaise Paris France; Ann Madonia Fine Arts Southampton NY. *Mailing Add:* 80 N Main St Southampton NY 11968

KOEHLER, RONALD GENE
SCULPTOR

b Cape Girardeau, Mo, Sept 30, 50. *Study:* Southeast Mo State Univ, Cape Girardeau, BS (art educ), 72, MAT, 75; Memphis State Univ, Tenn, with Harris Sorrelle, MFA (sculpture), 80. *Work:* Ark Arts Ctr, Little Rock; Del Mar Coll, Corpus Christi, Tex; Tenn All-State Artist Collection, Nashville; W Palm Beach Int Airport, Fla; Hawaii State Found on Culture & the Arts, Honolulu; Hechinger Tools as Art Collection, Washington, DC. *Comn:* sculpture installation, Our Lady of Victories Catholic Church, Cleveland, Miss, 91; Marble outdoor sculpture, Arrowmont Sch Arts & Crafts, Gatlinburg, Tenn, 97. *Exhib:* Suitcase Exchange Show, USA & New Zealand, 2004; Westmoreland Art Nat, Youngwood, Pa, 2012; Arts in Harmony, Elk River, Minn, 2012; 46th Nat Del Mar Coll, Tex, 2012. *Pos:* Int pres, Kappa Pi Int Hon Art Fraternity, 98-. *Teaching:* GA Instr design, Memphis State Univ, Tenn, 78-80; instr sculpture, Delta State Univ, Cleveland, Miss, 80-82, assoc prof sculpture & printmaking, 84-93; staff asst, Arrowmont Sch Arts & Crafts, Gatlinburg, Tenn, 82-84; prof art, Delta State Univ, 93-, chair art dept, 2007-. *Awards:* Visual Artist Fel-Miss Arts Comn, 91-92; Miss Humanities Teacher of the Year Award, 2008; Sculpture Award, Westmoreland Art Nat, Youngwood, Pa, 2010; 1st place, 3D Award, Southern Appalachian Art Guild Nat, Blue Ridge, Ga, 2008; Meri Award, Cooperstown Nat, NY, 2010. *Bibliog:* Featured artist, Fine Wood Working Mag, No 62, 1/87, Gallery section, Am Craft Mag, Vol 47, No 4, 8/87 & Woodwork Mag, No 23, 10/93; Arthur Williams (auth), Sculpture: Technique-Form-Content, Davis Publ, rev ed 95; Country Roads Mag, 12/99; Donald Meilach (auth), Wood Art Today, Schiffer Publ, 2004; Arthur Williams (auth), The Sculpture Reference, Sculpture Bks Publ, 2004-2005; Wood Art Today 2, Schiffer Publ, 2010. *Mem:* Int Sculpture Asn; Am Crafts Coun; Kappa Pi (int pres 98-). *Media:* Wood, Metal. *Publ:* Auth, Natural Dyes on Handmade Paper, Delta State Univ, 82; (ed) The Sketch Book, A Journal of Kappa Pi Intl Hon Fraternity, 98-2012. *Dealer:* Galeria Ortiz San Antonio TX; Art Under a Hot Tin Roof Memphis TN; Arts Company Nashville TN. *Mailing Add:* 400 S Bolivar Cleveland MS 38732-3745

KOEHLER-TRICKLER, SALLY JO
RETIRED ILLUSTRATOR

b. Burlington, Iowa, Jan. 7, 1948. *Study:* AA, Southeastern C.C., West Burlington, Iowa, 1976; BA, Western Ill. U., 1988. Cert. master gardener Iowa State U horticultured Dept., Ames, 2008. *Pos:* Commn. Contracts. FBI Agents came to Burlington to do extensive background check for "Q Clearance" to work on Line One (AEC Contract). Sr. Tech. Illustrator, JI Case Co., Burlington, 1973-. Constructing "To Scale" Exploded Isometric Drawings of Constrn. Equipment (also some Agr. Equipment): Elec. Harnesses, Hydraulic Sys., Engine parts, Loader Backhoe Buckets, Loader Lift Frame & Buckets, Sheet Metal Parts, Elec. Sys., Hydraulic Cylinders, etc., for Parts Catalogs, Svc. Manuals, & Operator Manuals. rep. tech. illustrating Burlington Cmty. HS Career Day ann. event, 1985-91.; Mem. pub. rels. com. United Way, Burlington, 1975, chmn. pub. rels. 1976-77, art designer, 1987. *Mem:* Burlington Engrs. Club (v.p. 1974-75, pres. 1975-76, chmn. HS counseling com. on career days, 1977-80), Allegro Motor Home Club Iowa, Phi Kappa Phi. Clubs: Good Sam (Big River Sams, Iowa) (sec./treas. 1985-87). *Interests:* Creative writing-poetry, fiction, landscape design, photography. *Publ:* Pub. History of Saints John and Paul Church (1839-2000), 2000. *Mailing Add:* 11904 44th St Burlington IA 52601

KOENIG, ELIZABETH
SCULPTOR

b New York, NY, Apr 20, 1937. *Study:* Sorbonne, Paris, 57; Wellesley Col, BA, 58; Yale Univ, MD, 62; Art Students League, New York, with John Hovannes, 63-64; Corcoran Mus Sch Art, with Heinz Warnecke & John Rood, 64-67. *Work:* Curator's Collection, Eugene O'Neill Mem Theater Found, Waterford, Conn; Art Students League, NY; Desert Stone, Marble Carving, Regional Ctr for Women in Arts, Westchester, Pa. *Comn:* Tenn marble carving, Washington Hebrew Cong, Washington, DC, 78; monumental bronze sculpture for front of Admin Bldg, George Meany Ctr Labor Studies, Silver Spring, Md, 82. *Exhib:* Ten Sculptors, Washington Womens Arts Ctr, Washington, DC, 77; solo exhibs, Foxhall Gallery, 77, 85 & 99, La Galerie Myrian H, Paris, France, 2006, Gallery Pont Neuf, Paris, 2011; retrospective 1963-1978 (auth, catalog), Lyman Allyn Mus, New London, Conn, 78 & Rotunda, Pan-Am Health Orgn, Washington, DC, 78; Finalist Exhib, Outdoor Sculpture Competition, Rockville Munic Gallery, Md, 78; 11th Ann Sculpture Conf, Meridian House Int, Washington, DC, 80; Sculpture & Prints, Cath Univ Am, 80; 35 Yr Retrospective, Foundation Henri Harpignies, Paris, France, 99. *Collection Arranged:* The Mystique of Metal, Art Barn, Nat Park Serv, Washington, DC, 85. *Pos:* delegate USA, L'Academie Internat des Arts et Lettres. *Awards:* First Prize for Sculpture, 70 & Second & Third Prizes for Sculpture, 71, Tri-State Regional Sculpture Exhib, Montgomery Co Art Asn; Silver Medal for Sculpture, Asn Merite Devouement Francais. *Bibliog:* Patricia Raymer (auth), From iron to gold, Washington's metal artists, Washingtonian Mag, 75; Robert Spring (auth), New projects: Sculpture for the George Meany Center, In: The Artists Foundry for Practicing Sculptors, Vol 5, No 1, 82. *Mem:* Artists Equity Asn, Washington, DC (vpres, 77-83); life mem Art Students League, NY; Int Sculpture Ctr; Assn Int des Arts Plastiques (UNESCO). *Media:* Stone, Bronze. *Interests:* Reading & Gardening. *Publ:* Auth, Monumental torso, Washington Artists News, 81; From Monet to Matisse at the Columbus Mus of Art, Confluences, 2012; Sculpture of Elizabeth Koenig, in Musis de Demain, Paris, France, pp 56-59, 2013. *Dealer:* Foxhall Gallery 3301 New Mexico Ave NW Washington DC 20016; Miller Gallery 2715 Erie Ave Cincinnati OH 45208. *Mailing Add:* 9014 Charred Oak Dr Bethesda MD 20817

KOENIG, PETER LASZLO
PAINTER, CURATOR, EDUCATOR

b Hungary, Sept 10, 1933. *Study:* Mass Coll Art, BFA, 59; Cranbrook Acad Art, MFA, 61; Harvard Univ, EdM, 71; Warsaw Acad Fine Arts; Boston Univ; Mass Inst Technol. *Work:* RI Coll, Providence; Univ NDak, Grand Forks; Weber State Coll, Ogden, Utah; Prahran Coll, Melbourne, Australia; Ctr Contemp Art, Great Falls, Mont. *Exhib:* Butler Inst Am Art, Youngstown, Ohio, 63; Boston Arts Festival, 64; Pa Acad Fine Arts, Philadelphia, 66; solo exhibs, Harvard Univ, Cambridge, Mass, 71, Ctr Contemp Art, Great Falls, Mont, 85, Univ Hawaii, 91, Fitchburg Mus, Mass, 92, Heritage Plantation, Sandwich, Mass, 92 & Mass Coll Art, 93; Salt Lake Art Ctr, Utah, 75; Cataumet Art Ctr, Mass, 98; Peter Paul Gallery, Fla, 2008. *Collection Arranged:* Utah Artist Today, Brigham Young Univ, Utah, 77; Rodger P Kingston: Photographs, Univ Ark, 80; Rituals of the Land, Art Complex Mus, Duxbury, Mass, 86; New Horizons: 19th Century Am Marine Painting (auth, catalog), Art Complex Mus, Duxbury, 88; Falmouth: A Visual Legacy, Cape Mus Fine Arts, Mass, 88; Hungarian Millenium Exhib, Art Ctr, Sarasota, 2000; Premiere Sarasota Artists, Temple Beth Israel, 2003. *Pos:* Dean, Prahran Col Art, Melbourne, Australia, 76-79; cur, Art Complex Mus, Duxbury, Mass, 85-89; art critic, Enterprise Newspaper, Mass & Bradenton Herald, Fla; exhib dir, Art Ctr Sarasota, Fla, 98-2003 & Peter Paul Gallery; dir, Twin Palms Studio. *Teaching:* Prof painting & drawing, RI Coll, Providence, 63-67; chmn art dept, Wheelock Coll, Boston, 67-71 & Weber Coll, Utah, 71-76; prof, Univ Ark, 79-82; lectr, Univ Hawaii, 90. *Awards:* Provincetown Workshop Fel, Mass, 61; McDowell Fel, 64; Fulbright Grant, 64-65; US Bicentennial Grant, 76. *Mem:* Am Asn Mus; New Eng Mus Asn; Coll Art Asn Am; Falmouth Artists Guild; Honolulu Acad Fine Arts; Art Ctr, Sarasota, Fla. *Media:* Acrylic, Photography, Conceptual Art. *Interests:* Sailing, Bicycling, Swimming, Film. *Publ:* Auth, Rituals of the Land: Native American Art of the Colorado Plateau, Art Complex Mus, 86; Falmouth: A Visual Legacy, Teaticket Press, 87; Lacuna, A Hist Vision, Twin Palms Studio, 2010; 50 Years on the Trail, Sarasota Visual Art Ctr, 99; New Horizons, Art Complex Mus, 88. *Mailing Add:* PO Box 1223 Osprey FL 34229

KOENIG, ROBERT J
MUSEUM DIRECTOR, EDUCATOR

b Jersey City, NJ, June 6, 1935. *Study:* Pratt Inst, BS (art educ), 57; Yale Univ, BFA, 59, MFA, 61; New Sch Soc Res; Columbia Univ Sch Gen Studies; Gen Elec Mgt Prog Mus Adminrs. *Exhib:* Wood, Fiber, Clay and Metal in African Art, The African Art Mus of the SMA Fathers, NJ, 1999; Eloquent Threads: The Language of African Textiles and Costumes; Perspectives on African Art, The African Art Mus of the SMA Fathers, NJ, 2000; Asanti Brass Miniatures from the Collections of AfrikaCentrum, Cadier en Keer, The Neth, 2001; Five Cultures of Africa: African Art from the Collections of the SMA African Art Mus, 2002; Design for Living Traditional Arts of Sub-Saharan Africa from the Collections of the SMA African Art Mus, 2002; Textile Art of the Bakuba: Velvet Embroideries in Raffia from the Collection of Sam Hilu, 2003; Beauty and the Beasts: Kifwebe Masks of the Songye, Luba and Related Peoples of the Congo, 2003. *Pos:* Exhib designer, Newark Mus, NJ, 61-63; asst dir, Morris Mus Arts & Sci, 69-76; from asst dir to assoc dir, Montclair Art Mus, NJ, 76-80, dir, 80-93; juror/evaluator, AAM Accreditation Comm, NJ State Coun on Arts & Inst Awards, 85-88; bd dir, NJ Mus Coun, 85-87, Long-range Planning Comn,

87-88; Md State Coun Arts, 87; Vietnam Mem Comp, 88; dir, Noyes Mus, Oceanville, NJ, 91-93 & African Art Mus, SMA Soc, Tenafly, NJ, 95-; pres, Composers Guild, NJ, 96-2001. *Teaching:* Instr art, Pub Schs, Union City, NJ, 63-69, Bloomfield Col, NJ, 89-90, Montclair State Col, NJ, 88-89, Univ Pa, 90 & Berkshire Sch Contemp Art, North Adams, Mass, 92; adj prof, Stockton State Col, Pomona, NJ, 92-93; assoc prof museology, Seton Hall Univ, 94-97; lectr Montclair State Univ, 97-; lectr Jane Voorhees Zimmerle Art Mus, Rutgers Univ, 97-. *Awards:* First Prize, Grad Painting, Yale Univ, 60; Excellence Award, NJ Art Dir's Club, 90; Silver Medal, The Song of the Loom, Leipzig Int Bk Exhib, 90. *Mem:* MAAM, Gov NJ; Am Asn Mus; Nat Trust His Preservation; NJ Mus Coun; AAMD; Nat Arts Club; Yale Club, New York. *Res:* traditional arts of sub-Saharan Africa. *Specialty:* works assoc with the SMA workshop at Ekiti, Nigeria under Father Kevin Carroll, SMA; African pottery and textiles. *Interests:* African, Asian, ancient Greek and Roman art; 20th century and contemporary art. *Collection:* African Art Mus of SMA. *Mailing Add:* 23 Bliss Ave Tenafly NJ 07670

KOESTENBAUM, WAYNE
WRITER, EDUCATOR
Study: Harvard Univ, BA; Johns Hopkins Univ, MA (creative writing); Princeton Univ, PhD. *Teaching:* Distinguished prof, Grad Sch English, City Univ of NY, currently. *Publ:* Auth, Jackie Under My Skin: Interpreting An Icon, 1995, The Milk of Inquiry, 1999, Cleavage: Essays on Sex, Stars, and Aesthetics, 2000, Andy Warhol, 2001, Moira Orfei in Aigues-Mortes, 2004, Model Homes, 2004, Hotel Theory, 2007, Humiliation, 2011; The Anatomy of Harpo Marx, 2012; Blue Stranger with Mosaic Background, 2012. *Mailing Add:* City University of NY Graduate Center 365 Fifth Ave, Room 4409 New York NY 10016

KOGAN, DEBORAH
PAINTER, ILLUSTRATOR
b Philadelphia, Pa, Aug 31, 1940. *Study:* Philadelphia Coll Art; Pa Acad Fine Arts, 58-62; Univ Pa, Albert C Barnes Found, 62-64. *Work:* Drexel Univ, Philadelphia, Pa; Libr Cong, Washington; Univ Minn, Minneapolis; Free Libr Philadelphia; Carnegie-Mellon Univ, Pittsburgh. *Comn:* Graphic murals, Chase Manhattan Bank, 69. *Exhib:* Pa Acad Fine Arts Biennial, 67 & 69; Philadelphia Artists, Philadelphia Mus Art, 73, 74 & 79; 110th Exhib Am Watercolor Soc, Nat Acad of Design, NY, 77; Am Women in Fine Arts, Moore Coll Art, Philadelphia, 77; Mus Philadelphia, 79; US-Israeli Exchange Exhib, Tel Aviv, 78; Albright Col, 80; Soc Illustrators, 90, 91, 92, 94, 95 & 98; also many solo exhibs. *Teaching:* Univ of Arts, Philadelphia. *Awards:* Tiffany Grant, 68; Drexel Citation, 87; Carolyn W Field Award for Children's Lit, 88; Int Reading Asn Award, 90; Penn Book Award, 91. *Bibliog:* 21 Women Artists, Muse, 79; Sixth Book of Childrens Book Authors and Illustrators, HH Wilson Publ, 91; Something About the Author, Gale, 93; and others. *Mem:* Artists Equity Asn (mem bd dir, 77-79); Women's Caucus for Art; Muse: Woman's Collab (mem bd dir, 77-80); Authors Guild; Soc Childrens Bk Writers & Illustrators. *Media:* Acrylic; Watercolor. *Publ:* Star Gazing Sky, Crown, 91; illus, Apple Picking Time, Crown Publ, 94; Jackrabbit, Crown Pub, 96; illus, The Barn Owls, Charlesbridge, 2000; auth, illus, Hokusai: The Man Who Painted a Mountain, Farrar, Straus & Giroux, 2001; Sweet Dried Apples: A Vietnamese Wartime Childhood, Houghton Mifflin, 96. *Mailing Add:* 810 Southampton Ave Wyndmoor PA 19038

KOHL-SPIRO, BARBARA
PRINTMAKER, PAINTER
b Milwaukee, Wis, Feb 10, 1940. *Study:* Univ Wis Madison, BS (art hist); Univ Wis Milwaukee. *Work:* Milwaukee Art Ctr. *Comn:* Painting, comn by Golda Meier, 77. *Exhib:* Wis Painters & Sculptors, Milwaukee Art Ctr, 65; Washington Art, Washington Armory, DC, 77 & 78; NY Show, Allen Park Gallery, 77; Janus Gallery, Washington, DC, 78; Alex Rosenberg Gallery, 78-79; Voices of Past, Women in Jewish Art, Jewish Community Ctr, Washington, DC, 79. *Teaching:* Asst trainer of docents in art hist, Milwaukee Art Ctr, 78-. *Awards:* Pub Television Auction Award for Best in Show, 77. *Media:* Color and Fabric on Paper; Oil on Canvas. *Collection:* Milton Avery oils, Morris Lewis, Dubuffet, Hockney, Ralph Fasanella, Wayne Thiebold, Hepworth, Suttman, Saul Steinberg. *Dealer:* Michael Lord Gallery Milwaukee WI. *Mailing Add:* 777 N Prospect Milwaukee WI 53202-4000

KOHLER, RUTH DEYOUNG
MUSEUM DIRECTOR, CURATOR
b Chicago, Ill, 1941. *Study:* Smith Col, Northampton, Mass, BA; Univ Hamburg, Ger; Kunsthochschule, Hamburg, Ger; Banff Sch Fine Arts; Univ Wis, Madison; Lakeland Col, LHD, 84. *Pos:* Dir & mem, Kohler Found, Inc, Wis, 60-, pres 85-; asst dir, John Michael Kohler Arts Ctr, Sheboygan, Wis, 68-72, dir, 72-; mem, Wis Arts Bd, Madison, 73-81 & chmn, 74-77; mem, Wis Am Revolution Bicentennial Comn, Madison, 74-77; mem visual arts panel, Nat Endowment Arts, Washington, DC, 75-, mem visual arts mus panel, 76-78, mem, Selection Panel for Percent Art Prog Madison, Wis, 86. *Teaching:* Instr printmaking, Univ Alta, Calgary, Can, 64-66. *Awards:* Fel, Wis Acad Sci, Art & Letts, Madison. *Mem:* Nat Coun on Educ for Ceramic Arts, 90; hon bd James Renwick Alliance, Smithsonian Inst, 90; hon mem Coll Fel Am Crafts Coun, 92. *Mailing Add:* 608 New York Ave Sheboygan WI 53081

KOHUT, LORENE
PAINTER
b La Port, Tex, Nov 16, 1929. *Study:* With Coulton Waugh & John Gould. *Work:* Court Gen Sessions, Washington, DC; Pa State Univ; Du Pont Co; Del State Coll; Wesley Coll; and others. *Exhib:* Ogunquit Arts Ctr 49th Nat, Maine, 69; Hudson Valley Art Asn, 42nd & 43rd Nat, White Plains, NY, 69-70; Nat Acad Design, NY, 70; Catharine Lorillard Wolfe Nat, NY, 80; Am Artist Prof League Grand Nat Exhib, 81. *Awards:* Gold Medal Oils, Hudson Valley Art Asn, 69; Gold Medal, Watercolor, Catharine Lorillard Wolfe Nat, 80; Gold Medal, Oil, Am Artist Prof League Grand Nat Exhib, 81. *Media:* Mixed Media, Alkyd. *Dealer:* Little Gallery Rock Shop Smithville TX 78957. *Mailing Add:* 706 Garwood St Smithville TX 78957

KOIS, DENNIS
MUSEUM DIRECTOR
b 1970. *Study:* Univ Wis, Milwaukee, BA (cum laude); NY Univ, MA (Mus Studies); Getty Mus Leadership Inst. *Pos:* Asst mgr design, Met Mus Art, New York; chief designer, Freer Gallery Art & Arthur M Sackler Gallery, Smithsonian Inst, Washington, 2001-06; exec dir, Grace Mus, Abilene, Tex, 2006-08, DeCordova Mus & Sculpture Park, Lincoln, Mass, 2008-; exec dir, DeCordova Mus & Sculpture Park, Lincoln, Mass, 2008-. *Teaching:* Adj prof, grad mus studies, George Washington Univ, 2002-07; Adj Prof, George Washington Univ, 2002-07. *Mailing Add:* DeCordova Mus & Sculpture Park 51 Sandy Pond Rd Lincoln MA 01773-2600

KOLASINSKI, JACEK J
NEW MEDIA ARTIST, EDUCATOR
Study: Studied history and philiosophy, Jagiellonian Univ, Krakow, BA (Int Relations); Fla Int Univ, Miami, BFA, MFA. *Exhib:* exhibitions include Teatro Colon, Buenos Aires, Argentina, Festival Int Cervantino, Guanajuato, Mexico, 61 Festival de Cannes-Short Film Corner, Cinema Politic, Barcelona, Spain, and Digital Fringe, Melbourn, Australia, and several others. *Teaching:* New media artist, asst prof of visual arts in the art and art history dept, Fla Internat Univ, department chair, currently. *Awards:* Kosciuszko Found Fellowship, Fla Cultural Consortium Fellowship in the media and visual arts. *Mailing Add:* School of Art+Art History Col of Architecture+The Arts Modesto A Maldique Campus 11200 SW 8th St VH216 Miami FL 33199

KOLISNYK, PETER
PAINTER, SCULPTOR
b Toronto, Ont, Nov 30, 1934. *Study:* Western Tech Sch Toronto, Ont, with Fred Fraser, Julius Griffith, Margaret Aitken & George Griffin, 51-54. *Work:* Art Gallery Ont, Toronto; Art Bank, Can Coun, Ottawa; Winnipeg Art Gallery, Man; Queen's Silver Jubilee Art Collection, Govt Ont, Toronto; Ukrainian Inst Mod Art, Chicago. *Comn:* Agnes Etherington Gallery, Queens Univ, Kingston, Ont; Peterboro Art Gallery. *Pos:* Cur, Cobourg Art Gallery, 64-69; trustee, Art Gallery Ont, 82-. *Teaching:* Dir & lectr art, Glendon Col, York Univ, Toronto, 75-; instr, Prison Arts Found, Kingston, Ont, 78 & Emily Carr Col Art, Vancouver, 82-. *Awards:* Sculpture Award, Ont Soc Artists, 72; Can Coun Sr Arts Grant, 75-76; Ont Arts Coun Grants, 75, 77-79 & 81-83. *Bibliog:* Clara Hargittay (auth), article, Art Mag, 5-7/82; David Nasby & Fern Bayer (coauth), Art for Architecture, Govt Ont, 82. *Mem:* Can Artists Representation Ont; Can Soc Painters Watercolour; Ont Soc Artists; Royal Can Acad Arts. *Media:* Watercolor; Miscellaneous. *Mailing Add:* c/o Ukranian Inst Mod Art 2320 W Chicago Ave Chicago IL 60622-4722

KOLLER-DAVIES, EVA
ASSEMBLAGE ARTIST, PAINTER
b St Peternov, Rumania, Jan 29, 1925; Can citizen. *Study:* Cent Tech Sch, 43; Ont Coll Art, Toronto, 68-70; Univ Toronto, 72-73. *Work:* Permanent collection, Ctr Arts, Vero Beach, Fla, 92; Art Gallery of Algoma, Sault Ste Marie, Ont, Canada. *Exhib:* Solo exhib, Indian River Community Coll Gallery, Fla, 86, Gallery of Brevard Community Coll, Melbourne Fla, 88, McAlpine Ctr Arts, Ft Pierce, Fla 89, Art Gallery Algoma, Sault Ste Marie, Ont, 2006; Five Abstract Artists, Gallery of Riverside Theatre, Vero Beach, Fla, 86; Fla Artists, Ctr for Arts, Vero Beach, 88; Ont Soc Artist, McDonald Gallery, Toronto, 88; Abstract Artists from the Permanent Collection, Ctr for Arts, Vero Beach, Fla, 96. *Bibliog:* Screens, Paintings, Works on Paper- A Review by Michael Burtch (dir & cur), Art Gallery of Algoma. *Media:* Acrylic, Mixed Media; 3D Screens

KOLODZEI, NATALIA
ADMINISTRATOR, CURATOR
b Moscow, Jan 8, 1974. *Study:* State Univ NJ, BA in Art Hist with hons, 98; Phi Beta Kappa. *Exhib:* Body Politics: Selections from the Kolodzei Collection of Russian & Eastern European Art, Resnick Gallery, Long Island Univ, 3-4/99; 4+4: Two Generations of Russian Avant-Garde, Mimi Ferzt Gallery, NY, 2001; New Identities New Forms: Contemp Russian Women Artists from the Kolodzei Collection, Georgetown Univ Art Galleries, Washington, DC, 3/2002; Women in Art: Three Generations of Women Artists, Long Island Univ, NY, 2003; A Retrospective of the Works by Petr Belenok, United Nations, NY, 2003; From Leningrad to St Petersburg: 25 Years of Art, Chelsea Art Mus, NY, 12/2003-5/2004; Finding Freedom: Forty of Soviet & Russian Art, Bergen Mus Art & Science, NJ, 2004 & Leepa-Rattner Mus Art, Fla, 2005; The Federal Assembly: A Project by Sergei Kalinin & Farid Bogdalov, Moscow Mus Modern Art, 2004 & Central Exhib Hall, St Petersburg, Russia, 2005; Oleg Vassiliev: Memory Speaks (Themes & Variations), State Tretyakov Gallery, Moscow, 2004 & State Russian Mus, St Petersburg, Russia, 2005; Shimon Okshteyn Dialogue with Objects, State Russian Mus, 2007; Parallel Play, Kolodzei Art Found, Chelsea Art Mus, 2008; From Non-Conformism to Feminism, Kolodzei Art Found, Chelsea Art Mus, 2009; Concerning the Spiritual Tradition on Russian Art, Kolodski Art Found, Chelsea Art Mus, 2011; plus many others. *Collection Arranged:* Kolodzei Collection of Russian & Eastern European Art. *Pos:* Exec dir, Kolodzei Art Found, Inc, Highland Park, NJ, 91-; adv bd, Russian Am Forum, NY, 95-; cur, Bergen Mus Art & Sci, Hackensack, NJ, 2000-08. *Awards:* Named Hon Citizen of State of Okla, Gov of Okla, 93. *Mem:* Am Asn for Advancement of Slavic Studies, Int Salon Soc (ambassador 1996-); Int Art Fund, Print Club NY; NY Russian Club; Golden Key Nat Hon Soc; AICA; Asn Art Historians, Russia; Hon Mem of the Russian Acad Arts; Art Table. *Publ:* auth, Unknown Segal at the Hermitage, Iskusstvo, 10-11/2002, 16; auth, James Rosenquist. Retrospective, Iskusstvo, 11-12/2003, 23; auth, First Illustrated Constitution of Russia, in: Art Constitution, Moscow, 2003, 14-15; auth, Four Visions: Transcultural New Jersey, in: Transcultural New Jersey: Diverse Artists Shaping Culture & Communities, Rutgers Univ, NJ, 2004-2005; Natalia Kolodzei (edit), Oleg Vassiliev: Memory Speaks, Palace Ed, 2004; coauth (with Tatiana Kolodzei), Our Collection. Some Facts, Sobranie, 2006, 108-115; auth, The American National

Exhibition of 1959, Pinakotheke, 22-23, 2006, 78-84; auth, Shimon Okshteyn, Dialogue with Objects, Palace Ed, 2007; auth, Vadim Vulnov: The State Hermitage under a Full Moon, State Hermitage Mus, 2009; auth, Dimitry Gerrman Poetry of Form, Palace Ed, 2009; auth, Olga Bulgakova, Knigi Wam, 2009; auth, Alexander Sitnikov, Knigi Wam, 2009. *Mailing Add:* 123 S Adelaide Ave Apt 1N Highland Park NJ 08904-1614

KOLOSVARY, PAUL PALKO See Palko Kolosvary, Paul

KOMAR, VITALY See Komar and Melamid

KOMAR AND MELAMID
PAINTER, PRINTMAKER
b Moscow, USSR, Komar Sept 11, 43, Melamid July 14, 45. *Study:* Stroganov Inst Art & Design, Moscow, USSR, 67. *Work:* Whitney Mus Am Art; Stedeliyk Mus Amsterdam; Guggenheim Mus, Mus Mod Art & Metrop Mus Art, NY. *Comn:* Murals, Liberty as Justice, NY Percent For Art Prog, 94; mural, Unity, First Interstate Bank Bldg, Los Angeles, Calif, 93. *Exhib:* Solo exhibs, Wadsworth Atheneum, Hartford, Conn, 78, Mus Mod Art, Oxford, Eng, Mus Decorative Art, Paris, France, 85, Neuen Gesellschaft für Gildende Kunst, Berlin, 88, Brooklyn Mus, 90; Counterparts and Affinities, Metrop Mus Art, NY, 82; Reallegory, Chrysler Mus, Norfolk, Va, 83; An Int Survey, Mus Mod Art, NY, 84; The Biennale of Sydney, Australia, 86; Documenta 8, Kassel, 87; Fifty Yrs of Collecting: An Anniversary Selection, Sculpture of the Modern Era, Solomon R Guggenheim Found, 87; FIAC Paris, 89; Brooklyn Mus, 90. *Teaching:* Instr visual art, Moskov Regional Art Schole, 68-76. *Awards:* Grant, Nat Endowment Arts, 82. *Bibliog:* Umberto Eco (auth), Bevente Breznev Cola, L'Espresso, 76; Robert Hughes (auth), Through the ironic curtain, Time Mag, 10/25/85; Gary Indiana (auth) Komar and Melamid confidential (cover story), Art in Am, 6/85; Jan Frazier (auth), Profile, The New Yorker, 12/86; Jean-Hubert Martin (auth), L'art da da da de Komar et Melamid, Art Press, N103, 5/86; Carter Ratcliff (auth), Komar and Melamid, Abbeville Press, 89. *Publ:* Coauths, The barren flowers of evil, 3/80 & In search of religion, 5/80, Artforum; Death Poems, NGBK-Nichen, Ger, 88

KOMAR AND MELAMID See Melamid, Alexander

KOMARIN, GARY
PAINTER
b New York, NY, Sept 14, 1951. *Study:* Albany State Univ, studied with Richard Stankiewicz, BA, 73; New Sch Social Res, 74; New York Studio Sch, studied with Paul George, 74; Art Students League, studied with Gabriel Laderman, 75; Brooklyn Mus Sch, 75; Boston Univ Sch Fine Arts, studied with Philip Guston, MFA (painting), 77. *Work:* AT&T, NY; Boston Univ; Stevens Corp, Ark; United Bank Houston; Prudential Ins Co; and others. *Comn:* Painting for Clarendon House Project, Liebman & Liebman, NY, 80; painting on paper, comn by chmn bd trustees, Kimball Art Mus, Ft Worth, Tex, 85; Chris Thompson album (cover painting), Atlantic Records. *Exhib:* Solo exhibs, Mus Art, Univ Ore, Eugene, 81, Maxwell Davidson Gallery, NY, 85, Helander Gallery, Palm Beach, 88, Brian Reddy, Little Silver, NJ, Sandler/Hudson Gallery, Atlanta, Ga, 91, Klarfeld/Perry Gallery, NY, 92 & others; East Village and NY-New Work (with catalog), Moos Art, Fla, 85; Best of Season, Helander Gallery, Fla, 86; Dog Days of Summer, Littlejohn Smith Gallery, NY, 86; Morris Mus Biennial, NJ, 88; and others. *Teaching:* Asst prof painting & drawing, Hobart & William Smith Cols, Geneva, NY, 77-78, Univ Ore, 80-81 & Southern Methodist Univ, Dallas, 81-84. *Awards:* Finalist, Int Art Competition, Los Angeles, 83; 1st Prize, 19th Ann Painting Competition, Houston, 83; Philip Hulitan Award, Soc of Four Arts, Palm Beach, 86. *Bibliog:* Carol Everingham (auth), A comical view of American dream lost, Houston Post, 11/85; Pam Perry (auth), Stories in paint, Atlanta Constitution, 11/85; W Zimmer (auth), The mentor shines through at show in Little Silver, 87, Summer splendors outside the city, 87, New York Times; Eileen Watkins, Surrealist loads canvas with images so viewer can find something new, New York Times, 87; and others. *Mem:* Coll Art Asn. *Media:* Oil on Canvas, Oil on Paper. *Dealer:* Klarfeld/Perry 472 Broone St New York NY 10012. *Mailing Add:* 259 Tophet Rd Roxbury CT 06783-1523

KOMODORE, BILL
PAINTER, EDUCATOR
b Athens, Greece, Oct 23, 1932; US citizen. *Study:* Tulane Univ La, BA, 55 & MFA, 57; Hans Hofmann Sch, Provincetown; also with Mark Rothko. *Work:* Whitney Mus Am Art; Des Moines Art Ctr, Iowa; Nat Gallery Art; Walker Art Ctr; Milwaukee Mus Art; Hamilton Gallery Art, Ont, Canada; Dallas Mus Art, Tex; Barrett Collection, Dallas, Tex. *Exhib:* Solo exhibs, Haydon Calhoun Gallery, Dallas, 61, Howard Wise Gallery, NY, 65 & 67, Automation House, NY, 73, DW Gallery, Dallas, 81, 83 & 84, Eugene Binder Gallery, Dallas, 87 & Studio Gallery, Brookhaven Col, 96; The Responsive Eye, Mus Mod Art, 64; Albright-Knox Art Gallery, Buffalo, NY, 65 & 68; Whitney Mus Am Art, NY, 65 & 68; 12 Artists from North Texas, Dallas Mus Fine Arts, 79; First Texas Triennial (with catalog), Contemp Arts Mus, Houston, 88; Texas II, San Francisco Mus Modern Art, 88; three-man show (McManaway, Komodore, Gummelt), Baylor Univ Gallery, Waco, Tex, 90; The Vessel, Dallas, Tex, 90; Bill Komodore/Jay Sullivan, Irving Arts Ctr Gallery, Tex, 91; Jansen-Perez Gallery, San Antonio, Tex, 92; The Establishment Exposed, Dallas Visual Art Ctr, 96; Content Drives Form: Recent Works of Bill Komodore, Meadows Mus, Dallas, Tex; Komodore, Art Mus South Tex, Corpus Christi, 1/99; Bill Komodore: Poetry in Paint, Pillsbury Peters Fine Art, Dallas, 2000; The Gaze, Gerald Peters Gallery, Dallas, 2005; Not Dead Yet: Persistence of the Figure in Contemp Art, Landmark Arts, Tex Tech Univ, 2006; Modalities of the Visible: A Survey of Contemp Art in North Texas, Forum Gallery, Brookhaven Coll Ctr for Arts, Dallas, 2002; Bill Komodore & Laurence Scholder, Art League, Houston, 2002. *Teaching:* Vis artist, Mary Washington Col, 73-76, Richland Col, Arts Magnet High Sch, Dallas, 77-78, Brookhaven Col, Dallas, 81-90, Dallas Theatre Ctr, 81-84 & Univ Tex, Dallas, 82-88; painter, prof, Southern Methodist Univ, 89-. *Awards:* Assistance League Houston, 97; First Prize, Whitney Mus (dir) David Ross, 97; Legends Award, Dallas Visual Arts Ctr, 97. *Bibliog:* Melissa Morrison (auth), article Dallas Morning News, 8/90; Dee Mitchell (auth), Article Dallas Morning News, 9/97; Janet Kuther (auth), Article Dallas Mooney News. *Media:* Oil, Watercolor. *Publ:* Illusr, Fishes of Lake Pontchartrain, Tulane Univ Press, 54; contribr, Contemporary American Painting and Sculpture, Univ Ill Press, 65; Young America, 1965, Whitney Mus Am Art, 65; auth, Komodore (color catalog), Dallas Visual Art Ctr, Meadows Mus, Dallas, Tex & Mus South Tex, Corpus Christi, 97. *Dealer:* Gerald Peters Fine Art 2913 Fairmount Dallas TX. *Mailing Add:* c/o Southern Methodist Univ Div Art Rm 1640 0AC Dallas TX 75275

KONG, YOUNGHEE See Doe, Willo

KONITZ, ALICE
SCULPTOR
b Essen, Germany, 1970. *Study:* Kunstakademie, Düsseldorf, Germany, Master Student, 1994, Akademiebrief, 1996; Calif Inst Arts, Valencia, CA, MFA, 1999. *Work:* Whitney Mus Am Art, New York; Saatchi Gallery. *Exhib:* Solo exhibs include Centric 65, Univ Art Mus, Long Beach, CA, 2004; group exhibs include Tirana Biennial, Tirana, 2001; Drawn from LA, Midway Contemp Art, Minneapolis, 2001; Int Paper - Drawings by Emerging Artists, UCLA Hammer Mus, Los Angeles, 2003; Run for the hills, Locust Projs, Miami, 2004; Bring the war home, Elizabeth Dee Gallery, New York, 2006; New Ghost Entertainment-Entitled, Or Gallery, Vancouver, 2006; New Ghost Entertainment - Entiltled, Kunsthaus Dresden, Dresden, Germany, 2006; Hug Fu, Daniel Hug Gallery, Los Angeles, 2007. *Dealer:* Hudson Franklin 508 W 26th St 318 New York NY 10001; Susanne Vielmetter Los Angeles Projects 5795 W Washington Blvd Culver City Los Angeles CA 90232

KONOPKA, JOSEPH
PAINTER
b Philadelphia, Pa, Oct 6, 1932. *Study:* Cooper Union, grad, 54; Columbia Univ, 55. *Work:* Butler Inst Am Art, Youngstown, Ohio; Nat Mus Am Art, Washington, DC; Mus Art, Brigham Young Univ, Utah; Tucson Mus Art, Ariz; Vatican Mus, Vatican City; Hickory Mus Art, Hickory, NC; NY Pub Libr; Archives of Am Art, Smithsonian Inst, Washington, DC; Biggs Mus Am Art, Dover, DE; Saginaw Art Mus, Mich; Springfield Art Mus, Springfield, Mo; Elmhurst Art Mus, Ill; Nat Air & Space Mus, Smithsonian Inst; Flint Inst Arts, Flint, Mich; Nat Mus, Warsaw, Poland; Noyes Mus Art, NJ; Mus of Flight, Seattle, Wash; Saginaw Art Mus, Saginaw, Mich; Naples Mus Art, Naples, Fla; Ringling Mus Art, Sarasota, Fla; Univ Alaska, Mus N, Fairbanks, Alaska; Mus Fine Art, St Petersburg, Fla; Ind State Univ; Mus Contemp Art, Fla; Kaua'i Mus, Lihue, Hawaii; Sheldon Mus Art, Neb; Owensboro Mus Fine Art, Ky; Mo Nay Art Mus, San Antonio, Tex; Navy Mus, Wash Navy Yard, Wash DC; Nev Historical Soc, Reno; Adirondack Mus, Blue Mountain Lake, NY; Mus Contemp Art, Jacksonville, Fla; Polish Historical Soc, Paris, France; NY Public Lib Performing Arts, Billy Rose Theatre Division; Brooklyn Hist Soc, Brooklyn, NY; Kenosha Pub Mus, Kenosha, Wis; Wyo State Mus, Cheyenne, Wyo; Muzeum Narodowe, w Krakowie, Krakow, Poland; Mus of the City of New York, NY; Swope Art Mus, Terre Hauto, Ind; Tenn State Mus, Nashville, Tenn; Mercer Mus Bucks Co Historical Soc, Doylestown, Pa; Nat Gallery of Iceland, Reykijavik, Iceland; Ocean Co Historical Soc Mus, Toms River, NJ. *Exhib:* Butler Inst Am Art, 74, 77, 79, 82, 84 & 87; Brooklyn Mus, 76, 78 & 81; Recent Acquisitions, 81, Drawing from Permanent Collections, 82 & On the 20th Century, 83, Monclair Art Mus, NJ; Atlantic City Art Ctr, 89, 90 & 96; Bergen Mus, Paramus, NJ 91; South Bend Regional Mus Art, Ind, 98; Harn Mus Art, Gainesville, Fla, 98; Selections from Permanent Collection, Ogunquit Mus Am Art, Maine, 99; The Human Factor, Sunrise Mus, Charleston, WVa, 2000; Molvane Art Mus, Collecting & Connecting, 2003; New Jersey Historical Soc, Changed Lives, 2nd Anniversary Sept 11, Sept-Nov, 2003; Univ Mus, Southern Ill Univ, Carbondale, Ill, 2004; Jersey City Mus, Constructing Am III: Industry & Modernity, 2005; Recent Acquisitions to the Swope Collection, Swope Art Mus, 2005; Recent Accessions on Exhibit, Springfield Art Mus, Ill, Dec-Jan, 2006; New Accessions, Anderson Fine Arts Center, summer 2006; Recent Accessions on Exhibit, Naples Mus Art, 2007; NJ Through Artists' Eyes, Newark Pub Libr, 2009; Summerlands: Works from the Permanent Collection, Noyes Mus Art, Oceanville, NY, 5-9/2011; A Lifetime of Giving, William J Dane Fine Print Collection, Newark Public Lib, 4-6/2011; Changed Lives, NJ Historical Soc, 2011; Elemental Arts, Earth, Fire, Water, Asheville Art Mus, North Carolina, 2012; Hurricane Sandy, Ocean Co Historical Soc Mus, Toms River, NJ, 2013. *Pos:* Scenic artist, NBC TV 52-2012, Late Night with David Letterman, 82-93, Late Night with Conan O'Brian, 93-2009, Late Night with Jimmy Fallon, 2009-. *Awards:* Purchase Awards, Newark Mus, 68 & NJ State Mus, 70; Medal Honor, NJ Painters & Sculptors Soc, 71. *Bibliog:* Articles, Arts Mag, 2/73 & 12/75; Sunday NY Times, 76 & Newark Star-Ledger, 10/79 & 1/82; article, NJ Art Form Mag, 3-4/81; article, Szymon Bojko, Polish-American & Polish Artists in Contemporary American Art, 2002; article, The Polish American Encyclopedia, 2012. *Mem:* Assoc Artists NJ (vpres, 77-85); Clifton Asn Artists, NJ; United Scenic Artists, Local 829 (52-); Atlantic City Art Asn. *Media:* Acrylic. *Res:* Smithsonian Institution, Archives of American Art, Newark Public Library. *Dealer:* Capricorn Gallery 10236 River Rd Potomac MD 20854. *Mailing Add:* 26 Snowden Pl Glen Ridge NJ 07028

KOO, JEONG-A
INSTALLATION SCULPTOR, ASSEMBLAGE ARTIST
Work: Guggenheim Mus, New York; Centre Pompidou, France. *Exhib:* Centre Pompidou, Musée National d'Art Moderne, Paris, 2004; Emergency Biennale in Chechnya, Vancouver Int Centre for Contemp Asian Art, BC, Can, 2006; Wherever We Go: Art, Identity, Cultures in Transit Phase 1, San Francisco Art Inst, 2007; Full House, Mus Contemp Art, Helsinki, 2008; 53rd Int Art Exhib Biennale, Venice, 2009

KOOB, PAMELA NABSETH
INDEPENDENT ART HISTORIAN, CURATOR
b Boston, June 28, 1948. *Study:* Stanford Univ, BA, 70; Harvard Grad Sch Edn, MAT, 71; Hunter Col, CUNY, MA, 97. *Exhib:* Edward Hopper's New York Movie (with catalog), 1998; A Century on Paper: Prints by Art Students League Artists (with catalog), 2002; A Permanent Record of What has been Accomplished: Highlights from the Permanent Collection, Art Students League of NY, Forbes Galleries, NY, 2004; Drawing Lessons: Early acad drawings from the permanent collection of the Art Studients League of NY (with catalog), 2009; Will Barnet & the Art Students League, 2010 (with catalog). *Pos:* curator, Art Students League of NY, 98-2013. *Awards:* Richard M Kaye Scholarship, Hunter Coll, NY, 97. *Mem:* Coll Art Asn; AAM. *Collection:* Permanent collection Art Students League of NY documents school's history. *Publ:* Giorgio de Chirico and America, Hunter Coll, 96; Edward Hooper's NY Movie (exhib catalog), Hunter Coll, 98; A Century on Paper, Art Students League of NY, 02; States of Being: Edward Hopper and Symbolist Aesthetics, Am Art, Vol 18 No 3, 52-77, 2004; Will Barnet and the Art Students League, Art Students League of Ny, 2010; 1875-2012: A History in Art-A Timeline of the Art Students League, NY, 2012. *Mailing Add:* 100 E Solitude Dr Jackson WY 83001

KOONS, DARELL J
EDUCATOR, PAINTER
b Albion, Mich, Dec 18, 1924. *Study:* Bob Jones Univ, BS, 51; Western Mich Univ, MA, 55; Eastern Mich Univ. *Work:* Butler Inst Am Art, Youngstown, Ohio; Mint Mus Art, Charlotte, Gov Mansion, Columbia, SC State Art Collection Mus Art, SC; Gibbes Gallery, Charleston, SC. *Comn:* Series of paintings hist scenes city of Greenville, comn by Tom Styron (dir Greenville Co Mus), 2004. *Exhib:* Acquavella Galleries, NY, 64 & 66; Springfield Mus Art Nat, Mass, 65; Soc Four Arts Nat, Palm Beach, Fla, 67; Solo exhibs, Mint Mus, Charlotte, NC, Wash Co Mus Art, Hagerstown, Md, Columbus Mus, Columbus, Ga, Jesse Besser Mus, Alpena, Mich; Art Embassies Prog, US State Dept, 90. *Pos:* Painter, currently. *Teaching:* Instr art, Homer Community Schs, 52-54; Bob Jones Univ, 55-98, drawing & painting instr, retired. *Awards:* Purchase Awards, Guild SC Artists, 63, Davis Assocs, Chattanooga, Tenn, 65 & Wake Forest Univ Gallery Contemp Art, 65. *Bibliog:* Steve Yates (auth), Greenville's noted barn painter, Sandlapper, 3/68. *Mem:* Upstate Visual Artists. *Media:* Watercolor, Acrylic. *Specialty:* fine arts, sculpture, ceramics. *Dealer:* Hampton III Gallery Wade Hampton Blvd Taylors SC 29687

KOONS, JEFF
PAINTER, SCULPTOR
b York, Pa, 1955. *Study:* Md Inst Coll Art, Baltimore, 72-75 & BFA, 76; Art Inst Chicago, Ill, 75-76. *Exhib:* Solo shows include Mus Contemp Art, Sydney, Australia, 95, Galerie jerome de Noirmont, Paris, France, 97, Guggenheim Mus Bilbao, Spain, 97,Anthony d'Offay Gallery, London, Eng, 98, Deste Found, Athens, Greece, 99, Deutsche Guggenheim, Berlin, Ger, 2000 & Gagosian Gallery, Los Angeles, 2000, Helsingin kaupungin taidemuseo, 2005, Gagosian Gallery, London, 2006, 2007, Luxembourg & Dayan, New York, 2011; Retrospective (with catalog), Stedelijk Mus, Amsterdam, The Neth, 92, San Francisco Mus Mod Art, Calif, 92, Staatsgalerie Stuttgart, Ger, 93, Aarhus, Denmark, 93 & Walker Art Ctr, Minneapolis, Minn, 93; A Survey 1981-1994, Anthony d'Offay Gallery, London, Eng, 94; group exhibs include Playpen & Corpus Delierium (with catalog), Kunsthalle Zurich, Switz, 96; a/drift, Ctr Curatorial Studies Mus, Bard Col, Annandale-on-Hudson, NY, 96; Art at Home - Ideal Standard Life (with catalog), Spiral Garden, Tokyo, Japan, 96 & Gallery Seomi, Seoul, Korea, 96; It's Only Rock and Roll: Rock and Roll Currents in Contemp Art, Phoenix Art Mus, Ariz, 97; Belladonna, Inst Contemp Arts, London, Eng, 97; Family Values: Am Art in the Eighties and Nineties (with catalog), Scharpff Collection, Hamburger Kunsthalle, Hamburg, Ger, 97; Autoportraits, Galerie Municipale du Chateau d'Eau, Toulouse, France, 97; Multiple Identity: Amerikanische Kunst 1975-1995 Aus Dem Whitney Mus of Am Art (with catalog), Kunstmuseum Bonn, Ger, 97 & Castello di Rivoli, Mus d'Arte Contemporanea, Rivoli, Italy, 97; Objects of Desire: The Modern Still Life (with catalog), Mus Mod Art, NY, 97; Futuro Presente Passato: La Biennale di Venezia (with catalog), Venice, Italy, 97; Envisioning the Contemp: Selections from the Permanent Collection, Mus Contemp Art, Chicago, Ill, 97-98; On the Edge: Contemp Art from the Werner and Elaine Dannheisser Collection (with catalog), Mus Mod Art, NY, 97-98; A House Is Not A Home, Ctr Contemp Art, Amsterdam, The Neth, 97; Dramatically Different (with catalog), Ctr Nat D'Art Contemporain de Grenoble, France, 97-98; Kunst, Arbeit (with catalog), Sudwest LB Forum, Stuttgart, Ger, 97-98; Art in the 20th Century: Collection from the Stedelijk Mus Amsterdam (with catalog), Ho-Am Art Mus, Seoul, Korea, 98; Tuning Up #5, Kunstmuseum Wolfsburg, 98; Rene Margritte and the Contemp (with catalog), Mus voor Mod Kunst, Oostende, Belg, 98; Urban, Tate Gallery, Liverpool, Eng, 98-99; Interno - Esterno/Alterno (with catalog), FENDI, NY, 98; A Celebration of Art, Hirshhorn Mus & Sculpture Garden, Washington, 99; Am Century, Part II, Whitney Mus Am Art, NY, 99; Innocence and Experience, Mus Mod Art, NY, 2000, Pop and After, 2000, Matter, 2000, MoMA 2000, 2000, Actual Size, 2000 & Collaborations with Parkett: 1984 to Now, 2001; Reflections, Monika Sprüth Philomene Magers, Munich, 2002, Penetration, Friedrich Petzel Gallery, New York City, 2002, Penetration, Marianne Boesky Gallery, New York City, Shopping, Tate Liverpool, 2002; Air, James Cohan Gallery, New York City, 2003; Leckerbissen, Fischerplatz-Galerie, Ulm, 2003. *Awards:* Name one of 10 Most Important Artists of Today, Newsweek mag, 2011. *Bibliog:* Roberta Smith (auth), Jeff Koons: Easyfun, NY Times, 99; Robert Hicks (auth), Jeff Koons brings art to the people, Villager Preview, 12/1/99; Robert Rigney (auth), Kitsch and Tell, Artnews, 3/2000. *Publ:* auth, The Jeff Koons Handbook, 93; coauth (with Thomas Kellein) Jeff Koons Pictures 1980-2002, 03; coauth (with Robert Rosenblum and David Sylvester) Jeff Koons Easy Fun Ethereal, 03. *Dealer:* Sonnabend 420 W Broadway New York NY 10012. *Mailing Add:* c/o Gagosian Gallery 980 Madison Ave New York NY 10021

KOONTZ, REX
EDUCATOR, ADMINISTRATOR
Study: American Col, Paris, BA, 1985; Univ Texas, Austin, MA (Art History), 1988, PhD (Art History), 1994. *Teaching:* Asst prof, Univ Texas, El Paso, 1995-2001, assoc prof, 2001; asst prof, Univ Houston, Sch of Art, 2001-07, assoc prof, 2007-, assoc dean graduate studies, currently, dir, currently. *Publ:* sr editor, Landscape and Power in Ancient Mesoamerica, 2001; (co-editor) Mexico (5th ed), 2002, (6th ed) 2008; (co-editor) Blood and Beauty: Organized Violence in the Art and Archaeology of Ancient Mesoamerica and Central America, 2009; (auth) Lightning Gods and Feathered Serpents: The Public Sculpture of El Tajin, 2009. *Mailing Add:* School of Art Fine Arts Buliding Room 100C/104B University of Houston 4800 Calhoun Rd Houston TX 77204

KOOPALETHES, OLIVIA ALBERTS
PAINTER, PRINTMAKER
b New York, NY. *Study:* The Cooper Union, New York, 43-45; study with Wallace Harrison, New York, 46-49; Atelier Fernand Leger, Paris, 49; Atelier Andre Lhote, Paris, 50; Roberto DeLamonica, 76-79, Krishna Reddy, New York Blackburn Workshop, 80 & Shou Ping Liao, 81, Tenafly, NJ. *Exhib:* Solo exhibs, On Paper, New City Libr, NY, 89, L'Atelier Gallery, Piermont, NY, Greek Consulate Cult Ctr, Greek Embassy, NY, 92, Gallery Interchurch Ctr, NY, 94, Intermission Gallery, John Harms Ctr, Englewood, NJ, 95 & Bergen Mus Arts & Sci, Paramus, NJ, 96, Gannon Univ, Schuster Gallery, Erie, Pa, 98-99, Arts Guild of Rahway, NJ, 2001, Pleiades Gallery, New York, 2001, Studio 4 West, NY, 2001, Audubon Artists, 2002, Belskie Mus, NJ, 2003, Maniotis Art Ctr, Boston, 2003 & Berlox Laboratories Corp, Wayne, NJ, 2004; League of Transient Beauty, Aspects of Flowers, Invitational, Lever House, NY, 92; Critical Eye, Am Soc Contemp Artists, Broome St Gallery, 92; Ridgewood Art Inst, NJ, 92; Nat Asn Women Artists Print Show (traveling), 92-93; Audubon Artists Ann Exhib, New York, 92, 95-96, 2000 & 2006; Invitational Exhib (auth, catalog), Pleiades Gallery, NY, 96; Nat Asn Women Artists (traveling), 96-99; Hunterdon Art Ctr, Clinton, NJ, 97; Painters Affiliate, Johnson & Johnson, New Brunswick, NJ, 97; City Without Walls, 18th Ann Metro Traveling Show, Newark, NJ, 99; Seton Hall, Newark, 99; Pleiades Gallery, New York, 2000; Am Soc Contemp Artists Ann Exhib, 2000, 2003-2004 & 2007; Jane Vorhees Zimmerli Art Mus, Rutgers Coll, New Brunswick, NJ, 2003; World Paper Challenger II, Dana Libr, Rutgers, Newark, NJ, 2003; Int Soc Experimental Artist De Vos Mus, Marquette, Ill, 2006; 13th Ann Edward House Art Ctr, Nyack, NY, 2006; Nat Asn Women Arts, 2006; Karpeles Libr Mus, Newburg, NY; Port of Call Gallery, Warwick, NY; Invitational, Consul of Greece Gallery, New York, 2007; Synagogue for the Arts, New York, 2007; Belskie Mus, Closter, NJ, 2007; Blue Hill Art Ctr, Pearl River, NY, 2007; 90th Annual American Society of Contemp Artists, NY, 2008; 66th Ann Audubon Artists, NY, 2008; 67th Ann Audubon Artists, 2009; 119th Annual National Association of Women Artists, Goggle Works, Reading, Pa, 2008; 19th Annual Michael Zakin Gallery, Small Works, Demarest, NJ, 2008; American Society of Contemp Artists, Manhatten Boro Pres Exhib Gallery, NY, 2008; NAWA in NJ, John Dana Libr, Rutgers Univ, Newark, NJ, 2008; 120th Ann Nat Asn Women Artists, Salmagundi Arts Club, NY, 2009; Salute to Women Artists, Bergen PAC Juried Show, Englewood, NJ, 2009; Salute to Women Artists, Art Ctr, Northern NJ, New Milford, NJ, 2009; 92nd Ann Am Soc Contemp Artists, Broome St Gallery, New York, 2009; 19th Juried Exhib, Int Soc Experimental Artists, Forest Hills Fine Art Ctr, Grand Rapids, Mich, 2010; 121st Nat Asn Women Artists, Nat Arts Club, New York, 2010; Audubon 69th, Salmagundi Arts Club, NY, 2011; Nat Asn Women Artists, Sylvia Wield and Pokim Gallery, NY, 2011; Celebrating Bergens Diversity, Art Center of Northern NJ, New Milford, NJ, 2011; Salute to Women in the Arts, Marcella Geltman Gallery, New Milford, NJ, 2011; Painting Affiliates, Bergen Commun Annex Bldg, Hackensack, NJ, 2012; Salute to Women in the Arts, Waltuch Art Gallery at Kaplan JCC on the Palisades, Tenafly, NJ, 2012; Celebrating Bergen County's Diversity, Art Ctr Northern Jersey, New Milford, NJ, 2012; Nat Asn Women Artists, Midday Gallery, Englewood, NJ, 2012; 71st Ann Audubon Artists Online, 2013; 124th Ann Nat Asn women Artists, Sylvia Wald & Pokim Gallery, 2013; Salute to Women in the Arts, Art Ctr Northern NJ, New Milford, NJ, 2013; The Art Ctr Northern NJ, Celebrating Bergen County's Diversity, New Milford, NJ, 2013; The Art Ctr of Northern NJ, Celebrating Bergen Co Diversity, New Milford, NJ, 2013; Salute to Women in the Arts, Art Ctr of Northern NJ, New Milford, NJ, 2013; 124th Ann Nat Assn Women Artists, Sylvia Wald, & Po Kim Gallery, NY, 2013; 71st Ann Audubon Artists online, 2013. *Pos:* Historian, Nat Asn Women Artists, 89-97; violinist Bergen Philharmonic Orch, Teaneck, NJ; Bergen Co Teen Arts Festival, Art Critique, 99-2005. *Teaching:* Monitor printmaking, Robert DeLamonica Art Ctr, 79-81, Shou Ping Lian Art Ctr, Tenafly, NJ, 81-82. *Awards:* Hon Mention, Montclair State Art Gallery; Grumbacher Silver Medal, Best in show, Salute to Women in the Arts, 93; Myra Biggerstaff Award, Nat Asn Women Artists 107th Ann, 96 & 108th Ann, 97; Am Soc Contemp Artists Award, 80th Ann Exhib, 98; Salute to Women in the Arts, Award of Excellence, Art Ctr Northern NJ, New Milford, NJ, 2002, 2nd Prize, 2005; Nat Asn Women Artists 117th Ann Dorothy Schweitzer Mem Adwards, Reading, Pa, 2006; Jami Taback Award, 88th Ann, Am Soc Contemp Artists, New York, 2006; Best in Show, Focus NJ, Art Center of Northern NJ, New Milford, NJ; 90th Am Soc Contemp Artist, 2008; 119th Ann Nat Asn Women Artists, 2008; 89th Ann Am Soc Contemp Artists, 2008; 1st Pl, Bergan Co Diversity, Marcella Geiman Gallery, New Milford, NJ; 3rd Pl, Salute to Women in the Arts, Marcella Geltman Gallery, New Milford, NJ; Marquis Who's Who in Am Art References Award in Graphics, Audubon Artists, New York, 2011; 1st Pl, Mixed Media, Celebrating Bergen County's Diversity, Art Ctr Northern NJ, New Milford, 2012; 123rd Ann Nat Asn Women Artists, Sylvia Ward and Pokim Gallery, NY, 2012; 70th Ann Audubon Arts Inc Exhib, 2012; 1st Pl, Mixed Media, Celebrating Bergen Co, Diversity, New Milford, NJ, 2013; 1st Pl, Celebrating Bergen Co Diversity, New Milford, NJ, 2013; 124th Ann Nat Assn Women Artists Miriam E Haperin Meml award, Sylvia Wald & Po Kim Gallery, NY, 2013. *Bibliog:* EC Lipton (auth), Art Speak, NY, 10/92; Evonne E Courtros (auth), Hellenic Times, NY, 2/94; David Messer (auth), article, Bergan Mus Newsletter, 9-12/96; Ed McCormack (ed), Immediacy to an Ancient Medium, Gallery & Studio, Nov-Dec 2003/Jan 2004; Joanne Mattera (auth), Encaustic Painting: Contemporary Expression

in the Ancient Medium of Pigment Wax, Watson Guptill. *Mem:* Nat Asn Women Artists (hist, 6/87-5/91); Am Soc Contemp Artists; Printmaking Coun NJ; Audubon Artists Inc, NY; Art Ctr Painting Affil NJ; Salute to Women in the Arts NJ; Hellenic Am Womes Soc of NJ; Art from Detritus, NY; Int Soc Experimental Artist (ISEA), Fort Worth, Tex; Artist Equity Asn, Inc, 2008. *Media:* Wax Crayon, Colored Pencil; Encaustics. *Publ:* Contribr, Pages of Revelation, Artbuilders Inc, 86; 100 Years: A Centennial Celebration of National Association of Women Artists, Nassau Co Mus Fine Arts, Roslyn Harbor, NY, 88. *Dealer:* Leader Associates Wayne NJ; Artvue Mahwah NJ. *Mailing Add:* 12 Cambridge Way Alpine NJ 07620

KOOYMAN, RICHARD E
CRAFTSMAN
b Grand Rapids, Mich, Oct 1, 1956. *Study:* Grand Valley State Univ, BFA, 79; Ohio State Univ, MFA, 82. *Exhib:* Objects Gallery, Chicago, 87, 88, 90 & 93; Detroit Gallery Contemp Craft, Detroit, 89 & 93; The Works Gallery, Philadelphia, Pa, 93; Smithsonian Craft Show, Smithsonian Inst, Washington, DC, 93 & 94; Twist Gallery, Portland, Ore, 93; Bennett Galleries, Knoxville, Tenn, 94; Nancy Sach Galleries, St Louis, Mo, 94. *Awards:* Mich Coun Arts, 89; Nat Endowments Arts, 89; Mich Gov Award Arts, 90. *Mem:* Am Craft Coun; Coll Art Asn; Nat Coun Educ Ceramic Arts

KOPF, SILAS
CRAFTSMAN
b Warren, Pa, 1949. *Study:* Princeton Univ, AB (archit), 72; with Wendall Castle, 74-76; Ecole Boulle, France. *Work:* Gannett Corp; Scovill Corp; pvt Collections of Anne & Ronald Abramson, Washington, DC, Walda & Sydney Bestoff, New Orleans, La, Janice & Robert Diamond, NY, Sylvia & Donald Gerson, Ft Myers, Fla and many others. *Comn:* Craft work, Steinway & Sons, NY. *Exhib:* Wisteriahurst Mus, Holyoke, Mass, 86; Workbench Gallery, NY, 86; A C E Crafts at the Armory, NY, 87; Artful Objects: Recent Am Craft, Ft Wayne, Ind, 89; solo exhibs, Gallery Henoch, NY, 90, 92, 95 & 2001; Conservation by Design (nat touring exhib), 95-97. *Collection Arranged:* Mus of Art & Design, NY; Smith Col, Northamton, Mass; Yale Univ, New Haven, Conn. *Awards:* Craftsman's Fel, Nat Endowment of Arts, 88; New Eng Found Arts Fel, 97. *Bibliog:* Articles in fine woodworking, Am Craft, NY Times, Boston Globe, Art in New Eng, La, Marqueterie (France) & Art and Practices of Marquetry (Britain). *Mem:* Furniture Soc. *Dealer:* Gallery Henoch 555 W 25th St New York NY. *Mailing Add:* 20 Stearns Ct Northampton MA 01060

KOPLOS, JANET
CRITIC, EDITOR
Study: Univ Minn, BA; Ill State Univ, MA. *Pos:* Mainichi Daily News, Tokyo; Arts & books ed; contrib ed, Fiberarts, Art Papers, New Art Examiner; sr ed, Art in America, NYC, 90-2008; guest ed, Am Craft, 2009. *Teaching:* adj prof, Parsons, New Sch Design, 2003-2009, Univ Arts, Pa, 2009-2010, RI Sch Design, 2012-; instr, Pratt Inst, 2010-2013. *Awards:* Recipient, Nat Endowment Arts, Art Critic's Fel; Phi Beta Kappa, Kappa Tau Alpha journalism hon; Hon Fel, Am Craft Coun 2010; Hall of Fame, Ill State Univ Coll Fine Arts, 2010. *Mem:* Coll Art Asn; Asn Int Critiques d'Art. *Publ:* Contemp Japanese Sculpture, 91; Collecting Ceramics Today (pamphlet), Microsoft Art Coll, 2002; coauth, Unexpected: Artists' Ceramics of the 20th Century, Laura De Santillana Works, 2002; Gyongy Laky, 2003; Teun Hocks, 2005; coauth, Makers: A Hist of Am Studio Craft, 2010; A Chosen Path: The Ceramic Art of Karen Karnes, Univ NC Chapel Hill, Press, 2010; Toshiko Takaezu from the Ceramic Research Center, Ariz State Univ, Tempe, 2011; Winifred Lutz, Between Perception & Definition, Abington Art Ctr, Jenkintown, Pa. *Mailing Add:* 987 Como Blvd E Saint Paul MN 55103

KOPLOWITZ, ALICIA
COLLECTOR
b Sept 12, 1953. *Pos:* Co-owner, Construcciones y Contratas SA (Cysca), 1989-1997; owner, Omega Capital, currently. *Awards:* Named one of Top 200 Collectors, ARTnews mag, 2004-13. *Collection:* Old masters & modern art. *Mailing Add:* Found Alicia Koplowitz Paseo de la Castellana 28-4 Madrid 28046 Spain

KOPPELMAN, DOROTHY
PAINTER, CONSULTANT
b New York, NY, June 13 1920. *Study:* Brooklyn Col; Am Artists Sch; Art Students League; studied Philosophy of Aesthetic Realism with Eli Siegel, founder, now with Ellen Reiss. *Work:* Yale Univ, New Haven, Conn; Hampton Univ, Va; Rosenzweig Mus, Durham, NC; Nat Mus Women Arts, Washington, DC; Savannah Coll Art Design, Ga; Wash Co Mus Art; Libr Cong. *Exhib:* Rina Gallery, 61; Museum Mod Art, New York City & Columbus Gallery Fine Art, 62; City Art Mus St Louis & Walker Art Ctr, 63; Baltimore Mus Art; Brooklyn Mus; NJ State Mus; San Francisco Art Inst; 161st Ann Juried Exhib, 86, 165th Juried Exhib, 90, Nat Acad Design, NY; Hudson Guild, 88 & 90; Susan Teller Gallery, 93 & 95; Drawing Ctr, 95; Audubon Juried Ann, 96 & 98, Levitan Gallery, 96; Atlantic Gallery, 97-98, 2000-2003, 2007, 2008; 175th Juried Exhib Nat Acad Design, NY, 2000; Beatrice Conde Gallery, 2000; Terrain Gallery, 61, 2002-2003 & 2005-2006, 2007, 2008, 2010. *Pos:* Dir, Terrain Gallery, 55-83 & Visual Arts Gallery, 62-64; pres, Aesthetic Realism Found Inc, 73-87. *Teaching:* Instr art, Adult Educ, Brooklyn Col, 52-75; consult Aesthetic Realism, 71-; instr, Nat Acad, Sch Fine Arts, 88, 89, 96 & 98; instr, Critical Inquiry, Aesthetic Realism Fedn, New York, 80-. *Awards:* Prize Painting, Brooklyn Soc Artists, 60; Tiffany Found Grant, 65-66; T Lindner Award for Painting, 96; Clara Shainess Award for Painting, 99. *Bibliog:* Emily Genauer (auth), article, NY Herald Tribune, 62; revs, Art News, 59, 61 & 62, NY Times, 62. *Mem:* NY Artist's Equity; Am Soc Contemp Artists. *Media:* Oil, Printmaking. *Res:* Frescoes of Piero della Francesca. *Specialty:* Contemp Art. *Publ:* Coauth, Aesthetic Realism: We Have Been There, 69; illusr, Children's Guide to Parents & Other Matters, 71, 2003, 2010; Van Gogh, Sunstorm, 84; Chardin, Tenn Tribune; Picasso's Guernica for Life, Tenn, Tribune; Opposites are Picasso's: Man with a Lamb, ASCA Newsletter, 2003; Frescoes of Della Francesca, at Sansepolcro, Italy, Artists Proof, 2008; Poems & Prints, Pierodella Press, 2000; Napolean Entering New York (forward, catalogue); Museo Napoleonico, Gangiemi Editore, 2011; Damned Welcome (forward), 2011. *Dealer:* Terrain Gallery 141 Greene St NYC 10013. *Mailing Add:* 141 Wooster St New York NY 10012

KOPRIVA, SHARON
PAINTER, SCULPTOR
b Houston, Tex, Feb 11, 1948. *Study:* Univ Houston, with J Alexander & J Surls, BS, 70, MFA, 81. *Work:* Mus Fine Arts, Sante Fe, NMex; Mus Fine Arts & Menil Mus, Houston, Tex; Lowe Mus, Miami, Fla; Oshman Collection; Mus Fine Arts, Dallas, Tex; New Orleans Mus Fine Arts; Ogden Mus, New Orleans; Mus Fine Arts, El Paso, Tex. *Comn:* Sculpture, ZZ Top, Billy Gibbons, Houston, 90; Grant, Mid Am, 92; Cultural Arts Coun, Houston, 92 & 95. *Exhib:* Mus Fine Arts, Santa Fe, NMex, 86; Ctr Contemp Art, Mexico City, 87; Mus SE Tex, Beaumont, 91; Mus Fine Arts, Houston, Tex, 94; Nat Mus Am Art, Washington, 96; Menil Mus 2001; Mus Fine Arts, Shanghai, China; Nat Mus Lima, Peru, 2006; Broken Bushes, Ogden Mus Fine Art, New Orleans, La; Blue Star, San Antonio, Tex, 2013; and others. *Pos:* Bd mem, Orange Show Found, Houston, 89-. *Teaching:* Teach fel, Univ Houston, 81; vis artist, Tex Tech & NDak State Univ, 90. *Awards:* First Place, Blaffer Gallery, Univ Houston, 88; Sculpture Grant, Diverse Works, Houston, 90; Texas State Artist Year 2005; Artist of the Year, ALH, 2002. *Bibliog:* S Bell (auth) & Gambrell (auth), articles in: Art Am, 87 & 89; Ed Hill (auth), article, Art Forum, 90; C Anspon (auth), Art News, 2000 & Sculpture, 2000; Houston Contemp Art, MFA Shanghai 2006; Sharon Kopriva, Ogden Mus, 2012; S Kalill (auth) Art Am, 2013. *Media:* Oil, Pencil; Bone, Paper-Mache, Bronze. *Dealer:* Colton Gallery Houston TX; Hall Barnett, New Orleans, La. *Mailing Add:* 1317 Arlington Houston TX 77008

KOPYSTIANSKY, IGOR
MULTIMEDIA ARTIST, PAINTER
b 1954. *Work:* Mus Modern Art, NY; Whitney Mus Am Art, NY; Metropolitan Mus, NY; Art Inst Chicago, Ill; Mus Fine Arts, Houston, Tex; Smithsonian Am Art Mus, Wash DC; Tate Modern, London; Center Pompidou, Paris, Fr; Musee d'Art Moderne de Saint-Etienne, Fr; AGNSW, Sydney, Australia; Folkwang Mus, Essen, Ger; Ludwig Forum Int Art, Aachen, Ger; MMk Frankfurt am Main, Ger; Deutsche Bank Coll, Frankfurt, Ger; Mus Modern Art, Palais Lichenstein, Vienna, Austria; Centre Contemp Art Luigi Pecci, Prato, Italy. *Comn:* sculpture, Univ Gelsenkirchen, Ger; sculpture, Deutsche Welle, Bonn, Ger. *Exhib:* Works by Igor and Svetlana Kopystiansky were exhibited at venues including: MoMA, NY, 2012, Metropolitan Mus, NY, 97, 2001, 2010-2011, Art Inst Chicago, 96-98, 2008, Mus Contemp Art Chicago, 99, Smithsonian Am Art Mus, 2010-11, Scottsdale Mus Contemp Art, Ariz, 2005, Fine Arts Ctr, UMass, Amherst, Mass, 2005, Ctr Pompidou, Paris, 2009, 2010, 2011, Ctr Pompidou Metz, 2011-2012, Musée d'Art Moderne de Saint-Etienne, 2010, Tate Modern London, 2011-2012, Tate Liverpool, 99, Whitechapel Art Gallery, London 99, MMK Frankfurt/Main, 99, 2010, 2011, Kunsthalle Düsseldorf, 92, 94, 95, Kunstmuseum Düsseldorf, 2000, Folkwang Museum, Essen, 2000, Sprengel Mus, Hannover, 2002, Kunsthalle Fridericianum, Kassel, 99, 2005-2006, Deichttorhallen Hamburg, 2011-2012, Kunsthalle zu Kiel, 2011-12, Kunstwerke Berlin, 99, Reina Sofia, Madrid, 94-95, S.M.A.K. Gent, 2009, GAMeC, Bergamo, 2011, Mus Modern Art EMMA, Finland, 2007, AGNSW, Sydney, 92, 2003, 2005, 2008, 2009, Kunsthalle Krems, Austria, 2012, MARCO, Vigo, Spain, 2007, Mus Modern Art, Palais Lichtenstein, Vienna, 89; Igor and Svetlana participated in international exhibs including Sculpture Projects Münster 97, Documenta 11, 2002, and biennials in Venice, 88, Sao Paulo, 94, Istanbul, 95, Johannesburg, 97, Lyon, 97, Liverpool, 99, and others. *Awards:* Fel, DAAD Artists Prog, Berlin, Ger, 90; Kathe-Kollwitz-Preis 2000, Akademie der Kunste, Berlin, Ger, 2000; Residences Int aux Recollets, Paris, 2008. *Bibliog:* Adam D Weinberg, Barry Schwabsky, Rene Block, Anthony Bond (auths), Igor & Svetlana Kopystiansky (Eng and Ger), Kunsthalle Fridericianum, Kassel and Fine Arts Ctr Univ Mass, Amherst, Mass, 2005; Gabriel Coxhead (auth), A Dual Perspective, The Financial Times, 2006; Anthony Spira, Barry Schwabsky (auths), Igor & Svetlana Kopystiansky, Espoo Mus Modern Art, Helsinki, 2007; John G Hanhardt, Philippe-Alain Michaud (auth), Kopystiansky, Musee d'Art Moderne de Saint-Etienne, Les Presses du Reel, 2010. *Media:* Installation, Painting; Video, Photography. *Interests:* videoing; sculpting; photography. *Mailing Add:* 526 W 26th St No 608 New York NY 10001

KOPYSTIANSKY, SVETLANA
MULTIMEDIA ARTIST, PAINTER
b 1950. *Work:* Mus Modern Art, NY; Whitney Mus Am Art, NY; Metropolitan Mus Art, NY; Art Inst Chicago, Ill; Mus Fine Arts, Houston, Tex; Smithsonian Am Art Mus, Wash DC; Tate Modern, London; Center Pompidou, Paris; Musee d'Art Moderne de Saint-Etienne, France; AGNSW, Sydney, Australia; Folkwang Mus, Essen, Ger; Ludwig Forum for Int Art, Aachen, Ger; MMK Frankfurt am Main, Ger; Deutsche Bank Coll, Frankfurt, Ger; Mus Modern Art, Palais Lichtenstein, Vienna, Austria; Centre Contemp Art Luigi Pecci, Prato, Italy. *Comn:* Univ Gelsenkirchen, Ger; Deutsche Welle, Bonn, Ger. *Exhib:* Works by Igor and Svetlana Kopystiansky were exhibited at venues including: MoMA, NY, 2012, Metropolitan Mus, NY, 97, 2001, 2010-2011, Art Inst Chicago, 96-98, 2008, Mus Contemp Art Chicago, 99, Smithsonian Am Art Mus, 2010-11, Scottsdale Mus Contemp Art, Ariz, 2005, Fine Arts Ctr, UMass, Amherst, Mass, 2005, Ctr Pompidou, Paris, 2009, 2010, 2011, Ctr Pompidou Metz, 2011-2012, Musée d'Art Moderne de Saint-Etienne, 2010, Tate Modern London, 2011-2012, Tate Liverpool, 99, Whitechapel Art Gallery, London 99, MMK Frankfurt/Main, 99, 2010, 2011, Kunsthalle Düsseldorf, 92, 94, 95, Kunstmuseum Düsseldorf, 2000, Folkwang Museum, Essen, 2000, Sprengel Mus, Hannover, 2002, Kunsthalle Fridericianum, Kassel, 99, 2005-2006, Deichttorhallen Hamburg, 2011-2012, Kunsthalle zu Kiel, 2011-12, Kunstwerke Berlin, 99, Reina Sofia, Madrid, 94-95, S.M.A.K. Gent, 2009, GAMeC, Bergamo, 2011, Mus Modern Art EMMA, Finland, 2007, AGNSW, Sydney, 92, 2003, 2005, 2008, 2009, Kunsthalle Krems, Austria, 2012, MARCO, Vigo, Spain, 2007, Mus Modern Art, Palais

Lichtenstein, Vienna, 89 ; Igor and Svetlana participated in international exhibs including Sculpture Projects Münster 97, Documenta 11, 2002, and biennials in Venice, 88, Sao Paulo, 94, Istanbul, 95, Johannesburg, 97, Lyon, 97, Liverpool, 99, and others. *Awards:* DAAD Artists Prog, Berlin, Ger, 1990; Kathe Kollwitz Preis 2000, Akademie der Kunste, Berlin, Ger, 2000; Residences Internationales aux Recollects, Paris, France, 2008. *Bibliog:* What is Contemporary Art? (catalogue), Rooseum, Malmo, 89; Adam D Weinberg, Barry Schwabsky, Rene Block, & Anthony Bond (auths) Igor & Svetlana Kopystiansky, Kunsthalle Fridericianum, Kassel and Fine Arts Ctr Univ Mass, Amherst, Mass, 2005; Gabriel Coxhead (auth), A Dual Perspective, Financial Times, 7/21/2006; Anthony Spira and Barry Schwabsky (auths), Igor & Svetlana Kopystiansky, Espoo Mus Modern Art, 2007; John G Hanhardt and Philippe-Alain Michaud (auths), Kopystiansky, Musee d'Art Moderne de Saint-Etienne, Les Presses du Reel, 2010. *Media:* Installation Sculpture, Painting; Video, Photography. *Interests:* sculpting; painting; videoing. *Mailing Add:* 526 W 26th St No 608 New York NY 10001

KORD, VICTOR GEORGE
PAINTER, INSTRUCTOR
b Satu Mare, Romania, Sept 16, 1935; US citizen. *Study:* Cleveland Inst Art; Yale Univ, BFA, 58, MFA, 60. *Work:* Whitney Mus Am Art, NY; Cleveland Mus Art, Cleveland; Aldrich Mus, Ridgefield, Conn; Madison Art Ctr & Univ Wis, Madison, Wis; Elvehjem Art Ctr, Univ Wis. *Exhib:* Chicago Art Inst, 62; solo exhibs, Richard Gray Gallery, Chicago, 67, Univ SFla, Tampa, 68, Galerie Ricke, Cologne, Ger, 70 & Univ Ill, Champaign, 70; Cleveland Mus Art, Ohio, 68; Lyrical Abstraction, Whitney Mus Am Art, NY, 71; New Am Abstract Painting, Vassar Col, Poughkeepsie, NY, 72; Invitation 77 - Ten Painters, Walker Art Ctr, Minneapolis, 77; Made in Virginia, Reynolds-Minor Gallery, Richmond, 84; group exhib, Kathryn Sermas Gallery, NY, 90; two-man show, Kathryn Sermas Gallery, NY, 90; and others. *Pos:* Co-ed, New Arts Examiner, Richmond Off, 83-87. *Teaching:* Univ Ill, Champaign, 60-65; Univ Wis, Madison, 65-81, chair, 79-81; chair & prof, Va Commonwealth Univ, Richmond, 81-87; prof art, Cornell Univ, Ithaca, NY, 87-. *Awards:* Guggenheim Fel, 62. *Mem:* Fed Arts Coun Richmond, Va (bd dir, 83-87); Am Abstract Artists. *Mailing Add:* 245 Henry St Brooklyn NY 11201

KOREN, EDWARD B
CARTOONIST, ILLUSTRATOR
b New York, NY, Dec 13, 1935. *Study:* Columbia Univ, BA, 57; Atelier 17, Paris, with SW Hayter; Pratt Inst, MFA, 64. *Hon Degrees:* Union Col, LHD, 84. *Work:* Fogg Mus, Cambridge, Mass; Princeton Univ Mus; RI Sch Design Mus; US Info Agency; Libr Cong; and others. *Exhib:* Exposition Dessins d'Humeur, Soc Protectrice d'Humeur, Avignon, France, 73; Art from the NY Times, Soc Illusr, NY, 73; Art from the New Yorker, Grolier Club, 75; Terry Dintinfass Gallery, NY, 75-77, 79 & 91; Koren: Prints and Drawings 1954-1981 Traveling Exhib, State Univ Albany, NY, 82-83; Virginia Lynch Gallery, Tiverton, RI, 99, 2000, 2001, 2002; Middlebury College Mus Art, 2006; Wallach Art Gallery, Columbia Univ, 2010; Luise Ross Gallery, NYC, 2010; Fleming Mus, Univ Vt, 2011; Big Town Gallery, Rochester, Vt, 2011. *Pos:* staff artist, The New Yorker Magazine. *Teaching:* Adj prof art, Brown Univ, 64-2006. *Awards:* Third Prize, Biennale Illusr, Bratislava, Czech, 73; Ten Best Childrens Bks of Yr, New York Times, 73; Prix d'Humour, Soc Protectrice d'Humour, Avignon, France, 76; John Simon Guggenheim Fel, 70-71. *Mem:* Authors Guild; Soc Am Graphic Artists. *Media:* Pen & Ink. *Publ:* Auth, The Hard Work of Simple Living, Chelsea Green, 98; Pet Peeves, 2000; Travelling While Married, Algonquin Books, 2003; auth, illusr, very Hairy Harry, Harper Collins, 2003; illusr, The New Legal Seafoods Cookbook, Broadway Books, 2003; Thelonius Monster's Sky-High Fly Pie, 2006. *Mailing Add:* Box 464 Brookfield VT 05036

KORENIC, LYNETTE MARIE
LIBRARIAN
b Berwyn, Ill, Mar 29, 1950. *Study:* Univ Wis, Madison, MFA, 79 MA, Libr Sci, 81, MA, Art History, 84. *Pos:* Asst art librn, Fine Arts Libr, Ind Univ, 82-84 & Arts Libr, Univ Calif, 84-88; head arts libr, Univ Calif, Santa Barbara, 88-. *Mem:* Art Libr Soc NAm (secy 83-84, vpres 89, pres 90, past pres, 91; Coll Art Asn; Am Libr Asn. *Res:* 18th, 19th and 20th century American art; history of photography. *Publ:* Coauth, Survey of Periodical Use in an Academic Art Library, 82, Grant Development Strategies for Large and Small Libraries, 90, ARLIS/NA Publ. *Mailing Add:* Univ Calif Arts Libr Santa Barbara CA 93106

KORMAN, SHARON
PAINTER
Study: State Univ NY, Oneonta, BS (educ), 1963-1967; Queens Coll, MS (educ), 67-70; studied watercolor with Lei Yu, 87-89; Nat Acad Design Sch Fine Arts, New York, 90-96. *Exhib:* Solo shows incl Risley Gallery, Litchfield, Conn, 98, Front St Gallery, Hamilton, Bermuda, 98, Terrace Gallery at the Dockyards, Bermuda, 98, Works Gallery, New York, 99, 2001, 2003, 2005, China 2000 Fine Art Gallery, New York, 2002, 2004; group shows incl Kent Gallery, Conn, 97. *Teaching:* Artist in residence, tchr, Masterworks Found, Bermuda, 98. *Mem:* NY Artists Equity Asn; Allied Artists Am; Wash Art Asn, Conn; Nat Acad (adv bd, 1994-2006, coun 1999-2006). *Media:* Oil on Linen. *Dealer:* Manhattan Arts Int 200 E 72 St New York NY 10021; China 2000 Fine Art 5 E 57th St New York NY 10022

KORN, HENRY
MUSEUM DIRECTOR, WRITER
b Sept 19, 1945. *Study:* Johns Hopkins Univ, AB, 68. *Pos:* Arts comn & found dir, City of Santa Monica, Calif, 86-90; cult affairs mgr, City of Irvine, Calif, 90-93; pres & mus dir, Guild Hall of East Hampton, NY, 93-99. *Teaching:* Adj instr, Johnson State Col, Vt, 84; practicum seminars on pub arts and cult diversity for local government agencies, 86-93; Dir Art & Cult, City of Beverly Hills, Calif, 99-; Dir, City of Beverly Hills Munic Gallery, 99-. *Awards:* Nat Endowment Arts Fel Fiction, 78; City Livability Award, US Conf Mayors, 89; Award of Excellence, Calif Parks & Recreation Soc, 91. *Bibliog:* Carissa Katz (auth), Guild Hall: a hot summer, East Hampton Star, 5/97; Robert Lipsyte (auth), Long on celebrity, short on charity, NY Times, 8/98. *Mem:* Mus Asn NY State. *Publ:* Contribr, Connoisseur, Art & Auction, LA Weekly; auth, Muhammad Ali Retrospective, 77, A Difficult Act to Follow, 82 & Marc Chagall, 85, Staten Island Advance & Congress Monthly

KORNBLATT, BARBARA RODBELL
DEALER
b Baltimore, Md, Jan 25, 1931. *Study:* Community Coll Baltimore, AA; Goucher Col, with Hilton Brown, BA. *Pos:* Dir, B R Kornblatt Gallery, Washington, DC; founder, dir, Fine Art, Baltimore; bd director, Shriver Hall, Baltimore, currently. *Teaching:* Lectr, Smithsonian Inst & Baltimore Hebrew Univ; leads art educ trips. *Awards:* served on art advisory panel for Internal Revenue Serv, 86-89. *Bibliog:* Articles in Sun, 5/26/76, News Am, 9/23/79 & Baltimore News Am, 11/2/80. *Mem:* Art Table. *Specialty:* Contemporary American sculpture, prints and painting. *Mailing Add:* c/o Shriver Hall Ste 105 3400 N Charles St Baltimore MD 21218-2698

KORNBLUM, MYRTLE
PAINTER, PRINTMAKER
b Chicago, Ill, Aug 18, 1909. *Study:* Washington Univ, St Louis; Univ Miami, Coral Gables, studied with Hans Hoffman. *Exhib:* City Art Mus, St Louis, Mo, 60-62; Print Club NY, 60; Art USA, Madison Sq Garden, NY, 60; Libr Cong, Washington, DC, 63; Silvermine Printmakers, New Canaan, Conn, 65; Atkins Mus Fine Art, Kansas City, Mo; Joslyn Mus, Omaha, Nebr; Solo exhibs, St Louis Artists Guild, 70-81 & Norton Gallery, St Louis, Chicago, Kansas City, Madrid & Haifa; and others. *Awards:* First Prize, New Testament Show, Temple Israel, St Louis Co, Mo, 70; Second Prize, 70 & First Energy Prize, 75, St Louis Artists Guild. *Mem:* St Louis Artists Guild; Acad Prof Artists; Community Women Artists. *Media:* Collagraph, Woodcut. *Mailing Add:* St Louis Artist Guild 2 Oak Knoll Park Saint Louis MO 63105-3008

KORNBLUTH, FRANCES
PAINTER, ASSEMBLAGE ARTIST
b New York, NY, July 26, 1920. *Study:* Brooklyn Col, BA, 40; Brooklyn Mus Art Sch, 55-59; Pratt Inst, MAE, 62. *Work:* Aetna & Cigna Collections, Hartford, Conn; Quinebaug Valley Community Col, Danielson, Conn; Doctor's Coun, NY; Gestalt Inst, Cleveland, Ohio; Hudson River Mus, NY; Chrysler Mus, Norfolk, Va; Altos de Chavon Found, Dominican Republic; pvt collections of Jamie Wyeth, Southern Island, Maine and other pvt collections in US, Can, Dominican Republic, Eng, Italy & Israel. *Comn:* pvt collections all over the US. *Exhib:* 158th Ann Exhib Pa Acad Fine Arts, Philadelphia, 63; 32nd & 42nd Conn Artists Ann, Slater Memorial Mus, Norwich, Conn, 75 & 85; Joan Whitney Payson Gallery Art, Portland, Maine, 83; 78th & 83rd Ann Exhib, Conn Acad Fine Arts, William Benton Mus, Storrs, 88 & 94; Conn Vision, Mattatuck Mus, Waterbury, 89; Prudence Crandall Mus, Canterbury, 93 & 94; Homer Babbidge Libr, Univ Conn, 96; solo exhib incl Artworks Gallery, Hartford, Conn, 69, 81, 91, Pradis Gallery, East Douglas, Mass, 97, Slater Mem Mus, Norwich, Conn, 2001; On Island, Women Artists Monhegan Univ New Eng, Portland, Maine, 2007; Thompson Community Gallery, Conn, May 2009; Putting it Together, Portland Mus Art, Maine, 2010; Challenge, Wit & Comfort, Fryeburg Acad, Maine, 2010; Older Artists, New Works at the Aurora Gallery, Worcester Art Mus, 2010; The Nature of Things, Audubon Soc, Pomfret, Conn, 2011; Selections: A Retrospective, Silver Circle Gallery, Putnam, Conn, 2012; Maine Women PioneersIII, Univ New England Art Gallery, 2013; The Nature of Things II, Audubon Soc, Pomfret, Conn, 2013. *Pos:* Estab & taught program for gifted elem in Thompson, Conn, 80-84. *Teaching:* Lectr art, Univ Conn, 70 & 71 & Annhurst Col, Woodstock, Conn, 79-80, Adelphi Univ, Garden City, NJ, Hofstra Univ, Hempstead, NY, Dowling Col, Oakdale, NY, Mills Col, New York City; instr & dir gifted educ, Thompson Pub Sch, Conn, 72-76. *Awards:* Knox Found Finalist for Commission, Hartford, 90; Miriam E Halpern Mem Award, 92; Shortell Award, 95; Award for Solo Exhib, Collages and Constructions, Slater Meml Mus, Norwich, 2001; Work on Paper Award, Conn Acad Fine Arts, Conn, 2004; and numerous others; Miriam E Halpern Mem Award Collage, 2010; Best in Show, Works on Paper, Slater Memorial Mus, Norwich, Conn, 2013. *Bibliog:* Jude Schwendenwein (auth), Color & Light Permeate Kornbluth Show, Hartford Courant, Conn, 6/15/91; Susan Wadsworth (auth), Frances Kornbluth: Paintings & Constructions, Art New England, Boston, Mass, 8-9/91; Alicia Craig Faxon (auth), Frances Kornbluth: Points of Departure, Art New Eng, Boston, Mass, 10-11/95. *Mem:* Nat Asn Women Artists; Conn Acad Fine Arts; Women Artists Monhegan Island. *Media:* Acrylic; Mixed Media; Constructions; Collage. *Interests:* Film, music. *Publ:* Monhegan: the Artists Island. *Dealer:* Lupine Gallery Monhegan Island ME 04852; Silver Circle Studio 85 Main St Putnam CT 06260. *Mailing Add:* 134 Buckley Hill Rd North Grosvenordale CT 06255

KORNETCHUK, ELENA
DEALER, HISTORIAN
b Ger, June 10, 1948; US citizen. *Study:* Univ Md, College Park, BA, 70; Univ Iowa, MA, 72; Georgetown Univ, PhD, 82. *Collection Arranged:* The Graphics of Estonia, Latvia and Lithuania, Russian Images Ltd, 78, Contemporary Russian Painting, 78 & Kaplan's Lithographs, 79; Retrospective of Anatolii Kaplan, Russian Images Ltd, Pittsburgh, 79. *Pos:* Partner, Masterworks Int, Chicago, 76-78; pres, International Images, Ltd (aka Russian Images, Ltd), Sewickley, Pa, 78-; lectr, contemp art in the USSR, Univ Pittsburgh, 85-; mem, bd dir, Carnegie-Mellon Univ Art Gallery, Pittsburgh, 85-; cur Eastern Europ Art, New Eng Ctr Contemp Art, Brooklyn, Conn, 86-. *Teaching:* Instr Russian lang, lit & cult, Univ Iowa, 70-72 & Univ Md, College Park, 73-75. *Mem:* Asn Advan Slavic Studies, Stanford, Calif, 71-; World Affairs Coun, Pittsburgh, 78-; Sweetwater Art Ctr, Sewickley, Pa (bd dir, 80-84); Asn Advan Baltic Studies, Mahwah, NJ, 82-; Am Coun Study Islamic Soc, Villanova, Pa, 85-; Am Latvian Artists Asn, NY, 85-. *Specialty:* Contemporary art from Russia, Latvia, Estonia, Bulgaria and other countries of Eastern Europe. *Collection:* Contemporary art from the USSR, Japanese wood engravings. *Publ:* Auth, Contemporary Russian

printmaking: An overview, Graphics Mag, 10-11/79; Contemporary Soviet prints: A national diversity, Print News, 10/80; Inars Helmust and the Latvian graphic tradition, spring 82, Nature printing: Robert Little and Renata Sawyer, spring 83, Prints today: Holland summer, 83 & The watercolors of Dzemma Skulme, spring 86, J Print World. *Mailing Add:* International Images Ltd 514 Beaver St Sewickley PA 15143-1779

KORNHAUSER, ELIZABETH MANKIN
MUSEUM DIRECTOR, CURATOR
b Tenafly, NJ, June 24, 1950. *Study:* Boston Univ, BA, 72, PhD, 88; State Univ NY, Cooperstown, MA, 76. *Work:* Wadsworth Atheneum Mus Art, Hartford, Conn; Brooklyn Mus, Long Island Hist Soc, Brooklyn, NY; Smith Coll Art Mus, Northampton, Mass; Yale Art Gallery, New Haven, Conn. *Collection Arranged:* Brooklyn Before the Bridge, 82-83; Ralph Earl, 91-92; Am Paintings at the Wadsworth Atheneum, 2 vols, 96; New Worlds from Old: Australia and Am 19th Century Land, 98-99; Alfred Stieglitz, Georgia O'Keeffe and Am Modernism, 99; Caldar in Connecticut, 2000. *Pos:* cur Am art, Wadsworth Atheneum, 83-95, deputy dir, chief cur, 95-99; acting dir, Wadsworth Atheneum Mus Art, 2000, chief cur, 2006-. *Teaching:* lectr Am art hist, Trinity Col, Hartford, Conn, 89-2000. *Bibliog:* John Updyke (auth), Alfred Stieglitz, Georgia O'Keeffe and American Modernism, NY Rev Books, Spring 99; James Fenton (auth), New Worlds from Old, NY Rev Books, Fall 99; Robert Hughes (auth), article, Time Mag. *Mem:* Arch Am Art; Am Studies Asn; Coll Art Asn; Am Asn Mus Dirs; AAMC. *Mailing Add:* Wadsworth Atheneum Mus Art 600 Main St Hartford CT 06103

KORNMAYER, J GARY
PAINTER, PHOTOGRAPHER
b Omaha, Nebr, 1934. *Study:* San Diego State Univ, 59-61; Nat Univ, San Diego, BA, 70, MA (audio-visual commun), 74. *Work:* Riverside Art Mus, Calif. *Comn:* Tex Hist, Nat Univ, San Diego, 73 & Am Hist of Slavery, 74; stations of cross, St Charles Borromeo Church, Morganton, NC, 98. *Exhib:* Solo exhibs, Soho Gallery, New York, 75-78, Inst Mex N Am Relaciones Cult, Mexico City, Inst Allende, San Miguel Allende, Mex, 80, San Diego Art Inst, 89, 92-93 & Tryon Art Ctr, NC, 96; Calif-Hawaii Biennial, Fine Arts Gallery, San Diego, 76; San Diego Art Inst, Calif; Upstairs Gallery, Tryon, NC, 96-2000; Village Gallery, Flat Rock, NC, 98; Tryon Arts Gallery, Tryon, NC, 2002; Conn Gallery, Lambrum, SC, 2002; Spartanburg Co Art Mus, Spartnaburg, SC, 2005. *Pos:* Photogr, Gen Dynamics Corp, San Diego, 58-60, sr audio-visual commun, 60-69, mgr graphics commun, 80-92; mem adv bd, Carolina Foothills Artisan Ctr, 99-2012. *Awards:* Distinctive Merit, San Diego Art Director's Soc, 65; Second Place, Fine Arts Gallery San Diego, 68; First Place Purchase Award, Riverside Art Mus, 70. *Bibliog:* Hedy O'Beil (auth), J Gary Kornmayer, artist, Arts Mag, 10/77; Hal Gray (auth), Horizons, Channel 39, 12/77; In the Public Interest, City of San Diego, Channel 2, 1/78. *Mem:* San Diego Fine Arts Soc-Art Guild (mem bd dir, 68-70); Span Village Art Asn (mem bd dir, 72-74, pres, 74-78); San Diego Art Inst (mem bd dir, 90-93, pres, 93-94); Upstairs Gallery (95-2009); Tryon NC Art Ctr (95-2009). *Media:* Mixed Media. *Dealer:* Upstairs Gallery PO Box 553 Tryon NC 28782; Carolina Foothills Artisan Ctr PO Box 517 Chester SC 29323. *Mailing Add:* 3350 River Rd Columbus NC 28722

KOROT, BERYL
VIDEO ARTIST
b New York, NY, Sept 17, 1945. *Study:* Univ Wis, 63-65; Queens Col, BA, 67. *Work:* Chase Manhattan; Kramlich Coll. *Comn:* Video opera, The Cave, with Steve Reich, 93; Video opera, Three Tales, with Steve Reich, 2002. *Exhib:* Solo exhibs, The Kitchen, New York, 75, Everson Mus, Syracuse, 75 & 79, Castelli Gallery, NY, 77 & Whitney Mus, 80, 86, John Weber Gallery, Text/Weave/Line, video, 1977-2010, Aldrich Mus Contemp Art, 2010, Dartmouth Coll, 2011, Jaffe Friede and Strauss Galleries, 2011, Bitforms Gallery, 2012; Group exhibs, Yesterday and After, Mus des Beaux Arts, Montreal, 80; Burden, Kos, Korot, San Francisco Art Inst, 81; Paintings, John Weber Gallery, 86; Videoskulptor, Kolnischer Kunstuerein, Zurichkunsthaus, Berliner Kunstverein, 89; Carnegie Inst Art, Points of Departure: Origins in Video, Pittsburgh, 90; 1993-94 The Cave Exhib Video Installation Tour: Whitney Mus, 93, Düsseldorf Kunsthalle, 94 Reina Sofia, Madrid, 94, Mus Moderne d'Ascq, Lille, 94, Jewish Mus, Paris, 2002, ZKM, 2008; 2 installations, Mass Coll Art, 99; video projection, Am Century Post 2, Whitney Mus, 2000 & 2006; video installation, Frankfort, History Mus, 2000; American Century at Whitney Mus, 2001; DMZ, S Korea, 2005,2008, Dachau 74-, CDAN Huesca, Spain, 2009, Indomitable Woman, Barcelona, 2010; Locks Gallery, Phila. Pa, 2011; Alterations, NYU Gallery, 2011; Travelling video opera, Three Tales, Cambridge Univ, 2002-2010, Vienna, Berlin, Amsterdam, Torino, Lisbon, London, Paris, NY, Charleston, Perth & Hong Kong, Koln Philharmonic, Essen Philharmonic, Laznia Nowa Theatre, Krakow, Poland, 2011; Dartmouth Coll, Jaffe-Friede Gallery, 2011; Bitforms Gallery, NY, 2012; The Cave and Three Tales, performances, Berlin, 2013; Whitworth Gallery, 2013; Abteiberg Mus, Ger, 2013. *Teaching:* Sch Visual Arts, 76-78; Montgomery Fel Dartmouth Col, 2000. *Awards:* Nat Endowment Arts Grant, 75, 77 & 79; NYSCA Grant, 78; John Simon Guggenheim Fel, 94; Anonymous Woman Award, 2008. *Bibliog:* Andrew Clements (auth), rev, The Guardian, 5/18/2002; Keith Potter (auth), rev, The Independent, 5/18/2002; Justin Davidson (auth), rev, NY Newsday, 10/13/2002, Mark Godfrey, 2007, Abstraction and the Holocaust; Katie Geha (auth), Artform Critics Pick, 2011; O'Neill Butler (auth), Art Forum, 2012; Art Critical, Joan Boykoff Baron & Reuben Baron, 2012. *Media:* Video, Computer. *Collection:* Kramlich Collection, Tate Mod, London, Hood Mus, Hanover, NH. *Publ:* Ed, Radical software, Vol I & Vol II, Gordon & Breach Sci Publ, 72-74; Video Art, Harcourt, Brace, Jovanovich, 1976. *Dealer:* Bitforms New York NY. *Mailing Add:* 114 Horseshoe Hill Rd Pound Ridge NY 10576

KOROW, ELINORE M See Korow-Bieber, Elinore Maria Vigh

KOROW-BIEBER, ELINORE MARIA VIGH
PAINTER, GALLERY DIRECTOR
b Akron, Ohio, July 31, 1934. *Study:* Cleveland Inst Art, with Rolf Stoll, Paul Riba & John Teyral; Sienna Heights Womens Col; Sawyer Coll Bus; world travel. *Work:* Hebrew Acad, Cleveland Heights, Ohio; Berkowitz Kumin Mem Chapel; Cleveland Play House Gallery; Bd Rm, Blue Cross/Blue Shield, Cleveland, Ohio; Cleveland Clinic Found; Kent State Univ, School Fashion & Kent Mus; Temple EmanuEl, Cleveland Heights, Ohio; First Congregational Church, Akron; Univ of Akron, Stitzlein Alumni Center, OH; The Sargent Laessig Mus Fine Arts, Hinckley, Ohio; Cuyahoga Valley Art Center, Cuyahoga Falls, Ohio. *Comn:* Rabbi Boruch Sorotzkin, Pres of Rabbinical Coll Telshe, Wickliffe, Ohio; George Hilden, Pres of Osco Drugs, Chicago; Jerome Weinberger, Pres Gray Drugs, Cleveland; Charles Walgreen, Pres Walgreen Drugs, Chicago; double oil portrait, Stitzlein Alumni Ctr, Univ Akron, Ohio, 98; Mrs Burton D Morgan, Kent State Univ; Cantor Irvin Bushman, Temple EmanuEl, Cleveland Heights, Ohio; Pres William Luntz, Luntz Corp, Canton, Ohio; Pres Stewart Turley, Eckert Drug, Clearwater, Fla; Producer Syd Friedman, Channel 35, Fairview Park, Ohio; and others. *Exhib:* Butler Inst Am Art, Youngstown, Ohio, 68-70; Nat Acad Design, NY, 73; World Trade Ctr, Am Artists Prof League, NY, 80; solo exhib, Chagrin Valley Little Theatre, Ohio, 80, Nat Acad Design, NY, 73; Miniature Painting Show, Bath, Ohio, 81; All Ohio-Canton Art Inst, 88; Boston Mills Nat Show, Peninsula, Ohio, 88; Mansfield Art Mus, 88; Invitational, Fairmont Fine Arts Ctr, Novelty, Ohio, 2002; Massillon Mus, 2002; Lynn Kottler Galleries, New York City, 1974; Stan Hywet Hall & Gardens, Akron, OH; Spring Exhib, Women's Art League of Akron, OH, 2006; Laurel Lake Gallery, Hudson, Oh, 2013; Laurel Lake Gallery, Hudson, Oh, 2013. *Pos:* Staff artist & designer, Am Greeting Corp, Cleveland, 57-58 & 71-73; owner, Elinore Korow: Portraits, Shaker Heights, Ohio, 1973-94, Akron, Ohio, 1994-. *Teaching:* Instr painting, drawing & portraiture, Eastern Campus Elders Prog, Cuyahoga Community Col, 79-, Univ Akron, 95-; lectr, Ancient Egypt, Cleveland Clinic Found: Oasis, 96; instr pastel & oil Cleveland Inst Art, Ohio, 2007; instr portraiture, Cuyahoga Valley Art Ctr, Cuyahoga Falls, Ohio, currently. *Awards:* 2nd Prize Geo Mayer Galleries, Akron, Ohio, 2000; Best in Show Award, First Annual Juried Show, Women's Art League, Akron, 2000; Honorable Mention Award, Akron Soc Artists and Womens Art League of Akron, Almond Tea Gallery, Chyahoga Falls, Ohio, 2000; Best of Show, Stan Hywet Hall & Gardens, Akron, OH; First Place, All Members Show, Cuyahoga Valley Art Ctr, Ohio, 2007; Best in Show, Womens Art League of Akron, Cuyhoga Valley Art Ctr, Cuyahoga Falls, Ohio; Honorable Mention, Sorelle in Arte II, Medina Co District Libr, Medina, Ohio; 2nd Place, Cuyahoga Valley Art Ctr Landscape Exhib, Ohio; 1st Place in Painting, Akron Gallery, Womens Art League, Oh, 2012. *Bibliog:* Review, Northern Ohio Live Mag; Guest Artist Interview & Viewing of Work, Cable Ch. 9, 10/4/2011. *Mem:* Charter mem Ohio Watercolor Soc; Women's Art League Akron (pres 99-2000); Am Portrait Soc; Am Artists Prof League; signature mem Akron Soc Artists; Am Pastel Soc; Akron Soc Artists; and others. *Media:* All, Oil, Pastel. *Specialty:* Senior Artists 55 and Older, 6 exhibs per year, monthly exhibs in all media. *Interests:* Music, concerts, live theater, travel; Portraits, Oil, Watercolor, Pastel, Silverpoint, Acrylic. *Collection:* Landscapes in Oil/Pastel on Ampersand Bord, Watercolor. *Publ:* Akron Life & Leisure. *Dealer:* Peninsula Art Acad 1600 Mill St W Peninsula Ohio 44264. *Mailing Add:* 923 Mayfair Rd Akron OH 44303

KORSHAK, YVONNE
HISTORIAN, EDUCATOR
b Chicago, Ill. *Study:* Radcliffe Col, BA, 58; Univ Calif, Berkeley, with D A Amyx, H Chipp, J K Anderson & J Bony, MA (classical archeol), 66, PhD (art hist), 73. *Collection Arranged:* Selections from the Adelphi Univ Art Collection (co-ed, catalog), 79. *Teaching:* Prof, Adelphi Univ, 75-, chairperson dept art & art hist, 79-82, dir mus studies prog, 79-. *Awards:* Award Merit, 88, President's Award, 90, Adelphi Univ; Award Merit, Am Ash Mus. *Mem:* Charter mem Long Island Art Historians Asn; Coll Art Asn Am; Archeol Inst Am; Asn Ancient Historians; Am Soc 18th Cent Studies. *Res:* Eighteenth-nineteenth century French painting; classical Greek art; iconography and hidden imagery. *Publ:* coauth, Selections from the Permanent Collections of the Arkansas Arts Center, 83; auth, Realism and Transcendent Imagery: Van Gogh's Crows over the Wheatfield, Pantheon 43, 85; Frontal Faces in Attic Vase Painting of the Archaic Period, Chica, 87; The Liberty Cap as a revolutionary symbol in America and France, Smithsonian Studies in Am Art, 10/87; "Paris and Helen" by Jacques Louis David: Choice and judgement on the eve of the French Revolution, Art Bull, 3/87. *Mailing Add:* 1025 Fifth Ave New York NY 10028

KORZENIK, DIANA
HISTORIAN, WRITER
b New York, NY, Mar 15, 1941. *Study:* Vassar Coll, Oberlin Coll, BA, 61; Columbia Univ, Art Hist Masters; Harvard Grad Sch of Educ, D Ed, 72. *Work:* Diana Korzenik Collection of Am Art Edn, Huntington Libr & Mus, San Marino, Calif; Drawn to Art, Am Antiquarian Soc. *Comn:* J P Getty Trust; Art-Making & Education. *Exhib:* 4 Decades of Painting (retrospective), Boston. *Collection Arranged:* Exhibitions on Nineteenth Century Am, 86 & Drawn to Art: Fruitlands, 88, Univ NH; Korzenik Collection of Am Art Education, Huntington Mus Libr, San Marino, Calif; Drawn to Art res, Am Antiquarian Soc. *Pos:* Prof emer, Mass Coll Art. *Teaching:* chair & prof art educ, Mass Coll Art, 72-95, Harvard Grad Sch Educ, 95-96, visiting lectr. *Awards:* City of Boston Pro Arts Serv in the Arts Award, 92; Am Libr Asn LEAB Award, 05; Bezalel award, Torah Acad Art Program, 2013. *Bibliog:* David Perkins (auth), Project Zero, J Aesthetic Educ; Howard Gardner (auth), Art, Mind & Brain & Artful Scribbles, Basic Bks Inc; Clair Golomb (ed), The Development of Artistically Gifted Children; Drawn to Art 19th Century American Dream, Univ Press New England, 86; Objects of American Art Education, Huntington Library Press, 2006. *Mem:* Mus Fine Arts; Ephemera Soc Am; Coll Art Asn; Women's Caucus Art; Am Antiquarian Soc; Mass Hist Soc. *Media:* Painter and writer on art. *Res:* History of Am Art edn. *Specialty:* The Art Connection (web gallery), Boston, Mass. *Publ:* Framing the Past,

Nat Art Educ Asn, 92; Art Making & Education, Ill Univ Press, 93; Gifted Child Artists, Ehrlbaum, 94; co-ed, The Cultivation of American Artists, Oak Knoll Press; auth, Drawn to Art, 86; Objects of American Art Education, Huntington Lib Press, 2004; Essays in Historic New Hampshire, 2010; New England Quarterly, 2011. *Dealer:* The Art Connection Boston MA. *Mailing Add:* 7 Norman Rd Newton MA 02161

KOSCIELNY, MARGARET
SCULPTOR, DRAFTSMAN
b Tallahassee, Fla, Aug 13, 1940. *Study:* Tex Woman's Univ, with Toni Lasalle; Univ Ga, BA (art hist) & MFA, with Irving Marantz, Joseph Schwarz, Charles Morgan; workshops with Gabor Peterdi, Arthur Deshaise, Kenneth Kerslake. *Work:* Jacksonville Art Mus; Ga Art Mus. *Comn:* Omni, Norfolk, Va, 75; Hyatt Hotel, Nashville, 76; Fla Senate, 78; Atlanta Airport, 80; AT&T, Jacksonville, 83; Stage Set Designs, The Magic Flute, Univ NMex, 87; Harsfield Int Airport, Atlanta, Int City Corp, Atlanta, John Portman, Omni Int, Norfolkd, Am Transtech, jacksonville, Pvt collections, Philadelphia, Paris, NY, Chicago. *Exhib:* Two-person exhib, Contemp Gallery, St Petersburg, 75; Four Jacksonville Artists, Cummer Gallery, Fla, 76; solo exhibs, Vanderbuilt Univ, Nashville, Tenn, 77, Univ Conn, 81 & Univ NMex, 87, Jacksonville Main Pub Libr, 2010; Flight Patterns, Third Floor Gallery, Atlanta, Ga, 80; and many others; The Fine Art of Drawing, Mus Fine Arts, Fla State Univ, 2008. *Pos:* Asst to dir, Cummer Gallery Art, 69-74; cur, Kamal Col, Jacksonville, Fla, 78-98. *Teaching:* Instr printmaking, Jacksonville Univ, 67 & Jacksonville Art Mus, 68. *Awards:* Nat Competition, Atlanta Airport Comn, 79; NEA Grant, Fla Art Coun, 75. *Bibliog:* Photos & Essays, Kalliope, 79. *Media:* Three-Dimensional Drawing, Assemblage, All Media. *Interests:* Music, physics, nat sciences, ballet. *Dealer:* www.margaretkoscielny.com. *Mailing Add:* 1254 Belvedere Ave Jacksonville FL 32205-7941

KOSHALEK, RICHARD
FORMER MUSEUM DIRECTOR
b Wausau, Wis, Sept 20, 1941. *Study:* Univ Wis, Madison; Univ Minn, Minneapolis, BA (archit), MA (art hist). *Collection Arranged:* 9 Artists-9 Spaces (auth, catalog), 70; Stephen Antonakos: Outdoor Neons, 75; Dan Flavin: Drawings, Diagrams & Spaces, 75; Larry Bell: The Iceberg & Its Shadow, 75; Robert Irwin: Continuing Responses, 75-76; The Great Am Rodeo (auth, catalog), 76-77; Ronald Bladen: Outdoor Sculpture Proposals, 78; Warburton Ave: The Architecture of a Neighborhood, 78; John Mason: Installations From the Hudson River Series, 78; Richard Serra: Elevator 80; and many others. *Pos:* Cur, Walker Art Ctr, Minneapolis, 67-72; asst dir, Nat Endowment Arts, Washington, 72-73; dir, Ft Worth Art Mus, 74-76; dir, Hudson River Mus, Westchester, NY, 76-80; dir, Mus Contemp Art, Los Angeles, 80-99; pres Art Ctr, Coll Design, Pasadena, Calif, 99-2009; dir, Hirshhorn Mus & Sculpture Garden, Smithsonian Inst, Washington, 2009-2013. *Awards:* Nat Endowment Arts Fel, 72; IBM Int Fel, 84; Durfee Found Fel, 92; Parkinson Spirit of Urbanism Award, Univ Southern Calif Archit Guild, 96; Chevalier des Arts et des Lettres, France, 99; Outstanding Achievement Award, Univ Minn, 2007. *Mem:* Art Prog, Chase Manhattan Bank; Yale Univ Coun Comt on Art Gallery & Brit Art Ctr. *Publ:* Auth, Midwest Photographers, Walker Art Ctr, 72

KOSINSKI, DOROTHY M
MUSEUM DIRECTOR
b Wallingford, Conn. *Study:* Yale Univ, BA, 1974; NY Univ, MA, 1977 & PhD, 1985. *Collection Arranged:* Passion for Art: 100 Treasures, 100 Years, Dallas Mus Art, Dialogues: Duchamp, Cornell, Johns, Rauschenberg, Matisse: Painter as Sculptor, Van Gogh's Sheaves of Wheat, 2007 & JMW Turner, 2008. *Pos:* Cur asst, Guggenheim Mus, New York, formerly; cur, Bruce Mus, Greenwich, Conn, formerly & Douglas Cooper Collection, formerly; independent cur, Kunstmuseum Wolfsburg, Kunstmuseum Basel & Royal Accad Arts, London, formerly; sr cur painting & sculpture & Barbara Thomas Lemmon cur European Art, Dallas Mus Art, 1995-2008; dir, Phillips Collection, Washington, 2008-. *Mailing Add:* Phillips Collection 1600 21st St NW Washington DC 20009

KOSLOW, HOWARD
PAINTER, ILLUSTRATOR
b Brooklyn, NY, Sept 21, 1924. *Study:* Pratt Inst, Brooklyn, with Alexander Kostellow, 44; Cranbrook Acad Art, Bloomfield Hills, Mich, 48; Sch Visual Arts, NY, 67; NY Studio, apprentice to Jean Carlu, 44-45. *Work:* Brooklyn Mus, NY; Mus Am Illus, New York, NY; Smithsonian Inst, Wash DC; Nat Postal Mus, Wash DC; NASA Mus, Wash DC; Smithsonian Nat Postal Mus, Wash DC. *Comn:* 26 indust paintings, Babcock and Wilcox Co, NY, 64; Apollo test stand, 65, Apollo 15 Launch, 71, Premiere Flight of Endeavour, Nat Aeronautics & Space Admin, Wash DC, 92; 55 commemorative US stamps, US Postal Serv, Wash DC, 1971-2011; 22 paintings, US Air Force, Wash DC, 1960-06. *Exhib:* Historical Art Coll, Nat Air and Space Mus, Wash DC, 1960-06; How Babcock & Wilcox Grows, Fine Arts Ctr Inc, Lynchburg, VA, 1965; Solo exhib, Art of Howard Koslow, Cedar Rapids Art Ctr, Cedar Rapids, Iowa, 1973; 105 Paintings, Greatest Military Heroes of America, Society of Illustrators, New York, 1986; Solo retrospective, Chelsea Ctr, East Norwich, NY, 1991; The Art of the Postage Stamp, Norman Rockwell Mus, Stockbridge, Mass, 2000; Ocean Co Artists Guild, Island Heights, NJ, 2008-11; Audubon Artists, Inc, Salmagundi Club, NY, 2010; Allied Artists of America, Nat Arts Club, NY, 2012. *Collection Arranged:* Remembering Our War Heroes, Ocean Co Artists' Guild, 2000; NJ Am Artists Prof League, 1999-2011. *Pos:* painter, NYC Studio, E. Norwich, NY, Toms River, NJ, 48-2011; freelance illusr, NY, Wash DC, Cheyenne, WY, 51-2011. *Teaching:* instr stamp design, Norman Rockwell Mus, Stockbridge Mass, 2001; lecture, seminar, The Art of the Stamp, Smithsonian Nat Postal Mus, 2012. *Awards:* Arts for the Parks Top 100, Nat Parks Acad Arts, 1990, 1999, & 2006; Best in Show, NJ Amer Artists Prof League, 2001 & 2003; Henry Dixons Jurors Award, Paint Am Assoc, 2008; Best in Show award, Ocean Co Artists Guild, Toms River, NJ, 2012. *Bibliog:* Howard Munce (auth), Easel to Industry, North Light, Fletcher Art, 72; Peggy & Harold Samuels (co-auths), Contemporary Western Artists, Southwest Art Publ, 82; Roger Launius & Bertram Ulrich (coauth), NASA: The Exploration of Space, Stewart, Tabori, & Chang, NY, 98; Walt Reed (auth), The llustrator in America, Watson Guptil Publ, 2001; James Dean & Bertram Ulrich (coauth), NASA: Art 50 Years of Exploration, Harry N. Abrams, Inc, 08. *Mem:* life mem Soc Illustrators, NY (1958-); Soc Am Historical Artists (1991-2011); NJ Am Artists Prof League (trustee, 1999-2011); Ocean Co Artists Guild (exhibitor, 2007-11); Audubon Artists Inc (2009-11). *Media:* Acrylic, Oil. *Collection:* Graphics, Picasso, Dali, Renoir, Christo, Carlu, Sternberg, Zuniga, Taylor Arms. *Publ:* contribr, The Art of Acrylic Painting, Grumbacher Lib, 69; ed, Tenth Annual of American Illustration, Hastings House, 69; illusr, The Ocean World of Jacques Cousteau (20 vol.), Danbury Press, 73; illusr, Toms River Artists Depict Military History of WWII, Ocean Co Observor, 99. *Dealer:* Meyer Fine Art Inc 2400 Kettner Blvd Ste 104 San Diego Calif 92101. *Mailing Add:* 1592 Goldspire Rd Toms River NJ 08755

KOSS, GENE H
SCULPTOR, EDUCATOR
b La Crosse, Wis, Nov 17, 1947. *Study:* Univ Wis, River Falls, BS, 74; Tyler Sch Art, Temple Univ, Philadelphia, MFA, 76. *Work:* The Lannan Found, Palm Beach, Fla; Univ Wis, La Crosse; Tyler Sch Art, Temple Univ, Philadelphia; One Canal Place, New Orleans; New Orleans Mus Art. *Comn:* Ceramic sculpture, Schie Eye Inst, Philadelphia, 76; steel & glass sculpture, Contemp Art Ctr, New Orleans, La; sculptural rondels for stained glass windows, Toura Synagogue, New Orleans, La. *Exhib:* Solo exhibs, Univ Southwestern La, Lafayette, 76, Newcomb Art Sch, Tulane Univ, New Orleans, La, 77, Perception Gallery, Houston, 86, Arthur Roger Gallery, New Orleans, La, 82, 84, 90, 92, 94 & 96, 98, 2001-2002, Newcomb Col/Tulane Univ, Dept Art, New Orleans, La, 86, Public Sculpture, Baton Rouge Gallery, La, 2002; Third Biennial Lake Superior Int Craft Exhibit, Tweed Mus Art, Minn, 75-77; Marietta Coll Crafts Nat, Ohio, 76; 55th Ann Exhib, Meadows Mus Art, Shreveport, La, 77; Glass Art Soc Invitational, Contemp Art Ctr, New Orleans, La, 85, Southern Abstraction, 88, Artists/Architects Collaboration Drawing and Models, 91 & Glass and Iron, 93; 3500 Yrs of Glassmakers, New Orleans Mus Art, La, 86, Contemp Crafts in the Urban Environment, 93 & 100 Yrs of Ceramic Art, 1894 - 1994: A Newcomb Faculty Retrospective, 94; Innovations I-Glass Sculpture, Masur Mus Art, Monroe, La, 91; The Vessel Transformed, Pensacola Mus Art, Fla, 92; Nat Glass Show, Judy Youens Gallery, Houston, Tex, 94; Outdoor Sculpture, Penland, NC, 95; Sculpture Object Functional Exposition, Chicago, 97; 20th Anniversary Exhib, Arthur Roger Gallery, New Orleans, 98; Int Cast Glass, Belvetro Gallery, Miami, Fla, 98; Between Grains of Sand and Microchips, Silverstein Gallery, NY, 2000. *Collection Arranged:* Louisiana Craftsmen Show, 77-78 & Glass & Ceramics Student Show, 77-78, Newcomb Art Sch, Tulane Univ, New Orleans. *Pos:* Cur, Nat Glace Sculpture Exhib, Perception Gallery, 84; exhib coordr, Glass Invitational Contemp Art Ctr, 84; reg coordr, Glass Art Soc Conf, New Orleans, La, 85; consult steel molds, Blenko Glass, Wheeling, WVa, 90. *Teaching:* Instr glass, Tyler Sch Art, Temple Univ, Philadelphia, summer 76; assoc prof to prof ceramics & glass, Newcomb Art Sch, Tulane Univ, New Orleans, 76-81 & 81-, Maxine and Ford Graham chair, currently; instr, mixed media sculpture, Pilchuck Glass Sch, Seattle, Wash, 93; adv, New Orleans Sch Glass Works, La, 90. *Awards:* Face-Wilson Art Found Travel Grant, Newcomb/Tulane Univ, New Orleans, La, 91-92; Research Grant, Tulane Grant Univ, New Orleans, La, 90; Necomb Found Fel Grant, Newcomb Col/Tulane Univ, New Orleans, La, 91 & 92; recipient Nat Endowment for the Arts award, New Orleans Community Arts award, Pace-Willson Art Found grant. *Bibliog:* Gene Koss (auth), Sculptural Glass, Glass Art Soc J, Process used in fabrication my sculpture, 85-86; Marcia Vetrocq (auth), Report from New Orleans: Marching On, Art Am, 97; Doug McCash (auth), Big Glass in the Big Easy, Glass, 97. *Mem:* Glass Art Soc; Am Crafts Coun; Nat Coun on Educ in Ceramic Arts; Contemp Art Ctr; La Crafts Coun (mem standards comt bd, 77-78). *Media:* Glass, Ceramics. *Publ:* Auth, The techniques of manufacture, In: Vasilike Ware: An Early Bronze Age Pottery Style in Crete, Paul Astroms Forlag, Sweden, 77; Gene Koss (auth), Sculptural Glass, Glass Art Soc J, Process used in fabrication my sculpture, 85-86; Marcia Vetrocq (auth), Report from New Orleans: Marching On, Art in America, 97; Doug Mc Cash (auth), Big Glass in the Big Easy, Glass, 97. *Dealer:* Perception Galleries Glass Art Houston TX; Arthur Roger Galleries New Orleans LA. *Mailing Add:* Tulane University Newcomb Art Dept 125C Waldenberg Art Ctr 6823 St Charles Ave New Orleans LA 70118

KOSSOFF, LEON
PAINTER
b London, Eng, 1926. *Study:* Royal Coll Art, London; St Martin's Sch Art; Bordugh Polytechnic. *Work:* Tate Gallery, London; Chicago Art Inst; Brit Coun, London; Art Gallery NSW, Australia; Cleveland Mus Art. *Exhib:* Venice Biennale (traveling), 95-96; solo retrospective, Tate Gallery, London, 96; Drawn To Painting, LACMA, 99, Poussin Landscapes by Kossoff, J Paul Gotty Mus, 99. *Publ:* Drawn To Painting, Richard Kendall, Merrell Publishers, 99. *Dealer:* La Louver 45 N Venice Blvd Venice CA 90291. *Mailing Add:* c/o LA Louver Gallery 45 N Venice Blvd Venice CA 90291

KOSTA, ANGELA
ASSEMBLAGE ARTIST, WRITER
Study: Louis Ritman, 64; Art Inst Chicago, 76-78. *Exhib:* Solo exhibs, Main St Art Gallery, Chicago, 65, Spectrum Gallery, 83 & San Diego Mus Art, 85-88, 94, 96 & 99; Yokohama Citizens' Gallery, Japan, 92; William Grant Still Art Ctr, Los Angeles, 93; Art Inst Nat, San Diego, 96 & 2001; Studio 21, San Diego, 2005-2006; Whitney Mus Am Art, Biannual, New York, 2006. *Awards:* Purchase Award, New Horizons Art, North Shore Art League, 77; Best of Show Awards, Artists Guild Ann, San Diego Mus Art, 87-88; San Diego Art Inst, 89 & 2001. *Bibliog:* Miller (auth), article, Los Angeles Times, 6/2/82; Lewinson (auth), article, San Diego Union, 4/7/83; Ollman (auth), article, Los Angeles Times, 11/20/87. *Mem:* San Diego Artists Guild; San Diego Mus Contemp Art. *Media:* Mixed Media; Collage, Painting. *Publ:* Paper art, Fiberarts Mag, 84; Abakanowicz retrospective, 11/6/84 & Judy Chicago's project, 7/7/85, San Diego Union; Banham by design, Reader, 4/24/86; Teacher/student interface: two views of education, Fiberarts Mag, 87

KOSTABI, MARK
PAINTER, SCULPTOR
b Los Angeles, Calif, Nov 27, 1960. *Study:* Fullerton Community Col, 78; Calif State Univ, Fullerton, 79-81. *Work:* Mus Mod Art & Guggenheim Mus, NY; Memphis Brooks Mus Art, Tenn; Metrop Mus, NY; Groninger Mus, Holland; Brooklyn Mus; Corcoran Gallery Ary; Nat Gallery Mod Art, Rome. *Comn:* Shopping bag design, Bloomingdales, NY, 86; mural, Palazzo dei Priori in Arezzo, Italy, 88; To See Through is Not to See Into (public sculpture), San Benedetto del Tronto, Italy, 88; album covers, Guns 'N' Roses -Use Your Illusion & Ramones -Adios Amigos. *Exhib:* Solo exhibs, Azabu Mus, Tokyo, 93, Seibu, Osaka, Japan, 93, Nicolae Gallery, Columbus, Ohio, 94, Hanson Gallery, New Orleans, 94, Studio Gastaldelli, Milan, 94, Sony Tower, Osaka, Japan, 94, Martin Lawrence Galleries, Newport Beach, Los Angeles, NY & San Francisco, 94, Parco, Tokorozawa & Kichijoji, Japan, 94, Giovanni Di Summa Gallery, Rome, Italy, 94, Meitetsu, Nagoya, Japan, 94, Arlene Bujuse Gallery, East Hampton, NY, 94 & Studio Spaggiari, Milan, 94; L'Immagine Galleria d'Arte Contemporanea, Arezzo, Italy, 98; Blu Art Arte Moderna, Alba Adriatica, Italy, 98; Martin Lawrence Galleries, Sherman Oaks & San Francisco, Calif, NY, 98, 99; Galerie Le Jardin des Arts, Jingumae & Aoyama, Toyko, 98; Galleria Pio Monti, Rome, 99; Palazzine Azzurra, San Benedetto de Tronto, Italy, 99; Studio G, Milan, 99; ArteCapital, Brescia, Italy, 2000; Trevi Flash Art Mus Int Contemp Art, Trevi, Italy, 2000; Guastalla Arte Moderna e Contemporanea, Forte dei Marmi, Italy, 2000; Temple Gallery, Temple Univ, Rome, 2000, George Billis Gallery, LA, 2006; Solo retrospective, Mitsukoshi Mus, Toyko, 92, Art Mus of Estonia, Tallinn, 98. *Pos:* Designer consumer prods, swatch watches, album covers, T-shirts, ties, glasses, lighters, book covers, puzzles, posters & ltd ed vases; producer, Inside Kostabi, NY; writer of monthly advice column, Ask Mark Kostabi, Artnet.com & Artists Pick, Shout Mag. *Teaching:* lectr, worldwide. *Awards:* Proliferation Prize, East Village Eye, 84. *Bibliog:* Walter Robinson (auth), Mark Kostabi at Hal Bromm, Art in Am, 84; features in many articles in the New York Times, People, Vogue, Vanity Fair, Playboy, Forbes, New York Mag, Artforum, Art in Am, ARTnews, Arts, Flash Art & Tema Celeste. *Media:* Oil on Canvas. *Publ:* Auth, Kostabi: The Early Years, Office Suite, Sadness Because the Video Rental Store was Closed & numerous others, self publ, 81; illusr, East Village 85, 85 & auth, Upheaval, 85, Pelham Press; Soho New York, Egret Press, 86; profiled on 60 Minutes, Eye to Eye with Connie Chung, A Current Affair, Nightwatch, The Oprah Winfrey Show, Lifestyles of the Rich & Famous, West 57th, CNN, MTV & numerous TV programs throughout Europe & Japan; I Did it Steinway (CD), 98; auth, Sadness Because the Video Rental Store Was Closed, Kostabi: The Early Years & Conversations with Kostabi. *Dealer:* Ronald Feldman 31 Mercer St New York NY 10013. *Mailing Add:* c/o Kostabi Worl 514 W 24th St New York NY 10011

KOSTECKA, GLORIA
PAINTER
b Bloomfield, NJ. *Study:* Am Art Sch, NY; Traphagen Sch Fashion, NY; Prosopon Shc Iconology, NY. *Comn:* St John The Baptist Orthodox Ch, Alpha, NJ. *Exhib:* Federated Art Asn Exhib, NJ State Mus Cult Ctr, Trenton, 77; Nat Soc Painters Casein & Acrylic 24th Exhib & Nat Audubon Soc Exhib, Nat Acad Galleries, NY, 77 & 78; Am Artists Professional League, Bergen Co Mus, NJ, 80; Nat Soc Painters Casein & Acrylic 28th Ann Exhib, Nat Arts Club, NY, 81 & 85. *Awards:* Travel Awards, Nat Soc Painters Casein & Acrylic, 81-85 & Wash Square Outdoor Art Exhib, 81-83. *Mem:* Nat Soc Painters Casein & Acrylic; Am Portrait Soc. *Media:* Acrylic, Pencil. *Mailing Add:* 23 Elmwood Dr Clifton NJ 07013

KOSTELANETZ, RICHARD
MEDIA ARTIST, WRITER
b New York, NY, May 14, 1940. *Study:* Brown Univ, AB (with honors), 62; Kings Coll, London, Fulbright Scholar, 64-65; Columbia Univ, MA, 66. *Work:* Book-Art Books: Mus Mod Art; Humanities Res Ctr, Univ Tex, Austin; Videotapes: Anthology Film Archives, NY; Franklin Furnace, NY; Visual Poetry, The Sackner Archive of Concrete and Visual Poetry. *Comn:* Videotapes Synapse, Syracuse Univ, 75; holograms, Cabin Creek Ctr, Work & Environ Studies, 78; audiotapes, Westdeutscher Rundfunk, 82, 83 & 89; audiotapes, Am Pub Radio, St Paul, Minn, 84; holograms, Dennis Gabor Lab, Mus Holography, 85. *Exhib:* Imaged Words & Worded Images, NY Univ, 70; solo exhibs, Video Writing, Anthology Film Archives, NY, 75 & 76, Visual poems, Nonsyntactic Prose, Minimal Fiction, Numerical Art, Chistopher Stephens, NY, Univ Toledo, 75-77; Audio Art, The Kitchen, NY, 78; Book Art, PS 1, Long Island City, NY & Tulsa Pub Libr, 78; Wordsand (retrospective work in several media), Simon Fraser Univ, Univ Alta, Cornell Coll, Iowa, Calif State Univ, Bakersfield, Miami Dade Community Coll, Vassar Coll, 78-81; Rik Gadella, Int Artists Books, 96; Fusion Arts, 2007; Books and Books, Miami, Fla, 2010; Kunstrerein, Amsterdam, Netherlands, 2011. *Collection Arranged:* Language & Structure in North Am, traveling exhib throughout Can & US, 75-77. *Pos:* Co-founder & publ, Assembling & Assembling Press, 70-82; stipendiat, DAAD Berliner Kunstperprogramm, Ger, 81-83. *Teaching:* Vis prof, Am studies & eng, Univ Tex, Austin, 77; Master Artist, Atlantic Ctr for the Arts, 2001; vis prof theater, grad fac, Hunter Coll, CUNY, 2002. *Awards:* Guggenheim Fel, 67; Visual Arts Grant, 76, 78, 79 & 85 & Media Arts Grant, 81, 82, 85, 86, 89 & 90, Nat Endowment Arts; Pollock-Krasner Fel, 2001. *Bibliog:* Tom Johnson (auth), Intermedia Lives, Village Voice, 10/4/76; George Myers Jr (auth), Scavenger Art & Richard Kostelanetz, An Introduction to Modern Times, Lunchroom, 82; SoHo: The Rise and Fall of an Artist's Colony, Routledge, 2003. *Mem:* Nat Artworkers; Found Independent Video & Film; Int Asn Art Critics. *Media:* Books, Print, Audio, Video, CD-Rom, Holography, Film. *Res:* Polyartistry; literary intermedia (sound & visual poetry). *Interests:* Words in various media, book art, audio, video, film, holography and others. *Collection:* Visual literature, paintings, drawings, black and white, cultural magazines' self-retrospectives. *Publ:* John Cage: A Documentary Monograph, 70, 91; Language and Structure in North America, 74; Wordworks: Poems New & Selected, 93; A Dictionary of the Avant-Gardes, 93; An ABC of Contemporary Reading, 95; Crimes of Culture, 95; John Cage: (ex)plain(ed), 96; Thirty-Five Yrs of Visible Writing, Koja, 2004; Micro of Stories, 2010. *Dealer:* www.minusspace.com

KOSTER, MARJORY JEAN
PRINTMAKER
b Grand Rapids, Mich, Feb 9, 1926. *Study:* Univ Mich Exten Night Sch, 47-64; Pratt Graphic Workshop, New York, summer 64. *Work:* Metrop Mus Art, NY; Brooklyn Mus Art, NY; also pvt collection of Harold Joachim; Detroit Art Inst, Mich; Grand Rapids Art Mus, Mich; and others. *Exhib:* Ann Exhib Prints & Drawings, Oklahoma Art Ctr, 67; 7th Ann Mercyhurst Coll Nat Graphics Exhib, Erie, Pa, 67; 3rd Nat Print & Drawing Exhib, Western Mich Univ, Kalamazoo, 68; 16th Nat Print Exhib, Brooklyn Mus, 68; 1st Nat Print Exhib, Honolulu, 71. *Mem:* Nat Inst Arts & Lett. *Media:* Woodcut. *Mailing Add:* 940 Maynard Ave NW Grand Rapids MI 49504-3659

KOSTIANOVSKY, TAMARA
INSTALLATION SCULPTOR
b Jerusalem, 1974. *Study:* Escuela Nacional de Bellas Artes, Argentina, BFA, 1998; Pa Acad Fine Arts, Philadelphia, MFA, 2003. *Exhib:* Solo exhibs, Nexus Gallery, Philadelphia, 2001, Univ Arts, Philadelphia, 2004, Philadelphia Mus Jewish Art, 2006, Black and White Gallery, New York, 2008; 5 into 1, Moore College Art & Design, Philadelphia, 2003; Back to the Front, Slought Found, Pa, 2004; Art with Accent: Latin Americans in the Mid-Atlantic States, Arlington Art Ctr, Va, 2005; The (S) Files 007, El Museo del Barrio, New York, 2007; El Ultimo Libro, Biblioteca Nacional de Buenos Aires, Argentina, 2008; Reinventing Ritual: Contemporary Art and Design for Jewish Life, The Jewish Mus, New York, 2009; Dali Dance, Godwin-Ternbach Mus, Queens Coll, NY, 2010. *Awards:* SOS Grant, Pa Coun on Arts, 2005; Pollock-Kranser Found Grant, 2008; Artist Pension Trust, Mex, 2009; Emerging Artist Fel, Socrates Sculpture Park, New York, 2009; NY Found Arts Fel, 2009. *Bibliog:* Holland Cotter (auth), New Latino Essence, Remixed and Redistilled, NY Times, 11/28/2004; Roberta Fallon (auth), Body Language, Philadlephia Weekly, 1/26/2006; RC Baker (auth), Bounty in the Barrio, The Village Voice, 11/14-20/2007; Cate McQuaid (auth), In exhibit devoted to meat, some offerings are a cut above, The Boston Globe, 7/2/2008

KOSTYNIUK, RONALD P
SCULPTOR, EDUCATOR
b Sask, July 8, 1941. *Study:* Univ Sask, BSc & BEd; Univ Alta, BFA; Univ Wis, MS & MFA. *Work:* Edmonton Art Gallery, Alta; Saskatoon Art Gallery, Sask; Kresge Art Found, Detroit, Mich; Can Coun Art Bank, Ottawa, Ont; Ft Lauderdale Mus, Fla; Glenbow Art Mus, Calgary; Univ of Calgary, Calgary; Univ of Saskatchewan, Saskatoon; Univ of Manitoba, Winnipeg; Mackenzie Art Mus, Regina; Winnipeg Art Gallery, Winnipeg; Univ of Lethbridge, Lethbridge; Alta Foundation for the Arts, Edmonton; Saskatchewan Allied Arts Board, Regina, Sask. *Comn:* Relief mural, exec off Paul Albertsen Ltd, Winnipeg; sculpture, Asn Bldg, Calgary; sculpture, City of Edmonton Recreational Complex, Edmonton; Silvermans, Winnipeg, Manitoba; Amoco Petroleum Ltd, Calgary, Alta. *Exhib:* Solo exhibs, Mem Univ, St John's, Nfld, 73, Sarnia Art Gallery, Ont, 74, Univ Moncton, NB, 74, Mt St Vincent Univ, Halifax, NS, 75 & Univ Calgary, Alta, 78; Kunst Int, Hippe Halle, Gmunden, Austria, 89; Art Concrete, Mus Archit, Wroclaw, Poland, 90; L'Idee-Systematisole Koncrete en Konstruktieve Kunst, Zoetermeer, The Neth, 90; Concept/Form, Cult Art Centrl Munic Athens, Greece, 91; City as a Memory, Chicago Athenaeum, Chicago; Sci in the Arts-Arts in the Sci, Hungraian Acad of Fine Arts, Budapest; Concrete Art, Mondriaanhaus Mus, Amersfoort, The Neth; Innovation, Kongresshous Mus, Gmunden, Austria; Int Constructive Art, Millenarium Ctr, Budpest; Int Overview of Constructive Art, Galerie Konkrete, Sulzberg, Ger. *Teaching:* Prof design & sculpture, Univ Calgary, Alta, 71-, head grad studies, dept art. *Awards:* Can Coun Arts Bursary, 69; Foreign Exchange Scholar, External Affairs Govt Can, 78; Killam Resident Fel, Univ Calgary, 79. *Bibliog:* Jan Van der Marck (auth), Relief sculpture, 69; John Stocking (auth), Relief sculptures, Arts Mag, 75; John Graham (auth), Kostyniuk's reliefs, Vie des Arts, 75; Marion Andres (auth), Kostyniuk's constructed reliefs, Art Post, 86; Virgil Hammock (auth) Prairie Visions: The art of Ron Kostyniuk, Art Focus, 92; Kay Burns (auth) Ron Kostyniuk: The Saskatchewan Road Map Series, Artichoke, 2000; Joan Kendrick (auth), Kostyniuk's Road Map Series, Art Focus #73, 2002. *Mem:* Royal Can Acad Art; Univ Art Asn; Can Conf of the Arts. *Media:* Plastics, Metals. *Publ:* Auth, The Evolution of the Constructed Relief 1913-1979 & Art and Sources, Univ Calgary; Neo-Constructions, Univ Calgary; An Antropomorphic Architecture, Univ Calgary; Saskatchewan Road Map Series, Univ of Calgary, 2001. *Mailing Add:* 4907 Viceroy Dr Calgary AB T3A 0V2 Canada

KOSUTH, JOSEPH
CONCEPTUAL ARTIST
b Toledo, Ohio, Jan 31, 1945. *Study:* Toledo Mus Sch of Design, 55-62; Cleveland Art Inst, 63-64; Sch of Visual Arts, New York, 65-67, New Sch for Social Research, New York, 71-72. *Hon Degrees:* LHD, Univ Bologna, 2001. *Work:* Mus of Mod Art, Solomon Guggenheim Mus & Whitney Mus Am Art, New York; Nat Gallery of Can, Ottawa, Ont; Tate Gallery, London, Eng. *Comn:* The Brooklyn Museum Collection: The Play of the Unmentionable, Grand Lobby, Brooklyn Mus, NY, 90; Ex Libris Frankfurt, 90; Ex Libris J F Champollion, Place des Ecritures, Figeac, France, 91; Ex Libris Robert Musil, City of Esslingen, 92; Paul Lobe Haus, Ger Parliament, Berlin, Ger, 2001; De iis quae ad speculum et in Speculo, Galelria Nazionale d'Arte Moderna, Rome, Italy, 2005. *Exhib:* Solo exhibs, Leo Castelli Gallery, NY, 88, Knoll Galleria, Budapest, 88, Galerie Le Gall Peyroulet, Paris, 89, Galeria Juana de Aizpuru, Madrid, 90, Galeria Comicos, Lisbon, 90, Margo Leavin Gallery, Los Angeles, 90, The Brooklyn Mus, NY, 90, Prague: Office of the President, Czechoslovakia, Prague Castle, 92, Smithsonian Inst, Hirshhorn Mus & Sculpture Garden, Washington, DC, 92, MIT List Visual Arts Ctr, Boston, 97, Van Abbemuseum, Eindhoven, The Neth, 2004, Sean Kellly Gallery, 2006. *Pos:* Rev critic, Arts Mag, New York, 67; Am ed, Art-Lang J, New York, 69-73; bd mem, Franklin Furnace, New York, currently. *Teaching:* Fac mem, Sch Visual Arts, New York, 687-85; prof, Hocschule für Bilden Künst, Hamburg, Ger, 88-90, Staatliche Akademie der Bildende Kunste, Stuttgart, 91-97, Kunstakademie Munich, 2001-2006 & Istituto Universitario di Architettura, Venice, Italy, currently. *Awards:* Chevalier de l'ordre des Artsw et des Lettres, French

Govt, 93; Decoration of Honor in Gold, Rep Austria, 2003. *Bibliog:* Catherine Millet (auth), Joseph Kosuth, Flash Art, 2-3/71; Elizabeth Baker (auth), JK: Information Please, Art News, 2/73; Bruce Boice (auth), Kosuth: two shows, Artforum, Vol II. *Publ:* Auth, The Play of the Unmentionable: An Installation by Joseph Kosuth at the Brooklyn Museum, New Press in asn with the Brooklyn Mus, NY 92; Podobenstvi (Ex Libris, Kafka)/Parable (Ex Libris, Kafka) Joseph Kosuth (exhib catalog), Off of the Pres, Czechoslovakia, Prague Castle, 92; A Room with 23 Qualities, Ed Cantz, Stuttgart, 92; Ex Libris, J F Champollion (Figeac), Artpress and Centre des Arts Plastiques, Paris, France, 91; Art after Philosophy and After: Collected Writings, 1966-1990, MIT Press, Mass, 91. *Dealer:* Sean Kelly Gallery. *Mailing Add:* 50 Pine St Fl 10 New York NY 10005-1527

KOTASEK, P MICHAEL
PAINTER, LECTURER
b Endicott, NY, Sept 2, 1962. *Study:* Syracuse Univ (studied under Jerome Witkin & Murray Tinkleman), BA, 1985; Private study from Burt Silverman, 1988-1990. *Exhib:* Philadelphia Watercolor Soc Ann Exhib, 1999, 2001-2003; Cooperstown Art Asn Ann Nat Exhib, Cooperstown, NY, 99, 2001-2002 & 2004; Am Artists Professional League, Salmagundi Club, NY, 1999, 2002, 2005; Art Asn Harrisburg, Harrisburg, Pa, 2003; Allied Artists of Am, Nat Arts Club, NY, 2003, 2005, 2006; Local Landscapes, Grenning Gallery, Sag Harbor, NY, 2005; 4 Artists Invitational, Harrisburg Art Asn, Harrisburg, Pa, 2006; Man and Nature, Grenning Gallery, Sag Harbor, NY, 2006; Spring Gala, New Britain Mus Art, Conn, 2007-2008; April Showers May Flowers, Grenning Gallery, Sag Habor, NY, 2007; Regional Exhib, Roberson Mus, Binghampton, NY, 2007; 10th Anniversary Show, Greening Gallery, Sag Harbor, NY, 2008. *Pos:* Freelance Illusr, 1985-1993. *Awards:* Henry Gasser Mem Award, Allied Artists of Am, NY, 2004; Frank C Wright Mem Award, Am Artists Professional League, NY, 2005; AAPL Medal of Hon, Am Artists Prof League, NY, 2002; Heitland Mem Award, Philadelphia Watercolor Soc, Bryn Mawr, Pa, 2003; Thomas Moran Mem Award for Watercolor, Salmagundi Club, NY, 2003; Award of Merit, Roberson Mus, NY, 2007. *Bibliog:* Int Showcase of Award Winners, Allied Artists of Am, Int Artist Mag (issue 36), 2004; Annette Hinkle (auth), Grenning Gallery: New Views of Old Haunts, Sag Harbor Express, 2004; Joshua Rose (auth), Man and Nature in the Hamptons, Am Art Collector (issue 9), 2006. *Mem:* Allied Artists Am (artist mem); Fine Arts Soc Southern Tier (artist mem). *Media:* Egg Tempera, Watercolor, Graphite Pencil. *Publ:* Every Picture Tells a Story, Watercolor Magic Mag, winter 2001. *Dealer:* Grenning Gallery 90 Main St PO Box 3049 Sag Harbor NY 11963. *Mailing Add:* 2600 Yale St Endicott NY 13760

KOTIK, CHARLOTTA
CURATOR, HISTORIAN
b Prague, Czech, Dec 13, 1940; US citizen. *Study:* Kunsthistorisches Inst, Univ Wien, 65; Charles Univ, Prague, BA (art hist), 66, MA (art hist), 68. *Collection Arranged:* Jiri Kolar: Transformations (auth, catalog), 78; On Paper, About Paper (auth, catalog), 80; Jennifer Bartlett (auth, catalog), 80; Figures: Forms and Expressions (auth, catalog), 81; Fernand Leger: Retrospective (auth, catalog), 82; John Cage: Scores and Prints (coauth, catalog), 82; Charles Clough, Recent Work (auth, catalog), 83; Second Western States Exhib (auth, catalog), 84; Expendable Ikon: Works by John McHale (auth, catalog), 84; Francois Morellet: Systems (auth, catalog), 84; Working in Brooklyn: Sculpture (auth, catalog), 85; Monumental Drawing: Works by 22 Contemporary Am (auth, catalog), 86; Third Western States Biennal (auth, catalog), 86; Working in Brooklyn: Painting (auth, catalog), 87; 4 Am: Aspects of Current Sculpture (auth, catalog), 89; Working in Brooklyn: Installations (auth, catalog), 90; Grand Lobby Installation Series (auth, brochures), 84-93; Louise Bargeois: Recent work, 45th Venice Biennale (brochure), 93; Louise Bargeois: Locus & Memory, Works 1982-1993, (coauth, catalogue) 1994. *Pos:* Cur asst, Jewish Mus, 58-61 & Nat Gallery, 61-64, Prague, Czech; assoc & asst cur, Nat Trust, Prague, Czech, 67-70; cur, Albright-Knox Art Gallery, Buffalo, 70-83; cur, Brooklyn Mus, NY, 83-, chair dept painting & sculpture, 92-. *Teaching:* Tutor fine arts, Empire State Col, Buffalo, NY, 77-79; adj asst prof, State Univ NY Buffalo, 79-83; instr art hist, Sch Visual Arts, NY, 90-. *Awards:* Frederick R Weisman Art Found Award for outstanding achievement in contemp art, 91; Munic Art Soc Cert of Merit for the Grand Lobby Ser, 91; Nat Endowment Arts & US Info Agency, selected to curate Louise Bourgeois, the exhib to represent US in the 1993 Venice Biennale. *Mem:* Adolph & Esther Gottlieb Found Inc, NY (bd dir); Art Table Inc; Nat Endowment Arts (panelist & field rep); Arts Action Coalition, NY (bd dir); City Arts Workshop Inc, NY (bd dir); Experimental Intermedia Found Inc, NY (bd dir). *Res:* Contemporary American art and architectural history. *Publ:* Co-auth, Contemporary Art 1942-72, Collection Albright-Knox, 72; Albright-Knox Art Gallery, Paintings and Sculpture from Antiquity to 1942, 78; Fernand Leger, Abbeville Press, 81; contrib auth, The Play of the Unmentionable: An Installation by Joseph Kosuth at The Brooklyn Museum, New Press, with Brooklyn Mus, 91

KOTOSKE, ROGER ALLEN
PAINTER, SCULPTOR
b South Bend, Ind, Jan 4, 1933. *Study:* Univ Notre Dame, Ind, 50-52; Univ Denver, Colo, BFA, 54, MA, 56. *Work:* Rockhill Nelson Gallery, Kansas City, Mo; State Univ NY Coll Oswego; Denver Art Mus; Franklin Mint, Philadelphia. *Comn:* Large outdoor sculpture, City of Denver, 68. *Exhib:* Artist Teacher Today USA, State Univ Oswego, NY; Solo exhibs, Pollock Gallery, Southern Methodist Univ, Dallas, 69 & James Yu Gallery, NY, 76; Report from Soho, Grey Gallery, NY, 76; Contemp Am Painting & Sculpture, Indianapolis Mus Art, 78; Ill Painters Traveling Exhib, 81-; 22nd Biennial Works on Paper Exhib, Univ Del, Newark, Del, 86; Int Exhib, Chinese Nat FA, Beijing, 87; Greater Midwest Int III, Mo, 88. *Teaching:* Prof art, Univ Denver, 58-68 & Univ Ill, Urbana, 68-. *Awards:* Purchase Awards, Nelson-Atkins Mus, 59 & State Univ Oswego, NY, 68. *Bibliog:* Meilach & Kowal (co-auth), Sculpture Casting, Crown Publ, 72; Meilach (auth), The Artist Eye, Regnery Press, 72; Verhelst (auth), Sculpture: Tools, Materials and Techniques, Prentice-Hall, 73 & 88. *Mem:* FATE. *Media:* Acrylic; Wood

KOUNS, MARJORIE
MURALIST
b Elmhurst, Ill, Aug 4, 1957. *Study:* Studied sculpture with Mary Rose Carroll, 78; Ill Wesleyan Univ, Bloomington, 79, Ed McCullough 75-79, Robert Irwin, 77. *Work:* Franklin Furnace Archive Inc, NY; Ben Franklin Univ Hosp, Berlin, Ger; Josephine Butler Parks Ctr, Wash DC; Ill Wesleyan Univ, Bloomington, Ill. *Comn:* Satellite Mural Proj, Mothers Ctrs, Hamburg, Stuttgart, Munich, Ger, 97; Docu murals, Nat Cong Neighborhood Women, Washington, DC, 97; Well Lit Chess Pieces, project for Washington Sq Park, New York City; Body as Canvas, New York City, Miami, Chicago, Los Angeles, Calif, & Shreveport Bossier, La; Shades of Shreveport, Shreveport Regional Arts Coun, 2010; mural design concepts, Let the Good Times Roll, Shreveport/Bossier Convention and Tourism Bureau Ctr, 2010. *Exhib:* Made by Hand, 4th UN Conf on Women, Beijing, China, 95; Trans Hands, UN Habitat, Taskisla Univ, Istanbul, Turkey, 96; Beijing-One Yr Later, UN Int Hq, NY, 96; solo show, USIS Am Haus, Berlin, Ger, 97; Art of Change, Times Sq Gallery, NY, 98; Sarkahc Neves (Seven Chakras) Pub Art Installation, Times Sq Gallery, NY, 99; Nurture Art, NY, 2000; Installation Room, P.S. 122, NY, 2000 26th and 27th Ann Small Works Show, NY, 2003-2004; Impromptu-Coolspace, Shreveport, La, 2011; Look But Don't Touch, East Bank Gallery, Bossier City, La, 2011; Body As Canvas-The Project-Woman Made Gallery, Chicago, 2011. *Pos:* Voice Actor, Public Artist. *Teaching:* ArtBreak Lead Artist, Shreveport, La, 2010-2012; Noel Community Arts Program, Shreveport, La, 2012. *Awards:* Materials for the Arts, H 2 Timeline, New York Dept Cult Affairs, 83; Starbucks Neighborhood Park Grant, NY, 2005; Nat Endowment for the Arts & Mayor's Inst on City Design with Shreveport Regional Arts Coun, 2011. *Bibliog:* Annabel Walker (auth), Hands off to writer-handsome work, Hong Kong Standard, 1/7/96; Rachel Hatch (auth), Taking Art to the Streets, Ill Wesleyan Mag, 2005. *Mem:* Artists' Circle, New York, NY; Northwest La Roster Artist. *Media:* Paint. *Mailing Add:* 15 Minetta St New York NY 10012

KOVATCH, JAK
PAINTER, SCULPTOR
b Los Angeles, Calif, Jan 17, 1929. *Study:* Univ Calif, Los Angeles, 46; Chouinard Art Inst, Los Angeles, 47-49; Calif Sch of Art, Los Angeles, 49-50; Univ Southern Calif, Los Angeles, 51; Los Angeles City Col, 55-56; Art Students League, spec study with Michael Ponce de Leon, 72 & 75. *Work:* Fogg Mus Art, Harvard Univ; Libr Congress; Joseph Hirshhorn Collection; Fairfield Art Collection, Town Hall, Conn; John Slade Ely House Collection, New Haven; Art Mus, Joinville, Brazil; Univ Miss; Boston Pub Libr, Print Collection, Boston, Mass. *Exhib:* Los Angeles Co Mus Art, 49, 54 & 55; Boston Mus Fine Arts, 54; Libr Congress, 54; Butler Inst Am Art, 54; M H de Young Mem Mus, San Francisco, Calif, 54; Mus Mod Art, NY, 56; Wadsworth Atheneum, Hartford, Conn, 58 & 72-76 & 79; Audubon Artists Inc, Nat Acad Galleries, NY, 73 & 78 & Nat Arts Club, NY, 79-95; Boston Ctr Arts, 76; Nat Acad Design Exhib, 77 & 80; Honolulu Acad Arts, Hawaii, 77 & 85; Print Club, Philadelphia, Pa, 78; Metrop Mus Art, Tokyo, Japan, 87 & 88; Taiwan, Rep of China, 88 & 91; Barbican Art Ctr, London, Eng, 89; Hammond Mus, North Salem, NY, 92; Lever House, NY, 95; Fed Hall, NY, 96; Salmagundi Club, NY, 97; Rensselaerville Inst, NY, 97; and 600 others. *Pos:* Student asst, Lynton Kistler Lithography Studio, Los Angeles, 52-53; animation dept, Walt Disney Prod Inc, Burbank, Calif, 53-54; Commercial Illustration, 57; mem selection comt, Conn Comn on the Arts, Percent for Art Prog, Hartford, 87-88. *Teaching:* Instr, Famous Artists Schs Inc, Westport, Conn, 57-59, New York City Col Exten Div, 59-60; prof design, Univ Bridgeport, Conn, 62-94; ethyl prof, Indust Design, 88-94; fac, Silvermine Sch Art, New Canaan, Conn, 94-. *Awards:* Merit Award, The Print Club of Albany, Inc, Schenectady Mus, NY, 92; Award, Stamford Mus, Conn, 94, 95 & 2000; Painting Award, New Britain Mus Am Art, Conn, 97; Mellon Fel, Vis Fac Prog, Yale Univ, 79-81, 83; Printmaking Grant, Conn Com Arts, 83, 84; Lifetime Art Achievement award, Westport Arts Adv Com, Westport, Conn, 2012; More than 180 Awards & Honors. *Mem:* Audubon Artists (dir graphics, 95); Artists Equity; Westport Arts Ctr Conn; Los Angeles Printmaking Soc; Silvermine Ctr Arts; Internat Sculpture Ctr; Nat Sculpture Soc INC; and others. *Media:* Miscellaneous Media; use of Etching inks for impasto passages in paintings, combined with oil washes on 300 LB hot press water color paper. *Interests:* Many years x-ray experience with the human figure-combined with experimental real or imaginary forms has had significant influence on images used in painting, graphics, and sculpture. *Dealer:* Silvermine Ctr for Arts Inc 1037 Silvermine Rd New Canaan CT 06840-0411. *Mailing Add:* 34 Sasco Creek Rd Westport CT 06880

KOVINICK, PHILIP PETER
WRITER, HISTORIAN
b Detroit, Mich, July 4, 1924. *Study:* Calif State Univ, Chico, BA & MA. *Collection Arranged:* The Woman Artist in the Am West, 1860-1960, 76; Canyons, Arroyos & Oases: Desert Landscape in Southern California, 1900-1985 (co-cur), 85; Reaching the Summit: Mountain Landscapes in Calif, 1900-1986, co-cur, 86. *Awards:* Western Heritage Award, Outstanding Art Book of Yr, 98. *Bibliog:* Nancy Moure, Pub in California Art, Vol 9. *Mem:* Collegium Western Art (pres); Laguna Art Mus Hist Collections Coun (charter mem); Archives Am Art; Huntington Libr Reader, San Marino, Calif; Getty Mus Reader, Los Angeles. *Publ:* auth, South Dakota's Other Borglum, South Dakota History, 71; coauth, Women artists: The American frontier, Art News, 12/76; An Encyclopedia of Women Artists of the American West, Univ Tex Press, Austin, 98; Publications in Southern Calif Art, Vol VI, Dustin Publs, Los Angeles, 99; Western Women Artists, Southwest Art 11/98; contribr, Grove's Encyclopedia of American Art Before 1914, 2000; auth, Woman Artist in The American West, 1860-1960 (exhib catalog), 76; contribr, A Seed of Modernism (exhib catalog), The Art Student's League Los Angeles, 2008; contrib, Sam Hyde Harris 1869-1977: A Retrospective, 2007; contrib, Scenic View Ahead: The Westways Centennial (exhib catalog), 2009; coauth, The Art & Life of Edwin Roscoe Shrader, 2010; contribr, Love Never Fails: The Art of Edouard and Luvena Vysekal, 2011; contbr, James Jarvaise and the Hudson River Series, 2012; auth, John Frost, Quiet Mastery, 2013. *Mailing Add:* 4735 Don Ricardo Dr Los Angeles CA 90008

KOWAL, CAL (LEE)
CURATOR, PHOTOGRAPHER
b Chicago, Ill, Sept 4, 1944. *Study:* Univ Ill, Chicago (art & art hist), 67; Ill Inst Technol, Inst Design, MS (photog), 71. *Work:* Art Inst Chicago, Ill; Cincinnati Art Mus, Ohio; De Cordova Art Mus, Lincoln, Mass; Miami Art Mus, Oxford, Ohio; Chase Manhattan-Ohio Banks, Cincinnati. *Comn:* Silkscreen, SHV NAm, Cincinnati, Ohio, 81; Collaborative Effort (with Peter Bodnar III), Louisville Water Tower Art Asn, 85. *Exhib:* National Photog Invitational, Anderson Gallery, Richmond, Va, 75; OK Art, Contemp Art Ctr, Cincinnati, Ohio, 76; Solo Exhibs: True-False, Carl Solway Gallery, Cincinnati, 83 & Univ Dayton, Ohio, 85; Representation Strategies in Contemp Photog, Southern Ill Univ, Carbondale, 85; 5 in Color: The Constructed Photograph, Warren Lee Ctr, Vermillion, SDak, 86; Group Exhibs: Mus of Contemp Photog, Chicago, 1994; Cincinnati Art Mus, Ohio, 2002; Wesleyan Art Mus, Ohio, 2007; Weston Art Gallery, Ohio, 2003; Aronoff Center, Cincinnati, Ohio, 2003. *Collection Arranged:* Daniel Brown Collection, Middlebury Col, Vt, 81; All Ohio Photography File, Art Acad Cincinnati, 83; Extended Vision (auth, catalog), Ponderosa, Inc, Dayton, Ohio, 84; Mus Contemp Photog, Columbia Col, Chicago, 94. *Teaching:* Sr fac photog & drawing, Art Acad Cincinnati, Ohio, 71-2002 (Retired); guest prof, Miami Univ, Oxford, Ohio, 76-78; vis artist, Sch Art Inst, Chicago, 84-85. *Awards:* Artist-in-Residence, Syracuse Univ, 77; Ohio Arts Coun Fel, 82; Soc Contemp Photog Award, Current Works, Kans, 85; Lifetime Achievement Award, ASMP (Cincinnati Chap), Ohio, 2002. *Mem:* Contemp Art Ctr (bd trustees); Soc Photog Educ (Midwest bd). *Media:* Mixed Media & Drawing; Photographic Assemblages. *Publ:* Auth, Book Full of Spoons, Rose-Pose Publ, 75; T-Shirts Are Tacky, 76; This Space Reserved, 79; Soft Color, portfolio, Self-Publ, Cincinnati, Ohio, 84; Unfamiliar House Series, 86. *Dealer:* Carl Solway Gallery Cincinnati Ohio. *Mailing Add:* 2543 Cleinview Ave Cincinnati OH 45206-2101

KOWAL, DENNIS J
SCULPTOR, WRITER
b Chicago, Ill, Sept 9, 1937. *Study:* Art Inst Chicago; Univ Ill, Navy Pier; Southern Ill Univ, BS, 61, MFA, 62. *Work:* Gillette Corp, Boston; Lakeforest Coll, Ill; Inst Contemp Art, Boston; Babson Coll, Wellesley, Mass; Bank New Eng Corp hq, Boston; Fed Reserve Bank, Boston; Newsweb Corp, Chicago; Boston Univ; DeCordova Mus, Lincoln, Mass; Ravinia, Lakeforest, Ill; Treviso, Italy; Hamilton, Ont; Perpignan, France; Vladimir, Russia; Tel Mond, Israel; Dunfermline, Scotland; Siming/Xiamen, China; Sarasota CofC, Van Wezel Performing Arts Hall, Fla; Sacred Heart Hosp & Allegheny Coll, Cumberland, Md; Mt Holyoke Coll, S Hadley, Mass; Sarasota Chamber of Commerce, Fla; Wentsworth Inst Tech, Boston, Mass; 5 Pt Park City of Sarasota, Fla. *Comn:* Photon II, Sarasota Season of Sculpture, 2000-01; Enigma, Sarasota Season of Sculpture, 2002-03; Remembrance, Temple Beth Israel, Longboat, Fla, 2004; Menorah, Fla Holocaust Mus, St Petersburg, Fla, 2004; Remnant Series 25, Sculpture, Key West, Fla, 2005; Iris, Sarasota Season of Sculpture, 2005-06; WOW II, Remnant Series #19, Ft Pierce, Fla, 2008. *Exhib:* Solo exhibs, Mead Art Mus, Amherst Coll, Mass, 78, NC Mus Art, Raleigh, 78, Gilbert Gallery Ltd, Chicago, Ill, 79, Boston Fine Arts Gallery, Mass, 84, Beaulieu Art Gallery, Cambridge, Mass, 88 & Mt Holyoke Coll Mus, Mass, 88; Mead Art Mus, Amherst Coll, Mass, 78; NC Mus Art, 78; Gilbert Gallery Ltd, Chicago, 79; Kristopher Lindsay Gallery, Sarasota, Fla, 94; John & Mable Ringling Mus Art, Sarasota, Fla, 94; pub sculpture, Navy Pier, Chicago; Sarasota Season of Pub Sculpture, 2000-03, 2005-06 & 2007-08. *Pos:* Artist-in-residence, Dartmouth Coll, 70-71, Univ Ga, 73, Amherst Coll, 77-78, Milton Acad, 77, Maudslay State Park, Newburyport, Mass, 88-90; vis artist, Pinellas Co Arts, St Petersburg, Fla; panelist Fla Arts Coun, 99; chmn, City of Sarasota Pub Art Comt, 2000-2003. *Teaching:* Prof sculpture, Columbus Coll Art, Ohio, 63-64, Frostburg Coll, Frostburg, Md, 64-65, Univ Ill, Champaign, 66-70 & Mass Coll Art, Boston, 71-72; vis lectr, Univ Ga, 73. *Awards:* Numerous awards, 70-; Artist-in-residence & Fel, Macdowell Colony, Peterborough, NH, 65 & 72, Yaddo, Saratoga Springs, NY, 70 & Vietnam Veterans Mem Commonwealth, Mass, 86-; Nat Endowment Arts Matching Grant, Babson Coll, Wellesley, Mass, 76; Vietnam Vets Mem Award Commonwealth of Mass, 86-90; Cultural Recognition Award Fla Dept of State, Millennium, Photon 11, 2000; Intersection Purchase Award, Sarasota, Fla, 2011; Brandeis Univ, Nat Womens Com. *Bibliog:* Rituals of celebrations, Dennis Kowal, Decade Mag, 79; 100 year philosophy, Sarasota Art Rev, 91; Dateline (Channel 4 with K Kirshner): public art, voodoo dolls and politics, Sarasota, Fla, 94; Symbols: Signs of Our Times, CG Jung Soc, 2000; plus others. *Mem:* Inst Contemp Art, Boston, Chicago; Boston Visual Artists Union; Pub Art Comt, City Sarasota, Fla (vchmn, formerly, chmn, currently); Sarasota Anglers Club; Int Game Fish Asn; Int Sculpture Ctr; Mangrove Fly Fishing Club; Coastal Conservation Asn; Carl Jung Soc. *Media:* Stone, Wood, Plastic, Steel, Aluminum, Mixed Media. *Collection:* artifacts; fossils; artwork. *Publ:* Contribr, Contemporary Wood Sculpture, 68, Contemporary Stone Sculpture, 69 & auth, Casting Sculpture, 72, Casting Sculpture (re-pub), Studio Ed, Bookstand Pub, 2011; Artists speak, NY Graphic Soc, 76; The Link, An Artist of Modern Time, Boston Univ Press, 88; Public Art in Greater Boston, Harvard Common Press, 88; Art, money & politics-public art, Sarasota Art Rev, 91; Cultural Wars - Critique and Affirmation Series #29, Artarget News, 97; Liberal Arts?, Forbes Pub, 99; Direct Metal Sculpture, Schiffer Pub, 2001; Dorsky Gallery, New York, Art in m, Art Forum, Art News; Alive is Good, Dennis Kowal, American Sculptor, DVD Documentary, 2010; Unconditional Surrender, Diamonds Along the Highway, PBS/WEDU TV 2012. *Dealer:* DJ Kowal Studios 508 Osprey Ave South Sarasota FL 34236. *Mailing Add:* 508 Osprey Ave S Sarasota FL 34236

KOWALKE, RONALD LEROY
PAINTER, PRINTMAKER
b Chicago, Ill, Nov 8, 1936. *Study:* Univ Chicago, 54-56; Art Inst Chicago, BFA, 54-56; Rockford Col, BA, 59; Cranbrook Acad Art, MFA, 60. *Work:* Mus Mod Art & Metrop Mus Art, NY; Libr Cong & Nat Gallery, Washington, DC; Rockford Col, Ill; Boston Pub Libr; The Contemp Mus, Honolulu; The Samuel P Hard Mus Art, Gainesville, Fla, 93. *Comn:* interior wall, The Europa Ctr Econ Study, Mannheim, Ger, 97; Windows of Fire, The Hawaii Convention Ctr, 98. *Exhib:* Nat Print Exhib, Calif Soc Etchers, San Francisco Mus Art, 65; 15th Ann Print Exhib, Brooklyn Mus, 66; New Directions 1982, Hawaii Artist League, Amfac Plaza Gallery, 82; Hawaii '82-Works on Paper, Univ Hawaii, Hilo, 82; Hawaii Craftsman '82, Amfac Plaza Gallery, 82; two-man exhib, Structures, Art Loft Gallery, Hawaii, 83; Easter Arts Festival, Ala Moana Art Ctr, Hawaii, 83. *Teaching:* Instr design, Northern Ill Univ, 60-61; instr drawing, design & printmaking, Swain Sch Design, New Bedford, Mass, 61-64; assoc prof art, Univ Hawaii, 69-72, prof, 72-. *Awards:* Purchase Awards, Honolulu Acad Arts, 69 & 71; Faculty Res Grant, Univ Hawaii, 69 & 70; Faculty Travel Grants, Univ Hawaii, 79 & 82; Spec Projects grant, Univ Hawaii, 90, Travel grant, 91; Distinguished Citizen award, Chopin Soc Hawaii, 93; fellowship Ctr Arts and Humanities, 94. *Bibliog:* Dantes Inferno: A Portfolio of Ten Etchings, Impressions Workshop, Boston, 70; Gentle Words and Gentle People: A Portfolio of Ten Etchings, Univ Hawaii, Honolulu, 71; Artists of Hawaii, Vol 11, Univ Hawaii Press, 77. *Mem:* Honolulu Printmakers. *Dealer:* Associated American Artists Inc 663 Fifth Ave New York NY 10022; Ferdinand Roten Inc 123 W Mulberry Baltimore MD 21201. *Mailing Add:* 1590 Ulupii St Kailua HI 96734-4443

KOWALSKI, LIBBY R
FIBER ARTIST, EDUCATOR
b Chicago, Ill, Jun 29, 1940. *Study:* Millikin Univ, BA, 62; Colorado State Univ, BFA, 79; Cranbrook Acad Art, MFA, 81. *Work:* Kresgie Art Mus, ELansing, Mich; Dowd Fine Arts Gallery, Cortland, NY; IBM, Southfield, Mich; Unisys, Washington; General Motors, Detroit, Mich. *Exhib:* Fiber Structure Nat, Downey Art Mus, Downey, Calif, 88; Black & White, Gayle Willson Gallery, Southampton, NY, 89; Small Works Invitational, Ctr Tapestry Arts, NY, 89; Fiber Explorations, State Univ NY, Stony Brook, 89; solo exhib: Space/Place/Fragment, Ctr Tapestry Arts, NY, 91; and others. *Teaching:* Prof weaving & surface design, State Univ NY, Cortland, 82-; fibers, Chautauqua Sch Art, summers 87-91; designer/owner, CTD Studio, Hand Weaving & Design Studio, New York, 89-; adj fibers, Grad Prog, Syracuse Univ, 91. *Awards:* Visual Artists Prog Grant, NY State Coun on Arts, 85; Computer Graphics, Stipend, Research Found State Univ New York, 86. *Bibliog:* Else Regensteiner (auth), Geometric Design in Weaving, Schiffer Publ, 86; Tom Milligan (auth), Libby Kowalski: her work (film), WSKG, 4/90. *Mem:* Am Craft Coun; Coll Art Asn. *Media:* Fibers. *Publ:* Contribr, Fiberarts Design Book, 80; contribr, Ithaca Women's Anthology, 89. *Dealer:* Yaw Gallery Birmingham Mich. *Mailing Add:* 32 Union Sq E Ste 216 New York NY 10003

KOWALSKI, RAYMOND ALOIS
PAINTER
b Erie, Pa, June 21, 1933. *Study:* Pa State Teachers Col, Edinboro; Cleveland Inst Art, BFA, 77. *Work:* State of Pa Educ Syst. *Exhib:* May Show, Cleveland Mus Art, 69-71 & 83; Preview 71, Mt St Joseph's Col, Cincinnati, 71; Butler Mus Show, Youngstown, Ohio; Solo exhibs, Green Mansion Gallery, Cleveland, 79, Bluffton Coll, Ohio, 79, Ohio Mus Beachwood, 87, Lmeek Gallery, Cleveland, Ohio, 2005; Ohio State Fair, 79; Willoughby Fine Arts Ctr, Ohio, 79; Shaker Hist Mus, 90. *Pos:* Designer, Am Greetings Corp, Cleveland, 59-65, art dir, 65-, managing art dir, 73-, dir, Creative Planning, 81, dir design, 83; Exec dir design, 85; consult, Carlton Cards Ltd, United Kingdom, 93-95. *Teaching:* Instr design, Cooper Sch Art, Cleveland, 69-70; instr painting for local art groups, 70-; guest critic, RI Sch Design, Sr Proj, 90; guest instr, Columbus Col Art & Design, Parsons Sch Design, 92; Cleveland Inst of Art; Ringling Sch Design. *Awards:* Award, Jewish Community Ctr Ann, Cleveland Heights, 79; Award, Erie Art Ctr Ann, Penn, 79; Ohio State Fair, 81; and others; Fine Arts Show Awards, B P Am Gallery, Cleveland Ohio, 87 & 88; Am Greetings Corp Fine Arts Show, Cleveland Playhouse Gallery. *Bibliog:* Helen Borsick (auth), article in Cleveland Plain Dealer Suppl, 68; Ray Kowalski--painter of houses, Wonderful World Ohio, 10/69; Ray Kowalski-House Painter, WKYC-TV, Cleveland. *Mem:* Soc Illusrs; Int Arts Comt-UNICEF, 96-97. *Media:* Acrylic, Collage, Watercolor, Digital imagery. *Specialty:* Graphic Design. *Interests:* Digital photography, landscape design. *Mailing Add:* 2429 Derbyshire Ct Cleveland OH 44106

KOZLOFF, MAX
PHOTOGRAPHER, WRITER
b Chicago, Ill, June 21, 1933. *Study:* Univ Chicago, BA, 53, MA, 58; Inst Fine Arts, NY Univ; Fulbright scholar, France, 62-63. *Exhib:* Solo exhibs, Holly Solomon Gallery, NY, 77 & 79-80, Marlborough Gallery, NY, 82, PPOW Gallery, NY, 93; Nat Ctr Performing Arts, Bombay, India, 96; Higher Pictures, NY, 2011; Art Inst, Chgo, 2013. *Pos:* Art critic, The Nation, 61-69; NY corresp, Art Int, 62-64; contrib ed, Artforum, 63-74, exec ed, 74-76. *Teaching:* Instr, Calif Inst Arts, 70-71 & Yale Univ, 74; prof photog, Sch Visual Arts, NY, 89-00; and many others. *Awards:* Pulitzer Fel Critical Writing, 62-63; Frank Jewett Mather Award Art Criticism, 66; Guggenheim Fel, 68-69; Nat Endowment Arts Criticism Fel, 84; Int Ctr Photog Writing Award, 90. *Media:* Color Photography. *Publ:* Renderings, Simon and Schuster, 1968; Auth, Cubism Futurism, 73; Photography and Fascination, 79; The Privileged Eye, 87; Duane Michals Now Becoming Then, Twelve Trees Press, 90; Lone Visions, Crowded Frames, Univ NMex Press, 94; NY Capital Photography, Yale Univ Press and Jewish Mus, 02; The Theatre of the Face, Portrait Photography Since 1900, Phaidon, 2007; Vermeer, A Study Contrasto, Rome, 2011. *Dealer:* Higher Pictures NY. *Mailing Add:* 152 Wooster St New York NY 10012

KOZLOWSKI, EDWARD C
PAINTER, DESIGNER
b Bridgeport, Conn, Mar 11, 1927. *Study:* Butera Sch Fine Art, 47; Whitney Sch Art, portrait with Simka Simkovitch, dipl, 51; Yale Sch Design, color with Josef Albers, BFA, 54. *Work:* Yale Univ, New Haven, Conn; Brittex; Citytrust; IBM; General Electric; Xerox; pvt collection of Al Pacino. *Exhib:* Conn Yale Artists, Yale AA Gallery, New Haven, 76; 2nd Ann Int Soc Arts, Foothills Art Ctr, Golden, Colo, 79; 27th Ann Nat Soc Painters Casein & Acrylic, Nat Arts Club, NY, 80; 3rd Ann, Salmagundi Club, NY, 80; 156th Ann, Nat Acad Design, NY, 81. *Pos:* Staff artist, Bridgeport Post, Conn, 47-54; advert designer, Int Silver Co, Meriden, Conn, 54-56;

dir packaging develop, Warner Packaging, Bridgeport, Conn, 56-64; owner, Edward C Kozlowski Design Inc, New York, 64-83. *Teaching:* Instr design, Pratt Inst, Brooklyn, 65-69 & Parson Sch Design, 83-86. *Awards:* Best Show, 20th Ann, Barnum Festival Soc, 80; Best Acrylics, 20th Ann, Barnum Festival Soc, 80; Frederick Lowey Award, Salmagundi Club, 81. *Mem:* Salmagundi Club; Conn Classical Arts; Am Inst Graphic Arts; Advertising Club Fairfield Co (pres, 64-65). *Media:* Acrylic, Watercolor; Conte, Pencil, Lithograph, ink. *Publ:* Coauth, The Package Designer Looks At Packaging Materials, Packaging Design, 64; Contribr, Changing Times, Indust Design, 75; Auth, Job Sheet: A Better Link Between Packager and Marketer, Product Mgt, 76. *Dealer:* Art/Place 400 Center St Southport CT; Moviehouse Gallery Main St Millerton NY. *Mailing Add:* 74 Columbine Dr Trumbull CT 06611-4603

KOZMON, GEORGE
PAINTER
b Cleveland, Ohio, Apr 22, 1960. *Study:* Cleveland Inst Art, Ohio, BFA, 82. *Work:* Cleveland Mus Art, Ohio; Erie Art Mus, Pa; DuPont, Detroit, Mich; IBM, Armonk, NY; Butler Inst Am Art, Youngstown, Ohio; and others. *Comn:* canvas (4ft x 6ft), Goodyear Tech Ctr, Akron, 85; Canvas (6ft x 10ft), Progressive Field, Cleveland Indians; painting on masonite (3ft x 5ft), Turner Construction, Columbus, 86; 5 (5ft x 8ft) canvases, Univ Hosp, Cleveland, 89; 9 paintings on aluminum, Key Corp, Cleveland, 99. *Exhib:* Gov Residence Invitational, Columbus, Ohio, 85; The Artist Obsessed: Architecture Perceived, Fendrick Gallery, Washington, DC, 866; Sande Webster Gallery, Philadelphia, 89 & 91; Solo exhibs, Quan/Schieder Gallery, Toronto, Robert Kidd Gallery, Thrive an artspace 2005; two-man exhib, Deson/Saunders Gallery, Chicago, 94 & Elevation art 2006, Groupshow on the Wall, Cleveland State Univ, 2006; Directors Choice Show, Virginia Miller Gallery, Miami. *Collection Arranged:* Thrive an artspace, 2004, 2005; Image System, Elevation Art, 2006; Cumahoga Community Coll, 2008. *Pos:* dir, Cain Park Art Festival, Cleveland Heights, Ohio, 97-; founder/owner, Thrive an artspace; independent cur, High art gallery. *Teaching:* Vis lectr, Mid Am Col, Art Asn, 84; instr, drawing & archit, Cleveland Inst Art, 85-96, life drawing, 2000-; Orange Art Center, 87-. *Awards:* Ohio Coun Individual Fel, 84-85; Ohio Arts Coun Visual Artists Fel, 84, 87, 91 & 95; Nat Endowment Arts Individual Artists Fel, 87-88; and others. *Bibliog:* Gerorge Kozmon (video), Goodyear, 84; A brush with buildings, Washington Post, 4/12/86; Am Artist watercolor, Evolving subject mater, 2003; and others. *Mem:* World Fedn Hungarian Artists; Cleveland Hungarian Am mus. *Media:* Acrylic on Paper & Canvas. *Publ:* Auth, Art in the Midwest, Am Artist, 84; City whites, Cleveland Mag, 84; Drawing a line of departure, Cleveland Mus Art, 84; On the wall, Cleveland State Univ, 2006; and numerous catalogues. *Mailing Add:* 360 Timberidge Tr Gates Mills OH 44040

KOZO
PRINTMAKER
b Osaka, Japan, June 18, 1937. *Study:* Keio Univ, Dipl Art, 60. *Work:* Mus Mod Art, Paris, France; Royal Libr Belg, Brussels; Mus Mod Art, Calcutta, India; Osaka City Mus, Japan; Keio Univ, Tokyo, Japan. *Comn:* Mural, Siege Social Fougerolle, Paris, France, 74; mural, Dresdner Bank, Frankfort, Ger, 79; mural, Siege Social Itocyu, Tokyo, Japan, 80; mural, Villas Presidentielles, Bagdad, Iraq, 82; mural, Dresdner Bank, Singapore, 85. *Exhib:* Salon de Mai, Mus Mod Art, Paris, France, 63-68; solo exhibs, Mus Chartres, France, 73, Cent Mus, Tokyo, Japan, 85 & Hakone Open-Air Mus (with catalog), Kanagawa, Japan, 92. *Awards:* Grand Prix de Serigraphie, Paris, France, 69; Grand Prix du Contemp Art, Tokyo, Japan, 71. *Bibliog:* Bernard Gheerbrandt (auth), Kozo Lavis, FRT Races, 83; Jacques Busse (auth), Dictionary of Art, E Benezit, 93. *Media:* Oil, Silkscreen. *Publ:* Sculptures of Crystal, Daum, 80; Post Cards, Posters, Nouvelles Images, 80; Ed, Tapestries, Robert Four, 82; Portfolio of Silkscreen, Multiple Impressions, 85; Kimono, Juraku, 86. *Mailing Add:* c/o John Szoke Graphics Inc 24 W 57th St Ste 304 New York NY 10019

KRAAL, LIES
PAINTER
b Rotterdam, Holland, July 23, 1937. *Hon Degrees:* 2005 Cola Award City of Los Angeles. *Work:* Laguna Mus Art, Calif; Panza Collection, Milano, Italy; La Coleccion Jumex, Mexico City. *Comn:* LA Coleccion Juniex Mus, Mexico City, 2002. *Exhib:* 2 Dimensions, Univ Tex, El Paso, 84; Exemplary Contemp, Univ Calif, Santa Cruz, 87, 88; Lies Kraal, Claremont Univ, Calif, 2000; Jumex Mus, Mexico City. *Teaching:* guest artist, Painting's Edge, Idyllwild Arts, Calif; resident, Chinati Found, Marfa, Tex, 2003; Vis Artist Residency Chinati Fond, Marfa, Tex, 2003. *Awards:* COLA Fel, City of LA Cultural Affairs Dept, 2005. *Bibliog:* Rosanna Albertini (auth), Lies Kraal, Claremont Grad Univ, 2000. *Media:* Acrylic. *Specialty:* Contemporary Art. *Dealer:* Susanne Vielmetter 5795 West Washington Blvd. Culver City, CA, 90232; Charlotte Jackson Fine Art 200 W Marcy St Ste 101 Santa Fe NM 87501. *Mailing Add:* 724 Milwood Ave Venice CA 90291

KRAFT, CRAIG ALLAN
SCULPTOR, CURATOR
b Ames, Iowa, Dec 7, 1949. *Study:* Univ Wis-Madison, BA & MA; Atlantic Ctr Arts (Stephen Antonokos-Artist Residence Prog), New Smyrna Fla, 88. *Work:* French Consulate, New Orleans, La; Dorsey Law Firm, Minneapolis, Minn; Zimmering & Zinn Inc, NY; Epco, Bensalem, Pa; Int Machinist Asoc, Washington. *Comn:* Maitland Surgical Ctr, Fla, 88; 30' acrylic & neon with cross faders, Rouse Co, Washington, 91; Five Famous Washingtonians in neon, Pennsylvania Ave Dev Corp, Washington, 93; auditorium marquee, 96, Falling Rising Man, Admin Bldg, 98, RI Sch Design. *Exhib:* DC Sculpture Now, Sumner Sch Mus, Washington, 89; Transformations, Washington Sq, Washington, 90; one-man show, Zenith Gallery, Washington, 90 & 94, Reston Art Ctr, Va, 92, Perry House Galleries, Arlington, Va, 97 & Traveling Light, Seto, Japan, 98; Electric Eclectic, Ctr Contemp Art, North Miami, Fla, 93; Outdoor Sculpture Competition Exhib, Western Carolina Univ, NC, 95; Pop Ups, Socrates Sculpture Park, Long Island City, 95-96; Convergence Art Festival & Intern Sculpture Conf, Providence, RI, 96. *Collection Arranged:* Light as a Helping Hand traveling exhib, 94. *Pos:* Artistic dir, Glen Echo Neon Restoration, Washington, DC, 90. *Teaching:* Instr neon/light sculpture, Int Sculpture Ctr Conf, 90, Smithsonian Inst, 90-. *Awards:* Neon Lit Art Nat Winner, St Publ, Cincinnati, Ohio, 88, 89, 90 & 96; Visual Arts Grant, Nat Endowment Arts & DC Arts & Humanities, 93 & Small Proj Grant, 97; Masterworks, Convergence XI, Providence, RI, 98. *Bibliog:* Personal interview, Channel 9 WUSA, 91; Christian Schiess (auth), Interviews with light artists, St Publ, 93; Fox News Network, Neon Exhibition-Craig Kraft, 94. *Mem:* Washington Sculpture Group. *Media:* Light Sculpture. *Publ:* Auth, Neon (instrnl video), 97. *Mailing Add:* 931 R St NW Washington DC 20001

KRAFT, STEVE
DESIGNER
b Los Angeles, Calif, Dec 5, 1946. *Study:* Univ Calif at Berkeley, B (Arch). *Work:* De Young Mus, San Francisco; Oakland Mus, Calif. *Comn:* Reception area work in cherrywood & glass, Osborne McGraw-Hill, Emeryville, Calif, 87; construction in steel & nylon, Saatchi & Saatchi, San Francisco, 88; collection case, Richard Diebenkorn, Healdsburg, Calif, 90; assemblage in red oak & steel, Bechtel Corp, Richmond, Calif, 91; furniture for private residence/studio, Wolf von dem Bussche, Berkeley, 96. *Pos:* Owner/design dir, Kraft Furniture, 78-. *Media:* Wood, Metal. *Mailing Add:* 4356 Coliseum Way Oakland CA 94601

KRAFT, YVETTE
INSTRUCTOR, PAINTER
b Jan 17, 1945, Wash DC. *Study:* Private student of the late Master Painter, Leon Berkowitz, 82-87; Studied at, Corcoran Coll Art & Design, with Master Painter William Christenberry, 92-2004. *Work:* Am Univ, Wash DC; Shiloh Baptist Church, Wash DC; George Washington Univ Hosp, Wash DC; Whitman-Walter Clinic, Wash DC; Embassy of Israel, Wash DC; Larry King, Boston, Mass; represented by Parish Gallery, Wash DC; Studio Gallery, Wash DC. *Exhib:* Solo exhibs, Maret Sch., Washington, 1987, Georgetown Montessori Sch., 1988, Horace Mann Sch., 1989, Fillmore Sch. of Arts, 1991, NIH, Clin. Ctr. Gallery, Bethesda, Md., 1995, Fondo del Sol Visual Arts Ctr., Washington, 1996, DC Arts Ctr., 1999, Nat. Coalition for Homeless, 2001, Studio Gallery, 2009,. *Pos:* adv. bd. New Art Examiner Mag., Washington, 85-86; Art dir. after-sch. program Georgetown Montessori Sch., 88; condr. art classes N St. Village, Wash DC, 2003-04; asst. mgr. Americana West Gallery, Wash DC; founder, dir. Project City People, 92-93; founder, Kraft Media Prize, Wash Project for the Arts (WPA). *Teaching:* art instr. Washington Home, Sr. Citizen Care Facility, 89-90; art instr. students with spl. needs Horace Mann Elem. Sch., 90; art instr. Southeast Asian Refugee Children, 4-H, Arlington, Va., 89-90; pvt. art instr. ages 2-17, 90-92; art instr. Janney Elem. Sch., 91, 98, 99; art instr. children and adolescents with emotional disorders Clara Aisenstein, MD, Child Psychiatrist, 93-96; art instr. Randle Highlands Elem. Sch., 94. *Awards:* Grantee, Cafritz Found, 90, 91; George Preston Marshall grant, 91; scholarship, Artists of Our Town, Corcoran Sch Art; Winter grant, Hattie M Strong Found, 91; Advanced Painting Scholar, Corcoran Sch Art, 92, Special Selection, Arts for Our Town program, 94. *Bibliog:* Arts Beat (feature), Washington Post, 12/93, 6/96, 9/98, 6/2001; City Paper (feature), Wash DC, 4/2001; Voice of America-Korean Service (video), 7/2001. *Mem:* Wash Project for the Arts. *Media:* Acrylic, Pastel. *Interests:* Jazz, Observing and Sketching People

KRAINAK, PAUL
PAINTER, CRITIC, ART SCHOOL ADMINISTRATOR
Exhib: Exhibited widely in the US including the Southeast Ctr for Contemporary Art, Winston-Salem, NC, Ukrainian Mus of Modern Art, Hyde Park Art Ctr Chgo, Fay Gold Gallery, Atlanta, Bernis Ctr for the Arts, Omaha, Artist Image Resource Ctr, Pittsburgh, Semaphore Gallery, NYC and NEXUS Gallery, Philadelphia. *Pos:* Artist, critic, chair art department, Bradley Univ, currently; lectured at the Acad of Fine Arts, Prague, Czechoslovakia, The Acad of Art, Bratislava, Slovakia, Acad of Fine Art and Design, China and Sch of Fine Art, Nanjing, China. *Publ:* Published by Indiana Univ Press, Afterimage, New Art Examiner, Dialogue, Sculpture Magazine and Artpapers (St. Louis Editor). *Dealer:* Ingrid Fassbender. *Mailing Add:* Bradley University Dept of Art Heuser Art Center 102 1400 West Bradley Ave Peoria IL 61625

KRAKOW, BARBARA L
DEALER
b Boston, Mass, June 9, 1936. *Study:* Boston Univ, BA, 58. *Collection Arranged:* Internat Contemporary Art, 45-. *Pos:* Pres, Harcus-Krakow Gallery, Boston, 64-83, Barbara Krakow Gallery, 83-; art adv panel, Internal Revenue Service, 80-84; membership comt, Art Dealers Asn Am, formerly; bd mem, Art Auction AIDS Action Comt, 85, co-chairperson, 86; cur, Ninth Ann Drawing Show, Boston Ctr Arts, 88. *Teaching:* Lectr, Harvard Arts Mus, 11/86. *Awards:* Honored by Boston YWCA, Tribute to Women Entrepreneurs, 86. *Mem:* Art Table Inc; Art Dealer Asn Am; Int Fine Print Dealer Asn. *Specialty:* Internat art 1945 to present, paintings, sculpture, drawings and prints. *Mailing Add:* Barbara Krakow Gallery 10 Newbury St Boston MA 02116

KRAMER, BURTON
ARTIST, DESIGNER
b New York, NY, 1932. *Study:* Inst Design, Ill Inst Technol, BSc (visual design), 54; Royal Coll Art, London, Eng, 55-56; Yale Univ Sch Fine Arts, MFA (design), 57; with Josef Albers, Paul Rand, Alexey Brodovitch & Bradbury Thompson. *Hon Degrees:* Ont Coll Art and Design, Can, Hon D, 2003. *Work:* Smithsonian Inst, North Am Life Assurance; Foundation for Constructive Art, Calgary, Alberta & pvt collections. *Comn:* Identity program design, Can Imperial Bank Com, Can Broadcasting Corp, Copps Coliseum, Reed Paper, Can Craft Coun, Teknion Furniture, Science North, Nat Res Coun Can, Onex Packaging, Gemini Group & St Lawrence Centre Arts. *Exhib:* Can Graphic Design, Tokyo, Japan, 75; Spectrum Can, Montreal, 76; VI Poster Biennale, Warsaw, Poland, 76; RCA Designers 78, Toronto, 78; Graphic Designer Can Best of '80's, Art Dirs Show, Toronto, 85; Logo Biennale, Ostend, Belgium, 94; Pekao Gallery, Toronto, 99; Peak Gallery, Toronto, 2001-2002; Kabat-Wrobel Gallery,

Toronto, 2003; Arta Gallery, Toronto, 2005; Fran Hill Gallery, Toronto, 2005; Siano Gallery, Philadelphia, 2006; CorBraun Gallery, Westport, Ont, Can, 2006; Oeno Gallery, Prince Edward Co, Ontario, Can, 2007; Gallery 1313, Toronto, 2007; Gallery Moos, Toronto, 2008, 2010. *Pos:* Chief designer, Halpern Advert, Zurich, Switz, 62-65; dir corp graphics, Clairtone Sound Corp, 66-67; pres, Kramer Design Assocs Ltd, Marketing Commun & Design, 67-2001. *Teaching:* Mem design fac, Ont Coll Art, 78-98. *Awards:* Graphic Designers Can, 85; Lifetime Achievement Award, Arts Toronto, 99; Order Ont, 2003. *Bibliog:* Article, Studio Mag, Toronto, 85; First Choice, Tokyo, 89; Idea Mag, Tokyo, 92. *Mem:* Royal Can Acad Art; fel Graphic Designers Can (pres, 75-77); Alliance Graphique Int. *Media:* Acrylic. *Interests:* Art, antiquities, architecture, music, books and travel. *Publ:* Auth & contribr, Top trademarks and symbols of the world, Milan, 74; auth & ed, Idea Mag, Tokyo, 75 & 85; auth, Canadian Interiors, Toronto, 75; Appl Arts Quart, 90; Essays on Design, 9/97; ColourSignals, 97-2009. *Dealer:* Oeno Gallery Ont; Gallery Moos Toronto Ontario Canada. *Mailing Add:* Kramer Design Assoc Ltd 103 Dupont St Toronto ON M5R 1O4 Canada

KRAMER, HARRY
PAINTER
b Philadelphia, Pa, Mar 20, 1939. *Study:* Philadelphia Coll Art, BFA in painting, 1962; Yale Univ, MFA in painting, 1965. *Work:* group exhib Hudson River Mus, Yonkers, NY, 1983, NY Studio Sch, 1985, Nat Acad of Design, 1994, 95, 96, 2001, US Embassy, Vienna, 2002, Ameringer and Yohe Fine Art, Boca Raton, 2002, 2003; pvt collections, Brooklyn Mus Art, Corcoran Gallery, Metrop Mus Art, Nat Acad of Design, Ketcham and McDougal Found, NJ, Detroit Inst of Art, Chase Manhattan Bank. *Exhib:* Solo exhibs: Brata Gallery, New York City, 1972, 55 Mercer Gallery, New York City, 1973, 74, 76, 81, Forum Gallery, Maryland, 1977, Ted Greenwald Gallery, New York City, 1983, Gruenebaum Gallery, New York City, 1985, 87, Charles Cowles Gallery, New York City, 1991, 94, 98, 2003, Bill Bace Gallery, 1993, Ameringer and Yohe, 2003 & 05, Ober Gallery, Kent, Conn, 2006. *Teaching:* Prof, Queens Coll, Flushing, NY, 1970; Instr, NY Studio Sch, 1968-73; NYU, 1968-69. *Awards:* Fel NY State Coun on Arts, 1973, 77; Fel Nat Endowment for Arts, 82; Faculty Res Grant Queens Col, 83, 94, 95, 96. *Mem:* Nat Acad (acad, 94). *Media:* Oil

KRAMER, LINDA LEWIS
PAINTER, COLLECTOR
b New York, NY, Mar 25, 1937. *Study:* Scripps Col, Claremont Calif, with Paul Soldner, BA, 59; Sch Art Inst, Chicago, MFA, 81; Graham Sch, Univ Chicago, 2008-2010. *Work:* Mus Contemp Art, Chicago; Purdue Univ, W Lafayette; Univ Ill, Carbondale; Allan Chasonoff Ceramic Collection, Mint Mus Art, Charlotte, NC; Mary & Leigh Block Mus Art, Evanston, Ill; Ill State Mus, Springfield, Ill; Smart Mus of Art, Univ Chgo. *Exhib:* Solo exhibs, "Three Cultures, Red, Yellow & Blue", Univ Ariz, Tucson, 84, Chicago Cult Ctr, 86, Still Light, Evanston Art Ctr, Luminous Light, Tough Gallery, Chicago, 93, Pool, Franklin Sq Gallery, Chicago, 94, Printworks Gallery, Chicago, 2008; Alternative Spaces, Mus Contemp Art, Chicago, 84; 80th Exhib, Art Inst, Chicago, 84; Material & Metaphor, Chicago Cult Ctr, 86; Retrospective, Hyde Park Art Ctr, Chicago, 99; Evanston Arts Coun, Noyes Cult Arts Ctr, 2003; Corbett vs Dempsey, 2005; Printworks Gallery, 2008; Retrospective, Unstable Variations, Evanston Art Ctr, Ill, 2013. *Pos:* Comt mem, Evanston Art Ctr Exhibs, 91-, prog dir art after 5, collectors; cur, Hyde Park Art Ctr, 2010; dir, 70+ Chicago Visual Artist History Oral Archives, 2010-2013. *Teaching:* Instr, Columbia Col, 93; Sch Art Inst, 95; Urban Gateways, Chicago, 96. *Awards:* Ill Arts Coun Grant, 84, 96; Levy Found Prize, 80th Chicago & Vicinity Exhib, 84, 89; Karolyi Found Grant, Vence, France, 89. *Bibliog:* Diane Douglas (auth), Material & Metaphor, Chicago Pub Libr Cultural Ctr, 86; Patty Carroll (auth), Spirited Visions, Univ Ill Press, 91; Ivy Sundell (auth), Art Scene Chicago, Crow Woods Pub, 2000; Linda Kramer: Retrospective, Hyde Park Art Ctr, Chicago, 99; Artist as Collector, N Ind Arts Asn, 2004. *Mem:* Mid-west Clay Guild (vpres, 86, treas, 90); Evanston Art Ctr (exhib comt, 96); Artemisia Gallery (bd, 97-); Art after 5- Chair-Evan AM Art Ctr, 2005. *Media:* Miscellaneous Media, Installations, Watercolor, Oil Painting. *Res:* dir Sandra Binioin of 70+ Chicago Visual Artist Oral History Archives 2010-2013, held at Ryerson and Burnham Libraries, Art Inst Chicago. *Collection:* Chicago imagists first and second generation, Hairy Who Sch. *Publ:* Auth, Natural & Cultural Energy, Leonardo Mag, 87; Retrospective Catalog, Hyde Park Art Ctr, Chicago, 99, Evanston Art Ctr, Ill, 2013; Unstable Variations, Linda Kramer Retrospective (45 pg color catalog). *Dealer:* Printworks 311 W Superior Chicago 60610; Corbett vs Dempsey 1120 N Ashland, Chicago 60622. *Mailing Add:* 370 Glendale Ave Winnetka IL 60093

KRAMER, LOUISE
MURALIST, SCULPTOR
b New York, NY. *Study:* Cooper Union, cert, 44; Hofstra Univ, BA, 68; Hunter Col, MA, 70. *Work:* Nassau Community Col, Hempstead, NY; Mus Fine Art, Univ Iowa, Iowa City; Brentwood High Sch, NY. *Comn:* Mural, Int Ladies Garment Workers' Union, Local 23-25, NY, 85. *Exhib:* Two Women Sculptors, RI Univ Gallery, Kingston; Emerging Real, Storm King Art Ctr, Mountainville; Solo exhib, Nassau Co Mus Fine Arts, Roslyn; Women Choose Women, NY Cult Ctr; Calif Coll Arts & Crafts Print Show, San Francisco Mus Art; Printmaking, New Forms, Whitney Mus, NY; AIR Gallery, NY, 75, 78, 81, 83 & 85; Working Women, Am Fedn State Co & Munic Employees; 18th Nat Print Exhib, Brooklyn Mus, 86. *Teaching:* Artist-in-residence, sculpture, Univ Iowa, Iowa City, 78; lectr sculpture, Arrandale Sch, Great Neck, NY. *Awards:* North Shore Community Arts Award, Great Neck, 75; Fel Printmaking, NY State Coun Arts, 76; Nat Endowment Arts Fel Printmaking, 76. *Bibliog:* Lizzie Borden (auth), Louise Kramer, Artforum, 72; Kate Linker (auth), Louise Kramer, Arts Mag, 5/77. *Mem:* Women in the Arts; Women's Caucus Arts. *Media:* Steel, Brass. *Dealer:* AIR Gallery 63 Crosby St New York NY 10012. *Mailing Add:* 26 Beaver St New York NY 10004

KRAMER, MARGIA
CONCEPTUAL ARTIST, MULTI-MEDIA ARTIST
b Brooklyn, NY, 1939. *Study:* Art Students League; Brooklyn Col, BA; Inst of Fine Arts, New York Univ, MA (art hist); performance/dance study with Yvonne Rainer & Simone Forti. *Work:* Mus Mod Art, NY; Allen Mem Art Mus, Oberlin, Ohio; New York Pub Libr; Univ Calif, San Diego; Temple Univ; Carnegie/Mellon. *Comn:* Secret (video), Ill Arts Coun, Chicago, 81; Progress (Memory) I (video), Visual Studies Workshop, Rochester, NY, 83; New Wozzeck (video) Jerome Found, 85; Obelisk for Raymond Williams (pub sculpture), Pub Art Fund Inc, NY, 88; I a Wo/Man (multi-media), San Francisco Artspace, 89. *Exhib:* Issue, Social Strategies by Women Artists, Inst Contemporary Arts, London, Eng, 80; Jean Seberg-The FBI-The Media, Mus Mod Art, NY, 81; Progress (Memory) II, Whitney Mus Art, 84; Surveillance, Los Angeles Contemp Exhibs (LACE), 87; Social Engagement: Women's Video in the 80's, Whitney Mus Art, 87; Democracy and Politics, Dia Art Found, 88; Committed to Print, Mus Mod Art, 88; A Different War: Vietnam in Art, Akron Art Mus, traveling exhib, 89-92; Making Their Mark: Women Artists move into the Mainstream 1970 to 1985, Cincinnati Art Mus, traveling exhib, 89-90. *Teaching:* Vis asst prof, painting & drawing, Duke Univ, 79-80; asst prof painting & drawing, Univ of Ill, Chicago, 80-81; asst prof film & video, Univ of Hartford, 83-84; artist-in-residence, Mass Inst Technol, 89. *Awards:* Woodrow Wilson Found Fel, 63; Bronx Coun Arts Grant, 76; NYC Dept Cultural Affairs Grant, 76; NEA Fel, 76, 82, 89; The Media Bureau of the Kitchen Grants, 80, 85; Comt Visual Arts Grants, 79, 85; NY State Coun on the Arts Grant, 81; Nat Endowment for Humanities Grant, 81; Ill Arts Coun Grant, 81; Eastman Fund Grant, 82; NY State Coun Arts CAPS Fel, 82; Jerome Found Grant, 85; NY State Coun Arts Grant, 86; Public Art Fund Comn, 88; NY Found Arts Fel, 87; Mass Coun Arts Grant, 88. *Bibliog:* Dore Ashton (auth), American Art Since 1945, 82; Lucy Lippard (auth), Get the Message? A Decade of Art for Social Change, 84 & A Different War: Vietnam in Art, 90; Branda Miller & Deborah Irmas et al (auths), Surveillance, 87; Deborah Wye (auth), Committed to Print, Social and Political Themes in Recent American Printed Art, 88. *Media:* Multi-media installations, books, video. *Interests:* 1980s political economy, art and politics, feminism, human rights, civil rights, social issues, censorship. *Publ:* auth, Essential Documents: The FBI File on Jean Seberg Part I, NY, 79, Part II, 80; auth, Jean Seberg/The FBI/The Media, NY, 81; auth, Andy Warhol et al: The FBI File on Andy Warhol, NY, Unsub Press, 88. *Dealer:* Printed Matter Inc New York NY

KRAMLICH, RICHARD & PAMELA
COLLECTOR
Study: Northwestern Univ, BA (hist), 1957; Harvard Univ, MBA, 1960. *Pos:* With, Kroger co, Cincinnati, 1960-64; joined, Gardner & Preston Moss, Boston, 1964, exec vpres, 1968-69; gen partner, Arthur Rock & Assoc's, 1969-78; co-founder & gen partner, New Enterprise Assoc's, Menlo Park, Calif, 1978-; founder, New Art Trust, 1997-; bd dirs, Celetronix, Decru, Fabric7Systems, Financial Engines, Force10 Networks, Foveon, Graphic Enterprises, Informative, Zhone Technol, Visual Edge Tech, Silicon Valley Bancshares, UCSF Found, Bay Area Video Coalition; vchmn bd dirs, San Francisco Exploratorium, currently. *Awards:* Lifetime Achievement Award 2001; Named one of Top 200 Collectors, ARTnews mag, 2004-11; Lifetime Achievement Award in Entrepreneurship & Innovation, Lester Ctr for Entrepreneurship & Innovation, Haas Sch Bus, Univ Calif, Berkeley, 2005. *Mem:* Nat Venture Capital Asn (pres, 1992-93, chmn, 1993-94). *Collection:* Contemporary art, especially video and film. *Mailing Add:* 3699 Washington St San Francisco CA 94118

KRANE, SUSAN
CURATOR, MUSEUM DIRECTOR
b Gary, Ind, June 8, 1954. *Study:* Carleton Coll, BA (magna cum laude), 1976; Columbia Univ, MA, 1978, Univ Colo, MBA, 2000; Exec Edu Program in Non-Profit Mgmt, Harvard Bus Sch, 2011. *Collection Arranged:* Max Weber: The Cubict Decade (auth, catalog), 1991; Equal Rights & Justice (auth, brochure), 1994; Tampering: Artists & Abstraction Today, (auth, brochure) 1994; Tangle of Complexes: Photography in Mexico, 1996; Enrique Chagoya, 1997; Nene Humphrey: A Wild Patience, 1998; Out of Order: Mapping Social Space (co-auth, catalog), 2000; Let's Walk West: Brad Kahlhamer, 2004; Flip a Strip, 2008; Crossroads of Am Photog (auth, catalog) 2008; Real and Hyper Real, 2009. *Pos:* Rockefeller Found Intern, Walker Art Ctr, Minneapolis, 1978-79; asst cur, Albright-Knox Art Gallery, Buffalo, NY, 1979-82, assoc cur 1983, cur 1983-87; cur, 20th Century Art, High Mus Art, 1987-95; dir, Univ Colo Art Mus, 1996-2001; dir, Scottsdale Mus Contemp Art, Ariz, 2001-08; exec dir, San Jose Mus Art, Calif, 2008-. *Teaching:* Adj prof art hist, State Univ NY, Buffalo, 1980-86; adj prof, Emory Univ, Atlanta, 1988-95; asst prof, Univ Colo, Boulder, 1996-2001. *Awards:* Norton's Curators' Fel, 1994. *Mem:* Art Table; Coll Art Asn; Asn of Art Mus Directors. *Specialty:* Mod & contemp art, archit & design. *Publ:* Hollis Frampton, MTT Press, 1986; Albright Knox Art Gallery: The Painting & Sculpture Collection, Hudson Hills, 1988; Lynda Benglis: Dual Natures, Univ Wash Press, 1990; Max Weber: The Cubist Decade, Univ of Wash Press, 1991; Brad Kahlhamer: Let's Walk West, 2004; At the Crossroads of American Photography: Callahan, Siskind, Sommer, Radius Books, 2008. *Mailing Add:* San Jose Mus Art 110 S Market St San Jose CA 95113

KRANKING, MARGARET GRAHAM
PAINTER, LECTURER
b Florence, SC, Dec 21, 1930. *Study:* Am Univ, Washington, DC, BA (summa cum laude, Clendenin Fellow in Art Hist), 52. *Work:* Fed Nat Mortgage Asn, AT&T & Wall St J, Washington, DC; US Gen Accounting Off; Marsh & McClennan cos; Nat Coun Educ, Washington, DC; Hospice Montgomery co, Md; Art in Embassies: Mission Off UN, Official Residence Ambassador to UN, Hon John Bolton; US Coast Guard Hall of Heroes; Florence Mus, SC; Freddie Mac; Fannie May; Philip Morris co; Univ Va. *Comn:* Portrait, Rear Admiral Harold C Train & Admiral Harry D Train II, comn by Mrs Harold C Train, Washington, DC, 71; portrait, Dr Cecile Bolton Finley, Univ Va, Mrs Joseph V Marcoux, Alexandria, Va, 79; Charles H Jones, 83 & Harry A Tow, 85, Water Pollution Control Fed, Washington, DC; Children's Nat Med Ctr, Washington,

DC; Navy Fed Credit Union Hq, Vienna, Va, 97. *Exhib:* 7th Ann Area Show, Corcoran Gallery Art, Washington, DC, 52; Maryland Biennial, Baltimore Mus Art, 74 & 76; Rocky Mountain Nat Watermedia Exhib, Foothills Art Ctr, Golden, Colo, 85, 86, 88 & 92; Retrospective, Florence Mus, 91; Shada Gallery Invitational, Riyadh, Saudi Arabia, 91; Bicentennial Exhib, Belle Grove Plantation, Middletown, Va, 94; Washington Co Mus Invitational, Hagerstown, Md, 96; Government House Invitational, Annapolis, Md, 97 & 98; Black Rock Ctr, Germantown, Md, 2002. *Pos:* Asst to head of publications, The Nat Gallery of Art, 52-53; official US Coast Guard artist, 86-. *Teaching:* Guest instr, Amherst Coll, Mass, 85; Woman's Club, Chevy Chase, Md, 97-2006. *Awards:* First Place, Area 87 Exhib Paintings & Graphics, Fairfax Co Coun Arts, Va, 87; Ross Family Award, Adirondacks Nat Exhib Am Watercolor, Old Forge, NY, 88; George Gray Award, US Coast Guard Art Prog, 91 & 98. *Bibliog:* Charles Sullivan (auth), Numbers at Play, Rizzoli, New York, 92; Christine Unwin (auth), The Artistic Touch I, II & III, Creative Art Press, 94, 96 & 98; Phil Metzger (auth), The North Light Guide to Materials and Techniques, 96 & The Artist's Illustrated Encyclopedia, 2001, North Light Bks. *Mem:* Transparent Watercolor Soc; Potomac Valley Watercolorists (pres, 81-83); Southwestern Watercolor Soc; Southern Watercolor Soc; Nat Watercolor Soc; Am Watercolor Soc; Houston Watercolor Soc; Baltimore Watercolor Soc; Western Fedn of Watercolor Socs; Wash Soc Landscape Painters. *Media:* Watercolor, Pastel. *Specialty:* Paintings, sculpture. *Publ:* Auth, The watercolor page, 5/88 & Add Watercolor Page, 10/2002, Am Artist Mag. *Dealer:* McBride Gallery 215 Main St Annapolis MD 21401. *Mailing Add:* 3504 Taylor St Chevy Chase MD 20815

KRANTZ, CLAIRE WOLF
MIXED MEDIA ARTISTS, WRITER
b Chicago, Ill, Jun 22, 1938. *Study:* Univ Ill, BS in Occpl Therapy, 61, Phi Kappa Phi, 58-59; Sch of the Art Inst of Chicago, BFA, 79; Stanford Univ, postgrad; Bag Factory, Johannesburg, S Africa, Artists' Residency Prog, 2006. *Hon Degrees:* Sch Inst Chicago, BFA, 1979. *Work:* Nat Mus Women in the Arts, Wash DC; Mus Contemp Art, Chicago; Moma, Books Donated by Franklin Furnace, NYC. *Exhib:* Solo Exhibs: Counterpoints, Reflections on India, Perimeter Gallery, Chicago, 2000; Paintings & Digital Media-Toomey, Tourell Gal, San Francisco, Calif, 2002; Jaua in Time + Memory, 1 Space, Chicago, 2002; Meditations on Ruin, Flatfile Gallery, 2004; Invented Travelogues, Flatfile Gallery, Chicago, 2007, Gordart Gallery, Johannesburg, S Africa; Group Exhibs: Bridges and Boundaries: African Americans and American Jews, Traveled, Jewish Mus, NY, 1999; Self Portraits, Printworks Gallery, Chicago, 2000-2001; Tangential Pleasures, Fine Arts Center, Highland PK, Ill, 2003; Drawing Conclusions: Works by Artist-Critics, NY Arts Gallery, 2003; Clark House Mus, 2004, Art in Embassies Prog, Jakarta, Indonesia. *Collection Arranged:* Beautiful (cur with Claire Prussian), Ukrainian Inst Modern Art, 1983; Bridges & Boundaries: Chicago Crossings (guest cur), Spertus Mus, Chicago; Ordinary/Extraordinary, Artists US of Home (Nancy Azara, cur), Wood St Gallery, Chicago, 1997; Response: Art & The Art of Criticism (cur with others), U Ill Gallery, Chicago, 2009. *Pos:* occupational therapist, 61-76; artist, writer, curator, 80-. *Teaching:* lectr, at var univs in the US, Europe, and Indonesia. *Awards:* Artist's Residency, Bag Factory; Special Assistance Grant, Ill Arts Council. *Bibliog:* Michael Coulson (auth), Landscapes for Imagining, The Weekender, Joburg, SA, 2006; Susan Senseman (auth), Java, in Time and Memory, Art Papers, 1-2/2003; Lisa Stein (auth), Artist's Profile: Claire Wolf Krantz, Painter, Chicago Tribune, 10/6/02. *Mem:* Chicago Art Critics Assoc; International Assoc Art Critics. *Media:* Photo, painting, computer images. *Specialty:* Perimeter paintings. *Interests:* Writing, curating, making art. *Publ:* Art in America; Flash Art; Art Papers; Chicago Artists News. *Dealer:* Perimeter Gallery 210 W Superior St Chicago IL 60654-3508; Toomey-Tourell Gallery 49 Geary St San Francisco CA 94108; A.I.R. Gallery 111 Front St #228 Brooklyn NY 11201. *Mailing Add:* 711 S Dearborn #401 Chicago IL 60605-2308

KRASHES, BARBARA
PAINTER
b New York, NY. *Study:* Art Students League, with Reginald Marsh, Julian Levi & Vaclav Vytlacil; NY Univ, BS; Hunter Coll, NY; Educ Alliance, with Chaim Gross; New Sch Social Res, NY. *Work:* Ulrich Mus Art, Wichita, Kans; St Lawrence Univ Mus, Canton, NY; Valley Bank, Springfield, Mass; Walter Kidde Constructors, Inc, Cincinnati, Ohio; Hood Mus Art, Dartmouth Coll, Hanover, NH. *Exhib:* Art: 1965, Am Express Pavilion, NY World's Fair; Am Abstract Artists, Riverside Mus, NY; Fordham Univ at Lincoln Ctr, NY; NY Univ; Hyde Collection, Glens Falls, NY; Tyler Art Gallery, SUNY, Oswego, NY; Myers Fine Arts Gallery, SUNY, Plattsburgh, NY; Brooklyn Mus, NY; Newark Mus, Newark, NJ. *Pos:* Art dir, Adult Educ Ctr, New York, 61-93. *Awards:* George B Bridgman Mem Scholar, Art Students League, NY. *Bibliog:* Art World Problems (tape), Today's World, Fordham Univ, 73. *Mem:* Fedn Mod Painters & Sculptors, Inc (past pres), NY; life mem Art Students League, NY; NY Artists Equity Asn, Inc. *Media:* Mixed-Media, Acrylic. *Publ:* The New York Arts Calendar (spec issue) for NY World's Fair Am Express Show, 65; Feigin Memorial Collection (catalog), St Lawrence Univ; Female Artists in the United States: A Research and Resource Guide to Women Painters 1900-1985, Nat Endowment Humanities; Experimental Works, Fedn Mod Painters & Sculptors, NY. *Mailing Add:* 77 W 85th St New York NY 10024-4161

KRASNYANSKY, ANATOLE LVOVICH
PAINTER, ARCHITECT
b Kiev, Ukraine, USSR, Feb 26, 1930; US citizen. *Study:* Kiev State Inst Fine Art & Archit, MA, 53. *Work:* Kiev State Artist's Union Collection, Ukraine, USSR; Dalzell Hatfield Gallery Collection (Int Watercolor Masters), Los Angeles; Stanford Univ, Palo Alto, Calif; Los Gatos Mus, Calif; Dyansen Galleries; Park West Gallery, Southfield, Mich; Termitage Mus. *Comn:* Restoration of Potemkin and Marble Palases, State, St Petersburg, Russia, 52-53; Central Art Pavilion, Exhibs Artists Union, State, Kiev, Ukraine, 55-58; Restoration of Historical Alexandria Park, State, Uman, Ukraine, 61-68; Metro Station Politechnical Inst, State, Kiev, Ukraine, 69; Ampitheatre & Corp Bldg, Renaissanse Guild Inc, Long Beach, Calif, 84-85. *Exhib:* Russian Artist's in USA, Stanford Univ, Palo Alto, 81 & contemp Russian Artists, UCLA; solo exhibs, Stanford Univ, Palo Alto, 82 & Dyansen Galleries, Beverly Hills & Coho, NY, 88-90; Contemp Russian Artists in Exile, Univ Calif, Los Angeles, 82; Russian Art in USA, Los Gatos Mus, Calif, 82; group & solo exhibs, Dyansen Galleries, Boston, San Diego, Washington & Tokyo, 88-91; and others. *Pos:* Principal archit designer, Inst Tech Aesthetics, Dept Interior Design, Kiev, Ukraine, 68-74; principal designer & art dir, Central Ukraine Pavilion Republican Exhibs, Kiev, 74; set designer, Universal Studios, Hollywood, 78-84; independent consult archit design & presentation, Univ Calif, Los Angeles, 83; dir design & art, Renaissance Guild Inc, Long Beach, Calif, 84. *Teaching:* Lectr aesthetic design & art, Kiev Inst Tech Aesthetic, Ukraine, 69-73. *Awards:* First Prize, Interiors and Art for Metro, Politechnical Inst, State, 60; Second Prize, Monument of Potemkin Uprising in Odessa, State, Ukraine, 65; ABC Certif Appreciation Prof Contrib Acad Award Shows, Hollywood, 76-77. *Media:* Watercolor, Acrylic. *Dealer:* Dyansen Galleries of USA 131 Varick St New York NY 10012; Park West Gallery 29469 Northwestern Southfield MI 48034. *Mailing Add:* 871 S Bundy Dr Los Angeles CA 90049

KRATE, NAT
PAINTER
b New York, NY, Aug 26, 1918. *Study:* WPA Art Sch, New York, 34-35; Pratt Inst, New York, 35-36; Art Students League, 36-38 & 46-47. *Work:* Berkshire Mus, Pittsfield, Mass; Mus Arts & Sci, Daytona Beach, Fla; Van Wezel Performing Arts Hall, Sarasota, Fla; Fla WCoast Symphony Hall, Sarasota. *Comn:* Thirteen wall murals, 1st Army Hq, Govs Island, NY, 42-43; 11 portraits, comn by different individuals, 80-93; ann report cover art, Fla Progress Corp, St Petersburg, Fla, 90. *Exhib:* Solo-shows, Becket Art Gallery, Mass, 78, Welles Gallery, Lenox, Mass, 81, Ana Sklar Gallery, Bal Harbor, Fla, 85, Foster Harmon Galleries Am Art, Sarasota, Fla, 86, 89, 92 & 94, Arvida Gallery, Longboat Key, Fla, 86, Longboat Key Art Ctr, Fla, 89 & Donn Roll Galleries, Sarasota, Fla, 94; Fla Figure Show, Brevard Mus, Melbourne, Fla, 93; 43rd Ann All Fla, Boca Raton Mus, Fla, 94; Fla Artist Group, Mus Arts & Sci, Daytona Beach, Fla 94; 4th Biennial Exhib, Huntsville Mus, Ala, 94; Retrospective, Ringling Coll Art, Sarasota, Fla, 2009. *Teaching:* Instr figures, Longboat Key Art Ctr, Fla, 84-86, Sarasota Art Asn, Fla, 86-87 & Ringling Sch Art & Design, Sarasota, Fla, 89-90. *Awards:* Silver Medal of Hon, Knickerbocker Artists USA, 93; Elizabeth Morse Genius Award, 94; Houser Award, Soc 4 Arts, Palm Beach, 95; Best in Show, Charlotte City, Art Guild, National Exchange, Punta Fla, 04. *Bibliog:* Carol Parker Rife (auth), Artful ways, Gulfshore Life Mag, 90; Profile & portfolio, Arts & Sci Quart, 92; Laura Stewart (auth), State artists show-cased, Daytona Beach News J, 94. *Mem:* Knickerbocker Artists USA; Fla Artist Group; Am Artists Prof League; Sarasota Co Arts Coun. *Media:* Oil. *Publ:* Mag illus, Fawcett Publ, New York, 48. *Dealer:* Donn Roll Galleries 1415 Main St Sarasota FL 34236; Mickelson Gallery 707 G St NW Washington DC 20001; Zenith Gallery 413 7th St NW Washington DC 20004. *Mailing Add:* Zenith Gallery 1111 Pennsylvania Ave NW Washington DC 20004

KRATZ, DAVID
PAINTER, ADMINISTRATOR
Study: New York Acad of Art, graduate, 2008. *Exhib:* Group shows Water on paper, New York Acad of Art, 2007, Manhunt, 2008, Studio 7 Fine Art Gallery Group Exhibition, Bernardsville, NJ, 2009, Take Home a Nude, Sotheby's, NY, 2009 (also curator), Water/Bodies, Eden Rock Gallery, St Barth's, 2009; Afternoon, MFA Diploma Show, won Vasari Prize for Best-in-Show. *Pos:* Pres, New York Acad of Art, 2009-. *Mailing Add:* New York Academy of Art 111 Franklin St New York NY 10013

KRAUS, JILL GANSMAN
COLLECTOR
b Philadelphia, Pa, Oct 25, 1952. *Study:* Carnegie Mellon Univ, BFA, 74; RI Sch Design, MFA, 77. *Pos:* Designer, Accesocraft, New York, 77-78, Cadoro, New York, 78-79; asst to dir, Monet Jewelry, 79-81; sr designer, Swank Inc, 81-85; product marketing mgr, Marvella, 85; vpres design & training, Swarovski Jewelry US Ltd, New York, 92. *Awards:* Named one of Top 200 Collectors, ARTnews mag, 2004 & 2010-13. *Mem:* Friends of the Carnegie Int (co-chmn, currently); Carnegie Mellon Univ (bd trustees, currently); World Studio Found (bd dir, currently); New Mus Contemp Art (bd trustees, currently); Pub Art Fund (bd trustees, currently); Mus Modern Art (bd trustees, currently). *Collection:* Contemporary art

KRAUS, PETER STEVEN
COLLECTOR
b Aug 12, 1952. *Study:* Trinity Coll, Hartford, Conn, BA (econ), 74. *Pos:* Partner, Goldman, Sachs & co, New York, 94, co-head fin, inst group, investment banking div, 98-2001, co-head pvt wealth mgt, 2001, co-head investment mgt div, 2001-2008, also managing dir & mem mgt comt; exec vp, mem mgmt com, Merrill Lynch & Co, Inc, 2008; chmn, AllianceBernstein Holding LP, 2008-. *Awards:* Named one of Top 200 Collectors, ARTnews mag, 2004 & 2010-13. *Mem:* Trinity Coll (Charter trustee, 98-); Calif Inst Arts (bd overseers, currently); Friends of the Carnegie Int (co-chmn, currently). *Collection:* Contemporary art. *Mailing Add:* Alliance Bernstein Holding LP 1345 Ave of the Americas New York NY 10105

KRAUS, (ERSILIA) ZILI
SCULPTOR, JEWELER
b Satchinez, Timisoara, Romania; US citizen. *Study:* Graphic Sketch Club, Philadelphia, Pa, 28-30; Nat Acad Design with Leon Kroll, 30-32; Barnes Found, Pa, 33-35; Samuel S Fleisher Art Mem with Frank Gasparro, 62-74; Inst Allende, San Miguel de Allende with Enrique Lopez, 72-81. *Work:* Cinnaminson Town Hall, NJ; Burlington Co Libr, Westhampton, NJ. *Comn:* Resurrection (mural), Calvin Presbyterian Church, Pa, 35; Yearbook (cover illustration), Columbia Univ Sch Pub Health & Admin, NY, 67. *Exhib:* Earth Edge, Painting, Montreal Mus Fine Art, Quebec, 56; Sculpture, Fleisher Art Mem, Philadelphia, Pa, 67-72; Sculpture, Woodmere Art Mus, Philadelphia, Pa, 68-86, jewelry, 80-85; Sculpture, Cheltenham

Art Ctr, Pa, 70-84; Sculpture, Da Vinci Art Alliance, Philadelphia, Pa, 72-84; Sculpture, Burlington City Cult & Heritage Comn, Mt Holly, NY, 84-87. *Collection Arranged:* Membership Show, Cinnaminson Art Centre, 66-67; Triboro Artists, Burlington Co Libr, 69; jewelry, Cheltenham Art Ctr, Pa, 85; jewelry, Woodmere Art Mus, Philadelphia, 83-92. *Pos:* Textile designer, Shapiro & Co, New York, 45-48. *Teaching:* Instr painting, Art League Long Island, Queens, NY, 50-51 & Northern Burlington City Region High Sch, Columbus, NJ, 64-65; instr beginning & advanced painting, Cinnaminson High Sch, NJ, 65-76. *Awards:* First Prize, jewelry (man's neckpiece), Woodmere Art Mus, Philadelphia, 83 & 91; Oscar d'Italia, sculpture, Accademia Italia, Italy, 85; Purchase, ring, Cheltenham Twp Art Ctr, Pa, 85. *Mem:* Woodmere Art Mus, Germantown, Pa; Leonardo Da Vinci Art Alliance, Philadelphia; Cheltenham Township Art Ctr, Cheltamham, Pa; Nat Mus Women Arts, Washington, DC. *Media:* Wood, Pastel; Metal, Gem Stones. *Interests:* Designing creative jewelry (men's and women's). *Publ:* Burlington Co Times, 91. *Mailing Add:* 4306 Pinetree Rd Rockville MD 20853-1317

KRAUSE, BONNIE JEAN
MUSEUM CONSULTANT
b La Crosse, Wis, Sept 20, 1942. *Study:* Viterbo Col, BA, 64; Southern Ill Univ, MS, 68. *Collection Arranged:* US Grant: Man of Peace, Man of War, traveling exhib, 83; Bits and Pieces: Southern Illinois Tradition in Rag Rugs, traveling exhib, 90; Olynthus 348 B C: The Destruction and Resurrection of a Greek City, traveling exhib, 92; New Deal Art: Images of Mississippi, 94-95, exhib & traveling exhib; Waves of the Future, 98. *Pos:* Dir, Ill Ozarks Graft Guild, Southern Ill Univ, 80-81, cur hist, Univ Mus, 81-85, sr develop specialist, 85-90; dir univ mus, Univ Miss, 90-2000. *Teaching:* Instr art marketing, Southern Ill Univ, 74-76. *Bibliog:* Palmer Hudson (auth) Mississippi Folklorist: Mississippi Folklife, Vol. 32, No 1. *Mem:* Ozark States Folklore Soc; Miss Hist Soc; Miss Folklore Soc. *Publ:* Family of the Hills: The Bridgemans of the Pine Hills, US Forest Serv, 85; coauth, German Americans in the St Louis Region 1840-60, Mo Hist Soc, 89; Auth, Bits and Pieces: The Southern Illinois Tradition in Rag Rugs, Mid-American Folklore, Vol XXI, No 1, Spring 93; The Mary Bure Mus, Oxford Mississippi, as a WPA Community Art Center, 39-42. *Mailing Add:* 141 Haw Creek Mews Dr Asheville NC 28805

KRAUSE, DOROTHY SIMPSON
PAINTER, COLLAGE ARTIST
b Mobile, Ala, Sept 22, 1940. *Study:* Montevallo Univ, BA, 60; Univ Ala, MA, 62; Pa State Univ, DEd, 68. *Work:* Smithsonian Am Art Mus, Washington, DC; Zimmerli Mus Rutgers Univ; DeCordova Mus; Boston Mus Fine Arts; Danforth Mus Art, Framingham, Mass. *Comn:* Mural, Trinity Place, Boston, 98; Herman Miller (mural), Holland, Mich, 98; murals, prints, Fed Reserve Bank, Boston, 2002-2003. *Exhib:* Solo exhibs, Ctr Creative Imaging, Camden, Maine, 94, NE Sch Photog, Boston, Mass, 94, Wellesley Coll, 95 & Dana Hall, 99; Univ Mass, Lowell, 99; Simmons Coll, 2000; Creiger-Dane Gallery, 2000; Art Complex Mus, Duxbury, Mass, 2001; Evos Arts Inst, Lowell, 2002; Fla Gulf Coast Univ, 2002; New Eng Sch Photog, 2003; Judi Rotenberg Gallery, Boston, 2003-07; Danforth Mus Art, Framingham, Mass, 2003; Havard Med Sch, Boston, 2006; Whistler House Mus Art, Lowell, Mass, 2007; S Shore Art Ctr, Cohasset, Mass, 2007; Landing Gallery, Rocklaind, Maine, 2007, 2009, 2011; Thayer Acad, 2010; 571 Projects, 2011-2012; Jaffe Ctr, Boca Raton, Fla, 2012. *Pos:* Artist-in-residence, Ctr Creative Imaging, 91-94; corp cur, Iris Graphics, Bedford, Mass, 93-98; consult, Hewlett-Packard, 2006-; vis artist, Am Acad, Rome, 2006; Von Hess vis artist, Univ Arts, Borowsky Ctr, Philadelphia, Pa, 2007; artist-in res, Jaffe Ctr Book Arts, 2012, Oceana Cruise Lines, 2012-2013. *Teaching:* Assoc prof art educ, Va Commonwealth Univ, Richmond, 69-74; prof computer graphics, Mass Coll Art, Boston, Mass, 74-2000, prof emer, 2000-. *Awards:* Frank Procter Whiting, Cooperstown Nat, 93; IDAA award, 2003. *Bibliog:* Colin Wood (auth), Dorothy Krause & the Trinity Place Project, Design Graphics, 9/98; Harald Johnson (auth) Mastering Digital Printmaking, 2002 & 2005; Jeremy Sutton & Daryl Wise (auths), Secrets of Award Winning Digital Artists; Richard Noyce (auth), Printmaking at the Edge, 2006; Bruce Wands (auth), Art of Digital Age, 2006; Steve Miller (juror), 500 Handmade Books, 2008; Lisa Cyr (auth), Art Revolution, 2009; Dorothy Krause (auth), Book and Art: Handcrafting Artists Books, 2009; Peter Thomas (auth), 1,000 Artists Books, 2012. *Mem:* Women's Caucus Art; Coll Art Asn; Boston Printmakers; Photog Resource Ctr; others. *Media:* Artist Books, Mixed Media. *Publ:* Fractal Design Painter, Creative Techniques, Hayden, 96; Painting with Computers, Rockport Publ, 96; The Painter 5 WOW! Book, Peachpit Press, 2002; Photoshop 5 Bible, 98 & Painter 5 Studio Secrets, 98, IDG Bks; Digital Art Studio, Watson-Guptill, 2004; Book and Art: Handcrafting Artists Books, North Light, 2010. *Dealer:* Landing Gallery Rockport ME; 571 Projects New York NY. *Mailing Add:* The Pilot House 3100 NE 48th St #912 Fort Lauderdale FL 33308

KRAUSE, GEORGE
PHOTOGRAPHER
b Philadelphia, Pa, Jan 24, 1937. *Study:* Philadelphia Coll Art. *Work:* Mus Mod Art, NY; Bibliot Nat, Paris; Libr Cong, Washington, DC; Philadelphia Mus Art; Houston Mus Fine Art. *Exhib:* Five Unrelated Photographers, Mus Mod Art, NY, 63; Solo exhibs, George Eastman House, Rochester, NY, 75, Mus Bellas Artes, Caracas, Venezuela, 76, Witkin Gallery, NY, 78, Houston Mus Fine Art, 78, Am Acad Rome, 79 & Pa Acad Fine Art, Philadelphia, 82; Solo Retrospective, Houston Mus Fine Art, 92. *Teaching:* Assoc prof photog, Bucks Co Community Col, Newtown, Pa, 73-75; prof photog, Univ Houston, 75-99, ret; dir photog workshops, Venice Photog Biennale, Italy, summer 79; artist-in-residence, Am Acad Rome, 79-80; hon prof photog, E Tex State Univ, 88. *Awards:* Guggenheim Found Grants, 67 & 76; Prix de Rome, 76; Nat Endowment Arts, 73 & 79; and others. *Bibliog:* Mark Power (auth), George Krause I, Monog Toll & Armstrong, 72; Nancy Hellebrand (auth), I Nudi-George Krause, Photo Rev, 80; Arno Minkkinen (auth), article, Contemp Photogr, 81; Anne Tucker (auth), George Krause: A Retrospective, Rice Univ Press. *Mem:* Am Acad Rome. *Media:* Silver Gelatin, Mixed Media. *Publ:* Illusr, The photographer's eye, 66 & Looking at pictures, 73, Mus Mod Art; auth, I Nudi (catalog), Mancini, 80. *Dealer:* Photographs Do Not Bend Gallery 3115 Routh St Dallas TX 75201; George Krause 291 E Summit Dr Wimberley TX 78676. *Mailing Add:* c/o PDNB Gallery 1202 Dragon St Ste 103 Dallas TX 75207-4000

KRAVIS, HENRY R
COLLECTOR
Study: Claremont-McKenna Coll, BA (econ), 1967; Columbia Univ, MBA, 1969. *Pos:* Partner, Bear Stearns, formerly; founding partner, Kohlberg Kravis Roberts, 1976-, sr partner 1987-; bd dir, PRIMEDIA Inc, 1991-; leadership coun & bd trustees, Claremont-McKenna Coll, Metrop Mus Art, Mount Sinai Hosp, currently; co-chmn, Partnership for NYC; chmn, Columbia Bus Sch Coun. *Awards:* Named on of Top 200 Collectors, ARTnews mag, 2004-13; Forbes 400: Richest Americans, 2006-; Bus People of Yr, Fortune Mag, 2010. *Collection:* Old Master drawings and paintings, Impressionist art, 20th-century art, French furniture. *Mailing Add:* Kohlberg Kravis Roberts & Co Ste 4200 9 W 57th St New York NY 10021

KRAVIS, JANIS
DESIGNER, ARCHITECT
b Riga, Latvia, Oct 20, 1935; Can citizen. *Study:* Sch Archit, Univ Toronto. *Exhib:* Royal Can Acad Arts, Nat Gallery Can, Ottawa, 70. *Awards:* Ont Tourist Accommodation Award, 67; Ont Eedee Design Award, 67; 25 Year Merit Award in Archit Excellence, Ont Asn Archit, 91. *Mem:* Ont Asn Architects; Asn Can Indust Designers; Royal Can Acad Art; Royal Archit Inst Can. *Mailing Add:* 38 Cedarbank Crescent Toronto ON M3B 3A4 Canada

KRAVIS, MARIE-JOSEE
COLLECTOR
b Ottawa, Ont, Can, Sept 11, 1949. *Study:* Univ Que, BA, 1970; Univ Ottawa, MA, 1973. *Hon Degrees:* Univ Windsor, Laurentian Univ, LLD. *Pos:* Financial analyst, Power Corp Can Ltd, 69-70; spl asst to solicitor gen, Govt Can, 71-73; sr economist, Hudson Inst, 73-76, exec dir, 76-94, sr fellow, 94-; bd mem & exec comt, Can Coun for Rsch on Social Sci & Humanities, 82-86, Can Govt Comn Adv Bd, 82-89, Consultative Comt on Financial Inst, Govt Que, 84-90; vchmn, Royal Can Comn on Nat Passenger Transp, 90-92; bd dirs, Ford Motor co, 95-, Vivendi Universal, 2001- & Interactive Corp, 2001-; pres & bd trustees, Mus Modern Art. *Awards:* Named one of Top 200 Collectors, ARTnews mag, 2004-12. *Mem:* Coun Foreign Relations, New York. *Collection:* Contemporary art, Impressionism, 20th century art & 18th century French furniture; Art Deco. *Mailing Add:* 625 Park Ave New York NY 10021

KRAVITZ, WALTER
SCULPTOR, PAINTER
b Chicago, Ill, Oct 25, 1938. *Study:* Art Inst Chicago, BFA (fel), 64; Syracuse Univ, MFA, 67. *Work:* Hirshhorn Mus, Washington. *Comn:* Suspended sculptures, Washington Conv Ctr, 86 & Niagara Falls, NY wintergarden; stairwell installation, Wash Proj Arts, 83; Muddy Branch Sch, Montgomery Co, Md; cabin, John Md Ice Rink, 90; Montgomery Coll Fine Arts Ctr, 92. *Exhib:* PS1, NY, 82; Franz Bader Gallery, Washington, 86-88; SE Ctr Contemp Art, 87; Corcoran Gallery Art, 92 & 94; Gallery K, Washington, 93 & 94; Sullivan Co Mus, NY, 93-96; and others. *Teaching:* Prof design & painting, Philadelphia Col Art, 69-74; prof painting & drawing, George Mason Univ, 76-. *Awards:* DC Comn Individual Artist Grant, 83, 87 & 89; Va Mus Fel, 88. *Mailing Add:* 614 A St SE Rear Washington DC 20003

KRAVJANSKY, MIKULAS
PAINTER, PRINTMAKER, DESIGNER
b Rudnay, Slovakia, May 3, 1928; Can citizen. *Study:* Acad Muzas Art, Bratislava, Slovakia, PSV, 57. *Hon Degrees:* Magister of Arts. *Work:* Simon Fraser Univ; White Mt Acad Arts; Wilfred Laurier Univ; Can Union Coll; and many others. *Comn:* Stucco mural, Nitra City Hall, Czech, 55; mobile sculpture, Dept Rec & Parks, Bratislava, 59; mural, Toronto City Hall, 69; mural, City of Napa, Calif, 96; mural, Humboldt Bay, Southport Landing, Calif, 97. *Exhib:* Binale of Fine Arts, Sao Paolo, Brazil, 57 & 61; Scenography, Int Cult Ctr, Cairo, Egypt, 66; ETC Opera Designs, Nat Opera, Budapest, Hungary, 67; Nat Canadian Exhib, Toronto, 72; Group of Contemporarists, tour of S Am cities, 72; Art Expo, Javitz Comr Ctr, New York, 80-88; solo exhibs, Dyansen Galleries, New York, Los Angeles, San Francisco, San Diego, New Orleans & Boston. *Pos:* Head scenographer, State Theatre, Presov, Czech, 59-64; head art & design dept, Czechoslovak TV, Bratislava, 64-68; artistic dir, Black Box Theatre Can, 69-78; owner, MK Publ co. *Teaching:* Lectr scenography, Acad Arts, Bratislava, 57-58; asst prof design, Acad Muzas Art, Bratislava, 65; asst master art-design, Humber Coll, Toronto, 69-75. *Awards:* Gold Medal, Bienale of Sao Paulo, 65, 67. *Bibliog:* Stage Design Throughout the World Since 1950; Harap, London, 60; Genesis (film), Gregor Film, Toronto; Artists of California, Mt Production, 93; Paintings the Towns, RJD Enterprises, Los Angeles, 97. *Media:* All Media; Intaglio Printing. *Mailing Add:* 7 Penny Lane Wasaga Beach ON L9Z 1N4 Canada

KREILICK, MARJORIE E
MOSAIC ARTIST, EDUCATOR
b Oak Harbor, Ohio, Nov 8, 1925. *Study:* Ohio State Univ, BA, 46, MA, 47; Cranbrook Acad Art, MFA, 52; apprentice to Gulio Giovanette, Rome, 56; Am Acad in Rome, FAAR, 63. *Work:* Joslyn Mus, Omaha, Nebr; Columbia Mus Art, SC. *Comn:* Marble pebble mural, Wonderland Shopping Ctr, Livonia, Mich, 59; ten marble murals, State Off Bldg, Milwaukee, 63; mosaic foucault pendulum, Augustana Univ, Sioux Falls, SDak, 67; marble mosaic mural, Mayo Clinic, Rochester, Minn, 69; marble mosaic pool, Telfair Acad Arts & Sci, Savannah, Ga, 73. *Exhib:* Palace of Expos, Rome; Minn Mus Art, St Paul; solo show, Archit League, NY; Fairweather Hardin Gallery, Chicago. *Pos:* Univ of Wisconsin, Madison, WI, 53-92. *Teaching:* Instr-docent design, Toledo Mus Art, 48-51; from instr to prof design-sculpture, Univ

Wis-Madison, 53-92, prof emer, 92-. *Awards:* Univ Wis Grant, 60; Prix de Rome, Am Acad in Rome, 61; Edwin Austin Abbey Fel, Am Acad in Rome, Italy, 61-63; Research Grant, Univ of Wis-Madison, 65, 70, 76, 79, 80, (mosaic studio asst); Univ of Wis-Madison Grant from Chancellor's Office for Design, 68. *Mem:* Nat Soc Mural Painters; Int Asn Contemp Mosaicists, Ravenna, Italy. *Media:* Marble Mosaic. *Publ:* Contribr, Art in Architecture, 69; Art in Architecture, Louis Redstone, 68, McGraw Hill Source Book of Architectural Ornament, Brent Brolin, 82, Van Nostrand Reinhold; Inquiring About Comunities, Robert Tabachnick, Holt, Rinhart, Winston; Friends Around the Corner, G.F. Kenney, Lyons, and Carnahan. *Mailing Add:* 2713 Chamberlain Ave Madison WI 53705-3719

KREITZER, DAVID MARTIN
PAINTER
b Ord, Nebr, Oct 23, 1942. *Study:* Concordia Coll, BS, 65; San Jose State Univ, MA, 67. *Work:* Santa Barbara Mus, Calif; San Diego Mus, Calif; Joseph Hirshhorn Found, Washington, DC; Sheldon Gallery, Univ Nebr; Bakersfield Mus, Calif. *Comn:* Woman's Place & US Army Corps of Engrs, covers for Atlantic Mag, 70; California & the War, cover for Motorland Mag, 70; Tristan und Isolde (opera posters), Seattle, 81; Ring des Nibelungen poster, Seattle Opera, 2009. *Exhib:* Solo exhibs, Am Art Since 1850, 68, Maxwell Gallery, San Francisco, Ankrum Gallery, Los Angeles, 71, 75, 77 & 79-81, Gumps Gallery, San Francisco, 81, Ring Festival, Seattle Opera, 2009; Benedictine Art Awards, NY, 69; 6th Mobile Ann, Ala, 71; Adelle Mus Fine Arts, Dallas, 83; Stary-Sheets Gallery, Los Angeles, 92. *Teaching:* Instr painting, San Jose State Coll, 68; instr life drawing, Poly State Univ, San Luis Obispo, Calif, 83. *Awards:* Ciba-Geigy Award, 71. *Bibliog:* Currant Mag, 6/75; Am Artist, 4/82. *Media:* Watercolor, Oil. *Dealer:* Summa Gallery 527 Amsterdam Ave NY 10024. *Mailing Add:* 1442 12th St Los Osos CA 93402

KREMER, SHAI
PHOTOGRAPHER
b Israel, 1974. *Study:* Camera Obscura Sch Arts, Tel Aviv, Israel, BA (Photography), 1998-2002 ; Sch Visual Arts, New York, MFA (Photography & Related Media), 2003-05. *Work:* Metro Mus Mod Art, New York; Mus Fine Arts, Houston; Mus Contemp Photography, Chicago. *Exhib:* Solo exhibs include Sch Visual Arts Eastside Gallery, New York, 2005, Synagogue Gallery, Carpentras, France, 2006, Julie M Gallery, Tel Aviv, Israel, 2008, Robert Koch Gallery, San Francisco, 2008, Julie Saul Gallery, New York, 2008; Group exhibs include Artic 6, Am Israel Cultural Found, Univ Gallery, Tel Aviv, Israel, 2004; See What I Mean, Visual Arts Gallery, New York, 2005; Focused, Photographic Ctr NW, Seattle, 2005; Emerging Photographers, Art & Commerce, New York, 2005; Infected Landscape, Julie Saul Gallery, New York, 2005; Art Chicago, Robert Koch Gallery, 2008. *Awards:* Am Israel Cultural Found, BA Accomplishment Grant, 2002, MFA Grant, 2004, 2005; Dean Award, Sch Visual Arts Photography Dept, 2005; NY Found Arts, Artist's Fel in Photography, 2008. *Mailing Add:* Julie Saul Gallery 535 W 22nd St New York NY 10011

KREMERS, DAVID
CONCEPTUAL ARTIST
b Denver, Colo, 1960. *Study:* Self-taught, Paris, 76-82. *Work:* San Francisco Mus Mod Art; Denver Art Mus; Panza Coll, Milano, Italy; Eli Broad Family Found, Santa Monica, Calif; Norton Coll, Santa Monica, Calif. *Exhib:* Facing the Finish (traveling), San Francisco Mus Mod Art, 91; The 8th Day, Landesmuseum, Linz, Austria, 93; Centennial Greetings, Denver Art Mus, Colo, 93; Veered Science, Huntington Beach Art Ctr, 95; solo show, ACME, Santa Monica, Calif, 95; Art Meets, Royal Acad, Copenhagen, 96; Boretum, Mondridan Found, The Neth, 98; In the Polka Dot Kitchen, Otis Col, 98. *Pos:* Distinguished Conceptual Artist, Caltech, 97. *Awards:* Colo Fedn for Art New Talent, Univ Colo, 94. *Bibliog:* Kenneth Baker (auth), David Kremers, Art News, 5/92; David Pagel (auth), Virtual reality, Los Angeles Times, 9/17/93; Louwrien Wijers (auth), Art meets science & spirituality in a changing economy, Acad Editions, 96. *Publ:* Contribr, Genetische Kunst-Kunstelisches Leben, PVS Verlager, 93; auth, Science Fair (exhib catalog), Thomas Solomon, 93; Growing reality, Zing Mag, 96; Delbruck paradox version 2, Art J, 96. *Dealer:* ACME 6750 Wilshire Blvd Los Angeles CA 90034. *Mailing Add:* 3031 S Ash St Denver CO 80222-6704

KREN, MARGO
PAINTER, EDUCATOR
b Houston, Tex, Dec 1, 1939. *Study:* Univ Wis, Madison, BS, 66; Univ Iowa, MFA, 79. *Work:* Acad Arts and Design, Tsinghua Univ, Beijing, China; Deakin Univ, Melbourne, Australia; Emprise Fin Corp, Wichita, Kans; Mariana Beach Mus Art, Kansas State Univ, Manhattan; NH Inst Art, Manchester, NH; El Paso Mus Art, El Paso, Tex; Hosp Trust Tower, Providence, RI; McAllen Int Mus, McAllen, Tex; Univ Ark, Fayetteville, Ark; Univ Idaho, Moscow; Univ Iowa, Iowa City; Univ Northern Colo, Greeley; University Oregon, Eugene; Univ S Carolina, Spartanburg; NY Pub Lib Print Room, NY; Portland State Univ, Ore; Sheldon Mem Arts Gallery, Lincoln, Neb; Yunnan Art Inst, Kunming, China; and many more; NY Public Libr, NY; Otterbein University, Westerville, Oh; Univ Northern Colo; Western Mich Univ, Kalamazoo; South Bend Regional Mus Art, South Bend, Tex. *Exhib:* Deutsch-Amerikanisches, Regenburg, Germany, 1988; Yunnan Art Inst, Kunming, Yunnan, People's Repub China, 1997; New Harmony Gallery Contemp Art, Ind, 98; Northern Mich Univ, Marquette, 2000; Iowa State Univ, Ames, 2001; Spencer Mus Art, Univ Kans, 2001; Olson-Larson Gallery, Des Moines, 2001; River Gallery, Chelsea, Mich, 2001; Vanderbilt Univ, Nashville, 2002; The Waiting Room, New Orleans, 2002; Kawsasaki Factory, Tokyo, Japan, 2007; Belger Art Ctr, Kansas City, MO, 2011; Lawrence Art Ctr, Kans, 2011; Nat Acad Fine Arts, India, 2012. *Pos:* Panelist, Arts Midwest/NEA Regional Visual Arts Fel Selection, 88; Mid-Am Art Alliance panelist, Nat Endowment Arts Regional Fels, 92, New Eng Found Arts, 96. *Teaching:* Prof painting, drawing, Kans State Univ, Manhattan, 71-2003, Jilin Coll Art, Changchun, China, 2005, prof emer; artists residencies, Ragdale Found, Lake Forest, Ill, 86, Va Ctr Creative Arts, Sweet Briar, 87 & Yaddo, Saratoga Springs, NY, 89; invited lectr, The Marianna Kistler Beach Mus Art, Kansas State Univ, Manhattan, Kansas, 2015. *Awards:* Nat Endowment Arts Grant, 82; Kans Gov Art Award, 89; Kans State Univ Distinguished Grad Fac Mem Award, 89-90; Kans Arts Comn Fel, 2000. *Bibliog:* Novelene Ross (auth), Margo Kren/Dreams and Memories, Women Artist News, winter 86-87; Andrew Svedlow (auth), Within the mask: contemplation of works by Georgia O'Keeffe and Margo Kren, Kans Quart, Vol 19, No 4, 87; Leland Warren (auth), Margo Kren: Intimate experience and spaces of paintings, Kans Quart, Vol 24, No 1, spring 93. *Mem:* Kansas City Artist Coalition (pres, 82-83); Nat Women's Caucus for Art; Coll Art Asn. *Media:* Oil, Acrylic. *Res:* Kluge-Ruhe Collection of Aboriginal Art, Australia, Univ Va, Charlottlesville, Va, 2003; study room going over drawings and prints of Picasso, Musee Nat Picasso, France, 2002. *Specialty:* Painting, drawing, printmaking. *Interests:* opera, exercise, international travel. *Publ:* Performance in Search of Illumination: Michael Meyers & Chicago Artist, Kans Quarterly Manhattan, Kans, 1985; Auth, Philomene Bennett, a Kansas City artist, 82 & Michael Meyers, a Chicago performance artist, 85, Kans Quart; Studio Visits, The Open Studio Press, 2009; Dances with Jazz, Jilin Coll Art, China; Snooks Jazz. *Mailing Add:* 2912 Tatarrax Dr Manhattan KS 66502-1978

KRENECK, LYNWOOD
PRINTMAKER, EDUCATOR
b Kenedy, Tex, June 11, 1936. *Study:* Univ Tex, BFA, 58, MFA, 65. *Work:* Fine Arts Gallery San Diego, Calif; McNey Art Inst, San Antonio, Tex; Print Collection, Philadelphia Mus Art; Mus Contemp Art Knoxville, Tenn; Art in Embassies Prog, US State Dept; Okla Art Ctr, Oklahoma City; High Mus, Atlanta; Royal Mus Art, Antwerp, Belg; Art Inst Chicago, Ill. *Exhib:* Libr Cong Nat Print Show, 75; Nat Invitational Print Exhib, Visual Arts Ctr, Anchorage, Alaska, 89; The Passionate Eye Group Show, Laguna Gloria Arts Mus, Austin, Tex, 92; three-person exhib, Kalamazoo Inst Arts, Mich, 92; Tex Select Invitational, Wichita Falls Fine Art Mus, 93; Nat Touring Screen Print Show, Boston Mus Fine Arts Sch, 93; Nat Printmaking Invitational, Univ Miami, Fla, 95; 177th Ann Exhib, Nat Acad Art & Design, New York, 2002. *Collection Arranged:* judge, 32nd Bradley Univ Int Print & Drawing Competition, Peoria, Ill, March 2009. *Teaching:* Prof printmaking, Tex Tech Univ, 65-; vis artist, Univ Ulster, Belfast, Northern Ireland, 95, Diocesan Sch, Auckland, NZ, 96, Seacourt Collab Press, Eng & Royal Acad Art, Gent, Belg, 2000; Frogman Print and Paper Workshop, South Dakota, 2011; asst printers in use of waterbase inks, Guanlon Print Base, China, 2010. *Awards:* Purchase Prize, Boston Printmaker's Ann Exhib, 78 & 79; Purchase Prize, Works on Paper Int Exhib, Auburn Univ, 86; Lifetime Achievement in Teaching Excellence, Southern Graphics Int Conf, 2006. *Bibliog:* EC Cunningham (auth), Printmaking, A Primary Form of Expression, Univ Colo Press, 92; Julia Ayres (auth), Printmaking Techniques, Watson-Guptill Publ, New York, 93; Glen R Brown (auth), J Print World, spring 95; Malone Yingxue (auth), Contemporary American Printmaking, Wampler, Jilin Fine Arts, China, 99; Isabel Howe (auth), Lynwood Kreneck-Printmaker, Texas Tech Univ Press, 2003; Roni Henning (auth), Water-based Screenprinting Today, Watson Guptill Publ, New York. *Mem:* Southern Graphics Coun; Boston Printmakers; Los Angeles Print Soc; Soc Am Graphic Artists; Calif Soc Printmakers (hon mem). *Media:* Screenprinting, Drawing. *Res:* Research and development of techniques for new water base screen print inks; Visiting Artist in Residence, Ohio State University, 1986 to enhance R&D; Various articles and manual published in 1988. *Publ:* Article, Sch Arts Mag, 88; The complete printmaker, McMillan & Co, New York, 89. *Dealer:* Charles Adams Gallery Kingsgate Shopping Ctr Lubbock TX. *Mailing Add:* 3209 45th St Lubbock TX 79413-3513

KRENS, THOMAS
MUSEUM DIRECTOR, EDUCATOR
b New York, NY. *Study:* Williams Col, BA, 1969; State Univ NY, Albany, MA, 1971; Yale Univ, MPPM, 1984. *Hon Degrees:* State Univ NY, DHL, 1989. *Collection Arranged:* The Restoration of Thomas Hart Benton, 1985; The Peggy Guggenheim Collection, Venice, Italy, 1988-. *Pos:* Trustee, Williamstown Regional Art Conserv Lab, 1983-85; strategic planning consult, Brooklyn Mus, 1984-86; consult Solomon R Guggenheim Mus, NYC, 1986-88; adv comt mus proj Nat Educ Asn, Am Fedn Arts, Washington; dir Solomon R Guggenheim Found, 1988-, sr advisor internat affairs, 2008-. *Teaching:* Asst prof art history Williams Col, Williamstown, Mass, 1972-80, dir artist-in-residence prog, 1976-80, dir mus art, 1981-88. *Awards:* Spec Prize Archit Patronage, Venice Archit Biennale, 2000; Order of the Aztec Eagle, Govt Mex, 2006; Cult Leadership Award, AFA, 2007. *Mem:* Asn Art Mus Dirs; Aspen Inst Italia; Soc Kandinsky Ctr/Georges Pompidou; Gesellschaft fur Moderne Kunst am Mus Ludwig; Coun For Relations; AFA; Yale Univ Coun (art gallery comt, Brit Art Ctr com). *Publ:* auth Jim Dine Prints, 1970-77, 1977; The Prints of Helen Frankenthaler, 1980; The Drawing of Robert Morris 1956-82, 1982; Robert Morris The Mind/Body Problem, 1994; The Great Utopia The Russian and Soviet Avant-Garde, 1915-32. *Mailing Add:* Guggenheim Museum 1071 5th Ave New York NY 10128-0112

KRENTZIN, EARL
SILVERSMITH, SCULPTOR
b Detroit, Mich, Dec 28, 1929. *Study:* Wayne State Univ, BFA, 52; Cranbrook Acad Art, MFA, 54; Royal Coll Art, London, Fulbright Fel, 57-58. *Work:* Detroit Inst Art, Mich; Cranbrook Galleries, Bloomfield Hills, Mich; St Paul Art Ctr, Minn; Jewish Mus & Mus Contemp Crafts, NY; Hirshhorn Mus, Washington, DC. *Comn:* Enamel plaque, Gloria Dei Lutheran Church, Detroit, 54; Menorah, Temple Israel, Detroit, 63; metal sculpture, Westland Shopping Ctr, Detroit, 65; plus many pvt comn of silver sculptures. *Exhib:* Solo exhibs, Kennedy Galleries, NY, 68-75, Detroit Inst Art, 78 & Oshkosh Mus, 82; NJ State Mus, Trenton, 70; Jewelry USA Traveling Exhib, Am Crafts Mus, 84-; Masters Am Metalsmithing Mus Ornamental Metalwork, Memphis, 88; Toys Designed by Artists, Ark Arts Ctr, Little Rock, 89-2005; Am Modernist Jewelry, 1940-1970, Fort Wayne Mus Art, Ind, 2008. *Teaching:* Instr art, Univ Wis-Madison, 56-60; vis prof silversmithing, Univ Kans, 65-66; vis prof metalwork, Fla State Univ, 69. *Awards:* Fulbright Fel, 57-58; Nat Decorative Arts Exhib, Wichita

Art Ctr, Kans, 66; Tiffany Grant, 66. *Bibliog:* Article, Am Mag, 11-12/82; Earl Krentzin: Artist, Silversmith and Alchemist, Silver Mag, 3-4/08. *Media:* Precious & Base Metals. *Interests:* Collecting art, antiques & old toys. *Publ:* Auth, Centrifugal casting, Craft Horizons Mag, 11/54. *Mailing Add:* 412 Hillcrest Grosse Pointe Farms MI 48236

KRESTENSEN, ANN M
CERAMIST, PAINTER
b Baltimore, Md, Apr 4, 1939. *Study:* Md Inst Art, 60. *Hon Degrees:* Md Inst Art, Hon BFA, 96. *Comn:* Ceramic vessels & triptych (silk painting), ALB Fed Bank, Las Cruses & Corrales, NMex, 85. *Exhib:* Baltimore Regional Show, Baltimore Mus Art, Md, 60; Everson Mus Gift Gallery Show, Everson Mus, Syracuse, NY, 82. *Pos:* Craft rep, NMex Arts & Crafts Fair, 79-81; Southwest Arts & Crafts Festival, 88-90. *Teaching:* Instr pottery, Acad Arts, Easton, Md. *Awards:* Merit Award, NMex Clay, 83; Jurors Choice, Acad Arts, Easton, 95; Best of Show, Acad Art Mus, Mem Show, 2003. *Mem:* Am Crafts Coun; Acad Art Mus, Easton, Md. *Media:* Clay, Painting. *Mailing Add:* PO Box 96 Bozman MD 21612

KRET, ROBERT A
MUSEUM DIRECTOR
Study: Univ Detroit, BA (Hist); State Univ NY, Oneonta, MA (Hist Mus Studies). *Pos:* Dir, Mus Soc Preservation of New Antiquities, Boston, formerly; exec dir, Ella Sharp Mus, Jackson, Miss, formerly; dir, Leigh Yawkey Woodson Art Mus, Wausau, Wis, 1994-98, Miami Univ Art Mus, Oxford, Ohio, 1998-2000, Hunter Mus Am Art, Chattanooga, Tenn, 2000-2009 & Georgia O'Keefe Mus, Santa Fe, 2009-. *Mem:* AAM (panelist, juror); Asn Art Mus Dirs. *Mailing Add:* Hunter Mus Am Art 10 Bluff View Chattanooga TN 37403

KRETSCHMER, MELISSA
SCULPTOR
b Santa Monica, Calif, 1962. *Study:* Art Ctr Coll Design, Pasadena, Calif, BFA, 86, MFA, 88. *Work:* Allianz, Berlin, Ger; Wadsworth Atheneum, Hartford, Conn. *Exhib:* Julian Pretto, NY; Gallerie Tschudi, Glarus, Switz; Art Miami '98, Fla; Long Beach Mus Art, Calif; Vereniging voor Culturele Informatie en Actueel Prentenkabinet, Hasselt, Belg; Wadsworth Atheneum, Hartford, Conn; PS1 Mus, Long Island City, NY; Caledonian Hall, Royal Botanic Garden, Edinburgh; Ace Gallery, Los Angeles, Calif; Geukens & De Vil, Knokke, Belgium; Galerie Frank, Paris; Eric Stark, NY. *Bibliog:* Saul Ostrow & David Pagel (auths), Assemblage, Bricollage and the I: Meg Cranston, Melissa Kretschmer and Maya Lin, Bomb Mag, No 35, spring 91; Juan Cruz (auth), Carl Andre/Melissa Kretschmer, Art Monthly, No 220, 10/98; Duncan MacMillan (auth), Reflected glory, Scotsman, 8/27/98; Collette Chattonpadhyay (auth), Exhibition Review, Sculpture Mag, 6/02; Kyle MacMillan (auth), Exhibit Clearly Compels, Denver Post, 2001; Lilly Wei (auth), Transparent Facade: From New York to Los Angeles, Catalogue Essay, Otis Art Inst Gallery, 99. *Media:* Glass, Tar, Beeswax, Printing Ink, parafin. *Publ:* Claude Briand-Picard (auth), Ready-Made Color: La Couleur Importee, Positions & MCA, 2002. *Dealer:* Arnaud Lefebvre 30 Rue Mazarine 75006 Paris France; Rule Modern & Contemp 111 Broadway Denver CO 80203; Geukens & De Vil Zeedijk 735 8300 Knokke Belgium; Ace Gallery 5514 Wilshire Blvd Los Angeles CA

KREUTZ, GREGG
PAINTER
b Wis, 1947. *Study:* NY Univ; Art Students League. *Exhib:* Solo exhibs at Newport Art Asn, Newport, RI, Grand Central Art Gallery, Fanny Garver Gallery, Madison, Wis; group exhibs at Salmagundi Club; Knickerbocker Artists; Hudson Valley Art Asn; Luminous Realism, Gallery at Shoal Creek, Austin, Tex; Eleanor Ettinger Gallery, NY; Audubon Artists; Allied Artists. *Teaching:* Teacher, Art Students League, NY, 1981-; workshop instr, Platte and Chisel Club, Chicago, Ill, formerly, Maitland Art Ctr, Orlando, Fla, formerly, Scottsdale Artist's Sch, Ariz, formerly, Fechin Inst, Taos, NMex, formerly. *Awards:* Allied Artist's Award; Advancement of Art Award; Catharine Lorillard Wolf Award; Grumbacher Award, Knickerbocker Artists; Frank C Wright Award, Hudson Valley Art Asn. *Publ:* Auth (play) Buttoms Up!; auth (play) Academia Nuts; auth, Problem Solving for Oil Painters, Watson Guptil, 1986; auth, Everything You Ever Wanted to Know About Oil Painting, Watson-Guptill, 1990. *Mailing Add:* c/o Eleanor Ettinger Gallery 24 W 57th St Ste 609 New York NY 10019

KREZNAR, RICHARD J
PAINTER, SCULPTOR
b Milwaukee, Wis, May 1, 1940. *Study:* Univ Wis, BFA; Brooklyn Col, MFA; Inst Allende, Mex. *Work:* Walker Art Ctr, Minneapolis; Milwaukee Art Mus, Wis; Univ Wis, Madison; Colgate Univ, Hamilton, NY; Sidney Lewis Best Co; and others. *Exhib:* Pa Acad Fine Arts, 63; Butler Inst Am Art, 65; Milwaukee Art Mus, 66; Wis Directions, Milwaukee Art Mus, 75; solo exhibs, Paley & Lowe Inc, 72 & OK Harris Gallery, NY, 74, 76 & 83, Jefferson Pub Libr, NY, 94, Atelier Gallery, NY, 94 & Stewart Int Airport, NY, 98, Del Art Ctr Gallery, Narrowsburg, NY, 99; Thorpe Intermedia Gallery, Sparkill, NY, 83; Mattingly-Baker Gallery, Dallas, Tex; Century of Alumni Art, Univ Wis, Milwaukee, 85; Del Arts Ctr Gallery, Narrowsburg, NY, 95; Nutshell Arts Ctr, NY, 96 & 98; Liberty Mus & Arts Ctr, NY, 97 & 98; Beck Gallery, Sullivan Co Mus, NY, 98; and others. *Teaching:* Instr studio art courses, Brooklyn Col, 64-73, asst prof, 74-79; instr, Parsons Sch of Design, 78; instr sculpture, Skowhegan Sch Painting & Sculpture, 78; instr sculpture, Philadelphia Col Art, 80-82 & Cooper Union, NY; vis artist, Univ Wis-Milwaukee, 84. *Awards:* Ford Found Purchase Award, 62 & 64; Prizes, Milwaukee Art Ctr, 62, Wis Salon of Art, 63 & Walker Art Ctr, 64. *Media:* Oil. *Publ:* auth At Home with Art, 99. *Mailing Add:* Mauer Rd Callicoon Center NY 12724-0218

KRIEG, CAROLYN
PHOTOGRAPHER, PAINTER
b Vancouver, Wash, Dec 14, 1953. *Study:* Westmont Col, 72-73, American Coll in Paris, 73-74, Portland State Univ, 74-75, Univ Calif, Santa Barbara, BA, 76; Marylhurst Col, 84-86; Univ Wash, 87-88. *Work:* Seattle Art Mus; Biblioteque Nat, Paris, France; Mus Comtemp Photog, Chicago; Portland Art Mus, Ore; Holter Mus Art, Helena, Mont; and others. *Comn:* Photo mural, Seattle Arts Comn, 90; Wash State Arts Comn, 90, 91, 93, 94, 96. *Exhib:* Solo exhibs, Seattle Art Mus, 94, Goddard Ctr Visual & Performing Arts, Ardmore, Okla, 96, Holter Mus, Helena, Mont, 96, Dahl Cent Gallery & Fine Arts, Rapid City, SDak, 97, Sun Valley Art Ctr, Idaho, 99, Art Mus Missoula, Mont, 2001; Women in Photog Int, Acad Fine Arts, Catania, Italy, 90-92; Mementos, William Reagh Los Angeles Photog Ctr, Calif, 93; Predatory Visions, St Lawrence Univ, Canton, NY, 94; NW Int Art Competition, Whatcom Mus Art, Bellingham, Wash, 96; Beyond Novelty, Mus Contemp Photog, Columbia Col, Chicago, 2003; Celebrating Women in the Arts, Frye Art Mus, Seattle, 2003; United States Embassy, Rangoon, 2002-2006. *Pos:* Vpres photo coun, Seattle Art Mus, Wash, 89-92; vis scholar/artist, Univ Mont, Missoula, 93. *Teaching:* Everett Community Col, Wash, 2001; Pacific Luth Univ, Tacoma, Wash, 2001, 2003 & 2006. *Awards:* Juror's Award Best of Show, Artquake, 93; Juror's Award, Current Works, Soc Contemp Photog, 95. *Bibliog:* Matthew Kangas (auth), Carolyn Krieg at Cliff Michel, Art in Am, 93; Rod Slemmons (auth), Documents NW: Interior Vision, Seattle Art Mus, 94, Predatory Visions, St Louis Univ, Richard F Brush Gallery, 94; Rod Slemmons (auth), Carolyn Krieg: A Photographic Survey, Traces and Memories, Holter Mus, of Art, Helena MT, 96; Rod Stemmons (auth), Carolyn Krieg: Predator, Prey & Prayer, Augen Gallery (catalog); International Invitational, Benham Gallery, Seattle, 90, Art Works for Aids, NW Aids Found, Seattle, 90; Paint Me a Poem: A Canvas of Words, King Co Pub Art Prog, King County Poetry and Art on Buses, Seattle, 99; Silver Anniversary Art Auction, Missoula Art Mus, 93, 96; Eye of the Camera: Photographs from the 3M Corporate Art Program, Heather Otis, 96, Ten Years 1986-1996, Laura Russo Gallery, 96,; New American Talent, Laura Trippi, Laguna Gloria Art Mus, Austin, Tex, 90; Positive/Negative National Exhibition, M K Wegmann, Slocumb Gallery, Johnson City, TN, 91; Twelfth Annual Works From the Heart, Cheney Cowles Mus, Spokane WA, 97 Human References, Marks of the Artist, Beth Sellars, Seattle Art Commn, 97; Society for Contemporary Photography, Current Works 1995, Leedy Voulkos Art Ctr, Kansas City, MO, 95; Seattle Poets and Photographers: A Millennium Reflection, Rod Slemmons, J T Stewart, Univ of Wash Press, Seattle Arts Commn, 99. *Mem:* Seattle Art Mus; Mus Northwest Art, La Conner, Wash. *Media:* Mixed Media; Acrylics. *Specialty:* Contemporary Art and Prints. *Dealer:* Augen Gallery 817 SW 2d St Portland OR 97204; Robischon Gallery 1740 Wazee St Denver CO 80202; SAM Gallery 1220 3rd Ave Seattle Wash 98101; Prographica Gallery 3419 E Denny Way Seattle WA 98122. *Mailing Add:* 23511 53rd Ave SE Bothell WA 98021-8040

KRIEGER, FAWN
SCULPTOR
Study: Parsons Sch Design, BFA, 1997; Bard Col, MFA, 2004. *Exhib:* The Moore Space, Miami; The Kitchen, New York; Univ Nev, Reno; Queens Mus, New York; Vox Populi, Philadelphia; MAP, Baltimore; Tilt Gallery, Portland; Nice & Fit Gallery, Berlin; Rose Art Mus, Boston; Neon fdv, Milan. *Awards:* Jerome Found Grant, 2007; Art Matters Found Grant, 2008. *Media:* Miscellaneous Media. *Mailing Add:* c/o Von Lintel Gallery 520 West 23rd St New York NY 10001

KRIEGER, FLORENCE
SCULPTOR, PAINTER
b New York, NY. *Study:* Cooper Union Art Sch, BA, 35; Nat Acad Fine Arts, 40; Art Students League, 45; study with Jose DeCreeft & Robert Brackman. *Comn:* Medals, Bd Educ, NY, 35; Art Students League, 63; steel & bronze scorpion & lion, Crewe Group of Companies, NY, 70; bronze wall hangings, Elisofon Gallery, NY, 75; bronze menorah & eternal light, Westminster Chapels, NY, 80. *Exhib:* The Dream, Riverside Mus, NY, 52; Peace, Allied Artists, NY, 55; solo exhib, Long Island Univ Gallery, Brooklyn, NY, 63; The Am, Nat Acad Design, NY, 75; Wind Song, Pacem in Terris Gallery, UN, NY, 79; Mother Love, Salmagundi Club, NY, 83; Pray for Peace, Knickerbocker Artists, NY, 84; Women, Audubon Artists, NY. *Pos:* Dir, Fine Arts Sculpture Co, NY; pvt lessons in painting, 86-90. *Teaching:* Instr sculpture, NY Sch Indust Art, 38-42 & Gallery 7, Brooklyn, 80-86. *Awards:* Merit Award, Riverside Mus, Civil Serv Comn, 52; Salmagundi Club Award, Second Ann Exhib, 79; Knickerbocker Mem Award, 34th Ann Exhib, 84; Merit Award, Brooklyn Mus. *Bibliog:* Close Up article, New York Post, 80; John Korez (auth), profile, Villager, 81. *Mem:* Catharine Lorillard Wolfe Art Club Inc; Knickerbocker Artists; Nat Asn Women Painters & Sculptors; Audubon Artists; Am Artists Prof League. *Media:* All. *Publ:* Auth, article, 90th Anniversary Catherine Lorillard Art Club, NY Times. *Dealer:* Ed Elisofon Galleries 115 E 9th St New York NY. *Mailing Add:* Gallery 7 & Art Studios 8759 19th Ave Brooklyn NY 11214

KRIEGER, RUTH M
PAINTER, PRINTMAKER
b Newark, NJ, May 17, 1922. *Study:* With Stuart Davis, 41; Moses Soyer, 42; Newark State Col, BA, 43. *Work:* State Mus, Trenton, NJ; Miss Art Asn, Jackson; Rosenberg Libr, Galveston, Tex; Burndy Engineering Co, Norwalk, Conn; Montclair State Col, NJ. *Exhib:* Conn Acad, Hartford Atheneum, Conn, 71; Audubon Artists, Nat Acad Gallery, NY, 71; Boston Printmakers, Boston Mus Fine Arts, Mass, 72; Ann Small Sculpture & Prints, Butler Inst, Youngstown, Ohio, 72; Assoc Artists of NJ, Montclair Art Mus, NJ, 74; Drawing Invitational, Hunterdon Co Art Ctr, Clinton, NJ, 81; Assoc Artists of NJ, Nabisco Galleries, Parsippany, NJ, 81. *Awards:* Clyde L Carnahan Award, 70 & 72; Second in Oils, Nat Acad New York, 70 & Conn Acad Ann, 71. *Mem:* Assoc Artists of NJ (pres 78-80, bd mem 74-); Artists Equity Asn of NJ. *Media:* Oils, Acrylic; Seriagraph, Cliche Verre. *Dealer:* Little Gallery Raleigh NC

KRIEGER, SUZANNE BARUC
PAINTER, LECTURER
b Jan 31, 1924. *Study:* Studied oil painting with Esphere Slobotkina; self-taught batik. *Work:* Nassau Community Col, NY; Schoenfeld Med Art Asn, New York, NY. *Comn:* Mural, Radium Treatment Room, Franklin Gen Hosp, Valley Stream, NY, 66; murals & decorations, Saddle Rock School Disco, Great Neck, NY 75; vignette for brochure, Designers Showcase, 84 & 85. *Exhib:* Parrish Art Mus, Southampton, NY, 68; Arts Festival, Nat Arts Pavilion, NY, 70; Festival of Arts, Brooklyn Mus; Art Exhib, Heckscher Mus, Huntington, NY; Versions of Our World Today, Donnell Libr, NY, 80; Salmagundi Club, NY; NY State Pre-Biennial Art Exhib, Lever House, NY, 83; Art Exhib of the 80's, Union Carbide Bldg, NY; Nassau Co Fine Arts Mus. *Pos:* Co own, 1st Co-op Gallery, Long Island, currently. *Teaching:* Instr arts & crafts, Creative Develop Prog, 7-11 Club, Great Neck, NY, 66-71 & Summer Wkshp, Saddle Rock Elem Sch, 66-72; instr seniors art, Continuing Educ Res Ctr, Queens, NY; art progs, Osborne Sch, Rye, NY, currently. *Awards:* First Prize Batik, Salmagundi Club, 75; Second Prize Watercolor, 44th Nat Art League Spring Exhib, 80. *Bibliog:* Jeanne Paris (auth), review, Long Island Press, 70; A Smith (auth), Wall with a view, New York Daily News; Malcom Preston (auth), Unusual work, Newsday, Long Island. *Mem:* Nat Asn Am Pen Women; Long Island Craftsman Guild; Nat Art League; Artists Net-Work Long Island. *Media:* Batik; Pen and Ink. *Publ:* Contribr, Little Neck Then and Now, Banner Publ, 84. *Dealer:* Glass Gallery 315 Central Park W New York NY 10025

KRIEGSTEIN, ZARA
PAINTER, PRINTMAKER
b Berlin, Ger, July 28, 52; US Citizen. *Study:* Accad Art, painting with Klaus Fussmann, MFA, 78. *Work:* Mus Fine Arts, Santa Fe; Univ NMex Mus; Univ WVa; Roswell Mus Art Ctr; Univ Phoenix Mus. *Comn:* The History of Jazz and Blues (2 panels), comn by Edward P. Bass, Ft Worth, Tex, 83; mural, Retirement Ctr, Berlin, Ger, 85; The Judicial History of New Mexico (4 panels), Santa Fe Munic Ct, 94-95. *Exhib:* Kunst Und Krieg - Art and Work 1939-1989, Hausder Kulturen der Welt, Berlin, Ger, 90; The Alcove Show, 90, 75th Anniversary Show, 92, New Mexico 93, 93, Mus Fine Arts, Santa Fe; Holocaust Exhib, Las Vegas Art Mus, 98; The Rainforest, Kaohsiung Mus Fine Arts, Taiwan, 2001. *Bibliog:* Bill Lasaroff (auth), Zara Kriegstein, Artscene, 89; Simone Ellis (auth), Santa Fe Art, Brompton Bks Corp, 93; Arthur Flowes & Anthony Curtis (auths), The Art of Gambling Through the Ages, Huntington Press, 99; Karoline Muller (auth), Torso, Verein der Berliner Kunstverein, 2003; Dr Robert Bell & Dr James Mann (auths), 15 Santa Fe Artists, Bell Tower Ed, 2005. *Media:* Acrylic, Oil, Etching, Lithography. *Publ:* Illusr, The Meaning of Life, Frauslimbic Press, 2007. *Dealer:* Argos Gallery 821 Canyon Rd Santa Fe NM 87501; McNish Gallery Oxnard College Campus Oxnard CA

KRIEMELMAN, SHEILA M
PAINTER, EDUCATOR
b Honolulu, Hawaii, Sept 15, 1941. *Study:* Univ Mo, BS (art educ), 63; Coll New Rochelle, MS (studio art), 83; Studies with Roy Lichtenstein, Larry Rivers & Eric Fischl, Long Island Univ, 87. *Work:* Bell Atlantic Corp, Paramus, NJ; Honolulu Acad Art, Hawaii; Iona Col, New Rochelle, NY; Quigley Publ, Larchmont, NY; and other corp collections. *Comn:* Wall mural (collab with Leroy Cox), Arthur Murray Studios, Wilmette, Ill, 77; wall mural, Willard Sch, Evanston, Ill, 78; canvas mural (17' x 12'), Mussavi Gallery, Soho, NY, 87. *Exhib:* Nat Asn Women Artists, 93-96; Art of the Northeast USA, Silvermine Galleries, Conn, 94; Dachau 1933-1945, Wildcliff Ctr Arts, New Rochelle, NY, 94; KOA Gallery, Honolulu, Hawaii, 95; Klutznik Mus, Washington, 97. *Teaching:* Assoc prof fine art, Iona Col, New Rochelle, NY. *Awards:* Best in Show, Mamaroneck Artists Guild Juried Show, 83; Molly Canady Award, Nat Asn Women Artists 104th Juried Show, 93; Grace Huntley Pugh Award (First Place), Mamaroneck Artists Guild 36th Ann Exhib, 94. *Bibliog:* Ed McCormack (auth), Sheila Kriemelman & the art of social witness, Artspeak, 4/94; Catherine Drillis (auth), Triumph of the human spirit, Manhattan Arts, 4/94; Deborah Scates (dir), Dachau, An Artists Response, Va Cable TV, 4/94. *Mem:* Nat Asn Women Artists; NY Soc Women Artists; NY Artists Equity; Coll Art Asn; Mamaroneck Artist Guild Inc (bd mem, 81-91). *Media:* Acrylic, Watercolor. *Publ:* Auth, Craighead, the litany of the great river, cross currents, Am Asn Relig & Intellectual Life, 92. *Mailing Add:* 148 Greene St New York NY 10010-3288

KRIENKE, KENDRA CLIVER See Daniel, Kendra Cliver Krienke

KRIMS, LES
ARTIST
b Brooklyn, NY, Aug 16, 42. *Study:* Cooper Union, New York, BFA, 64; Pratt Inst, Brooklyn, MFA, 67. *Work:* Mus Mod Art, New York; Nat Gallery Can, Ottawa; Musee Nat d'Art Moderne, Centre Georges Pompidou, Paris; George Eastman House, Rochester, NY; Bibliot Nat, Paris. *Exhib:* Le nu photographié (catalog), Galerie d'Art du Consul Gen Bouche-du-Rhone, Aix-en-Provence, France; Making Light: Wit and Humor in Phtography, The Francis Lehman Loeb Art Ctr, Vassar Coll, Poughkeepsie, NY, 2000; Photographs for Sick Kids, The Royal Hosp for Sick Children, Edinburgh, Scotland, 2001; The Peter C Bunnell Collection, Princeton Univ Art Mus, 2002; solo exhibs, Les Krims, Forum de l'Image, Toulouse, France, 2002 & Galerie Baudoin Lebon, Paris, France, 2007; Revelation: Representations of Christ in Photog, Hotel de Sully, Paris & The Israel Mus, Jerusalem, 2002; The Photographers Edge, Carl Solway Gallery, Cincinnati, 2002; Hexenwahn: Ängste der Neuzeit, (catalog), Deutsches Historisches Mus, Berlin, 2002; two-person exhib, Form and Femininity, The MacLaren Art Ctr, Barrie, Ont, 2003; Venus in Furs, Neue Galerie am Landsmus Joanneum, Graz, Austria, 2003; Galerie Baudion Lebon, Paris, France, 2007; Galerie Paci Arte, Brescia, Italy, 2007. *Teaching:* Prof art, Buffalo State Coll, 69-81, prof, 81-. *Awards:* State Univ NY Res Found Grant & Grant-in-Aid, 70 & 71; Nat Endowment Arts Fel, 71, 72 & 76; NY State Coun Arts Grant, 71, 73 & 75. *Bibliog:* Jacques Bloesch (auth), Jacques Désires de photographies, Le Scorpion Bleu, Geneva, 2001; Alain Roger (auth), Nus et paysages, Edits Aubier, 2001; Les Krims, (photo, mongr), Actes Sud, Arles, France, 11/2005. *Media:* Inkjet Print. *Publ:* Illusr, Grafisk Form Mag, 90; contribr & illusr, Det Iscenesatte Fotografi (by Mette Sandbye), Forlaget Politisk Revy, Copenhagen, Denmark, 92; illusr, Foto Taschenkalender, Atium Verlag/Michale Klant Publ, Heidelberg, Ger, 92; contribr & illusr, Images, Centre de la Photographie Geneve, Geneva, Switz, 93; Mollusk #2, Berlin, Ger, 2006. *Dealer:* Galerie Baudoin Lebon Paris France; Galerie Paci Arte Brescia Italy. *Mailing Add:* 187 Linwood Ave Buffalo NY 14209

KRINSKY, CAROL HERSELLE
EDUCATOR, HISTORIAN
b Brooklyn, NY, June 2, 1937. *Study:* Smith Col, BA, 57; NY Univ, MA, 60, PhD, 65. *Teaching:* Prof art hist, NY Univ, 65-. *Awards:* Millard Meiss Publ Award, 88; Design Arts Grant, Nat Endowment Arts, 94; Distinguished Teaching of Art Hist Award, Coll Art Asn, 2004; Frederic Lindley Morgan Chair, Univ Louisville, 2001; Distinguished Teaching Award, NY Univ, 2008; Senior Fulbright Specialist, 2006-2011. *Bibliog:* Sister Cities: Architecture & Planning in the Twentieth Century, Chicago & New York: Architectural Interactions, Chicago, Art Inst, p 55, 84; Chicago & New York: Plans & Parallels, Centennial Lectures, Art Inst Chicago, p 219, 83; St Petersburg on the Hudson: The Albany Mall, Art the Ape of Nature, p 771, New York, 81; State of the Field: Identity in Modern Architecture, Anales de investigaciones esteticas 85, Autumn, 2004; The Synagogues of Poznan, Polin 20, 2007; Stuyvesant Town/Peter Cooper Village, Site Lines: A Journ of Place, Fall 2007; Synagogue Architecture, YIVO Encyclopedia of Jews in Eastern Europe, Yale Univ Press, 2008; New York City: How its Port Shaped its Architecture, Port Cities, 2011; The Office Building Architecture of the Early 20th Century in NY, Entwicklung Zur Moderne, Hamburg, ICOMOS, 2012; Why Hand G of the Turin-Milan Hours Was Not Jan Van Eyck's Artibus et Historiae, 2014; New York, Typology-Hong Kong, Rome, NY, Buenos Aires, Zurich, ETH and Park Books, 2012; The Turin-Milan Hours: Revised Dating and Attribution, Journal of the Historians of Netherlandish Art, 2014. *Mem:* Soc Archit Historians (NY chap pres, 79-81, nat pres, 84-86); Coll Art Asn; Int Ctr Medieval Art; Columbia Sem on the City (co-chmn, 93-95); Byzantine Studies Conference, Soc Am City Regional Planning Hist; History of Netherlands Art. *Res:* Architecture in New York and Chicago; Synagogue architecture; Representing group identity in modern architecture; 15th C Flemish Painting. *Publ:* Vitruvius De Architectura, Wilhelm Fink Verlag, 69; Rockefeller Center, Oxford Univ Press, 78, Parts reprinted in Johanna Gibson, ed, Case Studies in Academic Writing, Addison-Wesley-Longman, 2002; Synagogues of Europe: Architecture, History & Meaning, Archit Hist Found, MIT Press, 84, rev ed New York, Dover Publ, 96; Gordon Bunshaft of Skidmore, Owings & Merrill, Archit Hist Found, MIT Press, 88; Contemporary Native American Architecture: Cultural Regeneration & Creativity, Oxford Univ Pr, 96

KROLL, DAVID
PAINTER
b Phoenix, Ariz, Feb 27, 1956. *Study:* San Francisco Art Inst, BFA, 80; Art Inst Chicago, MFA, 86. *Work:* First Nat Bank Chicago; Gund Collection, Cambridge, Mass; Microsoft Corp, Redmond, Wash; Philip Morris Mgt Corp, NY; Prudential Ins Co, Newark, NJ. *Exhib:* Solo exhibs, Sch Art Inst Chicago, 85, NAME Gallery, Chicago, 88, Betsy Rosenfield Gallery, Chicago, 89, 91 & 93, Betsy Rosenfield Gallery, Chicago Int Art Expo, 90 & Jamison/Thomas Gallery, NY, 92; Revelations: Artists Look at Religion, Gallery 2, Sch Art Inst Chicago, 91; Still Alive: Contemp Still Life, Rockford Coll Art Gallery, Ill, 91; Light, Milwaukee Inst Art & Design, 92; Artfair/Seattle, Betsy Rosenfield Gallery, Seattle, 92; From America's Studio: Drawing New Conclusions, Betty Rymer Gallery, Sch Art Inst Chicago, 92; May 1992, Betsy Rosenfield Gallery, Chicago Int Art Expo, 92; Nature Fabrilis, Steibel Modern, NY, 92; and others. *Teaching:* Vis artist painting, Art Inst Chicago, 86-91. *Bibliog:* Wade Wilson (auth), David Kroll, New Art Examiner, 12/91; Susan Snodgrass (auth), David Kroll at Betsy Rosenfield Gallery, Art Am, 1/92; Holland Cotter (auth), Nature Fabrilis, NY Times, 7/3/92. *Media:* Oil on Linen. *Mailing Add:* c/o Lisa Sette Gallery 4142 N Marshall Wy Scottsdale AZ 85251

KROLL, LYNNE FRANCINE
PAINTER, COLLAGE ARTIST
b San Mateo, Calif, Dec 18, 1943. *Study:* Brooklyn Community Coll, AAS, 63; Rockland Found Arts, 68; workshops with numerous masters, 79-2007; Ed Betts Master Class Watermedia Juried, 93, Wolf Kahn, 98, Anna Tomchyk, 99, Maggie Taylor's Digital Collage, 2002 & Jonathan Talbot's Collage-A New Approach, 2009. *Work:* Broward Co Main Libr, Ft Lauderdale, Fla; Coral Springs Med Ctr, Fla; Anne Kolb Nature Ctr, Hollywood, Fla; Jane Voorhees Zimmerli Art Collection, Rutgers Univ; Int Mus Ecollage & Assemblage, Mex; Artecolle, Mus & Gallery Collage Sergines, France; Yuko Nii Found WAH Ctr, Brooklyn, NY. *Comn:* Brass welded copper doors depicting external flame, Mania Nudell Holocaust Learning Ctr, Davie, Fla; brass welded copper doors, Belle Terre Bldgs, Coral Springs, Sunrise, Davie & Boca Raton, Fla, 77. *Exhib:* New Art, S Fla, Fel Recipients, Mus Contemp Art, Miami, 98; Nat Soc Painters in Casein & Acrylic, Salmagundi Club, New York, 98 & 2001-2006; Under the Influence, Ft Lauderdale Mus Art, 2000; Birth of Wisdom, Soc Layerists in Multimedia, Santa Fe, NMex, 2000; Millennium Collection, UN, 2002; Wish You Were Here, Cork Gallery, Lincoln Ctr Performing Arts, New York, 2002; Allied Artists Am, 89th, 90th, 91st, 95th, 96th, Ann, 2004-2009; Catharine Lorillard Wolfe Art Club, 107th Nat Exhib, Nat Arts Club, New York, 2003; In the Spotlight, and Award Winners Invitational, Nat Asn Women Artists, Fifth Ave Gallery, New York, 2003; Am Watercolor Soc 138th & 140th Ann Int Exhib, Salmagundi Club, New York, 2005-2006; Watercolor USA, Springfield Art Mus, Mo, 2006 & 2009; Springfield Art Mus, Mo; Western Colo Watercolor Soc 15th Ann Exhib, Ctr Art, Grand Junction, Colo, 2007; Southern Watercolor Soc 30th Ann Exhib, Colquitt Co Arts Ctr, Moultrie, Ga, 2007; Exploring Multiple Dimensions, Soc Layerists in Multimedia, Mus Art & Hist, Albuquerque, NMex, 2007; Nat Asn Women Artists 118th Ann Exhib, Monroe Ctr Arts, Hoboken, NJ, 2007; Rocky Mt Nat Watermedia Exhib, Foothills Art Ctr, Golden, Colo, 2008, 2009; 88th Ann Exhib, Nat Watercolor Soc; Riverside Art Mus, Calif, 2008; 67th Ann Exhib, Audubon Artists, Salmagundi

Club, New York, 2009; Nat Asn Women Artists 121st Ann Exhib, Nat Arts Club, New York, 2010; Fallbrook Art Ctr, 2nd Ann Signature Am Watercolor Exhib, 2011; Nat Watercolor Soc, San Pedro, Calif, 2012; Catharine Lorillard Wolfe Art Club, Salmagundi Club, NY, 2013. *Pos:* Judge, SC State Fair Fine Arts & Crafts, 2009; judge, I Love Watercolor, Goldcoast Watercolor Soc, Fla, 2012. *Awards:* South Fla Cult Consortium Fel Award, Nat Endowment Arts, 98; 1st Place Watermedia Award, Catharine Lorillard Wolfe Art Club Mem Exhib, 2006-2007; Art Students League NY Award, Audubon Artists 63d Ann Exhib, 2006; Dr Irving Silver Mem Award, Nat Asn Women Artists 115th Ann Exhib; Third Place, 16th Ann Nat Exhib, Western Colo Watercolor Soc, Grand Junction, Colo, 2008; Merit Award, WS of Ala, 68th Nat Exhib Talladega, 2009; Award of Excellence, TAWS 22nd Tri State Juried Watermedia Exhib, Leoyne Ctr Arts, 2010; Keith Crown Mem Award, Watercolor USA 50th Exhib, Springfield, Mo, 2011; Seligson Memorial award, Nat Assn Women Artists; Marquis Who's Who in Am Art References award in Collage & Mixed Media, Audubon Artists, NY, 2013. *Bibliog:* Artists Profile, Broward Cult Quart, Spring 98; Artists Profile, Art Trends Mag, Glycee Ed, 8-9/98; How Rutgers Women's Collection Grows, NY Times, 9/15/2002. *Mem:* Am Watercolor Soc; Nat Watercolor Soc; Nat Asn Women Artists; Soc Layerists Multimedia; Tex Watercolor Soc; Nat Asn Painters Casein & Acrylic; Catharine Lorillard Wolf Art Club; Nat Collage Soc; Fla Watercolor Soc; Audubon Artists; Allied Artists Am; Watercolor Hon Soc; Rocky Mountain Nat Watercolor Soc. *Media:* Mixed Media, Computer, Photography, Watercolor. *Publ:* Auth, Abstracts in Watercolor, 96, Painting: The Best of Watercolor Composition, 97 & Best of Watercolor I, II, III, 95-96 & 98, Rockport Publ; Best of Photography, Pub Photogrs Forum, 98-2002; Bridging Time & Space, Artwork & Essays on Layered Art, Soc Layerists Multimedia, 99; Collage in All Dimensions, Nat Collage Soc, 2006; Artistic Touch 4, 2009; Visual Journeys: Art in the 21st Century, Soc Layerists in Multi Media, 2010; A Walk into Abstract, Ebook, Sue St John. *Dealer:* Orlando Mus Art Gallery Gift Shop Orlando FL; Studio 19 Fine Art Ft Lauderdale FL. *Mailing Add:* 6943 Lost Garden Ter Parkland FL 33076

KROLOFF, REED
ADMINISTRATOR, EDUCATOR
Study: Univ Texas, grad; Yale Univ, grad. *Pos:* Dean, Ariz State Univ, formerly; editor-in-chief, Architecture mag, 1995; dean, Tulane Univ Sch Architecture, New Orleans, 2004-07; dir, Cranbrook Acad Art and Art Mus, Bloomfield Hills, Mich, 2007-2013; advisor, US Army Corps of Engineers, Ministry of Culture of Fed Govt of Mexico, Whitney Mus of American Art, Case Western Reserve Univ, History Channel, currently. *Teaching:* Prof, Ariz State Univ, formerly

KRONE, LARRY
PAINTER
b Chicago, Ill, 1970. *Study:* New York Univ, BS, 1993; Art Inst Florence. *Exhib:* Selections Fall '94: Installations, Drawing Ctr, New York, 1994; Imaginary Beings, Exit Art, New York, 1995; solo exhibs, North Gallery, Ringling Sch Art & Design, Fla, 1995, Automatic Art Gallery, Chicago, 1996, Forum for Contemp Art, St Louis, 1998, Mark Pasek Gallery, New York, 2000, William Shearburn Fine Arts, St Louis, 2002; So You Wanna be a Rock & Roll Star, Mus Contemp Art, Chicago, 1996; Current Undercurrent, Brooklyn Mus, 1997; Second New York State Biennial, New York State Mus, Albany, 1998; Almost Warm and Fuzzy, Tacoma Art Mus, Wash, 2000; Five by Five, Whitney Mus Am Art, New York, 2002 . *Awards:* NY Found Arts Fel, 2009. *Bibliog:* Kim Levin (auth), Voice Choices, Village Voice, 10/4/1994; Eddie Silva (auth), Book Smart, Riverfront Times, St Louis, 11-12/1995; Bill Arning (auth), Sleeping with the Avant Garde, Time Out New York, 1996; Jeff Daniel (auth), Mane Event, St Louis Post Dispatch, 12/11/1998

KRONSNOBLE, JEFFREY MICHAEL
PAINTER, EDUCATOR
b Milwaukee, Wis, Feb 9, 1939. *Study:* Univ Wis-Milwaukee, BS, 61; Univ Mich, Ann Arbor, MFA, 63. *Work:* Mus Fine Arts, St Petersburg, Fla; Addison Gallery Am Art, Andover, Mass; Nat Gallery Art, Washington, DC; Fla Capitol Bldg; New Orleans Mus Art; Morris Mus Art; and others. *Comn:* Portrait, Univ S Fla Med Sch; Notes on the 19th, 20th, and 21st Centuries: paintings by Jeffrey Kronsnoble. *Exhib:* Chicago & Vicinity Exhib, Art Inst Chicago, 61-63; Solo exhibs, New Orleans Mus Art, 67, Univ Fla, Gainesville, 75 & ACA Galleries, NY, 79, 81, 84 & 86; 25 Yr Retrospective Exhib, Polk Mus Art, Lakeland, Fla, 90. *Teaching:* Prof art (Emeritus), Univ Southern Fla, 1963-2006. *Awards:* Thomas B Clarke Prize, Nat Acad Design, New York, 80; William A Paton Prize, Nat Acad Design, New York, 81. *Bibliog:* Barbara Gallati (auth), Jefferey Kronsnoble, Arts, 12/81; Katherine Duncan (auth), Jeffrey Kronsnoble, A Retrospective, Catalogue Essay, Polk Mus Art; Jay Williams (auth), Notes on the 19th, 20th, and 21st Centuries: Paintings by Jeffrey Kronsnoble. *Media:* Mixed, Oil. *Dealer:* Clayton Galleries Tampa FL; Main Street Gallery Clayton Ga. *Mailing Add:* Clayton Galleries 4105 S MacDill Ave Tampa FL 33611

KRONZON, ZIVA
PRINTMAKER, SCULPTOR
b Haifa, Israel. *Study:* Bezalel Acad Art, Jerusalem, student. *Work:* Nat Mus Women in Arts, Washington, DC; Israel Nat Mus, Jerusalem, Israel; Sprengel Mus, Hanover, Ger; Herbert Johnson Mus, Ithaca, NY; Art Student League, NY. *Exhib:* Terra Interdicta II, Blanis Mus, Mongevideo, Uruguay, 96; Parer Sculr Jures, Gerhard Harcks House, Bremen, Ger, 97; Terra Interdicta I, Yad Levanim, Petach Tikva, Israel, 98; New Works, Ashdod Mus, Israel, 98. *Awards:* Herman Struck Prize, oil painting, Bezalel Acad Art, 88; HRCA Sculpture Award, Hudson River Mus, 89; Int Art Critic Award, Montecideo, Uruguay, 90. *Media:* Paper. *Publ:* Michael Brenson (auth), Ziva Kronzon, NY Times, 88; Martha Viale (auth), Infrequent Expressions, El Pais, Montevideo, 96; Karin Stelwag (auth), Lehm Und Blut, Stutgart Zeitung, 98. *Mailing Add:* 315 E 86th St Apt 20M New York NY 10028

KROPF, JOAN R
CURATOR, LECTURER
b Cleveland, Ohio, Aug 4, 1949. *Study:* Cleveland Art Inst; Cooper Sch Art; Cuyahoga Community Col; St Petersburg Jr Col; Eckerd Col, BA; Calif State Univ, MA;. *Collection Arranged:* Cancelled Graphic Plates, 75; Hiram College Graphics Show, 76; Erotic Art by Dali, 76; Dali's Anamorphoses, 77; Dali/Hasman Photog Exhib, 78; Important Dali Statements & Surrealist Documents, 79; Women: Dali's View, 79; Homage to Gala, 82; Secret Life Drawings, 82; Flor Dali, 83; Lucas Collection, 85; Dali's Divine Comedy, 85; Dali Sculpture, 86; Surrealist Drawings, 88; Many Faces of Dali-Lacroix Photographs, 89; The Alchemy of the Philosophers, 90; Dali's Graphic Art, 92; Homage to the Masters: Vision Nouvelle, 93; Dali The Early Years, 94; Dali by the Book, 96; Dali by Design, 97; Surrealism in Am, 1998; The Morse Adventure, 2000; Dali Objects/Dali Fetishes, 2002; Dali in Am Collection, 2004; Dali Revealed, 2005; Dali Under the Influence, 2005; Dali-Japan Retrospective, 2006; Dali by the Decades: Surreal Century, 2006; Women, Dali's View, 2007; Dali, Freud & Survealism, 2008-2009; Dali Through Glass, 2009; Dali: Gems, 2009; Salvador Dali: Liquid Desires, Australia, 2009. *Pos:* Asst deputy dir, Salvador Dali Mus, Cleveland, 71-75, dir, 76-82, cur, 83-89, co-exec dir, 90 & cur, collection, 92-, deputy dir, 2000-. *Mem:* Am Asn Mus. *Publ:* Auth, Secret Life Drawings, 82 & Flor Dali (photographs), 83, Salvador Dali Mus; auth, Dali's Divine Comedy, Surrealist Drawings, Docent Training Manual; Dali's Animal Crackers; collabr The Official Catalog of Graphic Works of Salvador Dali, Dali Japan, 99; Dali Objects, 2002; Dali, Japan, 2006; Dali, Centennial, Italy, 2004; Salvador Dali: Liquid Desires, Melbourne, Australia, 2009; Dali Mus Catalog of the Collection, 2011. *Mailing Add:* c/o The Dali Mus One Dali Blvd Saint Petersburg FL 33701

KRUEGER, LOTHAR DAVID
PAINTER, EDUCATOR
b Two Rivers, Wis, Sept 19, 1919. *Study:* Milwaukee State Teachers Col, Wis, BS, 42; Univ Wis-Madison, MS, 47; Univ Iowa, with Mauricio Lassansky in printmaking, grad, 50; Ohio State Univ, Columbus, grad art hist, 53. *Work:* Wis Mem Union, Madison; Am Inst Architects, Ark Arts Ctr, First Nat Bank Little Rock & Pulaski Savings & Loan, Little Rock, Ark. *Exhib:* 6 Ann Exhibs Art, Springfield Art Mus, Mo, 48-67; 9 Midwestern Delta Exhibs, Ark Art Ctr, Little Rock, 60-75; St Paul Art Ctr, 63 & 64-65; 10th Midsouth Exhib, Brooks Mem Gallery, Memphis, Tenn, 65; Ann, Ark Arts Ctr, Little Rock, 80; 22nd Ann, Oklahoma Arts Ctr, 80; and others. *Collection Arranged:* Am Inst Architects Art Collection, Ark Artist Exhib, traveling since 66; Arts, Crafts & Design Fair, Ark Distinguished Artists Collectors Exhib, 74. *Pos:* Vpres, Ark Educ Asn, 65-66, pres, 66-68. *Teaching:* Instr painting & drawing & ed, Northern Iowa Univ, Cedar Falls, 47-51; prof painting & drawing, Univ Ark, Fayetteville, 53-81, prof emer, 81-. *Awards:* First Place, Ark Artist Exhib, Am Inst Architects, 60-61 & 77; Honorable Mention, 12th Ann Delta Regional, Ark Arts Ctr, 69; Purchase Prize, Ark Arts Ctr, 80. *Bibliog:* Edgar A Albin (auth), An expert in abstract expressionism, Ark Democrat, 61 & The Arts, Sunday News & Leader, Springfield, Mo, 72. *Media:* Acrylic, Watercolor. *Mailing Add:* c/o North Dak Mus Art PO Box 7305 Grand Forks ND 58202

KRUG, HARRY ELNO
PRINTMAKER, EDUCATOR
b Oshkosh, Wis, Aug 20, 1930. *Study:* Univ Wis-Milwaukee, BFA; Univ Wis-Madison, MS. *Work:* Libr of Cong, Washington, DC; Nelson-Atkins Art Gallery, Kansas City, Mo; US Info Agency; Springfield Art Mus, Mo; Ohio Univ Galleries. *Exhib:* 22nd Am Color Print Exhib, Am Color Print Soc, 63; 6th Nat Print Exhib, Silvermine Guild Artists, New Canaan, Conn, 67; 19th Ann Exhib, Boston Mus Fine Arts, Mass, 68; Teacher-Artist Today, State Univ NY Coll Oswego, 69; Hopman, Krug, Ecker, Galerie Feursee, Stuttgart, 70. *Pos:* Crafts dir, Spec Serv, Ger. *Teaching:* Prof & chmn printmaking, Pittsburg State Univ, currently. *Awards:* Mid-Am Ann Purchase Award, Nelson-Atkins Art Mus, Kansas City, 60; Sonia Watter Award, Am Color Print Soc, Pa, 62; Prize for Graphics, Jersey City Mus, NJ, 68. *Bibliog:* Kenneth W. Auvil (auth), Serigraphy, Prentice Hall, 65; John Ross & Clare Romano (auth), The Complete Screenprint & Lithograph. 72; John Ross & Clare Romano (auth), The Complete Printmaker, Free Press, 72; Screen Printing, Watson-Guptill Publications, 73. *Mem:* Boston Printmakers; Philadelphia Print Club. *Media:* Serigraphy, Lithography. *Mailing Add:* 1113 S 220th St Pittsburg KS 66762-6851

KRUGER, BARBARA
CONCEPTUAL ARTIST, FILM CRITIC
b Newark, NJ, Jan 26, 1945. *Study:* Syracuse Univ, 65; Parsons Sch Design; Sch Visual Arts, 66. *Work:* Floor mosaics in five locations, Fisher Coll of Bus, Ohio State Univ, Columbus, 98; Op Ed page, The NY Times, 7/26/98; display windows, Saks Fifth Avenue, NY, 2000; Untitled, banner billboards at 8th Ave/42nd St and Washington St/West Side Hwy, Pub Art Fund & Whitney Mus Am Art, 2000. *Exhib:* Solo shows incl Monika Spruth Gallery, Koln, WGer, 87, 90, Nat Art Gallery, Wellington, New Zealand, 88, Mary Boone Gallery, NY, 89, 91, 94, 97, Galerie Bebert, Rotterdam, The Neth, 89, Fred Hoffman Gallery, Santa Monica, Calif, 89, Duke Univ Mus Art, Durham, NC, 90, Parrish Art Mus, Southampton, NY, Mus Contemp Art, Los Angeles, 99, Galerie Yvon Lambert, Paris, 99, Whitney Mus Am Art, NY, 2000, South London Gallery, 2001, Ctr Arte Contemp, Siena, Italy, 2002, Sprueth Magers Lee, London, 2003; group shows incl Castello di Rivoli, Turin, Italy, 89; Ctr Georges Pompidou, Paris, France, 89; Kalamazoo Inst Arts, Mich, 98; Ga Mus Art, Athens, 99; Galerie Yvon Lambert, Paris, 2000; Mus des Beaux-Arts, Lille, France, 2002, Schirn Kunsthalle, Frankfurt, Ger, 2002. *Collection Arranged:* Pictures and Promises, The Kitchen, NY, 81; Artists' Use of Language, Franklin Furnace, NY, 83; Creative Perspectives in Am Photography, Hallwall's Gallery, Buffalo, NY, 83. *Teaching:* Vis artist, Calif Inst Art, Art Inst Chicago & Univ Calif, Berkeley; prof art Univ Calif Los Angeles, currently. *Awards:* Creative Artists Serv Progr Grant, 76-77; Nat Endowments Arts Grant, 83-84; Golden Lion Award for Liftetime Achievement, Venice Biennial, 2005. *Bibliog:* Robert C Morgan (auth), Barbara Kruger, Arts Mag, 4/89; Carol Squires (auth), Diversionary (Syn) tactics/Barbara Kruger has a way with

words, Bijutsu Techo, 4/89; Therese Lichtenstein (auth), Barbara Kruger's After-Effects: The Politics of Mourning, Art and Text, 7/89; Frederick Garber (auth), Re Positioning: The Syntaxes of Barbara Kruger, Univ Hartford Studies in Lit, 9/89; Maia Damianovic (auth), Scandali a New York, Tema Celeste, Jan 98; David Frankel (auth), Barbara Kruger, Artforum, Feb 98; Carissa Katz (auth), Barbara Kruger: The Place of Art, The East Hampton Star, 7/23/98; Erica-Lynn Gambino (auth), Barbara Kruger, The Parrish Art Mus, Sculpture, 1/99; David L Jacobs (auth), Gendered Engendered, Camerawork, Oct 99; Suzanne Muchnic (auth), Barbara Kruger, Art News, Jan 2000; Lane Relyea (auth), Barbara Kruger, Artforum, Feb 2000; Diane Armitage (auth), Barbara Kruger Q & A, The Magazine (Santa Fe), May 2000; Anne Wehr (auth), Ism she lovely?, Time Out New York, 7/6/2000; Kim Levin (auth), Shortlist: Barbara Kruger, The Village Voice, 2000; Hilton Kramer (auth), Greed Is Really Bad, Says Designer Kruger, The New York Observer, 8/21/2000; Marie-Pierre Nakamura (auth), Barbara Kruger, Art Actuel, Sept 2000; Eric Miles (auth), Barbara Kruger, Tema Celeste, Oct 2000; Claire Bishop (auth), Interview with Barbara Kruger, Make, Dec 2000; Raphael Rubinstein (auth), Barbara Kruger at the Whitney Museum, Art in America, Mar 2001; and many others. *Media:* Mixed. *Publ:* Auth, Picture/Readings, 79; No Progress in Pleasure, 82; contribr, film criticism, Artforum. *Dealer:* Dorfman Projects 529 W 20th St New York NY 10011; Dranoff Fine Art 591 Broadway New York NY 10012; Guy Hepner LA 825 Kings Rd West Hollywood CA 90069; Rhona Hoffman Gallery 118 N Peoria St Chicago IL 60607; Ikon Ltd/Kay Richards Contemporary Art 2525 Michigan Ave Santa Monica CA 90404; Keitelman Gallery 9 rue de la Paille 1000 Brussels Belgium; Monika Sprüth Philomene Magers Schellingstrasse 48 80799 Munich Ger; RS&A Ltd 50b Buttesland St London N16BY UK; André Simoens Gallery Kustlaan 128-130 B-8300 Knokke Belgium; Simon Lee 12 Berkeley St London W1J 8DT UK; Yvon Lambert 108 rue Vieille du Temple F-75003 Paris France. *Mailing Add:* 24 Lancaster Ln Monsey NY 10952

KRUKOWSKI, LUCIAN
PAINTER, EDUCATOR
b Brooklyn, NY, Nov 22, 1929. *Study:* Brooklyn Col, BA, 52; Yale Univ, BFA, 55; Pratt Inst, MS, 58, Washington Univ, St Louis, PhD, 77. *Work:* St Louis Art Mus, Mo; Fogg Mus, Mass; San Francisco Art Mus, Calif. *Comn:* Outdoor wall painting, Nat Endowment Arts, St Louis, 72; outdoor wall painting, HBE Corp Bldg, St Louis, 83. *Exhib:* Staempfli Gallery, 58 & 62 & Cee-je Gallery, NY, 67; Loretto Hilton Gallery, 70, Moore Gallery, St Louis, 75 & 78 & Burns Gallery, St Louis, 81; Long Island Univ, NY, 85; Messing Gallery, St Louis, Mo, 92. *Teaching:* Prof art, Pratt Inst, 55-69, chmn dept fine arts, 67-69; prof art & dean, Sch Fine Arts, Washington Univ, 69-77, prof philos, 77-. *Mem:* Am Soc Aesthetics; Am Philos Asn. *Publ:* A basis for attributions of art, J Aesthetics Art Criticism, fall 80 & Artworks that end and objects that endure, winter 81; commentary on Beardsley's fiction as representation, Synthese 46, 81; Adorno & atonal music (rev), Bucknell, 84; Art and Concept, Univ Mass Press, 87; Aesthetic Legacies, Temple Univ Press, 92

KRULIK, BARBARA S
DIRECTOR, MUSEOLOGIST
b June 13, 1955. *Study:* Pa State Univ, Univ Park, BA (art hist), 76; Reinwardt Acad, Amsterdam Sch Arts, The Neth. *Collection Arranged:* Oil Sketches from the Ecole des Beaux Arts, 87; Painters by Painters, Portraits from the Uffizi Gallery, 88; 19th Century Polish Painting, 88; Women in Mex, 90; Helene Schjerfbeck: Finland's Modernist Rediscovered, 92; Hallowed Haunts: The Drawings & Watercolors of Charles Addams, 91-92; Darkness & Light: Swedish Drypoint Etchings, 93; Artists By Artists, Forum Gallery, 93; Sidney Simon: A Retrospective, Provincetown Art Asn, Mass, 95; Derriere Guard: An Exhibition, Kitchen Ctr Video, Music & Dance, NY, 97; Radical Views: George Grosz and Philip Evergood, Forum Gallery, NY, 98. *Pos:* Asst dir, 83-89, Nat Acad Design, interim dir, 89-90, deputy dir, 90-92; guest cur, New York City AIA Archit Design Awards exhib, 86, 87 & 90; assoc dir, Forum Gallery, 92-94; dir, Grad Sch Figurative Art, NY Acad Art, 94-97; mgr, Magpie Music Dance Co, 2001-; mgr, Warren & Consorten, 2006-. *Teaching:* Guest lectr, Fashion Inst Technol & Mus Studies Prog, 87 & 88; Univ Pa, continuing educ, 92, Kalamazoo Art Inst, 93; guest lectr, mus managment, Reinwardt Acad, Amsterdam, Neth, 99 & 2005. *Mem:* Am Asn Mus; Int Coun Mus; Initiative Group, Exhib Platform. *Publ:* Auth, Raphael Soyer, Forum Gallery, New York, 95; writer, Art Dealers Asn Am Report, summer 96 & spring 97; Marjukka Kaminen, Galleria Bronda, Helsinki, Finland, 98; Radical Views, Forum Gallery, NY, 98; Jules Pascin, Forum Gallery, NY, 2001; Sean Henry, exhib catalog, Berkely Square Gallery, London & Forum Gallery, NY, 2001; contribr, Patrick Huse & the object as data carrier, Stenersen Mus, Oslo, Norway, 2001; Charles Matton, Forum Gallery, 2002; From Monumentality to Intimacy, Diana Moore exhib catalog, Forum Gallery, NY, 2004; Questioning Beauty: attraction & repulsion in the art of Silvia B., Sculpture Magazine, 7/2005. *Mailing Add:* 2e Jacob van Campenstraat 112 II Amsterdam Netherlands 1073XX

KRUPA, ALFRED FREDDY
PAINTER, LECTURER
b Karlovac, Croatia, June 14, 71. *Study:* Acad Fine Arts Univ Zagreb, Croatia, MFA, 95; Tokyo Gakugei Univ, Inst for Art Res, Akira Itoh, Japan, non-degree postgrad study, 99; Inst for Educ of Repub of Croatia, Zagreb, prof, 2005. *Work:* TATE Britain Libr Spec Collection, London, England; Mus Contemp Art (MSU) - Collection RARA, Zagreb, Croatia; Silesian Mus in Katowice, Contemp Art Collection, Katowice, Poland; The Alfredo Guati Rojo Nat Watercolor Mus, Mex City, Mex; Franklin Furnace/MoMA Artist's Book Collection, New York; Metrop Mus Art, New York; Pratt Inst, New York. *Comn:* Portrait of Mayor I. Benic, City of Karlovac, Croatia, 94; Portrait of Prefect J. Jakovcic, Prefecture of Karlovac County, Croatia, 95; Portrait of Pres F. Tudjman, Kaarlovac County Prefect Office, Zagreb, Croatia, 96; Portrait of Head of Caputo Fund, Caputo Childrens Fund/Family Asn, Guatemala City, 2013; Royal Group Portrait (HM King Kigeli V), Royal House of Rwanda in Exile, Wash, DC, 2013. *Exhib:* Easter Eggs with a Reason Klovocevi Dvori Gallery/MGC-Zagreb, Croatia, 94; Croatian Watercolor Festival, Art Gallery Split, Croatia, 97; 3rd Croatian Watercolor Triennial, Gallery Zvonimir Gallery Vjekoslav Karas, A Salon Vladimir Becic, Karlovac, Slavonski Brod, Zagreb, Croatia, 2004; Drava Art Annale, Koprivnica Gallery-City Mus, Koprivnica, Croatia, 2006; Krupa & Krupa, Gallery Ulrich, Zagreb, Croatia, 2008; 3rd Int Exhib of the Chinese/Anshan Mus-Youth Palace Calligraphy and Ink Painting, Anshan, China, 2013; In One Stroke, Orange Regional Art Gallery, Orange, NSW, Australia, 2014; Exposure-2015, Louvre Mus, Paris, France, 2015. *Teaching:* lectr basis of design, Univ Zagreb, Fac Textile Technol, Croatia, 94-96; prof painting and drawing, Duga Resa Upper Secondary Sch, Graphic Design Dept, Croatia, 2004-2015. *Awards:* Councillor Spec Prize, 3rd Int Exhib of Chinese Calligraphy and Ink Painting, Int Chinese Calligraphy and Ink Painting Soc, 2013; Prince of Antioch Medal, Portrait Achievement, Caputo Childrens Fund/Family Asn, Guatemala City, 2013; Knight Grand Cross and Baron of the Royal Order of the Crown Rwanda, Portrait Achievement, HM Jean Baptiste King Kigeli V, Wash, 2013; Cert of Excellence, Artavita Contest, Artavita, Calif, 2015. *Bibliog:* Zvonimir Gerber (auth), Visnja Lasic (auth), Alfred Freddy Krupa, 2014; Dr. Wolf Tegethoff (auth), Dr. Benedict Savoy (auth), The Visual Artists of All Times and Peoples, 2014; Sonja Svec Spanjol (auth), Monograph A.F. Krupa, 2015. *Mem:* Croatian Asn Artists in Zagreb; European Asn of Univ Profs, London, England; Fel Int Chinese Calligraphy and Ink Painting Soc, (NAm Branch); Synapse Initiative-Australian Coun for Art; Int Soc for Educ Through Art, (Croatian Coun); Int Watercolor Soc (head operations, founding mem). *Media:* Ink, Oil. *Publ:* auth, Adoration, 2016

KRUPP, BARBARA D
CONCEPTUAL ARTIST, PAINTER
b Elyria, Ohio, July 1, 1942. *Study:* NY Sch Art, with Graham Nixon, Lowell Ellsworth AWS & Fred Leach AWS, 97. *Work:* Massillon Mus Art, Massillon, Ohio; Mansfield Art Ctr, Mansfield, Ohio; Osceola Bd City Commissioners, Osceola, Fla; Five Points Plaza Bldg & Mike Bieber, Sarasota, Fla; Collection of Disney World. *Comn:* 6 pieces Art Collection, John Calys, Leesbury, Va, 2006. *Exhib:* Not Just Another Perfect Face, Mansfield Art Ctr, Mansfield, Ohio, 97; Salon D'Out, Isabelle Duncan Mus, Paris, France; Poems of Reality, Ariel Gallery, New York, NY; Gasparilla Arts, Tampa Mus, Tampa, Fla, 2004; Colors, Orange Ctr for Contemp Arts, Orange, Calif, 2005; Blooms of Summer & Abstract Nature, Dabbert Gallery, Sarasota, Fla, 2006; A Couple of Visions, Dabbert Gallery, Sarasota, Fla, 2007; Toledo Mus Art, Oh, 2012; Restoration, Recycling, Remembering, Canton Mus Art, Oh, 2013. *Awards:* Best Show, Piegon Key Art Festival, 2004; Best Show, Marquette, Mich, 2006. *Mem:* Rockport Art Asn; NAIA; Ohio Arts & Crafts Counc. *Media:* Acrylic, Oil, Mixed media. *Publ:* 100 Southern Artists. *Mailing Add:* 2125 Seagrape Dr Vero Beach FL 32963

KRUSKAMP, JANET
PAINTER, JUROR
b Grants Pass, Ore, Dec 10, 1934. *Study:* Chouinard Art Inst, Los Angeles and pvt study. *Work:* Rosicrucian Egyptian Mus, San Jose & Triton Mus Art, Santa Clara, Calif; Springville Mus Art, Utah; Alexandria Mus Art, La; La Grange Col, Ga; Hist San Jose Mus, Calif, 2008; San Jose Women's Club, San Jose, Calif; and others. *Comn:* Seven paintings, Cowden Ranch, 74; painting, Burger King, 75; Challenge-Cook Brothers, 76; two paintings, Jet Air, Inc, 76; painting, Anning-Johnson & Co, 89; Bicentennial Event, comn by San Jose Bicentennial, 76; Bentley House Publ, 99. *Exhib:* Soc Western Artists Ann, M H De Young Mus, San Francisco, 71; Soc Western Artists, Rosicrucian Egyptian Mus, 72; Mainstreams, Marietta Col, Ohio, 75; solo exhibs, Rosicrucian Egyptian Mus Gallery, 70, 73, 76 & 86, Springville Mus Art, Utah, 78, San Jose Mus Art, 80 & Charles & Emma Frye Mus Art, Washington, 74; San Jose Mus Art, Calif, 80; Redding Mus Art, Calif, 80; and others. *Pos:* Artist, juror. *Teaching:* Pvt instr, 40 yrs. *Awards:* Trustees' Award & Andy Trophy, Grand Galleria Nat Art Competition, Seattle, 72, First Prize & Purchase Prize, 73; and others. *Bibliog:* Janice Loveos (auth), Janet Kruskamps America, Southwest Art, 6/75; Ted Bredt (auth), Beauty From the Commonplace, Calif Today; Robert Sher (auth), Portraits to Products, Abbink Comm Group, 2/2003. *Mem:* Los Gatos Art Asn (pres, 69); Nat Mus Women Artists (charter mem). *Media:* Oil, Egg Tempera, Watercolor, Acrylic. *Specialty:* Fine Art, Traditional. *Publ:* Painting From Your Own Photos... Another View, Northlight Mag, 2/79. *Dealer:* The Bentley Global Arts Group Austin Tex; Bentley Licensing San Ramon Ca

KU, FAY
PAINTER
b Taiwan. *Study:* Bennington Coll, Vt, BA; Pratt Inst, Brooklyn, MS (art hist), MFA. *Work:* Asian Am Art Ctr, New York; Contemp Mus, Honolulu, Hawaii. *Exhib:* Solo exhibs, Metaphor Contemp Art, Brooklyn, 2005, AIR Gallery, New York, 2005, Real Art Ways, Hartford, Conn, 2007, Gallery 10G, New York, 2007, Kips Gallery, New York, 2008, Brooklyn Pub Cent Libr, 2008, Sam Lee Gallery, Los Angeles, 2008; Women's Identities, Walter Wickiser Gallery, New York, 2005; Underneath, McCaig-Wells Gallery, Brooklyn, 2005; Summer Solstice, Gallery Boreas, Brooklyn, 2005; Good Housekeeping, Tribes Gallery, New York, 2005; Bearings: The Female Figure, PS 122 Gallery, New York, 2006; The Lady Doth Protest Too Much, Heidi Cho Gallery, New York, 2006; Little Monsters, AG Gallery, Brooklyn, 2006; Kid Pink Gloves, Chashama, New York, 2006; The Troubled Waters of Permeability!, Parker's Box, Brooklyn, 2007; Working Space, Cuchifritos, New York, 2007; Frolic: Humor & Mischief in New Taiwanese Art, 2x13 Gallery & Taipei Cultural Ctr, New York, 2007; Four Artists, Pratt Manhattan Gallery, New York, 2007. *Awards:* AIR Emerging Artist Fel, 2005; Urban Artists Initiative/NYC Proj Grant, 2007; Louis Comfort Tiffany Found Grant, 2008; NY Found Arts Deutsche Bank Fel, 2009

KUCHAR, KATHLEEN ANN
PAINTER, EDUCATOR
b Meadow Grove, Nebr, Feb 4, 1942. *Study:* Kearney State Coll, BA, 63; Ft Hays Kans State Coll, MS, 66; Brooklyn Mus Art Sch, Max Beckmann Mem scholar, 66-67, with Reuben Tam, 67; Wichita State Univ, MFA, 74; Santa Reparata Graphic Art Ctr, Florence, Italy, 91. *Work:* Wichita State Univ Art Gallery; Ft Hays State Univ

Art Gallery; Nebr Arts Collection; Crescent Cardboard co Collection; Biblical Arts Ctr, Dallas, Tex. *Exhib:* Watercolor USA, Springfield Art Mus, Mo, 68, 79, 80, 84, 85, 91 & 94; solo exhibs, Nat Design Ctr, NY, 68 & Biblical Arts Ctr, Dallas, Tex, 88; Am Watercolor Soc Exhib, NY, 79; group exhib, Ariel Gallery, NY, 88. *Teaching:* Instr art, Minden Pub Schs, Nebr, 63-65; assoc prof painting-design, Ft Hays State Univ, 67-78, prof, 78-2001. *Awards:* Pilot Award Outstanding Prof at Ft Hays State Univ, Hays, Kans, 80; Nat Endowment/Mid-Am Arts Fel, 86; Governor's Visual Artist, State of Kans, 93. *Bibliog:* Rev in Art News, 68 & Art Rev, 69; Female Artists, Past & Present, Women's Hist Res Ctr, Inc, 74; Rev in Manhattan Arts, 88; New York Art Rev, 88. *Mem:* Rocky Mountain Nat Watermedia Soc; Kans Watercolor Soc; Nat Watercolor Soc; Watercolor-USA-Honor Soc; Soc Layerists Multi-Media. *Media:* Acrylic; Watercolor Monotype. *Dealer:* Hand Artes Gallery Truchas NMex; Strecker-Nelson Gallery Manhattan KS

KUCHTA, RONALD ANDREW
MUSEUM DIRECTOR, EDITOR

b Lackawanna, NY, 1935. *Study:* Cape Cod Sch Art, Provincetown, Mass, 53-57; Kenyon Coll, Gambier, Ohio, BA, 57; Case Western Reserve Univ, Cleveland, Ohio, MA (art hist), 62; Mgt Inst, Cornell Univ, 79. *Collection Arranged:* Modern Mexican Painting, 70; Tantra (with catalog), 70; Interior Vision, European Abstract Expressionism, 1945-1960 (with catalog), 70; Animals in African Art (with catalog), 73; 15 Abstract Artists--Los Angeles, 73; New Works in Clay, 76; Provincetown Painters, 77; Diversions of Keramos: Am Clay Sculpture 1925-1950, 83; Robert Beauchamp: Am Expressionist, 84; Syracuse China Ctr Study Am Ceramics, 87; Continuity and Transformation, Contemp Japanese Ceramics, 92; Sublime Forms, Enigmatic Visions, CJCS, 98; Norwegian Clay & the Possible Superiority of Ceramics, 2005; Conversation with Three Famous Architects- IM Pei, Frank Gerhry & Santiago Calatrava, 2006; Familiar Encounters with Unforgettable Ceramics for Architectural Enhancement, 2006; Shin Sang Ho's Fired Paintings & the Korean Artists Evolution from Potter to Painter of Clay or Ceramist/Painter, 2007; Women Touch: Ceramics, 2007. *Pos:* Cur, Chrysler Art Mus, 61-68, Santa Barbara Mus Art, 68-74; dir, Everson Mus Art, 74-95; assoc, Loveed Fine Arts, NY, 95-; ed, Am Ceramics, NY, 95-; chmn, Longhouse Res Art Comt, E Hampton, NY, 97-; trustee Moca, NY, Watershed Ctr for Ceramic Arts, Edgecomb, Maine; trustee, Kulaev Cult Heritage Fund, Los Angeles, Calif, 2004; US Commissioner, 3rd World Ceramic Biennial, Korea, 2005. *Teaching:* Adj prof museology, Syracuse Univ, 74-94. *Awards:* Service to the Arts Award, Cult Resources Coun, Syracuse, 92; Award for Contributions to Am Art, Fonda del Sol Arts Ctr, 93; Commending dir, NY State Senate Resolution 317, Everson Mus Art, 95; Lifetime Acheivement Award in the Ceramic Arts, Nat Conf of Educators in the Ceramic Arts, Tampa, Fla, 2011. *Mem:* Am Asn Mus Dir; Int Coun Mus; Nat Arts Club, NY; Nat Conf Educ Ceramic Art; Int Acad Ceramics, 92; Friends of Contemp Ceramics. *Media:* Ceramics. *Res:* Int contemp ceramics. *Specialty:* Ceramic sculpture. *Collection:* Contemporary Ceramics. *Publ:* Acquired Identities: And Other Observations on Contemporary Ceramics by an Acquisitive Museum Director, Ceramics, Art & Perception, Sydney, 93; In the Beginning Was the Word: Takako Araki's Ceramic Bibles, Am Ceramics, Vol II, No 1, 93; The Past is Present-Ceramics at the End of the Twentieth Century, Ceramics Art & Perception, Sydney, Australia, 12/96; From the Earth: Clay, Water & Fire, 96; The Emergence of 6 Taiwan Artists, 96; The Persistence of Craft, Major Themes in Contemporary Ceramics, London, 2002; plus many others. *Dealer:* Loveed Fine Arts 575 Madison Ave New York NY 10022. *Mailing Add:* 60 Sutton Place S New York NY 10022

KUCKEI, PETER
PAINTER, STAINED GLASS ARTIST

b Husum, Schleswig-Holstein, Ger, May 25, 1938. *Study:* Staatliche Kunstschule Bremen, 61; Staatliche Akademie de bildenden Kuenste, Stuttgart, 63. *Work:* Landesmuseum Schleswig-Holstein, Ger; Kunsthalle Emden, Ger; Staatsgallerie Stuttgart, Ger; Mus Karlsruhe, Ger; Assoc Art Amsterdam, Holland. *Comn:* Stained glass windows, Maritim ProArte Hotel, Berlin, Ger, 95; Glaswork, Dorint Hotel, Berlin, Ger, 97. *Exhib:* Modus Vivendi 11 Ger Painters, Mus Wiesbaden, Ger, 85; Image of Shakespeare, Kunstforum Berlin, Ger, 86; solo exhibs, Landesmuseum Oldenburg, Ger, 88, Kunsthalle Wilhelmshaven, Ger, 89 & Staedtischer Kunstverein Paderborn, Ger, 92; Masterpieces from the Collection of Henri Nannen, Kunsthalle Emden, Ger, 90 & 96; The Large Format, Emsdettener Kunstverein, Ger, 93; Painting, Galerie Ricker, Heilbronn, Ger, 97; Galerie Kuckei & Kuckei, Berlin, Ger, 98; Galerie Schutte, Essen, Ger, 98; Between Inst & Construction, Galerie MB Art, Stuttgart, Ger, 98. *Teaching:* Drawing, Staatliche Akademie, Stuttgart, 86-87. *Awards:* DEUBAU Award, Ger, 79; BDA Award, Niedersachsen, Ger, 80 & 82; Walter Hesselbach Award, Ger, 80. *Bibliog:* W Hennig (auth), Monumente Documente, AM-Gruppe, 85; Dr J Schilling (auth), Drawings and Gouaches, Galerie Schueppenhaur, 86; Dr Peter Reindl (auth), Peter Kuekei Landesmuseum Oldenburg, 88. *Media:* Oil on canvas. *Publ:* Auth, Peter Kuckei San Francisco (portfolio), Nau-Verlag, Berlin, 95; Yan Geling, Peter Kuckei, San Francisco, 95. *Dealer:* Galerie Rieker Friedrich-Ebert-Brucke 74019 Heilbronn Germany; Galerie Kuckei & Kuckei Linienstr 158 (HOF) 10115 Berlin-Mitte Germany

KUCZUN, ANN-MARIE
PAINTER, ILLUSTRATOR

b Springfield, Mass. *Study:* Bay Path Jr Col, ABS; Univ Colo, Boulder. *Work:* Pratt Community Col, Kans; EF Hutton & Co, Colo; US West, Colo & Wyo; Ellsworth Hist Soc, Kans; US Embassy, Nicosia, Cyprus, Greece; Microsoft Corp, Wash. *Comn:* Bookcover, Roberts-Rinehart Inc, Boulder, Colo; bookcover, Natural Resources Ctr, Boulder, Colo; illus & bookcover, Island Press, Covelo, Calif. *Exhib:* Nat Arts Club, NY; solo-shows, Sangre De Cristo Arts Ctr, Pueblo, Colo, 88-89 & Andrew J Macky Gallery, Univ Colo, Boulder, 92; CU Art Galleries, Univ Colo, Boulder, 93; Colo Hist Mus, Denver, 94 & 98; Womens Studio Workshop Gallery, Rosendale, NY, 94; Colo Springs Art Ctr, 98; Denver Art Mus, Colo; Int Asn Pastel Socs, 98; Int Watermedia, Colo Springs, 2000; Dos Chappel Outdoor, Colo, 2003; Waterways, Canyon Gallery, Boulder Colo, 2008, 2012; The Ditch Proj, Dairy Art Ctr & Canyon Gallery, Boulder City Park, 2009; Canyon Gallery, Boulder, Colo. *Pos:* Freelance illusr, Univ Colo, John H Breck, Inc, Buxton Corp, WWLP/TV, Roberts Rinehart Inc Publ; pub, Roberts-Rhinehart Inc; Auth, designer, of Illustr book, cd, book, Holy Transfiguration of Christ Orthodox Cathedral; A guide to its Art & Architecture, 2004. *Teaching:* lectr, Boulder Valley Sch District, 75-79, Dairy Ctr Arts, 99, Univ Colo, Boulder, 79. *Awards:* 1st Prize, Sangre De Cristo Arts Ctr, Pueblo, Colo; Purchase Award, Pratt Community Col, Kans, 80; Art in Pub Places award, Colo Arts Coun, 97; Merit award, Int Asn Pastel Socs, 98; Gold award, Pikes Peak Art Asn, 2000; Best of Show, Pixelated Palette & Paintbrush, 2002. *Bibliog:* Durham Caldwell's Corner: Ann-Marie Kuczun, Wilbraham/Hampdem Times, Mass, 10/24/2002; Trendsetters (illustrated article), Art Business News, NYC, 2/3/2003; Digging the Old West: How Dams and Ditches Sculpted an American Landscape, Amazon Press, 2011. *Mem:* Colo Pastel Soc; Int Asn Pastel. *Media:* Watermedia, Pastel; Digital Collage. *Res:* Subject of gardens & figure sculptures that inhabit them by creating shadow-box depth collages using multi-layers of substractes & varied elevations of scale, depth & shapes with the intention to engage the viewer to try to decipher this puzzle of organic juxtaposed with the inorganic of living gardens & the sculptures that share the space of these gardens world wide. *Specialty:* Multimedia. *Interests:* Genealogy and travel, creating catalogs of art work. *Collection:* Exhib Quest, Denver, Colo; EF Hutton & Co Inc, Colo. *Publ:* Collage Techniques, Gerald Brommer, Watson-Guptill, 94; Open Studios (dir/catalog), 95 & 97; article, Women's Mag, 8/97; Bravo, 2000; illusr, Wilbraham-Hampden Times, 2002; illusr, Bus News, NYC, 2/2003; illusr, Historic Denver, INC, Spring, 2004; Colo Historical Society Archives, Denver, 2005; Boulder Daily Camera, 2008. *Dealer:* Artists Resource. *Mailing Add:* 930 Miami Way Boulder CO 80305

KUEHN, FRANCES
PAINTER

b New York, NY, Feb 16, 1943. *Study:* Douglass Col, Rutgers Univ, BA, Rutgers Univ, New Brunswick, MFA. *Work:* J B Speed Art Mus, Louisville, Ky; Weatherspoon Art Gallery, Univ NC; Power Inst, Univ Sydney, Australia; Allen Mem Art Mus, Oberlin, Ohio; NJ State Mus, Trenton; and others. *Comn:* Portrait for pvt collection, 72. *Exhib:* Whitney Mus Ann, 72 & Biennial, 73; solo exhibs, Douglass Coll Libr, 73, Max Hutchinson Gallery, 73 & 74 & A M Sachs Gallery, NY, 78, Phoenix Gallery, NY, 01, William Paterson Univ, Wayne, NJ, 02; Contemp Portraits by Well-Known Am Artists, Lowe Art Mus, Coral Gables, Fla, 74; Selections in Contemp Realism, Akron Art Inst, Ohio, 74; Mitchell Algus Gallery, NY, 2002; Artists on the Edge, Douglass Coll Libr, 2005; Hudson Guild, NY, 2010-2011; 100 Curators, 100 Days, Saatchi Online, 2012. *Teaching:* Artist-in-residence, Rice Univ, 80. *Awards:* NJ State Coun Arts Artist's Fel, 78-79; Nat Endowment Arts Artist's Fel, 82-83. *Bibliog:* Phyllis Derfner (auth), Frances Kuehn, Art Spectrum, 2/75; Lynn Miller & Sally Swenson (auths), Lives and Work, Talks with Women Artists, Scarecrow Press, 81. *Media:* Acrylic. *Mailing Add:* 789 W End Ave Apt 4D New York NY 10025-5417

KUEHNL, CLAUDIA ANN
GOLDSMITH

b Kenosha, Wis, Aug 11, 1948. *Study:* Philadelphia Coll Art, Pa, BFA, 70; State Univ NY Col, New Paltz, MFA, 74. *Exhib:* Contemp Am Gold-Silversmiths, Corcoran Gallery Art, Washington, DC, 72; Southern Tier Arts & Crafts Exhib, Corning Mus, NY, 74; Jewelry & Metal Objects from the Society of North Am Goldsmiths (Europ traveling show); Holstein Gallery, Palm Beach, Fla, 83; Gene Barth Gallery, Oklahoma City, 85; Cross Creek Gallery, Malibu, Calif, 86; Fergus-Jean Gallery, Columbus, Ohio, 89; Gayle Willson Gallery, Southampton, NY, 94; plus many others. *Teaching:* Asst prof, art appreciation, two dimensional design & drawing, Suffolk Co Community Col, Selden, NY, 75- & metalsmithing & jewelry, Southampton Col, NY, 76-79 & art dept drawing; tech mgr, Gesswein, Thailand, 89-90. *Awards:* Nat Endowment Arts Fel, Crafts, 75-76. *Mem:* Soc NAm Goldsmiths; Am Crafts Coun; NY State Craftsmen Inc. *Media:* Gold, Stone. *Publ:* Jewelry concepts, Technology, Oppi Untrach; auth, Murray Bouid, Jewelry Making; Metal Smith, spring 87. *Dealer:* Works Gallery Jobs Lane Southampton NY 11968; Works Gallery 1250 Madison Ave New York NY 10128. *Mailing Add:* Box 622 Quogue NY 11959

KUEMMERLEIN, JANET
FIBER ARTIST

b Dearborn, Mich, Jan 10, 1932. *Study:* Detroit Soc Arts & Crafts, 50-51; Cranbrook Acad Art, with Harry Osaki, 51-52. *Work:* Chicago Art Inst; Rochester Inst Technol; Ga Inst Technol; Smithsonian Nat Gallery Art; 3M Corp. *Comn:* Fiber relief sculpture, Gen Serv Admin, Richmond, Calif, 76; fiber mural, Williams Ctr, Tulsa, 80 & State Bar Calif, Sacramento, 80; fiber & sculpture, State Fed Savings, Tulsa, 82; fiber relief sculpture, Richardson-Vicks, Shelton, Calif, 83; fiber relief, Z J Loussac Libr, Anchorage, Alaska; fiber mural, DuPont, Wilmington, Del. *Exhib:* Five Fiber Artists, Sheldon Mem Gallery, Lincoln, Nebr, 63; Objects USA Traveling Exhib, US & Europe, 69; Forms in Fibre, Chicago Art Inst, 71; Am Craft Exhib, Dallas Mus, 72; Craft Invitational, San Diego Mus Fine Art, 74; Art in Worship, Mus Contemp Crafts, NY, 74; Women, Fiber, Clay & Metal, Bronx Mus, 77; Fiberworks, Cleveland Mus, 78. *Collection Arranged:* Contemporary Crafts (auth, catalog), Rockhurst Col, 64. *Awards:* Awards, Univ Kans, 65-69 & Am Inst Archit, 69-71, 75-79 & 88. *Bibliog:* Louise Schulteis (auth), Artist in fiber, Kansas City Star, 71; Irene Reynolds (auth), Fiber artist, Kansan Mag, 76. *Mem:* Mo Coun Arts; Am Craft Coun. *Media:* Fiber. *Publ:* Contribr, Textile Art in the Church, Abingdon Press, 71; contribr, Quilting, Patchwork, Applique, Trapunto, 74 & Soft Sculpture, 74, Crown; contribr, The Place of Art in the World of Architecture, Chelsea House, 80; contribr, Sewing Machine Craft Book, Van Nostrand Reinhold, 80. *Mailing Add:* 7701 Canterbury St Shawnee Mission KS 66208-3946

KUHLMAN, WALTER EGEL
PAINTER, EDUCATOR

b St Paul, Minn, Nov 16, 1918. *Study:* St Paul Sch Art, with Cameron Booth, 36-40; Univ Minn, BA, 41; Tulane Univ, 45-46; Calif Sch Fine Arts, 47-50; Acad Grand Chaumiere, Paris, 50-51. *Work:* San Francisco Mus Mod Art; Oakland Mus, Calif; NY Metrop Mus Art; Nat Mus Art, Washington, DC; Mus Mod Art, Rio de Janeiro; De

Saisset Mus, Santa Clara, Calif; Minn Mus Art; Laguna Mus Art, Calif; and many others. *Exhib:* Solo exhibs, The Carlson Gallery, Hist Survey of Bay Area Abstr Expressionist Art in San Francisco, 1945-1960, Calif Palace of the Legion of Hon, 56-64, Walker Art Ctr, Minneapolis, Stanford Univ Gallery, Santa Barbara Mus Art, Charles Campbell Gallery, San Francisco, 81, 83, 85 & Bolles Gallery, San Francisco; 20-yr Retrospective, De Saisset Mus, 69, 40-yr Retrospective, Sonoma State Univ Gallery; Petit Palais Mus, Paris; Painting & Sculpture in California: of the Moden Era, Smithsonian Inst; NY World's Fair; San Francisco Mus Mod Art; Group exhib, Period of Exploration 1945-1950, Oakland Mus, Calif, 73; UC Davis, Directions in Bay Area Painting, A Survey of Three Decades; traveling exhib, San Francisco Mus Mod Art, Laguna Arts Mus, Calif & Nat Acad Design, 95; Dark Ave Armory Ann Int Fine Print Exhib, NY, Virginia Mus Modern Art Am Paintings, Petit Palais Mus, Paris, Mus of Modern Art, Sao Paulo British Mus, London, Nat Mus Am Art, Phillip Memorial Gallery, Washington, DC, Oakland Mus Art, Calif, Laguna Mus of Art, Calif, 98, The Menil Collection, Houston, Cleveland Mus Art, Mus Modern Art, San Francisco Mus Modern Art, Salander O'Reilly Gallery, NY; and others. *Teaching:* Stanford Univ; Calif Sch Fine Arts; Univ NMex, 60-65; Univ Santa Clara, 66-69; prof painting & chmn dept art, Sonoma State Univ, Calif, 69-, emer prof. *Awards:* Fel, Cummington Found, Mass, 42, Graham Found, Chicago, 57, Calif Arts Coun, 83, Maestro Award; Calif Arts Coun Award, Outstanding Calif Working Artist & Teacher; Tiffany Found, NY; Graham Found, Chicago. *Mem:* Nat Acad Design. *Media:* Oil, Monoprints. *Mailing Add:* 45 Island Ct Walnut Creek CA 94595-1213

KUHR, ALEXIS
EDUCATOR, ADMINISTRATOR
Exhib: Show Off, Minnesota Faculty Artists Off-Campus, Rochester Art Ctr, 2000; All Systems Go, Tweed Mus of Art, Duluth, 2000; Gallery Joe, Phila, 2002; 55 Mercer Gallery, NY, 2000, 2001, 2002, 2003; Banfill-Locke Center for the Arts, Fridley, Minnesota, 2002. *Pos:* Juror, Minneapolis Col of Design, 2000, Waubonsee Community Col, Sugar Grove, Ill, 2001, Katherine Nash Purchase award, Univ Minnesota, 2001; Bd dirs, Midway Initiative Gallery, Minneapolis, 2002. *Teaching:* Assoc prof, dept art chair, Univ Minnesota, currently. *Awards:* McKnight Summer Research Fellowship, 1999; Minnesota State Arts Bd Fellowship in Painting, 2001. *Mem:* Col Art Asn

KUITCA, GUILLERMO
PAINTER
b Buenos Aires, Argentina, 1961. *Exhib:* Solo exhibs include Galeria Lirolay, Buenos Aires, 1974, Elizabeth Franck Gallery, Knokke-Le-Zoute, Belgium, 1985, Kunsthalle Basel, Switzerland, 1990, Witte de With Ctr Contemp Art, Rotterdam, The Netherlands, 1990, Galleria Gian Enzo Sperone, Rome, 1990 & 1996, Mus Mod Art, NY, 1991, Mus Contemp Art Montreal, 1993, Sperone Westwater, NY, 1993, 1994, 1995, 1997, 1999, 2002, 2005, Wexner Ctr Arts, Columbus, Ohio, 1994, Mus Alejandro Otero, Caracas, Venezuela, 1997-98, Ctr Art Hélio Oiticica, Rio de Janeiro, Brazil, 1999, Arts Club Chicago, 1999, Fond Cartier, Paris, 2000, Galerie Hauzer & Wirth, Zurich, 2001, Galeria Cardi & Co, Milan, 2002, LA Louver, Venice, Calif, 2002, Galeria Enrique Guerrero, Horacio, Mexico, 2002, Nat Mus Centro de Arte Reina Sofia, Madrid, 2003, MALBA Coleccion Costantini, Buenos Aires, 2003, Sala Muralla Bizantina, Cartagena, Spain, 2004, Hauser & Wirth, London, 2005, Sperone Westware, 2010; group exhibs include Art of the Fantastic, Indianapolis Mus Art (traveling), 1987; New Image Painting, America's Soc, NY, 1989; XX Bienal San Paulo, Brazil, 1989; Metropolis, Martin Gropius Bau, Berlin, 1991; Mito y Magia de los '80s, Mus Art Contemp, Monterrey, Mex, 1991; Documenta IX, Kassel, Germany, 1992; Latin Am Artists of the 20th Century (traveling), 1992; Cartographies (traveling), 1993-95; Mapping, Mus Modern Art, NY, 1994, Tempo, 2002, Contemp Voices, 2005; Art from Argentina 1920-1994, Mus Modern Art, Oxford, Eng, 1994; About Place, Art Inst Chicago, 1995; Sleeper, Mus Contemp Art, San Diego, 1995; Kwangju Biennale, Kwangju Mus Contemp Art, Korea, 1995; Carnegie Internat, Carnegie Mus Art, Pittsburgh, 1995; Distemper, Hirshhorn Mus & Sculpture Garden, Washington, 1996; Contemp Projects, Los Angeles County Mus Art, 1997; 4e Lyon Contemp Art Biennale, Halle Tony Garnier, Lyon, France, 1997; Wounds, Moderna Mus, Stockholm, 1998; XXIV Bienal de São Paulo, Brazil, 1998; Reality & Desire, Juan Miró Found, Barcelona, 1999; Arte Americana, Mus Art della Citta di Ravenna, Italy, 2000; F(r)icciones, Nat Mus Centro de Arte Reina Sofia, Madrid, 2000; 7th Internat Istanbul Biennial, 2001; Content is a Glimpse, Timothy Taylor Gallery, London, 2001, Inaugural Group Show, 2003; Galerie Hauser & Wirth, Zurich, 2002; Drawing Mod, Cleveland Mus Art, 2003; Home, Sweet Home, Galleria Cardi, Milan, 2004, ...So Fresh, So Cool!, 2004; El Mus del Barrio, NY, 2004; Interting the Map, Tate Liverpool, 2006; Mapping Space, Miami Art Mus, 2005; The 80s: A Topology, Mus Serralves, Portugal, 2006; Constructing a Poetic Universe, Mus Fine Arts, Houston, 2007; 52nd Internat Art Exhib, Venice Biennale, 2007. *Media:* Mixed Media. *Dealer:* Sperone Westwater New York NY. *Mailing Add:* c/o Speone Westwater 257 Bowery New York NY 10002

KULOK, BARNEY
PHOTOGRAPHER
b New York, NY, 1981. *Study:* Bard Coll, Annandale-on-Hudson, NY, BA, 2004. *Exhib:* Solo exhibs include Woods Studio, Bard Coll, 2004, Barbara Walters Gallery, Heimbold Visual Arts Ctr, Sarah Lawrence Coll, Bronxville, NY, 2005, Simple Facts, Nicole Klagsbrun Gallery, NY, 2007; group exhibs include Woods Studio, Bard Coll, 2002; Walls N'Things, Nicole Klagsbrun Gallery, NY, 2005. *Awards:* Manhattan Community Arts Funt Grant, 2002. *Mailing Add:* 4711 Vernon Blvd Long Island City NY 11101

KUMAO, HEIDI ELIZABETH
PHOTOGRAPHER, KINETIC ARTIST
b California, 1964. *Study:* Univ Calif, Davis, BA&BS, 88; Sch Art Inst Chicago, MFA, 91. *Work:* Philadelphia Mus Art; Mus Fine Arts, Houston; Ariz State Univ Art Mus. *Comn:* Installation of cinema machines, Washington Project for the Arts, Washington, DC, 93. *Exhib:* solo shows, Washington Proj Arts, Washington, DC, 93, Art in General, NY, 93, Hallwalls Contemp Art Ctr, Buffalo, NY, 94, Contemp Arts Center, Cincinnati, 96, Alternative Mus, NY, 97, Introductions, Braunstein-Quay Gallery, San Francisco, 98, Center for Arts Yerba Buena Gardens, San Francisco, 99, Lisa Sette Gallery, Scottsdale, Ariz, 99 Three Rivers Art Gallery, Pittsburg, Pa, 2001, Creative Capital Found, Emerging Fields, NY, 2004, Wired Wear, Mott Community Coll Art Gallery, Flint, Mich, 2005; Houston Ctr Photog, Houston, 96; Ariz State Univ Art Mus, 96; The Alternative Mus, NY, 97; Joan Miro Found, Barcelona, 98; Yerba Buena Ctr Arts, San Francisco, 98; Zoetropia, Zeum, San Francisco, 99; Womentek, Peninsula Fine Arts Ctr, Va, 2000; Arrested Development, Castle Gallery, Coll New Rochelle, NY, 2002; Still, Ann Arbor Film Festival, 2003; Listen to Me, Detroit, 2003; Tart, Klein Gallery, Chicago, 2004; Only Skin Deep: Changing Visions of the American Self, Int Ctr Photog, NY, 2004; Thought Crimes: The Art of Subversion, Diverseworks, Houston, 2005; Brides of Frankenstein, San Jose Mus Art, 2005; Nat Acad Mus, NY, 2006; Zero One, San Jose, Calif, 2006; Pixilerations, Providence, RI, 2008; Wing Luke Asian Art Mus, Seattle, 2009; Museo Universitario Arte Contemp, Mex, 2009. *Teaching:* Vis asst prof photog, Univ Maryland Baltimore County, 1991-92; res fellow arts, Univ Mich, Ann Arbor, 1995-96, Roman J Witt vis asst prof, 2001-03; vis asst prof photog, Syracuse Univ, 1992-95, 1997-98; instr, sculpture dept, RI Sch Design, 1997; adj faculty, dept art and art history, City Col NY, 1997; assoc prof, Sch Art & Design, Univ Mich, 2008-. *Awards:* Philadelphia Mus Art Purchase Prize, Print Club, 91; Creative Capital Grant, 2002; AAUW Post Doc Fel, 2007-2008; Governors Award for Art & Cult, 2008; Guggenheim Fel, 2009. *Bibliog:* Ann Barclay Morgan (auth), Heidi Kumao: tied, Artpapers, 5/94; Martha McWilliams (auth), Transformers, Washington City Paper, 10/22/93; Elizabeth Licata (auth), Heidi Kumao, Artforum, 94; and others. *Mem:* Coll Art Asn. *Media:* Photography. *Mailing Add:* Univ Mich Sch Art and Design 2000 Bonisteel Blvd Ann Arbor MI 48109

KUMLER, KIPTON (CORNELIUS)
PHOTOGRAPHER, LECTURER
b Cleveland, Ohio, June 20, 1940. *Study:* Cornell Univ, BEE, 63, MEE, 67; Mass Inst Technol, with Minor White, 68-69; Harvard Univ, MBA, 69; spec study with Paul Caponigro, 70. *Work:* Mus Mod Art, Metrop Mus Art, NY; Mus Fine Arts, Boston; Victoria & Albert Mus, London; Int Mus Photog, George Eastman House, Rochester, NY. *Comn:* Essay on Danish Archit in Frederiksted, St Croix, Landmark Soc, 75-76; Photog Surv, Del Water Gap, Nat Endowment Arts, 76-77. *Exhib:* Recent Acquisitions, Boston Mus Fine Arts, 74; Addison Gallery Am Art, 74; solo exhibs, NJ Mus, Trenton, 78, Photog Place, Philadelphia, 79, Cronin Gallery, Houston, 80, Harcus Krakow Gallery, Boston, 80 & Worcester Art Mus, Mass, 80; and others. *Collection Arranged:* Traveling Exhib, Nat Endowment Arts Survey Work, NJ, 77-78. *Teaching:* Instr photog, Project Inc, Cambridge, Mass, 69-72; instr advan photog, Maine Photog Workshops, Rockport, 77-80. *Awards:* Nat Endowment Arts Photog Survey Grants, Peters Valley, NJ, 76-77 & Boston Hist Survey, 80-81; Mass Coun Arts Photog Fel, 77. *Publ:* Contribr, Camera, Lausanne, Switz, 70; contribr, Popular Photography, 75; auth, Kipton Kumler: Photographs, 75 & Plant Leaves, 78, David Godine; contribr, Print Letter, Zurich, 77. *Dealer:* Marcuse Pfeifer Gallery 825 Madison Ave New York NY 10016; Harcus Gallery 7 Newbury Boston MA 02116. *Mailing Add:* 28 Beaver Pond Rd Lincoln MA 01773

KUN, NEILA
PHOTOGRAPHER
b Philadelphia, Pa, Feb 8, 1951. *Study:* Tyler Sch Art, Temple Univ, BFA, 72, MFA, 94. *Work:* Bibliotheque Nat, Paris, France; NY Pub Libr; Ctr Photog, Woodstock, NY; Lehigh Univ; Villanova Univ, Pa; Philadelphia Mus Art; Brooks Art Mus, Memphis, Tenn; Mus Modern Art/Franklin Furnace/Artist Book Collection, New York; St Louis Mus Art; Montclair Art Mus, NJ; Getty Art Ctr; Newark Pub Libr, NJ; Bryn Mawr Coll, Scott Collection, Bryn Mawr, Pa; Historic Soc of Pa. *Comn:* Sculpted obverse coin of the realm, Guyana one penny piece, Franklin Mint, Pa, 77; sculpted coin for Queen Elizabeth's silver anniversary for Brit Virgin Island, Franklin Mint, Pa, 79. *Exhib:* Works on Paper (catalog), Beaver Coll, 89 & 94; Mems Show, Philadelphia Art Alliance, Pa, 90; solo exhib, Muse Gallery, Philadelphia, Pa, 93; group exhib, Fachhochschule Bielefeld Fachbereich Design, Ger, 93 & Berman Mus, Ursinus Coll, Collegeville, Pa, 94; Light Source and Subject in Photographs, Univ Ia Mus Art, 2006. *Teaching:* Instr, De Ctr Arts Wilmington, 2001, Phoenixville Art Ctr, 2003-2005 & Montgomery Co Community Coll West, 2003-2010; workshop paste papers, Scattergood Sch, West Branch, Iowa, 2004; juror, Reflections Prog, (grades 1-12), Owen Roberts Sch, 2004; instr, Montgomery County Community Coll, Bluebell, Pa, 2010-2012; Montgomery Co Comm Coll, 2010-2013. *Awards:* Abbington Photo Show, 87; Award of Merit, Artists Equity Show, 88 & 94; Griffiths Award, MainLine Ctr Arts, 94; Friends Award, Widner Univ, Chester, Pa, 2002; Window of Opportunity Award, Leeway Found, 2004; Purchase Award, Philadelphia Mus Art, Perkins Art Ctr, 2005. *Bibliog:* One of a Kind, Artist's Book Traveling Show (exhib catalog), Spanish/English ed, 96; Daphne Landis (auth), Speaking for Themselves, The Artist of South Eastern Pennsylvania, 2003. *Mem:* Soc Photog Educ; Friends Photog; Artists Equity; Print Club, Philadelphia. *Media:* Non-Silver Processes Cyanotype, Gum Bicromate Prints, Photography. *Publ:* Article, Popular Photog, 2/90; Art Matters, Celebrating Philadelphia's Artist Legacy, Woodmere Art Mus, 2000; coauth (with Ava Blitz & Jennifer Schmidt), Art & Community 4, Visual Art Residency Prog, Del Ctr for Contemp Art, 2001-2002. *Mailing Add:* PO Box 170 Birchrunville PA 19421

KUNATH, FRIEDRICH
PAINTER
b Chemnitz, Germany, 1974. *Study:* Peter Mertes Stipendium, Kunstverein Bonn, Bonn, Germany. *Exhib:* Solo exhibs include The Mod Inst, Glasgow, Scotland, 2000, Blum & Poe, Los Angeles, 2004, 2006, Andrea Rosen Gallery, New York, 2005, 2007, Aspen Art Mus, Aspen, CO, 2008; Group exhibs include Green Room, San Diego, 1995; Inaugural Group Show, Blum & Poe, Los Angeles, 2003; Ring of Saturn, Rockwell Gallery, London, 2004; Looking at Words: The Formal Use of Text in Mod & Contemp Works on Paper, Andrea Rosen Gallery, New York, 2005; Exile: New

York Is A Good Hotel, Broadway 1602, New York, 2005; Bonanza, Jack Tilton Gallery, New York, 2006; Life on Mars: Carnegie Int Exhib, Carnegie Mus Art, Pittsburgh, 2008. *Dealer:* Blum & Poe 2754 S La Cienega Blvd Los Angeles CA 90034. *Mailing Add:* Andrea Rosen Gallery 525 W 24th St New York NY 10011

KUNC, KAREN
PRINTMAKER, EDUCATOR
b Omaha, Nebr, Dec 15, 1952. *Study:* Univ Nebr-Lincoln, BFA, 75; Ohio State Univ, MFA, 77. *Work:* Nat Mus Am Art, Smithsonian Inst, Washington, DC; Libr Cong, Washington, DC; Worcester Art Mus, Mass; Mus Mod Art, NY; Nat Art Libr, Victoria & Albert Mus, London; and others. *Comn:* Woodcut print, Madison Print Club, 94; Suite of Prints, Zimmerli Art Mus, Rutgers Univ, 95; Artist Book, Nat Mus Women Arts, Washington, 96; Label Image, Benziger Winery Imagery Series, Glen Ellen, 96; Artist's book, Women's Studio Workshop, NY, 98. *Exhib:* Solo exhibs, Columbus, Ohio Mus Art, 83, Sheldon Mem Art Gallery, Lincoln, Nebr, 84, Joslyn Art Mus, 95, Gallery APA, Nagoya, Japan, 95, Davidson Galleries, Seattle, 95, Felix Jenewein Gallery, Kutna Hora, Czech Repub, 96, Hafnarborg Inst Cult & Fine Art, Iceland, 96 & Galleria Harmonia, Jyvaskyla, Finland, 96, Galerie Dumont 18, Geneva, Switz, 2000; Group exhibs, World Print III, San Francisco Mus Mod Art, 80; Tradition & Innovation 1500-1989, Calif Palace Legion of Honor, San Francisco, 89; National Mus Women in Arts, Washington, 1991, Elvehjem Mus Art, Univ Wisconsin, Madison, 93, 9th Seoul Int Print Biennale, 94; Recent Acquisitions, Nat Mus Am Art, 95; Dressing the Text: The Fine Press Artists Book, Art Mus Santa Cruz Co, 95; Ibizgraphic 96, Int Biennial, Mus Art Contemp, Spain, 96; Carved Block Prints in the Americas, Graphic Studio Gallery, Tampa, 96; Sightlines, Int Invitational, Edmonton, Can, 97; Int Print Exhib, Portland Mus Art, 97; 8th Int Biennial, Taipei Fine Art Mus, Taiwan, 97; The Sense of Touch, Women Printmakers, Ceres Gallery, NY, 97; 4th Sapporo Print Biennale, Hokkaido Mus Mod Art, Japan, 98; 2nd Int Triennial Graphic Art, Prague, 98; Between Nature and Culture: American Prints, Felix Jenewein Gallery, Kutna Hora, Czech Republic, 99; Relativities, Bankside Gallery, London, 2000; Int Artists Print Exhib, Hyndai Arts Centre Gallery, Ulsan, Korea, 2001; 5th Am Print Biennial, Marsh Art Gallery, Univ Richmond Mus, Va, 2002; 4th Egyptian Int Print Triennale, Cairo and Alexandria, Egypt, 2003; VII Int Art Triennale Majdanek, State Mus, Lublin, Poland, 2004; Biennale Int d'Estampes Contemporaine de Trois-Rivieres, Quebec, Can, 2005; Book as Art: Twenty years of Artists' Books, Nat Mus Women in Arts, Washington, DC, 2006; and others; Represented in permanent collections Mus of Modern Art, NY, National Mus Am Art, Smithsonian Insti, Washington, Libr Congress, Washington, Worcester (Mass) Art Mus, Sheldon Memorial Art Gallery, Univ Nebraska, National Art Libr, Victoria and Albert Mus, London, Mus Modern Art, New York City, Brooklyn Mus Art, Fogg Art Mus Harvard Univ. *Pos:* Gallery dir, Univ Nebr, 88-91; research fellow Kyoto Seika Univy, Japan, 93; visiting artist Icelandic Coll Arts & Crafts, Rekyavik, 95; dir Mid-Am print coun conf, Printmaking Relevance/Resonance, 2004. *Teaching:* Prof printmaking, Univ Nebr, Lincoln, 83-97; vis asst prof, Univ Calif, Berkeley, 87; vis artist/teacher, Carleton Col, Northfield, Minn, 89; vis prof, Univ Mich, Ann Arbor, 99; artist-in-residence, Nagasawa Art Park, Tsuna, Japan, 2001; Willa Cather prof, Univ Nebr, 2003-. *Awards:* Sponsors Prize, 5th Sapporo Int Print Exhib, Japan, 2000; Artist of Yr Award, Nebr Gov Arts Award, 2000; Boston Printmakers NAm Print Exhib, 2000; Purchase award, Bradley Nat Print & Drawing Exhib, 2001; Lincoln Arts Coun Award, 2003; Sally R Bishop Master Faculty Fel, Ctr for Book Arts, 2005; Milw Art Mus Award, 2006; and others. *Bibliog:* Mendelowitz, Faber, Wakeham (co-auth), A Guide to Drawing, Wadsworth/Thomson Learning, 2005; Bob Nugent (auth), Imagery: Art for Wine, Imagery Estate Winery Art Collection, 2005; Hilda Raz (auth), Visionary Evidence, Davidson Galleries, 2005. *Mem:* Nat Acad NY; Soc Printmakers; Coll Art Asn; Nebr Art Asn; Calif Soc Printmakers. *Media:* Woodcut, Artist Books. *Collection:* Mirror of the Wood: A Century of the Woodcut Print in Finland, 2005. *Dealer:* Atrium Gallery 4729 McPherson Ave St Louis MO 63108; Davidson Galleries 313 Occidental Ave S Seattle WA 98104; Robischon Gallery 1740 Wazee St Denver CO 80202. *Mailing Add:* 1557 N 32nd Rd Avoca NE 68307

KUNCE, SAMM
CONCEPTUAL ARTIST, SCULPTOR
b Los Angeles, Calif, Oct 16, 1956. *Study:* San Francisco Art Inst, 86; Mason Gross Sch of the Arts; Bard Col, MFA, 89. *Work:* Mus Mod Art, NY; Mus Contemp Art, Chicago; Bauhaus Kunstlerbarten, Weimar, Ger; Mus Mod Art, Tusla, Slovenia. *Comn:* outdoor earthwork, Polish Cen Contemp Art, Oronsko, Poland, 98; outdoor earthwork, Bauhaus Univ, Weimer, Ger, 99; outdoor earthwork, Sacred Heart Univ, Fairfield, Conn, 2000; outdoor earthwork, S Eastern Cen Contemp Art, Winston-Salem, NC, 2000. *Exhib:* Living with Contemp Art, Aldrich Mus Contemp Art, Ridgefield, Conn, 95; Configura 2, Fishmarket Gallery, Ehrfurt, Ger, 95; Botanica, Tweed Mus (traveling), Duluth, Minn, 99; Samm Kunce, Thomas Ruben Gallery, Ger, 99; Samm Kunce: Dune, John Gibson Gallery, NY, 99; LIfe Cycles, S Eastern Cen Contemp Art, Winston-Salem, NC, 2000; Garden & Memory, Medici Palace, Rome, Italy, 2000; Samm Kunce: Rough, Gallery Contemp Art, Fairfield, Conn, 2000. *Awards:* Louis Comfort Tiffany Award, 97. *Bibliog:* Susan Harris (auth), Samm Kunce, Art in Am, 9/95; Susanne Altmann (auth), Samm Kunce, Kunstforum, 7/99; Tom McDonough (auth), Samm Kunce@John Gibson, Art in Am, 11/99. *Dealer:* John Gibson Gallery 568 Broadway New York NY 10012. *Mailing Add:* 25 Pierrepont St Apt 9 Brooklyn NY 11201-3383

KUNIN, JULIA
SCULPTOR, VIDEO ARTIST
Study: Wellesley Coll, Mass, BA, 1984; Rutgers Univ, NJ, MFA, 1993. *Exhib:* Ann Small Works Show, Sculpture Ctr, New York, 1988; Vulgar Realism, Hallwalls Contemp Art Ctr, Buffalo, 1989; Material Obsession, Soho Ctr for Visual Artists, New York, 1990; Six East Coast Sculptors, Colburn Gallery, Univ Vt, 1992; Crosscurrents of Influence, Brattleboro Mus, Vt, 1993; Pieces of Eight, Marymount Manhattan Coll, New York, 1996; The Grammar of Ornament, Memphis Coll Art, Tenn, 2001; Corporal Identity, Body Language, Mus Art & Design, New York, 2003. *Awards:* State Fel, NJ State Coun Arts, 1995; t Studio Ctr Fel, 1996; Marie Walsh Sharpe Art Found Grant, 2001; Pollock-Krasnfer Found Grant, 2008. *Bibliog:* Amra Brooks (auth), Must See Art, LA Weekly, 12/13/2006; Sabine Rothman (auth), Divine Inspiration, House and Garden Mag, 9/2006. *Dealer:* Greenberg Van Doren Gallery 730 Fifth Ave New York NY 10019

KUNIN, MYRON
COLLECTOR
Pos: CEO, vchm bd dirs, Regis Corp, Edina, Minn; pres, Curtis Squire Venture Capital Inc. *Mem:* Minn Inst Arts (lifelong trustee). *Collection:* Collector of old masters & contemporary art. *Mailing Add:* Regis Corporation 7201 Metro Blvd Edina MN 55439-2103

KUNSCH, LOUIS
PAINTER, COLLAGE ARTIST
b Bronx, NY, Dec, 1937. *Study:* Art Students League New York, 61-65, Sch Visual Arts, NY, 70-72. *Work:* Queens Borough Community Coll, New York; Printmaking Workshop, New York; Libr Cong, Capital Heights, Md. *Exhib:* Ball State Univ, Ind; Jamaica Arts Ctr; Berkshire Mus, Mass; Purdue Univ, Ind; solo exhibs, Main Street Gallery, Brewster, NY, 75, Long Beach Libr, 77, The Exhibitionists, Jamaica, 77, PS 1, Long Island City, 79, Queens Borough Libr, New York, 91 & 94 & LaGuardia Community Coll, NY, 92; Works on Paper, Gallery BAI, 95; Queens Mus Art, New York, 2000; Ink & Watercolor Works on Paper, Franklin 54 Gallery, New York, 2007. *Pos:* Bd dirs, Artists Talk On Art, New York. *Awards:* Ford Found Scholar, 64-65. *Mem:* Art Students League. *Media:* Ink & Watercolor on paper. *Dealer:* Franklin 54 Gallery 526 West 26 St New York NY

KUNSTLER, MORTON
PAINTER, ILLUSTRATOR
b New York, NY, Aug 28, 1931. *Study:* Brooklyn Col; Univ Calif, Los Angeles; Pratt Inst, cert, 50. *Hon Degrees:* Dr Fine Arts, Shenandoah Univ, Winchester, VA, 99. *Work:* USAF Mus, Boulder, Colo; San Mateo Co Historical Mus, Calif; US House Reps, US Senate & The White House, Washington, DC; Lowie Mus Anthrop, Berkeley, Calif; Nassau Co Mus Fine Arts, Roslyn, NY; Mus Am Hist, Smithsonian Inst, Washington, DC; Booth Western Art Mus, Cartersville, Ga; Nat Civil War Mus, Harrisburg, Pa. *Comn:* Paintings, National Geographic, Washington, DC, 66-69; six paintings, American Cyanamid, NJ, 71-76; four paintings, NY Bank for Savings, NY, 76; seven paintings, Rockwell Int, Pa, 80; Crum & Forster, 80; four paintings, US Army War Coll, Carlisle, PA, 89-06 ; Judge Advocate General LCS Alumni Asn, Va, 2011; numerous private commissions; Washington's Crossing, Mr and Mrs Thomas Suozzi, 2011. *Exhib:* Solo exhibs, Hammer Galleries, NY, 77, 79, 81, 82, 85, 86, 89, 92, 93, 95, 98, 2000, 2003, 2004 & 2006, USN Mem Mus, Washington, DC, 79 & 82 & Pittsburgh Ctr Arts, Pa, 81; Mus Westward Expansion, St Louis, 89; Dunnegan Gallery, Bolivar, Mo, 91; Nat Military Park, Gettysburg, 92; Hall Valor Mus, New Market Battlefield, Va, 92; NC Mus Hist, Raleigh, 95; Nassau County Mus Art, Roslyn, NY, 98, 2006, 2010-2011; Mus of the Confederacy, Richmond, VA, 2000; Nat Civil War Mus, Harrisburg, PA, 2002; Booth Western Art Mus, Cartersville, GA, 2005 & 2011; and others. *Awards:* Henry Timrod, Southern Culture Award from the Order of the Stars & Bars; Jefferson Davis, Southern Heritage Award; Pratt Inst Alumni Achievement Award. *Bibliog:* Long Island Jour, NY Times, 9/2/84, Crossing the Delaware, More Accurately, 12/23/2011; By George, Hes Got it! Newsday, 12/27/2011; Civil War Anniversary: I Feel That You're There: Mort Kunstler Tries to Convey Emotions of Conflict in Paintings, Atlanta Jour Constitution, 4/12/2011. *Media:* Oil, Watercolor. *Publ:* Images of the Civil War, Gramercy Books, 92; Gettysburg, Turner Publ, 93; The Am Spirit, Rutledge Hill Press, 94; Jackson and Lee-Legends in Gray, Rutledge Hill Press, 95; Images of the Old West, Park Lane Press, 96; Mort Kunstler's The Civil War, The North and The South, 97; Mort Kunstler's Old West-Cowboys and Indians, 98; The Confederate Spirit, Rutledge Hill Press, 2000; Gods & Generals, Greenwich Workshop Press, 2002; The Civil War Art of Mort Kunstler, Greenwich Workshop Press, 2004; Civil War Paintings of Mort Kunstler, Vol 1-4, Cumberland House, 2006-08; For US the Living-The Civil War in Paintings and Eyewitness Accounts, The Art of Mort Kunstler, Sterling, 2010. *Dealer:* Mort Kunstler Inc Cove Neck Rd Oyster Bay NY 11771. *Mailing Add:* Cove Neck Rd Oyster Bay NY 11771

KUNZ, SANDRA THURBER
PAINTER
b London, Conn. *Study:* Principia col; Art Students League. *Work:* Monmouth Mus; Morris Mus of Arts & Sci; Bergen Mus of Art & Sci; AT&T; Nabisco World Hq. *Exhib:* Nat Acad of Design, 90; Monmouth Co Arts Coun Juried Show, 95; New London Art Soc and Gallery, 96. *Awards:* The Tucker, Anthony & RL Day Award, Garden State Watercolor Soc; Shrewsbury State Bank Award, NJ Watercolor Soc; Watercolor Award, Long Beach Island, 99. *Mem:* NJ Watercolor Soc; Garden State Watercolor Soc; Princeton Art Asn; Ocean Co Artists' Guild; Monmouth Co Arts Coun. *Media:* Miscellaneous Media. *Publ:* article, The Best of Watercolor, 97. *Mailing Add:* 249 Daffodil Dr Freehold NJ 07728

KUOPUS, CLINTON
PAINTER, VISUAL ARTIST
b Detroit, Mich, Dec 8, 1942. *Study:* US Navy Photog Intelligence Sch, 63; Eastern Mich Univ, Mich State Univ, Wayne State Univ, Kent State Univ. *Work:* Mich Educ Asn; Hiram Coll, Ohio; J Walter Thompson Advert Agency; Lake Erie Coll Permanent Collection; Pub Collection, Cedar City, Utah. *Exhib:* Source Detroit Exhib, Cranbrook Mus Art, Bloomfield Hills, Mich, 76; May Show Exhibs, Cleveland Mus Art, Ohio; Butler Inst Am Art, Youngstown, Ohio, 79; 38th Cedar City Nat, Utah, 79; Print Collaboration-Stewart and Stewart, Detroit Inst Art 91 & Kansas City Art Mus, 91-92; Berkowitz Gallery, Univ Mich, 2009. *Pos:* Photog interpreter, US Navy, 62-66; fac dir exhibs, Parsons Sch Design, 83-2004. *Teaching:* Photog intelligence training petty off,

US Navy, 64-66; instr visual art, Bloomfield Hills Schs, Mich, 70-75; asst prof art, Lake Erie Coll, Painesville, Ohio, 75-80, 82-83; adj fac, Youngstown State Univ, 80-82 & Univ Akron, 81-82; foundations fac, Parsons Sch Design, dir of exhib, 83-2004, faculty in illusr, painting, and drawing. *Media:* Multimedia. *Dealer:* Stewart & Stewart Bloomfield Hills MI; Cass Lace Studio. *Mailing Add:* 1790 Poppleton Dr West Bloomfield MI 48324-1149

KURAHARA, TED N
PAINTER, EDUCATOR
b Seattle, Wash, July 16, 1925. *Study:* St Louis Sch Fine Arts, Washington Univ, with Paul Burlin, BFA, 51; Bradley Univ, Peoria, Ill, with Leon Engers, MA, 52. *Work:* Museo Civico, Taverna, Italy; Univ Sidney, Australia; Brooklyn Mus; Huntington Gallery, WVa; Malmo Konsthal, Malmo, Sweden; Columbia Univ, New York; Pratt Inst, Brooklyn, NY; Des Moines Art Ctr; Torgiano Civic Mus, Italy; Nat Gallery of Australia; Metropolitan Mus, NY. *Comn:* Comune Di Torgiano, Italy. *Exhib:* Woodside-Braseth Gallery, Seattle, 80; Anders Tornberg, Lund, Sweden, 81, 84, 91 & 98; Leif Stahle Gallery, Paris, France, 87; Anita Shapolsky Gallery, New York, 87-94; Kiyo Higashi Gallery, Los Angeles, Calif, 95, 97, 99 & 2002; Pardo-Lattuada Gallery, New York, 2002-05; Robert Pardo, Artefact Gallery, Milan, Italy & Zurich, Switz; Am Abstract Asn Group Shows, 2005 & 2007; Walter Randel Gallery, New York, 2007 & 2009; Gallery Astley, Sweden, 2009. *Pos:* Dir, Springfield Art Asn, Ill, 53-55 & Emily Lowe Gallery Hofstra Univ, Long Island, NY. *Teaching:* Prof art, Grad Fine Art, Pratt Inst, Brooklyn, NY, 70-2006, chairperson painting & drawing dept; 80-83, emeritus prof, 2008; retired, 2006. *Awards:* Yaddo Fel, 78; Guggenheim Found Grant, 85; Nat Endowment Arts Grant, 86. *Bibliog:* Donald B Kuspit (auth), Kuraharas Paintings, 84; J Sans (auth), A propos du travail de Kurahara, L'oeilk, Paris; Corinne Robins, Panel Paper, Asia Soc, New York, 2000; catalog essay Robert Lee, Asian Am Arts Ctr, New York, 2000; Janet Kopolos (auth), rev, Art in Am, 2008; Donald B Kuspit, Facing the Wall, Jonathan Goodman Rev, Artcritical.com, 2009. *Mem:* Abstract Am Artists. *Media:* Acrylic, All Media. *Dealer:* Mi Chou Gallery New York NY; Kiyo Higashi Gallery Los Angeles CA; Anders Tornberg Gallery Lund Sweden; Pardo-Lattuada Gallery New York NY; Artefact Gallery Milan Italy & Zurich Switz; Walter Randel Gallery New York NY; Leif Stahl Paris. *Mailing Add:* 78 Greene St New York NY 10012

KURHAJEC, JOSEPH A
SCULPTOR
b Racine, Wis, Oct 13, 1938. *Study:* Univ Wis, BS, 60, MFA, 62. *Work:* New Sch Social Res, NY; Espanol Mus Contemp Art, Madrid, Spain; Mus Mod Art, NY; Chicago Art Inst; Walker Art Ctr, Minneapolis, Minn. *Comn:* Bronze cone, Allan Stone, Purchase, NY, 71; bronze sculpture, Norman Shaifer, Brooklyn Heights, NY, 71. *Exhib:* Am Fedn Art Traveling Exhib, 64; Sculpture Ann, Whitney Mus Am Art, NY, 64, Young Am, 65; Espanol Mus Contemp Art, 69; Ten Independents, Guggenheim Mus, NY, 72; Basel Art, 76. *Pos:* owner, dir, Treadwell Mus Fine Art, NY. *Teaching:* Asst prof, Cornell Univ, 65-66; asst prof, Newark Sch Indust & Fine Art, 67-69; asst prof, Univ Wis-Stout, 71-73, State Univ NY, New Paltz, 73-74, Lo Studiolo, Rome, 74-83. *Awards:* Int Fur Designers Award, 83. *Mem:* Sculptors Guild, NY. *Dealer:* Treadwell Museum Fine Art Treadwell NY 13846. *Mailing Add:* 178 Rue Raymond Losserand Apt 3104 Paris 75014 France

KURLANDER, HONEY W
PAINTER, INSTRUCTOR
b Brooklyn, NY. *Study:* Parsons Sch Design; NY Univ; Pratt Inst, Brooklyn, BA. *Work:* De Seversky Conf Ctr, Greenvale, NY; Dietz Mus, Wasserberg, Ger; C W Post Coll Art Ctr, Brookville, NY; Gregory Mus Traveling Collection, Hicksville, NY; Reddon Collection, Paris, France. *Comn:* Western scenes of horses & oil drilling, Rotan-Mosle, Tulsa, Okla, 81; Waldorf Astoria, NY & Stanford Ct, Calif, Hospitality Valuation Serv Inc, Mineola, NY, 83-87; Roslyn, Turn of the Century (2 murals), Jolly Fisherman, Roslyn, NY, 84; Fulton Street Ferry Landing (mural), Thomas M Quinn & Sons Inc, Astoria, NY, 85; Mural, Comn by Friends Oyster Bay, E Norwich Libr. *Exhib:* Solo exhib, Adelphi Univ, Alumni House Gallery, Garden City, NY, 77 ; Exposition Intercontinental, The Palace, Monaco, 65; Traveling Art Exhib, Gregory Mus, Hicksville, NY, 70-; Long Island Artists, The Heckscher Mus, Huntington, NY, 66-68; First Int Art Competition, Am Artist Mag, Marion, Ohio, 78; NLAPW Nat Exhib, Goethe Hall, Sacramento, Calif, 78; Exhib of Oil Paintings, Salmagundi Club, NY, 78; Celebration of the Arts, Nassau Mus Fine Art, Roslyn, NY, 83; NLAPW Nat Biennial, Arlington, Va, 2000; 75th Ann Int Exhib of Fine Art, Miniature Painters Sculptors & Gravers Soc of Washington DC, 2008. *Collection Arranged:* Dietz Mus, Wasserberg, Germany; Grumbacher Collection, NYC. *Pos:* Freelance textile designer, 49-58; Freelance children's bk illustr, 50-60. *Teaching:* Instr of painting, E Meadow High Sch, New York, 58-60 & Kurlander Studio, Old Westbury, NY, 59-2000. *Awards:* Best of Show, Malverne Artists 28th Ann, Greenwich Savings Bank, 72; Best of show, excellence & first prize, NLAPW, 78-2000; Best of show, NY State Juried Art Exhib, Lever House, 87; Best of show, C W Post, 90. *Bibliog:* Tom Cullen (auth), Looking back-the art of success, Long Island Com Rev, 9/72; Jeanne Paris (auth), Many faces of nature, Newsday, 9/79; Malcolm Preston (auth), Two definitely modern realists, Newsday, 4/84. *Mem:* Nat League Am Penwomen; Salmagundi Club; Art League Nassau Co. *Media:* Acrylic, Oil. *Publ:* auth, Best of Flower Painting, North Light Books, 98. *Dealer:* Robley Gallery Old Northern Blvd Roslyn NY 11576; Garden City Galleries Ltd 923 Franklin Ave Garden City NY 11530. *Mailing Add:* 6185 Wooded Run Dr Columbia MD 21044

KURTZ, RICHARD
PAINTER
b. Newark, NJ, Nov 15, 1955. *Study:* Kenyon Coll, BA, 77; attended, Instituto de Artes Plasticas Taxco, Mex, 81-82; studied photog with Tetsu Okuhara, NY, 80, drawing with Phyliss Yampolsky, NY, 86. *Work:* de Young Mus, San Francisco, Calif; Ark Art Ctr, Little Rock, Ark; Thea Found, Little Rock, Ark; Clinton Found, Little Rock, Ark; Mus of Everything, London; David Lisboa Mini Mus Contemporary Art, Barcelona, Spain. *Exhib:* Hero, Ctr Contemp Art, Santa Fe, NMex, 2005; Diane and Sandy Besser Collection, de Young Mus, San Francisco, Calif, 2007; The End Game, Goldleaf Gallery, Santa Fe, NMex, 2009; Art Across Am, Clinton Lib, Little Rock, Ark, 2009; New Acquisitions, Ark Art Ctr, Little Rock, Ark, 2010; Paris Outsider Art Fair, Paris, 2013; NYC Outsider Art Fair, NYC, 2014; Roberta Britto Gallery, Sao Paolo, 2014; Faces and Figures in Self Art, Frances Lehman Loeb Art Ctr, Vassar Coll, NY, 2014. *Awards:* Artist Fellowship, NYC, 2012; Finalist, Erie Hoffer Book awards, 2011. *Bibliog:* Elizabeth Cook-Romero (auth), What Makes a Hero, Santa Fe New Mexican, 2005; Rebecca Chastende de Gery (auth), Drawing Discoveries, Raw Vision Mag, 2006, Seventh Heaven, Santa Fean Mag, 2007; Jon Carver (auth), End Game, The Mag, 2009; Douglas Fairchild (auth), Richard Kurtz End Game, Santa Fe New Mexican, 2009. *Media:* Oil, Acrylic, Mixed Media. *Publ:* auth, Seventh Heaven: The Alchemy of Richard Kurtz, Santa Fean Mag, 2007; contbr, Diane and Sandy Besser Collection (book), de Young Mus, 2007; auth, Richard Kurtz End Game, The Mag, 2009, Santa Fe New Mexican, 2009; auth, Heartbreak (book), Burning Books, 2010. *Dealer:* Koelsch Gallery 703 Yale St Houston TX 77007; Ricart Gallery 3900 NE 1st St Miami Fl 33137; Laura Steward Projects 664 Don Gaspar Ave Santa Fe NM 87505. *Mailing Add:* PO Box 9525 Santa Fe NM 87504

KURTZ, STEVE
EDUCATOR, ADMINISTRATOR
Study: PhD (Interdisciplinary Humanities). *Pos:* Founding mem, Critical Art Ensemble (CAE). *Teaching:* Assoc prof art, Carnegie Mellon Univ, formerly; with Univ Buffalo-SUNY, 2002-, prof, dept chair, currently. *Mailing Add:* University of Buffalo Department of Art 202 Center for the Arts North Campus Buffalo NY 14260-6010

KURTZMAN, TODJI
SCULPTOR
b San Francisco, 1970. *Study:* Univ Calif Santa Barbara, BA, 1993; NY Acad Art, 1998; San Francisco Acad Art, 1996. *Exhib:* Exhibs include Wires in Dynamic Movement, Silver Twinkie Gallery, San Francisco, 1996; Bronze Brass Silver and Flesh, Sculpture & Photography Exhibition, Go-Gallery, Portland, Ore, 2002; Are You Gandhi?, NUE Gallery, Portland, Ore, 2004; Am Dance Guild's Global Dance Today, Merce Cunningham Dance Space, New York, 2004; New Orleans Jazz Festival 2005, 2007; Hellfire Weenie Roast, Mark Woolley Gallery, Portland, 2006; Sacred Geometry, Water in the Desert, Portland, Ore, 2007. *Awards:* Proj Grant Recipient, Regional Arts & Culture Coun, Portland, Ore, 2003; George Sugarman Found Grant, 2005, 2007; Puffin Grant, Teaneck, NJ, 2008

KURYLUK, EWA
PAINTER, SCULPTOR
b Cracow, Poland, May 5, 1946. *Study:* Acad Fine Arts, Warsaw, MFA & MA, 70. *Work:* Biblio Nat, Paris; Graphische Sammlung Albertina, Vienna, Austria; Nat Mus, Warsaw, Poland; Kettle's Yard Mus, Cambridge, Eng; Bass Mus Art, Miami Beach, Fla. *Comn:* Wall piece, Nat Humanities Ctr, Res Triangle Park, NC, 89. *Exhib:* Textile Sculpture, Mus des Beaux Arts, Lausanne, Switz, 85; 40th Int Festival, Richard Demarco Gallery Edinburgh, 86; Membranes of Memory, Centro de Arte y Comunicacion, Buenos Aires, 86; Fourth Int Triennale Drawing, Mus Archit, Wroclaw, Poland, 88; Polish Women Artists and the Avant-garde, Nat Mus Women in Arts, Washington, 91; and others. *Pos:* Ed, Cahiers Litteraires, Paris, 82- & Formations, 83-, Private Arts, 92-. *Teaching:* Prof acad film, Lodz, 79-80, Inst Applied Theater Sci, Giesseh, WGer, 86, New Sch, New York, 88-, Univ Calif, San Diego, 92 & New York Univ, 94-. *Awards:* Rockefeller Fel, Nat Humanities Ctr, 88; Bronze Medal, 4th Int Triennale Drawing, 88; Asian Cult Coun Fel Japan, 91. *Bibliog:* Jan Kott, E White & E Grabska (coauths), The fabric of memory, Ewa Kuryluk: Cloth works 1978-1987, Formations, 87; Ewa Kuryluk, Drawings and Installations, ZPAP, Warsaw, 94; Janet Koplos (auth), Art and Textiles, Art in Am, 2/96. *Mem:* Int Art Critics Asn; PEN. *Media:* All Media, Cloth. *Mailing Add:* 504 W 110 St Apt 3A New York NY 10025

KURZ, DIANA
PAINTER, EDUCATOR
b Vienna, Austria; US citizen. *Study:* Brandeis Univ, BA (fine arts, cum laude); Columbia Univ, MFA (painting). *Work:* Bezirks-Mus Josefstadt Vienna, Austria; US Holocaust Mus, Washington, DC; Rowan Univ, NJ; Corcoran Gallery Art, Washington, DC; Rose Art Mus, Brandeis Univ, Mass; Brooklyn Botanic Garden, Brooklyn, NY; Jewish Mus, Vienna, Austria; Historisches Mus der Stadt Wien, Vienna, Austria; Yad Vashem Mus, Jerusalem, Israel. *Comn:* Mural, comn by Howard Finkelstein, NY, 85. *Exhib:* Solo Exhibs: Snug Harbor Cult Ctr, 82; Rider Col, 84; Alex Rosenberg Gallery, NY, 84; Palais de Justice, Aix-En-Provence, France, 86; Brooklyn Botanic Garden, 89; Mercer Co Community Col, 90; Thomas Ctr Gallery, Gainesville, Fla, 91; Austrian Consulate Gen, NY, 95; Santa Fe Gallery, Gainesville, Fla, 98; Trenton City Mus, NJ, 2002; Holocaust Mus & Study Ctr, Spring Valley, NY, 2003; St Joseph's Col, Patchogue, NY, 2003; Show Walls, NYC, 2008, Suffolk Co Community Coll, Long Island, 2010, Kingsborough Community Coll, NY, 2012, Palais Porcia, Vienna, 2015; Group Exhibs: Bergen Mus Art, NJ, 93; Trenton City Mus, NJ, 94; Clymer Mus, Wash, 95; Nat Mus Women Arts, 97; Jacqueline Casey Hudgens Ctr for the Arts, Ga, 2004; Tucson Mus d'Art, 2007; Morris Mus, NJ, 2008; Albany Inst Hist & Art, NY, 2009; Philadelphia Mus Jewish Art, 2010; Rowan Univ Art Gallery, 2011. *Teaching:* Lectr drawing, Philadelphia Col Art, 68-73; adj lectr art, Queens Col, NY, 71-76; vis prof art, Pratt Inst, 73; vis asst prof, Univ Colo, 78; vis asst prof art, State Univ NY Stony Brook, 79; Brooklyn Mus, 75; vis artist painting, Va Commonwealth Univ, 80; vis artist painting, Cleveland Inst Art, 80-81, Sch Art Inst Chicago, 87, Oxbow Sch Art, Mich, 88 & Vermont Studio Ctr, 90. *Awards:* Fulbright Grant, 65-66; Am Ctr Residency, Paris, 85-86. *Bibliog:* Lawrence Alloway (auth), catalog, Queens Col, 72; Lawrence Campbell, Art in Am, 5/84; Arlene Raven

(auth), catalog, Seton Hall Univ, 2002; Evelyn Torton Beck (auth), Feminist Studies, Spring 2009. *Mem:* NY Artists Equity Asn (bd dir). *Media:* Oil, Watercolor. *Publ:* Mother Massage, Dell Publ, 92; East meets west (article), Am Artist Mag, 12/92; cover illusr Attitudes Mag, Jewish Fed Pub, NJ, spring 2000. *Mailing Add:* 152 Wooster St New York NY 10012

KUSAMA, YAYOI
SCULPTOR, PAINTER
b Matsumoto City, Japan, 1929; US citizen. *Study:* Art Students League, NY, 1957; Kyoto Arts & Crafts Sch, Japan, 1959. *Work:* Chrysler Mus, Provincetown, Mass; Stedelijk Mus, Amsterdam. *Exhib:* Solo exhibs, Fuji Television Gallery, Tokyo, 1984, Missoni Boutique, Yura Kucho-Marion Seibu, Tokyo, 1985, Tamagawa-Takashimaya, Tokyo, 1986, Musee Municipal Dole, 1987, Soul Burning Flashes, Fuju Gallery, 1988, Ctr Int Contemp Art, NY, 1990 & Oxford Mus, Eng, 1990; Le Japon des Avantgarde, Centre Georges Pompidou, Paris, 1986; Japanese Art Today, San Diego Mus, 1986; Opening Show, Meguro Mus Art, Tokyo, 1987; Objet, Tsukashin Hall, Osaka, 1987; Second Int Contemp Art Fair, Los Angeles, 1988; Chicago Int Art Expos, 1988; Art-Kites Traveling Show, 1988-92; Mus Contemp Art, Finland, 1995; Ronald Feldman Gallery, NY, 1996; Victoria Miro Gallery, London, 2000; Geenberg Van Doren Gallery, NY, 2006. *Pos:* Pres & found, Japan Ed Co, 1977-. *Awards:* Praemium Imperiale Prize, Japan Art Asn, 2006. *Publ:* auth: Manhattan Suicide Addict, 1978, Christopher Homosexual Brothel, 1983, Lost in Swapland, 1992; Woodstock Phallus Cutter, 1988; Publ, Between Heaven and Earth, 1988; contribr articles to mag and newspapers. *Dealer:* Paula Cooper Gallery 534 W 21st St NY City NY 10011

KUSNERZ, PEGGY ANN F
EDITOR, HISTORIAN
b Detroit, Mich, Jan 12, 1947. *Study:* Univ Mich, BA (art hist), 71, MLS, 71, MA (Am cult), 82, PhD (Am cult), 92. *Collection Arranged:* Images of Old Age 1790 to Present (coauth, catalog), SITES Exhib, 79. *Pos:* Head librn exten serv & mus librn, Univ of Mich, head art, archit libr, 80-94, asst to dean, 94-97, lectr, 94-99, assoc editor, History of Photography, 01. *Teaching:* Art: Hist of Photog, Am Culture: Res Methods, Univ of Mich. *Mem:* Coll Art Asn; Am Studies Asn; Soc Photog Educators. *Media:* Photography. *Res:* History of photography. *Interests:* History of photography & panoramic photography. *Publ:* Ed, Architecture Library of the Future, Ann Arbor Univ of Mich Press, 89. *Mailing Add:* 804 Sycamore Ann Arbor MI 48104

KUTNER, JANET
CRITIC, WRITER
b Sept 20, 1937; US citizen. *Study:* Stanford Univ, 55-57; Southern Meth Univ, BA, 59. *Pos:* art critic, Dallas Morning News, 70-. *Awards:* Art Critics Award, Nat Endowment Arts, 76-77; Art Critics Fel, Nat Gallery Art, 91; Legend Award, Dallas Ctr for Contemp Art, 2005. *Mem:* Am Asn Mus; Int Coun Mus; Art Table. *Publ:* Coauth, David McManaway, Contemp Art Mus, Houston, 73; auth, James Surls, Tyler Mus Art, 74; various reviews of Texas exhibits for Artnews Mag, 75-. *Mailing Add:* Dallas Morning News Communs Ctr Dallas TX 75265

KUWAYAMA, GEORGE
CURATOR, HISTORIAN
b New York, NY, 1925. *Study:* Williams Col, BA; Inst Fine Arts, NY Univ; Univ Mich, MA, PhD. *Collection Arranged:* Arts Treasures from Japan (ed & auth, catalog), 65; Contemporary Japanese Prints (auth, catalog), 72; Ceramics of Southeast Asia (auth, brochure), 72; Ancient Ritual Bronzes of China (auth, catalog), 76; Chinese Jade from Southern California Collections (auth, catalog), 77; Chinese Ceramics: The Heeramaneck Collection (auth, catalog), 73; The Joy of Collecting: Far Eastern Art from the Lidow Collection (auth, catalog), 80; The Bizarre Imagery of Yoshitoshi (co-auth, catalog), 80; Far Eastern Lacquer (auth, catalog), 82; Japanese Ink Painting (ed & auth, catalog), 85; Shippo: The Art of Enameling in Japan (auth, catalog), 87; The Quest for Eternity: The Sculptural Development of Ceramic Funerary Figures in China (ed & contribr), 87; Imperial Taste: Chinese Ceramics from the Percival David Foundation, The significance of Chinese Ceramics in the East and West (ed & contribr), 89; Ancient Mortuary Traditions of China (ed), 91; New Perspectives on the Art of Ceramics in China (ed), 92; Chinese Ceramics in Colonial Mexico (auth, catalog), 97. *Pos:* Cur Oriental art, Los Angeles Co Mus Art, 59-69, sr cur Far Eastern art, 69-96, sr cur emer, 96-. *Teaching:* Instr Chinese painting, Univ Calif, Los Angeles, 62; instr Far Eastern painting, Univ Southern Calif, 63; Univ Hawaii, 2000. *Awards:* Freer Fel, Univ Mich, 55; Hackney Fel, Am Oriental Soc, 56; Inter-Univ Fel, Ford Found, 57. *Mem:* Asn Asian Studies; Chinese Art Soc; Japan Soc; Int House Japan; Coll Art Asn. *Res:* Far Eastern art and archaeology. *Publ:* Ed & contribr, The Great Bronze Age of China: A Symposium, Los Angeles Co Mus Art, 83; Archaeological Objects, Ceramics and Lacquer Works, Arts of Asia, 3-4/89; Beauty and Utility: the Lacquered Baskets of China, Orientations, 11-12/89; Watt and Ford, East Asian Lacquer: The Florence and Herbert Irving Collection, J Asian Studies, Vol 52, No 1, rev ed, 2/93; Qiangjin Lacquer, in Bulletin of the Oriental Ceramic Soc, Hong Kong, No 10, 92-94; Japan, Enamels, The Dictionary of Art, vol 17, pp 377-379, London, 1996; Chinese Ceramics in Colonial Peru, Oriental Art, vol XLVI, no 1, 2000; co-auth (with Anthony Pasinski) Chinese Ceramics in the Audiencia of Guatemala, Oriental Art, vol XLVIII, no 4, 2002; catalog entries in The Grandeur of Viceregal Mexico, Mus Fine Arts, Houston, 2002; Craig Clunas, rev Art in China, China Review Int, vol 6, no 1, 1999; Chinese Porcelain in the Viceroyalty of Peru, Denver Art Mus, 2009; Japanes Porcelain in the Audiencia of Guatemala, Kyushu Kinsei Joki Gakkai, Arita, p302-306, 2010. *Mailing Add:* Los Angeles Co Mus Art 5905 Wilshire Blvd Los Angeles CA 90036

KUWAYAMA, TADAAKI
PAINTER, SCULPTOR
b Nagoya, Japan, Mar 4, 1932. *Study:* Tokyo Univ Art, BFA, 56. *Work:* Albright-Knox Art Gallery, Buffalo, NY; Worcester Art Mus, Mass; Wadsworth Atheneum, Hartford, Conn; Larry Aldrich Mus, Ridgefield, Conn; Herron Art Mus, Indianapolis; Guggenheim Mus, New York; Mus Mod Art, New York; Akron Art Mus, Akron, Oh; Weatherspoon Gallery, Greensboro, NC; Indianapolis Mus Art, Ind; Vasser Coll Art Gallery, Poughkeepsie, NY; Birmingham Mus Art, Ala; and many others. *Exhib:* Systemic Show, Guggenheim Mus, NY, 66; Plus by Minus, Today's Half-Century, Albright-Knox Art Gallery, 68; Kunst Wird Material, Nationalgalerie, Berlin, 82; Gegenwart Ewigkeit, Martin Gropius Bau, Berlin, 90; Scream Against the Sky, Guggenheim Mus & San Francisco Mus Mod Art, 94-95; Stiftung fur Konkrete Kunst, Reutlingen, Ger, 95; Kawamura Mem Mus, Japan, 96; Third Mind, Guggenheim Mus, 2009; Out of Silence: Kuwayama Tadaaki, Nagoya City Art Mus, Aichi, Japan, 2010; 21st Century Mus Contemp Art, Kanazawa, Ishikawa, Japan, 2011, Gallery Yamaguchi Kunst-Bau, Osaka, Japan, 2011, White Tadaaki Kuwayama Osaka Project, Nat Mus Art, Osaka, Japan, 2011; Gary Snyder Gallery, NY, 2012; and many others. *Awards:* Nat Coun Arts Grant, 69; Adolph & Esther Gottlieb Found Grant, 86. *Bibliog:* Robert C Morgan (auth), Sculpture Mag, July/August, 2000. *Media:* Acrylic, Oil; Mixed Media. *Dealer:* Gallery Yamaguchi Osaka Japan; Renate Bender Munich Germany; Galeriekonig Germany; Gary Smyder New York. *Mailing Add:* 136 W 24th St New York NY 10011

KWAK, HOON
PAINTER
b Seoul, Korea, July 9, 1941; US citizen. *Study:* Fine Art Col, Seoul Nat Univ, BFA, 63; Calif State Univ, Los Angeles, MA, 80, Long Beach, MFA, 82. *Work:* Security Pac Nat Bank, Los Angeles; Exec Life Insurance, Los Angeles; Mod Art Mus, Seoul, Korea; Manatt, Phelps, Rothenberg & Tunney Co, Los Angeles; Bear Stearns & Co, Los Angeles. *Comn:* Paintings, Conrad Hilton, Chicago, 85 & Compri Hotel, Aurora, Colo, 85. *Exhib:* Spokane Nat exhib, Cheney Cowles Mem Mus, Spokane, 81; 6 Artists, Nagasaki Prefecture Mus, Nagasaki, Japan, 81; 61st Nat Watercolor Soc exhib, Palm Springs, Calif, 81; New Comers, 81 & Only Los Angeles, 86, Los Angeles Municipal Art Gallery; Show-1 Winter, 81, Additional Space Expose V, 82 & 1 To 1, 85, Rental Gallery, Los Angeles Co Mus Art. *Awards:* Purchase Award, Minot State Col, NDak, 81; Past Pres Award, Nat Watercolor Soc, 81; Invitational Exhib Award, Pensacola Col, 82. *Media:* Acrylic, Oil. *Mailing Add:* 23602 Clearpool Pl Harbor City CA 90710-1113

KWARTLER, ALEX
PAINTER
Study: Cooper Union, BFA, 2002. *Exhib:* Solo exhibs include John Connelly Presents, NY, 2005; group exhibs include Champion Fine Art, Brooklyn, NY, 2004; Barricade, Rivington Arms, NY, 2004; Dark Dreams, Johnen Galerie, Berlin, 2004; The Painted World, PS1 Mus, Long Island City, NY, 2005; Group Show, Bronson Tropics, Los Angeles, 2006; Take One, Glassell Sch Art, Houston, Tex, 2006; Abstraction, Mitchell Iness & Nash, NY, 2006; Late Liberties, John Connelly Presents, NY, 2007; Signs of Precarity, Klaus von Nichtsssgend Gallery, Brooklyn, NY, 2007; Powers of Ten, 96 Greene, NY, 2007; Destroy Athens, 1st Athens Biennial, 2007. *Bibliog:* Holland Cotter (auth), Sampling Brooklyn, Keeper of Eclectic Flames, NY Times, 1/23/04; Chiara Lunardelli (auth), On Now, On Soon, Flash Art, Fall 2005; Polly Apfelbaum (author), Alex Kwartler, ArtNews, 11/06

KWIECINSKI, CHESTER MARTIN
EDUCATOR, PAINTER
b Youngstown, Ohio, July 7, 1924. *Study:* Kansas City Art Inst, BFA & MFA; Kansas City Univ; Youngstown Univ. *Work:* Butler Inst Am Art, Youngstown, Ohio; El Paso Mus of Art, Tex. *Comn:* Historical murals, McSorley Colonial, Pittsburgh, Pa, 54; murals (with Bill Rakocy), Colonial House and Congo Rm, Youngstown, Ohio, 60 & Alberini Restaurant, Niles, Ohio, 65. *Exhib:* Mo State Fair, 49 & 50; Albright-Knox Gallery Art, Buffalo, NY, 52; El Paso Regional show, 76; Solo exhib, Butler Inst Art, Youngstown Ohio, 62. *Pos:* Mus dir, Abilene Fine Arts Mus, Tex, 73-80. *Teaching:* Instr, Warren City Schs, Ohio, 54-66; assoc prof painting, Col of Artesia, NMex, 67-71. *Awards:* Best Local Art, New Year Show, Butler Inst Am Art, 42; Purchase Award, Carlsbad Art Asn, NMex, 68; Purchase Award, Hobbs-LLano Estacado, Hobbs Art Asn, NMex, 69. *Mem:* Am Asn Mus; Tex Asn Mus; Permian Basin Mus Asn, 78. *Media:* Watercolor, Oil. *Publ:* Guest art ed, Abilene Reporter News, 74; auth, articles, Pigment & Form, 64

KWONG, EVA
SCULPTOR, CERAMIST
b Hong Kong, 1954. *Study:* Oxbow Summer Sch Painting, Saugatuck, Mich, 74; RI Sch Design, Providence, BFA, 75; Tyler Sch Art, Temple Univ, MFA, 77. *Work:* Cranbrook Art Mus, Bloomfield Hills, Mich; Finnish Craft Mus, Helsinki, Finland; Butler Inst Am Art, Youngstown, Ohio; Slippery Rock State Univ, Pa; Shigaraki Ceramic Cult Park Mus, Japan; Racine Art Mus, Racine, Wis; Minneapolis Inst Art, Minn; Wright State Univ, Dayton Ohio; Mint Mus Art and Design, Charlotte; Fule Int Ceramic Art Mus, Fuping, China; Ctr Disease Control and Prevention, Atlanda, Ga; Cleveland Art Asn, Cleveland, Ohio; Springfield Art Mus, Springfield, Ohio; Crocker Art Mus, Sacramento, Calif; B.W. Rogers Co, Akron, Ohio; Eskin Coll, Univ Iowa Art Mus, Iowa City; Archie Bray Found, Helena, Mont; South Bend Regional Art Mus, South Bend, Ind; St. Clair Superior Develop Corp, Cleveland, Ohio; Cleveland Clinic Arts and Med Program, Lutheran Hosp, Cleveland, Ohio. *Comn:* Bacteria, Diatoms and Cells, 2004 Nat'l Inst of Infections Disease Ctr for Disease Control of Preventions, Atlanta, GA; AsiaTown Trio, Pub Art Proj, St Clair Superior Corp, City of Cleveland, Midtown Cleveland & Asia Town Ctr, 2011; Growth, Regeneration, Remembrance & Healing, Cleveland Clinic, Lutheran Hosp, Cleveland, Ohio, 2011; Cleveland, The Wind Turbine City, Cleveland Airport, Cleveland, Ohio, 2012; Gazebo and landscape design, Comt for Public Art and Millcreek Develop, Cleveland, Oh; permanent sculpture installation with resident participation, Ring of Friendship, comn by Millcreek Develop, Cleveland, Oh. *Exhib:* Lill St Gallery, Navy Pier, Chicago, Ill, 91 & 92; solo shows, South Bend Mus Art, Ind, 93 & The Clay Place, Pittsburgh, Pa, 94; group shows, Everson Mus Art, Syracuse, NY, 93, Newark Mus, NJ, 93, Akron Art Mus, Ohio, 93, Cleveland State Univ, 93, Bellevue Art Mus, Wash, 93, Cleveland Mus

Art, 94 & Craft Mus, Columbus, Ohio, 94; McDonough Mus Art, Youngstown, Ohio, 96; Carleton Col, Northfield, Minn, 96; plus many others; Minneapolis Inst Art, Minn; others. *Teaching:* Instr for numerous drawing & ceramic workshops throughout US & abroad; part-time fac, Kent State Univ, 89-. *Awards:* Ohio Arts Coun Fel, 88, 94, 99 & 2004; Nat Endowment Arts, 88; Pa Coun Arts Fel, 85 & 87. *Bibliog:* Article, Monthly Craft Mag, Seoul, Korea, Vol 1, No 9, 54-55, 11/88; Barbara Tannenbaum (auth), Ohio Perspectives: 5 Sculptors, Akron Art Mus, 93; Tom E Hinson (auth), The Invitational: Artists of Northeast Ohio, Cleveland Mus Art, 94. *Media:* Clay, Paper. *Dealer:* William Busta Gallery 2021 Murray Hill Rd Cleveland OH 44106; Sherrie Galleries, 694 N High St, Columbus, OH 43215

L

LABLE, ELIOT
SCULPTOR
b Apr 24, 1937. *Study:* Ohio Univ, BA, 59; New Sch, 70-73; Brooklyn Mus Art Sch, 72-73. *Work:* City Art Mus Helsinki, Finland; Bd Educ; Pub Art for Pub Schs; Museo de Arte, Costarricense, Costa Rica; Mus Modern Art, Helsinki, Finland; Recuerdos, Flushing Town Hall, 2006. *Comn:* Coop Tech HS Comn; Root Mem Outdoor sculpture; Creative Path, Flushing Town Hall, Flushing, NYC, 2005; Queen Council Exhib, 2005; Bd of Dir Nurture, Art, Guggenheim Mus. *Exhib:* Reflections Ann, Aldrich Mus Contemp Art, 76; 55 Mercer St Gallery, 84 & 86-96; Gallerie Pelen, Helsinki, Finland, 87, 88 & 94; Gallerie Ostermahl, Stockholm, Sweden, 88; Contemp Mus Costa Rica (auth, catalog), 92; Impremo Atelier Print Show (auth, catalog), Helsinki, Finland, 92 & 94; Bothnia Ice Sculpture Competition (with catalog), Oulu Art Mus, Finland, 96; Cooptech Pub Comn, New York City, 99; Long Island City Art Frenzy, New York City, 2001; Chelsea Studio Gallery, New York City, 2002; Dam Struhltraber Gallery, NY, 2002; Queens Coun on the Arts Exhib, NY, 2003; and others. *Pos:* bd dirs, educ dir, Nurture Art. *Teaching:* Adj lectr, LaGuardia Col; mem fac, Brooklyn Mus Art Sch, 78-85, LaGuardia Col, 85-. *Awards:* Nat Endowment Arts Artist in Residence Grant, 83; Fulbright Grant, 94. *Bibliog:* Kivirinta (auth), Helsinki Sanomat, review, 1/92; Pessi Rautio (auth), Review Helsinki Sonomas, 94; Diane Nahas (auth), review, Woodside Queens Gazette, 5/95; Marja Salmela (auth), review, Helsingen Sonomat, 2/96; James Della Fiora (auth), review, The Villager, 5/96; Natasha Sweeten (auth), review, 11211, 2002. *Mem:* Fulbright Asn; adv, MAD Mus Art Design. *Media:* Welded Steel. *Collection:* PorkKana Col, Helsinki, Finland; Contemp Mus, Helsinki, Finland; City Mus, Helsinki, Finland; Contemp Mus, Costa Rica. *Publ:* Auth, Galerie (catalog), Pelin, 88 & 94; Contemporary Museum, Costa Rica (catalog), 92

LA BOBGAH, ROBERT GORDON
INSTALLATION SCULPTOR, VIDEO ARTIST
b Montreal, Que, Nov 22, 1936. *Study:* Concordia Univ, Montreal, BA, 62; Western Mich Univ, Kalamazoo, MA, 67. *Work:* Nat Gallery Alvethorpe, Libr Congress, Washington, DC; Nat Gallery Can, Ottawa; Philadelphia Mus Art; Andy Warhol Mus; Hijikata Tatsumi Mem Archive, Tokyo; Kazuo Ohno, Tokyo. *Comn:* Ceramic murals, Hamburg Bros, Pittsburgh, Pa, 77; stages of the cross in ceramic, Immaculate Conception Church, Clarion, Pa, 78. *Exhib:* Carnegie Inst Art, Pittsburgh, Pa, 87 & 92; Pittsburgh Biennial, Pittsburgh Ctr, 94; Brew House, Space 101, NEA, Pittsburgh, Pa, 98; Soc of Sculptors, Pittsburgh, Pa, 2002; Pittsburgh Filmmakers, Pa, 2005; Artists Upstairs, Pittsburgh, Pa, 2006; Solo exhib, Pa Ave Gallery, 2007; Pa Filmmakers Biennial, Pa, 2008; Pittsburgh Filmakers, Pa, 2010; Three Rivers Film Festival, 2011; Pittsburgh Filmmakers, PA, 2012; Art All Night, PGH, Pa, 2013. *Teaching:* Instr, Pittsburgh Ctr Arts, Pa, 88-91. *Awards:* Purchase Award, Erie Art Mus, 87; Jurors Award, Auburn Works on Paper, Ala, 86 & Westmoreland Mus Art, 86; Gloria Fitzgibbons Award, Pittsburgh, 92; Print Group Award, PGI, 2000; Fel, Pa coun on the Arts, 2007. *Bibliog:* Murry Horn, Monogr, Pittsburgh Biennial, 9/94; article, PGH City Paper, 2/2000; NEA Forecast Regional, Space 101, Catalogue, Pittsburgh, Pa, 98; Pittsburgh Filmmakers, Catalogue, Pittsburgh, Pa, 2007. *Mem:* Soc Sculptors, Pittsburgh; Pittsburgh Soc Artists; Philadelphia Print Club. *Media:* Mixed Media; Video. *Publ:* Coauth, The Paper Bird Handmade Book, pvt publ, 72; Book I: The Book of Unnameable Rites of Mystery, Unique Press, 2000; Book II: The House Song of the Theatrical Bamboo Cutter, Unique Press, 2003; Pittsburgh Post-Gazette, 6/2005; Pittsburgh City Paper, 6/2006, 5/2007 & 6/2008. *Dealer:* DeVechis Gallery Philadelphia PA; Gallerie Chiz, Pittsburgh, Pa; Space Gallery, Pittsburgh, PA. *Mailing Add:* 319 S Atlantic Ave Pittsburgh PA 15224-2310

LABONTE, DICK
PAINTER
b Battle Creek, Mich, 1921. *Study:* Colgate Univ, NMex; Chicago Acad Fine Arts, Ill; studied with Alfred Krakusin & John Hennigan. *Work:* Cocktails at White House, Pres & Mrs Bill Clinton; White House, Washington, DC; Cocktails at White House, Pres & Mrs George Bush; Schering-Plough Corp, NJ; Manasquan Libr, NJ; Borough Hall, Bay Head, NJ. *Comn:* Holiday on Wall St, McGraw Hill Publ, 79; Spring Lake 1892, Spring Lake Hist Soc, 92. *Exhib:* Anchor & Palette Gallery, Bay Head, NJ; William Ris Galleries, Stone Harbor, NJ; Foligraph Galleries, Falls Church, Va; Solo exhib, Anchor & Palette Gallery, Bay Head, NJ, Peck Sch, Morristown, NJ, Artists Guild Ocean Co, NJ, Main St Gallery, Manasquan, NJ; Lovelandtown Mus, Bay Head, NJ,; Schering-Plough Corp, NJ. *Teaching:* instr, NJ artists groups & sch's, currently. *Mem:* Manasquan River Group Artists, NJ; Artists Guild Ocean Co, NJ. *Media:* Acrylic, Oil. *Specialty:* Americana and nostalgia themes, NJ beach scenes. *Publ:* auth, Paintings of the Jersey Shore and More, Jersey Shore Publications. *Dealer:* LaBonte Prints Inc PO Box 96 Bay Head NJ 08742. *Mailing Add:* Anchor & Palette Gallery PO Box 96 45 Mount St Bay Head NJ 08742

LABRIE, CHRISTY
STAINED GLASS ARTIST, PAINTER
b Portsmouth, NH, June 24, 1943. *Study:* Boston Ctr Adult Educ; Sacred Heart Hosp Sch Nursing, Manchester; Boston Coll & Boston Univ (CEU courses). *Work:* Healing & Restoration off, Mission Ch, Boston; Carmelite Monastery, Concord, NH; LaSalette Shrine, Attleboro, Mass (lost in fire 99); St Anselm Coll, Manchester, NH. *Comn:* Numerous pvt comns. *Exhib:* Southhampton Glassworks & Galerie, Palm Beach, Fla; Sheafs Warehouse Mus, Portsmouth, NH. *Pos:* Licensed RN, CCS, quality reviewer & coding analyst, formerly; clinical res nurse, Peter Bent Brigham Hosp, Joslin Diabetes Found & USDA Human Aging at Tufts Univ, Boston, retired. *Teaching:* Instr, classes, lects & assembly, Archdiocesan Choir Boy Sch, Cambridge, Mass. *Awards:* Award Medal, Outstanding People of the 20th Century, Intl Biographical Centre, Cambridge, Eng, 98; and numerous other awards. *Mem:* Our Lady's Rosary Makers. *Media:* Stained Glass; Acrylic Paints. *Publ:* Illusr, cover artist, Yankee Mag, 1/76, Our Lady's Missionary, 10/76 & Soul Mag, 9-10/86; Christmas card, Healing & Restoration Ministry, 90-91; contribr, Randy the Rooster (children's bk) & Nursing spectrum, articles & crossword puzzles; coauth, several abstracts & papers publ in sci/med j

LACHAPELLE, DAVID
PHOTOGRAPHER
Study: Sch Visual Arts, NY; NC Sch Arts. *Exhib:* Staley-Wise Gallery, NYC, 1996, 2006, Tony Shafrazi Gallery, 1999, Fahey-Klein Gallery, LA, 2000, Femmes plus que femmes, Museu de Arte Brazileira, Sao Paolo, Brazil, 2000, Baldwin Gallery, Galleria Carla Sozzani, Milan, 2000, Fish Stick, Camerawork, Berlin, 2001, Photology, Villa Impero, Bologna, Italy, 2001, LaChapelle, Kunsthaus, Vienna, Austria, 2002, Moscow Photo Festival, James Gallery, Russia, 2003, Montblanc Internat., Rockfeller Ctr., NYC, 2003, Artists and Prostitutes, Deitch Gallery, 2005, Maruani & Noirhomme Gallery, Kanokke, Belgium, 2005, Reflex Gallery, Amsterdam, Netherlands, 2005, Kals Art Exhibition, Palermo, Italy, 2005, Tony Shafrazi Gallery, NYC, 2005, 2007, Maruani & Noirhomme Gallery, Paris, 2006, VIP: Very Important Portraits, Capodimonte Mus, Naples, Italy, 2006, Jablonka Gallery, Berlin, Germany, 2007, Men, War & Peace, Helmut Newton Found., 2007, Goss Gallery, Dallas, 2007, David LaChapelle: Heaven to Hell, Malba Mus., Buenos Aires, 2007, Heaven to Hell, Museo Brasiliero da Escultura, 2008, Delirium of Reason, Antiguo Colegio de San Ildefonso, Mex City, 2009, Post Modern Pop Photography, 2010, Thus Spoke LaChapelle, Galerie Rudolfinium, Prague, 2011, Burning Beauty, Fotografiska Museet, Stockholm, Sweden, 2012, Gas Stations, Maruani & Noirhomme Gallery, Brussels, 2013, American Cool, Nat Portrait Gallery, Wash DC, 2014, Beyond Earth Art, Cornell U: Johnson Mus Art, NY, 2014, Land Scape, 2013, Paul Kasmin Gallery, 2014, and many others. *Pos:* portrait photographer to many celebrities including Drew Barrymore, Jim Carrey, k.d. lang, Leonardo DiCaprio, Faye Dunaway, Tupac Shakur, Madonna, Uma Thurman, Marilyn Manson, Daniel Day-Lewis, Ewan McGregory, Cameron Diaz, Lil' Kim, Eminem, Britney Spears, Cher, Bjork, Angelina Jolie, Backstreet Boys, Elton John, Pamela Anderson, Whitney Houston, Mariah Carey, Jackie Chan, Sylvester Stallone, Donatella Versace, Ricky Martin, Jay Z; dir, numerous music videos. *Awards:* named Best New Photographer of Yr, French Photo and Am Photo magazines, 95; VH1 Fashion Award, Photographer of the Year, 96; Infinity Award Applied Photog, Int Ctr Photog, 97; Art Dir Club award for Best Book Design for LaChapelle Land, 1997, Cover of Yr award, Alfred Eisenstadt awards (Eisies), 1999; Best Cutting Edge Essay and Style Photography, Alfred Eisenstadt awards for Mag Photography (Eisie awards), 1998; Vito Russo award, GLAAD, 2004. *Publ:* auth, LaChapelle Land, 1996; Hotel LaChapelle, 1999; David LaChapelle, 2004; LaChapelle Land, Deluxe Ed, 2005; LaChapelle, Artists and Prostitutes, 2006; LaChapelle, Heaven to Hell, 2006; David LaChapelle: al Forte Belvedere, 2008; David LaChapelle, 2008; David LaChapelle: The Rape of Africa, 2009. *Dealer:* Paul Kasmin Gallery 293 Tenth Ave New York NY 10001; Galerie Alex Daniels Reflex Gallery Weteringschans 79A 1017 RX Amsterdam Netherlands; Jablonka Galerie Lindenstrasse 19 D 50674 Koln Ger. *Mailing Add:* Creative Exchange Agency c/o Steven Prancia 545 W 25th St 19th Fl New York NY 10001

LACHMAN, AL
PAINTER
b Bronx, NY, Oct 17, 1936. *Study:* Syracuse Univ, 53-54; Art Students League, 55-60; Sch Visual Arts, New York; studied with Robert Philipp & Americo DiFranza. *Work:* Walt Disney Corp Collection, Orlando, Fla; Hershey Corp Collection, Pa; Ford Motor Co, Detroit, Mich; Domino Pizza Collection, Detroit, Mich; Central Libr Denver, Colo; Disneyland Int; Mayer, Brown, Rowe & Maw, LLP; Stonebridge Bank & Sunbank; Northwest Airlines; Doylestown Hospital, Pa. *Exhib:* Pastels Only, Salmagundi Club, New York, 83; Cherry Creek Nat Art Show, Cherry Creek Found, Denver, Colo, 90; Las Olas Nat First Show, Las Olas Mus, Fla, 91; Gasparilla Nat Arts Show, Tampa Mus, Fla, 92; Boca Raton Art Show, Crocker Mus, Fla, 93; Nat Art Show, Bruce Mus, Greenwich, Conn, 94; Contemp Eye, Michener Mus, New Hope, Pa, 2005. *Collection Arranged:* Northwest Airlines; Walt Disney Corp Collection; Univ Ga Law Sch; Baptist Hosp, Fla; Sun Bank. *Pos:* Co-founder & dir bd ctrl, PSA for Pastels only, Nat Arts Club, New York. *Teaching:* instr, workshops int, currently. *Awards:* Best of Show, Las Olas Nat Art Show, Las Olas Mus Art, 91; Best of Show, Giffuni Mem Award, Pastel Soc Am Nat, 92; Best of Show, Naples Nat, Eden Found, 2000. *Bibliog:* P Sessler (auth), Artists Mag, F&W Publ, 94; Krachen (auth), Best of Pastel, North Light Bks, 96; P Metzger (auth), Artists Encyl, North Light Bks, 2000. *Mem:* Pastel Soc Am (dir bd control, formerly); Pastel Soc Can; Salmagundi Club; Pastel Soc Kans; Nat Drawing Asn. *Media:* Oil, Pastel. *Publ:* contribr, Pastel Interpretations, 95, Best of Pastel, 96, Artist Guide to Materials & Techniques, 96 & Artists Encyl, 2000, North Light Bks; Artists of the River Town, River Arts Press, 2002; Expressions: Drawings, Paintings & Thoughts, 2005; best of Color, 2006. *Dealer:* Lachman Gallery. *Mailing Add:* PO Box 100 Solebury PA 18963

LACKTMAN, MICHAEL
CRAFTSMAN, JEWELER
b Philadelphia, Pa, Mar 1, 1938. *Study:* Pa State Col, 57-61; Cranbrook Acad of Art, Bloomfield Hills, Mich, 61-63; Kunsthaandverskolen, Copenhagen, Denmark, 65-66. *Work:* Pa State Col, Millersville, Pa; Cranbrook Acad Art, Bloomfield Hills, Mich; Metrop Art Mus, NY; Chicago Art Inst; Philadelphia Art Mus; and others. *Comn:* Liturgical metalry, Redeemer Lutheran Church, Livermore, Calif, 71; Kiddusch cup, Brandeis Univ, Waltham, Mass, 63. *Exhib:* California Design VI, Crocker Art Mus, Sacramento, 69; California Design XI, Pasadena Art Mus, 71; Metal Experience, Oakland Art Mus, Calif, 71; 4th Int Jewelry Exhib, Schmuckmuseum, Pzorheim, Ger, 72; Diamond Today: Int Jewelry Exhib, NY, 75. *Collection Arranged:* The Brooklyn Mus; Art Inst Chicago; Philadelphia Art Mus; Met Mus Art; Oakland Art Mus; Dallas Art Mus; Milwaukee Art Mus; Newark Art Mus; Los Angeles Art Mus. *Pos:* Prof emeritus. *Teaching:* Asst prof design, Univ Calif, Berkeley, 66-73, Univ Chile, Santiago, 72-73; prof jewelry & metalsmithing, Univ Wis-Milwaukee, 73, art prof, 1973-95. *Awards:* Louis Comfort Tiffany Grant, 63; Ford Found Grant, 72-73; Nat Endowment Humanities Grant, 75. *Bibliog:* Articles & photographs of work, Art & Archit, 71 & Playboy Mag, 75. *Mem:* Am Craftsman Coun; San Francisco Bay Asn; Sterling-Silversmiths Guild Am; Scand-Am Found; Coll Art Asn. *Media:* Jewelry, Metals. *Mailing Add:* 573 Park Estates Sq Venice Park FL 34293

LACOM, WAYNE CARL
PAINTER, GRAPHIC ARTIST
b Glendale, Calif, Oct 11, 1922. *Study:* Art Ctr Sch, 42; Chuoinard Art Inst, 43-44; Jepson Art Inst, 45-46; Univ Calif Exten, 50. *Work:* Brand Libr Gallery, Glendale, Calif, Los Angeles Unified Sch Dist; Hawaiian Airlines; Lahaina Restoration Found; Village Gallery, Lahaina, Maui, Hawaii; Viva Gallery, Sherman Oaks, Calif; Bakersfield Mus Art. *Comn:* Bronze sculpture, Flamingo Hotel, Las Vegas, 70; painting, Hawaiian Airlines, Honolulu, 71; stained glass window, comn by Mr & Mrs Taub, Encino, Calif, 72; painting, Security Pacific Bank, Glendale, Calif, 75. *Exhib:* Artists of Los Angeles & Vicinity, Los Angeles Co Mus Art, Calif, 50; Watercolor Exhib, Santa Barbara Art Mus, Calif, 52; Pasadena Mus Art, Pasadena, Calif, 53; Denver Mus Art, Colo, 54; Cuernavaca Art Mus, Mex, 55; Lahaina Restoration Found Mus, Lahaina, Hawaii, 88; Heritage Mus, Calif Watercolorist, Santa Monica, Calif, 2004; Bakersfield Mus Art; Sullivan Goss Gallery, Santa Barbara, Calif. *Pos:* Pres, Int Art Serv, 78-. *Teaching:* Instr watercolor, Los Angeles Unified Sch Dist, Adult Educ, 47-78; instr, School of the Arts, E Los Angeles City Coll, 80-90. *Awards:* First Place, Glendale Art Asn, 48; Best of show, Catalina Art Fest, 89; Best of Show, Lahaina Town Exhib, Lahaina, Hawaii, 93 & 98. *Bibliog:* The Creative Hand (video), Los Angeles Unified Sch Dist, 73. *Mem:* Nat Watercolor Soc (pres, 65-66); Artists Educ Action (treas, 67-73). *Media:* Watercolor, Acrylic. *Publ:* Transparent Watercolor, 73 & Landscapes, 77, Davis Publ; Palette Talk, Grumbacher, 75; The California Style, Hillcrest Press, 85; The California Romantics, Artra, 86; McClelland & Last (auths), California Watercolors 1850-1970, Hillcrest Press, 2003. *Dealer:* Village Gallery 120 Dickenson St Lahaina HI 96761; Gordon McClelland PO Box 3564 San Clemente CA 92672. *Mailing Add:* 16703 Alginet Pl Encino CA 91436

LACY, SUZANNE
CONCEPTUAL ARTIST, WRITER
b Wasco, Calif, Oct 21, 1945. *Study:* Bakersfield Col, Calif, AA, 65; Univ Calif, Santa Barbara, BA (zoological scis, with honors), 68; Calif Inst Arts, MFA (social design), 73; Studied with Judy Chicago, Sheila de Bretteville & Allan Kaprow. *Comn:* Martk Taper Forum, Los Angeles, Calif, 73; Studio Watts Workshop, Los Angeles, Calif, 75-77; Nev Humanities Com, Las Vegas, 78; Law Enforcement Assistance Asn, Los Angeles, Calif, 79; Center Music Experiment, San Diego, Calif, 83. *Exhib:* Solo exhibs, Montgomery Gallery, Pomona Col, 83; Video Art: A History, Mus Mod Art, NY, 83; Committed to Print, Mus Mod Art, NY, 88; Full Circle (installation), Chicago, 93; Underground (installation), Three Rivers Art Festival, Pittsburgh, 93; The Roof is on Fire, Oakland, 94; Auto on Edge of Time, Snug Harbor Cult Ctr, NY, 94; Auto on the Edge of Time: A Retrospective of Works on Violence, Snug Harbor Cult Ctr, Staten Island, NY, 94; In a Different Light, Univ Art Mus, Berkeley, Calif, 95; Out of Action, Mus Contemp Art, Los Angeles, 98; and others. *Pos:* Mem nat adv bd, Art Dept, Carnegie Mellon Univ, 92-; artist-in-residence, Oakland Sharing Vision, 96-2000; city arts comnr, City of Oakland, Calif, 99-2001, mayor's task force edn, 99; mem adv bd, Attitudinal Healing Connection, Oakland, Calif, 2000-. *Teaching:* Minneapolis Col Art & Design, 85-86; Sch Art Inst Chicago, 86; vis artist, Carleton Col, 87; dean, Sch Fine Arts, Calif Col Arts & Crafts, 87-97; spec asst to pres serv learning, Ctr Art and Pub Life, Calif Col Arts and Crafts, 97-98, dir, 98-; mem edn and arts task force, Oakland Unified Sch Dist, Calif, 2001; mem supt's task force schs, Alameda Co Office Educ, 2001. *Awards:* Individual Artists Fel, Nat Endowment Arts, 79, 81, 85 & 92 & Media Arts Grant, 92; Guggenheim Fel, 92; Award Pub Serv, NY Benevolence Coun, 95; Grant, Surdna Found 96, 97 & 98, Inst Noetic Scis and Fetzer Inst, 98, Nathan Cummings Found, 98, 99 & 2000, Fleishhacker Found, 99, Tides Found, Potrero Neuvo Fund, 99, Levi Strauss Found, 99, Morris Stulsaft Found, 99, Richard and Rhonda Goldman Fund, 99 & Oakland Found Children and Youth, 99; Fel, Creative Works Fund, 98 & Flintridge Found, 2000; Lifetime Achievement award, Coll Art Asn, 2010. *Bibliog:* Jennifer Fisher (auth), Interperformance: the live tableaux of Suzanne Lacy, Janine Antoni, and Marina Abramovic, Art Jour, 97; Meiling Cheng (auth), Sacred naked nature girls, TDR: Jour Performance Studies, Summer/98; Katy Deepwell (auth), Suzanne Lucy on new genre public art, n.paradoxa 4, 99; Charles R Garoian (auth), Performing Pedagogy: Toward an Art of Politics, SUNY Press, 99; Nic Paget-Clarke (auth), An Interview with Suzanne Lacy: Art and Advocacy, In Motion Mag, 11/2000. *Mem:* Los Angeles Inst Contemp Art; The Woman's Bldg (mem bd, 74-79); Women's Caucus Arts (nat bd, 79-82). *Media:* Theatrical and Non-Theatrical Performance; Installation, Books and Video. *Publ:* ed, Mapping The Terrain: New Genre Public Art, Bay Press, 94; Affinities: Thoughts on An Incomplete History in The Power of Feminist Art, Abrams, 94; co-auth, Jo Hanson, Susan Steinman, WCA, 97; ed, Mapping the Terrain: New Genre Public art, Bay Press, Seattle, 95; auth, Prostitution notes, Veiled Histories: The Body, Place and Public Art, Critical Press, 97. *Mailing Add:* 28 Privateer St Apt 5 Marina Del Rey CA 90292-6761

LADDA, JUSTEN
INSTALLATION SCULPTOR, PAINTER
b Germany, 1953. *Work:* Mus Mod Art, New York; Israel Mus, Jerusalem; New York Pub Libr. *Exhib:* Solo exhibs include Time is Us, ABC No Rio, New York, 1980, Art & Fashion & Relig, Mus Mod Art, New York, 1986, 1+1=2, Israel Mus, Jerusalem, 1987, Galerie Lelong, New York, 1988, Simulation Meltdown, San Diego State Univ Art Gallery, 1988, Fuller Gross Gallery, San Francisco, 1990, is it? it is isn't it, Jay Gorney Mod Art, New York, 1990, Double Dig, 1992, Kings & Queens, Donna Beame Gallery, Las Vegas, 1996, Tempozan Temporary Mus, Osaka, Japan, 1996, Rear Views, Feature, New York, 1998, Mario DiAcono, Boston, 2007; group exhibs include Times Square Show, New York, 1980; 50th Anniv Exhib, Willard Gallery, New York, 1986; Avant-Garde in Eighties, Los Angeles County Mus Art, 1987; Quotations, Aldrich Mus Contemp Art, Ridgefield, CT, 1992, Here, 1998, Faith, 2000; Invitational Exhib, AAAL, 1997, Painting & Sculpture, 2001, Visual Arts, 2008; How Human-Life in Post Genome Era, Int Ctr Photog, New York, 2003; Constructed Image, Kent Gallery, New York, 2004; Downtown Show, Grey Art Gallery, New York, 2005; Figure it out, Hudson Valley Ctr Contemp Art, Peekskill, NY, 2005, Reverence, 2006. *Awards:* Acad Award Art, AAAL, 2008

LADOUCEUR, PHILIP ALAN
ADMINISTRATOR, DIRECTOR
b Syracuse, NY, Nov 6, 1950. *Study:* State Univ NY, MA, 80; studied with Kenneth Lindsay & Albert Boime. *Collection Arranged:* Teacher and Student, 95; Ohio and the Civil War, 96; Diverse Visions Invitational, 96; Waters, Classic Forms, 97; Jim Wallace & Laura; Leslie Cope Retrospective, 97; Ceramic Int Exhib, 98. *Pos:* Dir, Blanden Art Mus, 91-94 & Zanesville Art Ctr, 95-. *Mem:* Am Asn Mus; Coll Art Asn. *Mailing Add:* Zanesville Arts Ctr 620 Military Rd Zanesville OH 43701

LA DUKE, BETTY
ARTIST
b Bronx, NY, Jan 13, 1933. *Study:* Denver Univ, 50; Cleveland Inst Art, 51-52; Inst Allende, San Miguel, Mex, 53; Calif State Univ, Los Angeles, BA, MA. *Work:* Heifer Int, Little Rock, Ark; Medford Int Airport, Medford, Ore; Farmers Market, Martinsville, Va. *Comn:* Three Monkeys, Lion King Parade, Disney Land, Calif, 97; Dreaming Cows (7'x100' mural project), Heifer Int Global Village, Little Rock, Ariz, 2008; Famers Market (mural project), Martinsville, Va. *Exhib:* The Field Mus, Chicago; Hampton Univ Art Mus, Hampton, Va, 2000; Africa from Eritrea with Love, Dallas Mus of Art, Dallas, Tex, 2001; Africa: Myth, Magic and Reality, Hudgens Art Ctr, Duluth, Ga, 2001; Chattanooga African Am Mus Art, Chattanooga, Tenn, 2001; Dallas Mus Art, Tex, 2001; From Africa with love, William King Art Ctr, Abingdon, Va, 2002; Capitol Children's Mus, Washington, DC, 2003; Smith Robinson Mus, Jackson, Miss, 2003; solo circulating exhibs: Dreaming Cows, Heifer Int, Africa: Myth, Magic & Reality, Children of the World, Latin American Transitions, Surviving War, Dreaming Home, Chiapas Mexico: Land & Liberty, Celebrating Women's Creative Hands & Spirits; Emory Univ, Atlanta, Ga; Children's Mus Houston, Houston, Tex; NMex Univ Mus Arts, Las Cruces, NMex; Brauer Art Mus, Valparaiso Univ; Ore State Univ; Southern Ore Univ, Ashland, Ore, 2013. *Collection Arranged:* Hallie Ford Mus of Art, Willamette Univ, Salem, Oreg; Portland Art Mus, Oreg; Schneider Art Mus, So Oreg Univ, Ashland, Oreg; Waterloo Center for the Arts, Waterloo, IA; RI Mus Art (RISD); James E Lewis Mus Art, Baltimore, Md; Smith Robinson Mus Art, Jackson, Miss; Jordan Schnitzer Art Mus, Univ Ore, Eugene, Ore. *Teaching:* Art teacher, Stevenson Jr High, Los Angeles, Calif, 60-64; prof art, Southern Ore Univ, Ashland, 64-96, prof art emer, retired. *Awards:* Oreg Gov's Award for the Arts, 93; Ziegfield Award, Nat Art edn Asn, 96. *Bibliog:* Gloria Orenstein (auth), Multi Cultural Celebrations, The Paintings of Betty La Duke, Pomegranate, 90; Susan Ressler (auth), Women Artists of American West, 2003; Brian Varady(auth), Mc Farland Video, Africa Between Myth and Reality and An Artists Journey from the Bronx to Timbuctu, So Oreg Univ, 96; Ore Art Heritage Film, 2006; Sue Bumagin (auth), Paintings, Drawings, Murals of Betty LaDuke, Hefer Int, 2009. *Mem:* Art Coun/Africa Studies Asn; Internat Soc Educ Through the Arts/Nat Art Educ Asn. *Media:* Acrylic on Canvas, Murals, Wood Panels. *Res:* Work with Heifer Int, 2003-2007. *Specialty:* Environmental Sustainability. *Interests:* Women and Art in Non-Western societies and documenting Heifer Int Education Center projects to alleviate world hunger, Little Rock Arkansas; Projects related to hunger, malnutrition, and sustainable solutions with Valparaiso Univ, Indiana, Brauer Art Mus, Portland Oreg Art Mus, Willamette Univ, Haille Ford Art Mus, Schneider Art Mus, Ashland, Oreg, Benett Col, Greenboro, NC; local farms, farm workers. *Publ:* Companras: Women, Art & Social Change in Latin America, City Lights, San Francisco, 85; auth, Africa Through the Eyes of Women Artists, 90; Women Against Hunger, a Sketchbook Journey, Africa World Press, 97; Africa: Women's Art, Women's Lives, Africa World Press, 97; Women Artists: Multi Cultural Visions, Africa World Press, 97; Art Reflecting Life (filmed in Ore & Rwanda Africa); Dreaming Cows Mural Proj. *Dealer:* Hanson Howard Gallery Ashland OR. *Mailing Add:* 610 Long Way Ashland OR 97520

LAEMMLE, CHERYL
PAINTER
b Minneapolis, Minn, Aug 11, 1953. *Study:* Humboldt State Univ, BA, 74; Washington State Univ, MFA, 78. *Work:* Eli Broad Family Found; Metrop Mus Art & Chase Manhattan Bank, NY; Frederick R Weismann Found; Corcoran Mus Art, Washington, DC; Walker Art Ctr, Minneapolis; Gen Mills, Minneapolis, Minn; High Art Mus; Nat Mus Women in the Arts, Washington. *Exhib:* Solo exhibs incl Sharpe Gallery, NY, 84, 86, Holin Kaufman Gallery, Chicago, 86, Mus of Art, Wash State

Univ, Pullman, 90, Faye Gold Gallery, Atlanta, 92; group exhibs incl An Int Survey of Recent Painting & Sculpture, Mus Mod Art, NY, 84; From NY, Ace Contemp Exhib, Los Angeles, Calif, 88; Making Their Mark; Women a Move in the Mainstream 70-85, Cincinnati Art Mus, 89; Real Illusion, Whitney Mus Art at Equitable Ctr NY, 90; In the Looking Glass, Mint Mus Art, Charlotte, NC, 91; La Femme Surreal & the Frozen Narrative, Visual Arts Ctr, Calif State Univ, Fullerton, 91; I, Myself & Me, Twentieth Century & Contemp Self Portraits, Midtown Payson Galleries, NY, 92; Midtown Payson Gallery, NY 94; Duane Reed Gallery, St Louis, Mo, 98. *Awards:* Fel, Creative Artists Pub Serv Prog, 80; Vera G List Award, 84; Painting Fel, Nat Endowment Arts, 85-86 & 86-87. *Bibliog:* Lisa Peters (auth), article, Arts Mag, 5/83; Richard Armstrong (auth), article, Art Forum, summer 83; Ronny Cohen (auth), article, Art News, summer 83; William Zimmer (auth), Art walk, Village Voice, 4/1/86. *Media:* Oil. *Dealer:* Alan Brown Gallery Naples FL

LAESSIG, ROBERT
PAINTER, ILLUSTRATOR

b West New York, NJ, Nov 15, 1913. *Study:* Art Students League; also study in Ger. *Exhib:* Philadelphia Watercolor Soc, 64-70; Allied Artists, NY, 70-72; Pittsburgh Watercolor Show, 78; Ohio Watercolor Show, 78-79; Am Watercolor Show, 79. *Pos:* Pres, Robert Laessig Fine Arts Co, West Richfield, Ohio, 69-71 & Quail Ravine Studios, Inc, Peninsula, Ohio, 85-89; Senior art consultant Am. Greetings, Inc; painting represented in collections Norfolk Mus Art, Cleveland Mus Art, Springfield Inst Fine Art, Denver Mus Art; designer personal Christmas cards President Lyndon B Johnson, 1964-66, Gov Celeste, Ohio, 83-90; Pub of prints Art Beats, Salt Lake City; assoc with Gallery One, Mentor, Ohio. *Awards:* Prizes, Am Watercolor Soc, 70 & 71, Wichita Centennial, 70 & Pittsburgh Watercolor, 80; Pitts Watercolor Society, 81, award Mainstreams Marietta, Ohio, 83; Adirondack Nat Show, Old Forge, NY, 82-83; Gold medal, Ohio Watercolor Soc, 87 & 88; Lifetime Achievement award, Fairmount Ctr, Ohio, 2003; and numerous others. *Mem:* Nat Acad (assoc 64-94, academician, 94-); Dolphin Club; Am Watercolor Soc; Ohio Watercolor Soc; Am Watercolor Soc. *Mailing Add:* 26376 John Rd Olmsted Township OH 44138-1277

LAFAYE, BRYAN F
MUSEUM DIRECTOR, EDUCATOR

Study: La Col, BA, 91; Clemson Univ, MFA, 93. *Collection Arranged:* Will Henry Stevens (paintings; auth, catalog), Am Modernist, 95; Salvation on San Mountain (photos; auth, catalog), Neel & Springer, 96; Abstract Perceptions: Gary Chapman (paintings), 97; Leroy Archuleta: A to Z (NMex folk art), 97; On the Road: T H Benton(paintings), 98. *Pos:* Cur, Alexandria Mus Art, La, 94-96; dir, Univ Art Mus, Univ Southern La, Lafayette, 96-. *Teaching:* Instr drawing, La Col, Pineville, 94-96; inst art hist, La State Univ, Alexandria, 96; asst prof art hist, Univ SW La, Lafayette, 96. *Awards:* Exhib Award, Lannan Found, 95 & Los Angeles Div Arts, 98; Int Partnership Award, Am Asn Mus, 97-99. *Mem:* Am Asn Mus; La Asn Mus (first vpres); Southeastern Mus Conf. *Res:* American Modernism; Contemporary Art from the American South. *Publ:* contribr, Emery Clark, Univ Art Mus, 98. *Mailing Add:* Univ Southwestern La Univ Art Mus USL Drawer 42571 Lafayette LA 70504

LAFLEUR, LAURETTE CARIGNAN
PAINTER

b Manchester, NH, Nov 14, 1939. *Study:* Notre Dame Col, 80; NH Inst Art, 81. *Comn:* Individual paintings for collectors (series of 64 plus individual paintings consisting of child's toys). *Exhib:* Group exhibs, Ogunquit ME, 93-05, 2009-12, Saco Merchants Asn, 93-2007, Keene Ashuelot Park, 93-2007, Plymouth NH, Park Show, 93-2014, South Portland (Maine) Park Show, 94-2011, & 2013, Andover, Mass, Show, 94-2013, Prime Time, 99-2007, Kennebunk River Club, 2001, Carlyle Place, 2002-2004, Milford, NH, Park Show, 2003-2007, Lawrence Heritage Park Show, 2003, Keene Colony Mill, 2003-2010, Art Affair in the Country, 2005, 2007, 2010, 2011, Greeley Park Show, Nashua, NH, 2005-2006, Sharon Arts Miniature Show, 2005, Animal Rescue League Show, 2006; Hollis, NH Park Show, 2006-2007, Souhegan Valley Show, 2006-2007, Wilton Miniature Show, 2006-2007, Manchester Artists Asn Show, 1993-1995, 2010-2013, Art in Action, Londonberry, NH, 2014, Eliott Senior Care, 2014; solo exhibs, Barnes & Noble Bookstore, 96, Hooksett Pub libr, 99, Peterborough NH Libr, 2005, Keene City Hall, 2010; two-person exhibs, Keene, City Hall, 2003 & 2009, Chesterfield, Pub Libr, 2003, Chesterfield Granite Bank, NH, 2003, Jaffrey NH Civic Ctr, 2008, Conn River Bank, 2009. *Pos:* Artist, 76-; Cashier, Pru-Bache Securities, Manchester, 86; off mgr, Shockley & Assoc Advertising, Amherst, NH, 87-88; accounting clerk, State of NH Admin Serv, Concord, 93-96. *Teaching:* Instr basic drawing, Sr Citizens, Webster Woods Community, Hooksett, NH, 2008; instr basic drawing & painting, Hooksett Pub Libr, 2009-2014; instr, Villa Crest Assisted Living/Art Therapy, 2011-2013, Drawing & Acrylic Painting, Suncook Sr Ctr, 2012-2013. *Awards:* Recipient Awards; Manchester Park Shows, 85-86, Greeley Park shows, 88, Deerfield Fair, 93-95, Saco, Maine, 94, Am Mothers Inc, Augusta, Maine, 95, Andovers Art in the Park, 2005-2006, Art Affair in the Country, 2005-2006. *Mem:* Andover Artists Guild; Monadock Area Artists Asn; Manchester Artists Asn; Nashua Area Artists Asn. *Media:* Acrylic, Oil, Watercolor. *Res:* Genealogy res. *Interests:* Reading, snowshoeing, walking, sewing. *Mailing Add:* 11 Heather Dr Hooksett NH 03106-1538

LAFOGG-DOCHERTY, DEBORAH
PAINTER

Work: Under Moms Watchful Eye (poster), Sarasota Wildlife Art Festival, 2013. *Exhib:* solo exhibs: corner stone artist Cat's Meow Show; from mild to wild, Cornell Mus, Delray Beach, Fla; Marine and Wildlife Art Festival and Craft SHow, Memorial Park, Stuart Fla, 2015; Everglades Nat Park's Ernest F Coe Gallery, Visitors Center, 2015; 41st Ann Mount Dora Arts Festival, 2016; ArtiGras Fine Art Festival, Abacoa Town Ctr, Jupiter, Fla, 2016; Delray Affair, Downtown Delray Beach, 2016; Demos: Delray Art League, Delray Beach City Hall, 2016; Palm City Art Associates Inc, The Cummings Library, Donahue Room, Fla, 2016. *Teaching:* workshop/classes, Delray Center for the Arts, 2016; Hobe Sound Fine Arts League, Fla, 2016. *Awards:* Masters Circle award, Internat Asn of Pastel Societies, 2011; Second Place in drawing, Nat Wildlife Art Competition; Honorable mention in drawing, Ex Arte Equinus 5 Equine Art Competition, 2012; Third and Honorable mention Arthur Marshall Loxahatchee Visions Art Show, 2012; Second Place other media, Richeson 75 Landscapes, Seascapes and Architecture, 2013; Third Place Crest Theatre Art Exhib, Delray Beach, 2014; Third Place Sarasota Wildlife Art Festival, 2014; Marquis Who's Who in American Art References award in Pastel, Audubon Artists, 2014; Sidney Friedlander Memorial award, 10th Ann Northeast Nat Pastel Exhib, Old Forge, NY, 2014; First Place: Woemn Artists of the West Goes Wild online exhib of wildlife art, 2014; Finalist Animal & Wildlife category, Ann Pastel 100 Competition, Pastel Journal, 2014; Third Place Arthur Marshall Loxahatchee Visions Art Show, 2014; Finalist, Art Renewal Salon Ctr for the Arts in Wildlife/Animal Category, 2014; Two honorable mentions, animal/wildlife category, 16th Ann Pastel 100 Competition, Pastel Journal, 2015; Finalist, Art Renewal Salon Ctr for the Arts, wildlife/animal category, 2015; Second place, Beaux-Arts Realiste Pastel Internat Online Pastel Completion, 2015. *Bibliog:* (illustrator), Woodrat Jill. *Mem:* Artists for Conservation (signature mem); Pastel Soc Am (signature mem); Southeastern Pastel Soc (mem excellence); Audubon Artists; Soc Animal Artists (assoc mem); Oil Painters of Am (assoc mem); Internat Guild of Realism (mem excellence); Women Artists of the West (assoc mem); Salagundi Art Club (non-resident mem); Patel Soc of North Florida (mem excellence); Degas Pastel Soc. *Media:* Pastels. Oils, and Acrylics. *Publ:* Published in many newspapers and several magazines including Wildlife Art Mag, Wildscape Mag (UK) and Southwest and Wildlife art Mag online. *Mailing Add:* 12375 Military Trail #133 Boynton Beach FL 33436

LAFON, DEE J
PAINTER, SCULPTOR

b Ogden, Utah, Apr 23, 1929. *Study:* Weber State Col; Univ Utah, BFA, 60, MFA, 62; also with Francis de Erdley, Phil Paradise & Marquerite Wildenhain. *Work:* Utah State Fine Art Collection, Salt Lake City; Okla Art Ctr, Oklahoma City; Philbrook Art Mus, Tulsa, Okla; Univ Okla, Norman; Dillard Collection, Univ NC, Greensboro. *Comn:* Wood sculpture, Univ Okla, 72. *Exhib:* Am Drawing Bienniale, Norfolk, Va, 69; Int Miniature Prints Show, Pratt Graphic Ctr, NY, 70; Midwest Bienniale, Omaha, Nebr, 72; Solo exhibs, Springfield Art Mus, Mo, 78 & Goddard Art Ctr, Ardmore, Ore, 78. *Teaching:* Instr ceramics & drawing, Weber State Col, 62-64; assoc prof painting & drawing, ECent State Col, 64-, chmn dept art, 79-. *Awards:* Eight State Exhib Purchase Award, 70; Hon Mention, Midwest Bienniale, 72; Tulsa Regional Painting & Drawing Award, 72. *Mem:* Okla Designer Craftsman. *Media:* Oil, Multi-media. *Dealer:* Oklahoma Art Ctr 3113 General Pershing Blvd Oklahoma City OK 73118; Ben Pickard Gallery 541 NW 39th St Oklahoma City OK 73118. *Mailing Add:* 904 Tarkington Dr Norman OK 73071-0868

LAGORIA, GEORGIANNA MARIE M
MUSEUM DIRECTOR, CURATOR

b Oakland, Calif, Nov 3, 1953. *Study:* Gonzaga Univ, Florence, Italy, 1974; Santa Clara Univ, Calif, BA, 1975; Univ San Francisco, MA, 1978. *Collection Arranged:* The Candy Store Gallery (with catalog), 1980, Contemp Hand Colored Photographs (with catalog), 1981, Northern California Art of the Sixties (with catalog), 1982 & Artist and the Machine 1910-1940 (with catalog), 86, de Saisset Mus, Santa Clara, Calif; Judy Dater: Twenty Yrs, traveled through US & Spain, 1986; The Laila and Thurston Twigg-Smith Collection, 1993. *Pos:* Asst dir, de Saisset Mus, Santa Clara Univ, Calif, 1978-83, dir, 1983-86; dir, Palo Alto Cult Ctr, Calif, 1986-91, Contemp Mus, Honolulu, 1995-; adv bd, Wiegand Gallery, Coll Notre Dame, Belmont, Calif; consult, 1991-95. *Awards:* Publ Support Grant, Ahmanson Found, 1981; Nat Endowment Arts, 1985-86; NAS fel, Stanford Grad Sch Bus, 2002. *Mem:* ArtTable; Calif Asn Mus (bd, 1987-89); Western Mus Conf Am Asn Mus; Hawaii Mus Asn (pres, 2000-02); Asn Art Mus Dirs (2000-). *Res:* Modern and contemporary art, craft, and design with an emphasis on the West Coast. *Publ:* Contribr, Judy Dater: Twenty Years, Univ Ariz, 1986 & Persis Collection of Contemp Art, Honolulu Advertiser. *Mailing Add:* Contemporary Museum 2411 Makiki Heights Drive Honolulu HI 96822

LAGRANGE, PIERRE
COLLECTOR

b Belgium, 1962. *Study:* Solvay Brussels Sch Econ & Mgmt, MA (engring). *Pos:* With JP Morgan & Goldman Sachs, formerly; co-founder GLG Partners divsn, Lehman Brothers Int, 1995; co-founder & sr mng dir, GLG Partners LP, 2000-, bd dirs, 2009-. *Awards:* Named one of Top 200 Collectors, ARTnews mag, 2010-13. *Collection:* Postwar and contemporary art. *Mailing Add:* GLG Partners LP One Curzon St London United Kingdom W1J 5HB

LAGUNA, MARIELLA
PAINTER, PRINTMAKER

b New York, NY. *Study:* NY Univ (archit); New Sch; Brooklyn Mus Art Sch; Adelphi Univ; Pratt Graphic Ctr. *Work:* Rockefeller Family; Brooklyn Col; also in many pvt & indust collections. *Comn:* Portraits & wall paintings, pvt & indust. *Exhib:* Pa Acad Fine Arts, Philadelphia, 64; Allied Artists Am Ann, 64; Nat Acad Design Ann, 64; Salvatora Rosa, Naples, Italy, 72; Pallazzo Vechio, Florence, Italy, 72; and many others. *Pos:* Colorist, Lawrence Laguna Architect, 60-; interior designer (free lance). *Teaching:* Instr art, Baldwin, Oceanside, Rockville Centre Pub Schs continuing educ workshops, 57-; St Margret Sch, Va & Lincoln Ctr, NY. *Awards:* Gold Medal (First Prize), Hofstra Univ, 61; Medal of Honor, Nat Asn Women Artists, 67; Ann Award, Am Soc Contemp Artists, 83 & 89; and many others; 13 Resident Fels. *Bibliog:* Newspaper interviews, Taos, Long Island Press, News Day, San Jose Mercury News, Calif & others. *Mem:* Artist Equity of New York, Inc; Nat Asn Women Artists, Inc; New York Soc Women Artists; Contemp Artists; Nat Asn Women Artists. *Media:* Oil, Acrylic; Watercolor, Pastel. *Dealer:* Karol Kamin New York NY. *Mailing Add:* 1521 Wiley St Hollywood FL 33020-6522

LAHR, J(OHN) STEPHEN
PAINTER, EDUCATOR
b Lincoln, Nebr, Aug 5, 1943. *Study:* Univ Nebr, Lincoln, BFA, 68, with James Eisentrager, MEd, 72, EdD, 79. *Work:* Univ Nebr, Omaha; Joslyn Art Mus, Omaha; Pensacola Jr Col, Fla, 86. *Exhib:* Paper in Particular, Columbia Coll Gallery, Mo, 81, 82 & 83; Mid-Four Regional Competition, Nelson Gallery Art, Atkins Mus, Kansas City, Mo, 81 & 82; Watercolor Missouri, William Woods Col, Fulton, 83 & 84; two-person exhib, Joslyn Art Mus, Omaha, 83; Kans Watercolor Soc Ann Competition, Wichita Art Mus, 85; Pensacola Nat Landscape Exhib, 86; Ga Watercolor Soc Ann Nat Exhib, Macon Mus Arts & Sci, 89 & 92. *Collection Arranged:* Missouri Folk: Their Creative Images, Folk Arts Exhib, 82; Sichaun Fine Arts Acad Exhib, Fine Arts Gallery, Valdosta State Col, Ga, 86 & 89; Valdosta Work on Paper I and II, Fine Arts Gallery, 88-89; Artoberfest (juried exhib), Cult Arts Ctr, 91-94. *Pos:* State art dir, Nebr Dept Educ, Lincoln, 74-79. *Teaching:* Instr art, Lincoln Pub Sch, Nebr, 69-72 & Univ Nebr, Lincoln, 72-73; asst prof art educ & studio, Univ Nebr, Omaha, 78-80; asst prof art educ & painting, Univ Mo, Columbia, 80-85; assoc prof, head dept art & gallery dir, Valdosta State Col, Ga, 85-89, prof art dept, 91. *Awards:* Purchase Awards, Joslyn Art Mus, 80 & Univ Nebr, Omaha, 82; Pensacola Nat Purchase Award, 86. *Mem:* Nat Art Educ Asn; signature mem Am Watercolor Soc; Ga Art Educ Asn (bd mem); Ga Watercolor Soc; ASCD; Phi Delta Kappa. *Media:* Watercolor, Intermedia. *Res:* Methods of art instruction; Mixed Media Constructions; art educator profiles. *Publ:* Auth, Handbook for Art Education, Nebr Dept Educ, 78; Who teaches art: Report of recent surveys, In: Studies in Art Educ, Nat Art Educ Asn, 83-84; Health Hazards in the Artroom, EAEA J, 91; Missouri Folk: Their Creative Images (videographer) Libr of Congress, 84; Postmodernism: An Overview of Theory, Resources in Edn, 2000. *Mailing Add:* Valdosta State Univ Art Dept Valdosta GA 31698

LAHTINEN, SILJA (LIISA) TALIKKA
PAINTER, PRINTMAKER
b Lumivaara, Finland, 1954. *Study:* Helsinki Univ, BA & MA, 69; Atlanta Coll Art, BFA, 83; Coll Art, Md Inst, MFA, 86; Acad Int Greci Marino. *Hon Degrees:* Associated Acad, Acad Internacionale, Vinzaglio, Ital, 2002. *Work:* In the Spirit of Fluxes, Santa Barbara Mus Art, Calif; Peanut Gallery, Albany Mus Art, Ga; Excellent Ctr Art & Cult, Grover Beach, Calif; Saint-Marg-in-the-Woods Coll Gallery, Ind; Womens Studio Workshop, Rosendale, NY; Chatachoochee Mus of Art, Ga. *Exhib:* Solo exhibs: Ariel Gallery, NYC, 1987; Taide Art Gallery Helsinki, 1987, 1988, 1991, 1992; 350th Anniversary Swedish/Finnish Art, Atlanta, 1988; Callanwolde Arts Ctr, Atlanta, 1988; Morin-Miller Gallery, NYC, 1989; La Chapelle de la Sorbonne, Paris, 1990; Noitakaraja Show, Viljamakasiini, Ruovesi, Finland, 2006; Summer Show, Ronnvik Vinery, Laitikkala, Finnland 2007; Amsterdam Whitney Gallery, 2009, Artblend Gallery, Ft. Lauderdale, 2014; and numerous others; Albany Mus Art, 1994; Rutgers Nat, 1994; Stedman Gallery, City of Atlanta Gallery, Chastain Park, 1994; San Bernardino Art Mus, 1995; Color: The Divine Madness, Ward-Nasse Gallery, NY, 96; Myths, Milagros and Magic, Ward-Nasse Gallery, 96; Printmakers Renaissance, Rolling Stone Press Gallery, 96; Coca Cola Co: New Americans, Spruill Arts Ctr, 96; Fullgrown Art, Woodruff Arts Ctr, 96; Chattahoochee Valley Art Mus, La, Grange, Ga, 1997; Nuutti Galleria, Finland, Virrat, 2003-2005; Art Expo, Ward Nasse Gallery, NYC, 2008 ; Year Round Salon, Ward Nasse, 2008; Malmö Award Svenska Konstgalleriet, Malmö, Sweden, June 6-27, 2009; Not Just Pretty, Georgia Perimeter Coll, March 23-April 18, 2009; Int Show, Mus of the Americas, Florence, Itlay, Sept 2009; Year Round Salon, Ward-Nasse, 2009, 2010, 2010; Artists Haven Gallery, April Show, Fort Lauderdale, Fla, 2011; Ward-Nasse Gallery, NY, 2014. *Pos:* Artist, owner, Siljas Fine Art Studio, Marietta, Ga, 1987; Vpres, creative advisor Pentec Int Inc, Marietta, 1994-; owner, Siljas Summer Studio & Gallery, Ruovesi, Finland. *Teaching:* Instr, Teknillinen Oppilaitos, Lahti, Finland, 1969-1978; asst instr, Md Inst Col Art, Baltimore, 1986; instr, etching, painting, Atlanta Col Art, 1997. *Awards:* Int Art Competition Cert of Excellence in Printmaking, 88; State of Ga award, Women in Visual Arts, 97; Premio Alba, Meriti Artistici, Ferrara, Ital, 2003; Honorable mention, Women in Arts, Latin Mus Art, Miami, Fla, 2004. *Bibliog:* Susan Randall (auth), A guardian of the earth, Manhattan Arts Int, 1-2/94; Claude le Suer (auth), Nature and Mysticism in the Art of Silja T Lahtinen, Artspeak, 12/94; Joseph Merkel (auth), Silja Talikka Lahtinen, Karelian Girl, Artspeak, 1/95; Ruthie Tucker (auth), Art Acquisitor, Vol 6 No 1, summer 2008; Prof Antonio Malmo (auth), Grandi Maestri, Palermo, Italy, 2008. *Mem:* Orgn Independent Artists; Ga Artists Registry; Am Craft Coun; Roswell Fine Arts Alliance; WCA of Ga (found mem); Am Art Therapy Asn. *Media:* Oil, Acrylic on Canvas; Mixed Media. *Interests:* Shamanism. *Publ:* Contribr, Encyclopedia of Living Artists, Vols 2-10, Art Network Press, 87-96; Erotic Art by Living Artists, Directors Guild Publ, 88; The Art of Lovemaking, An Illustrated Guide, Prometheus Bks, 92; cover, Downtown, 5/26/93; contribr, The Guild, Gallery and Designers Editions, Kraus Sikes Inc, 94-96, 2003-05, 2009; Printworld Dir, 2005, 2008; contribr, New Art Int, 2006-2009; contribr, Guild, 2007-2008. *Dealer:* Ward-Nasse Gallery 178 Prince St New York NY 10012; Rolling Stone Press Gallery 432 Calhoun St Atlanta GA; Amsterdam Whitney Gallery 511 W 25th St New York NY; Artists' Haven Gallery 2757 East Oakland Park Blvd Ft Lauderdale FL 33306. *Mailing Add:* 5220 Sunset Trail Marietta GA 30068

LAI, WAIHANG
PAINTER, EDUCATOR
b Hong Kong, 1939. *Study:* Chinese Univ Hong Kong, BA, 64; Claremont Grad Sch & Univ Ctr, MA, 67. *Comn:* Painting of McBryde Mill, A&B Inc, 75 & 77. *Exhib:* Watercolor USA, Springfield Art Mus, Mo, 69; The Best in the West, Edward-Dean Mus, Calif, 70; Philadelphia Watercolor Club Exhib, Philadelphia Civic Ctr Mus, 72; Solo exhibs, Phoenix Art Mus, Ariz, 67, Kauai Mus, Hawaii, 71-72, 92-93 & 2003-2004, Kahana Kii Fine Art Gallery, 82, & Princeville Galleries, Hawaii, 85, Kilohana Galleries, Hawaii, 89, Kauai Mus, Hawaii, 92 & 93 & Art & Soul Gallery, Hawaii, 2001; Am Watercolor Soc Ann Exhib, 85; Kauai Com Coll Performing Arts Ctr Gallery, 98. *Teaching:* Vis prof art, Ariz State Univ, Tempe, summer 67; asst prof art, Maunaolu Col, Maui, Hawaii, 68-70; prof, Kauai Community Col, 70-04. *Awards:* First Place for Watercolor, Maui Co Creative Arts Exhib, Hawaii, 68; Bronze Medal Honor, Univ Hawaii Bd Regents, 92; Hon Excellence in Teaching Award, 93. *Mem:* Am Watercolor Soc; Philadelphia Watercolor Soc; Kauai Watercolor Soc (pres); Kauai Oriental Art Soc (pres, currently). *Media:* Watercolor, Acrylic. *Publ:* Auth, The Chinese Landscape paintings of Waihang Lai, 66; The Watercolors of Waihang Lai, 67 & Waihang Lai, Watercolor Calendar, 78; illusr, The Tao of Practice Success, 91; Advertisements for acupuncturists, 92. *Mailing Add:* PO Box 363 Lihue HI 96766

LAICO, COLETTE
COLLAGE ARTIST, PAINTER
b Shoreline, Wash. *Study:* Art Students League; Marymount Col, Haystack Mtn Sch Art & Crafts. *Work:* Northern Westchester Hosp, Mt Kisco, NY; Berman Mus Art, Collegeville, Pa; Bellevue Arts Mus. *Comn:* Paintings, Am Int Life Assurance Co, NY, 89. *Exhib:* Monmouth Mus Fine Arts, Monmouth, NJ, 87; ann exhib Silvermine Guild Gallery, 86-96; ann Nat Asn Women Artists, NY, 87-96; Conn Gallery, Marlborough, 88, 89 & 90; Greenwich Art Soc, 88-96; Hudson River Mus, Yonkers, NY, 89; solo show, Hammond Mus, North Salem, NY; ann Bedford Asn Art Show, 2003-2005; Cornell Mus, Delray Beach, Fla, 2008; Longmont Mus, Longmont, Colo, 2009. *Teaching:* Instr art/craft, Westchester Art Workshop, 71-86; instr colonial art/crafts, Westchester Comm Col, 76-80; instr quilting, Scarsdale Adult Sch, 79-92. *Awards:* Gerald Kandler Mem Award, Womans Club Whiteplains, 89 & Mamaroneck Artists Guild, 86; Elizabeth Morse Genius Award, 88 & Sara Winston Mem Award, 92, Nat Asn Women Artists; The Sharon Tietjen Award, Women Painters of Wash Juried Show, 2009. *Bibliog:* Dorothy Friedman (auth), Artist Explores "Arts", Greenwich Time, 1/19/90; Janet Koplos (auth), article, Advocate & Greenwich Time, 2/18/90; The Designers Sourcebook, Guild Publs, eds, 92-96. *Mem:* Silvermine Guild Ctr Arts; Katonah Mus Artists Asn; Katonah Mus (bd mem 2004-2006); Nat Collage Soc (signature mem, 2011-); Northwest Collage Soc; Seattle Co-Arts; Women Painters of Wash. *Media:* Mixed Media. *Mailing Add:* 350 N 190th St Apt 618-C Shoreline WA 98133

LAING-MALCOLMSON, BONNIE
MUSEUM DIRECTOR, PAINTER
b Seattle, Wash, Dec 16, 1952. *Study:* Pac Northwest Coll Art, BFA, 77; Mont State Univ, MFA, 91. *Pos:* Dir acad affairs & admis, Pac Northwest Col Art, 81-87; exec dir, Beall Park Art Ctr, Bozeman, Mont, 91-94, Paris Gibson Sq Mus Art, Great Falls, Mont, 94-. *Teaching:* Adj prof art appreciation & art hist, Mont State Univ, 93. *Mem:* Am Asn Mus; Mont Art Gallery Dir Asn; Mont Asn Mus. *Mailing Add:* c/o Paris Gibson Sq Mus Art 1400 First Ave N Great Falls MT 59401

LAIOU, ANGELIKI E
EDUCATOR
b Athens, Greece, Apr 6, 1941. *Study:* Univ Athens, 58-59; Brandeis Univ, BA (summa cum laude), 59-61; Harvard Univ, MA, 62, travel grants, 64-65, PhD, 66. *Pos:* Dir, Dumbarton Oaks, Washington, DC, 89-. *Teaching:* Instr, Univ La, New Orleans, 62; instr, Harvard, 66-69, asst prof, 69-72, prof Byzantine hist, 81-; assoc prof, Brandeis, 72-75; prof, Rutgers, 75-81; vis prof, Princeton, 81. *Awards:* Guggenheim Fel, 71-72 & 78-79; Rutgers Univ Res Coun grants; Am Coun Learned Soc Fel, 88-89. *Mem:* Phi Beta Kappa; Medieval Acad Am; Am Comt Byzantine Studies; Greek Comt Study South-Eastern Europe; Am Sch Classical Studies Athens. *Mailing Add:* 1735 32nd St NW Washington DC 20007

LAKE, RANDALL
PAINTER, PRINTMAKER
b Long Beach, Calif, Aug 2, 1947. *Study:* Acad Julian, Paris, 67; Univ Colo, BA, 69; Ecole Superieure Beaux Arts, Paris, 72; Atelier 17, Paris, 72-73; Univ Utah, MFA, 77. *Work:* Springville Mus Art, Utah; Am Embassy, Am Libr, Paris; Utah State Arts Collection. *Comn:* Oil paintings of Jerusalem, Mormon Church, Salt Lake City, 79; portrait Willard Eccles, Weber State Col, 81; portrait Nellie Tayloe Ross, Wyo State Capitol, Cheyenne, 82; portrait Dr Leonard W Jarcho, Univ Utah Med Sch, 83; Val A Browning, St Benedict's Hosp, Ogden, Utah, 85; Mayor Ted Wilson, City & Co Bldg, Salt Lake City, 86. *Exhib:* Salon D'Automne, Grand Palais, Paris, 70 & 72; Salon De Mai, Musee D'Art Mod, Paris, 72; Utah Painting & Sculpture, Mus Fine Arts, Univ Utah, Salt Lake City, 75-76; Intermountain Biennial, Salt Lake Art Ctr, 76; Assoc Utah Artists Bicentennial Exhib, Salt Palace, Salt Lake City, 76. *Pos:* Assoc dir, Guthrie Inst Fine Arts, 73-78, painter in residence, 80-. *Teaching:* Assoc instr, Univ Utah, 76-78; Scottsdale Artists' Sch, 92-93. *Awards:* First Place, Asn Utah Artists Bicentennial Exhib, 76; Purchase Award, Deseret News Show, 78, Utah Arts Co, 84; Gold Medal, April Salon, Springville Mus Art, 81; Purchase Award, Utah Arts Coun, 84. *Bibliog:* Genevieve Breerette (auth), A travers les galeries, Le Monde, 71; Lois Collins (auth), Painters of the Guthrie, Expression Mag, 81; Diane Casella Hines (auth), Randall Lake-traditional realist, Am Artist Mag, 2/3/84; article, Randall Lake-Revivalist, Southwest Art Mag, 9/85. *Media:* Oil, Pastel; Gouache. *Dealer:* John Pence Gallery 750 Post St San Francisco CA 94109. *Mailing Add:* 158 E 200 S Salt Lake City UT 84111-1556

LAKES, DIANA MARY
PAINTER
b Sussex, NJ, Aug, 12, 1948. *Study:* Russell Sage Coll, BA, 70; State Univ of NY, Albany, MSW, 71. *Work:* Musee D'Art Naif Max Fourny, Paris, France; Le Musee Int D'Art Naif, Quebec, Can; Theatre on the Lake, Chicago, Ill; Gallerie Je Reviens, Westport, Conn; pvt collection, Daryl Hannah; Int Ctr Naif Art, Modena, Italy; Cedar Rapids Mus Art, Edn/Study Coll, Ia; 3 White-Line Woodblock Prints, Am Family Children's Hospital, Madison, Wisc, 2014. *Comn:* painting in watercolor, Am Family Children's Hospital, Madison, Wisc, 2011. *Exhib:* Pittori Naifs a Guiglia, 5th Salone Int, Modena, It, 99; The Naive Painters in Castelvetro, Castelvetro, It, 2001; US Embassy, Montevideo, Uruguay, So Am, 2001; Gallerie Je Riviens, Wesport, Conn, 2001; solo exhibs, The Cedar Rapids Mus of Art, Cedar Rapids, IA, 2003, Leigh Yawkey Woodson Art Mus, Wausau, Wis, 2005; Rassegna Int d'Arte Naive, Bologna,

Italy, 2008-2009; Musée International d'art naif de Magog, Québec, Can, 2013. *Bibliog:* Se De Lee, Magic of Naive:1992, Sonje Mus of Contemp Art, 92; Jean Florman, Paintings, Ia City Press Citizen, 95; Auth: Amanda Pierre, Artist in Wonderland, Des Moines Register, 2002; Leigh Yawkey (auth), Two Artists, Two Visions, Two Approaches, (exhib catalog), Leigh Yawkey Woodson Art Mus, Wausau, Wisc, 2005. *Mem:* Wis Watercolor Soc. *Media:* Acrylic, Watercolor. *Mailing Add:* 1225 Edgehill Dr Madison WI 53705-1414

LALIN, NINA
PAINTER
b Mar 9, 1935. *Study:* Hofstra Univ, BA(art & english), 56; Art Students League, 70 & 80-82; studies with Barbara Nechis, Daniel Greene & Dong Kingman, 84, 86 & 87. *Work:* Am Labor Mus, Paterson, NJ. *Exhib:* Natural Forms, Soc Experimental Artists, Bradenton, Fla, 92; Forest Floor, Salmagundi Club, NY, 93; Rythems II, Ramapo Coll Gallery, NJ, 94; Two Women, Fairleigh Dickenson Gallery, Hackensack, NJ, 94; Natural Forms, Cork Gallery, NY, 94. *Teaching:* Art teacher, pvt studio work, 76-94, YMHA, Wayne, NJ, 91-92. *Awards:* Buckett Award, Greenwich Village Arts Show, 85; Merit Award, Soc Experimental Artists Soc, 92; Excellence Award, Salute, Cork Gallery, 94. *Bibliog:* Alexandra Shaw (auth), Salute to women in arts, Manhattan Arts Mag, 9/94. *Mem:* Salute Women Arts; Nat Asn Women Artists; Int Soc Experimental Artists. *Media:* Oil, Watercolor. *Dealer:* Shannon Art Gallery Wayne NJ 07470. *Mailing Add:* 10 Bonita Terr Wayne NJ 07470

LALLY, JAMES JOSEPH
DEALER, CONSULTANT
b Mt Vernon, NY, Apr 18, 1945. *Study:* Harvard Univ, BA, 67; Columbia Univ, MBA, 68, MIA, 70. *Pos:* Dir, Chinese Works of Art Dept, Sotheby Parke Bernet NY, Inc, formerly, dir, Sotheby Parke Bernet Hong Kong, Ltd, formerly; pres, Sotheby's NAm, formerly, J J Lally Co, currently. *Specialty:* Chinese works of art (ceramics, archaic bronzes, jades, sculpture, paintings and the minor arts). *Mailing Add:* JJ Lally & Co 41 E 57th St 14th Fl New York NY 10022

LAM, STEVEN
ADMINISTRATOR, EDUCATOR, CURATOR
Study: Trinity Univ, BA; Univ Calif Irvine, MFA. *Collection Arranged:* Spectral Evidence, Rotunda Gallery, Brooklyn, and 1A Space, Hong Kong, 2007-10; For Reasons of State, with Angelique Campens and Erica Cooke, The Kitchen, NY, 2008; Tainted Love, with Virginia Solomon, Visual AIDS, La MaMa Galleria, NY, 2009; SPACES, Cleveland, 2010; ...in a most dangerous manner, with Sarah Ross, 2010; co-curator with Saskia Bos, Free as Air and Water, The Cooper Union, 2009, The Crude and the Rare, 2010, Ruptures: Forms of the Public Address, 2012. *Pos:* art history instr, Sch Visual Arts, 2007-2012, assoc dean sch art, The Cooper Union, 2008-2013, dir sch art & design, assoc prof art & design, Purchase Coll, SUNY, NY, 2013-. *Bibliog:* The NY Times, Brooklyn Rail, Third Text, Flash Art, and others. *Mailing Add:* Purchase College Department of Art and Design 735 Anderson Hill Rd Purchase NY 10577

LAMAGNA, CARLO
EDUCATOR
Study: Coll Holy Cross, BA in English; Univ Mass, MA in art hist. *Teaching:* Prof & Chmn, art dept NYU. *Mailing Add:* NY Univ 82 Wash Sq East New York NY 10003

LA MALFA, JAMES THOMAS
SCULPTOR, EDUCATOR
b Milwaukee, Wis, Nov 30, 1937. *Study:* Univ Wis, Madison, BS, 60, MS, 61 & MFA, 62; studied sculpture with Leo Steppat & printmaking with Alfred Sessler. *Work:* Memphis Acad Art; Univ Wis, La Crosse; Neville Art Mus, Green Bay, Wis. *Comn:* Relief sculpture, Phillips Hall, Univ Wis, Eau Claire, 66 & Theater Bldg, Univ Wis Ctr, Marinette, 95; sacred sculpture, Wittenberg Univ, Ohio, 68; mural, Marinette City Hall, The 400, 2009; City of Menominee, Mich, 2010. *Exhib:* Springfield Art Ctr, Ohio, 67; Print & Drawing Nat, Minot State Teachers Coll, NDak, 70; 29th Northeastern Wis Art Ann, Green Bay, 70; 23rd Ohio Ceramic & Sculpture Ann, Butler Inst Art, 71; solo exhib, West Bend Gallery Art, 2000-2001; UW Marinette sculpture garden, 2000 & 2003; Northeastern Wis Tech Inst, 2003. *Pos:* Instr, art cur, Theater on the Bay Fine Art Gallery. *Teaching:* Instr visual arts, Univ Wis-Eau Claire, 63-66 & Wittenberg Univ, 66-69; asst prof, Univ Wis, Green Bay, 69-72; assoc prof, Univ Wis Ctr, Marinette, 72-. *Awards:* A System of Sculpture Invitational, Univ Wis, Milwaukee Art Dept, fall, 91; Best of Show, 52nd Annual Exhib, Neville Mus Art. *Bibliog:* JJ (auth), article, Art News, 4/64; Pierre Mornand (auth), Expositions diverses rev, Rev Mod, 11/71. *Mem:* Mendminee Area Arts Council. *Media:* Multimedia. *Res:* Notebooks of Leonardo da Vinci. *Specialty:* Local & Regional Art. *Interests:* Photography, Aviation. *Publ:* The Fischer Collection, Wis Acad Sci, Arts & Lett, 74; The Da Vinci Diaries, Marinette, Wis, 7/2007. *Dealer:* Art and Garden Gallery Stephenson Mich. *Mailing Add:* U Wis Ctr Marinette 750 W Bay Shore St Marinette WI 54143

LAMANTIA, JAMES
ARCHITECT, PAINTER
b New Orleans, La, Sept 22, 1923. *Study:* Tulane Univ La, BSArch, 43; Harvard Univ Grad Sch Design, BArch, 47; Skowhegan Sch, 47. *Work:* NO Mus Art; High Mus Atlanta; Colby Coll Mus, Maine; Miss Mus Art. *Comn:* Dairy & Belvedere, Central Park, NY. *Exhib:* Simonne Stern Gallery, New Orleans, 87; Am Acad Rome, 2008. *Pos:* Emer prof archit, Tulane Univ. *Teaching:* Held var teaching positions at several major univs. *Awards:* Prix de Rome, 48-49; Fulbright fel, Italy, 49-50; Fulbright prof archit, Univ Jordan, Amman, 78-79. *Bibliog:* Equal arts of James Lamantia, Arch Forum, 52. *Mem:* Am Inst Archit; Inst Fine Print Dealers Asn. *Media:* Oil, Acrylic. *Specialty:* Rare Archit Prints, drawings, books. *Collection:* Architectural drawings; Piranesi prints; Rare Architectural Books

LAMANTIA, PAUL CHRISTOPHER
PAINTER
b Chicago, Ill, Jan 20, 1938. *Study:* Art Inst Chicago, BFA, 66, MFA, 68. *Work:* Koffler Found Collection, Nat Collection Fine Arts, Smithsonian Inst; Dennis Adrian Collection, Chicago; Art Inst of Chicago, Ill; David & Alfred Smart Mus, Chicago; Cincinnati Mus Art, Ohio; and others; Mus Contemp Art, Chicago; DePaul Art Mus. *Exhib:* What They're Up To In Chicago Traveling Exhib, Nat Gallery Can, Ottawa, 72-73; North, East, South & Middle: An Exhib on Contemp Am Drawing, Corcoran Gallery Art & Ft Worth Art Mus, 75-76; Works on Paper, Art Inst Chicago, 77; solo retrospective, Hyde Park Art Ctr, Chicago, 82; Chicago Imagism, A 25 Yr Survey, Davenport Mus Art, Iowa, 94; Post-War Chicago Works on Paper & Sculpture, David & Alfred Smart Mus, Univ Chicago, Ill, 95; Art in Chicago, 1945-1995 (with catalog), Mus Contemp Art, Chicago, 96; Don Baum says' Chicago Has Famous Artists, Hyde Park Art Ctr, Chicago, 96; Cincinnati Collects, Contemporary Art Ctr, 2007; The Exquisite Snake, Block Mus, Northwestern Univ, Evanston, Ill, 2007; Twos: Dominican Univ, River Forest, Ill, 2010; Twos, Dominican Univ, River Forest, Ill, 2010; 40/40 Ukrainian Inst Modern Art, 2011; On & Of Paper, Selections from the Ill State Mus Collection, Ill State Mus, Chicago Gallery, James Thompson Ctr, 2011; Works on Paper, Elmhurst Art Mus, Elmhurst, Ill, 2011; Subconcious Eye, Ukrainian Inst Modern Art, 2013. *Collection Arranged:* Art Inst Chicago, Chicago, Ill; Mus Contemp Art, Chicago, Ill; Nat Mus Am Art, Smithsonian Inst, Wash DC; The Collection of Jean Dubuffet, Paris, France; Cincinnati Art Mus, Cincinnati, Ohio; The Figge Art Mus, Davenport, Iowa; The Wright Mus Art, Beloit, Wis; The Ukrainian Inst Mod Art, Chicago, Ill; The Milwaukee Art Mus; The Smart Mus, Chicago; The Block Mus, Evanston, Ill; Pa Acad Fine Arts, Philadelphia; Ill State Mus, Springfield, Ill; DePaul Univ Mus, Chicago, Ill; Contemporary Mus, Honolulu, Hawaii; The Madison Mus Contemp Art, Wis; Roger Brown Study Collection, Art Inst Chicago; Elmhurst Coll Art Collection, Chicago Imagist and Abstractionist Art, Elmhurst, Ill. *Teaching:* Creative Seminar Proj, Columbia Col, Chicago, Ill, 94 & 98, Cincinnati Acad Art, Art Inst Chicago, Loyola Univ Chicago. *Awards:* Logan Prize, Art Inst Vicinity Show, Chicago, 84. *Bibliog:* David Elliott (auth), Cunning painter of the smart set, Chicago Sun-Times, 3/29/81; Dennis Adrian (auth), Sight Out of Mind, Essays & Criticism on Art, UMI Research Press, 10/85; Lynn Gamell, Ernest Hartmann & Donald Kuspit (auths), Dreamworks: Artistic and Psychological Perspectives, State Univ, NY & Cornell Univ Press, 99; James Yood (auth), Paul Lamantia, New Art Examiner, Mar, 1996; Dennis Adrian (auth), Painting & Drawing, Paul Lamantia, Randolph Street Press, 2000; Jimmy Wright & David Sharpe (coauths), The Anxious Image, Painting Ctr, NY, 2004; Robert Cozzolino (auth), Art in Chicago, Resisting Regionalism, Transforming Modernism, Pa Accad Fine Arts, Philadelphia, 2007; Lynne Warren (auth), New American Paintings, No 83, 2009; Adriene Kochman (auth), Selections, From the Permanent Collection, Ukrainian Inst Art, 2011; Natalie Domchenko (auth), 40/40 Ukrainian Inst Modern Art, 2012; Robert Cozzolino (auth), Subconcious Eye Ukrainian Inst Modern Art, 2013. *Media:* Oil, Mixed Media, Drawing. *Res:* 70 plus Chicago Visual Artist Oral History Archive, 2010. *Interests:* World Travel. *Publ:* auth, Regions, Chicago Art Write Vol 1, Sch Art Inst Chicago, 86. *Dealer:* Packer Schopf Gallery 942 W Lake St Chicago Ill 60607. *Mailing Add:* 315 W Concord Pl Chicago IL 60614

LAMARCA, HOWARD J
DESIGNER, EDUCATOR
b Teaneck, NJ, July 11, 1934. *Study:* Cooper Union Art Sch, scholar, 52-56, cert graphic arts, 56; Columbia Univ, BFA, 60; Syracuse Univ, grad asst, 60-62, MFA, 62. *Collection Arranged:* James Gordon Irving-Painter, 71; Grant Reynard-Painter, 71; Charles Shedden, Sculptor-Ralph Didriksen, Painter, 71; George Fish, Painting-Shirley Yudkin, Paintings, 72; Marion Lane, Painting Retrospective, 72; Arnoldo Miccoli-Painter, 73; Sam Weinik-Painter, 74; Erna Will-Sculptor; Eleanor Smoler-Painter, 74; Batiks--Giovanna Bellia La Marca, Co Coll Morris, 76; Batik & Calligraphy Exhibit, Dwight-Englewood Sch, 85; Korean Graphic Design Exhib, Hillwood Mus, Brookville, NY, 98; NY Art Dir Club, 98. *Pos:* Advert art dir, Givaudan Advert, New York, 57-; dir, Bergen Community Mus, 71-74; sem dir Europ advert, Paris, France, Dusseldorf & Frankfurt, Ger, Zurich, Switz & Milan, Italy, 78-84; European Art Tour, Milano, Venice, Florence, Rome, 90. *Teaching:* Asst prof art, Trenton State Col, 74-80; assoc prof art, Co Col of Morris, 74; adj asst prof, Parsons Sch Design, 79-81; chmn art dept & prof art, C W Post Ctr, Long Island Univ, 80-; lectr, Musashino Art Univ Tokyo, Meiji Gakuin Univ, Yokohama & Tokyo, Hoseo Univ, Hanyang Univ & Kyung-yi Univ, Korea, 97. *Awards:* Graphics Design Award, New York, 79 & 81. *Mem:* Soc Scribes; Art Dir Club NY; Coll Art Asn Am; Am Inst Graphic Arts; Univ & Coll Design Asn. *Media:* Graphics, Calligraphy. *Publ:* Auth, An analysis of Gauguin's-What are We? Where Do We Come From? Where Are We Going?, Artist Mag, London, 3/62; An analysis of the facade of San Marco, Eleven Mag, spring 72; Some Thoughts on Design, City Univ New York, 74; Ethics & aesthetics, Focus, 76; Another Hillwood, Ventures in Res, 2/86. *Mailing Add:* Three Crescent Ave Cliffside Park NJ 07010

LAMARRE, PAUL
CONCEPTUAL ARTIST, SCULPTOR
b Detroit, Mich. *Study:* Univ Mich, BFA, 78. *Work:* ICA, London, Eng; New Mus Contemp Art, NY; Montecarotto Mail Art Mus, Italy. *Comn:* Bldg installation, comn by Andrew Klink, Los Angeles, 89-90; bldg installation, comn by Helen Jacobs, NY, 90. *Exhib:* one-person shows, Hallwalls, Buffalo, NY, 83 & Dooley Le, Cappellaine Gallery, NY, 92; Starving Artists Cook Book, Anthology Film Archives, NY, 89; EIDIA Show, Barbara Braathen, NY, 89; New Fabricants, Richard Green Gallery, Los Angeles, 90; Store Show, Richard/Bennett Gallery, Los Angeles, 91; Value, NY, 91; and others. *Awards:* CAPS Fel, New York, 82; Video Fel, New York Found, 87. *Bibliog:* Luca Neri (auth), Il Ricettario Dell Artista, Lei Mag, 89; Robert Mahoney (auth), Quiet desperation, Arts Mag, 89; Judd Tulley (auth), Art speak, Taxi Mag, 89; Hal Rubenstein (auth), Mirabella Mag, 91. *Mem:* Asn Independent Video & Filmakers; NY Artists Equity Asn; Media Alliance. *Media:* Installations, Video. *Publ:* Coauth, Starving Artists' Cook Book, EIDIA Publ, 91; Starving Artists' Banquet, NY Times, 92. *Mailing Add:* 426 E Ninth St No 1C New York NY 10009

LAMB, DARLIS CAROL
SCULPTOR, PAINTER
b Wausa, Nebr. *Study:* Univ Nebr, Omaha; Creighton Univ, Omaha; Red Rocks Community Col; studied sculpture with Stanley Bleifield, Lloyd Glasson & Francisco Zuniga; Columbia Pacific Univ, BA, MA. *Work:* Gannett Found, Denver; Nebr Hist Soc, Lincoln; First Fed Savings & Loan Asn of Lincoln, Omaha; Benson Park Sculpture Garden, Loveland, Colo; Am Lung Asn; Space Found, Colorado Springs, Colo; Colorado Springs Osteopathic Foundation, Colo; Rocky Mountain Health Facility, Loveland, Colo. *Comn:* Spirit of Health (sculpture, bas reliefs & medallions), Am Lung Asn, Colorado Springs & Denver, Colo, 84-89; sculpture, Loveland High Plains Arts Coun, Colo, 88, 2001, 2008; Hall of Fame Medal, Space Found, Colo, 97; Coll Osteopathic Found, 99. *Exhib:* Northern Am Sculpture Exhib, Foothills Art Ctr, Golden, Colo, 83, 84, 86, 87, 90 & 91; Catherine Lorillard Wolfe, NY, 83, 85, 89, 91, 93, 2004-2005; Nat Sculpture Soc, NY, 85, 91, 95, 97, 2003-06; 161st Exhib, Nat Acad Design Gallery, NY, 86; Allied Artists, NY, 92 & 95; Pen & Brush, NY, 93, 95, 96, 98 & 2000. *Teaching:* instr, terra cotta sculpture Ruidoso Art Sch, Ruidoso, NMex, 94, 95, Loveland Acad Fine Arts, Loveland, Colo, 1995, 96, Curtis Ctr for Arts & Humanities, Greenwood Village, Colo, 2000, 2001, St Mary's Acad, Denver, 1998. *Awards:* C Percival Dietsch Award, Nat Sculpture Soc, 91; Horse's Head Award Best Sculpture, Catharine Lorillard Wolfe Art Club, 94 & Hon Mention, 96 & Medal of Honor, 98 & 2005; Roman Bronze Award, Pen & Brush, 95; Bronze medal for Sculpture, 99; Harriet W Frishmuth Memorial Sculpture award, 2002; Paul Manship Memorial Sculpture award, 2001. *Bibliog:* Gary Michael (auth), article, Southwest Art Mag, 1/89 & 7/99; Betty Lane (auth), Footprints in the sand, Elan Mag, 5/90; Christina Reid (auth), Artists medal is out of this world, Villager, 7/17/97; Darlis Lamb, SWA Mag, 7/99; Focus Santa Fe, 8-9/2005; Sculptural Pursuit Mag, spring 2008; Am Art Collector Mag, 2/2008; Southwest Art Mag, 9/2010; Stan Shur (auth), Successful Women Speak Out, 2011; Southwest Art Mag, 7/2013. *Mem:* Catharine Lorillard Wolfe Art Club; North Am Sculpture Soc; Am Womens Art Asn. *Media:* Clay, Cast Metal; Watercolor, Oil. *Publ:* Bonnie McCune (auth), Darlis Lamb Stories in Sculpture, Denver Woman Mag, 6/7/2009; Sculpture of the Rockies, 97 Contemp Sculptors, Southwest Art Mag, Darlis Lamb, 2010, 2013. *Dealer:* Howard Mandville Kirkland, Wash; Ventura Fine Art, Santa Fe, NMex; Marta Stafford Fine Art Marble Falls TX; 3795 Gallery Doylestown Pa. *Mailing Add:* 5515 S Kenton Way Englewood CO 80111

LAMB, MATT
PAINTER, SCULPTOR
b Chicago, Ill. *Work:* Nat Treasury, Washington; Spertus Mus Judaica, St Xavier Coll & State of Ill Collection, Chicago; Vatican Mus, Italy; Mus Contemp Art, Ferrara, Italy. *Comn:* Life of Christ (9 tarps), Mannheim Cathedral, Ger. *Exhib:* Carl Hammer Gallery, Chicago, 90; Galerie Berlin, Ger, 92; Galeria Praxis Arte Int, Mexico City, 93; Galerie Kasten, Mannheim, Ger, 95; Madness & Matt Lamb, Fasshender Gallery, Chicago, 96; State of Ill Gallery, Lockport, Ill, 96; Rockford Art Mus, Ill, 97; Galeria Punto, Valencia, Spain, 97; Mus Contemp Art, Ferrara, Italy, 97; Fassbender Gallery, Chicago, 98. *Bibliog:* Michael Bonesteel (auth), Lamb of God, Carl Hammer Gallery, 90; James Yood et al (auths), Matt Lamb, Fassbender Gallery, 94; Donald Kuspit (auth), Madness and Matt Lamb, Fassbender Gallery, 96; and others. *Media:* Oil on canvas. *Mailing Add:* c/o Judy Saslow Gallery 300 W Superior Chicago IL 60610

LAMBERT, ED
PRINTMAKER, PAINTER
b Atlanta, Tex, Jan 27, 1949. *Study:* Tex Tech Univ, BFA & MFA. *Exhib:* Pratt Graphic Ctr Int Miniature Print Exhib, 75; Mach I Int Print Exhib, Metrop Mus Art, Miami, Fla, 75; Solo exhibs, M E's Gallery, Houston, 83 & Charlton Art Gallery, San Antonio, 86; Animal Magnetism, Nueva Street Gallery, San Antonio, 90. *Teaching:* Prof printmaking, Del Mar Col, Corpus Christi, Tex, 74-, chmn art dept, 80-. *Bibliog:* Joseph A Cain (auth), Profile, Art Voices South, 7-8/80; Dan Goddard (auth, rev), San Antonio Express News, 7/19/90. *Media:* Etching, Airbrush. *Dealer:* Nueva Street Gallery 507 E Nueva St San Antonio TX 78205. *Mailing Add:* 607 Del Mar Corpus Christi TX 78404

LAMBERT, PHYLLIS
ARCHITECT, DIRECTOR
b Montreal, Que, Jan 24, 1927. *Study:* Vassar Coll, BA, 48; Ill Inst Technol, with Myron Goldsmith & Fazlur Khan, MS (archit), 63. *Hon Degrees:* McGill Univ, DLitt, 86; Concordia Univ, LLD, 86; Univ Windsor, LLD, 89; Pratt Inst, DFA, 90; Queen's Univ, DCL, 90; Univ British Columbia, Dlitt, 92; Univ Victoria, LLD, 93; Univ New Brunswick, Dlitt, 95; Emily Carr Inst of Art and Design, Dlitt, 98; Univ Waterloo, LLD, 2000; Dartmouth Univ, Hon Dr, 2001; Spertus Inst of Jewish Studies, Hon Dr, 2001; Univ du Québec à Montréal, Hon Dr, 2002; Ryerson Univ, Hon Dr, 2004; Corcoran Coll Art & Design, DFA, 2007. *Work:* Saidye Bronfman Ctr, with Webb, Zerafa & Menkes, YWHA, Montreal, 63-68; Jane Tate House Renovation, with Arcop Assoc, Phyllis Lambert off & residence, Montreal, 74-76; Small Cinema, with Arcop Assoc, pvt house, Montreal, 75-76; Biltmore Hotel Renovation, with Gene Summers, Los Angeles, Calif, 76-77; 8 Housing Units, with Peter Lanken, 78; Restoration Project, Ben Ezra Synangogue Cairo, Egypt, 81-94; Can Ctr Archit, Consult Archit, with Peter Rose, Montreal, 84-89. *Comn:* Photographic Mission, with Richard Pare, 71-74, Court House: A Photographic Document, (exhib catalog), with Richard Pare, 77-80; Olmsted Parks Project (photogs Robert Burley, Lee Friedlander, and Geoffrey James), CCA, 88-94; Richard Lippold, Four Seasons Restaurant, New York, 58; Mark Rothko, Four Seasons Restaurant, New York 58-59. *Exhib:* Retrospective (auth, catalog), 4th Fl Gallery, Seagram Bldg, NY 77; Cooper-Hewitt Mus, NY, 83; Art Inst Chicago, 83; Nat Gallery Can, Ottawa, 84; Musee Nat d'art moderne, Ctr Georges Pompidou, Paris, 84; Montreal Mus Contemp Art, Chicago, 2001-2002. *Collection Arranged:* Joseph E Seagram & Sons Inc Collection, 54-; Can Indian Exhib, 69 & Aaron Siskind Exhib, 70, Saidye Bronfman Centre, Montreal; Seagram Plaza: Its Design & Use, Seagram Bldg, NY, 77; Can Ctr for Archit Collection, 79-99. *Pos:* Dir planning, Seagram Bldg, NY, 54-58; dir, Seagram Bicentennial Proj, Co Courthouse in the US, 74-; founder & dir, Can Ctr for Archit, 79-99, Interim dir, 2004-2005; comnr, Int Confederation Archit Mus, 79; project dir, renovation of Ben Ezra Synagogue, Cairo, Egypt, 81-94. *Teaching:* Lectr, Urban Studies Prog and Dept Hist, Concordia Univ, Montreal, 82-83; final yr reviews, École d'Archit, Faculté de l'aménagement, Université de Montréal, 85; adj prof, Sch Archit, McGill Univ, Montreal, 86- & final yr reviews, 89-92; assoc prof, Faculté de l'aménagement, École d'Archit, Univ de Montréal, 89-; guest prof, Atelier Triptyque, Faculté d'aménagement, École d'Archit et paysage, Univ de Montréal, 92; final yr reviews, Sch Archit, Univ Waterloo, Ontario, 93. *Awards:* 25-year Award Excellence, Am Inst Archit, 84; Gold Medalist, Royal Archit Inst of Can, 91; Hon Mem: Am Inst of Archit, NY Chap, 96; Life mem, Coun of the Ontario Asn of Archit, 2003; Fel of the Am Inst of Archit, Hon, 2003; Ville de Montreal and Heritage Montreal, 2007; Jane Jacobs Lifetime Achievement Award, Canadian Urban Institute, 2008; Iris Found Award, Iris Found, Bard Grad Ctr for Studies in the Decorative Arts, Design, and Culture, 2008. *Bibliog:* Paul Goldberger (auth), A Treasurehouse for Architecture, NY Times, 5/7/89; Various auth, Profiles darchitectes d'aujourd'hui; ARQ: La Revue d architecture, 12/95; Blair Kamin (auth), Talking frankly with Joan of Architecture, Chicago Tribune, 2/19/2002; The Architects Newspaper, 2007; Teri Wehn-Damisch (dir), Citizen Lambert: Joan of Architecture/Citizen Lambert: Jeanne d'architecture, Nat Film Bd Can, 2007. *Mem:* Royal Can Acad Arts; Soc du Patrimoine Urbain de Montreal (pres, 79); Soc Archit Historians (dir, currently); Int Confederation of Archit Mus (ICAM); Fonds d'investissement de Montréal (FIM), (pres, bd dir, 96-); Table de concertation, PPU centre-ville Ouest, Montreal (pres, 2006-). *Media:* Manuscript drawings, Photography, Literature pertaining to the art of archit in its broadest sense. *Interests:* the culture of architecture. *Collection:* Architectural drawings from the 16th century to the 20th century; photographs of the 19th and 20th century; manuscripts and books on architecture. *Publ:* Contribr, Court House, Horizon Press, spring 78; auth, The archit mus: "a founders perspective," J of the Soc of Archit Hist, 9/99; Mies Immersion, Mies in America, 2001; Love in the Time of the WTC, Log, 2004; Simmung at Seagram: Philip Johnson Counters Mies van der Rohe, Grey Room, 2005; Farnsworth on Mars? Or on the Commissioning and Stewardship of Buildings, Hunch, 2006; Building Seagram, Yale Univ Press, 2011. *Mailing Add:* Can Centre for Architecture 1920 Baile St Montreal PQ H3H 2S6 Canada

LAMBRECHTS, MARC
PAINTER, PRINTMAKER
b Lier, Antwerp, Belg, Sept 14, 1955. *Study:* Higher St Lucas Inst, Brussels, Belg; Art Sch, Bratislava, Czech (govt scholarships); Pratt Inst, New York. *Work:* Aldrich Mus Contemp Art, Conn; Flemish Community, Belg; Gemeentekrediet, Belg; Kidder & Peabody, New York; Terra's Interno, Tokyo, Japan; PROTEK Pharmaceutical, Bern, Switz; David & Lucile Packard Found, Los Altos, Calif; Saks Fifth Ave; Stichting Paulus Dommelhof, Eindhoven, Holland; Davidsfonds Nat, Belgium; SABENA Belg World Airlines; Soc Worldwide Interbank Financial Telecommun sc, Belg; IDB Commun Group; Redback Networks Inc, Sunnyvale, Calif; UN Belgian Mission, New York; Ensign-Brickford Industs Inc, Conn; and numerous other pvt & corp collections; Mint Mus Art (pvt collection), Charlotte, NC, 2008; Collection Edward Albee, NY. *Comn:* etchings, Leo Magits Found, Golflengthe Mag, 83; etchings, Free Univ Belg, 89 & 2006; portfolio-works on paper, GIMV Investment Co, Flanders. *Exhib:* Solo Exhibs: Gallery Fontainas, Brussels, Belg, 88; Arts Club Washington, DC, 89; Tibor de Nagy Gallery, New York, 91; Hugieia Art Gallery, Belg, 92; Crossroad-Paintings & Objects, Hugieia Gallery, Antwerp, 93; Recent Works, Galerie Laegveld, Hasselt, Belg, 94; Hugieia Gallery, Tongeren, Belg, 96; Galerie Faider, Brussels, Belg, 97; Gallery Moving Space, Ghent, Belg, 98; Joie Lassiter Gallery, Charlotte, NC, 99; Jeffrey Coploff Fine Art Ltd, New York, 2002; Salon des invités, Belg Moba Art, Brussels, Belg, 2003; A Walk Through Mini-mini Space, Joie Lassiter Gallery, Charlotte, NC, 2004; Recent Works, Van den Brande-Wauters, in asn with The Peak, Singapore, 2004; Sediments, Joie Lassiter Gallery, Charlotte, NC, 2005; Belgian King's Visit, Invitational exhib, UN Belg Mission, New York, 2007; Slivers of Reality, ARTHAUS, San Francisco, 2007; Salon des Invites Willem Elias, Brussels, Belgium, 2008; Lemmons Contemp, NY, 2008; Art Dirs Club Gallery, New York, 87; Recent Acquisitions, Aldrich Mus Contemp Art, Conn, 88; Hudson River Open '89, Hudson River Mus, New York, 89; Gallery Michel Dekeyser, Brussels, Belg, 90; 100 Yrs Belgian Art, L'Arc de Defence, Paris, France, 90; Art of Northeast USA, Silvermine Galleries, Conn, 91; VUB, Free Univ Brussels, Belg, 91; Abstracted Reality, Tibor de Nagy Gallery, New York, 93; Am Abstraction: A New Decade, Southern Alleghenies Mus Art, Loetto, Pa, 94; Ludmilla Baczynsky Gallery, New York, 96; 10th Anniversary, Gallery Moving Space, Ghent, Belg, 97; Elements of Style, ArtHaus, San Francisco, 98; Residual Value, Tyron Ctr Visual Art, Charlotte, NC, 99; Paper Products, ArtHaus, San Francisco, 2000; One Land, Eight Belgian Artists, Frieda & Roy Furman Gallery, Lincoln Ctr, New York, 2002; Le Bateau Fou, West Hampton, NY, 2003; Olympic Truce: Pieces of Peace, Olympic Arts Fest, 2004; In The Mix, Getting Real & No Contest, ArtHaus, San Francisco, 2005; Within Our Walls, Trizec Properties, Charlotte, NC, 2005; AAF Contemp Art Fair, New York, 2005-2006; four-person exhib, House Guests, Lemmons Contemp, New York, 2007; Group Exhib: Lemmons Contemp, NY, 2008; and many others. *Pos:* Cur, Eight Belgian Artists, Z Gallery, New York, 93 & 26 Am Artists, Campo & Campo, Antwerp, Belgium, 99; coordr, Higher Inst Arts, Antwerp in New York, 2001-2005. *Teaching:* Guest prof, Higher Inst Arts, Antwerp, Belgium, 99-2005. *Awards:* First Prize, Young Belgian Graphic Artists, Rotary Club, 81; Cert Excellence, printmaking, Int Art Competition, New York, 87; Medal, printmaking & Cert Excellence, small works, USA Major Art Competition, Los Angeles, 87; Olympic Truce: Pieces of Peace competition, Greek Embassy, Olympic Arts Festival, 2004. *Bibliog:* Revs In: NY Times, 6/91, Staten Island Advan, 5/91, Art News, 1/92, W E Knack, 11/93 & 11/2004, Trends, 9/93, The Hill, spring 96, NY Arts Mag, 11/98 & Arts & Entertainment, NC, 10/98; Alice Gray (auth), Art News, 1/92; Brooklyn Bridge, interview, 3/97; Financeel Economische Tijd, interview, 8/22/98; and many other revs & interviews. *Media:* Mixed Media; Etching. *Specialty:* Contemporary. *Dealer:* Joie Lassiter Gallery 318 E 9th St Charlotte NC 28202; Arthaus 1053 Bush St Suite #2 San Francisco CA 94109; Lemmons Contemporary Harrison St Ground Floor NY 10013

LAMBRIX, TODD
SCULPTOR
b Livingston, NJ, 1969. *Study:* Rutgers Univ, New Brunswick, NJ, BFA, 1998; RI Sch Design, MFA, 2001; studied with Kuehn, Tom Butter, Dean Snyder. *Work:* Pvt collections. *Exhib:* Solo exhib, Bristol-Myers Squibb Gallery, Princeton, NJ, Slater Mem Mus, Norwich, Conn, Phoenix Gallery, New York City, Utopia of One Sol Koffler Gallery, Providence, RI, 2001; RI Sch of Design, 2001. *Pos:* instr, Parsons New Sch of Design, 2005-. *Teaching:* instr, Raritan Valley Community Col, currently; instr Foundation Dept, RI Sch of Design, currently. *Awards:* VT Studio Residency Award, 1996; Sculpture Award, Ct Acad Fine Arts, 2000. *Mem:* Coll Art Asn. *Media:* Mixed; Wood and Metal. *Specialty:* Non-objective experimental

LAMENSDORF, JOAN
PAINTER, DESIGNER
Study: Catholic Univ of Am, BA; Studied with Dannielle Mick, Annette Hanna, Christina Debarry, Hollie Heller, Anne Kullaf & Al Lachman, Visual Arts Ctr NJ; Studied with Julie Friedman, Artspace Studios; Sch Visual Arts, New York. *Exhib:* Pfizer Gallery, Morris Plains, NJ, 2005; Madison Artist Studio Tour, Madison, NJ, 2006, 2009, 2010, 2011; Bernardsville Libr Juried Show, 2008; Tewksbury Juried Art Show, Oldwick, NJ, 2008, 2009; Artspace Gallery, Morristown, NJ, 2008; Ridgewood Art Inst Juried Show, Ridgewood, NJ, 2009; NJ Green Exhib, Art Coun Morris Area, 2009; Rivergarden Gallery, Works on Paper Exhib, Denville, NJ, 2009; Gaelen Juried Art Show, JCC Metrowest, Whippany, NJ, 2009, 2010 & 2011; Somerset Art Asn Juried Show, 2009; Audubon Artist Juried Exhib, Salmagundi Club, New York, 2009; Mountain Arts Juried Show, 2009; Wallflowers Gallery, 3 Person Show, 2009; Wallflowers Gallery, 2010; Catherine Lorillard Wolfe Art Club Juried Exhib, 2010; Speak Easy Galery, Boonton, NJ, 2010; Harding Gallery, Morristown, NJ, 2011; Gaelen Gallery East, W Orange, NJ, 2011. *Awards:* Hon mention, Tewksbury Juried Art Show, 2008; Award of Merit, MSHAC Juried Exhib, 2008; 3rd Prize, PSNJ Mem Show, 2008; Award of Merit, MSHAC Overlook Juried Exhib, 2009; Marquis Who's Who References award in Pastels, Audubon Artist Exhib, 2009; Hon Mention, Gaelen Juried Art Show, 2009; Award of Excellence, Somerset Art Asn Mem Show, 2010; PSNJ Award of Excellence, Pastel Soc NJ Juried Show, 2010; Hon mention, MSHAC Overlook Exhib, 2011; Best in drawing/pastels Category, Gaelen Juried Art Show, 2011. *Mem:* bd mem, Pastel Soc NJ; Visual Arts Cr NJ; Millburn-Short Hills Art Ctr; Somerset Art Asn; mem, Ctr Contemp Art. *Media:* Pastel, Oil, Collage. *Publ:* Vicnity Mag, Summer 2011. *Mailing Add:* 840 E Green St #504 Pasadena CA 91101

LAMM, LEONID IZRAIL
CONCEPTUAL ARTIST, PAINTER
b Moscow, Russia, Mar 6, 1928; US citizen. *Study:* Archit Acad, Moscow, 47; Graphic Acad, Moscow, MFA, 54. *Work:* Metrop Mus Art, New York; Solomon R Guggenheim Mus, New York; Stedelijk Mus, Amsterdam, Holland; Jewish Mus, New York; Tretiakovsky Gallery, Moscow. *Exhib:* SOTs-ART, The New Mus Contemp Art, New York, 86; Transit, State Russ Mus, 89; The Colors of Money, Musee de la Poste, Paris, 91; New Acquisitions, Stedelijk Mus Amsterdam, 91; From Gulag to Glasnost: Nonconformist Art from Soviet Union, 1956-1986, Jane Voorhees Zimmerli Art Mus, New Brunswick, NJ, 95; Russian Jewish Artists in a Century of Change 1870-1988, Jewish Mus, New York, 95; Temporarily Possessed, New Mus Contemp Art, New York, 95; Re-inventing the Emblem: Contemp Artist Recreated a Renaissance Idea, Yale Univ Art Gallery, 95; Russian Conceptual Art of the 1980's, Duke Univ Mus Art, Durham, NC, 96; Non-Conformist Art from Soviet Union 1956-1986, Stedelijk Mus, Amsterdam, 97-98; The Hall in the Hall, Herbert F Johnson Mus Art, Cornell Univ, Ithaca, NY, 97; Birth of an Image, Duke Univ Mus of Art, Durgham, NC, 98; Birth of an Image, Jane Voorhees Zimmerli Art Mus, New Brunswick, NJ, 2000; The State Russ Mus, St Petersburg, 2002; Abstraction in Russia, XX Century; Soviet Artists, Jewish Themes, Jane Vorhees Zimmerli Art Mus, New Brunswick, NJ, 2003; Global Village: the 1960's, Montreal Mus Fine Art, 2003-2004; Iakov Chernikhov & Leonid: Codes of Geometry, Nat Center Contemp Arts, Moscow, 2005; Leonid Lamm: From Utopia to Virtuality, The State Russian Museam, St Petersburg, 2009; The Ludvig Mus in The Russian Mus; The Forbidden Arts, The Dostinar Russian Avant-Garde, The Hillstrom Mus Art, Gustavus Adolphus Coll, 2009; Zglasnost & Soviet Non-Conformist Art from the 1980s Haunch of Venison, London, 2010. *Teaching:* Prof painting & drawing, Graphic Acad, Moscow, 62-73 & 76-82. *Awards:* Silver Medal, Int Book Fair, Leipzig, Ger Democratic Repub, 59; 2000 Outstanding People of the 20th Century Medal & Diploma, Int Biographical Ctr Cambridge, CB2 3QP, Eng, 98. *Bibliog:* John Bowlt (auth), A Catafalque of the Senses, Eduard Nakhamkin Fine Art, New York, 90; Donald Kuspit (auth), Leonid Lamm's Homage to Yakov Chernikhov, Howard Schickler Fine Art, New York, 94; Eleanor Heartney (auth), Leonid Lamm: Birth of an Image (exhib catalog), Duke Univ Mus Art, 98; Iakov Chernikhov (auth), Leonid Lamm: Codes of Geometry (exhib catalog), Nat Ctr Contemp Arts, Iakov Chernikhov Int Found, Moscow, 2005; Leonid Lamm: From Utopia to Virtuality, The State Russian Mus; St Petersburg, Russia (Exhib Almanac), 2009. *Mem:* Iakov Chernikhov Int Found, Moscow & Sofia, NY (co-dir). *Media:* Installation; All Media. *Dealer:* Westwood Gallery 758 Broadway 1st fl New York NY 10012; Sloan Gallery Oxford Office Bldg 1612 17th St Denver CO 80202; Guelman Gallery 7/7 Malaya Polyanka 109180 Moscow Russia; IZO Gallery 4 Davies St London W1K 3DL; Gallerie Blue Square, Wash. *Mailing Add:* 332 E 22nd St Apt 6B New York NY 10010

LAMONTAGNE, ARMAND M
SCULPTOR, PAINTER
b Pawtucket, RI, Feb 3, 1938. *Study:* Studied in Florence, Italy. *Comn:* 7-foot wood sculptures of Babe Ruth, 84 & Ted Williams, 85, Baseball Hall of Fame, Cooperstown, NY,; portrait of gov, Providence, RI, 87; life size wood sculptures of Larry Bird, Bobby Orr, Carl Yastrzemski, New Eng Sports Mus; life size bronze sculpture of Ted Williams, Ted Williams Mus, Hernando, Fla; life size wood sculpture of Gen George Patton, Patton Mus, Ft Knox, Ky. *Awards:* Russell Grinell Found Grant, 64. *Media:* Wood. *Mailing Add:* 405 Bungy Rd N North Scituate RI 02857

LAMONTE, ANGELA MAE
PAINTER
b New Britain, Conn, 1944. *Study:* Catan-Rose Inst Fine Arts,Cert, studied with Kazires Zoromskis, 67; Nat Acad Fine Arts, Study with Hugh Gumpel, 69; City Col, New York, MFA, 77; Bank St Col, MS, 82. *Work:* numerous private collections US & worldwide. *Exhib:* Malcolm King Faculty Exhib, Harlem State Off Bldg Gallery, 81; Art '84 Tobago, Int Art Convention, Trinidad-Tobago, Wis, 84; Boniface Gallery, Cathedral of St John the Divine, NY, 86; Gallery M, NY, 87; Gallery Art 54, NY, 88; Atlantic Gallery, NY, 1990, 92, 93, 96-2002, 2008; Multi-Media Arts Gallery, NY, 91-94; Atlantic Gallery, NY, 2003-2006; Atlantic Gallery, 2005, 2006; Apexart, NY, 2007; Atlantic Gallery, NY, 2007, 2008, 2009, 2011, 2012, 2013; AIR Gallery, New York, 2009, 2010, 2011, 2012, 2013; 2/20 Gallery, NY, 2011. *Pos:* Adv coun mem, New Century Artists Inc, New York, currently. *Teaching:* Prof art, painting & drawing collage, Malcolm King Col, New York, 79-89, chairperson art dept, 84-89. *Awards:* Louis La Beaume Award, Nat Acad Fine Arts, 70; Art Alumni Pres Award, City Coll New York, 83. *Mem:* Artists Equity, NY. *Media:* Oil; Multi-Media. *Publ:* Art exhibit to benefit Malcolm-King, New York Voice, 9/81; article, New Britain Herald, 9/86; article, Hartford Courant, 9/87; article, Amsterdam News, 1/88; article, New Britain Herald, 8/93

LAMOUREUX, MARIE FRANCE
ART DEALER, GALLERY DIRECTOR
b Montreal, Can, 1961. *Study:* Univ Montreal, Quebec, Can, 83; Univ Quebec, Rivieres, Quebec, Can, 91; Banff Sch Fine Arts, Banff, AB, 83. *Collection Arranged:* Exposition Speciale Du Canada, Mass, 2002; Nomadic Current: Louis Hughes, Lamoureux, 2004; Body & Soul, Gisele L'Epicier, Lamoureux, Ritzenhoff Gallery, Quebec, 2004; Today, The Light with Bertrand Tremblay, Ritzenhoff Gallery, Quebec, 2005; Modern Layers, Miklos Rogan, Lamoureux Ritzenhoff Gallery, Quebec, 2005; Paul Soulikias, J C Mayodon: Au Usuael Quiet, Retrospective, 2006; Bertrand Tremblay, IAF: The Earth, the Sea & the Sky, 2007. *Pos:* Art dir, Galerie Lamoureux Ritzenhoff, Montreal, Quebec, Can, 2000, 2006. *Bibliog:* Cynthia Ashton (auth), Libamah Review, Vandance Publ, 84; Max Wyman (auth), Review, Anna Wyman Dance Theatre, Vandance, 86; Robert Bernier (auth), Etablir Maîtres Demain, Parcours Informateur, 2004; Robert Bernier (auth), La Galerie Lamoureux Ritzenhoff, Marie-France Lamoureux, Parcours Art, Aug-Sept 2008. *Mem:* Consult, Nikken Art of Wellbeing. *Specialty:* Canadian emerging mid-career & established contemporary & Canadian masters. *Collection:* Canadian Masters & Canadian contemporary works. *Publ:* auth, Le Ballon Rouge (book), Ed Pierre Tisseyre, 89; auth, Du Pur Expressionism & Contemporain, L'Action Gam, 93 & 2004; auth, Le Nubisme (prog), Centaur Theatre, 97; auth, Le Nubisme (prog), Theatre Rideau Vert, 97; auth, Québec Art, Canadian Art, Its Vitality, Our Pride, 2006. *Mailing Add:* Galerie Lamoureux Ritzenhoff 1428 Sherbrooke West Montreal PQ H3G 1K4 Canada

LAMPASONA, EYDI
ARTIST
b Jan 9, 1955. *Study:* Fla Atlantic Univ, BFA, 99; Vt Col, Union Inst Univ, MFA, 2007. *Work:* Coral Springs Mus, Fla; art Collection Mus, Sergines, France; Int Mus of Collage, Mex City, Mex; Mus of Art, Ft Lauderdale, Fla. *Exhib:* 8th Ann Exhib, Huntsville Mus Art, Ala, 99; Under the Influence, Mus of Art, Ft Lauderdale, Fla, 2000; Solo exhibs, Selections, Coral Springs Mus, Fla, 2001, 2002; Wish you were here, Lincoln Ctr, NY, 2002; Eleventh Ann Int Exhib, Rosen Mus, Boca Raton, Fla, 2002; Eighty-second Ann Nat Watercolor Soc, Mont Serrat Col, San Pedro, Calif, 2002; All Mixed, Alliance for the Arts Ctr, Ft Myers, Fla, 2004; All Fla 55th Ann Exhib. *Teaching:* Art Instr, Coral Springs Mus of Art, 97-2002; art instr, summer art dir, Boca Raton Mus Art Sch, 2001-; educ, Golden Acrylic Paint Co, 2001-; instr, Boca Raton Mus Art, Boca Raton, Fla. *Awards:* Best in Show, Ninth Annual Int Exhib, 2001; Best in Show, Indoctrination, Fla Atlantic Univ, 2001; Second Place, Image, Boca Mus, 2003. *Bibliog:* Playbill, Palm Beach, Cover and Featured Artist, 98; State Port Pilot, NC, Art Review, Newspaper, 99; Sun Sentinel City Link, Art Review, Newspaper, 2000. *Mem:* Int Soc of Experimental Artists, (pres, 2004); Nat Watercolor Soc (signature mem); Nat collage Soc (signature mem); Soc of Layerists in Multi-media (signature mem); The Artists Assoc. *Media:* Mixed Media. *Interests:* gardening. *Publ:* Int Mag, Nat Publ, 2001; Contribr, Composition and Design, North Light Bks, 2003; The Art of Layering, Nelson/Dunaway, 2004; Collage in all Dimensions, Gardner, 2005

LAMUNIERE, CAROLYN PARKER
PAINTER
b Cleveland, Ohio, Nov 22, 1942. *Study:* Skidmore Coll, BA (art hist), 65. *Work:* Berkshire Mus, Pittsfield, Mass; Needham, Harper, Steers Advert, Chicago; Am J Psychiatry, Washington; Sybil & Stephen Stone Collection, Brocton Mus, Mass; Art in Embassies, Washington. *Exhib:* Through the Looking Glass, Reflected Images in Am Art, Hecksher Mus, Huntington, NY, 84; 100 Yrs, 100 Artists, Nat Asn Women Artists, NY & Franz Bader, Wash, 89; Earth, Sea, Sky, Adelphi Univ, Long Island, NY, 91; Elaine Beckwith Gallery, Jamaica, Vt, 98; Hand Artes Gallery, Truchas, NMex; Women Made Gallery, Chicago, Ill, 98; Joyce Robbins, Group Show, Santa Fe, NMex, 2000; Munson Gallery, 9/11 Group Show, Santa Fe, NMex, 2001; 9 Artists Revisited, Frederick, Md, 2006; Convergence Gallery, NMex, 2007, 2010, 2012; Patio Gallery, Las Cruces NMex, 2010, 2011. *Awards:* Michael Engel Award, Nat Soc Painters in Acrylic & Casein; Runner Up Governors Award, Md; 1st & 2nd Mural Awards, Sign of the times, Int Competition. *Mem:* Nat Soc Painters Acrylic & Casein, NY; Nat Soc Women Artists, NY. *Media:* Acrylic and Oil. *Specialty:* art (five arts). *Interests:* French Preservation. *Publ:* Contemporary Women Artists Calendar, Wash, Recreation Register; Better Homes & Gardens, 79 & 85; NY Times Gallery Guide, 81, 82 & 86; William & Mary Review, 92 & 93; The Best of Acrylic Painting, 97; Collectors' Guides, Santa Fe, Taos, NMex, 98-2002; 100 Southwest Artists; One Hundred Artists of the Southwest, 2005. *Dealer:* Hand Artes Gallery Truchas NM; Elaine Beckwith Gallery Jamaica VT; Convergence Gallery Santa Fe NM; Patio Gallery Las Cruces NM. *Mailing Add:* 2953 Plaza Blanca Santa Fe NM 87500

LANCASTER, VIRGINIA (GINNY) JANE
EDUCATOR, PAINTER
b Mulberry, Kans, Feb 7, 1930. *Study:* Santa Rosa Jr Col; Univ Calif, Berkeley; Sonoma State Univ. *Hon Degrees:* Teaching Degree, Fine & Applied Arts & Related Technologies. *Work:* Mendocino Co Mus, Willits, Calif. *Exhib:* Birds of a Feather, Marin Co Libr, San Rafael, Calif, 71, Some Things I Love, 72 & Kid Stuff, 73; View from the Air, Sonoma State Univ, Cotati, Calif, 72, 150 Yrs of Work by Sonomo Co Women Artists, 80 & Generations, 86; Japanese Arts, George & Elsie Wood Libr, St Helena, Calif, 80; Caprice, Santa Rosa Community Col, Calif, 83; Homage to Japanese Art, Finley Community Ctr, Santa Rosa, Calif, 98. *Teaching:* Art, Sonoma State Col, 73-74, Napa Valley Col, 74-81 & Santa Rosa Jr Col, 75-79. *Mem:* Watercolor Artists Sonoma Co. *Media:* Miscellaneous Media. *Interests:* Avid gardener, Flying Private Pilot (retired list); Interior Design: making curtains, slipcovers, and Historical Houses. *Publ:* Contribr of several articles in Directions Mag, 73-74. *Mailing Add:* 638 Wright St Santa Rosa CA 95404

LAND-WEBER, ELLEN E
PHOTOGRAPHER, EDUCATOR
b Rochester, NY, Mar 16, 1943. *Study:* Pembroke Coll, 61-63; Univ Mich, 64; Univ Iowa, BA (art hist), 65; Univ Iowa, MFA, 68. *Work:* Int Mus of Photog, George Eastman House, Rochester, NY; San Francisco Mus Mod Art, Calif; New Orleans Mus Art; Libr Cong, Washington, DC. *Comn:* Bicentennial Doc Proj on Archit of Courthouses in US (in collab with 23 other photogrs with assigned geog areas), Seagram's Inc, New York, 75-76. *Exhib:* Solo exhibs, San Francisco Mus Mod Art, 78, Bard Col, Annandale on Hudson, NY, 79, Focus Gallery, San Francisco, 80 & Shadai Gallery, Tokyo, 83, Views and Portraits of Turkey, Daley Civic Ctr, Chicago, 98, Portrait of Turkey, Southeastern Okla State Univ, Durant, Okla, 99 & To Save a Life: Stories of Holocaust Rescue, Humbolt State Univ First Street Gallery, Eureka, Calif, 2000; Portrait of Turkey: Ellen-Land Weber, Visual & Performing Arts Ctr Gallery, Southeastern Okla State Univ, Durant, Okla, 2000; Water in the West, First Street Gallery, Eureka, Calif, 2000; Fish On/No Fish: Hupa Tribal People & Trinity River Water, Morris Graves Mus, Eureka, Calif, 2001; Water in the West, FotoFest 2004, Williams Tower Gallery, Houston, Tex, 2004; Threads of Vision: Weaving a Life in Photog, Humboldt State Univ, Eureka, Calif, 2005; plus numerous others. *Teaching:* Instr photog, Univ Calif Extension, Los Angeles, 70-74; asst prof photog, Humboldt State Univ, Arcata, Calif, 74-79, assoc prof, 79-83, prof, 83-; prof emer art, Humboldt State Univ, 2006. *Awards:* Fel, Nat Endowment for Arts, 75, 79 & 82; Fel, Fulbright, 93-94; Grant, Polaroid Artist's Support, 90, 92 & 93; Humboldt State Univ Scholar of the Year, 2005. *Mem:* Soc for Photog Educ, mem since 73 to present (nat treas, 79-81, nat secy, 81-83). *Res:* Photographic digital imaging. *Interests:* Photography, Travel. *Publ:* Women of photography: an historical survey, San Francisco Mus of Mod Art, 75; Translations, Herbert F Johnson Mus, Ithaca, NY, 79; Courthouse, a Photographic Document, Horizon Press, 79; The Passionate Collector, photographs by Ellen Land-Weber, Simon & Schuster, 80; Photography and Art, Interactions Since 1946, Grundberg & Gauss, Abrams, 87; auth, To Save a Life: Stories of Holocaust Rescue, Univ Ill Press, 2000; Gettysburg Monuments: A Picture Album, 2014. *Dealer:* Craig Krull Gallery Santa Monica CA. *Mailing Add:* 790 Park Pl Arcata CA 95521

LANDAU, BARBARA DOWNEY
COLLECTOR
Pos: Editor, Rolling Stone, formerly. *Awards:* Named one of Top 200 Collectors, ARTnews mag, 2006-13. *Collection:* Renaissance painting and sculpture; 19th-century French and English painting

LANDAU, ELLEN GROSS
HISTORIAN, CRITIC
b Philadelphia, Pa, Feb 27, 1947. *Study:* Cornell Univ, BA, 69; George Washington Univ, MA, 74; Univ Del, PhD, 81. *Collection Arranged:* Am in the War: An Exhibit by Artists for Victory Inc (auth, catalog), Libr Cong, Washington, DC, 83; Jackson Pollock-Lee Krasner: Kunstlerpaare Kunstlerfreunde (auth, catalog), Kunstmuseum, Bern & Switz, 89; Lee Krasner's collages 1953-55 (auth, catalog), Jason McCoy Inc, 95-96; Pollock Matters, McMullen Mus, Boston Coll, 2007; Mercedes Matters: A Retrospective, 2009-2010. *Pos:* Res asst to chief cur, Corcoran Gallery Art, 69-71; asst cur hist properties, Nat Trust Hist Preserv, 73-76. *Teaching:* Prof art hist & chair, Case Western Reserve Univ, 82-, Andrew W Mellon prof humanities, 2002-. *Awards:* Rockefeller Found Fel, 78-79; Am Coun Learned Soc Fel, 85-86; Cleveland Arts Prize Lit, Women's City Club, 91; John S Diekhoff Award Distinguished Grad Teaching, Case Western Reserve Univ, 93; Inst Advanced Study, Mem 2004; Nat Endowment Humanities Fel, 2010-2011. *Mem:* Coll Art Asn; Mid-West Art His Soc; Am Cult Asn; Catalogue Raisonne' Scholars Asn; Asn Hist Am Art; Am Studies Asn. *Res:* Post 1945 American art; abstract expressionism; women's studies (gender issues); critical theory. *Interests:* Mex & Am Modernism, Philip Guston. *Publ:* Auth, Jackson Pollock, 89 & Lee Krasner: A Catalogue Raisonne, 95, Abrams; Reading Abstract Expressionism: Context and Critique, Yale, 2005, Pollock Matters ed, McMullen Mus, 2007; Mercedes Matter, Sidney Mishkin Gallery, Baruch Coll et al, 2009. *Mailing Add:* Dept Art Hist & Art Case Western Reserve Univ Mather House 11201 Euclid Ave Cleveland OH 44106-7110

LANDAU, EMILY FISHER
COLLECTOR, ADMINISTRATOR
b Glen Falls, NY. *Hon Degrees:* Yeshiva Univ, NY, PhD, 1998. *Pos:* Partner, Fisher Bros, New York, pres 1984-91; founding mem, Nat Mus Women Arts, 1987; trustee, Whitney Mus Am Art, New York, 1987-, vpres, 1990-, co-chmn contemp comt, 1994-; charter mem, US Holocaust Mem Mus, 1992; mem chmn's coun, Mus Mod Art, New York, 1992-, mem comt prints & illus bks, 1985-, mem comt painting & sculpture, 1997-; bd dirs, Site Santa Fe, 1994 & Georgia O'Keefe Mus, Santa Fe, 1996; founder, Fisher Landau Ctr for Treatment of Learning Disabilities. *Awards:* Decorated Chevalier, Order Arts & Letts, France; named one of Top 200 Collectors, ARTnews mag, 2004-2013. *Mem:* Metrop Club, Doubles, & Palm Beach Co Club. *Collection:* Contemporary American art. *Publ:* Contribr, Jasper Johns: The Screenprints (exhib catalog), 1996; Mishoo Cosmopolitan Cat (children's storybook), 2000

LANDAU, JON
COLLECTOR
Study: Brandeis Univ, 68. *Pos:* mgr for artists such as Shania Twain, Natalie Merchant, Bruce Springsteen, Train, Patti Scialfa; producer, albums for MC5, Livingston Taylor, Jackson Brown, Bruce Springsteen, formerly; founder & co-owner, Jon Landau Mgmt; critic, Crawdaddy!, Boston Phoenix, Rolling Stone & The Real Paper. *Awards:* Named one of Top 200 Collectors, ARTnews mag, 2004-12. *Collection:* Renaissance painting and sculpture; 19th-century French and English painting. *Mailing Add:* Jon Landau Management 158 Rowayton Ave Norwalk CT 06853

LANDAU, MYRA
PAINTER, MURALIST
b Bucharest, Romania; Mex citizen. *Study:* Studied with Oswaldo Goeldi, Authodactic engraving on metal in painting. *Work:* Mus Mod Art, Mexico; Pinqcoteca del Estado, Sao Paulo, Brazil; Casa de Las Americas, Habana, Cuba; Univ Veracruzana, Xalapa, Mexico; Casas de Cultura, Mexico; and others. *Exhib:* Mus Mod Art, Mexico City, 75 & 87; Centro de Estudios del er Mundo, Mexico City, 77; Casa de La Cultura, Recife-Pe, Brazil, 78; Gallery Arte Global, Sao Paulo, Brazil, 78; Mus Mod Art, Salvador, Brazil, 78; Mus Carrillogil, Mexico City, 79; Univ Metrop Mexico City, 80; Ctr Cult Mexique, Paris, 83; Instituto Italo, Latino Americano, Roma, Ital. *Pos:* Docente-Facultad de Artes Plasticas, 74-75; investigadora, Inst de Investigaciones; esteticas, Univ Veracruzana, 75-. *Bibliog:* Teresa del Conde (auth), 12 Expresiones plasticas de hoy, Bancreser, 11/88; Raul Renan & Berta Taracena (auth), Diez años de la Galeria Metropolitana, Univ Autonoma Metropolitana, 89. *Mem:* Foro de Arte Contemporaneo, Mexico City. *Media:* Linen, Pastels. *Publ:* Si Sabes Ver, Univ Veracruzana, 76; Textos Legirles Ritmos Ile Gibles, Univ Veracruzana, 85; Ritmos, Univ Autonoma Nacional de Mexico, 86. *Mailing Add:* Alfaro 6 Xalapa Veracruz Mexico

LANDFIELD, RONNIE (RONALD) T
PAINTER
b Bronx, NY, Jan 9, 1947. *Study:* Art Students League, 62-63, 94; Kansas City Art Inst, Mo, 63; San Francisco Art Inst, 64-65. *Work:* Mus Mod Art, Whitney Mus Art, Metrop Mus Art, NY; Hirshhorn Mus of Art, Washington; RI Sch of Design Mus, Providence; Walker Art Ctr, Minneapolis, Minn. *Comn:* Mural (painting 11 ft x 20 ft), Westinghouse Corp & I Chermayoff, Pittsburgh, Pa, 70. *Exhib:* Whitney Ann & Biennial Exhib of Am Painting, NY, 67, 69 & 73; Lyrical Abstraction, Whitney Mus of Am Art, 71 & Aldrich Mus of Contemp Art, Ridgefield, Conn, 71; Art for Your Collection, RI Sch of Design, Providence, 71; Recent Acquisitions, Mus of Mod Art, NY, 72; Solo exhibs, Andre Emmerich Gallery, NY, 73-75 & 75, Linda Farris, Seattle, Wash, 78, 79, 81, 84, 87 & 89, Sarah Rentschler Gallery, NY, 78 & 79, Medici-Berensen, Miami, Fla, 79, Stephen Rosenberg Gallery, NY, 94 & Nicholas/Alexander Gallery, NY, 94; Charles Cowles Gallery, NY, 80, 82-84; Hokin Gallery, Miami, Fla, 85 & 87; Hokin-Kaufman Gallery, Chicago, 85 & 87; Stephen Haller Fine Arts, NY, 87, 88, 89 & 90; Claudia Carr Gallery, 99; Salander - O Reilly Galleries, NY, 2000; Heidi Cho Gallery, NYC, 2005; Ronnie Landfield Paintings from 5 decades, Butler Inst Am Art, Sept-Nov 2007; Heidi Cho Gallery, NYC, 2007; LewAllen Gallery, Santa Fe, NM, 2009, 2011; Stephen Haller Gallery, New York, 2009, 2011. *Teaching:* Instr fine arts, Sch of Visual Arts, New York, 75-89; instr, Art Students League NY, 1994-. *Awards:* Gold Medal, San Francisco Art Inst, Calif, 65; Cassandra; Nat Endowment Arts, 83; Pollock/Krasner Foundation, Grants 1995, 2001. *Bibliog:* Noel Frackman (auth), article, Arts, Vol 50, No 1, 9/75; Phyllis Tuchman (auth), article, Art News, Vol 77, No 3, 3/78; Lisa Messinger (auth), The landscape in Twentieth-Century American art: selections from the Metropolitan Museum of Art, Rizzoli, NY, 91; Cohen Mark Daniel (auth) Ronnie Landfield: New Works on Paper, Claudia Carr Gallery, Exhibition Rev Mag, 4/99; Klaus Kertess (auth), Ronnie Landfield the Nature of Paint, 2009; Robert C Morgan (auth), Landfields Illuminations, 2007. *Mem:* Art Students League. *Media:* Acrylic, Watercolor. *Specialty:* Painting, Sculpture. *Publ:* Art News, Art Forum, NY Times, Art in America. *Dealer:* Stephen Haller Gallery 542 W26th St New York NY 10001; LewAllen Galleries 1613 Paseo De Peralta Santa Fe NM 87501 . *Mailing Add:* 31 Desbrosses St New York NY 10013

LANDIS, ELLEN JAMIE
CURATOR, HISTORIAN
b Chicago, Ill, May 6, 1941. *Study:* Univ Calif, Berkeley, BA; Univ Vienna, 60-61; New York Univ, Inst Fine Arts, MA. *Exhib:* Mus Menagerie, 91; El Couse, 91; Unbroken Threads, 92; Human Factor: Figurative Sculpture Reconsidered, 93; Man on Fire (auth, catalog), Luis Jimenez, 94; Zones of Experience: The Art of Larry Bell, 97; Tibet: Tradition & Change, 98; Silent Things, Secret Things: Still Life from Rembrandt to the Millennium, 99; Cast of Characters Figurative Sculpture, 2000; Picasso to Plensa, 2006. *Collection Arranged:* Homage to Rodin (coauth, catalog), Los Angeles Co Mus Art, Los Angeles, 67; Rodin Bronzes from the Collection of B Gerald Cantor (auth, catalog), Am Fedn Art, 70; Vincent Van Gogh, Baltimore Mus Art, 70; Four Am in Paris: The Collections of Gertrude Stein and Her Family, Baltimore Mus Art, 71; Early 20th Century European Masterpainters, 77, Indian Art Today (auth, catalog), 77, Metro Youth Art (auth, catalog), 77 & Albuquerque Artists I (auth, catalog), 77, Mus Albuquerque; Reflections of Realism (auth, catalog), 79 & Katachi: Form and Spirit in Japanese Art, 80, Albuquerque Mus; Here and Now, 35 Artist in New Mexico (auth, catalog), 81, West-Southwest (auth, catalog), 82, In Place, 82, Eve Laramee, 83, Hiroshige, 83 & Albuquerque Mus, Wilson Hurley, 85; Adventures West, 89; Printers Impressions, 90; Zones of Experience: the Art of Larry Bell, 97; Man on Fire, Luis Jimenez, 94; Tibet: Tradition & Change, 97; Picasso to

Plensa, 2006; Prelude to SPanish Modernism, From NY to Picasso, 2006; El Alma de Espagna, 2005. *Pos:* Cur, painting & sculpture, Baltimore Mus Art, 70 & 71, Albuquerque Mus, 77-2004; actg cur, Robert Gore Rifkind Collection, Beverly Hills, Calif, 72; bd dir, Actors Theater, Albuquerque, NMex, 79-81; bd adv, Artspace Mag, 78-93; art cur, Albuenque Mus, 77-; bd trustees, Comprehensive Art Publ, Ohio, 80-; mem, Writers Comt, Am Asn Mus; independent cur, 2004-2008; cur, Grounds for Sculpture, Hamilton, NJ, 2008-. *Teaching:* Lectr introd to art, Yuba Coll, Marysville, Calif, 76-77. *Awards:* The Chris Award, Homage to Rodin, Film Coun Greater Columbus, 69; Building Bridges Award, Univ NMex, 98; The Albuquerque Mus Dir's Award, 2000; Albuquerque Arts Alliance Bravos Award, 2000. *Bibliog:* Contemporary Personalities, Acad Italia' Delle Arti e Del Lavoro, 82. *Mem:* Coll Art Asn; Am Asn Mus; SW Art Hist Coun (pres, 92-98 & 2004-). *Res:* Centralized research in areas of 19th Century and 20th Century art. *Publ:* Coauth, The David E Bright Collection, Los Angeles Co Mus Art, Los Angeles, 67; Matisse in Baltimore, Television Spec, 71; Carl Redin (exhib catalog), 84 & Wilson Hurley: A Retrospective Exhibition (exhib catalog), Albuquerque Mus, 85

LANE, JOHN RODGER
ADMINISTRATOR, FORMER MUSEUM DIRECTOR
b Chicago, Ill, Feb 28, 1944. *Study:* Williams Col, BA, 66; Univ Chicago, MBA, 71; Harvard Univ, AM, 73, PhD, 76. *Hon Degrees:* San Francisco Art Inst, Hon Doc Fine Arts, 95. *Collection Arranged:* Stuart Davis: Art and Art Theory, Brooklyn Mus & Fogg Art Mus, 78; Modernist Art from the Edith and Milton Lowenthal Collection, Brooklyn Mus, 81; Robert Bourdon: Auto Rex, Carnegie Inst, 82; The Groups: Paintings by Archie Rand, Carnegie Inst, 83; Abstract Painting and Sculpture in Am, Carnegie Inst, San Francisco Mus Mod Art, Minneapolis Inst Art & Whitney Mus, 83-84; Carnegie International, Carnegie Inst, 85; Ross Bleckner, 1988 & Don Van Vliet, San Francisco Mus Mod Art, 88; Frida Kahlo, Diego Rivera, & Mexican Modernism from the Jacques & Natasha Gelman Collection, San Francisco Mus Mod Art, 96; Maria Botta: The SFMOMA Project, San Francisco Mus Mod Art, 95; Sigmar Polke: Recent Paintings and Drawings, Dallas Mus of Art & Tate Modern, 2002-03; Lothar Bumgarten: Carbon, Dallas Mus Art, 2004. *Pos:* Asst dir, Fogg Art Mus, 74; exec asst to dir, Brooklyn Mus, 75-78, adminr curatorial affairs, 79, asst dir curatorial affairs, 80; dir, Carnegie Mus Art, 80-86, San Francisco Mus Mod Art, 87-97; Eugene McDermott dir, Dallas Mus Art, 99-2008; trustee Fountain Valley Sch Colo Springs, 1999-2005; pres & CEO, New Art Trust, San Francisco, 2008-. *Teaching:* Teaching fel art hist, Harvard Univ, 73-75. *Mem:* Am Asn Mus; Int Coun Mus; Asn Art Mus Dirs; Williams Coll Mus Art (vis comt); Asn Art Mus Dir (trustee 2000-02). *Res:* 20th century American Art. *Publ:* Auth, New York: The Brooklyn Mus, Stuart Davis: Art and Art Theory, 78; co-ed (with Susan C Larsen), Abstract Painting and Sculpture in America 1927-1944, Carnegie Inst & Harry N Abrams, Inc, 83; co-ed (with Saskia Bos & John Caldwell), 1985, Dalls Mus Art 100 Years, 2003, Gerhard Richerter, 1965-04, Lothar Baugmarten: Carbon, 2004; contribr, The Barney A Ebsworth Collection Catalog, St Louis Art Mus, 87; Stuart Davis, American Painter, Metrop Mus Art, 91; exec ed, The Making of a New Museum, San Francisco Mus Mod Art, 95; co-ed (with Maria de Corral), Fast Forward: Contemp Collections for the Dallas Mus Art, 2007. *Mailing Add:* c/o San Francisco Mus Mod Art 151 Third St San Francisco CA 94103

LANE, MARION ARRONS
PAINTER, SCULPTOR
b Brooklyn, NY. *Study:* Brooklyn Mus Art Sch, with Manifred Schwartz & Reuben Tam; Pratt Inst, NY; Art Students League, with Morris Kantor; Wm Paterson Univ, NJ, BA; Rutgers Univ, with Leon Golub, MFA. *Work:* Bergen Co Mus, Paramus, NJ; Bloomfield Coll Mus, NJ; The Drawing Center, Viewing Prog, NY; Feminist Art Base, Elizabeth Sackler Center, Brooklyn Mus, NY. *Exhib:* Pleiades Gallery, NY, 76-77 & 2005-2007; Williams Ctr, Rutherford, NJ, 90; Nabisco Corp Hq, 95; Broome St Gallery, 96; Edward Williams Col, NJ, 99; Retrospective Exhib, Westbeth Gallery, 2000, 2006; Gov Island Art Fair, NY, 2011; Brooklyn Waterfront Artists Coalition, 2012; Carter-Burden Gallery, 2013. *Teaching:* Instr, art appreciation & drawing, Bergen Community Col, NJ, 80-86; art therapist, Manhattan Psychiatric Ctr, NY, 86-99. *Awards:* Edward Albee Found, NY, 1983; NJ State Council on The Arts Fellowships, 1983 & 1988; Richard Florsheim Art Fund Grant, 1999; Valparaiso Found Grant, Mojaca, Spain, 2002; Julia and David White Found Grant, Costa Rica, 2003; Residency Grant, Va Ctr for the Cult Arts, 2004; Resident Fellow, Rocky Neck Art Colony, Gloucester, Mass, 2007 & 2008. *Bibliog:* Hedy Obeil (auth), article, Arts Mag, 10/77; Deborah Jerome (auth), article, Record, 82; Eileen Watkins (auth), article, in: Newark Star Ledger, 4/86 & 9/90; article, NY Sun, 9/07. *Mem:* Life mem Art Students League. *Media:* Acrylic, Oil Paint; Sheetmetal, Fabric. *Interests:* Dance & nature. *Collection:* R. Sunshine, B. Feigen, N. Levine. *Publ:* Changing Perspectives, The Art of Marion Lane; Auth, Retrospective Catalog, 2000. *Dealer:* 14 Sculptors Gallery 332 Bleecker St Suite K35 New York NY 10014; Westbeth Gallery 463 West St New York NY 10014; Carter-Burdan Gallery 548 W 28th St #534 New York NY 10001. *Mailing Add:* 55 Bethune St G 119 New York NY 10014

LANE, MIHARU
PAINTER, PRINTMAKER
b Fukuoka, Japan, Apr 3, 1948; arrived in US, 58. *Study:* East Stroudsburg Univ, BA, 91; Marywood Univ, MFA, 95; also studied at Va Commonwealth Univ, 67-68, Md Inst Coll Art, Baltimore, 69, Calif Coll Arts and Crafts, Oakland, 69. *Work:* Monroe Co Court House, 90; Brooklyn Botanic Garden, NY, 84; Mus Modern Art, NY, 84; Wallops Island Marine Science Consortium, Va, 2011; East Stroudsburg Univ, Pa, 96-2011; Mus Chincoteague, Chincoteague, Va, 2012. *Exhib:* Solo exhibs, Madelon Powers Gallery, East Stroudsburg Univ, 80, 92, 2000, 2003, 2008, 2009, Meir Gallery, Ranana, Israel, 83, The Middleton Gallery, Annapolis, 83-85, Brooklyn Botanic Garden, NY, 84, Blair Acad, Blairstown, NJ, 93, Antoine Dutot Museum and Gallery, Del Water Gap, Pa, 96, 2000, 2009, Synagogue for the Arts, Tribeca, NY, 2004, Seruci Gallery, Marywood Univ, Scranton, Pa, 2008, Chincoteague Nat Wildlife Refuge, 2010-2011, Findings Gallery, 2011; Group exhibs, Everhart Mus, Scranton, 94; Susquehanna Art Mus, Visual Traditions, 95; Allentown Art Mus, 96; Md Inst Coll Art, 97, 2001-2002, 2004; Contemp Gallery, Marywood Univ, Scranton, 97; The Pahaquarry Paint Out, The Ridge and Valley Conservancy Gallery, Blairstown, NJ, 98-99; Hub & Kern Galleries, 98; Whittaker Center of Science and the Arts, Harrisburg, Pa, 2000; Women Artists of Pa, Antoine Dutot Mus and Gallery, 2002, NJ Landscapes, 2002, The Delaware River: The Big Picture, 2003; Flowers, Great Bear Golf and Country Club, Marshall's Creek, Pa, 2005; Music Motif, Celebration of the Arts, Del Water Gap, 2005; Marywood Univ Alumni Weekend Art Show, Scranton, 2006; Findings Gallery, Stroudsburg, Pa, 2001-2011; Red Queen Gallery, Onancock, Va, 2012. *Teaching:* Asst art prof, East Stroudsburg Univ, Pa, 96-2007; Assoc art prof, East Stroudsburg Univ, Pa, 2007, emer prof art, 2011-. *Awards:* East Stroudsburg Found Grant, 2005; fac develop & res grant, East Stroudsburg Univ, 2006-2008, 2009. *Mem:* Society for the Arts, board mem, East Stroudsburg Univ, Pa, 2007; Office of Multicultural Affairs, advisory board, East Stroudsburg Univ, Pa, 2005-2008; Pocono Arts Coun, Stroudsburg, Pa, 1995-2011; Eastern Shore Art League, Onancock, Va, 2013; Chincoteague Cultural Alliance, Va, 2013. *Media:* Oil, watercolor, pastel. *Res:* Painting on the Trail of the Hudson River Sch, 2006-2009. *Publ:* Gallery Guide, Clinton: Art Now Inc, 2004; Comparing Media from Around the World, Pearson Edn Inc, NY, 2006

LANE, ROSEMARY LOUISE
PRINTMAKER, SCULPTOR
b San Francisco, Calif, Dec 6, 1944. *Study:* Calif Coll Arts & Crafts, Oakland, with Ralph Borge, Robert Bechtle & Roy DeForrest, BFA, 66; Calif State Univ, Hayward, 70; Univ Ore, with Laverne Krause & Ken Paul, MFA, 73. *Work:* Univ Ore Art Gallery, Eugene; Brussels Art Mus, Belg; Fran Masereel Ctr Graphics, Kasterlee, Belg. *Comn:* Artwork, comn by Martha Dupont, The Sanctuary, Wilmington, Del, 89-90. *Exhib:* One-person exhib, Pa State Univ Invitational, 83, Prints & Cast Paper, Wilmington, 83 & Relics of Hope, 86, Art Loop, Wilmington, Del, 89, Inner Visions, Del State Arts Coun, Wilmington, 95; Int Print Biennial, Silvermine Guild Artists, New Caanan, Conn, 94; Art for Peace, Prints, Youth & Creative Arts Ctr, Troitsk, Russia, 94; Lane/Schwab (2 person exhib), John M Clayton Hall, Univ Del, Newark, 94; Okla State Univ, 97; Southern Graphics Coun Conf, Univ SFla, Tampa, 97. *Teaching:* Vis instr printmaking, Univ Ore, Eugene, 73-74; from instr printmaking, drawing & papermaking to assoc prof, Univ Del, Newark, 74-867, prof, 88-. *Awards:* Merit Award, Int Juried Art Exhib, Mussavi Gallery, New York, 85; Purchase Awards, 5th, 15th & 17th Nat Print & Drawing Exhib, Minot State Col, NDak; Art for Peace Grant, People to People Int, 94. *Bibliog:* Lisa Lyons (auth), Rosemary Lane, Artvoices, 1-2/80; Patricia Wright (auth), Rosemary Lane/Muse Gallery, Art Express, 12/81; Penelope Bass Cope (auth), Artist goes with her feminine instincts, Wilmington J, 11/83. *Mem:* Soc Am Graphic Artists; Los Angeles Printmaking Soc; Philadelphia Print Club; Int Graphic Arts Found. *Media:* Bichromate Prints; Handmade Paper Casts. *Mailing Add:* 50 Cummings Ct Bear DE 19701

LANE, WILLIAM
PAINTER
b Kalamazoo, Mich, Jan 12, 1936. *Study:* Univ Calif Los Angeles, BA, 58, MA, 61. *Work:* Home Savings & Loan Collection, Los Angeles, Calif; Security Pac Bank, Los Angeles, Calif; Toronto Dominion Bank, Los Angeles, Calif; Price, Waterhouse & Co, Los Angeles, Calif; 1st Independent Gallery, Santa Monica, Calif, 93. *Exhib:* Solo exhibs: Palos Verdes Art Mus, 69; La Jolla Mus Art, 67; Studio Cafe, Corona Del Mar, 88; St Luke's Episcopal Church, Long Beach, Calif, 89; 20th Century European & Am Watercolors, Long Beach Mus Art, Calif, 88; 6 + 35, FHP Hippodrome Gallery, Long Beach, Calif, 91; Seductive Geometry, Los Angeles Abstr Art, Olga Dollar Gallery, San Francisco, Calif, 91; Aspects of Figural Painting in Southern California, Tatistcheff Gallery, Santa Monica, Calif, 91; Schick Art Gallery, Skidmore Col, Saratoga Springs, NY, 95; Fig Gallery, Santa Monica, Calif, 96 & 99; Defined Edge, Century Gallery, Sylmari, Calif, 98. *Pos:* Art gallery dir, Rio Hondo Col, Whittier, Calif, 98-99. *Teaching:* emer prof art, Rio Hondo Col, Whittier, Calif, 69-; vis asst prof painting, Univ Calif Los Angeles, 76-77. *Awards:* Purchase Awards, City Art Festival, Los Angeles, 60, 66; Nat Endowment Arts Fel, 87. *Media:* Acrylic, Watercolor. *Specialty:* Paintings. *Dealer:* Fig Gallery Santa Monica CA. *Mailing Add:* 2203 E 10th St Long Beach CA 90804

LANG, CAY
PHOTOGRAPHER
b Long Beach, Calif, Feb 5, 1948. *Study:* Calif State Univ, Fresno, BA, 76; San Francisco Art Inst, MFA, 79. *Work:* Mediateque, Henin Veaumont, France; De Saisset Mus, Santa Clara, Calif; Los Angeles Co Mus Art; Bibliotheque Nat, Paris, France. *Exhib:* Laguna Beach Mus Art, Calif, 85; Camden Art Ctr, London, Eng, 85; Mus Mod Art, Ft Mason, San Francisco, 86; De Saisset Mus, Santa Clara, Calif, 88; Palais de Tokyo, Paris, 88. *Teaching:* Univ Calif Berkeley Exten, 90; Calif State Univ, San Francisco Exten, 90; Univ Calif, Davis, spring 91 & 92. *Awards:* Fel, MacDowell Colony, 87; Proj Grant, Polaroid Corp, 87; Visual Arts Fel, Am Pen Women, 88-89. *Bibliog:* Hans Eberhard Hess (auth), Blumenwunder aus Kalifornien, Phototecnik Mag, 4/86; Portfolio, Photo Design, 7/88; Evelyn Roth (auth), Body language, Am Photogr, 7/88. *Dealer:* Galerie Michele Chomette 24 Rue Beauborg 75003 Paris France; Benteler-Morgan Gallery, Houston, Tex

LANG, J T
PRINTMAKER, EDUCATOR
b Maple Shade, NJ, Dec 24, 1931. *Study:* Philadelphia Coll Art, cert; Tyler Sch Art, BFA, BS (educ) & MFA; Barnes Found, with Violette De Mazia; also with Toshi Yoshida, Hirooyuki Tajima & Yuji Abe, Tokyo. *Work:* Philadelphia Mus Art; Cincinnati Mus Art; Birmingham Mus Art; State Dept, Washington, DC; Philadelphia Libr Collection. *Comn:* Large ed/woodcut, Print Club Philadelphia, 65; Exodus (litho ser), Pearl Fox Gallery of Elkins Park, 71; color litho ed, La Salle Col, Philadelphia, 74; John Baptist de La Salle, La Salle Col, Philadelphia, 81. *Exhib:* Japan Print Soc Ann, Tokyo, 62, 63, 65 & 66; Solo print exhibs, Yoseido Gallery, Tokyo, 65 &

Birmingham Mus, Ala, 74; USA Print Workshop Exhib, Cincinnati, 67; Am Color Print Soc Ann, Philadelphia, 68-81. *Teaching:* Asst prof Western cult, Aoyama G Univ, Tokyo, 63-67; vis lectr printmaking, Tyler Sch Art, Philadelphia, 68-70; asst prof printmaking & Asian art hist, LaSalle Col, Philadelphia. *Awards:* Purchase Award, Pa Acad Fine Arts, 69; Outstanding Printmaker Award, Philadelphia Bd Educ, 73; Tyler Art Sch Award of Honor, 84. *Bibliog:* Dorothy Grafly (auth), Summer print show, Sun Bull, Philadelphia, 7/30/67; Richard L Bell (auth), Prints of J T Lang (video tape), Springfield High Sch, 4/71; Sally Ann Harper (auth), Lang/printmakers, La Salle Collegian, 3/27/73. *Mem:* Am Color Print Soc (coun mem, 72-); Philadelphia Print Club; Coll Art Teacher's Asn; Philadelphia Watercolor Club, 87-. *Media:* All. *Dealer:* Pearl Fox Gallery 104 Windsor Ave Melrose Park Philadelphia PA 19126

LANG, ROSALIE
PAINTER, EDUCATOR
b New York, NY, 1940. *Study:* Queens Coll, City Univ NY (painting), BA, 1962; Pratt Inst (painting, photog), MS, 1966; NY Univ (art educ res), EdD, 1973. *Work:* 3M Corp Collection, Mountain View, Calif; Bank of the West Collection, San Jose, Calif; Bethune-Cookman Univ Collection, Daytona Beach, Fla; Syntex Corp Collection, Palo Alto, Calif; National Academy of Sciences Art Collection, Washington, DC. *Comn:* Painting (exec conf rm), Syva Co, Palo Alto, Calif, 1980; Painting (main lobby), Motorola-Four Phase Systems, Cupertino, Calif, 1981; Painting (exec conf area), Pacific Bell, San Francisco, Calif, 1983. *Exhib:* NJ Artist - Composition '70 (invitational), Jersey City Mus, Jersey City, NJ, 1970; Discovery--Young NJ Artists (juried), Rutgers Univ Art Gallery, New Brunswick, NJ, 1971; Morris Mus Arts & Scis, Morristown, NJ, 1972, Contemp Landscape Painters Calif, Santa Cruz, Calif, 2010, 2011, Left Coast Annual, Sanchez Art Ctr, Pacifica, Calif, 2012; Solo exhibs: Sea Walls, NJ State Mus Art, Trenton, NJ, 1974; Paintings from the Gate Series, Rorick Gallery, San Francisco, Calif, 1982, 1983; Gate Series, Monterey Mus Art, Monterey Calif, 1983; Recent Paintings, Cabrillo Coll Art Gallery, Aptos, Calif, 1983; Painted Passages, Art Mus Los Gatos, Los Gatos, Calif, 1991; On the Rocks, Art Mus Los Gatos, 2007; A Fragile Beauty, Monterey Peninsula Coll Art Gallery, Monterey, Calif, 2013; Statewide Painting Exhib, Triton Mus Art, Santa Clara, Calif, 2013; Imagining Deep Time, Nat Acad Sciences, Wash DC, 2014-2015. *Teaching:* Asst prof, Col of NJ, Trenton, NJ, 1967-1976; Asst prof, San Jose State Univ, San Jose, Calif, 1976-1980. *Awards:* Nat Defense Educ Act Title IV Fel (doctoral studies in art & art educ), NY Univ, 1970. *Bibliog:* Lenore Greenberg (auth), State Exhibs Local Artist's Work, Somerset Spectator, Somerset, NJ, Jan 1974; Review of Ward-Nasse Gallery show, Arts Mag, Jan 1976; Alastair Dallas (auth), Fine, Unusual Art at Tait Mus, Los Gatos Observer (on-line), June 2007; Julianne Carroll (auth), Rock Solid, for artist Rosalie Lang, beauty is all in the details, Los Gatos Weekender/Silicon Valley Community Newspapers, Jan 2008. *Mem:* NY Univ Alumni Asn (1993-); Los Gatos Mus Asn (2007-). *Media:* Oil. *Publ:* Auth, Why Johnny Can't Do His Own Thing In His Art Work (article), Art Educ (NAEA), 1974; auth, A Critical Look At Textbooks For Consistency Between Theory and Practice (article), Studies in Art Educ (NAEA), 1974-1975; auth, Teaching Beliefs and Evaluation (article), Art Educ (NAEA), 1976

LANG, WENDY FRANCES
ADMINISTRATOR, PHOTOGRAPHER
b Cleveland, Ohio, Feb 15, 1938. *Study:* Skowhegan Sch Painting Sculpture, Maine, 54-56; Antioch Coll, BA (design), 61; Stanford Univ Grad Sch, MA (Hispanic-Am Studies), 63; Coll Mex, 63; Inst Hautes Etudes Am Latine, Paris, 64-65; Los Angeles City Coll, 73-77; Abram Freeman Occupation Ctr, 81; Calif State Univ, Northridge, 81-82. *Work:* Nara Mus, Japan. *Exhib:* Butler Inst Am Art, Youngstown, Ohio, 78; Canton Inst Art, Ohio, 78; Friends Photog, 78; Downey Mus Art, Los Angeles Ctr Photog Studies, 78; Tenth Ann Int Photog Meet, Arles, France, 79; San Francisco Camera Work, Herbert Asherman Gallery, Cleveland, Ohio; Clarence Kennedy Gallery, Cambridge, Mass; solo exhib, Cleveland Playhouse Gallery; and many others. *Pos:* Coordr, Photog Mus, Los Angeles, 80-81; photogr, var freelance, 84-; interpreter, Pasadena City Coll Hearing Impaired prog, 81-83; bd dir, Damien Proj, Los Angeles (treas, 90). *Teaching:* Instr, Los Angeles City Coll Community Serv, 79-82 & Parsons Workshops, 90-93. *Awards:* Outstanding Student Award, Los Angeles City Coll, 76. *Bibliog:* Photographic Artists & Innovators, 83. *Mem:* Soc Photog Educ; Friends Photog, San Francisco; Ctr Creative Photog, Tucson, Ariz; Int Ctr Photog, New York; Mus Photog. *Media:* Digital. *Interests:* travel, language, the arts, genealogy. *Publ:* Co-illusr, Ballet Box, RCA Records, 79; contribr & coauth, Sequences: Baptism of Eros II, Peterson's Photog, 6/79; cover photog, Wolf Mag Lett, spring 91 & fall 91; article, Manuscripts Mag, 99. *Dealer:* Getty Images. *Mailing Add:* 1231 Kipling Ave Los Angeles CA 90041-1616

LANGAGER, CRAIG T
PAINTER, SCULPTOR
b Seattle, Wash, July 5, 1946. *Study:* Minn State Univ, Bemidji, BS (art), 71; Univ Ore, Eugene, MFA (art), 74. *Work:* Brooklyn Mus Art, New York; Denver Art Mus, Colo; Metrop Mus Art, New York; Winnipeg Art Gallery, Manitoba, Can; Seattle Art Mus; Whatcom Mus History & Art, Bellingham, Wash; Tacoma Art Mus; Mus NW Art, La Conner; Jordan Mus, Univ Oregon, Eugene; NDak Mus Art, Grand Forks. *Comn:* One Percent for Art Purchase, Seattle Arts Comn, Wash, 78; wall relief, comn by Ann Gerber, Seattle, Wash, 79; sculpture, comn by Gordon Hanes, Winston-Salem, NC, 82; sculpture, Niagara Frontier Transportation Authority, Buffalo, NY, 82-83. *Exhib:* Solo Exhibs: Susan Caldwell Gallery, New York, 81 & 83-84; Inst Contemp Art, Boston, 82; Ruth Siegal Ltd, New York, 86; Bemidji State Univ, Minn, 86; William Traver Gallery, 91; Security Pac Gallery, Seattle, 91-92; ND Mus Art, Grand Forks, 2007-08; Painting & Sculpture Today, Indianapolis Mus Art, Ind, 82 & 86; New New York (with catalog), Fla State Univ, Metrop Mus & Art Ctr, Coral Gables, Fla, 82-83; Dialogues (with catalog), Winnipeg Art Gallery, 84; Body and Soul: Aspects of Recent Figurative Sculpture (with catalog), Contemp Art Ctr, Cincinnati, 85 & traveled 85-87, Art Mus Asn Am, San Francisco; Totems, Edith Baker Gallery, Dallas, 88; Small and Stellar, Ruth Siegel Ltd, New York, 89; 20th Anniversary of the Visiting Artist Prog, CU Art Galleries, Univ Colo, Boulder, 92; 5th Int Shoebox Sculpture Exhib, Univ Hawaii Art Gallery, Honolulu, 94; Recent NW Acquisition, Seattle Art Mus, 96; Recent Acquisitions, Blair & Lucky Kirk Collection, Mus NW Art, La Conner, 2005; On a Grand Scale, Whatcom Mus Hist & Art, Bellingham, 2009; Critical Messages: Contemp Northwest Artists on the Environment, Western Gallery, WWU & Hallie Ford Mus, Williamette Uiv, traveled to Boise Art Mus, 2010-2011; Wild/Life, Mus Northwest Art, 2011; Pruzan Coll, Tacoma Art Mus, 2013. *Pos:* Coordr, Earthworks: Land Reclamation as Sculpture Symp, King Co Arts Comn, Seattle, Wash, 78-79. *Teaching:* Chmn, fine arts dept, Cornish Inst, Seattle, Wash, 76-78; vis artist, sculpture, Syracuse Univ, NY, winter 82; Univ Colo, Boulder, spring 85; vis prof, sculpture & painting, Western Wash Univ, Bellingham, 89-90. *Awards:* Minn State Arts Grant, Minn Coun Arts, Minneapolis, 75; Whitney Found Grant, Dartington Coll Arts, Eng, 77. *Bibliog:* Kim Levin (auth), Craig Langager, Critical Distance-Cloning for a New Society, (catalog essay) Issues, New Allegory II, Inst Contemp Art, Boston, 82; Shirley Madill (auth), Dialogues, The Winnipeg Perspective 1984: Sherry Grauer, Craig Langager and John McEwen (catalog), 3-4, 9-15 & 35, Winnipeg Art Gallery, Manitoba, 84; Gerrit Henry (auth), Craig Langager at Ruth Siegel, Art in Am, 117, 7/10/86; Regina Hackett (auth), rev, Twenty Years, 1970-1990 Prints, and Installation by Craig Langager, Seattle Post-Intelligencer, C15, 11/20/91; 5th Int Sculpture Exhib (catalog), 69, Univ Hawaii Art Gallery, Honolulu, 94; Laura Reuter (auth), North Dakota Museum of Art, pages 48-49, NDak Mus, Grand Forks, 2008; Sarah Clark-Langager & William Dietrich (auth), Critical Messages: Contemp Northwest Artists on the Environment, WWU, Bellenghan, 2010. *Mailing Add:* 2970 N Shore Rd Bellingham WA 98226

LANGDO, BRYAN RICHARD
ILLUSTRATOR, WRITER
b Denville, NJ, Jan 7, 1973. *Study:* Art Student's League of NY, Studied with Harvey Dinnerstein, Michael Burban, Jack Henderson, Michael Pellitieri, 90-91, 92-95; Rutgers Coll, BA, 98. *Exhib:* The Original Art, Mus of Am Illus at the Soc of Illusr, 2002. *Teaching:* Instr, Somerset Art Asn, Bedminster, NJ, 2005-. *Media:* Watercolor, Pencil. *Publ:* Auth & illusr, The Dog Who Loved the Good Life, Henry Holt, 2001; illusr, Joe Cinders, Henry Holt, 2002; illusr, Cat and Dog, Harper Collins, 2005; illusr, Mummy Math: An Adventure in Geometry, Henry Holt, 2005; illusr, The Best Time of Day, Gulliver Bks, 2005; illusr, The Stuffed Animals Get Ready for Bed, Harcourt, 2006; illusr, Patterns in Peru: An Adventure in Patterning, Henry Holt, 2007. *Mailing Add:* 67 John St West Hurley NY 12491

LANGER, SANDRA LOIS (CASSANDRA)
ART APPRAISER, HISTORIAN, CRITIC, AUTHOR
b Woodridge, NY, Dec 18, 1941. *Study:* Univ Miami, BA, 67, MA, 69; NY Univ, PhD, 74. *Collection Arranged:* Beyond Survival: Old Frontiers, New Horizons; Robert R Presto Collection, Mus City of NY. *Pos:* Contrib critic, Art Papers, 74-79; independent art hist & critic, New York, 86; co-dir, Psych-Arts Soc, currently; exec appraiser, free-lance writer, critic, grants & publ adv, currently; contrib ed, Women Artists Book Review; HG & LR Int Rev; critic at large, Women's Art J; dir, Private Eye: Noir Arts Ltd; Cassandra Langer & Assocs Fine Art Appraisal Servs, currently; contribr, Women's Art J & Midwest Bk Rev; editor in chief, Painted Pony Productions; Womens Review of Books. *Teaching:* Asst prof mod-contemp art, Fla Int Univ, 73-78; asst prof to assoc prof, Univ SC, Columbia, 78-86; vis assoc prof, Hunter & Queens. *Awards:* Smithsonian Post-Doctorial Fel, Nat Mus Art, 84. *Bibliog:* Harper Collins (auth), A Feminist Critique, 96; auth, What's Right with Feminism, 2000; Rainbow Blues, Printed Paper Press, Lulu Books, 2014; All or Nothing: Romaine Brooks 1874-1970, Univ Wisc Press, 2015. *Mem:* Coll Art Asn; Int Asn Art Critics; Am Soc Journalists & Authors; Pen & Appraiser Asn Am; PEN. *Res:* Deconstructing Romaine Brooks; critical overview; contemporary art and criticism, feminism and post modernism; deco-noir connections between film & photography. *Interests:* film, photography, l & g studies, literature, critical thinking, biography, the environment. *Publ:* Co-ed & contribr, Turning points & sticking places: Feminist art criticism, Coll Art J, 91; Mother and Child in Art, Cresent/Random House Bks, 91; New Feminist Criticism Art, Identify, Action, 94; Joan Synder, Eva Hesse: The wisdom of Nothing, 2006; auth, My Love Affair with Romaie Brooks (H.L.L.Q. July), 2007; auth, Queer Heroic Portraits by Romaine Brooks (paper), Journal of Lesbian Studies, 2011; Behind the Mask: The Facist Heroism of Romaine Brooks Portaits, Clio Psyche Vol. 18, No. 3, 2011. *Mailing Add:* 32-22 89th St Apt 306 East Elmhurst NY 11369-2179

LANGFORD-STANSBERY, SHERRY K
ENVIRONMENTAL ARTIST, PAINTER
b North Platte, Nebr, Oct 29, 1944. *Study:* Pvt study with G Leslie Smith, 67-70, Kansas City Art Inst, 69-72. *Work:* Searcy Co Bank, Marshall, Ark; Tenneco, Houston, Tex. *Comn:* Great Blue Heron, NW Ark Audubon Soc, Fayetteville, Ark, 84; Red Wolf, Wolf Sanctuary, Eureka, Mo, 87; River Otters, Little Rock Zoo, 87; Mountain Lion, Little Rock Zoo, 92; Mexican Wolf, Wolf Sanctuary, Eureka, Mo, 92; and others. *Exhib:* Okla Wildlife Art Festival, Camelot Hotel, Tulsa, Okla, 82-91; Arts Crafts & Design Fair, Robinson Conv Ctr, Little Rock, Ark, 82-92; Art Happening, St Louis, Mo, 84-96; Cheyenne Audubon Wildlife Exhib, Conv Ctr, Cheyenne, Wyo, 85; Wildlife Art Walk, St Louis Zoo, Mo, 85-88; Nat Wildlife Art Fest, Doubletree Inn, Overland Park, Kans, 88-2000; and others. *Collection Arranged:* One-woman Exhibition, Fort Smith Art Ctr, 86 & 89. *Pos:* Litho-artist, Hallmark Cards, 62-64. *Awards:* Best of Show, Okla Wildlife Art Fest, 88 & 91; Best of Show, Nat Wildlife Art Exhib, 88, 94, 95, 96, 97, 98, 99, 2000; Artist of Year, Ark Wildlife Fed, 88, 91, 92, 94 & 95, 96, 97, 98, 2000; Best of Show, Red River Revel, Shreveport, La, 89; Best of Show, Best Bald Eagle, Best Pencil, Okla Wildlife Art Festival, 90. *Bibliog:* Doris Freyder (auth), Wildlife Artist, Ozarks Mountaineer, 10/82; Terry Horton (auth), article, Arkansas Out of Doors, 10/88. *Mem:* Eureka Springs Guild of Artists & Craftspeople. *Media:* Pencil, Watercolor. *Publ:* Illusr, Trees, Shrubs & Vines of Arkansas, Ozark Soc; A Shadow in the Forest, JB George, Vantage Press. *Dealer:* White Oak Studio PO Box 937Harrison AR 72602; Quicksilver The Nature Gallery 99 Spring St Eureka Springs AR 72632. *Mailing Add:* 309 Hwy 62-65 North Harrison AR 72601

LANGLAND, TUCK
SCULPTOR, EDUCATOR
b Minneapolis, Minn, Oct 6, 1939. *Study:* Univ Minn, BA (art), 61, MFA (sculpture), 64. *Work:* Ind Univ, Univ Notre Dame, South Bend; Midwest Mus Am Art, Elkhart, Ind; St Paul Acad & Summit Sch, Minn; Minn Mus, St Paul. *Comn:* Violin Woman (bronze), South Bend, Ind, 82; Polymnia (bronze), Ft Wayne, Ind, 84; Madeline Bertrand (bronze), Niles, Mich, 87; Flak Bait (bronze), Air & Space Mus, Smithsonian Inst, 94; Legacy (bronze), Goshen Ind Pub Libr, 97. *Exhib:* Solo exhibs, Small Bronzes, traveling, Eng, 77-78, Tweed Mus, Duluth, Minn, 78, Reflections, South Bend Art Ctr, Ind, 80, Mid-West Mus Am Art, Elkhart, Ind, 84; Concurrent Themes, South Bend Art Ctr, 87, SW Mich Coll, 94, Hillsdale Coll, Mich, 96 & Filli Gallery, Chi, 96; Cantigny, Ill, 94-98; Serravezza, Italy, 96; Chesterwood, Mass, 97; and others in US & Eng. *Teaching:* Asst lectr sculpture, Carlisle & Sheffield Cols o -Art; Eng: 64-67; asst prof sculpture; Murray State Univ, 67-71; assoc prof & Chmn dept fine arts, Ind-Univ; South-Bend, 71-82, prof, 82; vis lectr; Stoke-on-Trent, Eng, 77-78; Hoosier Salon Show, Indianapolis, 1980, 82, 84, 85, 86 (Outstanding Work in Sculpture awards), collections incl: Midwest Mus Am Art, Elkhart, Ind, Calhoun St Pedestrian Mall, Ft Wayne, Ind, Beatrice Foods, Chicago, Morris Civic Auditorium, S Bend, Univ Minn, Minneapolis, Ind Univ at South Bend, Notre Dame Univ, S Bend, Minnesota Mus Art, St Paul; nat exhib incl: Nat Acad of Design, New York City, 1982, 83, 99, Salmagundi Club, New York City, 1982, 83, 99, Terrace Gallery Show (Honorable Mention award), Palenville, NY, 1982, Audubon Artists, New York City, 1984, Nat Sculpture Society (Liskin Prize 1986), New York City, 1985; invitational exhib include: Royal Festival Hall, London, 1980, Promega, Madison, Wis, 1996, Lyme Acad, Conn, 1997, Chesterwood, Mass, 1997. *Awards:* Best of Show, Northern Ind Arts Asn, 83; Liskin Prize, Nat Sculpture Soc, 85; Outstanding Work in Sculpture, Hoosier Salon, 88, 90, 93, 94, 95, 98 & Best of Show, 97. *Mem:* Artists Equity; Fel, Nat Sculpture Soc; Nat Acad; Nat Sculptor's Guild. *Media:* Bronze. *Interests:* Choral singing, swimming. *Publ:* Auth, Practical Sculpture, Prentice Hall, Englewood Cliffs, NJ, 88. *Dealer:* Columbine Loveland CO; Sculpture Showcase New Hope PA. *Mailing Add:* 12632 Anderson Rd Granger IN 46530

LANGMAN, RICHARD THEODORE
GALLERY DIRECTOR
b Philadelphia, Pa, June 9, 1937. *Study:* Cornell Univ, 54-55; Univ Calif, Berkeley, BA (urban design), 60. *Collection Arranged:* Alice Neel, Paintings, 74; Clayton Pond, Paintings & Graphics, 74; Graphics of the 70's (Int Graphics Show), 75 & Craft Art (Nat), 77, Langman Gallery; Bruce Evans, Paintings, SICA, 78 & 80, Constructions, 80; Andy Warhol, Paintings & Graphics, 83. *Pos:* Dir, Langman Gallery, Jenkintown, Pa. *Specialty:* Contemporary painting and sculpture. *Mailing Add:* 218 Old York Rd Jenkintown PA 19046-3244

LANGSTON, MARY VIRGINIA
SCULPTOR, PAINTER
Study: Univ NC, BA (political sci & hist), 68; Corcoran Sch Art, 84-88 & 90. *Work:* Greenville Mus Art, NC; Contemp Art Mus, Monte Catini, Italy; archive Nat Mus Women in Arts, Washington, DC. *Comn:* Painting, Kathy Moore, Alexandria, Va; painting, Maggi Castelloe, Marshall, Va; painting, Paul Castelloe, Raleigh, NC. *Exhib:* Light in Tobacco Barn, Greenville Mus of Art, NC, 98; Centro Marino Marini, Pistoia, Italy, 2001; Light in Tobacco Barn, Danville Mus of Fine Arts & Hist, Va, 2003; 48th Paint Exhib, Hunterdon Mus Art, Clinton, NJ; Hope & Fear, Arlington Arts Ctr, Arlington, VA, 2007-2008; Clouds, Gallery 10, DC, 2009. *Pos:* Res asst, Nat Portrait Gallery, Washington, DC, 68-70; Int exhib coordr, Gallery 10 Ltd, DC, 2004-2010. *Awards:* Merit Award, The Athenaeum, Alexandria, 84; First Place, Cash Award, Peninsula Fine Arts Ctr; Resident fel, Va Ctr Creative Arts, Sweet Briar, Va, 94, 98 & 2006. *Bibliog:* Women Artists: Works from the Greenville Mus Art Collection, (exhib catalog), Greenville Mus Art, NC, 3/2001; Acceleration 30 years at high speed at Gallery 10, LTD, (exhib catalog), 2004; US Embassy, Banjul, The Gambia, Art in Embassies Prog, Dept State, 2005. *Mem:* Wash Sculptors Group; Gallery 10 LTD (exec bd, 2001-2009); Wash Proj Arts; Int Sculpture Ctr; Arts and Artists, Wash DC. *Media:* Installation Sculpture, Mixed Media. *Interests:* Travel, gardening. *Publ:* Coauth, The Light in the Tobacco Barn (catalog), Greenville Mus Art, 98; Clouds (catalog with Cole Swensen). *Dealer:* Gallery 10 Washington DC

LANIGAN-SCHMIDT, THOMAS
ASSEMBLAGE ARTIST, INSTRUCTOR
b Elizabeth, NJ, Jan 16, 1948. *Study:* Pratt Inst, Brooklyn, NY, 65-66; Sch Visual Arts, New York, 67; studied pvt with Jack Smith & Charles Ludlam, 70-74. *Work:* Metrop Mus Art, NY; Albright Knox Mus, Buffalo, NY; Mus d'Art Contemporain, Lausanne, Switz; Ludwig Mus, Aachen, Ger; Nelson Atkins Gallery, Kansas City. *Exhib:* Venice Biennale, The Pluralist Decade, USA Pavillion, Venice, Italy, 80; 20th Century Art from the Metrop Mus NY, Queens Mus, Flushing, NY, 83; Arte, Ambiente, Scena, Venice Bienale Italy, 84; Content: A Contemp Focus, Hirshhorn Mus & Sculpture Garden, Washington, DC, 84; Sacred Images in Secular Art, Whitney Mus, NY, 86; Contemp Diptychs, Whitney Mus (Equitable), NY, 87; Americana Installation, Groninger Mus, The Neth, 87; 1991 Biennial Exhib, Whitney Mus Am Art, NY, 91. *Pos:* Bd govs, Skowhegan Sch Painting & Sculpture, 91-. *Teaching:* Instr MFA prog, Sch Visual Arts, 89-; resident artists studio, Skowhegan Sch Painting & Sculpture, 91-. *Bibliog:* Robert Atkins (auth), The center show, Village Voice, 5/26/89; Roberta Smith (auth), The return of Tzarina Tatlina, NY Times, 4/24/92; Tzarina Tatlina, New Yorker, 4/92. *Media:* Scotch Tape, Plastic Wrap. *Publ:* Contribr, Ornamentalism, Robert Jensen & Patricia Conway (auths), Oitter/Crown, 82; Once a Catholic, Peter Occhigrasso (auth), Houghton/Mifflin, 88

LANSDON, GAY BRANDT
PRINTMAKER, JEWELER
b San Antonio, Tex, Dec 6, 1931. *Study:* Univ Houston, Tex, BFA, 65; Mus of Fine Arts Sch, Houston, 66-68; Sam Houston State Univ, MFA, 75. *Work:* Univ Houston, Univ Ctr; Sam Houston State Univ; Shell Oil Co; Xerox Corp; Price Waterhouse; and others. *Comn:* 16 paintings, comn by Dr Robert Stewart, Houston, 67; serigraph, comn by Jean Geeslin, Huntsville, Tex, 69; three printed fiber panels, Bellville State Bank, Tex, 72. *Exhib:* 15th Ann Tex Craftsman, Dallas Mus Fine Arts, 71; Colorprint USA, Lubbock, Tex, 75; Third Nat Print Exhib, Univ Southern Calif, Los Angeles, 75; 14th Midwest Biennial, Joslyn Art Mus, Omaha, Nebr, 75; Purdue Univ Small Print Exhib, 76; Five Texas Jewelers, Austin, 92; The Art of Jewelry, 94. *Teaching:* Instr art, Houston Mus Fine Arts, Tex, 69-71; art dept fac, Univ Houston, Cent Campus, 71-82, coordr printmaking, 76-82; mem fac continuing educ, Univ Tex, Austin, currently. *Awards:* Jurors' Merit Awards, SW Graphics Invitational, 72 & Dimension X, 76, Houston Art League; First Prize, Baytown Ann, 78. *Bibliog:* Kit Van Cleave (auth), Gay Lansdon: Mixed-media printmaking, Today's Art, 2/77. *Mem:* Soc N Am Goldsmiths. *Media:* Mixed. *Dealer:* Artisans Gallery at the Arboretum 10000 Research Blvd Suite 258 Austin TX 78759. *Mailing Add:* 11631 River Oaks Tr Austin TX 78753

LANYON, ELLEN
PAINTER, PRINTMAKER
b Chicago, Ill, 1926. *Study:* Art Inst Chicago, with Joseph Hirsch, BFA, 1948; State Univ Iowa, with M Lasansky, MFA, 1950; Courtauld Inst, Univ London, with Helmut Reuhman. *Hon Degrees:* DHL, Lincoln Col; Hon Doctorate, Sch Art, Inst of Chicago, 2007. *Work:* Art Inst of Chicago; Walker Art Ctr, Minneapolis; Nat Mus Am Art, Smithsonian Inst; Metrop Mus Art, NY; Brooklyn Mus, NY; Mus Contemp Art, Chicago; Milwaukee Art Mus; Denver Art Mus; Am Mus Art, Washington, DC; Nat Mus Women in the Arts, Washington, DC; Grand Rapids Mus, Mich; Boston Pub Libr; Libr Cong, Washington, DC; Mus Mod Art, New York; New York Pub Libr; Des Moines Art Ctr, Iowa; Nat Acad, New York; Univ Iowa Mus Art; Wash Co Mus Art; Walker Art Ctr, Minn; and many more. *Comn:* Mural, Workingmans Coop Bank, Boston, 1981; Mural, State Ill Bldg, Chicago, 1983; Art in Public Places (mural), Police & Court Facil, Miami Beach, Fla; Miami Beach, TMA, 1997; Mural, Rise of Chicago, Ill State Capitol, Springfield, 1989; Mural, Riverwalk Gateway, City of Chicago, 2000; Hiawatha LRT Murals, Minneapolis, 2003. *Exhib:* Solo exhibs: Zabriskie Gallery, NY, 1962, 1964, 1969, 1972; Richard Gray Gallery, Chicago, 1972, 1973, 1976, 1979, 1985; Odyssia Gallery, Rome, 1976; Odyssia Gallery, NY, 1980; Retrospective: Krannert Mus, Ill, McNay, San Antonio, Tex, Stamford Mus, Conn, Univ Tenn, 87-88, Printworks Gallery, Chicago, 1989, 1993, 1999, 2007, 2011; Struve Gallery, Chicago, 1990, 1993; Berland Hall Gallery, NY, 1992; Andre Zarre Gallery, NY, 1994, 1997; Transformations, 30 yr retrospective, Nat Mus for Women in the Arts, 1999, 2000, Chicago Cult Ctr, 2000, 2007; Valerie Carberry Gallery, Chicago, 2006, 2008, 2011, 6 Decade Retrospective (traveling), Brauer Mus, Valparaiso Univ, Ind, 2007, Pavel Zoubok, 2010, DePaul Art Mus, Chicago, 2012; group exhibs incl Art Inst Chicago, 1946-81, 2011; Corcoran Gallery Art Ann, 1961; The Figure, Mus Mod Art, NY, 1962; Landscape, Whitney Mus; Am Realism, San Francisco Mus Art, 1985; 25 yr retrospective (traveling), Krannert Mus, Univ Ill, 1987-88; Realism & Realities, Voorhees, Mus, Rutgers Univ, 1989; Pretto-Berland Hall, NY Struve Gallery, Chicago, 1990; Face to Face, Chicago Cult Ctr, 1992; Artists Sketchbook, Nat Mus Women Arts, 1994-95; Art in Chicago 1945-1995, Mus Contemp Art, Chicago, 1996; Contemp Classicism, Neuberger Mus of Art, 1999; Chicago Loop, Whitney Mus of Am Art, Stamford, Conn, 2000; Nat Acad Mus Bi-Annuals, 1999, 2001, 2003, 2005, 2007, 2009; Adam Baumgold Gallery, NY, 2002, 2004, 2012; Am Acad Arts & Letters-Invitational, 2004, 2011; Two person exhib, with Philip Pearlstein, Valerie Carberry, Chicago, 2011. *Pos:* Mem, Col Art Asn Bd Dirs, 1978-82; CAA Art Journal Ed Bd, 1979-92; Nat Acad of Design-Council Mem-2001-; Chair Ex Comm, 2004-2006. *Teaching:* Instr painting & dir, Ox Bow Summer Sch of Painting, Saugatuck, Mich, 1960-2008; vis artist-lectr, Stanford Univ, 1973 & Univ Calif, Davis, 1973 & 1980; vis artist & fel, Inst Arts & Humanistic Studies, Pa State Univ, 1974; vis artist, State Univ Iowa; instr painting, State Univ NY Purchase, 1978-, Parsons Sch Design, 1979-80 & Sch Visual Arts, 1980-83; instr painting, Cooper Union, 1979-82, assoc prof, 1983-92; instr painting, Anderson Ranch, 1994-96 & Vt Studio Sch, 1995, 1997, 2001. *Awards:* Nat Endowment Arts Grant, 1974 & 1987; Yaddo Fel, 1974-75, 1976 & 1998; Hereward Lester Cooke Found, 1981; Florsheim Found Grant, 1999; Puchase Am Acad Arts & Letters, 2004, 2010; Cassandra Grant, 1970; Hon Doc, Sch Art Inst, Chicago, 2007; Award, Nat Acad, 2009. *Bibliog:* Donald Kuspit (auth), Strange Games (catalog essay), 1987; Christopher Lyon (auth), Recent Drawings, 1990; Eleanor Heartney (auth), Monograph Essay, 1992; Lucy Lippard (auth), Under the Wing of Survival (catalog essay), 1983; Debra Bricker Balkin (auth), Transformations (catalog essay), 1999; Paintings of the 60's (auth) Franz Schultz Catalog Essay, 2005; Esther Sparks (auth), Ellen Lanyon, A Wonder Production, Brauer Mus, Ind, 2007; Michael Rooks (auth), At the Design of the Hat (catalogue, essay), 2008. *Mem:* Coll Art Asn (bd dir, 1977-81); Nat Acad (coun); Elected to the Century Asn NY 2005. *Media:* Acrylic, Prismacolor; Lithography. *Res:* 19th Century engravings & restoration. *Specialty:* Contemp paintings, drawings, prints. *Interests:* Collecting ephemera & turn of the century mechanical devices & inventions. *Publ:* The Weasel by Annie Dillard, 1982; White Walls, autumn 1982; Mirabai Versions by Robert Bly, 1984; Wonder Production, Vol 2, Landfall Press, 1971; The Wandering Tattler, Perishible Press, 1975; Index Print Studio, Cambridge, UK, 2003; Objects/Objectivity, 2 Person/P Pearlstein (catalog Interview by Irving Sandler); Persistence of Invention (catalog, Louise Lincoln essay, Rob Storr interview), 2012. *Dealer:* Printworks Ltd 311 W Superior Chicago IL 60610; Valerie Carberry Gallery 875 N Michigan Ave Chicago IL 60611. *Mailing Add:* 138 Prince St #4 New York NY 10012

LAPALOMBARA, CONSTANCE
PAINTER, DRAFTSMAN
b Brooklyn, NY, Dec 13, 1935. *Study:* Manhattanville Coll, BA, 57; Yale Univ, with William Bailey, 76-77; New York Studio Sch, 78; Tyler Sch Art, Temple Univ, MFA, 82. *Work:* Banca Commerciale Italiana, New York; Wells Fargo, New Haven, Conn; Enichem USA, New York; Italiana Gas Industriale, Milan; Soundview Care Center, New Haven, Conn; Southern New Eng Tel, New Haven, Conn; New Haven Pub Libr; New Haven Paint and Clay Permanent Coll, New Haven, Conn; Univ Conn Health Ctr, Farmington, Conn; New Britain Mus Am Art, New Britain, Conn. *Exhib:* Guido

io vorrei..., Palazzo Ducale, Mantua, Italy, 93; Ezra Stiles Coll, Yale Univ, New Haven, 2000; A Moveable Feast, Zeuxis, Westbeth Gallery, New York, 2003; Industrial Beauty, George Billis Gallery, New York, 2004; Bachelier Cardonsky Gallery, Kent, Conn, 2004; Italia, Brickwalk Gallery, West Hartford, Conn, 2005; Points of View, Kehler Liddell Gallery, New Haven, Conn, 2005; Between Perception & Invention, Sharon Arts Ctr, Peterborough, NH, 2005; Around the Corner, Fenn Gallery, Woodbury, Conn, 2005; New Haven, Gallery 195, Conn, 2006; The City, Whitney Humanities Ctr Gallery, Yale Univ, New Haven, Conn, 2007-2008; Perceptions, Univ Conn Health Ctr Gallery, Farmington, Conn, 2007; Summer in the City, George Billlis Gallery, New York, 2009; Water, Atlantic Gallery, 2010; Eat/Art, Atlantic Gallery, 2010; Wingspread Legacy, Courthouse Gallery, Ellsworth, ME, 2010; Conn Watercolor Show, John Slade Ely House, New Haven, Conn,; Pathways to Landscape, Ridgefield Guild of Artists, 2011; Static Verve, Rockwell Galleries, Ridgefield, Conn, 2011; Salty Dog Gallery, Southwest Harbor, ME, 2011; In Translation, Jonathan Edwards College, Yale Univ, 2011; Stonework: Artist's Encounters with Hard Places, Inst Libr, New Haven, Conn, 2012; The Gallery at Frenchmans Bay, Somesville, ME, 2012; Art Essex Gallery, Ct, 2012; Star Gallery, Northeast Harbor, ME, 2013. *Teaching:* Instr painting & drawing, Southern Conn State Univ, 84-85. *Awards:* Univ Fel, Temple Univ, 81-82; Grant, Schohaire Co Arts Coun, 98; Artists Fel, Conn Comn on the Arts, 2000; Heliker-LaHotan Residency Fel, 2010. *Bibliog:* Andrew Forge (auth), The Clarity of American Light (catalog), Gabbiano Gallery, 93; T O'Shaughnessy (auth), The Cleansing Breeze of Everyday Objects, Waterbury Republican, 99; John Hollander (auth) Landscape Painting, 1960-90: The Italian Tradition in Am Painting Catalog, Gibbes Mus, Charleston, SC; J Harris (auth), A Different Landscape, Italy-Italy Mag, 2003; M Mullarkey (auth), Industrial Beauty Review, New York Sun, 2004; J Birke (auth), Elm City, New Haven Register, 9/2005; C Tyler (ed), Artists Next Door, Partnership for Conn Cities (publ), New Haven, 2006; Norma Thompson, Rosanna Warren (auths), The City (exhib catalog), Whitney Humanities Ctr Gallery, Yale Univ, New Haven, Conn, 2007; Tamera Lenz Muente (auth), Everytown, USA, The Artists Mag, 9/2009; Painting Perceptions, 2010; Stephen Kobasa (auth), How the Sea Colors Itself, The New Haven Independent, 2011; Conn Art Scene, 2011. *Mem:* Conn Acad Fine Arts; Conn Watercolor Soc; Conn Women Artists; New Haven Paint & Clay. *Media:* Oil, Watercolor, Charcoal, Pencil. *Dealer:* Sandro Manzo-Gabbiano NY & Rome; Star Gallery Northeast Harbor ME. *Mailing Add:* 50 Huntington St New Haven CT 06511

LAPALOMBARA, DAVID
EDUCATOR, ADMINISTRATOR
Study: Oberlin Col, BA; Nova Scotia Col of Art and Design, MFA. *Exhib:* Art has been exhibited in Canada, Italy and several cities in the US. *Pos:* Contribr (tour guide) City Secrets: Rome; vis artist, American Acad, Rome. *Teaching:* Chair, interdisciplinary arts & humanities department, Antioch Col, formerly; prof Sch of Art, Ohio Univ, currently, dir Sch of Art, 2007-. *Awards:* Rome Prize Fellowship; Fulbright Fellowship, Italy. *Mailing Add:* Ohio University School of Art 528 Seigfred Hall Athens OH 45701

LA PELLE, RODGER
PAINTER, DEALER
b Philadelphia, Pa, July 31, 1936. *Study:* Univ Pa; Pa Acad Fine Arts. *Work:* Free Libr Philadelphia, Pa; Munson-Williams-Proctor Mus, Utica, NY; Mus Mod Art, New York. *Exhib:* Nat Exhib, Pa Acad Fine Art, Philadelphia, 58, Calif Palace of Legion Honor, San Francisco, 62 & San Francisco Art Mus, Calif, 63; La Pelle Galleries, 85-88, 92 & 94. *Pos:* Owner, Rodger La Pelle Galleries. *Awards:* Silver Medal, Cologne, Fed Repub Ger, 56; Cresson Traveling Scholar, Pa Acad Fine Art, 61; Moss-Graff Prize, Cheltenham Ann Exhib, 88; Lucy Glick Prize, 2001. *Mem:* Fel Pa Acad Fine Arts (past pres). *Media:* Oil, Pencil. *Specialty:* Contemporary painting, sculpture and graphics. *Publ:* Art Matters. *Mailing Add:* c/o La Pelle Galleries 122 N Third St Philadelphia PA 19106-1802

LA PIERRE, THOMAS
PAINTER, PRINTMAKER
b Toronto, Ont, Dec 28, 1930. *Study:* Ont Coll Art, AA, 56; Ecole Beaux Arts; Atelier 17, France, 55-56. *Hon Degrees:* AOCA; RCA. *Work:* Montreal Mus Fine Art, PQ; Art Gallery Mississauga, MacLaren Art Ctr; Art Gallery Hamilton, St Catherines & Art Gallery Ont, Ont; Art Gallery Ont; Art Gallery Peel. *Comn:* Graphite Portrait, Ms Lynne Walters, 74, Oil Portrait, Dr Archibald, 2001. *Exhib:* Sao Paulo Biennial, 63; Atlantic Provinces, 74; WCoast traveling exhib, Burnaby Art Gallery; Dimensions of Realism, Milan, Italy, 78; Sichuan Fine Art Inst, Chong Quing, China, 88; Rodman Hall, St Catherines, Ont, 88; Martin Sumers Art Gallery, NY, 89; The Arena of Heart and Mind, Works from 1972 to 1992 (with catalog), Art Gallery of Peel; Art Gallery of Ont; Art Gallery of Hamilton, Ont; MacLaren Art Gallery, Barrie, Ont; Art Gallery of Peel, Brampton; Art Gallery of Mississauga, Ont. *Teaching:* Instr figure drawing, painting & composition, Ont Col Art, 58-95. *Awards:* Woolfitt Award for Painting Watercolor, 89; Trillium Workshop Award for Painting in Watercolor, 93; Arts & Lett Club Award for Painting in Oil, 98. *Bibliog:* William McElcheran (auth), Dialogue with demons, Arts Can, 70; Robert Percival (auth), 20th Century mystic, Art Mag, 75; Paul Duval (auth), article in Art Mag, 76 & 77. *Mem:* Can Soc Painters in Watercolour; Royal Can Acad Arts. *Media:* Oil, Watercolor; Lithography. *Interests:* Travel, art study, nature(landscape). *Publ:* Limited edition bk, lithographs, drawings & paintings, 1975-1980. *Dealer:* Kinsman Robinson Galleries Toronto ON; Joan Ferneyhough Galleries 157 First Ave E North Bay Ontario Canada P1B 1J7 . *Mailing Add:* 2067 Proverbs Dr Mississauga ON L4X 1G3 Canada

LAPIN, ANNIE
PAINTER
b Washington, DC. *Study:* Yale Univ, BA (cum laude), 2001; Sch Art Inst Chicago, 2004; Univ Calif Los Angeles, Grad Sch Fine Art, MFA, 2007. *Exhib:* Painting Pots and Prints, Studio 54, New Haven, Conn, 2000; Yale Sch Art Exhib, Yale Univ, 2001; The Fall of the House, Calif State Polytechnic Univ, Pomona, 2005; Ann Group Show, Taylor de Cordoba, Los Angeles, 2006; New Wight Gallery, Univ Calif, Los Angeles, 2007; LA Now, Las Vegas Art Mus, 2008; solo exhibs, Angles Gallery, Santa Monica, 2008, Grand Arts, Kansas City, Mo, 2008, Pasdena Mus Calif Art, 2009; NewNow, Nerman Mus Contemp Art, Johnson County Community Coll, Overland Park, Kansas City, 2009. *Awards:* Artist-in-residence, Chatauqua Inst, NY, 2000, Burren Coll Art, Ballyvaughn, Ireland, 2002 & Grand Arts, Kansas City, Mo, 2008. *Bibliog:* Doug Harvey (auth), Some Paintings, LA Weekly, 1/9/2008; Kimberly Brooks (auth), The Painting Whisperer and the Anxiety of Abstraction, The Huffington Post, 5/17/2008; Leah Ollman (auth), Raw Confidence Painted on Canvas, Los Angeles Times, 5/30/2008; Alice Thorson (auth), Installation puts the wild back in nature, Kansas City Star, 7/19/2008. *Media:* Oil

LAPINSKI, TADEUSZ (A)
PRINTMAKER, EDUCATOR
b Rawa Mazowiecka, Poland, June 20, 1928; US citizen. *Study:* Acad Fine Arts, Warsaw, Poland, BA, 54, MFA, 55. *Work:* Academia Abertina Collection, Turin, Italy; Albertina Mus, Vienna, Austria; Bibliotheque Nationale, Paris; Calif Palace of Legion of Honor, San Francisco; Ctrl Inst Art, Beijing; Frick Collection, NYC; Hirshhorn Mus, Washington, DC; Libr of Congress, Washington, DC; and others. *Exhib:* Am Print in Venice, 77; Solo exhibs, Baak Gallery, Cambridge, Mass, 79, Bacardi Art Gallery, 79, Forum Gallery, Zagreb, Yugoslavia & Klevit Gallery, Washington, DC; Central Inst Art, Beijing, Peoples Repub China, 88; Mus City Torun, Poland, 92; solo exhibs, District Mus Art, Torun, Poland, 92, Sci Soc Plock Art Gallery, Poland, 93 & Dist Mus Zuhafdow, Poland, 94, Nat Mus of Art, Tien Jin, People's Rep China, Cork Gallery, Lincoln Ctr NY, Tadeusz Lapinski: Recent Lithographs, Kennedy Galleries, New York City, Gallery Lambert, Paris, Graphics by Lapinski, Mus Contemp Art, Sao Paolo, Brazil, Mus Modern Art, New York City, Tadeusz Lapinski Color Lithographs, Miami Mus Modern Art, Fla, House of Prints Gallery with Miro and Hass, Toronto, Can, Gallerie ULUS, Belgrade, Yugoslavia; 36th Biennale of Art, Venice, Italy. *Teaching:* Assoc prof lithography, Univ Md, 72-82, prof, 83-; instr, Grodzisk Mazowiecki, Poland, 56-63, 65-67; vis artist/lectr, Pratt Graphics Ctr, New York City, 63-64 & 68-69, Univ Brazil, Porto Alegre, 67-68. *Awards:* First Prize, Int Print Festival Vienna, 78; Second Prize, World Print, Paris, 80; Outstanding Achievement Award, 81 & Honor Awards, 86, Univ Md; Statue of Victory, World Prize Calvatone, Italy, 85. *Bibliog:* Fritz Eichenberg (auth), The Art of the Prints, Abrams, 77; Jane Haslem (ed), American Paintings and Graphics, Washington, DC; Lillian Dobbs (auth), Lapinski prints are unique, hard to find, Miami News, 11/16/79. *Mem:* Soc Am Graphic Artists; Painters Sculptors Soc of NJ (vpres, 72-76); Washington Printmakers Soc; Soc Graphic Arts, NY. *Media:* Lithography. *Dealer:* Jack Walsh Gallery Woodbine MD. *Mailing Add:* 10413 Eastwood Ave Silver Spring MD 20901

LAPKUS, DANAS
CURATOR, CRITIC
b Siauliai, Lithuania, Apr 4, 1964; US citizen. *Study:* Vilnius Art Acad, MA (art hist), 89; Univ Ill, Chicago, MA, 95. *Collection Arranged:* Death: Born in the USA, Lemont Lithuanian Art Mus, 93; The Form of My Life, Contemp Art Ctr, Vilnius, 96; Smuggled Art, Balzekas Mus, Chicago, 96 & Perfection in Exile, 97; Visions of Love, Chicago Cult Ctr, 98. *Pos:* Pub relations dir, Contemp Art Ctr, Vilnius, Lithuania, 89-90; chief cur, Balzekas Mus Lithuanian Cult, Chicago, 91-. *Mem:* Midwest Mus Coun; Chicago Registrars Comt; Lithuanian Am Fine Arts Asn (bd mem, 95-); Ethnic Cult Preserv Coun, Chicago (bd mem, 97-). *Publ:* Numerous contemp art articles in Draugas Daily Paper, 91- & Metmenys Mag, 93-

LA PLANT, MIMI
PAINTER, EDUCATOR
b San Francisco, Calif, Jan 7, 1943. *Study:* Santa Rosa Jr Col, AA, 72; Univ Calif, Berkeley, BA, 74; Humboldt State Univ, MA, 82; Univ Calif Santa Barbara, MFA, 91. *Work:* Morris Graves Mus; Coll the Redwoods, Calif; Humboldt St Univ, Calif. *Comn:* Monotypes, Bank of Del Mar, Calif, 83 & Prudential Life Insurance Co, & Bank of Colo, 84; six monoprints, Dow Chemical, San Diego, Calif; large monotype, ANA Hotel, Japan 85. *Exhib:* Crocker-Kingsley Ann, Crocker Mus, Sacramento, Calif, 86; West Coast Works On/Of Paper, 87 & 88; Locus, San Luis Obispo Art Ctr, 92; 3 Abstract Painters, Foxhall Gallery, Washington, DC, 92; Introductions 92, Weintraub, Sacto, Calif; Crazy for Color, Humbi Arts Coun, Cailf, 2003; Spring Series, Picante Gallery, Calif, 2007; My Life As an Artist, Mimi LaPlant, First St Gallery, Calif, 73-2010; Humboldt St Fac Show, First St Gallery, Calif, 2010. *Collection Arranged:* Martin Wong, The Eureka Years, Humboldt State, First St Gallery, 1999; John Pound, Waht Was I Thinking?! Humboldt State, First St Gallery, 2000. *Teaching:* Lectr painting, drawing, color theory, Humboldt State Univ, Ancata, Calif. *Awards:* Regents fel, Univ Calif, Santa Barbara; Assoc Faculty of Yr Award, Coll of the Redwoods, 2000; Best of Show, RAA Juried Show, 2002; Unsolicited award, Ingrid Nickelson Trust, 2011. *Mem:* Humboldt Arts Coun; The Ink People; Arcata Artisans Coop. *Media:* Oil, Acrylic; Monotype, Pencil, Mixed Media. *Interests:* Plein air, painting, gardening, teaching. *Publ:* Auth, Monoprint: Painting or Printing, Mendocino Art Ctr Mag, 7/87. *Dealer:* SFMOMA Artists Gallery San Francisco CA; Arcata Artisans Arcata CA; Arts & Crafts Cooperative

LAPLANTZ, DAVID
JEWELER, SCULPTOR
b Toledo, Ohio, June 12, 1944. *Study:* Bowling Green State Univ, with Hal Hasselschwert, BS (art), 66; Cranbrook Acad Art, with Richard Thomas, MFA, 69; Southern Ill Univ, with Alex Bealer, 70. *Work:* St Paul Art Ctr, Minn; Nat Mus Mod Art, Kyoto, Japan; Nat Mus Am Art, Smithsonian Inst, Washington, DC; Am Craft Mus; Schmuck Mus, Pforzheim, Ger; and others. *Comn:* Commemorative (scale model of house), Civil Rights Group, Detroit, 67; Smithsonian Mus, Wash; Nat Mus Modern Art, Kyon, Japan; Oakland Mus Art, Calif; Schmuck Mus, Pfarzheim, Ger. *Exhib:* For the Table Top, 80-83 & Contemp Am Jewelry: US Info Agency Arts Am, 85-87, traveling shows, Am Craft Mus; Gold as Gold-Alternative Materials in Am Jewelry, Renwick Gallery, Smithsonian Inst, Washington, DC, 81-84; Contemp

Jewelry-the Americas, Australia, Europe, Japan, Nat Mus Mod Art, Tokyo & Kyoto, Japan, 84; Jewelry USA, Nat Competitive Exhib, Am Crafts Mus & NAm Goldsmiths Soc, 84-86; Sixth Int Jewelry Ornament for the Head and Hair Competition, Pforzheim, Ger, 85-86; Gems & Jewels, New Acquisitions, Oakland Mus Art, 94-95; and others. *Teaching:* Instr, Inst Am Indian Arts, Santa Fe, NMex, 67-68, Flint Community Jr Col, Flint, Mich, 68-69, Kent State Univ, 77-78, Colo State Univ, 69-70, San Diego State Col, 70-71 & Humboldt State Univ, 71-2002, ret. *Awards:* Fulbright Scholar, New Zealand, 85; Merit Award, North Am Goldsmith Biennial Exhib, Phoenix Art Mus, Ariz; Scholar of the Year, Humboldt State Univ, 94. *Bibliog:* Articles in Crafts Horizons, 69-70 & 75, Goldsmith J, 80 & Art Craft Mag, 80; article, Ornament Mag, Vol V, No 4, 82; Chuck Evans (auth), Jewelry: Contemporary Design & Techniques, Davis Publ, 83; Peter Dormer & Ralph Turner (coauth), The New Jewelry-Trends and Traditions, Thames & Hudson, London, 85. *Mem:* Am Craftsman's Coun; Soc NAm Goldsmiths. *Media:* All. *Interests:* Custom cars, motorcycles, bikes. *Publ:* Contribr, Contemporary Jewelry, rev ed, 76; Jewelry Concepts & Technology, 83; auth, Artists Anodizing Aluminum, Press de LaPlantz, 88; ed, Jewelry Metalwork Survey, 1991, Press de LaPlantz, 91; contribr, Workshop Notes: Metals, Brynmorgan Press, 93. *Mailing Add:* 69A Las Estrellas Santa Fe NM 87507-4230

LAPOINTE, FRANK
PAINTER, PRINTMAKER
b Port Rexton, Nfld, May 11, 1942. *Study:* Ont Coll of Art, AOCA, 66. *Work:* Can Coun Art Bank, Pub Works, Canada; Univ Ore, Corvallis; Nat Gallery Can, Ottawa; Art Gallery Ont, Toronto. *Comn:* Nfld postcard ser: What do you think of Jack?, Mem Univ Art Gallery Jubilee Portfolio, St John's, Nfld, 75; stainless steel & aluminum mirror sculpture, Fed Bldg, Grand Falls, Nfld, 79; lithograph portfolio, Can Saltfish Corp, 81; lithograph ed, For Sale, Mem Univ, St Johns, Nfld, 85; lithograph ed, Contrasts, Nfld Teachers' Asn, 90; mural, Trinity Arts Ctr, NF, 2000; lithograph, The Stone Age, Nat Gallery of Can. *Exhib:* 5 Salon Des Vendanges De Cognac, Cognac, France, 85; 25 Yrs of Art, Nat Touring Show, Mem Univ Art Gallery, 86; Door as a Circular Passage, Mem Univ Gallery, St John's, Nfld, 86; Out of the Studio, Mem Univ Gallery, St John's, Nfld, 90; Nfld Art, Salle de la Renaissance, Bordeaux, France, 92; Hidden Values, Art Gallery Nova Scotia, Halifax, 94; Land And Sea, Queen's Univ, Belfast, Ireland, 95; Land And Sea Tour of Ireland, Cork, Waterford, Sligo & Dublin, 96. *Pos:* Asst cur & art specialist, Art Gallery, Mem Univ, St John's, Nfld, 70-72, cur, 72-73; resident printmaker, St Michael's Printshop, Nfld, 81-82; guest cur, Art Gallery, NS Halifax, 83; visual arts coordr, Sound Symp, St John's, Nfld, 83, 88 & 90; colour/design consult, Enterprise Nfld, 91-92; visual art cons, Rising Tide Asn, 97-2003. *Teaching:* Instr painting & printmaking, Dundas Valley Sch of Art, Dundas, Ont, 69-70, design & color, Cobot Col, St Johns, 93 & 94; lectr, aesthet design, Mem Univ, St John's, Nfld, 88, 90 & 91. *Awards:* Silver Medal, 67 & Bronze Medal, 68, Nfld Arts & Lett, Govt Nfld; Can Coun Grant, 77; Can Coun Grant, 86. *Bibliog:* Joe Bodolai (auth), Visit to Newfoundland, 75-76 & Peter Bell (auth), Frank Lapointe/Gerald Squires, 76-77, Artscanada; Peter Bell (auth), Oberheide, Wright, Lapointe, Vie des Arts, Montreal, winter 76; Visions Artists and the Creative Process, TV Ont, 82. *Mem:* Can Soc of Painters in Watercolor; St Michael's Printshop; CARFAC Nat Toronto; Nfld Sound Symp. *Media:* Watercolor, Acrylic; Lithography, Etching. *Dealer:* Red Ochre Gallery, 96 Duckworth St, St Johns, NL, A1C 1E7. *Mailing Add:* Box 11 Port Rexton NL A0C2H0 Canada

LA PORTA, ELAYNE B
PAINTER, PRINTMAKER
b Wilton, Conn. *Study:* Lesnick Sch Art with Steve Lesnick, 68-79; pvt study with Arnold Hitchcock, 68 & Cliff Segerblum, 68; Acad Fine Arts, Florence, Italy, 69. *Work:* Biblical Arts Ctr, Dallas, Tex; Villanova Univ, Pa, 91; St Bernadette Inst Sacred Art, Albuquerque, NMex; Nat Mus Cath Art & Hist, New York, Washington DC; Our Lady of Streets, St Vincent Plaza, Cath Charities of Las Vegas, Las Vegas, Nev; St Rose Dominican, Rose de Lima Campus, Henderson, Nev. *Exhib:* Biblical Arts Ctr, East Gallery, Dallas, Tex, 87; Univ New Orleans, La, 91; Paul VI Inst Arts, Washington, DC, 91; Marion Libr, Dayton, Ohio, 91; West Bend Gallery Fine Arts, Wis, 92; Billy Graham Sacred Arts Ctr, 93. *Awards:* Mother Teresa Award for Religious Folk Art, 2005. *Bibliog:* Beije Howell (auth), Historical biblical art by Elayne La Porta, Santa Monica Outlook, 10/80; Judee Quillum (auth), Elayne La Porta Artist, Art Voices South, 1/80; A D Hopkins (auth), Elayne La Porta Biblical Artist Las Vegas Review J, 11/83; Pam Lang (auth), Elayne La Porta, Artist, Neighbor, Philanthropist, BLVDS, Las Vegas, Nev, 12/2008-1/2009. *Mem:* Catholic Fine Arts Soc, NY; Catholic Artists of the 90's, NY; Midwest Asn Relig Talent Inc, Milwaukee, Wis; Int Registry Relig Women Artists, Fresno, Calif; Christians in the Visual Arts, Wenham, Mass; Nat Mu Women Arts. *Media:* Oil. *Specialty:* religious and native art; biblical, naive. *Dealer:* Billy Graham Ctr Mus Wheaton IL 60187. *Mailing Add:* 443 Blackridge Dr Henderson NV 89015

LARAMEE, EVE ANDREE
SCULPTOR, CONCEPTUAL ARTIST
b Los Angeles, Calif, Jan 6, 1956. *Study:* San Diego State Univ, BA, 78; San Francisco Art Inst, MFA, 80. *Work:* Albuquerque Mus Art, NMex; Mus Mod Art, NY; Fogg Mus, Harvard Univ, Cambridge, Mass; MacArthur Found, Chicago, Ill; Mus Contemp Art, Chicago. *Comn:* Site-specific installation, Zilkha Gallery, Wesleyan Univ, Middletown, Conn, 90; site-specific installation, Mus Contemp Art, Chicago, Ill, 92; pub art comn, San Diego State Univ, 97; Mass Inst Technol, List Visual Art Ctr, Cambridge, Mass, 99. *Exhib:* Galerie des Archives, Paris, France, 95; Venice Biennalle, 97; Mass Inst Technol List Ctr Visual Art, 99; Mass Mus Contemp Art, 2000; Getty Mus, Los Angeles, 2001; Koln Art Fair, Ger, 2002; Georgia Mus of Art, Athens, 2003; Kuntehalle Palazzo Liesfal, Basel, Switz, 2004. *Pos:* Artists Exhib Bd, Rotunda Gallery, Brooklyn; founding ed coun, Blast/Xart Found; bd dir, Int Artists Mus, Lodz, Poland. *Teaching:* Adj prof sculpture, NY Univ, 89-94; part-time prof art grad studies, RI Sch Design, 92-93; vis prof sculpture, Mass Inst Technol, Cambridge, 92; fac, Col Art, Md Inst, 94-96 & Cooper Union, 95; sculpture fac, Sarah Lawrence Col, 97-98, prof, 97-2001; Fairfield Univ, Dir of Visual Arts Prog 2001-2004; Md Inst Col of Art, Chair of Interdisciplinary Sculpture, 2004-. *Awards:* Fel, NY Found Arts, 89; sculptor-in-residence, Guggenheim Mus, 92; Nat Endowment Arts Regional Fel, 95, Educ & Access Grant, 98; NY Found for the Arts Grant, 2003; Pollock Krasner Found Grant, 2004; Mac Dowell Colony Fel, 2001, 2003, 2004. *Bibliog:* Nicolas de Oliveria, Nicola Oxley & Michael Petry (auths), Installation Art, Smithsonian Inst Press, 94; Making Sense: Five Installations on Sensation, The Katonah Mus, Katonah, NY, 96; A Permutational Unfolding: Eve Andree Laramee, Mass Inst Technol, 99; Linda Weintraub; In the Making, DAP Press, 2003; Jochen Gerz; Anthology of Art, Dumont Pub, 2003; Anna Hanigman; Questioning Authority; A Conversation with Eve Andree Laramee, Sculpture Mag July/Aug 2002; Jennifer MacGoregor Sugar Mud; Hudson River Projects, Wave Hill 2003; Steve Wilson, Information Art; Intersection of Art, Science, & Technol, MIT Press, 2001. *Mem:* Blast/The X Art Found, NY; Coll Arts Asn; Nat Speleological Soc. *Media:* All; Installation. *Res:* Environmental issues, place/space/site. *Specialty:* Art and Science. *Publ:* Auth, Notes on Sculpture, Albuquerque Mus, 83; The Eroded Terrain of Memory, Wesleyan Univ, 90; Inventing Wilderness: The National Parks, New Observations Mag, 91; Artists Project, J Contemp Art, 92; Wandering, Innerscapes; Anthology, of Artists Writing, Trieste, 98; A Permutational Unfolding: Art and the Culture of Science, Brazilian Nat Asn for Researchers in Visual Arts, 99; Only Questions- Interaction; Artistic Practice on the Network, Eyebeam/DAP Press, 2001; Netherzone; A Psychogeographical Force, Art Journal Mag, Fall 2004. *Mailing Add:* 126 Java St Brooklyn NY 11222

LARKIN, EUGENE
DESIGNER, EDUCATOR
b Minneapolis, Minn, June 27, 1921. *Study:* Univ Minn, BA & MA. *Work:* Mus Mod Art, New York; Nat Gallery Art & Libr Cong, Washington, DC; Art Inst Chicago; Addison Gallery Am Art, Andover, Mass; Nat Collection Fine Arts, Smithsonian Inst, Washington, DC; and others. *Comn:* Int Graphic Arts Soc; Gen Mills Corp; Bus Wk; Minneapolis Soc Fine Arts; US Info Agency. *Exhib:* US Info Agency Traveling Exhib to Iran, Italy, France, Spain & Ger; solo exhibs, Minneapolis Inst Art & Hamline Univ, 68; State Univ NY, Albany, 69; Univ Calif, Long Beach, 69; Univ Minn, 74, 78, 81, 87 & 91-92; Anderson & Anderson Gallery, 91-92 & 94. *Teaching:* Instr, Kans State Coll, Pittsburg, 48-54; head printmaking dept & chmn fine arts div, Minneapolis Sch Art, 54-69; prof, Design Dept, Univ Minn, Minneapolis, 69-91. *Awards:* Walker Art Ctr, 60 & Washington Watercolor & Print Exhib, 63; Rockford Biennial, 83; plus many others. *Mem:* Am Asn Univ Prof; Coll Art Asn Am. *Media:* Woodcuts, Lithographs, Oil. *Publ:* Auth, Design: The Search for Unity, William C Brown, 88. *Mailing Add:* 1016 W Washington St South Bend IN 46601

LARKIN, JOHN E, JR MD
COLLECTOR, PATRON
b St Paul, Minn, Nov 8, 1930. *Study:* Univ Minn, BS & MD; Harvard Univ. *Pos:* trustee, Minn Mus Am Art, Minn Inst Art; benefactor, Minn Inst Art, Minn Mus Art & Weisman Mus; accessions comt, Minneapolis Inst Art, 78-2009. *Awards:* Outstanding Achievement Award, Univ Minn, 2010. *Collection:* American art. *Mailing Add:* 7 Yellow Birch Rd Dellwood White Bear Lake MN 55110

LARMER, OSCAR VANCE
PAINTER, EDUCATOR
b Wichita, Kans, July 11, 1924. *Study:* Minneapolis Sch Fine Arts, cert painting; Univ Kans, BFA; Wichita State Univ, MFA. *Work:* Nelson Gallery of Art, Kansas City, Mo; Kans State Univ, Manhattan; Wichita State Univ, Kans; Wichita Art Asn Gallery; Kans Univ, Lawrence; Kans State Bank Collection, Manhattan, Kans; Emprise Bank, Wichita, Kans; Commerce Bank Collection, Manhattan, Kans; Emprise Bank Coll, Wichita, Kans; and others. *Comn:* Medallion, Wichita Center for Art, Centennial, Manhattan, 61; President's Medallion, Kans State Univ, 74; painting, Kans 4-H Found, Kans State Univ, 77; Gift Print Artist, Kans State Univ, Manhattan, Kans, 98. *Exhib:* Mid-Am Exhib, Nelson Gallery Art, Kansas City, Mo, 52-70; Watercolor USA, Springfield Art Mus, Mo, 57 & 68; Rocky Mountain Exhib, Denver Art Mus, Colo, 65; 45th Ann 17-State Exhib, Springfield, Mo, 75; Nat Watercolor Exhib, La Watercolor Soc, 76; Works of Art on Paper, Nat-Western Ann, Western Ill Univ, Galesburg, 76; Summer Invitational, Nelson Gallery of Art, Kansas City, Mo, 77, 79, 81, 84 & 86; Kansas Landscapes-Touring Invitational, 85-86; Burke Armstrong Gallery, Taos, NMex, 91-92; Kans Watercolor Soc Seven State Exhib, Wichita Art Mus, Kans, 98; Solo exhibs, Hutchinson Art Assoc, Shaeffer Art Mus, Barton Co Community Coll, Great Bend, Beach Art Mus, Kans State Univ, Manhattan & Columbian Gallery, Wamego, Kans, 98, Mural, First United Methodist Church, Manhattan, Kans; Kans Watercolor Nat Exhib, Wichita, Kans, 2012. *Pos:* Asst dir, Wichita Art Mus, Kans, 53-55. *Teaching:* Prof drawing & painting, Kans State Univ, Manhattan, 56-89, head art dept, 67-71, emer prof, 90-. *Awards:* Purchase Awards, Smoky Hills Art, Hadley Med Ctr, 77, Kans Watercolor Soc, United Bank & Trust, 77, Prairie Exhib, 83 & Showcase Manhattan, 90; Winner, Kansas Postcard Series No 13, 90. *Bibliog:* V W Bell (auth), The Kansas Art Reader, Univ Kans Press, 76. *Mem:* Nat Coll Art Asn; Mid-Am Coll Art Asn; Kans Watercolor Soc; Kans Fedn Art. *Media:* Watercolor, Oil. *Res:* Landscapes. *Specialty:* Fine arts. *Interests:* Light, color, composition & expression. *Collection:* many private collections. *Publ:* Coauth, A Foundation for Expressive Drawing, Burgess Publ, 83; auth, Kansas Masters, 2007. *Dealer:* Strecker-Nelson Gallery Manhattan, KS. *Mailing Add:* 2441 Hobbs Dr Manhattan KS 66502

LAROCCO, BEN
CRITIC, PAINTER
Exhib: Group exhibs include Wagmag Benefit Art Show, Front Room Gallery, Brooklyn, 2006; 183rd Ann: Invitational Exhib Contemp Am Art, Nat Acad Mus, New York, 2008. *Pos:* Mng art editor, critic, The Brooklyn Rail, currently. *Awards:* SJ Wallace Truman Fund Award, Nat Acad, 2008. *Dealer:* Galeria Janet Kurnatowski 205 Norman Ave Brooklyn NY 11222. *Mailing Add:* c/o The Brooklyn Rail 99 Commercial St #15 Brooklyn NY 11222

LARRAZ, JULIO F
PAINTER
b Havana, Cuba, Mar 12, 1944. *Work:* Westmoreland Co Mus Art, Greensburg, Pa; Archer M Huntington Art Gallery, Univ Tex, Austin; Pa State Univ, Philadelphia; Mus Arte Mod, Bogota, Colombia; Mus Monterrey, Mexico, 87. *Exhib:* Solo exhibs, Nohra Haime Gallery, NY, 83-86, 88-92, Foire Int d'Art Contemp, Grand Palais, Paris, 83, Museo de Monterrey, Mex, 87, Ron Hall Gallery, Miami, 91-93, Krannert Art Mus, Univ Ill, Urbana-Champaign, 92, Alonso Art, Artfi, Bogota, Colombia, 93, Alonso Art, Feria Iberoamericana de Arte, Caracas, Venezuela, 93, New Work, Marlborough Gallery, NY, 2006; Group exhibs, Work on Paper, Atrium Gallery, St Louis, 90; Prints, Collen Creco Gallery, Nyack, NY, 90. *Awards:* Cintas Found Fel, Inst Int Educ, 75; Am Acad Arts & Lett Award, 76. *Bibliog:* Barbara Duncan (auth), Lines of Vision, Washington, DC, 69; David Bourdon (auth), New York reviews Julio Larraz, Art Am, 3/87; Ruth Bass (auth), New York reviews Julio Larraz, Art News, 10/88; Edward Sullivan (auth), Julio Larraz, Hudson Hills Press, NY, 89. *Media:* Oil, Watercolor. *Publ:* Contrib, The Eye Witness to Space, Abrams, 70; illusr, The Perfect Wagnerite, Time-Life Bks, 72; The Whitehouse Enemies, New Am Libr, 73; contribr, Still the flypaper of politics, New York Times Mag, 74; New York Mag. *Dealer:* Nohra Haime Gallery 41 E 57th St New York NY 10022. *Mailing Add:* c/o Gary Nader Fine Art 62 NE 27th St Miami FL 33137

LARSEN, D DANE
CERAMIST, SCULPTOR
b Oct 21, 1950. *Study:* Harvard Univ, BA, study with William Reimann, Rudolf Arnheim & Buckminster Fuller; Univ Calif, Study with Ron Nagle; San Francisco State Univ, MA, study with Charles McKee, Hayward King, Dale Roush, Daniel Rhodes & Paul Soldner. *Work:* San Francisco State Univ Ceramics Collection; Carpenter Ctr for the Visual Arts, Harvard Univ, Cambridge, Mass; Oakland Mus, Calif; Prieto Gallery, Mills Col, Oakland. *Exhib:* Calif Ceramics & Glass, Oakland Mus; The Calif Craftsman, Monterey Peninsula Mus Art, Monterey, Calif; Marietta Coll Crafts Nat, Grover M Hermann Fine Arts Ctr, Marietta, Ohio; Designer-Craftsman Nat, Richmond Art Ctr, Calif; Calif Crafts X, E B Crocker Gallery & Mus, Sacramento; Nat Cone Box Show, Kans Univ Union Gallery, Lawrence. *Pos:* Consult & dir of ceramics prog, San Rafael City Recreation Dept, 77-. *Teaching:* Instr ceramics, Col of Marin, Kentfield, Calif, 76- & Columbia Jr Col, Calif, summer 77; Art Acad, San Francisco, Calif, 80-84. *Awards:* Cash Awards, Calif Craftsman, 76, San Jose Mus Art, 76 & 76 & Civic Arts Gallery, 77. *Mem:* San Francisco Potters Asn; Am Crafts Coun; Coll Art Asn. *Media:* Clay, Wood. *Dealer:* Meyer, Fort Mason Ctr San Francisco CA 94123

LARSEN, PATRICK HEFFNER
PAINTER, SCULPTOR
b Port Arthur, Tex, July 11, 1945. *Study:* Lamar Univ, BBA, 68; Sam Houston State Univ, teacher cert, 69; Stephen F Austin State Univ, MA, 70, MFA, 73. *Work:* Stephen F Austin State Univ, Nacogdoches, Tex; First Nat Bank of Ark, Little Rock; Univ Cent Ark, Conway. *Exhib:* Okla Art Ctr, Oklahoma City, 70 & 72; 16th & 17th Ann Delta Exhib, Ark Art Ctr, Little Rock, 73 & 74; Solo exhibs, Ft Smith Art Ctr, Ark, 75 & SArk Art Ctr, El Dorado, 76; 54th Ann Exhib, Meadows Mus of Art, Shreveport, La, 76; Rocky Mountain Ann Watercolor Exhib, Foothills Art Ctr, Golden, Colo, 77; Ariz Nat Painting Exhib, Scottsdale Art Ctr, Ariz, 77. *Teaching:* Asst prof painting, drawing, sculpture, watercolor & design, Univ Cent Ark, Conway, 70-80, assoc prof, 80-. *Awards:* First Place & Purchase Award, Fifth Ann Ark Artist Exhib, Southeastern Ark Art Ctr, 72; First Place in 19th Invitational Exhib of Ann Ark State Festival, 76; Top Award, 18th Ann Ark Oil Painting Exhib, 77. *Mem:* Nat Art Educ Asn; Ark Art Educ Asn. *Media:* Acrylic, Watercolor; Wood. *Mailing Add:* 6 Salem Rd Conway AR 72032-3388

LARSEN, SUSAN C
CURATOR, HISTORIAN
b Chicago, Ill, Oct 3, 1946. *Study:* Knox Col, Galesburg, Ill, 64-66; Northwestern Univ, BA, 68, MA, 72, PhD, 75; Graves Found Fel, 80. *Collection Arranged:* Abstract Painting and Sculpture in Am 1927-44 (auth, catalog), Mus Art, Carnegie Inst, Pittsburgh, Pa, 83; Edward Hopper, Whitney Mus, 89; Art in Place: 15 Years of Collecting, Whitney Mus, 89. *Pos:* guest lectr, series of lectures on Richard Diebenkorn, Los Angeles Co Mus Art, Los Angeles, 77; mem adv bd, Archives Am Art; chief cur, Farnsworth Art Mus, currently. *Teaching:* Asst prof hist of art, Carleton Col, Northfield, Minn, 74-75; from assoc prof to prof hist of art, Univ Southern Calif, Los Angeles, 75-; cur permanent collection, Whitney Mus Am Art, New York, 88-90; adjunct cur permanent collection, Whitney Mus Am Art, 90-91. *Mem:* Coll Art Asn Am; Am Studies Asn; Southern Calif Art Historians Asn. *Res:* Abstract art of the 1930's; WPA in New York City; contemporary art in California; American folk art. *Publ:* Coauth, A Conversation with Richard Diebenkorn, J Los Angeles Inst Contemp Art, summer 77; auth, exhib catalogue, Vija Celmins, Newport Art Mus, 12/79; Richard Tuttle, Baxter Art Gallery, 79; CY Twombly, Newport Art Mus, 10/81; Selections from 8 Collections (catalog), Mus Contemp Art, Los Angeles, 83; coauth, Art in Place, Whitney Mus Am Art, 89; regular contribr, Art News Mag, Artweek & Artforum. *Mailing Add:* c/o Farnsworth Art Mus 352 Main St Box 466 Rockland ME 04841-0466

LARSON, JUDY L
DIRECTOR
b Glendale, Calif, Mar 9, 1952. *Study:* Univ Calif, Los Angeles, BA, 74, MA, 78; Inst Lib Arts, Emory Univ, Atlanta, PhD, 98. *Collection Arranged:* Am Engravings before 1820 (with catalog), Am Antiquarian Soc, 79-84; Enchanted Images (auth, catalog), Santa Barbara Mus, 80; Am Illustration (auth, catalog), Glenbow Mus, 85-86; Georgia Printmakers, (auth, catalog), High Mus, Atlanta, Ga, 86. *Pos:* actg asst cur Los Angeles Co Mus Art, 78; Sr cataloger, Am Antiquarian Soc, Worcester, Mass, 78-85; cur Am Art, High Mus, Atlanta, Ga, 85-98; exec dir, Art Mus W Va, Roanoke, 98-02; dir, Nat Mus Women in Arts, Washington, 02-. *Teaching:* Lectr hist prints, Assumption Col, fall 84 & Emory Univ, spring 86-88. *Res:* 18th and 19th century American Painting, federal period printmaking & illustration 1880-1925. *Publ:* auth American Illustration 1890-1925, 86; Contribr, William M Harnett Metrop Mus Art, New York, 265-275, 92; ed, Graphic Arts & the South: Proceedings of the 1990 North American Print Conference, Univ Ark Press, 93; coauth, American Paintings at the High Museum of Art (exhib catalog), Hudson Press, 94

LARSON, KAY L
CRITIC, WRITER
b Cedar Rapids, Iowa, 1946. *Study:* Pomona Coll, Claremont, Calif, with Mowry Baden, BA (philos, art practice), 69. *Pos:* Art critic & writer, Real Paper, Cambridge, Mass, 72-75 & Village Voice, 79-80; assoc ed, ARTnews, 75-78; art critic, NY Mag, 80-94; freelance writer, NY Times, 94-; managing ed, Cur: The M Jour, 2003-. *Teaching:* Instr & adj prof, NY Univ, 90-98; Writing Tutor, Ctr Curatorial Studies, Bard Coll, Annandale-on-Hudson, NY, 2003-10. *Awards:* Nat Endowment Arts Critic Grants, 78 & 80; Japan Found Study Grant, 86. *Mem:* Int Art Critics Asn. *Publ:* Where the Heart Beats: John Cage, Zen Buddhism, and the Inner Life of Artists, Penquin Press, 2012

LARSON, PHILIP
PAINTER, SCULPTOR, PRINTMAKER
b Ventura, Calif, July 21, 1944. *Study:* Univ Minn, Minneapolis, BA, 66; Columbia Univ, PhD, 71. *Work:* Walker Art Center, Minneapolis; Inst Art, Guggenheim Mus; NY General Mill Hq, Minneapolis; Hq Chicago; 3M HQ. *Comn:* glass murals for shelters, Nicollet Mall, Minneapolis; outdoor service terrace, Mt Zion Temple, St Paul, 91; inlaid terrazo floor, River Centre, St. Paul, 99; Hiawatha Light Rail Line, Minneapolis, 2005, 2008. *Exhib:* Emergent Americans, Guggenheim Mus, NY, 81; Mus Art, RI Sch Design, 83; Thomson Gallery, Minneapolis, 83,94; Walker Art Center, 1994, 2000; Bockley Gallery, Minneapolis, 2008. *Collection Arranged:* DeKooning: Drawings & Sculptures (auth, catalog), 74; Naives/Visionaries (auth, catalog), 74; World Architecture in Minnesota (auth, catalog), 78; Prairie School Architecture in Minnesota, Iowa and Wisconsin (auth, catalog), 82. *Pos:* Cur, Walker Art Ctr, Minneapolis, 70-75; mem, Walker Art Ctr, Minneapolis; fellow grad sch arts & sciences, Columbia Univ. *Teaching:* Prof art & archit hist, Minneapolis Col Art & Design, 75-2012. *Awards:* European and American Nat Endowment for the Arts Fellowship, 79, 81. *Media:* Cast Iron, glass, screenprinting, welded bronze, aluminum, painting on paper. *Res:* Art & archit ancient to renaissance mediterranean, prints & drawings, 1880-present. *Publ:* 60 Scholarly articles on prints & drawings. *Dealer:* Bockley Gallery, Minneapolis. *Mailing Add:* 111-Marquette Ave S Apt 2002 Minneapolis MN 55401

LARSON, SIDNEY
EDUCATOR, MURALIST
b Sterling, Colo, June 16, 1923. *Study:* Univ Mo, AB & MA; Univ Okla; also with Thomas Hart Benton. *Work:* State Hist Soc, Mo; Munic Bldg, Jefferson City, Mo; Columbia Col; Columbia Pub Libr. *Comn:* Social History of Insurance, Shelter Ins Co, Columbia, Mo, 1959; Social History of Ceramics & Metal, Riback Industs, Columbia, 1967; mural, Munic Bldg, Jefferson City, Mo, 1985; mural, Guitar Bldg, Columbia, Mo; mural, Boone Co Courthouse, Columbia, Mo. *Pos:* Mus cur, State Hist Soc, Mo, 1961-. *Teaching:* Instr, Oklahoma City Univ, 1950-51; Univ Mo-Columbia, summers; prof art, Columbia Col, 1951-. *Awards:* Huntington Hartford Found, 1962; Distinguished Serv Award, State Hist Soc, Mo, 1989; Mo State Arts Coun Award, 1991. *Mem:* Nat Soc Mural Painters; Am Inst Conserv Hist Artistic Works. *Res:* Private, federal, state and municipal painting restorations. *Publ:* Auth, Introduction to Fred Shane Drawings, 1964; articles on Thomas Hart Benton, 1969, 1974 & 1975 & auth, Conservation of a Bingham, 1972, Mo Hist Rev; Chap in: Thomas Hart Benton Artist-Writer-Intellectual, 1989. *Mailing Add:* 1001 Rogers St Columbia MO 65216

LARSON, WILLIAM G
PHOTOGRAPHER, EDUCATOR
b North Tonawanda, NY, Oct 14, 1942. *Study:* State Univ NY, Buffalo, BS (art), 64; Inst Design, Ill Inst Technol, Chicago, MS (photog), with Aaron Siskind & Wynn Bullock, 67. *Work:* Mus Mod Art, New York; Philadelphia Mus Art; Los Angeles Co Mus Art; Baltimore Mus Art; Nat Gallery Can; J Paul Getty Mus; Inst Mus Photogr, George Eastman House; San Francisco Mus Art; Metrop Mus Art, New York; Hallmark Corp Art Collection. *Exhib:* Extending the Boundaries of Photog, Ctr Creative Photog, Tucson, 89; Artists Choose Artists, Inst Contemp Art, Philadelphia, 92; solo exhibs, Md Art Place, 94, RI Sch Design, 95, Krannert Art Mus, 96, Cepa Gallery, Buffalo, 99, Visual Studies Workshop, Rochester, 2000, Arcadia Univ, 2002, Renaissance Soc, 2002 & Art Inst Chicago, 2003; Flora, Los Angeles Co Mus Art, 98; The Color Tradition, J Paul Getty Mus, Los Angeles; Works from the Collection by Philadelphia Artists, Philadelphia Mus, 2000; group exhib, Univ Chicago, 2003, San Francisco Mus Art, 2004 & Howard Greenberg Gallery, New York, 2004; Hidden From Plain View, Metrop Mus Art, 4/18-9/4, 2007. *Teaching:* Prof & dept chmn photog, Tyler Sch Art, Temple Univ, Philadelphia, 67-; prof & dir grad studies photog & digital image, Md Inst Coll Art, prof emer, currently. *Awards:* Nat Endowment Arts, 71, 79, 86 & 92; Pa Coun Arts Fel, 83 & 88; Aaron Siskind Found Fel, 93; Guggenheim Fel, 82; Pew Fel, 2002. *Bibliog:* S Perloff (ed), Lexigraphic portraits by William Larson, The Photo Rev, 88; Bill Gaskins (auth), William Larson's Theatre du Monde, New Art Examiner, 10/94; Taken by Design, NY Times Bk Rev, 12/2002; Robert Hirsch (auth), Flexible Images, Exposure Vol 36: 1/2003; Eileen Neff (auth), rev, Artforum, 9/2003. *Media:* Photography and Video. *Interests:* Fly fishing. *Publ:* Photographing in the Studio, Hallmark Inc, 94; Photomontage, Rockport Publ; A Century of Photography, 2002; Taken by Design, 2003; Seizing the Light, A History of Photography, 2003. *Dealer:* Fern Shadd Photography 135 E 74th St New York NY; Charles Isaacs 19th & 20th Century Photography Malvern Pa

LARUE, JOAN MARRON
PAINTER
b Custer Co, Okla, Aug 19, 1934. *Study:* Univ Okla, BA (fashion art), 56; workshop study with Sergei Bongart, William Reese, Ben Konis, Don Puttman, Jon Zahourek & Bettina Steinke, Hollis Williford, Richard Schmid, Harley Brown & Michael Lynch, 80-88. *Work:* Robert S Kerr Conf Ctr, Poteau, Okla; Mercy Health Ctr, Baptist Health Ctr, Presby Health Ctr & Okla State Senate Press Ctr, Oklahoma City; Frye Mus, Seattle, Wash; Okla State Art Collection. *Comn:* Mural size paintings, Senate Rooms, Okla State Senate, Oklahoma City, 83; mural, McCauley Plaza, comn by Sisters of Mercy, Oklahoma City, 86; Mural size paintings, Mercy Birthplace Ctr, 88. *Exhib:* Solo exhibs, Ft Smith Art Ctr, Ark, 70 & Okla Mus Art, Oklahoma City, 75; Midland Stewart Haley Memorial Show, 88, 89, 91 & 92; Plein Air Painters Am, 88, 89, 90 & 92; Philbrook Mus, Tulsa, Okla, 90 & 92; Okla Soc Impressionalists Traveling Show, 90; Gilcrease Mus Show, Petroglyphs in Okla, 93; and others. *Teaching:* Prof fashion arts, Univ Okla, 60-65; instr fine art, Okla Mus Art, Oklahoma City, 65-75; instr workshops, NMex, Okla, Tex & Hawaii, 75-80. *Awards:* First Place, Scottsdale Art Sch; Best of Show, Wrass, Cheyenne, Wyo. *Bibliog:* M J Van Deventer (auth), Painter and palette, Okla Home & Garden, 83; Lorene Marvin (producer), Oklahoma Original, Educ Television, OETA, 84; M J Van Deventer (auth), Joan Marron, excited student of life, Art Gallery Mag, 85; Susan Mcgarry (auth), Southwest Art Mag, 8/89; Walter Gray, Painting on Location (film), TV-KAUT, 89. *Mem:* Fashion Group Int (secy, 60); Oklahoma City Art Guild; Soc Am Impressionists; Plein Air Painters Am; Okla Soc of Impressionists. *Media:* Oil. *Dealer:* Dodson Gallery 7660 N Western Oklahoma City OK

LARZELERE, JUDITH ANN
TAPESTRY ARTIST
b Ann Arbor, Mich, Mar 17, 1944. *Study:* Radcliff Col, 62-64; Univ Mich, BA, 67; Rutgers Univ, MFA, 74. *Work:* Mus Am Quilters, Paducah, KY; Am Craft Mus, NY; Radcliffe Col/Harvard Univ, Cambridge, Mass; Bristol Myers/Squibb, US Corp Office, Princeton, NJ; Fed Reserve Bank, Philadelphia, PA; First Nat Bank Boston, Boston, Mass; SAS, INC Cary, NC. *Comn:* P&B Textiles, Burlingame, Calif 1993; Bristol Myers/Squibb, US Corp Office, Princeton, NJ, 1993; Free Spirit Textiles, NYC, 2001; SAS, Inc, Cary, NC, 2001; NOVUS, Inc, Atlanta, Ga, 2002. *Exhib:* Quilt Nat, Athens, Ohio, 1981, 1983, 1985, 1987, 1989, 1999; Quilt Arts, A Contemp View, Mus Max Berg, Heidelberg, Ger, 1994; Intersections (3 person show), San Jose Mus Quilts, San Jose, Calif, 2000; Explorations (group exhib), Wesserling Textile Mus, Mulhouse, France, 2003; 30 Distinguished Quilt Makers of the World, Tokyo, Japan, 2003; Art Quilts, Newport Art Mus, Newport, RI; Material Matters Quilt Making in the 21st Century, Columbus Mus Art, Columbus, Ohio, 2008. *Pos:* Studio artist, 78-. *Teaching:* Penland Sch, NC, 90; Arrowmont Sch, Gatlinburg, Tenn, 90; Haystack Sch, Deer Isle, Maine, 98 & 2003; Banff Center, Calgary, Alberta, 91. *Awards:* Mass Cultural Coum, Individual Proj Grant, 1993; Best of Show, NY Quilt Festival, 1995; Taconic/Berkshire Trust, 1999, 2004; Mass Cultural Coun Grant, 1999; Niche Award, Niche Magazine, 2006. *Bibliog:* Visions Catalog, C&T Publ, 90, 94 & 98; New Wave Quilt Collections I & II by Setsuko Segawa, 91 & 93; Quilt Art A Contemporary View, Textilmuseum Max Berg Catalog, 94; 80 Leaders of the Quilt World, Nihon-Vogue, 94; Contemporary Quilts from the James Collection, AQS, 95; Quilts: A Living Tradition, Hugh Lauter Levin, 95; The Art Quilt, Hugh, Lauter, Levin, 97; The 30 Distinguished Quilt Artists of the World, Tokyo, Japan, 2003; Am Quiltmaking 1970-2003, Eleanor Levie (auth), 2004; Art Quilt Elements, Wayne Art Ctr, Wayne, Pa. *Mem:* Quilt Visions; Studio Art Quilt Asn. *Media:* Contemporary Quilts, Strong Color. *Interests:* gardening, canoeing, bird-watching. *Publ:* Auth, Beyond log cabin, Threads, Tauton Press, 2/86; contribr, Fiber Expressions: The Contemporary Quilt, Schiffer Publ, 87; America's Glorious Quilts, Hugh Lauter Levin, 87, Dennis Duke & Deborah Harding, 87; Fiberarts Design Book III, Lark Press, 88; auth, Quilting strip by strip, Threads, Tauton Press, 8/88; Threads Magazine, 1/86, 8/88, 8/90; Quilt Nat Catalog, 81, 83, 85, 87, 89, 98; Fiberarts Design Book III, Lark Press, 87, Book IV, 91; 88 Leaders in Quilt World Today, Japan, 94; Art in Embassies Prog, Bangkok, 2003; The Creative Force, SAQA, 2006

LASANSKY, LEONARDO
DRAFTSMAN, PRINTMAKER
b Iowa City, Iowa, Mar 29, 1946. *Study:* Univ Iowa, BGS, 71, MA, 72 & MFA, 72; also with Byron Burford & 15 Stuart Edie. *Work:* Brooklyn Mus, NY; Princeton Univ Mus; Philadelphia Mus Art; Achenback Collection, San Francisco; Nat Mus, Krakow, Poland; Libr of Cong, Washington, DC; Mus of Art, Grenchen, Switz; Minneapolis Inst Art; Nat Gallery of Art, Washington, DC; Hood Mus, Dartmouth Coll. *Comn:* Portrait, Christopher Columbus, James Ford Bell Libr. *Exhib:* Int Print Biennale, Krakow, Poland, 80; solo exhib, Dartmouth Coll, Hood Mus, 82; Premio Int, eiella, Italy, 87; Bienal de San Juan, Grabado Lationamericano, Puerto Rico, 88-98; Am Embassy, Belgrade, Yugoslavia, 89-90; Prefectural Mus Art, Fukuoka, Japan, 90; Nat Acad & Mus, New York, 95, 98 & 2009; Mus Art, Ball State Univ, 96. *Collection Arranged:* Espana: The Legacy of War: Works by Francisco Goya, 97; Africa: A Legacy in Memory, Material Differences, Mus for African Art, NY, 2004; Icons of Perfection: Figurative Sculpture from Africa, 2005-2006. *Pos:* Adv panel, Minn State Arts, 88-90; dir of exhib, Hamline Univ, 97. *Teaching:* Prof art, Hamline Univ, 72-2012, prof emeritus, 2012-, chmn fine arts div, 80-85, acting chmn art dept, 90-91; artist-in-residence, Dartmouth Coll, 82; chair studio arts & art hist dept, 95-2010; chair fine arts div, 98-; artist-in-residence, lifetime appointment, Hamline Univ, 2004-. *Awards:* Purchase Award, 5th Nat Hawaii Print Exhib, Honolulu, 80; Purchase Award, 4th Miami Int Print Exhib, Fla, 80; Distinguished Alumni Award, Univ Iowa, 81; Drawing Award, Berkshire Mus, Pittsfield, Mass, 82; Regis Found Grant, 2007-; Drawing Award, Nat Acad, 2009; and others. *Bibliog:* John Wilford Knopf (auth), The Mysterious History of Columbus, 91; NY Times, ed page, 1/2/91 & mag, Sect 6, 8/11/91; Columbus & The Age of Discovery, Morrow, 91. *Mem:* Nat Acad (mem comt). *Media:* Intaglio. *Publ:* Auth (introduction), Icons of Perfection: Figurative Sculpture from Africa, Hamline Univ Press, 2006. *Mailing Add:* Hamline Univ MS-0161 1536 Hewitt Ave Saint Paul MN 55104

LASCH, PAT
SCULPTOR
b New York, NY, Nov 20, 1944. *Study:* Queen Col, NY, BA, 70; Ga State, MFA, 90. *Work:* Queens Col, City Univ NY; Mus Mod Art, Metrop Mus Art, NY; Oberlin Mus, Ohio; Prudential Insurance Co, NJ; Rutgers Univ, New Brunswick, NJ. *Comn:* Hommage: 1929-1979 (sculpture), Mus Mod Art, NY, 79, Kiresky Art Mus, Lansing, Mich, 2000; Womens Mus, Washington; Nat Acad Design, NY. *Exhib:* Solo exhibs, AIR Gallery, NY, 73, 77, 79 & 80, Kathryn Markel Gallery, NY, 81, 84 & 85, Lerner Heller Gallery, NY, 81, Albright-Knox Gallery, Members' Gallery, Buffalo, NY, 84, McIntosh Drepdale Gallery, Washington, 85, Marilyn Pearl Gallery, NY, 88 & 90 & Paridiso, Il Ponte Gallery, Rome, Italy, NH Acad Design, New York City, 01; Contemp Women: Consciousness & Content, Brooklyn Mus Art Sch, NY 77; Out of the House, Whitney Mus Am Art Downtown, NY, 78; The Cooked & the Raw, Thomas Segal Gallery, Boston, Mass; Controlling Woman, Sculpture Ctr, NY, 93; Bad Girl Show, New Mus, NY, 94; 20 yr retrospective, AIR Gallery, NY, 94; Controlling Woman: aka True Love, Hampshire Gallery, Mass, 94; and other solo exhibs. *Pos:* Guest panelist, Soho Ctr Visual Arts, NY, 77; lectr, Art Inst Chicago, currently. *Teaching:* Parson's Sch Design, 78-88, RI Sch Design, 89-90 & Univ Mass, Amherst, 91-. *Awards:* Special Proj, NY St Coun Arts, 84-85; Pollock-Krasner, 87; New Eng Found Arts, 95; and others. *Bibliog:* Ellen Lubell (auth), When a good gallery folds, Village Voice, 4/11/85; Vivien Raynor (auth) article, NY Times, 10/4/85; Jeff Weinstein (auth), It's heaven when you, Village Voice, 10/22/85. *Mem:* Soc Fels AAR; Nat Acad. *Media:* Mixed. *Publ:* Auth, AIR, Artforum, 11/80, 70; If You Make A Mistake Put A Rose On It, 85. *Dealer:* Judy Goldman Fine Arts 11 Newbury St Boston MA; Marilyn Pearl Gallery New York NY 10012

LASCH, PEDRO
PAINTER, INSTALLATION SCULPTOR
b Mexico City, 1975. *Study:* Sch Visual Arts, New York, Fine Arts Found Prog, 1995; Cooper Union Advan Science & Art, BFA, 1999. *Exhib:* Solo exhibs include Polvo Gallery, Chicago, 2005, Queens Mus Art, New York, 2006; Group exhibs include Collaborative/MODE, Bronx Mus, New York, 2001; How Latitudes Become Form, Walker Art Ctr, Minneapolis, 2003; The Net of Two Tongues, Queens Mus Art, New York, 2004, Propia Vision/Our Vision, 2006; Social Capital, Whitney Mus Am Art, New York, 2004; Patriot, Contemp Mus, Baltimore, MD, 2005; CounterCampus, Baltimore Mus Art, 2005; When Artists Say We, Artists Space, New York, 2006; Civic Performance, Staller Art Gallery, Stony Brook, NY, 2006; The Nightly News, Luxe Gallery, New York, 2007; Primitivism Revisited, Sean Kelly Gallery, New York, 2007. *Teaching:* Asst Prof Practice, Drawing, Painting & Multimedia, Dept Art, Art History, & Visual Studies, Duke University. *Awards:* Howard Steinberg Award Painting, Cooper Union Advan Science & Art, New York, 1998; Ruth Gutman Epstein Award in Sculpture, New York Artists Equity Asn, New York, 1999; Leader of the Present Award, New York, 2006; Joan Mitchell Found Grant, 2007

LASKE, LYLE F
SCULPTOR, EDUCATOR
b Green Bay, Wis, May 10, 1937. *Study:* Univ Wis, Platteville, BS, 59; Univ Wis, Madison, MS, 61 & MFA, 65; Univ Minn, 68. *Work:* Plains Art Mus, Moorhead, Minn. *Exhib:* Solo exhib, Walker Art Ctr, Minneapolis, Minn, 66; Artists of Central NY, Everson Mus Art, Syracuse, 71; Draw and Small Sculpture Show, Ball State Univ, Ind, 74; Miss River Crafts Show, Memphis, Tenn, 77; Am Woodcarvers, Craft Ctr, Worchester, Mass, 78; New Handmade Furniture, Am Craft Mus, NY, 79; Beyond Folk, Minneapolis Inst Art, Minn, 84. *Teaching:* Instr, Wis State Univ, Platteville, 62-64; prof sculpture, Moorhead State Univ, Minn, 65-97, retired, 97; assoc prof, New York State Univ Col Oneonta, 70-71. *Media:* Wood. *Publ:* American woodcarvers, Craft Horizons, 4/78; Air-powered tools, Fine Woodworking, 1-2/79; Some abrasive facts, Fine Woodworking, 3-4/80; Woodworking: The New Wave, Crown Publ, 81; Fine Woodworking Techniques 3, The Taunton Press, 81. *Mailing Add:* 28433 Junco Dr Nevis MN 56467

LASKER, JOE (JOSEPH) L
PAINTER, ILLUSTRATOR
b Brooklyn, NY, June 26, 1918. *Study:* Cooper Union Art Sch, cert, 39; Escuela Universitaria de Bellas Artes, Mex, 48. *Work:* Whitney Mus Am Art, NY; Philadelphia Mus Art; Springfield Mus, Mass; Joseph H Hirshhorn Collection, Washington, DC; and others. *Comn:* Murals, US Pub Works Admin, Post Off, Calumet, Mich, 41, Milbury, Mass, 42 & Henry St Settlement Playhouse, NY, 48. *Exhib:* Pa Acad Fine Arts Ann, 47-53; Whitney Mus Am Art Ann, 47-58; Nat Acad Design Ann, NY, 47-82; Kraushaar Galleries, NY, 51-; and others. *Teaching:* Instr, College City, NY, 47; Assoc prof painting, Univ Ill, 53-54. *Awards:* Abbey Mem scholar, 46-47; Prix de Rome fel, 50-51; Guggenheim Fel, 54; Nat Inst Arts & Lett Grant, 68; Nat Acad Design, 80. *Bibliog:* 19 Young Americans, Life, 3/20/50; Goodrich & Bauer (auth), American art of our century, Praeger, NY, 61; Figurative Tradition, Whitney Mus Am Art, NY, 61; Mothers Can Do Anything, 1972(auth), He's My Brother, 1974(auth), Tales of a Seadog Family, (auth)1974, Merry Ever After (best illustrated children's book, NY Times, 1976, Notable Bk of Year Am Libr Asn 1977), (auth)1976, The Strange Voyage of Neptune's Car, (auth)1977, Lentil Soup, (auth)1977, Nick Joins In, (auth)1980, The Do-Something Day, (auth)1982, The Great Alexander the Great, (auth)1983, Tournament of Knights, (auth)1986. *Mem:* Nat Acad. *Media:* Oil, Watercolor. *Mailing Add:* c/o Kraushaar Gallery 74 E 79th Ste 9B New York NY 10021-0269

LASKER, JONATHAN
PAINTER
b Jersey City, NJ, 1948. *Study:* Sch Visual Arts, NY, 75-77; Calif Inst Arts, Valencia, Calif, 77. *Work:* Mus Ludwig, Cologne; The Corcoran Gallery of Art, Washington; The Hirshhorn Mus & Sculpture Garden, Smithsonian Inst, Washington; Wacoal Art Ctr, Tokyo; and others. *Exhib:* Fortieth Biennial Exhib of Painting, Corcoran Gallery Art, Washington, 87; Post-Abstract Abstraction, Aldrich Mus Contemp Art, 87; The Kaldewey Press, Thomas J Watson Libr, Metrop Mus Art, NY, 88; New Acquisitions,

Hirshhorn Mus & Sculpture Garden, Washington, 91; one-person exhibs, Ctr Contemp Art (with catalog), Rotterdam, 93, Galleri Lars Bohman, Stockholm, 94, Bravin Post Lee (with catalog), NY, 94, Galeria Soledad Lorenzo, Madrid, Spain, 95, LA Louver, Venice, Calif, 95, Galleria Milleventi, Turin, Italy, 97 & Galerie Thaddaeus Ropac, Paris, 2000; Am Painting Now (with catalog), Eva Menzio, Turin, Italy, 94; ARS 95 Helsinki, Mus Contemp Art, Helsinki, Finland, 95; Reconditioned Abstraction, Forum for Contemp Art, St Louis, 96; Pop/Abstraction, Mus Am Art, Pa Acad Fine Arts, 98; Mixed Bag: Summer Group Show, Schmidt Contemp Art, St Louis, 99; Arte Americana: Ultimo Decennio, Mus d'Arte della Citta di Ravenna, 2000; Kevin Bruk Gallery, Miami, Fla, 2001; Thomas Schulte, Berlin, 2002; Nat Acad Mus, NY, 2006. *Awards:* Nat Endowment Arts Fel, 87 & 89; New York Found Arts Fel, 89; Art award, Am Acad Arts and Letts, 2011. *Bibliog:* Gerhard Mack (auth), Jonathan Lasker im Kunstmuseum, Kunst-Bull, 6/98; Katy Siegal (auth), Jonathan Lasker: Selective Identity, ArtForum, 9/99; Kenneth Baker (auth), Odd Abstractions, San Francisco Chronicle, 10/28/2000. *Publ:* auth, Not a First, Kaldewey Press, 89; auth, Plastic Made Perfect: Measuring Mondrian: The New Math, Artforum, 9/95; auth, Jonathan Lasker: Complete Essays 1984-98, Edgewise Press, 98. *Mailing Add:* c/o Sperone Westwater 257 Bowery New York NY 10002

LASKIN, MYRON, JR
CURATOR, HISTORIAN

b Milwaukee, Wis, Apr 7, 1930. *Study:* Harvard Univ, AB, 52, AM, 54; Inst Fine Arts, NY Univ, PhD, 64. *Collection Arranged:* Fountainebleau, Nat Gallery Can, 73; J Paul Getty Mus. *Pos:* Cur Europ art, Nat Gallery Can, 1968-1984; cur paintings, J Paul Getty Mus, Malibu, Calif, 84-89. *Teaching:* Asst prof art hist, Washington Univ, 61-66. *Awards:* Italian Govt Grant, NY Univ, 59-60; Villa I Tatti Fel, 65-67, Kress Fel, 66-67, Harvard Univ. *Res:* Italian 16th and 17th century painting. *Publ:* Contribr, Burlington Mag, Art Bulletin, Arte Illustrata & others. *Mailing Add:* 17601 Tramonto Dr Pacific Palisades CA 90272

LASSITER, VERNICE B
PAINTER

b Nov 6, 1927. *Study:* Art Student League, with Joseph Hirsh, New York; Mobile Mus, pvt teachers; Workshops with famous teachers for many years; Studied with Henry Gasser, Max Carter, August Trovoahe, Robert Brackman, Valdi maris. *Work:* Am Nat Bank, Mobile, Ala; 3 mural size, Regions Bank, Mobile, Ala; Mitchel Collection, Mobile, Ala; Chatom Spring Hill Baptist Church, Chatom, Ala. *Comn:* Plexiglass, comn by pres of coll, Univ Ala, Mobile, Ala, 74; plexiglass, Springdale Travel Agency, Mobile, Ala, 76; regions bank, Hist Scenes, Mobile, Ala, 83; on linen, Springbank Baptist Church, comn by Wilcox Art Gallery, Chatom, Ala, 84; on linen, Hist Resort, First Commerce Bank, Chatom, Ala; mural sized oil painting on linen, Millry Ala Church, 2014. *Exhib:* Solo and group exhibs, Mobile Art Gallery, Mobile Pub Libr, Mobile Skyline Country Club, Mobile Womans Club, Battle House, Mobile, Ala, Montgomery Mus, Montgomery, Ala, Birmingham Mus, Ala, Sarasota Art Asn, Fla, Southeastern Ann, Atlanta, Chantel Gallery, Georgetown, DC, Edgewater Plaza Ann, Gallery 21, Birmingham, Ala, W Point Cown Art Gallery, and more; and 27 solo shows over Ala, Miss, and other states. *Teaching:* owner & instr, Vernice Lassiter Art Gallery, Springhill, Ala, 82-85; Mobile Art Mus. *Awards:* 1st, Best of Show, Gold Cup, Mobile Art Asn, Azelea Trail exhib, 60, 61; 1st & Best of Show, Deep South Folk Festival, 61; 1st & 2nd, Mobile Amarylis Show, Silver trophy, 65; Best of Show, Gold Medal in watercolor, 65; 1st in oil, Mobile Art Asn, 74. *Bibliog:* Mobile Press Register, articles for 20 years; US Sports Acad; Mobile Art Asn. *Mem:* Am Watercolor Soc; Mobile Art Asn. *Media:* Watercolor. *Interests:* Music, Writing

LASSRY, ELAD
PHOTOGRAPHER

b Tel-Aviv, Israel, 1977. *Study:* Calif Inst of Arts, BFA, 2003; Univ Southern Calif, Los Angeles, MFA, 2007. *Exhib:* Solo exhibs, Art Inst of Chicago, 2008, David Kordansky Gallery, Los Angeles, 2009, Massimo De Carlo, Milan, 2010, Sum of Limited Views, Contemporary Art Mus, St Louis, 2010, Luhring Augustine, NY, 2010, Galerie Francesca Pia, Zurich, 2011, White Cube, Hoxton Square, London, 2011, Tramway, Glasgow, Scotland, 2011; group exhibs, Contemporary Arts Mus, Houston, 2010, Ctr for Curatorial Studies, Bard Col, NY, 2010, Galleria Civica D'Arte Moderna e Contemporanea, Turin, Italy, 2010, Beverly Hills Municipal Gallery, 2010, Contemporary Art Gallery, Vancouver, 2010, Garage Ctr for Contemporary Culture, Moscow, 2010, Musee d'Art Contemporain de Bordeaux, 2010, 54th Int Art Exhib Biennale, Venice, 2011. *Mailing Add:* David Kordansky Gallery 3143 S La Cienega Blvd, Unit A Los Angeles CA 90016

LASTER, PAUL
CONCEPTUAL ARTIST

b Flint, Mich, Oct 14, 1951. *Study:* Univ Houston, Tex, 71-72; Fashion Inst Technol, New York, 76-80; New Sch for Social Res, New York, 81-84, with Lisette Model and Ian Wilson; Cooper Union, 84-85. *Work:* Art Inst Chicago; Whitney Mus Am Art, NY; Nat Mus Am Art, Smithsonian Inst, Washington; Los Angeles Co Mus Art, Calif; Brooklyn Mus Art, NY. *Exhib:* Solo exhibs, 91, The Greenberg Gallery, St Louis, 92, Hamiltons Gallery, London, 92, Galerie Baudoin Lebon, Paris, 92, Richard Levy Gallery, Albuquerque, 93, Mark Moore Gallery, Santa Monica, 93, Michael Klein Gallery, NY, 96 & photo solo (with catalog), 102 Prince St Space, NY, 97 & 98; The Photog of Invention, Nat Mus Am Art, Washington, DC, Mus Contemp Art, Chicago & Walker Art Ctr, Minneapolis, 89-90; Departures Photog 1923-90, Denver Art Mus, Joslyn Art Mus, Omaha & Pittsburgh Ctr Arts, 91-92; Dark Decor, San Jose Mus Art, Fla Gulf Coast Art Ctr, Belleair & The Alberta Coll Art, Calgary, 92-93; The Return of the Cadavre Exquis, The Drawing Ctr, NY, Corcoran Gallery Art, Washington & Carnegie Mus Art, Pittsburgh, 93-94; True Stories, Betsy Senior Gallery, NY, 94; Interventions, UBU Gallery, NY, 95; Collection in Context (with catalog), Thread Waxing Space, NY, 96; Smallest Show on Earth, Richard Levy Gallery, Albuquerque, NMex, 97; Affirm Identity (with catalog), Kingsborough Community Coll Art Gallery, Brooklyn, NY, 97; Empire State Pride Agenda Benefit, NY, 97; photo solo (with catalog), 102 Prince St Space, NY, 97 & 98; Emergency Art Fund, Pat Hearn Gallery, NY, 97; Obsession (with catalog), Rotunda Gallery, Brooklyn, NY, 97; Sex/Industry, Stefan Stux Gallery, NY, 97; 100, Holland Tunnel Proj Space, Brooklyn, NY, 98; Regarding Duchamp, Abraham Lubelski Gallery, NY, 98; A Brooklyn Salon, Rotunda Gallery, Brooklyn, NY, 98; The Winter Show, Charles Cowles Gallery, NY, 98; A Room with A View, Sixth at Prince Fine Arts, NY, 99. *Pos:* Adj cur photog, PS1 Mus, NY, 87-88; photog cur, Independent Curators, Inc, NY, 88-90. *Awards:* Nat Endowment Arts, 85 & 89; Art Matters, Inc, 88 & 89; Change, Inc, 89. *Bibliog:* Stuart Servetar (auth), article, New York Press, 2/7-13/96; Howard Halle (auth), article, Time Out/New York, 2/21-28/96; Paul D Miller (auth), WEBS, Axis Press, Brooklyn, NY, 99. *Media:* Miscellaneous Media. *Publ:* Auth, exhib catalog, Hirschl & Adler Modern, New York, 90; exhib catalog, Runkel-Hue-Williams, London, 91

LATHAN-STIEFEL, CAROLINE
INSTALLATION SCULPTOR, PRINTMAKER

Study: Brown Univ, Providence, BA, 1989; Maine Coll Art, Portland, MFA, 2001. *Work:* Jersey City Mus; NJ State Mus; Zimmerli Mus, NJ; NJ State Coun on the Arts; Newark Libr. *Exhib:* 100 NJ Artists Make Prints, NJ STate Mus, Trenton, 2002-04; Solo exhibs, Mendel Mus Libr, Princeton Univ, 2003, Atlanta Contemp Art Ctr, Ga, 2005, Powel House, Landmarks Contemp Projects, Philadelphia, 2008, Abington Art Ctr, Pa, 2008 & Del Ctr for Contemp Art, 2009; Personal Perspectives, Rutgers Univ, NJ, 2003; Projects, Islip Mus Art, NY, 2003; Running Rampant, Fe Gallery, Pittsburgh, 2004; Matter, SPACE Gallery, Portland, Maine, 2008; Hovering Above, Abington Art Ctr Sculpture Park, Pa, 2008. *Awards:* Rebay Teaching Artist Award, Guggenheim Mus Children's Program, 2001; NJ Print & Paper Fel, Brodsky Ctr, New Brunswick, 2002; Sculpture Fel, NJ State Coun on the Arts, 2003; Creative Capital Found Grant, 2005; Pollock-Krasner Found Grant, 2008. *Bibliog:* Catherine Fox (auth), Changing Faces, Atlanta J & Constitution, 6/4/1999; Mary Thomas (auth), Getting More Fiber, Pittsburgh Post-Gazette, 4/28/2004; Petra Fallaux (auth), Strands of Fabrication, Fiberarts Mag, 9-10/2004; Adriana Grant (auth), Intricate Netting, Seattle Weekly, 5/8/2007; Warren Seeling (auth), Young Approaches: Crossing/Crossing Out Categories, Surface Design J, 2008

LATTANZIO, FRANCES
PHOTOGRAPHER, EDUCATOR

b Detroit, Mich, Oct 2, 1949. *Study:* Univ Mich, BFA, 71, MFA, 73. *Work:* Bank of Ind & Vincennes Univ, Ind; Madison Plaza Corp & Hyatt Int Corp, Chicago; Ind State Univ, Terre Haute. *Exhib:* One-person exhib, Quincy Col, Ill, 86; Midwest Photograph Invitational VI, Univ Wis, Green Bay, 90; Creative Images, Indianapolis Art League, 88; The Known/The Unknown, Briscoe Gallery, Miss State Univ, 88; Hand-Manipulated Photog, Buckham Fine Arts Proj, Flint, Mich, 89. *Teaching:* Assoc prof photog, Ind State Univ, Terre Haute, 75-; adj asst prof photog, St Mary of the Woods Col, Ind, 80. *Awards:* Engraph Award, Engraph Inc, 81. *Bibliog:* Cheryl Bopp (auth), article, Arts Insight, 3/80. *Mem:* Coll Art Asn; Soc Photog Educ; Friends of Photog; Arts Illiana. *Media:* Silver Prints; Hand-colored. *Publ:* Illusr, Figurative Contexts, Turman Gallery, 83. *Mailing Add:* 1500 S Sixth St Terre Haute IN 47802-1638

LAU, JOSEPH LUEN-HUNG
COLLECTOR

b Hong Kong, 1951. *Study:* Univ Windsor, Can, BS. *Pos:* With Chinese Estates Holdings Ltd, Hong Kong, 1989-, exec dir, formerly, chmn & chief exec officer, 2006-; with Lifestyle Int Holdings Ltd, Hong Kong, 2001-, non-exec dir, currently. *Awards:* Named one of World's Richest People, Forbes; named one of Top 200 Collectors, ARTnews mag, 2007-13. *Collection:* Modern & contemporary art, especially Warhol. *Mailing Add:* Chinese Estates Holdings Ltd 26th Fl MassMutual Tower 38 Gloucester Rd Wan Chai Hong Kong

LAU, REX
PAINTER, PRINTMAKER

b Trenton, NJ, Feb 26, 1947. *Study:* Sch Visual Arts. *Work:* Met Mus Art, NY; Solomon R Guggenheim Mus, NY; Albright-Knox Art Gallery, Buffalo, NY; Yale Univ Art Gallery, New Haven; Libr Congress, Washington; Whitney Mus Am Art, NY. *Comn:* large panel painting, IBM Corp, Los Angeles, 85; large panel painting, Coca-Cola USA, Atlanta, 88. *Exhib:* Ten Narrative Paintings, Met Mus Art, NY, 83; Nueva Pintura Narrative, Museo Rufino Tamayo, Mexico City, 84; New Horizons in Am Art, Solomon R Guggenheim Mus, NY, 85; The Barry Lowen Collection, Mus Contemp Art, Los Angeles, 86; Selections from the Exxon Series, Solomon R Guggenheim Mus, NY, 87; A New Generation, the 1980s, Met Mus Art, NY, 88. *Awards:* Pollock-Krasner fel, 95. *Bibliog:* Stephen Westfall (auth), Rex Lau, Ruth Siegel Gallery, 85; Gerrit Henry (auth), Rex Lau, Art in America, 87; Donald Kuspit (auth), Rex Lau, Galerie Objecta, Munich, 92. *Media:* Oil. *Dealer:* Kouros Gallery 23 East 73rd St New York NY 10021; The Drawing Room East Hampton NY. *Mailing Add:* PO Box 697 Montauk NY 11954

LAUB, STEPHEN
SCULPTOR

b Oakland, Calif, July, 10, 1945. *Study:* Univ Calif, Berkeley, BA, 69, MA, 70. *Work:* Mus Mod Art; GOT A Gruppen AB (consortium), Stockholm, Sweden; Kunsthaus, Zurich, Switz; Fine Arts Mus, Houston, Tex; San Francisco Mus Modern Art. *Exhib:* Extended Photog, Fifth Biennale, Vienna Mus, Austria, 81; Venice Biennale 1984, Venice Exhib Hall, Italy, 84; Spatial Relationships, Mus Mod Art, NY, 85; Alles und noch viel mehr, Kunstmuseum, Bern, Switz, 85; Images of Am Pop Cult, Laforet Mus, Tokyo, 89; On the Edge: Photog & Sculpture, Cleveland Ctr Contemp Art, Ohio, 90; Ealan Wingate Gallery, NY, 91; Power: Its Icons, Myths, Indianapolis Mus Art, Ind, 91; Stephen Wirtz Gallery, 95; Invitational Exhib, Guild Hall, East Hampton, NY, 2005; Pacific Standard Time, Orange Co Mus Art, 2011-2013. *Teaching:* Assoc prof sculpture, Rutgers Univ, NJ, 87-. *Awards:* Fulbright Fel, Italy, 71-72; Artist's Fel, Nat

Endowment Arts, 78-79; Artist's Fel, NY Found Arts, 89-90. *Bibliog:* Willoughby Sharp (auth), Stephen Laub's Projections, Avalanche, 74; Roberta Smith (auth), Stephen Laub, NY Times, 3/25/88; Charles Hagen (auth), Stephen Laub at Koury Wingate, Artforum, summer 88; Janet Koplos (auth), Stephen Laub, sculpture, 9/10/91; State of Mind, Art in LA, 2011; Making WET, Leonard Koren, 2012. *Media:* Wood

LAUDER, EVELYN H
COLLECTOR
b Vienna, 1940. *Study:* Hunter Coll, BA. *Hon Degrees:* Muhlenberg Coll, Hon degree, 1996. *Pos:* Educ dir, Estée Lauder Cos, New York, 1959, vpres, sr corp vpres, 1989-; founder, Breast Cancer Res Found. *Awards:* Spirit Achievement Award, Albert Einstein Coll Med, 1991; Mary Waterman Award, Breast Cancer Alliance, 1998; Award for Excellence in Philanthropy, Sloan-Kettering, 2001; named one of Top 200 Collectors, ARTnews mag, 2004-12. *Collection:* Modern art, especially Cubism. *Publ:* Photogr, The Seasons Observed, 1994 & An Eye For Beauty, 2002. *Mailing Add:* Estee Lauder Cos 767 5th Ave New York NY 10153-0023

LAUDER, JO CAROLE
COLLECTOR
Awards: Named one of Top 200 Collectors, ARTnews mag, 2004-13. *Mem:* Ronald S Lauder Found (bd dir, currently); Mus Modern Art Int Coun (pres, currently); Mt Sinai Med Ctr (bd trustees, currently); Friends of Art & Preservation in Embassies (chmn, bd dir, currently). *Collection:* Late 19th and early 20th-century art, especially German and Austrian; decorative art; medieval art; arms and armor. *Mailing Add:* Mus Modern Art 11 W 53rd St New York NY 10019

LAUDER, LEONARD ALAN
ADMINISTRATOR, COLLECTOR
b New York, NY, Mar 19, 1933. *Study:* Wharton Sch, Univ Pa, BS, 1954. *Hon Degrees:* Conn Coll, DFA. *Pos:* Chmn, pres, Whitney Mus Am Art, formerly; with Estée Lauder, Inc, 1958-, exec vpres, 1962-75, pres, 1972-82, pres, chief exec off, 1982-99, chmn, 95-2009, chmn emer, 2009-; vchmn bd, CFTA, 1976-79; trustee, Aspen Inst for Humanistic Studies, 1978, chmn, 2007; bd govs, Joseph H Lauder Inst Mgt and Int Studies, 1983; bd dirs, Adv Comn on Trade Negotiations, 1983-87. *Awards:* Philanthropist of Yr, Greater NY Chap of Nat Soc of Fund Raising Execs, 1993; Am Art award, Whitney Mus Am Art, 1996; Am Spirit award, Nat Retail Fedn, 1998; Ellis Island Medal of Honor, 2000; named one of Top 200 Collectors, ARTnews mag, 2004-12. *Collection:* Modern art, especially Cubism. *Mailing Add:* Estée Lauder Cosmetics Inc 767 5th Ave New York NY 10153

LAUDER, RONALD STEPHEN
COLLECTOR, PATRON
b New York, NY, Feb 26, 1944. *Study:* Univ Paris, degree (French literature) 1964, BS (int business), 1965; Univ Brussels, cert, 1966. *Pos:* Bd dirs, Econ Develop Bd, NY, 1974-76; trustee, Mus Modern Art, new York, 1975-, bd chmn, 1995-; vis comt for Medieval Art, Metrop Mus Art, currently; chmn, NY State Rep Finance Comt, 1980-83, NY State Senate Adv Comn on Privatization, 1991-93, NY State Res Coun on Privatization & NY State Privatization Comn, 1995; dep asst secy defense, European & NATO Policy, US Dept Defense, 1983-86, Estee Lauder Int Inc, currently, Clinique Lab Inc, currently; trustee, Mt Sinai Med Ctr, 1981-; pres, Neue Galerie, New York, 2001-; US Ambassador to Austria, formerly. *Awards:* Ronald S Lauder Drawing Gallery, Mus Modern Art, 1984; Great Cross of Order of Aeronautical Merit with White Ribbon, Spain, 1985; Ordre de Merit, France, 1985; Distinguished Pub Serv Medal, Dept Defense, 1986; named one of the World's Richest People, Forbes Mag, 1999-2002; named one of the Top 200 Collectors, ARTnews mag, 2004-13. *Collection:* Late 19th and early 20th-century art, especially German and Austrian; decorative art; medieval art; arms and armor . *Publ:* Auth, Fighting Violent Crime in America, Dodd Mead, 1985. *Mailing Add:* Lauder Investments Inc Ste 4200 767 Fifth Ave New York NY 10153-0023

LAUF, CORNELIA
CURATOR, ART HISTORIAN
b May 26, 1961. *Study:* Oberlin Col, BA, 83; Columbia Univ, MA, 85; PhD, 92. *Collection Arranged:* Natura Naturata (An Argument for Still Life), Josh Baer Gallery, NY, 89; Flux Attitudes (auth, catalog), New Mus Contemp Art & Hallwalls, 92; The Wealth of Nations (auth, catalog), Warsaw, 92. *Pos:* Independent cur, 87-. *Teaching:* New Sch for Social Res, 95. *Awards:* Wolfgang Stechow Mem Prize, Oberlin Col, 81-82, Oberlin Coll Alumni Fel, 85-86; University Fel, 83-84, President's Fel, 84-86, Columbia Univ Travel Grant, 86, Samuel H Kress Fel, 89-90, Columbia Univ. *Publ:* Auth, Joseph Beuys, Seven Days (rev), 11/88; Franz Erhard Walther, Arts, 2/89; Talents and Gewgaws, Artscribe, 9-10/89; On reading some drawings of Reuys, Arts, 3/90; Collection Handbook, Guggenheim Mus, 92; Andre Cadere, Mus Mod Art, Paris & PSI, New York, 92

LAUMANN, LARS
VIDEO ARTIST
b Bronnoysund, Norway, 1975. *Study:* N Norwegian Art & Film Sch, Kabelvag, 93-95; Norwegian State Acad, Oslo, 95-2001. *Exhib:* Jours lounges et nuit lumineuses, Bergen Kunsthall, Bergen, 2003; Vekkero Skulpturpark, Oslo, 2004; The Atlantic, Kling & Bang, Reykjavik, 2005; solo exhibs, Vinterfestukekunstner, Ofoten Mus, Narvik, 2005, Entre Chienne et Louve, Le Commissariat, Paris, 2006, The Thick Plottens, Galuzin Gallery, Oslo, 2006, Morrissey Foretelling the Death of Diana, White Columns, New York & Vox Populi, Philadelphia, 2007, Ft Worth Contemp Arts, Tex, 2009; Cross My Heart, Torpedo Kunstbokhandel, Oslo, 2006; Giving People What They Want, The Glass Box, Paris, 2006; Peer In Peer Out, Scottsdale Mus Contemp Art, Ariz, 2007; EAST Int, Norwich Gallery, 2007; The Backroom/Societe Anonyme, Kadist Art Found, Paris, 2007; Monumeno Mori, Astrup Fearnley Mus Mod Kunst, Oslo, 2008; PopShop, MU Gallery, Eindhoven, 2008; Update, White Columns, New York, 2008; Report on Probability, Kunsthalle Basel, Basel, 2009; As Long As It Lasts, Marian Goodman Gallery, New York, 2009. *Bibliog:* Ray Huston (auth), How soon is now?, San Francisco Bay Guardian, 9/12/2007; Adrian Searle (auth), Toil and Rubble, The Guardian G2, 23-25, 4/8/2008; Matthew Higgs (auth), Emerging Artists, Frieze, 137, 1/2008; Paul Carey-Kent (auth), Tales from the wasteland, Art World, 113, 9/2008; Linda Yablonsky (auth), Part of the solution?, Art News, 92-93, 1/2009; Helen Sumpter (auth), article, Time Out, 44, 6/17/2009. *Mailing Add:* 21 Herald St London E2 6JT United Kingdom

LAURENCE, GEOFFREY F
PAINTER
b Paterson, NJ, 1949. *Study:* Byam Shaw, with Bridget Riley & Bill Jacklin, LCAD, 68; St Martins, with Frederic Gore & John Hoyland, BA, 71; NY Acad, with Eric Fischl & Vincent Desidirio, MFA (cum laude), 95. *Work:* London Borough of Camden, London, Eng; Mus Fine Art, Santa Fe, NMex; Mus Biblical Art, Dallas Tex. *Exhib:* Tolly Cobbold Touring Show, Eng, 78; 5th Int Kunstaustellung, Freiburg, Ger, 92; Dialogues with Visual Tradition, NY Acad, 98; The Am Scene, Taos Mus, 99 & 2000; Artists on the Edge, Yeshiva Univ Mus, NY, 2002; Representing Representation VI, Arnot Mus, Elmira, NY, 2003; 15, Las Vegas Mus, Nev, 2005; solo exhibs, Iswaswillbe, Meisel Arts Ctr, Denver, Colo, 2005, The Reality of Things: New Paintings and Drawings, LewAllen Contemp, N Mex, 2006; Inheritance, Skotia Gallery, Santa Fe, NMex, 2010. *Teaching:* instr anat & painting, Acad Realist Art, Seattle, 1999; instr fine art, Santa Fe, 2000; instr fine art, Gage Acad, 2000-2004; instr fine art, Armory Arts Ctr, West Palm Beach, Fla, 2003; instr anat drawing, Andreeva Portrait Acad, 2005; faculty, Santa Fe Sch Art, 2010-2013. *Awards:* Walter Erlebacher Award, 95; J Epstein Travel Award, 95; Robert Rauschenberg award, 2004; George S Garman, 2006. *Bibliog:* Malin Wilson (auth), Albuquerque J, 97; Wesley Pulka (auth), Albuquerque J, 97; Lynn Cline (auth), New Mexican, 98; Ori Z Soltes (auth), Fixing the World, Univ Press New Eng; D Dashmore (auth), Posen Libr Jewish Culture, 2013. *Media:* Oil. *Dealer:* 101 Exhibit Gallery Miami Fla. *Mailing Add:* 814 Camino de Monte Rey # 112 Santa Fe NM 87508

LAURIDSEN, HANNE
PAINTER, SCULPTOR
b Esbjerg, Denmark; US citizen. *Study:* Univ Calif, Berkeley, BA (art & art hist), 80; Univ Calif, San Diego, MFA, 82. *Work:* Mus Mod Art, NY; Paterson Mus, NJ; Buhl Collection, New York. *Exhib:* Arrivals, Guild Hall Mus, E Hampton, NY, 83 & Mem Exhib, 98-2006; Who is the Monster, Galleri Jansen & Norgaard, Copenhagen, Denmark & Galerie Gerry Salant, Paris, France, 84; Parrish Art Mus Juried Exhib, Southampton, NY, 94; Mixed Media Installation, Gallery Bai, Barcelona, 96; Black & White with Picasso, Matisse, Dubuffet, Goldstrom Gallery, NY, 98; Good Against Evil Installation, Goldstrom Gallery, 99; Exhibs in Denmark, 2005-. *Bibliog:* Hannes Universe, Channel 2TV, Denmark, 90; Marion Wolberg Weiss (auth), Artist of the Hamptons, Dans Paper, Bridge Hampton, NY, 3/14/97; The Seven Stations of OJ, Fox TV, Channel 5 News, 97. *Mem:* Guild Hall Mus, East Hampton, NY; Parrish Art Mus, Southampton, NY; Alliance Francaise. *Media:* Paintings, Sculpture, Photography. *Publ:* Auth, Shadows, High Performance, Los Angeles, spring-summer, 82. *Dealer:* H7L Studio 517 E 11 St New York NY 10000. *Mailing Add:* 517 E 11th St No 2 New York NY 10009

LAUSEN, MARCIA
EDUCATOR, DESIGNER
Study: Ind Univ, BFA (graphic design), 1981; Yale Univ, MFA (graphic design), 1985. *Pos:* Prin, Studio/lab, Chicago, currently. *Teaching:* Prof, dir, Sch of Art + Design, Univ Ill, Chicago, currently. *Awards:* Named a Fast Company Master of Design, 2004. *Publ:* Auth, Design for Democracy: Ballot + Election Design, 2007. *Mailing Add:* University of Illinois School of Art & Design MC 036 929 W Harrison St 106 Jefferson Hall Chicago IL 60607

LAUTTENBACH, CAROL L
PAINTER
b New Haven, Conn, Nov 26, 1934. *Study:* Washington Sch Art, (honors in oils & watercolors), 67. *Hon Degrees:* Washington Sch Art, Certificate Award, 1967. *Work:* Mus Des Duncan, Paris. *Comn:* Soundview Special Care Ctr, 76; Schiavone Corp, 80, Yale-New Haven Hosp, 82, New Haven Conn; Vet Mem Med Ctr, Meride, Conn, 84; Unholtz Corp, Wallingford, Conn, 84. *Exhib:* Conn Acad Fine Arts, Wadsworth Athenium, Hartford, Conn, 76; Int Art Competition, Palm Beach Art Galleries, New Orleans, La & Palm Beach Fla, 83; Grand Salon des Surindependants, Mus des Duncan, Paris; Nat Soc Painters in Casein & Acrylic, Am Acad & Inst of Arts & Letters, NY; Conn Acad Fine Arts, New Britain Mus Am Art, Conn, 93; New Haven Paint & Clay Club, John Slade Ely House, Conn, 94. *Teaching:* private instr, acrylic & painting. *Awards:* Grumbacher Silver & Gold Medal, Arts & Crafts Asn Meriden, Inc, 1983-84 & 1993; Beazley Realtors Award, Mt Carmel Art Asn, Hamden, 2000; Harvey Fuller Award, Arts & Crafts Asn Meriden, Inc, 2001; Mayor Carl Amento Award, Mt Carmel Art Asn, Hamden, 2002; Utrech Art Supplies Award - Hamden Art League, 2004; Dusa Chiropractic Center Award - Hamden Art League, 2005; Best Theme Award - Arts & Crafts Assn Meriden, 2005; Sara Cambria Meml Award, Arts & Crafts Asn Meriden Inc, 2008; Aurora Bellafronte Mem Award, Arts & Crafts Asn Meriden, 2009; Carol Murphy Realtor Award, Hamden Art League, 2010; Suzio Insurance Ctr Award, Arts and Crafts Asn Meriden, 2011. *Bibliog:* Drawing Anthology International, Regina Publ, 74. *Mem:* Conn Acad Fine Arts, Hartford; Shoreline Alliance for Arts, Guilford, Conn; Provincetown Art Asn, Mass; Int Soc Artists, Marion, Ohio; Wallingford Hist Soc (life mem); Guilford Art League; Madison Art Soc; Arts & Crafts Asn, Meriden; Nat Asn Professional Women, Garden City, NY. *Media:* Acrylic. *Specialty:* Fine Arts. *Interests:* Painting in realistic and palette knife acrylic. *Publ:* Guilford Courier, 3/10/2005; Record-Journal, Meriden, Conn, 2008; Int Biog Centre of Cambridge, Eng, 2008; and others. *Dealer:* Carriage House Gallery Ltd 23 Bostn St Guilford CT 06437; Frame Shop Gallery 147 Post Rd E Westport CT 06880; Mary Lous Fischer Gallery, LTD, 23 Boston St, Guilford, CT. *Mailing Add:* 39 Ridgewood Rd Wallingford CT 06492

LAVADOUR, JAMES
PAINTER
b Adams, Ore, 1949. *Work:* Seattle Art Mus, Wash; Portland Art Mus, Ore; The Heard Mus, Phoenix, Ariz; Wash State Arts Comn, Olympia; Seattle Arts Comn, Wash. *Comn:* Art in Public Places, Wash State Arts Comn, Olympia, 83, 85 & 87; NW Major Works Project, 89, Seattle Arts Comn, Wash. *Exhib:* Northwest Now, Tacoma Art Mus, Wash, 86; Crossed Cultures: 5 Contemp Native Northwest Artists, Seattle Art Mus, Wash, 89; Northwest Viewpoints: James Lavadour, Portland Art Mus, Ore, 90; Shared Visions: Native Am Sculptors and painters in the 20th Century, The Heard Mus, Phoenix, Ariz, 91; Land, Spirit, Power: First Nations at the National Gallery of Canada, Nat Gallery Can, Ottawa, Ont, 92. *Awards:* Ore Arts Fel, Ore Arts Comn, 86; Nat Printmaking Fel, Rutgers Univ, 90; Betty Bowen Mem Recognition Award, Seattle Art Mus, 91. *Bibliog:* Linda E Evans (auth), The Undiminished Landscape, Security Pacific Gallery, San Francisco, Calif, 90; Iona Chelette (auth), Northwest Southwest: Painted Fictions, Palm Springs Desert Mus, 90; Margaret Archuleta (auth), Shared Visions, The Heard Mus, 91. *Media:* Oil on Linen. *Mailing Add:* PO Box 1191 Pendleton OR 97801

LAVELLI, LUCINDA
ADMINISTRATOR
Study: Denison Univ, B (Psychology); Case Western Reserve Univ, M (Nonprofit Management), MFA (Theater Arts and Dance). *Pos:* Chairwoman, performing arts, dir dance, Hathaway Brown Sch, Shaker Heights, Ohio, 1981-93; dir Sch of Dance, then dir Sch of Dance, Theatre, and Arts Administration, Univ Akron, 1993-2002; provost, vice chancellor for arts and academics, North Carolina Sch of Art, 2002-06; dean, Univ Florida Col of Fine Arts, 2006-; active member of boards and arts organizations including the Laban Inst of Movement Studies, RiverRun International Film Festival, Alban Elved Dance Company, DanceCleveland and OhioDance, DanceAlive!, National Ballet, The Cade Mus Found, New World Sch of the Arts; advisory board member Univ Florida Performing Arts and the publication Dean and Provost; pres, Florida Higher Educ Arts Network, currently; secretary, International Council of Fine Arts Deans, currently. *Awards:* OhioDance award for service to the artform, 2005. *Mailing Add:* Dean's Office University of Florida College of Fine Arts 101 FAA PO Box 115800 Gainesville FL 32611-5800

LAVIN, IRVING
HISTORIAN
b St Louis, Mo, Dec 14, 1927. *Study:* Cambridge Univ, Eng, 48-49; Washington Univ, BA, 49; NY Univ, MA, 52; Harvard Univ, MA, 52, PhD (Sheldon Fel), 55. *Teaching:* Lectr hist art, Vassar Col, 59-62; from assoc prof to prof, NY Univ, 63-73; prof, Sch Hist Studies, Inst for Adv Study, 73-. *Awards:* Fulbright Fel, 61-63; Am Coun Learned Soc Fel, 65-66; Guggenheim Found Grant, 68-69. *Mem:* Fel Am Acad Arts & Sci; Corpus Ancient Mosaics Tunisia (mem steering comt, 69-); Nat Comt for the Hist of Art; Comite int d'histoire de l'art. *Res:* Art of late antiquity; Renaissance and Baroque sculpture. *Publ:* Auth, Bernini and the Crossing of Saint Peter's, Arts, Archaeol Inst Am & Coll Art Asn Am, 68; Five new youthful sculptures by Gianlorenzo Bernini and a revised chronology of his early works, 68, Bernini's death, 72 & Divine inspiration in Caravaggio's two St Matthews, 74, Art Bull; Bernini and the Unity of the Visual Arts, Oxford Univ Press, 80; Drawings by Gianlorenzo Bernini from the Museum der Bildenden Kunste, Princeton Univ Press, 81. *Mailing Add:* 56 Maxwell Ln Princeton NJ 08540

LAVIN, MARILYN ARONBERG
EDUCATOR, HISTORIAN
b St Louis, Mo, Oct 27, 1925. *Study:* Washington Univ, BA, 47, MA, 49; Univ Rome, cert, 52; Inst Fine Arts, NY Univ, PhD, 73. *Teaching:* Prof hist art, Princeton Univ, 75-; vis prof, Yale Univ, 78 & Univ Md, 79-80. *Awards:* Charles Rufus Morey Book Award, Coll Art Asn, 77. *Mem:* Coll Art Asn Am (mem bd dir, 79-83); Renaissance Soc. *Res:* Italian Renaissance painting with special interest in work of Piero della Francesco and history of fresco painting. *Publ:* Auth, The Corpus Domini Altarpiece of Urbino, Art Bull, 67; Piero Della Francesca: The Flagellation, Penguin, Viking, 72; 17th Century Barberini Documents & Inventories of Art, NY Univ Press, 75; Piero della Francesca's Baptism of Christ, Yale Univ Press, 81; The Eye of the Tiger: Department of Art & Architecture, Princeton Univ Press, 83. *Mailing Add:* 56 Maxwell Ln Princeton NJ 08540

LAVINE, STEVEN DAVID
EDUCATOR, WRITER, ADMINISTRATOR
b Sparta, Wis, June 7, 1947. *Study:* Stanford Univ, BA, 69; Harvard Univ, MA, 70, PhD, 76. *Pos:* Pres, Calif Inst Arts, 88-. *Teaching:* Asst prof Eng, Univ Mich, Ann Arbor, 74-81; fac chmn, Salzburg Seminar on Mus, 89. *Awards:* Ford Grad Prize Fel, Harvard Univ, 69-74, Charles B Dexter Traveling Fel, 72; Horace H Rackham Resident Fel; Univ Michigan Faculty Recognition Award, 80; Children's Freedom Award, Children's Mus Los Angeles, 2001; Class of 1923 Award, Univ Mich; 2005 Los Angeles Highlight Award, W.O.M.E.N. Inc Los Angeles. *Mem:* Input TV Screening Conf, Montreal, Can & Granada, Spain (selection panelist 85-86); Wexner Found, Columbus, Ohio (consult, 86-87); KCRW-FM Nat Pub Radio (bd dir, 89); Los Angeles Philharmonic (bd dir, 94-2004); J Paul Getty Mus (vis comt, 90-97); Los Angeles Cathedral (mem archit, selection jury, 96); Arts Coalition for Acad Progress, Los Angeles Unified Sch Dist (co-dir, 97); Asia Society, Southern, Calif (adv Committee, 98); Cotsen Family Found, (bd trustees, 2000); Am Coun on Educ (bd dirs, 2004); Villa Aurora Found European-Am Relations (bd dirs). *Publ:* Co-ed, The Hopwood Anthology: Five Decades of Am Poetry, Ann Arbor Univ Press, 81; The Writer's Craft, Mich Quart Rev 21, 82; International Jewish Writing: From the Bellagio Conference, Prooftexts 4, 84; Exhibiting Cultures: The Poetics and Politics of Mus Display, Smithsonian Inst Press, 91; Museums & Communities: The Politics of Public Culture, Smithsonian Inst Press, 92; Karp & Lavine, Exhibiting Cultures: The Poetics & Politics of Museum Display, Smithsonian Inst Press, 91; Karp & Levine, Museum & Communities: The Politics of Public Culture, Smithsonian Inst Press, 92. *Mailing Add:* California Institute of Arts Office of President 24700 McBean Pkwy Santa Clarita CA 91355-2397

LAW, JAN
PAINTER, ART DEALER
b Newton, Mass, May 24, 1946. *Study:* Mus Fine Arts, Boston, Mass, 59; Paris Am Acad, 79; Wellesley Col, 81; Pine Manor Col, BA, 82. *Work:* Paris Am Acad Art Gallery, Paris, France; Goddard Hosp, Brockton, Mass; Children's Hosp, Boston, Mass; Bay State Med Ctr, Springfield, Mass. *Exhib:* Solo exhibs, Jan Law Watercolors, Decorators Showhouse at Plympton Ct, Boston Jr League, Sudbury, Mass, 90, Jan Law Painting & Prints, Swain Gallery, Dover, Mass, 2000; Art Expo, Jacob Javits Conv Ctr, NY, 93, 98, 99 & 2000; Art Expo Europe Int Conv Ctr, Eng, 94; group exhibs, So this is Art, Wellesley, Mass, 95, Small Paintings, Medfield, Mass, 98, Art Show with Edna Hibel, Wellesley, Mass, 2002; Calif Art Expo, Int Conv Ctr, Calif, 98; Art Gallery, Framingham, Mass, 2008; Art Gallery, Wellesley Hills, MA, 2009-. *Teaching:* artist, painter, instr, drawing & painting, Children's Art Studio, Wellesley, Mass, 93-94. *Bibliog:* Margaret Fitzwilliam (auth), Happenings Artists Exhib, Wellesley Townsmen, 83; Victoria Fraza (auth), So they call this Art, The Tab, 95; Eric Shacker (auth), Artis Mag, Will Steigerwald Publ, 6-7/2005. *Media:* Acrylic, Oil, Watercolor. *Specialty:* Original paintings. *Interests:* Dancing, writing, yoga & politics. *Publ:* 34 paintings (art prints). *Dealer:* Jan Law Art 312 Washington St Bldg 2 #4 Wellesley MA 02481. *Mailing Add:* 312 Washington St Bldg 2 Apt 4 Wellesley Hills MA 02481

LAWALL, DAVID BARNARD
HISTORIAN, MUSEUM DIRECTOR
b Detroit, Mich, Aug 27, 1935. *Study:* Oberlin Col, BA, 56; Princeton Univ, MFA, 59 & PhD, 66. *Collection Arranged:* A B Durand 1796-1886 (auth, catalog), Montclair Art Mus, 71; Small Paintings Toward a Renewal of Classicism, 74-79, Anton Refregier (auth, catalog), 77, Image of Post-Modern Man, 79 & Ernest Fiene/Leon Kroll, New Still Life & Landscape Painting, 87, NY Gallery Show, 88, Univ Va Art Mus. *Pos:* Cur, Univ Va Art Mus, 71-85, dir, 85-90. *Teaching:* Instr, Univ Mo, Columbia, 60-61; instr, Ohio State Univ, Columbus, 61-64, asst prof, 64-68; assoc prof, Univ Va, Charlottesville, 69-. *Awards:* Fel, Nat Endowment Humanities, 69. *Mem:* NY Acad Art (exec bd, 81-90); Am Asn Univ Profs. *Publ:* Auth, Asher Durand: Art and Art Theory, 77 & Asher Durand: Catalog of Paintings, Garland, 78; ed, John Barber, 92. *Mailing Add:* 108 Bollingwood Rd Charlottesville VA 22903-1706

LAWLER, LOUISE
ARTIST
b Bronxville, NY, 1947. *Study:* Cornell Univ, BFA, 69. *Exhib:* Solo shows incl Aero Theater, Santa Monica, 79, Anna Leonowens Gallery II, 82, Matrix, Wadsworth Atheneum, Hartford, Conn, 84, Nature Morte, NY, 85, Maison de la Culture ed de la Communication de Saint Etienne, France, 86, Mus Mod Art, New York, 87, Galerie Yvon Lambert, Paris, 88, 90, 2003, 2007, Photo Resource Ctr, Boston, 89, Mus Fine Arts, Boston, Mus Fine Arts, Boston, 90, Metro Pictures, NY, 91, 94, 97, 2000, 2004, 2008, Sprengel Mus, Hannover, 93, Galleria Klemens Gasser, Bolzano, Italy, 94, Munich Kunstverein, 95, Hirshhorn Mus and Sculpture Garden, Wash, DC, 97, Skarstedt Fine Art, NY, 99, Neugerriemschneider, Berlin, 2000, Art & Pub, Geneva, 2001, Portikus, Frankfurt, 2003, Mus for Gegenwartskunst, Kunstmuseum Basel, 2004, Dia, Beacon, 2005, Wexner Ctr, Ohio, 2006; group shows incl Artists Space, NY, 78; Secessionist Mus, Vienna, 81; PS 1, NY, 83; Diane Brown Gallery, New York, 84; New Mus Contemp Art, New York, 85, 86, 90; Moderna Museet, Stockholm, 87; Mus Contemp Art, Los Angeles, 88; Nat Mus Am Art, Smithsonian Inst, 89; Carnegie Mus Art, Pittsburgh, 91; Whitney Biennial, Whitney Mus Am Art, 91, 2000, 2008, Visions from America, 2002; Museo d'Arte Moderna e Contemporanea di Trento, Italy, 92; Kunsthalle Wien, Vienna, 93; Mus Contemp Art, Chicago, 94, 2002; Ivan Doughert Gallery, Australia, 96; Photogrs Gallery, London, 97; Triennal di Milano, Italy, 99; Mus Mod Art, New York, 99; Margo Leavin Gallery, Los Angeles, 2003; Walker Art Ctr, Minneapolis, 2003; Nat Mus Art, Oslo, 2005; Mus Moderner Kunst, Austria, 2006; PS 1, New York, 2007; Sammlung Verbund, MAK, Vienna, 2007; Wexner Ctr, Ohio, 2006; Spruth Magers, London, 2007; BFAs Blondeau Fine Art, Serv, Geneva; Metro Pictures, New York, 2008; Spruth Magers, Berlin, 2009; Jumex Collection, Mex City, 2010; Art Inst Chicago, 2010; APower Plant, Toronto, 2010. *Dealer:* Art & Public 37 rue des Bains 1205 Geneva Switzerland; Blondeau Fine Art Services 5 rue de la Muse 1205 Geneva Switzerland; Metro Pictures 519 W 24th St New York NY 10011; Galerie Edward Mitterrand 52 rue des Bains 1205 Geneva Switzerland; Monika Sprüth Philomene Magers Schellingstrasse 48 80799 Munich Germany; Friedrich Petzel Gallery 535 W 22nd St & 537 W 22nd St New York NY 10011; Simon Lee 12 Berkeley St London W1J 8DT UK; Yvon Lambert 108 rue Vieille du Temple F-75003 Paris France

LAWRENCE, ANNETTE
CONCEPTUAL ARTIST, EDUCATOR
b Rockville Centre, NY, Jan 28, 1965. *Study:* Hartford Art Sch, Univ Hartford, BFA, 86; Md Inst Coll Art, MFA, 90. *Work:* Dallas Mus Art; Mus Fine Arts, Houston; Art Pace Ctr Contemp Art, San Antonio; Goldman Sachs & Co, NYC; Jack S Blanton Mus Art, Austin; Coin Toss, Cowboys Stadium, Arlington, Tex, Mar 2010. *Exhib:* Gender: Fact or Fiction, Laguna Gloria Mus Art, Austin, Tex, 92; Texas Collection, Modern Postmodern, Mus Fine Arts, Houston, 96; Finders/Keepers, Contemp Art Mus, Houston, 97; Art on Paper, Weatherspoon Art Gallery, Univ NC, Greensboro, 97; 1997 Whitney Biennial, Whitney Mus Am Art, NY, 97; Transparent/Opaque, Univ Mich Mus Art, Ann Arbor, 2000; Concentrations:36, Dallas Mus Art, Dallas, 2000; Theory Glassell Sch Art, Mus Fine Arts, Houston; audio visual: Recent Drawings by Annette Lawrence, Sweeney Art Gallery, Riverside, Calif, 2003. *Pos:* Artist in residence, Community Artists Collective, Houston, Tex, 90-91 & Proj Bridge,

Houston, Tex, 92-93. *Teaching:* Asst prof painting, Univ NTex, Denton, 96-, assoc prof, painting and drawing, 2002-, prof, 2009-. *Awards:* Cult Art Coun Houston Artist Award, 94; Awards to Artists, Kimbrough Fund, Dallas Mus Art, 94; Skowhegan Camille Cosby Award for African Am Artists, 96; Dozier Travel Award, Dallas Mus Art, 2010. *Bibliog:* Janet Kutner (auth), Annette Lawrence at Gerald Peters Gallery, Art News, 4/98; Valerie Laupe Olsen (auth), Annette Lawrence: Theory (monograph), 03; Charles Wylie (auth), Annette Lawrence Concentrations, Dallas Mus Art, 2000; Rachel Koper (auth), Annette Lawrence: Free Paper, The Austin Chronicle, 1/30/2009. *Media:* Mixed Media. *Dealer:* Talley Dunn Gallery 5020 Tracy St Dallas Tx 75205; Betty Cuningham Gallery 541 W 25th St New York NY 10001. *Mailing Add:* PO Box 3093 Denton TX 76202

LAWRENCE, JAMES A
PAINTER, PHOTOGRAPHER

b San Mateo, Calif, May 23, 1910. *Study:* Univ Calif, Davis, grad, 33; Art Ctr, Los Angeles, art & photog, with Barse Miller, Will Connell & Charles Kerlee, 35-37; Chouinard Art Inst, Los Angeles, with Phil Paradise & Ricco Lebrun, 38; Art Students League, 40; New York Sch Mod Photog; also with illusr Louis J Rogers, San Francisco, 34. *Work:* Ford Collection, Dearborn, Mich; Calif Hist Soc. *Comn:* Ford Times Publications 1948-1960, Inc, 60. *Exhib:* Solo exhibs, Reed Galleries, NY, 41, Gump Galleries, San Francisco, 43 & Univ Nev, 53; Golden Gate Int Exhib, San Francisco; Art Inst Chicago; Metrop Mus Art, NY; Los Angeles Co Mus Art; and others. *Pos:* Tech photogr, Pagano Inc, New York, 40-41; mem, Nev State Coun Arts, 67-71. *Teaching:* Guest instr watercolor, Stanford Univ, spring 48; also pvt students in watercolor at var periods. *Awards:* Cert Merit & Gold & Silver Medals, Golden Gate Int Exhib, 40-41; Am Artists Prof League, 42; Terry Art Inst Award; and others. *Mem:* Nat Watercolor Soc. *Media:* Watercolor. *Publ:* Contribr, Ford Times, Sunset Mag, US Camera & Carson Valley-Historical Sketches; photogr, Sunset Mag, Calif, 40-49; Calif Art Rev, 1st ed, 90. *Mailing Add:* Rock Creek Ranch 1198 Centerville Lane Gardnerville NV 89410

LAWRENCE, JAYE A
SCULPTOR, CRAFTSMAN

b Chicago, Ill, Jan 8, 1939. *Study:* Univ Ariz, BFA, 60; Ariz State Univ, MFA, 75. *Work:* Ariz State Univ Collection, Tempe; Pac Lutheran Univ Collection, Tacoma, Washington; Yuma Fine Arts Asn Collection, Ariz; Won Kwang Univ, Korea. *Exhib:* Teapot Image, Faith Nightingale Gallery, San Diego, Calif, 89; Return of the Magnificent 11, Cova Gallery, San Diego, 90; Hand Made for the Table, Folktree Collections, Pasadena, Calif, 91; Int Artist Exhib 92, Gallery 2000, Seoul, Korea, 92; Artisan Showcase, Newport Harbor Art Mus, Newport Beach, Calif, 93 & 94; Inaugural, Arveda Gallery, La Jolla, Calif, 96; Allied Craftsman, Hyde Gallery Grossmont Col, El Cajon, Calif, 96; Spectrum Revisited, Next Door Gallery, San Diego, Calif, 96; Brooch the Subject, Next Door Gallery, San Diego, Calif, 96; Artists chairs, Folk Tree Collections, Pasadena, Calif, 96. *Teaching:* Instr leather art, Grossmont Col, El Cajon, Calif, 81. *Awards:* Best of Show, 3rd Ann Phoenix Jewish Community Ctr Show, 69; Purchase Award, 4th Ann SWestern, 69; 12th Ariz Ann Award, 69; First Award Region XX, Tex Fine Arts Asn, Lubbock, Tex, 82. *Bibliog:* Marilyn Hagberg (auth), Jaye & Les Lawrence, 10/73 & Erik Gronborg (auth), Jaye Lawrence, 8/74, Craft Horizons; Carolyn Russell (auth), Rope forms sculpture, Daily Times Advocate, 4/28/74. *Mem:* Am Crafts Coun; Allied Craftsmen San Diego (corresp secy); COVA; NCECA. *Media:* Rawhide, Hog Casing; Wood. *Dealer:* Arveda Gallery 5624 La Jolla Blvd La Jolla CA 92037. *Mailing Add:* PO Box 5967 Carefree AZ 85377-5967

LAWRENCE, LES
CERAMIST, SCULPTOR

b Corpus Christi, Tex, Dec 17, 1940. *Study:* Southwestern State Col, Okla, BA, 62; Tex Tech Univ; Ariz State Univ, MFA (ceramics), 70. *Work:* Whitty Mus, San Antonio; Phoenix Art Mus, Ariz; E B Crocker Art Gallery, Sacramento, Calif; Pac Lutheran Univ, Tacoma, Wash; Ariz State Univ Collection, Tempe; Sheraton Hotel, Los Angeles, Calif; Southern Conn State Univ. *Exhib:* Les Lawrence, Southplains Col, Tex, 82; Am Crafts Traditions, San Francisco Airport, Calif, 84; Ceramic Festival II, Univ Art Collections, Ariz State Univ, 85; The Cup Exhib, Salem Art Asn, Ore, 86; 200 Tea Pots, Springfield Art Asn, Ill, 87; Birthday Party, Kohler Art Ctr, Sheboygan, Wis, 88; Ceramic Invitational, Sikes Gallery, Millersville Univ, Pa, 89; Visiting Artist, Monarch Tile Nat Exhib, San Angelo Tex Mus Art, Tex, 90; Ceramic Conjunction, Long Beach Mus Art, Calif, 77; Great Am Foot, Mus Contemp Crafts, NY, 78; Solo exhibs, Gallery 2000, Seoul, Korea, 92, San Diego Mus Art, Calif, 93 & Schneider Gallery, Chicago, 94; and others. *Teaching:* Instr ceramics-sculpture, Hardin-Simmons Univ, Abilene, Tex, 66-68; prof ceramics, Grossmont Col, El Cajon, Calif, 70-; vis artist, Northern Iowa Univ, Cedar Falls, 88. *Awards:* Tex Watercolor Soc 16th Ann First Purchase Award, San Antonio Art League, 67; First Purchase Award, Region 20 Tex Fine Arts Asn, 68; Calif Crafts IX Purchase for E B Crocker Art Gallery, 75; Distinguished Alumni, South Plains Col, Tex, 87. *Bibliog:* Les Lawrence, Ceramics Monthly, 4/74 & 4/93; Studio potter, San Diego Ceramics, 93; Susan Delainey (auth), Les Lawrence New Vision Ceramics, Ceramic Art & Perception, 93. *Mem:* Am Crafts Coun; Allied Craftsmen San Diego (secy, 74); Nat Coun Educ for Ceramic Arts. *Media:* Clay. *Dealer:* Lawrence Arts 2097 Valley View Blvd El Cajon CA 92019; Martha Schneider Gallery 230 W Superior St Chicago IL 60610. *Mailing Add:* 2097 Valley View Blvd El Cajon CA 92021

LAWRENCE, RODNEY STEVEN
PAINTER

b Flint, Mich, Feb 20, 1951. *Study:* Flint Community Jr Col; Univ Mich, BFA (magna cum laude), 73. *Work:* Kalkaska Memorial Hospital. *Comn:* Painting, First Nat Park Bank, Livingston, Mont, 74; illus, Dept Interior, Washington, 82; Hamilton Collector Plates, 88 & 92. *Exhib:* CM Russell Mus, Great Falls, Mont, 76-79; Nat Wildlife Art Show, Kansas City, 80; Birds in Art Nat Tour, Leigh Yawkey Woodson Mus, Wausau, Wis, 83; Wildlife: The Artist's View, 90 & 93; Art of the Animal Kingdom X, 2005 & XIII, 2008, 2010-2012, Bennington Ctr for the Arts; Birds in Art & National Tour, Leigh Yawkey Art Mus, 2005, 2008 & 2011; Soc of Animal Artist Exhib, 2009, 2011 & 2012. *Teaching:* Beartooth Wildlife Workshop, Big Timber, Mont, 92 & 95; Cedar Bend Farm Artist's Workshop, 94; Multiple ann artist's workshops, 1984-. *Awards:* Artist of the Year, Mich Ducks Unlimited, 79; Mich Artist of the Year, Mich United Conserv Club, 81; State Chmn Award, Mich Ducks Unlimited, 85-86; Conserv Awareness Awardm Kalkaska Soil & Water Conserv Dist, 94; Artist of the Year, LeBlanc Wildlife Art Festival, 94; Judges Excellence Award, Northern Wildlife Art Expo, 94, 95; Master Palette Award, People's Choice, Masterworks in Miniature, 2006. *Bibliog:* Subject of many TV interviews on work and awards won, 81-86; Am interview with wildlife artist Rod Lawrence, Small-Towner, 83; Go mid-west young man, Midwest Art, 84; Who's Who mag, 11/88; Traverse Mag, 11/89. *Mem:* Signature mem Soc Animal Artists; signature mem Nat Wild Turkey Found. *Media:* Acrylic on Panel, Oil. *Interests:* Plein air painting, teaching workshops, hunting, playing sports. *Publ:* Illusr, Fred Bear's Field Notes, The Adventures of Fred Bear, Doubleday, 76; Complete Guide to Walleye Fishing, Willow Creek Press, 80; The Pigeon River Country, Asn Pigeon River Country, 85; Bear Paw Tackle (catalog cover), 91; Painting Wildlife Textures, Step by Step, Northlight Bks, 97; Wildlife Painting Basics, Waterfowl & Wading Birds, Northlight Bks, 2000; Wildlife, Walter Foster Pub 2004: Animals, Walter Foster Pub, 2009. *Dealer:* Mill Pond Press; Twisted Fish Gallery. *Mailing Add:* 9320 M72 SE Kalkaska MI 49646-9780

LAWRENCE, SIDNEY S
PAINTER, WRITER

b San Francisco, Calif, 1948. *Study:* Univ Calif, Berkeley, BA (art hist), 72; Univ Calif, Davis, 72-74, MA, 80. *Work:* Longwood Univ Visual Art Ctr; Lehman Art Ctr, Brooks Sch; Artery Coll; Soc Calif Pioneers; Georgetown Libr. *Exhib:* Solo exhibs, Gallery K, Washington, DC, 83, 85, 88, 92, 96 & 2001, Braunstein/Quay, 97, Robert Lehman Art Ctr, Brooks Sch, Mass, 2001 & Dist Fine Arts, 2005 & 2008, Café Leopold, 2009; Univ Calif DC Ctr, 2013; Contemp Self-Portraits from the James Goode Collection, Nat Portrait Gallery, Washington, DC, 93; Beyond Likeness: Unconventional Portraits, Montgomery Col, Md, 94; Black Art, Rockville Arts Place, Md, 95; Rockwellian Times, 57 N Artspace, Washington, 2000; Complimentary Wisc Ave Studio, Wash, 2013. *Collection Arranged:* Roger Brown Retrospective 87-88, Hirshhorn Mus & Natl Tour, Washington, DC; Red Grooms, Houston Conwill, Boyd Webb, Alison Saar, Tony Oursler, Ron Mueck, Hirshhorn, 1984-2003; Ghirardelli: 150 Yr Show, Mus Italo-Am, San Francisco, 1999; Roger Brown Southern Exposure, Auburn Univ Nat Tour, 2007-2008. *Pos:* Pub affairs officer, Hirshhorn Mus & Sculpture Garden, Smithsonian Inst, Washington, 75-2003; DC corresp, artnet.com, 2004-10; arts consultant, Katzen Am Univ, 2005. *Awards:* Award of Merit Mus Italo-Am, Am Asn State & Local Hist, 2000. *Bibliog:* Pat Kolmer (auth), Sidney Lawrence: Wall Reliefs and Drawings, Wash Rev, 6-7/92; Joe Shannon (auth), Sidney Lawrence, Art Am, 7/96; Mark Jenkins (auth), Flat & 3-D, Wash City Papers, 2005; Lennox Campello (auth), 100 DC Artists, 2010. *Mem:* Int Asn Art Critics. *Publ:* Co-auth, Music in Stone: Great Sculpture Gardens of the World, Scala Bks, 84; contbr auth, Houston Conwill--Markings on the Sand, Hirshhorn Works 1989, Washington, 90; rev var shows for Art Am, Wall Street J, 2004-2013; auth, Roger Brown, George Braziller Inc, 2007, contbr auth, Washington Art Matters, 1940-90, 2013, Southern Exposure, Univ Ala Press, 2007. *Dealer:* Adah-Rose Gallery. *Mailing Add:* 1240 29th St NW Washington DC 20007

LAWRENCE, SUSAN
ART DEALER, CONSULTANT

b New York, NY, Dec 10, 1939. *Study:* Univ Kans, BA, 61. *Pos:* Dir, Lawrence Gallery, Kansas City, Mo, 76-84; co-dir, Batz-Lawrence Gallery, Kansas City, Mo, 84-88; Lawrence Fine Art, Kansas City, Mo, 88-97; bd dir, UM-KC Gallery Art, Kansas City, Mo, 88-93, Film Soc Greater Kansas City, 91-, & Ko-Arts, supporting Tango in Kansas City, 2000-; founder & mem dir, Film Soc Greater Kansas City; Susan Lawrence Fine Art, Kansas City, Mo, 98-; bd dirs, Print Soc, Nelson Atkins Mus Art, Kansas City, Mo, 2005-, vpres, 2008, 2010-. *Mem:* Kansas City Art Gallery Asn (pres, 83-84, treas, 86); Westport Gallery Asn, Kansas City, Mo (founder & pres, 78-83); Contemp Art Soc, Kansas City (secy, 86); Print Soc, Nelson Atkins Mus Art (vice pres 2008, 2010-2012). *Specialty:* Contemporary fine art, paintings and original prints by American and European artists, including regional artists. *Mailing Add:* 2525 Main St Ste 306 Kansas City MO 64108

LAWSON, JAMES EMMETT
PHOTOGRAPHER, PRINTMAKER

b Newport News, VA, Aug 8, 1957. *Study:* Chowan Univ, BS (studio art), 2004. *Work:* Gallery on the York, Yorktown, Va; Mathews Art Gallery, Mathews, Va; Creations, Hampton, Va; Crabcake House Restaurant, Poquoson, Va; Gallery at York Hall, Yorktown, Va. *Comn:* Watermen's Mus (comn sale), Yorktown, Va, 1995; PFAC Gift Shop, Peninsula Fine Art Center, Newport News, Va, 1996; Watermen's Mus Gift Shop, Yorktown, Va, 1996. *Exhib:* Senior Exhibition, Chowan Univ, Green Hall, Murfreesboro, NC, 2004; Summer Photography Exhibition, Yates House Gallery, Deltavillie, Va, 2005; Juried Photography Show, Gallery on the York, Yorktown, Va, 2005; Posquotank Art Council Photography Show, Posquotank Art Council, Elizabeth City, NC, 2006; SAL Photography Juried Show, Suffolk Mus, Suffolk, Va, 2006; Fall Colors, This Century's Gallery, Williamsburg, Va, 2006; 2007 Miniature Show, Gallery on the York, 2007; Jamestown 400th, Charles H Taylor Art Center, Hampton Va, 2007. *Collection Arranged:* Zoom in on Newport News Photo Contest, 2008; Collection with Newport News Tourism Develop Office, Zoom in on Newport News, 2008. *Pos:* Printmaker, Gallery on the York, 10/2004-6/2007; photogr, Phoebus Arts Factory, 5/2005-2/2007; photogr, Mathews Art Group, 6/2006-2007; creation photogr, 2007-2008. *Awards:* Outstanding Young Men Am, Gallery on the York, 1984; Hon Mention, Hist Triangle Art Show, 2007; Hon Mention, Operation Spruce Up, 97, 98; Hon Mention, Fall River Renaissance, 96; Best in Show Family Fun, Best in Show for Hist & Grand Prize, Newport Nwes Nat Tourism Week Photo Contest, 2000. *Mem:* AmeriCorps Alum (1996); Peninsula Fine Arts Center (2007); Creations (exhibiting artist, 2007); Mathews Art Group (photogr, 2007); Int Soc Poets (distinguished mem); Tidewater Artist Alliance (2008); Peninsula Fine Art Ctr Art League (2008); Phoebus Art Gallery (2009). *Media:* Photographer, Printmaking, Drawing. *Res:* Nature & it's relationship with the human figure. *Specialty:* Printmaking, Photog. *Interests:* Hiking, sailing, art, travel canoeing, history, landscapes, nature. *Publ:* Int Poet Soc 2 vols, Daily Press, 2000. *Mailing Add:* 534 Blount Point Rd Newport News VA 23606-2144

LAWSON, KAROL ANN
MUSEUM DIRECTOR, CURATOR
b Davenport, Iowa, Nov 10, 1958. *Study:* Sweet Briar Col, BA, 81; Univ Va, MA, 83, PhD, 88. *Collection Arranged:* Nobody Knows the Trouble I've Seen: The Paintings and Prints of Lamar Baker, Columbus Mus, Ga, 96; Exploring Identity, Maier Mus, Va, 2001; The View from Here: The Contemp Landscape, Maier Mus, Va, 2002; Women I Have Known: A Survey of Work by Benny Andrews, Maier Mus, 2003; All of Me: Margrit Lewczuk, Maier Mus, 2004; Heart of the Matter: Recent Work by Elizabeth Murray, Maier Mus, Va, 2005; Some Kind of Wonderful: Sculpture by Jim Clark & Tara Donovan, Maier Mus, Va, 2006; Humor's Lines, Maier Mus, Va, 2007; Language Arts, Sweet Briar, 2009; Body Image, Sweet Briar, 2010; Gods and Monsters, Sweet Briar, 2011; This Green Earth, Sweet Briar, 2012; Asia, Sweet Briar, 2012; The Artists Hand, Sweet Briar, 2013. *Pos:* rsch asst, Nat Mus Am Art, Smithsonian Inst, Wash DC, 1987-91; chief cur & dir collections, Columbus Mus, Ga, 1991-99; dir, Maier Mus Art, Lynchburg, Va, 1999-2007; interim dir, Sweet Briar Col Mus & Galleries, 2008-2009; dir, Sweet Briar Coll, Art Collections, Galleries, 2009-; dir, Sweet Briar Mus, 2011-. *Teaching:* instr, Univ Va, 82-84, St Mary's Col, Maryland, 1986, Randolph-Macon Woman's Coll, 1999-2007; adj asst prof, Sweet Briar Coll, 2008-2011, vis asst prof, Sweet Briar Coll, 2011-. *Awards:* pre-doctoral fel, Nat Mus Am Art, Wash, DC, 85-86; pre doctoral fel, John Carter Brown Libr, Providence, RI, 87; post doctoral fel, Huntington Libr & Art Collections, San Marino, Calif, 1992; fel mus practice, Smithsonian Inst, 2009. *Mem:* Am Asn Mus; Va Asn Mus; Southeastern Mus Conf; Coll Art Asn; Asn Historians Am Art; Asn Acad Mus & Galleries. *Res:* 19th, 20th centuries and contemp Am Art; early landscape imagery; mus ethics; Hist of mus, prof practices in mus, mus ethics. *Specialty:* American art. *Publ:* auth, Charles Willson Peale's John Dickinson: An American Landscape As Political Allegory, Proceedings Am Philos Soc, 92; auth, An Inexhaustible Abundance: The National Landscape Depicted in American Magazines 1780-1820, J Early Repub, 92; coauth, The (Im)Permanent Collection: Lessons From A Deaccession, Museum, Jan/Feb 2009. *Mailing Add:* Sweet Briar College Sweet Briar VA 24595-1115

LAWSON, THOMAS
PAINTER, WRITER
b Glasgow, Scotland, 1951. *Study:* Univ St Andrews, MA, 73; Univ Edinburgh, MA, 75; Grad Sch City Univ NY, Phil, 81. *Work:* Chase Manhattan Bank, NY; Brooklyn Mus, NY; Scottish Arts Coun, Edinburgh; City New York; Arts Coun Gt Brit, London; Hessell Coll, Bard Coll, NY; Hammer Museum, Los Angeles; QCC Gallery, City Univ NY, Tate, London. *Comn:* Temporary mural, Manhattan Munic Bldg, Dept Gen Serv, NY; temporary mural, Dunstan Soap Works, First Tyne Int, Gateshead, Eng, 90; sculpture, Circulo de Bellas Artes, Madrid, 91. *Exhib:* The Heroic Figure, Contemp Arts Mus, Houston, 84; Civic Virtues, City Univ Grad Ctr Hall, NY, 86; Sydney Biennale, Art Gallery NSW, 86; Painting, Brooklyn Mus, Brooklyn, 87; solo exhib, San Diego Mus Contemp Art, La Jolla, 87; A Forest of Signs, Mus Contemp Art, Los Angeles, 89; First Tyne Int, Gateshead, UK, 90; 10 Yr Survey Exhib, Third Eye Ctr, Glasgow, Scotland, 90; El Sueno Imperativo, Circulo Belles Artes, Madrid, 91; Monumental Propaganda, Independent Curs, NY & Moscow, 93; Painting in the British Arts Coun, UK galleries, 94-95; Sleeper, Edinburgh, 2001; Lax Art, Los Angeles, 2007; Participant, Inc, Pictures Generations, Metrop Mus Art, New York, 2009; Made in LA, Hammer Mus, Los Angeles, 2012. *Pos:* Cur consult, The Drawing Ctr, NY, 78-81; ed, Real Life Mag, NY, 79-91; co-ed, Afterall Journal, London & Los Angeles, 2002-2009; ed-in-chief, East of Borneo, Los Angeles, 2009. *Teaching:* Instr, Sch Visual Arts, NY, 81-89; vis artist, Calif Inst Arts, spring 87 & 89, dean, 91-; grad instr, Rhode Island Sch Art Design, 87 & 88. *Awards:* Nat Endowment Arts Fel, 82-83, 85-86 & 88-89; Ucross Found, 2003; Guggenheim Fel, 2009. *Bibliog:* Richard Martin (auth), article, 11/84 & Ronald Jones (auth), article, summer 85, Arts Mag; Jeanne Silverthorne (auth), Third Eye Centre (monogr & exhib catalog), Glasgow & Anthony Reynolds, London, 90; Scott Rothkopf (auth), Artforum, Apr, 2002; Christopher Miles (auth), Artforum, summer 2007. *Mem:* Coll Art Asn. *Media:* All. *Res:* Contemp Art. *Publ:* Jet Lag & Iron Hard Jets, The British Art Show (exhib catalog), 95; Allan McCollum, Art Press, Los Angeles, 96; Looking For Something to Read, Herald J, 2002; Mining for Gold, Selected Essays, 1979-1996, JRP/Ringier, Zurich, 2004; Real Life Magazine, Selected Writings 1979-1994, Primary Information, NY, 2007. *Dealer:* Anthony Reynolds Gallery 60 Great Marlborough St, London, WIF 7B5; David Kordarksy Gallery 3143 S La Cienega Blvd Unit A Los Angeles CA 90016. *Mailing Add:* 127 Wilton Dr Los Angeles CA 90004

LAWSON-JOHNSTON, PETER ORMAN
PATRON
b New York City, Feb 8, 1927. *Study:* Univ Va, 1951. *Pos:* Reporter, yachting editor, Balt Sun Papers, 1951-53; exec dir, Md Classified Employees Asn, Balt, 1953-54; pub info dir, Md Civil Def Agency, Pikesville, 1954-56; dir, Zemex Corp, New York City, 1960-, vpres 1966-72, vchmn 1972-75, pres 1975-76, chmn 1975-2003; dir, Feldspar Corp 1959-2003, sales mgr 1956-60, vpres sales 1961-66, vpres 1966-72, chmn1972-81. *Awards:* Gertrude Vanderbilt Whitney Award, Skowhegan Sch Painting & Sculptures, 1986; Lawrenceville Medal, Lawrenceville Sch, 1997. *Mem:* Trustee, Solomon R Guggenheim Mus, 1964, vpres bus admin 1965-69, pres 1969-95, chmn 1995-98, hon chmn 1998-; pres adv bd, Peggy Guggenheim Collection; dir, Harry Frank Guggenheim Found, 1968-, chmn 1971-2011, pres emer 2011-; partner, Guggenheim Bros, 1962-70, sr partner 1971-; Pilgrims of US, Carolina Plantation Soc, US Sr Golf Asn, Edgartown Yacht Club, Edgartown Reading Room Club, Jupiter Island Club, Brook Club, Yeamans Hall Club. *Publ:* Auth, Growing Up Guggenheim: A Personal History of a Family Enterprise, 2005. *Mailing Add:* 25 W 53rd St 16 New York NY 10019-5401

LAWTON, FLORIAN KENNETH
PAINTER, LECTURER
b Cleveland, Ohio, June 20, 1921. *Study:* Cleveland Sch Art, 42 & 48-50; John Huntington Polytech Inst, 48-49; Cleveland Col, 48-49. *Work:* Cleveland Mus Art; Miami Univ, Oxford, Ohio; pvt collection of King Kahlid, Saudi Arabia; Duramax Inc, Middlefield, Ohio; Hiram Col, Ohio; Charles Miller Jr. & Paul Miller families, S Russell, Ohio; and others. *Comn:* Cleveland Citiscape, Ohio Bell Tel Co, 79; Rotek Co, Hamburg, Ger, 88; Nat Engineering Co, Cleveland, Ohio; TRW Inc, Cleveland; Carret & Co, NY; Cleveland-Clinic, Cleveland, Ohio; and others. *Exhib:* Cleveland Mus Art, 78-84; Butler Mus Am Art Nat, Youngstown, Ohio, 77-88; Nat Watercolor Soc, All-West Traveling Exhib, Los Angeles, 77-80; Salmagundi Club, NY, 78-80; Ky Watercolor Soc, Owensboro Mus, 79; Retrospective, Butler Mus Am Art, Youngstown, Ohio, 89; Am Watercolor Soc, NY; Watercolor USA, Springfield, Mo; and others. *Pos:* Art consult, Cleveland, Ohio, 72-; adv, Orange Arts Coun, Ohio, 77-; critic, 82-. *Teaching:* Instr painting & watercolor, Cleveland Inst Art, 81-; instr watercolor, Orange Arts Coun, Ohio, 77-; pvt classes. *Awards:* Grand Buckeye Leaf Award, Nat Watercolor Soc, 81; Peoples Choice Award, Great Lakes Regional, 82; First Prize & Larry Quackenbush Award, Hudson Ann, 82; Ohio Watercolor Soc, 80-84, 86, 88; Boston Mills Ann First, 86-87, 88, 89. *Bibliog:* Modern art review, Revue Mod Desarts, Paris, France, 6/70; Amish Romance (doc film), Scripps-Howard TV, Hiram Col, 75. *Mem:* Ohio Watercolor Soc; Am Watercolor Soc; Ky Watercolor Soc; Pa Watercolor Soc; Nat Watercolor Soc; Hilton Head, SC Watercolor Soc. *Media:* Mixed, Watercolor. *Res:* hist of downtown Cleveland; Ohio canal system. *Publ:* Auth, Watercolor page, In: American Artist, Watson-Guptill, 70; featured artist, fine arts prints, Mill Pond Press, Venice, Fla; Artists Mag, 3/96; Artists Mag, 11/2000; Int Artists Mag, 1-2/2001. *Dealer:* Bonfoey Co Cleveland OH; Mill Pond Press Venice FL. *Mailing Add:* 410-29 Willow Cir Aurora OH 44202

LAWTON, JAMES L
SCULPTOR, EDUCATOR
b Louisville, Ky, July 28, 1944. *Study:* Louisville Sch Art, Ky; Murray State Univ, Ky, BS; Kent State Univ, Ohio, MFA. *Work:* Western Mich Univ, Kalamazoo; City Hartland, Mich; City of Detroit, Mich; Williamston Publ Sch, Mich; Am Asian Soc, NY; Eli and Edy the Broad Art Mus at MSU, East Lansing, Mich. *Comn:* Three Trusses Plus painted steel sculpture, Cass Park, City Detroit, 77-78; Past, Present, Future, 99, Williamston Publ Sch, Mich; Forest of Hands, Mason Pub Sch, Mason, Mich, 98. *Exhib:* Solo Exhibs: Otherwise Gallery, Lansing, Mich, 94; Fine Arts Gallery, DeWaters Art Ctr, Flint, Mich, 95; Group exhibs, New Regionalism, Detroit Artist Market, Detroit, 97; The Formal Issue: The State of Sculpture in Mich Univs, Midland Ctr for Arts, 03; Denison Univ Art Gallery, Granville, OH, 04 ; A Road Show, juried, Contemp Art Inst Detroit, 85-86, Traveling ; Invitational, Structure, Object Event, Art Ctr Battle Creek, Mich, 92; Saginaw Art Mus, Mich, 91; Summer Int Sculpture Ctr Exhib, Grounds for Sculpture, Hamilton, NJ, 2003; 1st Invitational Outdoor Sculpture Exhib, Brighton, Mich, 06-, 2nd Invitational, 2009-2011; Regional Biennial Juried Sculpture Exhib, Marshall M Fredericks Sculpture Mus, Saginaw, Mich, 2010; Evolutionary Artifacts Exhib, MSU Mus, Mich State Univ, E Lansing, Mich, 2011. *Collection Arranged:* cur, 2005-2006 Fringe Festival, Mich State Univ, E Lansing, Mich; cur, Art on the Edge & Beyond: MSU's Fringe Events 06-08, Mich State Univ, E Lansing, Mich. *Pos:* Co-cur, The 12th Biennial & Beyond Boundaries, Kresgo Art Mus, E Lansing, Mich, 91 & 92; co juror, Wassenberg Art Ctr Ann, Van Wert, Ohio, 94; producer, Mapa/Corpo 2: Interactive Ritual for the New Millenium, Whaton Center for the Performing Arts, E Lansing, Mich, 2007; moderator, The New Millenium and Art, MSU, E Lansing, Mich, 2007; speaker, 2nd Ann Visual and Performing Arts Conf, Athens, Greece, 2011, Vision and Perspectives: Global Studies in the 21st Century, Nanjing, China, 2011. *Teaching:* prof sculpture, Mich State Univ & Kresge Art Ctr. *Awards:* Best of Show, 22nd Ann Paint & Sculpting Competition, Lansing, Mich; Mich State Univ Grants, 68, 79, 90 & 94; '89 Coll Res Leave & Grant Awards; Best of Show, Mich Artist Exch; Battle Creek Art Ctr, Battle Creek, Mich; 1st Place Nat Sculpture Exch, Cen Mich Univ, Mt Pleasant, Mich, 84; Creative Inclusive Excellence Grant, Mich State Univ, E. Lansing, 2005, 2006, 2008; Univ RI Coll Arts & Letts Grant; Mich State Univ, East Lansing, Mich, 2012. *Bibliog:* Darlene B Damp (article), Saginaw News, Mich, 9/91; Leslie Cavell (auth), article, Lansing Capital Times, 12/93; Grace Schott (auth), article, Flint J, 3/95; Arthur Williams (auth), The Sculpture Reference, Sculpture Books Publ; Dennis Nowrocki (auth) Art in Detroit Public Places, Wayne State Univ Press; Christopher R. Young (auth), The Flint Journal, 9/04; Evolution and Martin Luther King, Jr: Different but the Same, State News, Mich State Univ, 2011. *Mem:* Int Sculpture Ctr; Detroit Artist Market; Contemp Art Inst Detroit. *Media:* All Media. *Interests:* contemp art addressing social & political issues along with new media/multimedia. *Mailing Add:* 3485 Zimmer Rd Williamston MI 48895-9184

LAXSON, RUTH
CONCEPTUAL ARTIST, PRINTMAKER
b Roanoke, Ala, July 16, 1924. *Study:* Auburn Univ; Atlanta Coll Art. *Work:* Mus Mod Art, NY; New York Pub Libr; Yale Univ; Getty Ctr, Malibu, Calif; Sackner Collection, Miami; Victoria & Albert Mus, Tate Gallery, London; Univ Alberta, Edmonton; Brown Univ; RI Sch Design; Emory Univ; Woodruff Lib; High Mus, Atlanta; UCLA, Irwin. *Comn:* 2 lithographs, Rolling Stone Press; 1 etching, Atlanta Printmakers Studio; 2 artists' books, Nexus Press. *Exhib:* Amerikanischer Buchkunst, Zeitgenssische Handpressendruke, Hamburg, 93; Int Survey Artists Bks, Atlanta Coll Art, 94; Installation-Arts Festival Atlanta, 95; Artist Page, Art Papers, 96; Int Traveling Exhib Artists' Bks, Am Fedn Arts, 98; The Next Word, Newberger Mus, State Univ NY, 98; Connections/Contradictions, Carlos Mus, Emory Univ, 98; Drawings & Books, The Contemp, Atlanta, 99; Identity in the New Millennium, Eyedrum, 2000; Expert Narrative in Artists' Books, La State Univ, Baton Rouge, 2000; Solo Exhib: paintings & drawings, Marcia Wood Gallery, 2002, Chairs Project, Emory Univ, 2003; Reading Material, Volume, NYC, 2004; Drawn in Georgia, MOCA, Ga, Atl, 2006; Life is a Page, Marcia Wood Gallery, Ga, 2008; RISD, Privideence, RI; UCLA, Irwin; Mus Contemp Art, Atlanta, Ga; Marcia Wood, Atlanta,

Ga. *Collection Arranged:* Life is a Page (with catalog), Marcia Wood Gallery, 2008. *Pos:* dir, artist, Press 63 Plus, Atlanta. *Teaching:* Vis artist, Agnes Scott Col, Atlanta, 91; Atlanta Col, 91-92; Univ Iowa, 96. *Awards:* Acquisitions Grants, Ga Coun Arts, 89 & 90; Resident Fel, Hambidge Ctr, 95; Arts Festival Atlanta Exhib, 95; Ga Women in the Visual Arts Grant, 97; CGR Scholarship, Hambridge Ctr, 98; Nexus Press Residency, 2000. *Bibliog:* Johanna Drucker (auth), The Century of Artists Books, 95; Pattie Belle Hastings (auth), interview, J Artists' Bks, 97; Jerry Cullum (auth), review, Re-Tell the Tale, 98; Rene Hubert (auth), The Cutting Edge of Reading: Artists' Books; Glen Harper (auth), Cat Life is a Page, M Wood Gallery, 2008. *Mem:* Atlanta Coll Art Alum; Atlanta Contemp Arts Ctr; Oglethorpe Mus, Atlanta; High Mus, Atlanta; Carlos Mus, Atlanta; Carlos Mus; Carlos Mus; Emory Univ. *Media:* Printmaking, Multimedia. *Res:* Religions of the World; The Alphabet & its Effect; The Auto Culture. *Specialty:* Marcia Wood Gallery, encaustic, works on paper, multi-media. *Interests:* Word art, visual poetry, garden as art. *Publ:* Imaging, 91; Some Things are Sacred, 91, Press 63 Plus Atlanta; Wheeling, 92; Measure up, 95; Letters to the Ether/Other, 96; Retell the Tale, Art Papers, 98; Muse Measures, 99; Mythos Chronos Logos, 2000; A Hundred Years of: Lex Flex, Nexus Press, 2003; Ideas of God, 2008; Press 63 Plus Atlanta; (Ho+Go)2 = It, Nexus Press, Atlanta, 86. *Dealer:* Marcia Wood Gallery Atlanta; Vamp & Tramp Birmingham Ala; Printed Matter New York. *Mailing Add:* 2298 Drew Valley Rd Atlanta GA 30319

LAY, PATRICIA ANNE
SCULPTOR
b New Haven, Conn, Aug 14, 1941. *Study:* Rochester Inst Technol, MFA; Pratt Inst, BS. *Work:* NJ State Mus, Trenton; Rochester Inst Technol; IBM; Rutgers Univ; Henie-Onstad Mus, Oslo. *Comn:* Montclair State Col, 85 & 96. *Exhib:* Solo Shows, Douglass Coll Women Artists Series, 73, NJ State Mus, 74, Jersey City Mus, 87 & Condeso/Lawler Gallery, NY, 92; Contemp Reflections, Aldrich Mus, Ridgefield, Conn, 75; Whitney Mus Am Art Biennial, 75; Structures: 13 NJ Artists, Montclair Art Mus, 84; Noyes Mus, NJ, 89; NY: Clay (traveling), Norway, 95-96; Six Artists: The 1990's, NJ State Mus, 96; Transcending Boundaries, Mi Qiu Modern Art Workshop, Coll Fine Arts, Shanghai Univ, China, 99; 1999 East and West, Soho 20 Gallery, 99; Lives and Works, The Exhibition, Ceres Gallery, NY, 2000; NJ Fine Arts Annual, Jersey City Mus, 2002; Wish You Were Here Too! AIR Gallery, NY, 2003; Altars, Icons and Symbols: Exploring Spirituality in Art, Noyes Mus, NJ, 2004. *Teaching:* Asst prof sculpture, State Univ NY Buffalo, 68-69; instr ceramics, Wagner Col, 69-71; lectr ceramics, Hunter Col, 71-72; prof sculpture & ceramics, Montclair State Univ, 72-. *Awards:* NJ State Coun Fel in Sculpture, 84 & 88; Am Scandinavian Found, 96. *Bibliog:* Leon Nigrosh (auth), Claywork, 75, 2nd ed, 86 & Low Fire: Other Ways to Work in Clay, 80, Davis Publ; Susan Peterson (auth), The Craft & Art of Clay, Prentice Hall, NJ, 92, 2nd ed, 95; J Arbeiter, B Smith & S Swenson (auths), Lives & Works: Talks with Women Artists, Vol II, Scarecrow Press, 96. *Media:* Clay, Metal. *Mailing Add:* 77 Grand St Jersey City NJ 07302

LAYNE, BARBARA J
INSTRUCTOR
b Seattle, Wash, Jan 12, 1952. *Study:* Univ Colo, BFA, 79; Univ Kans, MFA, 82. *Work:* SC State Art Collection, Columbia; Cent d'Art Graphique, Romainmotier, Switz; Fed Reserve Bank Richmond, Charlotte, NC. *Exhib:* The HUB, Lincolnshire, Eng, 2005; Montreal Centre Contemp Textiles, 2006; Int Biennale Design, France, 2006; The Canadian Embassy, Washington, DC, 2007. *Teaching:* prof fibers, Concordia Univ, Montreal, 89-. *Awards:* Hexagram Research Grant, 2003-2006; Principal Investigator, CFI Infrastructure Grant, 2004-2007; Social Science & Humanities Research Grant, 2005-. *Bibliog:* Betty Ann Brown (auth), Expanding Circles, 96; Kim Sawchuk (auth), Barbara Layne & Ingrid Bachmann, Parachute Mag, 96; Mark Newport (auth), Fiberarts, 98; and others. *Mem:* Coll Art Asn; Textile Soc Am. *Media:* Electronic Textiles. *Res:* Interactive textiles & wearable computing at the Hexagram Institute for Media Arts & Technology, Montreal. *Publ:* Auth, Paper Art in America, Leopold Hoesch Mus, Duren, WGer, 86; auth, Migrant Textiles, Telos Art Publ, 2001; auth, Barbara Layne (catalog), Portfolio Collection, Telos Art Publ, 2003. *Mailing Add:* Dept Studio Arts Concordia Univ EV2-823 1515 St Catherine W Montreal PQ H3G 2W1 Canada

LAYNE, MARGARET MARY
DIRECTOR
Pos: Exec dir, Huntington Mus Art, currently. *Mailing Add:* Huntington Mus Art 2033 McCoy Rd Huntington WV 25701-4999

LAZANSKY, EDWARD
PAINTER, EDUCATOR
b Brooklyn, NY, Oct 31, 1930. *Study:* Syracuse Univ, Syracuse, NY, BFA, 1952; Iowa Univ, Cranbrook Acad, 1953; Oberlin Coll, Oberlin, Ohio, MA, 1954; Ecole Des Beaux-Arts, Paris, France, studied with Maurice Brianchon, 1960-1961; Art Students League, studied with Edwin Dickinson, 1958-1960; La Sorbonne, Paris, studied with Andre Chastel, 1960-1961. *Work:* Archive Am Art (Smithsonian Inst), Washington, DC; Portrait (oil), Jason Leese, Paris, France, 1961. *Comn:* Portrait (oil), Edwin Dickinson, New York, NY, 1958; Portrait (oil), David K Gordon, New York, NY, 1959; Mural (figurative), Leonard Slatkes, New York, NY, 1980; Portrait (oil), Rachel Weast, Berkeley, Calif, 2005. *Exhib:* Painting Ann, Everson Mus, Syracuse, NY, 1952; Print & Drawing Ann, Butler Inst Am Art, Youngstown, Ohio, 1953; Print Ann, Brooklyn Mus, Brooklyn, NY, 1953; Ann (art), Allen Art Mus, Oberlin, Ohio, 1954; Doane Art Gallery, Denison Univ, 1954; Painting Ann, Nat Acad Design, New York, NY, 1976; Art Ann, Rubelle & Alan Shafler Gallery, Brooklyn, NY, 2002, 2005, 2007; Bertha Schaefer, Prince Street, March, James, Greene & Phoenix galleries, New Bedford Art Mus, 2004; Woodstock Art Mus, 2007; Kleinert-James Gallery, 2010-11. *Pos:* Theatrical Designer, United Scenic Artists, NYC, 1980-1990; and numerous TV, film, & stage productions. *Teaching:* instr, art & design, Swain Sch Design, New Bedford, Mass, 1965-1967; instr, Queens Coll, New York, NY, 1967-1969; prof, art & design, Pratt Inst, Brooklyn, NY, 1967-2012. *Awards:* First Prize, PTG, Syracuse Mus Ann, 1952; Scholar, Found des Etats-Unis, Harriet Hale Woolley Found, 1960; Henry Schnakenberg Prize, Art Students League, Henry Schnakenberg, 1960. *Bibliog:* Featurefilms of Sidney Lumet (dir), The Verdict, Paramount Films, 1980; Alan J Pakula (dir), Rollover, Independent Production, 1981; Francis Coppola (dir), The Cotton Club, Robert Evans (prod), 1982; Theater work of Richard Foreman (auth), Lines of Vision; Gertrude Stein (auth), The Making of Americans, Listen to Me, Dr Faustus Lights the Lights, Judson Poet's Theater, 1975-1976; George Balanchine (choreo), Jewels (Ballet), New York City Ballet, 1986. *Mem:* UFCT; United Scenic Artists. *Media:* Miscellanious Media. *Interests:* Violin, Hiking, Fossil, Collecting. *Dealer:* Arlene Freedman 201 East 66th St NY 10021. *Mailing Add:* PO Box 96 Woodstock NY 12498

LAZARUS, LOIS
PAINTER
b Brooklyn, NY, Aug 25, 1931. *Study:* Cooper Union, Art/Arch, 1952; Univ of Miami, BA, 1965; Hofstra Univ, MA, 1975. *Work:* San Francisco Mus of Mod Art, San Francisco, Calif; Los Angeles Mus of Mod Art, Los Angeles, Calif; El Paso Mus, El Paso, Tex; De Young, San Francisco, Calif. *Exhib:* New Painters, Archives of Venice Biernale Contemp Art, Venice, Italy, 1952; Los Angeles Co Painters, Los Angeles Mus of Mod Art, Los Angeles, CA, 1957-65; San Francisco col, San Francisco Mus, San Francisco, CA, 1957-73; Miami Painters, El Paso, El Paso, Tex, 1968; Norton Gallery, Palm Beach, FL, 1970; De Young Mus, San Francisco, CA, 1979-84; Retrospect, Pratt Inst, New York, NY, 2005. *Teaching:* adj prof painting, Pratt Inst, New York, NY, 2003-06, adj prof architecture, 2003-06. *Media:* All Media. *Publ:* Auth, contribr, With These Hands They Built A Nation, 1979; auth, contribr, Country Is My Music, 1983. *Mailing Add:* 792 Columbus Ave Ste 2E New York NY 10025

LAZZARINI, ROBERT
SCULPTOR
b Parsippany, NJ, 1965. *Study:* Parsons Sch Design, Grad, 85; Sch Visual Arts, NY City, BFA, 90. *Work:* Current/Undercurrent: Working in Brooklyn, Brooklyn Mus Art, 1997, The Whitney Biennial, Whitney Mus Art, 2002, first solo mus exhib, robert lazzarini, Va Mus Fine Arts, 2003-04 (Award for Best Exhib of Digital Art, Inter Asn Art Critics/USA, 2005). *Exhib:* Group exhibs, Intercourse, Mustar, Brooklyn, 94, Soup, 10, Brooklyn, 94, Second Independents Biennial, Galeria El Bohio, New York City, 94 & 96, Self Images, HBO Corp Gallery, New York City, 96, Gramercy Int, Gramercy Hotel, Gina Fiore Salon, New York City, 96, Genuine Fiction, W-139, Amsterdam, 97, Gramercy Int, Gramercy Hotel, Pierogi 2000, New York City, 97, Current/Undercurrent: Working in Brooklyn, NY Drawers, Gasworks Gallery, London, 97, The House, Manchester, 97, Invitational 98, Stefan Stux Gallery, New York City, 98, Multiple Sensations, Yerba Buena Ctr for the Arts, San Francisco, 2000, Haulin' Ass, Post, Los Angeles, 2000, Minutiae, Southeastern Ctr for Contemp Art, Winston-Salem, NC, 2000, Pierogi Flat Files, Block Artspace, Kansas City, Mo, 2001, Bitstreams, Brent Sikkema Gallery, New York City, 2001, Situated Realities: Works from Silicon Elsewhere, Md Inst Coll Art, 2002, On Perspective, Gallery Faurschou, Copenhagen, 2002. *Awards:* Visual Arts Grant, NY Found for Arts, 85 & 86

LE, AN-MY
PHOTOGRAPHER
b Vietnam, 1960. *Study:* Stanford Univ, BA, 82, MS, 85; Yale Univ Sch Art, MFA (photog), 93. *Work:* Mus Mod Art & Metrop Mus, NY; Mus Fine Arts, Houston; Mus Mod Art, San Francisco; Bibliotheque Nationale, Paris. *Exhib:* MFA Thesis Exhib, Art & Archit Gallery, Yale Univ, 93; Wings of Change: Images of Contradiction and Consensus, Dir Guild Am, Los Angeles, 93; Building, Dwelling, Thinking, Lowinski Gallery, NY, 94; Picturing Asia Am: Communities, Cult, Difference (traveling exhib), Hunt Gallery, Webster Univ, St Louis & Silver Eye Ctr Photog, Pa, 94-96; Picturing Communities, Houston Ctr Photog, 97; New Photog 13, Mus Mod Art, NY, 97; Re-Imaging Vietnam, Fotofest, 98; Vietnam, Scott Nichols Gallery, San Francisco, 99. *Pos:* Staff photogr, Compagnons du Devoir, France, 86-91; freelance photogr, 93-. *Teaching:* Asst, Photog Dept, Yale Univ Sch Art, 92; lectr photog, Art Dept, Stanford Univ, 96, Continuing Studies Dept, 97, Fordham Univ & NY Univ, 98; vis asst prof, Bard Col, 99. *Awards:* Blair Dickenson Mem Award, Yale Univ Sch Art, 93; Photog Fel, NY Found Arts, 96; John Simon Guggenheim Mem Found Fel, 97; Louis Comfort Tiffany Found Grant, 2009; Named a MacArthur Fellow, John D & Catherine T MacArthur Found, 2012. *Mailing Add:* 25 Monroe Pl Apt 2C Brooklyn NY 11201-2615

LE, DINH
PHOTOGRAPHER
Study: Univ Calif, Santa Barbara, BA (fine arts), 89; Sch Visual Arts full scholar, 90-92, New York, MFA (photog, digital imaging), 92. *Comn:* Accountability? (poster/postcard proj), Creative Time, NY & Los Angeles, 92; Race, Gender & Sexuality (poster proj), Painted Bride Gallery, Philadelphia, 93; Collaboration, Bronx Mus, Montefiore Family Health Ctr, NY, 96; Biography Memorial, Bronx Coun Arts, Woodlawn Cemetery, NY, 95. *Exhib:* Solo exhibs, Univ Ctr Art Gallery, Santa Barbara, Calif, 89, Art Studio Gallery, Santa Barbara, Calif, 89, Midtown Y Photog Gallery, NY, 90, Los Angeles Contemp Exhibs, 91, Visual Art Gallery, NY, 92 & Tyler Sch Art Gallery, Elkins, Pa, 92, Project 93: Dinh Q Le, 2011; Nat Mus Art, Kyoto, Japan, 92; Inst Contemp Art, Boston, 94; retrospective (traveling), Betteravia Gallery, Santa Maria, Calif, Elverhoy Mus, Solvang, Calif & Ro Snell Gallery, Santa Barbara, Calif, 94; San Francisco Mus Mod Art, 94; Points of Entry (traveling, with catalog), Friends Photog, Ansel Adams Ctr, San Francisco, Calif, 95; Portland Inst Contemp Art, Ore, 96; The Present (H)OUR, Oakland Mus, Calif, 96; A Labor of Love, New Mus, NY, 96; CEPA Gallery, Buffalo, NY, 97-98. *Awards:* Individual Fel, Art Matters Inc, NY, 92; Dupont Fel, Art Inst Boston, 94; Photog Fel, Nat Endowment Arts, 94-95. *Bibliog:* Karen Lipson (auth), An angry voice from Vietnam, NY Newsday, 12/8/92; Joanne Silver (auth), East and west woven into art, Boston Herald, 2/16/94; Cate McQuaid (auth), For Christ's sake, Boston Phoenix, 3/3/94. *Dealer:* CEPA Gallery 617 Main St Suite 201 Buffalo NY 14203. *Mailing Add:* 13055 Silver Creek St Moorpark CA 39021

LEA, STANLEY E
COLLAGE ARTIST, PRINTMAKER, PAINTER
b Joplin, Mo, Apr 5, 1930. *Study:* Pittsburg State Univ, BFA; Univ Ark, MFA. *Work:* Smithsonian Inst & Libr Cong, Washington, DC; Brit Mus, London; Inst Mex Norteamericano, Mex City; Mus Fine Arts, Houston. *Comn:* Collagraphs, Hyatt Regency Hotel, Houston, 72; paintings, Ft Worth Nat Bank, 73, Citizens Bank, Richards, Tex, 74, Am Nat Bank, Austin, 74 & USAA Bldg, San Antonio, 74; City of Hunstville (mural), Bradford Hotel, Dallas, Tex. *Exhib:* 48th Ann Soc Am Graphic Artists, New York, 67; Mainstreams Int, Marietta, Ohio, 68; Watercolor USA, Springfield, Mo, 69; 148th Ann Nat Acad Design, New York, 73; Nat Color Print USA, Lubbock, Tex, 74; and numerous others. *Teaching:* Prof printmaking & painting, Sam Houston State Univ, Huntsville, Tex, 61-93; vis prof, Mus Fine Arts, Houston, 68-71; retired 93. *Awards:* Casa Argentina Grant for Creative Work, Buenos Aires, 73; Award, 68th Nat Tex Fine Arts, 79; and others. *Bibliog:* Gerald F Brommer (auth), Art of Collage, Davis, Publ, Inc, 78 & Collage Techniques, 94; Betty Foster (auth), Biog Sketch, 87. *Media:* Mixed Media. *Mailing Add:* 3324 Winter Way Huntsville TX 77340

LEACH, ELIZABETH ANNE
ART DEALER, WRITER
b Salinas, Calif, Mar 2, 1957. *Study:* Scripps Col, Claremont, Calif, BA, 79; study with Arthur Stevens, Roland Reiss & Carl Hertel. *Collection Arranged:* Architecture of Monterey Peninsula (coauth, catalog), Monterey Mus, 76; Permanent Collection, Heathman Hotel, 84; co-cur, Curator's Choice, Ore Art Inst, 86; cur, Corporate Collections, Ore Business Committee Arts, Heathman Hotel, 86 & 89; cur, Photography Collection, Tonkin Torp Galen Marmaduke & Booth, 90. *Pos:* Asst dir, Galerie de Tours, Pebble Beach, Calif, 76; consult for archit survey, Hollywood Revitalization Comt, 78; dir, Elizabeth Leach Gallery, Portland, Ore, 81-, chair, Visual Arts Comt, Artquake, 87-89; adv bd, Artfair Seattle, 90-. *Bibliog:* Megan McMorran (auth), Leach Will Agree, Bus J Mag, 8/13/84; Dorothy Smith (auth), article, in: Daily J Commerce, 11/8/84; Stephanie Martin (auth), article, in: Pac Northwest Mag, 4/85; Randy Gragg (auth), A Gallery for Our Time, Oregonian, 5/91. *Mem:* Portland Ctr Visual Arts (bd mem, 84-); Ore Art Inst; Chair of Visual Art Comt Artquake, 87. *Specialty:* Contemporary fine art. *Publ:* Auth, Art as an investment, Inst Managers & Prof Women, 81

LEAF, JUNE
PAINTER, SCULPTOR
b Chicago, Ill, 1929. *Study:* Roosevelt Univ, Chicago, BA (art educ), 54; Inst Design, Chicago, MA (art educ), 54; DePaul Univ, LHD, 84. *Work:* Mus Mod Art, NY; Art Inst Chicago & Mus Contemp Art; Smithsonian Inst, Washington, DC; Madison Art Ctr, Wis; Coll Cape Breton, Sydney, NS, Can. *Exhib:* Torment, Whitney Mus Am Art, NY, 70; solo exhibs, Coll Cape Breton Art Gallery, Sydney, NS, 82, Dalhousie Art Gallery, Halifax, NS, 82, NDak Mus Art, 83, Optica Gallery, Montreal, Can, 85, Edward Thorp Gallery, NY, 85, 88, 95 & 97, A Survey of Painting, Sculpture and Works on Paper, 1948-1991, traveling, Wash Proj Arts, DC, 91 & Works on Paper, 1969-1970, Va Lust Gallery, NY, 91, Edward Thorp, New York, 2010; Edward Thorp Gallery, NY, 86-98; Phyllis Kind Gallery, Chicago, Ill, 89; Collector's Choice, Ctr Arts, Vero Beach, Fla, 92; Terra Firma-Five Immigrant Artists, Art Gallery, Mt St Vincent Univ, NS, Can, 93; Deplacements, La Chambre Blanche, Que, Can, 94; Prodigal Daughter, Rockford Coll Art Gallery, Ill, 95; Sniper's Nest: Art that has Lived with Way R Lippard, Bard Col, NY, 95; Small as a Way of Working, Owen Art Gallery, Mount Allison Univ, New Brunswick, Can, 96; Women Chicago Imagists, Rockford Art Mus, Ill, 96; Making Music, Champion Int Corp, Stamford, Conn, 97; Body Double, Winston Wachter Fine Art, NY, 98. *Pos:* Instr painting & drawing, Art Inst Chicago, 54-58, Parson Sch Art & Design, NY, 66-68. *Awards:* Can Coun Arts Award, 78 & 84; Nat Endowment Arts, 89; Alumni, Award, Chicago Inst Technol, 96. *Bibliog:* John Yau (auth), Original desire, ARTS Mag, 11/91; Nancy Stapen (auth), June Leaf's emphatically female figure Imagery, Boston Globe, 12/91; Let us now praise artist's artists, Art & Auction, 4/93. *Media:* All Media. *Mailing Add:* 7 Bleecker St New York NY 10012

LEAF, RUTH
PRINTMAKER, INSTRUCTOR
b New York, NY. *Study:* New Sch Social Res, New York, with Anthony Toney; Atelier 17 with William Stanley Hayter. *Work:* NY Univ; US Info Agency; Bowdoin Coll Mus Art; Colgate Univ; Portland Mus; Lib of Congress; Northeastern Univ; Mus Tex Tech Univ; Spencer Mus Art, Laurence, Kans. *Exhib:* Sala Exposiciones, Escuela Nac Artes Plasticas, 67; Boston Mus, 70; De Cordova Mus, Mass, 71; Soc Am Graphic Artists, NY, 71; Galerie Art & Gravure, Paris, 72; Northeast Col, Maine; The Print Center, New York City. *Collection Arranged:* permanent collection at Northeastern Univ; Queensborough Community Coll. *Pos:* Consult, Colby Col, Maine. *Teaching:* Instr intaglio, NShore Community Art Ctr, 69-. *Awards:* Purchase Awards, Libr Cong, 46, Hofstra Univ, 63 & Olivet Col, 67; Nassau Mus Prize, 94. *Bibliog:* Ron Perkins (auth), Artists at Work--Filmstrip 4, Jam Handy Sch Serv, 70; Interview with artist, Art in the World radio prog, Nassau Community Col. *Mem:* Soc Am Graphic Artists; Print Center, Philadelphia; Los Angeles Print Soc. *Media:* Graphics, Paper Works. *Publ:* Auth, Intaglio Printing Techniques, Watson-Guptill; Etching, Engraving & Other Intaglio Techniques, Dover. *Dealer:* Robin Ficara; Sondra Mayer; Carolin Silver; Dr Jane Spiegel. *Mailing Add:* 711 Boccaccio Ave Venice CA 90291

LEARSY, RAYMOND J
COLLECTOR
b Luxembourg. *Study:* Univ Pa. *Pos:* Appointee, Nat Endowment for the Arts, 1982-88. *Awards:* Named one of Top 200 Collectors, ARTnews mag, 2004-13; recipient Gertrude Vanderbilt Whitney Award for outstanding arts patronage & philanthropy (with Melva Bucksbaum), 2004. *Mem:* Whitney Mus Am Art; Woodrow Wilson Int Ctr for Scholars; Tate Gallery. *Collection:* Contemporary art. *Publ:* Auth, Over a Barrel: Breaking Oil's Grip on Our Future; auth, Oil and Finance: The Epic Corruption, 2006-2010; auth, Oil and Finance: The Epic Corruption Continues, 2010-2012; contbr, The Huffington Post. *Mailing Add:* 253 Amelia Union Rd Sharon CT 06069

LEARY, DANIEL
PAINTER, PRINTMAKER
b Glens Falls, NY, July 20, 1955. *Study:* Antioch Coll, Yellow Springs, Ohio, BFA, 79; Syracuse Univ, MFA, 96. *Work:* Metrop Mus Art, New York, NY; Libr Cong, Washington, DC; NY Pub Libr, New York, NY; Yale Univ Art Gallery, New Haven, Conn; Univ Indianapolis; Williams Coll Mus Art; Zimmerli Art Mus, Rutgers Univ, New Brunswick, NJ. *Exhib:* Solo exhibs, Printworks Ltd, 88, Hyde Collection, Glens Falls, NY, 90, Printworks Gallery, Chicago, 91, 95, Blanden Mem Art Mus, Ft Dodge, Iowa, 92, Bobbit Visual Arts Ctr, Albion Coll, Mich, 93, Sharon Campbell Gallery, Greenville, SC, 94, Western Mich Univ, 94, New Monotypes, Printworks Gallery, Chicago, Ill, 95, Self Portraits, Printworks Gallery, 2000, Greenville Co Fine Arts Center, SC, 2002, Landscapes, Tannery Pond Community Ctr Gallery, North Creek, NY, 2003, The Fine Art Ctr, Greenville, SC, 2008; Group exhibs, Bradford Art Mus & Galleries, West Yorkshire, Eng, 90; 50 at 50: Five Decades of Collecting, Hyde Coll, Glens Falls, NY, 2013; Face Forward: The Art of the Self Portrait, Printworks Gallery, Chicago, Ill, 2013; Self Portraits: Susanna Coffey, Susan Haputman, Daniel Leary, Elaine L Jacobs Gallery, Wayne State Univ, Detroit, Mich, 99; Expression: Portraits from the Permanent Collection, Plattsburgh State Art Mus, Suny Plattsburgh, 2009; Size Matters! Selections from the Permanent Collection, Zanesville Art Mus, Zanesville, Oh, 2010. *Awards:* New York Found Arts Fel, 88; Nat Endowment Arts, 89; Adirondack Community Coll Found Grant, 2009. *Bibliog:* Alan G Artner (auth), Leary portraits etched with discernment, Chicago Tribune, 1/6/89; Gordon Ligocki (auth), Young artist drawing powerful figures, The (Hammond, Indiana) Times, 8/24/90; Alan G Artner (auth), Leary drawings reflect rare craft, insight, Chicago Tribune, 10/4/91; contribr, The Lens of Poetry, Essays and Poems by William Bronk, 2011. *Media:* All Media. *Dealer:* Printworks Gallery 311 W Superior St Suite 105 Chicago IL 60610. *Mailing Add:* PO Box 384 Hudson Falls NY 12839-0384

LEATHERDALE, MARCUS ANDREW
PHOTOGRAPHER
b Montreal, Que, Sept 18, 1952. *Study:* Ecole Des Beaux Arts, Montreal, 70-73; Art Ctr, Los Angeles, BFA, 74; San Francisco Art Inst, BFA (hon student), 75-77. *Work:* Madison Art Ctr, Wis; Australian Art Gallery, Canberra; New Orleans Mus Art, La; Vienna Mus Mod Art, Austria; Art Inst Chicago, Ill. *Exhib:* Solo exhibs, London Regional Art Gallery, Ont, 83, Rheinisches Landes Mus, Bonn, Ger, 84, Greathouse Gallery, NY, 84, 85, 86 & 87, Claus Runkel Fine Arts, London, Eng, 88, Wessel O'Connor Gallery, NY, 89, Fay Gold Gallery, Atlanta, Ga, 90 & Fahey Klein Gallery, La, 90; Brent Sikkema, NY, 90; Arthur Roger Gallery, New Orleans, 91, NY, 92; Galerie del Conte, Milwaukee, 92; Galerie Bardamu, NY, 93. *Awards:* Nat Endowment Arts Award for Photog, 84. *Bibliog:* Brook Adams (auth), Marcus Leatherdale 1984-1987, Greathouse Gallery, New York, 88; Peggy Cypher (auth), Marcus Leatherdale, Arts, 89; Ali Anderson Spivy (auth), Argonaut, 94. *Dealer:* Fahey-Klein Gallery Los Angeles CA; Brent Sikkemma Fine Arts 155 Spring St New York NY 10012. *Mailing Add:* c/o Fahey Klein Gallery 148 N La Brea Ave Los Angeles CA 90036

LEAVENS, EVELYN
PAINTER
b Brooklyn, NY, Sept 25, 1924. *Study:* Monmouth Univ, NJ, 70's; Vt Studio Ctr, Vt, 90's; Studied with Neil Welliver, Malcom Marley, & Archie Road, 90's. *Work:* Pfizer, Inc, Parsippany, NJ; Hoffman-La Roche, NY; Simon & Schuster, NY; Estate of William "Count" Basie, Red Bank, NJ. *Comn:* various portraitures. *Exhib:* NJ State Mus, Trenton, NJ, 77-80; Morris Mus, Morristown, NJ, 85; Monmouth Coll, W Long Branch, NJ, 80; City Without Walls, Newark, 90; Small Treasures, Sue Berk Fine Art, New York, 97; R Cummings Gallery, Moscow, Vt, 99; Shore Inst of Contemp Art, Long Branch, NJ, 2007; Nat Juried Audubon Artists, Salmagundi Club, 2009; Retrospective, Monmouth Mus, NJ, 2010. *Pos:* lithographer, Graphics House, Manalapan, NJ, 1960s . *Teaching:* Watercolor demonstrator, Monmouth Reform Temple, Tinton Falls, NJ,a 2000; pvt teaching (design, oil, watercolor, pastel), Red Bank, NJ, 41-2009. *Awards:* Warner Lambert, NJ Watercolor Soc, 76; Fel, NJ State Coun of the Arts, 80, 85; Princeton Bank Award, Garden State WCS, 83; Hemlick Award, NJ Watercolor Soc, 83; Women of Achievement for Arts, Monmouth Co Adv Comn on Status of Women, 88. *Bibliog:* Fellowship Award, NY Times, 85; Showing City Without Walls, Newark Star Ledger; Joan Labanca, Creative Lunacy, Monmouth Co Art Coun, 2008. *Mem:* Guild of Creative Arts (founding mem), Shrewsbury, NJ; Monmouth Mus, Lincroft, NJ; Monmouth Co Art Coun, Red Bank, NJ; Art Alliance of Red Bank, NJ; Audubon Artists, New York. *Publ:* Auth & illusr, Boswell's Life of Boswells, Simon & Schuster, 58. *Dealer:* NEH Visual Art 57 Lennox Ave Rumson NJ 07760; Laurel Tracy Gallery 10 White St Red Bank, NJ 07701; James Yarosh Associates Fine Art Gallery 55 E Main St Holmdel NJ 07732

LEAVEY, JOHN CHRISTOPHER
PAINTER
b Bronx, NY, Mar 21, 1937. *Study:* studied under George Grosz, Robert Beverly Hale, Edwin Dickinson, Arts Students League, New York City, 55-61 (scholar, 60). *Hon Degrees:* Fel, Am Acad in Rome. *Work:* Museo Della Citta Roma; Hirschhorn Collection Nat Gallery, Washington, DC; Readers Digest Collection, Pleasantville, NY; Atelier-AJE, NY; Dickinson Col, Carlisle, Pa; Pfizer Co, NYC. *Comn:* mural, Am Acad Rome, 70; mural, Pfizer Co, New York City. *Exhib:* Annual Exhib, Nat Acad Design, NY, 61, 63, 78, 88 & 90; Anniversary, Mus Della Citta Roma, 70; 4 Am Painters, Am Acad Rome, 72; Audubon Artists, Nat Arts Club, New York City, NY, 94 -2009; 5 Landscape Painters, Mus Art, Springfield, Mass, 97; Blue Mountain Gallery, New York City, 80, 84, 87 & 89, 90-2005; Southern Vt Art Ctr, 96 & 98, 2003-2005; Bennington Mus, Bennington, Vt, 2007. *Pos:* Scenic Painter, Metropolitan Opera, 85-88, NYC; Paperhill Playhouse, NJ, 88-2001; O.L.L.I, 2004. *Teaching:* instr Renaissance Art & art history, St Stephens Sch, Rome, Italy, 72-73; instr painting landscapes, Southern Vt Art Cen, 2000-2002; instr, Renaissance Art, 2003. *Awards:* Prix de Rome 70-71; Louis Comfort Tiffany Grant, 65; B Altman Figure Prize Nat

Acad of Design, 88; RB McNeely Award, Audubon Artists, 95; Art Students League Award, Audubon Artists, 00. *Mem:* United Scenic Artists; Fel Am Acad Rome; Audubon Artists; Southern Vt Artists; Art Students League. *Media:* Oil, Acrylic. *Dealer:* Elaine Beckwith Gallery Jamaica VT; Blue Mountain Gallery New York NY

LEAVITT, THOMAS WHITTLESEY
MUSEUM DIRECTOR
b Boston, Mass, Jan 8, 1930. *Study:* Middlebury Col, AB, 51; Boston Univ, MA, 52; Harvard Univ, PhD, 58. *Collection Arranged:* New Renaissance in Italy (auth, catalog), Pasadena Art Mus, Calif, 58; Piet Mondrian (auth,catalog), Santa Barbara Mus Art, Calif, 65; Am Portraits in California Collections (auth, catalog), Santa Barbara Mus Art, 66; Brucke (auth, catalog), Cornell Univ, 70, Georg Kolbe (auth, catalog), 72; Seymour Lipton (auth, catalog), Herbert F Johnson Mus Art, 73; Directions in Afro-Am Art, 74; Painting Up Front (auth, catalog), Herbert F Johnson Mus Art, 81; Masters of Contemporary Art in Poland, 86; Agnes Denes, Cornell Univ, 92; Unto the Fifth Generation: The Vanderbilts as Artists (auth, catalog), Newport Art Mus, 95. *Pos:* Asst to dir, Fogg Art Mus, 54-56; exec dir, Fine Arts Comn, People to People Prog, 57; dir, Pasadena Art Mus, 57-63, Santa Barbara Mus Art, 63-68, Andrew Dickson White Mus Art, Cornell Univ, 68-72 & Herbert F Johnson Mus, Cornell Univ, 73-91; dir mus prog, Nat Endowment Arts, 71-72, mem mus adv panel, 72-75; trustee, Am Fed Arts, 72-91 & Newport Art Mus, 95-2001; interim dir, RI Sch Design Mus, Providence, 93-94, Newport Art Mus, RI, 94-95; interim dir, Menil Collection, Houston, Tex, 99-2000. *Teaching:* Lectr Am art, Univ Calif, Santa Barbara, 64-65; prof hist art, Cornell Univ, 68-92. *Awards:* Distinguished Serv to Mus Award, Am Asn Mus, 97. *Mem:* Coll Art Asn Am; Am Asn Mus (coun mem, 76-79, vpres, 80-82, pres, 82-85); Asn Art Mus Dirs (pres, 77-78); Independent Sector (bd mem, 80-84); Am Fedn Arts; Williamstown Regional Art Conserv Lab (pres, 85-87, bd dir, 88-91). *Res:* American 19th & 20th century painting. *Publ:* auth, Artists & Museums: Tensions and Intentions, Q A J Art, Cornell Univ, 5/89; intro in: Agnes Denes, Herbert F Johnson Mus Art, 92; many others; Let the Dogs Bark: George Loring Brown and the Critics, Am Art Rev, 74. *Mailing Add:* 25 Water Way Saunderstown RI 02874

LEBEJOARA, OVIDIU
PAINTER, SCULPTOR
b Ciupa Arges, Romania, Dec 14, 1952; US & Romanian citizen. *Study:* N Tonitza Sch Art, Bucharest, BFA, 73; Otis Parsons Inst Art, Los Angeles, BA, 88; Syracuse Univ, MA, 98. *Exhib:* Contemp Portraits, Barnsdall Art Ctr, Los Angeles Municipal Art Gallery, Calif, 96; Art Addiction, Int Art Gallery Stockholm, Sweden, 96-97; Ucci Gallery, New York, 96; Pasadena Art Space, Calif, 96; Retrospective Exposition, Minister Cult, Romania, 96; City Los Angeles Cult Affairs Dept, Munic Art Gallery, 97; Institut Int D'Arts Plastiques, Grand Prix Du Japon, Saporo, Japan, 97; Art World Gallery, SoHo, New York, 97; Absolut Chalk, a street festival in Pasadena, Calif, 97; New World Art Ctr, New York, 98; First Int Biennial Trevi Flash Art Mus, Palazzo Lucarini Trevi, Perugia, Italy, 98; Forth Ann Int Miniature Art Show, Seaside Art Gallery, NC, 98; Open Call Exhib S Calif Artists, City Los Angeles, Cult Affairs Dept, 98; Flecher Gallery, Woodstock, NY, 2000; The Millennium Art Collection, 2003; Limnar Gallery, New York, 2003; LA Mart Art, Los Angeles, 2004; Word Art Collection, Holland & Korea, 2004; Infusion Gallery, Los Angeles, 2005; Romanian Future, Viitorul Romanese, Romanian-Am Soc Art & Sci, Marriott Hotel, Los Angeles, 2006; NeoCon, Chicago, 2007; Exemplars Gallery, England; Artoteque, Sweden; Artist's Alley Gallery, San Francisco; Int Contemp Masters, S Nev Mus Fine Art, Las Vegas, 2012; Gora Gallery, Montreal, Canada, 2012; Galleria de Marchi, Little Treasures, Paola Trevistan curator, Bologna, Italy, 2012; See Me Art Show, NY, 2013, See Me, The Story of Creative Art Show, NY, 2013; Amsterdam Whitney Gallery, NY, 2013-2014; Salonul Int de Arta Temeuri editia a V-a, Bucharest, Romania, 2014; World Wide Art, Los Angeles Convention Center, 2014; Salonul Artelor Temeiuri Elogiul Frumusetii ca Infatisare a Binelui, Bucharest Romania, 2015. *Pos:* Artist, Siderma, Bucharest, Romania, 79-96, Los Angeles Signs & Graphics, 87-94 & Art & Signs, Burbank, Calif, currently. *Awards:* Award of Merit, Calif State Fair, 91; March Award of Merit, Int Art Gallery, Stockholm, Sweden, 96; Award Art, Int Art Mag, 2000. *Bibliog:* Interviews, Romanian TV-CLUJ, Ovidiu Suciv, 8/93, Dreptatea Newspaper, Pan Iserna, 10/93, Interview, Cotidianul II, Sanda Aronescu, 10/93 & Origini, Gabriel Stanesu, 2003; Origini (Roots), Romanian Art Mag, 94, 99 & 2000; George Nicolescu (auth), Mondo Mag, 96; Glendace News Press, 97; Cetatea Culturala, 2000; Art in Vogue, England; Creative Genius, Masters of Today. *Mem:* Am Pastelist Asn; Knickerbockers Artist Asn; Graphic Artists Guild, New York; New World Art Ctr, New York; Am Acad Arts & Sci (Romanian); Literart, Asn Romanian. *Media:* Oil, Acrylic; Tempera, Clay. *Publ:* Visalia Star, 91; Magazin Int, Universul, Micromagazin-Romanian Mag, Artspeak, The Villager, Actualite Departmentale Sub Ovest-French Mag, 95; Luceafarul Romanesc, Can, 97; Int Dictionary of Artists, St. Barbara; Int Contemp Masters V, World Wide Art Books Inc, Santa Barbara, 2012; Modern Masters Art Book, Art Approach, 2012; Art in Focus-NY, Art in America Annual Guide, 2012; Exposure Publications, 2012; Art Takes Square Publication, 2012; Amsterdam Whitney Facebook, ArtTour Int-The Best of the Int Arts Year, 2013; Modern Painters Magazine, Aesthetica Magazine, M Art Tour Magazine-Top 60 Masters of Contemp Art, Amsterdam Whitney (Facebook, Twitter, Blog, Pinterest, and Tumblr), Art Aquisitor Magazine, World Press, Instagram, ArtSlant, AW ArtInfo, 2013; Int Biographical Center, Cambridge, Eng, Outstanding People in the Arts Today, 2014; Int Contemp Masters, World Wide Art Books Inc, Santa Barbara, 2015; ArtTour Int Top 60 Masters of Contemp Art, 2015. *Dealer:* Exemplars Gallery England; Art in Focus. *Mailing Add:* 8306 Crenshaw Blvd Apt B Inglewood CA 90305-1721

LEBEY, BARBARA
PAINTER, PRINTMAKER, WRITER
b Newark, NJ, Feb 28, 1939. *Study:* Sarah Lawrence Col, BA, 59, Emory Univ Sch Law, JD, 70. *Work:* Princeton Univ Art Mus, NJ; Carter Presidential Ctr, Atlanta; Robert B Coggins Collection of Woman Artists, Marietta, Ga; Vanderbilt Collection; Newark Mus Art; Hunter Mus; Albany Mus, Ga, 90. *Comn:* Floral Still Life, comn by President & Mrs Jimmy Carter, 86; Seacoast Garden (painting), comn by Pat Conroy, 87; Springtime in Buckhead (commemorative print), Greater Atlanta C of C, Buckhead Sesquicentennary, 88; Walter B Ford Collection, 90. *Exhib:* Rablen West, Vero Beach, Fla, 90; Little Acorn Gallery, Dunwoody, Ga, 90; Leon Loard Gallery Fine Arts, Montgomery, Ala, 90; Foster Harmon Galleries, Sarasota, Fla, 92; Omell Galleries, London, St James, Eng, 92; and others. *Pos:* Bd dir, Ga Vol Lawyers Arts. *Awards:* Gold Medal, Artists in New Eng, Vt Co Arts, 85; Award of Merit, Robert B Coggins Collection, Trammel Crow Co, 88; Governor's Award for Ga Women in the Visual Arts, 97. *Bibliog:* Diana Brown (auth), Gardens of painted delights, Southern Homes, 87; Robert Nesbitt (auth), Artist realizes her dream, Inside Buckhead, 87. *Mem:* Atlanta Artists Club; Collectors Club, High Mus Art, Atlanta; Internat Women's Forum. *Media:* Oil, Watercolor; All Media. *Publ:* auth, Family Engagements, Longstreet Press, 2001

LEBOFF, GAIL F
PHOTOGRAPHER
b Brooklyn, NY, June 6, 1950. *Study:* State Univ Ala, 71-73; New York Univ, BS, 80, MA (studio art-photo), 82. *Work:* Coca-Cola Collection, Atlanta, Ga. *Comn:* Work in Genre of Art Work, comn by Poumans, Queens, NY, 85-86. *Exhib:* New Works, Bergen Mus Art & Sci, NJ, 83; Print Collection Color, Brooklyn Mus, NY, 84; Seeing is Believing, Alternative Mus, NY, 85; Images of Icon (traveling exhib), Johnson & Johnson, NJ, 86-87; Taking Liberty, NY State Mus, Albany, 86; Chairs, Witkin Gallery, NY, 87. *Teaching:* Instr, Sch Visual Arts, NY, currently. *Mem:* Women's Caucus Art; Soc Photogr Educ. *Mailing Add:* 451 Broome St No 12W New York NY 10013

LECHTZIN, STANLEY
GOLDSMITH, EDUCATOR
b Detroit, Mich, June 9, 1936. *Study:* Wayne State Univ, BFA; Cranbrook Acad Art, Bloomfield Hills, Mich, MFA. *Work:* Mus Am Crafts, NY; Detroit Inst Arts; Schmuckmuseum Pforzheim, Ger; Philadelphia Mus Art; Goldsmiths Hall, London; Yale Univ. *Comn:* Silver mace, Temple Univ, 66; Longwood Col, 74; paten, 41st Int Eucharistic Cong, Philadelphia, 76. *Exhib:* Solo exhibs, Mus Contemp Crafts, NY, 65, Lee Nordness Galleries, NY, 69, Int Jewelry Exhib, Tokyo, Japan, 73 & Goldsmiths Hall, London, 75; Philadelphia: Three Centuries of Am Art, Philadelphia Mus Art, Pa, 76; 20th Century Jewelry, Electrum Gallery, London, Eng, 85; Hong-ik Ann Exhib, Walker Hill Art Ctr Mus, Seoul, Korea. *Teaching:* Prof metalsmithing, Tyler Sch Art, Temple Univ, 62-, chmn metals/jewelry 62-, chmn dept crafts, 65-79 & 85-88. *Awards:* Nat Endowment Arts Craftsmen's Grant, 76 & 85; Pa Governor's Award in Crafts, 84; Art Achievement Award, Wayne State Univ, 94. *Bibliog:* Karl Schollmayer (auth), Neuer Schmuck, Ernst Wasmuth-Verlag, Ger, 74; C E Licka (auth), Stanley Lechtzin: Technic and the organic paradigm, Metalsmith, summer 82; Michael Dunas (auth), Conversations on Technology, Philosophy of the Physical, Metalsmith, summer 88. *Mem:* Soc NAm Goldsmiths (mem bd dir, 70-75); Am Crafts Coun; Coll Fels Am Crafts Coun. *Media:* Metal, Plastic. *Res:* Electroforming of gold jewelry; computer aided design & manufacture for crafts. *Publ:* Auth, Electrofabrication of metal, Craft Horizons, 64; contribr, Metal Techniques for Craftsmen, 68; auth, Museum of Contemporary Crafts (brochure), 69; contribr, Contemporary Jewelry, 70. *Dealer:* Helen Drutt Gallery Philadelphia PA. *Mailing Add:* PO Box 8816 Beech & Penrose Ave Elkins Park PA 19027

LECKY, SUSAN
PAINTER
b Los Angeles, Calif, July 19, 1940. *Study:* Univ Southern Calif, BFA; also Europ travel. *Work:* Los Angeles Co Mus; Bloomington Fed Savings & Loan, Bloomington, Pontiac & Streator Br; Mus Geometric and Mavi Art, Dallas, Tex. *Exhib:* Solo exhibs, Millikin Univ, Decatur, Ill, 83, Eastfield Coll, Mesquite, Tex, 85, Conduit Gallery, Dallas, Tex, 86, ETex State Univ, Commerce, Tex, 86, Brazos Gallery, Richland Coll, Callas, Tex, 91, Art Ctr, Waco, Tex, 92, LA Thompson Gallery, Dallas, Tex, 95, Irving Art Ctr, Tex, 98, Longview Mus Art, Tex, 2001, Art Centre Plano, Tex, 2001, Continental Gallery, Dallas, 2002, Brookhaven Coll, Dallas, 2006, Unity Theatre, Brenham, Tex, 2007, Discovery Garden Gallery, Dallas, Tex, & others; Looking at the Earth, Nat Air & Space Mus, Smithsonian Inst, Washington, 86-87; Masur Mus, La, 91, 93, 95-97, 2000, 2003; Abstraction II, Doshi Ctr Contemp Art, Harrisburg, Pa, 96; Horace Cardwell Competition, Meadows Gallery, Mus ETex, Lufkin, 96; 15th Ann Sept Competition, Alexandria Mus Art, La, 96; 3rd Ann Nat Exhib, State of Art Gallery, Ithaca, NY, 96; Decumano Secondo Verona, Italy, 97; Capino Veronese, Italy, 98; Warehouse Living Arts Ctr, Corsecann, TEx, 98-2002; Art with a Southern Draw, Mobile, Ala, 98, 99, 2001; Dishman Competition, Beaumont, Tex, 95-97, 2002; Art In the Metropolis, Ft Worth, Tex, 2001-2004, 2007-2009; Arthouse on Routh, Dallas, Tex, 2003-2004; Asn League of Houston Celebrates Tex Art, 2005-06 & 2008; Bath House Cultural Ctr, Dallas, 2006, 2009, 2011, 2012; Latino Cult Ctr, Dallas, Tex, 2008, 2011, 2013; 14th St Gallery, Plano, Tex, 2011; Haley-Henman Gallery Dallas, Tex, 2009-2010; Mus Geometric and Madi Art, Dallas, Tex, 2011; and many others. *Pos:* Restorer, Univ Ill Libr, 73-; art critic, New Art Examiner, 76-78; pub lect, Millikin, Decatur, Ill, 83, Eastfield Coll, Mesquite, Tex, 85, East Tex Univ, Commerce, 86, Univ Tulsa, 86, 99, Richland Coll, Dallas, 89, Tex Woman's Univ, Denton, 89, Webster Univ, St Louis, 91, Art Ctr, Waco, Tex, 92, Circolo della Kosa, Verona, Italy, 97; bd mem, The Friends of the Bath House Cultural Ctr, Dallas, Tex, chairperson public art, 2009-. *Teaching:* Vis artist, Univ Tulsa, Okla, 88 & 99. *Awards:* 60th Nat Windsor & Newton Award for acrylics, Cooperstown, NY, 95; People's Choice Award, Whitehorse Living Arts Ctr, Corsicana, Tex, 98; and others. *Bibliog:* Joe Kagle (dir), The Studios (video), Art Ctr, Waco, Tex, 92. *Mem:* Friends of the Bath House Cultural Ctr (pres & public art chairperson). *Media:* Acrylic, Colored Pencil. *Mailing Add:* 12116 Brookmeadow Ln Dallas TX 75218

LEDRAY, CHARLES
SCULPTOR
b Seattle, Washington, 1960. *Work:* Whitney Mus Am Art, New York; San Francisco Mus Mod Art; Mus Fine Arts, Boston; Des Moines Art Ctr, Iowa; Denver Art Mus. *Exhib:* Solo exhibs, Tom Cugliani Gallery, New York, 1993, Jack Hanley Gallery, San Francisco, 1994, Jay Gorney Mod Art, 1996, Inst Contemp Art, 2002-2003, Sperone Westwater, New York, 2003, 2007, Galerie Schmela, 2004, Mus Boijmans Van Beuningen, Rotterdam, Netherlands, 2009-2010, Mus Fine Arts, Houston, Tex, 2010-2011; group exhibs, Sweet Dreas, Barbara Toll Gallery, New York, 1991; Kim Light Gallery, Los Angeles, 1992; Villa Arson, Nice, France, 1993; Bernard Toale Gallery, Boston, 1993; Takashimaya, New York, 1994; Castle Gallery, Coll New Rochelle, 1994; Whitney Mus, Champion Plaza, Stamford, Conn, 1997; Dorsy Gallery, New York, 1999; Gorney Bravin & Lee, New York, 1999; Hudson Valley Ctr Contemp Art, 2004; Whitney Mus Am Art, New York, 2005; Mint Mus Art, Charlotte NC, 2006; Leila Taghinia-Milani Heller Gallery, New York, 2009; FLAG Art Found, New York, 2010. *Awards:* Louis Comfort Tiffany Found, 1993; Gorham Phillips Stevens Visual Arts Fel, Am Acad in Rome, 1997-1998; Acad Award, Am Acad Arts & Letters, 1998; Int Art Critics Assn, 2002. *Bibliog:* auth, Jed Perl, Group Dynamics, Art & Antiques, 1991; auth, Jerry Saltz, The 10 Commandments of Taste, Art & Auction, 1992; Keith Seward, review, Artforum, 1993; auth, Kim Levin, Voice Listings, The Village Voice, 1995; auth, Lynn Yaeger, Art...laMode, The Village Voice, 1997; auth, Art at the Millenium, San Francisco Examiner, 1997; auth, Ken Johnson, Contemplating Childlike Wonder, Long Past Childhood, The New York Times, 2005; auth, Robert Hobbs, Contemporary Cool & Collected: The Mint Mus, North Carolina, 2007; auth, Michele Rececchi, Ledray Mens Suits, Domus: Contemp Archit interiors Design Art, 2009; auth, Judith Shwartz, Confrontational Ceramic: The Atist as Social Critic, London, 2008. *Mailing Add:* Sperone Westwater Gallery 257 Bowery St New York NY 10002

LEE, BARBARA
COLLECTOR
b July, 1945. *Study:* Simmons Coll, BA. *Hon Degrees:* Boston Univ, MSW. *Pos:* Vchmn & dir, Inst Contemp Art, Boston, Mass; pres, Barbara Lee Family Found, Cambridge, Mass; founding chmn, contemp Arts prog, Isabella Stewart Gardner Mus, Boston, Mass; co-founder, The White House Project, 1997. *Awards:* George Alden Leadership Award; Opening Doors Award, Womens Inst for Housing Develop, 2003; named one of Top 200 Collectors, ARTnews mag, 2004-13; named one of 100 Women who Run this Town, Boston Mag. *Collection:* Modern and contemporary art by women. *Mailing Add:* 131 Mt Auburn St Ste 2 Cambridge MA 02138

LEE, BOVEY
PAINTER
b Hong Kong, June 11, 1969. *Study:* Chinese Univ Hong Kong, BA (Fine Arts), 91; Univ Calif Berkeley, MFA (Painting), 95; Pratt Inst, Brooklyn, NY, MFA (Digital Arts), 2000; Cone Editions, studied with Jon Cone, Master Printer (prof workshop), 2003. *Work:* Hong Kong Mus Art, Hong Kong; Art Mus, Chinese Univ Hong Kong. *Comn:* F P Journe, Hong Kong. *Exhib:* Contemp Hong Kong Painting, Fukuoka Art Mus, Fukuoka, Japan, 95; Hong Kong Art 1997, Mus Fine arts, Beijing, China, 97; Beyond Ethnic Stereotype, Kennedy Mus Am Art, Athens, Ohio, 2000; Digital: Printmaking Now, Brooklyn Mus Art, Brooklyn, NY, 2001; Unknown/Infinity, Legion Arts/CSPS, Cedar Rapids, Iowa, 2002; Tomorrow: Digital Art 2004, NY Hall Sci, New York, NY, 2004; Bing Lee & Bovey Lee at Mid Career, Asian Am Arts Centre, New York, NY, 2007; On Gossamer's Edge, Grotto Fine Art Gallery, Hong Kong, 2007-. *Pos:* Bd mem, Soc Contemp Craft. *Awards:* Urban Coun Fine Arts Award, Urban Counc, Hong Kong, 92; Jack K & Gertrude Murphy Fine Arts Fel, San Francisco Found, 94; Individual Artist Special Opportunity Stipend, Pa Coun Arts, 2004; Artist Opportunity Grant, Greater Pittsburgh Arts Counc, 2007; Mid-Career Artist, Asian Am Arts Center, 2007; Vira I Heinz Endowment Fel, 2007; Va Ctr Creative Arts Fel, 2007; Individual Artist Fel, Pa Coun on the Arts. *Bibliog:* Robert Hirsch (auth), Exploring Color Photography: From the Darkroom to the Digital Studio, 4th ed, McGraw-Hill, NYC, 2004; Carrie Patterson (auth), A Freedom to Mean, Calif State Univ, Fullerton, 2006; Murtaza Vali (auth), Bing Lee & Bovey Lee: Mid Career Artist Exhib, Asian Am Arts Center, NYC (pub online, www.artspiral.org), 2007; Andrea Moore Paldy & Rebecca Gallagher (coauths), Exploring Motion Graphics, Delmar Learning, 2007; Henry Au-yeung, On the Edge of Innocence, Grotto Fine Art Inc, Hong Kong, 2007. *Media:* Mixed Media, Paper cutouts, digital media, painting & drawing. *Dealer:* Grotto Fine Art Gallery Hong Kong

LEE, BRIANT HAMOR
HISTORIAN, EDUCATOR
b New Haven, Conn, May 6, 1938. *Study:* Carnegie-Mellon Univ; Adelphi Univ, BA; Acad de Belle Arti, Rome, Cert de Frequenza; Univ Italiana per Stranieri-Perugia; Ind Univ, MA; NY Univ; Mich State Univ, PhD. *Comn:* Over 100 theatrical productions, Scenographer, (in collaboration with staging dir); 25 theatrical productions, staging dir & scenographer, 64-. *Pos:* Design engineer, Kliegl Lighting, New York, 63-64; ed, J Empirical Research in Theatre, 80-85; prof emer, BGSU, 98. *Teaching:* Instr scenography, US Int Univ, San Diego, Calif, 62-63; asst prof scenography, Bradley Univ, Peoria, Ill, 67-68; prof theatre, Bowling Green State Univ, Ohio, 96. *Awards:* Undergrad Alumni: Asn Master Teacher Award Finalist, Bowling Green State Univ, 96-97. *Mem:* Am Theatre Asn; Speech Commun Asn; Am Soc for Theatre Res; Ohio Theatre Alliance; Ohio Community Theatre Asn. *Media:* Watercolor, Ink. *Res:* Late 18th century European theatre architecture and theatrical staging. *Publ:* Auth, Pierre Patte, Late 18th century lighting innovator, Theater Survey, 76; The origins of the box set in the late 18th century, Theatre Survey, 78; Corrugated Scenery, Oracle Press, 82; Understanding Microcomputers & Microcomputer Word Processing, Bowling Green State Univ, 85; European Post-Baroque Neoclassical Theatre Architecture, Mellon Press, 96; Play script adaptations include Macbeth, 85, Gemini, 85, Mid Summer's Night Dream, 86; Original plays include, A Thorn in Her Heart, 87, Silly Billy, 87. *Mailing Add:* 336 S Church St Bowling Green OH 43402-3719

LEE, CATHERINE
SCULPTOR, PAINTER
b Pampa, Tex, Apr 11, 1950. *Study:* San Jose State Univ, BA, 74. *Work:* Stadtische Galerie im Lenbachhaus, Munich; Mus Mod Art, NY; Tate Gallery, London; Mus Art, Carnegie Inst, Pittsburgh; US Dept State, Washington, DC; Irish Mus Mod Art, Dublin, Ireland; Musee Hotel des Arts, Toulon, France; Musee de Arte Moderne, St Etienne, France; Blanton Mus Art, Austin, Tex; Mus Fine Art Houston; Indianapolis Mus Art; Contemporary Austin, Austin, Tex; Mus Southwest; The McNay Mus, San Antonio, Tex; San Angelo Mus Fine Arts, Tex; Mus Southwest, Midland, Tex; Dallas Mus Art, Dallas, Tex; San Francisco Mus Art, San Francisco, Calif; Kroeller-Mueller Mus, Netherlands. *Exhib:* Selected Works, Albright-Knox Mus, Buffalo, NY, 87; Artists in the Abstract, Weatherspoon Gallery, Univ NC, Greensboro, 90; Biennale de Sculpture, Monte Carlo, Monaco, 91; Geteilte Bilder, Das Diptychon in der neuen Kunst, Mus Folkwang, Essen, Ger, 92; Stadtische Galerie im Lenbachhaus, Munich, 92; Neue Galerie der Stadt Linz, Austria, 92; Contemp Prints, The Tate Gallery, London, 94; 29th Ann Exhib of Art on Paper, Weatherspoon Art Gallery, 94; US Print/Grafilkkaa USA Garner Tullis Workshop, Retretti Art Ctr, Finland, 95; Mizuma Gallery, Tokyo, Japan, 95; Galerie Karsten Greve, Köln, Ger, 95, 2007, 2009, 2013; Serienbilder-Bilderserien, Städtische Galerie im Lenbachhaus, Munich, 96; ArtPace, A Found for Contemp Art, San Antonio, Tex, 96; Sonoma State Univ Art Gallery, 97; Galleri Weinberger, København, Denmark, 98; Bemis Art Found, Omaha, Nebr, 98; San Diego State Univ Art Gallery, 99; Lafayette Coll Art Ctr, Easton, Pa, 99; Galerie Lelong, NY, 99, 2007, 2012; Die Kunst der Gegenwart Im Lenbachhaus München, Städtische Galerie im Lenbachhaus, Munich, 99; Galeria Carles Taché, Barcelona, Spain, 2000; Lyman-Allen Art Mus, New London, Conn, 2000; Southwest Sch Art, San Antonio, Tex, 2004; Irish Mus Mod Art, Dublin, Ireland, 2005; Musee Hotel des Artes, Toulon, France, 2006; Musee de Arte Moderne, St Etienne, France, 2006; Galerie Lelong, NYC, 2007; Annely Juda Fine Art, London, 2008; Galerie Karsten Greve, Koln, Ger, 2009; Keramikmuseum Westerwald; Hohr Girenzhausen, Ger, 2011; Kunsthaus Wiesbaden, Ger, 2011; San Angelo Mus Fine Art, Tex, 2012; Mus Southwest, Midland, Tex, 2012; Old Jail Art Ctr, Albany, Tex, 2012; Grace Mus, Abilene, Tex, 2012; Noel Art Mus, Odessa, Tex, 2012; Galerie Lelong, NYC, 2012; Blue Star Contemporary Art Mus, San Antonio, Tex, 2014; Omi Internat Arts Ctr, Omi Fields, Ghent, NY, 2014; Galerie Karsten Greve, Paris, 2014; Galleri Weinberger, Kobenhavn, Denmark, 2015. *Teaching:* Artist-in-residence, Minneapolis Col Art & Design, Minn Inst Art, 82; vis asst prof, Univ Tex, San Antonio, 2000, lectr, 2010; adj asst prof, Columbia Univ, NY, 86-87. *Awards:* Creative Artists Pub Serv Prog Fel Painting, 78; Nat Endowment Arts, Painting Grant, 89. *Bibliog:* John Russell (auth), Bright young artists, New York Times, 5/18/86; Demetrio Paparoni (auth), A Conversation with Catherine Lee, Tema Celeste, 2/92; David Carrier & Helmut Friedel (auths), Catherine Lee, Outcasts, Stadtische Galerie im Lenbachhaus, Munich, 92; Carter Ratcliff & Faye Hirsch (auths), Catherine Lee, The Alphabet Works, Univ of Wash Press, 2d edit, 99; Elizabeth Ferrer, Francis Colpitt, Paula Owen (auths), Shards: The Work of Catherine Lee, Southwest Sch Art & Craft, San Antonio, Tex, 2004; Nancy Princenthal, Enrique Juncosa (auths), Catherine Lee, The Irish Mus Mod Art, Dublin, 2005; Gilles Altieri (auth), Catherine Lee, Musee Hotel des Artes, Toulon, France, 2006; Benjamin Genocchio (auth), The New York Times, 12/21/2007; Carla Esposito Hayer (auth), The Monotype, Skira, 2007; Rachel Cook (auth), Moving Fluidly Through the Landscape, The Austin Chronicle, 1/18/2008; Jeanne Clair Van Ryzin (auth), Three Questions with Catherine Lee, The Austin American Statesman, 2/21/2008; Stephen Westfall (auth), Art in America, 9/2008; Kathleen Whitney (auth), Catherine Lee, The Clad Works, Annely Juda Fine Art, London, 2008; Lilly Wei, Hearne Pardee, Stephen Westfall (auths), Catherine Lee/West Tex Triangle, Charta, Milan, 2012; Kathleen Whitney (auth), Catherine Lee, Constellations, Ceramics Monthly, 4/2014; Victor Cassidy, Catherine Lee, Always Inspired, Always at it, Ceramics Art and Perception Issue 99, 2015; Rachel Adams (auth), The Artist as Lens, Myriad Influences Inform the Work of Catherine Lee, Arts and Culture, Sept 2014; Elda Silva (auth) Selfies A Meditiation on Identity, San Antonio Express-News, 5/24/15; Best of San Antonio, Best Visual Artist: Catherine Lee, San Antonio. *Media:* Bronze; Oil; Ceramic; Works on Paper. *Dealer:* Galerie Karsten Greve 5 Rue Debelleyme 75003 Paris France; Galleri Weinberger Valkendorfsgade 13 Baghuset Copenhagen Denmark DK1151; Galerie Karsten Greve Wallrafplatz 5 Koln Ger; Annely Juda Fine Art 23 Dering St London England

LEE, DAVID (TZEH-HSIAN)
PAINTER, PHOTOGRAPHER
b Hupei, China, Mar 24, 1944. *Study:* NJ Inst Technol, MA, 69; Ridgewood Art Inst, 80 & 90. *Work:* Zhejiang Mus, Hangzhou, Zhejiang, China. *Exhib:* Allied Artists Am Ann Exhib, Nat Arts Club, NY, 87-89, 91, 93-94, 97, 99 & 2000; Pa Watercolor Soc Ann Exhib, Port Hist Mus, Philadelphia, 87; NJ Watercolor Soc 50th Anniversary Exhib, Montclair Art Mus, 88; Am Watercolor Soc Ann Open Exhib, Salmagundi Club, NY, 90 & 2000; Art Competition Winners, Artist's Mag, Cincinnati, 91; Watermedia, Challenge of Champions, 2003; Int Exhib of the Watercolor Art Soc, Houston, Tex, 2003. *Awards:* Bergen Mus Art & Sci Juror's Award, Open Juried Art Exhib, 83, 86 & 87; NJ Watercolor Soc Award, 44th Ann Open Exhib, 86; Winsor & Newton Award, Am Artist Prof League 60th Grand Nat Exhib, 88; and many others. *Bibliog:* Estelle F Sinclaire (auth), Watercolor Soc Show, Arts Tues, Princeton Packet, 10/2/84; Eileen Watkins (auth), Art (critique), Star-Ledger, 9/11/87; Carole Katchen (auth), Winning strategies for landscape painting, Artists Mag, 12/91. *Mem:* Allied Artists Am Inc; Am Artists Prof League Inc; Hudson Valley Art Asn; NJ Watercolor Soc (historian, 93-2000). *Media:* Watercolor. *Publ:* Add Asian accents for tranquility in watercolor magic, Artists Mag, 93; A Boy in the Field, in: The Best of Portrait Painting, 98 & Needle Works, in: Splash 6, 2000, North Light Bks; Lotus Pond, in: The Best of Watercolor, Rockport Publ, 99; Butterflies, in: The Best in Watercolor, Splash 8, North Light Bks, 2004; Birds & Butterflies, F&W Publ, 2008; Beijing Hatong, in: Splash 11, N Light Books, 2009. *Mailing Add:* 186 Hickory St Township of Washington NJ 07676

LEE, DORA FUGH
PAINTER, SCULPTOR
b Peking, China, Aug 16, 1930; US citizen. *Study:* With Prince Pu Ru, Chao Meng-chu & Yen Shao-Hsiang, Peking, China; additional study with sculptor, Pietro Lazzari, Washington. *Work:* China Inst, NY; Pearl Buck Found, Philadelphia; Smithsonian Inst & Nat Cathedral, Washington; The Willard Hotel, Washington; Johns Hopkins Medical Ctr, Baltimore, Md; Nat Portrait Gallery, Smithsonian Inst; and others. *Comn:* Sears House, Washington. *Exhib:* Watercolor USA, Springfield, Mo, 75; sculpture Mainstreams, Marietta Coll, Ohio, 76; Am Watercolor Soc Traveling Exhib, 76-92; Franz Bader Gallery, Washington, 76-96; Univ Md, 2009; Anhui, Beijing, China; Shenzhen, China, 2014. *Collection Arranged:* Portrait Gallery, Smithsonian Inst, Nat Mus. *Teaching:* Pvt lessons in Chinese traditional painting & calligraphy, Smithsonian Inst, Washington, 83-84; Chinese calligraphy, George Washington Univ, 82. *Awards:* Best of Show, 68, First Prize/Watercolor, 71 & 72, Montgomery Co Art Asn Traveling Exhib, Am Watercolor Asn, 76; North Light Award, Nat Sumei Soc, 85. *Mem:* Washington Watercolor Asn; Nat League Am Pen Women; Am Watercolor Soc. *Media:* Oil, Watercolor, Bronze. *Publ:* Treasures From Across the Sea, Literati Pu Ru's Work, 2010; Collected Letters of Philip Fugh, 2012. *Dealer:* Courtyard Gallery Beijing China

LEE, ELLEN WARDWELL
CURATOR
b Indianapolis, Ind, Feb 5, 1949. *Study:* Smith Col, Northampton, Mass, BA, 71. *Collection Arranged:* William McGregor Paxton, 79; The Aura of Neo-Impressionism: WJ Holliday Collection, 83; More than Red, White and Blue: Am Paintings from the Permanent Collection of Indianapolis Mus Art, 89; Seurat at Gravelines: The Last Landscapes, 90. *Pos:* Assoc cur painting & sculpture, Indianapolis Mus Art, 75-84, cur, 84-89 & sr cur, 89-91, chief cur, 91-. *Mem:* Am Asn Mus; Int Coun Mus. *Res:* Late 19th early 20th century American & European painting and sculpture. *Publ:* William McGregor Paxton, Nat Acad, Indianapolis Mus Art, 79; auth, The Aura of Neo-Impressionism: The WJ Holliday Collection, Indianapolis Mus Art & Ind Univ Press, 83; Seurat at Gravelines: The Last Landscapes, Indianapolis Mus Art, 90; Seurat Centenary (bk revs), Art J, Vol 51, No 2, 104-107, summer 92; Beyond the blackluster: Good exhibitions in small packages, Cur, Mus J, Vol 37, No 3, 172-184. *Mailing Add:* 3705 Spring Hollow Rd Indianapolis IN 46208-4169

LEE, ERIC MCCAULEY
MUSEUM DIRECTOR, HISTORIAN
b Clinton, NC, Feb 23, 1966. *Study:* Yale Univ, New Haven, Conn, BA, 88, MA, 91, PhD, 97. *Pos:* Asst cur paintings, Yale Cent British Art, New Haven, Conn, 95-96; acting dir Fred Jones Jr Mus Art, Univ Okla, Norman, 97-98, dir, 98; dir, Taft Mus Art, Cincinnati, 2007-2009, Kimbell Art Mus, Ft Worth, 2009-. *Teaching:* Asst prof art hist, Sch Art, Univ Okla, Norman, formerly. *Mem:* Asn Art Mus Dirs. *Publ:* co-auth, Fred Jones Jr Mus of Art at the Univ of Oklahoma: Selected Works, Univ of Oklahoma Press, 2004. *Mailing Add:* 333 Camp Bowie Blvd Fort Worth TX 76107

LEE, GERALDINE See Hooks, Geri

LEE, JAE RHIM
ENVIRONMENTAL ARTIST, DESIGNER
Study: Wellesley Coll, Mass, BA (psychology, Magna Cum Laude), 1998; Dept Visual & Environmental Studies, Harvard Univ, Cambridge, 2004; Mass Inst Technol, Cambridge, MA (Program Fel, visual studies), 2006. *Exhib:* Habitable Zone: Tools for Meditation and Rest, Exit Art, New York, 2005; Alternatives for Urination, The Studio Visit, Exit Art, New York, 2006; Green Skirt, Green Urinal, The Thread Counts Project, Gasp, Brookline, Mass, 2006; N=1=NPK=KIMCHI=N, Six, Space Other Gallery, Boston, 2006; Renegades: 25 Yrs of Performance, Exit Art, New York, 2007; Death Awareness Training Module 2, Spring Open Studios, Headlands Ctr for the Arts, Sausalito, Calif, 2007; N=0=Infinity: Infinity Burial Suit, Seamless: Computational Couture, Mus Sci, Boston, 2008; MIT FEMA Trailer Project, Tricks of the Eye, RI Sch Design, Providence, 2009. *Pos:* Res & fac asst, Kennedy Sch Govt, Harvard Univ, 2000-2005; facilitator & res fel, MIT Coun for the Arts, Cambridge, 2006-2007; founder & dir, MIT FEMA Trailer Project, Cambridge, 2008-. *Teaching:* Mentor, List Found Fel, MIT Coun for the Arts, Cambridge, 2006-2007; vis lectr, Visual Arts Program, Dept Archit, MIT, Cambridge, 2007-. *Awards:* Dirs Grant, MIT Coun for the Arts, 2005-2006, Grant, 2008; Grant for Emerging Fields, Creative Capital Found, 2009; Artist-in-residence, Headlands Ctr for the Arts, Sausalito, Calif, 2007. *Mailing Add:* MIT Visual Arts Program N51-319 265 Massachusetts Ave Cambridge MA 02139

LEE, JEESOO
PAINTER, INSTALLATION ARTIST
Study: Sungshin Women's Univ, Seoul, BFA, 2002; San Francisco Art Inst, 2004; SUNY New Paltz, MFA, 2006. *Exhib:* Newfangled, Smiley Art Gallery, New Paltz, NY, 2004; Open Space Rotunda, Fine Art Bldg, SUNY New Paltz, 2005; Curatorial Program Dorsky Gallery, Long Island City, NY, 2006; Tiberino Mus Contemp Art, Philadelphia, 2007; Garrison Art Ctr, 2008; BRIC Rotunda Gallery, Brooklyn, 2008; Nat Library Spain, Madrid, 2008; Michael Steinberg Gallery, New York, 2008; Abrons Arts Center, New York, 2009; Am Acad Arts and Letts Invitational, New York, 2009; Toomey Tourell Fine Art, 2009; Solo exhibs, SUNY Purchase, 2006 & C3 Gallery, New York, 2007. *Awards:* Patricia Kerr Ross Award, 2006; Fel, Abrons Arts Ctr, Henry Street Settlement AIR, New York, 2008. *Media:* Miscellaneous Media. *Mailing Add:* c/o Toomey Tourell Fine Art 49 Geary St San Francisco CA 94108

LEE, JOHN KEMP
ARTIST
b Hartford, Conn. *Study:* Dartmouth Col, BA; Maine Coll Art, BFA; Univ Pa, MFA. *Exhib:* Solo exhibs include Blue Mountain Gallery, Soho, NY City, 95, South Vt Univ Arts, Manchester, Vt, 98, Univ Wis, La Crosse, 99, Norwich Univ, Northfield, Vt, 2001, Aughinbaugh Art Gallery, Messiah Col, Grantham, Pa, 2002, Kouros Art Gallery, NY City, 2003, 2005; group exhibs include Nat Acad Design, NY City, 2006. *Teaching:* Adj asst prof studio art Dartmouth Col, Hanover, NH, 84-. *Awards:* Individual Artist grant, Vt Council ARts, 2000-2001

LEE, KATHARINE C
DIRECTOR
b Detroit, Mich, Dec 12, 1941. *Study:* Vassar Col, BA (art hist, magna cum laude), 63; Fulbright Scholar, 63-64; Harvard Univ, MA, 66; Knoxville Col, Il, Hon Dr Humane Letters, 96. *Collection Arranged:* Prairie School Furniture: Wright, Elmslie, Maher, 72, Art Deco: Trends in Design, 73, Collection of Contemporary Art of Mid-Am Club, Chicago, 76-78, Artists View the Law of the 20th Century (auth, catalog), 77, Renaissance Soc & Smart Gallery, Univ Chicago; Some Recent Art from Chicago (auth, catalog), Ackland Art Mus, Univ NC, 80. *Pos:* Asst cur, Toledo Mus Art, Ohio, 68-70; dir exhib, Renaissance Soc, Univ Chicago, 71-73, cur collections, Smart Gallery, Univ Chicago, 73-79; cur, Ackland Art Mus, Univ NC, Chapel Hill, 79-82; asst dir, Art Inst Chicago, 81-85, dept dir, 85-91; dir, Va Mus Fine Arts, formerly & Cleveland Mus Art, 2000-2005. *Teaching:* Mus course in hist mus & collection inst, Univ Chicago, 78; Getty Trust/Am Fed Art Mus Inst Fac, 91-93. *Awards:* Ford Found Grant in Mus Curatorial Training Internship, 66-68. *Mem:* Am Asm Mus (accreditation comn, 96-); AAMD (trustee, 96-, mem comt, 98-); CAA. *Mailing Add:* Va Mus Fine Arts 200 N Blvd Richmond VA 23220-4007

LEE, LARA
PRODUCER, FILMMAKER
b Brazil. *Study:* NY Univ. *Work:* Prufrock, B&W, 91, Neighbors, 92, Am Autumn Wind, 93, Synthetic Pleasures (full length documentary), 96, Architettura, Modulations-Cinema for the Ear (full length documentary), 98, Caipirinha Music Record Label, 97, Oblique (film) & Beneath the Borqa in Afghanistan, 2001, Caipirinha Music Record Label. *Exhib:* Munich Film Festival, Ger, 93; Breckenridge Festival of Films, Colo, 93; Univ Cincinnati Film Soc, 93; Humboldt Film Festival, Calif, 93; Women in Film, Hollywood, 94; Jerusalem Film Festival, Israel, 94; Bombay Int Film Festival, India, 94; S Beach Film Festival, Miami, 94; Int Outdoor Short Fest - Flickerfest, Australia, 95; Whitney Biennial, Whitney Mus Am Art, NY, 97; and many others. *Pos:* Producer & programmer, Sao Paulo Int Film Festival, 84-89; establisher film production company, Caipirinha Productions

LEE, LI LIN
PAINTER
b Jakarta, Indonesia, Oct 11, 1955; US citizen. *Study:* Univ Pittsburgh, BS, 78. *Work:* Ameritech Servs, Chicago; Arthur Anderson & Co, Chicago; Art Inst Chicago; Philip Morris Co Inc, NY; Prudential Ins Co Am, Newark, NJ. *Exhib:* Solo Exhibs, LaSorda-Iri Gallery, Los Angeles, 88, Reicher Gallery, Barat Col, Lake Forest, Ill, 89, Tilden-Foley Gallery, New Orleans, 89, E M Donahue Gallery, NY, 89, 90, 91 & 92, Li-Lin Lee, New Works, Richard Iri Gallery, Los Angeles, 90, Betsy Rosenfield Gallery, Chicago, 90 & 92; Artfair/Seattle, Betsy Rosenfield Gallery, 92; Wall Project, Sculpture Center, Benefit Exhib, NY, 92; The Rectangled Bank, E M Donahue Gallery, NY, 92; May 1992, Betsy Rosenfield Gallery, Chicago Int Art Expo, Chicago, 92; and others. *Bibliog:* S G (auth), Li Lin Lee at Blum Helman Gallery, LA Times, 5/89; John Yau (auth), Li Lin Lee at E M Donahue Gallery, Artforum, summer 89; John Brunetti (auth), Li Lin Lee at Betsy Rosenfield Gallery, New Art Examiner, 5/92. *Media:* Oil on Burlap, Enamel on Wood. *Dealer:* E M Donahue Gallery 560 Broadway No 304 New York NY 10012. *Mailing Add:* 853 W Lawrence Ave Chicago IL 60640-4212

LEE, MACK
ART DEALER
b 1952. *Study:* Hampshire Col, BA, 75. *Pos:* Own & dir, Lee Gallery, 81-. *Mem:* Asn Int Photog Art Dealers (bd mem, currently). *Media:* Photographs. *Res:* George Kendall Warren, James Wallace Black, Southworth & Hawes, Eugene Cuvelier, Adalbert Cuvelier, Gustave LeGray, Charles Negre, Henri LeSecq, Charles Marville, Edouard Baldus, Gertrude Kasebier, George Seeley, Karl Struss, Alfred Stieglitz. *Specialty:* 19th c Am, British & French photos; photo-secessionists & circle of Alfred Stieglitz; 20th c Am photos before 1980. *Publ:* Auth, Fifteenth Anniversary Show (exhib, catalog), Pvt Publ, 96; California in the 1930s, Photographs By Lange Levenson, and Noskowiak (exhib, catalog) pvt publ, 96; Camera Work, pvt publ, 12/97; Naturalist Photography 1880-1920, pvt publ, 9/98. *Mailing Add:* Lee Gallery 9 Mount Vernon St Winchester MA 01890

LEE, MARGARET F
PAINTER
b South St Paul, Minn, May 19, 1922. *Study:* Rochester Art Ctr, with Adolph Dehn, Arnold Blanch & Robert Birmelin, 60-74; John Pike Watercolor Sch, Woodstock, NY, 72; watercolor with Zoltan Szabo, 74; Japanese woodblock with Toshi Yoshida, 74; Univ Minn, BA (art), 75. *Work:* YMCA-YWCA Permanent Collection, Rochester, Minn. *Exhib:* Solo exhib, Augsburg Coll, Minneapolis, 73; 17th & 18th Int, Galerie Int, NY, 73-74; Mainstreams USA, Marietta Coll, Ohio, 74; Am Painters in Paris, French Ministry & Paris City Coun, 75; Arts of Asia Gallery, Rochester, Minn, 75-77; and others. *Teaching:* Lectr Japanese Sumi-e, Winona Art Ctr, Minn, 74; instr Japanese painting, Rochester Art Ctr, 74; (retired). *Awards:* First Place, Northern Lights 75, St Paul, 75; Award of Excellence, Arts Omnibus, 76, St Paul; Award, Midwest Watercolor Soc Exhib, Minn Mus of Art, St Paul, 77. *Mem:* Minn Artists Asn; Sumi-e Soc Am, NY; Twin City Watercolor Soc, Minneapolis, Minn. *Media:* Acrylic, Sumi Ink; Watercolor. *Dealer:* Southeastern Minn Visual Artists Gallery 16 First St SW Rochester MN 55901

LEE, MARY VIRGINIA
MURALIST, PAINTER
b Clinton, Okla, Nov 19, 1924. *Study:* Am Univ, 43-45. *Work:* Phillips Mem Gallery, Washington; St Laurence Cathedral, Amarillo, Tex. *Comn:* Stations of the Cross, 81 & 12th Chapter Revelations (mural), 81, Parish Church, Montalto, Parma, Italy; Stations of the Cross, Epiphany Church, Oklahoma City, Okla, 84; two stained glass rose windows, St Peter's Church, Guymon, Okla, 85; sanctuary mural, St Joseph's Church, Hong-Kong, 93. *Exhib:* New Mexico Artists, Okla Art Ctr, Oklahoma City, 51; Alcove Exhib, NMex State Gallery, Santa Fe, 54; Traveling Group Show, NMex State Gallery, Santa Fe, 55; Alcove Exhib, NMex State Gallery, Santa Fe, 57; and others solo exhibs. *Bibliog:* Peter Seracino Inglott (auth), The Art of Mary Virginia Lee, Arte Cristiana, Scvola Beato Angelico, Milano, Italy, No LXIX, 8-9/81. *Mem:* Nat Asn Women Artists; hon mem Kappa Pi. *Media:* Oil, Acrylic

LEE, NELDA S
DEALER
b Gorman, Tex, July 3, 1941. *Study:* Tarleton State Coll, AA, 61; N Tex State Univ, BFA, 63; Tex Tech Univ, Lubbock, grad study, 65 & San Miguel de Allende Art Inst, Mex, 65. *Work:* Delgado Mus Art, New Orleans, La; El Paso Mus Art, Tex. *Comn:* Portrait of late Sam Jones, Supt Rising Star Pub Sch, comn by Student Coun, 66; designed terrazo marble floors, Sweetwater High Sch, comn by Balfour Co, Tex, 67; student ctr, Tarleton State Univ, comn by Student Coun, Stephenville, Tex, 68. *Exhib:* Artist of SE in Tex, Delgado Mus Art, New Orleans, La, 64; Tex Fine Arts Asn Traveling Exhib, 64-67; Int Designer-Craftsmen Exhib, El Paso Mus, Tex, 65; Tex Watercolor Soc Exhib, Elizabeth Ney Mus, San Antonio, Tex, 67. *Collection Arranged:* President Carter's Inaugural Reception Exhib, The Capitol, Washington, DC, 77. *Pos:* Owner-operator, Nelda Lee Inc, 67-; mem, Tex Comn Arts, 93-99. *Teaching:* Chairperson art dept, Ector High Sch, Odessa, Tex, 63-68. *Awards:* First Place Sculpture, Artist of the SE in Tex, Delgado Mus of Art, 64; First Place Design, Int Designer-Craftsmen Exhib, 65; First Place Mixed-Media, Tex Fine Arts Exhib, 65. *Bibliog:* Scheryl Vannoy (auth), Texas art dealer stages exhibition at Capitol, San Angelo Standard Times, 77; article, SW Art Mag, 80; Carrie Steenson (auth), A rare work of art, Business Mag, 81. *Mem:* Am Soc of Appraisers; Tex Asn Art Dealers (pres, 79-91). *Specialty:* 18th to 20th century English and American masters. *Interests:* Scholarships funded for art students. *Publ:* Auth, History of Art in Odessa, Texas, Permian Basin Hist Ann, 69; coauth, Painter of a vanishing America, SW Art, 74. *Mailing Add:* PO Box 14438 Odessa TX 79768

LEE, NIKKI S
PHOTOGRAPHER, FILMMAKER
b Korea, 1970. *Study:* Fashion Inst Tech; NY Univ, MA (photog), 1998. *Exhib:* Solo exhibs include Leslie Tonkonow Artworks + Projects, NY, 1999, 2001 & 2003, Stephen Friedman Gallery, London, 2000, Gallery Gan, Tokyo, 2000, Mus Contemp Photog, Chicago, 2001, Yerba Buena Ctr Arts, San Francisco, 2001, Inst Contemp Art, Boston, 2001, Clough-Hanson Gallery, Rhodes Coll, Memphis, Tenn, 2002, Galeria Senda, Barcelona, 2002, Printemps de Septembre, Toulouse, France, 2003, Cleveland Mus Art, 2003, Numark Gallery, Washington, 2004, Kemper Mus Contemp Art, Kansas City, Mo, 2005, Galerie Anita Beckers, Frankfurt am Main, Germany, 2005, LT/Shoreham Gallery, NY, 2006; group exhibs include The Cultured Tourist, Leslie Tonkonow Artworks + Projects, NY, 1998, Process/Reprocess, 2000; The Calendar Project, Ctr for Curatorial Studies, Bard Coll, NY, 1999, Bodily Acts, 2001, The Volatile Real, 2001, Framing the Real, 2003, If It's Not Love, It's the Bomb, 2004; Generation Z, PS1 Contemp Art Ctr, Long Island City, NY, 1999, Greater New York, 2000; Reflections in a Glass Eye, Internat Ctr Photog, NY, 2000, Only Skin Deep, 2003, White, 2005; Gwangju Biennale, Gwangju, South Korea, 2000; The Likeness of Being, DC Moore Gallery, NY, 2000; Chelsea Rising, Contemp Arts Ctr, New Orleans, 2001; One Planet Under a Groove, Bronx Mus Arts, NY, 2001, Portraits & Places, 2004, How to Read, 2005; Open City, Modern Art Oxford, England, 2001; Fresh Albright Knox Art Gallery, Buffalo, NY, 2001, In Focus, 2004; Recent Acquisitions, Met Mus Art, NY, 2001; Liverpool Biennial, Tate Liverpool, England, 2002; One Planet Under a Groove, Walker Art Ctr, Minneapolis, 2002; open City, Museo de Bellas Artes de Bilbao, Spain, 2002; 8th Istanbul Biennial, Turkey, 2003; Exhibiting Signs of Age, Berkeley Art Mus, Univ Calif, 2003; Somewhere Better Than This Place, Contemp Arts Ctr, Cincinnati, 2003; White, Ctr Art & Visual Cult, Univ Md, Baltimore, 2003; Exhibiting Signs of Age, Colby Coll, Maine, 2004; Only Skin Deep, Seattle Art Mus, 2004; Sublime Audacity, Galeria Luis Serpa, Lisbon, 2004; Will Boys Be Boys?, Salina Art Ctr, Kans, 2004; Common Ground, Jewish Mus, NY, 2005, Jewish Identity Project, 2005; Only Skin Deep, San Diego Mus Art, 2005; Will Boys Be Boys?, Mus Contemp Art, Denver, 2005; Jewish Identity Project, Skirball Cult Ctr, Los Angeles, 2006; Will Boys Be Boys?, Indianapolis Mus Art, 2006; Tell Me a Story, Mus Photog Arts, San Diego, 2007. *Publ:* Projects, 1997-2001; Parts, 2002-05; AKA Nikki S Lee (film), 2006. *Mailing Add:* Leslie Tonkonow Artworks + Projects 535 W 22nd St New York NY 10011

LEE, SUNGMI
SCULPTOR
b Seoul, South Korea, 1977. *Study:* Emmanuel Coll, Boston, BFA, 2002; Md Inst Coll Art, Baltimore, Cert, 2003, MFA (sculpture), 2005. *Exhib:* Solo exhibs include C Grimaldis Gallery, Baltimore, 2006 & 2007; group exhibs include Gallery Korea Exhib, Gallery Korea, Embassy of the Republic of Korea, Washington, 2005; Washington Square Sculpture Invitational, Gallery 10 at Washington Square, Washington, 2005; Gallery 10 Sculpture Invitational, Gallery 10 Ltd, Washington, 2006; Bearable Lightness/Likeness, PS1 Contemp Arts Ctr, New York, 2006; Summer Show, C Grimaldis Gallery, Baltimore, 2006, The Dialectic of Line, 2007; Agents of Change: Women, Art & Intellect, Ceres Gallery, New York, 2007; 183rd Annual: Invitational Exhib Contemp Art, Nat Acad Mus, New York, 2008. *Awards:* SJ Wallace Truman Fund Award, Nat Acad, 2008

LEE, SUSIE J
VIDEO ARTIST
b Hersey, Pa. *Study:* Yale Univ, BS; Columbia Univ, MS; Univ Wash, MFA. *Work:* Colby Coll Mus Art; Boise Art Mus; Wing Luke Asian Mus; Wash State Svcs for the Blind; and many pvt collections. *Exhib:* Good n' Guilty, Kirkland Arts Ctr, 2000; solo exhibs, Animus, Northwest Asian Am Theatre, Seattle, 2001, Wait & Showers, Bemis Bldg, Seattle, 2002, Pending, Secluded Alley Works, Seattle, 2002, Frost, Phinney Ctr Gallery, 2003, Bound, 2003 & Fermata, 2006, CMA Gallery, Univ Wash, Refrain, Lawrimore Project, 2007, Indeterminancy, or the Observers Paradox, Rendezvous Theatre, 2008, Bodies of Water, Galleria Tiziana Di Caro, Salerno, Italy, 2008 & Shadow Playing, The Art Gym, Portland, 2009; Nat Juried Cup Show, Gallery 138, Kent, Ohio, 2001; I Scream, You Scream, Vt Clay Studio, Waterbury, Conn, 2001; Brace, The Sack Factory, Seattle, 2001; Inchoate, Prudential Ctr, Seattle, 2002; Preface, Kirkland Arts Ctr, 2002; The Last Judgment, Bumbershoot Festival, Seattle, 2003; Works in Progress, Jacob Lawrence Gallery, Univ Wash, 2004; XChange, Western Wash Univ, Bellingham, 2004; Coupling III, Ctr on Contemp Art, Seattle, 2005; Marking Territories, Portland Art Ctr, 2006; Perfect Landscape, Lawrimore Project, Seattle, 2007; Aqua Art Miami, Wynwood Dist, Miami Beach, 2007; Contested Ground, Northwest Mus Arts & Cult, Spokane, 2008; Ghost Light, Moore Inside Out, Seattle, 2009. *Teaching:* Instr chemistry & math, New York, NY & Milford, Conn, 95-97; resident artist, Kirkland Arts Ctr, 2001; teaching asst 3-D Design, Univ Wash, 2005, guest instr introduction to new media, 2006, guest artist landscape archit, 2007; teaching artist, Frye Art Mus, Seattle, 2007

LEE, THOMAS H
COLLECTOR
b 1944. *Study:* Harvard Univ, BA, 1965. *Pos:* With, First Nat Bank Boston, 1966-74, mgr high tech leading group, 1968-74, vpres, 1973-74; chmn, TH Lee Mezzanine; chmn & chief exec officer, TH Lee Putnam Ventures; founder, chmn, and chief exec officer, Thomas H Lee Partners, Boston, 1974-2005 & Lee Equity Partners LLC, New York, 2006-; nat adv bd, JP Morgan; dir, Metris Cos Inc, Miller Import Corp, Wyndham Int Inc, Snapple Beverage Corp, Gen Nutrition Cos, Playtex Products Inc, Vail Resorts Inc, 1993, Safelite Glass Corp, Vertis Holdings Inc, First Security Servs Corp; trustee, Intrepid Mus, Lincoln Ctr for Rockefeller Univ, NY Univ Med Ctr, Mus Modern Art, New York; vpres bd, Whitney Mus Am Art, currently. *Awards:* Named one of Top 200 Collectors, ARTnews mag, 2003-12. *Collection:* Modern and contemporary art; photography

LEE-SISSOM, E (EVELYN) JANELLE SISSOM
PAINTER
b Oakland, Calif, Feb 11, 1934. *Study:* Art Instruction, Inc; Watkins Inst; Univ Tenn. *Work:* Parthenon Galleries & Mus, Tenn State Mus & Opryland Hotel's Collection Tenn Art, Nashville; Sunkist Corp Off, Atlanta, Ga; Tenn Valley Authority Corp Offices & Visitors Ctr, Knoxville, Tenn. *Comn:* Painting, Cookeville General Hospital, Tenn, 81. *Exhib:* 26th Nat Soc Painters Casein & Acrylic, Am Acad & Inst Arts & Letters, NY, 79; 22nd Traveling, Nat Soc Painters Casein & Acrylic, 79-80; 2nd Ann Open, Salmagundi Club, NY, 79; Grand Nat, Am Artists Prof League, NY, 79 & 80; Solo exhibs, Parthenon Galleries, Nashville, Tenn, 79 & 81. *Awards:* Third Award, 17th Tenn All-State, 77; Grand Award, 13th Central S, 78; Lyzon Art Gallery, 16th Central South, 81. *Mem:* Assoc mem Nat Soc Painters Casein & Acrylic; Am Artists Prof League; Tenn Art League; Cumberland Arts Soc Cookeville Tenn (bd dir, 75-80). *Media:* Acrylics. *Publ:* Contribr, Tennessee Conservationist, Tenn Dept Conserv, 78; Int Soc Artists Communicator, Billboard Publ, 79; illusr cover, Key: Nashville, Silversmith, 82; contribr, Nashville, Advantage Publ, 83. *Mailing Add:* 1151 Shipley Church Rd Cookeville TN 38501-7730

LEEBER, SHARON CORGAN
ART DEALER, CONSULTANT
b St Johns, Mich, Oct 1, 1940. *Study:* Univ Wyo; Cent Mich Univ; Nat Open Univ, Washington, Trinity Univ. *Work:* Int Sculpture Park, Liberty Hill, Tex; Barnwell Art Ctr, Shreveport, La; Univ Tex, Arlington; Dallas Mus Fine Arts, Univ Tex, Dallas & Brookhaven Col, Dallas, Tex; Del Mar Col, Corpus Christi, Tex; Lone Star Park, Grand Prairie, Tex, 97; and others. *Comn:* Univ Tex, Arlington, 76; Arlington City Hall, Tex, 76; large welded male, Incarnate Word Col, San Antonio, Tex, 77; Veterans Meml Park, Irving, Tex, 2000; and others. *Exhib:* Tex Fine Arts Nat, Austin, 69; solo retrospective show, Elizabet Ney Mus, Austin, 71; Tex Sculpture & Painting, Dallas, 71; Dallas Art, City Hall, Dallas, Tex, 78; Big Name Artists Show, Dallas, 78 & 79; Johannesburg Mus Art, The Fashion Designers Group of SA, Crafts Coun of S Africa, Pretoria Technikron, S Africa; plus others. *Collection Arranged:* Curatorials: Two From Texas, Two From London, Read Stremmel Gallery, 88; The Italian Show, Crescent Gallery, Dallas, Tex, 88; Beaux Arts Ball Fine Arts, Dallas Mus Art, 90; Plaza of the America's Glass Collection, 92; Similarities, Beverly Gordon Gallery, Dallas, Tex, 92; Dale Chihuly Glass & Drawing Exhib, Plaza Gallery, Dallas, Tex, 92; Dale Chihuly at Gerald Peters Gallery, Dallas, Tex, 94. *Pos:* Pres, Archit Arts Co, 80-; trustee, Florentine Found Art, 85-86. *Teaching:* Instr photog, El Centro Col, Tex, 71-81, Univ Tex, Dallas, 76-77. *Awards:* Purchase Awards, Shreveport Mus, 69 & Dallas Mus Fine Arts, 78. *Bibliog:* Thelma Neuman (auth), The Mirror Book, 78; L Haacke (auth), Art is more comfortable, Dallas Times Herald, 3/30/78; High Profile - Dallas Morning News, 92. *Mem:* Int Women's Forum; Artists Equity Asn (secy, Dallas Chap, 72-73); Dallas Women's Forum; and others. *Media:* Welded Steel, Glass. *Interests:* Travel. *Publ:* Nat Asn Indust & Off Parks Publ Series: How to Acquire for Your Development, #5, 87. *Mailing Add:* 6410 Dykes Way Dallas TX 75230-1816

LEEDS, VALERIE ANN
CURATOR, WRITER
b Summit, NJ, Jan 22, 1958. *Study:* Univ Rochester, BA, 1979; Syracuse Univ, MA, 1981; City Univ New York, PhD (Douglass Fellowship in American Art, Dissertation Travel Fellowship), 2000. *Collection Arranged:* At the Water's Edge: 19th & 20th Century Am Beach Scenes, Tampa Mus of Art, 1989; The Portraits of Robert Henri,

Orlando Mus of Art, FL, 1994; An Am Palette: Works from the Beck Collection, Mus of Fine Arts, St. Petersburg, FL, 2000; Robert Henri: The Painted Spirit, Gerald Peters Gallery, NY, 2005; Andrew Wyeth: Am Master, Boca Raton Mus of Art, 2005; Simple Beauty: Paintings by Georgia O'Keeffe, Shelburne Mus, 2006; Marguerite Zorach: A Life in Art, Gerald Peters Gallery, NY, 2007; Charles Harold Davis: His Art and Career (in retrospect), Gerald Peters Gallery, NY, 2007; Harold Western: A Retrospective, Gerald Peters Gallery, NY, 2006; Shock of the Real: Photorealism Revisted, Boca Raton Mus Art, 2008; Edmund Lewandowski, Precisionism and Beyond, Flint Inst Arts, Mich, 2010-11; From NY to Corrymore: Robert Henri and Ireland, Mint Mus, Charlotte, 2011-12; The New Spirit and the Cos Cob Art Colony: Before and After the Armory Show, Greenwich Historical Soc, Conn, 2013; Southwestern Allure: The Art of the Santa Fe Art Colony, Boca Raton Mus Art, Fl, 2013-14; Spanish Sojourns: Robert Henri and the Spirit of Spain, Telfair Mus, Savannah, Ga, 2013-14; Along his Own Lines: A Retrospective of New York Realist Eugene Speicher, Dorksy Mus, SUNY New Paltz, NY, 2014-15; Charles H Davis: Mystic Impressionist, Bruce Mus, Greenwich, Conn, 2015. *Pos:* Cur assist, Whitney Mus of Am Art, New York, 1982-1984; Researcher & assoc, Spanierman Gallery, New York, 1984-1986; Cur exhibs, Tampa Mus of Art, 1987-1990; Cur Am Art, Orlando Mus of Art, 1990-1996; Independent cur, ed and writer, 1996-; Adjunct cur Am Art, Flint Inst of Arts, 2000-2010. *Teaching:* Adj prof, Eckerd Col, St. Petersburg, Fl, 2000. *Awards:* NEA Grant, NEA, 1995; Heinrich Boll Found Residency, Ireland, 2013. *Mem:* Assoc of Art Editors; Assoc Historians Am Art. *Res:* 20th century Am art. *Interests:* art of Robert Henri, Ernest Lawson & the Ashcan Sch. *Publ:* John Sloan: Still on the Am Scene, Art Connoisseur, Vol 4, Nov/Dec, 2007; Pictorial Pleasures: Leisure Themes and the Henri Circle, Life's Pleasures: The Ashcan Artists' Brush with Leisure, Detroit Inst Arts, 2007; The Worlds of John Sloan: Gloucester & Santa Fe, Mennello Mus Am Art, 2008; 101 Masterpieces of NYC: Must See Works of Art & Architecture in the NY Metropolitan Area, Alyson Books, 2009; Georgia O'Keeffe & the Faraway: Nature & Image; Nat Cowgirl Mus, Fort Worth, Tex, Georgia O'Keefe Mus, 2010, 2012; Edmund Lewandowski: Precisionism & Beyond, Flint Inst Arts, Mich, 2010; From New York to Corrymore: Robert Henri and Ireland, Mint Mus, Charlotte, NC, 2011; James Vullo: Deconstructing Urbania, Burchfield Penney Art Ctr, 2012; Seeking the Spirit Old Spain: Robert Henri and Spanish Themes, 1904-1924, Telfair Mus, Savannah, Ga, 2013; The New Spirit and the Cos Cob, Art Colony: Before and After the Armory Show, Greenwich Historical Soc, Greenwich, Conn, 2013; Far and Wide: The Travels and Art of Robert Henri, Laguna Art Mus, Calif, 2014; Along his Own Lines: A Retrospective of NY Realist Eugene Speicher, Dorksy Mus, SUNY New Paltz, NY; Charles H Davis: Mystic Impressionist, Bruce Mus, Greenwich, Conn, 2015. *Mailing Add:* 728 Sergeantsville Rd Stockton NJ 08559

LEESMAN, BEVERLY JEAN
PAINTER, WRITER

b Lincoln, Ill, Apr 22, 1953. *Study:* Ill State Univ, Normal, Ill, BS, 1976; Springfield Coll in Ill, Springfield, AA, 1973. *Comn:* Dinosaur Mural (3 walls), Gold Cup Gymnastics, Albuquerque, NMex, 2002-03; Southwest theme & faux walls, Andrew's, Albuquerque, NMex, 2001-02; Dragon Image in Watercolor for Kempo Karate Studio, Albuquerque, NM. *Exhib:* 18th Ann Exhibit, NE Watercolor Soc, Goshen, NY, 1994: 2003-2004; 2002 33rd River Road Show, La Art and Artists' Guild, Baton Rouge, La, 2002; Salmagundi Club 26th Ann Non-mem Juried Exhib, NY, 2003; 26th Int Exhib of WAS-H, Houston, Texas, 2003; Hilton Head Art Leaques Nat Juried Art Exhib, SC, 2003; Allied Artist of Am, NY, 2004; Catherine Lorillard Wolfe Art Club Juried Nat'l Show, NY, 2003-04; Watercolor West Brea, Calif, 2004; Taos Exhib of Am Watercolor VII, 2004, Taos, NMex. *Pos:* Art critic, Syracuse New Times, Syracuse, NY, 93-97. *Awards:* Dick Blick award, Aqueous Open, Dick Blick Supplies, 1995; Bd Dirs award, Fall 2002 Exhibit, NMex Watercolor Soc, 2002; 2nd place, 2002 33rd River Show, La Art & Artists' Guild, 2002; Am Artist Mag Award, Watercolor West, 2004; Richard Ochs Award, Northeast Watercolor Soc, 2004;. *Bibliog:* North Suburban Snapshot, Syracuse Herald Journal, 12/21, 94; Deidre Neilen (auth), An eye for detail: Beverly Leesman thrives on painting the complicated, Syracuse New Times, 2/15/95; Jewish Link, 2002. *Mem:* Am Artist Prof League (signature mem); Nat Asoc Women Artists; Juried mem of Watercolor West; Signature mem of Northeast Water CO, Soc; Mio Watercolor Soc (signature mem). *Media:* Watercolor, Egg Tempera. *Interests:* my family. *Collection:* private col. *Publ:* Art Critic, Syracuse New Times, 93-97; Watercolor Studio; Pleen Air Mag, 2004; Artist Mag, 2004-05; Best in Worldwide Landscape Artists, vol I book, Kennedy Publ

LEESON, TOM
PAINTER, SCULPTOR

b Chicago, Ill, Mar 16, 1945. *Study:* Ball State Univ, BS, 68, Univ Calif, Los Angeles, MA, 71. *Work:* Los Angeles Co Mus Art, Calif; Santa Monica City Coll Art Gallery, Calif. *Comn:* Painting comn by Lynda Resnick, Los Angeles, 86. *Exhib:* Current Concerns, Part 2, Los Angeles Inst Contemp Art, 75; The Object Observed, Los Angeles Munic Art Gallery, 78; Deja Vu: Masterpieces Updated, traveling exhib, Western Asn Art Mus, 83; Setting the Stage, Los Angeles Co Mus, 85-86; one person exhib, Ovsey Gallery, Los Angeles, Calif, 86, 89 & 95. *Teaching:* Vis lectr drawing, Univ Calif, Los Angeles, 77-79, lectr, 83-90, vis asst prof, 91-94; vis lectr drawing & sculpture, Univ Calif, Santa Barbara, 82. *Bibliog:* Howard Fox (auth), Setting the Stage, Los Angeles Co Art Mus Art, 85; David Helfrey (auth), Suspending disbelief, Visions Mag, Spring 88. *Media:* Oil, Acrylic; All Media. *Mailing Add:* 4748 W Washington Blvd Los Angeles CA 90016

LEET, RICHARD (EUGENE)
RETIRED MUSEUM DIRECTOR, PAINTER

b Waterloo, Iowa, Sept 11, 1936. *Study:* Univ Northern Iowa, BA, 58, MA, 65, with Ansei Uchima, Ted Egri, Paul R Smith & John Page; Univ Iowa, 61-64, with Stuart Edie & Robert Knipschild. *Work:* Mus Art, El Paso, Tex; Charles H MacNider Mus, Mason City, Iowa; Waterloo Munic Galleries, Iowa; Des Moines Art Ctr; Sioux City Art Ctr, Iowa. *Comn:* Art-in-State Bldg proj, 3 large paintings, Brenton Ctr, Iowa State Univ, Ames, Iowa, 95. *Exhib:* Ann Midyear Show, Butler Inst Am Art, Youngstown, Ohio, 69, 75 & 77; Midwest Biennial, Joslyn Art Mus, Omaha, 72, 74 & 76; Tweed Mus Art, Minn, 80; Mabee-Gerrer Mus Art, Shawnee, Okla, 87; Watercolor USA, Springfield Mus Art, Mo, 88, 94, 2002, 2004, 2006, 2007; Land of the Fragile Giants (touring), Brunnier Art Mus, Iowa State Univ, 94-96; Art-in-Embassies, Cambodia; Leet: 30 Yrs of Painting (retro), touring, 95-97; 57th Juried Exhbn, Sioux City Art Ctr, Iowa, 2001; over 67 solo exhibs & over 100s of invitational & group exhibs; Retrospective, Charles H MacNider Art Mus, Mason City, Ia, 2012; Clear Lake Arts Ctr, Iowa, May/June, 2013. *Pos:* Mus dir & founding dir, CH MacNider Mus, 65-2001. *Teaching:* Instr art, Oelwein Community Schs, Iowa, 58-65; instr painting & drawing, CH MacNider Mus, Mason City, Iowa, 65-85, watercolor and drawing workshops, 2004-. *Awards:* Esther & Edith C Younker Painting Award, Iowa Artist's Show, Des Moines Art Ctr, 78; Lifetime Distinguished Serv Award, Midwest Mus Conf, 95; Patron Purchase award, Watercolor USA, 2002, 2006, 2007. *Bibliog:* Mark Stegmaier (auth), An Artful Balance, Iowan Mag, spring, 88; Richard Leet: Artist/Administrator (exhib catalog), Charles H MacNider Mus, 95; The Art of the Matter, The Rotarion, 6/96. *Mem:* Iowa Arts Coun (mem coun, 70-76); Iowa Mus Asn (pres, 78-80, life mem, Hall of Fame, 2001); Iowa Watercolor Soc (signature mem). *Media:* Watercolor; Pastel Painting. *Collection:* Led Development of collection of Am Art as dir of MacNider Mus, 65-2001. *Publ:* Portfolio, Selections from the Yucatan Sketch Books of Lawrence Mills, 81; He Pulled Lots of Strings, Monograph accomp Bil Baird Mem Exhib, 88; auth & designer, 25 Selections American Art, Charles H MacNider Mus (collection catalog), 91; auth, Charles Atherton Cumming-A Deep Root for Iowa Art, Am Art Rev, vol 2, 4/97; contribr, American Puppetry, PT Dirks, 2004 & The Biographical Dictionary of Iowa, Hudson, Bergman & Horton, 2008. *Dealer:* Octagon Art Shop Ames IA; Clear Lake Arts Ctr Clear Lake IA; Dynamic Designs Mason City IA; Macnider Art Museum Shop, Mason City, Ia. *Mailing Add:* 1149 Manor Dr Mason City IA 50401

LEETE, WILLIAM WHITE
PAINTER

b Portsmouth, Ohio, June 12, 1929. *Study:* Yale Univ, BA, 51, BFA, 55 & MFA, 57. *Work:* De Cordova Mus, Lincoln, Mass; Cleveland Mus, Ohio; Worcester Mus, Mass; Univ Mass; Bank of America, Providence, RI; Providence Mayflower Trust Bank; Mechanics Nat Bank, Worcester, Mass; 180 Beacon St Corp, Boston; various pvt collections; Newport Mus, RI. *Exhib:* New Eng Contemp Artists, Boston, 63 & 65; Silvermine Guild, Conn, 66; Art in Embassies, Inst Contemp Arts, Boston, 66; Structured Art, De Cordova Mus, 69; Young New Eng Painters, John & Mabel Ringling North Mus, Fla; Portland Mus & Currier Gallery, Manchester, 69; Newport Art Asn, RI, 70, 75; Decordova Mus, Decordova Collects, Lincoln, Mass, 78; Hypergraphics Int 7, Kansas City, Mo, 85; Conn Coll Arts and Tech Symposium, 89, 91, 93; numerous exhibs at Univ of RI, Kingston incl Digital Prints, 00. *Teaching:* Assoc prof art, Univ RI, 57-74, prof, 74-95, prof emeritus, 95-. *Mem:* Coll Art Asn. *Media:* Acrylic, Digital. *Interests:* Digital painting, fracals. *Mailing Add:* 202 Silver Lake Ave Wakefield RI 02879-4291

LEFF, CATHY
DIRECTOR

b New York. *Study:* Sophie Newcomb Coll, Tulane Univ, New Orleans, Bachelors, 1973; Univ Miami, Bus Admin; Harvard Bus Sch, Cert Progs; Stanford Bus Sch, Cert Progs. *Pos:* Dir, Wolfsonian, Miami Beach, 1998-Present; publ, Jour Decorative & Propaganda Arts. *Mem:* Assoc Art Mus Dirs. *Mailing Add:* Wolfsonian Mus 1001 Washington Ave Miami FL 33139

LEFKOVSKY, ERIC AND LIZ
COLLECTORS

b. Detroit, Mich, Sept, 69. *Study:* Univ Mich, BA; Univ Mich Law Sch, JD. *Pos:* co-found, Lightbank; dir, InnerWorkings Inc, 2001; dir, Echo Global Logistics Inc, 2005; dir, MediaBank, LLC, 2006; founder & dir, Groupon, 2008. *Teaching:* prof, Univ Chicago Booth Sch Bus, Ill. *Awards:* Name one of Top 200 collectors, ARTnews Mag, 2012, 2013. *Mem:* Art Inst Chicago (bd trustees); Mus Contemp Art (bd trustees). *Collection:* contemporary art. *Publ:* auth, Accelerated Distribution, Easton Studio Press, 2007

LEGGETT, ANN VAUGHAN
PAINTER, PRINTMAKER

b New York, NY, Oct 6, 1941. *Study:* Sarah Lawrence Coll, Bronxville, NY, 58-60; Art Students League, New York, 60-63; apprenticeship with Frank Mason, 60-63. *Work:* Mus of the City of New York; Princeton Univ Library, NJ; Town Hall, West Tisbury, Mass; Wabash Coll, Crawfordsville, Ind. *Comn:* Portrait of Arnold Fischer, West Tisbury, Mass, 84; 7 Libyan Horseman (oil), Mission to U.N. of Libyan Arab Jamahiria, New York, 92. *Exhib:* Solo exhibs, Nat Arts Club, New York, 61, 74 & 86, 500th Anv Bartolome de las Casas, Princeton Univ Libr, NJ, 76, Wabash Coll, Crawfordsville, Ind, 78; Painting New York, Mus of the City of New York, 83; Two-man show, Union League Club, New York, 90; Hammond Mus, North Salem, NY, 2005. *Awards:* Best Vineyard Subject, Martha's Vineyard Agr Soc, Cattle Show & Fair, 65; 3 Montague Award Pastel, Nat Arts Club, Pastel Soc of Am, 74; Award for Portrait, Nat Arts Club, Bruce Stevenson, 76. *Mem:* Japanese Artists Asn of New York; Japan Soc; Asia Soc. *Media:* Oil, Miscellaneous Printmaking, Small Sculpture, Pastel. *Interests:* Gardening; Study of Japanese language and culture. *Publ:* Susan Meyer (auth), 20 Figure Painters, Am Artist/Watson-Guptill, 79; Carol Donnell Kotrozo, Art That Addresses Life, Southwest Art, 80; Kay Larson (auth) Italian Fantasies, New York Facts, New York Living Mag, 83. *Dealer:* Fielder & Fielder 440 North Rd Chilmark MA 02535; GC Lucas Gallery 884 Massachusetts Ave Indianapolis IN 46204. *Mailing Add:* 13-22 Jackson Ave Long Island City NY 11101

LEGRAND, YOLENE
PAINTER, MURALIST

b Port-Au-Prince, Haiti. *Study:* Art Students League, NY, with Kay Hazelip, Peter Homitzky, Leatrice Rose, 92-97; David Leffel Portrait Painting Workshop; Bill Behnken Printmaking Workshop. *Comn:* cityscape mural, St Paul RE, NY, 96. *Exhib:* Solo exhibs, La Maison Francaise Gallery, Columbia Univ, 95, Verve Art Gallery,

Leuven, Belgium, 96, NY Pub Libr, 96, Hamilton Landmark Gallery, NY, 99, L'Alliance Francaise, Washington DC, 99, Shea Stadium, NY, 2000, 101 Hudson St Gallery, Jersey City, NJ, 2000, Alliance Francaise de Miami, 2002, Dennis Public Libr, Dennisport, Cape Cod, Mass, 2004, Wellfleet Public Libr Art Gallery, Cape Cod, Mass, 2006, Univ Coll Art Gallery, Fairleigh Dickinson Univ, NJ, 2006, Hampton Bays Public Libr Art Gallery, Long Island, NY, 2006, Columbia Univ, Russ Berrie Med Sci Pavilion Gallery, 2007-2008 & New York Pub Libr, 2009, Embassy of Haiti, Wash DC, 2009, Durst Orgn Wall Show, NY, 2010, AARLCC us, Ft Lauderdale, Fla, 2010, Uniondale Libr Art Gallery, Long Island, 2010, Montclair Public Libr Art Gallery, NJ, 2012, Tompkins Square Libr Gallery, NY, 2013; group exhibs, Musee du Pantheon Nat Haitien, 99, Wet Paint, Newport Art Mus, RI, 2001, Salmagundi Club, Audubon Artists, 2002, Vanderbilt Gallery, Nantucket, Mass, 2002-2003, Am Mus of Nat Hist, 2004, Pen & Brush Club Juried Exhib, 2004-2005, Nicole Gallery, Chicago, 2005, Dorsey's Art Gallery, NY, 2005, Makeready Press Gallery, Montclair, NJ, 2006, Taiwan Ctr, NY, 2006; Salon Int du Pastel, Yvetot, France, 2007, Conn acad Fine Arts (juried), 2007, Manhattan Borough Pres's Office Gallery, NY, 2008, Salon Int du Pastel, Giverny, France, 2008, Am Mus Natural Hist, Caribbean Heritage, NY, 2008, Bearden Found Gallery, NY, 2008 & Asoc de Pintores Pastelistas, Spain, 2009; NY Pub Libr, 2009; Embassy of Haih, DC, 2009; Durst Org Wall Gallery, 2010; Uniondale Pub Libr Gallery, 2010; Taiwan Ctr Int Pastel Artists Invitational, NY, 2010; Wilmer Jenning Gallery, NY, 2010, 2012; Dorsey Art Gallery, 2011, 2012; Medgar Evers Coll, NY, 2011; Int Pastel Artists Invitational, Taiwan, 2012. *Teaching:* art teacher, Brooklyn Mus, 98-; artist-in-residence, Glen Ridge Elem Sch, 98-; instr, adult painting workshops. *Awards:* Lower Manhattan cult coun grant, 2000; Contribr to the World Art, Manhattan Borough Pres, 2004; LMCC Manhattan Community Arts Fund Grant, 2000; Proclamation Manhattan Borough Pres at City Hall, 2004; Toussaint L'Ouverture Bus Award (as Haitian-Am), 2005; Elaine & James Hewitt Mem Award in Oil, Audubon's 64th Ann Juried Exhib. *Bibliog:* Numerous newspaper articles, 95-98; News-Leader, NJ, 1/27/99; Haitian Times, 3/15/2000, 2/6/02; Miami Times, 9/12/02, 10/3/02; Miami Today, 9/12/02; The Miami Herald, 9/13/02, 10/4/02; Caribbean Life, 2009; South Fla Times, 4/2/2010; Amsterdam News, 7/15/2010; Harlem News Group, 7/2010; NY Beacon, 8/2010; France Amerique, 9/24/2010; NY TImes, 9/12/2010 & 9/19/2010; Caribbean Life 2/24/12. *Mem:* Art Students League NY; Audubon Artists, Inc (bd 1st vpres & treas, 2003-); Allied Artists of Am; Art du Pastel en France; Pastel Soc Am; Asn de Pintores Pastelistas Espanoles. *Media:* Oil, Pastel; Intaglio Print. *Interests:* Landscape. *Publ:* covers, Tribes Mag, fall 2005. *Mailing Add:* Studio # 807 32 Union Square East New York NY 10003

LEHMAN, ARNOLD L
MUSEUM DIRECTOR, CURATOR
b New York, NY, July 18, 1944. *Study:* Johns Hopkins Univ, BA, 65, MA, 66; Yale Univ, MPhil, 68, PhD, 74. *Collection Arranged:* Archit of World Fairs (auth, catalog), Dallas Mus Fine Arts, Tex, 72; Boom or Bust, Am Painting from World War I through 1939, 74; Art Deco, 74; Judaica from Am Collections, 75; The Vanderbilts: Collectors, 75; Am Magic Realists (auth, catalog), 76; World of Haitian Printing, (auth, catalog), 77; 50 Years of Cuban Painting, 77; Oskar Schlemmer (ed, catalog), 86, Benjamin West, 89; A Grand Design: The Art of Victoria & Albert Mus, 97. *Pos:* Chester Dale Fel, Metrop Mus Art, New York, 69-70; dir, Urban Improvements Prog, New York, 70-73; Parks Coun, New York, 73-74; dir, Metrop Mus & Art Ctr, Miami, Fla, 74-79, Baltimore Mus Art, Md, 79-97 & Brooklyn Mus Art, NY, 97-2015. *Teaching:* Lectr art hist, Cooper Union Sch Art & Archit, New York, 69-71; Hunter Coll, City Univ New York, 71-72; adj prof art history, Johns Hopkins Univ, Balt, 86-97. *Mem:* Am Asn Mus Dirs (pres, 90-91, trustee, 86-92). *Res:* American architecture and urban planning; American painting, 20th century; late 19th century French painting. *Publ:* Ed, Oskar Schlemmer, Abrams, 86; contribr, A Grand Design, Abrams, 97

LEHMAN, MAX
SCULPTOR
b Ft Knox, Ky, 1961. *Study:* Santa Fe Comm Coll, Media Arts Prog; Ariz State Univ, Media Arts Prog. *Work:* Ceramic Res Ctr, Ariz State Univ Art Mus; City of Phoenix Art mus, Ariz; Santa Fe Comm Coll, NMex; Kamm Teapot Found, Sparta, NC. *Exhib:* The Contemp Cup, Nat Invitational Exhib, Lillstreet Art Ctr, Chicago, 2005; What's Up Doc?, Kirkland Art Ctr, Kirkland, Wash, 2007; Renegade Ceramics Five Views From the West, Ariz State Univ Ceramic Res Ctr, Ariz, 2007; A Human Impulse, Ariz State Univ Ceramic Res Ctr, Ariz, 2008; All Fired Up, White Plains Mus Gallery, Westchester Arts Coun, NY, 2008; The Trouble with Boys & Girls, Mesa Art Ctr, Ariz, 2009; Tell Me a Story: Contemp Narrative Ceramics, UNI Gallery Art, Cedar Falls, Iowa, 2010. *Pos:* adj fac/IT coordr, Santa Fe Comm College, 2002-2005; web developer, Los Alamos Nat Labs, NMex, 2005-2006; webmaster, NMex Tourism Deptr, NMex, 2006-. *Teaching:* adj fac (web design & animation), Santa Fe Comm Coll, adj fac (ceramic sculpture), 2007-2008. *Media:* Ceramic, Mixed Media. *Mailing Add:* 19 Arroyo Nambe Santa Fe NM 87506

LEHR, JANET
DEALER
b New York, NY, June 7, 1937. *Study:* New York Univ, BA, 55; Brooklyn Law Sch, LLB/JD, 58. *Exhib:* 19th & 20th Century Landscape Photog, Munich State Mus, 78; Luminist Art, NGA, Washington, DC, 78; Robert Demachy, Yale Univ Art Mus, 81; History of Photog, Art Gallery New S Wales, Australia, 94; Horatio Ross, Scottish photographer 1850s, Yale Univ, Brit Ctr for the Arts, 93. *Pos:* Co-partner, Gallery 6M, 62-72; owner, Janet Lehr Inc, 72-; co-owner, Vered Gallery, East Hampton, NY, 88-. *Mem:* Founding mem Asn Int Photog Art Dealers; Antiquarian Booksellers Am. *Res:* Photographically illustrated books of the 19th century. *Specialty:* Fine vintage photographs of both the 19th and 20th century; exceptional contemporary; Milton Avery, Wolf Kahn, Leonard Baskin, Paul Georges and Rediscovery 1930-1950. *Publ:* Auth, Talbot's Role in the History of Photography, Antiquarian Bookman, J Chernofsky, 78; John Thomson, History of Photography, 1/80; and 32 catalogs. *Mailing Add:* 891 Park Ave New York NY 10021

LEHR, MIRA T(AGER)
PAINTER
b New York, NY, Sept 22, 1938. *Study:* Vassar Col, BA, 56; Boston Mus Sch, 57; Robert Motherwell & James Brooks, 68 & 69; Nieves & Billmyer, 60-80. *Work:* Univ Tex Mus, Tyler; Bass Mus, Miami Beach, Fla; Suntrust Banks, FL; Frances Lehman Loeb Art Center, Poughkeepsie, NY; Bacardi Collection, Miami, Fla. *Comn:* Large scale wall piece, Art Enterprises Inc, Chicago, 86; monoprints, Interterra Corp, Miami, 88; Stephanie Odegard Collection: Rugs, 2005. *Exhib:* A Century of Women's Achievements, La Worlds Fair, New Orleans, 85; Ann Hortt Mem, Ft Lauderdale Mus, Fla, 86 & 89; Ann Exhib Contemp Am Paintings, Soc of 4 Arts, Palm Beach, Fla, 87-90; Cuban Mus, Miami, Fla, 89; 6 Artists-NY/Miami, Mus of Contemp Art, Miami, Fla, 94; Elaine Baker Gallery, Boca Raton, Fla, 2003; Bernie Steinbaum Gallery, Miami, Fla, 2004; Miami/Dade Community Col, 2004; Fay Gold Gallery, Atlanta, GA, 2004; Flomenhaft Gallery, NY, 2005. *Pos:* Chmn, Continuum Inc, 80-89 & Art in Public Places, Miami Beach, Fla, 85-91; trustee, Art in Pub Places, Dade Co, 86-90. *Awards:* Purchase Award, First Ann Works on Paper, Univ Tex, 86; Purchase Award, Belmont Towbin Found, 90; Grumbacher Award, Nat Orgn Women Artists, New York, 93. *Bibliog:* Linda Nochlin (auth), article, Best Mag, 10/5/90; Elisa Turner (auth), Luria group poses lively dialogue, Miami Herald, 6/6/90; Andrew Delaplaine (auth), The Myriad Colors of Mira Lehr, YES Mag, Vol I, No 4, 8/5/94; Mira Lehr: Visual Imprints by Courtney Curtis; Florida Design, Florida Design, Inc, Winter, 2003/2004. *Mem:* Womens Caucus Art (bd dir, 83-86); Nat Asn Women Artists; Nat Asoc of Mus, 2005. *Media:* Acrylic, Mixed Media. *Dealer:* Elaine Baker Gallery; Gallery 608 Banyan Trail Boca Raton FL 33431; Fay Gold Gallery, Atlanta, GA; Flomenhaft Gallery, NY, NY. *Mailing Add:* 5215 Pine Tree Dr Miami Beach FL 33140

LEHRER, LEONARD
PAINTER, PRINTMAKER
b Philadelphia, Pa, Mar 23, 1935. *Study:* Philadelphia Coll Art, BFA, 56; Univ Pa, MFA, 60. *Work:* Mus Mod Art & Metrop Mus Art, NY; Nat Gallery of Art, Corcoran Gallery & Libr Cong, Washington; Philadelphia Mus Art. *Comn:* Paintings, Kreissparkasse, Hildesheim, Ger, 90. *Exhib:* Brooklyn Mus Print Show, 72; Solo exhibs, Utah Mus Fine Arts, 73 & 82 & Marian Locks Gallery, Philadelphia, 74, 77 & 84; Galerie Kuhl, Hannover, Ger, 79, 82 & 91; 4th Miami Int Print Biennial, 80; Myung Sook Lee Gallery, NY, 97; Crecloo Art Gallery, NY 2004; Albright Coll Freedman Gallery; Int Ctr Cult Mgt (ICCM), Salzburg, Austria; and others. *Pos:* chair, Nat arts adv comt, Col Bd, 93-06; trustee, Int Print Ctr, New York, 94-. *Teaching:* Prof art & chmn dept, Univ NMex, 70-74; prof art & dir, Sch Art, Ariz State Univ, Tempe, 77-90; chair, Dept Art & Art Prof, New York Univ, 91; dean, Sch Fine & Performing Arts, Columbia Col, Chicago, 01-. *Awards:* First Prize, Fourth Miami Int Print Biennial, 80; Heitland Found Prize, Celle, Ger, 80; Gold Medal Award, Nat Soc Arts & Letters, 81; Fulbright Scholar Grant to Greece, 01; Fulbright Sr Scholar AIA Grant to Greece, 03-; and others. *Bibliog:* VD Coke (auth), The Painter and the Photograph, Univ NMex Press, 72; Fritz Eichenberg (auth), The Art of the Print, Abrams, 76; EA Quensen (publ), The Art of Leonard Lehrer, WGer, 86. *Media:* Collage, Lithography. *Publ:* Auth, articles, Art J, 74; Coll Bd Review, 94; The Tamarind Papers. *Dealer:* Myungsook Lee Gallery New York NY. *Mailing Add:* Sch Fine & Performing Arts Columbia Col Chicago 600 S Michigan Ave Chicago IL 60605-1996

LEIB, CHRIS
PAINTER
Study: Univ Calif Berkeley, BA (Anthropology), 1989; San Francisco State Univ, Interactive Computer Art, Conceptual Design, Painting with Robert Bechtle, 1992; Acad Art Coll, San Francisco, Fine Art, 1993, 1996. *Exhib:* Solo exhibs include Downey Gallery, Santa Fe, 2000, Giacobbe-Fritz Fine Art Gallery, Santa Fe, 2001, 2002, San Francisco Pub Libr, 2004, San Francisco Mus Mod Art, Artists Gallery, 2005; Group exhibs include Sustainability, San Francisco Art Ctr Proj, 2000; Introduction, Hat Factory Artist's Salon, Gallery 22, San Francisco, 2001; Figures & Artifacts, Garden Gallery, Half Moon Bay, Calif, 2001; New Dialogues, Michael Martin Galleries, San Francisco, 2001; Groundswell Mural Proj Auction, White Columns Gallery, New York, 2003; Art for Aids, Sotherby's West, San Francisco, 2004; Art of the Book, Donna Seager Gallery, San Rafael, Calif, 2006, Delicious, 2006; In Real Time: Artists of Studio 212, Mina Dresden Gallery, San Francisco, 2007, Bedtime Stories, 2008; Drawing, Realist Works on Paper, A Mus Gallery, San Francisco, 2008. *Awards:* George Sugarman Found Grant, 2007. *Dealer:* Cain Schulte Gallery 101 Townsend St Suite 207 San Francisco CA 94107

LEIBER, GERSON AUGUST
PRINTMAKER
b Brooklyn, NY, Nov 12, 1921. *Study:* Art Students League; Brooklyn Mus Art Sch; DFA (hon), Bar Ilan Univ, Israel, 93. *Work:* Metrop Mus Art, NY; Whitney Mus Am Art, NY; Nat Gallery Art, Washington, DC; Libr Cong, Washington, DC; Boston Mus Fine Arts. *Comn:* Print eds, Asn Am Artists & Int Graphic Arts Soc. *Exhib:* Solo exhibs, Oakland (California) Mus, 60, New York City, 61-64, 68-69, 72, 76, 85, 95-96, 98-99; Am Prints Today, USA, NY, 59; Cincinnati Int Biennial, 60; Fine Arts Mus Long Island (NY), 91, Steinbaum-Kraus Gallery, 98, Denise Bibro Gallery, East Hampton, 2001, 2003, Guild Hall Mus, 2003; exhib in numerous nat and int; Am Prints, in Russia, Rome, Italy, Mexico City, Mex & Salzburg, Ger; Libr Cong Exhibs; and many others. *Pos:* vpres, Judith Leiber, Inc, New York City, 63. *Teaching:* Instr graphics & illus, Newark Sch Fine & Indust Art, 61-68. *Awards:* Tiffany Fels, 57 & 60; Purchase awards Brooklyn Mus, 53-66 & Hunterdon Co Art Ctr 6th nat print exhib, 1962 Soc Washington Printmakers prize, 62; Audubon Medals of Honor for Graphics, 63-65; Sonia Watter award Am Color Print Soc, 68, 1000 Purchase award Asn Am Artists, 68, John Taylor Arms Mem prize Nat Acad of Design, 71; Am Nat Print Exhib Prize, Assoc Am Artists Gallery. *Bibliog:* Frank Getlein (auth), Bite of the Print, Potter, 63; Hooten & Kaiden (auth), Mother and Child in Modern Art, Meredith Corp. *Mem:* Asn Nat Acad; Soc Am Graphic Artists (pres, 78-80); Audubon Artists. *Media:* Intaglio. *Publ:* Illusr, Crisis (poem), Oxhead Press, 69. *Mailing Add:* 446 Old Stone Hwy East Hampton NY 11937-3191

LEIBERT, PETER R
CERAMIST, SCULPTOR
b New York, NY, Mar 13, 1941. *Study:* Buffalo State Univ, BS (art educ), 63; Indiana Univ, MS (art educ), 67, MFA (ceramics, with distinction), 67. *Comn:* Wall relief, Conn Col, 93. *Exhib:* Solo exhibs, Portogallo Gallery, NY, 69, Cooper Union, NY, 71 & Kogei Gallery, Dobbs Ferry, NY, 74; Lyman Allyn Mus, New London, Conn, 80 & 96; New Port Art Mus, RI, 88; Pritman & Eams Gallery, East Hampton, Long Island, 88; NAC Gallery, Norwich, Conn, 88-96. *Teaching:* Artist in residence, Haystack Mountain Sch Crafts, Deer Isle, Maine, 78; prof ceramics, Conn Col, 67-, chmn dept art, 78-93; prof art. *Awards:* Purchase Prize, Rose Arts Festival, Norwich, Conn, 70-78 & 83; Best in Clay, 22nd Ann Exhib, 78 & First Prize for Sculpture, New Eng Regional Exhib, 83, Mystic Art Asn. *Mem:* Am Crafts Coun; Nat Coun Educ Ceramic Arts; Soc Conn Craftsmen. *Media:* Ceramics; Mixed. *Publ:* Illusr, Back to gum prints, Camera 35, 70 & A portfolio of photography, Pukka, 70; contribr, The artist as photographer, Conn Coll Alumni News, 71. *Mailing Add:* 201 Cummings Art Ctr Connecticut College Box 5473 270 Mohegan Ave New London CT 06320-4196

LEIBOWITZ, BERNICE
PAINTER, EDUCATOR
b Brooklyn, NY, Nov 2, 1929. *Study:* Hunter Col, BA, 50, MA, 53; Art Students League, 55. *Work:* Schering-Plough Collection, Madison, NJ, 81 & 82. *Exhib:* Affiliate Group Show, Newark Mus, NJ, 78; Art of the North East, Silvermine Art Guild, New Canaan, Conn, 90; The New Romanticism, Pleiades Gallery, NY, 90; Art From New York City, Hispano 20 Gallery, Barcelona, Spain, 90; Art Educators as Artists, Glassboro State Col, NJ, 90. *Pos:* Bd dir, Arts Ctr, 80-, chmn, 89-. *Teaching:* Instr fine art, Bergen Community Col, 74-. *Bibliog:* Meredith Hall (auth), Bernice Leibowitz' Haunting Images, Art Speak, 3/90; Eileen Watkins (auth), Celebration of Spring, Sun, Star Ledger, 2/87; Carnival of Color, Manhattan Arts, 11/87. *Mem:* Nat Asn Women Artists; Artists Equity. *Media:* Acrylic. *Mailing Add:* 144 N Terrace Pl New Milford NJ 07646-1208

LEICESTER, ANDREW JOHN
ENVIRONMENTAL ARTIST
b Birmingham, Eng, Mar 5, 1948. *Study:* Portsmouth Polytechnic, England, BA, 69; Manchester Polytechnic, England, MA, 70; Univ Minn, Minneapolis, MFA, 72. *Work:* Walker Art Ctr; Sheldon Mem Art Gallery. *Comn:* Riverwalk at Piers 3 & 5 (promenade and overlook), Philadelphia, Pa, 90; Genetic Eng Bldg (roof, facade and atrium), Iowa State Univ, Ames, 90; Zanja Madre (watergarden), Los Angeles, 92; Courtyard, Minn Hist Ctr, St Paul, 95; Ghost Series (5 ceramic murals) Pa Cent Sta, NY, 95. *Exhib:* Invitation, 75 & The River--Images of the Mississippi, 76, Walker Art Ctr; Proposals for Sawyer Point, Contemp Art Ctr, Cincinnati, 77; Artpark, Lewiston, NY, 78; Art on the Beach, Creative Time, Battery Park, NY, 80; Artists Gardens & Parks, Hayden Gallery, 81; Nature-Sculpture, Wurttembergischer, Kunstverein, Stuttgart, WGer, 81; The Artist As Social Designer, Los Angeles Co Mus Art, 85; The Texas Landscape 1900-1986, Mus Fine Arts, Houston, 86. *Pos:* Bd dir, Pub Art St Paul, Minn. *Teaching:* Instr sculpture & drawing, Carleton Col, Minn, 73-74; instr sculpture, Minneapolis Col Art & Design, 75-80; instr, Sch Landscape Archit, Univ Minn, St Paul, 85; vis fel, Royal Melbourne Inst Technol, Australia, 86. *Awards:* Fel, Minn Arts Bd, 80-81, Nat Endowment Arts, 81-82, Bush Found, 77, 83, 90, McKnight Found, 85 & Fed Transportation Authority, 95. *Bibliog:* John Beardsley (auth), The New Urban Landscape, Earthworks and Beyond, Abbeville Press, 89; Garth Rockcastle (auth), Ethics in Paradise, VIA Mag, Vol 10, 90; Donlyn Lyndon (auth), Conceiving a Courtyard, PLACES Mag, Vol 6, No 3, 90. *Media:* Mixed. *Publ:* Double Crossing, a George Washington Memorial for Dade County Courthouse, Flagler St, Miami, 87; Cincinnati Gateway, Main Entrance to Bicentennial Commons Part, Cincinnati, 88; Riverwalk at Piers 3 & 5, Delaware Avenue, Philadelphia, 90

LEIGH, HARRY E
SCULPTOR, PAINTER
b Buffalo, NY, Nov 7, 1931. *Study:* Albright Art Sch, dipl, 52; State Univ NY, Buffalo, BA, 53; painting with Richard Pousette-Dart, 56-60; Columbia Univ, MA, 59; TC Columbia Univ, prof dipl, 62; studied painting privately with Richard Pousette-Dart, 57-60; studied sculpture with Peter Voulkos, 59-60, NY. *Work:* Va Mus Fine Art, Richmond; Birchfield Penney Art Collection, Buffalo; Ulrich Mus Art, Wichita, Kans; John Dean, Tappan, NY; Pratt Inst, Brooklyn. *Comn:* Albany Int Airport, NY, 2008. *Exhib:* Albright-Knox Art Gallery, Buffalo, NY, 52, 53 & 57; Everson Mus, Syracuse, 61; OK Harris, NY, 72, 74, 78, 05, Sighting & Collection Selection, Anderson Gallery, Buffalo, NY, 93; Community of Creativity: A Century of Mac Dowell Colony Artists, Currier Gallery Art, Manchester, NH, 96; Nat Acad Design, NY, 97; Wichita Art Mus, Kans, 97; Interpreting the River, Blue Hill Cult Ctr, Pearl River, NY, 98; 26 sculptures, Artist in Their Studios, Rockland Ctr for Arts, Nyack, NY, 99; Silvermine Guild Art Ctr, 51st Ann Exhib, Art of the Northeast, New Canaan, Conn, 2000; John Davis Gallery, Hudson, NY, 2006-2007, 2010; Chautauqua 56th Ann Exhib, Selected by Director of Albright-Knox Gallery, Janne Siren, 2013. *Collection Arranged:* The Constructed Image, Rockland Center for Arts, West Nyack, NY. *Awards:* MacDowell Fel, artist-in-residence, 68-69, 70, 72, 74-75, 83 & 85-86; Yaddo Fel, artist-in-residence, 72, 79-80, 87, 90, 96, 2001-09; Creative Arts Prog Serv Fel, 78-79; Hand Hollow Found Fel, 80; artist-in-residence, Thorpe Intermedia Gallery, 88; John D and Catherine T MacArthur Found Residency at Yaddo, 2007; Space Prog grant, 2010; Residency, Marie Walsh Sharp Art Found, NYC, 2010-2011; The Richard Florsheim Art Fund Studio award, 2010-2011. *Bibliog:* Martin Last (auth), rev, Art News, 1/69; Elizabeth Frank Perlmutter (auth), article, Art News, 9/74; Grace Glueck (auth), Harry Leigh & Keith Long, NY Times, 5/12/78; and others. *Mem:* MacDowell Fel Comt (treas, 80-93). *Media:* Wood, Bricks; House Paint, Oil. *Dealer:* OK Harris 383 W Broadway New York NY 10012. *Mailing Add:* 340 Haverstraw Rd Suffern NY 10901

LEIGH, SIMONE
SCULPTOR
Study: Earlham Coll, Ind, BA, 1990. *Exhib:* SMIRK, Women, Art and Humor, Firehouse Gallery, Hempstead, NY, 2001; Ctr for African Am Art and NOEL Gallery, Charlotte, North Carolina, 2002; Nathan Cummings Found, New York, 2003; Steuben Gallery, Pratt Inst, Brooklyn, 2004; James E Lewis Mus Art, Morgan State Univ, Baltimore, 2005; Remnants and Relics: Reinterpretations in African Am Art, Jamaica Ctr for Arts and Learning, Queens, NY, 2005; solo exhibs, Momenta Art Gallery, Brooklyn, 2005, Rush Arts Gallery Project Space, New York, 2008, G Fine Art Project Room, Washington, DC, 2009 & In Practice, Sculpture Ctr, Queens, 2009; Brooklyn Divas, Corridor Gallery, NY, 2006; Red Badge of Courage, Newark Coun for Arts, Newark, NY, 2007; Visual Jury, Fine Art Work Ctr, Provincetown, Mass, 2007; Intransit, Moti Hasson Gallery, New York, 2008; Ethnographies of the Future, Rotunda Gallery, Brooklyn, 2008; Pulse, Taller Boricua, NY, 2009; The Pleasure of Hating, Lisa Cooley Fine Art, NY, 2009; 30 Seconds off an inch, Studio Mus Harlem, 2009; Herd Thinner, Charest-Weinberg Gallery, Miami, 2009; Else, Jack Tilton Gallery, 2010; Comedy and Tradgedy, Marvelli Gallery 2010; Bunny Redux, Andy Warhol Mus, Pittsburge, Pa, 2010. *Awards:* Kil God Fel, Watershed Ctr for Ceramic Arts, Maine, 2001; Wheeler Found Grant, 2004; Workspace Grant, Lower Manhattan Cult Coun, 2007; Visual Arts Grant, Astraea Found, 2007; Art Matters Found Grant, 2009; NY Found Arts Fel, 2009. *Media:* Miscellaneous Media. *Dealer:* Charest-Weinberg Gallery 250 NW 23rd St SPace 408 Miami FL 33127. *Mailing Add:* c/o G Fine Art 1350 Florida Ave NE Washington DC 20002

LEIGHTON, DAVID S R
ADMINISTRATOR
b Regina, Sask, Feb 20, 1928. *Study:* Queen's Univ, BA; Harvard Univ, MBA, DBA. *Hon Degrees:* Windsor Univ, LLD; Queen's Univ, LLD. *Pos:* Dir, Sch Fine Arts, Banff Ctr, 70-82; Dir, Nat Ctr for Mgt Res Develop, Univ Western Ont, 86-99; chmn, Nat Arts Ctr, Ottawa, 99-. *Teaching:* Prof, Univ Western Ontario, 56-70, 86-93. *Bibliog:* auth, co-auth, 9 books on Marketing; co-auth, Artists Builders & Dreamers, 83; co-auth, Making Boards Work, 97

LEIS, MARIETTA PATRICIA
PAINTER
b Newark, NJ. *Study:* Univ Calif, Santa Monica Community Coll, Parson, 78-82; Univ NMex, Albuquerque, MA, 85 & MFA, 88. *Work:* St Mary's Home, Manitowoc, Wis; Univ NMex, Health Servs & Div Continuing Educ Conf Ctr; Ross Labs, Columbus, Ohio; State Capitol, Santa Fe, NMex; Corrales Sr Ctr, Corrales, NMex; Albuquerque Art Mus, NMex; Resort at Summerlin, Las Vegas; Hudson Valley Hosp Ctr, Peekskill, NY; Harwood Mus, Taos, NMex; NMex State Libr, Santa Fe; MOCA, Hot Springs, Ark; and others. *Comn:* Fort Smith Conv Ctr, Alaska; bas relief mural, 1% for Art, NMex State Libr, Records, Archives, Santa Fe. *Exhib:* Solo exhibs, In Between Architectonic Artworks, Pt I, Univ MNex, Albuquerque, 88, Pt II, Dartmouth St Gallery, Albuquerque, 88, Marietta Patricia Leis: The Pentimento Series, Pac Int Art Gallery, Palo Alto, Calif, 91, Textures of Italy, Univ NMex Continuing Educ Conf Ctr, Albuquerque, 93, Illuminations, The Casements, City Cult & Civic Ctr, Ormond Beach, Fla, 94, Excerpts from the Marietta Robusti Tintoretto Story, Jonson Gallery, Univ NMex, Albuquerque, 96, Marietta Robusti Tintoretto Story, Patricia Carlisle Gallery, Santa Fe, NMex, 2001, W Valley Mus, Surprise, Ariz, 2001, Atmospheres: Inspirations from the Highlands, Gallery-in-the-field, Brandon, Vt, 2006 & Koelsch Gallery, Houston, Tex, 2008; Man & Nature, Stone House Gallery, Fredonia, Kans, 88; Pindar Nat Invitational, 5 Artists, Pindar Gallery, Soho, NY, 89; Graven Images, Chemeketa Community Col, Salem, Ore, 93; Two Artists, Clatsop Community Col, Astoria, Ore, 94; MOSTRA 94, Mus Ital Americano, San Francisco, 94; Two Views, Montana State Univ, Billings, 95; Visible Whispers, Univ Gallery of Bridgeport, Conn, 99; Past Influence / Present Use, Sun Valley Ctr for Arts, Vt, 2000; Crater Lake Centennial Exhib, Schneider Mus Art, Ashland, Ore, 2002; All That Glitters (with catalog), Islip Art Mus, East Islip, NY, 2003; 35th Nat Exhib, Palm Springs Desert Mus, Calif, 2004; Messing Around & Around, Spike Gallery, New York, 2005; Nat Biennial, Chattahoochee Valley Art Mus, LaGrange, Ga, 2006; Dante's Inferno, Museo ItaloAmericano, San Francisco, 2007; Harmonious Convergence, Museo ItaloAmericano, San Francisco, 2008; IATTDA, The Poly, Falmouth, Cornwall, Uk & Galeria de Arte Pintor Samora Barros, Albufeira, Portugal, 2008; Grants Pass Mus, Ore, 2009; Harlan Gallery, Seton Hall Univ, Pa, 2009; Long Island Mus, New York, 2009; Meadows Gallery, Univ Tex, Tyler, Tex, 2010; 105 Gallery, Albuquerque, NMex, 2010; Ctr Contemp Arts, Santa Fe, NMex, 2010; 2011 Park Fine Art Int Tour Show, Park Fine Art, Albuquerque, NMex, Han-Yan Gallery, Bejing, China, EW Culture Gallery, Seoul, Korea, Korea Int Art Fair, Almelek Gallery, Istanbul, Turkey, 2012; Environmental Considerations, Carr Gallery, Willard Arts Ctr, Id Falls, 2012; 10 by 10 Collect, Ctr Contemp Art, Santa Fe, NMex, 2012; Expo 31, BJ Spoke Gallery, Huntington, NY, 2012; Works on Paper, Abercrombie Gallery, MCNeese State Univ, Lake Charles, LA, Grey Gallery, NYU, 2012; 18th Ann Tex Nat, Cole Art Ctr, Old Opera House, Nacogdoches, Tex, 2012; Lo Studio dei Nipoi, Int Arts and Artists Hillyer Art Space, Wash DC, 2012; 2012 Park Fine Art Int Tour Show, Park Fine Art, Albuquerque, NMex, EW Culture Gallery, Seoul, Korea, Korea Int Art Fair, Almelek Gallery, Istanbul, Turkey; Going Green II, Crossing Art, Queens, NY; Two person exhib, Environmental Considerations, Carr Gallery, Willard Art Ctr, Id Falls, 2012; 10x10 Collect, Ctr Contemp Art, Santa Fe, NMex; Expo 31, b.j. Spoke Gallery, Huntington, NY, New Mus, NY, 2012; Works on Paper, Abercrombie Gallery, McNeese State Univ, Lake Charles, LA, Grey Gallery, NY, 2012; 18th Ann Tex Nat, Cole Art Ctr, Old Opera House, Nacogdoches, Tex, 2012; Earthly Pleasures, Walsh Gallery, Seton Hall Univ, South Orange, NJ, 2013; Green Abundance, Las Cruces Mus Art, NMex, 2013; 28th Int Exhib, Meadows Gallery, Univ Tex, Tyler, 2013; Intimate Visions, Leich Lathrop Gallery, Albuquerque, NMex, 2013; Sea and Sky, Liz Afif Gallery, Phila, Pa, 2013; Selections from the Permanent Coll, NMSU Univ Art Gallery, NMex, 2013; Miniatures, Albuquerque Mus Art, NMex, 2013. *Pos:* Lectr, including Vt, Tenn, Colo, NMex and others, 97-. *Awards:* Hon Distinction, Int Art Biennial-Mus, Hisico, Capranica, Italy; Artists Grant, ED Found, 94, 95 & 96; Artist

Grant, Connemara Conservancy, Dallas, Tex, 98; Artist-in-residence, Weir Farm Trust, Wilton Conn, 2000, Schneider Mus, Ashland, Ore, 2001, Footpaths to Creativity, Azores, Portugal, 2007 & Wassard a Elea, Ascea, Italy, 2008; Artist in Residence, Compelling Village, Doi Saket, Thailand, 2010; Artist in Res, Kemi Jarvi, Finland, 2011. *Bibliog:* O Reed, Jr (auth), Multimedia artist likes viewers touch, to feel her work, Albuquerque Tribune, 3/2/93; S Randall (auth), She works in every medium you can imagine, Albuquerque J, Bosque Beat, Metro Plus, 4/27/93; L Stewart (auth), Secret garden blooms in illuminating exhibit, Daytona Beach Sunday News J, 7/17/94; T Dingman (auth), Blue by Her, Albuquerque Sunday Jour, Arts & Culture Section F, 5/2005, 1-2; J Carver, Picturing Transcendence, Focus, 8-9/2006, 34-35; P Coyle (auth), Through the Eyes of Artists, Images of Albuquerque, 32-35, Vol 1, 2008; and others. *Mem:* Coll Art Asn. *Media:* Oil, All Media. *Publ:* Auth, Three Artists in touch, Albuquerque Journal, W Pulkka, 10/31/99; Alegacy Framed (brochure), Jonson Gallery, 96. *Dealer:* Roelsch Gallery Houston TX; Tinney Fine Art Nashville TN; Swapp-Price Projects Albuquerque NM; Leich Lanthrop Albuquerque NM. *Mailing Add:* 601 Aliso Dr SE Albuquerque NM 87108-3327

LEITAO, CATARINA
PRINTMAKER, SCULPTOR
b Stuttgart, Ger. *Study:* Univ Lisbon, Portugal, BA, 1993; Hunter Coll, New York, MFA, 1999. *Exhib:* Solo exhibs, Centro de Arte Moderna, 2002, Galeria Pedro Cera, Lisbon, 2004, 2006, 2009; Leaves of Grass Pillow, Tenri Cult Inst, New York, 2006; 50 Years of Portuguese Art, Calouste Gulbekian Found, 2007; Point of View, Museu da Cidade, Lisbon, Portugal, 2008; Pretty Tough: Contemporary Storytelling, Aldrich Contemp Art Mus, 2009; Open Book: An International Survey of Experimental Books, Eastern Mich Univ, 2010. *Awards:* Pollock-Krasner Found Grant, 2002; Marie Walsh Sharpe Art Found Grant, 2005; NY Found Arts Fel, 2009

LEITES, ARA (BARBARA) L
PAINTER, EDUCATOR
b Hamilton, Ohio, June 3, 1942. *Study:* Miami Univ, BFA, 1964 & MFA, 1967; studied with Judi Betts, Betty Lou Schlemm, Robert Wade, Milford Zornes, Louise Cadillac, Maxine Masterfield & Al Brouillette. *Work:* Springfield Art Mus, Mo; Dayton Art Inst, Ohio. *Exhib:* Cincinnati Art Mus Ann & Biennial, Ohio, 1966, 1967; Audubon Artists Ann Exhib, Salmagundi Club, NY, 1989, 1994, 1997, 1999; Nat Watercolor Soc Ann, Muckenthaler Cult Ctr, Fullerton, Calif, 1991, 2000; Foothills/Rocky Mountain Nat, Foothills Art, Colo, 1991, 1998, 2001-2003, 2007; Allied Artists Ann, Nat Arts Club, NY, 1994, 1996, 2004; Watercolor USA, Springfield Art Mus, Mo, 1997, 2000, 2011; Watercolor USA, Japan Exchange, 2010; Watercolor Hon Soc Biennial, Springfield Art Mus, Mo, 1997, 2011; Int Soc Acrylic Painters, 1997-2000, 2002-2012, 2013; NAPA UK, Westminster Gallery, London, 1999; Am Watercolor Soc, 1999, 2008, 2009, 2012; Soc Watercolor Artists-Ft Worth, 1993, 1995-97, 2000, 2001; Okla Nat Watercolor Soc, 1993, 1997, 1998, 2002, 2003-2005; Eastern Wash Watercolor Soc, 1997, 2002; San Diego Watercolor Soc, 2001, 1995; Pittsburgh Watercolor Soc, 1997, 1994, 1997, 1999-2001; Int Soc Experimental Artists, 1997-2001, 2003, 2004, 2012; Ariz Aqueous, 1992, 1994, 1996-1999, 2005, 2010; Philadelphia Watercolor Asn Soc, 1992, 1996, 1998, 2000; Northwest Watercolor Soc, 1999, 2000; Ariz Watercolor Asn, 1998, 1999, 2003, 2005; Soc Watercolor Artists, 1999, 2002-2003, 2006; Wyoming Watercolor Soc, 1999; Red River Watercolor Soc, 1997; Parkersburg Art Ctr, 1996, 1997; Western Colo Watercolor Soc, 1995, 1996; Northeast Watercolor Soc, 1993, 1996; Madison Avenue Art Gallery of Tenn, 1996; Calif Watercolor Asn, 1996, 2009, 2011; Soc Experimental Artists, 1992-1994, 1996-2004, 2012; Nat Congress of Art and Design, 1995; Mid-Atlantic Regional Watercolor Exhib, 1993-95; Watercolor Today, Conn, 1992. *Pos:* Bd dir, Woodstock Guild Craftsmen, NY, 1978-1979; co-dir, Kleinert Gallery, Woodstock Guild, 1978-1979; reg rep, Calif Watercolor Soc, 1998-, pres/treas ISAP, 2008-2013. *Teaching:* instr drawing, painting, Georgiana Bruce Kirby Photog Preparatory High Sch, 1998-2001 & 2005-2013, head visual arts dept, 1999-2001, workshops in acrylic, 2013, retired, 2013. *Awards:* Winsor Newton Award, Ky Watercolor Soc, 1996; Eastern Wash Watercolor Soc for Best of Show, 1997, Merit award, 2002; Swede Johnson Memorial Award, Rocky Mountain Nat, 1998; Chairman's award-Most Experimental Painting, Soc Watercolor Artists, 2002; Ga Peach award, Ga Watercolor Soc, 2002, Travel Show Selection, 1997; Best of Show award, Okla Nat Watercolor Soc, 2002, Tulsa Art Clubs award, 1997; Merit award, Eastern Wash Watercolor Soc, 2002; Watermedia, Int soc experimental Artist Houston, Tex, 2003; 23rd Adirondacks Nat Exhib Am Watercolors Award, Dr. Donald & Helen Budd Burness Memorial, 2004-2005; Texas Watercolor soc 56th Annual Nat Exhib Award, 2005-2006; Most Experimental award in Acrylics, ISEA; Jane Riley Bowers Mem Award, Texas Watercolor soc, 2009; ISAP Third Place, 2011, 2012; CA.W.A. Silver Medal, 2011. *Bibliog:* Edited by Dona LeCrone Walston, Fifty Years of Excellence - Tex Watercolor Soc, 1999; Finalist/Experimental Category, The Artist's Mag, Dec, 2000; International Artist, Feb/Mar, 2001; The Artist's Magazine, 2004; The Palette Magazine, issue 17, 3/2006-4/2006. *Mem:* Signature mem Nat Watercolor Soc; signature mem Am Watercolor Soc; signature mem Tex Watercolor Soc; signature mem Ky Watercolor Soc; signature mem Nat Soc Painters In Casein & Acrylic; signature mem Nat Acrylic Painters Asn; signature mem Audubon Artists, Inc; signature mem Miss Watercolor Soc; signature mem Ga Watercolor Soc; signature mem Watercolor Soc Ala; Federation Canadian Artists (former mem); Mont Watercolor Soc; signature mem Taos Nat Watercolor Soc; signature mem Pa Watercolor Soc; signature mem Rocky Mountain Nat Watercolor Soc; signature mem Soc Layerists in Mixed Media; Mo Watercolor Soc; signature mem CWA; signature mem ISAP. *Media:* Acrylic, Watercolor. *Interests:* skiing; paddle-boarding; carpentry. *Collection:* KMS Corp; Seattle Washington, 1992; Dos Puertos Restuarante; Mexico City, Mexico, 1994; Kastrea Corp; Mexico City, Mexico, 1994; Tane Internat'l; Mexico City, Mexico, 1995; Ascala SA, Mexico City, Mexico, 1996; Springfield Art Mus, Springfield, MO, 1997; NAPA Exhib-England; Alizadeh Toosi, BBC World Serv, Persian Section, Strand, London WC2B 4PH Timothy Clarke, Farthings/Seymour Place, Mile Path, Hook Heath, Gu 22 OJX, 1999; Angaria SA, Mexico City, Mexico, 2004. *Publ:* Contrib, Creative Watercolor: A Step By Step Process, 1995, Best of Watercolor, 1995, Best Abstracts, 1995, Best of Watercolor-Composition, 1997, Rockport Press; Splash 5, Northlight, Bks, 1998; Fifty Years of Excellence-Tex Watercolor Soc, 1999; Finalist/Experimental Catalog-Dec issue, pp 49; Chosen for inclusion in 2004 Limited Ed Calendar The Artists Magazine, 2003; The Art of Layering, Making Connections, 2004, The Soc of Layerists in Mult-Media, Finalist/Experimental Category-December issue The Artists Magazine, 2004; Watercolor Magic (feature article), 8/2006; contrib, The Creative Edge, Mary Todd Beam, Northlight, 2009. *Mailing Add:* 168 Oxford Way Santa Cruz CA 95060

LEITHAUSER, MARK ALAN
PAINTER, DESIGNER
b Detroit, Mich, June 22, 1950. *Study:* Wayne State Univ, BA, 72, MA, 73, MFA, 74. *Work:* Nat Gallery Art; Brooklyn Mus; Libr Cong. *Exhib:* Michigan Focus, Detroit Inst Arts, 74; Boston Printmakers Nat Show, DeCordova Mus, Lincoln, Mass, 76; 30 Yrs of Am Printmaking, Brooklyn Mus, 76; Nat Printmakers Show, Libr Cong, 77; In Celebration of Prints, Philadelphia Art Alliance, 80; Nat Print & Drawing Competition, Dulin Gallery Art, Knoxville, Tenn, 81; Am Perspective, 81 & Close Focus, 87, Nat Mus Am Art; Recent Acquisitions on Paper, Corcoran Gallery Art, 81; solo exhibs, Coe Kerr Gallery, 89 & 92, Chrysler Mus, 93 & Corcoran Gallery, 93; Refiguring Nature, Mus Contemp Art, Ft Worth, 91. *Pos:* sr cur, chief design, Nat Gallery Art, 74-. *Awards:* Purchase Award, Nat Print Show, Libr Cong, 75, Nat Printmakers Show, Nat Mus Am Art, 77 & Nat Print & Drawing Exhib, Dulin Gallery Art, 81; Leslie Cheek Design Award, 88; Presidential Design Award, 84, 88, 92 & 95. *Media:* Painting, Etching. *Dealer:* Hollis Taggart Gallery 48 E 73rd St New York NY 10021. *Mailing Add:* 3614 Idaho Ave NW Washington DC 20016

LEKA, DEREK
PAINTER
b Bridgeport, Conn, Nov 6, 1970. *Study:* Purchase Col, NY, BFA, 2005; Western Conn State Univ, Danbury, MFA, 2007. *Exhib:* Group exhibs include Erie Canal Mus, Syracuse, NY, 2002; Artspace, New Haven, 2005 & 2007; Art of the Northeast, Silvermine Guild Arts Ctr, Norwalk, Conn, 2008; 183rd Ann: Invitational Exhib Contemp Art, Nat Acad Mus, New York, 2008. *Teaching:* Instr, color. Silvermine Guild Arts Ctr, 2007, 2008, Southern Conn State Univ, 2008. *Awards:* Andrew Carnegie Prize, Nat Acad, 2008. *Mem:* Silvermine Guild Arts Ctr. *Mailing Add:* 393 Washington Ave West Haven CT 06516

LEKBERG, BARBARA
SCULPTOR
b Portland, Ore, Mar 19, 1925. *Study:* Univ Iowa, BFA & MA, with Humbert Albrizio. *Hon Degrees:* Simpson Coll, DFA, 64. *Work:* Montclair Mus Art, NJ; Des Moines Art Ctr, Iowa; Knoxville Art Ctr, Tenn; Whitney Mus Am Art; General Electric Collection, Fairfield, Conn. *Comn:* Three interior sculptures, Beldon-Stratford Hotel, Chicago, 53; three interior sculptures, Socony-Mobil Co, New York, 55; lobby relief, Riedl & Freede Advert, Clifton, NJ, 64; life-size figures, Bayfield Clark, Bermuda, 71 & 74; Orpheus (10 ft work), Simpson Coll, Iowa, 84; life-size figure, Trafalgar House Realty, New York, 86; Loie Fuller Dancing figure, Brookgreen Gardens, SC, 2005; and others. *Exhib:* Five Pa Acad Fine Arts Ann, Philadelphia, 50-62; Whitney Mus Ann, 52 & 56; New Talent, Am Fedn Arts Traveling Show, 59-60; Recent Sculpture USA, Mus Mod Art, New York, 59; solo exhibs, Sculpture Ctr, New York, 59, 65, 71, 75, 77 & 83, Traveling Exhib, Birmingham Mus Art, Ala & Columbia Mus Art, SC, 73, Percival Galleries, Des Moines, Iowa, 90, 95 & 2000, Harmon Meek Galleries, Naples, Fla, 97 & Century Asn, New York, 2001; Retrospective, Mt Holyoke Coll Mus, Mass, 78; Contemp Sculpture at Chesterwood, Stockbridge, Mass, 88-89, 94, 97, 2001 & 2004; British Mus, London, 94; Meguro Mus, Tokyo, Japan, 2001. *Teaching:* Fac, Coll New Rochelle, 80-84; Univ Arts, Phila, 81-2001; Nat Acad Design, New York, 90-95. *Awards:* Am Inst Arts & Lett Grant, 56; Guggenheim Found Fels, 57 & 59; Saltus Gold medal, Nat Acad, 90; Fel, Gold medal, Nat Sculpture Soc, 91; Grant, Richard Florsheim Art Fund, 98; and others. *Bibliog:* Wayne V Anderson (auth), American Sculpture in Progress 1930-1970, New York Graphic Soc, 75; Donald M Reynolds (auth), Masters of American Sculpture: The Figurative Tradition, Abbeville Press, 93; Nathan Cabot Hale (auth), Creative Welding, Overpress, 94; and others. *Mem:* Sculptors Guild; Nat Acad (acad, 90); Nat Sculpture Soc (sec, Fel, 91). *Media:* Bronze, Welded Steel. *Dealer:* Harmon-Meek Gallery Naples FL; Judith Leighton Gallery Blue Hill ME

LELAND, WHITNEY EDWARD
PAINTER, EDUCATOR
b Washington, DC, Apr 12, 1945. *Study:* Memphis Acad Arts, BFA; Univ Tenn, Knoxville, MFA. *Work:* Springfield Art Mus, Mo; Hunter Mus Art, Chattanooga, Tenn; Nat Mus Am Art, Smithsonian Inst, Washington, DC; Ark Art Ctr, Little Rock; Chase Manhattan Bank, NY. *Exhib:* solo exhib, Cumberland Gallery, Nashville, 90, Slemp Gallery, Mountain Empire Community Col, Big Stone Gap, Va, 93; 33rd Chautauqua Nat Exhib Am Art, Chautauqua, NY, 90; H20 Color Exhib, Crossman Gallery, Univ Wis, Whitewater, Wis, 93; Watercolor USA, Springfield Art Mus, Springfield, Mo, 94; The Tenn Twelve: Contemp Painting Today, Tenn State Mus, Nashville, Tenn, 94. *Teaching:* Asst prof, Univ Tenn, Knoxville, 70-78, assoc prof, 78-86, prof painting, 86-. *Awards:* Fel Grant, Nat Endowment Art, SE Ctr Contemp Art, 77; Nominee, Eighth Ann Awards Visual Arts, SE Conf Contemp Art, Winston-Salem, NC, 88; Arches & Rives Paper Award, Arjo Wiggins USA, Springfield Art Mus, 92. *Bibliog:* Bennett Schiff (auth), In a Tobacco City the Arts are Put in Place-Out Front, Smithsonian, Vol 9, No 10, 1/79; Don Kurka (auth), Southern Abstraction, Art Papers, Vol 8, No 2, 3-4/84; Faith Heller (auth), Ten Years of 'Southeast Seven': An Abundance of Individual Visions, Arts J, 1/88. *Media:* Acrylic, Watercolor. *Dealer:* Cumberland Gallery Nashville Tenn. *Mailing Add:* 2205 Maplewood Dr Knoxville TN 37920-2754

LEMAY, HARRY ADRIAN
PAINTER, INSTRUCTOR
b Lewistown, Pa, Dec 19, 1929. *Study:* US Merchant Marine Acad, BS (with hon), 52; Cooper Union, grad cert, 58, CCNY Masters, 74. *Work:* Libr Cong, Washington, DC; Mus Radio & Television Broadcasting, New York & Los Angeles. *Comn:* Graphic Design, Illus, Reader's Digest, Dell Books, New York, 59-65; Illus & Design, Columbia Record Club, New York, 60-63; Graphic Design, Life Mag, Prom, NY, 64; Package Design, Pfizer, Merk Sharf & Dome, New York, 64; Lighting Design, Carnegie Hall-Folklorico Filipino, New York, 73. *Exhib:* First Paperback Book Show, AIGA, New York, 59; 25 Year Retrospective, Kenny Gallery, Art & Design, New York, 80; Solo exhib, LaGuardia Community Coll, New York, 91; 5 Solo exhibs, 3 in NY, 1 in LA; 25 Group exhibs, 12 in NY, 13 in LA. *Pos:* Art dir, Mann Assoc, New York, 60-64; mgr art & production, RCA Victor Record Club, New York, 65-67; vpres creative, Capitol Record Club, Los Angeles, Calif, 67-69. *Teaching:* Instr theater arts, design, drawing, Art & Design, New York, 72-91; instr life drawing, graphic design, Sch for the Arts, Los Angeles, Calif, 93-97; instr life drawing, Rustic Canyon Park, La Brea Art Ctr, Los Angeles, Calif, 93-98. *Awards:* Best in Show, Suburban Art League, NY, 62. *Bibliog:* NBC TV Series (mongr), You're Part of Art, 70. *Mem:* Los Angeles Art (93-97); Art Students League NY (life mem); County Mus Am Art Philatelic Soc. *Media:* Acrylic, Oil, Educator, Lecturer. *Interests:* art book collecting; computer graphics; website design. *Publ:* Medley Mag, 65-66; Keynotes Mag, 67-69; Dr Cristina Carney (auth), LeMay Lines Through Time (monogr); Calif Quar, Univ Calif Davis, 81; Kiplinger's Personal Finance Mag, 2/98. *Dealer:* Jean Marc Gallery 906 N LaCienega Los Angeles, CA 90069. *Mailing Add:* 357 S Curson Ave #6B Los Angeles CA 90036

LEMAY, NANCY
PAINTER, GRAPHIC DESIGNER
b New York, NY. *Study:* Sch Visual Arts, BFA, 78; NY Univ, 84; Calif State Univ, MA in Communication Studies, 2012. *Comn:* Designer (logotype design), Art Direction Mag, 85. *Exhib:* Group exhib, Wings N Water Festival (poster winner), 90; Designer, Robey Theater Co, 2014. *Pos:* Graphic designer, JC Penney, 87-89; art dir, Catch A Rising Star, 89; graphic designer, WNBC TV News Graphics, 89-90; graphics engineer, NBC Network News Graphics, 90-91, KCOP TV News, Los Angeles, 91-94 & superv graphic designer, 94-2000; graphic designer, KNBC-TV, 2000-01; graphic artist, KABC TV, 2006-. *Teaching:* Instr, Rustic Canyon, Santa Monica, Calif, 2001- & Abram Friedman Occupational Ctr, Los Angeles, 2001-; instr, Studio Arts, Calif State Univ, Los Angeles, 2006-,; instr, Oasis, 2009. *Awards:* Recipient, 5 Los Angeles Area Emmy Awards, 96-99; Catharine Lorillard Wolfe Art Club's, 108th Ann Nat Juried Show, 2004; 3 Broadcast Designer Assn Awards; 4 Assoc Press Awards. *Mem:* Art Dir Guild; Nat Hon Soc; Phi Kappa Phi. *Media:* Oil, Acrylic, Collage, Watercolor & Photography. *Interests:* painting, bird watching, sculpture, photography. *Publ:* Contribr, MacWeek Mag, 89; Kiplinger's Personal Finance Mag, 2/98; featured artist, White Graphics, 2001. *Dealer:* Carol Sauvion Freehand 8413 W Third St Los Angeles CA 90048; Aarnon Gallery 603 E Green St Pasadena CA 91101

LEMIEUX, ANNETTE ROSE
CONCEPTUAL ARTIST, PAINTER
b Norfolk, Va, Oct 11, 1957. *Study:* Northwestern Conn Community Col, AA, 77, Hartford Art Sch, Univ Hartford, Conn, BFA, 80. *Work:* Mus Mod Art, Chase Manhattan Bank, Dannheisser, New York; Rooseum, Malmö, Sweden; Okla Art Mus, Okla City; Elaine Dannheisser Found, New York; Israel Mus, Jerusalem, Israel. *Exhib:* Solo shows incl Wadsworth Mus, Hartford, Conn, 88, Rhona Hoffman Gallery, Chicago, 90, Josh Baer Gallery, New York, 91 & 93, Stichting De Appel, Amsterdam, Holland, 92, Brooke Alexander Ed, New York, 93, Davis Mus & Cult Ctr, Wellesley Col, Mass, 94 & Kaiser Wilhelm Mus, Krefeld, Ger, 94; group shows incl Whitney Biennial, Whitney Mus Am Art, New York, 87 & 89; Currents, Inst Contemp Art, Boston, Mass, 87; Nat Mus Am Art, Smithsonian Inst, Washington, 89; Albright Knox Mus, Buffalo, NY, 89; San Francisco Mus Mod Art, Calif, 90; Corcoran Gallery, Washington, 90; Newport Harbor Art Mus, Newport Beach, Calif, 90; Oklahoma City Art Mus, Okla, 91; More Than One Photography, Mus Mod Art, New York, 92; Benefit Exhib, Leo Castelli Gallery, New York, 93; Giftland II: Extra-ordinary, Printed Matter Bookstore, 93; Milena Dopitova In Context, Inst Contemp Art, Boston, 94; The Ossuary, Luhring Augustine Gallery, New York, 94; Old Glory: The American Flag in Contemporary Art, Cleveland Ctr Contemp Art, 94. *Teaching:* Visiting artist & lecturer at mus, schools & organizations for the past 7 years. *Awards:* New York Fel for Painting, 87; Nat Endowments Arts Painting Grant, 87 & 91; Mies van der Rohe Stipendium, Kaiser-Wilhelm Mus, Krefeld, Ger, 92. *Bibliog:* Vivien Raynor (auth), What do clothes mean to an artist anyway?, NY Times, Conn ed, 6/13/93; Frank Merkling (auth), Unstylish in 'Fashion' at Aldrich, News-Times, Conn, 6/15/93; Bill Van Siclen (auth), Sex & politics mix in Brown exhibit, Art News, 2/94. *Publ:* Beyond Boundaries (Jerry Saltz, auth), Rizzolli, 86; Contribr, Unexpressionism (Germant Celant, auth), Rizzolli, 88; Memoirs of a Survivor, ZG Publ, Brooke Alexander Inc, 89. *Dealer:* Josh Baer Gallery 270 Lafayette St New York NY 10012; Baldwin Gallery 209 S Galena St Aspen CO 81611; Barbara Krakow Gallery 10 Newbury St Boston MA 02116

LEMIEUX, BONNE A
PAINTER
b Elmwood Park, Ill, Aug 3, 1921. *Study:* Los Angeles Art League, 82-83; Studied with Jake Lee, 82-83; Los Angeles Valley Col, 82-84. *Work:* City of Los Angeles Permanent Art Collection; Norwalk City Hall, Calif; Ernie Pyle Sch, Bellflower, Calif; Salvation Army Tabernacle, Hollywood; Univ Southern Calif. *Comn:* Portrait of Mayor, City of Norwalk, 90; Hist Bldg, Walleck, Shave, Stanard & Blender, Woodland Hills Calif, 90. *Exhib:* Women Painters W, Univ Del, Newark, 87; Am Contemp Masters Invitational, Dr Sun Yat-Sen Mem Hall, Taipei, Taiwan, 87; Old Bergen, Ky Highlands Mus, Ashland, 87; Artists Soc Int, E Co Performing Arts Ctr, El Cajon, Calif, 89; Seattle Art Mus, 96; San Bernardino Mus, Calif, 96. *Teaching:* Art instr watercolor, Creative Art Ctr, Burbank, 91-. *Awards:* Art Store & More Award, 86; Bronze Medal, Artists of the Southwest, 88; Best of Show, Ocean House Fine Arts Exhib, 96. *Bibliog:* David Kozinski (auth), Bonnie LeMieux, versatile artist, Artists Market, 76; Ernest Kay (ed), Bonnie LeMieux, The World Who's Who of Women, 86; Judy Shay (auth), Arts Glendale News Press, 89. *Mem:* Valley Watercolor Soc; Women Painters W; San Fernando Valley Art Club (vpres, 77 & pres, 78); Collage Soc; assoc mem Am Watercolor Soc. *Media:* Watercolor, Oil. *Mailing Add:* 22855 Belquest Dr Lake Forest CA 92630

LEMON, ROBERT S, JR
EDUCATOR, HISTORIAN
b Pittsburg, Kans, Oct 1, 1938. *Study:* Univ Mo, Kansas City, BA, 62; Ohio Univ, MA, 69 & PhD, 75. *Pos:* Mem, Orlando Airport Art Selection Comt, Orlando Aviation Authority, Fla, 83-89; mem, bd visitors, Cornell Fine Arts Mus, Rollins Col, 82-. *Teaching:* Prof art hist, Rollins Col, Winter Park, Fla, 73-, chmn, art dept, 80-99, chmn art dept Marshall Univ, 99-01. *Mem:* Southeastern Coll Art Conf (pres, 97-00); Coll Art Asn. *Res:* Twentieth century American painting and sculpture. *Publ:* Auth, An interview with Lowell Nesbitt, Art Voices South, 78; The Figurative Pretext: A Comparative Explication of the Fiction of Alain Robbe-Grillet and the Painting of the Photo Realists, University Microfilms, 80; American Printmakers of the 30's (exhib catalog), Cornell Fine Arts Mus, 81; Photo Realism: Logical evolution from post-painterly abstraction, Southeastern Coll Art Conf Rev, 87; Reliefs and Menhirs: The Sculpture of J G Naylor (exhib catalog), Univ Gallery of Gainesville, Fla, 88; Doris Leeper: A Retrospective (exhib catalog), Cornell Fine Arts Mus, 95. *Mailing Add:* Rollins Col 2676 Winter Park FL 32789

LENAGHAN, ANDREW
PAINTER
b New Brunswick, NJ, 1965. *Study:* Cornell Univ, BFA, 87; Brooklyn Col, MFA, 89. *Exhib:* It Figures, SFA Gallery, Stephen Austin State Univ, Nacogdoches, Tex, 96; Fac Exhib, NJ Asn Independent Schs, Gladston, 89; Watchung Art Ctr, NJ, 90; ADF/NY Sch Interior Design Exhib, Int Design Ctr, Long Island, 91; Roundabout Theater, NY, 93; solo exhibs, Gerorge Adams Gallery, 96, 96 & 98; Going Places, George Adams Gallery, NY, 96; Mixing Business with Pleasure: Selections from the George Adams Gallery NY, Sawhill Gallery, James Madison Univ, Harrisonburg, Va, 97; Reflections of Taste: Am Art from Greenwich Collections, Bruce Mus, Conn, 97; Robert Sandelson Gallery, London, 97; Illumination, George Adams Gallery, NY, 98. *Teaching:* Instr painting, Rutgers Prep Sch, Somerset, NJ, 88-92. *Bibliog:* Ruth Bass (auth), Realism: when a rose is a rose, Art News, 2/96 & Artist Mag (Tai Pei), 96. *Media:* Oil. *Mailing Add:* c/o George Adams Gallery 525 W 26th St New York NY 10001

LENKER, MARLENE N
PAINTER, COLLAGE ARTIST
b Clifton, NJ, Mar 07, 1932. *Study:* Fairleigh/Dickenson Univ, AA, 51; Montclair State Univ, MA, 76. *Work:* Bergen Mus, Paramus, NJ; Montclair State Col, Upper Montclair, NJ; St Barnabas Medical Ctr, Livingston, NJ; Pepsico Hq, Purchase, NY; Am Airlines, NY; Hoffman Laroche, NJ; Kidder Peabody, NY; Johnson & Johnson, NJ; Hewlett Packard, Tex & Calif; Smilow Cancer Hospital, New Haven, Conn; Yale New Haven Hosp. *Comn:* Okla State Bank, Okla; ASEA, Brown Boveri Inc, NJ; NJ Cent Power & Light; Guioiden Hq, NJ. *Exhib:* One-woman shows, David Gary Ltd, NJ, 83, Snug Harbor Cult Ctr, NY, 85, Adelle Taylor Gallery, Dallas, Tex, 86, Reece Galleries, NY, Bloomfield Cult Ctr, NJ, 91, David-Gary Gallery, NJ, 92, Art in Focus, NJ, 92, Forrest-Scott Gallery, NJ, 97 & Fredrick Clement Gallery, NJ, 98; group shows, Colorworks Gallery, Hilton Head Island, NC, 90, Hammond Gallery, Ohio, 93, Alva Gallery, New London, Conn, 2001, Mus New Art, Detroit, Mich, 2001, Intercultural Art Ctr Gallery, NY & many others; Miniature Invitational, Old Church Cult Ctr, Demarest, NJ, 90; Hummerick Mus, Cincinnati, Ohio, 90; Northcoast Collage Soc, Cincinnati Mus, Ohio, 90; Walton Art Ctr, Ark, 94; Jain/Maranuchi Gallery, NY, 94; David-Gary Gallery, NJ, 94; Gregory Gallery, Conn, 94; Williams Gallery, NJ, 95; Broadfoot & Broadfoot, NJ, 96; Nat Small Works, NJ, 96; Layer: Mining the Unconscious, Western NMex Univ, 96; Celtic Connections, Bradford Col, Mass, 98; Artium Gallery, Norwalk, Conn, 2000; Lippman Gallery, Short Hills, NJ, 2001; GJ Cloninger Gallery, NJ; Intercultural Art Ctr Gallery, NY, 2002; Abstractions, Forrest Scott Gallery, Milburn, NJ, 2002; Fire in the Heart, Schneider Mus Art Shland, Ore, 2003; Strata-Stratum, Mystic Arts Ctr, Mystic, Conn, 2004; On the Edge, Peninsula Fine Arts Ctr Mus, Newport News, Va, 2005; Connections, Art at the Cathedral, Lexington, Ky, 2006; Exploring Multiple Directions, Albuquerque Art Mus, NMex, 2007; Diane Birdsall Gallery, Old Lyme, Conn, 2007; Illuminations, Davis Art Ctr, Fort Myers, Fla, 2008; Altered Books Nat, Carghill Hall Gallery, Minneapolis, Minn, 2008; one-person shows, Chase-Freedman Gallerys, West Hartford, Conn, The Beth Shalom Rodfe Zedek, Synagogue, Chester, Conn, The Charter Oak Cultural Ctr, Hartford, Conn, 2006. *Pos:* Pres, West Essex Art Asn, 70-73. *Teaching:* Instr fine arts Caldwell Col, Caldwell, NJ, 77-79; lectr, Nat Acad, NY. *Bibliog:* Skye Griffith (auth), Lyrical Landscapes, Staten Island Advance, 85; J Taylor Basker (auth), Art Review, NY Art Forms, 87; Eileen Watkins (auth), A Sense of Special, Star Ledger, 89. *Mem:* Nat Asn Women Artists (selection jury, 82-83); Artists Equity - NY Chap; Soc Layerists in Multimedia (E Coast coord); North Coast Collage Soc; NJ Watercolor Soc; Soc Layerists in Multimedia. *Media:* Acrylic, Collage. *Publ:* Illusr, New Jersey Goodlife, Rene B Timpone, 88; contribr, New York Art Review, Krantz, 89; Layering (video) - An Art of Time and Space, 91; The Guild, Anniversary Ed, 95, 97 & 98; Bridging Time & Space, 99; The Art of Layering, Making Connections, 2004. *Dealer:* Harris Gallery, Houston, TX. *Mailing Add:* Lenker Studio 13 Crosstrees Hill Rd Essex CT 06426

LENNON, TIMOTHY
PAINTING CONSERVATOR
b Chicago, Ill, Sept 18, 1938. *Study:* Loras Col, BA; Univ Notre Dame, MA; Art Inst Chicago. *Pos:* Conservator, Art Inst Chicago, 80-. *Mem:* Fel Am Inst Conserv Artistic & Hist Works; Fel Int Inst Conserv Artistic & Hist Works. *Mailing Add:* Art Inst Chicago Michigan Ave at Adams St Chicago IL 60603

LEONARD, JOANNE
PHOTOGRAPHER, EDUCATOR
b Los Angeles, Calif, 1940. *Study:* Univ Calif, Berkeley, BA, 62; San Francisco State Coll, 63-64. *Work:* US State Dept; Am Arts Doc Ctr, Exeter, Eng; San Francisco Mus Art; Int Mus Photog, Rochester, NY; Stanford Univ Mus, Palo Alto; Crocker Art Mus, Sacramento, Calif; Oakland Mus; Univ Mich Bentley Lib. *Exhib:* One-person shows, MH de Young Mem Mus, 68, San Francisco Art Inst, 74, Calif, Laguna Gloria Art Mus, Austin, Tex, 80 & Orange Coast Coll Photo Gallery, Costa Mesa, 84, Photographs and Photo Collages, Jeremy Stone Gallery, San Francisco, Calif, 88, Not Losing her Memory: Stories in Photographs, Words an Collage, Univ Mich Mus Art, Ann Arbor, Mich, 92, Schlesinger Lib Womens' History, Radclife Coll, Cambridge, Mass, 95, Newspaper Diary, Trompe l'Oeil Photographs, Gallery Inst Humanites, Univ Mich, 2012; Group shows, Photo Trans Form, San Francisco Mus Mod Art, 81; San Francisco Mus Art, 71, 75, 82 & 85; Summer Light, Light Gallery, NY, 72; Seattle Art Mus, Wash, 76; Whitney Mus Am Art, NY, 78; Franklin Inst, Philadelphia, 83; Santa Barbara Mus Art, Calif, 82, 83 & 86; Detroit Inst Arts, 92; Univ Mich Mus Art, 92; Schlessinger Libr Gallery, Radcliffe Col, Cambridge, Mass, 95; Int Ctr Photog, NY, 97; Ceres at 20, Ceres Gallery, NY, 2003; The Art of Aging, Hebrew Union Col Mus, NY, 2003; About Face, Denise Bibro Gallery, NY, 2004; Disturbing the Peace, Bibro Gallery, NY, 2006; Art and Design at V and M Humanities Inst, Ann Arbor, Mich, 2007; View, Joseph Bellows Gallery, La Jolla, Calif, 2010; Oakland Mus Calif Art, Oakland, Calif, 2010; The View from Here, San Francisco Mus Modern Art, Calif, 2010. *Pos:* assoc, Women's Studies and Am Culture Programs, Univ Mich. *Teaching:* Lectr, San Francisco Art Inst, 73-75 & Mills Col, Oakland, Calif, 82-83 & 86; prof art, Univ Mich Sch Art, Ann Arbor, 78-2011, emerita, 2011-; Diane Kirkpatrick and Griselda Pollock Dist Univ Prof, Univ Mich, 2005. *Awards:* Phelan Award, 71; Nat Endowment, Photog Surveys Grant, 77; Josephine Nevins Keal Award, Univ Mich, 81; Individual Artist grant, Mich Council Arts, Univ Mich, 89; Mich Arts award, 98. *Bibliog:* HW Janson (auth), History of Art, Abrams, New York, 86; de la Croix, Tansey & Kirkpatrick (auth), Gardner's Art through the Ages, Harcourt, Brace & Javonovich, San Diego, 91; Lucy Lippard (auth), Lost & Found (catalog essay), 92; Joanne Leonard (auth), Being in Pictures: An Intimate Photo Memoir (forward by Lucy R. Lippard), Univ Mich Press, 4/2008; Newspaper Diary: Trompe l'Oeil Photographs (essay), Univ Mich Inst for Humanities, 2012; and many others. *Mem:* Soc Photog Educators; Coll Art Asn. *Interests:* Feminist art, photography, collage. *Publ:* Sexual Discourses: From Aristotle to AIDS 1989, Univ Mich Press, 92; Modern Fiction Studies, Vol 40, No 3, John Hopkins Univ Press, 94; Mich Feminist Studies, No 11, 96-97; M Hirsch (ed), The Familial Gaze, Univ Press, New Eng, 98; auth, Marlene and Me (essay), Changing Focus: Family Photography & American Jewish Identity, Scholar & Feminist Online, Ctr Rsch on Women, Barnard Coll, 2002; auth, Caring and Grieving: Part II, Mich Feminist Studies: Gender and Health, no. 11, pp 99-110, 2011; auth, Being in Pictures: A Commentary on Feminist Visual Narratives in the Digital Age, Vol. 45:1, pp 8-15, 2012; and many others. *Mailing Add:* Sch Art Univ Mich 2000 Banisteel Blvd Ann Arbor MI 48109

LEONARD, ZOE
PHOTOGRAPHER
b Liberty, NY, 1961. *Work:* Mus Contemp Art, Los Angeles; Mus Mod Art & Whitney Mus Am Art, NY; Philadelphia Mus Art, Pa; San Francisco Mus Mod Art, Calif; Univ Art Mus, Univ Calif, Berkeley. *Exhib:* One-person exhibs, Univ Art Mus/Pac Film Archives, Univ Calif, Berkeley, 91, Renaissance Soc, Univ Chicago, 93, Le Casa d'Arte, Milan, Italy, 95, Mus Contemp Art, N Miami, 97, Philadelphia Mus, Pa, 98, Centre National de la Photographie, Paris, France, 98 & Paula Cooper Gallery, NY, 99; Benefit Auction, New Mus Contemp Art, NY, 91; The Return of Cadavre (traveling exhib), Drawing Ctr, NY, Corcoran Gallery Art, Washington, DC, Found Contemp Art, Mexico City, Santa Monica Mus, Los Angeles & Forum Contemp Art, St Louis, Mo, 93; Sum of the Parts, Art Gallery Univ Hawaii, Manoa, 94; Nature Studies II, Univ Gallery Fine Arts Ctr, Univ Mass, Amherst, 95; Compulsion to Repeat: Repetition and Difference in Works from the Permanent Collection, Mus Contemp Art, Los Angeles, 97; Points of View: Photog from the Collection, Gallery 2, Univ Mass, Pac Film Archive, Univ Calif, Berkeley, 96; Gothic, Inst Contemp Art, Boston, 97; Whitney Mus Am Art Biennial, NY, 97; The Precious Image: Contemp Platinum Photog, Univ Art Gallery, Montclair State Univ, NJ, 98; The Mus as Muse: Artists Reflect, Mus Mod Art, NY, 99; many others in the US and abroad

LEONARDO, SHAUN EL C
PAINTER
Study: Bowdoin Coll, Brunswick, Maine, BA (vis arts & painting), 2001; San Francisco Art Inst, MFA (painting), 2005. *Exhib:* Solo exhibs, Lower Manhattan Cult Coun Swing Space Performance, New York, 2006, Real Art Ways, Hartford, Conn, 2007, RHYS Gallery, Boston, 2007, La Curtiduria, Oaxaca, Mex, 2008 & Rhys/Mendes, Minas Gerais, Brazil, 2009; Love Art & War, Emerging Arts Org, New York, 2003; Lucha Libre, Ice House Cult Ctr, Dallas, 2005; God Complex, RUSH Arts Gallery, New York, 2006; Masculine Box & Beyond, The LAB, San Francisco, 2006; Peekskill Proj, Hudson Valley Ctr Contemp Art, Peekskill, NY, 2006; Invade My Dreams, Taxter & Spengemann, New York, 2006; Emergency Room, PS1, Long Island, NY, 2007; Foam of the Daze, Smith-Stewart Gallery, New York, 2007; Hard Targets-Masculinity and American Sports, Los Angeles Co Mus Art, 2008; Heroic, Tenn State Univ, Nashville, 2008; An Intimate Affair, Ava Gallery, New York, 2009. *Awards:* Anne Bartlett Lewis Mem Prize, Bowdoin Coll, Brunswick, Maine, 2001; Swing Space Residency & Grant, Lower Manhattan Cult Coun, 2006; Smack Mellon Hot Picks, New York, 2007; Art Matters Grant (for residency in Mex), New York, 2007; New York Found Arts Fel, 2008

LEONG, LAMPO
PAINTER, EDUCATOR
b Guangzhou, Guangdong, China, July 3, 1961; US citizen. *Study:* Guangzhou Acad Fine Arts, China, BFA, 83; Calif Coll Arts, Oakland/San Francisco, MFA, 88; Cen Acad Fine Arts, Beijing, PhD, 2009. *Work:* Stanford Mus Art, Palo Alto, Calif; Asian Art Mus, San Francisco; Minneapolis Inst Arts, Minn; The Written Art Found, Frankfurt, Ger; Macao Mus Art; Guangdong Mus Art, China; granite medallion, City of San Francisco, 99; City Hall, Columbia, 2011. *Comn:* Paintings, Tokyo Westin, Japan, 94, Epcot Ctr, Disney World, Fla, 98; mural and paintings, Westin Surabaya, Indonesia, 96; murals, U Mo, Columbia, 2005; Cathay Bank, Los Angeles, 2008. *Exhib:* Solo exhibs, Rosicrucian Egyptian Mus, San Jose, 86, Luis De Camoes Mus, Macao, 86, Guangzhou Fine Arts Mus, Guangzhou, China, 88, Chinese Cult Ctr, San Francisco, 91, Cult Inst Macao, 98, DP Fong Galleries, San Jose, Calif, 2000, Western Ill Univ, Macomb, Ill, 2002, St Louis Univ Mus Art, St Louis, Mo, 2003, Suburban Fine Arts Ctr, Highland Park, ILl, 2003, Sam Houston State Univ, Huntsville, Tex, 2004, Lycoming Coll, Williamsport, Penn, 2004, Armstrong Atlantic State Univ, Savannah, Ga, 2005, Chapman Friedman Gallery, Louisville, Ky, 2005, Creative Macau, Macao, 2006, Univ Calif Berkeley, 2007, Sun Gallery, Minneapolis, Minn, 2006, 2008, Univ Mo, Columbia, 2009, Univ Calif Davis, 2010, Culver-Stockton Coll, Canton, Mo, 2011, Truman State Univ, Kirksville, Mo, 2012, MLB Designs, Kansas City, MO, 2012, Villanova Univ, 2013; Group exhibs, Art of China, Shanghai Mus Fine Arts, China, 97; Shining Stars: Four Cult Visionaries of Contemp Painting, Pacific Heritage Mus, San Francisco, 98; George E Ohr Nat Art Challenge, The Ohr-O'Keefe Mus of Art, Biloxi, MS, USA, 2002; Englewood Arts Nat Juried Art Show, Mus of Outdoor Arts, Englewood, CO, 2003, Suburban Fine Arts Center, Highland Park, Ill, 2003; Int Contemp Ink Painting, Changliu Art Mus, Taoyuan, Taiwan, 05; Question, Cantor Ctr for Visual Arts, Stanford, Calif, 2004; Media 1 Art Biennial, Medial Mus, London, 2005; Han Zi Reinvented: The Rhythm of Chinese Script, Calif State U, Fullerton, 2006; Taipei Internat Ink Painting Biennial, Nat Taipei U Tech, 2006; Int Modern Brush Painting, Chinese Cult Ctr of San Francisco, 2007; Culture Conflict? No Thanks! Raab Galerie, Beijing, China, 2008; 2nd Taipei Int Modern Ink Painting Biennial, Chung Shan Nat Gallery, Nat Dr Sun Yat-Sen Mem Hall, Taipei, Taiwan, 2008; 11th Nat Fine Arts Exhib, Shantou, Guangdong, China, 2009; From Nature to Mind: A Joint Exhib from New Intellectual Artists, Huantie Times Art Mus, Beijing, China, 2009; Sumi-E for Today: An Int Juried Exhib of Ink Paintings & Calligraphy; Exposicao de Coleccao de Arte do Macao Art Mus, Mus de Arte de Macao, 2010; 3rd Taipei Int Mod Ink Painting Biennial, Nat Mus Hist, Taiwan, 2010; Hong Kong & Macao Visual Art Biennial, Beijing World Art Mus, The China Millennium Monument, Beijing, China, 2010; China Int Gallery Expo, 2010; China World Trade Ctr, Beijing, China, 2010; Int Contemp Masters, Mus Southern Nev, Las Vegas, 2010; 31st Ann Paper in Particular Nat Exhib, Columbia Coll, Mo, 2010; Mobility and Memory: Macao's Proposed Artworks for the 54th International Art Exhib of the Venice Biennale, Museu de Arte de Macao, 2011; The Art of Writing: Contemporary Art from Three Cultures, Kurhaus Wiesbaden, Germany, 2011; East Meets West: An Exhibition of Paintings by Well-Known Asian American Artists, Foster Gallery, Univ Wisconsin, Eau Claire, 2011; Harvest: Artistic Creations from the Advisors and Honorary Master Painters of Guangzhou Painting Acad, Redtory Creativity and Arts Ctr, Guangzhou, China, 2011; Art Faculty Exhibit Celebrating the 30th Anniversary of the College of Art Education at the Guangzhou Academy of Fine Arts, Art Mus Guangzhou Acad Fine Arts, China, 2011; Multimedia Performance: Chinese Myths, Kauffman Ctr Performing Arts, Kansas City, Mo, 2012; Macao Contemp Drawings, Museu de Arte de Macau, Macao, 2012; Ink Painting Exhib and Symposium, Nat Dr. Sun Yat-Sen Mem Hall, Taipei, Taiwan, 2012; Donggang Digital Soc Mus, S Korea, 2012; Art Taipei 12, World Trade Ctr, Taipei, Taiwan, 2012; VAFA, 2012, Video Art for All Int Video Art Festival; Fundacao Oriente, Macao, 2012; Outstanding Works: Thirtieth Anniversary of Guangzhou Painting Academy, Univ MEga Ctr Art Mus, Guangzhou Acad Fine Arts, Guangzhou, China, 2012; Re-Ink: Invitational Exhib of Contemporary Ink and Wash Painting, 2000-2012; Hubei Mus Art, Wuhan & Today Art Mus, Beijing, China, 2013; Art Taipei 13, World Trade Ctr, Taipei, Taiwan, 2013. *Collection Arranged:* Asian-Am Contemp Art Exhibit, Chinese Cult Ctr, San Francisco, CA, 86; Chinese Artists in Academia, Columbia Art League, Columbia, Mo, St Louis Community College-Forest Park, St Louis, Mo, 2004; Am Eyes: Works from Art Prof at UM-Columbia, Guangdong Mus of Art, Guangzhou, China, 2004. *Pos:* Chair, Dept of Art, Univ Mo-Columbia, 2007-2009; distinguished rsch, hon master painter, Guangzhou Painting Acad, Guangzhou, Guangdong, China, 2011-. *Teaching:* Vis Asst Prof, brush painting, San Francisco State Univ, Calif, 96-2001; prof, painting, drawing & ink painting, Univ Mo-Columbia, 2001-; hon vis prof, Guangzhou Acad Fine Arts, Guangdong, China, 2009-; mfa mentor, Univ the Arts, Philadelphia, Pa, 2010-2011; hon vis prof, South China Normal Univ, Guangzhou, China, 2011-; Weiner dist prof, Missouri Univ Science and Tech, 2012-; hon visiting prof, Central China Normal Univ, Wuhan, China, 2012-. *Awards:* Cover Award, New Art Int, Woodstock, NY: Book Art Press, 2009; Ten Best Entries, Exposicao Ann de Artes Visuais de Macau, Macao, 2007, 2009, 2011, 2012; Gold Award, Creative Quarterly: The Joun Art & Design, No 18, New York, 2010; Best of Show & Founder Award, 48th Ann Exhib, Sumi-e Soc Am, McLean, Va, 2011; Front Cover, Creative Genius: 100 Contemporary Artists, London, UK, 2012. *Bibliog:* Betsy Crabtree (auth), A conversation with Chinese painter Lampo Leong, San Francisco Arts Monthly, 2/92; Manni Liu & Jung Park (auths), Bridging the old and the new Worlds, Asian Art News, Hong Kong, 9/97; Pat Berger (auth), intro, The Common Ground of Light and Gravity: Lampo Leong's Contemplation Forces, Chicago: Art Media Resources, Ltd, 98; Edmund Moy (auth), Chinese Calligraphy Meets Modern Computer Technology, Asian Week, San Francisco, 2000; Jenna Kaegel (auth), Global Expressions, Columbia Daily Tribune, 2002; Margey Fischer (auth), From Oppression to Expression, Vox Mag, publ by Columbia Missourian, Columbia, Mo, Vol 7, Issue No 52, p.2 & 7, 1/2005; Kevin Allton (auth), The Wild Calligraphy of Lampo Leong, Sublimation: Calligraphy by Lampo Leong, Creative Macau, Inst European Studies Macau, Macau Cultural Ctr, 2006; Michael Fleishman (auth), How to Grow as an Illustrator, Allworth Press, New York, 2007; Michael Fleishman, Drawing Inspiration: Visual Artist at Work, Clifton Park, New York, 2010; Tanya Sneddon, Cultural Connections: A Visit with Lampo Leong, Univ Mo Research Bd, 2009; Peter Russu (auth), Creative Genius: 100 Contemp Artists, London, Masters of Today, Ltd, 2012. *Media:* Modern Ink Painting, Calligraphy, Acrylic/Oil and Watercolor. *Res:* Current research is in comparative study of painting and calligraphy, and the spiritual expression of Sublime and grandeur in art. *Collection:* Contemporary ink paintings, chinese calligraphy. *Publ:* Auth, Lam-Po Leong's Paintings, Mus Macao Luis De

Camoes, 86; illusr, Brushstrokes-Styles and Techniques of Chinese Painting, Asian Art Mus San Francisco, 93; auth, The Common Ground of Light & Gravity, Chicago: Art Media Resources, Ltd, 98; auth, Learning the Art of Chinese Brush Painting: The Landscape, Nature in Art, Chinese Brush Painting, San Francisco, Calif, Asian Art Mus, 2001; auth, The Deconstruction & Reformation of Genes, The Artistic Trend of Modern Chinese Ink & Wash Works in the Late 20th Century, Modern Ink & Wash Painting Series IV, 2001; auth, Recoding the Roots: Genetic Reformation & Culture Synthesis in the Era of Globalization, Yishu Jour Contemporary Chinese Art, 2004; On Foundation, Essays from the National Symposium on Foundation Education by Top Ten Art Institutions in China, Beijing: China Youth Publ House, 2007; auth, The Purpose & Method of the Critique in Art Education, Fine Arts & Design, Nanjing Art Inst, Nanjing, China, 2010; auth, The Visual Forces of Curve, A Case Study in Chinese Brush Painting, Humanities & Art, Guizhou People's Publ, China, 2012; auth, Special Characteristics of the postmodern International Style in Art, Art Critic, Beijing, China, 2010; auth, Student-Centered Instructional Stategies in Art Educ, Calligraphy and Painting Educ, Hangzhou, Zhejiang: China Calligraphy Mag, 2010; auth, A Few Ideas for Chinas Reform in Higher Educ in Art Insp by Western Educ Concepts, Art Observation, Chinese Nat Acad Arts, Beijing, 2012; auth, The Nourishment of Creativity in the United States, Courage, Vision: Celebratory Essays for the 30th Anniversary of the College Art Education at the Guangzhou Academy of Fine Arts, Guangzhou, China, Guangdong, Higher Educ Press, 2012; auth, Important Factors in the US Art Coll Admission Application, China Art Educ, Nat Bureau Educ, Nanjing, China, 2012; auth, Utilizing Critical Thinking and Concept Mapping Skills to Enhance Artistic Creativity, China, 2013; auth, Lampo Leong: Contemplation, Forces, Truman State Univ, 2013

LEOPOLD, SUSAN
SCULPTOR, MURALIST
b Chicago, Ill, July 13, 1960. *Study:* Sch Visual Arts, BFA, 82. *Work:* Brooklyn Mus, NY; Chase Manhattan Bank; First National Bank Chicago, Ill; Bibliot Ctr, Firenze. *Exhib:* Solo exhibs: Carnegie Mellon Univ Art Gallery, Pittsburgh, 87; John Weber Gallery, NY, 95, 96; Saw Hill Gallery; James Madison Univ, Harrisonburg, Va; Peep Show, NY Kunsthalle; Miniature Environments, Whitney Mus Am Art, NY, 89; Rotunda Gallery, Brooklyn, NY, 95; Voyeur's Delight, Franklin Furnace, NY; Bare Bones - TZ Art, NY; Hosfelt Gallery, San Francisco; Nat Acad Mus, NY, 2006. *Teaching:* Artist-in-residence, Henry Street Settlement, NY, 94-95; prof, mixed media, Cooper Union, 96; Vis artist, archit, Pratt Inst, 96. *Awards:* Indo-Am Fel, 89; MacDowell Colony, 94; Djerassi Found, 96. *Bibliog:* David Rimanelli (auth), Susan Leopold at John Weber, Art Forum, 12/88; John Russell (auth), Some masterly work of microscopic stature, NY Times, 8/11/89; Ken Johnson (auth), Art in Am, 7/93. *Media:* All Media. *Publ:* A Labyrinthine World of Correlations, Aurea Found, 95. *Dealer:* John Weber Gallery 142 Greene St New York NY 10012. *Mailing Add:* c/o Jean Albano Art Gallery 215 W Superior Chicago IL 60610

LEPORE, JOAN
ARTIST
Study: The Yard School, (life drawing, anatomy & design), Montclair, NJ; Arts Student League, New York; NJ Center for Visual Arts (portraiture), Summit, NJ. *Exhib:* Monmouth Mus; Rider Univ; Cork Gallery, Lincoln Center, New York; Segreto Gallery, NMex; Louisa Melrose Gallery, Frenchtown, NJ; ISEA-Minnetrista Cultural Ctr, Muncie, Ind; Renee Foosner Gallery, Millburn, NJ; Nat Arts Club, New York City; Salmagundi Club, New York City; Banana Factory, Bethlehem, Pa; Ridgewood Art Inst, Ridgewood, NJ; Johnson & Johnson Corp, N Brunswick, NJ 2005; solo exhibs, Mirza Gallery, Fairfield, NJ, Korby Gallery, Verona, NJ, Gallery 9, Chatham, NJ, Robin Hutchins Gallery, Maplewood, NJ. *Awards:* Kent Day Coes, Allied Artists, 2003; Finalist, Artist Mag Experimental Category, 2002 & 2003; M-Shac Award of Excellence, 2003 & 2005. *Mem:* signature mem Nat Acrylic Painters Asn; signature mem Allied Artists; Int Soc of Experimental Artists; Soc of Layerists in Multi-Media; Nat Collage Soc; Am Watercolor Soc; Nat Watercolor Soc; Millburn-Short Hills Art Ctr; Morris Co Art Asn; Essex Watercolor Club; signature mem NJ Watercolor Soc; signature mem Nat Asn of Women Artists; signature mem Audubon Artists; signature mem Garden State Watercolor Soc. *Mailing Add:* 840 Vail Rd Parsippany NJ 07054

LERMAN, LEONID
SCULPTOR
b Odessa, Russia, 1953; arrived in US 80. *Study:* Professional Sch Mosaics and Wood Carving, Odessa, 70-71; VI Moukhina Coll Art and Design, Leningrad, MFA, 79. *Exhib:* Solo exhibs at CASE Mus Russian Contemp Art, Jersey City, NJ, 85, Paulo Salvador Gallery, NY, 86, Tradition 3 Thousand Gallery, NY, 87, On the Edge, Duke Univ Mus Art, Durham, NC, 88, Riskin-Sinow Gallery, San Francisco, Calif, 89, Sculpture Ctr Gallery, NY, 89, McKee Gallery, NY, 93, 94, 99, 2003, 2006, Complex Presentiment, Modernism, San Francisco, 94, Rochini Arte Contemporanea, Terni, Italy, 2002, Freedman Gallery, Albright Coll Ctr Arts, Reading, Pa, 2005; group exhibs include Menage Exhibition Hall, Leningrad, 78; Centre des Congres de Quebec, 82; Terminal NY, Brooklyn, 83; Sculpture Ctr Gallery, NY, 84, 85; Paulo Salvador Gallery, 84; Now Gallery, NY, 84; IMF, Washington, DC, 85; 13 Hour Gallery, NY, 85; Krain Club Gallery, NY, 87; Kenkeleba Gallery, NY, 87; Res Nova Gallery, New Orleans, La, 88; Transit: Russian Artists Between the East and West, Fine Arts Mus Long Island, NY, 89-90; Trietiakov Gallery, Moscow, Russia, 90; Old Symbols/New Icons in Russian Contemp Art, Stuart Levy Fine Art, NY, 93-94; Ideal Landscapes: Artists from the Former Soviet Union, de Saisset Mus, Santa Clara Univ, Calif, 94; Heroes and Heroines: From Myth to Reality, NJ Ctr Visual Arts, 95; 5 + 5, Ernest Rubenstein Gallery, NY, 95; Shaping Space: Drawings by Six Contemp Sculptors, Dunedin Fine Arts Ctr, Fla, 98; Red Square, Smack Mellon Studios, Brooklyn, NY, 99; Manifestations of the Human Spirit, Josha Lowenfels, The Baldacchino, NY, 1999-2000; Audrey Jones Beck Bldg, Mus Fine Arts, Houston, 2000; A Private Reading: The Book as Image & Object, Senior and Shopmaker Gallery, NY, 2001; Nat Acad Design Mus, NY, 2002; Drawing Today, New Arts Gallery, Litchfield, Conn, 2004; Am Acad Arts & Letts Invitational, New York, 2010. *Awards:* James Wilburt Johnson Sculpture Award, Washington, DC, 81

LERNER, ALEXANDRIA SANDRA
PAINTER
b Philadelphia, Pa. *Study:* Pa Acad Fine Arts, cert, 75; Philadelphia Coll Art, BFA, 76. *Work:* Philadelphia Mus Art, Pa; Rutgers Univ, NJ; Art Inst Chicago, Ill; Houghton Libr, Harvard Univ; Franklin Furnace Archive, New York; Southern Alleghenies Mus. *Comn:* Painting, Duke Energy Corp, Charlotte, NC. *Exhib:* 25 Pa Women Artists, Southern Alleghenies Mus, 79; Artists Books, Tweed Mus, Minn, 80; Speaking Volumes, AIR Gallery, New York, 80; Small Works, Washington Square East Gallery, New York, 81; Three Am Artists, ABF Gallery, Ger, 81; A Contemp Survey Art Books, Southern Alleghenies Mus, Loretto, Pa, 81; solo exhibs, Beyond the Garden Wall, Marian Locks Gallery, Philadelphia, 82, Philadelphia Art Alliance, 89 & Reflection, Morning and Evening, Harwood Mus of Art, Taos, NMex; Rutger's Nat, 85 & 86; Philadelphia Art Now, Philadelphia Mus Art, 90; Port Hist Mus, Philadelphia, 90; Harwood Mus, Taos, NMex, 91; Mangel Gallery, Philadelphia, Pa, 91; Contemp Landscape, Taos Art Asn, 93; Fenix Gallery, Taos, NMex, 96; Originals, Millicent Rodgers Mus, Taos, NMex, 2007. *Collection Arranged:* Erotic Art, Nexus Gallery, Philadelphia, 80; Bookworks (auth, catalog), Nexus Gallery, Philadelphia, 80; A Contemporary Survey Art Books (auth, catalog), Philadelphia Art Alliance, 81; Women in Art, William Penn Mus, Pa, 81. *Pos:* Co-dir, Artist Book Project, Nat Endowment Arts & Pa Council Grants, 80-; co-dir, SYNAPSE: A Visual Art Press, Pa, 80-; mem bd, New Art Examiner, 84-88; dir, McNeil Gallery, Philadelphia, 85-88; adv bd, Harwood Mus, Taos, NMex. *Awards:* Stedman Fund Purchase Prize, Rutgers Univ, 76; Philadelphia Mus Purchase Prize, Cheltenham Art Ctr, 80; Purchase Award, Art Inst Chicago, 81; Best of Show, Fall Arts, Taos, NMex, 99; Grant, Nat Endowment Art, 2001; Acclaimed Artist Award, Art in Pub Places, NMex State Univ, Las Cruces, 2002; Madiliene Martin Found Achievement Award, 2005. *Bibliog:* Ann Jarmusch (auth), The real realisme/Philadelphia's new image, Art News, 3/81; Miriam Siedel (auth), Sandra Lerner, New Art Examiner, 9/82; Martha Giever (auth), Artists books, alternative space or precious object?, Afterimage, 5/82; Edward Sozanski (auth), Works of Intensity by Sandra Lerner, Philadelphia Inquirer, 5/89. *Mem:* Found for Today's Art/Nexus (trustee, 76-); Philadelphia Art Alliance (chmn, 80-85); Fel Pa Acad Fine Arts; Citizens Arts in Pa; Artists Equity. *Media:* Mixed Media; Encaustic. *Publ:* Auth, Ruffled Passions, Visual Art Press, 80. *Dealer:* Fenix Gallery Thos NM. *Mailing Add:* PO Box 3172 Ranchos De Taos NM 87557

LERNER, LOREN RUTH
EDUCATOR
b Montreal, Que, Nov 4, 1948. *Study:* McGill Univ, BA, Honours Fine Arts, 1969; Univ Mich, MA, Hist Art, 1972; McGill Univ, MLS, 1975; Universite de Montreal, PhD, 1997. *Exhib:* Memories & Testimonies Montreal, Leonard & Bina Ellen Art Gallery, Concordia Univ (traveling exhib), 2002; Sam Borenstein, Montreal Mus Fine Arts (traveling exhib), 2005. *Pos:* Fine arts librn, Concordia Univ, Montreal, Que, 75-80, head libr media ctr & visual arts bibliographer, 81-91, spec servs & visual arts libr, 92-96 & assoc dean, res & grad studies, Faculty Fine Arts, 97-; chair, Dept Art Hist, Jan, 2000; res assoc, McCord Mus Can Hist, Sept 2003-Aug 2005. *Teaching:* Lectr, Dept Art Hist, Concordia Univ, 82-95 & assoc prof, 96-2003; Prof, 2004. *Awards:* Thirteenth George Wittenborn Mem Award, Univ Toronto Press, 91; Melva J Dwyer Award, 92 & 97; Joseph & Faye Tannenbaum Prize Scholar on Jewish Subject, Can Jewish Bk Awards, 2004. *Mem:* Art Libr Soc NAm (Can Regional Rep, 82-85); SHCY (Soc for the Hist of Children & Youth), Univs Art Asn Can. *Res:* Images of children in art. *Publ:* Coauth with Elizabeth Sacca, Visual Arts Reference and Research Guide, Perspecto Press, Montreal, 83; auth, Collection evaluation in fine arts libraries, in: Current Issues in Fine Arts Collection Development, Art Libr Soc NAm, Tucson, 84; Other disciplines and art: an overview based on oral evidence, Art Libr J, Vol XII, No 4, 87; Memoires et theses en histore de l'art Canadien & Annales d'histoire de l'art canadien, J Can Art Hist, vol X, No 1, 87, Vol XII, No 2, 88, Vol XIII, No 1, 90 & Vol XV, No 2, 94; co-ed, Art and Architecture in Canada: A Bibliography (Univ Toronto Press, 91 & Bibliography and Guide to Literature (Canadian film & video), 97, Univ Toronto Press; Sam Borenstein, Artist & Dealer: The Polemics of Post-Holocaust Jewish Cultural Identity, Can Jewish Studies (article) 12, 31-44, 2004; The Aron Mus at Temple Emanu-El-Beth Sholom, Montreal, Material Culture Review (article), 64, 8-19, fall 2004. *Mailing Add:* Concorida Univ Dept Fine Arts Rm VA-424 1455 de Maisonneuve Blvd W Montreal PQ H3G 1M8 Canada

LERNER, MARTIN
CURATOR, HISTORIAN
b Brooklyn, NY, Nov 14, 1936. *Study:* Brooklyn Col, BA, 59; Inst Fine Arts, New York, 62-65. *Collection Arranged:* Materpieces of the Art of India (with Richard Ettinghausen), Metrop Mus Art, 72; Indian Miniatures from the Jeffrey Paley Collection (auth, catalog), 74; Bronze Sculptures from Asia (auth, catalog), 75; Blue and White: Early Japanese Export Ware (auth, catalog), 76-77; Along the Ancient Silk Routes, Central Asian Art from Berlin, 82; Notable Acquisitions of Indian & Southeast Asian Art, Metrop Mus Art, 82; The Flame and the Lotus (auth, catalog), Metrop Mus Art, New York, 84; The Lotus Transcendent (auth, catalog), Metrop Mus Art, 91; Permanent Galleries South & Southeast Asian Art, Metrop Mus Art, 94. *Pos:* Asst cur Oriental art, Cleveland Mus Art, 66-72; vchmn in charge of Far Eastern art, Metrop Mus Art, NY, 72-76 & cur, Indian & Southeast Asian art, 76-; consult, Santa Barbara Mus Art, Akron Art Inst, Honolulu Acad Arts, and others; co-researcher for the Munson-Williams-Proctor Institute's 50th Anniversary reconstruction of the 1913 Armory Show; adv, for chaps on Asian Art in Dorra, H, Art in Perspective, NY, 72 & Gardner's Art Through the Ages, Sixth ed; consultant, Christie's, 2003-; Curatorial Ad for South and Southeast Asian Art 2004-. *Teaching:* Asst prof Oriental art, Univ Calif, Santa Barbara, 65-66 & Case-Western Univ, Cleveland, 68-71; lectr, Oberlin Col,

Princeton Univ, Phoenix Art Mus, Christie's NY, Utah Mus Art, Asia Soc in India and Nepal, 71 & 73, and others; Adj Prof Columbia Univ, 2004. *Res:* Indian and Southeast Asian art; American Modernist Art. *Publ:* The Flame and the Lotus, Abrams, 84; coauth (with W Felton), Thai and Cambodian Sculpture: From the 6th to 14th Centuries, Philip Wilson, 89; coauth (with W Felten), Entdeckungen: Skulpturen der Khmer und Thai (exhib catalog), Mus fur Ostasiatische Kunst, Koln, 89; coauth (with S Kossak), The Lotus Transcendent (exhib catalog), Metrop Mus Art, 91; Ancient Khmer Sculpture, New York, 94; and others. *Mailing Add:* Dept Asian Art Metrop Mus Art 1000 Fifth Ave New York NY 10028-0198

LERNER, SANDRA
PAINTER, COLLAGE ARTIST
b New York, NY. *Study:* Pratt Graphic Ctr, New York, 66-68; Hofstra Univ, BA, 78; studied painting with Leo Manso, Jerry Okomoto and Harry Sternberg, studied calligraphy & philos with Soshi Kampo Harada, Kampo Kaikan, Kyoto & Sumera, Japan, 81. *Work:* Aldrich Mus Contemp Art, Ridgefield, Conn; Jane Voorhees Zimmerli Art Mus, Rutgers Univ, NJ; World Study Mus, Fukuoka, Japan; Kampo Mus, Kyoto, Japan; Heckscher Mus, Huntington, NY; Radford Univ, Va; Mulenberg Coll. *Comn:* LAND (environ stage set for Eiko & Koma; with Eiko & Koma & Robert Mirabel), Rockefeller Found Multi-Arts Production Fund, 92; set design (Eiko & Koma), Japan Soc, 95; set design, Hiroshima Mus, Japan, 93; set design, Jacobs Pillow, Mass, 98; Redford Univ, Redford, Va. *Exhib:* Solo exhibs, Kauffman Gallery, Houston, Texas, 84, 86 & 91, Dubins Gallery, Los Angeles, Calif, 86, 87, & 89, Kampo Mus, Kyoto, Japan, 84 & 93, June Kelly Gallery, NY, 90, 92, 96, 2000, 2004, 2010, Anderson Gallery, Buffalo, NY, 92, Perimeter Gallery, Chicago, 92, Washington Art Asn Gallery, Conn, 97 & 2005, Zimmerli Mus, Rutgers, NJ, 98, Betty Parsons Gallery, 82, Kimberly Greer Gallery, Northpoint, NY, 2000, 2004, June Kelley Gallery, NY, 2010; Invitational Exhibs, Mino in Am, Mus of Fine Arts, Houston, 82 & Tokyo Mus, Japan, 84; Guild Hall Mus, Hampton, NY, 75, 83 & 87; Fundraiser Exhib, New Mus Contemp Art, NY, 85 & 86; Works on Paper, Dubins Gallery, Los Angeles, 87; Small Works, June Kelly Gallery, NY, 88; Free Spirits, Elaine Benson Gallery, Bridgehampton, NY, 91; Dubins Gallery, Los Angeles, 91; Perimeter Gallery, Chicago, 92 & 93; June Kelly: A Particular Vision, Anderson Gallery, Buffalo, NY, 94; A Woman's Place: Central Hall Gallery Artists in the 90's, Gallery North, Setauket, NY, 96; A Woman's Place: The Central Hall Gallery in the 70's, Mus at Stony Brook, NY, 96; The Shore Inst Contemp Arts, Long Branch, NJ, 2006; Ober Gallery, Kent, Conn, 2009; June Kelly, NY, 2009; Hidden Gems, 2009. *Pos:* Artist-in-residence, Nassau Co Bd Coop Educ, 75; art coordr, Friends Sch, Old Westbury, NY, 75-. *Teaching:* Lectr, Nassau Co Mus Fine Arts. *Awards:* Purchase Grant, Aldrich Mus Acquisition, Nat Endowment Arts, 78; Consult on Arts, NY State Senate Spec Comt Arts, 78-86; Stipend to lectr in Japan, Int Commun Agency Grant, 81; and others. *Bibliog:* Jennifer Dunning (auth), dance review, NY Times, 11/5/91; David McCracken (auth), rev, Chicago Tribune, 8/21/92; Margaret Moorman (auth), rev, ARTnews, 10/96; John Canady (auth), NY Times, 5/9/76; Lowery Sims (auth), catalog, 82; Donald Kuspit (auth), catalog, June Kelly Gallery, 90 & 92; Gladstone (auth), Art News, 3/2000; Mona Molarsky (auth), Art News, 2010; Johnson (auth), NY Times, 12/24/99-2004. *Media:* Oil, Acrylic; Mixed Media. *Specialty:* June Kelly Fine Arts Paintings, prints. *Publ:* and many others. *Dealer:* June Kelly Gallery 591 Broadway New York NY 10012

LERNER-LEVINE, MARION
PAINTER, PRINTMAKER
b London, Eng, Oct 1931; US citizen. *Study:* Univ Chicago, 47-50 ; Art Inst Chicago, study with Paul Wieghardt, Max Kahn, Vera Berdich, Adrian Troy & Laura Van Pappelandam, BFA, 54; Chicago Graphic Workshop, 53-55; Manhattan Graphic Ctr, NYC, study with Vijay Kumar, Fred Mershimer, Ben Rinehart, Takuji Hamanaka, 2000-06, James Hill, 2003; Belfast Yard, Printshop, Cambridge, England. *Work:* Citibank & Bank Am; Bates Coll Mus Art; Brooklyn Mus; US State Dept; Bryn Mawr Coll; Sprint World HQ; Bellevue Hospital Ctr, NY; Four Seasons Hotel, Beverly Hills, Calif; Lichtenstein & Levy, New York; Taipei Normal Univ (print collection), Taiwan; Sylvia Sleigh Coll, Rowan Univ, Glassboro, NJ; Mable S Douglass Lib, Rutgers Univ; Alta Bates Hosp, Berkeley, Calif. *Comn:* Printed Editions (6 etchings) for Orion Editions, NY, 85, 86, 88, 90, 91, 92, 94 & 96. *Exhib:* Solo exhibs, NY Univ, 78, Watercolors, Foundry Gallery, Washington, DC, 80 & Paul Klapper Libr, Queens Coll, NY, 81; Perlow Gallery, NY, 86; Carey Arboretum, 90; Prince St Gallery, NY, 71, 73, 75, 77, 79, 81, 83, 92, 95, 98, 2002, 2005, 2008, 2011; Bill Coffel Gallery (Monster Gallery), Brooklyn, NY, 2006; Watercolors: Wash Depot Gallery, Conn, 2006; Ernest Rubinstein Gallery, Educational Alliance Art Gallery, New York, 2008; Women Artists of the '70s Coops, Salena Gallery, Long Island Univ, Brooklyn; Dishman Art Mus, Lamar Univ, Beaumont, Tex; Rowan Univ Art Gallery, Glassboro, NJ, 2009, 2011; Int Print & Drawing Invitational, Nat Taiwan Normal Univ, Taipei, Taiwan, 2009; Bridge, Fyre Gallery, Braidwood, Australia, 2010; Traveling exhib, Reflections, Westgate Gallery, NY, Parking Ctr, NY, 2011-2012, Lindenwood, SW MO, State Universities, Coe Coll, Cedar Rapids, Iowa, and Pa Coll Art and Design, Lancaster, Pa, 2013; SAGA Council Exhib, Across the Waters, Callerie Recolte, Fukuoka, Japan, 2013. *Teaching:* Lectr watercolor, Sch Gen Studies, Brooklyn Coll, 76-80; instr drawing, Univ Calif, Los Angeles, 77; vis artist, Art Inst Chicago, 81 & Southeast Mo State Univ, 81; instr painting, Coll Staten Island, City Univ NY, 81-82; instr, watercolor, Educ Alliance Art Sch, NY, 98-2000. *Awards:* Adolf & Esther Gottlieb Grant in Painting, 81; Creative Artists Pub Serv Program Fel, 83; Nat Endowment Arts Fel, 86; Residencies, Yaddo Found, Saratoga Springs, NY, 79, 80, 82; Am Acad and Inst Arts & Letters, Award in Painting, 80. *Bibliog:* Carter Ratcliff (auth), art rev, Art News & Art Int, 71; Lawrence Campbell (auth), art rev, Art News, 73; Laurence Alloway (auth), The Nation, 77 & 88; Ruth Bass (auth), Art rev, Art News, 79; Anselm Hollo (auth), The Shelves of Paradise, Marion Lerner Levine's Watercolors, 79; June Cutler (auth), Marion Lerner Levine, Am Artist, 84; Cynthia Maris Dantzic (auth), 100 New York Painters, 2006; Manuel Macarella (auth), Pintamanuel, Blog review of Better than Ever, 2009; Betterthan Ever: Women Figurative Artists of the;70s Coop Galleries (catalogue), Essay by Hearn Pardee, Sharyn Finnegan, 2009; and others; William Corbett (auth), Reflections (catalogue), 2012-2013. *Mem:* Print Consortium; NY Artists Equity; Soc Am Graphic Artists (mem coun); Fedn Modern Painters and Sculptors; Artist's Fellowship; Print Connoisseur's Soc; Grace & Spiritus Chorale Brooklyn Heights. *Media:* Oil, Watercolor; Etching, Woodcuts. *Interests:* Choral singing, piano, botanical illus, photog. *Collection:* China and Porcelain, Metal Pitchers, Teapots, Lace, Books with Botanical Illustrations. *Publ:* Women's Art J, Vol 3, No 1, 82; Mystery in the Garden, 86; contribr, mems News Column (profiles), Assoc ed, Sagazine, Soc Am Graphic Artists Newsletter, 2006-2009. *Dealer:* Prince Street Gallery 530 W 25th St New York NY 10001. *Mailing Add:* 359 Sixth Ave Brooklyn NY 11215

LEROY, HUGH ALEXANDER
SCULPTOR
b Montreal, Quebec, Oct 9, 1939. *Study:* Montreal Mus Fine Arts, Sch Art & Design, studied with Arthur Lismer, 57-62; Sir George Williams Univ, Montreal, dipl, 60; McGill Univ, Montreal, studied with Louis Dudek, 76-77. *Work:* Nat Gallery & Can Coun Art Bank, Ottawa; Montreal Mus Fine Arts & Mus d'Art Contemporaine, Montreal; Ont Arts Coun, Toronto; Dept of Defense, Ottawa; Concordia Univ, Montreal. *Comn:* Sculpture, McGill Univ, Montreal, 73; sculpture, York Univ, Toronto, 74; sculpture, Fed Govt Can, Ottawa, 74; sculpture, Banff Ctr, Alta, 78; Ministry Govt Serv Public Works, New Justice Bldg, Ottawa. *Exhib:* Solo exhibs, Eye Level Gallery, Halifax, NS, 82, Self Seal, Wynick/Tuck Gallery, Toronto, 84, Wynick/Tuck Gallery, Toronto, 86, Toronto Sculpture Garden, 87, Jenny Rose-Le Bonheur, Olga Korper Gallery, Toronto, 89, Olga Corper Gallery, Toronto, Ont, 89, 90, 92 & 95 & Univ Waterloo Artspace Gallery, Ont, 95; Sculpture in a Garden, Art Gallery Ont, Toronto, 84; Installation Piece, Wynick/Tuck Gallery, Toronto, 86; Chinese Exchange Exhib, Zhejiang Acad, China, 86; 49th Parallel, NY, 89; Site/Memory, Cleveland Ctr Contemp Art, Cleveland & Macdonald Stewart Art Ctr, Guelph, 91. *Pos:* Dean, fine arts dept, Montreal Mus Sch Art & Design, 66-69; chmn, sculpture dept, Ont Col Art, Toronto, Can, 69-70; dir, MFA program, visual arts dept, York Univ, North York, Ont, 83-86. *Teaching:* Assoc prof, visual arts, York Univ, Toronto, 74-75, 77-78 & 81-89; sculpture instr, Banff Centre, Alta, 79; Nova Scotia Col Art Design, Halifax, 81; vis lectr, Importance of Intuition, Sheridan Col, Toronto, 85; A Search for Personal Imagery, Dundas Valley Sch Art, 85. *Awards:* First Purchase Prize, Can Pavilion, Expo '67, Can Coun, 67; UNESCO Fel, 68; Royal Can Acad Fel, 75. *Bibliog:* John Bentley Mays (auth), A Muscular Surge in Daring Hues, Globe & Mail, Toronto, 5/7/87; Christopher Hume (auth), Toronto Star (rev), 1/19/89; Donna Lypchuk (auth), Hugh LeRoy, Olga Korper Gallery, C Mag #21, spring 89. *Media:* Mixed. *Publ:* Contribr, What the Dickens--, Archit Canada, Toronto, 67

LEROY, LOUIS
PAINTER
b Yuma, Ariz, Aug 18, 1941. *Study:* Univ Ariz, with Andrew Rush, BFA, 70. *Exhib:* Chicano Affirmation & Resistance, White Gallery, Unic Calif, Los Angeles, 90. *Pos:* Owner, Salsa Graphics Studio, San Antonio, 80-. *Awards:* Chrystal Stairs Award, Asn Am Cult, 88-98. *Mem:* Asn Am Cult (Found bd mem, 85-). *Dealer:* Cruzitas Art Gallery San Antonio TX

LESHYK, TONIE
SCULPTOR, DRAFTSMAN
b Toronto, Ont, July 5, 1950. *Study:* Sheridan Coll Sch Design, Mississauga, Ont, dipl, high hons, 73; Ont Coll Art, dipl, high hons, 75, study with Colette Whitten & Ann Whitlock. *Work:* Art Bank, Can Coun Arts, Ottawa; Art Gallery Brant, Brantford, Ont. *Exhib:* Vancouver Art Gallery, BC, 74; Toronto-Los Angeles Exchange, Los Angeles Inst Contemp Art, 79; Small Sculpture (with catalog), 82 & The Shelter Drawings: Out of the Studio, 85, Harbourfront Gallery, Toronto; A Portrait Southern Alberta Art Gallery (with catalog), Lethbridge, Alta, 83; Shelter, Burlington Cult Ctr, 86; Scale, Alta Coll Art Gallery, Calgary, 86; Bollinger-Leshyk, Oakville Galleries, 87. *Collection Arranged:* Guest cur, ACT Powerhouse, Montreal-Toronto Exchange, 79; Artist's Choice, Glendon Gallery, Toronto, 80. *Teaching:* Artist-in-residence, Activity Ctr, Art Gallery Ont, Toronto, 79-82; instr, mixed media & visual arts, North York, Ont, summers, 83-88, head prog, 83 & 86; instr, Found Drawing I & III, Univ Guelph, 86-87. *Awards:* Design Can Award, 74; Ont Arts Coun Proj Award, 79 & 88; Can Coun Arts Grants, 83 & 86. *Bibliog:* Otto Rapp (auth), Tonie Leshyk at the Southern Alberta Art Gallery, Artmag, No 63/64, 83; Marshall Webb (auth), Ghost house: In memoriam to a worthy opponent, Vanguard, 4/84; Val Greenfield (auth), No peace, no shelter, C Mag, No 8, winter 86. *Media:* Plaster, Mixed Media. *Publ:* Auth, Your Skilled Weapon, self-publ, 85. *Mailing Add:* 338 Delaware Ave Toronto ON M6H 2T8 Canada

LESKO, DIANE
MUSEUM DIRECTOR, CURATOR
Study: State Univ NY, Binghamton, AB, 71, MA, 75, PhD, 81; Phi Beta Kappa. *Collection Arranged:* Jon Corbino: An Heroic Vision, 87; Gari Melchers: A Retrospective Exhib, 90; Frederick Carl Frieseke: The Evolution of an Am Impressionist, 2001. *Pos:* Cur collections, Mus Fine Arts, St Petersburg, Fla, 85-89, sr cur collections & exhibs, 89-94, asst dir, 93-94; dir, Telfair Mus Art, Savannah, Ga, 95-. *Teaching:* Asst prof art hist, Lycoming Col, Williamsport, Pa, 78-85. *Awards:* Harpur Coll Found scholar, 1968-71; SUNY-Binghamton grad fel in art hist, 1971-73; doctoral fel in art hist, 1978-79; Lycoming Coll Doctoral Dissertation grantee, 1981; fac prof devel grantee, summer 1982; recipient AAM Excellence in Peer Review Serv Award, 2004; Visionary Award, Savannah Area Tourism and Leadership Coun, 2004. *Mem:* Asn Art Mus Dirs; South East Mus Conf; Nat Organization of Women; Women's Caucus for Art; Coll Art Assoc. *Res:* Nineteenth and twentieth century European and American art. *Publ:* Auth, Il Faut Etre de Son Temps: Charles Negre as painter-photographer in mid-19th century France, Arts, 81; James Ensor, the Creative Years, Princeton Univ Press, 85; James Ensor and Symbolist Literature, Art J, 85; Jon Corbino: An Heroic Vision, 87; Gari Melchers: A Retrospective Exhib, 90; and others. *Mailing Add:* Telfair Mus Art PO Box 10081 Savannah GA 31412

LESLIE, ALFRED
PAINTER, FILMMAKER
b Bronx, NY, Oct 29, 1927. *Study:* NYU, 1947-1949. *Work:* Mus Fine Arts, Boston, Hirshhorn Mus, Wash, Mus Contemp Art, Chicago, 1984; Newport Harbor Art Mus, 1985; Boca Raton Mus Art, 1989; St Louis Art Mus, 1991; rep in collections of Metrop Mus Art, New York City, Stedelijk Mus, Amsterdam, Kunstmuseum, Basel, Moderna Museet, Stockholm. *Exhib:* Joseloff Gallery, Univ Hartford, 1991, Oil & Steel Gallery, NY, 1992, Manny Silverman Gallery, Los Angeles, 1995, Ameringer Yohe Fine Art, 2007. *Teaching:* Vis artist, Amherst Col, Youngstown State Univ; vis prof, painting Boston Univ. *Awards:* Recipient lifetime achievement award, Chicago Underground Film Festival; grantee Guttman Found for Avant-Garde Film, 1962. *Mem:* Nat Acad, Amer Acad Arts and Letters. *Publ:* films incl Pull My Daisy, 1959, The Last Clean Shirt, 1963, The Cedar Bar, 2002; auth of 100 Views Along the Road, 1988; founding ed, The Hasty Papers, 1959. *Mailing Add:* 313 E 6th St New York NY 10003

LESLIE, JIMMY
PAINTER, INSTRUCTOR
b Long Branch, NJ, Aug 18, 1967. *Study:* Monmouth Univ, BA, 1990; NY Acad Art, MFA, 1993; Monmouth Univ, Vermont Studio Ctr (scholarship), 1999. *Work:* Johnson & Johnson Health Care Systems, Skillman, NJ; First Baptist Church, Red Bank, NJ; Monmouth Medical Ctr, Long Branch, NJ. *Exhib:* Surroundings, Johnson & Johnson Hq, New Brunswick, NJ, 2002; Take Home a Nude Charity Art Auction, Sotheby's Auction House, NYC, 2003; Places & Spaces, Ocean City Arts Ctr, Ocean City, NJ, 2004; Interiors, Louisa Melrose Gallery, Frenchtown, NJ, 2004; Recent Exteriors, Potter Libr Gallery, Ramapo College, Mahwah, NJ, 2005; Small Landscapes, Mitchell Sanborn Gallery, Keyport, NJ, 2006; Asbury Artists, Asbury Scenes, The APeX Gallery, Asbury Park, NJ, 2007, Winter & Other Seasonal Moments, 2007. *Teaching:* Instr fine arts (assoc prof), St Johns Univ, Queens, NY, 1994-1999; instr, Brookdale Community Col, Lincroft, NJ, 1995-; instr, Monmouth Univ, W Long Branch, NJ, 1995-; owner/teacher, The Leslie Art Studio in the Jersey Shore Arts Ctr, Ocean Grove, NJ. *Awards:* Special Recognition, Figurative Small Works, Armory Arts Ctr, W Palm Beach, Fla, 1998; Special Recognition, All Media '99, Period Gallery Omaha, Nebr, 1999; Artist in Residency Award, Vt Studio Ctr, Johnson, Vt, 99. *Bibliog:* David Boyer (auth), Illuminating Show, Sunday Standard Times, New Bedford, Mass, 2003; Barbara Tompkins (auth), Gallery Highlights, Nouveau Mag, 2004; Jennifer Cattaui (auth), Art Stars, MAR Mag, Summer 2006. *Mem:* Monmouth Co Arts Coun; Shors Inst of Contemp Art. *Media:* Oil, canvas. *Interests:* Running; Surfing; Motorcycling. *Dealer:* APeX Gallery Cookman Ave Asbury Park NJ. *Mailing Add:* 15 Sickles Pl Shrewsbury NJ 07702

LESNICK, STEPHEN WILLIAM
PAINTER, INSTRUCTOR
b Bridgeport, Conn, Mar 22, 1931. *Study:* Silvermine Coll Art, BA, Art Career Sch, BA; also with Revington Arthur, Jon McClelland, Jack Wheat & Gail Symon; studied watercolor with Herb Olsen. *Work:* Elk's Western Helldorado Art Collection, Nev; Burndy Libr Arts & Sci, Norwalk, Conn. *Comn:* Indust paintings, Burndy Libr Art & Sci, 59; portrait of Gov mansion, comn by Gov Paul Laxalt, Carson City, 68; commemorative coin (Boulder Dam), Elks Lodge, Las Vegas, 71-78; medallion series, Nev State Mus, 77-. *Exhib:* All New Eng Art Exhib, Conn, 55; Layout & Design Int Art Competition, Japan, 63; Ann Conn Relig Art Exhib, 63 & 64; Ann Am Watercolor Soc Show, 68; Helldorado Western Art Exhib, Nev, 68; and thirty-three solo exhibs. *Pos:* Layout designer, Vacart Art Studio, Stamford, Conn, 60-65; art dir, Kelley & Reber Advert, Las Vegas, 65-66; illusr, EG&G, Inc, Las Vegas, 66-73; art ed, Las Vegas Sun, 70-; syndicated newspaper columnist, Art for Everyone; illusr, Marine Corps Gazette; one of founders, Las Vegas Art Mus; owner, Lesnick Art Products. *Teaching:* Instr art, Desert Art League, Boulder City, 65-66; instr art, Las Vegas Art League & Artists & Craftsmans Guild, Nev, 65-68 & Clark Co Community Coll; owner & instr, Lesnick Art Studio, Las Vegas, 65-. *Awards:* Conn Relig Show, Hallmark Greeting Cards, 63 & 64; First Prize, Nev Bicentennial Commemorative Medallion, Franklin Mint, 72; Purchase Prize, Barnum Fest; First Prize & Purchase Award, Helldorado Western Art Show; Region I Winner ($3000), Nat Arts in the Parks, 87; Purchase Award, Nat Arts Parks, 96; Juror's Choice Award, Paint the Parks, 2008; Grand Prize, Nat Paint Am Competition. *Bibliog:* Articles in Desert Scope, 69-71; Desert Valley Times. *Mem:* Nev State Watercolor Soc; Soc NAm Artists. *Media:* All Media. *Mailing Add:* 283 E Camellia Cir Mesquite NV 89027-5120

LETENDRE, RITA
PAINTER, PRINTMAKER
b Drummondville, Que, Nov 1, 1928. *Study:* Ecole Beaux Arts, Montreal; P E Borduas, Montreal. *Work:* Nat Gallery of Can; Mus Art Contemporain, Montreal; Art Gallery of Ontario; Mus Beaux-Arts, Montreal; Long Beach Mus Fine Arts, Calif; Rose Art Mus, Brandeis Univ, Waltham, Mass; Mus Que; San Diego Art Gallery; Algoma Art Gallery, Sault St Marie; Royal Bank of Can; Coopers Lybrand, NY; Blue Cross/Blue Shield, Mich; and others. *Comn:* Wall painting, Calif State Col, Long Beach, 65; mural, Greenwin of Toronto, 71; wall painting, Benson & Hedges, Neil-Wyick Col, Toronto, 71; mural, J D S Investment, Sheridan Mall, Pickering, Ont, 72; Via Rail, Toronto Transit Corp, 78. *Exhib:* Int des Arts, Mus Beaux-Arts, 60; 5 Festival di due Mondi, Spoleto, Italy, 62; IV Biennale Can Painting, Tate Gallery, London, Eng, 63; Can Pavilion Expo 67, Montreal, 67; Que Pavilion, World's Fair, Osaka, Japan, 70; Solo exhibs, Waddington & Gorce, Montreal, 97, Centre Culturel de Drummondville, 98, Galerie Madeline, Lacerte, Quebec, 98, Art Gallery of Algoma, Sault Ste Marie, Moore Gallery, Toronto & Simon Blais Gallery, Montreal; Achieving the Modern, Winnipeg Art Gallery, 92; Pastels du Quebec, Gallerie de L'UQAM, Montreal; La Crise De L'Abstraction, Les Annes 1950, Nat Gallery Can, 92; Art 2000, Stratford Art Gallery, 2000; Galerie Simon Blais, 2004-05 & 08. *Awards:* Le Prix de Peinture, Concours Artistique Que, 61; Cagnes sur Mer, France, 63; Que Bourse de Recherche, 67; Can Arts Coun Sr Grant Award, 71; Officire de l'ordre Nat du Quebec, 2002; Officire de l'ordre, Can, 2005. *Bibliog:* Jules Heller (auth), Printmaking Today, Holt, Rinehart & Winston, 71; Rita Letendre (auth), The Montreal Years 1953-1963, Concordia Art Gallery, 89; Gaston Roberge (auth), Rita Letendre: Woman of Light, Belle Publ, 97. *Mem:* Royal Can Acad Art. *Media:* Acrylic, Oil, Pastels. *Dealer:* Simon Blais Montreal. *Mailing Add:* 5420 Boul Saint-Laurent Ste 100 Montreal PQ H2T 1S1 Canada

LETHBRIDGE, JULIAN
PAINTER
b Colombo, Sri Lanka, 1947. *Study:* Winchester Coll & Cambridge Univ, Eng, 1960-69. *Work:* Metrop Mus Art, NY; Tate Gallery Contemp Art Soc, London; Nat Gallery of Art, DC; Whitney Mus Am Art, New York; Fogg Art Mus, Cambridge, Mass. *Exhib:* Solo Exhibs: Julian Pretto Gallery, NY, 1988, Daniel Weinberg Gallery, Los Angeles, 1989, Paula Cooper Gallery, NY, 1989, 1992, 1995, 1999, 2003, 2007, 2009, Stuart Regen Gallery, Los Angeles, 1991, Karsten Schubert Ltd, London, 1993, Schmidt Contemp Art, St Louis, 1996, Adelson Gallery, Colo, 1997-98, Marcel Sitcoske Gallery, San Francisco, 2003; Group Exhibs: include From Here, Karsten Schubert Ltd, London, 1995; Turner Runyon Gallery, Dallas, 1996; Susan Sheehan Gallery, NY, 1996; On Paper II, Schmidt Contemp Art, St Louis, Mo, 1996; 1950 Gallery, 1997; Paula Cooper Gallery, NY City, 1998; Fay Gold Gallery, Atlanta, 1998; Aspen Art Mus, 1999; Matthew Marks Gallery, NY City, 2000; Doug Lawing Gallery, Houston, 2001; Devin Borden Hiram Butler Gallery, Houston, 2004; Schmidt Contemp Art, St Louis, 2005; Looking Back: The White Columns Ann, White Columns, NY, 2009. *Teaching:* Vis lectr, visual and environ studies, Harvard Univ, 1999, 2001, 2004. *Awards:* Francis J Greenberger Award, 1988. *Bibliog:* Amy Eshoo (ed), 560 Broadway! A New York Drawing Collection at Work, 1991-2006, Yale Univ Press, New Haven, Conn, 2008; David Seidner (auth), Artist at Work: Inside the Studios of Today's Most Celebrated Artist, Rizzoli, p178-183, New York, 1999. *Dealer:* Paula Cooper Gallery 534 West 21st St New York NY 10011. *Mailing Add:* c/o Paula Cooper Gallery 534 W 21st St New York NY 10011

LETTENSTROM, DEAN ROGER
PAINTER, EDUCATOR
b Superior, Wis, Sept 12, 1941. *Study:* Univ Wis, Superior, BFA, 67; Univ Dallas, Irving, Tex, MA, 68; Skowhegan Maine, 68; Ohio State Univ, Columbus, Ohio, MFA, 69; MacDowell Colony, 73. *Work:* Chicago Art Inst Libr, Ill; Huntington Mus & Galleries, WVa; Tweed Mus Art, Duluth, Minn; Lutheran Brotherhood Co, Minneapolis; Ohio State Univ Galleries, Columbus. *Exhib:* Texas Painting & Sculpture, Dallas Mus Fine Arts, Dallas, Tex, 68; Solo exhibs, Five Yr Retrospective, Duluth, 90, St John's Univ, 93, Wis, 94; Nat Ann, Mo, 92; 38th Ann Nat, Calif, 92; Cheekwood Nat, 92; group tour, Stix, Wis, 93, Anderson & Anderson, Minneapolis, 93. *Teaching:* Assoc prof painting, Drake Univ, Des Moines, Iowa, 70-73; instr painting, Minneapolis Col Art Design, 77-78; assoc prof painting, Univ Minn, Duluth, 79-93, prof art, 94-. *Awards:* Honorable Mention, Nat PTG Exhib, Washington, Pa, 90; Wis State Arts Bd Develop Grant, 93; Honorable Mention, 7 State Regional, Duluth Art Inst, 94. *Mem:* Coll Art Asn Am. *Mailing Add:* Art Dept Univ Minn Duluth MN 55812

LEUNG, SIMON
CONCEPTUAL ARTIST
b Hong Kong, 1964. *Study:* Univ Calif, Los Angeles, BA (magna cum laude), 1987; Whitney Prog, 1988-89. *Exhib:* Solo exhibs include Pat Hearn Gallery, New York, 1996, Refusalon, San Francisco, 1997, Huntington Beach At Ctr, 1998, Santa Monica Mus Art, 2002; group exhibs include Whitney Biennial, Whitney Mus Am Art, New York, 1993; Venice Biennale, 2003. *Teaching:* Assoc prof studio art, Univ Calif, Irvine. *Awards:* John Simon Guggenheim Mem Found Fel, 2008. *Publ:* Co-ed, Theory in Contemp Art Since 1985, Blackwell, 2004. *Mailing Add:* Dept Studio Art Claire Trevor Sch Arts Univ Calif Irvine Irvine CA 92697-2775

LEVEE, JOHN H
PAINTER, SCULPTOR
b Los Angeles, Calif, Apr 10, 1924. *Study:* Art Ctr Sch & Chenard Sch, Los Angeles; Univ Calif, Los Angeles, BA, 48; New Sch Social Res, with Stuart Davis, Abe Rattner & Kunyoshi, 48-49; Acad Julian, Paris, grand prix, 51. *Work:* Mus Mod Art, Whitney Mus Am Art & Guggenheim Mus, NY; Corcoran Gallery Art, Washington, DC; Mus Mod Art, Paris; plus many others in pub & pvt collections. *Comn:* Wall, Architects, Chateau Vaudreuil, Paris, 71-72; walls, Bank Credit Com, Paris, 72-73; floor design, Sch Marne-le-Vallee, Paris, 75; walls & banners, Prudential Life Insurance Co, Los Angeles, 77; wall, (1700 sq ft), Coll Chateauchinon, France, 86. *Exhib:* Salon de May, Paris, 54-89; Corcoran Gallery Art, 56-58; New Acquisitions, 57 & Young Am Painters, 57-58, Mus Mod Art, NY; Whitney Mus Am Art, 57, 58 & 66; Salon de Realities, 58-98; Haifa Mus Art, Israel, 63; Phoenix Art Mus, Ariz, 64; Krannert Art Mus, Univ Ill, 65; Walker Art Ctr, Minneapolis, 65; Tel Aviv Mus, Israel, 69; Palm Springs Mus, Calif, 77; Comparisons, Paris, 80-2004; Salon des Grands et Juenes d' Aujour' hui 92-2004; Mus Saint Leo, France, 2004; and others. *Teaching:* Vis prof art, Univ Ill, 64-65, Washington Univ, 67, NY Univ, 67-68 & Univ Southern Calif, 70. *Awards:* Purchase award, Commonwealth Va Biannual, 66; Ford Fel, Tamarind Workshop, 69; First Grand Prix, First Biannual de Paris, 69; Four Prizes, Woolmark Found, 74-75. *Bibliog:* Calender of the Mus of Modern Art, 57; cover, Art In America, 57; Arts, 6/57; History of Modern Painting, 2008. *Media:* Acrylic, Mixed Media; Plexiglas. *Collection:* African, pre-Columbian and contemporary painting and sculpture. *Publ:* Abstract Expressionism, Le Masee, Paris, 2008. *Dealer:* Gallerie Callu-Merile 17 Rue des Beaux Arts Paris 6; Gallerie Le gall Peyroulet 18 Rue Keller Paris 11; Patrick Reynolds Le Masee Paris; Muller & Guipel 12 Rue Guenegoud Paris France. *Mailing Add:* 119 rue Notre Dame des Champs Paris France

LEVEN, ANN R
ADMINISTRATOR
b Canton, Ohio, Nov 1, 1940. *Study:* Brown Univ, AB, 62; studio work at RI Sch of Design; Harvard Bus Sch, MBA, 64; Fogg Mus. *Work:* Brown Univ. *Pos:* Financial asst, 67-69, asst treas, 70-72 & treas, 72-79, Metrop Mus Art, NY; Mus Aid Panel (mem), NY State Coun on the Arts, 77-79; adv comt, Art Dept, Brown Univ; trustee,

Artist's Choice Mus, 79-87; vpres, Chase Manhattan Bank, 79-83; trustee, Artists Choice Mus, 79-87 & NY Sch Interior Design, currently; staff liaison, Presidential Task Force Arts & Humanities, Nat Endowment Arts, 81; dir, Twyla Tharp Dance Found, 82-87 & Am Art's Alliance, 90-92; treas, Smithsonian Inst, 84-90; overseer, Hood Mus-Hopkins Ctr, Dartmouth Col, 84-91, chmn bd, 88-91; deputy treas, Nat Gallery Art, 90-94, treas, 94-. *Teaching:* Fac, Columbia Business Sch, 75-94. *Awards:* Minnie Nelen Hicks Prize, Brown Univ; NY State Outstanding Young Woman, 76. *Mem:* Womens Forum; Art Table; Am Asn Mus. *Publ:* Contribr, Cultural Institutions Across America: Functions and Funding; The Buck Starts Here: Enterprise and the Arts; coauth, Case Series on Metrop Mus Art, Harvard Bus Sch. *Mailing Add:* Nat Gallery Art Washington DC 20565

LEVENSON, DAN
CONCEPTUAL ARTIST
Study: Oberlin Coll, BA (fine art), 1994; Royal Coll Art, London, MFA (painting), 1997. *Exhib:* Solo exhibs include Sixtyseven Gallery, Brooklyn, 2003, White Columns, New York, 2003, Incident Report, Hudson, NY, 2008; group exhibs include Star67, Brooklyn, 2000, 2001; Good Words & Credentials, Columbia Univ, New York, 2003; Terrarium, Bronx River Arts Ctr, Bronx, NY, 2003; From New York with Love, Covivant Gallery, Tampa, Fla, 2004; Recent Acquisitions, Jason Rulnick Fine Art, New York, 2006, Geometric, Abstract & Geometric Abstraction, 2008; Cultivating Consciousness, Gallery NuLu, Louisville, 2007. *Awards:* Yaddo Fel, 2000, 2001, 2004 & 2006; NY Found Arts Grant, 2007; Pollock-Krasner Found Grant, 2007. *Mailing Add:* 339 2nd St Brooklyn NY 11215-2416

LEVENSON, RUSTIN S
CONSERVATOR, RESTORER
b Toledo, Ohio, July 19, 1947. *Study:* Wellesley Col, BA, 69; Fogg Art Mus, Harvard Univ, cert conserv, 72. *Pos:* Conservator, Can Conserv Inst, 73-74 & Nat Gallery Can, 74-77, Ottawa, Ont; asst conservator, Metrop Mus Art, New York, 77-80; pres & head conservator, New York Conserv Assoc, 80-; Fla Conserv Assoc, 86-. *Awards:* Am Libr Asn Excellence Prize, Distinction in Scholarship and Conservation Prize, Coll Art Asn, Boston Bookbuilders prize for design, 01, Seeing Through Paintings. *Mem:* Fel Int Inst Conserv; fel Am Inst Conserv (chmn Paintings group, 83-84); Nat Inst Conserv. *Publ:* Materials and techniques of early Quebec painters, J Can Art Hist, 83; A New Method for Loose Lining Contemporary Paintings, 87 & Emergency Conservation, 94, Am Inst Conserv; Seeing Through Paintings, Yale Univ Press, 2000; contbrib chpt, Authenticity in the Marketplace of Buying Selling and Collecting Visual Art, Oxford Univ Press, 2003; The Expert vs The Object, Oxford Univ Press, 2004. *Mailing Add:* 13291 Old Cutler Rd Miami FL 33156

LEVERING, ROBERT K
PAINTER, COLLAGE ARTIST
b Ypsilanti, Mich, May 22, 1919. *Study:* Univ Ariz, AB, 42; Art Inst Chicago, 43; Art Students League, 55-56; Brooklyn Mus Sch Art with Reuben Iam, 59-61. *Work:* USAF Collection, Pentagon, Washington, DC; also in pvt collections. *Comn:* Portraits of Kennedy, Eisenhower, U Thant, Martin Luther King & Dag Hamerskjold; portraits, pres Am Express; portraits, pres Wells & Fargo; and other public & pvt comns. *Exhib:* Seven exhibs, New York City Ctr Gallery; Soc Illustrators Gallery, NY; Brooklyn Mus, 61; Mikelson Gallery, Washington, DC, 68; NY Art Dirs Club Exhib, 69. *Teaching:* Guest critic & lectr, Parsons Sch Design, 65-70, instr painting & drawing, 76-93. *Awards:* Gold Medal, 69 & Merit Awards, Soc Illusr; Citation, NJ Art Dirs Club, 69; Soc Publ Designers Award, 69. *Media:* Oil; Graphics, Miscellaneous Media. *Publ:* Illusr, leading nat mag, bks, newspapers, advert & ed. *Mailing Add:* 433 E 84th St Apt 1 New York NY 10028-6358

LEVI, JOSEF
PAINTER
b New York, NY, Feb 17, 1938. *Study:* Univ Conn, BA, 59; Columbia Univ, 60. *Work:* Mus Mod Art, NY; Albright-Knox Gallery, Buffalo, NY; Aldrich Mus Contemp Art, Ridgefield, Conn; Krannert Art Mus, Univ Ill, Urbana; Des Moines Art Ctr; Corcoran Gallery, Washington, DC; Brooklyn Mus, NY; Newark Mus, NJ; and many others. *Exhib:* Solo exhibs, Stable Gallery, NY, 66 & 68-70, Art Club, Chicago, Ill, 67, Gertrude Kasle Gallery, Detroit, Mich, 71, AM Sachs Gallery, 75, 76 & 78, O K Harris Gallery, NY, 83, 85, 87, 90, 92, 94, 96 & 99, Harmon Meek Gallery, Naples, 96, 2001; Art Fair, Basel, Switz, 73; Mus Art, RI Sch Design, Providence, 76; Deja Vu: Masterpieces Updated, Western Asn Art Mus, 81-82; Westheimer Collection, Okla Art Ctr, Oklahoma City, 88; The Humanist Icon, Bayly Art Mus, Univ Va, 90; The Purloined Image, Flint Inst Arts, 93; Art After Art, Nassau Co Mus Art, 94; and others. *Teaching:* Artist-in-residence, Appalachian State Univ, Boone, NC, 69 & Pa State Univ, University Park, 76. *Awards:* Purchase Award, Univ Ill, Urbana, 66; Selected for New Talent USA, Art Am, 66. *Bibliog:* William Wilson (auth), In the eye of the beholder, Art News, 2/70; J Patrice Marandel (auth), Preface for Silkscreen Portfolio, Domberger, 71; Allen Ellenzweig (auth), Still life with art history: The collage paintings of Josef Levi, Arts Mag, 12/76; Martha Scott (auth), Josef Levi, Arts Mag, 3/85. *Mem:* New York Artists Equity Asn. *Media:* Acrylics, Graphite on Paper. *Dealer:* O K Harris 383 W Broadway New York NY 10021; Harmon-Meek Gallery Naples FL. *Mailing Add:* 353 W 57th St New York NY 10019

LEVIN, CAROL GELLNER
SCULPTOR
b Cincinnati, Ohio, Jan, 10, 1943. *Study:* Ind Univ, BA, 64; Univ Chicago, MA, 66; Corcoran Sch Art, 69-78. *Work:* Exec Off Bldg, Rockville, Md; Torpedo Factory Art Ctr, Alexandria, Va; Amnesty Int & Children's Defense Fund, Washington, DC; Strathmore Hall Arts Ctr, Rockville, Md. *Comn:* Ceramic sculpture, City Alexandria, Va, 83; Arts Coun Montgomery County, Md, 98. *Exhib:* Art This Way, Strathmore Hall, Rockville, Md, 91; Art in Embassies prog, US State Dept, 96-98; Everyday Life, Nat Sculpture Soc Exhib, 99; Nat Sculpture Soc Ann Exhib, Brookgreen Gardens, SC, NY, NY, 2000; Catherine Lorillard Wolfe Ann Exhib, NY, NY, 2000-2001; Invitational Exhib, Univ of Chicago, 2002; Invitational Exhib, Jane Haslem Gallery, Wash, DC, 2002 & 2004; Selden Gallery, Norfolk, Va, 2006; Wash Sculptors Group Exhib, 2007-08; Flanders 311 Gallery, Raleigh, NC, 2009; BBC World News Art Feature, 2009; Suffolk Mus, Suffolk, Va, 2009; Mus Am, DC, 2009-2010; Zenith Gallery, 2011. *Pos:* Artist-in-residence, Capitol Children's Mus, Washington, DC, 90. *Teaching:* tchr sculpture workshops, 2000-. *Awards:* Art League Awards, 94-95; Montgomery Co Artists Asn Grant, 96; Montgomery Co Arts Coun Grant, 96-97. *Bibliog:* Don Miller (auth), With tongue in cheek, Sculpture Review Mag, spring 86; Lab Sch Washington (auth), Sculpture: Carol G Levin, DC Area Artists, 93-; Ruth Palombo (auth), Clay sculptures reveal commonality of spirit, Gazette Newspapers, 10/93; The low down on high tech, The Washington Post, 9/26/99; Caution, Controversy Ahead, The Washington Post, 4/7/2000; Media appearance, Good Morning America, 2002; Donna Cedar Southwood (auth), Carol Gellner Levin, Elan Mag, 2007; Take the Day off with Public Television (media appearance), 2008; BBC World News (media appearance), 2009; Christo & Four Modern Creators of Environmental Art, Dennis Forbes, 2012. *Mem:* Nat Sculpture Soc; Artists Equity Asn; Wash Sculptors Group; Int Sculpture Ctr. *Media:* Ceramic, Bronze; Bonded Bronze, Concrete, Mixed Media. *Publ:* Auth, Sculptor's dilemma, Wash Post, 8/83; Auth, Good morning America, ABC, 4/2002; Auth, Life is Short, Wash Post, 3/2006. *Dealer:* Jane Haslem Gallery; Zenith Gallery. *Mailing Add:* 105 N Union St No 30 Alexandria VA 22314

LEVIN, DANA
PAINTER
b 1969. *Study:* New World Sch Arts, Miami, 86; Sch Art Inst Chicago, BFA (painting and drawing), 90; Florence Acad Art, Italy 2000. *Exhib:* Group exhibs, Artworks Gallery, San Francisco, 95; The Lenox Libr, Mass, 99; The Grenning Gallery, Sag Harbor, NY, 99, Vanitas, 2003; The Bert Gallery, Providence, RI, 2002, In Search of Beauty, 2004, Flora and Fauna, 2006; Realism Revisited, Panorama Mus, Bad Frankenhausen, Germany, Hirschl & Adler Galleries, NY, 2003; Still Classical, Westbeth Arts Gallery, NY, 2003; Nasters of the Florence Academy of Art, Eleanor Ettinger Gallery, NY, 2004, 2006, Winter Salon, 2004-2005, 2007, Autumn Salon, 2005,; Alumni Exhib, Florence Acad Art, Italy, 2005; The Boston Sch Legacy, The Banks Gallery, NH, 2006. *Teaching:* Drawing instr, Belvoir Terrace Summer Program, Lenox, Mass, 99; instr, Florence Acad Art, 2000-04; founder and instr, The New Sch Classical Art, Providence, RI, 2005-. *Awards:* Katharine A Lovell Memorial Award, 2006. *Mem:* Int Soc Realist Painters; Oil Painters of Am; Art Renewal Ctr. *Dealer:* Eleanor Ettinger Gallery 119 Spring St Ground Floor NY NY 10012; The Bert Gallery 540 S Water St Providence RI 02903; The Banks Gallery 126 State St Portsmouth NH 03801

LEVIN, GAIL
HISTORIAN, PHOTOGRAPHER, ARTIST
b Atlanta, Ga, 1948. *Study:* Sorbonne, Paris,; Simmons Col, BA (art hist),, Hon Dr, 96; Tufts Univ, MA,; Rutgers Univ, PhD (art hist), 76. *Hon Degrees:* Simmons Col, 96. *Work:* High Mus Art, Atlanta; Ctr for Photog, Woodstock, NY; Pollock-Krasner House, East Hampton, NY. *Exhib:* Solo exhibs, Mem Art Gallery, Univ Rochester, NY, 85, Cedar Rapids Art Mus, Cedar Rapids, Iowa, 86, Univ Iowa Mus Art, Iowa City, 87, Peale House Gallery, Pa Acad Fine Arts, Philadelphia, 87-88 & Univ Art Collections, Ariz State Univ, Tempe, Ariz, 88; Cress Gallery, Univ Tenn, Chattanooga, 95; Trustman Gallery, Simmons Coll, Boston, 95; Provincetown Monument Mus, Mass, 96; Cape Cod Mus Art, 2007; On NOT Becoming An Artist, Nat Asn of Women Artists, NYC, 2014; Collages and Stone Sculptures, Sandisfield Art Ctr, Sandisfield, Mass, 2015; Gail Levin, Scholar Rocks, El Museo Cult, Santa Fe, NMex, 2015; Gail Levin, Scholar Rocks, Squire Found, Santa Barbara, Calif, 2015; Gail levin: Food for Thought, Art from Scrap, Santa Barbara, Calif, 2015. *Collection Arranged:* Morgan Russell: Synchromist Studies, 1910-1922, Mus Mod Art, NY, 76; Synchromism and Am Color Abstraction, 1910-1925, Whitney Mus Am Art, 78; Abstract Expressionism: The Formative Years, traveling exhib, 78; Edward Hopper: Prints and Illustrations, 79 & Edward Hopper: the Art and the Artist, traveling exhib, 80; Visions of Tomorrow: NY and Am Industrialization in the 1920s-1930s, Isetan Mus Art, Tokyo & traveling, 88; Marsden Hartley in Bavaria (traveling exhib), Emerson Gallery, Hamilton Col, Clinton, NY, 89-90; Changing Cultures: Recent Artist Immigrants from China (traveling exhib), Baruch Coll Gallery, 91-92; The Poetry of Solitude: Edward Hopper's Drawings, Hunter Mus Art, Chattanooga, 95; Aaron Copland's Am, Heckscher Mus Art, Huntington, NY, 2000; Judy Chicago: Jewish Identity, Hebrew Union Col, Jewish Inst Relig Mus, NY, 2007; Theresa Bernstein: Artist of the 20th Century, James Gallery of the Grad Ctr of the City Uni of NY, 2013; touring five other venues. *Pos:* Cur, Edward Hopper Collection, Whitney Mus Am Art, 76-84. *Teaching:* Instr, New Sch for Social Res, 73-75; asst prof art hist, Conn Coll, New London, 75-76; vis asst prof, Graduate Sch, City Univ New York, 79-80; assoc prof, Baruch Coll, New York, 86-88; Will & Ariel Durant Prof Humanities, St Peter's Coll, Jersey City, NJ, 87-88; prof, Baruch Coll & grad ctr of City Univ, New York, 89-2007, distinguished prof, 2008-. *Awards:* Yale Univ Grant, 92-93; Nat Endowment Humanities Grant, 93-95 & 98-99; Am Nat Bank Chair of Excellence, Univ Tenn, 95-96; NY Times Notable Book of the Year, 1995; George Wittenborn Mem Award, Spec Mention, 96; Los Angeles Times Book Prize Finalist in Biography, 97; Hadassah-Brandeis Inst Res Grand, 2001; Schlesinger Libr Res Support Grant, 2005-2006; Hadassah Int Res Inst on Jewish Women at Brandeis Univ Res Award, 2006; Nat Endowment Humanities Grant, 2006; Senior Fulbright Scholar to Japan, 2006; Pollock Krasner Stonybrook Found Res Fel, 2006-2007; Getty Res Inst, Libr Res Grant, 2007; Nat Asn Women Artists Award Biog & Art Hist, 2007; Fulbright Distinguished Chair, Roosevelt Study Ctr, Neth, 2007-2008; Res Award, The Hadassah Int Res Inst on Jewish Women at Brandeis Univ, 2014; Distinguished Fulbright Chair, Col Fine Arts, Thiruvananthapuram, Kerala, India, 2015-2016. *Bibliog:* Auth, Marsden Hartley in Bavaria Univ Pres New England, 89. *Mem:* Int Asn Art Critics; PEN Freedom to Write; Coll Art Asn Am; Catalogue Raisonne Scholars Asn; Am Studies Asn. *Res:* Marsden Hartley Catalogue Raisonne; Yasuo Kuniyoshi. *Interests:* Twentieth century art; theory of biography. *Publ:* Theme and Improvisation:

Kandinsky and the American Avant-grade, 1912-1950, Blufinch Press, 92; Edward Hopper: An Intimate Biography, 95, 2nd expanded ed, 2007; Edward Hopper: A Catalogue Raisonne, WW Norton & Co Inc, 95; Hopper's Places, Univ Calif Press, 2nd ed, 98; Aaron Copland's American: A Cultural Perspective, Watson-Gupfill Pubs, 2000; co-ed & contribr, Ethics and The Visual Arts, 2006; auth, Becoming Judy Chicago: A Biography of the Artist, 2007; auth, Lee Krasner: A Biography, 2011; editor & lead auth, Theresa Bernstein: A Century in Art (lead essayist & editor), Lincoln, Nebr, 2013. *Mailing Add:* c/o Baruch Coll 1 Bernard Baruch Way B7-235 New York NY 10010

LEVIN, GOLAN
ARTIST
Study: Mass Inst of Tech, BS (art & design), 94, MS (arts & scis), 2000. *Exhib:* Solo exhibs at Moving Image Gallery, NY City, 2001, Bitforms Gallery, NY City, 2002, NTT InterCommunicationsCenter, Tokyo, Japan, 2006; group exhib include Whitney Biennial, Whitney Mus Am Art, 2004; Digital Sublime, Mus Contemp Art, Taipei, Taiwan, 2004; Interactions/Art and Technology, Am Mus Moving Image, NY City, 2004; Prix Arts Electronica, OK Centrum Gegenwartskunst, Linz Austria, 2004; The Algorithmic Revolution: On the History of Interactive Art, ZKM, Karlsruhe, Ger 2004; You Are Here: The Design of Information, Design, Mus, London, 2005; New Media: What, Neuberger Mus Art, Purchase, NY, 2005; OneDotZero9, Inst Contemp Art, London, 2005; ElectroScape, Duolun Zendai Art Mus, Shanghai, 2005; Rhizome ArtBase 101, New Mus Contemp Art, NY, 2005; Generator X Exhib, Nat Mus Art, Architecture and Design, Oslo, 2005; Tokyo Digital Arts Festival, Tokyo, Japan, 2005; Software Art, DeCordova Mus and Sculpture Pk, Boston, 2006; Whitney Mus Artport and Tate Online, Net Art Comn, 2006; Emacao Artificial 3.0 Biennial, Itau Cultural Inst, Sao Paolo, Brazil, 2006. *Pos:* Mem res staff, Interval Res Corp, 94-98; res asst, Mass Inst of Technol Media Lab, 98-2000; consult, Design Machine, NY, 2000-02; composer of numerous interactive and multimedia compositions, performances, recording and other works. *Teaching:* Adjunct prof, Columbia Univ, 2000; vis artist and lectr, Cooper Union Sch Art, 2001-02; adj fac Parsons Sch Design, 2001-03; asst prof electronic time-based art, Sch Art. Carnegie Mellon Univ, 2004-. *Awards:* Named New Artist Under 30, Print Mag, 2002; recipient Bronze Medal, ID Mag Interaction Design Award, 2002; named one of Top 100 Young Innovators, Mass Inst of Technol Tech Review, 2004; Award Distinction, Net Art, Prix Ars Electronica, 2004; Artist's Grant, Emerging Fields Category, Creative Capital Found, 2006. *Publ:* Composer numerous interactive and multimedia compositions, performances, recordings and other works

LEVIN, HUGH LAUTER
PUBLISHER
b Rye, NY, July 2, 1951. *Study:* Univ Pa, BA, 73, Wharton Sch, MBA, 84. *Pos:* Pres, Hugh Lauter Levin Assoc Inc, 74-; dir, Abrams Original Editions, 76-83, vpres, Harry N Abrams Inc, 81-83. *Mem:* Fine Art Publs Asn (treas, 82-85); Orgn Ind Artists. *Specialty:* Publication of illustrated books

LEVIN, KIM
CRITIC, CURATOR
Study: Vassar Col, AB; Yale-Norfolk Summer Sch Art; Columbia Univ, MA. *Exhib:* Exhibitions curated: CCA Ujazdowski Castle Warsaw, 92.; Nordic Biennial, Arken Mus Copenhagen, 96-97.; Henie-Onstad Kunstsenter, Norway, 93; Notes & Itineraries, Feldman Gallery, NY, 2006, traveled to museums in Europe, including Ludwig Mus, Budapest and KIASMA, Helsinki. *Pos:* NY corresp, Flash Art, 80-84; contribr, Village Voice, 81-2006. *Teaching:* Claremont Grad Sch Art, 87; vis prof, HISK, Antwerp, 01. *Awards:* Art/World Award for Distinguished Newspaper Criticism, 86; SECA Fel, San Francisco Mus Mod Art, 93; Annenberg/Getty Fel, 2004, 2011. *Mem:* Int Asn Art Critics (Am vpres, 84-90, Am pres, 90-92, int vpres, 92-96, int pres, 96-02). *Publ:* auth, Lucas Samaras, Abrams, 75; contribr, Theories of Contemporary Art, Prentice-Hall, 85; auth, Beyond Modernism, Harper & Row, 88; contribr, editor, Beyond Walls & Wars: Art, Politics & Multi-Culturalism, Midmarch Press, 92; Co-auth. Trans Plant; Living Vegetation in Contemporary Art (Hatje Cantz), 2000. *Mailing Add:* 52 W 71st St New York NY 10023

LEVIN, MORTON D
PRINTMAKER, PAINTER
b New York, NY, Oct 7, 1923. *Study:* City Univ NY, BS (art educ); studies in Paris, France; painting with Andre Lhote, sculpture with Ossip Zadkine, etching & engraving with Stanley W Hayter & etching with Federico Castellon; studied lithography, Pratt Graphic Arts Ctr, New York. *Work:* NY Pub Libr; Hist of Med Div, Nat Libr Med, Md; New Britain Mus of Am Art, Conn; Yale Univ Art Gallery, New Haven, Conn; Rochester Inst Tech, NY; Smithsonian Inst, DC; Ogunquit Mus of Am Art, Maine; Milwaukee Art Mus, Wisc; Crocker Art Mus, Calif; Achenbach Collection Legion of Honor, San Francisco, Calif. *Comn:* Mural, Stained Glass, L Natali Inc, 79. *Exhib:* 4th-7th Ann Nat Exhib of Prints, Libr Cong, 46-49; Nat Acad Design & Soc Am Etchers, Gravers, Lithographers and Woodcutters Inc, 46-48; 46th Ann Watercolor & Print Exhib, Pa Acad Fine Arts, 48; Salon de Mai, Musee D'Art Mod, Paris, France, 51; Biennale Int d'Arte Marinara, Pallazzo del Academia, Genoa, Italy, 51; solo exhibs, Galerie Breteau, Paris, France, 52, Winston Gallery, San Francisco, 77, 79-98; Winston Gallery, 2003-2008, 2009, 2011, 2012. *Teaching:* Founder, dir & instr printmaking & painting, Morton Levin Graphics Workshop, San Francisco, Calif, 72-91. *Awards:* Hon Mention, 21st Ann Northwest Printmakers, Seattle Art Mus, 49; Bryan Mem Prize, The Villager Travel Exhib, New York, 64; Third Prize, Washington Sq Art Exhib Inc, 64. *Bibliog:* Yellow Silk, J Erotic Arts, summer 90. *Media:* Etching, Woodcut; Watercolor, Oil. *Specialty:* Paintings: oils, acrylics, woodcuts, etchings. *Interests:* visual art. *Publ:* Contribr, Yellow Silk, No 34, summer 90; auth & illustr, A Fantasy of Beasts Revealed in Great Art, Egret Books, 2008. *Dealer:* Winston Gallery 414 Mason St Ste 704 San Francisco, CA 94102

LEVIN, ROBERT ALAN
GLASS BLOWER, SCULPTOR
b Baltimore, Md, Sept 25, 1948. *Study:* Denison Univ, Granville, Ohio, BFA, 71; Penland Sch Crafts, NC, 71; Southern Ill Univ, Carbondale, MFA, 74. *Work:* Corning Mus Glass, New York; Ebeltoft Glasmuseum, Denmark; Contemp Glass Mus, Madrid, Spain; High Mus Art, Atlanta, Ga; Mus Am Glass, Millville, NJ; Mus Art & Design, New York. *Comn:* Bus Awards, comn by Gov Jim Hunt, Raleigh, NC, 80 & 98; Entrepreneurial Sch Award, 94-2000; Awards, comn by Urban Land Inst, 2005 & 2008; Pub Art Sculpture, Town of Burnsville, 2011. *Exhib:* New Glass, Corning Mus Glass, New York, 79; Int Directions Glass Art, Art Gallery Western Australia, 83; Thirty Yrs New Glass, 1957-1987, Corning Mus Glass, 87 & Toledo Mus Art, 88; Am Glassmaking - The First Russian Tour, Steuben Glass, New York, Decorative Applied & Folk Art Mus, Moscow & Hermitage, Leningrad, 90; The First Ten Yrs, Glasmuseum, Ebeltoft, Denmark, 96; L'Chaim: A Kiddush Cup Invitational, Jewish Mus, San Francisco, Calif, 97; Celebrating Am Craft, Kunstindustrimuseum, Copenhagen, Denmark, 97; Hsinchu Int Glass Art Festival, Hsinchu Cult Ctr, Taiwan, 97; A World of Glass, Int Glass Exhib, Hadeland Glassverk, Jevnaker, Norway, 97; World Exhibition of Art Glass, Steninge Castle, Stockholm, Sweden, 99; Hot and Cool: Contemp Glass Work, touring via Exhibs USA, 2000; Extending the tradition: crafts from the Carolinas, Ogden Mus Southern Art, New Orleans, La, 2001; Glass Goblets, Kentucky Mus Arts & Design, Louisville, 2004; Power of Excellence, Southeastern Ctr Contemp Art, Winston Salem, NC, 2004; 4th Cheongju Int Craft Exhib, Cheongju Art Ctr, Korea, 2005; Humor & Whimsy, Racine Art Mus, Wis, 2006; Make It New, Asheville Art Mus, NC, 2007; Rooted in Craft: All Things Botanical, Sawtooth Ctr, Winston-Salem, NC, 2007; Goblet Exhib, The Works Gallery, Philadelphia, Pa, 2007 & Mus Arts & Design, New York, 2007-2008; For Real, the Art of Deceoption, Cabarrus Art Coun, NC, 2009; Down Home, Jewish Life in NC, NC Mus His, Raleigh, NC, 2010; Art in Pub Places, Bristol, Tenn, 2011; Fire on the Mountain: Studio Glass in Western NC, Asheville Art Mus, 2012; NC Glass 2012, Fine Art Mus, W Carolina Univ, Cullowhee, NC, 2012; Born from the Hand, Milton Rhodes Ctr Arts, Winston Salem, NC, 2013; Abstract, Harper Gallery, Presbyterian Coll, Clinton, SC, 2013. *Pos:* Artist-in-residence, Penland Sch, NC, 76-80 & Art Park, Lewiston, NY, 87. *Teaching:* Asst prof glass, Rochester Inst Technol, NY, 88; instr glass, Wanganui Coll, NZ, Penland Sch Crafts, Kilkenny, Ireland, 2008 and var workshops around the US. *Awards:* NC Arts Coun Fel, 80 & 96; NC Arts Coun Proj Grant, 89-90; S Arts Fed & Nat Endowment Arts Regional Visual Arts Fel, 95. *Bibliog:* Barbara Mayer (auth), Contemp Am Craft Art, 88; Susanne Frantz (auth), Contemp Glass, 89; Spillman & Frantz (auths), Masterpieces Am Glass, 90; Peter Layton (auth), Glass Art, 96; Leier, Peters & Wallace (auths), Contemporary Glass, Color, Light and Form, 2001; Object Lessons: Beauty & Meaning in Art, Guild Publ, 2001; Dona Z Meilach (auth), Wood Art Today, 2003; Ronni Lundy (auth), In Praise of Tomatoes, 2004; 500 Glass Objects, Lark Bks, 2006; Jeffrey B Snyder (auth), Wood Art Today 2, 2010; Best of America-Glass Artists-Vol II, Kennedy Pub, 2010; Ashley Rooney (auth), 100 Southern Artists, 2012. *Mem:* Am Crafts Coun; Piedmont Craftsmen Inc (bd trustees, 86-89); Glass Art Soc (bd dir, 91-94); Tri State Sculptors; Southern Highlands Craft Guild; Yancey Community Cult Resource Comn (2002-2010). *Media:* Glass; Mixed Media. *Publ:* New Zealand Crafts, winter 90; J Glass Art Soc, 91; Am Craft, 12/95-1/96 & 6-7/98; Craft Arts Int, Australia, No 59, 2003. *Dealer:* Blue Spiral Gallery 38 Biltmore Ave Asheville NC 28801. *Mailing Add:* 669 Upper Browns Creek Burnsville NC 28714

LEVINE, BARBARA
CURATOR, ASSEMBLAGE ARTIST
Study: San Francisco Art Inst, BFA (in photog) & MA (in museology). *Collection Arranged:* Out at the Library, San Francisco Pub Libr, 2005. *Pos:* Dir exhibs, San Francisco Mus Mod Art, 1989-2001; dep dir, Contemp Jewish Mus, 2001-2005; founder, Project b. *Publ:* Auth, Snapshot Chronicles: Inventing the American Photo Album, 2006; Around the World: The Grand Tour in Photo Albums, 2007 & Finding Frida Kahlo, 2009, Princeton Archit Press

LEVINE, EDWARD
PAINTER
b Detroit, Mich, Jan 10, 1928. *Study:* Wayne State Univ, Southlands Sch Design. *Work:* Ameritech, Detroit, Mich; Mich Bell Tel, An Ameritech Co, Detroit, Mich; Miller, Canfield, Paddock & Stone, Bloomfield Hills, Mich. *Exhib:* Solo exhibs, Xochipilli Gallery, Birmingham, Mich, 86, 88 & 90; Macomb Community Col, Mt Clemens, Mich, 87; Animal Life in Contemp Art, House of Reps, Washington, DC, 88; Urban Scenes of the 80's, De Waters, Flint, Mich, 88; Urbanology, Nat Exhib on Art & The City, Detroit, Mich, 89; and others. *Awards:* Silver Scarab, Scarab Club, 85. *Media:* Oil. *Mailing Add:* 700 Lockwood Rd Royal Oak MI 48067

LEVINE, ERIK
SCULPTOR
b Los Angeles, Calif, Oct 31, 1960. *Study:* Univ Calif, Los Angeles, 82; Calif State Univ, Northridge, 80-81. *Work:* Walker Art Ctr, Minneapolis, Minn; Mus Contemp Art, Los Angeles; High Mus Art, Atlanta, Ga; Albright-Knox Art Gallery, Buffalo, NY; Whitney Mus Am Art, NY; and others. *Comn:* Round House (sculpture garden), Walker Art Ctr, Minneapolis, Minn, 90; Faulconer Gallery, Grinnell Coll, 2001. *Exhib:* Enclosing the Void: 8 Contemp Sculptors, Whitney at Equitable Ctr, NY, 88; one-man shows, Louisiana Mus Mod Art, Humlebaek, Denmark, 89 & Fundacio Joan Miro, Barcelona, Spain, 89; 1989 Biennial Exhib, Whitney Mus Am Art, NY, 89; Awards in the Visual Arts 8, traveling, High Mus Art, Atlanta, Ga & La Jolla Mus Contemp Art, Calif, 89; CAC, Vassiviere, France, 92; Lenbachhaus, Munich, 93; Galerie Bernd Klueser, Munich, 93 & 95; Pfalz Galerie, Kaiserslautern, Ger, 98. *Awards:* Nat Endowment Arts, 87, 89; NY Fdn Arts, 87, 99; Guggenheim Fel, 92; Pollock Krasner, 86, 90, 99; Awards in the Visual Arts, 88. *Bibliog:* Renate Cornu

(auth), Erik Levine, Halle Sud, Barcelona, 89; Richard Armstrong, Richard Marshall, Lisa Phillips (auth), 1989 Whitney Biennial, Whitney Mus Am Art, 89; Michael Kimmelman (auth), Erik Levine at Diane Brown Gallery, NY Times, 89. *Dealer:* Galerie Bernd Klueser, Munich, Germany; Galerie Georges-Philippe & Nathalie, Vallois, Paris

LEVINE, GREGORY P A
EDUCATOR
Study: Oberlin Coll, BA, 1985; Princeton Univ, MA (art & archeol), 1990, PhD (art hist Japan), 1997. *Pos:* Ed adv bd, J Art Historiography. *Teaching:* Assoc prof Japanese art & archit, Univ Calif Berkeley. *Awards:* Nat Endowment for the Humanities Grant, 2001; Res Grant, Metrop Ctr Far Eastern Art Studies, 2003; Japan Found Fel, 2010; Guggenheim Found Fel, 2010. *Mem:* Coll Art Asn; Asn for Asian Studies; Japan Art Hist Forum . *Publ:* Auth, Daitokuji: The Visual Cultures of a Zen Monastery, Univ Wash Press, 2005; co-ed, Awakenings: Zen Figure Paintings from Medieval Japan, Yale Univ Press, 2007. *Mailing Add:* Univ California Dept Art History 416 Doe Library #6020 Berkeley CA 94720

LEVINE, LES
VIDEO ARTIST, MEDIA SCULPTOR
b Dublin, Ireland, Oct 6, 1935; US citizen. *Study:* Study, Cent Sch Arts & Crafts, London, Eng, 53-56. *Work:* Nat Gallery Can, Ottawa, Ont; Metrop Mus Art, Whitney Mus Am Art, Mus Mod Art, NY; Philadelphia Mus Art; Indianapolis Mus Art; Nat Gallery Australia, Canberra; Ludwig Mus, Koln, Ger; Walker Art Ctr, Minneapolis, Minn; Mus Contemp Art, Los Angeles, Calif; Getty Rsch Inst, Los Angeles, Calif; Irish Mus Modern Art, Dublin. *Comn:* Contact (sculpture), Gulf & Western Indust, 69. *Exhib:* Solo exhibs, Slipcover, Walker Art Ctr, 67, Star Garden, Mus Mod Art, NY, 67, I Am Not Blind, Wadsworth Atheneum, 76, Prayer Rug, Philadelphia Mus Art, 79, We Are Not Afraid, Lower Manhattan Cult Coun, NY Subways, 81, Blame God Inst Contemp Art, London, Eng, 85, Media Proj & Pub Advert, Mai 36 Gallery, Luzern, Switz, 88; Documenta, Kassel, Ger, 77 & 87; San Francisco Int Video Festival, 83; Committed to Print, Mus Mod Art, NY, 88; Consume or Perish & Pray for More, NY Found Arts, NY Subways, 89; Pub Mind: Les Levine's Media Sculpture and Mass Ad Campaigns, Everson Mus, Syracuse, 90; Ease Pain, NY Found Arts, NY, 92; Send Receive, The Language of Art, Kunsthalle Wien, Vienna, 93; Art Can See, Galerie der Stadt Stuttgart, Ger, 97; Celebrate Yourself, Brigitte March Galerie, Stuttgart, Ger, 2005; Truth=Beauty, Kunsthalle Goppingen, Goppingen, Germany, 2008; Authentic Desires, Nat Gallery of Canada, Ottawa, Canada, 2008, Mindful Media: Works from the 1970s, Irish Mus Modern Art, Dublin, 2011; Video Vintage, Centre Pompidou, Paris, France, 2012; Ends of the Earth, Mus Contemporary Art, Los Angeles, Calif, 2012. *Collection Arranged:* Open To New Ideas (organizer), Jimmy Carter Collection, Ga Mus Art, Athens, 77. *Pos:* Pres, Mus Mott Art, Inc, 71-. *Teaching:* Assoc prof, NY Univ, 71-72, Columbia Univ, NY, 78; video prof, William Paterson Coll, Wayne, NJ, 74-76. *Awards:* First Prize for The Star Machine, Sculpture Biennale, Art Gallery Ont, 68; Nat Endowment Arts Fel, 74 & 80; Gustav Klimt Award for Best Billboard, City of Vienna, 94; and others. *Bibliog:* David Bourdon (auth), Plastic art's biggest bubble, Life Mag, 8/69; Barbara Cavaliere (auth), Les Levine's ads---and more ads, Arts Mag, 3/81; Vivien Raynor (auth), Not Afraid in the Subway, New York Times, 5/21/82; and others; Tom Holert (auth), Information Soc, Artforum, 2013. *Mem:* Nat Arts Club (vp 84-); Architectural League of NY (vp 69-70). *Media:* Videotape; Gold, Multimedia. *Publ:* The poets' encyclopedia, Unmuzzled Ox, Vol 4, No 4, New York, 79; publ, Media: The Bio Tech Rehearsal for Leaving the Body, Alberta Coll Art, 79; Biennale van de la Critique, Palais des Beaux Arts, Antwerpen Charleroi, 79; auth, Handmade Etchings by Les Levine, Artist Profusions, 81; Blame God, Inst Contemp Art, London, Eng, 85; Ends of the Earth: Land Art to 1974, MOCA, LA & Haus Der Kunst, Munich, 2012. *Dealer:* Bridgette March Galerie Stuttgart Germany. *Mailing Add:* 20 E 20th St New York NY 10003

LEVINE, MARGE
PAINTER, INSTRUCTOR
b Brooklyn, NY July 30, 1934. *Study:* Fashion Inst Technol & Design, AAS, 1952; Studied with Richard McKinley, Albert Handell & Duane Wakeham, 2002. *Work:* Rider Univ, Lawrenceville, NJ. *Comn:* Mural, New Sch Monmouth Co, Hazlet, NJ, 1975. *Exhib:* Pastel Soc Am, Nat Arts Club, NY, 2006; 7th Nat Juried Exhib, Am Impressionist Soc, Tex, 2006; 30 Ann Exhib, Salmagundi Club, NY, 2007; 111th Open Exhib, Catharine Lorillard Wolfe Art Club, NY, 2007; 23rd Nat Juried Show, Nat Soc Artists, NY, 2007. *Pos:* Workshop demonstr, Guild Creative Arts, Shrewsbury, NJ, 4/29/2007; Monmouth Co Arts Coun, NJ, 10/17/2007. *Awards:* Dakota Art Award, Pastel Soc NMex, Dakota Pastels, 2002; Best of Genre, Nat NE Pastel Soc, 2005; Hon Mention, Pastel Soc Am, 2006; Scholar Award, Int Artist Pastel Socs//Tarbet, Urania Christy Tarbet, 2006; Hon Mention, Am Impressionist Soc, 2006; Merit Award, Pastel Painters Soc, Maine, 2007. *Bibliog:* Lynne Moss Perricelli (auth), Structure the Landscape, Am Artist Mag, 4/2006; John Genovese (auth), Arts & Culture, Night & Day Mag, 8/2006. *Mem:* Pastel Soc Am; Degas Pastel Soc; Pastel Painters Soc Cape Cod; Am Impressionist Soc Am; Plein Air Painters Jersey Coast. *Media:* Pastel. *Publ:* The Big Troll Book (illusr, contribr), Scholastic, 91; The Glass Menorah (illusr, bk), MacMillan Press, 92; Lifebirds (illusr, bk), Rutgers Press, 95; Am Artist Mag (illusr, contribr), 2006. *Mailing Add:* 108 Wesley Ave Atlantic Highlands NJ 07716

LEVINE, MARTIN
PRINTMAKER, EDUCATOR
b New York, NY, May 14, 1945. *Study:* State Univ NY, Buffalo, BS (art educ); Calif Coll Arts & Crafts, MFA (printmaking). *Work:* Libr Cong, Smithsonian Inst, Washington; Brooklyn Mus; Mus Fine Arts, Boston; Art Inst Chicago, Ill; Victoria & Albert Mus, London, Eng; and many others. *Comn:* Two etchings of hist landmark (with ADI Gallery, San Francisco), Clorox Co, Oakland, Calif, 76; etching for portfolio, Pratt Graphics Ctr, NY, 81 & 84; etching (facade), Union League Club, Chicago, 83; etching for portfolio, Brigham Young Univ, 93. *Exhib:* Nat Acad Design Ann Exhib, 74, 76-79, 86 & 96; 30 Yrs of Am Printmaking, Brooklyn Mus, NY, 76; Int Print Biennale, Cracow, Poland, 78, 86, 91 & 94; XV Int Bienal, Sao Paulo, Brazil, 79; Chicago & Vicinity, Art Inst Chicago, 81 & 85; Int Exhib, Kanagawa, Yokohama, Japan, 92 & 95; Int Biennale, Maastricht, The Neth, 93; Int Biennale, Belgrade, Yugoslavia, 94 & 96; Int Print Biennale, Varna, Bulgaria, 95. *Teaching:* Asst prof printmaking, Northwestern Univ, Evanston, 79-86 & State Univ NY, Stony Brook, 86-. *Awards:* Nat Endowment Arts Printmaking Fel, 77; NY Found Arts, 94 & 95; plus over 100 nat & int awards. *Mem:* Audubon Artists; Soc Am Graphic Artists (pres, 95-); Nat Acad. *Media:* Intaglio, Lithography. *Dealer:* Jonathan Greenberg Inc 1100 Madison Ave Suite 5K New York NY 10028. *Mailing Add:* Staller Ctr for Arts State Univ of NY Stony Brook Stony Brook NY 11794-5400

LEVINE, PHYLLIS JEAN
PAINTER
b Cleveland, Ohio, Jan 23, 1947. *Study:* Cuyahoga Community Col, AA, 71; Special study with Shirley Aley Campbell, 89-91. *Work:* Rocky River Pub Libr, City Hall, Ohio; Cuyahoga Community Col, Parma, Ohio. *Exhib:* 75th Ann Spring Show, Erie Art Mus, Pa, 98. *Media:* Acrylic on Canvas. *Mailing Add:* 301 Cornwall Rd Rocky River OH 44116

LEVINE, SHEPARD
PAINTER, EDUCATOR
b New York, NY, Feb 28, 1927. *Study:* Univ NMex, BA & MA; Univ Toulouse, France. *Work:* Parnassus Hall, Athens, Greece; Ore State Univ, Alumni Bldg, Bernard Malamud Room, Valley Libr OS, Univ Ore; Arkia Airlines, Israel; Salem Art Mus; Benton Co Public Libr, Corvallis, Ore. *Exhib:* Am Graphic Arts Asn; Brooklyn Mus; Henry Gallery, Univ Wash; San Francisco Mus Art; Portland Art Mus, Ore; Spokane Art Mus; and others. *Teaching:* Lectr to mus & pvt groups; prof art, Ore State Univ, formerly, emer prof, currently; retired. *Awards:* Purchase Award, Univ Ore. *Media:* Oil, Mixed media. *Interests:* Music & lit. *Mailing Add:* 3750 NW Hayes Ave Corvallis OR 97330

LEVINE, SHERRIE
PHOTOGRAPHER
b Hazelton, Pa, 1947. *Study:* Univ Wis, Madison, BFA, 1969, MFA, 1973. *Exhib:* Solo exhibs incl De Saisset Art Mus, Santa Clara, Calif, 1974, 3 Mercer St, NY City, 1977, Hallwalls, Buffalo, NY, 1978, The Kitchen, NY City, 1979, Metro Pictures, NY City, 1981, A and M Artworks, NY City, 1982, Baskerville + Watson Gallery, NY City, 1983, 1985, Richard Kuhlenschmidt Gallery, Los Angeles, 1983, 1985, Ace, Montreal, 1984, Daniel Weinberg Gallery, Los Angeles, 1986, 1990, Donald Young Gallery, Chicago, 1987, 1989, 1991, Rooseum, Sweden, 1992, Philadelphia Mus Art, 1993, Marian Goodman Gallery, NY City, 1994, Mus Contemp Art, Los Angeles, 1995, Margo Leavin Gallery, Los Angeles, 1996, Casino, Luxembourg, 1997, Art & Public, Geneva, 1998, Paula Cooper Gallery, NY City, 1999, 2000, 2001, 2003, 2004; group exhibs incl Artist Space, NY, 1977; The Kitchen, NY, 1980; PS1, NY, 1981; Vancouver Art Gallery, Chicago, 1982; Chicago Art Inst, 1983; Inst Contemp Art, Philadelphia, 1984, 1991; Whitney Biennial, 1985, 1989, 2008; Art Gallery of New South Wales, 1986; Los Angeles County Mus Art, 1987; Carnegie Mus Art, Pittsburgh, 1988; Hirshhorn Mus, Wash, DC, 1990; Mus Mod Art, NY City, 1992, 1996, 1999, 2000, 2001; Paula Cooper Gallery, NY City, 1994, 1998, 2002, 2004; New Mus, NY City, 1995; Mus Contemp Art, Miami, 1996; Tate Gallery, London, 1997; Whitney Mus Am Art, NY City, 1999, 2000; Met Mus Art, NY City, 2001; Mus Contemp Art, Basel, Switzerland, 2002; Walker Art Ctr, Minneapolis, 2003, 2005; Grey Art Gallery, NY Univ, 2005; Mus Contemp Art, Chicago, 2006; Perry Rubenstein Gallery, NY City, 2006; 53rd Int Art Exhib Biennale, Venice, 2009; Mayhem, Whitney Mus, NY, 2011. *Mailing Add:* 55 Hudson St New York NY 10013

LEVINE, TOMAR
PAINTER
b New York, NY, Mar 24, 1945. *Study:* City Coll New York, BA, 66; Brooklyn Coll NY, MFA, 74. *Work:* New York Acad Med; Chemical Bank, NY; AT&T, NY; Guy Carpenter & Co Inc, NY; INA Corp, NY. *Exhib:* New Am Still Life, Westmoreland Co Mus Art, Greensburg, Pa, 79; Painted Light, Reading Mus, Reading, Conn, 83; Artists' Choice: The First Eight Yrs, Artists' Choice Mus, NY, 84; Am Realism-20th Century Drawings & Watercolors, San Francisco Mus Mod Art, San Francisco, Calif, 85; 161st Ann Exhib, Nat Acad Design, NY, 86; Deutsch-Amerikanisches Inst, Munic Gallery, Regensburg, WGer, 88-89. *Teaching:* Instr, The New Sch for Social Research, NY. *Awards:* Yaddo Fel, 84; Fel, Va Ctr Creative Arts, 85; Cummington Community Arts, 91. *Bibliog:* Bill Sullivan (auth), Tomar Levine, Arts Mag, 83. *Mem:* NY Artists' Equity. *Media:* Egg Tempera, Acrylic Oil. *Mailing Add:* 191 Claremont Ave No 43 New York NY 10027-4033

LEVINSON, MIMI W
ASSEMBLAGE ARTIST, LECTURER
b Kenosha, Wis, June 6, 1940. *Study:* Carnegie-Mellon Univ, with Roger Anliker, BFA, 62; San Jose State Coll, Frick Scholar, 64. *Work:* Ga Railroad Bank Collection, Augusta; Mesa Vista Hosp, San Diego, Calif; New Delhi Handi Crafts Mus, India; Vista Hill Found; Kaiser Permanente San Ysidro Med Clinic, San Diego; Bauer Collection, San Diego, Mingei Escondito Judaica, 2009-2010. *Comn:* Stained glass wall mosaic, Casselhoff's, Pittsburgh, Pa, 62; painted fabric mural, Kaiser-Permanente, San Diego, Calif, 78; batiks, Hillcrest Psychotherapy Ctr, San Diego, Calif, 80. *Exhib:* Craftman's Guild Shows, Arts & Crafts Ctr, Pittsburgh, Pa, 66-67; Art Guild All Media, San Diego Mus Art, Calif, 75 & 81; Calif Crafts XI, EB Crocker Art Mus, Sacramento, 79; Exchange Exhib, Yokohama Art Ctr, Japan, 79; Textile Kunst, Krefeld, Fed Repub Ger, 88; Fibers Exhib, Brand Mus, Glendale, Calif, 91; solo exhibs, Jewish Community Ctr, San Diego, Calif, 91-92 & Wesley Palms Gallery, San Diego, Calif, 2004; Fibre Meets Fiber, Mansfield Mus, Eng, 92; Southwestern Coll Art Gallery, Allied Craftsmen, 2000; Spanish Village Art Ctr, 2000; San Diego Hospice, San Mus Art Artists Guild, 2000; Allied Craftsmen Next Door Gallery, 2001; Beyond Borders, South Western Coll, Calif, 2003; Small Images, San

Diego Calif, 2005; Allied Craftsman, Palomar Coll Boehm Gallery, 2005; Colorado Springs Univ Gallery, 2005; Small Images, San Diego, Calif, 2006; LaJolla Fiber Art, 2006-2007; Small Images, San Diego, Calif, 2008-2012; Mingi Int Mus, Judaica, 2009-2010; Retrospective, Wesley Palms Gallery, 2011-2012; San Diego Airport, 2013. *Teaching:* Instr art, Sunnyside Sch, Pittsburgh, Pa, 62-67; workshop leader batik-weaving, Convergence 76, Pittsburgh, Pa, 76; instr cult arts, Jewish Community Ctr, San Diego, Calif, 79-91; San Diego State Univ extended studies, 89-93; mgr, San Diego Japanese Friendship Garden, 92-98; guest lectr, 2003; instr Japanese Textile Dying, Mingei Int Mus Workshop, 2009. *Awards:* First Prize, Augusta Art Asn, 71; Third Prize, Weaver's Guild, 75; Purchase Prize, Small Images, 2003; Supply Award, Artists & Craftsmen, 2009. *Bibliog:* Dan Coyro (auth), Batik: How to turn wax and dye into art, The Sentinel, 75; Jan Jennings (auth), Natural history museum, San Diego Evening Tribune, 78; Elise Miller (auth), Womanism to surrealism, San Diego Mag, 79. *Mem:* Allied Craftsmen; Surface Design Asn; Calif Fibers (chmn, 77). *Media:* Batik, Mixed. *Res:* Preparation for Mus Lectures, 2002, 2003, 2005, Research for articles published; 2/2001 Arts de Mexico at the Minge International Mus in OBJECT 2001, Austrlia. *Specialty:* MM Crafts. *Interests:* Travel Asia. *Publ:* Contribr, Crafts 1976, Southern Calif Designer Inc, 76; Exotic Needlework, Crown, 78; Artes de Mexico: Mingei Int Mus, Object, 2001. *Dealer:* Next Door Art Gallery 2963 Beech St San Diego CA 92102. *Mailing Add:* 2119 29th St San Diego CA 92104-5505

LEVINTHAL, BETH E

MUSEUM DIRECTOR

b Oceanside, NY, Nov 21, 1951. *Study:* Hofstra Univ, BA (Graphic Design), 1973, MS (Elem educ), 1975. *Pos:* coodr sch, youth & family progs, Heckscher Mus Art, 1994-1996, coordr of educ, 1996-1997, dir of educ & pub progs, 1997-2000, exec dir, 2001-2006; dir, Hofstra Univ Mus, exec dir, 2006-; exec dir, Hofstra Univ Mus, 2006-. *Teaching:* Art instr, Huntington twp Art League, NY, 1987-1994; Jefferson Elem, Huntington, 1991-1992; adj instr, CW Post Coll, NY, 1998-2000; adj prof, Hofstra Univ, 2008-. *Awards:* George M Eastbrook Disting Serv Award, Hofstra Univ Alumni Asn; Malcolm Arth Fellow, 96. *Mem:* Fel Mid-Atlantic Asn of Mus; Am Asn Mus; LIAA; Art Table; Mus Asn New York. *Mailing Add:* Hofstra University Museum 112 Hofstra University Hempstead NY 11549

LEVINTHAL, DAVID LAWRENCE

PHOTOGRAPHER

b San Francisco, Calif, March 8, 1949. *Study:* Stanford Univ, AB, 70; Yale Univ, MFA, 73; Mass Inst Tech, SM, 81. *Work:* Mus Mod Art, NY; Corcoran Gallery Art, Washington, DC; Los Angeles Co Mus Art, Calif; Amon Carter Mus, Fort Worth, Tex; Nat Gallery NZ, Wellington. *Exhib:* Photog and Art, Los Angeles Co Mus Art, 87; Avant-Garde in the 80's, Los Angeles Co Mus Art, 87; Surrogate Selves, Corcoran Gallery, Washington, 89; Photog of Invention, Nat Mus, Washington, 89; Constructed Realities, Kunstverein, Munich, Ger, 89; Devil on the Stairs, Inst Contemp Art, Philadelphia, Pa, 91; More Than One Photog, Mus Mod Art, NY, 92; Instant Imaging Stories, Mus Mod Art, Vienna, Austria, 92; solo shows, Univ Art Mus, Univ NMex, Albuquerque, 95, Judah L Magnus Mus, Berkeley, Calif, 96, Philadelphia Mus Judaica, Pa, 97 & San Jose Mus, Calif, 99; Devoir de Memoire, Recontres Int de la Photographie, Arles, France, 97; Same Difference, Chapman Univ Guggenheim Gallery, Orange, Calif, 98. *Teaching:* Instr, photog, Univ Neada, Las Vegas, 75-76. *Awards:* Artists Grant, Nat Endowment Arts, 90-91; Guggenheim Fel, 95. *Bibliog:* Andy Gundberg & Kathy Gauss (coauths), Photo & Art & Anne Hoy (auth), Fabrications, Abbeville Press, 87; Terrie Sultan (auth), Surrogate Selves, Corcoran Gallery, 89. *Mem:* Coll Art Asn. *Publ:* Coauth (with Garry Trudeau), Hitler Moves East, Sheed Andrews & McMeel, 77; illustr, Modern Romance, Univ San Diego, 85; Centric 35: David Levinthal, Calif State Long Beach, 89; American Beauties, Laurence Miller, 90. *Dealer:* Gering Lopez Gallery 730 Fifth Avenue NY 10019. *Mailing Add:* 32 W 20th St New York NY 10011

LEVIT, HÉLOÏSE (GINGER) BERTMAN

ART DEALER, WRITER

b Philadelphia, Apr 2, 1937. *Study:* Univ Pa, BA in French, 1959; Univ Richmond, MA in French, 1975; Va Commonwealth Univ, MA in Art History, 1998; studies at Ecole du Louvre, Paris; La Sorbonne, Paris, Cert, 1994; Alliance Francaise, Paris, Cert; Università Stranieri di Perugia, Italy, 2007. *Work:* Horace Day, Carlyle House Garden, The Lyceum, Alexandria; William Fletcher Jones, Anne Perkins, Massey Cancer Ctr; Markel Corp; Hirshler Fleisher; Ann Newbold Perkins, The Hermitage at Cedarfield; Coll William & Mary, Va Mus Fine Arts. *Collection Arranged:* William Fletcher Jones, Horace Talmage Day, Fine Arts Am, Inc, 83, Capital One; William Fletcher Jones, Ginger Levit Atelier, 2006, 2008, 2009; Raoul Middleman: Westwood Club, Arts on the Square, 87; Paintings with Provenance, Richmond Symphony Designer House, 97, 2001, 2007, 2010; Paintings for the New Collector, 2005, 2007; Christine Lafuente: Luminosity, Incandescent Luminosity, 2005, 2007; Upon Reflection, Sept 2009; Painting Raffled World Affairs Council, 2004; Sheila Holland, September Song. *Pos:* dir, Fine Arts Am, Richmond, 82-84; dir, Arts on the Square, Richmond, 84-85; organizer, cons, Art-I-facts, 89-; dir, Ginger Levit Atelier, Richmond, 87-; art critic, correspondent, WRFK-FM & Va News Network; dir fund-raising & cmty outreach activities, Richmond Philharmonic; juror, Tidewater Artists' Assn, Spring 2003 Mystery Exhib; art journalist, Fine Art Connoiseur, Antique Week, Tidewater Women, Style Weekly, Antiques & The Arts Weekly. *Teaching:* lectr, Osher Inst of Lifetime Learning, Univ Richmond 2008-2011; lectr, Va Commonwealth Univ, 2011. *Awards:* Award, Va Press Women, 2001-2008; 1st, 2nd & 3rd Place, Va Press Women Communications Contest, 2003-2010; Ben Franklin award for cmty svc, Univ Pa, 1989; 1st place, Boudin Article, 2nd place, Sack & RAMA articles, 2008; Va Lawyers Weekly 2009 Influential Woman of Va Award; 1st place, German Expressionists Make their Way to Richmond, Antique Week, 2009; 1st place, Troubled Life Influenced Works of Gorky, Antique Week, 2010. *Bibliog:* Roy Proctor (auth), Richmond News Leader, 10/26/1991; A Fan of all Things French, Richmond Mag, 12/2001; Roy Proctor (auth), Sip Your Wine, Take Your Time, Welcome to Ginger Levit's atelier, Richmond Times-Dispatch, 4/6/2003; Bill McKelway (auth), Gifts from Underground, Richmond-Times Dispatch, 12/29/2007; Jo Lord (auth), Incandescent Luminosity on Display, 1/8/2008. *Mem:* Va Press Women; Richmond Symphony Orch League (PR chmn 1998-); La Table Francaise (dir 1998-); Accueil Francais de Richmond; Va Mus Find Arts Council Canvas & Collectors' Circle; Alliance Française de Richmond (program chairman); Young Audience of Va Steering Comt/ Richmond Regional Board 2008-09. *Res:* Pierre Bonnard and Edouard Vuillard and their Jewish Patrons; Edgar Degas' monotypes become etchings for the 1938 Blaizot "La Famille Cardinal"; Frank Myers Boggs: French or American?. *Specialty:* French Barbizon Sch painting from 1780 to New York Armory Show in 1913; French Impressionists; French Post-Impressionists; Nabis painters Bonnard and Vuillard; Regional American artists, 1900-1950 & contemporary; William Fletcher Jones, Larry Horowitz, Christine Lafuente; Horace Day. *Interests:* French paintings of the past 250 years. *Collection:* expatriate Frank Myers Boggs (Frank-Boggs), Frank-Will, Henri-Joseph Harpignies & William Fletcher Jones, Horace Talmage Day, Raoul Middleman, Christine Lafuente, Alfred Sisley, Katia & Hagues Claude Pissarro. *Publ:* Auth, Mainly Monet, Mid Atlantic Antiques Mag, 2000, East Coast Blockbuster Exhibition, 12/2001 & Less is more - Michelangelo at Atlanta's High Mus, 2001; auth, John Singer Sargent's Jewish Wertheimers, Richmond Jewish News, 2001; auth, John Singer Sargent's Jewish Wertheimers, Washington Jewish Week, 2001; auth, Touring the Brandywine Valley, Mid Atlantic Antiques News, 12/2002; auth, A golden legacy, Style Weekly, 2002; auth, American Impressionism at the Chrysler, Tidewater Women, 12/2002; auth, Strapped for Cash College, Antique Week, 12/3/2007; auth, Conversation with Sack Like an Advanced Course in Furniture, Antique Week, 5/26/2008, second place VPW CC; auth, Back to Boudin, Fine Art Connoisseur, Mar-Apr 2008; auth, Rembrandt: Master of Emotion, Tidewater Women, July 2008; auth, Boudin on the Beach, Tidewater Women, 1/2008, first place VPW CC; auth, The Age of Impressionism, Tidewater Women, 3/2008, second place VPW CC; German Expressionists Make Their Way to Richmond, Antique Week, Aug 10, 2009; Belcourt Castle: A Reminder of A Bygone Era in Newport, Antique Week, Aug 17, 2009; Frank Myers Boggs, An American in Paris, Fine Art Connoisseur, July-Aug, 2010. *Dealer:* Contract Associates 1519 West Main St Richmond VA 23220. *Mailing Add:* 419 Dellbrooks Pl Richmond VA 23238

LEVITT, HELEN

PHOTOGRAPHER, FILMMAKER

b New York, NY, 1918. *Work:* Mus Mod Art, Metrop Mus Art, NY; Boston Mus Fine Arts; Corcoran Gallery Art; Mus Fine Arts, Houston; Metropolitan Mus of Art, NY; Art Inst of Chicago, Ill; Whitney Mus of Am Art, NY. *Exhib:* Solo exhibs, Mus Mod Art, 43 & 74, Sidney Janis Gallery, 80, Corcoran Gallery Art, 80, Boston Mus Fine Arts, 83, Laurence Miller Gallery, 96, 2000 & Paris Photographie Centre, 01; Nat Mus Am Art, Washington, DC, 84; Dept Photog Galleries, Mus Mod Art, NY, 84-; Twentieth Century Photog, Mus Fine Arts, Boston, 84; The NY Sch (Parts 1 & 2), Corcoran Gallery Art, Washington, DC, 85 & Part 3, 86; Portraits from the Permanent Collection, Metrop Mus Art, NY, 86; Conclusive Beauty (with catalog), Whitney Mus Am Art, NY, 88; On the Art of Fixing a Shadow: One Hundred and Fifty Yrs of Photog (with catalog), Nat Gallery Art, Washington, DC & Art Inst Chicago, 89; Photog Until Now (with catalog), Mus Mod Art, NY, 89; The New Vision (with catalog), Metrop Mus Art, NY, 89; The Cherished Image, Nat Gallery Can, Ottawa, 89; Mus Mod Art, NY, 91, 94 & 95; Recent Acquisitions, Metrop Mus Art, NY, 96; History of Women Photographers (traveling exhib), NY Pub Libr, Nat Mus Women Arts, Washington, DC, Santa Barbara Mus, Calif & Akron Mus, Ohio, 96; NY Sch of Photog, Jan Kesner Gallery, Los Angeles, 98; Matrix/Berkeley Twenty Yrs, Berkeley Art Mus, Calif, 98. *Awards:* Guggenheim Fel, 59, 60, 80 & 81; Ford Found Fel, 64; Nat Endowment Arts Fel, 76; Master of Photog Award, Internat Ctr of Photog, 97; Outstanding Achievement in Humanistic Photog, Photog Adminrs. *Bibliog:* Walker Evans (auth), Quality: Its image in the arts, Atheneum, 69; John Szarkowski (auth), Looking at Photographs, Mus Mod Art, New York, 73; Roberta Hellman & Marvin Hosking (auths), Color Photographs by Helen Levitt, Grossmont Col, 80. *Publ:* Coauth (with James Agee), A Way of Seeing, Horizon, 81; Slide Show: The Color Photographs of Helen Levitt, 2005. *Dealer:* Jeff Fraenkel Gallery 49 Geary St San Francisco CA 94108. *Mailing Add:* c/o Laurence Miller Gallery 20 W 57th St New York NY 10019

LEVITZ, ILONA S

PAINTER, INSTRUCTOR

b Brooklyn, NY. *Study:* Vesper George Sch Art, Boston, Mass, 1965; Trinity Col, Private Tutorial, Hartford CT1970-1972; Hartford Art Sch, Univ Hartford, Studio Classes, 1975-1977; Wesleyan Univ, Grad Prog, Middletown, CT, 1978-1979. *Work:* Fierston Financial, West Hartford, Conn; Underwriters Servs, Farmington, Conn; COW Parade 2000, NY. *Exhib:* Juried Exhib, New Britain Mus Am Art, New Britain, Conn, 1982; 40th CT Artist Exhib, Silvermine Guild, Norwalk, Conn, 1983; Conn Vision, Mattatuck Mus, Waterbury, Conn, 1992; Three Women Artists, Jewish Community Center, W Hartford, Conn, 1994; Women in the Arts, Wave Gallery, New Haven, Conn, 1995; Open Studios Candlelight Weekend, Avon, Conn, 2003-2010; Hartford Jewish Community Center, W Hartford, Conn, 2009; New Hartford Art League, 2010. *Collection Arranged:* John Vivolo, folk artist, Hartford Ct Jewish Center, 1982; Chesire Art Asn, Chesire Art League, 1991; Art for the Cure, New Britain Mus Am Art, 2001; Joy of Art, Hosp for Spec Care, 2004. *Teaching:* Cezanne & Beyond, W Hartford Art League, 1995-2003; Master Class, Great Color, W Hartford Art League, 2003; Compos, Rhythem & Color Vision Painting, W Hartford Art League, 2004-2006; Master Class, Oh Henri, Farmington Valley Arts Center, 2008; Master Class, Color, Content, and Courage, W Hartford Art League, 2008-2009; Am Art Artist in Residence, New Britain Mus, 2010. *Awards:* Garfield Award, New Haven Paint & Clay, 1982; Best Drawing, New Britain Mus Am Art, 1985; Purchase Award, Wintonbury Art Asn, 1991. *Bibliog:* Stacy Stowe (auth), Is it Really Art?, NY Times, 1999; Patricia Rosoff (auth), A Wealth of Painterly Talent, Hartford Advocate, 2003; Will Steigerwald (auth), Northernlight, Artis, 10/2005; Jane Gordon (auth), A Painted Life, Home Living, 2006. *Mem:* Hartford Jewish Community Center (co-chmn cult arts comt), 1981-1983; Conn Acad Fine Art (bd mem), 1996-1999, (mem), 2005-2007; W Hartford Art League (bd mem), 1999-2002; Farmington Valley Ats Center (finance comt), 2003-2006, (bd mem), 2003-2009; Children's Art Educ Outreach Community (bd mem), FVAC, 2008, 2010; Studio Artists Asn (pres, 2011); Farmington Valley Arts Center, Conn. *Media:* Acrylic, Oil, Mixed Media. *Specialty:* Abstract paintings, mixed & acrylic media by I S Levitz. *Interests:* family, Arts activist, jazz, dance, theater, Hiking, Travel. *Dealer:* Ilona S Levitz 27 869 Farmington Ave West Hartford CT

LEVKOVA-LAMM, INNESSA
CRITIC, CURATOR
b Moscow, Russ; US citizen. *Study:* Leningrad Inst Film Eng, MD, 65; Moscow Inst Lang, 66-68. *Work:* Duke Univ Art Mus, Durham, NC; Int Kolodzey Found, NY. *Comn:* Jane Voorhees Zimmerli Mus of Art, NB, NJ; Shifting from Center to Margins: Moscow Conceptualism, 1980's-90's. *Exhib:* Women in Art Atrium Gallery, Morristown, NJ, 2000; Hackensack Art Ctr, NJ, 2001; Three Generations of Russian Women Artists, Salena Gallery, LI Univ Brooklyn Campus, 2002; 40 yrs of Soviet & Russian Art, The Bergen Mus Art, Paramus, NJ, 2003. *Collection Arranged:* Russian and Soviet Political Art, 87; Transit: Russian Art Between East and West (auth, catalog), 89; Back to Square One (auth, catalog), 91; After Perestroika (auth, catalog), 91. *Pos:* Freelance art critic, Literature Rev, Moscow, Russ, 64-81, Contempornia, NY, 88-91 & Flash Art, Milan, Italy, 91-97; pres, Imago Fine Art & Design Inc, NY, 98-. *Bibliog:* Dr Ekaterina Bobrinski (auth) Inessa Levkova-Lamm, Face of Squares: Mysteries of Kazimir Malevich, Pinakoteke, Moscow, Art Mag #51, 2004; Vladimir Salnikov (auth), Inessa Levkova-Lamm, Face of Square: Mysteries of Moscow, Kazimir Malevich, (The Collection #31) Pinakoteke, Moscow, 2004, 2005; Dr John Milner (auth), Innessa Levkova-Lamm, Mysteries of Kazimir Malevich, Pinkoteke, Moscow, 2004, Slavic Review, fall 2006. *Mem:* Int Asn Art Critics; Nat Writers Union. *Media:* Photography; Digital art. *Res:* Modern and contemporary art; Russian art of twentieth century. *Interests:* Revision of Kazimir Malevich's works. *Publ:* Auth, Rustislav Lebedev, Eduard Nakhamkin Fine Art, 90; coauth, Kultur in Stali Nismus, Edition Temmen, Ger, 94; Birth of an Image, Duke Univ Mus Art, NC, 98; Aufder Suche Nach Einer Neuen Indetiat, Ed Temmen, Ger, 98; auth, Face of Square: Mysteries of Kazimir Malevich, Pinkotheke, Moscow, 2004, The Art Magazine, Moscow, 2004 & The Collection, Moscow, 2005

LEVY, BERNARD
DEALER
b New York, NY, Feb 10, 1917. *Study:* NY Univ, BA, 37. *Pos:* Pres, Bernard & S Dean Levy Inc, 73-2001, chmn, 2001. *Bibliog:* On Madison Avenue, Fortune Mag, 12/47; Rita Reif (auth), Antiques, NY Times, 10/76; Douglas Villiers (auth), Next Year in Jerusalem, Viking Press, 76. *Mem:* Art & Antique Dealers League Am (pres, five yrs). *Specialty:* American paintings; American antique furniture; silver; English and American ceramics. *Publ:* An American Tea Party Colonial Tea & Breakfast Tables 1715-83; Opulence & Splendor - The New York Chair 1690-1830; Vanity & Elegance - The Dressing Table & Tall Chest in America 1685-1785. *Mailing Add:* Bernard & Dean Levy Inc 24 E 84th St New York NY 10028

LEVY, BUILDER
PHOTOGRAPHER
Study: Brooklyn Coll, BA, 1964; New York Univ, MA, 1966. *Exhib:* Solo exhibs include Coleman Intermediate Sch 271K, Brooklyn, NY, 1968, Int Ctr Photog, New York, 1989, Knoxville Mus Art, Tenn, 1992, Art Resources Transfer, New York, 1999, 2000, Hudson Guild Gallery, New York, 2007, O K Harris Gallery, New York, 2007, PhotoGraphic Gallery, New York, 2007, Doris Ulmann Galleries, Berea Coll, Ky, 2008, Univ Richmond Mus, 2008, Baldwin Photog Gallery, Murfreesboro, Tenn, 2008; group exhibs include Photog's Forum, Donnell Libr, New York, 1964; Rosenblum Collection, Queens Mus, New York, 1978; City Play, Mus City New York, 1988, Dressing for New York City Childhood, 2001; Benefit Auction, Silver Eye Ctr Photog Univ, Pittsburgh, 1992; Empire Beyond Great Wall, Am Mus Natural Hist, New York, 1994; Craven Gallery, West Tisbury, Martha's Vineyard, Mass, 2002; A R T Benefit Auction Exhib, Art Resources Transfer, 2003; Tropicalism, Jersey City Mus, NJ, 2006; Mongolia, Ruben Mus Art, New York, 2006; Road to Freedom, High Mus Art, Atlanta, 2008. *Awards:* John Simon Guggenheim Mem Found Fel, 2008. *Mailing Add:* Michael Ingbar Gallery 568 Broadway Basement New York NY 10012

LEVY, DAVID CORCOS
ART HISTORIAN, EDUCATOR
b New York, NY, Apr 10, 1938. *Study:* Columbia Coll, BA, 60; New York Univ, MA, 67, PhD, 79. *Hon Degrees:* Parsons Sch Design, DFA; Cedar Crest Coll, DFA. *Work:* Guggenheim Mus, New York. *Pos:* Exec dean, Parsons Sch Design, New York, 70-89; chancellor, New Sch Social Res, New York, 89-90; pres & dir, Corcoran Gallery Art, Washington, DC, 91-2005; pres, Educ Div, Cambridge Info Group, C Sotheby's Inst Art, currently. *Awards:* Chevalier des Arts & des Lettres, Repub France. *Mem:* Century Club, New York; Cosmos Club, Washington, DC

LEVY, MARK
WRITER, HISTORIAN
b New York, NY, June 24, 1947. *Study:* Clark Univ, BA, 68; Ind Univ, MA, 70, PhD, 77. *Pos:* Comnr, Alameda Co Art Comn, 85-86. *Teaching:* Asst prof, Kenyon Col, 74-79 & Univ Nev, 80-81; prof, Calif State Univ, Hayward, 81-; vis prof advan art theory, Grad Prog, San Francisco Art Inst, 84-89; vis prof grad prog consciousness dept, John F Kennedy Univ, 94-. *Awards:* Samuel Kress Dissertation Fel, 73; Nat Endowment Humanities Fel, 77; Fulbright-Hays Grant, summer 91. *Mem:* Int Asn Art Critics; Found Shamonic Studies. *Res:* World sacred art. *Publ:* Auth, The Shaman is a Gifted Artist, High Performance, fall 88; Rilke, Letters on Cezanne, San Francisco Rev of Books, fall 88; Squeak Carnwath, Artspace, 1/2/89; Wayang Kulit as a model for performance art, High Performance, summer 89; Technicians of Ecstasy: Shamanism & the Modern Artist, Bramble Books, 93; The Void of Art, summer 2005. *Mailing Add:* 5510 Golden Gate Ave Oakland CA 94618

LEVY, PHYLLIS
PAINTER
b Brooklyn, NY, June 20, 1927. *Study:* Cooper Union Art Sch, cert; San Francisco State, AB(art), MA(art educ); Colo Springs Fine Arts Ctr (scholar); Calif Sch Fine Arts (scholar). *Work:* Israel Mus, Jerusalem. *Exhib:* 15th Ann Watercolor, San Francisco Mus Art, Calif, 51; 26th Ann Women, San Francisco Mus Art, Calif, 51; Am Watercolor Drawings & Prints, Metrop Mus, NY, 52; Strathmore Hall Members Exhibs, 92, 93 & 94; Invitational, Strathmore Hall Arts Ctr Gallery, 93 & 94; Techno-Art, Rockville Arts Place, 94; Montgomery Co Art Asn Exhib, 94; solo exhibs, George Meany Ctr Labor Studies, 94 & Gaithersburg Coun Arts, Kentlands I Gallery, 94; plus many others. *Teaching:* Teacher art, Montgomery Co Pub Sch, 69-78. *Awards:* San Francisco Art Asn Prize, 51; Washington Watercolor Asn Award, 92; Montgomery Co Art Asn Award, 92 & 93. *Mem:* Artists Equity Asn; Rockville Arts Place; Montgomery Co Arts Coun. *Media:* Acrylic, Mixed Media. *Mailing Add:* 8100 Connecticut Ave # 405 Chevy Chase MD 20815

LEVY, STACY
SCULPTOR
b Philadelphia, NJ, 1960. *Study:* Yale Univ, New Haven, Conn, BA (sculpture), 1981; Skowhegan Sch Painting and Sculpture, Maine, 1988; Temple Univ, Philadelphia, MFA (sculpture), 1991. *Comn:* Capital Complex, Harrisburg, Pa, 1994; Arroyo: Fire and Police Station (sculpture), City of Philadelphia Dept Archit, Cecil Baker Assocs, Architects, 97; Cornerstones (sculputre), Seattle Art Comn, 1997; Wissahickon Food Web, Morris Arboretum Univ Pa, 1998; Confluences: Flows of the Schuylkill, Schuylkill River Park, Philadelphia; Pattern Book, Water Scroll and Bead Maze (installation), Children's Hospital at Montefiore, Carl Sagan Discovery Ctr, Bronx, NY, 2001; Lentic, Schuylkill Environ and Educ Ctr, Philadelphia, 2002; Acid Mine Drainage & Art, Vintondale, Pa, 2003; Watermap, Friend's Cent Sch, Ardmore, Pa, 2003; Waterlines, Del River Port Authority PATCO Line Art in Transit, Collingswood, NJ, 2004; Cloudstones, Seattle Arts Comn for Mineral Springs Park, 2004; Streamlines, NC Zoo, Ashboro, 2004; River Eyelash, Three Rivers Arts Festival, Pittsburg, Pa, 2005; Hillsborough Meander, Univ South Fla, Tampa, 2006; Lotic Meander, Ont Sci Ctr, Toronto, 2006; Tide Flowers, Hudson River Park, NY City, 2007; Moving Waters, Reading, Pa, 2007. *Exhib:* Solo exhibs include Abington Art Ctr, Jenkintown, Pa, 1991, Moore Coll Art, Philadelphia, 1991, Miami Dade Community Col, Miami, 1993, Rosen-Wolff Gallery, Univ Arts, Philadelphia, 1996, Larry Becker Contemp Art, Philadelphia, 1996, Inst Contemp Art, Philadelphia, 1998, John Michael Kohler Arts Ctr, Sheboygan, 2002, Lafayette Coll Art Gallery, Easton, Pa, 2005, Denison Musm Ohio, 2007; group exhibs include Royal Scottish Acad, Edinburgh, 1998-99; Hudson River Mus, Yonkers, NY, 1999; Southeastern Ctr Contemp Art, Winston Salem, NC, 2000; Cooper Hewitt Nat Design Mus, NY City, 2000; Nat Bldg Mus, Washington, DC, 2000; Mass Mus Contemp Art, North Adams, 2000; Snug Harbor Cult Ctr, Staten Island, NY, 2001; Kassel, Germany, 2001; Contemp Arts Ctr, Cincinnati, 2002; Santa Fe Art Inst, 2003; Armory Arts Ctr, Pasadena, Calif, 2004; Pittsburgh Craft Soc, 2006; Abington Art Ctr, Jenkintown, Pa, 2006; Wave Hill, Bronx, 2007. *Pos:* founder, Sere Ltd, 1986-. *Awards:* New Forms Regional Grant, 1992; Pew Fel of Arts, 1992; Pa Coun of Arts Fel, 1999; Nat Design Award for Environ, Cooper-Hewitt Mus, 2001; Excellence in Estuary Award, Partnership for the Del Estuary Inc, 2002. *Bibliog:* Sculpture Mag, Dec 2006; Landscape Archit Mag, Apr 2007. *Media:* Rain, Stone, Glass. *Mailing Add:* Sere Ltd 576 Upper Georges Valley Rd Spring Mills PA 16875

LEVY, S(TEPHEN) DEAN
DEALER, GALLERY DIRECTOR
b New York, NY, Nov 17, 1942. *Study:* Yale Univ, BA, 64. *Pos:* Vpres, Bernard & S Dean Levy, Inc, 73-. *Bibliog:* On Madison Avenue, Fortune Mag, 12/47; Rita Reif (auth), Antiques, New York Times, 10/76; Douglas Villiers (auth), Next Year in Jerusalem, Viking Press, 76. *Mem:* Art & Antique Dealers League. *Specialty:* American paintings, antique furniture, silver; English and American ceramics. *Publ:* Auth, An American Tea Party, Colonial Tea and Breakfast Tables 1715-1783; Opulence & Splendor, The New York Chair 1690-1830; Vanity & Elegance, The Dressing Table & Tall Chest in America, 1685-1785. *Mailing Add:* Bernard & Dean Levy Inc 24 E 84th St New York NY 10028

LEVY, TIBBIE
PAINTER
b New York, NY, Oct 29, 1908. *Study:* Cornell Univ, with Arshile Gorky, AB; Art Students League; Acad Grand Chaumiere & Acad Andre Lhote, Paris, France; NY Univ, JD. *Work:* Contemp Art Soc Gt Brit; Mus Mod Art, Madrid, Barcelona & Bilbao, Spain; Princeton Univ Mus; Cornell Univ Mus; plus 40 other mus. *Exhib:* Bodley Gallery, NY, 60-70; Galerie Ror Volmar, Paris, 61; Sala Nebli, Madrid, 62; Galeria Forum, Madrid, 63; Portal Gallery, London, Eng, 63 & 65; plus others. *Teaching:* Lectr art. *Media:* Oil. *Dealer:* Bodley Gallery 787 Madison Ave New York NY 10021

LEW, FRAN
PAINTER
b March 29 1946. *Study:* Brooklyn Col, with Philip Pearlstein, BA (hon in art), 66; Boston Univ Sch Fine & Applied Art, MFA, 68; Int Ctr Paintings & Costume Design, Palazzo Grassi, with Gregory Battcock, Archimedes Seguso, Venice, Italy, 78; Art Student's League, with Daniel Greene, Robert Beverly Hale & John Howard Sanden, 78-79; Reilly League Artists, NY, with Cesare Borgia, 79-84. *Work:* State of Israel, NY Consulate; Cornell Mus; Sherwin Miller Mus; Brooklyn Hist Soc; Maitland Art Center Mus. *Comn:* portrait, Interpub Group of Co, NY, 84; portrait, First Lady New York State, comn by Am Cancer Soc, NY, 86; portrait of Gov Mario M Cuomo, comn by coalition of Italo-Am Asn, NY, 90; portraits, comn by Tambrands Inc, Westchester, NY, 90; portrait, Dr Vincent du Vigneaud, Nobel Prize Laureate, 88. *Exhib:* Palazzo Grassi Int Ctr Painting & Design Exhib, Venice, Italy, 78; Salmagundi Club, 85, 86 & 87; Am Artists Mag Golden Anniversary Exhib, John Pence Gallery & Grand Cent Art

Galleries, 87; solo exhibs, Columbus Club, NY, 82, Manhattan Borough President's Art Gallery, 89, Pen & Brush Club, NY, 89 & Grand Cent Art Galleries, 90. *Teaching:* Instr art, Am Int Sch, Israel, 71-72; instr portrait drawing, Katonah, White Plains, NY, 80-82; art chmn, instr, Palisades Park Schs, NJ, 73-80. *Awards:* Gold Medal, Knickerbocker Artists, 84; Corporate Prize, Am Artist Mag Golden Anniversary Nat Competition, 87; Solo Award-Best Show, Pen & Brush Oil Exhib, 87. *Bibliog:* eds, Drawings in the Golden Anniversary National Art Competition, Am Artist Mag, 6/87; Edward Rubin (auth), article, Manhattan Arts, 10/89; quoted, portrait of Governor Mario M Cuomo, Am Artist Mag, 6/93. *Mem:* Knickerbocker Artists; Hudson Valley Art Asn; Catharine Lorillard Wolfe Art Club; Pen & Brush Club; life mem, Art Students League; Reilly League Artists . *Media:* Oil, Pastel, Charcoal. *Publ:* Member of the Issue, Northlight, 82; portrait, Governor Mario M Cuomo, James Barron (auth), The New York Times, 7/95. *Dealer:* Sandra Werther Ltd NY

LEW, WEYMAN
PAINTER, PRINTMAKER
b San Francisco, Calif, Feb 17, 1935. *Study:* Univ Calif, Berkeley, BS, 57; San Francisco Art Inst, with Jay deFeo, 65-66; Studied with Joan Brown, Ivan Majdrakoff. *Work:* MH de Young Mem Mus, San Francisco; Univ Calif Mus, Berkeley; Inst Arte Contemporaneo, Lima, Peru; Santa Barbara Mus Art, Calif; Oakland Art Mus, Calif; Brooklyn Mus; San Francisco Mus Mod Art, Calif. *Comn:* Univ Calif Mus, Berkeley, 74. *Exhib:* Over 40 solo exhibs, MH De Young Mem Mus, 70, Inst Contemp Art, Lima, Peru, 70, Santa Barbara Mus Art, 71, Art Gallery Greater Victoria, BC, Can, 72, Bonython Art Gallery, Sydney, Australia, 72-75, Sande Webster Gallery, Philadelphia, 72, 74, 77, 80 & 84 & Int Art Exhib Hall, Beijing, China, 91; and many others. *Pos:* Dir, Kelley Galleries, San Francisco, 68; guest cur, Nan Hai Arts Ctr, Calif, 90-92 & Chinatown Community Art Prog, San Francisco, 91 & 93. *Teaching:* Guest instr painting, drawing & serigraphy, MH de Young Mem Mus Art Sch, 70-71. *Awards:* Merit Award, San Francisco Art Festival, 80; Distinguished Award for Cult, Chinese Cult Found San Francisco, 91. *Bibliog:* Alfred Frankenstein (auth), 67 & Thomas Albright (auth), 68-70, San Francisco Chronicle; Arthur Bloomfield (auth), San Francisco Examiner, 68 & 70; Oriental Art Mag, Eng, Summer 91; Li Beige (auth), on Weyman Lew, Art Mag, China, 12/91; Guo Rui (auth), Weyman Lew, Four Seas Mag, Beijing, China, 1/92; and others; Nell Swartz (auth), MODA, San Francisco, 96. *Mem:* Calif Soc Printmakers; Chinese Cult Ctr (art adv bd), San Francisco; Asian Am Arts Found (art adv bd), San Francisco; Acad Art Coll (galleries & prom adv bd), San Francisco. *Media:* Etching, Pen and Ink. *Publ:* Auth, Weyman Lew Sketches Away, Triton Assocs, 81; ed, Contemporary Chinese Painting, Nan Hai co USA & Chinese Artists Asn, China Publ, 90; Of Peoples and Places, Chinese Cult Found San Francisco, 91; illus, Echoes of Oxford, Phillip Carlson, 91; Calif Graphics, Graphics Group, 74; Human Sexuality, Masters & Johnson, Little Brown, 85, 88; Art of Rock Posters, Presley to Punk, Abbeville Press, 88. *Dealer:* Sande Webster Gallery 2006 Locust St Philadelphia PA 19103; Robin Gibson Gallery 278 Liverpool St Sydney NSW 2010 Australia

LEWCZUK, MARGRIT
PAINTER
b 1952. *Study:* Queens Col, New York, NY, 52. *Exhib:* Solo exhibs, Brooklyn Mus, NY, 75, John Davis Gallery, Akron, Ohio, 82, Thorden Wetterling Gallery, Stockholm, Sweden, 87, Pamela Auchincloss Gallery, NY, 87, 89, 92 & 94, Dolan Maxwell Gallery, Philadelphia, Pa, 88 & Bjorn Wetterling Gallery, Gottenburg, Sweden, 91; Munson-Williams Proctor Mus, NY, 81; Faculty Invitational, Bennington Col, Vt, 83; Works on Paper, Allport Gallery, San Francisco, Calif, 89. *Pos:* Univ Conn, 99-. *Awards:* Nat Endowment Arts, 89. *Media:* Oil on Linen, Charcoal Pastel on Paper. *Publ:* Exhib Catalogues for Pamela Auchincloss Gallery, 87 & Thorden Wetterling Gallery, 87. *Mailing Add:* 79 Metropolitan Ave Brooklyn NY 11211-3932

LEWENZ, LISA
VIDEO ARTIST, PHOTOGRAPHER
b Baltimore, Md, Apr 1, 1955. *Study:* Philadelphia Coll Art, 73-74; Kans City Art Inst, 76-77; Art Inst Chicago, BFA, 78; Calif Inst Arts, MFA, 82. *Work:* New Eng Holocaust Found Collection, Boston; Mus Contemp Arts, Baltimore, Md; Hallmark Collections, Kans City; Tisch Photo Collections, New York Univ; Deutsches Historisches Mus, Berlin. *Comn:* John A Logan Col, Ill Arts Coun, Carbondale, 85; A Letter Without Words, Independent Television Serv, 95-99. *Exhib:* Solo exhibs, A View from Three Mile Island, San Francisco Camerawork, Calif, 87, A Letter without Words, 92 St Gallery, NY, 89, Gormley Gallery, Baltimore, Md, 91, E J Bellocq Gallery, Ruston, La, 91, Towards a More Perfect Union, Baltimore Mus Art, Md, 92 & Huntington Gallery, Boston, Mass, 92; Other Rooms, The Kunstraum, Washington, DC, 90; Visual AIDS, Mus Contemp Arts, Baltimore, Md, 90; Rotterdam Int Film Fest/CineMart, 96; IFFM/No Borders, NY, 96; PBS Nat Broadcast, 99; various film festivals incl Sundance, Berlin, Amsterdam, Vancouver, Edinburgh, Jerusalem & Gothenberg. *Collection Arranged:* Site Works, St Mary's Gallery, 87; Constructions, 90, Contemp Puerto Rican Painting, 90, Fifth Ann Nat Print & Drawing Exhibit, Gormley Gallery, 91. *Pos:* Dir, Unit One photog prog, Univ Ill, Champaign, 85-87 & Gormley Gallery, Col Notre Dame Md, Baltimore, 90-91; dir/coordr, site specific sem, St Mary's Col, Md, 87-88; dir, NoNet Productions, 94-. *Teaching:* Vis lectr photog, Minneapolis Col Art & Design, 84; vis asst prof photog, Univ Ill, Champaign-Urbana, 85-87 & New York Univ, 92; asst prof, St Mary's Col, Md, 87-88 & Col Notre Dame, Md, 89-93; vis asst prof, Rochester Inst Technol, 92; vis lectr, Cornell Univ, Johns Hopkins Univ, NY Univ, Rowan Univ, currently. *Awards:* Fulbright Hays Scholar, Sr Res Award Ger, Ger & Coun Int Exchange Scholars, 93 & 94; Nat Endowment Humanities Fel Berlin, 94; Fel, Anonymous Was a Woman Found, 98. *Bibliog:* Philadelphia Inquirer, 10/98; Los Angeles Times, 4/5/99; New York Times, 4/5/99. *Mem:* Soc Photog Educ; Md Art Place, Baltimore (exec bd dir, 88-92); Coll Art Asn; Baltimore Artists Housing Coop (co-pres, bd dir, 90-); Friends Photog. *Media:* Interdisciplinary Arts, Photography; Film, Video. *Publ:* Auth, 1984 A View from Three Mile Island, No Net Productions, 83; contribr, Nuclear Power, A Weapon for the Enemy, UCLA Press, 84; Visions Issue: Environmental Action, 85; Friends of the Earth J, 86

LEWIN, BERNARD
DEALER, COLLECTOR
b Ger; US citizen. *Study:* With Kurt Wagner, Berlin. *Exhib:* Ann shows, Castaneda, Cora, Coronel, Tamayo and others. *Pos:* Art dir, B Lewin Galleries, Palm Springs, Calif, 60-. *Awards:* Thirty-eighth Anniversary of Mexican Masters, Lifetime Achievement Award, City of Los Angeles; Lifetime Achievement Award, First Int Gallery Invitational, Chicago; Significant Contribution Award, City of Palm Springs. *Mem:* Art Dealers Asn. *Specialty:* Mexican masters, Tamayo, Siqueiros, Merida, R Martinez, R Coronel, Diego Rivera, Felipe Castenada, Gustavo Montoya and others. *Collection:* Mexican masters, American and European. *Mailing Add:* 254 E Lake Dr Palm Springs CA 92264-5582

LEWIS, CAROLE
SCULPTOR
b London, Eng, Dec 28, 1934; US citizen. *Study:* Hana Geber Workshop, apprentice to Hana Geber, 79-82, Art Students League, New York, with Gustave Rehberger; painting with George Jo Mess, Indianapolis, Ind; Aida Foster Sch, London, Eng; Greycotes Sch, Oxford, Eng. *Work:* Am Collection, Mus Int Art, Sophia, Bulgaria; Gen Electric Corp, Fairfield, Conn; Mus Hudson Highlands, Cornwall, NY; Starrett City Assoc, Brooklyn, NY; Seicomart Corp, Sapporo, Japan; and many other pub & pvt collections. *Exhib:* Group shows, Cleveland Mus Nat Hist, Ohio, 84; Cast Iron Gallery, Soho, NY, 91-93; Kyoto Gallery, Japan, 93; Krystal Gallery, Warren, Vt, 93-94; Wildlife in Midtown, Am Towers, NY, 94. *Awards:* Pietro & Alfrieda Montana Award, Nat Sculpture Soc, 91; Charles H Levitt Prize, Nat Asn Women Artists, 91; Vincent Glinsky Mem Award, Audubon Artists, 94. *Bibliog:* Sculpture: Technique, Form, Content, Williams, 94. *Mem:* Sculptors Guild; Nat Asn Women Artists; Fel Nat Sculptors Soc; Audubon Artists; Hudson River Contemp Artists. *Media:* Terra Cotta, Clay; Metal, Bronze. *Dealer:* Sculpture Ctr 67 E 69th St New York NY; Arlene McDaniel Galleries Simsbury CT

LEWIS, DAVID DODGE
PAINTER
b Houlton, Maine, Dec 21, 1951. *Study:* Univ Southern Main, BA (art educ), 70-74; Sch of Mus of Fine Arts, Boston, 74-75; Art Students League, New York, 78; East Carolina Univ, MA (painting), 80-81, MFA (painting), 84-87. *Exhib:* Stockton Nat Exhib, Haggin Mus, Calif, 97; 27th Bradley Nat Print and Drawing Exhib, Bradley Univ, Ill, 98; Vitreographs from the Littleton Studios, Blue Spiral Gallery, Asheville, NC, 99; Scene/Unseen, Eastern N Mex Univ, 99; Millennial Biennial: Nat Works on Paper, Univ Richmond, Va, 2000; Stone Tool Drawings, Longwood Ctr Visual Arts, Farmville, Va, 2001; The Sentient Object, McLean Project for Arts, Va, 2001; Hodges Taylor Gallery, Charlotte, NC, 2002; Biennial 2002, Peninsula Fine Arts Ctr, Newport News, Va, Faces/Reality, 2005; Americas 2000, Minot State Univ, NDak, 2004; Hand to Hand, Green Hill Ctr NC Art, 2005; Images, Pa State Univ, 2006; Va Artists, Hampton, Va, 2007. *Teaching:* Graphics instr Penland Sch Crafts, NC, 84 & 85, drawing instr, 93, 95 & 2000; intsr Mayland Technical Inst, Spruce Pine, NC, 84; asst prof fine arts Hampden-Sydney Coll, 87-93, assoc prof fine arts, 93-95, William W Elliot assoc prof fine arts, 95, prof, 2000-. *Awards:* Va Prize Arts, Prints and Drawings, 89; John Peter Mettauer Award Excellence in Res, Hampden-Sydney Coll, 92 & 2006. *Mem:* Coll Art Asn; South East Coll Art Conference; Va Art Hist Colloquium; Central Va Arts; Longwood Ctr Visual Arts; Va Mus Fine Arts. *Mailing Add:* 1004 Edmonds St Farmville VA 23901

LEWIS, DONALD SYKES, JR
PAINTER
b Norfolk, Va, Dec 13, 1947. *Study:* Randolph-Macon Coll, Ashland, Va, BA (fine arts); Univ Va, MA (hist of art). *Work:* Central Fidelity Bank, Norfolk, Va; Randolph-Macon Coll, Ashland, VA; Sears, Roebuck & Co, Chicago, Ill; First & Citizens Bank, Warm Springs, VA. *Exhib:* Second Ann Invitational Juried Show, Gallery II, Norfolk, 77; 57th Ann Nat Apr Salon, Springville Mus Art, Utah, 81; solo exhibs, Auslew Gallery, 82, Art Works Gallery, 94, Hermitage Found Mus, Norfolk, Va, 96 & Warm Springs Gallery, Va, 2000 & 2007; Randolph-Macon Coll, Ashland, Va 85; Twentieth Century Gallery, Williamsburg, Va, 85; Peninsula Fine Arts Ctr, Newport News, Va, 97; 20th Ann Juried Exhib, Pleades Gallery, New York, 2002; 25th Ann Open Non-mem Exhib, Salmagundi Club, New York, 2002; Am Artist Professional League Inc; 75th Grand Nat Exhib, Salmagundi Club, New York, 2003. *Pos:* Vpres, Auslew Gallery Inc, Norfolk, 73-76, dir, 76-83, pres, 83-95; adv comt, Chrysler Mus, 88-90; sec treas, Granby & Main Corp, 2004-05, pres, 2005-. *Teaching:* Instr Am art, Hermitage Mus, Norfolk, 75, 78 & 79 & Old Dom Univ, 75-76. *Bibliog:* Hampton Roads Virginia Guide to Visual Artists, Grunwald & Radcliff, 84. *Mem:* Chrysler Mus Art. *Media:* Oil. *Res:* Cataloging works of Herman Ottomar Herzog and his son, Lewis E Herzog. *Publ:* Auth, Emily Nichols Hatch (catalog), 74 & foreword, In: Carolyn Wyeth (catalog), 12/74, Auslew Gallery Inc; Herman Herzog, Southwest Art Rev, 75; contribr, Carolyn Wyeth Exhibition Catalogue, R W Norton Art Gallery, Shreveport, La, 1/76; auth, Herman Herzog (1831-1932), German landscapist in America, Am Art Rev, 7-8/76; American Paintings of Herman Herzog (exhib catalog), Brandywine River Mus, 9/12-11/22. *Dealer:* Warm Springs Gallery Warm Springs VA; Main St Fine Art and Antique Mall Kilmarnock VA; Green Leaf Gallery Inc NC; Gallery C Raleigh NC. *Mailing Add:* 708 Cavalier Dr Virginia Beach VA 23451

LEWIS, DOUGLAS
HISTORIAN, CONSULTANT
b Centreville, Miss, Apr 30, 1938. *Study:* Lawrenceville Sch, NJ, dipl, 56; Yale Col, BA, 59 & 60; Clare Col, Cambridge Univ, BA, 62, MA, 66; Yale Univ, MA, 63, PhD, 67; Am Acad Rome, Chester Dale fel, 64, dipl, 65. *Collection Arranged:* African Sculpture, 70, The Far North (Am Eskimo & Indian Art catalog), 73; The Drawings of Andrea Palladio Traveling Exhib (catalog), 81; Renaissance Small Bronze Sculpture and Associated Decorative Arts (catalog), 83; Renaissance Master Bronzes (with preface to catalog), 86; The Currency of Fame (catalog contributor), Nat Gallery Art, 94. *Pos:* David E Finley fel Venetian art, Nat Gallery Art, Washington, DC, 65-68; cur

sculpture, Nat Gallery Art, 68-2004; vchmn, Citizens Stamp Adv Comt, US Postal Serv, 85-2004; chmn, 2004-05; bd advisors, Oakley & Rosedown, La State Historic Sites; bd advisors, Natchez Literary & Cinema Celebration, Miss. *Teaching:* Asst prof baroque & romantic art, Bryn Mawr Col, 67-68; asst prof renaissance & baroque art, Univ Calif, Berkeley, spring 70; sem leader renaissance archit, Folger Inst, Renaissance Sem, Washington, DC, spring 72; adj prof, Renaissance & baroque art, Johns Hopkins Univ, 73-77; prof Renaissance art & archit, Univ Calif, Berkeley, fall 79; lectr, Iowa State Univ, Ames, 80; lectr, Georgetown Univ, 80-93; vis prof, Univ Md, 89-2003. *Awards:* Copley Medal, Smithsonian Inst, 81. *Mem:* Fel Am Acad in Rome; Soc Archit Historians; Coll Art Asn Am; Belg-Am Educ Found; Centro Palladiano, Vicenza; and others. *Res:* Art and architecture in Renaissance Venice; monographic studies on Michele Sanmicheli, Jacopo Sansovino, Andrea Palladio, Baldassare Longhena, Francesco Muttoni & Galeazzo Mondella (Moderno). *Interests:* John James Audubon; Architecture of American South. *Publ:* Auth, The Late Baroque Churches of Venice, 67 & Garland, 79; The Drawings of Andrea Palladio, Nat Gallery Art, 81 (rev ed, 2000); coauth, Renaissance Master Bronzes, SITES, 86; Nat Gallery Art Systematic Catalog, Renaissance Plaquettes. *Mailing Add:* 3600 Lower Centreville Rd Liberty MS 39645-8295

LEWIS, JEFFREY
PAINTER, EDUCATOR

b Brockport, NY, 1952. *Study:* State Univ NY, Brockport, BA; Univ Iowa, MA & MFA. *Work:* Del Mar Coll, Tex; Meridian Mus Art, Miss; Muscarelle Mus Art, Va; Trenton State Coll, NJ; Wesley Theological Seminary, Washington. *Exhib:* 183rd Ann: Invitational Exhib Contemp Am Art, Nat Acad Mus, New York, 2008. *Teaching:* Prof painting & drawing, Auburn Univ, Ala. *Awards:* Alden Bryan Prize in Painting, Nat Acad, 2008. *Media:* Encaustic, Silverpoint. *Dealer:* Thomas Deans Fine Art Atlanta Ga. *Mailing Add:* Dept Art 101 Biggin Hall Ctr Auburn Univ Auburn AL 36849

LEWIS, JOSEPH
COLLECTOR

b London, 1937. *Pos:* Founder, chmn & principal investor, Tavistock Group, Windermere, Fla; owner, Isleworth Golf & Country Club, Windermere, Fla & Lake Nona Golf & Country Club, Orlando; founder, Tavistock Cup. *Awards:* Named one of Top 200 Collectors, ARTnews mag, 2003-12; named one of World's Richest People, Forbes mag. *Collection:* Impressionism; modern art. *Mailing Add:* Tavistock Group Tavistock House PO Box 9000 Windermere FL 34786

LEWIS, JOSEPH S, III
ADMINISTRATOR, SCULPTOR

b New York, NY, Feb 22, 1953. *Study:* Hamilton Coll, NY, BA, 75; studied with John Ashbery, Allen Ginsberg & David Shapiro, grad writing sem, Brooklyn Col, NY; Md Inst Coll Art, Baltimore, MFA, 89; Mediation Training, Calif Lawyers for the Arts, Santa Monica, 98; Inst Management Learning Educ, Harvard Grad Sch Educ, Cambridge, Mass, 2005. *Work:* Studio Mus Harlem, NY; Mark Twain Bank, St Louis, Mo; Univ Colo, Boulder; State Univ NY, Potsdam; Experimental Print Workshop, NY; Anderson Ranch, Colo; Cite des Arts, Paris. *Comn:* Wind Chime, Riverside Arts Found, Calif, 95; The Twelve Principles, Long Beach Blue Line, Metrop Transit Authority, Los Angeles; The Wall of Dignity, Mayors Comt Arts & Culture, Baltimore. *Exhib:* Chant Acapella, Mus Mod Art, NY, 78; No Justice No Peace, Calif Afro-Am Mus, Los Angeles, 92; Primary Peoples Cols & Shapes, Univ Galleries, Ill State Univ, Normal, 93; Synesthesia: Sound & Vision, San Antonio Mus Art, Tex, 94; Equal Rights & Justice, High Mus, Atlanta, 94 & Smithsonian Inst, Washington, 95; Disciples of the Hood, Joe Lewis & The Neo-Ancestralist, Contemp Arts Ctr, Cincinnati, 96; Darkroom Projects, Milan, 99; Made in California, Los Angeles Co Mus Art; PhotoAlchemy, Sharadin Gallery, Univ Penn, Kutztown, 2000; Memory, Layers, Reflections, Substation, Singapore, 2001; Clairvoyance: Future Works by Joe Lewis, Kathleen Cullen Gallery, New York, 2007. *Collection Arranged:* The Times Square Show, NY, 80; Fashion Moda Store, Documenta VII, Kassel, Ger, 82; The Face of Jazz 1954-1984, Raymond Ross, Hamilton Coll, Clinton, NY, 84; The Gathering Storm: What is the Enemy Now, Md Art Place, Baltimore, 92; LA Freewaves (installations), The Geffen, Temporary Contemp/Mus Contemp Art, Los Angeles, 96. *Pos:* Publ, Appearances Mag & Press, NY, 76-89; dir, Fashion Moda, NY, 78-82; proj mgr, Jackie Robinson Found, NY, 87-90; adminr, Pub Art Prog, Cult Affairs Dept, Los Angeles, 92-94; proj mgr, Art for Rail Prog, Metrop Transportation Authority, Los Angeles, 94-95; chair, Dept Art, Calif State Univ, Northridge, 95-2001; dean, FIT Sch Art & Design, NY, 2001-2004; dean, prof, Sch Art & Design, NY State Coll Ceramics, Alfred Univ, 2004-2010; Dean, prof Claire Trevor Sch Arts, Univ Calif, Irvine, currently. *Teaching:* Vis asst prof art, studio, Carnegie Mellon Univ, Pittsburgh, 91-92; fac studio & theory, Calif Inst Arts, Valencia, Calif, 91-95; vis fac, New Genre Studio, Univ Calif, Los Angeles, 92. *Awards:* Fel, Thomas J Watson Found, 75; fel, New Genre, Nat Endowment Arts, 82; fel, New Genre, Md State Arts Coun, 92; fel, Photog, NY Found Arts, 2008. *Bibliog:* Lowery Stokes Sims (auth), The Mirror The Other: The Politics of Esthetics, Artforum, 90; Lucy Lippard (auth), Mixed Blessings: New Art in a Multicultural America, Partheon Books, 90; Tobey Crockett (auth), Joe Lewis at Robert Berman, Art in Am, 94; Julie Art (ed), Cultural Economics, 96; Urban Mythologies, The Bronx Represented Since the 1960's, The Bronx Mus, 99. *Mem:* Coll Art Asn, NY; Mus Contemp Art, Baltimore (bd vpres, 90-92); Side St Projs, Santa Monica, Calif (bd pres, 92-95); Mary Lind Found (bd mem, 98-2000 & treas, 99-); Am Soc Composers, Authors & Publ; Int Asn Art Critics; Calif Lawyer For the Arts (bd mem, 2000-); Nat Coun Art Admin (bd mem, 2000-); Jackie Robinson Found, Los Angeles (scholar comt). *Media:* Multimedia. *Publ:* Auth, How to commit suicide in South Africa: The work of Sue Coe, Artforum, 4/82; Jean Michel Basquiat, Contemporanea, 8/88; Soul shadows: Urban warrior myths: The work of Dawn Dedeaux, Artspace, 4/93; Radcliffe Bailey at Fay Gold, Art in Am, 3/95; Jim McHugh at the High Museum, Art in Am, 6/96; The Bronx Represented Since the 1960's, The Bronx Mus, 99. *Dealer:* Robert Berman Gallery 2525 Michigan Ave No C2 Santa Monica CA 90404. *Mailing Add:* Robert Berman Gallery 2525 Michigan Ave Santa Monica CA 90404

LEWIS, LOUISE MILLER
GALLERY DIRECTOR, EDUCATOR

b St Louis, Mo, Dec 4, 1940. *Study:* Univ Calif, Berkeley, BA, 63; Univ NMex, Albuquerque, MA (French), 66, MA (art history), 72. *Collection Arranged:* Contemporary Figuration: The Kamm Collection, 97; Patssi Valdez: Private Landscapes, 98; Akiko Arita: Exploring Native Culture in Japan, 98; Jane Dickson: Almost Home, 99; Editorial Drawings of the 20th Century, 2000; Lili Lakick, Sirens and other Neon Seductions, 2001; Von Dutch: An Am Original, 2002; Mus of Disappearance: Max Almy and Teri Yarbrow, 2003; Free Range: Seven Los Angeles Artists, 2003; Contemp Chinese Quilts, 2004; Suchen Hung: The Red Sea Series, 2004; African Art in the Life Cycle, 2005. *Pos:* Cur, Univ NMex Fine Arts Mus, 66-72, actg dir, 72; assoc dir, Calif State Univ Northridge Art Gallery, 72-80, dir, 80-. *Teaching:* Asst prof, Calif State Univ, Northridge, 72-79, assoc prof, 79-83, prof art hist, 83-, interdisciplinary humanities prog, 90-96. *Mem:* Art Table. *Res:* Art and the media. *Specialty:* International & Contemporary Art. *Publ:* Auth, California Video in Xle Biennale de Paris, Mus d'Art Mod, 80; Future Video: Max Almy, LAICA Journal, 83; Where Art the Daumiers of Video Art, Media Arts, 85; Generation of Mentors, Nat Mus Women, 94; Pattsi Valdez, Private Landscapes, 98; Lili Lapich: Sirens and other Neon Seductions, 2001; Free Range: Seven Los Angeles Artists, 2003. *Mailing Add:* California State Univ/Northridge Art Gallery 18111 Nordhoff St Northridge CA 91330-8299

LEWIS, MARCIA
METALSMITH, INSTRUCTOR

b Washington, DC, Oct 7, 1946. *Study:* Corcoran Sch, Washington, DC; San Diego Univ, Calif; Calif State Univ, Long Beach. *Work:* Mus Contemp Crafts, NY; Oakland Mus Art; Renwick Gallery Mus Am Art, Smithsonian Inst. *Exhib:* Int Handwerks Messe, Munich, Ger 71; Am Metalsmiths, DeCordova Mus, Lincoln, Mass, 73; Kunstindustri Mus, Copenhagen, Denmark, 73; Goldsmiths 74, Smithsonian Inst, Washington, DC, 74; Crafts of the NAmericas, Colo State Univ & Smithsonian Inst, 75; Calif Design 12, Los Angeles, 76. *Pos:* Apprentice goldsmith, Ingrid Hansen, Zurich, Switz, 71-72; asst silversmith, Tony Laws Studio Ltd, Londin, Eng, 72-73. *Teaching:* Instr metalsmithing & gen crafts, Univ Wis, Whitewater, 73-75 & San Jose State Univ, Calif, 75-76; assoc prof art, Long Beach City Col, Calif, 78-. *Awards:* Sterling Silversmiths Award, Design Competition, Silversmiths Guild, 69; George C Marshall Mem Fel, Denmark-Amerika Fondet, 72; Nat Endowment Arts Award, Washington, DC, 76. *Bibliog:* Beverly Edna Johnson (auth), Biographical, Los Angeles Times Home Mag, 72; Thelma Newman (auth), Containers, Crown Publ, 77; Oppi Untracht (auth), Jewelry Techniques for Craftsmen, Doubleday, 78. *Mem:* Soc NAm Goldsmiths. *Media:* Metal. *Publ:* Auth, Wearable aluminum ornaments, Calif State Univ, Long Beach, 77. *Mailing Add:* Dept Art Long Beach City Col 4901 E Carson St Long Beach CA 90808

LEWIS, MARY
SCULPTOR

b Multnomah, Ore, Jun 18, 1926. *Study:* Univ Ore, with Mark Sponenburgh, 45-50, BS (sculpture), 49; Ore Div Am Asn Univ Women Mabel Merwin fel, 50, Syracuse Univ, with Ivan Mestrovic, 50, tech asst to Mestrovic, 51-2/53, MFA, 53. *Work:* Obadiah (4' mahogany and copper bird), Backstage Restaurant, Torrington, Conn; Mother and Son (lifesize, rosewood) & alder tabernacle door, St John Medical Ctr, Longview, Wash, 84; Descent of the Holy Spirit (bronze relief, aumbry door), Trinity Cathedral Church, Sacramento, Calif, 96; Five Symbolic Bronze Reliefs, garden, St John Med Ctr, Longview, Wash, 2000; Mother & Child (lifesize), bronze, OHSU Ctr Women's Health Garden, Portland, Ore, 2006. *Comn:* Madonna and Child (4' diameter maple relief) St Joseph's Church Chapel, Roseburg, Ore, 78; The Holy Family (4'7″ by 2″ maple relief), St Frederic's Church, St Helens, Ore, 85; Mysteries of the Rosary (20 bronze reliefs), Peace Garden, The Grotto, Portland, Ore, 89 & 2005; Double front doors (4 insert relief panels, 2' x 5'6″, white oak), new church, David Richen (archit), Our Lady of Guadalupe Trappist Abbey, Lafayette, Ore, 2007-; The Columbia River (5'3″ by 2'5″ monkey pod wood), relief for donor wall, The Columbia Theatre for the Performing Arts, Longview, Wash, 2009-2010. *Exhib:* Artists of Oregon, Portland Art Mus, 51 & 69; 12th & 14th Ann New Eng Exhibs, Silvermine Guild Artists, New Canaan, Conn, 61 & 63; 62nd & 63rd Ann Exhib, New Haven Paint & Clay Club, John Slade Ely Ctr, New Haven, 63 & 64; Retrospective: 1944-2000, Fine Arts Gallery, Lower Columbia Coll, Longview, Wash, 81 & 2000; solo exhib, Liturgical Arts, Invitational Exhib, Marylhurst Coll, Ore, 84; Gallery Genesis, Chicago, Ill, 88; Works of Faith, First Presbyterian Church Gallery, Portland, Ore, 97-98 & 2005; Gifts of the Spirit invitational, First Presbyterian Church Gallery, Portland, Ore, 97 & 99; Retrospective, First Congregational United Church of Christ, Portland, Ore, 2011; Divergent Art, Lower Columbia Fine Arts Gallery, Longview, Wash, 2011; plus others. *Pos:* Staff artist, GAF Corp Photo Div, Portland, Ore, 70-76. *Teaching:* Asst prof art, Nat Coll Arts, Lahore, Pakistan, 58-60. *Awards:* Tiffany Traveling Scholar, 53; Fulbright Lectr, 58 & 59; Fel, Nat Coll Arts, Lahore, Pakistan, 98. *Bibliog:* Virginia Watson-Jones (auth), Contemporary American Women Sculptors, (illus), Oryx Press, 86,; Featuring The Little Yellow Dinosaur and artist, Stereo World, Nat Stereoscopic Asn Inc, Vol 28, No 2, 2001; Arthur Williams (auth), The Sculpture Reference and Beginning Sculpture (illus), 2004; Cathy Zimmerman (auth), Of Heart and Hands, 5/13/90 & Mary's Legacy, 9/25/2005, The Daily News, Longview, Wash; Abby Haight (auth), A Sculptor's Unfinished Journey, The Oregonian, 9/28/2006; Ed Langlois (auth), Sculptor: An Episcopalean's Influence on Catholic Art in Oregon, Catholic Sentinel, 2/4/2011, included on Sanctuary for Sacred Arts, Portland, Ore. *Mem:* Portland Art Mus. *Media:* Wood, Stone. *Publ:* Coauth & illusr, The Little Yellow Dinosaur, 71, illusr, In the Beginning--the Bible Story of Creation, Adam & Eve, Cain & Abel, 72, Jesus Christ, His Youth, Disciples, Miracles, 75, GAF View-Master; illusr, Mary Lewis, Sculptor, 1947-2011 (self-published), 2011. *Mailing Add:* 74394 Wortman Rd Rainier OR 97048

LEWIS, MICHAEL H
PAINTER, EDUCATOR
b Brooklyn, NY, Aug 10, 1941. *Study:* State Univ NY Col, New Paltz, painting with Ben Bishop, George Wexler & Ilya Bolotowsky, BS, 63, MFA, 75; Mich State Univ, MA, 64. *Work:* Fogg Mus Art, Harvard Univ; Albertina Mus, Vienna, Austria; Portland Mus Art, Maine; Art Bank Prog, U.S. Dept of State, Washington D.C.; Colby Coll Mus Art, Waterville, Maine. *Comn:* Oil portrait, comn by Edmund S Muskie, 83; cover paintings for The Magus of Strovolos, Homage to the Sun, Fire in the Heart and the Mountain of Silence (all by Kyriacos Markides), 86, 87, 90, 01; 6 Paintings, comn by Colby Coll Miller Libr, Waterville, Maine, 97. *Exhib:* Solo Exhibs: Uptown Gallery, NY, 80, 88, 91, 93, 95, 97, 2000, 03, 06; Steven Scott Gallery, Owings Mills, Md, 94, 98; Aucocisco Gallery, Portland, Maine, 2003, 04, 06, 08; Univ Mo, St Louis, 96; Colby Coll Mus Art, Waterville, Maine, 2000; Group shows, Fogg Art Mus, Harvard Univ, 87-89, 93, Vose Art Gallery, Boston, Mass, 2000, 03, 04; Aucocisco Gallery, Portland, Maine, 2003, 04, 06, 08, 09, 2010; Steven Scott Gallery, Owings Mills, Md, 92-98, 99, 2000-2006; Portland Mus Art Biennial, Maine, 98-99; Portsmouth Mus Fine Art, NH, 2010; Addison Gallery of Am Art, Andover, Mass, 2012; Art in Embassy Program, US State Dept, Manama Bahrain, 2012. *Pos:* Mem, Maine Arts Comn, 72-78, visual arts adv panel, 79-81, adv panel roster, 94-2004. *Teaching:* Instr art, Kingston City Pub Schs, NY, 64-66; prof painting & drawing, Univ Maine, Orono, 66-, chmn, Dept Art, 75-81, acting assoc dean col arts & sci, 81-83, chmn, Dept Art, 87-93. *Awards:* Video Work of Art Grant, Maine State Arts Comn & Maine Pub Broadcasting Network, 83; New Eng Found Arts/Nat Endowment Arts-Regional Fel, Visual Artists (drawing), 90-91. *Bibliog:* Alicia Anstead (auth), Artist Explores Winter in Orono in Colby Show, Bangor Daily News, 1/27/00; Phillip Isaacson (auth) Art Review, Maine Sunday Telegram, 5/9/2004; Kristen Andresen (auth), Michael Lewis' Landscapes Plumb Deeper Regions, Bangor Daily News, 2/7/06; Bob Keyes (auth), Michael Lewis Sees the Light, Maine Sunday Telegram, 6/11/06; Suzette McAvoy (auth), Transcending Nature, Maine Home & Design, Oct 2008; Bob Keyes (auth), Honor for the Soul of UHO Art, Maine Sunday Telegram, 5/20/12; Aislinn Sarnacki (auth), Painter Honored for Spreading Love of Art, Bangor Daily News, 5/11/2012. *Mem:* Maine Arts Comn (contemp artist devel prog comt, 99-2004). *Media:* Turpentine Wash (with Oils), Video. *Dealer:* Andy Verzosa Ancocisco Gallery 89 Exhange St Portland ME. *Mailing Add:* PO Box 323 Orono ME 04473

LEWIS, NAT BRUSH
PAINTER, INSTRUCTOR
b Boston, Mass, Dec 17, 1925. *Study:* Pembroke Col, Brown Univ & RI Sch Design, AB; Art Students League; watercolor with Mario Cooper; also with Henry Gasser Art. *Work:* Am Asn Univ Women, Somerset Hills, NJ; Bloomfield Art League, NJ; Bergen Mus Arts & Sci; Zhejiang Mus, China. *Exhib:* Am Watercolor Soc, NY; Am Artists Prof League Grand Nat; Salmagundi Club Exhib; Hudson Valley Art Asn; Philadelphia Watercolor Club; and others. *Pos:* artist-in-residence, Hillside High Sch, NJ. *Teaching:* Adj prof art, Seton Hall Univ, 84-; instr, pvt classes. *Awards:* Int Exhib Award, Philadelphia Watercolor Soc, 95-2000, Crest Award, 99; Grambacher Hall of Fame, 97. *Mem:* NJ Watercolor Soc (pres, 73-75); Am Artists Prof League; Hudson Valley Art Asn; Philadelphia Water Color Soc. *Media:* Watercolor, Oil. *Publ:* Palette Talk Mag, 83 & 97; Watercolor, Am Artist Publ, spring 93; The Best of Watercolor II & Painting Light and Shadow, Rockport Publ, 97; The Collected Best of Watercolor, 2002. *Mailing Add:* PO Box 287 Port Clyde ME 04855

LEWIS, PETER BENJAMIN
COLLECTOR
b Cleveland, Ohio, Nov 11, 1933. *Study:* Princeton Univ, AB, 55. *Pos:* pres, chief exec off, The Progressive Corp, Ohio, 65-2000, Mayfield Village, 65-94, chmn bd, 2000; trustee, Solomon R Guggenheim Mus, 93, chmn, 98. *Awards:* Named one of the Top 200 Collectors, ARTnews Mag, 2004. *Collection:* Contemporary art including American conceptual art. *Mailing Add:* Progressive Corp 6300 Wilson Mills Rd Cleveland OH 44143

LEWIS, RONALD WALTER
PAINTER, EDUCATOR
b Atlanta, Ga, Jan 27, 1945. *Study:* Ala Coll, BS (art & bus), 67. *Work:* Birmingham Mus Art, Ala; Fayette Art Mus, Ala; Jefferson State Col, Birmingham; Sylacauga Mus, Ala; Columbus Mus, Calif; Fine Art Mus of South, Mobile, Ala. *Exhib:* Ala Watercolor Soc, Birmingham Mus Art, 71-77; Dixieland Watercolor & Drawing Show, Montgomery Mus Art, Ala, 73; Watercolor USA, Springfield Art Mus, Mo, 73-74; Rocky Mountain Nat Watercolor, Golden, Colo, 76; Mainstreams, Marietta Coll, Ohio, 76-77; Southern Watercolor Soc, Nashville, Tenn, 77; and others. *Teaching:* Adj fac, Univ Montevallo. *Awards:* One hundred awards including Ala Watercolor Soc & Southern Watercolor Soc. *Bibliog:* Stevens (auth), Ronald Lewis Paintings, La Revue Mod, Paris, 9/73. *Mem:* Ala Watercolor Soc (vpres, 73-74); Birmingham Art Asn (mem bd, 76-); Southern Watercolor Soc; Am Watercolor Soc; signature mem, Am Watercolor Soc. *Media:* Acrylic, Oil, Watercolor. *Publ:* Illusr, My Country Roads & Pappa's Old Trunk, 11/81, Buck Publ co; Birmingham Mag, 7/83; Southern Accents Mag, winter 83; Artist's Mag, 4/90; Am Artist Mag, 3/97. *Dealer:* Dumonde Fine Art New York; Bryant Gallery New Orleans LA. *Mailing Add:* 2728 Ossa Wintha Dr Birmingham AL 35243

LEWIS, SAMELLA SANDERS
PAINTER, HISTORIAN
b New Orleans, La, Feb 27, 1924. *Study:* Hampton Inst, BS; Ohio State Univ, MA & PhD; Tunghai Univ, Taiwan; Fulbright fel, 62; Univ Southern Calif, 64-66; NY Univ Inst Fine Arts, 65; Hampton Univ, Va, LHD, 90. *Work:* Oakland Mus, Calif; Baltimore Mus Fine Arts; Va Mus Fine Arts, Richmond; High Mus, Atlanta, Ga; Atlanta Univ Mus Contemp Art. *Exhib:* Joseph Hirshhorn Collection, Palm Springs Mus, 69; Dimensions of Black, La Jolla Mus Art, 70; Two Generations of Black Artists, Calif State Univ, Los Angeles, 70; Smithsonian Inst Traveling Print Exhibs, 80-83; Print Club Invitational, Philadelphia, Pa, 83. *Collection Arranged:* Media, Style & Tradition - The California Artists, 81 & Wildlife Sculpture, A Bayou Heritage, 82, Calif Mus Afro-Am Hist & Cult; Artist-teachers, Univ Southern Calif, Santa Monica Place, 83; African Images in the New World, Los Angeles Calif, 83; Richard Hunt: Sculptures & Drawings, 86 & Jacob Lawrence: Paintings & Drawings, 89-91, Arts Am. *Pos:* Coordr educ, Los Angeles Co Mus Art, 69-70; ed-in-chief, Int Rev African-Am Art, 85; pres, Oxum Int, 87; art ed, Black Art Mag, 78. *Teaching:* Prof fine arts & head dept, Fla A&M Univ, 53-58; prof humanities & art hist, State Univ NY, 58-68; prof art hist, Scripps Col, 69, emer prof, 84-. *Awards:* NY State-Ford Found Grant, 65; Ford Found Research Grant, 81-82; Prof of Yr Award, Scripps Col, 84; Honor Award, Women's Caucus Art, 89. *Bibliog:* The Black Artists (film), Afrographics, 68; Focus, KNBC-TV, 68; article, Los Angeles Times, 70. *Mem:* Coll Art Asn Am; Nat Conf Artists (co-chairperson, 70-73). *Res:* African, Asian and Afro-American art. *Collection:* Rare African works, including Bakuba in the 1890's; Caribbean and African-American Works. *Publ:* Co-ed, Black Artists on Art, Vols I & II, 69 & 71; auth, Art: African American (textbk), Harcourt, 76; The Art of Elizabeth Catlett, Mus African Am Art, 84. *Dealer:* Alan S Lewis & Associates Fine Arts. *Mailing Add:* 1237 Masselin Ave Los Angeles CA 90019-2544

LEWIS, STANLEY
PAINTER
b 1940. *Study:* Wesleyan Univ, BA; Yale Univ, BFA, MFA. *Exhib:* Ecstasy and Silence, Del Coll Art & Design, 2000; Value and Presence, List Gallery, Swarthmore Coll, 2002; Member Show, Bowery Gallery, New York, 2003; Kazan Art Ctr, Am Univ Mus, Washington DC, 2007; Am Acad Arts & Letts Invitational, New York, 2009; Lohin Geduld Gallery, 2010. *Teaching:* Instr, Kans City Art Inst, 1969-86, Am Uni, Washington DC, Smith Coll, Mass, Parsons Sch Design, New York. *Awards:* Res & Training Grant, Smith Coll, 1987; Altman Prize, Nat Acad Design, 2002; Guggenheim Found Fel, 2005. *Dealer:* Lohin Geduld Gallery 531 W 25th St A New York NY 10001-5593. *Mailing Add:* c/o New York Studio School 8 W 8th St New York NY 10011

LEWIS, WILLIAM ARTHUR
PAINTER, EDUCATOR
b Detroit, Mich, Mar 20, 1918. *Study:* Coll Archit & Design, Univ Mich, BDesign, 48. *Work:* Butler Inst Am Art, Youngstown; Grand Rapids Mus Art; Univ Mich St Paul Art Ctr & Mus Art; Grinnell Coll. *Comn:* Acrylic paintings, Soc Mfg Engrs, Dearborn, Mich, 71 & Grand Rapids Jr Coll, 86; three portraits, 1st Unitarian Church, Ann Arbor, Mich, 90; watercolor, Zeppelin LZ4 over Landau, P Reusch Zeppelin Collection, Findlay, Ohio, 96; 2 pcs, US Navy Art Coll, 97; watercolor (steel indus), Pro Coil Coll, Canton, Mich, 98; 6 pcs, Mott Children's Hospital; U Mich, Ann Arbor, 2011; 2 pcs, Chelsea Community Hosp, Chelsea, Mich, 2012. *Exhib:* Five Ann Exhibs, Butler Inst Am Art, 54-65, 99; Drawing USA, Mus Mod Art, 56; Corcoran Gallery Biennial, Washington, & Am Fedn Art Tour, 57; solo exhibs, The Last Yr of the Civil War, Detroit Hist Soc, Mint Mus, Madison Coll, Va, Eastern Mich Univ, Dearborn Hist Mus & others, 62-65 & An Art Student in US Navy 1941-45, 43 watercolors & drawings, Clements Libr Am Hist Univ Mich, 95; Drawing USA, St Paul Art Ctr, 63 & 66; Romance of Transportation, 2 paintings, invited, Mich Art Train, 93-95; One Man's View: WWII through eyes of Bill Lewis (50 paintings, drawings), US Navy Hist Ctr, Washington, DC, 97; Fragments of the Great War, 1914-1918, Stamps Sch of Art and Design Univ Mich Ann Arbor, 19 paintings (of 47 acrylics and watercolors), 2015. *Pos:* Assoc dean, Sch Art, Univ Mich, Ann Arbor, 66-75 & 84-85; dir, Comn Accreditation, Nat Asn Schs Art, 72-75; chief reader, Advanced Placement Studio Art, Coll Bd-ETS, 78-81. *Teaching:* Prof art, Sch Art, Univ Mich, Ann Arbor, 57-86, prof emer, 85. *Awards:* Rackham Sch Grad Studies Fac Res Grants for Last Year of the Civil War, 60-62; JMW Turner, 64; Distinguished Alumnus, Univ Mich Sch Art, 93. *Bibliog:* Hazen Schumacher (auth), The Painting Professor, Univ Mich TV Studios, 62; Louise Bruner (auth), Feelings of an artist, Toledo Blade, 64; Joanne Nesbit (auth), War Painter, Univ Record, Univ Mich, 95; WWII Vet drawns to the past, AnnArbor.com, 5/23/2010. *Mem:* Fel Nat Asn Schs Art & Design; Mich Watercolor Soc. *Media:* Watercolor, Acrylics. *Res:* Photo hist. *Interests:* Urban & marine landscape of the Industrial Age, its wars & machines. Hist in photogr. *Collection:* 19th Century - early 20th century photography & stereographs of engineering, industrial, maritime & urban. *Publ:* Auth & illusr, The Civil War--A contemporary approach, Dimension, spring 62; illusr, cover & article, Limnos, summer 69. *Dealer:* River Gallery 121 Main St Chelsea MI 48118; Armstrong DeGraaf Fine Art 403 Water St Saugatuck MI 49453. *Mailing Add:* 2550 Traver Blvd Ann Arbor MI 48105

LEWIS, WILLIAM R
INSTRUCTOR, PAINTER
b Osceola, Iowa, Sept 23, 1920. *Study:* Drake Univ, BFA, 49; Univ Wash; Ariz State Univ, MA, 52. *Work:* Ariz Western Col, Yuma; Glendale Community Col, Ariz; Scottsdale Civic Ctr, Ariz; Valley Nat Bank, Phoenix, Ariz; Thunderbird Bank, Phoenix, Ariz; Southwest Savs, Phoenix, Ariz. *Exhib:* Ariz Ann, Phoenix Art Mus, 61-68; Butler Art Mus Ann Midyear Show, 62; Am Watercolor Soc Ann, 63-65; Southwestern Invitational, Yuma, 67-72; Watercolor USA Traveling Show, 68. *Teaching:* Chmn dept art, S Mountain High Sch, Phoenix, 54-81. *Awards:* Ariz Ann First in Watercolor, Phoenix Art Mus, 62. *Mem:* Ariz Watercolor Asn (pres, 63-64). *Media:* Watercolor. *Interests:* Collecting Jukeboxes and Radios. *Publ:* Prizewinning Watercolors, 64. *Mailing Add:* 313 E 15th St Tempe AZ 85281-6611

LEWTON, VAL EDWIN
PAINTER, DESIGNER
b Santa Monica, Calif, 1937. *Study:* Claremont Univ, Calif, MFA, 62. *Work:* Smithsonian Am Art Mus; Corcoran Gallery, Washington, DC; and others. *Comn:* Air shaft mural, DC Art Works, 88. *Exhib:* Ten Plus Ten, Corcoran Gallery Art, 82; solo exhibs, Plum Gallery, Kensington, Md, 83-85, Addison Ripley, Washington, DC, 90, 93 & 99; The Washington Show, Corcoran Gallery Art, 85; From the Anacostia to the

Potomac, WPA, Washington, DC, 89. *Collection Arranged:* Exhibition Designer for Robert Rauschenburg Retrospective, Nat Mus Am Art, 76; Decorative Designs of Frank Lloyd Wright, Renwick Gallery, 77; The Masterpieces of Louis Comfort Tiffany, Renwick Gallery, 89; Am in Paris, The Phillips Collection, 96; Calder-Miro the Phillips Coll, 2004; Jefferson's Academical Village, UVA Art Mus, 2009; Treasures Rediscovered, Chinese Sculpture, UVA Art Mus, 2010; Wedding Belles, Hillwood Mus, 2011; and others. *Pos:* Chief design & production, Nat Mus Am Art-Smithsonian Inst, 73-95. *Teaching:* Lectr art, Univ Calif, Riverside, 62-63 & Georgetown Univ, Washington, DC, 81-. *Awards:* Best in Exhib Design, Print Casebooks, 91-92. *Bibliog:* Harry Rand (auth), The watercolors of Val Lewton, Arts Mag, 5/80; and others. *Mem:* Am Asn of Mus. *Media:* Acrylic, Watercolor. *Publ:* Auth, Washington Review (column), 75-. *Dealer:* Addison Ripley Gallery 1670 Wisconsin Ave NW Washington DC 20007. *Mailing Add:* 1425 Manchester Ln Washington DC 20001

LEXIER, MICAH
SCULPTOR

b Winnipeg, Man, Nov 13, 1960. *Study:* Univ Man, Winnipeg, BFA, 82; Nova Scotia Coll Art & Design, Halifax, MFA, 84. *Work:* Art Gallery Ont, Toronto; Jewish Mus, NY; Vancouver Art Gallery, BC; The British Mus, London, England; Mus Contemp Art, Sydney, Aus; Nat Gallery Canada, Ottawa. *Comn:* Metro Hall, Toronto, 1992; Nat Trade Centre, Toronto, 97; Air Canada Centre, Toronto, 98; Agnes Etherington Art Ctr, Queens Univ, Kingston, Ontario, 1999; Toronto Transit Comn, Shepard/Leslie Subway Station, 00. *Exhib:* Un-Natural Traces, Barbican Art Gallery, London 91; Perspective 93, Art Gallery Ont, Toronto, 93; The Body as Measure, Davis Mus & Cult Ctr, Wellesley, Mass, 94; The Riddle of the Sphinx, Islip Art Mus, NY, 94; Alliances: The Family, Can Mus Contemp Photog, Ottawa, Ont, 94; Das Americas 11, Museu du Arte, de Sao Paulo, Brazil, 95; solo exhib, Open Studio Gallery, Toronto, Ont, 98, Robert Birch Gallery, Toronto, Ont, 98, McDonald Stewart Art Centre, Guelph (with catalog), 98, Charles H Scott Gallery, Emily Carr Inst Art & Design (with catalog), Vancouver, BC, 98, Dunlop Art Gallery (with catalog), Regina, Saskatchewan, 98, Musee de Art Contemp de Montreal, Quebec, 98, Trepanier Baer Gallery, Calgary, Whyte Mus Can Rockies, Banff, Alberta, Gitte Weise Gallery, Sydney, 99, Jack Shainman Gallery, NY, 99, Robert Birtch Gallery, Toronto, 2000, Agnes, Etherington Art Ctr Queen's U, Kingston, Ont, 2000, I Space Gallery Univ Ill, Chicago, 2000, Hallwalls, Buffalo, NY, 2000, Gitte Weise Gallery, Sydney, 2001, Gallery 111, (CD ROM), Univ Manitoba, Winnipeg, 2002, Jack Shainman Gallery, NY, 2003 & 05, Dazibao, Montreal, Quebec, 2004, Contemp Art Gallery, Vancouver, 2005, Michael Gibson Gallery, London, Ontario, 2006, Gitte Weise Galerie, Berlin, Germ, 2005 & 06; The World According to the Newest and Most Exact Observations, Tang Tchg Mus and Art Gallery, 2001; Light X Eight, The Jewish Mus, New York City, 2000; The Time of Our Lives, New Mus of Contemp Art, 1999; Making the Making, Apex Art, NY (brochure); Size Immaterial, Castle Mus, Norwich, Eng; Instant Criticism of Illusionism, Agnes Etherington Art Ctr, Kingston, Ontario; Open, Arcadia Univ Art Gallery, Glenside, Pa, 2004; Free Sample, Mt St Vincent Univ Art Gallery, Halifax, NS (catalogue), 2005; Funny Papers, Winnipeg Art Gallery, 2006. *Pos:* Bd mem, Eye Level Gallery, Halifax, NS, 84-86; organizer, Audio By Artists Festival, 84-86; bd mem, Power Plant, Toronto, 91-95. *Bibliog:* Robin Metcalfe (auth), Cross Reference, Confederation Ctr Art Gallery, 94; Michele Theriault (auth), Perspective 93, Art Gallery Ont, 93; M Fleming & N Tousley (auths), Book Sculpture, Oakville Galleries, 93; Sarah Milroy (auth), The art of brick and mortar, The Globe and Mail, Toronto, 11/3/2001; Eric Fredericksen (auth), Brick by Brick, Architecture Mag, NY, 3/2002; Michael Petry, Nicola Oxley & Nicolas de Oliveria (auths) Installation Art in the New Millennium, Thames & Hudson, 2003; Jerome Delgado (auth), Espaces Manipules, La Press, Montreal, Quebec, 10/21/2004; Christian Bok (auth), Still Counting, Canadian Art, (vol 22 no 1) Toronto, Ontario, Spring 2005; Gil McElroy, A Moment of Our Time: The Sculpture of Micah Lexier, Espace Sculpture (Issue #76), Montreal, Summer 2006. *Mem:* The Art Gallery of York Univ, Toronto, 1997 & 98 (bd mem); The Power Plant, Toronto, 1991-95 (bd mem); Eye Level Gallery, Halifax, 1984-86 (bd mem). *Media:* Sculpture. *Publ:* Co-ed (with Don Lander) Sound by artists, Art Metropole & Walter Phillips Gallery, spring 90; Making, Impulse, Vol 16, No 1, 91; Love Letters, Public 10, 94; An Artist & Books, Descant 90, The Book: Twenty Five Anniv, Part One, Vol 23, No 3, 95; A Minute of My Time, Gallery Largeness, Issue No 2, 10/96; If Then, Atopia Journal (issue 0.66), 2/2000; 9, 10, 11 Defile Vol 1 issue 1, Spring 2003; Lives & Works (4 consec texts), YYZ Mag, 5/2006. *Dealer:* Jack Shainman Gallery 560 Broadway 2nd Floor New York NY 10012; Birch Libralato 129 Tecumseth St Toronto Ontario M6J2H2; Trepanier Baer Gallery Suite 105 999 8th St SW Calgary Alberta T2R1J5; Gitte Weise Galerie Linienstrasse 154 Berlin Ger 10115. *Mailing Add:* 984 Queen St W 3rd Fl Toronto ON Canada

LEYRER, SHIRLEY D See Dani

LEYS, DALE DANIEL
EDUCATOR, DRAFTSMAN

b Sheboygan, Wis, Dec 10, 1952. *Study:* Yale Univ, 73; Layton Sch Art, Milwaukee, BFA, 74; Univ Wis, Madison, MA, 75, MFA, 77. *Work:* Evansville Mus Arts & Sci, Ind; Kentucky Fried Chicken, Louisville, Ky; A B Chandler Med Ctr, Lexington, Ky; Hyatt Regency Hotel, Frankfort, Ky; Hospital Corp Am, Nashville, Tenn; Budd Co, Shellbyville, Ky; Univ Ky, Mus Art; Nationsbank, Charlotte, NC. *Exhib:* Evansville Mus Arts & Sci, Ind, 77, 78 & 80; Ball State Univ Art Gallery, Muncie, Ind, 78 & 83; Rutgers Univ, NJ, 80; Greenville Mus, SC, 81; Davenport Mus, Iowa, 81; J B Speed Art Mus, Louisville, Ky, 82; Cheekwood Fine Arts Ctr, Nashville, Tenn, 84; Nat Drawing Invitational, Univ Tenn, Knoxville, 84 & Wake Forest Univ, Winston-Salem, NC, 88; Canton Art Inst, Ohio, 86; Univ SC, Columbia, 87; Univ Ark, Little Rock, 88; Marshall Univ, Huntington, WVa, 89; Dale Leys Recent Drawing, Heike Pickett Gallery, Lexington, Ky, 90; Univ Mo, Columbia, 92; Springfield Art Mus, Mo, 92. *Teaching:* Prof drawing, Murray State Univ, 77-. *Awards:* Drawing Award, State Univ NY, Potsdam, 77; Graphics Award, Mid States Exhib, Evansville Mus, 80; Purchase Award, Appalachian State Univ, Boone, NC, 83; 1986 Regional Competitive Exhib Award, Paducah, Ky, 86; Drawing Excellence Award, All Ky Art Exhibit, Lexington. *Bibliog:* Jerry Spieght (auth), Dale Leys: Ideas and his work, Sch Arts, 78 & Dale Leys, Art Voices S, 78; Dialogue Mag, 90; Art Papers, 91. *Media:* Mixed Media. *Mailing Add:* 1313 Lawson Ln Murray KY 42071-8203

LEYVA, ALICIA
PAINTER

b Mexico City, Mex, July 7, 1922. *Study:* Univ Nac de Mex; studies with Agapito Rincon Piña, 56-57; Inst Art de Mex, with Alfredo Guati Rojo, Erasto Leon Zurita & Manuel Arrieta, 72-74; studies with Fernando Casas, 77-79. *Work:* Patio de los Siete Príncipes, Oaxaca, Mex; Mus de la Zaragoza Alancón, Spain; Embajada de Mex, Madrid, Spain; Consulado de Mex, NY; La Pinacoteca de la Escuela Nac Preparatoria, Mexico City, Mex. *Comn:* Poster, Mex Red Cross. *Exhib:* Group exhibs throughout Mexico, 57-94; 31 solo exhibs, 69-94. *Teaching:* Imitation drawing, Inst Lestonac & Inst Asunción de Mex, formerly; art hist, Escuela Normal de Maestros; conferences & classes for 20 years. *Awards:* Medalla Sor, Juana Inés de la Cruz; Medalla Miembro, Fundador de las Bellas Artes de Mex; Pincel de Plata, Soc Acuarelistas. *Mem:* Soc Mexicana de Acuarelistas; Agrupación de Cataluña; Ky Watercolor Soc; AIPE-UNESCO. *Media:* Printed Literature. *Publ:* Illusr, History of Mexico, 58; Fomento Cultural de México; Artes de México, Arts & Artists Mag. *Mailing Add:* 3ra Cerrada San Bernabé No 42 San Jeronimo 10100 Mexico

LHOTKA, BONNY PIERCE
PAINTER

b La Grange, Ill, July 14, 1942. *Study:* Bradley Univ, BFA, 64. *Work:* United Banks, Rocky Mountain Energy, Midland Savings & Loan, Denver; First Nat Bank, Boise; Nat Conf State Legislations, Charles Swabb, IBM, US West United Air Lines, Johnson Space Ctr, Marriott Hotels. *Exhib:* Allied Artists Am, Nat Acad Design, NY, 74, 76 & 77; Nat Watercolor Soc, Palm Springs Desert Mus, Calif, 74-81; Am Watercolor Soc, Nat Acad Design, 77; Nat Acad Design Exhib, 77, 79 & 81; Solo exhib, Wyo State Art Gallery, Cheyenne, 79. *Teaching:* Instr abstract watermedia & acrylic, Colo Watercolor Soc, summer 77 & Colo Artist Workshops, summer 78. *Awards:* First Nat Top Ten, Am Artist Mag, 78; Strathmore Awards, Strathmore Paper Co, 79; Century Award of Merit, Rocky Mountain Watermedia Exhib, 81. *Mem:* Nat Watercolor Soc; Audubon Artists; Nat Soc Painters in Casein & Acrylics; Rocky Mountain Nat Watermedia Soc. *Media:* Watermedia; Acrylic. *Publ:* Contribr, Watercolor page, Am Artist Mag, 77; Watercolor, The Creative Experience by Nochis, North Light, 79; article, Southwest Art Mag,3/81; Creative Seascape Painting, Watson Guptill; The Guild 5, 6 & 7, Kraus Sikes Inc, Madison, Wis, 90-92. *Dealer:* Ruth Bachofnen Gallery 1926 Colorado Ave Santa Monica CA 90401. *Mailing Add:* c/o Jack Meier Gallery 2310 Bissonnet Houston TX 77005

LI, CHU-TSING
HISTORIAN

b Canton, China, May 26, 1920; US citizen. *Study:* Univ Nanking, China, BA (Eng Lit), 43; Univ Iowa, MA(Eng Lit), 49, PhD(art hist), 55; post-doctoral res, Harvard Univ, 59 & Princeton Univ, 60. *Pos:* Res cur, Nelson-Atkins Mus Art, Kansas City, 68-; vis prof fine arts, Chinese Univ, Hong Kong, 71-73, Grad Inst Art Hist, Nat Taiwan Univ, Taipei, 90-91; Andrew W Mellon vis prof fine arts, Univ Pittsburgh, Pa, 95. *Teaching:* From instr to prof art hist, Univ Iowa, Iowa City, 54-66; prof Oriental art, Univ Kans, Lawrence, 66-90, chmn, Dept Hist Art, 72-78, Judith Harris Murphy Distinguished prof art hist, 78-90, Judith Harris Murphy Distinguished Prof Art Hist Emer, 90-. *Awards:* Phi Tau Phi (Chinese Scholastic Hon Soc), Phi Beta Kappa (hon), Phi Beta Delta (Hon Soc Int Scholars). *Mem:* Coll Art Asn; Midwest Art Hist Soc; Asn Asian Studies. *Res:* Chinese painting of the Sung, Yuan, Ming, Ch'ing, and Modern Period. *Publ:* Auth, The Autumn Colors on the Ch'iao and Hua Mountains, 65 & A Thousand Peaks and Myriad Ravines: Drenwatz Collection, 74, Artibus Asiae; Liu Kuo-sung, Development of a Modern Chinese Artist, 69 & contribr, Five Chinese Painters: Fifth Moon Exhibition, 70, Nat Gallery Art, Taipei, Taiwan; auth, Trends in modern Chinese painting, Artibus Asiae, 79; ed, Chinese Scholar's Studio: Artistic Life in the Late Ming Period, London: Thames and Hudson, 87; ed, Artists and Patrons: Some Social and Economic Aspects of Chinese Painting, Seattle: Univ Wash Press, 89

LI, YING
PAINTER

Study: Anhui Teachers Univ, Hefei, China, 1977; Parsons Sch Design, New York, MFA, 1987. *Exhib:* Solo exhibs include Bowery Gallery, New York, 1990, 1992, 1994, Elizabeth Harris Gallery, New York, 1994, 1996, Cantor Fitzgerald Gallery, Haverford Coll, Pa, 1998, 2002, Marie Salant Neuberger Campus Ctr Gallery, Bryn Mawr Coll, Pa, 1999, ISA Gallery, Montecastello di Vibio, Italy, 1999, 2000, 2001, 2003, 2004, 2005, 2006, Painting Ctr, New York, 2001, 2004, 2006; group exhibs include Nat Young Artists Oil Painting Exhib & East China Regional Oil Painting Exhib, Nat Gallery Fine Art, Beijing, 1978-82, Int Calligraphy Exhib, 1989; Invitational, Bowery Gallery, 1987, 1988; Ann Invitational Exhib, Nat Acad Mus, New York, 1990, 1992, 1994, 2004 & 2008; Inaugural Group Show, Elizabeth Harris Gallery, New York, 1992, Works on Paper, 1993, Summer Group Exhib, 1993, January Exhib, 1995; Abstracted Reality, Tibor de Nagy Gallery, New York, 1993; Rhythm & Light, Painting Ctr, New York, 2000; Prospects: 6 Painters & the Landscape, Denise Bibro Gallery, New York, 2002; Work on Paper, Pa Acad Art, Philadelphia, 2003; Conversations in Paint, Painting Ctr New York, Andrews Gallery, Coll William & Mary, Va, Akus Gallery, Eastern Conn Univ & Cantor Fitzgerald Gallery, Haverford Coll, 2005. *Teaching:* Instr drawing & oil painting, Anhui Teachers Univ, 1977-81, asst prof fine arts, 1982-83; faculty, mem bd artistic develop, Int Sch Art, Umbria, Italy, 1999-; vis asst prof fine arts, Haverford Coll, Pa, 1997-2000, asst prof fine arts, 2000-2002, assoc prof fine arts, 2002-, chair fine arts dept, currently. *Awards:* Henry Ward Ranger Fund Purchase Award, Nat Acad, 2008. *Mailing Add:* 201 E 28th St Apt 7M New York NY 10016

LI-LAN
PAINTER
b New York, NY, Jan 28, 1943. *Study:* HS Performing Arts, New York. *Work:* Guild Hall Mus, E Hampton, NY; Ohara Mus Art, Kurashiki, Japan; Parrish Art Mus, Southampton, NY; William Benton Mus Art, Storrs, Conn; Heckscher Mus, Huntington, NY; The Sezon Mus Art, Karuizawa, Japan; Va Mus Fine Arts, Richmond; Weatherspoon Art Gallery, Univ NC, Greensboro; Ark Arts Ctr, Little Rock; Werner Kramarsky Coll, New York; Baltimore Mus Art, Baltimore, Md; San Diego Mus Art, San Diego, Calif; Am Embassy, Beijing, China. *Exhib:* Solo exhibs, Robert Miller Gallery, New York, 79, Nantenshi Gallery, Tokyo, Japan, 71, 74, 77, 80, 85, Asher/Faure Gallery, Los Angeles, 80, 82, O K Harris Gallery, New York, 83, 85 & 87, Franz Bader Gallery, Washington, DC, 89, William Benton Mus Art, Storrs, Conn, 90, Lung Men Art Gallery, Taipei, Taiwan, 93, Art Proj Int, New York, 94 & 96, Lin & Keng Gallery, Taipei, Taiwan, 95, 97, 2001 & 2006, Rutgers Univ, New Brunswick, NJ, 2002, Nabi Gallery, New York, 2004 & Jason McCoy Inc, New York, 2006, Jason McCoy Inc, New York, 2006, 2009; William Benton Mus Art, Storrs, Conn, 90; group exhibs, Yun Gee and Li-lan: Paintings by a Father & Daughter, Southampton Campus Fine Arts Gallery, Long Island Univ, NY, 1988, PS 1 Mus, New York, 92, New Mus Contemp Art, New York, 94, Ar Embassies Prog, US Dept State, Brussels, 2000, Taipei, Taiwan, 2000, The Parrish Art Mus, Southampton, NY, 2000, Guild Hall Mus, East Hampton, NY, 2000 & Lin & Keng Gallery, Beijing, China, 2007, 2008, Experiences of Passage: The Paintings of Yun Gee & Li-lan, Jason McCoy Inc, New York, 2008; Tina Key Gallery, Taipei, Taiwan, 2010. *Awards:* Artists Grant, Artists Space, NY, 88 & 90. *Bibliog:* David Ebony (auth), review, Art Am, 2/95; Phyllis Braff (auth), NY Times, 10/29/95; Alice Yang (auth, catalog), Art Projects International, 10/96; Joyce Brodsky (auth, catalog), 2001; Robert Berlind (auth), rev, Art in America, 1/2005; Peter Frank (auth), Two Exhibitions, Doublevision & Nabi, NY & Los Angeles, 2003-2004; Carter Ratcliff (auth, catalog), 2006; Scarlet Cheng (auth, catalog), 2006; Christine Kim (auth, cataglog), 2006; Tunghsiao Chou (auth, catalog). *Mem:* Artists Equity. *Media:* Oil, pastel, watercolor. *Interests:* writing, photography. *Publ:* Auth, Canvas with an Unpainted Part, An Autobiography, Asahi Newspaper Publishing, Tokyo, 76; Joyce Brodsky (auth), Experiences of Passage: The Paintings of Yun Gee and Li-lan 2008, Univ Wash Press, Seattle. *Dealer:* Jason McCoy Inc 41 E 57th St 11th Fl New York NY 10022; Tina Keng Gallery 1F No11 Lane 252 Sect1 Tunhua S Road Taipei 106 Taiwan. *Mailing Add:* 1F No 15 Ln Ruiguang Rd, Neihu Dist Taipei Taiwan

LIANG, LANBO See Leong, Lampo

LIAO, FRANK
PAINTER, CALLIGRAPHER
Study: Guangzhou Yangcheng Painting Art Sch; Studied with Li Rukuang. *Work:* Truewell Art Gallery, Flushing, NY; Confucious Gallery, NY; Hammond Mus, North Salem, NY; Salmagundi Club, NY. *Comn:* Peony Chinese painting, 86; Flower and Bird painting, GuangZhou, 88, 2009; Peony and Bee Chinese painting, Singapore, 96; landscape ink painting, Brooklyn, NY, 99. *Exhib:* Audubon Artists Ann, Salmagundi Club, NY, 2007, 2011. *Teaching:* instr Chinese painting, Maggie Studio Inc, 2010-2011. *Awards:* Marquis Who's Who in American Art References Award in Aquamedia, Audubon Artists, New York, 2011. *Mem:* New York Ling Nan Style Painting Soc; New York Int Chinese Art Asn; Am Soc Chinese Calligraphy; Audubon Artist Asn; Int Chinese Soc Photo and Art. *Media:* Watercolor, Chinese Painting. *Interests:* Stone Stamp Carving, Calligraphy. *Mailing Add:* 338 Van Sicklen St Brooklyn NY 11223

LIAO, SHIOU-PING
PAINTER, PRINTMAKER
b Taipei, Taiwan, Sept 2, 1936. *Study:* Nat Taiwan Normal Univ, Taipei, BA, 59; Tokyo Univ Educ, Japan, MA, 64; Ecole Nat Superienredes Beaux Arts, Paris, 65-68. *Work:* Nat Mus Mod Art, Tokyo, Japan; Victoria & Albert Mus, London, Eng; Musee Municipal d'Art Mod, Paris, France; Cincinnati Art Mus, Ohio; New York Pub Libr; Metrop Mus Art, NY. *Comn:* Mural, Cathy Hospital, Taipei, 76; mural, Howard Plaza Hotel, Taipei, 83. *Exhib:* Salon de Mai & Salon d'Antonne, Musee Municipal d'Art Mod, Paris, France, 68; Nat Print, Brooklyn Mus, NY, 70; Solo exhibs, Taft Mus, Cincinnati, 70, Calif Palace Legion Honor, San Francisco, 73, Mus Mod Art, Liege, Belg, 92 & Taiwan Mus Art, 92; Int Print Biennial, Nat Mus Mod Art, Tokyo, Japan, 70; Oversize Print, Whitney Mus Am Art, NY, 71; Int Print Exchange Exhib, Mus Art, Soeul, Korea, 79; Five from the Orient, Bergen Co Mus, Paramus, NJ, 81. *Collection Arranged:* Paintings by Leading Overseas Artist (auth, catalog), Hong Kong Mus Art, 82; Contemporary Printmaking Asn (auth, catalog), Singapore, 82; The Art of Shiou-ping Liao, Taiwan Mus Art, 92. *Teaching:* Vis prof printmaking, Tsukuba Univ, Japan, 77-79; Daemen Col, Amherst, NY, 78; adj prof painting & printmaking, Seton Hall Univ, NJ, 79-; vis prof, Nanjing Inst Art, Spring 91. *Awards:* Silver Medal, Salon des Artistes Francais, Paris, 65; De Cordova Mus Purchase Prize, Boston Printmaker Show, 71. *Bibliog:* The Art of Shiou-ping Liao, Taiwan Mus Art, 92. *Mem:* Soc Am Graphic Artists; Chinese Graphic Soc Taipei (bd dir, 74). *Media:* Mixed Media; Watercolor, Oil. *Publ:* Auth, The Art of Printmaking, 74 & Appreciation of Modern Prints, 76, Taipei Lion Art Book Co. *Mailing Add:* 284 Center St Englewood Cliffs NJ 07632-1601

LIBBY, GARY RUSSELL
MUSEUM DIRECTOR, AUTHOR
b Boston, Mass, June 7, 1944. *Study:* Univ Fla, studied with Jerry Uelsmann, AA, BA, studied with Philip Hultman, MA; Tulane Univ, studied with Leo Steinberg, MA with Jesse Poesch. *Collection Arranged:* Audubon: Birds & Animals, 75, The Third Empire Porcelains and Silver, 77 & Artistic Taste in Pre-Castro Cuba, (auth, catalog), 77, Mus Arts & Sci, Daytona Beach, Fla; 400 Years of Prints, Eight Cuban Masters, Sampson Hall Gallery, Stetson Univ, Deland, Fla, 77; Salon & Picturesque Photography in Cuba, 89; Chihuly: Form from Fire, 93; Celebrating Florida (auth, catalog), 95; Adams Rib: Sexual Mythology and The Roles of Women in Art, 97; Coast to Coast: The Contemporary Landscape in Florida (auth, catalog), 98; Dali over Daytona Paintings, Sculpture, Works on Paper by Salvador Dali, 2000; Young Am, 2001; Reflections I: Painting, 2009; Reflections II: Watercolors, 2012. *Pos:* Dir, Mus Arts & Sci, Daytona Beach, Fla, 77-2001, dir emer, 2001-; Dir 2003-2005; mem, Fla Arts Coun, 2005-2007, Cult Coun Volusia County, 2009-11; pres, Heritage Preservation Trust, 2007-2008; chair, Art & Entertainment, Halifax Area Advertising Authority & Volusia ECHO; mem, City of Daytona Beach Bd of Adjustment; trustee, Stetson Univ, Fla, 2008-2011; trustee, Univ Fla Found, Gainesville, Fla, 2012. *Teaching:* Instr, Tulane Univ, New Orleans, La, 68-71; asst prof humanities-art hist, Stetson Univ, 72-73, asst prof art hist surv, 72-77, vis prof, 77-85. *Awards:* Lifetime Achievement Award, Fla Asn Mus, 98; Lifetime Achievement Award, Fla Art Dirs Asn, 2000. *Mem:* Southeast Coll Art Conf; Coll Art Conf; Coll Art Asn; Am Asn Mus; Fla Mus Asn; Fla Art Mus Dirs Asn (pres-elect, 95-97); Fla Arts Coun (mem, 2005-2007). *Res:* Latin American: Cuban and Caribbean, 19th century English and American painting; Pre-Columbian ceramics; Florida art. *Collection:* Pre-Columbian, etchings, engravings, 19th century painting; Florida Art 19th-20th C. *Publ:* Ed, Alexander Archipenko: Themes and Variations, Mus Arts & Sci, Daytona Beach, Fla, 90; Treasury of Indian Miniature Painting, 93; Cuba: A History in Art, 98; ed, Celebrating Florida...Works of Art from the Vickers Collection, 95; auth, Coast to Coast: The Contemporary Landscape in Florida, 99 (Gold Medal, SEMC); Treasury of American Art, 2003; Reflections, Paintings of Florida 1865-1965, 2009; Reflections II Watercolors of Florida 1845-2012. *Mailing Add:* 723 N Oleander Ave Daytona Beach FL 32118

LIBEERT, MIMI & FILIEP J
COLLECTOR
b Belgium, 1953. *Pos:* Chmn, Libeltex (originally A Libeert & Sons), Belgium, 1990-; pres, Belgian Textile Fedn (Febeltex), 1998-2001 & European Apparel & Textile Org (Euratex), 2002-07, hon pres, 2007-; bd dirs, Brit Vita plc, currently; former independent non-executive dir, Picanol NV. *Awards:* Named one of Top 200 Collectors, ARTnews mag, 2008, 2010-13. *Collection:* Modern and contemporary art. *Mailing Add:* Euratex 24 rue Montoyer Bte 10 Brussels B-1000 Belgium

LIBESKIND, DANIEL
ARCHITECT
b Poland, 1946; naturalized, US. *Study:* Cooper Union, 70; Sch Comparative Studies, Essex, Eng, 72. *Hon Degrees:* Humboldt Univ, Berlin, Hon Dr, 97; Essex Univ, Eng, Hon Dr, 99; Univ Edinburgh, Hon Dr, 2002; DePaul Univ, Hon Dr, 2002; Univ Toronto, Hon Dr, 2004. *Work:* Victoria & Albert Mus, London, 96-; Jewish Mus, San Francisco, 98-; Jewish Mus, Berlin, 99; Felix Nussbaum Mus, Osnabrueck, 99; Westside Shopping & Leisure Ctr, Brunnen, Switz, 2001-; Imperial War Mus North, Manchester, Eng, 2002; German Military Mus, Dresden, 2002-; World Trade Ctr site, 2003-; London Metrop Univ, Grad Student Ctr, 2004; Dali Mus, Prague, 2004; Danish Jewish Mus, 2004; Bar Ilan Univ, Wohl Conv Ctr, Tel Aviv, 2005; Denver Art Mus, 2006. *Pos:* Head dept archit, Cranbrook Acad, 78-85; head, Inst Archit & Planning, Milan, Ital, 86-89; architect, Berlin, 90-2003 & NY, 2003-; designer, sets & costumes, Tristan, Opera Saarbrueken, 2001 & St Francis Assisi, Berlin Opera, 2003; cultural ambassador archit, CultureConnect Prog, US Dept State; Sr scholar, John Paul Getty Ctr; scholar, Royal Danish Acad & Am Israel Cultural Found. *Teaching:* Louis Sullivan prof, Chicago; Bannister Fletcher prof, Univ London; Louis Kahn prof, Yale Univ; Frank O'Gehry Ch, Univ Toronto; Cret ch, Univ Pa; guest prof, Harvard Univ, UCLA & Hochschule Weisensee, Ger. *Awards:* Golden Lion, Venice Biennale, 85; Award for Architecture, Am Acad Arts & Letters, 96; Citizen of Berlin Culture Prize, 96; Goethe Medallion for Cultural Contribution, 2000; Hiroshima Art Prize, 2001. *Mem:* European Accad Arts & Letters; Accad Arts; Fedn German Architects. *Publ:* auth, The Space of Encounter, Universe, 2001; auth, Breaking Ground: Adventures in Life & Architecture, Riverhead Books, 2004. *Mailing Add:* Studio Daniel Libeskind 2 Rector St 19th Fl New York NY 10006

LICCIONE, ALEXANDER
PAINTER, GRAPHIC ARTIST
b Rochester, NY, Jan 28, 1948. *Study:* Acad di Belle Art di Brera Milan, Italy Fine Art Int, 69-72; Fla Atlantic Univ, Boca Raton, BFA, 78. *Work:* Pvt collection, Brescia & Melfi (Potenza), Italy; (murals), CitiBank, NY; (ceramic statues), Dime Bank, NY; New Sch for Soc Res, NY Pub Libr, Avalanche Pictures, Financial Guaranty Ins Co, Cathedral Preparatory Seminary, NY; Teatro Contadino, Naples, Italy; ABC TV; Casa Argentina en Jerusalem Embassy, Israel; The Am War Libr Mus, Gardena, Calif; Academia Di Belle Arti Di Brera, Milan, Italy; Church and Friary of St Francis of Assis Chapel, New York; Alaska Aviation Heritage Mus; Blessed Kateri Tekakwitha, Catholic Church, New York; Beautiful Life, Drama TV Studio Stages, New York. *Comn:* TV announcer's box, Yankee Stadium; La Campagna Ristorante (Little Italy), NY, 93; Cent Properties Movie & Theatrical Co, NY, 93-94; murals, Limoncello/The Grotto, NY, 96; Am War Libr Mus, Gardenia, Calif, 2002. *Exhib:* Comedy Central, Harvard Lampoon, NY, 90; Comedy Central, ABC, NBC, CBS, and Universal Pictures, 90-2011; ABC TV, NBC TV, CBS TV, Universal Pictures & Guiding Light Soap Opera 90-2010; Apollo Prod, Comedy Hour, 93; NBC TV, Saturday Night Live, David Letterman, Conan O'Brien, NY, 90-2009; Michael Ingbar Gallery, NY, 93-98; Universal Film TV, Law & Order, NY, 93-2010; Instituto De Artes Visuais, Lisbon, Portugal, 94; Sex & the City, HBO, 2001; Sopranos, HBO, 2003; Special Victims Unit, 2003-2011; Two Weeks Notice (movie), Castle Rock Pictures, 2003; The Jury, 20th Century Fox, 2004; Rescue Me, Canterbury Prods, 2004-2010; The Webster Project, Warner Bros, 2005-9; MTV Networks, 2005-2011; Righteous Kill (film), 2007; The Taking of Pelham 123 (film), 2008; Cupid (film), 2008; I Hate Valentine's Day (film), 2008; Damages (tv show), 2008; Step-Up 3D (movie), 2009; Morning Glory (movie), Paramount, 2009; Son of No One, 2010; The Other Guys, 2009; Good Wife, TV, CBS, 2009-2011; Beautiful Life, TV Drama, 2009; Empire State, TV Movie, ABC, 2009; Arthur, Movie, Warner Bros, 2010; NBC TV, Saturday Night Live, 90-2011; Men in Black 3, Movie, 2011; New Years Eve, Movie, 2011;

Weekends at Bellevue, Movie, 2011; White Collar, Tv Series, 2010-2011; Unforgetable, TV Series, 2011; The Big C, 2012; Golden Boys, 2012; The Good Wife, 2012; Elementary, 2012; White Collar, 2012; Nicolodeon, 2012; Are we Officially Dating, 2013; The Following, 2013; Wolf of Wall St, 2013; Ironside, 2013. *Teaching:* Painting workshop, Ctr for the Arts, Vero Beach, Fla, 96. *Bibliog:* Am References Inc, Chicago, 87-90; Am Biog Inst, 91 & 92; Vincenzo Tanzj (auth), Antologia Dei Poettie D'Artisti Italiani, Rizzoli Publ, 95; Ricreatori Dell 'Abiente, 95. *Media:* Oil, Watercolor. *Publ:* Auth, Stereo (3-D) realism in oil, Nat Stereo World Mag. *Dealer:* Michael Ingbar Gallery 568 Broadway New York NY 10012. *Mailing Add:* 4 Heritage Lane Lagrangeville NY 12540

LICHACZ, SHEILA ENIT
PAINTER
b Monagrillo, Panama, Oct 9, 1942; US & Panamanian citizen. *Study:* Our Lady of the Lake Univ, San Antonio, Tex, BS, 65; Inter-Am Univ, PR, MA (educ), 68. *Work:* Palm Springs Desert Mus, Calif; Vatican Mus, Mus Contemp Religious Art, Vatican, 83; Vanidades Gallery, Miami, Fla, 92; Holyshrine of First Miracle, Cana in Galilee, Israel, 98; Domus Galilenea, Galilee, Isreal, 98 & 2005; St Saviour's Monastery, Old Jerusalem, Israel, 99; Franciscan Monastery/Meml Ch of Holy Land, Washington, DC, 2001; Our Lady of Mt Carmel Church, Panama City, Panama, 2005. *Comn:* Painting, presented to King Juan Carlos of Spain by Panamanian Govt; painting, presented to Pope John Paul II by Panamanian Govt, 83; painting, presented to president of Peru by Panamanian Govt, 86. *Exhib:* Solo exhibs, Feingarten Galleries, Los Angeles, 89, Arnold & Mabel Beckman Ctr, Nat Acads Sci & Eng, Irvine, Calif, 89, Art Gallery, Miami Herald, Fla, 92, Art Gallery, Dudley House, Harvard Univ, Cambridge, Mass, 93, Ctr Fine Arts, Miami, Fla, 94, Art Mus Am, Washington, 96, Cath Univ Santa Maria La Antigua, Panama City, 2002 & Smithsonian Ctr Latino Initiatives, Washington, DC, 2002-03; Expresion Plastica Latinoamerica, Habitante Gallery, Panama City, Panama, 90; Rediscovering the Americas, Bacardi Art Gallery, Miami, Fla, 91; The Spirit of Faith in Painting, Sculpture & Jewelry, Am Cath Mus, NY, 92; Exposicion Jerusalem: Taller Creativo de Artistas de America Latina y Miami Fla, Jerusalem Munic Art Gallery, 96; Rediscovering the Americas, Bacardi Art Gallery, Miami, Fla, 91; Segundo Salon de Artes Iberoamericano, Inst Mex dea Artes, La Asn de Agregados Culturales, Wash, DC, 93; Ctr Fine Arts, Miami Art Mus, Summit Americas, Fla, 94; Art Mus Am, Washington DC, 96; Art Gallery Brikel Ave, Miami, Fla, 97 & 98; The First Int Loan Exhib, Smithsonian Inst, Washington, DC, 97; Latin Artists visit Jerusalem, Fla Mus Hisp & Latin Am Art, Miami, Fla, 97; Ibero Am Traveling/Touring Art Show, Cult Inst Israel, 99; Espacio Venezuela Gallery, Miami Fla, 2001; Francisco De Paula Santander Gallery, Miami, Fla, 2002; Weisman Mus Art, Pepperdine Univ, Malibu, Calif, 2005. *Pos:* ambassador at large, Republic of Panama, 95-; vpres (special mission), Universidad Catolica, Santa Maria, La Antigua. *Awards:* Hispanic Achievement Award, Chicago, Ill, 96; Outstanding Alumna of Year (Awarded for Service to the Profession), Our Lady of the Lake Univ, San Antonio, Tex, 85. *Bibliog:* Ralph Luce (auth), Sheila Lichacz, Artist, Santa Fean Mag, 7/90; David Briggs (auth), Inspired works, Assoc Press, 20/3/92; Tara B Reddy (auth), Constructing religious faith through fragments of the past, Harvard Crimson, 2/18/93; Philip Eliasord (auth), Sheila E Lichacz, the spirit and soul of Latin America (catalog), 12/94; Fr James Heinsch (auth), God;s Paintbrush, Holyland, spring 99. *Media:* Pastel, Oil, Pre-Columbian Montage

LICHAW, PESSIA
PRINTMAKER, ARCHITECT
Study: Technion Tel-Aviv, Israel, BA, 64; Betzalel Acad, Jerusalem, 69-70; Art Students League, 76-80. *Work:* Jerusalem Mus; Art Students League, NY. *Comn:* Images reproduced, Marriott Hotel, Tex, 84, Hyatt Hotel, NY, 86 & Sheraton Hotel, Philadelphia, Pa, 88; Originals, Gurneys Inn, Montauk, NY, 87 & City Bank, NY, 88-90. *Exhib:* Duke Univ, NC, 80; Queens Mus, NY, 82; Gallery Sho, Tokyo, 87; Artful Framer, Honolulu, 90; Nassau Mus, Long Island, NY, 92-93. *Pos:* Architect, currently. *Awards:* Purchase Prize & Merit Scholar, 77; Mem prize, Nat Asn Women Artists, 84; 1st Prize, Nassau Mus, 93. *Bibliog:* Malcolm Preston (auth), Five approaches to graphics, Newsday, 2/7/80; Jeanne Paris (auth), Glen Cove's a gallery, Newsday, 4/18/80; Helen A Harrison (auth), Many shades of white, New York Times, 1/11/81. *Mem:* Nat Asn Women Artists; Artist Network Great Neck; Printmaking Workshop, NY; Art Students League, NY. *Media:* Monoprints

LICHTENSTEIN, MIRANDA
PHOTOGRAPHER
b New York, 1969. *Study:* Sch Art Inst Chicago, San Miguel de Allende, Mex City, 1989; Sarah Lawrence Coll, BA, 1990; Calif Inst Arts, MFA (Merit Scholar Award in Photog), 1993; Claude Monet Found, Giverny, France, Giverny Residency Prog & Fel, 2002. *Work:* Hirshhorn Mus & Sculpture Garden, Washington; Solomon R Guggenheim Mus, New York; New Mus Contemp Art, New York. *Exhib:* Solo exhibs include Three Day Weekend, LA, 1997, Steffany Martz Gallery, New York, 1998, LACE, 1999, Goldman Tevis, LA, 2000, 2001, Leslie Tonkonow, New York, 2001, Whitney Mus at Phillip Morris, New York, 2001, Dee/Glasoe, New York, 2002, Gallery Min Min, Tokyo, 2003, 2004, 2005, 2007, Mary Goldman Gallery, LA, 2003, 2006, Elizabeth Dee Gallery, New York, 2003, 2005, 2007, Hammer Mus, LA, 2006; group exhibs include Video Lounge, Art in General, New York, 1994; Spectacular Optical, Mus Contemp Art, Miami & Thread Waxing Space, New York, 1998; Playing Off Time, Adrich Mus Contemp Art, Ridgefield, Conn, 1999; Monster, Gracie Mansion, New York, 2000; Altoids Collection, New Mus Contemp Art, New York, 2001; Painting/Not Painting, White Columns, New York, 2001; Detourism, Renaissance Soc, Univ Chicago, 2001; Guide to Trust No 2, Yerba Buena Ctr Arts, San Francisco, 2002; Teenage Rebel, John Connelly Projects, New York, 2003; Afternoon Delight, Caren Golden Fine Art, New York, 2003; Currents: Recent Acquisitions, Hirshhorn Mus & Sculpture Garden, Washington, 2007. *Dealer:* Mary Goldman Gallery 932 Chung King Rd Los Angeles CA 90012. *Mailing Add:* c/o Elizabeth Dee 545 W 20th St New York NY 10011

LIDDELL, SIOBHAN
SCULPTOR
b Worksop, UK, 1965. *Study:* St Martins Sch Art, London, BFA, 1986. *Exhib:* Solo exhibs include Trial Balloon Gallery, New York, 1992, Thread Waxing Space, New York, 1993, Galerie Eric Dupont, Toulouse, France, 1995 & 2005, CRG Gallery, New York, 1999, 2002 & 2006, Hammer Mus, Univ Calif Los Angeles, 2000, Henry Moore Inst, Leeds, 2001; group exhibs include Witness Against Our Vanishing, Artists Space, New York, 1990; The Spatial Drive, New Mus, New York, 1992; Behind Bars, Thread Waxing Space, New York, 1992, Oh Shyness, 1993; Selections, Drawing Ctr, New York, 1993; Paula Cooper Gallery, New York, 1994; Biennial Exhib, Whitney Mus Am Art, New York, 1995; New Work, Hosfelt Gallery, San Francisco, 1999; Vapor, Marianne Boesky Gallery, New York, 2002; Bunch Alliance & Dissolve, Contemp Arts Ctr, Cincinnati, 2006 & 2007; Looking Back, White Columns, New York, 2006. *Dealer:* Galerie Eric Dupont 13 rue Chapon 73003 Paris France. *Mailing Add:* c/o CRG Gallery 535 W 22nd St New York NY 10011

LIDEN, HANNA
PHOTOGRAPHER
b Stockholm, Sweden, 1976. *Study:* Parsons Sch Design, NYC, BFA, 2002. *Exhib:* Group exhibs, You're Just a Summer Love but I'll Remember You When Winter Comes, 2005; Be In, The Volta Show, 2006; Noctambule, NYC, The Whitney Biennial, Whitney Mus Art, NYC, 2006; solo exhib, And in Her Shadow Death, Rivington Arms Gallery, NYC

LIEBER, EDVARD
PAINTER, FILMMAKER
b Rockville Centre, NY, Apr 11, 1948. *Study:* Manhattan Sch Mus, 66-68; Sch Visual Arts, New York, BFA, 76; studies with Robert Mangold & Richard Artschwager. *Work:* Mus Mod Art, NY; Ga Mus Art, Athens; Guild Hall Mus, East Hampton, NY; Chase Manhattan Bank, NY; Miele Corp, Guttersloh, Ger; Heckscher Mus Art, Huntington, NY. *Exhib:* Edvard Lieber Recent Work, Jason McCoy Gallery, NY, 1989; New York Collection 91-92, Albright-Knox Gallery, 91; The Perfect Likeness, Albany Mus Art, Ga, 93; Children in Crisis, Munchausen Mus, Goslar, Ger, 94; What's New, Heckscher Mus Art, Huntington, NY, 2000; Frontiers, Galería d'Art Horizon, Girona, Spain, 2004; Time and Chance, Galería d'Art Horizon, Girona, Spain, 2008; Acquisitions, Guild Hall Mus, East Hampton, NY, 2009-10; Horizon & 20, Galeria d'Art Horizon, Girona, Spain, 2012; Elaine de Kooning Portrayed, Pollock-Krasner House, East Hampton, NY, 2015. *Pos:* secy & cur to Elaine de Kooning, 82-89; secy & cur to Willem de Kooning 87-89. *Teaching:* Instr music & arts, Sch Visual Arts NY, 78-08; asst prof art hist, Cooper Union, NY, 93; instr masters of light, Sch Visual Arts, NY, 2001-03. *Awards:* NEA Solo Recitalist Award, 81; NY State Coun on the Arts award, 83; NY Found for the Arts Award, 93, 94; Found for Contemp Performance Arts, NY, 99. *Bibliog:* Mary Rawson (producer), Lyceum: Edvard Lieber, WQED-TV, 1/2/80; Amei Wallach (auth), Older works in a new light: Cy Twombly, Al Held, Edvard Lieber, Newsday, 1/26/90; Lawrence Campbell (auth), Edvard Lieber, Art in America, 7/90; Phyllis Braff (auth), Range of Interpretation of the Intuitive, NY Times, 11/30/1997; Dore Ashton (auth), Just Because I Don't Say Something, Mod Painters, winter 2000; Eudald Camps (auth), Forbidden Art, Diari de Girona, 7/2/2004; Ken Johnson (auth), A Painter and Places, NY Times, 8/7/2015. *Media:* Mixed Media. *Publ:* Contribr, Elaine de Kooning: Her world and persona, Christie's Newslett, 89; contribr, one Man Two Visions, Pergamon Press, 93; The 1940's, Washburn Gallery, 93; Willem de Kooning: Reflections in the Studio, Harry N Abrams Inc, 2000; Dear Jackson Pollock, Pollock-Krasner House, 2003; Elaine de Kooning Portrayed, Pollock-Krasner House, 2015. *Dealer:* Ekstrom & Ekstrom 417 E 75 St New York NY 10021; Galería d'Art Horizon Francese Ribera 22 E-17469 Colera Girona Spain

LIEBER, LOLA
ARTIST, GALLERY DIRECTOR
b Mukacevo, Czech (raised in Krakow, Poland), Mar 15, 23 (Holocaust Survivor), 1923. *Study:* Special study with John Pike, 74; Studies with Stefan Locos, 78. *Work:* Yad Vashem Holocaust Mus, Israel; San Francisco Mus Art; Lowdens Veterans Mus, Las Vegas; Kings Co Med Ctr, Brooklyn; SCC Libr, Brooklyn. *Exhib:* Portrait, Kings Co Med Ctr, Brooklyn, 65; Gordon Gallelry, Tel Viv, Israel, 72; Portrait, Ohr Somayach Educ Ctr, Monsey, NY, 95; Ghetto Scenery (portrait), Baby Togs Inc, New York, 99; and various other galleries, New York. *Bibliog:* Berger (auth), Bina Mag, Hamodia; Jewish Press, 65; Sullivan Co Democrat. *Media:* Oil, Watercolor, Woodcut, Restoration, Gallery Director, Art Dealer. *Dealer:* Lola's Art Gallery 4813 16th Ave Brookyln NY 11204. *Mailing Add:* 1530 54th St Brooklyn NY 11219

LIEBER, THOMAS ALAN
PAINTER
b St Louis, Mo, Nov 5, 1949. *Study:* Univ Ill, BFA, 71, MFA, 74. *Work:* Guggenheim Mus, Mus Mod Art, New York; San Francisco Mus Mod Art; Los Angeles Mus Mod Art; Tate Gallery, London; Cleveland Art Mus. *Exhib:* New Perspectives in Am Painting, Guggenheim Mus, 78-88; The Aesthetics of Grafitti, San Francisco Mus Mod Art, Calif, 78, Fresh Paint, 82; San Francisco Bay Area Paintings, Univ Nebr, Lincoln, 84; Contemp Am Monotypes, Chrysler Mus, Norfolk, Va, 85; Maine Collects, Farnsworth Mus, Rockland, Maine, 89; monotype, Tate Gallery, London, 94; Farnsworth Mus, Rockland, Maine, 2000; Hackett Freedman Gallery, San Francisco, 2003-2004. *Teaching:* Vis prof, Stanford Univ, 89 & Vt Studio Sch, Johnson, Vt. *Awards:* Nat Endowment Arts, 75; Invited Artist, Trillium Press, 2002. *Bibliog:* Robert McDonald (auth), Physically finds its place, 76 & Tom Liebers environmental paintings, 77, Art Week; John Russell (auth), Younger Americans, NY Times, 83. *Mem:* Nat Acad (acad, 94-). *Media:* Oil, Watercolor. *Dealer:* John Berggruen 228 Grant San Francisco CA; Friesen Gallery Seattle WA. *Mailing Add:* 2319 12th Ave San Francisco CA 94116-1907

LIEBERMAN, LAURA CROWELL
ADMINISTRATOR, CRITIC
b Oak Ridge, Tenn, Apr 7, 1952. *Study:* Pomona Col, 72; Swarthmore Coll, BA, 74. *Collection Arranged:* Atlanta Women Artists: A Personal Survey, Atlanta Art Workers' Gallery, 78; 36 Women Artists (co-ed, catalog), Peachtree Ctr Gallery, Atlanta, 78; Nine Diverse Directions: Atlanta, Ga Southern Coll, 83; Speaking Volumes, Am Mus of Papermaking, 2002; Artists of Heath Gallery, Mus Contemp Art of Ga, 2002. *Pos:* pres, Ga Alliance for Arts Education. *Awards:* Outstanding Ga Women in the Visual Arts, 92. *Bibliog:* Karen Wantuck (auth), Subjective (catalog), 78; Sherry Baker (auth), 36 women artists, Atlanta Gazette, 4/78; Clyde Burnett (auth), A personal survey, Atlanta J-Constitution, 7/78. *Mem:* Georgia Assembly of Community Arts Agencies; Georgia Asn of Mus & Gall (bd dirs); Am for the Arts. *Res:* Contemporary art in Atlanta, Georgia and the Southeast. *Specialty:* Georgia and Regional Artists. *Publ:* Co-ed, Other Harmonies, Atlanta Women's Poetry Workshop, 77; auth, Five Atlanta women artists, Southern Quart, Univ Southern Miss, 79; ed, Contracts for Artists, 83; and others; auth, William Christenberry: A Retrospective (catalog essay), 90; London to Atlanta: International Exchange (catalog), 91; ed, City Arts update (newsletter), 92; Artists of Health Gallery Catalog, 2002. *Mailing Add:* 2736 Whisper Trail Douglasville GA 30135-1406

LIEBERMAN, LOUIS (KARL)
SCULPTOR, DRAFTSMAN
b Brooklyn, NY, May 7, 1944. *Study:* Brooklyn Mus Art Sch, cert, 64; Brooklyn Col, BA, 62; RI Sch Design, BFA, 69. *Work:* Metrop Mus Art, New York; Staten Island Mus, Richmond, NY; Philadelphia Mus Art, Pa; Aldrich Mus, Ridgefield, Conn; Brooklyn Mus, NY; and others. *Comn:* Wall relief, Aldrich Mus Contemp Art, Ridgefield, Conn, 73; Wall relief, Kenan Ctr, NY State Coun on Arts, Lockport, NY, 73; and others. *Exhib:* Solo exhibs, Root Art Ctr, Hamilton Coll, Clinton, NY, 80, Harm Bouckaert Gallery, New York, 81, List Art Ctr, Hamilton Coll, Clinton, NY, 82, Ellen Price, New York, 82, John Davis Gallery, Akron, Ohio, 83 & 85, Columbus Mus Art Collectors Gallery, Ohio, 84 & John Davis Gallery, New York, 86; One Cubic Foot, Thomas J Watson Libr, Metrop Art Mus, New York, 83; A Sigh of Relief, Wilson Art Ctr, Rochester, NY, 87; Stephen Rosenberg Gallery, New York, 87-88; New Art on Paper, Hunt Paper Collection, Philadelphia Mus Art, Pa, 88; Paper Thick, Erie Art Mus, Pa, Art Mus, Santa Cruz, Calif, Hunter Mus, Chattanooga, Tenn, 88-89; Black, Gray and White, Henry Feiwel Gallery, New York, 89. *Pos:* Contribr art critic, New York Arts J, 78-79. *Teaching:* Adj lectr drawing, Brooklyn Coll, NY, 71-78; adj lectr sculpture/design, Lehman Coll, Bronx, 72-75; vis artist sculpture, Ill State Univ, Normal, 79; vis artist, Hamilton Coll, Clinton, New York, 82. *Awards:* New York Found Arts, 84-85; Pollock-Krasner Found, 87; Adolph and Esther Gottlieb Found, 89-90; and many others. *Bibliog:* Brian Riverman (auth), article, Dialogue, 7/84 & 8/84; Holland Cotter (auth) articles, Arts Mag, 11/85, Art Am, 1/87; Stephan Westfall (auth) article, Arts Mag, 2/87. *Media:* Multimedia

LIEBERMAN, MEYER FRANK
PAINTER, PRINTMAKER
b New York, NY, Aug 28, 1923. *Study:* Art Students League, with Reginald Marsh; Pratt Graphics Ctr, with Andrew Stasik. *Work:* Jewish Mus, NY; Presidential Residence, Jerusalem; Columbia Univ, NY; Brooklyn Col, NY; Woodstock Hist Soc, Woodstock, NY. *Exhib:* Drawing USA, Mus Mod Art, NY, 56; solo exhibs, Bodley Gallery, 78, Night Gallery, 81, Terrance Gallery, 81; Work Art Gallery, Saugerties, NY, 86; Unison Learning Ctr, New Paltz, 89 & 95; Woodstock Artists Asn, 94; Lieberman Gallery, 96 & 99; Art Soc Kingston, 2000; Woodstock Artist ASN, 2002; Coffey Cal Kington, 2003; Half Moon Studio, Saugeties, 2004; Coffey Cal Kington, 2005. *Teaching:* Instr drawing, painting & composition, Art Life Craft Studios, New York, 64-68; instr drawing, collage painting & composition, Temple Emanu-El, Yonkers, NY, 66-74; instr drawing, painting & composition, Flatbush Jewish Ctr, Brooklyn, 67-78; instr, Temple Emanuel, Kingston, NY, 78-80; Gifted & Talented Prog, Onteora School Dist, New York, 85-88, mentor, 2000; sr art prog, Woodstock, NY, 84-. *Mem:* Woodstock Artists Asn; Art Soc Kingston, NY. *Media:* Oil, Watercolor. *Mailing Add:* 397 Wilbur Ave Rm 306 Kingston NY 12401-6223

LIEBERMANN, PHILIP
PHOTOGRAPHER, EDUCATOR
b Brooklyn, NY, Oct 25, 1934. *Study:* Mass Inst Technol, BS & MS, 58, PhD (linguistics), 66. *Work:* Brooklyn Mus, NY; Mus RI Sch Design, Providence; Albright Knox Gallery, Buffalo, NY; Silver Bullet Gallery, Providence; Providence Athenaeum, RI; Happenhoffer Mus of Anthrop, Mass. *Comn:* Photographs, Book-Walking in Switzerland, The Mountaineers, Seattle, 85-87; US of the Alpine Tourist Comn; Alpine Parks of France & NW Italy, Mountaineers, 89; Switzerland's Mountain Inns, Countryman Press, 98 & 2000; Buddhist wall paintings of Mustang, Nepal, Getty Found; Haffenrepper Mus Arcanus, Tibet, Nepal, India, Laos; Tibetan & Himalayan Digital Libr Spec Collection. *Exhib:* Carl Siembab Gallery, Boston, 66; B Urdang Invitational Traveling Exhib, 84; Animal in Photog 1845-1985, Invitational Photographers' Gallery, London, 86; B Urdang Gallery 82, 84, 86, 89 & 92; Mus Rhode Island Sch Design, 94; OP Steker, Amsterdam, 96; AHaffenrepper Mus Anthrop, Mass, 2000; and others. *Pos:* Prof, Brown Univ. *Awards:* Young Photog Award, Time-Life, 65; Sullivan Award, J Banigan Sullivan, 84 & 86; Guggenheim Fel, 87. *Bibliog:* Contemp Art in Rhode Island, 2001. *Media:* Black & White Photography. *Specialty:* Contemporary Art. *Interests:* Mountain Climbing, Classical Music, Art. *Publ:* Coauth, Walking in Switzerland, Mountaineers, 87; photogr, Alpine parks, France & Italy, Mountaineers, 94. *Dealer:* Bertha Urdang 23 E 74th St New York NY 10021. *Mailing Add:* 141 Elton St Providence RI 02906

LIEBLING, JEROME
PHOTOGRAPHER, FILMMAKER
b New York, NY, April 16, 1924. *Study:* Brooklyn Col, with Walter Rosenblum, Milton Brown & Ad Reinhardt; New Sch Social Res, with Lew Jacobs & Paul Falkenberg; LLD Portland Sch Art, Maine. *Work:* Mus Mod Art, NY; Corcoran Gallery Art; Boston Mus Fine Art; Libr Cong; Minneapolis Inst Art. *Exhib:* The Photo League, Int Ctr Photog, NY, 78; Mirrors and Windows, Mus Mod Art, NY, 78; 14 Northeast Photographers, Boston Mus Fine Arts, 78; solo exhibs, Corcoran Gallery Art, 80, Fogg Art Mus, 82 & Portland Art Mus, Maine, 83; Am Children, Mus Mod Art, NY, 81; Northeast Perambulations, Addison Gallery, 82; Retrospective: Jerome Liebling Photographs, Minneapolis Inst Art, Minn, 95; Jerome Liebling Photographs, The Photographers Gallery, London, Eng, 95. *Teaching:* Prof photog & film, Univ Minn, Minneapolis, 49-69 & Hampshire Col, 70-83; prof, SUNY, New Platz, NY, 56-57; prof photog, Yale Univ, 76-77. *Awards:* Fels, Guggenheim Found, 77 & 81 & Nat Endowment Arts, 79. *Bibliog:* Estelle Jussim (auth), No 15, Friends Photog, 77; Alan Trachtenberg (auth), Jerome Liebling--Photographs, Univ Mass Press, 82. *Mem:* Soc Photog Educ (trustee, 73-78); Univ Film Study Ctr (vpres, 75-77). *Specialty:* Photography. *Publ:* Coauth, Face of Minneapolis, Dillon Press, 66; illusr, Photography Current Perspectives, Mass Rev, 77; The People, Yes (Photographs of Jerome Liebling), Aperture, New York, 94. *Dealer:* Howard Greenberg Gallery 120 Wooster St New York NY 10012. *Mailing Add:* 39 Dana St Amherst MA 01002

LIEBMAN, SARAH
EDUCATOR, PAINTER
b Brooklyn, NY. *Study:* Brooklyn Coll, BA, 76, with Sam Gelber & Jerome Viola, MFA, 78, with Philip Pearlstein & Lee Bonticou; Pratt Inst, Grad Fel Fine Art, 77, with Richard Bove & Dr Ralph Wickiser; Teachers Coll, Columbia Univ, EdM, 86, EdD, 90, with Justin Schorr & Maxine Green. *Exhib:* Mid East Traveling Exhib, Cult Affairs Ctr, US Embassy, Israel & Egypt, 81; Nat Asn Women Artists, 81-82; Ann Exhib, Catharine Lorillard Wolfe Art Club, NY, 82; Nat Coun Art Jewish Life, Lever House, NY, 83; Nat Asn Women Artists, Bergen Mus Art & Sci, Paramus, NJ, 83 & NY, 83-84; solo exhib, Macy Gallery, Columbia Univ, NY, 85. *Teaching:* Instr drawing & painting, Sephardic Community Ctr, 81-84; instr art hist appreciation, Brooklyn Coll, NY, 83-87; instr art hist, appreciation & drawing, Univ Conn, 91-92. *Awards:* Marilyn Freeman Award, Brooklyn Coll, 75; Elizabeth Elanger Award, Nat Asn Women Artists, 81; Binney & Smith Award, Catharine Lorillard Wolfe Art Club, 82. *Mem:* Nat Asn Women Artists; Nat Art Educ Asn; Audubon Artists; Artists Equity; Coll Art Asn. *Media:* Oil, Pastel, Painting & Drawing. *Collection:* Mary Private Collection. *Publ:* Adult Learners, Two Coll Art Prog. *Mailing Add:* 1255 North Ave #5R New Rochelle NY 10804

LIEBOWITZ, JANET
PAINTER, SCULPTOR
b New York, NY. *Study:* Art Students League; Am Art Sch; studied with Robert Reed, New Haven. *Work:* Elmira Col, NY; Bocour Artist Color Collection, NY; Butler Art Inst, Youngstown, Ohio; Albrecht Gallery, St Joseph, Miss; Griffith Art Inst, St Lawrence Univ, Canton, NY. *Exhib:* Artists Choice, Women for the Arts Found, NY, 77; Silvermine Gold of Art Ctr, Phoenix Gallery, NY; Elmira Col, NY; Wadsworth Atheneum, Hartford, Conn. *Collection Arranged:* Papyrus Abstracts, Westport Weston Arts Coun, 82; Selections in Contemp Art, Wesport Weston Arts Coun, 83. *Awards:* Painters prize, Painters & Sculptors Soc NJ, 68; Nat Asn Women Artists, NY; Reginald March Scholar Art Students League. *Bibliog:* Michael Benedict (auth), Art Int, 66; John Caldwell (auth), Art Forms of Paperwork, NY Times, 8/82. *Mem:* Nat Asn Women Artists; Penwomen, Boca Raton Chap; Lighthouse Gallery, Tequesta, Fla; Artists Equity; Prof Artist Guild of Boca Raton Mus, Fla. *Media:* All. *Dealer:* Silvermine Guild of Artists New Canaan Conn. *Mailing Add:* 7535 Fairfax Dr Fort Lauderdale FL 33321-4360

LIECHTENSTEIN, HANS-ADAM VON UND ZU, II
COLLECTOR
b Feb 14, 1945. *Study:* Univ St Gallen, Switz, Licentiate, 1969. *Pos:* Prince & head of state, Principality of Liechtenstein, 1989-. *Awards:* Named one of Top 200 Collectors, ARTnews mag, 2009-13. *Collection:* Old masters

LIECHTENSTEIN, MARIE AGLAE VON UND ZU
COLLECTOR
b Prague, Czech Rep, April 14, 1940. *Study:* Acad for Applied Arts, Univ Munich. *Pos:* Princess, Principality of Liechtenstein, 1989-; pres, Liechtenstein Red Cross. *Awards:* Named one of Top 200 Collectors, ARTnews mag, 2009-11. *Mem:* Soc for Orthopaedic Aid (hon pres, 1983-2005). *Collection:* Old masters

LIEPKE, MALCOLM T
PAINTER
b Minn, 1953. *Study:* Art Ctr Coll Design. *Exhib:* Solo exhibs include Albemarle Gallery, London, 1998, 1999, 2000, US Artists, 97, Phila, 1999, P&C Fine Arts, Washington, DC, 1996, Mendenhall Gallery, LA, 1996, 1999, Newbury Fine Arts, Boston, 1995, 1999, White OPak Gallery, Minneapolis, 1995, Art Asia, Hong Kong, 1992, 1993, 1994, 1995, Eleanor Ettinger Gallery, NY, 1989, 1991, 1994, 1996, 1998, 1999, 2000, 2001, Grand Central Gallery, NY, Kickerbocker Artists of NY, Hudson Valley Art Asn, Allie Artists, Pastel Soc Am, Nat Watercolor Soc. *Teaching:* Lectures in field. *Awards:* Rangor Purchase Award, Nat Acad Design. *Dealer:* Arcadia Fine Arts 51 Green St NY NY 10013. *Mailing Add:* c/o Eleanor Ettinger Gallery 24 W 57th St New York NY 10019

LIFSON, HUGH ANTHONY
PAINTER, EDUCATOR
b New York, NY, Nov 7, 1937. *Study:* Studio 10, with Irving Marantz, 53-59; Univ Wis, with Warrington Colescott & S Zingale, 55-56; Wesleyan Univ, with R Limbach, AB, 59; Ind Univ, 60; Pratt Inst, with Robert Richenberg, James McGarrell, 61 & Univ of Ind. *Work:* Cedar Rapids Mus Art, Iowa; State Univ NY, Postdam; Wesleyan Univ, Middletown, Conn; St Leo Coll, Fla; Davenport Munic Art Gallery, Iowa; Univ Iowa Hosp & Clinics; Kimmel Handing Nelson Ctr for Arts; Chain Griss Mus; Enduring Nights & Visions on September Attacks, NIH Sponsored. *Comn:* Environment, Cedar Rapids Art Ctr, Iowa, 69. *Exhib:* Mid Am Ann, St Louis Munic Mus, Mo, 68 & Nelson Atkins Mus, Kansas City, 84; solo exhibs, Ohio State Univ,

Columbus, 72 & Ward Nasse Gallery, NY, 78; USA The Figure, Mus Mod Art, NY; South Bend 20th Century Ctr, Ind, 81. *Collection Arranged:* Richard Kostelanetz, Carl Shorske, Alan Shestack, Larry Shiner. *Teaching:* Prof, Cornell Coll, Mt Vernon, Iowa, 84 & 86-2000, prof emer, 2000-. *Bibliog:* Richard Kostelanetz (auth), Metamorphosis, Assembling Press, 81. *Media:* Acrylics, Polyonics; Computer Graphics. *Publ:* Trobor Mag. *Dealer:* Wiederspan Gallery 1314 Mt Vernon Rd SI Cedar Rapids IA 52403; Hudson River Gallery 538 S Gilbert St Iowa City IA 52240. *Mailing Add:* 219 Sixth Ave N Mount Vernon IA 52314

LIGHT, KEN
PHOTOGRAPHER, EDUCATOR
b Bronx, NY, Mar 16, 1951. *Study:* Ohio Univ, Athens, Ohio, BGS, 73; San Jose State Univ, MFA (photog), 98. *Work:* San Francisco Mus Mod Art, Calif; Calif Hist Soc, San Francisco; Int Polaroid Collection, Boston; Fed Reserve Bank, San Francisco; Houston Mus Fine Arts; Int Ctr Photog; Center Creative Photog; NY Pub Libr; Nat Mus Am Art; Albin O Kuhn Libr; Bancroft Libr; Santa Barbara Mus Art; Univ Tex Dallas. *Comn:* Libr Congress, Am Folklife Ctr, 89 & 90. *Exhib:* Work, Oakland Mus, Calif, 77; Faces Photographed, San Francisco Mus Mod Art, 84; New Documentary Photog, USA Images Gallery, Cincinnati, Ohio, 89; San Joaquin Co Hist Soc & Mus Arts Sta, Tifton, Ga, 90; Mus Contemp Art, Morelia, Mex, 90; solo exhibs, The Eye Gallery, San Francisco, 91, Chovnick Gallery, New York, 91 & Pac Tel Corp Plaza Gallery, Walnut Creek, Calif, 92; Nev Mus Art-Weigand Gallery, 93; Italian Americans in the West, Libr Cong, 94; Track 16 Gallery, Santa Monica, Calif, 2005; Int Ctr Photog, 2005; SE Mus Photog, 2006; Smith Coll Gallery Art, 2008; Oakland Mus, 2012; San Francisco Mus Modern Art, Picturing Modernity, 2013; SE Mus Photog, 2013. *Teaching:* Fac photog, San Francisco Acad Art 76-96; adj prof, cur, Ctr Photography, Univ Calif, Berkeley, 83-; adj prof, Univ Calif, Berkeley Grad Sch Jour, 1983-; Reva and David Logan Prof Photojournalism, Univ Calif Graduate Sch Journalism, 88-, San Francisco Art Inst, 2000; Laventhol vis prof, Columbia Univ Grad Sch Journalism, 2012. *Awards:* Nat Endowment Arts Photogrs Fel, 82 & 86; Dorothea Lange Fel, 87; Thomas M Stoke Int Journalism Award, 90; Cannon Photo Esaysity Award, Univ Mo, 92; NPPA Res Grant, 96; Open Soc Inst Grant, 2005; Calif Book award, Gold Medal, Contbr to Publishing, Commonwealth Club, 2012. *Bibliog:* Mark Lapin (auth), Light on the Border, Photo District News, 88; Delta Time; Mississippi Photographs, 95; Tex Death Row, Univ Press Miss, 96; Aperture Witness in Our Time, Smithsonian, 2000; Coal Hollow, Univ Calif Press, 2007; With These Hands, 83; To The Promised Land, 88; Valley of Shadows & Dreams, Heyday Press, 2012. *Mem:* Soc Photog Ed; Am Fed Teachers; Nat Press Photographers Assn. *Media:* Photography. *Publ:* Contribr, The Circle of Life, Harper Collins Publ, 91; Mexico Through Foreign Eyes, WW Norton, 92; Time for a Witness, East Bay Guardian, 1/92; Granta, No 40, fall 92; Image Mag, San Francisco Examiner, 7/12/92; Coal Hollow, Univ Calif Press, 2/2005 & 2006; Valley of Shadows and Dreams, Hey Day, 2012. *Mailing Add:* 55 VIA Farallon Orinda CA 94563

LIGHT, MICHAEL RUDOLPH
PHOTOGRAPHER
b Clearwater, Fla, Aug 5, 1963. *Study:* Amherst Coll, BA (summa cum laude) 1986; San Francisco Art Inst, MFA (photog), 1993. *Work:* San Francisco Mus Mod Art; Los Angeles Co Mus; Getty Research Inst, Los Angeles; Victoria & Albert Mus, London; Am Mus Natural Hist, New York; Brooklyn Mus, New York; New York Pub Lib, New York. *Exhib:* Group Exhibs: Montreal Mus Fine Arts, 1999; Fondation Cartier, Paris, 2000; Getty Mus, 2001; Mito Art Tower, Japan, 2001 & 2006; Mus Mod, Salzburg, 2005; Colo Univ Art Mus, Boulder, 2005; Worcester Art Mus, Mass, 2006; LACMA, 2007, Musee de l'Elysee, Lausanne, 2008, Tang Mus, NY, 2009, Scottsdale Mus of Contemp Art, Ariz, 2009, De Young Mus, San Francisco, 2010, Getty Mus, Los Angeles, 2013, BALTIC Cent Cont Art, Newcastle UK, 2014, Contemp Jewish Mus, San Francisco, 2015, Art Gallery of Ontario, 2015; Solo Exhibs: Chrysler Mus, Norfolk, Va, 1995, Southeast MusPhotog, 1998, San Francisco Mus Mod Art, 1999, Hayward Gallery, London, 1999, Mus Contemp Art, Sydney, 2000, Am Mus Natural Hist, New York, 2000, Auditorium Arte, Rome, 2004, Casino Luxembourg, 2004, Nat Hist Mus Los Angeles Co, Calif, 2005, Nederlands Fotomuseum, Rotterdam, 2005, Hasselblad Ctr, Goteborg, Sweden, 2006, Knoxville Mus Art, 2008, Nevada Mus Art, Reno, 2008, Blue Sky Gallery, Portland Oreg, 2011; and many commercial gallery shows. *Teaching:* Instr, Deep Springs Coll, Calif, 2001 & 2006. *Awards:* Marin Arts Coun Grant, 1994; John Simon Guggenheim Mem Found Fel, Photog, 2007; Artadia Award, 2007; PDN Photo Ann Book Winner, 2015. *Bibliog:* John Sanford (auth), The Long Shadow, Los Angeles Times, 6/13/1999, Oliver Morton (auth), They Could See the Stars, Times Literary Supplement, London 8/20/1999, Anthony Lane (auth), The Light Side of the Moon, The New Yorker, 4/10/2000; Christopher Knight (auth), Puzzling Landscapes Happily Lost in Space, Los Angeles Times, 8/4/2000; Sharon DeLano (auth), On Photography: Darkness Visible, The New Yorker, 10/6/2003; Through the Lens, the Severe Beauty of Nuclear Test Blasts, The New York Times, 10/21/2003; Glen Helfand (auth), Critic's Picks: Michael Light, Artforum.com, 11/2003; Phillip Morrison (auth), Metaphorical Suns, Scientific American, New York, 1/2004; RC Baker (auth), Best in Show: Apocalypse Porn, The Village Voice, New York, 5/1/2006; Colin Westerbeck (auth), SUGAR, West Magazine, Sunday Los Angeles Times, 8/27/2006; Trevor Paglen (auth), BEST OF 2008/Some Dry Space/Michael Light, ArtForum 12/2008, Leah Ollman (auth), Michael Light: The Earth Is Reshaped, Los Angeles Times, 5/7/2010, Rebecca Horne (auth), In The Airlight With Michael Light, Wall Street Journal, 6/1/11, Jeff Gordinier (auth), Buzzed: Photographs by Michael Light, OUTSIDE Magazine, 6/2011, LyraKilston (auth), Economic Collapse/Michael Light, Wired.com, 9/13/2013, Vince Aletti (auth), Michael Light: Danziger Gallery, The New Yorker, 1/13/2014; Jordan Teicher (auth), The Decadence and Environmental Destruction of American Expansionism in Nevada, SLATE.com, 10/17/2014. *Media:* Photography. *Publ:* Ranch, Twin Palms Publ, NMex, 93; FULL MOON, New York, 1999 & 100 SUNS, New York, 2003, Knopf; Bingham Mine/Garfield Stack, Santa Fe, 2009 & L.A. Day/L.A. Night, Santa Fe, 2011 & Lake Las Vegas/Black Mountain, Santa Fe, 2014, Radius Books. *Dealer:* Hosfelt Gallery 260 Utah St San Francisco CA 94103. *Mailing Add:* PO Box 460428 San Francisco CA 94146

LIGHTNER, KURT
PAINTER, SCULPTOR
b Troy, Ohio, 1971. *Study:* Columbus Coll Art & Design, Ohio (Found Scholar, Fine Arts Scholar), 1989-93; Sch Visual Arts, New York (MFA Merit Scholar, Alumni Scholar, Paula Rhodes Mem Award), 2002-04. *Exhib:* Solo exhibs include Spotlight Gallery, Acme Art Co, Columbus, Ohio, 1992, Beaton Hall, Columbia Coll Art & Design, 1993, Roy G Biv Gallery, Columbus, 1998, Studio 972, Columbus, 2001, Ohio Art League, 2002, Clementine Gallery, New York, 2004, 2006 & 2008, Kemper Mus Contemp Art, Kansas City, 2006; group exhibs include Unframed First Look, Lehman Maupin Gallery, New York, 2003; Strange Fiction, Visual Arts Gallery, New York, 2003, The World in Everything/Everything in the World, 2004; Queens Int, Queens Mus Art, NY, 2004; Greater New York, PS 1 Contemp Art Ctr, New York, 2005; Garden, Visual Arts Ctr Richmond, Va, 2006; LIC, NYC, Socrates Sculpture Park, Long Island City, NY, 2007. *Awards:* Purchase Award, Greater Columbus Arts Coun, 2001; Reed Arts Award, Ohio Art League, 2001; Pollock-Krasner Found Grant, 2007. *Dealer:* Clementine Gallery 623 W 27th St New York NY 10001. *Mailing Add:* 4215 43rd Ave Long Island City NY 11104

LIGHTON, LINDA
SCULPTOR
b Kansas City, Mo, Mar 10, 1948. *Study:* Monterrey Inst Technol, Mex, 65-66; Fontainbleau Sch Fine Arts, France, 67; Factory Visual Arts, Seattle, Wash, 71-74; Western Wash State Col, Bellingham, 75; Univ Idaho, Moscow, 75-77; Kansas City Art Inst, BFA, 87-89. *Work:* also pvt collection of the Crown Prince of Brunei; H&R Block World Hq, Kansas City, Mo; Spence Mus, Lawrence, Kansas; Sprint Corp, Kansas City, Mo; Daum Mus, Sedalia, Mo; Johnson Co Community Col, Overland Park, Kans; Int Ceramic Mus, Icheon, Korea; Fule Int Ceramic Mus, Fuping, China; Nelson Atkins Mus Art, Kansas City, Mo; Kemoer Mus Contemporary Art, Kansas City, Mo; Ariana Mus, Geneva, Switzerland. *Comn:* Truman Med Ctr, Kansas City, Mo. *Exhib:* 1st World Bienniale Ceramics, Incheon Korea, 2001; Devine Porcelain, Vallauris, France, 2004; Int Bienniale de Manises, Valencia, Spain, 2005; 20th Int Ceramic Festival, Incheon, Korea, 2006; Int Acad Ceramics, Riga, Latvia, 2006; Boundless Joy, Carter Art Ctr, Penn Valley Col, Kansas City, Mo, 2008; Int Acad Ceramics Exhib, Xian Convention Ctr, Xian, China, 2008; Am Mus at Fule Int Mus, Fuping, China, 2008; Bridge Art Fair, Kathleen Cullen Gallery, New York, 2008; solo exhibs, Strecker Nelson Gallery, Manhattan, Kans, 2008. *Pos:* adv bd, Nat Coun Edn Ceramic Arts; bd dir, Rev Arts Mag & Kansas City Ballet; dir, Lighton Int Artists Exchg Program at Kansas City Artists Coalition, Kansas City, Mo; mem nat comt, Kemper Mus Contemp Art, Kansas City; bd mem, Kansas City Jewish Mus; mem, Int Acad Ceramics. *Awards:* Honorarium-Amerika Haus, Berlin, Ger, 94; Int Workshop Ceramic Arts, Tokoname, Japan, 96; Grant, Int Geramic Symposium, Hungary, 2003; Mo Arts Award, Gov Jay Nixon, St Joseph, Mo; Mallin Artists Award, Kansas City Artists Coalition, Kansas City, Mo; Binyami Found, Ceramic Artists of Israel, Tel Aviv, Israel, 2005; Int Ceramic Mus, Fuping, China, 2007. *Bibliog:* Diane Timmerman (auth), Flower power, Kansas City Home Design, Vol 1, 10/96; Roderick Townley (auth), The Winding Road to Her Creativity, Kansas City Home Design, 9/99; Joshua Rose (auth), Working to Build Bridges, Kansas City Jewish Life, 97. *Mem:* Nat Coun Educ Ceramic Arts; founding mem, Kansas City Contemp Art Ctr, Kans; Kansas City Artist Coalition; Arts Partners of Kansas City (dir, bd mem & secy); Int Acad Ceramics, Carouge, Switz. *Media:* Clay. *Publ:* Auth, numerous articles, Nat Coun for Educ of Ceramic Arts J. *Dealer:* Sherry Leedy Contemporary Art 2004 Baltimore Ave Kansas City MO 64108. *Mailing Add:* 4620 Charlotte Kansas City MO 64110-1535

LIGON, GLENN
PAINTER
b Bronx, NY, 1960. *Study:* RI Sch Design, 80; Wesleyan Univ, BA, 82; Whitney Mus Independent Study Prog, 85. *Work:* Boston Mus Fine Art & List Art Gallery, MIT, Boston; Mus Mod Art & Whitney Mus Am Art, NY; Carnegie Mus Art, Pittsburgh; Hirshhorn Mus & Sculpture Garden, Washington, DC; Philadelphia Mus Art. *Exhib:* Solo exhibs, White Columns, NY, 91, Wadsworth Atheneum, 92, Max Protetch Gallery, NY, 92, 93 & 94, Whitney Mus Am Art at Philip Morris, NY, 92, Hirshhorn Mus & Sculpture Garden, 93 & Ruth Bloom Gallery, Santa Monica, 94, Brooklyn Mus of Art, 96, San Francisco Mus Mod Art, Calif, 96, Ezra and Cecile Zilkha Gallery, Middletown, Conn, 97, Inst Contemp Art/Univ of Pennsylvania, 1998, St Louis Art Mus, 2000, The Studio Mus in Harlem, NY, 2001, Kuntsverein Munich, Ger, 2001, D'Amelio Terras, NY, 2001, Anthony Meier Fine Arts, San Francisco, Calif, 2002, D'Amelio Terras, NY, 2003, The Power Plant, Canada, 2005, The Andy Warhol Mus Pittsburgh, 2006, Regan Projects, Yvon Lambert, Paris, France, 2006, Powerhouse, Memphis, 2008, Thomas Dane Gallery, London, 2009, Michael Stevenson Gallery, South Africa, 2010, Whitney Mus 2011, Los Angeles County Mus of Art, 2011; Galerie Gilles Peyroulet, Paris, 94; Dark O'Clock, Museu de Arte Moderna de Sao Paulo, Brazil & Plug In Inc, Winnipeg, Manitoba, Can, 96; Biennale of Sydney: Jurassic Technologies Revenant, Art Gallery of New South Wales, Sydney, Australia, 96; La Biennale di Venezia, XLVII Esposizione Int D'Arte, Venice, Italy, 97; XXIV Bienal de Sao Paulo: Nucleo Historico: Antropofagia e Historia de Canibalismos, Brazil, 98; 3rd Kwangju Biennale: Man + Space, Kwangju, South Korea, 2000; group exhib: Skin Deep, Numark Gallery, Washington, DC, 2003, An Am Legacy: Art from the Studio Mus, The Parrish Art Mus, Southhampton, NY, 2003, Influence, Anxiety, and Gratitude, MIT List Visual Art Ctr, 2003, On the Wall: Wallpaper and Tableau, The Fabric Workshop and Mus, Philadelphia, Pa, 2003, Family Ties, Peabody Essex Mus, Salem, Mass, 2003, The Disembodied Spirit, Bowdoin Coll Mus of Art, Maine, 2003, Open House, Brooklyn Mus of Art, 2004, Singular Forms, Solomon R. Guggenheim Mus, NY, 2004, Drawing from the Modern, 1975-2005, Mus of Modern Art, NY, 2005-06, Skin Is a Language, Whitney Mus of Modern Art, NY, 2006, At Home, Yvon Lambert Gallery, NY, 2007, Across the Divide: Reconsidering the Other, Illinois State Mus, 2008-09, The Matrix Effect, The Wadsworth Atheneum Mus of Art, Conn, 2009-10, This Girl Bends: Art and Feminism Since 1960, Williams Coll Mus of Art, Mass, 2010, Collecting Biennial, Whitney Mus of American Art, NY, 2001, Face Off: Portraits by Contemporary Artists, Lyman Allyn

Art Mus, Conn, 2011. *Awards:* Dewar's Young Artists Recog Award, 90; Fel, Art Matters Inc, 90; Grant, Joan Mitchell Found, 96; Acad Award in Art, Am Acad Arts and Letters, 2006; Joyce Alexander Wein Artist Prize, 2009; US Artists Fellowship, Los Angeles, 2010. *Bibliog:* Laura Cottingham (auth), The pleasure principal, Frieze, 5/93; Ralph Rugoff (auth), Panic in the tower: Who's afraid of the Whitney, Los Angeles Weekly, 5/7/93-5/13/93; Roberta Smith (auth), A 24 hour-a-day show on gaudy, bawdy 42nd Street, New York Times, 7/30/93. *Mem:* Nat Acad. *Dealer:* D'Amelio Terras 525 W 22nd St New York NY 10011. *Mailing Add:* c/o Regen Projects 633 N Almont Dr Los Angeles CA 90069

LIJN, LILIANE
SCULPTOR, WRITER
b New York, NY, Dec 22, 1939. *Study:* Ecole de Louvre, Paris, Sorbonne, Paris. *Hon Degrees:* Univ Warwick, D Litt (Doctor of Letters), 2005. *Work:* The Brit Coun; Chicago Inst; Bibliot Nat, Paris; Mus Fine Arts, Bern; Victoria and Albert Mus, London; British Mus, London; Tate Gallery, London; Solar Beacon, a sci-art installation of heliostats on the towers of the Golden Gate Bridge; Light Pyramid, a beacon for the Queen's Diamond Jubilee, which was commissioned by Park Trust and MK Gallery, Milton Keynes; plus many others; One of six artists short-listed to produce a sculpture for the Fourth Plinth in Trafalgar Square; performed Crossing Map on Deutschlandradio. *Comn:* Extrapolation, Norfolk & Norwich Triennial Festival, Norwich, 81; Zigzag Blues, Churchill Plaza, Basingstoke, 87; Carbon Black, Nat Chemical Labs, London Argo, 88, NH Schroder, Poole Dorset, 88; Inner Light (24' x 7' Welsh slate, neon), comn by Kumagai Gumi (UK) Ltd & Ranelagh Developments for Prudential Insurance hq, Reading, 92; Dragon's Dance, Marks & Spencers for Culverhouse Cross, Cardiff, 94; Earth Sea Light Koan, St Mary's Hosp, Isle of Wight, 97; Inner Light, St Thomas' Hospital, London, 98; Zero Gravity Koan, Commune di Umbertide, Italy, 2004; Starslide, Evelina Children's Hospital, London, 2005. *Exhib:* Exhib, Mus d'Art Mod, Paris, 67 & Electra, 83; 20th Century Drawings & Watercolors, Victoria & Albert Mus, London, 85; Livres d'Artistes, Centre George Pompidou, Paris, 85; Liliane Lijn: Poem Machines 1962-1968, Nat Arts Libr, Victoria & Albert Mus, London, 93; Art Unlimited, South Bank Ctr Exhib, touring, 94; Catalyst for Care, Wellcome Found, 94; British Abstract Art II, Angela Flowers Gallery, London, 95; Liliane Lijn: Her Mothers Voice (with catalog), Eagle Gallery, London, 96; Chimeriques Polymeres, Mus d'Art Mod de la Vill de Nice, 96; Rubies & Rebels, Concourse Gallery, Barbican & touring, 96; Liliane Lijn: Poem machines & other book works, Nat Libr Gallery, Wellington & Govett-Brewster Gallery, New Plymouth, NZ, 98; solo exhib, Koans, Gallerie Lara Vincy, Paris, 97, Koans Shirley Day Gallery, London, 2000, Force Fields, Mus of Contemp Art, Barcelona, Hayward Gallery, London, 2000, Dream Machines, South Bank Nat Touring Exhib, UK, 2000; Light and Memory, Centro per l'Art Contemporanea, Rocca di Umbertide; Claudio Nardi, Florence, 2002; Liliane Lijn Works 1959-1980, Mead Gallery, Univ of Warwick, Coventry, 2005; Austin Desmond Fine Art, Eng & Co Gallery, London, 2006; Riflemaker becomes Indica, Ritlemaker Gallery, London, 2006; Nyehaus Gallery, NY, 2007; Stardust, Ritlemaker Gallery, London, 2008; Poor.Old.Tire.House, ICA, London, 2009; RCM Gallery, Paris, Images Moving Out Onto Space, Tate St Ives; DLA Piper series: Constellations, Tate Liverpool; Cartias: Histoires, Paraboles et Reves, Musee de Picardie, Amiens, France; William Burroughs CAN YOU ALL HEAR ME? October Gallery, London; Graphic Constellations: Visual Poetry and the Properties of Space, Ruskin Gallery, Cambridge; Light Years, Sir John Soane's Mus; Gallery One, New Vision Centre; Signals and Indica, Tate Britain; Ecstatic Alphabets/Heaps of Language, MOMA, NY; Cosmic Dramas, mima, Middlesbrough; Earth Body Art, Museo Santa Croce, Umbertide. *Awards:* LFVPA Prod Award, 97=6; Art Council of England, International Artist Fellowship Residency, Space Sciences Lab, Berkeley Univ of CA, 2005; Calouste Gulbenkian Funding Award, 2006. *Bibliog:* Phillipa Scott (auth), New Sculpture (catalog), Gillian Jason Gallery, London, 90; David Mellor (ed), The Sixties Art Scene in London (catalog), Phaidon Press, London, 93; Art in the Electric Age, Frank Popper, Thames & Hudson, London, New York, Editions Hazon, Paris, 93; Light & Memory, Thane & Hudson Ltd, London, 2002; Liliane Lijn: Works 1959-1980, Sarah Shalgosky (ed), Mead Gallery, Coventry, 2005. *Media:* All Industrially Used Materials. *Publ:* Auth, What is art?, Ostrich No 9, Northumberland, 9/73; Six Throws of the Oracular Keys, Ed de la Nepe, Paris, 82; Crossing Map, Thames & Hudson, 83; Imagine the Goddess, A Rebirth of the Female Archetype in Sculpture, Leonardo, Vol XX, No 2; Body and Soul: Interactions between the Material and the Immaterial in Sculpture, Vol 31, No, 1, 5-12, Leonardo, 98. *Mailing Add:* 28 Camden Sq London United Kingdom NW1 9XA

LILES, CATHARINE (BURNS)
PAINTER, PATRON
b Macon, Ga, 1944. *Study:* Wesleyan Coll BFA (magna cum laude), 79; Mercer Univ, MLS, 89; with Constantine Chatov, Rhett English; UGA, Corona, Italy. *Work:* Univ Tex Med Sch, Houston; Art by Am Women, Louise & Alan Sellars Collection, Indianapolis, IN; King & Spalding Attys, Washington, DC; Arnall Golden Gregory Atty, Macon, Ga; City of Macon, France. *Comn:* Macon Symphony, Southern Bell; Macon Cherry Blossom Festival; Mercer Med Sch. *Exhib:* People & Places, Middle Ga Coll, 81; Faces and Figures, Mercer Univ, 82; Pittura dal Muro, JH Webb Gallery, Macon, Ga, 84; Group Exhibs: Who Am I?, Mus Arts & Scis, Macon, Ga, 83; Paintings by Am Women, Mus Arts and Scis 83; Brenau Coll, Gainesville, Ga, 91; Etowah Art Coun, Cartersville Moultrie Art Ctr&Kennesaw Coll, Marrietta Ga, 92; Art by An Women, Brenau Col, Gainesville, Ga, 91; Knowsville Mus Art, Tenn, 92; St Petersburg Mus Art, Fla, 93; Macon Memories, 50 Years at the Mus, Mus of Arts & Sciences, Macon, Ga, 06 & 07; Solo Exhibs: Macon Arts, 2007, 2014; Middle Georgia Asn, 2008; Catharine Liles: A Retrospective Art Exhibit, Wesleyan Coll (12 pg catalogue), 2014. *Pos:* Owner & pres, Markwell Inc, Healthcare Marketing Liles & Assoc, 1982-2001, retired; past pres, Macon Arts Alliance; past pres, Macon Mus Arts & Scis. *Teaching:* Instr figure drawing & portrait painting, Mercer Univ, 1/83-9/83. *Awards:* Best in Show Print, Addy Award, Ad Club Central Ga, 87 & 88; Outstanding Alumni Award, Wesleyan Coll, 91; Cultural Award, Macon Arts Alliance. *Bibliog:* Paul E Sternberg (auth), Paintings by American Women: Selections from the Collection of Louise & Alan Sellars, 89 & Art by American Women, 91. *Mem:* Macon Arts Alliance; assoc mem Am Watercolor Soc; Middle Ga Art Asn; assoc mem Nat Watercolor Soc; Ga Watercolor Soc. *Media:* Watercolor, Oil. *Publ:* Project MLS, Mercer Univ, 85-89; Marketing Plan Macon Arts Alliance, 89; contribr, Drafting Volunteer Talent, A Case Study for the Macon Arts Alliance. *Mailing Add:* PO Box 6218 Macon GA 31208

LILES, RAEFORD BAILEY
PAINTER, SCULPTOR
b Birmingham, Ala, July 20, 1923. *Study:* Birmingham-Southern Col, 41-43, 46-47; Auburn Univ, BSEE, 49; Atelier Fernand Leger, Paris, France, 49-51. *Work:* Musee d'Art Mod, Eliat, Israel; Andrew Dickson White Mus Art, Cornell Univ; Corcoran Gallery Art, Washington, DC; Amos Andersons Konstmuseum, Helsingor, Finland; Alfred Khouri Collection, Norfolk Mus, Va; Boston Coll Mus Art, Mass; Birmingham Mus Art, Ala; Grey Art Gallery, New York Univ, NY; New Sch Social Research, NY. *Comn:* Silk screen series, East Hampton Gallery, NY, 67; also pvt collections. *Exhib:* Salon d'Art Independent & Art Libre, Paris, 51; Salon Nouvelle Realite, Mus Mod Art, Paris, 55; Mirco Salon d'Avril, Iris Clert, Paris, 56; Obelisk Gallery, London, 71; Birmingham Mus, 72; Andre Zarre Gallery, 76; Univ Ala, 77; Univ Montevallo, Ala, 77; Univ Ala, Tuscaloosa, 83; Solo shows, Gallery 8, Paris, 51, East Hampton Gallery, NY, 67, Gibbes Art Gallery, Charleston, SC, 75, Univ Ark, Little Rock, 78, EM Donahue Gallery, NY, 93, 95, 97, & 99, Jennifer Harwell Art Gallery, Birmingham, Al, 2007, 2008, 2009. *Awards:* Prize, Students of Leger, 51; First Prize, Alpine Gallery, 58. *Bibliog:* Turpin (auth), L'Orleanais Dans Les Art, 52; Orinese (auth), Tour D'Expositions Combat, 55; Brown (auth), Review of expositions, Art Mag, 68. *Mem:* Birmingham Art Asn; Ala Watercolor Soc. *Media:* All Media. *Interests:* Gourmet cooking, travel. *Publ:* Illus, The Stars and Stripes (M'aide French-English Phrase Dictionary), Darmstadt, Germany, 1953; Illus, Sex Quake: Art after the Apocalypse, Venice Biennale, 1993 & Gallery Guide, NYC, 1995. *Dealer:* Don Harwell Jenniferharwell art Gallery Birmingham AL. *Mailing Add:* 235 Inverness Ctr Dr Birmingham AL 35242

LILJEGREN, FRANK
PAINTER, INSTRUCTOR
b New York, NY, Feb 23, 1930. *Study:* Art Students League, with John Groth, Dean Cornwell, Frank J Reilly, Arthur Schwieder & Saul Tepper. *Work:* Manhattan Savings Bank, NY; Am Educ Publ Inst, NY; New Britain Mus Am Art, Conn; Art Students League, NY; Univ Mus, Southeast Mo State Univ, Cape Giradeau, Mo; Ft Wayne Mus Art (permanent collection); St. Francis Univ, Ft Wayne, Ind, (Permanent Collection). *Comn:* Pastel Portrait, First Presby Church, Van Wert, Ohio; Pastel of the Brumback Libr, Van Wert, Ohio. *Exhib:* Nat Acad Designs, NY; Coun Am Artists Soc, Lever House, NY, 64 & 67; Salmagundi Club, NY, 64-68; Acad Artists Asn, Springfield Fine Arts Mus, Mass, 66-70; OS Ranch Exhib, Tex, 77-80; Ft Wayne Mus Art, Ind, 79. *Teaching:* Instr painting, Westchester Co Art Workshop, White Plains, 66-77, Art Students League, 73-74, Wassenberg Art Ctr, Van Wert, Ohio, 77-80, Wright State Univ, 81-. *Awards:* Allied Artists Am Awards; Frank V Dumond Award, Salmagundi Club, 65 & 67; Medal of Merit for Oil Painting, Today's Art Mag, 71. *Bibliog:* Jo Mary McCormick-De Guyton (auth), Frank Liljegren and his old friends, Am Artist Mag, 2/72; Ralph Fabri (auth), Medal of merit winner in 58th A A A annual, Today's Art Mag, 3/72; Linda Evans (dir), Frank Liljegren - How Much is an Artist Worth - My Mentor, Myself, 93; Your Country (doc), with Eric Olson, Channel 21, Fort Wayne, Ind, 2/5/2007; documentary with Rick Cartwright (dir), Univ St Francis, Fort Wayne, Ind, 11/2006. *Mem:* Allied Artists Am (corresp secy, 67, exhib chmn, 68-76, pres, 70-72, dir, 72-76); Artists Fel; Salmagundi Club; life mem Art Students League. *Media:* Oil, Pastels, Pencil. *Specialty:* Still Lifes in Oils & Pastels. *Interests:* Visiting Mus, Reading Biographies about Artists. *Dealer:* Liljegren Galleries 203 S Cherry St Van Wert OH 45891-2006. *Mailing Add:* 203 S Cherry St Van Wert OH 45891-2006

LILYQUIST, CHRISTINE
EGYPTOLOGIST, CURATOR
b Glendale, Calif, Aug 15, 1940. *Study:* Pomona Col, BA, 62; NY Univ, MA, 65, PhD, 71. *Collection Arranged:* Dir, Dendur Temple Installation, Metrop Mus Art, NY, 72-78, dir, Egyptian Reinstallation, 72-83, consult, Renovation of the Cairo Mus, 75-77 & cur, Mus Consortium for the Exhib Treasures of Tutankhamun, 75-79. *Pos:* Asst cur Egyptian dept, Metrop Mus Art, New York, 70-72, assoc cur in charge, 72-74 & cur, 74-88, sen res cur, 88-91; consult, New York City Dept Park & Rec (Cleopatra's Needle), 78-80; rsch assoc, NY U IFA for Mendes Excavations 91-2010; Lila Acheson Wallace research cur in Egyptology, 91-2010. *Mem:* Egypt Exploration Soc; Am Res Ctr in Egypt. *Res:* Minor arts technology, Egypt's relations with neighbors. *Publ:* Ed, Tutankhamun Exhib Publ, Metrop Mus Art, New York, 76; auth, Ancient Egyptian Mirrors: From the Earliest Times Through the Middle Kingdom, Munchner Aegyptologische Studien 27, 79; auth, Studies in Early Egyptian Glass, Metrop Mus Art, 93; auth, Egyptian Stone Vessels, Metrop Mus Art, 95; auth, The Tomb of Three Foreign Wives of Tuthmosis III, 2006. *Mailing Add:* Metrop Mus Art Fifth Ave at 82nd St New York NY 10028

LIM, CHOONG SUP
INSTALLATION SCULPTOR
b Jincheon, Chungcheongbuk-do, Korea, 1941. *Study:* Seoul Nat Univ, BFA, 1960; Brooklyn Mus Art Sch (Max Beckmann Mem Scholar), 1973; NY Univ, MFA, 1993. *Work:* Metrop Mus Art, New York; Hirshhorn Mus, Smithsonian Inst, Washington; NY Asian Am Arts Ctr, New York; Kyung Gi-Do Mus, Korea; Shoes or Not Shoes Mus, Belgium; Samsung Mus Mod Art, Seoul, Korea; Sandra Gering Gallery, NY; Kukje Gallery, Seoul, Korea. *Comn:* pvt collection, comn by Mrs. Ken Marks, Potomac, MD; pvt collection, comn by Mrs. Robert Solon, NY; pvt collection, comn by Mr and Mrs Miles Stutchin, NY; pvt collection, comn by Mr. and Mrs. David Rabinowitz, Kings Point, NY; pvt collection, comn by Mr. Name June Paik, NY. *Exhib:* Solo Exhibs: include Kujke Gallery, Seoul, 1991, 1995, 1999, 2005; Sandra Gering Gallery, New York, 1992, 1997; Dorothy Golden Gallery, Los Angeles, 1993;

Neuberger Mus Art, Purchase, NY, 1993; Samsung Mus Mod Art, Seoul, 2000; Rodin Gallery, Seoul, 2000; Sabina Lee Gallery, Los Angeles, 2005; Habitual Habitat, Sabina Lee Gallery, Los Angeles, CA; Asian Am Arts Ctr, New York, 2006; Kukie Gallery, Seoul, Korea, 2006; Atelier, 705 Seoul, Korea, 2008; Group Exhibs: include Sandra Gering Gallery, New York, 1990, 1993; Beyond Acculturation, Tenri Cultural Inst, NY, 2005; New York Eviction Blues, Asian Am Arts Center, NY, 2005; Armory Show, Sandra Gering Gallery, NY, 2005; Points of Compass, Havana, Cuba, 2008; Shoes or Not Shoes Mus, Kruishoutem, Belgium, 2008; Multiple Parts, Dorothy Goldeen Gallery, Venice, Calif, 1994; Passion & Compassion, Asian Am Arts Ctr, New York, 1996, Below Canal Sept 11, 2002, 2004, New York Eviction Blues, 2005; Recent Acquisitions 1992-96, Hirshhorn Mus, Smithsonian Inst, Washington, 1997; Gurim Village Project I, 1st Earth Festival, Young-am, Korea, 2000; At the Crossroads, Korean Cult Serv, New York, 2003; Dreams & Reality, Smithsonian Int Gallery, Washington, 2004. *Teaching:* Vis prof studio art, Seoul Nat Univ Grad Sch, Korea, 1997, Korean Nat Univ Art, 1999-2000. *Awards:* Space Prog Grant, Marie Walsh Sharpe Found, 1991-92; NY State Coun Arts Grant, 1994; Woo-Kyung Found Art Award, 1998; Pollock-Krasner Found Grant, 2006-07. *Bibliog:* Claude Bouyeure (auth), Quatre Artistes de la Fondation Whanki (pages 37-40), Cimaise, 1-3/1981; Grace Glueck, Gallery Watch: A Trip to the Chicken Coop, NY Observer, 7/1995; Holland Cotter (auth), Art in Review: Personal Jokes (C25), NY Times, 7/25/1997; Kim Levin (auth), Village Voice (page 14), 8/5/1997. *Mailing Add:* 467 Greenwich St 2nd Fl New York NY 10013

LIM, WON JU
INSTALLATION ARTIST, SCULPTOR

b Gwang Ju, South Korea, Mar 14, 1968; US Citizen. *Study:* Woodbury Univ, BA, Burbank, Calif, 92; Art Ctr Coll of Design, Pasadena, Calif, MFA, 98. *Work:* Hammer Mus, Los Angeles, Calif; Honolulu Acad Arts, Hawaii; La Colección Jumex, Mex City, Mex; Vancouver Art Gallery, Can; T-B A21 Thyssen-Bornemisza Art Contemp, Vienna, Austria; Mus of Contemporary Art, Los Angeles, Calif. *Comn:* installation, Honolulu Acad Arts, Hawaii, 2006; installation, Vancouver Art Gallery, Can, 2002; installation, Guy & Myriam Found, Geneva, Switzerland, 2008. *Exhib:* Solo exhibs, Won Ju Lim: Longing for Wilmington, Mus für Gegenwartskunst, Siegen, Germany, 2001, Won Ju Lim, DA2 Domus Artium, Ctr Contemp Art, Salamanca, Spain, 2005, Won Ju Lim: In Many Things to Come, Honolulu Acad Arts, Hawaii, 2006, 24 Seconds of Silence, Ullens Ctr Contemp Art, Beijing, China, 2008, Untitles Silence, Jaffe-Fried Gallery, Dartmouth Coll, Hanover, NH, 2011, Raycraft Is Dead, Saint Louis Art Mus, Mo,, 2014, Yorba Buena Center for the Arts, San Francisco, Calif, 2015; Group exhibs, Zwischenwelten, Mus Haus Esters, Krefeld, Germany, 2004, For Excellence: 11 Korean Artists in America, Mus of Art, Seoul, South Korea, 2009, Dialogue: Art/Architecture, Los Angeles/Paris, MAK Center for Art and Architecture, Los Angeles, Calif, 2013, Permanent Collection: A Selection of Recent Acquisitions, Mus of Contemporary Art, Los Angeles,, 2013; Ein-Leuchten, Mus der Moderne Salzburg, Austria, 2004; Vanishing Point, Wexner Ctr Arts, Ohio State Univ, Columbus, Ohio, 2005; Lichtkunst aus Kunstlicht, ZKM Mus fur Neue Kunst, Karlsruhe, Germany, 2005; Idilio, DA2 Domus Artium, Ctr Contemp Art, Salamanca, Spain, 2007; Archit, Art & Landscape Biennial of the Canaries, Fuerteventura, Spain, 2006; All Inclusive A Tourist World, Schirn Kunsthalle, Frankfurt, Germany, 2008; Second Nature: The Valentine-Adelson Collection, Hammer Mus, Los Angeles, Calif, 2009. *Teaching:* lectr sculpture, Univ Calif Los Angeles, 2003-2006; vis instr new genre, Otis Coll Art & Design, Los Angeles, Calif, 2001; Freund Teaching Fellow, Washington Univ in Saint Louis, Mo, 2013-14; vis lectr, Univ Calif San Franciso, 2015. *Awards:* Phillip Morris Visual Artist Grant, 2000; emerging Artist Fel, Calif Community Found, 2004; Korea Arts Found of Am for Visual Arts, 2005; Rockefeller Found Media Arts Fel, ReNew Media, 2007; Freund Fellowship, 2013, Creative Capital Funds, 2014, COLA Fellowship grant, 2015. *Bibliog:* Mark Prince, Won Ju Lim, Flash Art, 2002; John Welchman, Won Ju Lim's Shadow World, DA2 Domus Artium, Ctr Contemp Art, Salamanca, Spain, 2005; Terry R Meyers, Won Ju Lim, Modern Painters: International Arts and Culture, 2006; Judith Collins, Sculpture Today, Phaidon Press Inc, New York, 2007; Hans Werner Holzwarth, Art Now Vol 3, Taschen, Cologne & Berlin, 2008; Lee Ambrozy, Won Ju Lim, Artforum, Vol XLVII, 2/2009; Hans Werner Holzwarth, 100 Contemporary Artists, Taschen, Cologne & Berlin, 2009; Tumlir, Jan, Won Ju Lim: The Newness of Cities, 2011; Triggs, Sarah, Studio Life: Rituals, Collections, Tools, and Observations on the Artistic Practice, 2013; Akademie X, 2014. *Dealer:* Patrick Painter Inc 2525 Michigan Ave #B2 Santa Monica CA 90404; Galerie Max Hetzler Zommerstrasse 90/91 Berlin Germany 10117; Pilar Parra & Romero Conde de Aranda 2 Madrid Spain 28001

LIMA, JACQUELINE (DUTTON)
PAINTER, DRAFTSMAN

b Niagara Falls, NY, Oct 28, 1949. *Study:* Swain Sch Design, New Bedford, MA, BFA, 78; Brooklyn Col, City Univ New York, MFA, 80. *Comn:* Hand painted wearable buttons, Rotunda Gallery, Brooklyn, NY, 85; 22' Circular ceiling mural, comn by New York Bd Educ & New York Sch Construction Authority, 96; A Family Portrait, Collection of John & Diane Herzog, 97; Infinite Collection of Flory Gardner, 98. *Exhib:* One-person Exhib, Fairleigh Dickinson Univ, Becton Hall Gallery, Teaneck, NJ, 3/98; Law Offices of Fredy H Kaplan, 26 Broadway, NY, 97; Art from the Ridge, L Gallery, Moscow, Russ & Berlin, Ger, 98; Time and Place, Kleinert/James Art Ctr, Woodstock, NY, 98; Object & Photo (Process the Image), Eklektikos Gallery, Georgetown, Washington, DC & East Ashland, Phoenix, Ariz, 98; Kentler Int Drawing Space, Red Hook, Brooklyn, 98. *Collection Arranged:* On the Waterfront, Kentler Int Drawing Space, 97; Members Exhib, Plymouth Church Pilgrims, Brooklyn, NY, 91, 92 & 93. *Pos:* Dir, Blue Mountain Gallery, NY, 91-98; cur, Brooklyn Water Front Artists Coalition, 88-93, exhib, Brookwood Child Care, Brooklyn, NY, 92 & 93; art therapist, Psychiatric Inpatient Prog, Coney Island Hosp, Brooklyn, NY, 92-95. *Teaching:* Instr, Hist & Theory Design Workshop, MFA Prog, Brooklyn Col, City Univ New York, 94-96; instr landscape drawing & painting, Western Carolina Univ, Cullowhee, 97; instr drawing, computer graphics/illus, New York Art World, Desktop Publ, Avant Garde Film, Fairleigh Dickinson Univ, Teaneck, NJ, 94-98. *Awards:* Charles W Shaw Award, Brooklyn Col, 79 & 80; Dr Maury Leibovitz Art Award, Lotos Club, Artists Welfare Fund, 86. *Bibliog:* Review of the World is Round, Contemporary Panoramas, Vivian Raynor, The New York Times, Jan 89; Review, Jed Perl (auth), The New Criterion, May 90; Jed Pearl (auth), Gallery Going Four Seasons in the Art World, The New Criterion, Harcourt Brace Jovanovich, 5/91. *Mem:* Brooklyn Waterfront Artists Coalition (bd dir, 85 & 86, rec secy, 87, vpres, 88, pres, 89, consult, 90-94). *Media:* Oil and graphite, acrylic. *Publ:* Crysalis J of the Reproduction of Who Would Have Ever Thought, spring 88; Crossings, An Artists Book ed by Nedd: Heller, 91 & 92. *Mailing Add:* 353 Van Brunt St Brooklyn NY 11231-1245

LIMONT, NAOMI CHARLES
PRINTMAKER, PAINTER

b Pottstown, Pa. *Study:* Pa Acad Fine Arts, BFA; Pratt Graphic Ctr, with Michael Ponce de Leon; Barnes Found; Univ Pa, BFA; Tyler Sch Art, with Romas Viesulas, MFA; also with Jerome Kaplan. *Work:* Philadelphia Mus Art & Pa Acad Fine Arts; Yale Univ; Eastern Mennonite Col, Va; Univ Southern Calif; Rutgers Univ, NJ. *Comn:* Mural, St Christopher's Children's Hosp, Philadelphia, 65; Creation (folio of prints), Philadelphia Print Club, 67; Folio '76 (bicentennial folio), Graphics Guild, Cheltenham, Pa, 75; Folio of Prints, The Centennial of Sun Printing Co, 80. *Exhib:* Int Biannual Print Show, Print Club, 77; Nat Print Exhib, Cedar City, Utah, 78; Eye on the Seventies, Philadelphia Mus Art, 79; Int Miniature Print Exhib, NY, 79; Structures, Rosenwald Gallery, Van Pelt-Dietrich Libr, Univ Pa, Philadelphia; and others. *Teaching:* Artist-in-residence, Lock Haven State Col, 81; instr graphics, Abington Art Ctr, 84-89. *Awards:* Sun Oil Award, Earth Art Exhib, 75; Stella Drabkin Award & Bronze Medal, Am Color Print Soc, 76; Grumbacher Award, 81, Guild Book Workers, Del Valley Guild Book Workers. *Bibliog:* Bagnell & Sosin (coordrs), The Tyler Show working women artists from Tyler School of Art, Samuel Paley Libr, Temple Univ, 73; review, Art News, 9/80; review, Art Voices, 3-4/81. *Mem:* Philadelphia Watercolor Club; Guild Bookworkers. *Mailing Add:* c/o Gallery Saint Martin Homestead Village 1954 Kestrel Ct Dr Lancaster PA 17603

LIN, CYNTHIA
ILLUSTRATOR, PAINTER

b Taiwan. *Study:* Univ Calif, Berkely, BA (art, with high distinction & honors), 1986; Univ Iowa, MA (painting), 1989, MFA (painting), 1990; Am Acad in Rome, vis artists & scholars prog, 1999. *Exhib:* Solo exhibs include Women & Their Work, Austin, Tex, 1997, Conduit Gallery Annex, Dallas, 1998, Sally Sprout Gallery, Houston, 1998, Meadows Mus Art, Southern Methodist Univ, Dallas, 2000, Satellite Space, Univ Tex, San Antonio, 2001, DiverseWorks Subspace, Houston, 2001, Devin Borden/Hiram Butler Gallery, Houston, 2001, Michael Steinberg Fine Art, New York, 2008; group exhibs include New York Statements, Art in General, New York, 1995; Selections from the Permanent Collection, Dallas Mus Art, 2001-02, 2005; Hair Stories, Adam Baumgold Gallery, New York, 2002; Realistic Means, Drawing Ctr, New York, 2002; Slowness, Dorsky Gallery, New York, 2003-04; The Topography of Absence, Asian-Am Arts Ctr, New York, 2004; The Luster of Silver: Contemp Metalpoint Drawings, Telfair Mus Art, Savannah, Ga, 2006; Ann Invitational Exhib Contemp Art, Nat Acad Mus, New York, 2008. *Pos:* instr, Morehead State Univ, Ky, 1990. *Teaching:* Teaching fel, Univ Iowa, Iowa City, 1988-89; vis asst prof, Dartmouth Coll, NH, 1991; assoc prof art, Southern Methodist Univ, Dallas, 1991-2002; vis artist, Cooper Union, New York, 2002-03; guest faculty, Sarah Lawrence Coll, Bronxville, NY, 2004-. *Awards:* Yaddo Visual Artist Fel, 1991 & 2004; MacDowell Colony Visual Artist Fel, 1994; Otis Dozier Travel Grant, Dallas Mus Art, 2001; Hall Farm Ctr Arts & Educ Fel, 2005; Djerassi Resident Artist Prog Visual Artist Fel, 2006; John Simon Guggenheim Mem Fel, 2006

LIN, MAYA Y
SCULPTOR

b Athens, Ohio, Oct 5, 1959. *Study:* Yale, BA, 81, MA (archit), 86, Hon Dr Fine Arts, 87. *Work:* Los Angeles Co Mus Art; Vietnam Veterans Mem, Washington, DC, 1981 (Twenty-five Year Award, AIA, 2007). *Exhib:* Solo exhibs and installations incl Industrial Ecology, Bronx Community Paper Co Munic Art Soc, NY, 97, Recent Work, Gagosian Gallery, Beverly Hills, Calif, 99, Maya Lin: Between Art and Archit, Cooper Union, Arthur A Houghton, Jr Gallery, NY, 2000, Systematic Landscapes, Henry Art Gallery, Univ Washington, 2005, Confluence Project, 2006; group exhibs incl Am Women Artists - Par II, The Younger Generation, Sidney Janis Gallery, NY, 84; Jane Voorhees Zimmerli Art Mus, Rutgers State Univ, NJ, 85; Civil Rights Memorial, Montgomery, Ala, 86; Avant-Garde in the Eighties, Los Angeles Co Mus Art, 87; 60's-80's Sculpture Parallels, Sidney Janis Gallery, 88; Group Exhib, Rosa Esman Gallery, NY, 90; Urban Mythologies: The Bronx Represented Since the 1960s, The Bronx Mus of the Arts, NY, 99; Powder, The Aspen Art Mus, Colo, 99; The cultural Desert, Bentley Gallery, Mayo Clinic Scottsdale, Mus of Contemp Art, Ariz, 2002. *Pos:* Design consult, Cooper-Lecky Partnership, Washington, DC, 81-82; archit designer, Peter Forbes & Assocs, Boston, 83, Batey & Mack, San Francisco, 84; archit apprentice, Fumihiko Maki & Assocs, Tokyo, 85; design assoc, Peter Forbes & Assocs, NY, 86-87; Maya Lin Studio, NY, 87-. *Teaching:* Archit studio instr, Phillips Exeter Acad, summer 82; head teaching asst, Yale Art Hist Dept, 84-85; vis prof, Yale Col Seminar, 86; vis lectr, Harvard Univ, Sch Landscape Design, Cambridge, Mass, 88; Resident in Fine Arts Am Acad, Rome, 98; vis lectr, Portland Arts and Lects, 97, TED Conf, 99. *Awards:* Henry Bacon Mem Award, AIA, 84; Nat Medal Arts award, Nat Endowment for the Arts, 88 & 2010; Design 100 - Elements of Style, Metrop Home, 90; Am Acad of Arts and Letters, award in Archit, 96; LVMH, Sci pour L'Art Award, 96; Finn Juhl Award, Wilhelm Hansen Found, Copenhagen, 2003; Nat. Medal of Arts, 2009. *Bibliog:* Alice Hall (ed), Vietnam Mem, Nat Geographic, 5/85; Jonathan Coleman (auth), Time Mag, 11/6/89; Boundaries (auth), 2000. *Mem:* Natural Resources Defense Counc (bd mem, NY, 98-); Nat Acad Design; Nat Acad Arts and Letters. *Mailing Add:* c/o Gagosian 980 Madison Ave New York NY 10021

LIN, SARA
PAINTER, CALLIGRAPHER
b Taiwan, Mar 25, 1940. *Study:* Worldjournal Coll, 66-70; Dr Ma Sing-Foon Calligraphy, 82-90; Jason Chang art studio, NY, 96. *Work:* Nat Hist Mus, Taipei, Taiwan. *Comn:* Bearo's Italian Restaurant, Conn, 2000; Terence Cardinal Cooke Healthcare Ctr, 2003; Taiwan Cult Ctr, Taipe Econ & Cult Office, NY, 2006. *Exhib:* Sara Lin's Pastel Exhib, Lin's Studio, Brooklyn, NY, 99; Pastel Soc Am Ann Exhib, Nat Art Club, Manhattan, NY, 99, 2003, 2005; Am Artist Prof League Ann Exhib, Salmagundi Club, Manhattan, NY, 2002-2004; Audubon Artist Inc Ann Exhib, Salmagundi Club, Manhattan, NY, 2002-2005; Allide Artists Am Inc Exhib, Nat Art Club, Manhattan, NY, 2004. *Pos:* Pastels demonstr, N Am Pastel Artists 4th Ann Show, 2002-2004; exhib ch, N Am Pastel Artists Exib, 2003-2006; juror selection, Taiwan Ctr Int Pastel Juried Exhib, 2005-2006; exhib chmn, NTD TV Childrens Art Competition, 2006. *Awards:* Grumbacher Gold Medal, Conn Pastel Soc 10th Ann Exhib, 2003; President's Award, Am Artists Prof League, NY, 2004; Art Spirit Found Dianne B Bernhard Award of Merit, Life, Audubon Artists Art Soc, 2005. *Bibliog:* Jason Chang (auth), Pastel World of Jason Chang, G&P Coll Marshall Wei, 99. *Mem:* Pastel Soc Am (signature mem); AudubonArtists Inc (full mem); Am Artists Prof League; NY Chinese Calligraphy Arts Soc; N Am Pastel Artist Asn (exhib chair). *Media:* Pastels, Chinese Painting. *Dealer:* Taiwan Cult Ctr 137-44 Northern Blvd Flushing NY 11354. *Mailing Add:* 1215 8th Ave Brooklyn NY 11215

LINCOLN, JANE LOCKWOOD
PAINTER, PRINTMAKER
b Exeter, NH, Mar 17, 1950. *Study:* St Lawrence Univ, BA (studio), 72; Cape Sch Art, 84-87; Art New England, with Wolf Kahn, 91; Mass Coll Art & Design, MFA, 2011. *Work:* Cahoon Mus Am Art, Cotuit, Mass; Cape Cod Mus Art, Dennis, Mass; 4 panel mural, McCarthy House, Sandwich, Mass; Dartmouth Hitchcock Med Center (4 print installation), Lebanon, NH; Provincetown Art Assn and Mus, Provincetown, Mass. *Comn:* Landscape, comn by H Zimmerman, New Seabury, Mass, 2000; Landscape, comn by J Budd, Dover, Mass, 2000; Landscape, comn by R Hallagan, Dover, Mass, 2002; Landscape, comn by C Goldberg, Tamarac, Fla, 2004; 6 print series, comn by J Borak, Guilford, Conn, 2005. *Exhib:* Three Sisters, Manchester Inst, NH, 96; Cape Mus Natural History, Brewster, Mass, 98 & 2004; Visions, Cape Cod Community Coll, Barnstable, Mass, 98, Generations, 2000; Biennial Alumni, St Lawrence Univ, Canton, NY, 98; Fields of Color, Cahoon Mus Am Art, Cotuit, Mass, 99, Signature, 2000 & Snow Birds, 2003; Pastel Show Ellison Ctr for Arts, Duxbury, Mass, 2000; Signature, Cape Mus Fine Arts, Dennis, Mass, 2003; Illuminations, Mass Gen Hospital, Boston, 2002-03; solo exhib (62 landscapes), Cranberry Bogs, Cape Cod Mus Art, Dennis, Mass, 2005-2006; Cahoon Mus Am Art, Cotuit, Mass, 2005; Wynne-Falconer Gallery, Chatham, Mass, 2005; Visions and Voices of the Outer Cape, Provincetown Art Asn & Mus, Mass, 2007; Cove Gallery, Wellfleet, Mass, 2009; America the Beautiful, 2011; MFAWC Thesis Show, Provincetown Art Asn & Mus, Provincetown, Mass, 2011, Mass Art, Boston, Mass, 2012; Reawakenings, Cahoon Mus Am Art, Cotuit, Mass, 2012; Bridges, Duxbury Art Complex, Duxbury, Mass, 2012; Color Notations, Clove Gallery, 2012; Bromfield Gallery, Boston, Mass, 2013; AE Backus Mus and Gallery, Fort Pierce, Fla, 2013; Stamford Art Assn, Stamford, Conn, 2013; ArtWorks Gallery, New Bedford, Mass, 2013; Gallery Ehva, Provincetown, Mass, 2013; Brush Art Gallery, Lowell, Mass, 2013; Cahoon Mus Am Art, Cotuit, Mass, 2013; Cove Gallery, 2014; Elliott Mus, Stuart, Fla, 2014; Kenise Barnes Fine Art, Larchmont, NY, 2014; State House, Boston, Mass, 2014; Creative Arts Ctr, Chatham, Mass, 2014; Cape Cod Mus Art, Dennis, Mass, 2014; Provincetown Art Assn & Mus, Provincetown, Mass, 2014; Cotuit Ctr Arts, Cotuit, Mass, 2015; Cahoon Mus Am Art, Cotuit, Mass, 2015; Court House Cultural Ctr, Stuart Fla, 2015; Kentler Internat Drawing Space, Brooklyn, NY, 2015. *Collection Arranged:* Calculated Color (cur), Higgins Art Gallery, Cape Cod Community Col, West Barnstable, Mass, Sept 3-Oct 3 2008. *Teaching:* color theory, Falmouth Artists Guild, 89-2000, abstract, 2003; lectr color mixing, Barnstable Pub Schs, 95-2000 & Cahoon Mus Am Art, 99; lectr color, Cape Cod Community Coll, Barnstable, 2003; lectr color theory, Cape Cod Art Asn, Barnstable, 2004; color theory, Duxbury Art Assn, Mass, 2006, 2012. *Awards:* Best Pastel, Falmouth Artists Guild, Falmouth, Mass, 2006; 32nd Annual Faber Birren Nat Color award Show, Stamford Art Assn, Conn, 2012, 33rd Ann Faber Birren Nat Color award Show, 2013; Artists Residency, Va Ctr Creative Arts, Amherst, Va, 2014. *Bibliog:* Exploring color with Jane Lincoln, The Pastel J, 2003; Jane Lincoln: Applying Color Theory to Painting the Landscape, The Pastel J, 2003; On Defining Personal Style, Pastelagram, Pastel Soc Am, Winter 2003; Color for Color's Sake, Cape Cod Life Arts Ed, 2009; Bridges: Expanding the Image, American Artist, 2012; Striking Color, Scott Gargan, Pulse, 2013; Deborah Forman (auth), Contemporary Cape Cod Artists: On Abstraction, 2015. *Mem:* Pastel Painters Soc Cape Cod (sig mem); Printmakers Cape Cod. *Media:* Pastel, Oil, White-Line Woodblock Prints, Acrylic. *Publ:* Coauth, Two for the Road, Am Artist,92; contribr, Exhibits Add Some Color, Boston Globe, 96 & Lifestyle & Arts, Cape Cod Times, 99; illusr, Take in Some Local Color-Spyglass, Cahoon Mus, 99; contribr, Guide, Art in Am, 2000; My At, My SPace, My Love, Cape Cod Mag, 2009; Featured artists profile, Cape Cod Life, 2009. *Dealer:* Cove Gallery Box 482 Wellfleet MA 02667; Kentler Internat Drawing Space 353 Van Brunt St Brooklyn NY 11231; Kingston Gallery 450 Harrison Ave #43 Boston Mass 02118. *Mailing Add:* 441 Central Ave East Falmouth MA 02536

LINCOLN, LOUISE
MUSEUM DIRECTOR, EDUCATOR
b Baltimore, Md. *Study:* Bryn Mawr Col, BA, 1969; Univ Del, MA, 1972. *Pos:* Editor, Minn Inst Arts, 1977-80, asst curator, 1980-94, associate curator, 1984-87, curator, African, Oceanic and New World Cultures, 1988; dir, DePaul Univ Art Mus, currently, adj faculty mem Museum Dept History of Art & Archit DePaul Univ, currently; adj prof art history Univ Saint Thomas, Saint Paul, 1994-. *Awards:* Scholarly Contribution award, Am Asn Mus Curators, 1993. *Mem:* Coll Art Asn; Am Asn Museums; Asn Academic Museums and Galleries; Am Anthropological Asn; Native Am Studies Asn; Pacific Arts Asn; African Studies Asn. *Specialty:* Art of Chicago. *Publ:* Consultant, writer World Book Encyclopedia, 1992; auth Finished Beauty, Southwest Indian Silver, 1983, Assemblage of Spirits: Idea and Image in New Ireland, 1987, Visions of the People: A Pictorial History of Plains Indian Life, 1992 (Wittenborn award, 1993); Re: Chicago, 2011; contributes articles to professional journals. *Mailing Add:* DePaul University Art Museum 935 W Fullerton Ave Chicago IL 60614

LINDAHL, TONI
PAINTER
b Paterson, NJ, Nov 8, 1949. *Study:* NY Univ, MA. *Work:* Volvo-White Corp Hq; Duke Univ; Lowes Co; Centura; Glaxo Inc. *Comn:* Pastel paintings, Sheraton Hotel, Greensboro, NC, 84; Pastel paintings, Hilton Hotel, Altamonte, Fla, 85; Pastel paintings, Wachovia Bank-Trust Co, Winston-Salem, NC, 90; Pastel paintings, Women's Hosp, Chapel Hill, NC, 2000. *Exhib:* Danville Art Mus, Danville, Va; Art on paper Exhib, Weatherspoon Gallery, UNCG; NC in NY, Nat Arts Club, New York; invitational, Greenhill Ctr NC Art, Greensboro, NC; Pastel Soc Am Exhib, Nat Arts Club, New York; Butler Inst Am Art, Ohio. *Teaching:* Vis artist, Greenhill Ctr NC Art. *Awards:* Nat Juried Exhib Award, numerous awards; Master Pastelist Award, Pastel Soc Am; Joseph U Giffuni Found Award; Award for Best Pastel, Salmagundi Arts Club, 85; Best in Show, Henley Southwestern Spectrum, 91. *Mem:* Greenhill Ctr NC Art; NC Pastel Soc; Assoc Artists Winston-Salem; Degas Pastel Soc; Pastel Soc Am. *Media:* Pastel Artist. *Interests:* Environmental issues. *Publ:* The Best of Pastels, Portrait Inspirations & Floral Inspirations, Rockport Publ; Pratigue des Arts (feature article). *Dealer:* American Art Resources 3262 Sul Ross St Houston TX 77098; Green Hill Center for North Carolina Art 200 N Davie St Greensboro NC 27401. *Mailing Add:* 546 Birch Creek Rd Mc Leansville NC 27301

LINDEMANN, ADAM
COLLECTOR
b 1962. *Study:* Amherst Coll, BA (Spanish lit); Yale Univ Law Sch, JD. *Pos:* Founder, pres & chief exec officer, Mega Communications co, NY, 1998-2005; appointee, Bush-Cheney FCC Adv Comt, 2001; prin, IKEPOD, Tan Tan Bo Puking LLC, 2005-; opened art gallery, Venus Over Manhatten, 2012. *Awards:* Named one of Top 200 Art Collectors, ARTnews mag, 2006-12. *Collection:* Contemporary art; African art; 20th-century design. *Mailing Add:* Venus Over Manhatten Gallery 980 Madison Ave 3rd Fl New York NY 10075

LINDEMANN, EDNA M
MUSEUM DIRECTOR, EDUCATOR
b Buffalo, NY. *Study:* Univ Buffalo, BS (art, dist); Albright Art Sch; Northwestern Univ, MA (magna cum laude), 40; Cranbrook Acad Art; Columbia Univ, EdD, 56. *Collection Arranged:* Burchfield Int Exhib, 68; 150 Years of Portraiture in Western NY, 81; Charles Clough: Selections 1972-81, 83; Charles Cary Rumsey, Sculptor: 1879-1922, 83; Niagara Falls, New Impressions, 85; Burchfield and His Colleagues, 89. *Pos:* Dir cult affairs, State Univ NY, Buffalo, 65-68; dir, Burchfield Art Ctr, 68-85, emer dir, 85-; Burchfield-Penney Art Ctr Coun, 68-; chmn, Gallery, Asn NY State, 70-72, mem bd dir, 72-77. *Teaching:* Instr art educ, NY Univ, 49-56; prof design, State Univ NY, Buffalo, 56-85, emer prof, 85-. *Awards:* Focus Award for Outstanding Contribution to Cult Affairs, Western New York-Buffalo Courier Express, 76; Achievement Award, Am Asn Univ Women, 83; Citizen of Yr Award, Buffalo News, 85. *Mem:* Gallery Asn NY State (found mem & chmn, 72-75); Burchfield Art Ctr, Buffalo, NY (found dir, dir emer current); Art Appraisers Asn; Am Asn Mus; Buffalo & Erie Co Botanical Gardens Soc (bd dir, 86-). *Res:* A comparative analysis of museums devoted to one artist or a small group of artists in the United States, Canada and worldwide; Charles E Burchfield and other Western NY artists. *Publ:* Auth, Our Legacy of Art in Western New York, 72; ed, Edwin Dickinson, 77; Roycroft: Spirit for Today, 77; The American Landscape: Paintings by Allen D'Arrangelo, 79; Auth, Burchfield and his Colleagues: Artist/Dealer/Collector, 89. *Mailing Add:* PO Box 249 West Falls NY 14170-0249

LINDENBERG, MARY K
PAINTER, INSTRUCTOR
b New York, NY, Feb 2, 1921. *Study:* Hunter Col, BA, 42; Phi Beta Kappa; Pi Mu Epsilon; Magna Cum Laude. *Work:* numerous pvt collections. *Comn:* Christmas Cards, 92 & 93, Courage Cards; Calendars for Am Press, 67, 79, 81, 83, 90, 95. *Exhib:* Brockton Art Mus, Mass, 80; Newport Art Mus, RI, 81; Three-person Show, Providence Art Club, RI, 85; RI Watercolor Soc, Pawtucket, 88; Bierstadt Art Soc, New Bedford, Mass, 88, 93 & 95. *Pos:* Co-founder, Mass Art Week, 57-, New Bedford, Mass, Art Week, 81. *Teaching:* Instr watercolor, New Bedford YWCA, 78-92, Southeastern Mass Univ, 85. *Awards:* First Prize, Brockton Art Mus, 80; Prize for watercolor, Greater Fall River Art Asn, 90; First Prize for drawing, Bierstadt Art Soc, 88; First Prize, Middleboro Art Soc, 87; First Prize, Magic Palette Gallery, 95; First Prize, Westport Art Group, 89. *Bibliog:* Eleanor Roth (auth), Do artists have special perceptions?, AIM Mag, 74; article, Surprising ingredient of creativity, Living Mag, Singapore, 79. *Mem:* Bierstadt Art Soc; Marion Art Ctr; Westport Art Group; Renaissance Art Gallery Fall River. *Media:* Watercolor, Acrylic, Drawing, Abstract Collage. *Publ:* Auth, mem issue, North Light Mag, 80, 83 & 91; Variations on a theme of nature, Palette Talk Mag, 84; Getting started in teaching, Draw Mag, 86. *Dealer:* Lopoukhine Gallery Inc 125 Newbury St Suite 4 Boston MA 02116. *Mailing Add:* 20 Emerald Dr North Dartmouth MA 02747

LINDER, CHARLES KEATING
SCULPTOR
b Pittsburgh, Pa, 1967. *Study:* San Francisco Art Inst, BFA, 90; Univ Calif, Berkeley, MFA, 97; studied with David Nash & Larry Jordan; self taught. *Exhib:* Solo exhib, Brian Gross, San Francisco, Calif, 2000, Paula Boettcher Galerie, Berlin, Ger, 2002, Post Gallery, Los Angeles, Calif. *Pos:* found, Alternative Gallery, Refusalon, San Francisco, Calif, currently. *Awards:* Murphy Cadogar Award; Marian Hahn Simpson Fel, Univ Calif, Berkeley; Sobel Award, San Francisco Art Inst. *Mem:* Soc of Independent Artists. *Media:* Metal

LINDGREN, CARL EDWIN
PHOTOGRAPHER, HISTORIAN
b Coeburn, Va, Nov 20, 1949. *Study:* Univ Miss, BAE, 72, MEd, 77, EdS, 93; Coll of Preceptors, London, FCP, 93; UNISA, DEdu, 99. *Work:* Ctr for Study of Southern Cult, Univ Miss; Ctr for Faulkner Studies, SE Mo State Univ. *Comn:* A Jefferson Collection, Ctr for Faulkner Studies. *Exhib:* Passing Shadows, Faulkner & Yoknapatawpha Conf, Ctr for Study of Southern Cult, 91 & 92, Cossett Gallery, Memphis, Tenn, 92 & Manduri Univ Mus, India, 93; Southern Delight, Fairfax Gallery, London, 93; various showings throughout US, Russia, India and Europe, 2002-04; Faulkner's Mem, 2010. *Pos:* Atlantic Chapter coordr, Royal Photographic Soc; prof photographic history, Am Coll Genealogy, Heraldry, and Documentary Sciences. *Teaching:* Lectr photo, Univ Miss, 79-81, darkroom tech, 91-93; prof hist, Am Military Univ. *Bibliog:* Rowan Oak, Royal Soc Arts J, 92; Dr Burl Hunt (auth), Passing shadows, Art Papers, 93; Penni Bolton (auth), From Oxford Street to Oxford; Ole Miss Alumni Rev, 93. *Mem:* Fel Royal Soc Arts, Eng; assoc Indian Int Photog Coun, Madra, India; mem Photog Soc Am; fel, World Acad Art & Sci; Royal Photographic Soc. *Media:* Black and White photography. *Res:* Faulkner & Ole Miss hist art studies. *Publ:* Illusr, Rowan Oak and Yoknapatawpha, The Cape Rock, 91; illusr & auth, The regional photographer, Photog Soc Am J, 92; auth, Teaching photography in the Indian school, Photo Trade Dir, 92; Enigmatic presence, Royal Soc Arts J, 93; illustr, Monuments to the past, Ole Miss Alumni Rev, 93. *Dealer:* Thompson Gallery; The Underground Photographer. *Mailing Add:* 10431 Hwy 51 Courtland MS 38620

LINDGREN, CHARLOTTE
SCULPTOR
b Toronto, Ont, Feb 1, 1931. *Study:* Univ Mich, BS; Can Coun studies in Finland, Sweden & Eng. *Work:* Canada Mus Civilization, Ottawa; Can Dept External Affairs, Ottawa; York Univ, Toronto; Winnipeg Art Gallery; Confederation Ctr Art Gallery, Charlottetown, PEI; McLaughlin Gallery, Oshawa; Art Gallery of Nova Scotia, Halifax. *Comn:* Ten Light Nets, Queen's Col, Nfld, 68; IBM Headquarters Conference Room, Toronto, 68; Discovery, Expo '70, Can Pavilion, Osaka, Japan, 70; Receptor, CBC Bldg, Montreal, 74; Weir, Fed Fisheries Bldg, Yarmouth, 77. *Exhib:* Montreal Mus Fine Arts, 66; Am Fed Arts, Threads of Hist, 66-69; Nat Art Gallery, Ottawa, 67; Art Gallery of Ont, 74; Can Cult Centre, Paris, France, 76; Harbourfront, Toronto, 80; IV Triennale, Poland, 81; Barbican Centre, London, Eng, 82; Mikrocosmo, Spain, Denmark, Ger, 83-85; Cool Sixties, Canadian Mus Civilization, Ottawa 2005. *Pos:* Mem adv arts panel, Can Coun; consult, Nat Capitol Commission, 78, Pangnirtung Tapestries, 78-81; vpres, Royal Can Acad Arts, 78-81; cur, The Knot Exhib, Mary Black Gallery, Halifax. *Teaching:* Mem fac, NS Col Art & Design, 78-79 & 81-82 & Banff Ctr Fine Arts, 79; vis prof, Royal Col Art, London, 83, 85 & 91. *Awards:* Haystack Sch Scholar Award, 64; Can Coun Arts Award, 65; First Prize Award, Perspective Competition Centennial Comn, Govt Can, 67; Ont Arts Coun Award, 87; presentation grant, Nova Scotia Arts Council; Golden Jubilee Medal, Queen Elizabeth II, 2002. *Bibliog:* C Fraser (auth), article, 6/66 & J Graham (auth), article, 7/71, Arts Can; L Rombout (auth), article, Vie des Arts, winter 67; J Murray (auth), article, Arts Atlantic, winter 80. *Mem:* Royal Can Acad Artists; Can Artists' Representation (NS rep). *Media:* Miscellaneous. *Mailing Add:* 1557 Vernon St Halifax NS B3H 3M8 Canada

LINDQUIST, EVAN
PRINTMAKER, EDUCATOR
b Salina, Kans, May 23, 1936. *Study:* Emporia Kans State Univ, BSE, 58; Univ Iowa, MFA, 63. *Work:* Whitney Mus Am Art, NY; Uffizzi, Florence, Italy; Albertina Mus, Vienna, Austria; Nelson-Atkins Art Mus, Kansas City; Art Inst Chicago. *Comn:* Print Club of Albany, 2007. *Exhib:* Prints by Seven, Whitney Mus Am Art, NY, 71; Boston Printmakers Ann Exhib, 71-75; Opera Bevilacqua La Masa, Venice, Italy, 77; two-men circulating exhib, Ark Arts Coun, 79-81; Gallerie V Kunstverlag Wolfbrum, Vienna, Austria, 79; Ark Arts Ctr, Little Rock, 83, 86, 87 & 2002; and others. *Pos:* Staff artist, Emporia State Univ, 58-60. *Teaching:* Prof printmaking & drawing, Ark State Univ, Jonesboro, 63-2003; Emer prof Art, 2003-. *Awards:* More than 60 awards including Boston Printmakers, 71-74 & Potsdam Prints, NY State Univ Potsdam, 72; Lifetime Achievement Award, Ark Arts Coun, 04; Distinguished Alumni Award, Emporia State Univ, 04; Lifetime Achievement award, Soc Am Graphics, NY, 2010. *Bibliog:* Julia S. Ayres, Printmaking Techniques, Watson-Guptill Pubs, 93; Robert Malone, Yingxue & Scott Wampler, Contemporary American Printmaking, Jilin Fine Arts Pub House, 99; Benny Shaboy, Evan Lindquist, StudioNotes, Benicia, 99-2000. *Mem:* Boston Printmakers; The Print Club, Philadelphia; Soc Am Graphic Artists; Southern Graphics Coun. *Media:* Engraving, Woodcut. *Dealer:* The Old Print Shop NYC; Sara Howell Gallery Jonesboro Ark; Old Print Gallery Wash DC; M2 Gallery Little Rock Ark. *Mailing Add:* 4300 Hickory Lane Jonesboro AR 72401

LINDQUIST, GREG
PAINTER
b Wilmington, NC, 1979. *Study:* NC State Univ, BA summa cum laude (design & English), 2003; Pratt Inst, MFA, 2008. *Exhib:* Missing Link, Schafler Gallery, Pratt Inst, New York, 2006; Site Matters: Brooklyn Represents, Brooklyn Arts Coun, 2007; solo exhibs, McCaig-Welles Gallery, Brooklyn, 2007, Elizabeth Harris Gallery, New York, 2008, Coll Design Gallery, NC State Univ, 2008 & Brooklyn Acad Music, 2009; Urban Landscapes, Elizabeth Harris Gallery, New York, 2008; Frozen Moments: Architecture Speaks Back, Ministry Transportation Project, Laura Palmer Found, Tbilisi, Georgia, 2010. *Pos:* Artist asst, Ryan McGinness, New York, 2005-07; res intern, Mus Mod Art, 2006-07; contribr, Brooklyn Rail, 2007-. *Awards:* Pollock-Krasner Found Grant, 2008; Milton & Sally Avery Found Grant, 2009. *Bibliog:* Mario Naves (auth), Brooklyn in Ruins, New York Observer, 3/21/2007; John Goodrich (auth), Factory Guy, New York Sun, 2/21/2008; Ann Landi (auth), Urban Landscapes at Elizabeth Harris, Art News, 9/2008

LINDQUIST, MARK
SCULPTOR, PHOTOGRAPHER
b Oakland, Calif, May 16, 1949. *Study:* New England Coll, BA, 71; Pratt Inst; Fla State Univ, MFA, 90. *Work:* Metrop Mus Art, NY; Victoria & Albert Mus, London, Eng; Smithsonian Am Art Mus, DC; The Art Inst of Chicago, Ill; Philadelphia Mus Art; and others. *Comn:* Sculpture, Brockton Art Mus, Mass, 85; 3 sculptures, Nations Bank Corp Hq, Charlotte, NC, 93; Installation of Totemic Triad, Bank of Am Corporate Headquarters, Charlotte, NC, 2010. *Exhib:* Solo exhibs, Ten-Year Overview, Greenville Co Mus Art, SC, 79, Brevard Art Mus, Melbourne, Fla, 86, Franklin Parrasch Gallery, NY, 89, Gail Severn Gallery, Ketchum, Idaho, 92, Snyderman Gallery, Philadelphia, 92 & Dorothy Weiss Gallery, San Francisco, Calif, 93, Revolutions in Wood: Mark Lindquist 25 yr Retrospective Hand Workshop Art Ctr, 95, Nat Mus Am Art, 96, Mark Lindquist: Forty Year Retrospective, Gadsen Arts Ctr, Quincy, Fla, 2010 ; The Art of the Turned Bowl, Renwick Gallery, Smithsonian Inst, 78; The Poetry of the Physical, Am Craft Mus, NY & traveling, 86-88; Mus Fine Arts, Boston, 91; Am Crafts: The Nation's Collection, Renwick Gallery, Smithsonian Inst, 92; Del Art Mus, 93; The Art of the Woodturner, High Mus Art, Atlanta, Ga, 93; Beyond Nature: Wood into Art (with catalog), Lowe Art Mus, Miami, Fla, 94; The White House Collection Am Art, Renwick Gallery, Smithsonian Inst, 95; The Founders' Circle Collection Inaugural Exhib & The Jane and Arthur Mason Collection, Mint Mus Craft and Design, Charlotte, NC 2000; Wood Turning in N Am since 1930, Renwick Gallery, Smithsonian Inst, Yale Univ & Minneapolis Inst Arts, 2001-2002; Kanazawa World Craft Forum, Kanazawa, Japan, 2003; Devos Art Mus, Marquette, Mich, 2005; The Presence of Absence, SOFA, Chicago, Ill, 2006; Am Masterpieces of Southern Craft & Traditional Art, Southern Arts Fedn (touring), 2007; Icons: A Tribute to Mel Lindquist, SOFA, Chicago, 2008; Soul's Journey: Inside the Creative Process exhib & documentary film, The Ctr for Craft Creativity & design, Hendersonville, NC, 2008; Turning Wood in New Hampshire: Mel and Mark Lindquist, Currier Mus Art, Manchester, NH, 2009; A Revolution in Wood: The Bresler Coll, Smithsonian Am Art Mus, Wash DC, 2010; The Tool at Hand, Milwaukee Art Mus, 2011-2013; Against the Grain: Wood in Contemporary Art, Craft and Design, Mint Mus, Charlotte, NC, Mus Arts and Design, NY, 2012-2013, Across the Grain: Turned and Carved Wood, Fuller Craft Mus, Brockton, Mass, 2013. *Teaching:* Instr welding & three-dimensional design, New Eng Col, 70-71; head of woodworking, Craft Ctr, Worcester, Mass, 77-78; assoc prof, Sch Archit, Fla A&M Univ, 88-89. *Awards:* MacDowell Colony Fel, NH, 79; Hon bd member, James Renwick Alliance, 96; Fel, Am Craft Coun, 2007; and others. *Bibliog:* Nancy Means Wright (auth), Mark Lindquist: The Bowl Is a Performance, Am Craft Mag, 10/11/80; Robert Hobbs (auth), Mark Lindquist: Revolutions in Wood, (exhib catolog) 25 yr retrospective at Hand Workshop Art Ctr, Richmond, Va & Renwick Gallery of the Smithsonian Inst, 95; Terry Martin (auth), Mark Lindquist: Pioneer of the Unexpected, Am Woodturner, 2010; and others. *Mem:* Phi Kappa Phi. *Media:* Wood, Photography. *Publ:* Auth, Spalted Wood, 77, Turning the Spalted Bowl, 78 & Harvesting Burls, 84, Fine Woodworking Mag; Sculpting Wood, Davis Press, 86. *Dealer:* Lindquist Studios Gallery. *Mailing Add:* 311 Glory Rd Quincy FL 32352

LINDROTH, LINDA
PHOTOGRAPHIC ARTIST, CURATOR
b Miami, Fla, Sept 4, 1946. *Study:* Douglass Col, BA (art), 68; Rutgers Univ with Leon Golub, MFA (art), 79; also with Gordon Matta Clark & Garry Winogrand. *Work:* Mus Mod Art, Metrop Mus Art & Mus City New York; Bibliot Nat, Paris; NJ State Mus, Trenton; Polaroid Corp; High Mus Art, Atlanta; Ctr Creative Photog, Tucson, Ariz; Yale Univ; First Bank Boston. *Exhib:* Solo exhibs, Newark Mus, NJ, 85-86, City Spirit Artists/The New Haven Found, 86 & Photo Structures 1982-1986, Aetna Inst Gallery, Hartford, Conn, 87; Pub Space in the New Am City/Atlanta 1996 Design Competition, Nexus Contemp Art Ctr, 94; Strokes of Genius: Mini Golf by Artists, DeCordova Mus, Lincoln, Mass, 95; 1994-95 Weir Farm Vis Artists, Aldrich Mus Contemp Art, Ridgefield, Conn, 95; 25 Years of Feminism, 25 Years of Women's Art, Rutgers Univ, New Brunswick, NJ, 96; Beyond the Picture Plane, Conn Comn Arts, Hartford, 96; Natural Immersion, Boston Ctr Arts, 96; Fellowship Exhib, Conn Comn on the Arts, Hartford, 2001; The Bunker with Craig Newick When the Earth Meets the Sky, Creative Arts Workshop, 2002. *Pos:* Founder & dir, Gallery Jazz Inc Art Gallery, New Haven, Conn, 84-87; guest cur, Aetna Inst Gallery, Hartford, 87; co-curator, Pump House Gallery, Hartford, 90-93; Pub Art Comn for Conn Children's Medical Ctr, Hartford, 95-96; coordr fine arts lectr series, Quinnipiac Univ, Hamden, CT, & asst & adj prof fine art, 98-; consultant & interior designer, Artspace Hartford and Artspace Norwich, Live/Work space for Artists, 96-99. *Teaching:* Instr photog, Douglass Col, New Brunswick, NJ, 77-79. *Awards:* Gold Award, Wilmer Shields Rich Awards for Excellence in Commun, 95; Fel Painting, Conn Comn Arts, 95-96; Nat Endowment Arts Regional Fel in Photog, New Eng Found Arts; Finalist, Howard Found, Brown Univ Fel in Art, 2001; Grant, Te Found, Inc, 2002. *Bibliog:* Judy Birke (auth), Art Review, New Haven Register, 10/16/94; Jude Schwendenwien, Art Review, Art New Eng, 12/95; Patricia Rosoff, Seeking to Recapture Paradise Lost, Hartford Advocate, 5/9/96; Linda Lindroth,(auth), Books and Articles. *Publ:* Contribr, New Jersey Photography, 74 & Photographic Process as Medium, 76, Rutgers Univ; Artists Books USA, Independent Cur Inc, 78; Virtual Vintage The Insider's Guide to Buying and Selling Fashion Online, Random House, 2002. *Mailing Add:* 219 Livingston St New Haven CT 06511-2209

LINDSAY, ARTURO
SCULPTOR, PAINTER
b Colon, Panama, Sept 29, 46; US citizen. *Study:* Cent Conn State Univ, BA, 70; Univ Mass, MFA, 75; New York Univ, doctoral studies ongoing. *Work:* Nat Union Cuban Writers & Artists, Havana; Slater Mem Mus, Norwich, Conn; Barnett-Aden Collection, Washington, DC; Royal-Athena Galleries, NY; Univ Mass, Amherst. *Comn:* Homage to our Musicians (mural), Craftery Gallery, Hartford, 78; Cinque (mural), Amistad Cult Resource Ctr, Hartford, 78. *Exhib:* Through Young Black Eyes, Wadsworth Atheneum, Hartford, 72-73; Caribbean Festival Arts, Nat Union Cuban Writers & Artists Mus, Havana, Cuba, 79; Black & Hispanic Art in Conn, Slater Mem

Mus, Norwich, 80; Art in the Southwest, African Am Mus, Dallas, 81; Artists of the 80's, Los Angeles Co Mus, 83; Houston Artists, Midtown Art Ctr, 84; African Am Art in Pub & Pvt Collections in Atlanta, The High Mus, 84; Caribbean Art: African Currents, Mus Contemp Hispanic Art, Soho, NY, 86; Encuentro de Escultura, Museo de Arte Contemporaneo, Panama City, Panama; Plexus, Santuary of Saitria, Sardinia, Italy. *Pos:* Dir & owner, Galeria Arturo, Hartford, Conn, 79-83; exec dir, Midtown Art Ctr, Houston, 83-84; asst dir, Royal-Athena Galleries, New York & Beverly Hills, 84-. *Teaching:* Instr, Univ Hartford, Univ Conn & NH Col. *Awards:* First Prize, Atlanta Life Ann Exhib & Competition, Atlanta Life Insurance Co, 81. *Bibliog:* Jay Whitsett (dir), Looking Better, Conn Pub Television Show, 78; James Miller (auth), Ancestry & the Art of Arturo Lindsay, Int Rev of African Am Art, 85. *Mem:* Int Sculpture Ctr; Coll Art Asn Am; Nat Conf Artists; Art Against Apartheid; Plexus. *Media:* Cast Metal; Multi-Media. *Mailing Add:* 4026 Birchwood Cove Decatur GA 30034-5251

LINDSTROM, GAELL
PAINTER, EDUCATOR
b Salt Lake City, Utah, July 4, 1919. *Study:* Univ Utah, BS; Calif Coll Arts & Crafts, MFA; also with Roy Wilhelm, Gloucester, Mass. *Work:* Utah State Univ; Southern Utah State Col. *Comn:* Murals, Southern Utah State Coll & Cedar City Pub Libr; mosaic mural, Utah State Univ Forestry Bldg, 61. *Exhib:* Am Watercolor Soc, 53 & 57; Calif Watercolor Soc, 57. *Collection Arranged:* Maynard Dixon Exhib, Southern Utah State Col, 55; Nat Ceramic Exhib, 57 & 58 & Nat Painting Exhib, 58, Utah State Univ. *Teaching:* Prof art, Southern Utah State Col, 53-56, Utah State Inst Fine Arts, 57-61 & Utah State Univ, 57-85. *Awards:* Prizes & Purchase Awards, Utah State Fair, 52-54; Utah State Art Inst, 54; Am Watercolor Soc, 57. *Mem:* Am Watercolor Soc; Nat Watercolor Soc. *Media:* All. *Mailing Add:* 825 Lava Pt Dr Saint George UT 84770-8725

LINDT, NIKKI
PAINTER
Study: Gerrit Rietveld Acad, Amsterdam, BFA, 1995; Yale Univ, MFA (painting & printmaking), 1997. *Exhib:* Solo exhibs include Gallery Four53, Brooklyn, 2002, 1:46 Exhib Space, Brooklyn, 2007; group exhibs include Postcards from the Edge, Sperone Westwater Gallery, New York, 2003; Lightshow, Clocktower Art Space, Brooklyn, 2003; Drawn to Drawing, Art Inst Chicago, 2005; Natural Reaction, Space B, New York, 2005; Small Works Exhib, 80 Washington Square East Galleries, New York, 2006; Nature Works, 1:46 Exhib Space, Brooklyn, 2007; Heskin Contemp, New York, 2008. *Teaching:* Vis critic, Art Inst Chicago, 2005; adj prof, Hudson County Community Coll, Jersey City, 2006-07. *Awards:* Cult Grant, Mama Cash, Netherlands, 2001; Environmental Cult Award, Milieudienst, Amsterdam, 2002; Pollock-Krasner Found Grant, 2007. *Mailing Add:* 151 Driggs Ave Apt 2 Brooklyn NY 11222-4215

LINHARES, JUDITH
PAINTER
b Pasadena, Calif, Nov 21, 1940. *Study:* Calif Coll Arts & Crafts, Oakland, BFA, 63, MFA, 70. *Work:* Calif Palace Legion of Honor; Butler Inst Am Art, Youngstown, Ohio; Frederick Wiseman Found, Los Angeles; Achenbach Found, San Francisco Mus Mod Art; Mills Coll Art Gallery, Oakland; and others. *Comn:* Airport, City of San Francisco. *Exhib:* Solo exhibs, Gallery Paule Anglim, San Francisco, 78, 80, 83, 84, 85, 89, 94 & 2003, La State Univ Art Gallery, Baton Rouge, 79, Nancy Lurie Gallery, Chicago, 81, 89 & 90, Concord Gallery, NY, 82 & 83, Ruth Seigel Gallery, NY, 85, L A Louver, Venice, Calif, 86 & 88, Julie Sylvester Editions, NY, 89, Sonoma State Univ, Calif, 94, Edward Thorp Gallery, New York City, 97, 2001 & 2006, Jancar Gallery, Los Angeles, 2007; group exhibs, Market Street Project, Newport Harbor Art Mus, Newport Beach, Calif, 73; Calif: 3 by 8 Twice, Honolulu Acad Art, Hawaii, 78, Triton Mus, Santa Clara, Calif, 89; 500 Yrs Since Columbus, Triton Mus, Santa Clara, Calif, 92; Conversation, ART Inc, New York City, 2000; Distilled Life, Bard Col, Hudson, NY, 2000; Figures of Invention, Hartwick Coll Art Gallery, Oneonta, NY, 2000; Exurbia, Gallery Luisotti, Santa Monica, Calif, 2001; Pulp Fiction, Sanoma State Univ, Calif, 2001; The Pilot Hill Collection, Croker Art Mus, Sacramento, Calif, 2002; Arrested Development, Castle Gallery, Coll New Rochelle, NY, 2002; Figures of Inventions, The Work Space, NY, 2003; Charmed, The Lower Eastside Girls Club, NY, 2004; Multiflorous: A Spring Affair, Edward Thorp Gallery, NY, 2005, Seaworthy, 2006-07; Nat Biennial Watercolor Invitational, Parkland Coll, Champaign, Ill, 2005; Unsung, Nicole Klagsbrun Gallery, New York, 2007; Invitational Exhib Visual Arts, AAAL, New York, 2008. *Teaching:* Sch Visual Arts. *Awards:* Adaline Kent Award, San Francisco Art Inst, 76; Nat Endowment Arts Grant, 79 & 87; Fel, Guggenheim, 97 & 98; Anonymous Was A Woman Grant, 99; Civitella Ranierei Residency Grant, 2006; Acad Award, Am Acad Arts & Lett, 2008. *Media:* Oil on Canvas, Gouache on Paper. *Dealer:* Gallery Paule Anglim 14 Geary St San Francisco CA 94108. *Mailing Add:* Edward Thorp Gallery 210 Eleventh Avenue New York NY 10001

LINHARES, PHILIP E
CURATOR
b Visalia, Calif, Aug 8, 39. *Study:* Calif Coll of Arts & Crafts, BFA, MFA, 66; post-grad study in Florence, Italy, 72. *Exhib:* San Francisco Mus of Art, Calif, 65; Nev Art Gallery, Reno, 77; La Mus, Copenhagen, Denmark, 77; Solo exhibs, Berkeley Gallery, San Francisco, 70, Lone Mountain Coll, San Francisco, 77 & Oakland Mus, 79; and others. *Pos:* Curatorial asst, Oakland Mus of Art, Calif, 67; dir exhib, San Francisco Art Inst, Calif, 67-77; artist-in-residence, South of Market Cult Ctr, San Francisco, 77-; dir, Mills Col Art Gallery, 78-. *Publ:* Auth, articles in Currant Mag, 75-76; California Communication, Sydney Biennale Exhib catalogue, Australia, 76. *Mailing Add:* c/o The Oakland Mus Art Dept 1000 Oak St Oakland CA 94607-4892

LINK, LAWRENCE JOHN
PAINTER, EDUCATOR
b Oklahoma City, Okla, Sept 2, 1942. *Study:* Univ Okla, BA, 65, MFA, 68. *Work:* San Francisco Mus Art; Smithsonian Inst; Osaka Univ Arts, Japan; Chase Manhattan Bank, New York; Ore State Univ Mus. *Comn:* Lithographs, World Print Orgn, 74. *Exhib:* 2nd Ann Hawaii Nat Prints Exhib, Honolulu Acad Arts, 73; World Print Competition 73, San Francisco Mus Art, 73; Nev State Mus, 75; Corcoran Gallery, Washington, DC, 75; solo exhib, Fred Jones Mem Mus, Okla, 78; Bold Statements: Painting, Southeastern Ctr Contemp Art, NC, 80; Pontiac Art Ctr, Mich, 83; Robert L Kidd Gallery, Birmingham, Mich, 87; Art Communications Int Juried CD-ROM, 95; Pre PostModern II, Patricia Swope Mem Gallery, Ohio, 2000; Bobbit Visual Arts Ctr, Mich, 2000; Mich Masters, Delta College, Bay City, Mich, 2005; Edmonton Contemp Arts Soc, Edmonton, Alberta, Can, 2004, 2012; San Francisco Mus Art, 2012. *Pos:* Mich ed, New Art Examiner, 83-; juror, W MI Biennial, 2007; editor, ArtCrit.org. *Teaching:* Prof, Western Mich Univ, 77-2007. *Awards:* Purchase Award, World Print Competition, 73; Ageless Creativity award, Ringling Coll, 2013. *Bibliog:* Article, Information Technology, The Chronicle of Higher Education, 7/8/92; article, Higher Ed Still a NeXT Priority, NeXTWORLD, summer 92; article, Digital Gallery, Digital Video, 3/94. *Media:* Acrylic, Video. *Interests:* Sports, Literature. *Publ:* Auth, Comment, Am Craft, 8/86; Walter Darby Bannard, Arts Mag, 10/86; The problem of imitation, New World, 10/87; Font styles, ClarisWorks J, 10/92; Start thinking about fonts, ClarisWorks J, 2/92; 3-D Text Tips, Digital Video, 12/94; Apollo on the muck, Newcrit, 1/2000, Susan Roth's Toughness, 4/2001 & Ideas don't matter, 4/2002; Slippery Slope of Hope, Newcrit, 6/2005. *Mailing Add:* 3382 Sandra Dr Kalamazoo MI 49004

LINK, PHYLLIDA K
PAINTER, EDUCATOR
b New York, NY. *Study:* Sorbonne, Paris, France, art cert, 80; City Univ NY, BA, 83, MA, 87. *Work:* Pen & Brush Club; Nat Arts Club; Avanti Gallery, NY; New York Pub Libr; Glyptothek Mus, Copenhagen, Denmark. *Exhib:* Staten Island Mus, NY, 83; Pastellists-Women, Pen & Brush Club, NY, 84-89; Lever House Gallery, Pastel Soc Am Mems, NY, 87; Nabisco Gallery, Pastel Soc of Am Mems, East Hanover, NJ, 88; Milburn Playhouse Gallery, Pastel Soc Am Mems, Milburn, NJ, 90; Riverdale Art Gallery, NY, 97, 2005 & 2007-08, 2009-10, 2011-12. *Teaching:* Adj prof, St Peter's Col, Jersey City, NJ, 86- & Am 19th and 20th Century Art, Hudson Co Community Col, Jersey City, NJ, 88-93. *Awards:* New York Pub Libr Award for Best Libr Exhib Ann, 79; Pastel Soc of Am Salmagundi Club, NY, 81; Cert, Lever House, NY, 82. *Mem:* Pen & Brush Club; Nat Arts Club. *Media:* Acrylic. *Specialty:* figurative, abstract art. *Publ:* City Univ NY Newsletter, 83; Saint Peter's Coll Newsletter, 93; Hudson Co Community Coll Newsletter, 93; St Peter's Campus Newsletter, 96-98 & 2000. *Dealer:* Riverdale Art Gallery 4572 Manhattan College Parkway Riverdale NY 10471

LINK, VAL JAMES
JEWELER, EDUCATOR
b Shreveport, La, Apr 28, 1940. *Study:* Cranbrook Acad Art, Bloomfield Hills, Mich, MFA; Univ Tex, Austin, BFA; Del Mar Jr Col, Corpus Christi, Tex, AA. *Work:* Ark Art Ctr Mus, Little Rock; Sarah Campbell Blaffer Gallery, Univ Houston; Mus Contemp Crafts Touring Exhib, NY; Denver Art Mus & Am Crafts Coun Touring Exhib. *Comn:* Sic Holloware & jewelry works, comn by Mr C A Harlan, Birmingham, Mich, 67-68; commemorative cup, comn by Univ Houston for Mrs Sarah Blaffer, 73; sculptural awards, Am Petrol Inst, Washington, DC, 73 & 74; seven major jewelry pieces, comn by Kenneth Helfand, Mill Run, Pa, 74-75; and others. *Exhib:* The Goldsmith 70 Exhibition, Minn Mus Art, St Paul; Inter-D III, Crafts 74 Int, McAllen Int Mus, Tex, 74; Reprise, Int Exhib Metalsmithing Work, Cranbrook Acad Art, 75; Contemp Metalcrafts, Clifford Gallery, Pittsburgh Arts & Crafts Ctr, Pa, 77; Soc NAm Goldsmiths Nat Metalsmith 77, Phoenix Art Mus, Ariz & Henry Gallery Fine Arts, Univ Wash, Seattle, 77; Am Goldsmiths--Now, Soc NAm Goldsmiths, Steinberg Gallery, Wash Univ, 78; and others. *Teaching:* Instr jewelry & metal, Interlochen Arts Acad, Mich, 67-70; assoc prof & head jewelry & metal area, Univ Houston, 70-. *Awards:* First Place, 15th Tex Crafts Exhib, Dallas Mus Fine Arts, 71; Ark Art Ctr Mus Purchase Award, 71-72. *Bibliog:* Lisa Hammel (auth), Thank technology, New York Times, 6/20/70; Murray Bovin (auth), Photographic representation of work, In: Silversmithing, Bovin Publ, 4th ed, 73. *Mem:* Soc NAm Goldsmiths; Sterling Silversmiths Guild Am; Am Contemp Arts & Crafts Slide Libr; Am Crafts Coun; Tex & Houston Designer Craftsmen. *Media:* Gold, Silver. *Mailing Add:* 5531 Darnell St Houston TX 77096-1101

LINKER, KATE PHILIPPA
CRITIC
b New York, NY, July 22, 1952. *Study:* Radcliffe Col, BA (magna cum laude), 72; Columbia Univ, 73. *Exhib:* Cur, Difference: on Representation & Sexuality, The New Mus, NY, 85. *Pos:* Assoc ed, Tracks J, New York, 75-77. *Teaching:* Prof Postmodern Theory, Grad Prog, Photog & Related Media, Sch Visual Arts, New York, 97-. *Mem:* Int Asn Art Critics; Coll Art Asn. *Publ:* Auth, Meditations on a goldfish bowl: Autonomy and Analogy in Matisse, Artforum, 10/80; Public sculpture, Parts I & II, Artforum, 3/81 & 6/81; On Representation and sexuality, Parachute, 9-11/83; contribr, Love for Sale: The words and pictures of Barbara Kruger, Abrams, 90; Vito Accons, Rizzoli, 94. *Mailing Add:* 227 W 17th St New York NY 10011

LINN, JUDY
PHOTOGRAPHER
b Detroit, Mich. *Study:* Pratt Inst, NY, BFA, 1969. *Work:* Getty Collection, Los Angeles, Calif; Detroit Art Inst; Dallas Mus Fine Art. *Exhib:* Dallas Mus Fine Arts, Tex, 1976; 4 Photographers, Padigione d'Arte Contemporanea, Milan, Italy, 1980; solo exhibs, PS 1, Long Island City, NY, 1980, Susanne Hilberry Gallery, Birmingham, Mich, 1982, Leonard's Artspace, Modesto, Calif, 1985, 55 Mercer Street Gallery, New York, 1986-89, Stone Ridge Library, NY, 1992, Feature, Inc, New York, 1995, 1997, 2000, 2001, 2007, RTp, Cokkie Snoiei, Rotterdam, 2003, Fotomuseum, Antwerp, 2004, White Room, White Columns, New York, 2005, Atlanta Contemp Art Ctr, 2008; NY, New Wave, PS 1, Queens, 1981; Recent Work, Susane Hilberry Gallery, Birmingham, 1982; Flowers, Detroit Art Inst, Mich, 1985; Chain Reaction, Gallery 55, NY, 1985; India Observed, Sandra Berler Gallery, Chevy Chase, Md, 1986; The Animal Show, Photocollect, NY, 1987; Gallery Onetwentyeight, New York,

1987, 1993, 1994, 1995, 1996, 1997, 1998, 1999, & 2001; No Trumpets, No Swans, Pratt Manhattan Gallery, 1988; 10 Steps, Muranushi Lederman Gallery, New York, 1992; Whitney Biennial, 1995; Feature Inc, NY, 1995, 1998, 1999, 2000, 2003, 2008; Autobiography, Cranbrook Art Mus, Bloomfield Hills, Mich, 1996; Sooi/Differences, Xa 104 Roadside Mus, Hiroshima, 1997; Visitors, Calif Inst Arts, 1999; New York, 100, Ataka Mus, Naruto City, Japan, 2000; In the Lake, Malca Fine Arts, New York, 2001; Trade, White Columns, New York, 2005; Under the Skin: Tattoos and Contemporary Culture, Asheville Art Mus, NC, 2006; People Take Pictures of Each Other, LaMontagne Gallery, Boston, 2007; Am Acad Arts and Letts, 2009. *Teaching:* Adj asst prof photogr, Pratt Inst, Brooklyn, NY, 1974-85. *Awards:* Artist Grant, Bob & Stephanie Scull, 1985; Line II Publ Grant, 1986; Annoymous was a Woman Grant, 2006; Peter S Reed Grant, 2007; Purchase Prize, Am Acad Arts and Letts, 2009. *Bibliog:* Oriole Farb (auth), article, Mass Rev, summer 1974; Patti Smith (auth), Babel, Putnam, NY, 1978; Sam Wagstaff (auth), A Book of Photographs, Grey Press, 1978. *Dealer:* Gallery Onetwentyeight 128 Rivington New York NY 10002. *Mailing Add:* 252 Elizabeth St New York NY 10012

LINN, STEVEN ALLEN
SCULPTOR
b Chicago, Ill, May 3, 1943. *Study:* Univ Ill, BS (floricult & ornamental hort). *Work:* Indianapolis Mus Art; Milwaukee Art Mus; Bayley Art Mus; Albany Art Mus, Ga; Mus Arts Decorative Lausanne, Switz; Nat Baseball Hall Fame; Mus Craft & Folk Art, Los Angeles, Calif; Mus Art and Hist, Anchorage, Alaska; Long Beach Art Mus, Long Beach, Calif; Mint Mus, Charlotte, NC; Natl Liberty Mus, Philadelphia, PA. *Comn:* One Colorado Plaza, Pasadena, Calif, 91; Louis & Susan Meisel Outdoor Sculpture Collection, Sagaponic, NY, 92; Fair Dept Stores, Worcester, Mass; Verrerie Ouvrier D'Albi, France, 96. *Exhib:* Rochester Mem, 79; Newport Art Mus, 79 & 86; Milwaukee Art Mus, 81; Corcoran Gallery Art, 82; Nat Baseball Hall Fame, 85; Mus D'Art Et Histoire, Geneva, Switz, 96; Aperto Vetro, Fondazione Levi Palazzo Giustinian Lolin, Venice, Italy, 98; Sofa, Chicago, 2000; Agropolis Mus, Montpellier, France, 2000; Musee de Design et D'Arts Appliques Contemporain, Luasanne, Switz, 2003; Blown Away, Flint Inst Art, Flint, Mich, 2009; Fort Wayne Mus Art, Ind, 2015. *Teaching:* Lectr theatre design, Smith Col, Northampton, Mass, 68-69; tech instr sculpture, Univ Calif, Santa Cruz, 71-74; asst prof, Pratt Inst, Brooklyn, NY, 86-; Cerfav, Vanne-le-chatel, France, 2000-. *Awards:* Ward Sculpture Prize, Berkshire Mus, 68; Rome Prize, Am Acad in Rome, 75; MacDowell Colony Fel, 80; Pollock-Krasner Found Award, 85. *Bibliog:* Arthur Williams (auth), Glass: State of the Art II, 88; Cover, Art Today Mag, Summer 89; Nancy Kapitanoff (auth), Works pay tribute to special leaders, Los Angeles Times, 5/24/92; Lise Ott (auth) Steve Linn, Ceramique et Verre, 9-10/94; Creative Glass, Kracun & McFadden, 2010; Contemp Kiln Formed Glass, Keith Cummings, 2009; Martha Drexler Lynn, Sculpture, Glass & Am Mus; Blown Away, Int Glass 21st Century, Flint Inst Art, 2009; Habatat Gallery (auth), Steve Linn Documentary Sculpture, 2015. *Media:* Bronze, Glass, Wood. *Dealer:* Gallerie H D Nick 30250 Aubais France; Habatat Gallery, 4400 Fernlee, Royal Oak, MI; Galerie Place des Arts, Montpellier, France. *Mailing Add:* 78 Ave Des Embruscalles 34270 Claret France

LINS, PAM
SCULPTOR
b Chicago, Illinois, 1960. *Study:* Univ Minn, BA, 1983; Hunter Coll, New York, MFA, 1993. *Work:* The West Collection, Oaks, PA. *Exhib:* Solo exhibs include Momenta Art, Brooklyn, NY, 1999, Ten in One Gallery, New York, 1999, 2001, 2003, Mercer Union Ctr Arts, Toronto, 2003 ; group exhibs include Projs, Sculpture Ctr, New York, 1993; Up Close, HF Johnson Mus Art, Cornell Univ, 1993; Working in Brooklyn, Brooklyn Mus Art, NY, 1997; New Mus Benefit, New Mus Contemp Art, New York, 1999; Hang Time, White Columns, New York, 1999; New York Projs, Delfina Arts, London, 2000; Wattage & Friendship, DeChira/Stewart, Berlin, Germany, 2001. *Awards:* John Simon Guggenheim Mem Found Fel, 2008; Howard Foundation, 2007. *Mailing Add:* Rachel Uffner Gallery 47 Orchard St New York NY 10002

LINTAULT, ROGER PAUL
ADMINISTRATOR, EDUCATOR
b New York, NY, June 13, 1938. *Study:* State Univ NY New Paltz, BS (art) with distinction, 60; Southern Ill Univ, MFA (sculpture & ceramics), 62. *Work:* Honolulu Acad Arts, Hawaii; Mus Contemp Crafts, NY; Warner Brothers Records, Los Angeles, Calif; Calif State Univ, San Bernardino. *Exhib:* Craftsmen USA, Los Angeles Co Mus Art, Calif, 66; Looking West 1970, Joslyn Art Mus, Omaha, Nebr, 70; Solo exhibs, Esther-Robles Gallery, Los Angeles, 75, Architectural Dreams and Visions, Ctr Gallery, Calif State Univ, 81; Calif State Univ, San Bernardino, 79 & Fullerton, 81; Janus Gallery, Los Angeles, 79; Contemp Bronze, Calif State Univ, San Bernardino, 87; Phantoms of Function: Evolution of Art in the Utilitarian, Riverside Art Mus, Calif, 91; Table, Lamp and Chair, Am Inst Archit, Inst Bus Designers, Ore Sch Arts & Crafts, Portland, 91. *Teaching:* Asst prof art, Univ Hawaii, Honolulu, 65-68; lectr art, Calif State Univ, Long Beach, 68-69; prof art, Calif State Univ, San Bernardino, 69-, chmn dept, 72-77 & 97-. *Awards:* First & Purchase Prizes, All Calif Art Exhib, Nat Orange Show, 74. *Bibliog:* Don Woodford (auth), Truth, illusion and Roger Lintault, 4/26/75, Artweek; Louis William Fox (auth), article, Artweek, 1/13/79; Suzanne Muchnic (auth), article, Ten tales of architecture, Los Angeles Times, 2/9/79. *Media:* Metal, Cast, Miscellaneous Media. *Mailing Add:* c/o Dept Art Calif State Univ 5500 University Pkwy San Bernardino CA 92407-2397

LINTON, HAROLD
PAINTER, ADMINISTRATOR
b Pittsburgh, Pa, Oct 1, 1947. *Study:* Lowe Sch Art, Syracuse Univ, BFA, 69; Univ Wash Sch Art, grad study with Spencer Moseley, 69-70; Sch Art & Archit, Yale Univ, grad study with Al Held, MFA, 72. *Work:* Muskegon Mus Art, Mich; Syracuse Univ, NY; Yale Univ, New Haven, Conn; Childrens Hosp, Detroit, Mich; Pittsburgh Rehab Inst, Pa. *Comn:* Shaped canvas, Handleman Corp, Clawson, Mich, 77; shaped canvas in main lobby, Beaumont Hosp, Royal Oak, Mich, 95; shaped canvas on ceiling, Temple Israel, West Bloomfield, Mich, 95; shaped canvas in lobby, Birmingham Temple, Farmington Hills, Mich, 95; shaped canvas, reception area, US Embassy, Helsinki, Finland, 96-97. *Exhib:* Solo exhib, I Irving Feldman Gallery, West Bloomfield, Mich, 85, 87 & 90; Harold Linton Paintings: 76-86, Muskegon Mus Art, Mich, 87; Handleman Collection, Oakland Univ-Meadowbrook Art Gallery, Rochester, Mich, 88; Form & Content, Janice Charach Mus Gallery, West Bloomfield, Mich, 92; Abstract Image Makers, Cincinnati Mus Art-Chidlaw Gallery, Ohio, 93; Self Portraits, Muskegon Mus Art, Mich, 95. *Collection Arranged:* Artwork can be found in numerous public, private and mus collections. *Teaching:* Prof art & archit, Lawrence Technol Univ, 74, creator, BFA Degree Prog Archit Illus, 91-92; asst dean, Col Archit & Design, Lawrence Technol Univ, 91-98, chmn Dept Art and Design; prof, color & design, Univ Art & Design, Helsinki, Finland, 96-97; prof art, Bradley Univ, 1998-2005, chmn Art Dept, 1998-2005, Caterpillar prof art, 2001-2005; prof. dir Sch of Art, George Mason Univ, 2005-. *Awards:* George Hess Mem Award, Syracuse Univ, 68; Ellen Battell Stoeckel Fel Grant Painting, Yale Univ, 68; Publishers Grant, Texts on Color, Design & Drawing, Van Nostrand Reinhold, 82, 85, 88, 90, 91, 94 & 96; William Rainey Harper Award for Dept Excellence, Bradley Univ; Nat Competition first prize award and commission for a large relief construction work of art entitled "Fortunes of Nature" for the Richard M DeVos Ctr and Grad Sch of Bus Administration, Grand Rapids, Mich. *Bibliog:* Charles Wallenschlager (auth), Basic Visual Concepts & Principles, WC Brown, 91; M Portillo & JH Dohr (auth), A study of color planning criteria used by noted designers, J Interior Design Educ & Res, 93. *Mem:* Nat Asn Schs Art & Design; Coll Art Asn; Am Soc Archit Perspectives; Inter-Soc Color Coun; Color Marketing Group; Nat Art Educ Asn; Abstract Image Makers; Found for Art, Theory and Educ. *Publ:* Coauth, Architectural Sketching in Markers, Van Nostrand Reinhold, 90; auth, Color Consulting, Van Nostrand Reinhold, 92; Sketching the Concept, McGraw-Hill/Design Press, 93; Color Forecasting, Van Nostrand Reinhold, 94; Portfolio Design, WN Norton & Co, 96, 4th edition, 2012. *Dealer:* I Irving Feldman Gallery 6606 Pleasant Lake Ct West Bloomfield MI 48331. *Mailing Add:* School of Art Col of Visual and Performing Arts George Mason Univ Art & Design Bldg Room 2050E 4400 University Drive MS 1C3 Fairfax VA 22030

LINZY, KALUP
FILMMAKER
b Florida, 1977. *Study:* Skowhegan Sch Painting & Sculpture, Maine, 2002; Univ S Fla, Tampa, BFA, 2000, Abroad Prog, Paris, 2001, MFA, 2003. *Exhib:* Solo exhibs include Le Petit Versailles, New York, 2004, Taxter & Spengemann, New York, 2005, 2006, Miami Beach, 2007, PS1 Contemp Arts Ctr, Long Island, NY, 2006, Context Galleries, Derry, North Ireland, 2007; two-person exhibs include Romo Gallery, Atlanta, (With Charles Nelson), 2006; group exhibs include 4th Ann Valentine's Peepshow, Hyde Park Gallery, Tampa, Fla, 2002; Benaddiction, Goliath Gallery, New York, 2004; African Queen, Studio Mus Harlem, New York, 2005, Frequency, 2005; Uncertain States of Am, Moscow Biennial, 2007; Playback, Mus Mod, Paris, 2007; Television Delivers People, Whitney Mus Am Art, New York, 2007; Bedtime Stories, Red House, Syracuse, NY, 2008; Summer Mixtape, Exit Art, New York, 2008; Prospect 1, New Orleans, 2008. *Awards:* Louis Comfort Tiffany Found Grant, 2005; John Simon Guggenheim Mem Found Fel, 2007; Creative Capital Found Grant, 2008

LIOTTA, JEANNE
FILM DIRECTOR
b NYC, 1960. *Exhib:* Solo exhibs at Whitney Biennial; Whitney Mus Art, 2006; Int Film Festival, Rotterdam; Pacific Film Archives, Berkeley, Calif; Anthology Film Archives, NYC; Mus Mod Art, NYC. *Pos:* Vis artist Bard, San Francisco Art Inst; dir (films), Blue Moon, 1988; Soma Sema, 1988; Open Sesame, 1989; Fungus Eroticus, 1990; Dervish Machine, 1992; CiCi N'est Pas, 1997; What Makes Day & Night, 1998; Mukitkara, 1999; Struck by the Hand, 2001; Window, 2001; L'air du Temps, 2003; One Day This May No Longer Exist, 2005. *Teaching:* Film instr Sch, Mus Fine Arts, Boston. *Awards:* Fel MacDowell Colony, 2002; grantee Jerome Found, NY State Coun Arts Experimental Television Center. *Mailing Add:* SMFA Boston 230 The Fenway Boston MA 02115

LIPMAN, BETH
GLASS BLOWER, SCULPTOR
b Philadelphia, 1971. *Study:* Mass Coll Art, Boston, 1990; Tyler Sch Art, Temple Univ, Philadelphia, BFA, 1994. *Work:* Smithsonian Am Art Mus; Brooklyn Mus Art; Corning Mus Glass, NY; John Michael Kohler Arts Ctr, Sheboygan, Wis; Mus Am Glass, Millville, NJ; Milwaukee Art Mus, Wis; RISD Mus, Providence, RI. *Comn:* BNO Design, New York. *Exhib:* Solo exhibs include Heller Gallery, New York, 2001 & 2004, Mangel Gallery, Philadelphia, 2002, John Michael Kohler Arts Ctr, Sheboygan, Wis, 2003, Mus Am Glass, Wheaton Village, NJ, 2004, Fuller Craft Mus, Brockton, Mass, 2004-05, RIS Mus, Providence, RI, 2008, Heller Gallery, 2010; group exhibs include Glassworks: Emerging Artists, Brooklyn Mus Art, 2000; Glass Express, DUMBO Art Ctr, Brooklyn, 2000; Good Business is the Best Art, Bronx Mus Art, NY, 2000; Under the Influence, Islip Art Mus, NY, 2001; Glass America, Heller Gallery, New York, 2002, Sculpture Objects & Functional Art (SOFA), 2003, 2004; Mus Glass, Tacoma, Wash, 2005; Mus Glass, Tacoma, Wash, 2010; ICA, Portland, Maine, 2010. *Pos:* Art/industry coordr, John Michael Kohler Arts Ctr, 2005-2010. *Teaching:* Instr, Corning Mus Glass, Penland Sch Drafts, Parsons Sch Design, New York Univ, LIU, Bard Grad Ctr Decorative Arts. *Awards:* Peter S Reed Found Grant, 2000; Creative Glass Ctr Am Fel, 2001; Nat Endowment Arts Grant, 2001; Prof Advancement Grant, NH State Coun Arts, 2001; Ruth Chenven Found Grant, 2002; Wis Visual Arts Fel, 2008. *Dealer:* Heller Gallery 420 W 14th St New York NY 10014; Cade Tompkins Proj 198 Hope St providence RI 02906. *Mailing Add:* N6366 Hwy 32 Sheboygan Falls WI 53085

LIPPARD, LUCY ROWLAND
WRITER
b New York, NY, Apr 14, 1937. *Study:* Smith Col, BA, 58; NY Univ Inst Fine Arts, MA, 62. *Hon Degrees:* Moore Coll Art, Hon DFA, 1972; San Francisco Art Inst, Hon DFA, 1985; Maine Coll Art, Hon DFA, 1994; Mass Coll Art, Hon DFA, 1998; Chicago Art Inst, Hon DFA, 2003; Nova Scotia Coll Art & Design; Bowdoin Col, Hon

DFA, 2008; Santa Fe Univ Art & Design, Hon DFA. *Pos:* Freelance writer, cult critic, cur; co-found WEB, Ad Hoc Women Artist's Comt, Heresies Collective Artists Call Against US Intervention in Cent Am, Political Art Documentation/Distbn; Bd, Ctr Environmental Art, Nevada Mus Art. *Teaching:* Vis prof, Sch Visual Arts, New York, Williams Col, Univ Queensland, Australia & Univ Colo, Boulder; lectr in field. *Awards:* Mather Award Coll art assoc; Art Table Award, 99; Southwest Book Award, 2002; Athena Award from RISD, 2004; Lifetime Achievement Award (WCA/CAA), 2007; Curatorial Excellence Award, Bard Coll Ctr for Curatorial Studies, 2010; Distinguished Feminist award, Coll Art Asn, 2012; First award, Elizabeth Sakler Ctr, Brooklyn Mus, 2012; Carolyn Baucroft History prize, Denver Public Libr, 2011; Ira Anastacio Dominguez Book prize, NMex Historical Soc, 2011. *Bibliog:* Florence Pierce: In Touch With Light, 98. *Res:* politics of land use conceptual art; Native American art. *Interests:* Local history. *Publ:* Auth 21 bks, incl, Eva Hesse, 76, Partial Recall, 92 The Pink Glass Swan, 95, The Lure of the Local, 97, Florence Pierce: In Touch With Light, 98, On the Beaten Track, 99; Author: Pop Art, 66, The Graphic work of Philip Evergood, 66; Changing: Essays in Art Criticism, 71; ed, Surrealists on Art, 70, Dadas on Art, 71; Tony Smith, 72; Six Yrs: The Dematerialization of the Art Object, 73; From the Ctr: Feminist Essays on Women's Art, 76; Sol Le Witt, 78, (with Charles Simonds) Cracking (Br Werden), 79; The Sch of Paris, 65, (novel) I See/You Mean, 79; Ad Reinhardt, 81; contribr, monthly columns Village Voice, 81-85; Overlay: Contemp Art and the Art of Prehistory, 83; Get the Message? A Decade of Art for Social Change, 84; Mixed Blessings: New Art in a Multicultural Am, 90; A Different War: Vietnam in Art, 90; contrib ed,: Art in Am; founding editor El Puente de Galisteo, 97; Village Voice In These Times, Z Mag, also numerous articles to mag, anthologies, and mus catalogs, 64-; curator 50 exhibs; performer in guerrilla and street theater; auth, Down Country: The Tano of the Galisteo Basin, 1250-1782, 2010. *Mailing Add:* 14 Avenida Vieja Galisteo NM 87540

LIPPINCOTT, LOUISE
MUSEUM DIRECTOR, CURATOR
Study: Yale Univ, BA (art hist); Princeton Univ, PhD (European hist). *Collection Arranged:* Pittsburgh Revealed, 1997; Light! The Industrial Age, 1750-1990; Fierce Friends: Artists & Animals, 1750-1990. *Pos:* Assoc cur paintings, J Paul Getty Mus, Los Angeles, formerly; cur fine arts, Carnegie Mus Art, Pittsburgh, 1991-, chief cur, 2006-, co-dir, 2008-. *Publ:* Auth, Selling Art in Georgian London: The Rise of Arthur Pond, 1983; Edvard Munch Starry Night, 1987; Alma Tadema Spring, 1990. *Mailing Add:* Carnegie Mus Art 4400 Forbes Ave Pittsburgh PA 15213-4080

LIPPMAN, IRVIN M
MUSEUM DIRECTOR
b 1948. *Study:* Univ Denver, BFA; Univ Tex, Austin, MA (Art Hist). *Pos:* Staff lectr, Nat Gallery Art, Washington, 1977-82; chief pub affairs, Amon Carter Mus, Ft Worth, Tex, 1983-88, asst dir, 1988-94; exec dir, Columbus Mus Art, Ohio, 1994-2002; pres, exec dir, Mus Art, Ft Lauderdale, Fla, 2003-. *Mem:* Asn Art Mus Dirs. *Mailing Add:* Mus Art Ft Lauderdale 1 E Las Olas Blvd Fort Lauderdale FL 33301

LIPPMAN, JUDITH
GALLERY DIRECTOR, EDUCATOR
b New York, NY, June 11, 1929. *Study:* Syracuse Univ, BA, 49. *Collection Arranged:* Maryland Art in Legislative Spaces (auth, catalog), 80 & Maryland Art & Artists (auth, catalog), 81, Gen Assembly Md. *Pos:* Guest lectr, Col Notre Dame, Md, 74-76; dir & cur, 20th Century Am Art, Meredith Gallery Contemp Art, Baltimore, 77-; mem, Artistic Properties Comn, State of Md, 77-80; Capitol arts coordr, Gen Assembly Md, 80-; lectr, New Sch Social Res, New York, 80-81, Johns Hopkins Univ, 83-, Md Inst Col Art, 85. *Mem:* Am Inst Architects; Artists Equity Asn. *Specialty:* Contemporary American art and fine crafts. *Publ:* Coauth, Gene Davis, Ed Baynard, Dorothy Gillespie, 80, Arts Gallery. *Mailing Add:* Meredith Gallery Contemp Art 809 N Charles St Baltimore MD 21201

LIPPMAN, MANDY
CONSULTANT, WRITER
b Baltimore, Md, Sept 23, 1956. *Study:* George Washington Univ, BA, 78; Parson's Sch Design, AAS, 81. *Collection Arranged:* Baltimore Off of KPMG/Peat Marwick (law off of Melnicove, Weiner, Smouse & Garbis); Artist Designed Furniture, Norton Gallery Art, W Palm Beach, Fla, 86. *Pos:* Dir, Meredith Gallery, Baltimore, Md, 81-87; self-employed consultant, 88-; bd mem, James Renwick Alliance, 90. *Teaching:* Instr, Md Inst Art, Baltimore, 83, Visit the Artist, Jewish Community Ctr, Washington, DC, 89 & Contemp Art in Washington, Smithsonian, 90. *Mem:* James Renwick Alliance. *Collection:* Contemporary American crafts, prints and paintings (1970 to present). *Publ:* Auth, The new art furniture: Functional creativity, Home Mag, 11/90. *Mailing Add:* 6605 Paxton Rd Rockville MD 20852

LIPPMAN, SHARON ROCHELLE
CURATOR, ART HISTORIAN
b New York, NY, Apr 9, 1950. *Study:* Art Students League, 66-68; HS Art & Design, 68; Mills Col, City Coll New York, BA(art hist), 72; NY Univ, MA (cinema studies), 76, grad studies, 87; New Sch Social Res, 68-70; Columbia Univ, 70. *Work:* Suffolk Co Legislature, 90-97; Dept Interior, Fort Wadsworth, NY 2001. *Comn:* Homage to NY-LI Baymen (mural), 85, Sunday in the Park (mural), Art Without Walls Inc, NY, 92; Art Therapy Program, Various Hospitals; Image of Home, Polish Consulate, NY, 2000; South St Seaport, By Land, By Sea, NY, 2005; Safari Adventure (art mural game), NY Univ Pediatrics, 2012, Creatures of the Deep, Art Therapy Game, 2012. *Exhib:* Holocaust Art, Polish Consulate, NY, 2002; Homage to the NY Skyscraper, Battery Park, 2002; Central Park: Peace-Quiet, Central Park, 2003; Nassau Co Detention Ctr, Within These Walls, 2003; W Islip/Bellport Libraries, Spiritual Energy, 2005; Caged Free, Nassau County, Detention Ctr, 2005; Mus Without Walls-Rhapsody in Art, South St Seaport, New York City, 2006; Museum Without Walls-Food as Art, Battery Park, NYC, 6/2008; Pen to Brush Art/Writing Prog, West Islip Pub Libr, 3/2008; Mus Without Walls Memories: 9/11 City-Country, Battery Park, NYC, 6/2009; Into the Woods, S Country Libr, NYC; Inner Worlds, S Country Libr, 3/2009; Mus Without Walls- Am Dream-War-Peace Space & H2O, Intrepid Mus, New York, 2010; Three-3 Artists 3 Views, Art Exhib, S Country Libr, Bellport, 2010; Bugs and Bones, Islip Public Lib, 2011; Kim Turner Art Exhib, W. Islip Public Lib, 2011; Katie Curran Artist, Bayport Bluepoint Lib, 2011; Mus Without Walls, Central Park Zoo, NY, 2011; Veterans and Art, Battery Park, NY, 2011; 4 Women Artists, 5 Country Lib, Bellport, NY, 2011; Two Generations: Gerald Ginsburg & Max Parrott, Bayport Bluepoint Lib, NY, 2012; Photographer: Tina Daube, Islip Lib Gallery, 2012; New Ideas: Artist A New, West Islip Lib Gallery, 2012; Mus Without Walls: Bridges, South St Seaport, NY, 2012; Mus Without Walls, Bridges II, South St Seaport, 2013; Loving, Robert Panetta and Kim Turner, Islip Public Lib, 2012; Melvin Bellinger, Emerging Artist, West Islip Public Lib, 2012; Emily Schaab, Emerging Artists, South Country Library, Bellport, NY, 2012; Mus Without Walls, Not Sch Art, South St Seaport, Brooklyn, Bridge, 2012; Mus Without Walls, TIME, Battery Park/Central Park, 2013; The Russians Precoming, Bluepoint, Bayport Public Libr, 2013; Real Men Write Poetry, Sayville, NY, 2013; Horseplay, Belmont Racetrack, NY, 2013; Bluepoint, Bayport Lib, 2013; Islip Lib, 2013; Babylon Lib, 2013. *Collection Arranged:* Mus Without Walls (auth, catalog), Pub Space-Heckscher State Park, 85-86; Color Me/Color Blind, Helen Keller Ctr for the Blind, 93; Blind Illusions, Pub Space-William Rodgers Bldg, NY, 94; Home Sweet Home, William Rodgers Bldg, 94; The Illustrative Eye, 94 & Quietplaces, William Rodgers Bldg; Holocaust-The Polish Experience, Polish Consulate, NY, 98; Mus Without Walls, Yesterday, Today & Tomorrow, Bryant Park, New York, 2007, Wallace Exhib, 2007. *Pos:* Exec dir, Art Without Walls Inc, Sayville & New York, 85-; art therapist, cur, historian, artist & filmmaker, currently. *Teaching:* Instr painting/drawing, sculpture & filmmaking, Sara Sch Creative Art, 76-85; instr painting-drawing, art therapy, art history, Art Without Walls Inc, Sayville, NY, 85-. *Awards:* Suffolk Co News Inspiration Award, 90; Suffolk Co Proclamation, 93; Newsday Leadership Award, 94; Nat Poetry Press Award, 96; Nat Women's Hist Month Award, 96; Long Island Hall of Fame, 2004; Suffolk Co News, Inspiration Award, 2005; LI Hall Fame Honorary Bench, Bethpage State Park, NY, 6/2009; Brooklyn Borough Proclamation, Art Without Walls Inc, Mus Without Walls Day, Pres Marty Markowitz, 2012. *Mem:* Coll Art Asn; Mus Mod Art; Metrop Mus Art; Univ Film Asn; Whitney Mus Am Art; Guggenheim Mus; Jewish Mus; Americans for the Arts. *Media:* Paint, Film. *Res:* Combine the social, aesthetic and historical elements of art theories with cultural and creative development through the ages. *Specialty:* Public Space. *Interests:* Expanding non-traditional Am art 1930-present and social/historical int art; emerging & outsider art, holocaust art. *Publ:* Auth, University Poetry Press, Nat Poetry Press, 68; Patterns, Idlewild Press, 68; Still Waters, Island Light Press, 83; America at the Millennium, Poetry, 2000. *Dealer:* Art Without Walls, Inc

LIPPMANN, JANET GURIAN
PAINTER, GALLERY DIRECTOR
b New York, NY, May 10, 1936. *Study:* Brooklyn Col, with Ilya Bolotowsky, Ad Reinhardt, Kurt Seligman, John Russell, Mark Rothko & Burgoyne Diller, BA (art educ), 56, MA (art educ), 60; NY Univ, with Knox Martin. *Work:* Reader's Digest Asn, Inc; Nat Arts Club; Newington Cropsey Mus; numerous pvt collections. *Exhib:* Solo Exhibs: River Gallery, Irvington-on-Hudson, NY, 91; Nat Arts Club, NY, 91, 94, 98, 2001, 2002, & 2008; Conoisseur Gallery, Rhinebeck, NY, 92, 93, 94; Goodman Gallery, Southampton, NY, 91-92; RVS, Southampton, NY, 91; Nature Nutures, State Univ NY, 94, The Sky Above, The Earth Below, 2001; Newington Cropsey Mus, 2003; Irvington-on-Hudson Publ Libr, 2005, 2011; Sunnyside Fed S&L, Irvington, 2006; Freshman Fine Arts, Beacon, NY, 2007; Nat Arts Club, 2008; 3 Generations of Artists, Greenburgh Public Libr, 2012, Part II, Larchment Public Libr, 2013. *Collection Arranged:* Columbia Univ Med Ctr; Bank of NY. *Pos:* Founder, pres & dir, The River Gallery, Irvington-on-Hudson, NY, 74-89; founder, pres & dir, Janet Lippmann Fine Arts, 89-; artist in res, Nat Arts Club, NY, 1991-. *Teaching:* Instr art, New York City, Cincinnati & Westchester Publ Sch, 56-74; Instr, Children's Art Series, Mt Vernon, 64-71; pvt instr, Adult Art Classes, Tarrytown, NY, 71-73; UFT Retiree Programs, 2006-2014. *Awards:* Nat Arts Club Award, 89; Hudson Valley Art Asn, 99; Art Spirit Found Award for pastel 2003, 2004 & 2009. *Mem:* Nat Arts Club, NY; Salmagundi Club; Artists Fel Pen & Brush Club, NY; Hudson Valley Art Asn; Pastel Soc Am; Catherine Lorillard Wolfe Club; Pen & Brush; North Am Pastel Asn. *Media:* Oils, Pastels. *Specialty:* Paintings by American and international artists; Contemporary Realism by Living Am artists. *Interests:* Gardening, travel. *Publ:* Auth, Painting in Giverny, Am Artist, 3/88; Giverny Revisited, Am Artist, 11/91; Rivertains Enterprise, 8/08; Gallery & Studio, 1/2008; Janet Lippmann Paintings, 86-2006. *Dealer:* Janet Lippmann Fine Art

LIPSKY, PAT
PAINTER, WRITER
b New York, NY, Sept 21, 1941. *Study:* Cornell Univ with Alan Solomon, BFA, 63; Art Students League, 63-64; Hunter Col, with Tony Smith, MA, 68; Arts Studio League with Charles Alston. *Work:* Hirshhorn Mus & Sculpture Garden; Whitney Mus Am Art, NY; San Francisco Mus Fine Arts; Walker Art Ctr; Brooklyn Mus; Wadsworth Atheneum; Blanton Mus Art, Univ Tex at Austin; MFA Houston, Fogg Art Mus; Brooklyn Mus; and others; Ft Lauderdale Mus Art; Indianapolis Mus Art. *Exhib:* solo exhibs, Fairleigh Dickinson Univ, Rutherford, NJ, 68, Andre Emmerich Gallery, NY, 70, 72, 74, 75, Everson Mus Art, Syracuse, 71, London Arts Gallery, Detroit, 71, Berenson Gallery, Bay Harbor Island, Fla, 74, 76, Deitcher O'Reilly Gallery, NY, 76, Andre Zarre Gallery, NY, 78, 91, Promenade Gallery, Hartford, Conn, 87, Virginia Miller Gallery, Coral Gables, Fla, 94, Lori Bookstein Fine Art, NY, 97, Elizabeth Harris Gallery, 99, 2001, 2003, 2004, 2006, Cathedral of St John the Divine, 2006, Pat Lipsky: Twenty Years, Acme Fine Arts, Boston, 2015; Chase Manhattan Bank, NY, 67, Allan Stone Gallery, NY, 69; Larry Aldrich Mus, Ridgefield, Conn, 70, 72, 74; Phoenix Art Mus, 70; Kansas State Univ, Manhattan, 70; Whitney Mus Am Art, NY, 71; Tyler Mus Art, Tex, 71; Cranbrook Acad Art Mus, Bloomfield Hills, Mich, 73; Grand Rapids Art Mus, Mich, 74; San Francisco Art Inst, 74; Toldeo Mus Art, Ohio, 74; Moravian Coll Art Gallery, Bethlehem, Pa, 77; Sarah Rentschler Gallery, NY, 79;

Univ Mass, Amherst, 87; Ruth Siegel Gallery, NY, 88; CS Schulte Gallery, Millburn, NJ, 92, 93, 94; Tribe Gallery, NY, 98; Snyder Fine Arts, NY, 96; Duke Univ, Durham, NC, 2004, 2006; DC Moore Gallery, NY, 2004, 2011; Nat Accad Mus (183 invitational), 2008; Gallery Selections, Boca Raton Mus, Fla, 2009; Spanierman Modern, 2009; and many others. *Pos:* Mem adv coun, Col Art & Archit, Cornell Univ, 88-93. *Teaching:* Instr, Fairleigh Dickinson Univ, 68 & Hunter Col, 72; vis artist, San Francisco Art Inst, 74; instr, State Univ NY, Purchase, 79-80; assoc prof, Hartford Art Sch, Univ Hartford, 83-2002; tchr, Art Students League, 2010, 2011, 2012, 2013. *Awards:* Va Ctr Creative Arts Fel, 86 & 93; NY Found Arts Fel, 92; Grant, Winsor & Newton Paint Co, 92; Grant Gottlieb Found, 99; Grant Pollock-Krasner, 2000, 2008; Purchase Prize, Hassam Speicher, Am Acad Arts & Letters, 2001; Edwin Palmer Mem Prize, Nat Accad Mus, 2008. *Bibliog:* Carol Damian (auth), Coral Gables, Artnews, 5/94; Charles Bernstein (auth), Pat Lipsky Sutton, Art Papers, 7/94; Across generational bounds, New York Times, 96; David Cohen, Gallery Going, NY Sun, 2004; Ken Johnson (auth) Art in Review, NY Times, 4/4/2004; Vicky Perry (auth), Abstract Painting, Concepts, and Techniques, Watson Guptill, pp. 15, 58, & 82, 2005; Stephen Westfall, Pat Lipsky at Elizabeth Harris, Art in Am, 2005; Karen Wilkin (auth), Pat Lipsky at Elizabeth Harris, Art in Am, 2007; David Fraser Jenkins (auth), Seeing Color, Lipsky & Piper, British Jour of Stained Glass, 2007; Karen Rosenberg (auth), Where have all the Paintings Gone? To the Nat Accad, NY Times, Vol 30, page E4, 2008; Swartz-Turfle, Harry (auth), When Beauty is Enough, Daily Gusto, 2/09; Piri Halasz (auth), From the Mayors Doorstep, No 79, pgs 45-6, 6-7/2008; Daniel Kunitz (auth), The Grab Bag Anthology, The New York Sun, pg 17, 6/5/2008; Karen Wilkin (auth), Anywhere in Between, The New Criterion, 6/2003; David Cohen (auth), Afterlife of an Ideal, NY Sun, 6/29/2006; Stephen Westfall (auth), Review of Exhibitions, Art in Am, 2/2005; Cate McQuaid, The Boston Globe, Artists Committed to Technique and Color, Critics Picks, The Boston Globe, March 12, 2015; Pat Lipsky lecture and video, Art Students League of NY, What Happened to the Art World? 2014; 28 Color Relief Print, published by Ribouli Digital, 9/2014, Contrast and Context, Shown Print Fair of Chelsea, 2014. *Media:* Oil on Linen, Acrylic on Canvas. *Specialty:* American 19th & 20th Century, Contemporary. *Interests:* Gothic Architecture, Stained Glass Windows. *Publ:* Karen Wilkin, Pat Lipsky at Elizabeth Harris Art in Am (page 170), 3/2007; Highlights, Cornell Architecture Art Planning, News 06, pg 23, 2009; East Hampton Star, The Last Act, 6/10/2010; Thomas Armstrong, A Singular Vision, 2012. *Mailing Add:* 410 W 24th St New York NY 10011

LIPTON, BARBARA B
EDUCATOR, CURATOR

b Newark, NJ. *Study:* Univ Iowa, BA (art hist); Univ Mich, studied Oriental art with James Plummer, MA; Rutgers Univ, MLS. *Exhib:* Solo photog exhib, Newark Mus, NJ, 78, Tibet, Pub Libr, Middletown, NJ, 2010, Wearable Art, Festival of the Arts Juried Exhib, Monmouth Co, NJ, 2010; Images of the Alaskan Eskimo, New Eng Found Arts, 80-82; Anchorage Mus, 81; Am Mus Nat Hist, NY, 81. *Collection Arranged:* Whaling Days in New Jersey (auth, catalog), 75 & Survival: Life and Art of the Alaskan Eskimo (auth, catalog), 77-78, Newark Mus, NJ; Arctic Vision: Art of the Canadian Inuit (traveling exhib, auth, catalog), Govt Can, 84-86; Treasures of the Tibetan Mus, 88; Village Life in Rajasthan (photog exhib), 2006-07. *Pos:* Art libr dir, Newark Mus, NJ, 70-75, spec proj consult 76-82; asst dir, Castle Gallery, Col New Rochelle, 83-84; guest cur, Govt Can, 84-86; dir, Jacques Marchais Mus Tibetan Art, 85-97; cons curator, Jacques Marchars Mus Tibetan Art, 2002; co-pres, Arts Council, Atlantic Highlands, NJ, 2011-2012, chair exhib comt, 2012-. *Teaching:* Instr, sch continuing ed, Pratt Univ, Brooklyn, NY, 79; instr eskimo art, New Sch, New York, & Univ Vt, 86; Drew Univ, 98, New Sch NY, 98 & State Univ NY, 98; instr Native Am art, Drew Univ, 97; instr Asian art, New Sch, New York, 98-, Tibetan art, 2003; instr Tibetan art, SUNY, Purchase, 2003. *Mem:* Explorers Club; Newark Mus Speakers Bureau Art Alliance of Monmouth Co. *Res:* Whaling history; life and art of the Alaskan and Canadian Eskimo; New Jersey history; archival Eskimo films; Tibetan art and history. *Interests:* photography, textiles, Buddhist art. *Collection:* Eskimo art and artifacts. *Publ:* Coauth, Westerners in Tibet, Newark Mus, 73; auth, John Cotton Dana and the Newark Museum, 79; exec producer, Village of No River (film), 81; Tibetan Visual Art in White Lotus, 91; Treasures of Tibetan Art, Oxford Univ Press, 96; auth, Survival: Life and Art of the Alaskan Eskimo, Morgan & Morgan, 1976; Arctic Vision: The Art of the Canadian Inuit, Canadian Arctic Producers, 1984; Whaling Days in New Jersey, The Newark Mus; village Life in Rajasthan, Scribbulations, LLC, 2010. *Mailing Add:* 10 Ocean Blvd Apt 8D Atlantic Highlands NJ 07716

LIPTON, LEAH
HISTORIAN, CURATOR

b Kearny, NJ. *Study:* Douglass Col, Rutgers Univ, BA, 49; Harvard Univ, MA, 50. *Collection Arranged:* Around the Station: The Town and the Train (with catalog), 78 & Family Connections: Portraits by Chester Harding (auth, catalog), 81, Danforth Mus Art, Framingham, Mass; A Truthful Likeness: Chester Harding and his Portraits (auth, catalog), Nat Portrait Gallery, 85; Charles Hopkinson: Pictures from a New England Past (auth, catalog), Danforth Mus Art, 88-89; Three New England Painters: Hosmer, Pooke, Woodward (auth, catalog), Danforth Mus Art, 91. *Pos:* Bd dir & adj cur Am Art, Danforth Mus Art, 80-. *Teaching:* Prof art hist, Framingham State Col, Mass, formerly, emer prof, currently. *Awards:* Distinguished Serv Award, Framingham State Col. *Mem:* Coll Art Asn; Soc Archit Historians; Am Studies Asn. *Res:* 19th and 20th century American art & architecture; portrait painting in America especially New England; life and career of Chester Harding (1792-1866); American women artists, 1900-1940. *Publ:* Auth, William Dunlap, Samuel F B Morse, John Wesley Jarvis & Chester Harding: Their careers as itinerant portrait painters, 81, The brief life of the Boston Artists' Association, 1841-1851, 83 & Chester Harding and The Life Portrait of Daniel Boone, 84, Am Art J; Chester Harding in Great Britain, Antiques, 84; Yankee Painters in the South, Southern Quart, 88; The Boston Five: Pioneers of Modernism in Massachusetts, Am Art Review, 94. *Mailing Add:* Dept Art Framingham State Col 100 State St Framingham MA 01701

LIPTON, SONDRA
PAINTER, SCULPTOR

b New York, NY, Apr 24, 1929. *Study:* NY Univ, sculpture with Vincent Glinsky. *Work:* Pres Lyndon B Johnson Libr & in private collections of Mrs Pierre du Pont II, Paul Mellon, Mrs Seward Mellon, Jacqueline Kennedy Onassis, Mrs Sybil Harrington. *Comn:* Mr & Mrs Ralph Baruch; Mr William Rondina. *Media:* Oil on Wood, Oil on Paper. *Mailing Add:* 419 E 57th St New York NY 10022

LIPTON-SAHLMAN, SONDRA See Lipton, Sondra

LIPZIN, JANIS CRYSTAL
FILMMAKER, PHOTOGRAPHER

b Colorado Springs, Colo, Nov 19, 1945. *Study:* Ohio Univ, BFA; NY Univ; Univ Pittsburgh, MLS; San Francisco Art Inst, MFA; Pittsburgh Filmmakers Workshop. *Work:* Carnegie Mus Art, Pittsburgh; Di Rosa Found Napa, Calif; C Richard & Pamela Kramlich, Coll Media Art; Berkeley Art Mus, Univ Calif Berkeley; Cal Arts, Valencia, Calif. *Comn:* Berkeley Art Mus, Berkeley, CA, 2003-2010; San Francisco Cinematheque Sink or Swim, Site Specific Projection: Naval Compression: Prelude, 2001. *Exhib:* Mus Mod Art, NY, 85, 91 & 97; PS 1, NY, 88; Art Gallery Ontario, Can, 90; Pacific Film Arch, Berkeley, Calif, 90, 95, 99; Stadtkino, Vienna, Austria, 92; Yerba Buena Ctr Arts, San Francisco, Calif, 94; De Young Mem Mus, San Francisco, 95; Chinese Taipei Film Archive, Taipei, Taiwan, 2003; Whitney Mus Am Art, 2000; Berkeley Art Mus, Calif, 2010; Edinburgh International Film Festival, 2010; San Francisco International Film Festival, 2010; Big Muddy Film Festival, 2013; Crossroads Festival, 2013; Venice Biennale, 2013. *Pos:* Media cur, Anne Bremer Mem Libr, San Francisco Art Inst, 74-76, chair dept filmmaking, 85-91 & 2004-2005; bd dir, Canyon Cinema Coop, 81-83; contribr ed, Artweek, 81-84; bd dir, Found Art in Cinema, San Francisco, 83-90; consult, Univ Wis, Milwaukee, 91; admin cons, Calif Conf Am Assn Univ Professors, 2013-. *Teaching:* Asst prof art in film & photog, Antioch Col, 76-80; prof filmmaking, San Francisco Art Inst, 78-2009, dir undergrad studio prog, 94-96; vis artist, San Francisco State Univ, 81, Univ Cincinnati, 2011, Calif Arts, 2012, Otis Coll Art & Design, 2013. *Awards:* Ohio Arts Coun Individual Artist Grant, 78; Nat Endowment Arts Individual Artist Grant, 83; NEA Inter/Arts, New Genres with Sonoma Co Found, 90-91; Director's Choice, Black Maria Film Festival, 2006, 2010, 2013; 2nd Jury's award, Montreal Underground Film Festival, 2013. *Bibliog:* Manohla Dargis (auth), The eight & narrow, Village Voice, 89; Steve Anker (auth), Testament to an orphaned art, Blimp Film Mag, Vienna, 92; Brian Frye (auth), Seasonal Forces, 95; Kathy Geritz (auth), I Came into an 8 MM World, Big as Life, MoMA Catalog, 99; Chun-Hui-Wu (auth), Totally Control, Film Appreciation Journal, Taipei Chinese Film Archive, 2001; Kathy Gertiz & Steve Anker (auths), Radical Light, 2010; Shira Segal (auth), Home Movies and Home Birth, Indian Univ Press, 2012. *Mem:* Canyon Cinema Coop; NY Filmmakers Coop; Calif AAUP; Lux London; Scratch Cinema Paris. *Media:* Photography, Film, Video. *Collection:* Richard & Pamela Kramlich Collection, Rene & Veronica di Rosa Collection, Carnegie Mus, Pittsburgh, Anne Bremer Libr, San Farncisco Art Inst. *Publ:* Auth, Looking for gems, Artweek, 81; Tribute to James Broughton, San Francisco Int Film Festival catalog; Addressing urban issues, Artweek, 83; Some Thoughts on Super-8 at the Close of the 20th Century (catalog), Viva 8 Festival, London, 96; Vaca Valley Visions: A Sense of Time and Place (catalog), Vacaville Mus, 96; Why Didn't I Work in Granite, Radical Light, Berkeley Art Mus, 2010; Made by human Hands, Small Windows: The 2d San Francisco Art Inst, 8MM Film Festival Catalog, 2001; Time Present, Gunvor Nelson Exhib, Konst Mus, Sweden, 2012; A Materialist Film Practice in the Digital Age, Millenium Film Jour, 2012. *Dealer:* Canyon Cinema Inc 145 9th St San Francisco CA 94107; NY Filmmakers Coop 175 Lexington Ave New York NY 10016; Light Cone Paris; Lux London. *Mailing Add:* 2434 Bloomfield Rd Sebastopol CA 95472

LIS, JANET
PAINTER, ILLUSTRATOR

b Cleveland, Ohio, Jan 9, 1943. *Study:* Cleveland Inst Art, scholar, 57-61; Ohio Univ Sch Fine Arts, BFA, 65. *Work:* Hollywood Mus Art, Fla; Southeastern Ctr Contemp Art; Lauren Rogers Mus, Miss; Brevard Co, Fla Art Pub Places Prog, Savanna's Clubhouse, Merritt Island; State of Fla Art Pub Bldg Prog, Fla Regional Off Bldg, Miami; Phil Desind Colls; Butler Inst Am Art. *Comn:* First United Methodist Church & First Church of Nazarene, Pompano Beach, Fla; First Baptist Church, Pampano Beach, FL. *Exhib:* Watercolor USA, 80 & 81; Piedmont Biennial, Mint Mus, Charlotte, NC; Ga Watercolor Soc Exhib, Columbus Mus Art, 81; Aqueous, Ky Watercolor Soc, 81; Realist Invitational, Southeastern Ctr Contemp Art, 83; Mainstream Am, 87 & 88 & Ann Mid-year Show, Butler Inst Am Art; San Diego Watercolor Soc Ann, 89; Watercolor Soc Ann 93. *Teaching:* Boca Mus, Boca Raton, Fla. *Awards:* Purchase Awards, Southeastern Ctr Contemp Art, 79, Eastman Mem Found, Lauren Rogers Mus, 79; Cash Awards, Watercolor USA, 80, Arts Assembly of Jacksonville, 81 & Ann Mid-year Show, Butler Inst Am Art, 88; Mitchell Graphics Award, Fla Watercolor Soc Ann, 93. *Bibliog:* Lorraine Huber (auth), The colorful world of Janet Lis, Fiesta Mag, 9/75; Mary Crowe Dorst (auth), article, Art Voices, 11-12/81. *Mem:* Southern Arts Fedn; Fla Watercolor Soc. *Media:* Acrylic on Paper. *Interests:* Painting tropical environments, writing & illustrating children's books. *Publ:* A Treasure Book of Poems for Young Readers, author & illustrator. *Mailing Add:* 12 Sunset Ln Pompano Beach FL 33062

LISAIUS, FRED A
PAINTER, EDUCATOR

b Glenridge, NJ, Sept 16, 1959. *Study:* RI Sch Design, BFA (honors), 81; Special study with Chris Van Allsberg, RI Sch Design, 80. *Work:* City of Everett Wash, Pub Art Coll, Everett, Wash; Evergreen Hospital, Pub Art Collection, Kirkland, Wash; Nordstrom, Pub Art Collection, Chicago, Ill. *Comn:* 30x4 ft mural, Evergreen Hosp, Kirkland, Wash; 8x3.5 ft mural, Mayo Clinic, Jacksonville, Fla; 6x4 ft Mural, Park Nicolett Cancer Ctr, Nicolett, Minn; 5x3 ft mural, Swedish Hosp, Seattle, Wash; 14x34 ft mural, Nordstrom, Chicago, Ill. *Exhib:* 36th Ann Puget Sound Exhib, Frye Art Mus, Seattle, Wash, 94; Whatcom Co Int Exhib, Whatcom Mus, Bellingham,

Wash, 2000; Transitions, Seattle Art Mus Gallery, Wash, 2001; Consumibles, Seattle Ctr, Wash, 2002; EAFA, Bellevue Art Mus, Bellevue, Wash, 2003; Place, Ga Univ, Milledgeville, Ga, 2009; Kindred, Bellevue Coll, Bellevue, Wash, 2009. *Teaching:* prof painting, Bellevue Coll, Wash, 2001-2007. *Awards:* Key to City, City of Bellevue, Wash, 2005. *Mem:* Wash State Artists Roster, 2007-2009; Eastside Asn Fine Arts, Wash, 2002-2009. *Media:* Acrylics & oil on convas or wood panel. *Dealer:* Linda Hodges Gallery 316 1st Ave Seattle Wash 98104; Circa Gallery 210 North 1st St Minneapolis MN 55401; Schomburg Gallery 2525 Michigan Ave Santa Monica CA 90404

LISK, PENELOPE E TSALTAS
PAINTER, PRINTMAKER
b New York, NY, June 16, 1959. *Study:* Bryn Mawr Coll, Pa, AB (fine art printmaking), 81, with Fritz Janschka; Cranbrook Acad Art, Bloomfield Hills, Mich, MFA (printmaking), 85, with Steve Murakishi. *Work:* Detroit Inst Art, Mich; Nelson Atkins Mus, Kansas City, Kans; Newport Harbour Art Mus, Calif; Cranbrook Acad Art Mus, Bloomfield Hills, Mich; Muskegon Mus Art, Mich. *Exhib:* Solo exhibs, Oceans, Fackenthal Pethick Gallery, The Baldwin School, Bryn Mawr, PA, 2015, Limited Impressions, Cabrini Coll, 88, Chilton Co, 90, Radnor, Pa, Episcopal Acad, Merion, Pa, 2002 & First Friday, Main Line, 2007; Drawing '89, Trenton State Coll, NJ, 89; Centennial Exhib, Baldwin Sch, 89; four-person exhib, Villanova Univ, Pa, 90; Pavillion Gallery, Mem Hosp, Pennsauken, NJ, 92; Women's Caucus for Art, Jun Gallery, Philadelphia, 94; group exhibs, Main Line Art Ctr, Artists Equity & Print Exchange III-VI, Philadelphia, 94-2000; The Episcopal Acad, Merion, Pa, 2002, 2014; Woodmere Art Mus, Morris Arboretum, 2012; Morris Arboretum, Phila, PA, Home Tweet Home, Designer Birdhouses. *Collection Arranged:* Centennial Exhib, Baldwin Sch, 89; 125th Anniv, Baldwin Sch Exhibs. *Pos:* Gallery asst, Noel Butcher Gallery, Philadelphia, Pa, 85-87; assoc develop dir, Chester Springs, Studio, Chester Springs, PA, 2004. *Teaching:* Instr, The Baldwin Sch, Bryn Mawr, Pa, 85, 2012, substitute teacher, 2014-2015, artist in res, The Baldwin Sch, camp mgr, 98-2005. *Awards:* Purchase Prize, Nat Drawing, Mercer Co Cult & Heritage Comn, 87; 2nd Prize-Painting, Impressions VIII, Main Line CofC & Sun Oil Co, 88; Mary Costanza Award in Painting, Main-Line Art Ctr, 2005. *Mem:* Artists Uniting Religion & Art; Main Line Art Ctr; Community Art Ctr; Chester Springs Studio. *Media:* Painting, Printmaking. *Interests:* blogging. *Publ:* Print Zero Studies, Seattle. *Mailing Add:* 2421 N Feathering Rd Media PA 19063

LITTLE, JAMES
PAINTER, PRINTMAKER
b Memphis, Tenn, July 21, 1952. *Study:* Memphis Acad Arts, BFA, 74; Syracuse Univ, MFA (fels), 76. *Work:* Ark Arts Ctr, Little Rock; Everson Mus Art; Brooks Mus Art; Twentieth Century Fund, NY; Mrs Raffaella de Ussia Collection, Mex; and others. *Comn:* Oil painting, Stephen Mallory Assoc, NY, 77. *Exhib:* Solo exhib, Everson Mus, 76; Works on Paper, Albright-Knox Art Gallery, 83; Liz Harris Gallery; Chrysler Mus; Alice Bingham Gallery, Memphis; RI Mus Art, Directions in the 1990's, 90; Nat Acad Mus, NY, 2006; and many others. *Teaching:* Asst drawing, Syracuse Univ, 74-76; instr drawing & painting, Memphis Acad Arts, 77-78. *Awards:* Creative Artists Pub Serv Grant, 81; Joan Mitchell Found Grant, 2009. *Media:* Oil on Linen or Canvas. *Dealer:* June Kelly Gallery 591 Broadway New York NY; Sid Deutsch Gallery 29 W 57th St New York NY. *Mailing Add:* 315 Seventh Ave New York NY 10001-6005

LITTLE, KEN DAWSON
SCULPTOR
b Canyon, Tex, April 8, 1947. *Study:* Tex Tech Univ, BFA, 70; Univ Utah, MFA, 72. *Work:* Art Pace, San Antonio; Phoenix Art Mus; Contemp Arts Found, Honolulu; Lannan Found, Palm Beach; Mus Contemp Craft; Ariz State Univ; Utah Mus Fine Art; plus many others. *Comn:* Woodland Park Zoo (outdoor work), Seattle Art Comn, Wash, 91. *Exhib:* Solo exhibs, Cheney Cowles Art Mus, Spokane, Wash, Portland Ctr Visual Arts, Ore, 86, Fabric Workshop, Philadelphia, Pa, 89, Diverseworks, Houston, Tex, 91, 94, Forum for Contemp Art, St Louis, 97, Amarillo Art Mus, Tex, 97, Ctr for Contemp Art, Fort Worth, Tex, 98, Finesilver Gallery, San Antonio, 99, City Mus, St Louis, 2000, Galveston Art Ctr, Tex, 2001, Hotel Pupik, 2001, Schrattenberg, Austria, 2001, Southwest Sch for Art and Craft, San Antonio, 2003, Salt Lake Art Ctr, Utah, 2003; Art Pace, San Antonio, 95; Forum Contemp Art, St Louis, 97; Finesilver Gallery, San Antonio, Tex, 99; Galveston Art Ctr, Tex, 2000; Field Mus, Chicago, 2002; Fabric Workshop, Philadelphia, 2003; Art House, Tex Fine Arts Asn, Austin, 2003; and many others. *Collection Arranged:* Daniel Jacobs, NYC; McDonald's Corp, Sacramento, Calif; Richard Nelson Gallery, Univ Calif at Davis; Microsoft Corp, Seattle. *Teaching:* Grad teaching asst, Univ Utah, 71-73; instr art; Univ South Fla, 72-74; asst prof, Univ Mont, 74-78, Univ Okla, Norman, 80-85; vis prof, Alfred Univ, NY, 78 & Univ Calif, Davis, 79; assoc prof, Univ Mont, Chmn, 78-80; prof, Univ Tex, San Antonio, 88-. *Awards:* Western States Arts Found Fel, 77; Nat Endowment Arts Fel, 82-83 & 88-89; Art Pace Found AIR Fel, 95; Artist/Ondustry Residency Grant, John M Kohler Art Ctr, Wis, 98; BorderArt/GrensKunst Artist Residency Exchange Grant, Ger, 01; Virginia Groot Found Award for Excellence in Sculpture, 01, 02. *Bibliog:* Elizabeth Skidmor Sasser (auth), Ken Little at the San Antonio Art Inst, Artspace Mag, Vol 8, No 3, 84; Dave Hickey (auth), Ken Dawson Little: A Bestiary of Damaged Goods, Art Space Mag, summer 85; Glen R Brown (auth), Focus: Ken Little, Meaning in Masquerade, Sculpture Mag, Vol 17, No 7, summer 98. *Media:* Mixed. *Dealer:* Finesilver Gallery San Antonio TX. *Mailing Add:* PO Box 830085 San Antonio TX 78283-0085

LITTLE, STEPHEN
MUSEUM DIRECTOR
Study: Cornell Univ, BA; Univ Calif Los Angeles, MA; Dept History of Art, PhD. *Pos:* Cur, Asian Art Mus, 1989-1994; Pritzker cur of Asian art, Art Inst Chicago, 1994-2002; dir & pres, Honolulu Acad Arts, 2002-. *Mem:* Asn Art Mus Dirs. *Mailing Add:* Honolulu Academy of Arts 900 S Beretania St Honolulu HI 96814

LITTLE CHIEF, BARTHELL
PAINTER, SCULPTOR
b Lawton, Okla, Oct 14, 1941. *Study:* Cameron Univ, Lawton, Okla; Univ Okla, Norman. *Work:* Southwestern Mus Los Angeles, Calif; Southern Plains Mus, Anadarko, Okla; Cahokia Mounds Hist Site, Collinsville, Ill; Mus Art, Univ Okla, Norman; Okla Hist Soc, Oklahoma City. *Comn:* Terra-cotta sculpture, US Dept Interior, Washington, DC, 69; tempera painting, US Dept Interior, Washington, DC, 81; fiberglass sculpture, US Dept Interior, Washington, DC, 85. *Exhib:* Am Indian Artist, Philbrook Art Mus, Tulsa, Okla, 78; Vestiges and Resurgence, Morris Mus, Morristown, NJ, 79; Am Contemp Paintings Traveling Exhib, SAm, 79; Solo exhib, Mus Art, Univ Okla, Norman, 79; Am Indian Art 1980's, Native Am Ctr Living Arts, Niagara Falls, NY, 81; Winter Camp, Nat Cowbow and Western Heritage Mus, Okla City, 99 & 2002. *Awards:* 1st Prize Sculpture, 95, Printmaking, 97, 3rd Prize, Sculpture, 96, Printmaking, 89, 94 & 95, Grand Award, 99, Red Earth Indian Art Show, Olka City, Okla; Grand Award, 91, 1st Prize Painting, 93, 2nd Prize, 95, 1st Prize Sculpture, 95 & 97 & 2nd Prize Sculpture, 95 & 96, Cherokee Nat Hist Mus, Tahlequah, Okla; 1st Painting, 2nd Bronze Sculpture, 2nd Stone Sculpture, 96, 1st Bronze Sculpture, 2nd Painting, 98, Schemitzun Indian Art Show, Harford, Conn; 1st Painting, Native Am Art Show, Jackson Hole, Wyo, 98. *Mem:* Kiowa Tia-Piah Soc; Descendents of the 7th US Cavalry Troop L. *Media:* Tempera, Gouache; Alabaster, Bronze. *Interests:* Hot Rods and Harley Davidson. *Publ:* Auth, Kiowa Voices, Tex Christian Univ Press, 83. *Dealer:* Barbara Gallery 135 Palace Ave Sante Fe NM 87501. *Mailing Add:* Rt 3 Box 109A Anadarko OK 73005

LITTMAN, BRETT
GALLERY DIRECTOR
Study: Univ Calif, San Diego, BA (philos). *Pos:* Chmn, Brooklyn Arts Coun Visual Arts Panel, 95-98; assoc dir, UrbanGlass, Brooklyn, NY, 95-2001; co-exec dir, Dieu Donné Papermill, New York, 2001-03; dep dir, PS1 Contemp Art Ctr, Long Island City, NY, 2003-07, mng dir, PS1 Radio Sta, 2003-04; exec dir, Drawing Ctr, New York, 2007-. *Mem:* Glass Art Soc (co-chmn, Bridge to the Future Conf, 2000); Int Art Critics Asn. *Publ:* co-dir & co-producer (film), Puro Party: Celebrating a Genocide, Deep Dish TV, 92; assoc producer (film), Pretty Vacant, by Jimmy Mediola. *Mailing Add:* Drawing Ctr 35 Wooster St New York NY 10013

LITTRELL, DORIS MARIE
DEALER
b Apache, Okla, Apr 30, 1928. *Pos:* Owner, Okla Indian Art Gallery, currently. *Specialty:* Native American arts, with emphasis on Oklahoma Indian artists and craftsman

LITWIN, RUTH FORBES
PRINTMAKER, PAINTER
b Omaha, Nebr, Apr 14, 1933. *Study:* San Antonio Col, Tex, 50; Richland Col, Dallas, 78; Southern Methodist Univ, Dallas, with Wilbert Verhelst, 79, Brookhaven Col, Dallas, Tex, with Don Taylor, 91-96; Western Ky Univ, Seminars with Ivan Schieferdecker & Laurin Northesen, 91; Washington Univ Workshop, Dallas, Tex, studied with Peter Marcus, 94 & 96 & Dawn Guernsey, 94. *Work:* Mem Ctr Holocaust Studies, Dallas; Nat Mus Women Arts, Washington, DC; AH Belo Corp, Texas Instruments, Brookhaven Col, Dallas; North Lake Col, Irving, Tex; Legacy, Willow Bend, Plano, Tex, 2009. *Comn:* Memorial (cast bronze) & Eternal Light (cast bronze), Mem Ctr Holocaust Studies, Dallas, 83; Sculpture, Jewish Home for the Aged, 88; Off Residence of the US Ambassador to Angola, Honorable Cynthia Efird, US Dept of State, 2005; Residence of the US Ambassador to Republic of Congo, Honorable Alan and Carolyn Gastham, US Dept of State, 2009; Off Residence of US Ambassador to Bermuda, Hon Grace W Shelton, US Dept State, 2010. *Exhib:* Nat Mus Women Arts, Washington, DC, 91; Masur Mus Art, Monroe, La, 92; Nat Competition, S Bend Art Ctr, Ind, 92; retrospective, Northlake Col, Irving, Tex, 92; Wichita Falls Mus & Art Ctr, Tex, 93; Tom Peyton Mem Arts Festival, Alexandria, La, 93; Wise Women Speak, Nat Open, Dallas, 94; Global Focus: Women in Art and Cult, UN Fourth World Conf Women, Beijing, China, 95; La State Univ Nat Exhib, Baton Rouge, 98; Univ Richmond Mus, Va, 2000; North Lake Col, 2001; Irving Arts Center, 2003; and many others. *Awards:* Purchase Award, Brookhaven Col, 96; Northlake Col, 2002; Rowena Elkin Award, 97; Soc Int des Beaux-Arts Prix, 98; Calendar Award, Figurative Sculpture, Tex Sculpture Asn, 2006. *Bibliog:* Rachel Amado Bortnick (auth), Spreading the Message of Tolerance, 94; Bridget Knight (auth), article, Wichita Falls Times Record News, 94; Wade Wilson (auth), Master strokes in printmaking, 95; Mike Jacobs (auth), Triumph over Tragedy, 148 & 149. *Mem:* Tex Fine Arts Asn (dir, 78-79, pres, 80-82, state bd, 82-86); Dallas Visual Art Ctr, (charter mem, 81); Int Sculpture Asn; Mid Am Print Coun; Women's Caucus Art (bd mem, 84-86, vpres prog, 86); Embassies Prog Washington, DC, Angola Embassy; Tex Sculpture Asn. *Media:* Printmaker; Sculpture. *Interests:* Live theater, movies, reading & yoga. *Publ:* Auth, Tough Issues in Women's Art, The Washington Post, Washington, DC, 2/22/91; Univers de Arts, Le Mag de L'Information Artistique, 9/88 & 10/99

LIU, JEN
PAINTER
b Smithtown, NY, 1976. *Study:* Oberlin Coll, BA (creative writing), BA (studio art, with high honors), 1998; Calif Inst Arts, MFA (fine arts & integrated media), 2001. *Exhib:* Solo exhibs include Knitting Factory, LA, 2001, Freezing Cold Gallery, 2001, Upstream Gallery, Amsterdam, 2004, 2005, 2008, Lizabeth Oliveria Gallery, LA, 2005, 2007, Rotterdam Art Fair, 2006, Division Mus Ceramics & Glassware, New York, 2007, DePauw Univ, Ind, 2007; group exhibs include An Interest in Life, Apex Art, New York, 2003; Through the Gates: Brown vs Bd of Education, Calif African Am Mus, LA, 2004; 100 Artists See God, Inst Contemp Art, London, 2004, traveling through 2006; Open Video Call, Artists Space, New York, 2005; Peekskill Project

2006, Hudson Valley Ctr Contemp Art, Peekskill, NY, 2006; Dream of Today, Steve Turner Contemp, LA, 2007; The Violet Hour, Henry Art Gallery, Seattle, 2008. *Media:* Watercolor. *Dealer:* Upstream Gallery Van Ostadestraat 294 1073 TW Amsterdam The Netherlands. *Mailing Add:* 1723 Lucretia Ave Los Angeles CA 90026-1705

LIU, KATHERINE CHANG
PAINTER, CURATOR
b Kiang-si, China; US citizen. *Study:* Univ Calif, Berkeley, MS, 66. *Work:* Lew Allen Contemporary, Santa Fe, NMex, 98 & 99; Watercolor Biennial, Parkland Coll Gallery, Ill, 98; Rosaline Koener Gallery, NY, 2000; Gail Harvey Gallery, Calif, 99; AMA Gallery, Finland, 6/01; Chrysler Mus, Va; Virginia Mus; Utah State Univ Art Mus; Palm Springs Desert Mus, Calif; Chiaroscuro Contemporary Art, Santa Fe, NMex. *Exhib:* Chicago Navy Pier Int Art Fair, 94; Taiwan Art Educ Inst Invitational, 94; Rosenfeld Gallery, 94; JJ Brookings Gallery, 96; Hong Kong Univ Sci & Technol, 96; plus many others; Solo Exhibs: Egelund Gallerie, Copenhagen, Denmark, 2002; Galerie Parsi Parla, Lyon, France, 2004; Jenkins Johnson Gallery, 2005, Architettosmith, Rome, italy, 2010; Art Miami, 2002-2005; Art Copenhagen, 2002-2005; Art Paris, 2002-2005; Duality, LewAllen Contemp, Santa Fe, 2006; Reduction/Addition, Gail Harvey Gallery, Santa Monica, 2007; Sole juror, Western Fedn Exhib (competition of 7 western states), 2008; Art Santa Fe, 2008; Parcours de l'Art, Provence, France, 2008; USA, Korea, Japan International, Asto Mus, Calif, 2008; State of Art Nat Biennial, Parkland Col, Ill, 2009; Teacher/Mentor/Muse Exhibit, Valley Inst Visual Arts, Los Angeles, 2009; Gwang Wha Moon Int Art Fair, Seoul, Korea, 2009; Asto Mus, Los Angeles; 60th Ann Nat Found of China, Beijing, 2009; 1st Shanghai Int Watercolor Biennial, Shanghai, China, 2010. *Pos:* Invited juror & lectr for over 75 nat & regional exhibs & orgns; cur, LewAllen Contemp, Santa Fe, 2003-04; cur, Jenkins Johnson Gallery, San Francisco, 2005; cur, Gail Havey Gallery, Santa Monica, Calif, 2006; sole juror, Southern Watercolor Regional Exhib, Dallas, 2010 & Calif Watercolor Asn An Show, San Francisco, 2011; Nat Watercolor Soc Pres Emiritus Invitational, Los Angeles, 2010; juror, Int Society Acrylic Painters, 2012; Int Watermedia Masters, 3rd Biennial Exhib, Nanjing, China, 2012; co-chair, Nanjing Internat, Internat Biennial Exhib and Conf in Contemporary Watermedia, 2013; Spring Invitational Chiaroscuro Contemporary Art, Santa Fe, NMex, 2013. *Teaching:* Instr watercolor, Western Va Mus Arts, 75-79, Conejo Valley Art Mus, 80-82 & watercolor groups, US & Abroad; instr intensive studies seminar, Taos, NM, 98-2010. *Awards:* Second Award, Nat Watercolor Soc, 79; Best show, Nat Watercolor Soc mem Show, 84; Gold Medal, Allied Artists Am, New York, 86; Lifetime Achievement award, Watercolor USA Hon Soc, 2012. *Bibliog:* Emilia Siltavuori (auth), Sweden, 7/21/01; Mia Tykkylainan (auth), The Possibility of a Slow Paced Life, The Art of Katherine Chang Liu, Gallerie Ama, 7/12/01; Ryon Harms (auth), Painting the Layers of Katherine Chang Liu, Los Angeles Daily News, 4/7/03; Peter Frank (auth), LA Weekly, 2007. *Mem:* Watercolor USA Hon Soc; Nat Watercolor Soc. *Media:* Painting, Monotype; Mixed Media. *Collection:* Inst of Contemp Art, Lyon France; Chrysler Mus; Va Mus; Palm Springs Desert Mus. *Publ:* Auth, The California Romantics, Robert Perine, Artra Publ, 87; Exploring Painting, Davis Publ; Painting the Spirit of Nature, Watson-Guptill; Watercolor and Collage Workshop, Watson-Guptill. *Dealer:* Sandra Walters Internat Hong Kong; Jenkins Johnson Gallery San Francisco CA & Chelsea New York; Galerie Parci Parla Lyon France; Chiaroscuro Contemporary Gallery Santa Fe NM; AMA Gallery. *Mailing Add:* 1338 Heritage Pl Westlake Village CA 91362

LIVERANT, GIGI HORR
PAINTER
b Portsmouth, NH, Apr 10, 1950. *Study:* Paier Coll of Art, BA, 1972; Studied under Robert Brackman, 1971-1973. *Work:* Lyman Allyn Mus, New London, Conn; Conn Col, New London, Conn; Pfizer, Groton, Conn; Aetna Insurance Co, Hartford, Conn; Conn Savings Bank, New Haven, Conn; Three Rivers Community Col, Conn; Smilow Cancer Ctr, New Haven, Conn; New Haven Paint and Clay Club, New Haven, Conn. *Comn:* Mural, Old Lyme Inn, Old Lyme, Conn, 1976; Mural, Conn Savings Bank, New Haven, Conn, 1978; CowParade, CowParade Inc, NY, 2000; CowParade, CowParade Inc, Boston, Mass, 2006. *Exhib:* Pastel Soc of Am, Hermitage Foundation Mus, Norfolk, Va, 1982; Illumination, Lyman Allyn Mus, New London, Conn, 1983; Gigi Horr Liverant, Slater Mem Mus, Norwich, Conn, 1992; Gigi Horr Liverant, Lyman Allyn Mus, New London, Conn, 1996; Chester Gallery, Chester, Conn, 1998; Norwich Arts Council Gallery, Norwich, Conn, 2006; Kehler Liddell Gallery, New Haven, Conn, 2007, 2010, 2012; Cooley Gallery, Old Lyme, Conn, 2013; Alexey Von Schlippee Gallery, Groton, Conn, 2014. *Awards:* Hurlimann Armstrong Award, Pastel Soc of Am, M Hurlimann Armstrong, 1979; Bd Dirs Award, Kansas Pastel Soc, 1988; Art Spirit Found, Pastel Soc of Am, Dianne B Bernhard, 2000; Pastel Jour 100 Finalists, 2002; Second Prize Conn Women Artists, 2002; Best of Show, Conn Pastel Soc, 2002; First Prize Conn Acad Fine Arts, 2003; Andrew Giffuni Meml award, Pastel Soc Am, 2009; Richard McKinley Mentorship award, Pastel Soc Am, 2013; Best in Show, Conn Acad Fine Arts, 2014. *Bibliog:* Claudia Becker (auth), Vibrant Renditions of Everyday Objects, Women in the Arts, 1995; Judy Birke (auth) A Sense of Possibility, New Haven Register, 2004; Beth Dufresne (auth), Portrait of the Artist As a Commuter, New London Day, 2005; Judy Birke (auth), Vibrant Visions, New Haven Register, 2007; Laura Beach (auth) Nature or Nurture?, Newtown Bee Arts and Antique Weekly, 2006; Visual Opposites Make for Engaging Kehler LIddell Exhib, New Haven Register, 2010; Hank Hoffman (auth), Spaced Out, New Haven Register, 2010; Spaced Out, New Haven Register, 2010; Deborah Secor (auth), Night and Day, Pastel Journal, 2012. *Mem:* Conn Women Artists 1983-2015; Conn Pastel Soc 2000-2015; Pastel Soc of Am 1979-2015; Conn Acad of Fine Arts; Pastel Painters Soc of Cape Cod. *Media:* Pastel, Oil, Acrylic. *Dealer:* Cooley Gallery Old Lyme Conn; Granary Callery Tisbury Mass. *Mailing Add:* 43 School Rd Colchester CT 06415

LIVESAY, THOMAS ANDREW
MUSEUM DIRECTOR, EDUCATOR
b Dallas, Tex, Feb 1, 1945. *Study:* San Francisco Art Inst, 63-65; Univ Tex, Austin, BFA, 68, MFA, 72; Harvard Univ, 78. *Collection Arranged:* Five Austin Artists (with catalog), 74; The Amarillo Competition, 75 & 77; Charles Burchfield Selected Works (with catalog), 75; Henri Matisse Etchings, 75; Am Masters, 75; Warren Davis Retrospective (with catalog), 75; Am Images, 76, with Nat Endowment for the Humanities; Young Texas Artists Series, 76-78. *Pos:* Tech staff, Univ Tex Art Mus, Austin, 66-70; cur, Elisabeth Ney Art Ctr, Austin, 70-73; dir, Longview Mus & Art Ctr, Tex, 73-75; cur, Amarillo Art Ctr, 75-77, dir, 77-80; asst dir admin, Dallas Mus Fine Arts, 80-85; dir, Mus NMex, 85-2000; dir, Whatcom Mus Hist & Art, Bellingham, Wash, 2000-2007; exec dir, La State Univ Mus Art, Baton Rouge, 2007-. *Teaching:* Univ Okla, MLS/me prog, 87-; adjunct prof art hist & mus studies, La State Univ, 2009. *Awards:* Roy Crane Award Fine Arts, Univ Tex, Austin, 68; Centennial Hon Roll, Am Asn Mus, 2006; Teaching exceelence, Coll Liberal Studies, Univ Okla, 99; Edgar L Hewett Award, NMex Asn Mus, 2007. *Mem:* Am Asn Mus (bd trustees, 87-90, 2004-2007); Tex Asn Mus (pres, 83-85); LA Asn Mus, (vpres 2010-). *Res:* Twentieth century American art with particular emphasis on sculpture. *Interests:* Photography, sculpture. *Publ:* Coauth, Larson-Walsh-Sculpture, 74; auth, Young Texas Artists Series, 78; American Images, 78; coauth, Made in Texas, 79; auth, Russell Lee, 79; Ruth Abrams, New York Univ, 86. *Mailing Add:* LSU Museum of Art Shaw Center for the Arts 100 Lafayette Street Baton Rouge LA 70801

LIVET, ANNE HODGE
ADMINISTRATOR, CRITIC
b Ft Worth, Tex, 1941. *Study:* Wellesley Col, Mass, 59-61; Univ Tex, Austin, 61-62; Tex Christian Univ, Ft Worth, BA, 72, MA, 74. *Collection Arranged:* Brazos River: a Television Exhibition with Robert Rauschenberg, Viola Farber and David Tudor, Ft Worth Art Mus, 77, The Record as Artwork: from Futurism to Conceptual Art (ed & contribr, catalog), 77 & Stella Since 1970 (ed, catalog), 78; David McManaway: Works-Twenty Years (auth, catalog), Univ Gallery, Meadows Sch Arts, Southern Methodist Univ, Dallas, 79; The Works of Edward Ruscha (auth, catalog), San Francisco Mus Mod Art, Calif, 81; Infotainment, 18 Artists from New York (auth, catalog); Art Against AIDS (ed, catalog); The New Urban Landscape (co-cur & auth, catalog), World Financial Ctr. *Pos:* Dir performing arts, Ft Worth Art Mus, 74-78 & cur, 75-78; co-founder with Stephen Reichard, Livet Reichard Co Inc, 79-. *Awards:* Nat Endowment Arts Fel Mus Prof, 76; Inst for Art & Urban Resources Fel, New York, 78-79. *Publ:* Ed & contribr, Contemporary Dance, Abbeville Press, 78; Contemporary Art Southeast, Vol II, No 2, 79; contribr, All Sweet Things, Bomb Mag, winter 98 & Looking Up, Pub Art Fund, 99. *Mailing Add:* c/o Livet Reichard Co Inc 306 W 38th St 7th Fl New York NY 10018

LIVICK, STEPHEN
PHOTOGRAPHER
b Castleford, Eng, Feb 11, 1945; Can citizen. *Study:* Self-taught. *Work:* Can Mus Contemp Photog, Ottawa; Mus Mod Art, NY; George Eastman House, Rochester, NY; Carnegie Mus Art, Pittsburgh, Pa; Corcoran Gallery Art, Washington. *Exhib:* Solo exhibs, George Eastman House, Rochester, NY, 75 & 77, Nat Film Bd Can, Ottawa, 76, 77, 82 & 83, Baltimore Mus Art, 78, McIntosh Gallery, Univ Western Ont, London, 81, 93, MacDonald Stewart Art Ctr, 83, 94 & Can Mus Contemp Photog, Ottawa, 92; Persona (with catalog), Nickle Arts Mus, Calgary, 82; Seeing People, Photogrs Gallery, London, Eng, 84; Contemp Canadian Photog, Nat Gallery Can, Ottawa, 85; Corcoran Gallery Art, Washington, DC, 89; Portside Gallery, Yokohama, Japan, 98. *Awards:* Several grants, Can Coun & Ont Arts Coun. *Bibliog:* David Scopic (auth), Gum Bichromate Book, 91; Calcutta, Can Mus Contemp Photog, 92; Livick Metaphorical Transformations, 97; and others. *Media:* Gum Bichromate Printing. *Dealer:* Deleon White Gallery 1096 Queen St W Toronto ON Canada M6J 1H9. *Mailing Add:* 22A Maitland St 3rd Fl London ON N6B 3L2 Canada

LIVINGSTON, CONSTANCE KELLNER
COLLAGE ARTIST, SCULPTOR
b Brooklyn, NY. *Study:* Tyler Sch Fine Art, Temple Univ, MFA, 44; studies with Philp Evergood, 50, Victor Candell, 70. *Work:* Ardsley Gallery Libr, NY. *Comn:* Sculpture-lucite & bronze, Patent Lawyers Asn, New Haven, Conn, 79. *Exhib:* Photog & Sculpture, Mus Gallery, White Plains, NY, 85; Nat Acad Galleries, NY, 85; Hudson River Mus, Westchester, NY, 85 & 90; Stamford Mus, Conn, 90; Katonah Mus, NY, 93; NY Soc Women Artists, NY, 93-94. *Teaching:* High sch educ art, Metrop Mus Art, 79-83. *Awards:* Famous Artist Award, Nat Asn Women Artists; Audubon Artists Medal, Audubon Artists; First Prize Sculpture, Mamaroneck Artists. *Mem:* Nat Asn Women Artists; Silvermine Guild Artists; Art Place Gallery; Art Initiatives; Artists Equity Asn. *Media:* Collage; Lucite, Welded Steel. *Mailing Add:* One Sheldrake Ln New Rochelle NY 10804

LIVINGSTON, MARGARET GRESHAM
ADMINISTRATOR, PATRON
b Birmingham, Ala, Aug 16, 1924. *Study:* Vassar Col, AB, 45; Univ Ala, MA, 46. *Pos:* Chmn bd, Birmingham Mus Art, 78-86, exec comn, 78- & chmn comp on collections, 86-. *Awards:* Silver Bowl Award for Contrib Arts, Birmingham Festival Arts, 67; Woman of Year, Birmingham, Ala, 86. *Mem:* Am Asn Mus. *Interests:* Art history, education, board administration & organization and publication of museums. *Collection:* American graphics and drawings. *Mailing Add:* 12 Country Club Rd Birmingham AL 35213

LIVINGSTON, VALERIE A
EDUCATOR, MUSEUM DIRECTOR
b Pittsburgh, Pa. *Study:* Univ SFla, BA (art hist), 77; Fla State Univ, MA (art hist), 80; Univ Del, PhD (art hist), 89. *Collection Arranged:* W Elmer Schofield: Proud Painter of Modest Lands (auth, catalog), Moravian Col, 88; Encountering the Narrative in the Work of Florence Putterman (auth, catalog), Susquehanna Univ, 93; Intimate

Perceptions: Aesthetic Considerations of Photography Through the Microscope, Susquehanna Univ, 93; Chronicles of Pa Plain People, 94; Joseph Priestly in Am: 1794 to 1804 (coauth, catalog), Dickinson Col, 94; James Fitzgerald: Spiritual Transformation, 97; Masters of the French Poster, Susquehanna Univ, 97; Public & Private Eyes: FSA Photography in Pennsylvania, 98; Monhegan Modernists: 1940-1970 from the Collection of John M Day, Susquehanna Univ, 2002; Cognac, Cafe & Clluture: The Art of the French Poster, Susquehanna Univ, 2003. *Pos:* Prof art hist, chmn art dept, mus dir. *Teaching:* Adj prof art hist, Moravian Col, 86-90; assoc prof art hist & head art dept, Susquehanna Univ, 90-, dir Lore Degenstein Gallery, 92-. *Mem:* Coll Art Asn; Am Asn Mus; Mid-Atlantic Asn Mus; Asn Coll & Univ Mus & Galleries; Asn Historians of Am Art. *Res:* American art; early 20th century & federal portraiture; abstract expressionist sculpture (Herbert Ferber); contemporary feminist painters; Pennsylvania Impressionists (W Elmer Schofield). *Specialty:* American Art; Decorative Arts; French Posters. *Publ:* Auth, W.Elmer Schofield: Proud Painter of Modest Lands, Moravian Col, 88; Encountering The Narrative in The Work of Florence Putterman, 93; Joseph Priestley in America, Dickinson Col, 94; Hans Moller Purveyor of Color: 1905-2001, 2002; Beyond Description: Abstraction in the Oil Paintings of James Fitzgerald, Monhegan Mus, 2001. *Mailing Add:* 444 N New St Bethlehem PA 18018

LIVINGSTONE, BIGANESS
PAINTER
b Cambridge, Mass, 1926. *Study:* Mass Coll Art, BFA (painting), 50; Univ Wis, Madison, MFA (painting), 80. *Work:* Chase Manhattan Bank Collection, NY; Merrimack Co Courthouse, NH; Neville Mus, Wis; Radcliffe Coll, Cambridge, Mass; Engineering Bldg, Univ Wis, Madison; Mass Coll of Art, Office of the Pres; Goldberg moser O'Neill Advt, Calif; and others. *Comn:* Mural, Cranwell Chapel, Lenox, Mass, 67. *Exhib:* DeCordova Mus, Lincoln, Mass, 58 & 60; Fitchburg Art Mus, Mass, 77; Arts & Sci Mus, Nashua, NH, 77; Bergstrom-Mahler Mus, Neenah, Wis, 78; Elvehjem Mus, Wis, 84; Minneapolis Art Mus, 86; Milwaukee Art Mus, 86; David Barnett Gallery, Milwaukee, 91-93; Claudia Chapline Gallery, Stinson Beach, Calif, 95; Crocker-Kingsley, Crocker Mus, Sacramento, 2000; Rahr-West Mus, Monitowoc, Wis, 2000; Allen/Thomas Gallery, Neenah, WI, 2001; City Hall, Benicia, Calif, 2004; The Art Foundry Gallery, Sacramento, 2005; San Francisco Mus Mod Art, Point Mason, Calif, 2008; MC O'Rourke Gallery, Benicia, Calif, 2010. *Pos:* Regional dir, City Spirit Grant, NH Comn Arts, 75; mem, adv bd, Cudahy Gallery, Milwaukee Art Mus, 84-85; mem, panel & artists grant awards, Wis Arts Bd, 86; juror, Fairfield City Gallery, Fairfield, CA, 2005. *Teaching:* Prof art, Univ Wis, Fox Valley, Drawing & painting, 76-93, emer prof, 93-. *Awards:* Grant, Bunting Inst Independent Study, Radcliffe Coll, Mass, 65; Univ Wis Painting Grants, 89 & 90; Grant: The George Sugarman Found, Inc, 2003; and others. *Bibliog:* Bartlett Hayes (auth), Tradition becomes innovation; Who's Who in American Education, Nat Reference Inst, 93. *Mem:* Soc Inst Fels, Radcliffe Coll, Mass; Mass Coll Art N Calif Alumni. *Media:* Acrylic, Oil. *Dealer:* San Francisco Mus Modern Art Artists Gallery Bldg A Ft Mason Ctr San Francisco CA 94123

LIZ-N-VAL
SCULPTOR, PAINTER
b Liz, Poland; Val, USSR. *Work:* Kassel Documenta Arch, Ger; Ludwig Mus, Cologne, Ger; Staats Galerie Grafische Sam Mlung, Stuttgart, Ger; Whitney Mus Am Art, NY; Detroit Inst Arts. *Comn:* Mural, Urban Jungle, 8 BC Club, NY, 85; Liz-N-Val Head, Steven Spielberg, NY, 87. *Exhib:* El Mundo De Mickey Mouse (with catalog), Cuartel Conde Duque, Madrid & Barcelona, 94-95; Liz-N-Val Fractal Realities, World Wide Web, Paris, 96; Liz-N-Val, New Breed of Art, MoMa, Pontiac, Mich, 2/2000; Liz-N-Val, Er-Ruptions, Gallery X, Harlem, NY, 5/2000; Art of Mail(ing), Wexler Ctr Arts, Columbus, Ohio, 9/2000; Solo exhibs, All Shook-Up, James Fuentes Gallery, NY, 2000, Liz-N-Val Monk Room, Monk Gallery, Brooklyn, 2002, Liz-N-Val Selected Art Sites, Henrybuilt, NYC, 2006, Liz-N-Val Selections from 3 Decades, GalleryOneTwentyEight, 2010; New Breed of Art, Mus New Art, Detroit, MI, 2001; Gefasse, Galerie Gesellschaft, Berlin, Ger, 2001; Hybrid @ Brooklyn Art and Hist Ctr, 2002; Kaboom Mus of New Art, Detroit, Mich, 2002; Smallworks Show, NY Univ, 2003; Sharjan Int Biennial, UAE, 2003; Space Travelers, Tribes Gallery, NY, 2004; Merry/Peace, Sideshow Gallery, Brooklyn, NY, 2004; Beautiful Dreamer, Spaces Gal, Cleveland, Oh, David Gibson (cur), 2005; X-Tremist, Gal X Istanbul, 2005; ABC No Rio Benefit, Deitch Project, 10/2005; Democracy Project, Art Ctr Gal, Missouri State Univ, 2006; ATOa Auction, Chelsea Mus, 2006; Blast, Holland Tunnel Gallery, 2007; Small Works, NY Univ Gallery, 2007; War is Over, Sideshow Gallery, 2007; Power Room, Diva Street Container Show, 2007; Nurture Art, Cue Found, 2007; Summer Show, Gallery 128, 2007; Liz-N-Val of Cabbages & Kings, Real Form Project Space (cur David Gibson), 2007; Puma Project, Serpentine Gallery, London, J Armleder cur, 2007; Peace, Sideshow Gallery, R Timpiero cur, 2008; Ides of March, ABC No Rio, 2008; Urban Sounds, Interactive Social Sculpture, 2008; CPS 22, 22 Central Park South, 2008; Funky Pop, 58 Gallery, Jersey City NJ, Gerald Jackson cur, 2008; Heroes, Usdan Gallery, Bennington Coll, G Handman cur, 2008; It's a Wonderful Life, Richie Timpieri, Side Show Gallery, 2009; Me Me Me Pool Fair, Windham Hotel, 2009; Unnatural Acts, 437 Gallery, Chris Twomy cur, 2009; My Heroes, Jack the Pelican Gallery, David Gibson cur, 2009; The Better Half, Educ Alliance, Jeffrey NoMure and David Gibson cur, 2009; Storm/Rainbow, Jack the Pelican, Brooklyn, NY, 2009; Pool Art Fair, Gershwin Hotel, 2010; Pop-Am cur by Michael Richardo, Trattoria Cinque, 2010; Ides of March Abc No Riot & the Biennial, 2010; Liz-N-Val Selections from 3 Decades, Gallery Onetwentyeight, 2010; Mystical Figureists cur by Paul cabezas, Soto Velez Gallery, 2010; Wet cur by Eliott Lessing, McCarren Park Brooklyn, 2010; Open Portfolio cur by Elga Wimmer, Chelsea Mus, 2010; Planet Alert, Gallery OneTwentyEight, 2011; The Massive Show, The Orchard Windows Gallery, 2011; Under Subway Video-Art Night, Local Project, 2011; Painting With Pictures, Art Jail, 2011; Pool Art Fair, Gershwin Hotel, 2011; Apocalypse Now, Sideshow Gallery, 2011; Face Book Show, Mona, Detroit, 2011. *Collection Arranged:* Art Quake Event, First Art-Genes Mus, 92; Decay & Growth, First Portable Am Mus, 93; Art Quake/Art After Post-Mod, First Art-Genes Mus, 93; Sex Quake-Art After Apocalypse, Show in the Form of a Book, Dia Printed Matter, 93; Mus Collection Part I, Art Mag, Venice, 96. *Teaching:* Liz; Instr getting from A to B, Sch Mus Fine Arts, Boston, 69-74; What Is Art?, Mass Col Art, Boston, 74-77. *Bibliog:* Eleanor Hartney (auth), Trash or Treasure, Art News, 88; Tracy Gray (auth), Liz-N-Val Signatures, New Art Int, 88; Grady Turner (auth), Liz-N-Val-Feted-N-Validated, Flashart, 1/2000; Interview by Lily Faust, Art Police, 2003; David Gibson, Catalogue, New Work, 2002; Pool Art Addict, M MacInnis, Daily News, 3/13/2004; Sarah Valdez (auth), 2004 Art in America, Space Travelers, 12/2004; Stephan Maine (auth), Artnet-Brooklyn Beat; Barbara Rosenthal (auth), Art After Art Event, Art Circles, 10/2004; Mary Hrbacek (auth), Tribes Gallery's Space Travellers, NYARTS Mag, 7-8/2004; Chris Twomey (auth), Liz-N-Val, NYARTS Mag, 10-11/2006; Steven Psyllos (auth), Selected Articles, NYARTS Mag, 10-11/2006; Natalie Hegert (auth), Liz-N-Val, Selections from 3 Decades, Artslant, 5/10/2010. *Mem:* Mus Abstract Realism (dir, 90-). *Media:* Interactive Media. *Specialty:* Abstractrealism. *Interests:* Inventors of abstractrealism. *Publ:* Liz-N-Val New Work, catalog, 2002; Space Travelers@Tribes Gallery (catalogue), 2004; Museum of Truth & Beauty@Pool Addict (Catalogue), NY, 2004; Mus Art After ART, A Collection Catalog, 2009; Liz-N-Val, Selections from 3 Decades catalog, Gallery Onetwentyeight, 2010

LIZAMA, SILVIA
ADMINISTRATOR, EDUCATOR, PHOTOGRAPHER
b Havana, Cuba. *Study:* Barry Univ, BFA; Rochester Inst of Technology, MFA (Photog). *Comn:* Metro Dade Art in Pub Places, Charles Deering Estate, Miami, Fla, 1999. *Collection Arranged:* Art work in collections:American Express, Archer M. Huntington Art Gallery, Univ Tex, Austin, Art in Pub Places, Miami and Orlando, Fla, Burdines, Centrust Banks, Consejeria de Cultura, Cantabria, Spain, Fondo del Sol, Washington, DC, Galeria Nina Menocal, Mexico, Lehigh Univ, Bethleheim, Pa, Lowe Art Mus, Cuban Mus Collection, Miami, Mosquera Collection (private), Fla, Miami Dade Pub Library, Mus Art Fort Lauderdale, Norton Mus Art, West Palm Beach, Prudential Bache, Samuel T. Harn Mus Art, Gainsville, Southeast Banks, Southeast Mus Photog, Dayton Beach. *Pos:* Prof Photog, chair dept fine arts, Barry Univ, dept fine arts and photog, Miami Shores, Fla, currently. *Awards:* Awarded South Fla Cultural Consortium Grant, 1992, Southern Arts Federation/NEA Regional Visual Arts Fellowship Grant, 1993, Ambassador Jean Wilkowski Int Fellowship, Barry Univ, 2009. *Publ:* Work appears in the following publ: Darkroom Expression, Eastmand Kodak Publ, 1984, Photographic Retouching, 1987, Outside Cuba/Fuera de Cuba, Rutgers Univ Publ, 1989, Aperture141 Cuba: Image and Imagination, 1995, Breaking Barriers, Mus of Art Fort Lauderdale, 1997, Espacio C: Arte Contemporaneo, Camargo, Espana, 2006, Reflections: The Sensationalism of the Art from Cuba by Alexis Mendoza, 2009, Puertas a la Imaginacion, Miami, 2011. *Mailing Add:* Department of Fine Arts Barry University 11300 NE 2nd Ave Miami FL 33161

LLEWELLYN, ROBERT
PRINTMAKER, EDUCATOR
b Baltimore, Md, May 9, 1945. *Study:* Baltimore City Community Col, AA, 66; Morgan State Univ, BA, 68; Md Inst Coll Art, MFA, 72. *Work:* Baltimore Mus Art, Md; Smithsonian Inst, Nat Gallery Art, & Nat Inst Health Washington; NY Pub Libr, NY. *Exhib:* Contemp Am Prints, Albrecht Mus, Mo, 86; Intergrafia '91, Bur Art Exhib, Cracow, Poland, 91; Earth Views 31, Rockville Art Pl, Md, 93; solo exhibs, Gomez Gallery, Md, 94; State of the Art, Md Art Pl, Md, 95; 18th Int, Kanagawa Perfectural Gallery, Japan, 95. *Teaching:* Prof printmaking, Frostburg State Univ, Md, 72-. *Bibliog:* Nicomeotes Aravz (auth), Amnesis Art, Lascaux Publ, 88; Robert Llewellyn, New Art Examiner, 3/89; Art Diary International, Giancarlo Politi Ed, 92. *Mem:* Am Print Alliance; Md Printmakers; Coll Art Asn. *Dealer:* Walter Gomez/Gomez Gallery 836 Leadenhall St Baltimore MD 21230. *Mailing Add:* 12213 Bedford Rd NE Cumberland MD 21502-6811

LLOYD WEBBER, ANDREW
COLLECTOR
b London, Mar 22, 1948. *Hon Degrees:* Knighted, 1992; created hon life peer, 1997. *Pos:* Composer (Broadway plays), Joseph and the Amazing Technicolor Dreamcoat, 1968, 1973, 1991, 2003; producer (Broadway plays), Joseph and the Amazing Technicolor Dreamcoat, 1973, 1974, 1978, 1980, 1991; composer & orchestrator (Broadway plays), Jesus Christ Superstar, 1970, composer & producer, 1996, 1998, 2012; composer (Broadway plays), Jeeves, 1975; composer & producer (Broadway plays), By Jeeves (revision of Jeeves), 1996; producer, Jeeves Takes Charge, 1975; producer (film version), The Phantom of the Opera; composer, The Beautiful Game, 2000, The Woman in White, 2004; producer & orchestrator (films), Jesus Christ Superstar, 1973, Evita, 1996, composer, orchestrator (Broadway plays) Evita, 1976, (stage version Broadway plays), 1978, (revival Broadway plays), 2012. *Awards:* Named a Living Legend Grammy, 1989; created Knight in Queen's Honours Birthday List, 1992; elevated to peerage in New Years Honours list, 1997; Grammy Awards, 1980, 1983, 1985, Triple Play Award, Am Soc of Composers, 1988; City and Music Ctr of Los Angeles, 1991; Praemium Imperiale Award for music, 1995, Richard Rodgers Award for contrib to musical theatre, 1996; Bernard Delfont award for contrib to show business, 1997; Acad award, 1997; named one of Top 200 Collectors, ARTnews mag, 2004-12; Kennedy Ctr Award for Achievement in the Arts, 2006; Best Contemp Classical Composition for Requiem; Special Award, Soc London Theatre, 2008; Woodrow Wilson Award. *Bibliog:* Auth, The Complete Phantom of the Opera, 1987, The Complete Aspects of Love, 1990, Sunset Boulevard: From Movie to Musical, 1993. *Mem:* Royal Coll Music. *Collection:* 18th to 20th-century British & American painting, especially Pre-Raphaelite; German Expressionism

LO, BETH (ELIZABETH)
CERAMIST, EDUCATOR
b Lafayette, Ind, Oct 11, 1949. *Study:* Univ Mich, Alpha Lambda Delta Scholar, 68, James B Angell Scholar, 69-70, BGS, 71; Purdue Univ, 67; State Univ NY, Alfred, 71; Eastern Mich Univ, 72; Univ Mont, Teaching Asst, 72-74, MFA (ceramics), 74. *Work:* Univ Wash Med Ctr, Seattle; Yellowstone Art Ctr, Billings, Mont; Hallmark Card

Corp Ceramics Collection; Univ Mont & Missoula Mus Arts; also several pvt collections. *Exhib:* Baltimore Mus Art, 86; solo exhibs, Clark Fork Gallery, Missoula, Mont, 90, Holter Mus Art, Helena, Mont, 92, MIA Gallery, Seattle, Wash, 93 & 96, J Maddux Parker Gallery, Sacramento, Calif, 93 & 96 & Missoula Mus Arts, Mont, 95; New Orleans Mus Art, 94; Cult Connections, Spaces Gallery, Cleveland, Ohio, 95; Beyond the Rock Garden (with catalog), Wing Luke Asian Mus, Seattle, 96; Magic Mud, NW Ceramics Invitational (touring Idaho), 96; Nat Coun Educ Ceramic Arts Cup Show, Chicago Art Expo, Navy Pier, 96. *Pos:* Commercial art work, including album covers, magazine illustration, promotional material, backdrops & archaeological drawings, currently. *Teaching:* Instr high-fire pottery, raku, dung firing & introductory art, Bitterroot Community Art Proj, 73-77, co-founder, 75-; fine arts camp instr, Univ Mont, Missoula, summer 74, vis asst prof ceramics, 85-86, asst prof art, 86-90, assoc prof art, 90-96, prof art, 96-; porcelain workshop, Creative Arts Workshop, New Haven, Conn, 85; vis artist, Bismarck Jr Col, NDak, 85-86; demonstrator, Nat Coun Educ Ceramic Arts Conf, Cincinnati, Ohio, 90; lectr, Univ Wash, Seattle, 93 & 96, Wing Luke Asian Mus, Seattle, 96; workshop & lectr, Calif State Univ, Chico, 93 & SW Crafts Ctr, San Antonio, Tex, 93; panelist, Nat Coun Educ Ceramic Arts, New Orleans, 94 & Mont Arts Coun Fel Awards, 96; organizer & coordr, Woodstack '95 (symp & summer prog), 95; co-chair & panelist, NGO Forum on Women, Beijing, China, 95. *Awards:* Indiv Artist Fel, Mont Arts Coun, 86; Visual Arts Fel, Nat Endowment Arts, 95; Sch Fine Arts Distinguished Fac Award & Merit Award, Univ Mont, 95; US Artists Hoi Fel, 2009. *Bibliog:* Susan Biskeborn (auth), Artists at Work: 25 Northwest Glassmakers, Ceramicists & Jewelers, Alaska Northwest Bks, 90; Ceramics Monthly, 5/95; Ron Glowen (auth), rev, Artweek, 12/96. *Media:* Clay, Mixed Media. *Dealer:* MIA Gallery Seattle WA; J Maddux Parker Gallery Sacramento CA. *Mailing Add:* 408 Village Pl Missoula MT 59802

LOBDELL, FRANK
PAINTER
b Kansas City, Mo, 1921. *Study:* St Paul Sch Fine Art, Minn, 38-39; Calif Sch Fine Art, 47-50; Acad Grande Chaumiere, Paris, 50-51. *Work:* Los Angeles Co Mus, Stanford Mus, San Francisco Mus Art & Oakland Mus Art, Calif; Nat Gallery, Washington, DC; Am Acad & Inst Arts & Letters, NY; Nat Mus Am Art, Smithsonian Inst, Washington, DC; Nat Acad Design, NY; numerous others. *Exhib:* Solo exhibs: Lucien Labaudt Gallery, 49; Galerie Anderson-Mayer, Paris, 65; San Francisco Mus Art, 69; Wiegand Gallery, Coll Notre Dame, Belmont, Calif, 81; San Francisco Mus Modern Art, 81; Stanford Univ Mus Art, 92; Art Exchange, San Francisco, 2000, others; 3rd Biennial of Sao Paulo, Brazil, 55; Int Art of a New Era, Osaka, Japan, 58; Martha Jackson Gallery, 58, 60, 63, 72, 74; Kompas 4, West Coast USA, Van Abbemuseum, Eindhoven, 70; 32nd Biennial Am Painting, Corcoran Gallery Art, Washington, DC, 71; San Francisco Mus Art, 83; IPA Gallery, Boston, 92; Office of Mayor, City Hall, San Francisco, 93; Escape from the Vault: The Contemp Mus Collection Breaks Out, Contemp Mus, Honolulu, 2002; Group exhibs: Salon du Mai, Paris, 50; III Sao Paulo Biennial, 55; Whitney Mus Am Art, 62-63, 72; Guggenheim Mus, New York City, 64; Univ Ill, 74, 15; Calif Modernists, Fresno Art Mus, 95; represented in permanent collections, San Francisco Mus Art, Oakland Mus Art, Los Angeles Co Mus, Nat Gallery Washington, DC. *Pos:* vis artist/artist-in-residence NY Studio Sch Drawing, Painting & Sculpture, 86, Yale Univ Sch Art, 92, Tyler Sch Art, Temple Univ, 93, numerous others. *Teaching:* Prof art, Stanford Univ, 66-; California Sch Fine Arts, 57-65. *Awards:* Nealie Sullivan Award, San Francisco Mus Art, 60; Gold Medal for Distinguished Achievement in Painting Medal, Am Acad & Inst Art & Letts, 88, Acad Purchase Award, 1992, 1994; elected to Nat Acad Design, 98. *Bibliog:* Michel Tapie (auth), Frank Lobdell, David Anderson, Paris, 66; Walter Hoppe (auth), Frank Lobdell 1948-1965, Pasadena Art Mus, 66; Gerald Nordland (auth), Frank Lobdell, San Francisco Mus Art, 69. *Mem:* Nat Acad. *Media:* All. *Publ:* Frank Lobdell: The Art of Making and Meaning, (catalog) Hudson Hills Press, 2003; Landauer, Susan (auth), The San Francisco School of Abstract Expressionism, Berkeley: Univ Calif Press, 1996; Natsoulas, John et al (auths), The Beat Generation Galleries and Beyond, Davis, Calif: John Natsoulas Press, 1996; Plagens, Peter (auth), Sunshine Muse, New York: Praeger, 1974; others; numerous catalogs & brochures

LOBELLO, PETER
SCULPTOR, GRAPHIC ARTIST
b New Orleans, La, Nov 18, 1935. *Study:* Sch Archit, Tulane Univ, 53-55, Newcomb Sch Art, 54-55. *Work:* Aldrich Mus Contemp Art; Geneva Mus Art, Switz; Phoenix Art Mus; Plains Art Mus, Moorhead, Minn; New Orleans Mus Art; New Mus, NYC; Am Telegraph & Tel, NYC; Univ Minn; Jones New York & Philadelphia. *Comn:* Sculptures, Chateau Bellereve, Geneva, 74, Villa Savoia, Geneva, 76 & Hyatt Hotels Corp, NY, 80; bronze sculpture for Privy Coun Chamber, New Istana Palace, Bandar Seri Begawan, 84; Atrium sculpture, Madison Equities and Gery Advertising, NY, 85; Anodized aluminum lobby sculpture, One Paydras Plaza, New Orleans, 86. *Exhib:* Contemp Reflections 73, Aldrich Mus Contemp Art, 73; Selections from the Art Lending Service, Mus Mod Art Penthouse Gallery, NY, 78; Prospectus: 1970s, Aldrich Mus Contemp Art, 79; Robert Kidd Gallery, Detroit, 80; 21st Midwestern Invitational, Plains Art Mus, Moorhead, Minn, 80; Alexander Rosenberg Gallery, NY, 80; Inaugural Show, Alexander Carlson Gallery, NY, 80; Rutgers Univ, 83; Sarah Y Rentschler Gallery, NY City, 84; Wood, Water and Stone, 909 Third Ave, NY, 85; Sculptures Contemporaries, Galerie Les Hirondelles, Tennay/Coppet, Geneva, Switzerland, 87, Un Choix de Plus, 89; Miriam Walmsley Gallery, New Orleans, La, 1990-1991; Galerie Patrick Cramer, Geneva, 1998. *Bibliog:* Paul Goldberger (auth), 42nd St: The Grand Hyatt, New York Times, 9/22/80; Isabel Forgang (auth), At home with sculptor Peter Lobello, New York Daily News Tonight, 10/15/80; Ada Louise Huxtable (auth), Architecture view: Two new triumphant hotels, New York Times, 10/19/80. *Mailing Add:* 47-15 36th St Long Island City NY 11101

LOCHNAN, KATHARINE A
CURATOR, WRITER
b Ottawa, Can, Aug 18, 1946. *Study:* Univ Toronto, BA, 68, MA, 71; Courtauld Inst, Univ London, Eng, PhD, 82; Univ Calif, Berkeley, cert mus mgt, 87, Ryerson Polytechnical Inst, cert bus admin, 91. *Pos:* Cur asst, Royal Ont Mus, 68-69; asst cur, Art Gallery Ont, 69-75, cur prints & drawings, 76-95, sr cur & R Fraser Elliot cur prints & drawings, 95-, deputy dir research, 2005-; volunteer asst, Brit Mus, 75-76; sr assoc fel, Massey Col, 94-; rev bd, Can Cult Property Export, 97-. *Teaching:* Fine Arts Dept, Univ Toronto, spring 93-96. *Awards:* J Paul Getty Trust Scholar, 87; Award of Merit, Ryerson Polytechnical Inst, 91. *Mem:* Print Coun Am (bd mem, 80-82); London House Asn Can (chmn bd, 81-84); William Morris Soc Can (vpres, 84-85); Toronto Hist Bd (vpres, 93-); Opera Atelier (bd mem, 94-). *Res:* 19th century French and English art, William Morris and Arts and Crafts Movement, Eng & French Symbolism. *Interests:* Archit restoration, drawing & painting, gardening & farming. *Collection:* European prints, British ceramics & Canadian antiquities. *Publ:* Auth, The Etchings of James McNeill Whistler, Yale Univ Press, 84; Whistler's Etchings and the Sources of His Etching Style, 1855-80, Garland Publ, 88; ed, The Earthly Paradise: Arts & Crafts by William Morris & his Circle in Canadian Collections, 93; co-auth, The Lithographs of James McNeill Whistler, Vol 1, Art Inst Chicago, 98; ed, Turner, Whistler, Monet, Tate Publ, 2004; ed, Painting Towards the Light: The Watercolours of David Milne, Douglas & McIntyre, 2005. *Mailing Add:* 21 Mackenzie Crescent Toronto ON M6J 1S9 Canada

LOCKE, MICHELLE WILSON
CURATOR
b Dallas, Tex, June 10, 1947. *Study:* Trinity Univ, San Antonio, Tex; Univ Tex, Austin, BFA. *Pos:* gallery dir, Tex A & M Univ, Corpus Christi. *Teaching:* Art appreciation, Del Mar Coll, Corpus Christi, Tex, 91-98. *Mem:* Am Asn Mus; Coll Art Asn; Tex Asn Mus. *Res:* Fifteenth Century French illuminated manuscripts. *Specialty:* Modern and Contemporary Art of the Region. *Publ:* Auth, Transitions in the Permanent Collection: The Legacy Continues 97-2006, Art Mus S Tex, 2006. *Mailing Add:* 1902 N Shoreline Dr Corpus Christi TX 78401

LOCKE, STEVE
PAINTER
b Cleveland, Ohio, 1963. *Study:* Boston Univ, BS (Bus Admin-Marketing), 1984; Mass Coll Art, Boston, BFA, 1997, Michael Doherty Fel, 1999-2001; Skowhegan Sch Painting & Sculpture, Maine, Artist's Fel, Summer 2002. *Exhib:* Solo exhibs include Patricia Doran Gallery, Boston, 2000, Boston Ctr Arts, 2005, Artists Found Main Gallery, Boston, 2005, Mazmanian Gallery Framingham State Coll, Mass, 2005, Lillian Immig Gallery Emmanuel Coll, Boston, 2007; two-person exhibs include Rhys Gallery, Boston, (with Youshi Li), 2006; group exhibs include Red, Fogg Mus Art, 2001; Bernard Toale Gallery, Boston, 2001; Boston High Tea, AramonaStudio, New York, 2004; Visual Dialogue, Schiltkamp Gallery, Worcester, Mass, 2007. *Awards:* Art Matters Grant, 2008. *Dealer:* RHYS Gallery 401 Harrison Ave Boston Massachusetts 02118. *Mailing Add:* Steve Locke Studio 1391 Hyde Park Avenue Boston MA 02118

LOCKHART, SHARON
PHOTOGRAPHER, FILMMAKER
b Norwood, Mass, 1964. *Study:* San Francisco Art Inst, BA; Art Ctr Coll Design, Pasadena, MFA. *Work:* Boijmans Van Beuningen Mus, Rotterdam, Holland; Eli Broad Family Found, Santa Monica, Calif; Whitney Mus Am Art, NY; Mus Contemp Art, Los Angeles, Calif; Mus Mod Art, San Francisco, Calif. *Comn:* Photograph, BMW. *Exhib:* Solo shows incl Blum & Poe, Santa Monica, Calif, 2001, 2006, Mus Contemp Art, Chicago, Ill, 2001, Mus Contemp Art, San Diego, Calif, 2001, Barbara Gladstone Gallery, NY, 2003, 2006, Fabric Workshop & Mus, Philadelphia, 2004, Gio Marconi, Milan, Italy, 2005, Fogg Art Mus, Cambridge, Mass, 2005, Walker Art Ctr, Minneapolis, 2006, Arthur M Sackler Mus, Harvard Univ, 2006, Secession, Vienna, 2008, Kunsverein, Hamburg, Ger, 2008; group shows incl Whitney Biennial, Whitney Mus Am Art, NY, 97 & 2000; Sharon Lockhart, Kemper Mus, Kansas City, 98; Cinema Cinema: Contemp Art & the Cinematic Experience, Van AbbeMuseum, Eindhoven, 99; Pub Offerings, Mus Contemp Art, Los Angeles, 2001, 2004; Art Gallery Ontario, Toronto, 2000; Chac Mool Gallery, Los Angeles, 2001; Mus Contemp Art, Chicago, 2001, 2003; Galerie Volker Diehl, Berlin, 2001; Mus für Neue Kunst, Karlsruhe, Ger, 2003; Vedanta Gallery, Chicago, 2003; Int Cooperation Admin Boston, 2004; New Dirs/New Films, Mus Mod Art, NY; Metrop Mus Art, New York, 2005, 2007; Sydney Biennale, 2006; Japanese Am Nat Mus, Los Angeles, 2007; Carnegie Int, Carnegie Mus Art, Pittsburgh, 2008. *Awards:* Rockefeller Found Fel, 2000; John Simon Guggenheim Mem Found Fel, 2001; Creative Capitol Grant, 2002; Alpert Award in the Arts nominee, 2002; Radcliffe Inst Fel, Harvard Univ, 2007-2008. *Bibliog:* Howard Halle (auth), Next Wave: 4 Emerging on Paper, 3/98; Roberta Smith (auth), Renew, NY Times, 3/98; Bernice Reynard (auth), Sharon Lockhart Photographers "Goshogaoka" (catalog essay), Blum & Poe, 4/98. *Media:* Film. *Publ:* Filmmaker, Shaun Khalil, A Woman Under the Influence, 96; Truce: Echoes of Art in an Age of Endless Conclusions, 97. *Dealer:* Blum & Poe 2754 S La Cienega Blvd Los Angeles CA 90034; Carole Lieff Gallery 2925 Sycamore Canyon Rd Santa Barbara CA 93108; Barbara Gladstone Gallery 515 W 24th St New York NY 10011

LOEB, MARGARET & DANIEL S
COLLECTOR
b 1962. *Study:* Columbia Univ, AB (econ), 1984. *Pos:* Assoc, EM Pincus & co, 1984; sr vpres distressed debt dept, Jefferies & co, 1991-93; vpres high-yield sales, Citigroup Inc, 1994; founder and chief exec officer, Third Group LLC, New York, 1995-. *Awards:* Named one of Top 200 Collectors, ARTnews mag, 2006-13. *Collection:* Postwar and contemporary art; feminist art. *Mailing Add:* Third Point LLC 390 Park Ave New York NY 10017

LOEHLE, BETTY BARNES
PAINTER
b Montgomery, Ala, Mar 21, 1923. *Study:* Auburn Univ, Ala, 40-42; Harris Sch Art, Nashville, Tenn, 42-46; Evanston Art Ctr, Ill, 63-67. *Work:* Ga Council Arts & Humanities, Atlanta; DeKalb Community Col, Clarkston, Ga; R J Reynolds Tobacco Co, Winston-Salem, NC; Coca-Cola Int, Atlanta. *Exhib:* Hunter Ann, Hunter Mus Art, Chattanooga, Tenn, 77; Piedmont Show, Mint Mus, Charlotte, NC, 77; Artists in Ga, High Mus, Atlanta, 78; Southern Watercolor Soc, 76-79, 81-85 & 89; Ala Watercolor Soc, 79-81, 83, 85, 89, 93 & 94; Ga Watercolor Soc, 79 & 81-87, 93 & 94; Ky Watercolor Soc, 81, 83, 85 & 94; Art in Ga, Albany Mus, Ga, 81. *Awards:* Purchase Award, Olin Mills Corp, Hunter Mus, 77; Hans Hofman Award, Southern Watercolor Soc, 79; Award, Southern Watercolor Soc, 80, Ga Watercolor Soc, 80, 82, 83, 85, 87 & 88. *Bibliog:* Pat Hetzler (auth), Betty Barnes Loehle, Art Voices Mag, 5-6/81. *Mem:* Artists Assocs Inc (pres 78 & 79); Atlanta Artists Club; Southern Watercolor Soc; Ala & Ky Watercolor Socs; Ga Watercolor Soc (bd dir, 80-87). *Media:* Mixed. *Dealer:* Little House on Linden Gallery 2915 Linden Ave Homewood Al 35209. *Mailing Add:* 1800 Clairmont Lake #401 Decatur GA 30033

LOEHLE, RICHARD E
PAINTER, ILLUSTRATOR
b Atlanta, Ga, 1923. *Study:* Atlanta Coll Art, 40; Harris Sch Art, grad cert, 48; Evanston Art Ctr, Ill, 67. *Work:* High Mus Art; Montgomery Mus Art, Ala; Ala Watercolor Soc, Birmingham; Ga Coun Arts & Humanities; Chicago Artists Guild. *Comn:* Produce portraits of yr's four inductees to Ga Aviation Hall of Fame. *Exhib:* Ga Artists Show, High Mus, 74 & 76; Southern Watercolor Soc, Columbus Mus, 78 & 82; Ga Watercolor Soc, Macon Mus, 82; Ky Watercolor Soc, Owensboro Mus, 83; Southern Watercolor Soc, Asheville Mus, NC, 83; and others. *Awards:* Purchase Prize, Dixie Ann, Montgomery Mus Art, 72; Best in Show, Atlanta Arts Festival, 73 & Southern Watercolor Soc, 80 & 83. *Bibliog:* Edith Coogler (auth), Prize-winning artist, Atlanta Constitution, 6/28/70; S Coleman & C Anderson (auths), article, Southern Watercolor Soc Newslett, 83; Richard and Betty Loehle, Parallel Careers, Nat Television, Mod Maturity, No 252. *Media:* Oil, Acrylic; Watercolor. *Publ:* Coauth, Great American Depression Book of Fun, Harper & Row, 81. *Dealer:* Portrait Brokers of Am Inc 36 Church St Birmingham AL 35213. *Mailing Add:* 1800 Clairmont Lake #401 Decatur GA 30033

LOESER, THOMAS
SCULPTOR
b Boston, Mass, May 27, 1956. *Study:* Haverford Col, BA (sociology and anthropology), 79; Boston Univ, BFA (furniture design) (magna cum laude), 82; Univ Mass, North Dartmouth, Mass, MFA, 92. *Work:* Mus Art, RI Sch Design, Providence; Cooper Hewitt Mus, Brooklyn Mus, NY; Mus Fine Arts, Boston; Yale Univ Art Gallery, New Haven; other pvt collections; Mus Fine Arts, Houston; Elvejhem Mus Art, Madison, Wis; Milwaukee Mus Art. *Exhib:* Furniture by British Am & French Designers, Victoria & Albert Mus, London, Eng, 84; Material Evidence, Smithsonian Inst, Washington, DC, 85; Furniture for Postmodern Age, Queens Mus, NY, 85; New Furniture in Am, Mus Fine Arts, Boston, Mass, 89 & 91; Art That Works, Mint Mus Art, Charlotte, NC, 90; one-person show, Peter Joseph Gallery, NY, 92, 95, & 96, Art Mus RI Sch Design, 93, Milwaukee Art Mus, 93, Ark Art Ctr Decorative Arts Mus, 93 & Leigh Yawkey Woodson Mus, Warsaw, Wis, 93; Additions, Distractions, Multiple Complications and Divisions, Peter Joseph Gallery, NY, 95; A Passion for Wood, Gallery Functional Art, Santa Monica, Calif, 95; 5: Fifth Anniversary Exhib, Peter Joseph Gallery, NY, 96; Wisconsin Triennial, Madison Art Ctr, 96; Sculpture, Objects and Functional Art, Navy Pier, Chicago, Ill, 97 & 98; In Case, Pritam & Eames Gallery, East Hampton, NY, 97; Re-evolution, Soc Arts & Crafts, Boston, Mass, 97; Am Craft, Renwick Gallery, Washington, DC, 97; Contemp North Am Furniture - A Survey of the Furniture Makers Art, Neuberger Mus Art, NY, 97; Small Works, Pritam & Eames Gallery, East Hampton, NY, 98; Brooklyn Mus, NY, 98; Please Be Seated, Yale Univ Art Gallery, Conn, 99; The Making of American Masterpiece, Yale Univ Art Gallery, Conn, 2000; Defining Craft, American Craft Mus, Ny, 2000; Solo Exhibitions, Leo Kaplan Gallery, NY, 2001 & 2005; The Makers Hand: American Studio Furniture, 1940-1990, Mus of Fine Arts, Boston, 2003; Internationaler Waldkunstpfad 2004: Expeditionen (Forest Art Path), Darmstadt, Germany, 2004; Disequilibrium, Leo Kaplan Gallery, NY, 2005; Old Friends, New Work: 25 Yearrs of Studio Furniture, Soc of Arts and Crafts, Boston, 2006; Wis Triennial, Madison Mus of Contemporary Art, 2007; Dept of Art, Quadrennial Exhibition, Chazen Mus of Art, 2008. *Collection Arranged:* Yale Univ Art Gallery, Conn, Renwick Gallery-Smithsonian Institution, DC, Mus of Art and Design, NY, Mus of Fine Arts, Houston, Tex, Mus of Fine Arts, Boston, Mus of Art-RI Sch of Design, Milwaukee Mus of At, Cooper-Hewitt Mus, NY, Mus of Art and Design, NY & Brooklyn Mus, NY. *Pos:* Bd trustees, Haystack Mountain Sch, Maine, 88-97; juror, Festival at the Lake Crafts Show, Oakland, Calif, 90 & Ill Arts Coun, 91; panelist, Nat Endowment Arts, 92. *Teaching:* Instr fine arts, RI Sch Design, 87-88; instr, Swain Sch Design, New Bedford, Mass, 87 & Univ Wis, Madison, 91-92, asst prof art, 92-96, assoc prof art, 96-2002, prof art, 2002-, chair, currently; numerous lectures & workshops at various univs & insts; adj prof, Calif Col Arts & Crafts, Oakland, 89-90. *Awards:* Visual Artists Fel Grant, Nat Endowment Arts, 84, 88, 90 & 94; Finalist, Biennale Award Competition, Louis Comfort Tiffany Found, 97; Grad Sch Res Award, Univ Wis, Madison, 98-99; Univ Wis Arts Inst Emily Mead Baldwin Bell Bascom Professorship in the Creative Arts, 97-98, Creative Arts award, 2004; Univ Wis Kellett Mid-Career award, 2006; Wis Arts Bd Visual Arts Fellowship, 2006. *Bibliog:* Christine Temin (auth), The fine art of furniture, Boston Globe Mag, 2/18/96; Caitlin Kelly (auth), Art meets craft, Art & Antiques, summer 96; Dan Mack (auth), The Rustic Furniture Companion: Traditions, Techniques, and Inspirations, Lark Books, Asheville, NC, 96. *Media:* Wood, All Media. *Publ:* Auth, Speakeasy, New Art Examiner, 9/92. *Dealer:* Pritam & Eames Gallery Easthampton NY; Leo Kaplan Gallery, New York. *Mailing Add:* 2826 Lakeland Ave Madison WI 53704

LOEWER, HENRY PETER
WRITER, ILLUSTRATOR
b Buffalo, NY, Feb 13, 1934. *Study:* Albright Art Sch, Univ Buffalo, with Lawrence Calcagno & Anne Coffin Hanson, BFA, 58. *Work:* Hunt Inst for Botanical Doc, Carnegie-Mellon Univ, Pittsburgh, Pa; Catskill Art Soc, Hurleyville, NY. *Exhib:* Int Exhib of Botanical Drawings, Hunterdon Art Ctr, Clinton, NJ, 77; 4th Int Exhib of Botanical Art, Carnegie-Mellon Univ, Pittsburgh, Pa, 77-78; Solo exhib, Horticultural Soc of NY, 77. *Awards:* First Place, Garden Writers Am, 81, 84 & 92. *Media:* Pen and Ink, Watercolor. *Publ:* Illusr, Wildflower Perennials for Your Garden, Hawthorn, 76; auth & illusr, Gardens by Design, Rodale, 86; A World of Plants, Abrams, 89; The Wild Gardener, 91; The Evening Garden, 93. *Mailing Add:* 185 Lakewood Dr Asheville NC 28803

LOFTUS, PETER M
PAINTER
b Washington, DC, Oct 27, 1948. *Study:* Md Inst Coll Art, BFA, 71; Univ Pa, 74. *Work:* Glen C Janss Collection; San Jose Mus Art, Calif; Hunter Mus, Chattanooga, Tenn. *Exhib:* Am Realism: 20th Century Drawings & Watercolors, San Francisco Mus Mod Art, traveling exhib, 85; Contemp Am Realism, Columbus Mus Arts & Sci, Ga, 85; The Realist Landscape, Robeson Art Ctr Gallery, Rutgers Univ, 85; The Subject is Water, Newport Art Mus, 88; The Face of the Land, Southern Allegheny Mus Art, 88; New Horizons in Am Realism, Flint Inst Arts (traveling exhib with catalog), 91. *Teaching:* Vis lectr painting, Univ Calif, Santa Cruz, 76-88. *Bibliog:* Fredy Kaplan (auth), Portfolio of regional landscapes, Am Artist, 2/84; Alvin Martin (auth), American Realism: 20th Century Drawings & Watercolors, Abrams, 86; West Art & the Law, West Publ Co, 87. *Mem:* Coll Art Asn Am. *Media:* Watercolor, Oil. *Dealer:* Fischbach Gallery 24 W 57 St New York NY; Contemporary Realist Gallery 23 Grant 6th Floor San Francisco CA 94108. *Mailing Add:* 729 Western Dr Santa Cruz CA 95060-3032

LOGAN, FERN H
PHOTOGRAPHER, GRAPHIC ARTIST
b July 6, 1945. *Study:* Pratt Inst, 63-65; State Univ NY, BS, 91; Art Inst Chicago, MFA, 93. *Work:* AC Buehler Library, Elmhurst Col, Ill; Harlem State Office Bldg, Schomburg Ctr Res Black Cult, Bellevue Hosp Ctr, NY. *Exhib:* Solo exhibs, Artist Portrait Series, Gallery 62, NY, 85 & Memories in Non-Silver, Delta Arts Ctr, Winston-Salem, NC, 88; Imagining Families, Smithsonian Inst, Washington, DC, 94; Spectra '97 Nat Photo Biennial, Silvermine Guild Galleries, New Canaan, Conn, 97; Myth Am, Urban Inst Contemp Artists, Grand Rapids, Mich, 97; Digital Sorcery, Ctr Photo, Woodstock, NY, 98. *Pos:* Sr graphic designer, Equitable Life, 78-83; owner, Logan Photog & Design Studios, 83-89. *Teaching:* Lectr, photogr & graphics, Mich Tech Univ, 89-92; asst prof, Elmhurst Col, 92-95 & Southern Ill Univ, 95-. *Awards:* Sponsored Project Grant, Artist Portrait Series, NY Coun Arts, 85; Parks, Chavez King Teaching Fel, Mich Tech Univ, 89-92; Arts Fel Grant, Digital Portraits, Ill, 98. *Bibliog:* Norman Schreiber (auth), Pop photo snapshots, Popular Photog, 2/85; Deborah Willis (auth), Black Photographs 1940-1988, Garland, 88; Lara Farb (auth), Gumbo Ya Ya, Midmarch Press, 95. *Mem:* Soc Photog Ed. *Publ:* Illustr, Six Decades at Yaddo, Yaddo Publ, 86; contribr, I Too Sing America, Workman Publ, 92; I Hear a Symphony, Anchor Bks, 94. *Mailing Add:* 1 Loblolly Lane Carbondale IL 62901

LOGEMANN, JANE MARIE
PAINTER
b Milwaukee, Wis, Nov 12, 1942. *Study:* Layton Sch of Art, Milwaukee, Wis, 61; Univ Wis, Milwaukee, BA, 63. *Work:* Stanford Univ Art Mus, Calif; The Jewish Mus, NY; James Michener Collection, Univ Tex, Austin; Allen Mem Art Mus, Oberlin Col, Ohio; Guggenheim Mus, NY. *Exhib:* AAA, Ulrich Mus, Wichita, Kans, 92; Collecting for the 21st Century: Recent Acquisitions: The Jewish Mus, NY, 93; Aishet Hayil, Yeshiva Univ Mus, NY, 93; Drawings, Leo Castelli Gallery, NY, 94; The Persistence of Abstraction, Noyes Mus, NJ, 94; plus many others. *Collection Arranged:* Diversity-NY Artists (auth, catalog), Univ RI, fall 85; Am Abstract Artists: New Work: New Mem, 87. *Bibliog:* Peter Frank (auth), revs, Artnews, 11/79 (auth), revs, Print Collector's Newslett, 11/82; Helen A Harrison (auth), NY Times, 6/89; William Zimmer (auth), NY Times, 8/28/94; Lilly Wei (auth), Art in Am, 5/95. *Mem:* Am Abstract Artists (mem bd dir, 86-). *Media:* Oil, Watercolor. *Publ:* Auth & illusr, Abstracts-Book III, 78; ed, Ecology and feminism issue, Vol 4, Art Heresies, 81; Art in New York Today: Idea Mag, Toyko, Japan, 8/88; Letters/Words: Jane Logemann; Naomi Spector; Hebrew Union Coll Publ, 8/94. *Mailing Add:* 35 Bond St New York NY 10012

LOHRE, THOMAS GEORGE, JR
PAINTER, SCULPTOR
b Covington, Ky, July 17, 1953. *Study:* Univ Ky, 71-73; Northern Ky Univ, BA, 76. *Work:* Beringer Crawford Mus, Covington, Ky; portrait Jesus, Mary & Joseph, Covington Cath High Sch, Park Hills, Ky; portrait St Agnes, St Agnes Grade Sch, Ft Wright, Ky; portrait Henry Williams, Over-the-Rhine Sr Ctr, Cincinnati, Ohio; portrait, Thomas More Col, Crestview Hills, Ky. *Comn:* 29 Portraits, Newport Storefront Restoration Proj, Ky, 96. *Exhib:* The Art of Tom Lohre, Carnegie Art Ctr, Covington, Ky, 80, HEREArt ART@-D2 exhib, NY, 99, The Great Tomaso Show, Visual History Gallery, Cincinnati, 02; One man show, Artists Asn, Nantucket, Mass, 88. *Pos:* Asst to Ralph Wolf Cowan, Portrait Painter, 80-81. *Awards:* Second Place Painting, Summer Fair, Cincinnati, Ohio, 78; Second Place, Fitton Art Ctr, 94; Grant, City Newport, Main St Restoration Comt, 96. *Bibliog:* Owen Findsen (auth), Lohre Mixes Art, People and Fantasy, Cincinnati Enquirer, 6/28/81; Terri Schierberg (auth), Thos Lohre Fine Artist and Landscape Painter, Northern Ky Univ Mag, 95; Steven Ramos (auth), Master Painter of Newport, City Beat, Cincinnati, 96. *Mem:* Northern Ky Heritage League; Friends Baker-Hunt Found, Covington, Ky. *Media:* Oil on canvas; Robotics. *Publ:* Auth, Greenwich Village Guidebook, St Martins Press, 94. *Dealer:* Visual Hist Gallery 3437 Michigan Cincinnati OH 45208. *Mailing Add:* 619 Evanswood Pl Cincinnati OH 45220

LOK, JOAN M
PAINTER
b Hong Kong, Apr 2, 1962. *Study:* Hong Kong Polytechnic Univ, 83; Baruch Col, BBA, 88; Strayer Univ, MBA, 2005. *Work:* Mus Chinese Australian Hist, Melbourne; Walt Disney World Co, Orlando, Fla; New Longon Arts Soc & Gallery, New London, Conn; Philippines Chinese Cult Ctr, Manila; Lingnam Art Asn Am, NY. *Comn:* calligraphy, Harrah's, Las Vegas. *Exhib:* Masters of Oriental Brush Painting, Raya Gallery, Victoria, Australia, 90; 20th Anniversary Exhib, Chinese Cult Ctr, Manila, Philippines, 96; Sumi-e Across Border, John B Aird Gallery, Toronto, Can, 96; Lingham Art Asn Exhib, Chinese Cult Inst, Boston, Mass, 97; Female Chinese Am Artists, Confusius Plaza Gallery, NY, 2001; 40th Anniversary juried exhib, Strathmore Hall Arts Ctr, Bethesda, MD, 2003; Solo exhib, Focus on China, Frelinghuysen Arboretum, Morristown, NJ, 2004, Mind to Paper, Slayton House Gallery, Columbia, MD, 2005. *Pos:* Vpres, Lingram Art Asn Am, NY, 92-94; Nat Pres, Sumi-e Soc Am, Wash, DC, 2002-. *Teaching:* instr, Plaza Art Materials, Towson, Md. *Awards:* Grumbacher Gold Medallion Award, Sumi-e Soc Am, 35th Annual juried show, Grumbacher Watercolors, 98; Best in Watercolor Award, Art for Art's Sake Exhib, Conn Audubon Soc, 99; Grand Prize Winner, Nat Cherry Blossom Festival, Art Contest, 2005. *Bibliog:* Mao-fen Yu (auth), Joan Lok - Artist of Cherry Blossom World J, 11/5/04; Susan DeFond (auth), Memory Blossoms Into a Winning Entry, Washington Post, 4/3/2005; Oksana Dragan (auth), HK-Born Artist Paints National Cherry Blossom Festival Poster, Voice of Am News, 4/11/2005. *Mem:* Sumi-e Soc Am, (nat pres, 2002-); Lingham Art Asn Am, (vpres, 92-94); Glastenburg Art Guild; Edison Arts Soc; Asn Chinese Calligraphy Am. *Media:* Sumi-e, ink & watercolor on rice paper. *Collection:* Delicate watercolor and ink on rice paper of floral and landscape combining Eastern and Western Styles. *Publ:* contribr, Best of Flower Painting, North Light Books, 97; contribr, Always Bright, Vol II, Painting by Chinese Am Artists, Homa & Sekey Books, 2001; contribr, Sumi-e Quarterly, Sumi-e Soc Am, 2002-05; back cover artwork, Sakura Celebration, 2005. *Dealer:* Radiant Brush GAllery PO Box 6271 Columbia MD 21045. *Mailing Add:* PO Box 6271 Columbia MD 21045

LOMAHAFTEWA, LINDA JOYCE
PAINTER, INSTRUCTOR
b Phoenix, Ariz, July 3, 1947. *Study:* Inst Am Indian Arts, Santa Fe, NMex; San Francisco Art Inst, BFA & MFA. *Work:* Ctr Arts Indian Am, Washington, DC. *Exhib:* Riverside Mus, NY, 65; Mus NMex, Santa Fe, 65-66; Ctr Arts Indian Am, 67-68; San Francisco Art Inst Spring Show, 70-71; Scottsdale Nat Indian Art Exhib, Ariz, 70-71. *Teaching:* Asst drawing, San Francisco Art Inst, 70; painting instr, Asn Am Indian Arts, San Francisco, summer 72; asst prof Native Am studies, Calif State Col, Sonoma, 72-; lectr, Native Am Studies, Univ Calif, Berkeley, 74-76; instr painting, Inst Am Indian Arts, Santa Fe, NMex, 76-. *Awards:* Hon Mention for Oil Painting, Mus NMex, 65; First Place in Graphic Arts Purchase Award, Ctr Arts Indian Am, 67; Third Place in Drawing, Scottsdale Nat Indian Art Exhib, 70. *Bibliog:* Lloyd E Oxendine (auth), 23 contemporary Indian artists, Art in Am, 7-8/72. *Media:* Acrylic, Oil. *Publ:* Illusr, Indian Mag, 71; Weewish Tree, Am Indian Historian Press, 71; contribr, Art in Am, 72. *Mailing Add:* c/o Joyce Robins Gallery PMB 458 7 Avenida Vista Grande Ste 7B Santa Fe NM 87509-9207

LOMBARDI, DON DOMINICK
ARTIST
b Bronx, NY, Dec 16, 1954. *Study:* Empire State Col, BS, 95. *Work:* The Library of Congress, Washington, DC; Empire State Coll, SUNY, Saratoga Springs, NY; Los Angeles Co Mus Art; Wueens Mus Art, Queens, NY. *Exhib:* All Of A Piece, Katonah Mus Art, NY, 95; Inked, Marshall Arts, Memphis, Tenn, 2005; Parl Sharpe Contemp Art, New York, 2006; Skin City, The Art of the Tattoo, Arts Ctr, St Petersburg, Fla, 2007; Deep Pop, Kenneth Chapman Gallery, Iona Coll, New Rochelle, NY, 2008; Apocalyptic Pop, Dorsky Curatorial Prog, Long Island City, NY, 2008; The Post Apocalyptic Tattoo, A Ten Year Survey of Art of D Dominick Lombardi, Blue Star Contemp Art Ctr, San Antonio, Tex, 2008; Graffoos & Tattoos, ADA Gallery, Richmond, Va, 2008; Post Apocalyptic Tattoo, Gallery Milieu, Tokyo, Japan, 2008; Toyota vs Godzilla, Artlexis Gallery, Brooklyn, NY, 2009; Post Apocalyptic Tattoo, Housatonic Mus Art, Bridgeport, Conn, 2009; Hidden World, Central Gallery, Univ Mass Amherst, Mass, 2010. *Collection Arranged:* The Waking Dream, Castle Gallery, 98; Obsession Fool, Pelham Art Ctr, 98; Over the Top, Shore Inst Contemp Art, Long Branch, 2005; East vs West, Lab Gallery, Roger Smith Hotel, New York, 2005; Reality Show, Lab Gallery, Roger Smith Hotel, 2005; Critics Select II, Shore Inst Contemp Art, Long Branch, NJ, 2005; Speaking in Strings, Ken Butler & Kurt Coble, Lab Gallery, Roger Smith Hotel, New York, 2006; Bom: How art can disrupt, reorient or destroy, Galeria Janet Kurnatowski, Brooklyn, NY, 2008; Nature Calls, The Shore Inst Contemp Art, Long Branch, NJ 2005. *Pos:* Critic, Sculpture Mag (& feature writer), DC, 99-, NYArts Ma,g 2004-, NYTimes, 98-2005, dart (US ed), Toronto, 2005-, resolve40.com, 2007, cultruecastch.com, 2006-, Art in Asia, New York, Seoul, 2007-. *Teaching:* Adj art prof, Westchester Community Col, Vallhalla, NY. *Awards:* Dorothy Mayhail Mem Award, Stamford Mus, 97; spl opportunity stipend, NY Found for the Arts, 97; resident, Reykjavík Art Mus, Iceland, 01; Emily Hall Tremain Found Grant, Intelligent Design Proj, 2006; Excellence in Arts award, 1st Ann Friends of SICA Award dinner, 2005; New Am Paintings, number 32, Northeastern, the Open Studio Press, Mass, 2001; SOS, NY Found Arts, Garrison Art Ctr, New York, 99, 2010. *Bibliog:* William Zimmer (auth), Narratives in Charcoal and Ink, The NY Times, 12/1/2002; Katherine Gass (auth), Refigured South Shore Arts Center, Art New England, 9/2002; William Zimmer (auth), The 20th Century, Two View Points in Sculpture and Collage, The NY Times, 1/18/1998; Germain Keller (auth), rev of Painter's Forms, ZING, issue 20, Nov 2005; Jill Conner (auth), Dominick Lombardi, Post Apocalyptic Tattoo, NYARTS mag, 2005; Ben Davis, A Future Present, artnet.com, 2005; Dan Goddard (auth), Grotesquely charming mutants are artist's glimpse into the future, San Antonio Express, Feb 2008; Michael Johnson (auth), San Antonio Report, The Post Apocalyptic Tattoo, A Ten Year Survey, NYARTS mag, 2008; Mary Hrbacek, Apocalyptic Pop, M Mag, Feb 2009; Michael Wilson (auth), Apocalyptic Pop, Time Out New York, 2009; Christopher Hart Chambers (auth), Hot Tattoos on Graphic Acyion in Brooklyn Gallery, culturecatch.com, Mar 2009; Stanford Kay (auth), Nostalgia for the Present, d'ART Int, 2009; Robert C Morgan (auth), WHITHOT mag, D Dminick Lombardi, Housatonic Mus, 2010. *Mem:* AICA. *Mailing Add:* 186 Prospect Ave Valhalla NY 10595-1831

LONDON, ALEXANDER
COLLECTOR, PUBLISHER
b Paris, France; US citizen. *Study:* Lycee Montaigne, Paris; Univ Pa, MSChE; Columbia Univ, PhD Program. *Pos:* Pres, Marstin Printing Corp, 69-; publ (with catalog), Trade Publ, 70-; exec dir, Imprimerie Centrale Commerciale, Paris, 70-. *Awards:* Forty five typographical & printing design awards, 56-98; spec awards for illus in Kalevala, 54 & design of Holocaust catalog, 79, Grolier Bk Club. *Mem:* Printing Industry Metrop, NY; Assoc Graphic Arts. *Collection:* French Impressionists; French Montparnasse; American contemporary, botanicals & wildlife animation. *Publ:* Illusr, Kalevala, 54; contribr & graphic designs var art catalogs, art mag, bks & printed materials. *Mailing Add:* 350 Central Park W No 10 New York NY 10025

LONDON, ANNA
GRAPHIC ARTIST, SCULPTOR
b Poland, July 2, 1913; US citizen. *Study:* Brooklyn Col, BA, 33; Columbia Univ, MA, 35; Ruth Leaf Workshop, 70-75. *Work:* Firehouse Gallery, Nassau Community Col, Garden City, NY; Berkshire Mus, Pittsfield, Mass; Queens Borough Community Col, Queens, NY. *Exhib:* CW Post Col, Greenvale, NY, 73 & 78; Heckscher Mus, Huntington, NY, 75; Parrish Mus, Southampton, NY, 79; Cork Gallery, Lincoln Ctr, NY, 80-90; Hudson River Mus, NY, 85; and others. *Awards:* Purchase Awards, Firehouse Gallery & Berkshire Mus; Prize, Nat Asn Women Artists. *Bibliog:* Ruth Leaf (auth), Intaglio Printmaking Techniques, Watson-Guptill, 76. *Mem:* Nat Asn Women Artists; Nat Mus Women Arts, Washington. *Media:* Monoprints; Clay, Computer prints. *Interests:* Exploring computer art. *Dealer:* Graphic Eye Gallery 402 Main St Port Washington NY 11050. *Mailing Add:* 33 Larch Dr New Hyde Park NY 11040

LONDON, BARBARA
CURATOR
b Glen Cove, NY, July 3, 1946. *Study:* Hiram Col, Ohio, BA, 68; Inst of Fine Arts, New York Univ, MA, 72. *Collection Arranged:* Projects: Video I-XXXII, 74-81, Loren Madsen, 75, Peter Campus, 76, Nam June Paik, 77, Bookworks, 77 (Sachs Gallery), Projects: Shigeko Kubota, 78, Video Viewpoints, 78-90, Laurie Anderson, 78, Donald Lipski, 79, Video from Tokyo to Fukui and Kyoto (auth, catalog), 79 & Sound Art, 79, Mus Mod Art, NY, Music Video 85, Bill Viola, 87, Barbara Steinman, 89, Gary Hill, 90; Tony Cokes, 91, Thierry Kuntzel, 91, Jana Sterbak, Mus Mod Art, 92. *Pos:* Asst int prog, Mus Mod Art, NY, 71-73, curatorial asst dept of prints & illus bks, 73-77, cur video prog, 77-. *Teaching:* Film Dept, NY Univ, 79-82. *Awards:* Fel, Nat Endowment Arts, 88. *Publ:* Auth, Video Letter of Shuntaro Tanileawa and Shuji Terayama, Camera Obscura, Los Angeles, 90 & Fall, 91; A Few Reflections on High Definition Video and Art, HDTV, Union Square Press, New York, 90; Gary Hill, Image Forum, Tokyo, 91; Electronic Explorations, Art in America, 5/92; Techno-Visions: Tradition and the Avant-Garde, Art 20/21 & Earthly Paradise: The Paintings of Po Kim, Seoul, Korea, 92

LONDON, NAOMI
SCULPTOR
b Montreal, Que, Oct 3, 1963. *Study:* Marianopolis Col, dipl, 83; Concordia Univ, BFA, 87; Univ Southern Calif, Los Angeles, MFA, 92. *Work:* Montreal Mus Fine Arts, Que; Stewart Hall Art Gallery, Pointe Claire, Que; Can Coun Art Bank, Ottawa, Ont; Musee d'art de Joliette; Musee d'art contemporain de Montreal. *Exhib:* One-woman shows, La Chambre Blanche, Que, 92, Brewery Arts Complex, Los Angeles, Calif, 92, Galerie Samuel Lollouz, Montreal, Que, 92, 95 & 97, Galleri Kilen, Lulea, Sweden, 94 & Agnes Etherington Art Ctr, Kingston, Ont, 95, Stichting Kunst & Complex, Rotterdam, The Neth, 98; Fall from Fashion (with catalog), Aldrich Mus Contemp Art, 93; Snow Sculpture Symp, Lulea Sweden, 94; Knit, Mus Textiles, Toronto, Ont; A-Dress: States of Being, Winnipeg Art Gallery, Man, 95; Young Contemporaries, London Regional Art & Hist Mus, London, Ontario, 96; Bereft, Hallwalls Contemp Art Ctr, Buffalo, NY, 96; L'oeil du collectionneur, Musee d'art contemporain de Montreal, 96; Sprawl, Mercer Union, Toronto, Ontario, 97; Nouvelles acquisitions Pret d'oeuvres d'art, Musee du Quebec, 97; Naomi London & Penelope Stewart, Open Studio, Toronto, Ontario, 99; The Poetics of Aging, Art Gallery of Hamilton, Ontario, 99; Weaving the World, Yokohama Mus Art, Japan, 99. *Teaching:* Instr contemp sculpture, Concordia Univ, 93-96; fine arts instr, Dawson Col, Montreal. *Awards:* Short Term Grant, Can Coun, 94; Proj Grant, Conseil des Arts et des Lettres du Que, 94; Prix Rene Payant, Musee d'art contemporian, Univ Montreal, 95. *Bibliog:* James Campbell (auth), Naomi London, Galerie Samuel Lallouz, 92; Pierre Landry (auth), The origin of things, Musee d'art Contemporain, 94. *Media:* Mixed Media, Drawing. *Publ:* L'origine des choses (exhib catalog); Discursive Dress (exhib catalog), John Micheal Kohler Art Ctr, Sheboygan, Wis, 94; Dispersions indentitiaires: videogranies recents du Que (exhib catalog), Art Gallery Ont, Toronto, 95; Necessary Grief; Naomi London - Grieving Equipment (exhib catalog), Agnes Etherington Art Ctr, Kingston, Ont, 95; London Life Young Contemporaries 1996 (exhib catalog), London Reg Art & Hist Mus, Ont, 96; Sweets, Hope and the Passage of Time: Three Projects, 2005; Wordsmiths, 2006. *Mailing Add:* 2712 rue Coleraine Montreal PQ H3K 1S7 Canada

LONG, A MITCHELL
PAINTER
Study: Univ Arts, Philadelphia, BFA, 1994; La State Univ, MFA (painting), 1998. *Work:* New Orleans Mus Art; Tampa Mus Art; Walt Disney co; Deland Mus Art, Fla; Orlando City Hall, Fla. *Exhib:* Hyde Park Gallery, Tampa, 1989; Am Artist Gallery, Philadelphia, 1993-95; Ann Connelly Gallery, Baton Rouge, La, 1998-99; Sylvia Smith Gallery, New Orleans, 1999; Oestricher Fine Arts, La, 2003-04; New Orleans Mus Art, 2005. *Awards:* Stobart Found Grant, Boston, 1999; Segal Found Grant, 2005; Pollock-Krasner Found Grant, 2005 & 2008; Joan Mitchell Found Grant, New York, 2006

LONG, CHARLES
SCULPTOR
b Long Branch, NJ, 1958. *Study:* Philadelphia Coll Art, BFA, 1981; Whitney Independent Study Prog, 1981; Yale Univ, New Haven, Conn, MFA, 1988. *Exhib:* Solo exhibs, Shoshana Wayne Gallery, Santa Monica, Calif, 1996, 1998, 1999, 2001, 2003, 2005, Tanya Bonakdar Gallery, NY, 1996, 1997, 2004, 2006, 2007, Galerie Camargo Vilaca, Sao Paulo, Brazil, 1997, Galerie Nathalie Obadia, Paris, 1997, London Projs, 1997, Sperone, Milan, 1998, Bonakdar Jancou Gallery, New York, 1998, St Louis Art Mus, 1998, Sak's Fifth Ave Proj, Los Angeles, 1999, Orange County Mus Art, Calif, 2002, SITE Santa Fe, 2005, 2004; group exhibs, Living with Contemp Art, Aldrich Mus Contemp Art, 1995, The Best of the Season, 1997, Pop Surrealism, 1998; Defining the Nineties, Mus Contemp Art, Miami, 1996; Transformal, Wiener Secession, Vienna, 1996; Now Here, La Mus Mod Art, Humlebaek, Denmark, 1996; Whitney Biennial, Whitney Mus Am Art, New York, 1997, 2008; Performance Anxiety, Mus Contemp Art, Chicago, 1997, Transmute, 1999, New Acquisitions, 2001, Original Language, 2001, Atmosphere, 2004; Crossings, Kunsthalle Wien, Austria, 1998; Open Ends, Mus Mod Art, New York, 2000; Greater NY, PS1 Contemp Art Center & Mus Mod Art, New York, 2000; A Decade of Collecting, Harvard Univ Art Mus, 2000; New Prints 2001, Int Print Center, New York, 2001; Art/Music, Mus Contemp Art, Sydney, 2001; Gone Formalism, Inst Contemp Art, Philadelphia, 2006; The Uncertainty of Objects & Ideas, Hirshhorn Mus & Sculpture Garden, Washington, 2006; Transitional Objects, Neuberger Mus Art, Purchase, NY, 2006; Nina in Position, Artists Space, New York, 2008; Invitational Exhib Visual Arts, AAAL, New York, 2008. *Teaching:* John Edwards Jr endowed chair, Skowhegan Sch Painting & Sculpture, Maine, 2005; res artist, Anderson Ranch Arts Ctr, Colo, 2006. *Awards:* Nat Endowment Arts, 1994; Guggenheim Fel, 1997; Pollock-Krasner Found Grant, 1999 & 2002; Award of Merit Medal for Sculpture, AAAL, 2008. *Bibliog:* Raphael Rubinstein (auth), Raphael Rubinstein on Charles Long, Gana Art, 5-6/96; Noel (auth), Stereolab, Bunnyhop, Issue 7, 1996; Mark Van de Walle (auth), Back to the future: Charles Long & Stereolab, Parkett, No 48, 1996. *Dealer:* Tanya Bonakdar Gallery 521 W 21st New York NY 10011. *Mailing Add:* 192 E Third St Apt 2-D New York NY 10009

LONG, MEREDITH J
DEALER
b Joplin, Mo, Sept 14, 1928. *Study:* Univ Tex, BA, 50, Law Sch, 50-51, 53-54. *Exhib:* Mary Cassatt, Prints and Drawings from the Artist Studio, 11/10/2000-12/29/2000; Childe Hassam, An American Impressionist, 1/11/2000-2/5/2000; Americans at Home and Abroad 1870-1920, 3/26/71-4/9/71; Frederick Church, Romantic Landscapes and Seascapes, 11/9/2007-12/5/2007. *Pos:* Pres, Meredith Long & Co, Houston, 57-. *Mem:* Art Dealers Asn Am; Am Fedn Arts; Am Asn Mus; Cult Arts Coun Houston; Archives Am Art (bd mem); Houston Art Dealers Asn (Pres 1982-84); Contemp Arts Mus (bd mem 1970-76); Alley Theatre (bd mem 1975-); Cultural Property Advisory Comm, US State Dept, 2003-2007. *Specialty:* 19th and 20th century American art; Am modern, contemp, and sporting art. *Interests:* Art dealer. *Publ:* Ed, Americans at Home and Abroad Catalogue, 71; Tradition and Innovation--American Paintings 1860-1870, 74; Americans at work and play, 1845-1944 (catalog), 80. *Mailing Add:* 2323 San Felipe Houston TX 77019

LONG, PHILLIP C
MUSEUM DIRECTOR
b Tucson, Ariz, 1942. *Study:* Tulane Univ, BA, 65. *Hon Degrees:* Art Acad of Cincinnati, Hon PhD Art History, 2007. *Pos:* Dir, Taft Mus Art, Cincinnati, Ohio, formerly, dir emeritus, currently. *Mem:* Asn Art Mus Dirs

LONG, ROSE-CAROL WASHTON
HISTORIAN, EDUCATOR
b New London, Conn, Mar 1, 1938. *Study:* Wellesley Coll, BA, 59; Yale Univ, MA (hist art), 62, PhD (hist art), 68. *Collection Arranged:* Twentieth Century Prints, Godwin-Ternbach Mus, 83. *Teaching:* Lectr, Queens Coll, City Univ NY, 67-69, asst prof, 69-78, assoc prof, 79-83, prof art hist grad ctr 84-2013, exec officer PhD prog, 85-2000; prof art hist, resident art prof, Grad Center, City Univ, NY, 2013-. *Awards:* Nat Endowment Humanities Fel, 72-73; Am Coun Learned Soc Grant, 72-73 & 82-83; Guggenheim Fel, 83-84; CUNY Rsch Award, 96-97, 97-98, 2004-05; J Clawson Mills Art History Fel, Met Mus Art, 2000-2001. *Mem:* Coll Art Asn; Am Fedn Arts; Historians Ger Cent Europ Art (pres, 97-2001, treas, 2001-); Soc Historian Eastern Europ & Russ Art. *Res:* Pioneers of 20th century abstract painting; Kandinsky; German Expressionism; art in the Weimer Republic, photog. *Publ:* Contribr, German Expressionist Prints and Drawings, Vol 1, The Robert Gore Rifkind Ctr, Los Angeles Co Mus Art, 89; auth & ed annotation, German Expressionism: Documents from the End of the Wilhelmine Empire to the Rise of National Socialism, GK Hall, Macmillan, 93 & Univ Calif Press, 95; Nationalism of Internationalism? Berlin Critics & the Question of Expressionism, Acts of the XXVIII International Congress of the History of Art, Vol III, Berlin, 93; auth, Vom Marchen zur Abstraktion: Kandinsky 1910 - Avantgarde oder regressiver Modernismus?, In: Der Fruhe Kandinsky, 1900-1910, Brucke Mus, 94; Kandinsky re-visited, Art J, fall 96; George Grosz, Otto Dix and the Philistines: The German-Jewish Question in the Weimar Republic, Experiment 9, 2003, From Metaphysics to Material Culture: Painting and Photography at the Bauhaus, Bauhaus Culture: From Weimar to the Cold War, Univ Minn Press, 2006; auth, Brücke and German Expressionism: Reception Considered, Brücke: The Birth of Expressionism in Dresden and Berlin, 1905-1913, NY: Neue Galerie, 2009; auth & co-ed, Of Truths Impossible to Put in Words: Max Beckmann Contexualized, Bern, Switzerland, AG, 2009; auth & co-ed, Jewish Dimensions in Modern Visual Culture: Antisemitism, Assimilation, Affirmation, 2009; Modernity as Anti-Nostalgia: The Photograph Books of Tim Gidel and Moshe Vorobeichic and the Eastern European Shetl, Ars Judaica 7, 2011; auth, Brucke, German Expressionism and the Issue of Modernism, New Perspectives on Brucke Expressionism: Bridging History, Christian Weikop, ed., Ashgate, 2011; auth, August Sander's Portraits of Persecuted Jews, Tate Papers, 19, 2013; auth, Contructing the Total Work of Art: Painting and the Public in Vasily Kandinsky: From Blaue Reiter to the Bauhaus, 1910-1925, NY, Neue Galerie, 2013. *Mailing Add:* 161 W 15th St No 6J New York NY 10011

LONG-MURPHY, JENNY
ART DEALER, CONSULTANT
b Ft Worth, Tex, June 26, 1955. *Study:* Finch Col, AA, 75; Sarah Lawrence Col, Bronxville, BA, 77. *Pos:* Asst dir, Meredith Long Contemp, New York, 77-79, dir, 79-80; mgr, Adam L Gimbel Gallery, New York, 81-83; adminr, Christie, Manson & Woods Int, Am Paintings Dept, 84-86; adminr, Meredith Long & Co, Houston, Tex, 86-91; bd, Blaffer Gallery, Univ Houston, 88-94; consult. *Specialty:* 19th and 20th century American Art. *Mailing Add:* c/o Meredith Long & Co 4517 Oleander St Bell Aire TX 77401-5118

LONGHAUSER, ELSA
MUSEUM DIRECTOR
Study: Studied Art Hist, Univ Pa. *Pos:* Dir, Paley and Levy Galleries at the Moore Col of Art and Design, Philadelphia, formerly; curator, Moore Col of Art and Design, formerly; exec dir, Santa Monica Mus Art, 2000-. *Publ:* Auth, Self-Taught Artists of the 20th Century, 1998. *Mailing Add:* Santa Monica Museum of Art Bergamont Station G1 2525 Michigan Ave Santa Monica CA 90404

LONGHURST, ROBERT E
SCULPTOR
b Latham, NY, Feb 23, 1949. *Study:* Adirondack Community Col, AS, 69; Kent State Univ, BA (archit), 75. *Work:* Adirondack Mus, Blue Mountain Lake, NY; Mus Art & Design, NY; Am Financial Corp, Cincinnati, Oh; Amoco Corp, Chicago, Ill; ANA Hotel, Tokyo, Japan; and many others. *Comn:* Sticks & Stones (environ construct, wood & granite) pvt residence, Lake Placid, NY, 89; Blast (14' high granite & stainless steel), Ensign-Bickford Ind, Simsbury, Conn, 92. *Exhib:* One-man shows, Randall Galleries, NY, 82 & Louis Newman Galleries, Beverly Hills, Calif, 86. *Awards:* Friends Am Art, Butler Inst Am Art, 79; Helen Eisler Mem Award, Audubon Ann, 80. *Bibliog:* Alice Gilborn (auth), Reaching for Perfection, Adirondack Life, 9/83; Dick Burrows (ed), A New Twist, Fine Woodworking, 8/91; Ken Fieldhouse (ed), Landmarks, Landscape Design, J Landscape Inst, 2/93. *Mem:* Int Sculpture Ctr, Washington, DC. *Media:* Wood, Stone. *Mailing Add:* 407 Potterbrook Rd Chestertown NY 12817

LONGO, VINCENT
PAINTER, PRINTMAKER
b New York, NY, Feb 15, 1923. *Study:* Cooper Union, Cert 46; Brooklyn Mus Art Sch, 49-50. *Work:* Libr Congress, Washington, DC; Mus Mod Art, Brooklyn Mus Art, Whitney Mus Am Art, NY; Nat Gallery Art, Washington, DC; Met Mus, New York City, NY; Amerada Hess, NY; Biblioteque Nationale, Paris, France; Braniff Airlines; Chemical Bank, NY; Ciba-Geigy Found, NY; Corcoran Gallery Art, Wash Dc; and many others. *Comn:* Enameled steel balustrade, Ronald Reagan; Cesar Pelli Terminal, Nat Airport, Washington, DC, 1996. *Exhib:* Two Decades of Am Prints, Brooklyn Mus, NY, 69; solo retrospectives, 15 Yr Print Retrospective, Corcoran Gallery & Detroit Inst Art, 70; Whitney Mus Painting Ann, NY, 71; Am Drawings, Whitney Mus, NY, 73; Fogg Mus, Libr of Cong, Metrop Mus Art, NY Mus Fine Arts, Boston Mus Mod Art; one-person shows Alfred Univ, 1978, Andrew Crispo, New York City, 1980, Adam Gimbel Gallery, New York City; Color in the Graphic Arts, Libr Congress, Washington, DC, 74; Thirty Years of Am Prints, Brooklyn Mus, NY, 76; Am Prints Process & Proofs, Whitney Mus, NY, 81; Condeso/Lawler Gallery, New York City, 1984, 85, 87, 89, 90, 93, Hunter Coll Art Galleries, Career Retrospective, 2003; The Persistence of Painting, Ulrich Mus, Wichita, Kans, 92; Painting, Print Retrospective, Hunter Coll Art Galleries, 2003; Butler's Fine Art, East Hampton, NY, 2005; Optical Simulations, Yellow Bird Gallery, Newburgh, NY, 2005; Wooster Arts Space, NY, 2007; Group exhibs, Am Abstract Artists: Tribute to Esphyr Slobodkina, Painting Ctr, NY, 2008, Color, Southwest Minn State Univ Art Mus, Marshall, Minn, 2009, Nat Acad Mus, NY, 2009. *Pos:* Prof emer, inaugural older Phyllis and Joseph Caroff chair fine arts; asst dir Yale Univ Summer Art School, Norfolk, Conn, 1955-59, dir, 1969. *Teaching:* Prof art, Bennington Col, Bennington, Vt, 57-67, Hunter Col, NY, 67-2001. *Awards:* Fullbright Fel, 51; Fel Guggenheim, 71; Grant Nat Endowment Arts, 73; Citation for Prof Achievement, Cooper Union, 1973; Morenon Memorial prize, Exhib Contemporary Art, Nat Acad, NY, 2009. *Bibliog:* Gene Baro (auth), Print Retrospective (catalog essay), Corcoran Gallery, 70; Judith Goldman (auth), American Prints: Process & Proofs; Louis Lomonaco (auth), Artes et Metier Graphique, Flammarion, 92; Judy Karabenick (interviewer) Retrospective Catalog Interview with Michael Brenson, 2003. *Mem:* Am Abstract Artists; Nat Acad. *Media:* Acrylic, Printmaking, Etchings, Woodcuts. *Publ:* Auth, A Debate on Abstraction (exhib catalog), Hunter Col, 88; Abstraction and Immanence, Hunter Col. *Dealer:* Condeso-Lawler 76 Greene St New York NY 10012; Eric Firestone Gallery East Hampton NY

LONGO-MUTH, LINDA L
PAINTER, INSTRUCTOR
b Nyack, NY, 1948. *Study:* Independent Study, Rome, Italy, 69; Southern Conn Univ, New Haven, BS, 70; independent study, Paris, France, 71; Montclair State Univ, NJ, MA, 75. *Work:* Cathedral St John the Divine, NY; Assoc Neurologists, Plainfield, NJ; Global Petroleum Corp, Waltham, Mass; Nat Multiple Sclerosis Soc; Helen Hayes Hosp. *Exhib:* NY Acad Sci, 92; World Trade Ctr, NY, 92 & 93; Paine Webber Corp Gallery, 93; Ueno Royal Mus, Tokyo, 94; Hakone Open Air Mus, Mt Fiji, Japan, 94; Birmingham Mus, Ala; IBM Gallery Sci & Art, 92-2010; Piermont Flywheel Gallery, NY. *Pos:* Bd advs, Resources for Artists with Disabilities, NY, 90-92 & bd dir, 92-; art advocate for artists with physical disabilities, Art's Coun Rockland, 93-94. *Teaching:* Instr studio art, Ramapo Central Sch Dist, Suffern, NY, 70-87; lectr, Mus Mod Art, Edward John Noble Ctr Symp Women Artists Disabled, 91 & Ramapo Col, Ramsey, NY, 94; symposium, Mus Modern Art, NY. *Awards:* Zvita & Joseph Akston Found Award, 91 & Dorothy Seligson Mem Award, 92, Nat Asn Women Artists; Guy Forde Mony Penney Award, Helen Hayes Hosp, 92. *Bibliog:* Robert Samuels (auth), Showing the true colors, in a new career, Gannett Newspapers, 7/2/89; Susan Leavitt (producer), video, CBS Affiliate WJW Life choices television prog, 91; Leslie Boyd (auth), Rockland artist profile in courage, Gannett Newspapers, 12/26/91. *Mem:* New York Artists Equity; Artists Space, NY; Nat Asn Women Artists; Arts Coun Rockland, Spring Valley, NY; NY Soc Women Artists. *Media:* Acrylic-on-Canvas. *Publ:* Contribr, NJ Rehab mag cover, 12/89; Mental and Physical Disability Law Reporter, Am Bar Asn, Washington, DC, Vol 16, No 3, 5-6/92. *Mailing Add:* 4 Reina Ln Valley Cottage NY 10989

LONGOBARDI, PAM
PAINTER, PHOTOGRAPHER
b NJ, 1958. *Study:* Exch student, Univ Utah, 78; Univ Ga, BFA (studio art), 81; Mont State Univ, Bozeman, MFA, 85. *Work:* Tweed Art Mus, Duluth, Minn; Kennedy Art Mus, Athens, Ohio; Deloitte-Touche and Freeman-Hawkins Attorneys, Atlanta, Ga; Corcoran Gallery Art, Washington, DC; Saks Fifth Ave, Atlanta, Ga; Benzinger Winery, Sonoma, Calif. *Comn:* Painting, Imagery Series Wine Label, 95 & 05; Paintings, MBL Life Assurance Corp, 95; Painting, Atlanta Hartsfield Int Airport. *Exhib:* Solo exhibs, San Francisco Mus Mod Art Rental Gallery, Calif, 90, Artemisia Gallery, Chicago, 90, Inst de Estudios Norte Americanos, Barcelona, Spain, 91, Kathryn Sermas Gallery, NY, 91 & 92, Lowe Gallery, Atlanta, 91, 93, 94 & 98, Santa Monica, Calif, 92, Czech Cult Ctr, 93, Animal/Beautiful (catalog), Lowe Gallery, Atlanta, Ga, 98, World World, Lowe Gallery, Atlanta, Ga, 2000, Visible/Invisible, Hartsfield Int Airport Atrium, Atlanta, Ga, 2000, Beyond the Frame, Knoxville Mus Art, Tenn, 2000, Damp Edge, Pearl of the Third Mind, collaboration with C Dongoski, Gallery Art, Univ Northern Iowa, Cedar Falls, Iowa, Pearl of the Third Mind, collaboration with C Dongoski, Gusto House Gallery/Free Space, Kobe, Japan and Thin Line Drawn, collaboration with C Dongoski, Bergen Gallery, Savannah Coll Art & Design, Savannah, Ga, 2002, Worlds within Worlds, Jacksonville Mus Mod Art; USA: Within Limits, Documenta Galeria de Arte Ctr for Book Arts, Sao Paulo, Brazil, 94; 3 Americans, Crossing Space, Portoguard, Venice, Italy, 96; Art and Science Int Exhib, 90th Anniversary Tsinghua Univ Global Symposium, Nat Mus Fine Art, Beijing, China, 2001; Barrister's Gallery, New Orleans, La, 2002; Art Chicago 2002 at Navy Pier, Fay Gold Gallery, Navy Pier complex, Chicago, Ill, 2002; Skin; Contemp Views of the Body, Jacksonville Mus Mod Art, Jacksonville, Fla, 2003. *Teaching:* Vis artist, Chicago Art Inst, 86, Dartmouth Col, Hanover, NH, 88, Univ Chapel Hill, NC, 88, Univ Northern Iowa, Cedar Falls, 89, Mason Art Ctr, San Francisco, 89 & La State Univ, Baton Rouge, 90; assoc prof art, Univ Tenn, Knoxville, 87-97, Ga State Univ, currently; assoc prof painting, Ga State Univ, 97-, assoc dean fine arts, 2001-2003; assoc prof art, Ga State Univ, 97-. *Awards:* SAF/Nat Endowment Arts Visual Arts Fel, 94; Visual Artist Fel, Tenn State Arts Comn, 96; Juror's Choice Award, Red Clay Survey, Huntsville Mus Art, Huntsville, Ala; Ga State Univ Sch Art and Design Summer Rsch Grant, Atlanta; Finalist, Atlanta Hartsfield Airport T-Terminal Comn Competition; Chancellor's Award for Rsch and Creative Achievement, Univ Tenn, 98; Major Pub Art Comn, Atlanta's Med Examiner's Facility, Fulton Co Arts Coun; Ga State Sch Art & Design Summer Rsch Grant, Atlanta; All Star Ball Comn, Metro Atlanta CofC and Atlanta Cult Affairs, 2000; Research Initiation Grant, Coll Arts & Scis, Ga State Univ, Atlanta; TABOO Project Grant, Requiem exhib, Nexus Contemp Art Center, Atlanta; Finalist, Atlanta Hartsfield Airport E-Concourse Expansion Comn Competition, 2001; Outstanding Faculty Res Award, Ga State Univ, Atlanta, 2005; and others. *Bibliog:* Peggy Cyphers (auth), Pam Longobard, NY in Review, ARTS, summer 91; Carny Ladislav (auth), Pam Longobardi, Profil, Bratislova, Slovakia, 93; Peter Frank & Jerry Cullum (auths), Appeals, Oaths & Queries: Objects & Installations by Pam Longobardi (catalog), 94. *Mem:* Coll Art Asn; Southeastern Ctr Contemp Art. *Media:* Mixed Media; Copper. *Res:* Relationship between humans & animals eco-feminism. *Specialty:* Contemporary Art. *Interests:* Scuba, snorkeling, surfing and yoga. *Collection:* Atlanta Hartsfield International Airport; Tweed Art Mus, Minnesota; Corcoran Museum of Art, Washington, D.C. *Publ:* Contribr, Scientific American, Vol 250, No 4, 84; Infinity Mag, Vols 2, 3, 4 & 5, 84-86; auth & contribr, Images of nature and power: Named and nameless, Vol 2, Peabody Review, 90; contribr, Divided World, La State Univ Printmaking Dept, 90; The Persistence of Myth, Wycross Press, Auburn, Ala, 90. *Dealer:* Metaphor Contemp Art Brooklyn NY; Sandler Hudson Gallery Atlanta Ga; Tinney Cannon Contemporary Art Nashville TN. *Mailing Add:* 1090 NE Standard Dr Atlanta GA 30319

LONGSTRETH, JAKE
PAINTER
b 1977. *Study:* Lewis & Clark Coll, Ore, BA, 1999; Calif Coll Arts, San Francisco, MFA, 2005. *Exhib:* Cream from the Top, Benicia Arts Ctr, Calif, 2005; Material World, Alliance Francaise, San Francisco, 2006; Real Space, Mahan Gallery, Columbus, Ohio, 2007; Manifest Destination, EgoPark Gallery, Oakland, 2008; One To Many, Partisan Gallery, San Francisco, 2009. *Awards:* Murphy & Cadogan Fel Award, 2004; Kimmel Harding Nelson Ctr for the Arts Fel, 2007; Pollock-Krasner Found Grant, 2008. *Bibliog:* Kenneth Baker (auth), Landscapes, real and imaginary, seen in the light of day, San Francisco Chronicle, 1/6/2007; Frank Cebulski (auth), Jake Longstreth at Gregory Lind, Artweek, 3/2009

LONGVAL, GLORIA
PAINTER, CERAMIST
b Tampa, Fla, Feb 7, 1931. *Study:* Am Art Sch, New York, NY, with Raphael Soyer, 51-52; Art Students League, with Robert Brackman, 52-53; Nat Acad Design, with Robert Philip, 55-58. *Work:* Los Angeles Co Mus; Museo Nacional, Palacio de Bellas Artes, Havana, Cuba; Riverside Art Mus, Calif; Latino Mus History, Art & Cult, Los Angeles; Wifredo Lam Cent, Havana, Cuba; San Diego Art Mus; Am Mus Ceramic Arts, Pomona, Calif, 2013. *Comn:* Drawing for Int Decade of Women, Woman Tours, Los Angeles, Calif, 75; portrait (oil), Boris Pillin, Los Angeles, 76; portrait, Sharon Davis, Los Angeles, 77; portrait (oil), Dr Gerald Newmark, Los Angeles, 80; portrait (oil), Polia Pillin, Los Angeles, 76; Commissioned illustration for publication of poetry, Idiosyncrasies, poet Suzanne Lummis, LA, Calif, 89. *Exhib:* One-person show, Paideia Gallery, Los Angeles, 62-65; San Bernadino Col Mus, Los Angeles, 85; Del Bello Gallery, Toronto, Can, 86; Downey Mus, Calif, 87; Group Exhib: Women's Sensibilities, Women's Art Registry of Minn (WARM), Minneapolis, 1986; April Sgro-Riddle Gallery, Los Angeles, 88; Radford Univ, Va, 90; Lancaster Mus, Calif, 90; Museo Nacional, Palacio de Bellas Artes, Havana, Cuba, 91; Latino Mus History, Art & Cult, Los Angeles, 95; Exploring a Movement: Feminist Visions in Clay, Laband Art Gallery, Loyola Marymount Univ, LA, Calif, 95; Group exhib: Feminist Visions in Clay, Loyola Marymount Univ, LA, 1995; Group exhib: Personae-Southern Calif Figurative Art, Calif State Univ, LA, 1985; London Univ, Eng, 96; Riverside Art Mus, Calif, 97; Group exhib and auction: Robert Feraud Gallery and Auction House, Montauban, France, 2006; Los Angeles Municipal Art Gallery, Calif, 2008; Taos Art Mus Taos, NMex, 2011; Doin It in Public: Feminism and Art at The Woman's Building, Otis Col Art and Design, Calif, 2011-2012; Oral History and Art in Taos, Okla State Univ, 2012; Women Artists of the Permanent Coll: Mid-Nineteenth Century to the Present Day, 2013; Riverside, Art Mus, Los Angeles, Calif. *Pos:* Vpres, Los Angeles Artcore, 86-87 & contrib ed, 86; visual arts adv, Los Angeles Poetry Festival, 90-96; cur, Latin Diaspora, Art n Barbee Gallery, Los Angeles, 92; bd dir, Brewery Art Asn, 99-2001. *Teaching:* Instr painting, Sch Fine Arts, Univ Judaism, 68-71; guest instr, Los Angeles Children's Mus, 87-88; guest artist, Yosemite Park, 94-97; lectr, Galeria, Las Americas, Los Angeles, 93 & Brandeis Univ Women, Los Angeles, 2002. *Awards:* First Hon Mention, Nat Acad Allied Artists Am, 59; First Prize, Multi Media Mini, San Bernardino Co Mus, 83. *Bibliog:* Betty Ann Brown (auth), Yesterday and Tomorrow, Calif Women Artists, 89; Margaret Lazzari (auth), Curriculum Viva, Visions Art Quart, 92; Al Martinez (auth), Rising Voices-Profiles in Leadership, LA, Calif, 93; Shifra M Goldman (auth), Dimensions of the Ams, 94. *Mem:* Brewery Art Asn Los Angeles; Comn Feminile de Los Angeles. *Media:* Acrylic, Oil. *Publ:* Doin it in Public: Feminism and Art At the Woman's Building, 2011; Remarkable Women of Taos, NMex, 2013. *Dealer:* Rima R Ralff 230 Lower Las Colonias Rd El Prado NM 87529

LONIDIER, FRED SPENCER
PHOTOGRAPHER, EDUCATOR
b Lakeview, Ore, Feb 19, 1942. *Study:* Yuba Coll, Marysville, Calif, AA, 62; San Francisco State Coll, BA, 66; Univ Calif, San Diego, MFA (photog & mixed media), 72; also with David Antin. *Work:* Long Beach Mus Art, Calif; Faith Flam, Studio City, Calif; Oakland Mus, Calif; New Mus Contemp Art, New York; Southern Calif Libr Social Studies & Research; Los Angeles Video Libr, Calif; Univ Calif, San Diego, Special Collections Libr, 98; Studio for S Calif Hist, Los Angeles, 2006. *Exhib:* Solo exhibs Rutgers Univ Labor Educ Ctr, New Brunswick, NJ, 78, 85-86, Ironworkers Union, Local 657, 86, Univ & Coll Labor Educ Asn, 86, Calif Fedn Teachers, 89 & 91, Walter/McBean Gallery, San Francisco Art Inst, 92, Gallery of Art, Univ of N Iowa, 97, Mission Cult Ctr for Latino Arts, San Francisco, 2000, Side St Projects, Los Angeles, Calif, 2001, Blue Oyster Gallery, Dundin City, NZ, 2002 & Truck-trailer traveling exhib to the maquiladora zones, 2003, Harcourt House Arts Centre, Edmonton, Can, 2005; Pressing Engagements: Socially Oriental Photog (catalog), Tuttle Gallery, McDonough Sch, Md, 89; Visual Sociology, Mendenhall Gallery, Whittier Coll, Calif, 90; Work Prints: The Eye of the Photojournalist, Rough Gallery, 90; Int Ctr Photog, Midtown, New York, 93; Inst Contemp Art, Boston, 93; Laguna Art Mus, Calif, 94; High Mus, Atlanta, Ga, 95; Exit Gallery, Univ of Nevada, 98; ACME Art Co, Main Gallery space, Columbus, Ohio, 2000; group exhibs, NAFTA, ACME Art Gallery, Main Gallery Space, Columbus, Ohio, 2000, At Work: The Art of California Labor (with catalog), SFSU Art Gallery, 2003 & inSite, 2005; and many others. *Pos:* Consult Eye Gallery, San Francisco, Calif, 85. *Teaching:* Prof, visual arts dept, Univ Calif San Diego, 72-2006. *Awards:* Nat Endowment Arts Fel, 80-83; Best Entry Award, S Shenere Gallery, Los Angeles, Calif, 2002-2003. *Bibliog:* Fred Glass (auth), A-V reference shelf, Labor Studies J, Vol 20, No 1, spring 95; Jim McVicker (auth), Labor link TV gives unions a voice on cable channels, The Worker, UFCW Local 135, 2/96; Fred Lonidier (auth), Dateline: San Diego, Calif, labor link TV, Community Media Rev, Vol 19, No 2, 96; Kate Callen (auth), Photographs that make a point, UCSD Perspectives, San Diego, summer 2001; Grant Kester (auth), Conversation pieces: diabolical encounters in modern art, Chapter five: community and communicability, UC Press, 2002. *Mem:* Coll Art Asn Am; Univ Coun/AFT. *Media:* Photo, Text, Video & Slide. *Interests:* installation art concerning class struggle. *Publ:* Coauth, Union Made: Artists Working with Unions, Upfront, NYPADD, New York, winter 83-84; Working with unions, Culture in Contention, Real Comet Press, Wash, 85; Working with Unions II, Democratic Communications in the Info Age, Garmond Press, Can, 92; Letters to the ed, Labor Studies Forum, spring 96; Setting aside our differences, Rethinking Marxism, Vol 8, No 4, summer 96; auth, UC Hates Unions II: Labor Relations at the Univeristy of California, New Indicator, 2002; Corporations in Societies, The Grenoble Res Center, CIESIMA, Grenoble, France, 2002. *Mailing Add:* Univ Calif San Diego Visual Arts Dept 9500 Gilman Dr La Jolla CA 92093-0084

LOOK, DONA
SCULPTOR
b Mequon, Wis, 1948. *Study:* Univ Wis, Oshkosh, BA, 70. *Work:* Philadelphia Mus Art; Arkansas Arts Ctr, Little Rock; Erie Art Mus, Pa; Am Craft Mus, New York; The White House & MCI Telecommunications Corp, Washington, DC. *Exhib:* Am Crafts Coun Shows, 81-98; Philadelphia Craft Show, Philadelphia Mus Art, 85 & 86; Baskets, Chicago Int New Art Forms Expos, Perimeter Gallery, Ill, 92; Baskets by Regional Artists, Neville Pub Mus, Green Bay, Wis, 92; The Space Within: Contemporary Basketry in the Midwest, Waterloo Mus Art, Iowa, 93; Sixth Ann Basketry Invitational, Sybaris Gallery, Royal Oak, Mich, 95; Perimeter Gallery, Chicago, 96; New Baskets: Expanding the Concept, Craft Alliance, St Louis, Mo, 97; Celebrating American Craft, Danish Mus Decorative Art, Copenhagen, Denmark, 97; Threads: Contemporary American Basketry, Barbican Ctr, London, Eng, 98. *Pos:* Art instr, Dept Educ, Sydney & Tamworth, NSW, Australia, 76-78; partner, Look & Heaney Studio, Byron Bay, NSW, Australia, 78-80; studio artist, Algoma, Wis, 80-. *Awards:* Craftsmen Award, Philadelphia Craft Show, 86; Nat Endowment Arts/Arts Midwest Fel, 87; Fel Nat Endowment Arts, 88; US Artists Windgate Fel, 2009. *Bibliog:* Craft Today: Poetry of the Physical, Am Craft Mus, 86; Dona Look, Am Craft Mag, 85; Jack Lenor Larson (auth), The Tactile Vessel, Erie Art Mus, 89. *Media:* Fiber. *Publ:* Meeting Ground: Basketry Traditions & Sculptural Forms, The Forum (catalog), St Louis, Mo, 90; The Traveler's Guide to American Crafts, East of the Mississippi, Dutton, New York, NY, 90; Fiberarts Design Book Four, 91 & Fiberarts Design Book Five, 95, Lark Books; Auth, International CRAFTS, Thames & Hudson, Ltd, London, Eng, 91; No: Nouvel Objet, Design House, Seoul, Korea, 97. *Mailing Add:* 4504 Turkey Ln East Apt 204 Algoma WI 54201-9698

LOONEY, DANIEL STEPHEN
PAINTER
b Watertown, S Dak, Apr 16, 1946. *Study:* Univ Idaho, BS (finance), Moscow, Idaho, 68. *Comn:* An Old-Fashioned Christmas Eve (watercolor, pen & ink) Boise, Idaho, 2014; Historic Idaho City Bell Tower (watercolor, pen, & ink) Idaho City, Idaho, 2014; Hyde Park Happy Hours (acrylic on rag paper) Boise, Idaho, 2014; Evening in Paris (watercolor) Boise, Idaho, 2013; Roseberry after a Summer Rain (watercolor) Reno, Nev 2014; McCall Summer (acrylic, pen, & ink) Friendswood, Tex, 2014; 8th Street Autumn Reflections (mixed media on masonite) Boise, Idaho, 2013; Kokanee Spawn (acrylic on canvas) Boise, Idaho, 2013; Mt McGowan Spring Meadow (acrylic on canvas) Boise, Idaho, 2013; An Early Idaho Autumn (acrylic on canvas) Boise, Idaho, 2013. *Exhib:* Idaho Watercolor Soc, Nat Gallery of Art, DC, 82; Dan Looney-Idaho Artist, Dr L Willems Inst, Hasselt, Belgium, 82; Elkhorn Art Festival, Sun Valley, Idaho, 82; Park City Art Festival, Park City, Utah, 82; Boise Art Festival, Boise, Idaho, 97; Dan Looney Gallery, McCall Idaho, 2000-2008; Art & Roses, Boise, Idaho, 2010-2014; Boise Baroque Orchestra, Boise, Idaho, 2011-2013; Boise's Art in the Park, 2012-2014. *Pos:* owner & artist, Dan Looney Art and Creative Services, Boise, Idaho, currently. *Teaching:* instr painting & design, Coll S Idaho, Twin Falls, Idaho, 94-95; instr water media, Dan Looney Gallery, 2004-2013. *Awards:* Cash Award, 40th Ann Exhib for Idaho Artists, Boise Gallery Art, Idaho, 76; Merit Award, 41st Ann Exhibit for Idaho Artists, Boise Gallery Art, Boise, Idaho, 77; Merit Award & Artist of the Month, NW Watercolor Soc, Everett, Wash, 82; Nominee, Idaho Governor's Award for Excellence in the Arts, 2008, 2010. *Bibliog:* Colleen Birch-Maile (auth), Portrait-Dan Looney, Boise Mag, 87; Idaho State Bar, Dan Looney, The Advocate, 2004; Amelia Nielsen-Stowell, Artist for All Seasons, Tamarack Life, 2008. *Media:* Mixed Media. *Interests:* Chess, History. *Publ:* auth, ARTWORKS, publ by Dan Looney, 99

LOPINA, LOUISE CAROL
PAINTER, PRINTMAKER
b Chicago, Ill, Nov 24, 1936. *Study:* Chicago Art Inst; Purdue Univ, BS; study with Lawrence Harris & Don Dennis AWS. *Work:* Cincinnati Nat Hist Mus & Cincinnati Club, Cincinnati; Cincinnati Club; Hartwood Club; Nissequoque Golf Club, St James, Long Island, NY; G & R Tackle co; Dana Pointe Yacht Club; Colo State Univ Vet Teaching Hosp; Bank of Smithtown; Ken Stewarts Lodge, Bath, Ohio, 2002-2003; San Bernardino Co Mus; The Dog Mus. *Comn:* Diorama Backgrounds: Asistencia Mission, San Bernardino Co Mus, 92; Vol III, IV & V (illus), comn by Russell Annebel; 125th Anniversary painting, Am Kennel Club, NY; official painting, Mission San Juan Capistrano. *Exhib:* Solo exhibs, Air Univ Libr, Montgomery, Ala, 77, Christ Church Little Gallery, Kettering, Ohio, 80, The Cincinnati Club, Ohio, 81, Nissequoque Golf Club, St James, Long Island, NY, 86 & Nat Mgt Asn, Local Chapter, Newport Beach, Calif; Soc Animal Artists Exhibs, anns 72-90; Nature Interpreted, Cincinnati Mus Natural Hist, 80, 82 & 84; Wondrous Wildlife, Cincinnati Zoo, 83; Outdoor Expo, Albany, NY, 85; Nature of the Beast, Southern Alleghenies Mus Art, 86; Prestige Gallery: 1st & 2nd Ann Original Art Showcase, Can, 89-90; Whaletail, East African Wildlife Soc, 91; Artist's Registry Exhib, Dog Mus, 92 & 94; Wildlife West Art Festival, San Bernardino Co Mus Found, 92-94; The Contemp Canine: Works from the Artists Registry, The Dog Mus, St Louis, Mo, 94, 96-98; Natural Selections IV, J MacArthur Beach State Park; 2000 Ky Nat Wildlife Exhib, Henderon Fine Art Ctr; Artists Focus on Calif Skies, Calif Art Club, 2002; Impressions of New Eng, Bennington Ctr for the Arts, 2002-2003; Small Works Big Impressions, Soc Animal Artists, Wildlife Experience, Parker, Colo, 2007-; Painting the California Landscape, Mission San Juan Capistrano, 2006-09; San Dimas Spirit of the West, San Dimas Wildlife Exhib, 2012. *Collection Arranged:* oil paintings, Ken Stewarts Lodge, Bath, Ohio, 02, 03. *Pos:* owner, Wildbrook Studio. *Teaching:* Instr drawing & painting, USAF Acad-Officer's Wives Club, 72-75. *Awards:* Best in Show, Nat Nature Art Exhib, 78-79 & 82; Selection for commemorative print, Snow Leopard Symposium, India, 85; Best in Show, San Clemente Art Club, Winter Juried Exhib, 2002, Spring Juried Exhib, 2003. *Bibliog:* Al Rosen & Faith Every (dirs), Louise Lopina's Art on the Wild Side, television feature program, 2/78; article, A sampling of assorted artists, Dayton Mag, 5-6/81. *Mem:* Nat Audubon Soc; Nature Conservancy; Soc Animal Artists (past exhib co-chmn); San Clemente Art Asn; S Calif Plein Air Painters Assoc; Laguna Plein Air Painters Asn. *Media:* Oil, Watercolor, Pastel. *Specialty:* Original paintings; Dog limited edition; prints. *Interests:* Landscaping with California native plants. *Publ:* Reptiles and Amphibians of Aullwood & Wild Flowers of Aullwood, Nat Audubon, 78; View from the top: Snow leopards, Color Print, 82; Old English Sheepdogs, 85, 92 & 97; Shetland Sheepdogs, 88 & 99; Bulldog, 90; Rottweiler, 92; Yellow Labrador & New Foundland, 96; Golden Retriever, 95; Australian Shepherd, 2001; Illustrated Vol 3,4,5, 6 & 7 Russell Annabel's Trouble is where you find it, Head for the Hills. *Dealer:* Wildbrook Studio; Black Hawk Gallery Saratoga Wyoming. *Mailing Add:* c/o Wild Brook Studio 7 Calle Agua San Clemente CA 92673

LORBER, D MARTIN H B
CONSULTANT, HISTORIAN
b Macon, Ga, July 22, 1943. *Study:* Univ NC, BA, 65; City Coll New York, BS, 91. *Interests:* Japanese Swords & Fittings; Korean, Song ceramics. *Publ:* Auth, Japanese Sword Fittings, 5/77 & Japanese Buddhist Paintings, 7/78, Arts of Asia; coauth, 100 Masterpieces from the Collection of Dr Walter Ames Compton, Christie's, 2/92; Parts I, II & III, In: Japanese Swords & Swords Fittings, Christie's, 92; auth, Japanese arms and armour at the Metropolitan Museum of Art, Orientations, 10/92; Japanese Buddhist Paintings in the NY Museums, Int Asian Art Fair Catalogue, 3/2001. *Mailing Add:* 304 E 20th St New York NY 10003-1813

LORBER, RICHARD
CRITIC, EDUCATOR
b New York, NY, Dec 9, 1946. *Study:* Columbia Coll, with Meyer Schapiro & Lionel Trilling, BA (lit & art hist), 67; Columbia Univ, with Meyer Schapiro & Linda Nochlin, MA (art hist), 70, EdD (art), 77. *Pos:* Ed, Dance Scope Mag, 74-; contrib ed, Arts Mag, 75-; community liaison, Mus of Mod Art, 76-77; critic & contribr, Artforum, Arts Mag, 77-; adv panelist, NY State Coun on Arts, 78-; proj dir, Nat Video Clearinghouse, 79-; consult, Electronic Arts Intermix, 81; pres, Fox-Lorber Assoc Inc, 81-2001; co-chmn, Winstart TV and Video, 96-2001; pres, Koch Lorber Films, 2002-; pres & ceo, Lorber HT Digital (Alive Mind), 2007-. *Teaching:* Instr art hist, Parsons Sch of Design, 74-77; asst prof art & art educ, Grad Sch of Educ, NY Univ, 77-79. *Publ:* Coauth, The Gap, McGraw-Hill, 68; auth, articles in Arts in Soc & Filmmakers Newsletter, 77; contribr, Video Art, Dutton, 78; article, Videodance, Millenium Film J, 12/81

LORBER, STEPHEN NEIL
PAINTER, PHOTOGRAPHER
b New York, NY, Aug 30, 1943. *Study:* Pratt Inst, BFA; Brooklyn Col, MFA; Yale Univ, Stoekel fel, 64. *Work:* Chicago Art Inst; Okla Art Ctr, Oklahoma City; Western NMex Univ, Silver City; Roswell Mus & Art Ctr, NMex; Am Tel & Tel Co; Chase Manhattan Bank, NY; and others; Harvard Univ Library; Queen Sofia Found, Madrid; Univ of Ill; US Dept of state; Nat Inst of Health; Art Mus of S Tex. *Exhib:* Solo exhibs, Milliken Gallery, NY, 81, 83, 85, & 2010, Dubins Gallery, LA, 83, Delahunty Gallery, Dallas, TX, 77 & 78, Sachs Gallery, NY, 74, 75, 76, 77, 78; Contemp Arts Ctr, NY, 82; John Szoke Gallery, NY, 87; Goddard Ctr Arts, Ardmore Okla, 89; Chicago Int Art Expos, 89 & 90; Group exhibs, The Kitchen, NY, 94, Addison Ripley Fine Art, Wash DC, 99, Roswell Mus, NMex, 2000, Oklahoma City Mus Art, 2006; Guild Hall, South Hampton, NY, 94; Mus de la Ciudad, Madrid, Spain; and others; Orlando Mus Fine Arts, Fla; Paul Roberson Gallery, Rutgers Univ, Newark, NJ, 2013; Still Life 1970s, Yale Univ Art Gallery, Still Life 1970s, New Haven, Conn, 2013; Am Acad Arts & Letts, NYC, 2014. *Awards:* Artist in Residence Grant, Roswell Mus & Art Ctr, NMex; Yaddo Fel, 71 & 75; Nat Endowment Arts Fel, 76-77; Hassam, Speicher, Betts, and Symonds Purchase award, Acad of Arts & Letts. *Bibliog:* Allen Ellenweog (auth), Arts Mag, 9/77; Stephen Yoskowitz (auth), Arts Mag, Vol 55, No 9, 5/81; Kramer, Hilton, NY Times, Dec 21, 71, Photo; Kramer, Hilton, NY Times, June 9, 73, Photo; Kramer, Hilton, NY Times, Dec 15,73; Martin, Richard, Arts & Artists, Gt Brit, Nov, 73; Brown, Richard, Arts Mag, Feb, 74; Ratcliff, Carter, Art Int, Apr, 75, Vol XIX, No 5 Photo; Hoestry, Ingelborg, Art Int, May, 75, Vol XIX, No 5 Photo; Henry, Garrit, Art News, Summer, 76; Kramer, Hilton, NY Times, Apr, 22, 77; Brody, Jacqueline, Print Coll Newsletter. *Media:* All. *Dealer:* Pace Editions NY; Bluehaven Press NY. *Mailing Add:* 709 County Rte 60 Greenwich NY 12834

LORD, ANDREW
SCULPTOR
b Rochdale, Eng, 1950. *Study:* Coll Art, Rochdale, 66-68; Cent Sch Arts & Crafts, Studied with Gilbert Harding-Green & Bonnie van de Wetering, London, 68-71. *Work:* Mus Art, Dallas, Tex; City Art Gallery, Leeds, Eng; Mus Beymans van Beuningen, Rotterdam; Mus Contemp Art, Los Angeles; Mus & Art Gallery, Portsmouth, Eng; and others. *Exhib:* Int Ceramics 72, Victoria & Albert Mus, & traveling exhib, London, 72; Postmodern Prints, Victoria & Albert Mus, London, 90; Act Up Benefit Exhib, Matthew Marks Gallery, NY, 91; Group show, Gagaosian Gallery, 92; Drawings 30th Anniversary Exhib, Leo Castelli Gallery, NY, 93; Solo exhib, Galerie Bruno Bischofberger, Zurich, 92, Carnegie Mus Art, Pittsburgh, 93, Gagaosian Gallery, NY 94; and many others. *Pos:* De Porceleyne Fles, Netherlands, formerly. *Teaching:* Vis lectr, Bath Acad Art, Eng, 75-80. *Awards:* British Coun Scholar, 74. *Bibliog:* Jerry Saltz (auth), Andrew Lord at 65 Thompson St, Art in America, 2/93; Peter Schjeldahl (auth), Nostalgie de la Boue, The New Yorker, 12/92; Peter Schjeldahl (auth), Excellent pot, Voice, 12/92. *Mailing Add:* c/o Baldwin Gallery 209 S Galena St Aspen CO 81611

LORD, CAROLYN MARIE
PAINTER, INSTRUCTOR
b Los Angeles, Calif, Oct 6, 1956. *Study:* Painting Workshops, with Millard Sheets, George Post, Rex Brandt, Robert E Wood, 76-83; Principia Col, Elsah, Ill, BA (fine arts), 78; San Francisco Tapestry Workshop, with Jean-Pierre Larochette, 81, Bay Area Classical Art Atelier Workshop, 2011-2012. *Comn:* Lodi Mem Hosp, Lodi, Calif; St. Josephs Hosp, Lodi, Calif; Los Angeles Athletic Club, Los Angeles, Calif. *Teaching:* La Romita Sch Art, Terni, Italy, 91; Mendocino Art Ctr, Calif, 96; Saddleback

Community Coll, 97, 98, 99 & 2000; Pacific Boychoir Acad, Oakland, Calif, 2004-2008. *Mem:* Nat Watercolor Soc; Calif Art Club; Thunderbird Found Arts. *Media:* Watercolor on Paper. *Publ:* California Light: A Century of Landscapes, Rizzoli Int, 2011. *Dealer:* Knowlton Gallery Lodi Ca; Bingham Gallery Mt Carmel Vt; GeorgeStern Fine Art Los Angeles Ca; Calabi Gallery Petaluma Ca; Figurehead Gallery. *Mailing Add:* 1993 DeVaca Way Livermore CA 94550

LORD, MICHAEL HARRY
DEALER, CURATOR
b Milwaukee, Wis, Nov 19, 1954. *Study:* Univ Wis-Milwaukee. *Pos:* Asst to dir, Irving Galleries, 68-77; owner & dir, Michael H Lord Gallery, 78-. *Mem:* Milwaukee Art Dealers Asn (pres, 81-); Wis Coalition Arts & Human Needs (bd dir, 83-). *Specialty:* Contemporary American art; masters in photography and sculpture. *Mailing Add:* Michael H Lord Gallery 1090 N Palm Canyon Dr Palm Springs CA 92262

LORELLI, ELVIRA MAE
SCULPTOR, PAINTER
b Upland, Calif. *Study:* Pomona Col, BA, 50; Claremont Grad Sch, Scripps Col, MA (art educ), 61; Claremont Grad Sch & Univ Ctr, MA (art), 69; Otis Art Inst, with Charlie White, Don Kingman, Renzo Femci & Joseph Martinek, 71-75, Pietra Santa, Italy, with Martini Pasqualini, Gigi Guadanuchi, Bigi Rinaldo & Bernice Schachter, 93-95. *Hon Degrees:* MA (art educ), Claremont Grad School, 61; MA (art), Claremont Grad School and Univ Ctr, 69. *Work:* Trona High Sch, Calif; Barstow Centennial Park, Calif; Mojave Valley River Mus, Barstow, Calif; Southwest Trading Post, Lake Arrowhead, Calif; Shoppers Lane Gallery, Convina, Calif; Schiffman Gallery, Hesperia, Calif; Little Red Caboose Originals, Barstow, Calif. *Comn:* Murals, Methodist Church, 84, Barstow, Calif; stained glass window, St Joseph Church, Barstow, 86; bronze reliefs, Rotary Club, Barstow, 90; sculptures, St Philip Neri, 96; sculptures, bronze relief, Montara Sch, Barstow, Calif, 99. *Exhib:* Around the World, Nat Art Appreciation Soc, New Orleans, 84; Chaffee Community Art Show, Ont Mus & Gallery, Calif, 86; Fine Arts Inst Ann Art Show, Mus Art, San Bernardino Co, Calif, 87; Sixth Ann Fine Arts Show, SW Sculptors Asn, Victoriville, Calif, 88; Calico Fine Arts Show, Calico Ghost Town, Calif, 84-97; JD Pelan Exhib, Los Angeles; Neberrys Spring Fine Art Festival; Searles lake Art Show, Trona, Calif; Indios Pilot Club of the Golden Sands int Invitational; Lorains Coffee Shop, Barstow, 2004-2005; Art by the Lake, Big Bear, Calif, 2005-2006; Barstow Chamber of Commerce, Calif, 2006; Idle Spurs Restaurant, Barstow, Calif, 2006; and others. *Pos:* Judge, Ft Irwin Ann Art Show & Barstow Ann Mardi Gras Parade. *Teaching:* Dept head art, art instr & prof, Barstow Community Col, 62-82; pvt painting & sculpture instr, El Mae Studio, Barstow, Calif, 62-97; instr art, Univ Calif, Riverside, 78-87, Chapman Col, 79-84 & Am Vets Home, Barstow, Calif, 96-2006; gate instr, Barstow Middle Sch, 96. *Awards:* Nat Art Appreciation Soc, 84; Artist of the Month, Holiday Inn, 93; Calico Ann Fine Arts Exhib, 96. *Bibliog:* Bill Deselms (auth), Desert Dispatch Feature, 90; Desert Dispatch, 93 & 96. *Mem:* SW Sculptors; Gem Carvers Guild Int; Fine Arts Inst; Chaffee Community Art Asn; Barstow Artists Guild (pres). *Media:* Bronze, Stone, Oils, Watercolor. *Res:* Art with and without music. *Interests:* Photography, bowling, line-dancing, hiking & gardening. *Publ:* Artists USA Inc, 1977-78; Directory of Portrait Artists, Am Portrait Soc, 85; Art at Pomona Galleries of the Claremont Colleges 1887 to 1987

LORENZ, MARIE
ARCHITECT, SCULPTOR
b Twenty-Nine Palms, California, 1973. *Study:* RI Sch Design, Providence, BFA, 1995; Arques Sch Traditional Boatbuilding, Sausalito, Calif, BFA, 1997; Salzburg Int Summer Acad, Public Interventions Seminar, Salzburg, Austria, 2002; Yale Sch Art, MFA, 2002; Skowhegan Sch Painting & Sculpture, Maine, 2002. *Exhib:* Solo exhibs include Icknield Port Loop, Ikon Gallery, Birmingham, England, 2007, Navigation, Artpace, San Antonio, Tex, 2007; group exhibs include Space 1026, Philadelphia, 2001; De Fetal, KR Space, New York, 2003; Video Whoopee Cushion, Harvard Univ, 2004; Emerging Artist Fel Exhib, Socrates Sculpture Park, Queens, New York, 2004; Fearless Vampire Killers, Casey Kaplan, New York, 2005; Action Adventure, Canada Gallery, New York, 2006; Eternal Flame, Red Cat, Los Angeles, 2007; 700 Club, Columbia Univ, LeRoy Neiman Gallery, New York, 2007; Till I Die, Spencer Brownstone Gallery, New York, 2007. *Awards:* Norfolk Prize Sculpture, Grant Public Art New Haven, 2001; Hayward Prize, Am Austrian Found, 2002; Joseph H Hazen Rome Prize, Am Acad Rome, 2008

LORING, JOHN
PAINTER, PRINTMAKER
b Chicago, Ill, Nov 23, 1939. *Study:* Yale Univ, BA, 60; Ecole des Beaux Arts, Paris, 61-64; printmaking with Johnny Friedlaender, Paris, 62-64. *Hon Degrees:* Pratt Inst, Hon DFA. *Work:* Metrop Mus Art, Whitney Mus Am Art, Mus Mod Art, NY; Art Inst Chicago; Boston Mus Fine Arts; Yale Univ Art Gallery. *Comn:* Mural, US Customs Serv, Main Hall, US Customhouse, World Trade Ctr, NY, 74; three posters, NY Cult Ctr, 74; murals, Prudential Life Insurance Co, Eastern Home Off, Woodbridge, NJ, 76; outdoor mural proj, Nat Endowment Arts, Scranton, Pa, 77; murals, Nat Hq, Western Savings, Philadelphia, 79. *Exhib:* Silkscreen: History of a Medium, Philadelphia Mus Art, 71; Realism Now, NY Cult Ctr, 72; Solo exhibs, Baltimore Mus Art, 72 & Long Beach Mus Art, Calif, 75; Biennale of Graphic Art, Ljubljana, Yugoslavia, 73 & 77; Intergrafia 74 & 76, Krakow, Poland; Painting & Sculpture Today, Indianapolis Mus Art, 74; Silkscreen Prints, Chicago Art Inst, 75; Pace Editions, NY, 77. *Pos:* Art ed, Deleg World Bulletin, UN, 72; contribr, Print Collector's Newsletter, 73-75 & Art in Am, 77-; assoc ed & contribr, Arts Mag, 73-; contrib ed, Archit Digest, 76-; design dir & sr vpres, Tiffany & Co, 79-. *Teaching:* Distinguished vis prof art, Univ Calif, Davis, 77. *Awards:* Fourth Prize, Intergrafia 74, Krakow; Edith Wharton Award, Design & Art Soc, New York, 88. *Bibliog:* Ellen Lubell (auth), John Loring, 2/74 & Mario Amaya (auth), John Loring, 2/78, Arts Mag; Robert Hughes (auth), Murals without walls, 6/79. *Mem:* Chelsea Arts Club, London. *Media:* Oil; Photo Silkscreens. *Publ:* A Tiffany Christmas, Doubleday, 97; Tiffany's 20th Century, 98; Tiffany Jewels, 99; Paulding Farnham, 2000; Tiffany's Lost Genius, 2000; Magnificent Silver, 2001; Louis Comfort Tiffany at Tiffany & Co, 2002; Tiffany Flora & Tiffany Fauna, 2003; Tiffany in Fashion, 2003. *Mailing Add:* 350 W 43rd St Apt 38E New York NY 10036-6470

LOSIER, MARIE
FILM DIRECTOR
b Boulogne, France, 1972. *Exhib:* Group shows: Tribecca Film Festival; Int Film Festival; Rotterdam; Seoul Film Festival, Lausagne Film Festival; York Underground Film Festival; Lake Placid Film Festival; Whitney Biennial, Whitney Mus Art, 2006; Chick-chick, 2000; The Touch Retouched, 2001; Loula Meets Charlie, 2002; Marie-Onette, 2002; Broken Blossoms, 2002; The Passion of Joan of Arc, 2002; Sanitarium Cinema, 2002; Mike Kuchar is on My Roof, 2003; Lunch Break on the Xerox Machine, 2003; Bird, Bath & Beyond, 2003; Electrocute Your Stars, 2004; Eat Your Makeup!, 2005; The Ontological Cowboy, 2005; Flying Saucey!, 2006. *Pos:* Film programmer, Fr Inst, Alliance Francaise, NYC, 2000; dir (films), 2000-2006. *Awards:* Grantee Nat Art Studio Club Grant, 1997; NY State Coun Arts, 2004. *Mailing Add:* French Inst 22 E 60th St New York NY 10022

LOTRINGER, SYLVERE
WRITER
b Paris, France, Oct 15, 1938; US citizen. *Study:* Sorbone Ecole Pratique des Hautes Etudes, Paris, BA & MA, 65, PhD 67. *Exhib:* Too Sensitive to Touch, No Wave Cinema, Whitney Mus Am Art, NY, 97. *Collection Arranged:* Artaud, Galerie Optica, Montreal, 93. *Pos:* Sr mellon critic, CAL Arts, Calif, 90-91; vis critic, Art Ctr, Pasadena, 91-99; consult, Mus Mod Art, New York, 96 & Banff Ctr, Alta, Can, 97-98. *Teaching:* Prof French Lit & Philo, Columbia Univ, 72-2009, prof emeritus. *Bibliog:* Under the Sign of Semiotexte, Critique, 94. *Media:* Text, Video. *Publ:* Auth, Photography & Death, Interrupted Life, New Mus Contemp Art, 91; Art & The Commodification of Theory, Flash Art, Milan, 91; auth, Nancy Spero, Phaedon Press, London, 96; Becoming Duchamp, Crossings, Kunsthalle, Wien, Austria, 98; Consumed by Myths, Premises, Guggenheim Mus Soho, N, 98. *Mailing Add:* Columbia University 522 Philosophy Hall New York NY 10027

LOTZ, STEVEN DARRYL
PAINTER, GALLERY DIRECTOR
b Los Angeles, Calif, Dec 28, 1938. *Study:* Univ Calif, Los Angeles, BFA, 61; Univ Fla, Gainesville, with Hiram Williams, MFA, 63; Acad Fine Arts, Vienna, Austria, 65-66. *Work:* Jacksonville Art Mus, Fla; Orlando International Airport; His Royal Highness, Prince Phillip, London; Alachua Pub Libr, Gainesville, Fla; Universal Studios, Orlando. *Comn:* Fla Solar Energy Ctr; Walt Disney World, Fla. *Exhib:* Appalachian State Univ, NC, 90; Stetson Univ, Deland, Fla, 88; Univ of Tampa, Fla, 89; Atlantic Ctr Arts, New Smyrna Beach, Fla, 95; Univ NFla, Jacksonville, 97. *Teaching:* Asst prof drawing & painting, Jacksonville Univ, Fla, 66-68; chmn, Univ Cent Fla, Orlando, 68-78, prof drawing & painting 68-; vis exchange instr, Edinburgh Col Art, 78-79 & 80-81. *Awards:* First Prize, Jacksonville Arts Festival, 65; First Prize, Ocala Arts Festival, Ocala Nat Bank, 69; State Fla Grant. *Bibliog:* Roger Ortmayer (dir), Space Cathedral (film), CBS TV, New York, 72; Frank Martin (auth), article, Art Voices South, 11-12/79; Egberdien Van Rossum (auth), article, Bres 99 Mag, 4/83. *Media:* Oil, Acrylic. *Mailing Add:* 626 Lake Ave Orlando FL 32801-3914

LOU, LIZA
SCULPTOR
b New York, 1969. *Study:* San Francisco Art Inst. *Exhib:* Solo exhibs include Santa Monica Mus Art, 1998, Bass Mus Art, Miami, 1998, 2001, Kemper Mus Contemp Art, Kansas City, 1998, Renwick Gallery, Smithsonian Inst Am Art, Washington, 2000, Deitch Projects, New York, 2002, Galerie Thaddaeus Ropac, Paris, 2004, White Cube, London, 2006, L&M Arts, New York, 2008, Galerie Thaddaeus Ropac, France, 2010; group exhibs include A Labor of Love, New Mus, New York, 1996; Art Through the Eye of the Needle, Henie Onstrad Kunstsenter, Norway, 2001; Give and Take, Victoria & Albert Mus, London, 2001; Un Art Populaire, Fondation Cartier, Paris, 2002; Domestic Odyssey, San Jose Mus Art, Calif, 2004; Splat, Boom, Pow: Cartoons in Contemp Art, traveling, 2004; Translation, Palais de Tokyo, Paris, 2005. *Awards:* MacArthur Found Fel, 2002. *Mailing Add:* c/o Elizabeth Schwartz Deitch Projects 76 Grand St New York NY 10013

LOU, RICHARD A
EDUCATOR, ADMINISTRATOR
Study: Southwestern Col, Chula Vista, Calif, AA, 1981; Calif State Univ, Fullerton, BA, 1983; Clemson Univ, SC, MFA, 1986. *Exhib:* Exhibitions include Berkeley Arts Ctr Juried Exhibition, 1986, Number 95, performance, Seaport Village, San Diego, Calif, 1988, Who I Am Not, Irvine Fine Arts Ctr, 1990, Unearthing the Future, Centro Cultural De La Raza, San Diego, 1996, Picante: Latino Influence on American Culture, Athens Inst for Contemporary Art, Ga, 2004, Gas, Food, and Lodging, Dalton Gallery, Agnes Scott Col, Ga, 2005, Fiber Arts Biennial, Dong-A Univ, South Korea, 2006, EYEDRUM Gallery, Atlanta, Ga, 2007 and many others. *Pos:* Co-founder, mem Save Our Centro Coalition, San Diego, Calif, 1999-. *Teaching:* Photography instructor, Southwestern Col, Chula Vista, Calif, 1988-89; art instructor, Donovan Correctional Facility, Otay Mesa, Calif, 1990; photography instructor, Grossmont Col, Le Mesa, Calif, 1989-90; Prof Art, San Diego Mesa Col, 1990-2001, chair art dept, 1993-96, prof and chair dept art drama, 1998-2001; vis prof (sabbatical from Mesa Col), Clemsen Univ, 1997; prof, chair dept art, Georgia Col & State Univ, Milledgeville, Ga, 2001-07; prof, chair dept art, Univ Memphis, 2007-. *Mailing Add:* University of Memphis Department of Art Art & Communications Bldg 211 Memphis TN 38152-3088

LOVEJOY, MARGOT R
MEDIA ARTIST, AUTHOR, EDUCATOR
b Campbellton, NB, Can, Oct 21, 1930. *Study:* Mt Allison Univ, with Alex Colville & Lauren Harris, 47-49; Univ Academie Julian, Paris, 49; St Martins Sch Art, London, cert (design & illus), 50; Pratt Graphics Ctr, New York, with Ponce de Leon, Stasik & Zimilies, 66-71. *Work:* Getty Inst; Bibliotheque Nat, Paris; Dresden Mus, Ger; Hunterian Mus, Glasgow; Mus Mod Art New York. *Exhib:* Solo exhibs PS1 Mus, Inst Contemp Art, 87, Labyrinth, East End Arts, Philadelphia, 88, Alternative Mus, 90, Islip Art Mus, NY, 92, 99, Arronson Gallery, Philadelphia, 93 & Queens Mus Art, 95; Committed to Print, Mus Mod Art, NY, 88; Philadelphia Print Club Invitational, Pa, 89; At the Intersection of Cinema & the Book, Granary Books Gallery, NY, 92; Mostra da Gravura Mostra Am, Curitiba, Brazil, 92; Contacts/Proofs, Jersey City Mus, 93; Academic Spirit, NY State Mus, Albany, 93; La Disparition de L'Alphabet (with catalog), Galerie Toner, Paris, 94; Site Readings, Granary Books Gallery, NY, 94; Gallery, NY, 94; TURNS Project Inst Contemp Art, Taiwan, 2001; Whitney Biennial, 2002; Queens Mus, NY, 2002; ZKM, Germany, 2003; Madrid Media Lab, Spain, 2003; Laboral Center, 2009; CONFESS Project, Neuberger Mus, 2009; Stephan Stoyanov Gallery, NY, 2011. *Teaching:* Instr, Pratt Graphics Ctr, New York, 72-79 & Parsons Sch Design, New York, 75-78; prof visual arts, State Univ NY, Purchase, 78-2007, emer 2007. *Awards:* NY State Coun Arts Individual Artist Support Grant, 86; John Simon Guggenheim Fel, 87; Arts Int Grant, Queens Mus, 95; Distinguished Teaching of Art Awad, Coll Art Asn, 2007; NYSCA Grants; Gregory Millard Fellowship, NYFA. *Bibliog:* Artists of conscience, Art News, 4/92; Nancy Princenthal (auth), Cinematic books, Artist's Book Beat, Print Collector's Newslett, Vol XXV, No 4, 9-10/94; Christine J Russo (auth), Afterimage, 10/94. *Mem:* Coll Art Asn. *Media:* Projection Installation; Mixed Media. *Publ:* Auth, Postmodern Currents: Art & Artist in the Age of Electronic Media, UMI Press, 89 & Prentice Hall, 92 & 97; Labyrinth, 91, The Book of Plagues & Paradoxic Mutations; Manifestations, Galerie Toner, Paris; Multiple Worlds: An Int Survey of Artists' Books (exhib catalog), Atlanta Coll Art Gallery, Ga, 1-3/94; Art and the Computer, Encyclopedia of Computer Science, 4th ed, Ralston Reilly, London, 2000; auth, Digital Currents: Art in the Electronic Age, Routledge, 2004; ed, Context Providers: Conditions of Meaning in Media Arts, 2011. *Mailing Add:* 166-04 81st Ave Jamaica NY 11432-1204

LOVELL, MARGARETTA MARKLE
HISTORIAN, CURATOR
b Pittsburgh, Pa, 1944. *Study:* Smith Coll, BA, 66; Univ Del, MA, 75; Yale Univ, PhD, 80. *Collection Arranged:* Am Painting, 1730-1960: A Selection from the Collection of Mr & Mrs John D Rockefeller, 3rd, Nat Mus Western Art, Tokyo, 82; William Morris: The Sanford and Helen Berger Collection, Univ Mus, Univ Calif, Berkeley, 84; Venice: The Am View, 1860-1920, Fine Arts Mus San Francisco & Cleveland Mus, 84-85; Celebrating William Morris, Huntington Libr & Art Galleries, Pasadena, Calif, 96-97. *Pos:* Cur asst, Yale Univ Art Gallery, 72-75; cur Am Art, Fine Arts Mus San Francisco, 81-85; guest cur, Berkeley Art Mus, 84; guest cur, Huntington Libr Art Galleries, 96-97. *Teaching:* Acting instr, hist art, Yale Univ, 77-80, asst prof 80-81; asst prof, Univ Calif, Berkeley, 81-85, asst prof hist art, 85-90, assoc prof hist art, 92-2003, prof hist art, 2003- & Jay D McEvoy prof Am art, 2007-; vis assoc prof, Univ Mich, fall 89; Duane A & Virginia S Dittman prof Am studies, Coll William & Mary, 90-92; vis assoc prof art & archit, Harvard Univ, fall 98; Distinguished vis prof art & art hist, Stanford Univ, fall 2001. *Awards:* Ralph Henry Gabriel Prize, Am Studies Asn, 81; Nat Endowment Humanities Res Fel, 89-90; Huntington Libr, R Stanton Avery Disting Fel, 94-95; Charles Eldredge Prize, Smithsonian Am Art Mus, 2006; Guggenheim Fel, 2007-. *Publ:* A Visitable Past: Views of Venice by American Artists 1860-1915, Univ Chicago Press, 89; Food photography and inverted narratives of desire, Exposure v 34: 1/2 summer 2001; Art in a Season of Revolution: The Artist, the Artisan, and the Patron in Early America, Univ Pa Press, 2005. *Mailing Add:* Dept Hist Art - 416 Doe Libr No 6020 Berkeley CA 94720-6020

LOVELL, WHITFIELD M
PAINTER
b New York, NY, 1959. *Study:* Cooper Union Sch Art, New York, BFA, 1981. *Work:* Metrop Mus Art, NY; Libr Congress, Div Prints & Photographs, Washington, DC; New Sch Soc Res, NY; Ark Arts Ctr Found, Little Rock; Bronx Mus, NY; Nat Mus Am Art, Washington; Seattle Art Mus; Montclair (NJ) Art Mus. *Exhib:* Solo exhibs, Harlem Sch Arts, NY, 1987, Jersey City Mus, NJ, 1988, Lehman Coll Art Gallery, NY, 1993, SE Ctr Contemp Art, Winston-Salem, NC, 1997, DC Moore Gallery, NY, 1997, Andy Warhol Mus, Pittsburgh, Pa, 1998, Univ N Tex Art Gallery, Denton, 1999, Neuberger Mus, NY, 2000, DC Moore Gallery, NY, 2000, 2002, 2006 Studio Mus in Harlem, NY, Rutgers Univ, NJ, 2001, Tubman Mus, Ga, 2001, Knoxville Mus Art, 2001, Zora Neale Hurston Nat Mus Fine Arts, Eatonville, Fla, 2003, John Michael Kohler Arts Ctr, Sheboygan, Wis, 2005; The Family, Goddard Riverside Ctr, NY, 1992, The Animal Show, 1994; Ctr Fine Arts, Miami, Fla, 1992; Allen Mem Art Mus, Oberlin, Ohio, 1992; Portraits/Retratos, Intar Gallery, NY, 1993; Duke Univ Mus Art, Durham, NC, 1993; Current Identities: Recent Painting in the US, traveling, Cuenca Bienal, Equador, 1993-96; Page 9: Artists Books Show, 450 Broadway Gallery, NY, 1994; Trees, Midtown Payson Galleries, NY, 1994; Identity Crisis, Puffin Found, NY, 1994; Empowerment: The Art of African Americans, Krasdale Gallery, White Plains, NY, 1994; Consecrations; The Spiritual in the Time of AIDS, Mus Contemp Relig Art, St Louis, Mo, 1994; Resisting Categories, City Without Walls, Newark, NJ, 1995; Murder, Wolfson Gallery, Miami Dade Col, Fla, Thread Waxing Space, NY, & Bergamot Station Arts Ctr, Santa Monica, Calif, 1995; It's How You Play the Game, Exit Art/First World, NY, 1995; African-Am Works from the Permanent Collection, Ark Arts Ctr, Little Rock, 1995, Nat Drawing Show, 1996, About Face, 2001; Inaugural Exhib, DC Moore Gallery, NY, 1995, Starting with Flowers, 1996, Food For Thought: A visual Banquet, 1998, Self-Made Men, 2001, The Way They See It, 2003, Everyday Mysteries, 2004; Dia de los Muertos, Lawndale Art Ctr, Houston, Tex, 1996; Round 3 Installations, Proj Row Houses, Houston, Tex, 1996; This is Why We Sing, Atrium Gallery, Morristown, NJ, 1997; Real: Figurative Narratives in Contemp African Am Art, Bass Mus Art, Miami Beach, Fla, 1997; Havana Biennal, Cuba, 1997; An Assessment of Contemp Figuration, David Klein Gallery, Birmingham, Mich, 1997; Major African-Am Artwork Exhib, Craven Gallery, W Tisbury, Mass, 1998; Urban Mythologies: The Bronx Represented Since the 1960s, Bronx Mus Arts, NY, 1999, Recent Acquisitions, 2001, Collection Remixed, 2005; Soho 20, NY; Yale Univ Art Gallery, 2000; A Shriek from an Invisible Box, Meguro Mus, Tokyo, 2001; The Culture of Violence, Samuel Harn Mus Art, Gainesville, Fla, 2003; Modern Storytellers, Met Mus Art, NY, 2003; Invitational Exhib Painting & Sculpture, Am Acad Arts & Lett, NY, 2004; African Am Masters, travelling, 2003-05; A History of Color, Greenville County Mus Art, SC, 2004-05; Africa in Am, Seattle Art Mus, 2005; Legacies, NY Hist Soc, 2006. *Awards:* Mid-Atlantic Nat Endowment Arts Regional Fel, 92; Andy Warhol Mus Residency, 98; Artist-in-Residence, Univ N Tex, Denton, 99; named a MacArthur Fellow, John D and Catherine T MacArthur Found, 2007; Nancy Graves Found Grant, 2009. *Bibliog:* Sallie Gaines (auth), Rundown row houses as art, San Francisco Examiner, 4/28/96; Joel Weinstein (auth.) Sculpture, 2001; Eduardo Costa (auth), Report from Havana: the installation biennial, Art Am, 3/98; Cynthia Nadelman (auth.) Art News, 2000; Princenthal, Nancy (auth.) A World in One Room, Art in America, 2001. *Mem:* Nat Acad. *Publ:* Auth, The Bronx Celebrates Whitfield Lovell (exhib catalog), Lehman Coll Art Gallery, New York, 93. *Dealer:* DC Moore Gallery 724 5th Ave New York NY 10019. *Mailing Add:* 405 E 13th St Apt 3 New York NY 10009

LOVING, CHARLES R
MUSEUM DIRECTOR, CURATOR
b Waukesha, Wis, Jun 2, 1957. *Study:* Univ Wis, BFA, 1980; Univ Utah, MFA, 1982; Univ Utah, MA, 1985. *Pos:* Asst coordr, Utah Arts Coun, Salt Lake City, 1982-84; asst dir, Utah Mus of Fine Arts, 1984-; juror, Park City Arts Festival, Utah, 1985-90; grants reviewer, Inst Mus Serv's, Wash, 1988-89; dir, cur, Snite Mus Art, Univ Notre Dame, modern sculpture, 1999-. *Mem:* Am Asn Mus (state rep, currently); Utah Fundraising Soc; Asn Art Mus Dirs. *Mailing Add:* U Notre Dame Snite Mus Art PO Box 368 Notre Dame IN 46556

LOVING, RICHARD MARIS
PAINTER, PRINTMAKER
b Vienna, Austria, 1924. *Study:* Fieldston Sch, Riverdale, NY, 39-42; Bard Col, Annandale, NY, 43-44; New Sch Soc Res, 46. *Work:* Art Inst Chicago; Joslyn Art Mus, Omaha, Nebr; First Nat Bank Chicago; Kemper Art Collection, Chicago; Mus Contemp Art, Chicago; Block Mus, Evanston, Ill; Smart Mus, Univ Chicago, Ill. *Comn:* Enamel triptych, Concordia Col, River Forest, Ill, 67; enamel & stainless wire, Graver Water Conditioning, Union, NJ, 68; vitreous enamel mural, Union Tank Car Corp, Chicago, 70. *Exhib:* Collector's Choice Exhib, Joslyn Art Mus, Omaha, Nebr, 68; Contemp Art in Midwest, Univ Notre Dame, 69; Karlsruhe-Chicago, Karlsruhe, WGer, 79; Chicago; Some Other Traditions, 83-85; Traveling Exhib, Abstract-Symbol-Image, Ill Arts Coun; Lerner Heller Gallery, NY, 82; Printworks Gallery, Chicago, Ill, 2003; Nat Acad Mus, NY, 2006; Evanston Art Ctr and The Art Ctr Highland Park, Ill, 2007; Brauer Mus, Ind. *Pos:* Founding ed, Chicago-Art-Write. *Teaching:* Prof painting & drawing, Sch Art Inst Chicago, 63-; Prof emer, Sch Art Inst, Chicago. *Awards:* Nat Endowment Arts Fel. *Media:* Oil on Canvas or Wood Panel, Vitreous enamel paintings, Drawing. *Dealer:* Print Works Gallery Chicago

LOWE, HARRY
ADMINISTRATOR, DESIGNER
b Opelika, Ala, Apr 9, 1922. *Study:* Auburn Univ, BA, 43, MFA, 49; Cranbrook Acad Art, 51 & 53. *Collection Arranged:* Stuart Davis Memorial, Smithsonian Am Art Mus, Washington, DC, Art Inst Chicago, Univ Calif Art Galleries, Los Angeles & Whitney Mus Am Art, NY, 65, The Charles Sheeler Exhibition, Philadelphia Mus Art & Whitney Mus Am Art, 69; Deputy Commissioner, US Exhib, Venice Biennale, 66. *Pos:* Dir, Tenn Fine Arts Ctr, Nashville, 59-64; cur, Dept Exhib & Design, Smithsonian Am Art Mus, 64-72, asst dir opers, 72-74, asst dir, 74-81, acting dir, 81-82, deputy dir, 82-84, deputy dir emer, 84; Smithsonian Am Art Mus, 2007-. *Teaching:* Prof art, Auburn Univ, 49-59; fac, Sem for Hist Adminrs, Williamsburg, Va, 65, 67-71. *Mailing Add:* 802 A St SE Washington DC 20003

LOWE, J MICHAEL
SCULPTOR, EDUCATOR
b Cincinnati, Ohio. *Study:* Ohio Univ, BFA; Cornell Univ, MFA. *Work:* Butler Inst Am Art, Ohio; State Univ NY Coll, Potsdam; St Lawrence Univ, NY; Tyler Mus, Tex; Del Mar Coll, Tex. *Comn:* St Lawrence Univ, 85. *Exhib:* San Diego Art Inst, Calif, 87 & 90; San Bernardino Co Mus, Calif, 89; NE Mo State Univ, 96 & 98; Lafayette Art Asn, La, 98; NW Art Ctr, NDak, 98; Art Forms Gallery, Manyunk, Pa, 99; Ann Drawing & Small Sculpture Show, Del Mar Coll, Corpus Christi, Tex, 2000 & 2004-2006; Schweinfurth Mem Art Ctr, Auburn, NY, 2001-2002, 2013; The Studio, Middleburg, Va, 2004; Visual Arts Soc, Tex, 2006; N Am Sculpture Exhib, Golden, Colo, 2006; Cooperstown Art Asn, 2007, 2009, 2013; Lakeside-Statewide exhib, Oswego, NY, 2009; Palace Theatre Gallery, Corning, NY, 2009; State of the Art Gallery, Ithaca, NY, 2007, 2011; The Spotlight Gallery, Corning, New York, 2010, 2012, 2013; Wells Coll, Aurora, NY, 2010; Seneca Co Arts Coun, Seneca Falls, NY, 2010; Fredrick Remington Art Mus, Ogdensburg, NY, 2010; The Arts Council of the Southern Finger Lakes, Corning, NY, 2011, 2012, 2013; CSMA Ann Open Show, 2011; Valdosta State Univ, Valdosta, Ga, 2012; Handwerker Gallery, Ithaca Coll, Ithaca, NY. *Teaching:* Instr fine arts, St Lawrence Univ, 66-67, asst prof, 67-72, chmn dept, 71-87, assoc prof, 72-78, prof, 78-, GL Flint prof, 97-2004; prof emer, GL Flint, 2004. *Awards:* Purchase Awards, Tyler Mus Art, 70, Butler Inst Am Art, 72, Clinton Co Govt Bldg, 76 & Sculpture, Del Mar Col, 2005; Second Award Sculpture, Cooperstown Art Asn, 91; Heymann Assoc Award, Lafayette Art Asn, 98; MacFadden-Dier Award, No Country Regional Exhib, NY, 2001; Cooperstown Art Asn, 2007. *Bibliog:* Dictionary of American Sculptors: 18th Century to the Present, Apollo Press. *Mem:* Int Sculpture Ctr. *Media:* Welded Metal. *Mailing Add:* 315 Blackstone Ave Ithaca NY 14850

LOWE, JOE HING
PAINTER
b Guangdong, China, July 13, 1933. *Study:* with Bill Lawrence - 1957; with Lajos Markos - 1960; with Daniel Greene - 1962. *Work:* Univ Texas at Dallas, Tex; Union Co College, Cranford, NJ; US Navy Combat Artist Gallery, Washington, DC; Guangdong Mus of Art, Guangzhou, China; The Institute Mus of Chicago, Ill. *Comn:* Charles Rosendahl (portrait), comn by Vice Adm Charles Rosendahl, Lakehurst, NJ; Arleigh Burke (portrait), comn by Adm Arleigh Burke, Washington, DC, 1969; Hon Mark A Constantino (portrait), comn by Hon Mark A Constantino, Brooklyn, NY, 1975; George Barrowclough, comn by Dr & Mrs. Keith Brodie, Durham, NC, 2004; Dr. Robert Goldman (portrait), comn by Dr. Robert Goldman, Chicago, Ill, 2006. *Exhib:* Joe Hing Lowe Nostalgic Sentiments, Guangdong Mus of Art Guangzhou, China, 2002; Allied Artists of Am, Museum of Texas Tech Univ, Lubbock, Tex, 2003; Allied Artists of Am, Huntsville Mus of Art, Huntsville, Ala, 2004; Allied Artists of Am, Bergstrom-Mahler Mus, Neenah, Wis, 2004; Allied Artists of Am, Danville Mus of Fine Art, Danville, Va, 2004. *Teaching:* instr oil & pastels, portrait/figure, Ridgewood Art Inst, Ridgewood, NJ, 1980-. *Awards:* Exceptional Merit, Pastel Soc of Am, Kalikow Award, 1989; Award for Excellence, Allied Artists of Am, Dianne B. Bernhard, 2001; Award for Excellence, Hudson Valley Art Asn, Dianne B. Barnhard, 2002; Portrait Award, Pastel Soc of Am, 2004. *Bibliog:* Kristina Feliciano (auth), The Best of Pastel 2, Quarry-Rockport Publishers Inc, 1998. *Media:* Charcoal, Oil, Pastel Painting, Watercolor. *Publ:* auth, How to Paint Portrait in Pastel, Watson Guptill, 1972 & 1976. *Mailing Add:* 36 Greaves Pl Cranford NJ 07016

LOWE, SARAH
CURATOR, WRITER
b Buffalo, NY, 1956. *Study:* Vassar Col, Poughkeepsie, NY, BA, 80; Grad Sch & Univ Ctr, City Univ New York, MPhil (dissertation fel), 89 & PhD, 96 & studied hist with Linda Nochlin, 96. *Collection Arranged:* Consuelo Kanaga: An Am Photographer (catalog), Brooklyn Mus, 93; Social Studies/Public Monuments, Ctr Photog Woodstock, NY, 93; Tina Modotti: Photographs (catalog), Philadelphia Mus Art, 95; Tina Modotti and Edward Weston: The Mexico Experience, Barbican Galleries, London, England, 2003. *Pos:* Mem bd dir, Lower E Side Printshop, NY, 95-97; co-chmn, Coll Art Asn Panel, Exile, Expatriation, and Relocation: Artists and Writers in Mexico, 1910-1950, Los Angeles, 99. *Teaching:* Adj asst prof, Hunter Col, City Univ, NY; BA & MA adv, Gallatin Sch, NY Univ. *Awards:* Dept Fel (PhD prog art hist), Grad Sch & Univ Ctr, City Univ NY, 84 & 85; Eliza Buffington Fel Grad Res, Vassar Col, Poughkeepsie, NY, 87; Kristie A Jayne Fel (PhD prog art hist), Grad Sch, City Univ NY, 92. *Mem:* Art Table Inc; Coll Art Asn; Latin Am Art Asn; Women Writing Women's Lives. *Res:* European, American and Latin American art of the 19th and 20th centuries; history of photography; printmaking and works on paper; feminist theory and criticism; contemporary art; Italian Renaissance art. *Publ:* Auth, The House that Jack Built: The Politics of Domesticity (exhib catalog), Foreman Gallery, Hartwick Col, Oneonta, NY, 87; Frida Kahlo, Universe Books, NY, 91; Fixing form: The still lifes of Tina Modotti, Hist Photog, Vol 10, No 3, fall 94; guest ed, Hist Photog, 9/94; contribr, The Diary of Frida Kahlo, Harry N Abrams, New York, 95; Itinera, IIR Gallery, New York, 12/2002; Edward Weston: Life Work, Lodima Press, 2003. *Mailing Add:* 497 Pacific St No 4A Brooklyn NY 11217

LOWENTHAL, CONSTANCE
HISTORIAN, CONSULTANT
b New York, NY, Aug 29, 1945. *Study:* Brandeis Univ, BA, 67; Inst Fine Arts, NY Univ, AM, 69, PhD, 76. *Pos:* Asst mus educator, Metrop Mus Art, NY, 78-85; exec dir, Int Found Art Res, NY, 85-98; bd dir, Int Art & Antiques Loss Register, Ltd, 91-94, Ctr Educ Studies, 91-; writer, Art Crime Update, Wall Street J, 88-97; dir, Comn Art Recovery, World Jewish Cong, 98-2001; pres, Constance Lowenthal, Inc, consult art provenance issues & ownership disputes, New York, 2000-. *Teaching:* Fac mem art hist, Sarah Lawrence Coll, Bronxville, 75-78. *Publ:* Auth, Lorenzo Ghiberti, Encycl Britannica 3, 74; Conrat Meit's Judith and a Putto at Brou, Marsyas, 74; Rev of Limewood Sculptors of Renaissance Germany, M Baxandall (auth), Renaissance Quart, 83; Recovering Looted Jewish Cultural Property, Resolution of Cultural Property Disputes, The Permanent Court of Arbitration, Peace Palace Papers, 2004; The Good Carver Conrad, Apollo Mag, 2007

LOWMAN, NATE
CONCEPTUAL ARTIST
b Las Vegas, 1979. *Study:* NY Univ, BS, 2001. *Exhib:* Solo exhibs include Maccarone Inc, New York, 2005, Midway Contemp Art Ctr, Minneapolis, 2006; group exhibs include Summer Program, Apex Art, New York, 2003; A Matter of Facts, Nicole Klagsbrun Gallery, New York, 2003; Drunk vs Stoned, Gavin Brown's Enterprise, New York, 2004; I Love Music, Creative Growth, Oakland, Calif, 2004; Bridge Freezes Before Road, Gladstone Gallery, New York, 2005; Greater New York, PS1 Contemp Art Ctr, New York, 2005; Uncertain States of America, Astrup Fearnley Mus Mod Kunst, Oslo, 2005; Slow Burn, Galerie Edward Mitterand, Geneva, 2006; Whitney Biennial, Whitney Mus Am Art, New York, 2006; Unmonumental: The Object in the 21st Century, New Mus Contemp Art, New York, 2007. *Dealer:* Galerie Edward Mitterand 52 rue des Bains 1205 Geneva Switzerland. *Mailing Add:* c/o Maccarone 630 Greenwich St New York NY 10014

LOWRY, GLENN D
MUSEUM DIRECTOR
b New York, NY, Sept 28, 1954. *Study:* Williams Coll, BA (magna cum laude), 76; Harvard Univ, MA, 78, PhD (For Lang Area Studies Fel, 78-79, travel grants, 80-81), 82. *Hon Degrees:* PhD Fine Arts, Pennsylvania Academy of Fine Arts, 2000. *Collection Arranged:* From Concept to Context: Approaches to Asian & Islamic Calligraphy (coauth, catalog), Freer Gallery Art, Smithsonian Inst, 86; A Jeweler's Eye: Islamic Arts of the Book from the Vever Collection (coauth, catalog), Arthur M Sackler Gallery, Smithsonian Inst, 88; Timur & Princely Vision: Persian Art & Culture in the Fifteenth Century (coauth, catalog), Arthur M Sackler Gallery, Smithsonian Inst & Los Angeles Co Mus Art, Calif, 89; Variations on a Script: Islamic Calligraphy from the Vever Collection, Arthur M Sackler Gallery, Smithsonian Inst, 90. *Pos:* Res asst, Clark Inst, 1976, Archeol Survey, Amalfi, Italy, 1980; researcher, Islamic Collection, McGill Univ, 1976-77; asst cur, Islamic Art, Fogg Art Mus, Cambridge, Mass, 1978-80; cur, Oriental Art, Mus Art, RI Sch Design, 1981-82; dir, Joseph & Margaret Muscarelle Mus Art, 1982-84; cur, Near Eastern Art & coordr, Curatorial Dept, Arthur M Sackler Gallery & Freer Gallery Art, Smithsonian Inst, 1984-90; dir, Art Gallery of Ontario, Toronto, 1990-95; dir, Mus Mod Art, New York, 1995-. *Teaching:* Instr, Wellesley Coll, 1981; Andrew S Keck vis prof, Am Univ, 1990. *Awards:* Naumburg Book Award, Williams Col, 1975, Karl E Weston Prize for Distinction in the Arts, 1976; Spec Exhib Fund Award for Timur & Princely Vision, Smithsonian Inst, 1987, Scholarly Studies Award, 1990; Chevalier de l'ordre de Merite Arts and Letters, Fr Govt, 1994; Named one of Contemporary Art's 100 Most Powerful Figures, ArtReview mag, 2009. *Mem:* Asn Art Mus Dirs; Can Asn Mus Dirs; Coll Art Asn; Am Acad Arts & Sci. *Publ:* Auth, The house of Timur, Asian Art, Vol 2, No 2, 1989; Humayun's tomb: Form, function and meaning in early Mughdal architecture, Muqarnas, Vol 4, 1987; Fatehpur-Sikri-urban structures and forms, In: Proceedings to the International Symposium on Fatehpur-Sikri, Marg Publ, 1987; Art of the Ancient Near East In: Asian Art in the Arthur M Sackler Gallery, 1987; Iskandar Mirza and Early Timurid metalware, Orientations, 9/86. *Mailing Add:* Mus Mod Art 11 W 53rd St New York NY 10019-5498

LOY, JOHN SHERIDAN
PAINTER
b St Louis, Mo, Nov 4, 1930. *Study:* Colorado Springs Fine Art Ctr, Colo; Wash Univ Sch Fine Arts, BFA, 54; Cranbrook Acad Art, Bloomfield Hills, Mich, MFA, 58. *Work:* Munson-Williams-Proctor Inst, Utica, NY; Utica Col, NY; Lincoln-Rochester Bank Collection, Rochester, NY; Hayes Nat Bank, Clinton, NY; Savings Bank Utica. *Exhib:* solo exhib, Kirkland Art Ctr, Clinton, NY, 92, Bonsack Gallery, St Louis, 98 &Gallery 15, Rochester, NY, 02; Cooperstown Art Asn Ann, NY, 95; Albany Inst Hist & Art Regional, NY, 96; Cazenovia Col, Cazenovia, NY, 97; Retrospective exhib, Kirkland Art Ctr, Clinton, 2005, Part 2, Kirkland Art Ctr, Clinton, 2011; Albany Inst Hist and Art Regional, NY, 2008. *Pos:* Prog dir, Peoples Art Ctr, St Louis, 59; gallery dir, Munson-Williams-Proctor Inst Sch Art, Utica, NY, 78-86. *Teaching:* Instr drawing, Wash Univ, 59; instr drawing & painting, Munson-Williams-Proctor Inst, 60-91; instr drawing, Hamilton Col, 92. *Awards:* First Painting Prize, Cooperstown Art Asn, 71, 74, 76 & 77; Grand Prize, Cooperstown Art Asn, 83; Residency, Cite Int des Arts, Paris, 91. *Media:* Oil. *Mailing Add:* 13 Fountain St Clinton NY 13323

LOZOYA, AGUSTIN PORTILLO
PAINTER
b Mexico City, Mex, Nov 29, 1960. *Work:* Mus Raly, Montevideo, Uruguay; Mus de Arte Contemporaneo de Monterrey, Nuevo Leon; Mus de Chopo, Galeria Arvil & Oscar Roman, DF, Mex. *Exhib:* Clasisismo en Mexico, Centro Cult Arte Cont, Mexico City, 90; Recauderias e Inhumanidades, Mus del Chopo, Mexico City, 90; 100 Pintores Mexicanos (with catalog), Mus de Arte Contemporaneo de Monterrey, NL Monterrey, 93; Autorretrato Anos 90, Mus de Arte Moderno, Mexico City, 96; The Richness of Diversity, Susquehanna Art Mus, Pa, 97. *Awards:* Fund for Artist Colonies, Mid Am Arts Alliance, 88; Intercambio de Residencias, Fonca, Mex, Nat Endowment Arts & Can Coun, 94. *Bibliog:* Luis Carlos Eherich (auth), Figuraciones y Desfiguros, Ed Diana, 89; various auths, Nueva Plastica Mexicana, Attame Ed, 97. *Mailing Add:* 3a De Guayaquil No 40 Frac Las Americas Naucalpan 53040 Mexico

LUBAR, KATHERINE
PAINTER
Wash, DC, Aug, 29, 1969. *Study:* Meadows Sch Fine Arts, SMU, Dallas, Tex, BA, 1993; City & Guilds of London Art Sch, London, UK, postgrad diploma, 1999. *Work:* Mus of MADI and Geometric Art, Dallas, Tex; Dept of Educ and Employment (of the UK). *Exhib:* American MADI Artists, Mus of MADI and Geometric Art, Dallas, Tex, 2004; Celebration of Geometric Art, Salon Borbonico de San Nicola la Strada, Naples, touring to Mus of MADI and Geometric Art, Nples, Italy, Dallas, Tex, 2004-05; Summer Exhib, Royal Acad, London, UK, 2006; Dorian Gray, Vegas Gallery, London, UK, 2007; Vivid Identities: Works by Wayne Mok and Katherine Lubar, Victory Gallery, Portland, 2012; Discerning Eye, Mall Galleries, London, UK, 2014; Pop Living, Schwartz Gallery, London, UK, 2015; Griffin Gallery Open, Griffin Gallery, London, UK, 2015. *Collection Arranged:* Happy Days, John Jones Project Space, London, 2007; Polarities, RR Gallery, St Peter's Church, London, 2014. *Awards:* Special Reserve, About Vision Competition, Gallery London, 2002; shortlisted, Celeste Art Prize, 2007; shorltisted, Liquitex Painting Prize, Griffin Gallery, London, 2014. *Bibliog:* Susan Nickalls (auth), No Cell Out in Virtual Prisons of the Mind, Edinburgh Evening News, 2000; Agnieszka Mlicka (auth), The Intangible Made Physical, Cherwell, 2006. *Mem:* The Colour Group of Great Brit. *Media:* Mixed Media. *Mailing Add:* Studio 9 Acme Studios Vigers Ct Plough Close 733 Harrow Rd London United Kingdom NW10 5BQ

LUBELL, ELLEN
CRITIC, WRITER
b Brooklyn, NY, Apr 7, 1950. *Study:* StonyBrook Univ, with Lawrence Alloway, BA, 71. *Collection Arranged:* Cur, Private gone Public, SOHO20 Gallery, NY, 85. *Pos:* Contrib ed, Arts Mag, 72-79; dir, Landmark Gallery, NY, 73-75; ed/publ, Womanart Mag, Brooklyn, 76-78; art critic, Soho Weekly News, NY, 77-79; free lance contribr, Art Am, 81-84; art writer, ed, publicist, Village Voice, NY, 84-91; free lance contribr, Newsday, 88-91; dir communs, Inform, NY, 91-95, Child Care Action Campaign, NY, 95-99; free lance contribr, Newark Star-Ledger, 96-97; dir of Pub relations, The Children's Aid Soc, 1999-2011; freelance writer, ed, publicist, 2011-. *Teaching:* Instr art criticism & art journalism, Sch Visual Arts, NY, 79-80. *Awards:* Art Critics Fel, Nat Endowment Arts, 78. *Bibliog:* Corinne Robins (auth), The women's art magazines, Art Criticism, Vol 1, No 2, 79; Cynthia Nadelman (auth), Women artists: Self-images, Art News, 82; Grace Glueck (auth), Private gone public, NY Times,

6/28/85; The Power of Feminist Art 94, Harry N. Abrams, NY; Ed by N Bronde and M D Gaward. *Mem:* Editorial Freelancers Asn. *Res:* To explore the relationship between fine arts and popular culture and the meaning of this differentiation in contemporary society. *Interests:* The endurance of creativity. *Publ:* Auth, Whatever happened to the women's artist movement, Womanart Mag, 77; Can museums collect contemporary sculpture? Soho Weekly News, 79; Park Slope: An Overview (catalog), Brooklyn Mus, 80; The corporate collector, 84 & Dia Foundation shaken, 85, Village Voice; Politics before culture in the Bronx, 87, Village Voice; Corporations and art: they mean business, 90, Variety; A new gallery scene grows in Chelsea, 97, The Star Ledger; ed, Mike Cockrill: The Awakening (essay in book), 2011; ed, Double Crescent, Campaign, Prospect 2, Irfan Onurmen (exhib catalogues), 2011; Fondation Beyeler (essay), Sculpture Review, 2012; Light of Liberty (essay), Sculpture Review, Summer, 2012; Making the Connection (essay), Sculpture Review, Winter, 2012; What Drives Attacks on Sculpture (essay), Sculpture Review, Spring, 2013

LUBER, KATHERINE
MUSEUM DIRECTOR
Study: Yale Univ, BA; Univ Tex, MA; Bryn Mawr Coll, PhD (art history); Johns Hopkins Univ, MBA, 2005. *Pos:* John G Johnson curator, Dept European Paintings, Phila Mus Art, 1993-2002; founder, Seasoned Palate, 2005; Kelso dir, San Antonio Mus Art, 2011-. *Awards:* Fullbright Scholar in residence, Kunsthistorisches Mus, Vienna. *Mailing Add:* San Antonio Museum of Art 200 W Jones Ave San Antonio TX 78215

LUCAS, BONNIE LYNN
PAINTER, INSTRUCTOR
b Syracuse, NY, Sept 20, 1950. *Study:* Wellesley Col, BA, 72; Rutgers Univ, MFA, 79. *Work:* Zimmerli Art Mus, Rutgers Univ; New York Pub Libr Print Collection. *Comn:* Temple Soc Concord (synagogue), Syracuse, NY, 88; Commissioned Assemblage (To Life). *Exhib:* Solo exhibs, Leverett House, Harvard Univ, 76, Kathryn Markel Gallery, NY, 79 & Avenue B Gallery, NY, 85, 86 & 87, Souyun Yi Gallery, NY, 91 & Edith Blum Gallery, Coll of the Atlantic, Bar Harbor, Maine, 94; People 81, Hudson River Mus, Yonkers, NY, 81; Basic Needs, Islip Mus, East Islip, NY, 85; The Doll Show: Artist's Dolls & Figurines, Hillwood Art Gallery, CW Post, Long Island Univ, 85; Tangents: Art in Fiber, Md Inst, Coll Art, Baltimore, MD, 87; Frontiers in Fiber: The Americans, NDak Mus Art, 88; Alice and Look who else, Through the looking Glass, Bernice Steinbaum Gallery, NY, 88; Love and Charity: The Tradition of Caritas in Contemp Painting, Sherry French Gallery, NY, 89; Assemblages from the Permanent Collection, Jane Voorhees Zimmerli Art Mus, Rutgers Univ, New Brunswick, NJ, 89; group exhibs, Good-bye to Apple Pie: Contemp Artists View the Family in Crisis, DeCordova Mus, Lincoln, Mass, 92, USA Today, Dutch Textile Mus, Tilburg, The Neth, traveling, 93 & Home is Where the Art is, or, Hybrid Affairs, Nat Arts Club, NY, 96; Bonnie Lucas & Steven Hardy, Gallery Rebolloso, Minneapolis, Minn, 95. *Teaching:* Lectr, Montclair State Col, NJ, 83 & Jane Voorhees Zimmerli Art Mus, Rutgers Univ, 84; vis artist, Appalachian Univ, Boone, NC, 87, Univ Ariz Tempe, 88; Workshop artist, Artpark, Summer, 88, Md Inst Col Art, Baltimore, 92; instr, Parsons Sch Design Continuing Educ, New York, 88-94, Md Inst Col Art, Baltimore, 92; vis artist, Am Acad Rome, 89, Col of the Atlantic, Bar Harbor, Maine, 94, Carleton Col, Northfield, Minn, 95; instr, Art Dept, City Col New York, 96-. *Awards:* Stevens Traveling Fel, Wellesley Col, 89; Grant, Art Matters Inc, 90. *Bibliog:* Joan Marter (auth), Review, Arts Mag, Summer, 87; Michael Brenson (auth), Cosmopolitan Artworks along suburban byways, NY Times, 8/4/89; articles & reviews in var publ. *Media:* Oil, Watercolor. *Mailing Add:* 37 Spring St New York NY 10012-5723

LUCAS, CHARLIE
PAINTER, SCULPTOR
b Pinklily, Ala, 1951. *Study:* Self taught. *Work:* Birmingham Airport, Ala. *Exhib:* Outside: Artist from Alabama, Montgomery Mus Fine Art, Ala, 91; Orphans in the Storm, Chatahoochee Valley Art Mus, Lagrange, Ga, 92 & Tucson Mus Art, Ariz, 94; Passionate Visions, New Orleans Mus Art, La, 93. *Pos:* Vis artist, Montgomery Mus Fine Arts & other various institutions. *Bibliog:* Dan Rathers, 60 Minutes, CBS News, 93. *Media:* Metal, Sculpture. *Dealer:* Robert Haardt Gallery. *Mailing Add:* c/o Anton Haardt Gallery 2714 Coliseum St New Orleans LA 36104

LUCAS, CHRISTOPHER
CONCEPTUAL ARTIST
b Durham, NC, Nov 13, 1958. *Study:* Yale Summer Sch Music & Art, 79; Kans Univ, BA, 80. *Work:* High Mus Art, Atlanta, Ga; Carnegie Mus Art, Pittsburgh, Pa; Bayer, Pittsburgh, Pa; Chase Manhattan, NY; Prudential Insurance Company of America. *Comn:* Ill-Saw Sculpture Park, Korea, 97. *Exhib:* Solo exhibs, John Good Gallery, NY, 86, 87, 89 & 92, Paolo Baldacci Gallery, NY, 95, Guy McIntyre Gallery, NY, 98 & Mario Diancono Gallery, Boston, 2003; Primal Abstractions, Mario Diancono Gallery, Boston, 92; Galleria Nazionale d'Arte Moderna, San Marino, 93; Spazio Atac, Rome, 96; and others. *Awards:* Fel, Nat Endowment Arts, 87-88; Pollock-Krasner Found, 88; Fulbright Fel, Repub of Korea, 90-91. *Bibliog:* Joshua Decter (auth), Christopher Lucas, Arts Mag, 4/92; Kunie Sugiura (auth), BT-Bijutsu Tecno, Japan, 4/92; Janet Koplos (auth), Christopher Lucas, Art in Am, 6/92. *Media:* Wood, Paint

LUCAS, GEORGETTA SNELL
PAINTER
b Harmony, Ind, July 25, 1920. *Study:* Ind State Univ, BS, 42; Butler Univ, MS, 64; Ind Univ & John Herron Sch Art, 60-65. *Work:* Ind Univ/Purdue Univ Med Ctr & Indianapolis Public Sch Collection; Ind State Univ Permanent Collection, Terre Haute, Ind; Nat Asn Women Artists; Jane Voorhees Zimmerli Art Mus, Rutgers Univ, NJ. *Comn:* Noah Loading Ark, mural, comn by William Plummer, Frankfurt, Ger, 74; Reflections, memorial oil painting, M S D Perry Admin, Indianapolis, 78; Masonic Lodge No 1-1809, comn by Bridgeport Lodge No 163, Ind, 90. *Exhib:* NY World's Fair, Bourbon St Gallery, La Pavilion, 64; Nat Asn Women Artist traveling show, Fine Arts Acad, Calcutta, India, 65; Nat Asn Women Artist show, Casino Municipale Gallery, Cannes, France, 66; Mid State Exhib, Evansville Mus, Ind, 70; 100th Yr Celebration Show, Nat Asn Women Artists, Jacob Javits Bldg, NY, 89; Nat Biennial 1994 Art Show for Nat League of Am Pen Women, Lincoln Ctr, NY, 94. *Pos:* Ind State Art chmn, Alpha Delta Kappa, 73-77; pres, Ind Artists/Craftsmen Inc, 79-84 & 87-89, Ind Fedn Art Clubs, 86-87; art chmn, Gov Int Platform Asn, 83-2000; Ind State pres, Nat League Am Pen Women, 98. *Teaching:* Inst art, Plainfield City Schs, Ind, 46-49 & 50-52; Metrop Sch Dist of Wayne, Indianapolis, 52-68; Metrop Sch Dist of Perry Twp, Indianapolis, 68-81; lectr, Int Platform Asn, Wash, 75, 77-78, 82 & 84, Art Educators Asn Ind, 76, Prof Educators Ind Conv, 78, Ind Fedn Art Clubs, 88 & Ind Sch Women's Asn, 88. *Awards:* Indiana Artist/Craftsmen, 74; Silver Award, Int Platform Art, 78; Best of Show, Nat League Am Pen Women, 83 & 97 & Ind Fedn, Art Club Exhib, 97. *Bibliog:* Leonidas Smith (auth), Hoosier artist, Indianapolis Star Mag, 8/65; Donald Frick (auth), Batik-Filmstrip-TV Cube, Indianapolis Mus Art, 74; Mary Slayton (auth), Shares love of art, music, The Plainfield Messenger, 5/17/90. *Mem:* Nat Asn Woman Artist; Nat League Am Pen Women (Ind art chmn, 84-96); honorary life mem, Ind Artist/Craftsmen Inc (pres, 79-84 & 87-89); Int Platform Asn (chmn art comt, 86-); honorary life mem Ind Fedn Art Clubs (pres, 85-87); life mem, Ind State Teachers Asn; World Craft Coun. *Media:* Watercolor, Oil. *Publ:* Illusr, Why So Sad, Little Rag Doll?, E C Seale, 63; contribr, Former Harmony resident receives VIP treatment, Brazil Daily Times, 8/3/67; Georgetta Snell Lucas art work presented to ISU, The Tribune, 73; Art teachers to see demonstration, Daily Herald, 3/22/76; cover art, Biennial Issue, Nat League Am Pen Women Mag, 6/94

LUCCHESI, BRUNO
SCULPTOR
b Lucca, Italy, July 31, 1926; US citizen. *Study:* Inst Arte, Lucca, MFA, 53. *Work:* Pa Acad Fine Arts, Philadelphia; Dallas Mus Fine Arts; Ringling Mus, Sarasota, Fla; Hirshhorn Mus, Washington, DC; Whitney Mus Am Art, NY; Bank Am, NYC; and numerous others. *Comn:* Sculptures, Trade Bank, NY; Cornell Univ; Yale Univ; Amer Sch Ballet, NYC; San Paolino Church, Lucca, Italy. *Exhib:* Whitney Mus Am Art, NY; Pa Acad Fine Arts; Corcoran Gallery Art, Washington, DC; Nat Inst Arts & Lett; Brooklyn Mus, NY; plus others; Solo exhibs incl Prince Arthur Gallery, Toronto, On, Can, 77, Foster-Harmon Gallery, Sarasota, Fla, 80, 86, Shirlee Raushbach Gallery, Bay Harbor, Fla, 83, Blue Hill Cult Ctr, Pearl River, NY, 84, Casey Gallery, Scottsdale, Ariz, 86. *Teaching:* Instr, Acad Fine Arts, Univ Florence, Italy, 50-57; instr, New Sch Social Res, 60-70; Nat Acad of Design, New York City, 70-80. *Awards:* Watrous Gold Medal, Nat Acad Design, 61; Gold Medal, Nat Arts Club, 63; S F B Morse Medal, Nat Acad Design, 65; Lion of S Marco award Holion Cult Soc, New York City, 81; and others. *Bibliog:* Bronzes Spotlight Exhibitions, New York Herald Tribune, 11/26/61; Dorothy Adlow (auth), Bruno Lucchesi, Christian Science Monitor, 1/26/62; Bruno Lucchesi, Arts Mag, 68, 71, 75; Bronze Realists, Time, 6/1/70; Michael Brenson (auth), Bruno Lucchesi, New York Times, 2/3/84; Art from Life, New York Times, 11/29/85; David Finn (auth), Brunco Lucchesi: Sculptor of the Human Spirit, Hudson Hills Press, 89, Bruno Lucchesi, Ruder Finn Press, 03, Bruno Lucchesi: Celebrating the Beauty of Everyday Life, Ruder Finn Press, 09. *Mem:* Sculptors Guild; Artists Equity Asn; Nat Acad; Am Asn Univ Prof. *Publ:* Co-auth (with Margit Malmstrom), Terracotta, Watson-Guptill Pubs, 77; co-auth (with Margit Malmstrom), Modeling the Head in Clay, Watson-Guptill Pubs, 79; co-auth (with Margit Malmstrom), Modeling the Figure in Clay, Watson-Guptill Pubs, 80. *Dealer:* Forum Gallery 745 Fifth Ave New York NY 10151. *Mailing Add:* 30 5th Ave No 4J New York NY 10011-8859

LUCE, C(HARLES) BEARDSLEY
CONCEPTUAL ARTIST
b Phoenix, Ariz, June 15, 1947. *Study:* Amherst Col, BA, 69, Univ Wash, MAT, 71. *Work:* The City of Seattle, Seattle Art Mus, Wash; Libr Cong, Washington, DC; Prudential Insurance Co, Newark, NJ; Bell Tel Co & Gen Elec Co, Chicago, Ill; NYNEX, NY; Sackner Archive of Concrete & Visual Poetry, Miami, Fla. *Exhib:* The Cyclonic Collapse of the Teahouse, 78 & Aether House, 79, Seattle Art Mus; Luise Ross, NY, 84; Fuji Art Salon, Tokyo, Japan, 85; Stokker-Stikker Gallery, NY, 86; Gracie Mansion, NY, 90-91; Dessont Saunders, Chicago, 91; Luise Ross, 92, 96, 99; plus others. *Pos:* Dean etymology, Inst Study of Etymological Lessons, NY, 79 & chmn, art dept. *Awards:* Art Matters, 89; John Simon Guggenheim Fel, 91. *Bibliog:* John Paoletti (auth), Charles Luce: Light truths, Arts Mag, 4/82. *Media:* Mixed. *Dealer:* Luise Ross 568 Broadway 4 Flr New York NY 10012. *Mailing Add:* 360 W 36th St 5NW New York NY 10018

LUCERO, MANUEL F
CERAMIST
b San Diego, Calif, May 26, 1942. *Study:* San Jose Univ, BA (art), 65, MA(art), 67; San Francisco Art Inst, post-grad study, 92-93. *Work:* Beswick Collection, Los Angeles, Calif; Oakland Art Mus & Antonio Prieto Mem Collection, Mills Col, Oakland, Calif; Ceramic Monthly Collection, Columbus, Ohio. *Comn:* Brian Wash Laundromat, San Francisco. *Exhib:* Solo exhibs, Calif State Univ, Chico, 70 & 75, Univ Nev, Las Vegas, 76; Introductions, Gallery Paule Anglim, San Francisco, Calif, 93; White: 10 in 10, San Francisco Art Inst, Calif, 94; Forecast: Shifts in Direction (with catalog), Mus NMex, Santa Fe, 94; Next to Nothing (with catalog), Ctr Arts at Buena Gardens, San Francisco, 94; La Panaderia, Mex DF, 95; Oakland Mus of Calif, Inst Contemp Art, San Jose, 96; Diego Rivera Gallery, San Francisco, 99. *Teaching:* Prof art, Calif State Univ, Chico, 68-; vis artist & instr, Univ Nev, Las Vegas, 76. *Awards:* Ceramic Monthly Award, 71; Ceramic Int Award, Alberta Col, Calgary, 73; Nat Endowment Arts Fel, 93. *Bibliog:* David Bonetti (auth), Still life, new fife at introductions, San Francisco Examiner, 7/16/93; Kenneth Baker (auth), Next to nothing, San Francisco Chronicle, 9/17/94; Rebecca Solnit (auth), Next to nothing, Art Issues, 11/94. *Dealer:* Gallery Paule Anglim 14 Heary St San Francisco CA 94108. *Mailing Add:* University of California, Chico Dept Art & Art History Ayres Hall 107 400 W First St Chico CA 95929

LUCEY, JACK
GRAPHIC ARTIST, ILLUSTRATOR
b San Francisco, Calif, Feb 11, 1929. *Study:* Acad Art Col, San Francisco, 55; San Francisco Art Inst, 59; San Francisco State Univ, BA, 76. *Work:* USAF Mus, Nellis, Nev; Naval Aviation Mus, Pensacola, Fla; Hall of Justice Bldg, San Francisco; Trans World Airlines, NY; USAF Artist Prog, Andrews AFB, Washington. *Comn:* Murals of Alaska, Pac Orient Lines, San Francisco, 72; London Illus, Trans World Airlines, NY, 74; Irish Countryside Paintings; Irish Tourist Bd, Dublin, 75; US Coast Guard Aircraft Scene, US Coast Guard Air Sta, San Francisco, 77. *Exhib:* 29th Ann Soc Western Artists, MH De Young Mus, San Francisco; San Francisco Art Festival, Civic Ctr, 76; Zellerbach Invitational, Zellerbach Plaza, San Francisco, 76; Industrial Graphics Int, San Jose, 77; Watercolor Technique, Marin Co Watercolor Soc, Mill Valley, Calif, 77; Third Falkirk Ann, Falkirk Cult Ctr, San Rafael, Calif, 78; Solo exhib, Agura Art, Collection of 36 paintings and Drawings Representing California Agriculture Today, Calif Mus Design & Industry, Los Angeles, 86. *Collection Arranged:* Veterans Mem Mus, 79; one-man shows, Sport's Art, Zellerbach Art Mus, 80 & Aviation Art, Bohemian Club, San Francisco, Calif, 81. *Pos:* Graphics artist, Shell Oil Co, San Francisco, 52-56; art dir, Independent J, San Rafael, Calif, 56-; courtroom artist, CNN, San Francisco Bureau, ABC-TV, NBC News-TV, KRON TV-4 & KGO TV-7, San Francisco. *Teaching:* Instr illus, Col Marin, 75-; instr art, Acad Art Col, San Francisco, 76-77; instr graphics, Indian Valley Col, Novato, Calif, 78-. *Awards:* First Place Illus, San Jose State Univ, Calif, 77. *Mem:* Coll Art Asn; Soc Western Artists; San Francisco Soc Commun Arts; Artists in Print; North Bay Advert Commun; US Air Force Artist, Washington, DC. *Media:* Oil, Watercolor, Pen & Ink. *Publ:* Illusr, The Alamo, Reader's Dig, 73; San Francisco Giants, San Francisco Mag, 78; Chemical facts of life, Standard Oiler Mag, Standard Oil of Calif, 78. *Dealer:* Allport Assoc Gallery 1000 Magnolia Ave Larkspur CA 94939. *Mailing Add:* 84 Crestwood Dr San Rafael CA 94901

LUCHS, ALISON
CURATOR, HISTORIAN
b Washington, DC, Oct 5, 1948. *Study:* Vassar Col, Poughkeepsie, NY, BA, 70; Johns Hopkins Univ, Baltimore, PhD, 76. *Collection Arranged:* Early European Sculpture, (permanent collection), 99-2002; Desiderio da Settignano (exhib), 2006-2007; Tullio Lombardo (exhib), 2009. *Pos:* Res asst, Ctr Advan Study Visual Arts, Washington, 80-83, asst cur sculpture, 82-89, assoc cur early European sculpture, 89-; cur, Early European Sculpture, 96-. *Teaching:* Asst prof, Swarthmore Col, Pa, 76-77; asst prof, Syracuse Univ, NY, 77-80. *Awards:* Robert H Smith Res Leave Grant, 88 & 98; Ailsa Mellon Bruce Nat Gallery Art Curatorial Sabbatical Fel, Ctr Advan Study History of Arts, 92-93, 2003; Samuel H Kress Found Grant & CAA Millard Meiss Grant, 94-95. *Mem:* Ital Art Soc; Coll Art Asn; Renaissance Soc. *Res:* Medieval, Renaissance & baroque sculpture, especially Italian. *Specialty:* European & Am Art, medieval to modern. *Publ:* The Convent of Sta Maria Maddalena de'Pazzi and its Works of Art, Florence, 90-91; Coauth, Western Decorative Arts, Part I, Nat Gallery Art & Cambridge Univ Press, 93; auth, Tullio Lombardo and Ideal Portrait Sculpture in Renaissance Venice, 1490-1530, Cambridge Univ Press, 95; auth, Lorenzo From Life? Renaissance Portrait Busts of Lorenzo de Medici, The Sculpture Jour, 2000; auth, Woman in Anguish, Artibus et, 2003; entries Encyclopedia of Sculpture, 2004; Tullio Lombardo & Venetian High Renaissance Sculpture, exhib catolog, 2009; The Mermaids of Venice: Fantastic Sea Creatures in Venetian Renaissance Art, 2010. *Mailing Add:* c/o Sculpture Dept Nat Gallery Art 2000B S Club Dr Landoyer MD 20785

LUCIANO, MIGUEL
INSTALLATION SCULPTOR
b San Juan, Puerto Rico, 1972. *Study:* Univ Fla, New World Sch Arts, BFA, 1997; Univ Fla, Gainesville, Fla, MFA, 2000. *Exhib:* Solo exhibs include Grinter Int Gallery, Univ Fla at Gainesville, 1999, Taller Boricua Gallery, New York, 2001, Newark Art Mus, NJ, 2003, New York Univ, 2003; Group exhibs include Seamless, Samuel P Harn Mus Art, Fla, 2000; Fulton Gardens, The Kitchen, New York, 2000; Aim 22, Bronx Mus Arts, New York, 2002; Haciendo Patria, CFA Gallery, Chicago, 2002; The S-Files, El Mus Del Barrio, New York, 2002; Critical Consumption, Rotunda Gallery, Brooklyn, 2003; Funky Fall Line, Chelsea Art Mus, New York, 2003; American Dream, Ronald Feldman Fine Arts, New York, 2003. *Awards:* Prof Develop Fel, Coll Art Asn, New York, 2000; Joan Mitchell Found Grant, 2007. *Mailing Add:* Cue Art Foundation 511 W 25th St Ground Floor New York NY 10001

LUCKNER, KURT T
CURATOR
b Stafford Springs, Conn, Dec 29, 1945. *Study:* Georgetown Univ, AB (art hist); Stanford Univ, MA (art hist). *Collection Arranged:* Silver for the Gods: 800 Years of Greek and Roman Silver (int loaned exhib), Toledo Mus Art, Ohio, Nelson Gallery, Kansas City, Mo & Kimball Mus Art, Ft Worth, Tex, 77-78. *Pos:* Asst cur ancient art, Stanford Univ Mus, summer 69; curatorial asst, Toledo Mus Art, Ohio, 69-70, asst cur, 70-73, cur ancient art, 73-. *Mem:* Coll Art Asn; Archaeol Inst Am (pres, Toledo Chap, 71-75). *Publ:* Auth, Art of Egypt-part I, Vol 14, No 1 & part II, Vol 15, No 3, Greek vases: Shapes & uses, Vol 15, No 3, African art, Vol 16, No 2 & Greek gold jewelry, Vol 17, No 1, Toledo Mus News. *Mailing Add:* 3452 Kenwood Blvd Toledo OH 43606-2807

LUDMAN, JOAN HURWITZ
WRITER, RESEARCHER
b Brooklyn, NY, Feb 1, 1932. *Study:* Barnard Coll, BA, 53; C W Post Coll, Long Island Univ, MA, 71. *Comn:* Essay, Mem Art Gallery, Univ Rochester, NY; Essay, New Britain Mus Am Art, Conn. *Pos:* Assoc, Mason Fine Prints, Glen Head, NY, 72-86. *Res:* American and European original prints; compiling catalog, Raisonne paintings of Fairfield Porter. *Publ:* Coauth (with Lauris Mason), Print Reference Sources: A Select Bibliography 18th-20th Centuries, 75, 2nd ed, 79 & The Lithographs of George Bellows: A Catalogue Raisonne, 77, Kraus-Thomson Orgn Ltd; contribr, Cecile Shapiro, auth, Fine Prints: Collecting, Buying and Selling, Harper & Row, 76; co-ed (with Lauris Mason), Print Collector's Quart: An Anthology of Essays on Eminent Printmakers of the World, 77, Kraus-Thomson Orgn Ltd; auth, Fairfield Porter: A Catalogue Raisonne of his Prints, Highland House Publ Inc, 81; Fairfield Porter: A Catalogue Raisonne of his Paintings, Watercolors and Pastels, Hudson Hills Press, 99, 01. *Mailing Add:* 11758 Grove Ridge Ln Boynton Beach FL 33437

LUDTKE, LAWRENCE MONROE
SCULPTOR
b Houston, Tex, Oct 18, 1929. *Study:* Univ Houston, BS; Coppini Acad Fine Art, San Antonio, with Waldine Tauch. *Work:* USAF Acad; Central Intelligence Agency Hq; White House; Pentagon; Lifesize Bronzes, Lyndon B Johnson Libr. *Comn:* Charging Bronze Rams, Johnson & Johnson Inc, San Angelo, Tex, 66; Dr Denton Cooley (bronze bust), St Lukes Hosp, Houston, 69; Eddie Wokecki (bronze bas relief), Rice Univ, Houston, 69; Pieta (bronze group), St Marys Sem, Houston, 74; Fiona O'Donnell (bronze bust), comn by Dr Manus O'Donnell, Houston, 74; works comn by President Ronald Reagan, John Wayne, General Robinson Risner, Maury Maucrick, Robert Kennedy and Martha Mitchell. *Exhib:* Nat Cowboy Hall of Fame. *Teaching:* Scottsdale Artist Sch, 89. *Mem:* Fel Nat Sculpture Soc; Coppini Acad Fine Arts; Royal Acad Brit Sculptors (corresp mem). *Media:* Bronze, Marble. *Mailing Add:* 10127 Whiteside Ln Houston TX 77043-4302

LUDWIG, ALLAN I
PHOTOGRAPHER, ART HISTORIAN
b New York, NY, June 9, 1933. *Study:* Yale Univ, with Josef Albers, Charles Seymour, Jr & Erwin R Goodenough, Edmund S Morgan, BFA, 56, MA, 60, Bollingen Found fel, 60-63, PhD, 64; Junior Sterling fel, Yale Univ, 62-63. *Work:* Mus Fine Arts, Houston, Tex; San Francisco Mus Mod Art; Espace Photographique de Paris; Tokyo Inst Technol; Mus Mod Art, Metrop Mus, NY; Mus Photog Arts, San Diego; Yale Univ Art Gallery; Chrysler Mus, Norfolk, Va; New Orleans Mus Art; Los Angeles Co Mus Art, Calif; Ctr Creative Photog, Tucson, Ariz; Libr Cong & Smithsonian Inst, Washington, DC; The Walker Art Ctr, Minneapolis; The Boston Athenaeum, Boston; Kiyosato Mus of Photographic Arts, Kiyosato, Japan; The Archives of American Art, Washington, DC; Am Acad, Rome. *Exhib:* Solo exhibs, Twining Gallery, NY, 87, Shaidai Gallery, Tokyo, Japan, 87, Cepa Gallery, Buffalo, NY, 87, White Columns, NY, 87 & 88, O'Kane Gallery, Houston, Tex, 88, XYZ Gallery, Ghent, Belg, 89, Farideh Cadot Gallery, NY, 88 & 90, Northern Light Gallery, Ariz State Univ, Tempe, 90, Galerie Farideh Cadot, Paris, France, 91, Pamela Auchincloss Gallery, NY, 92 & 94, Gallery 954, Chicago, 94, Gallery at 777, Los Angeles, 94, Cepa Gallery, Buffalo, 95, Chrysler Mus, Norfolk, Va, 95 & 2000, Hudson River Mus Westchester, Yonkers, 95, Houston Ctr Photog, 95, Kemper Mus Contemp Art, 97, Ricco/Maresca Gallery, NY, 99; group exhibs, Insect Politics, Hallwalls, Buffalo, NY, 90, Animals, Houston Ctr for Photog, Tex, 90, Photog: 1980's Discovery & Invention, Art, 21-90, Basel, Switz, 90, Natural History & Formaldehyde Photog, Musee Zoologique de l'Universite Louis Pasteur, Strasbourg, France, 90, Natur Mus Senchenberg Forschungs Institut, Frankfort, Fed Repub Ger, 91, Ricco-Maresca Gallery, New York, NY, 2000 & 2002, List Gallery, Swarthmore Col, Pa, 2004, Farideh Cadot Gallery, Paris, 2005, Albin D Kuhn Libr Gallery, Univ Md, 2006; Women Series, New Mus, NY, NY & Parko Gallery, Tokyo, Japan, 93; Narcissism: Artist's Reflect Themselves, Calif Ctr Arts Mus, Escondido, Calif, 95; retrospectives, Kemper Mus Contemp Art, Kansas City, 96-97, Chrysler Mus, Norfolk, 98, The Mus of photog Helsinki, Finland, Invisible Light, 99; Ricco/Maresca Gallery, NY, 2001-02; Marion Ctr, Coll of Santa Fe, Santa Fe, NMex, 2001; Extraordinary Bodies: Photographs from the Mütter Mus (traveling exhib), List Gallery, Swarthmore Coll, Pa, 2005, Albin O Kuhn Libr Gallery, Univ Md, 2006 & The Albuquerque Mus Art Hist, 2007; Richard R Brush Art Gallery & Permanent Collection, St Lawrence Univ, Canton, NY; A Celebration of Global Art, The Inspiration Art Exhib, Jerusalem, Israel, 2007; Outside/Inside, Artbreak Gallery, Williamsburg, Brooklyn, NY, 2008. *Collection Arranged:* Repulsion: The Aesthetics of the Grotesque, Alternative Mus, 86. *Pos:* Chmn bd, Alternative Mus, New York, 78-83, mem exec bd, 83-88; dir, Ludwig Portfolios, 81-88. *Teaching:* Instr, RI Sch of Design, Yale Univ, Dickinson Coll, Syracuse Univ. *Awards:* Joan Addison Porter Prize, Yale Univ, 64; For Book Graven Images, Asn State & Local Hist, 66-67; Photog Fel, NJ State Coun Arts, 89-90; Grant, Agfa Corp, 90; Nat Endowment Arts Fel, 91; Am Coun Learned Socs Fel. *Bibliog:* Photography 150 Years: Its Light and Shadow, Coll of Art, Nihon Univ, Tokyo Inst Technol, 178, 89; Kunstforum, 142-145, 3-4/90; Kath McQuaid (auth), Photo Surrealism, South End News, 2/15/90; Brooks Johnson (auth), Tableau Mort, Bull Chrysler Mus, summer 95; Brooks Johnson (ed), Photography Speaks: 150 Photographers On Their Art, Ed,; Brooks Johnson, Aperture Foundation, 304 & 305, 2004. *Mem:* Asn Gravestone Studies. *Media:* Installations using Photographs. *Res:* I am currently writing a book on Mummies, mannequins, wax figures, dolls, puppets, automatons and robots & essays on New York City neighborhoods. *Publ:* Auth, Graven Images, Wesleyan Univ Press, 66, 75 & 99; Holy Land USA, The Clarion, summer 79; Beyond Photography I, II, 81-82 & Seeing Is Believing, 12/85-1/86, Alternative Mus; Sermons in Stone, Franco Maria Ricci, 11/84; Repulsion: The Aesthetics of the Grotesque, Alternative Mus, 86. *Dealer:* Artbreak Gallery Grand St Williamsburg Brooklyn NY. *Mailing Add:* 55 Prince St New York NY 10012-3432

LUECKING, STEPHEN JOSEPH
SCULPTOR, EDUCATOR
b Belleville, Ill, Aug 11, 1948. *Study:* Quincy Col, Ill, BFA, 70; Bradley Univ, Peoria, Ill, grad study, 71; Miami Univ, Oxford, Ohio, MFA, 73. *Work:* Ill State Mus, Springfield. *Comn:* Miami Sun Reservoir (with Margaret Lanterman), Miami Univ & Nat Endowment Arts, Oxford, Ohio, 80; State Ill, 89, 90, 95 & 96; Upwells, Univ Ill, 90; Caparo Steel, Farrell, Pa, 95; Chem-Life Bldg, Univ Ill. *Exhib:* Ill State Mus, Springfield, 78; Art Inst Chicago, 79; Contemp Arts Ctr, Cincinnati, 80; Chicago Cult Ctr, 81; Rockford Art Mus, 89; Roy Boyd Gallery, Chicago, 90; Mus Contemp Relig Art, 94; Snite Mus, Notre Dame Univ, 96. *Collection Arranged:* Seven Sculptors, 78

& Stuart Court Installations (auth, catalog), 81-82, DePaul Univ; Paul Caponigro & Charles Ross, Archaeoastronomy Am Conf, St John's Col, 79. *Pos:* Reviewer & essayist, New Art Examiner, 86-; Visual Arts Panelist, Ill Arts Coun 87, & 88. *Teaching:* Asst prof, Purdue Univ, West Lafayette, Ind, 74-76; prof, chair, DePaul Univ, Chicago, 76-; vis artist, Sch Art Inst Chicago, 79 & 86. *Awards:* Clussman Prize, Art Inst Chicago, 78; project grants, Ill Arts Coun, 78, 80 & 81; Pougialis Award, Columbia Col, 81. *Bibliog:* Alan Artner (auth), The Nation: Chicago, Art News, summer, 77; Holliday T Day (auth), Chicago Invitational, Art Am, 11/78; Wendy Hoffman-Yuni, article, New Art Examiner, 3/79. *Media:* Steel, Iron. *Publ:* Contrib, Sculpture Mag, 89-90; Am Crafts, 90; Am Ceramics, 91-92. *Dealer:* Roy Boyd 215 West Superior Chicago IL 60610. *Mailing Add:* 1934 W Bradley Pl Chicago IL 60613-3614

LUFKIN, MARTHA BG
WRITER
b Boston, Mass, May 7, 1954. *Study:* Phillips Exeter Acad, Grad, 72; Yale Univ, BA (political Sci, magna cum laude), 76; Oxford (Eng) Univ, MLitt in Politics, 79; Columbia Univ, JD, 82. *Pos:* assoc, Shearman & Sterling, New York City, 82-87 & Bingham, Dana & Gould, Boston, 87-92; pvt practice, probate, estate planning, art, and non-profit, Lincoln, 92-; legal writer, 95-; atty, Clark, Hunt, Ahearn & Embry, Cambridge, Mass, Estate Planning, Art Law, Non-Profit Law, 2008. *Teaching:* Lectr, Lawsuits concerning Nazi-looted art & stolen antiquities, var venues, 2002-. *Awards:* Sr Scholar Hertford Coll, Oxford Univ, 78-79; Harlan Fiske Stone Scholar Columbia Law Sch, 82; Distinguished Speaker Award, Brandeis Osher Inst, 2006. *Publ:* Auth, humor column, Huffington Post, 2013-,Lincoln J 92(Humor prize New Eng Press Assoc 96, 97); Alfred Hitchcock Mystery Mag, 95, 97, 2007, 2011; US legal corr, art law corr The Art Newspaper, 97-; contribr, Art Antiquity and Law, J Cultural Property, written about art law, musuem, and non-profit law claims by Italy and Egypt to recover antiquities looted from their soil, lawsuits related to Nazi-looted art & many other scholarly legal articles

LUINO, BERNARDINO
PAINTER
b Latina, Italy, Mar 27, 1951. *Study:* Acad di Belle Arti, Rome & Florence, Italy, MA. *Comn:* Mural, Presso II Centro Incontri Marentino Fiat, Torino, Italy. *Exhib:* Solo exhibs, Galleria Lo Zibetto, 80, Galleria II Fante di Spade, 82, Milan, Italy; Biennale di La Spezia, La Spezia, 80; VII Nat Biennial of Figurative Art, Piacenza; I Int Biennial of Graphic Art, Museo Civico Riva del Garda, Centro Int, della Grafica Venezia, Trento, 82; Grafica Ital Contemporanea, Quadriennale Nazionale d'Arte di Roma, traveled USA and Can, 82; XXIV Biennale Nazionale d'Art, Palazzo della Permanente, Milan, Italy, 89. *Media:* Oil on Panel. *Publ:* Illusr, Luino, Fotolito Savaresi, 85. *Mailing Add:* c/o Gallery Henoch 555 W 25th St New York NY 10001

LUISI, JERRY
SCULPTOR, INSTRUCTOR
b Minneapolis, Minn, Oct 7, 1939. *Study:* Nat Acad Design, cert, 68-72; Art Students League. *Work:* NY State Gov Mansion, Albany; Agriculture Hall Fame, Kansas City, Mo; Nat Acad Design, NY. *Comn:* BASF Corp, Parsippany, NJ, 81-83; Armento Archit Arts, Buffalo, NY, 87; Franklin Mint, 88; Medallic Art, 89; Reseal, NY, 89. *Exhib:* Nat Acad Design 70, 74 & 81; Allied Artists Am, 71, 72 & 75; Nat Sculpture Soc, 74-; Mus Fine Arts, Springfield, Mass, 77; Salmagundi Club, 80 & 81; Artists Prof League, NY, 89; and others. *Pos:* Deleg, Fine Arts Fedn, New York, 78-80; ed sculpture, Aristos Mag, 83. *Teaching:* assoc prof, Fine Arts Prog, Fashion Inst Technol, 72- & Nat Acad Design, 79-82. *Awards:* Greenshields Found Grant, 72 & 75; Anna Hyatt Huntington Award, Hudson Valley Art Asn, 80; John Gregory Award, Nat Sculpture Soc, 80; and others. *Bibliog:* Articles, Nat Sculpture Rev, fall 80. *Mem:* Nat Sculpture Soc; Acad Artists Asn; life mem Art Students League; Artists Prof League, New York. *Media:* Clay, Bronze. *Mailing Add:* 36 E 36th St New York NY 10016

LUKASIEWICZ, NANCY BECHTOLD
ADMINISTRATOR, TAPESTRY ARTIST
b Berkeley, Calif, Dec 17, 1950. *Study:* Carnegie-Mellon Univ, BFA, 73; Univ Ga, MFA (with hons), with Glen Kaufman, 75. *Work:* Dow Chemical Co, Horgan, Switz. *Comn:* Tapestry, Dow Chemical Co, Midland Mich, 73; 4 panel tapestry, Jaworksi, Athens, Ga, 81. *Exhib:* Fiber Structures Int, Carnegie Mus, Pittsburgh, 75; Regional Invitational, Nexus Contemp Art Ctr, Atlanta, 79; solo exhib, Reece Mus, Johnson City, Tenn, 81; Athens Artists, Savannah Coll Art, Ga, 83; Habitat Show I, State Botanical Garden, Athens, Ga, 90. *Pos:* Fiber artist, 69-81; dir, Lyndon House Art Ctr, Athens-Clarke Co, Ga, 77-. *Awards:* Ga Coun Arts Proj Grants, 78-96; Athens Cult Award, Clarke Co, Ga, 88. *Bibliog:* Catherine Fox (auth), Review, Atlanta J Constitution, 79; Focus women, Athens Banner-Herald, 94. *Mem:* Handweavers Guild Am; Ga Mountain Crafts; Ga Asn Mus & Galleries. *Publ:* Auth, Directory of Resources Georgia Handweavers, Ga Coun Arts, 78. *Mailing Add:* 350 Belmont Rd Athens GA 30605-4904

LUKASIEWICZ, RONALD JOSEPH
PRINTMAKER, ADMINISTRATOR
b Pittsburgh, Pa, Apr 20, 1943. *Study:* Carnegie-Mellon Univ, BFA; Univ Ga, MFA. *Work:* Pittsburgh Pub Schs, Pa; Dow Chemical Co, Midland, Mich; City of Athens, Ga; Bankers Trust Co, NC; and others. *Comn:* Suite of serigraphs, 73 & bound book of serigraphs, 73, Dow Chemical Co, Midland, Mich; modular sculpture, Scorpio Rising Workshop, Farmington, Ga, 73; modular sculpture, City of Athens, Ga, 77; suite of serigraphs, Thornet Furniture, Dallas, 81. *Exhib:* 10th Ann Piedmont Graphics Exhib, Mint Mus of Art, Charlotte, NC, 73; Assoc Artists Ann Show, Carnegie Mus, Pittsburgh, Pa, 73; Medals, Banners, Ribbons, Pittsburgh Arts & Crafts Ctr, Pa, 74; Ga Nat, Lyndon House Galleries, Athens, 76; Moving Parts & Captured Light, The Third Floor, Atlanta; Spectrum I, Lyndon House Art Ctr, Athens, Ga, 80; Western Carolina Univ, Cullowhee, NC, 81; Corvoll Reese Mus, 86; Color as Theory, Goethe Inst, Atlanta, Ga, 88; and others. *Pos:* Dir cult activities, Athens, Ga, 74-76; preparator, Ga Mus of Art, Univ Ga, 76-87; dir, Climax Press, 83-. *Awards:* Purchase Award, Assoc Artists of Pittsburgh, Pittsburgh Pub Schs, 72; Award, Lyndon House Art Ctr, 81. *Bibliog:* D Miller (auth), Exhibit review, Pittsburgh Post Gazette, 74; J Chappell (producer), Scorpio Rising (16mm film doc), 74; Screen Printing Today, WGTV Television, 74. *Mem:* Coll Arts Asn; Asn Artist of Pittsburgh; Athens Art Asn. *Mailing Add:* 350 Belmont Rd Athens GA 30605-4904

LUKE , GREGORIO
MUSEUM DIRECTOR
Pos: Cult Inst Mex, Los Angeles; dir, Mus Latin Am Art, Long Beach, 99-. *Awards:* Recipient Mayoral Citation, Wash, DC, 92; Irving Leonard Award, Hispanic Soc of Libr of Congress, 95; Educ Award, March of Dimes, 2001. *Mailing Add:* Mus Latin Am Art 628 Alamitos Ave Long Beach CA 90802

LUKIN, SVEN
PAINTER
b Riga, Latvia, Feb 14, 1934. *Study:* Univ Pa. *Work:* Albright-Knox Art Gallery, Buffalo, NY; Los Angeles Co Mus Art; Larry Aldrich Mus, Ridgefield, Conn; Univ Tex, Austin; Whitney Mus Am Art, NY; and others. *Exhib:* Univ Ill, Urbana, 1965; Torcuato di Tella, Buenos Aires, Arg, 1965; New shapes of Color, Stedelijk Mus, Amsterdam, The Neth, 1966; Univ Colo, Denver, 1967; Painting: Out From the Wall, Des Moines Art Ctr, Iowa, 1968; New Work, Los Angeles Co Mus Art, 1978; Gallery Face, Tokyo, 1987; Mus Foreign Art, Riga, Latvia, 1987; and others. *Awards:* Guggenheim Fel, 1966; Pollock-Krasner Found Grant, 1990, 2007. *Bibliog:* Sam Hunter (ed), New Art Around the World, Abrams, 1966; Allen S Weller (auth), The Joys & Sorrows of Recent American Art, Univ Ill, 1968; Gregory Battcock (ed), Minimal Art: a Critical Anthology, Dutton, 1968

LUKKAS, LYNN C
VIDEO ARTIST
b Minneapolis, Minn, May 6, 1956. *Study:* Univ Minn, BFA, 82; RISD, MFA, 88. *Exhib:* When Night Cries, Intermedia Arts Gallery, Minneapolis, Minn, 92; Unter(halt)una, Franklin Furnace Arch, NY, 93; Yield the Body, Walker Art Ctr, 93; WE, Alice Rogers Gallery, St Johns Univ, Collegeville, Minn, 93; When Night Cries, St Johns Univ-Coll St Benedict, 94; Through the Body, Weisman Mus Art, Minneapolis, 96; Cleveland Performing Art Festival, 98; McKnight Found Fel Exhibn, Minn, 2000; One City Festival, Capetown, South Africa, 2001. *Teaching:* Asst prof, St Johns Univ, Collegeville, Minn, 88-95; asst prof, media art, time and interactivity, dept art, Univ Minn, 2000-. *Awards:* Jerome Found Travel Study Grant, 93, 2000; Nat Endowment Arts, 93; Minn State Arts Award Fel, 95; Bush Found Fel, 96-97; Women Film Makers Grant Media Artists Resource Ctr, 96; McKnight Found Fel, 99. *Media:* Video, Electronic Media. *Publ:* Auth, The Oculus Projects, Coll Arts Asn Jour, 1/2000. *Mailing Add:* 1915 Fremont Ave S Apt 1 Minneapolis MN 55403

LUM, KEN (KENNETH) ROBERT
CONCEPTUAL ARTIST, PHOTOGRAPHER
b Vancouver, BC, Sept 26, 1956. *Study:* Simon Fraser Univ, with Jeff Wall & Ian Wallace, BGS, 80; Univ BC, MFA, 85. *Work:* Kunst Mus Luzern, Luzern, Switz; Mus Boymans-Van Beuningen, Rotterdam, Neth; Städtische Galerie im Lenbachhaus, Munich, Ger; Frac Bretagne, Frac Loire, France; Nat Gallery Can, Ottawa. *Comn:* Functional sculpture, Art Gallery Ont, Toronto, 94. *Exhib:* Solo exhibs, Kunst Mus Luzerne, Luzern, 91, Badischer Kunstverein, Karlsruhe, 93, Stadtische Galerie im Lenbachhaus, Munich 93, Stills Gallery, Edinburgh, 95, Camden Arts Centre, London, 95 & Frac Haute Normandie, Rouen, 96, Agency Contemp Art, Philip Nelson Gallery, London, 98; Carnegie Int, Carnegie Mus Art, Pittsburgh, Pa, 91; Sydney Biennale, Art Gallery NSW, Sydney, Australia, 92; Johannesburg Biennale, 97; Sao Paulo Biennale, 98. *Teaching:* Asst prof, Univ BC, Vancouver, 90-; guest prof, Kunstakademie, Munich, Ger, 92, L'Ecole des Beaux-Arts, Paris, 94-97. *Awards:* Killam Res Prize, 98; Outstanding Alumni Award, Simon Fraser Univ, 97. *Publ:* Auth, Speculations, Imschoot Ltd, 93. *Dealer:* Andrea Rosen Gallery 130 Prince St New York NY 10012. *Mailing Add:* University of Pennsylvania School of Design 102 Meyerson Hall, 210 S 34 St Philadelphia PA 19104

LUMBERS, JAMES RICHARD
PAINTER
b Toronto, Ont, Oct 8, 1929. *Study:* Ont Coll Art, Toronto, OCA, 50. *Work:* Ont Govt; Tenn-Ness Antiques; Sun Oil Co; and numerous other corp & pvt collections in USA, Canada, Bermuda & Europe. *Comn:* Portraits, Former Prime Minister John Diefenbaker, 72, Chief Dan George, 73, 83 & 85, The Toronto Symphony Orchestra, 85, Hockey Greats: Gordie Howe, Sr & Wayne Gretzky, 91, Sir Edmund Hillary, 92, Joe Montana, 92; 4 paintings, Royal Can Mounted Police; painting, Home of Lucy Maud Montgomery, Univ Prince Edward Island, 2005. *Exhib:* Solo exhib, Royal Ont Mus, Toronto, Can; Ont Sci Ctr, Toronto; Kennedy Galleries Inc, NY, 72; Nature Can, Nat Mus Can, 73, 76-78; Sportsman's Edge Gallery, NY, 78; McMichael Can Collection, Toronto Dominion Ctr; Le Moyne Art Found, Tallahassee, Fla, 78; Several tours & exhib, Can, 85-97, 2000; and many others. *Pos:* Pres, Miroarts Publ Inc. *Teaching:* Lectr, many art groups. *Awards:* Statue, Juvenile Diabetes Found, 90; Winner of the Can Collectible of the Year, 91. *Bibliog:* Can Press, 89; Documentaries on PBS (Fla); Moments in Time-The Art of James Lumbers, 95; BBS Network Interviews, 96; The Art of James Lumbers, 95. *Mem:* ret mem, Soc Animal Artists, NY; Explorers Club, NY. *Media:* Acrylic. *Res:* Can Hist-native people of the north. *Specialty:* Contemp painting. *Collection:* Tenness Antiques Ltd, Toronto. *Publ:* Over 300 works in ltd eds; Art Bus News, 87-95 & 2000-2002; Art Impressions (feature), autumn 93; Can Art Buyers Guide (feature), 93. *Dealer:* Gallery Andrea, 7019 E Main St, Scottsdale, AZ, 85251

LUMMUS, CAROL TRAVERS
PRINTMAKER, ETCHING
b Hyannis, Mass, Nov 2, 1937. *Study:* Colby Sawyer Col, New London, NH, AA, 57; Mass Coll Art, Boston; Univ of Geneva, Switz; study color with Hannes Beckmann (Bauhaus), Dartmouth Col, Hanover, NH. *Work:* Univ Wis, Madison, Wis; Lund-Wassmer Springville Mus Collection, Salt Lake City, Utah; Arts Bank, Concord,

NH; Theodore Milton Wassmer Collection, Fairview Mus, Utah Snow Col, Ephraim; Ogunquit Mus Art, Harold Shaw Collection. *Comn:* Southern Editions, 78. *Exhib:* Solo Exhibs, Manchester Inst Arts, NH, 75-77; NH Col, Manchester, NH, 80; LA Galleria, San Mateo, Calif, 84; Gallery of Am Crafts, NC, 86; A.V.A. Gallery, Hanover, NH, 86, Lebanon, NH, 2013, Silvermine Guild Art, New Canann, Conn, 86, Bretanos, New York, NY, 86, Sharon Art Center, Sharon, NH, 92, 2010, Centerville Hist Mus, Centerville, Mass, 2007-2014; Gallery Z, Providence, RI, 2004, 2007, 2008; Colby Sawyer Col, New London, NH, 76, 94 & 2009; Royal Soc Miniature Painters & Gravers, World Exhib, London, Eng, 95; Cove Gallery, Wellfleet, Mass, 2003; Gallery Z, Providence, RI, 2004; Barn Gallery, Ogunquit, Maine, 2006; Group exhibs, Currier Mus Art Manchester, NH, 78, Saint Gaudens Natural Hist Site, Cornish, NH, 92, Mini Painters and Gravers Soc, Wash DC, 93, 95, 97, Royal Soc Mini Painters & Gravers, London, Eng, 95, Prints of the Year, Concord, NH, 97-2013, Cove Gallery, WellFleet, MA, 2003, Family Tree Gallery, Portsmouth, NH, 2004, Univ NE Portland, ME, 2005, Barn Gallery, Ogunquit, ME, 2006; Karl Drerup Art Gallery, Plymouth, NJ, 2009, 2013; Raising the Bar, Mus Art, UNH, Durham, NH, 2010; Francesca Anderson Fine Art Exhib, Lexington, MA, 2010; Leaving an Impression, Craft Ctr Concord, NH, 2012; Contemporary Arts of the Piscatequa, Berwick, Me, 2014. *Pos:* Illusr, Cincinnati Mag, Ohio, 64-67, Yankee Mag, 93-94. *Awards:* Oil award, Fitchburg Mus Art, Mass, 73; Rosmond DeKalb Award, Currier Mus Art, 75; Miniature Painters & Gravers, Washington, 93 & 96; Ga Miniature Society, Marietta, Ga, 98. *Bibliog:* Ellwyn F. Hayslip (auth), Career in Crafts, Deer Run Books, 97. *Mem:* League NH Craftsmen; Cape Cod Performing Arts Asn; NH Comn Arts (advisory panel); Silvermine Guild Arts, Conn; Nat Asn Women Artists, NY; Ogunquit Art Collaborative, ME. *Media:* Intaglio print. *Interests:* Italian Language, Opera, Cross Country Skiing. *Collection:* Gayle Lennard, NY Plus Numerous; Harold Shaw Ogunquit Me. *Publ:* Illusr, Editiones del Norte (cover/book), Hanover, NH, 68. *Dealer:* League of New Hampshire Craftsmen, Concord, NH; The Spectrum of Am Arts and Crafts 369 Old Kings Highway Brewster Mass 02631; Cove Gallery Wellfleet, MA. *Mailing Add:* PO Box 525 Barnstable MA 02630

LUMPKIN, LIBBY
MUSEUM DIRECTOR
Study: Univ Houston, BA (History); Univ Tex, Austin, MA (Art Hist); Univ NMex, Albuquerque, PhD. *Pos:* dir mus studies prog & asst prof art hist, Calif State Univ, formerly; consult exec dir, Las Vegas Art Mus, 2005-2007, dir, 2007-. *Teaching:* Asst prof art hist & cur, Donna Beam Fine Art Gallery, Univ Nev; vis prof, U NMex, Yale Univ, Univ Calif Santa Barbara

LUMSDEN, IAN GORDON
DIRECTOR
b Montreal, Que, June 8, 1945. *Study:* McGill Univ, Montreal, BA, 68; Mus Mgt Inst Univ Calif, Berkeley, 91. *Collection Arranged:* The First Decade (with catalog), Confedn Ctr Art Gallery & Mus, Charlottetown, PEI, 75; Wallace S Bird Mem Collection (with catalog), Beaverbrook Art Gallery, Fredericton, NB, 75; Bloomsbury Painters & Their Circle (US & Can traveling exhib), 76-78; The Queen Comes to New Brunswick: Paintings & Drawings by Molly Lamb Bobak (Can traveling exhib), 77-78; Drawings by Jack Weldon Humphrey (Can traveling exhib), 77-79; The Murray and Marguerite Vaughan Inuit Print Collection (Can traveling exhib), 81-82; 20th Century British Drawing, Beaverbrook Art Gallery, 86; Drawings by Carol Fraser 1948-1986 (Can traveling exhib), 87-88; Gainsborough in Canada (with catalog), 91; Early Views of British North Am, Can traveling exhib (with catalogue), 94; Sargent to Freud: Modern British Paintings & Drawings in the Beaverbrook Collection (with catalog), 98; A New Brunswick Tilogy (with catalog), Suzanne Hill, Toby Graser, Kathy Hooper, Ctr Cult Menda Olimpo, Yucatan, Mex, 2001; Colour of the Seasons (with catalog), New Brunswick Mus, 2010. *Awards:* Above & Beyond Award, City of Fredericton, NB, 98; J Paul Getty Trust Scholar, Mus Management Inst, 91; The Brit Coun Visitors' Grant, 78, 91, 96; Research Fel Mod Art, Nat Gallery of Canada, 2003-2004; Fel Canadian Mus Asn, 2010; Commemorative Medal for the Golden Jubilee of Hermajesty Queen Elizabeth II, 2003. *Mem:* Atlantic Prov Art Gallery Asn (chmn, 70-72); Can Mus Asn (secy-treas, 73-75); Can Art Mus Dirs Orgn (treas 73-75, 2d vpres 75-77, 1st vpres 77-83, pres 83-85, treas 98-); Secondary Art Sub-Comt for NB Schs; Am Asn Mus; Can Soc for Decorative Arts (nat coun 99-); Gallery Connexion, Fredericton(pres bd of dirs). *Res:* 19th & 20th century Canadian art; 20th century British painting. *Publ:* Auth, Warkov, No 66 & Forrestall: de l'expressionnisme a l'hyperrealisme, No 67, Vie des Arts; Artist in New Brunswick: George Neilson Smith, Can Antiques Collector, 5-6/75; L'agrandissement du Beaverbrook, Vie des Arts, Vol XXIX, No 116, 84; Art and Music in New Brunswick, In: New Brunswick Ship Portraiture in the Nineteenth Century: an Examination of the Work of John O'Brien, William Gay Yorke & Edward John Russell, Ctr Can Studies Mt Allison Univ, New Brunswick, Vol 3, pp 35-51, 87; Sargent to Freud, Mod British Paintings & Drawings in the Beaverbrok Art Gallery, 98; Beaverbrook Art Gallery, Selected Works, Beaverbrook Art Gallery, 2000

LUND, JANE
PAINTER
b New York City, NY, 1939. *Study:* Pratt Inst; Queens Coll, New Sch Social Research. *Work:* Nelson Gallery Found, Kansas City, Mo; de Saisset Mus, Santa Clara, Calif; De Cordova Mus, Lincoln, Mass; Boston Mus Fine Art, Mass; Mus Fine Arts, Springfield, Mass; PA Acad Art, Phila, Pa; Dan Forth Mus Art, Framingham, Mass; Davidson Collection, Art Inst Chgo, Ill; Ark Art Ctr, Little Rock, Ark. *Exhib:* Self-Amused: The Contemp Artist As Observer and Observed, Fitchburg Art Mus, Mass, 93; Seventh Triennial Exhib, Fuller Mus Art, Brockton, Mass, 93; Invitational Exhib Painting & Sculpture, Am Acad Arts & Letts, New York, 94; Nothing Overlooked: Women Painting Stillife, Contemp Realist Gallery, San Francisco, Calif, 95; Jane Lund: New Pastel Paintings, Forum Gallery, New York, 97; The Figurative Impulse, Kendall Art Gallery, Miami Dade Community Coll, Fla, 98; Contemp Am Realist Drawings: The Jalane & Richard Davidson Collection, Art Inst Chicago, 99-2000; Transforming the Commonplace-Master of Contemp Realism, Susquehanna Art Mus, Harrisburg, Pa, 2003; Precision, Forum Gallery, Los Angeles, 2003; 179th Ann Invitational Exhib, Nat Acad Design, New York, 2000, 2004; Jane Lund: My Work, Forum Gallery, New York, 2005; The Feminist Figure, Forum Gallery, New York, 2007; An Eye for Detail, Forum Gallery, Los Angeles, Calif, 2007; The Figure Revealed, Kalamazoo Inst Arts, Kalamazoo, Mich, 2008; As Others See Us: The Contemporary Portrait, Brattleboro Mus, VT; Then & Now: Contemporary Artists Revisit the Past, Arkell Mus, Canajoharie, NY; Inspiring Floures, Butler Inst Am Art, Youngstown, Oh, 2010; Jane Lund: Homebody, Danforth Mus Art, Framingham, Ma, 2012; Uncommon Ground, Forum Gallery, NY, 2012. *Teaching:* Instr drawing, Berkshire Community Coll, Pittsfield, Mass, 72-81, Smith Coll, 99-. *Awards:* Fel, Mass Coun Arts & Humanities, 79 & Bunting Inst Radcliffe Coll, 85-86; Artist's Fel, Nat Endowment Arts. *Bibliog:* A realist portfolio, New Eng Monthly, 10/85; New American Paintings, Open Studios Press, 96; cover and feature article, Am Artist, 3/99, Pastel J, 10/2006; others. *Mem:* Pastel Soc Am. *Media:* Highly Finished Pastels, Watercolor Constructions. *Dealer:* Forum Gallery 730 Fifth Ave Ste 201 New York NY 10019. *Mailing Add:* 366 Norton Hill Rd Ashfield MA 01330

LUNDBERG, THOMAS ROY
ARTIST
b Belle Plaine, Iowa, June 3, 1953. *Study:* Univ Iowa, BFA, 75; Ind Univ, MFA, 79. *Work:* Am Craft Mus, NY; Indianapolis Mus Art; Chase Manhattan Bank, NY; Kaiser Found, Health Plan of Colo, Denver. *Exhib:* Craft Today USA, Mus des Arts Decoratif, Paris & European Tour, 89-92; Conversations: Textiles about Textiles, The Textile Mus, Washington, 94; Contemp Fiber from St Louis Collections, St Louis Mus, 95; 5th Int Triennial of Miniature Textiles, Mus d Angers, France, 96, 97, 6th Int Triennial, 99-2000; Art in Fiber, Indianapolis Mus Art, 97; The Cutting Edge: Contemp Quilts, Am Craft Mus, NY, 97; Nos Plus Belles Histoires Brodees, Mus Nat des Art et Traditiones Populaires, Paris, 99. *Teaching:* Prof fiber art, Colo State Univ, 79-. *Awards:* Western States Arts Fedn Regional Fel, NEA, 95; Covisions Award Colo Coun on the Arts, 96, 2000. *Bibliog:* Barbara Lee Smith (auth) Celebrating the Stitch, Taunton Press, Newton CT, 91; Anne Morrell (auth) Contemporary Embroidery, Studio Vista, London, 94; Lippard, Lucy et al (auths) Parallaxis: 55 Points of View, Western States Art Fedn, 96. *Mem:* Surface Design Asn. *Media:* Embroidery, Fiber. *Dealer:* Hibberd McGrath Gallery 101 N Main Breckenridge CO 80424; Mobilia 358 Huron Ave Cambridge MA 02138. *Mailing Add:* 806 Sandy Cove Lane Fort Collins CO 80525-3383

LUNDBERG, WILLIAM
ASSEMBLAGE ARTIST, FILMMAKER
b Albany, Calif, 1942. *Study:* San Jose State Univ, Calif, BA (art), 64; Univ Calif, Berkeley, MA (art), 66. *Work:* Guggenheim Mus, NY; Mus Art, RI Sch Design; Mus Contemp Art, Univ Sao Paulo, Brazil; Mus Mod Art, Niterio, Brazil; numerous others, pub & pvt. *Exhib:* Solo exhibs, Whitney Mus Am Art, NY, 82, Carnegie Inst Mus Art, Pittsburgh, Pa, 84, Emily Davis Gallery, Univ Akron, Ohio, 87, Langford Archit Gallery, Tex A&M Univ, College Station, Tex, 89, Ctr Res Contemp Art, Arlington, Tex, 91, Solar Grandjean de Montigny, Centro Cult da PUC, Rio de Janeiro, Brazil, 92, Mus Contemp Art, Univ Sao Paulo, Brazil, 92 & Blanton Mus, Univ Tex Austin, 99; group exhibs, Bill Lundberg-Regina Vater, Bridge Ctr Contemp Art, El Paso, Tex, 90, World Disorder, Cult Space, NY, 91, Trance Medial, Austin, Tex, 91, Installation, Mexic-arte, Austin, Tex, 92, Funiarte, Cult Inst Rio de Janeiro, 93, 34th Ann Invitational, Longview Art Mus, Tex, 93, Old & New Masters of Super-8 & Anthology Film Archives, NY, 94; Mirrors Edge, BildMusseet, Umea, Sweden, Vancouver Art, 2000-; Alternative Currents, McKinney Ave Contemp, Dallas, 2001; and many others. *Teaching:* Instr, New Eng Col, Arundel, Eng, 71-74; Md Inst Col Art, Baltimore, 83; Parsons Sch Design, New York, 84-85; assoc prof, Univ Tex-Austin, 85-2000, prof, 2000-. *Awards:* Fel New Genre, Nat Endowment Arts, 91; Fulbright Fel, Mus Contemp Art, Sao Paulo, 92; Teaching Excellence Award, Coll Fine Arts, 93; Fac Res Award, Univ Tex, 94; and many others. *Media:* Film, Video. *Mailing Add:* 4901 Caswell Ave Austin TX 78751

LUNDEEN, GEORGE WAYNE
SCULPTOR
b Holdrege, Nebr, 1948. *Study:* Hastings Col, Nebr, LBA, 71; Univ Ill, MFA (sculpture), 73; Acad de Belle Arte, Italy, 74; Artist-in-residence Texas Agr & Mechanical Univ, Coll Station, 78-79. *Hon Degrees:* Univ Nebr, PhD, 1999. *Work:* Nebr State Collection, Kearney; People's Republic China, Nat Gallery, Peking; Holdrege, Nebr; Botanical Gardens, Wichita, Kans; City of Carmel, Calif. *Comn:* lifesize Robert Frost, Dartmouth Col, 96; Jack Swigert, Statuary Hall, Capitol Bldg, Washington, DC, 97; Lewis & Clark monument, Great Plains Art Mus, Lincoln, Nebr, 2004; monument, Coors Field, Denver, 2005; High Plains Heritage Ctr, Chadron, Nebr, 2002; and others. *Exhib:* Solo exhibs incl: O'Brien's, Scottsdale, Ariz, Driscol's, Denver, Vail, Trails West, Laguna Beach; works incl(bronze sculptures) Michelle (Nat Acad Art Watrous Gold medal 82), Promise of the Prairie (Holdrege Nebraska award 83), Fulbright-Hays grantee, Florence, Italy, 73-74, Mem Nat Sculpture Soc (Bronze medal 81, 84, Silver medal 82), Allied Artists Am (Montana award 82); recipient, Pioneer award, Neb legislature, 95, Distinguished Nebraskan, Gov Neb, 95; North Am Sculpture Exhib, Foot Hills Art Ctr, 79-86; Allied Artists Am Ann, NY, 80-87; Nat Sculpture Soc Ann, NY, 80-88; Nat Acad Design Ann, NY, 80-86; Am Western Art Exhib, Peking Arts Gallery, China, 81. *Pos:* Fulbright-Hays Scholar, Florence, Italy, 73-74; artist-in-residence, Tex A&M Univ, 78-79. *Awards:* Art Castings of Colorado Award, NAm Sculpture Exhib, 83; N Am Sculpture Exhib, John Cavenaugh Mem Award, 86; Allied Artists Members & Assocs Award, 87; Pioneer award, Legislature of Nebr, 92; Distinguished Nebraskan, State of Nebr, 95; and others. *Bibliog:* John Jellico (auth), G W Lundeen, Artist of the Rockies & Golden West, spring 81; M Lantz & T Morgan (auths), The western art of 12 western sculptors, Nat Sculpture Review, fall, 80; Libby James (auth), George Lundeen, Southwest Art, 5/83; Judy Hughs (auth), the Sculpting Lundeens, Southwest Art, 8/93. *Mem:* Nat Sculpture Soc; Allied Artists Am; Nat Acad. *Media:* Bronze. *Mailing Add:* c/o Loveland Sculpture Gallery 338 E Fourth St Loveland CO 80537

LUNDER, PETER & PAULA H
COLLECTOR
Study: Colby Coll, 1956. *Hon Degrees:* Colby Coll, DFA, 1998; Thomas Coll, DSc in Bus Adminstration, 2010. *Pos:* Mem bd govs, Colby Coll Mus Art, 1995-, current lifetime overseer and mem, Colby Mus of Art Governing Bd and Acquisition Com; founder, Kenilworth, Inc; co-chmn, pres, CEO, Dexter Shoe Co; former limited ptnr, Boston Red Sox; bd chmn Pan Am Shoe Co ; pres, OCSAP Ltd; former mem, Babson Coll Corporation Bd; former vice chairman National Bd, Smithsonian Institution; commissioner emeritus, Smithsonian American Art Mus (SAAM); chmn, The Lunder Found; mem, Dana-Farber Cancer Institute Visiting Com. *Awards:* Named of on Top 200 Collectors, ARTnews mag, 2009-11. *Collection:* American Impressionism and modernism; 19th-century and Western art

LUNDIN, NORMAN K
PAINTER, EDUCATOR
b Los Angeles, Calif, 1938. *Study:* Sch Art Inst Chicago, BA, 61; Univ Chicago, 61; Univ Cincinnati, MFA, 63; Univ Oslo, Norway, 63. *Work:* Mus Mod Art, NY; Detroit Inst Arts; Brooklyn Mus Art; Seattle Art Mus; Achenbach Found; Fine Arts Mus, San Francisco; Yale Univ. *Comn:* Set design, Dark Elegies, Pacific NW Ballet, Kennedy Ctr for Performing Arts, Wash, DC. *Exhib:* Solo exhibs, Allan Stone Gallery, NY, Space Gallery, Los Angeles, Stephen Haller Fine Art, NY, Long Beach Mus Art, Calif, (catalog), Schmidt Bingham Gallery, NY, Am Realism, San Francisco Art Mus, (catalog), Sources of Light, Henry Art Gallery, Seattle; Whitney Mus Am Art, NY; Barnsdale Gallery, Los Angeles Munic Mus; Seattle Art Mus; Koplin Gallery, Los Angeles; Francine Seders Gallery, Seattle. *Pos:* Vis artist, Hornsey Col Art, London, Eng, 69-70, Ohio State Univ, Columbus, 75, San Diego State Univ, 78, Brighton Col Art, Eng, 79 & Univ Tex, San Antonio, 82. *Teaching:* Prof art, Univ Wash, Seattle, 64-. *Awards:* Grants, Fulbright Found, 63-64, Ford Found, 78-79 & Nat Endowment Arts, 83; Wash State Visual Artists Fel, Tiffany Found. *Bibliog:* Bruce Guenther (auth), Fifty Northwestern Artists, San Francisco Chronicle Books, 83; Lynn Gamwell (auth), West Coast Realism, Laguna Beach Mus Art, 83; Robert Flynn Johnson (auth), Norman Lundin: A Decade of Drawing & Painting, Univ Wash Press, Long Beach Mus Art, 90; At 60 Norman Lundin, Frye Art Mus, Seattle; Richard V West, Bruce Guenther, David Brody (auths), Norman Lundin: Selecting From Three Decades of Drawing & Painting, Univ Wash Press. *Media:* Oil, Acrylic. *Dealer:* Schmidt-Bingham Gallery 41 E 57th St New York NY 10022; Francine Seders Gallery Seattle; Koplin Gallery 6031 Washington Blvd Culver City CA 90232. *Mailing Add:* 3419 E Denny Way Seattle WA 98122

LUNDSFRYD, TINE
PAINTER
b Falster, Denmark. *Study:* Jaruplund Hoejskole, Flensborg, 1983-84; Antroposofisk Selskab, Copenhagen, Denmark, 1984-87; Studied with Carsten Dinnsen, Denmark, 1984-87; NY Studio Sch, 1990-92; Parsons Sch Design, MFA (painting), New York, 1995. *Exhib:* Kunstnernes Efteraarsudstilling, Copenhagen, 1987; Kunstnernes Paaskeudstilling, Aahus, Denmark, 1989; CAA Exhib, Hunter Col, NY, 1993; MFA Thesis Exhib, Parsons Sch Design, New York, 1995; Lyric Art for the North, Unibank Gallery, Am-Scandinavian Soc, New York, 1996; solo exhibs, Multimedia Cafe, Copenhagen, 1996, Told-og Skattestyrelsen, Denmark, 1996, SID Uddannelsescenter, Denmark, 1996, Nysted Raadhus, Denmark, 1996, ISA Monte Castello di Vibio, Italy, 1999 & 2000, Corpus Christi Church, New York, 2001, Artpage Gallery, Williamsburg, New York, 2001, Lori Bookstein Fine Art, New York, 2004 & 2007 & Danish Consulate Gen, New York, 2005,; The Lightbox by Richard Hume, Williamsburg Art and Hist Ctr, New York, 1997; Artspace Available, Art in General, New York, 1999; Brooklyn Artists, Brooklyn Mus Art, 1999; Artpage Gallery, New York, 2000 & 2001; Elsa Mott Ives Gallery, New York, 2002; CMP Gallery, Wash, 2002 & 2003; I-20 Gallery, New York, 2002 & 2003; Lori Bookstein Fine Art, New York, 2002, 2004, 2005, 2007 & 2009; Sideshow Gallery, New York, 2004; Benefit Auction, NY Studio Sch, 2005-2006; 181st Ann Exhib of Contemp Am Art, Nat Acad Art, New York, 2006; We-Are-Familia, Collete, Paris, 2007; 6 Danish Artists in New York, Trygve Lie Gallery, New York, 2008; Cult Award, Am Scandinavian Soc, 2000; Purchase Prize, Am Acad Arts and Letts, 2008; Am Acad Arts and Letts Invitational, New York, 2009. *Bibliog:* Mario Naves (auth), A slow burn, 10/2002, The vision thing triumphs, honoring logic, courting chaos, 5/2003 & Danish artist Tine Lundsfryd delineates true abstraction, 10/2004, New York Observer; Dodie Kazanjian (auth), The purist: painter Tine Lundsfryd is seeking true abstraction, Vogue, 9/2004; New York as art metropolis, Børsen, 3/24/2006. *Media:* Oil. *Mailing Add:* Lori Bookstein Fine 138 10th Ave New York NY 10011-4727

LUNEAU, CLAUDE
SCULPTOR
b Paris, France, 1935; Can citizen. *Work:* Can Coun Art Bank; Laurentian Univ, Sudbury; Windsor Art Gallery; Holdbrooks Holdings, Toronto; Mus Civilization, Ottawa. *Exhib:* Solo exhibs, Mira Godard Gallery, Toronto, Ont, 82 & 84, Olga Korper Gallery, Toronto, Ont, 86, 88, 91, 93 & 96, Moosart Gallery, Miami, Fla, 86 & Koffler Gallery, Toronto, Ont, 93; Glenbow Mus, Calgary, Alta, 83; Olga Korper Gallery, Toronto, Ont, 86, 88 & 89; Equinox Gallery, Vancouver, BC, 88; Robertson Galleries, Ottawa, Ont, 88; 49th Parallel, NY, 89; Structure: Claude Luneau & Greg Murdock, Gallery/Stratford, Ont, 90. *Awards:* Can Coun Project Cost Grant, 83, 84 & 85; Ont Arts Coun Material Assts Grant, 83 & Traveling Cost Grant, 86. *Bibliog:* Christopher Hume (auth), Essays in whimsy, 8/14/82, Heavy Metal, 8/31/84, Toronto Star; From the Heart: Folk Art in Canada, McLelland & Stewart, Toronto, 83; Peter Day (auth), Claude Luneau, Can Art, spring 86

LUNNEY, KEVAN
FIBER ARTIST
b Stuttgart, Ger, 1959. *Exhib:* Solo exhibs, Noyes Mus, Oceanville, NJ, 2012, Mini Textile Art, Kherson, Ukraine, 2013, Monmouth Mus, Lincroft, NJ, 2015; Group exhibs, 728 Gallery, Phila, Pa, 2012, Sanitas Ctr, Gaberone, Botswana, Africa, 2012, Quilt Expo en Beaujolais, Sur Anse, France, Parc Expo de Villefranche sur Saone, 2012, Global Health Odyssey Mus of the Ctrs for Disease Control and Prevention, Atlanta, Ga, 2012, Visions Gallery, San Diego, Calif, 2012, Audubon Artists Online Ann Exhib, 2012, and many others. *Collection Arranged:* Fiber Revolution, Belskie Mus Art & Sci, 2005, Johnson & Johnson World Headquarters, New Brunswick, NJ, 2006; Art Concentrated, Acad Music, Spotswood, NJ, 2007, 2008, 2009, 2010, Somerset Arts Asn, Bedminster, NJ, 2007, Belskie Gallery of Art & Sci, 2007; Naked Truth, Arts Guild of Rahway, Rahway, NJ, 2007; Botswana Quilts from Fiber Revolution & Kalahari Quilters, Johnson & Johnson, 2010; Omnifarious Art Show, Straube Ctr, Pennington, 2010; Visual Thoughts, Morris Mus, Morristown, NJ, 2011; Straube Ctr, Pennington, NJ, 2014. *Teaching:* instr, Ctr Contemporary Arts, Bedminster, NJ. *Awards:* Surface Design award, Wayne Art Ctr, Art Quilt Elements, 2012; Marquis Who's Who in Am Art References award in Collage & Mixed Media, Audubon Artists, New York, 2012; Audubon Artists, 2013. *Bibliog:* Studio Art Quilters Associates, Portfolio 15, 16, 17, 18, 19; Karey Patterson Bresenhan (auth), Creative Quilting, Journal Quilt Project, Quilting Arts LLC, 2006; Why Innovation Matters (interview by Monica Moses, with David Revere McFadden) American Craft American Craft Council, Vol 72, pp 96, 2012. *Mem:* Fiber Revolution; Audubon Artists; Studio Art Quilters Asn; Surface Design Asn; Textile Study Group NY. *Media:* Stitch, Paint, Metal Leaf. *Publ:* Studio Art Quilters Associates Portfolio 15, 16, 17, 18, 19, 20, 21, 1000 Dog Portraits by Robynne Raye, Why Innovation Matters (Interview by Monica Moses, with David Revere McFaddem) American Craft Council, Vol 72, pp 96, 2012; SAQA Art Quilt Collector, Issue 1. *Dealer:* Maria Elena Kravetz Gallery Cordoba Argentina

LUNSFORD, JOHN (CRAWFORD)
HISTORIAN, CURATOR
b Dallas, Tex, Apr 15, 1933. *Study:* Harvard Univ, AB (Eng lit), 54; Columbia Univ, MA (pre-Columbian art hist & archaeol), 67. *Collection Arranged:* The Clark and Frances Stillman Collection of Congo Sculpture (with catalog), 69; Arts of Oceania (with catalog), 70; The Romantic Vision in Am (with catalog), 71; African Art from Dallas Collections (with catalog), 72; The Gustave and Franyo Schindler Collection of African Sculpture (with catalog), 75; Nora and John Wise Collection of Pre-Columbian Art, 76. *Pos:* Cur, Dallas Mus Art, 68-80, sr cur, 80-86; dir, Meadow Mus, Southern Methodist Univ, 96. *Teaching:* Adj prof art hist, Southern Methodist Univ, Dallas, 67-96. *Res:* The arts of pre-Columbian Meso-America and West and Central Africa; pre-Columbian Central and South America; native American art. *Mailing Add:* c/o Meadows Mus Southern Methodist Univ Dallas TX 75275

LUNTZ, IRVING
DEALER
b Milwaukee, Wis, Jan 9, 1929. *Study:* Northwestern Univ. *Pos:* Pres & dir, Irving Galleries, Inc, Palm Beach, Fla, 59-. *Mem:* Art Dealers Asn Am; Appraisers Asn Am. *Res:* Nineteenth and twentieth century American and European painting; sculpture and graphics; photography. *Specialty:* Modern and contemporary painting, sculpture and photography. *Mailing Add:* 332 Worth Ave Palm Beach FL 33480

LUPORI, PETER JOHN
SCULPTOR
b Pittsburgh, Pa, Dec 12, 1918. *Study:* Carnegie-Mellon Univ, BFA, 42; Univ of Minn, MS (educ), 47; studied with Joseph Bailey Ellis & John Rood. *Work:* The Walker Art Ctr, Minneapolis, Minn; Ball State Teachers Coll Art Gallery, Muncie, Ind; North Hennepin Community Coll Art Gallery, Fridley, Minn; Albert Lea Pub Libr, Minn; Minn Alumni Asn Art Gallery, IDS Ctr, Minneapolis; Normandale Jr Col, Minn; Coll of St Catherine, St Paul, Minn. *Comn:* Creation (ceramic bas-relief), Westminster Presbyterian Church, Minneapolis, 82; St Joseph tryptich (ceramic bas-relief), St Joseph Hosp, Dickinson, NDak, 84; Bishop Whipple (bronze), St Cornelia Church, Morton, Minn; Pentecost & Christ Welcoming (bronze) & 3 bronze reliefs, Univ St Thomas, St Paul, Minn, 96; 7 ft Madonna (bronze), Coll St Catherine, 98; St Joan of Arc, Bronze, Church of St Joan Arc, Minn, 2000. *Exhib:* Ann Assoc Artist of Pittsburgh, Carnegie Inst of Art, Pa, 40-62; Biennial Exhib of Paintings & Prints, Walker Art Ctr, Minneapolis, 47-49; 1st Biennial Exhib Prints & Drawing, Minneapolis Inst of Arts, 50, 52-54; Six-State Sculpture Exhib, Walker Art Ctr, 47, 51; Ann Local Artists Exhibs, Minneapolis Inst of Arts, 47-48, 50-52; 16th Ceramic Ann Nat Exhib, Syracuse, NY, 51; Fine Arts Exhib, Minn State Fair Art Gallery, St Paul, 46-; Solo exhib, St Paul Mus of Art, 52; Retrospective 1936-1993, Coll St Catherine, St Paul, Minn, 93. *Teaching:* Instr sculpture, Univ of Minn, Minneapolis, 46-49; asst prof, sculpture, Col of St Thomas, St Paul, Minn, 49-51; prof sculpture, The Col of St Catherine, St Paul, 47-92; Ceramic Sculpture, Northern Clay Ctr, Minneapolis, Minn, 92-. *Awards:* 2nd award in sculpture, Prix de Rome, NY, 41; Carnegie Inst Prize for Sculpture, Asn Artists Pittsburgh, 49; Emily Arsenberg Award, Asn Artists Pittsburgh, 62; total of 40 sculpture awards, 37-. *Mem:* Soc Minn Sculptors; Minn Artists Asn. *Media:* Ceramic, Bronze, Wood. *Interests:* Fishing, Traveling, Coin Collecting. *Mailing Add:* 5118 12th Ave S Minneapolis MN 55417

LUPPER, EDWARD
PAINTER, PUBLISHER
b NJ, Jan 4, 1936. *Study:* With Wesley Lea, Frenchtown, NJ; Trenton Jr Coll; Parsons Sch Design, New York; Calif Coll Arts & Crafts, Oakland; San Francisco Art Inst; San Francisco State Coll; M H de Young Mem Mus Sch, 78. *Work:* Los Angeles Maritime Mus; Healdsburg Mus and Hist Soc; George Ohr, O'Keefe Mus, Miss. *Comn:* Two paintings, Scott Newhall Collection, 80 & 82; Annedeen Hosiery Mills, 88. *Exhib:* Baltimore Mus Art, 55; San Francisco Mus Art, 60; Am Embassy, Belg, 77-78; solo exhib, Debruyne Fine Arts, Naples, Fla, 2001-2004; Rick Moore Fine Art, Santa Fe, NMex, 2003-2005; America's Best Paint, Naples, Fla, 2002-2003; DeBruyne Fine Arts, 2004-2006; Rancho Mirage Public Libr, 2008. *Pos:* Artist, card line, Posters, Sunrise Publ, 88-95; artist, Great Am Puzzle co, 97-98; Maggie Needlepoint co, 98-99. *Teaching:* Puzzle line, bits & pieces, 2002-2003; artist, Giclé Fine Art Prints, 2004-2007; www.lupperart.com, 2008-. *Awards:* Huntington Hartford Found Fel, 64; Courage Cards Art Search Award, 2000-2001; Courage Exclusive Art Card Award for

the internet, 2003, 2007-2010. *Bibliog:* Articles, San Francisco Chronicle, 60, San Francisco Examiner, 62 & 65, Seattle Times, 71, Naples Daily News, 86 & Naples Times, Fla, 86-92. *Media:* Casein, Oil. *Publ:* Auth, articles In: Playgirl, 74, Apartment Life, 9/74, Popular Gardening Indoors, 77, Eaton Paper Corp, 77-78, Sunrise Publ, 79-80, Gulfshore Life & Naples Guide, 86 & 91-92, Am Artist, 88, Artist Mag, 89 & Focus Mag, Fla, Desert Art Scene Mag, 2011-2012; brochure, Delta Shiva Corp, 87-88; auth (catalog), America's Best Paint, Naples, FL, 2001 & Naples Daily News, 3/2003; auth, The Bottom Line 2005, The Carousel Mag, 7/2005; The Press-Enterprise, 2004; Cathedral City Sun, 2007; Gulf Shore, MAGA2ine, 11/2009; Palm Desert Patch Network World Class Artists, Online News Interview, Arts & Entertainment, 2011. *Dealer:* Debruyne Fine Art 275 Broad Ave S Naples FL 34102; Richard Danskin Galleries 73-111 El Paseo Palm Desert CA 92260. *Mailing Add:* 69-784 Wakefield Rd Cathedral City CA 92234

LUQUE, JOSE ANTONIO
CRITIC, CURATOR

b Mexico City, Mex, June 5, 1954. *Study:* Facultad de Filosofia y Letras, UNAM, lic en hist, 84. *Collection Arranged:* Mexican Art Renaissance, Nagoya City Art Mus, Japan, 89; Le Fete de la Mort, Musee de la Botanique, Brussels, 93; Orozco, Rivera y Siqueiros Ctr, Cult de Delem, Lisbon, 95. *Pos:* Deputy dir & fine arts dus, Instituto Nacional de Bellas Arts, Mexico City, 82-86, Mus Mod Art, Instituto Nacional de Bellas Artes, 87-88 & Palace Fine Arts Mus, Mexico City, 93-94. *Publ:* Auth, La ilusion de lo real: realismos/hiperealism, Instituto Nacional de Bellas Artes, 88; Raices de Oaxaca: Tamayo, Nieto, Toledo, Casa de Tiempo, 92; Aguila y sol, pintura Mexico, siglo XX, 93 & Oaxaca, magia de Mexico, 93, Europalia; Os grandes mestres: Orozco, Rivera, Siqueiros, Fund das Descobertas, Lisbon, 95. *Mailing Add:* Calle Dos 17A-1 San Pedro de los Pinos 03800 Mexico

LUSKER, RON
PAINTER, DESIGNER

b Chicago, Ill, Jan 28, 1937. *Study:* Sch Art Inst Chicago, 54-60; Univ Ill, Chicago Circle, Ill State Gen Assembly scholar, 57-62; Univ Chicago, 62-63; Southern Ill Univ, Carbondale, BA, 65, MFA, 66. *Work:* Univ NC; Price Waterhouse, Chicago; Chase Manhattan; Southern Ill Univ; Aldrich Mus Contemp Art; Corcoran Gallery Art, DC; Aldrich Mus Contemp Art, Ridgefield, Conn. *Exhib:* 14th Ann Painting & Sculpture Exhib, Peoria Art Ctr, Ill, 66; 70th Ann Midwest Painting Exhib, Art Inst Chicago, 67; Convocation Arts, Sculpture, State Univ NY Albany, 68; 4th Ann Art Exhib Sculpture, Staten Island, 69; Eastern Seaboard Regional 3rd Ann Sculpture Exhib, 70; plus others. *Teaching:* Instr art, Southern Ill Univ, Carbondale, 65-67; asst prof art, State Univ NY Stony Brook, 68-72; assoc prof art, Kingsborough Community Col, 72-74. *Awards:* Grad Sch for Sculpture Fel & Grant in Aid, State Univ NY Stony Brook, 69 & 70. *Bibliog:* Malcolm Preston (auth), Assemblages display intellectual fantasy, Newsday, 5/21/69; Claire White (auth), Exhibition review, Craft Horizons, 6/70; Albert Boime (auth), Cosmic artifacts: The work in lucite of Ron Lusker, Art J, winter 72. *Mem:* Am Craftsmen Coun; Coll Art Asn Am; Ctr Study Democratic Insts. *Media:* Acrylic, Oils. *Publ:* Auth, New York: The season in sculpture, 8/70, The green meadow school, 8/70, The jewelry of Marci Zelmanoff, 12/70 & Attitudes, Brooklyn Museum, 70, Craft Horizons Mag. *Mailing Add:* 85 Mercer St New York NY 10012

LUTES, JIM (JAMES)
PAINTER

b Ft Lewis, Wash, Dec 5, 1955. *Study:* Wash State Univ, BA, 78; Art Inst Chicago, MFA 82. *Work:* Mus Contemp Art & Art Inst Chicago; Mus Contemp Art, Ghent, Belg; Domaine de Kerguehennec, Locmine, France; Ill State Mus, Springfield; Progressive Corp, Pepper Pike, Ohio. *Exhib:* Chicago & Vicinity Show, Art Inst Chicago, 84; 39th Corcoran Biennial (catalogue), Corcoran Gallery Art, 84-86; Viewpoints (catalogue), Walker Art Ctr, 85; Whitney Biennial (catalogue), Whitney Mus, 87, 2006; Why Paint, The Renaissance Soc, Univ Chicago, 92; solo exhibs, Dart Gallery, 86, 87, 88, 91 & 92, Guy LeDune Contemp Art, Brussels, Belg, 93, Vera Van Laer Gallery (catalogue), Knokke-Heist, Belg, 93, Zolla Lieberman Gallery, Chicago, 94, 96 & 99, Mus Contemp Art (catalogue), Chicago, 94, Mus van Hedendaagse Kunst (catalog), Ghent, Belg, 95 & Ctr Creative Studies, Detroit, 96; Abstract Chicago, Evanston Art Ctr, 95; Pulp Fiction, Gallery A, Chicago, 95; Faculty Biennial, Univ Galleries, Normal, Ill, 95; Art Chicago: 1945-1995, Mus Contemp Art (catalog), Chicago, 96; Zolla/Lieberman Gallery Inc, Chicago, 96, 97, 98 & 99; Art Chicago 1997, Navy Pier, Chicago, 97; Linda Hodges Gallery, Seattle, Wash, 97; Denaturalized, Mus Contemp Art, Chicago; Les Objets Contiennent l'Infiniti, Ecole Superiure des Beaux-arts de Tours, France, 98; Zolla Lieberman Gallery, Chicago, Ill, 99; Whitney Biennial, Whitney Mus Am Art, 2010. *Teaching:* Vis artist, Art Inst Chicago, 83-95 & 98; adj assoc prof abstract painting, Univ Ill, Chicago, 95; assoc prof, Ill State Univ, Normal, 95-99; assoc prof, Sch Art Inst Chicago, 98-. *Awards:* Ill Arts Coun Grant, 85, 99; Seven Awards in Visual Arts, 88; Nat Endowment Arts, 93; Louis Comfort Tiffany Found Award, 93; Guggenheim Found Fel, 2010. *Bibliog:* Kathryn Hixson (auth), Arts Mag, p 107-108, 4/91; Alan Artner (auth), Is Painting Dead, Chicago Tribune, 4/92; Robert Frank (auth), Kuntsforum Int, Bd 119, pages 178, 336, 392, 92; Alan Artner (auth), MCA's Three for all, Chicago Tribune, 12/11/94; Alan Artner (auth), Lutes delivers own brand of Commentary, Chicago Tribune, 11/7/96; Susan Snodegrass (auth), Art in Am, 2000. *Media:* Oil, Acrylic. *Dealer:* Valerie Carberry Gallery 875 N Michigan Ave Ste 2510 Chicago IL 6061. *Mailing Add:* Valerie Carberry Gallery John Hancock Ctr 875 N Michigan Ave Suite 2510 Chicago IL 60611

LUTNICK, HOWARD W
PATRON

b New York, NY. *Study:* Haverford Col, BA (econ), 83. *Pos:* With Cantor Fitzgerald, New York City, 83-, pres & Chief Exec Officer, 91-, chmn, 96-; founder, chmn, pres & Chief Exec Officer, eSpeed, 99-; speaker in field, currently; trustee, Solomon R Guggenheim Mus, currently; bd managers, Zachary & Elizabeth M Fisher Ctr Alzheimer's Disease Res, Rockefeller Univ; bd trustee, exec comt, Intrepid Mus Found; bd managers, Haverford Col; bd dir, Tate Gallery Projects Ltd, Tate Mus. *Awards:* Recipient Distinguished Pub Serv Award, Dept Navy. *Mailing Add:* eSpeed Inc 115 E 59th St New York NY 10022

LUTZ, MARJORIE BRUNHOFF
PAINTER, SCULPTOR

b Cincinnati, Ohio, Jan 25, 1933. *Study:* Art Students League, with Sidney Simon; Duke Univ, Empire State Coll, BA, Summit Univ La, MA, Sculpture Ctr, NY. *Work:* Tuttleman Collection, Merion, Pa; David Whitcomb Collection, Hudson, NY; Morgan Sculpture Gardens, Ctr Hall, Pa; Southern Vt Art Ctr, Manchester, Vt. *Comn:* Early Bird, Todd Hunter Develop Corp,; Welded steel abstract, Taft Steel Corp, NY, 81; Helios, David Whitcomb, Hudson, NY; La Petite Francaise, Dixon Collection, Dorset, Vt; Gaia, Alexander White Collection, Old Chatham, NY, Carl Sweet Winery, Sacramento, Sting Ray, 2000. *Exhib:* Solo exhibs, Southern Vt Art Ctr, 84, Elm St Gallery, Manchester, Vt, 96; Group exhibs, Ginofor Gallery, Cambridge, NY, 90-99; The Sculpture Works, Santa Fe, NMex, 2000; Four Winds Gallery, Santa Cruz, NMex, 2000; Munson Gallery, Santa Fe, NMex; Grace Fine Art Gallery, Morristown, NJ; Art is Okay, Alberquerque. *Teaching:* Instr sculpture, Southern Vt Art Ctr, Manchester, Vt, 85-95, pvt instrn 95-. *Awards:* Doris Kriendler Mem Award, Am Soc Contemp Artists, 83. *Bibliog:* American Artist Illustrated Survey of American Contemporaries; Am Dictionary of Sculptors. *Mem:* Am Soc Contemp Artists; Southern Vt Art Ctr, (bd dir, 88-93, vpres, 88, pres, 89-92); Screen Dir Guild. *Media:* Stone, Wood, Watercolor on paper. *Publ:* Archit Dig, 7/94. *Dealer:* Grace Fine Arts 142 South St Morristown NJ 07960. *Mailing Add:* 16 Brilliant Sky Dr Santa Fe NM 87508

LUTZ, WINIFRED ANN
ENVIRONMENTAL ARTIST, INSTALLATION SCULPTOR

b Brooklyn, NY, May 6, 1942. *Study:* Cleveland Inst Art, BFA, 65; Atelier 17, with Stanley William Hayter, 65; Cranbrook Acad Art, MFA, 68. *Work:* Cleveland Mus Art; Albright-Knox Art Gallery; Chicago Art Inst; Desert Mus, Palm Springs, Calif; Crocker Gallery, Sacramento; Newark Mus, NJ; Int Paper Corp, NY; Jan van Eyck Akademie, Maastricht, Neth; Mount Holyoke Coll Art Mus, Mass; Nat Bank of Chicago; Philadelphia Mus Art, PA; Ackland Art Mus; Univ N Carolina Chapel Hill; Cranbrook Acad Art Mus, MI; Wustum Mus of Fine Arts, WI; Abington Art Center, PA; The Mattress Factory, Pittsburgh, PA. *Comn:* sculpture, Harrisburg Mem, Commonwealth Pa, 93; sculpture garden, The Mattress Factory, 92-97; sculpture garden Ctrs for Disease Control, Atlanta, Ga, 98-2000; sculpture, American Philosophical Soc Mus, Philadelphia, Pa, 2007-8. *Exhib:* Solo exhibs, Paper Reliefs, Am Craft Mus, NY, 75, Marilyn Pearl Gallery, 77-79, 84-85, 86, 88 & 90, New Am Paperworks, Int Traveling Invitational Exhib, 82-86, Paper as Image, Arts Coun of Gt Brit, 83 & Dolan-Maxwell Gallery, Philadelphia, 90, Gallery Joe, 2000-4, Zabriski Gallery 02,07; Int Biennale Paper Art, Leopold-Hoesch Mus, Duren, Ger, 86 & 88; Light Cycle, Visual Arts Ctr of Alaska, Anchorage, 86; A Point of View--A Vista, Hewlett Gallery, Carnegie-Mellon Univ, Pittsburgh, 86; Paper Art, Mus Provencial, Hasselt, Belg, 88; Paper Makes Space, Nordyllandi Kunst, Denmark, 89, Grand Lobby Installation, Brooklyn Mus, 90; A Natural Order, Hudson River Mus, Yonkers, NY, 90; Flour to Ceiling/Surface to Edge, Cranbrook AcadArt Mus, 92; The Prison as Site, Historic Eastern State Penitentiary, Phila, 95; Correspondence/Congruence, The Contemp Arts Ctr Cincinnati, Ohio, 95; Nature Morte: Contemp Still Life, Am Mus Pa Acad Fine Arts, 96; Threshold, ICA Univ Pa, 97; The Best of the Season, Aldrich Mus Contemp Arts, Ridgefield, Conn, 99; Invisible Sky & Drawing Dock Creek, American Philosophical Soc, Ind Nat Hist Park 07-8. *Teaching:* Asst prof sculpture, Yale Sch Art, 75-81, assoc prof, 81-82; assoc prof sculpture, Tyler Sch Art, 82-99, Laura Carnell prof, 99-08. *Awards:* Nat Endowment Arts Fel, 84; Creative Time Inc Project Grant, 89; Pa Coun Arts, 89; Francis J Greenburger Found, 90; Pen Fel Arts, 92. *Bibliog:* Bloemink (auth), A Natural Order, Hudson River Mus, 90; Claudia Gianni (auth), The Garden by Winifred Lutz, photos by John Charloy, Mattress Factory, Pittsburgh, 97; Mac Griswold (auth), Brodding Forest as Artists Medium, NY Times, 11/30/97; Janet Koplos (auth), Stillness, Dieu Donne Papermill Inc, NYc; Garrison Roots (auth), Designing the Worlds Best Public Art, Images Pub Group, Australia, 02; Tom Csaszar (auth), Perception's Nature: The Sculptures of Winifred Lutz, Sculpture Mag, Vol 21, #7, 9/2002. *Mem:* Coll Art Asn (Dist Teaching Visual Arts, 99). *Media:* All. *Publ:* Auth, Felting, Am Crafts Mag, 8-9/80; Casting to Acknowledge the Nature of Paper, Int Conf Hand Papermakers, Carriage House Press, 81; appendix of Non-Japanese Fibers for Japanese Papermaking, Weatherhill, 83; Surface is A function Of distance, catalog essay, the Detroit Inst Arts Founders Soc, 88; Shrinking To Expand, Carriage House Press, 88; Flux & Interruption/Contingencies in the Field, Gallery Joe, 04; Flood Paper, Hand Papermaking, vol. 26, no. 1, 2011. *Dealer:* Gallery Joe 302 Arch St Philadelphia PA 19106; Zabriskie Gallery 41 East 57 St NY 10022. *Mailing Add:* 2316 Terwood Rd Huntington PA 19006-5509

LUZ, VIRGINIA
PAINTER

b Toronto, Ont, Oct 15, 1911. *Study:* Cent Tech Sch. *Work:* Robert McLaughlin Gallery, Oshawa, Ont; Can Dept External Affairs; Can Embassies; J S McLean Collection; London Art Mus; also in many pvt collections. *Exhib:* Ont Soc Artists, 45-83; Can Women Artists Show (traveling exhib to NY & Can), 47-49; Can Soc Painters in Watercolour, 47-75; Can Tours; Can Group Painters; Tribute to Ten Women, Sisler Gallery, Toronto, Ont, 75; and others. *Teaching:* Instr illus, Cent Tech Sch, Toronto, 40-74, dir art, 69-74. *Mem:* Ont Soc Artists; Royal Can Acad; Can Soc Painters in Watercolour. *Media:* Watercolor

LYFORD, CABOT
SCULPTOR, PAINTER
b Sayre, Pa, May 22, 1925. *Study:* Skowhegan Sch Art, summer 47; Cornell Univ, BFA, 50; Sculpture Ctr, New York, 50-51. *Work:* Lamont Gallery, Exeter, NH; Addison Gallery Am Art, Andover, Mass; Wichita Mus, Kans; Indianapolis Mus, Ind; New Eng Ctr Continuing Educ, Durham, NH; Ogunquit Art Mus; Portland Mus Art, Maine; Hunter Mus, Chattanooga, Tenn; over 150 pvt collections. *Comn:* Sculpture, Mt Sunapee Summit, NH, 64; Harbor Sculpture (black granite), Portsmouth, NH, 75; black granite whale, Prescott Park, Portsmouth, NH, 79; sculpture, Voc Tech, Stratham, NH, 83; Albacore Park Submariner Mem, Portsmouth, NH; Berwick Sch, ME; and others. *Exhib:* Addison Gallery, Andover, Mass; Fitchburg Art Mus; Univ NH; Midtown Gallery, NY; Ogunquit Mus, Maine; Theme Sculpture Bronze, New Bedford Whaling Mus; Mus of Art, Portland, ME. *Teaching:* Instr sculpture, Phillips Exeter Acad, NH, 63-86. *Awards:* Prizes, City Manchester, 70 & NH Architects Asn, 71 & 74-77; Sculpture Prize, Nat Acad Design, 90. *Media:* Stone, Wood, Bronze; Watercolor. *Publ:* Contribr, Contemporary Stone Sculpture, 71. *Dealer:* Greenhut Gallery Portland ME; Harbor Square Gallery, Rockland ME. *Mailing Add:* 4 Fish Pt Rd New Harbor ME 04554

LYLE, CHARLES THOMAS
ADMINISTRATOR
b Duluth, Minn, July 16, 1946. *Study:* Univ Minn, James Wright Hunt scholar, 67-68, BA (cum laude), 68; Univ Del, Hagley fel, 68-70, MA (Am hist), 71. *Collection Arranged:* supervised or curated over 40 exhibs at the institutions when serving as director. *Pos:* Dir, Monmouth Co Hist Asn, Freehold, NJ, 71-78 & Hist Soc Del, 80-90; dir mus, Nat Trust for Historic Preservation, 78-80; dir, Md Hist Soc, Baltimore, 90-93; exec dir, Boscobel Restoration, Inc, Garrison, NY, 95-2005; Exec dir, Webb-Deane-Stevens Mus, Wetnersfield, Conn, 2006-. *Teaching:* Vis instr, Mus Studies Dept, Univ Del; instr Am decor arts prior to 1900, Lincroft, NJ, 75-76; preserv prog, Gouchen Col, Towson, Md, 93-94; pub progs, Bard Grad Ctr Studies Decorative Arts, NY, 97. *Awards:* Scholar Am Friends, Attingham Summer Sch, 77. *Interests:* American architecture and decorative arts; house and garden restoration; The American R, revolution, historic house restoration, and house museum interpretation; colonial revival period. *Mailing Add:* 27 Tecumseh Rd West Hartford CT 06117

LYNCH, FLORENCE
GALLERY DIRECTOR
Study: BS; MA in Art Admin. *Pos:* With Salvatore Ala Gallery; independent cur, Japan, Ger, France, The Neth, Italy; found, cur, Florence Lynch Gallery, New York City. *Awards:* Named one of Seven Emerging Young Dealers in Chelsea, NY Arts Mag, 1999. *Mailing Add:* Florence Lynch Gallery 147 W 29th St New York NY 10001

LYNCH, MARY BRITTEN
PAINTER, COLLAGE ARTIST
b Pruden, Ky, 35. *Study:* Univ Tenn, Chattanooga, BA; Provincetown Workshop, Mass, studied with Leo Manso & Victor Candell; Univ Tenn, Knoxville, 65; Long Island Univ, Southampton, NY, grad study, 89, with Eric Fischl, Larry Rivers, Robert Dash, Miriam Schapiro & April Gornik. *Work:* Coca Cola, South Central Bell, Atlanta; Mohawk Industries, Ga; TJX Corp, Mass; Forrest City Enterprises, Ohio; Campbell Co Hist Mus, Tenn; TVA, Knoxville, Tenn; McGraw Hill Publ, NY; TSM Corp, MA; Cong Office, DC; Miss State Womens Coll; Univ Tenn at Chattanooga; Nashville Metro Int Airport, Nashville, Tenn; Hotel Martinique, Bahamas. *Comn:* posters, Gerald Brommers & Crystal Prod, Los Angeles, Calif, 2009. *Exhib:* Okla Arts Ctr, Oklahoma City, 74; Nat Watercolor Soc, Calif, Am Watercolor Soc, NY; Miss State Coll for Women; State Univ NY; Purdue Univ; Northern Nat, Nicolet Col, Wis; Nat Women in Arts Mus Arch, Washington, DC; Smithsonian Inst Archives; Vanderbilt Univ, Nashville, Tenn; Southern Watercolor Society, 2007; San Diego 27th Am Watercolor Exhib, 2007. *Pos:* Ba degree Fine Arts Grad Study, UT Knox, Long Island Univ, S Hampton, NY; Visual Arts Adv Panel Tenn Arts Comn; Juror, NC, Va, Tenn, Ga, 90-98, Idaho Watercolor Soc, 2000, WVa, 2001. *Teaching:* Instr watercolor & acrylics, Hunter Mus Art, Chattanooga, 69-77, Watercolor Workshop, Univ Tenn, Chattanooga, 75, 85 & 86 & Chattanooga Christian High Sch, 80-86, Girl's Preparatory Sch & Baylor Sch summer progs, Chattanooga; WVa workshop instr, 2002; Idaho Watercolor Workshop, 2000, Boise & Coeur d'Alene Idaho. *Awards:* Cash Award 91 & Purchase Award, 92, Tenn Watercolor Soc; Purchase, Cash Award & Medal, Ky Watercolor Soc, 96; Purchase Award, Nat Watercolor Soc, Calif, 94, Rocky Mountain Nat, 2001, 2002 & 2006, Ga Watercolor Exhib, 2000-2008, Adirondacks Nat Award; Ga Watercolor Society, 2007, 2010; Central South, 2007 & 2009; San Diego Int Award, 2007; Am Watercolor Trave, 2008. *Bibliog:* Southern Artisans (film for TV), 73. *Mem:* Founder Tenn Watercolor Soc (founder, 69, treas, 70, vpres, 71, pres, 72-); Watercolor USA Honor Soc (mem chmn); Am Watercolor Soc, NY; Ga Watercolor Soc; Southern Watercolor Soc; Rocky Mountain Nat Watercolor Society. *Media:* Watercolor, Acrylic, Collage. *Res:* Minimalism, ancient walls. *Specialty:* Landscapes, Collage. *Interests:* Books & Tennis. *Publ:* Contribr, Am Artist Mag Watercolor, 90, Feature, 9/2009; Artists Mag, 94, 96 & 2000; Collage Techniques, Brommer, 94; 100 Ways: Still Life & Florals, 2005; Best of Drawing, North Light Publishing, 2007. *Dealer:* Art4Business Inc Philadelphia PA; C Smith Consultants Phoenix AZ; E C May Alexandria Va; EDL Atlanta. *Mailing Add:* 1505 Woodnymph Tr Lookout Mountain GA 30750-2633

LYNCH, MATTHEW
ARTIST
b Ind, 1969. *Study:* Ball State Univ, BFA, 92; Syracuse Univ, MFA, 95. *Exhib:* Exhib incl, Highwayscape, Weber State Univ, Ogden, Utah, 97, An Investigation of Trans-Archit in Western Am, 97, Rise Overrun, Plan B Evolving Arts, Santa Fe, 97, L'Arche, Ecole Nationale d'Art, Cergy, France, 98, SPARCH, Bemis Ctr Contemp Arts, Omaha, 98, Ship from the Desert, Maschinenhalle, Potsdam, Ger, 98, Moorgs Project, 98, Free Basin, Hyde Park Arts Ctr, Chicago, 2000, Spec, Renaissance Soc, Univ Chicago, 2001, Mood River, Wexner Ctr Arts, Columbus, Ohio, 2002, Documenta XI, Kassel, Ger, 2002, Session the Bowl, Deitch Projects, NY, 2002, Whitney Biennial, Whitney Mus Am Art, NY, 2004, InSITE, San Diego, 2005. *Pos:* co-found & mem, SIMPARCH, 96-; Ctr Land Use Interpretation, LA, 99 & 2003; L'Ecole Nationale d'Art, France, Columbus Col Art & Design, Ohio, 2001; Documenta XI, Kassel, Ger, 2002. *Teaching:* Lectr, Concordia Univ, Montreal, Can, formerly; lectr, Weber State Univ, Ogden, Utah, 97; resident, Brandenburgischer Kunstverein, Potsdam, Ger, 98; lectr Univ Utah, Salt Lake City, 99; asst prof, fine arts Col Design, Archit, Art & Planning, Univ Cincinnati, 2002-. *Awards:* Pollock-Krasner Grant, 97; NMex Arts Cou Grant, 97; Creative Capital Grant, 2002. *Mailing Add:* 1328 Pullan Ave Cincinnati OH 45223

LYNCH, PERRI
INSTALLATION SCULPTOR, ENVIRONMENTAL ARTIST
Study: Evergreen State Coll, BA, 1994; Univ Wash, BFA (printmaking), 2001; Cranbrook Acad Art, MFA (printmaking), 2001. *Comn:* Imbrication, Lake City Civic Core, Seattle, 2005; Straight Shot, Warren G Magnuson Park, Seattle, 2006; Entrance Gate, Am Pavilion, Tamil Nadu, India, 2007. *Exhib:* Working Documents, Speakeasy Gallery, Seattle, 1997; Northwest Fine Arts Competition, Phinney Ctr Gallery, Seattle, 1998; Drop It Like It's Hot, Cranbrook Art Mus, Bloomfield Hills, Mich, 2000; Wight Biennial, New Wight Gallery, Los Angeles, 2001; Precisely Known Completely Lost, Jack Straw New Media Gallery, Seattle, 2003; Art-Urban Parks-Art, City Space Gallery, Seattle, 2004; Artist Trust: 20 Years, Seattle Art Mus, 2007. *Pos:* Vis art, Coll Creative Study, Detroit, 2005, Wash State Univ, Pullman, 2005 & Elon Coll, NC, 2007. *Teaching:* Instr, Pratt Fine Arts Ctr, Seattle, 2001; lectr, Univ Wash Sch Art, Seattle, 2001; dir Auroville India Study Abroad Prog, Univ Wash, 2005 & Univ Mass, Amhurst, 2006; grad mentor, TransArt Inst, Linz, Austria, 2007. *Awards:* Project Grant, Univ Wash Sch Art, Seattle, 1996; Spl Projects Grant, King County Arts Commn, 2002; Project Grant, Land Surveyors Asn Wash, Renton, 2004; GAP Award, 2004 & Fel Award, 2006, Artist Trust for Wash State; Fulbright Grant, 2010. *Bibliog:* A Engelson (auth), Lost and Found, Seattle Weekly, 9/2/2003; C DeLaurenti (auth), The Score, The Stranger, 3/18/2004; M Kangas (auth), Young Talent Leaves Paper Trail, Seattle Times, 4/22/2005; L Dillon (auth), Straight Shot, Sculpture Mag, 10/2007. *Mailing Add:* 4701 SW Admiral Way Seattle WA 98116

LYNCH, ROBERT L
ART ASSOCIATION ADMINISTRATOR
b Plymouth, Mass. *Study:* Univ Mass, Amherst, BA (Eng), 71. *Pos:* Exec dir Arts Exten Serv div continuing educ, Univ Mass, Amherst, 74-84; pres & CEO, Nat Assembly Local Arts Agencies, 84-96; pres & CEO, Ams for the Arts, Washington, 96-, founder Ams for the Arts Action Fund, 2005. *Mailing Add:* Americans for the Arts 6th Fl 1000 Vermont Ave NW Washington DC 20005

LYNCH, THOM
PAINTER, MURALIST
b Newark, NJ, Jan 17, 1947. *Study:* Self taught. *Comn:* mural restoration, Summit Playhouse, 2002. *Exhib:* Palmer Mus, Springfield, NJ, 95, Berkeley Heights Pub Libr, NJ, 95, Am Cyanamid, Princeton, NJ, 95, Berks Arts Coun, Reading, Pa, 97, Brion Gallery, Lambertville, NJ, 99; A Blast of Color, Watchung Arts Ctr, NJ, 94, Faces of Change, 94, Between a Thought and a Thing, 96, End of the Millennium, 96 & Anthropomorphic, 99; Ariel Gallery, Soho, NY, 90, Basile-Spingarn Gallery, Matawan, NJ, 91, Calif Mus of Art / Burbank Ctr, Santa Rosa, Calif, 95, Resurgam Gallery, Baltimore, 96, Simon Gallery, Morristown, NJ, 97, Orange Bear Music Club & Gallery, NY, 98; Berkshire Artisans, Pittsfield, Mass, 99, Trenton City Mus, NJ, 99, 2001; The Toy Show, Artists for Art, Scranton, Pa, 2000, It's Alive, Brion Gallery, 2000; Int Forum Art Initiative, Moscow, Russia, 2002; The Peace Mus, Chicago, 2003. *Collection Arranged:* curator,The World With Perforations, International Stamp Art Exhibit, Watchung Art Ctr NJ, 97. *Awards:* Grant, Union City Heart, 2001. *Bibliog:* A Fringe Benefit for the Gallery's Faithful, NY Times, 95; Into the 90's, Suburban Cable/NJ Public TV, 95; Diverse Artists Rally Around Common Themes, Courier News, 99; New Art Group Comes Alive, The Times of Trenton, 2000; New Art Group Finds a Common Thread and Develops a Theme, Star Ledger, 2000; Robert Henkes (auth), The Crucifixion in American Art, McFarland & Co, 5/2003. *Mem:* New Art Group. *Media:* Acrylic. *Dealer:* Brion Galleries 1293 Rt 179 Lambertville NJ 08853. *Mailing Add:* PO Box 195 Pottersville NJ 07979

LYNCH-NAKACHE, MARGARET
PAINTER, SCULPTOR
b Hartford, Conn, Dec 17, 1932. *Study:* RI Sch Design, BFA, 54; Beaux-Arts, Paris, cert, 56; Atelier Chapelain-Midy. *Work:* L'Ambassade du Liban, Paris; Our Lady Victory Church, Centerville, Mass; Les Embrunts, Les Essembres, France; Georgetown Univ Hosp, Washington; Inst Keguruan Dan Ilum Pendidikan, Yogyakarta, Indonesia. *Comn:* Blown Tulips, Sargi, Dakar, Senegal, 78; Paris Cityscape, Cameron, Royal Oak, Mich, 78; Roses, Dagommer Cie, Paris, 78; Madonna, Ostronic, Potomac, Md, 79; Green Dunes, McDonald, Wellesley, Mass, 83. *Exhib:* One-person show, La Galerie du Meridien, Paris, 79, Hunter House, Vienna, Va, 82 & Georgetown Univ Hosp, Washington, 85 & 87; Long Branch Nature Ctr, 81; Cape Cod Art Asn, 83; Sandscape Gallery at Munson Meeting, Chatham, Mass, 88; Oliver Bldg, Boston, 92 & 93; Old Selectman's Building Gallery, West Barnstable, Mass, 95; Waterstone's Booksellers, Boston, Mass, 96; Boston Athenaeum, 98; Boston Athemaeum, 2003; A to Z, CoSo, Boston, 2006. *Pos:* Artist, Universal Films, New York, 56-57 & Girl Scouts USA, Hq New York, 59-61; artist-in-residence, Art Barn, Washington, DC, 79; pres, Network For Artists, Kindred Art Collection & Host Exhib Ltd, McLean, Va, 79-85. *Awards:* Second Place, Cape Cod Art Asn, 56; Second Place, McLean Art Club, 79; Second Place, Dennis Art Festival, 81; Purchase Prize, Herdon Fine Art Exhib, 89. *Bibliog:* L Chauvin (auth), Margaret Nakache, Galerie Jardin des Arts, 2/75; E Holgren (auth), Whisperings and sharings, Alexandrian Mag, spring 78; J de Recqueville (auth), Carnet des arts, Paris-Tel, 1/79. *Mem:* McLean Proj

Arts (bd mem, 88-91); Copley Soc Boston. *Media:* Watercolor, Oil, Bronze. *Publ:* Contribr, Cadette Girl Scout Handbook, Girls Scouts USA, 63; auth, Art royalties, Int Herald Tribune, 5/16/77; Art game letters, Washington Post Mag, 11/5/78. *Dealer:* Copley Soc Boston 158 Newbury St Boston MA 02116. *Mailing Add:* PO Box 68 West Hyannisport MA 02672

LYNDS, CLYDE
SCULPTOR, PAINTER
b Jersey City, NJ, June 22, 1939. *Work:* Nat Mus Am Art, Washington, DC; Butler Inst Am Art, Youngstown, Ohio; Wadsworth Atheneum, Hartfield, Conn; New York Univ; Marion Koogler McNay Art Inst, San Antonio, Tex; NJ State Mus, Trenton; Newark Mus, Newark, NJ. *Comn:* Sculptures, Foley Sq Fed off Bldg, New York, 97, Eastern Conn State Univ, Willimantic, 98, AT&T Network Opers Ctr, Bedminster, NJ, 99, IRS Cent Computing Facility, Martinsburg, WVa, 98, NJ State Capitol Plaza, Trenton, 98, US Courthouse, Montgomery, Ala, 99 & Greater Hartford Arts Coun, Conn, 2000; Rutgers Univ, Camden, NJ, 2007; Rutgers Univ Bus Sch, Newark, NJ, 2009. *Exhib:* Solo exhibs, Babcock Galleries, New York, 69, 71, 73 & 75, Corcoran Gallery Art, Washington, DC, 73, OK Harris Works Art, New York, 86, 88, 91, 94 & 2001, NJ State Mus, Trenton, NJ, 93 & Butler Inst Am Art, Youngstown, Ohio, 94 & 08; Aldrich Mus, Conn, 88; La Mus de la Civilization, Que, Can, 89; Stadtmuseum, Dusseldorf, Fed Repub Ger, 90; Univ Calif, 90; Nicaf, Yokohama, Japan, 92-93. *Awards:* First Prize, Monmouth Coll, 68; First Prize & Medal Hon, Painters & Sculptors Soc, NJ, 68; NJ State Coun Arts Fel, 84; Fels, NJ State Coun Arts, 84 & 89; Nat Design award, GSA, Washington, DC, 97. *Bibliog:* Harry Rand & Eleanor Heartney (auths), Buddha Seat, Sculpture Catalog, 4/89 & 7/90. *Media:* Stone, Light, Glass. *Publ:* Frederick Morgan (auth), Drawings, Poems of the Two Worlds, Verona, Italy. *Dealer:* OK Harris Gallery 383 W Broadway New York NY 10012; Gallery Camino Real 608 Banyon Tr Boca Raton FL 33431. *Mailing Add:* 20 Franklin Ave Wallington NJ 07057

LYNN, JUDITH
PAINTER, ILLUSTRATOR
b Chicago, Ill. *Study:* Los Angeles Conservatory of Music, 59-62; Univ Vienna, Austria, third in class, 64; Fashion Inst Technology, 87-91. *Hon Degrees:* Hon teaching degree, Conservatory de Musica Marcay, Venezuela, 84-85. *Work:* Ateneo De Los Teques, Venezuela. *Exhib:* solo exhib Casa de la Cultura, Marcay, Venezuela, 84; Simbolos de la Menthe, Galeria EuroAmericano, Caracas, Venezuela, 84; Mus opening, Bayside Historical Soc, Bayside, NY, 97; Watercolor Exib, The Pen & Brush Club, NY, 2001; The Gallery at Lincoln Ctr, NY, 2002-2004. *Awards:* 3rd place oils & acrylics, IV Salon Imagen Annual, Salon Imagen Y Grumbacher, 84. *Bibliog:* Anne Louis Volkenborn (auth), Realism is the Theme of new Exhibits Opening in Caracas, The Daily Journal, Caracas, Venezuela, 1/18/84; Christina Assai (prod), Juventud Venezolano, TV-Concert with Paintings-Judith Lynn, 84; Dan Paolantonio (dir/prod), Documentary: The Italian Fascination, Flaming Cesar Film Co, England, 87. *Mem:* Am Watercolor Soc; Nat Mus Women in the Arts. *Media:* Watercolor, Acrylic. *Publ:* Recuento- Volumen II- Numero 7, Arte Plural Magazine, Caracas; Ademas de Soprano, Pintora, El Aragueno, Maracay, Venezuela, 2/1/85. *Mailing Add:* 2109 Broadway New York NY 10023-2106

LYNNE, NINAH & MICHAEL
COLLECTOR
b 1941. *Pos:* Atty, Barovick & Konecky; partner, Blumenthal & Lynne, 1960-80; counsel, New Line Cinema, 1980-90, bd dirs, 1983-2008, chief operating officer & pres, 1990-2001, co-chmn & co-chief exec officer, 2001-08; exec producer (films), Lord of the Rings: The Fellowship of the Ring, 2001, Lord of the Rings: The Two Towers, 2002, Lord of the Rings: The Return of the King, 2003, Who the #$%& is Jackson Pollock?, 2006, Hairspray, 2007 & The Golden Compass, 2007. *Awards:* Named one of Top 200 Collectors, ARTnews mag, 2004-13. *Mem:* mem, NY Bar Asn; bd mem, Mus Mod Art, Citymeals-on-Wheels, Am Mus Moving Image, Drawing Ctr; chmn, Mus Comt of Guild Hall East Hampton. *Collection:* Contemporary art

LYON, GILES ANDREW
PAINTER
b New York, NY, June 30, 1967. *Study:* Sch Visual Arts, New York, 84-85; Rochester Inst Technol, NY, 85-86; RI Sch Design, Europ hons prog, Rome, BFA, 89; Glassell Core Fel, Mus Fine Arts, Houston, 89-91. *Work:* Mus Fine Arts, Houston; also pvt collections of Edward Albee, Barret Collection, Christophe de Menil & Walter Hopps. *Comn:* Painting, Edward F Albee Found, Montauk, Long Island, 92; painting, Crowley, Mark & Douglas Attys at Law, Houston, 93; painting, Ambassador Hotel, Providence, RI, 94. *Exhib:* Core Fels Exhib, Alfred Glassell Sch Art, Mus Fine Arts, Houston, 90 & 91; Drawing from Tex, Mus Fine Arts, Houston, 91; The Big Show, Alfred Glassell Sch Art, Mus Fine Arts, Houston, 91; solo exhibs, Mus Art Guise, Houston, 92, Lynn Goode Gallery, Houston, 92, 94 & 96, Nine Freudenheim Gallery, Buffalo, NY, 94, Cuadrante 2, San Miguel de Allende, Mex, 96, Alexandre De Folin, NY, 97, Drawing Room, Area, Brooklyn, NY, 97, Angstrom Gallery, Dallas, Tex, 98, Feigen Contemp, NY, 99, 2002, 2004, Drawings from the Home Front, Mixed Greens, 2006; Conventional Forms/Insidious Visions, Alfred Glassell Sch Art, Mus Fine Arts, Houston, 93; Tex Contemp: Acquisitions of the 90's, Mus Fine Arts, Houston, 93; Dots & Lines, 8th Floor Gallery, NY, 96; Fascination, Lobby Gallery, Deutsche Bank, NY, 96; Buttered Side Up, Hallwalls Contemp Arts Ctr (catalog), Buffalo, NY, 96; The Exchange Show (with Arena & Pierogi 2000), NY, 96; Greater NY, Mus of Morder Art, 2000, New Plasma, Folin/Riva, NY, 2001; featured artist, Mixed Greens, New York City, 2003; Syncopated Rhythms Ensemble Improvisation, Clifford Chance, NY, 2004; Scene Stealers, curated by Nina Arias and Jose Diaz, Ingalls & Associates, Miami, Fla, 2005; Bibbidi-Bobbidi-Boo!, Bielefelder Kunstverein, Bielefeld, Ger, 2006; Pop surrealists, Gallerie Schuster, Berlin, Ger, 2007; Learning by Doing: 25 Years of the Core Program, Mus Fine Arts Houston, 2008; Fortress of Solitude, Brooklyn Fire Proof, New York, 2009; Uncertain Terrain, Knoxville Mus Art, 2010. *Collection Arranged:* Mus Fine Arts, Houston; Edward Albee, NYC; The Barrett Collection, Dallas; Ross Bleckner, NYC; Christophe de Menil, NYC; Walter Hopps, Houston, Tex. *Pos:* Artist-in-residence, Edward F Albee Found, Montauk, NY, 91 & Univ Tenn, Knoxville, 2009. *Teaching:* Vis artist/lectr var univ & schs. *Awards:* Nat Endowment Arts Fel Grant, Mid-Am Art Alliance, 94; Artist in Res, Edward F Albee Found, Montauk, NY, 91; Core Fel, Glassell Sch Art, Mus Fine Arts, Houston, 89-91. *Bibliog:* Elizabeth McBride (auth), Giles Lyon: Beauty and the blob, 9/94 & Elizabeth Licata (auth), Giles Lyon, Nina Freudenheim, 1/95, ArtNews; Frances Colpitt (auth), Report from Texas: Going against the grain, Art Am, 4/95; Tom Moody (auth), Giles Lyon, Lynn Goode, ArtForum, 5/95; Carol Kino (auth) The Emergent Factor, Art in America, 7/2000; Grady T Turner (auth) Beautiful dreamers: emerging American painters, Circa 2000, Flash Art, Jan/Feb 2000; New American Paintings, No 32, Open Studios Press, Wellesley, Mass, 3/2001; Giles Lyon, The New York Times, E40, 5/2002; James Kalm (auth), Brooklyn Dispatche, The Brooklyn Rail, 7/2009. *Media:* Acrylic, Water-based Mediums. *Dealer:* Lynn Goode Gallery 2719 Colquitt Houston TX 77098

LYON, ROBERT F
SCULPTOR, EDUCATOR
b Queens, NY, Sept 3, 1952. *Study:* Mercer Co Community Col, AA, 72; Coll NJ, BA 74; Tyler Sch Art, MFA, 77. *Work:* New Orleans Mus Art; La Arts & Sci Ctr, La State Univ, Baton Rouge; John Michael Kohler Arts Ctr, Sheboygan, Wis; Lamar Dodd Art Ctr, LaGrange, Ga. *Comn:* Bronze & terra cotta reliefs, Pioneer Place Plaza, Portland, 89; Earth Day Commemorative Sculpture, City of Baton Rouge, La, 95. *Exhib:* Two-person invitational, Sam Houston State Univ, Huntsville, Tex, 91, Troy State Univ, Ala, 2003; Clay Alabama Invitational, Univ Montevallo, 95; Solo Exhibs: Millsaps Col, Jackson, Miss, 96; Chattahoochee Valley Art Mus, LaGrange, Ga, 97; Bradley Univ, Peoria, Ill, 98; Univ SC, Spartanburg, 2001; McKissick Mus, Columbia, SC, 2003; McKissick Mus, Columbia, SC, 2003; Univ Ga, Athens, 2004; Francis Marion Univ, Florence, SC, 2008; Teaching Art: A Regional Faculty Invitational, Columbus Mus, Ga, 98; three-person exhib, Blue Spiral 1 Gallery, Asheville, NC, 2000; Univ Ark, Little Rock, 2000; Triennial, SC State Mus, Columbia, SC, 2004; 20th Anniversary Art Exhib, SC State Mus, Columbia, SC, 2008; LaGrange Nat, Lamar Dodd Art Center, LaGrange, Ga, 2008. *Pos:* Vpres & bd dir, Baton Rouge Gallery, 93-94; conf coordr, Sculpt-Fest 94, Baton Rouge, La, 94; nominations comt Nat Asn Schs Art & Design; bd dir, Southeaster Col Art Conf. *Teaching:* Prof art sculpture, La State Univ, 78-95; prof & chair dept art, Auburn Univ, 95-97, Univ SC, 97-2002, prof sculpture, 2002-. *Awards:* Visual Artists Fel, Nat Endowment Arts, 84. *Bibliog:* Dorothy Biner (auth), Robert Lyon, Melding, Clay & Wood, Ceramics Art & Perception, Issue #52, Sidney, Australia, 2003; Gary Dickey (auth), Robert F. Lyon: A Convergence of Arts, Turning Points, 2008. *Mem:* Int Sculpture Ctr; Southeastern Coll Art Conf (co-chair 2001 conf); Am Asn Woodturners, Woodturning Center. *Media:* Wood. *Collection:* University of Texas; Louisiana Arts & Science Center; New Orleans Museum of Art. *Publ:* Coauth, Vasilikeware: An Early Bronze Age Pottery Style in Crete, Paul Astroms Forlag, 79. *Dealer:* Blue Spiral 1 Asheville NC; City Art Gallery Columbia SC. *Mailing Add:* Univ S Carolina Dept of Art McMaster Col Columbia SC 29208

LYONS, AL
DIRECTOR
b Memphis. *Study:* Univ Memphis, BBA (Accounting). *Pos:* Pres, Bodine Co, Collierville, Tenn, 1995-2007; interim dir, Brooks Mus Art, Memphis, 2008. *Mem:* Vp bd trustees, Brooks Mus Art; bd dirs, Ballet Memphis; Memphis in May; RiverArtsFest; Collierville CofC. *Mailing Add:* Memphis Brooks Museum of Art 1934 Poplar Avenue Memphis TN 38104

LYONS, BEAUVAIS
PRINTMAKER, EDUCATOR
b Hanover, NH, Feb 24, 1958. *Study:* Alfred Univ, 77; Univ Wis, Madison, BFA, 80; Ariz State Univ, MFA, 83. *Work:* Philadelphia Mus Art; Kohler Art Libr, Madison, Wis; Univ SDak-Vermillion; Smith Coll Rare Book Collection, Northampton, Mass; Smithsonian Am Art Mus; Block Mus, Northwestern Univ, Evanston, Ill. *Exhib:* Selections from the Hokes Archives, Print Club, Philadelphia, Pa, 92; Carnegie Mellon Univ, Pittsburgh, Pa, 94 & 2001; St Lawrence Univ, Canton, NY, 94, 2001 & 06; State Univ NY, Buffalo, 95; Erie Mus Art, Pa,95; Vanderbilt Univ, 2002; Solo exhibs:Hokes Medical Arts, Open Studio, Toronto, Ont, Can, 2008; Hokes Medical Arts, Universite du Quebec a Trois Rivieres, Que, Can, 2008; George & Helen Spelvin Folk Art Collection, Univ Art Gallery, Univ Mass Dartmouth, New Bedford, Mass, 2009; others; Mus Am Philosophical Soc, Philadelphia, Pa, 2010. *Pos:* Dir, Hokes Arch, 83-. *Teaching:* Vis asst prof art, Weber State Col, Ogden, Utah, 84-85; asst prof, Univ Tenn, Knoxville, 85-89, assoc prof, 89, Ellen McClung Berry prof, 96-2005, 2007-2009, Chancellor's prof, Univ Tenn, Knoxville; Fulbright lectr, Art Acad Poznan, Poland, 2002; Chancellor's prof, UT Knoxville, 2011-. *Awards:* Southern Arts Fedn/Nat Endowment Arts Regional Fel, 88; Southeastern Coll Art Conf Award for Creative Achievement, 94; Fulbight Fel, Poznan Acad of Art, 2002; UTK Chancellor's Award for Research & Creative Achievement, 2006. *Bibliog:* Lawrence Weschler (auth), Mr Wilson's Cabinet of Wonder, Pantheon Bks, 95; Linda Hutcheon (auth), Irony's Edge: The Theory and Politics of Irony, NY & London Routledge, 95; Roy R Behrens (auth), History in the Making, 70-77, Print mag, 5-6, 97; Beaurais Lyons: folk art fabricator, Folk Art Messenger, Vol 15, No 1, spring 2002. *Mem:* Southern Graphics Coun, SGC Int (ed Graphic Impressions); Coll Art Asn; Am Asn Univ Profs; Soc Metavisual Studies. *Media:* All Media. *Publ:* Auth, The excavation of the apasht: Artifacts from an imaginary past, Leonardo J, Vol 18, No 2, 85; Speakeasy, New Art Examiner, Vol 17, No 5, 1/90; Artistic Freedom and the University, Art J, Vol 50, No 4, winter 91; The Art of the Trickster, Archaeology, 3-4/94, Vol 47, No 2. *Mailing Add:* Sch Art-Univ Tenn 1715 Volunteer Blvd Knoxville TN 37996-2410

LYONS, CAROL
PAINTER, PRINTMAKER
b Brooklyn, NY. *Study:* Art Students League, 60's; studies in painting with Chaim Gross, in 3-D composition with David Smith & in watercolor with Zoltan Szabo & Edgar Whitney; City Coll NY, BS (educ), MS (educ). *Work:* Victoria & Albert Mus, London; Jane Voorhees Zimmerli Mus, Rutgers Univ, NJ; Hermitage, Russia; IBM Collection, Westchester Co, NY; Omni Mag, pvt collection; New York City, 5th Ave Pub Libr Print Collection; Spencer Mus, Kans; His Royal Highness Duke of Gloucerter; Buren Town Hall, Netherlands; ADP Douglas Crest Vineyard; Nat Yiddish Bk Ctr; Carnegie Corp; Eli Lilly, Mem Sloan-Kettering; Virtual Mus Collection, Nat Sept 11 Mem & Mus of the World Trade Ctr. *Comn:* Watercolors painting, comn by Mrs M Huebner, Dobbs Ferry, NY, 93; watercolors painting, comn by Mr & Mrs Cloder, Pelham, NY, 93; watercolors painting, comn by Dr & Mrs B Klutchko, Hastings, NY, 93; watercolors painting, comn by Dr & Mrs Paul Hertz, Briarcliff Manor, NY, 94; watercolor, comn by Sothebys Real Estate, 96; Rockefeller Collections; more than 25 pvt commissions for watercolors, pvt collections. *Exhib:* Audubon Art Club, Nat Arts Club, NY, 80; Ann Juried Show, Berkshire Mus, Pittsfield, Mass, 82; solo exhib, Nicholas Roerich Mus, NY, 89; By the Riverside, Mus London, 90; Big Paintings, Nat Asn Women Artists, Javits Bldg, NY, 94; Nat Asn Women Artist, West Broadway Gallery, Soho, NY, 94; Artgroup of Yonkers, Studioalvianarte, Castel di Sangro, Italy, 94; Chautauqua Inst, NY, 96; Palatine Village Hall, Pallatine, Ill; Whittier City Hall, Whittier, Calif; 911 Woodblock Remembrances; Knickbocker Art Club, New York; Lorillard Wolf Art Club, New York; Catharine Laramie Wyo, 2004; Print Zero Seattle, Wash; Donnell Libr Ctr, New York, 2005. *Pos:* owner, Carol Lyons Studio. *Teaching:* Daring Drawing, Art in the Elem Sch, New York City, Irvington, NY, New York, NY. *Awards:* Best in show, Womanart Gallery, NY, 80; Bronze Medal, Mus of the Duncans, Paris, 81. *Bibliog:* Robert Fisher (auth), The Zen of watercolor, Am Artist, 90; Fred Nold (dir), Interview-Carol Lyons, Cable Channel 19-WDMC, 90; Michael Ward (auth), Letter from the editor, Artists' Mag, 11/94. *Mem:* Nat Archives Mus Women Arts; Bklyn Mus Archives; Albany Print Club, NY; Artists Equity, New York City; Barenforum.org-(global); and others; Int Soc Experimental Artists. *Media:* Watercolor, Handprint, Woodblocks, Water-based Media. *Res:* New York public library & prints. *Interests:* Reading, piano. *Publ:* Cover artist & contribr, The New Spirit of Watercolor, 89 & Watercolor Magic-Risk It, 93, F & W Publ; Watercolor '90, Watson Guptil, 90

LYONS, FRANCIS E, JR
ART DEALER, LECTURER
b Detroit, Mich, Feb 14, 1943. *Study:* Oakland Univ, BA, 68; City Coll San Francisco, studied archit, 73; Montgomery Col, Md, 74; Towson State Univ, Md, 88; Am Craft Coun, New York, 93. *Pos:* Co-founder, Xochipilli Gallery, Rochester, Mich, 70-72; gallery rep & nat mgr, Marson Galleries, Baltimore, Md, 74-81; owner, Frank Lyons Collection, Glens Falls, NY, 81-; consult & interim dir, Venable-Neslage Gallerie, Washington, 92-93, 2002. *Teaching:* Lectr, prints & printmaking, numerous cols, univs & art ctrs, 76-. *Specialty:* 19th and 20th century prints and photographs; Japanese ukiyo-e and sosaka-hanga; Am European early photography. *Mailing Add:* PO Box 2306 Glens Falls NY 12801

LYONS, JOAN
PHOTOGRAPHER
b New York, NY, Mar 6, 1937. *Study:* Alfred Univ, BFA, 57; State Univ NY, Buffalo, MFA, 73. *Work:* Visual Studies Workshop, Rochester, NY; Ctr Creative Photog, Tucson, Ariz; Mus Mod Art, NY; San Francisco Mus Mod Art; Minneapolis Art Inst. *Exhib:* In Sequence, Mus Fine Arts, Houston, 82; Facets of the Collection, Mus Mod Art, San Francisco, 83; Solo exhib, Ctr Creative Photog, Tucson, 84; Beyond Words, Art of the Book, Mem Art Gallery, Rochester, 86; Evocative Presence, Mus Fine Arts, Houston, 88; La Camera Ciega, Mus Art Contemp, Seville, Spain, 88; New Photomontage, Cranbook Acad Art, Bloomfield Hill, Minn, 88. *Pos:* Dir, Visual Studies Workshop Press, 72-. *Teaching:* Adj instr visual studies, Visual Studies Workshop, 75-, State Univ NY, Brockport, 86-. *Awards:* CAPS Fel, NY, 75 & 81. *Bibliog:* Tom Dugan (auth), Photography Between Covers, Light Impressions, 80; Ann Tucker (auth), Target Collection, Mus Fine Arts, Houston, 84; Joan Foncuberta (auth), Phot Visions No 15, Barcelona, Spain. *Mem:* Soc Photog Educ. *Publ:* Auth Ten self-pub artist's bks, 72-; ed, Artist's Books, a Critical Anthology & Source Book, Visual Studies Workshop Press, 86. *Dealer:* Visual Studies Workshop 31 Prince St Rochester NY 14607. *Mailing Add:* 176 Rutgers St Rochester NY 14607

LYONS, LISA
HISTORIAN, CONSULTANT
b Minneapolis, Minn, Dec 13, 1950. *Study:* Northwestern Univ, Evanston, Ill, BA (art hist), 72; Columbia Univ, New York, MA (art hist), 73. *Collection Arranged:* Scale & Environment: 10 Sculptors (contribr, catalog), 77, Nicholas Africano, 78, Eight Artists: The Elusive Image (auth, catalog), 79, Close Portraits (auth, catalog), 80, The Anxious Edge (auth, catalog), 82, Wegman's World (auth, catalog), 82, Walker Art Ctr, Minneapolis; 39th Biennial Cont Painting (auth, catalog), 85, Corcoran Gallery Art, Washington, DC; Nicholas Africano: Innocence & Experience (auth, catalog), 91, Siah Armajani: The Poetry Garden & Recent Works, 92 & Chris Burden and Lynn Davis, 92, Lannan Found, Los Angeles, Calif; Percept, Image, Oject, 94; Facts and Figures, 94. *Pos:* Fel, Toledo Mus Art, Ohio, 73-74; Rockefeller Found Fel, Walker Art Ctr, Minneapolis, 75-77, asst cur, 77-78, cur, 79-82; dir acquisitions, Mus Fund, Minneapolis, 83-89; dir art progs, Lannan Found, Los Angeles, Calif, 89-. *Publ:* Auth, Henri Matisse: 1914-1917, Arts Mag, 5/75; An interview with James Byrne, Studio Int, 5-6/76; contribr, The river: Images of the Mississippi, Walker Art Ctr, 76; auth, Chuck Close, Rizzoli Int Publ, 87; Siah Armajami: the poetry garden, Design Quart, MIT Press, 94. *Mailing Add:* 2000 DeMille Dr Los Angeles CA 90027

LYSHAK, FRANCIE
PAINTER, PHOTOGRAPHER
b Detroit, Mich, June 3, 1948. *Study:* Wayne State Univ, BFA, 1970; Pratt Inst, MPS, 1978; Col for Creative Studies. *Work:* Bronx Children's Psychiatric Ctr, Bronx, NY. *Exhib:* 1st Ann Prize Competition, Provincetown Art Asn, Provincetown, NY, 1983; 4th Ann Competition, Mus of Hudson Highlands, Cornwall-on-Hudson, NY, 1985; Art Quest '86 (cur, B Haskel), Los Angeles, Calif, 1986; Juried Exhib, Denisa Bibro Fine Art, NY, 1996; Invitational Exhib, Air Gallery, NY, 1997; Faber Birren Nat Color Award Show, 2009; DNA Gallery, East Side, Provincetown, 2011; Carter Burden Gallery, NY, 2014. *Pos:* Creative Arts Supervisor, Bronx Child Psychiatric Ctr, 1979-2010; art therapist, pvt practice, 2007-. *Teaching:* Adjunct prof, Art Therapy, Col New Rochelle, 2008. *Awards:* Hon Mention. 1st Ann Prize Competition, Alice Neel, Juror, 1983; Research Award, Am Art Therapy Asn, 2007; 4th Pl Award, Faber Birren Nat Color Show, 2009. *Bibliog:* Joe Vojtko (auth), Science & Art of Pain Management, 1/15/1998; Ocean of Infinite Metaphor, Review Mag , 10/1/1998; Bruce Moon (auth), Working with Images, 2002; Gary Indiana (auth), One Brief Scuzzy Moment, New York Mag, 12/6/04. *Mem:* Am Art Therapy Asn; New York Art Therapy Asn. *Media:* Oil, Photography. *Res:* Art therapy for adolescents with post traumatic stress disorder. *Interests:* Therapeutic application of fine art. *Publ:* Auth, The Secret Art & Healing from Sexual Abuse, Safer Soc, 1999; coauth, The Creative Art as a Response to Resistance to Change (review), Human Sci Press; co-auth, Art Therapy for Adolescents with Postraumatic Stress Disorder Symptoms, J Am Art Therapy Asn. *Dealer:* Carter Burden Gallery 548 W 28th St #534 New York NY 10001. *Mailing Add:* 32 E 2nd St Apt 20A New York NY 10003

LYSUN, GREGORY
PAINTER, RESTORER
b Yonkers, NY, Oct 24, 1924. *Study:* Art Students League, with Louis Bouche, Edwin Dickinson, John Groth, Robert Beverly Hale & Reginald Marsh, 47-53. *Work:* Art Students League; New Britain Mus Am Art, Conn; De Cordova Mus, Lincoln, Mass; Butler Inst Am Art, Youngstown, Ohio. *Comn:* Portrait of Ruth Taylor, Westchester Community Serv Coun, Inc, White Plains, NY, 75; restoration work of 6 paintings by Edward Gay, comn by Mrs S Gay Linville, Scarsdale, NY, 81; restoration work of painting by John Steuart Curry, comn by Eugene Curry, Armonk, NY, 81; restoration of John Stewart Curry's Portrait of a Gypsy, Jefferson Co Hist Soc, Oskaloosa, Kans, 82; restoration work of the Pieta, statue, comn by St Joseph's Church, Bronxville, NY, 91. *Exhib:* 35 Yrs in Retrospect, 36-70, Butler Inst Am Art Midyear Show, 71; 67th Ann Exhib Conn Acad Fine Arts, Wadsworth Atheneum Mus, Hartford, Conn, 77; Art Teachers Juries Exhib, Neuberger Mus, State Univ NY, Coll at Purchase, 77; From the 1920's to the Present, Works from the League's Permanent Collection, Art Students League, NY, 77; Directors Choice Exhib, selections from DeCordova Mus, Lincoln, Mass, 78; Ann Allied Arts Am, 85; 75th Nat Exhib, Conn Acad Fine Arts, William Benton Mus, Storrs, Conn, 88; Exhib Paintings & Sculpture, Berkshire Art Asn, Berkshire Mus, Pittsfield, Mass, 98; Allied Artists Am Mem Exhib, Butler Inst Am Art, Youngstown, Ohio, 2001; 73rd Grand Nat Exhib of Am Artists Profl League, Salmagundi Club, 2001. *Teaching:* Instr painting & drawing, Westchester Art Workshop, Co Ctr, White Plains, NY, 69-, Pelham Art Ctr, 78- & State Univ NY Col, Purchase, 82-; instr painting & drawing & chmn, Dept Art, Fairview-Greenburgh Community Ctr, Greenburgh, NY, 72-. *Awards:* Alice Collins Dunham Award, Best Portrait, 73rd Nat Exhib, Conn Acad Fine Arts, 83; Conn Acad Prize, 76th Ann Exhib, Conn Acad Fine Arts, 86; 64th Grand Nat Exhib Director's Award, Am Artists Prof League, New York, NY, 92; Continuing Education's Outstanding Fac Award, State Univ NY Purchase, 96; and others. *Bibliog:* Helen Ganz Spiro (auth), Art students follow teacher's example, 82 & Painter takes students to a different world, 83, Gannett Westchester Newspapers; M Stephen Doherty (auth), Different Strokes, Am Artist Mag, 12/99; Nelly Edmondson Gupta (auth), In Front of the Easel to Capture Not Just an Image, But Spirit, NY Times, 4/21/02. *Mem:* Life mem Art Students League; Allied Artists Am (hon); Life Fel Am Artists Prof League; Conn Acad Fine Arts; Hudson Valley Art Asn. *Media:* Oil. *Publ:* Auth, The construction of a painting, Palette Talk, 79; illusr, The Best of Oil Painting, 96 & Landscape Inspirations, 98, Rockport Publ. *Mailing Add:* 481 Winding Rd N Ardsley NY 10502-2701

LYTLE, RICHARD
PAINTER, EDUCATOR
b Albany, NY, Feb 14, 1935. *Study:* Cooper Union; Yale Univ, BFA & MFA; also with Josef Albers. *Work:* Mus Mod Art, New York; Yale Art Gallery; Nat Collection Art, Washington, DC; Minneapolis Mus Fine Arts; Rockefeller Mansion Mus. *Comn:* Concrete relief mural, Fairfield Univ, 65. *Exhib:* 16 Americans, Mus Mod Art, New York, 59; Seattle World's Fair, 62; Whitney Mus Am Art Ann, New York, 63; Art: USA: Now, SC Johnson Collection, World Tour, 63-; solo exhibs, De Cordova Mus, Lincoln, Mass, 74 & Green Gallery, Yale Univ Sch Art, New Haven, Conn, 2006; Hopkins Ctr, Dartmouth Col, 86; plus others. *Teaching:* Instr art, Yale Univ, 60-63, assoc prof, 66-81, prof 81-, actg dean, Yale Sch Art, 80-81, 90 & 94, prof emer, currently; dean, Silvermine Coll Art, 63-66. *Awards:* Fulbright Grant to Italy, 58; Prof Achievement Citation & Augustus St Gaudens Award, 85, Cooper Union. *Bibliog:* Art: USA: NOW, Viking Press, 63; 16 Americans, Mus Mod Art, 59; Artist Next Door, The partnership for conn cities Inc. *Media:* Oil, Watercolor. *Dealer:* Herbert Palmer Gallery Los Angeles CA; New Arts Gallery Litchfield CT; Marianne Boesky Gallery New York NY. *Mailing Add:* 14 Sperry Rd Woodbridge CT 06525

M

MAAS, MARION ELIZABETH
PAINTER
b Brooklyn, NY, Feb 27, 1930. *Study:* Pratt Inst, BS, 51; New York Univ; Frank Reilly Sch Art. *Exhib:* The Garden, Mill Pond House, St James, LI, NY, 89; 100 Yrs 100 Works Nat Asn Women Artists traveling exhib, Islip Art Mus, East Islip, NY, 89, Fine Arts Mus, Mobile, Ala, 89, Chattanooga Regional Mus, Tenn, 89, Longview Mus Art,

Tex, 89, Kirkpatrik Art Ctr, Oklahoma City, 90; Centennial Celebration, Jehangir Art Gallery, Bombay & Baroda, India, 89-90; Art Coun Port Washington (19 pieces), Port Washington Libr, 2003. *Teaching:* WYCA Manhattan, 1958-59. *Awards:* Best in show, Nat Art League, 86; First Prize, Nat Asn Women Artists, 87. *Mem:* Nat Asn Women Artists; Catharine Lorillard Wolfe Art Club; Nat Art League. *Media:* Acrylic, Oil, Watercolor, All Media. *Mailing Add:* 85-57 67th Rd Rego Park NY 11374

MABRY, NATHAN
SCULPTOR
Study: Kansas City Art Inst, Mo, BFA, 2001; Univ Calif, LA, MFA, 2004. *Exhib:* Solo exhibs: Filter Gallery, Kansas City, 2000; Aspen Mus Art, Colo, 2006; Cherry and Martin Gallery, LA, 2006; groups exhibs: Gordon Gallery, Yountville, Calif, 2000; The Cube, Kansas City, 2001; Jan Weiner Gallery, Kansas City, 2001; I am Human and I Deserve to Be Loved, Overtones Gallery, LA, 2003; Cornceptual Popstraction, cherrydelosreyes, LA, 2004; Thing: New Sculpture from LA, Hammer Mus, 2005; The Beginning of the End of the Beginning, Bucket Rider Gallery, Chicago, 2006; Bold Moves, House of Campari, LA, 2006; Red Eye: Los Angeles Artists from the Rubell Family Collection, Miami, Fla, 2006; Aspects, Forms and Figures, Bellwether, NY, 2007. *Mailing Add:* 2712 S La Cienega Blvd Los Angeles CA 90034-2642

MACADAM, BARBARA A
EDITOR
Pos: Freelance writer, 83-; assoc ed, Review: Latin Am Lit & Arts, currently; sr ed, ARTnews Mag, currently. *Mailing Add:* ARTnews Mag 48 W 38th St New York NY 10018-0042

MACARAY, LAWRENCE RICHARD
PAINTER, EDUCATOR
b Elsinore, Calif, May 8, 1921. *Study:* Whittier Col, BA, 51; Calif State Univ, Long Beach, MA, 55. *Work:* Bowers Mus, Santa Ana, Calif; San Bernardino Co Mus Art; Bertrand Russell Peace Found, Nottingham, Eng; Spectrum Press, Orange, Calif; pvt collection of art critic, William Wilson, Los Angeles Times; De Saisset Mus, Santa Clara, Calif,. *Comn:* Location oil paintings of Eng & Ireland, 75; Art Shelter Pgm, Brea, Calif, 97. *Exhib:* New Talent, NY, Los Angeles Co Mus Art, 71-72; Bertrand Russell Centenary Art Exhib, Nottingham, 73; Southern Calif Regional Print & Drawing Exhib, 73, 74 & 76; Long Beach Mus Art, 80; Joslyn Ctr Arts, Torrance, Calif, 82; Grants Pass Mus Art, Ore, 83; Prize Winner, La Mirada Festival of the Arts, 84; Solo exhib, Joslyn Fine Arts Gallery, Torrance, Calif, 85; El Camino Coll Exhib, 87. *Pos:* Art & travel ed, Torrance Press-Herald, Calif, 63-70. *Teaching:* Prof drawing & painting, El Camino Col, 62-88. *Awards:* Prize for Art Unlimited, Downey Mus Art, Calif, 74; Southern Calif Exposition Prize, Del Mar, 74; All Calif Art Exhib Prize, 76. *Bibliog:* Dictionary of American Painters, Sculptors & Engravers by Fieldings, 86; Davenport's Art Reference, 87-96; Smith's Printworld Directory, Bala Cynwyd, Pa, 82-2013. *Media:* Oil. *Publ:* Auth & illusr, Sketches from an Irish detour, Yankee Doodlers, 76; illusr, Yarns & tales from the Great Smokies, The Cataloochee Press, 78; auth & illusr, The DeSombre House, Orange Blossoms Into Art, Wordwise, 94. *Dealer:* Ruskin Fine Arts 3936 Walgrove Ave Los Angeles CA 90066. *Mailing Add:* 780 N Malden Ave Fullerton CA 92832

MACAROL, VICTOR GEORGE
ARTIST, PHOTOGRAPHER
Study: Peabody Inst, Johns Hopkins Univ, Baltimore, post-grad study, 68-69. *Work:* NJ State Mus, Trenton; Zimmerli Art Mus, New Brunswick, NJ; Kunsthaus, Zurich, Switz; Mus de l'Elysée, Lausanne, Switz; Biblio Nat, Paris; Noyes Art Mus, Oceanville, NJ. *Exhib:* Solo exhibs: Galerie 147, Basel, Switz, 1978; Galerie zur Stockeregg, Zurich, Switz, 1981; NJ State Mus, Trenton, 1984; Paterson Mus, NJ, 92; Galerie FOMA, Hradec Kralove, Czech Repub, 92; Hunterdon Art Mus, Clinton, NJ, 93; St Joseph's Univ Gallery, Philadelphia, 94; Galerie Mesmer, Basel, Switz, 98; Galerie Michel Ray, Paris, 01; Goldsmiths Gallery, Lambertville, NJ, 03; Front Room Gallery, Singapore, 03; Pep No Name Galerie, Basel, Switz, 2006, Galerie Mesmer, Basel, Switzerland, 2008; Group exhibs: 20th Century Am Photogrs, Galerie zur Stockeregg, Zurich, Switz, 1981; 4th Biennial: NJ Artists, NJ State Mus, Trenton, 1983; Acquisitions Recentes, Mus de l'Elysee, Lousanne, Switz, 91; Images of Flatiron Building, Berry-Hill Gallery, NY, 91; Five Yrs of Collecting Photographs, Mus Mod Art, Ljubljana, Slovenia, 96; Mensch-Focus-Ort, Galerie Arte, Basel, Switz, 96; NJ Artists from the Collection of Contemp Am Art, Noyes Art Mus, Oceanville, NJ 96; Spuren, Galerie Mesmer, Basel, Switz, 98; Schwarz auf Weiss, Galerie Mesmer, Basel, Switz, 99; Life of the City, Mus Modern Art, NY, 02; Contemp Am Artists, Singapore, 2004; 30th Anniversary Exhib, Barron Arts Center, Woodbridge, NJ, 2007; Accrochage, Galerie zur Stockeregg, Zurich, Switzerland, 2010; Contemporary Photog Exhib & Auction, Christie's Zurich, 2011; Zurich Univ, Switzerland, 2011; Biksady Galerie, Budapest, Hungary, 2011. *Awards:* Fel Award, NJ State Arts Coun, 82 & 86; Distinguished Artist Award, NJ State Arts Coun, 87. *Bibliog:* David L Shirey (auth), Art Sampler, NY Times, 5/81; John Caldwell (auth), Modernism in Morristown, NY Times, 8/81; Sally Friedman (auth), Macarol's Photo Treasures, Princeton Pack, NJ, 10/84; Vivien Raynor (auth), From Portraits to Available Forms, NY Times, 3/86; Patricia Malarcher (auth), State Awards Fellowships, NY Times, 8/86; Vivien Raynor (auth), A Celebration of Prints, NY Times, 8/91; Vivien Raynor (auth), Photos from Seasons of Life, NY Times, 11/92; Victoria Donohoe (auth), Macarol Exhibits at St. Joseph's University, Phila Inquirer, 11/94; Wendy Heisler (auth), A Witty Reflection of the World, Princeton Pack, NJ, 4/97; Martina Wohlthat (auth), Kunst in Basel, Basler Zeitung, Switz, 4/98; Jacqueline Falk (auth), Galerien Ausstellungen Wahrend der Kunstmesse, Basler Zeitung, Switz, 6/99; Daniel Shearer (auth), Invisibility in the Moment, Princeton Packet, NJ, 7/99; William Gordon (auth), Picture Perfect, The Star-Ledger, NJ, 4/02; Cheah Ui-Hoon (auth), Unmistakable 'American Feel,' The Business Times, Singapore, 5/03; Francoise Monnin (auth), Rencontres Impromptues, Bale, Suisse, 8/08. *Media:* Multimedia. *Mailing Add:* 34 Van Houten St Apt 304 Paterson NJ 07505

MACAULAY, DAVID ALEXANDER
DESIGNER, ILLUSTRATOR
b Burton on Trent, Eng, Dec 2, 1946. *Study:* RI Sch Design, BArchit, 1969. *Work:* Cooper Hewitt Mus, New York; Toledo Mus Art; Mus Art, RI Sch Design. *Exhib:* Ann Int Exhib Children's Bk Illus, Bologna, Italy, 1976-77; 200 Years Am Illus, Mus of Hist, New York, 1977; Buildingbooks, 1977 & Drawing the Line, 1978, Montclair Art Mus, NJ; Children's Book Art, Monterey Peninsula Mus Art, Calif & Triton Mus Art, Santa Clara, Calif, 1978-79. *Pos:* Free lance graphic designer & illusr, 1972-. *Teaching:* Instr 2-dimensional design, RI Sch Design, 1974-76, adj prof illus, 1976-85, chmn dept, 1977-79; vis lectr, Yale Univ, 1978-79; vis instr drawing, Brown Univ, 1982; vis prof art, Wellesley Col, 1985. *Awards:* Caldecott Hon Medal, Am Libr Asn, 1974 & 1978; Deutscher Jungenbuchpreis (Best non-fiction picture book), Ger, 1975; Medal, Am Inst of Archit, 1978; MacArthur Fellow, John D and Catherine T MacArthur Found, 2006. *Bibliog:* Paul Goldberger (auth), Schede/Libri, Abitare, Edtrice Segesta, Milan, 5/1976 & How to build a castle, New York Times, 11/1977; Stefan Kanfer (auth), Books, Time Mag, 11/1977. *Mem:* Providence Preserv Soc (trustee). *Media:* Pen & Ink. *Publ:* Auth & illusr, Cathedral, The Story of Its Construction, 1973, City, A Story of Roman Planning and Construction, 1974, Underground, 1976, Rome, Antics, Shortcut, Black and White (Caldecott Medal), Great Moments in Architecture, 1978, Motel of the Mysteries, 1979, Help Let Me Out, 1982, Mill, 1983, The Amazing Brain, 1984 & Baaa, 1985, The Way Things Work The New Way Things Work, 1998, Building Big, 2000 Houghton Mifflin; and many publications internationally

MACAULAY, THOMAS S
ENVIRONMENTAL ARTIST, SCULPTOR
b Marshfield, Wis, Jul 2, 1946. *Study:* St Olaf Col, BA, 68; Univ Iowa, MA, 70, MFA, 71. *Exhib:* Solo exhibs, Twining Gallery, NY, 87, Harvard Univ, Cambridge, Mass, 88, Ind Univ, Bloomington, 89, Contemp Mus, Honolulu, 90, Univ Colo, Boulder, 90, La Pietra, Honolulu, 91 & Case Western Reserve Univ, 92. *Teaching:* Prof sculpture, Wright State Univ, Dayton, Ohio, 73-. *Awards:* Fel, Guggenheim Mem Found, 84; Fel, Asian Cult Coun, 87; Fel, Fulbright Scholar Research, Japan-US Educ Comn, 91. *Bibliog:* Donald Kuspit & Betty Collings (coauth), Macaulay's Sculptural Views of Perceptual Ambiguity, Dayton Art Inst, 86; Donald Kuspit (auth), Thomas Macaulay: The Circle Squared, Univ Del, 90; Ann Bremner (auth), Thomas Macaulay A Year, Southern Ohio Mus, 90. *Mem:* Artist's Organization (pres, 87-92). *Media:* Outdoor Environments, Indoor Environments. *Res:* outdoor concrete forms & plant materials; commercial cardboard box forms & indoor environmental installations. *Publ:* Auth, Hawaii Architect: Art in Architecture, Hawaii Coun-Am Inst Architects, 3/90. *Mailing Add:* 5510 Scarff Rd New Carlisle OH 45344

MACBIRD, ROSEMARY (SIMPSON)
PAINTER
b St Joseph, Mo, Nov 19, 1921. *Study:* Art Inst Chicago, 41-43; also with Robert Wood, 82, Zoltan Szabo, 82 & Charles Reid, 83. *Comn:* Watercolors, Santa Barbara Bank, Calif, 81, Lawrence Stewart, Phoenix, Ariz, 82, Norman G Oliver, Hollywood, Calif, 83, Bonnie & Alan Kay, Los Angeles, 90 & Barbara Alter, Newport Beach, Calif, 92. *Exhib:* Knickerbocker Artists Ann Exhib, Salmagundi Club, NY, 83-84; Catherine Lorillard Wolfe Women Artists of Am, 84-85; Allied Artists Am Ann Exhib, Nat Arts Club NY, 84-85; US Dept Immigration & Naturalization Serv Centennial Art Exhib, Images of Am Immigration, a three yr traveling exhib, Georgetown Univ Art Gallery, Washington, DC, Ellis Island NY, Atlanta Fulton Co Libr, Ga, John F Kennedy Mus & Libr, Boston, Mass, Transamerica Tower, San Francisco, Calif, Natural Hist Mus, Los Angeles, Calif, 91-93; Audubon Artists 52nd Ann Exhib, Nat Arts Club, NY, 94; Salmagundi 1994 Non-Member Art Exhib, Salmagundi Club, NY; 1994 Alumni Traveling Art Show, Sch Art Inst Chicago, 94; and others. *Awards:* Santa Fe Fed Bank Purchase Award, Watercolor West Ann Exhib, 80; Grumbacher Gold Medal & Cash Award, Knickerbocker Artists Ann Exhib, 83; Best Watercolor Artist in Show Award, Art-a-Fair Festival, 89; Windsor Newton Watercolor Award, Audubon Artists 1994 Exhib, Nat Arts Club, New York & Salmagundi Exhib, Salmagundi Club, New York, 94; and others. *Mem:* Nat Watercolor Soc (bd mem). *Media:* Watercolor, Oil. *Dealer:* Tidelands Publications 28912 Canyon Rim Dr Trabuco Canyon CA 92619. *Mailing Add:* c/o Lu Martin Galleries 372 N Coast Hwy Laguna Beach CA 92651

MACCLINTOCK, DORCAS
SCULPTOR, WRITER
b New York, NY, July 16, 1932. *Study:* Smith Col, AB; Univ Wyo, AM; Lyme Acad Coll of Fine Arts. *Work:* Smith Col; Hiram Blauvelt Art Mus. *Comn:* Trophy, Collie Club Am Found, 88. *Exhib:* Animal Imagery, St Hubert's Giralda, 87-89; Wildlife Images, Central Park Zoo Gallery, NY, 90; Art & the Animal, Soc Animal Artists, Cleveland Mus Natural Hist, 91; Algonquin Park, Can, 95; Witte Mus, San Antonio, Tex, 96; Shot Tower Gallery, Columbus, Ohio, 97; Disney's Animal Kingdom, Orlando, Fla, 98, 2000-07; Wildlife Art, Sharon Arts Ctr, Peterborough, NH, 98; Art of the Animal Kingdom, Bennington Ctr Arts, Vt, 98-2007; Cleveland Mus of Nat History, 99; Wildlife Exp, Parker Co, 2002; Nat Sculpture Soc Ann, SC and NY, 2002; two-person exhib, Hiram Blauvelt Art Mus, Oradell, NJ, 2003; Hiram Blauvelt Art Mus, Oradell, NJ, 2004; Art of the Animal Kingdom IX, Bennington Ctr Arts, Vt, 2004-07; Catharine Lorillar Wolfe Art Club 108th Ann Exhib, NY 2004-07; Art and the Animal, The Neville, Public Mus, Green Bay, Wis, 2008; The Art of Conservation, NJ, 2008; Art and the Animal, Rolling Hills Wildlife Adventure, Salina, Kans, 2009; Birds in their Habitat, Conn Audubon, 2010. *Pos:* cur affil, Peabody Mus, Yale Univ, New Haven, Conn. *Awards:* Children's Book Award, NY Acad Sci, 74; Smith Coll Medal, 87; Anna Hyatt Huntington Award, Catharine Lorillard Wolfe Art Club, 2004; Bott-Borghi-Bransom Legacy Award, Soc Animal Artists, 2007. *Mem:* Soc Animal Artists Inc (mem exec bd, 76-, jury, 76-95); Am Soc Mammalogists; Auths Guild; Artists for Conservation. *Media:* Bronze. *Publ:* Auth 11 books incl, A Raccoon's First Year, Scribners, 82; African Images, Scribners, 85; Phoebe the Kinkajou, 85; Red Pandas, 88; Animals Observed, 93; A Natural History of Raccoons, 2003. *Mailing Add:* 33 Rogers Rd Hamden CT 06517

MACDONALD, BETTY ANN KIPNISS
PRINTMAKER, WRITER
b NY, 1936. *Study:* Adelphi Univ, BA, 58; Columbia Univ, MA, 60; Chinese Inst, 66-68. *Work:* Libr Cong; Mus Mod Art, Buenos Aires, Arg; Am Cult Ctr, New Delhi, India; New Orleans Mus Art; Montgomery Mus Art, Ala; NY Pub Libr; White House, Washington, DC; Cheremeteff Collection, Book Chamber Internat, Moscow, Russia; Portland Art Mus, Oreg; Nat Mus of Women in the Arts; Univ Richmond Mus, VA; Washington Co Mus Fine Art, Hagerstown, MD; Jane Voorhees Zimmerli Art Mus, Rutgers Univ, NJ; Montgomery Mus Fine Arts, Ala; Miss Mus Art; Boston Public Libr; House of Humour and Satire, Gabrovo, Bulgaria. *Comn:* Murals, comn by Washington Women's Investment Club, Washington, DC, 89, Community of Creative Non-Violence. *Exhib:* Los Angeles Printmaking Soc Exhib, Univ HI, Hilo, HI, 85; Prizewinners Exhib, Judicial Ctr, Fairfax, Va, 85; one-person shows, Dept Interior, Geological Survey, Reston, Va, 89, Washington Printmakers Gallery, Washington, 89, Bird-In-Hand Gallery, Washington, 92, 94 & 98; Univ Brazil, 94; Nat Mus Women Arts, 94-95; Book Chamber Int, Moscow, Russia; House Humor and Satire, Gabrovo, Bulgaria, 10, 12 & 16; Mus Modern Art, Buenos Aires, Argentina. *Teaching:* Instr art, Montshire Mus, 76-83, Lebanon Col, 83-84, Smithsonian Inst, 85-95 & Corcoran Gallery Art, 96. *Awards:* First Prize Printmakers VII, Wash Women's Art Ctr, 85; Past Pres Award, Mus Fine Arts, Springfield, Mass, 83; Book as Art VI and VII, Nat Mus Women in the Arts, Washington, 94, 95; Purchase Award Prize, Delta Nat Small Prints Exhib, Ark State Univ, 2001; Best in Show in Small Prints, Big Impressions, Md Fedn Arts Cir Gallery, Annapolis, Md, 2002; First Prize Graphics, Int Exhib on Fine Art Miniature, 2005; Second Prize, Getaway to The Rockies Art Aurora Artists Guild, Colo, 2007; Equal Merit Award, Lorton Arts Found, 2010; Hon Mention, Alexandria, Va, 2010-2011. *Bibliog:* Pamela Kessler (auth), Washington Post, 3/18/88; Mary McCoy (auth), Washington Printmakers Gallery, Washington Post, 8/22/91; Saiden Pakraven (auth), Washington Printmakers Gallery, Washington Post, 1/17/02; Paul Cassidy (auth), J Print World, 8/2/2004. *Mem:* Life mem Art Student League; Soc Am Graphic Artists; Wash Printmakers Club. *Media:* Etchings, Monoprints, Drypoints, Watercolor, Drawing, Pen & Ink. *Res:* Seven Deadly Sins (series): The Viewer is taken on a journey into twilight worlds of the imagination. *Specialty:* Sculpture, paintings, drawings, printmaking. *Interests:* Writing press releases of exhibits at the National Gallery of Art, Nat Portrait Gallery, Am Art Mus, for the Journal of the Print World, reading. *Publ:* Contribr, Tilt: An Anthology of New England Women's Writing and Art, New Victoria Publ, 75; Orig Print Calendar, Wash Area Printmakers, 87-2012; William & Mary Rev, 92-2003; book cover, Adagio for Trumpet and Strings, Precipice, Contrasts and Kaleidoscopic Changes, Arsis Press; press review writer, J Print World, 2008-. *Dealer:* River Gallery 400 E 2d St Chattanooga TN 37403; Somerhill Gallery Venable Ctr 303 S Roxboro St Durham NC 27701-3628; The Old Print Barn 343 Winona Road Meredith NH 03253; League of New Hampshire Craftmen, Concord, Hanover, North Country Littleton. *Mailing Add:* PO Box 1202 Mc Lean VA 22101

MACDONALD, BRUCE K
ARTIST, HISTORIAN
b New York, NY, June 6, 1933. *Study:* Trinity Coll, BA, 61; Harvard Univ, MA, 67 & PhD, 73. *Exhib:* Spirit Door, Soruba Samadhi Gallery, Asheville, NC, 6/2000; When...Now?, Artworks, Asheville, 7/2001; Closed...Open, The New Art Ctr, Newton, Mass, 9/2001; Original Nature, 16 Patton, Asheville, 6/2003. *Collection Arranged:* Photographs Before Surrealism, Mus Mod Art, NY, 68; Nineteenth Century Painting from the Mus de Arte de Ponce, Mass Inst Technol, 74. *Pos:* Dir exhibs, Mass Inst Technol, Cambridge, Mass, 74-75; dean, Sch Mus Fine Arts, Boston, Mass, 76-93, first pres, 93-94, pres emer, 94-. *Teaching:* Instr, Univ Mass, Boston,72; vis fac mem, Harvard Univ, 76. *Mem:* Photogr Resource Ctr, Inc (bd trustees, 76-86); Cambridge Multicultural Arts Ctr (bd dir, 83-85); Pro Arts Consortium (pres, 92-93); New Art Ctr (bd gov 94-96). *Media:* Oil on Panel. *Publ:* Contrib auth, Brassai, Mus Mod Art, 68; The Quarry by Gustave Courbet, Boston Mus Fine Arts Bull, 69; Nineteenth Century Painting from the Museo de Art de Ponce, Mass Inst Technol, 74; contribr, Visual Dharma: The Buddhist Art of Tibet, Shambala, 75. *Mailing Add:* 87 Dalby St Newton MA 02458

MACDONALD, CARROLL
PAINTER
Study: Bennett Coll, Millbrook, NY, 60-62. *Exhib:* Solo shows incl Paris-NY-Kent Gallery, Conn, 90-97, 1998-2005, Paul Mellon Art Ctr, Choate-Rosemary Hall Wallingford, Conn, 97, New Arts Gallery, Litchfield, Conn, 2006; group shows incl Nat Arts Club, New York, 70, 74, 76, 79; Pastel Soc Am, New York, 72; Nat Acad Design, New York, 84; Almquist Gallery, New Preston, Conn, 86; NOW Gallery, New York, 87; Mattatuck Mus, Waterbury, Conn, 89; Paris-NY-Kent Gallery, 90-97, 1998-2005; Westport Art Ctr, 95; Century Club, New York, 2001, 2002, 2003, 2005, 2006. *Teaching:* Grace Church Sch, NY, 63-67. *Awards:* Purchase Award, Art Students League NY, 82; First Prize, New Britain Mus Am Art, Conn, 92. *Media:* Oil. *Dealer:* Morrison Gallery 8 Old Barn Rd Kent CT 06757. *Mailing Add:* 144 Curtis Rd Bridgewater CT 06752

MACDONALD, ROBERT R
DIRECTOR, HISTORIAN
b Pittsburgh, Pa, May 11, 1942. *Study:* Univ Notre Dame, BA, 64, MA, 65; Univ Pa, MA, 70. *Exhib:* The Face of Genius: Images of Eugene O'Neill, 87; On Being Homeless: Hist Perspectives, 87; Within Bohemia's Boarders: Greenwich Village (1830-1930), 90; Broadway, 125 Urs Musical Theater, 91; Gaelic Gotham; A History of the Irish in NY, 96; Bernice Abbott: Changing NY, 97; NY Begins, 98. *Collection Arranged:* New Haven Colony Furniture (ed, catalog), New Haven Hist Soc, 72; La Portrait Gallery (ed, catalog), 81 & Sun King: Louis XIV and the New World (ed catalog), 84, La State Mus. *Pos:* Dir, New Haven Hist Soc, 71-74, La State Mus, 74-85 & Mus City NY, 85-. *Teaching:* Assoc fel Am civilization, Yale Univ, 73-74; instr mus studies, Tulane Univ, 81; lectr mus studies, NY Univ, 86-. *Awards:* Order of Arts & Lett, French Repub, 85; Order of Isabella Catolica, Govt Spain, 85. *Mem:* Am Asn Mus (pres, 85-87); Am Asn State & Local Hist (mem coun, 78-80). *Res:* American folk art, social and cultural history. *Mailing Add:* c/o Museum of the City of New York Fifth Ave at 103rd St New York NY 10029

MACDONALD, SCOTT
CRITIC, EDUCATOR
b Easton, Pa, Oct 10, 1942. *Study:* DePauw Univ, BA, 64; Univ Fla, MA, 66, PhD, 70. *Teaching:* Asst prof humanities, Univ Fla, 69-70; from asst prof to prof film & Am lit, Utica Col, 71-, dir, Art Gallery, presently. *Res:* Research regarding avant-garde filmmakers. *Specialty:* Upstate New York artists whose work poses a challenge to the local Utica-Rome community. *Publ:* Auth, The expanding vision of Larry Gottheim's films, 78; Surprise, The films of Robert Huot, Quart Rev Film Studies, 80; Interview with Taka Iimura, Part 1, Art & Cinema, 80; Interview with Robert Huot, Afterimage, 80; and others. *Mailing Add:* 5 Sherman St New Hartford NY 13413-2611

MACDONALD, WILLIAM L
HISTORIAN, WRITER
b Putnam, Conn, 1921. *Study:* Harvard Coll, AB, Harvard Univ, AM & PhD (Emerton Fel, Shaw Fel, Morse Fel, Vet Nat Scholar). *Teaching:* Instr, assoc prof, Yale Univ, 56-65; AP Brown prof, Smith Coll, 65-80; independent scholar, 80-. *Awards:* AD Hitcock Prize, Soc Archit Historian, 86 & 96; George Wittenborn Award, 96; Int Book Award, Am Inst Architects, 97; Getty scholar, Getty Ctr for Fine Arts & Humanities, 85-86. *Mem:* Fel Am Acad Arts & Sci; Soc Archit Historians (dir, 58-64); Am Asn Archit Bibliogr; Lifetime Fel Am Acad Rome. *Res:* History of architecture and urbanism; ancient, early Christian, Baroque & American architecture. *Publ:* Auth, The Pantheon: Design, Meaning and Progeny, 76, 2nd printing, 2002; assoc ed & contribr, Princeton Encyclopedia of Classical Sites, 76; auth, Piranesi's Carceri: Sources of Invention, 79; The Architecture of the Roman Empire, Vol 1, rev ed 82, Vol 2, 86; Hadrian's Villa (with John Pinto), 95 & La Villa Adriana (with John Pinto), 97; Northampton Massachusetts Architecture, 76; Early Christian & Byzantine Architecture, 62

MACDONELL, CAMERON
PAINTER, MURALIST
b Elmira, NY, 1938. *Study:* Coll Educ, State Univ NY, Buffalo, BS (art educ); studied with John Davidson, Mort Grossman, Larry Calcognio & Trevor Thomas; independent study, Santa Barbara, Calif. *Work:* IBM. *Comn:* pvt collections. *Exhib:* Solo exhibs, Mansfield State Coll, 1967, People Series, Cape Code, Arnot Art Mus, 1982; Santa Barbara Mus Art, Calif; Our Town Gallery, Santa Barbara, 74; Goleta Galleria, Calif, 75; two-person show, Two Rivels Gallery, Roberson Mus, Binghamton, NY, 68; Artists Gallery, Elmira, NY, 79-81; Clemens Ctr, Elmira, NY, 83; Chemung Canal Gallery, 88; Group exhibs: 76, regional group shows, Arnot Art Mus, Elmira, NY, 76-79; Life Drawing, Renderings, Gmeiner Art Gallery, Wellsboro, Pa, 1986, 2008, 2010; Community Art Elmira, NY, 2011-2014. *Pos:* Art dir marketing develop, Art Frame Publ, Santa Barbara, Calif, 70-76; mgr Econoline advert, Asn Retarded Children, Elmira, NY, 77-81; graph artist, 81-90; tech dir, NY State Div Youth, 1982; designer, Art made famous publ, Santa Barbara, Calif, formerly. *Teaching:* Instr, Corning Sch Dist, 1975-1977; instr, Arnot Mus, Elmira, NY, 1981-1990; instr, Studio 605, 84-90 & 96; Basic drawing, Adventist sch, 2006, acrylic painting, 2007, marionetts, puppets, 2013. *Awards:* Silver Medallions, Bicentennials, City of Santa Barbara & Co of Santa Barbara, 76; Artistic Serv Award, OMRDD, NY, 79; Citation, State of New York, Arts In the Park, 80; Best in Show Drawing, NY State Art Teachers Convention, 1989; grant, NY Coun Arts, 66. *Bibliog:* Larry Griffis, Jr (auth), World of art, Buffalo Courier Express, 61; Trevor Thomas, Buffalo Evening News, 62; Lee Batten (auth), California Artists, Art Fame Publ, 75; Tom Page (auth), Brush with Greatness, Elmira Star Gazette, 1/91; Artist City Hall Exhibi, John P Cleary, 2008. *Mem:* Southern Tier Arts Asn (co-chmn, 79-80); Founder of the Arts in the Park, An Ann Event, Elmira, NY; NY State Art Teachers Asn (1980); Community Arts of Elmira (life mem). *Media:* Woodcuts, Oil, Collages Acrylic. *Interests:* Combining traditional religious art with contemp, design sets for MDA ann telethon. *Collection:* IBM Collection, Binghamton, NY. *Publ:* contribr, Reflections, 72 & illusr, Salvang, 75, Art Fame Publ. *Dealer:* The Sturdivant Gallery 912 Southport St Elmira NY 14904; Art & Frame Gallery Hofman St Elmira NY 14901; Community Arts Ctr Elmira Inc. *Mailing Add:* Studio 605 605 Yale St Elmira NY 14904

MACDOUGALL, ANNE
ART DEALER, PAINTER
b Winchester, Mass, Apr 27, 1944. *Study:* Abbot Acad; Randolph-Macon Woman's Col, AB (art); Syracuse Univ, grad study in art. *Work:* Boston Univ, Mus Fine Arts, Boston; Va Mus Fine Arts; DeCordova Mus, Lincoln, Mass; Indianapolis Mus; Worcester Art Mus, Mass; Springfield Art Mus, Mo. *Exhib:* Boston Printmaker's Nat, 74, 76 & 77; Nat Print, Trenton State, 79; Drawings, DeCordova Mus, 80; Nat Print & Drawing, NDak State, 81; Addison Gallery Am Art, 81; Grand Cent Galleries, NY, 89; Luise Ross Gallery, NY, 94. *Pos:* Dir, GW Einstein Gallery, NY. *Awards:* Va Ctr Fel, 78; MacDowell Fel, 80; Purchase Award, Berkshire Mus, 81. *Bibliog:* Meryle Secrest (auth), article, Washington Post, 4/5/75; Paul Ciano (auth), article, Jewish Advocate, 2/8/78 & 6/81; Dr John Driscoll (auth), The American Landscape Book, 98. *Mem:* Art Table, NY; Boston Printmakers; Boston Visual Artists Union; Cambridge Art Asn (vpres, 72-73); Int Fine Print Dealers Asn. *Media:* Watercolor. *Specialty:* Modern & GNT Am Paintings, works on paper. *Mailing Add:* 98 Riverside Dr New York NY 10024

MACDOUGALL, PETER STEVEN
ARTIST, SCULPTOR
b Willimantic, Conn, Oct 23, 1951. *Study:* Northwestern Conn Community Col, 70-72; Alfred Univ, New York, BFA, 75; Wichita State Univ, Kans, MFA, 77. *Work:* Downey Mus Art, Downey, Calif; Elrich Mus, Wichita State Univ; Nelson Gallery, Alfred Univ, NY; and others. *Exhib:* Copperstown Ann, Copperstown Art Asn, NY,

79-80; Fingerlakes Show, Mem Art Gallery, Rochester, 80; Everson Mus, Syracuse, NY, 80; Artworks Gallery, Hartford, Conn, 81; Univ Dallas, Irving, Tex, 81; and others. *Teaching:* Instr ceramics, Wichita Art Asn, 76-78; asst prof, State Univ NY, Oswego, 78-82; asst prof, Middle Tenn State Univ, 82-87. *Awards:* Craft Award, Northwestern Community Col, 72; Jury Award, Hartford Civic Art Show, 75; Third Place, Adirondack Invitational, 81. *Mem:* Coll Arts Asn; Nat Coun Educ Ceramic Arts; Am Craft Coun. *Media:* Clay. *Dealer:* Hanover Gallery New York NY. *Mailing Add:* PO Box 119 Round Pond ME 04564

MACGAW, WENDY
SCULPTOR
b Detroit, Mich, Nov 16, 1955. *Study:* Univ Mich Sch Art, BFA, 77; Cranbrook Art Acad, MFA, 79. *Work:* Detroit Inst Arts, Albert Kahn & Asn, Architects. *Exhib:* Young Americans: Award Winner, Am Craft Mus, NY, 82; Steel-Glass Sculpture: Wendy MacGaw, Detroit Int Art, Mich, 85; Invitational Metal Show, 3 Rivers Art Fest, Pittsburgh, Pa, 85; Glass Am, Heller Gallery, NY, 85; Mich Nat Endowment Art Fest, 1965-85, Detroit Focus Gallery, 86; Detroit Artists: Update, Cranbrook Art Mus, Bloomfield Hills, 86; Detroit Artists Artemesia, 88; Glass, 88. *Pos:* Co-owner, Artpack Serv, Detroit, Mich, 84-; mem, Speech, Detroit, 84. *Teaching:* Asst prof design, Ctr Creative Studies, Detroit, 79-; instr fine arts, 3-D Design, Wayne State Univ, Detroit, 83-84; instr art & writing, Detroit Inst Art, Mich, 83-84. *Awards:* Award winner, Young Americans: Metal, 80; Nat Endowment Arts Fel, 82-83 & 86-87; Creative Artist Grant, Mich Coun Arts, 84-85; Mich Coun Arts, 88-. *Mem:* Detroit Focus; Founders Soc Detroit Inst Arts. *Media:* Metal, Glass. *Mailing Add:* 28201 Wellington St Farmington MI 48334-3266

MACGREGOR, GREGORY ALLEN
PHOTOGRAPHER
b La Crosse, Wis, Feb 13, 1941. *Study:* Univ Calif, San Francisco, MA (photog), 71; with Jack Welpott & Don Worth. *Work:* San Francisco Mus Mod Art, Calif; Oakland Mus, Calif; Chicago Art Inst, Ill; Mus Mod Art & Whitney Mus, NY. *Exhib:* On the Go, Fine Arts Mus, San Francisco, Calif, 78; Recent Work, OK Harris Works of Art, NY, 79 & 82; San Francisco Mus Mod Art, 82, 83, 87 & 88; The Calif Trail, Arch Mus, St Louis, Mo, 90, Nev Hist Soc Mus, 91 & Dept Interior Mus, Washington, 97; The Oregon Trail, Wash State Hist Mus, Tacoma, 95 & Ore State Hist Mus, Portland, 96; Explosions, Nichols Gallery, San Francisco, 96; Overland, the California Emigrant Trail, Managed by the California Humanities Council, 91-; Lewis and Clark, Traveling Nat Exhib, 2003-2007. *Teaching:* Asst prof & chmn photog, Lone Mountain Col, San Francisco, Calif, 70-78; prof photog, Calif State Univ, Hayward, 80-84, prof art, 80-, art dept chmn, 90-93. *Awards:* Oakland Artist Fel Award, 90. *Bibliog:* Ted Hedypath (auth), The real as surreal, Artweek, 2/25/80; Jim Hughes (auth), Proofsheet, Popular Photog, 6/80; Mark Levy (auth), article, Images & Issues, 10/82. *Mem:* Soc Photog Educ. *Publ:* contribr, Darkroom Dynamics, Curtin-London, 79; auth, Explosions, Headlands Press, 80; article, Art Comn, 6/83; illusr, Darkroom Mag, Vol 4, No 8, 82; Overland, The California Emigrant Trail, Univ NMex Press, 96; auth, Lewis & Clark Revisited, Univ Washington Press. *Dealer:* O K Harris 383 W Broadway New York NY 10012; Equivalents Gallery 1822 Broadway Seattle WA. *Mailing Add:* 6481 Colby St Oakland CA 94618-1309

MACHIORLETE, PATRICIA ANNE
PAINTER, CRAFTSMAN
b Jersey City, NJ. *Study:* Fairleigh Dickinson Univ, BS, 67; Art Ctr NJ, 81; also workshops with Barbara Nechis & Arthur Barbour. *Work:* Allied Signal Corp, Morris Township, NJ; Pub Serv Elect & Gas Co, Newark, NJ; NJ Am Water Co, Short Hills, NJ; Drakes Cakes, Wayne, NJ; The Lanid Corp, Parsippany, NJ. *Comn:* 3 Water Colors, comn by Mr Neil Vanderdusen, Pres, Sony Corp Am, Mendham, NJ, 86. *Exhib:* 15th Ann Salmagundi Club, 84 & 89 & Knickerbocker Artists, 84 & 89, NY; one woman show, Beneficial Mgt Corp Gallery, Peapack, NJ, 87; NJ Watercolor Soc, Monmouth Mus, Lincroft, NJ, 88-91; NAWA Travel Exhib, Mus Southwest, Sewanee, TN, 91-92; 71st Ann Nat Watercolor Soc, Brea Civic Ctr, Calif, 91; 49th Ann Audubon Artists, Nat Arts Club, NY, 91. *Pos:* Newsletter ed, NJ Watercolor Soc, 91-; bd dir, Nat Asn Women Artists, 91-93, catalog chairperson, currently. *Teaching:* Children's Workshops for Pub librs. *Awards:* Monmouth Mus Award, 46th Annual NJ WC Soc Exhib, 88; Grumbacher Medallion, Leonardo Da Vinci, 83; First Prize, 60th Anniversary Exhib, Essex Watercolor Soc, 93. *Mem:* Nat Asn Women Artists (bd dir & chairperson, 91-93); Garden State Watercolor Soc; Miniature Soc, NJ; Essex Watercolor Soc; NJ Watercolor Soc (bd dir, 91-, rec secy, 98-). *Media:* Watercolor; Furniture Painting. *Publ:* The Artist's Mag, 6/93. *Mailing Add:* 37 Sunlet Bnd Johns Island SC 29455-5681

MACHLIS, SALLY GRAVES
EDUCATOR, ADMINISTRATOR, PAINTER
Study: Univ Washington, BA (Art Educ), 1973; Univ Idaho, MFA (Painting), 1986. *Exhib:* Solo exhibitions include Truth and Fables at Arizona Western Col, Yuma, 2006, UC Art Gallery, Univ Montana, Missoula, 2006, Univ Ctr Gallery, Nat Chiayi Univ, Taiwan, 2007, The Art Ctr, Nat Yunlin Univ, Taiwan, 2007; The Chiayi Series at Herrett Ctr for Arts and Sciences, Twin Falls, Idaho, 2008, Univ of Idaho Prichard Gallery, Moscow, Idaho, 2008, Jacklin Arts and Culture Ctr, Post Falls, Idaho, 2009, ARC Gallery, Chicago, 2010; Group Exhibitions include Pleasure Craft, Tacoma Art Mus, 2001, 2001 Idaho Triennial Exhibition, Boise Art Mus, 2001, Toxic Landscape, Pa, NJ, and Havana, Cuba, 2002, Reveal/Conceal, Eastern Washington Univ, Cheney, 2006, Under Cover, Urban Inst for Contemporary Arts, Grand Rapids, Michigan, 2006, Prior Knowledge, Chase Gallery at City Hall, Spokane, 2008. *Pos:* Freelance illustrator, US Nat Park Service, 1974-75; co-author, illustrator of eight children's environmental books published by Dog Eared Publications, Madison, Wis, 1977-90; Artist-in-residence, Artists in Educ Program, Idaho Public Schools, Idaho Commission on the Arts, 1987-93; instructor, Visual Art for Boise Public Schools, Idaho Public Television, Idaho Commission on the Arts, 1988-90; bd dir, Arts for Idaho, 2004-; mem at large, Idaho Commission on the Arts, 2001-06, commissioner, 2006-; vis artist, Nat Chiayi Univ, Taiwan, 2007; invited juror and reviewer for several outreach services. *Teaching:* Elementary art teacher, K-6, Ben Rush Elementary Sch, Kirkland, Washington, 1975, Montowese Elementary Sch, North Haven, Conn, 1976-77; instructional asst, dept art, Univ Idaho, Moscow, Idaho, Drawing, Painting and Design, 1984-86, art instructor, Idaho Quests (summer enrichment program for gifted teens), 1985, instructor continuing educ program, painting and drawing, 1984-90, workshop instructor, Art in the Classroom, Celebrating the Arts Program, 1988, instructor drawing and painting, 1992-93, dir of Foundation Drawing Program, Col Art and Architecture, 1993-2000, asst prof art educ, adj asst prof art, 1993-99, asst prof art and art educ, 1999-2000; assoc prof, art and design and art educ, Univ Idaho, Col of Art & Architecture, Art and Design Program, Department of Curriculum and Instruction, Col of Educ, 2000-, chair art and design, 2000-04, 2010-. *Awards:* Idaho Art Educ Asn, Teaching and Service award, 1998; Mayor's award in the Arts, City of Moscow for Art Educator, 2000; Sabbatical Leave award, Visiting Artist Taiwan, 2007; Best of Show, Creative Quarterly: the Journal of Art and Design #14, NY, 2009. *Mem:* Women's Caucus for Art; Nat Art Educ Asn; Idaho Art Educ Asn; Idaho Alliance for Art Educ; Col Art Asn. *Mailing Add:* Art and Design Program University of Idaho PO Box 442471 Office AA 116 Moscow ID 83844-2471

MACIEJUNES, NANNETTE V
MUSEUM DIRECTOR
b Columbus, Ohio. *Study:* Denison Univ, Granville, Ohio, BA (art hist); Ohio State Univ, MA. *Pos:* Chief cur, Columbus Mus Art, 1984-89, 1990-2002, acting exec dir, 2002-2003; cur, Dixon Gallery & Gardens, Memphis, 1989; dir, Columbus Mus Art, Ohio, 2003-. *Awards:* Charles E Burchfield Found, 1997. *Mailing Add:* Columbus Mus Art 480 E Broad St Columbus OH 43215

MAC INNES, DAVID HAROLD
PAINTER, PRINTMAKER
b Troy NY June 29, 1926. *Study:* Cleveland Inst Art, 1949; Post grad studies: Western Reserve Univ, Cleveland Ohio, 1951; Carnegie Mellon Inst, Pittsburgh, Pa, 1954; Am Indian Inst Art (Printmaking workshop), Santa Fe, NMex, 2007; Palos Verdes Art Center, Rancho Palos Verdes, Calif. *Comn:* film, graphic design, editing, filming, LW Frohich Presents, Comn by Becton Dickinson and Parke Davis, 1972; art dir & communication design, IBM, Comn by Atlantic Richfield and Kidder Peadbody, 1980; TV and print, AT&T, US Postal and NY Telephone, 1990. *Exhib:* 27th New Eng Int, Silvermine, Conn, 1958; Art Directors Who Paint, Art Directors Club NY Gallery, New York, NY, 1991; Solo Exhibs: A Walk in the Park, Larchmont Art Gallery, Larchmont, NY, 1993; In Retrospect: David Mac Innes, Oresman Gallery, Larchmont, NY, 1995; David Mac Innes Paintings & Graphics, Palos Verdes Art Center, Rancho Palos Verdes, Calif, 2007; Expect the Unexpected, Mamaroneck Artist Guild, Larchmont, NY, 1994; Los Angeles Center for Digital Arts, 1/2008; Juried Show, Palos Verdes Art Center, 2008. *Pos:* Art dir and group supervisor, LW Frolich, Inc, NY, 1961-1972; Senior art dir, Consumer and Pharmaceutical Agencies, 72-80. *Teaching:* Guest Art Lectr, Calif Art Educ Asn Conference, Pasadena, Calif, 2007; Instr (various guest positions in Pittsburgh, Cleveland & NY). *Awards:* 1st Award, Artists in Industry, Pittsburgh Chamber of Com, 1956; 1st Place, LW Frolich Presents, LW Frolich Corp, 1960; 1st Award, Big Apple Show, Western Gallery, NYC Univ, 1960; 1st Place (Expect the Unexpected), Mamaroneck Artist Guild, 1994; 2nd Award, Palos Verdes Art Center Ann Show, 2003. *Mem:* NY Art Dirs Club (bd mem, treas, student scholar award comt), 1992-1995; life mem, Los Angeles Co Mus Art, 2002-; Calif Art Educ Asn, 2003-; Mus Latin Am Art, Long Beach, Calif, 2003-; Los Angeles Co Art Educ Coun, 2004-; Los Angeles Center for Digital Arts, 2008-. *Media:* Miscellaneous Media. *Interests:* Fusing and kilnforming diachronic glass, digital photography, painting. *Publ:* Trish Jochen (auth), David Mac Innes: Artist, Moon Tide Media, 2008. *Dealer:* Palos Verdes Art Center Gallery 5504 Crestridge Rd Rancho Palos Verdes CA 90275. *Mailing Add:* POB 4711 Palos Verdes Peninsula CA 90274-9622

MACK, CHARLES RANDALL
HISTORIAN, COLLECTOR
b Baltimore, Md, May 23, 1940. *Study:* Univ NC, Chapel Hill, AB, 1962, PhD (hist art), 1972. *Collection Arranged:* Classical Art from Carolina Collections (auth catalog), Columbia Mus Art, SC & NC Mus Art, Raleigh, 74; A Campus Collects (auth catalog), Univ SC Mus, Columbia, 80; H Robert Bonsack: Figure Studies, Goethe Inst, Atlanta traveling exhib, 81-82; Turned to Tradition: Southeastern Folk Pottery Today (auth catalog), Columbia Mus Art, SC, 88; Paper Pleasures: Five Centuries of Drawings and Watercolors (auth catalog), Univ SC Mus, Columbia, 92-94; Two Traditions in Transition: Folk Potters of E Germany and Am South, McKissick Mus, Univ SC, Columbia, 98; Bunzlauer Style (auth catalog), Georgia Mus of Art, Athens, 2002; Enamelware Art, McKissick Mus, Univ SC, Columbia, 2003; Bonsack: Centenary Celebration (auth catalog), McMaster Gallery, Univ SC, Columbia, 2003. *Pos:* VPres Southeastern Col Art Conf, 2000-03, pres, 2003-2004. *Teaching:* Prof ancient & Renaissance art, Univ SC, Columbia, 70-2005, William J Todd, Dist Prof Emer Italian Renaissance, 92-2005. *Awards:* Am Coun Learned Soc Trav Grant, 82, 89; Nat Endowment Humanities Grant, 84, 89; Am Phil Soc Grant, 94; Southeastern Coll Art Conf Research & Publ award, 98, Exhib & Catalog award 93. *Mem:* Am Coll Art Asn; Southeastern Coll Art Conf (pres 75-76, bd mem 84-87, pres 2003-2005); Southeastern Chap Soc Archit Historians (bd mem 84-87, pres 91-92). *Res:* Fifteenth century Italian art and architecture; Southeastern folk pottery; Bunzlauer style pottery from eastern Germany. *Collection:* Bunzlauer ceramics from Eastern Germany, Southeastern folk pottery. *Publ:* Pienza: The Creation of a Renaissance City, Cornell Univ, 87; Roman Remains: John Izard Middleton's Visual Souvenirs of 1820-23, Univ SC Press, 97; Looking at the Renaissance: Essays Towards Contextual Appreciation, Univ Mich Press, 2005; auth, Talking with the Turners: Conversations with Southern Folk Potters, Univ SC Press, 2006; European Art in the Columbia Mus Art, including the Samuel H Kress Collection, vol 1: The Thirteenth through the Sixteenth Century, Univ SC Press, 2009. *Mailing Add:* 122 Woodrow St Columbia SC 29205-3134

MACK, DANIEL R
DESIGNER, CRAFTSMAN
b Rochester, NY, Dec 23, 1947. *Study:* Univ Toronto, BA, 70; The New Sch, New York, MA, 75; self-taught woodworker. *Work:* Cooper Hewitt Mus; Am Craft Mus; Mus Fine Arts, Houston; Mus Fine Arts, Boston; Yale Art Gallery. *Exhib:* Am Craft Mus, 87, 91 & 92; Cooper Hewitt Mus, 92 & 2008. *Teaching:* Teacher rustic woodworking, Anderson Ranch Arts Ctr, Snowmass, Colo, 87-93 & Omega Inst Holistic Studies, 97-. *Awards:* Fel, NY Found Arts, 86 & 90; Fel, Mid-Atlantic Arts Found, 88. *Bibliog:* Rustic revival, Washington Post, 5/85; William Bryant Logan (auth), Rococo rustic, House & Garden, 11/86; many other articles in national magazines. *Media:* Natural Form Wood. *Publ:* Auth, Making Rustic Furniture, Sterling/Lark, 92; The Rustic Furniture Companion, Lark, 96; Simple Rustic Furniture, Lark, 99; Log Cabin Living, Gibbs-Smith, 99; Rustic Garden Structures, Lark, 2005; The Adirondack Chair, STC, 2008; The Hammock, STC, 2008. *Mailing Add:* 14 Welling Ave Warwick NY 10990

MACKENZIE, DAVID, IV
PAINTER
b Los Angeles, Calif, Nov 8, 1942. *Study:* Orange Coast Col, Costa Mesa, Calif, AA; San Francisco Art Inst, BFA & MFA; also with Ron Nagle & Tom Holland. *Work:* Oakland Mus Art, Calif; Mills Collage Art Gallery, Oakland, Calif; Oakland Mus, Calif; San Francisco Mus Mod Art, Calif. *Exhib:* Solo exhibs, San Francisco Art Inst, 73, Grapestake Gallery, San Francisco, 75, 76 & 80, A Ten Yr Survey, Bluxome Gallery, San Francisco, 83 & Angeles Gallery, Santa Monica, Calif, 89; 18 Bay Area Artists, Art Mus, Univ Calif, Berkeley, 75; Whitney Biennial, Whitney Mus Am Art, 75; Tough Stuff, San Francisco Mus Mod Art, 83; Bay Area Painting, San Francisco, 84; Sheldon Mem Art Gallery, Univ Nebr, Lincoln; Natural Order, Art in General, NY, 91; Painting Show, Ridge St Gallery, 96; Transport, NY, 97; Process & Image, Eklektikos Gallery, Washington, DC, 98; The Art of Absolute Desire, NY, 99; Straight Painting, NY, 2000; Viewpoints of Recent Developments in Abstract Painting, NY, 2001; Dialog and Discourse, NY, 2001. *Pos:* Guest cur, Los Angeles Inst Contemp Art, Los Angeles, 76, San Francisco Art Inst, 78 & Dialog and Discourse, Friends Acad, 2001; guest organizer, San Francisco Art Inst, 83. *Awards:* Nat Endowment Arts Grant, 75. *Bibliog:* Peter Frank (auth), On the Trail of the Exxon National, Nat Arts Guide, Vol 3, No 1, 81; Thomas Albright (auth), Art in the San Francisco Bay Area 1945-1980, Univ Calif Press; & others. *Mem:* Ridge St Gallery. *Dealer:* Angles Gallery Santa Monica CA. *Mailing Add:* 315 Columbia St Brooklyn NY 11231

MACKENZIE, HUGH SEAFORTH
PAINTER, ETCHER
b Toronto, Ont, June 19, 1928. *Study:* Ont Coll Art; Mt Allison Univ, BFA. *Work:* Montreal Mus Fine Arts, PQ; Art Gallery Ont & Univ Toronto, Toronto; Univ Waterloo; London Art Gallery, Ont; House Commons, Ottawa; and others. *Comn:* Portrait of LB Pearson, Dept State, Ottawa, 68. *Exhib:* Solo exhibs, Morris Gallery, Toronto, 63-77, Univ Waterloo, 75, Carleton Univ Art Gallery, Ottawa, 95 & Galerie Dresdnere, Toronto, 95; Montreal Mus Fine Arts, Que, 64 & 70; Lithographs in collabr with NS Coll Art, Nat Gallery Can, 71; Bau-Xi Gallery, Toronto, 81-83, 85-86, 88, 90, 92-93, 97, 99-2000, 2002 & 2004; Hart House, Univ Toronto, 87; Peterborough, Art Gallery, 88; Robert McLaughlin Gallery, Oshawa, Ont; Gallery Lambton, Sarnia, 2002; Bau-Xi Gallery, Toronto, 2006, 09; Bau-X, 2011; and others. *Teaching:* Instr art, Ont Coll Art, 68-91; retired. *Awards:* JWG Forster Award, Ont Soc Artists, 61; Can Coun Award, 70; AJ Casson Award for Teaching Excellence, Ont Coll Art Alumni Asn, 91. *Bibliog:* Hale (auth), article, Arts Mag, 2/70; Duval (auth), High Realism in Canada, Irwin Clarke & Co, Ltd, 74; Michael Bell (auth), Transitions - Hugh MacKenzie: Painter/Etcher, Carleton Univ Art Gallery. *Mem:* Royal Can Acad. *Media:* Oil, Etching. *Dealer:* Bau-Xi Toronto. *Mailing Add:* 84 MacPherson Ave Toronto ON M5R 1W8 Canada

MACKILLOP, ROD
PAINTER, EDUCATOR
b Northampton, Mass, June 15, 1940. *Study:* Tufts Univ, BA, 61, MFA, 68; Sch Boston Mus Fine Arts, with Jan Cox & Jason Berger, dipl, 68. *Work:* Ashville Art Mus, NC; Duke Univ; Davidson Col, NC. *Exhib:* 47th Ann Painting & Sculpture Competition, Southeastern Ctr Contemp Art, Winston-Salem, 79; Large Painting Invitational, Southeastern Ctr Contemp Art, Winston-Salem, 81; NC Artists Exhib, NC Mus Art, Raleigh, 84; Southern Exposure, Alternative Mus, NY, 85; solo exhibs, Asheville Art Mus, NC, 89, St Johns Mus Art, Wilmington, NC, 89 & Hickory Mus Art, NC, 90. *Pos:* Head art dept, Roxbury Latin Sch, Mass, 65-73. *Teaching:* Prof painting & art criticism, Univ NC, Charlotte, 73-. *Awards:* Purchase Awards, Mint Mus, 79 & 81, Weatherspoon Art Gallery, 84. *Bibliog:* Jane Kessler (auth), Rod MacKillop (article), Art Papers, 7-8/82; Jon Meyers (auth), Rod MacKillop (exhib rev), New Art Examiner, 5/86; Jane Kessler (auth), Rod MacKillop/Paintings 1972-1989, Asheville Art Mus, 89. *Mem:* Coll Art Asn; Friends of Art, Charlotte, NC. *Media:* Acrylic Paint. *Dealer:* Hodges Taylor Gallery 119 E 7th St Charlotte NC 28202. *Mailing Add:* 1918 Ewing Ave Charlotte NC 28203-5767

MACKINTOSH, SANDRA
SCULPTURE, COLLAGE ARTIST
b Detroit, Mich, July 2, 1944. *Study:* Ctr Creative Studies, Detroit, Mich. *Work:* Guggenheim Mus; Brooklyn Mus, NY; Newark Mus, NJ; Union Bank Switz, Zurich; Shearson Lehman, NY; Hood Mus, Dartmouth Col, NH. *Exhib:* Collage: The State of the Art, Bergen Mus Art & Sci, Paramus, NJ, 85; McNay Art Mus, San Antonio, Tex, 85; Constructed Sculpture in Wood, Brooklyn Mus, 92. *Collection Arranged:* Collection of Fox and Cook Archiecture Firm Ny, 2004. *Pos:* Dir, E Market St Gallery, Red Hook, NY. *Bibliog:* Maureen Mullarkey (auth), The Nation, 12/19/88. *Media:* Wood, Stone, Iron. *Dealer:* Cordier & Ekstrom 417 E 75th St New York NY 10021. *Mailing Add:* 54 Joy Rd Woodstock NY 12498

MACKLOWE, LINDA & HARRY
COLLECTORS
b 1938. *Study:* Univ Ala, NY Univ, Sch Visual Arts, New York. *Pos:* Founder, chmn, and chief exec officer, Macklowe Properties, Inc, New York, 1960-2008; chmn emeritus, 2008-. *Awards:* Named one of Top 200 Collectors, ARTNews mag, 2005-10. *Collection:* Contemporary art. *Mailing Add:* Macklowe Properties 767 5th Ave 21st Fl New York NY 10153

MACMURTRIE, CHICO
SCULPTOR, KINETIC ARTIST
b NMex, 1961. *Study:* Univ Ariz, BFA; Univ Calif, Los Angeles, MFA. *Pos:* Founder and artistic dir, Amorphic Robot Works, 1991-. *Bibliog:* Neva Chonin (auth), Culture Jamming, San Francisco Bay Guardian, 4/3/1996; Robert Gibbons (auth), Robots Take Center Stage at New York Exhibit, Reuters, 7/24/2003; Rachel Metz (auth), Mingling with Metal Men, Wired Mag, 3/21/2005; Rita Delfiner (auth), Cheep Living 'Apartment for Birds' Floats in East River, New York Post, 10/31/2007. *Mailing Add:* 111 Pioneer St Brooklyn NY 11231-1610

MACNAUGHTON, MARY DAVIS
MUSEUM DIRECTOR, EDUCATOR
Study: Scripps Col, BA (art history); Columbia Univ, MA & PhD (art history). *Pos:* Dir, Ruth Chandler Williamson Gallery, currently. *Teaching:* Assoc prof art history, Scripps Col, currently. *Awards:* Nat Endowment for Arts Mus Prof Grants; Southern Calif ArtTable Distinguished Women in the Arts Award, 2001. *Mailing Add:* Scripps College The Ruth Chandler Williamson Gallery 1030 N Columbia Ave Claremont CA 91711-6344

MACNEILL, FREDERICK DOUGLAS
PAINTER
b Boston, Mass, Sept 28, 1929. *Study:* Vesper George Sch Art, 52-54, with Alphonse J Shelton, 69 & Arthur Safford, 70. *Work:* First Nat Bank, John Hancock Life Insurance Co & First Church Christ Scientist, Boston; Otis Elevator Co, NY; Raytheon Corp, Lexington, Mass. *Exhib:* Southern Vt Art Ctr, Manchester, 82; solo exhib, Guild Boston Artists, Mass, 82-84; Hudson Valley Art Asn, Westchester Co Ctr, White Plains, NY, 85; Arts for the Parks, Jackson, Wyo, 91, 92 & 94; Mystic Int Exhib, Conn, 92; Grand Teton Natural Hist Asn, Jackson, Wyo, 93; Top 100 Art for the Park, 2004; and others. *Pos:* Instr, Needham Art Ctr, Mass, 83-83. *Awards:* Helen Van Wyk Gold Medal, Rockport Art Asn, 2002; Mareeret Pearson Gold Medal, Rockport Art Asn, 2002; Maurice E Goldberg Meml Award, Rockport Art Asn, 2002; Alden Bryan Award, North Shore AA Asn, 2006; Popular Vote Award, Rockport AA, 2006; Art Whole Supple Award, N Shore Art Asn, 2006; Bernard Corey Mem Award, Rockport Art Asn, 2006-2007. *Bibliog:* Article in Yankee Mag, 78; Print Catalogue, NY Graphic Soc Ltd, 84; article in Boston Globe, 95. *Mem:* Guild Boston Artists; Allied Artists Am; Am Artists Prof League; Rockport Art Asn; Hudson Valley Art Asn. *Media:* Oil, Watercolor. *Specialty:* traditional. *Publ:* Best of Oil Painting, Rockport Pub; Best of Watercolor, Rockport Pub; Art From the Park, North Light Pub; Landscape Inspirations, North Light Pub; Painting Textures, Rockport Pub; illusr book & cover, The Crucifixtion in American Art, Macfarland Publs; Catching the Light. *Dealer:* Guild of Boston Artists Boston MA; Powers Gallery Acton MA; Gallery on the Green Woodstock VT; Mastcove Gallery Kennebunkport ME. *Mailing Add:* 23 Dana Rd Concord MA 01742

MACPHERSON, KEVIN
PAINTER
b NJ, Apr 9, 1956. *Study:* N Ariz Univ, BFA, 78; Scottsdale Artists Sch, 86-. *Exhib:* Plein Air Painters Am, 87, 88, 89, 90, 91 & 94-; solo exhibs, Taos Art Gallery, NMex, 89 & Redfern Gallery, Calif, 94 & 96-98; Taos, Impressionist Show, 89, 90, 91 & 92; Ctr Arts Southwest, Santa Fe, NMex, 90; Am Art in Miniature Invitational, Gilcrease Mus, 94; Alumni Invitational Show, Northern Ariz Univ, 94; Greenhouse Gallery, 96 & 98. *Teaching:* Taos Art Inst, 7/89; oil painting workshops, Scottsdale Artists' Sch, 90-98; Macpherson workshop, 91-98. *Awards:* Best of Show, Amarillo Nat Landscape Competition, 87; Stacey Scholar, 90; Best Landscape, Oil Painters Am, 92. *Bibliog:* Artists' worth watching (article), Art Talk, 2/88 & 11/94; Focus, Santa Fe, 8-9/93; SW Profile, 5/93; and others. *Mem:* signature mem, Plein Air Painters Am (pres); master signature mem Oil Painters Am. *Media:* Oil. *Publ:* Artist Mag, 10/93 & 10/98; Fill Your Oil Paintings with Light and Color, Northlight Publ, 1/98; Landscape Painting Inside & Out, North Light Publ; Reflections on a Pond, Studio Escondido Publ, 2005. *Dealer:* Studio Escondido Taos NM; Redfern Gallery Laguna Beach CA. *Mailing Add:* 12 Clint Rd Taos NM 87571

MAC WHINNIE, JOHN VINCENT
PAINTER, SCULPTOR
b Rockville Centre, NY, Apr 22, 1945. *Study:* Southampton Col, NY, BA (magna cum laude), 71; studied with Fairfield Porter, Larry Rivers & Ilya Bolotowsky. *Work:* Guggenheim Mus; Brooklyn Mus; Phillips Collection; Walker Art Ctr; Parrish Art Mus. *Exhib:* Summer Loan Exhib, Metrop Mus Art, NY, 79; Art in Am Since World War Two, Guggenheim Mus, 79; 24th Ann Contemp Am Painting Exhib, Lehigh Univ, 79; Am Drawing in Black and White, Brooklyn Mus, 81; Am Acad & Inst Arts & Lett, NY, 81; Human Figure in Contemp Art, New Orleans Mus Contemp Art, 82; Poets and Artists of the Region, Guild Hall, East Hampton, NY, 82. *Awards:* First Prize Painting, Parrish Mus, Southampton, NY, 71; Excellence in Painting, Heckscher Mus, Huntington, NY, 74. *Bibliog:* David Shapiro (auth), Transcending photography, Art Int, 76. *Media:* Oil, Encaustic. *Dealer:* Marlborough Gallery New York NY

MADAN-SHOTKIN, RHODA
PAINTER
b New York, NY. *Study:* Pratt Inst, BFA, 59; Carl Schmalz Workshops 78-79; Charles Reid Workshops, 80-85. *Work:* Discovery Mus, Bridgeport, Conn; Fairfield Art Collection, Conn; Ctr Financial Studies, Fairfield Univ, Conn; Zimmerli Art Mus, New Brunswick, NJ. *Exhib:* Nat Asn Women Artists Traveling Exhib, 83-86; Ann

Open Exhib, Salmagundi Club, NY, 83; Womens Art Exhib, Purdue Univ, West Lafayette, Ind, 84; 100 Yrs/100 Works, Fine Arts Mus South Mobile, Ala & Longview Mus Art, Tex, 89-90; Flowers & Figures, Fairfield Univ Ctr Financial Studies, 90; solo exhibs, Greene Art Gallery, Guilford, Conn, 93, 2001, Galerie Jamault, France, 2001, In the Light, Rockwell Art Gallery, Wilton, Conn, 2005, In the Light II, Rockwell Art Gallery, Wilton Conn, 2007; Gallery Zoma, Greenwich, Conn, 2008; Greene Art Gallery, Guilford Ct, 2009, 2010, 2011; Juried Pres Show, Kent Art Asn, Conn, 2012; Foodies, Art Ctr, Westport, Conn, 2012. *Awards:* Mildred Reilly Mem, 83, Gene Alden Walker Award, 85 & 99 & Martha Reid Mem Award, 87, Jared Phillip Apple Mem Award, 2003, Nat Asn Women Artists; Koenig Art Prize, Brush and Palette Club, New Haven, Conn; Miriam Shorr Award for Watercolor, Nat Asn Women Artists, 2014. *Bibliog:* Thomas F Potter (auth), Art topics, Meriden Record J, 88-89; Shirley Gonzales, Watercolor's maturity, New Haven Register, 89; Judy Birke (auth), Other Interesting Works, New Haven Register, 2002. *Mem:* Nat Asn Women Artists; Conn Watercolor Soc; New Haven Paint & Clay Club; Westport Art Ctr. *Media:* Watercolor. *Publ:* Contribr, Pulling Your Paintings Together, Watson-Guptill, 85. *Dealer:* Rockwell Art Gallery 236 Post Rd East Westport Ct 06880. *Mailing Add:* Five Brookside Dr Westport CT 06880

MADDEN-WORK, BETTY I
PAINTER, HISTORIAN

b Chicago, Ill, Nov 12, 1915. *Study:* Am Acad Art, Chicago; Northwestern Univ; Univ Ill, BFA; Inst Design, Chicago; with Herb Olson, Spain & Italy; John Pellew, Ireland & Eng; Tom Hill, Mex; Zornes, Vt. *Work:* City of Springfield, Ill; Repub China; Ill Col; Lincoln Col; Caterpillar Tractor, Peoria; pvt collections. *Comn:* 7 paintings, Springfield Mayor's Awards Arts, 98. *Exhib:* Midwest Watercolor Soc, 81, 86 & 89; Ill Dept of Transportation, 81 & State Fair Professional, 81, 85 & 90; Fla Celebration of Women, 84; Solo exhibs, Western Ill Univ, Macomb, 78 & Caterpillar Tractor Co, Peoria, 79; S Ill Med Sch, 92; Sangamon State Univ, 91 & 94. *Collection Arranged:* Arts and Artifacts of Illinois. *Pos:* Com artist & illusr, Consolidated Bk Publ, Chicago, 44-46; com artist, Evans, Work & Costa Advert, Springfield, Ill, 55-59; fashion illusr, SA Barker Co, Springfield, 59-61; tech asst art dept, Ill State Mus, 61-63, cur art, 63-78; calligrapher, Ill Supreme Ct, 80-2003. *Teaching:* Instr art, Art Asn, Springfield, 78-94 & Ft Myers Beach, Fla, 85-90. *Awards:* Springfield Pacesetters Achievements in the Arts Award, 69; City Purchase Award, Springfield, 83; First Prize, Fla, SW Regional, 85 & 88; Midwest Water Color Soc Award, 86. *Bibliog:* Betty Madden Work: Building on a Wet-into-Wet Base, Am Artist, Watercolor, 92. *Mem:* Ill Artisans; Springfield Art Asn; signature mem Transparent Watercolor Soc Am; Prairie Art Alliance; Delta Kappa Gamma (hon). *Media:* Watercolor, Ink. *Res:* Arts, crafts and architecture of Ill. *Interests:* Art history, painting, calligraphy. *Publ:* Auth, Art, Crafts and Architecture in Early Illinois, Univ Ill Press, 74; Living Museum, articles, Ill State Mus, 63-78

MADDOX, JERALD CURTIS
CURATOR, HISTORIAN

b Decatur, Ind, June 9, 1933. *Study:* Ind Univ, AB, 55 & MA, 60; Harvard Univ, 60-61. *Hon Degrees:* Corcoran Sch Art, Hon Dr Fine Art, Wash, DC, 97. *Work:* Int Mus Photog, George Eastman House, Rochester, NY; Libr Cong, Washington, DC. *Collection Arranged:* Am Photography: The Sixties, Univ Nebr Art Galleries, 66; Creative Photography 1869-1969, Libr Cong, Washington, DC, 70. *Pos:* Asst to dir, Univ Nebr Art Galleries, 63-66; head curatorial section, Prints & Photog Div, Libr Cong, 66-78, cur photog, 66-, collections planner & coordr, 78-87; consult photog, Northern Va Community Coll, 77. *Teaching:* Instr art hist, NY State Univ Col New Paltz, 62-63. *Awards:* Mus Prof Fel, Nat Endowment Arts, 74. *Mem:* Coll Art Asn; Soc Photog Educ (treas, 68-73). *Res:* History and criticism of photography. *Publ:* Auth, Essay on a tintype, 1/69 & Creative photography, 1869-1969, 1/71, Quart J Libr Cong; Photography in the first decade, Art Am, 7/8/73; How much is a photograph worth, After Image, 2/75; The Pioneering Image: Celebrating 150 years of American Photography, 6/89. *Mailing Add:* 4514 Highland Ave Bethesda MD 20814

MADDOX, JERROLD WARREN
EDUCATOR, PAINTER

b Ft Wayne, Ind, Mar 6, 1932. *Study:* Ind Univ, BS, 54 & MFA, 59. *Exhib:* Recent Painting USA: The Figure, Mus Mod Art, NY, 62-63; Moods of Light, Am Fedn Art, 63-64. *Teaching:* Asst prof humanities, Monteith Col, Wayne State Univ, Detroit, 60-63; lectr painting & drawing, Regional Col Art & Crafts, Hull, Eng, 64; asst prof painting & drawing, Univ Ky, Lexington, 64-66; asst prof drawing & painting, Amherst Col, Mass, 66-69; assoc prof drawing & painting, Reed Col, Portland, Ore, 69-70; assoc prof drawing & painting, Ind Univ, Bloomington, 70-74; head prof, Kans State Univ, Manhattan, 74-; dir, Pa State Univ, University Park, 80-84, prof, 84-. *Mem:* Coll Art Asn Am; Nat Coun Art Adminr (chmn, 82); Nat Asn Sch Art & Design. *Media:* Oil. *Publ:* Coauth, Images and Imagination: an Introduction to Art, 65. *Mailing Add:* 1495 W Pine Grove Rd Pennsylvania Furnace PA 16865-9422

MADONIA, ANN C
CURATOR, ADMINISTRATOR

b New York, NY. *Study:* Hunter Col, City Univ New York, AB, 72, MA, 77; Hofstra Univ, cert (appraisal), 79. *Collection Arranged:* Am Profile: Drawings by Norman Rockwell (auth, catalog), 80; Selected Paintings from Charles August Ficke Collection (auth, catalog), 80; Mexican Colonial Paintings in the Davenport Art Gallery, 83; Lindley Am Collection, 84; Paul Norton Retrospective (auth, catalog), 85; Harute-Out Here: Swedish Immigrant Arts Midwest Am, 85; Quad City Art Showcase (competitive exhib; auth, catalog), 86; Intent Artist (auth, catalog), 87; Am Drawing Biennial (competitive exhib), 90, 92, 94, 96 & 98; Spirit of the South, 92; Sculpture of Alexander Galt, 92; Gifford Beal: Picture-Maker (co-auth, catalog), 93; Drawings and Watercolors by Hans Grohs (with catalog), 95; The European Phoenix: Selections from the Lania Collection of Contemporary Prints (with catalog), 96; Facing the Past: Portraits from the Permanent Collections (with catalog), 99; O'Keeffe in Williamsburg: A Re-Creation of the Artist's First Public Exhibition in the South (essay, catalogue), 2001; O'Keefe's Photo Essay, 2001; William & Mary Collects II, a Celebration, 2003. *Pos:* Cur collections, Davenport Mus Art, Iowa, 79-88; cur collections, Muscarelle Mus, Col William & Mary, Williamsburg, Va, 89-; actg dir, 2002-. *Teaching:* Adj instr art hist, Col William & Mary, Williamsburg, Va, 94-95 & 2003-2005. *Awards:* Curator's Award for Exhib, Southeastern Mus Conf, for Facing the Past: Portraits from the Permanent Collections, 98-99. *Mem:* Am Inst Conservation Artistic & Hist Works; Am Asn Mus; Coll Art Asn; Asn Art Mus Cur. *Res:* American art. *Publ:* Auth, Davenport: 1836-1936--The Centennial Mural, 80, Ralph Albert Blakelock--poet of the landscape, 80, Limners and likenesses, 81, & The Mexican Colonial Collection, 83, Bulletin, Davenport Mus Art; Early contributions by Swedish painters in America (essay), In: Harute-Out Here: Swedish Immigrant Artists in Midwest America (exhib catalog), 85; Rubens Peal still life, Thomas Hart Benton lithographs, Bulletin, Davenport Mus Art, 86; Intent of the Artist (exhib catalog), 87; auth, Facing the Past: Portraits from the Permanent Collection (exhib catalog), 99; co-auth, Gifford Beal: Picture-Maker (exhib catalog), 99, co-author, Faith, Spirit, and Tradition (exhib catalog), 2000; Georgia O'Keeffein Williamsburg, 2001. *Mailing Add:* Col William & Mary Muscarelle Mus Art PO Box 8795 Williamsburg VA 23197-8795

MADSEN, LOREN WAKEFIELD
SCULPTOR

b Oakland, Calif, Mar 29, 1943. *Study:* Reed Col, Portland, Ore, 61-63; Univ Calif, Los Angeles, BA, 66, MA, 70. *Work:* Mus Mod Art, NY; Georges Pompidou Ctr, Paris; Hirshhorn Mus, Washington, DC; Israel Mus, Jerusalem; Los Angeles Co Mus Art, Calif; Mus Contemp Art, San Diego, Calif. *Comn:* Brookhollow Atrium, San Antonio, Tex, 84; Horton Plaza, San Diego, Calif, 85; Chevy Chase Metro Bldg, Chevy Chase, Md, 85; Untitled, La Guardia Community Col, NY, 91; JR Kinschicyo Sta, Tokyo, Japan, 97; and others. *Exhib:* One man show, Mus Mod Art, NY, 75; Sculpture Made in Place, Walker Art Ctr, Minneapolis, Minn, 76; David McKee Gallery, NY, 76, 77, 82, 86, 90, 92, 96 & 98; Art First, London, 98; Six Billion Monkey, SUNY, Stony Brook, 99; Apex Art CP, NY, 99; Mus Contemp Art, San Diego, 00. *Teaching:* Instr painting & sculpture, Sch Visual Arts, New York, 87-88. *Awards:* New Talent Award, Mod & Contemp Art Coun, Los Angeles Co Mus Art, 75; Nat Endowment Arts Fel Grant, 76 & 80; Hon Mention, Vietnam, Veterans Mem Competition, 81. *Media:* Wood, Steel. *Mailing Add:* c/o McKee Gallery 745 5th Ave New York NY 10151

MADSEN, METTE B
PAINTER

b New York, NY, Apr 6, 1955. *Study:* Calif Coll Art & Sci, BFA, 78. *Work:* Smithsonian Inst, Washington, DC. *Exhib:* Old Masters-New Master, Vox Populi Gallery, NY, 84; East Village, Ctr Contemp Art, Montreal, Can, 85; Best & Brightest from East Village & Soho, Barbara Gillman Gallery, Miami, Fla, 86; Focus NY, Moosart Gallery; Embellishment of the Statue of Liberty, Benefit for Cooper-Hewitt Mus & Smithsonian Inst, NY, 86. *Media:* Oil on Canvas. *Mailing Add:* 184 Bowery St 2nd Fl New York NY 10012

MADSEN, ROY PAUL
SCULPTOR, AUTHOR

b Chicago, Ill. *Study:* Univ Ill; Univ Wyo; Univ Southern Calif, PhD; Am Acad Art, Chicago. *Comn:* William Shakespeare Sculpture, Old Globe Theater, San Diego, Calif. *Exhib:* Nat Sculpture Soc; Allied Artists; Audubon Artists; Hudson Valley Art Asn; Loveland Ann Sculpture Invitational; Temecula Wildlife Art Exhib; Redlands Mus Wildlife Exhib; Mountain Oyster Club Invitational. *Teaching:* Syracuse Univ; prof emer, San Diego State Univ. *Awards:* Pietro & Alfreda Montana Award, Katherine Thayer Hobson Award, Michael Gressel Award, Hudson Valley Art Mus; Pres Award, Am Artists Prof League; John Spring Art Found Award, Nat Sculpture Soc; Elliot Liskin Award, Audubon Artists; Best of Show Award, Temecula Wildlife Art Exhib; Alfred Mitchell Award, La Jolla Art Asn; Screen Director's Guild Fellow Award; Huntington Hartford in Sculpture. *Mem:* Allied Artists; Am Artists Prof League; San Diego Mus Art Artists' Guild; Audubon Artists; Hudson Valley Art Asn (elected sculptor mem); Nat Sculpture Soc. *Media:* Wax and Bronze. *Interests:* writing, foreign affairs, environmentalism. *Publ:* auth, The Impact of Film, Animated Film & Working Cinema; auth, articles in Southwest Art & Wildlife Art. *Dealer:* Prentice Gallery 45110 Main St Mendocino Ca 95460. *Mailing Add:* 6431 Lake Adlon Ct San Diego CA 92119

MADURA, JACK JOSEPH
PAINTER, INSTRUCTOR

b Chicago, Ill, Feb 6, 1941. *Study:* Murray State Univ, BS (art), 64 & MA (art educ), 66; Northern Ill Univ, with Robert Kabak, MFA (painting), 70. *Work:* Sun Yat-Sen Univ, Guang Zhou, Republic of China; Kemper Insurance, Chicago, Ill; Cincinnati Bell, Ohio; Northern Ill Univ, DeKalb; Ill State Mus, Springfield; and others. *Comn:* Portrait of Ill, New State Libr, 90 & Ill State Mus, 92. *Exhib:* Chicago State Univ Flat Show, 74; Am Printmakers, London, Eng; Watercolor USA, Springfield Art Mus, Mo, 75, 77-78 & 80-81; Art Polish Am, St Louis, Mo; Solo exhib, Ill State Mus, 78; and others. *Teaching:* Instr drawing & painting, Somerset Community Col, Ky, 66-68; prof art, Lincoln Land Community Col, 70-. *Awards:* Awards for Watercolor, Ill State Fair Prof Show, 75, 76, 77, 82, 84 & 91; First Place, Strawn Gallery, Ill Col; Mayors Award for Outstanding Visual Artist, Springfield, Ill, 91. *Bibliog:* Janet Taylor (dir), An interview with Jack Madura, Sangamon State Univ, Springfield, Ill; Jack Madura in his Studio, TV Interview, Springfield Area Arts Coun; Jerry Speight (auth), Jack Madura Watercolorist, School Arts. *Mem:* Ala & Ky Watercolor Socs. *Media:* Watercolor. *Mailing Add:* Dept Art Lincoln Land Comm Col Shepherd Rd Springfield IL 62708

MADY, BEATRICE M
PAINTER, ARTIST

b New York, NY. *Study:* Univ Dayton, Ohio, BFA; Pratt Inst, MFA, Brooklyn, NY. *Work:* Johnson & Johnson, New Brunswick, NJ; Sydney & Francis Lewis Found, Richmond, Va; Drew Univ, Madison, NJ; Arenol Chemical Corp, NY; Dayton Art Inst, Dayton, Ohio; Pfizer, Morris Plains, NJ; Bristol-Myers Squibb, Plainsboro & Lawrenceville, NJ; Janssen Pharmaceutical, Titusville, NJ; Ortho Dermatological, Skillman, NJ; Capital Health Med Ctr, Pennington, NJ; The Provident Bank of New Jersey Headquarters, Iselin, NJ. *Exhib:* Solo exhibs, Jersey City Visual Arts Gallery, NJ, 88, Caldwell Coll Gallery, NJ, 91, Johnson & Johnson Gallery, New Brunswick, NJ, 92, Johnson & Johnson Consumer Product Div, Skillman, NJ, 93, Rabbet Gallery, New Brunswick, NJ, 96 & Maurice M Pine Gallery, Fairlawn, NJ, 97, Rotunda Gallery, Jersey City, NJ, 2010, Discover Jersey Arts, Gallery Artist, 2010, Windows on Columbus Gallery, Jersey City, NJ, 2012; Group exhibs, Ten Yr Anniversary Exhib, Rabbet Gallery, New Brunswick, NJ, 94; Alternate Visions, Seton Hall Univ Law Sch, Newark, NJ, 95; Three Abstract Artists, Watchung Art Ctr, Watchung, NJ, 96; Merck Corp Hq, Whitehouse Station, NJ, 97; Lines of Direction, Ben Shahn Gallery, Wayne, NJ, 98; For the Sake of Beauty, City Without Walls Gallery, Newark, NJ, 98; Silent Poetry, Seton Hall Law Sch, Newark, NJ, 2000; Snap to Grid, Los Angeles Ctr for Digital Art, Calif, 2007; Inaugural Exhib, Mus of Friends, Walsenburg, Colo, 2007; Cathedral Arts Festival, Grace Church Van Vorst, Jersey City, NJ, 2008; Reason, Faith & Imagination, Art St Gallery, Dayton, Ohio, 2008; Catherdral Arst Festival, Grace Church Van Vorst, Jersey City, NJ, 2009; Herstory, The Brenman Gallery, Jersey City, NJ, 2010; Introducing the Heights, The Distillery Gallery, Jersey City, NJ, 2010; In Her Strength, Brennan Gallery, Jersey City, NJ, 2011; Womens History Month, Rotunda Gallery, Jersey City, NJ; India From my Window, Watchung Arts Ctr, Watchung, NJ; The Female Eye, Brennan Gallery, Jersey City, NJ, 2012; Refocus on Art, NJ Arts Incubator, West Orange, NJ; Rites of Spring, Gallery at 14 Maple, Morristown, NJ, 2013; Spring Photography Exhib, Grace Church Van Vorst, Jersey City, NJ, 2013; New Beginnings, Rabbet Gallery, New Brunswick, NJ, 2013. *Teaching:* Prof computer graphics-graphic design, St Peter's Univ, Jersey City, NJ, 98-; prof computer graphics, Parsons Sch of Design, New York, 2001-. *Awards:* Ford Found Grant, 78; Painting Fel, NJ State Coun Arts, 85; Kenny Fel, 2003, 06, 08, 2011, 2012, & 2014. *Bibliog:* Courtney Slevin (auth), Beatrice Mady, Contemp Art Univ Collection, 4/6/87; Vivien Raynor (auth), City without walls expands its reach, NY Times, 7/7/96; Ralph Bellantoni (auth), Artists revel in the abstract, Courier News NJ, 2/96; Debora Rosenthal (auth), The First Underground Show, Art in Am, New York, 11/84; Summer Dawn Hortillosa (auth), Her Travels Inspire Artist Beatrice Mady, The Jersey Jour, Jersey City, NJ. *Mem:* Coll Art Asn; Kappa Pi; Pro Arts. *Media:* Oil, Digital. *Publ:* Footprints & Memories (artists book); Land of the Shogun (artists book); Peru in Photographs and Digital Prints (artists book). *Dealer:* Rabbet Gallery 21 Reed St New Brunswick NJ 08901. *Mailing Add:* 106-108 Hopkins Ave Jersey City NJ 07306

MAEDA, JOHN
ADMINISTRATOR, GRAPHIC ARTIST

b Seattle, 1966. *Study:* Mass Inst Technol, BS, 1988, MS; Tsukuba Univ Inst Art & Design, Japan, PhD (Design Science), 1992; Ariz State Univ, MBA, 2006. *Hon Degrees:* Md Inst Coll Art, DFA, 2003. *Exhib:* Solo exhibs include Design Machines, Axis Gallery, Tokyo, 1995, Deconstructing Cyberspace, Axis Gallery Annex, 1995, Paper & Computer, Ginza Graphic Gallery, Tokyo & Dai Nippon Duo Dojima Gallery, Osaka, 1996, one-line.com, Ginza Graphic Gallery, 1999, maeda@media, Inst Contemp Art, London & Calif Inst Arts & Crafts, San Francisco, 2000, Post-Digital, Cristinerose Gallery, New York, 2000 & Food, 2003, Towards Post Digital, NTT Inter-Communication Ctr, Tokyo, 2001, NATURE + Eye'm Hungry, Found Cartier, Paris, 2005; group exhibs include NHK Heart Exhib, Bunkamura Gallery, Tokyo, 1996; Organic Computation, NY Art Dir's Club, 1999; Design Triennale, Cooper-Hewitt Nat Design Mus, 2000; 010101: Art in Technological Times, San Francisco Mus Mod Art, 2001; Workspheres, Mus Mod Art, New York, 2001. *Collection Arranged:* Work is in the permanent collections of Mus of Modern Art, San Francisco Mus of Modern Art, and Cartier Foundation in Paris. *Pos:* Dir, Aesthetics & Computation Group, Mass Inst Technol, formerly, co-dir, SIMPLICITY, formerly; assoc dir, Mass Inst Technol Media Libr, formerly; pres, RI Sch Design, 2008-2013; trustee, Smithsonian Cooper-Hewitt Nat Design Mus; mem TED Brain Trust, Proctor & Gamble Design Advisory Bd; design partner, Kleiner Perkins Caufield Byers, 2013-. *Teaching:* Assoc prof, design & computation, Mass Inst Technol, formerly, E Rudge & Nancy Allen prof media arts & sciences, formerly. *Awards:* Multimedia Asn Japan Grand Prix, Interactive Prize, 1995; Gold Prize, Tokyo Type Dir's Club, 1996, Interactive Prize, 1998; Interactive Prize, Japan Ministry Culture, 1998; Gold Prize, ID Mag, 1998; Gold Prize, NY Art Dir's Club, 1998; Yahoo 15 Master Graphic Designers, 1999; Esquire Mag 21 Geniuses, 1999; Best Book in Computer Sci, Am Asn Publ, 2000; DaimlerChrysler Design Prize, 2000; ResFest Mag 10 to Watch, 2001; Muriel Cooper Prize, Design Mgmt Inst, 2001; Köln Designer of Yr, 2001; Nat Design Award, Smithsonian Inst, 2001; Mainichi Design Prize, 2002; Fast Co Mag 20 Masters of Design, 2004; Raymond Loewy Found Prize, 2005; named to New York Art Director's Club Hall of Fame, 2009; AIGA medal, 2010. *Publ:* Reactive Square, Ditigalogue Co, 1995, Flying Letters, 1996, 12 o'clocks, 1997, Tap, Type, Write, 1998; Design by Numbers, Mass Inst Technol Press, 1999; maeda@media, Thames & Hudson, 2000, Creative Code, 2004; The Laws of Simplicity, 2006; @johnmeada, picked as one of the 140 Best Twitter Feeds of 2011 by TIME Magazine; Redesigning Leadership, 2011. *Mailing Add:* Kleiner Perkins Caufield Byers 2750 Sand Hill Rd Menlo Park CA 94025

MAGDEN, NORMAN E
FILMMAKER, VIDEO ARTIST

b Cleveland, Ohio, Apr 21, 1934. *Study:* Cleveland Inst Art, BS, 57; Case Western Reserve Univ, MA, 58, PhD, 74. *Work:* Cleveland Mus Art; Butler Inst Am Art, Youngstown, Ohio; Canton Mus Art, Ohio. *Exhib:* Int Film Competition, London Amateur Film Festival, Eng, 84; Canadian Film Festival, Montreal, 86; Multi-Image Performance Works Traveling Exhib, 73-96. *Pos:* Art Critic, Akron Beacon J, 66-67; film panel, Ill Arts Coun, 77-79; pres, Mimesis Inc, Ill, 78-93. *Teaching:* Prof media arts, Northern Ill Univ, 67-93; prof & dept head, Dept Art Univ Tenn, Knoxville, 93-. *Awards:* Short Film Showcase, Nat Endowment Arts, 79-80; Fel, Ill Arts Coun, 89-90. *Mem:* Coll Art Asn. *Media:* Media Arts Performance. *Publ:* Auth, Peerless Motor Co Plant No 1, 1906-1909, Hist Am Bldg Survey, 73; illusr, Pennis Oppenheim Retrospective, Mus Mod Art, Paris, 80; Auth, Robert Morris Meets Post Modernism, New Art Examiner, 86; illusr, Carnival, American Style, Mardi Gras at New Orleans, Univ Chicago Press, 90. *Mailing Add:* Univ Tenn Dept Art 1715 Volunteer Blvd Knoxville TN 37996-2410

MAGEE, ALAN
PAINTER, SCULPTOR

b Newton, Pa, May 26, 1947. *Study:* Tyler Sch Art, 65-66; Philadelphia Coll Art (now Univ Arts), 67-69. *Work:* Columbus Mus Art, Ohio; Fine Arts Mus San Francisco; Newark Mus & Rutgers Mus Art, NJ; Portland Mus Art & Farnsworth Art Mus, Maine; Norton Gallery Art, Fla; Art Inst Chicago; Boston Mus Fine Arts; Nat Portrait Gallery; US Senate. *Comn:* Illus novels, Graham Greene & Bernard Malamud, Pocket Bks, NY, 74; cover paintings for Time Mag, 78, 79, 81, 82 & 85; portfolio of paintings for the Atlantic: The Walls Around Us, 87; mural, Earth Sci Bldg, Univ Maine, 97; mural, Maine State House, 2000; portrait, Senate Majority Leader George Mitchell, US Senate, Capital Bldg, Washington, DC. *Exhib:* Solo exhibs, Edith Caldwell Gallery, San Francisco, 92-93, 95-97, Kodak Ctr Creative Imaging, 92, San Jose Mus Art, Calif, 93, Newport Art Mus, RI, 94, Hollis Taggart Gallery, NY, 99, Berlin Philharmonic, Berlin, Ger, 2000, Hackett-Freedman Gallery, San Francisco, Calif, 2000, Forum Gallery, New York, 2001, 2003, 2005-2007, James A Michener Art Mus, Doylestown, Pa, 2003, Frye Art Mus, Seattle, Wash, 2005, Sordoni Art Mus, Pa, 2006, Goethe Inst, New York, 2006, Ctr Maine Contemp Art, Rockport, Me, 2007, Raab Gallery, Berlin, Ger, 2007, Forum Gallery, 2010, George Krevsky Gallery, San Francisco, Calif, 2011; Group exhibs, Fresno Art Ctr, Calif, 85; Meckler Gallery, Los Angeles, 86; Am Acad & Inst Arts & Letters, NY 87; Art and the Law (with exhib catalog), ann traveling exhib, 89, 90; traveling retrospective, Farnsworth Art Mus, Ringling Sch Art & Design, Cheekwood Ctr for the Arts, James A Michener Mus Art, 91-92; and many others. *Teaching:* Ctr Creative Imaging, 93 & 94. *Awards:* R&H Rosenthal Award, Am Acad Arts & Letts, 81; Am Bk Award, 82; Leo Meissner Prize, Nat Acad Design, 90. *Bibliog:* John Canaday (auth), A dazzling new realist painter, Saturday Rev Mag, 12/80; Theodore F Wolff (auth), The emergence of a gifted artist, Christian Science Monitor, 10/26/82; John Russell (auth), article in the New York Times, 10/22/82; Edgar Allen Beem (auth), Alan Magee, Arts Mag, 10/86; Maureen Mullarkey (auth) NY Rev mag, 4/15/2000; John B. Yellott (auth), Alan Magee, Am Artists Quarterly, 11/2005; Beyond Recognition: The Art of Alan Magee, Sordoni Art Gallery, Wilkes Univ, 2007; Alan Magee: From the Underground River, Ctr Maine Contemp Art, 2007; Carl Little (auth), Alan Magee: From the Underground River, Art New England, 9/2007; Gerard Hagerty (auth), Alan Magee, Art News, 2/2007; Brita Konau (auth), The Real and the True, Maine Home and Design, 4/2011; Robert Stanton (auth), The Art of Social Critique (anthology), Shawn Bingham ed.; and many others. *Media:* All Media. *Publ:* Stones and Other Works, Harry N Abrams; Alan Magee 1981-1991, Farnsworth Art Mus; Alan Magee, Inlets, Joan Whitney Payson Gallery Art; Archive: Alan Magee Monotypes, Spectrum Concerts, Berlin, 2000; auth, Paintings, Sculpture, Graphics Forum, 2004; Barry Lopez (auth) Resistance (with monotypes by Alan Magee), Knopf, 2004. *Dealer:* Forum Gallery New York NY; George Krevsky Gallery San Francisco Ca; Turner Carroll Gallery Santa Fe NMex; Dowling Walsh Gallery Rockland Me; Greenhut Gallery Portland Me. *Mailing Add:* 476 Pleasant Point Rd Cushing ME 04563-9507

MAGEL, CATHARINE ANNE
SCULPTOR, PAINTER

b La Grange, Ill, Nov 13, 1956. *Study:* Kansas City Art Inst, BFA, 79; NY State Coll Ceramics, Alfred Univ, MFA, 82; Int Sch Art, Todi, Italy, 89. *Work:* Het Kruithuis Mus, Neth; Kansas City Art Inst, Mo; NY State Coll Ceramics; Archie Bray Found, Helena, Mont; Southern New Eng Telephone, New Haven, Conn. *Comn:* ceramic walkways & benches, Arts in Transit, St Louis, Mo, 96; bus, Bi-State Develop Agency, St Louis, Mo, 96-97; mosaics, Mo Dept Conserv; carved brick wall, Cloud Co Hist Soc Mus, Concordia, Kans, 2006; sculpture, S Station, St Louis; Metro Arts and Transit, Metro Station Forset Park, DeBalivere Station Mural, St Louis, Mo, 2015; others. *Exhib:* Solo exhibs, Paul Mellon Art Ctr, Walingford, Conn, 86, Creative Arts Workshop, New Haven, 87, & Fontbonne Col, St Louis, 96 & City Mus, St Louis, Mo, 97 & Mitchell Mus at CedarHurst, Mt Vernon, Ill, 2000; Muscarelle Mus Art, Coll William & Mary, Williamsburg, Va, 93; Ceramics Now, Downey Mus Art, 94; Ceramics, Fontbonne Col, St Louis, 95; Signs of the Cross, Forum Contemp Arts, St Louis, Mo, 95; Common Materials/Uncommon Ideas, Elliot Smith Contemp Art, St Louis, Mo, 97; The Figure in Clay and Fiber, New Bedford Art Mus, Mass, 97; Ceramic Work, Gallery Int, Baltimore, Md, 2005; Solo exhib, Ceramic Sculptures & Works on Paper, Univ St Louis Gallery, Visio, 2005, Uncommon Experience/Common Ground, Regional Arts Comn, St Louis, Mo, 2005; Remix, Art St Loius, St Louis, 2011; group show Dao Art Gallery, Xian, China, 2012; Solo exhib Bruno David Project Space, 2015; Group exhib Finder Arts Ctr, Nanjing, China, 2015. *Collection Arranged:* American Ceramic Mus, Fuping, China, 2012. *Pos:* Artist-in-residence, Ciudad Colony, the David & Julia White Artist Colony, Costa Rica, 2003, Vt Studio Ctr, 2006; Anderson Ranch, Showmass, Colo, 90; gallery assoc, Pro-art Gallery, St Louis, 92-93. *Teaching:* sculpture, Trumbull Col, Yale Univ, 83-84 & Lindenwood Univ, St Charles, Mo, 2005; instr drawing, NY State Col Ceramics, 89; beginning sculpture or 3/D design, Wichita State Univ, 90; instr ceramic sculpture, Maryville Univ, 94-95; instr scenic painting, Webster Univ, St Louis, Mo, 95-2002; the art of sculpture luminaria, St Louis Mus, St Louis, Mo. *Awards:* Fels, Nat Endowment Arts, 86 & Conn Comn Arts, 86. *Bibliog:* St Louis Design Magazine, St Louis, Mo, 2003 & 2004. *Media:* Paintings, Works on paper, Ceramic Sculpture. *Specialty:* Fine Art. *Mailing Add:* 985 E Essex Ave Saint Louis MO 63122

MAGENTA, MURIEL
COMPUTER ARTIST, VIDEO ARTIST
b New York, NY, Dec 4, 1932. *Study:* Queens Col, BA, 53; Johns Hopkins Univ, MA (art hist), 62; Ariz State Univ, MFA, 65, PhD, 70. *Work:* Univ Art Collections, Ariz State Univ, Tempe; Valley Nat Bank, Phoenix; Prudential Life Insurance, Scottsdale. *Comn:* video columns installation, Ariz State Univ Foundation, Sky Song Innovation Ctr, Scottsdale, Ariz, 2008. *Exhib:* Coiffure Carnival, video/sculpture installation, Kansas City Art Inst, Mo, 91, Gallery 10, Wash, 91, Madrid Int Festival of Films by Women, Spain, 91, Europ Film Festival, Osnabruck, Ger, 91, Median Operative Berlin, Ger, 92; United Nations Fourth World Conference on Women, Beijing, China, 95; 5th Electro-Video Clip of ACREQ, Montreal, Que, Can, 96; Token City Multimedia Installation (auth, catalog), Ariz State Univ Art Mus, Tempe, 97; Inter-Soc Electronic Arts 97, Sch Art Inst Chicago, Ill, 97; Minn Nat Print Biennial, Univ Minn, Minneapolis, 98; Token City, Electronic Rituals, Intermedia Art Gallery, Minneapolis, 99; Token City, Dream Centenary CG Grand Prix, Aizu, 99; Tokyo, 99; Progress of the World's Women, United Nations Building, NY, 2000; Token City, Cyberslag Electronic Festival, Groingen, The Neth, 2000; Coiffure Carnival Sculpture (permanent installation) Galvin Theater Lobby, Ariz State Univ, Tempe, 2002; Times Square Installation, Computing Common Gallery, Ariz State Univ, 2003; Times Square, Brooklyn Int Film Festival, Brooklyn Mus Art, NY; Galvin Playhouse, Ariz State Univ, Tempe Ariz, 2005; Tempe Center for the Arts, Tempe, Ariz, 2007 & 2009. *Pos:* Exec ed & designer, Hue Points Women's Caucus for Art Newsmag, 82-84; Woman Image Now: Arizona Women in Art J, Ariz State Univ, 80-90; resident artist fel, multimedia/electronic imaging, Inst Studies Arts, Ariz State Univ, 91-; proj dir, The World's Women On-Line, Website, 95-; project dir, curator, Momentum: Women/Art/Technology, 2009-. *Teaching:* Prof inter-media art, Ariz State Univ, 69-; vis artist-in-residence studio art, Univ Wis, Madison, summer 79, St Mary's Col, Notre Dame Univ, 84; vis artist, curator, Rutgers Univ, 2010-2012. *Awards:* Ariz Siggraph Asn Award, 86; Grants for sculpture, film, video, computer arts, 74, 76, 79, 82-84, 86, 88, 91-92, 94-95, 2000, 2002-2004; Mid-Career Achievement Award, Woman's Caucus for Art, 91; Life Time Achievement Award, Women's Caucus Art, 2002; NEA grant, Momentum: Women/Art/Technology with Inst for Women and Art, Rutgers Univ. *Bibliog:* N Broude (auth), The Power of Feminist Art, Harry N Abrams, 94; J Heller (auth), North American Women Artists of the 20th Century: A Biographical Dictionary, Garland, 95; M Lovejoy (auth), Postmodern Currents: Art and Artists in the Age of Electronic Media, Prentice Hall, 96. *Mem:* Coalition Women's Art Orgn (nat vpres, 78-80); Women's Caucus Art (nat pres, 82-84); Coll Art Asn; Women in Animation; Inter-Soc Electronic. *Media:* Installation, Computer, Video, Computer Animation. *Interests:* art & tech. *Publ:* Auth, Photographic Essay, Women Artist News, Eyewitness Nairobi: United Nations World Conference of Women, Nairobi, Kenya, 86; Woman Image Now: Arizona State University, Women's Studies Quart, 87; Coiffure Carnival: Muriel Magenta, Exhib Catalog Ctr Arts, 90; Coiffure Carnival, Women Arts Mag, Women Artists Slide Libr, London No 39, 3-4/91; co-exec ed, Muriel Magenta & Dan Collins, The Simulated Presence: A Critical Response to Electronic Imaging, 93; Token City Multimedia Installation (exhib catalog) Ariz State Univ Art Mus, Tempe, 97. *Dealer:* V TAPE Toronto. *Mailing Add:* 8322 E Virginia Scottsdale AZ 85257

MAGID, JILL
CONCEPTUAL ARTIST, INSTALLATION SCULPTOR, VIDEO ARTIST
b Bridgeport, Conn, 1973. *Study:* Lorenzo di Medici Sch, Florence, 94; Cornell Univ, BFA, 95; Mass Inst Technol, MS (Visual Studies), 2000; Rijksakademie van Beeldende Kunsten, Amsterdam, 2001-02. *Exhib:* Solo exhibs include Mus Van Loon, Amsterdam, 2002, Galerie van Gelder, Amsterdam, 2003, Galerie L'Observatoire, Brussels, 2004, Tschumi Pavilion Gronigen, Netherlands, 2005, Tech Univ Eindhoven, Netherlands, 2005, Stedelijk Mus Bur Amsterdam, 2005, Sparwasser, Berlin, 2007, Center Art Santa Monica, Calif, 2007, Gagosian Gallery, New York, 2007, Stroom & Dutch Ministry Interior, The Hague, 2008, Whitney Mus Am Art, New York, 2010; group exhibs include Evidence Locker, Tate Mus Liverpool, Eng, 2004; Kunstrai, Galerie van Gelder, Amsterdam, 2004, And the Story Begins, 2005; Berlin Art Fair, 2005; Lost and Found, Art in General, New York, 2006; The Dotted Line, Rotunda Gallery, Brooklyn, NY, 2007; The Armory Show, New York & Yvon Lambert Gallery, Paris, 2008; Under the Influence, Center Cur Studies, Bard Coll, Annandale-on-Hudson, NY, 2008. *Teaching:* Lectr, Univ Pa, Philadelphia, 2006, Parsons Sch Design, New York, 2007; vis artist in sculpture, Cooper Union, New York, 2006 & 2008. *Awards:* Walter King Stone Memorial Prize, Cornell Univ, 97; Jacob K Javits Fel, 98; Mass Inst Technol Coun Arts Grant, 99 & 2000. *Dealer:* Galerie van Gelder Planciusstraat 9 A 1013 MD Amsterdam The Netherlands

MAGLIOZZI, RON
CURATOR
Collection Arranged: Pixar: 20 Years of Animation, Mus Mod Art, 2005-2006. *Pos:* Supv, Celeste Bartos Int Film Study Ctr, 1976-; head, Int Fedn of Film Archives Documentation Comn, 1991-1996; asst cur dept film, Mus Mod Art. *Teaching:* Instr, NYU, Columbia Univ, East Anglia & George Eastmen House Archive, 1981-. *Publ:* Ed, Treasures from the Film Archive, Scarecrow Press, 1988; prodr, Let's Go In To A Picture Show, Le Giornate del Cinema Muto, 2006. *Mailing Add:* 11 W 53 St New York NY 10019

MAGNAN, OSCAR GUSTAV
PAINTER, SCULPTOR
b Cienfuegos, Cuba, Dec 16, 1937. *Study:* San Alejandro, Habana, Cuba, with Mateo Dela Torriente, MFA; Oxford Univ, Eng, Master in aribus; Sorbonne, with Dufrenne, PhD (aesthet). *Work:* Brit Mus; Libr Congress; Smithsonian Inst; RCA Corp; NY Univ; and others. *Comn:* Three panel mural, Univ Autonoma, Dom Repub, 68; bronze statue, Haina, Dom Repub, 68. *Exhib:* Salzburg Int Biennial, 64; Solo exhibs, Palazzo Strozzi, Florence, Italy, 66 & Galerie Motte, Paris, 70; Int Fair, Basle, Switz, 72; Inter-Kunst-Infomaturien, Dusseldorf, Ger, 72; New Jersey Selects, Squibb Corp, Princeton, NJ. *Pos:* Dir art gallery, St Peter's Col, 72-, cur mus, 73-. *Teaching:* Prof aesthet-sculpture, St Peter's Col, Jersey City, NJ, 77-. *Awards:* Can Coun Fel, 64; Cintas Found Inst Int Educ Fel, 66; Guggenheim Found Fel, 68; Hereward Lester Cooke Found. *Mem:* Am Abstract Artists; Artists Fel. *Media:* Acrylic, Oil; Aluminum, Bronze. *Publ:* The Art of Oscar Magnan, Ramparts, 64; Le Figaro, Litteraire, Paris, 7-20-26/70; Searching for Truth, Jersey J, 89. *Dealer:* Susan Teller Gallery 568 Broadway New York NY. *Mailing Add:* 50 Glenwood Ave Jersey City NJ 07306-4606

MAGNIER, SUSAN & JOHN
COLLECTORS
b Fermoy, County Cork, Ireland, Feb 10, 1948. *Pos:* Owner, Coolmore Stud, Fethard, County Tipperary, Ireland; co-owner, Manchester United Football Club, 2000-05; mem, Senate of Ireland, formerly. *Awards:* Named one of Top 200 Collectors, ARTnews mag, 2004-13; named 9th Richest Man in Ireland, Sunday Times' Rich List, 2007. *Collection:* 18th-century British painting; 20th-century Irish art; equestrian art; modern art. *Mailing Add:* Coolmore Stud Fethard Ireland

MAGNO, LIZ
SCULPTOR, CONCEPTUAL ARTIST
b Philadelphia, Pa, Feb 3, 1938. *Study:* Univ Arts & Montclair State Univ, BA & grad study; Moore Coll Art; New York Univ. *Comn:* Outdoor sculpture, Mayfair Sculpture in the Park, Allentown, Pa, 87, 89 & 94; outdoor sculpture, Pa State Univ, Reading, 88, 91 & 93; mural, Paolo Di Matheis Arts Fest, Piano Veterale, Italy, 89; outdoor sculpture, Burlington Co Col, Pemberton, NJ, 93-94; sculpture, Mayfair 10th Anniversary, 96. *Exhib:* Noyes Mus, Oceanville, NJ, 94; Reading Art, Freedman Gallery, Albright Col, Pa, 94; Contemp Women Artists, Freyberger Gallery, Pa State Univ, Berks Campus, Reading, 94; Decentered (traveling exhib), 96; Contemp Arts Corridor (traveling exhib), 97. *Pos:* Freelance maskmaker/theatre designer. *Teaching:* Artist in residence, var Pa schs, Pa Coun Arts, Arts Educ Prog. *Bibliog:* Stan Schaffer (auth), Low tech - high interest, Morning Call, 11/21/91; Marilyn J Fox (auth), Natural order, Reading Eagle, 7/25/93; Susan Chase (auth), Profile: Liz Magno - Lehigh Valley Woman Mag, 1-2/97. *Mem:* Int Sculpture Ctr. *Media:* All Media. *Dealer:* Maria Feliz Gallery and Sculpture Garden 60 W Broadway Jim Thorpe PA 18229. *Mailing Add:* 4601 Aspen Dr Walnutport PA 18088-9472

MAGNOTTA, FRANK
PRINTMAKER
Study: Hope Coll, Mich, BA, 1992; Univ Ill, MFA, 2003; Skowhegan Sch Painting & Sculpture, 2003. *Exhib:* Solo exhib, White Columns, New York, 2001; Greater New York, PS1 Contemp Art Ctr, 2005; Twice Drawn, Tang Mus, Skidmore Coll, 2006; New New York Drawing, Richmond Ctr, Western Mich Univ, 2007; American Soil, Nerman Mus Contemp Art, Kans, 2007; Beyond Words, Kohler Arts Ctr, Wis, 2010. *Awards:* Rema Hort Mann Found Grant, 2002; Pollock-Krasner Found Grant, 2005; NY Found Arts Fel, 2005, 2009

MAGOON, NANCY & ROBERT
COLLECTOR
Awards: Named one of Top 200 Collectors, ARTnews mag, 2009-10, 2013. *Collection:* Contemporary art. *Mailing Add:* 277 Danielson Dr Aspen CO 81611

MAGSIG, STEPHEN
PAINTER
Study: Ferris State Col, AA, 74; Coll Art & Design, Ctr Creative Studies, 85. *Exhib:* Solo exhibs include Young & Rubicam, Detroit, Mich, 90; Feigenson/Preston Gallery, Birmingham, Mich, 92; Lemberg Gallery, Birmingham, Mich, 95; Images of NY, Chuck Levitan Gallery, NY City, 96, Urban Landscapes, 97; Mercury Gallery, Boston, 97; Ten Year Retrospective, Meadow Brook Art Gallery, Oakland Univ, Rochester, Mich, 97; Street Scenes, Lemberg Gallery, Birmingham, Mich, 98, Urban Landscapes, 2001; Views of NY, Manhattan Athletic Club, NJ, 2001; City Views, George Billis Gallery, NY, 2001, 2003, 2005; New Paintings, David Klein Gallery, 2006; group exhibs include Detroit Artists Market, 90, Images Unfold: Contemp Screens, 92, 93, Sketchbooks, 94; Eye for Art II, Detroit Inst Arts, 91; Friends for Focus, Detroit Focus Gallery at ARTPACK, Farmington Hills, Mich, 93; In, On, and Around the Box, Willis Gallery, Detroit, 95, 96; Gallery, 84, NY City, 95; Lemberg Gallery, 98; Gallery Henoch, NY City, 99; Urban Aesthetics, Bender Fine Art, Atlanta, Ga, 2000; Manhattan Contrasts, NY Historical Soc, 2000. *Awards:* Polk Purchase award, 2000

MAHAFFEY, MERRILL DEAN
PAINTER, INSTRUCTOR
b Albuquerque, NMex, Aug 12, 1937. *Study:* Mesa Col, Colo, AA, 1957; Calif Coll Arts & Crafts, 1958; Sacramento State Col, BA, 1959; Ariz State Univ, MFA, 1966. *Work:* Ariz State Univ; Phoenix Art Mus; Tucson Fine Arts Ctr; Mus Am Art; Colorado Springs Fine Arts Ctr. *Exhib:* Solo exhibs include Scottsdale Ctr Arts, Ariz, 1970, Northern Ariz Univ, Flagstaff, 1981, Fresno Ctr Arts, Calif, 1981, Portland State Univ, Ore, 1981, Tucson Art Mus, Ariz, 1982, Colo Springs Fine Arts Ctr, 1983, Meredith Long Gallery, Houston, Tex, 1984, Fishbach Gallery, NY, 1985, Mus of the Am West, Houston, Tex, 1985, Univ Utah Mus Fine Art, 1987, Foothills Art Ctr, Golden, Colo, 1991, Elaine Horwitch Gallery, Scottsdale, Ariz & Santa Fe, NMex, 1981-1991, Chandler Fine Arts Ctr, Ariz, 1992, Montana Art Gallery Dirs' Asn, 1993, Suzanne Brown Gallery, Scottsdale, Ariz, 1994-98 & 2000, Charlene Cody Gallery, Santa Fe, NMex, 1998, Mesa Southwest Mus, Ariz, 2000, Palm Springs Desert Mus, 2000, Vanier Gallery, Tucson, Ariz, 2001-03, Bentley Gallery, Scottsdale, Ariz, 2004, Sky Harbor Internat Airport, Phoenix, Ariz, 2004; group exhibs include Joslyn Mus Biennial, Omaha, Nebr; Newport Art Mus, 1979; Mus Am Art, Washington, DC, 1979; San Francisco Mus Mod Art, 1979; Sierra Nev Mus Art, 1981; RAFT Exhib, Scottsdale Ctr Arts, Ariz, 1984; Denver Mus Nat Hist, 1985; NY Acad Art, 1986; C Grimaldis Gallery, Baltimore, 1986; Capturing the Canyon, Mesa Southwest Mus, Ariz, 1987; Contemp Landscape Painting of the West, Rockwell Mus, 1987; Joanne Lyons Gallery, Aspen, Colo, 1990; Rocky Mountain Nat Park, Colo, 1990; Jan Cicero

Gallery, Chicago, 1991; Sherry French Gallery, NY, 1991; Eiteljorg Mus Invitational, Indianapolis, 1992; Artists of Am, Western Heritage Ctr, Denver, 1993-94; Susan Duvall Gallery, Aspen, Colo, 1994; Mulvaine Art Mus, Topeka, Kans, 1994; Foothills Art Ctr, Golden, Colo, 1996; Sangre de Cristo Ctr Arts, Pueblo, Colo, 1997; Century of Art, Grand Canyon Nat Park, 2000; Gerald Peters Gallery, Santa Fe, NMex, 2000. *Teaching:* Instr painting & art hist, Phoenix Col, 1967-83; art instr Ariz State Univ, Tempe, 1963-66, Western State Coll, Gunnison, Colo, 1966-68, Phoenix Community Coll, 1968-82; lectr & writer art hist Am West. *Media:* Acrylic, Oil. *Publ:* Auth, Merrill Mahafley Monumental Landscapes, Northland Press, 79. *Dealer:* Duley Jones Gallery 7100 E Main St Scottsdale AZ 85251; Telluride Gallery Fine Arts 130 E Colorado Ave Telluride CO 81435; Piñon Fine Art 2510 W Main St Littleton CO 80120. *Mailing Add:* 1707 E Earll Dr Phoenix AZ 85016-7619

MAHLKE, ERNEST D
SCULPTOR, EDUCATOR
b Madison, Wis, Sept 15, 1930. *Study:* Univ Wis, BS & MS; Inst Allende, Univ Guanajuato, Mex, MFA. *Work:* State Univ NY Oneonta; and many pvt collections. *Exhib:* Smithsonian Inst Traveling Exhibs, 55, 57 & 58; Smithsonian Inst, 55, 61 & 62; Cooperstown Art Asn Nat Ann, NY, 61-82, 66-81 & 89; Artists of Cent NY Regional Ann, Munson-Williams-Proctor Inst, Utica, NY, 68-79; solo exhibs, Two Rivers Gallery, Binghamton, NY, 72, The Art Ctr, Albany, NY, 76 & State Univ NY Oneonta, 80; Drawing & Small Sculpture Show, Ball State Univ Art Gallery, 75, 79, 81 & 82; Sculpture 75 Nat, 75; Major Albany Sculpture Sites, 82; Art Faculty Invitation, State Univ NY, Oneonta, 95. *Pos:* Pres, Wis Designer Craftsmen, Milwaukee, 62; mem bd, Oneonta Art Ctr, NY, 77. *Teaching:* Assoc prof sculpture, State Univ NY Oneonta, 62-78, prof, 78-93. *Mem:* Am Craftsmen's Coun. *Media:* Wood, Metal. *Dealer:* Gallery 53 Cooperstown NY 13326. *Mailing Add:* Mary Brown Hill Rd Laurens NY 13796

MAHLMANN, JOHN JAMES
PUBLISHER, ADMINISTRATOR
b Washington, DC, Jan 21, 1942. *Study:* Boston Univ, BFA, 62, MFA, 63; Univ Notre Dame, summer 62; Pa State Univ, EdD, 70. *Pos:* Asst exec secy, Nat Art Educ Asn, Washington, DC, 69-71, exec dir, 71-82; ed, Art Educ, 70-81 & Art Teacher, 71-80; exec ed, Design for Arts Educ, formerly; exec dir, Music Educators Nat Conf, 82-. *Teaching:* Grad asst, Boston Univ, 62-63; grad asst & res asst, Pa State Univ, 63-64, instr, 66-67, dir gallery, Art Educ Dept, 66-67; asst prof, Tex Tech Col, 67-69. *Mem:* Music Educators Nat Conf; Rotary; Am Soc Asn Exec. *Mailing Add:* 10703 Cross Sch Rd Reston VA 22091-5105

MAHON, ROBERT
PHOTOGRAPHER
b Wilmington, Del, Dec 28, 1949. *Study:* Univ Del, BA, 72. *Work:* Mus Mod Art, Metrop Mus Art & New York Pub Libr, New York; Humanities Res Ctr, Austin, Tex; Philadelphia Mus Art, Pa; Fogg Mus, Harvard Univ, Boston, Mass; and others. *Exhib:* Big Pictures by Contemp Photographers, 83, Permanent Collection Exhib, 84-86, Multiple Images, 93, Mus Mod Art, NY; Recent Acquisitions, NY Pub Libr, 85; Philadelphia Mus Art, 89 & 95; A Force of Repetition, NJ State Mus, 90; Guggenheim Mus, Soho, 94; Newark Mus, NJ, 2003; Philosophy Box, New York City, 2005; Schotland Gallery, NJ, 2007; Witherspoon Gallery, NJ, 2008. *Awards:* Guggenheim Grant, 85-86; Rutgers Ctr Innovative Printmaking Fel, 96. *Publ:* Illusr, These Trees Stand, 81, & Between the Lions, 86, Carol Joyce; Themes and Variations, Station Hill Press, 82; auth & illusr, Tribute to Minor White, Aperture, 84; illusr, I-VI, John Cage, 90. *Dealer:* Schotland Gallery 123 Main St Flemington NJ 08822. *Mailing Add:* PO Box Q Stockton NJ 08559

MAHONEY, JOELLA JEAN
EDUCATOR, PAINTER
b Chicago, Ill, June 11, 1933. *Study:* Art Inst Chicago, 51; Inst Allende, San Miguel, Mex, 54 & 55, Northern Ariz Univ, Flagstaff, BS (art & english), 55; Claremont Grad Sch, Calif, Fel, MFA (painting), 65. *Work:* Sedona Mus Art, Ariz; Sohio Corp, Houston, Tex; Am Express Office, Phoenix, Ariz; Claremont McKenna Coll, Calif; Northern Ariz Univ; Sedona Arts Ctr, Permanent Collection; West Valley Art Mus, Phoenix, Ariz; Pomona Valley Hospital; Am Embassy, Indonesia, Bhutan. *Comn:* Painting, Mutual Life Insurance, Newport Beach, Calif, 75; painting, comn Weldon Diggs-Atty, Upland, Calif, 87; painting, Univ LaVerne, Laverne, Calif, 84; painting, comn by F. Elliot for Mrs Wilhelmina Holladay, Nat Women's Mus Art, Washington, DC, 2006; painting, comn by C. Perrin, Mus Northern Ariz, Flagstaff, 2006. *Exhib:* Art-in-Embassies Prog, US State Dept, Bhutan, Lybia & Indonesia, 70-90; Jamison Gallery, Santa Fe, NMex, 74; Laguna Beach Invitational, Laguna Beach Mus Art, Calif, 75; solo exhibs, NAU Art Gallery, Flagstaff, Ariz, 80 & Austin Gallery, Scottsdale, Ariz, 84; 5 Arizona Artists, Van Buren-Hazelton Cutting Gallery, Boston, Mass, 88; Red Stone Gallery, 89 & 96; 30 yr retrospective, West Valley Art Mus, Phoenix, Ariz & Riverside Community Coll, Calif, 97, Claremont Graduate Univ Art Dept Gallery, Univ La Verne, Harris Art Mus, Northern Arizona Univ Art Mus; Blue Mt Gallery, Chelsea, New York, 2002-2003; Sedona Artist Invitational, 2003; Chaffey Art Mus, Rancho Cucamonga, Calif, 2004; Ariz Treasures, 70 yrs or better, West Valley Art Mus, Surprise, Ariz, 2006; Develop Motif, Presentation, Kerr Cult Ctr, Scottsdale, Ariz, 2006; 50 yr retrospective, Grand Canyon Nat Park, Historic Kolb Studio, Grand Canyon Asn, 2006-2007, Coconino Ctr for Arts, Flagstaff, Ariz; New Work, West Valley Art Mus, Phoenix, Ariz, 2008; Classic Works, Northern Trust Bank, Phoenix, Ariz; Group exhib, The Painting Ctr, New York, 2009; Painting Residency, Painted Desert- Petrified Forest Nat Park, Ariz, 2009; Painting Residency, Hubbell Trading Post Nat Hist Site, Ariz, 2010; Greatest Earth on Show exhib, Phippen Art Mus, Ariz, 2010. *Pos:* Bd dir, Sedona Mus Art, Ariz, 89-; docent, Mus Northern Ariz, Flagstaff, 89-; art comn, City of Sedona, Ariz, 90-. *Teaching:* Prof art, Univ LaVerne, LaVerne, Calif, 64-98, prof emer, 98-; guest prof, Univ La Verne, Athens, Greece, 96; artist-in-residence, Northern Ariz Univ, 97; interim co-coordr, Northern Ariz Univ, Sch Fine Arts, 2000. *Awards:* Outstanding Alumnae Award, painting, Northern Ariz Univ, 96; Achievement in Art, painting, Scripps Coll, Fine Arts Found, Claremont, Calif, 97; Joella Jean Mahoney Endowed Scholarship in painting, Univ La Verne, Calif, 2001; Artist's Award, Manhattan Arts Int 20th Anniversary Competition, 2003; Sedona Mayor's Award for Lifetime Achievement in Painting, 2008. *Bibliog:* Morneen K Bratt (auth), Oil on Canvas (catalog), Northland Press, 85; Cal Poly Univ, Women's Work, Univ Press, 86; Mystery Ridge (painting), National Mus Women in the Arts mag, Washington, DC; Phil & Marian Kovinick (auth), Encyclopedia of Women Artists, Univ Tex Press; 40 Years Retrospectives 1962-20002, Introduction by Joel Eide, PhD Dir Emerita, Fine Art Mus, Northern Ariz Univ. *Mem:* Sedona Arts Ctr; Coconino Ctr Arts, Flagstaff, Ariz; Mus Northern Ariz; PETA; SPCA; Nat Orig of Women. *Media:* Oil, Watercolor. *Res:* Paintings that honor the earth and hold up the beauty and mystery of natural SW Canyon, landforms, figurative themes, classical. *Interests:* Hiking, horseback riding. *Publ:* Monsoon Evening at Oracle (image), Gov Bruce Babbitt's State-of-the-State Report, 1985; Sedona Rhythms (show poster), Ann Jazz on the Rocks Concert Gala, Sedona, Ariz, 2006. *Dealer:* Lawrence S Green 310 Apple Ave Sedona AZ 86336. *Mailing Add:* 495 Smith Rd Sedona AZ 86336

MAHONEY, MICHAEL R T
HISTORIAN, EDUCATOR
b Worcester, Mass, Jan 24, 1935. *Study:* Phillips Acad, 53; Yale Univ, BA, 59; Courtauld Inst, Univ London, PhD, 65. *Pos:* Mus cur, Nat Gallery Art, Washington, DC, 64-69, ed, 68-69. *Teaching:* Prof art hist, Trinity Col, Hartford, 69-. *Res:* Seventeenth century art. *Publ:* Auth, Drawings of Salvator Rosa, Garland, 77; coauth, Wadsworth Atheneum Paintings II: Italy and Spain, Hartford, 91. *Mailing Add:* Trinity Col Dept Fine Arts Hartford CT 06106

MAHR, ERIKA
ARTIST
b New York, NY, 1982. *Study:* Univ Fla, BFA, 2004; Hunter Coll, MFA, 2007. *Exhib:* Works of Art on Paper, Long Beach Found Arts, NJ, 2008; Inventive Structures: Books Beyond the Codex, Hilles Gallery, CAW, Conn, 2010. *Awards:* Tony Smith Award, Hunter Coll, 2009; NY Found Arts Fel, 2009. *Bibliog:* Judy Birke (auth), Clever CAW Exhibit re-invents books as objets d'art, New Haven Register, 2010; Allison Pitt (auth), Between the LInes, Astoria Times, 2010

MAI, JAMES L
PAINTER, EDUCATOR
b Cheyenne, Wyo, Mar 8, 1957. *Study:* Univ Wyo, BFA, 82, MFA, 85. *Work:* Univ Wyo Art Mus, Laramie; Wyo State Mus & Art Gallery, Cheyenne. *Comn:* Indianapolis Chamber Orchestra Comn, 2000. *Exhib:* Faber Birren Color Exhibition, Stamford Mus, Conn, 97; ANA 27, Holter Mus Art, Helena, Mont, 98; Nat Exhib, Muse Gallery, Philadelphia, 99; 3rd National Exhibition, Gallery West, Alexandria, Va, 2000; Hunter Mus Art, Chattanooga, Tenn, 2001; 9th National, Art Ctr Northern NJ, New Milford, 2001; Myth, Imagination, Legends, Art Spaces Gallery, Calif, Md, 2001; Greeley Sq Art Gallery, NY, 2001; Exclusively Contemp, Eleven East Ashland Gallery, Phoenix, Ariz, 2001; others. *Pos:* Registr & curatorial asst, Univ Wyo Art Mus, Laramie, 1980-85; gallery dir, Univ Wyo Gallery 234, Laramie, 1985-86. *Teaching:* Vis lectr design, Univ Wyo, Laramie, 1986; asst prof painting, Wenatchee Valley Col, Wash; assoc prof, dept chair Graceland Univ, Lamoni, Iowa, 1996-2000; assoc prof art, coord found, Ill State Univ, Normal, 2000-. *Mem:* Coll Art Asn; Am Soc Aesthetics; Found in Art, Theory & Educ. *Media:* Acrylic, Oil. *Mailing Add:* Ill State Univ Sch Art Campus Box 5620 Normal IL 61790

MAIDOFF, JULES
PAINTER, PRINTMAKER
b New York, NY, May 6, 1933. *Study:* City Coll New York, BS, 55, MA, 56; New York Univ, advan study with Estaban Vicente. *Work:* Des Moines Art Ctr, Iowa; Rose Mus, Waltham, Mass; Mus Spirito Santos, Lisbon, Portugal; Mus Masaccio, S Giovanni, Italy; City of Pisa, Italy. *Exhib:* Solo exhibs, Contemp Art Mus, Pisa, 77, 20 Yrs in Italy, Mus Masaccio, S Giovanni, Italy, 93, Mus Spirito Santos, Lisbon, 94; Americans Abroad, Covent Garden, London, 89; Self Portraits with Family, Galleria Ciovasso, Milan, 91; Palazzo Dei Sette, Orvieto, Italy, 96-97; Pinocateca, City of Fabriano, 6/97. *Pos:* Artist & designer, Asterisk Assoc, New York, 60-73; artist & founder dir, Studio Art Ctr Int, Florence, Italy, 75-; Avore Cult Ctr, Oporto, Portugal, 98; juror, Nat Prize Italy, City of Serra, di San Quirico, 98. *Teaching:* Head art dept, painting & drawing, Studio Art Ctr Int, Florence, Italy, 75-97. *Awards:* Fulbright Grant; Stearns Award, City Coll New York. *Bibliog:* Mario De Michelli (auth), Jules Maidoff, 20 Years in Italy (monogr), City of S Giovanni, 93; Carol Becker (auth), Work on the 5 years 91-96, Palazzo Dei Sette, 12/96. *Mem:* Coll Art Asn; Nat Asn Schs Art Design; Asn Am Coll Univ Progs Italy; Asn Indep Sch Art. *Media:* All Media

MAIER, MARYANNE E
PAINTER
b Rochester, NY. *Study:* With Dana Gibson Noble, 75-77; Paier Coll Art, dipl (fine arts), 77; with Charles Gruppe, 81 & Sam Barber, Cape Cod, 2006. *Hon Degrees:* Fine Arts Degree (hon), Paier Coll Art. *Work:* Juried shows in New England, NY, Fla. *Comn:* Various institutions, banks, restaurants & mus. *Exhib:* Am Painters in Paris Exhib, 77; Audubon Artists, Nat Acad Galleries, New York, 79; Mus Art & Sci, Bridgeport, Conn, 80; Hudson Valley Art Asn, White Plains, NY, 80; Seascapes of New Eng, Hartford State Capitol, Conn, 83; Cape Cod Gallery, 2006; Woodmont, Conn, 2007; Art Ctr, Sarasota, 2011; Bird Key Yacht Club, Sarasota, Fla, 2012. *Pos:* Artist, writer, demonstrator, lectr. *Teaching:* Art instr, Post Acad Art, Cheshire, Conn & Milford Acad, Milford, Conn. *Awards:* Judge's Spec Award, Bridgeport Art League, 79; Best Painting, Sarasota Visual Arts; First Prize, Rockport Art Asn; Best of Show, Salmagundi, NY; Nat League for Am Penwomen, 2007; Sarasota Fla, 2010; Milford Fine Arts, Conn, 2010. *Bibliog:* Edward Meaney (auth), Family life, Lynn Item News, Mass, 76; Lynn Doherty (auth), In her eyes all the world is a canvas, Milford Citizen,

80; She loves the rock, New Haven Register, 2007. *Mem:* Nat League Am Pen Women; Conn Classic Arts; Milford Fine Arts; life mem Kent Art Asn; Salmagundi Club; Art Ctr Sarasota. *Media:* Oil, Acrylic. *Interests:* Seascapes & children. *Mailing Add:* 159 Kings Highway #13 Milford CT 06460

MAIER-AICHEN, FLORIAN
PHOTOGRAPHER
b Stuttgart, Germany, 1973. *Study:* Hoegskolan for Fotografi och Film Gothenborg, Sweden; Univ Essen, Germany; Univ Calif, Los Angeles, MFA, 2001. *Exhib:* Solo exhibs include Blum & Poe, 2002, 2004, 2006, Gallery Min Min, Tokyo, Japan, 2003, 2004, Baronian-Francey, Brussels, Belgium, 303 Gallery, NY, 2006, Mus Contemp Art, Los Angeles, 2007; group exhibs include Galeri Gufot, Gothenburg, Sweden, 1997; Art in the City, Stockholm, Sweden, 1998; Can, Blum & Poe, 2000, 2003; Vision Embraces the World, Echo Park Projects, Calif, 2001; Snapshot: New Art from Los Angeles, Univ Calif Los Angeles, Hammer Mus, 2001; Constructed Realities, Grand Art, Kansas City, Mo, 2002; Anti-Form: New Photographic Work from Los Angeles, Soc for Contemp Photography, Kansas City, 2002; Bernier/Eliades, Athens, Greece, 2003; Daniel Hug Gallery, Los Angeles, 2004; Set up: Recent Acquisitions in Photography, Whitney Mus Am Art, NY, 2005, Whitney Biennial, 2006; Photography 2005, Victoria Miro Gallery, London, 2005; The Blake Byrne Collection, Mus Contemp Art, 2005; USA Today, Saatchi Gallery, London, 2006. *Dealer:* Blum & Poe Gallery 2754 S La Cienega Blvd Los Angeles CA 90034. *Mailing Add:* 303 Gallery 525 W 22nd St New York NY 10011

MAILMAN, CYNTHIA
PAINTER, EDUCATOR
b Bronx, NY, Dec 31, 1942. *Study:* Pratt Inst, BS, 64; Art Students League; Brooklyn Mus Art Sch; Rutgers Univ, MFA, 78; Video Cert, Studio Prod & Portapak Prod courses, Community Television, Staten Island, NY, 94. *Work:* Everson Mus, Syracuse; Staten Island Mus; The Jane Voorhees, Zimmerli Art Mus, New Brunswick, NJ; Prudential Life Ins Co, Newark, NJ; NJ State Mus, Trenton; The Port Authority NY & NJ; The Queensborough Community Coll Gallery, Queens, NY. *Comn:* Mural, Citywalls Pub Arts Coun, Staten Island, New York, 77; mural, World Trade Ctr, Port Authority, New York; Cow Parade, New York, 2000. *Exhib:* Solo exhibs, SOHO 20 Gallery, New York, 74, 76, 78, 80, 83, 86 & 99, Everson Mus Art, Syracuse, NY, 81, Maurice M Pine Free Pub Libr, Fairlawn, NJ, 81, Fairleigh Dickinson Univ, Edward Williams Coll, NJ, 82, Manhattanville Coll, New York, 85, New House Gallery, Staten Island, New York, 87, Staten Island Visions, 88, Staten Island Inst Arts & Scis, 2000 & Eco: Illuminations, Staten Island Mus, 2000; Works from the Permanent Collection, Staten Island Mus, New York, 87; Open Studio Tour & Show, 87; Staten Island Invitational, Newhouse Ctr, New York, 89; Summer on Broome, SOHO 20 Gallery, New York, 89; The John Noble Collection, SINY, 90; Women Printmakers, Queensborough Community Coll Gallery, 91; Women & Am Dream Machine, Coll Staten Island & Taking Art to Heart, Snug Harbor Cult Ctr, New York, 92; Women for Choice, Woman's Caucus Art Int, New York, 92; Resolutions, Affirmations, Acclamations, Art Lab, Snug Harbor, Staten Island, New York, 92; Hallelujah Invitational, Ceres Gallery, New York, 93; The Pushpin Show, SOHO 20 Gallery, New York, 94; Island Views, Newhouse Ctr, Staten Island, New York, 98; Spring Arts Festival, Unitarian Church, Staten Island, New York, 2002; two-person exhib, Gifted Twist Gallery, Staten Island, New York, 2004; Small Works, SoHo 20 Chelsea, New York, 2005; The Reality Show, Viridian Artists, New York, 2006; Ideas/Images/Structures, SoHo 20, Chelsea, New York, 2006; Claiming Space, Am Univ, Washington, DC, 2007. *Collection Arranged:* Mural, Dow Jones, NJ. *Pos:* Lectr, 77-; Ci Huval Coun Found/CETA Artists proj, 78-80; adj art instr, Livingston Coll, NJ, 78-80. *Teaching:* Instr art, Queensborough Community Coll, 80-85, adj asst prof, 85-2005, retired. *Awards:* Group Studio Arts Tours Grant, Staten Island Coun Arts, 87; Individual Artists Grant, NY State Coun Arts, 87; Encore Grant, Staten Island Coun Arts & Humanities & NY State Coun Arts, 2000. *Bibliog:* Eric Maisel (auth), Artists Speak-A Sketchbook, Harper San Francisco, 93; Henry Abrams (auth), The Power of Feminist Art, Broude & Garrard, 94; Seeing Ourselves, F Borzello, Thames & Hudson, 98. *Mem:* NY Womens Caucus Art; Coun on Arts Staten Island; SOHO 20 Artists; Mud Land Soc for Renaissance Stapleton; Community Bd #1; Bd Member SI, NY. *Media:* Acrylic, Mixed Media. *Interests:* Bird watching, traveling, reading, guitar playing, community activist. *Dealer:* Soho 20 Chelsea, 511 W 25th St, New York, NY 10005. *Mailing Add:* 52 Broad St Staten Island NY 10304

MAINARDI, PATRICIA M
HISTORIAN, CRITIC
b Paterson, NJ, Nov 10, 1942. *Study:* Vassar Col, AB, 63; Columbia Univ, 63-65; New York Studio Sch, 65-66; Brooklyn Col, City Univ New York, MFA, 76; Hunter Col, MA, 80; City Univ New York, MPhilos, 81, PhD, 84. *Pos:* Ed, Women & Art, 71-72; ed, Feminist Art J, 72-73, contrib ed, 73-74, reviews ed, 87-89; dir, Goddard MFA Visual Arts Prog, 78-81; contrib ed, Arts Mag, 79-; bd dir, Col Art Asn, 91-95; pres, Asn Historians 19th Century Art, 93-96; ed bd, Art Bulletin 91-, chair, 94-; co-chair, Columbia Univ Seminar on Women & Soc, 94-96. *Teaching:* Vis lectr, Pratt Inst, Mass Col Art, 73 & 74, Brooklyn Col, 76-78, Sch Visual Arts, 77 & Goddard Col, 77-81; asst prof, Harvard Univ, 84-85; prof, Brooklyn Col & Grad Sch, City Univ New York, 85-; vis prof, Univ Queensland, Australia, 88, Princeton Univ, 92, Williams Col, 94. *Awards:* Chester Dale fel, Nat Gallery Art, 81-82; Tools of Res Grant, NEH, 89; Paul Mellon Vis Sr Fel, Ctr Advan Study, Nat Gallery Art, 90; Grant-in-Aid, Am Coun Learned Soc, 89. *Mem:* Coll Art Asn; Int Asn Art Critics; Am Hist Asn. *Publ:* Quilts: The Great American Art, Miles & Weir, 78; Art & Politics of the Second Empire, Yale Univ Press, 87; The End of the Salon, Cambridge Univ Press, 94. *Mailing Add:* 602 Carlton Ave Brooklyn NY 11238-3407

MAIOR, PHILIP
SCULPTOR
Study: Mott Community Col, 67-69; Aquinas Col, Grand Rapids, Mich, 71-72. *Work:* Lincoln Ctr Sculpture Garden, Ft Collins, Colo. *Exhib:* NAm Sculpture Exhib, Foothills Art Ctr, Golden, Colo, 90; Colo Open, Foothills Art Ctr, Golden, 94; Poudre Valley Art League, Lincoln Ctr, Ft Collins, Colo, 94; Governor's Invitational, Loveland Mus, Colo, 94; Allied Artists Am, NY, 94. *Awards:* Best of Show, Poudre Valley Art League, 90; Foothills Art Ctr Award, NAm Sculpture Exhib, 90; Best of Show, Colo Open, 94. *Media:* Clay. *Dealer:* Carol Siple Gallery 1401 17th St Denver CO 80202. *Mailing Add:* 1034 Blue Spruce Loveland CO 80538-2861

MAISEL, DAVID
PHOTOGRAPHER, ENVIRONMENTAL ARTIST
b New York, NY, Apr 22, 1961. *Study:* Princeton Univ, BA (visual arts, art hist), 79-84; Harvard Univ, MA (architecture) 88-89. *Work:* Metrop Mus Art, NY; Int Mus Photog, George Eastman House, Rochester, NY; Rose Art Mus, Brandeis Univ, Waltham, Mass; Brooklyn Mus Art, NY; Baudoin Coll Art Mus, Maine. *Exhib:* Collection Visions: Twelve Contemp Photogrs, Rose Art Mus, Waltham, Mass, 86; New Acquisitions, New Work, New Directions, Int Mus Photog, George Eastman House, Rochester, 89; Selected Photographs from the Permanent Collection, Brooklyn Mus Art, NY, 89; The New Am Pastoral: Landscape Photog in and Age of Questioning, Int Mus Photog, George Eastman House, Rochester, NY, 90 & Whitney Mus Am Art, Equitable Ctr, NY, 90; Landscapes of Consequence, Aldrich Mus Contemp Art, Ridgefield, Conn, 91; Managing Eden, Ctr Photog, Woodstock, NY, 2003; Treading Water, Soc Contemp Photog, Kansas City, Mo, 2003; Diversions & Dislocations; California's Owens Valley, Ctr Land Use Interpretation, LA, 2004; reGenerations: Environmental Art in California, Armory Crt Arts, 2004; No Man's Land: Contemp Photogrs and Fragile Ecologies, Halsey Gallery, Inst Contemporary Art, Coll Charleston, SC, 2004; New Turf, Robert Hull Fleming Mus, Univ Vt, 2005. *Pos:* vpres bd dirs, Photo Alliance, 2002-04. *Teaching:* Instr photog, Cambridge Sch Weston, Mass, 84-85, Santa Fe Photog Workshops, 91; Int Ctr Photog, New York, 92-. *Mem:* Advert Photog Am. *Media:* Photographic prints. *Mailing Add:* David Maisel Photography 100 Ebbtide Ste 320 Sausalito CA 94965

MAISNER, BERNARD LEWIS
PAINTER
b Paterson, NJ, June 21, 1954. *Study:* Cooper Union Coll Art, New York, BFA, 77. *Work:* Philadelphia Mus Art; Pierpont Morgan Libr & Philip Morris, Inc, NY. *Exhib:* Solo exhibs, Kathryn Markel Gallery, NY, 82 & 85, Stux Gallery, NY, 88; New Drawing in Am, The Drawing Ctr, NY, 84; Words-Pictures, Bronx Mus Art, NY, 84; Written Imagery, Fine Arts Mus Long Island, Hempstead, NY, 84; Precious, Grey Art Gallery, NY Univ, 84; Gold Illuminators, Metrop Mus Art, NY, 85; The Shape of Abstraction, Stux Gallery, Boston, 86. *Teaching:* Guest lectr, medieval manuscript illumination technique, Cloisters Mus & Metrop Mus Art, NY, 77- & J Paul Getty Mus, Malibu, Calif, 83. *Awards:* Best in Show Award, 77 & Jurors' Award, 86, New York Univ Small Works Show. *Bibliog:* Calvin Thompkins (auth), Artists' books, New Yorker Mag, 1/25/82; Lorraine Karafel (auth), Maisner exhibition--Markel Gallery, Arts Mag, 3/83; Grace Glueck (auth), Religion makes an impact, NY Times, 4/7/85; Arlene Raven (auth), Spirited, Village Voice, 3/8/88; Judy Schwendenwein (auth), Bernard Maisner, Art News, summer 88. *Media:* Painting, All Media. *Publ:* Auth, My molding, flowing conception of image and how it affects the universe, Tracks, A Journal of Artists' Writings, spring 77. *Mailing Add:* 56 Mount St Bay Head NJ 08742-4632

MAJDRAKOFF, IVAN
PAINTER, ASSEMBLAGE ARTIST
b New York, NY, June 19, 1927. *Study:* Cranbrook Acad Art, with Wallace Mitchell. *Work:* Univ Minn Gallery; Minneapolis Inst Art; Cranbrook Art Mus, Bloomfield Hills, Mich. *Comn:* Black & white photo collage, Bronx State Hosp, NY, 71; Masonite outdoor mural, San Francisco Art Comn. *Exhib:* Pa Acad Art, Philadelphia; Detroit Art Inst, Mich; Walker Art Ctr, Minneapolis; San Francisco Mus Art; Drawing Exhib, Mus Mod Art, NY; Mass Inst Technol, 83; Solo exhib, Cranbrook Mus, Bloomfield Hills, Mich, 86; Oakland Mus, 97. *Pos:* Actg dir, Univ Art Gallery, Univ Minn, 52-55; dir, Stanford Univ Gallery, 62. *Teaching:* Instr drawing & painting, San Francisco Art Inst, 57-97, prof emer, 98-; instr drawing, Stanford Univ, 57-58 & 68-69. *Bibliog:* Al Wong (auth), Portrait of Ivan (film), 68. *Media:* Acrylic, Ink

MAJESKI, THOMAS H
PRINTMAKER, EDUCATOR
b Council Bluffs, Iowa, Sept 14, 1933. *Study:* Univ Omaha, BFA, 60; Univ Iowa, with Mauricio Lasansky, MFA, 63. *Work:* Philadelphia Mus Art, Pa; Sheldon Mem Art Mus, Lincoln, Nebr; Joslyn Mus, Omaha, Nebr; Mus Voor Schone Kunsten, Antwerp Belg; Guangzhou Acad Fine Arts, People's Rep China; and others. *Comn:* Opera Omaha 25th Annv Print Edition. *Exhib:* Prints, Watercolors & Drawings, Pa Acad Fine Arts, Philadelphia, 65; 17 State Exhib, Springfield Art Mus, Mo, 74; Colorprint USA, Tex Tech Univ, Lubbock, 74; Int Miniature Print Competition, Pratt Graphics, New York, 83; solo exhib, Sioux City Art Ctr, Iowa, 95; Univ Tex, Pan Am, 2002; Laredo Art Ctr, Tex, 2006. *Teaching:* Prof printmaking, Univ Nebr Omaha, 63-, Reagents prof, 89, prof art & prof emer, 99. *Awards:* Purchase Awards, Philadelphia Print Club, 67; Univ Nebr Teaching Excellence Award; Regents Prof, 89. *Bibliog:* The Print Collector's Newsletter, New York, 60, 5/82. *Media:* Monotypes, Wall constructions. *Mailing Add:* 1315 Silver St Ashland NE 68003-1843

MAJOR, JAMES
ADMINISTRATOR
Study: Western Ill Univ, BME; Univ Iowa, MA; Univ Wis, PhD. *Pos:* Conducted and given presentations and clinics at state, regional, national and international music conventions and festivals. *Teaching:* Prof choral and music educ, chair music educ div, Sch of Music, Ohio State Univ, Columbus, formerly, emeritus status, currently; with, Illinois State Univ, 1995-, dir Choral Activities, formerly, dir Sch of Music, formerly, dean Col of Fine Arts, currently. *Publ:* Published articles in the Journal of Research in Music Education, Choral Journal, and the Journal of Music Teacher Education. *Mailing Add:* Office of the Dean College of Fine Arts Illinois State Univ Campus Box 5600 Center for Visual Arts 116 Normal IL 61790-5600

MAJORE, FRANK
PHOTOGRAPHER
b Richmond Hill, NY, Feb 9, 1948. *Study:* Philadelphia Coll Art, BS, 69. *Work:* Albright Knox Art Gallery, Buffalo, NY; Boston Mus Fine Arts; Brooklyn Mus; Los Angeles Co Mus Art; Whitney Mus Am Art, NY. *Exhib:* 1985 Biennial Exhib, Whitney Mus Am Art, NY, 85; Avant-Garde in the Eighties, Los Angeles Co Mus Art, 87; The Photog of Invention, Nat Mus Am Art, Washington, 89; Pleasures and Terrors of Domestic Comfort, Mus Mod Art, NY, 91; This Sporting Life, 1878-1991, High Mus Art, Ga, 92; solo exhibs, Butler Inst Am Art, 91, John & Mabel Ringling Mus Art, 91; Commodity Image, Int Ctr Photog, NY, 93. *Awards:* Tiffany Award, 93; Photog Fel, Aaron Siskind Found, 93, John Simon Guggenheim Found, 96. *Bibliog:* Andy Grundberg (auth), Images that represent deep bites of forbidden fruit, NY Times, 1/26/86; Richard Martin (auth), Frank Majore, Arts Mag, 2/88; Ileen Sheppard (auth), Frank Majore: Dreamsville, Ringling Mus Art, 91. *Media:* Photography

MAKANOWITZKY, BARBARA
PAINTER
Study: Art Students League, NY; San Francisco Art Inst, Calif. *Exhib:* 11 solo exhibs; Juried & Invitational Exhibs: 37th Ann Juried Summer Exhib, Maine Art Gallery, Wiscasset, Maine, 94; Pastels Only, Sharon Art Center, Sharon, NH, 96; Land, Sea, Skyline, Jo Anne Chappel Gallery, San Francisco (mems only), 96; Four Man Exhib, Maine Art Gallery, Wiscasset, Maine, 98; Thirteenth Ann Exhib of the Pastel Soc of Am, NY, 2002; and numerous other juried shows in New Eng, Calif, NY and Washington, DC. *Teaching:* instr workshops, Sharon Arts Center, NH. *Bibliog:* Master Painters World Pastel Showcase, International Artist, 12/05-1/06; Pastel Journal, 7-8/2005. *Mem:* Signature mem, Pastel Soc Am (PSA). *Media:* Pastel. *Interests:* Favorite subject to paint is the sea. *Dealer:* Big Sur Gallery Carmel CA; The Ventana Gallery Big Sur CA

MAKI, COUNTESS HOPE MARIE
PAINTER
b St Joseph, Mo, Jan 14, 1938. *Study:* Self-taught. *Work:* Numerous pvt collections. *Comn:* Masters of Art (4 x 8 ft oil painting), comn by His Eminence Prince John, Ormiston Palace, Tasmania, Australia, 92; Horses (4 x 12 ft oil painting), comn by Jerry Grimes, Santa Rosa Beach, Fla, 94. *Exhib:* Solo exhib, Arts-Inter Salon Int Des Sekneurs de L'Art, Chateauneuf du Pape, France, 94; Salon Int des Seigneurs de L'Art, Palais des Congres Marseille, 94; Montserrat Gallery, New York. *Teaching:* Art instr, Okaloosa Walton Jr Coll, Fla, 66-68, television art show, Channel 6-Ft Walton Beach, Fla, 73-75 & Pensacola Jr Coll, Fla, 78-88. *Awards:* Women's Inner Circle Achievement Award, Am Biog Inst; Most Admired Woman of the Decade, Bd Int Res Am Biog Inst; Community Leader of Am, 86; Best New Poet, Am Poetry Asn & Amherst Soc, 87, 88 & 89; Coat of Arms, Grand Duchy of Avram, Prince John, Tasmania, Australia, 89, Countess Title, 94; Int Art Award, Salon Int Des Seigneurs de L'Art, France, 94; Key of Success Award, Excellence in the Arts. *Mem:* Int Biog Asns, Cambridge, Eng; Int Platform Asn; hon mem Res Bd Advisors for Am Biog Inst. *Media:* Oils, Mixed Media. *Publ:* Illusr, Create-a-book, Merchant of Memory & Trader Jon: His Life; auth, Hope and Freedom, Statue of Liberty & Ellis Island Spec Collection. *Dealer:* Overseas European Corp PO Box 7152 Freeport NY 11520. *Mailing Add:* 3985 Langley Ave Pensacola FL 32504

MAKI, ROBERT RICHARD
SCULPTOR, PAINTER
b Walla Walla, Wash, Sept 15, 1938. *Study:* Western Wash State Col, BA, 62; Univ Washington, MFA, 66; San Francisco Art Inst Summer Workshop, 67. *Work:* Western Wash Univ, Outdoor Sculpture Collection, Bellingham; Henry Art Gallery, Univ Washington; Stanford Univ; Nat Collection Am Art, Washington, DC; Seattle Art Mus; Whatcom Mus Art, Wash; Mus Art, Wash State Univ; Kemper Art Mus, St Louis, Mo; Kent State Univ. *Comn:* Seattle-Tacoma Int Airport; Expo Ctr, Portland, Ore; Wash State Univ, Pullman, Wash; Fed Bldg/Courthouse, Eugene, Oreg; Evergreen State Col, Olympia, Wash; Trimet, City of Portland, Ok; Wake Forest Univ, Winston-Salem, NC. *Exhib:* West Coast Now, Portland Art Mus & De Young Mus, 68; solo exhibs, Richmond Art Ctr, 67, Michael Walls Gallery, San Francisco, 69, Seattle Art Mus, Wash, 73 & 84, Montana State Univ, 73, Portland Ctr Visual Arts, Ore, 74, Southeastern Ctr Contemp Art, Winston-Salem, NC, 78, Richard Hines Gallery, Seattle, Wash, 79 & 81 & Maki/Maki, World Trade Ctr East, Seattle, 99; Reality of Illusions, Herbert F Johnson Mus Art, Cornell Univ, 79; Images & Latitude, Mona Bismark Estate, Paris, France, 88; Ishikowa Perfectual Mus Art, Japan, 88; Lannon-Cole Gallery, Chicago, Ill, 92; Maki/Maki, Butters Gallery, Portland, Ore, 94; Robert Maki = Wood & Steel, Bryan Ohno Gallery, Seattle, 98; Essential Abstraction, The Evergreen State Coll, Olympia, Wash, 2005; Cross Section, Prographica, Seattle, Wash, 2011. *Pos:* Guest lectr at many schs & mus nationwide, 66-. *Teaching:* Hon lectr, Univ Wash, Seattle, 66-68; guest artist, Humboldt State Univ, Calif, 74; Rockefeller Artist-in-Residence Fel, Wake Forest Univ, 79; St Cloud State Univ, Minn; NY Univ; Univ Idaho, Pocatello; NC Sch Arts, Winston-Salem; Montana State Univ, Bozeman; Ariz State Univ, Tempe; Univ Oreg, Eugene. *Awards:* Hon Alumni Fel, Western Wash Univ, Bellingham, 93; Purchase Award, Wright Found, 80; Nat Endowment Arts Senior Sculpture Fel, 68, Drawing, 85 & Sculpture, 79; King Co Hon Award, 90; Grantee Nat Endowment Arts, 68, 79, 85; Alumni of Century, Western Wash Univ, Wash, 2008. *Bibliog:* Peter Selz & Tom Robbins (auth), West Coast report: The Pacific Northwest today, Art Am, 11-12/68; Jan Van de Marck (auth), Robert Maki at Center for Visual Arts, Art Am, 9-10/74; Bruce Guenther (auth), 50 NW Artists, 83; Matthew Kangas (auth), Limitless Geometry: Robert Maki Sculpture, Vol 17, No 8, 10/98; Sculpture Mag; Felicia Gonazles (auth) Maki/Maki - double vision, Met Living, Vol 2 No 3, 10/2000; Robert Maki, exhit catalog, Seattle Art Mus, 73; Robert Maki, exhib catalog, Richard Hines Gallery, Seattle, 79; Matthew Kangas (auth), Epicenter, Midmarch Art Press, New York, 2005. *Media:* All. *Mailing Add:* 9154 NE Eglon Rd Kingston WA 98346

MAKI, SHEILA A
PRINTMAKER, PAINTER
b Sudbury, Ont, Aug 31, 1932. *Study:* Univ BC, Can, 67; Camden Arts Ctr, London, Eng; George Brown Coll, Toronto, Canada. *Work:* Hamilton Art Gallery; Kitchener-Waterloo Art Gallery; Metrop Mus & Art Ctr, Miami, Fla; Ore State Univ; Cornell Univ, Ithaca, NY; Nat Mus Civilization, Ottawa; Robert McLaughlin Gallery, Oshawa; Art Gallery of Northumberland, Cobourg, Can; WKP Gallery, North Bay, Can; Burnaby Art Gallery, Burnaby, BC, Can; Ontario Gov Ministry of Educ. *Comn:* Circling Around, (portfolio), Merritt Publ, Toronto. *Exhib:* Printmakers '82, Art Gallery Ont, Toronto, 82; Gloucester Co Coll, Sewell, NJ; Int Print Soc, New Hope, Mass; Woodstock Pub Art Gallery, Woodstock, Ont; Glenhyrst Art Gallery of Brant, Brantford, Ont, 88; WKP Kennedy Gallery, North Bay, Ont, 89; Robert McLaughlin Gallery (auth, catalog), Oshawa, Ont, 94; Grimsby Art Gallery, Ont, 96; Wilfrid Laurier Univ, Waterloo, 2000; and others. *Pos:* Visual artist. *Teaching:* Guest artist, var seminars. *Bibliog:* Elaine Sills (article), Art in a Dream, Home Decor, Can, 81; Mary Mason (auth), Artist, Glendon Univ, 85; Franz Geierhaus (article) J of the Printworld, fall 90; Joan Murray (auth), McLaughlin Gallery. *Mem:* Heliconian Club, Toronto (exec mem, 75-80 & 83-86, treas, 93-95 & secy, 86-88. *Media:* Serigraphy, Miscellaneous; Acrylic. *Dealer:* Venturgraph Int. *Mailing Add:* c/o Venturgraph Int 19-400 Esna Park Dr Markham ON L3R 3K2 Canada

MAKLANSKY, STEVEN V
CURATOR
b New York, NY, Nov 13, 1963. *Study:* Sir Jon Cass Sch Art, London; Tulane Univ, BA, 85; NY Univ, MA, 88. *Collection Arranged:* Masterpieces from the Permanent Collection, 93; Asserting Equality, A Photographic Legacy of African-Am Identity, 93; Double Exposure, 94; Camaraderie - The Latent Sociology of Photo-History, 95; E J Bellocq, New Orleans, 96. *Teaching:* Vis prof hist photog, Univ New Orleans, 96. *Mem:* Oracle-Photog Curators Group; La Asn Mus; Nat Endowment for Humanities. *Publ:* Auth, Asserting Equality, 10/93, Double Exposure-repairing photographs, 4/94, Modest Witness, the unknown photographer, 7/94, Photography by the Numbers, 10/95, Arts Quart Mag; Handbook to the collection, New Orleans Mus Art, 96. *Mailing Add:* c/o New Orleans Mus Art One Collins Diboll Cir PO Box 19123 New Orleans LA 70124

MAKLER, HOPE WELSH
ART DEALER
b Philadelphia, Pa, Mar 24, 1924. *Study:* Drexel Univ, BS; Bryn Mawr Coll & Univ Pa, MA; Barnes Found. *Pos:* Owner & pres, Makler Gallery, Philadelphia, currently. *Specialty:* Twentieth century painting and sculpture

MAKSYMOWICZ, VIRGINIA ANN
SCULPTOR, WRITER
b Brooklyn, NY, Feb 19, 1952. *Study:* Brooklyn Coll, City Univ, New York, with Lucas Samaras, BA, 73; Brooklyn Mus Art Sch, 73-74; Univ Calif, San Diego, with Allan Kaprow, Eleanor Antin & Newton & Helen Harrison, MFA, 77. *Comn:* Mural, BACA Downtown Cult Ctr, 78 & sculpture, NY Botanical Gardens, 79, Cult Coun Found, NY; St Thomas Episcopal Church, Lancaster, Pa, 2005; NY Botanical Gardens; Coll Wooster, Ohio; Mesa Coll & Univ Calif, San Diego; Allen Art Mus, Oberlin, Ohio; many pvt collections. *Exhib:* Lightweight Works, Mitchell Mus, Mt Vernon, Ill, 95; Cameo Appearances, St Joseph's Univ, Philadelphia, Pa, 98; The Physical boundaries of this world, Ceres Proj Room, NY, 2002; Garden of Earthly delights, Phoenix Proj Room, NY, 2003; Accumulated Intention, DePauw Univ, Ind, 2003; Corners, Mus Contemp Art, Ft Collins, Colo, 2003; Sheltered, Williams Art Ctr, Lafayette Coll, Easton, Pa, 2005; Searching for Patterns, Ctr Art Gallery, Calvin Coll, Grand Rapids, Mich, 2006; Stations of the Cross, Narthex Gallery, Saint Peter's at Citicorp, NY, 2007; Reconstructuring a Feminist Past, Mus Modern Art, New York, 2007; Structure & Metaphor, Delaware Center Cont Arts, 2008; Aesthetic Distance, Michener Mus, Doylestown, Pa, 2009; Constructed Visions, Woodmere Mus, Pa, 2010; Previously Occupied, Art on the Avenue, Phila, Pa, 2011; Fragile Boundaries, Del Ctr Contemporary Art, 2012. *Collection Arranged:* African Objects & Ethnobotany Collection (with catalog), NY Botanical Garden, 79; Time, Form, Nature, Mind, 10 on 8, NY, 86; 24 Canadians in NY, Amos Eno Gallery, NY, 86; Funny Girls: Women, Humor, and the Visual Arts, Maria Feliz Gallery, Jim Thorpe, Pa, 93. *Pos:* Exec dir, Amos Eno Gallery, New York, 83-86; articles ed, Art & Artists, New York, 86-89. *Teaching:* Vis asst prof sculpture, Oberlin Coll, Ohio, 80-81; vis sculptor, Wayne State Univ, Detroit, 81-82; vis artist, Minneapolis Coll Art Design, 90; vis asst prof art, Franklin & Marshall Coll, Lancaster, Pa, 91-96; adj prof art, Moore Coll Art & Design, Philadelphia, 96-98; asst prof art, Franklin & Marshall Coll, Lancaster, Pa, 2000-06, assoc prof art, 2006-. *Awards:* Artist Fel in Sculpture, Nat Endowment Arts, 84-85; Artist Fels, Art Matters Inc, 88, Mellon Found, 2006, 2012 & Vt Studio Ctr, 2007; visiting artist, Am Acad in Rome, 2006, 2012. *Bibliog:* Human body as metaphor, NY Times, 88; Political art with style & decorum, review of women, Philadelphia Inquirer, 92 & 96; A Rich Exhib of Paper Possibilities, NY Newsday, 94; Modern Perspective into Italy's Art, Los Angeles Times, 98; Yes Virginia, Phillips Mus (catalog essay), 2002; The Physical Boundaries of this World, Sculpture Mag, 2003; Married to Art and Each Other, NY Times, 2008; Couples, Newsday, NY, 2008; Wall to Wall, The Philadelphia Inquirer, 2011; Fanfare for Maksymowicz, KPBS TV. *Mem:* Coll Art Asn; Women's Caucus Art; Int Sculpture Ctr. *Media:* Sculptural installation. *Interests:* Political and social issues. *Publ:* contribr, Sculpture Mag, Encyl Sculptor, Art & the Pub Sphere, Women Artist News, Atlanta Art Papers & Art & Artists. *Dealer:* TandM Arts Philadelphia PA; Sculpturesite Gallery San Francisco CA. *Mailing Add:* 3719 Lancaster Ave Philadelphia PA 19104-2334

MALAMED, LYANNE
PAINTER
b Alton, IA, 1931. *Study:* Briar Cliff Coll, Sioux City, IA, BA, 53; Univ IA, Iowa City; studied with Eugene Ludins & Mauricio Lasanski. *Work:* Bristol-Myers Squibb Co; Johnson & Johnson Corp Hq, New Brunswick, NJ; Rider Coll, Lawrenceville, NJ; Rutgers Inst Health, New Brunswick, NJ; Johnson Pharmaceuticals, Titusville, NJ.

Exhib: Solo exhibs, Haverford Coll, Haverford, Pa, 90, Mercer Co Community Coll, Trenton, NJ, Marymount Manhattan Coll Gallery, 97, Rabbet Gallery, New Brunswick, NJ, 99, Hunterdon Mus Art, Clinton, NJ, 2000, Atrium Gallery, Chubb Group Ins Co, Warren, NJ, 2001, Somerset Art Asn, Bedminster, NJ, 2004, Arts Counc the Morris Area, 2005; Carnegie Ctr, Princeton, NJ; Morris Mus, NJ; Artists League of Central NJ; Gallery at Bristol-Myers Squibb, Lawrenceville, NJ; Douglass Coll, New Brunswick, NJ. *Awards:* Fel, NJ State Coun on Arts, 85-86; First prize, NYC Ctr Gallery; First prize, Des Moines Art Ctr. *Media:* All Media. *Publ:* Eternal Woman Paintings and Drawings

MALDRE, MATI
PHOTOGRAPHER, EDUCATOR
b Geestacht, Ger, Apr 3, 1947; US citizen. *Study:* Univ Ill, with Joseph Jachna, BA (design), 69; Inst Design, Ill Inst Technol, with Aaron Siskind, Arthur Siegel & Charles Swedlund, Encycl Britannica grant, 70-72, MS (photog), 72; also with Paul Caponagro, Jerry Uelsmann, Nathan Lyons & Les Krims. *Work:* Int Mus Photog, George Eastman House, Rochester, NY; Australian Nat Mus & Libr, Canberra, ACT, Australia; Art Inst Chicago; Ill State Mus, Springfield, IL; Norton Simon Mus, Pasadena, Calif. *Comn:* photog and prod of ltd ed photo montage of The Old Dome and the New Campus, Chicago State Univ Found, 1982; photog of Beverly Hills/Morgan Park, Beverly Area Planning Asn & Chicago Architecture Found, Chicago, 1985-6; photog for Art in Architecture Program, State of Ill Capital Develop Board, 1995; photog and exhib develop, Walter Burley Griffin in Am, Chicago Arch Found, 1996; photog, Chicago Bungalow, Chicago Department of Housing and Chicago Arch Found, 2001. *Exhib:* Solo Exhibs: Chicago Bungalow, Chicago Architecture Found, Santa Fe Building, Atrium Gallery, 2001-2003; Walter Burley Griffin in Am: Photographs by Mati Maldre, Mac Nider Mus, Mason City, Iowa, 1999; Mati Maldre Photographs: 1968-2008, Beverly Arts Center, Chicago, Ill, 2008; Taken by Design: Photos from the Institute of Design, 1937-1971, Art Inst Chicago, 2002; Beyond Architecture: Marion Mahony and Walter Burley Griffin, Power House Mus, Sydney, NSW, Australia, 1999. *Pos:* Photogr & lab technician, Encycl Britannica, Chicago, 70-74; consult photog & graphics, Chicago Urban Corps, 72-; photog, US Dept Interior, Historic Am Building Survey on US Industrial Heritage, Jeanette, PA Project, 1990-91; photog and consult, Chicago Urban Corps; photog and consult, Westinghouse, Inc; photog and consult, Compton's Encyclopedia; photog and consult, Chicago Landmarks Commission. *Teaching:* instr, 1972-75, asst prof 75-84, prof, 84-2007, emer, 2008, Chicago State Univ Art, Chicago, Ill,. *Awards:* Faculty Excellence Award, Chicago State Univ, 81, 85, 89, 91, 96; Ind Project Grant, Nat Endowment for the Arts, Design Arts, 92; Grant, Graham Found for Advanced Studies, 88, 92, 95. *Bibliog:* Paul Grap (auth), Photographs Capture Special Beauty of City's Far Southwest Side Secret, Chicago Tribune, 1986; Lee H Bey (auth), Chicago Sun Times, 2001; Local Photographer Displays 40 Years of Art at BAC, 2008. *Mem:* Soc Photo Educ; Photo Society Art Inst Chicago; Chicago Architecture Found; Landmarks Preservation Council of Illinois; Walter Burley Griffin Society Am (bd member); Ridge Hist Society (bd member). *Media:* Black and White. *Publ:* The Prairie School: Design Vision for the Midwest, Art Inst Chicago Mus Studies, (pages 172 and 180), 1995; cover and photos, Reflections no. 9, Journal Sch Archit, Univ Ill, Urbana, 1993; The Griffins in Australia and India, Melbourne Univ Press, Australia, 1998; Rebuilding an Architect, (pages 38, 39, 40, 41, & 42), Reader, Dec, 2002; auth, Walter Burley Griffin in am, Univ Ill Press, Chicago, 2001. *Mailing Add:* 1727 W 104th Pl Chicago IL 60643-2807

MALEN, LENORE
VIDEO ARTIST, PHOTOGRAPHER
Exhib: Solo exhibs, Beaver Coll, Pa, 1981, RI Sch Design, Providence, 1992, Univ Vt Francis Colburn Gallery, 1998, Slought Found, Univ Pa, 2004, CUE Art FOund, 2007, Zilkha Gallery, Wesleyan Univ, 2008; Burning in Hell, Franklin Furnace, NY, 1991; SITEseeing, Islip Mus Art, NY, 1992; Game Show, Bellevue Art Mus, Wash, 1999; Paradise/Paradox, New Rochelle Coll, NY, 2003; Orion's Belt, Univ Nev, 2007; Global Warning: Artists Tackle Climate Change, Wesleyan Univ, 2009. *Pos:* Exec ed, Coll Art Asn Art J, 1990-96. *Teaching:* Instr, Beaver Coll, Pa; adj instr & prof, Univ Arts, Philadelphia, Queensborough Cmty Coll, Marymount Manhattan Coll, Cooper Union, NY, RI Sch Design; assoc prof, New Sch Univ Parsons Sch Design, 1992-. *Awards:* Yaddo Residency Fel, 1994, 1998, 2001; Hand Hollow Found Fel, 1998; Blue Mountain Ctr Fel, 2003; NY Found Arts Fel, 2009; Guggenheim Meml Fel, 2009. *Bibliog:* Peter Schjeldahl (auth), Soiling the Nest, Village Voice, 5/2/1995; Jane Ingram Allan (auth), Cecilia Vicuna and Lenore Malen, Sculpture, 10/1999; Nancy Princenthal (auth), Willing Spirits: Art of the Paranormal, Art in Am, 2/2006

MALENDA, JAMES WILLIAM
ENAMELIST, EDUCATOR
b Kingston, Pa, Sept 14, 1946. *Study:* Miami Dade Community Col, 69; Kent State Univ, BFA, 71; State Univ NY, MFA, 75. *Work:* Roberson Ctr Arts & Sci, Binghamton, NY; Univ Ga, Athens; Nordenfjeldske Kunstridustrimuseum, Trondheim, Norway; House of Humour and Satire, Gabrovo, Bulgaria. *Comn:* Advent Wreath, St Paul's Cathedral, Peoria, Ill, 80; Crucifix, Salem Lutheran, Peoria, Ill, 80; Medallions-Putnam, Rothberg, Bradley Univ, Peoria, 85; Wall Sculpture, Reading Tube Co, Reading, Pa, 90. *Exhib:* Enameling: Art and Industry, Nat Ornamental Mus, Memphis, Tenn; Int Exhib Enameling Art in Japan, Tokyo CentMus, & Ueno Royal Mus, 81, 83 & 85; Wine, Cooper-Hewitt Mus, NY, 85; Die Kugel-Glas & Metall, Deutsche Goldschmiedehaus, Hanau, Ger, 86; Masterworks Enamel 87, Taft Mus, Cincinnati; L'Art de L'Email, 10th Biennale Int, Limoges, France, 90. *Teaching:* Instr enamel & metal, Mohave Community Col, Kingman, Ariz, 75-76; assoc prof, Bradley Univ, Peoria, Ill, 76-78 & Kutztown Univ, Pa, 87-. *Awards:* Enameling Award, Thompson Enamel Co, 90; Artists Fel, Ill Arts Coun, 84 & 86; Pa State System Grant, 90. *Mem:* Distinguished mem Soc NAm Goldsmiths. *Media:* Enamel, Metal. *Publ:* Coauth, A Sculptural breakdown of static three dimensional form through multi-positioning, Leonardo, Vol 19, Issue 4, 86; auth, A breakdown of static 3-D form through multi-positioning, Glass on Metal, Vol 5, nos 2 & 3, 4-6/86. *Dealer:* Gallery 500 Church/Old York Rd Elkins Park PA 19117. *Mailing Add:* Dept Art Educ/Crafts Kutztown Univ Kutztown PA 19530

MALER, LEOPOLDO MARIO
CONCEPTUAL ARTIST, EDUCATOR
b Buenos Aires, Argentina, Apr 2, 1937. *Study:* Univ Buenos Aires, law degree, 60; Univ Col, London, post-grad study, 62. *Work:* Nat Gallery Mod Art, Santo Domingo, Dominican Repub; Mus Tamayo, Mexico City; Hara Mus, Tokyo; Mus Nacional de Bellas Artas, Montevideo, Uruguay; Miami-Dade Community Col, Fla; sculpture, Universidad Nacional de San Martin, Buenos Aires, 2015. *Comn:* Bookabulary (performance), Int Bk Fair, Miami, 85; 394 Words (performance), CLAAS, Miami, 85; Marble monument, 1st Latin American Symposium Sculpture, Santo Domingo, 85; Life-Death (installation), Argentine Pavilion, Venice Biennale, Italy, 86. *Exhib:* Sao Paulo Biennale, Brazil, 77; Hayward Annual, Hayward Gallery, London, 78; Screams & Dreams, Ctr Inter-Am Realtions, New York, 82; 3 Argentine Artists, Hara Mus, Tokyo, 82; 7 in the 80's, Metrop Mus, Miami, 85; Museo de las Casas Reales, Santo Domingo, Dominican Repub, 86; one man show: Artodelharte, Mus Modern Art, Santo Domingo, 2005, Intoxications, Mus of Contemp Arts, Puerto Rico, 2009. *Pos:* Producer art progs, Brit Broadcasting Corp, London, 67-77; dean art, Parsons Sch Design Affil, Dominican Repub, 86. *Teaching:* Lectr, Middlesex Polytech, London, 72-75. *Awards:* 1st Prize, Sao Paulo Biennale, Brazil, 77; Guggenheim Found Fel, 77-78. *Bibliog:* Amina Harris (producer), Maler's Requiem, Brit Broadcasting Corp, 79; Seward Lucie Smith (auth), Art Now, Morrow, 81; Gregory Batecock (auth), The Art of Performance, Dutton, 84. *Media:* Performance, Three-Dimensional Objects, Installations. *Dealer:* Leila Tachinia Milani 1082 Madison Ave New York NY 10028

MALER, M LEOPOLDO MARIO
SCULPTOR
b Buenos Aires, Arg, Apr 2, 1937. *Study:* Univ Buenos Aires, law, 60; Int Asn Comparative Law, France, 62. *Work:* Tamayo Mus, Mex; Hess Collection, Napa, Calif; Fundacion San Telmo, Buenos Aires, Arg. *Comn:* Monument, Seoul Olympic Comt, Korea, 88; monument, Mayor of Madrid, Spain, 92; monument for World Cup, Folk Village, S Korea, 2002. *Exhib:* 1st Biennale of Latin American Art, Sao Paulo, Brazil, 78; Echoes & Reflections, Ctr Interamerican Relations, NY, 82; Venice Biennale, Italy, 86; Otros Diluvios, Cult Ctr, Buenos Aires, Arg, 87; Latin American Art, Mus OAS, Washington, DC, 90; and others. *Pos:* Prog producer, BBC World Serv, London, 62-77; dir, Napa Contemp Arts Found, 88-94. *Teaching:* Vis prof art, Middlesex Polytechnic, London, 71-74; dean design, Parsons Sch Design, Santo Domingo, 83-85. *Awards:* First Prize, Sao Paulo Biennale Art, 77; Guggenheim Fel, 77; Medal Art Merits, Madrid, Spain, 91. *Bibliog:* BBC's Arena (dir), Maler's Requiem (film), BBC, 79; Edward Lucie-Smith (auth), Art Now, 85; Jorge Glusberg (auth), Maler, New York Univ, 87. *Media:* Recycled Metals, Wood. *Interests:* psychology, sailing, ecology. *Collection:* Laffont Collection, Hess Collection, Helft Collection. *Dealer:* Norah Haime Gallery

MALLIN, JUDITH YOUNG
WRITER, COLLECTOR
Study: Syracuse Univ, NY, 56; NY Univ, 57 & 87. *Pos:* Lectr, Courtauld Inst, London, 91; Art Inst, Chicago, 92; Sch Visual Arts, 92; estab, The Young Mallin Archive, 92. *Awards:* Who's Who in East. *Res:* Surrealism; women artists of the forties, creativity and aging. *Collection:* Surrealist, women artists of the forties. *Publ:* Auth, Muriel Streeter, Anna Howard Gallery, 90; Virgil Thomson's Swan Song, Avenue Mag, 90; Juliet Man Ray, London Ind & Quest, NY, 92; Edward James, Quest, NY, 92; View: Parade of Avant-Garde 1940-47, Thunders Mouth Press, NY, 92. *Mailing Add:* 719 Greenwich St New York NY 10012

MALLIN, SHERRY & JOEL
COLLECTORS
Study: Cornell Univ, BS; Columbia Univ, LLB; NY Bar, 1961. *Pos:* Atty, Joel Mallin LLP, New York; Chmn, Aldrich Mus, Conn. *Awards:* Named one of top 200 collectors, ARTnews mag, 2004-13. *Mem:* Manhattan Theater Club. *Collection:* Modern & contemporary art, particularly sculpture

MALLORY, RONALD
PAINTER, SCULPTOR
b Philadelphia, Pa, June 17, 1939. *Study:* Univ Colo, BA, 51; Univ Fla, BArch, 55; Sch Fine Arts, Rio de Janeiro, with Roberto Burle Marx, 56; Acad Julian, Paris, 57. *Work:* Mus Mod Art, Whitney Mus Am Art, NY; Albright-Knox Mus, Buffalo, NY; San Francisco Mus Mod Art; Inst Contemp Art, Philadelphia; Smithsonian Inst, Washington, DC; many others. *Comn:* Port Authority NY, World Trade Ctr, 83; Allied Lyons Corp, London, 88. *Exhib:* Mus Mod Art, 66 & 68; Larry Aldrich Mus, Ridgefield, Conn, 67 & 68; Torcuato di Tella, Buenos Aires, Arg, 69; Univ Calif, Los Angeles, 69; Solo exhibs, Stable Gallery, NY, 66, 67, Esther Robles Gallery, Los Angeles, Bonino Gallery, NY, 72, 73, Salon Annuciatta, Milan, Italy, 72, 73, Hansen Fuller Gallery, San Francisco, 73, Iris Clert, Paris, 901 Canyon Road Gallery, Santa Fe, NMex, 96 & Mitchell Algus Gallery, NY, 2001; Whitney Mus Am Art; World Trade Ctr, NY, 86; Mus Mod Art, NY & San Francisco; Whitney Mus Sculpture Ann; Milwaukee Art Ctr; Hayward Gallery, London; San Jose Mus Mod Art; Many others. *Pos:* Artist consultant, Bunker Hill Proj, Los Angeles; cur, C Project (holograms), NY & Miami, 95-98. *Teaching:* Instr, Univ Calif, Berkeley, 72; guest lectr, San Jose Univ, Calif; artist-in-residence, Univ Calif, Berkeley, 72. *Awards:* Pollock-Krasner Grant, 99; Artists Fel, 99. *Bibliog:* Larry Aldrich (auth), New Talent USA, Art in Am (rev), 7/8; John Gruen (auth), The galleries-a critical guide, New York Herald Tribune, 3/26; Peter Schjeldahl (auth), New York Letter, Art Int, Arts Mag & In the Galleries. *Mem:* Artists Equity. *Media:* Holograms. *Dealer:* Mitchel Algos Gallery 25 Thompson St New York NY 10013; Bonino Gallery 48 Great Jones St New York NY

MALLOY, BARRY
PHOTOGRAPHER
Study: Sch Art Inst Chicago, BFA, 1962, MFA, 1964; Hunter Coll, City Univ NY, PhD (admin), 1981. *Exhib:* Solo exhibs include Synagogue for the Arts Gallery, New York, 2001, 55 Mercer St Gallery, New York, 2001; group exhibs include Lower East Side Printshop, New York, 1970, 1978, 1981; Pratt Graphics Ctr Gallery, New York, 1972; Ctr Int Art, New York, 1976; Organization Independent Artists, New York, 1982; PS1 Contemp Art Ctr, New York, 1988; 183rd Ann: Invitational Exhib Contemp Art, Nat Acad Mus, New York, 2008. *Pos:* Crafts dir, Ft Tilden, NY, 1966-67. *Teaching:* Art teacher, New York City Bd Educ, 1967-77, instr in-service courses, 1979, spec educ curriculum develop, 1980, teacher trainer, 1980-81; instr photo-printmaking, Lower East Side Printshop, New York, 1975, 1979-82; guest instr, Coll New Rochelle, NY, 1980; adj instr, Hunter Coll, New York, 1986-87, Manhattanville Coll, 2003-. *Awards:* 3rd Prize for Painting, Chicago Sun-Times Show, 1963; Fulbright Travel Grant, 1975; Visual Arts Serv Grant, Nat Endowment Arts, 1977. *Mailing Add:* 2819 Brighton 6th St Brooklyn NY 11235

MALO, TERI (A)
PAINTER, PRINTMAKER
b Whitinsville, Mass, July 20, 1954. *Study:* Emmanuel Col, with Michael Jacques, BA, 76; Univ Mass, Amherst, with John Townsend & Fred Becker, MFA, 78. *Work:* Philadelphia Mus Art; IBM Inc, Rose Art Mus Brandeis Univ, Waltham, Mass; DeCordova Mus, Lincoln, Mass; Newport Art Mus, RI. *Exhib:* Philadelphia Int Print Exhib, Philadelphia Mus Art, 79; solo exhibs, Pucker Gallery, Boston, 79, 80, 82, 83-92 & 96, JRS Gallery, Providence, RI, 86, 88, 92 & 95, Art Collectors Gallery, NY, 81, Danforth Mus, 98 & Mus Work and Cult, 2001; Miami Int Print Exhib, Fla, 80; Silvermine 13th Nat Print Exhib, 80; Prints, Heritage Mus, Sandwich, Mass, 82; Jerusalem to Boston, Mitchell Mus, Mt Vernon, Ill, 83; Prints & Pots, Newport Art Mus, 85; Danforth Mus, 88 & 92. *Teaching:* Instr studio arts, Danforth Mus, 78-, fine arts, Buffalo State Col, NY, 90-91. *Awards:* Blanche E Colman Award, 98. *Mem:* Fenway Studios Inc. *Media:* Oil, Watercolor; Monotype. *Dealer:* Crane Collection Gallery 564 Washington St Wellesley MA 02181; Powers Gallery 342 Great Rd Acton MA 01720. *Mailing Add:* Malo Studio 103 30 Ipswich St Boston MA 02215

MALONE, JAMES HIRAM
PAINTER, WRITER
b Winterville, Ga, Mar 24, 1930. *Study:* Morehouse Col, AA, 50; Ctr Creative Studies Coll Art and Design, with Sarkis Sarkesian, AA, 59. *Work:* Pavilion Int, Montreal, Can; Knokke-Heist Mus, Knokke-Heist, Belgium; New York Fales Library, 1996; Teaching Mus South, 1999; Paul Jones Collection; Larry and Brenda Thompson Collection. *Comn:* Malone's Atlanta Book, Atlanta newspapers, Ga, 86-88; Wall mural, Atlanta Centennial Olympic Park Corp, 96; Urban Renewal Hist Makers, NY RepoHist Asn, 97; Walt Disney scenery, 01; Mural, Washington Park Libr, Atlanta, 2004; Vine City Tree Trunk deco public art, Atlanta, 2006. *Exhib:* Solo exhibs, Neighborhood Art Ctr, Atlanta, 85, C W Hill Sch Gallery, 90 & Alma Simmons Mem Gallery, Atlanta, 94-96; Encore Invitational Exhib, Giving Art Back To The Community, Atlanta Projs Hq Off, Atlanta, 94; A Peanut Extravaganza, Art and Imagery of the Peanut Exhib (A nutty show), Albany Mus Art, Ga, 94; Atlanta Res Auburn Ave African Am Hist Gallery, 96; City Hall East Gallery; RepoHistory Installation, 98; McPheeter's Art Gallery, 99; Gallery on the Greene, 2000; Teaching Mus South, 2003; Contemp Studious Biennial, 2003; Homecoming: 20th Century, City Gallery East, 2005; and others. *Pos:* Graphic designer, Northgate Advert Agency, 68-80; art dir, artist-in-residence, Contemp Studios, 59-62; graphic designer, Atlanta Newspaper, 81; advertising designer, Atlanta J & Constitution, Ga, 84; fine arts chmn, Black Arts Network and Advocacy, 86; ad hoc comn, Nat Black Arts Fest, 88; publ, Literacy Cartoon Simply Apply Yourself, Southeastern Publ, Atlanta, GA, 90-; columnist, Atlanta News Leader, 91. *Teaching:* instr mgr Spec Serv Arts/Crafts Shop, SC, 52; instr Contemp Art Studios, Detroit, Mich, 63; Instr art basics, Your Heritage House, Detroit, 70; instr Fisher YMCA, Detroit, Mich, 71; instr, Nexus Art Ctr, Atlanta, 94; instr Highland Park Jr Col, Detroit, Mich, 73; instr Metrop College, Atlanta, Ga, 2000. *Awards:* 1986 Bronze Jubilee, WPBA 30 Pub TV, 86; Hon Art Award, Ctr for Creative Studies Coll Art and Design Alumni Exhib, 86; Art Award, Art With a Southern Drawl Exhib, Mobile Col, 93; Art Award, Atlanta Centennial Olympic Park, 97; Annie L McPheeters Community Medallion, Atlanta, 98; Sr Art Award, Million Man March, 98. *Bibliog:* Richard Gincel (auth), Artist's work enlivens TAP offices, Atlanta J/Constitution Newspaper, 94; Bo Emmerson (auth), Uncovering Buttermilk Bottom, Atlanta J Constitution, 95; Estella Zavala (auth), Writer Pushes Multiethnic Art for Disadvantaged Youngsters, Wave Newspapers, Calif, 95; Malone's Colorful World, Donna Angle(auth), Millionaire Magazine, 8/2000; Express Yourself Felicia Feaster (auth), Creative Loafing, 2000; Bold Strokes of Affection H M Cauley (auth), Atlanta Journal/Constitution 2002; Who's Who in Black Atlanta, 2004-2005. *Mem:* Visual Vanguard Art Asn; Nat Conf Artists, Atlanta; Int Black Writers Group, Atlanta; Contemporary Artists Detroit, 2006; Keep Atlanta Beautiful Board, 2006; Grove Park Arts Alliance (pres), 2006. *Media:* Acrylics, Enamel. *Publ:* Auth, Anthology of Black Writers Poetry: Word Up, Beans & Rice Publ, 90; illusr/writer, No-Job Dad, Victory Press, Monterey, Calif, 92; Street Beat Newspaper Column, Atlanta News Leader, College Park, Ga, 92; contribr, Something About the Author, Gale, 96; Jones Family Cart, Ahkeelah's Press, 97; and others. *Mailing Add:* 1796 North Ave NW Atlanta GA 30318-6441

MALONE, PATRICIA LYNN
PAINTER
b Kansas City, Mo, Dec 3, 1930. *Study:* Kansas City Jr Coll, 48; Kansas City Art Inst, 49-51; Univ Tulsa, 78-80. *Work:* Oklahoma Art Ctr, Oklahoma City; Transco Energy Corp, Houston, Tex; Hallmark-Crown Ctr, Kansas City, Mo; Univ Tulsa, Okla; McGraw Hill Publ co, New York; Crowe Donlevy, Hall, Estill, Hardwick & Nelson, McGraw Hill. *Comn:* Painting, Cancer Care Ctr, 88; Logsdon Woody, 89; painting, Fed Judge Dana Rasure for Fed Ct House, Tulsa, Okla, 99; Day Break, Bartlesville. *Exhib:* Watercolor USA, Springfield Mus, Mo, 81, 83 & 89; Am Watercolor Soc, Salmagundi Club, New York & Canton Mus, Ohio, 82-88; Midwest Watercolor, Neville Pub Mus, Green Bay, Wis, 83-86; Miniature Art Soc Fla, 93; Miniature Painters Soc Washington, DC, 93-94; and others. *Awards:* Phyllis France Award, Midwest Watercolor Soc, 85; First Place Watercolor, 4th Ann, Phillips Petroleum, 88; Third Place Still Life, Miniature Painters Soc, Washington, DC; First place Painting, Women's Show. *Bibliog:* Watercolor '87, Am Artist Mag, 87; Ward (auth), New Spirit of Watercolor, North Light Bks, 89; Albert-Wolf (auth), Splash 91, North Light Bks; and others. *Mem:* Am Watercolor Soc; Nat Watercolor Soc; Watercolor Soc; Nat Watercolor Okla; Okla Visual Artist Coalition. *Media:* Watercolor, Pastel. *Dealer:* M A Doran Gallery 3509 S Peoria Tulsa OK; Art South, Philadelphia PA; Art4Business.com. *Mailing Add:* 3139 S Sandusky Ave Tulsa OK 74135

MALONE, PETER
PAINTER
b New York, NY, 1950. *Study:* Teachers Col, Sch Visual Arts, Columbia Univ, BFA, 77, MA, 83. *Work:* Elizabeth de C Wilson Mus, Manchester, Vt; Munson Williams Proctor Inst, Utica, NY. *Exhib:* Stilled Life, Islip Mus, East Islip, NY; Southern Vt Arts Ctr, Manchester, Vt; Kirkland Arts Ctr, Clinton, NY. *Pos:* Gallery dir, Kingsborough Community Coll, City Univ New York, 2000-. *Teaching:* Adj asst prof, Kingsborough Community Coll, City Univ New York, 84-. *Awards:* Res grant, Profl Staff Cong, City Univ New York, 98 & 2002. *Media:* Oil on Linen. *Mailing Add:* Kingsborough Community Coll Art Gallery 2001 Oriental Blvd Brooklyn NY 11235

MALONE, ROBERT R
PAINTER, PRINTMAKER
b McColl, SC, 1933. *Study:* Furman Univ; Univ NC, BA; Univ Chicago, MFA; Univ Iowa. *Work:* Central Academy Fine Arts, Beijing; Humana Inc, Ky; Seven-Up Co, Mo; Emerson Electric Co, Mo; Gen Am Ins Co, Mo; NY Pub Libr; Calif Palace Legion Hon, San Francisco; Philadelphia Mus Art; Smithsonian Inst & Libr Cong, Wash. *Comn:* several editions of intaglio & relief prints, Ferdinand Roten Galleries, Baltimore, Md, 66-69; two editions intaglio & relief prints, De Cinque Gallery, Hollywood, Fla, 67; color etching, Ill Arts Coun, 1st Print Comn, 73; several editions of lithographs, Lakeside Studio, Lakeside, Mich, 71-80; Capital Develop Bd, State Ill, 94-95; Sculpture for Third Millennium, Ill, 1994-95. *Exhib:* Solo exhibs, Elliot Smith Gallery, St Louis & Merida Galleries, Louisville, KY, 85 & 87, Rapp Gallery, Louisville, 90, 92, 93 & 96; New Talent in Printmaking, AAA Gallery, NY, 68; Biennial Print Exhib, Calif State Col, Long Beach, 69; Bienniale Int L'Estampe 1970, Mus Mod Art, Paris, 70; 26th Ann Exhib Boston Printmakers, De Cordova Mus, 74; Currents 29: Drawing in St Louis (with catalog), St Louis Art Mus, 85. *Teaching:* Assoc prof painting & printmaking, Wesleyan Col, Macon, Ga, 61-68; assoc prof printmaking, WVa Univ, Morgantown, 68-70; assoc prof printmaking, Southern Ill Univ, Edwardsville, 70-75, prof, 75-2000, prof emeritus, 2000-; prof emeritus, Southern Ill Univ Edwardsville. *Awards:* Recent Am Graphics Purchase Award, Univ Wis-Madison, 75; Southern Ill Univ Sr Res Scholar Award, 75 & 84; Purchase Award, Sixty Sq Inches, Purdue Univ, 94. *Bibliog:* Prize-winning Graphics, book 7, 1967; Motive Mag, 1968, 1969; Sun Courier Journal & Louisville Times, 11/2/69; Charleston Daily Mail, 07/21/70; New Art Examiner, Apr, 1975; Basic Design, Systems, Elements, Applications, 1983; West End Word, 2/7/85; NY Art Review, 1988; Marks from the Matrix, Normal Editions Workshop, Ill State Univ, 2007. *Mem:* Coll Art Asn Am; Southern Graphics Coun. *Media:* Oil, Acrylic; Lithography, Monotype. *Res:* The Redevelopment and Advancement of the Photo-Gelatin Process, 1975-76; Ford Fel, 1977; New Problems with Surface and Illusion in Printmaking, 1977-80; A Re-examination of large scale group portraits for the 1980's, 1982-86; A Contemporary view of the human condition, 1984-85. *Specialty:* Paintings. *Interests:* running; weight lifting. *Publ:* Contemporary American Printmakers, 1999. *Dealer:* Yvonne Rapp Gallery 2117 Frankfort Ave Louisville KY 40206. *Mailing Add:* 600 Chapman St Edwardsville IL 62025-1260

MALPEDE, JOHN
PERFORMANCE ARTIST, DIRECTOR
b Wichita Falls, Tex, June 29, 1945. *Study:* Univ Wis, BA, 68. *Work:* Out of the Public Eye, 84; Too Many Questions, 84; South of The Clouds, 86; No Stone for Studs Schwartz, 87; LAPD Inspects San Francisco, 89-90; Jupiter 35, 89-90; LAPD Inspects the Twin Cities, 91; LAPD Inspects Amsterdam, 91; LAPD Inspects London, 91; Call Home, 91-93; Give Up All Your Possessions and Follow Me, 93; Dead Dog & Lonely Horse, 94-95; Standing Up and Falling Down, 95; Bronx Train, 95; I Was Sleeping with My Eyes Open, 95; Avec Motard, 96; Pre-Existing Conditions, 97; Temporary Quarters (Hit & Run), 97; co-dir Ping-Pong, 99; GET, 99; Agents & Assets, 2000. *Exhib:* Solo performance, Same or Different, 81, Olympic Update: homelessness in Los Angeles, 84-85. *Pos:* Artistic dir, Los Angeles Poverty Dept, Theater, 86-; self-employed artist, NY Univ, 84-85. *Teaching:* Vis distinguished prof performance, Miami-Dade Community Col, 91; vis asst prof performance, Dept World Arts & Cult, Univ Calif, Los Angeles, 94; teacher, MFA Dir's Prog & Calif Col Arts and Crafts; vis fac mem, Amsterdam Sch for Advanced Research in Theater and Dance Studies, 95-96; vis dir dept undergrad drama, Tisch Sch Arts, NY Univ, 95; vis artist, Movement Research, 93, 95; vis fac, Columbia Col, Chicago, 92, Sch Art Inst Chicago, 90. *Awards:* Adelaide Kent Award, San Francisco Art Inst, 87; Visual Arts Grant, Nat Endowment Arts, 88; Bessie Creation Award, Dance Theater Workshop, Los Angeles, Calif, 89; NY State Coun on Arts grant; NEA grant; Calif Arts Coun grant; Dance Theater Workshop Bessie Creation Award; Adeline Kent Award, San Francisco Art Inst; Durfee Sabbatical Grant & Los Angeles Theater Alliance Ovation Award for work with Los Angeles Poverty Dept. *Bibliog:* Thomas Lebhardt (auth), John Malpede, Southern Calif Performance Issue, Mime J, 91. *Mem:* Coll Art Asn; Nat Performance Network (mem, steering comt 90-92); Los Angeles Festival (mem, steering comt, 93); City of Los Angeles Cult Affairs Dept (mem arts adv comt, 90-91); Liberty Hill Community (funding bd, 94); Peter Sellars' Old Stories New Lives Found; Social and Pub Art Resource Ctr. *Publ:* Co-dir, producer video LAPD Inspects the Twin Cities, 92; prodr video The Hunger Artist on Sports Incredible, (The Kitchen grant), 84. *Mailing Add:* PO Box 26190 Los Angeles CA 90026

MALTA, VINCENT
INSTRUCTOR, PAINTER
b Brooklyn, NY, Apr 9, 1922. *Study:* Art Students League. *Work:* Univ of Minn; Philadelphia Mus; Immaculate Heart Col; Birmingham Mus Art. *Exhib:* Brooklyn Mus Biennial Print Exhib, 52; Metrop Mus Nat Exhib of Watercolors, 52; Pa Acad Fine Arts, 53; Brooklyn Mus Int Watercolor Exhib, 53; Nat Acad of Design, 53; Three-man show, Art Students League, 94. *Teaching:* Instr fine arts, painting, Art Students League, 66-. *Awards:* Emily Lowe Award, 52; Louis Comfort Tiffany Found Award, 54; Betti Salzman Award, Nat Arts Club, 77. *Bibliog:* Marlene Schiller (auth), Return of the art spirit, Am Artist Mag, 3/78; Art Showcase, Manhattan Cable TV, 5/25/83 & 10/12/83. *Mem:* Artist Equity; Artists' Fel Inc, NY. *Media:* Mixed. *Mailing Add:* 1960 60th St Brooklyn NY 11204

MALTZMAN, STANLEY
PAINTER, PRINTMAKER
b New York, NY, 1921. *Study:* New York Phoenix Sch Design, degree, 48. *Work:* Schenectady Mus, NY; Hudson River Mus, Yonkers, NY; Carnegie-Mellon Univ; Mus Fine Arts, Springfield, Mass; Greene Co Savings Bank, Greenville, NY; and others; Met Mus Art, NY; US Coast Guard Mus, New London, Conn, 2006. *Comn:* Steuben Glass, Corning, NY; Danbury Mint, Norwalk, Conn; Fed Land Bank & Smith & Wesson, Springfield, Mass. *Exhib:* Berkshire Mus, Pittsfield, Mass, 79; Am Watercolor Soc, NY, 80; Monotypes, The Painterly Print, NY, 86 & Pastel Soc Am, 94; Pretty Deadly Poisonous Plants of Forest, Field & Garden, Bruce Mus, Conn, 95; Allied Artists Am, Nat Arts Club, 97; Gifts of Winter exhib, Carnegie Mellon Univ, 2000; Butler Inst Art, Ohio, 2004; Prof Artists League, 2006; Audubon Artists, 2006; Invitational Artist, Arts Ctr, Old Forge, NY, 2008; Pastel Exhib, Bennington Ctr for the Arts, Vt, 2008; Em Plain Air, Debbie Davis Gallery, NY, 2008. *Collection Arranged:* Color Fields from the Evening Sky, 83; Inspirations from Nature, Elliot Mus, Stuart, Fla, 96. *Pos:* Cur, Greenville Comm Libr Gallery, 97-98. *Teaching:* Instr drawing & pastel, Hudson Valley Workshops, 87-; Arts in Educ Serv, Questar III & Boccs, 96; instr, watercolor & drawing workshops, Greenville Libr, 2005; instr, Arts Ctr, Old Forge NY, 2007; instr, View, Old Forge, NY. *Awards:* First Prize, Conn Acad Fine Arts, 76; Ball State Univ Award, 81; Drawing Prize, Berkshire Mus, Pittsfield, Mass; Childehassam Fund Purchase Award, Am Acad Arts & Letts; Gold Medal, Graphics, Hudson Valley Art Asn; Gold Medal, Graphics, Am Artists Prof League; Silver medal, Audubon Artists, 2011; Rooney Etc award, View, Old Forge, 2013. *Bibliog:* Article, Am Artist Mag, 4/86; Kaatskill Life Mag, spring 96; Artists Mag, 98; Artful Mind Mag, 2013. *Mem:* Greene Co Coun Arts, Catskill, NY (visual arts coun); Pastel Soc Am; Am Artists Prof League, Hudson Valley Art Asn; Audubon Artists; All Arts Matter, Greenville, NY (hon mem bd dirs). *Media:* Watercolor, Pastel, Graphics. *Specialty:* Contemporary Landscape. *Interests:* Landscapes of the Masers, the various kinds of papers work on, ornithology. *Collection:* Prints, drawings, watercolors of the 20th century. *Publ:* Sounds of Mystery-Sounds of a Distant Drum, Holt, Rinehart, Inc, 67; Botanical Arts & Illustration, Carnegie-Mellon Univ, 77-78; Printworld Directory, 82, 83, 84 & 85; The Crayon, Olana Newsletter; Drawing Nature, Northlight Books, 95; The Best of Flower Painting, Materials & Techniques, 97; Drawing Trees, NLight Bks, 99; Buildings & Barns, North Light Bks, 99; The Artful Mind, 5/2006; The Art of Stanley Matzman, Sketches & Studies in Pencil, Pastel & Watercolor, 2006; Art Times, Apr-May, July-Aug 2007; Pencil Box, Northlight Bks, 2007; Art Jour America, Landscapes, North Light Books, 2012. *Dealer:* Stahley Maltzman Studio and Gallery Freehold NY; Roshkowska Gallery Windham NY. *Mailing Add:* PO Box 333 Freehold NY 12431

MANCHANDA, CATHARINA
CURATOR
b Germany; arrived in US, 1990. *Study:* Univ Stuttgart, Germany, BA (art history), 1990; Univ Del, MA (art hist), 1993; City Univ NY, PhD, 2005. *Collection Arranged:* The Sketchbooks of George Grosz, Harvard Univ Art Mus, 1992 & 1993; Between War & Utopia: Prints & Drawings of the German Avant-Garde, 1905-1933, Philadelphia Mus Art; Gerhard Richter: 40 Years of Painting, Mus Mod Art, New York; Models & Prototypes, Kemper Art Mus, St Louis, 2006, Beauty & the Blonde: An Exploration of Am Art & Popular Culture, 2007. *Pos:* Curatorial intern, Harvard Univ Art Museums, Cambridge, Mass & Solomon R Guggenheim Mus, New York, formerly; curatorial fellow, Philadelphia Mus Art, 1993-95; curatorial asst, Mus Mod Art, New York, 1999-2002; cur, Mildred Lane Kemper Art Mus, Washington Univ, St Louis, 2006-08; sr cur, Wexner Ctr Arts, Ohio State Univ, Columbus, 2008-. *Awards:* Samuel H Tress Travel Fel; Getty Libr Res Grant. *Mailing Add:* Wexner Ctr Arts Ohio State Univ 1871 N High St Columbus OH 43210

MANCINI, JOHN
PAINTER
b Comiso, Italy, Jan 9, 1925; US citizen. *Study:* Scuola d'Arte, Comiso, Italy, dipl; Liceo & Acad di Belle Arti, Palermo, Italy, BA; Art Students League; Columbia Univ. *Work:* Galleria Della Acad, Palermo, Italy; Bank Am & Wells Fargo Bank, San Francisco; Mus Ital Art, Stone Park, Ill; Galeria de Colecionistas, Mexico City; Hespe Gallery, San Francisco, Calif; Herbert Palmer Gallery, Los Angeles, Calif; Wellington Mgt Co, Boston, Mass; pvt collections incl, Robert Doran, Chestnut Hill, Mass, Harry & Gwen Schlough, Hillsborough, Calif, Chuck Silverman, Houston, Tex & David Himmelberger, Palo Alto, Calif. *Comn:* Frank Carrubba, Palo Alto, CA. *Exhib:* Crocker Mus Art, Sacramento, Calif, 67; Palace of Fine Art, San Francisco, 68; Heritage Gallery, Los Angeles, Calif; Mus Ital-Am, San Francisco, Calif; Gallery Europa, Palo Alto, Calif. *Pos:* Art dir, R W Graphics, Palo Alto, Calif, 66-70 & Mancini Design, Mountain View, Calif, 70-90; Mancini Fine Art, San Mateo, Calif. *Teaching:* Art teacher painting, Scuola d'Arte, Comiso, Italy, 49-51. *Awards:* Gold Medal, Ital-Am Artists in USA, 77; Environ Protection Agency, San Francisco, 80; US Embassy, Bucharest, Rumania, 90-. *Bibliog:* E M Polley (auth), John Mancini, Artforum, 65; Thomas Albright (auth), John Mancini, San Francisco Chronicle, 73; R L P (auth), Los Angeles Times, 84; and others. *Media:* Oil, Acrylic. *Interests:* Travel to Rome, Florence for Renaissance Art. *Collection:* R Doran, Willington Mandg Co, R&C Schlough, R McKenzie, C Silverman. *Publ:* NY Graphics Soc Pub Group. *Dealer:* Hespe Gallery San Francisco CA 94123; Gallery Europa, Palo Alto CA 94301; Himmelberger Gallery San Francisco. *Mailing Add:* 604 Connie Ave San Mateo CA 94402

MANCUSO, LENI
PAINTER, GRAPHIC ARTIST, COLLAGE ARTIST, WRITER
b New York, NY. *Study:* Brooklyn Mus Art Sch; Art Students League; Pratt Inst, NY; New Sch Univ, NY. *Work:* Newberry Collection, Detroit, Mich; First Nat Bank Boston; Portland Mus Art, Maine; Kresge Gallery, Ann Arbor, Mich; Mich Bell Tel; NH State Art Bank; US State Dept, Washington, DC; John Day Collection of Monhegan Art, ME. *Exhib:* Wadsworth Atheneum, Hartford, Conn, 78; Solo exhibs, Lamont Gallery, Exeter, NH, 72, Univ Maine Art Mus, Orono, Maine, 77, Currier Art Gallery, Manchester, NH, 81, St Anselm Col, Goffstown, NH, 87, Manchester Inst Arts, NH, 87, Maine Arts Commn, Augusta, Maine, 95, Jubilant Light, Maine Ctr for Contemp Art, Rockport, Maine, 96; Maine Coast Artists, 78, 79 & 96; Leighton Gallery, 91; Danforth Gallery, 94; Maine Arts Comn, 95; Castine Arts Asn, Maine, 99-2000; Trinity Gallery, Castine, Maine; Galerie am Neuen Palais, Potsdam, Ger, 2003; Ctr for Maine Contemp Art, 2004-2005. *Teaching:* Instr painting & head art dept, Proctor Acad, Andover, NH, 55-60; instr painting & watercolor, Currier Gallery Art Sch, Manchester, NH, 62-70; instr painting & compos, St Paul's Sch, Concord, NH, 67-75. *Awards:* Watercolor Prize, Portland Mus Art, Maine, 61 & Currier Gallery Art, NH, 68 & 81; First Prize, Danforth Gallery, 94. *Bibliog:* T Rawson (auth), Leni Mancuso at Manchester Institute, Art/New Eng, 3/87; Beyond Tradition, Bar Harbor News, 93; Kenneth Greenleaf (auth) For Mancuso, It's not light, but reflection, Maine Sunday Telegram, 6/2/96; Carle Little & Arnold Skolnick (eds), The Art of Maine in Winter, Down East Bks, Rockport, Maine, 2002; Robert Post (auth), Understanding Maine Winter, Down East Bks, 2003; C. Little & A. Skolnick (eds.), The Art of Monhegan Island, Down East Bks, Rockport, ME, 2004. *Mem:* NH Art Asn; Deer Isle Artists' Asn; Coll Art Asn; Union Maine Visual Artists; Maine Coast Artists. *Media:* Watercolor, Casein, Acrylic, Oil. *Interests:* poems. *Publ:* In Rothkos's Cave, 20 original drawings and poems, Puckerbrush Rev Porfolio # 6, Winter/Spring 98; 12 books, 2 CDs of poems composed; Flight of the Monarch (cover image), isis Journey, 2012. *Mailing Add:* PO Box 303 Castine ME 04421-0303

MANDEL, JOHN
PAINTER
b New York, NY, Dec 6, 1941. *Study:* Pratt Inst, BFA, 64. *Work:* Nat Gallery Australia; Pa State Univ. *Exhib:* Whitney Mus Am Art Painting Ann, 69 & 72; The Contemp Figure, A New Realism, Suffolk Mus & Carriage House at Stony Brook, NY, 71; In Sharp Focus, Sidney Janis Gallery, NY, 72; Indianapolis Mus Ann, Ind, 72; Solo exhibs, Max Hutchinson Gallery, NY, 71-73, 75 & 79. *Pos:* Assoc dean, Sch Art & Design, Calif Inst Arts. *Teaching:* Instr painting, grad & undergrad sch, Pratt Inst, 71-76; instr painting, Calif Inst Arts, 72-. *Awards:* Paul Mellon Fel, 79. *Bibliog:* John Canaday (auth), Art: The figure as defined by Mandel, 11/21/71 & Art: In Mandel's Art, superb control, 4/28/73, New York Times. *Mailing Add:* c/o Calif Inst Arts Art Sch 24700 McBean Pkwy Valencia CA 91355

MANDEL, MIKE
PHOTOGRAPHER, ARTIST
b Los Angeles, Calif, Nov 24, 1950. *Study:* Cal State, Northridge, BA, 72; San Francisco Art Inst, MFA, 74. *Work:* Mus Mod Art, NY; San Francisco Mus Mod Art; Bibliot Nat, Paris, France; Mus Fine Arts, Houston; Calif Inst Photog, Univ Calif, Riverside; and others. *Comn:* Hearth (wood tile mosaic mural), NY, 93; 5 skaters, City San Jose, Calif, 94-96; Waiting, San Francisco Int Airport, 96-99; Atlanta Fed Ctr, Gen Serv Admin, Ga, 99-. *Exhib:* Evidence, San Francisco Mus Mod Art, 77; New Photog 5, Mus Mod Art, NY, 89; Making Good Time, Calif Mus Photog, Riverside, 90; Phelan Award Winners, San Francisco Camerawork, 90; Add Noise, Contract Design Ctr, San Francisco, Calif, 92; Sprung in die Zeit, Berlinische Galerie, Mus Moderne Kunst, Photographie und Architektur, Berlin, Ger, 92-93; The Turk & the Jew, World Wide Web, 96-97; Scene of the Crime, Armand Hammer Mus, Univ Calif, Los Angeles, 97; The Artists Book II, Fine Art Ctr, Taos, 98; 25/25, Southern Exposure, San Francisco, 99. *Teaching:* Instr photog, Cabrillo Col, Aptos, Calif, 83-93, Calif Col Arts & Crafts, 92-93; vis assoc prof photog, Sch Art Inst Chicago, 93-94; prof electronic imaging, Wash State Univ, Pullman, 95-; lectr, Univ Mass, Boston, 98, Mass Col Art, Boston, 98- & Sch Mus Fine Arts, Boston, 98-. *Awards:* Nat Endowment Arts Grants, 73, 76 & 88; Calif Arts Coun Grants, 78 & 80; Fulbright Fel, 97. *Publ:* Auth, Baseball-Photographer Trading Cards, 75; coauth, Evidence, 77; auth, San Francisco Giants: An Oral History, 79; coauth, Headlands: The Marin Coast at the Golden Gate, Univ NMex Press, 89; auth, Making Good Time, Calif Mus Photog, Univ Calif, Riverside, 89. *Mailing Add:* 124 Maplewood St Watertown MA 02472

MANDELBAUM, ELLEN
STAINED GLASS ARTIST, PAINTER
b New York, NY. *Study:* Ind Univ, AB, 60, MFA, 63; study with James McGarrell, Ludwig Schaffrath, Jochem Poensgen & Albinus Elskus. *Work:* Shoreham-Wading River Libr, Long Island, New York; Living Art Found, New York; Ind Univ, Bloomington; Nishida Mus, Toyama, Japan. *Comn:* Greater Baltimore Med Ctr, Md, 93; chapel windows, Adath Jeshurun Synagogue, Minnetonka, Minn, 95; 30' window wall, SC Aquarium, Charleston, 2000; 28 windows, Marian Woods Convent, Hartsdale, NY, 2001; Har Shalom, Potomac, Md, 2003; Toni Sikes (residence), 2003; B'Nai Shalom, Olney, Md, 2004; Susana Simon, Dir, Queens Coll Art Ctr, 2004; painted hanging window, comn by Alexandra Deluise, Queens Coll Art Ctr, 2004; Window of Hope, Interfaith Chapel, Robert Packer Hosp, Sayre, Pa, 2006; Kol Shalom Synagogue, Rockville, Md, 2012. *Exhib:* Solo exhibs, Painting & Glass Art, Queens Coll Art Ctr, New York, 98, Painting With Light, Community Gallery, 2010; Int Exhib, Centre Int Du Vitrail, Chartres, France, 89; Hudson River Mus, Yonkers,

NY, 90; Personal Visions Invitational, New Glass Workshop, New York, 91; The Glass Canvas, Soc Arts & Crafts, Boston, 93; Layers of Experience, Women's 4th Int Stained Glass Workshop, Park Tower Gallery, Tokyo, 95; Crawford Munic Art Gallery, Cork, Ireland, 97; GlassWorks, Gallery on the Hudson, New York, 2000; Int Women's Contemp Stained Glass, Foothills Art Ctr, Golden Colo, 2000; Reflections on Glass, Am Bible Soc, 2002-2003; Sense of Place, Toronto, 2004; Art & Archit, Omni Gallery, Uniondale, NY, 2005; Small Works: Big Ideas, Women's Studio Ctr, Long Island City, New York, 2005; En Quete Des Lumieries Dumonde, The Search for the Light of the World, Musee Suisse Du Vitrail Romont Schweizer Glas Malerei Mus, Romont, Switz, 2005; Light Listened: Art & Glass, Queens Coll Art Ctr, Flushing, New York, 2006; Women's 9th Int Stained Glass Workshop, Glass Artists Gallery, Sydney, Australia, 2006. *Pos:* Owner, Ellen Mandelbaum Glass Art, 81-. *Teaching:* Docent exhibs, Whitney Mus Am Art, 64-66; lectr mod painting, Hunter Coll, 64-67; instr, glass painting & archit glass classes & workshops, Ellen Mandelbaum Glass Art Studio. *Awards:* Judges Choice, Stained Glass Asn Am, Toronto, 85; Visual Art Award of Excellence, Mod Liturgy Mag, 87 & 89; Ministry and Liturgy, Best of Show, 2001-2002; Syracuse Residential Art Award, Stained Glass Asn, 2011. *Bibliog:* Synagogue with a view, Stained Glass, winter 95; Christopher Peterson (auth), The Art of Stained Glass, Rockport Press, 98; An artists statement: A Solo Exhib, Stained Glass Quart, Vol 93, No 2, summer 98; Ellen Mandelbaum: Painting and Glass Art (catalog), Queens Coll Art Ctr, New York, 98; Lynn Nesmith (auth), South Carolina Aquarium, Archit Record, New York, 2000; Claudia Rowe (auth), Spiritual reflections in bits of glass, NY Times, Westchester ed, 1/20/2002; Still doing good work, Environment & Art Lett, 3-4/2003; Marian Woods (auth), Kate/Gross Stained Glass Quart, spring 2003. *Mem:* Stained Glass Asn Am; Am Glass Guild. *Media:* Stained Glass. *Publ:* Dada & surrealism show at the Museum of Mod Art, Artforum, 68; Contribr, Glass Art in Architecture, Thoughts & Ideas, Poensgen, Dusseldorf, 88; auth, The Venice Chapel: Matisse's Legacy in Stained Glass, New York, 88; New Glass, The Painterly Alternative, Professional Stained Glass, 92; Masterclass, Glass Craftsman, 12/96; Working with a Stained Glass Artist, Faith and Form, 2002. *Mailing Add:* 39-49 46th St Long Island City NY 11104-1407

MANDELBAUM, LYN
PAINTER, PRINTMAKER
b New York, NY, Sept 7, 1950. *Study:* Tyler Sch Art, Rome, 70-71, Philadelphia, BFA, 72, MFA, 74. *Work:* Philadelphia Mus Art; Otis Libr, Los Angeles; New York Libr; Jean Brown Arch, Tyringham, Mass. *Comn:* Mural, Byblos Discoteque, Marigot, St Martin, 81. *Exhib:* Mus Mod Art, NY, 73; Images - Dimensional - Movable - Transferable, Akron Art Inst, Ohio, 73; Fed Reserve Bd, Washington, DC, 74; Pa State Univ Mus Art, 74; Photo-Synthesis, Johnson Mus Art, 76; two-person exhib, 14 Sculptors Gallery, NY, 80; solo exhib, Foundations Gallery, NY, 82. *Pos:* Founder & dir, Eastern Shore Press, Philadelphia, 74-76 & Street Ed Inc, New York, 79-; pres, Island Magic Inc, New York, 82-. *Teaching:* Lectr printmaking, Philadelphia Col Art, 76-78; instr, Tyler Sch Art, 77-78. *Awards:* Purchase Award, Univ Del, Newark, 71. *Media:* All. *Publ:* Auth, Moderate Expectations, 78 & Anita's Revenge, 78, pvt publ; Consider Yourself Lucky, Street Ed Inc, 79; Notes: Keep a Candle Burning, pvt publ, 80; Say, Street Ed Inc, 82. *Mailing Add:* 20 Desbrosses St New York NY 10013-1704

MANDERS, SUSAN KAY
ARTIST
b Burbank CA Dec. 9. 1948. *Study:* Univ Guadalajara, BA, 1969; Calif State Univ, postgrad, UCLA, Otis Parsons, LA, postgrad, 1985; Royal Col, London, 1987; Silicon Digital Art. *Work:* Steel Sculpture, Harry Ross Industries, 2003. *Exhib:* UN World Conference on Women, Beijing, 1996 (LA, NY, Chicago, Beverly Hills, Irvine, San Francisco, New Orleans, 1990); US artist Athens (Greece) Summer Olympic Games, 2004. *Pos:* Consultant in field; Docent UCLA; Tuesday's Child; Pillars of Hope Project, San Fernando Valley Co Fair, 1995. *Teaching:* Instr, Art Experience School & Gallery (owner & dir), Studio City, Calif, 1978. *Mem:* Am Asoc of Univ Women; LA Art Asn; Beverly Hills Art Assoc; Hills Art Asn; Nat Mus Women in the Arts; Nat Univ Women; LA Co Mus of Art; Dada, La; Mus Conte Coun; Women in Animation; Nat Asn Univ Women; Vidamation Asn (bd dirs). *Mailing Add:* 4132 Fulton Ave Sherman Oaks CA 91423

MANDZIUK, MICHAEL DENNIS
COMPUTER ARTIST
b Detroit, Mich, Jan 14, 1942. *Study:* Self taught. *Work:* Minn Mus Art, St Paul; Borg Warner Corp, Chicago; Kemper Ins Collection, Long Grove, Ill; Art Ctr Collection, Park Forest, Ill; Springfield City Collection, Ill. *Exhib:* Tex Fine Arts Asn Travel Shows, 71-72 & 74; Boston Printmakers Nat, 72-74; Minn Mus Art Drawing Biennial, St Paul, 73; Butler Inst Am Art, Youngstown, Ohio, 73-75; solo exhibs, Welna Gallery, Chicago, 74 & Ukrainian Inst Mod Art, Chicago, 75; Hunterdon Nat Print Show, 74; Okla Art Ctr Nat Print Show, 74; 22nd Art Conf, Univ Mich, 74; Mitchell Art Mus, Mt Vernon, Ill, 75; Battle Creek Art Ctr, Mich, 76. *Pos:* Artist-craftsman juror, Ann Arbor St Art Fair, 71; Retired graphic specialist, Ford Motor Co, formerly, 97; Developing computer graphic images. *Awards:* Best of Show Award; Old Capt Art Fair Award, Springfield, Ill, 73-74; Detroit Artist Market, 71-72. *Media:* Computer Images. *Mailing Add:* 7191 Kolb St Allen Park MI 48101

MANERA, ENRICO ORLANDO
SCULPTOR, PAINTER
b Asmara, Italy, Apr 4, 1947. *Study:* Liceo Artistico, Acad Fine Arts, Rome, 67. *Work:* Museo D'arte Moderna, Spoleto, Italy; Galleria D'arte Moderna Rondanini, Rome, Italy; Museo Nazionale Della Grafica, Rome, Italy; Palazzo Del Governo, Bari, Italy; Archivio Storico Della Biennale Di Venezia, Venezia, Italy. *Comn:* Sculpture, Mus Mod Art, Spoleto, Italy, 79; painting, Salzano Inst, Rome, Italy, 80 & Puglie Region, Bari, Italy, 82; sculptures (five), Valadier Inst, Rome, Italy 84; sculpture, Colaco Real Estate/Land Developer, Calif, 90. *Exhib:* Pop Art in Italy, Palazzo Collicola, 80 & Norma Jean, Mus Mod Art, 82, Spoleto, Italy; Tribute to Man Ray, Art Inst, Rome, Italy, 81; Visioni Imperiali, Cortina Inst, Rome Italy, 90; Arte Rome 90, Palazzo Del Congressi, Italy. *Collection Arranged:* Guido Io Vorrei, Palazzo Ducale Mantova, 93; Messuno Tocchi Caino, Gillo Dorfles, European Parliament, Bruxelles, 93; Palazzo Esposizioni, Rome, 94; Contact Duccio Trombadori (catalog), Galleria Cortina, Rome, 93. *Awards:* Eight Premio Pittura, Martina Franca, Salvatore Basile, 80. *Bibliog:* Carmine Benincasa (auth), La Tavola Di Paro, Selecta, 6/79; Ruggero Marino (auth), Pop Art Don't Surrender, Il Tempo, 5/80; Arturo Carlo Quintavalle (auth), L'Assassino ê IL Mercante, Corriere Della Sera, 2/88. *Publ:* Next-Contact, Gillo Dorfles, Joyce E Co, Rome, 93; Principali Mostre in Italia, City Hall, Rome-Palazzo Deue Esposizioni-Rome, Italy, 93; Quelli Che Contano Those Who Count, Marsilio Editori, Venice, 94. *Mailing Add:* 120 Morningside Dr San Francisco CA 94132

MANES, BELLE
PAINTER
b New York, NY. *Study:* Cooper Union, BFA, 78. *Hon Degrees:* Cooper Union, BFA. *Work:* General Electric, Unimin Corp; Pfizer Chemical; Cochran Corp; Chubb Insurance; Sanford Bernstein & Sons. *Exhib:* Katonah Gallery, Conn, 88, 2001; Art Place Gallery, Conn, 92; Faber Birren Color Award Show, Conn, 93 & 94, 2002; Broome St Gallery, NY, 95; Lehman Coll Gallery, NY, 96; Northern Westchester Ctr for Arts, 2002; Flinn Gallery, Conn, 2005; Hammond Mus, 2007; Brooklyn Mus, 2007. *Teaching:* Instr art, Plainfield Community Ctr, NJ, 56-59 & privately, White Plains, NY, 62-64; mentor, Pratt Inst, 78. *Awards:* Medal Honor, Nat Asn Women Artists, 79; Top Silvermine Award, New England Show, 81. *Bibliog:* Johnathan Goodman (auth), Belle Manes at Branchville SOHO, Art News, 3/94; Vivian Raynor (auth), Artists and curators with country roots, NY Times, 1/95; William Zimmer (auth), Community expressed in mixed media, NY Times, 12/95; Sally Aldrich (auth), Katonah Mus, Interviewing Belle Manes, 2001. *Mem:* Nat Asn Women Artists; Silvermine Guild; Contemporary Artists Guild. *Media:* Oil, Acrylic. *Dealer:* Branchville Soho Gallery RR Sta Rtes 7 & 102 Ridgefield CT 06829. *Mailing Add:* 1097 North St White Plains NY 10605

MANGEL, BENJAMIN
DEALER
b Philadelphia, Pa, Jan 12, 1925. *Pos:* Owner, Benjamin Mangel Gallery, Philadelphia, Pa. *Specialty:* Contemporary paintings and sculpture. *Mailing Add:* 1108 Saint Andrews Rd 1714 Rittenhouse Sq Bryn Mawr PA 19010-1936

MANGEL, DEBORAH T
ART DEALER, CURATOR
b Philadelphia, Pa. *Study:* Temple Univ, BA (art hist, summa cum laude). *Collection Arranged:* Annual Holliday Crafts Exhib, Paley Mus PCT & S, Philadelphia, 92-; one screen 2 souls 4 Hands (with catalog), Art in City Hall, Philadelphia, 96. *Pos:* Pres, Mangel Gallery, Philadelphia, 70-, Pa Acad Fine Arts, 83; dir mus shop, Paley Design Ctr PCT & S, Philadelphia, 92-. *Bibliog:* Karen Heller (auth), The art of the sale, Philadelphia Inquirer, 9/17/89; Edward J Solanski (auth), Art, Philadelphia Inquirer, 10/18/96; Edward Higgins (auth), Leader of a New Movement, Art Matters, 10-96. *Mem:* Friends Philadelphia Mus Art; Collector's Circle, Pa Acad Fine Arts, Philadelphia; Arts Adv Bd, Univ City Sci Ctr, Philadelphia. *Specialty:* Contemporary art. *Mailing Add:* 1108 St Andrews Rd Bryn Mawr PA 19010

MANGLANO-OVALLE; IÑIGO
SCULPTOR
b Madrid, Spain, 1961. *Study:* Williams Col, Mass, BA (art hist), 83; Art Inst Chicago, MFA (sculpture), 89. *Work:* Mus Contemp Art, MacArthur Found, First Nat Bank & Linc Group, Chicago; Bohen Found, NY. *Exhib:* Solo exhibs, Assigned Identities, Centre Gallery, Miami-Dade Col, Fla, 91, Balsero, Mus Contemp Art, Chicago, 97, WooferWoofer, Contemp Arts Ctr, Cincinnati, Ohio, 97, The El Nino Effect, ArtPace Found Contemp Art, San Antonio, Tex, 97, Garden of Delights, Southeastern Ctr Arts, Winston-Salem, NC, 98, Inst Vis Arts, Univ Wis, Milwaukee, 99, Max Protetch Gallery, New York City, 00, 03, Cranbrook Art Mus, Bloomfield Hills, Mich, 01, Barcelona Pavilion, Mies van der Rohe Found, Barcelona, 02; From America's Studio: Drawing New Conclusions & Los Encuentros, Betty Reimer Gallery, Art Inst Chicago, Ill, 92; Bookmarks, Northern Ill Univ Art Gallery, 92; Latin Am Art in Miami Collections, Lowe Art Mus, Univ Miami, Fla, 94; Xicano Progeny: Redefining the Aesthetic - Towards a New Vision of Am Cult, Mex Mus, San Francisco, 95; Correspondences/Korrespondenzen, Chicago Cult Ctr, 95; Art in Chicago 1945-1995, Mus Contemp Art, Ill, 96; Contemp Art Collections, Nelson Fine Arts Ctr, Ariz State Univ Art Mus, Phoenix, 98; Mus Contemp Art, San Diego, 00; Whitney Mus Am Art, New York City, 01; Mus Modern Art QNS, Long Island City, NY, 02; and many others. *Collection Arranged:* The Bohen Found, NYC; Guggenheim Found, NYC; MacArthur Found, Chicago; Whitney Mus Am Art; Art Inst Chicago; Mus Contemporary Art, Chicago & San Diego; ArtPace, San Antonio; Metrop Bank and Trust Collection, Highland Hills, Ohio; The Refco Collection, Chicago; The Linc Collection, Chicago; Fundacion Cisneros, Caracas, Venezuela. *Awards:* Artist Fel Award, Ill Arts Coun, 92 & Spec Proj Award, 93; Visual Artist Fel, Nat Endowment Arts, 95; Int Artist Residency Fel, ArtPace Found, San Antonio, 97; Media Arts Residency, Henry Art Gallery, Univ Wash, Seattle, 98-00; Media Arts Award, Wexner Ctr for the Arts, Columbus, Ohio, 97-01; John D and Catherine T MacArthur Found Fel, 01. *Bibliog:* Bonnie Clearwater (auth), Studio Visit, Trans, Vol 1, No 3 & 4, 97; Victor Zamudio-Taylor (auth), Where is the bleeding heart?, Atlantica, No 15, 82-91, spring 97; Miwon Kwon (auth), For Hamburg: Public art and urban identities, Kunst auf Schritt und tritt, image pg 95, Kulutrbehorde Hamburg, 97. *Mailing Add:* c/o Max Protech Gallery 245 8th Ave New York NY 10011

MANGO, ROBERT J
PAINTER
b Chicago, Ill, Jan 20, 1951. *Study:* Art Inst Chicago, 65-69; Univ Ill, BFA, 70-73, MFA, 75-76; Univ NMex, MFA, 73-74. *Work:* Pvt corp & pub collections throughout the US & Europe. *Exhib:* Solo exhibs, Loyola Univ Art Gallery, 79, Merchants Manufactures Club Am, Chicago, 81, Gallerie Chastain, NMex, 83, Dillon Gallery,

NY, 95, Gallery Radost, Prague, Czech Repub, 97, Gallerie Orangerie, St Paul de Vence, France, 97 & Gallerie Miro, Prague, Czech, 98. *Pos:* Owner & dir, Neo Persona Gallery, NY, 83-90. *Teaching:* Instr, Thorthan Community Col, 75-77, Seton Hall Univ, East Orange, NJ, 82-84 & Caldwell Col, Montclair, NJ, 84; dept head sculpture, Loyola Univ, Chicago, 77; Seton Hall Univ, E Orange, NJ, 82-84. *Bibliog:* Scott MacMillan (auth), Is It Art? (interview), Prague Bus J, 6/97; Prague Post Rev, 6/97; Robert Forrester, Jr (auth), Theshold Prague Rev, 6/97. *Mailing Add:* 178 Duane St New York NY 10013

MANGOLD, SYLVIA PLIMACK
PAINTER
b New York, NY, Sept 18, 1938. *Study:* Cooper Union, cert, 1959; Yale Univ Art Sch, BFA, 1961. *Work:* Albright-Knox Art Gallery, Buffalo, NY; Yale Univ Art Gallery; Mus Mod Art, Whitney Mus Am Art, NY; Weatherspoon Art Gallery, Greensboro, NC; Walker Art Ctr, Minneapolis, Minn; Utah Mus Fine Arts; Brooklyn Mus; Detroit Inst Art. *Exhib:* Solo shows incl Young Hoffman Gallery, Chicago, 1980, Nocturnal Paintings, Contemp Arts Mus, Houston, 1981, Paintings, Brooke Alexander Inc, 1982, 1984, 1986, 1989, 1992 & 1995, Rhona Hoffman Gallery, 1985, Tex Gallery, Houston, Brooke Alexander, NY, Fuller Goldeen Gallery, San Francisco, 1987, Annemarie Verna Galerie, Zurich, 1991 & 1997 New Van Straaten Gallery, Chicago, 1992, Herbert F Johnson Mus Art, Cornell Univ, NY, 1998, Alexander & Bonin, NY, 2000 & 2003; group shows incl A Contemp View of Nature, Aldrich Mus, Ridgefield, 1986-87; 15th Anniversary, Flander's Contemp Art, Minneapolis, 1987; Annemarie Verna Galerie, Zurich, 1988, Measure/Mass, 2001, Retrospektiv III, 2002; Landscape Anthology, Grace Borgenicht Gallery, NY, 1988; The Unnatural Landscape, Fay Gold Gallery, Atlanta, 1988; The Transformative Vision; Contemp Am Landscape Painting, Three Rivers Arts Festival, Pittsburgh; Making Their Mark, Women Artists Move into the Mainstream, 1970-1985, Cincinnati Art Mus, New Orleans Mus Art, Denver Art Mus & Pa Acad Fine Art, 1989; A Decade of Am Drawing 1980-1989, Daniel Weinberg Gallery, Los Angeles, 1989; Yale Collects Yale, 1950-1993, Yale Univ Art Gallery, Conn, 1993; Building a Collection, Mus Fine Arts, Boston, 1993; Block/Plate/Stone: What a Print Is, traveling, 1994; Inspired by Nature, Neuberger Mus Art, Purchase, NY, 1994; Karo Dame, Aargauer Kunsthaus Aarau, Austria, 1995; Private Worlds, Aspen Art Mus, Colo, 1996-97; Queens Artists, Queens Mus Art, NY, 1997; Selections from the Collection, Mus Mod Art, NY, 1997; Afterimage, Mus Contemp Art, Los Angeles, 1999, WACK! Art & the Feminist Revolution, 2007; Alexander & Bonin, NY, 1999, Still, 2000, (Self) Portraits, 2001, Land & Sea, 2003, Early Works 1965-75, 2004; Northern Light, Danese Gallery, NY, 2002; Ann Exhib, Nat Acad Design, 2002, 2006; Lyrical Landscapes, Widener Gallery, Trinity Col, Hartford, Conn, 2003; Mirror Tenses, Univ Gallery, Fine Arts Ctr, Univ Mass, Amherst, 2003; Watercolor Worlds, Dorsky Gallery, Long Island City, NY, 2004; Picasso to Thiebaud, Cantor Ctr for Visual Arts, Stanford Univ, Calif, 2004; Building & Breaking the Grid, Whitney Mus Am Art, NY, 2005; Incorrigible, Sentimental, Kerlin Gallery, Dublin, 2005; Plane Figure, Kunstmuseum Winterthur, 2006; Twice Drawn, Tang Teaching Mus & Art Gallery, Skidmore Col, NY, 2006; Ann Exhib of Contemp Am Art, Nat Acad Mus, NY, 2007; LeWitt x 2, traveling, 2007-08. *Pos:* Sr painting critic, Yale Univ, 1995-98 & 2000. *Teaching:* Instr drawing, Sch Visual Arts, New York, 1970, instr painting, 1970-71 & 1974-82. *Awards:* Nat Endowment for the Arts Fel, 1974; Edwin P Palmer Mem Prize, Nat Acad Mus, NY, 2006, William A Paton Prize, 2007; Cooper Union Pres's Citation for Art, NY, 2007; Paintings, Sculpture, Works on Paper Award, Am Acad Arts & Letts, 2010. *Bibliog:* Michael Florescu (auth), Sylvia Plimack Mangold, Arts Mag, 3/1984; Michael Brenson (auth), Sylvia Plimack Mangold, New York Times, 11/22/1985; Jeanne Silverthorne (auth), Sylvia Plimack Mangold, Brooke Alexander Gallery, Artforum, 3/1986; Kenneth Baker (auth), Gestures that work or don't, San Francisco Chronicle, 5/12/1987; John L Ward (auth), American realist painting, 1945-1980, UMI Research Press, Ann Arbor, Mich, 1989. *Mem:* Nat Acad. *Media:* Oil, Drawings. *Publ:* Auth, Inches and Field, Lapp Princess Press Ltd, New York, 1978; Project for Artforum, two moods, Sylvia Plimack Mangold, Artforum, 2/1988. *Dealer:* Alexander & Bonin 132 Tenth Avenue New York NY 10011

MANGOLTE, BABETTE M
FILMMAKER, PHOTOGRAPHER
b Montmorot, France, Oct 11, 1941. *Study:* La Sorbonne, Paris, BA, 64; Ecole Nat Photographique & Cinematographie, Paris, 64-66. *Work:* Mus Mod Art, NY; Mus G Pompidou, Paris; New York Pub Libr; Australian Nat Libr, Canberra. *Pos:* Assoc prof, Visual Arts Dept, Univ Calif, San Diego, 89-. *Awards:* Prix de la Lumiere, Toulon Film Festival, France, 75; CAPS Fel, NY, 76; Pre-production Grant, NY State Coun Arts, 86. *Mem:* Asn Independent Video & Filmmakers; Media Alliance. *Mailing Add:* 319 Greenwich St New York NY 10013-3339

MANHART, MARCIA Y
ADMINISTRATOR, CURATOR
b Wichita, Kans, Jan 14, 1943. *Study:* Univ Ariz, Tucson, with Maurice Grossman, 62; Univ Tulsa, Okla, with Duayne Hatchett, Tom Manhart & Alexandre Hogue, BA, 65, MA, 71. *Work:* Okla State Art Collection, Okla Arts Ctr, Oklahoma City; Ark Arts Ctr, Little Rock; Fred Jones Mem Mus Art, Univ Okla, Norman; Philbrook Mus Art, Tulsa; Univ Tulsa. *Exhib:* Southwestern Craftsmen Biennial, Mus Int Folk Art, Santa Fe, NMex, 65, 67, 71 & 75; Craftsmen USA '66, Dallas Mus Fine Arts, Tex, 66; Ceramic Nat, Everson Mus, Syracuse, NY, 68; Manharts, Fred Jones Mem Mus Art, Norman, Okla, 73; Ceramics Invitational, Little Gallery, Mus Contemp Crafts, NY, 74; Ann Print, Drawing & Crafts Exhib, Ark Arts Ctr, Little Rock, 74 & 76. *Collection Arranged:* Our Oklahoma Indian Heritage: The Old Ways, 76; Traders Cargo from the China Sea: The Gillert Collection of Southeast Asian Ceramics, 78; Nature's Forms--Nature's Forces: The Art of Alexandre Hogue, 84; The Eloquent Object, 87; The Sanford and Diane Besser Collection, 92. *Pos:* Dir, Alexandre Hogue Gallery, Univ Tulsa, Okla, 67-69; dir educ, Philbrook Art Ctr, Tulsa, 72-77, asst dir, 77-83, actg dir, 83-84, exec dir, 84-. *Awards:* One-man Award, Southwestern Crafts Biennial, Mus Int Folk Art, 71; George Wittenborn Mem Award; Harwelden Award, Tulsa Arts & Humanities Coun, 89. *Bibliog:* Garth Bethel (auth), Manharts, Craft Horizons, 74; Research and education, In: Your Portable Museum, Am Crafts Coun, 75; John Conrad (auth), Contemporary Ceramic Technique, Prentice-Hall, 79. *Mem:* Art Mus Asn; Asn Art Mus Dirs. *Media:* Clay, Porcelain. *Res:* Contemporary art in craft media. *Publ:* Auth, Alexandre Hogue: Nature's Forms/Nature's Forces, 84; The Search is Over Enter Janet Kardon, Art Today, 89; A Neglected History: 20th Century American Craft, 90; Objects and Drawings, The Sanford and Diane Besser Collection, 92; Charting a new educational vision-craft in the machine age (essay), 94. *Mailing Add:* Philbrook Art Ctr PO Box 52510 Tulsa OK 74152

MANHART, THOMAS ARTHUR
EDUCATOR, CERAMIST
b Canon City, Colo, July 16, 1937. *Study:* Univ Hawaii; Univ Tulsa, BA & MA. *Work:* Ark Arts Ctr, Little Rock; Fred Jones Mem Art Mus, Univ Okla, Norman; Philbrook Art Ctr, Tulsa; Okla State Art Collection, Okla Art Ctr, Oklahoma City; Tulsa Performing Arts Ctr, Okla. *Exhib:* Nat Decorative Arts Exhib, Wichita, Kans, 61, 64 & 66; Southwestern Crafts Biennial, Santa Fe, NMex, 65, 72 & 75; Craftsmen USA, Dallas & NY, 66; Regional Prints, Drawings & Crafts Exhib, Little Rock, 67 & 75; Nat Craftsmen's Exhib, Wichita, 68, 70 & 72. *Pos:* State rep, Am Craft Coun, 66. *Teaching:* Instr ceramics, Univ Tulsa, 61-68, asst prof, 69-73, assoc prof, 74-91, prof, 91-. *Awards:* Nat Decorative Arts Exhib Medal of Honor, Wichita Art Asn, 66; Nat Merit Award, Craftsmen USA, Am Crafts Coun, 66; Okla State Art Collection, Okla Arts & Humanities Coun, 73. *Bibliog:* Gar Bethel (auth), Manharts, Craft Horizons, 74; Okla designer craftsmen exhib, Ceramics Monthly, 75. *Mem:* Am Crafts Coun; Okla Designer Craftsmen; Tulsa Designer Craftsmen (pres, 68). *Media:* Clay and Fibers. *Publ:* Contribr, Profile, Am Crafts Coun, 60; Craft Horizons, 66, 68 & 74-75, Cimarron Rev, 69, Tulsa Univ Alumni Mag, 69 & Ceramics Monthly, 75. *Mailing Add:* 5318 E Fifth St Tulsa OK 74112-2812

MANHOLD, JOHN HENRY
SCULPTOR
b Rochester, NY; Aug 20, 1919. *Study:* Univ Rochester, BA; Washington Univ, St Louis, MA; New Sch, with Chaim Gross & Manolo Pasqual; also with Ward Mount. *Work:* City of West Orange, NJ; Memorial Sloan-Kettering Hosp, NY; Pyrofilm Corp, Whippany, NJ; A J Levera Assocs, Madison, NJ; Jacques Piccard Inst, Bern, Switz; Toyotara Yamada collection, Nagoya, Japan; Allen Hofricter collection, NY; Sass Mus, Albuquerque, NMex. *Comn:* Bronze bust, Kallman Assocs, Jersey City, NJ; four bronze busts, Coll Med & Dentistry NJ, Newark, 69-70 & 78; bronze figure, Bernard Koven, 71; bronze bust, SASS Mus, Albuquerque, NMex, 2004. *Exhib:* Group exhibs, Allied Artists Am, 66; Audubon Artists Am, 67-69; Mainstreams '68 & '71, Grover M Hermann Fine Arts Ctr, Ohio, 68 & 71; Nat Sculpture Soc, 69; Am Artists Prof League, 70-72; and others. *Pos:* Dir sculpture, Ringwood Manor Asn Arts, 68-70, 1st vpres, 70-71. *Teaching:* semester course, Introductory Sculpture, Univ S Fla, 2010; Pvt instr, currently. *Awards:* Medal Honor, Sculpture, State of NJ, 68; First Prize, Paris Int, 70; Second Prize Patrons Award, Painters & Sculptors Soc NJ, 71; John Subkis Award, Nat Arts Club, 71; and others. *Bibliog:* David Leis (auth), Pictures in Life Mag, 69; Pierre Morand (auth), La section Americaine de la Salon del'arte Francaise, La Rev Mod, 70; Ruth Ann Williams (auth), Art of the Oranges, NJ Music & Art, 72. *Mem:* Acad Artists Asn; Am Artists Prof League; Nat Arts Club; Knickerbocker Artists; West Valley Art Mus (2006). *Media:* Marble, Bronze. *Interests:* Precious metals, jewelry

MANILOW, LEWIS
COLLECTOR, PATRON
b Chicago, Ill, Aug 11, 1927. *Pos:* Pres, Mus Contemp Art Chicago, 76-81; mem of bd, Beaubourg Found, 78-. *Collection:* Contemporary art, Mannerist prints and Turkish rugs

MANN, C GRIFFITH
CURATOR
Study: Williams Coll, BA (hist & art hist), 1991; Johns Hopkins Univ, MA (art hist), 1995, PhD (hist medieval art), 2002; Mus Leadership Inst; 2006, J Paul Getty Mus, LA, CCL Fel, 2011. *Collection Arranged:* Mything Persons: Historic Figures in Legends East & West, Walters Art Mus, Baltimore, 1998, The Book of Kings: Art, War & the Morgan Library's Medieval Picture Bible, 2002-03, Sacred Arts & City Life: The Glory of Medieval Novgorod, 2005-06, Treasures of Heaven: Saints, Relics, and Devotion in Medical Europe, The Cleveland Mus Art, The Walters Mus, The British Mus, 2010-2011. *Pos:* From asst to full cur medieval art, Walters Art Mus, Baltimore, formerly, co-dir curatorial div, formerly, asst dir curatorial affairs & dir curatorial div, 2007-08; chief cur, Cleveland Mus Art, 2008-2010; deputy dir and chief cur, 2010-. *Mem:* AAM; AAMC; CAA; ICMA; ICOM. *Publ:* Treasures of Heaven: Saints, Relics, and Devotion in Medieval Europe, New Haven: Yale Univ Press, 2010; Exporting China: The Collecting Tastes of William and Henry Walters, Collecting China: The World, China, and a History of Collecting, Vimalin Rujivarcharakul, Univ Del Press, 2010; Oxford Dictionary of the Middle Ages, Robert Bjork, ed. Oxford Univ Press, 2010. *Mailing Add:* The Metropolitan Museum of Art Dept Medieval Art and The Cloisters 1000 Fifth Ave New York NY 10028

MANN, CURTIS
PHOTOGRAPHER
b Dayton, Ohio, 1979. *Study:* Univ Dayton, BS (mechanical engring), 2002; Columbia Coll, MFA, 2008. *Exhib:* Solo exhibs, O Gallery, Univ Dayton, 2005, Kusseneers Gallery, Antwerp, 2008, Mus Contemp Art, Chicago, 2009; Hokin Gallery, Columbia Coll, Chicago, 2007; Are We There Yet, Hyde Park Art Ctr, Chicago, 2008; MP3 II: Midwest Photographers Project, Mus Contemp Photog, Chicago, 2009; Whitney Biennial, Whitney Mus Am Art, 2010. *Awards:* Nat Crystal Apple Award, Soc Photog Educ, 2006; Weisman Project Grant, Columbia Coll, Chicago, 2008; Leopold Godwosky Jr Award, Boston Univ, 2009. *Bibliog:* Alan Artner (auth), Journeying

Beyond a Vacation, Chicago Tribune, 8/2008; Margaret Hawkins (auth), Mann's Altered Photos Reflect, Chicago Sun Times, 2/2009; Cate McQuaid (auth), All the Way Down to the Details, Boston Globe, 4/2009. *Mailing Add:* Kavi Gupta Gallery 835 W Washington Blvd Chicago IL 60607

MANN, FRANK
PAINTER, GRAPHIC ARTIST
b Washington, DC, Apr 22, 1950. *Study:* George Wash Univ, Washington, with painter Gene Davis, BS, 79; Pratt Inst, Brooklyn, NY, MFA, 82. *Work:* Mus Mod Art, NY; Guggenheim Mus, NY; Corcoran Gallery Art, Washington; Nationalgalerie, Berlin, Ger; Mus contemp Art, Nice, France. *Comn:* Window drawing, Artist's Space, NY, 89; mural, Dept Cult Affairs, NY, 90; mural, NY State Coun Arts, Binghamton, NY, 90; outdoor mural, Art Around Park, NY, 92; Project for St. Cyrits Church, NY, 97. *Exhib:* Contemp Sensibilities, Cie, Mod et Contemporain, Paris, France, 91; Painting Today, Mus Mod Art, Buenos Aires, Arg, 91; First Int Biennial, Trevi Flash Art Mus Int Contemp Art, Trevi, Italy, 98; Similar Shapes in Painting and Sculpture, Walter Wickiser Gallery, NY, 98; Venice Italy Palazzo Correra a Santa Fosca, Italy, 98; Printmaking Today, Corcoran Gallery Art, Washington; Driven to Abstraction (invitational), Brother Chapman Gallery, I and Col, New Rochelle, NY, 2005. *Pos:* Exec dir, Collab Projs, NY, 87-88; proj dir, Basic Arts Network, NY, 91-92; bd dir, Artist Equity, NY, 2000-01; vpres, Artists Equity, NY, 2003-2005; vpres, The Am Soc of Contemp Artists, NY, 2003-2005. *Teaching:* Guest lectr, Corcoran Sch Art, Washington, 78-79, Pa State Univ, Reading, 86-87, Pratt Inst, Brooklyn, 87-88 & Parsons Sch Art & Design, NY, 96-97; Parsons Sch of Design The New Sch Univ, NY, 96-99; Pvt Studio Instr, Painting and Drawing, 98-present; guest lectr, Iona Col, New Rochelle, NY, 2005. *Awards:* NY State Coun Arts, 89; Nat Endowment Arts, New Arts Prog, 89; New York City Dept Cult Affairs, 90; The Lorenzo IC Maonifico Medal in Painting, Biennale Invt'l Dell'Ante Contemporanea, Florence, Italy, 2001. *Bibliog:* Marcello Llorens (auth), Frank Mann, Mind of a Visionary, Art Al Dia, NY, 90; Mitchell Corber (dir), Eye of the Painter (film, 28 minutes), Pub Broadcasting System, 91; Susan Scutti, Painting the Velocity of Intuition, Cover Mag, 43, Vol 12, No 2; Franklin Sirman's, Notes to an Exhib, ASCA Art Bulletin, 2004. *Mem:* Drawing Soc, NY; Artists Equity, NY; Collab Projs, NY (prog dir, 87-88); Am Soc Contemp Artists, NY; Contemp Artists Guild, NY; The Assoc D' Art Int'l, Mirabel, France. *Media:* Oil on Canvas. *Publ:* contribr, Works of Art on Paper with George Nelson Preston, Mus Mod Art, Buenos Aires, 90 Night Rider, illustrated, Redstone Press, 90; Midnight Review, Rio Arts Proj, 91; illusr, Nerves, Domestic Press, New York, 91; contribr, Contemporary sensibilities, Cie Modern et Contemporain, Paris, France, 91; The Optical Machine: Some Observations on Artistic Vision, nap text(s), Vol 3, No 1, p 1, 98; ASCA, The Am Soc of Contemporary Artists, (Essay), 2003. *Dealer:* Walter Wickiser 568 Broadway New York NY 10012; Kim Foster Gallery, 529 West 20th St, 1st FL, NY, NY, 10011. *Mailing Add:* 212 E 34th St No 3E New York NY 10016

MANN, JAMES ROBERT
CURATOR, CRITIC
b Columbia, SC, Oct 5, 1956. *Study:* The Citadel, BA, 78; Univ SC, PhD, 85. *Collection Arranged:* Art After Post-Modernism, 97; George Sturman Collection of African Art (auth, catalog), 98; Domenic Cretara Retrospective Exhibition, 98; Wm Thomas Thompson Retrospective Exhibition, 98; Asian Art Now, 2000; Eli Leven Retrospective Exhibition (auth, catalog), 2000. *Teaching:* prof Am Poetry, Fed Univ Rio de Janeiro, Brazil, 87-88; prof Brit Poetry, Catholic Univ Arg, Buenos Aires, 88-89; lectr Am Culture, Univ Grenoble, France, 90-91. *Publ:* auth, Metaphysical Ptg of Lani Irwin, Am Arts Quart, 94, Bruno Civitico' s Paintings, 95; auth, catalog, Holocaust Exhibition, Las Vegas Art Mus, 98. *Mailing Add:* Las Vegas Art Museum Ste 100 3065 S Jones Blvd Las Vegas NV 89146

MANN, JEAN (ADAH)
CERAMIST, SCULPTOR
b Schenectady, NY, June 27, 1927. *Study:* Mannes Coll Music; Hunter Coll, sculpture with Irma Rothstein; Donald Mavros Studio, 4 yr apprenticeship, 64, Chinese Brush painting with Jongsoon Chung, Kiln Building and pottery with Gerry Williams; Glaze Chemistry with Yvonne LaFean & Dr Louis Navias. *Hon Degrees:* Master Craftsmen/Educator, Soc for Connecticut Crafts, Conn. *Work:* Metrop Mus Art, NY; Smithsonian Inst Hist & Technol Dept, Washington, DC; Mus Art & Archeol, Univ Mo, Columbia; Mus Haaretz, Ceramics Mus, Tel Aviv, Israel; Everson Mus Art, Syracuse, NY; Yale Univ Art Gallery, 10 pieces, New Haven, Conn; Martin Luther King Jr Ctr Non-Violent Social Change, Atlanta; Hammond Mus, North Salem, NY; Southern Conn, New Haven; Schenectady Mus, Schenectady, NY; Housatonic Mus Art, Bridgeport, Conn; Cyrenius Booth Libr, Newtown, Conn. *Exhib:* Solo exhibs, Hammond Mus, North Salem, NY, 75, 77, 82, 85, 88-89, 93-95, 99, 2001, Silvermine Guild, New Caanan, Director's Choice Invitational, Conn, 76 & 2000, The Galerie, Chester, Conn, 81 & 82, GWS Gallery, Southport, Conn, 87, Atelier Gallery, New Milford, Conn, 89, Weslayan Potters, Middletown, Conn, 89 & Variations, Riverton, Conn, 92; Silvermine Guild, New Canaan, Conn, 76-; Mark Twain Libr Art Show, Redding, Conn, 84-91; Mendelson Gallery, Washington Depot, Conn, 87; Exhib Contemp Netsuke, Yamada Co, Tokyo, Japan, 88; Ceramics - The Oriental Influence, Farmington Valley Ctr, Fisher Gallery, 89; Cyrenius Booth Lib, Newtown, Conn, 2003; Cyrenius Booth Libr, 2008; Barn Gallery, 2009, 2010, 2011, 2012, & 2013. *Pos:* Artist & studio tchr. *Teaching:* Wheel, hand methods, sculpture, carving porcelain & painting with underglazing, Rescue: Vis Artist Prog, Danbury & Southbury, Conn, 69; carving porcelain, Brookfield Craft Ctr, Conn, 81-82; demonstrator Netsuke carving, George Walter Vincent Smith Art Mus, Springfield, Mass, 84; Phoenix Workshop, Goffstown, NH; co-instr with Gerry Williams, Adult Edn, Newtown Heritage Village, The Kick Wheel Studio, New Fairfield, Conn. *Awards:* Artist Award, The Galerie, Conn Comn Arts, 81; Master Craftsman & Educator, Soc Conn Crafts, 96; Society of Creative Arts of Newtown Award, SCAN Annual Juried Show, 2004; Andrew J Alexander Award, Candlewood League of Artists, 2006. *Bibliog:* Betty K Leavitt (auth), Netsuke-She, J Int Netsuke Collectors Soc, 83; Betty K Leavitt & C Randall (coauths), Netsuke: Superlative Pieces, Netsuke Kenkyukai Conv, 83; Diane Dowling (dir), Artist Jean Mann (film), Com Cast, 89; and others. *Mem:* Silvermine Guild; Am Crafts Coun; Brookfield Craft Ctr; Soc Conn Crafts; New Haven Paint & Clay Club; Oriental Brush Artists Guild; Candlewood League of Artists; Kent Art Assoc (elected artist). *Media:* Porcelain. *Specialty:* porcelain, wall sculptures. *Interests:* Carving, reading, photography. *Publ:* Auth, Tools for Carving Porcelain, Vol 4 No 1, 78, winter 75-76 & Highfired Copper Reds on Porcelain, Vol 8 No 1, 23, winter 79-80, The Studio Potter; photo & ltr, Arts of Asia, 9-10/92; interview & photo, The Studio Potter, Vol 25 No 1, 97, 12/96. *Dealer:* Barn Gallery New Fairfield CT; Silvermine Guild New Canaan CT. *Mailing Add:* c/o The Kick Wheel 154 State Rte 39 Danbury CT 06812-4203

MANN, KATINKA
SCULPTOR, PHOTOGRAPHER
b New York, NY, June 28, 1925. *Study:* Univ Hartford Art Sch, Conn; Pratt Graphic Arts, New York. *Work:* Brooklyn Mus, Guggenheim Mus, Mus Mod Art Study Collection, New York; Polaroid Int Corp, Boston; Williamsburg Savings Bank & Russ Togs Inc, New York; San Francisco Mus Mod Art; Islip Art Mus; Heckscher Mus, Huntington, NY; Hillwood Art Mus, Greenvale, NY; Muhlenberg Coll, Allentown, Pa; Am Abstr Artists Print Portfolio 50th & 60th Anniv. *Exhib:* Solo exhibs, Cent Hall Gallery, 74-84, Hansen Gallery, New York, 76-79 & Heckscher Mus, Huntington, NY, 77 & 84, AIR Gallery, Ulrich Mus Art, Konica Gallery, Tokyo, Art Gallery Port Washington Libr, NY, 96, Space 504 Gallery, New York, 98 & Heckscher Mus Art, Bryant Libr, Roslyn, NY, 2001; Aldrich Mus Contemp Art, 78; Ulrich Mus Art, Wichita, Kans; NJ State Mus, Trenton; Nikon, NY; Konica Gallery, Tokyo, Japan; Condeso/Lawler Gallery, NY; Toward the New, Hillwood Art Mus, Allentown, Pa, 2000; Tabletop 2002, Hofstra Mus, Hempstead, NY; El Instituto Nacional de Bellas Artes, San Miguel de Allende, Mex, 2003; Artitst, Neighbors, Friends, Heckscher Mus Art, Huntington, NY, 2003; Earth Gallery, Rutherford, NJ, 2012. *Pos:* Co-chmn & bd mem, Prof Artists Guild, 72-73; treas, Am Abstr Artists, 89-96 & 2002-; Elizabeth Found Art, NY Studio Program, NY, 2009-. *Awards:* Judith Leiber Co Purchase Award, Soc Am Graphic Artists, 69; Polaroid Corp Award, 83; Residency, Marie Walsh Sharp Art Found, Space Prog, Brooklyn, 2008-2009, Elizabeth Foun Art, New York Studio Prog, New York, 2009-2013; Vega Residency, Va Ctr Creative Arts, Amherst, Va, 2013. *Bibliog:* Art in the World, Rinehart Press, 75; articles, NY Times, 77, 81, 85 & 96; Helen Harrison (auth), Photographs That Confound, Central Hall Gallery; Valerie Natsios (auth), Katinka Mann: An Alternative, NY Times; Phyllis Braff (auth), Originality Stands Out in Sculptural Variety; Helen Harrison, 2000 & Phillis Braff, 2001, NY Times; Am Abstr Artists Journal, #4, 2000; Janie Welker (auth, cur), Hechscher Mus Art, (exhib brochure), Huntington, NY, 2001; Hofstra Art Mus, Hempstead, NY, 2002; Martin Art Gallery, Women Artists, Past and Present, Catalog, 2002; The Morning Call, Go Art, Abstr Demand Attention, Feoff Gehman, 2002. *Mem:* Am Abstr Artists (treas, 89-96 & 2002-2013); Prof Artists Guild (vpres, 69-71); Artists Equity Asn; Prof Women Photogr. *Media:* Reliefs. *Dealer:* Central Hall Gallery 386 West Broadway New York NY 10012. *Mailing Add:* 290 9th Ave Apt 13H New York NY 10001

MANNINO, JOSEPH SAMUEL
SCULPTOR
b Chicago, Ill, 1950. *Study:* Knox Col, Galesburg, Ill, BFA, 1971; Southern Ill Univ, Carbondale, MFA, studied with Robert Arneson. *Work:* Crocker Art Mus, Sacramento, Calif; Renwick Gallery, Smithsonian Inst, Washington, DC; Southern Alleghenies Mus, Loretto, Pa; Univ Ala, Birmingham. *Exhib:* San Angelo Mus, Tex; Everson Mus Art, Syracuse, NY; Mus Modern Art, San Francisco, Calif; Bruce Gallery, Univ Pa, Edinboro, 2000; solo exhib, Arlington Arts Ctr, Va, Three Rivers Art Festival, Pittsburgh, Pa, Montpelier Cult Arts Ctr, Laurel, Md, Crocker Art Mus, Sacramento, Calif. *Teaching:* Instr, sculpture, ceramics, Carnegie-Mellon Univ, 86-. *Awards:* Individual Fel Award, Pa Coun Arts; Wash State Art Comn Award, Medical Lake, Wash; Artist-in-Residence Award, Kohler Arts Ctr, Sheboygan, Wis. *Mem:* Nat Coun on Educ for Ceramic Arts; Coll Art Asn; Soc of Sculptors, Pittsburgh, Pa. *Media:* Clay, Stoneware, Porcelain, Terra Cotta. *Specialty:* Large scale ceramic sculptures. *Mailing Add:* Carnegie Mellon University School of Art 5000 Forbes Ave Pittsburgh PA 15213

MANNOR, MARGALIT
PHOTOGRAPHER, CONCEPTUAL ARTIST
b Tel-Aviv, Israel, Nov 16, 1940. *Study:* Hebrew Univ, Israel, 60-63, Avni Inst Fine Arts, Tel Aviv, cert, 64-69; studied photography with Rae Russel, cert, NY, 76-77. *Work:* Brooklyn Mus, Mus City New York, Jewish Mus, NY Pub Libr, NY; Mus Fine Arts, Houston; Israel Mus, Jerusalem; Tel Aviv Mus, Israel; The British Mus, London; Haifa Mus Modern Art, Israel; Mishkan Le Omanut Ein Harod, Israel; Hudson River Mus, Yonkers, NY; Ashdod Mus, Coreine Maman Mus, Ashdod, Israel; Ashdod Art Mus, Monart Ctr, Ashdod, Israel; Bertha Urdang Collection, Jerusalem. *Exhib:* People 81, Hudson River Mus, Yonkers, NY, 81; Inaugural Exhib, Hudson River Mus, Yonkers, NY, 82 & Exhib, 83 & 85; Member Choice, Albright-Knox Art Gallery, Buffalo, NY, 86-92; solo exhibs, Ein Harod Mus, Israel, 91 & Negev Mus, Beer Sheva Israel, 95; Modern Times Through the Concerned Eye, Katonah Mus Art, 92; All-of-a-Piece, Katonah Mus Art, NY, 95; Photog, Mus Fine Arts, Houston, 96; Women of the World, A Global Collection of Art, White Columns Gallery, NY, 2000; Landscapes of Israel, The Jewish Mus, NY, 2000; photopleshet, The Corinne Maman Mus, Ashdod, Israel, 2003; The Philistines are Coming-Photography by Margalit Mannor, Yeshiva Univ Mus, NY, 2004; Inside No 6, Ashdod Art Mus, Monart Center, Ashdod, Israel, 2005; Bread, Daily & Divine, The Israel Mus, Jerusalem, 2006; Bread/Lechem, Yeshiva Univ Mus, New York, 2008; The Last Book, Mus Nat Libr Spain, Madrid, 2008, Nat Libr Argentina, 2008, Zurich, Swizerland, 2010; The Ten Plus Group-Myth and Reality, Tel-Aviv Mus Art, Israel, 2008; Floor Rag, Memoire de Lavenir, Paris, 2010; Souvenier Art, De Tournement, Scalamata Exhib Hall, Venice, Italy, 2009; Art to the Point, Katonah Mus Art, NY, 2012; The Spectrum of Sexuality, Hebrew Union Coll Mus, NY, 2012; 20th Anniv Israeli Branch of Internat Artists Mus, NY, 2013; Seventh Day Revisiting Shabbat, Hebrew Union Coll Mus, NY, 2014; Evil:

A Matter of Intent, Hebrew Union Coll Mus, NY, 2015. *Awards:* First Prize, Grand Prix Int, La Principalite de Monaco, 71; Solo Prize Photog, People 81, Hudson River Mus, 81; Photog Prize, All-of-a-Piece, Katonah Mus Art, 95. *Bibliog:* Donald Kuspit (auth), Margalit Mannor, Art Forum, NY, 9/90; Mordechai Omer (auth), The Presence of the Absent (exhib catalog), Tel Aviv Univ, 5/91; William Zimmer (auth), 51 selections out of 1000, NY Times, 6/11/95; Shlomit Shakked (auth), Beheaded Ready (exhib catalog), Bineth Gallery, Tel Aviv, 11/98; Calendar Art Selects(picture & text), The New York, 3/18/2008; Around Town(picture & text), Time Out New York, Feb 21-27, 2008; Sima Robinowitz (auth), Water-Stone Rev, A Literary Ann vol 12, Hamline Univ, Bread/Bred in Cocordance, 2009; Yeshiva University Museum: The First 35 Years (Picture & Text), 2010. *Media:* Mixed Media, Installation, Photography. *Interests:* June 2010 photographed the Design Mus Holon, Israel Archit by Ron Arad. *Mailing Add:* 28 Sage Terr Scarsdale NY 10583

MANOLAKAS, STANTON PETER
PAINTER
b Detroit, Mich, Jul 25, 1946. *Study:* Univ Southern Calif, BA, 69. *Work:* Marriott Corp, Newton, Mass; Bechtel Industries Corp Collection, San Francisco, Calif; Datum Inc, Anaheim, Calif; Callagher & Heffernan, San Francisco, Calif; Wolverine Bronze, Roseville, Mich. *Comn:* Historic Boston Suite, Marriott Corp, 87. *Exhib:* Los Angeles Co AFL-CIO Exhib, Calif, 82-90; Calif Traditional Artists, Mus Natural Hist, San Bernardino, 83; City Art Exhib, Millard Sheets Gallery, Pomona, Calif; Second Ann Southern Calif Hist Fair, Heritage Sq Mus, Los Angeles; Dossin Great Lakes Mus, Detroit, Mich; Featured Artist Grand Opening Ave Maris Gallery, Domino's Farms Ann Arbor Mich, 2000. *Awards:* First Place, Union Artist Exhibit, Los Angeles Co AFL-CIO, 89. *Bibliog:* Julia Ayres (auth), Paper the Critical Support, Watercolor 87 Am Artist, 1/87. *Media:* Watercolor. *Publ:* Auth, A Visual Odyssey Through America's Past, Watercolor 90 Am Artist, 9/90. *Dealer:* Gallery 131 Glendale CA; Art Angles Orange CA; Progressive Art & Frame Design Clawson MI. *Mailing Add:* 2500 Las Flores Dr Los Angeles CA 90041

MANSARAM, P
PHOTOGRAPHER, PAINTER
b Mount Abu, India, 1934. *Study:* Sir J J Sch Art, Bombay, India, 54-59; State Acad Fine Arts, Amsterdam, fel, 63; Ryerson Polytech, Toronto, Can, cert (motion picture prod), 70; visual studies workshop, Rochester. *Work:* Gemeente Mus, The Hague; Nat Gallery Mod Art, New Delhi, India; Mem Univ Gallery, St Johns, Nfld; NY Pub Libr; Art Gallery Mississauga; Air India, Electrografia Mus Int, Cuenca, Spain; Art Gallery of Hamilton, Royal Ontario Mus, Toronto. *Comn:* 8 posters on India destinations (lasergraphic images), comn by Air India; Faculty Club, McMaster Univ, 2004, Dhoomimal Art Gallery New Delhi, 2006, Ed Video Media Art Center, Guelph, 2012, JM (now Ashok jain) Gallery, NY, 2012, Art Gallery of Mississauga, 2013, A Space Galllery, Toronto, 2014, Center 3, Hamilton, 2015. *Exhib:* Solo exhibs, Gallery de Drie Hendricksen, Amsterdam, The Neth, 64, Burlington Art Ctr, 89, 95; Pundole Gallery, Bombay, India, 92; St Naubert Arts & Cult Ctr, Winnipeg, 97. *Awards:* First Prize, Bombay State Art Exhib, 59, First Prize, Colour & Form Soc award, Toronto, 75, Award of Recognition, by Mosaic, 2012. *Bibliog:* Manmohan Saral (auth), Kala Khete. *Mem:* Colour & Form Soc (pres, 78-79, lifetime mem); Bombay Art Soc, life mem. *Media:* Mixed Media, film and video. *Res:* Created Mansaram's Art of the Rocks, Site Specific Project in Progress, Mt Abu, India, 1997-. *Publ:* Contribr, Art-Life Mag, 2/4/86; Colour Documentation of 40th Anniversary Art Exhib of Color & Form Soc, Mississauga, 92; Lalit Kala Contemporary Mag, Issue 48, India; Kala Deergha Mag, 4/15/15. *Mailing Add:* 298 Gardenview Burlington ON L7T 1K6 Canada

MANSFIELD, ROBERT ADAMS
SCULPTOR, EDUCATOR
b Chicago, Ill, May 4, 1942. *Study:* Minneapolis Sch Art & Design, 61-62; St Cloud State Univ, BA, 68; Univ Mass, Amherst, MFA, 70. *Work:* Univ Mass, Amherst; Smith Coll Mus Art, Mass; San Diego State Univ; St Cloud State Univ, Minn. *Exhib:* Abstract Painting of 70's, DeCordova Mus, Lincoln, Mass, 71; Nat Juried Exhib, Austin Mus Art, 79; 13th Ann, Marietta Col, Ohio, 80; North Am Sculpture Exhib, Golden Coll Art Ctr, Colo, 80; Corpus Christi Coll Mus, Tex, 81; and others. *Collection Arranged:* New Directions, Univ Mass, 69; Twombly & Diao, Hampshire Col, 71; Arthur Hoener, San Diego State Univ, 76; Jerome Liebling Photographs, San Diego State Univ, 78. *Teaching:* Instr art, Smith Col, 70-71; asst prof art, Hampshire Col, 71-79; assoc prof art & head sculpture dept, San Diego State Univ, 76-. *Awards:* Second Prize, Southern Calif Expos, Del Mar, 77; Best of Show, Marietta Col, 80. *Bibliog:* Mary Vercauteren (auth), Robert Mansfield, Holyoke Transcript, 4/12/73; Edward Silver (auth), Elliptical construction, Advocate, 12/4/75; Susan Muchnic (auth), Sculpture is alive and well, Los Angeles Times, 1/22/79. *Mailing Add:* Sch Art Design & Art Hist San Diego State Univ 5500 Campanile Dr San Diego CA 92182-4805

MANSHIP, JOHN PAUL
PAINTER, SCULPTOR
b New York, NY, Jan 16, 1927. *Study:* Harvard Univ, AB, 48; with George Demetrios; Brera Acad, Milan. *Work:* Nat Collection Fine Arts, Washington, DC; Long Beach Art Mus, Calif; New Britain Mus, Conn; Hamilton Col, Clinton, NY. *Comn:* Baptism of Christ, Baptistry, St John Martyr, NY, 63; Pentecost (fresco), Chapel Sisters of St Joseph, Pawtucket, RI, 65; Stations of cross, St Clements Church, Warwick, RI, 66; Resurrection (with Margaret Cassidy), St Anthony's Church, Springfield, Mass, 71; portrait of Judge O'Connor, Worcester Co Courthouse, 72. *Exhib:* Newhouse Gallery, 82; Gallery on the Green, 88. *Pos:* Pres, Rockport Art Asn, 81-85. *Teaching:* Instr drawing & painting, Marymount Col, New York, 63; instr, Minnetonka Art Ctr, 78. *Awards:* Ranger Fund Purchase Award, Nat Acad Design, 65; Gold Medal, Burckhardt Acad, Rome, 78; Rockport Art Asn, 83 & 94; Nat Arts Club, 91; North Shore, 93. *Mem:* Am Watercolor Soc; Nat Soc Mural Painters (secy, 72-75); North Shore Art Asn (dir, 70-72); Artists Equity NY; Salmagundi Club; and others. *Media:* Oil, Watercolors; Bronze. *Publ:* Auth, Paul Claudel, Commonweal, 55; Raphael, Cath Encycl Youth, 64; Paul Manship, Abbeville, 90; Sculptors of Cape Ann, Nat Sculpture Mag, 97. *Dealer:* Leonarda di Mauro Gallery New York NY

MANSION, GRACIE
ART DEALER
b Braddock, Pa, Oct 22, 1946. *Study:* Clarion State Col, 64-66; Montclair State Col, BA, 79. *Exhib:* Small Works Show, 80 Wash Sq E, NY, 80; Neo York (collab with Judy Rifka), Univ Art Mus, Santa Barbara, 84. *Collection Arranged:* Harvard Bus Sch. *Pos:* Dir, Gracie Mansion Gallery, 82-. *Bibliog:* Peter Bach (auth), Gracie Mansion's Art Alive, Taxi Mag, 9/87; John Carlin (auth), Gracie's new mansion, Paper, 5/89; John Jost (dir), All the Vermeers in New York (film), 90 & (play & TV), 92. *Mem:* Art Table. *Specialty:* Contemporary art. *Publ:* Articles, Gracie Mansion, New York Talk, 9/84, 10/84 & 11/84; New York Woman Mag, 7-8/87, 9/87 & 4/88; Hope Batey & Deborah Gimelson, Gracie Mansion Manhattan Catalog, Fall/Winter

MANSPEIZER, SUSAN R
SCULPTOR
b New York, NY. *Study:* Art Students League, Corcoran Sch Art, 66-68; City Coll New York, BA, 62, MA, 66. *Work:* Greenburgh Pub Libr, Elmsford, NY; Off Bldg, Chappaqua, NY; Alumni & Friends of La Guardia High Sch. *Exhib:* New Members, Silvermine Guild Artists, New Canaan, Conn, 90; Hudson River Mus, Grace Glueck, Juror, Yonkers, NY, 90; Kirkland Art Ctr, Clinton, NY, 91; Southwest State Univ, Marshall, Minn, 91; Silvermine Guild of Artists, New Canaan, Conn, 92; Viridian Gallery, NY, 87, 90 & 93; two-person show, Berkshire Artisans, Pittsford, Mass, 94; Onward Gallery-Nihom Bashi (exhib catalog), Tokyo, Japan, 9/94. *Teaching:* Instr drawing, Col of New Rochelle, NY, 74-75; instr collage, painting & drawing, Art Ctr of Northern NJ, 90-. *Awards:* Sculpture Invitational, Pelham Art Ctr; Ivan Karp, Best in Show, Soho Gallery 54, 88; Second Prize Sculpture, Katonah Libr, 93. *Bibliog:* Vivian Raynor (auth) rev, NY Times, 3/90 & 9/90; Cornelia Seckel (auth), rev, Art Times, 11/98. *Mem:* The Gallery at Hastings-on-Hudson, 79; Mamaroneck Artist Guild, 79-90; Viridian Gallery, 85-90; Artist Equity, 90; Silvermine Guild Artists. *Media:* Wood, Metal. *Publ:* Auth, Onward Gallery-Nihom Bashi (exhib catalog), Tokyo, Japan, 9/94; NY Art & Antique Guide Book, International Art Reference Inc, 94. *Dealer:* Walter Wickiser Gallery Inc 568 Broadway New York NY 10012. *Mailing Add:* 67 Autumn Ridge Rd Pound Ridge NY 10576

MANTER, MARGARET C
PAINTER
b Providence, RI, Feb 20, 1923. *Study:* RI Sch Design, 42; Syracuse Univ, NY, BFA, 46; Workshops with Barse Miller, Ed Betts & Chen Chi, 66-72, Edward Betts, Virginia Cobb & Maxine Masterfield, 82-89. *Work:* Coll of Atlantic, Bar Harbor, Maine; Thomas Col, Waterville, Maine; Univ Maine, Machias; Eastern Maine Med Ctr, Bangor; Central Maine Power Co, Augusta. *Exhib:* Maine Coast Artists, Rockport, Maine, 88 & 89; Nat Asn Women Artists, NY, 89 & 90; Western Ill Univ, 90; Watercolor USA, Springfield, Mo, 91; Soc Experimental Artists, Bradenton, Fla, 92; Union of Maine Visual Artists, Gilley Mus, 2002; Experimental Artists, Travis City, Mich, 2001; Collage Exchg, New Zealand, 2002; and many others. *Teaching:* Instr watercolor, YMCA, Bangor, Maine, 70-80; Instr design, Univ Maine, Orono, 80-. *Awards:* Purchase Award, Central Maine Power Exhibit, Central Maine Power Co, 90; Cer Award, Int Soc Experimental Artists, 2000. *Bibliog:* Hollerbach & Schlemm (auth), Best of Watercolor Vol I & II, 99. *Mem:* Nat Asn Women Artists; Union Maine Visual Artists; Int Asn Experimental Artists. *Media:* Watercolor, Miscellaneous Media. *Publ:* Best of Watercolor, Rockport Publ, Mass, 96

MANUAL, ED HILL & SUZANNE BLOOM
PHOTOGRAPHER, VIDEO ARTIST
b Springfield, Mass, Aug 30, 1935; Suzanne Bloom: b Philadelphia, Pa, Nov 25, 1943. *Study:* Ed Hill: RI Sch Design, BFA, 57; Yale Univ, MFA, 60; Suzanne Bloom: Pa Acad Fine Arts, BFA, 65; Univ Pa, MFA, 68. *Work:* Mus Contemp Photog, Chicago; Los Angeles Co Mus Art; San Francisco Mus Mod Art; Int Mus Photog, Rochester, NY; Int Ctr Photography, NY. *Comn:* Site specific installation, Fotofeis & Scottish Arts Coun, Inverness, Scotland, 93; Cult Arts Coun Houston & Harris Co, Houston, Tex, 96; The Protracted Image, FotoFest, 2002. *Exhib:* Signs, The New Mus Art, NY, 85; Photog & Art, Los Angeles Co Mus Art, 87; Solo-shows, Forest/Products, Contemp Arts Mus, Houston, Tex, 91, Mus Contemp Photog, Chicago, Ill, 92, NY Int Ctr Photog, 93 & Scottsdale Ctr for the Arts, Ariz, 94; Wasteland, Fotografie Biennale, Perspektief, Rotterdam, The Neth, 92; Renewing Our Earth, US Pavilion, Taejon, Korea, 93; Forest of Visions, Knoxville Mus Art, 93; Photography's Multimpe Roles, Mus Contemp Photog, Chicago, 88; 6th Bienal Int de Pintura, Cuenca, Ecuador, 88; Two Worlds; the Collaboration of Ed Hill and Suzanna Bloom, Int Ctr Photog, NY, 2002. *Teaching:* Prof art, Univ Houston. *Awards:* Rockefeller Interdisciplinary Arts Fel, Nat Endowment Arts, 87; Artists' Fel Photog, Nat Endowment Arts, 92; Visual Artists Pub Proj, Nat Endowment Arts, 93; Pub Art and Urban Design, Cult Arts Coun, Houston and Harris Co, 96. *Bibliog:* Mark Dery (auth), Art & technology, Artnews, 2/93; Stephen Hobson (auth), Manual et in Arcadia Ego, Perspektief 47/48, 94; Anne Barclay Morgan (auth), Art & technology, Art in Am, 4/94. *Mem:* Soc Photographic Educators; Coll Art Asn. *Media:* Digital Photography, Video. *Dealer:* Moody Gallery 2815 Colquitt Houston TX 77098. *Mailing Add:* 2520 White Oak Dr Houston TX 77009

MANUELLA, FRANK R
DESIGNER, CONCEPTUAL ARTIST
b New York, NY. *Study:* Cooper Union Advan Sci & Art, BFA; Pratt Inst, MS. *Work:* NY Univ; McAllen Int Mus; Univ Tex; Pan Am, 2000; Int Mus Art & Sci. *Comn:* Mural, McAllen Int Mus, 83; mural, Harlingen, Tex, 91; mural, City of McAllen, Tex, 2000. *Exhib:* Solo exhib, Int Mus Art & Sci, McAllen, Tex, 2006. *Pos:* Pres, F R Manuella Associates, currently. *Teaching:* Asst prof light & color, Pratt Inst, 75-82;

prof art, Univ Tex, 82-2000; master prof art & design, Univ Tex, 2000-, prof emeritus. *Awards:* Outstanding Faculty Award, Univ Tex, Pan Am Univ, 87, 90 & 95; Merit Award, McAllen Int Mus, 88; Govs Award for Outstanding Serv, 89; Grant, Fulbright-Hays, 94. *Bibliog:* Carompsun, NY Times Mag, 12/1/68; Karen Fisher (auth), Five careers, Cosmopolitan Mag, 3/69; Reviews & previews, Art News, 1/71; Dr N Moyer (auth), Fine Arts Review, Festiva/The Monitor, 6/9/2006; Voices of Art Mag, spring/summer 2006. *Mem:* Univ Tex (fac senate, 88-94); Univ Press Univ Tex (bd mem grad faculty). *Media:* Site-Specific, Mixed Media Installation

MANVILLE, ELSIE
PAINTER
b Philadelphia, Pa, May 11, 1922. *Study:* Tyler Sch Fine Arts, Temple Univ, BFA, BS. *Work:* Temple Univ, Philadelphia; Butler Inst Am Art; Guild Hall Permanent Collection, East Hampton, NY; Univ Iowa. *Exhib:* Butler Inst Am Art, 56; Walker Art Ctr, 58; Dallas Mus, 63; 30 Yr Retrospective Exhib, Snug Harbor Cult Ctr, Staten Island, 83; The Art of Flowers, Moravian Col, 84; Focus on Realism, Glenn C Janss Collection, 85; Hermitage Found, Norfolk, Va, 85; Tyler Sch Fine Arts, Pa, 88; Butler Inst Am Art, 98. *Teaching:* Adj instr, Fashion Inst Technol. *Awards:* Purchase Award, Butler Inst Am Art, 78; Nat Endowment Arts Visual Artists Fel, 81 & 85; NY Fedn Arts Grant, 90. *Bibliog:* Paintings reproduced, Arts Mag, 6/75, 4/78 & 2/82, Art News, 10/78 & New York Times Art & Leisure Guide, 2/28/82. *Media:* Oil, Oil Pastel. *Mailing Add:* 9 Dean St Brooklyn NY 11201

MAPES, DORIS WILLIAMSON
PAINTER
b Russellville, Ark, June 25, 1920. *Study:* Little Rock Jr Coll; Hendrix Coll, Ark; Ark Arts Ctr, Little Rock; Rex Brandt's Sch Painting, cert, Corona del Mar, Calif; also with George Post, Millard Sheets, John C Pellew, Louis Freund, Edgar A Whitney, Robert E Wood, John Pike & Robert Andrew Parker, 72. *Work:* Winthrop Rockefeller Gallery, Petit Jean, Ark; Ark Coll Mus, Batesville; Am Found Life Ins Co, First Nat Bank & Ark Arts Ctr, Little Rock; Advan Indust, Blythville, Ark; Pres Clinton, White House, Washington; Historic Mus Ark, Little Rock, Ark; Ark Art Ctr, Little Rock, Ark; Springfield Art Mus, Springfield, Mo; Clinton Presidential Libr, Little Rock, Ark. *Exhib:* Mid-Southern Ark Arts Ctr, 71-89; Watercolor USA, Springfield, Mo, 75; Southern Watercolor Soc, Cheekwood Mus, Jackson, Miss, 77; solo exhib, Univ Ark, Little Rock, 78; Celebrating Ark Women Artists, Russell Senate Bldg, Washington, 91, 93 & 96; Celebrating Ark artist of the Future 95, Fed Bldg, Little Rock, Ark, 95; Louie's Unique Framing and Gallery, 2011, 2012; S Ark Arts Ctr, El Dorado, Ark, 2013. *Teaching:* Oil & watercolor painting, Dansarts Sch, Little Rock, Ark, 68-86; oil painting, Bella Vista Fine Arts Ctr Ark, 71; watercolor, Miss Co Coll, Blytheville, Ark, 72-73; Air Force Base, Little Rock Ark, 82-83. *Awards:* Top Show, Ark State Festival Arts, 68 & 75; First Award, Southern Artists Asn, 72; First Award, Mid-Southern Watercolorists 74 & 85; Top Award, Mid-Southern Watercolorists, 74, 84 & 85. *Bibliog:* La Revue Mod des Arts, Paris, France, 3/75; Some Remarkable Women of Arkansas, 77; Arts & Voices South, 7/79. *Mem:* Mid-Southern Watercolorists (pres, 70-72); Southwestern Watercolor Soc; assoc mem Am Watercolor Soc. *Media:* Mixed Media, Watercolor, Acrylic & Oil. *Publ:* Art News, 9/94. *Dealer:* Louie's Gallery 1509 Mart Little Rock AR 72202. *Mailing Add:* 622 N Bryan Little Rock AR 72205

MARABLE, DARWIN WILLIAM
HISTORIAN, CRITIC
b Los Angeles, Calif, Jan 15, 1937. *Study:* Univ Calif, Berkeley, BA, 60; San Francisco State Univ, MA (hist art), 72; Univ NMex, PhD (hist photog), 80; studied with Beaumont Newhall & Van Deren Coke. *Collection Arranged:* Visual Dialogue Found Revisited 1968-2000; JJ Brookings Gallery, San Francisco, Calif; The Crucifixion in Modern Art, Hearst Art Gallery, St Mary's Coll, Moraga, Calif, 92; Vilem Kriz Meml Exhib, 96; Irwin Art Ctr, Coll Arts & Crafts, Oakland, Calif; John Spence Weir: Surreal Spaces, 2006; Diablo Valley Coll Art Gallery, Pleasant Hill, Calif. *Teaching:* Lectr art hist, San Francisco State Univ, 76-77 & 82 & St Mary's Coll, Moraga, Calif, 90-92; lectr hist photog & criticism photog, Univ Calif, Berkeley Exten, 95-2004 & 2008; San Francisco Art Inst, 77, 2001 & Acad Art Univ San Francisco, Calif, 2001, 2006; Osher Lifelong Learning Inst at CSU, East Bay, 2011-. *Bibliog:* Julian Cox (auth), Edmund Teske Memory and Synthesis, Hist Photog, 95; numerous citations. *Mem:* Soc Photog Educ; Hist Photog Group; Friends Photog San Francisco, Calif; Photo Alliance, San Francisco, Calif. *Res:* Surrealism & American Photography; Crucifixion in 20th Century Art; Visual Dialogue Found, San Francisco. *Interests:* Travel, Genealogy, Photography. *Publ:* Auth, Leland Rice's Photographs of the Berlin Wall, Shadow & Substance, 90; interview, Oliver Gagliani, Photo Metro, 12/92; Capturing Chaos, the Photomontages of John Heartfield, Wash Times, 8/94; The Crucifixion in Photography, Hist Photog, Autumn 94; Visual Dialogue Found, Black & White Mag, 2001; Luc Tuymans: To Clarify and Visualize, The World & I Online, Wash DC Times, 2010; Jack Welpott, a homage, Zone Zero, 2010; and others. *Mailing Add:* 166 Valley Hill Dr Moraga CA 94556

MARAIS
PAINTER
b New York, NY. *Study:* Acad de la Grande Chaumiere, Paris & self-taught. *Work:* J Aberbach Collection, Long Island, NY; Hugo Perls, NY Collection; Dr Milton Reder, New York; UNICEF Collection, New York; Theodora Settele Collection, New York. *Exhib:* Galerie Chantepierre, Aubonne, Switz, 72; Galerie Int, New York, 75; Cafe de la Paix Exhib, Paris, 79; PubTV Channel 13, 79-80; Galerie St Placide, Paris; Salon des Nations, Paris, 84. *Mem:* Visual Artists & Galleries Asn; Nat Soc Lit & Arts. *Media:* Oil. *Publ:* Art Diary, 82 & 83

MARAK, LOUIS BERNARD
CERAMIC SCULPTOR, EDUCATOR
b Shawnee, Okla, Sept 9, 1942. *Study:* Univ Ill, Champaign-Urbana, BFA, 65; Alfred Univ, MFA, 67. *Work:* Krannert Art Mus, Univ Ill, Urbana; Western Gallery, Western Wash State Coll, Bellingham; Utah Mus Fine Arts, Univ Utah, Salt Lake City; Henry Art Gallery, Univ Wash, Seattle; Los Angeles Co Mus Art, Calif; Oakland Mus, Calif; Renwick Gallery, Wash DC; Fine Arts Mus, San Francisco; DeYoung Mus, San Francisco. *Exhib:* San Francisco Art Inst Centennial Exhib, MH De Young Mem Mus, 71; Calif Ceramics & Glass, Great Hall, Oakland Mus, 74; Northern Calif Clay Routes: Sculpture Now, San Francisco Mus Mod Art; Am Porcelain: New Expressions in an Ancient Art, Renwick Gallery, Nat Collection Fine Arts, Washington, DC, 80; Int Tea Party, Contemp Crafts Gallery, Portland, Ore, 84; Inaugural Exhib, New Am Crafts Mus, New York, 86; Ceramics from the Smits Collection, Los Angeles Co Mus Art, Calif, 87; Fired with Enthusiasm, an exhib contemp soup tureens, Campbell Mus, Camden, NJ, 87; Beyond Words: The Book as Metaphor for Art, Vol 2, Calif Crafts Mus, San Francisco, 90; 500 Yrs Since Columbus, Triton Mus Art, Santa Clara, Calif, 92; and others; International Art Teapot Exhib, County Yingge Ceramics Mus, Yingge Jen Taipei, Taiwan, 2002; The Yixing Effect: Echoes of the Chinese Scholar, Holter Mus Art, Helena, Mont, 2006; The Diane & Sandy Besser Collection, Fine Arts Mus San Francisco, Calif, 2007. *Pos:* vis artist, Am Academy in Rome, 1995. *Teaching:* Instr art, Keuka Coll, New York, 67-69; prof art, Humboldt State Univ, Arcata, Calif, 69-2006 (Emeritus). *Awards:* Nat Endowment Arts Craftsmen's Fel Grant, 75; Artist Fel Grant, Calif Arts Coun, 94; Fel of the Am Crafts Coun, 2009. *Bibliog:* Lloyd Herman (auth), American Porcelain: New Expressions in an Ancient Art, Timber Press, 81; Paul J Smith and Edward Lucie-Smith (coauth), Craft Today: Poetry of the Physical, Weidenfeld & Nicolson, 86; Martha Drexler Lynn (auth), Clay Today, Contemporary Ceramists & Their Work, Chronicle Books & Los Angeles Co Mus Art, 90. *Mem:* Am Craft Coun. *Media:* Ceramics. *Mailing Add:* 1110 Freshwater Rd Eureka CA 95503-9558

MARANDER, CAROL JEAN
PAINTER, GRAPHIC ARTIST
b Minneapolis, Minn, Dec 30, 1950. *Study:* Colo State Univ, BFA (with honors), 73; Coll Santa Fe, Albert Handell, pastel workshop, 82. *Work:* Comlinear Corp Gallery, Fort Collins, Colo; Micro Motions, Boulder, Colo. *Comn:* Pastel paintings, Marriott Hotels, Charlotte, NC, Trumball, Conn, 90, Omaha, Nebr, 92; pastel painting, Tucson Nat Resort & Spa, Ariz, 91; pastel paintings, US Post Off, Norman, Okla, 92. *Exhib:* 12th & 13th Ann Exhib, Pastel Soc Am, NY, 84 & 85; 75th Ann Exhib, Allied Artists Am, NY, 88; Exposition Int, Societe des Pastellistes de France, Compiegne, 88; Biennial Exhib, 88, Fine Art Calendar Artists Exhib, 89, Viva l'amour Artists Invitational, 91, Loveland Mus & Gallery, Colo; one-woman show, Colorscapes, Loveland Mus & Gallery, Colo, 90. *Pos:* Graphic designer, Colo State Univ, Fort Collins, 76-99, coodr of graphic & web design, 99-2006. *Awards:* Ann & Richard Sauter Award, 12th Ann Exhib, Pastel Soc Am 84; First Place Other Media, Colo Artists Asn State Show, 86. *Mem:* Pastel Soc Am (signature mem); Allied Artists Am. *Media:* Pastel. *Mailing Add:* 1400 Elm St Fort Collins CO 80521-1623

MARASCO, ROSE
PHOTOGRAPHER, EDUCATOR
b Utica, NY, Dec 25, 1948. *Study:* Syracuse Univ, BFA, 71; Goddard Coll, with Todd Webb, MA, 81; Visual Studies Workshop, MFA, 91, with Nathan Lyons & Frank Gohlke. *Work:* Polaroid Int Collection; Portland Mus Art; Davis Mus & Cult Ctr, Wellesley Coll; NY Pub Libr Photog Collection; Fogg Art Mus, Harvard Univ; Univ New Eng; Smithsonian Nat Mus Am Hist; Fidelity Collection. *Comn:* Percent for Art Grant, Harrington Elementary Sch, Maine; Aegean Cult Exchange US, 97; Open House, Portrait Mus Art, 2002. *Exhib:* Solo exhibs, Farnsworth Mus, Rockland, Maine, 92, Davis Mus & Cult Ctr, Wellesley Coll, 95, Latvia Photog Mus, Riga & Domestic Objects Sarah Morthland Gallery, NY, 98, Leafing, Sarah Morthland Gallery, 2000, Circles, Sarah Morthand Gallery, 2003, Domestics Objects: Past & Present, Univ Southern Maine, 2004-2005, Univ Western Brittany, France, 2008, Projections, Houston Ctr for Photography, 2010-2011, New York: Pinhole Photos, Meredeth Ward Fine Art, 2014; Group exhibs, Photokina '88, Polaroid Inst Exhib; Perspectives, Portland Mus Art, Maine, 88 & 2001; Exhib Photo, Berkshire Mus, Pittsfield, Mass, 92; Marlborough Gallery, 98; Photographing Maine 1840-2000, Maine Coast Artists, 2000; The Long View, Norma Marin Collection, Univ Maine Mus Art, 2005. *Collection Arranged:* Todd Webb-Photographs, Univ Southern Maine Art Gallery, 81; Work from Five Decades-Todd Webb (auth, catalog), New Eng Found Arts, Cambridge, Mass. *Pos:* disting prof art, Univ Southern Maine, 2000-, distinguished prof art, 2010-. *Teaching:* Instr & dept head photog, Munson-Williams-Proctor Inst, 74-; assoc prof art, Univ Southern Maine, 79-2000; instr photog, Portland Sch Art, Maine, 81-87. *Awards:* Polaroid Materials Grant, 86; Maine Arts Comn Artists' Fel, 90; Maine Humanities Coun Major Grant, 90-91; Womens Studio Workshop Fel, 94; Good Idea Grant, Maine Arts Comn, Project Maine/France Grant, Univ Southern Maine, 2006. *Bibliog:* Lucy R Lippard (auth), The Lure of the Local, The Mar Press, 97; Vince Aletti (auth), The Village Voice, 2/4/98; The New Yorker, 2/23/98; Deborah Martin (auth), Dear Print Fan, Harvard Univ Art Mus, 2001; Apile Gallant & Mimi Hellman (auths), Undomesticated Intentions, Coll Mus Art, 2003. *Media:* Photography. *Publ:* Auth, A personal reflection based on the SPE Questionnaire: Teaching and Learning, Exposure 20:1, 3/82; How to make slides of your artwork, In: The Percent for Arts Handbook, Maine Arts Comn, 85; The silhouette craft of Kaye Housel, In: The World and I, 87; Looking at Photographs, In: 20th Century Photographs from Collection of the Bowdoin Coll Mus Art (exhib catalog), 88. *Dealer:* Meredith Ward Fine Art 44 E 74th St Ste G New York NY

MARCHESCHI, (LOUIS) CORK
SCULPTOR, EDUCATOR
b San Mateo, Calif, Apr 5, 1945. *Study:* Coll San Mateo, 63-66; Calif State Col, Hayward, 66-68; Calif Coll Arts & Crafts, Oakland, MFA, 70; also with Mel Ramos & Paul Harris. *Work:* Bochum Mus, WGer; Milwaukee Art Ctr; Mus Mod Art. *Comn:* Principle Group, Des Moines, Iowa, 91; Victoria Peak, Hong Kong, 93; Ft Lauderdale Airport, 94; Rowan Col, NJ, 94; Louisville Sci Ctr, 94; and others. *Exhib:* Solo exhibs, Kunsthalle Dusseldorf, Ger, 76, Milwaukee Art Ctr, Wis, 76, Hanson-Cowles Gallery, Minneapolis, Minn, 77, Tubingen Mus, Ger, 78, Van Abbe Mus, Endhoven, The Neth 78, Nat Gallery, Berlin, Ger, 78 & Braunstien Quay, 95; New Mus, NY, 80;

Rutgers Mus, 83; Paris Mus Mod Art, 84; Nat Gallery, West Berlin, 84; Braunstein Quay, San Francisco, 92; Morgan Gallery, Kansas City, Mo, 92; and others. *Teaching:* Assoc prof art & intermedia, Minneapolis Col Art & Design, 70-85 & San Francisco Art Inst, 87-92. *Awards:* Minn State Arts Coun Grant, 75; Bush Found Grant, 78; DAAD Berlin Artist Prog Grant, 78; Nat Endowment Art, 82-83. *Bibliog:* Paul Owen (auth), Energy works (16mm film), 71; Merike Weiler (auth), Art Can article, 73; Heiner Hepper (auth), Cork Marcheschi (film), Ger Pub Broadcasting, 75; George Tapley (auth), article in Arts Mag, 83. *Media:* Electricity, Found Objects. *Collection:* Art deco objects and architectural period writings. *Publ:* Auth, Objects for producing visual phenomena with high-voltage electricity, 73; Heat, light and motion, 74; Neon, 75; Energy as Sculpture, Prof Kornelia V Berswordt (catalog), Mus Glaskasten, Marl, Ger, 91. *Dealer:* Modernism 236 8th St San Francisco CA 94103. *Mailing Add:* 192 Connecticut San Francisco CA 94107-2415

MARCHINI, CLAUDIA H
PAINTER, MURALIST
b Lima, Peru, Feb 3, 1959; US Citizen. *Study:* Memphis Coll Art, BFA, 87; Univ Tex, MFA, 89. *Comn:* Images of Ore, Ore Advocates Arts Found, Ore State Capital Bldg, Salem, 94; mural, Asante/Three Rivers Community Hospital, Grants Pass, Ore, 2001; large paintings, Lung Clinic-Center for Sleep Medicine, Grants Pass, Ore, 2006. *Exhib:* Crosscut Biennial, Portland Mus Art, Ore, 93, Oregon Biennial, 95; Expo Sicion de Pinturasy Esculturas, Mus Nac, Lima, Peru, 98; The End, Tacoma Art Mus, Wash, 99; NMex Photogr, Eastern NMex Univ, 99; Millennium Madonna, Grants Pass Mus Art, Ore, 2000; 20th Ann NW Int Art Competition, Whatoom Mus, Bellingham, Wash, 2000; Negotiating Identities in the African World, Schmucker Gallery, Gettysburg Col, Pa, 2007; Solo Exhib: Darfur Series, Listen Here Galleries, Grants Pass, Ore, 2008; Art Celebrating the Making of Wine, Grants Pass Mus Art, 2008; Fragments from the Past, Onda Gallery, Portland, Ore, 2008; Art of Love, Harper-Howell Gallery, Grants Pass, Ore, 2008; Home Sweet Home, Wiseman Gallery (RCC), Grants Pass, Ore, 2008; Painting on Canvas, Infusion Gallery, Los Angeles, 2009; Principles of Forms, Firehouse Gallery, Ore, 2009; 61st Southern Ore Art Show, Firehouse Gallery, Ore, 2009; Ann Mem Exhib, Grants Pass Mus Mus Art, 2009. *Pos:* Teaching Asst, Sat Sch for Children, Memphis Col Art, Memphis, Tenn, 86; Grad Asst, Univ Tex San Antonio, Tex, 2008; Art Inst (volunteer), St. Anne Catholic Sch, Grants Pass, Ore, 2006; Part Time Adminr, Lung Clinic-Center for Sleep Med, Inc, 1990-; Full Time Painter, Studio Location: 140 Rustic Canyon-Grants Pass, Ore, 1990-. *Awards:* Second Place, Lucy Lippard, 97; First Place, Southern Ore Art Exhibit, Am Asn Univ Women, 2000; Individual Artist Fel Grant, Ore Arts Comn, 2000; First Place, Pacific Northwest Exhib, Rogue Gallery, Medford Ore, 2002; Best Exhib of the Year, Homage to Slaves (sneak preview), Josephine County, Ore, 2003; Second Place Painting, 56th Ann Southern Ore Art Exhib, AAUW, Grants Pass Mus Art, 2003; Semi finalist, Nat Portrait Gallery, Outwin Boochever, 2009; Portrait Competition, Smithsonian Inst, DC, 2009. *Bibliog:* Marcia Goren Weser (auth),Interesting Group Show Marks Gallery Closing, San Antonio Light, 8/2/89; Soledad Garcia (auth), Claudia Cilloniz Entre Piedray Pintura, Cosas Mag, 1/97; Jeremias Gamboa (auth), Hibridaciaires de Claudia Cilloniz, Visto Bueno Mag, 4/98; Rocio Rios (auth), Arte Peruano Expone en Grants Pass, El Centinela, Portland, 1999; Barbara Baily (auth), Downtown Galleries Display Engaging Shows, Daily Courier, 6/2000; Arts Council of Southern Oregon News, Summer, 2000; Winners of the 53rd Annual Southern Ore Art Show, Daily Courier, Grants Pass, Ore, 2000; Carmen Martin-Stiles, Buscando America, Radio interview, Portland, Ore, 2008. *Mem:* Josephine County Cultural Coalition (bd treas), 2004. *Media:* Oil on Marble. *Interests:* Hiking, nature. *Dealer:* San Francisco Mus Modern Art Rental Gallery San Francisco CA. *Mailing Add:* 874 NE 7th St Grants Pass OR 97526

MARCIARI-ALEXANDER, JULIA
MUSEUM DIRECTOR
Study: BA in Art History & French, Wellesley Coll; MA in History of Art, PhD in History of Art, Yale U; MA in French Literature, NYU. *Pos:* asst curatorial paintings & sculpture, Yale Ctr British Art, 1997-2008; deputy dir curatorial affairs, San Diego Mus Art, 2008-2013, interim co-dir, 2009-2010, interim deputy dir educ, 2010-2011; exec dir, Walters Art Mus, Baltimore, Md, 2013-. *Mailing Add:* Walters Art Museum 600 N Charles St Baltimore MD 21201

MARCLAY, CHRISTIAN
VISUAL ARTIST
b San Rafael, Calif, 1955. *Study:* Ecole Superieure d'Art Visuel, Geneva, 1975-77; Boston Mass Coll Art, BFA, 1977-80. *Work:* Whitney Mus Am Art, New York; Tate Mod, London, England; Metrop Mus Art, New York; Mus Mod Art, New York; Kunst Mus, Switzerland; and others; Ctr Georges Pompidou, Paris. *Exhib:* Solo exhibs include PS1 Contemp Art Ctr, NY City, 1987, Tom Cugliani Gallery, NY, 1988, 1989, 1990, 1991, Gelbe Musik, Berlin, 1988, Maureen Paley Interim Art, London, 1991, Galerie Jennifer Flay, Paris, 1992, Fawbush Gallery, NY, 1994, Venice Biennial, 1995, Whitney Mus Am Art, 1997, Paula Cooper Gallery, 1999, 2001, 2002, 2005, 2006, 2008, New Mus Contemp Art, 2000, Gallery Koyanagi, 2001, Mus Contemp Art, Chicago, 2001, Mus Contemp Art, Miami, 2002, Philadelphia Mus Art, 2003, Tate Mod, London, 2004, Eyebeam, NY City, 2005, MIT List Visual Art Ctr, 2006, Moderna Museet, Stockholm, Sweden, 2006, White Cube, London, Eng, 2007, High Mus Art, Atlanta, Ga, 2007, Musée d'art Moderne et Contemporain, Geneva, Switzerland, 2007, 2008, Fraenkel Gallery, San Francisco, 2008, Found for Contemp Art, Montreal, Can, 2008, Video Quartet, Nasher Mus Art, Durham, NC, 2009, Christian Marclay, PS1, Contemp Art Ctr, Long Island City, NY, 2009, Fourth of July, Paula Cooper Gallery, NY, 2010, Christian Marclay: Festival, Whitney Mus Amer Art, NY, 2010, Goya Contemp, Md, 2010; group exhibs include New Music Am, Wash Proj for Arts, Wash, DC, 1983; Palud No 1, Lausanne, Switzerland, 1986; City Gallery, NY, 1986; Tom Cugliani Gallery, NY, 1987; Paul Kasmin Gallery, NY, 1988; New Mus Contemp Art, NY, 1989; Andrea Rosen Gallery, NY, 1990; Whitney Biennial, 1991, 2002; Am Ctr, Paris, 1992; Contemp Arts Ctr, Cincinnati, 1993; Cleveland Ctr Contemp Art, 1994; Venice Biennial, 1995, 1999; Milwaukee Art Mus, 1995; Auckland Art Gallery, New Zealand, 1996; Centre PasquART, Biennial, Switzerland, 1997; Rupert Goldsworthy Gallery, NY, 1998; Tokyo Opera City Art Gallery, 1999; Hayward Gallery, London, 2000; Paula Cooper Gallery, NY, 2000; Valencia Biennial, Spain, 2001; Angel Row Gallery, 2003; Palais de Tokyo, Paris, 2004; Walter Phillips Gallery, Alberta, 2005; Mus der Moderne Salzburg, Austria, 2006; Mus Contemp Art, N Miami, 2007; Mori Art Mus, Tokyo, Japan, 2007; PS1 Contemp Art Ctr, 2007; Moderna Mus, Stockholm, Sweden, 2006; Paula Cooper Gallery, NY, 2006; Galerie Art & Essai, Université de Rennes, Rennes, France, 2008; The Record, Nasher Mus Art, Duke Univ, Durham, NC, 2009; Collecting History: Highlighting Recent Acqusitions, Mus Contemp Art, Los Angeles, Calif, 2009; Haunted: Contemp Photog/Video/Pergormance, Solomon R Guggenheim Mus, NY, 2010; 54th Int Art Exhib Biennale, Venice, 2011. *Awards:* Found for Graphic Arts in Switzerland Award, 2003; The Kitchen Spring Gala Benefit, Honoring Christian Marclay, New York, NY, 2008; The Larry Aldrich Award, Ridgefield, Conn, 2009; Named one of 10 Most Important Artists of Today, Newsweek mag, 2011. *Bibliog:* Valérie Mavridorakis (ed), Christian Marclay: Snap!, Le Presses du Réel, Geneva, 2009; Jean-Pierre Criqui, Christian Marclay Replay (exhib catalogue), JRP Ringier, Paris, 2007. *Dealer:* Paula Cooper Gallery 534 W 21st St New York NY 10011. *Mailing Add:* c/o Paula Cooper Gallery 534 W 21st St New York NY 10011

MARCUS, ANGELO P
DEALER, COLLECTOR
b 1947. *Study:* Cairo Univ, MA. *Pos:* Pres, Eagle Art Gallery, Inc, currently. *Mem:* Nat Cowboy Hall Fame. *Specialty:* Western art. *Collection:* Olaf Wieghorst, Frank McCarthy, Robert Lougheed, William Whitaker, George Marks, John Clymer, Don Crowley, James Bama & Norman Rockwell. *Publ:* Wall Street Journal. *Mailing Add:* c/o Eagle Art Gallery 1250 Prospect La Jolla CA 92037

MARCUS, GERALD R
PAINTER, PRINTMAKER
b New York, NY, 1946. *Study:* Art Students League, New York, with Jean Liberte, Julian Levy, Sol Wilson & Jacob Lawrence, 1963-68; City Coll NY, BA, 1968. *Work:* Standard & Poor Inc; Am Reinsurance Co Inc; Columbia Presby Hosp; Art in Embassies Prog, US State Dept; Albany Print Mus. *Exhib:* Solo exhibs, Paul Klapper Art Ctr, Queens Coll, NY, 1983 & Griffith Menard Gallery, Baton Rouge, La, 1984; Adirondack Life, Lake Placid Art Ctr, 1989 & 90; Trenton City Mus, NJ, 1993; Stockton Nat, Haggin Mus, Calif, 1996; 40th Ann Nat Print Exhib, Hunterdon Art Ctr, Clinton, NJ, 1996; Soc Am Graphic Artists 68th Ann Exhib, 2000 & 2004; Humanity, Printmaking Coun NJ, 2001; A Movable Feast, Zeuxis Westbeth Gallery, NY 2003; September 11th Memorial Portfolio, Am Print Alliance; New Prints 2005/Winter, Int Print Ctr, NY, 2005; 15th Biennial Exhib, Purdue Univ, 2006; Prague/New York, Hollard Soc, Prague, 2006; 74th Member's Exhib, Soc Am Graphic Artists, Old Print Shop, NY, 2007; Field Report, Boston Printmakers, Gordon Col, 2008; Delta Nat Small Prints Exhib, Ark State Univ, 2008; Penned, Md Inst, Coll Art, Baltimore, 2008; Iowa Biennial Archives, Univ Iowa, 2007; Wesbeth Galleries, 2007; Los Angeles Printmaking Soc, Old Town Gallery, Tustin, Calif, 2007; Col Design Iowa State Univ, 2007; Kellog Univ Art Gallery, 2009; Fyre Gallery, Braidwood, Australia. *Awards:* Claire Romano Prize for Etching. *Bibliog:* Cynthia Nadelman (auth), rev, Art News, summer 82; Stephanie Rauschenbusch (auth), Finding the Catskills, Prospect Press, 11/23/86; Artzine, Review of solo show, May 2003; John Goodrich (auth), review, New York Sun, 2/9/2006. *Mem:* Art Students League; Soc Am Graphic Artists (pres). *Media:* Oil, Watercolor; Etching. *Dealer:* Concept Arts Gallery 1031 S Braddock Ave Pittsburgh PA 15218; Prince St Gallery 520 W 25th St New York NY 10001

MARCUS, GWEN E
SCULPTOR
b New York. *Study:* NY Univ; RI Sch of Design; Art Students League; Nat Acad Design; studied with Clemente Spampinato, Bruno Lucchesi, Edgar Whitney & Isaac Soyer. *Hon Degrees:* Hon, BS. *Work:* Chi Mei Mus, Taiwan; Brookgreen Gardens, SC; Champs Hill, Sussex, Eng; Stamford Hospital, Conn; First Nat Bank, Miss. *Exhib:* Kerygma Gallery, Ridgewood NJ, 99-2009; Chi Mei Mus, Taiwan, 2001-2014; Frank T Sabin Gallery, London, Eng, 2001-2005; Champs Hill, W Sussex, Eng, Cavalier Gallery, Greenwich, Conn, Greenberg Fine Art Gallery, Santa Fe, NMex, 2009-2014, Morris & Whiteside Galleries, Hilton Head, SC, 2001-2014; Cheryl Newby Gallery, Pawleys Island, SC, 2014; Brookgreen Gardens, SC, 2007-2014; Morrison Gallery, 2012-2014; Southport Gallery, Conn, 2014. *Pos:* Bd mem & fel, Nat Sculpture Soc. *Teaching:* Brookgreen Gardens, SC, 2012; Scottsdale Artists Sch, 2013. *Awards:* Gold Medal, 93 & Centennial Award, 96, Catharine Lorillard Wolf, 93; Gold Medal Am Prof League, NY, 94, 96, 2005, 2008; Gold Medal, Allied Artist Am, Inc, NY, 96; Gold Medal, Audubon Artist, NY, 97 & 2007, Leonard Meiselman award for Realistic Sculpture, 2012; Josephine Beardsley Sander Mem Award, Allied Artist Am, Inc, NY, 99; Gold Medal Hon, Hudson Valley Art Asn, NY, 2000; Am Artists Fund Award, Am Prof League, NY, 2001, The Helen G Oehlea Memorial award, 2012; The Pietro & Alfrieds Montana Mem Award, Allied Artist Am, New York, 2007; Richard L Marini Award, Audubon Artists, New York, 2007; Allied Artists Am Mem & Assoc Award, New York, 2008; Harriet W Frishmuth Mem Award, Catharine Lorrillard Wolfe Art Club, New York, 2009; Kathryn Thayer Hobson Mem Award, Am Artists Prof League, New York, 2009; CAAS Award, Hudson Valley Art Assoc, 2010; Pietro & Alfrieda Montana Memorial Award, Hudson Valley Art Asn, NY; Marquis Who's Who in American Art References Award in Sculpture, Audubon Artists, New York, 2011; Lelia Gardin Sawyer Award, Catharine Lorillard Wolfe Art Club, New York, 2011; Leonard I Meiselman award, Catharine Lorillard Wolfe Art Club, NY, 2012; Agop Agopoff Memorial award, Am Professional League, NY, 2013; Claude Parsons Memorial award, The American Professional League, 2013; Agop Asopoff Memorial award, Hudson Valley Art Assn, At the Lyme Art Assn, CT, 2013; First Place award for Sculpture, Catharine Lorillard Wolfe Art Club Mem Show, NY. *Mem:*

Am Medallic Sculpture Asn (bd dir, 96-99); Hudson Valley Art Asn, 2002, 2012, 2013, 2014; Nat Sculpture Soc (fellow bd mem, 2003-2014); Audubon Artists, 2005 & 2007; Am Prof League, 2008-14. *Media:* Bronze. *Interests:* travel, music. *Publ:* Am Art Collector, 2007; Gwen Marcus Sculptor, Book. *Mailing Add:* 401 E 80th St Apt#19E New York NY 10075

MARCUS, IRVING E
PAINTER, EDUCATOR
b Minneapolis, Minn, May 17, 1929. *Study:* Univ Minn, BA, 50; Univ Iowa, MFA, 52. *Work:* Oakland Mus Art, Calif; Butler Inst Am Art, Youngstown, Ohio; Yale Univ Art Gallery, New Haven, Conn; Nelson Gallery, Univ Calif, Davis; Minneapolis Inst of Art, Minneapolis, Minn; Allen Art Mus, Oberlin, Ohio; Crocker Art Gallery, Sacramento, Calif; Reed Coll, Portland, Ore; Wake Forest Univ, Winston-Salem, NC; New Britain Mus Am Art, New Britain, Conn; S Tex Mus, Corpus Christi, Tex, San Jose Mus Art, Calif; also many pvt collections. *Comn:* Var revs in mags. *Exhib:* Solo exhibs, Zara Gallery, San Francisco, 78 & 80, Artspace, Crocker Art Mus, 78 & 88, Southeastern Ctr Contemp Art, Winston-Salem, NC, 79, Joseph Chowning Gallery, San Francisco, 85 & 91, Kathryn Sermas Gallery, 90, Sacramento State Univ Gallery, 2006, Flatlanders 3, Nelson Gallery, Univ Calif Davis, 2010, b. sakata garo, 2013; Welcome to the Candy Store, Crocker Art Mus, Sacramento, Calif, 81; Seven Artists in California, Gallery Takano, Tokyo, Japan, 85; Vertigo: The Poetics of Dislocation, San Francisco Art Inst, Calif, 87; John Natsoulas Gallery, Davis, Calif, 93; Joseph Chowning Gallery, San Francisco, Calif, 95; Solomon Dubnick Gallery, Sacramento, Calif, 2003; The Pilot Hill Col, Crocker Art Mus, Sacramento, Calif, 2003; The Airplane Show, 2015, b. sakata garo; group show, 2015; 30 Painters to Collect, 2015, The Blueline Gallery, Roseville. *Teaching:* Instr art, Oberlin Coll, 55-56, Univ Hawaii, 56-57 & Blackburn Coll, 57-59; prof painting & printmaking, Sacramento State Coll, retired, chmn dept art, 66-69; artist-in-residence, Wake Forest Univ, NC Sch Arts, Winston-Salem, 79. *Awards:* Prizes, Denver Mus Art, 52 & 58 & Crocker Art Mus, 63. *Bibliog:* Thomas Albright (auth), An extraordinary artist, San Francisco Chronicle, 2/11/73; Thomas Albright (auth), Bay area mythmakers, Art Gallery Mag, 11/74; various reviews in mags. *Media:* Painting, Drawing. *Dealer:* b. sakata garo 923 20th St Sacramento Ca. *Mailing Add:* 601 Shangri Lane Sacramento CA 95825

MARCUS, MARCIA
PAINTER, LECTURER
b New York, NY, Jan 11, 1928. *Study:* NY Univ, BA, 47; Art Students League, 54, with Edwin Dickinson. *Work:* Whitney Mus Art, New York; Philadelphia Mus Art; Univ Colo, Boulder; Hirshhorn Mus; Neuberger Mus; and others. *Comn:* Var pvt & pub portrait comns. *Exhib:* Young Artists, Whitney Mus Art, 60; Woman Choose Women, NY Cult Ctr, 73; Everson Mus, Syracuse, 75; Canton Art Inst, 84; Benton Gallery, 86; 100 Yrs Creativity: The MacDowell Colony, Currier Gallery, NH, 96. *Pos:* Vis critic, 64-90. *Teaching:* Adj instr painting, Cooper Union Sch Art, New York, 70-71; assoc prof painting & drawing, La State Univ, Baton Rouge, spring 72; instr, Vassar Coll, 73-74; vis artist, Cornell Univ, spring 75, Syracuse Univ, 76 & Purdue Univ, 77-78; asst prof, RI Sch Design; assoc prof, Univ Iowa, 79-80; adj assoc prof, Queens Coll, 81, Ohio State Univ, winter 83, Univ Calif, spring 89 & Chautauqua Inst, 90. *Awards:* Ingram Merrill Award, 64 & 77; artist-in-residence, RI Sch Design, Ford Found, 66; Nat Endowment Arts, 91; Pollock Foundation, 93. *Bibliog:* Paul Cummings (auth), Smithsonian Archives Interview, 75; Noel Frackman (auth), The Attic Mind of Marcia Marcus, Arts, 9/75; Alexander Russo (auth), Profiles of Women Artists, Univ Press, 84. *Media:* Oil, Pastel, Charcoal. *Interests:* reading, movies. *Publ:* Art and the Law Catalogues, West Publ, 81; 25 Year Retrospective, Canton Art Inst, 84; auth, Mutiny and the Mainstream: Talk that changed Art 1975-1990, MidMarch Arts Press, 92. *Mailing Add:* 80 N Moore St 16J New York NY 10013

MARCUS, ROBERT (MRS) P
COLLECTOR, PATRON
b New York, NY, July 10, 1923. *Study:* Northwestern Univ; Parsons School of Design, NY. *Pos:* Bd Dir, Palm Beach Coun Arts; founder, Mus Am Folk Art, NY. *Mem:* Philarmonic Orchestra Fla; Fla Cult Action Alliance. *Collection:* American Folk Art (exhibited in 11 museums as: Two Centuries of American Folk Art: Masterworks From the Collection of Mr & Mrs Robert Marcus) North American, Latin American & European Art. *Mailing Add:* 208 Sandpiper Dr Palm Beach FL 33480-3327

MARDEN, BRICE
PAINTER, PRINTMAKER
b Bronxville, NY, Oct 15, 1938. *Study:* Boston Univ, BFA, 58-61, with Reed Kay, Arthur Hoener & Hugh Townley; Yale-Norfolk Summer Sch Music & Art, 61, with Bernard Chaet & Jon Schueler; Sch Art & Archit, Yale Univ, MFA, 61-63, with Esteban Vicente & Alex Katz. *Work:* Mus Mod Art, Whitney Mus Am Art, NY; Walker Art Ctr, Minneapolis, Minn; Ft Worth Art Ctr, Tex; Stedelijk Mus, Amsterdam; and others. *Exhib:* Solo shows incl Wilcox Gallery, Swarthmore, Pa, 64, Bykert Gallery, New York, 66, 68-70, 72-74, Galerie Yvon Lambert, Paris, 69, 73, Galleria Francoise Lambert, Milan, Italy, 70, 73, Konrad Fischer, Dusseldorf, 71-73, 75, 80, Gian Enzo Sperone, Turin, Italy, 71, 77, Locksley-Shea Gallery, Minneapolis, 72, 74, Jack Glenn Gallery, Corona del Mar, Calif, 73, Cirrus Gallery, Los Angeles, 74, Sable-Castelli Gallery, Toronto, Can, 74, Contemp Arts Mus, Houston, 74, Loretto Hilton Gallery, St Louis, 74, Ft Worth Art Mus, Tex, 74, Minneapolis Inst Arts, 75, D'Allesandro/Ferranti, Rome, 75, Solomon R Guggenheim Mus, New York, 75, Sperone Westwater Fischer, New York, 76, Max Protech Gallery, Wash, 77, Bell Gallery, Providence, 77, Jean and Karen Bernier, Athens, 77, Pace Gallery, New York, 78, 80, 82, 84, Kunstraum, Munich, 79, Inst für Moderne Kunst, Nurnberg, 79, Ink, Zurich, 80, Stedelijk Mus, Amsterdam, 81, Daniel Weinberg Gallery, Los Angeles, 84, Mary Boone Gallery, New York, 87, Mary Boone/Michael Werner Gallery, New York, 88, 89, Gallery Montenay, Paris, 88, Anthony d'Offay Gallery, London, 88, Van Straaten Gallery, Chicago, 89, Galerie Michael Werner, Cologne, 90, Kunsthalle im Kulturhaus Palazzo, Baselland, Switzerland, 91 Kunstmuseum, Basel, 92, St Louis Art Mus, 93, Mus Fur Gegnwartskunst, 93, Mus Friedericianum, Kassel, 93, Kunsthalle, Bern, 93, Secession, Vienna, 93, Stedelijk Mus, Amsterdam, 93, Stattliche Graphische Sammlung, Munich, 97, Kunstmuseum Winterthur, Switz, 97, Wexner Ctr Arts, Columbus, Ohio, 97, Fogg Art Mus, Mass, 97, Whitney Mus of Am Art, NY, 98, Carnegie Mus Art, Pittsburgh, 99, Miami Art Mus, 99, Hirshhorn Mus, 99, Dallas Mus Art, Tex, 99, Serpentine Gallery, London, 2000, Drawing the Line, The Maier Mus of Art, Randolph-Macon Woman's Coll, Va, 2001, Boston Univ Alumni Gallery, 2002, Matthew Marks Gallery, NY, 2003, Akira Ikeda Gallery, NY, 2005, A Retrospective of Paintings & Drawings, San Francisco Mus Mod Art, 2007; Group exhibs, Whitney Mus Am Art Ann, NY, 69, 77 & 83; Modular Painting, Albright-Knox Art Gallery, Buffalo, 70; Painting, New Options, Walker Art Ctr, 72; Documenta 5, Kassel, Ger, 72; Guggenheim Mus, NY, 75; A New Spirit in Painting, Royal Acad Arts, London, 81; Affinities, Hayden Gallery, Mass Inst Technol, Cambridge, 83; Paintings, Galerie Maeght Lelong, NY, 83; Anthony d'Offay Gallery, London, 88; Matthew Marks Gallery, NY, 91, 93, 95, 2002; Dia Ctr for the Arts, 91; The Tate Gallery, London, 91; Kunstmuseum Basel, 93; Kunsthalle Bern, 93; Biennale Di Venezia, Venice, Italy, 97; Staatliche Giraphische Sammlung, Munich, 97; William Hayes Fogg Art Mus, Cambridge, 98; Miami Art Mus, Fla, 99; Mixing Memory and Desire, Neues Kunstmuseum, Lucerne, 2000; Age of Influence, Reflections in the Mirror of Am Culture, Mus Contemp Art, Chicago, 2000; Etchings, Margo Leavin Gallery, LA, 2001; Serpentine Gallery, London, 2001; Repetition in Discourse, The Painting Center, NY, 2001; Auras and Epitaphs, First Public Sch of Hydra, 2002; Drawing the Line: A Retrospective, Maier Mus Art, 2002; Rocks and Art, Nature Found and Made, Chambers Fine Art, NY, 2002; Looking East, Boston Univ Art Gallery, 2002; Attendants, Bears, and Rocks, Matthew Marks Gallery, NY, 2003; Forty Years, Richard Gray Gallery, Boston Univ, 2003; The Stage of Drawing: Gesture and Act, The Drawing Ctr, NY, 2003; Singular Forms (Sometimes Repeated), Guggenheim Mus, NY, 2004; A Minimal Future? Art as Object, Mus Contemp Art, LA, 2004; Not Exactly Photographs, Fraenkel Gallery, San Francisco, 2004; An Empty Space, Akira Ikeda Gallery, NY, 2005; Contemp Voices, Mus Mod Art, NY, 2005; Imagineless Icons: Abstract Thoughts, Gagosian Gallery, London, 2005. *Pos:* security guard, Jewish Mus, 63-64; gen asst to Robert Rauschenberg, 66; painting instr, Sch Visual Arts, NY, 69-74. *Bibliog:* Jeremy Lewison (auth), Brice Marden: Prints 1961-1991, 91; Brenda Richardson (auth), Brice Marden Cold Mountain, 92; Klaus Kertess (auth), Brice Marden: Paintings & Drawings, 92. *Mem:* Am Acad Arts & Letts; Nat Acad. *Media:* Oil. *Dealer:* Matthew Marks Gallery New York NY 10021. *Mailing Add:* 6 St Lukes Pl New York NY 10012

MARENOFF, SUSAN EVE
MUSEUM DIRECTOR
b 1965. *Study:* SUNY Binghamton, B in Bus Mgmt. *Pos:* Various sales positions through vice pres Madison Square Garden; NY/NJ venue dir FIFA Women's World Cup soccer tournament, 98; dir global mktg Women's Tennis Asn Tour, 99; gen mgr, New York Power, NY, 2000-03; chief mktg officer, exec vice pres bus develop, Intrepid Sea Air & Space Mus, NYC, 2003-05, interim exec dir, 2005, exec dir, 2006-2011, pres, 2011-. *Mailing Add:* Intrepid Sea Air Space Mus W 46th St and 12th Ave Pier 86 New York NY 10036

MARET, RUSSELL
DESIGNER, PUBLISHER
Pos: Resident printer, Press, Tuscany Alley, formerly; monotype & linotype compositor, Firefly Press, Somerville, Mass, formerly; artist-in-residence, Ctr Bk Arts, formerly. *Teaching:* Instr & lectr, Ctr for Bk Arts, New York, Ctr for Contemp Printmaking, Norwalk, Conn, Cathedral St John the Divine, New York, La Casa del Libro, San Juan, La Escuela de Artes Plasticas, San Juan. *Awards:* Rolland Rome Prize, Am Acad in Rome, 2010. *Publ:* Designer, Meditation on Saviors, 1994, Color, 1995, Incidents, 1996, The Eclipse of the Moon, 1998, Kuboaa Press; Courting Couples, 2000 & The Stations of the Cross, 2001, Ctr for Bk Arts; The Drunken Boat, 2003; Retracing the Day, 2006; Prometheus Bound, 2007

MARGO, ADAIR
ADMINISTRATOR, GALLERY OWNER
Study: Vanderbilt Univ, BA (art hist); studied Renaissance art & Italian, Florence, Italy; NMex State Univ, MA (art hist). *Pos:* Founder, owner, Adair Margo Fine Art (formerly Adair Margo Gallery), El Paso, Tex, 1985-; chmn, Pres's Comt on Arts & Humanities, Washington, 2001-; chmn, Tex Commission on the Arts, formerly; chmn exhibs for USA, Mid-Am Arts Alliance, formerly; bd dirs, Humanities Tex, formerly. *Teaching:* Instr art hist, NMex State Univ & Univ Tex, formerly. *Awards:* Presidential Citizens Medal, 2008. *Mailing Add:* Presidents Comt on Arts & Humanities Ste 526 1100 Pennsylvania Ave NW Washington DC 20506

MARGOLIS, RICHARD M
PHOTOGRAPHER, ARTIST
b Lorain, Ohio, June 10, 1943. *Study:* Univ Americas, Mexico City, 64, Kent State Univ, BS, 69; Visual Studies Workshop, 72; Rochester Inst Technol, MFA, 78. *Work:* Mus Mod Art, NY; Victoria & Albert Mus, London, Eng; Bibliotheque Nat, Paris, France; Int Mus Photog, Rochester, NY; Yale Univ Art Gallery, New Haven, Conn; and others. *Comn:* Treasures of Imperial Austria, photographed medieval armor & armory, Landeszeughaus-Graz, Austria (exhib catalog), Mus Fine Arts, Houston, 91; photographs, Rochester Int Airport. *Exhib:* Solo exhibs, Foto,NY, 76, George Eastman House, Rochester, NY, 79, Bridges-Symbols of Progress, Rochester's Big Trees, Spectrum Gallery, Rochester, 90, Nat Acad Sci, Washington, DC, 90 & Rochester's Pub Art Dawson Gallery, 92; St Lawrence Univ, Canton, NY, 77; Carpenter Ctr, Harvard Univ, Cambridge, Mass, 78; Creative Artists Pub Serv Prog Photog Show, Whitney Mus Am Art, NY, 78; Mem Art Gallery, Rochester, NY, 79; Eng Landscapes, Camden Arts Ctr, London, Eng, 81; Foto, NY, 83; Queens Mus Art, 91; Paul Cava Gallery, 93; String Room, Weus Col, 96; Phot-Eye Gallery, Santa Fe, NMex, 98; Family Gatherings, Fototage, Wiesbaden, Germany, 2009. *Collection Arranged:* Personal Landscapes, Rochester Landscape in Various Media, Artworks Gallery, 80;

Francis Murray & H Jones, Gallery 696, Rochester, 81; Photography-Art of the State (auth, catalog), State Univ NY, Brockport, 83 & NY State Mus, 83; New York Bridges, 86; Computers and Photography, Pyramid Art Center, Rochester NY, 89. *Teaching:* Instr photog, Penland Sch Crafts, 79, 80, 86, 90 & 94; adj instr photog, Nazareth Col, Rochester, NY, 79-81; asst prof photog, State Univ NY, Brockport, 81-88; vis artist, Chautauqua Inst, 83. *Awards:* Agr Lift Grant, 89; Grant, NY State Coun Arts, 90; Artist Award for Contrib to Community, AGR, 94; Artwalk Founders Award, 2008. *Bibliog:* Owen Edwards (auth), Raveling the knot, Saturday Rev, 4/28/79; Owen Edwards (auth), The complex complex, Am Photographer, 6/81; Contemporary Photographers, 82-86; A Photographer's Vision, Upstate, 90. *Mem:* Soc Photog Educ (chmn, Northeast region, 83 & 85); Photogr Heritage Asn, (founder & chair); Nat Trust Hist Preservation; Soc Indust Archeol; Neighborhood of the Arts, 2000-. *Media:* Traditional black & white photography. *Specialty:* traditional large format photography. *Publ:* Bridges-Symbols of Progress Exhib Catalog, 91; Boat Houses on the St Lawrence River (Poster); Photography, Art of the State, 1983; Catalog: Family Gatherings Seder Tables, 2007; ArtisanWorks: A Guided Tour, 2009. *Mailing Add:* 250 N Goodman St Rochester NY 14607

MARGULIES, MARTIN Z
COLLECTOR
b Feb, 1938. *Pos:* Pres, Martin Z Margulies Found, Inc; owner, Martin Z Margulies Sculpture Park, 1994-, Margulies Collection at the Warehouse, Miami, Fla, 1999-; co-founder, Overtown Youth Ctr, Miami, Fla, 2003-; bd dirs, Arts for Learning, Miami, Fla. *Awards:* Named one of Top 200 Collectors, ARTnews mag, 2004-13. *Collection:* Modern and contemporary art; photography. *Mailing Add:* 445 Grand Bay Dr Key Biscayne FL 33149

MARI, M
PAINTER, PRINTMAKER
Study: Atlanta Sch Art, BFA; Butler Univ; Ga State Univ; Principia Col. *Work:* Mus Contemp Crafts, Slide Libr, NY; Vogue Fabrics Libr, Conde Nast, NY; Hunter Mus, Chattanooga, Tenn; Lily Endowment, Indianapolis, Ind. *Comn:* Batik wallhanging, Emory Univ, Atlanta, Ga; sculptured fabric wall relief, Kennedy Ctr, Tampa, Fla, 86; triptych, diptych, monoprints, Hyatt Regency, Albuquerque, NMex, 90; triptych, Dewitt Embassy, 90. *Exhib:* Midstates Painting Exhib, Evansville Mus Art, 72-74; Am Fiber Art, Ball State Univ, 74; Fibers Invitational, Austin Peay State Univ, 74; Spoleto Festival, 77; The Dyers Art, Cincinnati, Ohio, 78; Southern Graphics Coun Invitational, 86. *Teaching:* Instr batik, silkscreen & fabric painting, Ind Univ, Indianapolis, 69-72, instr painting & drawing, 72-77; instr painting, Herron Sch Art, 72. *Awards:* Objects 71, Textile Award, IMA, 71; Purchase Award, Bardstown Invitational, Ky, 73; Southeastern Arts Festival Painting Award, Atlanta, Ga, 70; Purchase Awards, Dekalb Coun for Arts Invitational, 84 & 85. *Bibliog:* Dona Meilach (auth), Contemporary Batik & Tie Dying, Crown, 73; Joanifer Gibbs (auth), Batiks Unlimited, Watson-Guptill, 74. *Mem:* Surface Design Int; Am Crafts Coun. *Media:* Oil on Canvas. *Publ:* Peachtree Papers, 85. *Mailing Add:* 2080 NW Bolton Rd Atlanta GA 30318-1106

MARIA, LEVYA
CURATOR
Pos: Cur of Permanent Collections, Art Mus of the Ams, currently. *Mailing Add:* Art Museum of the Americas 201 18th St NW Washington DC 20006

MARINCOLA, MICHELE D
ADMINISTRATOR, EDUCATOR
Study: RI Sch Design, 76-78; Brown Univ, Providence, BA (Ancient studies), 81; New York Univ Inst Fine Arts, MA (with cert conservation), 90. *Pos:* Asst Dept European Decorative Arts & Sculpture, Mus Fine Arts, Boston, 81-86; intern, Conservation Lab, Brooklyn Mus Art, 87-88, The Menil Collection, Houston, 88, Sculpture & Painting Lab, Bayerisches Nat Mus, Munich, 89-90 & Lab di Barbara Schleicher, Florence, Italy, 90; conservators apprentice, Objects Conservation Dept, Metrop Mus Art, 88-89, conservation asst, 90, asst conservator The Cloisters, 90-95, assoc conservator The Cloisters, 95-2001 & conservator The Cloisters, 2001-2002; dep dir admin & bldgs, Inst Fine Arts New York Univ, 2008, interim dir, 2008-2009. *Teaching:* Adj lectr, Williams Coll, Mass, 92; adj asst prof, Mus Studies Prog, New York Univ, 95-2000; adj prof conservation, Inst Fine Arts, New York Univ, 2000-2002, Sherman Fairchild chmn & prof conservation, 2002-. *Mem:* Am Inst for Conservation; Int Inst for Conservation. *Publ:* Coauth (with Anne Poulet & Stephen Scher), Gothic, Renaissance and Baroque Medals from the Museum of Fine Arts, Boston, The Medal, No 9, 79-105, 86; auth, The Examination and Treatment of a Pre-Columbian Scale, Art Conservation Training Programs Conf, Kingston, Ont, 5/7-8/87; co-ed (with Ellen Pearlstein), Loss Compensation: Technical & Philosophical Issues, Objects Specialty Group Session, Vol 2, Am Inst for Conservation, 94; auth, A Standing Virgin in the Cloisters: The Conservation and Restoration of a Medieval Alabaster, Metrop Mus Art Bull, 38-45, winter 98; The Surfaces of Riemenschneider's Sculpture, Tilman Riemenschneider: Master Sculptor of the Late Middle Ages (exhib catalog), 100-116, 99; coauth (with R Stein, J Kimmel & F Klemm), Observations on Cyclododecane as a Temporary Consolidant for Stone, Jour Am Inst for Conservation, Vol 39, No 3, 335-369, spring 2001. *Mailing Add:* New York Univ Inst Fine Arts Conservation Center 14 E 78th St New York NY 10021

MARINER, DONNA M
PAINTER, WRITER
b Warren, Pa, Aug 6, 1934. *Study:* Art Inst Sch, 45; Studied with W Peterson, Edinboro Col; Ben F Stahl & John Kuller; Dr Baptist, Clarion Col, 65-75; studied with A Sanders, 69; Famous Artist Sch, Westport, Conn, 74; Penn State, 83-84; Long-Ridge Writer Group Sch, 94-95. *Work:* Mariner's Art Gallery, Warren, Pa; Clinton Wilder Mus, Irvine, Pa. *Comn:* Portraits in pastel, pvt collections, 72-94; wood carvings, Warren Co Comnrs Off, Pa, 78 & 79; wood carving and oil paintings, Gulf Oil Co, Cleveland, 79-81; clipper ships, seascapes, still lifes, oils & pastels, comn by M Glotz, Warren, Pa, 88-91; Still lifes & hist railroad sta scenes, C Gerber, Wilcox, Pa, 93-96; large oils of Electro-Glide Classic of Harley-Davidson motorcycles, also done in pencil sketches for DW Mariner of Warren, Pa, 2007-2008. *Exhib:* Warren Art League Shows, 68-94; Bradford Art Festival, 69-70, 76, 82 & 85; Int Chautauqua Art Shows, NY, 76 & 78; 4th Can Int Corning Exhib, Toronto, 80; Am Artist Mag Nat Competition, New York, 86; and others. *Pos:* publicity chmn, Warren Art League & Warren Art League Summer Art Festival, 89-93, historian, 88-94; student consult, Long Ridge Writer Group Sch, 95-. *Teaching:* Instr painting, Warren Art League, 72-75, Warren Art League, 74-94 & Mariner's Art Studio, 76-; instr crafts, Warren Art League, 80-90; instr, home studio, 2006-. *Awards:* Master Pastels, 84-96; Master of Oils, 86-99; Golden Poet Award, 87-94; Outstanding Achievement, 90. *Bibliog:* Elaine Rhodes (auth), Artist returns to work, Warren Times Observer, 6/82; E Gallenstein (auth), Artist, carver and writer, Chip Chaps Mag, 86; Dianne Anderson (ed & auth), Mariner honored, Warren Times Observer, 6/15/94 & 8/17/93. *Mem:* Warren Art League; Nat Woodcarvers Asn; Int Soc Poetry; World of Poetry; Nat Libr Poetry; Poetry Guild; Famous Poets Soc; Int Artistic Asn (1980-). *Media:* Pastels, Oils. *Interests:* Poetry. *Publ:* Auth, Quick tips, perfect blenders, Am Artist Mag, 12/82; Last Farewell to Dixie, World of Poetry, 1/11/91 & In: Where Dreams Begin, 8/4/92; Summer arts festival, Dailey Press, Warren Times Observer, Corry Evening J, Jamestown Post J & Titusville Herald Paper, Pa, 7/92; Falling In Love, In: Outstanding Poets 1994, Nat Libr Poetry, 1/8/94; Warning, No Cats Allowed, Short Short Story Competition, 9/20/94; Paradise, Poetry Guild, 12/28/97; Paradise, publ American Art at the Millennium & Best Poems and Poets of 20th Century; plus numerous others. *Dealer:* Girtons 16 Hertzel St Warren PA 16365; Such'a Deal Gallery Rte 62 North Warren Pa. *Mailing Add:* PO Box 563 Warren PA 16365-0563

MARION, ANNE WINDFOHR
PATRON, ADMINISTRATOR
b Fort Worth, Tex, Nov 10, 1938. *Study:* Univ Tex, attended, Univ Geneva. *Pos:* Chmn, Burnett Oil co & Georgia O'Keeffe Mus, Santa Fe; pres, Burnett Ranches Ltd, 6666 Ranch, Guthrie, Tex, Burnett Found, Forth Worth, Tex; trustee, Kimbell Art Mus; trustee, former chmn & pres, chmn acquisition com, Mod Art Mus, Forth Worth; past trustee, Mus Mod Art, New York; mem bd regents, Tex Tech Univ; dir emeritus & hon bd mem, Nat Cowboy Hall of Fame; mem exec comt, Forth Worth Stock Show; hon bd mem, West Heritage Ctr. *Awards:* Great Woman of Tex, Fort Worth Bus Press, 1993; Charles Goodnight award, 1993; Golden Deed honoree, Fort Worth Exchange Club, 1993; Fern Sawyer award, Nat Cowgirl Hall of Fame, 1994; Gov award for excellence in the arts, NMex, 1996; Boss of the Plains award, Ranching Heritage Ctr, 2003; named one of Top 200 Collectors, ARTNews mag, 2003-12. *Mem:* Tex & SW Cattle Raisers Asn; Am Quarter Horse Asn. *Collection:* 17th- and 18th-century European art; modern and contemporary art; Taos art. *Mailing Add:* Burnett Ranchers Ltd PO Box 130 Guthrie TX 79236

MARION, JOHN LOUIS
COLLECTOR
b New York, NY, Nov 27, 1933. *Study:* Fordham Univ, BS, 1956; Columbia Univ, post grad, 1960-61. *Pos:* Sotheby Parke Bernet Inc, New York, 1960-, dir, 1965-, vpres, 1966-70, exec vpres, 1970-72, pres, 1972-87; chmn bd, Sotheby's Inc, 1975-, hon chmn, currently; bd dirs, Sotheby Holdings Inc, London, Mus NMex Syst. *Awards:* Named one of Top 200 Collectors, ARTnews mag, 2003-12. *Mem:* Appraisers Asn Am; Vintage Club; Shady Oaks Club; Eldorado Club; Lotos Club. *Collection:* 17th- and 18th-century European art; modern and contemporary art, Taos art

MARIONI, DANTE
GLASS BLOWER
b Mill Valley, Calif, 1964. *Exhib:* Solo exhibs include Traver/Sutton Gallery, Seattle, 1987, 1989, Studio 5 Seibu, Tokyo, 1990, Betsy Rosenfield Gallery, Chicago, 1992, Robert Lehman Gallery, 1993, Heller Gallery, NY City, 1994, 1996, 2000, 2003, Margo Jacobsen Gallery, Portland, Oreg, 1995, Contemp Art Niki, Tokyo, 1997, Riley Hawk Gallery, Columbus, Ohio, 1998, Susan Duval Gallery, Aspen, 1999, 2002, Holsten Gallery, NY City, 2000, Howard Yezerski Gallery, Boston, 2001, Mus Northwest Art, Washington State, 2002, Martha Connell Gallery, Atlanta, 2003, Marz Saunders Gallery, Chicago, 2004, Master Works Gallery, Aukland, New Zealand, 2004, Buschlen Mowatt, Vancouver, BC, 2005, Dane Gallery, Nantucket, 2005, Maurine Littleton Gallery, Washington, DC, 2005, Recent Glass Works, Wade Wilson Art, Tex, 2010; group exhibs include Greenwood Gallery, Seattle, 1984; Mandarin Gallery, Tacoma Wash, 1985; Traver/Sutton Gallery, Seattle, 1986; Beaver Gallery, Canberra, Australia, 1987; Am Embassy, Prague, 1988; Am Craft Mus, 1989, 1990; Bellevue Art Mus, Wash, 1991; Heller Gallery, NY City, 1991; LewAllen Gallery, Santa Fe, 1991, 1992, 1993; Gallery Nakama, Tokyo, 1992; William Traver Gallery, Seattle, 1992, 1996; Carnegie Mus Art, Pittsburgh, 1993; Seattle Art Mus, 1995; Susan Duvall Gallery, Aspen, 1996; Mus Fine Arts, Boston, 1997; Cleveland Mus Art, 1997; Image Gallery, Palm Desert, Calif, 1997; Galleria Marina Barovier, 1998; Aperto Vetro, Venice, 1998; Howard Yezerski, Boston, 1999; Jenkins Johnson Gallery, San Francisco, 2000; Lane Gallery, Del Mar, 2003; Marx Saunders, Chicago Sofa, 2005, 2006; Liuligongfang Mus and Gallery, Shanghai, 2006; Scottish Gallery, Edinburgh, Scotland, 2006; Everhart Mus, Scranton, Pa, 2006. *Teaching:* instr, Pratt Fine Arts Ctr, Seattle, 1985, Niijima Glass Art Ctr, Japan, 1989-92, Pilchuck Galls Sch, Stanwood, Wash, 1990-2003, Haystack Sch, Deer Isle, Maine, 1991, 1992, 1996, SUWA Glass Mus, Nagano, Japan, 1996; asst tchr, Pilchuck Glass Sch, 1987, Haystack Sch, Deer Isle, Maine, 1987; tchr, Penland Sch Crafts, NC, 1988, 1996, Wanganui Summer Sch, 1989, Fujikawa Craft park, Japan, 1990, Toyama Glass Art Inst, Japan, 1993, RI Sch Design, 1993, Kent State, Cleveland, 1999, Miami Univ, 2000, Northlands Creative Glass, Lybster Scotland, 2001, 2006, Canberrs Sch Art, Australia, 2005. *Awards:* Louis Comfort Tiffany Found Award, 1987; Outstanding Achievement in Glass, Urban Glass Award, NY City, 1997; 1st Place-Reticello,

Ebeltoft Mus, Denmark, 2002; represented in permanent collections Cincinnati Mus Art, Columbia Mus Art, SC, Corning Mus Glass, NY, Japanese Nat Mus Mod Art, Tokyo, LA County Mus Art, Nat Mus Art, Renwick Gallery, Smithsonian Inst, Wash, DC, New Zealand Nat Mus, Carnegie Mus Art, Yokohama Mus Art, Japan. *Bibliog:* Waggoner, Shawn (auth), Dante Marioni: Upholding the Vessel Tradition, Glass Art, winter/1994; Kangas, Matthew (auth), Dante Marioni: Apprentice to Tradition, Am Craft, 2/1994; Dante Marioni, Seattle's Standard Bearer, Glass and Art, winter/1997. *Publ:* auth, Blown Glass, Hudson Hill Press. *Dealer:* Pismo Gallery 433 E Cooper Rd Aspen CO 81611; Maureen Littleton Gallery 1667 Wisconsin Ave NW Washington DC 20007; Marx Saunders Gallery 230 W Superior St Chicago IL 60610; Dane Gallery 28 Ctr St Nantucket MA 02554; Holsten Gallery 3 elm st Stockbridge MA 01262; Howard Yezerski Gallery 14 Newbury St Boston MA 02116; Charlotte Jackson Fine Art 200 W Marcy St #101 Santa Fe NM 87501; Hawk Galleries 153 E Main St Columbus OH 43215; Tom Riley Gallery 2026 Murray Hill Rd Cleveland OH 44106; Davis & Cline Galleries 525 A Street #1 Ashland OR 97520; The Bullseye Connection Gallery 300 NW 13th Ave Portland OR 97209; Concept Art Gallery 1031 S Braddock Ave Pittsburgh PA 15218; Buschlen-Mowatt Gallery 1445 W Georgia St Main Floor Vancouver BC V6G 2T3. *Mailing Add:* c/o William Traver Gallery 110 Union St 2nd Fl Seattle WA 98101

MARIONI, PAUL
SCULPTOR, GLASS BLOWER

b Cincinnati, Ohio, July 19, 1941. *Study:* Univ Cincinnati, BA, 67. *Work:* Corning Mus Glass; Hessisches Landesmuseum, Darmstadt, WGer; Oakland Mus; Yamaha Corp, Tokyo; Mus Am Craft, NY. *Comn:* Light columns, Port Authority, Pier 69 Hq, Seattle, 93; The Further I Look, the More I See, Eye Clinic, Univ Med Ctr, Seattle, 93; shelter, Veterinary Teaching Hosp, Pullman, Wash, 96; pillars, Burbank Police/Fire Dept, 97; Water Equals Light, Seattle City Light, 97. *Exhib:* New Glass: A Worldwide Survey, Corning Mus Glass, World Tour, 78-82; 200 Objects, Corning Mus Glass, Russ Tour, 90-91; Int Conf on Environ Glass, Corning Mus Glass, NY, 93; 100 Yrs - Calif Crafts, Oakland Art Mus, Calif, 93; V Internationales, Glasmuseum Frauenau, Ger, 95; Light Interpretations: Menorah Invitational, Jewish Mus, San Francisco, 95; Pilchuck Pioneers, William Traver Gallery, Seattle, 95; cast glass, Contemp Crafts Gallery, Portland, Ore 96; Trashformations, Watcom Mus, Bellingham, Wash, 97. *Pos:* Dir, Canyon Cinema, San Francisco, 72-74; coordr glass prog, Summervail, Vail, Colo, 79-84; dir, Glass Art Soc, 84-86. *Teaching:* Lectr art, San Francisco Art Inst, 73-75; asst prof, San Francisco State Univ, 74-78; fac, Pilchuck Sch, Stanwood, Wash, 74-96. *Awards:* Nat Endowment Arts Grants, 75-76, 82 & 88; First Prize Archit, Fragile Art, 83. *Bibliog:* Otto Rigan (auth), New Glass, Simon & Schuster, 76; Narcissus Quagliata (auth), From Mind to Light, Mattole Press, 76; Julie Hall (auth), Tradition and Change, Dutton Press, 78. *Mem:* Glass Arts Soc; Northwest Glass Artists. *Media:* Glass. *Dealer:* Walter-White Gallery 7th & San Carlos PO Box 4834 Carmel CA 93921; William Traver Gallery 110 Union St Seattle WA 98101. *Mailing Add:* 4136 Meridian Ave No 1 Seattle WA 98103

MARIONI, TOM
SCULPTOR

b Cincinnati, Ohio, 1937. *Study:* Cincinnati Art Acad, 55-59. *Hon Degrees:* Soc Ind Artists, PhD, 70. *Work:* Mus Mod Art, NY & San Francisco. *Comn:* Logo, Western Asn Art Mus, 69; pub sculpture, Marin Co Civic Ctr, 88. *Exhib:* Sound Sculpture As, Mus Conceptual Art, 70; De Marco Gallery, Edinburgh, Scotland, 72; White Chapel, London, Eng, 72; Student Cult Ctr, Belgrade, Yugoslavia, 74; Solo exhibs, Foksol Gallery, Warsaw, Poland, 75, Mod Art Gallery, Vienna, Austria, 79, Pellegrino Gallery, Bologna, Italy, 79, Kunst Mus, Bern, Switz, 80 & Ctr G Pompidou Mus, Paris, 80. *Collection Arranged:* All Night Sculptures, Mus Conceptual Art, 73; Art Against War, San Francisco Art Inst, 84; Elegant Miniatures from San Francisco, Belca House, Kyoto, Japan. *Pos:* Cur art, Richmond Art Ctr, 68-71; dir, Mus Conceptual Art, 70-84; ed, Vision, Oakland, 75-82. *Teaching:* Instr, Univ Calif, Berkeley, 79, Los Angeles, 86. *Awards:* Nat Endowment Arts, 79, 80 & 84; J S Guggenheim Grant, 80; Travel Grant, Asian Cult Coun, 86. *Bibliog:* Bill Berkson (rev), Artforum, 5/86; David Winter (rev), Artnews, 4/86; Terri Cohn (auth), Tom Marioni Sacred Geometry, Sculpture Mag, 3/98; and others. *Mem:* San Francisco Art Inst (bd dir, 74-). *Media:* Wood. *Specialty:* Contemporary Art. *Interests:* Jazz. *Collection:* Glassware. *Publ:* The Return of Abstract Expressionism, 69; The San Francisco Performance, 72; Notes & Scores for Sounds, 72; Vision (California), 75, Vision (Eastern Europe), Vision (New York City), Vision (Word of Mouth), 80 & Vision (Artist Photographs), 81; Writings on Art 1969-1999, Crown Point Press; Beer, Art & Philosophy, Crown Point Press, San Francisco, Calif, 2003; Fabliaux, Crown Point Press. *Dealer:* Margarete Roeder 545 Broadway New York NY; Paule Anglim 14 Geary St San Francisco. *Mailing Add:* 657 Howard San Francisco CA 94105

MARISOL
SCULPTOR

b Paris, France, 1930. *Study:* Ecole Beaux Arts, 49; Art Students League, 50; New Sch, Hans Hofmann Sch, 51-54; Moore Coll Art, Philadelphia, Hon DFA, 69, RI Sch Design, Providence, Hon Dr Arts, 86; State Univ NY, Buffalo, Hon DFA, 92. *Work:* Mus Mod Art, NY; Whitney Mus Am Art, NY; Albright-Knox Art Gallery, Buffalo; Mus De Arte Contemporaneo, Caracas, Venezuela; Nat Portrait Gallery, Washington, DC; Rose Art Mus, Brandeis Univ, Waltham, Mass; Hakone Open Air Mus, Japan; Art Inst Chicago; and others. *Exhib:* Solo exhibs, Sidney Janis Gallery, NY, 66, 75, 84 & 89, Boca Raton Mus Art, Fla, 88, Galerie Tokoro, Tokyo, 89, Nat Portrait Gallery (with catalog), Washington, DC, 91, Tenri Gallery, Cult Inst New York, NY, 92, NJ Ctr Visual Arts (with catalog), NJ, 92 & Marlborough Gallery (with catalog), NY, 98; Forms in Wood, Am Sculpture of the 1950's, Philadelphia Art Mus, 85; The Artist's Mother: Portraits & Homages, Heckscher Mus, Huntington, NY & Nat Portrait Gallery, Washington, 87; Urban Figures, Whitney Mus Am Art at Philip Morris, 88; Body Language: The Figure in the Art of Our Time, Rose Art Mus, Waltham, Mass, 90; Figures of Contemp Sculpture (1978-1990): Images of Man, Isetan Mus Art, Tokyo, Dakimoru Mus Art, Osaka-Umeda & Hiroshima City Mus Contemp Art, 92; The League at the Cape, Provincetown Art Asn & Mus, Mass, 93; Lateinamerikanische Kunst im 20 Jahrhundert, Mus Ludwig & Josef-Haubrich Kunsthalle, Cologne, Ger, 93; Museo de Arte Contempo Ranio, Caracas, Venezuela, 96; Latin Viewpoints: into the Mainstream, Nassau Co Mus Art, NY, 97; The Feminine Image (with catalog), Nassau Co Mus Art, NY, 97; Coming Off the Wall, Susquehanna Art Mus, Pa, 98; Rep in permanent collections at Mus Modern Art, New York City, Whitney Mus Am Art, Albright-Knox Gallery, Buffalo, Hakone Open Air Mus, Tokyo, Nat Portrait Gallery, Washington, Harry N Abrams Collection, New York City, Yale Univ Art Gallery, Art Inst Chicago, Metrop Mus, New York City, numerous others; pub installation Am Merchant Mariner's Memorial, Promenade Battery Park Pier A, Port of NY, New York City; and others. *Awards:* 11th Annual Art Comn Awards, Excellence in Design for Am Merchant Mariner's Mem, Art Comn City New York, 92; Medal of Honor, Nat Arts Club, New York, 95; Gabriela Mistral Inter-Am Prize for Cult, Org Am States, 97; and others. *Bibliog:* Margaret R Lunn (auth), Marisol, NJ Ctr Vis Arts, Harvard Printing Co, 93; Roberta Bernstein (auth), Marisol, Art Lift Ltd, NY, 95; Willo Doe (auth), Interview with Marisol, Space, 82-87, 7/97. *Mem:* Am Acad Arts & Letters, 78; Nat Acad. *Publ:* Contribr, Robert Bernstein & Yoshiaki Turo (auths), Marisol, Galerie Tokoro, Tokyo, 89; Carol Anne Munsun (ed), Pop Art: The Critical Dialogue, Univ Mich Res Press, Ann Arbor, 89; Contemporary American Women Artists, Cedco Publg, San Rafael, 91; Nancy Grove (auth), Magical Mixtures: Marisol Portrait Sculpture, Smithsonian Inst Press for Nat Portrait Gallery, 91; Margaret Lunn (auth), Marisol, NJ Ctr Visual Arts, Harvard Printing Co, 92; and many others. *Mailing Add:* 427 Washington St 7th Fl New York NY 10013

MARK, PHYLLIS
SCULPTOR, ENVIRONMENTAL ARTIST

b New York, NY. *Study:* Ohio State Univ; New Sch Social Res, sculpture study with Seymour Lipton. *Work:* Dickerson-White Mus, Cornell Univ; Allentown Mus Art, Pa; RCA Collection; Corcoran Gallery Art, Washington; Ft Wayne Mus Art, Ind; and others. *Comn:* Birmingham Ctr, Mich, 75; Land Sail installation, Hofstra Univ Mus, 90. *Exhib:* Sculpture as Jewelry, Inst Contemp Art, Boston, 73; Works on Paper by Women Artists, Brooklyn Mus, 75; Cast Iron Gallery, 92 & 93; Washington Square Atrium, 93; Soho 20 Gallery, NY, 93, 94 & 95; FFS Gallery, NY, 94, 95 & 96; Guild Hall, East Hampton, NY, 95; Solo exhibs, Ivoryton, Conn, 96, Roger Williams Park, Providence, RI, 96, Stamford Mus, Conn, 96 & Lever House, NY, 96. *Pos:* Bd dir, Soho 20 Gallery, 86- & Artists Representing Environ Arts; ed, The Guild Reporter, Sculptors Guild, 86. *Awards:* Ind Arts Comn & Nat Endowment Arts Grant, 79. *Bibliog:* Ed McCormack, Artspeak, 3/92; Rose Slivka, East Hampton Star, 92, 94 & 95; Williamsport Sun Gazette, 95; and others. *Mem:* Artist Rep Environ Art (mem bd dir & treas, currently); Women's Caucus for Art; Sculptors Guild (bd mem & vpres publs, currently). *Media:* Painted Aluminum, Stainless Steel. *Publ:* Auth, Zen Kustlers Aus New York (exhib catalog), Reinesche Post Rev, 89. *Dealer:* Soho 20 Gallery New York NY 10013. *Mailing Add:* 801 Greenwich St New York NY 10014-1842

MARKARIAN, ALEXIA (MITRUS)
PAINTER, SCULPTOR, DESIGNER

b Binghamton, NY. *Study:* Art Students League, drawing & anatomy studies with Robert Hale; Broome Community Coll, State Univ NY, Binghamton, AB. *Work:* Chattahoochee Valley Art Asn, La Grange, Ga. *Comn:* Small Shade Pavilion (sculpture), Cal Trans/City Heights Community Develop Corp, Garden Art Proj Site Specific Pub Art, San Diego, 93. *Exhib:* Solo Exhibs: Free Fall, Univ St Louis, 88; Dietrich Jenny Gallery, San Diego, 89; Artists Union Gallery, Moscow, USSR, 90; Oneiros Gallery, San Diego, 91; Terra Obscura, Traveling USA & Can, 91-93; Red Venus Gallery San Diego, 94; Heart in a Fist, Simay Space, San Diego, 2001; Paintings & Works on Paper, 2000-2008; Earl & Birdie Taylor Libr, Mark-Elliott Lugo (cur), San Diego, 2008; Group Exhibs: Riverside Mus Art, Calif, 86; 8th Ann Invitational Drawing Show, E Mark-Elliott Lugo (cur), San Diego Visual Arts Prog, Earl & Birdie Taylor Libr, San Diego; 2008; National Midyear Show, Butler Inst Am Art, Youngstown, Ohio, 86-87; Five Women Artists: A Southern California Perspective, traveling, USA & Can, 86-88; Fla Nat, Fla State Univ, Tallahassee, 88; On the Horizon: Emerging in California, Fresno Arts Ctr & Mus, 88; Bestiary, Women's Bldg, Los Angeles, Calif, 88; Artists Union Gallery, Moscow, USSR, 90; Calif Ctr Arts, Escondido, 93; Centro Cult, Tijuana, Mex, 94; Munic Art Gallery, Los Angeles, 95; Temporary Situations, Mira Costa Coll, 96; Hello Again, Oakland Mus Art, Calif, 99; Three Plus Three, Oceanside Mus Art, Oceanside, Calif, 2000; Schneider Mus Art, Ashland, Ore, 2000; Pure Painting, San Diego Visual Arts Prog, Earl & Birdie Taylor Libr, San Diego, Calif, 2006; Protea Gallery, San Diego, Calif, 2012; 7 Deadly Sins, Mesa Coll Art Gallery, San Diego, Calif, 2012; Cannon Art Gallery, Carlbad, Calif, 2013. *Pos:* Lectr, San Diego Art Inst Artist Series, 89-90; Isomata Master Class Series, painting, Idyllwild, Calif, 92; lectr, Art Mus Greater Victoria, BC, Can, 93; set designer, Mac Wellmans play A Murder of Crows, San Diego, Calif, 93; originator & producer, Phototropolis: Contemp Photog, Int Photo Exhib, San Diego, Calif, 95; designer, Cinewest Productions film, Love Always, 96. *Awards:* Bellinger Award, Gebbie Found, Chatauqua Exhib, 85; First Award, Fine Arts, Int Soc Airbrush Arts, Pasadena, Calif, 85; Permanent Collection Purchase Award, La Grange Nat, Ga, 88; Artists Fel, Calif Arts Coun, 90. *Bibliog:* Tony di Gessu (prod), interview, Channel 51-TV, San Diego, Calif, 10/26/85; Bill Van Siclen (auth), Art in Rhode Island, Providence J-Bull, 2/86; Leah Ollman (auth), At the Galleries (article), Los Angeles Times, 2/12/88, 10/1/89 & 11/20/91; Robert L Pincus (auth), articles, San Diego Union Tribune, 10/19/89, 6/15/90, 12/91, 8/20/92, 6/24/93, 3/16/2000, 8/31/2000, 5/31/2001, 6/29/2006, 6/15/2008, 6/11/2009; Art in America, Rev of Exhibs, 4/90; Elizabeth Kidd (auth), Outlook Mag, Vol III, issue 2, (article), Edmonton Art Gallery, 92; Gene Grey (auth), Living (article), Binghamton Press, 2/92; Mus Mod Art San Francisco, Mus Store Catalog, Winter, 96; Susan Subtle (auth), San Francisco Focus, Gift of Garbage (article), 97; Tessa Decarlo (auth), Art & Leisure, article, NY Times, 6/22/97; Seattle Post Intelligencer, Fashion, 2002; Dona Z Meilach (auth), Art Jewlery Today, Schiffer Publ Ltd, 2003. *Mem:* San Diego Art Inst (bd dir, 81-82); Artists Equity (vpres, 84-86); Artists Guild San Diego Mus Art (corresp secy, 84). *Media:* Acrylic, Miscellaneous Media. *Publ:* Illusr, The Red Flower, Crossing Press, 88; contribr, Art Jewelry Today, Schiffer Publ, 2003; auth, illustr, Midnight Auto, 2008; auth, illustr, Woosh, 2008. *Mailing Add:* 1702 Primrose Dr El Cajon CA 92020-5649

MARKEL, KATHRYN E
DEALER
b Richmond, Va, Oct 19, 1946. *Pos:* Co-owner, Kathryn Markel Gallery, New York, currently. *Media:* Work on Paper. *Specialty:* Specialty work on paper by contemporary American artists. *Mailing Add:* 22 Hobart St Bronxville NY 10708

MARKER, MARISKA PUGSLEY
PAINTER, WRITER
b San Francisco, Calif. *Study:* With Leon Berkowitz, Robert Newmann, Hank Harmon, Horace Day, Daniel Greene, Albert Handell, Henry Hensche, and others. *Work:* Nat Mus Fine Arts, Valletta, Malta; The White House Artists Easter Collection, Smithsonian Inst, Washington, DC; Fed Reserve Bd Governors Collection, Washington, DC; Dulin Gallery Art, Knoxville, Tenn; and others. *Comn:* Container Corp Am. *Exhib:* Two-person exhib, Nat Mus Fine Arts, Valletta, Malta, 76; solo exhibs, Fed Reserve Bd Governors, Washington, DC, 81 & 84, Va Beach Art Ctr, 83, Gilpin Gallery, The Atholl Series, 88, among others; Continuum V, Dulin Gallery Art, Knoxville, Tenn, 84; US State Dept Art in Embassies Prog, US Embassy, Muscat, Oman, 86-90; and others. *Pos:* Bd mem, Art League Alexandria, Va, 69-70; artist-in-residence, Hollin Meadows Sch, Fairfax Co, Va, 86. *Teaching:* Instr puppet classes, William Rockhill Nelson Gallery Art, Kansas City, Mo, 40's; instr painting, Vet Admin Hosp, Kansas City, Mo, 50's; lectr, contemp Am folk art, Alexandria Lyceum, Va, 78 & Va Mus, 80. *Awards:* Judged, Maine Artists, The Next Generation, Washington, DC, 90, for Maine Arts Comm & Maine State Soc. *Bibliog:* The Markers at the Museum of Fine Arts, Times Malta, 10/20/76; Teresa Annas (auth), Energetic Marker creates art with depth, 9/4/83; John Levin (auth), Illuminating images, a unique technique, 9/8/83; Pam Frese & Ansley Valentine, Mariska Marker (film), Coll of Wooster, Ohio, 2005; and others. *Media:* Miscellaneous media. *Res:* Max Schallinger, a rediscovered artist. *Publ:* Auth, Korean arts have a great potential, Feel of Korea, Holl M Corp, 66; Pebbles in the Pond, 5/20/94; also feature articles in Kansas City Star, catalogs for Northern Va Fine Arts Asn & var mag articles, 2000-2003. *Mailing Add:* 9082 Belvoir Woods Pkwy Fort Belvoir VA 22060

MARKETOU, JENNY
VIDEO ARTIST
b Athens, Greece. *Study:* Univ Athens, Greece, BA, 80; Corcoran Sch Art, Washington, DC, BFA, 82; Pratt Inst, Brooklyn, MFA, 86. *Comn:* Astoria: Dreams of New York, Metrop Transit Auth, NY, 92. *Exhib:* 114 + 114, Univ SFla Contemp Art Mus, Tampa, 93; solo exhibs, Western Front Gallery, Vancouver, BC, 95, Gallery Anadiel, Old City, Jerusalem, Israel, 96, Aria Kappatos Gallery, Argostoli, Kefalonia, Greece, 97 & In Situ, Snug Harbor, Staten Island, NY, 97; The Invisible Force: Nomadism as Art Practice, Polk Mus Art, Lakeland, Fla, 95; Ethereal Images, Southeast Mus Photog, Daytona Beach Community Col, 96; Artist's Messengers of Peace, Eretz Israel Mus, Tel Aviv, 96; En Route to MEX, ART & IDEA, Old Mexico City, Mex, 96; Int Showcase, Women and the Art of Multimedia, Nat Mus Women Arts, Washington, DC, 97; I Can Not Take My Eyes Off You (video proj), The Sculpture Garden, NY, 97; Projected Sites, Sixth Biennial Arts & Technol, Cummings Art Ctr, Conn Col, New London, 97. *Awards:* Visual Arts Fel Photog, Nat Endowment Arts, Washington, DC, 91; Found Hellenic Cult Grant, 96; Resident Artist Fel, Ariz State Univ, 97 & Banff Ctr Arts, Alta, Can, 97. *Bibliog:* Sania Page (auth), Women Beyond Borders, Antikenmuseum & Sammlung, 96; Rosa Martinez (auth), Manifesta I, Witte de With Mus Contemp Art, 96; Roy Ascott & Robert Rindler (auths), Techno-Seduction, Cooper Union, 97. *Mailing Add:* c/o Jayne H Baum Gallery 26 Grove St Suite 4C New York NY 10014

MARKLE, GREER (WALTER GREER MARKLE)
MUSEUM DIRECTOR, HISTORIAN
b Port Arthur, Tex, Apr 12, 1946. *Study:* Univ Wyoming, BFA, 68; Univ Utah, MA, 76; Univ Ore, PhD, 99. *Collection Arranged:* Contemp Am Prints and Drawings, UMFA Traveling, 78; Utah Wilderness Photography, traveling, 78; Potter and Prints, Sun Valley Ctr, 81; Will Martin Retrospective, Schneider Mus Art, 87; Art of the Orient: Schneider Mus Art, Zundel Col, 88. *Teaching:* Instr art hist, Univ Utah, Salt Lake City, 76-78; lectr art admin, Radcliffe Col, Cambridge, Mass, 78-82; asst prof art hist, S Ore State Col, Ashland, 86-; prof, S Ore Univ. *Mem:* Coll Art Asn; Ore Advocates Arts; Am Asn Mus. *Res:* Contemporary Am art and Italian Renaissance art; Diego Rivera's portrait of America: Marxism and Montage. *Publ:* Auth, Marilyn Levine and photorealism, Ceramics Monthly, 76; Utah wilderness photography, Utah Arts Coun, 78; Potters & prints, Sun Valley Ctr, 81; Handbook for traveling exhibitions, Cambridge, Mass. *Mailing Add:* Southern Oregon State Col Art Dept Ashland OR 97520

MARKLE, SAM
DEALER, SCULPTOR
b Winnipeg, Man, 1933. *Study:* Self-taught. *Work:* Nat Art Bank, Ottawa; McLaughlin Mus, Oshawa. *Comn:* Neon installations (with Jack Markle), Alcan Aluminum, Head Off, Toronto, 70; United Trust, Head Off, 72, Famous Players Theatre, Four Seasons Hotel, 73, Sunoco Bldg, 73 & Concourse & Plaza, Hudson Bay Co, 73, Toronto, 74. *Exhib:* Solo exhibs, Pop Sign Art, Gallery Pascal, 64, Alpha 64, Four Seasons Hotel, 64 & Flower & Garden Show & Electric Gallery, Toronto, 71; New Media, Art Gallery Ont, 71; Espace V Gallery, Montreal, 74. *Pos:* Dir, Electric Gallery, Toronto. *Mem:* Prof Art Dealers Can (vpres, 75-78); Can Conf Arts. *Media:* Neon tubing. *Specialty:* Electric art exclusively. *Mailing Add:* The Brothers Markle Inc 3530 Pharmacy Ave Toronto ON MIW 257 Canada

MARKMAN, RONALD
PAINTER
b Bronx, NY, May 29, 1931. *Study:* Yale Univ, BFA, 57 & MFA, 59. *Work:* Brooklyn Mus, NY; Art Inst of Chicago, Ill; Hirshhorn Mus & Sculpture Garden, Smithsonian Inst, Washington, DC; Metrop Mus of Art, NY; Mus of Mod Art, NY; Cincinnati Art Mus; Cornell Univ Art Mus; Libr Congress; Indiana Univ Art Mus; Univ Alberta, Canada. *Comn:* Christmas Card, Mus Mod Art, 68; Drawing, Rockland State Hosp, NY, 72; five murals, Riley Children's Hosp, 86; Ortho Childcare Ctr, Raritan, NJ, 91. *Exhib:* Recent Acquisitions Show, Mus Mod Art, 59 & 66, Young Am, Whitney Mus Am Art, 60, Am Inst Arts & Letts, 77 & 89, NY; Young Am, Whitney Mus Am Art, 60; Chicago Biennial Print & Drawing Show, Art Inst Chicago, 64; Pa Acad Fine Arts Ann, 67, Tyler Sch Art, 76, Philadelphia; Am Painting, Butler Inst, Youngstown, Ohio, 67; Print Biennial, Brooklyn Mus, 68; Humor, Satire and Irony, New Sch for Social Res, 72; Indianapolis Mus Art, 72 & 74; Work by Students of Josef Albers, Harvard Univ, 74; Solo exhibs, Kanegis Gallery, Boston, 59, Terry Dintenfass Gallery, NY, 65-66, 68, 71, 76, 79, 82 & 85, Dart Gallery, Chicago, 80, & King Gallery, Indianapolis, 83 & 86; Mitchell Gallery, St John's Col, Annapolis, MD, 2005. *Teaching:* Instr, Univ Fla, 59, Art Inst Chicago, 60-64 & Indiana Univ, 64-95, retired, 95-. *Awards:* Fulbright Fel, 62-63; Lilly open faculty fel, 89; Ind Arts Comn, 90, 93; Center for New Television, 92; Honorable Mention, Ohio Film Festival, 95. *Mailing Add:* 1623 St Margaret's Rd Annapolis MD 21401

MARKOWITZ, MARILYN
PAINTER, PRINTMAKER
b New York, NY. *Study:* Colo Col, BA, 63; Univ Colo, Boulder, MA, 71. *Work:* State of Colo Art in Pub Places, Univ Colo, Colorado Springs & Boulder. *Comn:* Painting, State of Colo, Colorado Springs, 81. *Exhib:* Solo exhibs, Brena Gallery, Denver, Colo, 75, Albatross Gallery, Boulder, Colo, 79, Carson-Sapiro Gallery, Denver, Colo, 80, Univ Colo, Colorado Springs, 82, Art Resources Gallery, Denver, 83, Western Nebr Art Ctr, Scotts Bluff & Reiss Gallery, Denver, 86; Hassel-Haesler Gallery, Denver, 92; Art of Craft, Denver, 93; Pinache, Denver, 94; Univ S NMex, 96; Nat Collage soc, Elyria, Ohio, 97; Curtis Ctr Arts & Humanities, Greenwood, Colo, 97; New World Art Ctr, NY, 98; Laura Knott Gallery, Bradford Col, Haverhill, Mass, 98; Alchemy, Nabisco Gallery, East Hanover, NJ, 200; plus many others. *Teaching:* Instr art, Dist No 11 Colorado Springs, 63-69 & Univ Colo, 70-71. *Awards:* Award, Boulder Fine Art Ctr, 71 & 72; Nat Asn Women Artists Award, 77, 79, 85 & 86; Art in Pub Places Award, State of Colo, 81. *Bibliog:* Am Artists Mag, 6/78; Very Important Women, Denver Mag; One Source: Sacred Journeys. *Mem:* Nat Asn Women Artists; Layerist Soc Am; Nat Asn Women Artists. *Media:* Acrylics, Oil; Sand. *Publ:* Contribr, La Revue Moderne, Paris, France, 80; Layering, an art of time and space, Empire Mag, 91; Very important women, Denver Post; One Source: Sacred Journeys, 97; Bridging Time and Space, 98

MARKOWSKI, EUGENE DAVID
PAINTER, SCULPTOR
b St Louis, Mo, Sept 16, 1931. *Study:* Washington Univ Sch Fine Art, BFA, 60; Univ Pa Sch Fine Art, MFA, 61. *Work:* Minn Mus Art, St Paul; Lauren Rogers Mus Art, Laurel, Miss; Philip Morris Corp & First & Merchants Bank, Richmond, Va; NY Bank for Savings; Guaranty Savings & Loan, Charlottesville, Va. *Comn:* Chapel, Holy Comforter Roman Cath Church, Charlottesville, Va, 82; stained glass windows, St Mary's Roman Cath Church, Lovingston, Va, 83; sculpture (wood), St George's Roman Cath Church, Scottsville, Va, 83; painting, Civil War Trust, Washington DC, 92. *Exhib:* Northern Ill Univ Nat Drawing Competition, 71; Nat Drawing Competition, Minn Mus Art, 71; Int Print & Drawing Competition, Alta Coll Art, 72; Regional Painting Competition, Montgomery Mus Fine Arts, 75; Novumn Gallery Ltd, Basel, Switz, 92; Frank Bustamante Gallery, NY, 91; and others. *Pos:* Art critic, Cablevision, Charlottesville, 72-; chmn, studio art dept, Univ Va, 86-; chmn Studio, Trinity Univ, Washington, DC, 91-. *Teaching:* Asst prof painting, Univ Pa, 61-68 & Montgomery Coll, Rockville, Md, 68-70; assoc prof painting, Univ Va, Charlottesville, 70-87; prof art, Trinity Univ, Washington, DC, 88-. *Awards:* Drawing Award, Smithsonian Inst, 81; Sesquicentennial Associateship, Res Italy, Univ Va, 85; Fulbright Fel, research in India, Coun Int Exchange Scholars, 86. *Mem:* Coll Art Asn Am; assoc mem Int Ctr Art Intelligence; Fullbright Asn. *Media:* Oil on Canvas; Wood. *Res:* Monuments and people of India. *Interests:* Photography, music, travel. *Publ:* Auth, The Art of Photography: Image and Illusion, Prentice-Hall, 84; Art Fraud and authentication, Harry N Abrams, 2001. *Dealer:* Novumn Gallery Ltd Binningerstsrasse 82-88 Basel-Alischwil Switzerland; Artisans Gallery 4834 MacArthur Blvd NW Washington DC 20007; Voltz Gallery Poligono 2 Parcela 26 07340 Alaro Baleares Spain; Studio Gallery 2108 R St NW DC 20008. *Mailing Add:* 4706 Foxhall Crescents NW Washington DC 20007

MARKS, MATTHEW STUART
ART DEALER
b New York, NY, Nov 14, 1962. *Study:* Columbia Univ 80-82, with Milton Resnick; Bennington Col, BA, 85. *Collection Arranged:* From the Collection of Matthew Marks, Am Prints 1860-1960 (auth, catalog), Bennington Col, 85; British Modernist Prints 1900-1950 (auth, catalog), 85 & Je suis le cahier: The Sketchbooks of Picasso (auth, catalog), 86, Pace Gallery, NY. *Pos:* Consult, Pace Gallery, New York, 82-86; trustee, Bennington Col, Vt, 85-89; dir, Anthony d'Offay Gallery, London, 87-89; pres, Matthew Marks, Inc, 81-89 & 90-; bd mem, Merce Cunningham Dance Co, 93-96. *Bibliog:* Rising Stars Under 40, Art News, 95; Portrait of the Dealer as a Young Man, Out, 11/97; and numerous articles in art mags. *Res:* 19th and 20th century European and American art; contemp Am art & European art. *Publ:* Auth, Henry Farrer's early etchings of New York, Imprint, 82; Provincetown prints, Print Collector's Newlett, 84; The graphic work of Lucian Freud, Print Quart, 86. *Mailing Add:* 523 W 24th St New York NY 10011

MARKS, ROBERTA BARBARA
SCULPTOR, COLLAGE PAINTER

b Savannah, Ga. *Study:* Univ Miami, Fla, BFA, 80; Univ S Fla, MFA, 81. *Work:* Victoria & Albert Mus, London, Eng; Galerie du Manoir, La Chaux-de-Fonds, Switz; AT&T Corp, Philip Johnson Bldg, NY; IBM Corp, Jacksonville, Fla; NMex Mus Fine Arts, Santa Fe; Ball State Univ, Ind; Mus of Arts & Scis, Santa Fe, NM; Notre Dame Univ, Ind; Rochester Inst Tech, NY; Smithsonian Instn, Washington; Arkansas Art Ctr; numerous others. *Exhib:* Craft Multiples, Renwick Gallery, Smithsonian Inst, Washington, DC, 75; 1976 Biennial Exhib, Mint Mus Art, Charlotte, NC, 76; A Painter and a Ceramist, Galerie Du Manoir, Switz, 78; 50 National Women in Art, Edison Community Coll Mus Fine Art, Ft Myers, Fla, 82; The Primal Vessel, Garth Clark Gallery, Los Angeles, 83; Southeastern Ctr for Contemp Art, Winston-Salem, NC, 85; Key West Art & Hist Soc, E Martello Mus & Gallery, 85; New Gallery, Univ Miami, Fla, 87; Katie Gingras Gallery, Milwaukee, Wis, 87; Helander Gallery, Palm Beach, Fla, 88; Galerie Scapa, Bern, Switz, 88; Deux Femmes', East Martello Mus, Key West, Fla, 90; paintings, Roberta B Marks, Biel, Switz, 90; one artist exhib, Lucky Street Gallery, Key West, Fla, 87-2004, Barbara Gillman Gallery, Miami, Fla, 91 & 94, Galerie Arte Krone, Biel, Switz, 94 & Galerie Jones, Cortaillod-Neuchatel, Switz, 95, 98, 2003, Key West Mus Art & History, 2003; group exhib, Art Miami 95, Miami Beach, Fla, 95, Oxidation/Burial project, I/O Gallery, New Orleans, La, 97, Women's Art, Woodenhead Gallery, Key West, Fla, 98, Art in the Park, 98 & Fort Zachary Taylor, Key West, Fla, 98, Anderson Contemp Art, Santa Fe, 2004. *Collection Arranged:* Lake Superior Int Craft Exhib, Tweed Mus Art, Univ Minn, 72-75 & 77. *Pos:* Cur, The Valley of Oaxaca: The Zapotecs, Ceramic Sculpture, Univ S Fla, Tampa, 81; cur, Two-Dimensional Key West E Martello Mus, Key West, Fla, 85. *Teaching:* Vis artist ceramics, Univ SFla, Tampa, 76; instr ceramics, Rochester Inst Technol, NY, 76, Art Inst Chicago, 77, NC State Univ, Raleigh, 81, Nat Coun Educ for Ceramic Arts, Boston Univ, Mass, 84, Brookfield Craft Ctr, Conn, 85 & Univ Wis, Milwaukee, 87; Fla Key Comm Col, Key West, Fla, 96-; Armory Art Ctr, Palm Beach, Fla, 2002; Anderson Ranch Art Sch, Snowmass, Colo, 2004. *Awards:* Best in Show, Florida Craftsmen, Ceramic Monthly Publ, 73; Purchase Award, Am Crafts Coun, Am Bankers Insurance Co, 76; Merit Award, Ceramic League, Miami, Fla, 79; Lloyd E Herman Merit Award, Smithsonian's Renwick Gallery, Washington, DC, 81; Visual Artists Fel S Fla, 90. *Bibliog:* Judi Bradford (auth), Deux Artists, Solares Hill (pp 26-27), 3/90 & Letting go (pp 26-17) 11/92; Anita Geiser-Coref (auth),Neue Bilder, Ger, 93; Barbara Bowers (auth), Roberta Mark: Collages, Tropic Keys Mag, 1/94. *Mem:* Artists Equity Asn Inc; Am Crafts Coun; Nat Coun Educ Ceramic Arts; World Crafts Coun; Fla Craftsmen; Int Sculpture Ctr. *Media:* Assemblage, Collage, Mixed Media, Painting. *Specialty:* Contemp Art. *Publ:* Auth, International Leaders of Achievement, Cambridge, Eng, 88-90. *Dealer:* Garth Clark Gallery 24 W 57th St New York NY 10019; Barbara Gillman Gallery, Miami, FL; Diane Zolotow Key West Fla; Galerie Jones Weuchatel Suisse; Galerie Jonas Neuchatel Suisse. *Mailing Add:* 1800 Atlantic Blvd Apt C-440 Key West FL 33040

MARKSON, EILEEN
LIBRARIAN

b New York, NY, Mar 13, 1939. *Study:* Lewis & Clark Col, BA, 60; Ecole du Louvre, Institut de Phonetique, Paris, France, 62; New York Univ, MA, 64; Queens Col, MLS, 73. *Pos:* Dir lect prog, Archaeol Inst Am, 66-73, asst secy-treas, 68-73; head, Art & Archaeol Libr, Bryn Mawr Col, 73-96 & Rhys Carpenter Libr Art, Archaeol & Cities, 97-; copy ed, Art Documentation, 97-. *Mem:* Art Libr Soc N Am (exec bd, 85-86); Archaeol Inst Am. *Interests:* Classical archaeology; Dutch seventeenth century painting; Impressionism. *Publ:* Auth, Atlas of the Greek World (rev), Art Documentation, 2/82; co-auth, Archaeology resources in libraries: are they accessible?, Art Libr J, 12/87; auth, Raymond M Holt, Planning Library Building and Facilities: From Concept to Completion (review), Metuchen Scarecrow Press 89, Art Documentation, Winter issue, vol 9 no 4; Frances Van Keuren, Guide to Research in Classical Art and Archaeology, Chicago and London; Am Libr Asn 91 (review), Art Documentation, Summer issue, vol 11, no 2, 92; coauth, Claireve Grandjouan, Hellenistic Relief Molds from the Athenian Agora, Princeton, NJ: Am Sch Classical Studies at Athens, 89 (Hesperia: Supplement XXIII). *Mailing Add:* Rhys Carpenter Libr for Art Archaeology & Cities Bryn Mawr Col 101 N Merion Bryn Mawr PA 19010

MARKUSEN, THOMAS ROY
CRAFTSMAN, SCULPTOR

b Chicago, Ill, Jan 1, 1940. *Study:* Univ Wis, Madison, BS, 65, MS, 66. *Work:* Am Craft Mus, NY; Lannan Found Art Mus, Palm Beach, Fla; Wustum Mus Fine Arts, Racine, Wis; Hand Workshop Gallery, Richmond, Va; Vatican Mus, Rome; and others. *Comn:* Sculpture Bed, Elson, Atlanta, GA, 80; Altar set, Newmen Oratory, Brockport, NY, 75-76; Altar set, First Universalist Church, Syracuse, NY, 88. *Exhib:* Contemp Am Silversmiths & Goldsmiths, Corcoran Gallery, Washington, DC, 73; Int Goldsmiths & Weavers, Albright-Knox Art Gallery, Buffalo, NY, 74; 275 Yrs of Am Metalsmithing, Mus Contemp Crafts, NY & Cranbrook Acad Arts Mus, Bloomfield Hills, Mich, 75; Solo exhib, Craft Company Sixth, Rochester, NY, 84; 41st Int Eucharistis Exhib of Liturgical Arts, Civic Ctr, Philadelphia, 76; Solid Wrought Iron, Southern Ill Univ Mus & Art Gallery, Carbondale, 76; Arts/Objects USA, Lee Nordness Gallery & Johnson Wax Found, NY, 76; and others. *Pos:* Dir & organizer metal exhib, Fine Arts Gallery, State Univ NY Col, Brockport, 71-78; guest lectr metalsmithing, Univ Wash, Mont State Univ, Va Commonwealth Univ, Syracuse Univ, State Univ NY Col, New Paltz, US Embassy-Mexico & Seventh World Craft Conf, Mex, 75-77; Chairman, 85. *Teaching:* Instr crafts, Univ Wis, Madison, 65-66; asst prof metalsmithing, Radford Col, Va, 66-68; assoc prof metalsmithing, State Univ NY Col, Brockport, 68-80, prof, 80-. *Awards:* Fac Res Fel, State Univ NY Res Found, 71 & 79; Craftsmen Fel, Nat Endowment for the Arts, 75; Tech Res Grant, Soc N Am Goldsmiths & Nat Endowment for the Arts, 77. *Bibliog:* Leon Nigrosh (auth), Forged iron today, Craft Horizons, 2/76; Jack O'Field (filmmaker), Hands: The Arts & Crafts of America, Raymond Lowry Int Productions, 76; Dona Z Meilach (auth), Decorative, Sculpture Ironwork, Crown, 77; Katherine Pearson (auth), American Craft, Stewart, Tabori Chang. *Mem:* World Crafts Coun; Am Craftsmen Coun; Artist & Blacksmiths Asn of N Am; Soc N Am Goldsmiths; NY State Craftsmen. *Media:* Metal, Wood. *Mailing Add:* 17218 Roosevelt Hwy Kendall NY 14476-9762

MARLATT, MEGAN BRONWEN
PAINTER

b Indianapolis, Ind, 1957. *Study:* Memphis Coll Art, Tenn, BFA, 1981; Skowhegan Sch Painting & Sculpture, Maine, 1985; Rutgers Univ, MFA, 1986. *Comn:* Site-specific asphalt & grass painting, Louisville Visual Art Asn, Ky, 91; fresco mural, Charlottesville City Hall Annex Bldg, Va, 91; site-specific asphalt & grass painting, Atlanta Arts Festival, Piedmont Park, 91; site-specific asphalt painting, Hillwood Mus, CW Post Campus, Long Island Univ, NY, 93; fresco mural, Emmanual Episcopal Church, Rapidan, Va, 96. *Exhib:* Solo exhibs include Clough-Hansom Gallery, Rhodes Col, Memphis, Tenn, 1983, Artemisia Gallery, Chicago, 1985, Yvonne Rapp Gallery, Louisville, Ky, 1991, Univ Ark, 1991, DC Arts Ctr, 1992, Art Nurnberg 8, 1993, Pyro gallery, Ky, 2003, Les Yeux du Monde Gallery, Charlottesville, Va, 2005, Dupree Gallery, Pa, 2005, Anthony Giordano Gallery, Dowling Col, NY, 2005; group exhibs include Metro Show, City Without Walls, Newark, NJ, 1986; Emerging Artists, Princeton Fine Arts Gallery, NJ, 1987; New Forces, Ceres Gallery, NY, 1988; Embracing Mysteries, Souyun Yi Gallery, NY, 1989; Mythic Moderns, Real Art Ways, Hartford, 1989; Object D'Art, Va Mus Fine Arts, Richmond, Va, 1990, Touch, 1993; The Street, The Slogan, The Artist, DC Arts Ctr, Washington, 1990; 3 Women in the South, Robinson/Willis Gallery, Nashville, Tenn, 1990; Annual Cite' Artists' Show, Cite' Int des Artes, Paris, 1992; 10 Steps, Muranushi Lederman Inc and Horodner Romley Gallery, NY, 1992; Recycled Ideas, Craven Arts Gallery, NC, 1993; Fresco, Elan Vital Gallery, Boston, 1995; Larry and Co, The Univ Memphis Art Mus, 1997; A New Naturalism, Snyder Fine Art, NY, 1997; All Media Group Show, The Turtle Gallery, Deer Isle, Maine, 1998; Spirit and Earth, Bernard Maisner Fine Art Gallery, Bay Head, NJ, 1999; Fresco/Fresh, Educational Alliance Art Gallery, NY, 2001; Danko-Marlatt-Schaffer, Murray State Univ, Ky, 2001; Viterbo, Montserrat Coll Arts, Boston, 2002; Holiday Show, Erin Devine Gallery, Louisville, Ky, 2002; 500 Works on Paper 1922-2002; Gary Snyder Fine Arts, 2002; Al Fresco, Contemp Art in Plaster and Pigment, Schiavone/Edward Contemp Art, Baltimore, 2004. *Pos:* Adj fac, Ocean Co Col, Toms River, NJ, 1987-88; assoc prof art, Univ Va, Charlottesville, from 1988, prof art, currently; panelist, Southeast Col Art Conf, Memphis, Tenn, 1992 & Col Art Asn, NY, 1994; juror, Asn Artists Winston-Salem, NC, 1995. *Teaching:* Artist-in-residence, Watershed Ctr Ceramic Arts, North Edgecomb, Maine, 1990, Cite Int Arts, Paris, 1992 & Va Mus Fine Arts Affiliate Prog, 1993, Va Ctr for Creative Arts, Sweet Briar, Va, 2000, Art Space, Big Tancook Island, Canada, 2004; vis artist, Hampton Univ, Va, 1992, Randolph-Macon Women's Col, Lynchburg, Va, 1999, Montserrat Col Art, Italy, 2002; vis artist & juror, Vanderbilt Univ, Nashville Tenn, 93. *Awards:* Fel Exchange Prog & Summer Res Grant, Univ Va, 90; Nat Endowment Arts Fel Painting, 95; Artist Fel, Va Comn Arts, 96; Summer Res Award, Univ VA, 2002. *Bibliog:* Ann Glenn Crowe (auth), Art papers, Objects Art, 2/91; Thomas Kliemann (auth), Nurnbergerer zeituing, Art Nurnberg 8, 4/24/93; Michael Becker (auth), Nurnberger nachrichten, Art Nurnberg 8, 4/24/93. *Publ:* Contribr & critic, Modern art, the individual vs the community, Arts Quart, spring 88. *Mailing Add:* PO Box 488 Orange VA 22960

MARLIEB, WILLIAM (BILL) FRANKLIN
PAINTER

b New York, NY, Feb 15, 1929. *Study:* Sch Industrial Art, NY, 44-48; New Sch, New York, 48-50; Studied color & design with Leo Russell and Judith Epstein, New York, 48-49. *Work:* Butler Inst of Am Art, Youngstown, Ohio; Nassau County Mus Art, Roslyn Harbor, NY; Carnegie Art Ctr, Oregon City, Ore; Ore Jewish Mus, Portland, Ore; Canby Station Mus, Carby, Ore; Wilsonville Public Lib, Wilsonville, Ore. *Exhib:* exhibs in New York, Philadelphia, Naples & Palm Beach, Fla, and various Portland, Ore art shows & galleries; Portland Mus Art; Wallflower Gallery; Full Moon Art Gallery, Gig Harbor, Wash; Aurora Artisan, Aurora, Ore. *Pos:* pres, General Media Fine Arts, New York, 82-97; pres & creative dir, Tilley Marlieb & Alan Adv Agency, 78-82. *Teaching:* Weekly acrylics classes, Wilsonville, Ore, 2000-2015. *Awards:* various local art show awards including 1st, 2nd & 3rd Prize, Carnegie Art Ctr, Oregon City, Ore, Aurora Art Show, Aurora, Ore, Lake Oswego Art Show, Lake Oswego, Ore, and more. *Media:* Acrylics on Canvas, Contemporary Folk Art & Abstract. *Dealer:* Wallflower Galleries 288 NW 1st Ave Canby OR 97013; Portland Art Mus Rental/Sales Gallery; Elliot Tower 10th & Jefferson Portland Ore; Full Moon Art Gallery 3155 Harborview Dr Gig Harbor Wash 98335; The Aurora Artisan 21680 Main St NE Aurora Ore 97001

MARLOR, CLARK STRANG
HISTORIAN, COLLECTOR

b Camden, NJ, Nov 18, 1922. *Study:* Carnegie-Mellon Univ, BFA, 45; Univ Mich, MA, 46; NY Univ, DEduc, 61. *Collection Arranged:* John Barnard Whittaker (with catalog), 68 & Eleanor C Bannister (with catalog), 71, Adelphi Univ; Benjamin Eggleston, Long Island Hist Soc, 75. *Teaching:* Prof, Adelphi Univ, 56-86. *Bibliog:* Marlor (auth), Society of Independent Artists: 1917-1944, Cloth, 84; Marlor (auth), Salons of America: 1922-1936, Cloth, 91. *Mem:* Salmagundi Club (mem, libr comt & bicentennial comt). *Res:* 19th century American artists. *Collection:* American artists of the 19th and early 20th centuries. *Publ:* John B Whittaker, Brooklyn artist, Antiques, 11/71; A quest for independence: the SIA, Arts & Antiques, 81; The Society of Independent Artists: Exhibition Record and History, 84; Salons of America, 1922-1936, 91; Brooklyn Index of Artists, 92; and others. *Mailing Add:* 35 Prospect Park W Apt 6C Brooklyn NY 11215

MARLOW, AUDREY SWANSON
PAINTER, DESIGNER

b New York, NY. *Study:* Art Students League, with Robert Brackman, Robert Beverly Hale & Raphael Soyer, 51-55. *Work:* NY Univ, City Hall, NY; Middle Island Pub Libr, Long Island; Sr Citizens Complex, Newark, NJ; Little Flower Children's Servs, Wading River, NY. *Comn:* Millicent Fenwick, comn by Regency Housing Partners,

Newark, NJ, 86; Harrison J Goldin, NY Comptroller, NY, 86; Monsignor John Fagan with 7 members of family, Quoque, NY, 88; Mother Katharine Drexel & 3 children, comn by Monsignor Fagan, Hanging at St Theresa of the child Jesus Convent, wading River, NY, 90; Mother Franceska Seidliska & 3 children, St Theresa of the Child Jesus Convent, 93. *Exhib:* Hudson Valley Artists, White Plains, NY, 79, 81, 83, 85, 88-90; Nat Acad Design, NY, 80 & 85; one-person show, Salmagundi Club, NY, 85; Parish Art Mus, Southampton, NY, 86; Pastel Invitational, Palais Rameau, Lisle, France, 88; Sumner Mus, Washington, 92. *Pos:* Package designer & illus, Prince Matchabelli Perfume Co (freelance), 57-68; textile designer, RS Assocs, New York, 60-72. *Teaching:* Design, Phoenix Sch Design, 72-73; demonstrs, pastel, Catharine Lorillard Wolfe Art Club, 85 & Hudson Valley Artists, 88. *Awards:* Five Awards, Salmagundi Club Shows, 78; Gold Medal, Nat League Am Pen Women, Cork Gallery, Lincoln Ctr, 85; Pastel Soc Am, Artists Professional League, 87. *Mem:* Am Artists Prof League; Knickerbocker Artists; Hudson Valley Artists; Pastel Soc Am; Nat League Am Pen Women (pres 80-82). *Media:* Multimedia. *Publ:* Illus, Breads of Many Lands, 66 & 4 H Club Bakes Bread, J Walter Thompson Advert Agency, 66; Anna Smith Strong and the Setauket Spy Ring, Peter Randall, 91. *Mailing Add:* 147 Northside Rd Wading River NY 11792

MARLOWE, WILLIE
PAINTER, EDUCATOR

b Whiteville, NC, Jan 17, 1943. *Study:* Summer study, Pa Acad Fine Arts, 64; East Carolina Univ, BS, 65; Univ Idaho, MFA, 69; Post-graduate study, Mexican Cult & Civilization, Merida, Mex, Peace Univ, Raleigh, NC, 93. *Work:* Wexford Arts Centre, Ireland; Albany Inst Hist & Art, NY; State Univ NY Art Mus, Albany; Schenectady Mus, NY; Greenville Mus Art, NC; Fondo del Sol, Visual Arts Centre, Washington, DC; Rocky Mount Art Center, Rocky Mount, NC; Tula State Lev Tolstoy Pedagogical Univ, Tula, Russia; Emily Harvey Found, Venice, Italy; East Carolina Univ, Greenville, NC; Adirondack, SUNY, Queensbury, NY; Rutgers Univ, NJ; Ballinskellias, Ireland. *Comn:* Modular installation, Greenhut Gallery, Albany, NY, 93; modular paintings, Art Gallery Ltd, New Bern, NC, 2000. *Exhib:* Solo Exhibs: Mint Mus Art, Charlotte, NC, 71; Schenectady Mus, NY, 75; Crosscurrents, Greenville Mus Art, NC, 82 & 97 & 10 Yr Retrospective, Wexford Arts Centre, Ireland, 98; Fondo del Sol Visual Arts Center, Wash, DC, 2002; Ai Genovesi, Venice, Italy, 2008;Hallspace Gallery, Boston, Mass, 2011, A Survey:1977-2010, Opalka Gallery, Sage College of Albany, The Arkell Mus, Gallery C, Raleigh, NC, Carrie Haddad Gallery, Hudson, NY, 2011, Feneex Ctr Gallery, Saratoga Springs, NY, 2012, Red Dot Gallery, Sacramento, Calif, 2013, Atelier Cross, Rijeka, Croatia, 2015; Group exhibs, Fire and Ice, Attleboro Mus, Mass, 98; Annual Juried Exhib, Nexus Gallery, New York City, 98-99; Int Art Expo, Masterpiece Art Center, Taipei, Taiwan, 98 & Post Millennial Musings, Artemisia Gallery, Chicago, Ill, 2000; Reprize, Int Invitational Show, Wexford Arts Ctr, Wexford, Ireland, 2002; AIR Gallery, NY, 2001, 2004, 2005, & 2008; Art Upstairs, Wexford, Ireland, 2007; Opalka Gallery, Sage Coll Albany, 2007; Virgo Girl, Bow St Gallery, Cambridge, Mass, 2009; Miniature, 2010, Castle Mus, 2010; Zagreb, ULS Art Asn of Zapresic, Croatia, 2010, 2011, 2012; Archtypology, Int Show in Sarajevo, Zagreb, Cres, Berlin, Boston, Joliette, Canada; Abstract Blue Hill Cultural Ctr, Pearl River, NY, 2012; Ceres Gallery, NY, 2013-15; Synesthia, Arts Ctr of the Capital Region, Troy, NY, 2013; Nat/International, Liz Long Gallery, Chgo Urban Resource Art Ctr, Chgo, Ill, 2013; The Legacy of Emily Harvey, Archivo Emily Harvey, Venice, Italy, 2013; 15 Art 20, European Artists Asn, Hameenlinna, Finland, 2013; Papyri, Archivo Emily Harvey, Venice, Italy, 2012; Galerie Doxa, Cesky Krumlov, Czech Republic. *Collection Arranged:* Stamp Act, Int Mail Art Show, Sage Coll of Albany & traveled to Barbados & West Indies, 87; Pony Express, Int Mail Art Show, Sage Coll of Albany & Wexford Art Centre, 88; Project House, Int Mail Art Show, Russel Sage Coll of Albany, 93; Project House II, Int Mail Art Show, Russel Sage Coll of Albany, 93. *Pos:* Partners of the Americas, Lectures at the US Embassy & at Colleges in Barbados, Bridgetown, Barbados, West Indies, 86; vis artist, Univ Ga Studies Abroad Program, Cortona, Italy, 89; vis artist, Wexford Arts Ctr, Wexford, Ireland, 98; artist-in-residence, The Millay Colony for the Arts, Austerlitz, NY, 99; International Artist Residency Program, Cill Rialaig, Ballinskelligs, Ireland, 2005; vis artist, Tula Univ, Russia, 2006; int artist residency, Emily Harvey Found, Venice, Italy, 2006, 2008, 2010; Milkwood Internat Residency, Cesky Krumlov, Czech Republic, 2014, Atelier Cres, Cres Town, Croatia, 2015. *Teaching:* Prof Emeritus, dept visual arts, Sage Coll of Albany, NY, 77-2008, chair, 79-81; Sage at Oxford, Somerville Coll, Oxford Univ, Eng, 92; Celtic Connections, Sage Coll Int Studies abroad program, Trinity Coll, Dublin, Ireland & Straithclyde Univ, Glasgow, Scotland, 2001. *Awards:* Lewis Swyer Mem Award, 95; FJ Carlson Mem Award, 95; Purchase Award, Schenectady Mus, NY, 98; Fac Res Develop Grant, The Sage Colls, 78, 81, 84, 91 & 95; Strategic Opportunity Stipend, The Art Ctr of Capital Dist, Troy, NY, NY Found for Arts, 91-93, 96, 98, 99, 2002, 2003, 2006, & 2008, 2011; Woman's Roundtable award in Visual Arts, ECU, 2013; Les Urbach Lifetime Achievement award, Albany Ctr Gallery, NY, 2014. *Bibliog:* Nancy Norman, Arts panorama (interview), WMHT TV, 88; Bernice Steinbaum, The definitive American contemporary quilt (interview), Bernice Steinbaum Gallery, NYC, 91; Chuck Welch (auth), Eternal network, Univ Calgary Press, 95; Zoran Krusvar, Atetier Galerie, Rijeka, Croatia (interview). *Mem:* WCA; Orgn for Women Artists; Fulton St Gallery; Artists' Equity; Albany Ctr Gallery (bd dir, 96-2000, chmn arts comt, 97, mem arts comt, 97-2000); Albany Inst Hist & Art (99-); Artemisia Gallery, Chicago (2001-03). *Media:* Miscellaneous Media, Painting. *Res:* Paintings inspired by archaeology, research into Celtic mythology & stone monoliths. *Specialty:* Contemporary Art. *Interests:* Travel, visual poetry. *Collection:* Indian & Persian miniatures. *Publ:* Illusr, Healing, Color Cover Vol 2, Sacramento, Calif, 93; contribr, Reticular 44, Visual Poetry, Buchlabor, Germany, 93, Spinne - A Visual Poetry Publication, Dusseldorf, Germany & Common Sense, Almanac of Art & Literature, Kowalski & Tarlatt, 97; Willie Marlowe, 1977-2010, Catalogue for Retrospective Exhib (32 pg, color), Opalka Gallery, Sage Col Albany, 2011. *Dealer:* Artforms Gallery 5 New Karner Rd Guilderland NY 12084; Gallery C Wade Ave Raleigh NC 27607; Martinez Gallery 3 Broadway Troy NY 12180; Denis Collins Gallery Wexford Ireland; Robert Ray Sacramento Ca. *Mailing Add:* 820 Cortland St Albany NY 12203

MARONEY, DALTON
SCULPTOR

b Greenville, Tex, July 9, 1947. *Study:* E Tex State Univ, BS, 69; Univ Okla, MFA, 72. *Work:* Arco, Dallas, Tex & Anchorage, Alaska; Prudential, Newark, NJ; IBM, Washington, DC. *Exhib:* Solo exhibs, Dallas Mus Art, Tex, 83-84, D W Gallery, Dallas, Tex, 87, San Antonio Art Inst, Tex, 89 & Dalton Maroney Gallery, Pittsburg State Univ, Pittsburg, Kans, 96; Excellence '86 & '87, Tex Sculpture Asn, Dallas, Tex, 86 & 87; 2D/3D Frito Lay Corp, Plano, Tex, 87; Magic & Ritual Objects, Alexander Hoague Gallery, Univ Tulsa, 87; 10th Ann Exhib, Austin Vis Arts Asn, Tex, 87; Third Coast Review: A Look at Art in Texas, traveling exhib, Aspen Art Mus, Colo, 87-88; Renwick Gallery, Nat Mus Am Art, Washington, DC, 89; The Vessel, Dallas, Tex, 90; Woodworks, Arlington Mus Art, Tex, 90. *Pos:* Asst dir, John Michael Kohler Arts Ctr, Sheboygan, Wis, 72-73. *Teaching:* Asst prof art, Morningside Col, Sioux City, Iowa, 73-76; instr, Pittsburg State Univ, Pittsburg, Kans, 76-77; asst prof, Univ Tex, Arlington, 79-84, assoc prof, 84-. *Awards:* Visual Arts Fel, Nat Endowment Arts, 86-87. *Bibliog:* Jana Vander Lee (auth), article, Art Space, summer, 82; Susan Freudenheim (auth), Making art against the current, Tex Homes, 4/84 & Dalton Maroney at the Dallas Museum, Art Am, summer 84. *Mailing Add:* 2601 Burning Tree Ct Arlington TX 76014

MARQUIS, RICHARD
CRAFTSMAN

b Bumblebee, Ariz, 1954. *Study:* Univ Calif, Berkeley, MA, 72. *Work:* Am Craft Mus & Corning Mus Glass, NY; Los Angeles Co Mus Art, Calif; Philadelphia Mus Art, Pa; Seattle Art Mus, Wash; Smithsonian Inst, Washington, DC; Auckland (New Zealand) Art Mus. *Exhib:* Am Glass Today, Oakland Mus, 79; one-person exhibs, Foster White Gallery, 86, Dowse Art Mus, Wellington, NZ, 87, Betsy Rosenfield Gallery, Chicago, 87, 89, 91, 93 & 94, Kurland/Summers Gallery, Los Angeles, 87, 88 & 91, Auckland Art Mus, NZ, 89, Louise Allrich Gallery, San Francisco, 89 & Sandra Ainsley Art Forms, Toronto, Can, 90 Ellery Brown Gallery, Seattle, 94, 99, 2001, Cafe Florian, Venice, 98, Galerie Rob Van Den Doel, The Hague, The Neth, 2000; New Glass, Gallery Nakama, Tokyo, 89; Craft Today: USA Int Touring Exhib, Am Craft Mus, 89-91; Chicago Int New Art Forms Expo, Betsy Rosenfield Gallery, 92; Elliott Brown Gallery, Seattle, Wash, 94, 96 & 98; Boston Mus of Fine Arts, 97; Los Angeles Co Mus of Art, 2000; Seattle-Tacoma Airport, Washington, 2001. *Awards:* Nat Endowment Arts Grants, 74, 78 & 84; Univ Calif-Los Angeles Research Grants, 79, 80, 81 & 82; Senior Fulbright Grants, NZ, 81 & 88; Distinguished Aliorvus award, Univ. Calif., Berkeley, 2000; Outstanding Achievement in Glass, Urban Glass, Brooklyn. *Bibliog:* Frantz, Susanne K. (auth) Marquis at the Caffe Florian, American Craft Magazine, 99. *Mem:* Fel Am Crafts Coun. *Publ:* Tina Oldknow (auth, monogr), Richard Marquis Objects, Univ Wash Press, 97

MARRAN, ELIZABETH
PAINTER, EDUCATOR

Study: Hamilton Coll, grad; Cranbrook Acad Art, MFA (painting). *Work:* Fogg Art Mus, Harvard Univ; Boston Pub Libr. *Exhib:* Solo exhibs include OHT Gallery, Boston, 2003; group exhibs include Spare: Works on Paper, OHT Gallery, Boston, 2003; 183rd Ann: Invitational Exhib Contemp Am Art, Nat Acad Mus, New York, 2008. *Teaching:* Asst prof, Dept Art, Univ Mass, Boston, 1987-. *Awards:* Mary & Maxwell Desser Mem Award, Nat Acad, 2008. *Dealer:* OHT Gallery 450 Harrison Ave #57 First Fl Boston MA 02118. *Mailing Add:* 44 Alpine St Cambridge MA 02138

MARRERO, MARLO R
PHOTOGRAPHER, SCULPTOR

b Bristol, Conn, Nov 18, 1969. *Study:* Univ Conn, with William E Parker, BFA, 92; Hartford Art Sch, with Mary Frey & Ellen Carey, MFA, 97. *Exhib:* Don't I Know You?, LACPS, Los Angeles, 94; The Ubiqustous Bead, Bellevue Mus Art, Wash, 96; Rebellious Bead, Mus of Southwest, Midland, Tex, 97. *Teaching:* instr photog, Central Conn State Univ, New Britain, 98 & Miss Porter's Sch, Farmington, Conn, 98-. *Awards:* Art Matters Fel, Art Matters Found, 95; Visual Arts Grant, Conn Comn of Arts, 2000. *Mem:* Coll Art Asn; Soc Photog Educ; Circles, Ctr for Photog (dir, 98-99). *Media:* Fibers. *Publ:* contribr, Coll Artists Visual Excess, Hartford Courant, 96, CT Student Wins Right to Reinstate Censored Artwork, Nat Campaign For Freedom of Expression, 96, Art Exhib Unites Three Artists, Hartford Courant, 98 & Marlo Marrero's Constellation, EL Extra News, 99

MARRON, DONALD BAIRD
COLLECTOR

b Goshen, NY, July 21, 1934. *Study:* Baruch Sch Bus, 1957. *Hon Degrees:* Baruch Coll, City Univ New York, LLD; Long Island Univ, LLD. *Pos:* Investment analyst, NY Trust co, New York, 1951-56; with Lionel D Edie Co, New York, 1956-58; mgr res dept, George O'Neill & Co, 1958-59; pres, DB Marron & Co Inc, New York, 1959-65, Mitchell Hutchins & Co Inc (merger with DB Marron & Co Inc, 65), New York, 1965-69, pres, chief executive officer, 1969-77; co-founder, Data Resources Inc, 1969-79, chmn, formerly; dir, NYSE, 1974-81; gov & vchmn, Securities Indust Asn, 1974-77; pres, PaineWebber Inc (merger with Mitchell Hutchins & co Inc, 1977), 1977-80, chief exec officer, 1980-2000, chmn bd, 1981-2000; gov, NASD, 1997-2001; chmn, chief exec off, and founder, Lightyear Capital, LLC, New York, 2000-; chmn, UBS Am, 2000-2003, Collegiate Funding Serv's, 2004-2006 & Ctr Study Presidency; bd mem, Fannie Mae 2001-2006 & Shinsei Bank 1999-2005; mem adv bd, UBS Art Collection; mem bd overseers & mgr's, Mem Sloan-Kettering Cancer Ctr; trustee, Charles A Dana Found, Ctr Strategic & Int Studies (private sector co-chmn, Nat Comn on Retirement Policy); bd dir, New York Partnership; mem, Gov's Sch & Bus Alliance Task Force, New York; pres emer, Mus Mod Art, New York; former mem pres comn, The Arts & The Humanities; vchmn, Calif Inst Art. *Awards:* Named one of Top 200 Collectors, ARTnews mag, 2004-13. *Mem:* Coun on Foreign Relations. *Collection:* Modern and contemporary art. *Mailing Add:* Lightyear Capital LLC 9 West 57th St New York NY 10019

MARRON, JEAN See LaRue, Joan Marron

MARRON, PAMELA ANNE
PAINTER
b Hackensack, NJ, Nov 16, 1945. *Study:* Parsons Sch of Design, AA, 1965-1968; Max Beckman Scholar, Brooklyn Mus, 1969-1970; Stanford Univ (postgrad), 1970. *Work:* Southern Vt Art Ctr Mus, Manchester, Vt; Yoder Brothers Int, Barberton, Ohio; Factory Point Bank, Manchester, Vt; Richard Heileman & Dr Abe Madkour, Manchester, Vt; Vt State House, Montpelier, Vt, 1992; Southern Vt Mus Collection, 2003-2004; Schenectady Mus, 2004; Omni Corp, NY City; Lotus Corp, Cambridge, Mass; Yoder Brothers Int, Barberton, Ohio. *Comn:* Numerous Comns private collection, 1980-2005; Katharina Rich Perlow Gallery, New York City, 96-2004; Ole Moon Gallery, Breckenridge, Colo, 2004. *Exhib:* Solo shows: Stratton Arts Festival, Stratton Mountain, Vt, 1981-1994; Castleton State Coll, Castleton, Va, 1986; North Star Gallery, Manchester, Vt, 1988-2002; Avanti Gallery, Lambertville, NJ, 1990; Cove Gallery, Wellfleet, Mass, 1991-1997; Chaffee Art Center, Rutland, Vt, 1994; Artisans Gallery, Brattleboro, Vt, 2006; Hopkins Ctr, Dartmouth College, 77-85; Landscape Groups, Norwich Univ, Northfield, Vt, 1980; Berkshire Mus, Pittsfield Mass, 1981; AVA Gallery, Hanover, NH, 84; Castleton State College, 86; Pinder Gallery, New York City, 87; Landscape Solos, Nicholas Roerich Mus, NYC, 1990; Vt State House, Montpelier, Vt, 1992; Grayson Gallery, Woodstock Vt, 1999; Southern Vt Ctr, Manchester, Vt, 2006; Redux Gallery Dorset, Vt, 2006; Kerygma Gallery, Ridgewood, NJ. *Teaching:* Instr art, Southern Vt Col, Bennington, Vt, 1981-1982. *Awards:* Jay Conway Award, Jay Conway Fund, Southern Vt Arts Ctr, 87 & 90; Basin Harbor Artist Residency Prog, 97; Southern Vt Art Ctr Jurors Award, 98; Women Artist Calendar, 99. *Bibliog:* Mary Hard Bort (auth) Art & Soul, Gallery Press LLC, 2000; Susan Sargent (auth) The Confort of Color, Manchester Vt & Bull Finch, 2003. *Mem:* Stratton Arts Festival (art comt), 1978-1980; Southern Vt Art Ctr (juror), 2005; Southern Vt Art Ctr (art comt), 2006; Nat Mus Women in the Arts, Washington DC, 2006; Cheffee Art Ctr, Rutland Vt; Vt Coun on Arts, S Vt Art Center (art comt, numerous art exhibs). *Media:* Oil. *Specialty:* Vt Landscapes. *Interests:* swimming, tai chi, traveling. *Publ:* Architectural Digest, 98. *Dealer:* The Redux Gallery Dorset VT 05251; Vt Artists Gallery Brattlelovo Vt; Southern Vt Art Ctr. *Mailing Add:* PO Box 563 Dorset VT 05251

MARROW, JAMES HENRY
HISTORIAN, EDUCATOR
b New York, NY, Mar 27, 1941. *Study:* Univ Minn, BA (magna cum laude), 63; Columbia Univ, MA, 66, PhD (with distinction), 75. *Teaching:* Assoc prof hist art, State Univ NY, Binghamton, 70-76 & Yale Univ, 76-80; prof, Univ Calif, Berkeley, 80-91, Princeton Univ, 91-. *Mem:* Coll Art Asn Am. *Res:* Northern European art of the late Middle Ages and early Renaissance, with special interest in religious iconography, manuscript illumination and early prints. *Publ:* Coauth, The James A de Rothschild Collection at Waddesdon Manor: Illuminated Manuscripts, Office Livre, 77; coauth, Medieval and Renaissance Manuscripts at Yale: A Selection (exhib catalog), Yale Univ Press, 78; auth, Passion Iconography in Northern European Art of the Late Middle Ages and Early Renaissance, Van Ghemmert, 79; coauth, Hans Baldung Grien: Prints and Drawings (exhib catalog), Yale Univ Press, 78; auth, Simon Bening in 1521: A group of dated miniatures, Liebaers Festschrift, 84. *Mailing Add:* 104 Library Pl Princeton NJ 08540

MARSH, CHARLENE MARIE
ARTIST, PAINTER
b Muncie, Ind, May 19, 1956. *Study:* Ind Univ, Bloomington, BA, 79, BA, 86. *Work:* Evansville Mus Arts & Sci; Minnetrista Cult Ctr, Muncie; Harrison Steel Castings Co, Attica, Ind; Ind Orthopaedics & Sports Med, PSC, Indianapolis; Indianapolis Mus Art; The White House, Washington; Brown Co Community Found; Indianapolis Mus Art, Ind; Ind State Mus, Ind. *Comn:* Art in the Classroom, Purdue Univ, West Lafayette, Ind, 95; Tufled Tapestry, Minnetrista Cult Ctr, Muncie, Ind, 97 & Purdue Univ, West Lafayette, Ind, 98; West Baden Springs Historic Site, 2001; Brown Co Pub Libr, Nashville, Ind, 2002. *Exhib:* Solo exhibs, Campus Community Art Ctr, Ind Univ, Bloomington, 91, Bellevue Gallery, Bloomington, Ind, 91 & 93, John Waldron Arts Ctr, Bloomington, Ind, 94, Univ Indianapolis, 95, Minnetrista Cult Ctr, Muncie, Ind, 97 & Ft Wayne Mus Art, 99; Northern Indiana Art Asn, Munster, IN, 94, 96, 98, 2000, 2001, 2002, 2004; 34th Mid-State Craft Exhib, Evansville Mus Arts & Sci, Evansville, Ind, 95-96; Nat Mus Women in Arts Ind Chap Exhib, Nat Women's Mus, Washington, DC, 99-2000; Gov's Residence, Indianapolis, 2002-03; Whispers to Shouts, Ind State Mus, Ind, 2005; Fiber Surfaces & Structure, Mobile, Ala, 2005; 42nd Ann Coconut Grive Arts Festival, Coconut Grove, Fla, 2005. *Pos:* Bd dir, Bellevue Gallery, 92-. *Teaching:* Instr oil painting, John Waldron Arts Ctr, Bloomington, Ind, 92-98. *Awards:* First Prize, Pittsburgh Ctr Arts, 95; Best of Show, Three Rivers Arts Festival, Pittsburgh, 96; Gold Medal Award, Westmoreland Arts & Heritage Nat Competition, Youngwood, Pa, 97; Past pres award, Northern Ind Arts Asn, 2002; Best of Show, 23rd Contemp Crafts, Mesa, Ariz, 2001; IAC prog grant, 1999-2000, 2002-03. *Bibliog:* Jean Robertson (auth), Infinity of Form: Indiana Fiber Art, Fiberarts Mag, 4/92; Steve Mannheimer (auth), Fiber art exhibits beg the questions, what's a female aesthetic, Ind Star, 1/17/93; Kathleen Mills (auth), Nature's soldier Marsh puts spirit into tapestries, Bloomington Herald Times, 7/29/92; Lydia Finkelstein (auth), Artists Marsh, Sage exhibiting to national audiences, Bloomington Herald Times, 6/23/96; film (producer-Ron Prickel), Continuing the Legacy of Art in Brown County, Emmy award winner; Laura Lane (auth), Angels Above, Bloomington Hoosier Times, 11/18/2001. *Mem:* Brown Co Arts Alliance; Brown Co Studio Tour; Brown Co Arts & Cult Comn; Indiana Artists Club; Hoosier Salon; Indiana Heritage Arts; Indiana Plain Air Painters Mus. *Media:* Hand Dyed Wool & Metallic Yarns Tufted onto Cotton Backing; Oil on Cotton on a Wood Panel. *Publ:* Auth, Celebration of hand hooked rugs, In: Raindrops on a Pond, 91, Rughooking magazine, In: Interconnections, 92, Celebration of hand hooked rugs II, In: Driftnels, 92 & Celebration of hand hooked rugs III, In: Season of Dread, 93, Stackpole Books; Portfolio, Arts Indiana, Ann M Stack, 93; Portfolio, American Craft, 95. *Dealer:* Charlene Marsh Studio & Gallery

MARSH, DAVID FOSTER
EDUCATOR, PAINTER
b Salkum, Wash, Jan 24, 1926. *Study:* Cent Wash Univ, BA; Univ Ore, MS. *Work:* Westminster Col, Fulton, Mo; Inst Mexicana-N Am, Guadalajara, Mex. *Exhib:* NW Watercolor Soc Exhib, 58, 62 & 77; NW Ann, 63 & 66. *Teaching:* Prof drawing & painting, Western Wash Univ, 57-92, dean, Fine and Performing Arts, 83-85, emer prof, 92-. *Mem:* Coll Art Asn; Nat Art Educ Asn

MARSH, FREDRIK
PHOTOGRAPHER
b Quantico, Virginia, 1957. *Study:* Ohio State Univ, BFA (Photog), 1980, MFA (Printmaking), 1984. *Work:* Mus Contemp Photog, MPP Collection, Columbia Coll, Chicago. *Exhib:* Solo exhibs include Univ Notre Dame, Ind, 2000, Gallery Sink, Denver, 2003, Tex Tech Univ, Lubbock, 2004, Univ Arts, Philadelphia, 2006, 9th Int Photo Gathering, Aleppo, Syria, 2007; group exhibs include Latest Develop, Huntington Mus, WVa, 2000; Trading Places, Ohio State Univ, Columbus, 2003; Photographers, ART-Galerie, Siegen, Germany, 2005; Image as Evidence, Dayton Vis Arts Ctr, Ohio, 2006; Nat Prize Show, Kathryn Schultz Gallery, Cambridge, Mass, 2007; Heroes of Horticulture, George Eastman House, Rochester, NY, 2007; FotoFest, Fine Print Auction, Houston, Texas, 2008. *Awards:* Ford Found Award, Ohio State Univ, 1983; Arts Midwest/NEA Fel, 1985; Prof Devel Assistance Award, Ohio Arts Coun, 1988, Individual Artist Fel in Photog, 1991, 2004, Artists Projects Grant, 2002, Individual Excellence Award in Photog, 2007; Artists Projects Grant, Sächsichen Ministeriums für Wissenschaft und Kunst, Dresden, Ger, 2003; Individual Artist Fel in Photog, Greater Columbus Arts Coun, 2004, 2007, Spec Projects Grant, 2007; John Simon Guggenheim Mem Found Fel, 2008

MARSH, THOMAS A
SCULPTOR
b Cherokee, Iowa, May 7, 1951. *Study:* Layton Sch Art, Milwaukee, Wis, BFA (painting), 74; Univ Southern Calif, aesthetics with John Hospers, 76-77; Calif State Univ, Long Beach, MFA, sculpture with Kenneth Glenn & Stephen Werlick, 77; also with Milton Hebald, Rome, Italy. *Work:* Univ San Francisco Rossi Libr, Calif; St Mary's Hosp Libr, San Francisco; Calif Mfrs Asn, Sacramento; Calif State Univ, Long Beach; Mus Tex Tech Univ. *Comn:* Surfing monument (6' Bronze figure), Santa Cruz, 91; 10 bronze panels, 3'x4' each, Pine St, San Francisco, 91; bust, Richard M Lucas Ctr, Stanford Univ Med Sch, Palo Alto, Calif, 92; Goddess of Democracy (12' bronze monument), proj leader, Portsmouth Sq, San Francisco, 94; 7' bronze figure, Shrine St Joseph Church, Santa Cruz, Calif, 97; Bronze bust, St Mary's Church, Sacramento, Calif, 97; bust of Betty White & a figure of Dick Van Dyke, Acad Television & Scis Hall of Fame Sculpture Garden; 7' figure of John the Baptist at the Mission Church, San Juan Bautista Calif, 2000; 7' figure of St Joseph, Patron of the Unborn at Shrine of St Joseph Santa Cruz, Calif; 6 1/2 life size portrait bronze figure, Amgen, Inc Thousand Oaks Calif, 2002; bronze bust Sonoma State Univ Rohnert Park, Calif, 2003; 10' Crucifix 10' Cross, 6' Corpus St Joachim's Catholic Church, Madera, Calif, 2003; 7' bas reliefs. Resurrection Catholic Church, Aptos, Calif; Victims of Communism Mem, Washington, DC, 2007. *Exhib:* Solo exhibs, Civic Courtyard, Bracciano, Italy, 78, Alliance Francaise, San Francisco, 82 & Univ San Francisco, Calif, 85 & 87; Sioux City Connection, Sioux City Art Ctr, Iowa, 84; Interfaith Religious Art, Judah L Magnes Mus, Berkeley, Calif, 86; About Faces: A Celebration of the Portrait, Walnut Creek Civic Arts Gallery, Calif, 87 & Bay Area Bronze, 88; The Goddess of Democracy, 91; Yerba Buena Center, San Francisco. *Pos:* Bd dir, Chinese Democracy, Educ Found, San Francisco, Calif, 92- & Acad Art Univ, 92-. *Teaching:* Instr sculpture, Calif State Univ, Long Beach, 78-79 & San Francisco, 79-80, Calif; instr anatomy & sculpture, Acad Art Univ, San Francisco, Calif, 81-2000, coordr MFA prog, 83-85. *Awards:* Elizabeth Greenshields Found Fel, 77; Outstanding Contrib Chinese Democracy Award, Serv Ctr Chinese Democracy, 91. *Bibliog:* Artweek (exhib rev), 2/21/91; San Jose Mercury News, 3/10/92; NY Times, 6/5/94; Humanist Art Rev, 1/2001; Nat Rev Online, 6/2007. *Media:* Bronze, Wood. *Mailing Add:* 198 Peliso Ave Orange VA 22960

MARSHALL, BRUCE
PAINTER, ILLUSTRATOR
b Athens, Tex, Dec 23, 1929. *Study:* Univ Ariz, Tucson; Southern Ariz Sch of Art (full scholar). *Work:* First Cavalry Mus, Ft Hood, Tex; Hill Univ History Complex, Hillsboro, Tex; San Jacinto Monument, Tex; The Alamo, San Antonio; Nat Infantry Mus, Ft Benning, Ga; Inst Tex Cultures, Univ Tex, San Antonio. *Comn:* Gen Achibald Gracie Jr (portrait), Gracie Mansion, NY, 63; Portrait of Dick Dowling, Dowling Sch, Houston, 70, comn by Sons of Confederate Veterans; paintings, Inst Texan Cult, Univ Tex, San Antonio, 70-75; Tex Citizen Soldier (mural), Tex Nat Guard for Nat Infantry Mus, Ft Benning, Ga, 76; Ten Historic Texans (cover painting), Southwestern Bell Telephone Co, 79-80; Tom Lubbock (portrait), W Tex Mus Asn, 83; Patriots, (painting), Dallas Baptist Univ, 92; plus many others. *Exhib:* Smithsonian Inst, Washington, DC, 54; First Cavalry Mus, Ft Hood, 72, Univ Ariz, 73, Llano Estacado Mus, 75; Rotunda, Tex State Capitol, Austin, 75, 76, 84 & 95; Chamizal Nat Mem, El Paso, Tex, 77; Mus of the Big Bend, Alpine, Tex, 77; Tex Navy Exhib, Tex State Archives & Libr, 78; Star of the Repub Mus Washington State Park, Tex, 78; The Alamo, 81; Le Musee de l'Historie de l'Homme, Brussels, Belg, 83; John E Conner Mus, Kingsville, Tex, 85-86; Cannon House Office Building, Wash, DC, 88; War Mem Mus, Va, 91-92. *Pos:* Auth & illusr, The Texas Star, 72-73; assoc ed, Military Hist Tex & South West, 72-88. *Awards:* Knighted by King Peter II, Yugoslavia, 66; Artist of the 65th Legislature, Tex, 77; Artist in Res, Tex Navy Asn, 90; National Artist, Confederate States of Am from Sons of Confederate Veterans. *Bibliog:* Margaret Taylor Dry (auth), article, Austin American Statesmen, 74; Robert St Johns (auth), article in Argosy Mag, 78; Frank Woods (auth), article in Austin Mag, 80; Bess Whitehead Scott (auth), article, Austin Homes & Gardens, 80; Ned Polk (auth), article, The Westerner, 87; Thomas W Knowles (auth), They Rode for the Lone Star-The Saga of the Tex Rangers, 99. *Mem:* Scots of Austin (past pres); Hood's Tex Brigade Asn (past pres); Sons of Confederate Vets (past lt comdr & mem bd dirs

Houston camp, Austin camp, Tex div, Trans-Miss dept); Confederate Hist Asn of Belgium (chargé d' affairs, 2001-); Former Tex Rangers Asn; Tex Navy Asn (bd dirs). *Media:* Watercolor, Oil. *Specialty:* Historical subjects. *Interests:* Hist & reading. *Publ:* Illusr, Military History of Texas and the Southwest, Presidial Press, 71-78; The Texas Rangers: Their First 150 Years, Encino, 75; History of Hood's Texas Brigade, Hill Coll, 78; Kent Biffles Texana Column, Dallas Morning News, 94-99 & 03; auth & illusr, Uniforms of the Republic of Texas, 98, Uniforms of the Alamo and the Texas Revolution, 2003; Southwestern Historical Quarterly, 2005; auth & illus, City of Silver, 2008. *Dealer:* Westart PO Box 161616 Austin TX 78716. *Mailing Add:* 11204 Ranch Rd 1826 Austin TX 78737-3506

MARSHALL, JAMES DUARD
PAINTER, PRINTMAKER
b Springfield, Mo, Sept 29, 1914. *Study:* Kansas City Art Inst, Mo, dipl painting, 40, with Thomas Hart Benton; Colo Col, BA (art), 45, with Boardman Robinson, Lawrence Barrett & Ricco Lebron; Univ Denver, MA (art), with Julio de Deigo & Ruth Reeves. *Work:* Libr of Cong, Washington, DC; Tex Fine Arts Asn, Austin. *Comn:* Murals, History of Missouri (7 ft x 30 ft), Pub Libr, comn by City of Neosho, Mo, 39; Children's Stories (500 ft long), Officer's Wives Nursery, Ft Worth, Tex, 52; Beginning of a New Day (two 4 ft x 6 ft mosaics), Jones Store, Prairie Village, Kans, 62. *Exhib:* San Francisco Mus of Art Ann, 38; Philadelphia Print Club Ann, Pa, 40, 45 & 52; Solo exhibs, Santa Fe Art Mus, NMex, 43 & Oklahoma City Art Ctr, 43; Carnegie Inst Int, Pittsburgh, 45; Denver Art Mus Ann, 45-47; Nat Acad of Design, NY, 46; Under the Influence, The Students of Thomas Hart Benton, Albrecht Kemper Mus Art, St Joseph, Mo, 93; Fifteen Colo Artists (Fifty Yr Reunion, 1998), Elizabeth Schlosser Gallery, Denver, 98. *Pos:* Chmn art dept, Ft Worth Children's Mus, Tex, 51-53; crafts dir, US Army, Ger, 54-60; asst to Thomas Hart Benton, Truman Libr & New York Power Authority Murals, 60. *Teaching:* Mem, Fed Teaching Prog, Fayetteville, Ark, 33-34; teacher summer & Saturday classes, Kansas City Art Inst, 36-40; asst prof drawing & painting, Univ Denver, Colo, 46-51; instr summer art sessions, Kansas City Univ, 63. *Awards:* Hon Mention, Denver Ann, Colo & Philadelphia Print Club, 46; Benedictine Art Awards, New York, 70-74. *Media:* Lithography, egg tempera painting; Woodcut

MARSHALL, JOHN
PAINTER, INSTRUCTOR
b St John's, Nfld, Oct 20, 1957. *Study:* Univ of the South, study with Edward Carlos, 78-81; Mid Tenn State Univ, with David Le Doux, Jim Gibson, BFA, 83; Univ NC, Greensboro, with Walter Barker, MFA, 85. *Work:* Weatherspoon Art Gallery, Greensboro, NC; Meridian Mus Art, Miss; Nines Community Coll District, Marie Hull Gallery. *Comn:* Sculpture, Campus of Meridian Community Col. *Exhib:* Art Wave, William Carey Coll Gallery Gulfport, Miss, 88; Art on Paper, Weatherspoon Art Gallery, Greensboro, NC, 89; solo exhibs, General Art Gallery, 94, Miss Art Colony, 95, Jones Jr Col, 96, Horne-Marshall Gallery, 96, Sylvia Schmidt Gallery, New Orleans, 97, Marie Hull Gallery, Miss, 98 & Architectural Gallery, Miss State Univ, 98. *Collection Arranged:* 80's Images from North Carolina, 87, Visions of Flowers, 87, Southern Idiom: 3 Views, 88 & Stephanie Dinkins: Retro, 88, Meridian Mus Art, Miss; Jacob Drachler - Retrospective, Meridian Mus Art, 89; Homer Casteel: Early Figurative Years (essay, catalog), Meridian Community Col, 89; Casteel & His Students (auth, catalog), Meridian Mus Art, Miss, 98. *Pos:* Cur asst, Weatherspoon Art Gallery, 83-85, cur, 86; dir, Meridian Mus Art, 86-89. *Teaching:* Cur & instr, Meridian Community Col, 86-. *Awards:* Best of 3-D Design, Art Wave, 88; Art Education of the Year, 96; Lamplighter Award, Meridian Community Col, 96. *Mem:* Weatherspoon Art Asn; Coll Art Asn; Meridian Coun Arts. *Media:* Oil, Mixed Media. *Dealer:* Sylvia Schmidt Gallery New Orleans LA; Horne-Marshall Gallery Meridian MS. *Mailing Add:* 9361 Collinsville Lake Dr Collinsville MS 39325

MARSHALL, JOHN CARL
CRAFTSMAN
b Pittsburgh, Pa, Feb 25, 1936. *Study:* Cleveland Inst Art, BFA; Syracuse Univ, MFA. *Work:* Everson Mus, Syracuse, NY; Chicago Art Inst, Ill; Am Craft Mus New; Syracuse Univ, NY; Mukhina Sch Art & Design, St Petersburg, Russia; and others. *Comn:* Gold Bowl, Hendricks Chapel, Syracuse, NY, 69; Series of 5 large silver sculptures, Patrick Lannan, 84; coffee tea service, Anne Gould Hauberg, Seattle, Wash, 87; eight flatware designs for Bloome Collection, Seattle, Wash, 88; star rose quartz sphere sculpture, White Rose Found, Calif, 91. *Exhib:* Masterworks of Am Jewelry since 1950, Victoria & Albert Mus, London, 85; Hong-ik Metalcrafts Asn Exhib, Walker Hill Art Ctr Mus, Seoul, Korea, 88; Craft Today USA, premiere opening Musee Des Art Decoratifs, Paris, France & toured major Europ cities, 89; Art that Works, The Decorative Arts of the Eighties Crafted in Am, toured maj US cities 2 yrs, 90; Solo exhib, Nat Ornamental Metals Mus, Memphis, Tenn, 91; Fortunoff Silver Competition III, Silver New Forms & Expressions, New York, NY, 91. *Teaching:* Asst prof metalworking, design & enamel, Syracuse Univ, 65-70; Asst prof, Univ Wash, 70-75, prof, 75-. *Awards:* Nat Merit Award, Am Craftsmen Coun, Craftsmen USA, 66; Thomas C Thompson Prize 45th Ceramic Nat Competition, 68; Am Metalcraft Award, Nat Enamels Exhib, 70. *Bibliog:* C E Licka (auth), Sublime passages and other reflections: The work of John Marshall, Am Craft Mag, 85; John Marshall: A Conversation with Patterson Sims, Metalsmith Mag, 91. *Mem:* Am Craftsmen Coun; Soc N Am Goldsmiths; Soc Am Silversmiths; Fel Am Crafts Coun. *Media:* Gold, Silver. *Mailing Add:* 5618 75th Ct W Tacoma WA 98467-4512

MARSHALL, KERRY JAMES
DESIGNER, PAINTER
b Birmingham, Ala, Oct 17, 1955. *Study:* Otis Art Inst, Los Angeles, Calif, BFA, 78. *Hon Degrees:* Otis Art Inst, D, 99. *Work:* Mus Contemp Art, Chicago, Ill; Whitney Mus Am Art, NY; San Francisco Mus Modern Art, Calif; Los Angeles Co Mus Art, Calif; Corcoran Mus Art, Washington, DC. *Exhib:* Solo exhibs, James Turcotte Gallery, Los Angeles, 83, Pepperdine Univ, Malibu, 84, Koplin Gallery, 85 & 91, Studio Mus Harlem, 86, Terra Incognito, Chicago Cult Ctr, 92, Jack Shainman Gallery, NY, 93, 95, 99, 2004, 2006 & 2008, Koplin Gallery, Santa Monica, Calif, 93, Cleveland Ctr Contemp Arts, 94, Addison Gallery Am Art, 97, Phillips Acad, Andover, Mass, 97 & Orlando Mus Art, Fla, 98, Cheekwood Mus Art, Nashville, 2000, Greg Kucera Gallery, Seattle, 2002, Mus Contemp Art, Chicago, 2003, Camden Arts Ctr, London, 2005-06, Wexner Ctr, Columbus, Ohio, 2008; Drawings III, Koplin Gallery, Santa Monica, 93; Markets of Resistance, White Columns Gallery, NY, 93; 43rd Biennial of Contemp Am Painting, Corcoran Gallery Art, Washington, DC, 93 & The Corcoran Collects, 98; Bridges & Boundaries: Chicago Crossings, Spertus Mus, Chicago, 94; Saddlebrook Coll Art Gallery, Mission Viejo, Calif, 94; About Place: Recent Art of the Americas, Art Inst Chicago, 95 & A Century of Collecting, 2003; No Doubt: African-Am Art of the 90's, Aldrich Mus Contemp Art, Ridgefield, Conn, 96; Whitney Biennial, Whitney Mus Am Art, NY, 97; The Corcoran Collects: Selections from the Permanent Collection, Corcoran Gallery Art, Washington, DC, 98; Postcards from Black Am: Contemp African-Am Art, De Beyerd, Breda, Amsterdam, 98; Collectors Collect Contemp: 1990-1999, Inst Contemp Art, Boston, 99; Trouble Spot: Painting, Mus Contemp Art Antwerp, Belgium, 99; Other Narratives: Fifteen Yrs, Contemp Arts Mus, Houston, Tex, 99 & Splat Boom Pow: The Influence of Comics in Contemp Art, 2003; Age of Influence: Reflections in the Mirror of Am Cult, Mus Contemp Art, Chicago, 2000; Illusions of Eden: Visions of the Am Heartland, Madison Art Ctr, Wis, 2001; Perceptual Experience, Frye Art Mus, Seattle, 2002; Venice Biennial, 2003; Comic Release: Negotiating Identity for a New Generation, traveling, 2003-04; The Undiscovered Country, Hammer Mus, Los Angeles, 2004; Drawing from the Modern, 1975-2005, Mus Mod Art, New York, 2005; A Historic Occasion, Mass Mus Contemp Art, 2006; Portraiture Now: Framing Memory, Smithsonian Nat Portrait Gallery, Washington, 2007-08. *Pos:* Production designer, Praise House & Hendrix Proj, 91; exhib comt mem, Randolf St Gallery, Chicago, Ill, 92-. *Teaching:* Art instr, Los Angeles City Col, 80-83; art fac, Los Angeles Southwest Col, 81-85; adj asst prof, Sch Art & Design, Univ Ill, Chicago, 93-94, assoc prof, 95-. *Awards:* Resident Fel, Studio Mus Harlem, 85; Fel, Art Matters Inc, 90; Nat Endowment Arts Visual Art Fel, 91; Ill Arts Coun Visual Arts Grant, 92; Tiffany Found Grant, 93; John D and Catherine T MacArthur Found, 97; Distinguished Artist Fellowship and Stillwater Found Grant, Coll Fine Arts, Univ Tex, Austin, 2004; Residency Award in visual arts, Wexner Ctr Arts, Ohio, 2006; Skowhegan Medal Painting, 2008. *Bibliog:* Gallery review, NY Times, 2/12/93; Art review, Los Angeles Times, 4/24/93; Up from the streets, Artweek, 4/28/93; Howard Halle, Portraits of the artists (the Whitney Biennial), Time Out NY, 3/20-27/97; Christopher Knight, Kerry James Marshall (Doc), Art & Antiques, 9/97; Garrett Holg, Stuff your eyes with wonder, Art News, 3/98; Alan Artner, Broader canvas: painter Kerry James Marshall is finding new ways to say what he wants to say, Chicago Tribune, 5/3/98; Holland Cotter, In civil rights ferment, a conflicted nostalgia, NY Times, 10/2/98; Grace Glueck, Kerry James Marshall at Jack Shainman, NY Times, 4/9/99; Shaila Dewan, Too much for words, Houston Press, 6/10-16/99; Kenneth Baker, Through the past, mournfully: Marshall's art revisits civil rights era, San Francisco Chronicle, 11/23/99; Artist joins in students' search for their identities, Southampton Press, 1/3/2000; James Myer, Impure thoughts: the art of Sam Durant, Artforum, 4/2000; writer, dir, The Doppler Incident, 97. *Mem:* Ill Arts Coun. *Publ:* Auth, article, Visions Quart, fall 91; article, Los Angeles Times, 3/15/91; production designer, NUNU, 90; production designer, Prairie House, 91. *Dealer:* Jack Shainman Gallery 513 W 20th St New York NY 10011. *Mailing Add:* 4122 S Calument Ave Chicago IL 60653

MARSHALL, ROBERT LEROY
EDUCATOR, PAINTER
b Mesquite, Nev, Dec 15, 1944. *Study:* Brigham Young Univ, BA, 66, MA, 68; studies in Europe, primarily Spain & England. *Work:* Mus of the Southwest, Midland, Tex; Brigham Young Univ, Provo, Utah; Webster Oil Co, Springfield, Mo; Springville Mus, Utah; Shell Oil. *Exhib:* Watercolor West; Watercolor USA, Springfield, Mo; Utah Coun Arts, Salt Lake City; Am Watercolor Soc, NY; Butler Inst Am Art; Scottsdale Biennial, Ariz. *Teaching:* Prof painting & drawing, Brigham Young Univ, 69-, chmn dept art & design, 76-81. *Awards:* Purchase Award, Watercolor USA, Webster Oil Co. *Mem:* Nat Watercolor Soc; Nat Coun Art Adminrs; Springville Mus Art (mem bd dir, 77-). *Media:* Watercolor, Oil. *Mailing Add:* Dept Visual Arts Brigham Young Univ Provo UT 84602

MARSTON, JD
PHOTOGRAPHER
b NY, Jan 30, 1948. *Study:* Emerson Col, BS/SP, 70. *Work:* The Colo Col, Colo Springs; Ohio Wesleyan Univ, Delaware, Ohio; Sierra Club, San Francisco; MCI; Texaco; Lucent Technols; JD Marston Photography Gallery. *Comn:* This Land is Sacred, US Forest Service, Colo, 90; Healing Waters, Sisters of the Holy Redeemer, Pa, 99. *Exhib:* Creative Impulse, The Colo Col, 95; Homage to Ingmar Bergman, Birger Sandzen Gallery, Lindsborg, Kans, 97; L'Itimerances L'Art Fixe En Movement, Arles, France, 01; Recipients of the Ansel Adams Award, Sierra Club Gallery, Calif, 01. *Pos:* Artist in Residence, The Colo Col, Colo Springs, 93. *Teaching:* Vis Prof, The Colo Col, 94; Vis Prof, Ohio Wesleyan Univ, Delaware, Ohio, 95. *Awards:* Ansel Adams Award, Sierra Club, 92; Ernst Haas Scholarship, Anderson Ranch, 92. *Mem:* Am Soc Media Photogs. *Media:* Black and White, Silver Gelatin Photography. *Specialty:* photography of JD Marston. *Publ:* auth, Vince Bzdek, Meditations in Black & White, Denver Post, 92; The Waiting, Lenswork Quarterly, 94, Personal Themes, 99. *Dealer:* Joan Sapiro Art Consultants 4750 E Belleview Littleton CO 80121. *Mailing Add:* JD Marston Photography 117 E 37th Ave PMB 376 Loveland CO 80538

MARTEL, RICHARD
CONCEPTUAL ARTIST, EDITOR
b Bagotville, Provide, Que, July 7, 1950. *Study:* Univ Laval, Que, BA, 75 & Hon MA, 79. *Exhib:* Workshop Art, Dokumeusa 7- OFAJ, Kassel, 82; Casscades, Galerie Du Musée, Que, 84; Europékunstruction in Memoriam Ugorugg Maciunas, Festival, Que, 84; La Pluie Au Nicaragua, La Lieu, Centre en Art Actuel, Oue, Can, 84; So Bor Dination, Galerie Donguy, Paris, France, 85; Mohouaec, Musée Du Que, Can, 86;

Defrinazione, Centro Int Multimedia, Salerno, Italy, 86; Multimedia Exhib Musso del Sannio, Beneveito, Italy, 86. *Pos:* Pres, Editions Intervention, 78-; vpres, AEPOQ, 82-85. *Teaching:* Instr art, Univ Que, Chicicouimi, Can, 78-82. *Awards:* Soutien A La Création, Govt du Que, 82 & 85. *Media:* Performance Art. *Publ:* Illusr, 78-, auth, Activitiés Artisques, 1978-1982, 83 & Art Société Quebec, 1975-80, 82, Editions Intervention. *Dealer:* Le Lieu Centre Rn Art Actuel 629 St Jean Quebec PQ G1R 4P7 Canada. *Mailing Add:* 221 Lavingueur Quebec PQ G1R 1B1 Canada

MARTER, JOAN
HISTORIAN, CURATOR

b Philadelphia, Pa, Aug 13, 1946. *Study:* Temple Univ, BA, 68; Univ Del, MA, 70, PhD (art hist), 74. *Collection Arranged:* Vanguard Am Sculpture 1913-1939 (guest cur & coauth, catalog), Rutgers Univ Art Gallery, 79; Design in Am: The Cranbrook Vision 1925-1950, Detroit Inst Arts & Metrop Mus Art, 83; Beyond the Plane, Am Constructions 1930-1965, NJ State Mus, 83; Alexander Archipenko Constructions (auth, catalog), Blum Art Inst, Bard Coll, 85; Alexander Calder: Artist As Engineer (auth, catalog), Mass Inst Technol, 86; Theodore Roszak: The Drawings, (auth, catalog), Elvehjem Mus Art, 92; Dorothy Dehner Retrospective, Katanoh Mus Art & Corcoran Gallery Art, 93-94; Women and Abstract Expressions (with catalog), Baruch Coll & Guild Mus, 97; Off Limits: Rutgers & The Avant Garde 1957-63 (ed, catalog), Newark Mus, 99; Pop Art & After, Zimmerli Art Mus, 2008. *Pos:* Critic, Arts Mag, 77-82, Sculpture Mag, 90-, Art J 90- & Woman's Art J, 92-; ed in chief, Woman's Art J, 2006-. *Teaching:* Prof art hist, Rutgers Univ, 77-, distinguished prof art hist, 2000-, dir curatorial studies prog, 89-, dir grad studies art hist, 94-97 & grad prog dir, 2006-2009, bd govs prof, 2013-. *Awards:* Res Coun Grants, Rutgers Univ, 77-2010; Charles F Montgomery Prize, Decorative Arts Soc, 84; George Wittenborn Award, Art Libr Soc, 85; John Sloan Mem Found Grant, 89; Diamond Achievement Award, Temple Univ, 94; Best Exhibn Outside New York City, Int Asn Art Critics, 99; Grad Tchg Excellence Award, Northeastern Asn Grad Schs, 99; Getty Rsch Inst Libr Grant, 2002; Pollock-Krasner Found/Stony Brook Res Fel, 2004-2005; Univ Del Alumni Wall of Fame, 2004; Lifetime Achievement Award, Nat Women's Caucus for Art, 2011. *Mem:* Coll Art Asn; Women's Caucus for Art; Int Asn Art Critics (mem USA sect); Art Table. *Res:* 20th century art; American sculpture; Women studies; Contemporary art. *Publ:* Auth, Jose De Rivera Construction, Madrid, 80; articles in Am Art J, Art J, Arts Mag & Sculpture, Woman's Art J; Alexander Calder, Cambridge Univ Press, 91 & 97; Theodore Roszak Drawings, Univ Wash Press, 92; Dorothy Dehner, Sixty Years of Art, Univ Wash Press, 93; ed, Postwar Sculpture in Europe and America, Art J, winter, 94-95; auth, Off Limits: Rutgers University and the Avant-Garde 1957-63, Rutgers Univ Press, 99; co-auth, American Sculpture in the Metropolitan Museum of Art, Vol II, Metropolitan Mus Art, 2000; ed, Abstract Expressionism: The International Context, Rutgers Univ Press, 2007; editor-in-chief, Grove Encyclopedia of American Art, Oxford Univ Pres, 2010. *Mailing Add:* 220 Madison Ave New York NY 10016

MARTIN, ALEXANDER TOEDT
EDUCATOR, PAINTER

b Kinderhook, NY, Mar 11, 1931. *Study:* Albright Art Sch, cert, 52; Univ Buffalo, BFA, 57; Tulane Univ, MFA, 63. *Work:* Neuberger Mus, State Univ NY Col, Purchase; Whitney Mus Am Art, Union Carbide Corp, Salomon Brothers, NY; Schenectady Mus, NY; Continental Transport Inc, White Plains, NY; Dow Jones, NY; Marist Coll Collection, Poughkeepsie, NY. *Exhib:* Albright-Knox Art Gallery, Buffalo, 59; Southeastern Exhib, Delgado Mus, New Orleans, La, 63; Wadsworth Atheneum, Hartford Conn, 66; Convocation of Arts Exhib, State Univ NY, Albany, 69; Cooperstown Ann, NY, 75; Plaza Gallery, State Univ NY Central, Albany, 82; solo exhib, Barrett House, Poughkeepsie, NY, 83 & Tom James Gallery, Westwood, NJ, 96; The New Response, Contemp Hudson River Painters Exhib, Albany, Poughkeepsie & NY, 86; James Cox Gallery, Woodstock, NY, 91-96; Maris Col, 2001. *Teaching:* Prof painting & drawing, State Univ NY Col, New Paltz, 63-96, emer prof, 96-. *Awards:* First Prize Painting, Schenectady Mus, 58 & Cooperstown Ann, 75. *Bibliog:* Hilton Kramer (auth), article in NY Times, 3/25/78; article, Am Artist, 5/82. *Media:* Oil, Watercolor, Pastel. *Publ:* Auth, Painting the Landscape, Watson Guptill, 85. *Dealer:* James Cox Gallery Woodstock NY

MARTIN, BILL
PAINTER, SCULPTOR

b South San Francisco, Calif, Jan 22, 1943. *Study:* Acad Art, San Francisco, Calif; San Francisco Art Inst, BFA, 68, MFA, 70. *Work:* San Francisco Int Airport; AT&T, NY; Owens Corning, Toledo, Ohio; Glenn C Janss Collection Boise Art Mus, Idaho; Levi Strauss, San Francisco, Calif; and others. *Exhib:* Baja, San Francisco Mus Mod Art, 75; Ninth Biennale de Paris, Musee d'Art Modern de la Ville, Paris, France, 75; University Show, State Univ NY, Postdam, 77; Triennial Invitational of India, 78; Painting and Sculpture Today, Indianapolis Mus Art, Ind, 78; New Am Painting (world traveling show), New Mus, NY, 79-80; Art in Bay Area 1945-1980, Oakland Mus, Calif, 85; Am Realism, San Francisco Mus Art, 85; one-person shows, Nancy Hoffman Gallery, NY, 82, 76 & 79-80, Joseph Chowning Gallery, San Francisco, 83, 85, 87, 89 & 92, Univ Nev, 88, Chabot Col, Calif, 90, Kabutoya Gallery, Tokyo, Japan, 91, Atrium Gallery, San Francisco, 92; Art of Fantasy & Science Fiction, Del Art Mus, 89; Watercolor USA Springfield Art Mus, Mo, 89; West Coast Works on Paper, Humbolt State Univ, Calif; Exhibition 48, Southern Utah State Univ, 89; Paper in Particular, Columbia Col, Mo, 90; From the Studio Oakland Mus, Calif. *Teaching:* Instr painting, Acad Art, San Francisco, Calif, Univ Calif, Berkeley, Univ Calif, San Jose, 73, Col of Marin, Kentfield, Calif, 75-78 & Col of Redwoods, Mendocino, Calif, 83-. *Awards:* Grant to Artists, Louis Comfort Tiffany Found, 70; Artist's Fel; Nat Endowment Arts. *Mem:* Mendocino Art Ctr (bd of dir); Ft Braggs Ctr Art. *Media:* Oil, Bronze; Gouache, Watercolor. *Publ:* Contribr, Visions, 77, auth, 1969-1979 Bill Martin Paintings, 79; American Realism, Abrams; Arts of the San Francisco Bay Area, Univ Calif Press; auth, Joy of Drawing, Watson-Guptill Publ. *Dealer:* Joseph Chowning Gallery 1717 17th St San Francisco CA 94103. *Mailing Add:* 33611 Navarro Ridge Rd Albion CA 95410-9705

MARTIN, CAMERON
ARTIST

b Brooklyn, NY, 1970. *Study:* Brown Univ, BA (art & semiotics), 94; Whitney Mus Am Art, Ind Study Program, NY, 96. *Work:* exhib in group shows at Home, Bellevue Art Mus, Wash, 1994 Whitney Biennial, Whitney Mus Am Art, 2004. *Exhib:* Solo exhibs, The Future Lasts Forever, Howard House, Seattle, 99, Future Views, Tate, NY, 99, Angstrom Gallery, Dallas, 2000, Three Pictures, Howard House, Seattle, 2001, New Paintings, Kevin Bruk Gallery, Miami, 2001, Standstill, Artemis Greenberg Van Doren Gallery, NY, 2002, Never Rider, Gallery Min Min, Tokyo, 2003, Clear Skies, Artemis Greenberg Van Doren Gallery, NY, 2004, A Turn Pale, Gallery Min Min, Tokyo, 2004; group exhibs, Home Northwest Ann, Ctr Contemp Art, Seattle, 95, Images Lost & Found, Chassie Post Gallery, NY, 96, Apartments, Artra, Milan, Italy, 97, Landscapes, Meyerson Nowinski Gallery, Seattle, 98, Open, Tate, NY, 98, Other Paintings, Huntington Beach Art Ctr, Calif, 99, Twice Born: Beauty, Mills Gallery, Boston, 2000, Flat File, Bellwether Gallery, Brooklyn, 2000, Three Painter, Lawrence Rubin Greenberg Van Doren Fine Art, NY, 2001, Guide to Trust No 2, Yerba Buena Ctr Arts, San Francisco, 2002, Linger, Artemis Greenberg Van Doren Gallery, NY, 2002 Everybody Knows This is Nowhere, Kevin Bruk Gallery, Miami, 2002, City Mouse/Country Mouse, Space 101, Brooklyn, 2003, How Come, Stux Gallery, NY, 2003, Nature Boy, Elizabeth Dee Gallery, NY, 2003, Giverny, Salon 94, NY, 2003, Colored Pencil, KS Art, NY, 2004, About the House, Howard House, Seattle, 2004, Stay Inside, Shoshana Wayne Gallery, Santa Monica, Calif, 2004. *Awards:* Samuel T Arnold Fel, 94; Recipient Pollock-Krasner Found Award, 2000; Artists Giverny Fel & Residency, France, 2001; Guggenheim Found Fel, 2010. *Mailing Add:* Van Doren Waxter Gallery 23 E 73rd St New York NY 10021

MARTIN, CHESTER YOUNG
PAINTER, SCULPTOR

b Chattanooga, Tenn, Nov 2, 1934. *Study:* Univ Chattanooga, BA, 61. *Work:* Smithsonian Inst; Brit Mus, London; Royal Swed Coin Cabinet, Stockholm; First Am NB Collection, State of Tenn, Nashville; Art Hist Mus, Vienna. *Comn:* Rose Inn (oil painting), Ga-Pac Corp, Crossett Div, Crossett, Ark, 73; Centennial mural, Chattem Inc, Chattanooga, Tenn, 74; The Sixth Day (bronze relief sculpture), 81, Brookgreen Gardens Wildlife Medal, Brookgreen Gardens, Murrells Inlet, SC, 83; Congressional Gold Medal, Gen. Colin Powell, 91; White House commemorative silver dollar, US Mint, Philadelphia, 92; Congressional Gold Medal, Andrew Wyeth, Artist, 92. *Exhib:* Medialia Gallery, New York, Feb-April, 2005; Seaside Art Gallery Miniature Exhib, 2005-2013; Int Exhib of Art Medals at Medici Palace, Florence, 83; Int Medals Exhib, Glasgow, 2012. *Pos:* Sculptor & engraver, US Mint, Philadelphia, 86-92. *Awards:* Purchase Award, Julius Wile Sons & Co, New York, 75; 16th Tenn All-State Artists' Exhib First Purchase Award, First Am Bank Nashville, 76; Medallic Sculpture Award, Am Numismatic Asn, 93. *Bibliog:* Ed Reiter (auth), World food day medal, NY Times, 84; George S Cuhaj (auth), Chester Martin: A life of art, The Numismatist, 93 & Chester Y Martin: Painter and Sculptor, The Medal, Brit Art Medal Trust, 94. *Mem:* Fed Int de La Medaille; Am Medallic Sculpture Asn (vpres, 87); Mem Int Medallic Fed, Paris. *Media:* Oil, Watercolor, Sculpture (including Medallic Art). *Interests:* Modern languages. *Dealer:* Seaside Art Gallery Nags Head NC; Medialia Gallery New York NY. *Mailing Add:* 4110 Sunbury Ave Chattanooga TN 37411-5232

MARTIN, CHRIS
PAINTER

b Washington, DC. *Study:* Yale Univ, 1975. *Work:* Lannan Found; Progressive Corp. *Exhib:* Solo exhibs, Thread Bldg Gallery, NY, 1980, Mary Delahoyd Gallery, NY, 1985 & 1987, Philippe Briet Gallery, NY, 1988, John Good Gallery, NY, 1990 & 1992, Jimenez & Algus Gallery, Brooklyn, NY, 1991, Bernard Toale Gallery, Boston, 1995 & 2006, Mario Diacono Gallery, Boston, 1996, Pierogi Gallery, Brooklyn, 1997, Bill Maynes Gallery, New York, 1998, Galapagos Art and Performance Space, Brooklyn, 2000-01, Sideshow Gallery, Brooklyn, 2005, Daniel Weinberg Gallery, Los Angeles, 2006-07, Mitchell-Innes & Nash, 2008-09; Penultimate Salute, A Place Apart Gallery, Brooklyn, 1984; Twelve from New York, Yale Sch Art, Yale Univ, New Haven, Conn, 1986; Brooklyn Mus, NY, 1987; Words as Symbols, Aldrich Mus, Conn, 1990; Visions/Revisions: Selections from the Contemp Collection, Denver Art Mus, 1991; Max Protech Gallery, New York, 1992; Arena Gallery, New York, 1993; Bernard Toale Gallery, Boston, 1994; Elizabeth Harris Gallery, New York, 1997; N3 Project Space, Brooklyn, 1998; Pierogi Gallery, Brooklyn, 1999; New York Studio Sch, 2000; Geoffrey Young Gallery, Great Barrington, Mass, 2001; Gallery 817, Philadelphia, 2002; Newhouse Ctr Contemp Arts, Staten Island, 2003; Studio 18 Gallery, New York, 2004; Rosenwald-Wolf Gallery, Philadelphia, 2005; Am Acad Arts and Letts Invitational, New York, 2006, 2009; Artspace, New Haven, Conn, 2008; Saatchi Gallery, London, 2009. *Awards:* Richard & Linda Rosenthal Award, 1987 & Purchase Prize, 2009, Am Acad Arts and Letts; Nat Endowment Arts, 1990 & 1993; Fel, NY Found for Arts, 1996; Pollack-Krasner Found Award, 1999; Fel, John Simon Guggenheim Mem Found, 2002. *Bibliog:* Chris Martin, NY Times, 4/27/1990; Roberta Smith (auth), Chris Martin, NY Times, 4/27/1990. *Mailing Add:* 284 Graham Ave Brooklyn NY 11211

MARTIN, DAN J
ADMINISTRATOR, EDUCATOR

Study: Western Mich Univ, BA, 1976; City Univ of NY, Brooklyn Col, MFA, 1982. *Pos:* Promotions dir, Dept Theatre, Western Mich Univ, Kalamazoo, 1976-80; managing dir, CSC Repertory, New York City, 1981-84; marketing dir, Walnut St Theatre, Philadelphia, 1984-85; coordinator, Grad Program in Arts Mgt, Sch Theatre Arts, Univ Akron, Ohio, 1989-92; dir, Inst for Mgt of Creative Enterprises, Carnegie Mellon Univ, 1992-, dir, Arts and Culture Observatory, 2002-06, assoc dean, Col of Fine Arts, 2009-2011, interim dean, 2011-2012, dean, 2012-, Stanley and Marcia Gumberg prof, 2012-. *Teaching:* Asst prof, Sch Theatre Arts, Univ Akron, 1989-92; prof, assoc dean, Heinz Col; vis prof Univ of Bologna & Univ Montreal. *Mailing Add:* 6316 Jackson St Pittsburgh PA 15206

MARTIN, DIANNE L
PAINTER, PRINTMAKER
b Boston, Mass, Apr 8, 1940. *Study:* RI Sch Design with Robert Hamilton, BFA, 65; Univ Iowa, with Byron Burford, MA, 67. *Work:* Pepsico; Pfizer; JC Penney; Wilmington Trust Co; David Rockefeller Jr; Credit Suisse; Warburg Pincus. *Comn:* watercolor painting, Spence Sch, NYC, 03. *Exhib:* Works on Paper, Brooklyn Mus, NY, 75; Juried Ann, Queens Mus, NY, 85; In Search of the Am Experience, Mus Nat Arts Found Nat Competition, 89; Fables of La Fontaine, Inst for Am Univ Aix En Provence, Temple Univ, Rome, Md Inst, Univ Wash, 2003-04; Interchurch Ctr, NY, 2002, 2009; Noho Gallery, NY, 2003; Siren Song Gallery, Greenport, NY, 2009; East End Arts Council Gallery, Jamesport, NY, 2011; Winners Show, East End Arts Council, Riverhead, NY, 2012. *Pos:* Dir, Spence Gallery, 92-2005. *Teaching:* Chmn, Art Dept, Spence Sch, NY, 72-95. *Awards:* Resident fel, Va Ctr Creative Arts, 96. *Mem:* Nat Asn Women Artists; Manhattan Graphics Ctr. *Media:* Watercolor, Monotypes, Intaglio Prints. *Collection:* David Rockefeller Jr, Pfizer Inc, Pepsico, JC Penney, Warburg Princess. *Mailing Add:* 27-15 41st Ave Long Island City NY 11101

MARTIN, DORIS-MARIE CONSTABLE
DESIGNER, SCULPTOR
b New York, NY, July 5, 1941. *Study:* Miami-Dade Community Col, S Campus, Miami, Fla, AA, 71; Univ Miami; Univ NC, Asheville, BA, 76; Penland Sch Crafts, NC; Arrowmont Sch Crafts, MA, 81; Goddard Col, MA (sculpture), 80; Univ NC, Greensborough, MFA, 89. *Work:* Miami-Dade Community Col; Durham Art Guild, M Biddle Gallery for the Blind, NC State Mus, Raleigh; Chrysler Mus, Norfolk, Va; Miami Herald, Fla; Univ NC, Asheville; and others. *Comn:* Soft sculpture, Unitarian/Universalist Church of Asheville, 78. *Exhib:* Ann Painting & Sculpture Exhib, Mint Mus, Charlotte, 73 & 76; Marietta Coll Int, Grover M Hermann Fine Arts Ctr, Ohio, 76 & 77; Springs Mills Traveling Show, Ft Mill, SC, 77 & 78; Solo exhibs, Chrysler Mus, 73 & Beyond Craft: Fiber-Form-Fabric, Univ NC, Asheville, 75; and many others. *Teaching:* Instr soft construction sculpture, Asheville Art Mus, 76-, instr beginning printmaking, 77-, instr watercolor, drawing & painting, currently; vis artist, Western NC & Ashville sch system, 70-. *Awards:* Best Sculpture, Craft Work 76, Am Crafts Coun, 76; Best Sculpture & One-Man Show, Durham Arts Guild, Inc, Allied Arts Ctr, NC, 76; Award for Sculpture, Springs Mills Traveling Show, 75 & 77. *Bibliog:* R Clermont (auth), Poloities & Expositions Diverses, Les Editions de la Revue Moderne Des Arts, Paris, France, 73; article, Miami Herald, 76. *Mem:* Am Crafts Coun; Fla Craftsmen, Miami; Western NC Fibers/Handweavers Guild; Handweavers Guild Am; NC Art Soc; and others. *Media:* Fiber. *Publ:* Contribr, Shuttle, Spindle & Dyepot, Handweavers Guild Am, 76. *Mailing Add:* 65 Woodland Rd Asheville NC 28804

MARTIN, DOUG
PAINTER
b Newton, Kans, Dec 10, 1947. *Study:* Kans State Univ, BFA; Univ Nebr, MFA. *Exhib:* William Rockhill Nelson Gallery Art, Kansas City, 72; St Louis Art Mus, Mo, 72; Sheldon Art Gallery, Lincoln, Nebr, 75; Robert Hull Fleming Mus, Univ Vt, 81; solo exhibs, Oscarsson Hood Gallery, NY, 81 & Edward Thorp Gallery, NY, 82; Aldrich Mus Contemp Art, Ridgefield, Conn, 81; Herbert Johnson Mus, Ithaca, NY, 81; Krannert Art Mus, Univ Ill, Champaign, 86; Ruschman Art Gallery, Indianapolis, 87; Sherry French Gallery, NY, 88; The Hyde Collection, Glens Falls, NY, 90. *Pos:* Vis artist, Cornell Univ, Ithaca, NY, 81-, Colo Mountain Col, Vail, 75, 76 & 78-81, Univ Ill, Champaign, 86; asst to dir, Yaddo, Saratoga Springs, NY, 84-88. *Awards:* NY Found for Arts Grant in Painting, 89. *Media:* Oil

MARTIN, FLOYD W
HISTORIAN, EDITOR
b Gainesville, Ga. *Study:* Carleton Coll, BA, 73; Univ Iowa, MA, 75; Univ Ill, Urbana-Champaign, PhD, 82. *Pos:* Mem bd dir, Southeastern Col Art Conf, 86-89 & 2002-06, vpres, 2008-2011, pres 2011-; chair, Dept Art, Univ Ark, Little Rock, 94-95, 2005 & 2012. *Teaching:* Prof art Hist, Univ Ark, Little Rock, 82-; inaugural prof, Univ Ark, Sch Pub Serv, Clinton, 2003-06. *Awards:* Award of Distinction, Little Rock Arts and Humanities Promotion Comn, 96; Exemplary Achievement Award, Southeastern Coll Art Conf, 99 & Pres's Award for Serv in Arts, 2005. *Res:* Art history, esp British 1750-1850. *Publ:* Contribr, Art J, 83; Contemporary Designers, Macmillan, 84; Victorian Britain, Garland, 88; Design for Arts in Education, 91; Encyclopedia of World Biography, 94; The Eighteenth Century: A Current Bibliography, 92; ed, Southeastern Coll Art conf Rev, 91-98 & 2007; Albion, 94, 2000 & 2001; contribr, Encyclopedia of Arkansas History and Culture, 2006, 2009. *Mailing Add:* Univ Ark at Little Rock 2801 University Ave Little Rock AR 72204

MARTIN, FRED THOMAS
PAINTER, EDUCATOR
b San Francisco, Calif, June 13, 1927. *Study:* Univ Calif, Berkeley, BA, 49, MA, 54; San Francisco Art Inst, with David Park, Clifford Still & Mark Rothko. *Work:* Whitney Mus Am Art, Mus Mod Art, NY; San Francisco Mus Mod Art; Oakland Mus of Calif. *Exhib:* Solo exhibs, MH DeYoung Mus, San Francisco, 54 & 64, San Francisco Art Inst, 72 & San Francisco Mus Mod Art, 58 & 73; San Francisco Mus Art Ann, 50-60; Whitney Mus Am Art, 70 & 73; Rena Bransten Gallery, San Francisco, 84; Frederick Spratt Gallery, San Jose, 96; Ebert Gallery, San Francisco, 97-2001, 2003; Han Art, Montreal, 98; Oakland Mus of Calif, 2003; Gallery Denovo, Sun Valley, ID, 2007-2011; 183rd Ann Invitational, Nat Acad, NY, 2008; Art Foundry Gallery, Sacramento, Calif, 2009, 2011; Ever Gold Gallery, San Francisco, 2014; SZ Art Center, Beijing, 2014. *Pos:* Dir, San Francisco Art Inst, 65-75, dean, 83-92; contrib ed, Art Week, 77-92. *Teaching:* Profr art hist, painting & drawing, San Francisco Art Inst, 79-; adj prof image & process, Dept of Arts & Consciousness, JFK Univ, Berkeley Campus, 96-2008. *Awards:* Nat Found Arts Artists Grant, 70-71. *Bibliog:* Dan Tooker (auth), article, Art Int, 11/75. *Media:* Miscellaneous. *Publ:* Auth, Beulah Land, A Book of Etchings, Hansen Fuller & Crown Press, 74; A Travel Book, Arion Press, San Francisco, 76; From an Antique Land, Green Gates Press, Oakland, Calif, 79; Lesson from the Masters, 2009, A Tarot Book, 2010; A Picture Book, 2012. *Dealer:* Han Art Montreal Que Can; Gallery DeNovo Sun Valley ID; Carlson Gallery Palm Desert Ca. *Mailing Add:* 4096 Piedmont Ave #116 Oakland CA 94611

MARTIN, JANE
PAINTER, DRAFTSMAN
b Montreal, Que, Mar 31, 1943. *Study:* Bishop's Univ, Lennoxville, Que, BA (Hons), 65; Carleton Univ, Ottawa, Ont, MA, 66. *Work:* Nat Gallery, Ottawa; Can Coun Art Bank, Ottawa, Ont; City of Ottawa; Art Gallery Greater Victoria; Winnipeg Art Gallery; The Art Gallery of Ontario. *Exhib:* Solo exhibs, Whitewater Gallery, North Bay, 85, Berkeley Castle Works 1984-1987, Toronto, 87, Gallery 101, Ottawa, 89, Gathie's Cupboard/Emblems/Transfigurations, Gallery 101, Ottawa, 89, Open Space, Victoria, 91, Rose Show, Toronto, 93, Ewen's Christmas Cabinet (and Rose Garden Tour), Toronto, 96, Gathie's Cupboard (1988-1998), Carleton Univ, Ottawa, 99, Juniper's Roses, Juniper, Ottawa, 2003, Dear Heart, *new*, Toronto; Ottawa Art Gallery, Ottawa, 2004, Rose Show: Rose Paintings and Garden Tour, Toronto, 2005, Something Happened, The Red Head Gallery, Toronto, 2008, The Roses are Just Moving into Fabulosity, The Red Head Gallery, Toronto, 2010, WE, The Red Head Gallery, Toronto, 2011; Wrapture, Ufundi Gallery, Ottawa, 90; Nat Gallery Can, Ottawa, 90; Eve's Eden: Problems in Paradise, Toronto, 94; The Four Show, Toronto, 95; Odd Bodies, Nat Gallery Can, Ottawa, Toronto & Calgary, 96-2000; Something Happened, The Read Head Gallery, Toronto, 2008; Deviant Detours, Kunsthaus, San Miguel de Allende, Mexico, 2009; Temperatura al Tope, Centro Cultural Ignacio Ramirez El Nigromante, San Miguel de Allende, Mexico, 2009; The Matter of Loss, Art Gallery of Ontario, Toronto, Canada, 2009; Cases, Red Head Collective, upArt, Gladstone Hotel Toronto, 2009; Insomnia, Nuit Blanche, The Red Head Gallery, Toronto, 2009; Time Shift, with Peter Dykhuis, Bill Ralph, Samantha Mogelonsky, Lynn Kelly, and Ram Samocha, The Red Head Gallery, Toronto, 2010; re(Verb), Arts Count, Ottawa, 2011; Being She with Sarah Anne Johnson, Nina Levitt and Meryl McMaster, 100th Anniversary of Woman's Coll Hospital, Gladstone Hotel, Toronto, 2011; An Embarassment of Riches: The Collection in Focus, curators: Diana Nemiroff and Sandra Dyck, CUAG, Ottawa, 2012; In Support of Now: 60 Years of the Associates Championing Contemporary Art at the AGGV, Victoria, BC, curated by Mary Jo Hughes and Toby Lawrence, 2012; Heart of the Moment: Selections from the Permanent Collection, OAG's 25th Anniversary Exhib, The Art Gallery of Ottawa, 2013. *Pos:* Artist-in-residence, Ont Arts Coun Project, 77; coordr, SAW Gallery, Ottawa, 78; co-founder, Can Artists' Representation Copyright Collective, 88; founding bd, Can Reprography Collective, 88-93. *Teaching:* Lectr, UAAC Conf, Concordia Univ, Montreal, 81, Univ Ottawa, 81 & Powerhouse Gallery, Montreal, 81. *Awards:* Canada Council and Ontario Arts Council Grants. *Bibliog:* Susan Crean (auth), Berkeley Castle Works 1984-1987, Can Art, fall 87, Body Language, 89; Lisa Rochon (auth), Portraits of suffering, Globe & Mail, 5/28/87; Joyce Nelson (auth), The Sacrament of the Flesh, Wrapture, Open Space, Victoria, 91; Conley, Christine, and Michael Bell (auths), Jane Martin Gathie's Cupboard 1988-1998, Ottawa, 1999; Nancy Beael, National Gallery prints, drawings live up to exibit's Odd Bodies title, Ottawa Citizen, 1/12/96; Renee Baert, Medical Imprints, Ottawa Art Gallery, 2004. *Mem:* Can Artists Representation/Le Front Artistes Can (nat coun, 77-79, nat rep 89-91). *Media:* Oil, Prisma color. *Publ:* Illusr, 77 Best Canadian Stories, Oberon, 77; auth, Who judges whom, Atlantis, 79; illusr, Stories of Quebec, Oberon, 80; auth, Woman Visual Artists on Canada Council Juries, Can Artists Representation/Le Front Artistes Can, 81; illusr, Fat Woman, General, 82. *Mailing Add:* 21 Rose Ave Toronto ON M4X 1N7 Canada

MARTIN, KNOX
PAINTER, SCULPTOR
b Barranquilla, Colombia, Feb 12, 1923; US citizen. *Study:* Art Students League, 4 yrs. *Work:* Corcoran Gallery Art, Washington; Mus Mod Art, Whitney Mus Am Art, NY; Mus Art, Austin, Tex; Univ Calif, Berkeley; Weatherspoon Art Gallery, Greensboro, NC; Mus Art, Baltimore, Md; Art Inst, Chicago, Ill; Mus Art, Dallas, Tex. *Comn:* 19 story wall painting, City Walls, Inc, West Side Hwy, NY, 1971; wall painting, Mercor, Inc, Merritt Complex, Ft Lauderdale, Fla, 1972; wall painting, Houston & McDougal Streets NY, 1979; wall painting, Nieman Marcus, White Plains, NY, 1980; John Wayne Mural, John Wayne Sch, Brooklyn, 1982. *Exhib:* Whitney Mus Am Art, NY, 1972; Art Students League, NY, 1985, 1986, 1994, 1998, 2004, 2005 & 2006; Int Sch Art, Italy, 1990-92; many retrospectives, Art Students League, NY, 1992; Tibor De Nagy, NY, 1992; Gremillion Gallery, Houston, Tex, 1993, 1995 & 1998; Macon Fine Art Ltd, 1995; Benny Smith Gallery, Nelsonville, NY, 1996; Janos Gat Gallery, NY, 1997, 2000, 2001 & 2003; Rivington Gallery, London, 1999; LightHouse Mus, Tequesta, Fla, 1999; Noel Fine Arts, NY, 2004; Salander-O'Reilly Galleries, NY, 2004; Ann Exhib Group Show, Nat Acad Mus, NY, 2005; Woman: Black & White Paintings, Woodward Gallery, New York, 2010. *Teaching:* Asst prof drawing & painting, Yale Univ, 1965-70; instr, Art Students League, NY, 1972-; instr, Univ Minn, NY Univ & Internat Sch Art, Umbria, Italy. *Awards:* Nat Endowment Arts, 1972; Creative Artists Pub Serv, 1978; Pollock-Krasner Found Grant, 1990 & 2008; Goetlieb Award, 1991. *Bibliog:* George Parrino (auth), Knox Martin, The Deadalian Work, 1972; H Kramer (auth), rev, NY Times, 10/25/75; G Brown (auth), Knox Martin Retrospective, Arts, 12/75; G Henry (auth), review, Art News, 1/76; Vivian Raynor (auth), article, NY Times, 10/29/96; Arthur Danto (auth), Adventures in Pictorial Reason, 1999; Julio Congora (auth) Knox Martin: Black & White, 2001; Edward Leffinwell (auth), Knox Martin at Janos Gat, Art in Am, 10/03. *Mem:* Visual Artists Group Asn; Nat Acad. *Dealer:* Janos Gat Gallery 1100 Madison Ave New York NY 10028. *Mailing Add:* 128 Ft Washington Ave Apt 8-J New York NY 10032

MARTIN, LLOYD
PAINTER
Study: RI Sch Design, 80. *Exhib:* Solo exhibs include AS220 Gallery, Providence, RI, 85, Gallery One, Providence, RI, 91, Hunt Cavanaugh Gallery, RI, 93, Trustman Gallery, Boston, Mass, 97, Lenore Gray Gallery, RI, 98, 2000, 2002, 2005, Stephen Haller Gallery, NY City, 2001, 2002, 2003, 2004, 2006, Spheris Gallery,

Walpole, NH, 2002, 2004, 2005, Urban Shelter, Pawtucket, RI, Roshkowska Gallery, Windham, NY, 2003, 2004,; group exhibs include Bristol Art Mus, RI, 79, 80, 82; Imagination, Peconic Gallery, Riverhead, NY, 93; Lenore Gray Gallery, 95, 98, 2005; Native Gallery, RI, 96; NY Studio Sch, 2000; Aesthetic Boundaries, Stephen Haller Gallery, NY City, 2001, Constant Aesthetic, 2001, Surface Fragments, 2002, Narrative Abstraction, 2003, Coda, 2003, Focal Point, 2005, Solstice, 2006; Brattleboro Mus, Vt, 2002; Mead Art Mus, Amherst, Mass, 2003; 2 x 2 x 2 Grimshaw Gudewicz Art Gallery, Falls River, Mass, 2004; Spheris Gallery, Vt, 2005; Eye on Art 54 Greenwich Ave, 2006; Gallerie Pierre, Taichung, Taiwan, 2006. *Awards:* Painting Fellowship, RI State Council Arts, 96, 99, Drawing Fellowship, 2000. *Mailing Add:* c/o Stephen Haller Gallery 542 W 26 St New York NY 10001

MARTIN, LORETTA MARSH
CARTOONIST, CALLIGRAPHER
b Plymouth, Ind, Jan 22, 1933. *Study:* Art Inst Chicago, BAE, 55; Univ Notre Dame, MA, 68; Famous Artists Schs, 68 (cert com art). *Work:* Many pvt collections in US & other countries. *Comn:* Calligraphy for Granaderos de Galvez, (presented to the King of Spain) 86. *Exhib:* Solo exhib, First Unitarian Church, South Bend, Ind, 62; Northern Ind Artists; Alumni Asn Art Inst Chicago; Artists 70 & 71, Citrus Co, Fla; El Paso Centennial Mus. *Pos:* Asst cur, El Paso Mus Art, 74-86. *Teaching:* Art instr, Grapevine Sch Art, Grapevine, Tex. *Mem:* Ft Worth Calligraphers Guild; Trinity Arts Guild. *Media:* All Media. *Interests:* Repair/restoration of objects d'arte: ceramic, porcelain, papier mache, etc. *Publ:* Graphic work included in Mangan Publ. *Mailing Add:* Martin Art Studio 1437 Simpson Hurst TX 76053

MARTIN, LUCILLE CAIAR
PAINTER, MURALIST
b Carlsbad, NMex, June 7, 1918. *Study:* With La Vora Norman; Frederic Taubes Workshops, Cloudcroft & Ruidoso; Merlin Enabnit Art Sch, Chicago, dipl; workshop with Olaf Wieghorst, Puerto Vallarta, Mex, dipl, 75. *Work:* Carlsbad Libr & Mus, NMex; Houston Med Ctr, Tex; Univ Ariz, Tucson. *Comn:* Jordan River (mural), Hillcrest Baptist Church, Carlsbad, 62; Sacred River (mural), First Baptist Church, McCrory, Ark, 63; El Capitan (mural), Security Savings & Loan, Carlsbad, 64; NMex State Bird-Roadrunner, Young Democrats for Gov Off, State Capitol, Santa Fe, 64; roadrunner painting, comn by Gov Campbell for aircraft carrier Constellation, 64. *Exhib:* Fla Int Art Exhib, Lakeland, 52; Nat Palo Duro Art Show, WTex State Univ, Canyon, 64; Nat Sun Carnival Art Exhib, El Paso Mus Art, 64; solo exhib, NMex State Univ, Las Cruces, 65; Boulder City Art Festival, Nev, 70; BPO Elks 385, Tucson, 90-2000. *Pos:* Artist, Leanin' Tree greeting cards, reproduced by Boulder, Colo, 70-2000. *Teaching:* Workshops, Nev, Carlsbad, NMex & Tucson, Ariz. *Awards:* Grand Sweepstakes, Tri-State Art Exhib, El Paso, 57; First Place, Carlsbad Area Art Asn Exhibs, 64, 65 & 66; First Place, Nat Parks Show, 73, 75 & 76. *Bibliog:* Articles in NMex Newspapers & El Paso Times, 64 & 65; Elena Montes (auth), Lucille Martin's art, NMex Mag, 4/65 & 10/88. *Mem:* Charter mem Carlsbad Area Art Asn; Tucson Art Ctr. *Media:* Acrylic, Oil. *Publ:* Contribr, NMex Mag, 54 & 65 & Ariz Highways Mag, 3/70. *Dealer:* Two Coats Southwestern Gallery Tucson AZ

MARTIN, LYS
PHOTOGRAPHER, CURATOR
b Lafayette, La, Mar 3, 1957. *Study:* Univ Miss, Oxford, BA (summa cum laude), 79; Art Inst Chicago, BFA, 83, MFA, 86. *Work:* Art Inst Chicago; Mus Contemp Art. *Exhib:* Solo Exhibs, Artemisia Gallery, Chicago, 86; Moming Gallery, Chicago, 87; Vanitas, Chicago Pub Libr Cult Ctr, 90; Wade Wilson Gallery, Chicago, 90; Ross Wetzel Studios, Chicago, 93; Art Detour, Ojai, 96, 2000 & 2001; Ojai Art Stroll, Cherubs, 98; Trendz, 2000; Inner Alchemy, Ojai Creates! Ojai, Calif, 2006; Art Expo, 89, 90 & Selections, 90, Wade Wilson Gallery, Chicago; Personal Political: Sexuality Self-defined, Sch Art Inst Chicago, 90; Photo Projects, White Columns, NY, 90; Contrasts, John Michael Kohler Art Ctr, Sheboygan, Wis, 91; Still Alive: Contemp Still Life, Rockford Art Col, Ill, 91; Light, Milwaukee Inst Art & Design, Wis, 92; TRINE, Parkland Coll Art Gallery, Champaign, Ill, 92; Picture This, Benefit Exhib & Auction, Renaissance Soc Chicago, Ill, 92; New Gallery, Houston, Tex, 92; Small Works, Hal Katzen Gallery, NY, 93; Artlantic City, Randolph St Gallery, Chicago, 93; Positive Images, Somism Found, Daley Ctr, Chicago, 93; Twenty Artists Under Twenty Four Inches, Hal Katzen Gallery, NY, 93; Is There Still Life in Chicago, Sazama Gallery, Chicago, 94; Art of Communication, Gallery Cafe, Chicago, 94; Women Photographers, New Gallery, Houston, 94; Camera Obscura/Obscura Camera, Betty Rymer Gallery, Sch Art Inst, Chicago, 94; Blast Exhib & Auction, 102 Greene St, New York City, 93, TZ Art & Co, NY, 94; Introductions, New Gallery, Houston, 93; Art Detour 2, Can Studio, Ojai, 96; The Visionary Show, Ojai Ctr for Arts, Ojai, Calif, 96; 11th Ann Hearts & Flowers Exhib, The Folk Tree Gallery, Pasadena, Calif, 98; Open a Book and Fall In, Ojai Ctr for Arts, 2000; Oak St Etalier, 2000; Touch of Light Gallery, 2001; Tula Hatti, Ojai Calif, 2001; Touch of Light Gallery, 2004. *Collection Arranged:* Polaroid & Polaroid Derived Imagery, 88, John Plouf & Howard Miller, 88 & Investigations, 90, MoMing Gallery, Chicago. *Pos:* Secy, Dept of Prints and Drawings, Art Inst Chicago, 84-87; co-cur, MoMing Gallery, 87-89; asst dir, Feigen Inc, 87-88; co-dir, Betsy Rosenfield Gallery, Chicago, 88-94. *Teaching:* Visiting Artist, Grad Critique Panelist, Sch Art Inst Chicago, 94; guest lectr, Col DuPage, Glen Ellyn, Ill, 94; artist-in-residence, Ragdale Found, Lake Forest, Ill; Life Drawing, San Antonio Sch, Ojai, CA, 2003. *Awards:* Unendowed Merit Scholar, Art Inst Chicago, 85 & 86; Spec Assistance Grant, Ill Arts Coun, 86; Community Arts Assistance Grant, Chicago Off Fine Arts, 90 & 91. *Bibliog:* Patricia C Johnson (auth), Galleries Host Their Annual Introductions, Houston Chronicle, 1 & 14, sec D, Friday, 7/9/93; Mark Frohman (auth), Home Shopping Art, Publ News, 7/28/93; Tina Wasserman (auth), Sense of Place (catalog, reproduc), Gahlberg Gallery Arts Ctr, Coll DuPage, 94; Art Spirit Focus for Gallery Debut, Ojai Valley News, Pg A-8, June 18, 2004; Ojai Creates! hosts Lys Martin Show, Ojai Valley News, Pg A10, June 30, 2006 (photo); Arts Calendar, Ojai Valley News, Pg A8, July 7; Pg A10, July 14 (photo); pg A8, July 21 (photo); pg A10, July 28 (photo); pg A10, Aug 25, 2006. *Media:* Photography, Mixed Media. *Collection:* Gallery Mem show, BAT (Buenaventura Art Gallery), Ventura CA, 2002; Angels Around the World, Gardens of the World, Thousands Oaks CA, 2004. *Publ:* Contribr, Poetry, Seams, Vol 2, No 3, 86; Artist's Pages (collab), Primer, No 3, 89; Project Pages, WhiteWalls, No 26, fall & winter 90; Video Trine: Lys Martin, for Arts Sake, #22, 93; and many others. *Dealer:* Touch of Light 311 N Signal St Ojai CA 93023. *Mailing Add:* PO Box 82 Ojai CA 93024

MARTIN, MARGARET M
PAINTER, EDUCATOR
b Buffalo, NY, 1940. *Study:* Boston Univ, BFA; watercolor workshops with John Pike, Robert E Wood, John Pellew, Rex Brandt & Milford Zornes. *Hon Degrees:* Honorary Doctor of Fine Arts Degree, D'Youville Col, Buffalo, NY. *Work:* Burchfield Penny Art Mus & Adam's Mark Hotel, Buffalo, NY, Jacksonville & Daytona Beach, Fla; Taiwan Art Inst, Taipei; Roswell Park Cancer Inst, Buffalo, NY; Niagara Falls, Ont, Can City Hall. *Comn:* Painting, Lockport Savings Bank, NY, 90; Connors & Vilardo, Buffalo, NY, 94; paintings, Lancaster Opera House, NY, 96, 97; mural, D'Youville Col, Buffalo, 2001; painting, Cheektowaga Cen Sch Dist, Cheektowaga, NY, 2007. *Exhib:* Am Watercolor Soc, 70-73, 78-79, 83, 86, 88-89, 94, 96, 2002; Nat Arts Club, NY, 74-97; Republic China/USA/Australia Watermedia Exhib, 94; Wet & Fresh: A Survey of Current Watercolor in Western NY, Burchfield-Penny Art Center, 2004; and others. *Collection Arranged:* Buffalo Seminary; Colby Art Collection, 20th Anniversary Exhib Coll, 04. *Pos:* Designer, Wagner Folding Box, Buffalo, NY, 62-64; art dir-designer, Manhardt-Alexander, Inc, Buffalo, NY, 64-77; freelance graphic designer & illusr, 77-80; Watercolor classes & workshop sessions in many areas of US & Can. *Teaching:* prof fine artist, MMMartin Studio, 80-. *Awards:* Hardie Gramatky Mem Award, Am Watercolor Soc, 83; Catharine Lorillard-Wolfe Gold Medal Honor Watercolor, 85; Transparent Watercolor Award, Knickerbocker Artists, 90; Mary LaGreca Mem Watercolor Award, Hudson Valley Art Asn, 2006; and others. *Bibliog:* Splash, F&W Publ, 90, 92, 98; Watercolor 90, Am Artist, spring 90; The Best of Watercolor, Rockport Publ, 95; The Human Element, Am Artist, Watercolor, Winter, 2008. *Mem:* Am Watercolor Soc; Nat Transparent Watercolor Soc; Nat Watercolor Soc; Nat Arts Club; Catharine Lorillard Wolfe Art Club; and others. *Media:* Watercolor, Architecture/Floral/Landscape. *Specialty:* Watercolor paintings (architectural, still-life, industrial, and marine subjects). *Publ:* Contribr, Painting with the White of Your Paper, F&W Publ, 95; The Best of Flower Painting, 96 & No More Wishy Washy Watercolor, F&W Publ; auth, Make a value judgement, Watercolor Magic, fall 96; contribr, AWS Isolating the Moment, Buffalo Spree, David Laurence Publ, fall 2005; auth, The Human Element, Am Artist, Watercolor, winter 2008; contrib auth, Margaret M Martin, Watercolor Secrets, F&W Publ, 2009. *Dealer:* House Gallery, 4300 N Sewell Ste 201, Oklahoma City, Okla, 73119; Tidewater Gallery, 1038 Moore St, Swansboro, NC, 28584; Albright-Knox Art Gallery, Rental Sales Gallery, 1285 Elmwood Ave, Buffalo, NY, 14222. *Mailing Add:* 69 Elmwood Ave Buffalo NY 14201

MARTIN, MARY FINCH
PAINTER, GALLERY DIRECTOR
b Glens Falls, NY, Sept 7, 1916. *Study:* Pvt tutoring with Isabel La Freniere. *Exhib:* Rockport Art Asn, Mass, 71; Hamilton-Wenham Art Show, S Hamilton, Mass, 74; Newbury Art Asn, Mass, 75; Gloucester & Cape Ann Exhib, Gloucester, Mass, 72; N Shore Art Asn, Gloucester, Mass. *Pos:* Art dir, Harbor Gallery, Mass, 71-91. *Mem:* Rockport Art Asn; N Shore Art Asn. *Media:* Oil. *Mailing Add:* 730 SW Munjack Cir Fort Pierce FL 34986-3455

MARTIN, ROGER
PAINTER, WRITER
b Gloucester, Mass, 1925. *Study:* Boston Mus Fine Arts Sch (honors). *Hon Degrees:* Montserrat Col, DFA, 94. *Work:* Pvt collections in New Eng, NY, the West Coast, Europe, Japan, Switz, S Africa; Cape Ann Hist Asn, Gloucester, Mass; Boston Pub Libr; Fogg Art Mus; Harvard Univ, Cambridge, Mass; Rubin & Rudman, Boston. *Comn:* Graphic art, D C Heath & Co, Allyn & Bacon, Beacon Press, 65-68 & United Church Teaching Pictures; designed cases & executed carvings, C B Fisk Pipe Organs, Harvard Univ & Pohick Church, Lorton, Va, 65-69; House of Hope Presby Church, St Paul, Minn, 79; Stanford Univ, 83; Presby Church, New Bern, NC, 85. *Exhib:* Solo exhibs, Trinity Coll, Hartford, 61, Carl Siembab Gallery, Boston, 69, So Vermont Art Ctr, Manchester, 70, Rockport Art Asn, Rockport, Mass, 83, Orphanos Gallery, Boston Mass, 88, Montserrat Coll Art, 90; Westend Gallery, Gloucester, Mass, 95; Acacia Gallery, Gloucester, Mass, 98; Cape Ann Hist Asn, 98. *Teaching:* Instr design & drawing & head freshman dept, New Eng Sch Art, Boston, 67-69; instr design & painting to chmn foundation prog dept, Montserrat Coll Art, Beverly, Mass, 69-90, prof emer, 91, assoc prof, 90-, mem found fac, bd trustees, 92-93. *Awards:* Poet Laureate, Rockport, Mass, 90-98. *Bibliog:* Article, Gloucester Daily Times, 5/83. *Media:* Oil; Prints, Woodcut. *Res:* local history. *Interests:* gardening. *Publ:* Contribr, illus in New Yorker Mag, Atlantic Monthly & NY Times; articles & illus in Child Life Mag & textbks; contribr, Gloucester Daily Times, Mass, 89-98; Boston Sunday Globe, Mass, 92-94; Rockport Remembered: An Oral History, 97 & A Rockport Album: Photographs of Bygone Days, 98, Curious Traveller Press, Gloucester, Mass; Rockport Recollected, Real Stories From Real People, 2001. *Dealer:* David Hall Fine Art Dover Mass. *Mailing Add:* 29 Penryn Way Rockport MA 01966

MARTIN, WALTER
SCULPTOR
b Norfolk, Va, 1953. *Exhib:* Solo exhibs, PPOW, NYC, 84, 86, 88-89, 91-92, 94, 96, 98, 2001, The Chrysler Mus, Norfolk, Va, 93, Moriarty Gallery, Madrid, 96, Alejandro Sales Gallery, Barcelona, 97, Espacio Caja de Burgos, Spain, 99, Dis, Momenta, Brooklyn, 99, Loss of Experience, Santa Barbara Arts Forum, Calif, 2000, Travelers, Moriarty Gallery, Madrid, 2003, PPOW, NYC, 2003, Phona Hoffman Gallery, Chicago, 2004, Mario Mauroner Contemp Art Salzburg, 2004, Cold Front, PPOW Gallery, NYC, 2005; Group exhibs, Behind The Stacks: 4th Annual Artists Books, Kathryn Markel Gallery, NYC, 84; Sculpture, Objects & Related Drawings, Art Palace, NYC, 85; Esbo Mus of Art, Helsinki, 88; Gothenburg Art Gallery, Sweden, 89;

Writ in Water, Solo Press/Solo Gallery, NYC, 90; Dead Heroes, Disfigured Love, Lorence Monk Gallery, NYC, 91; Art/Functional Art, Turbulence, NYC, 93; The Body Human, Nohra Haime Gallery, NYC, 94; Revisiting the Landscape, Calif Center for Arts, Escondido, 95; The Subverted Object, Ubu Gallery, NYC, 96; The Chalkboard Chronicles, TZArt & Co, NY, 97; No Small Feat: Investigations of the Shoe is Contemp Art, Rhona Hoffman Gallery, Chicago, 97; Seeing Money, Rotunda Gallery, Brooklyn, 98; True West, PPOW, NYC, 99; Plastic Monuments, Centro Municipal de Exposiciones Subte, Montevideo, Uruguay; Animas!, The Rotunda Gallery, Brooklyn, 2001; Miami Art, PPOW Gallery, NYC, 2003-2004; Hot Summer in New York, Sean Kelly Gallery, NYC, 2003; MetroSpective at City Hall Park, Public Art Fund, NYC, 2003; The Art Show, PPOW Gallery, NYC, 2004; ARCO Galeria Moriarty, Madrid, 2004-2005; Arts for Transit Along the Way, UBS Gallery, NY, 2005; CIGE, China Int Gallery Expos, 2006; Art Brussels, MAM Mario Mauroner Contemp Art, Belgium, 2006; Bienal de Zamora, Claustro del Colegio Universitario, Zamora, Spain, 2006; Double Take, Schroeder Romero Gallery, NYC, 2006; Little Disasters, Mauroner RoomnumberOne, Vienna, 2006; installations include 911, The Schulman Sculpture Garden, NY, 88, Changing Places, Metro Tech Center, Public Art Fund Brooklyn, 96, A Gathering, MTA Arts for Transit Program, NYC, 1997-2000, Forbidden Door, Bloomberg LP, Public Art Fund, NY, 2001, Travelers, Grand Central Terminal, MTA Arts for Transit, NYC, 2002-2003, Wilshire/Normandie Metro Rail Station, MTA Metro Art, Los Angeles, 2005, MetroSpective at City Hall Park, NYC, 2003. *Bibliog:* Mark Shannon (auth), Review of Exhibition at PPOW, ARTS Magazine, 2/1985; Laura Maggi (auth), A New York, Una Galleria Minimalista, Casa Vogue, June/1988; Josef Woodard (auth), Space and Matter, The Independent, 4/1990; Poderoso caballero, Babelia (El Pais), 2/1995; Josephine Gear (auth), Changing Places, Review, 11/1996; Christopher Chambers (auth), Picks, NY Arts, 3-4/1998; Paul Laster (auth), Brooklyn Spice, Artnet.com, 10/1999; Rob Wilson (auth), Walter Martin & Paloma Muñoz, Sculpture Magazine, Summer/2001; Tomas Paredes (auth), Walter Martin & Paloma Muñoz: Cuentos de Invierno, El Punto, 2/2003; Michael Kimmelman (auth), A seasonal migration of cultural scope, NY Times, 8/8/2003; Alan G Artner (auth), McElheny succumb to glass' seductiveness, Chicago Tribune, 2/27/2004; Jessica Dawson (auth), Reflecting on a cultural divide, Washington Post, 10/6/2005; Amy Simon (auth), Ars 06, Artforum, 4/2006; Rachel Somerstein (auth), The Weather Inside is Frightful, Artnews, 10/2006. *Media:* miscellaneous

MARTIN, YOUNGHEE CHOI
PAINTER, DRAFTSMAN

b Seoul, Korea, Aug 20, 1954. *Study:* Brooklyn Mus Art Sch, 73; Yale Univ Summer Sch Music & Art, 76; RI Sch Design, Hon BFA, 77. *Work:* Norma Series, Salome Series, Poppea, The Magic Flute Series, The Waste Land Series, landscape paintings; The Aenied Series; In The Wilderness. *Exhib:* Creative Artists Pub Serv Prog Award Winners, Munson-Proctor Art Ctr, Utica, NY & Bard Col, 81; Operatic Themes by Two Artists, Alexandre Hogue Gallery, Univ Tulsa, Okla, 85; Inaugural Exhibit: Chronicling Time, Pastel Soc Am Art Showcase, NY, 93, Subjective Projections, 94, Art Showcase V, 95 & As Subjective as Possible, 97; Violent Nature, Gallery 28, New Eng Sch Art & Design, Boston, 94; 20th Century Oil Painting in Korea, Han Ga Ram Mus, Seoul, Korea, 94; 4th Nat Painting Competition, Cheekwood Mus Art, Nashville, Tenn, 94; Invitational Drawing Exhib, Smith Col, Northhampton, Mass, 96; 173rd Ann Exhib, Nat Acad Mus, NY, 98; Drew Univ, Madison, NJ, 98; solo exhib, Simon Gallery, Morristown, NJ, 98; Areum, Kyoto City Mus, Japan, 99; Voila! Le Monde Dans La Tete, Mus Art Modern Ville Paris, France, 2000; The Heart of Light, Nabi Gallery, Sag Harbor, NY, 2000; Donaldson Gallery, Miss Porter Sch, Farmington, Conn, 01; Florence Bienale, Italy, 02; Maurice Arlos Fine Art, NY, 02; Gallery Horikawa, Kobe, Japan, 02; Rich & Strange, Nobi Gallery, 2004; Bamidbar, 55 Mercer Gallery, 2005. *Collection Arranged:* Yonsei Univ, Seoul; Carpenter Design Group, NY; Bond Market Asn, NY; Bryn Mawr Col, Pa; Korea Merchant Bank, Seoul; Memorial Sloan Kettering, NYC. *Pos:* co-cur, Art Showcase, Bond Market Asn, 93-01; Full time Artist. *Awards:* Creative Artists Pub Serv Prog Painting Fel, 81; Nat Endowment Arts Painting Fel, 83; Vt Studio Ctr Award, 2000. *Bibliog:* Martica Sawin (auth), The drawings of Younghee Choi Martin, Visions and Revisions catalog, 97; Interview with painter: Younghee Choi Martin, Flora Mag, No 5, 12/99; Louis Finkelstein (auth), Women view: two generations of women artists from New York, Haverford Col, 2000; Eric Ernst (auth), Korean innovators on display at Nabi Gallery, SouthHampton Press, 5/25/2000; Joel Silverstein (auth) Oil Painting by Younghee Choi Martin, an Artist odyssey through the Waste Land, catalog, 2004. *Media:* Oil, Charcoal, Pencil. *Publ:* Oil Painting by Younghee Choi Martin an Artist Odyssey, Nobi Press. *Dealer:* Jeong Song Gallery Seoul Korea; Gallery horikawa, Kobe Japan; Nobi Gallery, NYC, NY. *Mailing Add:* 144 W 27th St No 9F New York NY 10001

MARTINE, DAVID BUNN
PAINTER

b Southampton, NY, 1960. *Study:* Inst Am Indian Arts, Santa Fe, NMex, Certificate Prog, 1983; Univ Okla, BFA (Advert Design), 1982; Cent State Univ, M Ed (Art Educ), 1984. *Work:* Children's Mural, Challenge Am Grant Joint Proj, Family Preservation Ctr, Shinnecock Reservation, Southampton, NY; Am Friends Service Comt, New York; Shinnecock Nation Cultural Ctr and Mus, Southampton, NY. *Exhib:* exhibs include In Beauty It Is Begun, Metrop Mus Art, New York, 1973; Rider With No Horse, Gallery Manhattan Borough Pres, New York, 1988, Jamaica Arts Ctr, NY, 1988, Minor Injury Gallery, Brooklyn, 1988; Circle of Power, Am Indian Community House Gallery/Mus, 1992, Southampton, NY, 1992, New York Mix, 2005; Whaling: A Cultural Odyssey, Sag Harbor Whaling & Historical Mus, NY, 2001. *Teaching:* Adult Educ, Beginning Drawing, Southampton Cultural & Civic Ctr, 1990; Long Island Indian History Class, Long Island Univ, Southampton, NY, 1997-98. *Awards:* Joan Mitchell Found Grant, 2007. *Mailing Add:* PO Box 1285 Southampton NY 11969

MARTINEZ, ALFRED
PAINTER

b Ennis, Tex, Dec 24, 1944. *Study:* Southern Methodist Univ, Dallas, BFA, 68; Syracuse Univ, MFA, 71. *Comn:* Invisible-Lips (painting), comn by Gerry Dorman, NY, 81; Electric Fans (painting), comn by William Maxwell, NY, 82; Mystery (painting), comn by Gray L Cooper, Austin, Tex, 85; painting, Venetian Blinds, SLS, comn by Jeff Russell; painting, Venetian Blinds, comn by Richard Pitts. *Exhib:* Dallas Mus Fine Arts Ann, 63; Artist-Initiate, Bronx Mus Arts, 78; Artists Books--Franklin Furnace, Walker Art Ctr, 81; History of Art Works Gallery Coop, Wadsworth Atheneum, 81; Prints Benefit, Ctr Inter-Am Arts, NY, 82; Appalachian Nat Drawing Competition, Appalachian Col, NC, 83; Movin-Light, Kamikaze Rock Club, NY, 84; Exploit/Expose, Kentler Int Drawing Space, Brooklyn, NY, 91; William Benton Mus, Storrs, Conn, 92; group exhib, Slater Mem Mus, Norwich, Conn, 93; one-person exhib, Sensate Light, Univ Gallery, Cent Conn State Univ, New Britain, 94; and others. *Teaching:* From assoc prof art to prof, Univ Conn, West Hartford, 73-86, dir, Campus Art Gallery, 81-86. *Awards:* Traveling Artist Fel, Syracuse Univ, 69; Res Grant, Univ Conn, 74; Vis Artist Grant, Castle Gallery, Coll New Rochelle, Artists Space Inc, 80. *Bibliog:* Robyn Brentano & Mark Savitt (auths), One Hundred and Twelve Workshop, 112 Green Street, NY Univ Press, 81; Roger Winter (auth), Introduction to Drawing, Prentice-Hall, 83; Susanna Sheffield (auth), Alfred Martinez's Sensate Light, Cent Design/Cent Conn State Univ, New Britain. *Mem:* Film/Video Arts, NY. *Mailing Add:* 9 Chatham Sq Third Flr New York NY 10038-1027

MARTINEZ, CARLOS
DIRECTOR

b 1963. *Study:* Calif State Univ, Grad, 1986. *Pos:* Exec dir, Fresno Art Mus, Calif, 2004-; prog officer, James Irvine Found, 2002-2004; vpres of community investments, United Way of Mass Bay, 2000-2002; exec dir, La Alianza Hispana, 1997-2000. *Mailing Add:* Fresno Art Museum 2233 N 1st St Fresno CA 93703

MARTINEZ, DANIEL JOSEPH
CONCEPTUAL ARTIST

b Los Angeles, Calif, 1957. *Study:* Calif Inst Arts, BFA. *Comn:* Art work in bus shelters, Los Angeles, Calif, 1990; Public art work, NY, 1990. *Exhib:* Performances, Barnsdall Music Mus series, Los Angeles, 1988, Santa Monica Mus Art, Calif, 1988, Los Angeles Festival premier, Los Angeles, 1990; solo exhibs include Abstraction Gallery, Los Angeles, 1987, Mus Contemp Art, Mex City, 2000, The Project, New York, 2001, 2004, San Francisco Camerawork, 2002, The Project, Los Angeles, 2002, ArtPace, San Antonio, 2005, LACE, 2006; group exhibs include Centro Cultural de La Raza, San Diego, Calif, 1985; Trans Am Ctr Gallery, Los Angeles, Calif, 1986; Arts Ctr, Boston, Mass, 1987; Venice Biennale, 1993; Whitney Biennial, Whitney Mus Am Art, New York, 2008; Seeing, Los Angeles County Mus Art, 2001; The Show That Will Show That a Show is Not Only a Show, The Project, Los Angeles, 2002; Only Skin Deep, Int Ctr Photog, 2003; Indelible Images, Mus Fine Arts, Houston, 2005; An Image Bank for Everyday Revolutionary Life, REDCAT, Los Angeles, 2006; Cairo Biennial, 2006; In Someone Else's Skin, Ctr Curatorial Studies, Bard Coll, NY, 2007; Divine Violence, The Project, New York, 2007; Nina in Position, Artists Space, New York, 2007; Arte Vida: Actions by Artists of the Americas, 1960-2000, El Mus del Barrio, New York, 2008; Disorderly Conduct: Recent Art in Tumultuous Times, Orange County Mus Art, Newport Beach, Calif, 2008. *Teaching:* Asst prof studio art, Univ Calif, Irvine. *Awards:* Rockefeller Found Grant Conceptual Performance, 1987; Nat Endowment Arts, 1989; US Artists Broad Fel Visual Arts, 2007. *Dealer:* Robert Berman Gallery 2525 Michigan Ave C2/D5 Santa Monica CA 90404. *Mailing Add:* Studio Art Dept 3212 ACT Univ Calif Irvine Irvine CA 92697-2775

MARTINEZ, DAVID
COLLECTOR

b Mexico, 1957. *Study:* Inst Technol de Monterrey, Mexico, BSEE; Harvard Bus Sch, MBA. *Pos:* Founder & mng partner, Fintech Advisory, Inc, New York & London, 1987-. *Awards:* Named one of Top 200 Collectors, ARTnews mag, 2008-13. *Collection:* Modern and contemporary art. *Mailing Add:* Fintech Advisory Inc Ste 3805 375 Park Ave New York NY 10152

MARTINEZ, ERNESTO PEDREGON
MURALIST, ARTIST

b El Paso, Tex, Feb 26, 1926. *Study:* Self-taught. *Comn:* Mural, Pre-Columbian Mexico, Cafeteria Bowie High Sch, El Paso, Tex, 76; murals, Congressional Medal of Honor, Veteran's Clinic, El Paso, 77, 95; mural, The Resurrection, main altar, St Joseph's Catholic Ch, Houston; murals, Love of Country & Disabled Am Veterans, Veterans Hosp, NMex; mural, Labyrinth of the Americas, Univ of Tex, El Paso; mural, Desert Storm, Jr League of El Paso, 91-92. *Exhib:* Solo exhibs, NMex State Univ, 74, Univ Tex, El Paso, 74, Chamizal Nat Mus, 74-75 & Officer's Clubs, Univ Colo, 75; Exhib for First Ladies of US & Mex, Chamizal Nat Mus, El Paso, 77; Wight Gallery, Univ Calif, Los Angeles; Smithsonian Art Mus, Washington, DC. *Teaching:* Art consult, Boy Scouts Am, 60-; prof Mex-Am Art, El Paso Community Col, 74-; instr free classes for underprivileged & sr citizens; artist-in-residence, Chicano Studies dept, Univ of Tex, El Paso. *Awards:* Artist of Year, Lulac Coun, 74 & 79; City Coun Recognition, El Paso, 77; Tex Navy Admiral, Gov Tex; selected Tex State Artist in two-dimensional works of art, Senate of State of Tex, 97-98. *Bibliog:* Interview world television, Mexico City, 78; Art Diary, 82; Commander Veterans of Foreign Wars. *Media:* Acrylics, Watercolors. *Publ:* Auth, articles on Pre-Columbian Art, El Paso Newspaper, 85-86; art articles, El Paseno Newspaper. *Mailing Add:* 7140 Villa Hermosa El Paso TX 79912-2221

MARTINEZ-CANAS, MARIA
PHOTOGRAPHER

b Havana, Cuba, May 19, 1960. *Study:* Philadelphia Coll Art, Pa, BFA, 82; Sch Art Inst Chicago, Ill, MFA, 84. *Work:* Int Ctr Photog, NY; Bibliotheque Nationale, Paris, France; Mus Latin Am Art Orgn Am States, Washington, DC; Los Angeles Co Mus Art, Calif; Ctr Creative Photog, Tucson, Ariz; Chrysler Mus, Norfolk, Va. *Exhib:* Solo exhibs, Chrysler Mus, Norfolk, 92, Southeastern Ctr Contemp Art, Winston-Salem, NC, 93, Cronologias: 1990-1993, Iturralde Gallery, Los Angeles, Calif, 94, Catherine Edelman Gallery, Chicago, Ill, 95, 99, 03, Piedras, Iturralde Gallery & Catherine Edelman, Los Angeles, Calif, 97, Mus Art, Fort Lauderdale, Fla, 02, Julie Saul Gallery, NY, 02; SFla Cult Consortium Fel Exhib, Ctr Fine Arts, Miami, 93; Tampa Mus Art, 93; Fac Exhib, Lowe Art Mus, Univ Miami, Fla, 93; Photog by Cintas Fellows, Art Mus, Fla Int Mus, Miami, 93; Fredric Snitzer Gallery, Miami, Fla, 99, 00, 02; and others. *Collection Arranged:* Bibliotheque Nat, Paris; Ctr for Creative Photog, Tucson, Ariz; Ctr Cult Art Contemp, Mex City; Chase Manhattan Bank; City of Orlando; Haverford Col, Pa; Int Ctr Photog, NY; Int Mus Photog, Rochester, NY; JP Morgan Bank, NYC; Lehigh Univ, Bethlehem, Pa; Light Work, Syracuse, NY; LA Co Mus Art; Miami Art Mus; Mus d'Art Mod de la villa de Paris; Mus Mod Art; Nat Mus Am Art, Smithsonian Inst; San Francisco Mus Mod Art; St Louis Art Mus; Prudential Insurance Co, NY; Whitney Mus Am Art, NY; Tampa Mus Art. *Awards:* Grant, Photog Fel, Nat Endowment Arts, 88-89; Artist-in-Residence, Light Works, Syracuse, NY, 90; Visual & Media Artists Fel, SFla Cult Consortium, 92-93; Grant, Metro-Dade Art in Pub Places Comn, Miami, 94; Grant, Nat Mus Women in the Arts, Washington, DC, 00. *Bibliog:* Cloe Cabrera (auth), Former Cuban artists form images in black and white, Tampa Trib, 7/13/93; Helen L Kohen (auth), Fellowship winners share their talents, Miami Herald, 7/24/93; Helen L Kohen (auth), Photos are linked by Cuban heritage, Miami Herald, 10/30/93; Elisa Turner (auth), Two Centuries of Latino Art, The Miami Herald, 12/9/2001; Elisa Turner (auth), Identity Crisis: Maria Martinez-Canas, The Miami Herald, 5/22/2002. *Dealer:* Catherine Edelman Gallery 300 W Superior Chicago IL 60610; Iturralde Gallery 154 N Brea Ave Los Angeles CA 90036. *Mailing Add:* 2011 SW 10th St Miami FL 33135

MARTINO, NINA F
PAINTER
b Philadelphia, Pa. *Study:* Temple Univ, Tyler Sch Art, BFA; Instituto Allende, Univ Guanajuato, Mex, MFA; L'Acad di Belle Arti, Firenze, Italia (Embassy Scholar) Diploma; Pa Acad Fine Arts, Scholar; Moore Coll Art, Philadelphia, Pa; Studied with Giovanni Martino, NA, AWS & Eva Martino. *Work:* Mex-NAm Inst, Mexico City; Utica Coll, NY; Montgomery Coll, Pa; Woodmere Mus, Chestnut Hill, Pa; Butler Inst Am Art, Ohio; Acad Fine Arts, Florence, Italy; Villanova Univ, Pa; Penn Wynne Sch, Philadelphia, Pa. *Comn:* Seascape (oil), Mercantil de Irapuato, Mex, 80; landscape (oil), Mercantil de Irapuato, Mex, 80; Watercolor: Bullfighter in Action, Corona Beer Co, San Miguel Agency, Mex; Portraits (2), Los Ricos Hacienda, San Miguel Allende, Mex; Murals (2), Corona Beer Co, Ocean Waves Breaking & Atotonilco Creek & Portrait Comn, Irapuato, Mex; Posters of Musicians incorporated in Landscapes, Tourism of Guanajuato, Mex; Landscapes, Austin Coal Co, Canton, Ohio. *Exhib:* Woodmere Mus, Pa; Villanova Univ, Pa; Philadelphia Artists, Pa; Audubon Artists, 79; Butler Inst Am Art, 79; Martino Family: A Legacy of Excellence in Painting, Mus Civic Center, Philadelphia, 80; 4 Martinos 2 Generations-Villanova Univ, Pa, 93; Solo Exhibs: Michelet Gallery, Zona Rosa, Mex City; Mexican-N Am Inst Cult Relations Gallery, Mex City; Whitfield Gallery, SMA, Guarajuato, Mex; Fine Arts Nat Inst, SMA, Guanajuato, Mex, Paintings by Nina Martino, Whitfield Galleries, 2007, Retrospective, 2008, Retrospective 60 Yrs, Instituto Allende, San Miguel Allende, Mex, 2010, Martino Family, Newman Galleries, Phila, Pa, 2010; Group: Traveling Instrs Exhib, Guanajuato & Queretero Mus, Mex; Exhib Profs/Instrs, Univ Guanajuato, Mex; 8 Women Instituto Allende, Gto, Mex; Homage to the Martino Family, SMA, Mex, 2002, 2003-2010. *Collection Arranged:* Woodmere Art Mus, Philadelphia, Pa; North Am-Mex Inst Cult Affairs, Mexico; Austin Coal Co, Ohio; Cervezas Modelo, S.A. de C.V., Mex; Butler Inst Am Art, Ohio; Pa Acad Fine Arts, Philadelphia. *Teaching:* Grad & undergrad instr, painting & drawing, Inst Allende, Mex, 77-80; lectr, Rosemont Coll, 2010-2012. *Awards:* Antonio Cirino Mem Award, Allied Artists Am, 94, Len G Everett Memorial award, 97; Klein Family Award, Cheltenham Ctr, 95; Joan & Thomas Holmes Award, Phillips Mill, 95, George S Hobensack Jr award, 96; Salmagundi award, Audubon Artists, NY, 2000, Stephan Hirsch Mem award, 2001; Best in Show, Pa Acad Fine Arts, 2001, Berthe Goldberg Mem prize, 2004, Painting award, 2006, Lucy Glick Painting award, 2012; Jack Bookbinder Memorial award, PAFA, 2006, Painting award, 2006, 2008; Memorial award, Phillips Mill, Pa, 2009; Silver Medal of Hon, Audubon Artists Am, NY, 2010, Jack Richeson Painting award, 2011; Loan of Painting, US Embassy in Bandar Seri Begawan, 2011-2014. *Bibliog:* James McClelland (auth), The Martinos: A Legacy of Art (book), 2010. *Mem:* Fel Pa Acad Fine Arts; Allied Artists Am, NYC; Audubon Artists Am, NYC; Invitation Canton Mus Ohio celebrating 100 Years Allied Artists of Am, 2015. *Media:* Oil. *Dealer:* Schwarz Gallery 18th & Chestnut Sts Philadelphia, PA; Whitfield Galleries 5th Ave New York NY. *Mailing Add:* 1435 Manor Ln Blue Bell PA 19422

MARTINOS, DINOS
COLLECTOR
Pos: Head, Thenamaris Ships Mgt, Athens, Greece. *Awards:* Named one of Top 200 Collectors, ARTnews mag, 2004-12. *Collection:* Antiquities; modern and contemporary art; icons. *Mailing Add:* Thenamaris Ships Mgmnt 16 Athinas & Verrou S Athens 166 71 Greece

MARTINSEN, IVAR RICHARD
PAINTER, EDUCATOR
b Butte, Mont, Dec 9, 1922. *Study:* Mont State Col; Univ Ore; Univ Wyo. *Exhib:* Wyo Artists Traveling Exhib, Sheridan & Laramie; Scottsbluff, Nebr; Sheridan Inn Gallery, 75-76, 78 & 79. *Pos:* founder & bd mem, Martinsen Gallery, Sheridan Col; ret 85. *Teaching:* Prof art & chmn humanities div, Sheridan Col, formerly. *Awards:* Prizes, Wyo-Nebr Exhib, 58 & 59 & Wyo State Fair, 60. *Mem:* Sheridan Artist Guild; Wyo State Art Asn. *Mailing Add:* 452 Falcon Ridge Dr Sheridan WY 82801

MARTON, PIER
VIDEO ARTIST, EDUCATOR
US citizen. *Study:* Univ Calif, Los Angeles, BFA (cum laude), 76, MFA (film, video), 79; also in Paris. *Work:* Inst Contemp Arts, London, Eng; Nat Gallery Can, Ottawa; Long Beach Mus Art, Calif; Carnegie Mus, Pittsburgh; Mus Mod Art, NY. *Exhib:* Biennale de Paris, Mus Art Mod, Paris, France, 80; Mus Mod Art, NY, 85, 86 & 91; Video & Language, Am Mus Moving Image, NY, 89; The Eye and the I, Whitney Mus Am Art, NY, 89; Passage de l'Image, Beaubourg, Ctr George Pompidou, Paris, 89; Video Installations, Spertus Mus, Chicago, 90 & The Art Barn, Utah Arts Coun, Salt Lake City, 91; Performances for video, MOA Theatre/Video Gallery, Carnegie Mus Art, Pittsburgh, 94; JEW (video installation), part of Witness & Legacy (traveling), 95-2000; Sao Paolo/Paris Biennials, AFI, Mus Modern Art, Whitney Mus; The Other Man's Show, Jewish Mus; The Kitchen, Beaubourg & Musee d'Art Modern, Paris; Retrospective, Ramat Gans Mus, Israel. *Pos:* Dir, Found Art Resources, 81-83. *Teaching:* Asst prof film, video & photog, Occidental Col, 78-79 & 82-83; vis lectr video, Univ Calif, Los Angeles, 80-83 & Art Inst Chicago, 84; vis artist, Minneapolis Col Art & Design, 84-85; asst prof, Sch Art Inst Chicago, 85-90, chmn video area, 86-87; instr art hist & photog, Victor Valley Community Col, Calif, 91; vis assoc prof, Carnegie Mellon Univ, 93-95; fac editing, web & multimedia design & digital imaging, Pittsburgh Filmmakers, 95-97. *Awards:* Northwest Area Found Grant, 85; Media Arts Grant, 86 & Regional Fel Award, 87, Nat Endowment Arts; Ill Arts Coun, 87 & 90; Mem Found Jewish Cult Grant Award, 89. *Bibliog:* Lorri Zipay (ed), Artists' Video: An International Guide, EAI, Cross River Press, 91; Robert Raczka (auth), Pier Marton, The New Art Examiner, 5/94; Margot Lovejoy (auth), Post Modern Currents, Prentice-Hall, 96. *Mem:* Found Art Resources (bd dir, 81-82). *Media:* No Media. *Publ:* Auth, Ephemera No 3, U Carrion, Amsterdam, 79; Cahiers du cinema No 5, Cahiers, Paris, 81; Dreamwork No 4, Human Sci Press, 81; La Opinion, Los Angeles, 11/92-5/93. *Dealer:* Mus Mod Art New York NY; Electronic Arts Intermix New York NY

MARTON, TUTZI
PAINTER, SCULPTOR
b Bucharest, Romania, US citizen. *Study:* Acad Journalism, Budapest, grad, 71; silk screening, Salvator Fiume, Italy, 86; woodblock printing, Zhejiang Acad Fine Arts, Hangzhou, China, grad, 88. *Hon Degrees:* Fellow of American Biographical Inst; (hon fellow) Anglo-American Academy, Cambridge, 80. *Work:* Nat Arch, Washington, DC; Mus Art State Fla; Mus de Petit Format, Couvin, Belgique; Vatican, Rome; Mus Music & Ethnology, Haifa, Israel; private colls US, South Am, Australia, Austria, Belgium, Can, China, Ger, Greece, Hungary, Italy, Netherlands, others; Mus of History, Augustin Bunea, Romania, 2003. *Comn:* portrait His Holiness Pope John Paul II, Vatican, Rome; portrait Frank Sinatra, Hollywood, Calif; portrait Princess Redwing, RI. *Exhib:* one-person show, Kar Gallery Fine Art, Toronto, 78; Ann Show, Mus Art, Long Beach, NY, 79 & 81; Mus Petit Format de Papier, Exposition Int, Couvin, Belgique, 87; 6th Ann Int Exhib Miniature Art, Toronto, Can, 91; Mus of History, Augustin Bunea, Romania, 2003. *Collection Arranged:* (priv col) Romanian Library of NY, Foreign Press Association, NYC. *Pos:* Critic, 69-71. *Awards:* First Prize, Ann Show, Mus Art, Long Beach, 1981; Ioan & Maria Constantinescu Grant, Fondatia Cult Neth, 1981; I Passatore Award of Romana, Italy, 1982; Hon mention in Camerata Blajeana, Romania, 2003. *Mem:* Int Asn Art, UNESCO, Paris; Artists Equity Asn; For Press Asn, NY, 81; hon fellow Anglo-Am Acad. *Media:* Mixed Media, Oil; Precious Metal. *Res:* Bible, Art, Working with Metal. *Interests:* Art, music and museums. *Dealer:* Zois Shuttie Wallase Ave New York NY 10462. *Mailing Add:* 110 Riverside Dr Apt 7B New York NY 10024-3732

MARTONE, MICHAEL
PHOTOGRAPHER
b New York, NY, Nov 8, 1941. *Study:* Self-taught. *Work:* Mus Mod Art, NY; Fogg Mus, Harvard Univ; High Mus Art, Atlanta; Musee De L'Elysee Lausanne, Switz, 90; Major purchase of photogr, Musee De Elysee, Lausanne, Switz, 96. *Comn:* AIR Light Work, Syracuse Univ, NY, 78. *Exhib:* Die Welt Ausstellung der Photographie, Akad der Kunste, Berlin, 64; New Acquisitions, Mus Mod Art, NY, 70; Multiple Image Show, Mass Inst Technol, Cambridge, 72; New Acquisitions, Fogg Mus, Harvard Univ; solo exhibs, Hirshhorn Mus, Washington, DC, 79, photographs, Print Dept, Fogg Mus, Harvard Univ, 87 & Robert Menschel Gallery, Syracuse Univ, NY, 89; Fifth Vienna Biennale Contemp Photog, Austria, 81; The Foundation Select Collection, Musee De Elysee, Lausanne, Switz, 94. *Teaching:* Instr & artist-in-residence, Photo Dept, Tisch Sch Arts, New York Univ, 86. *Awards:* Purchase Awards, Art Festival Atlanta, 66 & 67; Photog Fel Grant, Nat Endowment Arts, 75; AIR Exhibitor & Lectr Grant for Light Work, Syracuse Univ, 78. *Bibliog:* A D Coleman (auth), Latent image, Village Voice, New York, 4/71 & article, New York Times, 3/74; Fred McDarrah (auth), Martone Show, Village Voice Rev, 85; A D Coleman (auth), Michael Martone Ripe for Rediscovery, Art News Mag, 11/96. *Publ:* Auth, Dark Light, Lustrum Press, 74; contribr, Creative Camera Mag, 74; The Grotesque in Photography, Summit Press, 78; Light Readings, Oxford Univ Press, 79; Altered photographs, Art News Mag, 81. *Mailing Add:* 342 E 15th St New York NY 10003-4028

MARTONE, WILLIAM ROBERT
PAINTER, INSTRUCTOR
b Wilmington, Del, Nov 30, 1945. *Study:* Pa Acad Fine Arts, Cressen Traveling Scholar, certif, 68; Univ Pa, BFA, 69, MFA, 91; pvt study with Morris Blackburn, 65-73, Walter Stuempfig, 66-68, Franklin C Watkins, 69-72 & Julian Levi, 77-80. *Work:* Ronald Reagan Mus, Santa Barbara, Calif; US State Dept, Gen Serv Admin; White House, Washington, DC; Vatican Art Gallery, Vatican City; also many pvt collections. *Comn:* Portrait of Fredrick Joseph Kinsman, Third Episcopal Bishop, comn by Mr & Mrs Charles Proctor, Warren, Ohio, 72; San J Caleb Boggs, comn by Sen & Mrs J Caleb Boggs, Wilmington, 73; Joe Frazier (portrait), comn by Cloverlay, Philadelphia, 74; Joe Frazier & Family, 81; Portraiture & landscape, Poet Prodns, Disney Studios/Touchstone Pictures; M Lavoisier, Lavoisier Libr, DuPont Co; Dean A

J Santoro, Widener Law Sch. *Exhib:* Ann Exhib, Nat Acad Design, NY, 67 & 75; Pa Acad Fine Arts, 75 & 79; Cottage Tour, Rehoboth Art League, Del, 75; solo exhibs, Grand Opera House, Wilmington, Del, 77 & Hardcastles, Wilmington, Del, 79; Rockwood Mus, Wilmington, Del, 81; Univ Delrs; Philadelphia Art Alliance; Philadelphia Mus Art; Butler Inst Am Art, Youngstown, Ohio. *Pos:* Account exec, Southam Assocs, 87-88 & Kimble & Melody Advertising & Media Features, 89-90; William Martone & Assocs, 90. *Teaching:* Instr, Howard Pyle Studios, Wilmington, Del, 69-85; instr portraiture, Pa Acad Fine Arts, 73-81; instr art & chmn upper sch dept, Wilmington Friends Sch, 74-77; instr adv/graphic design & typography, Art Inst Philadelphia, 86; instr vis arts & literacy & dir pre-intensive prog, Arts & Educ Intensive/Urban Educ Found, 90-91. *Awards:* First Prize, Philadelphia Watercolor Club, 72; First Prize, Chestertown Arts League, Wash Col, 77, 79 & 85; First Prize Oils, Soc NJ Artists, 79; and others. *Mem:* Del Archaeol Soc; Fel Pa Acad Fine Arts; Philadelphia Watercolor Club (bd dir, 72); Int Soc Artists; assoc Am Inst Conserv, Washington, DC. *Media:* Oil, Watercolor

MARTYL,
PAINTER, MURALIST
b St Louis, Mo, Mar 16, 1917. *Study:* Washington Univ, AB; Colorado Springs Fine Arts Ctr, with Arnold Blanch & Boardman Robinson. *Work:* Whitney Mus Am Art, New York; Art Inst Chicago; Colorado Springs Fine Arts Ctr; Los Angeles Co Mus; St Louis Art Mus; Hirshhorn Mus & Sculpture Garden, Washington, DC; Brooklyn Mus; Miyagi Prefecture Mus Art, Japan; Calif Palace Legion Honor, San Francisco; Pa Acad Fine Arts; Ill State Mus; DuSable Mus, Chicago; Arnot Gallery, Elmira, NY; Greenville, SC Mus; Peace Mus, Chicago; Davenport Munic Art Gallery, Iowa; Washington Univ, St Louis; Univ Ariz; Nat Mus Am Art, Washington, DC. *Comn:* Recorder of Deeds (mural), comn by Sect Fine Arts, Washington, DC, 43; Darkness into Light (mural), Unitarian Church, Evanston, Ill, 62; 22 projections for Pierrot Lunaire, Fine Arts Quartet, Ill, 62; portraits, James Franck, Chandrasekar, Harry Kalven, Univ Chicago. *Exhib:* Am Drawing Biennial XXIV, Norfolk Mus Arts, 71; one-person shows, Art Inst Chicago, 76, Fairweather-Hardin Gallery, 77, 81, 83 & 88, Ill State Mus, 78, Lake Forest Col, 79 & Brooklyn Mus, 86; Oriental Inst Mus, Chicago, Ill, 87; Gibbes Mus, Charleston, SC, 88; Ill State Mus Art Gallery, Chicago, 90; Tokyo Expo, 90; Printworks Gallery, Chicago, 95, 97, 99, 2002, 2004, 2007; and others. *Pos:* Art ed, Atomic Sci Bull, 45-72; exec comt, Artists Equity Asn Chicago, 58-69; bd dir, Arts Club; adv bd, Ragdale Found. *Teaching:* Instr painting, Univ Chicago, 65-70; artist-in-residence, Tamarind Inst, Univ NMex, 74. *Awards:* Logan Award & Medal, 50 & William Bartels Award, 57, Art Inst Chicago; Am Inst Archit Hon Award, 62; Artist in Residence, Ucross Found, Wyo, 2008. *Bibliog:* George McCue (auth), Martyl, St Louis Dispatch, 69; interview (film), WTTW Pub TV, 79; Michael Bonesteel, article, New Art Examiner, 83; Hist Channel, The Dooms Day Clock, 2003; Alan Artner, Chicago Tribune, 2007; Wall Paper Mg, April 2009. *Mem:* Arts Club Chicago; Renaissance Soc (pres, 70-71); Oxbow Sch Art. *Media:* Acrylic; Ink. *Specialty:* works on paper. *Interests:* Music & Gardening. *Publ:* Contribr, Methods and Techniques of Gouache Painting, 46; auth, Cliches, old and new, St Louis Post-Dispatch, 67; New Art Examiner--Fred Sweet, 68; introd to The Ste Genevieve Artists Colony & Summer sch Art, James G Rogers Jr, 98; Oral Hist, Art Inst Chicago, 2007. *Dealer:* Printworks 311 W Superior Suite 105 Chicago IL 60610; Thea Burger Assoc PO Box 842 Barnard VT 05031. *Mailing Add:* 645 S Meacham Rd Schaumburg IL 60193

MARUYAMA, WENDY
DESIGNER
b La Junta, Colo, July 11, 1952. *Study:* San Diego State Univ, BA, 75; Rochester Inst Tech, MFA, 80. *Work:* Oakland Mus Art, Calif; Univ Art Mus, Univ Ariz, Tempe; Macy's, Miami, Fla; Am Craft Mus, NY; and many pvt collections. *Comn:* Linda Cohn, Phoenix, Ariz; Michael & Nina Zagaris, Modesto, Calif; Marion Lee, Portola Valley, Calif; Alice Zimmerman, Nashville, Tenn; Ronald & Anne Abramson, Washington; Don Thomas & Jorge Cao, NY. *Exhib:* Solo exhibs: New Art Forms Expo, Joanne Raap Gallery, Chicago, 90; The Ingrained Image, Riverside Art Mus, Calif, 90; Signs of Support, John Michael Kohler Arts Ctr, Sheboygan, Wis, 90; Artists Design Furniture, Eve Mannes Gallery, Atlanta, 90; Gallery NAGA, Boston, Mass, 91; Peter Joseph Gallery, NY, 92 & 95; Margolis Gallery, Houston, Tex, 96; Virginia Breier Gallery, San Francisco, Calif, 97; Gallery NAGA, Boston, Mass, 97; Joanne Rapp Gallery, Scottsdale, Ariz, 98; Oceanside Art Mus, Calif, 99; Leo Kaplan Moder, NY, 2000; Brad Grad Ctr Studies Decorative Art, NY, 2000; Pacific Rim: Japan, Calif Crafts Mus, San Francisco, Calif, 93; Hybridization: Contemp Northern Calif Craft, 1975-Present, Oliver Art Ctr, Calif Coll Arts & Crafts, Oakland, 93; Functional Sculpture, Indigo Gallery, NY, 94; Masterworks Two, Peter Joseph Gallery, NY, 94; Breaking Barriers: Recent Am Craft, Am Craft Mus, traveling exhib, 95; World Urushi Cult Coun Exhib, Fujita Corp, Tokyo, 96; Talking to Myself: Cult, Fantasy and Domestic Condition, Porter Troupe Gallery, San Diego, Calif, 2001; Ariz State Univ Art Gallery, Tempe, 2001. *Pos:* Designer & maker contemp furniture, Comns & Speculative Work, 79-; artist-in-resident, Artpark, Lewiston, NY, 83, Carnegie-Mellon Univ, Pittsburgh, Pa, 84, Boston Univ, Mass, 84, Ind State Univ, Evansville, 84, La Napoule Art Found, France, 92, Buckinghamshire Col, High Wycombe, Eng, 94; bd trustees, Haystack Mountain Sch Crafts, 94-. *Teaching:* Instr metalworking & jewelry design, Crafts Ctr, San Diego State Univ, Calif, 73-75 & grad asst metalworking prog, 75; head, woodworking & furniture design prog, Appalachian Ctr Crafts, Tenn Technol Univ, Smithville, 80-85 & Calif Col Arts & Crafts, Oakland, 85-89; artist-in-residencies, Artpark, Lewiston, NY, 83, Carnegie-Mellon Univ, Pittsburgh, Pa, 84, Boston Univ, Mass, 84 & Ind State Univ, Evansville, 84; assoc prof, head, woodworking & furniture design prog, San Diego State Univ, Calif, 89-. *Awards:* Artists Fels, Nat Endowment Arts, 82, 84, 86, 90 & 92 & Tenn Arts Comn, 83; Metropolitan Home/Kraus Sikes Merit Award,89; Fulbright Grant, Eng, 94; Residency Grant, Nat Endowment Arts/Japan-US Friendship Comn, 95; Grants-in-Aid, San Diego State Univ, 96 & Rsch Scholar, Creative Activities Grant, 2000; Office Int Exchange Grant, 2000; Japan-US Friendship Comn Grant, 2000; Mini Grant, Adams Humanities, 2001. *Bibliog:* Daniel Mac Alpine (auth), Woodshop News, 12/93; Candice Miles (auth), Nothing Ordinary, Pheonix Home & Garden, 11/94; Barbara S Greene (auth), Peter Joseph Gallery an Art Furniture Affair, Woodshop News, 3/94; Candice Miles (auth), Nothing ordinary, Phoenix Home and Garden, 11/94; Stylemakers, San Diego Union Tribune, 8/11/96. *Mem:* Am Crafts Coun; World Urushi Cult Coun. *Media:* Furniture Design, Wood. *Publ:* Wendy's place, San Diego Union, 8/27/89; Crackerjack creations, Newsweek, 1/29/90; Art rev, Atlanta J & Constitution, 2/12/90; Back to the Past, Southern Accents Mag, 5/90; Contemporary Crafts for the Home, Kraus Sikes Inc, 90. *Mailing Add:* San Diego State Univ Sch Art Design Art Hist 5500 Campanile Dr San Diego CA 92182-4805

MARX, MADDY See Segall-Marx, Madeleine (Maddy Marx)

MARX, ROBERT ERNST
PRINTMAKER, PAINTER
b Northeim, Ger, 1925. *Study:* Univ Ill, BFA, 51, MFA, 53; study & travel in Ger, Austria, Italy, Switz & France, 1 yr. *Work:* Mus Mod Art, NY; Philadelphia Mus Art; Dallas Mus Art, Tex; Seattle Art Mus; Hirshhorn Mus, Washington, DC; and many others. *Exhib:* Franz Bader Show, Baway Found, Vienna, Austria, 76; Art of Poetry, Nat Collection Fine Arts, Smithsonian Inst, 76; Premio Int Biella, l'Incisione, Italy, 76; Davidson Galleries, Seattle, Wash; US Embassy Gallery, Belgrade, Yugoslavia, 83; Davidson Gallery, Seattle, Wash, 95; Int Biennial Exhib Portrait Drawing, Tuzla, Yugoslavia; Int Exhib Graphic Art, Kustveilein, Zufrechen, WGer; Int Biennial Exhib Graphic Art, Ljubljana, Yugoslavia; Trinity Gallery, Atlanta, Ga, 2007. *Pos:* Artist attached to USIA exhib in Prague & Bratislava, Czech, 65; dir, Flint Inst Art, 57 & Impressions Workshop, Boston, 69. *Teaching:* Instr, Univ Wis, 53; chmn dept art, Flint Jr Col, 56; instr, Sch Art, Syracuse Univ, 58; assoc prof art, State Univ NY Binghamton, 66-69; assoc prof, State Univ NY Col Brockport, 70-72, prof, 72-89, distinguished prof, 89, retired, 90; instr, Fulbright Sch Art, Delhi Univ, India, 84; lectr wkshp, Art Dept, Drake Univ, Des Moines, Iowa, 85. *Awards:* Grand Diploma Drawing, Third Int Biennial Exhib Portrait Drawings & Graphics, Tuzla, Yugoslavia, 84. *Bibliog:* Sebby Jacobson (auth), article, Times-Union, 11/22/85. *Media:* Etching; Oil on Canvas. *Dealer:* Davidson Galleries Inc 313 Occidental Ave S Seattle WA 98104; Trinity Gallery 315 E Paces Ferry Rd Atlanta GA 30305. *Mailing Add:* 80 Nunda Blvd Rochester NY 14610-2840

MARX, SUSAN & LARRY
COLLECTORS
Pos: Founder, SLM Spec Needs Fund, 2006. *Awards:* Named one of Top 200 Collectors, ARTnews mag, 2009-13. *Collection:* Postwar and contemporary art, especially Abstract Impressionism and works on paper

MARZANO, ALBERT
PAINTER, DESIGNER
b Philadelphia, Pa, Aug 22, 1919. *Study:* Philadelphia Graphic Sketch Club; Philadelphia Plastic Club. *Comn:* Murals, Dept Pub Health, Philadelphia, 67 & 69; portrait Riccardo Muti, Friends & Admirers Maestro Riccardo Muti, Philadelphia, 78; portrait Louis A DeSimone, Grand Lodge Pa, Order Sons Italy, Philadelphia, 81; portrait John Cardinal Krol, Archbishop Philadelphia, Grand Lodge Pa, Order Sons Italy, 84; portrait Rabbi Joshu Toledano, Congregation Mikveh Israel, 85. *Exhib:* Ann Mid-Year Show, Butler Inst Am Art, Youngstown, Ohio, 60; Solo exhibs, St Joseph's Coll, Philadelphia, 70, La Salle Coll, Philadelphia, 71, Philadelphia Sketch Club, 74, Waldron Acad, 75 & Episcopal Acad, 77; plus others. *Teaching:* Instr drawing & painting, Sons Italy in Am, Philadelphia, 65-70. *Awards:* Gold Medals, Philadelphia Art Dirs Club, 54, 55 & 56; Gold Medal, Haddonfield Art Ctr, NJ, 59; Gold Medal, Nat Soc Painters in Casein, 61. *Mem:* Philadelphia Art Alliance. *Media:* Mixed. *Mailing Add:* 1949 Locust St Philadelphia PA 19103-5730

MARZOLLO, CLAUDIO
SCULPTOR
b Milan, Italy, July 13, 1938; US citizen. *Study:* Columbia Col, BA. *Work:* Windsor Art Gallery, Ont; Neiman-Marcus Exec Off, Dallas, Tex; Mus Sci & Indust, Chicago; Ft Wayne Mus Art, Ind. *Comn:* Kinetic piece, ARCO Hq, Philadelphia, 74. *Exhib:* Loan Exhib, Everson Mus, Syracuse, NY, 72; Solo exhibs, Tafts Mus, Cincinnati, Ohio, 74, traveling exhib, Nat Acad Sci, Washington, DC, 77; Illum, Whitney Mus Am Art, NY, 74; New Acquisitions, Windsor Gallery Art, Ont, 75; The Logic & Nature of Color, Akron Art Inst, Ohio, 75; Hudson River Mus, Yonkers, NY, 76; Solo exhib, Virginia Beach Arts Ctr, 79. *Teaching:* Instr three-dimensional design, Sch Visual Arts, New York, 74 & Univ Bridgeport, Conn, 75-77; Mather vis scholar, Case Western Reserve Univ, Cleveland, 75; vis artist, US Military Acad, West Point, 78-. *Bibliog:* Joseph Horning (dir), Metamorphoses (film), Ohio Arts Comn, 75. *Media:* Plexiglas, Aluminum. *Mailing Add:* 437 Lane Gate Rd Cold Spring NY 10516

MASHECK, JOSEPH DANIEL CAHILL
HISTORIAN, CRITIC
b New York, NY, Jan 19, 1942. *Study:* Columbia Univ, AB, 63, MA, 65, Dublin Univ (Trinity C), MLitt, 2001, Columbia, PhD, 73, study with Dorothea Nyberg, Meyer Schapiro & Rudolf Wittkower. *Exhib:* Small Works, NY, 79; A More Store, Tilton Gallery, NY, 83-84; The New Portrait, PS1, Long Island City, NY, 84; Dealers and Critics, MO David Gallery, NY, 85; Off the Wall, Kamikaze Club, NY, 86; Joseph Masheck and Peter Plagens, Hofstra Univ Mus, 89; Dan Devine: Consumer Matrix; Dublin Paintings, Hofstra Univ, 95; Critics as Artists, Andrew Zarre Gallery, NY, 95; Post War Am Art: The Novak O'Doherty Coll, Irish Mus Modern Art, Dublin, 2010-11. *Collection Arranged:* Richard Serra Drawings, Visual Arts Mus, NY, 1974; Ed Moses Drawings, 1958-1976; Frederick S Wight Art Gallery, Univ Calif, 1976; Beat Art: Drawings by Gregory Corso, Jack Kerouac, Peter Orlovsky, Philip Whalen & others, Rare Bk & Manuscript Libr, Columbia Univ, 1977; Critical Perspectives, PS 1, Long Island City, NY, 1982; Thomas Nozkowski: Drawings of the '70s, Gallery Nature Morte, NY, 1983; Smart Art: New Work from New York, Jose Luis Sert Gallery, Carpenter Center Visual Arts, Harvard Univ, 1985; Smart Art Too,

Cooperative Gallery, NY, 1985; The Joseph Masheck Collection of Contemp Art, Rose Art Mus, Brandeis Univ, 1986; Makarevich's Second Level of Feeling: A Work of Perestroika Contextualized, Rosenberg Gallery, Hofstra Univ, 2001-2002; Tendril Ornament: Diffused or Universal Axinn Libr, Hofstra Univ, 2002; Photo-Architecture: Diurnal/Nocturnal, Gallery 128, NY, 2003. *Pos:* Ed in Chief Artforum Mag, 77-80; contrib ed, Art in Am Mag, 87-2012; ed consult, New Observations; bd dir, Crosby St Proj, 95-96; adv bd, Annals of Scholarship, 98-; columnist, Boston Rev, 85-87; consult ed, Brooklyn Rail, 2004-; adv bd, Art in Translation, 2009-. *Teaching:* Lectr, Maidstone (Kent) Col Art, Eng, 68-69; preceptor art hist, Columbia Col, Columbia Univ, New York, 69-71; instr art hist, Barnard Col, 71-73, asst prof, 73-83; lectr visual studs, Harvard Univ, 83-86; vis prof art hist, Hunter Col, spr & fall 84; assoc prof art hist, Hofstra Univ, 87-94, prof, 94; vis prof art hist, Columbia Univ, New York, summer 2002; adj prof, art hist, Fordham Univ, 2003; vis prof hist of art. *Awards:* Samuel H Kress Found, fell, 68-69; NEA, fel, 72-73, 75-76; Soc fel in the Humanities, Columbia Univ, 77-78; Reva & David Logan Grant for New Writing on Photography, Bost Univ, 85; research grant, Malevich Soc, 2003; Centenary Fell, Edinburgh Coll Art, 2006-2010; Visiting Fell, St. Edmunds Coll, Cambridge Univ, 2011. *Mem:* Am Asn Univ Profs; Coll of Arms, London (hon armiger); Int Asn Art Critics; Soc Antiquaries of Scotland (fell). *Res:* Abstract modern and contemporary, art and architecture. *Interests:* General Art History, Modernism, Abstract Painting, Criticism, Art and Religion. *Publ:* Historical Present: Essays of the 1970s, U M I Research Press, 84; Smart Art, Willis, Locker & Owens, 84; Modernities: Art-Matters in the Present, Penn State Press, 93; Building-Art: Modern Architecture Under Cultural Construction, Cambridge Univ Press, 93; Van Gogh 100, Greenwood Press, 96; ed, introd Arthur Wesley Dow, Composition 1899; 1913, Univ Calif Press, 97; Marcel Duchamp in Perspective, rev ed, Da Capo Press, 2002; C's Aesthetics, Slought Found and Bryn Mawr Coll., 2004; The Carpet Paradigm: Integral Flatness from Decorative to Fine Art, Edgewise Press, 2010; Le Paradigme du Tapis, Jacques Soulillou, Musee d'Art Moderne et Contemporain, Geneva, 2011; (Texts on) Art, The Brooklyn Rail, 2011; Adolf Loos: The Art of Architecture, IB Tauris Press, 2013. *Mailing Add:* 290 9th Ave 3A New York NY 10001-5724

MASIH, LALIT K
PAINTER

b Almora, India, 1932. *Study:* Syracuse Univ, 56-60; Long Island Univ, NY, MFA (fine arts & design), 80-85; studied with Harold Stevens, Stan Brodsky, Arnold Siminoff & Milford Zornes, Rex Brandt, Robert E Wood. *Work:* Friends Nassau Co Mus; many pvt collections. *Exhib:* Am Watercolor Soc; Nat Watercolor Soc; Salmagundi Club; Allied Artists, Audubon Artists; other regional and nat watercolor exhibs. *Teaching:* instr, watercolor workshops & demonstrations, currently. *Awards:* Winsor & Newton Award, Am Artists Prof League, 89; Silver Medal of Honor, Audubon Artists, 97; Jane Peterson Mem Award, Allied Artists of Am, 2000; Walser Greathouse Medal 2005; and numerous others. *Mem:* Am Watercolor Soc; Nat Watercolor Soc; Am Artists Prof League; Salmagundi Club; North East Watercolor Soc; Allied Artists; Audubon Artists. *Media:* Watercolor. *Specialty:* Landscapes, street scenes & harbors. *Publ:* Watercolor Magic, Simple by Design, Apr 2005

MASLEY, CAITLIN
GRAPHIC ARTIST, INSTALLATION SCULPTOR

Study: Univ Ariz, MFA, 1997. *Exhib:* Solo exhibs include ArtistsSpace, New York, 1999, Babylon's Wet Dream Billboard Proj, 2001, Sara Meltzer Gallery, New York, 2001, Galleri 5, Copenhagen, 2002, 2004, Sidewalk Proj, DUMBO Arts Festival, New York, 2003, Lower Manhattan Cult Coun Swing Space, New York, 2006-07; group exhibs include Greater New York, PS 1 Contemp Arts Ctr, New York, 2000; Open Range, Greenberg Van Doren Gallery, New York, 2004; New Foundland, Priska C Juschka Fine Art Gallery, New York, 2005; Draw_drawing_2, London Biennale, 2006; Weak Foundation, Momenta Art, New York, 2006; Future Nomad, Vox Populi, Philadelphia, 2007. *Awards:* Emerging Artist Fel, Socrates Sculpture Park, 2002; Pollock-Krasner Found Grant, 2007. *Mailing Add:* 238 Carlton Ave Brooklyn NY 11205-4002

MASNYJ, YURI
PAINTER, SCULPTOR

b Washington, 1976. *Study:* Cooper Union, BFA, 98. *Exhib:* solo shows, On Our Black Rainbow, Sutton Lane, London, 2004, A World of Interiors, Metro Pictures, NY, 2004; 126a, Brooklyn Front Gallery, 2001; Ballpoint Inklings, Geoffrey Young Gallery, Mass, 2002; Shallow Interiors, Rivington Arms Gallery, NY, 2002; New Topography, 2003; From Here On, Guild & Greyskhul, NY, 2003; Drawings, Metro Pictures, NY, 2003; International Paper, Hammer Mus, Univ Calif, Los Angeles, 2003; Happy Days Are Here Again, David Zwirner, 2004; Radical Vaudeville, 2005; The Night Has a Thousand Eyes, 2005; Greater NY, PS 1 Mus Modern Art, Long Island City, NY, 2005; Landings, Susan Inglett Gallery, NY, 2005; Square Dance, Galerie Jacky Strenz, Frankfurt, Germ, 2005; Whitney Biennial: Day for Night, Whitney Mus Am Art, NY, 2006; NY Drawings, Travesia Cuatro, Madrid, 2006

MASON, EMILY
PAINTER

b NY City, 1932. *Study:* Bennington Col, 50-52; Cooper Union, NY City, BFA; Wheaton Col, Mass, DFA (hon), 2000. *Exhib:* Exhibs incl Grace Borgenicht Gallery New York City, Landmark Gallery New York City, Walker-Kornbluth Gallery Fairlawn NJ, Thomas Babeor Gallery San Diego, MB Modern New York City, Va Lynch Gallery Tiverton RI, Mugar Art Gallery Colby-Sawyer Col; rep in collections of Springfield (Mass) Mus, Rockefeller Group New York City, Ciba-Geigy Chemical Group Ohio; subject of Emily Mason: At the Heart of Abstraction, by David Ebony, 2002; The Filter Element, David Ebony, 2nd Book in Production. *Teaching:* teacher, Hunter Col, New York City. *Awards:* Grantee Fulbright Fel, Acad delle Belle Arti, Venice, 56. *Mem:* Nat Acad (acad). *Media:* Oil on Canvas. *Interests:* Plants, Reading. *Dealer:* David Findlay Jr NY; LewAllen Santa Fe, NMex. *Mailing Add:* 263 Stark Rd Brattleboro VT 05301

MASON, FRANCIS, JR
ADMINISTRATOR, WRITER

b Jacksonville, Fla, Sept 9, 1921. *Study:* St John's Col, Annapolis, Md, BA, 43; grad study art hist with Nikolaus Pevsner, Birkbeck Col, Univ of London, 61-64. *Pos:* Dance critic, Hudson Rev, 50-55, WNXC radio, New York, 51-55 & WQXR radio, New York, 79-; Cult attache & exhibs off, US Info Agency Foreign Serv, 54-64; chief US exhibs to Russia & E Europe, US Info Agency, 65-67; pres Experiments in Art & Technol, New York, 68; asst dir, Pierpont Morgan Libr, New York, 75-87, acting dir, 88, consult on endowment campaign, 88-92; ed, Ballet Rev, 79-. *Mem:* New York Studio Sch Drawing, Painting & Sculpture (chmn emer, 1969-1972); Century Asn NY. *Publ:* Ed, Steuben, Seventy Years of Glassmaking, Praeger, 74; co-auth, Balanchine's Complete Stories of the Great Ballets, Doubleday, 77; 101 Stories of Great Ballets, Doubleday, 77; I Remember Balanchrine, Doubleday, 90. *Mailing Add:* 46 Morton St New York NY 10014-4021

MASON, JOHN
SCULPTOR

b Madrid, Nebr, Mar 30, 1927. *Study:* Otis Art Inst, Los Angeles, 49-52; Chouinard Art Inst, Los Angeles, 53-54. *Work:* Art Inst Chicago; Los Angeles Co Mus Art; San Francisco Mus Art; Mus Contemp Crafts, NY; Nat Mus Mod Art, Kyoto, Japan; and others. *Comn:* Ceramic relief, Palm Springs Spa, Calif, 59; ceramic relief, Tishman Bldg, Los Angeles, 61; ceramic doors, Sterling Holloway, South Laguna, Calif; City of Boise, Idaho, 82; City of Sacramento, Calif, 82; and others. *Exhib:* Solo shows include Pasadena Art Mus, Calif, 60 & 74, Frank Lloyd Gallery, Calif, 2007; group shows include Whitney Mus Am Art, 64, 73 & 76; Kompas 4, Van Addemuseum Eindhoven, The Neth, 69; Nat Mus Mod Art, Kyoto, Japan, 71; and others. *Teaching:* Assoc prof art, Univ Calif, Irvine, 67-73, prof art & chmn dept studio art, 73-74; prof studio art, Hunter Col, New York, 74-85. *Awards:* Ford Found Award, 67th Am Exhib, Art Inst Chicago, 64; Univ Calif Award, Creative Arts Inst, 69-70; and others. *Bibliog:* John W Mills (auth), The Technique of Sculpture, Reinhold Corp, NY, 65; John Coplans (auth), John Mason--Sculpture, Los Angeles Co Mus Art, 66; Susan Peterson (auth) The Craft and Art of Clay, 00, 03. *Media:* Ceramics. *Dealer:* Frank Lloyd Gallery 2525 Michigan Ave B5B Santa Monica CA 90404. *Mailing Add:* 1521 S Central Ave Los Angeles CA 90021

MASON, LAURIS LAPIDOS
ART DEALER, WRITER

b New York, NY, Apr 21, 1931. *Study:* Syracuse Univ, AB, 52; State Univ NY, New Paltz, MS, 55. *Pos:* Dir, Mason Fine Prints, 72-. *Specialty:* American & European original prints. *Publ:* Auth, Print Reference Sources: A Select Bibliography, 18th-20th Centuries, 75, second ed, 79; coauth (with Cecile Shapiro), Fine Prints: Collecting, Buying & Selling, co-ed (with Joan Ludman), auth, Print Collector's Quarterly: An Anthology of Essays of Eminent Printmakers of the World & coauth (with Joan Ludman), The Lithographs of George Bellows: A Catalogue Raisonne, KTO Press, rev ed 92, auth Missionary Mary L Proctor, the doors, Fine Print Press, 14. *Mailing Add:* Country Club Tower Apt 1112 10777 W Sample Rd Coral Springs FL 33065

MASON, MOLLY ANN
SCULPTOR, ENVIRONMENTAL ARTIST

b Cedar Rapids, Iowa. *Study:* Univ Iowa Sch Art, BFA (magna cum laude, Phi Beta Kappa, studio art & art hist), MA (sculpture, ceramics), MFA (sculpture, ceramics). *Work:* Univ Central Fla, Orlando; Univ Northern Iowa, Cedar Falls; City of Alexandria, La; City of W Palm Beach, Fla; City of Albuquerque, NMex; Kirkwood Coll, Cedar Rapids, Iowa, 2009; % For Art, State Utah, Ogden-Weber Applied Tech Coll; 2 Major bronze, stainless, glass and stone sculptures, 2011. *Comn:* Stainless Steel/Copper Sculpture, City of Brisbane, Australia; Bronze/Copper Sculptures, Royal Caribbean Cruise Lines; Stainless Steel/Copper Sculpture, Michener Mus, Doylestown, Pa; Bronze/Kiln-Formed Glass Sculptures, Northwest Valley Med Ctr, Tucson, Ariz; 2 major sculptures, water feature & pool for Conf Center, Stainless Steel/Bronze Kiln-Formed glass, Kirkwood Coll, Cedar Rapids, Iowa, 2009. *Exhib:* Minneapolis Inst of Arts, Minn, 79; Soho 29 Gallery, NY, 87, 89, 92, & 95; Quietude Garden Outdoor Sculpture Gallery, NJ, 90 & 96; Elaine Benson Gallery, Bridgehampton, NY, 90 & 96; Gallery COM & Art Space Niji, Kyoto, Japan, 92; Sculpture Showcase Gallery, New Hope, Pa, 94-2002; Sculpture on the Grounds, Rockville Civic Ctr, Md, 95 & 96; James A Michener Mus Art (with catalog), Doylestown, Pa, 98-99; Johnson Atelier's Sculpture Mus, 99; Contemp Sculpture Chesterwood Mus, Stockbridge, Mass, 2000, 2001; Tadu Gallery, Santa Fe, NMex, 2005; and 15 other solo exhibs. *Teaching:* Prof sculpture, Univ Minnesota, Morris; asst prof, Southern Illinois Univ, Edwardsville, IL; asst prof sculpture, Univ NMex, & Tulane Univ, New Orleans, La; State Univ NY, Stony Brook, NY. *Awards:* Am Asn Univ Women Found Fel; Fel, Lilly Found; Fulbright Fel, Japan; and 45 other awards. *Bibliog:* Elizabeth Blair (auth), Scale, Spirit and Energy: Contemporary Sculpture thrives in Yugoslavia's Symposium, Int Sculpture Mag; Jules Heller (auth), Twentieth Century North American Women Artists, Garland Press; Stephen Paul Miller (auth), rev New York solo exhib, Cover Arts NY Mag; Molly Mason: Sun and Shadow, James Michener Mus Art; Virginia Watson Jones (auth), Contemporary American Women Sculptors, Oryx Press; Jules Heller (auth), North American Artists of the Twentieth Century, Garland Press, NY; Adelphi Univ, NY, Sculpture Catalogues; and 80 others. *Mem:* Coll Art Asn; Int Sculpture Ctr; Sculptors Guild, NY; Washington Sculptors Group, Wash, DC. *Media:* Metal, kiln formed glass; ceramic tile cast concrete, water features. *Dealer:* Art 4 Business, 161 Leverington Ave, Philadelphia, PA, 19127; Art & Sculpture Consulting at: art and sculpture US; The Guild at guild.com; Contract Art, 11 Halls Rd, Old Lyme, CT, 06371. *Mailing Add:* 24 Waterview Dr Port Jefferson NY 11777

MASON, NOVEM M
SCULPTOR, EDUCATOR

b North Wildwood, NJ, Nov 22, 1942. *Study:* NC State Univ Sch Design, BA (archit), 68; ECarolina Univ Sch Art, MFA, 74. *Work:* Relief sculpture, ECarolina Univ; Southern Univ, Shreveport, La; West Tex Mus, Lubbock, Tex. *Comn:* Sculptural screen, Southern Bank, Richmond, Va, 76; relief sculptures, Richmond Fredericksburg

Petersburg Railroad, Richmond, Va, 77, Southern Univ, 80 & First Fed Savings & Loan, Lake Charles, La, 81; entrance sculpture, Mid-States Wood Preserving Inc, Simsboro, La, 82. *Exhib:* Anderson Gallery Summer Invitational, Richmond, Va, 76; Three Artists, Wyly Tower Gallery, Ruston, La, 81; Alumni Masonic Temple Studios, Anderson Gallery, Richmond, Va, 83; Canal Place/Art Place, Contemp Art Ctr, New Orleans, La, 86; Sculpture '86, Houston Mus Fine Arts, Tex, 86; The Red Clay Survey, Huntsville Mus Art, Ala, 88; Louisiana Artists, Louisiana Arts & Sci Ctr, Baton Rouge, 89; Art in Park, Lubbock, Tex, 90; Outstanding is Their Swamp, Sangre De Cristo Arts Ctr, Pueblo, Colo, 90. *Collection Arranged:* Drawing nude: Coll of Faset I Seay, Atlanta, GA, 72; Painting still life: Coll of Augustus W Mason, Morehead City, NC, 73; Sculpture, Bust: Coll of John J Armstrong, Glen Cove, NY, 73; Sculpture, Relief: Coll of sch of Art East Carolina Univ Greenville, NC, 74; Sculpture screen: Coll of Southern Bank, Richmond, VA, 75-76; Sculpture Relief: Coll of Richmond Fredrickburg Railroad, Richmond VA, 77; Sculpture abstract: Coll of A W Mason, Morehead City, NC, 77; Sculpture, screen: Coll of Woodsmith, Inc, Ruton, LA, 80; Sculpture Relief: Coll of First Federal Savings and Loan, Lake Charles, LA, 81; Sculpture Relief: Coll of AD Mazisys, Air, Ruston, LA, 82; Sculpture, Abstract: Coll of Mid States Wood Preservers, Inc, Simsboro, LA, 82; Sculpture, conceptual: Coll of Ken Willis, Glen Allen, VA, 84; Sculpture, Abstract: Coll of Dr Joseph Strother, Clayton, GA, 90; Sculpture, abstract Coll of Jack Lewis, Ruston, LA, 90; Sculpture abstract: Coll of West Texas Mus, Lubbock, Tex, 91; Sculpture, abstract: Coll of Masuil Mus of Art Monroe, LA, 92. *Pos:* Partner, artist & designer, Design Collaborative, Richmond, Va, 74-79; designer & artist, Woodsmith, Ruston, La, 79-85. *Teaching:* Asst prof art, Va Commonwealth Univ, Richmond, 68-79; assoc prof art, La Tech Univ, Ruston, 79-88, prof, 88-90; prof, Univ NC, Greensboro, 90-. *Awards:* Summer Res Grant, La Tech Univ, 88; Juror's Choice Award, Huntsville Mus Art, 88; Design Educ of the Year Award, Carolina's Chap of Am Soc Interior Designers, 95; Sch Human Environ Scis Outstanding Teacher Award, 2002. *Mem:* Southern Asn Sculptors; Coll Art Asn Am; Tex Sculpture Asn; Am Soc Interior Designers; Int Interior Design Asn; Interior Design Educators Coun. *Media:* Wood; Mixed. *Mailing Add:* Dept Interior Architecture 259 Stone Bldg Unc-G Greensboro NC 27412-5001

MASON, WALLY
MUSEUM DIRECTOR
b Ohio. *Study:* Beloit Coll, BA; Ind Univ, MFA. *Pos:* dir, Univ Maine Mus, 1996-2007; dir, Haggerty Mus, Marquette Univ, 2007-; dir, Selby Gallery, Ringling Sch Art & Design, formerly. *Teaching:* Prof art courses, Western Mich Univ, Univ Vt, Univ S Fla, Univ Idaho, Univ Maine. *Mailing Add:* Haggerty Museum of Art Marquette University 530 N 13th St Milwaukee WI 53233

MASSAD, GEORGE DANIEL
PAINTER, EDUCATOR
b Oklahoma City, Okla. *Study:* Princeton Univ, BA in English, 1969; Univ Chicago, MA in English, 1977; Univ Kans, MFA in Painting, 1982. *Work:* Met Mus Art, NY; Art Inst Chicago; Philadelphia Mus Art; Smithsonian Am Art Mus; Milwaukee Art Mus; Philbrook Mus Art, Tulsa, Okla; Ark Art Ctr, Little Rock; and others; Pa Accad Fine Arts. *Exhib:* Solo Exhibs: Tatistcheff Gallery, NY, 86; Pa Accad Fine Arts, Philadelphia, Pa, 91; Franklin & Marshall Col, Lancaster, Pa, 92; Allentown Art Mus, Allentown, Pa, 97; Forum Gallery, NY, 2001 and 2006; Univ Richmond 2002; Things Found Along the Way, Lancaster Mus Art, Lancaster, Pa, 2003; Huntington Mus Art, WVa, 2003; Philbrook Mus Art, Tulsa, 2006; Palmer Mus Art, State College, Pa, 2008, Minds Eye, Ark Art Ctr, 2012; Group Exhibs: Mid-Four, Nelson-Atkins Mus Art, 83; AM Realism, San Francisco Mus Modern Art, 85; Realism Today, Nat Acad Design, NY 87, New Acquisitions, Nat Mus Am Art, Wash DC, 88; 20th Centruy Drawing & Sculpture, Cummer Mus Art, Jacksonville, Fla, 89; Am Modern Still-Life, Snite Mus, Univ Notre Dame, 98; Contemp Am Realist Drawings, Art Inst Chicago, 99; New Acquisitions, Philadelphia Mus Art, 2000; About Face, Ark Arts Center, Little Rock, Ark, 2001; Representations: The Art of Drawing, Skidmore Col, 2002; Transforming the Commonplace, Susquehanna Mus Art, Harrisburg, Pa, 2003; Poem, Demuth Found, Lancaster, Pa, 2004; Graphic Masters, Highlights from the Smithsonian Am Art Mus, 2003-5. *Pos:* Artist-in-residence, Lebanon Valley Coll, Annville, Pa, 93-; trustee, Suzanne Arnold, Found, 97-. *Teaching:* adj prof, art & English honors prog, Lebanon Valley Col, Pa, 84-. *Awards:* Pa Council on the Arts; Pollock-Krasner Found; Nat Endowment for the Arts. *Bibliog:* Thomas Bolt (auth), Daniel Massad, Arts Mag, Vol 60, 1986; Ronny Cohen (auth), G Daniel Massad, Artforum, summer 95; John Loughery (auth), Silent History, Forum Gallery & Univ Richmond Mus, 2001; Lynne Perricelli (auth), The Meaning of Things, Am Artist, 10/2006; Leo Mazow (auth), Tatistcheff Gallery & Lebanon Valley Col, 1998; Christine Kallenberger (auth), Philbrook Mus Art, 2006. *Mem:* Coll Art Asn. *Media:* Pastel. *Dealer:* Forum Galley 745 Fifth Ave New York NY 10151. *Mailing Add:* Art & Art History Dept Lebanon Valley College Annville PA 17003

MASSARO, KAREN THUESEN
CERAMIST, LECTURER
b Copenhagen, Denmark; US citizen. *Study:* State Univ NY, Buffalo, BSEd, 66; Univ Mass, Amherst, 67-68; Univ Wis, Madison, with Don Reitz, MFA, 72. *Work:* Nat Gallery Art, Washington; Milwaukee Art Mus; Wustum Mus, Racine, Wis; Univ Wis, Madison; Decorative Arts Mus, Little Rock, Ark; Topeka & Shawnee Co Pub Libr Collection. *Exhib:* Solo exhibs, Kresge Art Gallery, Univ Mich, E Lansing, 79, Rochester Art Ctr, Minn, 80, Winfield Gallery, Carmel, Calif, 92, Porter Col, Univ Calif Santa Cruz, 95, Perimeter Gallery, Chicago, 2001, Pence Gallery, Davis, Calif, 2001, Artist of Yr Exhib, Co Gov Center, Santa Cruz, Calif, 2003; A Discerning Passion, Forum for the Visual Arts, Tex Tech Univ, Lubbock, 94; Ten Outstanding Women Ceramists, Univ Wis, Eau Claire, 96; Nat Coun Educ Ceramic Arts Ceramic Nat, Las Vegas, Nev, 97; The Common Object, Calif Coll Arts & Crafts, Oakland, Calif, 97; Tea Bowl Invitational, San Francisco Craft & Folk Art Mus, San Francisco, Calif, 98; A Survey: Two Artists in Mid Career, Karen Thuesen Massaro & Joel Leivick, Mus Art Hist, Santa Cruz, 2000; Gallery Eight, LaJolla, Calif, 2003; Taking Measure: Am Ceramic Art in New Millennium, World Ceramic Exposition, Yeoju, Republic of Korea, 2001; Sidney Myer Fund Int Ceramics Exhib & Competition, Shepparton Art Gallery, Australia, 2002. *Collection Arranged:* Guest Cur, Time & Place: Fifty Years of Santa Cruz Studio Ceramics, Mus of Art Hist, Santa Cruz, CA, Exhib 97, catalog pub 96 with same title; Revealing Influences: Conversations with Bay Area Artists, Mus of Craft & folk Art, San Francisco, CA, 2003; 21st Century Ceramics in the US & Can cur by Bill Hunt, Columbus Coll of Art & Design, OH, 2003; Fabrication, Bruce Gallery of Art, Edin Boro Univ of PA, 2004. *Pos:* Vis artist, Kohler Artist Ed, Kohler Co, Wis, 84-; guest cur, Mus Art Hist, Santa Cruz Co, Calif, 96-97. *Teaching:* Vis fac mem fine art & art hist, Beloit Col, Wis, 72-77; vis artist ceramic arts, Ohio State Univ, 77; vis fac mem, Scripps Col, Claremont, Calif, 80; lectr, Univ Calif, Santa Cruz Exten, 95. *Awards:* Purchase Prize, 51st Exhib Wis Crafts, Milwaukee Art Ctr, 72; Best in Ceramics & Outstanding Wis Craftsman, Beaux-Arts Designer-Craftsman 72 & Columbus Mus Fine Arts, 72; Honorable Mention & Patron Purchase, Wichita Nat All Media Crafts Exhib, 88; Santa Cruz Co Art of Yr, 2003; Viewpoint: Ceramics 2001, Grossmont Col, El Caton, CA, First Prize; Form Follows Function, Lill St Gallery, Chicago, Third Prize, 2004. *Bibliog:* Ceramic Art Taipei, Taiwan, profile by Lin Chen-Long, 70, 71, Spring 2003; The Craft Art of Clay by Susan Peterson, 2003; Making Marks, Robin Hopper. *Mem:* Nat Coun Educ Ceramic Arts (exhib chmn, 78-80). *Media:* Porcelain, Other Clay. *Res:* History of ceramic arts, studio ceramics by American women 1875-present. *Specialty:* Ceramics, painting, sculpture. *Interests:* Painting on abstract assemblage of 3-D ceramic forms. *Dealer:* Perimeter Gallery Chicago IL. *Mailing Add:* 617 Arroyo Seco Santa Cruz CA 95060

MASSEY, ANN JAMES
PAINTER, GRAPHIC ARTIST
b Evanston, Ill, Nov 9, 1951. *Study:* Art Acad El Paso, 1970; Ramon Froman Sch Art, 1974; Univ Texas, El Paso, 70-71; Paris Am Acad, 78; Schuler Sch Fine Art, 90. *Work:* El Paso Mus Art, Huthsteiner Fine Arts Trust & Providence Mem Hosp, El Paso, Tex; Helen of Troy, LTD, El Paso. *Comn:* Portraits of Student of the Week, El Paso Electric Co, 82; Two Portraits, comn by Peter DeWetter (former Mayor), El Paso, 90; Portrait, Dr Reuben McDaniel, Austin, Tex, 1990; Tribute to Rob, comn by Robert Hoy, Jr, El Paso, Tex, 2005. *Exhib:* Carlsbad Mus & Art Ctr, NMex, 92; Am Drawing Biennial III, Muscarelle Mus Art, Williamsburg, Va, 92; retrospective, Chamizal Nat Mem, El Paso, Tex, 96; Expoarte 96, Fine Arts Mus Pronaf, Cuidad Juarez, Chihuahua, Mex, 96; The Miniature Art Soc, Fla Silver Anniversary Int Miniature Art Show, St Petersburg Mus Art, 2000; Royal Scottish Acad 176th Ann Exhib, McLellan Galleries, Glasgow, Scotland, 2002; Catharine Lorillard Wolfe Art Club 107th Ann Open Juried Exhib, Nat Arts Club, NY, 2003; 3rd Worldwide Exhib Fine Arts in Miniature, Smithsonian Inst, Arts & Indust Bldg, Wash, DC, 2004; The Am Artist's Prof League 78th Grand Nat Exhib, Salmagundi Club, NY, 2006; Soc Women Artists Ann Exhib, Mall Galleries, The Mall, London, 2007. *Pos:* Owner, The Montwood Gallery, El Paso, Tex, 74-78 & Massey Fine Arts, Santa Teresa, NMex, 92-94; pres, United Kingdon Coloured Pencil Soc, UK, 2004-2006, hon pres, 2007-. *Teaching:* Pvt drawing, instr, El Paso, 75-1994; Pvt consult & workshop instr, 1992-. *Awards:* Best Show, $6500 Purchase Prize, Ann EPAA Exhib, Sierra Med Ctr & El Paso Mus Art Asn, 91; First Place Drawing Pastel & Scrimshaw, Miniature Art Soc Fla 20th Int Miniature Art Show, Clearwater, Fla, 95; Barbara Tate Award, Soc of Women Artists 141st Ann Exhib, London, UK, 2002. *Bibliog:* Victor Martinez (auth), Pencil pusher opts for Paris, El Paso Times, 1/20/94; Sandra Angelo (auth), Colored pencil artists get it together, Am Artist Mag, 3/94; Deborah Martin (auth), Coming Home, El Paso Herald Post, 7/8/96. *Mem:* Signature mem Soc Women's Artists, Eng; Am Artists Prof League; signature mem Colored Pencil Soc Am & UK; Catharine Lorillard Wolfe Art Club. *Media:* Oil, Wax Pencil. *Publ:* Contribr, New things to expand your knowledge, Artists Mag, 9/93; Perfect Pencil Renderings, Artists Mag, 5/1993; The Best of Colored Pencil 1993-1995; David Hockney's Secret Knowledge (book review), Art Renewal Ctr, 2004. *Mailing Add:* 4 rue Auguste Chabrieres Paris 75015 France

MASSEY, CHARLES WESLEY, JR
PRINTMAKER, EDUCATOR
b Lebanon, Tenn, Aug 21, 1942. *Study:* Mid Tenn State Univ, BS, 64; Univ Ga, MFA (honors), 72. *Work:* Pushkin Mus, Moscow, USSR; Bradford City Art Gallery, Eng; Libr of Cong, Washington, DC; Whitney Mus Am Art, NY; Corcoran Mus Art, Wash; and 81 others. *Exhib:* Am Drawings III & IV, Smithsonian Traveling Exhib, 81-85; 1st & 2nd Int Print Exhibs, Seoul, Korea, 81-82; Boston Printmakers Nat Print Exhib, 81-84 & 86; Int Print Triennale, Cracow, Poland, 91, 94, 97 & 2000; curated exhib, Colorprint USA, 88, 91, 94, 98 & 2002; Nat Acad Design 177th Ann Exhib, NY, 2002; and approx 500 other int and nat exhibs since 1971. *Pos:* Univ prof art, Ohio State Univ, 74- & chairperson dept art, 82-88. *Teaching:* Instr art printmaking, Univ Ga, Athens, 72-74; prof printmaking, Ohio State Univ, 74-. *Awards:* Ohio Arts Coun Fel Grant, 81 & 86-94; Purchase Awards, Philadelphia Print Club, 81 & 19th Oulin Nat, Knoxville, 87; Nat Endowment Arts Grant, 82; Nat Exhib Trenton, NJ, 88. *Bibliog:* Albert Christ-Janer (dir), Artist--Charles Massey, Jr, Printer (film), Univ Ga, 71. *Mem:* The Print Center, Philadelphia; Boston Printmakers; Coll Art Asn; Columbus Art League (pres, 82-92); Southern Graphics Coun; Mid-Am Print Coun; Am Print Alliance. *Media:* Lithography, Drawing. *Publ:* Illusr, The Complete Screenprint & Lithography, Macmillan & Free Press, 74; Sing with Understanding, Broadman Press, 80; J Higher Educ, OSU Press, 83; Realizing the obvious: everything counts, Taipei Fine Art Mus, 12/2001; Prints and politics: everything counts, J of Am Print Alliance, Vol 10, Spring/2002. *Mailing Add:* 93 E Lincoln St Columbus OH 43215-1563

MASSEY, JOHN
COLLAGE ARTIST, CONCEPTUAL ARTIST
b Toronto, Can, July 6, 1950. *Study:* Ont Coll Art, AOCA, 74. *Work:* Ydessa Hendeles Art Found, Toronto; Stedelijk Mus, Amsterdam, Holland; Fonds Nat D'Art Contemporain, Paris; Nat Gallery Can, Ottawa; Albright-Knox Art Gallery, Buffalo. *Comn:* Because its Twue, video comn, Dundas Square, 2007. *Exhib:* Das Goldene

Zeitalter, Wurttembergischer Kymstverein, Stuttgart, 91; Canada: Une Nouvelle Generation, Musee de L'Abbaye, St Croix, France, 93; The Body/Le Corps, Kunsthalle Bielefeld, Ger, 94; Press Enter, Power Plant, Toronto, 95; La Luxure, Centre Georges Pompidou, Paris, 97; Biennale of Sydney, Artspace, Art Gallery NSW, Australia, 96; Ydessa Hendeles Art Found, 2000; New Photog, Olga Korper Gallery, Toronto, 2002; Canadian Mus Contemp Photog, 2004; Canadian Cultural Center, Paris, 2005; Beyond Cinema: The Art of Projection, Hamburger Bahnhof, Berlin, 2006; Univ Toronto Art Centre, 2006; Projections, Univ Toronto Galleries, 2007; Cinema Paradiso, Australian Center for Contemp Art, Melbourne, 2007; Morris and Helen Belkin Art Gallery, Vancouver, 2007; Yesterdays Tomorrows, Musee d'art Contemporain de Montreal, 2010; Marburg! The Early Bird! Marburger Kunstrerein, Germany, 2010; Elastic Frames, Transmission Gallery, Glasgow, 2011; La Biennale de Montreal, Montreal, 2014. *Teaching:* asst prof John H Daniels Faculty Architecture, Landscape, and Design, Univ Toronto. *Awards:* Gershon Iskowitz award, 2001. *Bibliog:* Didier Ottinger (auth), The Jack Photographs, ou L'Ubiquite du Parachute Regard, 94; David Rimanelli (auth), Naked House, Bailey Fine Arts, 2004; Daniele Cohn (auth), Nons n'irons plus au bois, Centre Culturel Canadien, 2006. *Media:* Digital Photography. *Dealer:* Georgia Scherman Projects 133 Tecumseth St Toronto Ontario M6J 2H2. *Mailing Add:* 201/R Christie St Toronto ON M6G 3B5 Canada

MASSEY, TIM
EDUCATOR, ADMINISTRATOR
Exhib: For The Love of Dogs, Savannah Col of Art and Design, Savannah Gallery, Atlanta, 18th Annual Art Show At the Dog Show, Kistler Mus Art, Kansas State Univ, Foyer Gallery, Border Crossings: International Juried Exhibition, Hartwick Col, The Ink Stop, Ithaca, NY, 40th Annual National Works On Paper and Small Sculpture Show, Del Mar Col, Corpus Christi, Texas, National Printmaking Show, curated by David Jones, founder of Anchor Graphics, Beverly Arts, Chgo, Shrine, TVUUC Gallery, Knoxville, Footlong, Runnels Gallery, Eastern New Mexico Univ, Portales and others. *Teaching:* Chair, Assoc prof art, gallery dir, Col of Brockport, State Univ NY (SUNY), currently. *Mailing Add:* The College of Brockport 122 Tower Fine Arts 350 New Campus Drive Brockport NY 14420

MASSEY, WALTER E
ADMINISTRATOR, EDUCATOR
Study: Morehouse Col, BS (math & physics), 1958; Washington Univ, MA, 1966, PhD, 1966. *Pos:* Physicist, Argonne Nat Lab, 1966-68, dir, 1979-84; dean, Brown Univ, 1975-79; dir, Nat Sci Found, Washington, DC, 1991-93; sr vpres acad affairs, Univ Calif System, 1993-95; pres, Morehouse Col, Atlanta, 1995-2007, pres emeritus, 2007-; pres, Sch of the Art Inst of Chicago, 2008-; chmn, Bank of America Corp, 2009-10. *Teaching:* Asst prof physics, Univ Ill, Urbana, 1968-70; assoc prof, Brown Univ, 1970-75, prof, 1975-79; prof, Univ Chicago, 1979-93. *Mailing Add:* School of the Art Institute of Chicago Office of President 37 S Wabash Ave Chicago IL 60603

MASSIE, ANNE ADAMS ROBERTSON
PAINTER
b Lynchburg, Va, 1931. *Study:* St Mary's Coll, Raleigh, NC, 50; Randolph Macon Woman's Coll, Lynchburg, Va, BA, 52, studied with Everett Raymond Kinstler, John Pike, Charles Reid, Rex Brandt, Alex Powers, Glenn Bradshaw, & Pierre Daura. *Work:* Randolph Coll; St John's Episcopal Church; Hotel de Ville, Rueil-Malmaison, France; Lynchburg Coll; Va Episcopal Sch; Va Ctr for the Creative Arts; Jones Memorial Libr; EC Glass High Sch; Old City Cemetary, Lynchburg, Va; James River Day Sch; Va State Bar Assn; CentraHealth Hosp. *Exhib:* Parkland Coll Art Gallery; Nat Acad Design; Nat Arts Club; solo exhibs, Lynchburg Art Club, Joyce Petter Gallery, Saugatuck, Mich, Twentieth Century Gallery, Williamsburg, Va & Lynchburg Fine Arts Ctr, 2000, Butler Inst Am Art, 2001 & 2007; Acad Fine Arts, Lynchburg, Va, 2008, 2011; Les Yeux du Monde, Charlottesville, 2012. *Teaching:* EC Glass High Sch, Lynchburg, 55-59. *Awards:* Gold Medal Hon, Am Watercolor Soc, 93; Best in Show, Nat League Am Pen Women, 94; Best in Show, Va Watercolor Soc, 92, 97, Founders award, 2nd place, 2014; Water Media Medal Hon, Catharine Lorillard Wolfe Club,; Gold Medal of Honor, Audubon Artists, 2006; Geneviere Cain Award for Watercolor, Nat Arts Club, 2011. *Bibliog:* Rachel Wolfe (ed), Splash 4 & Splash 5; Chris Unwin (auth), The Artistic Touch; Christopher Schink (auth), Colorlight; The Best of Watercolor, Rockport Publ. *Mem:* Nat Arts Club; Allied Artists Am; Catharine Lorillard Wolfe Art Club; Fel, Va Ctr Creative Arts; Nat Watercolor Soc; Audubon Artists; Am Watercolor Soc; Watercolor USA Hon Soc; Watercolor W; Dolphin fel, Am Watercolor Soc; Va Watercolor Society; Southern Watercolor Soc; Foothills Art Ctr; Nat League Am Pen Women; Rocky Mountain Nat Watercolor Soc. *Media:* Watercolor, Oil. *Interests:* Book club, tennis, historic preservation, gardening. *Publ:* numerous publications including Splash 4, Artistic Touch, Color & Light, The Best of Watercolor, The Artist's Mag, Palette Mag. *Mailing Add:* 3204 Rivermont Ave Lynchburg VA 24504

MASSIE, LORNA
PRINTMAKER
b Milwaukee, Wis, Dec 27, 1938. *Study:* Layton Sch Art, Milwaukee; Smith Col; Univ Calif, Berkeley, BA, 61; Marshall Glazier, New York, 67; Woodstock Sch Art, 74-76; Albert Handell Sch, 77; Art Students League, 78. *Work:* Woodstock Hist Soc. *Exhib:* Print Club Albany, 95; Allied Artists Am, 96; Audubon Artists, 96; Acad Artists, 96; Northeast Regional Exhib, 96; and others. *Awards:* Philip Isenberg Award for Graphics & Drawing, Knickerbocker Artists, 91; Nicholas Reale Mem Award Graphics, Allied Artists Am, New York, 93; Atlantic Papers Award, Audubon Artists, 96. *Bibliog:* Who's Who Am Women; Art Print Index; Art Network Encyl Living Artists. *Mem:* Woodstock Artists Asn; Albany Print Club; Women's Studio Workshop. *Media:* Serigraphs. *Mailing Add:* 452 Whitfield Rd Accord NY 12404

MASTELLER, BARRY
PAINTER, CRAFTSMAN
b Los Angeles, Calif, Apr 21, 1945. *Study:* Studied painting & life drawing under Walter Craig Titus, 62-65. *Work:* Monterey Mus Art, Monterey Conf Ctr, Calif; San Jose Mus Art, Calif; Gonzaga Univ, Seattle, Wash; Syntex Corp, Palo Alto, Calif; Bank of America, San Francisco, Calif; Santa Cruz Mus Art & History; Palm Springs Mus; Crocker Mus. *Comn:* Paintings, Home Fed, Los Angeles, 85, Coldwell Banker, Philadelphia, 85, Pebble Beach Corp, Calif, Stouffer Corp, Los Angeles, 86 & Hyatt Regency, Chicago, 88. *Exhib:* Solo exhib, Monterey Conf Ctr Art Comn, 79 & 94, San Jose Mus Art, 82, Monterey Mus Art, 75, 83 & 94 & Shaklee Corp, San Francisco, 89 & 94, Patricia Rovzar Gallery, 2006, Trajan Gallery, Calif, 2006, Campton Gallery, NY, 2006, Dubuque Mus Art, 2007, WireGrass Mus Art, 2007; Group exhibs: Newport Harbor Art Mus Invitational, 88 & 94; Bank of Am World Hq, San Francisco, 94; Lisa Parker Fine Art, NY, 96-97; Emmie Smock Gallery, San Francisco, 97; Tamara Bane Gallery, Beverly Hills, 97; Nelson-Rovzar Gallery, Kirkland, Wash, 99; Patricia Rovzar Gallery, 2001-2003; Caldwell/Snyder Gallery, New York, NY, 2000-2001, 2003-2005; Trajan Gallery, Carmel, Calif, 2003 & 2006; Mus of Southwest, Midland, Tex, 2005; Anderson Fine Art Ctr, Ind, 2005; Campton Gallery, NY, 2005-2006; Monterey Mus Art, Calif, 2006; Patricia Rovzar Gallery, Seattle, Wash, 2006; Grace Mus, Abilene, Tex, 2007; Elenor D Wilson Mus, Hollins Univ, Roanoak, Va, 2009; US Embassy, Kathmandu, Napal, 2010-2013. *Pos:* dir/cur, Pacific Grove Art Ctr, Calif, 81-83; owner, Masteller/Shadow Graphics, 80-89; owner/dir, Claypoole-Freese Gallery, 89-2003. *Awards:* Best of Show, Ann Monterey Mus Art; Best of Show, Members Exhibit Pacific Grove Art Ctr; First Place Award, Monterey Co Competitive; Best of Show, Beacon House Competitive. *Bibliog:* Michael Gardner (auth), Artists taps subconscious, San Jose Mercury, 81; Richard Reilly (auth), Mastellers dreamy strokes, San Diego Union, 81; Irene Lagorio (auth), Mastellers seriocomic paintings, Monterey Herald, 83; Rick Deragon (auth), Let There Be Light, 90; Dominique Nahas (auth), Ecstatic Reserve in the work of Barry Masteller; Kathleen Moody (auth), 2002 Catalog Essay. *Mem:* Artists Equity; Int Inst Conservation Hist Artistic Works; Santa Cruz Art League. *Media:* Watercolor, Oil; Drawing; Monotype. *Publ:* Exhibition Catalogs, Caldwell/Snyder, 2000-2002; Exhibition Catalogs, Campton Gallery, NY, Trajan Gallery, Carmel, Calif & Patricia Rovzar Gallery, Seattle, Wash, 2006; Boulevards (catalog, essay) by Donald Kuspit, 2007. *Dealer:* Patricia Rovzar Gallery Seattle WA; Trajan Gallery Carmel CA. *Mailing Add:* PO Box 397 San Juan Bautista CA 95045

MASTER-KARNIK, PAUL
MUSEUM DIRECTOR, CRITIC
b New York, NY, Nov 20, 1948. *Study:* Rutgers Univ, BA, 70, MA, 71, PhD, 78; NY Univ, cert (mus studies), 79. *Collection Arranged:* Expressionism in Boston, 1945-85, DeCordova Mus, 85. *Pos:* Art critic, Staten Island Advan, Newhouse Publ, 76-81; dir, New Jersey Ctr for Visual Arts, 81-84; De Cordova Mus, 1984-2007. *Teaching:* Adj prof cult & art hist, Rutgers Univ, New Brunswick, NJ, 71-78; adj prof mus studies, New York Univ, 80-84. *Awards:* Nat Endowment Arts Critics Fel, 80-81. *Mem:* Am Asn Mus; Asn Art Mus Dirs. *Res:* Methods and styles of contemporary art criticism; social history of the art museum; contemporary American art. *Publ:* Auth, Art criticism in the suburban context, Artview, Vol 3, No 1, 79; Philip Pearlstein: Progress of a Painter (exhib catalog), 82, American Realism 1930's/1980's: A Comparative Perspective (exhib catalog), 83 & William Zorach: Sculpture and Drawings (exhib catalog), 83, NJ Ctr Visual Arts. *Mailing Add:* DeCordova Museum and Sculpture Park 51 Sandy Pond Rd Lincoln MA 01773

MASTERFIELD, MAXINE
PAINTER
b Los Angeles, Calif, July 21, 1933. *Study:* Cleveland Inst Art, grad 55. *Work:* First Chicago Trust of Ariz & St Joseph Children's Ctr, Phoenix; Nat Watercolor Soc; Bancohio Nat; Ohio Savings & Loan; Laguna Beach Mus Art; Chicago Bank of Ill; 3M Corp, Minneapolis; Cleveland Clinic. *Exhib:* Watercolor USA, Springfield Art Mus, Mo, 68 & 77; Nat Acad Design, 76; Aqueous Open, Arts & Crafts Ctr, Pittsburgh, Pa, 76-79; Butler Midyear Exhib, Butler Inst Am Art, Youngstown, Ohio, 77; Rocky Mountain Nat Watermedia, Foothills Art Ctr, Golden, Colo, 77-79; Nat Watercolor Soc, Los Angeles, 77-79; Ky Watercolor, Owensboro Mus Fine Arts, Ky, 78 & Mid-Am Art Exhib, 79; C G Rein Galleries, 87-2009; Sexton Gallery, Ft Lauderdale, 97-98; Wells Fargo Sarasota, Fl, 2014; Golden Image, Sarasota, Fl, 2014. *Teaching:* Watercolor workshops, worldwide, 80-; pvt instr, Masterfield Studio, Sarasota, Fla. *Awards:* Purchase Award, Nat Watercolor Soc, 78; High Winds Medal, Am Watercolor Soc, 81; Grand Buckeye Leaf Award, 82, Silver Buckeye Leaf Award, 83 & Award of Excellence, 86, Ohio Watercolor Soc. *Mem:* life mem Am Watercolor Soc, 76; Fla Watercolor Soc, 87; Ky Watercolor Soc, 76; Soc Experimental Artist; Int Soc Experimental Artist (found & lifetime mem, 92-2000 & 2006-). *Media:* Watercolor, Enamel, Acrylic. *Publ:* Illusr, Watercolor Bold and Free, 80, Creative Seascape Painting, 81, auth, Painting the Spirit of Nature, Watson-Guptill; Exploring Color, North Light Bks; auth, painting in the Spirit of Nature, 83; Painting In Harmony with Nature, 90. *Dealer:* The Look Gallery Minneapolis MN; Golden Image Sarasota FL Wells Fargo. *Mailing Add:* 5075 Robinsong Rd Sarasota FL 34233-2249

MASTERS, DEBORAH
SCULPTOR
Study: Bryn Mawr Coll, BFA, 1974; NY Studio Sch, MFA, 1979. *Work:* Long Island Univ; Port Authority; Brooklyn Mus. *Exhib:* Solo exhibs include Gallerie Hirondelle, New York, 1987, Gracie Mansion Gallery, New York, 1990, LedisFlam Gallery, New York, 1990, 1993, Cantor Fitzgerald Gallery, Haverford Coll, Haverford, Pa, 1994, Queens Mus, Bulova Space, Queens, 1996, Maurice Arlos Gallery, New York, 2002, Smack Mellon Gallery, Brooklyn, 2002, Storm King Art Ctr, Mountainville, NY, 2007 ; Group exhibs include In a Dark Vein, Sculpture Ctr, New York, 1989; In Honor of Mary, Bill Bace Gallery, New York, 1990; Drawing in NY, LedisFlam Gallery, New York, 1992; 2nd Dimension: Sculptors' Drawings, Brooklyn Mus, 1993, New

Acquisitions, 1997; Socrates Sculpture Park, 1997; Drawings & Paintings, Bond Market, New York, 1999; Art for Animals, Pierogi 2000, Brooklyn, 2002; Merry, Sideshow Gallery, Brooklyn, 2004; NYSS Drawings by Sculptors, Sculptors' Studio, Brooklyn, 2006; Big Jeff, Piero's Jesus, & Aaron, Sculpture Invitational, Columbus, Ind, 2007

MASTRANGELO, BOBBI
SCULPTOR, ENVIRONMENTAL ARTIST
b Youngstown, Ohio, May 16, 1937. *Study:* State Univ NY, Buffalo, BS cum laude, 59; State Univ NY, Stony Brook, 69-79; studied printmaking with Dan Welden, John Ross, Clare Romano, Tim Ross & Gail Cohen Edleman. *Work:* Islip Art Mus, East Islip, NY; Baltimore Md Pub Works Mus; Suffolk Co Water Authority, Oakdale, NY; Nat Asn Women Artists Permanent Collection, Zimmerli Art Mus, Rutgers Univ, New Brunswick, NJ; Heckscher Mus, Huntington, NY; The Moscow Collection of World Manhole Covers; Nassau Community Coll, Garden City, NY. *Exhib:* Solo exhibs, NY Hall Sci, Flushing, 94, Grateworks, Toast Gallery, Port Jefferson, NY, 2003, Underfoot: Manhole and other covers, Attleboro Industrial Mus, Mass, 2004, Baltimore Pub Works Mus, 96, Toho Water Authority, 2011, Manhole Messages, Islip Art Mus, MacArthur Airport, Ronkonkoma, NY, 2013; Group exhibs: Winners showcase Smithtown, NY Arts Council, 99; NY Collects Buffalo State, Burchfield Penney Art Center, 2004; Transformation of Matter into Art, NY, Acad Sci, 92; City Views, Staller Ctr Arts, State Univ NY, Stony Brook, 92; Listen to the Earth, Hamilton Col, Clinton, NY, 95; Gwinnett Environ Ctr, Buford, Ca, 2010; A Way With Words, Heckscher Mus, Huntington, NY, 2012; Sculpture the Ultimate Process, Orlando Mus Art, 2012; Best of the Best, Orlando Mus Art's First Thursdays: Fla June, 2014. *Pos:* Judge, 11th Ann Cong Art Competition, Riverhead, NY, 92. *Teaching:* Paper making, Bd Coop Servs, Suffolk Co, NY, 87-94; Title One Tutor, Smithtown, NY, 89-99; artist-in-residence, NY Middle Sch, Port Jefferson, 98; writing teacher, Smithtown, NY, 98 & 99. *Awards:* Spec Opportunity Stipend, NY Found Arts, 92 & 94; Eve Helman Award Work on Paper, 92 and Aida Whedon Mem Award, 97, Nat Asn Women Artists, NY; Maryvale High Sch Hall of Fame for Achievement in the Arts and Environment, 94; Paul Harris Fel, Rotary Int, 96; First Prize for sculpture, Osceola Ctr for the Arts, Kissimmee, Fla, 2005 & 09; Best of Show: Inside/Out, Orlando, Museum of Art's 1st Thursday, May, 2014. *Bibliog:* Phil Mintz (auth), Going in circles, Newsday, 9/98; Sara Muller (TV reporter), Grate Works, News 12, 10/98; Michael Ollove (auth), Finding beauty in the grate beyond, Balt Sun, 9/2001; Caryn Eve Murray (auth), Cover Girl, Newsday, 12/2002; Beauty under Foot, TV Park, Moscow, (auth), 2003; Stephen Koenig (auth), Maryvale Alumma Featured in Art Display, Buffalo, NY, Cheektowaga Times, 2004; Sam Edsell, (Interview, http://mentalcontagion.com/issue0709/causeandeffect.html); Artsyshark.com, 2010; Sally Hansell (auth), Passion for Paper, Fiber Arts Mag, 2010. *Mem:* Art & Sci Collabrs Inc, Staten Island, NY; Nat Asn Women Artists; Nat Mus Women Arts; Friends of Dard Hunter; NAWA Fla Chap; Solivita Artisans Guild. *Media:* Sculpture relief, mixed media, fiber art. *Interests:* Creating Grate Works of Art, a Novel Group (book club), Poetry, creative writing, walking, singing, Zumba Gold Dancing, travel, foreign languages & culture. *Publ:* Auth, Grate works, Time Capsule, 11/1995; Manhole Covers, Oxymoron, The Fringe, Arts & Sci Ann, 98; WUCF-TV Artisode # 108 Grate Works of Art, 11/2013; Turning Manhole Covers into Art by Barbara Sieminski, The Municipal.com, 1/2015, Q and A with a Grate Artist by Mary Joye Today and Tongith Magazine, 5/2015. *Mailing Add:* 747 Coronado Dr Poiniana FL 34759

MASULLO, ANDREW
PAINTER
b Elizabeth, NJ, Sept 6, 1957. *Study:* Rutgers Univ, BA, 1979. *Work:* Capital Group, NY; Cartin Collection, Hartford, Conn; Montgomery Mus Fine Art, Ala; NY Pub Libr; Sackner Archive of Concrete & Visual Poetry, Miami Beach, Fla. *Exhib:* Word as Image: American Art 1960-1990, Milwaukee Art Mus, 1990; Solo shows, Thomas Ammann Fine Art, Zurich, 1999, Feature Inc, NY, 2010, Steven Zevitas Gallery, Boston, 2011, Daniel Weinberg Gallery, Los Angeles, 2011; Around About Abstraction, Weatherspoon Mus, Greensboro, NC ; Am Acad Arts & Letts Invitational, NY, 2010; Whitney Biennial, Whitney Mus Am Art, NY, 2012. *Awards:* Pollock-Krasner Found Grant, 1988; CAPS Grant, Ny State Coun on Arts, 1989; Art Award, Am Acad Arts and Letts, 2010. *Bibliog:* Carol Kino (auth), Painting by Numbers, to Whitney Biennial, NY Times (reproductions, Mar 25 page AR21); Nuit Banai (auth) Review, Artforum (reproduction, Feb page 232); Roberta Smith (auth), Andrew Masullo: Recent Paintings, NY Times, Art in Review (Nov 25, page C36). *Dealer:* Gallery Paule Anglim 14 Geary St San Francisco CA 94108; Daniel Weinberg Gallery 6363 Wilshire Blvd Suite 104 Los Angeles CA 90048; Steven Zevitas Gallery 450 Harrison St Suite 47 Boston MA 02118. *Mailing Add:* Feature Inc 131 Allen St New York NY 10002

MATARANGLO, ROBERT PATRICK
VIDEO ARTIST, MURALIST
b South Amboy, NJ, Mar 17, 1947. *Study:* Montclair State Univ, MA, 99; Vt Coll, MFA, 2002. *Comn:* Exterior, Long Branch Chamber, West End LB, NJ, 2000; Interior, Siperstein's, Middletown, NJ, 2002; Exterior, Long Branch, NJ, 2006; Exterior, Health Farm, Middletown, NJ, 2003; Exterior, Herr Family Days Restaurant, Ocean Grove, NJ, 2004. *Exhib:* Solo exhib, Monmouth Univ Gallery, Long Branch, NJ, 2003; Ion animation Festival, Culver City, Los Angeles, 2004; Mardi Gras Film Festival, Sidney, Australia, 2006; Monmouth Co Arts Coun, Monmouth Mus, Lincroft, NJ, 2006. *Pos:* Bd dirs, Art Alliance, Red Bank, NJ, 2000-2004; Animation Club Adv, Monmouth Univ, Long Branch, NJ, 2002-2004; vpres, Shore Inst Contemp Art, Long Branch, NJ, 2003-2004. *Teaching:* Adj prof, art hist, Ocean Co Coll, Toms River, NJ, 99-2002; adj prof, art, Brookdale Community Col, Lincroft, NJ, 99-; adj prof, Monmouth Univ, Long Branch, NJ, 2002 & 2004. *Awards:* Best Local Animation Award, Garden State Film Festival, 2003, 04, 05; Champion of the Arts, Monmouth Co Arts Coun, 2004; Best Animation, Coney Island Film Festival, 2005. *Bibliog:* Steven Bove (auth), His Path to Joy, Asbury Park, Press, 2005; Linda DeNicola (auth), Video Mountain Arts Festival, The Hub, 2005; Robert Scott (auth), Tiny Tents, Cottage Style (mag), Harris Publs, 2005. *Mem:* Black Box, Asbury Park, NJ; Freedom Film Soc, Red Bank, NJ; Monmouth Co Arts Coun, Red Bank, NJ (bd dirs 2002-2004); Shore Inst Comtemp Arts, Red Bank, NJ (vpres 2003-2004). *Media:* Video Animation

MATELLI, TONY
INSTALLATION SCULPTOR
b Chicago, 1971. *Study:* Alliance Independent Colls Art, New York, independent study, 1991; Milwaukee Inst Art & Design, BFA, 1993; Cranbrook Acad Art, Mich, MFA, 1995. *Exhib:* Solo exhibs include Ten in One Gallery, Chicago, 1997, 2000, Basilico Fine Arts, New York, 1997, 1999, Univ Buffalo Art Gallery, 1999, Sies & Hoeke Gallery, Dusseldorf, Germany, 2000, 2003, Leo Koenig Inc, New York, 2001, 2007, 2008, Gian Enzo Sperone, Rome, 2002, Emmanuel Perrotin Gallery, Paris, 2002, 2005, Kunsthalle Wien, Vienna, 2004, Andrehn Schiptjenko, Stockholm, Sweden, 2006, Gary Tatinsian Gallery, Moscow, 2008, Green Gallery East, Milwaukee, 2009, Stephane Simoens Contemp Fine Art, Belgiu, 2010; group exhibs include Pop Surrealism, Aldrich Mus Contemp Art, Conn, 1998; Yesterday Begins Tomorrow, Bard Coll Curatorial Studies, NY, 1998; Small World, Mus Contemp Art, San Diego, 2000; Greater NY, PS1 Contemp Art Ctr, Long Island City, NY, 2000, Into Me, Out of Me, 2006; The Americans, Barbican Ctr, London, 2001; PLOP: Recent Projects of the Pub Art Fund, New York, 2003; The Fourth Sex, Mus Contemp Art Chicago, 2003; Metamorphosis, John Michael Koehler Arts Ctr, Wis, 2004; Five Billion Years, Swiss Inst, New York, 2004; I Am As You Will Be: Skeletons in Art, Cheim & Read, New York, 2007; Undone, Whitney Mus Am Art at Altria, New York, 2008; Infinitesimal Eternity, Images Madein the Face of Spectacle, yale Sch Art, Conn, 2009; The Effect of Mod Art on Green Circles, Vanmoerkerke Collection, Belgium, 2009; Realismus: Das Abenteurer der Wirklichdeit, Germany, 2010; Buy-Self, CAPC, Bordezux, France, 2010; Both Sides of the Pulaski, Fine Art in Space, Long Island City, NY, 2010. *Awards:* NY Found Arts Grant, 1998. *Bibliog:* Frederic Montornes (auth), Una Lucha por la supervivencia, Exit Express, 2008; Katie Sokoler (auth), The Armory Show, Gothamist, 2009; David Ebony (auth), Art in America, 2009; Jacquelyn Davis (auth), Critics Picks, Stockholm, 2010; Ken Johnson (auth), Ahoy from Nudes, a Pirate & Scrooge McDuck, New York, Times, 2010. *Mailing Add:* 390 McGuiness Blvd Brooklyn NY 11222

MATHER, TIMOTHY WAYNE
EDUCATOR, SCULPTOR
Teaching: Assoc prof, dir, Henry Radford Hope Sch of Fine Arts, Ind Univ, currently. *Mailing Add:* Indiana University Henry Radford Hope School of Fine Arts 1201 E Seventh St, Room 123 Bloomington IN 47405-7509

MATHEWS, NANCY MOWLL
HISTORIAN, CURATOR
b Baltimore, Md, Feb 11, 1947. *Study:* Goucher Col, BA, 68; Cleveland Mus Art, fel, 70-71; Case-Western Reserve Univ, MA, 72; NY Univ Inst Fine Arts, Goldwater fel, 73-74, PhD, 80. *Collection Arranged:* Mary Cassatt: The Color Prints (auth, catalog), 89-90; Maurice Prendergast (auth, catalog), Prestel, 90; Charles Prendergast (auth, catalog), 93; Maurice Prendergast: The State of the Estate, 98-99. *Pos:* Randolph-Macon Womans Col, 77-; Eugenie Prendergast cur, Williams Col Mus Art, currently. *Teaching:* Assoc prof, Randolph-Macon Womans Col, 77-87; lectr, Williams COl, 88-. *Awards:* Katherine Graves Davidson Award, 80; Smithsonian Postdoctoral Fel, 82; and others. *Mem:* Coll Art Asn; IFA Alumni Asn; Am Asn Mus; Catalogue Raisonne Scholars Asn. *Res:* 19th & 20th century European and American painting; impressionism; Mary Cassatt; Maurice & Charles Prendergast; Gauguin; Women artists. *Publ:* Ed, Cassatt and Her Circle: Selected Letters, Abbeville Press, 84; Cassatt: A Retrospective, Levin, 96; auth, Mary Cassatt: A Life, Yale, 98; Maurice Prendergast: The Art of Leisure, 99. *Mailing Add:* Williams Col Mus Art Main St Williamstown MA 01267

MATHIAS, THELMA
CONCEPTUAL ARTIST, SCULPTOR
b New York, NY. *Study:* High Sch of Music & Art, NY; Univ Mich, BA; NY Univ, MSW. *Work:* Yeshiva Univ Mus, NY; Islip Art Mus, Long Island, NY; Stadtisches Mus, Kleve, Ger; Artists Mus, Lodz, Poland; Art/OMI, Ghent, NY; De Libris, Book Transformed, El Mus Cult, Santa Fe, 2005; Baroque & Neo-Baroque, Cont Art Center, Salanomica, Spain, 2005; Art from Detritus, Fairleigh Dickinson Univ, NJ, 2006; Ctr Contemp Art, Santa Fe, NMex, 2009; Mus Modern Art; FF Artists Books, NY; Galerie Analix Forever, Geneve; Hewlett Packard Corp, Palo Alto, Calif; Cabrini Hospice, NY; Oppenheimer Capital Corp, NY; Bank of America, San Fran, Calif; Stadtisches Mus, Kleve, Germany; McDonalds Corp, Oakbrook, Ill. *Comn:* Bulgaria, NY, Elizabeth Found. *Exhib:* cur, Stilte, Mus Silence, Amsterdam, 1999; Elements 2000, Here Art, New York City, 2000; Lugares Encantados, Islip Art Mus, Long Island, NY, 2000; Los Montanas, Ricardo Flores Ctr, Oaxaca, Mex, 1995; Under the Floorboards, BWA, Lublin, Poland, 1998; My Fathers List, Yeshiva Univ Mus, New York City, 1995; Pulling of the Threads, Newark Mus, NJ, 1999; Dumbo Double Deuce, New York City, 2001; The Puffin Room, New York City, 2001; Longview Mus Fine Arts, Texas, 2001; The London Biennale, Eng, 2000; Art Indust, Santa Fe, NMex, 2002; Words in the Dust, Phil Place, Santa Fe, NMex, 2004; Stories Retold, Box Gallery, Santa Fe, NMex, 2004; Gallerie Jurgen Richter, Frankfurt, Germany, 2007; Subversive Stiching, Belen, NMex; Axle Contemporary, Sante Fe, NMex, 2010-2011; Studio Two, Santa Fe, NMex, 2011; Exchange with Sol LeWitt, Mass MOCA, Mass, 2011; Odes & Offerings, Convention Ctr Gallery, Santa Fe, NMex, 2012; Solo exhib, Highland Univ, NMex, 2012; Artists Book Exhib, King St James Mus, Budapest, Hungary, 2013. *Collection Arranged:* cur, Sculpture Addressing Social Issues, Artist Talk Panel, NY, 93, Bearing Witness, 94; cur, Repair Work, Deutsche Bank, NY, 94; cur, After 50 Years, City Hall, NY, 95; cur, Performance Night, Gallery 128, NY, 98; Analix Forever Galerie, Geneva. *Pos:* Guest speaker, Barnard Col, NYC, 2000, Islip Art Mus, Long Island, 2000, Cont Art Mus, Mexico City, 98; cur, Curious Ephemera,

Oaxaca Mus, Oaxaca, Mex 2002. *Teaching:* Panelist, NMex Dept Cult Affairs, Arts grants org. *Awards:* Nat Endowment for the Arts, 80; Puffin Found Grant, 93; Ctr Book Arts, Residency Grant, 98. *Bibliog:* Robert C. Morgan (auth) 4:45 AM, Art in America, 2/96; Dan Bishoff (auth), Pulling of the Threads, Newark Star Ledger, 4/99; Joel Silverstein (auth) Elements 2000, Review, 3/2000; Jan Adlmann (auth), Stitching the Image, NYArts Mag, 11/2004; Zane Fisher (auth), Who Needs Louise, Santa Fe Reporter, 9/2004; Jane Collins (auth), The Hem, Sumpter, SC, 2003; THE Mag, Santa Fe, NMex, 2004; Kathryn M Davis (auth), Axle Revew, The Mag, Santa Fe, NMex, 2011. *Mem:* Asn Video & Filmmakers; Orange Peel Pubs (pres 93-96); Artists Equity; Santa Fe Coun Arts; Nat Womens Caucus Art. *Media:* Embroidery, Textual, Cultural Discards, Bronze, Cast Paper, Wax, Textiles,(embroidery), Mundane Objects. *Specialty:* Contemp Art. *Interests:* Buddism, travel, semiotics, writing, non fiction, dance, culture, international politics, history, yoga, ballet, and much more. *Publ:* Contrib, Feminist Performance Art, R Wyler & Co, 93; co-auth, Repair Workbook, Orange Peel Press, 94, Mail Performance, Watermark Press, 98; auth, An Earth Shattering Experience, 2001; auth, Poesa, Orange Peel Press, Santa Fe, NMex, 2009. *Dealer:* Jurgen Richter Frankfurt, Germany; Axle Contemporary, Sante Fe, NMex. *Mailing Add:* PO Box 32106 Santa Fe NM 87594

MATHIS, BILLIE FRITZ
PAINTER, CONCEPTUAL ARTIST
b Lindale, Ga, Apr 16, 1936. *Study:* Art Instruction Inc; studied with noted watercolorists, Paris for painting. *Work:* Promina; Cobb Bd of Educ Collection; Peachtree Ctr, Atlanta, Ga; Foster Higgons, Inc, Atlanta, Ga; also pvt collections. *Comn:* Plantation Resorts, Fla; Post Properties, Contel Corp, Pvt Collector, Germ; Reinhardt Col, Waleska, Ga. *Exhib:* Butler Inst Am Arts 53rd Nat, Youngstown, Ohio; Atlanta-Savannah Exhib, Visual Arts; Marietta Cobb Mus Art; Marietta/Cobb Collection Tours, Abstein Gallery; Gallery 300/SAGA; Celebrate the Arts, Marietta Cobb Mus Art; Marietta Cobb Mus Art; Across the Borders, Atlanta/Can, Md Fedn, New Orleans Int; solo exhib, St Augustine, Fla; solo exhib, Cherokee Arts, Ga; group exhib, Metro Montage, I, II, & III, Marietta, Ga. *Awards:* Featured Artist, Marietta-Cobb Mus Arts Masterpiece Ball, 96. *Mem:* Nat Women in Arts; Asn Allied Artists; Atlanta Artist Soc; Asn Am Watercolor Soc; signature mem Ga Watercolor Soc (area dir); Visual Arts Coun; Cherokee Arts, Arts Alliance of Ga. *Media:* Mixed Media, Watercolor. *Publ:* Contribr, Georgia Artists, Mountain Prod, 88; artist, Am References; illustr, cover, AirBorne Mag; Break of Day, Lufrnint Publ, 11/97; Through My Window, Children's Poems, Lufraint Publs; Watercolor Video & DVD, Painting Loose, A Lesson in Watercolor. *Dealer:* Frame Works Gallery 1205 Johnson Ferry Rd, Marietta GA 30068; Artistic Frames, Jasper, Ga; Creations Gallery, Canton, GA. *Mailing Add:* 110 Cedar Ct No 3090 Waleska GA 30813-4604

MATHIS, EMILE HENRY, II
DEALER, COLLECTOR
b Superior, Wis, Feb 25, 1946. *Study:* Dominican Col, Univ Wis, Superior, BFA, MFA. *Collection Arranged:* J A McN Whistler, (etchings & lithographs), 81; Rubber stamps by contemp Am artists, 81; 19th Century French Etching, 82; British printmakers of late 19th & early 20th century; Western Africa (sculpture), 91; Fibre & Utilitarian Objects, 92; Sir Francis Seymour Haden (etchings), 93; Whistler & Haden (etchings), 93; 5 Centuries of Printmaking; 19th & 20th century Am and European paintings, 99; Objects of ritual and reverence from various W African cultures, 2000; African objects of utility, 2002. *Pos:* Asst dir, La Porte Gallery, Racine, 70-71; dir, New Gallery One, Racine, 71-72; gallery owner, Mathis Gallery, Racine, 72-; mem bd dir, Wustum Mus Fine Art. *Teaching:* Instr art, Sheboygan Sch Syst, Wis, 68-69. *Mem:* Racine Urban Aesthetics; Am Asn Mus. *Specialty:* Old and modern masters, contemporary graphics, paintings, fine prints and African sculpture. *Interests:* 18th century American furniture, Spanish colonial religious art, commemorative medals & medallions. *Collection:* American nineteenth and twentieth century contemporary drawings and paintings. *Mailing Add:* 328 S Main St Racine WI 53403

MATISSE, JACKIE (JACQUELINE) MATISSE MONNIER
PAINTER, SCULPTOR
b Neuilly-sur-Seine, France, July 12, 1931; US citizen. *Exhib:* Drachen, Rhein Landesmuseum, Bonn, Ger, 81; Traveling exhib, Philadelphia Mus Art, 81; one-person exhibs, Fundacion Miro, Barcelona, Spain, 85, Magic Hair & Bottled Dream, Galerie Satellite, Paris, France, 93, Jacqueline Matisse Monnier, Kiallitasa, Bartok 32 Galeria, Budapest, Hungary, 98; Art that Flies, Dayton Art Inst, 90; Zero Gravity, 91; Les Artists Decident De Jouer, 91; Magic Hair & Bottled Dreams, Galerie Satellite, Paris, 93; Rolywholyover A Circus for Mus, Los Angeles, 94, Houston 94, NY, 94, Japan, 94-95, Philadelphia, 95; Happy End, Galerie Satellite, Paris, France, 96; 10 Jours d'Art Contemporain, Chateau de Nemours, Nemours, France, 97; From One Point to Another, L'Atelier Soardi, Nice, France, 97; Odeurs Une Odyssee, Passage de Retz, Paris, France, 97; Kitetail Cocktail, Goldie Paley Gallery, Philadelphia, PA, 99; Art that Soars, Mengei Int Mus, San Diego, Calif, 2000; Echigo Triennale, Art Front Gallery, Tokyo, Japan, 2001; Art Flying in and out of Spae, Va Tech, 2002; Art Volant dan l'Escape et Ailleurs, Virtual Reality Project, Chalon Sur Saone, France, 2003. *Bibliog:* Newman (auth), Kite Craft, Crown Publ Inc, 74; Jean-Michel Folon, Aquiloni, Alice Editions, Switz, 76; Suzi Gablik (auth), Cosmic kites, Art in Am, 11/80; Jackie Matisse (auth), The Blue Book, Ed de l'Onde, 97. *Media:* Miscellaneous Media. *Publ:* Art That Flies, 91; Eric et Marc Dumage (auth), Certs-Volants L'art en Ciel, Ed Alternatives, 96. *Dealer:* Jack Tilton Gallery 24 W 57th St New York NY 10019. *Mailing Add:* 23 Rue du Buisson Villiers-sous-Grez 77760 France

MATSUBARA, NAOKO
PRINTMAKER, PAINTER
b Kyoto, Japan, 1937. *Study:* Kyoto Acad Fine Arts, BFA, 60; Carnegie-Mellon Univ, MFA, 62; Royal Coll Art, London, 63. *Hon Degrees:* Chatham Univ, Pittsburgh, Pa, Dr Fine Art, 2009. *Work:* Brit Mus, London; Mus Fine Arts, Boston; Tokyo Nat Mus Mod Art; Cincinnati Mus Art; Libr Cong; Royal Ont Mus, Toronto, Can; Carnegie Mus Art, Pittsburgh; White House, DC; Smithsonian Inst, DC; Yale Univ Art Gallery, Conn; and many more. *Comn:* Mural, Kyoto Univ Hosp, 59; mural, Carnegie-Mellon Univ, Pittsburgh, 62; woodcut print, Smithsonian Inst, Washington, 67; woodcut print, Boston Winter Festival, 69; Solitude (portfolio), Aquarius Press, NY, 71; mural for new YMCA lobby, Oakville, Ont, 2002; three large works for the window, Royal Ont Mus, Toronto, 2007; A Giant Tree (large woodcut collage),Chatham Univ, 2009; mural, Aquatic Movement, Jeux d'eau, City of St. Catharines, Ontario, 2012; mural, Fragrance, SPIC Internat, Kamakura, Japan, 2014. *Exhib:* Takashimaya Art Gallery, Tokyo, Japan, 87; Vancouver Art Gallery, BC, 90; Hart House Gallery, Univ Toronto, 90; Oriental Mus, Durham, Eng, traveled to Ireland & Wales, 91-92; Japan Festival Prints Show, Spirit Sq, Charlotte, NC, 94; Davidson Galleries, Seattle, Wash, 95; Casa de la Cultura Oaxaquena, Mex, 95; World Artists for Tibet, Gallery at 678, NY, 98; Yamaso Gallery, Kyoto, Japan, 99; Through the Medium of Wood, Japan Found Gallery, 2001; Tree Spirit (with catalog), Royal Ont Mus, Toronto, Can, 2003; 35 Yrs in Can: Recent Works by Naoko Matsubara, Prince Takamado Gallery, Can Embassy, Tokyo, 2007; Carnegie Mus Art, Pittsburgh, 2009; The Art Gallery, Chatham Univ, 2009; Odori (Dance), Abbozzo Gallery, Oakville, ON, 2012; Gallery Tsutsui, Tokyo, 2012; UNAC Salon, Tokyo, 2013; Hirano no Ie Eieito Kyoto, 2014; Dancing with Wood: 50 Years of Woodcuts by Naoko Matsubara, AbbozzoGallery, Toronto, ON, 2015. *Teaching:* Instr woodcut, Pratt Graphic Art Ctr, 65-67; instr woodcut, Univ RI, 67-68; asst prof woodcut, Univ Victoria, BC, summer 77; asst prof woodcut, Univ Guelph, Ont, 84; vis instr, Inuit Workshop, Cape Dorset, 85. *Awards:* Kegon award, Hangain Ten, Shiko Munakata, 63; Samuel Gold Award, Soc Am Graphic Artists, 68; Soc Am Graphic Artists Awards for Excellence, 84; CBC TV Documentary Video, 90; Distinguished Achievement Award, Carnegie Mellon Univ, Pittsburgh, 2010. *Bibliog:* Fritz Eichenberg (auth), Naoko Matsubara, Xylon, Switz, 70; Joan Stanley-Baker (auth), The woodcuts of Munakata and Matsubara, Art Gallery Greater Victoria, 76; Franz Geirhaas (auth), The Creative Act Paths to Realization, Int Print Soc, 84; Arlene Gehmacher & Klaas Ruitenbeek (auths), Tree Spirit, The Royal Ont Mus, Toronto, 2005. *Mem:* Soc Am Graphic Artists; Royal Can Acad Arts. *Media:* Woodcut, Acrylic, Collage, Paper Sculpture. *Interests:* Hiking, Travel, Tai Chi, Meditation, Reading. *Publ:* Nantucket Woodcuts, 68, Boston Impressions, 70, Barre Publ, Kyoto Woodcuts, 78, Kodansha Int, Ltd, Tokyo; Hagoromo (portfolio), Pinetree Press, 86; Tibetan Sky, 30 color woodcuts on Tibet, Bayeux Arts, Can, 97; Tokonoma (ltd ed portfolio based on Eng haiku by James Kirkup), The Old Press, Eng, 99; Tales of Days Gone By, ALIS, Tokyo, Japan, 2003. *Dealer:* Gallery Tsutsui Tokyo Japan; The Tolman Collections Ltd Tokyo Japan & New York, NY; Abozzo Gallery CS Gallery Toronto; Azuma Gallery Seattle WA. *Mailing Add:* 324 Coral Terr Oakville ON L6J 4C4 Canada

MATSUDA-DUNN, PAMELA
PAINTER
b Hawaii. *Study:* Univ Hawaii; Reed Coll; Pacific NW Coll Art. *Work:* Coll NJ. *Exhib:* Exhibs include Snapshot, Contemp Mus, Baltimore, 2000-01, Aldrich Mus, Ridgefield, Conn, 2002; Fresh, NURTUREart, Brooklyn, 2003; Raid Proj, Spring Armory Show, New York, 2004; This is for Real: War & Contemp Audience, Stony Brook Univ, Stony Brook, NY, 2004; Sticker Throw, KCDC Skate Shop, Brooklyn, 2004; Art-o-Mat, Whitney Mus Am Art, New York, 2004-05, Mus Contemp Art, Los Angeles, 2004-05; Evidence & Residues: An Investigation of Contemp Drawing, Ind State Univ, Terre Haute, Ind, 2007; Booked, ABC No Rio, New York, 2007; Pool Art Fair, Hotel Chelsea, New York, 2007. *Awards:* Lower Manhattan Cultural Coun Swing Space, 2005-06; George Sugarman Found Grant, 2007

MATSUMOTO, ROGER
PHOTOGRAPHER
b Honolulu, Hawaii. *Study:* Self taught in primary medium. *Work:* Philadelphia Mus Art; Utah Mus Fine Art; Salt Lake City Int Airport; Libr Philadelphia; Buddy Holly Ctr, Lubbock, Tex; Univ Sciences, Philadelphia. *Exhib:* Illuminance, Lubbock Fine Arts Ctr, Lubbock, Tex, 97; Ann Photog Exhib, Phillips Mill, New Hope, Pa, 98; Photog 18, Perkins Ctr Arts, Moorestown, NJ, 99; Current Works 2000, Soc Contemp Photog, Kansas City, Mo, 2000; From the Collection/Philadelphia Area, Philadelphia Mus Art, 2000; Works on Paper, La Univ Union Art Gallery, Baton Rouge, La, 2002; Award Winners II, Biggs Mus Am Art, 2002; Alternative Process, Soho Photo Gallery, New York, 2004; Illuminince, Buddy Holly Art Ctr, Lubbock Texas, 2004; The Silver Garden, Philadelphia Mus Art, 2005; The Camera Club London, 2006; Challenge Exhib, Fleisher Art Mem, Philadelphia, 2007; Camera Work Gallery, Portland, Ore, 2011; Photog 31, Perkins Ctr Arts, Moorestown, NY, 2012; Delaware Art Mus Centennial Exhib, 2013; Perkins Ctr Arts Collingwood, NJ, 2013; Fotto Photo, NY, 2013; Foto Photo Gallery, Huntington, NY, 2013; Photo 33, Perkins Ctr Arts, Moorestown, NY, 2014. *Pos:* Artist fel, Del Div Art, 2001. *Awards:* Group 4 Award, Foundry Art Ctr, St Charles, Mo, 2007. *Media:* Palladium prints. *Mailing Add:* 205 LaSalle Way Newark DE 19711

MATTEO, DOROTHY
ARTIST, ILLUSTRATOR
b Summit, NJ, Dec 21 1940. *Study:* Newark Sch of Fine & Indust Art, Cert, 1963; Ocean Co Col, Fine Art, 1974-1977; Sch of Visual Art, Silk Screen. *Work:* Hallmark, Meaning of Life (watercolor), Kansas City, Mo; Wonderful World of Oz (scarecrow sculpture), Los Angeles, Calif; Jesus Christ Superstar, Radio WABC (poster), NY. *Comn:* Private homes (murals, portraits & paintings), NJ. *Exhib:* Solo Exhibs: Ocean County Public Libr, 2006; Point Pleasant Libr, 2006, Georgian Court Col, 2006; Lavallette Libr, 2006; Toms River Libr, 2007, Summit Art Ctr, Summit, NJ, Loft, Red Bank, NJ, NJ Resources Wall, 2009; Ocean Co Artists Guild, 2009, 2010; Summit Art Ctr Members' Show, 65; New & Young Show, Ocean County Artists' Guild, 78; The Loft Gallery, Red Bank, NJ, 99; Women Artists of Ocean County, Jackson Public Libr, 2002; 20th State Juried Exhib, Ocean County Artists' Guild, 2005; 2005 Biennial, Noyes Mus, Brigantine, NJ, 2005; Group Show: Women Artists of Ocean Co, 2006-2007; Tropicana Hotel, Atlantic City, NJ; Ocean Co Artists Guild, Juried Show, 2013. *Collection Arranged:* Beach Series, 2008-2009; Sepia Series, 2009-2012;

Mullica Series, 2011-; Brides Series, 2012. *Pos:* graphic artist & campus photographer, Ocean Co Coll, 88; industrial designer, Lakewood, NJ, 89-2002; Art dir, nat marketing firm, 2001; exec asst, Ocean Co Artist Guild, Island Heights, NJ, 2006; J&B Direct Mail Marketing. *Teaching:* Instr, Spectrum Inst Sch of Art, 1970-1971, Toms River Adult Educ, Jackson, NJ. *Awards:* Hallmark (student exhib), Hallmark Cards, 1958; Dynamic Graphics, 1978; Most Prominent Woman in Advertising, WABC Poster Contest, 89; Third pl Ocean Co Coll Juried Show, 2005; Honorable Mention, OCAG, 2008; 2nd Pl, OCAG, 2009, 2nd Pl, 2013. *Mem:* Ocean Co Artists Guild (exec asst); Shore Inst of Contemp Art; Trac, Toms River, NJ; Noyes Mus, Oceanville, NJ; John F Peto Mus, Island Heights, NJ. *Media:* Oil, Mixed Media, Sculpture, Prints. *Mailing Add:* 123 Swan Blvd Toms River NJ 08753

MATTERNES, JAY HOWARD
PAINTER, ILLUSTRATOR
b Corregidor, Philippines, Apr 14, 1933; US citizen. *Study:* Carnegie Mellon Univ Coll Fine Arts, Mellon Found scholar & BFA, 55. *Work:* Cleveland Mus Natural Sci, Ohio; Carnegie Mus, Pittsburgh; Bedloe Island Mus Immigration, NY; Smithsonian Inst, Washington; Am Mus Natural Hist, NY, 93. *Comn:* Morristown Revolutionary War Mural, Nat Park Serv, NJ, 75; fossil primate murals & Paranthropus mural, Hall of Human Biology, Am Mus Natural Hist, 89-93; Reconstruction of fossil mammals, Hall of Fossil Mammals, Am Mus Natural Hist, 89-94; Homo habilis Utilizing Stone Tools (mural), Gunma Mus Nat Hist, Japan, 95; The Sculpting of the Clay Bison of Tuc d'Audoubert in France (mural), Gunma Mus Nat Hist, Japan, 96. *Exhib:* Art & the Animal, Royal Ont Mus, Ottawa, Can, 75; Nat Acad Western Art at Cowboy Hall Fame, Oklahoma City, 79; Leigh Yawkey Woodson Art Mus, Wausau, Wis, 80, 81 & 83; bird art, Royal Scottish Acad, Edinburgh; Brit Mus, London, 82; Ancestors, Mus Natural Hist, NY, 84; First Western Art Classic, Minnetonka, Minn, 84; Soc Illusrs, NY, 84, 86 & 88; Commonwealth Inst, London, Eng, 85 & 86; Game Conservation Int, San Antonio, Tex, 87; Australian Mus, Sydney, 88. *Pos:* Self-employed free-lance artist, 60-. *Awards:* Merit Award, 68 & Gold Medal, 82, Art Dir Club Wash; Award Merit, Soc Animal Artists, 79. *Bibliog:* Dr LB Leakey (auth), The Dawn of Man (film TV), 65 & Dr Clark Howell (auth), Man Hunters (film TV), 68, Nat Geographic Soc; John Heminway (auth), The Three Million Year Clue (film TV), Survival Anglia Ltd, 76. *Mem:* Artists Equity Asn; Soc Animal Artists; Nat Cowboy Hall Fame. *Media:* Oil, Acrylic; Charcoal, Pencil. *Publ:* Illusr, American Cowboy, 72 & Vanishing Wild Life of North America, 74, Nat Geographic Soc Bk Div; A New Look at Early Man in North America, World Yr Bk, 73; Lost Empires, Living Tribes, 82 & Peoples & Places of the Past, 83. *Mailing Add:* 4328 Ashford Ln Fairfax VA 22032-1435

MATTESON, IRA
SCULPTOR, DRAFTSMAN
b Hamden, Conn, June 26, 1917. *Study:* Art Students League, with Arthur Lee, 37-42, also with William Zorach, 46-51; Nat Acad, with John Flanagan, 46-47. *Work:* Akron Art Inst, Ohio; Cleveland Mus Art; Chrysler Mus, Provincetown, Mass; Norfolk Mus, Va; Akron Univ, Ohio. *Comn:* Figure-Bend, Cascade Plaza, Akron, 77; Back, Case Western Reserve, Univ Cleveland, Ohio, 81. *Exhib:* Kent State Univ; Akron Univ, 88. *Pos:* Prof emer, 85-. *Teaching:* Fac, Sch Art, Kent State Univ, Kent, 68-87. *Awards:* Prix de Rome, Am Acad Rome, 53-55, Louis Comfort Tiffany, 56 & 60; Ohio Arts Coun Grant, 78. *Media:* Wood, Paper. *Interests:* trees, apples, figures, heads. *Publ:* Dialogue, 4/88. *Mailing Add:* PO Box 603 Thetford VT 05074

MATTHEWS, HARRIETT
SCULPTOR, EDUCATOR
b Kansas City, Mo, June 21, 1940. *Study:* Sullins Jr Col, Bristol, Va, AFA; Univ Ga, BFA & MFA; with Leonard DeLonga. *Work:* S Maine Law Libr; Colby Coll Art Mus & Libr; Key Bank, Portland, Maine; Bristol K-8 Sch, Bristol, Maine; Portland Mus Art, Maine; Farnsworth Mus, Rockland, Maine; Univ Ga Mus, Athens, Ga. *Comn:* Designed awards for the Maine Arts & Humanities Comn, 69; outdoor sculpture, Kennebec Valley Vocational Tech Inst Per Cent for Art, 86; Univ Maine Law Libr, 93. *Exhib:* One-person shows, Vanderbilt Univ, 74, Treat Gallery, Bates Col, Lewiston, Maine, 79, Univ S Maine, Gorham, 82, Montpelier Cult Arts Ctr, Laurel, Md, 83, Colby Coll Art Mus, 87, 92, 96, 2001 & 2007, Perspectives, Portland Mus Art, Maine, 90 & June Fitzpatrick Gallery, Portland, Maine, 97 & 2001, Jonathan Frost Gallery, Rockland, Maine, 2015; Payson Gallery, Westbrook Col, Portland, 85; Maine Coast Artist Gallery, 89; Dean Valentgas Gallery, Portland, Maine, 89; Anita Shapolsky Gallery, NY, 91; Frick Gallery, Belfast, Maine, 91-92; Univ Ga Art Gallery, 2005; and others. *Teaching:* Vis instr sculpture, Univ Okla, 64-65; from instr to assoc prof sculpture I-VI & drawing I-II, Colby Col, 66-85, prof, 85-; prof art, Colby Col, Waterville, Maine, prof emeritus, 2014. *Awards:* Colby Travel Grants, 71, 76, 78, 81, 85, 87 & 90; Colby Mellon Grant, 80; Ingram Merrill Grant, 80. *Bibliog:* Virginia Watson-Jones (auth), Contemporary Women Sculptors; Arthur Williams (auth), Sculpture: Technique, Form, Content. *Mem:* Coll Art Asn. *Media:* Welded Metal, Cast Metal, Wood. *Interests:* Archeol

MATTHEWS, ROBERT
DRAFTSMAN
b Wilson, NC, 1974. *Study:* Univ Tenn, Knoxville, BFA (painting); Va Commonwealth Univ, MFA (painting & printmaking). *Work:* NC Mus Art, Raleigh; Philadelphia Mus Art; Pa Acad Fine Arts; De Young Mus, San Francisco. *Exhib:* Solo exhibs, Middle Tenn State Univ, 1998, Univ Arts Gallery 817, Philadelphia, 2003, Philadelphia Art Alliance, 2004, Gallery Joe, Philadelphia, 2005, 2007 & 2010, Sarah Moody Gallery, Univ Ala, 2007; Greater Philadelphia, Paley & Levy Galleries, Moore Coll Art, 2002; Drawing for It, Spector Gallery, Philadelphia, 2003; Arcadia Works on Paper, Arcadia Univ, Glenside, Pa, 2004; Torrid, Kutztown Univ Sharadin Art Gallery, 2005; 181st Ann Invitational Exhib Contemp Art, Nat Acad Mus, New York, 2006; On the Mark!, Turchin Ctr for Arts, Appalachian State Univ, NC, 2007; Spot Check, Pa Acad Fine Art, 2008; The Philadelphia Story, Woodmere Art Mus, 2009. *Awards:* Pa Coun Arts Fel, 2004 & 2008; Philadelphia Mus Art Purchase award, 2004; Pew Ctr for Arts Fel, 2009. *Bibliog:* Roberta Fallon (auth), Sketches-See Spots Run, Philadelphia Weekly, 2003; Edward J Sozanski (auth), Imagination Abounds in Arcadia Show, Philadelphia Inquirer, 2/6/2004; Susan Hagen (auth), Pencil Him In, City Paper, 4/14-21/2005; Chris Berendt (auth), A Portrait of Family, Sampson Independent, 6/16/2009

MATTHEWS, WILLIAM (CARY)
PAINTER
b NY, May 28, 1949. *Study:* San Francisco Art Inst, 69. *Work:* Eiteljorg Mus, Indianapolis, Ind; Buffalo Bill Hist Ctr, Whitney Gallery, Cody, Wyo; Gene Autry Mus, Los Angeles, Calif; Nat Cowboy Hall Fame, Okla City, Okla; Denver Art Mus, Colo; Phoenix Art Mus; Joslyn Art Mus; Gilcrease Art Mus. *Comn:* Ann Bluegrass Festival poster, Telluride, Colo, 84-90 & 93-96; anniversary poster, WestFest, Copper Mt, Colo, 92-93 & 96; numerous designs, Warner Western Records, Nashville, Tenn, 92-96; Canyon de Chelly (commemorative post card), US Postal Serv, 94; twelve watercolors, Ritz-Carlton Hotel, Aspen, Colo, 94. *Exhib:* Solo exhibs, Am Quarter Horse Mus, Amarillo, Tex, 94 & Nev Mus Art, Reno, 96; Prix de West, Nat Cowboy Hall Fame, Okla City, Okla, 95; Covering the West, traveling, 95-96; Great Am Artists, Cincinnati Mus Ctr, Ohio, 96; Buffalo Bill Invitational, Buffalo Bill Mus, Cody, Wyo, 96. *Pos:* Guest lectr, Nev Mus Art, Reno, 96-97. *Teaching:* Instr watercolor, Western Folklife Ctr, Reno, Nev, 96. *Awards:* William E Weiss Purchase Award, Buffalo Bill Hist Ctr, Cody, Wyo, 94; J Schram Prize, Schramsberg Vineyards, 92. *Bibliog:* M J Van Deventer (auth), William Matthews: A painter of cowboy images, Persimmon Hill, autumn 93; Dyan Zaslowsky (auth), William Matthews, Southwest Art, 3/95; Don Hagerty (auth), 100 Leading Contemporary Painters & Sculptors of the American West, Northland Publ (in press). *Media:* Watercolor. *Publ:* Auth, Buckaroo: Visions and Voices of the American West, Simon & Schuster, 93; Cowboys & Images: The Watercolors of William Matthews, Chronicle Books, 94; auth, William Matthews: Working the West, Chronicle Bks, 2007. *Dealer:* Spanierman Gallery NY; Nedra Matteucci Fenn Galleries Santa Fe; Simpson Gallagher Gallery Cody WY; Claggett Re Gallery Vail CO; Goodwin Fine Art Denver CO

MATTICK, PAUL
EDUCATOR, CRITIC
b 1944. *Study:* Harvard Univ, PhD, 1981. *Pos:* Ed, Int J Polit Econ, 1987-2004; art critic, Arts, Art in Am & Artforum. *Teaching:* Prof philos, Adelphi Univ, 1989-. *Publ:* Auth, Social Knowledge, Hutchinson, 1986; Art in Its Time, Routledge, 2003; coauth (with Katy Siegel) Artworks: Money, Thames & Hudson, 2004. *Mailing Add:* Adelphi Univ Dept Philosophy Alumnae Quad Annex 300 Rm 1 PO Box 701 Garden City NY 11530-0701

MATTINGLY, JAMES THOMAS
PRINTMAKER, PAINTER
b Southgate, Calif, Mar 14, 1934. *Study:* San Jose State Univ, with Fred Spratt, Terry Frost, Ken Auvil, Jeff Bowman, Robert Collins & Robert Freemark, BA, 63, MA (art), 66. *Work:* Montreal Mus Fine Arts; Honolulu Acad Arts; Coos Art Mus, Coos Bay, Ore; Wash State Arts Comn, Seattle; Gilkey Print Ctr, Portland Art Mus, Oreg. *Comn:* Box (wood sculpture), comn by Glenda Melton, Salem, Ore, 80; Theatrical Heartscape (mural), comn by Mid-Valley Arts Coun, Elsinore Theatre, Salem, Ore, 84; Coup Stick VI (sculpture), comn by Scott Casebeer, Salem, Ore, 97; Technicolor Coho Buck Salmon in the City (mixed media sculpture), Salem, Ore, 2005. *Exhib:* Northwest Prints 82, Portland Art Mus, Ore, 82; solo exhib, Renshaw Gallery, Linfield Col, Ore, 92, Monmouth Series, Hamersly Libr, Western Ore Univ, 2003, Focus Gallery, AN Bush Gallery, Salem Art Asn, Ore, 2002; NW Print Coun Group Show, Pierce Coll Gallery, Los Angeles, Calif, 93; Hunterdon Art Ctr, Print Exhib, Clinton, NJ, 80 &93; Sitka Art Invitational, Jack Longman Forestry Ctr, Portland, 93, 94, 95 & 96; Cult Identity, Western Ore Univ, Monmouth, 2002; Beyond Seeing, Northwest Print Coun, Interstate Firehouse Cult Ctr, Portland, Ore, 96; Traveling exhib, Cooper Village Mus & Art Ctr, Anaconda & Custer Co Art Ctr, Miles City, Mont, 96; Election HQ, Seattle, Wash, 11/96; XXVII Fed Int Des Soc D'Amateur D'Ex Libris Congress, Boston, 2000; Cambridge Bookplate, Boston Pub Libr, Boston, Mass, 8/2000; Hamersly Libr, Western Ore Univ, Monmouth, Oreg, 12/2000-3/01; Pacific States Biennial Nat Print Exhib, Univ Hawaii, Hilo, 2002-03; Coos Art Mus, Coos Bay, Ore, 2003; Contemp Print Exhib, Univ Wollongong, Australia, 2003; Cascade Print Edition Exchange Exhib, Ore State Univ, Corvallis, Ore, 2005; solo exhib, Governor's Ceremonial Off, State Capital Building, Salem, Ore, 2005; Mary Lou Zeek Gallery, Monmouth Series Landscapes, Salem, Ore, 2005; Retrospective Show, Salem Art Asn, Salem, Ore, 2006; From America, Mus Contemp Art, Minsk, Belarus, 2006. *Pos:* prof emer in art, Western Oregon Univ, Ore. *Teaching:* Asst art, San Jose State Col, 63-66; instr, Alta Col Art, Calgary, 66-68; prof, Western Ore State Col, 68-94, art dept head, 78-86 & 89-90. *Awards:* Reid Mem Award, Int Exhib Graphics, Montreal Mus Fine Arts, 71; Statewide Serv Travel Award, 74 & Visual Arts Resources Award, 77, Mus Art, Univ Ore; Fac Hon Award, Western Ore State Col, Monmouth, 85; All Ore Juried Art Ann, Salem, 89, 90, 91. *Mem:* Salem Art Asn, Ore (mem bd dir, 77-90); Northwest Print Coun (pres, 83-85, mem bd dir, 82-83, 85-); Hon Life Mem, Northwest Print Coun, Portland, Ore, 98. *Media:* Intaglio printmaking, painting, Mixed media. *Res:* Digital photography. *Interests:* Fly fishing, travel. *Publ:* Auth, Professional Concerns, A Handbook for the Apprentice Professional Visual Artist, pvt publ, 96, Rev 98, 2003 & 2004; auth, Standing on the Water Like a Dragonfly, pvt publ, 2006. *Dealer:* Prints Arts Northwest 416 NW 12th Ave Portland OR 97209; May Lou Zeek Gallery 335 State St Salem OR 97301

MATYAS, DIANE C
AUTHOR, PRINTMAKER
b Pittsburgh, Pa, Nov 28, 1961. *Study:* Cornell Univ, BFA, 84; Vermont Studio Sch, 86, Cornell, MFA, 89; Studies at Columbia Univ, Sch Bus, Ctr Non-Profit Mgt, 2006. *Work:* Sculpture, City of Mesa, Ariz. *Comn:* Monkey Puzzle (sculpture), Philadelphia, Pa, 87; Water (mural, oil), Staten Island Childrens Mus, 92; Desert Pergola (sculpture), Mesa, Ariz, 93. *Exhib:* Alliance in the Park, Philadelphia, Pa, 87; New Visions Gallery, Ithaca, NY, 88; AIR Gallery, NY, 88; ARC Gallery, Chicago, Ill, 92;

Columbus Circle, NY subway installation, 92. *Pos:* prog developer/instr, Homeless Art Proj, Queens Mus, NY; instr, Studio in a School Asn, NY, 91-92; Educ Dir, Noble Maritime Collection, 99-2002, prog dir, 2002-2005; Mus Dir of Exhib & Programs, Staten Island Mus, 2005-; exhibs curated: Show & Tell: Cynthia Von Buhle, 2007, Spanish Camp: This Was Our Paradise, 2007, Making Things Go, 2008, Contact: 1609, 2009. *Teaching:* instr printmaking, Cornell Univ, 89-; instr painting & design, Wagner Col, 94. *Awards:* Cornell Fac Medal of Art, 84; Sculpture Grant, Pa Coun Arts, 87; Grant, The Greater New York Art Develop, 88. *Bibliog:* Helen A Harrison (auth), Young artist offers works of maturity, NY Times, 3/2/86; Karin Lipson (auth), Works of young & emerging artists, Newsday, 3/86; Thomas Hine (auth), The Philadelphia Inquirer, 7/27/87. *Media:* Intaglio, Pastel, Graphite, Charcoal. *Publ:* Thoughts on Public Sculpture: The Work of Petah Coyne, 88 & The 1988 Venice Biennale, Q Mag, 88; auth & illusr, The Terrible Captain Jack Visits the Museum, Noble Maritime Collection, NY, 2007. *Mailing Add:* 22 Livingston Ct Staten Island NY 10310-1630

MATZKIN, ALICE ROSALINDA
PAINTER, WRITER
b Los Angeles, Calif, Nov 18, 1939. *Work:* Smithsonian Inst, DC. *Comn:* portrait, Chelsea Clinton, Congressional Club for White House, DC, 1999; portrait, Larry Hagman, Los Angeles, 2000. *Exhib:* 20th Century Am, Smithsonian, DC, 2006; Am Women, Smithsonian, DC, 2002-2003; Mirror of the Mind, Fort Collins Mus Contemp Art, Colo, 2002; juried exhib, Carnegie Art Mus, Oxnard, Calif, 2002; Alice Matzkin Retrospectives, Ventura Co Mus Art, 2001; Powerful Beauty, Images of Ventura Co Women, Calif, 2005; The Struggle for Justice, Smithsonian, DC, 2010. *Teaching:* art dept dir & instr, Abraham Joshua Heschel Day Sch, 1976-1984; adj instr, Los Angeles & Orange Co Comm Coll, 1983-1986; prog co dir, Expressive Arts, Manor West Psychiatric Hospital, 1984-1986. *Awards:* Bronze, Independent Pub Book Award, The Art of Aging, 2010; Silver nautilus Book Award, Art of Aging, 2010. *Bibliog:* Naked Old Women, Ms Mag, 2000; The Oprah Winfrey Show, Aging Gracefully, Harpo Produc, 2001; Oompth TV, Art of Aging, 2009; Focus on the Masters, Donna Granata, 2005; Beautiful Minds, Nat Ctr Creative Aging, 2011. *Mem:* Ojaj Studio Artists. *Media:* Acrylic, Paint. *Interests:* Aging, Portraits. *Publ:* auth, Art of Aging, Sentient Pub, 2009; auth, Ms Mag, 2000; auth, Aging Today, Am Soc on Aging, 2009; auth, Celebrate the Vitality of Aging Through Art, Journ of Longevity, 2007

MAUGHELLI, MARY L
PAINTER, PRINTMAKER
b Glen Lyon, Pa, Nov 20, 1935. *Study:* Univ Calif, Berkeley, BA & MA; Pratt Graphic Ctr. *Work:* Fresno Art Mus, Calif; Helene Wurlitzer Found, Taos, NMex; Univ NMex Tamarind Prints, Albuquerque. *Exhib:* 85th Ann San Francisco Art Inst Exhib, San Francisco Mus Art, 66; Prints USA Malmo, Konstall, Sweden, 85; Beyond NY, AIR Gallery, NY, 89-2001; Condition: Human, AIR Gallery, 89-2003; solo exhibs, Silhouette Symbol & Spirit, Fresno Art Mus, Calif, 98, Women Symbols & Memories, ARC Gallery, Chicago, 2009, Being a Woman Paintings: Then and Now, Gallery 25, Fresno, Calif, 2009; Female, Feminine, Feminist, Orlando Gallery, Tarzana, Calif, 2003; Persistent Image 2006, Tulare Historical Mus, Tulare, Calif; Explorations Gallery 25, Fresno, Calif, 2006; Five Foot Two, Arc Galley, Chicago, Ill, 2007; Artists and Issues that Matter, Arc Gallery, Chicago, Ill, 2008; Women, Symbols, & Mem, ARC Gallery, Chicago, Ill, 2009; Wish You Were Here 9, AIR Gallery, New York, 2010; Women & Girls Zone Gallery, Osaka, Japan, 2010; Its Our Nature, S. Printmaker Thoreau Center for Sustainability, San Francisco, Calif, 2010; Wish You Were Here, AIR Gallery, 2011; Evocative Images, Past and Present, Gallery 25, Fresno, Calif, 2011; AIR Gallery, NY, 2011-2015; Early Work, Abstract Non-Objective Painting & Monotypes, Fig Tree Gallery, Fresno, Calif, 2012; New Work, CS Printmakers Exhib, Triton Mus, Santa Clara, Calif, 2012; Aging, Zone Gallery, Osaka, Japan, 2012; Gallery 25, 40th Anniversary, Fresno Art Mus, 2014; Fig Tree Gallery, Fresno, 2015. *Teaching:* Prof art, Calif State Univ, Fresno, 62-98, prof art emer, 98-; lectr design, Univ Calif, Berkeley, summer 63. *Awards:* Fulbright Fels, Italy, 59-61; Helene Wurlitzer Found Fel, Taos, NMex, summer 76, 77, 83, 86 & 91; artist-in-residence, Hambidge Ctr, Rabun Gap, Ga, 95, 2006, 2011; artist-in-residence, Mishkenot Sha'ananim, Jerusalem, Israel, 96; Jentel artist-in-residence, Banner, Wyo, 2006; Dorland Mountain Arts Colony Temecula, Calif, 2010. *Bibliog:* David Hale (auth), Her Free Floating Figures Defy Gravity, Convention, Fresno Bee, 5/31/98; David Hale (auth), Mary Maughelli: Her Style Remains Ageless, Fresno Bee, 3/11/90; Donald Munro (auth), Personal J, Fresno Bee, 11/13/2003; Mary Lou Aguirre (auth), Making Figures of Expression, News, Fresno Bee (southvalley), page 2 illus, 9/29/2006; Donald Munro (auth), Maughelli's art wows'em again, Fresno Bee, Spotlight, pages K1, k2 illus, 6/17/2007; Art for Thought, Gallery 25, Fresno; Video Interview, Univ Southern Calif, Los Angeles, 2011; Video in Archives, USC, Douglas Coll, Rutgers Univ NJ, Mus Women in the Arts, Wash DC. *Mem:* Coll Art Asn; Calif Soc Printmakers; Women's Caucus for Art; Southern Calif Women's Caucus for Art; Gallery 25, Fresno, Calif. *Media:* Mixed Media, Oil, Collage. *Publ:* D Munro (auth) 7 Things to Do, p.4, Fresno Bee, 4/29/11. *Dealer:* Fig Tree Gallery 644 Van Ness Ave Fresno CA 93721; AIR Gallery 111 Front St #228 Brooklyn NY 11201. *Mailing Add:* 1114 W Keats Ave Fresno CA 93711

MAURER, EVAN MACLYN
MUSEUM DIRECTOR
b Newark, NJ, Aug 19, 1944. *Study:* Amherst Col, BA, 66; Univ Minn, MA, 68; Univ Pa, PhD, 74. *Collection Arranged:* The Native Am Heritage (auth, catalog), Art Inst Chicago, 77; The Rising of a New Moon, 86; Visions of the People, Minneapolis Inst Arts, 92. *Pos:* Cur & asst to dir, Minneapolis Inst Arts, 71-73, dir & chief exec officer, 88-; cur art, Art Inst Chicago, 73-81; dir, Univ Mich Mus Art, 81-88. *Teaching:* Vis prof primitivism & mod art, Univ Chicago, 76; lectr primitivism, mod art & mus studies, Art Inst Chicago, 78-81, assoc prof, 81; prof art hist, Univ Mich. *Awards:* Recipient medal of Chevalier Order of Arts and Letters, French Govt, 2004. *Mem:* Coll Art Asn; Am Asn Mus; Am Asn Mus Dirs

MAURER, NEIL
PHOTOGRAPHER
b New York, NY, Jan 12, 1941. *Study:* Brown Univ, BA, 62; RI Sch Design, MFA, 75. *Work:* Mus Mod Art, NY; Corcoran Gallery Art; San Antonio Mus Art; Mus Art, RI Sch Design; Libr Cong. *Exhib:* Solo shows, Marcuse Pfeifer Gallery, NY, 88, Art Forum Gallery, Quito, Equador, 91, New Gallery, Houston, Tex, 92, Martin-Rathburn Gallery, San Antonio, Tex, 96 & Silver Eye Ctr Photog, Pittsburgh, Pa, 96; Houston Ctr Photog, Tex, 95; Kobe Aid Fund, Tokyo, Japan, 96. *Teaching:* Asst prof, Div Art & Design, Univ Tex, San Antonio, 78-84, assoc prof, Div Visual Arts, 85-. *Awards:* Fulbright-Hays Grant, 75-76; Fulbright-Hays Sr Lectr Photog, Cent Univ, Quito, Equador, 91; Fel Award Photog, Mid-Am Arts Alliance/Nat Endowment Arts, 95

MAURO, ROBERT F
EDUCATOR, PRINTMAKER
b Englewood Cliffs, NJ, Oct 2, 1951. *Study:* Glassboro State Col, BA (art educ), 73; Pratt Inst, MFA (printmaking), 78. *Work:* Stedman Gallery Rutgers Univ, Camden, NJ; Univ Mich, Ann Arbor; Newark Pub Libr, NJ. *Comn:* 3-D serigraph, Subaru Am, Cherry Hill, NJ, 82; 3-D serigraph, Corning Glass, Philadelphia, Pa, 82; 3-D serigraph, PNB, Philadelphia, Pa, 83. *Exhib:* Korea Int Print Competition, Seoul, 80; Print Club Biennial Int, Philadelphia Print Club, Pa, 86; Artlink Prints, Artlink Contemp Space, Ft Wayne, Idaho, 8; Scan, Franklin Inst, Philadelphia, Pa, 93; Scan, Silicon Gallery, Philadelphia, Pa, 95. *Pos:* Chmn fine arts, Beaver Col, Pa, 78-. *Teaching:* Assoc prof printmaking, Beaver Col, Glenside, Pa, 78- & chmn, 93-. *Mem:* Philadelphia Print Club. *Media:* Computer Imaging. *Dealer:* Rosenfeld Gallery Arch St Philadelphia PA. *Mailing Add:* 805 Jamestown Rd Turnersville NJ 08012

MAURY, RICHARD
PAINTER
b Washington, DC, Nov 6, 1935. *Study:* Corcoran Sch Art, Washington, DC; Art Students League, NY; Acad di Belle Arti, Florence, Italy. *Work:* Metrop Mus Art, NY; New Britain Mus Am Art, Conn; Arnot Mus Art, Elmira, NY; Flint Mus, Mich; rep in collections of Am Express Co, Arnot Art Mus Elmira NY, Mus Art NY City, New Britain (Conn) Mus Art, Fogg Mus Cambridge Mass. *Exhib:* The Figure in Am Art Since Midcentury, Silvermine Metro Ctr, Stamford, Conn, 88; New Britain Invitational, New Britain Mus, Conn, 89; Exquisite Painting, Orlando Mus Art, Fla, 91; Acad Inst Exhib of Painting & Sculpture, Am Acad & Inst of Arts & Letters, NY, 91; Midyear Invitational, Butler Mus Art, Youngstown, Ohio, 92; Ann Exhib, Nat Acad Design, NY, 92; Rerepresenting Representation, Arnot Mus Art, Elmira, NY, 93; one-man show, Greenville Co Mus, SC, 93; Forum Gallery New York City, 2001-03, Forum Gallery Los Angeles, 2003; Art Students League New York City, Flint (Mich); Uffizi Gallery Florence Italy. *Bibliog:* Margaret Matthews (auth), Richard Maury, Am Artist, 9/85; Jason Kaufman (auth), Realism rising, Atelier Mag Int Art; Thomas Hoving (auth), My eye, Connoisseur, 2/90. *Mem:* Nat Acad (acad). *Media:* Oil Colors, Charcoal. *Mailing Add:* c/o Forum Gallery 730 5th Ave Ste 201 New York NY 10019

MAUSSION, PIERRE EDOUARD See Edouard, Pierre

MAVIGLIANO, GEORGE JEROME
ADMINISTRATOR, EDUCATOR
b Chicago, Ill, Oct 24, 1941. *Study:* Western Ill Univ, BA, 64; Northern Ill Univ, MA, 67. *Pos:* Assoc dean, Coll Commun & Fine Arts, Southern Ill Univ, 86-94. *Teaching:* Assoc prof art hist, Southern Ill Univ, 70-; prof emer, 97-. *Awards:* Nat Endowment Arts Expansion Arts Grant, 77; Smithsonian Inst Fel, 81; Nat Endowment Humanities Summer Sem Award, 81 & 85. *Res:* New Deal art programs; art of the Capitol. *Publ:* Auth, A Matter of History: New Deal and the Arts (exhib catalog), 73; On Painting, Sculpture and Architecture, Stipes, 73; Fred Myers, Woodcarver, Southern Ill Univ, 80; The Federal Art Project: Holger Cahill's Program of Action, Art Education, Vol XXXVII, No 3, 5/84; The Chicago Design Workshop: 1939-1943, J Decorative & Propaganda Arts, No 6, fall, 87; The Federal Art Project in Illinois: 1935-43, Southern Ill Univ, 90; Heather Becker (auth), The Illinois Art Project: An Overview, 84-86, Chronicle Bks, 2002. *Mailing Add:* 405 Marcia Carterville IL 62918-1555

MAVROMATIS, DIMITRI
COLLECTOR
Pos: investment banking and asset management business. *Awards:* named one of Top 200 Collectors, ARTNews Mag, 2011, 2012, 2013. *Collection:* postwar and modern art

MAVROUDIS, DEMETRIOS
SCULPTOR
b Thasos, Greece, Nov 18, 1937. *Study:* Jersey City State Col, BA; Teachers Col, Columbia Univ, MA & EdD. *Comn:* Bronze sculptures, Bus Comt for Arts, Esquire, 73-76; sculpture, Lifestyles Mag, 77; ESG Enterprises, 86; mosaic of Madonna & Child in St Constantine & Helen's Greek Cathedral, Richmond, Va, 87. *Exhib:* Albright-Knox Art Gallery, Buffalo, NY, 70 & 71; Artists-in-Residence Traveling Exhib, Del Art Mus, Wilmington, 75 & 76; Sculpture in the Fields, Storm King Art Ctr, Mountainville, NY; Solo exhibs, Philadelphia Art Alliance, Pa, Anchorage Hist & Fine Arts Mus, Alaska & Alaska State Mus. *Pos:* Artist-in-residence, NJ Coun Arts, 71-73. *Teaching:* Asst prof sculpture, NY Univ, 69-71 & Teachers Col, Columbia Univ, 67-69 & 73-74; assoc prof sculpture & artist-in-residence, Univ Richmond, Va, 74-86. *Awards:* Dow Purchase Award, Columbia Univ, 69. *Mem:* Am Foundrymen's Soc; Nat Art Educ Asn; Coll Art Asn. *Media:* Cast Metal, Wood. *Mailing Add:* 1808 Belleau Dr Richmond VA 23235-4214

MAWDSLEY, RICHARD
SILVERSMITH, GOLDSMITH
b Winfield, Kans, July 11, 1945. *Study:* Emporia State Univ, BSE, 67; Univ KS, MFA, 69. *Work:* Am Crafts Mus, NY; Mus Fine Arts, Boston; Renwick Gallery, Smithsonian Inst, Washington; Yale Univ Art Gallery, New Haven, Conn. *Exhib:* Minn Mus Art, 70 & 78-80; Cocoran Gallery Art, 72; solo exhibs, Helen Drutt Gallery, Philadelphia, 77,

Ornamental Metal Mus, Memphis, Tenn, 87 & Mobilia Gallery, Cambridge, Mass, 92; Vatican Mus, Italy, 78; Nat Mus Am Art, Smithsonian Inst, Washington, 81; Mus Fine Arts, Boston, 84-86 & 87-90; Oakland Mus, 84-86 & 87-90; Victoria & Albert Mus, 85; Philadelphia Mus Art, 86-87; Nat Mus Mod Art, Tokyo & Kyoto, 87-90; Grand Prix des Metiers d'Art, Int Invitational Exhib, Acad Royal Arts, Toronto & Salon des Metiers d'Art, Montreal, 88; 1988 Hong-iK Metalcrafts Asn Ann Exhib, Invitational Exhib, Walker Hill Art Ctr Mus, Seoul, Korea, 88; Explorations: The Aesthetic of Excess, Am Craft Mus, NY, 90; Stedlijk Mus, Amsterdam, The Neth, 95; America's Smithsonian (traveling), 96-98; Intl Invit Exhib, Brooching It Diplomatically: A Tribute to Madeleine K Albright, Helen Drutt Gal, Phila, PA, Het Kruithuis, Mun Mus Contemp Art's, Hertogenbosch, Netherlands, Mus Art & Design, Helsinki, Finland, Tarbekunstimuuseum, Tallin, Estonia, Am Craft Mus, NY, Villa Croce, Mus Contemp Art, Geneva, Italy, Kunstgewerbemusuem, Berlin, Germany & Schmuckmusem, Pforzheim, Germany, 1998-2001; cur exhib, Attitude & Action! North American Jewelry, Univ Cent England, Birmingham Inst Art & Design, Eng & DESIGNyard Gal, Dublin, Ireland, 2000; Generating Connections Emerging Jewelry Artists & Mentors, Soc Arts & Crafts, Boston, Mass, 2002; A View From America: Contemp Jewelry, Gold Treasury Mus, Melbourne, Australia, 2004; Think Small, Ill State Mus, Chicago Gallery, James R Thompson Ctr, Ill State Mus, Springfield, & Ill State Mus, Lockport Gallery, 2005-06. *Pos:* Fellow, Am Craft Council, 98-; pres, Soc North Am Goldsmiths, 87-89. *Teaching:* Prof emeritus, Southern Ill Univ, Carbondale. *Awards:* Artist Fel in Crafts, Ill Arts Coun, 87-88, 97-98, 2000-01; Artist Fel Grant, Nat Endowment Arts, 77-78 & 94-95; Distinguished Alumni, Emporia State Univ, Kkansas, 93. *Bibliog:* Janet Koplas (auth), Richard Mawdsley Tubular Fantasies, Am Craft Mag, vol 43, no 2, April/May, 1983; Susan Barahal (auth), Richard Mawdsley New Work: Architectural series, Metalsmith Mag, Vol 13, No 4, fall 92; Susan Grant Lerwin (auth), One of a Kind American Art Jewelry, Harry N Abrams, New York, 94; Helen W English Drutt (auth), Jewelry of Our Time: Art Ornament and Obsession, Rizzoli, New York, 95; Howard Risatti (auth), Skilled Work: American Craft in the Renwick Gallery, Smithsonian Inst Press, Wash, DC, 1998. *Mem:* Soc NAM Goldsmiths (pres, 87-89). *Media:* Metals

MAXERA, OSCAR
PAINTER, ASSEMBLAGE ARTIST
b Buenos Aires, Arg, Jan 12, 1930. *Study:* Acad Fine Arts, Arg, cert, 55. *Work:* Solomon R Guggenheim Mus (5 paintings), NY; Westport Mus, Conn, 77; Mus Mod Art, Buenos Aires, 82; Centro Argentino de Relaciones Internacionales, Buenos Aires, 79; Co-Art, New York, NY, 94; Solomon R Guggenheim Mus; Yale Univ Art Gallery, New Haven, Conn, 2003; Lawrence Univ Arts Center, Wisconsin, 94 & 95; and many more in pvt collections. *Comn:* Artists of the World, Meibner Edition, Lufthansa, Hamburg, 83. *Exhib:* One-man shows, Nice Gallery, 68, 70 & 71, Ctr Cult San Martin, 72, Lirolay Gallery, 73, Van Riel Gallery, Buenos Aires, 74, Westport Pub Libr, 77 & Sarmiento Gallery, Buenos Aires, 80; Mus Mod Art, Buenos Aires, 69-79; Mus Mod Art, Paraguay, 74; Solomon R Guggenheim Mus, 87 & 88; Ergane Gallery, NY, 90; La Mama Galleria, NY, 92; Gubala Gallery, New York, 94-95; Silvermine Guild Arts Ctr, 95; New York Radiance, Lawrence Univ Art Ctr, Appleton, Wis, 95; Gallery Korea, New York, 95. *Teaching:* Acad Fine Art, Meeba, Buenos Aires, 57-60; Prof fine art, Buenos Aires, Argentina, 55-60. *Awards:* First Prize, Salon for Newcomers Fine Arts, 68; First Prize, Vincente Lopez Munic Salon, 70; Second Prize, San Antonio de Areco Salon, 73; 2000 outstanding people of the 20th century, Int Biographical Ctr, Cambridge, Eng, 98. *Bibliog:* Arte D'Oggi (auth), Ultime Tendenze Nell, Gillo Dorfles, Italy, 74; Fifty Years of Collections: Painting Since World War II, Guggenheim Mus, 87; K G Saur (auth), Allgemeines Künstlerlexikon, Munchen Leipzig, 93; and others. *Media:* Collage, Acrylic, Oil. *Interests:* Art research & reading. *Publ:* Nueva Historia de la Pintura y Escultura en la Argentina, 3d ed, 99-2000; Fifty Years Collecting Paintings, Guggenheim Mus, NY, 1987-88. *Dealer:* Galerie Mourlot New York; Diego Salazar Gallery Long Island City NY 11101. *Mailing Add:* 334 E 90th St No 3 C New York NY 10128-5185

MAXFIELD, ROBERTA MASUR
SILVERSMITH
b Chicago, Ill, Oct 30, 1952. *Study:* Northern Ill Univ, with Eleanor Caldwell & Lee Peck, BFA, 74, MA, 75; Ind Univ, with Alma Eikerman, MFA, 77. *Work:* Ill State Mus, Springfield; Village Art Collection, Oak Park & River Forest High Sch, Ill. *Exhib:* Goldsmiths Show, Phoenix Art Mus, Ariz, 77; Ill Craftsmen, Ill State Mus, Springfield, 79; Everyday Metal Exhib, Nat Ornamental Mus, Memphis, Tenn, 80; Young Americans Metal, Am Crafts Mus, NY 81; Calso, traveling, 81; Alma Eikerman Retrospective Exhib, Ind Univ Art Mus, 85; Soc Arts Crafts Pa, 85; Scent Bottle Exhib, Signature Gallery, Mass, 85. *Awards:* Honorable Mention, Soc N Am Goldsmiths, 77; Purchase Award & Third Place, Village Art Fair, Village Art Comt, 79; Honorable Mention, Ill Crafts Exhib, Ill State Mus, 80. *Bibliog:* Craft Horizons, Am Coun Crafts, 4/77. *Mem:* Soc N Am Goldsmiths. *Media:* Sterling Silver. *Mailing Add:* 461 W Hillcrest Dr Dekalb IL 60115-2377

MAXIM, DAVID NICHOLAS
PAINTER, GRAPHIC ARTIST
b Los Angeles, Calif, May 11, 1945. *Study:* Univ Calif Los Angeles, BA, 66, MA, 68. *Work:* San Francisco Mus Mod Art; Mus Fine Moderne Kunst, Frankfurt, Ger; British Mus, London,; Graphische Sammlung Albertina, Vienna; Brooklyn Mus, NY. *Exhib:* Bilder fur Frankfurt, Deutschen Architectur Mus, Frankfurt, Germ, 85; Ten Americans, Carnegie Inst Art, Pittsburgh, Pa, 88; Kunstverein, Heidenheim, Ger, 93; Painted Philosophy, Univ Calif, Berkeley Mus, Danville, 94. *Awards:* Grant, Judwig Vogelstein Found, 95. *Bibliog:* Jan Butterfield (auth), David Maxim (exhib catalog), Galerie Sander, 91; August & Dorothy Friedman (coauths), Maxim's paint machines, Downtown, New York, 4/8/92; Nicole Blunt (auth), Heroes and Giants, 96 & David Naxim: Drawings, Walsworth Publ, 98. *Media:* Acrylic & Mixed Media on Canvas; Drawing Media. *Publ:* Coauth, Painted Philosophy (exhib catalog), 94. *Mailing Add:* 224 Guerrero St San Francisco CA 94103

MAXWELL, DAVID OGDEN
PATRON
b Philadelphia, Pa, May 16, 1930. *Study:* Yale Univ, BA, 52; Harvard Univ, LLB, 55. *Pos:* insurance comnr to admin and budget secy, State of Pa, 67-70; gen counsel, HUD, Wash, 70-73; pres, Chief Exec Officer, Ticor Mortgage Insurance Co, 73-81; Chief Exec Officer, Fannie Mae, Wash, 81-91; bd dir, Centre Partners. *Mailing Add:* 5335 Wisconsin Ave NW Ste 440 Washington DC 20015-2052

MAXWELL, JANE HOFFMAN
ARTIST
b Framingham, Mass, Mar 16, 1964. *Study:* Middlebury Coll, BA, 86. *Exhib:* Hubert Gallery, New York, 2007; Campton Gallery, New York, 2008; Caldwell Snyder Gallery, San Francisco, 2009; Mauger Mod Art, London, Eng, 2009. *Awards:* Mixed Media Award, Newburyport Juried Show, 2000; Jurors Choice Award, Attleboro Arts Mus, 2006. *Bibliog:* contrbr, Holly Harrison & Paula Grasdal (auths), Collage for the Soul, Rockport Books, 2003; contribr, Holly Harrison & Paula Grasdal (auths), Collage Sourcebook, Quarry Books, 2005; contribr, Lynne Perella (auth), Beyond Paper Dolls, Stampington & anp, 2006; contribr, Terry Taylor (auth), Artful Paper Dolls, Lark Books, 2006; contribr, Mixed Media Collage, Quarry Books, 2008. *Mem:* New Art Ctr (Bd mem), Newton, Mass, 2006-2009; Inst Contemp Art (mem dirs circle), Boston, Mass, 2005-. *Media:* Mixed media. *Dealer:* Caldwell Snyder Gallery 341 Sutter St San Francisco CA 94108; Campton Gallery 451 W Broadway New York NY 10012; Lanoue Fine Art 160 Newbury St Boston MA 02116. *Mailing Add:* 167 Lake Ave Newton MA 02459

MAXWELL, PETER
FOUNDATION DIRECTOR, DESIGNER
b Easton, Pa, May 2, 1930. *Comn:* The Ballinglen Ctr, The Ballinglen Arts Found Ltd, Ballycastle, Co Mayo, Republic of Ireland. *Pos:* Pres & found, Maxwell & Maxwell, 60-75, Maxwell Communications, 75-80 & Maxwell's Business, 80-; co-owner, Dolan-Maxwell, Inc, Philadelphia, 84- & New York, 88-90; co-founder, Artist in Rural Ireland Fund, Pa & Ballinglen Arts Found, Co Mayo, Eire, 92-. *Mem:* Int Fine Print Dealers Asn. *Specialty:* Modern and contemporary works on paper, distinguished mod & contemp work of art. *Publ:* Publ, Susan Rothenberg, The Prints, A Catalog Raisonne, 87; Roger Vieillard, 88; The Sculpture of Bill Freelend, 89; The Ballinglen Experience, 97; Am Artists in Rural Ireland, Ballinglen Experience, 226, Cheryl Warrick, 2008. *Mailing Add:* 2046 Rittenhouse Sq St Philadelphia PA 19103

MAY, DANIEL STRIGER
DEALER
b Decatur, Ill, Sept 5, 1942. *Study:* State Univ NY, Buffalo, BA, 64, MBA, 66 & MEd, 68. *Pos:* Dir, Jackson Hole Art Gallery, 70-72; owner & dir, May Gallery, Jackson, Wyo, 72-; owner, May Gallery, Scottsdale, Ariz, 78-, Danela Gallery, Scottsdale, Ariz, currently. *Specialty:* Fine American paintings and sculpture; contemporary jewelry

MAYER, BILLY (WILLIAM) ROBERT MAYER
SCULPTOR
b St Paul, Minn, June 28, 1953. *Study:* Univ Minn, BFA, 76; Pa State Univ, MFA, 78. *Work:* Frederick Weisman Collection, Los Angeles, Calif; Muskegan Art Mus, Mich; Univ Galleries, Univ Minn. *Comn:* Outdoor sculpture, Holland, Mich, 83; large-scale sculpture, Howard Miller Inc, Zeeland, Mich, 85; outdoor sculpture, Christ Community Church, Spring Lake, Mich, 88. *Exhib:* West Mich Art Exhib, Muskegon Mus Art, 86; Signs, Times and Writing on the Wall, Detroit Inst Art, Mich, 87; Appalachian summer sculpture competition, Appalachian State Univ Gallery, Boone, NC, 88; two-person exhib, Muskegon Mus Art, Mich, 88 & Rochester Art Ctr, Minn, 90; solo exhib, Grand Rapids Art Mus, Mich, 89; SW Tex State Univ, 90. *Pos:* Chmn art dept, Hope Col, Holland, Mich, 88-. *Teaching:* Instr ceramic/sculpture, Hope Col, 78-79, asst prof, 79-85 & assoc prof, 85-. *Awards:* Merit Award, Whirlpool Sculpture, Krasl Art Ctr, St Joseph, Mich, 85; Merit Award, W Mich Regional, Muskegan Mus Art, 88. *Media:* Clay, Welded Metal. *Mailing Add:* Hope Col PO Box 9000 Holland MI 49422-9000

MAYER, EDWARD ALBERT
SCULPTOR, EDUCATOR
b Union, NJ, Oct 30, 1942. *Study:* Brown Univ, Providence, RI, BA, 64; Univ Wis, Madison, MFA, 66. *Work:* Milwaukee Art Mus, Wis; Huntington Galleries, WVa; Rose Art Mus, Waltham, Mass; Ohio State Univ; NMex State Univ; and others. *Comn:* Ohio Bldg Authority, Columbus, 74. *Exhib:* Sao Paulo Bienal, 85; Zolla Lieberman, Chicago, 85; Burchfield Art Ctr, Buffalo, 88; Pub Art Works, San Rafael, Calif, 89; Haenah Kent Gallery, NY, 93; Univ Albany, Mus 2005; Zabriskie, 2005. *Teaching:* Asst prof art, Carthage Col, Kenosha, Wis, 66-70; prof sculpture, Ohio Univ, Athens, 70-83; vis sculptor, Tyler Sch Art, Rome, Italy, 73-74; prof, Univ Albany, 83-; prof art, sculpture, chmn, currently. *Awards:* Nat Fel, Nat Endowment Arts, 78, 79 & 86; Ava Fel, 83; NYFA in Sculpture, 86; ISC Outstanding Educator, 2006. *Bibliog:* Helen Harrison (auth), review, New York Times, 3/28/93; Grace Glueck (auth), review, New York Times, 11/11/2005; Leigh Ann Miller (auth), review, Art in America, 2/2006; and others. *Media:* All. *Dealer:* Zabriskie Gallery, 41 E 57th St New York NY 10022. *Mailing Add:* State Univ NY Dept Art Albany NY 12222

MAYER, MARC
MUSEUM DIRECTOR
b Sudbury, Ont, Can, 1956. *Study:* McGill Univ, BA (art hist; with honors), 1984. *Pos:* Production asst, ARTnews, New York, 1986; asst dir, 49th Parallel Ctr Contemp Can Art, 1986-90; head of visual arts, Can Embassy, Paris, 1990-93; corresp, Rizzoli's Jour Art, New York, 1990-91; cur, Albright-Knox Art Gallery, Buffalo, NY, 1994-98; dir, Power Plant Contemp Art Gallery, Toronto, 1998-2001; dep dir art, Brooklyn Mus, 2001-2004; dir, Musée d'Art Contemporain de Montréal, 2004-09; dir & chief exec officer, Nat Gallery Can, Ottawa, 2009-. *Mem:* Asn Art Mus Dirs (exec comt, chmn pub affairs comt, 2008-10); Can Art Mus Dirs Orgn (exec comt, treas, 2005-07). *Mailing Add:* Nat Gallery Can 380 Sussex Dr Ottawa ON K1N9N4 Canada

MAYER, MONICA P
WRITER, CONCEPTUAL ARTIST
b Mexico City, Mex, Mar 16, 1954. *Study:* Escuela Nacional de Artes Plasticas, BA (visual arts), 78; Goddard Col, MA (sociology of art), 80. *Work:* Mus de Arte Contemporaneo, Aguascalientes; Mus Int de Electrografia, Cuenca, Spain; Mus Nacional de la Estampa, Mexico City. *Exhib:* Novela Rosa o me Agarro el Arquetipo, Mus Carrillo Gil, Mexico City, 87; EMPA, Mus Univ del Chopo, Mexico City, 95; Binomio: Electrografia, Mus Casa Diego Rivera, Guanajuato, 96, Nat Gallery, Kingston, Jamaica, 96 & Casa Cultura Candido Mendes, Rio de Janeiro, Brazil, 97. *Bibliog:* Florisa Calderon (producer), La Casa de la tia Arte, Producciones Volcan, 96. *Mem:* Anglo Mex Cult Inst (bd mem, 95-98); Pinto mi Raya. *Media:* Performance. *Publ:* Auth, A Brief Story of Almost 10 Years of Applied Conceptual Art, Pinto mi Raya, 98; La Muestra (de performance), 98, Nunca ha visto un performance?, 98 & Concursus de arte sobre obesos y enanos, 98, El Universal. *Mailing Add:* Gonzales de Cosio 17 Mexico 03100 Mexico

MAYER, ROSEMARY
SCULPTOR, GRAPHIC ARTIST
b Ridgewood, NY, Feb 27, 1943. *Study:* State Univ Iowa, Iowa City, AB, 64; Brooklyn Mus Art Sch, 65-67; Sch Visual Arts, New York, 67-69. *Work:* Sidney Lewis Collection, Richmond, Va; Herbert Johnson Mus, Cornell Univ, Ithaca, NY; Allen Mem Art Mus, Oberlin Col, Ohio; Hartwick Coll Collection, Oneonta, NY. *Comn:* Spell (temp outdoor work with weather balloons), Queens Coun Arts & Greater Jamaica Develop Coun, 77; Balloon, Rose Hill Property Assoc, NY, 78; plans for Orfeo, Soho Baroque Opera Co, NY, 82. *Exhib:* One-person shows, AIR Gallery, 73, Whitney Mus Am Art Resources Ctr, NY, 75, 55 Mercer St, NY, 79, Cornell Univ, 80 & Locrian Mode, Interart Ctr, NY, 80; Times Square Show, NY, 80; Moontent (outdoor installation), Lansing, NY, 82; Pam Adler Gallery, NY, 85; Long Island Univ, Brooklyn, NY, 93 & 2005; Bowery Poetry Club, New York, 2007; LaGuardia Community Coll, 2009; and others. *Pos:* Art writer & reviewer, Arts Mag, 71-73 & Art Am, 74-75. *Teaching:* Vis artist painting, Art Inst Chicago, 74; vis artist painting & drawing, Hartwick Col, Oneonta, 76; Artist's Workshop Program, Nat Endowment Arts, 81; lectr art, Baruch Col, City Univ NY, 87-91; adj prof, Long Island, Univ NY, 88-2009; adj lectr art, La Guardia Community Col, NY, 92-2009, lectr art, 2009-. *Awards:* Creative Artists Pub Serv Grant, NY State Coun Arts, 76-77, 80-81 & 82; Nat Endowment Arts Grant, 79-80; Pollock Krasner Found, 87 & 88. *Bibliog:* Bruce Kurtz (auth), Rosemary Mayer, Art in Am, 3-4/77; Valentin Tatransky (auth), Rosemary Mayer, Arts Mag, 4/78; Ballerini & Milazzo (eds), Pontormo's Diary/Rosemary Mayer, 82; Reagan Upshaw (auth), Rosemary Mayer, Art in Am, 10/85. *Media:* Fabric, Rag Vellum; Watercolor, Pencil. *Publ:* Auth, Those, White Walls, winter 80; Pontormo's Diary, Out of London Press, 82; Moontent, White Walls, winter 83; Luxe, Beauty and Critique, TSL Ltd, 83; Some of my stories, Heresies, no 23, 88. *Mailing Add:* 59 St Marks Ave Brooklyn NY 11217

MAYER, SONDRA ELSTER
ART DEALER, ART APPRAISER
b New York, NY, July 12, 1933. *Study:* Syracuse Univ, BA, 54; Columbia Univ, MA, 55; Mus Mod Art, 57-58; Pratt Inst, 68; Art Students League, 72. *Work:* Los Angeles Co Mus Art, Los Angeles; Syracuse Univ Lowe Gallery, NY; MacDowell Colony Collection, Peterborough, NH; Portland Art Mus, Ore; Crocker Nat Bank, San Francisco, Calif. *Comn:* Greeting card design, Mus Mod Art, New York, 76 & 78; design for Star & Snowflake Jewelry, Metrop Mus Art, New York, 77 & 81; greeting card design, UNICEF, 79 & 81; greeting card design, Cartier, 85. *Exhib:* Philadelphia Print Club; Boston Printmakers Ann, DeCordova Mus, Lincoln, Mass, 79; Current Works, Everson Mus, Syracuse, NY, 80; Heckscher Mus, Huntington, NY, 79-82; Int Miniature Show, Seoul, Korea, 80; Queens Mus, 81; and others. *Pos:* Asst dir, Printmaking Studio Sch, 75-84; rep, Petersburg Press, 84-86; owner & dir, Sondra Mayer Fine Art; art writer, Great Neck Record, Anton Community Newspapers, Sunstorm, Long Island Heritage, The World and I. *Teaching:* Instr printmaking, Ruth Leaf Studio, Douglaston, NY, 76-90; instr, Great Neck Adult Educ prog, 2006-2007. *Awards:* MacDowell Colony fel, Peterborough, NH, 78; Leila Sawyer Mem Prize in Graphics, Nat Asn Women Artists, 79; Graphics Award, Firehouse Gallery, Garden City, NY, 81. *Mem:* Artists Equity New York; Philadelphia Print Club; MacDowell Colony Fels. *Media:* Etching, Intaglio. *Specialty:* Contemporary and modern art in all media with a special interest in master graphics; appraisals, collection advice, purchasing archival storage & framing. *Interests:* Contemporary Art, cosmology, theatre and literature. *Collection:* Contemporary Art; Books, art books, contemporary signed first editions, pop-up books. *Publ:* Illusr, Intaglio Printmaking Techniques, Watson-Guptill, 76; contribr, Graphis Ann, Graphis Press, 78-79; and others. *Mailing Add:* Six Wooleys Ln Apt A32 Great Neck NY 11023

MAYER, SUSAN MARTIN
EDUCATOR, MUSEOLOGIST
b Atlanta, Ga, Oct 25, 1931. *Study:* Am Univ; Univ NC, BA (art); Univ Del; Ariz State Univ, MA (art educ); Atelier Grande Chaumier, Paris; Kans State Univ. *Exhib:* Earthly Delights: Garden Imagery in Contemp Art, Ft Wayne Mus Art, 88; solo show, Galveston Arts Ctr, 90; In the Beginning, Art Mus Beaumont, Tex, 93; Genesis Through Revelation, RH Love Contemp Art Gallery, Chicago, 93. *Teaching:* Coordr mus educ, Huntington Art Gallery, Univ Tex, 70- & art fac, 71-. *Awards:* Mus Educators Award, Nat Art Educ Asn, 83; Distinguished Serv Award, Nat Art Educ Asn, 91. *Mem:* Nat Art Educ Asn; Tex Art Educ Asn; Tex Asn Mus; Am Asn Mus. *Media:* Oil. *Publ:* coauth, (with B Reese & A Mayer), Texas, Trillium Press, 87; auth, Art Works, Holt Rinehart & Winston, 89; Museum Education: History, Theory & Practice, Nat Art Educ Asn, Reston, Va, 89; Museums & Art Education, In: Inside Art: culture, Theory, Expression, WS Benson & Co, Austin, Tex, 92; Educating the Public, Art Papers, 93. *Mailing Add:* Dept Art Univ Texas at Austin Austin TX 78712

MAYERI, BEVERLY
SCULPTOR
Study: Univ Calif, BA, 67; San Francisco State Univ, MA, 76. *Work:* Canton Art Inst, Canton, Ohio; Nat Mus of Hist, Taipei, Taiwan; Long Beach Parks and Recreation, Long Beach, Calif; Los Angeles Arts Comn, Los Angeles, Calif; Los Angeles Co Mus of Art, Decorative Arts Dept. *Exhib:* Solo exhibs, Ivory/Kimpton Gallery, San Francisco, Calif, 81 & 83, Garth Clark Gallery, NY, 85 & 87, San Jose Inst Contemp Art, Calif, 90, Dorothy Weiss Gallery, San Francisco, 90, 92, 94, 96 & 98 & Robert Kidd Gallery, Mich, 93, Robert Kidd Gallery, San Francisco, Calif, 2000, Dorothy Weiss Gallery, San Francisco, Calif, 2000 & Susan Cummins Gallery, Mill Valley, Calif, 2002; Renwick Gallery, Smithsonian Inst, Washington, DC, 81; Signet Arts Gallery, St Louis, Mo, 84; Robert L Kidd Gallery, Birmingham, Mich, 86 & 93; Fresno Arts Ctr & Mus, Calif, 87; Euphrat Gallery, De Anza Col, Cupertino, Calif, 88; Esther Saks Gallery, Chicago, 88 & 90; Dorothy Weiss Gallery, San Francisco, Calif, 90, 92 & 94; 500 Yrs Since Columbus (with catalog), Triton Mus Art, Calif, 92; The Clay Figure, Dorothy Weiss Gallery, San Francisco, 93; The Nude in Clay (with catalog), Perimeter Gallery, Chicago, 95; Beauty and the Beast, Sybaris Gallery, Mich, 96; group exhibs, About Face, The Clay Studio, Philadelphia, PA, 2001, Figure It Out: A Ceramic Sculpture Invitational, Calif State Univ, Chico, CA, 2001, Head Ceramic Sculpture on a Heroic Scale, SSAC, San Antonio, Tex, 2002, Major Figures, Ferrin Gallery, lenox, MA, 2002; and others. *Teaching:* invited lectr, Scripp's Col, Claremont, CA, 99; invited lectr & workshop, Cuesta Col, San Luis Obispo, CA, 2002; invited workshop, San Diego State Univ, San Diego, CA, 2002; invited speaker, CCACA, Natsoulas Gallery, Davis, CA, 2002; and others. *Awards:* Nat Endowment Arts, 82 & 88; Individual Artist Grant, Marin Arts Coun, 87; Recognition Grant, Virginia A Groot Fedn, 91; Grant, Marin Arts Coun Individual Artist, San Rafael, CA, 2002. *Bibliog:* Marcy Timberman (auth), Review shorts, Artweek, San Jose, Calif, Vol 21, 3/90; Victor Cassidy (auth), Beverly Mayeri, Am Ceramics, NY, Vol 8, No 4, 12/90; Stephen Luecking (auth), Beverly Mayeri, Am Crafts, NY, Vol 50, No 6, 12/90-1/91; Debra Koppman (auth), Beverly Mayeri, Artweek Previews, San Jose, CA, 2002; and others. *Publ:* Numerous articles in New Art Examiner, Artweek, Ceramics Mo, Am Craft, Am Ceramics, 88-90. *Mailing Add:* 201 Eldridge Ave Mill Valley CA 94941

MAYES, ELAINE
PHOTOGRAPHER, VIDEO ARTIST
b Berkeley, Calif, Oct 1, 1938. *Study:* Stanford Univ, BA, 59; San Francisco Art Inst, with Paul Hassel, John Collier & Minor White. *Work:* San Francisco Art Inst; Mus Mod Art & Metrop Mus Art, NY; Minneapolis Inst Arts, Minn; Oakland Mus, Calif; and many others. *Exhib:* Photographs from Collection of Sam Wagstaff, Corcoran Gallery Art, DC, Grey Gallery, NY Univ, St Louis Mus, Mo, Seattle Mus Art, Wash & Berkeley Mus Art, Calif, 78-79; Ft Wayne Ind Mus Art, 88; Sandra Berler, Chevy Chase, Md, 80, 82, 84, 88, 90 & 96; Friends of Photog, 97; Monterey Art and Hist Asn, 01; Contemp Mus, Honolulu, 2003-04; Metrop Mus, 2005; Int Fototage, Cologne, 2005; Roded Rok Hall of Fame, Cleveland, 2005-06; Robert Burge, NY, 2007; Robert Burge, NY, 2007; Into the Sunset, Mus Mod Art, NY, 2009; Steven Kasher Gallery, New York, 2009; Who Shot Rock, Brooklyn Mus, New York, 2009; Mus Mod Art, San Francisco, 2010. *Pos:* prof Emer, Tisch Sch of Arts, New York City, currently. *Teaching:* Instr photog & filmmaking, Univ Minn, 68-70; assoc prof film & photog, Hampshire Col, 71-81 & Bard Col, 82-84; Chmn, Dept Photog, Tisch Sch Art, NY Univ, 84-2001, prof photog, prof emer, 2001-. *Awards:* Nat Endowment Arts, 71 & 78; CAPS, 82; Guggenheim, 91 & 92; Atherton Foun, 2002. *Mem:* Soc Photog Educ. *Media:* photography, video. *Collection:* Avon Collection, NY; Metropolitan Mus, NY; Getty Mus of Art, Calif; Boston Mus Fine Arts; Denver Mus Art; Philadelphia Mus Art; San Francisco Art Inst. *Publ:* Contribr, Faces: A History of Photographic Portraiture, Chanticleer Press, New York, 77; A Book of Photographs, by Sam Wagstaff, New York, 78; San Francisco Viewed, Chronicle Books, 85; The Cat in Photography, 90; Animal Attractions, Abrams, 94; Leg, 88; It Happened In Monterey, 03; and others; K: No Hawaii, Photographs of/from/about Hawaii, 2009. *Dealer:* Robert Burge New York NY; Steven Kasher Gallery New York NY; Morrison Hotel Gallery New York NY

MAYFIELD, SIGNE S
CURATOR
b Woodbury, NJ. *Study:* Univ Calif-Berkeley, BA (art hist), 65; George Washington Univ, MA Prog, Higher Education. *Collection Arranged:* David Park: Fixed Subjects, 94; Dominic DiMare: A Retrospective (tour), 97-99; Of Princely Courts & Pleasure Gardens: Indian Miniatures, 97-98; The Print is Cast, 99; The Thought of Things: KiffSlemmons (tour), 2000; Big Idea: The Maquettes of Robert Arneson (tour), 2002; Jim Campbell: Seeing Digital, 2004; The Gift: Surimono Prints from Bay Area Coll, 2005; Ideo Prototypes the future, 2006; Correspondence: Masami Teraoka & Ukiyo-e, 2007; Nathan Oliveira: The Painter's Bronzes, 2008; The Miniature Worlds of Bruce Metcalf (tour), 2008; Treasures from The Mexican Mus: A Spirited Legacy, 2009-; In the Realm of Nature: Bob Stocksdale & Kay Sekimachi (tour), 2014. *Pos:* Independent cur, 2010-; Cur, Palo Alto Art Ctr, 89-2010. *Mem:* Achenbach Graphic Arts Coun (bd dir), 90-97. *Publ:* Directions in Bay Area Printmaking: Three Decades; Christopher Brown: Works on Paper, 94; Dominic Di Mare: A Retrospective, 97; The Thought of Things: Jewelry by Kiff Slemmons, 2000; Big Idea: the Maquettes of Robert Arneson, 2002; Jim Campbell: Seeing Digital, 2004; Robert Brady: Sculpture 1989-2005; Nathan Oliveira: The Painter's Bronzes; The Miniature Worlds of Bruce Metcalf; In the Realm of Nature: Bob Stocksdale & Kay Sekimachi

MAYHEW, RICHARD
PAINTER
b Amityville, NY, April 3, 1934. *Study:* Art Students League; Brooklyn Mus Art Sch, studied with Edwin Dickinson and Reuben Tam, 51; Columbia Univ, New York, NY. *Work:* Whitney Mus Am Art; Nat Mus Am Art, Smithsonian Inst; Brooklyn Mus; Mus Mod Art; Nat Acad Design; and many others. *Exhib:* Butler Art Inst, Youngstown,

Ohio, 61; Univ Ill, 63; Hamilton Col, Clinton, NY, 1974, Montclair State Col, NJ, 1975; retrospective, Studio Mus, NY, 78; solo exhibs, San Jose Mus Art, 80, Pa State Univ Mus, 83 & Young Gallery, San Jose, 85; Group shows: Brooklyn Mus, Whitney Mus, Nat Acad of Design, Carnegie Inst, Chicago Art Inst, San Francisco Mus Art, NY Cult Ctr, New York City, Gallery Modern Art, New York City, Butler Inst, Ohio, Chicago Art Inst, Am Acad Arts and Letters, New Sch Social Res, Smith Col, San Francisco Mus Art, Pa Acad Fine Arts, Hampton Univ Mus, Va, 1986; Midtown Galleries, NY, 82-87. *Teaching:* Instr art, Brooklyn Mus Art Sch, 63-68 & Art Students League, 65-71; instr, Smith Col, 69-70; asst prof, Hunter Col, 71-75; San Jose State Univ, 1975-76; prof, Pa State Univ, 77-. *Awards:* Recipient Macdowell Colony award, 58; recipient Childe Hassam purchase award, 1963-64, purchase award Ford Foundation, 62, Henry Ward Ranger purchase award, 64, National Inst Arts and Letters award, 65; Benjamin Altman Award, Nat Acad Design, 70; Butler Institute award, 74; Merit Award, Nat Acad Design, 77; Grumbacher Gold Medal, Nat Acad Design, 83. *Mem:* Nat Acad; MacDowell Colony Asn. *Media:* Oil, Watercolor. *Dealer:* Midtown Payson Galleries 745 Fifth Ave New York NY 10151; Braunstein/Quay Gallery 545 Sutter St San Francisco CA 94115. *Mailing Add:* c/o Alitash Kebede Gallery 170 S La Brea Ave Los Angeles CA 90036

MAYHEW, TIMOTHY DAVID
PAINTER, DRAFTSMAN
b St Clair, Mich, 1952. *Study:* Univ Mich (undergrad studies through 74); Wayne State Univ, Doctorate, 78; studied landscape painting with Clyde Aspevig, 95, Matt Smith, 97-2007, Skip Whitcomb, 2007-09; studied wildlife painting with Bob Kuhn, 2000-07. *Work:* Mus Fine Arts, Boston; Fogg Art Mus, Cambridge, Mass; Univ NMex, Mus Fine Arts, Albuquerque; Straus Center for Conservation, Cambridge, Mass; Tamarind Inst, Albuquerque; Nat Gallery of Art, Wash DC; Nat Mus Wildlife Art, Jackson Hole, Wy; Philadelphia Mus Art; Woodson Art Mus, Wausau, Wisc. *Exhib:* Group shows, Am Art in Miniature, Thomas Gilcrease Mus, 94, 2004 & 2006-09; Duo Exhib, Cheyenne Frontier Days Old West Mus, Cheyenne, Wyo, 97; Behind the Line, Fogg Art Mus, Cambridge, Mass, 98; Gala & Miniature Show, Univ Wyo Art Mus, Laramie, Wyo, 98-99; Western Visions, Nat Mus Wildlife Art, Jackson, Wyo, 2004-13; Metalpoint Drawings, Mus Fine Arts, Boston, 2006; Birds in Art, Woodsen Art Mus, Wausau, Wis, 2010-11, 2013; Masters in Miniature, Trailside Galleries, Jackson, Wyo, 2011, 2013; Solo exhib, The Paintings and Drawings of Timothy David Mayhew, Nat Mus Wildlife Art, Jackson, NY, 2010; Beaux Arts, Scottsdale, Ariz, 92-2013; Saks Galleries, Denver, Colo, 2012; Laumeister Fine Art, Bennington Ctr Arts, Vt, 2012; Cheyenne Frontier Days Old West Mus Western Art Show, Cheyenne, Wyo, 2013. *Pos:* Prof artist (self employed), 1978-. *Teaching:* Vis instr, old master drawing materials & tech, Fogg Mus Art, 94-2012; instr, Scottsdale Ariz School. 2008. *Awards:* Robert Kuhn Award, Western Visions Exhib, Nat Mus Wildlife Art, Jackson, WT, 2010; Certificate of Recognition, Legislature NMex, July, 2011; Artistic Excellence Award, Southwest Art Mag, 2011. *Bibliog:* Edward Saywell (auth), Behind the Line, Harvard Univ Art Mus Bull, 98; Penley Knipe (auth), Grounds on Paper, Straus Center for Conservation, 98; Betty Johnson (auth), Wildlife Art, N Co Times, 2007; VP Sant, EA Powell III, (auths), Nat Gallery of Art, 2008. *Mem:* Plein Air NMex (2006-); Nat Acad Prof Plein Air Painters (signature mem, 2007-09). *Media:* Oil; Natural red chalk; Metalpoint; Natural black chalk, Natural white chalk, Natural yellow chalk. *Res:* Traditional Old Master Drawing Materials & Tech. *Publ:* Contribr, Touchstone, 200 Years of Artists' Lithographs, Harvard Univ Art Mus, 98; contribr, The Restoration of Drawings, Books and Other Roy Perkinson Works of Art on Paper, Getty Conserv Inst, 2006; auth, Natural Black Chalk in Traditional Old Master Drawings, Joun of the Am Inst for Conservation, Fall/Winter 2010; Steatite and Calcite Natural White Chalks in Traditional Old Master Drawings, Jour of the Am Inst for Conservation, 2012. *Dealer:* Rose John 7215 Dellwood Ct Farmington NM 87402. *Mailing Add:* Atelier Cedar Ridge 7215 Dellwood Ct Farmington NM 87402

MAYNARD, WILLIAM
PAINTER, EDUCATOR
b Brookline, Mass, Dec 31, 1921. *Study:* Mass Coll Art; Sch Mus Fine Arts, Boston, dipl, 50. *Work:* Boston Mus Fine Arts; Springfield Mus Fine Arts, Mass; Fairleigh Dickinson Univ; Fitchburg Mus Fine Arts; Tufts Univ; Mus Arts & Sci, Macon, Ga. *Exhib:* Shore Studio Galleries, Charles Childs Gallery & Vose Gallery, Boston; De Cordova Mus, Lincoln, Mass; Busche Reisinger Mus, Cambridge, Mass; J H Webb Gallery, Macon, Ga, 85. *Pos:* Chmn dept fine arts, New England Sch Art & Design, 74-. *Teaching:* Instr drawing & painting, Boston Mus Fine Arts, 60-67; instr painting, New Eng Sch Art & Design, formerly. *Mem:* New Eng Watercolor Soc; Provincetown Art Asn; Copley Soc; Brookline Soc Artists. *Media:* Watercolor, Acrylic. *Mailing Add:* 72A Commercial St Provincetown MA 02657

MAYNE, THOM
ARCHITECT
b Waterbury, Conn, Jan 19, 1944. *Study:* Univ Southern Calif, BArch, 68; Harvard Univ, MArch, 78. *Work:* Archit one-man exhib incl Cheney Cowles Mus, Spokane, Wash, 1989, San Francisco Mus Modern Art, 1990, Laguna (Calif) Art Mus, 1991, G201 Gallery, Ohio, 1991, Mus of Contemp Art, 1982 Mus Modern Art, San Francisco, 1983, Calif Mus Sci. and Indust, 1984 Cooper-Hewitt Mus, NY City, 1988 Deutsches Architektur Mus, Frankfurt, 1989. *Comn:* archit projs incl Sequoyah Educ and Res Ctr, Santa Monica, 1977 (Progressive Archit award 1974); Flores Residence, 1979 (Progressive Archit award 1980); Sedlak Residence, 1980 (Am Inst of Archits award 1981); Western Melrose Off Bldg, 1981 (Progressive Archit award 1982); Hermosa Beach Central Bus Dist (Progressive Archit award 1984); 72 Market St Restaurant, 1983 (Am Inst of Archits award 1985, CCAIA award 1986); Bergren Residence, 1984 (Am Inst of Archits award 1985, CCAIA award 1986, Nat Am Inst of Archits award 1986); Cedar Sinai Comprehensive Cancer Ctr, Los Angeles, 1988 (Progressive Archit award 1987, Am Ins of Archits award 1988, CCAIA award 1989),; Arts Park Performing Pavilion, 1988 (Progressive Archit award 1989); Leon Max Showroom, Los Angeles, 1988 (CCAIA award 1990, Archit Record Interior award 1990); Club Post Nuclear, Laguna Beach, Calif, 1988; Berlin Wall Competition, 1988; Expo '90 Folly, Osaka, Japan, 1989; The Emery Ctr Performing Arts, 1989; Temple Univ Commodity Credit Corp, Philadelphia, 1989; Politix, 1990 (Am Inst of Archits award 1990); Salick Health Care Corp Hdqs, 1990 (Am Inst of Archits award 1992, CCAIA award 1993); Visual Performing Arts Sch at Thomas More Col, Crestview, NY, 1990; MTV Studios, Los Angeles, 1990, Higashi Azabu Tower, Tokyo, 1991; Disney Inst and Town Ctr Competition, Orlando, Fla, 1991; Cranbrook Acad Gatehouse Competition (Pilkington Planar prize 1993); Spreebogen Master Plan, Berlin, 1993, Check Point Charlie Off Bldg, Berlin, 1993. *Exhib:* Solo exhibs, 2 AES Gallery, San Francisco, 88, Walker Arts Ctr, Minneapolis, 89, Gallery of Archit, Los Angeles, 89, Contemp Arts Ctr, Cincinnati, 89, Graham Found, Chicago, 90, Aedes Galerie and Archit Forum, Berlin, 90, Fenster Archit, Frankfurt, Ger, 90, Gallery MA, Tokyo, 90, G201 Gallery, Ohio, 91, 1-Space Gallery, Chicago, 92, Sadock & Uzzan Galerie, Paris, 1992, Diane Farris Gallery, 93; group exhibs, Umwelt Galerie, Stuttgart, Ger, 1978, The Archit Gallery, Venice, Calif, 1979, Inst Contemp Arts, London, 83, Archit Assoc, London, 83, Nat Acad of Design, New York City, 83, 88, G A Gallery, Tokyo, 85, 87, 90, Max Protech Gallery, New York City, 85, 86, IDC, New York City, 86, Axis Gallery, Tokyo, Milan, Paris, 88, Pacific Design Ctr, Los Angeles, 88, Australia Ctr for Contemp Arts, Victoria, 88, Aedes Galerie für Archit und Raum, Berlin, 88, Kirsten Kiser Gallery, 88, 89, Visual Arts Ontario, Toronto, 88, Gallery Functional Art, Santa Monica, Calif, 89, US Info Agency, Moscow, 89-90, Lameier Sculpture Park, St Louis, 89, Gwenda Jay Gallery, Chicago, 90, Sadock & Uzzan Galerie, 191, Bannatyne Gallery, Santa Monica, 91, ROM Galleri for Arkitektur, Oslo, 92, 65 Thompson St Gallery, New York City, 92. *Pos:* Mem fac, UCLA Sch Art and Archit, Santa Monica, Calif, 72-; bd dir, Southern Calif Inst Archit, 83-; archit Morphosis. *Teaching:* Vis fac, Calif State Col, Pomona, 71, Miami Univ, Ohio, 82, Wash Univ, St Louis, 84, Univ Tex, Austin, 84, Univ Pa, 85, Columbia Univ, New York City, 86, Harvard Univ, 88, Clemson Univ, 91, Yale Univ, 91, UCLA, 86, 92, Univ Ill, Urbana-Champaign, 92-93, Tech Univ, Vienna, Austria, 93, Berlage Inst, Amsterdam, 93, Hochschule für Andgewandt Kunst, Vienna, 91, 93; Adj prof, UCLA, 93; lectr in field. *Awards:* Rome Prize fel, Am Acad Rome, 87; Archit award, Am Acad Arts & Letts, 92. *Mem:* Am Instit of Archit; Nat Acad; Am Acad Arts & Letts. *Publ:* contributor articles to prof jour

MAYO, MARGARET ELLEN
CURATOR
b Charlottesville, Va, May 18, 1944. *Study:* Randolph-Macon Women's Col, AB, 66; Rutgers Univ, PhD, 73. *Collection Arranged:* Ancient Portraiture: The Sculptor's Art in Coins and Marble, 80 & The Art of South Italy: Vases From Magna Graecia (auth, catalog), 82, Va Mus; Wealth of the Ancient World: The Nelson Bunker Hunt and William Herbert Hunt Collections (coauth, catalog), 83. *Pos:* Res assoc, Iconographical Lexicon, Rutgers Univ, 73-76; dir, Summa Galleries, Beverly Hills, 76-78; cur, Ancient Art, Va Mus, 78-. *Mem:* Archaeol Inst Am; Soc Promotion Hellenic Studies. *Res:* Greek art; Greek and south Italian vase-painting. *Mailing Add:* Va Museum Fine Art 200 N Blvd Richmond VA 23220-4007

MAYO, MARTI
MUSEUM DIRECTOR, CURATOR
b Bluefield, WVa, Oct 17, 1945. *Study:* Am Univ, BA, 70, MFA, 74. *Collection Arranged:* Vernon Fisher Story Paintings & Drawings (auth, catalog), 80; The New Photography (auth, catalog), 80; Placements and Performances: Works for Washington, 80; Other Realities: Installations for Performance (auth, catalog), 81; 4 Painters: Jones, Smith, Stack, Utterback (auth, catalog), 81; Robert Morris: Selected Works 1970-1980 (auth, catalog), 81; Paintings by Pat Steir (auth, catalog), 83; Michael Tracy: Requiem Para Los Olvidados (auth, catalog), 83; Southern Fictions, 83; Recent works of Robert Helm, 84; Paintings by Mark Tansey, 85; Barbara Kruger: Striking Poses, 85; Robert Rauschenberg: Work from Four Series, 86; Works of Joseph Glasco, 86; Images on Stone: Two Centuries of Artists Lithographs, 87; 6 Artists: 6 Idioms, 88; Gael Stack: A Survey 1974-1989, 89; Reinventing Reality: Five Tex Photogrs, 90. *Pos:* Asst dir, Jefferson Place Gallery, Washington, DC, 73-74; coordr exhib, Corcoran Gallery Art, DC, 74-80; cur, Contemp Arts Mus, Houston, 80-86; dir, Blaffer Gallery, Univ Houston, 86-94, dir, chief cur, 1994-2007; vpres Cultl Arts Coun Houston/Harris Co; mem rev panel Inst of Mus & Libr Servs; panelist Nat Endowment for Arts, Tex Comn on Arts. *Teaching:* Contemp art & criticism, Glassell Sch Art, Mus Fine Arts, Houston, 84-86; Art since 1960, Univ Houston, 86-91. *Mem:* Am Asn Mus; Coll Art Asn; Asn Art Mus Dirs; Am Fedn Arts (bd trustees). *Publ:* Auth, Robert & Morris: Selected Works 70-80 (exhib catalog), 81; Robert Rauschenberg: A Chronology (exhib catalog), Contemp Arts Mus, Houston, 86; Joseph Glasco: 1948-1986 (exhib catalog), Contemp Art Mus, Houston, 86; Gael Stack (exhib catalog), Univ Houston, 88; Northwest x Southwest: Painted Fictions (exhib catalog), Palm Springs Desert Mus, 90; and others

MAYO, PAMELA ELIZABETH
CONSULTANT, FINE ART APPRAISER
b Richmond, Va, June 18, 1959. *Study:* Longwood Col, BFA, 81. *Collection Arranged:* Lue Osborne & Cordray Simmons, Am Regionalists (auth, catalog), 80; Am, the Sporting View, Sporting Art (ed, catalog), 85; The Art of Doris Spiegel (auth, catalog); A Critical Eye, 2008. *Pos:* Dir & appraiser, Gallery Mayo Inc, Richmond, Va, 81-95; appraiser fine art, 86-. *Mem:* Int Soc Appraisers; Phi Kappa Phi. *Specialty:* Late 19th-early 20th century American art. *Mailing Add:* 710 Washington St Sewickley PA 15143

MAYO, ROBERT BOWERS
ART DEALER, COLLECTOR
b Phoenixville, Pa, 1933. *Study:* Art Students League, 49; Chicago Art Inst, 51; Richmond Prof Inst (Va Commonwealth Univ), BA, 59. *Collection Arranged:* Thomas Sully & His Contemporaries, 78; Mrs Susan Waters, 19th Century Itinerant Painter, 79; Am Paintings from Virginia Collectors, 81; Am: The Sporting View (auth, catalog), 85. *Pos:* Cur, Jamestown Festival Park, Va, 59-61; exhibs designer, Arch

Hist, Raleigh, NC, 61-66; dir, Valentine Mus, Richmond, 66-75; coordr & dir, Am Art Studies Group, Richmond, formerly; owner, Gallery Mayo Inc, currently. *Teaching:* Guest lectr, NY Hist Soc, Cooperstown, summer 72 & Longwood Coll, Farmville, Va, 79. *Mem:* Am Asn Mus (nat coun, 73-77); SEastern Mus Conf Inc (pres, 74); Va Mus Fedn (vpres, 72-73); Antiquarian Soc Richmond (pres, 74-75); Collector's Circle, Va Mus Fine Arts; Am Soc Appraisers (formerly). *Specialty:* 19th & 20th century Am art. *Interests:* Collector of early American Sporting Art - 19th & early 20th century. *Collection:* Am Sporting Art; 19th & early 20th century American art. *Publ:* Auth, Exhibit techniques for small museums, Mus News, 73; Painting collection of the Valentine Museum, Mag Antiques, 73; America: The Sporting View, 85. *Mailing Add:* 11758 River Crest Dr Gloucester VA 23061

MAYRS, DAVID BLAIR
PAINTER, EDUCATOR
b Winnipeg, Man, May 2, 1935. *Study:* Vancouver Sch Art, dipl (hon), 57. *Work:* Vancouver Art Gallery; London Pub Libr & Art Mus, Ont; Etherington Art Ctr. *Exhib:* New Talent Show, Vancouver Art Gallery, 64; Young Contemporaries, London Art Mus, Ont, 65; Canadian Group of Painters, Montreal Mus Fine Art, 67; Nat Gallery Can Bi-Ann, 68; Young Vancouver Artists, Victoria Art Gallery, 68; H Marc Moyens Collection, Corcoran Gallery Art, 69; West Coast Artists, Sadie F Bronfman Ctr, Montreal, 75; BC Artists, Vancouver Art Gallery, 83; Mus Modern Art, Toyama, Japan, 87. *Teaching:* Instr painting & silkscreen, Emily Carr Col Art, Vancouver, 67-. *Awards:* Purchase Award, Burnaby Art Gallery Print Show, 71. *Media:* Acrylic. *Mailing Add:* 440 Ellis St North Vancouver BC V7H 2G6 Canada

MAYS, PETER
GALLERY DIRECTOR
Pos: Contributing writer, art critic, Pittsburgh Buss, gallery dir, Clark Gallery, chmn Steering Com, Community Technology and Discovery Ctr, Los Angeles, formerly; dir development and supplementary educ services, Galef Inst, Los Angeles, formerly; joined, Los Angeles Art Asn, 2005, exec dir, currently. *Mailing Add:* Los Angeles Art Association 825 N La Cienega Blvd Los Angeles CA 90069

MAYS, VICTOR
PAINTER, ILLUSTRATOR
b New York, NY, 1927. *Study:* Yale Univ, BA, 49. *Work:* De Grummond Collection of Children's Book Illus, Univ Southern Miss; Kerlan Collection, Univ Minn; Peabody Mus, Salem, Mass; Mystic Seaport Mus; Submarine Force Mus; Conn River Mus. *Comn:* Illusr for children's bks, major US publ, 55-. *Exhib:* Mystic Seaport, Conn, 79-82; Peabody Mus, 81; Mariners Mus, 85-86; Md Hist Soc, 89; Mystic Maritime Int, 90-2007; Mystic Seaport Mus, 92-94; Frye Art Mus, Seattle, 97; Cummer Mus, Fla, 98; Cape Mus Fine Arts, Mass, 2001; Cornell Mus, Fla, 2011; Mobile Mus, Ala, 2012; Mus Southeast Tex, 2012; Mus South Tex, 2012; Haggin Mus, Calif, 2013; Coos Art Mus, Oreg, 2013; Minn Marine Art Mus, 2013. *Awards:* Best in Show, Mystic Seaport Mus, Conn, 80, First & Second Prize Watercolor, 81 & Best in Show, Mystic Int Marine Art Exhib, 83, Award of Excellence, 86, 87, 97, 2000, 2002, 2008, 2009, & 2011. *Bibliog:* Bound for Blue Water, Jinishian, 2003; Romance of the Sea (film), CPTV, 2001. *Mem:* Am Soc Marine Artists (fellow). *Media:* Watercolor. *Publ:* Auth & illusr, Fast Iron, 53, Action Starboard, 55, Dead Reckoning, 65. *Dealer:* Kirsten Gallery Roosevelt Way NE Seattle WA 98103; Mystic Maritime Gallery Mystic CT 06355; Sylvan Gallery Main St Wiscasset ME 04578; Edwards Studio Block Island RI 02807. *Mailing Add:* 10 Shoreland Dr Apt 313 Belfast ME 04915

MAYTHAM, THOMAS NORTHRUP
FINE ARTS CONSULTANT
b Buffalo, NY, July 30, 1931. *Study:* Williams Coll, BA, 54; Yale Univ, MA, 56. *Exhib:* Alvan T Fuller Collection, Boston Mus Fine Arts; Eighteenth Cent Venetian painting, Boston Mus Fine arts; Hidden Treasures, Boston Mus; Ernst Ludwig Kirchner Retrospective, Seattle Art Mus; Great Am Paintings from the Boston and Metro Art Mus, Nat Gallery, Washington, DC, St Louis & Seattle Art Mus. *Collection Arranged:* Ernst Ludwig Kirchner Retrospective (148 works), Seattle Art Mus, Pasadena Art Mus & Boston Mus, 68-69; Great Am Paintings from the Boston & Metropolitan Mus (100 paintings, with catalog), Nat Gallery Art, City Art Mus, St Louis & Seattle Art Mus, 70-71; and others. *Pos:* Asst, Wadsworth Atheneum, summer 55; res asst, Prof Carroll L V Meeks, Yale Univ, summer 56; asst in dept paintings, Mus Fine Arts, Boston, 56-57; head dept paintings, Boston Mus, 57-67; assoc dir, Seattle Art Mus, 67-74; dir, Denver Art Mus, 74-83, consult, 83-. *Teaching:* Lectr, mus, clubs, groups & art asns, Boston, Seattle, Denver, Nat Gallery, Wash & Portland Art Mus, Maine & Ore. *Awards:* Governors Art Award, Colorado; Governors Art Award, Seattle-Tacoma Airport Art Proj. *Mem:* Am Asn Mus; Humanities Inst Univ Colo (bd mem); Asn Art Mus Dirs; Int Exhib Found; Colo Coun on Arts and Humanities; United Arts Fund. *Publ:* Auth, articles in Boston Mus Bull, Antiques & Can Art; ed, American Painting in the Boston Museum & Metropolitan Museum of Art (catalog), Vols I & II, 68; auth, TV Prog for Nat Educ TV, produced by Boston Mus & WGBH-TV; Heritage Am Art (Slide/Tape) Publ Metro Mus Art, 77-. *Mailing Add:* 3882 S Newport Way Denver CO 80237

MAZER, MIKE
PAINTER, ARTIST
b Boston, Mass, May 17, 1936. *Study:* Studied with Betty Lou Schlemm, AWS, DF, Robert Wade, AWS, John Stobart, Joseph Mcgurl. *Work:* New Bedford Free Pub Libr, Mass; US Coast Guard, Washington, DC; Tabor Acad, Marion, Mass; Mass Dept of Environ Protection; Marion Art Ctr, Mass; New Bedford Art Mus, Mass; New Bedford Whaling Mus, Mass; Mattapoisett Historical Soc & Mus; Mass Maritime Acad, Buzzards Bay, Mass. *Comn:* Painting art work for Festival of Trees invitation, New Bedford Art Mus, Mass, 2006. *Exhib:* Watercolor USA, Springfield Art Mus, Mo, 2003; Taos Nat, Watercolor Exhib, Taos Art Mus, 2004 & 2007-09; 11th Ann Marine Art Exhib, Coos, Art Mus, Ore, 2004; Am Soc Marine Artist, 13th Nat, Vero Beach Art Mus, Fla, 2004; Mississippi Grand Nat'l Exhib, Miss, Mus of Art, Jackson, 2004; Nat Watercolod Soc exibs, 2007; Zeeland Maritime Mus, Vlissingen. Holland, 2009; solo exhib, New Bedford Art Mus, 2006-07, Cape Cod Mus Art, 2009; New Bedford Whaling Mus, 2010; Am Soc Marine Artists, 2011-2013; and over 500 nat exhibs, exhibs in 37 mus. *Pos:* Pres, New England Watercolor Soc, 2004-2007. *Awards:* Best in Show, Miss Grand Nat, 2003; Best in Show, RI WC Soc, 2004 & 2006; Frank C Wright Mem Award, AAPL, 2004; 1st Place Canton Art Assoc, Canton, Mass, 2004; Best in Show, Stoughton Art Assoc, Mass, 2004; Special Recognition, 7th Ann Realism Int Exhib, Upstream Gallery, Omaha, Nebr, 2005; Founder's Award, Philadelphia, 2005; Best of Show, Arts Affair, Quincy, Mass, 2006; Paint the Parks, Top 100, 2008; Paint Am Top 100, 2009, 2010, 2011; 1st pl, North Shore Arts Asn, 2010; 1st pl Cape Cod Art Asn, All New England Exhib, 2010; Award of Excellence, 2010; Taos Soc Watercolorists Nat, Tex, 2010; Howard Curtis Mem Award, Excellence in Marine Painting, North Shore Arts Asn, 2010; and over 100 total awards. *Bibliog:* The Standard Times, South Coast Today, Newpaper, Written by David B Boyce, 7/18/2001, 8/25/2004; South Coast Artist Mike Mazer's Work Exhibited Across the Country, Wicked Local, 2012. *Mem:* New England Watercolor Soc; Acad Artists Asn; Nat Soc Artists; The Salmagundi Club; Allied Artists Am; Watercolor USA (hon soc); Am Artists Prof League (fel); Pa Watercolor Soc; Transparent Watercolor Soc Am; Taos Nat Soc Watercolorists; over 37 signature mem in nat and int soc. *Media:* Watercolor Painter. *Publ:* Contemp Am Marine Arts, 2002, 2004, 2011; Splash 9 Tips & Techniques, North Light Bks, F & W Pub, 2006; Splash 10, North Light Bks, 2008; Artistic Touch 4, Creative Arts Press, 2010, Artistic Touch 5, 2012; Image of New Bedford Whaleman Statue (cover), A Bold and Hardy Race of Men, Univ Mass Press, 2013. *Dealer:* Roger's Gallery, Mattapoisett MA. *Mailing Add:* 7 Holly Woods Rd Mattapoisett MA 02739

MAZZE, IRVING
SCULPTOR, MEDALIST
b New York, NY. *Study:* With Beth Sutherland, 72; with Hermann Gass & Richard Hahn, 77. *Work:* Residenz Mus Munzsammlung, Munich; Cabinet Medailles, Bibliot Nat, Paris; Proust Mus, France. *Comn:* Citrine portrait, comn by Alice Whitfield, NY, 74; moonstone portrait, comn by Louise Benton, Chicago, 75; moonstone portrait Marcel Proust, comn by Mr & Mrs Milton Stern, Long Island, 75; crystal engraving, comn by James Van Aken, NY, 83; topaz engraving, comn by John Sinkankas for Smithsonian Inst, 84. *Exhib:* Sculpture Showcase Gallery, Pa, 95; Mus d'Art & d'Histoire, Neuchatel, 96; Residenz Mus, Munich, 96; Isao Gallery, Nara, Japan, 96; Gallery Heian, Kyoto, 96; Rock & Hamper Gallery, NY, 97; Mus Beelden aan Zee, The Neth, 98. *Pos:* Consult engraved gemstones, Dept Mineralogy, Am Mus Natural Hist, 79-. *Bibliog:* Beverly Philip Mazze (auth), The making of a gem engraver, Lapidary J, 6/73; John Sinkairkas (auth), Gem Cutting, Van Nostrand Reinhold, 84; Ingrid Weber (auth), Geschnittene Steine des 18, bis 20, Jahrhunderts, Deutscher Kunstverlag, 96. *Mem:* Am Medallic Sculpture Asn; Royal Soc Arts; Fedn Int Medaille. *Media:* Gemstone

MCADOO, CAROL WESTBROOK
CERAMIST, PAINTER
b Colonial Heights, Va, Dec 28, 1937. *Study:* Self taught. *Work:* Lauren Rogers Mus, Laurel, Miss; NCNB Art Collection, Charlotte, NC; P Hanes Collection, Winston-Salem, NC; AT&T Corp; Coca-Cola Corp. *Comn:* Mag cover, Brown's Guide to Georgia, Atlanta, 73. *Exhib:* Piedmont Painting & Sculpture, Mint Mus Art, Charlotte, NC, 71; 4th Realist Exhib, Southeastern Ctr Contemp Art, Winston-Salem, NC, 72; Rogers Mus Exhib, Lauren Rogers Mus, Laurel, Miss, 72; Solo exhibs, Mint Mus Art, Charlotte, NC, 73 & Wilson Arts Coun, NC, 75; Soc Four Arts, Palm Beach, Fla, 73; Catherine Lorillard Wolfe, Nat Arts Club, NY, 80. *Teaching:* Private lessons. *Awards:* 3rd Place, Cape Coral Nat Exhib, 71; Purchase Award, Lauren Rogers Mus, 72; 1st Place Painting, 23rd Ann Poplar Lawn Art Festival, 81. *Mem:* Nat Soc Painters Casein & Acrylic; South Cobb Arts Alliance; SEastern Ctr Contemp Art. *Media:* Clay; Acrylic. *Publ:* Auth, Reflections of the Outer Banks, Island Publ House, 76. *Dealer:* Edward L Greene Box 265 Manteo NC 27954. *Mailing Add:* c/o Edward L Greene Box 265 Manteo NC 27954

MCALLISTER, GERALDINE E
GALLERY DIRECTOR
b Asher, Okla, Sept 22, 1925. *Study:* Univ Calif, San Diego, BA, 72, MFA, 74. *Pos:* Dir, Mandeville Gallery, Univ Calif, San Diego, 75-. *Mem:* Nat Soc Arts & Lett; Univ Calif & San Diego Alumni Asn (pres). *Mailing Add:* 1705 Malden St San Diego CA 92109-2207

MCCABE, ELSIE CRUM
MUSEUM DIRECTOR
Study: Barnard Coll, New York, grad, 1981. *Pos:* Sr litigator, Shearman & Sterling, New York, formerly; chief of staff for Mayor David N Dinkins, 1990-93; co-founder, Nat Urban Technol Ctr, 1995; pres, Mus African Art, New York, 1997-. *Mem:* Asn Art Mus Dirs. *Mailing Add:* Museum of African Art 1280 5th Ave Apt 20A New York NY 10020

MCCABE, MAUREEN M
COLLAGE ARTIST
b Quincy, Mass, June 12, 1947. *Study:* RI Sch Design, Providence, BFA, 69; Cranbrook Acad Art, Bloomfield Hills, Mich, MFA, 71. *Work:* RI Sch Design; Wadsworth Atheneum, Hartford, Conn; Kogod Collection, Washington, DC; Hollis Taggart Galleries; Barry Friedman, NY; Michael Monroe, Bellevue, Wash. *Exhib:* One-person shows, Gallery K, Washington, DC, 72, 75, 79, 82, 84, 87 & 95, Allan Stone Gallery, NY, 72, 75, 77, Phyllis Kind Gallery, Chicago, 78, Lyman Allyn Art Mus, New London, Conn, 81, Marianne Deson Gallery, Chicago, 84, Barry Friedman, Ltd, 85, Sackler Gallery, Stamford, Conn, 90, Cooley Gallery, Old Lyme, Conn, 95, 2011, Mattatuck Mus, Conn, 96, Perimeter Gallery, Chicago, 98, Network Gallery, Cranbrook Acad Art, Pontiac, Mich, 99, ALVA Gallery, New London, Conn, 2000, 2003, Kouros Gallery, New York City, 2001, 2003, Vose Gallery, 2005, Bellevue Mus,

2006, Parthenon Mus, 2007-2008; Museo Tamayo, Mexico City, 85; Excavating Cult, Brattleboro Mus & Art Ctr, Vt, 96; Metaphor for Ireland, Boston Univ, Fuller Bldg Gallery, Mass, 97; Art Chicago 1998, Barry Friedman Ltd, Navy Pier, Chicago, 98; Allan Stone Gallery, New York City, 2000; 9th Int Exhib Contemp Collage, Paris, France, 2002; Realism Now, Vose Galleries, 2003; Art Athina, Contemporary Art Fair, Greece, 2003; Remembering Marc and Komei, Katzen Arts Ctr, Am Univ Mus, 2006; The Image in the Box, Hollis Taggart Galleries, NY, 2008-2009; Hollis Taggart Galleries, Art Wynwood Internat Contemporary Art Fair, Miami, Fla, 2014. *Teaching:* Prof studio art, Conn Col, New London, 71-2011, retired. *Awards:* Residence Grant, Cite des Arts, Paris, 77-78; Individual Artist Grant, Conn Comn Arts, 80; MacDowell Fel, 88; Rockefeller Fel, Bellagio, Italy, 88; John S King Fac Teaching Award, Conn Col, 97-98; named Joanne Toor Cummings prof studio art, 2001. *Media:* Mixed Media. *Mailing Add:* 50 Old Norwich Rd Box 346 Quaker Hill CT 06375

MCCAFFERTY, JAY DAVID
VIDEO ARTIST, PAINTER

b San Pedro, Calif, Feb 21, 1948. *Study:* Los Angeles State Col, BA; Univ Calif, Irvine, MFA. *Work:* Los Angeles Co Mus Art; Long Beach Mus Art. *Exhib:* Solo exhibs, Grapestake Gallery, San Francisco, 78 & Cirrus Gallery, Los Angeles, 79, Mark Moore Gallery, Santa Monica, Calif, 2005; Baudoin Lebon, Paris, France, 80; Los Angeles Co Mus Art, 81; Cirrus Gallery, Los Angeles, 85 & 90; Works Gallery, Long Beach, Calif, 89; Mark Moore Gallery, Santa Monica, Calif, 94-96, 99; Video, J Paul Getty Mus, Calif, 2008; Museo Nat Ctr De Arte Reina Sofia, 2010. *Teaching:* Vis lectr art, World Campus Afloat, Chapman Col, 1974-2008; instr to prof, Los Angeles Harbor Col, Wilmington, Calif, 1976-2014; instr, Claremont Col Grad Sch Art, 78; vis lectr, Univ Calif, Irvine, 80. *Awards:* New Talent Award, Los Angeles Co Mus Art, 74; Nat Endowment for Arts Fel, 76. *Bibliog:* Joseph Youth (auth), Los Angeles, Art Int, 1/75; article, Art News, 9/83; article, Rick Gilbert (auth), Art Week, 2004. *Media:* Sun, Paper, Video. *Dealer:* Cirrus Gallery 409 S Manhattan Pl Los Angeles CA 90001. *Mailing Add:* 1017 Beacon St San Pedro CA 90731

MCCALL, ANN
PAINTER, PRINTMAKER

b Toronto, Ont, Dec 12, 1941. *Study:* McGill Univ, Montreal, BA, 64; Univ Pittsburgh, 71-73; Concordia Univ, Montreal, BFA, 78. *Work:* DeCordova Mus, Lincoln, Mass; Vancouver Art Gallery, BC; Winnipeg Art Gallery, Man; Can Coun Art Bank, Ottawa; Mus Lodz, Poland; McGill Univ, Rare Books Library, McGill Univ, La Bibliotheque National de Quebec, Montreal, Loto Quebec, Montreal; Thomas More Inst, Montreal. *Comn:* Edition (100) of Prints for Les Femmeuses Exhibition, Pratt & Whitney, Montreal. *Exhib:* Solo exhibs, Galerie Clair0Obscur, Montreal, 2004, Musee Pierre-Boucher, Trois-Rivieres, 2005, Galerie Jean-Claude Bergeron, Ottawa, 2005, Malaspina Printmakers,Vancouver, 2005, Night Series, Collagraphs at Galerie St Ambroise, Montreal, 2008, Galerie Jean Claude Bergeron, Ottawa, 2008, Artist's Proof Gallery, Alberta Printmakers' Soc, Calgary, 2009, Nature decoupee, Atelier Alain Piroir, Montreal, 2010, Galerie Jean-Claude Bigeron, Ottawa, Arborescence, Centre d'expositions di Repentiary, 2014, Convergence, Callagraphs, Galerie Jean-Claude Bergeron, 2014, Duo exhibition: Galerie 3C, Montreal, 2014; Group exhibs, Cracow Print Biennale: Cracow, Poland, 78, 80, 88; Rockford Int, Ill, 79, 81, 83; World Print III, San Francisco, 80; Norwegian Int Print Biennial, Frederikstad, Norway, 80, 82, 84; Biennale Graphic Art, Ljubljana, 81, 83; 7th & 8th British Int Print Biennial, Bradford, Eng, 82, 86; Listowel Int Print Biennale, Ireland, 86; Premio de Grabado Maximo Rames, Ferrol, Spain, 87, 90; Int Print Bienale, LVIV, Russia, 90; McClure Gallery, Montreal, 99; M Gibson Gallery, London, Ont, 98-2002; Gallery 418, Montreal, 2003; Time Remembered, Time Past, Boston Printmakers Mems, 2004; Exposition, Instituto Cultural de Peru, Lima; Biennale for Gravure, Sarcelles, Invited artist, 2009; Ottawa Sch Art, Int Juried Print Exhib, 2009; The Print Show, Galerie John B Aird, Toronto, 2014; Hibernus, Royal Canadian Acad Arts, 2014. *Teaching:* Saidye Brontman Centre for the Arts, Montreal, Silkscreen Printing, 92-2005. *Awards:* Purchase Award, Burnaby Biennale, BC, 77; Merit Awards, Boston Printmakers Exhib, 77 & 83; Grant, Atelier de Ile, Val David, Québec, 02; Co-winner, Martin O'Hara Award, Thomas More Inst Exhib, Montreal, 2008; Purchase Award, Ottawa Sch Art Int Exhib Miniature Prints, 2010. *Bibliog:* Diana Nemiroff (auth), article, Vie des Arts, 78; Virginia Nixon (auth), article, The Montrealer, 82; CBC Radio Interview, Exhibition at Gallerie Clair-Obscur, 2004. *Mem:* Boston Printmakers; Print & Drawing Coun Can; Visual Arts Ont; Royal Can Acad Arts (pres); Regroupement pour la promotion de l'art imprimé; Print Consortium; Print Coun Australia. *Media:* Acrylic; Silkscreen; Collagraphy; Mixed Media. *Interests:* Incorporating weather patterns into works through nature based imagery and symbols. *Dealer:* La Guilde Graphique 9 St Paul Ouest Montreal Que Can; Open Studio 401 Richmond St Toronto Ont Can; Galerie Jean-Claude 150 St Patrick St Bergeron Ottawa; Malaspina Printmakers Granville Island Vancouver BC

MCCALL, ANTHONY
FILMMAKER, CONCEPTUAL ARTIST

b London, Eng, Apr 14, 1946. *Study:* Whitgift Sch, Croydon, Eng, 1956-64; Ravensbourne Coll Art & Design, Bromley, Kent, Eng, 1964-68, BA (first class hons), 1968. *Work:* Royal Belgium Film Arch, Brussels; Arts Coun of Gt Brit, London; Mus of Mod Art, NY; Whitney Mus Am Art, NY; Ctr Georges Pompidou, Paris. *Comn:* Designing a Virtual Art Mus, 1996. *Exhib:* Documenta, Kassel, Ger, 1977; Film as Film, 1910 to the Present, Kunstverein, Cologne, 1978; Int Film Theory Conf 5, Univ Wis-Milwaukee, 1979; Edinburgh Int Film Festival, 1980; Berlin Film Festival, 1981; Whitney Mus Am Art, NY, 2001, 2004; Tate Modern, London, 2002; Gagosian Gallery, London, 2004; Sean Kelly Gallery, NY, 2007; Eclipse, BAM Fisher, Brooklyn Acad Music, 2012. *Pos:* founder, Anthony McCall Assoc, 1979; founder, & managing partner Narrative Rooms LLC, 1996. *Teaching:* Instr, London Col Printing, 1970-71; vis lectr avant-garde film theory, New York Univ Dept of Cinema Studies, 1977. *Awards:* Marie-Josi Prize 5th Int Experimental Competition, Knokke, Belg, 1975; Creative Artists Prog Serv Grant, 1976; Film Production Grant, New York State Coun Arts, 1981; John S Guggenheim Mem Found Fel, 2008. *Bibliog:* Annette Michelson & P Adams Sitney (coauth), A on Knokke and the independent filmmaker, Artforum, 5/75; Jane Weinstock (auth), The subject of argument, Downtown Rev, Vol 1, No 1; E Ann Kaplan (auth), Feminist approaches to history, psychoanalysis and cinema in Sigmund Freud's Dora, Millennium Film J, fall/winter 1981; and others. *Publ:* Flim, Line Describing a Cone, 1973; author: (article) Visitors Online. *Mailing Add:* 11 Jay St New York NY 10013

MCCALLUM, CORRIE PARKER
INSTRUCTOR, PAINTER

b Sumter, SC, Mar 14, 1914. *Study:* Univ SC, cert fine arts, 36; Boston Mus Sch, with Karl Zerbe. *Work:* La State Univ, Baton Rouge; SC Arts Comn, State Collection; Columbia Mus Arts, SC; Ford Motor Co; Mint Mus Art; and others. *Comn:* Mural, Home Federal Bank, 62. *Exhib:* Contemp Artists of SC (with catalog), Greenville Mus; Solo exhib, Concourse Gallery, State St Bank, Boston, Mass, 71; Art in Transition, Boston Mus Fine Arts, 77; Southeastern Contemp Art, Winston Salem, NC, 88; Gibbes Mus Art, Charleston SC, 89; Spoleto Festival USA, 91 & 92; solo retrospective, Gibbes Mus Art, 94. *Pos:* Emer printmaker, Southern Graphics Coun, 84. *Teaching:* Cur art educ for Charleston Co, Gibbes Art Gallery, 60-69; instr painting & drawing, Newberry Col, SC, 69-71; instr painting, drawing & printmaking, Col Charleston, 71-79. *Awards:* Purchase Prize for Drawing, Mint Mus Graphics Ann, 64; Painting Award, Guild SC Artists Ann, 65; Scientific Educ Found Grant for Travel & Study Around the World, 68. *Bibliog:* Jack Morris (auth), Contemp Artists of South Carolina, 70; Art in Transition, Boston Mus, 77. *Media:* All Media. *Publ:* Illusr, Dutch Fork Farm Boy, & 50 Years Along the Way, 68, Univ SC; coauth, A Travel Sketchbook, R L Bryan Co, 71; Corrie McCallum, A Life in Art, 94; Expressions: Images and Poems, Gibbes Mus Art, 97. *Dealer:* Kunstsalon Wolfsberg Bederstrasse 109 Zurich Switz; Halsey-McCallum Studio 20 Fulton St Charleston SC 29401

MCCANNEL, LOUISE WALKER
COLLECTOR

b Minneapolis, Minn, Nov 20, 1915. *Study:* Smith Col, BA; Minneapolis Sch Art. *Pos:* Bd mem, Walker Art Ctr, Minneapolis, currently. *Collection:* Contemporary American sculpture and painting

MCCARDWELL, MICHAEL THOMAS
GRAPHIC ARTIST, PAINTER

b Shelbyville, Ky, Aug 30, 1949. *Study:* Murray State Univ, BFA, 71; Morehead State Univ, MA, 74; Univ Louisville, tchg cert, 76. *Work:* Evansville, Ind Mus Arts and Sci. *Exhib:* JB Speed Mus Eight State Show, JB Speed Mus, Louisville, 85, Ky Art Exhib, 86; 38th Mid-State Art Exhib, Evansville Mus Arts and Sci, Ind, 85, 38th Mid-State Art Exhib, 85, 5th Ann Realism Today, 87; July Juried Exhib, Floyd Co Mus, Ind, 86, 88, 89, 96; Brand Libr Art Galleries, Glendale, Calif, 87-88; Visions VI Int, Cathedral Found, Cincinnati, 96, 2000. *Teaching:* Art teacher, Henry Co High Sch, 78-2005, Spalding Univ, 2003, KCTCS, 2005-2006, Ky Arts Mktg Prog, 2007. *Awards:* Junta Woods Aiken Purchase Award, Evansville Mus, 85; First Place Drawing Award, Cathedral Basilica of the Assumption, 96; Al Smith grantee Ky Arts Coun, 98; fel Nat Endowment for the Humanities, Western Ky Univ, 92 & Rollins Coll, 94; Owensboro Mus, 2006. *Mem:* Ky Hist Ctr (community scholar, 2006-2008). *Media:* Pen, Pencil, Oil. *Mailing Add:* 579 Hinkle Lane Shelbyville KY 40065

MCCARRON, PAUL
ART DEALER, ART APPRAISER

b Mason City, Iowa, June 15, 1933. *Study:* Art Inst Chicago, BA, 58, MFA, 59. *Mem:* Int Fine Print Dealers Asn. *Res:* 16th to 20th century fine prints and drawings; Rembrandt; 16th century Italian prints; 17th century mezzotints; Martin Lewis. *Publ:* Auth, Martin Lewis: The Graphic Work (catalog) & Martin Lewis: Catalogue of the Retrospective Exhibit, Kennedy Galleries, 73; The Prints of Martin Lewis (catalog Raisonne), 95. *Mailing Add:* PMB 601 123 Town Square Pl Jersey City NJ 07310-1756

MCCARTER, JOHN WILBUR, JR
RETIRED MUSEUM DIRECTOR

b Oak Park, Ill, March 2, 1938. *Study:* Princeton Univ, NJ, AB, 60; London Sch Econ, postgrad, 61; Harvard Univ, MBA, 63. *Pos:* Consultant, vice pres, Booz Allen and Hamilton, Inc, Chgo, 63-69; sr vice pres, 87-97; White House fel, Washington, 66-67; dir, Budget and Dept Fin, State of Ill, Springfield, 69-73; vp DeKalb AgResearch, Ill, 73-78, dir Ill 75-86, exec vp, Ill, 78-80, pres Ill, 81-82; pres, CEO, DeKalb-Pfizer Genetics, 82-86; pres DeKalb Corp, 85-86; pres, CEO Field Mus, Chgo, 96-2012, pres emeritus, 2012-; bd dirs, Divergence Inc, WW Grainger Inc, Janus Emeritus trustee, Chgo, Pub TV Station Channel 11, chmn, 89-86, trustee, Princeton Univ, 83-87, Nat Recreation Found, emeritus trustee Univ Chgo, bd govs, Argonne Nat Lab, regent, Smithsonian Inst. *Awards:* fel, Am Acad Arts and Scis. *Mem:* fellow American Academy of Arts and Sciences. *Mailing Add:* Field Museum 1400 S Lake Shore Dr Chicago IL 60605

MCCARTHY, CHRISTINE M
DIRECTOR

b Hartford, Conn. *Study:* Providence Coll, BA, 89; Syracuse Univ, MA, 92. *Pos:* Asst dir, ICA, Boston, 94-98; dir admin planning, ICA, 98-2001; exec dir, PAAM, Provincetown, Mass, 2001-. *Teaching:* adj prof, Cape Cod Community Coll, 2002-2003 & Boston Univ, 2002-. *Mem:* AAM; New England Mus Asn. *Specialty:* Am Art 1899-. *Collection:* Over 3,000 works, all media, from 1899-. *Publ:* George McNeil: Bather's, Dancer's, Abstracts, Provincetown Art Asn, 2002; James Gahagan Hank Jenson, Provincetown Art Asn Mus, 2002; Fine Arts Work Centers, Provincetown Arts, 2002-03; Am Art Rev, 2006; Herman Maril, An Artist's Two Worlds, 2008; Anne Peretz, Search for the Real: Hans Hofmann and His Student, 2009; Robert Motherwell: Beside the Sea, 2012. *Mailing Add:* Provincetown Art Asn & Mus 460 Commercial St Provincetown MA 02657

MCCARTHY, DENIS
PAINTER
b New York, NY. *Study:* Cooper Union, 59-64; Yale Univ, BFA & MFA, 64-66. *Work:* Work in pvt collections only. *Exhib:* Stable Gallery, NY, 69; Painting Ann, 70 & Biennial Exhib, 73, Whitney Mus Am Art; Reese Palley, NY, 70; Exhib, O K Harris, NY, 72; Warren Benedek Gallery, NY, 73; Spring Exhib, Aldrich Mus, Ridgefield, Conn, 73; Paula Cooper Gallery, NY; Michael Wyman Gallery, Chicago, 74; Univ Maine Portland, 75; Automation House, NY, 76; Hundred Acres Gallery, NY, 77; NY Acad Sci, 78; solo exhibs, Stable Gallery, NY, 70, 55 Mercer Gallery, NY, 78 & NY State Col, Old Westbury, NY, 80; Times Square Gallery, NY, 96; Leubsdorf Gallery, NY, 97, 2002; Times Square Gallery, NY, 2000. *Teaching:* Instr drawing, Sch Visual Arts, New York, 67-72 & New York Univ, 76-77; instr painting & printmaking, Hunter Col, 71-. *Mailing Add:* Hunter Col Dept Art 695 Park Ave New York NY 10021

MCCARTHY, PAUL
VIDEO AND PERFORMANCE ARTIST, SCULPTOR
b Salt Lake City, 1945. *Study:* Univ Utah, 1966-68; San Francisco Art Inst, BFA (painting), 1969; Univ Southern Calif, MFA, 1973. *Work:* Luhring Augustine Gallery, 97-98 & 2002. *Exhib:* Solo exhibs, LACE, 1979, 1982, Rosamund Felson Gallery, LA, 1986-87 & 1990-91, Air de Paris, 1994, 1996, Mus Mod Art, New York, 1995, Blum & Poe, Santa Monica, 1995, 1999, Galerie Hauser & Wirth, Zurich, 1997, 2001-2002, 2007, 2009, 2011, 2012, 2013, Mus Contemp Art, LA, 2000, Deitch Projects, New York, 2001, New Mus Contemp Art, New York, 2001, Tate Liverpool, 2001, Kunstverein Hamburg, 2001, Nat Mus Contemp Art, Oslo, 2003, Tate Mod, London, 2003, Whitechapel, London, 2005, Moderna Museet, Stockholm, 2006, Maccarone Gallery, New York, 2007, Whitney Mus Am Art, New York, 2008, Quilting Sessions, Warsaw Poland, 2009, Salt Lake Art Ctr, Utah, 2009, Fondazione Nicola Trussardi, Milan, Italy, 2010, Charles Riva Collection, Bruxelles, Belgium, 2011, Hammer Mus, Los Angeles, 2011, Kukje Gallery, Seoul, 2012, The Box, Los Angeles, Calif, 2012; Venice Biennale, 1993, 1995, 1999, 2001, 2013; Whitney Biennial, Whitney Mus Am Art, New York, 1995, 1997, 2004; Performing Bodies, Tate Gallery, London, 2000; Open Ends, Mus Mod Art, New York, 2000, Drawings from the Modern, 2005, Transforming Chronologies 2, 2006, Live/Work, 2007; Painting at the Edge of the World, Walker Art Ctr, Minneapolis, 2001, Walk Around Time, 2002, Mythologies, 2005; Extreme Connoisseurship, Harvard Univ Art Mus, 2001; Video Acts, PS1 Contemp Art Ctr, 2002, Inst Contemp Art, London, 2003; Point of View, New Mus Contemp Art, New York, 2004; 100 Artists See God, traveling, 2004; Artist's Favourite, Inst Contemp Art, London, 2004, Surprise Surprise, 2006; White, Int Ctr Photog, New York, 2004; Big Bang, Ctr Pompidou, Paris, 2005, LA-Paris, 2006; Domestic Violence, Reina Sofia, Madrid, 2005; Panic Attack!, Barbican Ctr, London, 2007, Martian Museum of Terrestrial Art, 2008; Looking Back: The White Columns Annual, White Columns, New York, 2008; Target Practice: Painting Under Attach 1949-78, Seattle Art Mus, Calif, 2009; Where Do We Go from Here? Bass Mus Art, 2009; 200 Artworks-25 Years, Seoul, Hangaram Mus, 2010; American Exuberance, Rubell Family Collection, Miami, Fla, 2011; Recollecting Performance, LACE Los Angeles Contemporary Exhibs, Los Angeles, Calif, 2011; The Box, Painting, Los Angeles, Calif, 2012; Fruits of Passion, Centre Georges Pompidou, Paris, Fr, 2012; This Will Have Been: Art, Love, & Politics in the 1980s, Boston, Mass, Inst Contemporary Art, 2013; The Humors, Perry Rubenstein Gallery, Los Angeles, Calif, 2013; WS, Park Ave Armory, NY, 2013. *Teaching:* Instr, performance, video, installation & art hist, Univ Calif, Los Angeles, 1982-2002. *Awards:* Skowhegan Medal for Sculpture, Skowhegan Sch Painting & Sculpture, 2009. *Bibliog:* Holland Cotter (auth), The American Fairy Tale, Fun House Style, Paul McCarthy: WS Turns a Magic Mirror on Excess, NY Times, 6/27/2013; and many others. *Mailing Add:* c/o 1301PE 6150 Wilshire Blvd 8 Los Angeles CA 90048

MCCARTY, LORRAINE CHAMBERS
PAINTER, INSTUCTOR
b Detroit, Mich, 1920. *Study:* Detroit Art Acad, Wayne State Univ, with G Alden Smith; Meinzinger Art Acad; Stephens Col, with Albert Christ-Janer, also with Glen Michaels, Emil Weddidge, Robert Wilbert & Adolph Dehn. *Work:* Butler Mus Am Art, Youngstown, Ohio; Smithsonian Nat Air & Space Mus, Fed Aviation Admin, Washington, DC; Northwood Inst, Midland, Mich; Int Women's Air & Space Mus, Ohio; and others. *Comn:* Painting, Bohn Copper & Brass, Detroit; painting, R L Polk Co Int Hq, Detroit, 73; painting, Wyandotte Paint Products, Troy, Mich, 74; murals, Int Women's Air & Space Mus, Ohio, 77 & Lear Siegler, 88; mural (24 x 52 ft), General Dynamics Landsystems, Mich. *Exhib:* Butler Mus Am Art Ann, 67 & 70-74; Womanart, Saginaw Mus Arts, Mich, 74; Fed Aviation Admin, Washington, DC, 77; Dayton Art Inst, Ohio, 78; Battle Creek Art Ctr, Mich, 78; Smithsonian Air & Space Mus, DC, 80-82; Flint Inst Traveling Exhib, 83; and 43 solo exhibs. *Pos:* Mem, Arts Cult Coun, Oakland Co, Mich, 75-; designer & adv, Int Women's Air & Space Mus, Ohio. *Teaching:* Instr painting, Flint Inst Arts, 70-; instr, Grosse Pointe War Mem, Mich, 70-79 & Birmingham Bloomfield Art Asn, currently; instr oil painting, Art Ctr, Pontiac, Mich, 75-; res artist, Stephens Col, Mo. *Awards:* 1st Place Educ Series, NFLCP Hometown USA, 84; 1st Prize, Poster Competition, Pontiac Gen Hosp, Mich, 89; MCA Grant, Design Consult, Oakland Tech Ctr, Mich, 90. *Bibliog:* Joy Hakenson (auth), Abstract artists focus on a real world, Detroit News, 79; Corinne Abatt (auth), Flight's romance captured, Birmingham Eccentric, Mich, 79; Cheryl Beller (auth), Take off just beginning, Royal Oak Daily Tribune, 79. *Mem:* Mich Acad Arts, Sci & Lett; Mich Watercolor Soc; Detroit Soc Women Painters & Sculptors; Scarab Club, Detroit; and others. *Media:* Acrylic, Oil. *Publ:* Dir, The Artist in You, 42 Show TV Series, aired nationally. *Mailing Add:* 1112 Pinehurst Ave Royal Oak MI 48073

MCCAULEY, ELIZABETH ANNE
HISTORIAN, WRITER
Study: Wellesley Col, BA, 72; Yale Univ, MA, 75, PhD, 80. *Pos:* Asst dir, Univ NMex Art Mus, 78-80. *Teaching:* Asst assoc prof art hist, Univ Tex, Austin, 80-88; assoc prof, Univ Mass, 88-94, prof, 95-. *Awards:* Mus Prof Grant, Nat Endowment Arts, 82-83; Getty Postdoctoral Fel, 85-86; Guggenheim Fel, 98-99. *Mem:* Coll Art Asn. *Res:* History of photography; 19th & 20th century European art. *Publ:* contribr, Eakins and the Photograph: Works by Thomas Eakins and His Circle in the Collection of the Pennsylvania Academy of Fine Arts, Smithsonian Inst, 94; Olympe Aguado Photographe 1827-1894, Mus de Strasburg, 97; coauth, The Museum and the Photograph, Clark Art Inst, 98; auth, Geschickte Fotografen': Daguerreotypien und Portraits der Familie Bisson, Mus Folkwang, 99, Le realisme et ses detracteurs, Mus Carnavalet, 2000, Edward Steichen: Artist, Impresario, Friend & Auguste Rodin, 1908 & 1910: The Eternal Feminine, In: Modern Art & Am: Alfred Stieglitz and his New York Galleries, 2001. *Mailing Add:* Univ Mass Boston Dept Art Boston MA 02125

MCCAULEY, GARDINER RAE
ADMINISTRATOR, PAINTER
b Oakland, Calif, Aug 8, 1933. *Study:* Calif Coll Arts & Crafts, studied with Hamilton Wolf, 48-51; Univ Calif, Berkeley, BA, 55, MA, 57, studied with Milton Resnick, David Park, Esteban Vicente, Erle Loran & Corrado Marca-Relli. *Exhib:* Ann Exhib of San Francisco Art Asn, San Francisco Mus Art, 55-57; Bay Area Invitational, Calif Palace of the Legion of Honor, San Francisco, 58; solo exhibs, Berkeley Gallery, San Francisco, 64 & Columbia Art League Galleries, 81; Artists of Ore, 67, 70, 72; Spectrum, Portland Art Mus, Ore, 70; Stephens Faculty, Merril Chase Gallery, Chicago, 74; Marymount Manhattan Col, NY, 78; Area Painters, Art Gallery, Univ Mo-Columbia, 78; and others. *Pos:* Crafts dir, US Spec Serv, France & Ger, 59-62; exec dir, Montalvo Ctr Arts, Saratoga, 82-89. *Teaching:* Lectr drawing, Univ Calif, Berkeley, 62-65; instr art, Univ Santa Clara, Calif, 64; asst prof painting & drawing, Lewis & Clark Coll, Portland, Ore, 66-72; head dept art, painting & drawing, Stephens Coll, Columbia, Mo, 72-82; vis artist, Barnfield Coll, Eng, 80. *Awards:* Juror's Prize, San Francisco Art Asn Ann, San Francisco Mus Art, 63; James D Phelan Found Award, Calif Palace of Legion of Honor, San Francisco, 65; Firestone-Baars Found Grant, 80. *Bibliog:* Joanna Magloff (auth), From the Berkeley Gallery, 12/63, Elizabeth Polley (auth), San Francisco: Gardiner McCauley & Howard Margolis, 3/64, Artforum; Anita Ventura (auth), Pop, Photo & Paint, Arts Mag, 4/64. *Mem:* Nat Coun Art Adminrs; Coll Art Asn Am; Mid-Am Coll Art Asn; Am Asn Univ Profs. *Media:* Acrylic, Oil. *Publ:* Auth, Introduction to Masayuki Imai: Ceramic Art, Saratoga Villa Montalvo, 85. *Mailing Add:* 14181 Gochine Dr Nevada City CA 95959

MCCHESNEY, MARY FULLER See Fuller, Mary (Mary Fuller McChesney)

MCCLANAHAN, JOHN D
PAINTER, EDUCATOR
b Salina, Kans. *Study:* Bethany Col, Lindsborg, Kans, BFA; Univ Iowa, Iowa City, MFA. *Work:* Art Mus, Univ Iowa, Iowa City; Weatherspoon Art Gallery, Univ NC, Greensboro; Mint Mus Art, Charlotte, NC; Baylor Univ, Waco, Tex; Seguin Art Ctr, Tex; Gates Gallery, Port Arthur, Tex; Hong Kong, Baptist Coll, Hong Kong, China. *Exhib:* One-man exhib, Mint Mus Art, 71; Mid-Am Art Exhib, Owensboro, Ky, 79, 82 & 86; Baylor Univ, 81, 83, 2010; Art Ann Two, Okla Art Ctr, Oklahoma City, 81; Biennial Nat Small Painting Exhib, Mullaly-Matisse Galleries, Birmingham, Mich; Kans Nat Small Painting Exhib, Ft Hays State Univ, Kans, 84 & 87; 2nd Ann Int Exhib Miniature Art, Del Bello Gall, Toronto, Can, 87; 30th Ann Delta Art Exhib, Ark Art Ctr, Little Rock, Ark, 87; Retrospective Exhib, Baylor Univ, Tex, 95; 29th Ann Rocky Mountain Nat Watermedia Exhib, Foothills Art Ctr, Golden, Colo, 02; Vision Int Art Ctr of Waco, 02; Weathersby Fine Arts Gallery; La Coll, Pineville, La. *Pos:* dir, Allbritton Art Inst, 98-. *Teaching:* Instr painting, Stephen F Austin State Univ, Nacogdoches, Tex, 64-67; from asst prof to assoc prof painting, Queens Col, Charlotte, NC, 67-76, chmn dept art, 75-76; prof painting, Baylor Univ, Waco, Tex, 76-, acting dir visual arts, 85-89, chmn dept art, 89-; dir, Allbritton Art Inst, 98-. *Awards:* Purchase Prizes, Tex Painting & Sculpture Exhib, 77 & 82 & Fifth Biennial Five State Exhib, 79. *Mem:* Coll Art Asn Am; Tex Fine Arts Asn. *Media:* Water Media, Collage. *Mailing Add:* Baylor Univ Sch Art Waco TX 76798-7263

MCCLEARY, MARY FIELDING
COLLAGE ARTIST, EDUCATOR
b Houston, Tex, Feb 27, 1951. *Study:* Tex Christian Univ, Ft Worth, BFA, 72; Univ Okla, Norman, MFA, 75. *Work:* San Antonio Mus Art, Tex; El Paso Mus of Art, El Paso, Tex; Mus Fine Arts, Houston, Tex; Art Mus Southeast Tex, Beaumont; Crystal Bridges Mus Am Art, Bentonville, Ariz. *Exhib:* Solo exhibs, Watson/de Nagy & Co Gallery, Houston, Tex, 80, 82, 83, 85, 86 & 89, Lynne Goode Gallery, Houston, 92 & 95, Adair Margo Gallery, El Paso, Tex, 93, 2000 & 2003, Scriptural References, Amarillo Mus Art, Amarillo, Tex, Moody Gallery, Houston, Tex, 2006, 2008, 2011, Grace Mus Art, Abilene, Tex, 2011; Works by Texas Woman, Nat Mus Women Arts, Washington, DC, 88; Mid-American Biennial Art Exhib, Nelson Atkins Mus, Kans City, 89; Altered Egos, Hallswalls Gallery, Buffalo, NY, 97; Word as Art; Contemp Pendings, Gallery at Am Bible Soc, NY 2000; A Broken Beauty, Laguna Mus of Art, Laguna Beach Calif; The Next Generation: Contemp Expressions of Faith, Mus Biblical Art, NY, 2005; I Love the 'Burbs, Katonah Mus Art, NY, 2006; Texas 100, El Paso Mus Art, 2006; Damaged Romanticism: A Mirror of Modern Emotion, Blaffer Gallery, Univ Houston, 2008-9; Grey Gallery, NY Univ, 2008-9; Parrish At Mus, Southampton, NY, 2008-9. *Pos:* Gallery dir, Stephen F Austin State Univ, 79-82. *Teaching:* regents prof art, Stephen F Austin State Univ, Nacogdoches, Tex, 75-2005, prof Emeritus. *Awards:* First Place Award, Houston Area Exhib, Blaffer Gallery, Univ Tex, 77; Mid-America Alliance/Nat Endowment Arts Fel, 88-89; Texas Artist of the Year, Art League of Houston, 2011. *Bibliog:* Wayne Roosa (auth), A Fullness of Vision: The Collages of Mary McCleary, Image: J Arts & Religion, summer 99; Dana Friis-Hansen & Gregory Wolfe (auths), Mary McCleary: Beginning with the Word, Galveston Art Ctr, 2000; James Romaine (auth), Objects of Grace: Essays & Interviews on Creativity & Faith, Sq Halo Books; Terrie Sultan (auth), Damaged Romanticism, D. Gileds Ltd, 2008. *Media:* Mixed Media on Paper, Collage. *Publ:* It Was Good; Making Art to the Glory of God, Square Halo Books, Baltimore, Md, 2007; After Paradise, Square Halo Books, Baltimore, Md, 2006; Mary McClearly: A Survey, Art League of Houston, 2011. *Dealer:* Moody Gallery 2815 Colquitt Houston TX 72098; Flatbed Press Austin TX. *Mailing Add:* 4005 Raguet Nacogdoches TX 75965

MCCLELLAN, DOUGLAS EUGENE
PAINTER
b Pasadena, Calif, Oct 10, 1921. *Study:* Art Ctr Sch, Los Angeles, Calif; Colorado Springs Fine Arts Ctr, with Boardman Robinson & Jean Charlot; Claremont Grad Sch, MFA. *Work:* Los Angeles Co Mus Art; Los Angeles Co Fair Asn; Pasadena Art Mus. *Exhib:* Libr Cong, 48; San Francisco Mus Art, Calif, 49-52; Los Angeles Co Mus Art, 49-55; Metrop Mus Art, NY, 50; Pa Acad Fine Arts, Pa, 53; Corcoran Gallery Art, Washington, DC, 53; Pacific Coast Biennial, 55; Carnegie Inst of Technol, Pittsburgh, Pa, 55 & 57; Whitney Mus Am Art, NY, 57; Solo exhibs, Felix Landau Gallery, 53-59, Pasadena Art Mus, 54 & Univ Calif, Riverside, 55. *Teaching:* Instr, Chaffey Col, 50-59, Otis Art Inst, Los Angeles, Calif, 59-61, Scripps Col & Univ of Calif, Santa Cruz; prof art, Univ Calif, Santa Cruz, 70-. *Awards:* Painting Prize, Los Angeles Co Mus Art, 50 & 53; Nat Orange Show, 54. *Mailing Add:* 4150 Glen Haven Rd Soquel CA 95073-9580

MCCLENDON, MAXINE NICHOLS
PAINTER
b Leesville, La, Oct 21, 1931. *Study:* Univ Tex, Austin; Tex Women's Univ; Univ Tex, Pan Am. *Work:* Mus NMex; IBM Collection; Lauren Rogers Mus Art, Laurel, Miss; Ark Arts Ctr, Little Rock; Int Mus Art & Sci, McAllen, Tex; Northwestern Univ Med Ctr, Chicago; Caterpillar Corp, Peoria, Ill; Tex Instruments, Dallas; Ark Mus Fine Arts, Little Rock; and others. *Comn:* Tex Instruments, Houston, 79; Union Bank of Switz, 80; Hyatt Regency Hotel, Ft Worth, Tex, 81; Continental Plaza, Ft Worth, Tex, 82; panels, Four Corners, Dallas, Tex, 86. *Exhib:* 16th Tex Crafts Exhib, Dallas Mus Fine Arts, 74; 8th & 9th Ann Southwestern Area Exhibs, Mus Southwest, Midland, Tex, 74 & 75; Fourth Nat Crafts Exhib, Marietta Coll, 75; Invitational Biennial, Beaumont Art Mus, Tex, 76; 19th nat, El Paso Mus Art, Tex, 76; McAllen Int Mus, 76; SW Craft Ctr, Tex Designer/Crafts Ctr, San Antonio, 78; solo exhib, Adelle M Gallery, Dallas, 80, Amarillo Art Ctr, Tex, 82, Univ Tex Pan Am, 94; group exhib, Invitational Red, Int Mus Art & Sci, McAllen, Tex, 2006. *Pos:* Cur, Mex folk art, McAllen Int Mus, 74-80. *Teaching:* Drawing instr, McAllen Int Mus, 89-91; drawing instr, pvt studio, 91-. *Awards:* Best in Exhib, 6th Ann Prints, Drawings & Crafts, Ark Art Ctr, 74; Judges Award, Fourth Marietta Nat, 75; Award of Excellence, Houston Designer/Craftsman, 76; and many others. *Mem:* Am Crafts Coun (state rep, 76-80); Tex Designer/Craftsmen (pres, 73-74). *Media:* Acrylic, Oil. *Dealer:* J Siegler 9410 Blue Jay Way Irving TX 75063. *Mailing Add:* 2018 Sharyland Rd Mission TX 78572

MCCLENNEY, CHERYL ILENE
ADMINISTRATOR
b Chicago, Ill, July 18, 1948. *Study:* Art Inst Chicago, BFA, 69. *Work:* Solomon R Guggenheim Mus, NY. *Pos:* Cur coordr, Solomon R Guggenheim Mus, 70-74; asst prog dir, Mus Collab Inc, 74-76; asst comnr, New York City Dept Cult Affairs, 76-78; dir mus prog, Nat Endowment Humanities, 78-83; asst dir prog, Philadelphia Mus Art, formerly, vpres external affairs,currently. *Teaching:* Instr, Art Inst Chicago, 68-69. *Mem:* Am Asn Mus; Am Asn State & Local Hist; African-Am Mus Asn. *Mailing Add:* Philadelphia Mus Art PO Box 7646 Philadelphia PA 19101-7646

MCCLURE, THOMAS F
SCULPTOR, EDUCATOR
b Pawnee City, Nebr, Apr 17, 1920. *Study:* Univ Nebr, BFA, 41; Wash State Col, 41; Cranbrook Acad Art, MFA, 47. *Work:* Seattle Art Mus; Syracuse Mus Fine Arts, NY; Detroit Inst Arts; Wright Mem Ctr, Beloit Col, Wis; DeWaters Art Mus, Flint, Mich. *Comn:* Welded bronze relief, Victor Gruen Assocs, Eastland Shopping Ctr, Detroit, 56; cast bronze relief, DeWaters Art Ctr, 58; welded bronze free standing sculpture, Albert Kahn Assocs, Univ Mich Undergrad Libr, Ann Arbor, 59; ten cast bronze relief sculptures, Congregation Shaarey Zedek, Detroit, 69; large cast bronze sculpture, Mich Blue Cross Bldg, Detroit, 74; and others. *Exhib:* Pa Acad Fine Arts Ann, Philadelphia & Detroit, 58; Contemp Sculpture 1961, Cincinnati Art Mus & John Herron Art Inst, 61; Drawings USA, St Paul, Minn, 61; solo exhibs, Gilman Galleries, Chicago, 68, 70 & 75, Arwin Gallery, Detroit, 76, Flint Inst Art, 78, Elaine Horwitch Gallery, Sedona, 87; Neon & Kinetic Art, Mus Neon Art, Los Angeles, 87. *Teaching:* Instr design, Sch for Am Craftsmen, Alfred, NY, 47-48; asst prof drawing & design, Univ Okla, 48-49; prof sculpture, Univ Mich, 49-79. *Awards:* Prize in Sculpture, 12th Nat Ceramics Ann, Syracuse, 47; Founders Prize in Sculpture, 45th Mich Artists Ann, Detroit, 54; Bicentennial Sculpture Competition Award, Pa State Col, 76. *Media:* Metal. *Specialty:* Painting; sculpture. *Publ:* Dennis Kowal (auth), Sculpture Casting, Crown Publishers, NY; Nicholas Roukes (auth), Plastics in Sculpture, Watson Guptill Pub; Lewis G Redstone (auth), Public Art-New Directions, McGraw Hill Book Co; Norman Gesky (auth), The American Painting Collection of the Sheldon Memorial Art Gallery. *Dealer:* Jordan Rd Gallery 395 Jordan Rd Sedona AZ 86336

MCCOLLUM, ALLAN
SCULPTOR, PAINTER
b Los Angeles, Calif, 1944. *Work:* Mus Mod Art; Metrop Mus Art; Chicago Art Inst; Los Angeles Mus Contemp Art; Detroit Inst Art; and many others. *Exhib:* Solo exhibs, Each and Every One of You, La Salle de Bains, Lyon, Fr, 2010, 2011, Perfect Vehicles, Art & Public, Geneva, Switz, 2011, Drawings, JGM, Galerie, Paris, Fr, 2011, The Shapes Project: Perfect Couples, Barbara Krakow Galler, Boston, Mass, 2012, Allan McCollum: The Book of Shapes, Galerie MFC-Michle Didier, Paris, Fr, 2013, The Shapes Project, JGM Galerie, Paris, Fr, 2013, and many others; Group exhibs, The Wilderness, Miami Art Mus, Miami, Fla, 2011, CLAP, Hessel Mus Art, Bard Coll, Annandale on Hudson, NY, 2011, The Wilderness, Miami Art Mus, Fla, 2011, Picture No Picture, Carriage Trade, NY, 2011, Silence and Time, Dallas Mus Art, Tex, 2011, Situation NY 1986, Art & Public, Cabinet PH, Geneva, Switz, 2011, Pacific Standard Time: Crosscurrents in LA Painting and Sculpture, 1950-1970, J Paul Getty Mus, Getty Ctr, Los Angeles, 2012, Volume! Museu d'Art Contemporani de Barcelona, Spain, 2012, Hirschfaktor-Die Kunst des Zitierens, Mus fur Neue Kunst & Medienmuseum, Karlsruhe, Ger, 2012, Object Fictions, James Cohan Gallery, NY, 2012, Dark Matters, Hirshorn Mus, Wash DC, 2012, The Way We Live Now, Brooke Alexander Gallery, NY, 2012, THANKS: 50th Anniversary Exhib, Carl Solway Gallery, Oh, 2012, This Will Have Been: Art, Love, & Politics in the 1980s, Mus Contemporary Art, Chicago, Ill, Walker Art Ctr, Minn, 2012, The Last Days of Pompeii: Decadence: Apolocalypse, Resurrection, Cleveland Mus Art, Cleveland, Oh, 2013, 55th Int Art Exhib, Biennale, Venice, 2013, and many others. *Teaching:* visiting prof, Immaculate Heart Coll, Los Angeles, Calif, 72-74, Fla State Univ Art Dept, Tallahassee, Fla, 75-76, Rhode Island Sch Design, 88-89, Univ S Fla Sch Art & Art History, Tampa, Fla, 2004, Mass Inst Tech, Cambridge, Mass, 2004-2005; practicum supervisor, Bard Coll Ctr Curatorial Studies, Annandale-on-Hudson, NY, 2002-2004; adj asst prof, Columbia Univ Visual Arts Dept, NY, 2002-; senior critic in sculpture, Yale Univ Sch Art, New Haven, Conn, 2007-. *Awards:* Nat Endowment Arts, 87, 88, 89 & 90; Adolph and Esther Gottlieb Found Grant, 2005. *Bibliog:* Mathilde Roskam (auth), Allan McCollum at the Van Abbemuseum, Eindover, Flash Art, 1/2/90; Dorothy Spears (auth), Allan McCollum, Artform, summer 90; Kim Levin (auth), Allan McCollum, Village Voice, 3/20/90. *Media:* Miscellaneous Media. *Mailing Add:* 63 Greene St New York NY 10012-4372

MCCONNELL, BRIAN E
EDUCATOR, ADMINISTRATOR
Study: Dartmoth Coll, AB (Classical Archaeology-Dept Classics), 1980; Brown Univ, PhD (Classical Archaeology-Dept Classics), 1985; Certification, licensure, Register of Professional Archaeologists, 2002. *Pos:* Conducted archaeological field research in Sicily for over two decades. *Teaching:* Vis asst prof, Connecticut Col, 1987-1988, 1990, 1991, Brown Univ, 1990, 1992, Tufts Univ, 1991-1992, Univ Michigan Ann Arbor, 1993-1994, Middlebury Col, 1994-1995, Emory Univ, 1998-1999, Univ Dayton, 2001-2002; instructor, Mediterranean Ctr for the Arts and Sciences, Italy, 2003, 2010; instructor foreign study program, Univ Dayton School of International Business, 2003; asst prof, dept visual arts and art history, Florida Atlantic Univ, Boca Raton, Florida, 2003-2008, on sabbatical leave, 2009-2010, assoc prof, 2008-, interim chair, 2012-. *Mem:* Col Art Assn; Archaeological Inst of America (mem European Com). *Publ:* Several publications that focus on the art and architecture of the Archaic and Classical periods at ancient Palike and the historiography of early explorations of the island's cultural and natural resources. *Mailing Add:* Dept Visual Arts & Art History Dorothy F Schmidt College of Arts & Letters Florida Atlantic Univ 777 Glades Rd AH118 Boca Raton FL 33431

MCCONNELL, WALTER
CERAMIST
b Philadelphia, PA, 1956. *Study:* Univ Conn, BFA (Ceramics & Painting), 1978; NY State Coll Ceramics, Alfred Univ, MFA (Ceramics), 1986. *Exhib:* Solo exhibs include Mark IV Gallery, Lincoln, NE, 1989, Windows on White, New York, 1990, Artemisia Gallery, Chicago, 1992, Gallery Raw Space, Chicago, 1991, Northern Clay Center, Saint Paul, MN, 1993, John Slade Ely House, New Haven, CT, 1995 ; Group exhibs include Five Sculptors, Cent Conn State Univ, New Britain, CT, 1993 ; 49th Scripps Ceramics Annual, Lang Gallery Scripps Coll, Claremont, CA, 1993 ; New Work, Artspace Gallery, New Haven, CT, 1994; Art City, A Community Residency Proj, Pawtucket, RI, 1994; Personally Defining Clay, New Orleans Contemp Art Ctr, New Orleans, LA, 1994 ; RAW Space, Real Art Ways, Hartford, CT, 1995; Sights in the Sound, Special Olympics Sculpture Invitational, New Haven, CT, 1995 ; Gifts for the 21st Century, Artspace Gallery, New Haven, CT, 1995; The Eight Triennial, Fuller Mus Art, Brocton, MA, 1996; Cooled Matter, Columbus Coll of Art & Design, Columbus, OH, 1999 . *Teaching:* Assoc Prof Ceramic Art, Alfred Univ. *Awards:* Louis Comfort Tiffany Found Grants, 2008. *Mailing Add:* 1 Saxon Dr Alfred NY 14802

MCCORISON, MARCUS ALLEN
LIBRARIAN
b Lancaster, Wis, July 17, 1926. *Study:* Ripon Col, BA, 50; Univ Vt, MA, 51; Columbia Univ, MS, 54; Coll Holy Cross, LHD, 92; Univ Vt, Hon DLitt, 92; Clark Univ, Hon LittD, 92. *Work:* Navy Federal Credit Union, US Coast Guard Hall of Heroes; The Florence Mus, SC; Marsh McLelland, Washington, DC; Nat Institutes of Health; Children's Nat Hosp, Washington, DC. *Collection Arranged:* A Society's Chief Joys (auth, catalog), Grolier Club, Newberry Libr, Univ Calif, Los Angeles, 68-70. *Pos:* Librn, Kellogg-Hubbard Libr, Montpelier, Vt, 54-55; chief rare bk, Dartmouth Col, Hanover, NH, 55-59; head spec collections, Univ Iowa, Iowa City, 59-60; librn, Am Antiq Soc, Worcester, Mass, 60-91, dir, 67-89, pres, 89-92, pres emer, 93; trustee, Fruitlands Mus, 80-89, Old Sturbridge Village, 81-92 & Historic Deerfield, 91, Newberry Libr, 92- & Am Printing Hist Asn, 98-2003; bd mgrs, Lewis Walpole Libr, Yale Univ, 95. *Awards:* Ripon Col, Distinguished Alumni Award, 89; Columbia Univ, Sch Lit Serv, Distinguished Alumni Award, 92; Laureate, Am Printing Hist Asn, 98. *Bibliog:* The 1764 Catalogue of The Redwood Library, Yale, 65; History of Printing in America, Isabela Thomas (auth), 70. *Mem:* Century Asn; Rare Bk Sect, Asn Coll & Res Libr (chmn, 65); Independent Res Libr Asn (chmn, 72-73 & 78-80); Grolier Club (councilor, 79-84); Bibliog Soc Am (pres, 80-84); Washington Soc Landscape Painters. *Res:* History of American printing, publishing, book trades, including American prints. *Interests:* American prints in all media prior to year 1877. *Collection:* American prints of the 18th and 19th century. *Publ:* Auth, Vermont Imprints, 1777-1820, Am Antiq Soc, 63; 1764 Catalogue of the Redwood Library, Yale Univ Press, 65; ed, The history of printing in America, Imprint Soc, 70

MCCORMICK, DANIEL
ENVIRONMENTAL SCULPTOR
Study: Coll Environmental Design, Univ Calif, Berkeley, grad; studies with James Turrell. *Comn:* Silt Trap Installation, Olema Creek, Point Reyes Nat Recreation Area, Calif, 2002; The Watershed: An Ecological Installation, Sleepy Hollow Creek, San Anselmo, Calif, 2002; Flood Plane Wall, Erosion Sculpture & Urban Run-Off Basket (watershed sculptures), Arroyo Seco, Calif, 2005; Willow Basket Sculpture, Olema Creek Watershed, Golden Gate Nat Recreation Area, Point Reyes, Calif, 2006. *Exhib:* Solo exhibs include Meridian Gallery, San Francisco, 2007, Bolinas Mus, 2008. *Awards:* George Sugarman Found Grant, 2007; Puffin Found Grant; Headlands Affiliate Award, Marin Arts Coun. *Mailing Add:* 219 Scenic Rd Fairfax CA 94930

MCCORMICK, PAM(ELA) ANN
SCULPTOR
b Grand Rapids, Mich, Jan 7, 1946. *Study:* San Jose State Univ, BA, 72, study with Sam Richardson, MA, 72; Stanford Univ, post-grad study in art hist, 76. *Comn:* Floating water sculpture, Artists Representing Environmental Art, NY, 84; Drawing Water from a Rock, Cent Park, NY, 84; World Win, water sculpture, Harbor Festival, NY, 85; Apollo Muses, sculpture, comn by Lila Tyng, NY, 86; Sculpture in the Mall, Corcoran Art Gallery & Wash Sculptors' Group, Washington, 86. *Exhib:* Aldrich Mus (with catalog), Ridgefield, Conn, 85; Ann Photo Auction, Ctr Photog, Woodstock, NY, 91; Solo exhibs, Mus NY, 91, Unison Gallery & Learning Ctr, New Paltz, NY, 91 & Artopia Gallery, NY, 97; Blast Art Benefit, X-Art Found, 93; Children's Mus Manhattan, NY, 93; Atropia Gallery, NY, 95; Unison Gallery, New Paltz, NY, 96; Puffin Room, NY, 97; Sculpture Symposium on the Mall, Corcoran Gallery & Wash Sculptors Group, 86; and others. *Awards:* Nat Endowment Arts Fel, 74; Pollock Krasner Found, grant, 90; Lila Wallace Int Artist Grant, 94. *Bibliog:* Viboon Leesuwan (auth), Pam McCormick, Thai News, Bangkok, 10/21/94; Jon Kalish (auth), A work of art even fish love, NY Newsday, 8/13/94; Carter Ratcliff (auth), Art in Am, 2/96. *Mem:* Int Sculpture Soc; Artists Representing Environmental Arts; Artists Equity. *Media:* Water, Stone. *Publ:* Illusr, Palace Peeper, Gilbert & Sullivan Soc, New York, 12/85

MCCOUBREY, SARAH
PAINTER
b New Haven, Conn, Sept 5, 1956. *Study:* Univ Pa, BA, BFA, MFA, 81. *Exhib:* One-man shows, More Gallery, Philadelphia, Pa, 85, Leslie Cecil Gallery, NY, 89, Comfort Gallery, Haverford Col, Pa, 90, Robert Brown Contemp Art, Washington, DC, 90, Pa Acad Fine Arts, Philadelphia, 97 & Stone Quarry Art Park, Cazenovia, NY, 98; BAUhouse Gallery, Baltimore, Md, 90; Cheekwood Nat Contemp Painting Competition, Tenn, 91; Botanical Gardens & Fine Arts Ctr, Cheekwood, Nashville, Tenn, 91; Robert Brown Gallery, Washington, DC, 92, 93 & 97-98; Twilight Intervals, Patricia Shea Gallery, Santa Monica, Calif, 93; Border to Border, Larson Biennale Nat Drawing Exhib, Trahorn Gallery, Austin Peay State Univ, Clarksville, Tenn, 93; Matrilineage: Women, Art and Change, Altered Space, Syracuse, NY, 93; The Hill Becomes the Valley - Central New York Landscape Paintings, Eberson Mus, Syracuse, NY, 94. *Teaching:* Instr painting, Corcoran Sch Art, Washington, DC, Syracuse Univ, NY, 91-. *Awards:* Nat Endowment Arts Grant, 89; Artist's Colony Fel, Millay Colony, Austerliz, NY, 96; Saltomstall Found Award, 97. *Bibliog:* Washington Post, 12/18/93; New Art Examiner, summer 94; Art Papers, 3-4/94. *Media:* Oil. *Mailing Add:* c/o Robert Brown Gallery PO Box 53307 Washington DC 20009-9307

MCCOY, KATHERINE BRADEN
DESIGNER, EDUCATOR
b Decatur, Ill, Oct 12, 1945. *Study:* Mich State Univ, BA, 67. *Comn:* Poster & catalog, Detroit Inst Arts, 73-76; archit signage & graphic design, Pontiac Silver Dome, Mich, 75-79; package design & signage, Tivoli Ltd, Birmingham, Mich, 77; environ design, Univ Mich, 78-79. *Exhib:* Commun Graphics Shows, Am Inst Graphic Arts Gallery, NY, 72, 76 & 79, Five Yrs of Posters, 79 & Covers Show, 79; Artists in Residence, Cranbrook Acad Art, Bloomfield Hills, Mich, 78; Station 100, Chicago, 78-81. *Collection Arranged:* Knoll and Herman Miller: The Development of Contemporary Furniture (auth, catalog), Cranbrook Acad Art, 75 & Design in Michigan (auth, catalog), 77; International Graphic Design Education, Icograda Chicago, 78. *Pos:* Designer, Unimark Int, Detroit, 67-68; sr designer, Chrysler Corp Identity Off, Detroit, 68-69; sr designer, Omnigraphics, Boston, 69-70; sr designer, Designers & Partners, Detroit, 70-71; partner, McCoy & McCoy, Detroit, 71-; bd ed, Indust Design Mag, 76-. *Teaching:* Co-chmn, Dept Design, Cranbrook Acad Art, 71-. *Awards:* Industrial Design Excellence Award, 80; I Award, Interiors Mag, 80; Showroom of the Year Award, Inst Business Designers, 80. *Bibliog:* Articles, Graphic Design Educ, 81, Interiors Mag, 82 & Novum Grebrauschgraphik, 82. *Mem:* Indust Designers Soc Am (pres, 83-84); Am Inst Graphic Arts; Soc Typographic Arts. *Publ:* Auth & ed, Projects and Processes, Cranbrook Acad Art, 76; Design in Michigan, Wayne State Univ Press, 78. *Mailing Add:* PO Box 2001 Buena Vista CO 81211

MCCOY, MICHAEL DALE
DESIGNER, EDUCATOR
b Eaton Rapids, Mich, Sept 16, 1944. *Study:* Mich State Univ, BA, 66; Wayne State Univ, MA, 68. *Work:* Am Inst of Graphic Art, NY; Cranbrook Acad Art Mus, Bloomfield Hills, Mich; Cooper Hewitt Mus, NY; Philips Design Ctr, Neth; JIDA, Tokyo. *Comn:* Archit graphics, Pontiac Silverdome, Mich, 76; furniture, Knoll Int, NY, 78; Experimental dealership design, Chrysler Corp, Detroit, 78; interior design, Univ Mich, 79; furniture, Interior Ctr, Tokyo. *Exhib:* Commun Graphics, Am Inst Graphic Arts, NY, 74, 76 & 79; Cranbrook Art Mus, 77, 78 & 83; Cooper-Hewitt Mus Design, NY, 81; Progressive Archit Furniture Exhib, 81. *Pos:* Partner, McCoy & McCoy Design Consult, Bloomfield Hills, Mich, 71-. *Teaching:* Co-chmn design dept, Cranbrook Acad Art, Bloomfield Hills, Mich, 71-. *Awards:* Ann Design Rev Awards, Indust Design Mag, 71-80; Print Casebooks Award, Print Mag, 76-78; Design Excellence Award, Industrial Designers Soc Am, 80. *Bibliog:* Cranbrook comes back, 9/82 & Office of the year, 5/83, Interiors Mag. *Mem:* Indust Design Soc Am. *Publ:* Coauth, Problem Solving in the Man-Made Environment, Cranbrook Acad Art, 74. *Mailing Add:* PO Box 2001 Buena Vista CO 81211

MCCOY, PAT A
WRITER, CRITIC
b Seattle, Wash. *Study:* Ctr Mod Psychoanalytic Studies; NY Univ with Ross Bleckner, Achille Bonito Oliva & Gillo Dorfles, 83; PhD, Applied Linguistics, NY Univ, 2011. *Work:* Curated, The Inscribed Image, 1988, Specific Metaphysics, 1989, Body, Mind and Spirit, 1994, Into the Psychic Landscape, 1996. *Pos:* Art lectr to mus, univs & galleries, New Arts Prog, Pa & Atlantic area, 91-; ed text(s) journal; vis artists, Pa Acad Fine Arts, 93, Moore Col Art, 94 & Mus Am Art, 95. *Teaching:* Lectr Engl, City Univ NY, 85-88 & John Jay Col Criminal Justice, 88-91; clinical spec educator, NY, 95-; NY Univ, 1998. *Awards:* Mid-Atlantic Grant, 92; Nat Endowment Art Grant, 92; Pew Charitable Trust, 93; Deans Grant for Graduate Rsch, NYU, 2006. *Bibliog:* Barry Schwabsky (auth), The Widening Circle: Consequences in Contemporary Art, 97. *Mem:* Asn Int Des Critiques D'Art; NY State Coun Humanities; Orthopsychiatry Asn. *Res:* Cultural study & analysis pertaining to art, psychoanalysis & aesthetics, "interior of individual" in post modern & modern eras; social & emotional learning in education. *Publ:* Auth, East Village: dead or alive, Artscribe Mag, 87; Disrupted narrative, 88 & Modern lexicon, 89, Arts Mag; Art Criticism Today (Round Table ed), M/E/A/N/I/N/G, 92; Innovations in Child Mental Health-rev, J Mod Psychoanalysis, 92; Bricks and Mortar: Social and Emotional Learning the the School Curricula in Readings, Jour Orthopsychiatry, 1998. *Mailing Add:* 630 E 14th St Apt 3 New York NY 10009

MCCOY, T FRANK
PAINTER, EDUCATOR
b Wichita, Kans, Jan 27, 1925. *Study:* Kans Univ, BFA, 1950, MFA, 52; Academie Des Beaux Arts, Liege Belgium, (summa cum laude), 51. *Work:* Columbia-Greene Community Col, Columbia-Greene, NY; Bank IV, Emporia, Kans; F & M Bank & Trust, Tulsa, Okla; Rennecote Corp, Stanford, Conn; Emprise Bank Collection, Wichita, Kans. *Comn:* many pvt comn work, Mass. *Exhib:* Silvermine Guild 9th Ann New Eng Exhib, Silvermine Guild, New Canaan, Conn, 38; All New Eng, Cape Cod Art Asn, Barnstable, Mass, 75, 86. *Teaching:* prof drawing, Univ of Mass, 58-91; prof painting, Dartmouth, formerly. *Awards:* Friends Award for a Seascape, Silvermine Guild 10th Nat Exhib, 59; First Prize in Oil, Audubon Artists 39th Ann Exhib, 81; Emily Lowe Found Award, Audubon Artists 44th Ann Exhib, 86. *Mem:* Audubon Artists. *Media:* Oil, Watercolor. *Mailing Add:* PO Box P56 Dartmouth MA 02748

MCCRACKEN, PHILIP
SCULPTOR, PAINTER
b Bellingham, Wash, 1928. *Study:* Univ Wash, BA; sculpture with Henry Moore, Eng, 54. *Work:* LaConner School District, Wash; King County District Courthouse, Issaquah, Wash; City of Seattle, Wash; Bartlett Square, Tulsa, Okla; Anacortes Public Library, Wash. *Comn:* Norton Bldg, Seattle, 59; Kankakee State Hospital, Kankakee, Ill, 61; Swinomish Indian Tribal Ctr, LaConner, Wash, 64; Gus Hensler Mem, City of Anacortes, Wash, 66; United Nations Asn, New York, 68; Seattle First Nat Bank, Mt Vernon, Wash, 74; Fed Bldg, Gen Services Admin, Seattle, 76; King Dome, Seattle, 78; City Hall, Everett, Wash, 80; LaConner Sch District, Wash, 98, 2000; Wash State Resources Ctr, 2010. *Exhib:* Solo exhibs, Willard Gallery, New York, 1960, 65, 68, 70, Seattle Art Mus, 61, Washington State Capitol Mus, Olympia, 64, Victoria Mus, BC, 64, La Jolla Mus Art, Calif, 70, Anchorage Mus Art, 70, Tacoma Art Mus, 80, Kennedy Galleries, New York, 85, Lynne McAllister Gallery, Seattle, 86, Valley Mus Northwest Art, LaConner, Wash, 93, Whatcom Mus, Bellingham, Wash, 94, Schneider Mus Art, Southern Ore State Col, Ashland, 97, Monterey Mus Art, 99, Port Angeles Fine Arts Ctr, 2001, Kurt Lidtke Gallery, Seattle, Wash, 2001, Mus Northwest Art, LaConner, Wash, 2004; group exhibs, CSA Gallery, Christchurch, New Zealand, 96, Spanierman Gallery, New York, 98 & 2003, Seattle Art Mus, Wash, 2001, The Art & Culture Ctr, Fallbrook, Calif, 2002, Gordon Woodside/John Braseth Gallery, Seattle, Wash, 2005, Portland Art Mus, Portland, Ore, 2012-2013. *Collection Arranged:* Univ Oreg Mus, Eugene; Whitney Mus Am Art, NYC; Int Minerals & Chemicals Corp, Skokie, Ill; Henry Art Gallery, Seattle; St Louis Art Mus; Sarah Werner, Aspen, Colo; Mr. & Mrs. Milton Trafton, Seattle; Mr. & Mrs. Langdon Simons, Seattle; Mr. & Mrs. Robert Sarkis, Seattle; Mr. & Mrs. Lawrence Martz, NYC; Anne Gould Hauberg, Seattle; Mr. & Mrs. William Haseltine, Gearhart, Oreg; Morris Graves, Lolita, Calif; Mr. & Mrs. Bill Gates, Seattle. *Awards:* Ruth Nettleton Award, 54; Univ Wash Art Prize, 54; Norman Davis Purchase Award, 57; Certificate for Superior Design & Execution, Am Inst Arch, 60; Governor's Award Washington State Artist of the Year, 64 & 94; Irene D Wright Memorial Award, 65; Cornish College of the Arts Lifetime Achievement Award, 99; and others. *Bibliog:* Dore Ashton (auth), Modern American Sculpture, Abrams, 67; Faith Medlin (auth), Centuries of Owls, Silverline, 67; James J Kelly (auth), The Sculptural Idea, Burgess Press, 70; Colin Graham (auth), Philip McCracken, Univ Wash Press, 80; Donald W. Thalacker (auth), The Place of Art in the World of Architecture, 80; Reproductions - NY Times, Jeopardy Literary Mag, 87, NY Herald Tribune, Long Island Press, Seattle Times, Seattle Post-Intelligencer, Northwest Arts, Sat Review of Literature, Time Mag, Art News, Art in America; James M Rupp & Mary Randlett (auth), Art in Seattle's Public Places, Univ Wash Press, 92; Delores Tarza Ament (auth), Iridescent Light, Univ Wash Press, 2002; Delorez Tarzan Ament (auth), 600 Moons: 50 Years of Philip McCracken's Art, Marquand Books, 2004; and others. *Media:* All Media. *Dealer:* Winfield Gallery Carmel CA. *Mailing Add:* 5029 Guemes Island Rd Anacortes WA 98221

MCCRAY, DOROTHY WESTABY
PAINTER, PRINTMAKER
b Madison, SDak, Oct 13, 1915. *Study:* State Univ Iowa, BA (painting and art history) 37, MA, 39; Calif Coll Arts & Crafts, MFA, 55; studies in Europe, 62-90. *Hon Degrees:* DHL, Western NMU, 01. *Work:* Smithsonian Inst; Worcester Art Mus, Mass; El Paso Mus, Tex; Western NMex Univ Gallery; Fine Arts Mus, Santa Fe, NMex; Governor Gallery, Santa Fe, Univ NM Art Gallery. *Exhib:* 20-21 Int Watercolor, Art Inst Chicago, 41-42; Dallas Print Soc, Dallas Mus, 60; US Off Info Traveling Show, Europe, 71-72; one-man show, Richard Levy Gallery, Albuquerque, NMex, 92; Printmaking in NMex, Mus NMex, Santa Fe, 92; one-man retrospective, Western NMex Univ, Silver City, 93. *Teaching:* From instr to emer prof art, Western NMex Univ, Silver City, 48-81. *Awards:* Purchase Awards, Print Drawing Ann, Mus NMex, 56 & 57; Francesca Wood Award, Am Color Print Soc, 60; NMex Gov Award for Excellence & Achievement in Art, 92. *Bibliog:* Clinton Adams (auth), Printmaking in New Mexico, Univ NMex, 91; David Acton (auth), The Stamp of Impulse: Abstract Expressionistic Prints, Worcester Art Mus. *Media:* Oil; Intaglio, Lithography. *Dealer:* Atelier 108 Silver City NM 88061. *Mailing Add:* PO Box 322 Silver City NM 88062

MCCREADY, ERIC SCOTT
ADMINISTRATOR, EDUCATOR
b Vancouver, Wash, Mar 14, 1941. *Study:* Univ Ore, BS, 63, BA, 65, MA, 68; Univ Pavia, Italy, BA, 65; Univ Del, PhD (art hist), 72; Wintherthur Summer Inst. *Pos:* Dir, Huntington Art Gallery, Univ Tex, 79-89 & Portland Develop Prog, 92-. *Teaching:* Asst prof art hist, Bowling Green State Univ, 72-75; asst prof, Univ Wis-Madison, 75-79; assoc prof, Univ Tex, Austin, 79-89; assoc prof & vpres develop & pub affairs, Univ Ore, 96-97. *Awards:* Knight First Class, Order of St Olaf. *Mem:* Soc Archit Historians (mem decorative arts chap); Mid-West Art Hist Soc; Victorian Soc Am. *Res:* American art; decorative arts. *Publ:* Auth, The Nebraska State Capitol: Its Design, Background and Influence, Nebr State Hist Soc, 74; Tanner and Gilliam: Two American black painters, Negro Lit Forum, 74; Richard Taliaferro: 18th Century Virginia Architect, Univ Ore Press, 77; Bertram Goodhue: Master of many arts (rev), J Soc Archit Historians, 78; Huntington at 25, Univ Tex Press, 86. *Mailing Add:* c/o Univ Ore Portland Ctr 70 NW Couch St Ste 207 Portland OR 97209-4038

MCCUE, HARRY
PAINTER, PRINTMAKER
b New York, NY, Sept 27, 1944. *Study:* Pratt Inst, with Romano, Blaustien & McNeil, BFA, 67; Univ Colo, Boulder, with Roland Ries & William T Wiley, MFA, 69. *Work:* Univ Colo, Boulder; Cornell Univ; Univ Pa, Edinboro; Maritime Mus, Ft Schuyler, NY; City of Ithaca, NY; Univ Maine; Ithaca Coll, Sch Bus; Countess IngeVon Der Schulenberg, Hanover, Ger; Wichita Art Ctr, Wichita, Kans; The office of Senator Hilary Clinton, Washington, DC, 2004-2009; Purdue Univ Galleries, Lafayette, Ind; Herbert F Johnson Mus, Cornell Univ. *Comn:* Set design (collabr, D Smyth), Cornell Dance Group, Ithaca, NY, 84; cart design & construction, Mystic Seaport Mus, Conn, 84; design carriage, NY State Hist Soc, Cooperstown, 85; design pastel drawings & prints, New Statler Hotel Complex, Cornell, Ithaca, NY. *Exhib:* Solo exhibs, Art Gallery, Adelphi Univ, 80, Schweinfurth Mus, Auburn, NY, 86 & Herbert F Johnson Mus, Cornell Univ, NY, 87 & Wells Col, Aurora, NY, 96, Harry McCue Kendall, Ithaca, NY, 2011; Group exhibs, Elmira Col, NY; New Vision Gallery, Ithaca, NY, 86-90; Edinboro Univ, Pa, 87; Arnot Mus, Elmira, NY, 96; Parkside Nat Small Print Exhib, Univ Wisc, 2003; Wichita Art Ctr, Kans, 2004; Purdue Univ, Lafayette, Ind, 2004, 2007, 2008; Everson Mus Biennial, Syracuse, NY, 2006; Finger Lakes Biennial, Rochester Mus Art Gallery, 2007; Art on Paper, Maryland Fed Arts, Annapolis, Md, 2008; Light in Winter, Upstairs Gallery, Ithaca, NY, 2008; 16th Mini Print Show, Binghamton, Univ, Binghamton, NY, 2008; Wright State Univ, Dayton, Ohio, 2008; Altgeld Gallery, Northern Ill Univ, DeKalb, Ill, 2008; Susquehanna Univ, Selinsgrove, Pa, 2008; Art in Motion, Finger Lakes, 2009; Made in New York, Schweinfurth Mus, Auburn, NY, 2009; New York Soc Etchers First, Nat Exhib Intaglio Prints, Nat Arts Club, NY, 2011; Community Arts Partnership Ann, Ithaca, NY, 2011, 2012, 2013; Herbert F Johnson Mus, Cornell Univ, 2011. *Pos:* prof emeritus, Ithaca Coll. *Teaching:* Instr painting, drawing & printmaking, State Univ NY, Geneseo, 69-72; instr drawing, printmaking & painting, Ithaca Col, 73-77, chmn art dept, 77-2010, assoc prof 87-2000, prof 2001-2010, emer, 2010. *Awards:* Lodestar Grant, Ithaca Coll, 84; Most Meritorious Fac, Ithaca Coll, 95; Featured Artist/Lectr, Rochester Mem Art Gallery, Rochester, NY, 2007. *Bibliog:* Wellikof (auth), American Historical Supply Catalog, Schocken Press, 84; Sherry Chayat (auth), rev, Syracuse Herald Mag, 8/3/86; Patricia Morrisrow (auth), Robert Mapplethorpe, Random House, 95. *Mem:* Community Arts Partnership, Tompkins Co; Southern Graphics Coun; Finger Lakes Art Trail; NY Soc Etchers. *Media:* Intaglio Prints, Oil. *Specialty:* Representational Art. *Interests:* Hist, farming & carriages. *Collection:* Prints by early 20th century artists. *Dealer:* Rochester Mem Art Gallery Rochester NY; Studio/Gallery 2423 Skinner Rd Lodi NY 14860. *Mailing Add:* 2423 Skinner Rd Lodi NY 14860

MCCULLOCH, FRANK E
PAINTER, PRINTMAKER
b Gallup, NMex, Aug 24, 1930. *Study:* Univ NMex, BA, 53; Princeton Univ, 53-54; MA, NMex Highlands Univ, 55; Inst Allende, Mex, MFA, 65. *Work:* Amarillo Art Ctr, Tex; Mus Albuquerque; Roswell Mus & Art Ctr, NMex; Mus Fine Arts, Univ NMex, Albuquerque; Inst Allende, San Miguel, Mex. *Comn:* Don Quixote Proj, One Percent For Arts Prog, Albuquerque, 82; acrylic, Cent Bank Cooperatives, Denver, 83; oils, Albuquerque Conv Ctr, City of Albuquerque. *Exhib:* Southwest Biennial, Mus NMex, Santa Fe, 63, 67, 74 & 76; solo exhibs, Roswell Mus & Art Ctr, NMex, 79, Governors Gallery, State Capitol, Santa Fe, 81, Munson Gallery, Santa Fe 84 & 88, RSV Gallery, Southampton, NY, 83, Dartmouth St Gallery, 88-89, 91, 98, 2001-03 & 2006-07, Conrad Gallery, Galveston, Tex, 91, La Galleria del Carraresi (Civic Mus), Treviso (Venice) Italy, 91, Cline Art Gallery, Santa Fe, 94, 2001 & 2004-05, Cline Fine Arts Gallery, Scottsdale, Ariz, 2006 & Matrix Gallery, 2007; Here & Now, Mus Albuquerque, 80; 46th Ann Midyear Exhib, Butler Inst Am Art, 82; Artists of Albuquerque, Mus Albuquerque, NMex, 90; 50 yr retrospective, NMex Highlands Univ; retrospecitve Mus Albuquerque, 2008; Summer Dene Gallery, 2009; and others. *Teaching:* Mem fac art, pub schs, Albuquerque, 56-85, Inst Allende, Mex, 63-65, Univ NMex, 70-73 & Southern Methodist Univ, 77, full time artist. *Awards:* Honoree of Year, Magnifico Show, Albuquerque, 94; Artist of Year, Albuquerque Arts Alliance, 93; NMex Gov's Arts Award, 2001; Distinguished Alumnus of Year, NMex Highlands Univ, 2002. *Bibliog:* Sandy Ballatore (auth), article, NMex Mag; Mary Carrol Nelson (auth), article, Southwest Art; Frank McCulloch Colores feature, Pub Television, 86 & 94. *Mem:* Albuquerque Arts Bd, 88; Capitol Arts Bd, Santa Fe, 93; Mus Albuquerque (acquisition bd); Nat Hispanic Ctr (collections bd). *Media:* Acrylic, Oil; All Media. *Interests:* Southwestern art history, musician and performer, research Hispanic folk music of New Mexico and Mexico. *Publ:* Auth, Raymond Jonson, Artspace, 81; Paranoid Dreams & Parallel Schemes (collected poems), 83; JD Robb (auth), Folk Music of New Mexico; Adams (auth), Printmaking in New Mexico; The Landscape (Dartmouth St Gallery). *Dealer:* Dartmouth St Gallery New Mexico; Matrix Gallery Albuquerque NM; Summer Dene Gallery Albuquerque NM; Winterowl Gallery Santa Fe NM. *Mailing Add:* 608 11th St Albuquerque NM 87102

MCCULLOUGH, DAVID WILLIAM
PAINTER, SCULPTOR
b Springfield, Mass, Dec 28, 1945. *Study:* Boston Inst of the Arts, Mass, 63-64; Aspen Sch of Contemp Art, Colo, summer 68, with Wilbur Neiwald & Doris Cross; Kansas City Art Inst, Mo, BFA (printmaking, painting), 70; Univ Mich, 69, with printmaker, Emil Weddige; Calif Inst of the Arts, 70, with Allan Kaprow & Dick Higgins. *Work:* Continental Insurance Co, NY; Sony Corp, Parkridge, NJ; Joslyn Art Mus, Omaha; Indianapolis Mus Art; Kemper Insurance Co, Chicago. *Comn:* Sculptural fountain, Am Petrofina Oil Co, Dallas, 74; three monumental sculptures, Tex Comn Arts & Humanities, 74. *Exhib:* Dallas Mus of Fine Arts Bicentennial, 71; Okla Art Mus, Oklahoma City, 71; South by SW Exhib, Ft Worth Art Mus, 72; Tyler Mus of Art, 74; Beaumont Art Mus, Tex, 75; Joslyn Art Mus, Omaha, Nebr, 76; Amarillo Art Ctr, 77; and others. *Teaching:* Artist-in-residence video-audio, Western Wash State Col, Bellingham, 76; artist-in-residence painting & sculpture, Santa Fe Contemp Art Sch, NMex, 76; lectr, Kansas City Art Inst, 82, Minneapolis Sch Art & Design. *Awards:* First Prize, Painting/Sculpture Biennial, Dallas Mus of Fine Arts, 71; First Prize, Univ Tex, Arlington, 76; Best of Show, Meadows Art Mus, Shreveport Art Guild, La, 77. *Bibliog:* Museum People, KERA-TV film, 74; Victoria Melcher (auth), David McCullough, Arts Mag, 1/76; Sarah Burns (auth), David McCullough, Arts Mag, 1/82. *Media:* Acrylic; Sand, Mixed. *Dealer:* Virginia Miller Galleries 169 Madiera Ave Coral Gables FL 33134; Patrick King Contemporary Art 427 Massachusetts Ave Fort Wayne IN 46204. *Mailing Add:* c/o William Campbell Contemporary Art 4935 Byers Ave Fort Worth TX 76107

MCCULLOUGH, EDWARD L
SCULPTOR; INSTRUCTOR
b Danville, Ill, Sept 18, 1934. *Study:* Ill State Univ, BS, 62, MS, 66. *Work:* Univ Iowa Mus Art, Iowa City; Fed Reserve Bank, Chicago; State of Ill Bldg, Chicago; Univ Notre Dame, South Bend, Ind; Luther Col, Decorah, Iowa; Monticello Sculpture Park, Godfrey, Ill. *Comn:* outdoor sculpture, Eastern Ill Univ, Charleston, 98; outdoor sculpture, Ctrl Ill Regional Airport, Bloomington, Ill, 2002; outdoor sculpture, Chicago Police Hdqr Bldg, 2002; outdoor sculpture, S Ill Univ, Sch Medicine, Springfield, 2005; outdoor sculpture, Dominican Univ, River Forest, Ill, 2006; outdoor sculpture, Kanakee Comm Coll, Ill, 2011; outdoor sculpture, Hines Va Med Ctr, Ill, 2011. *Exhib:* One-person shows, Loyola Univ, Chicago, 88, McLean Co Arts Ctr, Bloomington, Ill, 2001 & Spring Arbor Col, Mich, 2005; Sculpture Project, Nat Group Show, Univ Notre Dame, South Bend, Ind, 96; Pier Walk 98, Nat Group Show, Navy Pier, Chicago, 98; Second Biennial Nat Group Sculpture Show, South Bend Regional Airport, Ind, 2000-02; Cliff Dwellers, Chicago, 2009. *Teaching:* Adj fac, 3-D design art Columbia Col, Chicago, Ill, 91-. *Awards:* Nat Endowment Arts Fel, 81-82; Tech Grant, Ill Arts Coun, 84. *Bibliog:* Tom Butler (auth), The Elegy Series, Mitchell Mus, 87; Alec Nicolescu (auth), Songs, Kean Col, NJ, 95. *Mem:* Chicago Artists Coalition. *Media:* Metal Welded. *Dealer:* Lee Hansley Gallery 225 Glenwood Ave Raleigh NC 27603; Heike Pickett Gallery 400 E Vine St Lexington KY 40507; Sculpture Site SF Convention Ctr Plaza 201 Third St Ste 102 San Francisco CA 94103. *Mailing Add:* 421 N First St Cissna Park IL 60924-9789

MCCULLOUGH, SARAH CASH See Cash, Sarah

MCCURDY, MICHAEL CHARLES
ILLUSTRATOR, WRITER
b New York, NY, Feb 17, 1942. *Study:* Sch Mus Fine Arts, Boston; Tufts Univ, Medford, Mass, BFA, 64, MFA, 71. *Work:* New York Pub Libr; Boston Pub Libr & Mus Fine Arts, Boston; Univ Tex, Austin; Penmaen Press archive Univ Conn. *Comn:* Print, Lincoln Conserv Comn, Mass, 81; print, Art Soc, Cleveland Mus Natural Hist, 81; Albany Print Club, NY, 86; Rochester Print Club, 92. *Exhib:* Solo exhib, Michael McCurdy & Penmaen Press, Boston Athenaeum, Mass, 76; The Artist & the Book, Wenneger Graphics, Boston, 82; Int Exhib of Wood Engraving, Hereford City Art Gallery, Eng, 84; Univ of Mo Libr, 88; Elizabeth Stone Gallery, Birmingham, MI, 92; Club Odd Volumes, Boston, 99; and others. *Collection Arranged:* Boston Public Libr Archive of Prints and Books; Univ Conn, Storrs, Archive of Penmar Press Ltd Ed. *Teaching:* Instr drawing, Boston Sch Mus Fine Arts, 66-67; instr drawing & graphics, Concord Acad, Mass, 72-75; instr fine printing, Wellesley Col, Mass, 76. *Awards:* Bronze Medal, Book Award, Die Schonste Bucher Aus Aller Welz, Leipzig, 83; Ten Best Illustrated Children's Books, New York Times, 86, 96; Literary Light, 2002, Boston Pub Libr. *Bibliog:* Fritz Eichenberg (auth), article, Illus 63 Mag, Ger, 76; Mary Peterson (auth), Penmaen Press, NAm Rev, 81; Eunice Agar (auth), Michael McCurdy and Penmaen Press, Am Artist, 84; Tamara Tragakiss (auth), Michael McCurdy, 2006. *Mem:* Soc of Printers, Boston. *Media:* Book Arts, Wood Engraving. *Publ:* Illusr, American Buffalo, Arion Press, 92; Giants in the Land, Houghton Mifflin, 93; Singing America, Viking, 95; The Signers: The 56 Stories Behind the Declaration of Independence, Walker, 2002; The Train They Call the City of New Orleans, Putnams, 2003; The Founders, Walker, 2005; Walden, Shambhala, 2004; Tales of Terror, Knopf, 2005; Knee-Deep in Blazing Snow, Word Song, 2005; Tales of Adam, Steerforth Press, 2005 & So Said Ben, Creative Ed, 2007; ed & illusr, Escape From Slavery: The Boyhood of Frederick Douglass, Alfred Knopf, 94; auth & illusr, Trapped by the Ice, Walker, 97 & An Alonquian Year, Houghton Mifflin, 2000. *Mailing Add:* 103 Reeds Landing Springfield MA 01109-2054

MCDANIEL, CRAIG MILTON
EDUCATOR, PAINTER
b Norfolk, Va, Sept 14, 1948. *Study:* Univ Pa, BS, 70; Univ Mont, MFA, 75; Ohio State Univ, MFA (painting), 86. *Work:* Sheldon Swope Art Mus, Terre Haute, Ind; Southern Ohio Mus, Portsmouth. *Exhib:* Focus: Craig McDaniel, Gov Ohio's State Residence, Columbus, 87; In Indiana, Indianapolis Art Mus, 91, 95 & 2001; Craig McDaniel & Anita Bracalante, Ind Arts Comn, 91; two-person shows, South Bend Regional Art Mus, Ind, 93, New Harmony Gallery Contemp Art, Ind, 93 & Jan Cicero Gallery, Chicago, 95; solo exhibs, Ind Univ, 97 & Ft Wayne Mus Art, 99; Jan Cicero Gallery, Chicago, 99. *Collection Arranged:* Hurry Sundown: The 1930's (catalog with

Jean Robertson), 79; Six Guns and Tomahawks (catalog with Jean Robertson), 81; The Last Laugh, 83; Object As Subject (exhib catalog), 89; Exploring Maps (catalog with Jean Robertson), 92; Native Streams (catalog with Jan Cicero), 96. *Pos:* Founding dir (with Jean Robertson), Southern Ohio Mus & Cult Ctr, Portsmouth, 78-84; dir progs dept, Columbus Mus Art, Ohio, 85-88; dir, Turman Art Gallery, Ind Stat Univ, 88-94. *Teaching:* Prof painting & mem fac, Sch Grad Studies, Ind State Univ, Terre Haute, 88-. *Awards:* Merit Award, Water Tower Ann, Louisville Visual Arts Asn, 91; Visual Artist Fel, Ind Arts Comn, 91 & 92; Award of Excellence, 48th Ann Wabash Valley Exhibit, Swope Art Mus, 92. *Bibliog:* Sarah Rogers Lafferty (auth), Selections: Six in Ohio, Contemp Arts Ctr, 82; Portfolio: Craig McDaniel, Arts Ind, 10/91 & 9/95; Portfolio: The Gettysburg Review, spring 96. *Media:* All. *Publ:* Auth, Under Intense Scrutiny (exhib catalog), Turman Gallery, 90; coauth, Artists Explore the Map, Midwest Quarterly, spring 96 & Painting as a Language: Materials, Techniques, Form, Content, Harcourt, 2000. *Mailing Add:* Ind State Univ Dept Art Fine Arts Bldg 108 Terre Haute IN 47809

MCDANIEL, WILLIAM HARRISON (HARRY)
SCULPTOR
b Wichita, Kans, Oct 29, 1959. *Study:* Warren Wilson Col, 79; Coll Atlantic, 80-81; Creative Arts Workshop, 85. *Work:* AD 2000, New Haven, Conn; Brevard Co Health Dept, Titusville, Gla; Fla Atlantic Univ, Boca Raton; UNLA-Kellogg Ctr, Hendersonville, Nebr; Robert Morgade Libr, Stuart, Fla. *Comn:* Sculpture, Md-Nat Capital Parks & Planning Comn, Redland, Md, 88; wooden wall sculpture, Fair Haven Woodworks, Fair Haven, Conn, 94; mobile, Moore Co Regional Hosp, Pinehurst, NC, 99; outdoor sculpture, Fla State Univ, Tallahassee, 2005; outdoor sculpture, New River Trail State Park, Pulaski, Va, 2003. *Exhib:* NC Fel Recipients 93/94, Southeastern Ctr Contemp Art, Winston-Salem, NC, 94; NC Artists Exhib, Fayetteville Mus Art, 95; Souvenirs from My Visit to Am, Urban Inst Contemp Arts, Grand Rapids, Mich, 95 & Spirit Sq Ctr Arts & Educ, Charlotte, NC, 96; Images of the Human Spirit, Asheville Art Mus, NC, 95; Am Artifacts, DC Arts Ctr, 2001; and others. *Pos:* Mgr, Highwater Studio Coop, Asheville, NC, 90-91; webmaster, 98-2003. *Awards:* Alternate Visions Proj Grant, Alternate Roots-Atlanta, 93; Visual Arts Fel, NC Arts Coun, 93 & 98; Award of Excellence, Roanoke Art Show, Art Mus WVa, 97. *Bibliog:* Susan Wadsworth (auth), Review: Connecticut circumscribed, Art New Eng, 10/86; Michela Oberlaender (auth), Review: Tri-State sculptures exhibition, Art Papers, 7/90; Tom Patterson (auth), McDaniel's "Souvenirs" scrutinize our US values, Charlotte Observer, 9/15/96. *Mem:* Tri-State Sculptors. *Media:* All Media, Wood. *Mailing Add:* 95 Cumberland Cir Asheville NC 28801

MCDEAN, CRAIG
PHOTOGRAPHER
b Manchester, England, 1964. *Pos:* Photog, i-D & The Face, London, formerly; contrib, W, Vogue, Another Mag, New Yorker, others; photog campaigns for Armani, Gucci, Yves Saint Laurent, Estée Lauder, others. *Awards:* Infinity Award, Int Ctr Photog, 2008. *Publ:* I Love Fast Cars, Powerhouse Books, 1999; Lifescapes, Steidl/Dangin, 2004

MCDERMOTT, DAVID WALTER
PAINTER
b 1952 Hollywood, Calif, 1952. *Study:* Univ Syracuse, 1970-74. *Exhib:* Solo exhibs include Massimo Audiello Gallery, NY, 1985, 1986, 1987, 1988, Pat Hearn Gallery, NY, 1986, Galleria Lucio Amelio, Naples, 1986, Frankfurter Kunstverein, Germany, 1986, Robert Miller Gallery, NY, 1989, 1992, Sperone Westwater Gallery, NY, 1990, 1992, Fraenkel Gallery, San Francisco, 1990, 1992, Gian Enzo Sperone, Basel, Switzerland, 1991, Fay Gold Gallery, Atlanta, 1991, Galerie Philippe Rizzo, Paris, 1992, Torch Gallery, Amsterdam, 1994, 2004, Temple Bar Gallery, Dublin, Ireland, 1997, Provincial Mus Modern Art, Belgium, 1997, Galerie Jerome de Noirmont, Paris, 1998, 2000, 2002, Akureyri Art Mus, Iceland, 2003, Cheim & Read Gallery, NY, 2006; group exhibs include James Graham & Sons Gallery, NY, 1995; Robert Miller Gallery, NY, 1995; Biennial, Whitney Mus Am Art, NY, 1995; Marlborough Gallery, NY, 1996; Royal Hibernian Acad, Ireland, 1997; Guy Mc Intyre, NY, 1998; Triskel Art Ctr, Cork, Ireland, 1998; Irish Mus Modern Art, Dublin, Ireland, 1998; The White Chapel Gallery, London, 2000; Boutique le Printemps, Paris, 2000; Edwynn Houk Gallery, NY, 2001; Mus Modern Art, Ostende, 2001; Robinson Gallery, NY, 2002; Musee des Beaux Arts de Tourcoing, 2003; Akureyri Art Mus, 2003; Cheim & Read, NY, 2004; Galerie Jerome de Noirmont, Paris, 2006. *Pos:* Mem, McDermott & McGough, currently. *Mailing Add:* c/o Cheim and Read Gallery 547 W 25th St New York NY 10001

MCDONALD, SUSAN STRONG
PAINTER, PRINTMAKER
b Rochester, NY, Aug 18, 1943. *Study:* Sweet Briar Col, BA, 65; studied with Kathan Brown, 68-71; Yoshida Hanga Acad, 71-74; Univ Minn, MA (art hist), 1996; Univ Minn, PhD (art hist), 2002. *Work:* Walker Art Ctr, Minneapolis Inst Art & Univ Minn Gallery, Minneapolis; Michael C Rockefeller Gallery, Fredonia, NY; Western Regional Post Off, San Francisco; WARM (Women's Art Registry of Minn), 12 Artists, Weisman Mus Art, Minneapolis, 2006. *Comn:* YWCA Award Prints, St Paul, 89. *Exhib:* Photoetchings from Crown Point Press, Ames Gallery, Berkeley, 71; Oakland Mus Art, 74; Japan Printmakers Asn Ann Exhib, Tokyo, 75; Portrait of an Artist, Minneapolis Inst Art, 81; Five Minneapolis Artists, Tweed Mus Art, 82; WARM: A Landmark Exhib, Minn Mus Art, St Paul, 84; Women's Art Registry, 86; solo exhib, Soho 20, Invitational, 87, 4th Ann Minn Artists' Exhib, 87, Kew Studios, London, Eng, 88 & Hogarth Club London, 88, Out of Control: Artists Bks, ARC Gallery, Chicago, 90; Out of Bounds, Phipps Center Arts, Hudson, Wis, 2002. *Pos:* Scientific illusr, Univ Calif, Berkeley, 69-71; muralist, Wall Painting Artists Inc, 78-81. *Teaching:* Instr, Int Sch Sacred Heart, Tokyo, Japan, 71-74, Metrop State Univ, Minneapolis, Minn, 79-90, North Hennepin Community Coll, 83-2009, Split Rock Arts Prog, Univ Minn, 84-89. *Awards:* CUE Award, City Minneapolis, 82; WARM Mentor Scholarships, 83, 86 & 89; One month residency fel for printmaking, Ucross Found, 87. *Bibliog:* Diane Hellekson (auth), Using the figure, 1/85 & Margot Kreil Galt (auth), Delving into the self and finding the bones of us all, 1/86, Artpaper; Sharon Zweigbaum (auth), Susan McDonald tackles Lay issues, Vol 3, No 5, FAN, 5/86; Joanna Inglot (auth), WARM A Feminist Art Collective in Minn, Univ Minn Press, 2007; Harold B Stone (auth), Life Drawing, Thomson Delmar Learning, P 117, 2007. *Mem:* Founding mem Womens Art Registry Minn; Traffic Zone Center Visual Art. *Media:* Oil, Encaustic. *Res:* Koshiro Onchi: Taisho modernist. *Interests:* Botanical painting. *Publ:* Auth, State: State of the art/art: Art of the state, Craft Connection, 75; Harmony Hammond: A ten year retrospective, 81, In the studio, 83 & Fitting into the fifties, 83, WARM J; Making art: Political and personal change, 84 & Mystery in art, 12/85, Exhibition or Carnival, 4/86 & Ritual & Tradition, Vol 6, No 8, 4/87, Art paper. *Dealer:* Traffic Zone Center for Visual Arts 250 Third Ave #324 Minneapolis MN 55401; Marta Echazarreta Work of Art Gallery

MCDONNELL, JOSEPH ANTHONY
SCULPTOR, PAINTER
b Detroit, Mich, Oct 20, 1936. *Study:* Univ Notre Dame, with Ivan Mestrovic, BFA & MFA; Acad Belli Arte, Florence, Italy; Harvard Sch Design. *Work:* Milwaukee Pub Mus; Snite Mus, Univ Notre Dame; Art Inst for the Permian Basin, Odessa, Tex; Flint Art Inst. *Comn:* Sculpture fountain, Montgomery Co, Fenwick Park, Silver Spring, Md, 88; suspended sculpture, IBM, East Fishkill, NY, 89; sculpture, Nexus Properties Inc, Trenton, NJ, 90; wall sculpture, Durst Orgn, NY, 91; Univ Washington Campus, 2000; Bill & Melinda Gates Found, 2002. *Exhib:* Solo exhibs, McNay Art Inst, San Antonio, Tex, 64, Flint Art Inst, Mich, 64, Katonah Gallery, NY, 79, Century Asn, NY, 84 & Nardin Gallery, NY, 97; Snite Mus, Univ Notre Dame, 80; Nat Acad Design, 92; Andre Emmerich, NY, 93-95; Foster White, Seattle, 2001. *Pos:* Critic & asst ed, Artworld, 84-94. *Teaching:* Instr, Col New Rochelle, NY, 82-83. *Awards:* Award, New Eng Silvermine Exhib, 76 & 77; Sculpture Award, Jazz at Lincoln Ctr, New York, 96. *Bibliog:* Louis G Redstone (auth), New Directions in Shopping Centers and Stores, McGraw-Hill, 73; Vivian Raynor (auth), Westchester sect, NY Times, 10/9/94; Sean Simon (auth), Art Speak, NY, 12/97; Donald Kuspit & David Finn (auths), Joseph McDonnell, Univ Wash Press, 2004. *Mem:* Sculptors Guild; Century Asn. *Media:* Multi. *Publ:* Auth, monthly sculpture revs, Art World, 84-94. *Dealer:* Weber Fine Art 17 Bonneface Cir Scarsdale NY. *Mailing Add:* 946 Federal Ave E Seattle WA 98102

MCDONNELL, PATRICIA JOAN
MUSEUM DIRECTOR
b Minneapolis, March 30, 1956. *Study:* Mills Coll, BA (German Studies), 1978; Brown Univ, MA (Art History), 1985, PhD (Art History), 1991. *Pos:* Prof training coordr, Art Mus Asn Am, San Francisco, 1978-1983; asst to dir, Mus Art, RI Sch Design, Providence, 1984; cur, Frederick R Weisman Art Mus, Univ Minn, 1991-2002; chief cur, Tacoma Art Mus, 2002-2006; dir, Ulrich Mus Art, Wichita State Univ, 2007-. *Mem:* Coll Art Asn (bd mem). *Publ:* contrib, A Sexual Immensity Even: Marsden Hartley and the Wilhelmine German Military (pgs 211-213), Frames of Ref: Looking at Am Art 1900-1950, Whitney Mus Am Art in assoc with Univ Calif Press, 1999; co-ed with Rob Silberman, World Views: Maps and Art, Frederick R. Weisman Art Mus with Univ Minnesota Press, 1999; On the Edge of Your Seat: Popular Theater and Film in Early 20th Century Art, Frederick R. Weisman Art Mus with Yale Univ Press, Minneapolis, 2002; Portrait of Berlin: Marsden Hartley and Urban Modernity in Expressionist Berlin (pg 38-67), Wadsworth Atheneum with Yale Univ Press, Hartford, Conn, 2003; Painting Berlin Stories: Marsden Hartley, Oscar Bluemner, and the First Am Avant-Garde in Expressionist Berlin, Peter Lang Publ, NY, 2003. *Mailing Add:* Ulrich Museum of Art Wichita State Univ 1845 Fairmount St Wichita KS 67260

MCDOWELL, WAYNE
PAINTER
Exhib: Solo exhibs, Access and Vehicles, Southeast Mo State Univ, Cape Girardeau, Mo, 91; The Involuntary Arc, North Fourth Collection, Wilmington, NC, 2000, The Cage Series, 2001; Simmons Wright Gallery, Wilmington, 2002: Miss Gulf Coast Community Col, 2003; Chase Gallery, Wilmington, 2003; Cameron Art Mus, Wilmington, 2004; Hodges Taylor Gallery, Charlotte, NC, 2005; Buchanan Gallery, Galveston Island, Tex, 2005; Bald Head Island Corp, NC, 2005; Lee Hansley Gallery, Raleigh, NC, 2005; Greenhill Ctr, Greensboro, NC, 2005; Fayetteville Art Mus, NC, 2006; Chase Gallery, Boston, 2007; Group exhibs, Simmons Wright Gallery, NC, 2002; No Boundaries Int Artist colony, Acme Art Studios, NC, 2002, 2003, 2004; Chase Gallery, Wilmington, NC, 2003; Hodges Taylor Gallery, Charlotte, NC, 2003; Cameron Art Mus, Wilmington, NC, 2004; The Artist Gallery, Wilmington, NC, 2004; Chase Gallery, Boston, 2004, 2006; Fayetteville Mus Art, NC, 2005; Green Hill Ctr for NC Art, Greensboro, NC, 2005; Water Water TAG Gallery, Wilmington, NC, 2006; Bennett Street Gallery, Atlanta, Ga, 2006; Three Hounds Gallery, Wilmington, NC, 2006; Lee Hansley Gallery, NC, 2006. *Media:* acrylic, oil

MCDUFF, FREDRICK H
PAINTER, PRINTMAKER
b Birmingham, Ala, Oct 20, 1931. *Study:* Art Student's League, NY. *Work:* Pvt collections of Mrs Ronald Reagan, Burt Reynolds, former Gov & Mrs Pierre Dupont & Mrs Ethel Kennedy. *Exhib:* Catalog Raisonne 1982-1992 of Serigraphs, Va, 93. *Publ:* Cover illusr, Impressions, 10/88; cover illusr, Potomac Life, 3-4/91

MCELHENY, JOSIAH
SCULPTOR
b Boston, 1966. *Study:* RI Sch Design, BFA, 88. *Exhib:* Solo exhibs include Henry Art Gallery, Seattle, 99, 2008 Isabella Stewart Gardner Mus, Boston, 99, Johnson Country CC, Overland Park, Kans, 2001, Centro Galego de Arte Contemporanea, Spain, 2002, Mod Mus, Stockholm, 2007, Mus Mod Art, New York, 2007, Mus Nat Ctr Art Reina Sofia, 2009; Group exhibs, Site Santa Fe, NMex, 2001; Whitney Biennial, Whitney Mus Art, NY, 2000; Saatchi Gallery, London; Wexner Ctr Arts, Ohio. *Teaching:* vis

faculty, Univ Nev, 2000; vis sculpture critic, Yale Univ Sch Art, 2001-2003, 2005-2010. *Awards:* Louis Comfort Tiffany Found Award, 95; Bagley Wright Fund Award, Seattle, 98; MacArthur Fellow, John D and Catherine T MacArthur Found, 2006. *Media:* miscellaneous. *Mailing Add:* c/o Donald Young Gallery 224 S Michigan Ave Chicago IL 60604

MCELROY, JACQUELYN ANN
PRINTMAKER, EDUCATOR
b Rice Lake, Wis, June 28, 1942. *Study:* Univ Minn; Univ Mont, BA, 65, MA, 66, MFA, 67. *Work:* Dulin Gallery Art, Knoxville, Tenn; Pillsbury co, Minneapolis; Winnipeg Art Gallery, Man, Can; Plains Art Mus, Moorhead, Minn; Okla Art Ctr, Oklahoma City; and others. *Comn:* Nat Touring Exhib in Honor of Lewis & Clark's 260th Anniversary. *Exhib:* Midwest Biennial Exhib, Joslyn Mus, Omaha, Nebr, 74; 62nd Ann Spring Salon, Springville Art Mus, Utah, 87; NJ Art Ctr Nat Show, 88; Critical Choices, Univ Art Galleries, Univ SDak, 90; Mid-Am Print Invitational, South Bend Art Ctr, Ind, 94; 35th Midwestern Invitational, Rourke Art Ctr, Moorehead, Minn, 94; Oscar Howe Art Ctr, Mitchell, SDak, 94; On Common Ground: Oscar Howe Art Ctr, Mitchell, SDak, Dahl Fine Arts Ctr, Rapid City, Sunset Mus, Gettysburg, SDak Mus Art, Brookings, Old Courthouse Mus, Sioux Falls & Dakota Prairie Mus, Aberdeen, 95; Midwestern Invitational, Rourke Gallery, Moorehead, Minn; Mind's Eye Gallery, Dickinson, NDak, 99; Bismarck Art & Galleries Asn, NDak, 2006; and others. *Teaching:* Prof art hist & printmaking, Univ NDak, Grand Forks, 68-2000, asst dean, 79-84 & 91-92, chmn visual arts, 86-2000; Retired prof emer. *Awards:* Purchase Awards, Art & the Law, Minn Mus & Western Publ co, 80, Challenge of the Land, Pillsbury co, 81 & Tempo Gallery, Appleton, Wis, 83. *Bibliog:* Just Plain Art, Plains Art Mus Publ, Minn, 90. *Mem:* North Valley Arts Coun. *Media:* Serigraphy. *Interests:* Writing murder mysteries. *Dealer:* Rourke Art Gallery 523 S Fourth Moorhead MN 56560; Browning Arts 22 N 4th Grand Forks ND 58201. *Mailing Add:* 770 Ashley Ln NE Thompson ND 58278-9636

MCENEANEY, SARAH
PAINTER
b Munich, Ger, 1955. *Study:* Philadelphia Coll Art, 1973-75; Pa Acad Fine Arts, 1975-79. *Exhib:* Solo exhibs include Samuel S Fleisher Art Mem, Philadelphia, 1985, More Gallery, Philadelphia, 1987, 1988, 1992, 1993, 1994, 1996, 1997, Morris Gallery, Pa Acad Fine Arts, 1990, Inst Contemp Art, Philadelphia, 2004, Tibor de Nagy Gallery, NY City, 2006; group exhibs include Chongqing and Tianjin, China, 1986; Pa Acad Fine Arts, 1987; Southern Alleghenies Mus Art, 1989; State Mus Pa, Harrisburg, 1990; Del Art Mus, Wilmington, 1991; Allentown Art Mus, Pa, 1992; Bryn Mawr Coll, 1993; Michael Klein Inc, NY City, 1994; Rosemont Coll, Pa, 1996; Moore Coll Art and Design, 1997; Boston Univ, 1997; Arcadia Univ; Luckman Gallery, Cal State; Wash Univ Gallery Art, St Louis, Mo; Weatherspoon Art Mus; Univ Buffalo Art Gallery, NY. *Pos:* Mem bd. overseers, Inst Contemp Art, Univ Pa; exec bd mem, Vox Gallery, Philadelphia. *Teaching:* Brooklyn Coll, Fairfield Univ, Conn, Middlebury Coll, Vt, Calif Coll Art, San Francisco, Sch Visual Arts, NY City, Univ Pa, Calif Coll Art, San Francisco, Moore Coll Art, Tyler Sch Art, Univ of Arts, Univ Pa; res fac artist Skowhegan Sch Painting and Sculpture, Maine; instr, Pa Acad Fine Arts. *Awards:* Anonymous Was a Woman Grant; Joan Mitchell Found Grant; Pew Fel in Arts; Pa Coun on Arts Fel; Distinguished Alumni Award, Pa Acad Fine Arts, 2007. *Media:* Egg Tempera. *Dealer:* Adam Baumgold Gallery 74 East 79th St NY City NY 10021. *Mailing Add:* c/o Tibor de Nagy Gallery 724 Fifth Ave New York NY 10019

MCEWEN, ADAM
SCULPTOR, PAINTER
b 1965. *Study:* Christ Church Col, Oxford Univ, BA, 1987 (english lit); Calif Inst of Arts, 1991. *Exhib:* Solo exhibs include Much Better, 17 Rosebery Ave, London, 2002, Sleeper, Edinburgh, Scotland, 2002, Alessandra Bonomo Gallery, Rome, 2003, The Wrong Gallery, NY, 2003, The McAllister Inst, NY, 2003, History is a Perpetual Virgin..., Nicole Klagsburn Gallery, NY, 2004, Jack Hanley Gallery, San Francisco, 2006; group exhibs include Grapeshot Bullseye Harvest, Attache Gallery, London, 2001, Free Coke, Greene Naftali Gallery, NY, 2001, Art Transplant, British Consulate in NY, 2001, Yes We're Excerpts, Andrew Kreps Gallery, NY, 2002, Happy Birthday newspaper project, Gavin Brown's Enterprise, NY, 2002, I See A Darkness, Blum & Poe, LA, 2003, Melvins, Anton Kern Gallery, NY, 2003, A Matter of Facts, Nicole Klagsbrun Gallery, NY, 2003; I Love Music, Creative Growth Gallery, Calif, 2004, The Chaim Soutine: Tattoo Project, Frieze Art Fair, London, 2004, I'll Be Your Mirror: Hotel Project at Frieze Art Fair, 2004, Situational Prosthetics, New Langton Ctr for Arts, San Francisco, 2005, Post Notes, Inst Contemp Art, London, 2005, in words and pictures, Murray Guy, NY, 2005, OK/OKAY, Swiss Inst Contemp Art, NY, 2005; Take it Furthur, Andrew Mummery Gallery, London, 2005, Bridge Freezes Before Road, Barbara Gladstone Gallery, NY, 2005, Drunk vs Stoned 2, Gavin Brown Enterprise, 2005, Star Star: toward the center of attention, CAC Contemp Arts Ctr, Cincinnati, 2005, Superstars, Kunsthalle Wien, Vienna, Austria, 2005. *Collection Arranged:* A Fete Worse Than Death, 2004; Couldn't Get Ahead, Independent Art Space, London, 2004; Power, Corruption and Lies, Roth Horowitz, NY, 2004; Interstate, Nicole Klagsburn Gallery, NY, 2005. *Mailing Add:* c/o Nicole Klagsbrun 303 W 18th St Apt A New York NY 10011

MCFADDEN, DAVID REVERE
CURATOR
b 1947. *Study:* Univ Minn, BA (magna cum laude), 1972 & MA, 1978. *Collection Arranged:* The Education of Craftsmen: Silver, 1975; Exotic Entrepreneurs:Trade with the Orient, 1976; Cooper-Hewitt Collections of Decorative Arts (auth, catalog), 1978-84, Scandinavian Modern: 1880-1980 (auth, catalog), 1982, English Majolica, 1982, Tiffany Studios Metalwork, 1983, Design in the Service of Tea, 1984 & Wine: Celebration and Ceremony, 1985; L'Art De Vivre, 1989; Flora Danica, 1990. *Pos:* Cur, Minneapolis Inst Arts, 1974-78 & Cooper-Hewitt Mus, 1978-1997; chief cur & vice pres programs & collections, Mus Arts & Design, 1997-. *Teaching:* Instr MA program, Cooper-Hewitt/Parsons Sch Design, 1982-. *Awards:* Knight First Class, Order of Lion of Finland, 84; Knight Commander, Order of Northern Star, Sweden, 88; Chevalier, Ordre des Arts et des Lettres, France, 89. *Mem:* Worshipful Co Goldsmiths; Decorative Arts Soc; Soc Silver Collectors; founder Decorative Arts Asn. *Res:* Nineteenth century decorative arts and ceramics; twentieth century design. *Publ:* Auth, Recent Acquisitions in Silver: A Petrie and D Willaume, 1975, An Aldobrandini Tazza: A Preliminary Study, 1977 & Scandinavian Modern Design 1880-1980, 1984, Minneapolis Inst Bull; L'Art De Vivre: Decorative Arts and Designs in France 1789-1989, 1989. *Mailing Add:* 2 Columbus Cir New York NY 10019-1800

MCFADDEN, MARY
COLLECTOR, DESIGNER
b New York, NY, Oct 1, 1938. *Study:* Columbia Univ: Traphagen Sch of Design; Int Fine Arts Coll, Miami, Dr (fine arts), 84. *Hon Degrees:* Hon Dr, Rhode Island Sch Design. *Work:* Lannan Found, Palm Beach, Fla; Metrop Mus Art Costume Inst, NY; Fashion Inst Technology, NY; Golden Eye Exhib, Cooper Hewitt Mus, New Delhi, India. *Exhib:* The Golden Eye, Cooper-Hewitt Mus, NY, 85; Retrospective: Allentown Mus, Pa, 2005; Dixon Mus, Memphis, Tenn, 2006; More Coll Art, Philadelphia, Pa, 2008; Retrospective Nat Mus for Women in the Arts, DC, 2009; Mass Art Boston, 2010. *Collection Arranged:* Biet Giorgis Trust, Lannan Found. *Pos:* Ed, Vogue Mag, S Africa, 65-68 & US, 71-74; contribr, Rand Daily Mail, 69-70; pres & cur, Lannan Found, Palm Beach, Fla, 74-82; chmn & chief exec officer, Mary McFadden Inc, 74- & Mary McFadden Jewels, 78-; chmn, Mary McFadden Collection. *Teaching:* Instr fashion, Fashion Inst of Technol, New York, 76; instr chic, Hunter Coll, 77; instr style, Cooper-Hewitt Mus Decorative Arts & Design, New York, 77; lectr, Smithsonian Inst, Archit League, New York, Syracuse Univ, Duke Univ, Brooklyn Mus, Metrop Mus Art, New York, Newark Mus, NJ, Sackler Mus, Washington, DC, Polish Mus, Southampton, NY, Rubin Mus, New York, NY Univ Acad Med, Preservation Soc, Newport, RI & Westbury Gardens, Long Island, NY, Nat Mus Women in the Art, DC, Bing Auditorium, Los Angeles Contemp Mus Art, Calif; Lyfordcay Club, NassauBahamas; Syracuse Univ, NY. *Awards:* First Living Landmark Excellency Design, NY Landmarks Conserv, 94; Women in Urban Leadership, Marymount Manhattan Coll, 96; Designer of the Decade & Beyond, Philadelphia Breast Health Inst & Fashion Group Int; Gold Coll, Bactria Schythian. *Media:* Silk, Polyester, Metal-Cast, Mixed Media. *Interests:* travel, archaeology. *Collection:* Ancient artifacts Egypt, Greece & Madagascar; Africa; Oriental artifacts & furniture; contemp Am art, including painting by Tom Wudl, Robert Mangold, sculpture by Kenneth Shores & Isamu Noguchi; Indian 16th-19th century miniatures, ancient textiles, 13th-16th century Buddhist paintings & sculpture, Japan, Korea, Mongolia, China, Tibet & Vietnam; Gold Collection, Pre-Columbian, Indian, 3rd century BC-2nd century AD Roman & Greek, Pre-Columbian, Costa Rica, Columbia, Peru, China. *Publ:* Auth, var articles on Iran, Haiti, Madagascar, Ethiopia Burma, India, Kashmir, Usbzcistan-Tashkent & Easter Island, Vogue USA, 71; Mirabella, 89; auth, High Priestess of High Fashion, Bunker Hills Publ; Ritzolli, 2012; A Lifetime of Design, Collecting and Adventures, Rizzoli, 2013. *Mailing Add:* 525 E 72d St New York NY 10021

MCFARLAND, LAWRENCE D
PHOTOGRAPHER
b Wichita, Kans, Sept 1, 1942. *Study:* Kansas City Art Inst, Mo, BFA (photog), 73; Univ Nebr, Lincoln, MFA (photog), 76. *Work:* Ctr Creative Photog, Tucson; Int Mus Photog George Eastman House, Rochester, NY; Mus Mod Art, NY; Amon Carter Mus, Ft Worth, Tex; Carpenter Ctr Arts, Harvard, Cambridge, Mass; Houston Mus Fine Arts; Nev Mus of Art, Reno; High Mus of Art, Atlanta; Los Angeles Co Mus of Art. *Exhib:* Solo shows, Int Mus Photog, Rochester, NY, 80, Etherton Gallery, Tucson, Ariz, 82, Lone Star Gallery, Austin, Tex, 83 & 85, Nexus Gallery Photog, Atlanta, Ga, 83, Gallery Milepost Nine, Ariz Western Col, 84, SRO Gallery, Tex Tech Univ, 88, Trans Avant-Garde Gallery, Austin, Tex, 90 & Fotofest Int, Coll Mainland, Texas City, Tex, 94, Dragomanni Gallery, Coll of the Mainland, Tex City, Tex, 94, Dragomanni Gallery, Castiglion Florentino, Italy, 97, Blue Sky Gallery, Portland, Ore, 99; Road & Roadside, Chicago Art Inst, Ill, 87; Past/Present, Mus Fine Art, Houston, Tex, 92; 1992 New Orleans Triennial (catalog), New Orleans Mus Art, La, 92; Icons of the West, William Campbell Contemp Art, Ft Worth, Tex, 94; Real Vision/Photographs from the Southwest, Colo Gallery Arts, Arapahoe Community Col, 94; Canon Land Visions, Amon Carter Mus, Ft Worth, 95; Western Panoramas Städtisches Mus Simeon Trift Simeonslipfutz Trier, Ger, 95; Nev Mus of Art, Univ, Nev, Reno, 99; Visual Studies Workshop, Rochester, NY, 2000; Pine Manor Col, Chestnut Hill, Mass, 2001. *Pos:* Self-employed artist, 79-; co-dir, Etherton Ed, Tucson, Ariz, 83-. *Teaching:* Asst prof photog, Colo Mountain Col, Leadville, 78-79; assoc prof photog, Univ Tex, Austin, 85-. *Awards:* Nat Endowment Arts Fel, 78-79, 84-85 & 90-91; Guggenheim Found Fel, 2010. *Mem:* Soc Photog Educ. *Publ:* Contribr, Working papers, Am Photogr, 8/89; Memories carved in American west landscapes, Brutus, Tokyo, Japan, 8/15/89; Parting shots, Am Photogr, 11/89; Arizona Photographers: The Snell & Wilmer Collection, Ctr Creative Photog, Univ Ariz, 90; Amon Carter Museum Photography Collection (catalog), 93. *Dealer:* Ethenton Gallery 135 S Sixth Ave Tucson AZ. *Mailing Add:* 1702 Ravey St Austin TX 78704

MCGAHEE, DOROTHY BRAUDY See Braudy, Dorothy

MCGEE, BARRY
PAINTER
b San Francisco, Calif, 1966. *Study:* San Francisco Art Inst, BFA (painting & printmaking), 1991. *Exhib:* Solo shows include Maseu Lasar Segall, Sao Paulo, Brazil, 1992, Ctr for Arts, Yerba Buena, San Francisco, 1994, K&T Lionheart Ltd, Boston, 1995, Regards, Walker Art Ctr, 1998, Hoss, Rice Univ Art Gallery, Houston Tex, 1999, The Buddy System, Deitch Projects, New York, 1999 & One More Thing, 2005, Alleged Galleries, Tokyo, 2000, UCLA Hammer Mus, 2000, Gallery Paule Anglim, 2004 & 2006, Fondazione Prada, Milan, Italy, 2004, Rose Art Mus, Brandeis Univ, Boston, 2004, Stuart Shave/Mod Art, London, 2005, Nicolai Wallner Gallery,

Copenhagen, 2006, Watari Mus Contemp Art, Tokyo, 2007, Redcat, Los Angeles, 2007, Baltic Ctr Contemp Art, New Castle, UK, 2008; group shows include Big Jesus Trashcan, Victoria Room, San Francisco, 1995; Post No Bills, Acme Gallery, Oakland, Calif, 1995; Degenerate Art, The Lab, San Francisco, 1995; City Folk, Holly Solomon Gallery, NY, 1996; Wall Drawings, The Drawing Ctr, NY, 1996; John Berggruen Gallery, San Francisco, 1997, A Way With Words, 2003; Art From Around the Bay Area, San Francisco Mus Modern Art, 1998; Indelible Market, Inst Contemp Art, Phila, 2000; Made in California, LA County Mus Art, 2000; Street Market, Deitch Projects, 2000, Widely Unknown, 2001; Venice Biennale, 2001; Liverpool Biennial, England, 2002; Drawing Now: Eight Propositions, Mus Modern Art, NY, 2002; Scribble and Scripture, Roberts & Tilton, LA, 2003; Outerspace Hillbilly, The Luggage Store, San Francisco, 2003; Surf Style, 111 Minna Gallery, San Francisco, 2003; Ten By Twenty, Yerba Ctr for Arts, 2003; Gallery Paule Anglim, 2004; Beautiful Losers, Contemp Arts Ctr, Cincinnati, 2004; On Line, Louisiana Mus, Denmark, 2005; Spank the Monkey, Baltic Ctr Contemp Art, Gateshead, UK, 2006; Am Art in China, Mus Contemp Art Shanghai, China, 2007; Carnegie Int, Carnegie Mus Art, Pittsburgh, 2008. *Awards:* Lila Wallace Readers Digest Travel Grant, 1994; SECA Art Award, San Francisco Mus Modern Art, 1996; Louis Comfort Tiffany Found Grant, 1999. *Media:* Graffiti Artist. *Dealer:* Deitch Projects 76 Grand St New York NY 10013. *Mailing Add:* c/o Gallery Paule Anglim 14 Geary St San Francisco CA 94108

MCGEE, J DAVID
DIRECTOR, EDUCATOR
b Chelsea, Mass, Mar, 7, 1945. *Study:* Ind Univ, MA & PhD (Kress Found Scholar) 80. *Pos:* From asst prof to assoc prof art hist, Ind-Purdue Univ, Ft Wayne, 80-87, chair dept, 84-87; chair dept, Grand Valley State Univ, 88-. *Mem:* Coll Art Asn; Soc Archit Historians. *Res:* Medieval art and theory. *Publ:* Auth, Early Vaults of Saint-Etienne, Beauvais, Soc Archit Historians, 86; John Scotor Erigena and Some Carolingian and Ottonian MSS, Mediavistik, 88; Iconograph, of Rose Window at Saint-Etienne, Beauvais, Grand Valley Review, 89. *Mailing Add:* Dept Art & Design Grand Valley State Univ 1 Campus Dr Allendale MI 49401

MCGEE, WINSTON EUGENE
PAINTER, EDUCATOR
b Salem, Ill, Sept 4, 1924. *Study:* Univ Mo, BJ, 48 & MA, 49; Univ Wis; Ecole Superieure Beaux-Arts, 50-51; Atelier-M Jean Souverbie, French Nat Acad, 51; Fulbright Scholar to Paris, 51. *Work:* Whitney Mus Am Art, NY; Calif Palace of Legion of Honor, San Francisco; Philadelphia Mus Art; Smithsonian Inst, Washington, DC; Indianapolis Mus Art, Ind. *Comn:* Relief painting, Mo State Hist Soc, Columbia; mural, Trinity Cathedral, Cleveland, Ohio; mural, David Leach estate, Madison, Ohio; Sara Beck Mem, Lake Erie Col, 78; Calif Wall, ceramic mural, Turlock Centennial Found, Calif. *Exhib:* Solo exhib, Mitchell Mus, Mt Vernon, Ill, 74; 50th Yr Anniversary Traveling Show, Cleveland Mus, 68; Lincoln Fine Arts Ctr Dedication Exhib, 70; Atelier II, La Defense, Paris, France, 78; Calif State Univ-Stanislaus, Turlock, 78; Abante Fine Arts Gallery, Portland, Ore, 88, 92, 94 & 97; Craighead Green Gallery, Dallas, Tex, 98. *Pos:* Head, Dept Art, Lake Erie Col, 52-69; actg chmn art, Cleveland State Univ, 69-72, fac in painting, 72-76; prof & chmn art dept, Calif State Univ, Stanislaus, 77-93, prof emer, 98-. *Awards:* Cleveland Mus May Show Jury Award, 68; Annie McEntree Norton Award Painting & Graphic, Univ Mo; Gold Medal, Academie Italia delle Arti, 84; Res & Creative Grant, CSUS, 86. *Bibliog:* Articles, Graphic Artists, 72 & 75; article in Mo State Hist Soc Bulletin, 9/75; Materials & Techniques of 20th Century Artists, Cleveland Mus Art, 77. *Mem:* Cleveland Coun Arts; Cleveland Art Community; New Orgn for Visual Arts; fel Int Inst Arts & Lett (Switz). *Media:* Oil, Acrylic. *Publ:* Urban Crafts, PBS-TV, 76; Winston McGees Abstract Images, Art Seen, David Howard Production, San Francisco Ctr Visual Studies, 92; California Wall (film), Winsu Prod, 88; Winston McGee, Orchard Series, Abante Publ, Portland, Ore, 94. *Dealer:* Abante Fine Arts Gallery 204 SW Yamhill Portland OR; Craigheads Green Gallery 2404 Cedar Springs Dallas TX

MCGILL, CHARLES
PAINTER, SCULPTOR
Study: Sch Visual Arts, New york, BFA, 1986; Md Inst Coll Art, Baltimore, MFA (Ford Found fel), 1989; Skowhegan Sch Painting & Sculpture, Maine. *Work:* Brown and Willimaons Tobacco co; Bridge Country Club, NY; Synchronal Corp; and var pvt collections. *Exhib:* The Heads, Va Tech Univ, 1987; Works on Paper, JB Speed Mus, Louisville, Ky, 1988; solo exhibs, Norfolk Gallery Art, Va, 1988, Sch 33 Art Ctr, Baltimore, 1989, Barbara Ann Levy Gallery, New York, 2000, Bronx Community Coll, 2003, Alfred State Univ, NY, 2006; Art and Architecture, Albright Knox Mus, Buffalo, 1990; The Red Show, Barbara Ann Levy Gallery, New York, 1998; Night of a Thousand Drawings, Artists Space, New York, 2002; The Envelope, Please! New York Univ, 2003; For the Love of the Game: Race and Sport in African-American Art, Wadsworth Atheneum Mus, Hartford, Conn, 2007; From Africa to America: Visual Reflections on the African Diaspora, Brother Kenneth Chapman Gallery, Iona Coll, 2009. *Pos:* Dir, Arthur M Berger Art Gallery, Purchase, NY. *Teaching:* Instr drawing, Manhattanville Coll, Purchase, NY. *Awards:* Art Matters Found Grant, 2009; NY Found Arts Fel, 2009. *Bibliog:* Steve Purchase (auth), Works on Paper, Evening Sun, Baltimore, 1/19/1989; Ken Johnson (auth), Club Negro, NY Times, 5/26/2000; Douglas F Maxwell (auth), Picking CHerries - Art Miami Top Ten List, D'Art Int Mag, 2010. *Publ:* Illusr, The Six-Spoke Approach to Golf, Lyons Press, 2005. *Mailing Add:* 2900 Purchase St Purchase NY 10577

MCGILVERY, LAURENCE
BOOK DEALER, PUBLISHER
b Los Angeles, Calif, May 21, 1932. *Study:* Pomona Col, BA, 54. *Pos:* Mem adv bd, Artbibliographs Mod, Santa Barbara, 73, Who's Who in Am Art & Am Art Dir, 78. *Mem:* Art Libr Soc of NAm; Antiquarian Booksellers Asn Am. *Res:* Art periodical indexes and art bibliographies. *Specialty:* books & periodicals with emphasis on modern and contemporary art. *Publ:* Auth, Artforum, 1962-1968: A Cumulative Index to the First Six Volumes, McGilvery, 70; auth, The 21st Century Countdown Calendar, Countdown Enterprises, 98-2000; auth, The ArtForum Index (online version); coauth, several other bibliographies; The Frayed Knot and Other Sublime Tales, in press. *Mailing Add:* PO Box 852 La Jolla CA 92038

MCGINNIS, CHRISTINE
PAINTER, PRINTMAKER
b Philadelphia, Pa. *Study:* Pa Acad Fine Arts; Fleisher Art Mem. *Work:* Mus Nat Sci, Philadelphia; Civic Ctr Mus, Philadelphia; Free Libr Philadelphia; Am Embassy, Dublin, Ireland; Pa Acad Fine Arts. *Exhib:* Philadelphia Art Mus Regional Exhib, 64; Brooklyn Art Mus 14th Nat Exhib, NY, 65; Am Express Pavillion, NY World's Fair, 66; Libr Cong 20th Nat, Washington, DC, 67; Washington Art Mus, 77-81; Art Expo Traveling Show, 80-83; One-person shows, Roger LaPelle Galleries, 82, 84, 86, 89, 90, 93 & 97; Touchstone Gallery, Washington, DC, 88; Phoenix Gallery, NY, 88; Rose Lehrman Art Ctr, Harrisburg, Pa, 95. *Teaching:* Fleisher Art Memorial, Philadelphia; Sch Art League, Philadelphia; Wynne Art Ctr, Philadelphia. *Awards:* Award, Albany Print Club, 68; First Prize, Pa Acad, 74; Second Prize, Allentown Mayfair Festival, 92; Fellowship Prize, PAFA, 00. *Bibliog:* Margaret Holbern Ellis (auth), The Care of Prints and Drawings, 78; The Woodmere Art Museum: Index to the Permanent Collection, 86. *Mem:* Fel, Pan Am Festival Asn & Pa Acad Fine Arts. *Media:* Acrylic, Graphics. *Publ:* Illusr, Ctr City Mag, 63; Promenade Mag, 68; Audubon Mag, 70; Decor Mag, 78; Imfad Cat, 77-80. *Dealer:* Rodger LaPelle Galleries, Philadelphia. *Mailing Add:* 5929 Devon Pl Philadelphia PA 19138

MCGINNISS, JIM
SCULPTOR
b Bloomfield, NJ, 1932. *Study:* self taught. *Work:* Stairway to Dedication, New Hope Fire Co, New Hope, Pa; Jump'n for Joy, Pearl S Buck Hist House, Penn; Yesterday Shadows, Entrance to Doyles Town hos, Doylestown, Pa. *Comn:* Replica model, New Hope CofC, New Hope, Pa, 2001; Fiddler on the Roof, Village Art Works, Lahaska, Pa, 2004. *Exhib:* Solo exhib, Mary Anthony Gallery, SoHo, New York, 99; Trenton City, Mus NJ, 2000; Byer's Choice Limited Corp Ctr, Chalfont, Pa, 2001; Da Vinci Art Alliance Juried Exhib, Philadelphia, Pa, 2001; Ellarslie Trenton NJ City Mus, 2006; NOVA Gallery, 2005; Selma Burke Sculpture Show, 2005; Artsbridge at Phillip's Mill, 2006; Mary Anthony Galleries, New York. *Awards:* First place Award, Metuchen Cult Arts Comn; First place Award, Plainfield Festival of Art; Second place Award, Franklin Arts Coun; Hon by Speaker House Representatives for Stairway to Dedication (sculpture), Pa Capitol Bldg, 9/24/2006. *Mem:* Artsbridge, Lambertville, NJ; Art & Cult Coun Bucks Co, Pa. *Media:* Bronze, Kinetic Sculpture. *Specialty:* Early life. *Dealer:* Lahaska Fine Art 5785 York Rd Lahaska PA 18931. *Mailing Add:* 103 Stoney Hill Rd New Hope PA 18938

MCGLAUCHLIN, TOM
SCULPTOR
b Beloit, Wis, Sept 14, 1934. *Study:* Univ Wis, BS, 59, MS (art), 60; pottery with James McKinnell, Univ Iowa, 62; Oriental art hist, Univ Washington, 66-67. *Work:* Corning Mus Glass, NY; Toledo Mus Art, Ohio; Musee des Arts Decoratifs de la Ville de Lausanne, Switz; Nat Mus Mod Art, Kyoto, Japan; Kunst Mus, Dusseldorf, WGer; and others. *Comn:* Clouds of Joy (23' glass sculpture), Webstrand Ltd, Toledo, Ohio, 84; glass sculpture, Glass Capitol Columns, Crosby Gardens, Toledo, 86; glass & stainless steel sculpture, A Mountain for Toledo, Rotary Club Toledo, 88. *Exhib:* Glass Aus USA, Glasmuseum Frauenau, WGer, 79; Am Glass Now II, touring Japan, 80; Glass: Artist and Influence, Detroit Art Inst, 81; Nat Mus Mod Art, Kyoto, Japan, 81; Thirty Yrs of New Glass, 1957-1987, Corning Mus Glass, NY, 87; Int Exhib Glass 88, Kanazwa, Japan; and others. *Pos:* Chmn art dept, Cornell Col, Mt Vernon, 68-71. *Teaching:* Prof art, Cornell Col, Mt Vernon, Iowa, 61-71; prof & dir glass prog, Toledo Mus Art, 71-84. *Awards:* Ohio Arts Coun Grant, 79. *Bibliog:* Glass at Wagman, St Louis Globe Democrat, 4/23-24/82; Losken M Feuerzauber (auth), Glas aus USA, Kunst und Handwerk, WGer, 11-12/79. *Mem:* Glass Art Soc; Am Crafts Coun; Int Sculpture Ctr. *Media:* Glass; Steel. *Mailing Add:* 2527 Cheltenham Toledo OH 43606

MCGLOTHLIN, FRANCES G
COLLECTOR
Pos: Bd mem, Va Mus Fine Arts, 1998-2008. *Awards:* Named one of Top 200 Collectors, ARTnews mag, 2009-11. *Collection:* 19th- and 20th-century American art, especially American Impressionism. *Mailing Add:* 20489 Carson Ln Bristol VA 24202

MCGLOTHLIN, JAMES W
COLLECTOR
b 1940. *Study:* William & Mary Coll, LLB; Bar: Va, 1964. *Pos:* Chief financial officer, United co, Big Rock, Va, 1970-; dir, Birmingham Steel Corp, CSX, 1989-; bd dirs, King Pharmaceuticals, Summit Fund, Massey Energy, Basset Furniture Industries Inc, Va Business Higher Educ Coun. *Awards:* Named one of Top 200 Collectors, ARTnews mag, 2006-10. *Collection:* 19th- and early 20th-century American art, especially American Impressionism. *Mailing Add:* United Company Inc PO Box 1280 Bristol VA 24203-1280

MCGLOUGHLIN, KATE
PRINTMAKER, PAINTER
b Kingston, NY, 1962. *Study:* Univ Ariz, with Robert Colescott, BFA (painting & drawing), 85; Woodstock Sch Art, with Robert Angeloch, 95. *Hon Degrees:* Master Printmakers, WSA. *Work:* Schenectady Mus, NY. *Comn:* Ann Membership Print Woodstock Artists Asn, 1992, 2000; Ann Collector's Prints, Friends of the Woodstock School Art, 1997. *Exhib:* Int Mini Print Expos, Juniper Gallery, Napa Valley, Calif, 92; Print Club Albany Nat Exhib, Schenectady Mus, 92; State of the Art 93, New Eng Fine Arts Inst, 93; National Works on Paper, Univ Tex, 93; Printworks 98, Barrett House Gallery, Poughkeepsie, NY, 98. *Collection Arranged:* Relief Prints in Woodstock, Kleinert James Gallery, Woodstock, NY. *Pos:* Bd dir, Woodstock Sch Art,

94-99, dir, 96-. *Teaching:* Instr monotype, Woodstock Sch Art, NY, 93-, instr lithography, 96-, head printmaking dept, 2003; instr watercolor, Il Chiostro d Toscana, Italy, 98-2001. *Awards:* Sidney Laufman Award, Woodstock Artists Asn, 95, Rudolph Galleries Award, 97, Frederick-Fiolic award, 97, Jacobs-Towbin award, 2001; Kuniyoshi Fund Award, Woodstock NY, 96. *Bibliog:* Bonnie Langston (auth), Woodstock's Next Generation, Kingston Freeman, 8/94; Raymond J Steiner (auth), 4 contemporary printmakers, Art Times, 9/94; Dakota Lane (auth), Bright rises and stark ramps, Woodstock Times, 4/98; Journal of Print World, Book Review, Winter 2003. *Mem:* Woodstock Artists Asn. *Media:* Relief printing, monotype, watercolor, oil. *Res:* 11 Century Mosgics of Torcello. *Publ:* A Walk in the Woods: Selected Etchings, Lithographs, and Block Prints 1991-1996, Precipice Publ, West Hurley, NY, 2002. *Dealer:* Sarah Stitham PO Box 1397 Olivebridge NY 12461. *Mailing Add:* Woodstock Sch Art 2470 Rte 212 PO Box 338 Woodstock NY 12498

MCGLYNN, JOSEPH MICHAEL
PAINTER
b Jersey City, NJ. *Study:* Mechanics Inst, NY, 63-65; Art Students League, NY, 76-81; Ridgewood Art Inst, NJ, 97; studied with Mario Cooper, Dan Greene, and Charles Vickery, 76-81 & 93-98. *Work:* United States Coast Guard Collection Museum, Wash DC; Johnson & Johnson Corporate Headquarters, New Brunswick, NJ; Salmagundi Curators Collection, NY. *Comn:* Tea Clipper on the High Seas, Howard Boswell Engineering, Englewood, NJ, 1976; US Coast Guard Cutter Hamilton, US Coast Guard Red Beech, 41 ft Patrol at Dawn, 1981, Jim Ward, Wash DC, 1985; Aboard the Tall Ship, Jim Ward, Wash DC, 1992; 72″ x 36″ oil, Dutch Canal, New Amsterdam, Wilbert Weber, Vlissingen, The Netherlands, 2009; 72″x36″ oil, Half Moon on the Hudson River, Wilbert Weber, Vlissingen, The Netherlands, 2009. *Exhib:* United States Coast Guard Art, Officers Club, Governors Island, NY, Federal Hall/US Customs House, NY, 1988-1995; George Gray Commemoration, Nat Arts Club, NY, 1998; American Seascapes, Gallery Gee 71, Amsterdam, Holland, 2003; American Artists Professional League, Noyes Mus, Oceanville, NJ, 2004; Hudson Valley Art Assn, Newington Cropsey Mus, Hastings on Hudson, NY, 2004-2006; Olde NY, Fraunces Tavern Mus, NY, 2009; 400th Anniversary Dutch in Manhatten, Zeeuws Maritiem Mus, Vissingen, Netherlands, 2009-2010; McGlynn at the Salmagundi, Salmagundi Mus, NY, 2011. *Pos:* vice pres, Portrait Soc NJ, Ridgefield, 1979-1980; trustee, American Artists Professional League, NY, 1999-2000, vice pres, 2005-2013. *Teaching:* instr oil landscape, Westchester Country Club, Rye, NY, 1983-1988; demonstrator marine in oil, Salmagundi Gallery, NY, 2004; instr plein air landscape, Outdoor Oil Wkshps, Cape Ann, Mass, 2003-2004. *Awards:* Best in Show, NJ Portrait Soc, 1981; Best in Show, Purchase award, American Artists Professional League, Johnson and Johnson, 2002; Edmond F Ward award, Hudson Valley Art Assn, 2005; Antonio Cerino Landscape award, Salmagundi Club, 2006; Salmagundi Club award, Salmagundi Spring Auction, 2008. *Mem:* Salmagundi Club NY (art comt, 2004-current, curators comt, 2011-2014, admission comt, 2012-2013); American Artists Professional League NJ (trustee, 1998-1999, vice pres 2005-2013); Portrait Soc Am; Artists Fellowship NY; Am Soc Marine Artists; Internat Soc Marine Painters. *Media:* Acrylic, Oil, Watercolor. *Dealer:* State of the Arts 4 Wonson St Gloucester MA 01930; Salmagundi Club and Salmagundi Club Patrons Gallery 47 Fifth Ave New York NY 10003; Galarie Gee 71 Burg Vd Minnelaan 7/3211 A S Geervliet The Netherlands. *Mailing Add:* PO Box 703 Oradell NJ 07649

MCGLYNN, MARY ASPINWALL
PAINTER, SCULPTOR
b Warren, OH. *Study:* Nat Acad Design, 1994; Art Students League NY, 1978; Studied with Raymond Kinstler, Charles Vickery, Daniel Greene, Mario Cooper, 1971-1978. *Work:* United States Coast Guard Mus, Wash DC; Oradell Public Library, Oradell, NJ; Salmagundi Club, NY. *Comn:* 30″x48″ oils, Guardian of the Sea, United States Coast Guard, Wash DC, 2002; 60″ x 36″ oils, Rough Surf, Tom & Debbie Requier, Gloucester, Mass, 2005; Bass Rocks Seascape, J Magner, Gloucester, Mass, 2006; Oradell Public Library, Friends of the Library, Oradell, NJ, 2008; 1798 Maiden Lane & Williams St Wharf, Zeuws Meritiem Mus, Vissingen, The Netherlands, 2008. *Exhib:* United States Coast Guard Art Program, Federal Hall and US Customs House, NY, 1988-1995; Hudson Valley Art Asn Annual, Newington Cropsey Mus, Hastings on Hudson, NY, 1994-2002; George Gray 90th Commemorative, Nat Arts Club, NY, 1996; Regional Open Show, Blauvelt Art Mus, Oradell, NJ, 2000; American Seascapes, Galerie Gee 71, Amsterdam, Holland, 2003; American Artists Professional League, Noyes Mus, Oceanville, NJ, 2004; 400th Anniversary-Dutch in America, Zeeuws Maritiem Mus, Vissingen, The Netherlands, 2009-2010; McGlynn at the Salmagundi, Salmagundi Mus, NY, 2011. *Pos:* bd dirs, awards judge, recording sec, American Artists Professional League, Toms River, NJ, 1996-2003; bd dirs, correspondence sec, Salmagundi Club, NY, 2003-2004, chmn admissions, 2004-2013. *Teaching:* instr portraiture, Golden Meadow Artists, New Orleans, LA, 1976-1977; instr oil painting, Hackensack Bd Educ, Hackensack, NJ, 1978-1994, instr watercolor, 1978-1994; prestige art, Oradell, NJ, 1995-2001. *Awards:* Best in Show, Barrons Art Ctr, American Artists Professional League, NJ, 1999; Best Seascape Painting, Hudson Valley Assn, 2000; Joseph and Daisy Salomon award, Joseph and Daisy Salomon, Pastel Soc Am, 2002; Special Presidents award, J & J Corporate Gallery, 2002. *Mem:* Salmagundi Club of NY (corresponding sec, 2003-2004, chmn admissions, 2004-2013); American Artists Professional League NJ Chapter (recording sec, 1996-2003); Hudson Valley Art Assn (historian, awards chmn, 1997-2000); Portrait Society of NJ (recording sec, 1976-1977). *Media:* Acrylic, Oil, Clay, Stone, Watercolor, Pastel. *Dealer:* Salmagundi Club Patrons 47 Fifth Ave New York NY 10003; Galerie Gee 71 3211 AS Geervliet Amsterdam The Netherlands; State of the Arts 4 Wonson St Gloucester MA 01930. *Mailing Add:* 737 Greentree Lane Oradell NJ 07649

MCGOUGH, CHARLES E
PRINTMAKER, EDUCATOR
b Elmhurst, Ill, Aug 2, 1927. *Study:* Southwestern Univ; Ray Vogue Commercial Art Sch, dipl; Univ Tulsa, BA & MA; NTex State Univ; also with Hardin Simmons. *Work:* Boston Mus; Philbrook Mus; Dallas Mus Fine Arts; Little Rock Mus Fine Arts. *Comn:* Genre mural, Southern Hills Country Club, Tulsa, Okla, 56; mural, ETex State Univ, Commerce, 63; mural, Goodfellow AFB, San Angelo, Tex, 64; several graphic works, First Nat Bank, Dallas, Tex, 65; several graphic works, Southwestern Life Ins Co, Dallas, 67. *Exhib:* Nat Serigraph Ann, Brooklyn Mus Art, 63; Drawing USA, Walker Art Ctr, 66; Nat Print Ann, Boston Mus Fine Arts, 67; Southwest Print & Drawing Ann, Dallas Mus Fine Arts, 67, 68 & 70; Nat Print & Drawing Ann, Okla Art Ctr, 69-72. *Pos:* Owner, McGough Advert Co, 45-50; art dir, Crane Advert, Tulsa, 50-52. *Teaching:* Instr art, N R Crogier Tech High Sch, Dallas, 52-56; prof & head art dept, ETex State Univ, 56-. *Awards:* Graphic Purchase Award, Boston Univ Mus Show, 65; Southwest Print & Drawing Ann Award, Dallas Mus Fine Arts, 67; Graphic Purchase Award, Nat Print Ann, Okla Art Ctr, 71. *Mem:* Southwest Print & Drawing Soc; Tex Asn Schs Art. *Media:* Graphics. *Publ:* Auth, Print painting, Dallas Morning News, 67; Serigraphy, Dallas Times Herald, 68; Serigraph & the total image, Tex Trends Art Educ, 68. *Dealer:* Cushing Galleries 2723 Fairmount St Dallas TX 75201. *Mailing Add:* 1603 Walnut St Commerce TX 75428-3347

MCGOUGH, PETER THOMAS
PAINTER
b 1958, Syracuse, 1958. *Study:* Univ Syracuse, 1976; Fashion Inst Tech, 1978. *Exhib:* Solo exhibs include Massimo Audiello Gallery, NY, 1985, 1986, 1987, 1988, Pat Hearn Gallery, NY, 1986, Galleria Lucio Amelio, Naples, 1986, Frankfurter Kunstverein, Germany, 1986, Robert Miller Gallery, NY, 1989, 1992, Sperone Westwater Gallery, NY, 1990, 1992, Fraenkel Gallery, San Francisco, 1990, 1992, Gian Enzo Sperone, Basel, Switzerland, 1991, Fay Gold Gallery, Atlanta, 1991, Galerie Philippe Rizzo, Paris, 1992, Torch Gallery, Amsterdam, 1994, 2004, Temple Bar Gallery, Dublin, Ireland, 1997, Provincial Mus Modern Art, Belgium, 1997, Galerie Jerome de Noirmont, Paris, 1998, 2000, 2002, Akureyri Art Mus, Icleand, 2003, Cheim & Read Gallery, NY, 2006; group exhibs include James Graham & Sons Gallery, NY, 1995; Robert Miller Gallery, NY, 1995; Biennial, Whitney Mus Am Art, NY, 1995; Marlborough Gallery, NY, 1996; Royal Hibernian Acad, Ireland, 1997; Guy Mc Intyre, NY, 1998; Triskel Art Ctr, Cork, Ireland, 1998; Irish Mus Modern Art, Dublin, Ireland, 1998; The White Chapel Gallery, London, 2000; Boutique le Printemps, Paris, 2000; Edwynn Houk Gallery, NY, 2001; Mus Modern Art, Ostende, 2001; Robinson Gallery, NY, 2002; Musee des Beaux Arts de Tourcoing, 2003; Akureyri Art Mus, 2003; Cheim & Read, NY, 2004; Galerie Jerome de Noirmont, Paris, 2006. *Pos:* Mem, McDermott & McGough, currently. *Mailing Add:* c/o Chem and Read Gallery 547 W 25th St New York NY 10001

MCGOWIN, ED (WILLIAM EDWARD)
PAINTER, SCULPTOR
b Hattiesburg, Miss, June, 2, 1938. *Study:* Univ Southern Miss, BS, 61; Univ Ala, MA, 64. *Work:* Whitney Mus Am Art & Guggenheim Mus, NY; Hirshhorn Mus, Nat Collection Fine Arts & Corcoran Gallery, Washington, DC; Ogden Mus Southern Art. *Comn:* Sculpture, Dallas Rapid Transit Authority, Tex, 94; NY Supreme Court, Queens, 98; Univ Iowa, Cedar Falls, 2003; sculpture, Ft Lauderdale, Fire Rescue, 2006; sculpture, Rockville Town Sq, Md, 2008; Art Garden Comn, Mississippi Mus Art, Jackson, 2011. *Exhib:* Group exhibs, Whitney Mus Am Art, NY, 66 & 76, Corcoran Gallery of Art (with catalog), Washington, DC, 75, Guggenheim Mus, NY, 83, Miss Mus Art, (with catalog), Miss, 89, Art What Thou Eat, Edith Blum Gallery (with catalog), Bard Coll, NY, 90, Beyond Realism: Image & Inigma in Am Art (with catalog), Southern Alleghenies Mus, Loretto, Pa, 92, In the Ring (with catalog), Snug Harbor Cult Ctr, NY, 93, Thirty Something (with catalog), Fine Arts Mus South Mobile, Ala, 94, Southern Trade, Brenau Univ, Gainsville, Ga, 2005, 45 from Litchfield, Bachelier-Kardonsky, Kent, Conn, 2006, The Mississippi Story, Miss Mus Art, Jackson, Miss, 2007, O What a Night, Ogden Mus, New Orleans, La, 2009, Art Park 74-84, SUNY Buffalo, NY, 2010, Wash Color and Light, Corcoran Gallery Art, Wash DC, 2011, Best of South, Greg Thompson Gallery, Little Rock, Ark, 2012; solo exhibs, Baltimore Mus Art (with catalog), 72, Int Painting Exhib, Cagnes Sur Mer, France, 76, Mus Mod Art, Paris, 78, Contemp Art Ctr, New Orleans, La, 82, PS1, New York, NY & Cranbrook Acad Art Mus, Bloomfield Hills, Mich, 83, Ctr For Fine Arts, Miami, Fla, 87, Boca Raton Mus Art (with catalog), Fla, 91, Paris, NY, Bangkok Gallery, Thailand, Anderson Gallery, Buffalo, NY & Silpakorn Univ, Bangkok, Thailand, 94, Grey Gallery, New York Univ, NY, 95, Miss Mus Art, Jackson, Miss, 2000, Mobile Mus Art (catalog), Ala, 2006, PSI, MOMA, Long Island City, NY, 2006, Ogden Mus Southern Art, New Orleans, La, 2007, Flint Inst Art, Mich, 2008; Moode Gallery, Univ Ala, 2007; OCW Coll, Niceville, Fla, 2007; Tallinn Icunsethoone, Estonia, 2008; Gallery Jan Colle, Ghent, Belgium, 2009; Miss Mus, Jackson, Miss, 2009; Herron Inst Art, Indianapolis, Ind, 2010; Katzin Gallery, Am Univ, DC, 2010; Banned in DC, Vanetta 244, Brooklyn, NY, 2013; Wash Art Matters, Katzen Gallery, Am U, Wash DC, 2013. *Pos:* prof emeritus, State Univ, NY. *Teaching:* Prof, State Univ NY, Old Westbury, 1976-2003. *Awards:* Grants, Nat Endowment Arts, 67, 76 & 80, Cassandra Found, 72. *Bibliog:* Jane Livingston Corcoran (auth), True Stories, Gallery Art, Washington, 75; Susan Freudenhime (auth), The Southern Voice, Ft Worth Art Mus, Tex, 81; Eleanor Heartney (auth), Ed McGowin at Gracie Mansion, Art in America, 141-142, 3/87; Helen L Kohen (auth), Center for the Fine Arts Tempts Eye, Mind, Imagination, The Miami Herald, 2/87; Timothy Eaton (auth), Ed McGowin Painting, Boca Raton Mus Art, Fla, 91; Patama Jantrapinan (auth), Unlocking Art's Secret, The Nation, Bangkok, 2/94; Racial Profiling, Style Weekly, Richmond, Va, 2/2003; Artful Travelers Still Making Magic After All These Years, The Gazette, Bethesda, Md, 2004; Confronting the Souths Complexities, Atlanta Jour-Constitution, 2004; Gunn's Fund Raiser, Litchfield Co Times, Conn, 2005; Ed McGowin, Namechange, Mobile Mus Art, Ala, 2006; Thomas B Harrison (auth), Fall Colors, Press Register, Mobile, Ala, 10/2006; Megan Heuer (auth), Art News, 2008; Carol Azizian (auth), The Art of Reinvention, Flint J, 7/2008; The Art Garden

Blossoms, Clarion Ledger, Jackson, Miss, 2011; In Good Hands, The Clarion Ledger, Jackson, Miss, 2011; William Ferris (auth), The Storied South, 2013; Sean Cohen (auth), Wash Art Matters, 2013. *Mem:* Century Asn NY. *Media:* Mixed Media. *Interests:* Am untrained artists of 20th century. *Dealer:* Gracie Mansion Gallery 54 St Marks Pl New York NY 10009; Barbara Gillman Gallery Miami Fla; Osuna Gallery Bethesda Md; Greg Thompson Little Rock Ar. *Mailing Add:* 96 Grand St New York NY 10012

MCGRAIL, JEANE KATHRYN
PAINTER, PHOTOGRAPHER
b Minneapolis, Minn, May 1, 1947. *Study:* Univ Wis, River Falls, BS, 70; Cranbrook Acad Arts, MFA, 72; Sch Art Inst, Chicago. *Work:* Univ Wis, Milwaukee; Miami-Dade Pub Libr, Fla; Univ Chicago; Nat Mus Women Arts, Washington, DC; Mus Sci & Indust, Chicago; Oakton Coll. *Exhib:* Nat Mus Women in Arts, Washington; Mini Print Int Cadaques, Adogi Taller, Galleria Fort, Spain, 2000-2014; Blue, Northeastern State Univ Gallery, Chicago & Space 900 Gallery, Chicago; 14th Mini Print Int Exhib, Binghamton, NY, 2000; Visions Toward Wellness, Macy Gallery, NY, 2000; 24th Ann Invite Drawing, Norman R Eppink Art Gallery, Emporia, Kans; Red, Oakton Community Coll; Ukrainian Mus, 2003; Lake Co Community Coll, Ill, 2003; Chautauqua Natl Exhib, NY, 2004; Ukrianian Mus Modern Art, Chicago, 2004; Rockford Coll Art Gallery, 2006; Phipps Ctr, Hudson, Wis, 2006; Inspiring Change: Global Warming, Chicago, 2007; Viridian Artists Inc, New York, 2009; Best of Best, Art Alliance, Peabody Mus, Oak Brook, Il, 2010; Pres Gallery, Truman Coll, 2011, 2012; Arc Gallery, Chicago, 2013. *Pos:* Ed, CAG Newslett, Miami, Fla, 78-80; exec bd dir, CWCA, 92-95. *Teaching:* Pvt instr; adj fac, Truman Coll, 96-2012, & DePaul Univ, Chicago, 2008, photog adv. *Awards:* Award, Art Auction Exhib, N Miami, Fla, 80; Chicago Cult Arts CAAP Grant, 92; TCIA-art Institute of Chicago, 2004; Scholar, CTS Chgo, 2012. *Mem:* Chicago Artists Coalition; Women's Caucus for Arts; Nat Asn Photoshop Profs; Coll Art Asn; Chicago Prof Photogs Asn; Sierra Club (exec comt, formerly, sec prairie group); Soc of Photog Educators. *Media:* Printmaker, Digital Imaging, Photography. *Publ:* Best of Printmaking, IBID Collections; auth, Touching the Edges of Winter, 2008; Fierce with Reality, 2009. *Dealer:* Space 900 Group 1040 West Huron LLW Chicago IL 60622. *Mailing Add:* 1S035 Euclid Ave Oakbrook Terrace IL 60181

MCGREW, BRUCE ELWIN
PAINTER
b Wichita, Kans, Oct 20, 1937. *Study:* Wichita State Univ, Kans, BFA; Univ Ariz, MFA, 64. *Work:* Nat Park Serv, Three Rivers, Calif & Haleakala Nat Park, Maui, Hawaii; Univ Minn, Morris; Univ Kansai, Osaka, Japan; Univ Ariz, Law Sch. *Comn:* oil landscape, Georgetown Leather, Washington, DC, 77; watercolor, Pennie Edmonds Law Firm, NY, 77. *Exhib:* Kiosko del Arte, Hermosillo, Mex, 78; Maggie Kress Gallery, Taos, NMex, 79; Marion Locks, Philadelphia, 81; Colorado Springs Fine Arts Ctr, Colo, 81; Univ Ark, Fayetteville, 81; and others. *Teaching:* Instr painting & drawing, Univ Minn, Morris, 64-66; prof art, Univ Ariz, Tucson, 66-; artist-in-residence, Nat Park Serv, Sequoia & Kings Canyon Nat Park, Three Rivers, Calif, summer 75 & Haleakala Nat Park, Maui, Hawaii, summer 76; mem staff watercolor workshop, Summervail Art Workshop, Vail, Colo, summer 77; mem staff drawing & watercolor workshop, Univ Tex, El Paso, 4/78 & Guadalajara Summer Sch, Univ Ariz, 79. *Awards:* Fac Res Support in Humanities & Sociology, Univ Ariz, Tucson, 72-73; Purchase Awards, 13th Ann Cedar City Exhib, Utah, 74 & Ninth South Western Invitational Yuma Fine Arts Asn, Ariz, 75. *Media:* Watercolor, Oil. *Publ:* Contribr, Oracle: A Voluntary of Poems and Prints, Oracle Press, 74. *Dealer:* Marion Locks Gallery 1524 Walnut Philadelphia PA 19102. *Mailing Add:* PO Box 160 Oracle AZ 85623

MCGUIRE, MAUREEN
DESIGNER, STAINED GLASS ARTIST
b Flushing, NY, July 13, 1941. *Study:* NY State Coll Ceramics, Alfred Univ, BFA, 63; Pope Pius XII Inst, Florence, Italy (affil Rosary Col, Ill), Cardinal Spellman scholar & MA, 64; workshop, with Ludwig Schaffrath, Berkeley, Calif, 75. *Comn:* Design for large tapestry, La Casa De Cristo Lutheran Church, Paradise Valley, Ariz; leaded stained glass windows & laminated glass screen wall, St Matthew's United Methodist Church, Bowie, Md; faceted glass window, skylights, mosaic walls, exterior concrete bas relief sculptures, interior design, furniture design incorporating flower display system, St Francis Cemetery Resurrection Mausoleum; commercial installation: 15 faceted glass windows, Paradise Valley Mall, Paradise Valley, Ariz; residential installation: leaded glass window & light fixtures, Logan Van Sittert residence, Phoenix; and many others. *Pos:* Apprentice designer-craftsman, Glassart Studio, Scottsdale, Ariz, 64-69; independent artist-designer, Phoenix, 69-. *Awards:* Honor Awards, Nat Conf Relig Archit, 68 & Interfaith Forum Relig, Art & Archit, 79. *Bibliog:* Ann Patterson (auth), Stained glass: The art, Ariz Repub, 9/30/79. *Mem:* Stained Glass Asn Am; Interfaith Forum Relig, Archit & Arts; Am Craft Coun; Ariz Stained Glass Asn. *Media:* Leaded and Faceted Stained Glass; Mosaics in Glass. *Publ:* Auth-illusr, The case for the independent designer, Stained Glass Quart, 4/80. *Mailing Add:* 924 Bethany Home Rd E Phoenix AZ 85014-2147

MCGUIRE, RAYMOND J
PATRON
Study: Harvard Univ, AB, MBA, JD. *Pos:* Co-Head Global Investment Banking Citigroup, Inc; Managing dir, mergers & acquisitions group, First Boston Corp, Wasserstein Perella & Co Inc, Merrill Lynch, Morgan Stanley; trustee, Int Ctr Photog; trustee, Whitney Mus Am Art, mem investment comt; trustee, NY Presbyterian Hosp; chmn bd dir, Studio Mus; trustee, Lincoln Ctr; trustee NY Pub Libr; chmn bd, De La Salle Acad. *Mailing Add:* Citigroup 388 Greenwich St New York NY 10013

MCHAM, SARAH BLAKE WILK
HISTORIAN, EDUCATOR
b Boston, Mass. *Study:* Inst d'Art et Archéologie, Paris, France, 65-66; Smith Col, BA, 66; Inst Fine Arts, New York Univ, PhD, 77. *Teaching:* Asst prof art hist, Rutgers Univ, 78-84, assoc prof, 84-86, chmn, 86-90, prof, 92- & chmn, 96-99. *Awards:* Am Philoso Soc Grant, 81, 86 & 2000-01; Am Coun Learnd Soc, 84; Gladys Krieble Delmas Grant, 81, 2000 & Publ Subvention Grant, 93; Inst Advanced Study, Princeton Univ, NJ, 2001-01. *Mem:* Coll Art Asn; Renaissance Soc Am; Ital Art Soc. *Res:* Italian Renaissance sculpture and painting. *Publ:* The Chapel of St Anthony in Padua and the Development of Venetian Renaissance Sculpture, Cambridge Univ Press, 93; Looking at Italian Renaissance Sculpture, Cambridge Univ Press, 98, 2d ed, 2000; Donatello's bronze David and Judith as Metaphors of Medici Rule in Florence, Art Bull, Vol 83, 2001; La scultura esterna di Santa Maria dei Miracoli, S Maria dei Miracoli, Instituto Veneto, 2002; Renaissance Monuments to Favourite Sons, Ren Studies, Vol 19, No 4, 458-86, 9/2005; Structuring communal history through repeated metaphors of rule & The interior decoration of the Palazzo della Signoria, in: Renaissance Florence: A Social History, Cambridge Univ Press, 2006; Now and Then: Recovering a Sense of Different Values, Depth of Field, The Place of Relief in the Time of Donatello, 305-50, 2007; A Padua, Bassano, & Treviso, Venice and the Veneto, Cambridge Univ Press, 207-51, 2007; Reflections of Pliny in Giovanni Bellini's Woman with a Mirror, Artibus et Historiae, 58, 157-71, 2008; Oedipal Palimpsest, Source, Notes in the History of Art, 27, No 4, 37-46, summer 2008. *Mailing Add:* Dept Art Hist Voorhees Hall Rutgers Univ 71 Hamilton St New Brunswick NJ 08901-1248

MCILVAIN, DOUGLAS LEE
EDUCATOR, SCULPTOR
b Mt Holly, NJ, July 26, 1923. *Study:* Tyler Sch Fine Arts, Temple Univ, BFA & BS, Tyler Sch Fine Arts Rome; New York Univ, MA (art educ); also with Raphael Sabatini, Jose De Creeft & Bruno Lucchesi. *Work:* Monmouth Univ, NJ; Merrill Lynch, Princeton, NJ; Tyler Sch Fine Arts Rome; Stanford, Conn Forum; Georgian Ct Univ, NJ. *Comn:* Four portraits, Health Hall of Fame, 80; Bell Tel Labs, 82; Portrait, Roosevelt Hosp, 89; Statue for ARC, NJ, 91; portrait, Mahatma Gandhi, 94; and others. *Exhib:* Pa Acad Art, 60; Morris Mus, NJ, 82; Art Expo, NY, 83; Monmouth Mus, NJ, 85-88, 92 & 94; Phoenix Gallery, NY, 92; Guild Creative Arts, 92; Lever House, NY, 95; and others. *Pos:* Art designer, Monmouth Mus, 78-79. *Teaching:* Assoc prof art, Georgian Ct Univ, 68-86; instr sculpture, Longboat Key, Fla, 98-2008; Seabrook and Scan, 2001-2004. *Awards:* First Prize, Jersey City Mus, 61; First Prize, Red Bank Festival Arts, 61-62, 64-65, 67, 69-71 & 73; First Prize, Guild of Creative Arts, 89; Best of Show Award, Longboat Key, Fla, 2000. *Mem:* Sculpture Asn NJ, vpres; Guild Creative Arts; Art Alliance; Am Asn Univ Prof; Int Sculpture Ctr. *Media:* Bronze, Wood. *Publ:* Bound Secret, 2010

MCILVAIN, FRANCES H
PAINTER, INSTRUCTOR
b Newark, NJ, May 11, 1925. *Study:* Tyler Sch Art, Temple Univ, BFA & BS, 47, Temple Univ Rome, with Charles LaClair, 65; Philadelphia Mus Sch Art, with W Emerton Heitland, 48; with Mario Cooper, 75, Nicholas Reale, 80, Marilyn H Phyllis, 89 & Louise Cadillac, 98. *Work:* Temple Univ, Philadelphia, Pa; Bell Laboratories, Holmdel, NJ; Continental Group Computer Hq, Conn; Firmenich Corp, Princeton, NJ; Nabisco Brands, E Hanover, NJ; Off of Senator John O Bennett, Majority Leader, State House, Trenton, NJ, 94-98. *Comn:* Mural of Noah's Ark, First Presbyterian Church, Red Bank, NJ, 60; paintings, Atchison Sch, Tinton Falls, NJ, 70 & 81; mural, Monmouth Mus, Lincroft, NJ, 80. *Exhib:* Am Watercolor Soc, NY, 65-70; Garden State Watercolor Soc, Princeton, NJ, 81-2000; Art Expo, NY, 83; Ann Open Show, NJ Watercolor Soc, 85, 88-93, 88-89; Philadelphia Watercolor Soc, 94; Georgian Ct Univ, Lakewood, NJ, 2003; Longboat Rey Art Ctr State Show, 2003-06; Seabrook Village Art Shows, Tinton Falls, NJ, 2012. *Pos:* Halsted & Van Vechten/Advert, 52-58. *Teaching:* Instr art, Rancocas Valley Regional High Sch, Mt Holly, NJ, 47-53; instr, Seabrook Village, Tinton Falls, NJ, 2001-2003; instr art, Tinton Falls Sch, NJ, 63-83, SCAN Learning Ctr, Eatontown, NJ, 2003-06. *Awards:* Monmouth Arts First Prize, 83, Second Prize, 85; Best in Show, 88; Excellence Award, Garden State Watercolor, 93; Garden State 2000 Best in Show; Third Prize, Guild of Creative Arts, Shrewsbury, NJ, 2005; First Prize, Longboat Key Art Ctr, Fla, 2005 & 06; color fin award, 1st Ann NJ Pastel Show, Guild of Creative Arts, Shrewsbury, NJ, 09. *Bibliog:* Watercolours in a Weekend, Godsfield Press; Hazel Harrison (auth), David and Charles Publishers, London, 2000. *Mem:* Guild Creative Arts, (bd mem, 75-98); Am Watercolor Soc; NJ Watercolor Soc (1st vpres, 79-86, pres, 92-94); Garden State Watercolor Soc; Soc Experimental Artists. *Media:* Acrylic, Oil, All Media, Watercolor. *Publ:* Auth, Splash 3, North Light Books; Best of Watercolors, Rockport Press. *Mailing Add:* 612 Sandy Cove Tinton Falls NJ 07753

MCILVANE, EDWARD JAMES
STAINED GLASS ARTIST, GLASSBLOWER
b New York, NY, July 5, 1947. *Study:* St John's Univ, New York, BS (Art Educ), 75, RI Sch Design with Dale Chihuly & James Carpenter, MFA (Glass), 78. *Work:* Pilchuck Sch, Stanwood, Wash; Patrick Lannon Found, Palm Beach, Fla. *Comn:* Lobby windows, Temple Beth-El, Providence, RI, 82; chapel windows, Good Shepherd of Hills, Cave Creek, Ariz, 84; exec off windows, Bank of Boston, Mass, 85; two leaded glass skylight windows, Ctr Law & Soc, Stonehill Coll, N Easton, Mass, 90; Lobby windows, Presby World Hq, Louisville, Ky, 92. *Exhib:* Young Americans in Clay & Glass, Mus Contemp Crafts, NY, 78; Das Bild in Glas (with catalog), Hessiches Landsmuseum, Darmstadt, W Ger, 79; Art in Craft Media: The Haystack Tradition, traveling exhib, 81; 3-Dimensions, Univ Tex, El Paso, 85; A History of Excellence, Newport Art Mus, RI, 87. *Teaching:* Instr stained glass, Haystack Mountain Sch Crafts, 77 & RI Sch Design, 78-; prog coordr, stained glass, Pilchuck Sch, 78. *Awards:* Crafts Fel, 80 & Design Fel, 86, RI State Coun Arts; Visual Artists Fel, Nat Endowment Arts, 83. *Bibliog:* K & F Breydert (auths), Ars Pro Deo, SMI,

Paris, 86; Kemp & Perron (auths), Architectural Ornamentalism, Whitney Libr Design, 87. *Mem:* Am Crafts Coun. *Media:* Stained Glass. *Publ:* Contribr, artist's statement, In: Art in Craft Media, Bowdoin Coll Press, 81; auth, New perspectives on glass in architecture, Glass Art Soc J, 87. *Mailing Add:* 329 Pomfret Rd Brooklyn CT 06234

MCINERNEY, GENE JOSEPH
PAINTER
b Easton, Pa, Jan 6, 1930. *Work:* Miniature Art Soc NJ, Nutley; Fred Clark Mus, Carversville, Pa; Meadowbrook Sch, Philadelphia, Pa. *Comn:* Bicentennial Calendar, Northampton Co, Pa, Bicentennial Comn, 75. *Exhib:* Miniature Painters, Sculptors & Gravers Soc, Washington DC Arts Club, 72 & 73; Nat Soc Painters in Casein & Acrylic, NY, 72-75 & 98-2007; Mainstreams Int, Marietta, Ohio, 72 & 73; Butler Inst Am Art, Youngstown, Ohio, 84, 85 & 86; 20th Century Realism, Philip Desind Collection, Southbend Mus, 94. *Pos:* Adv panel, Winsor & Newton Artists, 93-95. *Awards:* Mainstreams Award of Excellence, Marietta Coll, 72; Don Selchow Award, Northeast Watercolor Soc, 95; Howard Mandell Award, Nat Soc Painters in Casein & Acrylic, 2002. *Bibliog:* Art, Gene McInerney, La Rev Mod, 11/72; Gene McInerney Lehigh Valley Painter, (PBS Channel 39, 7:30), 2/05/2007. *Mem:* Nat Soc Painters in Casein & Acrylic. *Media:* Acrylic, Watercolor, Oil. *Publ:* Taking Advantage of Acrylics, Watercolor, An Am Artist Publ, fall 91; Maximum Impact, The Artist's Mag, May 99; Reproductions of Oil & Acrylic Paintings, Bruce Mcgaw Graphics, 2003; The Delicate Engineer, Am Artist, 10/2006. *Mailing Add:* Gene McInerney Studio 315 Brodt Rd Bangor PA 18013-9236

MCINTOSH, GREGORY STEPHEN
PAINTER
b Ojai, Calif, May 7, 1946. *Study:* Santa Clara Univ, BA, 68 & MA, 71. *Work:* Libr Cong, Washington, DC; Muskegon Mus Art, Mich; Calif Palace Legion Hon & San Francisco Mus Mod Art; Los Angeles Co Mus Art, Arco Ctr Arts, Calif Confed Arts & Cedar Sinai Med Ctr; Oakland Mus, Calif; Calif Arts Counc, Sacramento, Calif; Univ Art Mus, Univ Calif, Santa Barbara, Calif; Miami Beach Fine Arts Comn, Miami Beach, Fla; Aurora Pub Art Comn, Aurora, Ill. *Comn:* Jazz at Ojai, Commemorative Fine Art Posters, 81 & 82; mural, US Post Off, 83; US Olympic Comt fine art commem poster, 84. *Exhib:* Solo exhibs, Ojai Art Ctr Gallery, Calif, 88, Park Gallery, Ft Lauderdale, Fla, 88, Jewish Community Ctr, Cleveland Heights, Ohio, 89, Waterstreet Gallery, Mystic, Conn, 89, Springfield Art Asn, Ill, 89 & Bernard's Township Libr, Basking Ridge, NJ, 89, Nocturnes, Marina Gallery, Morro Bam, Calif, 2010, Nocturnes II, Nikko Gallery, Palm Springs, Calif, 2010; Boca Raton Mus Art Festival, Fla, 88, 90, 91, 92, 96 & 97; Artist Show, Novometro Gallery, Cleveland, Ohio, 90; Miami Beach Festival Art, Fla, 91, 92, 97 & 98; Calif Gold Coast Watercolor Soc Ann Competition, Ojai Ctr Arts, 92; Art & Healing, Lipsett Gallery, Nat Ins Health, Bethesda, Md, 92; Oakbrook Ctr Invitational, Ill, 96 & 98; Old Orchard Invitational, Skokie, Ill, 96 & 98; Dreams & Visions, Ojai Ctr Arts, Calif, 96 & 97; Talking to the Creator, Appleton Art Ctr, Wis, 96; N Shore Art League Nat, North Brook, Ill, 97; Key Biscayne Art Festival, Fla, 97; Fort Lauderdale Mus Art Festival, Fla, 97 & 98; Arti-Gras 97, North Palm Beaches Fine Arts Bd, Fla, 97 & 98; The Big Little Show, Ojai Ctr Arts, Calif, 98; Open Spaces: The Ojai Landscape, Ojai Ctr Arts, Calif, 98; The Art of Healing Exhib, Lipsett Gallery, Nat Inst Health, Washington, 98; Ladislaus Gallery, Palm Desert, Calif, 2003; Atmospheric Expressions, Nikki Contemp, Palm Desert, Calif, 2004; Featuring Function, Wag Artworks, Chicago, 2004; The Blues, Inspire Fine Arts, Chicago, 2005; Land Forms, San Luis Obispo Art Ctr, San Luis, Calif, 2005; Tabula Rasa, San Luis Obispo Art Ctr, San Luis, Calif, 2005; Introduction, San Luis Obispo Art Ctr, San Luis, Calif, 2005; Vignettes, Marina Gallery, Morro Bay, Calif, 2008; New Views, Firefly Gallery, Paso Robles, Calif, 2008; Paintings, McMean Gallery, San Luis Obispo Art Ctr, San Luis, Calif, 2008; Vignettes II, Cambria Libr, Cambria, Calif, 2009; Color of Autumn, Paso Robles Art Asn, Paso Robles, Calif, 2009; Brushstrokes, San Luis Obispo Mus Art, Calif, 2009, 2010, 2011; The High Season, Morro Bay Art Asn, Calif, 2010; Nocturnes, Marina Gallery, Morro Bay, Calif, 2010; Parks Imagined: Capturing the Dream, Cent Coast Natural Hist Mus, Morro Bay, 2010; Affaire in the Gardens, Beverly Hills, Calif, 2010, 2011; Beacon 4: Art & Soul, 2011; The Blues, Art Central Gallery, San Luis Obispo, Calif, 2012; McIntosh Prints, Nikko Contemp Gallery, Palm Desert, Calif, 2012; Allied Arts Ann, Cambria Ctr Arts, 2012; The Beverly Hills Art Show, Beverly Hills, Calif, 2012, 2013; Beacon 6: Awaken the Spirit, San Luis Obispo, Calif, 2013; Body Parts, Art Central Gallery, San Luis Obispo, Calif, 2013; Love, Art Central Gallery, San Luis Obispo, Calif, 2013; Palette Talent, Morro Bay Ctr Arts Annual, Morro Bay, Calif, 2013. *Collection Arranged:* Calif Arts Coun; Aurora Pub Arts Commn, Ill; City of Miami Beach, Fine Art Commn, Fla; Ventura Co Historical Mus, Venice, Calif; Univ Art Mus, Univ Calif. *Teaching:* asst prof, ret. *Awards:* Various awards, City of Miami Beach Fest Art, Fla, 91, 92, 97 & 98; Drawing Award, 97 & Cur Award Recognition, 98, Ft Lauderdale Mus Fest Art, Fla; First Place Award, Ojai Ctr Arts, Calif & Miami Beach Fine Arts Bd, Fla, 98; First Place Award in Drawing, Scottsdale Ctr for Arts, Ariz, 2002; and many others; Comt Award, Hyde Park Art Exhib, Chgo, 2002; Painting Award, Color of Autumn, 2009; Painting Award, Brushstrokes, 2010; 1st Pl Award in drawing prints & graphics, Affaire in the Gardens, Beverly Hills, Calif, 2010, 2011; Purchase Award, Beacon 4 Exhib, San Luis Obispo, Calif, 2011; Drawing and Printmaking award, Beverly Hills Art Show, Calif, 2012, 2013. *Bibliog:* McIntosh sky scapes will be displayed at Maturango Museum during March, Daily Independent, 3/87; Beate Bermann-Enn (auth), In Search of Landscape Lost, Art Scene vol 8 no 4, 12/88; Best Pastel, Rockport Publ, Mass, 96. *Mem:* Pastel Soc Am (full mem, 90). *Media:* Gouache & Pastel on Paper, Oil on canvas, monotype. *Dealer:* Anca Colbert Fine Art Ltd. *Mailing Add:* PO Box 572 Cayucos CA 93430-0572

MCIVER, BEVERLY
PAINTER
b Geensboro, SC. *Study:* NC Cent Univ, BA (painting & drawing), 1987; Pa State Univ, MFA (painting & drawing), 1992. *Exhib:* Elain Jacobs Gallery, Detroit, 1999; Weatherspoon Art Gallery, Greensboro, NC, 1999; YADDO Writers and Visual Artist Invitational, Art in General, NY, 2000; solo exhibs, Loving in Black and White, Greenhill Ctr for NC Arts, 2000, Life is Good, Joseph Gross Gallery, Tucson, 2000, Kent Gallery, NY, 2003, 2004 & 2006, Mammy, How I Love You, C Grimaldis, Gallery, Baltimore, 2003, 40 Acres Art Gallery, Sacramento, 2004, New Paintings, Pacini Lubel Gallerym Seattle, 2005, Recent Paintings, Tyndall Galleries, Chapel Hill, NC, 2005, Raising Renee, Addison Gallery of Am Art, Phillips Acad, Andover, Mass, 2006 & Raising Renee and Other Themes, NC Cent Univ Art Mus, 2007; Black Face/White Face, LewAllen Contemp, Santa Fe, 2001; Baltimore Mus Art, 2002; HairStories, Scottsdale Mus Contemp Art, 2003; Narrative Visions, C Grimaldis Gallery, Baltimore, 2004; Pacini Lubel Gallery, Seattle, 2004; Summer Camp, Patricia Faure Gallery, Los Angeles, 2004; The Nature of Craft and the Penland Experience, Mint Mus Art, Charlotte, NC, 2004; Am Acad Arts & Letts Invitational, New York, 2009. *Teaching:* Prof, Pa State Univ, NC Cent Univ, NC State Univ, Duke Univ & Ariz State Univ-Tempe. *Awards:* Res and Creative Activity Award, Ariz State Univ, Tempe, 2003; Disting Alumni Award, Pa State Univ, State Coll, 2003; Louis Comfort Tiffany Award, New York, 2004; Artist of Yr Award, Scottsdale Cult Coun, 2004; Purchase Award, Am Acad Arts and Letts, 2009; Anonymous Was a Woman Award; Guggenheim Found Fel. *Bibliog:* Joe Shannon (auth), Report from Arizona, Art in Am, 2002; Paula Wasley (auth), Behind the makeup, ART news, 11/2006; Irving Sandler (auth), Beverly McIver and photoexpressionism, Beverly McIver: Invisible Me, 2006. *Media:* Oil. *Dealer:* Lewallen Galleries 1613 Paseo de Peralta Santa Fe NM 87501. *Mailing Add:* Ariz State Univ-Tempe PO Box 871505 Tempe AZ 85287-1505

MCKAY, RENEE
PAINTER
b Montreal, Que; US citizen. *Study:* Inst Pedagogique, Montreal, Can; McGill Univ, Montreal, Can, BA, 41; studied with Ben Shahn, Morris Davidson & Joe Jones. *Work:* Slater Mem Mus, Norwich, Conn; Norfolk Mus, Va; Butler Inst Am Art, Youngstown, Ohio; Lydia Drake Libr, Pembroke, Mass. *Exhib:* Open Ann, Newark & Montclair, NJ; Nat Asn Women Artists Traveling Show, Butler Inst Am Art, Youngstown, Ohio; Nat Asn Women Artists Ann & Audubon Ann, Nat Acad Galleries, NY; Nat Asn Women Artists, Lever House & Union Carbide, NY; Weyhe Gallery, NY, 79. *Teaching:* Instr art, Peck Sch, Morristown, NJ, 55-57. *Awards:* Watercolor Award, 75 & Oil Award, 80, Audubon Artists; Acrylic Award, Nat Soc Painters Casein & Acrylic, 83; and others. *Mem:* Audubon Artists (pres, 79-80); Artists Equity Asn (vpres, 79-81); Nat Asn Women Artists (adv bd, 74-76); Nat Soc Painters Casein & Acrylic; Nat Arts Club; and others. *Media:* Acrylic, Watercolor

MCKEAN, MICHAEL JONES
INSTALLATION SCULPTOR, EDUCATOR
b Truk Island, Micronesia, 1976. *Study:* Marywood Univ, BFA, 2000; Alfred Univ, MFA, 2002. *Exhib:* Young Artists, New York, Gardo Gallery, Pa, 2000; solo exhibs, Robert Turner Gallery, Alfred, NY, 2001, SUNY Purchase Coll, NY, 2002, San Diego Mesa Coll, Calif, 2003, Mezzanine Gallery, Del, 2004, Bemis Ctr for Contemp Art, Omaha, 2005, Grand Arts, Mo, 2006, Univ Ill, Springfield, 2008, Art Verona, Italy, 2009; Yankee Clay: Ceramic Artists of the Norhteast, Slater Mus, Conn, 2002; New Colors, Station 29 Gallery, RI, 2003; Biomimicry, Univ Ind, 2004; Glassell Sch Art, Mus Fine Arts, Houston, 2005-06; Preview Exhib, Bemis Ctr for Contemp Art, Omaha, 2008; Objet Petit A, Spoke Gallery, Chicago, 2009. *Teaching:* Asst prof sculpture, Va Commonwealth Univ, Richmond, 2006-. *Awards:* Stephen L Barstow Fel, Central Mich Univ, 2003; Eliza Prize, Mus Fine Arts Houston, 2005; Nancy Graves Found Award, 2005; Va Mus Fine Arts Fel, 2010; Artadia Found Fel, 2010; Guggenheim Found Fel, 2010. *Bibliog:* Michael Fressola (auth), Evocative, Romantic, Intricate, Staten Island Advance, 8/10/1998; David Pencek (auth), Slater Expands It's Future, Norwich Bulletin, Conn, 6/21/2002; Alice Thurson (auth), AMbitious Avenue of the Arts, Kans City Star, 1/11/2003; Emily Mitchell (auth), Chasing Rainbows, Houston Mag, 208, 5-6/2005; Karen Rosenberg (auth), The Discipline of Astronomy and Wind, NY Times, 9/28/2007. *Dealer:* Horton Gallery 504 W 22nd St New York NY 10011; Inman Gallery 3901 Main St Houston TX 77002-9614

MCKEE, DAVID MALCOLM
ART DEALER
b Cumbria, Eng, Oct, 8, 1937. *Pos:* Dir, David McKee Gallery, currently. *Mem:* Art Dealers Asn Am. *Specialty:* Postwar and contemporary painting and sculpture, mainly American, including Philip Guston, Jake Berthot, Harvey Quaytman, Sean Scully & William Tucker. *Mailing Add:* McKee Gallery 745 Fifth Ave New York NY 10151

MCKEE, HUNTER
PAINTER
b Long Branch, NJ, 1950. *Study:* Boston Univ, 1970-71; Mass Coll Art, 1972, 1974, studied with George Nick; Brookdale Community Coll, Lincroft, NJ, AA, 1979. *Exhib:* Solo exhibs include Monmouth Beach Cult Ctr, NJ, 2003, West Long Branch Pub Libr, NJ, 2003, 2007, Orange St Fine Art, Nantucket, 2004, 12 Orange St Fine Art, Nantucket, 2005, Art Alliance, Red Bank, NJ, 2007; two-person exhib with David Halliday, 12 Orange Fine Art, Nantucket, 2006; group exhibs include Ann Statewide Juried Exhib, Art Alliance, Red Bank, NJ, 2000, 2003, 2004, 2005, 2007; X Gallery, Nantucket, 2001; Juried Art Show & Sale, Monmouth County Arts Coun, NJ, 2002, 2005; Beauregard Fine Art, Rumson, NJ, 2003, 2004, 2006, 2008; 12 Orange Fine Art, Nantucket, 2007; Ann Invitational Exhib Contemp Am Art, Nat Acad Mus, New York, 2008. *Awards:* 2nd Prize, Brookdale Community Coll Alumni Asn Juried Art Show, 2008. *Mem:* Art Alliance Red Bank, NJ. *Media:* Oil

MCKEE, RENEE CONFORTE
DEALER
b Belgrade, Yugoslavia; US citizen. *Study:* Mt Holyoke Col, BA (magna cum laude); Univ Paris I, Sorbonne; Ecole du Louvre, Paris. *Pos:* Admin asst, Marlborough Gallery, New York, 68-72; dir & co-owner, David McKee Gallery, New York, 74-. *Specialty:* Contemporary American art. *Mailing Add:* c/o McKee Gallery 745 Fifth Ave 4th Fl New York NY 10151

MCKENZIE, ALLAN DEAN
EDUCATOR, HISTORIAN
b Pendleton, Ore, Aug 17, 1930. *Study:* San Jose State Univ, BA (com art), 52; Univ Calif, Berkeley, MA (art hist), 55; Inst Fine Arts, NY Univ, PhD (art hist; Fulbright Scholar), 65. *Teaching:* Instr medieval art, NY Univ, 57-64; asst prof medieval & classical art, Univ Wis, Milwaukee, 64-66; assoc prof medieval art, Univ Ore, 66-74, prof, 74-90, emer prof, 90-. *Awards:* Consultation Grant, Icon Preservation Task Force, State Alaska & US Park Serv, 89; First Recipient of Earl L Hain Award for Distinguished Serv to Learning in Retirement (LIR) Prog, Univ Ore, 94; Outstanding Contributions to Learning in Retirement, 95. *Mem:* Coll Art Asn, 57-86; Archeol Inst Am (Eugene Chap pres & secy, formerly); Int Ctr Medieval Art; Medieval Acad Am, 75-82; Am Asn Advan Slavic Studies. *Res:* Russian and Byzantine painting; Medieval art. *Publ:* Auth, Greek & Russian Icons, Northwest, 65; Russian Art: Old and New, Univ Ore, 68; Provincial Byzantine painting in Attica, Cahiers Arch, 82; Russian Icons in the Santa Barbara Museum of Art, 82; Mystical Mirrors, Icons of Russia, Maryhill Mus Art, 86; Sacred Images & The Millennium; Christianity & Russia (AD 988-1988), 88; Toronto's Unique Crusaders Icon, Studies in Honor of Thomas F Mathews, 2009. *Mailing Add:* 2705 Lincoln St Eugene OR 97405

MCKENZIE, DAVE
PAINTER
b Kingston, Jamaica, 1977. *Study:* Univ Arts, Philadelphia, BFA, 2000; Skowhegan Sch Painting & Sculpture, Maine, 2000. *Exhib:* In/SITE/Out, Apexart, New York, 2001; Freestyle, Studio Mus Harlem, New York, 2001 & Figuratively, 2004; Material World, Susquehanna Art Mus/VanGo, Harrisburg, Pa, 2001; Something/Nothing, Art in General, New York, 2001 & Video Marathon, 2002; Listening to New Voices, PS1 Contemp Art Ctr, Long Island City, NY, 2002; Dave McKenzie Show, Queens Mus Art, NY, 2002 & Queens Int, 2002; Videodrome II, New Mus Contemp Art, New York, 2002; Videos in Progress, RI Sch Design Mus, 2003; In Practice, Sculpture Ctr, Long Island City, NY, 2003; 24/7, Contemp Art Ctr, Vilnius, Lithuania, 2003; Open House, Brooklyn Mus Art, NY, 2004; Together is Forever, Susanne Vielmetter Los Angeles Projects, Culver City, Calif, 2004; Portrait as a Ghost, Savage Art Resources, Portland, Ore, 2005; Haven't Seen You in a Minute, Gallery 40000, Chicago, 2006; Tomorrow will be Better, Small A Projects, Portland, Ore, 2007; Just Kick It Till It Breaks, The Kitchen, New York, 2007; IPO: New Objects, New Audiences, Whitney Mus Am Art, New York, 2007; Momentum 8, Inst Contemp Art, Boston, 2007. *Pos:* Bd govs, Skowhegan Sch Painting & Sculpture, New York. *Teaching:* Artist in residence, Skowhegan Sch Painting & Sculpture, Maine, 2000, PS1 Nat Studio Program, New York, 2001-02, Studio Mus Harlem, New York, 2003-04. *Awards:* William H Johnson Prize, 2005; Art Matters Found Grant, 2009; US Artists Rockefeller Fel, 2009. *Mailing Add:* Skowhegan Sch Painting & Sculpture 200 Park Ave Ave Ste 1116 New York NY 10003-1503

MCKENZIE, MARY BETH
PAINTER
b Cleveland, Ohio, July 30, 1946. *Study:* Mus Fine Arts, Boston, 64-65; Cooper Sch Art, 65-67; Nat Acad Design, 69-74. *Work:* Hesse Collection; Danish Bank, Mus of City of NY, Metrop Mus, NY; Butler Inst Am Art, Youngstown, Ohio; Nat Mus Women in Arts, Nat Mus Am Art, Smithsonian Inst, Washington, DC; NY Hist Soc. *Exhib:* Solo exhibs, Nat Arts Club, 76 & FAR Gallery, 80, NY; Frank Caro Gallery, NY, 88; Joseph Keiffer Gallery, 91; Union Co Col, NJ, 98; self portrait exhib, Looking at You, Metrop Mus Art, 2001. *Teaching:* Instr painting, Nat Acad Design, 81-; Art Students League, NY, 96-. *Awards:* Greenshields Found Grant & Stacey Found Grant, 78; Thomas B Clarke Prize, Nat Acad Design Ann, 81; Isaac N Maynard Prize, Nat Acad Design, 90 & 97. *Bibliog:* Harvey Stein (auth), Artists Observed, Harry Abrams, 86. *Mem:* Nat Acad; Allied Artists; Audubon Artists; Pastel Soc Am. *Media:* Oil. *Interests:* theater, literaure. *Publ:* Auth, A Painterly Approach, Watson-Guptil, NY, 87. *Mailing Add:* 525 W 45th St Apt 3 New York NY 10036-3415

MCKIE, TODD STODDARD
PAINTER
b Boston, Mass, Apr 25, 1944. *Study:* RI Sch Design, BFA (painting), 66. *Work:* Philip Morris, USA; Mass Inst Technol; Fogg Mus, Cambridge, Mass; Lincoln Ctr for the Performing Arts & Chase Manhattan Bank; Mus Fine Arts & Wellington Mgt Co, Boston, Mass. *Comn:* Mural (90ft x 40ft), City of Boston, 72; mural (7' x 60'), Mass Bay Transportation Authority, 96. *Exhib:* Eat Art, Contemp Art Ctr, Cincinnati, Ohio, 72; Boston Collects Boston, Mus Fine Arts, 73; Works on Paper, Fogg Art Mus, Harvard Univ, Cambridge, Mass, 74; Biennial Exhib, Whitney Mus Am Art, NY, 75; Painted in Boston, Inst Contemp Art, 75; Boston Watercolor Today, Mus Fine Arts, Boston, 76; Collectors Collect Contemp, Inst Contemp Art, Boston, 77; Rose Art Mus, Brandeis Univ, 90. *Awards:* Colman Award, Blanche E Colman Found, 72; Creative Artists Fel, Mass Arts & Humanities Found, 74 & 89. *Bibliog:* Carl Belz (auth), The grid and the buffet, Art Am, 3/72; David Greenberg (auth), Big art, Running Press, Philadelphia, 77. *Media:* Oil, Drawing, Sculpture. *Dealer:* Gallery Naga 67 Newbury St Boston MA 02116; Carver Hill Gallery 338 Main St Rockland ME. *Mailing Add:* 82 Holworthy St Cambridge MA 02138-4510

MCKIM, GEORGE EDWARD
PAINTER, GRAPHIC ARTIST
b Wilmington, NC. *Study:* Va Commonwealth Univ, BFA, 77; E Carolina Univ, MFA, 85; Skowhegan Sch Painting & Sculpture, study with Bell Jensen, Judy Pfaff, Peter Saul & Judith Shea. *Exhib:* NC Artist Triennial, NC Mus Art, 84, 87, 90, 93 & 96; Tampa Triennial, Tampa Mus Art, 85. *Media:* Acrylic, Oil on Canvas. *Publ:* Contribr, New American Paintings, Open Studio Press, 98. *Dealer:* Lee Hansley Gallery 16 W Martin St Suite 201 Raleigh NC 27601. *Mailing Add:* 2720 Wayland Dr Raleigh NC 27608

MCKINLEY-HAAS, MARY
PAINTER, DESIGNER
b St Louis, Mo. *Study:* Smith Col, BA; Studio & Forum Stage Design; Nat Acad Design: Art Students League with Norman Lewis. *Work:* Fontbonne Col, St Louis; Nat Mus Women Arts, Washington, DC; Northern Trust, Naples, Fla; Tari Women's Cult Ctr, New Guinea; Leon Templesman & Son, NY; Associated Textiles, NY. *Exhib:* Solo exhibs, Tarlowe Gallery, Westhampton Beach, NY, 74, Fontbonne Gallery, St Louis, Mo, 77, Gallery Yssa (Ludlow-Hyland), NY, 79, Vered Gallery, East Hampton, NY, 81, The Neth Bankt Ludlow-Hyland Gallery, New York, 81, Univ Tex, Austin, 88 & 92, RVS Fine Art, Southampton, NY, 90, TSS Gallery, NY, 92, TAI Gallery, NY, 99 & Ezair Gallery, New York, 2007; Group Show: Design 70, Contemp Stage Design USA, Lincoln Ctr, NY, 74; Parish Art Mus, Southampton, NY, 75, 76, 78 & 81; Guild Hall, East Hampton, NY, 76, 78, 81, 85 & 96; Medeci-Berenson Gallery, Miami, Fla, 81; Water Mill Mus, Water Mill, NY, 83 & 92; Five Hampton Painters, Vered Gallery, East Hampton, NY, 85; Nabisco Brands Gallery, East Hanover, NJ, 89; Queens Coll Art Ctr, NY, 91; Art by Design, Dorothy Chandler Pavillion, Los Angeles, 93; Stony Brook Univ Art Gallery, NY, 94; Elite Gallery, Moscow, Russ, 95; Nat Mus Women Arts, Washington, DC, 96; Soho 20 Gallery, NY, 98; Canajoharie Lib Art Ctr, Canajoharie, NY, 2000; Weill Cornell Med Libr, NY, 2002; Noho NY Art Walk, 2004-2005; Venezuelan Consulate 2006-2007; Westbeth Gallery, New York, 2009; Office Manhattan Borough President, New York, 2010, 2013; and others. *Pos:* Head, Costume Design Dept, ABC-TV, NY, 68-73; costume designer, CBS-TV, NY, 75-77. *Bibliog:* Helen Thomas (auth), Arts Reviews (review with black & white reproduction), Arts Mag, 9/79; Phyllis Braff (auth), From the Studio (review with black & white reproduction), East Hampton Star, 8/20/81; Jose Alaniz (auth), Nature's Growth through a Kaleidoscope (article with black & white reproduction), Daily Texan, 10/26/92; Scott Dietsch (auth) The Beauty and Danger of Lava on Exhibit, The Villager, 4/28/99; Art Pick, New York Post, 4/28/99; and several others; Christine Lyons (auth), Honoring the Artists of the Hamptons-Mary McKinley Haas; Eileen Watkins (auth), A Few Stars Shine Out from the Crowd (Rev), Newark Sunday Star Ledger, 2/5/95. *Mem:* United Scenic Artists; Women Arts Found; NY Artists' Equity. *Media:* Oil, Mixed Media; Monotype. *Publ:* Auth, Designing Shadows, In: Dark Shadows Almanac (bk), Promegranate Press, 95. *Mailing Add:* 284 Lafayette St Loft 5B New York NY 10012

MCKNIGHT, THOMAS FREDERICK
PAINTER, PRINTMAKER
b Lawrence, Kans, Jan 13, 1941. *Study:* Wesleyan Univ, Middletown, Conn, BA (art); Columbia Univ. *Work:* Davison Art Ctr, Wesleyan Univ; NY State Mus, Albany; Smithsonian Inst, Wash; Metrop Mus Art, NY; White House, Wash; Clinton Libr, Little Rock, Ark; New Britain Mus Am Art, New Britain, Conn. *Comn:* Poster & print, US Constitution Bicentennial, 89; prints, America's Cup, 92; paintings & prints, Urban Fair, Kobe, Japan, 93; White House Christmas card, Pres & Mrs Clinton, 94, 95 & 96. *Exhib:* Solo Exhibs; Basel Art Fair, 75-77; Tomic Galerie, Dusseldorf, Ger, 76; Hartmann Gallery, Munich, Ger, 77; Newport Art Asn, RI, 81; Seibu, Tokyo, Japan, 89; Davison Art Ctr, Weslyan Univ, 88; Kobe Munic Mus, Japan, 92; and many others. *Teaching:* Lectr, Crystal Cruise Lines. *Awards:* Distinguished Alumnus Award, Wesleyan Univ, 98. *Bibliog:* Thomas McKnight's World, Abbeville Press, 87; Thomas McKnight: Windows on Paradise, Abbeville Press, NY, 90; Annie Gottlieb (auth), Thomas McKnight: Voyage to Paradise A Visual Odyssey, Harper, San Francisco & Treville, Tokyo, 93; Francesco Colonna (auth), Thomas McKnight's Arcadia, Vendome Press, NY, 2006. *Media:* Casein, Serigraphy, Acrylics. *Interests:* Alchemy, neo-platonism, archetypal psychology, Venice and Greece. *Publ:* auth, Thomas McKnight, Scribners, 84. *Dealer:* Thomas McKnight LLC 315 Riggs St Bldg A Unit One Oxford CT 06478. *Mailing Add:* PO Box 98 Litchfield CT 06759

MCKOY, VICTOR GRAINGER
SCULPTOR
b Fayetteville, NC, Apr 21, 1947. *Study:* Clemson Univ, BS (biology), 70, Sch Archit, two years. *Work:* Charleston Mus, SC; Ward Found Mus, Salisbury State Col, Md; Gibbes Art Gallery, Charleston, SC; Sanderling Inn, Duck, NC; Dover Corp, NY. *Exhib:* Birds of the Wood, Am Mus Nat Hist, 74; Expressions of Nature in Art, Greenville Mus Art, SC, 75 & Columbia Mus Art, SC, 75; Bird Sculpture Birmingham Mus Art, Ala, 76; Solo exhibs, Hammer Galleries, NY, 76, Gibbes Art Gallery, SC, 84, Coe Kerr Gallery, NY, 84, Brandywine River Mus, Chaddsford, Pa, 93 & Brook Green Gardens, 99; The Artist and the Animal, High Mus Art, Atlanta, Ga, 77; Wild Am, Kodak Gallery, NY, 78; Birds in Art, Leigh Yawkey Woodson Art Mus, 85. *Bibliog:* Margaret Pridgen (auth), When Wooden Birds Take Wing, Clemson World, fall 90; James Kilgo (auth), The Birds of Grainger McKoy, Georgia Rev, spring 93; Edward Sozanski (auth), The Real McKoy, Philadelphia Inquirer Mag, 7/23/93; James Kilgo (auth), The Sculpture of Grainger McKoy, Wyrick & Co, 99. *Media:* Wood, Bronze, Sterling. *Mailing Add:* 490 N Kings Hwy Sumter SC 29154-8655

MCLEAN, JAMES ALBERT
EDUCATOR, PRINTMAKER
b Gibsland, La, Nov 25, 1928. *Study:* Southwestern La Inst, AB, 50; Southern Methodist Univ, BD, 53; Tulane Univ, MFA with J L Steg, 61. *Work:* Seattle Mus Art, Wash; High Mus, Atlanta, Ga; Brooklyn Mus, NY; Olivet Col, Mich; Minot State Col, ND. *Exhib:* 33rd, 35th, 36th & 38th Northwest Printmakers Int, Seattle Mus, Wash,

62, 64, 65 & 67; 14th, 15th, 19th & 20th Nat Print Exhibs, Brooklyn Mus, 64, 66, 74 & 76; Nat Print & Drawing Exhibs, Minot State Col, 73-76; Colorprint, USA, Tex Tech Univ, Lubbock, 74-76; Spec Interest Group on Computer Graphics, 88; Postive/Negative Exhib, ETenn State Univ, 88; Small Print Exhib, Purdue Univ, 88; SIGGRAPH, 88, 89; Artware, Cebit, Hanover, WGer, 89. *Teaching:* Assoc prof gen art, LaGrange Col, Ga, 63-66; prof printmaking, Ga State Univ, Atlanta, 66-94. *Awards:* Purchase Award, Northwest Printmakers Int, 64, Western NMex Univ Nat Print Exhib, 73 & Minot State Coll Nat Print & Drawing Exhib, 76; First prize, Glassboro State Col, 90. *Bibliog:* Illus in: Fritz Eichenberg (auth), The Art of the Print, Abrams, 76, Gene Baro (auth), 30 Years of American Printmaking, Brooklyn Mus. *Media:* Silkscreening. *Mailing Add:* 1256 Dunwoody Knoll Dr Atlanta GA 30338

MCLEAN, RICHARD
PAINTER
b Hoquiam, Wash, 1934. *Study:* Calif Coll of Arts & Crafts, Oakland, BFA, 58; Mills Col, Oakland, Calif, MFA; studied with Richard Diebenkorn. *Work:* Satin Doll, pvt collections, Oakland Mus, Calif; Smithsonian Inst; Whitney Mus Am Art, NY. *Exhib:* Whitney Mus Am Art, 70; Expo 70, Osaka, Japan; Documenta 5, Kassel, Ger, 72; This is Am, Aarhus Kunstmuseum, Aarhus, Denmark, 2001; Solo exhib, Valparaiso Univ, Ind, Univ Omaha, Neb. *Teaching:* instr, painting, drawing, San Francisco State Univ, 63-96. *Awards:* Nat Endowment for Arts, 85; Alden Bryan Meml Award for Trad Landscape Painting, Nat Acad Invitational Exhib Contemp Art Awards, 2010 . *Media:* Acrylic, Oil, Watercolor. *Specialty:* Equine and canine subjects, landscapes. *Mailing Add:* 20530 Crow Creek Rd Hayward CA 94552

MCLEOD, CHERYL O'HALLORAN
PAINTER, INSTRUCTOR
b Nov 12, 1944. *Study:* Indiana Univ, Pa, BS (art educ), 66; Boston Univ, Sch Fine Arts, 67; Mass Coll Art, 83-84; studies with Daniel Greene, Albert Handel & Robert Cormier. *Work:* Delta Corp Services, Parsippany, NJ; Cogen Technol, East Brunswick, NJ; Libr Co-op Inc, Edison, NJ; Oklahoma City Allergy Clinic, Okla; Butler & Stein Attys, Tucson, Ariz; Farley & Bernathy, LLC Law Offices; plus others. *Comn:* still life, Domestic Clutter. *Exhib:* one-woman exhibs, Georgian Court Col, Lakewood, NJ, 94, Swain Gallery, Plainfield, NJ, 95, Barron Arts Ctr, 96, Union Co Arts Ctr, Rahway, NJ, 97, Lucca's Backroom Gallery, Metuchen, NJ, 98, Palmer Mus, Springfield, NJ, 98, Children's Specialized Hosp, Mountainside, NJ, 98, Aberjona River Gallery, Winchester, Mass, 2005 & 2008; Arts Ctr Northern NJ, New Milford, 93; Winter Thoughts, Barron Arts Ctr, 93; Jersey City State Col, 93; Art Educators of New Jersey, Newark Mus, NJ, 94; Lever House Gallery, NY, 95; Exhib, Salmagundi Club, NY, 95 & 96; Catherine Lorillard Wolfe Art Club, NY, 95 & 97; Deleware Arts Alliance, Narrowsburg, NY, 2000. *Teaching:* Pvt & group instr, Studio-The Art Alcove, The Villages, Fla. *Awards:* Paul Bransom Award, Grand Nat Shows, Am Artists Prof League, 93; The Raymond Chow Memorial Award, Am Artist Prof League, 2003; Merit Award, Wilmington Arts Coun, 2006; and others. *Bibliog:* Constance Flavell Pratt & Janet Monafo (auths), The Best of Pastels, Rockport Publ, 96, Best of Pastels 2, 98; Landscape Inspirations (Quarry bk), Rockport Publ, 1/98. *Mem:* Fel Am Artists Prof League; Delta Phi Delta; signature mem, Pastel Society of America. *Media:* Pastel, Oil. *Interests:* Art educ, painting. *Collection:* pastel landscapes, kitchen art, southwest landscapes. *Publ:* The Best of Pastels 2, Rockport Pubs, 99; Landscape Inspirationa, Rockport Pubs, 88. *Dealer:* Swain Galleries 703 Watchung Ave Plainfield NJ 07060; The Art Alcove 1232 Carvello Dr The Villages FL 32162

MCMANN, EDITH BROZAK
PAINTER, SCULPTOR
b Totowa, NJ. *Study:* Sch Am Ballet, New York; George Balanchine's NYCB, 1950-1957; Westchester Art Workshop, studied sculpture with Leslie Dor, 76-84; Art Students League, studied printmaking with Michael Ponce De Leon, New York, 77; State Univ NY, studied painting with Roger Hendricks, BPS, 84; Coll New Rochelle, NY, MA (studio art), 89; Silvemine Coll Art, (internship), 89. *Work:* Nat Mus Women Arts, Washington, DC; Libr & Mus Performing Arts, Lincoln Ctr, New York; Harvard Theatre Collection, Dusey Libr, Cambridge, Mass; San Francisco Performing Arts Libr & Mus, San Francisco, Calif; Lawrence & Lee Theatre Research Inst, Columbus, Ohio; Nat Resource Ctr for Dance, Univ Surrey, UK; UCI Libr, Irvine, Calif. *Comn:* portrait, plaster sculpture, Trudy Paul, 74; Remembrance, dance sculpture, Francesca Corkel, 75; sectional abstract acrylic on canvas, Linda Rodregues, 94. *Exhib:* Solo exhib, Dance in Art, Gutman Gallery, White Plains, NY, 90; Hudson River Contemp Artists, Hammond Mus, Salem, NY, 93; Mamaroneck Artists Juried, 91-2010, Westbeth Gallery, New York, 94; Townhouse Gallery, Stamford, Conn, 2001-2010; Stamford Art Invitational, Tower Perrins Gallery, Stamford, Conn, 2002; Faber Birron, 2009. *Awards:* Cert of Merit award, Dance in Art, Sen Nick Spano, 89; Cert of Merit award, 17th Ann Art Exhib, US State Assembly, Richard Brodsky, 89; Letter of Appreciation, Greenburgh Art Exhib, US Sen Pat Moynihan, 89-90; and numerous others from 79-present. *Bibliog:* Reporter Dispatch, White Plains, NY, 5/73; The Enterprise, Westchester, NY, 11/89; Greenburgh Art & Cult, NY, 12/90; NYC Ballet Newsletter, New York, 3/2000; The Advocate, Greenwich Times, 1/14/2007. *Mem:* Mamaroneck Artist Guild, Inc (bd dirs, 90-91); Stamford Art Asn; Allied Artists Am Inc; Nat Mus Women Arts; Katonah Mus. *Media:* Painting, acrylic, all media, oil, watercolors, sculpture clay, digital art. *Interests:* Interpreting dance into realistic stylized & abstract works of art. *Publ:* Auth, Dance in Art, 2005; auth, Portrait of a Dancer, Video Artists Int, 2006; auth, Remembering Lincoln, Kirstein Ballet Soc, 2007. *Dealer:* Mamaroneck Artists Guild Gallery 126 Larchmont Ave Larchmont NY 10538; Townhouse Gallery 39 Franklin St Stamford CT 06901. *Mailing Add:* 10 Burkewood Rd Hartsdale NY 10530-2933

MCMANUS, JAMES WILLIAM
SCULPTOR, GALLERY DIRECTOR
b Glenwood Springs, Colo, Jan 1, 1942. *Study:* Colo State Univ, BFA, 65; Univ Washington, MFA, 67. *Work:* Oakland Art Mus; San Diego Art Mus, Calif; Reading Art Ctr, Eng; Henry Art Mus, Univ Washington; 3M Corp, Chicago. *Comn:* Expo '74, Spokane, Wash; Admin Bldg, Wash State Hwy Comn, Olympia; Electro-Develop Corp, Seattle. *Exhib:* Six-man traveling exhib, Brit Art Coun, 73-75; Allrich Gallery, San Francisco, 77; Selected Works 1967-1977, de Saisset Mus, Univ Santa Clara, Calif, 77; Calif State Univ, Fresno, 77; Allrich Gallery, San Francisco, 79; Oakland Art Mus, 81. *Collection Arranged:* California Realism, 19th & 20th Century Comparison, 78; Mel Ramos, 79; Stanton Macdonald Wright, 80; Adja Yunkers, 80; Rodin's Burghers of Calais, 81; Alice Hutchins Survey, 82. *Teaching:* Teaching asst, Univ Wash, 67, instr art, 67-68; prof art & gallery dir, Calif State Univ, Chico, 68-; vis prof art, High Wycombe Col Art, Eng, 71-72. *Awards:* Fac Res Grant, Calif State Univ, Chico, 69; Fulbright-Hays Grant, Eng, 72. *Bibliog:* John Marlowe (auth), article, Current Art Mag, 6/75; James W McManus (30 min video tape), Calif State Univ, Chico, 77; Kevin Star (auth), article, San Francisco Examiner, 11/18/79; and others. *Media:* Bronze, Steel, Aluminum. *Dealer:* Allrich Gallery 251 Post St San Francisco CA 94133. *Mailing Add:* 5200 Trafalgar Sq Paradise CA 95969-6675

MCMILLAN, CONSTANCE
PAINTER, ILLUSTRATOR
Study: Bennington Col, painting with Karl Knaths & sculpture with Simon Moselsio, BA, 46; Mills Col, painting with William Gaw & ceramic sculpture with Antonio Prieto, fel, 53-55, MA, 55. *Exhib:* Slusser Gallery, Univ Mich, Ann Arbor, 80; Pindar Gallery, NY, 85; Il Mercate Galleria, Milan, Italy, 86; Galleria 9, Cologne & Spe-resta Del Carline, Bologna, Italy, 86; Solo exhibs, Cornerstone Gallery, Conn, 86-89, Atlantic Gallery, NY, 87 & Phoenix Gallery, NY, 89. *Teaching:* instr painting, design & art hist, Emma Willard Sch, Troy, NY, 52-53; instr painting & design, Angell Sch, Ann Arbor, 62-63. *Awards:* First Prize, Morris Gallery, New York, 56; Grad Fel, Mills Col, Calif. *Mem:* Ann Arbor Art Asn. *Media:* Oil, Gouache; Charcoal, Pastel. *Publ:* Illusr, Chikka, 62, Ponies for a King, 63, Reilly & Lee; illusr, Memory of a Large Christmas, Norton, 62; drawing reproduced record cover, Gateway Summer Sounds, Folkways Records, 82. *Dealer:* Phoenix Gallery 568 Broadway New York NY

MCMILLAN, STEPHEN WALKER
PRINTMAKER, PHOTOGRAPHER
b Berkeley, Calif, Dec 21, 1949. *Study:* Hornsey Coll Art, London, Eng, 70-71; Univ Calif, Santa Cruz, AB, 72, BFA, 75. *Work:* Brooklyn Mus, NY; Achenbach Collection, San Francisco; Oakland Mus, Calif; Mem Mus, Petah-Tiqua, Israel; US Embassy, Tokyo, Japan; Portland Art Mus; Stanford Univ Libr, Palo Alto, Calif; and others. *Exhib:* 4th Int Biennial Print Exhib, Taipei Fine Arts Mus, Repub China; 21st Nat Print Exhib, Brooklyn Mus, 78; 17th Bradley Nat Print & Drawing Exhib, Lakeview Mus, Peoria, Ill, 79; 31st Ann Boston Printmakers Exhib, De Cordova Mus, Lincoln, Mass, 79; New Aquisitions, Achenbach Collection, San Francisco, 80; Prints from Kala Inst, Newcastle Art Gallery, NSW, Australia, 87. *Awards:* 4th Prize, 3rd Kochi Int Triennial Exhib Prints, Ino-cho Paper Mus, Kochi, Japan; Purchase Award, San Francisco Art Comn, 78, Davidson Gallery, Seattle, Wash, 78 & Los Angeles Printmaking Soc, 78; James D Phelan Art Award Printmaking, San Francisco Found, 95. *Mem:* Calif Soc Printmakers; Boston Printmakers. *Media:* Etching, Lithograph

MCMILLEN, MICHAEL C(HALMERS)
ENVIRONMENTAL ARTIST, SCULPTOR
b Los Angeles, Calif, Apr 6, 1946. *Study:* Calif State Univ, Northridge, BA; Univ Calif, Los Angeles, MA & MFA. *Work:* Australian Nat Gallery, Canberra; Art Gallery New South Wales, Australia; Los Angeles Co Mus Art; Oakland Mus, Calif; Guggenheim Mus, NY. *Exhib:* Eight Artists from Los Angeles, San Francisco Art Inst, Calif, 75; Sounds: Environments by Four Artists, Newport Harbor Art Mus, Newport Beach, Calif, 75; Biennial of Sydney, Art Gallery New South Wales, Australia, 76; Los Angeles in the 70s, Ft Worth Art Mus, Tex, 77; Solo exhibs, Inner City, Los Angeles Co Mus, Los Angeles, 77 & Whitney Mus Am Art, NY, 78; Eight Artists: The Elusive Image, Walker Art Ctr, Minneapolis, 79; Art in Los Angeles-The Mus as Site, Los Angeles Co Mus, 81; New Perspectives in Am Art: Exxon Nat Exhib, Guggenheim Mus, 83; 38th Corcoran Biennial: Exhibition of Am Painting, Corcoran Gallery Art, 83. *Teaching:* Lectr at var inst, 74-. *Awards:* travel grant, Biennale of Sydney, Australia Coun, 76; Nat Endowment Arts Fel, 78; Young Talent Award, Los Angeles Co Mus Art, 78. *Bibliog:* Melinda Wortz (auth), Inner City of the Mind, Art News, 2/78; Christopher Knight (auth), Some recent art and archit analogue, Los Angeles Inst Contemp Art J, 2/78; Christopher Knight (auth), Michael C McMillen, Arts & Archit, Fall 81. *Publ:* Auth, True confessions, Los Angeles Inst Contemp Art J, 75; contribr, Choke, Choke Publ, 76; auth, Special effects breakdown, Los Angeles Inst Contemp Art J, 77. *Dealer:* 45 N Venice Blvd Venice CA 90291. *Mailing Add:* c/o LA Louver Gallery 45 N Venice Blvd Venice CA 90291

MCMILLIAN, RODNEY
SCULPTOR, PAINTER
b Columbia, South Carolina. *Study:* Univ Virginia, BA Foreign Affairs, 1991; Sch Art Inst Chicago, BFA, 1998; Skowhegan Sch Painting & Sculpture, Skowhegan, ME, 2000; Sch Art Inst Chicago, 2000; Calif Inst Arts, MFA, 2002. *Work:* Whitney Mus Am Art, Studio Mus Harlem, New York; UCLA Hammer Mus, Mus Contemp Art, Los Angeles; Orange County Mus Art, Newport Beach, CA; Städtisches Mus Abteiberg, Mönchengladbach, Germany; Saatchi Gallery, London. *Exhib:* one-man shows, Main Gallery, Valencia, CA, 2000, Gallery Adamski, Aachen, Germany, 2002, on comfort, 2004, Susanne Vielmetter LA Projs, Los Angeles, 2003, Miami Beach, 2006, Galleria Estro, Padova, Italy 2005, Neuer Aachener Kunstverein, Aachen, Germany, 2007; Laundromat Show, Butler's Laundromat, Skowhegan, Maine, 2000; Plus, Gallery D301, Valencia, CA, 2001; Urban Aesthetics, Cali African Am Mus, Los Angeles, 2003; Veni Vidi Video, Studio Mus Harlem, New York, 2003, Frequency, 2005, Philosophy of Time Travel, 2007; Now is a good time, Andrea Rosen Gallery, New York, 2004; Happenstance, Harris Lieberman, New York, 2005; Everybody Dance Now, EFA Gallery, New York, 2006; Uncertain States of America, Serpentine Gallery, London, 2006; USA Today, Royal Acad Art, London, 2006; Silicone Valley, PS1 Contemp Art Ctr, Long Island, NY, 2007; On A Porch, Laxart, Los Angeles, 2007; Stop Look Listen - Exhib Video Works, Herbert F Johnson Mus Art, Ithaca, NY, 2007;

Disorderly Conduct: Recent Art in Tumultuous Times, Orange County Mus Art, Newport Beach, CA, 2008; MÄNNERFANTASIEN II, COMA Ctr Opinions Music & Art, Berlin, 2008. *Awards:* Fel, Visual Arts, US Artists, 2008. *Dealer:* Adamski Gallery Contemp Art Passstraße 14 Aachen Germany 52070; Susanne Vielmetter Berlin Projs Holzmarktstrasse 15/18 Bogen 48 Berlin Germany 10179; Galleria Estro Via San Prosdocimo 30 Padova Italy 35139; Susanne Vielmetter LA Projs 5795 W Washington Blvd Culver City CA 90232; Finesilver Gallery Houston 3913 Main St Houston TX 77002; Finesilver Gallery San Antonio 816 Camaron No 1 02 San Antonio TX 78212. *Mailing Add:* c/o Susanne Vielmetter Los Angeles Projects 6006 Washington Blvd Culver City CA 90232

MCMILLIAN, RODNEY
PAINTER, INSTALLATION ARTIST
b Columbia, SC. *Study:* Univ Va, Charlottesville, BA, 1991; Sch Art Inst Chicago, BFA, 1998; Skowhegan Sch Painting and Sculpture, 2000; Calif Inst Arts, Valencia, MFA, 2002. *Exhib:* solo exhibs, Gallery A-402, Valencia, 2002, Finesilver Gallery, San Antonio, 2002, Susanne Viemetter Los Angeles Projects, 2003, 2006 & 2007, Gallery Adamski, Aachen, Germany, 2004, Galleria Estro, Padua, Italy, 2005, Triple Candle, New York, 2005, The Kitchen, New York, 2008 & Inst Contemp Art/Boston, 2009; Track 16, 2002; Calif African Am Mus, 2003; Andrea Rosen Gallery, New York, 2004; Cheekwood Mus Art, Nashville, 2004; UCLA Hammer Mus, 2005; Centre Contemp Art, Warsaw, 2005-2008; Astrup Fearnley Mus Art, Oslo, 2005-2008; Mus Contemp Art Los Angeles, 2006; Royal Acad Art, London, 2006; Herbert F Johnson Mus Art, Cornell Univ, 2007; Studio Mus, Harlem, NY 2007; Whitney Biennial, 2008; Geffen Contemp, Mus Contemp Art, 2008; Rubell Collection, Miami, 2009. *Awards:* William H Johnson Prize, 2007; Art Matters Found Grant, 2008; Broad Fel, US Artists, 2008. *Media:* Acrylic, Oil. *Mailing Add:* c/o Susanne Vielmetter Los Angeles Projects 6006 Washington Blvd Culver City CA 90232

MCMULLAN, JAMES BURROUGHS
ILLUSTRATOR, GRAPHIC ARTIST
b Tsingtao, China, June, 14, 1934; US citizen. *Study:* Cornish Art Sch, Seattle, Wash; Pratt Inst, NY, BFA, 58. *Work:* Libr Cong, Washington. *Exhib:* Push Pin Retrospective, The Louvre, Paris, France, 70; Century of Am Illustration, Brooklyn Mus, NY, 72; Maps Show, Mus Natural Hist, NY, 77; Int Poster Biennale, Polish Mus, Warsaw, 84; World's Most Memorable Posters, UNESCO, Grand Palais, Paris, 86; Five Masters of the Contemp Poster, Lowell Gallery, NY, 87; solo exhibs, Giraffics Gallery, East Hampton, NY, 88 & Margo Feiden Gallery, NY, 88; Art of Illustration Show, Headley-Whitney Mus, Lexington, Ky, 88; Twenty Best Am Illustrators, Seoul, Repub Korea, 88. *Pos:* Illusr, Push Pin Studios, NY, 65-68. *Teaching:* Instr illus, Sch Visual Arts, NY, 71-84, instr drawing, 82-, master degree prof, 84-85. *Awards:* Gold Medal, 81, Hamilton King Award, 87 & Silver Medal, 88, Soc Illusrs; ANDY Award, Advert Club NY, 88. *Bibliog:* Richard Coyne (auth), James McMullan, Communication Arts Mag, 5-6/74; Michael Patrick Hearn (auth), The Art of the Broadway Poster, Ballantine Bks, 80; Ko Noda (dir), The Art of James McMullan, Van Gough Video, 83; S Chwast & S Heller (ed), The Art of New York, 84; S Heller (auth), Innovators of American Illustration, Van Nostrand Reinhold, 86; My life in the theater, Print Mag, 5/6/88. *Mem:* Am Inst Graphic Arts (dir, 74-76, vpres, 76-77); Soc Illusrs; Am Illus (adv bd, 85-); The Century Asn, 94. *Media:* Watercolor. *Publ:* Ed, Realism in illustration; auth, Revealing Illustrations, Watson-Guptill, 81; The Gant ad, How Mag, 1/85; High-Focus Drawing, Overlook Press, 95. *Mailing Add:* 207 E 32nd St New York NY 10016

MCNALLY, SHEILA JOHN
EDUCATOR, HISTORIAN
b New York, NY, Dec 10, 1932. *Study:* Vassar Col, BA; Univ London; Univ Kiel; Univ Munich; Harvard Univ, PhD, 65. *Pos:* Prin investr, Excavations Diocletian's Palace, Split, Yugoslavia, 68-; dir, Excavations, Akhmim, Egypt, 78-. *Teaching:* Prof art hist, Univ Minn, Minneapolis, currently. *Awards:* Fulbright Res Grants, Ger, 53-54 & Yugoslavia, 67-68. *Mem:* Coll Art Asn (bd dir, 75-79); Midwest Art Hist Soc; Archaeol Inst Am; Libyan Soc; Women's Archaeol Caucus. *Res:* Late Roman art. *Mailing Add:* 124 Bedford St SE Minneapolis MN 55414-3526

MCNAMARA, JOHN
PAINTER
b Cambridge, Mass, Feb 16, 1950. *Study:* Mass Coll Art, BFA (painting), 71, MFA (painting), 77. *Work:* Mus Fine Arts, Boston; Rose Art Mus, Brandeis Univ; Metrop Mus Art, NY; Honolulu Acad Fine Art; Visual Art Ctr MIT, Cambridge, Mass; Tucson Mus of Art; JB Speed Mus, Louisville, Ky. *Exhib:* Rose Art Mus, Waltham, Mass, 78; Boston Now, Inst Contemp Art, Boston, 81-83; solo exhibs, Exhib Space, NY, 82, Stavaridis Gallery, Boston, 83-85, 87 & 89, & Bess Cutler Gallery, NY, 84-86 & 88; Tucson Mus Contemp Art, Ariz, 92-96; Metrop Mus of Art, NY, 88; Painting in Boston 1950-2000, 2002-03; Clark Gallery, Lincoln, Mass, 2002; Bick Ebert Gallery, San Francisco, 2002; In Our Hands installed in the Barrel Gallery, HDLU, Zagreb, Croatia, 2013; Livin'-Large: Works from the 1980's, Tucson Art Mus, 2015. *Teaching:* Instr, sr lectr, Mass Col Art, San Francisco Art Inst & Univ Calif, Berkeley. *Awards:* Mass Arts & Humanities Grant, 80-83, 86, & 89; Nat Endowment Arts Fel, 81; Awards in Visual Arts II Fel, 82. *Bibliog:* Theodore Wolff (auth), The home forum, Christian Sci Monitor, 4/7/83; Nancy Stapen (auth), John McNamara, artforum, 1/88; David Bonetti (auth), John McNamara, Art News, 2/88. *Mem:* Berkeley Breakfast Club. *Media:* Oil on Canvas

MCNAMARA, MARY JO
HISTORIAN, EDUCATOR
b Troy, NY, Jan 23, 1950. *Study:* Vassar Col, AB, 72; Stanford Univ, MA, 75, PhD, 83. *Pos:* Cur, Vassar Col Art Gallery, 76-78. *Teaching:* Instr art hist, Vassar Col, Poughkeepsie, NY, 76-78; lectr, Univ Wis, Milwaukee, 78-79; instr, Oberlin Col, Ohio, 79-80; acting asst prof, Univ Calif, Irvine, 80-83; vis asst prof, Univ Calif, Riverside, 84; asst prof, Wayne State Univ, 84-92 & State Univ NY, Potsdam, 93-. *Awards:* Cantor-Fitzgerald Res Grant, 75-76. *Mem:* Coll Art Asn; Asn Historians 19th Century Art. *Res:* Modern Art. *Publ:* Coauth, Rodin's Burghers of Calais, Cantor-Fitzgerald Group, Los Angeles, 77. *Mailing Add:* 498 River Rd Potsdam NY 13676

MCNAMARA, WILLIAM PATRICK, JR
PAINTER, PRINTMAKER
b Shreveport, La, Sept 3, 1946. *Study:* Centenary Coll La, BA, 69; NMex Highlands Univ, MA, 72. *Work:* Centenary Coll La; First Nat Bank, Shreveport, La; Ark Art Ctr, Little Rock; Springfield Art Mus; Phillips Petroleum Co, Tulsa, Okla. *Exhib:* Delta Art Exhib, Ark Arts Ctr, Little Rock, 80 & 84-88; Watercolor USA, 80 & 82-87 & A View from the Mountain, 89, Springfield Art Mus, Mo; Butler Inst Am Art, 82 & 83; Rocky Mountain Nat Watermedia Exhib, Foothills Art Ctr, Golden, Colo, 85; Watercolor West Nat, Riverside Nat Mus, Redlands, Calif, 85; Nat Watercolor Soc, Brea, Calif, 87 & 91; Watercolor Retrospective, Ark Arts Ctr, Little Rock, 89. *Teaching:* Instr drawing & composition, Centenary Col La, 73-76. *Awards:* Award Merit, Watercolor USA, Springfield Art Mus, Mo, 80; SMMA Purchase Award, The Monumental Image, Springfield Art Mus, Mo, 86; Binney-Smith Award, Nat Watercolor Soc, Brea, Calif, 87. *Bibliog:* M Stephen Doherty (auth), Watercolor today: Ten contemporary artists, Am Artist, 2/83; Elizabeth B Leonard (auth), Painting the Landscape, 84 & Mary Suffudy (ed), Sketches Techniques, 85, Wastson-Guptill; Dan Morris (auth), McNamara Ventures into Monumentalism, Ark Gazette, 6/86; Donald Harrington (auth), Songs of sunlight & water, Ark Times, 7/89. *Mem:* Watercolor USA Honor Soc; Nat Watercolor Soc. *Media:* Watercolor. *Publ:* Auth, Watercolor page, Am Artist, 5/83. *Dealer:* Capricorn Galleries 4849 Rugby Ave Bethesda MD 20814; M A Doran Gallery 3509 S Peoria Tulsa OK. *Mailing Add:* HC-33 Box 52 Pettigrew AR 72752

MCNAMARA-RINGEWALD, MARY ANN THERESE
PAINTER, ILLUSTRATOR
b Hempstead, NY, April 11, 1935. *Study:* Fordham Univ, BS, 57; Adelphi Univ, MSA, 72; Parsons School of Design (illus), 73-75; Salve Regina Univ, 2003; Salve Regina Univ, Nat Bd Educ Certification (Expressive Arts Therapy), 2004. *Work:* Fordham Univ, New York City; Adelphi Univ, Garden City, NY; St. Michaels Maritime Mus, Md; Yupo Corp, Chesapeake, Va & Japan; Doubleday, New York City. *Exhib:* Solo exhibs include Fordham Univ, 54, Andonia Gallery, Massapequa, NY, 74, Isis Gallery, Islip, NY, For the Birds, Salisbury, Conn, 78, Harguen Gallery, Port Jefferson, NY, 79, Adelphi Univ, Garden City, NY, 92, Wohlfarth Gallery, Washington, 94-95, SpanBauer Gallery, Naples, Fla, 96, Naples Philharmonic, Fla, 92, Gallery 44, Millbrook, NY, 97-98; group exhibs include Acad of Arts, Easton, Md, 93. *Collection Arranged:* Kennedy Gallery, Key West, Fla, 97-99; Chesapeake Coll, Md, 98-99. *Pos:* owner, pres, South Shore Creative Arts Ctr, Massapequa, NY, 75; illusr, Doubleday, Inc, New York; art adv bd, Chespeake Coll, Wye Mills, Md, 95-, lectr, 98-99, 2000; symposium coord, Hofstra Univ, NY; copyist prog, Nat Gallery, Washington, DC, 97-2005. *Teaching:* Elem sch art tchr, Dept Educ, Freeport, NY, 57-58, Farmingdale, NY, 67; jr and high sch art tchr, Massapequa Sch Dist, NY, 70-90; lectr, Naples Philharmonic, 92. *Awards:* Outstanding Young Women of Am, Massapequa, NY, 69; Nat Middle Sch Teachers Art, Massapequa, NY, 88-89; Tobasco Book, Annapolis, St. Michael Mus, 93; Hon Mention, Plein Air, Easton, Md; and others. *Mem:* Nat League of Am Pen Women, Wash, DC (pres Naples Fla bd 96); Working Artist Forum, Easton, Md; Am Assoc Univ Women (pres Long Island, NY 69); Annapolis Md Plein Air Painters; Bonita Springs Fla Art Asn; St Michaels Md Art League. *Media:* Oil, Etching, Watercolor. *Res:* Analysis of East coast architecture, 88; Comparison of color theory, 98. *Interests:* Art, music, gardening & poetry. *Publ:* Illus, From a Lighthouse Window, Chespeake Maritime Mus, 92. *Mailing Add:* Marafour 5493 Anderby Dr Royal Oak MD 21662

MCNANY, TIM
PHOTOGRAPHER
b Newark, NJ, Dec 5, 1955. *Study:* Boston Univ, BA, 79; Ctr Media Arts, New York, 89-90; New Sch, New York, with George Tice, 96. *Comn:* Landscapes & Location Portraits (black/white & color prints), comn by Tim Gill, Maplewood, NJ, 97. *Exhib:* Am Soc Media Photogr Fine Art Competition, Bergen Mus Art & Sci, Paramus, NJ, 94 & 95; Johnson & Johnson Nat Art Show (with catalog), Hunterdon Mus, Clinton, NJ, 94; Garden State Int, Watchung Art Ctr, NJ, 98; Montclair State Univ Nat Small Works, NJ, 98; solo exhibs, Presidents Gallery, Drew Univ, Madison, NJ, 98. *Teaching:* Instr photog, Ann St Sch, Newark, NJ, 98; invitational resident photogr, Paris, 99. *Awards:* Emmy Nomination, 94; Telly Award, 96; First Place, Am Soc Media Photogr, 98. *Bibliog:* Eye on TV, Star-Ledger, 10/31/92; Mitch Seidel (auth), Media lensmen's exhibition, Star-Ledger, 9/24/93; Susan Poor (auth), ASMP/NJ winners, Photo Distric News, 3/98. *Mem:* Int Ctr Photog; Advertising Photogr New York. *Media:* Black & White, Color. *Dealer:* Thistledown Gallery 1405-1 Third Ave Spring Lake NJ 07762

MCNEIL, HENRY S, JR
COLLECTOR
Awards: Named one of Top 200 Collectors, ARTnews mag, 2009-11. *Collection:* Contemporary art, especially Minimalism

MCNETT, DENNIS
SCULPTOR, GRAPHIC ARTIST
Study: Old Dominion Univ, Va, BFA, 2000; Pratt Inst, New York, MFA, 2004. *Exhib:* Inky and Stinky, Lombardi Gallery, Austin, Tex, 2008; INprint, SCA Contemp Art, Albuquerque, 2008; Brooklyn Block Party, Adhoc Art Gallery, New York, 2008; The Detournements of Wynn Miller, Exibit A Gallery, Los Angeles, 2009; Barnstormers, Joshua Liner Gallery, New York, 2010. *Pos:* Printer, Branx-x Editions, 2001-05. *Teaching:* Adj asst prof, Pratt Inst, 2010-. *Awards:* NY Found Arts Fel, 2009. *Publ:* Contribr, illus, Juxtapoz Mag, 2007, Complex Mag, 2008, Inked Mag, 2009, Bliss Mag, 2009

MCNICKLE, THOMAS GLEN
PAINTER
b New Castle, Pa, Oct 17, 1944. *Study:* Edinboro Univ, BS (art), 66, MEd (studio), 72. *Work:* Butler Inst Am Art; Hoyt Inst Fine Art, New Castle, Pa; Vero Beach Mus of Art, Fla. *Comn:* US Air, Pitts, PA; Cox Comm, Atlanta, Ga; Bank of AM, Charlotte,NC; Pfizer Corp, Cleveland, Ohio; Price Waterhouse, Charlottle, NC. *Exhib:* Am Artists Prof League Grande Nat, NY, 82 & 83; Views of Youngstown, Butler Inst Am Art, 82; Audubon Artists Ann, Nat Arts Club, NY, 83, 84 & 85; Am Watercolor Soc Ann Exhib, 84; Watercolor USA, Springfield, Mo, 84 & 85. *Collection Arranged:* Forty Watercolors (auth, catalog), from collection Butler Inst Am Art, 82; Hoyt Nat Painting Show (auth, catalog), 84 & 85. *Teaching:* Instr art, Neshannock Twp Schs, New Castle, Pa, 66-98; private workshops watercolors, 79-. *Awards:* Award Excellence, Black Forest Inst, Exhib, 82; Second Prize Watercolor, Terrance Gallery Nat Exhib, 82; Ford Motor Co Fund Award, Mich Watercolor Soc Ann, 85; Outstanding Alumni Awards in the Arts, Edinboro Univ, 92. *Mem:* Nat Watercolor Soc; Pa Soc Watercolor Painters; Pittsburgh Watercolor Soc (bd dir, 83); Am Watercolor Soc. *Media:* Oil. *Dealer:* Thomas G McNickle 107 Fayette NF Road Volant PA 16156; Jerald Melberg Gallery Charlotte NC; David Findlay Fine Art, NYC; James Gallery, Pitt, PA. *Mailing Add:* RR 3 Volant PA 16156-9803

MCNUTT, JAMES CHARLES
MUSEUM DIRECTOR
Study: Harvard Univ, BA (English), 1972; Univ Tex, MA (English), 1977, PhD (Am Civilization), 1982. *Pos:* site reporter, Nat Endowment for Arts; Asst instr, Univ Tex, 1978-1982; res assoc, Inst Texan Cultures, San Antonio, 1982-1985, dir res, 1985-1986, dir res & collections, 1986-1993, asst exec dir for planning, 1993-1995; dir, NC Mus History, Raleigh, 1995-1999; pres & exec dir, Witte Mus, San Antonio, 1999-2006; pres & chief exec officer, Nat Mus Wildlife Art, Jackson Hole, Wyo, 2006. *Teaching:* Adj asst prof, dept hisotry, NC State Univ, Raleigh, NC, 1995-. *Awards:* Tex Com for Humanities, 1984; Nat Endowment for Arts, 1986; LJ Skaggs & Mary C Skaggs Found, 1984; Inst Mus Serv, 1990; Sprint Inc, 1997. *Mem:* Mem, Am Asn Mus (bd dirs); Am Folklore Soc; Am Studies Asn; coun, Tex Folklore Soc, 1986-1988, bd dirs, 1989-1990; NC Folklore Soc; NC Literacy & Hist Asn. *Mailing Add:* National Museum of Wildlife Art PO Box 6825 Jackson WY 83002

MCOWEN, C LYNN
ART DEALER, COLLECTOR
b Long Beach, Calif, July 12, 1953. *Study:* Calif State Univ, BA, 77; studied with Master Painter, People's Republic of China, 85-86; pvt study with Calvin J Goodman in Art Marketing. *Pos:* Dir graphics & printing, East End Arts & Humanities Coun, Childrens Inst Res & Design Ctr, 77-79; graphic illusr, State Univ NY, Stony Brook, 79-84. *Mem:* UCLA Art Coun. *Specialty:* Contemporary paintings, prints & drawings from the People's Republic of China. *Collection:* Variety of paintings, prints, drawings & sculpture done by contemporary artists from the People's Republic of China. *Dealer:* Mayoon Fine Asian Art 6409 W 6th St Los Angeles CA 90048

MCPHEE, SARAH COLLYER
HISTORIAN, EDUCATOR
Study: Harvard Univ, AB, 82; Columbia Univ, MA (art hist), 88; Columbia Univ, PhD (art hist), 97. *Pos:* Ed, writer, Metrop Mus Art, 84-86. *Teaching:* asst prof, Emory Univ, Art Hist Dept, 95-2001, assoc prof, 2001-; Vis assoc prof, Columbia Univ, Dept Art Hist & Archaeology, 2003-04. *Awards:* Fel Guggenheim Mem Found, 2004. *Mem:* Inst for Advanced Study. *Publ:* Co-auth: Drawings from the Roman Period 1704-1714, 99; auth: Bernini and the Bell Towers: Architecture and Politics at the Vatican, 2002. *Mailing Add:* Art His Dept Emory Univ 128 Carlos Hall Atlanta GA 30322

MCPHERSON, BRUCE RICE
EDITOR, PUBLISHER
b Atlanta, Ga, Oct 12, 1951. *Study:* Brown Univ, AB, 73; Annenberg Sch Commun, Univ Pa, 75. *Pos:* Ed & publ, McPherson & Co (Documentext, Treacle Press), 74-. *Mem:* PEN (Am Ctr). *Res:* Avant-Garde, 1958-present, principally United States, especially concerned with happenings, fluxus, performance art, cinematography and related areas. *Publ:* Art & Discontent: Theory at the Millenium, 91, Crisis in Cultural Identity, 92, The Triumph of Anti-Art: Conceptual and Performance Art in the Formation of Post-Modernism, 2005, 2012; Ed, More than Meat Joy: Complete Performance Works and Selected Writings, by Carolee Schneemann, 79 & 97, Something Else Press: An Annotated Bibliography, by Peter Frank, 82, Documentext; Essential Brakhage: selected writings on filmmaking by Stan Brahage, 2001; Essential Deren: collected writings on Film by Maya Deren, 2005; Telling Time: Essays of a Visionary Filmmaker, by Stan Brakhage, 2003; Art, Love, Friendships: Marina Abramovic & Ulay, Togther & Apart, Thomas McEvilley, 2010; Yves the Provocateur: Yves Klein & Twentieth Century Art, Thomas McEvilley, 2010. *Mailing Add:* PO Box 1126 Kingston NY 12402-0126

MCPHERSON, CRAIG
PAINTER, PRINTMAKER
b Wichita, Kans, Sept 29, 1948. *Study:* Univ Kans, BFA, 70. *Work:* Metrop Mus Art, & Whitney Mus Am Art, NY; Brit Mus London; Art Inst Chicago; Cleveland Mus Art; Fine Arts Mus San Francisco; Art Gallery New South Wales, Sydney, Carnegie Mus Art, Pittsburgh, Lib of Congress, Washington, Hunterian Gallery Art, Glasgow and 30 others. *Comn:* Twilight: The Rivers & Bridges of Manhattan (mural), Am Express Co, NY, 85-86; Harbors of the World (mural), Am Express Co, NY, 87-92; paintings, Corp Lobby, World Financial Ctr; Nat Gallery of Art, Washington, 2014, Fitzwilliam Mus, Cambridge, Eng, 2015. *Exhib:* Recent Acquisitions, Nat Gallery Am Art, Washington, 85; Recent Acquisitions, Metrop Mus Art, NY, 85; 162nd Ann Exhib, Nat Acad Design, NY, 87; Tradition & Innovation: 1500 to Present, San Francisco Mus Fine Arts, 89; Diamonds Are Forever, NY Pub Libr, Inst Contemp Art, Boston, Seiba Dept Store, Tokyo, Taipei Fine Arts Mus, Taiwan, Denver Art Mus, Albright-Knox Mus, Buffalo, Southeastern Ctr Contemp Art, NC, 90; NY, NY, The Fitzwilliam Mus, Cambridge, Eng, The Hunterian Mus, Glasgow, Scotland, 94 & 98, Darkness into Light (retrospective), 98, From Goya to Johns, McNay Mus (exhib catalog), 2004, Impressions of NY, NY Hist Soc, 2005, Born of Fire, Westmorland Mus, 2006; Steel, The Frick Mus, Pittsburgh, Pa, 2008; At the Heart of Progress, Ackland Mus, 2009; Wichita Art Mus at 75, Wichita, Kans, 2011; Burnishing the Night, Chicago Art Inst, 2015, Nightfall, Virginia Mus Fine Arts, Richmond, 2015. *Pos:* Dir, Kans Cult Arts Comn Mobile Gallery, Wichita Art Mus, 71-73; mgr, Mich Artrain, Mich Coun Arts & Nat Endowment Arts, 73-74; cur, Mobile Gallery (Wichita Art Mus/NEA/Kans Cultural Arts Comm grants), Art Now, 70-71, Happy Birthday Picasso, 71-72, Un Saludo a las Artes Mexicana, 72-73, Art of the Plains and NW Coast Indians, 74-75, NY New Realism Gallery G Witchita, Kans, 75. *Bibliog:* Heller, Chwast (auth), The Art of NY, 83; Wax (auth), Mezzotint, 90; John Arthur (auth), Craig McPherson (exhib catalog), Mary Ryan, 1/93; Masello (auth), NY Art in Public Places, 99; Craig Hartley (auth), Darkness Into Light (exhib catalog), The Fitzwilliam Mus, Cambridge, Eng, The Hunterian, Glasgow, Scotland, 98-99; Ramirez (edit), Painting the Town, 2000; From Goya to Johns (exhib catalog), McNay Mus, 2004; Symmes (auth), Impressions of NY (exhib catalog), 2005; Jones (auth), Born of Fire (exhib catalog), 2006; Riggs, Timothy (auth), At the Heart of Progress (exhib catalog), Ackland Mus, 2009; Wichita Art Mus at 75, 2011. *Media:* Oil; Mezzotint. *Dealer:* Forum Gallery 730 Fifth Ave New York NY 10019

MCPHERSON, LARRY E
PHOTOGRAPHER, EDUCATOR
b Newark, Ohio, 1943. *Study:* BA, Columbia Col, Chicago; MA, Northern Ill Univ, 1978. *Work:* Mus Mod Art, NY; Art Inst Chicago & Exchange Nat Bank, Chicago, Ill; Int Mus Photog at George Eastman House, Rochester, NY; New Orleans Mus Art, La; Mus Fine Arts, Houston; Dayton Art Inst, Ohio; Birmingham Mus Art, Ala; Milwaukee Mus Art, Wisc; plus others. *Exhib:* Solo exhibs, Art Inst Chicago, Ill, 69, 78 & 81, Dayton Art Inst, Ohio, 92; Vision and Expression, George Eastman House, Rochester, NY, 69; Mirrors & Windows, Mus Mod Art, NY, 78; Farbwerke, Kunsthaus Gallery, Zurich, Switz, 80; Contemp Am Color, Galerie Rudolf Kicken, Koln, Ger, 80; Color as Form: A History of Color Photog, Corcoran Gallery & George Eastman House, 82; The Nature of the Beast, Hudson River Mus, Yonkers, NY, 89; 1992 Trienial, New Orleans Mus Art, 92; New Faces and Other Recent Acquisitions, Art Inst Chicago, Ill, 97; Visualizing the Blues, the Dixon Gallery and Gardens, Memphis, Tenn, 2000; plus others. *Teaching:* Assoc prof photog, Univ Memphis, Tenn, 78. *Awards:* Nat Endowment Arts Fel Photog, 75 & 79; Guggenheim Fel Photog, 80; Tenn Arts Commn Ind Artist Fel Photog, 96. *Bibliog:* Candida Finkel (auth), review, Afterimage, 10/78; Elaine King (auth), article, Camera Mag, 80; History of Photography, Spring 93; Wendy McDaris (auth) Visualizing the Blues, 2001. *Mem:* Soc Photog Educ. *Publ:* Memphis, Santa Fe, NMex, Center for American Places, 2002; Beirut City Center, Gottingen, Germany, Steidl, 2006; The Cows, Gottingen, Ger, Steidl, 2007

MCREYNOLDS, (JOE) CLIFF
PAINTER, INSTRUCTOR
b Amarillo, Tex, Jan 26, 1933. *Study:* San Diego State Univ, BA, 59, MA, 60. *Work:* Chicago Art Inst; Music Corp of Am, Time Warner; Northern Trust co, Chgo. *Comn:* Portrait of pres, Mesa Coll, San Diego, Calif, 75. *Exhib:* Drawings USA Traveling Exhib, Minn Mus Art, St Paul, 75; Alternative Realities, Mus Contemp Art, Chicago, Ill, 76; Calif Painting & Sculpture--the Modern Era, San Francisco Mus Mod Art, 76; Juried Drawing Exhib, Chicago Art Inst, 77; Fourth Triennial--India Traveling Exhib, New Delhi, 78 & Tokyo, Japan, 79; For God's Sake--Cliff McReynolds, San Jose Mus Art, Calif, 83; Downey Mus Art, Calif, 87; Venice Arts Festival Venice, Calif, 88; Biola Univ La Mirada, Calif, 88; SDTYAE (traveling), Yukohama, Japan, 92; solo exhib, Taylor Libr, San Diego, 2001; and others. *Pos:* Illusr, Psychol Today, 70-73, Esquire Mag, 73, Visions, 77 & Omni Mag, 78-79. *Teaching:* Instr drawing, Mesa Coll, San Diego, 69-96. *Awards:* Best in Show, Del Mar Exhib, 63; Best in Show, All Calif Exhib, 63 & First Prize, Calif-Hawaii Regional, 72, Fine Arts Gallery, San Diego; First Prize, Small Images, Spanish Village, San Diego, 97-99. *Bibliog:* Marilyn Hagberg (auth), McReynolds--sharp satirist, San Diego Mag, 2/67; State of the Arts, Dr Gene Edward Veith Jr, 91; Karen L Mulder (auth), Inklings, The Art of Cliff McReynolds, 5/98. *Mem:* Christians in the Visual Arts. *Media:* Oil, Pencil. *Publ:* Auth, All Things New, Revelation Art, 80; Wonders of the Visible World, Critique of America 3/88; Making Art and Eating Too, The Forum, 93. *Mailing Add:* 6311 Dowling Dr La Jolla CA 92037

MCREYNOLDS, KIRK See St Maur, Kirk

MCROBERTS, SHERYL ANN
SCULPTOR
b Kalamazoo, Mich, Aug 14, 1950. *Study:* Augsburg Col, BA (art), 73; St Cloud State Univ, MA (sculpture), 76; Ind Univ, MFA (sculpture), 78. *Work:* Missoula Mus Arts, Mont; Doane Coll Art Gallery, Crete, Nebr; Normandale Community Coll Art Collection, Bloomington, Minn. *Comn:* Fed Reserve Bank, Minneapolis, 90; Artstop, Powderhorn Park Neighborhood, Minneapolis, 91; St Cloud State Univ, Minn, 92; Fergus Falls Community Col, Minn, 93; Franconia Sculpture Park, Schafer, Minn, 99. *Exhib:* Wyoming: The Cowboy State, (traveling), 87; Sculpture to Touch, New Art Ctr, Washington, 87; Nicolaysen Mus, Univ Mont, 88; Forum Gallery, 91; MC Gallery, 92-94 & 96. *Teaching:* Asst prof sculpture, Doane Col, 80-84; Univ Wyo, 84-89; instr sculpture, Normandale Community Col, 89-. *Awards:* Ford Found Grant, 78; A Question of Scale Purchase Award, Missoula Mus Arts, 86; Fulbright Grant for Scholars, Fulbright Comn, 96. *Bibliog:* Karl Vokmar (auth), Review, Northern Lights Mag, 87; Mary Abbe (auth), Review, Minneapolis Star & Tribune, 89; Arthur Williams (auth), Sculpture Fundamentals, 89. *Mailing Add:* Normandale Community Col 9700 France Ave S Minneapolis MN 55431-4399

MCSHEEHY, CORNELIA MARIE
PRINTMAKER, PAINTER
b Floral Park, Long Island, New York, Aug 10, 1947. *Study:* Mass Coll Art, Boston, BFA, 69; State Univ NY, Albany, MA, 72. *Work:* Libr Cong, Washington, DC; Mus Fine Arts, Boston; State Univ NY, Potsdam; Art Inst Chicago, Ill; Tex Tech Univ, Lubbock; Univ Okla; and numerous others. *Exhib:* Boston Printmakers, De Cordova Mus, Lincoln, Mass, 73; Print Exhib, Libr Cong, 75; Mus Fine Arts, Boston, 76; New Am Graphics 2 & 3, Madison Art Ctr, 82-84; Printed by Women, Port Hist Mus, Philadelphia, 83; Brit Int Print Biennial, WYorkshire, 86; Contemp Am Prints, US Consulate, Leningrad, Russia, 86; Wild, Wild Wit, Boston, 87; Cameron Univ, 88; SUNY-Albany, NY, 88; Printmakers, Anold Gallery, Newport, RI, 92; Fac Biennial Exhib, Mus Art, RI Sch Design, 92 & 95; Small Works Exhib, Woods-Gerry Gallery, RI Sch Design, 93; Colorprint USA 25, Tex Tech Univ, Lubbock, 94; Albany Alumni Artists, Univ Art Mus, State Univ NY, Albany, 94; Feminism in the Arts of the 70's, Univ Art Mus, State Univ NY, Albany, 95; Colorprint USA Spanning the States in '98, Tex Tech Univ, Lubbock, Tex, 98; Berkshire Comminuty Coll, Pittsfield, Mass, 99; Left/Right-Right/Left, Pacific Northwest Coll Art, Portland, Oreg, 99; Art Bank Program Exhib, US Info Agency, Dept of State, Washington, DC, 2000. *Pos:* prof Fine Arts Printmaking, RISD. *Teaching:* Instr printmaking, Mass Coll Art, Boston, 72-75; asst prof, Brown Univ, 76-77; prof, RI Sch Design, 77-, head printmaking prog, 78-89; prof, Fine Arts/Printmaking. *Awards:* Nat Endowment Arts Grant Printmaking, 75-76; Mellon Rac Res Grant, Polaroid Corp Grant, 85, 86, finaist, Mass Coun Arts, 87; John R Frazier Award Excellence in Teaching, RISD, 94. *Bibliog:* Nancy Stapen (auth), article, Boston Herald, Mass, 11/20/87; Christine Temin (auth), Boston Globe, Mass, 11/20/87; John Pantalone (auth), Newport This Wk, RI, 11/19/92. *Mem:* Boston Printmakers; MacDowell Colony Fel; Mus of Fine Arts Boston. *Media:* Printmaking; Painting, Mixed Media; Sculpture. *Publ:* The Collograph, Free Press, NY, 80. *Mailing Add:* 77 Barney St Rumford RI 02916

MCTWIGAN, MICHAEL
CRITIC, EDITOR
b Lincoln, Nebr, July 9, 1948. *Study:* Lake Forest Col, Ill, BA (anthrop), 71; Columbia Univ, postgrad studies, 76-77. *Pos:* Ed asst, Craft Horizons Mag, New York, 72 & 74-78; asst ed, Art Quart, Metrop Mus, New York, 78-79; sr ed, Watson-Guptill Publ, New York, 79-81; ed, Indust Design, New York, 82-83; ed, Am Ceramics Mag, New York, 82-. *Awards:* Art Critics Fel, Nat Endowment Arts, 80. *Mem:* Decorative Arts Soc of Soc Archit Historians; Coll Art Asn. *Res:* Post-World War II sculpture in the new craft media of clay, glass and fiber; architecture, decorative arts and portraiture. *Publ:* Auth, Heroes and Clowns (sculpture of Robert Arneson exhib catalog), Allan Frumkin Gallery, 79; William Daley: Duality in Clay, Am Craft, 80; First things first, 82 & The fruitful mysteries of Graham Marks, 82, Am Ceramics; An interior exchanges: Cynthia Carlson and Betty Woodman, Arts Mag, 82. *Mailing Add:* 51 Prospect Pl Brooklyn NY 11217-2801

MCVICKER, CHARLES TAGGART
PAINTER, INSTRUCTOR
b Canonsburg, Pa, Aug 31, 1930. *Study:* Principia Col, BA, 52; Art Ctr, Coll of Design, BPA, 57. *Work:* US Capitol, US Hist Soc & US Air Force, DC; Princeton Univ; Soc Illusr, NY; Trenton City Mus; Rutgers Univ Art Mus. *Exhib:* NJ Artists, Newark Mus, 64; NJ Ann, NJ State Mus, Trenton, 70; Illusr Ann, Soc Illusr, NY; NJ Art Dirs Ann, Newark; Am Watercolor Soc Ann, Nat Acad, NY; Nat Audubon Artists; Watercolor, USA. *Collection Arranged:* Retrospective, Coll of NJ; Major Exhib, Ellarslie, Trenton City Mus; Two person show, Sawmill Gallery, Stockton, NJ. *Teaching:* Assoc prof illus, Pratt/Phoenix, New York, 79-84; asst prof art, Trenton State Col, 85-2005. *Awards:* Ralph Fabri Medal, NAPAC Exhib, 91; Merrill Lynch Award, GSWS, 96; Watercolor USA Awards, 98, 99, 2000, 02; Adirondacks Nat Exhib, 2011. *Mem:* Soc Illusr (pres, 76-78); Am Watercolor Soc; Audubon Artists, 88-; Princeton Artists Alliance (founder); Garden State Watercolor Soc (pres, 2006-2007); Nat Watercolor Soc; Watercolor Hon Soc. *Media:* Oil, Acrylic. *Interests:* Jazz Pianist. *Publ:* Illusr, Addie and the King of Hearts, Knopf Publ, 76; The Soccer Book, 76 & The Circus Book, 78, Random House; Guard of Honor, Franklin Libr, 78; Internat Artist, 03. *Mailing Add:* 26 Old Orchard Ln Princeton NJ 08540

MEAD, GERALD C, JR
COLLAGE ARTIST, EDUCATOR
b Hamburg, NY, Aug 16, 1962. *Study:* State Univ Col, Buffalo, NY, BA (psychology), 85, BS (design), 86; Univ Buffalo, NY, MFA (visual studies), 2008. *Work:* Albright-Knox Art Gallery, Buffalo, NY; Castellani Art Mus, Niagara Falls, NY; George Eastman House, Int Mus Film & Photography, Rochester, NY; Burchfield-Penney Art Ctr, Buffalo, NY; Ore State Univ, Corvallis, Ore. *Comn:* poster design, Buffalo Ensemble Theatre, NY, 92; cover design, VOICES Mag, Buffalo, NY, 99; poster design, Buffalo United Artists, NY, 2000. *Exhib:* Rochester-Finger Lakes Exhibition, Rochester Mem Art Gallery, NY, 94; Western NY Exhibition, Albright-Knox Art Gallery, Buffalo, NY, 94; 72nd Ann Spring Show, Erie Art Mus, Erie, Pa, 95; World in a Match Box, Grand Central Art, Melbourne, Australia, 97; Three Rivers Arts Festival, Carnegie Mus Art, Pittsburgh, 2000; Regional 2000, Arnot Art Mus, Elmira, NY, 2000; SUNY Brockport, NY, 2002; Daemen Coll, Amherst, NY, 2002; solo exhib, Castellani Art Mus, Niagara Falls, NY, 2004, Cedar Arts Ctr, Corning, NY, 2006; Upstate Invitational, Rochester Contemp, NY, 2006; SUNY Fredonia, 2009. *Collection Arranged:* Roycroft Desktop (decorative art), 95; EB Green, Buffalo's Architect, 97; Buffalo's Grain Elevators (photography, painting), 97; James KY Kuo: A Retrospective (painting), 98; Art of the Chair: WNY Furniture Design (decorative art), 2000; Nancy Belfer: Textile Art, 2001; Wet & Fresh: A Survey of Current watercolor, 2004; Cindy Sherman, WNY collections (photography), 2005; Extraordinary Forms: Binational Clay, 2007; Retrospective of Masterworks by Frances Crohn, 2007; Feasting Eyes: Artist Take on Food, 2008; Pastel Perfect: A Survey at Pastel Artists, 2009. *Pos:* Cur, Burchfield-Penney Art Center, Buffalo, NY, 87-2005; auditor, NY State Council on the Arts, New York City, 93-96; field reviewer, Inst Mus & Libr Serv, Washington, DC, 97-2005; reviewer, Am Asn Mus, Washington DC, 2000-; art writer, Artvoice, Buffalo, NY, 2000-; Cur, Charles E Burchfield Nature & Art Ctr, W Seneca, NY, 2008. *Teaching:* Adj lectr design, State Univ Coll Buffalo, NY, 98-; adj lectr visual studies, Univ Buffalo, NY, 2006-. *Awards:* First Place, Carnegie Art Ctr Nat Exhib, 93; Gold Medal, Seymour H Knox Found, 97; Fine Arts Merit Award, Creative Quarterly, 2007; Silvery Addy Award, Advertising Club Buffalo, 2010. *Bibliog:* Robert Hirsch (auth), Exploring Color Photography, Brown & Benchmark, 97; John Valentino (auth), Photographic Possibilities, Focal Press, 2001; Becky Koenig (auth), Color Workbook, Prentice Hall, 2009. *Mem:* Big Orbit Gallery (bd pres, 95-); CEPA Gallery (adv bd 96-); Buffalo Arts Studio (bd mem, 2003-); Buffalo United Artists (bd mem, 2003-); Buffalo Arts Comn (bd mem, 2004-). *Publ:* editor, EB Green: Buffalo's Architect, Buffalo Sate Coll Found, 97, The Inanimate: 12 Artists on Still Life, 98, Craft Art from Western New York, 98; The Art of the Chair: Western New York Furniture Design, Buffalo State Coll Foun, 2000; editor, Wet & Fresh: A Survey Current Watercolor in Western New York, Buffalo State Coll Found, 2004; auth, Handmade in Buffalo, Niagara Conv & Visitors Bureau, 2010. *Dealer:* Art Dialogue Gallery One Linwood Ave Buffalo NY 14209. *Mailing Add:* 209 Woodward Ave Buffalo NY 14214

MEADE, FIONN
CURATOR
Study: Bard Coll Ctr for Curatorial Studies, MA; Columbia Univ, MFA (creative writing). *Pos:* Asst cur, Univ Wash Henry Art Gallery, Seattle & Bard Coll Ctr for Curatorial Studies & Hessel Mus Art; cur, Sculpture Ctr, New York. *Mailing Add:* 44-19 Purves St Long Island City NY 11101

MEADER, JONATHAN (ASCIAN)
PRINTMAKER, PAINTER
b Aug 29, 1943; US citizen. *Work:* Whitney Mus Am Art, Metrop Mus Art, NY; Corcoran Gallery Art, Nat Collection Fine Art, Hirshhorn Mus, Washington, DC; and others. *Comn:* Serigraphs, Off Equal Employment Opportunity, 73; lithographs, Washington Printmakers' Workshop Proj, 74; serigraph, Washington Print Club, 75. *Exhib:* One-person shows, Corcoran Gallery Art, Dupont Ctr, 69, Green Panther Gallery, Frankfurt, Ger, 82, Fla Southern Col, 82, Seven Young Artists, Corcoran Gallery Art, Washington, DC, 72; Baltimore Mus, 72; Illumination, San Francisco, Calif, 80; Sylvia Ullman Gallery, Cleveland, Ohio, 80; Zenith Gallery, Washington, DC, 80; House of Artists, Moscow, USSR, 89; and many others. *Awards:* Stern Family grant, 70; Washington Printmaker's Proj, 74; Printmakers Grant, Nat Endowment Arts, 74. *Bibliog:* Dreamtime, The Washingtonian, 4/75; Paul Richard (auth), Making it as an artist, The Washington Post, 10/77. *Media:* Mixed. *Collection:* Fantasy and surrealism: Klinger, Milton. *Publ:* Auth, The Unicorn, Viking Press, 80; illusr, The Unicorn Calendar, Pomegranite Press, 80 & 82; Auth, The Wordless Travel Book, 10 Speed Press; In Praise of Women, Celestial Arts Press. *Mailing Add:* PO Box 97 Mill Valley CA 94942-0097

MEADOWS, JASON
SCULPTOR
b Indianapolis, 1972. *Study:* Sch Art Inst Chicago, BFA, 94; Univ Calif, LA, MFA, 98. *Exhib:* Solo exhibs, ROOM 702, LA, 97; Marc Foxx, LA, 2000, 2002-2003, 2005; Studio Guenzani, Milan, Italy, 2000, 2002; Corvi-Mora, London, Eng, 2001, 2003-2004; Tanya Bonakdar Gallery, NY, 2001-2002; Els Hanappe Underground, Athens, Greece, 2003; Group exhibs, Some of you who are now reading..., New Works Gallery, Chicago, 95; Brighten the Corners, Marianne Boesky, NY, 98, Down to Earth, 99; Caught, 303 Gallery, NY, 99; Mise en Scene, Santa Monica Mus Art, 2000; Brown, The Approach, London, 2001; Project, Tanya Bonakdar Gallery, NY, 2002, Painting on Sculpture, 2003; Youngstars, Krinzinger Projekte, Vienna, Austria, 2002; I Assassin, Wallspace, NY, 2004; SPF: Self Portraits, Angles Gallery, Santa Monica, 2004. *Collection Arranged:* Cur, The Thought That Counts, Sister, LA, 2004

MEADOWS, PATRICIA B
CURATOR, CONSULTANT
b Amarillo, Tex, Nov 12, 1938. *Study:* Univ Tex, BA, 60; additional studies with Ramon Froman, Julius Zsohar, William Henry Earle & Victor Armstrong. *Work:* Harlingen Court House, Tex; State Bar Tex Hq, Austin; Univ Tex Health Sci Ctr, Tyler. *Collection Arranged:* Presenting Nine (auth, catalog), Dallas, Tex, 84; Critic's Choice (auth, catalog), Dallas, Tex, 84-95; Texas Women (catalog), 88-89 & Texas: reflections, rituals (catalog), 90-91, Nat Mus Women Arts, Washington; Establishment Exposed (catalog), 96; Texas Sculpture Garden, Hall Off Park, Frisco, Tex. *Pos:* Co-founder & dir, D-Art Visual Art Ctr, Dallas, 81-99, pres bd dir, 82-85, cur, 90-97; bd dir, Arts Dist Management Asn, Dallas, Tex, 85-91, Tex State Comn, Nat Mus Women Arts, 86-98, Artists Sq Design Team, 88-90 & Mid-Am Alliance, Kansas City, Mo, 90-93; exhib dir, Texas Women, Nat Mus Women Arts, Washington, 87-89; acquisition comn, Dallas Mus Art, 88-92; founder & cur, The Collectors, Dallas, Tex, 89-96; adv bd, Univ Tex, Austin, Sch Fine Arts, 90-91; pres, Dallas Art Dealers Asn, 97-99; sr vpres, sr cur & collection mgr, Hall Collection, 99-2008; pres, Art Connections, 94-. *Awards:* Serv to the Arts Award, Tex Fine Arts Asn, 84; James K Wilson Award, 88; Legend Award, Dallas Visual Art Ctr, 96. *Mem:* Tex Sculpture Asn; Nat Mus Women Arts (bd of dir, Texas Committee); Tex Asn Mus; Emergency Artists' Support League (co-founder, 92-); Dallas Mus Art; Nasher Sculpture Ctr; Int Sculpture Ctr (bd of dir, 2008-). *Collection:* Art Shirer; Eliseo Garcia; Sherry Owens; Marty Ray; Randy Brodnax; James Watral; Karl Umlauf; Jerry Daniel; Margaret Ratelle; Heather Marcus; David Iles; Norman Kary; Andrea Rosenberg. *Mailing Add:* 2707 State St Dallas TX 75204

MEAGHER, SANDRA KREBS
PAINTER, PHOTOGRAPHER
b NY. *Study:* Smith Coll, BA, 58; Art Students League, 73-80; Silvermine Guild, Conn, 86; Robert Reed, one-on-one Sem, 87-92; Ctr Contemp Printmaking. *Work:* Town of Fairfield, Conn; pvt collection, Stoneleigh-Burnham Sch. *Exhib:* Art/Place, Southport, Conn, 92-; Breaking the Rules, Katonah Mus, Katonah, NY, 2001; Art of

the Northeast, Silvermine Guild Arts Ctr, New Canaan, Conn, 2005-. *Awards:* First Prize (Breaking the Rules), Katonah Mus Tri-State Competition, 2001; Carol Eisner Sculpture Award, Art of the Northeast, 2003. *Bibliog:* Vivian Raynor (auth), In Pelham, Artists Who Take to the Rd, NY Times, 92; Lorraine Gengo (auth), Me Talk Pretty Art One Day: Fiery Female Artists Bring their Dialogue Project to Silvermine, County Weekly, Fairfield, Conn; Meagher Brings Conumble Art Artplace, the Hour. *Mem:* Silvermine Guild Art Ctr (chmn, Inst Visual Artists, 89); Art Place (pres, 2005, 2009); Art Students League (life mem); Rowayton Arts Ctr; Katonah Mus Artists Asn. *Media:* Charcoal, Acrylic, Mixed Media. *Interests:* Abstract. *Publ:* Auth, Nora, Cross Roads Press, 91. *Dealer:* Art/Place Fairfield Conn. *Mailing Add:* 8 Craw Ave Norwalk CT 06853-1603

MECKSEPER, JOSEPHINE
SCULPTOR
b Lilienthal, Germ, 1964. *Study:* Studies at Hochschule der Kunste, Berlin, 86-90; Calif Inst Arts, Valencia, MFA, 90-92. *Exhib:* Solo exhibs, Shine oder Jedem das Seine, Galerie Reinhard Hauff, Stuttgart, 2001; Lustgarten, Borgmann Nathusius Galerie, Cologne, 2002; Josephine Meckseper, Elizabeth Dee Gallery, 2003; IG Metall und die kunstlichen Paradiese des Politischen, 2004; Elizabeth Dee Gallery, New York, 2005; The Bulletin Board, White Columns, NY, 2005; Int Project Room (with Galerie Reinhard Hauff), ARCO, Madrid, 2006; Josephine Meckseper, Galerie Reinhard Hauff, Stuttgart, 2007; Josephine Meckseper (with catalogue), Kunstmuseum Stuttgart, Stuttgart, 2007; Group shows, Tattoo Collection, Andrea Rosen Gallery, NY, 92; This Is Your Home, Stuyvesant Town, NY, 94; Wheel of Fortune, Lombard-Fried Fine Arts, NY, 95; Mixing Messages: Graphic Design in Contemp Culture, Cooper-Hewitt, Nat Design Mus, NY, 96; Super Freaks: Post Pop and the New Generation, Part 1: Trash, Green Naftali, NY, 98; Overflow, D'Amelio Terras, Marianne Boesky Gallery & Anton Kern Gallery, NY, 99; Flea Market, Gavin Brown's Enterprise, NY, 2000; Wine, Women & Wheels, White Columns, NY, 2001; In the Public Domain, 2003; American Idyll, 2004; Girls on Film, Zwirner & Wirth, NY, 2005; Whitney Biennial, Whitney Mus Am Art, 2006, 2010; This Ain't No Fooling Around, Rubicon Gallery Contemp Art, Dublin, 2006. *Mailing Add:* c/o Elizabeth Dee Gallery 545 W 20th St New York NY 10011

MEDEL, REBECCA ROSALIE
SCULPTOR, ENVIRONMENTAL ARTIST
b Denver, Colo, 1947. *Study:* Ariz State Univ, Tempe, BFA (environ design), 70; Fiberworks, Ctr for Textile Arts, Berkeley, Calif, cert, 79; Univ Calif, Los Angeles, MFA, 82. *Work:* Mus des Arts Decoratifs, Lausanne, Switz; Mus de la Tapisserie, Aix-en-Provence, France; Art Inst Chicago, Ill; Longhouse Reserve, East Hampton, NY; Denver Art Mus, Colo; Wustun Mus, Racine, Wisc; Found Toms Pauli, Lausanne, Switzerland; Philadelphia Mus Art. *Comn:* pvt collectors, Scottsdale, Ariz, St Louis, Mo & Chapel Hill, NC. *Exhib:* The 20th Century Textile Artist, Art Inst Chicago, Ill, 99; Contemp Art of Linear Construction (with catalog), Yokohama Mus Art, Japan, 99; Made in Calif 1900-2000, Los Angeles Co Mus Art, 2000; The Art of Containment, Hunterdon Mus, Clinton, NJ, 2002; Fibertart Int, Soc Contemp Arts, Pittsburgh, 2001; Small Works, Long House Reserve, East Hampton, NY 2002; solo exhib, Continuity & Change, Thirteen Moons Gallery, Santa Fe, NMex, 2003; Blue, Mobilia Gallery, Boston, Mass, 2004; Nat Gallery of Irish Craft Council, Kilkenny, Ireland, 2005; Art & Infinity, Santa Fe Community Col, NMex, 2006; Tapisserie, Anger, France, 2007; Beyond Boundaries, Arthur Ross Gallery, Univ Pa, Philadelphia, 2008; Sessions, KCC Gallery, Tokyo, Japan, 2010; Sleight of Hand, Denver Art Mus, 2011. *Teaching:* Asst prof fibers, Tenn Technol Univ, Smithville, 83-; assoc prof, Univ Calif, Los Angeles, 89-91, prof, Tyler Sch Art, Philadelphia, 95-, emeritus prof, 2011. *Awards:* Bronze Medal, Fifth Int Triennal, Cent Mus Lodz, Poland, 85; Southern Arts Fedn Fel, 85; Nat Endowment Arts, 86 & 88; Pew fel in the Arts, 99; Fel Pa Coun on the Arts, 2001 & 2007; McRight Award for Contemp Art, Delaware Art Mus, 2000. *Bibliog:* Artweek, Oakland, Calif, 9/13/90; Nouvel Object III, Design House Publ, Seoul, Korea, 97; Article in fiber arts, Textile Plus & British Crafts, 98-99; Am Style, Baltimore, Md, fall & winter 2000. *Media:* Embellished Digital Prints. *Mailing Add:* 7134 Potomac St Riverside CA 92504

MEDENICA, BRANKO
SCULPTOR, RESTORER
b Darmstadt, Fed Repub Ger, July 17, 1950; US citizen. *Study:* Birmingham-Southern Coll, BA, 72; Univ Miss, MFA, 75; Richard MacDonald Master Class, 98;. *Work:* Arch Am Art, Washington, DC; Univ Miss, Oxford. *Comn:* Duty Called (cast bronze), State Ala, Montgomery, 85; Coll Cullman (cast bronze), City Cullman, Ala, 88; Aspirations (stainless steel), comn by Dr Sam Barker, Birmingham, 91; Centurion (cast bronze), Fraternal Order Police, Birmingham, 92; Jesse Owens (cast bronze), Oakville, Ala, 96; Wings of Triumph (cast bronze), Auburn, Ala, 2008; Horse Power (polychrome steel, Barber Racetrack, 2010. *Exhib:* Nat Sculpture '74 Traveling Exhib, 74; 1st Ala Sculpture Show, Mobile Mus, 80; Outdoor Sculpture Invitational, Univ Ala, Tuscaloosa, 82; The Fiery Furnace: Cast Metal Sculpture, Sloss Mus, Birmingham, 90; Chariscuro, Light & Dark, Montgomery Mus Art, Ala, 94; River Gallery, Chattanooga, 96; others. *Pos:* Co-founder, Birmingham Arts Comn, 80; chair long range planning comt, Bham Arts Comn, 81-83; chair visual arts adv panel, Ala State Coun Arts, 82-86. *Teaching:* Birmingham Southern Coll, 95; Univ Ala Birmingham, 96; Jefferson State, 2008. *Awards:* Addy Award, 71. *Bibliog:* George Inser (dir), Forging Art Through Friendship (film), City of Birmingham, 89; Mary Jean Parson (auth), Accessible art, Birmingham Mag, 89; Jesse Holland (auth), Gift honors UAB's aspirations, Post-Herald, 91. *Mem:* Nat Sculpture Soc; Int Sculpture Soc. *Media:* Cast Metal, Welded Metal, Installation Sculpture. *Specialty:* painting and sculpture. *Interests:* Skiing. *Publ:* Auth, Old George: The Restoration Process by Branko Medenica. *Dealer:* Dale Chambliss Gallery Destin FL. *Mailing Add:* 2300 Peacock Ln Birmingham AL 35223

MEDINA, JUAN
PAINTER
b Mexico City, Mex, Sept 19, 1950. *Exhib:* SNBA Salon, Carrousel Du Louvre, Paris, France, 99-2008; Art en Capital, Grand Palais, Paris, France, 2008; AAPL 8th Grand Nat Exhib, Salmagundi Club, New York, 2008; AAA 95th Ann Exhib, Nat Arts Club, New York, 2008. *Awards:* Mérite et Dévouement Français Silver Medal, SNBA Salon, 99; Silver Medal, Societe Nationale des Beaux-Arts, 2005. *Bibliog:* Julie Boteler (auth), The Language of Juan Medina, AMB Publ Co/Bryant Galleries, 2002. *Mem:* Societe Nationale Des Beaux-Arts; Arts Renewal Ctr; Int Guild of Realism. *Media:* Oil, Misc Media. *Dealer:* Bryant Galleries 3010 Lakeland Cove Suite A Flowood MS 39232; Bryant Galleries 316 Royal St New Orleans LA 70130

MEDVEDOW, JILL
MUSEUM DIRECTOR
b New Haven, Conn, Oct 4, 1954. *Study:* Colgate Univ, BA, 76; NY Univ, Inst Fine Arts, MA, 78. *Hon Degrees:* Montserrat Coll Art, Hon Dr, 98. *Collection Arranged:* Honey, I'm Home, Midtown Art Ctr, Houston, Tex, 85; Outside New York: Seattle, New Mus, NY, 86; Dorit Cypis: The Body in the Picture (catalog), Isabella Stewart Gardner Mus, Boston, Mass, 93; Denise Marika: New Works (with catalog), Isabella Stewart Gardner Mus, Boston, 94; Juan Munoz: Potrait of a Turkish Nan Drawing (with catalog), Isabella Stewart Gardner Mus, Boston, 95. *Pos:* Artist-in-residence, Blue Mountain Ctr, 86 & 90; Prog developer, WGBH Educ Found, Boston, Mass, 89-92; freelance consult to museums regarding pub programming; consult, Nat Endowment Arts; dep dir progs & cur contemp art, Isabella Stewart Gardner Mus, Boston, Mass, 93-97; Ellen Matilda Poss dir, Inst Contemp Art, Boston, 98-. *Awards:* Writer-in-residence, Blue Mountain Ctr, NY, 84-86; fel critical writing, Seattle Arts Comn, 85. *Mem:* Art Table; Am Asn Mus; Coll Art Asn. *Publ:* Auth, A View from the outside: The art of Nancy Spero and Elaine Reichek, Cocafolio, Ctr Contemp Art, 85; coauth, Back to basics: media arts centers in the 80's return to their roots, Visions, spring 87; auth, Daniel Reeves, Video Currents, spring 87; coauth, Review of Hard Core: Power, Pleasure and the Frenzy of the Visible, The Independent, 91; ed, The Eye of the Beholder, Isabella Stewart Gardner Mus, 94. *Mailing Add:* Institute of Contemporary Art 100 Northern Ave Boston MA 02210-1802

MEEK, J WILLIAM, III
DEALER, CONSULTANT
b Aberdeen, Md, Nov 8, 1950. *Study:* Fla Southern Col, BA, 72; Johns Hopkins Univ, MA, 2011. *Collection Arranged:* curated more than 300 exhibitions, more than 80 museums in 27 states. *Pos:* Asst dir, Harmon Gallery, Naples, Fla, 72-77; dir-owner, Harmon-Meek Gallery, 78-; bd mem, Richard Florsheim Art Fund, Tampa, Fla, 85-95, von Liebig Art Ctr, Naples, Fla, 2003-8. *Awards:* 10 Paul Harris Fel, Rotary Int; Contrib to Visual Arts Ann Award, Artists Equity Asn, 99; Stars in the Arts: United Arts Council of Collier Co, Fla, 2006; Svc to the Arts award, Southern Alleghenies Mus Art, PA, 2012. *Mem:* Fel Royal Soc Arts, London; Nat Arts Club, NY. *Specialty:* Paintings, drawings and sculpture by major American artists of the 20th century. *Collection:* Private collection of 20th century American art. *Mailing Add:* Harmon-Meek Gallery 599 9th St Nò Ste 309 Naples FL 34102

MEEKER, BARBARA MILLER
EDUCATOR, PAINTER
b Peru, Ind, Dec 31, 1930. *Study:* DePauw Univ, BA; also with Jack Pellew, Ed Betts, Edgar A Whitney, Claude Croney, Charles Reid, Ed Fitzgerald, Frank Webb, Millard Sheets, Robert E Wood, Miles Batt, Dong Kingman, Glen Bradshaw & Virginia Cobb. *Work:* DePauw Univ Art Ctr Print Collection, Greencastle, Ind; Purdue Univ, Calumet & Hammond Pub Schs, Ind; Tri-State Col, Angola, Ind; Oak Park River Forest High Sch, Ill; Lake Co Pub Libr; Ind Bell Telephone; Nat Easter Seal Soc; Community Hosp, Munster, Ind; St Catherine Hosp, E Chicago, Ind; Oak Park-River Forest HS, Oak Park, Ill; Whiteco Corp, Merrillville, Ind. *Comn:* Viking Eng. *Exhib:* Ft Wayne Art Mus; Lafayette Art Mus; Artist Guild Chicago Watercolor Show, Rocky Mountain Nat Watercolor Exhib, Denver; Contemp Artists Ind, Indianapolis; Ind State Mus Invitational, Indianapolis; Nat Watercolor Oklahoma, Okla City; Watercolor USA; retrospective, NIAA, Munster, Ind. *Collection Arranged:* Calumet Collection, Purdue Univ; DePauw Univ Collection; Sand Ridge Bank Art Collection; Northern Ind Pub Svc Co Art Collection. *Pos:* Mem art comn, Ind State House, 63-65; bd dir, Midwest Watercolor Soc, 83-85 & VSA Arts, Ind, 2000-05; coordr, Very Special Arts, Ind, 88-89, 90 & 91; mem art com, Town of Munster Public Art Comt, 2003-; bd dir, NIAA, 94-2000. *Teaching:* Emer prof freehand drawing & painting, Purdue Univ, Calumet, 65-86. *Awards:* Jury Prize Distinction, Indianapolis, 84; Nat Watercolor Okla, 87; Midwest Watercolor, 97; Community Leader Award (class of 1952 reunion), DePauw Univ, 2007. *Bibliog:* Hawkins & McClarren (auth), Indiana lives, Hist Rec Asn, 67; J L Collins (auth), Women Artists in America, Les Krantz. *Mem:* signature mem, Ky Watercolor Soc; life mem & signature mem, Midwest Watercolor Soc; Chicago Artists Coalition; N Coast Collage Soc; life mem Northern Ind Arts Asn (bd dir, 95-2001). *Media:* Watercolor, Collage, Acrylic, Silver & Gems Jewelry. *Interests:* Gardening, traveling. *Publ:* Auth, Freehand Drawing, 72, 2nd ed, 75, 3rd ed, 80; contribr, Complete Guide to Creative Watercolor, 88. *Dealer:* Heart To Heart Gallery Munster IN; The Steeple Gallery St John IN. *Mailing Add:* PO Box 3204 Munster IN 46321

MEEKS, DONNA MARIE
ADMINISTRATOR, PAINTER
b Louisville, Ky, Jan 14, 1960. *Study:* Univ Louisville, Kentucky, BA (honors, drawing), 82, MAT, 84; Univ Wis, Milwaukee, MFA (painting, sculpture), 86. *Work:* Hoyt Inst Fine Arts, New Castle, Pa; Wabash Coll Art Dept; Kirkland Fine Arts Ctr, Millikin Univ; Cape Townsend Artists' Workshops, Algoma, Wis; Coca-Cola Bottling Co, Elizabethtown, Ky; Fundacion Torre Pujales, Corme, La Coruna, Galicia, Spain; Art Mus Southeast Texas, Beaumont; Brandywine Workshop, Phila, Pa. *Exhib:* Nat Works on Paper, Univ Gallery, St John's Univ, Jamaica, NY, 95; Nat Exhib, Denise Bibro Fine Art, Soho, 97; Nat Showcase Exhbn Alternative Mus, Soho, 99; Critics

Choice Dallas Visual Art Ctr, Tex, 99; Beefcake/Cheesecake: Sex, Flesh, Money and Dreams, Orange Co Ctr for Cont Art, Santa Ana, Calif, 2001; Cerebral Candy, Lankershim Art Gallery, N Hollywood, Calif, 2004; Go Figure, Circle Gallery, Maryland Federation of Art, Annapolis, 2004; Oct Int Competition, Montgomery Art Ctr, West Palm Beach, Fla, 2004; 7th Ann All Media Exhib, Touchstone Gallery, Washington, DC, 2005; 19th Ann Int Juried Show, NJ Ctr Visual Arts, Summit, NJ, 2005; Transcribing the Human Form, Campbell Hall Gallery, Western Ore Univ, 2007; Extremely Superficial, Dangen Art Gallery, Nashville, Tenn, 2007; Skin Deep: Recent Works by Donna Meeks, Northwestern State Univ, Natchitoches, La, 2008; Painting, Foundry Art Ctr, St Charles, Mo, 2008; The Big Show, Lawndale Art Ctr, Houston, Tex, 2009, 2010; Skin Deep: Recent Works by Donna M Meeks, Univ Tex, Permian Basin, Odessa, Tex, 2012; Upshot x3, Houston Community Coll Central Campus, Houston, Tex, 2013. *Pos:* Cur educ, Tarble Arts Ctr, Eastern Ill Univ, Charleston, 87-93; dir educ, Am Acad Art, Chicago, 93-95; chmn, Art Dept, Lamar Univ, Beaumont, Tex, 95-. *Teaching:* Instr, Eastern Ill Univ, 87-93; prof, Dept Art, Lamar Univ, Beaumont, Tex, 95-. *Awards:* First Place Monetary Award, Works on Paper, Houston, 96; Provocative Symbolism Award, 2nd Annual Musky Nat, Muskingum Col, Ohio, 96; First Place, Small Works '98, Sam Houston State Univ, Huntsville, Tex, 98. *Bibliog:* Lois Michel (auth), Magical, mystical aura ect, Naperville Sun, 88; James Auer (auth), Gall exhib include kitchen sink, Milwaukee J, 89; Art symposium hailed a success, Leavenworth Times, Kans, 91; Cecelia Johnson (auth), Here & Hereafter: Artists explore questions of life, death and mortality in exhibit, Issue: The Arts Mag of the Art Studio Inc, 2003. *Mem:* Coll Art Asn; Nat Asn Schs Art & Design; Nat Coun Arts Adminr; Tex Asn Schs Art. *Media:* Oil, Egg Tempera, Mixed. *Publ:* auth, The allegorical imperative (or why paint when the copy store is open twenty-four/seven), Visual Resources, Vol XV, No 2 fall 99; auth, Some Thoughts on Jesse Stuart and Emmanuel Kant: New Passageways in Men of the Mountains, Jack London Newsletter, Vol 16, No 1, Jan-Apr 1983; auth, Do We Know Our ABC's: Art, Bridges and Community, issue: The Arts Mag of the Art Studio Inc, Vol 9, No 9, 6/2003; auth, Then & Now: A Half Century of Alumni Art, winter/sprig 2005; auth, Off Ramp: A Guide to Arts & Culture Adventures in Southeast Texas, winter/spring 2005. *Mailing Add:* Lamar Univ Dept Art PO Box 10027 Beaumont TX 77710

MEHN, JAN (JAN VON DER GOLZ)
PRINTMAKER
b Chicago, Ill, Aug 26, 1953. *Study:* Kansas City Art Inst, Mo, Calif Coll Arts & Crafts, Oakland, BFA, 79, Ariz State Univ, Tempe, MFA, 87. *Work:* Auburn Arts Ctr, Ala; Univ Tex, San Antonio; Ariz State Univ, Tempe; Kansas City Art Inst, Mo; Calif Coll Arts & Crafts, Oakland; Rutgers Univ, NJ. *Exhib:* 31st Ann San Francisco Art Festival, Calif, 77; 13th Nat Print Exhib, Silvermine Guild Art, New Canaan, Conn, 80; 28th Nat Print Exhib, Hunterdon Art Ctr, Clinton, NJ, 84; 6th Miami Int Print Exhib, North Miami Mus, North Miami, Fla, 84; 37th Boston Printmakers, Rose Art Mus, Waltham, Mass, 85; Prints: Washington, The Phillips Collection, Washington, 88; Ariz State Univ Alumni, 99; Anchor Graphics, Ill, 99. *Pos:* Printers asst, De Soto Workshop, San Francisco, 79-80; Conserv aid, Nat Arch, Washington, 88-89; preparator, Sackler Gallery Art, Smithsonian, 89-90, Wash Proj Arts, Washington, 90; Studio Mgr, DePaul Univ, Chicago, 98-. *Teaching:* Instr drawing & printmaking, Ariz State Univ, Tempe, 84-87; instr monotype, Arlington Arts Ctr, Va, 88 & Pyramid Atlantic, Washington, 89; Va Mus, Richmond, 90-91; asst prof, Bradley Univ, Peoria, Ill, 91-92; DePaul Univ, Chicago, 98-00. *Awards:* Artist's Grant, District Columbia Arts & Humanities, 89; Artist's Grant, State Ill Arts Coun, 95; Change Found Grant, 00; Mid Atlantic Arts Foundation/NEA Grant, 1988. *Bibliog:* JoAnn Lewis (auth), At the Phillips, Wash Post, 9/17/88; Daniel Barbiero (auth), Atlanta Art Papers, 1-2/89; Michael Welzenbach (auth), Wash Post, 4/7/90. *Mem:* Southern Graphics Conf; Mid-American Print Alliance. *Media:* Monotypes, Mixed Media. *Dealer:* Chipp-D Gallery 2905 Broadway Long Beach CA 90803. *Mailing Add:* 2711 S 59th Ct Cicero IL 60804

MEIER, RICHARD ALAN
ARCHITECT
b Newark, NJ, Oct 12, 1934. *Study:* Cornell Univ, BArch, 57. *Hon Degrees:* Univ Naples, Italy, Doctor (hon), 1991; NJ Inst Tech; New Sch Social Res; Wheaton Col; Pratt Inst; The New Sch, NY City, Doctor (hon), 1995. *Work:* High Mus, Atlanta; Mus Contemp Art, Barcelona, Spain; Mus TV & Radio, Beverly Hills, Calif; US Fed Courthouse, Islip, NY. *Comn:* High Mus Art, Atlanta, Ga; Douglas House; J Paul Getty Mus & Fine Arts Ctr, comn by J Paul Getty Trust, 84; Mus Decorative Arts; Frankfurt City Hall, The Hague; Des Moines Art Ctr additions; UCLA, vis design critic, 87, 88 & 89; Ara Pacis Mus, Rome, 2006. *Exhib:* Modernism Gallery, San Francisco, 80; Wadsworth Atheneum, Hartford, Conn, 80; High Mus Art, Atlanta, 80; Max Protetch Gallery, NY, 80; Harvard Univ, 80; Knoll Int, Tokyo, Japan, 88; October Gallery, London, Eng, 90; Royal Palace, Naples, Italy, 91; Galerie Nationale de Jeu de Paume, Paris, 99; Archit Inst, Rotterdam, 2001; Mus Applied Art, Frankfurt, Ger, 2003; High Mus Art, Atlanta, 2003-2004; Modena Forum, Italy, 2004; Richard Meier Retrospective, MARCO Mus, Monterrey, Mex, 2011. *Pos:* principal architect, Richard Meier & Assocs, NY, 1963-1980; mem adv coun, Col Art, Archit & Planning, Cornell Univ, Ithaca, NY, 71-; Resident architect, Am Acad in Rome, 73-74; juror, Int Competition, Convention Hall, Nara, Japan, 92. *Teaching:* Adj prof, Cooper Union, 64-73; William Henry Bishop vis prof, Yale Univ, 75 & 77; Eliot Noyes vis design critic, Harvard Univ, 80 & 81; vis design critic, Univ Calif, Los Angeles, 87, 88 & 89; vis prof, Cornell U, 2000-. *Awards:* Pritzker Archit Prize, 84; Royal Gold Medal, Royal Inst Brit Architects, 88; Gold Medal, Am Inst Architects, 97; Praemium Imperiale Award, Japan Art Assoc, 97; AIA Twenty five Year Award, 2000; World Archit Award, 2001; Legend Award, 2004; Frate Sole Int Award for Sacred Archit, 2004; Gold Medal Archit, AAAL, 2008. *Bibliog:* Richard Meier Architect, Rizzoli, 84; Wesner Blaser (auth) Richard Meier: Bldg for Art, 89; Gloria Gerace (ed), Getty Center Design Process, J Paul Getty Trust, 91. *Mem:* Nat Acad; fel Am Inst Architects; Int Acad Archit; Century Club New York; Am Acad & Inst Arts & Letts; hon fel Royal Inst Brit Architects. *Publ:* Coauth, Five Architects: Eisenman/Graves/Gwathmey/Hejduk/Meier, Wittenborn Co, 72; Richard Meier, Architect: Buildings and Projects 1966-1976, Oxford Univ Press, 76; Richard Meier, Architect, Rizzoll, 84; Richard Meir, Architect 2, Rizzoll, 91; and others. *Mailing Add:* Richard Meier & Partners 475 10th Ave 6th fl New York NY 10018-1120

MEIRELES, CILDO
SCULPTOR
b Rio De Janeiro, Brazil, 1948. *Work:* Ctr Pompidou, Paris; Mus Mod Art, New York; Tate Mod, London. *Exhib:* Solo exhibs, Mus Arte Mod, Salvador, Bahia, Brazil, 1967, Mus Mod Art, New York, 1990, New Mus Contemp Art, New York, 1999, Miami Art Mus, 2003, Mus Vale do Rio Doce, Sao Paulo, Brazil, 2006; Il Salao Arte Mod do Distrito Federal, Brasilia, Brazil, 1965; Information, Mus Mod Art, New York, 1970, New Perspectives in Latin Am Art, 2007; Latin American Spirit, Bronx Mus, NY, 1989; Rhetorical Image, New Mus Contemp Art, New York, 1990; Face à l'Histoire, Ctr Georges Pompidou, Paris, 1996, Face of History, 1997; Heterotopias, Reina Sofia, Madrid, 2000, Versiones del Sur, 2001; Open Systems, Tate Mod, London, 2005; Arte Vida:, El Mus del Barrio, New York, 2008; 53rd Int Art Exhib Biennale, Venice, 2009. *Awards:* Prince Claus Found Award, Netherlands, 1999; Velazquez Prize, Ministerio de Cult, Spain, 2008; Ordway Prize, Creative Link Arts & New Mus Contemp Art, New York, 2008. *Mailing Add:* Galerie Lelong 528 W 26th St New York NY 10001

MEISEL, LOUIS KOENIG
DEALER, HISTORIAN
b Brooklyn, NY, Sept 4, 1942. *Study:* Tulane Univ, BA, 1964; Columbia Univ; New Sch Social Res. *Collection Arranged:* Photo Realism 1973, Stuart M Speiser Collection (with catalog), Smithsonian Inst; Photo-Realism, Guggenheim Mus; and 50 others. *Pos:* Pres, Eminent Publications, NYC, 1964-1978; owner, Meisel Gallery, New York, 1967-1972; pres Louis K Meisel Gallery, NYC, 1973-; partner Susan P. Meisel Gallery, NYC, 1983-, Meisel Real Estate, NYC, 1988-; co-partner Bernarducci Meisel Gallery, NY, 2001-. *Bibliog:* Les Levine (auth), New dealer, Arts Mag, 1/74; Judy Beardsall (auth), Louis Meisel, Art Gallery Mag, 9/73; Mel Ramos (auth), Pop Fantasies: The Complete Paintings, Watson-Gaptil, 2006. *Mem:* International Soc Appraisers and Appraiser Asn America. *Res:* Photo realism. *Specialty:* Photo realism. *Publ:* Auth, 15 Years of Photorealism, Horizon Mag, 11/80; Richard E Estes, H N Abrams, 86; Clarice Cliff-The Bizarre Affair, H N Abrams, 88; Charles Bell, The Complete Paintings 1970-1990, H N Abrams, 91; Photo Realism Since 1980, H N Abrams, 93; The Great American Pin-up: Köln Germany, Benedikt Taschen Verlag, 95; auth, Photorealism, N H Abrams, Inc, 80; coauth, The Best of American Girlie Magazine, Benedikt Taschen Verlag, 97; coauth, The Edward Runci Collection: Pin Up Poster Book, Collectors Press, Inc, 97; co-auth, Gil Elvgren-All His Glamorous American Pin-Ups, Benedikt Taschen Verlag, 99; auth, Photorealism at the Millennium, N H Abrams, Inc, 2002; auth, Photorealism in the Digital Age, N H Abrams, 2013. *Mailing Add:* Louis K Meisel Gallery 141 Prince St Ground Floor New York NY 10012

MEISEL, SUSAN PEAR
PAINTER, PRINTMAKER, PHOTOGRAPHER
b New York, NY, Apr 16, 1947. *Study:* Barnard, 66; Parsons Sch Design, 68; Sch Visual Arts, 70; NY Univ, 2002-03. *Work:* Larry Aldrich Mus, Richfield, Conn; Ft Wayne Mus, Ind; State Dept, Washington, DC; numerous Am Embassies world wide. *Comn:* Libr Cong, Washington, DC; Smithsonian Inst, Washington, DC; Comsat Corp Hq, Washington, DC; Independence Hall, Philadelphia, Pa; The Excelsior Hotel, Rome; The Olaffsson Collection, Omea, Sweden; Coca Cola Bottling Co. *Exhib:* 10 yrs of Printmaking, Ft Wayne Mus, Ind, 80; 10 yrs of Printmaking, Tomasulo Gallery Union Coll, NJ, 81; Transworld Art, NY; Galerie Le Portrail, Heidelberg, Germany; Bay Harbor Gallery, NY; The Wickersham Gallery, NY. *Teaching:* Art teacher, UN Int Sch, 90-97. *Bibliog:* Judy Beardsall (auth), Susan Pear Meisel, Arts Mag, 5/78; Robert Voskowitz (auth), Susan Pear Meisel(catalog), Ft Wayne Mus. *Media:* Acrylic on Canvas. *Publ:* auth, The Hamptons, Harry N Abrams, 2000; auth, Hampton Pleasures, Harry N Abrams, 2004; auth, Gourmet Shops of NY, Rizzoli, 2007; Fresh from the Farm, Rizzoli, 2010. *Mailing Add:* c/o Louis K Meisel Gallery 141 Prince St New York NY 10012

MEISELMAN, MARILYN NEWMARK See Newmark, Marilyn

MEISSNER, ANNE MARIE
ADMINISTRATOR
Study: Oxford Univ, St Ann's Col, cert, 68; Univ Mich, Ann Arbor, MSW, 67; Univ Calif-Berkeley, BA, 79. *Pos:* Dir, San Francisco Art Comm Gallery, 87. *Mem:* Art Table (co-chair, prog comt, 91); Non-Profit Gallery Asn, San Francisco Bay Area (vpres & bd dir); Art Span/Open Studios San Francisco. *Mailing Add:* 1673 Sacramento St San Francisco CA 94109-3718

MEISTER, MARK J
INSTITUTE DIRECTOR, ART HISTORIAN
b Baltimore, Md, June 26, 1953. *Study:* Washington Univ, AB (art & archeol), 74; Univ Minn, MA (art hist & museology), 76. *Pos:* Dir, Mus Art & Hist, Port Huron, Mich, 78-79, Midwest Mus Am Art, Elkhart, Ind, 79-81 & Mus Art, Sci & Indust, Bridgeport, Conn, 86-89; exec dir, Children's Mus, St Paul, Minn, 81-86; exec dir, Archaeol Inst Am, Boston, Mass, 89-. *Teaching:* Adj lectr museology, Kenyon Col, Gambier, Ohio, 77; lectr art hist, Ind Univ, South Bend, 80-81. *Awards:* Nat Endowment Humanities Museology Fel, 76-77; Kress Fel, 77; Bush Found Summer Fel, 83. *Mem:* Am Asn Mus; Am Coun Learned Socs; Archaeol Inst Am; Soc Am Archaeol; US Comt/Int Coun Monuments & Sites. *Publ:* Ed, Selections Art & Artifacts from the Kenyon College Collection (catalog), 77; auth, The man who painted Lake Gervais Tornado, Minn Hist Mag, 77; Midwest Photo 80 & 81, Midwest Mus Am Art; ed, American Artists Abroad (exhib catalog), 86 & Milton Avery (exhib catalog), Mus Art, Sci & Indust, 87; co-ed, Archaeology on Film, Kendall/Hunt Publ Co, 94. *Mailing Add:* Archaeological Inst of Am 656 Beacon St Boston MA 02215-2010

MEISTER, MICHAEL WILLIAM
HISTORIAN, EDUCATOR
b West Palm Beach, Fla, Aug 20, 1942. *Study:* Harvard Col, BA, 64; Harvard Univ, MA, 71, PhD, 74; Univ Pa, Hon MA, 79. *Exhib:* Cooking for the Gods, Newark Mus, 95-96; Multiple Modernities, PMA, 2008. *Pos:* Cur, South Asia Art Archive, 78-. *Teaching:* Asst prof art hist, Univ Tex, Austin, 74-76; asst prof, Univ Pa, 76-79, assoc prof, 79-88, grad chmn hist of art dept, 78-79 & 86-90, prof, 88- & chmn hist of art, 94-; prof, W Norman Brown Univ, Pa, 2002-. *Awards:* Smithsonian Develop Grant, 81; Studies Awards, Am Inst Pakistan, 94 & 96; Interpretive Res Grant, J Paul Getty Trust, 96-98. *Bibliog:* SARAS Bull, No 3. *Mem:* Am Comt South Asian Art (mem bd dir, 76-79 & 83-86); Am Inst Indian Studies; Asn Asian Studies; Comt Art and Archeol; Coll Art Asn. *Res:* South Asian art, particularly Hindu temple architecture, sculpture and iconology. *Publ:* Ed, Encyclopedia of Indian Temple Architecture, Vols 1 & 2, Princeton Univ Press, 83, 86, 88 & 91; Discourses on Siva, Univ Pa Press, 84; On the Development of a Symbolic Architecture: India, Res 12, 86; Making Things in South Asia, Univ Pa, SAsia Dept, 88; Coomaraswamy: Essays in Early Indian Architecture, 92; Essays in Architectural Theory, 95. *Mailing Add:* Hist Art Dept 201 Jaffe Bldg Univ Pa Philadelphia PA 19104

MEJER, ROBERT LEE
PAINTER, EDUCATOR
b South Bend, Ind, Nov 8, 1944. *Study:* SBend Art Ctr with Joseph Wrobel; Ball State Univ, BS; Miami Univ with Robert Wolfe, Jr, MFA; Kent State Univ with Nathan Oliveira & Milton Resnick, 73; Kalamazoo Art Inst with Harvey Breverman, 75; Oxbow Summer Sch Art with Leon Golub, Joe Wilfer & Richard Haas, 76-78 & 81; Notre Dame Univ with Michael Ponce de Leon, 79; Wash Univ with Ed Paschke & Sam Gilliam, 80; Univ Chicago with Vera Klement, 86; Skidmore Coll with Hugh O'Donell, 96, Dan Wezden, 2001, 2002. *Work:* Kemper Insurance Co, Chicago; Hallmark Cards, Mo; Quaker Oats Corp, Chicago; Neville Pub Mus, Wis; Springfield Art Mus, Mo. *Comn:* Serigraphs, AFA Press, Lakeside, Mich, 98. *Exhib:* Retrospective 1969-1979, Quincy Art Ctr, Ill, 79; 51st Nat Midyear Painting, Butler Inst Am Art, 87; Int One of a Kind: Monotypes, Sigma Gallery, NY, 90; 24th Bradley Nat Print & Drawing Competition, Ill, 93; Dakota's Int Artwork on Paper, Univ SDak Art Gallery, Vermillion, 94; Greater Midwest Int, Cent Mo State Univ, 96; 44th mid-state juried, Evansville Mus Arts, Ind, 99; 11th Nat Western Colo Watercolor, 2001; 1st Invitational ISEA Gross Innovation Juried, Wales, 2003-2005; 20th Penn Watercolor Juried, Lancaster Mus, 2007; 33rd Nat Okla Watercolor invitational, Omniplex Sci Mus, Okla, 2007; 17th Biennial Ill drawing/watercolor, 2009. *Collection Arranged:* Mid-Am Print Coun Exhib, 95, 2008, Gray Gallery, Quincy Univ; Douglas Craft: Works on Paper, 97; Quincy Univ Alumni Comm Art Exhib, 2009. *Pos:* Gallery asst, Ball State Art Gallery, Ill, 62-66; gallery cur, Quincy Univ, 68- & chair arts dept, 91-94, chair div fine arts, 94-99, prog coord, 99-; gallery asst, Quincy Art Ctr, Ill, 70- & chair exhibs comt, 76-80 & 89-95. *Teaching:* Instr painting & drawing, Ball State Univ, summers 66 & 67; instr drawing, Miami Univ, 66-68; prof art, Quincy Univ, 68-, distinguished prof art, 2001-; instr, John Wood Community Col, 75-76; vis res fac, Skidmore Col, Summer Six II, NY, 82-96, 2001, 2002. *Awards:* City of Quincy Individual Artist Award, 90; Fel, Vt Studio Ctr, 96; Quincy Univ Serv Award, 97; Quincy Trustees Award, Scholarly Achievements, 98-99; Quincy Univ Distinguished Prof Art, 2001. *Bibliog:* Julia Ayers (auth), Monotypes, Watson-Guptill, 91; Helen Dobbyn (producer, dir & ed), Artscape: Bob Mejer, Quincy Univ, 1/28/96; Nita Leland (auth), Exploring Color, Watson-Guptill, 98; Betty Lou Schlenny (auth), Abstracts in Watercolor, Rockport, 96; Mark Mehaffey (Auth), creative in watercolor workshop, Northlight, 2005; Rachel Rubin Wolf (ed), Splash 11, Northlight, 2010. *Mem:* Life mem Quincy Univ Found; Quincy Art Ctr (bd dir, 76-80, vpres, 76 & 89-95); life mem Transparent Watercolor Soc; Watercolor USA Honor Soc; Mid-Am Print Coun; Signature mem Nat Watercolor Soc; Nautilus Fel of the Invitational Soc of Experimental Artists. *Media:* Watercolor, Monotypes. *Specialty:* Contemporary artists. *Publ:* Illusr, Salt-Lick Mag, 68-71; illusr, Riverword Mag, Vols 1, 2, & 3, 77. *Mailing Add:* 619 Meadow Lark Quincy IL 62301-5943

MELAMED, DANA
PAINTER
b Israel. *Study:* Ort Technicum, Givatayim, Israel, 1990; Tel Aviv Art Design Ctr & Tel Aviv Sch Visual Art, 1995. *Exhib:* Solo exhibs, Priska C Juschka Fine Art, New York, 2006 & 2007; group exhibs include Edward Hopper House, Nyack, NY, 2003, 2004, 2005; Cooper Union Residency, Cooper Union, New York, 2005; The Reasonably Straight Digital Photog Show, Old Church Art Ctr, Demarest, NJ, 2005; New Found Land: Inaugural Group Show, Priska C Juschka Fine Art, New York, 2005; Frames of Mind, Bernnan Gallery, Justice william Bernnan Court House, Jersey City, 2006; Go North, New Yorker!, Peekskill Project 2006, Hudson Valley Ctr Contemp Art, Peekskill, NY, 2006; Lost Horizon, Herter Gallery, Univ Mass, Amherst, 2008; Future Tense: Contemp Views/Post-Utopian Landscape, Neuberger Mus Art, New York, 2008; Ann Invitational Exhib Contemp Art, Nat Acad Mus, New York, 2008

MELAMED, HOPE See Winter, Hope Melamed

MELAMID, ALEXANDER
PAINTER
b Mascow, July 14, 1945. *Study:* Moscow Art Sch, 1958-60; Stroganov Inst Art & Design, Moscow, 1962-67. *Work:* Nat Ctr Contemp, Moscow Branch, Moscow. *Exhib:* Solo exhibs include Mus Contemp Art, Detroit, 2008; Group exhibs include East Art Mus, Karl Ernst Osthaus Mus, Germany, 2005. *Dealer:* Ronald Feldman Gallery 31 Mercer St New York NY 10013

MELBERG, JERALD LEIGH
ART DEALER, COLLECTOR
b Minneapolis, Minn, Aug 17, 1948. *Collection Arranged:* 1977, 1979 & 1981 Biennial Exhibition of Piedmont Painting & Sculpture (ed, catalog), 77, 1978, 1980 & 1982 Biennial Exhibition of Piedmont Crafts (ed, catalog), 78 & Romare Bearden 1970-1980 (ed, catalog), 80, Mint Mus Art, Charlotte, NC; Seymour Lipton: Sculpture (ed, catalog), 82; Herb Jackson: Drawings (ed, catalog), 83; Ed Buonagurio: Recent Paintings (auth, catalog), 83. *Pos:* Dir, Hampton III Gallery, Ltd, Greenville, SC, 73-74; exec dir, Anderson Co Arts Coun, SC, 75-76; cur exhib, Mint Mus Art, 77-84; owner, Jerald Melberg Gallery Inc, 84-. *Bibliog:* Wolf Kahn (auth), New Landscapes, 91; Arless Day (auth), Constructing the best of all possible worlds, Recent Collages, 93; Charles Basham (auth), View from the studio, New Pastel Landscapes, 94. *Mem:* Int Coun Mus; Am Asn Mus; assoc Smithsonian Inst, Washington, DC. *Res:* Herb Jackson, Wolf Kahn, Romare Bearden. *Specialty:* Classic Contemp Art. *Collection:* Paintings, sculpture, graphics by United States artists, graphics by nationally known American artists, and early 20th century works. *Mailing Add:* c/o Jerald Melberg Gallery 625 S Sharon Amity Rd Charlotte NC 28211

MELBY, DAVID A
PAINTER, PHOTOGRAPHER
b Wichita, Kans, June 8, 1942. *Study:* Kansas City Art Inst; Wichita State Univ, BFA, 67; Univ Nebr, MFA, 70. *Work:* Am Express Corp, Salt Lake City; McDonald Corp, Chicago; Mulvane Art Mus, Topeka, Kans; Sheldon Mem Art Gallery & Sculpture Garden, Lincoln, Nebr; Mus Nebr Art, Kearney; and others. *Comn:* Plains People, 78. *Exhib:* A Sense of Place, Joslyn Art Mus, Sheldon Mem Art Gallery, Mid-Am Arts Alliance & others, 73; Nat Small Works Exhib, York Univ, NY, 79, 80, 83 & 84; Gwenda Jay Gallery, Chicago, Ill, 89; Am Myth, Sioux City Art Ctr, Iowa, 90; Spirit of the Landscape: The Landscape of the Spirit, Mitchell Mus, Mt Vernon, Ill, 91; Western Ill Univ, Macomb, 94; St Mary Col, Leavenworth, Kans, 97; Leavenworth Mus Art, 2000; and others. *Collection Arranged:* Artists Behind Bars, Jewish Community Ctr, Kansas City, Mo, 76; In Respect of Space, 79, Groups: A Public Face, 79 & Gold Rush: Work of Hal Parker, 80, Swan River Mus; Points of View: Six Artists, St Mary Col, 81; Mixed Metaphors: Visual Affinities, 2000; Points of View, Leavenworth Mus Art, Leavenworth, Kans, 2001. *Pos:* Artist in residence, US Fed Penitentiary, Leavenworth, Kans, Nat Endowment Arts, 75-76; dir exhibs, Swan River Mus, Paola, Kans, 79-80; dir, Bedyk Gallery, Kansas City, Mo, 85-86; dir Leavenworth Mus Art, Leavenworth, Kans, 2000-01. *Teaching:* Instr drawing & painting, Iowa State Univ, Ames, 70-75; instr painting, drawing & photog, St Mary Col, Kans, 80-82; instr, Nelson Atkins Mus, Kansas City, 83-84 & Kansas City Art Inst, 90-91. *Awards:* First Prize, Kansas Two, Kans Arts Comn, 82; Award Merit, Mid-Four Exhib, Nelson Atkins Mus, 82; Fel (painting) Mid Am Arts Alliance, Nat Endowment Arts, 86. *Bibliog:* Knut Forsundrsund (auth), article, Fotografi, 11/77; Victoria Melcher (auth), Kansas City: Dizzying directions, Art News, 10/80; David Knaus (auth), article, Art Gallery, 4-5/84; Marilyn Propp (auth), article, New Art Examiner, 10/86. *Mem:* Kansas City Artists Coalition; Kans Grass Roots Arts Asn; Leavenworth Co Arts Coun (exec coun); and others. *Media:* Oil; Black & White Photo. *Specialty:* Painting, Photography. *Collection:* Nineteenth and twentieth century European, American and native American art, American folk art, Photography. *Publ:* Contribr, A Sense of Place: The Artist and the American Land, Mid-Am Arts Alliance, 73; co-dir, videotape, Artist in Residence Prog, US Bur Prisons, 76; contribr, Poets on Photography, Dog Ear Press, 81; The Kansas Landscape, Kansas Dept Econ Develop, 85; New York Art Review, 88; Forum, 1-2/90. *Dealer:* Hallar Gallery 4540 Main St Kansas City MO 64111. *Mailing Add:* c/o David Melby Fine Arts PO Box 508 Leavenworth KS 66048

MELCHERT, JAMES FREDERICK
SCULPTOR, EDUCATOR
b New Bremen, Ohio, Dec 2, 1930. *Study:* Princeton Univ, AB; Univ Chicago, MFA; Univ Calif, Berkeley, MA; ceramics with Peter Voulkos. *Hon Degrees:* San Francisco Art Inst, Hon Dr; Coll Art, Md Inst, Hon Dr. *Work:* Mus Mod Art, San Francisco; Mus Mod Art, Kyoto, Japan; LA Co Mus Art; Oakland Mus Art, Calif; Stedelijk Mus, Amsterdam. *Comn:* Ceramic tile mural, New Biology Bldg, Mass Inst Technol, Cambridge, 92; bronze wall sculpture, Biomedical Res Bldg, Case Western Reserve Univ, 94; San Francisco Int Airport, 2014. *Exhib:* Abstract Expressionist Ceramics, Univ Calif, Irvine, 66; Contemp Am Sculpture, Whitney Mus Am Art, NY, 66, 68 & 70; Documenta 5, Kassel, Ger, 72; Solo exhibs, Galerie Fignal, Amsterdam, 78, San Francisco Art Inst, Calif, 81; Calif Painting & Sculpture, San Francisco Mus Mod Art & Nat Collection Fine Arts, Washington, 77; Words at Liberty, Mus Contemp Art, Chicago, 77; One Hundred Yrs of Am Ceramics, Syracuse Mus, NY & Renwick Gallery, Washington, 80; California Sculpture, San Francisco Mus Mod Art, 86; Holly Solomon Gallery, NY, 91; European Ceramic Work Ctr, Denbosch, The Neth, 98; World Contemp Ceramics, Inchon, Korea, 2001; Contemp Am Ceramics, Nat Mus Mod Art, Kyoto, 2002; Secret History of Clay, Tate, Liverpool, 2004. *Pos:* Dir visual arts prog, Nat Endowment Arts, 77-81; dir, Am Acad Rome, 84-88. *Teaching:* Chmn dept ceramics, San Francisco Art Inst, 61-64; prof art, Univ Calif, Berkeley, 65-76 & 81-92; vis sculptor, Univ Wis-Madison, spring 71. *Awards:* Artist Fel, Nat Endowment Arts, 73; Award of Distinction, Nat Coun Art Adminrs, 89; Hon Doctorate, San Francisco Art Inst, 84; Disting Alumnus Award, Coll Environ Design, Univ Calif, Berkeley, 99. *Bibliog:* Nancy Princethal (auth), Jim Melchert at Holly Solomon, Art in Am Mag, 12/91; Marsha Miro (auth), Jim Melchert, Mister-In-Between, Am Ceramics Mag, Vol 12, No 2; Gerry Williams (ed), James Melchert: Conversations, Studio Potter Mag, 6/97. *Media:* Clay. *Dealer:* Gallery Paule Anglim San Francisco; Paul Kotula Projects Detroit. *Mailing Add:* 6077 Ocean View Dr Oakland CA 94618

MELIKIAN, MARY
PAINTER
b Worcester, Mass. *Study:* RI Sch Design, Providence, BFA, 55; Columbia Univ Teachers Col. *Work:* Worcester Mus Art, Mass; Mint Mus, Charlotte, NC; Yerevan Mus, Armenia; Vassar Coll Art Mus; Art for US Embassies, State Dept; Centre Human Rights, UN, NY. *Exhib:* Nat Arts Club NY, 69 & 70; Galerie de Tours, San Francisco & Ankrum Gallery, Los Angeles, 70, Calif; Retrospective, Centenary Coll, Hackettstown, 75; Solo exhibs, Bodley Gallery, NY, 78 & 81, Quadrangle Gallery, Dallas, 80 & Dorsky Gallery, NY, 86; Group exhib, Nicholas Gallery, Palm Beach, Fla, 79; Elaine Benson Gallery, Bridgehampton, NY, 91. *Collection Arranged:* A

Retrospective, Along the Way, paintings by Melikian 50 year span, Nat Arts Club, 2008. *Pos:* Asst designer, Fuller Fabrics, NY, 56; asst dir, Grand Cent Moderns, New York, 60-61; dir pub rels, Grand Cent Art Galleries, New York, 61-67. *Teaching:* Instr art, Nutley High Sch, 57-60. *Awards:* First Prize, Kit Kat Club, 61, Armenian Student Asn, 61 & 62 & Women's Nat Repub Club, 70, 72, 73 & 75; Spirit of Art Award, 107th Artists Mem Exhib, Nat Arts Club, 2006; Gold metal for pastel, 11th Artist Mem Exhib, Nat Arts Club. *Bibliog:* Colette Roberts (auth), article, France-Am; N Stepanian (auth), Paintings of Mary Melikian, Voice of Am, 68; Anna Avedisian (auth), The Heart Remembers, Ararat Mag, 92. *Mem:* Parrish Art Mus, Southampton, NY; Guild Hall, East Hampton, NY; Nat Arts Club, NY. *Media:* Watercolor, Oil. *Interests:* human rights, theology & music. *Publ:* Auth, articles, Ararat Mag. *Mailing Add:* 429 E 52nd St Apt 27H New York NY 10022

MELLON, MARC RICHARD
SCULPTOR, MEDALIST

b Brooklyn, NY, Oct 17, 1951. *Study:* Brooklyn Col, BA (fine arts), 74; Art Students League, with Robert Beverly Hale, 75; Nat Acad Design, with Gaitano Cecere, 75. *Work:* Smithsonian Inst Nat Portrait Gallery, Washington DC; Nat Art Mus Sport, Indianapolis; Salmagundi Mus, NY; Elliot Mus, Jupiter, Fla; Brookgreen Gardens, Am Numismatic Soc; The British Mus; Butler Inst of Am Art; Nat Mus Am Illustration; Smithsonian Inst Nat Mus Am Hist. *Comn:* Alton Ochsner MD (statue), Ochsner Med Found, New Orleans; Kate Smith (statue), Spectrum Arena, Philadelphia; Generations, New Learning Ctr, Westport, Conn; The Planting (bas-relief), Glick Jewish Community Ctr, Indianapolis; Pres Bush (bust) Bush Sch Govt, College Station, Tex; Pred Lee Yeng-Hui (bust), Chi Mei Mus, Taiwan, 99; Pope John Paul II (bust), Vatican Collection, 2001; NCAA Centennial (sculpture), Indianapolis, 2006; Stringer-Rainey Fountain, Anderson Univ, 2008; Official 2009 Presidential Inaugural Medal, portrait of Barack Obama; George Eastman State Univ of Rochester, 2009. *Exhib:* Solo exhibs, Minds, Moods & Movement, Nat Arts Club, NY & The Figure in Motion, Elliot Mus, Stuart, Fla; Artists of Am, Colo Hist Mus, Denver, 2000; World Leaders, NSS, NY; Newington-Cropsey Mus Ann Exhib, Hastings-on-Hudson, NY; Paul Mellon Art Gallery, Choate Rosemary Hall, Wallingford, Conn, 2006. *Awards:* John Gregory Mem Prize, NSS, 84; Mod Art Prize, Salmagundi Club Ann Exhib, 98; Artist in Tribute, Hudson Valley Art Asn Ann Exhib, 98; Brooklyn Coll CUNY Alumni Asn Distinguished Achievement in the Arts, 2005; Salmagundi Club Purchase Prize, 2008. *Bibliog:* Adam Gopnick (arts ed), New Yorker Mag, 87; Steven Doherty (ed), Am Artist Mag, 91; Conneticut Man Sculpts Inaugural Medal, Newday Danbury News-Times, 2009. *Mem:* Nat Arts Club; Salmagundi Club; Artists Fel Inc (pres 90-98); NSS; Audubon Artists; Am Renaissance for the 21st Century (adv bd); Nat Mus Am Illustration (adv bd); Portrait Soc Am (comt mem); Century Asn. *Media:* Bronze. *Publ:* auth, Art Ideas-Values & Achievement in Sculpture, 97; contribr, Art Ideas, 98. *Dealer:* Cavalier Galleries 405 Greenwich Ave Greenwich CT 06896. *Mailing Add:* 61 Pheasant Ridge Rd Redding CT 06896

MELLOR, MARK ADAMS
PAINTER, GALLERY DIRECTOR

b Chicago, Ill, Oct, 28, 1951. *Study:* Univ Bridgeport, Conn, AA, 76; Illusr Workshop, Tarrytown, NY, cert, 83; Tony Van Hasselt Watercolor Workshop, 2001. *Work:* Quaker Oats co, Chicago, Ill; Westport Town Art Collection & Stamford Town Hall, Conn; Aetna, Hartford, Conn; Pepsico, NY; Middlebank, Middletown, Conn. *Comn:* Historic watercolor painting, Westport, Conn, 80. *Exhib:* Conn Watercolor Soc Exhib, Wadsworth Atheneum Hartford, 76-77; 112th Am Watercolor Soc, Traveling Exhib, Frye Mus, Seattle, Wash, Tweed Mus Art, Univ Minn, Duluth, & Springfield Art Ctr, Ohio, 79-80; New Haven Paint & Clay Ann, John Shade Ely House Gallery, Conn, 86; 5th New Eng Ann, Green Art Gallery, Guilford, Conn, 86; Solo exhibs, Max's Art Supplies, 90 & Fairfield Libr Gallery, 91; Conn Watercolor Soc Ann, Univ Hartford, 92; Conn Acad Fine Arts, Norwich Mus, Norwich. *Pos:* Illusr asst, Fred Otnes Illusr, W Redding, Conn, 76-96; Artist Gallery Owner, Oak St Gallery, Boothbay Harbor, Maine, 96-. *Teaching:* Watercolor demonstrations, Westport Nature Ctr Ann, Fairfield Adult Educ & Fairfield Pub Libr, 90-92. *Awards:* Art Friend Prize, Conn Watercolor Soc Mem Exhib, 80; Am Watercolor Soc Award, 112th Ann Traveling Exhib, 80. *Mem:* Conn Watercolor Soc; New Haven Paint & Clay Club, 85; Conn Acad Fine Arts, 90; Conn Classic Arts, Trumball (juror awards); Boothbay Region Art Found, 98-. *Media:* Watercolor. *Publ:* Auth, The watercolor page, Am Artist Mag, 1/84. *Dealer:* Oak Street Gallery, 35 Oak St. *Mailing Add:* 35 Oak St Boothbay Harbor ME 04538

MELNICK, ROBERT Z
DIRECTOR

b New York City. *Study:* Bard Coll, BA (Am History), 1970; New York State Coll Environ Sci & Forestry, MLA (landscape archi), 1975. *Pos:* Vis Sr Prog Officer for Grants Prog, Getty Ctr; interim dir, Jordan Schnitzer Mus Art, Univ Ore, currently. *Teaching:* Prof & dean, Sch Archi & Allied Arts, Univ Ore, formerly. *Mailing Add:* Jordan Schnitzer Museum of Art University of Oregon 1223 University of Oregon Eugene OR 97403

MELTON, TERRY R
PAINTER, ADMINISTRATOR

b Gooding, Idaho, Nov 20, 1934. *Study:* Idaho State Univ, BA, 58; Univ Ore, MFA, 64. *Work:* Portland Art Mus, Ore; Yellowstone Art Mus, Billings, Mont; Salt Lake Art Ctr, Salt Lake City, Utah; Mus Art, Univ Ore, Eugene; Boise Art Mus, Idaho; Colorado Springs Fine Arts Ctr, Colo. *Exhib:* 5 State Invitational, Univ Wyo Mus Art, Laramie, 66; solo exhib, Salt Lake Art Ctr, 70 & Univ Tex Pan Am, Edinburg, Tex, 95; Invitational, Idaho State Univ, Pocatello, 74; group show, Steinbaum-Krauss Gallery, NY, 93; Hallie Ford Mus, Salem, Ore, 2003. *Pos:* Regional rep, Nat Endowment for Arts, 75-84; exec dir, Western States Art Fedn, 84-90 & McAllen Int Mus, 93-96. *Awards:* Governor's Art Award, Mont Arts Coun, 91. *Media:* All Media. *Mailing Add:* 3860 Oak Hollow Ln SE Salem OR 97302

MELTZER, JULIA
VIDEO ARTIST

Study: Brown Univ, BA; Rensselaer Polytechnic Inst, MFA. *Exhib:* Exhibs and screenings include PS 122, New York, 2002; The Project, Los Angeles, 2002; Pacific Film Archive, Berkeley, Calif, 2003, 2005, 2007; New York Video Festival, 2003; San Francisco Int Film Festival, 2004; Toronto Int Film Festival, 2004, 2005; A Secret Service, Hayward Gallery touring exhib, London, 2006; San Francisco Cinemateque, Yerba Buena Arts Ctr, 2006; Calif Biennial, Orange County Mus Art, Newport Beach, Calif, 2006; Yerab Buena Ctr Arts, San Francisco, 2007; Gene Siskel Film Ctr, Chicago, 2007; Redcat, Los Angeles, 2007; Whitney Biennial, Whitney Mus Am Art, New York, 2008. *Pos:* founder & dir, Clockshop, Los Angeles, 2003-; media artist with David Thorne. *Awards:* Paul Robeson Fund for Independent Media Grant, 2001; Puffin Found Grant, 2004; Media Arts Fel, Rockefeller Found, 2004, Technical Assistance Grant, 2006; Fulbright Fel, 2005-06; Durfee Found Grant, 2007; Art Matters Grant, 2007; Louis Comfort Tiffany Biennial Award, 2007. *Mailing Add:* Julia Meltzer & David Thorne 2806 Clearwater St Los Angeles CA 90039

MENCONI, MICHAEL ANGELO
GLASSBLOWER, SCULPTOR

b La Grange Ill July 21, 1977. *Study:* The Studio of the Corning Mus Glass, 1996-2001; Contemp Studio of Glass Art, 2003-2008; Studied with Stuben Crystal and Lino Tagliapietra, Corning Mus Glass, 1997. *Work:* Corning Mus Glass; Nat Liberty Mus, Philadelphia; Mass Coll Art & Design; Mus Art, Wash State Univ; Ohio State Univ Glass Collection for Study. *Comn:* wall installation, comm by Manja Gupta, Ill, 2004; wall installation, lighting, comm by John Fleming, Ill, 2005; Whisper, comm by Wilson Jackson, Penn, 2009; Merleto/Lace, comm. by Deno Papageroge, Can, 2006; From the Sea, comm by Al Utack, Tex, 2007. *Exhib:* Group exhibs, Internat Juried Exhib, Glass Art Soc 34th Ann Conf, New Orleans, 2004; SOFA New York, Mattsons Fine Art, 2008, 2009; SOFA Chicago, Mattsons Fine Art, Chicago, 2008, 2009; Transcensions, Nat Liberty Mus, Penn, 2010. *Collection Arranged:* cur, Transcensions, Nat Liberty Mus, 2010. *Pos:* Art dir, Contemp Studio of Glass Art, 2003-2008. *Teaching:* gaffer, instr, Hands on Glass, Corning, NY, 1998-2001; gaffer, Patterson Glasswords, Mundelein Ill, 2001-2003; guest teacher, Mass Coll Art & Design, Boston, 2010. *Bibliog:* James Kennedy (auth), Best of America Glass Artists Vol2, Kennedy Pub, 2010; Las Vegas Mgmt, Internat hot glass invitational, Blue Hair Media, 2009; Sergei Litvinenko (auth), Technology of Fusing, Vitraznaja Masterskaja, 2005; Goerge Kennard (dir), Fantastico, Independent Prod, 2004. *Mem:* Glass Art Soc; Art Alliance for Contemp Glass; James Renwick Alliance; Am Craft Coun; Corning Mus Glass. *Publ:* auth, The Cold Collar Pick Up, Glass Line/ Jim Thingwold, 2004; auth, Making Switchback Reverse Balls, Glass Line/ Jim Thingwold, 2004; auth, Making Bow-Tie Reverse Balls, Glass Line/ Jim Thingwold, 2004; auth, Making A Clover Leaf by Reversal, Glass Line/ Jim THingwold, 2005; auth, Montage with Medallions, Glass Line/ Jim Thingwold, 2005. *Dealer:* Eclectric Image Gallery Suite 19 the Shops at Wailea Maui Hawaii 96753; Avalon Gallery 425 East Atlantic Ave Delray Beach FL 33483; The Glass Menagerie 37 East Market St Corning NY 14830

MENDELSON, HAIM
PAINTER, PRINTMAKER

b Semiatich, Builsk, Poland, Oct 15, 1923; US citizen. *Study:* Am Artists Sch, 36-40; Saul Baizerman Art Sch, 40-43; pvt study with Saul Baizerman, 43-52; Educ Alliance Art Sch, 46. *Work:* Contemp Drawing Collection, Minn Mus Art, St Paul; Print Collection of NY Pub Libr; Print Collection of St Vincent Col, Latrobe, Pa; Griffiths Art Ctr of St Lawrence Univ, Canton, NY; Edwin A Ulrich Mus, Wichita State Univ, Kans; Flint Inst Fine Arts, Flint, Mich. *Comn:* Dansk Designs, 80. *Exhib:* The Artist as Reporter, Mus Mod Art, NY, 40-41; Nat Acad of Design, NY, 65, 68, 75, 77 & 90; 10th Nat Exhib of Prints & Drawings, Okla Art Ctr, 68; Fedn of Mod Painters & Sculptors (traveling exhib), Gallery Asn NY, 76-78; Prints USA, Pratt Graphics Ctr Traveling Exhib, 82-85; Prominent Print Makers, Mo Western State Col, 88; East Coast Prints, Adrian Col, Mich, 88; Artists Proof, Arts Coun Gallery, Winston-Salem, NC, 88. *Pos:* Dir, Hudson Guild Art Gallery, New York, 71-72 & 73-94. *Teaching:* Instr painting & drawing, City Col New York, 61-64; teacher, City & Country Sch, New York City, 64-91. *Awards:* Dr Maury Leibovitz Spec Merit Award, 87; Special Distinction Award, Graphics, Int Art Biennale Malta, 95; Award, Graphics, Audubon Artists New York Cent, 96; Florsheim Found Grant, 99. *Bibliog:* Article, The New Yorker, 6/70. *Mem:* Fedn of Mod Painters & Sculptors (pres, 74-); The Print Consortium; Audubon Artists; Am Soc Contemp Artists. *Media:* Oil, Acrylic; Intaglio. *Publ:* Auth, Mezzotint, Prize Winning Graphics Book III, Allied Publ, Ft Lauderdale, Fla, 65. *Dealer:* Susan Teller Art Gallery New York City NY. *Mailing Add:* 234 W 21st St New York NY 10011

MENDENHALL, JACK
PAINTER, INSTRUCTOR

b Ventura, Calif, Apr 7, 1937. *Study:* Calif Coll Arts & Crafts, BFA, 68 & MFA (painting), 70. *Work:* Univ Calif Art Mus, Berkeley; Oakland Mus, Calif; RI Sch Design Mus Art, Providence; Butler Inst Am Art, Ohio; Va Mus Fine Arts, Richmond; Pohang Iron & Steel co, Seoul, South Korea; Evergreen Holding Group, Downsview Can; AT&T, Chicago, Ill; plus numerous other pvt & corp collections, US & Europe. *Comn:* Rainbows, Waldo Tunnels, Calif Div Hwy, San Francisco, 70. *Exhib:* Amerikanske Realister, Panders Kunstmuseum, Sweden, 73; Tokyo Biennale 74, Japan, 74; New Photo Realism, Wadsworth Atheneum, Hartford, Conn, 74; solo exhibs, O K Harris Gallery, New York, 74-2002, 2006, 2011; Realist Painting in California, John Berggruen Gallery, San Francisco, 75; Watercolors & Drawings, Am Realists, Meisel Gallery, New York, 75; The Photorealists, Holmes Gallery, Ctr Arts, Vero Beach, Fla, 2000; Contemp Am Landscapes: An Urban & Rural Perspective, MA Doran Gallery, Tulsa, Okla, 2001; As Real As It Gets: Super Realism & Photo-Realism, Tucson Mus Art, Ariz, 2002; Ann Realism Invitational, Jenkins Johnson Gallery, San Francisco, 2003-2005; Am Photorealism (traveling exhib, with catalog), Iwate Mus Art, Japan, 2004; Exactitude III, Plus One Gallery, London,

England, 2006, Exactitude V, 2009; Shock of the Real Photorealism Revisited, Boca Raton Mus Art, Fla, 2008-2009; Beyond Realism, Galerie De BelleFeulle, Montreal, 2012, Photorealism, 2013; Adornment, Belger Arts Ctr, Kans City, Mo, 2013; Photorealism Revisited, Okla Mus Art, 2013; Photorealism: 50 Yrs of Hyperrealistic Painting: Kunsthalle Tubingen, Ger, 2012; Traveling, Museo Thyssen Bornemisea, Madrid, Spain, Birmingham Mus and Art Gallery, Musee d'Ixelles, Belgium, 2012. *Teaching:* Prof painting & drawing, Calif Coll Arts & Crafts, 70-. *Awards:* Purchase Award, San Francisco Art Comn, 70. *Bibliog:* William C Seitz (auth), The real and the artificial: Painting of the new environment, Art in Am, 12/72; Linda Chase (auth), Les hyperrealistes Americans, Paris, Ed Filipacchi, 73 & Hyperrealism, Rizzoli, New York, 75; Ellen Lubell (auth), article, Arts Mag, 2/75; Gregory Battcock (auth), Superrealism, A Critical Anthology, EP Dutton, New York, 75; Edward Lucie-Smith (auth), Superrealism, Phaidon Publ, Oxford, Eng, 79; Christine Lindsay (auth), Superrealist Painting and Sculpture, WIlliam A Morrow & co, New York, 80; Louis K. Meisel (auth), Photorealism, 80, Photorealism Since 1980, 93 & Photorealism At The Millennium (with Linda Chase), 2002, Harry N Abrams, New York. *Media:* Oil, Watercolor. *Publ:* Seeing Photographically: Photorealist Paintings, The Syndey and Walda Besthoff Collection (exhib catalog), New Orleans, La, 2004; Louis K. Mesiel & Linda Chase (auths), American Photorealism (exhib catalog), Iwate Mus Art, Japan, 2004; Louis Meisel (auth), Photorealism in the Digital Age, Abrams Press, 2014. *Dealer:* O K Harris Gallery 383 W Broadway New York NY 10012. *Mailing Add:* 5824 Florence Terr Piedmont CA 94611

MENIL, GEORGES & LOIS DE
PATRON, COLLECTOR
Study: Georges de Menil: AB Harvard, PhD Mass Inst Technol, 62/68; Lois de Menil: AB Wellesley, 60; Univ Paris (law), 62; Harvard Univ, PhD, 72. *Pos:* Lois de Menil: vis comt, Harvard Univ Art Mus, 75-, Int Coun, Mus Mod Art, NY, 75-, Nat Gallery Art, Washington, vchmn trustees coun, 78-97, trustee, vchmn, NY, Dia Ctr Arts, 84-96 & trustee, World Monuments Fund, 91-; chmn, Ctr for Khmer Studies. *Collection:* 20th century painting & sculpture, African Art. *Mailing Add:* Box 417 Fishers Island NY 06390

MENSCHEL, ROBERT BENJAMIN
PATRON
b New York, NY, Jul 2, 1929. *Study:* Syracuse Univ, BS, 51; NYU, grad sch bus admin, 54. *Hon Degrees:* Syracuse Univ, LLD, 91. *Work:* Mus Modern Art; Metropolitan Mus; Nat Gallery Art. *Pos:* trustee, mem exec comt, Guild Hall, East Hampton, chmn bd, formerly; bd adv, Grad Sch Inst Int Bus Pace Univ, formerly; Mem, New York Stock Exchange, New York City, 50-51; specialist, HW Goldsmith & Co, 51-54; staff, Goldman, Sachs & Co, 54-66, general partner, institutional sales, 66-78, ltd partner, 79-2000, sr dir, 2000, 08-09; mem, Pres Clinton's comt on the arts & humanities; trustee, investment comt, Inst Advanced Study, Princeton, bd trustees, treas, Chess in the Sch, New York City; hon trustee bd, former bd pres, Dalton Sch, New York City; mem exec bd, NY chap Am Jewish Comt, NY; life trustee, former mem bd, exec comt, earned income comt, New York Pub Libr, New York City; former bd dir, Parks Coun; vpres bd trustees, mem fin & exec comt, Temple Emanu-El, NY; mem bd trustees, NY Presbyterian Hosp; former trustee, former mem exec & investment comts, Syracuse Univ; former trustee, mem exec, investment & develop comts, Montefiore Hosp; former managing dir, Horace W Goldsmith Found; former bd dir assoc, YM-YWHA; chm bd trustees, former chmn photog comt, former pres, mem finance, investment, ann fund, marketing & exec comts, Mus Modern Art

MENSES, JAN
PAINTER, PRINTMAKER
b Rotterdam, Neth, Apr 28, 1933; Can citizen. *Study:* Rotterdamse Kunst Akademie; hon degree, Univ Delle Arti, 81 & Acad Bedriacense, 84. *Work:* Mus Mod Art & Guggenheim Mus, New York; Art Inst Chicago; Brooklyn Mus; Ryksmuseum, Amsterdam, Holland; Victoria & Albert Mus, London; Vatican Mus, Rome. *Comn:* Mural, Montreal Holocaust Mem Ctr, Can. *Exhib:* Montreal Mus Fine Arts, 61, 65 & 76; 5th & 7th Biennial Can Painting, 63 & 68 & 1st & 2nd Biennial Can Watercolors, Drawings & Prints, 64 & 66, Nat Gallery Can, Ottawa; 20 New Acquisitions, Mus Mod Art, New York, 66; 9th & 11th Int Exhib Drawings & Engravings, Lugano, Switz, 66 & 72; Rotterdam Art Found, The Neth, 74; Univ BC, Vancouver, 81; Mead Art Mus, Amherst, Mass, 83; Marywood Coll, Scranton, Pa, 85; Esperanza Gallery, Montreal, 88-89; Galerie La Magie D'Art, Toronto, 1991 ; Blom & Dorn Gallery, Hartford, Conn, 92, 96-97 ; The DBD Gallery, Santa Monica, Calif, 99; and more. *Teaching:* Vis lectr, var Can univs. *Awards:* Gold Medal, Accademia Italia Delle Arte, Italy, 80; Gold Medal, Int Parliament USA, 82; Gran Premio Delle Nazioni, Italy, 83; Golden Flame of World Parliament Award, 86; Ish Shalom Award, Jerusalem, 93. *Bibliog:* Jan Menses--Peintre et prophete, Johathan, 82; La peinture de Jan Menses: Kaddish, Klippoth Tikkoune, Tribune Juive, Montreal, 83; Jan Menses: Exile and Redemption (film), Can Broadcasting Corp, 85. *Mem:* Royal Can Acad Arts; Soc Artistes en Arts Visuels de Que; Accademia Italia Delle Arte, Italy; Accademia D'Europa; Accademia Delle Nazione; Jewish Am Acad Arts & Sci. *Media:* Tempera, Acrylic. *Specialty:* Menses Mus, Safed, Israel, bookcollecting, Chinese & Japanese art

MENTHE, MELISSA
LIBRARIAN, PHOTOGRAPHER
b Hackensack, NJ, June 16, 1948. *Study:* Montclair State Col, NJ, BA; Rutgers Univ, MLS. *Pos:* Reference librn, Art Dept, Newark Pub Libr, NJ, 71-76 & Rutgers Univ, New Brunswick, 76-82. *Awards:* Nat Endowment Arts Grant, 81. *Mem:* Art Libr Soc NAm; Asn Coll & Res Libr, Am Libr Asn; Coll Art Asn; Spec Libr Asn; Indust Photographers NJ. *Res:* Methodology in history of photography. *Interests:* History of photography, incunabula & fine printing, historic preservation. *Mailing Add:* PO Box 1246 Paramus NJ 07653-1246

MEREDITH, MICHAEL
ARCHITECT
Study: Syracuse Univ, BA (archit), 1994; Harvard Univ, MA (archit, Fredrick Sheldon Fel), 2000. *Exhib:* The Elevator Gallery, New York, 1997; Archit League NY, The Urban Ctr, New York, 1998; Open Studio, Chinati Found, Marfa, Tex, 2000; Nat Bldg Mus, Washington, DC, 2002; Munic Arts Soc, New York, 2003; Mercer Union Contemp Art Mus, Toronto, 2004; Henry Urbach Archit, New York, 2005; Tate, London, 2006; ICFF, New York, 2006; Cooper Hewitt Design Triennale, New York, 2006; PS1/Mod Mus Art, New York, 2007; Design Triennale, Design Life Now, ICA Boston, 2007; Whitney Mus, New York, 2008; XXII World Congress Archit, Torino, Italy, 2008; Venice Biennale, Experimental Archit Padiglione Italia Pavilion, 2008; Scottsdale Mus Art, 2008-09; Mus Mod Art, New York, 2009; Art Inst Chicago, 2009. *Pos:* Architect, SLA Architects, 1994-96, Storefront for Art and Archit, 1995-98 & Richard Gluckman Architects, 1996-98,; writer, critic, Artforum Mag, 2002-04; principal, MOS, design off, 2003-. *Teaching:* Teaching asst, Harvard Univ, Grad Sch Design, 1998-99, vis design critic, 2003-04, asst prof archit, 2004-07 & assoc prof archit, 2007-; prof, Boston Archit Ctr, 1999; lectr, Muschenhiem Fel, Univ Mich, Sch Archit, 2000-01; asst prof, Univ Toronto, 2001-04; vis design critic, Ohio State Univ, Knowlton Sch Archit, 2009. *Awards:* ID Award Best in Catergory, Huyghe & LeCorbusier Pupper Theater, 2005; Archit award, Am Acad Arts & Letts, 2010. *Mem:* Am Inst Architects

MERFELD, GERALD LYDON
PAINTER, SCULPTOR
b Des Moines, Iowa, Feb 19, 1936. *Study:* Am Acad Art, with William Mosby, 54-57. *Work:* Marietta Col, Ohio; McDonough Collection Am Art; US Navy Arch; John Deere & Co; Mus Contemp Impressionism, Conn. *Exhib:* Hope Show, Butler Inst Am Art, 72, 74, 76, 78, 80 & 82; Allied Artists Am Ann, NY, 75-77, 80; Hudson Valley Art Asn, 75, 81, 82, 86 & 90; Knickerbocker Artists, 75, 85, 86, 87 & 89; Civic Fine Arts Asn, Sioux Falls, SDak, 77; Vanishing Landmark Exhib, Springfield Art Mus, Mo, 77; Artists of the Rockies & Golden West Retrospective Exhib, Sangre de Cristo Arts Ctr, Pueblo, Colo, 83; Audubon Artists, NY, 73-90; Am Artists Prof League, NY, 89; Butler Inst Am Art, 81-83; Akron Soc Artists Grand Exhib, 91 & 92; North West Rendezvous Exhib, 96, 98, 99, 2000-07; Colo Gov Invitational, 97, 98 & 99; Western Colo Ctr Arts, 2008; Bradford Brenton Biennial, 2008; NW Rendezvous, 96-2010. *Pos:* Studio asst, Dean Cornwell, New York, 57-60; combat artist, US Navy, Vietnam, 69 & Mediter, 71. *Awards:* Louis E Seley Gold Medal, Salmagundi Club, 71; Okla Mus Art Award, 75; First Prize, Hope Show Butler Inst Am Art, 80; First Prize, Drawing, Butler Inst Am Art, 83; Gold Medal of Hon, Am Artist Prof League, 89. *Bibliog:* Betty Harvey (auth), Gerald Merfeld, Artists of the Rockies & Golden West, fall 81; Ron Ranson (auth), Modern Oil Impressionists, 92; Betty Harvey-Manson (auth), Gerald Merfeld, Southwest Art, 7/96; Charles Movalli (auth), Gerald Merfeld's Teaching Tenets, Am Artist Mag, 12/78; Peggy & Harold Samuels (auth), Contemporary Western Artists; Fielding's Dictionary Am Painters, Sculptors & Engravers. *Mem:* Northwest Rendezvous Group (NWR); Sangres Art Guild (bd dirs). *Media:* Oil, Pastel. *Dealer:* Brookwood Gallery Westcliffe. *Mailing Add:* 2302 Muddy Rd Westcliffe CO 81252

MERGEL, JEN
CURATOR
Study: Harvard Univ, BA (visual & environmental studies), 1998; Bard Coll Ctr for Curatorial Studies, MA, 2005. *Collection Arranged:* Accumulations, 2007-2008, Tara Donovan, 2008-2009 & Acting Out: Social Experiments in Video, 2009, Inst Contemp Art, Boston. *Pos:* Cur fel, Phillips Acad Addison Gallery Am Art; cur asst, Inst Contemp Art, Boston, 2005-, asst cur, 2007-2008, assoc cur, 2008-2010; Beal cur contemp art, Mus Fine Arts, Boston, 2010-. *Mailing Add:* Museum Fine Arts Ave of the Arts 465 Huntington Ave Boston MA 02115-5597

MERHI, YUCEF
INSTALLATION SCULPTOR, VIDEO ARTIST
Work: Orange Co Mus Art, Calif; Museo ALejandro Otero, Venezuela; Museo de Arte Contemporaneo, Venezuela; Ateneo de Valencia, Venezuela; and var pvt collections. *Exhib:* III Salon Pirelli, Museo De Arte Contemporaneo, Caracas, Venezuela, 1997; VI Bienal Internacional de Poesía Experimental, Museo del Chopo, Mex, 1998; CIN-O-MATIC, New Mus Contemp Art, New York, 2001; El Museo's Bienal / The (S) Files, El Museo del Barrio, New York, 2002; Correspondences: Poetry and Contemporary Art, Hunterdon Mus Art, NJ, 2003; Hypermedia, Orange Co Mus Art, calif, 2004; solo exhibs, Orange Co Mus Art, Calif, 2005, Universidad de Los Andes, Venezuela, 2008, Boston Cyberarts Festival, 2009, Galeria La Otra Banda, Venezuela, 2010; AIM 25, Bronx Mus Arts, New York, 2005; The Labyrinth Wall: From Mythology to Reality, Exit Art, New York, 2008. *Pos:* Dir new media, White Box, New York, 2009-10. *Teaching:* Instr digital art, Embassy of Spain, Fundacion Chacao, Caracas, Venzeula, 2006, Universidad de Los Andes, Merida, Venezuela, 2009-10. *Awards:* New York Found Arts Fel, 2009. *Bibliog:* Ken Johnson (auth), Art in Review: Neo, NY Times, 7/28/2000; Ulf Ziegler Erdmann (auth), In the Theater of the Dolls, Art in Am, 4/2001; Holly Myers (auth), Still Searching for the Best Use of Technology, Los Angeles Times, 7/19/2002; Marjorie Delgado (auth), Un poeta errante en Estambul, El Nacional, Venezuela, 9/27/2007; Christiane Paul (auth), Digital Poetic Meltdown, New York Arts Mag, 2009

MERIDA, FREDERICK A
ART DEALER, PRINTMAKER
b Indianapolis, Ind, Mar 10, 1936. *Study:* Kansas City Art Inst, Mo, 54-57; Brooklyn Mus Sch, NY, 57-59; New Sch Social Res, New York, 57-59. *Work:* Columbia Mus Art, SC; Libr Cong, Washington, DC; JB Speed Mus, Louisville, Ky. *Exhib:* 11th & 13th Ann Boston Printmakers, Boston Mus Fine Arts, 58 & 60; Pasadena Art Mus, Calif, 58; 15th Ann, Pa Acad Fine Arts, Philadelphia, 61; Prints 1962, State Univ NY,

Potsdam, 62; 8 State Ann, JB Speed Mus, Louisville, Ky, 85 & 87. *Collection Arranged:* Melville Price Retrospective 1920-1970, 70, Rookwood: A Historical Survey, 71, Biggest Show of Little Painting, 73 & Kentuckian Painters Invitational, 75, Frame House Gallery, Louisville, Ky; Black Artists Ann, 1980-1985, Nat Black Artists, Gallery One, 1st Nat Bank, Louisville, Ky. *Pos:* Dir, Frame House Gallery, Louisville, Ky, 69-75, dir bus art develop & asst to pres, 75-77; owner & dir, Merida Gallery, Louisville, Ky, 77-; cur corp art collection, Hilliard Lyons Ctr, Louisville, Ky, 88-92 & CSI, Paducah, Ky, 96-97, 2003-05. *Awards:* Pennell Purchase Prize, Libr Cong, Washington, 57; Purchase Awards, Nelson Gallery Art, Kansas City, Mo, 60 & JB Speed Mus, Louisville, Ky, 85, 87. *Bibliog:* Ira Simmons (auth), Art and money, Scene Mag, Louisville Times, 2/8/86. *Mem:* Am Soc Appraisers (chap pres, 85-86); Appraisers Asn Am. *Specialty:* Contemporary art; 19th century American and European paintings. *Publ:* Ed, Art Gallery Guide of Louisville, Merida Gallery, Inc, 68-69. *Mailing Add:* Merida Galleries PO Box 53 Farmington KY 42040-0053

MERIDA, MARGARET BRADEN
CRAFTSMAN, INSTRUCTOR

b Louisville, Ky, Jul 26, 1937; Am citizen. *Study:* Univ Louisville, Ky, BS (high honors), 59, MAT, 71; Nat Endowment Fel, George Wash Univ, 66. *Work:* Aetna Oil Collection, Louisville, Ky; CSI, Ky. *Exhib:* Quiltmaking Trends, Evansville Mus Art, Ky, 77; solo exhib, Appalachian Ctr, Smithville, Tenn, 2000; Womans Hands, Arts Coun, Berea, Ky, 2005. *Pos:* owner, Farmington Fiberarts, 98-. *Teaching:* Instr, Jefferson Co Publ Schs, Louisville, Ky, 64-90; instr, Gov's Scholars, Ky, 85-90; instr, Visual Arts Magnet Sch, Jefferson Co, Ky, 87-90; instr, Murray State Univ, Ky, 2000-. *Awards:* Purchase Award, Art Ctr Annual, Aetna Oil, 60; Best in Show, Louisville Craftsman Annual, 77; Best in Show, Ky Craft Marketing Prof, 2005. *Mem:* Ky Craft Marketing Prog, 98-; Ohio Designer's Craftsmen 2004-. *Media:* Fibers, Wearable art & quilted wall pieces. *Dealer:* Appalachian Fireside Gallery Main St PO Box 87 Berea KY 40403; Ky Artisans Ctr Berea KY 40403; Pear Tree Gallery 36840 Detroit Rd Avon OH; Rivers Bend Gallery First St Parksville MO 64152

MERKEL, JAYNE (SILVERSTEIN)
HISTORIAN, CRITIC

b Cincinnati, Ohio, Sept 28, 1942. *Study:* Simmons Col, with Wylie Sypher, BS, 64; Smith Col, with Henry-Russell Hitchcock, MA (art hist), 68; Univ Mich, with Leonard K Eaton, 66-68. *Collection Arranged:* Early Works: Alexander Calder (auth, catalog), Taft Mus, 72; Drawn by Cincinnati (auth, catalog), Archit Drawing Collection of the Cincinnati Hist Soc, Contemp Arts Ctr, 80; 1930's Remembered, Part I, The High Style, Taft Mus, 82; In Its Place, the Architecture of Carl Strauss & Ray Roush, Contemp Arts Ctr, 85; Peter Eisenman: An Architecture of Absence, Contemp Arts Ctr, 86-87. *Pos:* Cur, Contemp Arts Ctr, Cincinnati, 68-69; dir educ, Taft Mus, Cincinnati, 69-74; archit critic, Cincinnati Enquirer, 77-88; reviewer, Artforum, 80-90; art & archit critic, WGUC-FM (pub radio), 83-88; contrib ed, Inland Archit, 84-93; ed, Oculus Mag, 94-02; contrib ed & mem ed bd, Archit Design Mag, London, 2000-; mem ed advisory bd, Architects Newspaper, 2005; contr ed, Architectural Record, 2006. *Teaching:* Instr art hist, Art Acad Cincinnati, 73-78; vis instr art hist, Miami Univ, 78-79 & 81-82; asst prof Eng (writing), Univ Cincinnati, 88-91; dir, grad prog archit & design criticism, Parsons Sch Design, New Sch, 92-96; vis prof, Rhode Island Sch of Design, 99. *Awards:* Special citation for writing, ed & criticism from NY Chap, Am Inst, 98; Fellow Inst for Urban Design, New York, 99-; Harry B Rutkins Award, NY chap Am Inst Architects, 2001; Inst Hon for Collaborative Achievement, Am Inst Architects (nat), 2003; Emmy Award Amer Academy Television Arts & Sciences for Scriptwriting for The Gateway Arch A Reflection of America, St. Louis 2007. *Mem:* Coll Art Asn; Soc Archit Historians; Archit League; Century Asn. *Media:* Print. *Res:* Contemporary American architecture, art and criticism; Contemp Am archit, art & criticism. *Publ:* articles & reviews, Am Inst Archit J, 78, Prog Archit, 80-82, 88-89, Artforum, 81-90, Inland Archit, 83-92, New Art Examiner, 83 & 88, Connoisseur, 84, Dialogue, 84-86, Art in Am, 86-94, 2006, Competitions, 92 & Design Book Review, 93-94, Oiulis, 94-2002, Architechural Design, 99-, Archit Record, 2006-, Archit Newspaper, 2004-, NY Times ONline, 2010; Intro to Kliczkowski's Hariri & Hariri, Casas Int 48, Asppan, Buenos Aires, 97; Pasanella + Klein Stolzman + Berg (an architectural monograph), Rockport Publ, 99; Chap, In: Modernism and Modernization in Architecture, Acad Ed, London, 99; Richard Dattner, Images Publishing, Malgrave, Australia, 2000; Eero Saarinen, (monograph), Phaidon Press, London, 2005; Chap in Archit in Cincinnati, with Sue Ann Painter, Beth Sullebargr & Alice Weston, Ohio Univ Press, Athens, Ohio, 2006; Intro Balmori, Seoul, Korea, C3 Pub, 2007; Univ Cin: Architectural Transformation, Cin RAF Press, 2007; and others. *Mailing Add:* 60 Gramercy Park N 7B New York NY 10010

MERKL, ELISSA FRANCES
PRINTMAKER, PAINTER

b Colorado Springs, Colo, July 2, 1949. *Study:* Marymount Coll, with Robert J Lee, John Hull & John Lotchtefeld, BA (fine arts), 71; NJ Ctr Visual Arts, with David Finkbeiner, 74. *Work:* Nabisco Hq, East Hanover, NJ; St Hubert's Giralda (Geraldine R Dodge Collection), Madison, NJ; Nat Bank Detroit, Mich; America the Beautiful, Township Art Collection, Millburn, NJ; Fed Reserve Bank, Chicago. *Exhib:* Solo Exhibs: Johnson & Johnson World Hq, New Brunswick, 96; Childrens Specialized Hosp, Mountainside, NJ, 96; The Show Bistro, NJ, 2000; Monmouth Beach Cult Ctr, NJ, 2002; Les Malamut Gallery, NJ, 2002; Gallery 50, Bridgeon, NJ, 2006; Potpourri, Westfield Art Gallery, NJ, 2006; Expressions Through Contours, M Christina Geis Gallery, Georgian Ct Univ, Lakewood, NJ, 2007; The Layered Look, Interchurch Center, NY, 2007, Take a Walk on the (not so) Wild Side II, Edn Ctr, Frelinghuysen Arboretum, Morristown, NJ, 2013, Wings, Tales, & Scales, Greater Columbus Convention Ctr, Oh, 2013; Int Mini Print, Taller Galeria Fort & Trvl Cadaques, Spain, 86, 87 & 97; CL Wolfe Nat, Nat Arts Club, New York, 88 & 91; Animals in Art, La State Univ Sch Vet Med, Baton Rouge, 92; We Love NY, Lever House, New York, 96; Small Pictures, Great Harmony Exhib, Nagano, Japan, 98; Small Works, Hopper House Art Ctr, Nyack, NY, 2001; Northeast Prints, 2001; William Paterson Univ, NJ, 2001; Open Juried Show, Pen & Brush, New York, 2001; Int Miniature Print, Graphics Ctr, Conn, 2001-2002; Int Juried Miniature Show, Paper Mill Playhouse, NJ, 2001 & 2003; Agora Gallery, Soho, 2002; Monmouth Festival of the Arts, NJ, 2003 & 2005; Nat Juried Miniature Print Exhib, Arts Coun Creede, Colo, 2003; Color, Gallery Petite, Clinton, NJ, 2004; Women Art juried exhib, Summit Coll Club, NJ, 2004; Current Printmaking, Printmaking Currents, Old Church Cult Ctr, NJ, 2004; Wild for Wildlife, Columban Park Zoo, Lafayette, Ind, 2005; Prints 2005, Springfield Art Mus, Mo, 2005; Take a Walk on the (not so) Wild Side, Wisner House, Summit, NJ, 2005; Monmouth Co Arts Coun Juried Show, Monmouth Mus, NJ, 2006; Nat Open Juried Show & Audubon Artists Nat Juried Show, Salmagundi Club, New York, 2006; Juried Members Show (traveling exhib), Printmaking Coun NJ, Somerville, NJ, 2006; Small Works Nat Juried Show, Sullivan Muncie Cult Ctr, Ind, 2006; Int Juried Miniature Art Show, Hillard Soc, Wells, Somerset, Eng, 2006; Int Masnj Juried Show, World Fine Art Gallery, New York, 2006; Invitational Group Show: Menagerie, Rahway Arts Guild, NJ, 2008; 8th National Small Print Show, Creede, Co, 2008; Annual State Juried Show, Bernardsville Libr, NJ, 2008; Monmouth Mus, 2008, 2010; Millburn Short Hills Arts Ctr Mem Shows, Madison Pub Libr, 2008, Paper Mill Playhouse, 2009, 2010, 2011; Art in the Park, Montclair Art Mus, NJ, 2009; NJ Visual Arts Ctr Mem Shw, Summit, NJ, 2009; Visions Art Exhib, Overlook Hospital, Summit, NJ, 2011; 3rd Ann Nat Pet Fine Art Show, Irving, Tex, 2011; Small Matters of Great Importance: Interior/Exterior, Edward Hopper House Art Center, Nyack, NY, 2011; Grand Nat Exhib, Am Artists Prof League Show, Salmagundi Club, NY, 2011; Art Takes Times Square, NY, 2012; All Things Colorado, Poudre Studio Galleries, Colo, 2013. *Pos:* Publicity chair, NJ Ctr Visual Arts, 74 & 75; newsletter ed, Art Gallery South Orange, 78-; co-chair/adv art fair, Millburn-Short Hills CofC, 79-; art exhib chair, Millburn-Short Hills Arts Ctr, 88-90, pres, 98-2001; ed & pub, Cult Events of NJ, 2001-; visual arts critiquer, Teen Arts Festivals, 95-; juror, judge area shows, 94-. *Teaching:* Demonstr serigraphy, Area Art Asn NJ, 72-, lectr marketing art, 94-; guest artist, Kids in Business, Newark Pub Schs, 2001-02. *Awards:* First Prize Graphics, Mamaroneck Art Guild Nat, 91; First Prize Prints, Nev Art Asn Nat Miniature, 93; Award for Artistic Achievement, Art Fair 94 & 96, Millburn-Short Hills CofC, 94; Awards of Merit, Old Church Cult Ctr, NJ, 2001; H M Caldwell Coll Juried Show, NJ, 2001; Skylands Juried Show, NJ, 2002; Jane Law Studio & Gallery Miniature Show, NJ, 2002; Awards of Merit, Millburn-Short Hills Arts Ctr Mems Show, Bedminster Libr, 2004-2005; First Place Exterior/Architecture, Miniature Art Soc Fla Int Juried Show, 2006; Award of Merit, Carlisle Arts Learning Ctr Small Works Show, Carlisle, Pa, 2006; First Place, Renaissance Art Gallery Small Works Juried Show, WVa, 2006; Honorable Mention, Graphics, Int Juried Miniature Show, Painters, Sculptors & Engravers Soc, Washington, DC, 2006; 3rd Place, Lucky 13 Nat Juried Show, Mesquite Art Gallery, Nev, 2006; Honorable Mention, Visual Arts Center NJ, Members' Show and Save, 2008; Award of Merit, M-Sh Arts Center Members' Show, Overlook Hospital, 2007; Merit Award, W Essex Art Asn, Caldwell Coll, NJ, 2009; Award of Excellence, W Essex Art Asn, Caldwell Coll, NJ, 2010; First Place, Nat Pet Fine Art Show, Irving, Tex, 2011. *Bibliog:* Mary La Motta (dir), Art al Fresco (video), TV 36, 91; Eileen Watkins (auth), New venue for representational art, Star Ledger, 94; Jean Galler (auth), Artists life work meshes together in exhibit: silk screen print process called lost art, Star Ledger, 1/96; Mary Windhorst (auth), Overlook Shows Work of Riv & Merkl, Independent Press, 2003; Marylou Marano (auth), Works of acclaimed artist Ellisa F Merkl at Westfield Art Gallery, Westfield Leader, 11/16/2006; Kim Predham (auth), Artist's display shows she's queen of the screens, Ocean Co Observer, 4/20/2007. *Mem:* NJ Ctr Visual Arts; Westfield Art Asoc; Printmaking Coun of NJ; Milburn-Short Hills Art Ctr. *Media:* Acrylic; Serigraphy. *Publ:* Illus, Add a Little Love Cookbook, Pacelle Press, 74; auth, Bicentennial Coloring Book, private publ, 75; Color Images from Nikon, NJ Music & Arts, 75; contribr, Art Lovers Cookbook, NJ Ctr Visual Arts, 76. *Mailing Add:* 325 Morristown Rd Gillette NJ 07933

MEROLA, MARIO
SCULPTOR, PAINTER

b Montreal, Que, Mar 31, 1931. *Study:* Ecole des Beaux Arts de Montreal, dipl, 52; Ecole Superieure des Arts Decoratifs de Paris, 53. *Hon Degrees:* Diplome, Ecole Des Beaux-Arts, Montreal. *Work:* Mus d'Art Contemp & Mus Fine Arts, Montreal; Nat Gallery, Ottawa; Mus Munic, Brest, France; Mus Quebec; Carleton Art Gallery; Mus Fine Arts, Budapest. *Comn:* Mural, Mazenod Seminary, Ottawa, 65; fountain, Expo 67, Montreal, 67; two murals, Quebec Govt, Osaka, Japan, 70; stained glass, Montreal subway, 79; Monumental Door, Nagyiatad, Hungary, 89; plus over 100 comn. *Exhib:* Solo exhibs, Luminous Reliefs, Mus Fine Arts, Montreal, 65, Mus du Quebec, 71, Constructions, 1950-1976, Mus d'Art Contemp, Montreal, 76, Mus Munic, Toulouse, France, 77, Mus Munic, Brest, France, 78, Muvezsetek Hasa, Pecs, Hungary, 91 & Ady Endre Gymnazium, Nagyatad, Hungary, 92, Mus des Beaux-Arts de Sherbrooke, 2009-2010; Affect-Effect, La Jolla Mus, Calif, 68; New Tendency, Mus d'Art Contemp, Montreal, 78; Made in Canada, Nat Libr Can, Ottawa, 84; Bibliotheque Nationale du Quebec, 2002; Musee des Beaux-Arts de Sherbrooke, 2010; 54th Int Venice Biennale. *Collection Arranged:* Galerie D'Arts Contemporain. *Teaching:* Prof fine arts, Ecole des Beaux Arts, Montreal, 60-69; prof drawing, Univ Que, Montreal, 69-91. *Awards:* First Prize, murals, Can Pavilion, Brussels, 57 & Inst d'Hotellerie, Can Govt, 73; First Prize, sculpture, Int Sculpture Meeting, St-Jean-Port-Jolie, 84; Hon Citizen, City Iri, South Korea. *Bibliog:* Jacques de Roussan (auth), Mario Merola, Ed Lidec, 70; L Letocha (auth), Mario Merola, Formart, 72; Robert Melancon (auth), L'espace de la ville, Liberté, 82; A Metchnikov (auth), Mario Merola, Fini-Infini, 92. *Mem:* Royal Can Acad Art; Conseil de la Sculpture du Quebec; hon mem Conseil de la Peinture du Quebec; Int Sculpture Ctr. *Media:* Polymer on Wood, acrylic on canvas. *Publ:* Graphies, 13 Dessin, 97; Ombres/Shadows, 76-98; Dessings, Encres et Poemes, 98; Sculptures/Structures, 2005; Rehefs Lumineux, 2005; Peintures, Studio 216, 2010; Dessiros Oublies, 2010; Figures Imprevisibles, 2010; Ode A Tiepolo, 2010. *Dealer:* Gallerie d'Arts Contemp. *Mailing Add:* 216 Somerville Montreal PQ H3L 1A3 Canada

MEROMI, OHAD
VIDEO ARTIST, SCULPTOR
b Kibbutz Mizra, Israel, 1967. *Study:* Kalisher Sch Art, Tel Aviv, Israel, 1985; Bezalel Acad Art & Design, Jerusalem, BFA, 1992; Columbia Univ, Sch Arts, Vis Dept, NY, MFA, 2003. *Exhib:* Solo exhibs include Avivit, Israel Mus, Jerusalem, 1995, The Didactic Exhibition, Dvir Gallery, Tel Aviv, Israel, 1996, Classrooms, Spring Gallery, Philadelphia, 1998, Villa 2, Ctr Regional d'art Contemp, Region Languedoc-Roussillon, France, 1998, Villa 3, Nathan Gottesdiener Found Israeli Art Prize, Tel Aviv Mus Art, 1999, Cyclops, Tal Esther Gallery, Tel Aviv, 2004, Cyclops 2, Harris Lieberman, New York, 2005, PS1, New York, 2006; group exhibs include Israeli Proposal, Artifact Gallery, Tel Aviv 1992; Photog, Dvir Gallery, Tel Aviv, 1997; Wish List, Israel Mus, Jerusalem, 2000; Helena, Helena Rubinstein Pavilion, Tel-Aviv Mus Art, 2001; Lod Road, Israel Pollack Gallery, Kalisher, Tel Aviv, 2003; Who is the Protagonist, Guild & Greyshkul Gallery, NY, 2004; Power, Reading Power Sta, Tel Aviv, 2005; Uncertain States Am, Astrup Fearnley Mus, Oslo, Norway, 2005; Mercury In Retrograde, De Appel gallery, Amsterdam, Netherlands, 2006. *Awards:* Mary Fisher Award, Bezalel Acad Art & Design, Jerusalem, 1992; Israeli Art Prize, Nathan Gottesdiener Found, Tel Aviv Mus, 1998; Hadasa & Refael Klachkin Award, Am Israel Cult Found, 2002; Israeli Minister Cult Award, 2002; Found Contemp Arts Grant, 2008. *Dealer:* Harris Lieberman Gallery 89 Vandam Street New York NY 10013

MERRILL, HUGH JORDAN
PRINTMAKER, PAINTER
b Olney, Md, Apr 28, 1949. *Study:* Md Inst Coll Art, BFA, 73; Yale Sch Art & Archit, MFA, 75. *Work:* Mus Mod Art, NY; Sackler Mus, Harvard Univ, Cambridge, Mass; Yale Univ Mus Art, New Haven, Conn; Davenport Mus Art, Iowa; Cranbook Mus Art, Mich. *Comn:* Nova Huta Rising, Works Festival, Edmonton, Alta, Can, 95; Sanford-Kimpton Health Facility, Columbia, Mo. *Exhib:* Lucky Dragon, Nelson Atkins Mus, Kansas City, Mo, 85; Palace Fine Arts, Krakow, Poland, 93; Life Cycles, Santa Barbara Contemp Art Forum, Calif, 93; Rosa Luxemberg Suite, Navy Pier Exhib, Chicago, Ill, 93; Transparent Motives, New Orleans Mus, La, 95; Portrait of Self (auth, catalog), Community Proj, Kemper Mus, Kansas City, Mo, 98; Collected Prints, Nelson-Atkins Mus, Kansas City, Mo, 98; Daum Mus, Sedalia, MO,; Touch, Morgan Gallery, KC, MO, 2005; Tides, Import Conference Pozan Poland. *Pos:* Pres, Southern Graphics Coun, 92-94; vpres, Mus Without Walls, Jewish Mus Fedn, 98-; Exec Dir Chameleon Arts & Youth Develop. *Teaching:* Prof paint & print, Kansas City Art Inst, 76-. *Bibliog:* Auschwitz Sky, New Letts Mag, 98; Lynn Allen & Phylis McGibbons (auths), Best in Printmaking, 98; Printmaking by Richard Noyce. *Mem:* Coll Art Asn; Southern Graphics Counicl Berzinger Winery Collection, Donald Kuspit. *Media:* Mixed Media. *Publ:* Auth, Post Print Stacking Claim, Contemp Impressions, 94; coauth, Content as creativity, Printmaking Today, 95. *Mailing Add:* c/o Jan Weiner Gallery 3014 Eveningside Dr Topeka KS 66614

MERZBACHER, GABRIELLE & WERNER
COLLECTOR
b Germany, 1928; arrived in Switzerland, 1949; arrived in US, 1949; arrived in Switzerland, 1964. *Pos:* Ptnr, Mayer & Hoffman & Max Pick, Inc, New York, 1953-64; co-founder, Werner & Gabrielle Merzbacher Collection, Zurich, Switz, 1972-; owner, Mayer & Cie AG, Switz, 1989-. *Awards:* Named one of Top 200 Collectors, ARTnews mag, 2003-12. *Collection:* 20th-century art, especially Fauvism and German Expressionism. *Mailing Add:* Bergrasse 22 Zurich 8700 Küsnacht ZH Switzerland

MESA-BAINS, AMALIA
SCULPTOR
b Santa Clara, Calif, July 10, 1943. *Study:* San Jose State Univ, BA (painting), 66; San Francisco State Univ, MA, 71; Wright Inst, MA, 80, PhD, 83. *Exhib:* Solo exhibs, INTAR Gallery, NY, 87, Artspace, Phoenix, 90, Whitney at Philip Morris, 93, William Coll Mus Art, Williamstown, Mass, 94 & Steinbaum Krauss Gallery, New York, 95; Emblems of the Decade: Borders, La Reconquista: A Post Columbian New World Exhib, 3rd Int Biennial, Istanbul, Turkey, 92; Revelations: Hispanic Art of Evanescence, Cornell Univ, Ithaca, NY, 93; Queen of the Waters, Mother of the Land of the Dead: Homanje to Tonatzin/Guadalupe, Ante Am, Queens Mus Art, NY, 93; Venus Envy Chapter One, Whitney Mus Am Art at Philip Morris, 93; Grandmother Is That You, States of Loss: Migration, Displacement, Colonialism & Power, Jersey City Mus, NJ, 94; and others. *Pos:* Comnr of art, City of San Francisco, formerly; proj mgr, consent decree staff development, Div Integration, San Francisco Unified Sch Dist, 83-90; SPARC mural training proj, Los Angeles, 85-86; consult arts, INTAR-Hispanic Art Ctr, NY, 85-87, Ariz Comn Arts, 90, Tex Coun Arts, 90, Sci Educ Youth Found, Audubon Soc, 89-90; adv bd, Mex Mus, San Francisco, Calif, publ adv bd, Studio Mus Harlem, NY; producer/host, Community Affairs, Latin Tempo, KPIX-TV, Channel 5, San Francisco, 86-88; lectr/speaker, numerous mus, insts & exhibs, 88-93; sr res assoc, Far West Labs, San Francisco, 90-; dir, Bd Ctr Arts, Yerba Buena Gardens, San Francisco, Calif, 93-96, Galeria de la Raza, San Francisco, Mission Community Legal Defense, San Francisco & Visual & Pub Art Inst, Calif State Univ, 96-. *Teaching:* Bilingual, ESC & multicult educ, Elem Div, San Francisco Unified Sch Dist, 71-83; Univ Calif Regents Professorship, Irvine, 93. *Awards:* Golden Palm Award, INTAR Hispanic Arts Ctr, 91; Distinguished Serv Field Award, Asn Hispanic Arts, 91; Distinguished MacArthur Fel, John D & Catherine T MacArthur Found, 92. *Publ:* Auth, Grandma is that you, San Francisco Camerawork Quart, Photog & Belief, 91; Acts of Memory: The Alternative Chronicle of Mildred Howard, San Francisco Art Inst, 91; Chicano Chronicle & Cosmology: The Works of Carmen Lomas Garza, Laguna Gloria Mus, Austin, Tex, 91; The Real Multiculturism: A Struggle for Authority & Power in: Different Voices: A Social, Culture & Historical Framework For Change in the American Art Museum, New York, 92; Redeeming Our Dead: A Homanaje a Tenochtitlan, William Col, Williamstown, Mass, 92. *Mailing Add:* 326-A Capp St San Francisco CA 94110-1808

MESCHES, ARNOLD
PAINTER, EDUCATOR
b Bronx, NY, Aug 11, 1923. *Study:* Art Ctr Sch; Chouinard Art Inst; Jepson Art Inst; self-taught in fine arts. *Work:* High Mus Art, Atlanta, Ga; San Francisco Mus Art; Nat Gallery Art, Washington, DC; Los Angeles Co Mus Art; Albright-Knox Gallery, Buffalo, NY; Metrop Mus Art, New York; Whitney Mus Am Art, New York; and others. *Comn:* Murals, Temple Isaiah, Los Angeles, 73 & Bank of Am, Beverly Hills, Calif, 75; portraits, Frederick Weisman, Los Angeles, Gordon Hampton, Los Angeles, Billie Milam, Los Angeles & Richard Weisman, Seattle, Wash. *Exhib:* Solo exhibs, Civilian Warfare Gallery, New York, 84; Jack Shainman Gallery, Washington, DC, 87; Inst Contemp Art, Philadelphia, PA, 94; PS1 MOMA, Long Island City, NY, 2002-03, Jacksonville Mus Mod Art, Fla, 2004, Skirball Mus, Los Angeles, Calif, 2004, Univ Gall, Univ Buffalo, New Orleans Contemp Art Ctr, 2004, Harn Mus, Gainesville, Fla, 2005, Ogden Mus, New Orleans, 2006 & Dorsch Gallery, Miami, Fla, 2008, 2010; Frost Mus, Fla, 2010; Weatherspoon Mus, Greensboro, NC, 2010; Retrospective exhib, Arnold Mesches: A Lifes Work at The Freedom Tower, Miami-Dade Coll, Miami, Fla, 2013. *Pos:* Art dir, Frontier Mag, 54-60; courtroom artist, Walter Cronkite/CBS, 69-71; master artist, Atlantic Ctr Arts, New Smyrna Beach, Fla, 2005-2006. *Teaching:* Instr painting & drawing, Univ Southern Calif, summer 50; instr & dir, New Sch Art, Los Angeles, 55-58; instr, Otis Art Inst, 63-67, Otis/Parsons Art Inst, 75-84, Los Angeles & Univ Calif Exten, Los Angeles, 72-77; guest prof, grad sch, Rutgers Univ, New Brunswick, NJ, 85- & vis lectr, 87-88; instr advan painting & drawing, Parsons Sch Design, New York, 86; instr grad painting, NY Univ, 88-; instr, NY Univ, 88-2002; prof grad painting, Univ Fla, Gainesville, 2003-2011. *Awards:* Nat Endowment Arts Grant, 82; NY Found Arts, 91; Artist-in-residence, Altos de Chavon, Dominican Republic, 94; Pollock-Krasner Found Grant, 2002, 2009; Art Critics of America, 2004; Hon Doc, Univ Fla, 2009. *Bibliog:* Eleanor Heartney (auth), Arnold Mesches, ARTnews, 92; Edward Sozanski (auth), Art in America, 97 & Inst Contemp Art, Philadelphia Inquirer, 94; Willaim Zimmer (auth), Arnold Mesches: From Columbus to 2000, NY Times, 98; Eleanor Heartney (auth), Art in America, NY Times; Robert Storr (auth), UCF Gallery, Univ Central Fla (catalog), Orlando, Fla, 2007; Paula Harper (auth), Art in Am, 2007; and others. *Media:* Acrylic, Collage. *Publ:* Municipal Art Gallery Catalog, 83, Selections from the 80's, Castellani Art Gallery 88, Burchfield Art Ctr Catalog, 88 & Painting History, Inst Contemp Art, 94; Anomie: 1492-2000 (exhib catalog), Neuberger Mus Art, State Univ NY, Purchase, 98 & Selby Gallery, Ringling Sch Art & Design, Sarasota, Fla, 98; Echoes: A Century Survey (catalog), Ore Jewish Mus, 2000; Arnold Mesches A Painting History 1940-2003 (catalog), Jacksonville Mus Mod Art, 2003; auth, The FBI Files, Hanging Loose Press, New York, 2004; Robert Storr & Phong Bui, the Brooklyn Rail, 2010; Arnold Mesches: A Life's Work (280 pg book), Cement Hse. *Mailing Add:* 1602 SW 35th Pl Gainesville FL 32608

MESIBOV, HUGH
PAINTER, PRINTMAKER
b Philadelphia, Pa, Dec 29, 1916. *Study:* Fleischer Mem Art Sch, Philadelphia, 34-35; Pa Acad Fine Arts, Philadelphia, 35-37; Albert C Barnes Found, Merion, Pa, 36-40. *Work:* Metrop Mus Art & NY Univ Collection Contemp Am Art, New York; Philadelphia Mus Art & Nat Archives, Philadelphia; British Mus, London, Eng; Albert C Barnes Found, Merion, Pa; Whitney Mus Am Art; Philadelphia Mus Art, Pa; Pa Acad Fine Arts,; Carnegie Libr, Pittsburgh; Worcester Mus Art; Libr Cong; and many others; Smithsonian Mus Art, DC. *Comn:* Mural design, Benjamin Franklin High Sch, 37-40 & Bennett Hall, Univ Pa, Work Progress Admin Art Proj, 37-40; mural, Steel Indust, US Treas, US Post off, Hubbard, Ohio, 41; paintings & color lithograph, NY Hilton Art Collection, 62; acrylic on canvas mural, Job, Temple Beth El, Spring Valley, NY, 72. *Exhib:* Nabisco Brands Gallery, East Hanover, NJ, 91 & 98; Ellen Sragow Gallery, New York, 91-2006; The Wartime Shipyard, Susan Teller Gallery, New York, 91-2006, 2010; Krasdale Gallery, White Plains, NY, 93, 96, 2000 & 2002; retrospective, Rockland Arts Ctr, 97; Industrial Realism, Susan Teller Gallery, 97; Baltimore Mus Art, Md, 2000; Fleisher Mus, Phila, 2001; Woodmere Mus Art, Phila, 2002; Recent Monotypes & Watercolors, Susan Teller Gallery, 2002; Reba and David Williams Collection, New York, 2003; Cummer Mus & Gardens, Jacksonville, Fla, 2003; Blue Hill Cult Ctr, Pearl River, NY, 2003; Am Mural Studies 1935-1962, Teller Gallery, New York, 2004; Nat Acad Mus, New York, 2005; Phoenix Art Mus, Ariz, 2005; A Ninetieth Birthday Exhib, Susan Teller Galelry, 2006; Under the Influence, Am Artists Look at Picasso, Susan Teller Gallery, 2006; The Am Scene: Prints from Hopper to Pollock, The British Mus, 2008; Djanogly Art Gallery, Nottingham, England, 2009; Brighton Mus Art, England, 2009; Whitworth Art Gallery, Manchester, England, 2009; Surrealist Painting & Work on Paper, 42/45; Seeing Trees, Blue Hill Art & Cult Ctr, NY; Uptown Gallery, NJ. *Teaching:* Art therapist, Wiltwyck Sch Boys, NY, 57-66; prof art, Rockland Community Coll, Suffern, NY, 66-88, prof emer, 93. *Awards:* Suny Fel Grant Research Award, 67; Thornton Oakley Mem Prize, Philadelphia Watercolor Club, 68 & 76; Rockland Co Exec Arts Award, NY, 88; New York State Gov's Art Award, 90; Individual Artist Award, NY State Coun Arts, 95; Achieved nat recognition for experimental work in printmaking. *Bibliog:* Robert Delany & Richard Connely (dirs), Experience of the Artist - Hugh Mesibov (video tape), Rockland Community Coll, NY; Five Artists from the 1930's and 1940's (catalog & monogr), Midtown Galleries, New York, 88; Linda Shopes (dir), audio tape & interview, Pa Hist & Mus Comn, Harrisburg, 90; Archives of American Art (video tape), Smithsonian Inst, Washington, DC, 90. *Mem:* Rockland Ctr Arts; Rockland Coun Arts; Artists Equity, NY; Whitney Mus Am Art; Fairlawn Art Asn, NJ; Hopper House Art Ctr, Nyack, NY. *Media:* Acrylic, Watercolor. *Res:* Pennsylvania Art Project, painting, printmaking and mural work; co-inventor of Carborundum Print and inventor of Color Carborundum Print. *Interests:* Gardening. *Dealer:* Susan Teller Gallery 568 Broadway New York NY; Sragow Gallery 73 Spring St New York NY. *Mailing Add:* 4 Margetts Rd Chestnut Ridge NY 10952

MESLAY, OLIVIER
CURATOR, MUSEUM DIRECTOR
Dec 4, 1956. *Study:* Paris-Sorbonne Univ, BA, 1981, MA, 1982; Ecole du Louvre, MA, 1983; Inst Nat du Patrimoine, grad, 1993. *Pos:* curator British, American and Spanish paintings, Mus du Louvre, Paris, 1993-2006, chief curator Louvre Lens, 2006-2009; sr curator European and American art, Barbara Thomas Lemmon curator European art, Dallas Mus Art, 2009-, interim dir, 2011, assoc dir curatorial affairs, 2012-. *Teaching:* prof, Ecole du Louvre, 1997-2006. *Awards:* fellow, Clark Art Inst, Williamstown, Mass, 2000-2001; Chevalier des Arts et Lettres, 2009. *Publ:* D'Outre Manche (auth), L'art britannique dans les Collections Publiques Francaises, 1999; Turner (auth), L'incendie de la peinture, 2006. *Mailing Add:* Dallas Museum of Art 1717 North Harwood Dallas TX 75201

MESSER, DAVID JAMES
MUSEUM DIRECTOR
b San Diego, Calif, Aug 25, 1942. *Study:* Birmingham-Southern Col, BA; Purdue Univ, MS. *Pos:* Dir dept mus studies, Vincennes Univ, Ind, 76-79; cur exhibs, Beaumont Art Mus, Tex, 79-85; dir, Mus East Tex, Lufkin, 85-87 & Bergen Mus, Paramus, NJ, 87-. *Mailing Add:* Bergen Mus Art & Sci 327 E Ridgewood Ave Paramus NJ 07652

MESSERSMITH, HARRY LEE
SCULPTOR, MUSEUM DIRECTOR
b Buckhannon, WVa, Aug 7, 1958. *Study:* Stetson Univ, De Land, BFA, 81; Univ Fla, Gainesville, MFA, 83, Crealde Sch Art, Winter Park, Fla, 84-85, Penland Sch, NC, 94, 2004, 2011; Atlantic Ctr for the Arts, New Smyrna Beach, Fla, 99. *Work:* Daytona Beach Justice Ctr, Fla; Volusia Co Public Sch, Fla; New Smyrna Beach Libr, Stetson Univ; DeLand City Hall, Fla; Mus Fla Art. *Comn:* Life size busts (five, bronze), Stetson Univ, De Land, Fla, 87-2008; life size statue (bronze), Iverson Technol, Ellburn, Ill, 89; Volusia Co Coun, De Land, 90; bronze sculpture, Cincinnati Playhouse, Ohio, 2009. *Exhib:* The Bronze Exhibit, Milan, Italy, 2000; Epcot & Disney World, Ann Int Garden Festival Sculpture Installation, 2000-07. *Collection Arranged:* De Land Nat Sculpture Exhib, Triennial juried competition, 91. *Pos:* Artist in educ, Volusia Co Schs, Fla, 86-89; exec dir, De Land Mus Art Fla Inc, 89-95, Lighthouse Gallery & Sch Art Inc, Fla, 95-96. *Teaching:* Artist in educ, traveling throughout Volusia Co, Fla, 86-89; instr art, Stetson Univ, De Land, Fla, 83-2005; instr ceramics, Daytona Beach Community Col, 88-89; Univ Ctrl Fla, 01-02. *Awards:* Best of Show Awards, Stetson Univ Homecoming, 78 & De Land Mus Art, 88. *Bibliog:* Margaret Linger Pearson (auth), Heroic Measures, Sch Arts Mag, Davis Publ Inc, 4/91. *Mem:* Int Sculpture Ctr; Coll Art Asn; Fla Craftsman Inc; Fla Pyrotechnic Arts Guild; Martha Vineyard Art Asn. *Media:* Cast Bronze, Metals, Cast glass. *Dealer:* Robert Lombard Contemporary Art. *Mailing Add:* 726 N Boston Ave Deland FL 32724

MESSINA, CHARLES
ARTIST
b Wilmington, DE, Jan 6, 1950. *Comn:* John A. Travalini, various, 78-2006; Albert Vitri, Landscape, watercolor, Greenville, DE, 98; Anthony Fusco, Portrait, oil, New Castl, DE, 99; John Adamson, Indian Setting, oil, Elsmere, DE, 2002; Mary Bensen, Row Homes, oil, Wilmington, DE, 2003; Diane Dufaj, Angels, oil, Wilmington, DE, 2004. *Exhib:* Federal Fel Exhibit, Federal Building, Wilmington, DE, 89; Local Artists Exhibit, Convention Ctr, Wilmigton, DE, 2003; Vendemmia da Vinci, sponsored by Societa da Vinci, Wilmington, DE, 2004. *Pos:* Owner, C Messina Art Studio, Wilmington, DE, 98-. *Bibliog:* Lex Bayard (auth), Mike Tyson (Boxing), Del Marva Beach Bull (from front page); Mus & Gall, The News Journal, 12/4/98; Berland Bruce, $1 Launched Artist's Brush with Fame, The News Journal, 5/12/99. *Publ:* Walkers Mill, Brandywine Deleware Today, 98; Little Italy, www.discoverlittleitaly.com, 2003; RE/Max Sunvest Michael A DiFonzo, 2004. *Mailing Add:* 1902 W 6th St Wilmington DE 19805

METCALF, BRUCE B
JEWELER, WRITER
b Amherst, Mass, Sept 30, 1949. *Study:* Syracuse Univ, BFA, 72; Tyler Sch Art, Temple Univ, Philadelphia, MFA, 77. *Work:* The Montreal Mus Fine Arts; Philadelphia Mus Art; Renwick Gallery, Nat Mus Am Art, Washington; Cooper-Hewitt Nat Mus Design, NY; Mint Mus Craft & Design, Charlotte, NC; Mus Arts & Design, NY; Nat Mus Scotland, Edinburgh; Mus Fine Art, Houston; Mus Fine Arts, Boston; Metrop Mus Art; Victoria & Albert Mus, London; Design Mus, Helsinki, Finland; Newark Mus, NJ. *Exhib:* Forms in Metal - 275 Yrs of Am Metalsmithing, Mus Contemp Crafts, NY, 75; Good as Gold, Renwick Gallery, Smithsonian Inst, 81; Ohio Perspectives: New Work in Clay, Glass, Textiles, and Metal, Akron Art Mus, 88; Ornamenta 1: Int Exhib of Contemp Jewelry Art, Schmuck Mus, Pforzheim, Ger, 89; Jewelry Arsenals, Nat Mus, Zurich, Switz, 91; Modern Jewelry 1964-1991: The Helen Williams Drutt Collection, Mus Appl Arts, Helsinki, Finland, 92; Facet '93: International Biennial of Jewelry, Kunsthal Rotterdam, The Neth, 93; Jewelry in Europe & Am: New Times, New Thinking, Craft Coun Gallery, London; Jewelry Moves, Nat Mus Scotland, Edinburgh, 98; Defining Craft I, Am Craft Mus, NY, 2000; An Inaugural Gift: The Founders' Circle Collection, Mint Mus of Craft & Design, Charlotte, NC, 2000; Corporal Identity - Body Language, Frankfurt Mus für Angewandte Kunst, Ger, 2003; Jewelry by Artists, The Daphne Farago Collection, Mus Fine Arts, Boston, 2007-; The Miniature Worlds of Bruce Metcalf, Palo Alto Art Ctr, Calif, & nat tour, 2008-2010; Royal Coll Art vis artists collection, Victoria & Albert Mus, London, 2008; Odyssia: Contemp Craft & Drawing, Chiwoo Craft Mus, Seoul, Korea; Venus Adorned, Nat Craft Gallery of Ireland, Kilkenny, Ireland, 2011. *Collection Arranged:* New Ohio Jewelry, Massillon Mus, Ohio, 90; Revising Classicism: The Language of Antiquity in Contemporary Furniture and Ceramics, Hicks Art Ctr, Newtown, Pa, 93; organizing cur, The Art of Gold, Exhibits USA, 2003. *Pos:* Soc NAm Goldsmiths, nominating comt chair, 87, bd dir & secy, 98-2002. *Teaching:* Temporary instr jewelry/metals, Colo State Univ, Ft Collins, 77-78; instr, Mass Col Art, Boston, 79-80; assoc prof, Kent State Univ, Ohio, 81-91; sr lectr, Univ Arts, Philadelphia, 94-95, 98-99, 2007, 2010, 2011, & 2012. *Awards:* Ohio Arts Coun Crafts Fel, 83, 84 & 88; Fulbright Comn Teaching & Res Fel, Korea, 90; Pew Fel Arts, 96; PEW Fel Spl Opportunity Stipend, 2002. *Bibliog:* Cheryl White (auth), Focus: Bruce Metcalf, Am Craft, 10-11/90; C E Licka (auth), Focus: Bruce Metcalf between darkness and light, Metalsmith, winter 90; Ulysses Dietz (auth), Ohio Metals: A Legacy, Interalia/Design Books, 93; Cindi Strauss (auth), Ornament as Art: Avant-Garde Jewelry (from the Helen Williams Drutt collection), Stuttgart:Arnoldsche, 2007; Andy Lim (ed), Compendium Finale of Contemp Jewellery, Cologne, Darling Publ, 2008. *Mem:* Am Crafts Coun; Soc NAm Goldsmiths. *Media:* Miscellaneous Media. *Res:* History of 20th century studio craft. *Specialty:* Contemporary American Crafts. *Publ:* Replacing the myth of modernism, Am Craft, 2-3/93; On the nature of jewelry, Metalsmith, winter 93; The Problem of the Fountain, Metalsmith, summer 2000; The Hand: At the Heart of Craft, Am Craft, 8-9/2000; Embodied Sympathy, Metalsmith, Summer 2002; coauth (with Janet Koplos), Makers: A History of American Studio Craft, Univ NC Press, 2010; Art Glass Conundrum, Glass Art Soc, 2009; Corning, New York, 2010; Critical Discourse 3: State of the Craft, Furniture Soc, 2009. *Dealer:* Snyderman Gallery 303 Cherry ST Philadelphia PA. *Mailing Add:* 116 Leedom Ave Bala Cynwyd PA 19004

METCALFE, ERIC WILLIAM
VIDEO ARTIST
b Vancouver, BC, Aug 22, 1940. *Study:* Univ Victoria, BFA, 70. *Work:* Art Bank Can, Ottawa; Nat Gallery Can; Akad Kunst, West Berlin; Univ Calgary, Alta; Art Gallery Ont. *Comn:* Multi-media performance, 78 & video performance, 83, Music Gallery, Toronto. *Exhib:* Chair Show, Art Gallery Ont, 74; From This Point of View, Vancouver Art Gallery, 77; Off the Wall, A Space, Toronto, 77; Chair Show, And/Or, Seattle, 79; Manner SM, Vancouver Art Gallery, 82; Okanada, Akad Kunste, West Berlin, 83. *Pos:* Dir & cur performance art, Western Front, 73-. *Awards:* Bursary, 73 & Video Production Award, 77, 80 & 83, Can Coun; JVC Corp Third Video Festival Award, 80. *Bibliog:* Balkind Shadbolt (auth), Visions, Douglas & McIntyre, 83; Peggy Gane (auth), Parachute, Colour Video, 83. *Media:* Video, Performance. *Mailing Add:* Western Front Soc 303 E Eighth Ave Vancouver BC V5T 1S1 Canada

METZ, FRANK ROBERT
PAINTER, DESIGNER
b Philadelphia, Pa, July 3, 1925. *Study:* Philadelphia Mus Sch, with Ezio Martinelli; Art Students League, with Will Barnet. *Work:* Olsen Found, Guilford, Conn; Ball State Teachers Col, Muncie, Ind; Philadelphia Mus Art; Mass Inst Technol; Charles Pfizer Co; AT&T; Deutsche Bank. *Comn:* Coll Tec Industries NC. *Exhib:* Solo exhibs, Alonzo Gallery, 74, 77 & 79, Haber Theodore Gallery, 84 & 85, Gross McCleaf Gallery, Philadelphia, Pa, 87 & Minor Mem Libr, Roxbury, Conn, 95, 2005; Monhegan Artists, Allentown Mus, Pa, 74; Retrospective, Gross McCleaf Gallery, 85; From the Landscape, Washington Art Asn, Conn, 9g; Randall Tuttle Fine Arts, Woodbury, Conn, 99; Cent High Sch Alumni Exhib, Woodmere Art Mus, Philadelphia, 2002; Group exhibs, Potter & Slack Gallery, Washington, Conn, 2003-2004; Frost Gully Gallery, 40th Anniversary Show, 2006. *Pos:* Art dir, Simon & Schuster, 50-95. *Bibliog:* Jules Perel (auth), Landscape drawings of Frank Metz, Am Artist, 5/62; Doreen Managan (auth), Landscape paintings of Frank Metz, Am Artists, 3/78 & Twenty Oil Painters and How They Work, Watson-Guptill, 78; Paul Bacon (auth), articles, Arts Mag, 3/84 & 4/85; Carl Little & Arnold Skolnick (coauths) Art of the Maine Islands, Down East Books; Landscapes & Inspiration, New Milford Times, 6/24/2005. *Media:* All Media. *Specialty:* Landscapes of Maine. *Interests:* Travel & Sketches. *Dealer:* Judith Selkowitz Art Advisory Services Inc 530 Park Ave New York NY 10021; Frost Gully Gallery Freeport ME; RVS Gallery, Southampton, NY. *Mailing Add:* 800 W End Ave Apt 6C New York NY 10025

METZGER, EVELYN BORCHARD
PAINTER, SCULPTOR
b New York, NY, June 8, 1911. *Study:* Vassar Col, AB, 32, with C K Chatterton; Art Students League, with George Bridgman & Rafael Soyer; also George Grosz, sculpture with Sally Farnham, Guzman de Rojas in Bolivia & Demetrio Urruchua in Arg. *Work:* Fine Arts Gallery San Diego, Balboa Park, Calif; Ariz State Mus, Tucson; Lyman Allyn Mus, New London, Conn; Univ Mo-Columbia; Butler Inst Am Art, Youngstown, Ohio; and others. *Exhib:* 19 solo exhibs, Galeria Muller, Buenos Aires, 50, Gallerie Bellechasse, Paris, 63, Washington Co Mus Fine Arts, Hagerstown, Md, 99- & Ann Norton Sculpture Garden, West Palm Beach, 2001; Norfolk Mus Art, Va, 65; Mex-Am Cult Inst, Mexico City, 67; Van Diemen-Lilienfeld Gallery, NY, 66; Bartholet Gallery, NY, 73; Arsenal Art Gallery, NY, 83; Nat Mus Women Arts, Washington, DC, 97, 02; Joan Whelan, NY, 97; Cornell Univ, 98; Curzon Gallery, Boca Raton, Fla, 2003. *Pos:* Hon dir, Vassar Art Gallery. *Bibliog:* Aymel Seghers (auth), New York News (and cover), Arts Rev, 4/63; M L D'Otrange Mastai (auth), An American flowering, 5/63 & Evelyn Metzger--recent works, 12/66, The Connoisseur; Nancy Heller & Brett Topping (auths), The Aged of Grandeur and a Woman Who Lived It, Nat Mus Women Arts, 95. *Mem:* Artists Equity Asn; Am Fedn Art; Arch Am Art. *Media:* Oil. *Mailing Add:* 815 Park Ave New York NY 10021

METZGER, ROBERT PAUL
CURATOR, DIRECTOR
b Detroit, Mich. *Study:* Wayne State Univ, BA, MA; Columbia Univ, with T Reff; Univ Calif, Los Angeles, with Fred Wight, PhD; Am Film Inst, with Jean Renoir. *Pos:* Cur, Lydia Winston Malbin Collection of Art, New York, 74-76; dir art, Stamford Mus, Conn, 76-; dir, Reading Mus, currently. *Teaching:* Asst prof art hist survey, Univ Detroit, Mich, 65-66; assoc prof Am art hist, Univ Bridgeport, Conn, 77-. *Awards:* Univ Calif Arts Coun Traveling Grant, 69; Mich State Univ Art Hist Res Grant, 74. *Mem:* Coll Art Asn Am. *Res:* Biomorphism in the 20th century, American painting and sculpture 18th through 20th century, Reuben Nakian. *Publ:* Ed, Directory of American Periodicals, Oxbridge Press, 76; auth, Karl Struss, American Cinematographer, 76, Nakian's Place in History, 77 & The Case for Pop Art as Neo-Dada, 78, Stamford Mus. *Mailing Add:* c/o Reading Mus 500 Museum Rd Reading PA 19611

MEW, TOMMY
PAINTER, CONCEPTUAL ARTIST
b Miami, Fla, Aug 15, 1942. *Study:* Fla State Univ, BS, MA; NY Univ, PhD. *Work:* Am Tel & Tel, NY; Jacksonville Art Mus, Fla; Moderna Mus, Stockholm; McDonald's Corp Collection; Macon Mus Arts & Sci; and others. *Exhib:* Solo exhibs, Montgomery Mus Fine Arts, Ala, 70 & Miss Mus Art, 79; Paintings, Mus Art, Macon, Ga, 72; Rockefeller Arts Ctr, NY; High Mus Art, Atlanta, 76; Nat Gallery Can, Ottawa, 77; Gallery 34, Kassel, Ger; and others. *Pos:* Dir, Fluxus West/South East. *Teaching:* Grad asst art, Fla State Univ, 64-65; asst prof art, Troy State Univ, Ala, 66-68 & Jacksonville Univ, Fla, 68-70; prof painting & chmn art dept, Berry Col, 70-; vis artist & lectr drawings, Nat Endowment Arts, 72 & Univ Tulsa, 81. *Awards:* Grant, Cowperthwaite Corp, 72 & Ga Coun Arts, 80. *Bibliog:* Annette Kuhn (auth), Scar art, Village Voice, 75; Peter Frank (auth), Auto-art-and how, Art News, 76; Alan Storey (auth), Tommy Mew, Art Voices S, 3/78. *Mem:* Coll Art Asn; Southeastern Coll Art Asn; Popular Cult Asn South; Nat Art Educ Asn; Am Fedn of the Arts. *Media:* Acrylic; Mixed. *Interests:* Running; Racing. *Publ:* Ed & contribr, Third Floor Love Poems, 66 & auth & ed, Le Voyage, 68, Troy State Press; ed & contribr, Dramatika, New York Press, 70; ed & contribr, Scartissue, Troy State Press, 76; auth, Ray Johnson, Coll Art Asn J, 77; contribr, Intermedia Mag, Can, 77. *Dealer:* Marney Rhodes 111 Saddle Mt Rd Rome GA 30161

MEYER, EDWARD HENRY
PATRON
b New York City, Jan 8, 1927. *Study:* Cornell U, BA, 1949. *Pos:* With Bloomingdale's div Federated Dept Stores, 1949-51; with, Biow Co, 1951-56; with, Gray Global Group, NYC,1956-, exec vpres 1963-68, pres 1968-, Chief Exec Officer, chmn,1970-; bd dir, Ethan Allan Interiors Inc, Harman Internat Industries Inc, Jim Pattison Group Inc,. *Mem:* Trustee, Solomon R Guggenheim Mus & NY Univ Med Ctr; bd mem, Am Mus Natural History & Film Soc fo Lincoln Ctr; Econ Club, Univ Club, Harmonie Club, Century Country Club, Atlantic Golf Club

MEYER, JAMES SAMPSON
WRITER, HISTORIAN
b Springfield, Mass. *Study:* Yale Univ, BA, 84; Inst Fine Arts, NY Univ, MA, 86; Johns Hopkins Univ, PhD, 95. *Collection Arranged:* What Happened to the Institutional Critique? (auth, catalog), Am Fine Arts, NY, 93. *Teaching:* Instr 20th century art, Sch Visual Arts, NY, 90-94; asst prof contemp art & criticism, Emory Univ, Atlanta, Ga, 94-. *Bibliog:* Christopher Reed (auth), Postmodernism & the Art of Identity, Concepts Mod Art, Thames & Hudson, 94; Barry Schwabsky (auth), Mel Bochner: thought made visible 1966-73, On Paper, 9-10/96. *Mem:* Coll Art Asn. *Res:* American art 1955-1975; specifically mimimalism; conceptualism; institutional critique; contemporary art. *Publ:* Auth, AIDS & Postmodernism, Arts Mag, 92; The functional site, Platzwechsel, Kunsthalle, Zurich, 95; Ellsworth Kelly: Sculpture for a large wall, 1957, Matthew Marks Gallery, 98. *Mailing Add:* Art History Dept Carlos Hall Emory Univ Atlanta GA 30322

MEYER, JERRY DON
HISTORIAN, EDUCATOR
b Carbondale, Ill, Nov 19, 1939. *Study:* Southern Ill Univ, Carbondale, BS, 62, MA (art hist), 64; New York Univ, Inst Fine Arts, PhD (art hist), 73. *Teaching:* Prof art hist, Northern Ill Univ, 68-2001 asst chair, 85-2001, prof emer, 2001-. *Mem:* Coll Art Asn; Midwest Art Hist Soc; Am Acad Religion. *Res:* Late 18th & 19th century English & American Art, 20th century art. *Publ:* Auth, Benjamin West's Chapel of Revealed Religion, Art Bull, 75; Benjamin West's St Stephen altar-piece, Burlington Mag, 76; Benjamin West's window designs for St George's Chapel, Am Art J, 79; The Woman Clothed with the Sun: Two Illustrations to St John's Revelation by William Blake, Studies in Iconography, Vol 12, 88; Profane and Sacred: Religious Imagery and Prophetic Expression in Postmodern Art, J Am Acad Relig, Vol 65/1, 97. *Mailing Add:* Sch Art Northern Ill Univ Dekalb IL 60115

MEYER, JOSHUA
PAINTER
b Lubbock, Tex. *Study:* Bezalel Acad Art & Design, Jerusalem, BA, 1995; Yale Univ, New Haven, MA, 1996. *Exhib:* Solo exhibs, Jewish Community Ctr, New Haven, Conn, 2001, Joseph Slifka Ctr, New Haven, 2003, Goldman Gallery, Hebrew Coll, 2004, Bronfman Ctr, New York, 2006, Philadelphia Mus Jewish Art, Pa, 2007; ARTcetera, Boston Ctr for the Arts, 1998; Int Exhib, San Diego Art Inst, 2003; Faith Alive, Univ Mass Healey Libr, Boston, 2006; Smaller is Better, Schiltkamp Gallery, Clark Univ, 2007; 35th Ann Exhib, Masur Mus Art, Monroe, La, 2008. *Pos:* Steering comt & bd dirs, Berkshire Inst for Music & Arts, 2003-, vis artist, 2005 & 2008-09; vis artist, Hebrew Coll, 2004 & 2006. *Awards:* Trumbull Fine Arts Award, 1996; Pollock-Krasner Found Grant, 2008; Mass Cult Coun Painting Fel, 2010. *Bibliog:* Denise Taylor (auth), Artist finds his inspiration in the time before creation, Boston Globe, 8/26/2004; Judy Birke (auth), Heavily textured 'Becoming' draws from primitive energy, New Haven Register, 5/21/2006; Dorothy Robinson (auth), The Knives Have It, Philadelphia Metro, 5/2/2007. *Dealer:* Rice Polak Gallery 430 Commercial St Provincetown MA 02657

MEYER, MELISSA
PAINTER
b New York, NY, 1947. *Study:* New York Univ, BS, 68, MA, 75. *Work:* Mus Mod Art, Metrop Mus Art & Solomon R Guggenheim Mus, NY; Aldrich Mus Contemp Art, Ridgefield, Conn; Ark Art Ctr, Little Rock; Rose Art Mus, Waltham, Mass; Tampa Mus Art, Fla; Brooklyn Mus, NY. *Exhib:* Solo exhibs, J L Becker/East End Gallery, Provincetown, Mass, 88, Holly Solomon Gallery (with catalog), 91, 93 & 96, Miller Bloch Fine Art, Boston, Mass, 91, 94 & 96, Montgomery Glasoe Fine Arts, Minneapolis, Minn, 93 & 96 & Galerie Renee Ziegler, Zurich, 93, Deven Golden Fine Art, NY, 97, Ibel Simeonov Gallery, Ohio, 98, Rebecca Ibel Gallery, Ohio, 2000, 2004 & 2006, Elizabeth Harris Gallery, NY, 2001, 2002, 2003, & 2005, Emily Davis Gallery, Myers Sch of Art, 2003, NY Studio Sch, 2006-2007, List Gallery, Swarthmore Coll, 2007, Lennon, Weinberg, Inc, NY, 2009; Painting, Nina Freudenheim Gallery, Buffalo, NY, 94; Embraceable You, Selby Gallery, Ringling Sch Art & Design, Sarasota, Fla, 94; About Color, Charles Cowles Gallery, NY, 94; Contemp Prints, Allez les Filles Gallery, Columbus, Ohio, 94; The Permanent Collection: Recent Acquisitions, San Jose Mus of Art, Calif, 95; Abstract Women, Ibel Simeonov, Ohio, 96; Large Scale Abstract Paintings, Neuberger Mus of Art, Purchase, NY, 97; Garner Tullis: The Art of Collaboration, AAP Gallery, Pittsburgh, PA, 98; Artists as Teachers, Lobby Gallery, Merrill Lynch Financial Center, NY, 99; Paper Abstractions, Gallery@49, NY, 2000; 2001 Invitational Exhibition, American Acad of Arts and Letters, NY; Made in Tribeca, Galerie Albrecht, Munich, Ger, 2002; AbstractNewYork, Klein Art Gallery, Philadelphia, 2003; 179th Annual Invitational, Nat Acad Design, NY, 2004; Pure Paint, Henry Gregg Gallery, NY, 2005; Water Color One, Rose Burlington Gallery, NY, 2006; Paper, Lennon, Weinberg, Inc, NY 2007, Flowchart, 2008, Before Again, 2009, Ends and Means, 2010; Summer Reverie Invitational, William Siegel Gallery, Santa Fe, 2009; 40, Texas Gallery, Houston, 2010. *Teaching:* Vis artist, Univ Iowa, 85, Syracuse Univ, 85 & 86, Art Inst Chicago, 85, Ft Hays State, Hays, Kans, 86, Middlebury Col, Vt, 86 & Univ Buffalo, 86, Univ of Maryland, 94, Memphis Coll of Art, 2000, Univ of Akron, Myers Sch of Art, Ohio, 2003, Royal Acad of Arts, London, England, 2005, Columbus Coll of Art and Design, Ohio, 2006; instr, Parsons Sch Design, New York, 82-91, Bennington Col, Vt, 82 & 85, Provincetown Art Mus, 85 & 86, Columbia Univ, 89, RI Sch Design, 92 & 94, Vt Studio Ctr, 92 & Sch Visual Arts, New York, 93-, Nat Acad of Design, NY, 2003-. *Awards:* CAPS Grant, 81-82; Grant in Painting, Nat Endowment Arts, 83-84 & 93; Grant, New York Found Arts, 92; Yaddo, 94, 95, 97, 99, 2000, 2001, 2003, & 2005; The American Acad in Rome Vis Artist, 2004; Eric Isenburger Annual award, 2008; Pollack-Krasner Found Grant, 2009. *Bibliog:* Nancy Stapen (auth), Galleries/the vast canvas of abstraction, Boston Globe, 4/21/94; Joan Altabe (auth), Super-realism colors superb abstract show, Sarasota Herald-Tribune, 8/26/94; Mary Ann Marger (auth), A mission in abstract, Sarasota Times, 8/26/94; Art Smart, Avenue, February, 1991; The New York Times, Westchester, Edition, 7/26/98; Abstract Art Online, February, 2002, Gallery Views/Chelsea & October 30, 2003. *Mem:* Nat Acad. *Publ:* Illusr, Ms Mag, 12/73; coauth, Femmage, Heresies, spring 78; illusr, Parnassus: Poetry in Review, 83; Kimura at Ruth Siegel, Arts, 4/85; Provinceton Arts, fall 86, summer 87 & 88; Garner Tullis and the Art of Collaboration, text by David Carrier, Copenhagen and NY, 98; The Art of Encaustic Painting, text by Joanne Mattera, Watson-Guptill Publications, NY, 2001; Abstract Painting: Concepts and Techniques, Vicky Perry, Watson/Guptill Publications, NY, 2005

MEYER, MILTON E, JR
PAINTER
b St Louis, Mo, Nov 26, 1922. *Study:* Wash Univ, BSBA, 43; St Louis Univ, LLB, 50; NY Univ, LLM, 53; also studied with George Carlson, 83 & Daniel E Greene, 84. *Work:* Byron White Federal Courthouse, Denver; Cherry Hills Country Club, Denver, Colo; Roaring Fork Club, Basalt, Colo; Denver Zoo, Colo. *Comn:* Fed Court Appeals, 10th Circuit, Denver, Colo, 94. *Exhib:* Mem shows, Pastel Soc W Coast, 90-95 & Ann Open Exhib, 91-95; 19th, 20th, 21st, 22nd, 23rd & 24th Ann Open Exhib, Pastel Soc Am, NY, 91-96; Denver Rotary's Artists Am Show, Colo, 2000. *Pos:* Chmn, Denver Rotary's Artists Am, Colo, 90-92; art consult, 10th Circuit Court of Appeals, Denver, 94; secy, Int Am Portrait Soc, 94. *Awards:* Second place (pastel) All-Media Competition, Artist's Mag; Award Merit, Pastel Soc Am, San Francisco, 96; Silver Award, Int Asoc Pastel Socs, Placerville, Calif, 2002; First place, Pastel Soc Colo, 2002; Master Circle, Int Asn Pastel Soc, 2005. *Bibliog:* Starr Yelland (auth), Work of Milton Meyer, CBS (TV), Denver, 7/89; Carole Katchen (auth), A Traveller's Mood, Focus, Santa Fe, 8/92; Carole Katchen (auth), Filling in the Blanks, The Artist's Mag', 7/94; co found, Int Asn Pastel Soc, 93. *Mem:* Pastel Soc Am & W Coast; Knickerbocker Artists; Salmagundi Club; Int Asn Pastel Soc (co-found, masters cir). *Media:* Pastels. *Interests:* Foreign Travel and Subject matter. *Publ:* Auth, Approaching Photo Realism with Pastels, Am Artist, 11/92; Harnessing the spirit of water, The Artist's Mag, 12/98; contribr in various art publ of Quarto, Rockport Publishing and F&W Publ; auth, Picture perfect, Artist Int, 11-12/99; Selected pastels of Milton Meyer, Meyer, Meyer & McNeil, 2000

MEYER, MORRIS ALBERT
PAINTER
b Lebanon, Pa, Oct 14, 1936. *Study:* Pa State Univ, BSME, 58. *Comn:* Painting (3 children), comn by Mr & Mrs Harry Gardner, Dublin, Ohio, 94; painting (2 boys), comn by Elizabeth Coley, Dublin, Ohio, 96; painting (house 38 x 50), comn by Mr & Mrs Jon Tabor, Delaware, Ohio, 98; Rocky Mountain Nat Watermedia Exhib, 94, 97, Grand Exhib, 96, 97; Adirondacks Nat Exhib Am Watercolors, 96, 97. *Exhib:* Realism, Parkersburg Art Ctr, WVa, 95, 96, 97 & 98; Watercolor USA, Springfield Art Mus, Mo, 96 & 97; Taos Nat Exhib Am Watercolor, Taos Art Mus, NMex, 97; Ariz Aqueous, Tubac Ctr Arts, 98; Watercolor Ohio 98, 96, 97, 99, 2000, Canton Mus Art, 98. *Pos:* Artist, US Coast Guard, 94-. *Teaching:* Instr watercolor painting, pvt lessons, 98. *Awards:* Bloomsbury Award, Windsor Newton, 96; Award of Excellence, Trin Found, Strathmore, 96; Purchase/Gold Medallion, Brown Forman, 98; Best of Show, First Place. *Bibliog:* Betty Lou Schlemm (auth), People In Watercolor, Rockport Publ, 96; Webster Schlemm (auth), Best of Watercolor II, Rockport Publ, 97. *Mem:* Nat Watercolor Soc (signature mem); Ohio Watercolor Soc (signature mem); NW Watercolor Soc (signature mem); Watercolor Hon Soc (Watercolor USA), (signature mem); Pa Watercolor Soc (signature mem); Ala Watercolor Soc. *Media:* Watercolor. *Publ:* Auth, Keeping clutter under control (art), Artist Mag, 4/98. *Mailing Add:* 8636 Gavington Ct Dublin OH 43017

MEYER, SEYMOUR W
SCULPTOR
b Great Neck, NY. *Study:* With Louise Nevelson. *Work:* Arlen Industs, NY; Mus Mod Art, Rio de Janeiro, Brazil; Tel-Aviv Mus & Bat-Yam Mus, Israel; Temple Beth-El, Great Neck, NY; Fine Arts Mus, Long Island; and others. *Comn:* NY Inst Technol Libr, Old Westbury, NY; Isreal Tennis Ctr, Ramat Hashiron, Israel. *Exhib:* Metrop

Mus Art, NY, 76; D Justin Lester Gallery, Los Angeles, Calif, 78-80; Royal Acad, London, Eng, 79; Galeria of Sculpture, Palm Beach, Fla, 79-80; Engel Gallery, Jerusalem, 81; Art in Embassies, US State Dept, 85-; Exec Mansion, Albany, NY, 94-2000. *Pos:* Bd Trustees, NY Inst Technol; fel, Am Col of Surgeons. *Awards:* First Place, National Physicians Art; Two Valentine Mott Medals. *Mem:* Am Fedn Arts; Mus Mod Art NY; Sculptors League of NY; Guggenheim Mus; Prof Sculptors Guild. *Media:* Bronze. *Dealer:* J Richards Gallery Eaglewood NJ 07631. *Mailing Add:* 495 E Shore Rd Great Neck NY 11024

MEYER, SUSAN E
EDITOR, WRITER

b New York, NY, Apr 22, 1940. *Study:* Univ Perugia, 60; Univ Wis, BA, 62; NY Univ, MA, 2007. *Pos:* Managing ed, Watson-Guptill Publ, NY, 63-70; ed in chief, Am Artist, NY, 71-79, retired; ed dir, Am Art & Antiques, NY, 78-80 & Am Artist, Art & Antiques & Interiors & Residential Interiors, NY, 79-80; treas, Art Table, 81-85; founder & pres, Roundtable Press, Inc, 81-2002. *Teaching:* Adj prof, Empire State Coll/Union Coll, 76-78, NY Univ, 98-2000. *Awards:* Acad Women Achievers of YWCA, NY, 78. *Mem:* Artists Fel (trustee, 78-85); Art Table (treas, 81-85). *Publ:* James Montgomery Flagg, 74; America's Great Illustrators, 78; Norman Rockwell's People, 81; Treasury of the Great Children's Books Illustrators, 83; Mary Cassatt, 90; Norman Rockwell's World War II, 91; Edgar Degas, 94; Suyvesant High Sch, The First 100 Years, 2004. *Mailing Add:* 20 E Ninth St New York NY 10003

MEYERHOFF, ROBERT E
COLLECTOR

b Jan 1924. *Hon Degrees:* Achievements include establishing Meyerhoff Scholars Prog at Univ Md Baltimore Co, 88. *Pos:* Pres, Henderson Webb Inc, Md; owner Fitzhugh Farm, Phoenix. *Awards:* Named Philanthropists of the Year (with wife Jane), United Way of Central Maryland, 2001; named one of Top 200 Collectors, ARTnews Magazine, 2004. *Mem:* Jockey Club, Thoroughbred Owners & Breeders Asn (Outstanding Md Owner-Breeder 99); Mem of corp Metrop Mus Art, New York City. *Collection:* modern & contemporary art, especially postwar Am abstraction; collection is pledged to Nat Gallery of Art, Washington. *Mailing Add:* 3615 Blenheim Rd Phoenix MD 21131

MEYERS, AMY
MUSEUM DIRECTOR

Study: Univ Chicago, BA, 1977; Yale Univ, PhD (Am Studies), 1985. *Exhib:* Exhibs in Huntington Libr, Art Collections, Botanical Gardens, yale Ctr British Art. *Pos:* Researcher, Dumbarton Oaks, Washington; cur am art, Henry E Huntington Libr, San Marino, Calif; dir, Yale Ctr British Art; vice chair, Huntington Rep Asn Research Insts Hist Art, 1995-2000; editor, Empire's Nature, Classic Essays on Photog. *Teaching:* Adj Prof Art Hist, Yale Univ; adj fac, Calif Inst Tech. *Mem:* Coll Art Asn; Asn Art Mus Dir. *Specialty:* British art. *Publ:* Margaret Pritchard (coed), Empire's Nature: Mark Catesby's New World Vision, Univ NC Presss, Chapel Hill, 98; ed, Art & Sci Am, Issues of Representation, The Huntington, San Marino, 98; ed, Knowing Nature: Art & Sci in Philadelphia, 1740-1840, Yale Univ Press, New Haven, 2011. *Mailing Add:* Yale Ctr Brit Art PO Box 208280 1080 Chapel St New Haven CT 06520-8280

MEYERS, DALE (MRS MARIO COOPER)
PAINTER, INSTRUCTOR

b Chicago, Ill, 1922. *Study:* Corcoran Gallery Sch Art; Art Students League; watercolor with Mario Cooper; graphics with Seong Moy. *Work:* Space Mus, Smithsonian Inst; Palace of the Legion of Honor, San Francisco; Nat Air & Space Mus, Wash; Nat Acad Design, NY; Art Students League, NY; Portland Mus, Maine. *Comn:* Apollo 11 Moon Flight (painting), 69 & Project Viking (landing on Mars), 75, NASA, Nat Gallery Art, Washington; ecology paintings, Environ Protection Agency, Wash, 72; paintings, US Coast Guard, 84, 85 & 87. *Exhib:* Smithsonian Inst, Washington, 62-63; 200 Yrs of Watercolor Painting in Am, Metrop Mus Art, NY, 66; Nat Acad Design, 68-; Eyewitness to Space, Nat Gallery Art, 70; int watercolor exhib Can, US, Gt Brit, 1991-94, Chung Cheng Gallery, Taipei, 1994. *Pos:* Ed newslett, Am Watercolor Soc, 62-79, chmn awards, 67-79, chmn traveling exhibs & scholarships, 78-92; academician, Nat Acad Design, 79. *Teaching:* Instr watercolor, Kefauver Sch Art, Washington, DC, 61-62 & Art Students League, 79-; workshops in NMex, Calif, Maine, NY, Tex, Pa, Fla, Colo, Wyo, Ore, Ohio, Vt, Wis & Tenn, 70-77, 79, 81 & 88; lectr, Nat Acad & Parson's Sch Design, NY. *Awards:* Silver Medal, Allied Artists, 93; Medal of Hon, Salmagundi Club, 94; Medal, Dolphin Fel, 2000. *Mem:* Allied Artists Am (pres, 75-78); Am Watercolor Soc (pres 1992-, hon mem Miami chpt); dolphin fel Am Watercolor Soc (pres, 92-); hon mem Soc Mex de Acuarelistas; fel Royal Soc Arts, Gt Brit; Nat Acad. *Media:* Watercolor. *Publ:* Contribr, Eyewitness to Space, Abrams, 71; Nat Sculpture Rev, 77; Watercolor Bold & Free & Let the Medium Do It, Watson Guptill, 80; auth, The Sketchbook, Van Nostrand Reinhold, 83; contribr, Exploring Color, North Light Publ, 85. *Mailing Add:* Art Students League 215 W 57th St New York NY 10019

MEYERS, MICHAEL
SCULPTOR, PAINTER

Study: Univ Colo Boulder, Bachelor of Design, 1987; Mills Coll, Oakland, Calif, MFA, 2000. *Exhib:* Solo exhibs include Mesa State Coll's Johnson Gallery, Grand Junction, Colo, 2001, Colo State Univ, Pueblo, 2005, Jackson St Gallery, San Francisco, 2006, Johansson Projs, Oakland, Calif, 2007; group exhibs include MFA 2000, Mills Coll Art Mus, Oakland, Calif, 2000 ; Experimental Archit & Cultivated Landscape, Red Door Gallery, Oakland, Calif, 2001; Geographic Premonitions, Richmond Art Ctr, Richmond, Calif, 2006; Close Calls, Headlands Ctr Arts, Sausalito, Calif, 2007. *Awards:* Trefethen Award, Mill Coll, 1999, Nell Sinton Award, 1999; Pollock-Krasner Found Grant, 2007. *Mailing Add:* Johansson Projs 2300 Telegraph Ave Oakland CA 94612

MEYERS, MICHAEL K
PERFORMANCE ARTIST, PAINTER

b Chicago, Ill, Sept 28, 1939. *Study:* Drake Univ, Des Moines, Iowa, BS, 61; Coll Med, Univ Ill, cert, 65; Univ Iowa, MA (painting), 67. *Exhib:* Wattle and Daub Storefront and Street Theater, Int Performance Archives, Mus Mod Art, NY, 75; Short Plays for a Man on the Moon, Mus Mod Art, NY, 78; Cranbrook Acad Art, Bloomfield Hills, Mich, 81; An Illustrated History of the World, Joslyn Mus, Omaha, 82; Performance Space, Art Inst Chicago Sch, 83; Hefner Hall, Art Inst Chicago Sch, 84; Performance, Ind State Univ, 93; Drawing Exhib, Chicago Cult Ctr, 93; God's Brain, Chicago Cult Ctr, 93; Looking for Paradise, Pauline Oliveros Studio, Kingston, NY, 93; God's Brain, Dixon Place, NY, 93; and others. *Teaching:* Instr painting, Univ Iowa, Iowa City, 70-72; assoc prof art, Kansas City Art Inst, Mo, 72-83; prof performance/time arts & chair first year prog, Sch Art Inst Chicago, 83-. *Awards:* Nat Endowment Arts Individual Artist Fel, 80, 87 & 90; Sch Art Inst Chicago Fac Grant, 85-87, 90 & 91; Ill Arts Coun Individual Artist Grant, 86-88 & 91. *Publ:* Auth, Wasps and whales, Chouteau Review, Kansas City, 80; Scenes from an illustrated history of the world, 81, Teaching in the midwest, 81, High Performance Mag; Vacillation, Kans Quart, Manhattan, 85; Reconstructing the Temple from Memory, Whitewalls, Chicago, autumn, 86; Short pieces and performance fragments, J Dramatic Theory & Criticism, fall 90. *Mailing Add:* c/o Sch Art Inst First Yr Prog 37 S Wabash Chicago IL 60603

MEYERS, RONALD G
EDUCATOR, CERAMIST

b Buffalo, NY, Nov 4, 1934. *Study:* State Univ NY, Coll Buffalo, BS, 56, MS, 60; Sch Am Craftsmen, Rochester Inst Technol, with Frans Wildenhain, MFA, 65. *Work:* High Mus Art, Atlanta; Lamar Dodd Art Ctr, LaGrange, Ga; SC Arts Comn, Columbia. *Exhib:* Guild Prize Winners, Columbia Mus Art, SC, 71; Southeastern Crafts, Greenville Mus Art, SC, 74; 25 Southeastern Artists, High Mus, Atlanta, 75; Artist-Craftsmen Invitational, Southeastern Ctr Contemp Art, Winston-Salem, NC, 76; Tribute to Hands, Springfield Art Asn, Ill, 78; Drinking Companions, J M Kohler Art Ctr, Sheboygan, Wis, 79. *Teaching:* Asst prof ceramics, Univ SC, Columbia, 67-72; assoc prof, Univ Ga, Athens, 72-. *Awards:* Best of Show, Mid-South Ceramic & Crafts, 71 & SC Craftsmen, 71; Guild Purchase Award, Columbia Mus, 71. *Media:* Clay. *Mailing Add:* 180 Hidden Hills Ln Athens GA 30605-4202

MEYERSOHN, ELIZABETH
PAINTER, EDUCATOR

Study: Smith Coll, Northampton, Mass, BA, 1980; Yale Sch Art, New Haven, MFA (painting), 1982. *Work:* Bay State Med Ctr, Springfield, Mass; New York Sun; ABC News, New York; Dana-Farber Inst, Boston; and var pvt collections . *Exhib:* Solo exhibs, Springfield Mus Art, 1989, Mount Holyoke Coll Art Mus, 1991, Eli Marsh Gallery, Amherst Coll, 1993, Vertical Gallery, Rensselaer Polytechnic Inst, NY, 1999, Drury Gallery, Marlboro Coll, Vt, 2001, Wash Art Asn, Conn, 2003, and Richmond Art Ctr, Conn, 2007; A Pastoral Eye, Somerville Art Mus, Mass, 1994; 4 Women, Perspective Fine Art, New York, 1995; Pastels Only, Pastel Soc New York, 1999; Eleven Realists, Painting Ctr, New York, 2001; Changing Prospects: The View From Mount Holyoke, Mount Holyoke Coll Art Mus, 2002; Women Fac, Oresman Gallery, Smith Coll, 2010. *Teaching:* Instr painting, Amherst Coll, RI Sch Design, Assumption Coll, Mount Holyoke Coll, Westfield State Coll, and Brandeis Univ, 1982- ; lectr drawing & painting, Smith Coll, 2003-. *Awards:* Mass Cult Coun Grant, 1994; Purchase Prize, Bank Western Mass, 1997; Mellon Found Res Grant, 2003; Northampton Arts Coun Grant, 2006; Pollock-Krasner Found Grant, 2008. *Bibliog:* Grace Glueck (auth), Hymning the Mountain in Many Views, NY Times, 9/13/2002; Amanda Gordon (auth), The Story of Painting, New York Sun, 2/3/2003; Roger Boyce (auth), Painting, Art New England, 11/1/2004; Larry Parnass (auth), When Sky Proves No Limit, Daily Hampshire Gazette, 7/5/2004; Kerry O'Keefe (auth), Conversations about Painting, Artful Mind, 3-4/2009. *Publ:* Contribr, cover, Alumane Quarterly, Smith Coll, 1992 & Mass Rev, 2002. *Mailing Add:* 30 Williams St Northampton MA 01060

MEZZATESTA, MICHAEL
HISTORIAN, MUSEUM DIRECTOR

b New York, NY, June 9, 1948. *Study:* Columbia Col, BA, 70; NY Univ Inst Fine Arts, MA, 74, PhD, 80. *Collection Arranged:* Henri Matisse, Kimbell Art Mus, 84; Leonid Tishkov-Creatures (coauth, catalog), Duke Univ Mus Art, 93; Moscow Conceptualism, Duke Univ Mus Art, 95. *Pos:* Cur Europ art, Kimbell Art Mus, Ft Worth, 80-86; dir, Duke Univ Mus Art, 87-. *Teaching:* Adj prof art hist, Duke Univ, 87-. *Res:* Italian Renaissance; Baroque; 20th century. *Publ:* Auth, Dmitri Plavinsky, Ferzt, 95; Victor Hugo Irazabal, Art News, 95. *Mailing Add:* Duke Univ Museum Art PO Box 90732 Durham NC 27708

MHIRE, HERMAN P
MUSEUM DIRECTOR, CURATOR

b Lafayette, La, Nov 23, 1947. *Collection Arranged:* Louisiana Bicentennial Exposition, Maison de Radio, France, Paris, 76; Henry Botkin: Paintings, Drawings & Collages 1928-1981 (coauth, catalog), 82 & Senegal: Narrative Paintings (coauth, catalog), 85, Univ Art Mus, Lafayette, La; A Century of Vision: Louisiana Photography 1884-1984 (auth, catalog), La State Mus, 84; Village Architecture in Jordan (contribr, catalog), Mus Anthrop, Univ Kans, 86; Baking in the Sun: Visionary Images from the South (contribr, catalog). *Pos:* Guest cur, Lafayette Natural Hist Mus, La, 75-84; dir, Gallery Sch Art & Archit, Univ Southwestern La, 77-83 & Univ Art Mus, 83-; founder and pres, Festival Int de Louisiane, 87-89. *Teaching:* Instr drawing & printmaking, Sch Art & Archit, Univ Southwestern La, 77-. *Awards:* Gold Medal Award, La Bicentennial Exposition, US Dept Com, 76. *Mem:* Am Asn Mus; Southeastern Mus Conf; La Asn Mus. *Publ:* Contribr, Contemporary Works on Paper, 84, Univ Art Mus, Lafayette, La, 84. *Mailing Add:* 1500 Myrtle Pl Lafayette LA 70506-2538

MIAOULIS, IOANNIS NIKOLAOS
MUSEUM DIRECTOR
b Athens, Greece, July 24, 1961; came to US, 1980. *Study:* Tufts Univ, BSME, 83, MA, 86, PhD, 87; MIT, MME, 84. *Pos:* pres, dir, Mus Sci, Boston, 2003-; served on advisory coun, NASA; Elected mem Mass Tech/Eng Educ Advisory Bd, chair, elected mem, Mass, Math & Sci Educ Bd, 1995-99, Tufts Alumni Coun, Medford, 1994-2002, elected coun mem, Pompositticut Sch, Stow, Mass, 1993-98, trustee Tufts U, Wellesley Coll, mem, Nat Mus and Libr, Services Bd, 2006. *Teaching:* asst prof mechanical eng, Tufts Univ, Medford, Mass, 87-93, assoc prof, 93-97, assoc dean eng, 93-94, dean sch eng, 94-2002, prof 97-2002, interim dean, Sch Arts & Sci, 2001, assoc provost, 2001-2002. *Awards:* Inventors' Asn award, New Eng, 90; Presidential Young Investigator award, NSF, 91; Community & Leadership award, Toastmasters Int, Mass, 95; William P Desmond award, Citizens' Educ Resource Ctr, Mass, 96; Jaycees Outstanding Young Leader award, 99; Outstanding Svc Alumni award, Tuffi Univ, 2003; Sophia award, Hellenic Inst, 2004; NASA Exceptional Public Svc medal, 2006. *Mem:* ASME; AAAS; Am Soc Eng Educ; ASTK; Materials Rsch Soc. *Mailing Add:* Museum of Science 1 Science Park Boston MA 02114

MICCOLI, ARNALDO
PAINTER, COLLAGE ARTIST
b 1938. *Study:* Istituto d'Arte G Pellegrino Lecce, Italy, 60; Acad Fine Arts, Rome, Italy, 63; Univ Social Studies, Rome, 64; Acad Tiherina, Rome. *Work:* Mus Mod Art-Republica di San Marino, Italy; Pinacoteca Provinciale, Lecce, Italy; Webb & Athey Corp, NY; Bill Evans & Son Inc, Santa Monica, Calif; Kay Home Ctr, Lodi, NJ. *Exhib:* Nona Quadriennale Nazionale, Palazzo dell'Esposizioni, Rome, Italy, 65; Arnaldo Miccoli Paintings, Bergen Community Mus, Paramus, NJ, 68; NJ State Mus, Trenton Mus, 71; Int Art Show, Republica di San Marina State Mus, Italy, 74; Vereniging Volksuniversiteit Mus, Rotterdam, 86; Faces, Germanow Gallery, Rochester, NY, 87. *Awards:* Gold Medal, Citta di Mentana, Mentana City, 65. *Bibliog:* Toti Carpentiery (auth), Una storia Americana, Terzocchio, 83; Carlo Munari (auth), Metropolitan Apocalypse, Nuovo Sagittario, Milan, 85; A Sala & R Barletta (coauths), Arnaldo Miccoli, Capone Editore, 89. *Media:* Oil

MICHAEL, GARY
PAINTER, WRITER
b Denver, Colo, Apr 17, 1937. *Study:* Denver Univ, BA; Colo Univ, MA; Syracuse Univ, with Sydney Thomas, PhD. *Work:* Denver Pub Libr Permanent Collection, Colo; Denver Art Mus; Mus Natural Hist, Denver; Colorado Springs Fine Arts Ctr, Colo; Miron Collection, Poughkeepsie, NY. *Comn:* Mural, Perlmack Corp, Regent Plaza, Denver, 75; bus panel design, Bill & Dorothy Harmsen Collection, Denver, 78 & Saks Gallery, Denver, 86. *Exhib:* Solo exhibs, First of Denver, Farraginous V, 76, United Bank, Denver, 75 & 76, The Fleeting Moment, Saks Gallery, Denver, 86, The Diamond and Other Wonders, Gary Michael Studio, 88 & Western Co Art Ctr, Grand Junction, Colo, 89; Northern Colo Invitational Art Exhib, 79; Pastel Soc Am, NY, 79; Faces and Places, Denver Nat Bank, 82; Of Lilies and Ladies, Kontny Studio, Englewood, Colo, 83; Visual Arts Ctr, Boulder, Colo, 90; Currents & Collossi, Huntsman Gallery, Aspen, Colo, 90. *Pos:* Demonstrating artist, Spree Arts Festival, 75-; lectr & demonstr, Grumbacher, New York, 77-; contribr ed, Southwest Art, 88; fac mem, Art Students League, 91-. *Teaching:* Prof humanities, Metrop State Coll, Denver, 70-73; instr painting, Colo Univ, Denver, 75-76. *Awards:* Popular Vote Award, Pastel Soc Am Ann Exhib, 79; Merit Award, Colo State Fair, Pueblo, 79; cash award, Nat Pastel Exhib, Kans Pastel Soc; and others. *Bibliog:* Joan Gould (auth), Academician turned artist, Southwest Art, 5/75; Irene Clurman (auth), Farraginous artist, 11/76 & Marjorie Barrett (auth), Traditional artist with a rebellious streak, 11/79, Rocky Mountain News. *Mem:* Pastel Soc Am; Plein Ari Artists Colo. *Media:* Pastel, Oil. *Specialty:* American Art. *Publ:* Auth, Dorothy Mandel: Her woodcut magic, Am Artist, 1/79; The Art Institute of Chicago at 100, Denver Post, 8/26/79; Markings, Southwest Art, 3/81; Imagination in realist painting, Am Artist, 1/83; cover, Learning From the Pros, Watson-Guptill, Pastel Techniques, 2002. *Dealer:* Adamson-DuVannes Gallery 484 S Vicente Blvd Los Angeles CA 90048. *Mailing Add:* 3009 E Tenth Ave Denver CO 80206

MICHAELS, BARBARA L
HISTORIAN, WRITER
b New York, NY, Oct 4, 1935. *Study:* Cornell Univ, BA, 57; NY Univ Inst Fine Arts, MA, 62; City Univ New York, PhD, 85. *Pos:* Gallery asst, Samuel M Kootz Gallery, NY, 58-63; asst cur, Mus Mod Art, NY, 73-76; guest cur, Gertrude Käsebier Traveling Exhib, 92-95. *Teaching:* Adj lectr art hist, NY Univ, 76-86. *Bibliog:* Gretchen Garner (auth), Gertrude Kasebier & Helen Levitt, Art J, Winter, 92. *Mem:* Coll Art Asn; Authors Guild; ArtTable. *Res:* Big Dealer (s): Sam Kootz, Picasso, and the NY Art World. *Publ:* Auth, An introduction to the dating and organization of Eugene Atget's photographs, Art Bull, 9/79; Gertrude Käsebier: The Photographer and Her Photographs, Harry N Abrams Inc, 92; New light on F Holland Day's pictures of African Americans, Hist Photog, winter 94; auth catalog, On Charles Sheeler, The Camera Work that Wasn't, and Others that Might have Been, Camera Work: A Centennial Celebration, catalogue for Camera Work exhibition, James A Michener Art Mus, Phot Review, vol 26, 1 & 2, Doylestown, Pa, 2003; auth, An Affinity for Architecture: Philip Trager's Photographs of Buildings, 2006. *Mailing Add:* 336 Central Park W New York NY 10025-7111

MICHAELS, GLEN
ASSEMBLAGE ARTIST, PAINTER
b Spokane, Wash, July 21, 1927. *Study:* Yale Sch Music, 50-52; Eastern Wash Coll Educ, BA, 57; Cranbrook Acad Art, with Zoltan Sepeshy, MFA, 58. *Work:* Am Inst Archit, Detroit Chap; Kresge Found; Kirco Corp, Troy, Mich; Jacobson's, Birmingham, Mich; Univ Mich Alumni Ctr, Ann Arbor; Wall & Pool Floor, Wm Beaumont Hosp, Royal Oak, MI, 96; 20 ft Assemblage, tile, metal and wood, Shifman Library, Wayne State Univ, Detroit, Mich, 2002, Wayne State med Ctr, 2003, Tile, Metal & wood, Ford Hospital (lobby), Detroit, Mich, fused glass pool floor looby, Henry Ford Memorial Libr, Dearborn, Mich, 2004; tile mural, Wayne State Univ, Detroit, Mich, 2003; waterfall wall, Tile, Lawrence, and Idell Wisberg Cancer Treatment Center, Southfield, Mich, 2004; oil portrait, John Crissman, Md Dean of Med, Wayne State Univ, Detroit, Mich; assemblage bas relief, Karmanos Cancer Center, Detroit Med Center, Detroit, Mich, 2007. *Comn:* fused glass pool, Mich State Mus, Archives & Libr, Mich, 90; Baldwin Pub Libr, Birmingham, Mich, 92-; Oil portrait, The Hon Avern L Cohn, Detroit Fed Court, Mrs Elmore Leanord, Glenn Davis, MD, Dean of Medicine, Mich State Univ, East Lansing, Mich, 2006; royal oak wall, Beaumont Hospital Imaging Center, 2000; portrait bust Ernest Goodman bronze, 2000; The Honorable John Feikens, US District Court, Detroit, Mich; tile and bronze mural, Providence Hospital, Southfield, Mich. *Teaching:* Supvr art for children, Cranbrook Acad Art, 59-65; asst prof sculpture, Wayne State Univ, 67-69 & Univ Windsor, 70-71. *Awards:* Kresge Grant, Detroit People Mover Station, 87; Artist of the Year Award, Mich Art Train, 90; Hon Affil Mem Fine Arts, Am Inst Archit, Mich Chap. *Bibliog:* Nordness (auth), Objects: USA, Viking Press, 70; The Confectioner's Art, Am Craft Coun, 89; Joann Lucktov (auth), The Art of Mosaic Design, Rockport Publ. *Media:* Bronze, Fused Glass, Oil. *Publ:* John Canaday (auth), NY Times, 62; Dorothy Rodgers (auth), A Chateau the sound of music built, Look Mag, 67; Art in Archit, Am Inst Archits, 80; Archit Rec, 80-81; Am Craft Mag, 6-7/92; Wall Street Journal, 2008. *Dealer:* Robert Kidd Gallery, Birmingham, Mich. *Mailing Add:* 4800 Beach Rd Troy MI 48098

MICHAELS-PAQUE, J
PAINTER, SCULPTOR
b Menominee, Mich. *Study:* Layton Sch Art, Milwaukee, Wis, scholar, 55-57; Marquette Univ, 56-57; Milwaukee Inst Art & Design, 92. *Work:* Nat Mus Am Art & Nat Collection Fine Arts, Washington; Objects USA, Johnson Wax Co, Racine, Wis; Wis Elec Co, Einhorn Assocs Inc, Beck Carton Co & Unitarian Church, Milwaukee; Univ Mus, Ill State Univ, Normal; Arrowmont Sch Art, Gatlinburg; SCJ Insurance Serv, Pleasanton, Calif; St Norbert Col, De Pere, Wis; Golda Meier Collection, Univ Wis, 2006; Richard Deavnlex Collection, Longport, NJ, 2006; Hispanic Chamber of Com Collection, Milwaukee, Wis, 2007; Ko-Thi Dance Co Collection, Milwaukee, Wis, 2007; Racine Wisconsin Art Mus. *Comn:* Janis Salon, Pfister Hotel, Milwaukee, Wis, 92; Terry Hueneke, Milwaukee, Wis, 93; Beck, Chaet, Loomis, SC, Milwaukee, 96; H Arnold Arch Firm, Denver, 98; Mary Nohl Kohler Mus, 2006. *Exhib:* Solo exhibs, Australian Nat Univ Sch Art, Dayton Art Inst, 81, Ariel Gallery, Chicago, 83, Univ Notre Dame, 89, Cardinal Stritch Univ, 95 & Wis Lutheran Col, Milwaukee, 2000; The Third Dimension Milwaukee Art Mus, 89; Antipodean Afterimages, Blatz Gallery, Milwaukee, 90; Inclinations, Godschalx Gallery, St Norbert Col, De Pere, Wis, 91; 50th Anniversary Fac Invitational, Arrowmont Sch Art, Gatlinburg, 95; Full of Herself, Cedarburg, Wis Cult Ctr; Int Expos Sculptural Objects & Functional Art, Chicago, Ill, 2000; Themselves, Schlueter Art Gallery, Wis Luth Col, Milwaukee, 2001-02; Arrowmont Sch Arts & Crafts, Gatlinburg, 2006; Sculptural Kinetic Books, JMP Gallery, 2005-2007; HGA Handweavers Guild of Am Exhib, Tampa, Fla, 2008. *Pos:* Adv bd, Milwaukee Art Mus, currently & Artists Working Edn, Inc, 99-2008; cur, Internos Gallery Milwaukee, 95, Miad Milw Inst Art & Design, 93-98, 2001, 2003, 2007; Artists Working in Educ Bd (AWE), 2007; juror, HGA exhib, St Petersburg, Fla, 2008. *Teaching:* Vis artist, Miami Univ, Ohio, 81, Dayton Art Inst, 81, Kawashima Textile Sch, Kyoto, Japan, 83 & Bellas Artes, San Miguel de Allende, Mex, 85, Univ Queensland, St Lucia, Australia, 88, Univ Notre Dame, 89, San Diego Book Arts, 2007; instr art dept, Cardinal Stritch Col, 90-, workshops/seminars for Handweavers Guild Am, American Univ, Washington, 92; vis artist, Viterbo Col, La Crosse, Wis, 92, Australian Nat Univ, Canberra, Brisbane, Univ Tenn Arrowmont Sch Arts & Crafts, 90-98, 2001, 03, 04, 05, 06; consult corp art, currently; Milwaukee Inst Art & Design, 93-96, 2003-2005; Scripps Col, Claremont, Calif, 2005; Sonoran Collective for Paper & Book Arts, Tuson, Ariz, 2005; The Clearing, Ellison Bay, Wis, 96, 2003-2007; Southern Calif Hand Bookbinders of San Francisco, 2006; Alverno Col, Milwaukee, WI, 2006; San Diego Book Arts, Calif, 2007. *Awards:* Fac Develop Award, Cardinal Stritch Col, Milwaukee, 93 & 94; Nat Endowment Humanities & Wis Humanities Coun Grants, 95; Roundt's 45 Corp Grant, 2000; Gary Goberville Mem Fel, Ragdale Found, 2006; Ragdale Foundation Goberville Memorial Fellowship, 2006-2007; NEA Grant, Charlotte, NC, 2008; and others. *Bibliog:* Feature article, Herald, CNI Newspapers, 94; Louis Blinkhorn (auth), Art Imitates Life, Milwaukee J, 2/12/95; James Auer (auth), Relating through the Rhombus, Milwaukee Jour Sentinel, 5/3/2000; Milwaukee Mag, lifestyle sect, 2006; Paul Zelanski (auth), Shaping Space: Dynamics of 3 Dimensional Design, 2007. *Mem:* Am Crafts Coun; Int Guild Journalists, Auths & Photogrs; Wis Painters & Sculptors; Handweavers Guild Am; Int Sculpture Ctr. *Media:* Flexible Linear Material, Mixed Media, 3D Artworks. *Res:* Exploring the reclamation and transformation of unpretentious materials into lightweight, large scale reliefs and sculptures. *Interests:* Research, writing, creating, dogs. *Publ:* Auth, reviews for Textile Fibre Forum, Australian Periodical, 92; Shuttle, Spindle & Dyepot (series of 4 articles), Art Approach to Bus, 93; Improvisation (article), Fiberarts, 94; Colored Threads, Fiberarts, 94; Lifecasting monograph, pvt publ, 96. *Dealer:* Snyderman Gallery 303 Cherry St Philadelphia PA 19106. *Mailing Add:* 4455 N Frederick Ave Milwaukee WI 53211

MICHAUX, HENRY GASTON
EDUCATOR, SCULPTOR
b Morganton, NC, Jan 19, 1934. *Study:* Tex Southern Univ, with John T Biggers, BFA, 59; Rochester Inst Technol, advanced design, 63; Pa State Univ, EdM, 60, EdD, 71. *Work:* NC State Mus, Raleigh; JB Speed Mus, Louisville, Ky; HC Taylor Gallery (A&T State Univ), Greensboro, NC; Univ Mus, Tex Southern Univ, Houston; BellSouth, Louisville, Ky; Tex Southern Univ, Houston, Tex; A&T State Univ, Greensboro, NC; Slave Ship Barrier (bronze), African Am Mem Monument, State Capital Bldg, Columbia, SC. *Comn:* Ceramic Mural on Medicine, comn by Dr & Mrs Carrol, Houston; coffee set (hand thrown), comn by John T Biggers, Houston; welded steel gift for Graduating High School, Houston Pub Sch, Tex, 69; stainless steel award, comn by James Oxygen & Welding, Hickory, NC, 75; ceramic sculptural representation of Justice, comn by atty Eddye L Lane, Columbia, SC, 94; Barrier

(bronze) at Af Am Monument, S Carolina Budget and Control Board, Columbia, SC, 2006. *Exhib:* Houston Mus Art, Tex, 56; Competitive Invitational, Henri Studio Galleries, NY, 64; Afro-Am Artists, Denver Art Mus, Colo, 69; Afro-Am Artists: North Carolina USA, N Mus Art, Raleigh, 80; Dimensions and Directions: Black Artists of the South, Jackson State Coll Mus, Miss, 80. *Pos:* Pres, Caldwell Arts Coun, Lenoir, NC, 75-76; organizer/planner, Ann Indoor/Outdoor Sculpture Competition, Lenoir, NC, 86; African Am monument com, State SC, 96-2000, adv com, selections recommendation com & designed prospectus adv com. *Teaching:* Prof sculpture, Tex Southern Univ, Houston, 68-70; prof ceramics, Appalachian State Univ, Boone, NC, 72-76; prof sculpture & ceramics, SC State Univ, Orangeburg, 78-96 (retired 96). *Awards:* Purchace Award, 9th Ann Black Artists' Exhib, Louisville Chap Links Inc, 88. *Bibliog:* Carolina Camera, feature story (film), WBTV Television, Charlotte, NC, 8/4/80; Biggers & Simms (coauths), Black Art in Houston, Univ Tex. *Mem:* Nat Asn Sch Art & Design; Am Crafts Coun; Nat Coun Educ Ceramic Arts; Sculpture Int; Nat Art Educ Asn. *Media:* Clay, Stainless Steel. *Interests:* 3-D art. *Publ:* Illusr, Folk Tales and Ghost Stories, Jourdan Atkinson, 57; auth, An Accommodational Esthetic: Precursor For One Legitimate Black Esthetic in African Rock Art Traditions, J Black Studies, 12/77; Black Art: Recognition, Nourishment, Celebration, Greensboro Asn Preservation Black Art, 78. *Mailing Add:* 310 Mulungu Pl NW Lenoir NC 28645-4234

MICHAUX, RONALD ROBERT
ART DEALER, GALLERY DIRECTOR
b Springfield, Mass, Aug 8, 1944. *Collection Arranged:* On Their Own, Robert Castagna, The Art Complex Mus, Duxbury, Mass. *Pos:* Dir, Rolly-Michaux Galleries, Boston. *Specialty:* 20th century Europ masters & contemporaries, including paintings, sculpture, graphics & rare etchings; French Impressionists and Post-Impressionists. *Mailing Add:* c/o Rolly-Michaux Galleries LTD 290 Dartmouth St Boston MA 02116

MICHELS, ANN HARRISON
PAINTER, CONCEPTUAL ARTIST
b Newark, NJ. *Study:* Colby-Sawyer Col, AA, 51; Skidmore Col, BS (fine arts), 53. *Work:* IT&T Inc, NY; PNC Bank, Edison, NJ; Rollins Col, Fla; Skidmore Col, Saratoga Springs, NY; Prudential Securties Inc, Short Hills, NJ. *Comn:* mural, Landscape in Oil, comn by A Gary Shilling Inc, NY, 90-92. *Exhib:* N E Watercolor Soc-18th Ann Exhib, Trotter's Mus, Goshe, NY, 94; Ridgewood Art Inst First Grand Nat, Bergen Mus Art & Science, Paramus, NJ, 95-96; Catherine Corillard Woiff Open Show, National Arts Club, NY, 95-96; Audubon Artists Inc, Federal Hall, Wall St, NY, 96, Salmagundi Club, NY, 2000; AAPL (NJ) 60th Anniversary Show, Papermill Playhouse Gallery, Milburn, NJ 96; Nat Asn Women Artists Inc - The Heart of the Artists, Art Ctr Sarasota, Sarasota, Fla, 2000. *Pos:* pres, The Essex Watercolor Club, 94-96. *Teaching:* art instr, Cartaret Sch, W Orange, NJ, 53-54. *Awards:* Award of Merit, Essex Watercolor Club, 96. *Mem:* Fel Am Artists Prof League Inc; Audubon Artists Inc; Nat Asn of Women Artists Inc (newsletter editor, 98-99, bd mem, 96-2001); North Shore Art Asn, Gloucester, Mass; Garden State Watercolor Soc Inc. *Media:* Acrylic, Watermedia. *Publ:* Illus, Snowy Egret Greeting Cards, Audubon Inc, 75; auth, Member of the Issue, North Lights Mag, 93. *Dealer:* Chetkin Gallery 308 Morris Ave Spring Lake NJ 07762. *Mailing Add:* 6 Benson Ct Short Hills NJ 07078

MICHELS, EILEEN MANNING
EDUCATOR, ART HISTORIAN
b Fargo, NDak, 1926. *Study:* Univ Minn, BA, magna cum laude, 47, MA, 53, MA, 59, PhD, 71; Inst Fine Arts, NY Univ, 50-51; Sorbonne, Paris, 56-57; Am Sch Classical Studies, Athens, Greece, 80. *Work:* books & articles are in various libr. *Collection Arranged:* Edwin Hugh Lundie, FAIA (auth, catalog), 72; An Architectural View: 1883-1974, the Minneapolis Soc of Fine Art (auth, catalog), 74. *Pos:* Art librn, Univ Minn, 48-53, gallery cur & dir asst, 54-56; freelance cur, Minneapolis Inst Arts, 73-74 & Minn Mus Art, 72-73, assoc dir, 73-74. *Teaching:* asst prof, Univ Wisc, River Falls, 66-70; Vis asst prof art hist, Stanford Univ, 72-73; assoc prof & chair dept, Univ St Thomas, 78-88, prof, 89-92, adj prof, 92 & prof emer, 96. *Awards:* Phi Beta Kappa, 47; Fulbright, Paris, 56-57; Vincent Sully Jr Res Grant, Archit Hist Found, 94; Nat Endowment for Humanities Grant, 80; Fellow, Soc Archit Historians, 2012. *Mem:* Soc Archit Historians (dir, 76-79, secy 82-86), co- found, Minn Chapter, 73, treasurer, 73-86; Coll Art Asn. *Res:* Nineteenth and twentieth century architecture; American art, especially Harvey Ellis, Frank Lloyd Wright. *Publ:* Auth, Edwin Hugh Lundie, FAIA (exhib catalog), Minnesota Mus Art, St Paul, 72; An Architectural View: Minneapolis Society of Fine Arts 1883-1974, Minneapolis Inst Arts, 74; A Landmark Reclaimed, Minn Landmarks, 77; Reconfiguring Harvey Ellis, Beavers Bond Press, 2004; harveyellisfacts.com, 2007-; Eileenmanningmichaels.com, 2007-. *Mailing Add:* 2183 Hendon Ave Saint Paul MN 55108

MICHELS, KATHRYN
PAINTER, PHOTOGRAPHER
b Gary, Ind, August, 14, 1961. *Study:* Western Ill Univ; Studied with Larry Lombardo, 2009-present. *Exhib:* Shanghai Zhujiajiao Int Watercolor Biennial, China, 2012; Shanghai Traveling Exhib, Children's Palace and Oriental Pearl Tower, China, 2013; Pa Watercolor Soc 34th Ann Int Exib, Warren, Pa, 2013; Baltimore Watercolor Soc Mid-Atlantic Exhib, Stevenson, Md, 2013; Harrisburg Art Assn Int Exhib, Harrisburg, Pa, 2013; Baltimore Watercolor Soc Mid-Atlantic Exhib, 2014. *Awards:* 1st Place Watercolors, Figuratively Speaking, 2012; Grand Prize, Everylife Art Contest, Kakkis Found, 2011, 2012; 2nd Place, Harrisburg Int Art Show, Tracey Meloni, 2013; Merchandise award, Baltimore Watercolor Soc, M Graham and Co, 2013. *Mem:* Pa Watercolor Soc (signature mem); Baltimore Watercolor Soc (signature mem); Nat League Am Pen Women (dual juried mem); Daily Painters of Pa; Harrisburg Area Art Asn. *Media:* Watercolor. *Mailing Add:* 128 East Emaus St Middletown PA 17057

MICHELSON, ERIC MICHAEL
PAINTER
b Manhasset, NY, 1954. *Study:* State Univ, NY; Stony Brook, BA, 76; Art Student League, studied with Robert Phillipp, Ted Jacobs, Stanley Michelson. *Work:* Plaza Hotel, NY; Art Students League, NY; Hypernon Hotel, NY. *Exhib:* Art Students League, Main Street Gallery, Eva Monte Gallery, New York City, 1997; Weill Art Gallery, New York City, 2000; and others. *Awards:* Len Everett Mem Award, oils, Salmagundi Club, NY, 1999. *Mem:* Audubon Artists, NY, (vpres, currently). *Specialty:* Large figurative works, portraits and NY Living, 2001. *Mailing Add:* 32 Union Sq E Rm 1216 New York NY 10003

MICHOD, SUSAN A
PAINTER
b Toledo, Ohio, Jan 3, 1945. *Study:* Smith Col; Univ Mich, BS; Pratt Inst, MFA. *Work:* Mus Contemp Art, Chicago, Ill; Ill State Mus, Springfield; Owens-Corning Fiberglass, Toledo, Ohio; Chase Manhattan Bank & Xerox Corp, NY. *Comn:* Shared Space (painted installation), Bronx Mus, NY, 83; painting with construction, Indust Trust & Savings Bank, Muncie, Ind, 84; mural, Regeneration, Rush-Pres St Luke's Hosp, Chicago, Ill, 91. *Exhib:* Painting and Sculpture Today, Indianapolis Mus Art, 76; Pattern Painting, PS1, Flushing, NY, 77; Jan Cicero Gallery, Chicago, 77-; Andre Zarre Gallery, NY, 78-79; Mus Contemp Art, Chicago, 79; Usable Art, State Univ NY, Plattsburg, 81; Susan Caldwell Gallery, NY, 81-83; The Chair Show, Thorpe Intermedia Gallery, Syracuse, NY, 82; Chicago Now, Brentwood Gallery, St Louis, Mo, 82; Wilson Galleries, Anderson Univ, Anderson, Ind, 92; Artemisia Gallery, Installation Show, Chicago, 93; Fragile Landscapes, Chicago Cult Ctr, 97; Stable Studios, Chicago, 2002; Florence Biennale, Ital, 2003; Andre Zorre Gallery, NY, 2003; Whitney Mus Am Art, NYC, 2006. *Teaching:* Instr painting, Chicago Acad Fine Arts, 69-74, Columbia Col Pougealis Apprentice Prog. *Awards:* Purchase Prize, Ill State Mus, 74; Purchase Prize, Carleton Coll Exhib, 75. *Bibliog:* John Russell (auth), Art, New York Times, 7/10/81; Ronny Cohen (auth), rev, Art News, Vol 81, No 9, 11/82; Judith Kirschner (auth), rev, Artforum, 3/83. *Media:* Acrylic, Watercolor

MICK, DANNIELLE
EDUCATOR, PAINTER
b Bronxville, NY, Jan 28, 1955. *Study:* Art Students League, NY; Nat Acad Fine Art, New York, NY; New Sch Parsons, New York, NY; Chicago Inst Art, Chicago, Ill; Studied with Wolfe Kahn, PSA, Elizabeth Mowry, PSA, NY, Robert Burridge, Richard McKinley, PSA. *Work:* Kean Univ, Union, NJ; Embassy of Uzbekistan. *Exhib:* Allied Artists 93rd Ann Open Juried Exhib, 2006; 110th Ann Juried Exhib, Catharine Lorillard Wolfe Art Club, NY, 2006; Audubon Artists 64th Ann Open Juried Exhib, Salmagundi Club, New York, NY; Ridgewood Art Inst 26th Regional Open Juried Show, 2006; Pastel Soc NJ 1st Juried Exhib, 2006; Int Artists Exhib, Taipei, Taiwan, 4/2007; Salmagundi Art Club Ann Juried Exhib (for non mems), 5/2007; Am Artist Prof League, NYC, 2007; Ridgewood Art Inst 27th Ann Open Juried Show, 2007, 2008; Audubon Artists Open Juried Exhib, NYC, 2007, 2008; Pastel Soc NJ 2nd Juried Exhib, 2007, 2008; Salmagundi Art Club Ann Juried Exhib (non mems), NYC, 2008; Catharine Lorillard Wolfe Arts Club, New York, 2008, 2013; Mayo Ctr for the Arts Exhib, Community Theatre, NJ, 2007-2009 & 2012; Audubon Artist Juried Exhib, 2009; Int Asn Pastel Societies, 22nd Biennial Juried Exhib, 2013; George Segal Gallery, Montclair State Univ, 2014; Internat Asn of Pastel Artists (IAPS) 26th Juried Exhib, 2015. *Pos:* Studio dir, Lakeside Art Studio, NJ. *Teaching:* instr (private & group): Visual Art Center, Summit, NJ; Somerset Art Asn, Bedminster, NJ; Creative Hands, Madison, NJ; Millburn-Short Hills Art Center; Scotch Plains Asn; Roxbury Art Asn; educator, Newark Mus, Newark, NJ, Ctr Contemp Art, Bedminster, NJ, Lakeside Art Studio, Parsippany, NJ. *Awards:* Award of Merit, Paper Mill Playhouse, 2004; Award of Excellence, Paper Mill Playhouse, 2005; Pastel Soc Am Award, 2006; Medal of Hon, Grand Prize-Pastel, Catharine Lorillard Wolfe Arts Club, 2006; Audubon Art Students League Award, Salmagundi Club, 2006; Award of Excellence, Pastel Soc NJ, 2006; Second Place, Somerset Art Asn, 2005-2006; Conn Pastel Soc Award; Salmagundi Arts Club, Conn Pastel Soc Award, 2007; Hon mention, Millburn Short Hills Art Ctr, 2007, Award of Merit, 2008; Hon Mention, Pastel Soc of NJ, 2007; Best in Show, Mayo Ctr Performing Arts, 2011; Internat Asn of Pastel Societies 22nd Biennial Juried Exhib, 2013; Pastel Painters Soc of Cape Cod, For Pastels Only 2014 Juries Exhib, 2014; Richeson75 Internat Landscape, Seascape & Architecture Juries Exhib Finalist & Meritorious, 2014; Richeson75 Internat Small Works 2014 Top 75 Finalist, 2014. *Bibliog:* Independent Press, NJ, 2005; Star Ledger, NJ, 1998, 2005-2006; Vicinity Mag, NJ, 2005-2006; Parsippany Life, NJ, 9/2006, 2008, 2010; Parsippany Monthly, NJ, 8/2006; Daily Record, NJ, 2008; The Daily Record, 2012, 2013. *Mem:* Audubon Artists Am (bd dirs); Pres, Pastel Soc of NJ; Allied Artists of Am; signature mem, Catharine Lorillard Wolfe Arts Club; signature mem, Pastel Soc NJ (pres, 2008-2010); Pastel Soc Am. *Media:* Acrylic, Pastel. *Publ:* Pastel Jour, 2000, 2001; Nat Arts Club, NY, 2002; NY Times, 2003; Courier News, NJ, 2004; Independent Press, NJ, 2005-2008, & 2012; Parsippany Monthly, NJ, 2006; Parsippany Life, NJ, 2004-2012; Southwest Art Mag, 2012; Jersey Shore Mag, NJ, 2010-12; Lakeside Reflections by Danielle Mick, 2014; Jersey Women Artists Now: Contemporary Visions at Montclair State Univ. *Mailing Add:* 6 Absecon Rd Parsippany NJ 07054

MICKENBERG, DAVID
MUSEUM DIRECTOR, HISTORIAN
b Brooklyn, NY, Apr 24, 1954. *Study:* Colgate Univ, BA, 76; Univ Wis, Milwaukee, MA (art hist), 79. *Collection Arranged:* Romantic Prints, Ind Mus Art, Indianapolis, 80; Ritual Power and Function (auth, catalog), 82, Winslow Homer: The Civil War Years, 83, Impressionism: Post-Impressionism (auth, catalog), 83 & Songs of Glory (auth, catalog), Okla Mus Art. *Pos:* Asst cur, Picker Art Gallery, Hamilton, NY, 74-76; coordr, Adult Educ Prog & asst dir, Indianapolis Mus Art, Ind, 79-81; exec dir, Okla Mus Art, Oklahoma City, 81-86; dir, Mary & Leigh Block Gallery Northwestern Univ, Evanston, Ill, 86-2001, Davis Mus and Cult Ctr, Wellesley Coll, Mass, 2001-2010 & Taubman Mus Art, Roanoke, Va, 2010-. *Teaching:* Teaching asst, Univ Wis, 76-79.

Awards: Dean's Scholarship, Ind Univ, 80-81. *Mem:* Coll Art Asn; Am Asn Mus; Int Ctr Medieval Art. *Res:* Romanesque and Gothic architecture; contemporary prints; painting and sculpture. *Publ:* Maurice Prendergast (editor) (exhib catalogue) Large Boston Public Garden Sketchbook, 1981; editor, auth: (exhib catalogue) Songs of Glory: Medieval Art from 900 to 1500, 1985. *Mailing Add:* 110 Salem Ave SE Roanoke VA 24011

MICKISH, VERLE L
EDUCATOR, ILLUSTRATOR
b Greeley, Colo, Sept 27, 1928. *Study:* Colo State Col, BA, 51; Univ Northern Colo, MAE, 55; Ariz State Univ, EdD, 70. *Hon Degrees:* Prof Emeritus, GA State Univ, 98. *Work:* State Artist; General's Headquarters Squadron, AFMF, US Marine Corps, 51-53. *Comn:* Acrylic painting, Great Moments in Music Corp, Atlanta, Ga, 83; Acrylic painting, Eastminster Presbyterian Church, 2000. *Exhib:* Georgia Ann Exhib, High Mus Art, Atlanta, 83-85; 3 solo exhibs; 32 national juried exhibs; 20 corporate collections; 28 private collections; one man art exhib, 60 Year Retrospect, 78 pieces, Univ Northern Colo, 2010; 110 Emory Med Cartoons; GWS Nat Watercolor Exhib, 2013. *Pos:* Presented over 800 workshops and keynote addresses, 56-present; Chmn, Int Cultural Arts, Nat Asn Partners of the Americas, 76-77; mem, Int Olympics Acad Comt, 78-80; mem Prof Standards Comt, Nat Art Educ Asn, Reston, Va, Southeastern mem 76-, vpres, 86-88. *Teaching:* Art dir K-12, Boulder Valley Pub Sch, Colo, 58-71; prof art, Ga State Univ, Atlanta, 71-96; presentation of over 800 workshops throughout US, Canada, Europe & Brazil since 1961. *Awards:* Nat Art Educator of the Year, Nat Art Educ Asn, 83; Distinguished Ga Educator, Ga Univ Syst, 83 & 96; Nat NAEA Art Fellow, 93; Nat NAEA Distinguished Service Award, 2002; Lifetime Achievement Award, GAEA, 2002; Nat Retired Art Educator of the Yr, 2006. *Mem:* Ga Art Educ Asn (pres, 79-81). *Media:* Acrylic, Watercolor. *Interests:* Painting, illustrating, cartooning. *Publ:* created over 300 illustrations used in magazines, books, & CD jacket cases, 61-2010; Auth, Creative Art-Junior High Grades, Pruett Press, 62; illusr, Corn for the Palace, Prentice-Hall, 63; 16 cartoons in School Arts magazine, 2004-05; monthly cartoon in Emory Hospital Newsletter, 2004-09; 66 drawings, Musterseed. *Mailing Add:* 5374 Pheasant Run Stone Mountain GA 30087-1235

MIDDAUGH, ROBERT BURTON
PAINTER
b Chicago, Ill, May 12, 1935. *Study:* Univ Ill, 54-55; Art Inst Chicago, BFA, 64. *Work:* Art Inst Chicago; Boston Mus Fine Art; Los Angeles Co Mus; Phoenix Art Mus; Worcester Art Mus, Mass. *Comn:* Prehistoric Project (permanent educ display, with Martyl Langsdorf & Prof Robert Braidwood), Oriental Inst, Univ Chicago, 68. *Exhib:* Chicago & Vicinity Show, Art Inst Chicago, 64, 66 & 73-85; Ill Biennial Exhib, Krannert Art Mus, Urbana, 65; solo exhibs, Kovler Gallery, Chicago, 65, 67, 69, Martin Schweig Gallery, St Louis, 70, 72, 79, 83, Univ Wis, 76, 81-82, Fairweather Hardin Gallery, Chicago, 77, 80, 83, 85, Rockford Art Mus 87, Zaks Gallery, Chicago, 92093, 97, Printworks Gallery, Chicago, 2006, 2010; Ill Exhib, Ill State Mus, Springfield, 66, 68, 69 & 71; Am Painting Exhib, Va Mus Fine Arts, Richmond, 66; 162nd Ann Exhib, Pa Acad Fine Arts, Philadelphia, 67. *Collection Arranged:* Coopers & Lybrand; Brinson Partners; Sonnenschein; Nath & Rosenthal. *Pos:* Asst cur, Art Collection First Nat Bank Chicago, 71-78, cur, 79-83; archivist, Chicago Park Dist, 98-2005. *Awards:* Purchase Prize, Am Acad Arts & Lett, 75. *Mem:* Arts Club Chicago. *Media:* All. *Publ:* Contribr, Buying Art on a Budget, Hawthorn, 68; contribr, Living World History, Scott Foresman. *Dealer:* Printworks 311 W Superior Chicago IL 60610. *Mailing Add:* 1121 S Central Ave Burlington IA 52601

MIDDLEBROOK, DAVID A
SCULPTOR, EDUCATOR
b Jackson, Mich, May 1, 1944. *Study:* Albion Col, BA, 66; Univ Iowa, with Jerry Rothman, Paul Soldner & Stuart Eddie, MA, 69, with Don Reitz, Byron Burford & Hans Braeder, MFA, 70. *Work:* Univ Wash Mus Art, Seattle; Koehler Mus, Sheboygan, Wis; San Jose Mus Art, Fresno Mus, Oakland Mus Art & San Francisco Mus Art, Calif; and others. *Comn:* Earth Sample (stone & marble), Thrust IV, Inc, Mt View, Calif, 85; Black Water, Bell Savings, San Jose, Calif, 85; Time Shadow, Sacramento Light Rail, 86-87. *Exhib:* Nine Calif Artists, Everson Mus Art, Syracuse, NY, 78; A Century of Ceramics in US, Smithsonian Mus, traveling, DC, 78-80; NCCR: Sculpture Now, San Francisco Mus Mod Art, 79; Joshua Wedgwood Invitational, Philadelphia Mus Art, 80; Illusionism in Am, Los Angeles Co Mus Art, Los Angeles, 80; Reconstructions, San Jose Mus Art, 81; Klein Gallery, Chicago, 81 & 82; one-person show, Fresno Mus, 83; RAU Sculpture Court, Johannesburg, 83; Asn Gallery, Capetown, 83; Ree Schonlau Gallery, Omaha, 85; Arvada Ctr Arts & Humanities, Colo, 85. *Teaching:* Asst prof art, Univ Ky, Lexington, 70-74; prof art, San Jose State Univ, 74-; vis prof art, Notre Dame Univ, 72 & 76, Mills Col, Oakland, Calif, 77; artist-in-residence, Darwin Community Col, Australia, 80, Shefield Polytechnic, Eng, 81; vis artist, SAfrica, 82. *Awards:* Westinghouse res award, Koehler Mus, Purdue Univ, 73; Nat Endowment for Arts artist grant, 77; Lucy Stern fel, Mills Col, 78; Environmental Improvement Award of Distinction, Assoc Landscape Contractors Am, 85. *Bibliog:* Elsbeth Wood (auth), Handbuilding, McGraw Hill, 78; Harvey Brody (auth), Low Fire Ceramics, 80; Susan Peterson (auth), Modern ceramic concerns, 81. *Mem:* Nat Conf Educ Ceramic Art; Coll Art Asn; Am Crafts Coun. *Dealer:* Klein Gallery 356 Huron Chicago IL 60610. *Mailing Add:* 18404 Montevina Rd Los Gatos CA 95030-9105

MIDDLEMAN, RAOUL FINK
PAINTER
b Baltimore, Md, Apr 3, 1935. *Study:* Johns Hopkins Univ, BA, 55; Pa Acad Fine Arts, 59-61; Brooklyn Mus Art Sch, 61. *Work:* Nat Acad Design; resp in permanent collections at ABC Network, Baltimore Mus Art, Corcoran Gallery, Frye Mus Art, Johns Hopkins Hosp Nat Acad of Design, Metrop Mus Art, NY Pub Libr, Syracuse Univ, Towson Univ, Univ, Md. *Exhib:* Solo exhibs, Landscapes & Portraits of the Ardeche, Scott-McKennis Gallery, Richmond, Va, 80, Yale Norfolk Summer Sch, 80, Boston Univ, 81, Grimaldis Gallery, Baltimore, 81-84, 78, 79, 99 & 2001, Water Gap Art Gallery, Walpack Ctr, NJ, 82, William Capro Gallery, New Bedford, Mass, 83 & Swanston Fine Arts, Atlanta, 88, Umbrian Summer, Kouros Gallery, 2007, Pop to Plein Air, Grinaldis Gallery, 2007, Scraps of Self, Prince Georges Community Coll, 2010, City Limits, American Univ, Katzen Gallery, 2012; MB Modern, NY, 2000; Rodger LaPelle Galleries, Philadelphia, 2001, Bavarian Paintings, Murnau, Ger, 2001, Maryland Art Place, Baltimore, 2002; group exhibs, Nat Acad Design, 1990, Md Inst, 1989-90, Gaumann Cicchino Gallery, 1989, Ingber Gallery, 1989, Bendann Gallery, 1989, Swanston Fine Arts, 1988, Haus der Kunst, 1986, Kornbluth Gallery, 1985, Steven Scott Gallery, and others; Kouos Gallery, NY, 2004; Roger Lapelle Galleries, Philadelphia, Pa, 2005; Grimaldis Gallery, 2005. *Pos:* pres, Nat Acad Design, 1998-01. *Teaching:* Chmn painting dept, Md Inst Col Art, Baltimore, 75-78; resident dir, summer landscape painting prog, Md Inst Col Art, 81-83; vis critic, Vt Studio Sch Summer Prog, 85; act dir, Hoffberger Sch Grad Painting, Maryland Inst, 98-99. *Awards:* Pres, Nat Acad Design, NY. *Bibliog:* Gerrit Henri (auth), rev in Art News, 72; Pat Mainardi (auth), rev in Art in Am, 7/74; H O Beil (auth), Arts Mag, 5/85. *Mem:* Nat Acad. *Media:* Oil, Watercolor. *Dealer:* MB Modern Gallery 41 E 57th St New York NY 10022; C Grimaldis Gallery 523 N Charles St Baltimore MD 21201. *Mailing Add:* 943 N Calvert St Baltimore MD 21217

MIDDLETON, JOHN S
COLLECTOR
Study: Amherest Coll, 1977. *Pos:* Owner, McIntosh Inns, Bradford Holdings, and Double Play, Inc; co-owner, Philadelphia Phillies; bd trustees, Penn Med. *Awards:* named one of Top 200 Collectors, ARTNews Mag, 2011, 2013. *Collection:* 19th and 20th-century art .

MIECZKOWSKI, EDWIN
PAINTER
b Pittsburgh, Pa, Nov 26, 1929. *Study:* Cleveland Inst Art, BFA, 57; Carnegie Inst, MFA, 59. *Work:* Cleveland Mus Art; Robert Hull Fleming Mus, Vt. *Exhib:* Solo exhibs include Cleveland Inst Art, 65, Robert Hull Fleming Mus, 74, New Gallery, Cleveland, 74, Tyler Sch Art, Pa, 74, Mansfield Art Ctr, Ohio, 75, Ellen Myers Inc, NY, 76, Akron Art Inst, Ohio, 77, Tanglewood Downtown, NY, 78, Cleveland Ctr Contemp Art, 81, 85, 90, Kaber Gallery Ltd, NY, 82, Neo-Constructivism, Great Northern Corp Ctr, Ohio, 87, Brenda Kroos Gallery, Columbus, Ohio, 88, Scarab Gallery, Cleveland, 95, Visual Paradox: Transforming Perception, Lew Allen Contemp, Santa Fe, N Mex, 2006, 2007; group exhibs include Vibrations Eleven, Martha Jackson Gallery, NY, 64; The Responsive Eye, Mus Modern Art, NY, 65; Inst Contemp Art, London, England, 66; Second Arts Festival, Albright Knox Gallery, Buffalo, NY, 68; The Square in Painting, Am Federation Art, NY, 69; Grids, Inst Contemp Art, Univ Pa, 72; Materials and Techniques of 20th Century Artists, Cleveland Mus Art, 76; Construction and Color, Myers Fine Arts Gallery, State Univ NY, Plattsburgh, 78; Visual Logic II, Parsons Sch Design, NY, 80; Kaber Gallery Ltd, NY, 83; American Purism Since 1945, Marylyn Pearl Gallery, NY, 84; Eight Sculptors, Cleveland Ctr Contemp Art, 90; William Busta Gallery, Ohio, 97; Harmonic Forms on the Edge: Geometric Abstraction in Cleveland, Cleveland Fine Arts Found, Beck Ctr for Arts, 2001. *Mem:* Founding mem Anonima Group; Nat Organization Visual Artists, Cleveland. *Media:* Acrylic

MIEZAJS, DAINIS
PAINTER, INSTRUCTOR
b Kaucminde, Latvia, Mar 11, 1929. *Study:* Ont Coll of Art, 56. *Work:* Nat Gallery of Can, Ottawa, Ont; Art Gallery of Ont, Toronto; Mus Fine Arts, Montreal, Que; Art Gallery of Winnipeg, Man; Vancouver Art Gallery, BC. *Comn:* Series of 18 paintings, Trans-Can Pipeline, Toronto, Ont, 71. *Exhib:* Ann Can Soc of Painters in Watercolors, 61-78; Can Painters in Watercolor & Am Watercolor Soc Exchange Show, 73; Can Painters in Watercolor & Watercolor Soc of Japan, 77. *Collection Arranged:* Across Canada in Watercolor, Art Gallery of Ont, 69-71. *Teaching:* Instr drawing & painting, Ont Col of Art, Toronto, 60-, chmn fine art, 83-; dir landscape, Madawaska Valley Sch Art, Maynooth, Ont, 65-. *Awards:* Merit Award, Can Soc of Painters in Watercolor Ann; Purchase Awards, Can Soc of Painters in Watercolor. *Bibliog:* F Barwick (auth), Pictures from the Douglas Duncan Collection, Univ Toronto Press, 75. *Mem:* Can Painters in Watercolor (dir, 65-67); Latvia Soc Artists (vpres, 62-64). *Media:* Watercolor, Tempera. *Mailing Add:* c/o General Delivery Maynooth ON K0L 2S0 Canada

MIGLIACCIO, ANTHONY J
PAINTER, EDUCATOR
b Long Branch, NJ, Jan 24, 1948. *Study:* Trenton State Col, BA (indust ed & tech), 1970; Kean Univ, MA (art educ), 1975. *Work:* EPA Bldg, Washington, DC; Georgian Ct Univ, Lakewood, NJ. *Exhib:* Nat Arts Club State Exhib, 77; NJ Signature Artist Exhib, Noyes Mus; MCAC State Juried Show, Monmouth Mus, Lincroft, NJ, 2005-2009; Audubon Artists 64th Ann Nat Juried Exhibition, Salmagundi Club, NY, 2006-2009; Nat Juried Exhib, Painters & Sculptors Soc, NY; Solo exhib, Frederick Gallery, Allenhurst, NJ, 2005, Georgian Ct Univ, 2010, Noyes/Seaview Galloway, NJ, 2011. *Pos:* former pres, Art Administrators NJ, 97; former pres, Art Educators NJ, 98; delegate, NJ Eastern Regin Assembly, Nat Art Education Asn, 98; bd dirs, NJ Sch Arts, 99-2001; chm, NJ Core Curric Content Studies, Vis & Performing Arts, 2000; former pres, Alliance Arts Education, NJ, 2000. *Teaching:* art instr, Monmouth Regional High Sch, Tinton Falls, NJ, 70-82; printmaking instr, Monmouth Univ, W Long Branch, NJ, 86-88; supv, Vis Info Servs, Fort Monmouth, NJ, 88-91; art & music supv, Montville Pub Schs, NJ, 91-92; art & music supv, East Brunswick Pub Schs, NJ, 92-98; dir vis & performing arts, Red Bank Regional High Sch, Little Silver, NJ, 98-. *Awards:* Geraldine R Dodge Found Painting Fel, 2002; Award for Oils, NY Nat Juried Show, Audubon Artists, 2008. *Mem:* Plein Air Painters, Jersey Coast; Monmouth Co Arts Coun; Noyes Mus (NJ signature mem); Guild of Creative Art (NJ exhib artist mem); Audubon Artists (NY exhib artist mem). *Media:* Landscape Oil Painting. *Dealer:* Veranda Fine Art & Gift Gallery Fair Haven NJ 07704; Frederick Gallery 3rd Ave Spring Lakes NJ 07762; Stillwell House Art & Antiques Manalapan NJ 07726. *Mailing Add:* 580 Patten Ave Apt # 41 Long Branch NJ 07740

MIGNOSA, SANTO
CERAMIST, SCULPTOR
b Siracusa, Italy, Nov 14, 1934; Can citizen. *Study:* Scuola d'Arte, Italy, Cert; Inst Statale d'Arte Firenze, Italy, Dipl: NY State Univ Alfred, MFA. *Work:* Univ Calgary Art Gallery, Can; Govt of Alta Art Found, Can; Govt of Tenn Ceramic Collection; Pall Mall of Can Art Collection; Art Centrum, Prague, Czech. *Exhib:* Smithsonian Inst, Washington, DC; Int Ceramic Exhib, Calgary, 73, Memphis Acad Art, 73; Tenn Int Ceramic Exhib, 73; Alta Govt Exhib, Atlanta, Ga, 75, Japan Tour, 79; Exhib of Miniatures Int Acad Ceramics, Kyoto & Tokyo, Japan, 80-81. *Collection Arranged:* Int Ceramic 73, Calgary, Can; Nat Ceramic 76, Calgary, Can. *Pos:* Co-chmn, Nat Ceramic Exhib, Calgary, Can, 75-76; Co-founder & vpres, Alta Potters, Asn, formerly; Co-founder, W Coast Clay Asn, Vancouver, BC, 93; bd dir & exhib comt & chmn, Seymour Art Gallery, North Vancouver, 93-94; dir, sculptor Soc BC, 94. *Teaching:* Instr ceramics & sculpture, Kootenay Sch of Art, Nelson, BC, 60-68; assoc prof ceramics, Univ Calgary, Alta, Can, 69-89 (ret). *Awards:* Gold Medal, Int Ceramic Exhib, Ostend, 58, Silver Medal, Prague, 61 & Second Prize Ex-Aequo, Calgary, 73, Int Acad Ceramics; Achievement Awards, Gov Alberta, 70 & 72. *Bibliog:* Al Riegger (auth), Featured Artist, Ceramic Mo, 63; article in, La Revue Mod des Arts et de la Vie, 67. *Mem:* Alta Potters' Asn (vpres, 70-71); Int Acad Ceramics, Geneva, Switz (coun mem). *Media:* Clay. *Mailing Add:* 571 N Dollarton Hwy North Vancouver BC V7G 1N3 Canada

MIHAESCO, EUGENE
PAINTER, ILLUSTRATOR
b Bucharest, Romania, Aug 24, 1937; Switz citizen. *Study:* Fine Art Inst, Bucharest, BA, 59. *Work:* Cooper-Hewitt Mus, NY; Republic's Art Mus, Bucharest, Romania; Musee des Arts, Decoratifs de la Ville, Lausanne, Switz. *Exhib:* Bienal Sao Paulo, Sao-Paulo Mus, Brazil, 63; Art of the Times, Musee des Arts Decoratifs, Louvre, Paris, France; The Statue of Liberty, Ctr Pompidou, Beaubourg, Paris, France, 76. *Teaching:* Assoc prof illus, Pratt Inst, 81-82. *Awards:* Best Illus, 1977 Show, Am Inst Graphic Arts; Best Cover, News Paper Guild, 83; Gold Medal, Ann Show, Art Dirs Club, NY, 85. *Bibliog:* Deborah Phillips (auth), Eugene Mihaesco, Arts News, No 5, 81; Steven Heller (auth), Eugene Mihaesco, Arts, No 10, Vol 58, 84 & Graphis, No 238, 85. *Media:* Pastel; Pen & Ink. *Publ:* Ed artist, NY Times, 71-86; illusr, 12 covers, Time Inc, 78-86; 57 covers, New Yorker Mag, 72-86. *Mailing Add:* 25 Tudor City Pl No 1423 New York NY 10017-6819

MIHICH, VELIZAR See Vasa

MIK, AERNOUT
VIDEO ARTIST, INSTALLATION SCULPTOR
b Groningen, Netherlands, 1962. *Study:* Acad Minerva, Groningen, 1983-88; Ateliers '63, Haarlem, Netherlands, 1987-88. *Exhib:* Solo exhibs include Witte de With, Rotterdam, 1990, Deweer Art Gallery, Belgium, 1992, 1995, Dutch Pavillion, Venice Biennale, 1997, 2007, Mus Ludwig, Cologne, 1999, 2004, Inst Contemp Art, London, 2000, Living Art Mus, Reykjavik, 2002, The Project, LA, 2003, Cleveland Mus Art, 2003, The Project, New York, 2004, Haus der Kunst, Munich, 2004, Ctr Contemp Image, Geneva, 2005, New Mus, New York, 2005, Hammer Mus, LA, 2006; group exhibs include Still Moving, Nat Mus Mod Art, Kyoto, 2000; The People's Art, Witte de With, Rotterdam, 2001; Loop-Alles auf Anfang, PS1 Contemp Art Ctr, New York, 2001; Post-Nature, Venice Biennale, 2001; Ce Qui Arrive, Foundation Cartier, Paris, 2002; This Much is Certain, Royal Coll Art, London, 2004; Suburban House Kit, Deitch Projects, New York, 2004; Fade In, Contemp Arts Mus, Houston, 2004; Art Unlimited, Art Basel, Switzerland, 2006. *Awards:* Kunstverein Hannover Prize, 1993; Sandbergprijs, Amsterdams Founds voor de Kunst, 1998; Heininkenprize, Amsterdam, 2002. *Dealer:* Deweer Art Gallery Tiegemstraat 6A B-8553 Otegem Belgium ; Carlier Gebauer Markgrafenstrasse 67 D-10969 Berlin Germany

MIKUS, ELEANORE
PAINTER
b Detroit, Mich, July 25, 1927. *Study:* Art Students League; study in Cent Europe; Univ Denver, BFA & MA. *Work:* Mus Mod Art, Whitney Mus Am Art, NY; Victoria & Albert Mus, London; Los Angeles Co Mus Art; Indianapolis Mus Art, Ind; Nat Gallery Art, Washington, DC; Honolulu Acad Arts, Honolulu, Hawaii; Univ Ariz, Tucson, Ariz; Norton Smith Mus, Pasadena, Calif; and others; Currier Mus Art. *Exhib:* Solo Exhibs: Pietrantonia Gallery, 60, Pace Gallery, 63-65 Okharris Gallery, NY, 70-74; Claudia Carr, NY, 98 & 2000; Mitchel Algus, NY, 98 & 2003; Drawing Center, NY, 2006-2007; Marlborough, NY, 2008; Arnot Art Mus, Elmira, NY, 2009; Group Exhibs: Mus Modern Art, NY, 1974; Los Angeles County Mus, 1984; Johnson Mus, Ithaca, NY, 1979-1994, & 1983; Tucson Mus Art, 2006; Blanton Mus, Austin, Tex, 2008; Zentral Bibliothek of Zurich, Switzerland, 2010; Rugby Art Gallery & Mus, Warwickshire, Eng, 2011. *Teaching:* Asst prof painting, Monmouth Col, 66-70; vis lectr painting, Cooper Union, 70-72; lectr painting, Cent Sch Art & Design, London, Eng, 73-77; assoc prof, Cornell Univ, 79-92, prof art, 92, emer prof, 94-; prof, Rome Prog, 89; prof emeritus, Cornell Univ, NY. *Awards:* Guggenheim Fellow, 66-67; Tamarind Fel in Lithogrpahy, 68; McDonell Fel in Painting, 69; Research Grant, Cornell Univ, 2001; Yaddo Grant in Drawing/Painting, 2004. *Bibliog:* Mark Daniel Cohen (auth), The Critical State of Visual Art in NY Paintings 1960's-1990's, Review Mag,; Eleanor Heartney (auth), Art in America, 1999; Robert Ayers (auth), Eleanore Mikus at the Drawing center, Nov-Feb 2007. *Mem:* Nat Asn Women Artists. *Media:* Oil, Paper Folds, Acrylic. *Specialty:* Contemporary art. *Interests:* Music, reading, gardening, history. *Publ:* Eleanore Mikus (auth), Shadows of the Real, Hobbs/Bernstock, Groton House, Itaca, in assoc with Wash Univ Press, Seattle & London, 91; coauth with Luis Camnitzer, The Drawing Papers #65 from Shell to Skin. *Dealer:* Marlborough Gallery 40 W 57th NYC 10019

MILAN, WARDELL, II
PHOTOGRAPHER
b Knoxville, Tenn, 1978. *Study:* Univ Tenn, BFA (Photog & Painting), 2001; Yale Univ, MFA (Photography), 2004. *Work:* Mus Mod Art, New York; Whitney Mus Am Art, New York; Studio Mus Harlem, New York. *Exhib:* Solo exhibs include Taxter & Spengemann Gallery, New York, 2005, 2008, Samson Proj, Boston, 2006, Franklin Arts Works, Minneapolis, 2008; Group exhibs include Homemade World, Reconstructed Images in Photograph, Rush Arts Gallery, New York, 2004; Notorious Impropriety, Samson Proj, Boston, 2004; Greater New York, PS 1 Contemp Art Ctr, New York, 2005; Being There, Cuchifritos, New York, 2005; Frequency, Studio Mus Harlem, New York, 2005, Midnight's Daydream, 2007; 25 Bold Moves, House of Campari, New York, 2006; Queens Int, Queens Mus Art, New York, 2006. *Awards:* Louis Comfort Tiffany Found Grants, 2008

MILANT, JEAN ROBERT
DEALER
b Milwaukee, Wis, Dec 27, 1943. *Study:* Univ Wis, Milwaukee, BA & BFA, 66; Tamarind Lithography Workshop, Los Angeles, 69, Univ NMex, Albuquerque, MA, 70;. *Work:* Norton Simon Mus; Amon Carter Mus. *Exhib:* No Shoes on the Carpet, Cirrus Gallery, 2009. *Pos:* Dir & owner, Cirrus Ed Ltd, 70- & Cirrus Gallery Ltd, 70-; mem bd, Los Angeles Inst Contemp Art, 74-76; vpres, Los Angeles Visual Arts & Grunwald Ctr, UCLA, 2003-. *Teaching:* Instr UC Long Beach, 71-. *Awards:* Tamarind Master Printer, 69. *Bibliog:* Bruce Davis (auth), Made in LA the Prints of Cirrus, Lacma; Proof: The Rise of Printmakers in S Calif, Getty Pub. *Mem:* LACMA; MOCA; LACE; MOMA; Grunwald Ctr. *Specialty:* Contemporary painting, sculpture, performance, environments of Southern California artists; publisher of lithographs and screenprints of noted California artists. *Publ:* Ed, Artists/Prints 76-77, Contemp Art Publ Inc, 78. *Mailing Add:* 542 S Alameda St Los Angeles CA 90013

MILBOURN, PATRICK D
PAINTER, ILLUSTRATOR, PORTRAIT PAINTER
b Omaha, NE, Sept 19, 1950. *Study:* Self taught; Studied Aaron Shikler-David Levine painting group (mem), 1979-. *Comn:* Painting (feature articles), Time Mag, New Yorker, Sports Illus, Entertainment Weekly, House & Garden, Forbes, NY Mag, Bus Week, 1978-2006; Cover art (40 murder mystery novels), Putnam, Ballantine, Fawcett & Random House Publs, 1990-2002; Beaux Arts Ball posters, Green Co Coun on Arts, 1999-2006; portrait, Dir Soc Illustrators, NY, 2002; many other portrait comns, 1980-. *Exhib:* Soc illusrs, NY, 1986, 1995; Nat Acad Design (juried), 1990, 1992; Salmagundi Club (juried), NY, 1992, 1993, 1995; Pastel Soc Am, NY, 1996, 1997,1999, 2001; Am Acad Arts & Letters (juried), NY, 1998; Butler Inst Am Art, 2010; Solo exhib, Guggenheim Pavilion, NY, 2015. *Teaching:* masters art lecture, Syracuse Univ. *Awards:* Master Pastelist, Pastel Soc Am, Nat Arts Club, NY, 94; Pastel Award, 21st Ann Juried Exhib, Salmagundi Club, 1998; Balin Award, 24th Ann Juried Exhib, Salmgundi Club, 2000; Strathmore Paper Award, 29th Ann Juried Exhib, Pastel Soc Am, 2001; and many more. *Bibliog:* Best of Pastel, Quarry Books of Rockport Publs, Gloucester, Mass, 1998; Best of Portrait Painting, North Light Books, F&W Publs, Cincinnati, Ohio, 1998; Best of Watercolor-Vol 3, North Light Books F&W Publs, Cincinnati, Ohio, 1999; Watercolor Expressions, Quarry Publs, Rockport Publ, Gloucester, Mass, 2000; Chronogram Magazine of Art, Culture & Spirit, Kingston, NY, 12/2005, cover art; Almanac Weekly, Ulster Publ, Kingston, NY, 10/27/2005; Art Times Journal, CSS Publ Inc, Patrick Milbourn at the M Gallery, 6/2006. *Mem:* Pastel Soc Am (signature mem); Soc of Illusrs; Green Co Coun on the Arts; Thomas Cole Nat Hist Site; Olana Frederick Church Nat Hist Site. *Media:* Acrylic, Oil, Pastel, Miscellaneous Media. *Specialty:* landscape painting, portrait painting. *Collection:* illustration art from 1870s to 1950. *Publ:* many publ, 93-2003. *Dealer:* M Gallery Catskill NY 12414. *Mailing Add:* 27 Franklin St Catskill NY 12414

MILES, CHRISTINE M
MUSEUM DIRECTOR, ADMINISTRATOR
b Madison, Ind, Mar 2, 1951. *Study:* Boston Univ, BA (fine arts), 73, George Washington Univ, MA, 82, Mus Mgt Inst, Berkeley, 85. *Pos:* Curatorial asst, Mus City New York, 73-75; dir, Mus Gallery, South St Seaport Mus, New York, 75-77, Fraunces Tavern Mus, New York, 80-86 & Albany Inst Hist & Art, New York, 86-. *Mem:* Am Asn Mus; Fedn Hist Serv (bd mem, 87-); Gallery Asn NY State (bd mem, 88-); Mus Asn NY. *Mailing Add:* Albany Inst History & Art 125 Washington Ave Albany NY 12210-2296

MILES, ELLEN GROSS
HISTORIAN, CURATOR
b New York, NY, July 28, 1941. *Study:* Bryn Mawr Col, BA, 64; Winterthur Summer Inst, 67; Yale Univ Grad Sch, MPh, 70 & PhD, 76. *Pos:* Pub relations asst & registr, Corcoran Gallery Art, Washington, DC, 64-66; asst to dir, Nat Portrait Gallery, Washington, DC, 71-77, assoc cur, 77-84, cur, dept painting & sculpture 84-94 & chair dept painting & sculpture, 94-2010, emeritus cur, 2010-. *Mem:* Coll Art Asn; Asn Historians Am Art; Omohundro Inst. *Res:* Eighteenth and nineteenth century American portrait painting; profile portraits. *Publ:* coauth (with Richard H Saunders), American Colonial Portraits: 1700-1776, Smithsonian Press, 87; auth, Saint-Memin and the Neoclassical Profile Portrait, Smithsonian Press, 94; auth, American Paintings of the Eighteenth Century, Nat Gallery Art/Oxford Univ Press, 95; coauth (with Carrie Rebora Barratt), Gilbert Stuart, Metrop Mus Art, 2004; auth, George & Martha Washington, Portraits from the Presidential Years, Univ Press of Va, 99

MILES, SHEILA LEE
PAINTER, INSTRUCTOR
b Indianapolis, Ind, Aug 10, 1952. *Study:* Purdue Univ, West Lafayette, Ind, BA, 73, MA (painting), MA (drawing), 74; Hans Hoffman Sch Art, Provincetown, Mass, 74. *Work:* Purdue Univ, West Lafayette, Ind; Yellowstone Art Mus, Billings, Mont; Hockaday Ctr Arts, Kalispell, Mont; Mus Fine Art, Univ Mont, Missoula; Ray

Graham Collection, Albuquerque, NMex; Deaconness Hosp, Billings, Mont; Fed Reserv Bank, Minneapolis. *Comn:* Missoula Int Airport, Mont; Missoula in Motion, 5 paintings, Mssoula; Miriam Sample Collection, Susan O'Conner, Don Todd, Evelyn Wertheim, Ossie Abrams & David Orser; Ray Graham Coll, Albuquerque, NMex. *Exhib:* Provinctown Art Asn & Mus, Mass, 74-78; Solo exhibs, Custer Co Art Ctr, Miles City, 84, Yellowstone Art Ctr (with catalog), Billings, 84, 99, Missoula Mus Arts, 86, 2003 & Paris Gibson Sq, Great Falls, 86, Mont; Coal Tax Collections, Yellowstone Art Ctr, Billings, Mont, 86; Owings-Dewey Fine Art, Santa Fe, NMex, 86, 87 & 88; retrospective (with catalog), Univ Mont, Missoula. *Collection Arranged:* Edwin Dickinson, 76; Richard Diebenkorn, 89-90; Beth Lo, 90; Freeman Butts 90. *Pos:* Gallery dir, Provincetown Art Asn & Mus, 75-77 & Mont State Univ, 85-86; artist-in-residence, Mont Arts Coun-Custer Co Art Ctr, 83-84; cur, Yellowstone Art Mus, 86-90; dir exhibs, Univ Montana Mus Art & Cult, Mont, 99-2000. *Teaching:* Instr drawing & painting, Mont State Univ, Billings, 80-82 & 85; instr painting, Mont State Univ, Bozeman, 85-86, Univ Mont, Missoula, 92-97; pvt instr art; chair visual arts, Desert Acad, Santa Fe, NMex, 2007-. *Awards:* Individual Artists Fel, Mont Arts Coun, 84; Purchase Award, Coal tax grant, Yellowstone Art Ctr, Mont Arts Coun, 84; Grant, Adolph and Esther Gottlieb Found, 1999. *Bibliog:* Chris Meyers (auth), Sheila Miles, Billings Gazette, 80-2002; Dan Rubey (auth), Artweek, San Francisco, Calif, 84; various auths, The Missoulian, Missoula, Mont, 86, 92-2005; Mus of Art & culture, UM, Simone Ellis, auth. *Mem:* Arts Advocacy. *Media:* Oil, mixed media, collage. *Interests:* Painting, drawing, printmaking, clay. *Mailing Add:* 5 Sunset Rd Santa Fe NM 87507

MILEWICZ, RON
PAINTER
b Brooklyn, NY. *Study:* Cornell Univ, BA (art hist, Sampson Fine Arts Prize), 1983; Columbia Univ, MArchit (William Kinnes Traveling Fel), 1986; NY Studio Sch, 1990-95. *Exhib:* Solo exhibs include Washington Art Asn, Conn, 1999, Hartell Gallery, Cornell Univ, 2000, George Billis Gallery, New York, 2002, 2003 & 2005; group exhibs include Bowery Gallery, New York, 1995; Small Works, 80 Washington Sq East Galleries, New York, 1998 & 2000; Vertigo: from the top of the World Trade Center, NY Studio Sch, New York, 1998, On the City: Urban Realities & Fantasies, 2000, Beckoning Vision: Ann Alumni Exhib, 2001, The Continuous Mark, 2005; Selections, Albright-Knox Mus, Buffalo, 2003; Inaugural Exhib, George Billis Gallery, New York, 2004, Industrial Beauty, 2004; New York Night, Elizabeth Harris Gallery, New York, 2004; Ann Invitational Exhib Contemp Art, Nat Acad Mus, New York, 2008. *Teaching:* NY Studio Sch, New York. *Awards:* Speyer Found Scholar, NY Studio Sch, 1992-93, Charles H Revson Found Fel, 1994, Vera List Endowment Scholar, 1994 & Hohenbert Travel Grant, 1994; Cornell Coun Arts Grant, 1999. *Dealer:* George Billis Gallery 511 W 25th St Ground Fl New York NY 10001. *Mailing Add:* 3752 85th St Jackson Heights NY 11372

MILEY, LES
CERAMIST, SCULPTOR
b Petersburg, Ind, Nov 1, 1934. *Study:* Purdue Univ, ceramics with Bill Farrell; Ind State Univ, BA & MA; Southern Ill Univ, with Nicholas Vergette & Brent Kington, MFA. *Work:* Axner Pottery Inc, Oviedo, Fla; Sheldon Swope Mus, Terre Haute, Ind; NY Stock Exchange, NY; Evansville Mus Arts & Sciences, Inc; Jane B Owen Collection, Houston, Tex & New Harmony, Ind; Gov Daniels Collection, Gov Mansion, Ind, 2007; Am Mus Ceramic Art, Pomona, Calif; Univ Evansville. *Comn:* Citizen's Bank, Evansville, Ind, 88; Archit ceramics, Robert L Blaffer Found New Harmony, Ind, 2005; Wall Plates, Old Nat Bank, Ind, 2005, Sculptures. *Exhib:* Solo exhibs, Johnson Center Fine Arts, Franklin Coll, Ind, 2007, Bauer-Suhrheinrich Gallery, Evansville, Ind, 2012, Melvin Peterson Gallery, Univ Evansville, 2012; Nat Tureen Exhib, R Bahr Gallery, New Albany, Ind, 99; Dinner Works, Louisville Visual Art Asn, 2000; The Regionalists, Mus Art, Owensboro, Ky, 2001; Capitol Arts Alliance Invitational, Bowling Green, Ky, 2002; 21st Century Ceramics Invitational Columbus, Ohio, 2004; Am Ceramic Soc Invitational Indianapolis, Ind, 2004; AMACO/BRENT NCECA Invitational Indianapolis, Ind, 2004; Color in Music, Ohio Valley Art League, Henderson, Ky, 2008; Art of the Contemp Craftsman, St Francis Coll, Ft Wayne, Ind, 2008; Hand of the Potter, Ella Sharp Mus, Jackson, Mich, 2008; Masters of Art, Hoosier Salon Gallery, Ind, 2008; Making it in the Midwest-Those Who Stayed, Ind State Mus, 2009; Owensboro Mus Art Invitational, Owensboro, Ky, 2009. *Pos:* Dir, Blafter Foundation ceramic workshop, New Harmony, Ind, 67-. *Teaching:* Prof art, Univ Evansville, 61-, chmn dept, 65-66 & 69-99. *Awards:* Purchase Award, 44th Wabash Valley Art Exhib, Sheldon Swope Mus, 86; Artist of Yr, SW Ind Arts Coun, 96; Purchase Award, 35th Mid-States Craft Exhib, Evansville Mus, 97. *Bibliog:* Thomas Schafer (auth), Pottery Decoration, 75 & Jack Troy (auth), Salt-Glazed Ceramics, 77, Watson-Guptill; R Burkett (auth), Glen Nelson's Ceramics, A Potters Handbook, 12/90; Phil Rogers (auth), Ash Glazes, 91; Robin Hopper & Daniel Rhodes (auths), Clay and Glazes for the Potter, 2000; Robin Hopper (auth) Making Marks, 2004. *Mem:* Nat Coun Educ Ceramic Arts; Hoosier Salon, Ind. *Media:* Clay, Watercolor. *Mailing Add:* 1212 S Plaza Dr Evansville IN 47715-5145

MILEY, RANDOLPH BENTON
EDUCATOR, ADMINISTRATOR, PAPERMAKING
Study: Hinds Community Col, AA (Art), 1975; Univ Southern Mississippi, BFA (Art Edu), 1977; Mississippi Col, MEd (Art Edu), 1982; Fla State Univ, PhD (Art Edu), 1994. *Exhib:* featured in several exhibitions 1973-2004. *Collection Arranged:* Permanent collections include Hinds Community Col, Mississippi Commissioner of Agriculture, Vision Clinic of Vicksburg, Mississippi, Cassino's Florist of Vicksburg, Mississippi, Deposit Guaranty Nat Bank of Vicksburg and Greenville, Mississippi, Coca-Cola Co of Vicksburg, & Merchant's Nat Bank of Vicksburg. *Pos:* Bd dir Louisiana Art Edu Asn, 1995-99, Northeast Louisiana Arts Coun, 1996-99, Friends of the Monroe Civic Theatre, 1997-99, Mississippi Alliance for Arts in Edu, 2003-06 (also higher edu com chair, 2003-06). *Teaching:* Student teaching, Rowan Junior High Sch, Jackson, Mississippi, 1977; secondary art teacher, Brinkley Junior High Sch, Jackson, 1977-78, art instructor, Hinds Community Col, Vicksburg, Mississippi, 1978-83; secondary art teacher, Keystone Heights Senior High Sch, Fla, 1986-89; graduate teaching asst in art edu, department of art edu, Fla State Univ, 1989-90; asst prof art, art edu, Northeast Louisiana Univ, 1990-96, assoc prof art, art edu, 1996-99, art dir Very Special Arts Festival, 1992-; assoc prof, department of art, Mississippi Col, 1999-2003, chair, 1999-, prof 2003-. *Awards:* Mississippi Art Edu Asn/Nat Art Edu Asn Bill Poirier Outstanding Art Educator of the Yr, 1985, 2000; Appreciation award, Ouachita Christian Sch, 1993; Louisiana Art Edu Asn Art Educator of the Yr for Higher Edu, 1994; Louisiana Roster Art, 1998; Man and Youth award, Boys & Girls Club of West Monroe, 1999; Outstanding Contributions Within the Profession, Louisiana Art Edu Asn, 1999, Mississippi Art Edu Asn Higher Edu Division Art Educator of the Yr, 2005, nat Art Edu Asn, Newsletter Editor award, 2006. *Mem:* Mississippi Art Edu Asn, Pres-elect, 1982-84, pres 1984-86, newsletter editor, 2004-06; mem Warren Country Teachers Organization, Fla Art Edu Asn, Fla Inst for Art Edu, Louisiana Alliance for Art in Edu, Vicksburg Art Asn, Louisiana Art Edu Asn, Twin City Art Found, Nat Art Edu Asn. *Mailing Add:* Mississippi Col Department of Art PO Box 4020 Aven 410A Clinton MS 39058

MILHOAN, RANDALL BELL
PAINTER, DESIGNER
b Overton, Nebr, Feb 24, 1944. *Study:* Kearney State Teachers Col, 64; Univ Nebr, Lincoln, BFA, 68; Univ Calif, Santa Barbara, Calif Regents Scholar, 70; Mont State Univ, 77; Arizona Western Col, 84-93. *Work:* Sheldon Mem Gallery, Lincoln, Nebr; Joslyn Mus, Omaha, Nebr; San Antonio Art Inst, Tex. *Comn:* Mural, Colo Arts Coun, Vail, 85; murals, Vail & Beaver Creek, Colo; mural, Town of Vail, Colo, 94; mural, Phillips '66, 96. *Exhib:* Joan Robey Gallery, Denver, Colo, 88; Cabrillo Gallery, Santa Cruz, Calif, 88; J Cotter Gallery, Vail, Colo, 88; Milhoan Studios, Vail, Colo; Santa Fe Pottery, Denver, 96; and others. *Collection Arranged:* Santa Fe Festival of Arts, NMex, 81; Colo Artists, Craftsman Asn Ann, Arvada, Colo, 85; Beaver Creek Arts Festival, 92. *Pos:* Dir, Colo Mountain Col, 70-84; founder & dir, Summervail Workshop for Art & Critical Studies, 71-85, pres & exec dir, Summervail Workshop Found, Inc, 84-85; dean, San Antonio Art Inst, 85-86; vpres, Int Marketing & Media, 86-88; owner/designer & pres, Milhoan Studios, Vail, Colo, 89-; exec dir, Vail Arts Coun, 93; Chm, Visioning Committee, Minturn, Colo, 2003-. *Teaching:* Instr advan studies & spec proj painting, Colo Mountain Col, Vail, 70-85; instr 2-dimensional studies, San Antonio Art Inst, 85-86. *Awards:* Purchase Award, Tenth Midwest Biennial, 68; Purchase Award, Crossroads Ctr, 94. *Bibliog:* Mark Huffman (auth), Milhoan's contribution to the local CMC, Vail Trail, 2/24/84; Irene Clurman (auth), Artists, teachers, converge at Vail workshop, Rocky Mountain News, 7/29/84; Paul Soderberg (auth), Little towns, Art-Talk, 8-9/91. *Mem:* Coll Art Asn Am; Vail Valley Arts Coun; Art Pub Places (bd mem); Yuma Symp (adv bd). *Media:* Acrylic, Oil. *Specialty:* Contemp AM Paintings & Am Folk & Primitive Art. *Collection:* Contemporary American fine arts and crafts; primitive toys; masks from around the world. *Publ:* The American Painting Collection of the Sheldon Memorial Art Gallery. *Dealer:* J Cotter Gallery PO Box 385 Vail CO 81658. *Mailing Add:* 483 E Gore Creek Dr PO Box 1114 Vail CO 81658

MILLARD, CHARLES WARREN, III
DIRECTOR, WRITER
b Elizabeth, NJ, 1932. *Study:* Princeton Univ, BA; Harvard Univ, MA & PhD. *Pos:* Asst dir, Dumbarton Oaks, 64-66; dir, Washington Gallery Mod Art, 66-67; cur 19th century European art, Los Angeles Co Mus Art, 71-74; art ed, Hudson Rev, 72-87; chief cur, Hirshhorn Mus & Sculpture Garden, 74-86; dir, Ackland Art Mus, NC, 86-93. *Teaching:* Adj prof art hist, Johns Hopkins Univ, 82-86 & Univ NC Chapel Hill, 86-93. *Mem:* Assn Art Mus Directors (AAMD). *Res:* Nineteenth century French sculpture, particularly Degas and Preault; various topics in modern painting and sculpture. *Publ:* Auth, Sculpture of Edgar Degas, Princeton Univ, 76; and many other articles & rev in var periodicals, including Hudson Review, Jour Aesthetics and Art Criticism, others; Auguste Préault: Sculpteur Romantique 1809-1879, Gallimard, 97. *Mailing Add:* 444 Cedar Club Cir Chapel Hill NC 27517

MILLEA, TOM (THOMAS) FRANCIS
PHOTOGRAPHER
b Bridgeport, Conn, Sept 30, 1944. *Study:* Univ Western Conn, BA, 66; studied with Paul Caponigro & H Jonathon Greenwald, 67-73. *Work:* Mus Mod Art, NY; Victoria & Albert Mus, London, Eng; Ctr Creative Photog, Univ Ariz, Tucson; Oakland Mus; Philadelphia Mus Art; Australian National Gallery, Canberra; New Zealand National Mus, Wellington; and many others. *Exhib:* Solo exhibs, Friends Photog, Carmel, Calif, 78, DeSaisset Art Mus, Santa Clara, Calif, 80, Arco Ctr Arts, Los Angeles, 80, Camden Arts Ctr, London, 81, Galerie au Poisson Rouge, Praz, Switz, 81, Ctr Creative Photog, Tucson, 82 & The Malone Gallery, Rochester, NY, 86; New Orleans Mus Art, 84; Light Gallery, NY, 84; The Weston Gallery, Inc, Carmel, Calif, 84; Monterey Peninsula Mus Art, 85; The Platinum Print, NJ State Mus, Trenton, 86; The Western Landscape (traveling), Int Ctr Photog, NY, 86; Polaroid Int Collection Exhib, 86; and many others. *Pos:* Cinematographer, Robert Fulton Co, Danbury, Conn, 68; photographer, United Aircraft, Sikorsky, Stratford, Conn, 68-69. *Teaching:* Instructor & guest lecturer at many universities, workshops and galleries, 75-84. *Awards:* Ruttenberg Grant, 82 & Publ Workshop Grant, 83, Friends Photog; Polaroid Grant, 85. *Bibliog:* John Hafey & Tom Shillea (auths), The Platinum Print, Rochester Inst Technol, 80; interview, New Pictorialist Soc, 83; Alan Plone (auth), The Life and Work of Tom Millea, Vis Art Films Inc, 84; rev, Rochester City Newspaper & Democrat & Chronicle, Rochester, NY, 12/85. *Mem:* Friends Photog; Soc Photog Educ. *Media:* Platinum, Palladium. *Publ:* Auth, The Technique of Platinum and Palladium, Platinum Workshops, 76; Death Valley Photographs (poster), Sunlight Graphics, 83. *Dealer:* Light Gallery 724 Fifth Ave New York NY; Weston Gallery Carmel CA. *Mailing Add:* c/o Winfield Gallery PO Box 7393 Carmel CA 93921

MILLER, ANELLE
DIRECTOR, ILLUSTRATOR
Study: Parsons Sch Design, grad (illustration and design). *Pos:* Asst art dir Aramis, Estee Lauder Companies, 1978, head creative team Orgins, formerly; exec dir, Soc of Illustrators, NY, currently; ptnr, Orginal Women. *Mem:* Friends of Materials for the Arts; Friends of Art and Design (bd mem). *Mailing Add:* Society of Illustrators 128 E 63rd St New York NY 10065

MILLER, ARTHUR GREEN
EDUCATOR, HISTORIAN
b New York, NY, May 19, 1942. *Study:* Colby College, Dept Art, 1964; Skowhegan Sch Painting & Sculpture, 1964, Harvard Univ, PhD, 69. *Collection Arranged:* Maya Rulers of Time (auth catalog), Tikal Architectural Sculpture, Univ Mus, Univ Pa, 86. *Pos:* Dir, Maya Art prog, Univ Mus, Univ Pa, 79-82; dir of studies, Ecole des Hautes Etudes, Paris, 88-. *Teaching:* Instr, asst prof art hist, Yale Univ, 68-73; prof, Latin Am art hist & archeology, Univ Md, Coll Park, 83-2003. *Awards:* Fulbright scholar, Ecole du Louvre, Paris, 64-65; fel Guggenheim Found, 73-74; Centennial Prize, Soc for Am Archaeol, Paris, 74; Grants, Nat Endowment Arts, 79, Nat Endowment Humanities 89-92; Disting Univ Scholar, Univ Md, 99. *Bibliog:* Esther Pasztory (auth), Mural painting of Teotihuacan J, Soc of Archit Hist, ArtBulletin, 74; Clemency Coggins (auth), On the Edge of the Sea, Am Antiquity, 83; William Fash (auth), Maya Rulers of Time, Am Antiquity, 88. *Mem:* Coll Art Asn; Soc for Am Archaeology. *Res:* Art history and archeology of pre-hispanic and early colonial Latin American; interaction between image and text communication systems. *Publ:* Auth, The Mural Painting of Teotihuacan Mexico, Dumbarton Oaks, 73; ed, The Codex Nuttall: A Picture Manuscript from Ancient Mexico, Dover Publ, 75; auth, On the Edge of the Sea, Dumbarton Oaks, 82; ed, Highland-Lowland Interaction in Mesoamerica: Interdisciplinary Approaches, Dumbarton Oaks, 83; auth, Maya Rulers of Time: Architectural Sculpture from Tikal, Guatemala, Univ Pa, 86; Living with the Dead, Mural Painting of Oaxaca, Mexico, Cambridge Univ Press, 95. *Mailing Add:* Alfonso De Cossio 3 / 8-C Sevilla Spain

MILLER, BRAD
CRAFTSMAN, CERAMIST
Study: Univ Ore, BFA (ceramics & graphics), 74, MFA, 77. *Work:* Los Angeles Co Mus; Denver Art Mus; Brooklyn Mus, NY; Renwick Gallery, Smithsonian Inst, Washington; Southern Alleghenies Mus Art, Loretto, Pa. *Exhib:* Seattle Art Mus, 79; Nat Gallery Art, Renwick Gallery, Smithsonian Inst, Washington, 80; solo exhibs, Arvada Ctr Arts & Humanities, Colo, 88, Mill St Gallery, Aspen, Colo, 91 & 93, Anderson Ranch Arts Ctr, Snowmass Village, Colo, 91, Margo Jacobsen Gallery, Portland, Ore, 93, Robischon Gallery, Denver, 94 & Univ Nebr, Lincoln, 94, Margo Jacobsen Gallery, Portland Ore, 99, Robischon Gallery, Denver, Colo, 2000; Colorado Artists: Recent Acquisitions, Denver Art Mus, 96; Altered States, Ctr Visual Arts, Metrop State Col, Denver, 96; Current, Robischon Gallery, Denver, 96; LongHouse Foundation, East Hampton, NY, 96; New Visions in Clay, Mendocino Art Ctr Gallery, Calif, 96; Bellas Artes Santa Fe, NMex, 97; Rivers, the Foothills Art Ctr, Golden, Colo, 2000. *Pos:* Exec dir, Anderson Ranch Arts Ctr, Snowmass Village, Colo, 84-92. *Teaching:* Ceramics prog dir, Anderson Ranch Arts Ctr, Snowmass Village, Colo, 80-84, instr, 91, workshop, 94 & 96; vis artist, RI Sch Design, Providence, 87, Spring Island, Beaufort, SC, 93 & Univ Ore, Eugene, 95; workshop, Penland Sch Crafts, NC, 89 & Ore Sch Arts & Crafts, Portland, 95; vis prof ceramics, Univ Ga Studies Abroad, Cortona, Italy, fall 94. *Awards:* Artist Recognition Award, Colo Fedn Arts, 92; Visual Artists Fel, Nat Endowment Arts, 94. *Bibliog:* Laura Dixon (auth), Bradley Miller, Ceramics Monthly, 12/95; George Melrod (auth), Back to nature, Art & Antiques Mag, 2/96; Rose Slivka (auth), From the studio, East Hampton Star, NY, 6/6/96. *Dealer:* Robischon Gallery 1740 Wazee St Denver CO 80202

MILLER, DANIEL DAWSON
PRINTMAKER, SCULPTOR, PAINTER
b Pittsburgh, Pa, July 7, 1928. *Study:* Lafayette Col, BA, 51; Pa State Univ, summers with Hobson Pittman; Pa Acad Fine Arts, 55-59; Univ Pa, MFA, 58. *Work:* Pa Acad Fine Arts, Philadelphia; Philadelphia Mus Art; Rutgers Mus, New Brunswick, NJ; Wilmington Soc Fine Arts, Del; Dickinson Col, Carlisle, Pa; Univ Maine; Cent Mo State Univ. *Exhib:* 11 Modern Am Artists, Rahr Mus, Manitowoc, Wis, 63; 158th-162nd Ann Exhib, Pa Acad Fine Arts, Philadelphia, 63-67; Artist's House, Philadelphia, 2001-2002 & 2007; Solo exhibs, Peale House, Pa Acad Fine Arts, 67, Drexel Inst, 68, Rutgers Mus, Rutgers Univ, 70, Univ Maine, 72 & Rosenfeld Gallery, Philadelphia, Pa, 81, 84 & 92; Artists House, Philadelphia, 2007, 2008 & 2010; Philadelphia Mus; Pa Acad of the Fine Arts; Rutgers Mus. *Pos:* Asst dean fac, Pa Acad Fine Arts, 83-86, actg dir, 84-85, head painting dept, 86-92, chmn grad sch, 98-13. *Teaching:* Instr, Pa Acad Fine Arts, 64-; instr art & head fine arts dept, Eastern Col, St Davids, Pa, 64-85; instr woodcut, Pa Acad Fine Arts, 83-. *Awards:* Prize for Oil, Del Ann, Del Soc Fine Arts, 60; May Audubon Post Prize, 61, Bertha M Goldberg Mem Award, 70 & 75, Leona Karp Brauerman Prize, 76 & Percy Owens Award, 86, Fel Pa Acad Fine Arts. *Mem:* Philadelphia Watercolor Club; Am Color Print Soc. *Media:* All. *Interests:* Travel. *Dealer:* Artist's House 57 2nd St Philadelphia PA 19106; Turtle Deer Isle ME; Chapter Two Corea ME; Littlefield Winter Harbor ME. *Mailing Add:* PO Box 41 Christiana PA 17509

MILLER, DENISE
MUSEUM DIRECTOR, EDUCATOR
b Chicago, Ill. *Study:* St Xavier Univ, BA, 80, MBA, 86; Univ Chicago & Northwestern Univ. *Exhib:* Pub-Pvt, Works by Contemp Commercial and Fine Art Photogrs, incl Sheila Metzner, George Hurrell, Mary Ellen Mark, Victor Skrebneski, Robert Mapplethorpe, David Seidner, Burt Glinn, William Coupon & Barbara Karant, 86-87; Frank Gohlke: Landscapes from the Middle of the World-- Photographs 1972-1987, 87; Contemp Photographs from Japan, 88; Changing Chicago: Close Up, Photog Essays on Family and Community (co-ed, catalog), 89; Fire Sites--Defense-Deterrence-Bargaining Chips--Photogrpahs by Emmet Gowin, David Graham, David Hanson, Richard Misrach, Patrick Nagatani & Barbara Norfleet, 89; Linda Connor: Spiral Journey (auth, catalog), 90; Anthony Dyrek: Poland Under Martial Law, 90; Mus Contemp Photog, Columbia Col, Chicago, 92-98. *Collection Arranged:* Permanent Collection, Mus Contemp Photog, 59-. *Pos:* Dir, Mus Contemp Photog, Chicago, 86-; bd mem, Etant Donnes, Fr Am Fund Contemp Art, 97. *Teaching:* Instr mus & curatorial practices, Columbia Col, Chicago, 85-; instr bus admin, Graham Sch Mgt, St Xavier Col, Chicago, 86; principle prof mus studies, Columbia Col, Chicago, 86-. *Mem:* Am Asn Mus; Art Mus Asn Am; Coll Art Asn; Soc Photog Educ; Int Coun Mus. *Res:* Contemporary art and photography, 59-. *Publ:* Auth & ed, Open Spain/Espana Abierta: Contemporary Documentary Photography in Spain, Lunwerg Editores, Barcelona & Madrid, 92; Within this Garden: Photographs by Ruth Thorne Thomsen, Aperture, NY, 93; auth, City of Secrets: Photography of Naples by Jed Fielding, Takarajima Bks, NY, 97; auth & ed, Photography's multiple roles: art, document, market, science, DAP Inc, 98. *Mailing Add:* Mus Contemp Photog 600 S Michigan Ave Chicago IL 60605-1901

MILLER, DOLLY (ETHEL) B
PAINTER, COLLAGE ARTIST
b Johnstown, Pa, June 14, 1927. *Study:* Brooklyn Col, NY, BA (chemistry); NY Univ, MA (Fr lit); art hist, The Sorbonne & the Louvre, Paris, France; studied painting with Andre Lhote, Paris; Art Students League, with Julian Levi; also with Leo Manso, NY Univ. *Work:* Johnson & Johnson, Surgico, Inc, Piscataway, NJ; The Friends Acad, Locust Valley, NY. *Exhib:* One-person shows, Vt Conserv Arts, 84, Culinary Inst, Montpelier, 85, N Country Hosp Gallery, Newport, 85, Vt Coun Arts Montpelier, Cornelia St Cafe, Greenwich Village, NY; Northeast Open, Worcester, Mass, 86; N Country Hosp, Newport, Vt, 88; Wickwire Gallery, Lyndon State Col, Lyndonville, Vt, 90; The League at the Cape, Provincetown Art Asn, Mass, 93; Inaugural Invitational, Ctr Gallery, Newport, Vt, 94. *Awards:* Candidates for Art Award, Am Acad Nat Inst Art, New York, 76; Salmagundi Club Award, Nat Acad Galleries, 79; Vt Studio Sch Residency Grant, 86. *Mem:* Audubon Artists, Inc; Art Students League New York; Art Resources Asn Vt. *Media:* Oil. *Mailing Add:* 39 N Park St Apt 2E Lebanon NH 03766

MILLER, ELAINE SANDRA
PAINTER, PRINTMAKER
b Philadelphia, Pa. *Study:* Drexel Univ, BS, 51; Cheltenham Ctr Arts, with G Noble Wagner, Jimmy Leuders & Paul Gorka, 71-84. *Work:* Siemens Corp Int; Rion Corp LTD, Tokyo, Japan; Nat Asn Women Artists (Permanent Millennium Collection), New York, NY, 2000; Free Libr Phila; Villanova Univ, Pa. *Exhib:* Solo exhib, Philadelphia Art Alliance, 81; Nat Mus Am Jewish Hist, Philadelphia, 92; Nat Soc Painters in Casein & Acrylic, NY, 92, 2007; Am Color Print Soc; 2nd Worldwid Femenist Expo, Balt, MD, 2001; United Nations (UNIFEM) Women's History Month, NY, 2002; Holocaust Mus, Houston, Tex, 2010. *Teaching:* Teacher art, Forman Hebrew Day Sch, Pa, 80-82; Philadelphia Sch Sys, 81-82. *Awards:* 2nd Prize, Woodmere Art Mus, Philadelphia, Pa, 2006. *Mem:* Am Color Print Soc; Artists Cult Exchange (pres, 87-90); Nat Asn Women Artists; Artists Equity; Nat Soc Painters in Casien & Acrylic. *Media:* Acrylic; All Media. *Publ:* Auth, Best of Acrylic Painting, 97 & Creative Inspirations, 98, Rockport Publ. *Mailing Add:* 1003 Indian Creek Rd Jenkintown PA 19046

MILLER, ELEANOR GRACE
PAINTER, INSTRUCTOR
b Teaneck, NJ, Oct 4, 1947. *Study:* Monmouth Coll, BA, 1970; Nat Accad Design, 1972. *Work:* Art in Public Places, NY. *Comn:* Mural, Am Cancer Soc, Airmont, NY, 2004. *Exhib:* Springfield Fine Arts Mus, Springfield, Mass, 1993; Women Artists 1994, Goodman Gallery, Southampton, NY, 1994; Viridian 30th Ann Exhib, Viridian Gallery, NY, NY, 1997; Red, ROCA, W Nyack, NY, NY, 2006; Gaga, NY, 2009; Bayer Pharmaceuticals, NJ, 2011; Rockefeller Gallery, NY, 2012; Blue Hill, NY, 2013; Montclair State Univ, NJ, 2014. *Teaching:* Instr, painting, ROCA, W Nyack, NY, 1987-; instr, Pelham Art Center, Pelham, NY, 1992-; adj prof, painting, St Thomas Aquinas Coll, Sparkill, NY, 2002-. *Awards:* Anna Hyatt Huntington Award, Catherine Lorillard Wolfe Club (CLWAC), Nat Arts Club, 1992; Best in Show, Springfield Art League, Springfield Fine Arts Mus, 1993; Gamblin Artists award, NY, 2010. *Bibliog:* Edward N (auth), Paintings so Lifelike, Poughkeepsie Jour, NY, 2003; Watson T (auth), A Rich Semi-Reality, Newcritics.com, 2009; Miller J (auth), Black And Still Life, culturemob.com, 2010; Mary Elen Marks (auth) Profile Eleanor Miller, Hook, NY, 2014. *Mem:* Salmagundi Club, 2007-. *Media:* Painter, acrylic oil. *Dealer:* Renaissance Fine Art Gallery 20B Mountainview Ave Orangeburg NY 10962; The Outside in Piermont 249 Ferdon Ave Piermont NY 10968. *Mailing Add:* 64 W Clarkstown Rd New City NY 10956

MILLER, (RICHARD) GUY
SCULPTOR
b Pittsburgh, Pa, 1947. *Study:* City & Guilds of London Art Coun, Eng, with Ennis Fripps, 58; Art Students League, New York, with Will Barnet & Robert Hale; Pratt Inst, Brooklyn, NY, with Calvin Albert, MFA, 65. *Work:* State Univ NY Coll New Paltz; Pratt Inst, Brooklyn; New Sch, NY; Bennington Col, Vt; Long Island Hall Fame, Stony Brook, NY; and others. *Comn:* Stainless steel wall sculpture, New Sch, NY, 74; free standing stainless steel dual form, Sky Island Club, Plainview, NY, 79; free standing painted steel sculpture, Atrium, Jericho, NY, 85; free standing brass sculpture, Tower Apartment, Fort Lee, NJ, 87; brass wall sculpture, NY, 88; and others; free standing cast aluminum sculpture, Sedona, Ariz, 2000. *Exhib:* Cochise Col, Douglas, Ariz, 87; Copper Village Art Mus, Anaconda, Mont, 88; Missoula Mus Art, Mont, 88; Orr's Bailey Art Asn, Orr's Island, Maine, 89-92; Maine Arts Festival, Thomas Point, Maine, 92; AIDS Project, Ann Auction, 94-2000; and many others. *Pos:* Bd dir, Huntington Township Art League, 78; chmn, Orr's Bailey Art Assoc, 89-99. *Teaching:* Instr sculpture, Pratt Inst, Brooklyn, summer 64; prof art, Monmouth Col, West Long Branch, NJ, 64-65, prof sculpture, 66-69; artist-in-residence, Friends

World Col, Lloyd Harbor, NY, 77-79. *Awards:* Tiffany Found Grant, 66; MacDowell Colony Found Fel, 68; Sculptor of the Year Award, Long Island Hall Fame, Sky Island Club, 79; and others. *Bibliog:* Discription of Sculpture, 11/86 & Clint Hagen (auth), Miller, 9/92, Time Rec; Brian Bixler (auth), Flotsam and jetsam, Fla Today, 1/91; Doug Hubley (auth), Art by Association, Times Rec, 7/98; and others. *Mem:* Art Students League, NY; Huntington Twp Art League, NY (bd dir, 78-81); Orrs Bailey Art Asn (chmn bd dir, 90-2000). *Media:* Stainless Steel; Lucite. *Res:* Sculptural habitat. *Dealer:* Marie Scott Palm Springs CA. *Mailing Add:* 78 Prospect St New Paltz NY 12501

MILLER, HARVEY S SHIPLEY
PATRON
b Philadelphia, Pa, Sept 28, 1948. *Study:* Swarthmore Coll, BA, 70; Harvard Univ, JD, 73; Phi Sigma Kappa. *Collection Arranged:* Russian Avant Garde & The Judith Rothschild Found Contemp Drawings Collection, Mus Mod Art; Jacque Villon Cubist Prints, Philadelphia Mus Art. *Pos:* Assoc, Debevoise & Plimpton, New York City, 73-75; mem, prints & drawings & photographs trustees adv comt, Philadelphia Mus Art, 74-, trustee, 85-, investment comt, 89-95, exec, develop & exhib comt, 93-96, chmn, 125th ann campaign, 99-2002, vchmn, 2004-; trustee, NY Studio Sch, 74-80, Univ the Arts, 79-86; bd dir, Once Gallery, Inc, 74-75, Wildlife Preserv Trust Int, Inc, 90-95; cur, dir, dept collections & spec exhib Franklin Inst, Philadelphia, 75-81; bd gov's Print Club, Philadelphia, 76-87; vis comt, on photog George Eastman House, Rochester, NY, 76-78; exec bd dir, Fabric Workshop, Philadelphia, 76-86; bd assoc, Swarthmore Coll Librs, Philadelphia, 78-86; exec bd, Citizens for Arts in Pa, 80; treas, dir, Arcadia Found, Norristown, Pa, 81-; bd overseers, Univ Pa Sch Nursing, 81-, Edith C Blum Art Inst Bard Coll, 84-87; assoc trustee, Univ Pa, 81-95; chmn adv bd, Inst Contemp Art Univ Pa, 82-84; vpres, Energy Solutions Inc, New York, 82-84; bd dir, mem corp, MacDowell Colony, New York City, 82-85; trustee, vchmn comt on instruction, Pa Acad Fine Arts, 82-91, trustee emer, 91-, chmn collections & exhib comt, 85-87; trustee, Milton & Sally Avery Arts Found, New York, 83-, secy, 96-; pres, chief exec off, dir, Daltex Medical Scis Inc, 83-86, dir exec comt, 83-94, chief operating off, vchmn, 86-91, pres, chief operating off, 91-93; mem, Mayor's Cult Adv Coun, Philadelphia, 87-91; mem collections comt, Hist Soc Pa, 91-93 & councilor trustee, 92-93; chmn, Mayor's Art-in-City Hall Prog Philadelphia, 92-94; trustee, The Franklin Inst, Philadelphia, 93-95, Philadelphia Mus Art, 85-, exec comt, 93-96; trustees coun, Nat Gallery Art, Wash, 95-2000, 2001-2006; mem vis comt, photographs Metrop Mus Art, 96-, vis comt modern art, 98-; trustees' comt on drawings, Mus Modern Art, 96-, trustee, 2003-, Prints & Illustrated Books, 2001-; San Francisco Mus Modern Art, (mem photog accessions comt, 97-2002); mem vis comt, modern art Metrop Mus Art, 98-; adv bd The Highlands Hist Soc, 99-; arts adv comt, Fund for the Waterworks, 99-2001; founding mem, bd trustees, Maltz Jupiter (Fla) Theatre, 2001-2005; trustee, Arcadia Univ, 2002-2005; bd dir, Am Patrons of the Tate Gallery, 2003-2006; charter mem, The Drawings Group, Los Angeles Co Mus Art, 2003-; mem drawings comt, Los Angeles Mus Contemp Art, 2003-; bd trustees, Whitney Mus Am Art, 2004-, chmn comt, on drawings, 2004-; bd overseers, Hammer Jus, Los Angeles, 2004-2005; trustee, Ursinus Coll, 2004-, Point Found, 2004-; collections comt, Harvard Univ Art Gallery, 2006-; founders coun, Williams Inst on Sexual Orientation & Publication UCLA, 2006-; dir, Salyburg Festival Soc, 2006-; adv bd, Wash Studio Sch, 2007-. *Awards:* Named 1st non-Russian recipient of Diploma of Merit, Russian Ministry of Culture, 2002. *Mem:* Fel The Pierpont Morgan Libr; Coll Physicians Philadelphia; Am Bar Asn; Asn Bar of City of NY; Athenaeum, Libr co Philadelphia; Am Philosophical Soc; Hist Soc Pa; Philadelphia Art Alliance; Union League of Philadelphia; Harvard Club NY; Swarthmore Club Philadelphia; George Pompidou Arts Cult Found (mem exec comt, 2006-). *Publ:* Auth, Milton Avery: Drawings and Paintings, 76, It's About Time, 79; auth, ed, New Spaces: Exploring the Aesthetic Dimensions of Holography, 79; coauth, Rapid Inactivation of Infectious Pathogens by Chlorhexidine-coated Gloves, 92; contribr, articles to prof jours

MILLER, JOAN
PAINTER, COLLAGE ARTIST
b New York, NY, 1930. *Study:* Brooklyn Mus with Gregorio Prestopino, 47; Parsons Sch Design; Tyler Sch Art Temple Univ, BFA, 52. *Work:* Butler Inst, Youngstown, Ohio; Slater Mem Mus, Norwich, Conn; Philadelphia Mus Art, Lending Libr, Pa; many pvt collections, US and abroad. *Exhib:* Group drawing & painting shows, Cocoran Gallery, Washington, DC, 53 & Brooklyn Mus, NY, 55; Nat Asn Women Artists, Nat Acad, New York, 65-80; 4-person invitational exhib, Port Wash Libr, NY, 70; Benson Gallery, Bridgehampton, NY, 86, 88 & 90; Clayton-Liberatore Gallery, Bridgehampton, NY, 95; Parrish Mus, Southhampton, NY, 96; Gallery BAI, Soho, New York; group invitation exhib, Palazzo Vecchio, Florence, Italy; Gayle Willson Gallery, Southampton, NY, 2002; Toronto Art Fair, 2008-2010; Chicago Art Fair, 2009; Guild Hall, East Hampton, NY; solo exhibs, Graphic Eye Gallery, Port Wash, NY, 75 & 77 Phoenix Art Gallery, New York, 78, 81 & 83, Books & Co, 92, Donnell Libr, New York, 92 & Southampton (NY) Coll, 2002, Walter Wickiser Gallery, New York, 2009, Retrospective Show, Walter Wickiser Gallery, 2011. *Collection Arranged:* pvt collections in US and Europe. *Awards:* Cash award, Soc Painters Casein, Nat Arts Club, 69; several cash awards, Nat Asn Women Artists. *Mem:* Nat Asn Women Artists (graphic jury, 85-88, painting jury, 2005-2007). *Media:* Acrylic on Canvas, Collage on Paper. *Publ:* Reproduction of work in book Intaglio Printmaking Techniques by Ruth Leaf, Watson Guptill, 76. *Dealer:* Walter Wickiser Gallery New York. *Mailing Add:* 1192 Park Ave New York NY 10128

MILLER, JOAN VITA
MUSEUM DIRECTOR, ADMINISTRATOR
b New York, NY, Jan, 1946. *Study:* Syracuse Univ, BA (art hist), MA (art hist); independent res in Italy. *Collection Arranged:* New York Eleven, 74; Louise Nevelson (auth, catalogue), 74; Gertrude Stein and Her Friends (auth, catalogue), 75; Wreck, 75; The Long Island Art Collector's Exhibit (auth, catalogue), 75; European Masters in Portraiture, 76; An Exploration of Photography 1839-1976 (auth, catalogue), 76; The Arts of China, 77; Marsden Hartley, 1877-1943, 77; Double Exposure: Alfredo Valente as Photographer and Collector, 78; The First 4000 Years: The Ratner Collection of Judaean Antiquities, 79; Realist Space, 79; African Sculpture: The Shape of Surprise, 80; Auguste Rodin, 80 & 81; Rodin: B Gerald Cantor Collection, Metrop Mus Art (auth, catalog), 86. *Pos:* Asst dir, Michael Rockefeller Arts Ctr, State Univ NY Col, Fredonia, 71-72; dir gallery & cur permanent collection, CW Post Art Gallery, CW Post Col, 73-80; dir, BG Cantor Sculpture Ctr, NY, 80-83, cur B G Cantor Collections, 83-89; mus & gallery mgr, CW Post Col, Long Island Univ, 76-80. *Mem:* Am Asn Mus; Coll Art Asn. *Mailing Add:* c/o Dr Gary Marotta PO Box 41810 Lafayette LA 70504

MILLER, JOHN FRANKLIN
ADMINISTRATOR
b Hagerstown, Md, June 4, 1940. *Study:* St Johns Col, Annapolis, BA, 62; Yale Univ, with Edgar Munhall, 65; Univ Md, with Ruth Butler, 69-72. *Work:* Hampton Nat Historic Site, Md; Stan Hywet Hall Foundation, Ohio. *Pos:* Resident cur, Hampton Nat Historic Site, Md, 72-75, admin, 76-79; cur of educ, Stan Hywet Hall Foundation, Akron, Ohio, 79-80, exec dir, 81. *Mem:* Am Asn Mus; Nat Trust for Hist Preserv; Am Asn State and Local Hist; Intermuseum Conserv Asn (trustee, 81). *Res:* European and domestic architecture of the late 17th and early 18th centuries and its influence in America. *Mailing Add:* Edsel & Elinor Ford House 1100 Lake Shore Rd Grosse Pointe MI 48236

MILLER, KATHRYN
PAINTER, PRINTMAKER
b Philadelphia, Pa, June 21, 1935. *Study:* Univ NC, BA, 57; Ga Southern Col, 69; Savannah Coll Art & Design, Ga, 79-80. *Work:* Waycross Junior Col, Ga; Savannah Coll Art & Design; Marion Co Mus, SC. *Comn:* Delta Corp, Hilton Head Island, SC, 84 & 86; Mus Nat Hist, NY, 95. *Teaching:* Instr, Armstrong State Col, Savannah, Ga, 87-88 & Trenholm Artists Guild Workshop, 88. *Awards:* Second Place, Mandarin Art Asn, 86; Award of Distinction, Tarpon Springs, 89; First Place Graphics, Atalaya Art Festival, 90 & 91. *Mem:* Ga Watercolor Soc; Southeastern Watercolor Soc; SC Crafts Asn; Savannah Art Asn; Hilton Head Art Asn. *Media:* Watercolor; Copper Etching, Oil. *Dealer:* Signature Gallery of Savannah 303 W Saint Julian St Savannah GA 31401. *Mailing Add:* 2 S Stillwood Ct Savannah GA 31419

MILLER, MARC H
CURATOR, WRITER
b New York, NY, June 28, 1946. *Study:* Univ Calif, Riverside, BA, 67; NY Univ, Inst Fine Arts, MA, 71, PhD, 79. *Collection Arranged:* Punk Art (auth, catalog) Wash Proj Arts, 78; Unforgettable Moments, ABC No Rio Gallery, 82; Television's Impact on Contemp Art (auth, catalog), Queens Mus, 86; Archit Models from the Last Decade (ed, catalog), Queens Mus, 87; Lafayette, Hero of Two Worlds (ed, catalog), Queens Mus, 89; Remembering the Future: The New York World's Fair From 1939 to 1964, Queens Mus (contrib catalogue), 89; Louis Armstrong: A Cultural Legacy, Queens Mus Art (ed Catalogue), 94. *Pos:* Prog dir, Art-New York, Inner Tube Video, 81-85; contrib ed, East Village Eye, New York, 82-86; cur, Queens Mus, NY, 85-91; mus consult, 91-. *Teaching:* Instr art hist, Sch Visual Arts, New York, 76-80; asst prof, St John's Univ, NY, 82-85. *Awards:* Smithsonian Inst Fel, 74 & 76. *Res:* 19th and 20th Century art reflecting broader political and social phenomenon. *Publ:* Auth, 25 years of Space Photog, Nieuwe Revu, Holland, 81; co-auth, ABC No Rio Dinero: the Story of a Lower East Side Art Gallery, Collaborative Proj, Inc, 85; The Panorama of New York City: A History of the World's Largest Scale Model, The Queens Mus, 90; Looking at Jazz, Cobblestone, 10/94. *Mailing Add:* 188 8th Ave Brooklyn NY 11215-2225

MILLER, MELISSA WREN
PAINTER
b Houston, Tex, Mar 3, 1951. *Study:* Univ NMex, BFA, 74. *Work:* Mus Fine Arts Houston; Hirshhorn Mus and Sculpture Garden, Wash DC; Dallas Mus Art, Dallas, Tex; Modern Art Mus Fort Worth, Fort Worth, Tex; Nat Mus Women in the Arts, Wash DC; Blanton Mus Art, Austin, Tex. *Exhib:* Solo shows incl Melissa Miller: A Survey 1978-1986 (with catalog), Contemp Art Mus, Houston, 81, Fort Worth Mus, Tex & Art Mus STex, Corpus Christi, 81, Tex Gallery, Houston, 83, 85, 95, Holly Solomon Gallery, New York, 84, 85, 95, Albright Knox Art Gallery, Buffalo, 86, Yellowstone Art Ctr, 89, Ga State Univ Art Gallery, Atlanta, 90, Kimbell Art Mus, Ft Worth, Tex, 91, Dallas Visual Art Ctr, 99, St Edwards Univ, Austin, 2001, Dunn and Brown Contemp, Dallas, 2002, Betty Moody Gallery, Houston, 2003, Galveston Art Ctr, Tex, 2003, Mary Baldwin Coll, Stanton, Va, 2004, Kans State Univ, 2004, Ringling Sch Art and Design, Sarasota, Fla, 2004, Betty Moody Gallery, Houston, 2008, Grace Mus, Abilene, Tex, 2011; group shows incl Whitney Biennial Exhib, Whitney Mus Am Art, 83; Biennial III, San Francisco Mus Mod Art, 84; Venice Bienniale, Italy, 84; Fresh Paint, Mus Fine Art, 85; Hirshhorn Mus, Smithsonian Inst, Wash, DC, 86; James Corcoran Gallery, Los Angeles, 87; Nat Mus Women in Arts, 88, 89; Am Acad Inst Arts Letters, New York, 90, 92; Holly Solomon Gallery, New York, 91; Corcoran Gallery Art, Wash, DC, 93; Mus Fine Arts, Houston, 95, 2000; Calif Ctr for Arts Mus, Escondido, 96; Whitney Mus Am Art at Champion, Stamford, Conn; Belles Artes Gallery, Santa Fe, 2001; Arlington Mus Art, Tex, 2004; Galleria del Instituto de Artes Plasticas de la Universidad Veracruzana, Mex, 2004; Austin Art Mus, Laguna Gloria, 2005; Frolick Gallery, Portland, Ore, 2006; Sarafim Sch Fine Arts, Southwestern Univ, Georgetown, Tex, 2007; Selby Gallery, Ringling Sch Art and Design, Sarasota, 2007; New Britain Mus Am Art, Conn, 2007. *Pos:* Distinguished vis prof art, SMU, 90. *Teaching:* Instr, Laguna Gloria Art Mus Sch, Austin, 78-80, Skowhegan Sch Painting and Sculpture, Maine; distinguished vis prof art, Southern Methodist Univ, Dallas, 90-91, 2000; vis lectr, Univ Tex San Antonio, 95, 99; Elizabeth Kirkpatrick Doenges instr, Mary Baldwin Coll, Stauton, Va, 2000; assoc prof art, Univ Tex, Austin, 2000-2011. *Awards:* Nat Endowment Arts Grants, 79, 82 & 85; Anonymous Was A Woman Found Award, 2004; Tex State Artist of the Year, Art League Houston, 2008, Tex Comn Arts, 2011. *Bibliog:* Roni Feinstein (auth), Melissa Miller: The uses of

enchantment, Arts, summer 84; Michael Brenson (auth), In Melissa Miller's Wild Kingdom Lurks a World of Wonder, NY Times, 7/86; Katherine Gregor (auth), Melissa Miller's Animal Kingdom, Artnews, 12/86; Eleanor Harvey (auth), Melissa Miller, New Paintings, Dunn and Brown Contemp and Moody Gallery, 2002; Michael Duncan (auth), Melissa Miller at Moody, Art in Am, 12/2003; Susie Kalil (auth) & Michael Duncan (auth), Melissa Miller, Univ Tex Press, 2007. *Media:* Oil, Acrylic, Gouache. *Dealer:* Moody Gallery 2815 Colquitt Houston TX 77098; Talley Dunn Gallery Contemporary 5020 Tracy St Dallas TX 75205. *Mailing Add:* 167 N Tumbleweed Tr Austin TX 78733-3222

MILLER, MICHAEL STEPHEN
PRINTMAKER, PAINTER
b Baltimore, Md, June 29, 1938. *Study:* East Carolina Univ, BS, 62; Pa State Univ, MA, 64. *Work:* Art Inst Chicago, Ill; Brooklyn Mus, NY; Philadelphia Mus Art, Pa; Springfield Art Mus, Mo; Seoul Mus of Art; Mus Contemp Photog. *Exhib:* Extraordinary Realities, Whitney Mus, NY, 75; Solo Exhibs: Frumkin & Struve Gallery, Chicago, Ill, 1983; Keumsan Gallery, Seoul, 2002, 2004; Walsh Gallery, Chicago, 2005; Conceptual Comics, Phillips Gallery, Banff Art Ctr, Can, 2007, Voices, Gallery Sun Contemp, Seoul, 2010, New Prints, Int Print Center, NY, 2011; 19 Print Biennial, 77 & 22nd Print Biennial, 80, Brooklyn Mus, NY; Site-Oriented Installations, Klein Gallery, Chicago, Ill, 83; Chicago Sculpture Int, Chicago Art Expo-Navy Pier, 83; Chicago Emerging Visions, Paine Art Ctr, Oshkosh, Wis, 85. *Collection Arranged:* VI Mostra De Gravura, Prints from Chicago, Curitiba, Brazil, 85; Mus Contemp Art, Chicago; Banff Art Ctr, Can; Skopelos Art Found, Skopelos, Greece. *Pos:* Chmn Grad Div & Prof Printmaking; Prof, Dept Printmedia, Sch Art Inst Chicago, 1973-; Sr Adv, Int Relations, SAIC, 1994-2006. *Teaching:* Instr printmaking, Middle Tenn State Univ, Murfreesboro, 64-67 & Southern Ill Univ, Carbondale, 68-69; asst prof printmaking, Univ Del, Newark, 69-73; prof printmaking, Art Inst Chicago, Ill, 73-. *Awards:* Artists Grant, Nat Endowment Arts, 79; DeWitt Award, 74th Chicago & Vicinity Exhib, Art Inst Chicago, 82; Visual Artists Grant, Ill Arts Coun, 86. *Mailing Add:* 1808 W Wabansia Ave Chicago IL 60622

MILLER, NICOLE
WRITER
Pos: "Arts Beat" columnist, Wash Post; visual arts columnist, for Sunday Source. *Mailing Add:* Wash Post 1150 15th St NW Washington DC 20071

MILLER, RODNEY E
ADMINISTRATOR
Study: West Texas State Univ, BM; Indiana Univ, MM; Ill State Univ, PhD. *Pos:* Don Basilio in Barber of Seville, Chautauqua Opera, NY, formerly. *Teaching:* Dir, vocal studies, NY University, formerly; dean, Col of Fine Arts & Humanities, Univ Nebraska, Kearney, formerly; dean, Col of Fine Arts, Wichita State Univ, Kansas, currently. *Interests:* 20th Century American Vocal Music, both popular and classical, as well as administrative theory as it applies to American Higher Educ. *Mailing Add:* Wichita State University 1845 Fairmount Wichita KS 67260

MILLER, RUTH ANN
PAINTER
b Columbia, Mo, Dec 7, 1930. *Study:* Univ Mo, BA, 54; Art Students League, 55-56; studied with Esteban Vincente & Earl Kerkam, 55-58. *Work:* Dela Art Mus, Wilmington; Corcoran Gallery; Bryn Mawr Col, Philadelphia; Ndak Mus Art, 1993. *Exhib:* Ann-juried, Baltimore Art Mus, Md, 61; solo exhib, NY Studio Sch Gallery, 79 & 88; Vision and Tradition, Morris Mus, Morristown, NJ, 87; Colby Coll Mus Art, Waterville, Maine, 88; Am Acad Inst Arts & Letts, NY, 89; Nat Acad Design, 167th Ann, NY, 92-95. *Teaching:* Painting-drawing, NY Studio Sch, 73-; painting-drawing, Univ Hartford, Conn, 75-78; painting-drawing, Int Sch Art, Todi, Italy, 89; painting-drawing, Parsons, Grad Painting, NY, formerly; Parsons Sch Design, New York City, 1991-93. *Awards:* Ingram Merrill Grant, 81, 95. *Bibliog:* Robert Godfrey (auth), In Praise of Space, Art Dept Westminster, 76; Hearne Pardee (auth), Vision and Tradition, NJ State Coun Arts, 88; Andrew Forge (auth), On Ruth Miller's Still Life Painting, New York Studio Sch, 88. *Mem:* Bowery Gallery, NY; Wash Art Asn, Conn; Nat Acad (academician). *Media:* Oil, Watercolor

MILLER, TRACY A
VIDEO ARTIST
b Cincinnati, Ohio, May 23, 1966. *Study:* Art Acad Cincinnati, BFA (painting), 90; Sch Art, Univ Cincinnati, MFA (electronic art), 93. *Exhib:* Interactive Experience, Inter CHI 93, RAI Cong Ctr, The Neth, 93; Mediatheque Lounge, ISEA 94, Helsinki, Finland, 94; Visual Surge, Studio San Guiseppe, Coll Mt St Joseph, Cincinnati, Ohio, 94. *Teaching:* Instr media studios, Columbus Col Art & Design, Ohio, 94-; artist-in-residence media art, Southern Ohio Mus & Cult Ctr, Portsmouth, 95. *Awards:* Isabel Wolfstein Travel Grant, Univ Cincinnati, 93; Project Grant, Ky Found Women, 94; Individual Artist Fel, Ohio Arts Coun, 95. *Mem:* Int Animated Film Soc; Asn Independent Video & Filmmakers Inc; Coll Art Asn. *Media:* Computer Based Interactive. *Publ:* Contribr, Multimedia CD-Rom, Siggraph 94, ACM Siggraph, 94; 1000 add One Frame, European Media Art Festival, Pool-Processing, 94. *Mailing Add:* c/o Columbia Col Art & Design 107 N 9th St Columbus OH 43215

MILLER, VIRGINIA IRENE
GALLERY DIRECTOR
b Tampa, Fla, May 29, 1943. *Study:* Miami Dade Community Coll, AA, 69; Univ Miami, BA (art hist & psychology), 73. *Pos:* Art consult, organizer, dir numerous art exhib for leading charities, financial instits, Dade Co, Fla, 69-73; owner & dir, Virginia Miller Galleries, Inc, Coconut Grove, Fla, 74-84; pres & dir, MACH I, Metrop Mus and Art Ctr, Coral Gables, 79-80; owner & dir, ArtSpace/Virginia Miller Galleries, Coral Gables, Fla, 81-; guest lectr, Miami-Dade Community Coll Ctr Continuing Educ of Women, 84, Univ Miami, 85 & Fla Int Univ, 85. *Awards:* Dedicated Service Award, Greater Miami Chap Am Red Cross, 90; Merrick Award of Excellence, Allen Morris Co & Coral Gables CofC, 2008-2009. *Mem:* Coral Gables Gallery Asn (pres); Greater Miami Chap Am Red Cross (dir, 90-96); Friends Lowe Art Mus (dir) ; Art Dealers Assn S Fla (secy & treas). *Specialty:* Contemporary fine art with a specialty in Latin American, Chinese master and mid-career artists, 19th and 20th Century American and European art. *Publ:* art writer, Women's Almanac newspaper, 1978-79. *Mailing Add:* Artspace Virginia Miller Galleries 169 Madeira Ave Miami FL 33134

MILLETT, CAROLINE DUNLOP
DESIGNER, CONSULTANT
b Kansas City, Mo, Feb 14, 1939. *Study:* Univ Edinburgh, 59-60; Univ Wis, BA, 61; Stanford Univ, MA, 63. *Collection Arranged:* Coordinator, US Contribution Sao Paulo Bienal, 73. *Pos:* Cult attache, Brasilia, 69-70; film dir, US Information Agency, 73; asst adv arts, Dept State, 74-80; adv arts, US Info Agency (USIA). Univ Arts, 81-; vpres, Philadelphia Col Art, 84-; pres, Millett Enterprises, 1985-1991, Millett Design, 1992-2013. *Teaching:* Assoc prof US cultural hist, Univ Sao Paulo, Brazil, 66-69; adj prof, Univ Pa, 92-2005. *Publ:* columnist, Ranch and Cove, Narrative Style (home design columns), 2004-2005; Broad St Review (cultural commentary, art and design critiques), 2008-2013; auth, with E. Ashley Rooney, Today's Historic Interiors, Schiffer Publishing Co, 2011; auth, Re-Designing Design, 2012. *Mailing Add:* 317 N 33rd St Philadelphia PA 19104-2549

MILLIE, ELENA GONZALEZ
CURATOR
b Greenwich, Conn. *Study:* Univ NC, BA, 64. *Collection Arranged:* Travel Then & Now, 70, The Paper Weapon (auth, catalog), 76, On View, 79 & Am & European Posters (auth, catalog), 80; 19th Century Am Book and Magazine Posters, 89. *Pos:* Cur, Libr Cong, 65-. *Publ:* Auth, Charlot, L'As des Comiques, 68, coauth, Tomorrow night, East Lynne, 80 & auth, Posters: A collectible art form, 82, Libr Cong Quart J; College poster art, Art J, 84; Jan Sawka, a Selected Retrospective (exhib catalog), Coll New Paltz, NY, 89; The Polish Poster, 95; French Posters from World War I, 96. *Mailing Add:* Library of Congress 101 Independence Ave SE Washington DC 20540

MILLIKEN, GIBBS
PAINTER, EDUCATOR
b Houston, Tex, Dec 15, 1935. *Study:* Scheiner Inst; Univ Colo; Trinity Univ, BSc; Cranbrook Acad Art, MFA. *Work:* Cranbrook Acad Art; Montgomery Mus Fine Arts, Ala; Serv League, Longview, Tex; Butler Inst Am Art. *Exhib:* San Antonio Artists, Witte Mus, 60-68; Tex Ann Painters & Sculptors, Witte Mus, Corpus Christi, Beaumont Mus & Dallas Mus Fine Arts, 62-66; Bucknell Univ, 67; Tex Fine Arts Comn, Hemisfair, San Antonio, 68; and many others. *Pos:* Asst, Univ Colo Mus, formerly; artist, photographer, asst cur, cur & head dept exhibs, Witte Mem Mus, San Antonio, formerly. *Teaching:* Instr painting & drawing, Cranbrook Acad Art, Bloomfield Hills, Mich, 64 & 65; instr art, Univ Tex, Austin, 65-69, asst prof, 69-73, assoc prof, 74-82, prof, currently. *Awards:* Grumbacher Award, Tex Watercolor Soc, Witte Mem Mus, 64, Naylor Award, 66 & Freeman Purchase Prize, 67; and many others. *Mem:* Am Fedn Arts; Am Asn Univ Prof; Men of Art Guild; Contemp Artists Group. *Mailing Add:* 434 Ridgewood Rd Austin TX 78746-5522

MILLIN, LAURA J
MUSEUM DIRECTOR
b Elgin, Ill, June 11, 1954. *Study:* Evergreen State Coll, BA (Interdisciplinary Studies), 1978. *Pos:* Dir, On the Boards, Seattle, 1979; art dir, City Fair, Metrocenter YMCA, 1980; dir, Ctr on Contemp Art, 1981; co-owner, Art in Form Bookstore, 1981-1989; co dir, 3d int festival of films by women dirs, Seattle Art Mus, 911 Contemp Arts, 1988; auction coordr, Allied Arts of Seattle, 1989; cur, Radio COCA, Ctr on Contemp Art, Seattle, 1986, co cur, 1981, 1983; dir, Visual AIDS, Missoula Mus Arts, 1989; exec dir, Missoula Mus Arts, Mont, 1990-. *Mailing Add:* Art Mus Missoula 355 N Pattee St Missoula MT 59802

MILLOFF, MARK DAVID
PAINTER, SCULPTOR
b Miami, Fla, June 19, 1953. *Study:* Conn Col, New London, BA, 75; Md Inst Coll Art, MFA (painting), 77. *Work:* Fogg Mus, Harvard Univ, Cambridge, Mass; Minneapolis Art Inst; Atlantic Richfield, Los Angeles; Chase Manhattan Bank, NY; Prudential Insurance Co; Berkshire Mus, Pittsfield, Mass. *Exhib:* Aviary, Mus Mod Art, NY, 82; Fel Winners Exhib, Rose Art Mus, Brandeis Univ, Waltham, Mass, 82; Dogs, Chicago Mus Contemp Art, 83 & Hood Mus, Dartmouth Col, Hanover, NH, 84; Drawing, Minneapolis Art Inst, 83; Inaugural Exhib, Dog Mus Am, NY, 83; Contemp Drawing, Brockton Mus Art, Mass, 85; retrospective, Berkshire Mus, Pittsfield, Mass, 86; The Clocktower, NY, 86. *Awards:* Mass Coun Drawing Fel, 82; Nat Endowment Arts Fel Sculpture, 84. *Bibliog:* Jon Friedman (auth), Reinventing the heroic: The work of Mark David Milloff, 12/81 & Lisa Peters (auth), Mark Milloff, 5/83, Arts Mag; Christine Temin (auth), Perspective, Boston Globe, 10/10/85. *Media:* Pastels, Oils. *Dealer:* Stux Gallery 411 West Broadway New York NY

MILLS, AGNES
PRINTMAKER, SCULPTOR
b New York, NY. *Study:* Cooper Union Art Sch, dipl; Pratt Inst, BFA; NY Univ Sch Archit; Art Students League; Design Lab; studied with Raphael Soyer, Chaim Gross, Yasuo Kuniyoshi, Ruth Leaf, Harry Gottlieb, Krishna Reddy & Betty Holliday. *Work:* Libr Performing Arts, Friends Tampa Ballet; Univ Maine, Amhurst; Calif Sch Arts & Crafts, Oakland; C W Post Col; Lincoln Ctr Performing Arts; Boca Raton Mus Art. *Comn:* Mural, Wakefield Collection, Long Beach, Calif; Portraits Inc, NY; Family Portrait, Grand Collection, 92. *Exhib:* Seattle Art Mus Ann, 74; Friends Tampa Ballet, 82; Deja Vu Gallery, 90; Works in Progress, 92; Boca Raton Mus, 92; and others. *Pos:* Art dir, Mills Agency Inc. *Teaching:* Art coordr & art instr, NShore Community Art Ctr, Great Neck, NY, 57-82. *Awards:* First Prize in Printmaking, Washington

Miniature Prints & Sculpture, 70; Purchase Prize, Hunterdon Co Art Mus, 72; Purchase Award, Nassau Community Col, 74; Purchase Prize, Nat Asn Women Artists, 81; Goldie Paley Award, 82. *Bibliog:* Article, Art News Mag, Oct, 81; New York Times, Mar, 81; Playbill, City Ctr Theatre, Mar, 81; Palm Beach Post, 3/91. *Mem:* Print Club; Nat Asn Women Artists; Artists Equity. *Media:* Color Etching, Cast Paper; Colograph, Monoprint. *Dealer:* Nuance Gallery Tampa FL 33609. *Mailing Add:* 337 Neva St Sebastopol CA 95472-3665

MILLS, LEV TIMOTHY
PRINTMAKER, DESIGNER
b Wakulla Co, Fla, Dec 11, 1940. *Study:* Fla A&M Univ, BA (art educ); Univ Wis, Madison, MA & MFA; Slade Sch Fine Art, Univ London, Eng; Atelier 17, Paris, France, with Stanley W Hayter. *Work:* High Mus Art, Atlanta; Victoria & Albert Mus, London; Libr of Cong, Washington, DC; Bibliot Nat, Paris; Mus Mod Art, NY. *Comn:* Three glass mosaic designs, Ashby St Subway Sta, City of Atlanta, Metrop Atlanta Rapid Transit Authority, 78; atrium floor design, City Hall, Atlanta, 88; mixed media work, Atlanta Pub Schs, 88. *Exhib:* Slade Centenary Exhib, Royal Coll Art, London, 71; Artists in Ga, High Mus Art, Atlanta, 74; 20th Century Black Artist, San Jose Mus Art, 76; Retrospective, Studio Mus in Harlem, NY, 75; Miss Mus Art, Jackson; Birmingham Mus Art, Ala; and others. *Pos:* Art consult & mem bd trustees, Art Festival of Atlanta Inc, 77-. *Teaching:* Instr gen art, Everglades Jr High, Ft Lauderdale, Fla, 62-68; asst prof printmaking, Clark Col, Atlanta, 73-78; assoc prof art, Spelman Col, Atlanta, 79. *Awards:* Outstanding Postgrad Fel, Univ Wis, 69; Europ Study & Travel Fel, Ford Found, 70; Bronze Jubilee Award for Cult Achievement, City of Atlanta, 78. *Bibliog:* Pat Gilmour (auth), Lev Mills, Arts Rev, London, 72; Lewis & Waddy (coauth), Black artists on art, Contemp Crafts Inc, Calif, 76; Samella Lewis (auth), Graphic Processes, Art: African American, Harcourt, Brace Jovanovich Inc, New York, 78. *Mem:* Nat Coll Art Asn; Black Artists Atlanta. *Media:* Mixed Media. *Publ:* Auth, I Do, A Book of Etchings & Poems, Cut Chain Press, 71. *Dealer:* Assoc Am Artists 663 Fifth Ave New York NY 10022. *Mailing Add:* 3128 Valleydale Dr SW Atlanta GA 30311-3064

MILNES, ROBERT WINSTON
SCULPTOR, EDUCATOR
b Washington, DC, April 1, 1948. *Study:* Claremont Men's Col, BA (philosophy, fine arts), 70; Univ Wash, MFA, 74; Univ Pittsburgh, PhD, 87. *Work:* Smithsonian Inst, Renwick Gallery; Erie Art Mus, Pa; Seattle Arts Comn; Nelson Fine Arts Ctr, Ariz State Univ; San Jose Mus Art, San Jose State Univ; La State Univ Mus. *Comn:* Sculpture, comn by Mr & Mrs Warner Bacon, Erie, Pa, 81; sculptures & wall mounted plates, Aqui Restaurant, San Jose, Calif, 97, 2000, 2005. *Exhib:* Solo shows, Theo Portnoy Gallery, NY, 79 & 80, Erie Art Mus, Pa, 83, Tercera Gallery, Los Gatos, 2000; Richmond Art Ctr, 2004 Two Person Show; Brookhaven Comm Coll, 2012. *Pos:* Dir, Sch Art & Design, San Jose State Univ, 1990-2005; Dean, Col Visual Arts & Design, Univ N Tex, 2006-2014. *Teaching:* Instr ceramics, Penland Sch Crafts, NC, 72 & 79; prof, Edinboro Univ, 74-86, art dept chmn, 81-86; dir, Sch Art, La State Univ, Baton Rouge, 87-90. *Awards:* Juror Award, Erie Art Ctr, 83; Jurors award, Louisiana Festival of the Arts, Mazur Mus, Alexandria, La, 90; Bautzer Development Award, CSU, 2003; Best of Tex Ceramics, 2011. *Bibliog:* Leon Nigrosh (auth), Ceramic Sculpture, 91; Po Zhou (auth), American Ceramic Artists Today, 98; Susan Peterson (auth), The Craft & Art of Clay, 3rd ed, 99; Dan Tom (auth), Heads for Thought, Ceramics Monthly, Sept 2000. *Mem:* Coll Art Asn; Nat Coun Arts Adminrs (past pres); Nat Asn Sch Art & Design (mem. accreditation comn, 1991-97, exec com board directors, 2000-05, vpres, 2002-05, pres, 2009-2011); Vice chair, Comm Advisory Bd, KERA-FM Public Broadcasting, 2009-2011, chair, 2012-2013. *Media:* Ceramics, Copper. *Res:* Higher educ accreditation; arts programs. *Specialty:* sculpture, ceramics. *Interests:* mountainbiking. *Publ:* The Impact of State Governing Board Policies on Fine Arts Programs in Post-Secondary Education, (dissertation), Univ of Pittsburgh, Pa. *Mailing Add:* 1426 Camino Robles Way San Jose CA 95120

MILONAS, MINOS (HERODOTOS MILONAS)
PAINTER, SCULPTOR
b Heraklion, Greece; US citizen. *Study:* Los Angeles Pierce Col, Woodland Hills, Calif, AA, 68; Calif State Univ, Northridge, with Fritz Faiss, Hans Burkhardt, Walter Gabrielson, Robert Bassler, Donald S Strong & Dolores Yonkers, BA (art), 70 MFA, 72; Univ Wash, Seattle, with George Tsutakawa & Everett Dupen. *Work:* Calif State Univ, Northridge; Hellenic Cult Ctr, Long Island City, NY; Cypriot Consultate, Young Broadcasting Inc & Girsberger Inc, NY. *Comn:* St Demetrios Cathedral, Seattle, Wash, 75; Int Drawing Biennale, Cleveland Eng, 82. *Exhib:* Solo exhibs, West Broadway Gallery, New York, 79, 81-84; Kreonides Gallery, Athens, Greece, 84, Cypriot Consulate, NY, 90; Group exhibs, Stockton Nat 85; Hagin Mus, Stockton, Calif, 85-86; North Dakota Print & Drawing Ann, Univ of NDak, Grand Forks, 87; Paper in Particular, Columbia Coll, Mo, 89; 35th Ann Drawing & Small Sculpture Show, Ball State Univ, Muncie, Ind, 89; Ctr Contemp Art, Rethymnon, Crete, Greece, 2003; Melina Merkouri, Athens Munic Cult Ctr, Greece, 2003; and others. *Teaching:* Teaching asst sculpture, Univ Wash, Seattle, 70-71, instr, 71-72. *Awards:* Poncho Sculpture Award, Univ Wash, Seattle, 71; 3 Merit Awards, 5th & 7th Ann Nat Greek Art Exhib, Springfield, Mass, 87 & 89; and others. *Bibliog:* Ball State Univ Art Gallery (producer), Artists Forum Video, 89; Minos Milonas-Art is: 500 Definitions (video), Art Seen, Ctr Visual Studies, San Francisco, 90; George Agelides (auth), No to the commerciality of art, Nat Herald, 90; Abraham Ilein (auth), The message is more than the medium, Art Speak, 90; George Tomko (auth), Minos Milonas emerges as a major abstract painter, Manhattan Arts, 90; and others; Minos Milonas-Multimedia Artist-Video Art Seen-Center for Visual Studies, San Francisco. *Mem:* NY Artists Equity Asn Inc. *Media:* Oil; Gouache. *Interests:* Music; Poetry; Traveling; Philosophy. *Publ:* The Small Caravan, collection of short stories, Athens, Greece, 62; An Ode to my Ancestors, The Greek-Am Rev, New York, 89; Sunset Over New Jersey, Nat Libr Poetry, Md, 96; Gaining and Losing - A Manifesto, Mod Poetry Soc, Fla, 96; Celestial Quest - Best Poems of the Nineties, Nat Libr Poetry, Md, 96; 33 books of poetry in Greek, 2 books of poetry in English, 3 books of bi-lingual poetry, 1990-2007; autobiography, 2005. *Mailing Add:* 790 11th Ave No 39A New York NY 10019

MILTON, PETER WINSLOW
PRINTMAKER
b Lower Merion, Pa, Apr 2, 1930. *Study:* Yale Univ, with Josef Albers, BFA, 54, MFA, 62. *Work:* Mus Mod Art, Metrop Mus, NY; British Mus, London; Nat Gallery Art, Washington, DC; Tate Gallery, London. *Exhib:* Primera Bienal Americana de Artes Graficas, Mus La Tertulia, Cali, Colombia, 71; Solo exhibs, Corcoran Gallery Art, Wash, DC, 72 & Drawing Toward Etching, Brooklyn Mus, 80; Extraordinary Realities, Whitney Mus Am Art, 73; Norsk Internasjonal Grafikk Biennale, Gamlegyen, Norway, 74 & 92; 4th Int Exhib Original Drawings, Mus Mod Art, Rijeka, Yugoslavia, 74; Frank Kyle Gallery, London; Inter Exhib Found, Traveling Retrospective; Jack Rutberg Fine Arts, Los Angeles, 2001; Ayle Gallery, 2006; Old Print Shop, New York, 2008. *Teaching:* Instr drawing & basic design, Md Inst Col Art, Baltimore, 61-68; instr printmaking, Yale Univ Summer Sch Music & Art, 70; artist-in-residence, Dartmouth Col, winter 1983, Rockefeller Found, Bellagio, Italy, 1990, Pasadena (Calif) City Col, 1999, Weber State Univ, Ogden, Utah, 2004. *Awards:* Rockefeller Found Residency, Bellagio, Italy; Medal of Honor, Lvov, USSR, 90; Exequo Award, Graphic Triennial, Crakow, Poland, 91, 94, 2003; Commendary award Miniprint Exhib, Finland, 1998, Hon award Int Biennial, Varna, Bulgaria, 1997; Int Triennial Graphic Arst, Poland, 2003; Miniprint exhib, Finland, 2004; Special Jury Award, Int Biennial, Varna, 2005. *Bibliog:* Harriet Shapiro (auth), All realism is visionary: A reach into the ambiguous realm of Peter Milton, Intellectual Digest, 11/72; Piri Halasz (auth), The metaphysical games of Peter Milton, Art News, 12/74; Kneeland McKnulty (auth), Peter Milton: Complete Etchings 1960-1976, Impressions Workshop Inc, Boston, 77; Theodore F Wolff (auth), What Links Duper & Milton, The Many Masks of Modern Art, 89. *Mem:* Nat Acad. *Media:* Etching, Engraving. *Dealer:* Franz Bader Gallery 2124 Pennsylvania Ave NW Washington DC 20037; Impressions Workshop 27 Stanhope St Boston MA 02116

MIM, ADRIENNE CLAIRE SCHWARTZ
SCULPTOR, PAINTER
b Brooklyn, NY, Feb 4, 1931. *Study:* Brooklyn Mus Art Sch & Brooklyn Col, NY, 50; Hofstra Univ, 65. *Work:* Mus Section, Guild Hall, East Hampton, NY; Sculpturesites, Amagansette, NY. *Comn:* Murals, Southampton Col, NY, 69; Robert & Joan Tausik-Pinto, East Hampton, NY. *Exhib:* Parrish Mus, Southampton, NY, 69; Heckscher Mus, Huntington, NY, 77; Wards Island, NY, 80; Brooklyn Mus, 81 & 84; Fordham Univ, Lincoln Ctr, NY, 81; Soho 20, NY, 85-88; Benton Gallery, Southampton, NY, 86, 89 & 90; and others. *Teaching:* Asst instr painting, Parrish Art Mus, 66-67; adj prof sculpture, Southampton Col, NY, 73-74. *Awards:* Fel, MacDowell Colony, 72-74; Helen B Ellis Mem Prize, Nat Asn Women Artists, 80; Silver Medal, Audubon Artists, 80. *Bibliog:* Carrie Rickey (auth), Stalking the wild sculpture, Village Voice, 7/1/80; Vivienne Wechter (interviewer), WFUV Radio, 6/81; Alexander Russo (auth), Profiles on Women Artists, Univ Pub of Am Inc, page 181-191, 85; Phillis Braff (auth), Messages in on the edge, NY Times, 6/90. *Mem:* Fedn Mod Painters & Sculptors; Nat Asn Women Artists; Sculptors Guild; Soho 20. *Media:* Fiberglass, Steel; Oil, Mixed Media. *Publ:* Auth, Helicomodmim, pvt publ, 79; illusr, Area Sculpture: Ward Island, Artists Representing Environmental Art, 80; Sculpturesites, Roger Wilcox, 81; Appearances, Independent Publ, 12/81; illusr, Appearances, Independent Publ, 12/81. *Dealer:* Roger Wilcox Sculpturesites Box 534 Amagansette NY 11930. *Mailing Add:* 69 Skimhampton Rd East Hampton NY 11937

MIN, YONG SOON
SCULPTOR, EDUCATOR
b S Korea, Apr 29, 1953. *Study:* Univ Calif-Berkeley, BA, MA, MFA, 79; Independent Study Prog, Whitney Mus, 81. *Comn:* Sculpture, Pub Art Fund, 88; sculpture, Creative Time Inc, 90; sculpture, Jamaica Art Ctr; sculpture, Univ Southern Maine; sculpture, Real Art Ways, 93; Percent for Art, NY, 93. *Exhib:* Committed to Print, traveling, Mus Mod Art, NY, 88; Pub Art Fund, City Hall Park, NY, 88; Creative Time, Art in the Anchorage, Brooklyn, NY, 90; The Decade Show, New Mus, Mus Contemp Hispanic Arts & Studio Mus Harlem, 90; Across the Pacific, Queens Mus, NY & Kumho Mus, Seoul, Korea, 93-94; Asia/Am: Identities in Contemp Asian Am Art, The Asia Soc, NY, 94; solo exhib with Allan deSouza, Camerawork, London, 94; Plan: Photog Los Angeles Now, Los Angeles Co Mus Art, 95; Thinking Print, Mus Mod Art, 96; Crossing Over/Changing Places, Corcoran Gallery Art, Washington, DC, 97; Thinking Print: Books to Billboards, Henry Art Gallery, Seattle, Wash, 98; All You Can Eat, City Market, Los Angeles, 98; Not on Any Map, Betty Rymer Gallery, Sch Art Inst, Chicago, 99. *Collection Arranged:* Mus Modern Art, NYC. *Teaching:* Instr printmaking & drawing, Univ Ohio, 81-84; asst prof arts, Univ Calif, Irvine, 93-99, assoc prof studio art, 99-. *Awards:* Artists Fel Grant, Nat Endowment Arts, 89-90; Bellagio Res, Rockefeller Found, 97; Fac Res Award, Univ Calif, Irvine Sch Art, 97-98. *Bibliog:* Shirley Hune (ed), Asian Americans: Comparative & Global Perspectives, Wash State Univ Press; Arlene Raven (ed), New Feminist Criticism, HarperCollins, 94; Elaine Kim (ed), Writing Self Writing Nation, Third Women Press, 94. *Mem:* Asian Am Arts Alliance (bd mem, 87-); Artist Space (bd mem, 91-); Women's Caucus for Art (bd mem, 92-). *Media:* Glass, Mirror, Photo-based Imagery, Paper. *Publ:* Auth, DMZ XING (exhib catalog), Real Art Ways & Smith Coll Mus Art, 94; Fermenting Kimchi (exhib catalog), Korean Am Mus, 98; Fermenting Kimchi (exhib catalog), Korean Am Mus, 98. *Mailing Add:* 8518 Saturn St Los Angeles CA 90035

MINCEMOYER, CARIN
INSTALLATION SCULPTOR
b Milton, Pennsylvania, 1972. *Study:* Temple Univ, Rome, Study Abroad Prog, 1993; Carnegie Mellon Univ, Pittsburgh, BFA (Painting), 1994; State Univ NY Buffalo, MFA (Art), 2005. *Exhib:* Solo exhibs include Turmoil Room, Pittsburgh, 1997, 3 Rivers Arts Festival Gallery, Pittsburgh, 2003, ODD Gallery, Dawson City, Yukon

Territory, Canada, 2007; group exhibs include Earth Wise, Forbes Gallery, Pittsburgh, 1994; 15 Minutes+, Andy Warhol Mus, Pittsburgh, 1998, SuZan, 1999, 92nd Ann Exhib, 2002; Inhibition Prohibition Exhib, Carnegie Mus Art, Pittsburgh, 1999; Biennial, Pittsburgh Ctr Arts, 2003, 2008; Habitat, Kipp Gallery, Indiana, Pa, 2007; You Are Here, SPACE Gallery, Pittsburgh, 2008; In the Making, Fe Gallery, Pittsburgh, 2008. *Pos:* Exhib Preparator, Phil Fraley Productions, Pittsburgh, 2007-Present. *Teaching:* Graphic Design Instr, Art Inst Online, Pittsburgh, 2006; Adjunct Instr, Indiana Univ Pa, Pittsburgh, 2007. *Awards:* Pittsburgh Found Individual Artist Award, 2003; Outstanding Student Achievement Contemp Sculpture Award, Int Sculpture Ctr, 2005; Pollock-Krasner Found Grant, 2007

MINDICH, ERIC
PATRON
Pos: Sr exec, ptrn, Goldman Sachs Group, Inc; founder, Eton Park Capital Mgt, 2005-; leadership coun, New Am Found; trustee, Whitney Mus Am Art

MINEAR, BETH
WEAVER, TAPESTRY ARTIST
b Evanston, Ill, Aug 31, 1939. *Study:* Skidmore Col. *Work:* Nat Inst Health, Bethesda, Md; Sulzer-Ruti Corp, Switz. *Comn:* Wall rug, Sulzer-Ruti Corp, Switz, 85, 87 & 96; wall rug, Scribner, Hall & Thompson, Washington, 88; and many pvt comns. *Exhib:* Philadelphia Craft Show, Pa, 87 & 89; Am Craft at the Armory, NY, 88 & 89; Washington Craft Show, 88 & 93; traveling mus show, Art that Works: The Decorative Arts of the Eighties, 90-93; Creative Arts Ctr Fiber Show, Chatham, Mass, 96; and others. *Awards:* Merit Award, Guild Am Crafts Awards, 87; Grant, DC Comn Arts & Humanities, 92. *Bibliog:* Bill Henry (auth), Artist profile, Hill Rag, 88; Maryann Ondovcsik (auth), Artist profile, Matter Mag, 90. *Mem:* Cape Mus Fine Arts, Dennis, Mass; Creative Arts Ctr, Chatham, Mass; Am Crafts Coun, NY. *Media:* Fiber. *Mailing Add:* PO Box 2165 Orleans MA 02653-6165

MINEO, JEAN
GALLERY DIRECTOR
Study: Rochester Inst Tech, BFA; American Univ, MA (arts mgt). *Pos:* Exec dir, New Art Center in Newton, Newtonville, Mass, 1994-2003; coordr, Jamaica Plains Open Studios, 2006-2010; dir, Boston Sculptors Gallery, 2006-; chair, Medfield Cultural Council. *Specialty:* Contemporary sculpture, Northeast artists. *Mailing Add:* Boston Sculptors Gallery 486 Harrison Ave Boston MA 02118

MINGWEI, LEE
PAINTER, ARTIST
b Taichung, Taiwan, 1964. *Study:* Calif Coll Arts and Crafts, BA (textile arts), 93; Yale Univ, MFA (sculpture), 97. *Exhib:* Solo exhibs, Isabel Percy West Gallery, Calif, 93, Lombard-Freid Fine Arts, NY, 97, 2000, 2003, The Fabric Workshop and Mus, Philadelphia, 98, Whitney Mus Am Art, NY, 98, Cleveland Ctr for Contemp Art, 99, Davis Mus, Wellesley Coll, 2000, Ft Lauderdale Mus Art, 2000, Isabella Stewart Gardner Mus, Boston, 2000, Eslite Gallery, Taipei, 2002, Rice Univ Art Mus, Houston, 2002, Harvard Univ, Mass, 2003, Mus Modern Art, NY, 2003, Bunker Mus Contemp Art, 2004, Mus fur Ostasiatische Kunst, Cologne, Germany, 2005, Albion Gallery, London, 2006, Queensland Gallery Modern Art, Australia, 2006, Sherman Galleries, Sydney, 2006, Neuberger Mus Art, NY, 2006, Taipei Mus Art, 2007, Chicago Cultural Ctr, 2007; group exhibs, Reflection, Yale Art and Archit Gallery, New Haven, 97; Money for Art, Refusalon, San Francisco, 97; Plural Speech, White Box, NY, 98; AsiaPacific Triennial, Queensland Art Gallery, Australia, 99; Worthless, Moderna Galerija Ljubljana, Slovenia, 2000; The Shrine Project, Taipei Beinnial, Taiwan, 2000; Male Pregnancy Project, Mus Contemp Art, Taipei, 2001, Fiction Love, 2004; The Gift, Scottsdale Mus Contemp Art, Ariz, 2002; Mind Space, Ho-AM Art Mus, Seoul, 2003; The Magic Makers, Des Moines Ctr Art, Ohio, 2003; Away from Home, Wexner Ctr Arts, Columbus, Ohio, 2003; Whitney Biennial, Whitney Mus Am Art, NY, 2004; This Storm We Call Progress, Arnolfini Ctr Arts, Bristol, Eng, 2005; Spice Box, Contemp Jewish Mus, Calif, 2005; We Are the World, El Museo Nacional Centre de Arte Reina Sofia, Madrid, 2005; Zhua-Zhou Project, Between the Lakes: Artists Respond to Madison, Mus Contemp Art, Madison, Wis, 2007; Echigo-Tsumari Art Triennial, Japan, 2006; Memory of Fabric, Liverpool Biennial - Int Festival of Contemp Art, Eng, 2006; 1.5, Queens Mus Art, NY, 2007. *Mailing Add:* c/o Lombard Freid Projects 518 W 19th St New York NY 10011

MINICK, ROGER
PHOTOGRAPHER, WRITER
b Ramona, Okla, July 13, 1944. *Study:* Univ Calif, Berkeley, BA (hist), 69; Univ Calif, Davis, FMA, 86. *Work:* Mus Mod Art, Metropolitan Mus Art, NY; San Francisco Mus Mod Art; Los Angeles Co Mus Art; Houston Mus Fine Arts. *Comn:* Photo Survey, Nat Endowment Arts, 77, 78 & 80; Paramount Theater, Lancaster-Miller, Berkeley, 82. *Exhib:* Solo exhibs, Delta and Ozark Photographs, Friends of Photography, 71, Delta Photos, Int Ctr Photog, NY, 75, Ozark Photographs, Univ Art Mus, 75, Hunter Mus Art, Tenn, 75, Sightseers Series, Grapestake Gallery, San Francisco, Calif, 81, Jan Kesner Gallery, 97, 2000; Am Photogrs and National Parks, Corcoran Gallery, 81, Amon Carter Mus, Ft Worth, 82 & Los Angeles Co Mus Art, 83; Espejo: Photographs of the Mexican-American Community, Ctr Creative Photog, Tucson, 83; Photog in Calif: '45 to 80, San Francisco Mus Mod Art, 84 & Ctr Georges Pompidou, Paris, 85; Jan Kesner Gallery, LA, 96, 97, 98, 99; Yancey Richardson Gallery, NY, 98; LA County Mus Art, Calif, 2000; Friends of Photography, San Francisco, 2001; Oakland Mus, Calif, 2001; Mus Photographic Arts, San Diego, 85, 2004; George Eastman House, Rochester, NY, 2004. *Teaching:* Dir & instr photog, Asn Students Univ Calif Studio, Berkeley, 66-75; instr, Ansel Adams Workshop, Yosemite, 74, 75, 76 & 82, Owens Valley Workshop, Sacramento Delta, Calif, 79 & 81; instr photog, Acad Art Col, San Francisco, 86-. *Awards:* Am Inst Graphic Arts Award, New York, 70; Guggenheim Fel, 72; Nat Endowment Arts Grant, 77, 78, 80; Gyorgy Kepes Grant in Photography, 88. *Bibliog:* A D Coleman (auth), Light Readings, Oxford Univ Press, 79; Hal Fischer (auth), article, Art Forum, summer 81. *Publ:* Auth, Delta West: Land and People of Sacramento-San Joaquin Delta, 69 & Hills of Home: Rural Ozarks of Arkansas, 75, Scrimshaw Press; contribr, American Photographers & the National Parks, Viking Press, 81; auth, Paramount Theater, Lancaster-Miller, 82; coauth, In the Fields, Harvest Press, 82

MINKKINEN, ARNO RAFAEL
PHOTOGRAPHER
b Helsinki, Finland, 1945. *Study:* Wagner Coll, BA (english), 1963-67; New Sch for Social Res, 1971-72; Sch Visual Arts, 1971-72; RI Sch Design, MFA (photog), 1972-74. *Exhib:* Solo exhibs include Spectrum Gallery, Tucson, Ariz, 1972, Gallery for Creative Photog, Copenhagen, 1973, Photographic Mus Finland, 1974, 1984, Forografiska Museet at Moderna Museet, 1976, Yuen Lui Gallery, Seattle, 1979, 1982, Robert Klein Gallery, Boston, 1983, Galerie Viviane Esders, Paris, 1986, Port Art Mus, Finland, 1987, Barry Friedman Ltd, New York, 1988, Bannister Gallery, RI, 1989, Peri Ctr Photog, Turku, Finland, 1990, Available Light Gallery, Jacksonville, Fla, 1991, Mus Mod Art, Nice, France, 1991, Images Ctr Photog, Cincinnati, 1992, Les Parvis, Tarbes, France, 1993, Akehurst Gallery, London, 1994, Pori Art Mus, Finland, 1995, Sundsvall Museet, Sweden, 1996, Am Cult Ctr, Prague, 1998, Met Mus Photog, Tokyo, 2000, Finland Univ, Hancock, Mich, 2001; group exhibs include Soho Photo Gallery, New York, 1972; Marcuse Pfeifer Gallery, New York, 1978; Keene State Coll, NH, 1980; Santa Barbara Mus Art, 1982 ; Theatre Antique, Arles, France, 1983; Mus Rimbaud, Charleville, France, 1984; Victor Barsokevitsch Mus, Finland, 1986; Circulo de Bellas Artes, Madrid, 1987; Burden Gallery, New York, 1988; French Cult Ctr, Brussels, 1989; Univ North Fla, 1990; Boston Ctr for Arts, 1991; Boston Ctr for Arts, 1991; Kerava Art Mus, 1992; L'Acquario Romano, Rome, 1993; Mus Fine Arts Boston, 1994; Basel Art Fair, 1995, 2000; Wash Ctr Photog, 1996; Belem Cult Ctr, Lisbon, Portugal, 1997; Skopelos Ctr Photog, Greece, 1998; Park Ave Armory, New York, 1998; Ctr Creative Photog, Tucson, 1999; Djanolgy Art Gallery, Nottingham, Eng, 2001; Robert Kelin Gallery, 2001. *Pos:* Copywriter, Quinn & Johnson/BBDO, Boston, 1982; creative dir, Crosson, Wolf & Partners, Boston, 1986. *Teaching:* Asst prof, Mass Inst Tech, 1977; vis artist, Philadelphia Coll Art, 1981; fac, Univ Arts & Design Helsinki, 1984, docent photog, 1992; tchr, Lahti Inst Design, 1984; grad fac, Rockport Coll; assoc prof art, Univ Lowell (now Univ Mass Lowell), 1988-93, prof, 1993-. *Awards:* New Eng Found for Arts, Boston, 1991; Order of Lion First Class, Helsinki, Finland, 1992; Grand Prix du Livre, 25th Recontres d'Arles, France, 1994; Scritture d'Acqua, Salsomaggiore, Italy, 1996; Silver Key/Still Not There, Trebianka Solvice Film Festival, 1998. *Dealer:* Barry Friedman Ltd 515 West 26th St New York NY 10001 ; Robert Klein Gallery 38 Newbury Street Boston MA 02116. *Mailing Add:* c/o Tibor de Nagy Gallery 724 Fifth Ave New York NY 10019

MINKOWITZ, NORMA
SCULPTOR
b New York, NY, Oct 19, 1937. *Study:* Cooper Union Art Sch, 58. *Hon Degrees:* Fel, Am Crafts Council. *Work:* Nat Mus Art/Renwick Gallery Smithsonian Inst, Washington, DC; Mus Arts and Design & Metrop Mus Art, NY; Wadsworth Antheneum, Hartford, Conn; Erie Art Mus, Pa; Charles A Wustum Mus Fine Arts, Racine, Wis; Philbrook Mus Art, Tulsa, Okla; Mint Mus Art, Charlotte, NC; Kwan Mus, Korea, DeCordora; Contemp Mus, Honolulu, HI; Detroit Inst Art, Mich; Philadephia Mus Art, PA; Denver Art Mus, Colo; MH de Young Mem Mus, San Francisco; Montreal Mus Art; Houston Mus Fine Arts; Mus Int Folk Art, Santa Fe, NMex. *Exhib:* Solo exhibs: The Body As Vessel, Bellas Artes Gallery, NY, Bellas Artes, Santa Fe, 2007, Snyderman/Works Gallery, Phila, Pa, 2013; group exhibs include The Tactile Vessel, Erie Art Mus, Erie, Pa, 88; Exploring the Figure in Sculptured Forms, Newport Art Mus, RI, 90; The Female Form in Contemp Art, Wadsworth Atheneum, 90; Modern Design 1880-1990, Twentieth Century Art, Metrop Mus Art, NY, 92; 5th Int Shoebox Sculpture Exhib (catalog), Univ Hawaii, 94; Fiber Five Decades from the ACM, Am Craft Mus, NY, 95; Out on a Limb, Bellas Artes Gallery, Santa Fe, NMex, 96; 9th Int Triennial Tapestry, Lodz, Poland, 98; Weaving the World, Contemp Art of Linear Construction, Yokohama Mus Art, Japan, 99; Miniatures, Mus Art Design, Helsinki, Finland, 2000; US Dept State, Lome, Toga; Trienniala Form and Contents: Mus Für Angewandte Kunst, Frankfurt, ger, 03; Chicago Anthenaeum 2003, Mus Arts & Design, New York City; Fiber Art: Following the Thread, Smithsonian Archives Am Art, 02; Wadsworth Atheneum, Tradition/Transitions; Metrop Mus Art, 2007; Intertwined, Lieberman Collection, Mus Arts & Design, New York, 2010. *Collection Arranged:* Mus Art, RI Sch Design; M H DeYoung Mem Mus, Calif; Contemp Mus, Hawaii; Kwang Ju Mus, Korea; Mus Int Folk Art, Mass; DeCordova Mus Art, Mass; Detroit Inst Art; Mathers of Pattern, Comm on the Arts, Grant Winners, 2009; Metrop Mus Art, New York. *Awards:* Artquest First Place Fiber, Artquest 86, Nat Competition, 86; Visual Arts Fel Grant, Nat Endowment Arts, 86; Purchase Award, Conn Comn Arts, 92; Named 100 Oustanding Conn Women, United Nations, 2000; Conn Comn on Arts Fellowship Grant, 02; Master of the Medium Award, James Renwick Alliance, 2009. *Bibliog:* Oral History Program Art News, Smithsonian Archives Am Art, 2002; Dottie Indike (auth), Nouvel Object IV, 9/2002; Portfolio Coll, Norma Minkowitz, Telos Art Publ, 2004. *Mem:* Am Crafts Coun (mem Coll fel); Conn Comn Arts. *Media:* Miscellaneous Media, Fiber, Paper, Mixed Media. *Res:* Smithsonian, Archives Am Art, Oral History Program, 2002. *Specialty:* fine arts. *Collection:* contemp art. *Publ:* contribr, Art News, Fiberarts, Surface Design; Sofa Catalog Essay, 2004; Sculpture Mag, 2005. *Dealer:* Brown Grotta Gallery Wilton Conn 06897; Snyderman/Works Gallery 303 Cherry St Pa. *Mailing Add:* 25 Broadview Rd Westport CT 06880

MINSKOFF, EDWARD & JULIE J
COLLECTORS
Study: Mich State Univ, undergrad; Univ Calif, MBA. *Hon Degrees:* Michigan State Univ, Hon PhD in Bus, 2009. *Pos:* Chief financial officer, Olympia & York; founder & chmn, Edward J Minskoff Equities Inc; chmn endowment, pediatric oncology, and trustee, NY Univ Med Ctr; bd dirs, NY Univ Med Ctr Cancer Inst; vice chmn & bd trustee, NY Univ Medicine Found; adv bd mem, NY Univ Real Estate Inst; bd trustee, Mus of Contemp Art; mem chmn's circle, Carnegie Hall; bd mem, Partnership for

NYC; real estate develop adv bd mem, Columbia Univ Graduate Sch of Arch and Planning; mem mixed/use coun, Urban Land Inst; mem. real estate coun, Metropolitan Mus of Art; founding mem, Friends of Modern Art, Metropolitan Mus of Art; mem steering com, Lincoln Ctr for the Performing Arts; dir, Realty Found of NY. *Awards:* Named one of Top 200 Collectors, ARTnews mag, 2006-12. *Mem:* Asn for a Better New York (exec comt); Real Estate Bd NY (gov); Asn of Builders and Owners. *Collection:* Postwar, Pop and contemporary American and European art. *Mailing Add:* 1325 Ave of Americas 53rd St New York NY 10019

MINSKY, RICHARD
CONCEPTUAL ARTIST, BOOK ARTIST

b New York, NY, Jan 7, 1947. *Study:* Brooklyn Col, BA (cum laude), 68; New Sch Social Res, 69-71; Brown Univ, MA, 70. *Work:* Victoria & Albert Mus; Hirshhorn Mus & Sculpture Garden; New York Pub Libr Rare Book Room; Nat Gallery Art; Getty Ctr; Metrop Mus Art; Yale Univ; Arts of the Book Coll; Art Inst Chicago; and many more. *Comn:* Leather & ivory binding for The Unicorn Tapestries, Metrop Mus Art, NY, 76; binding on Sha'arei Tefiloh, Donglomur Found, Villanova, Pa, 76; Program Book, White House, Washington, 77; binding for Buckminster Fuller's Tetrascroll, Universal Limited Art Ed, West Islip, NY, 77; Gracie Mansion regist, Gracie Mansion Conservancy, NY, 85; Brooklyn Mus Regist, 90. *Exhib:* Solo exhibs, Zabriskie Gallery, NY, 74 & 88, Allan Stone Gallery, 81 & Twining Gallery, NY 90, 25 Yr Retrospective, Harper Collins Gallery, NY, 92, Louis K Meisel Gallery, NY, 2002, Oberlin Col, 2002, Minn Ctr Book Arts, Minneapolis, 2003 & Syracuse Univ, 2005, Yale Univ, 2010; The Object as Poet, Renwick Gallery, 77 & Mus Contemp Crafts, NY, 77; The Artist and the Book, Dayton Arts Inst, Ohio, 78; Int Leather Arts Exhib, Sawtooth Ctr Visual Design, Winston-Salem, NC, 84; The First Decade, NY Pub Libr, 85; Bookworks by Photographers, Watson Libr, Metrop Mus Art, NY, 86; A Survey of Bk Arts, Queens Mus, Flushing, NY, 87; The Eloquent Object, Philbrook Mus, Tulsa, Okla, 87, Chicago Pub Libr Cult Ctr, Mus Fine Arts, Boston & Oakland Mus, Calif, 88, Va Mus Fine Arts & Orlando Mus Art, 89; Invitational Exhib, Benton Gallery, Southampton, NY; Book Making: Practical & Provocative, Painted Bride, Philadelphia; Completing the Circle: Artists' Books on the Environment (traveling exhib), Minn Ctr for Book Arts, 92; Redefing the Book, Brainstein/Quay Gallery, San Francisco, 95; Love, Arlene Bujeje Gallery, East Hampton, NY, 96; Legible Forms (traveling exhib); Legible Forms, Contemp Art Ctr Va, 99; Not for Publication, Hillwood Mus, Long Island Univ, NY, 2001; Love and/or Terror, Univ Ariz Mus Art, Tucson, 2003; Beyond Reading: Contemp Book Art, Ellipse Art Ctr, Arlington, Va, 2003; The Book at the Back of the Mind, Rutgers Univ, NJ, 2004; What's in a Book, Katonah Mus Art, 2004; Somewhere Far from Habit: The Poet and the Artist's Book, Pierre Menard Gallery, Cambridge, 2009; Beaten and Bound, Lubeznik Ctr for the Arts, Mich City, In, 2012. *Collection Arranged:* Book Artchitecture, Watson Libr, Metrop Mus Art, NY, 85; The Bookworks of Tom Phillips, Ctr Bk Arts, NY, 86; The Effects of Time, Bookworks: London, Jean de Gonet, Ctr Bk Arts, NY, 87; Book Arts in the USA, Ctr Bk Arts, NY & nine venues in Africa & S Am under US Info Agency sponsorship, 90-92; Out of Bounds, Creative Arts Workshop, New Haven, Conn, 94; Open for Action, Ctr Book Arts, New York, 2003. *Pos:* Founder, Ctr Book Arts, 74, pres, 74-78, chmn, 74-82 & 2002-2008, cur, 85-86, pres, 90-98. *Teaching:* Instr book arts, Sch Visual Arts, New York, 77-; instr, Experimental Book Purchase Coll, NY, 2010. *Awards:* Nat Endowment Arts Fels, 77-81; Grant, Pollock-Krasner Found, 96. *Bibliog:* Ed McCormack (auth), From neo-conceptual to bodies, Artspeak, 4/21/81; Rose Slivka (auth), Richard Minsky, Arts Mag, 5/88; Caroline Seebohm (auth), Richard Minsky, At Home with Books, Clarkson Potter, 95. *Mem:* Ctr Bk Arts; Guild of Bookworkers; College Art Asn; Art Libr Asn North Am; Am Printing Hist Asn. *Media:* Books; Gold, Gems. *Res:* Art & cognition; history of the book art movement; Am book covers, Asn hist of Am art. *Specialty:* Book art. *Publ:* Contribr, The decade: Change and continuity, Craft Horizons, 6/76; Innovation from Tradition in the Book Arts, Am Craft, 93; auth, Minsky in London, pvt publ, 80; Minsky in Bed, pvt publ, 96; American Decorated Publishers' Bindings 1870-1929, 2006, vol.2, 2009, vol.3, 2010; The Second Life Art World (SLART), 2007; American book Covers 1875-1930, George Braziller Publ, 2010; auth, The Book Art of Richard Minsky: My Life in Book Art, George Braziller Publ, 2011; The Book Cover Art of Thomas Watson Ball, 2012. *Dealer:* Allan Stone Gallery 113 E 90th St New York NY; Zabriskie Gallery 41 E 57th St New York NY; Louis K Meisel Gallery, 141 Prince St NY. *Mailing Add:* 413 County Rte 22 Hudson NY 12534

MINTICH, MARY RINGELBERG
SCULPTOR, CRAFTSMAN

b Detroit, Mich. *Study:* Albion Col; Ind Univ, BA; Queens Col; Univ Tenn; Univ NC, Greensboro, MFA. *Work:* Everson Mus Art, Syracuse, NY; Mint Mus Art, Charlotte, NC; RJ Reynolds; St Johns Art Mus, Wilmington, NC; Nations Bank; SC State Art Collection; Am Express. *Comn:* Sculpture, NC Arts Coun, Waterworks Gallery, Salisbury, 84; Capitol Ctr, Raleigh, NC; Cent Charlotte Asn, Charlotte, NC. *Exhib:* Mint Art Mus, Charlotte, NC; McKissick Mus, Columbia, SC, 81; Greenville Mus Art, SC, 81; Southeastern Ctr Contemp Art, Winston-Salem, NC; NC Mus Art, Raleigh; Clemson Univ; Columbia Mus, SC; Atlanta Arts Festival, Ashville Mus; SC State Mus. *Teaching:* Sacred Heart Col, 67-73; Penland Sch Crafts, 72; prof sculpture, design & metals, Winthrop Univ, 72-. *Awards:* Purchase Awards, Ceramics Nat & 8th Regional Piedmont Crafts Exhib; Purchase Award, SC, The State of the Arts, SC Arts Comn. *Mem:* Tri-State Sculptors; Int Sculpture Ctr; Piedmont Craftsmen Inc. *Media:* Multimedia. *Dealer:* Hodges Taylor Gallery 227 N Tryon St Charlotte NC. *Mailing Add:* PO Box 913 Belmont NC 28012

MION, PIERRE RICCARDO
ILLUSTRATOR, PAINTER

b Bryn Mawr, Pa, Dec 10, 1931. *Study:* George Washington Univ; Corcoran Gallery Sch of Art, Montgomery Col, with Elliot O'Hara; also privately with Norman Rockwell. *Work:* Nat Geographic; Smithsonian Air & Space Mus; Smithsonian Mus Nat Hist. *Comn:* Team portrait of Apollo astronauts, Nat Geographic Soc; paintings of space futures, Look Mag, 69; mural, Antarctica, Nat Air & Space Mus, Washington, DC; stamp, Va Statehood, US Postal Serv; postcards incl Blairhouse, US Postal Serv, The Whitehouse, 89, Jefferson Mem, 89 & Washington, DC, Bicentenial, 91; and several other stamps. *Exhib:* Nat Ann Watercolor Exhib, Smithsonian Inst, 51 & 63; Robots to the Moon, Hayden Planetarium, NY, 63; Artist & Space, Nat Gallery Art, Washington, 69; Space Art, Smithsonian Inst Air & Space Mus, 71 & Hudson River Mus, Yonkers, NY, 72; Solo exhibs, Acad of the Arts, Easton, Md, 72 & Metropolis Bldg Asn, Washington, 76; Int Space Art Show, Utrecht, The Neth, 86; Nat Geographic 100 Yrs Show, Soc Illusrs, NY, 88; Int Space Art Show, Madrid, Toledo, Seville, Barcelona, Spain, 90; Nat Geographic Art Show, Soc Illusr, NY, 2000; 5 Pieces in 100 Years of National Geographic Illustration, Norman Rockwell Mus, Stockbridge, Mass, Traveling thru the US; Northern Ariz Watercolor Soc, Sedona, 2011, 2012. *Collection Arranged:* numerous one-man shows. *Pos:* Art dir illus, Creative Arts Studio, Washington, DC, 57-60; vpres art-design, Northern Sci Indust Exhibs, 64-66. *Teaching:* Instr illus, Marine Corps Inst, Washington, DC, 53-54; instr watercolor, Bethesda, Md, 81-82; instr watercolor, Pagosa Springs, Colo, 2002-2010; instr, Watercolor Portrature, Sedona Arts Center, Sedona, Ariz, 2011, 2012. *Awards:* Award of Excellence, Int Edit Design Competition, 81; Award, Soc Publ Designers; Merit Award, Art Dirs Club; First Prize, Watercolor, Waterford Show, 86; Best Lodoun Co Artist, Waterford, 89, 90 & 95; 1st Place in Juried Exhib, Pagosa Springs, 2006, 2010; Award of Excellence, Northern Ariz Watercolor Soc, 2012; People's Choice award; Sedona Art Mus, Artist of the Month, 2014. *Bibliog:* Pierre Mion presents one-man show, Baltimore Sun, 72; Mary Runde (auth), Intensity brings detail to Mion's paintings, Star-Democrat, 72; Artist's cards get post office's stamp of approval, Washington Post, 89; Kudosaz, Sedona Monthly, Newspaper Biography, 2012; and many others. *Mem:* Soc Illusrs; Int Asn Astronomical Artists; Northern Ariz Watercolor Soc; SAGA. *Media:* Acrylic, Oil; Gouache, Watercolor. *Specialty:* Western Art. *Interests:* Travel; Model Railroading; Camping, 4x4 Wheeling. *Collection:* NASA, Smithsonian Nat Air & Space Mus; Nat Geographic; US Marine Corps Combat Art Collection. *Publ:* Illusr, The squalus is down, Reader's Digest, 68; All-girl team tests the habitat, 71 & First colony in space, 76, Nat Geographic; The Titanic, 86 & Mission to Mars, 88, Nat Geographic; Nile River Temples, 95; Population Supplement, Nat Geographic, 98; and many others. *Dealer:* Wild Spirit Gallery Pagosa Springs Colo. *Mailing Add:* 5975 La Privada Dr Cornville AZ 86325

MIOTKE, ANNE E
PAINTER, EDUCATOR

b Milwaukee, Wis, Aug 31, 1943. *Study:* Mount Mary Col, Milwaukee, BA, 65; Univ Wis-Milwaukee, with John N Colt & Laurence Rathsack, MS, 70 & MFA, 73. *Work:* Scripps, Howard Corp Hq, Cincinnati; Gilberts Commonwealth Asn, Reading, Pa; Deloitte, Haskins & Sells, Cincinnati; IBM, Los Angeles; and many others. *Comn:* Still life painting (publ as mus poster), Paine Art Ctr & Arboretum, Oshkosh, Wis, 92; Homage: Brooks Stevens painting and edited print, Milwaukee Chap, Young Presidents' Orgn, 93; Corporate Portrait (still life), The Jansen Group Inc, Milwaukee; Miller Art Mus, Sturgeon Bay, Wis. *Exhib:* J B Speed Art Mus, Louisville, 74; one-person shows, Dorothy Bradley Gallery, Milwaukee, 78, 81, 83, 85, 87, 89 & 91; Wustrum Art Mus, Racine, 69, 71-73, 93-2005; Yeiser Art Ctr, Paducah, Ky, 96; Tory Folliard Gallery, Milwaukee, Wis, 93, 95, 97, 99, 2001 & 2005; Charles Allis Art Mus, Milwaukee, Wis, 2004; and many other group and solo exhibs. *Pos:* Bd mem, Milwaukee Area Teachers of Art, 67-70; contrib ed, Midwest Art, 75-77. *Teaching:* Instr art, Mount Mary Col, Milwaukee, 70-72 & Layton Sch Art & Design, Milwaukee, 73-74; asst, Univ Wis-Milwaukee, 72-73; prof fine art, Art Acad Cincinnati, 74-92; adj prof, Milwaukee Inst Art & Design, 92-2005; adj prof, Mount Mary College, Milwaukee, Wis, 2005-. *Awards:* Nat Endowment Arts Vis Specialist Grant, Milwaukee Art Mus, 75-79; Nat Endowment Arts Guest Cur Grant, John Michael Kohler Arts Ctr, Sheboygan, Wis, 79; Ohio Arts Coun Fel, 80-81 & 88-89. *Mem:* Coll Art Asn Am; Am Asn Univ Prof; Phi Kappa Phi. *Media:* Watercolor, Mixed. *Res:* Reverse glass painting research for the Milwaukee Art Mus & the Jon Michael Kohler Arts Ctr, Sheboygan, Wis. *Collection:* Am Bank, Beechwood, Ohio; IBM, Los Angeles, Calif; Miller Brewing Co, Milwaukee, Wis; The Univ Wis, Madison; The Charles A Wustum Mus Fine Arts, Racine, Wis. *Publ:* Contrib ed, Midwest Art, 75-77; contribr, Glass/Backwards (exhib catalog), John Michael Kohler Arts Ctr, Sheboygan, Wis, 79. *Dealer:* Tory Folliard Gallery 233 N Milwaukee St Milwaukee WI 53202; Edgewood Orchard Galleries Peninsula Players Rd Fish Creek WI 54212; Grace Chosy Gallery 1825 Monroe St Madison WI 53711. *Mailing Add:* 4791 N Elkhart Ave Whitefish Bay WI 53211-1002

MIOTTE, JEAN
PAINTER

b Paris, France, 1926. *Study:* Ateliers Montparnasse. *Work:* Guggenheim Mus, NY; Cooper Hewitt Mus, Mus Mod Art, Smithsonian Inst, Nat Mus Design, NY; Bayrisch Staatsgoldesammlung, Munich; Mus D'Art Moderne, Paris; Ludwig Mus, Cologne; and others. *Comn:* Sculpture, Pub Sch Marcq-en-Baroel, France, 77; sculpture, Pub Sch, Orleans, France, 77; mural, rue Emile Zola, Paris, 91. *Exhib:* Kunstverein Cologne, 62; Kunst in Europe 1920-60, Cult Ctr Mechelen, 76; solo exhibs, N Mus, Singapore, 83, N Mus O/Hist, Taipeh, 83, Striped House Mus, Tokyo, Japan, 84, Seibu Mus, Tokyo, 90, Palais des Arts, Toulouse, 92, Mus Dunkirchen, 93 & Mus Les Cordeliers, Chateauroux, 94, Columbia Univ, Maison Francaise, NY, 1994, Mucsarnok Mus, Budapest, 1996, Wilhelm Hack Mus, Budapest, 1997, Nat Arts Club, NY, 1998, Mus d'Art Moderne et d'Art Contemp, Galeries Dufy et Mossa, Nice, France, 1998, Mus d'Art & d'Histoire, Fribourg, Switz, 1999, Jan van der Togt Mus, Amsterdam, 1999, Mus am Ostwall, Dortmund, Ger, 2000, Castle Prague, 2000, Mus Ludwig, Koblenz, Ger, 2000, Aboa Vetus Ars Nova Mus, Turku, Finland, 2000, Mus Contemp Art, Villa Heiss, Ger, 2000, Mus Brno, Czech Republic, 2002; Memoires de la Liberte, Ctr Poupidou, Paris, 91; Bard Col, Procter Art Ctr, NJ, 94; Musee d'Art Moderne et d'Art Contemporain, Nice; Wilhelm-Hack-Mus, Ludwighafen. *Teaching:* prof Tourcoing Beaux Arts, 1 yr. *Awards:* Ford Found Grant, 61. *Bibliog:* J L Chalumeau (auth), Fragment, Miotte Coll, Passeport, Paris, 90; M Pleynet (auth), Cercle d'Art, Miotte, Paris, 93; Karl Ruhrberg (auth), La Difference, Paris, 98; Himes, Pleynet, Tan Swie (auth), La Difference, Paris, 1988; M Pleynet (auth), Gimpel &

Weitzenhoffer, 1988; C Himes (auth), SMI, Paris, 1977; A Verdet (auth), Keeser, Hamburg, 1996; C Morgan (auth), Guy Pieters, St Paul de Vence, 2000; Ingo Bartsch, Beate Reifenscheid (auth), Mus Ludwig, Coblence Mus am Ostwall, Dortmund, 2000; Kingsley (auth), Mus Turku, 2000; JC Lambert (auth), Mus Dunkerque, 1991; Mus Dunkerque, 1991; H Paalman (auth), Mus Amstelveen, 1999; J Yau (auth), Nat Arts Club, New York, 1998; H Gercke (auth), Mus Chateauroux, 1994. *Media:* Acrylic, Oil, Etching, Lithographic. *Dealer:* Chapel Art Ctr Cologne & Hamburg Ger; Galerie von Braunbehren Munchen Ger; Galerie Wild, Frankfurt; Galerie Helene Lamarque, Paris; Galerie Guy Pieters, St Paul de Vence; Galerie Walter Bischoff, Stuttgart

MIR, ALEKSANDRA
CONCEPTUAL ARTIST
b Lubin, Poland, 1967. *Study:* Schillerska/Gothenburg Univ, Sweden, 87; Sch Visual Arts, BFA, New York, 92; New Sch Soc Res, New York, 96. *Exhib:* Solo exhibs, Life is Sweet in Sweden, Trixter, Gothenburg, 95, Pick UP (oh baby), Lyd/Galerie, Copenhagen, 97, City Forest (prototype), Tompkins Sq Park, NY, 98, Conspiracy Night, Swiss Institute, NY, 99, Gavin Brown's enterprise, NY, 2001, Corp Mentality, Lukas & Sternberg, NY, 2002, Naming Tokyo (part II), Swiss Inst, NY, 2003, Happy Holidays, The Wrong Gallery, NY, 2003, The Big Umbrella, NY, PS1 Contemp Art Ctr, NY, 2004, New Commission, Fundacion NMAC, Montenmedio, 2005, Gravity, Space Soom, Arts Catalyst, The Roundhouse, London, 2006, The Meaning of Flowers, Gaviak, Art Basel Miami Beach, 2006, Newsroom 1986-2000, Mary Boone Gallery, NY, 2007, White House, 2008, Plane Landing-Photography, Galerie Laurent Godin, Paris, 2009, The Church, Galeria Joan Prats, Barcelona, 2009; Empires without States, Swiss Inst, NY, 99; Democracy!, Royal Coll Art, London, 2000; COPY, Roth Horowitz Gallery, NY, 2002; The Twentieth Anniversary Show, Gavin Brown's Enterprise, NY, 2003; Sandwiched, Jacob Fabricius, NY, 2003; Power, Corruption & Lies, Roth Horowitz, NY, 2004; California Earthquakes, Daniel Reich Gallery, NY, 2004; Whitney Biennial, Whitney Mus Am Art, 2004; Monuments for the USA, CCAC Wattis Inst, San Francisco, 2005; Organized Movement, Andrew Kreps Gallery, New York, 2005; Hiding In the Light, Mary Boone Gallery, New York, 2006; USA Today, Royal Acad Arts, London, 2006; The Big Easy, ACC Galerie Weinmer, 2007; Making a Scene, Fondazione Morra Greco, Naples, 2008; The End, Andy Warhol Mus, Pittsburgh, 2009; Entrance Strategies, San Francisco Mus Mod Art, 2009; Making Worlds, 53rd Int Venice Biennial, Italy, 2009; Retro-Retro Tech, San Jose Mus Art, 2010. *Bibliog:* David Pagel (auth), Passionate Red-State Manifesto, Los Angeles Times, 7/7/2006; Alex Gartenfeld (auth), Postcards from Europe, Interview Mag, 6/18/2009; Holland Cotter (auth), In Numbers, NY Times, 1/28/2010. *Mailing Add:* c/o Andrew Roth 160 A E 70th St New York NY 10021

MIRAGLIA, ANTHONY J
EDUCATOR, PAINTER
b Militello Rosmarino, Sicily, Italy, Feb 10, 1949; US citizen. *Study:* Cleveland Inst Art, BFA (painting), 73; Syracuse Univ, MFA (painting), 75. *Work:* Southern Alleghenies Mus Art, Loretto, Pa; Kenneth C Beck Center Visual/Performing Arts, Lakewood, Ohio; The Cabot Corp, Boston, Mass; Matsui Corp, Cleveland, Ohio; Nat City Bank Corp, Cleveland, Ohio. *Exhib:* The May Show, Cleveland Mus Art, Ohio, 72; Regional Juried Exhibition, Rochester Mem Art Gallery, NY, 75; Dedication & Inaugural Exhibition, Southern Alleghenies Mus Art, Loretto, Pa, 76; 40th Ann Mid-Year Show, Butler Inst Am Art, Loretto, Pa, 76; La Grange Nationa XV, La Grange, Ga, 90; Texas National 99, Austin State Univ, 99; National Juried Exhibition, Artforms Gallery, Philadelphia, Pa, 99; Concerning the Spiritual in Art, New Bedford Art Mus, Mass, 2000. *Pos:* acad adv Mediterranean studies, Univ Mass, 99-. *Teaching:* prof painting, Univ Mass, 75-. *Mem:* Mus Fine Arts. *Media:* Mixed Media. *Mailing Add:* 105 Gaffney Rd Dartmouth MA 02748

MIRAGLIA, PETER F
ARTIST, PHOTOGRAPHER
Study: Univ Rochester, BA (fine arts/photography), 76; Rochester Inst Tech, 73-75; George Eastman House, Rochester, NY, 73-75. *Work:* Baltimore Mus Art, Md; Calif Mus Photog; Dayton Art Inst, Ohio; The Print Center, Philadelphia; Villanova Univ, Pa; Phila Mus Art, Pa; PNC Bank; Lehigh Univ, Bethlehem, Pa; Rowan Univ, Glassboro, NJ; The Ctr for Photog, Woodstock, NY; Movavian Coll, Bethelhem, Pa; many others. *Exhib:* Contemp Philadelphia Artists, Philadelphia Mus Art, 90; Beyond Aesthetics: Artworks of Conscience, Alternative Mus, NY, 91; Pennsylvania Photographers, Allentown Art Mus, 93; Focus 94, Ctr for Photog Art, Carmel, Calif, 94; Pittsburgh Filmmakers Gallery, 97; Biennial 98, Del Art Mus, 98; Int Competition, Print Center, Philadelphia, 2000; About Face, Del Ctr Contemp Arts, 2000; Pennsylvania Award Winners, Lancaster Mus Art, 2001; Krasdale Gallery, New York City, 2001; Phoenix Gallery, New York City, 2001; Print Center, Philadelphia, 2002; Univ of Arts, Philadelphia, 2002; Del Ctr for Contemp Arts, Wilmington, 2002; JMS Gallery, Philadelphia, 2004, 2007; Allentown Art Mus, 2005; Villanova Univ Art Gallery, 2006; Speer Gallery/Shipley Sch, Bryn Mawr, Pa, 2007; Los Angeles Ctr Digital Art, 2009; Forward Thinking, 2009; The Print Ctr, Phila, 2012; Orange Co Ctr Contemp Art, Calif, 2012; St Joseph's Univ Art Gallery, Phila, 2012; Del Art Mus, 2012; F-Stop Gallery, 2012; Photo Ctr Northwest, 2012; Les Rencontres d'Arles Photographic, 2012; Los Angeles Ctr Digital Art, 2013; United Photo Industries Gallery, Brooklyn, NY, 2013. *Awards:* Pa Coun on Arts Visual Arts Fel, 87, 97, 99 & 2005; Artist Space Individual Artist Grant, NYC, 88; Nat Endowment Arts Visual Arts Fel, 88; First Prize, Photo Review Nat Competition, 94; Finalist The Ctr for Documentary Studies/Honickman Book Prize in Photogr, 2002 & 2004; Photograohy Award, Forward Thinking Mus, 2009. *Bibliog:* Anne d'Harononcourt (auth), Contemp Philadelphia Artists, Philadelphia Mus Art, 90; Jeanne Nugent (auth), Beyond Aesthetics: Artworks of Conscience, The Alternative Mus, NYC, 91; Burton Wasserman (auth), Peter Miraglia - A Photographer's Photographer, Art Matters, 2/94; Nela Principe-Nelson (auth), Portraits-interview with Peter Miraglia, Photographer's Forum, 2000; Helene Ryesky (auth), The Work of Peter Miraglia, The Photo Review, 2000; Dede Young (auth), About Face, Del Center for Cont Arts, 2000; D Dominick Lombardi (auth), Krasdale Exhibit Review, The Sunday NY Times, 5/27/2001; Victoria Donohoe (auth), Peter Miraglia, review with reproductions, The Phildelphia Inquirer, 2002; R B Strauss (auth), Peter Miraglia / DCCA, Art Matters, 2002; Edward Sozanski; (auth) Portrait of Kerala, The Philadelphia Inquirer (philly.com), 3/26/2004; Victoria Donohoe (auth), Etheral India in Photographs, Philadelphia Inquirer, 11/19/2006; Burton Wasserman (auth), Mirror Images, Art Matters, Philadelphia Inquirer, 11/2006; Amanda McKenna (auth), Portraits from India, City Paper, Philadelphia, 11/8/2006; Random Acts of Time (catalog), Orange Co Ctr Contemp Art, Calif, 2012; F-Stop Mag (portrait issue), 2/2012; Online Jour Art Criticism, 2012; Del Art Mus Centennial Exhib, 2012; Bruce Wasserman (auth), Photographic Portraitist Par Excellence, Art Matters, 2012. *Media:* Gelatin silver prints, Archival pigment prints. *Mailing Add:* 208 Catharine St Philadelphia PA 19147

MIRAN, PATRICIA MARIE
PAINTER, PRINTMAKER
b Seattle, Wash, Apr 6, 1951. *Study:* Calif Coll Arts & Crafts (scholar), 1970; Art Students League (scholar, 1971-1972), Diploma, 1974; Excelsior Coll, BS, 2001; Studied with: Robert Beverly Hale, Robert Schulz, Jack Faragsso, Frank Mason, Earl Mayan, Vincent Malta, Robert Brackman, Jacob Lawrence, Michael Ponce de Leon, Frank Liljegren & Robert de Lamonica. *Work:* Ctr Arts, Homer, NY, May-Sept 2008. *Exhib:* Ann Exhib, Art Students League, New York, NY, 1970-1974; Veteran Artist Outdoor Exhib, Lincoln Ctr, New York, NY, 1971; Ann Exhib, Salmagundi Club, New York, NY, 1975; Group exhib, Whitney Mus Am Art, 1975; The Bank Show, Owego, NY, 2008; Ann Exhib, Arts Coun Southern Finger Lakes, Corning, NY, 2009, 2010, 2011, 2012, 2013, 2014; Bank Show, Owego, NY, 2008, 2009, 2011, 2012, 2013, 2014. *Awards:* Grant, Art Educ for Co Youth, Tioga Co Coun Arts, 1994-1996. *Mem:* Tioga Co Coun Arts; Am Artist Prof League; Studio Program; Arts Coun Southern Finger Lakes. *Media:* Oil, Graphics, Pastels, Watercolor,. *Interests:* Horseback riding, fencing, skiing, poetry & short story writing, photography. *Mailing Add:* 21 Lincoln St Waverly NY 14892

MISHLER, JOHN MILTON
ARTIST, EDUCATOR
b Cairo, Ill, Sept 25, 1946. *Study:* Orange Coast Coll, Calif, AA, 66; Univ of Calif, San Diego, AB, ScM, 67-71; Univ of Oxford, Eng, DPhil, 78; Royal Coll Pathologists, 92. *Exhib:* Art of the State, State Mus of PA, Harrisburg, 99, 2001; Annual Juried Exhib, Woodmere Art Mus, Philadelphia, Pa, 2000 & 2001; Ellarslie Open, Trenton City Mus, NJ, 2001; Non-members Exhib, Salmagundi Club, NY, 2002, 2008-2011; Allied Artists Am, 2004; Nat Juried Exhib, Red River Valley Mus, Vernon, Tex, 2004; Ariz Aqueous XX, Tubac Ctr of the Arts, Tubac, Ariz, 2005-2007; Nat Exhib, Calif Watercolor Assoc, San Francisco, Calif, 2005; Ann Exhibs: Audubon Artists, NY, 2005, 2007-2013, Conn Acad of Fine Arts, 2005, 2008, 2009; Nat exhib, Okla Watercolor Asn, 2005-2010; Nat exhibs: Acad Artists Asn, Mass, Chautauqua Center Visual Arts, NY, 2006; Pennsylvania Watercolor Soc, 2008; Pittsburgh Watercolor Soc, 2007 & 8; Rhode Island Watercolor Soc, 2002, 2007, 2009; Ann Int Exhib, Art Asn Harrisburg, Pa, 2003, 2005, 2009, 2011, 2012. *Teaching:* Prof, Univ Mo, Kansas City, 83-89, Univ MD, East Shore, 89-94 & Del Valley Coll, PA, 94-2008. *Awards:* Pres Award, non-mem show, Salmagundi Club, NY, 2002; Best of Show, 18th Annual Juried Show, Louisville Art Assoc, Co, 2003; Winston Churchill Award Painting, Mo Watercolor Soc, Mo, 2005; Ursus Abstract Award, Tubac Center Arts, Ariz, 2006; Arches Paper Award, Okla Watermedia Soc, 2007; Art Students League of New York Award, Ann Exhib, Audubon Artists Inc, 2007; Hon Mention, Non-Member Show, Salmagundi Club, 2008; Peter Jones Memorial Award for Innovative Watercolor, Audubon Artists, 2008; 2nd prize prints & graphics, Art Asn Harrisburg, 2009; Gold Medal of Hon aquamedia, Audubon Artists, 2010; Dick Blick Art Award, Audubon Artists, 2011. *Mem:* Mo Watercolor Soc (signature mem, 2005); Tubac Ctr for the Arts (signature mem, 2007); Baltimore Watercolor Soc (signature mem, 2008); Audubon Artists (elected mem, 2008); Conn Acad Fine Arts (signature mem 2009); Taos Nat Soc Watercolorists (signature mem 2009); Rhoad Island Watercolor Soc (signature mem, 2009). *Media:* Watermedia, Graphics. *Collection:* Robert Pierson private collection, 2004-2006. *Dealer:* Chapman Galleries Doylestown PA

MISRACH, RICHARD LAURENCE
PHOTOGRAPHER
b Los Angeles, Calif, July 11, 1949. *Study:* Univ Calif, Berkeley, BA, 1971. *Work:* Mus Mod Art, NY; Mus Mod Art, San Francisco; Metrop Mus, NY; Los Angeles Co Mus Art; Whitney Mus Am Art, NY; Nat Gallery Art, Washington; Mus Fine Arts, Houston. *Comn:* Photography, Am Tel & Tel, Washington, 1978; Time Mag (cover), 7/4/88; High Mus Art, Atlanta, 1998-99; Mod Conservancy, 1999. *Exhib:* Solo exhibs, Ctr Georges Pompidou, Mus Art Mod, Paris, 1979 & Mus Fine Arts, Houston (traveling), 1996; group exhibs, Am Images, Corcoran Gallery Art & traveling, 1979; Mirrors & Windows, Mus Mod Art (traveling), NY, 1979-80; Beyond Color, San Francisco Mus Mod Art, 1980; Whitney Biennial, Whitney Mus Am Art, NY, 1981; Los Angeles Co Mus Art, 1983; Honolulu Acad Arts, 1984; 10-year retrospective, Friends Photog, Carmel, 1984; Bravo 20: A National Park Proposal, Traveling exhib, Friends Photog, San Francisco, 1990; Mus Contemp Art, Chicago, 1997; San Jose Mus Art, 1998; Berkeley Mus, 2002; Art Inst Chicago, 2007; Contemp Mus Honolulu, 2007. *Teaching:* Instr photog, Assoc Students Studio, Univ Calif, Berkeley, 1971-77; vis lectr landscape archit, Univ Calif, Berkeley, 1982; vis lectr, dept art, Univ Calif, Santa Barbara, 1984 & Calif Arts, 1991. *Awards:* Nat Endowment Arts Photog Fel, 1973, 1977, 1984 & 1992; Friends Photog Ferguson Grant, 1976; Koret Israel Prize, 1993; Kulturpreis for Lifetime Achievement in Photog, 2002; Lucie Award for Achievement in Fine Art, Int Photog Awards, 2008. *Bibliog:* David Fahey (auth), Interview with Richard Misrach, G Ray Hawkins Newslett, 1979; Carter Ratcliff (auth), Richard Misrach: Words and images, Print Collectors Newslett, 1-2/80; Irene Borger (auth), Richard Misrach, Exposure Mag, 1980. *Publ:* Contribr, Graecism Portfolio, 1983, Grapestake Gallery; auth, Desert Cantos, Univ NMex Press, 1987; Richard Misrach: 1975-1987, Gallery Min, Tokyo, 1988; Bravo 20: The Bombing of the American West, John Hopkins Univ Press, 1990; Crimes and Splendors: The

Desert Cantos of Richard Misrach, Bulfinch Press, 1996; auth, The Sky Book, Arena Edits, 2000; auth, Richard Misrach: Golden Gate; auth, Pictures of Paintings, Blind Spot, Powerhouse, 2002; auth, Chronologies, Fraenkel Gallery, 2005; auth, On the Beach, A Picture, 2007. *Dealer:* Fraenkel Gallery 49 Geary St San Francisco CA; Pace/MacGill Gallery E 57th St New York NY; Marc Selwyn Fine Art 6222 Wilshire Blvd Los Angeles CA. *Mailing Add:* 1420 45th St Emeryville CA 94608

MISSAKIAN, BERGE ARTIN
PAINTER
b Alexandria, Egypt, Nov 6, 1933; Can citizen. *Study:* Cornell Univ, BA, 59; Concordia Univ, BFA, 64; Bur Cartooning, dipl, 68. *Work:* Air Canada, Montreal West City Hall, Que; Hamazkain Cult Asn, Toronto; Mekhetariste Mus, Vienna, Austria; Inst Fur Armenische Fragen-Munchen, Munich, Ger; Armenian Libr & Mus, Watertown, Mass. *Comn:* Painting, comn by Montreal West Centennial, Que, 97. *Exhib:* Un Printemps en Art, Musee Vaudreuil-Soulanges, Montreal, 93; Int Miniatures, Seaside Gallery, Nags Head, NC, 98; Winton Park, Fairfield, Conn, 95; Monty Stabler Galleries, Birmingham, Ala, 98 & 2004; Armenian Libr & Mus, Boston, 2003; Musee Laurier, 2007; Seaside Art Gallery, 2008. *Pos:* Consult art show, Tekeyan Cult Asn, Montreal, 92-93. *Awards:* First Choice, Lambeth Art Fest, Ont, 89; Peoples Choice, Int Art Festival, London, Ont, 90; Seaside Gallery Hon Award, Int Miniature, 94. *Bibliog:* Sally MacDougall (auth), Ontario impressions, London Free Press, 88; Louis Bruens (auth), Qui Donc est Missakian?, La Palette, 92; Bernard Daoust (auth), The Fruit of Sharing, Parcours Arts, 95; Mary Ellen Riddle (auth), Missakian - Jazz, The Coast, Art Beat, Nags Head, NC; James R Nelson (auth), Missakian puts energy in images, The Birmingham News, 2001; Nancy Snipper (auth), Artist jazzes up every canvas, The Chronicle, 2002; J Jancsurak (auth), Colors of Jazz, Art Business News, 2005; Anne-Marie Lavigne (auth), Missakian, Ellington & Picasso, Parcours, 2007. *Mem:* SCA. *Media:* Acrylic, Canvas. *Publ:* Auth, Paul Gaugin: Where do we come from? & Group of seven-creators of Canadian art, Mag Art, 90; Clement: painter of time & space, Mag Art, 91; Henry Matisse: retrospective-Mus Mod Art, New York & Three Laurentians: three artists' view, Laurentian Mag, Laurentian Mag, 93. *Dealer:* Seaside Art Gallery 2716 S Virginia Dare Tr Nag's Head NC 27959; Galerie Lamoureux Ritzenoff 1428 Sherbrooke West Montreal PQ Canada H3G 1K4. *Mailing Add:* 9 Northview Montreal West PQ H4X 1C8 Canada

MISSAL, JOSHUA M
ART DEALER, CONSULTANT
b Hartford, Conn, Apr 12. *Study:* Univ Rochester, BM, 37, MM, 38; London Inst, Hon DM, 72. *Pos:* Dir & owner, Gallery M, Farmington, Conn, 70-76 & Missal Gallery Ltd, Scottsdale, Ariz, 76-85, Missal Art Assocs, Scottsdale, Ariz, 85-88 & Mesa, Ariz, 95-98. *Teaching:* assoc prof interrelated arts, Wichita State Univ, 52-70. *Mem:* Am Fedn Art; Appraisers Asn Am. *Specialty:* Consultations. *Publ:* auth, American art--the continuing boom, Art Talk, 12/81 & articles on art collecting, World Fine Art, 82-83. *Mailing Add:* 262 E Brown Rd Apt 205 Mesa AZ 85201

MISSAL, STEPHEN J
EDUCATOR, ILLUSTRATOR
b Albuquerque, NMex, Apr 23, 1948. *Study:* Wichita State Univ, BFA, 70, MFA, 72; Marymount Col, 72; Studied forensic art with Karen T Taylor, Betty Pat Gatliff. *Work:* New Britain Mus Am Art, Conn; Jefferson Federal Savings & Loan Gallery, Meriden, Conn; Ulrich Mus, Wichita, Kans; Ariz Pub Serv, Phoenix; and pvt collections; pvt collections, Frank Sinatra, Joshua Logan (dir), Samuel Arkoff (dir/producer), Gary Owens (TV personality), Itzhak Perlman (violinist) & Sikorsky Family. *Comn:* Packard Deli at the Borgata (mural), 89; Shakespeare Festival (mural), Scottsdale Ctr Arts, 82; Jed Nolans (mural), Scottsdale, 82. *Exhib:* 9th Ann Ark Competition, Pine Bluff, 76; Festival 8, Scottsdale Ctr Arts, Ariz, 85; Springfield Mus Art, Nat Competitive Exhib, Utah, 85; Wilde Meyer Gallery, Nat Competitive Exhib, Scottsdale, Ariz, 87; Nat Forest Serv Centennial Competitive Exhib (touring), 91; Wyoming Wildlife Stamp Contest Exhib, 94; CAC Regional Exhib, Tucson, Ariz, 97; Sterberg Mus Natural History, 99; Leprecon Regional Sci-Fi/Fantasy Art Show, 2001. *Pos:* Primary illusr, Scottsdale Progress, 79-, TSR-Wizards of the Coast, Call of Cihulhu; paintings, Raising Arizona, 20th Century Fox, Dino Discovery, Scholastic Books, and others; Forensic reconstruction artist, Maricopa Med Examiners office & Forensic Lab, 2010-. *Teaching:* Instr, White Mountain Sch, Littleton, NH, 72-74; instr, Northeast Mo State Univ, Kirksville, Mo, 74-77; vis instr painting, drawing & design, Scottsdale Community Col, Ariz, 79-87 & Phoenix Col, 84-; Prof, Art Inst of Phoenix, 97-. *Awards:* Purchase Awards, Tulsa Invitational, 72 & 14th Ann Midwest Exhib, 76; Best Drawing, Scottsdale Ctr Arts, 77; Nat Forest Serv Centennial Competition Touring Exhib, 91; Best Exhib, Coppercon Sci-Fi Show, 2001. *Mem:* Ariz Watercolor Soc; Ariz Artist's Guild. *Media:* Oil, Pen & Ink, Prismacolor, Acrylic. *Interests:* Forensic art. *Publ:* Illusr, numerous periodicals & newspapers; Auth, Drawing for Animation, Delmar Publ, 2003; (auth) Exploring Character Design, Delmar Pub, 2005. *Mailing Add:* 6255 E Earll Dr Scottsdale AZ 85251

MITCHEL, JULIO
PHOTOGRAPHER
b Havana, Cuba, 1942; US citizen. *Study:* Studied photog with Lisette Model. *Work:* Mus Mod Art, Int Ctr Photog, NY; Int Mus Photog/Eastman House, Rochester, NY; Musee de L'Elysee, Lausanne, Switz; Mus Mod Art, Valencia, Spain. *Exhib:* Solo exhib, Recontre Int, Arles, France, 89, Muse de L'Elysee, Lausanne, Switz, 90, Galerie Vier, Berlin, Ger, 90, Mus Mod Art, Valencia, Spain, 91; More Than One Photog, Mus Mod Art, 92. *Teaching:* Fac, Sch Visual Arts, Cooper Union Art Sch & New Sch, NY. *Awards:* Fel, NY State Coun Arts, 72; Fel, NY Found, 82 & 88; Fel, Nat Endowment Arts, 82 & 92. *Bibliog:* A D Coleman (auth), Light Readings, Oxford Univ Press, NY, 81; Ralph Quinke (dir), About Julio Mitchel, NDR TV Network, Hamburg, Ger, 90. *Publ:* Auth, Triptych, Parkett, 89; Do You Love Me?, IVAM, 91. *Mailing Add:* 161 Columbia Heights Brooklyn NY 11201

MITCHELL, DEAN LAMONT
PAINTER
b Pittsburgh, Pa, Jan 20, 1957. *Study:* Columbus Coll Art & Design, BFA, 1980, MFA, 1994. *Work:* Nelson-Atkins Mus Art, Kansas City, Mo; Margaret Harwell Art Mus, Poplar Bluff, Mo; St Louis Art Mus, Mo; Miss Art Mus, Jackson; Nat Parks Found, Jackson, Wyo; Kemper Mus Contemp Art, Kansas City, Mo; Nerman Mus Contemp Art, Overland Park, Kans; Beach Mus Art, Manhattan, Kans; Canton Mus Art, Ohio; Autry Nat Ctr, Burbank, Calif; Phoenix Art Mus, Phoenix. *Comn:* Jazz Mural (4 ft x 140 ft) Vista/Allis Plaza Hotel, Kansas City, Mo, 84-85; five historical Kansas City scenes, Mo Art Coun, 85. *Exhib:* Miniature Invitational, Tampa Mus Art, Fla, 89; Miniature Art Soc Fla 15th Intern Exhib, St Petersburg Mus, 90; Nat Acad Design, 165th Ann, NY, 90; Arts for the Parks, Wild Life Am West Art Mus, Jackson Hole, Wyo, 90; Artist of Am, Colo Hist Mus, Denver, 91-92; Gallery of Fine Art, New Orleans, 2006. *Collection Arranged:* Everythings a Portrait, Cornell Mus Art Am Cult, 2008; Imperfect Beauty, A Point of Reflection, Ctr Visual Arts, Denton, Tex, 2008; Backbone, Images of Africa Am Men, Miss Mus Art, 2006; Dean Mitchell, Visions with Heart & Soul, Leepa Rattner Mus Art, 2010; Space, People, and Places, Canton Mus Art, 2010. *Teaching:* Instr, figure drawing, Kansas City Art Inst, 8-12/90. *Awards:* Hardie Gramatky Mem Award, Am Watercolor Soc, 90; Best in Show, June Baumgardner Geldart, Min Art Soc Fla, 90; Allied Artist Gold Medal, 91; Gold Medal, Am Watercolor Soc, 1998; Gold Award, Southern Watercolor Soc, 2006; Thomas Moran Award, Salmagundi Club non-mem, 2008; Silver medal, Am Watercolor Soc, 2010; Award of Excellence, Shanghai Zhujiajiao Internat Watercolor Biennial Exhib, 2012. *Bibliog:* James Edwards (auth), Dean Mitchell Artist, 90; Mike Smith (dir), Coming Home (film), Globalvision/Greenwich workshop, 92; Ann Saunders (auth), Coming Home, Bay Arts Alliance, 92. *Mem:* Am Watercolor Soc; Allied Artist Am; Nat Watercolor Soc; Nat Soc Painters Casein & Acrylic; Miniature Art Soc Am. *Media:* Oil, Watercolors. *Publ:* Auth, article, Artist Mag, F & W Publs, 84; Am Artist, Billboard Publs, 89; US Art, Frank Sisser, 89; Southwest Art, CBH Publ, 91; Being An Artist, North Light Books, 92. *Dealer:* Cutter & Cutter Fine Art Galleries 120 Charlotte St Saint Augustine Fl 32084; Astoria Fine Art 35 E Deloney Jackson Hole WY 83001; J Willott Gallery 73190 El Paseo Ste 1 Palm Desert CA 92260. *Mailing Add:* 101 S 12th St #607 Tampa FL 33602

MITCHELL, DIANNE
PAINTER
b Joliet, Ill. *Study:* Univ Hartford, Conn, Art Sch, with Rudolph Franz Zallinger, 82-83; Florence Acad Art, Florence Italy, 2005-2006. *Work:* US Coast Guard Collection. *Comn:* Diamond T Trucks Inc, 96; Conn Transport Magazine Covers, 92-94; Thousand Oaks New West Symphony, 2002-2003. *Exhib:* Ann Exhib, Salmagundi Club, NY, 84; Nat Midyear Exhib, Butler Inst Am Art, Youngstown, Ohio, 84; 100 Nat Finalists, Grand Cent Art Galleries, NY, 85; Egg Tempera and Watercolor Exhibition, Esther Wells Collection Galleries, Laguna Beach, Calif, 86; Am Watercolor Soc, 87; one-woman shows, Lake Tahoe Visitors' Ctr, 88 & 89, & US Coast Guard Exhib, Governor's Island, NY, 90; Focus Gallery Group Show, Cambria, Calif, 99-2001; Portrait Arts Ltd, Boston, MA, 87-88; and others. *Teaching:* Egg Tempera Workshop, King's Beach, Calif, 92 & 97; painting on safari, Kenya, Africa, 92. *Awards:* Lo Manaco Studio Award, Pastel Soc Am, 82; 1st Prize Watercolor, 2nd Prize Watercolor & Best of Show, Emerald City Classic, Nepenthe Mundi Soc, 86; George Gray Award, US Coast Guard, 89; 1990 Commemorative Print Competition Winner, Lake Tahoe Summer Music Festival. *Mem:* Pastel Soc Am; Nat Mus Women Arts; Pastel Soc Am, 80-2005, signature mem. *Media:* Oil, Egg Tempera. *Publ:* Illusr, Spinning: Where to begin, Shuttle Spindle & Dyepot Mag, 85; illusr & auth, One Egg, Over Medium, Am Artist Mag, 86; US Coast Guard Recruiting Brochure & Poster, 90. *Dealer:* Esther Wells Collection 1390 South Coast Highway Laguna Beach CA 92651; Miden Lane Zantman Galleries San Francisco Carmel Palm Desert CA

MITCHELL, JEFFRY
PAINTER, SCULPTOR
b Seattle, Wash, June 10, 1958. *Study:* Univ Dallas, Irving, BA, 80; Tyler Sch Art, Temple Univ, Philadelphia, Pa, MFA, 88. *Work:* Fogg Mus Art, Boston; Philadelphia Mus Art; Seattle Art Mus; Mus Fine Arts, Boston; Contemp Mus, Honolulu. *Exhib:* Foreign Artists Working in Japan, Gallery R, Seto, Japan, 83; Northwest Ann, Ctr Contemp Art, Seattle, 89; Installation Socrates Proj, Long Island City, Queens, NY, 91; solo exhibs, Seattle Art Mus, 90 & My Spirit, Workspace Gallery, New Mus Contemp Art, NY, 92; The Art of Microsoft, Henry Art Gallery, Univ Wash, Seattle, 93; Garden of Delights, Tacoma Art Mus, 95. *Pos:* Vis artist, RI Sch Design, Providence, 97, Harvard Univ, Cambridge, 94 & Mont State Univ, Missoula, 98. *Teaching:* Instr drawing & printmaking, Cornish Col Arts, Seattle, 89-91; vis lectr ceramics, painting & drawing, Univ Wash, Seattle, 93-95 & 97. *Awards:* Artist Trust Grant, 94; Art Matters Inc Grant, NY, 94; Joan Mitchell Found Grant, 2009. *Bibliog:* Eric Frederickson (auth), Hello, I'm Sorry, The Stranger, 2/6/97; Frances DeVuono (auth), Jeffrey Mitchell, Artweek, 4/97; Jordan Biren (auth), Transgressive Prints, Reflex, spring 89. *Media:* Works on Paper, Ceramics. *Dealer:* Elliot Brown Gallery 619 N 35th St No 101A Seattle WA 98103

MITCHELL, JOAN ELIZABETH See Robertson, Joan Elizabeth Mitchell

MITCHELL, KATHERINE
PAINTER
b Memphis, Tenn, Oct 25, 1944. *Study:* Atlanta Coll Art, BFA, 68; Tyler Sch Art, Rome, 68; Ga State Univ, MVA, 77. *Work:* Ark Art Ctr, Little Rock, Ark; JB Speed Mus, Louisville, Ky; High Mus Art, Atlanta; Michael C Carlos Mus, Atlanta; Mus Contemp Art, Ga; and others. *Comn:* Variations on a Theme of Modules (ceramic tile murals), Metrop Atlantic Rapid Transit Authority Station. *Exhib:* The Avant-Garde: 12 in Atlanta (catalog), High Mus Art, 79; Hassam Fund Purchase Exhib, Am Acad & Inst Arts & Letters, NY, 79; Artists in Ga, Albany Mus Art, 90; 9 Women in Ga (catalog), Nat Mus Women Arts, Wash 96; Artists of Heath Gallery, MOCA, Ga, 2002; Contemp Southern Drawings, High Mus Art, Atlanta, Ga, 2004; Labyrinthe, Factory,

Kunst Halle, Krems, Austria, 2006; Places of Memory & Dreams (catalog), MOCA, Ga, 2011-2012; Trading Places, High Mus Art, 2012; Retrospective (catalog), City Gallery Chastain, Atlanta, 91, 10 Yr Retrospective, Atlanta Contemp Art Ctr, 2005, 32 Yr Retrospective (catalog), Atlanta City Gallery East, 2007, Marking Time, Contemp Drawings GA Artists, Brenau Univ Galleries, Gainesville, 2001, Spirited Calligraphy, Welch Sch Art & Design, Ga State Univ, Atlanta, 2010; Places of Memory and Dreams, Mus Contemporary Art Ga, Atlanta, 2011-2012; Drawing Inside the Perimeter, High Mus Art, 2013; Cross-References, Visual Arts Gallery, Emory Univ, 2014. *Teaching:* Sr lectr drawing & painting, Emory Univ, 80-2009. *Awards:* Hassam Fund Exhib Purchase Award, Am Acad & Inst Arts & Lett, 79; Southern Arts Federation/Nat Endowment Arts Regional Fel Award, 92; Working Artist Proj Grant, MDCA, Ga, 2010-2011. *Bibliog:* John Howett (auth), Katherine Mitchell at Atlanta College of Art, Art in Am, 1/82; Katherine Mitchell: Paintings, Heath Gallery, Atlanta, Ga, 86; Amy Jinkner-Lloyd (auth), Katherine Mitchell at Chastain & Heath, Art Am, 2/92; Laura Lieberman (auth), Katherine Mitchell: A Retrospective and Recent Work, Art Papers, 2/92; Diana McClintock (auth), Katherine Mitchell, Atlantic Art Papers (5-61), 2007. *Mem:* Hambidge Center Creative Arts & Sci (fel). *Media:* Acrylic, Mixed Media. *Res:* Abstract painting & drawing. *Specialty:* Contemporary art. *Interests:* creating new systems and patterns. *Publ:* Katherine Mitchell: A Retrospective, essay by Glenn Harper, City Gallery, East Atlanta, Off Cult Affairs, 1974-2006; Contribr, Katherine Mitchell: A Retrospective (catalog), essay by John Howett, Atlanta, 91; 9 Women in Georgia, Nat Mus Women in Arts, 96; Working Artist Project: 2010-2011, text by Judith Rohrer, Mus Contemp Art Ga, 2012. *Dealer:* Sandler Hudson Gallery Atlanta. *Mailing Add:* 80 Stratford Pl NE Atlanta GA 30342

MITCHELL, MACEO
PAINTER
Study: Wayne State Univ, Detroit, Mich, BFA; Univ IA, MA, 1969. *Exhib:* Solo exhibs, Nine Arts, Gallery, Antwerp, Belgium, 1995, Bill Hodges Gallery, NY, 1998 & 2002, Galerie Michele Guerin, Limetz-Villez, France, 1999, Iandor Fine Arts, Inc, Newark, NJ, 1999; group exhib, Arnold Klein Gallery, Royal Oak, Mich, 1996; Pen & Brush Inc, Black Hist Celebration & Exhib, NY, 2002; Art in the Atrium, Morristown, NJ, 2003; Pastel Soc Ann, Nat Arts Club, NY, 2003; Flight, Mehu Gallery, NY, 2003. *Teaching:* instr, Pastel Soc Am, Nat Arts Club, New York City, currently; instr, elem to col level art, formerly. *Mem:* IA Print Group (IPG); signature mem, Pastel Soc Am (PSA). *Media:* Pastels

MITCHELL, MARGARETTA K
PHOTOGRAPHER, WRITER
b Brooklyn, NY, May 27, 1935. *Study:* Smith Coll, BA (magna cum laude), 57; Boston Mus Sch, 58; Escuela de Bellas Artes, Madrid, Spain, 59; Univ Calif, Berkeley, MA, 85. *Work:* Int Ctr Photog, New York; Performing Arts Libr & Mus, San Francisco, Calif; Bancroft Libr, Univ Calif, Berkeley; Royal Print Collection, Windsor, Eng; Oakland Mus, Calif; San Francisco Mus Mod Art; New York Public Libr. *Comn:* Mural, Anixter Corp, San Francisco, Calif, 74; mural, Amax Corp, San Francisco, Calif, 74; mural, San Francisco Art Comn, Calif, 78; posters, Portal Publ, 90; Berkeley Symphony, 99; Chappelet Vineyard, St Helena, 90. *Exhib:* San Francisco Mus Mod Art, Calif, 78; Recollections: Ten Women of Photography (auth, catalog), Int Ctr Photog, 79; Dance for Life (auth, catalog), Oakland Mus, Calif, 85; Michael Shapiro Gallery, San Francisco, 89 & 94; Bouquet's to Art, Deyoung Mus, 91; Witkin Gallery, New York, 91-92; Pepper Gallery, Boston, 93; Scheinbaum & Russek, Santa Fe, 94; New York Pub Libr, 96; Nat Mus Women Arts, Washington, DC, 96; Akron Mus Art, Ohio, 97; Santa Barbara Mus Art, 97; Cheekwood, Nashville, 2001; Mechanics Inst Libr, San Francisco, 2002; Univ San Francisco, 2002; MTSU, 2006; Univ Southern Calif, 2007; Smith Coll, 2007; Photocentral, 2009; View Point, 2010; Spectrum, 2010; Photo Gallery, Oakland, 2013; Photo Gallery, 2013; Photo Central, 2009. *Pos:* Pres & nat bd dir, Am Soc Media Photog, Northern Calif Chap, 90-92. *Teaching:* Instr photog, Univ Calif Extension, 76-78, 2001 & 2003, City Coll San Francisco, Calif, 80-81 & Univ Calif Santa Cruz Extension, 2001 & 2003-2007; Calif Coll Arts & Crafts, Oakland, 86; Univ Calif, summer session, 86; Friends Photog, summer workshop, 87-88; workshop, Carleton Coll, April, 88; instr, Acad Art, San Francisco, 90-95; DeAnza Coll, 2006-2011; Hawaii Photo Retreats, 2007; Photo Central, 2013. *Awards:* Nat Endowment Arts Mus Grant, 78-79; Calif Coun Arts Grant, Berkeley Art Ctr, 81-82; Grant, L J & Mary C Skaggs Found, 81; Oakland Cult Arts, 2010; Inst for Historical Study, 2011. *Bibliog:* New Photography, Prentice-Hall, 209-13, 83; Encore Mag, fall 85; Focus Mag, April, 85; A History of Women Photographers, Abbeville Press, 94. *Mem:* Am Soc Media Photog; Inst Hist Study. *Media:* Black & White, Color, Photography. *Res:* Photographers, particularly rediscoveries; Art and California history; dance. *Interests:* Photography, gardening, reading, traveling & yoga. *Publ:* Coauth, To A Cabin, Grossman Publ, 73; auth, intro, After Ninety, Univ Washington Press, 77; auth, essays, Contemp Photogr, St Martin's Press, New York, 82; Dance for Life, Elysian Eds, 85; Flowers, Elysian Eds, 91; auth, intro, The Eternal Body, Chronicle Bks, 94; Ruth Bernard: Between Art and Life, 2000; auth, intro, Under One Sky, Stanford Univ Press, 2004; The Face of Poetry, 2005; auth, intro, In Search of True North, 2007; Fire, Ruin, Renewal, The Phoenix Firestorm Project (film), 2011. *Dealer:* Robert Tat San Francisco CA. *Mailing Add:* 280 Hillcrest Rd Berkeley CA 94705

MITCHELL, N DONALD
ADMINISTRATOR, DEALER
b Mt Vernon, NY, Mar 5, 1922. *Study:* Wichita State Univ; Abbe Inst, Monterey Peninsula Col, art hist, painting with George DeGroat & Fay Hopkins. *Pos:* Vpres, Universal Arts, Inc, Carmel, Calif, 60-; dir, Zantman Galleries, Ltd, Carmel, 60-; co-owner, Highlands Gallery, Carmel, 60-. *Specialty:* Quality works, mostly representational, in all media, styles and techniques

MITCHELL, ROBIN
PAINTER, EDUCATOR
b Los Angeles, Calif, Sept 29, 1951. *Study:* Calif State Univ, Northridge, 68-70; Univ Calif, Los Angeles, 70-71; Calif Inst Arts, BFA, 72 & MFA, 74. *Work:* Security/Pac Corp Collection, Los Angeles, Calif; Flour Corp, Irvine, Calif; Kaufman/Broad-Paris Collection, France; Tuttle & Taylor Collection, Los Angeles, Calif. *Exhib:* Solo exhibs, Comsky Gallery, Los Angeles, 74, Baum-Silverman Gallery, Los Angeles, 81, Jan Baum Gallery, Los Angeles, 83, 84, The Living Room, Santa Monica, Calif, 2001, Jancar Gallery, Los Angeles, 2007, Code Paintings, Craig Krull Gallery, Santa Monica, Calif, 2007; Surface Tension, Santa Barbara Contemp Arts Forum, Calif, 95; Division of Labor: Women's Work in Contemp Art, Mus Contemp Art, Los Angeles, 95; Teeming, Post Gallery, Los Angeles, 96; Blessings & Beginnings, Skirball Cult Ctr, Los Angeles, 96; Feminist Directions 1970/1996 (catalog), Sweeney Art Gallery, Univ Calif, Riverside, 96; City of Los Angeles Exhib, Los Angeles Munic Art Gallery, 98; group exhibs, City of Los Angeles (COLA) Exhib, Munic Art Gallery, Barnsdall Art Park, Los Angeles, 98, Luminous, Ikon Gallery, Santa Monica, 2000, LA Post Cool, San Jose Mus Art, San Jose, Calif, 2002, The Importance of Being Earnest, Occidental Coll Galleries, Los Angeles, 2002, LA Post Cool, Tinseltown, domestic setting, Ben Maltz Gallery, Otis Coll Art, Los Angeles, Calif, 2003, Off the Wall: Murals, Armory Northwest, Armory Arts Ctr, Pasadena, Calif, Immodesty, Another Year in LA, Los Angeles Calif, 2006, Works On/Of Paper, The Brewery Proj, Los Angeles, Calif, 2007, Some Paintings: The Third Los Angeles Weekly Ann Biennial, Track 16 Gallery, Santa Monaci, Calif, 2008; Ikon Gallery, 2000; Importance of Being Ernest, Occidental Coll, 2001; Robin Mitchell: New Paintings, Craig Krull Gallery, Santa Monica, Calif, 2009; Robin Mitchell Paintings, Craig Krull Gallery, Santa Monica, Calif, 2010; Robin Mitchell Treasures Maps, Craig Krull Gallery, Santa Monica, Calif, 2011. *Teaching:* Vis artist studio art, Claremont Grad Sch, 79 & 83; lectr, Univ Southern Calif, 81- & Univ Calif at Irvine, 87- 92, Univ Calif, Santa Barbara, 93-95; asst adj prof, Pasadena City Coll, spring 97-; assoc fac, Art Dept, Santa Monica Coll, summer 98-. *Awards:* Visual Artist Fel (painting), Nat Endowment Arts, 87; Visual Artists Award for Anonymous was a Woman, 96; City of Los Angeles Artist Grant, 97-98; Calif Community Found Fel Visual Artist, Mid-Career Award, 2006. *Bibliog:* Norma Broude & Mary Degarard (eds), The Power of Feminist Art, The American Movement of the 1970's, History & Impact, Abrams Publ, 94; Michael Duncan (auth), LA rising, Art Am, 12/94; Susan Muchnic (auth), The kindness of strangers, Los Angeles Times, 8/30/96; David Pagel (auth), Robin Mitchell at Craig Krull Gallery, Around the Galleries (calender sect) Los Angeles Times, 7/13/2007; Constance Mallinson (auth), Robin Mitchell at Jancar Gallery, Art in Am, 2007; Christopher Miles (auth), Robin Mitchell at Craig Krull Gallery, LA Weekly, 2009. *Mem:* Coll Art Asn. *Media:* All. *Publ:* Auth, Susan Rankaitis, spring, 91, Patrick Nickell & Michael Gonzalez, fall, 92 & Renee Petropoulos, summer 94, Visions. *Dealer:* Craig Krull Gallery Santa Monica Ca. *Mailing Add:* 2614 Euclid Apt E Santa Monica CA 90405

MITCHELL, SHANNON DILLARD
CURATOR, ADMINISTRATOR
b Anchorage, Alaska, Oct 5, 1958. *Study:* Colo Col, BA, 80; Southern Methodist Univ, MA (arts admin) & MBA, 84. *Collection Arranged:* Paintings by Clementine Hunter, Ark Colls, 93; Adrian Brewer: Arkansas Artist (contribr, catalog), 96; Edwin Brewer Retrospective, Univ Ariz, Little Rock, 96; 20th Century African Am Art from the Darrell Walker Collection (contribr, catalog), 96. *Pos:* Dir, NS Haley Mem Libr & History Ctr, 81-82; asst to dir & cur asst, San Antonio Mus Art, 84-86; gallery cur, Univ Ark, Little Rock, 90-. *Teaching:* Adj asst prof mus studies, Univ Ark, Little Rock, 90-. *Mem:* Am Asn Mus; Southeastern Mus Conf; Ark Mus Asn. *Mailing Add:* Dept Art Univ Ark 2801 S University Little Rock AR 72204-1099

MITCHELL-INNES, LUCY
ART DEALER
Study: Courtauld Inst Art, BA & MA. *Pos:* Research asst, Henry Moore Found; dir contemp art & sr vpres, Sothebys, 1981-1994; dir & owner, Mitchell-Innes & Nash, 1996-; pres, Art Dealers Asn Am, formerly. *Mem:* Art Dealers Asn America (former pres). *Mailing Add:* Mitchell-Innes & Nash 1018 Madison Ave New York NY 10075

MITCHNICK, NANCY
PAINTER, EDUCATOR
b Detroit, Mich, Apr 25, 1947. *Study:* Wayne State Univ, BFA, 72, grad work, 72-73; Hunter Coll, 74-75. *Work:* Citibank, N Am, New York; Detroit Inst Arts; Edward Duffy Co, Detroit; J B Speed Mus, Louisville, Ky; Wayne State Univ, Detroit, Mich. *Comn:* Numerous pvt portrait comns. *Exhib:* Solo shows incl Willis Gallery, Detroit, 73, Susanne Hilberry Gallery, Birmingham, Mich, 80-84 & 91, Hirschl & Adler Mod, New York, 83 & 86 & John Berggruen Gallery, San Francisco, 85, Cue Found, NY, 2003; group shows incl American Still Life: 1945-83, Houston Mus Contemp Art, Buffalo Fine Arts Acad, Albright-Knox Art Gallery, Neuberger Mus, State Univ NY, Purchase, 83-84; Still Life-Landscape: New Approaches to Old Tradition, Gloria Luria Gallery, Bay Harbor Island, Fla, 86; Objects Observed, Summit Art Ctr, NJ, 86; Selected Member's Gallery Works, Albright-Knox Member's Gallery, Buffalo, NY, 86; Contemporary Screens, Art Mus Asn Am, Contemp Art Ctr, Cincinnati, Ohio, Lowe Art Mus, Coral Gables, Fla, City Art Gallery, Raleigh, NC, Toledo Mus Art, Ohio, Des Moines Art Ctr, Iowa, 86-88; Anita Freedman Gallery, New York, 91. *Teaching:* Instr painting, Wayne State Univ, 71-73 & Bard Coll, 77-86; instr, Calif Inst Art, 86-98; vis artist, dept visual and environ studies, Harvard Inst Arts, 94-95, sr preceptor, 98-99, Rudolf Arnheim lectr, studio arts, currently. *Awards:* CAPS grant, NY State Coun Arts, 76-77; Nat Endowment Arts, 86-87; Pollack Krasner Found Grant, 90; Guggenheim Fel, 90-91; Phi Beta Kappa Teaching Prize, Harvard Univ, 2001. *Bibliog:* Dr June Taboroff (auth), Edward W Duffy & Co, Art Auction, 10/84; New York Times, 1/24/86; Arts Mag, 3/86. *Media:* Acrylic, Oil; Gouache on Paper. *Mailing Add:* 24 Quincy St Cambridge MA 02138

MITTY, LIZBETH J
PAINTER, PRINTMAKER
b New York, NY, Oct 28, 1952. *Study:* State Univ NY, Stony Brook, 69-71; Univ Wis, Madison, BS, 73, MFA, 75. *Work:* Metrop Mus Art, NY; Newark Mus, NJ; Mint Mus, Charlotte, NC; Nassau Mus, Roslyn, NY; Queensborough Community Coll, Queens, NY; US State Dept, Va; Fidelity Investment, Boston; Greenpoint Bank, NY; Prudential Investments, NJ; NY Heart Found, NY; Blue Cross, Blue Shield, NY; Trierenberg Holdings, Traun, Austria. *Exhib:* Long Island Landscape Painting in the Twentieth Century, Mus Stonybrook, NY, 90; Nassau Mus, Roslyn, NY, 93; Steven Rosenberg Gallery, NY, 94; solo exhib, Cheryl pelavin Gallery, NY, 98, 2002, 2005 & 2008; Traun, Austria, 2006; Milwaukee, Wis, 2007; and others. *Teaching:* Instr painting & drawing, Lake Erie Coll, 75-76, Ohio State Univ, 76-77 & State Univ NY, New Paltz, NY, 91-; Hofstra Univ, 96-98. *Awards:* Best Show, Lyndon House, Athens, Ga, 78; Adolph & Esther Gottlieb Found Grant, 95. *Bibliog:* Grace Glueck (auth), rev, NY Times, 83; Edward Lucie-Smith (auth), American art now, Morrow, Inc, 85; Ronald Pisano (auth), Long Island Landscape Painting in the Twentieth Century, Little Brown Co, 90; NY Times weekend sect, Ken Johnson, 2001, Milwaukee Jour Sunday arts section, San Francisco Jour Sunday Arts section, NY Mag Art in Rev, 2001. *Media:* Acrylic, Oil; Monoprint. *Dealer:* Cheryl Pelavin Fine Arts 13 Jay St New York NY 10013. *Mailing Add:* 418 State St Brooklyn NY 11217

MIYAMOTO, WAYNE AKIRA
PAINTER, PRINTMAKER
b Honolulu, Hawaii, Sept 6, 1947. *Study:* Rensselaer Polytech Inst, 65-68; Univ Hawaii, BA & BFA, 70, MFA, 74. *Work:* Univ Alaska, Fairbanks; Contemp Mus, Honolulu; State Found Cult & Arts; Hawaii Honolulu Acad Arts; Fort Hayes State Univ, Kansas; Rutgers Univ, NJ; Portland Art Mus, Ore; Contemp Mus, Knoxville, Tenn; Univ Richmond Mus, Va; Nat Acad Fine Arts, Hangzhou, China; Assoc Premio Int Biella L' Incisione, Torino, Italy; Contemp Mus Asilah, Morocco; Int Print Triennial Soc, Cracow, Poland; State Mus Lublin, Poland; Nat Mus, Cluj-Napoca, Romania; Nat Mus, Hanoi, Vietnam; Grinnell Col, Iowa; Art Inst Boston and Lesley Col, Mass, Kohler Art Libr, Madison, Wisc, Miami Univ, Ohio; Univ Arizona, Tucson; Naestved Mus, Denmark; Bibliotheca Alexandrina, Egypt. *Exhib:* Silvermine Int, 90, 92 & 94; 65th Nat Print Exhib, Soc Am Graphic Artists, NY, 93; Int Print Triennial, Cracow, Poland, 94; 3rd Bharat Bhavan Int Biennial Prints, Bhopal, India, 95; Inter-Kontakt-Grafik '95, Int Triennial Graphic Art, Prague, Czech Repub, 95; 45th N Am Print Exhib, Boston Printmakers, Duxbury, Mass, 95; Millennial Biennial Nat, Univ Richmond Mus, Va, 2000; VI Miedzynarodowe Triennale, Int Print Exhib, Majdanek 2000, Majdanek Mus, Lublin, Poland; Int Print Biennial, Varna, Bulgaria, 2001; Ecco Homo, 2000, Clemson Univ, SC; Prints USA, Springfield Mus Art, Mo, 2001; Int Biennial Cluj, Nat Mus, Cluj-Napoca, Romania, 2001; Biennial Int Print Comp, Edmonton, Alberta, Can, 2002; Global Matrix Int Exhib, Purdue univ, Indiana and Wright State Univ, Dayton, Ohio, 2002; 12th Space Int Print Biennial, Seoul, Korea, 02; Boston Printmakers N Am Biennial, Boston, 03; Honolulu Printmakers 75th Anniversary, Honolulu Acad Arts, 03; 4th Minn Nat Biennial, Univ Minn, 04; Boston Printmakers, Duxbury, Mass, 04; 4th Lessedra World Art Print Ann, Sofia, Bulgaria, 2005; Nat Exhib, Society of Am Graphic Artists, NYC, 2005; Korean Contemp Printmakers Asn Int Exhib, Seoul, Korea, 2006; Solo Exhibs: Univ NMex, Gallup, 2006; Univ Houston, Clear Lake, Tex, 2007; Contemp Mus, Honolulu, 2008; Bienn Exhib, Topeka, Kansas, 2008; Harnett Bien, Richmond, Va, 2008; 13th Intranet Trien, Lodz, Poland, 2008; Intranet Bien, Alexandria, Egypt, 2008; 8th Biennial, Bhopal, India, 2008; 1st Intl Exhib, Yunnan Mus, Kunming, China, 2008; Soc Am Graphic Art, Ormond Mus, Fla, 2008; Compact Prints, No. Queensland, Australia, 2008; Americas Biennial, Iowa City, Iowa, 2008; SGC Nat Exhib, Columbia Coll, Chicago, 2009; Contemp Mus, Honolulu, 2009; MAPC, Morgan Conservatory, Cleveland, OH, 2009. *Pos:* Visual art consult & acquisition comt, State Found Cult Arts, Island Hawaii, 81-; exec bd, Hawaii Alliance Arts Educ, Honolulu, 88-89; Friends of Univ Hawaii-Hilo Art, 81-, vpres, 85-88; artist-in-residence, 11th Asilah Int Cult Festival, Morocco, 88; artist-in-residence, The Printmaking Workshop, New York, 90; Vis artist, Chicopee, Mass, 2002; Vis artist China Acad Art, Hangzhou, China, 2005; Vis artist, VASE, Houston, Tex, 2007; Vis artist, Appalachian State Univ, Boone, NC, 2007; Vis artist, Sch Vis Arts, NY, 2007; Vis artist, Univ W. Bohemia, Pilsen, Czech Republic, 2008; vis artist & Harkness Fel, School Fine Arts, Univ Canterbury, Christchurch, New Zealand, 2008; juror, Schaeffer Challenge, Maui Arts & Cult Ctr, Kahului, Hawaii, 2008; vis artist, Montclair State Univ, NJ, 2009; vis artist, Print Council, Branchburg, NJ, 2009; vis artist, Manhattan Graphics Ctr, NYC, 2009; artist in res, Serie Project, Austin, Tex, 2009. *Teaching:* Art Dept, Univ Hawaii, Hilo. *Awards:* Purchase Awards, State Found Cult Arts, Honolulu, 71, 74, 75, 87, 91 & 92; Juror's Award, Print Club, Philadelphia, Pa, 88; Purchase Awards, Honolulu Acad Arts, 92; Purchase Award State Found on Culture and the Arts, 97Pur; Purchase Award Univ Richmond Mus, Va, 2000; Univ Medal, Excellence in Scholarly and Creative Activities, Univ Hawaii at Hilo, 2005; Purchase Award, Alice C. Sabatini Gallery, Topeka, Kansas, 2006; Irwin Rosenhouse Award, Soc Am Graphic Artists, Ormond Beach, Fla, 2008; 2 purchase awards, State Found, Hawaii, 2008. *Mem:* Honolulu Printmakers Asn (mem bd & treas, 71-72); Print Club, Philadelphia; Northwest Print Coun; Southern Graphics Coun; Coll Art Asn; Boston Printmakers; The Print Consortium; Fla Printmakers Asn; Mid-Am Print Soc; Soc Am Graphic Artists. *Media:* Painting; Intaglio Printmaking. *Res:* Multiple Plate Printmaking; Gestural mark and digital imagery; digital applications and works on paper. *Publ:* Auth, Unique art of Akaji, Honolulu Star Bull Advertiser, 76; Lee Chesney, 25 Years of Printmaking, Univ Presses Fla, Gainesville, 78; ed, Pacific States Regional Print Exhib (exhib catalog), Univ Hawaii, Hilo, 82; Pacific States Regional Print & Drawing Exhib, (exhib catalog), Univ Hawaii Hilo, 83, 84, 85 & 86; ed, Pacific Rim Internet Print Exhib Series, Univ Hawaii, Hilo, 93. 95, 97, 99, 01, 05. *Mailing Add:* University of Hawaii Art Dept Office MC 395-1A 200 W Kawili St Hilo HI 96720-4091

MIYASAKI, GEORGE JOJI
PRINTMAKER, PAINTER
b Kalopa, Hawaii, Mar 24, 1935. *Study:* Calif Coll Arts & Crafts, BFA & BAEd, 57 & MFA, 58. *Work:* San Francisco Mus Art, Calif; Brooklyn Mus Art, NY; Mus Mod Art, NY; Art Inst Chicago; Pasadena Art Mus, Calif. *Teaching:* Prof art, Univ Calif, Berkeley, 64-. *Awards:* John Simon Guggenheim Fel, 63-64; Nat Endowment Arts, 80-81 & 85-86. *Bibliog:* Rudy Turk (auth), George Miyasaki, monograph, 81. *Mem:* Nat Acad. *Dealer:* Stephen Wirtz Gallery 49 Geary St San Francisco CA. *Mailing Add:* Magnolia Editions 2527 Magnolia St Oakland CA 94607

MNUCHIN, STEVEN T
PATRON
Study: Yale Univ, BA. *Pos:* Various mgt positions in tech div Goldman Sach, 85-2001, exec vpres, chief info off, 2001-2002; vchmn, Eng as Second Language Investments Inc, 2003; Chief Exec Officer, mem mgt comt, SFM Capital Mgt LP, 2003-04; chmn, co-Chief Exec Officer, Dune Capital Mgt LP, 2004-; Kmart (now Sears Holding Corp) (bd dir, currently). *Mem:* Yale Devel Board; Hirshhorn Mus & Sculpture Garden; Riverdale Co Sch, OCD Found; NY Presbyterian Med Ctr, (bd trustees, 2004-); Whitney Mus Am Art, (trustee, currently)

MOAKLEY, PAUL
PHOTOGRAPHER, CURATOR
Study: St Johns Univ, BA. *Pos:* Photo editor, Photo District News; sr photo editor, Newsweek; cur, Alice Austen House Mus, Staten Island, NY; guest editor, OjodePez, 2009-. *Mailing Add:* c/o Alice Austen House Museum 2 Hylan Blvd Staten Island NY 10305

MOBLEY, KAREN R
PAINTER, ADMINISTRATOR
b Cheyenne, Wyo. *Study:* Univ Wyo, BFA, 83; Univ Okla, MFA, 87. *Work:* NMex State Univ; Wyo State Mus; Nicolaysen Art Mus. *Comn:* Grandview Elementary Sch, Washington State Arts Comn; Bear Necessities, Spokane, Ronald McDonald House. *Exhib:* New Am Talent, Laguna Gloria Art Mus, Austin, Tex, 92; Wyo State Mus, 94; Wyo Arts Coun Gallery, 95; Casper Col, Wyo, 95; Univ Wyo, 95; Mont State Univ, 96; N Idaho Col, 99; Spokane Art Sch, 2000; Whitworth Col, 04; Kress Gallery, 04; JM Thamm Gallery, 2010; Clearstory, 2012. *Collection Arranged:* Ocho Inspiraciones, 89; Comics, 89; Painting Divergence (catalog), 90; The Computer Art Show, 91; The River, 2000; Metal, 2010. *Pos:* Dir, Univ Art Gallery, NMex State Univ, Las Cruces, NMex, 87-93; Nicolaysen Art Mus, Casper, Wyo, 93-97; Arts Dir, City of Spokane, Spokane Arts Comn, 97-2012, dir Spokane Arts Fund, 2012-2013, program mgr 2013-. *Teaching:* Whitworth Col, Spokane, Wash, 2006, 2008, 2010, 2012. *Awards:* Best show, Sangre de Cristo Art Ctr, 89; Individual Artist Grant, Wyo Arts Coun, 94; Women of Achievement for Arts & Culture award, Spokane YWCA, 2000. *Bibliog:* Drawings, Puerto del Sol/NMex State Univ, 88; Drawings, Caldera, 94; Poems, Caldera, 96; Tom West, Catalog for Nicolaysen Art Mus, 98; Pub Art Site, Spokane. *Mem:* Am Asn Mus; Coll Art Asn; Washington State Arts Alliance; Rotary Club of Spokane. *Media:* Mixed Media, Painting. *Dealer:* Art at Work Spokane WA. *Mailing Add:* 3515 S Lee Spokane WA 99203

MOCK, MARTHA L
CURATOR
b Chicago, Ill, Nov 3, 1946. *Study:* Coll Wooster, BA, 68; NY Univ, MA, 70; State Univ NY, Buffalo, MFA, 81. *Collection Arranged:* Ansel Adams: 100 Photographs, 79-80, August Sander: Photographs of an Epoch, 80, The Spirit of an Am Place, 80-81, The New West: Photographs by Robert Adams, 81, Am Frontiers: The Photographs of Timothy H O'Sullivan 1867-1874, 81-82, Danny Lyon: Pictures from the New World 1962-1982, 82, Frederick H Evans: The Desired Haven, 82, Minor White, 83 & Tibet: The Sacred Realm, Photographs 1880-1950, 83, Philadelphia Mus Art; The Golden Age of British Photography 1839-1900, 84-85; All Am, photogr by Burk Uzzle, 84-85; Twelve Photographers Look at Us, 87; Emmet Gowin photogr, 90. *Pos:* Assoc cur photogr, 85. *Awards:* Visual Arts Prog Critics Fel, Nat Endowment Arts, 79. *Mem:* Soc Photog Educ. *Publ:* Auth, Tibet: The Sacred Realm, Photographs 1880-1950, Millerton, 83; All American: Photographs by Burk Uzzle, St Davids, 84; Twelve Photographers Look at Us, Philadelphia Mus Art Bull, 84; Emmet Gowin Photographs, Philadelphia Mus Art, 90. *Mailing Add:* 406 E Main St Roaring Spring PA 16673-1353

MODE, CAROL A
PAINTER
b St Louis, Mo, Mar 27, 1943. *Study:* Washington Univ, BFA, 65, Summer Art Inst, 80; Vanderbilt Univ, 81-82. *Work:* Tenn State Mus, Nashville; Hosp Corp Am, Nashville; Northern Telecom, Vanderbilt Hosp, Nashville; Nynex, Nat; Bell South, Nashville, Tenn. *Comn:* Billboard painting, IDS, Nashville; Tenn State Mus Collection, Nashville. *Exhib:* 47th Ann Nat Midyear Exhib, 83 & 50th Nat Am Midyear Show, 86, Butler Inst An Art; Clemson Nat Print & Drawing Exhib, Clemson Univ, SC, 85; solo exhibs, Transfigurations, Tenn Fine Arts Mus, Nashville, 85, Tenn Arts Comn Gallery, Nashville, 88 & 96, Leu Gallery, Belmont Univ, Nashville, Tenn, 91, & Cumberland Gallery, Nashville, 95; 21st Bradley Nat Print & Drawing Exhib, Biennial, Bradley Univ, Peoria, Ill, 87; 6th Ann Summer Lights Exhib, Metro Arts Comn, Nashville, 89-91; Christoph Merian Stiftung, Basel, Switz, 95; and others. *Awards:* Artist Residency/Christoph Merian Fel, 95-96; Individual Artist Fel, Tenn Arts Comn, 96. *Mem:* CAA. *Media:* Acrylic, Oil. *Dealer:* Cumberland Gallery 4107 Hillsboro Circle Nashville TN 37215. *Mailing Add:* 421 Moss Creek Ct Nashville TN 37205-2828

MODI-VITALE, LYDIA
MUSEUM DIRECTOR, CURATOR
b New York, NY, Jan 6, 1917. *Study:* Scholar Award, Art Students League, New York; apprentice of Hans Hoffman, New York; internship, Museo Nac de Hist, 45-46 & Museo Nac de Antropologia, 58, Mexico City; studies in art conserv & restoration, Univ Calif, Davis, 70. *Collection Arranged:* Early Am Folk Art, Nat Art Gallery,

Washington, DC, 68; Art Nouveau, 68, 150 videotape exhibs, 70-78, Process Art, Wynn Bullock, 72, Six from Castelli's, 74, New Deal Art: California, 76, The Graham Nash Exhibit of Rare and Vintage Photography, 78, De Saisset Gallery, Univ Santa Clara, Calif; Bill Viola: An Instrument of Simple Sensations & The Vatican Collection with the De Young Mus, Mus Italo Americano, 83-84. *Pos:* Dir, Triton Mus, San Jose, Calif, 66-68 & De Saisset Mus, Univ Santa Clara, Calif, 68-78; consult, 78-; cur, Museo Italo Americano, 83-84; asst dir, Vorpal Gallery, San Francisco, 84, consult, 87-; bd dir, Archeoclub d'Italia, currently; proj dir, Soma Int Galleries, San Francisco, 95-; cur, Mus-Legion of Hon, 82. *Awards:* Adolph's Found Grant, 74, Calif Arts Comn Grant, 74; Nat Endowment for the Humanities Grant & exten, 74 & 75. *Mem:* Western Asn of Am Mus (exec secy, 69-71); Am Asn Art Mus; Bay Area Lawyers for the Arts; Archeoclub d'Italia. *Publ:* ed catalogs, Twenty Color Photographs: Light Abstractions, Wynn Bullock, 72, Fletcher Benton: Selected Works 1964-74, 74 & Scholder Collects Scholder 1965-75 Retrospective, 75, de Saisset Art Gallery & Mus; co-ed, James W McManus: Survey of Selected Works 1967-77, De Saisset Art Gallery & Mus, 77

MOE, KIEL K
ARCHITECT
Study: Univ Cincinnati, BArch, 2001; Univ Va Sch Archit, MArch, 2002; Harvard Univ Grad Sch Design, MDesS, 2003. *Exhib:* Ford Calumet Ctr, Ill, 2004; Art Inst Chicago, 2006; Boston Soc Architects, 2006-2007; Northeastern Univ, 2008. *Pos:* Architect, MOE, 1998-, Hargreaves Associates, 2003, WW, 2003-2004 & Garofalo Architects, 2004-2005. *Teaching:* Teaching asst, Univ Va Sch Archit, 2001-2002 & studio instr, 2002; res asst, Harvard Grad Sch Design, 2002-2003; vis asst prof, Univ Ill Sch Archit, 2004-2005; asst prof, Syracuse Univ Sch Archit, 2005-2006 & Northeastern Univ Sch Archit, 2006-. *Awards:* Res grant, Syracuse Univ Ctr Excellence, 2005, Boston Soc Architects, 2006, Northeastern Univ Provost, 2008, Am Inst Architects, 2008; Gorham P Stevens Rome Prize, Am Acad in Rome, 2010. *Bibliog:* Michael Brill (auth), Coming to Our Senses, Interiors, 12/1997; Peter Sherwood (auth), Moving Towards Sustainability, Interior Design, 10/13/2003; Alan Hess (auth), A Crystalline Cave, Turned Inside Out, San Jose Mercury News, 5/25/2003; J Hernandez (auth), San Deigo Waterfront Urban Design Competition, Competitions Mag, 2005. *Publ:* Auth, Compelling yet Unreliable Theories of Sustainability, J Architectural Edn, Vol 60, No 4, 24-30, 5/2007; Integrated Design in Contemporary Architecture, Princeton Architectural Press, 2008; Plastic Rheologies: From the Molecular to the Territorial, In: Architecture and Plastic (auth, Billie Faircloth), Princeton Architectural Press, 2009; Thermally Active Surfaces in Architecture, Princeton Architectural Press, 2010. *Mailing Add:* Northeastern University School of Architecture 151 Ryder Hall Boston MA 02115

MOFFIT, CHUCK
SCULPTOR
b West Bend, Wis, 1969. *Study:* Univ Nev, Reno, BA, 1992; Claremont Grad Univ, MFA (sculpture), 2000. *Comn:* Bayside Fire Station, City of San Diego, 2008; pub gathering place, Mira Costa Coll, 2008. *Exhib:* Nev Biennial, Weigand Mus, Reno, 1992; El Corazon Sangriento, Front Door Gallery, Univ Nev, 1993; solo exhibs, Sierra Arts Found, Reno, 1995, East Gallery, Claremont Grad Univ, Calif, 2000, Sheppard Gallery, Univ Nev, Reno, 2001, Boehm Art Gallery, Palomar Coll, San Marcos, Calif, 2010 ; SITE's First Ann Nat Competition, Loyola Law Sch, Los Angeles, 1996; Both, Claremont Grad Univ, Calif, 1998; Inland Specific, Univ LaVerne, Calif, 2000; Thing: New Sculpture from Los Angeles, UCLA Hammer Mus, 2005; Wittgenstein's Bath, Sierra Arts Found, Reno, 2008; Baker's Dozen, Torrance Art Mus, Calif, 2009. *Awards:* Jurors Prize, Nev Biennial, Reno, 1992; Sierra Arts Found Artist Endowment, 1994; Western Sculpting Supply Award, Foothills Art Ctr, Golden, Co, 1996; Pollock-Krasner Found Grant, 2008. *Bibliog:* Louise Roug (auth), Object Lessons, Los Angeles Times, 1/2/2005; Chris Lee (auth), Art Parties, Resculpted, Los Angeles Times, 12/21/2006; David Pagel (auth), Baker's Dozen, Los Angeles Times, 10/9/2009. *Mailing Add:* PO Box 502 Mount Baldy CA 91759

MOGAVERO, MICHAEL
PAINTER
b Rochester, NY, Nov 4, 1950. *Study:* Buffalo State Univ, BS, 73; Hoffberger Sch Painting, Md Inst Art, MFA, 75. *Work:* Rochester Mem Art Gallery, NY; Lowe Mus Art, Univ Miami, Fla; Minneapolis Mus Art, Minn; Prudential Insurance, Princeton, NJ; Artco Int, Geneva, Switz. *Exhib:* Md Biennial, Baltimore Mus Art, 74 & 75; Maryland Artists-A New Look, Baltimore Mus Art, 79; one person-exhibs, Gallery Six Friedrich, Munich, Ger, 83, Gallery Corinne Hummel, Basel, Switz, 85, Oscarsson Siegeltuch Gallery, NY, 86 & 87, Carol Getz Gallery, Miami, Fla, 88, Ruth Siegel Gallery, NY, 89, Lyons Matrix Gallery, Austin, Tex, 93 & Craighead-Green Gallery, Dallas, 95 & 97; San Francisco Mus Art, 87; Phizer Inc, Mus Mod Art, NY, 92; Fay Gold Gallery, Atlanta, Ga, 94; Eve Mannes Gallery, Atlanta, 94; New Works on Paper, Lyons Matrix Gallery, Austin, 95; Lynn Goode Gallery, Houston, 95; Valerie Miller Gallery, Palm Desert, Calif, 96; New Works by UT Faculty, Lyons Matrix Gallery, Austin, Tex, 96; Artspace, San Antonio, Tex, 96; Lyons Matrix Gallery, Austin, Tex, 98. *Teaching:* Assoc prof, Univ Tex, Austin, 84-. *Awards:* Individual Fel, NY Found Arts, 85. *Bibliog:* Kathryn Gregor (auth), Arts, Third Coast Mag, 85 & 88-89; Annette Carlozzi (auth), 50 Texas Artists, Chronicle Books, 86; John R Clarke (auth), Michael Mogavero at Lyons Matrix, Art in Am, 4/94. *Media:* Acrylic, Oil on Canvas. *Dealer:* Craighead-Green Gallery 2404 Cedar Springs Suite 700 Dallas TX 75201; Lyons Matrix Gallery 1712 Lavaca Austin TX 78701. *Mailing Add:* Univ Tex Austin Dept Art & Hist Coll Fine Arts 1 Univ Station D1300 Austin TX 78712

MOGENSEN, PAUL
PAINTER, PRINTMAKER
b Los Angeles, Calif, Dec 3, 1941. *Study:* Yale Univ, 62, Univ Southern Calif, BFA, 63. *Work:* Mus Mod Art, NY Pub Libr, NY; High Mus Art, Atlanta, Ga; Houston Mus Fine Arts, Tex; Wadsworth Atheneum, Hartford, Conn; Fogg Mus Art, Harvard Univ, Cambridge, Mass; Walker Art Ctr, Minneapolis, Mn; Menil Collection, Houston, Tex. *Comn:* Bykert Gallery, NY, 67, 68, 69, 75. *Exhib:* Modular Painting, Albright-Knox Art Gallery, Buffalo, NY, 70; A View of a Decade, Mus Contemp Art, Chicago, 77; Retrospective, Houston Mus Fine Arts, 78-79; Mary Boone Gallery, NY, 78; Edward Thorp Gallery, 87 & 88; Piccolo Spoleto Festival, Charleston, SC, 92; Reflex, Secession Mus, Vienna, Austria, 94; Art Et Industrie, NY, 97; Galerie Thomas Schulte, Berlin, 2002; A Minimal Future, Mus Contemp Art, Los Angeles, 2004; Lawrence Markey Gallery, San Antonio, Tex, 2012; The Whitebox, NY; Am Acad Arts & Scis, 2014. *Awards:* John Simon Guggenheim Mem Found Fel, 76; Nat Endowment Arts, 80; Pollock-Krasner Found Grant, 88; Harris Rosenstein, ARTnews. *Bibliog:* Carter Ratcliff (auth), Paul Mogensen at Thorp, Art Am, 87; Klaus Kertess (auth), Painting Order, Secession Mus, Vienna, Austria, 94; Richard Kalina (auth), Paul Mogensen, Art Am, 97; James Mayer (auth), Minimalism, 2000. *Publ:* Paul Mogensen Housten Mus Fine Art (catalog), 79; Secession Mus (catalog), Vienna, 94. *Dealer:* Lawrence Markey Gallery San Antonio TX. *Mailing Add:* 159 Mercer St New York NY 10012

MOHLE, BRENDA SIMONSON
ART DEALER, ART APPRAISER
b Dallas, Tex, May 9, 1959. *Study:* Univ Tex, Austin, BA, 80. *Pos:* Art adv, Newman Gallery, 81-84; art adv & gallery dir, Omni Art, 84-87; docent, Dallas Mus Art, 85-95; art consult, (art appraiser & pvt dealer) Signet Art, 87-. *Awards:* Outstanding Member of the Year, 98. *Mem:* Int Soc Appraisers; Dallas Mus Art; Appraisers Asn Am; Am Soc Appraisers. *Specialty:* Corporate work including late 19th century European work through contemporary American. *Mailing Add:* 2644 Newcastle Dr Carrollton TX 75007

MOHR, MANFRED
PAINTER
b Pforzheim, Ger, June 8, 1938. *Study:* Kunst & Werk, Schule, Pforzheim, 57-62; Beaux Art, Paris, 63-66. *Work:* Wilhelm-Hack Mus, Ludwigshafen, Ger; Mus D'Art Mod, Centre Pompidou, Paris,; Tel Aviv Mus, Israel; Stadt Mus Monchenglad Bach, Ger; Staats Galerie Stuttgart, Ger. *Exhib:* Solo exhibs, Mus D'Art Moderne, 71, Wilhelm-Hack Mus, 87, Reuchlin Mus, 88, Stuttgart Mus, 94; Printed Art-A View of 2 Decades, Mus Mod Art, NY, 80; Digital Vision, Everson Mus, 87; Josef Albers Mus, Bottrop Ger, 98. *Awards:* Golden Nica, Prix ARS Electronica, 90. *Bibliog:* Nadin, Keiner, Kurtz (monogr), Waser, Zurich, 94; M Dworschak (auth), Der Zeit, 10/31/96. *Mem:* NY Artists Equity; Am Abstract Artists. *Media:* Computer. *Dealer:* Teufel Cologne Germany; Mueller-Roth Stuttgart Germany. *Mailing Add:* 20 N Moore St New York NY 10013

MOIR, ALFRED
COLLECTOR, CURATOR
b Minneapolis, Minn, Apr 14, 1924. *Study:* Harvard Univ, AM, 49, PhD, 53; Univ Rome, 50-51. *Collection Arranged:* Drawings by Seventeenth Century Italian Masters from the Collection of Janos Scholz, 74; European Drawings, Santa Barbara Mus Art, 76 & 96; Old Master Drawings from the Feitelson Collections, 83; Old Master Drawings from the Collection of John & Alice Steiner, 86; Van Dyck's Antwerp, 91; Old Master Drawings, UCSB Art Mus & Santa Barbara Mus, 95, 2001-2002 & 2006-2007. *Pos:* Chmn, Dept Art, Univ Calif, Santa Barbara, 63-69; art historian in residence, Am Acad Rome, 69-70 & 80; adj cur, Univ Art Mus, 74-, UCSB, 74-96; dir, Univ Calif Educ Abroad Prog, Italy, 78-80; consult cur, Santa Barbara Mus Art, 97-2009. *Teaching:* From instr to assoc prof hist art, Newcomb Col, Tulane Univ, 52-62; from assoc prof to prof, Univ Calif, Santa Barbara, 62-91, prof emer, 91-. *Mem:* Soc Archit Historians; Renaissance Soc; Medieval Acad Am; Southern Calif Art Historians; Soc of Fels, Acad in Rome; Ateneo Veneto, Venice (Italy); and others. *Res:* Italian baroque art, particularly Caravaggio and his followers; drawings; Van Dyck. *Collection:* 16th to 18th century European drawings. *Publ:* The Italian Followers of Caravaggio, Harvard, 67; Caravaggio & His Copyists, New York Univ Press, 77; auth, Caravaggio, Abrams, 82 & 89; Van Dyck, Abrams, 94; and others. *Mailing Add:* 4706 Falstone Ave Bethesda MD 20815

MOJSILOV, ILENE KRUG
PAINTER
b St Paul, Minn, May 3, 1952. *Study:* Univ Minn, BFA, 74, MFA, 77; Ryusei Sch, Ikebana, studied with Kosen Otsubo, lic, 84. *Work:* Maki Gallery, Tokyo. *Exhib:* Tweed Mus Art, Duluth, Minn, 76; 37th & 38th Salon de Jeune Peinture, Grand Palais, Paris, 85 & 86; L'Ambiente Gallery, NY, 86 & 87; No Name Gallery, Minneapolis, 88; Bockley Gallery, 91; Wilensky Arts Gallery, 91-93; and others. *Pos:* Artist-in-residence, Asn Confluences, Paris, 84-85, La Vie des Formes, Chalon-sur-Sarbone, France, 90. *Teaching:* Instr painting, Tucson Mus Art Sch, 77-78; artist-in-residence, Minn State Arts Bd, 86-; instr, Walker Art Center, 88-. *Bibliog:* Yuri Akita (auth), New painting, Ikebana Soc, 8/83; Sandra Kwock-Silve (auth), From classical to avant-garde, Paris Free Voice, 4/85. *Mem:* Minn Alliance Arts in Educ; Minn Citizens for Arts. *Media:* Oil, Gouache. *Publ:* Auth, Performance and the mass media, Art Network (Japan issue), spring 84. *Mailing Add:* 4130 Blaisdell Ave S Minneapolis MN 55409-1513

MOLDENHAUER, SUSAN
MUSEUM DIRECTOR, CURATOR
Study: N IL Univ, BFA, 1974; Pa State Univ, MFA, 1982. *Pos:* Gallery mgr, Sch Visual Arts, Pa State Univ; exec dir, Second Street Gallery, Charlottesville, Va; cur mus progs, Univ Wyo Art Mus, Laramie, 1991-96, asst dir, 1996-2000, interim dir, 2000-02, dir, chief cur, 2002-. *Mailing Add:* Univ Wyo Art Mus Centennial Complex 2111 Willett Dr PO Box 3807 Laramie WY 82071-3807

MOLDROSKI, AL R
PAINTER, EDUCATOR
b Terre Haute, Ind, Aug 27, 1928. *Study:* Ind State Univ, BS; Mich State Univ, MA; Southern Ill Univ, grant; Md Inst Art, Post Masters. *Work:* Paintings & paper sculpture in Fla & NY. *Exhib:* Pa Acad Fine Arts; Detroit Mus Art; City Art Mus, St Louis; De Waters Art Ctr; Boston Festival Arts; and many others. *Pos:* Ill Spec Events Comn.

Teaching: Lectr art, Southern Ill Univ, formerly; asst prof, Glenville State Coll, formerly; from instr to prof art, Eastern Ill Univ, formerly, prof emer, currently; exchange prof, Portsmouth Polytech Fine Arts, Portsmouth, Eng & Wyzsza Szkola Roiniczo-Pedagogiczna w Siedlch, Poland. *Awards:* Tiffany Found Grant; Purchase Award, Pa Acad Fine Art; Mary Richart Mem Award in Painting & Art Directors Award, Detroit Mus Art; and many others

MOLESWORTH, HELEN
CURATOR
Collection Arranged: Bodyspace, Baltimore Mus Art, 2001; Work Ethic, Baltimore Mus Art, 2003-2004; Part Object Part Sculpture, Wexner Ctr for Arts, 2005; Twice Untitled and Other Pictures (looking back), Wexner Ctr for Arts, 2006. *Pos:* Chief cur exhibs, Wexner Ctr for Arts, Ohio, 2002-2007; Maisie K & James R Houghton cur contemp art & head dept mod & contemp art, Harvard Univ Art Mus, 2007-2009; chief cur, Inst Contemp Art, Boston, 2009-; sr critic, Yale Sch Art; co-founding ed, Documents. *Teaching:* Instr, Bard Ctr for Curatorial Studies, SUNY Old Westbury & Cooper Union Sch Art. *Mailing Add:* 32 Quincy St Cambridge MA 02138

MOLINARI, GUIDO
PAINTER, SCULPTOR
b Montreal, Que, Oct 12, 1933. *Study:* Ecole Beaux-Arts, Montreal; Sch Art & Design, Montreal Mus Fine Arts. *Work:* Kuntsmuseum, Basel, Switz; Mus Mod Art, Guggenheim Mus & Chase Manhattan Bank, NY; Nat Gallery Art, Ottawa, Ont. *Comn:* Murals, comn by Dept of Pub Works, Ottawa for Vancouver Int Airport, BC, 68 & Dept Nat Defence Hq Bldg, Ottawa, 72. *Exhib:* 4th Guggenheim Int Exhib, NY, 64; The Responsive Eye, Mus Mod Art, 65; Canada: Art Aujourdui, Rome, Paris, Lausanne, Bruxelles, 68; Venice 34th Biennial, Italy, 68; Can 101, Edinburgh, Scotland, 68; Retrospective Exhib, Nat Gallery, Ottawa, Montreal, Toronto & Vancouver, 76; 15th Anniversary Paris Biennial, Mus Mod Art, Paris & Seibu Art Mus, Tokyo, Japan, 77-78; Contemp Can Painters Exhib, Dept External Affairs World Tour, 77-78. *Pos:* Founder & pres, L'Actuelle, 55-57. *Teaching:* Head painting sect, Sir George Williams Univ, 70-. *Awards:* Robertson Award, Montreal Mus Fine Arts, 65; Guggenheim Mem Found Fel, 66; Bright Found Award Painting, 68. *Bibliog:* Gros Plan (film), Radio-Can, Montreal, 71. *Mem:* Academician Royal Can Acad Arts; Soc Esthetique Experimentale, Paris; Soc Color Res, Nat Coun Res (dir, 72). *Publ:* Coauth, Debats sur la Peinture Quebecoise, Univ Montreal, 71. *Mailing Add:* 3288 Saint Catharine St E Montreal PQ H1W 2C6 Canada

MOLLETT, DAVID
EDUCATOR, ADMINISTRATOR
Study: New York City Studio Sch, studied, 1970; Reed Col, Portland, Oregon, BA (Art), 1972. *Exhib:* Solo shows in every major public exhibition, Alaska; group exhibitions throughout the US. *Collection Arranged:* Collections include Portland (Oregon) Art Mus & Trenton State Col, NJ. *Awards:* Individual Artist Fellowship, Alaska State Council on the Arts, 1982, 1988; Camargo Found Fellowship for a residency in Cassis, France, 1992

MOLNAR, MICHAEL JOSEPH
PAINTER, INSTRUCTOR
b Hazleton, Pa. *Study:* Luzerne County CC, studied comml art, 1968-70; Md Inst Coll Art, BFA, studied under Joseph Sheppard, 1975; studies with Vincent Civiletti, 1977; studies with Joseph Sheppard, 1988; Schuler Sch Fine Art, Balt, studied with Ann Schuler, 1990-91. *Exhib:* Mid-West Mus Am Art, Elkhart, Ind, 1998; Evergreen House, Johns Hopkins Univ, Balt, 1998; Butler Inst Am Art, Salem, Ohio, 1998; invitational, Ea Sierra Art Found, Genoa, Nev, 1999; Allied Artists Am ann exhibn, Nat Arts Club, 2000; invitational, John Pence Gallery, San Francisco, 2008; Rittenhouse Fine Art Gallery, 2003; Eleanor Ehinger Gallery, Tromp L'oeil Soc Exhib, 2003; Woodson Art Mus, Visual Deceptions Exhbns, 2003; Phoenix Art Mus, Fashion's Art of Illusion, 2003; Trompe L'Oeil: The Art of Illusion Traveling Exhib, 2006-2007; Legacy: A Tradition Lives On Traveling Exhib, 2006-2007; The Jule Collins Smith Mus of Art, Auburn, Ala, 2006-2007. *Pos:* asst to Leonard Bahr, Md Inst Col Art, 73; with commercial art dept, Luzerne Co Community Col. *Teaching:* pvt teaching & research Old Master techniques, 77-90; instr painting, drawing & sculpture, Luzerne Co Community Col, 80-2006. *Awards:* First Prize, Pa Coll of Technol, 2002; 3rd Place-Portrait, Portrait Arts Festival Metrop Mus NY, 2003; Gary Erbe Award, Allied Artist of Am, 2005. *Bibliog:* Art Review, 2005; Legacy: A Tradition Lives On, 2005; American Artist Magazine, 2005. *Mem:* Am Soc Classical Realism; Allied Artists Am; Knickerbocker Artists; Scottsdale Art Sch; Am Soc Portrait Artists. *Media:* Oil. *Specialty:* realism. *Interests:* Painting. *Dealer:* John Pence 750 Post St San Francisco CA 94109; Eleanor Ettinger Gallery 119 Spring St New York NY 10012; Robert Wilson Gallery MA. *Mailing Add:* 1772 Hudson Dr Weatherly PA 18255

MOMENT, JOAN
INSTRUCTOR, PAINTER
b Sellersville, Pa, Aug 22, 1938. *Study:* Univ Conn, BS, 60; Univ Colo, with Roland Reiss & William Wiley, MFA, 70. *Work:* E B Crocker Art Mus, Sacramento, Calif; Blue Cross of Southern Calif, Los Angeles; NY State Develop Corp, NY; Oakland Mus, Calif; Allen Mem Art Mus, Oberlin Col, Ohio; and others. *Comn:* City of Sacramento, Sacramento Metrop Art Comn, Calif, 90-97. *Exhib:* Contemp Am Art Biennial, Whitney Mus Am Art, NY, 73; One-person show, Whitney Mus Am Art, 74, Crocker Art Mus, Sacramento, Calif, 81, Quay Gallery, San Francisco, Calif, 82, Southeastern Ctr Contemp Art, Winston-Salem, NC, 84, Rena Branston Gallery, San Francisco, 85, Glass Gallery, Univ NC, Chapel Hill, 86 & Solomon Dubnick Gallery, Sacramento, 92; A Moment Becomes Eternity; Flowers as Image, Bergen Mus Art, NJ, 93; Building a Collection: Recent Acquisitions, Crocker Art Mus, Sacramento, 94; Choices: Recent Acquisitions, Oakland Mus, Calif, 94; Sexy: Sensual Abstraction in Calif Art, 1950's-1990's, Contemp Artists Collective/Temporary Contemp, Las Vegas, 95; Jay Jay Gallery, Sacramento, Calif, 2002; Cent Acad of Fine Art, Beijing, China, 2003; and others. *Teaching:* prof art, Calif State Univ, Sacramento, 70-; vis artist, Univ Colo, Boulder, 75, Univ Mont, Missoula, 77, Diablo Valley Col, Pleasant Hill, Calif, 78, Bard Col, Milton Avery Grad Sch Arts, 85, Syracuse Univ, NY, 85, Univ NC, Chapel Hill, 86, Princeton Univ, NJ, 87 & Sonoma State Univ, Rohnert Park, CA; guest lectr, Eastern Wash State Col, Chency, 73, Wash State Univ, Pullman, 74, Claremont Grad Sch, Calif, 80, Solano Community Col, Fairfield, Calif, 82, Univ of Reno, Nev, 83 & Cent Acad Beijing, China, 2003; vis assoc prof, East Carolina Univ, Greenville, 84; lectr, Crocker Art Mus, Sacramento, CA, 94. *Awards:* Rockefeller Artist-in-Residency Fel, 84; Meritorious Performance Award, Calif State Univ, Sacramento, 86. *Bibliog:* Kenneth Baker (auth), Studio, show a bright light in dark times, San Francisco Chronicle, 7/5/92; Jeff Kelly (auth), California dreaming: From the studio at the Oakland Museum, Art Week, Vol 23, No 22, 8/20/92; Randal Davis (auth), Hybrid hits & misses paintings by Joan Moment, Soonja Kim & Hideo Sakato, Sacramento News & Review, 11/12/92; and many others. *Media:* Acrylic on Wood Panel, Canvas & Arches Paper. *Dealer:* Jay Jay Gallery 2906 Franklin Blvd Sacrament CA 95818. *Mailing Add:* 1424 35th St Sacramento CA 95816

MOMIN, SHAMIM M
CURATOR
Study: Williams Col, BA (Art Hist), 1995; Whitney Independent Study Prog; City Univ New York, PhD (Art Hist). *Collection Arranged:* Diablo Robleto: Say Goodbye to Substance, Whitney Mus at Altria, 2003; Will Boys Be Boys?: Examining Adolescent Masculinity in Contemp Art, 2004-07; co-cur: Whitney Biennial, 2004, 2008; cur: No Ordinary Sanctity, 2005; Banks Violette: Untitled (auth, catalog), 2005; Raymond Pettibon, 2005-06; Andrea Zittel: Small Liberties, 2006; Terrence Koh (co-auth, catalog), 2007. *Pos:* Asst cur, mgr br progs Whitney Mus Am Art, New York, formerly, assoc cur, 2003-, branch dir, cur Whitney Mus Am Art at Altria, 2000-. *Teaching:* Vis prof contemp art, NY Univ, 2005; adj prof contemp art, Williams Col Semester in New York prog, 2007

MONAGHAN, KATHLEEN MARY
DIRECTOR
b Waterville, Maine, Sept 6, 1936. *Study:* Univ Calif, Santa Barbara, BA, 78, MA, 81. *Collection Arranged:* Faces & Figures: European Drawings, Santa Barbara Mus Art, 81, Am Modernism 1910-1945, 81, The Gloria & Donald B Marron Collection Am Prints, 81, Rufino Tamayo-The Pre-Columbian, 82. *Pos:* Dir br mus, Whitney Mus Am Art, New York, 85-93, assoc cur, 92-93; dir, The Hyde Collection, Glen Falls, NY, 94-99; exec dir, Fresno Met Mus, 99-. *Awards:* Rubinstein fel, Whitney Mus Am Art, NY City, 78. *Mem:* Am Asn Mus Dir; Am Asn Mus; Int Comt Exhib Exchanges; Western Asn Art Mus; Southern Calif Art Historians Asn. *Res:* 19th-20th century American art; 18th century British art; Joseph Wright of Derby. *Publ:* contribr, Donald Marron Print Collection, SBMA, 80; The Stirling Morton Collection, SBMA, 81; auth, Elements, Whitney Mus Am Art, 87; Abstraction Before 1930, Whitney Mus Am Art, 91; Nature's Bounty, Whitney Mus Am Art, 93

MONAGHAN, WILLIAM SCOTT
PAINTER, SCULPTOR
b Philadelphia, Pa, Nov 1, 1944. *Study:* Yale Univ, BA; Harvard Grad Sch Design, MA. *Work:* Addison Gallery Am Art, Andover, Mass; Brockton Fuller Mem Art Mus, Mass; Fed Reserve Bank, Boston; Hyatt Hotel, Boston; Aldrich Mus Contemp Art, Ridgefield, Conn. *Comn:* Sculpture, Boston 200 Bicentennial Art Collection, 76. *Exhib:* Sculptors' Workshop Show, Addison Gallery Am Art, 74 & Berkshire Mus, Pittsfield, Mass, 75; solo exhib, Inst Contemp Art, Boston, 75; Contemp Reflections, Aldrich Mus Contemp Art, 76; Davidson Art Mus, Wesleyan Univ, Conn, 77; Two-man show, Soho Ctr for Visual Artists, NY, 77. *Mem:* Boston Visual Artists' Union. *Mailing Add:* 165 Perry St New York NY 10014-2382

MONAHAN, MATTHEW
SCULPTOR
b Eureka, Calif, 1972. *Study:* Cooper Union, BFA, 1990-94; Studies at Gerit Rietveld Acad, Amsterdam, 93. *Work:* AkzoNobel Art Found; Art Inst Chgo, Ill; Boijmans Van Beuningen, Rotterdam, Netherlands; De Ateliers, Amsterdam, Netherlands; Fries Mus, Leeuwarden, Netherlands; Hammer Mus, Los Angeles, Calif; Los Angeles Co Mus Art; Los Angeles MoCA; MoMA, San Francisco, Calif, NY; Stedelijk Mus, Amsterdam, Netherlands; TATE Modern, London; Bank of Netherlands, Amsterdam; Saatchi Coll, London; Centraal Mus Utrecht, Netherlands. *Exhib:* Solo shows, Anton Kern Gallery, NY, 1997, 2002, 2003, 2005, 2008, 2010, & 2012; Fools Gold, The Bank of Netherlands, 1998; Artist is Proof, Buro Leeuwarden, Neth, 1999; Gozaimas, Bur Stedelijk, 2000; Nameless Man for Not-Even-Anywhere, Galeries Fons Welters, Amsterdam, 2002 & 2005; Civilized Spl Zone, Chinese European Art Ctr, Xiamen, 2002; Container, Art Basel Miami, 2003; Mus Mod Art, London, 2006; Los Angeles Mus Contemp Art, 2007; Massimo de Carlo, Milan, Italy, 2010; Galerie Fons Welters, Amsterdam, Netherlands, 2011; Contemporary Arts Ctr, Cincinnati, Oh, 2011; Contemporary Art Gallery, Vancouver, BC, 2012; Stuart Shave Modern Art, London, 2012; Kaikai Kiki, Tokyo, Japan, 2012; Group shows, Night at Life, NY, 1997; Exterminating Angel, Galerie Ghislaine Hussenot, Paris, 1998; Subreal/The Human Condition, LA Int Biennial, Inmo Gallery, Los Angeles, 1999; I Love NY, Anton Kern Gallery, 2001; Mean Mercy, Tent, Rotterdam, 2001; Free-Standing, Beaver Coll Art Gallery, Philadelphia, 2001; To Be Recycled, Six Months, Los Angeles, 2004; Remembering, Univ Calif, Riverside Gallery, 2004; Whitney Biennial: Day for Night, Whitney Mus Am Art, 2006; USA Today, Royal Acad, London, 2007; Life on Mars: Carnegie Int, Carnegie Mus Art, Pittsburgh, 2008; Martian Museum of Terrestrial Art, Barbican Ctr, London, 2008; California Maximalism, Nyehaus, NY, 2009; Francisco Mus Modern Art, San Francisco, Calif, 2009; Mineral Spirits, Inst Contemporary Art, Univ Pa, 2010; Eisenberg, Bard Coll, NY, 2010; Outside the Box, Hammer Mus, Los Angeles, Calif, 2010; Statuesque, Nash Sculpture Ctr, Dallas, Tx, 2011; Proof: The Rise of Printmaking in Southern Calif, Norton Simon Mus, Pasadena, Calif, 2011;

Tracing the Century: Drawing from Tate Collection, Tate Liverpool, 2012; Exquisite Corpses: Drawing and Disfiguration, MoMA, NY, 2012; The Bronze Age, Massimo de Carlo, Milan, Italy, 2013; 55th Int Art Biennale, Venice, 2013. *Awards:* Fel de Ateliers, Amsterdam, 1994-96; Fonds BK Grant, Kitakysuhu, Japan, 2000; Chinese European Art, Ctr, Xiamen, 2002. *Mailing Add:* c/o Anton Kern Gallery 532 W 20th St New York NY 10011

MONDINI-RUIZ, FRANCO
ARTIST
b San Antonio, Tex 1961. *Study:* BA in English, St Mary's Univ, San Antonio, Tex, BA in English 1982; JD, St Mary's Univ, San Antonio, Tex, 1985. *Work:* group exhibs incl, Arlington Mus Art, 1991; Laguna Gloria Art Mus, Austin, 1997; Simply Beautiful, Contemp Art Mus, Houston, 1997; Collective Visions, San Antonio Mus Art, 1998; Material World, Austin Mus Art, 1998; Whitney Biennial, Whitney Mus Am Art, New York City, 2000; Mus Contemp Art, Helsinki, Finland, 2001; UCLA Fowler Mus Cult Hist, 2004-05. *Exhib:* Solo exhib incl, Infinito Botanica, ArtPace, San Antonio, 1996, Tableau Vivant, The Alamo, San Antonio, 1998, New Painting y Mas, Galeria Ortiz, San Antonio, 1999, Infinito Botanica: NY, Ctr Curatorial Studies, Bard Col, 1999, Mexique, El Museo del Barrio, New York City, 2000, Untitled Grid No 7, New Mus Contemp Art, New York City, 2001, Infinito Botanico: St Louis, Des Lee Gallery, Washington Univ, 2001, SHOP, Jessica Murray Projects, Brooklyn, 2001, Dust in the Wind, NY Pub Art Fund, 2002, Market Squared, Galeria Ortiz, San Antonio, 2002, Nacho de Paz (and Other TexMex Miracles), Frederieke Taylor Gallery, New York City, 2002, Pan in the Park, Laumeier Sculpture Park, St Louis, 2003, Infinito Botanico: Los Angeles, UCLA Fowler Mus Cult Hist, 2004-05. *Pos:* Atty USAA; owner Infinito Botanica and Gift Shop, San Antonio, 1995-98; ArtPace Artist in Residency Prog, 1996; Tryon Ctr Artist Residency Prog Charlotte, NC, 2003. *Awards:* New Forms Regional Initiative Grant, 1994, ArtPace General Grant, 1999, Pollock-Krasner Found Grant, 2000, Joan Mitchell Found Grant, 2001, Creative Capital Found Grant, 2001, Creative Capital Found Supplemental Grant, 2002, Penny McCall Found Fel, 2002, Jules Guerin Rome Prize Fel for Visual Arts, Am Acad in Rome, 2004-05

MONET, DIANE L.
PAINTER
b Bronxville, NY, July 6, 1960. *Study:* Nat Univ Mex, Summer Study, 80; New York Univ, BS, 82. *Work:* Albright Knox Mus, Buffalo, NY; Salon des Artistes Independents, Paris. *Comn:* oil paintings, many collectors, US, France, Japan, Yonkers Historical Soc, 90-2011. *Exhib:* Mitsukoshi Dept Store Galleries, Tokyo, Sendai, Hiroshima, Takamatsu, New River Art Gallery, Naples, Fla, Galerie Manumo, Paris, France; Asia Fine Art, Hong Kong. *Teaching:* instr, Christ Church, Bronxville, NY, 88-95. *Bibliog:* Bill Fallon (auth), Profits and Passions, Westchester City Bus Journal, 1/19/2009; Tom Hall (auth), Diane Monet Exhibit, 1/26, For Artist Diane Monet, 1/31, It Was All Smiles At Dm Reception, 2/13, Diane Monet's Incessant Dream, 3/8, The Examiner, 2011. *Mem:* Rotary Int. *Media:* Oil. *Specialty:* fine art. *Interests:* international travel, languages, animal welfare. *Collection:* paintings privately owned by international collectors. *Publ:* contribr, Promenades autour de l'art Contemporain, Salon des Independants, 2001. *Dealer:* Asia Fine Art Hong Kong

MONFORTE, IVAN
PERFORMANCE ARTIST
b Mexico. *Study:* Univ Calif Los Angeles, BA, 1996; New York Univ, MFA, 2004. *Exhib:* Calif Inst Arts, Valencia; MAK Ctr for Art and Archit, Los Angeles; Bronx Mus Art; New Fest 2005; Haven Artspace; Longwood Art Gallery. *Awards:* Art Matters Found Grant, 2008

MONGRAIN, CLAUDE
SCULPTOR
b Shawinigan, Que, 1948. *Study:* Ecole des Beaux-Arts de Montreal, 66-69. *Work:* Mus des Beaux-Arts de Montreal; Can Coun Art Bank, Ottawa; Musee d'Art Contemporain de Montreal; Nat Gallery Can, Ottawa; Mus de Que. *Exhib:* Solo exhibs, Olga Korper Gallery, Toronto, Ont, 85, 90 & 93, Claude Mongrain; Deuvres Recentes, Concordia Art Gallery, Concordia Univ, Montreal, Que, 87, Art Gallery Windsor, Ont, 88, Galerie Christiane Chassay, Montreal, Que, 89, Accelerateur de particules, Galerie Obscure, Montreal, Que, 91, Deux Monuments a une etoile Filante, Toronto Sculpture Garden, Ont, 91 & Zapping, Galerie Aline Vidal, Paris, France, 92; Espaces Int, CREDAC, Centre d'Art Contemporain, Ivry-Sur-Seine, France, 90; L'art de l'installation, Mus d'Art Contemporain, Montreal, Que, 90; Singulier/Pluriels, Galerie de L'UQAM, Montreal, Que, 92; Ameriques, Centre Lotois d'Art Contemporain, FIGEAC, France, 92; Vues d'Ensemble, CIAC, Montreal, Que, 92. *Awards:* Materials Assts Grants, Can Coun, 71, 73, 76, 85 & 86; Work Grant, 80, Bourse de Que, 87, Que Ministry Cult Affairs. *Bibliog:* Trevor Gould (auth), Claude Mongrain, No 14, C Mag, Toronto, summer 87, 65-66; Jerry McGrath (auth), Art in the Soo, Sans Demarcation, Vanguard, 2-3/88, 10-13. *Publ:* Contribr, Le Dessin Errant (catalog), Dalhousie Art Gallery, Halifax, 88

MONGRAIN, JEFFREY
SCULPTOR
Study: Univ Minn, BFA, 1978; Southern Ill Univ, MFA, 1981. *Work:* San Antonio Mus Art; Mus Arts & Design, New York; Smithsonian Mus Air & Space Divsn; Mus Fine Art, Tallahassee; Sarhjah Mus, United Arab Emirates; and many more. *Exhib:* San Angelo Mus Art, Tex, 2001; Univ Mus, Edwardsville, Ill, 2002; 8th Triennial, Mus Arts & Design, New York, 2003; Newcastle Regional Art Mus, Australia, 2004; Nat Mus Catholic Art, New York, 2005; Boston Soc for the Arts, Mass, 2006; Mus Fine Art, Tallahassee, Fla, 2007; Racine Mus Fine Art, Ill, 2008; Contemp Jewish Mus, San Francisco, 2009; Mus Contemp Ceramics, Dominican Repubic, 2010. *Awards:* NY Found Arts Gregory Millard Fel, 2009. *Bibliog:* Robin L Rice (auth), rev, Philadelphia Inquirer, 2001; Ken Johnson (auth), rev, NY Times, 2002; Barbara A MacAdams (auth), rev, ARTnews mag, 2004; Christine Temin (auth), rev, Boston Globe, 2005

MONK, NANCY
MIXED MEDIA ARTIST
b Minneapolis, Minn, 1951. *Study:* Colo State Univ, BFA, 73; Univ Minn, MFA, 76. *Work:* Corning Mus Glass, New York; Mod Int Glaskunst, Ebeltoft, Denmark; Los Angeles Co Mus Art, Calif. *Comn:* Venice Collaborative, Beach Boxes, 2002, Breeze, 2008, Rambla Vista, 2009, Ocean Front, 2009. *Exhib:* New Glass: A Worldwide Survey, Corning Mus Glass, New York, 79; Int Glass Exhib, Reria Int de Ceramica Vidrio, Valencia, Spain, 82; Int Glass Exhib, Mod Int Glass Mus, Elbeltoff, Denmark, 86; Long Beach Art Mus, 88; Handmade in Pasadena, Alfred Univ, NY State Coll Ceramics, 91; Sam Francis Gallery, Crossroads Sch, Santa Monica, Calif; Site Specific, Armory Ctr Arts, Pasadena, Calif; Part to the Whole, Lobend Gallery, Loyola Marymount Univ, Los Angeles; Solway-Jones Gallery, Los Angeles, 2003; The Brewery Project, Los Angeles, Calif, 2004; Irvine Fine Arts Center, 2004; Shakespeare as Muse, Schneider Mus Art, 2004; Pillowtalk, Ruth Bachofner Gallery, 2007; Hausguests, Haus Gallery & Brewery Project, Los Angeles, Calif, 2007; Enlightened Development, A&D Mus, Los Angeles, Calif, 2007; Inside/Outside, SCIART West, Camarillo, Calif, 2008; solo exhibs, Koplin Gallery, Los Angeles, Calif, 82, Los Angeles Junior Arts Ctr, Barnsdall Park, Calif, 84, NY Experimental Glass Workshop, Brooklyn, New York, 93, Clairemont Grad Sch East Gallery, 93, Jan Kesner Gallery, Los Angeles, 96, Person and Thing, Craig Krull Gallery, Santa Monica, Calif, 99, Portraits, Craig Krull Gallery, 2001, Assorted Spring, Harris Gallery, Univ LaVerne, Calif, 2002, Craig Krull Gallery, Baroque, 2004; Santa Barbara Contemp Arts Forum, Syncopation, Santa Barbara, Calif & Made in Pasadena, Craig Krull Gallery, 2006, Painting Over, Craig Krull Gallery, 2009, Black Matter, Craig Krull Gallery, 2012; The Wildflowers, Desanso Gardens, Sturt Haaga Gallery, 2013. *Teaching:* Instr, Minneapolis Coll Art & Design, 76-77 & Pasadena City Coll, 89-; instr, Mount San Antonio Coll 2007-2012. *Awards:* Nat Endowment Arts, 86 & 89; City of Pasadena Artist Fel, 92; Emergency assistance grant, Adolf & Esther Gottlieb Found, 2001; Beach Box Proj, 2005 & Breeze Proj, 2007, Venice Collaborative, Venice, Calif; Jeanne Ward Travel Grant, Pasadena Community Coll, 2005. *Bibliog:* K Moriyama (auth), Glassware Designed by Nancy Monk, Japan Interior Design; Suzanne K Frantz (auth), Contemporary Glass; Victoria Milne (auth), "Nancy Monk", Glass, No 52, summer 94; Ingrid Calame (auth), "Nancy Monk", Art Issues, No 43, summer 96; Christopher Miles (auth), The Part to the Whole, 2000; Nancy Monk at Craig Krull, Modern Painter, fall 2006; Ashley Emmenegger (auth), NANCY MONK Painting Over, THE, 4/2009. *Dealer:* Craig Krull Gallery 2525 Michigan Ave Bldg B3 Santa Monica CA 90404. *Mailing Add:* 444 S Euclid Apt 9 Pasadena CA 91101

MONK, ROBERT EVAN, JR
CURATOR
b New York, NY, Aug 20, 1950. *Study:* Pratt Inst, Brooklyn, NY. *Collection Arranged:* Dimitry Merinoff, Paintings: 1950-1970, Clocktower, NY, 80. *Pos:* Cur, Merinoff Estate, 74-84 & Leo Castelli Gallery, 74-84; pres, Lorence Monk Gallery, New York, 85-92; sr vpres & dir contemp art, Sotheby's New York, 92-97. *Teaching:* Instr, Sotheby's Educ Prog. *Media:* Paintings, Drawings; Sculpture. *Mailing Add:* Gagosian Gallery 980 Madison Ave New York NY 10021

MONKS, ALYSSA
PAINTER
Study: Boston Col, BA, 99; NY Acad Art, MFA, 2001; Parsons Col, NY, 94; Lorenzo de'Medici, Florence, 98. *Exhib:* Solo Exhibs: Sarah Bain Gallery, Calif, 2003, 2004, 2005, 2006, 2007, DFN Gallery, 2006 & 2008, NY, David Klein Gallery, 2010; Group Exhibs: Paint the Town Red, Rene Lezard, NY, 2001; Separate Visions, Sarah Bain Gallery, Calif, 2001, 8x10 2001, Interiors, 2002; NY Acad Art, 2001, 2006; Figures, J Cacciola Gallery, NJ, 2003; Annual Realism Invitational, Jenkins Johnson Gallery, Calif, 2005; DFN Gallery, 2005; An Assessment of Contemporary Figuration, David Klein Gallery, Mich, 2006. *Pos:* Asst to Damian Loeb, NY City, 2001. *Teaching:* Artist-in-residence, Fullerton Col, Calif, 2006; instr painting, NY Acad Art, 2003-. *Awards:* Stylus Grant, Boston Col, 99; Artplosian Grant, Boston Col, 99; Travel Grant (to Normandy, France), Forbes Found, 2001; Greenshields Grant for Painting, Elizabeth Greenshields Found, Quebec, 2003, 2004, 2006. *Dealer:* Sarah Bain Gallery 411 W Broadway Suite C Anaheim CA 92805; DFN Gallery 210 11th Ave 6th fl NY 1001

MONNIER, JACQUELINE MATISSE See Matisse, Jackie (Jacqueline) Matisse Monnier

MONROE, BETTY IVERSON
EDUCATOR
b Ames, Iowa, May 3, 1922. *Study:* Iowa State Univ, BS, 44, MS, 50; Univ Mich, MA, 64, PhD, 73. *Collection Arranged:* Chinese Ceramics in Chicago Collections, 82-83. *Teaching:* Asst prof art hist, Wash Univ, St Louis, 66-67; asst prof, Northwestern Univ, 68-74, chmn dept, 74-78, assoc prof, 74-. *Mem:* Coll Art Asn; Midwest Art Hist Soc; Am Comt S Asian Art. *Res:* Asian art history; Japanese painting. *Publ:* Ed & translr, Japanese Painting in the Literati Style, Weatherhill, New York & Heibonsha, Tokyo, 74; auth, Chinese Ceramics in Chicago Collections, Northwestern Univ Press, 82. *Mailing Add:* PO Box 1700 Iowa City IA 52244-1700

MONROE, DAN L
MUSEUM DIRECTOR
Pos: Dep dir, Alaska State Mus System, 1974-84; dir, Portland Art Mus, 1984-92; exec dir & CEO, Peabody Essex Mus, Salem, Mass, 1994-; mem, Lijang Studio. *Mem:* AAM; Asn Art Mus Dirs. *Mailing Add:* Peabody Essex Mus East India Sq 161 Essex St Salem MA 01970

MONROE, GERALD
PAINTER, EDUCATOR
b New York, NY, Aug 17, 1926. *Study:* Art Students League; Cooper Union; NY Univ, BA, 67, MS, 68, EdD, 71. *Work:* NY Univ Collection; NJ State Mus; Newark Mus, NJ; Port Authority NY & NJ. *Exhib:* Solo exhibs, Cooper Union Art, New York City, 67, 69, Loeb Ctr, NY Univ, 71, Glassboro State Col, NJ, 71, William Paterson State Col, Wayne, NJ, 73, NJ State Mus, Trenton, 75, Wagner Col, Staten Island, NY, 76, Newark Mus, NJ, 78, Bell Gallery, Greenwich, Conn, 79, Elaine Benson Gallery, Bridgehampton, NY, 80, 82, 87, 92, 94, ETS Campus, Princeton, NJ, 83, Southampton Col, NY, 86, Benton Gallery, Southampton, NY, 86, 88, 93, Bologna-Landi Gallery, East Hampton, NY, 93, Donohue/Sosinski Art, New York City, 96, 98, 2001; Michael Steinberg Fine Art, 2005; Group exhibs, Aldrich Mus, Ridgefield, Conn, 74, Finch Coll Mus, New York City, 73, NJ State Mus, Trenton, 73, Va Ctr Arts, Sweet Brair, 79, Parrish Art Mus, Southampton, NY, 81, 90, 98, 2000, Max Hutchinson Gallery, New York City, 83, Guild Hall Mus, East Hampton, NY, 87, Benton Gallery, East Hampton, NY, 89, Bergen Co Mus, NY, 93, Arlene Bujese Gallery, East Hampton, NY, 95, Vered Gallery, East Hampton, NY, 97. *Collection Arranged:* NJ State Mus; Newark Mus, NJ; NY Univ; Finch Coll Mus; Port Authority NY & NJ; Macalester Coll; Otis Elevator; Lanvin Corp; Best Products; Smith-Barney; mural, Glassboro High Sch, NJ. *Pos:* Assoc prof art, Glassboro State Col, 68-86; artist-in-residence MacDowell Colony, Va Ctr Arts, Ossabaw Island Project. *Awards:* Nat Endowment for Humanities Fel, 73-74, Grant, 75; Ossabaw Island Proj, 77; Va Ctr Creative Arts, 78; and others. *Media:* Oil. *Res:* Influence of left-wing politics on art; strategies for drawing instruction; artists during the Great Depression. *Publ:* Auth articles in Art J, Arch Am Art J, Studio Int & Art in Am; illusr, Am Artist. *Dealer:* Michael Steinberg Fine Art, 526 26 St, New York, NY

MONTALTO, LEAH
PAINTER
b Boston, 1979. *Study:* Haifa Univ, Israel, 2000; Cleveland Inst Art, BFA (painting, Portfolio Scholarship Grant), 2002; Brown Univ, Collegiate Teaching Cert, 2004; RI Sch Design, MFA (painting), 2004. *Exhib:* Solo exhibs include Art Bias Gallery, Cleveland, 2003, E Gordon Gallery, Cleveland, 2005 & 2006; group exhibs include Cold Exchange, Ice House Gallery, Akron, Ohio, 2000; Reinbarger Gallery, Cleveland Inst Art, 2001 & 2002; Sol Koffler Gallery, RI Sch Design, 2003 & 2004; Visual Aids, Robert Miller Gallery, New York, 2005; New World Orders, Juvenal Reis Gallery, New York, 2006; Gongju Int Art Exhib, Limlip Mus, Seoul, 2006; Ann Invitational Exhib Contemp Art, Nat Acad Mus, New York, 2008. *Teaching:* Teaching asst, RI Sch Design, 2002-03, instr, 2003-04; adj prof, Univ Conn, 2004-05; asst prof, State Univ NY, Purchase, 2005-06, Sarah Lawrence Coll, 2006-. *Awards:* Albert Murray Fine Arts Educ Grant, 1999; Mary Seymour Brooks Scholar, 2000; Frances Wise Lang Painting Scholar, 2001; Grad Fel, RI Sch Design, 2002, Award of Excellence, 2003, Excellence in Teaching Award, 2004; Individual Develop Grant, United Univ Professions, 2006; Julius Hallgarten Prize, Nat Acad, 2008

MONTANO, LINDA (MARY)
CONCEPTUAL ARTIST, VIDEO ARTIST
b Saugerties, NY, Jan 18, 1942. *Study:* Villa Schifanoia, Florence, MA (sculpture), 66; Univ Wis, Madison, MFA (sculpture), 69; Hobart Welding School, 69. *Work:* Mus Mod Art. *Exhib:* How to Become a Guru, Womens Bldg, Los Angeles, 75; Learning to Talk, Univ Calif, San Diego, 76; Talking About Sex: For My Father, Kitchen, NY, 80; Mitchell's Death, Mus Mod Art, NY, 81; Palm Reading, Real Art Ways, Hartford, Conn, 82; Readings: Visual Collaborations, Chicago Art Inst, 83; Seven Yrs of Living Art: Wearing Only One Color Each Yr, Speaking in a Different Accent Each Yr, Listening to One Tone Seven Hours a Day (Doing Art-Life Counseling and Reading palms at the New Mus Once A Month), 84-91; Another Seven Yrs of Living Art: An Experience of the Seven Chakras with Seasonal Astral Visits to the Chagall Chapel, UN, 91-98. *Collection Arranged:* Schiffler Collection. *Teaching:* Instr performance, San Francisco State Univ, 78-79, San Francisco Art Inst, 79-80, Womens Bldg, 81 & Chicago Art Inst, 83, Univ Tex, Austin, 91-98. *Awards:* Fels, Nat Endowment Arts, 77 & 85; Women's Studio Workshop Grants, 82 & 83; Fel, NY State Found Arts, 86. *Bibliog:* Moira Roth (auth), Towards a history of college performance, Arts Mag, 12/78; Marcia Tucker (auth), Not just for laughs, New Mus, 11/81; Tony Whitfield (auth), Dressing up, acting out, Live Mag, 82. *Media:* Performance; Video; Books; Singing. *Collection:* Schiffler Collection. *Publ:* Contribr, High Performance, 77- & auth, Art in Everyday Life, 80, Astro Artz; co-ed, Fuse Mag, Franklin Furnace, 82; auth, Before and after art-life counseling, Women's Studio Workshop, 83; auth, Performance Artists Talking in the Eighties, 2000; Lett from Linda M Moutane, 2005. *Mailing Add:* 9 John St Saugerties NY 12477

MONTEITH, CLIFTON J
CRAFTSMAN, SCULPTOR
b Detroit, Mich, July 8, 1944. *Study:* Mich State Univ, BFA(painting & educ), 68, MFA (painting), 74. *Work:* Art Inst Chicago; Am Craft Mus, NY. *Exhib:* Art Expo, Carl Hammer Gallery, Chicago, Ill, 91; Preferred Seating, Wetsman Collection, Birmingham, Mich, 91; solo show, Miami Univ Mus, Oxford, Ohio, 92 & Interlochen Ctr Arts, Mich, 97; Of Tops and Bottoms, Ohio Designer Craftsman Traveling Exhib, 93; The Chair as Art, Gallery Functional Art, Santa Monica, Calif, 93; Carlm Hammer Gallery, 94; Tamarack Craftsman Gallery, Omena, Mich, 95; Hershey Mus, Pa, 96; Contemp NAm Furniture-A Survey of the Furniture Makers Art, Newberger Mus Art, Purchase, NY, 97; The Chair Show, Southern Highland Craft Guild, Asheville, NC, 97; Evolution in for Exhib, Arrowmont Sch Arts & Crafts, Gatlinburg, Tenn, 98. *Pos:* Owner furniture making bus, 84-. *Teaching:* Instr painting, drawing & sculpture, 68-84; guest lectr, Univ Mich Sch Art, Ann Arbor, 87, Calvin Col, Grand Rapids, 90 & Parnham Col, Dorset, Eng, 93; lectr, S Ohio Mus, 93, Takumi-Jyuku Wood Working Sch, Japan, 94, Far East Soc Architects & Engineers, Japan, 94, Osaka Designers' Col, Japan, 94, Int House Japan, 94 & Dennos Mus, Mich, 95; instr, Haystack Mountain Sch Crafts, Deer Isle, Maine, 96, Penland Sch Crafts, NC, 97, Anderson Ranch, Snowmass, Colo, 98 & Ore Col Arts & Crafts, Portland, 98. *Awards:* Nat Endowment Arts, 92; Fel, US-Japan Friendship Comn, 94; Fel, Japan Found, 99. *Bibliog:* Daniel Mack (auth), Making Rustic Furniture, Lark Books, Asheville, NC, 92; US News & World Report, 11/92; Ralph Kylloe (auth), Rustic Traditions, Gibbs Smith, 93. *Dealer:* Carl Hammer Gallery 200 W Superior St Chicago IL 60610. *Mailing Add:* 20341 Fowler Lake Ann MI 49650

MONTEITH, MATTHEW
PHOTOGRAPHER
b Howell, Michigan, 1974. *Study:* Int Ctr Photog, New York, Gen Studies, 1995; Yale Univ, MFA, 2004. *Exhib:* Solo exhibs include Galerie de la Butte, Cherbourg-Octeville, France, 2002, 779 Galerie + Editions, Paris, 2003, Prinz Galerie, Kyoto, Japan, 2004, Hotel Nord Pinus, Arles, France, 2005; group exhibs include Small Works, PS 122, New York, 1999; Ville/Visages, Regional Ctr Cherbourg-Octeville, Normandy, France, 2000; Advance Notice, Int Ctr Photog, New York, 2002; Pictures for People Like Us, Wallspace Gallery, New York, 2003; Art & Com Festival Emerging Photogrs, New York, 2004; Stilled Life, Placemaker Gallery, Miami, 2004; Let's Talk About, Larissa Goldston Gallery, New York, 2006; Clinic, Les Nuits Blanches & Paris Photo, Paris, 2006. *Awards:* Abigail Cohen Rome Prize, Am Acad Rome, 2008. *Dealer:* Rosier Gallery 98 San Pablo Ave San Francisco CA 94127. *Mailing Add:* 140 16th St Brooklyn NY 11215

MONTESINOS, VICKY
PAINTER, PRINTMAKER
b Mexico City, Mex. *Study:* Studied with Jose Bardasano, Mex; studied with Quinquella Martin, Buenos Aires. *Exhib:* Solo exhib, Galeria Rosana, Mexico City, Mex, 71; Espana Pintura Contemporanea Mex 77, Madrid, 77; Int Expos, Rotterdam; Int Expos, Tokyo; Clayton R Betts Gallery, San Francisco

MONTGOMERY, STEVEN
SCULPTOR, PHOTOGRAPHER
b Detroit, Mich, 1954. *Study:* Grand Valley State Coll, Mich, BA, 1976; Tyler Sch Art, Temple Univ, MFA, 1978. *Work:* Metrop Mus Art, New York; Smithsonian Inst; Corcoran Gallery Art; Newark Mus, NJ; Mus Art & Design, New York; and many more. *Exhib:* Young Americans, Tucson Mus Art, Ariz, 1978; Philadelphia Clay, Tyler Sch Art, Temple Univ, 1981; Contemporary Ceramics, Hecksher Mus, Huntington, NY, 1983; A Passion Vision, Decordova Mus, Lincoln, Mass, 1984; Selections 41, Drawing Ctr, New York, 1988; 20th Ceramic Nat Exhib, Everson Mus Art, 1990; solo exhibs, Garth Clark Gallery, New York, 1991, Ok Harris Gallery, New York, 1996, 1998, 2000, 2003, 2006-07, Everson Mus Art, Syracuse, 1998, Dorothy Weiss Gallery, San Francisco, 1999, Newcomb Art Gallery, Tulane Univ, 2003, Daum Mus Contemp Art, Sedalia, Mo, 2006; Drawings '94, Sheraton Art Ctr, Kutztown Univ, 1994; Clay into Art, Metrop Mus Art, New York, 1998; Taipei County Yingge Mus, Taiwan, 2004; Single Object/Still Life, Katonah Mus Art, NY, 2008. *Awards:* NY Found Arts Fel, 1990, 2003, 2009; Pollock-Krasner Found Grant, 1998. *Bibliog:* Kay Larson (auth), Stalking the Wild Sculpture, Village Voice, 6/14/1980; Robert Ellison (auth), The 20th Ceramic National, Am Craft, 7/1990; Rita Reif (auth), Fantasy Machines from Technology's Dark Side, NY Times, 12/6/1998

MONTOYA, MALAQUIAS
ART EDUCATOR, ARTIST
b Albuquerque, June 21, 1938. *Study:* Univ Calif, Berkeley, BA, 70. *Pos:* Commerical artist, silkscreener, 62-68; foreman silkscreen dept Circo Inc, 63-66. *Teaching:* Art instr Laney Col, Berkeley, 69-70, Contra Costa Col, Richmond, Calif, 71; art workshop dir Alameda Co Neighborhood Arts Program, 74-81; lectr Chicano Studies Dept, Univ Calif, Berkeley, 60-74, full prof, 90-, cooperating faculty, 96-. *Mailing Add:* PO Box 6 Elmira CA 95625

MONTROSE-GRAEM, DOUGLASS J
MUSEUM DIRECTOR, PAINTER, POET, MUSIC MAKER
b Scotland; US citizen. *Study:* Piarist Col, BA (humanities), 54, LSE Economics, English Lit, 55; NY Inst Finance, MA, 61. *Hon Degrees:* MBA, 65. *Collection Arranged:* Domjan, NY Metrop Mus, 70-73; Turner Collection, 74-; Genius Unfolding, Annotated Proofs of JMW Turner, Ringling Coll, 2012; A Collector with Vision, 2012. *Pos:* Founder & dir, Turner Mus, Denver, Colo, 72-; chief exec, The Rainbow, A Space in Eight, Cultural Complex Sarasota. *Teaching:* Lectr on the work of Turner & Moran, currently. *Awards:* Founder's Award, Turner Mus, 74; Award for Excellence, Cambridge, Gt Brit, 75 & 85; One Thousand Great Americans, Honoree IBC, Cambridge, UK, 2003, 2004. *Bibliog:* Gerald Frank (auth), Douglas Graham's Dream, The Local, 89; Gerald W Bracey (auth), A Turner for the Better, Travel & Leisure, 91; David Alan (auth), Turners Cosmic Optimism Shines in Denver Mus, Colo Daily, 91; LinkedIn, 2013. *Mem:* Turner Soc, London (vpres, 78-2005, bd mem, 2013-, life mem, vpres Independent Turner Soc, 2013-); DAV (life mem); St. Andrew's Soc, Colo (life mem). *Media:* Watercolor, Tempera, Mixed Media. *Specialty:* Thomas Moran, Hokusai, JMW Turner. *Interests:* art collecting, bridge. *Collection:* Turner and Moran; most varied and extensive Turner works on paper outside England. *Publ:* Auth, Turner and Moran, 77 & Turner's Hand: The Master Touch, 78, Turner Mus; Turner on Paper, In: Joseph Mallord William Turner, Dixon Gallery & Gardens, Memphis, Tenn, 79; auth, Love Beginnings (poems, illus), pvt publ, 80; Turner's Cosmic Optimism, 90 & Turner's Angels, 91, Turner's Rainbows, 92, Turner's Children, 93, Turner's Powerful Allegories, 94; Five Master Classes in Art & Music, In: Turner's Liber Studiorum, 95; Turner & Renoir, 2003; auth & illustr, Sarah Angel, 2007; and others; Turner's Annotated Proofs-An Education in the Creative Process, 2012; Plus! 2012; Thesaurus of Positive Plus Words, Concepts, profusely illustrated

MOODY, ELIZABETH C
DEALER, GALLERY DIRECTOR
b Memphis, Tenn, Nov 20, 1944. *Study:* Univ Ky, Lexington, BFA, 66. *Pos:* Dir & owner, Moody Gallery, Houston, 75-. *Specialty:* Contemporary American: art, paintings, sculpture, photography, original works on paper. *Mailing Add:* Moody Gallery 2815 Colquitt Houston TX 77098

MOON, JAYE
SCULPTOR
b Seoul, South Korea. *Study:* Sangmyung Women's Univ, Seoul, BFA (sculpture), 1989; Pratt Inst, MFA (sculpture), 1994. *Exhib:* Out of Print, Pratt Inst LIbr, New York, 1996; Night of 1,000 Drawings, Artists Space, New York, 1996; Outer Boroughs, White Columns, New York, 1999; Hunter Coll Times Sq Gallery, NEw York, 2003; Dumbo Arts Ctr, Brooklyn, 2004. *Awards:* Pollock-Krasner Found Grant, 2006; NY Found Arts Fel, 2009

MOON, JIM (JAMES) MONROE
PAINTER, PRINTMAKER
b Graham, NC, June 7, 1928. *Study:* Cooper Union, 45-48; Acad Vannucci, Italy, cert, 55; Richmond Prof Inst William & Mary, BFA, 57; grad study at Mex City Coll, 57; Boston Mus Sch 58-59; Columbia Univ, 66-67. *Work:* Mus Mod Art, NY; NC Mus Art, Raleigh; Peggy Guggenheim Mus, Venice, Italy; Winston-Salem Pub Libr, NC; Northwood Inst, Midland, Mich; Hamilton Mus, Can; Duke Univ & Cent NC Univ, Durham; and others. *Exhib:* Solo exhibs, Watkins/Fair Contemp Arts, NY, 80, la Gallerie, Am Coll Paris, 81, Galleria Regina Cornaro, Asolo, Italy, 81, Alber Galleries, Philadelphia, 81, Calvert Collection, Washington, 83, Calvert Gallery, Palm Beach, Fla, 83 & Palm Beach Int Airport, West Palm Beach, Fla, 92; Mus Cuauhnahuac, Mex, 95; Skopje Macedonia, Nat Gallery, 2006. *Pos:* Pres Asolare Foundation. *Teaching:* Instr fine arts, Hofstra Univ, New York, 60-61; head dept visual arts, Barber Scotia Coll, NC, 65-66 & NC Sch Arts, Winston-Salem, 67-71; pres, Asolare Fine Arts Acad, 96-. *Bibliog:* William E Ray (auth), ArtScene, coming to a theatre near you, 2-3/88 & Alice R Gray (auth), An artist for all seasons, Vol X, No 1, 1-3/92, Palm Beach Co Coun Arts, Fla; John Chapman (ed), Jim Moon, Five Essays on His Painting, 94; and others. *Mem:* Soc Konaks, Republic of Macedonia. *Media:* Egg Tempera, Oil; Serigraphy. *Mailing Add:* C/O Asolare Fine Arts Acad 687 Callahan Hill Rd Lexington NC 27292

MOON, MARC
PAINTER, INSTRUCTOR
b Middletown, Ohio, Apr 6, 1923. *Study:* Appl Art Acad. *Work:* Canton Art Inst; Masillon Mus, Ohio; Richmond Mus, Va; Springfield Mus, Mo; Taylor Mem Libr, Cuyahoga Falls, Ohio. *Comn:* Mural, Canton Hall of Fame, Canton Hist Soc, Ohio, 70; mural, Lawson Milk Co, 75; McDonalds Restaurants, Akron, Ohio, 79. *Exhib:* Am Watercolor Soc, NY, 66-70; Nat Acad Design, 74; Watercolor USA, Springfield Mus, 74; Butler Art Inst, Youngstown, Ohio, 75; Nat Soc Painters Casein & Watercolor, NY, 81. *Teaching:* Instr watercolor, Hilton Leech Art Sch, Sarasota, Fla, 68-76, Marc Moon Gallery, Akron, Ohio, 82-84, Fort Meyers Branch Art Asn, 84. *Awards:* Mario Cooper Award, Am Watercolor Soc; Best in Show, Va Beach Art Asn; Purchase Award, Watercolor USA. *Bibliog:* R Fabri (auth), Medal of Merit, Todays Art, 66. *Mem:* Am Watercolor Soc; Ohio Watercolor Soc; Nat Soc Painters Casein & Acrylic; Rockport Art Asn; Allied Artist Am. *Media:* Watercolor, Acrylic. *Publ:* Auth, Watercolor page, Am Artist Mag, 74

MOONELIS, JUDITH C
SCULPTOR, CERAMIST
b Jackson Heights, Queens, NY, May 30, 1953. *Study:* Tyler Sch Art, Temple Univ, Philadelphia, BFA, 75; NY State Coll Ceramics, Alfred Univ, MFA, 78. *Work:* Pa Acad Fine Arts, Philadelphia; Renwick Gallery, Smithsonian Inst, Washington, DC; NY State Coll Ceramics, Alfred Univ, NY; Ill State Mus, Springfield; Everson Mus, NY; Am Craft Mus, NY. *Comn:* Sculpture, Heckscher Mus, NY, 83. *Exhib:* Solo exhibs, Heckscher Mus, Huntington, NY, 83, Rena Bransten Gallery, San Francisco, Calif, 85 & 88, Va Commonwealth Univ, 90, Swarthmore Col, PA, 92 & Hillwood Art Mus, Long Island Univ, NY, 93, John Elder Gallery, NY, 98; Sculpture, Pa Acad Fine Arts, Philadelphia, 86; A Passionate Vision: Daniel Jacobs Collection, DeCordova Mus, Lincoln, Mass, 84; Twenty Artists, Newport Harbor Art Mus, Calif, 85; Poetry of the Physical, Am Craft Mus, NY & traveling, 86-87; The Eloquent Object, Philbrook Art Mus, OK & traveling, 87-89; Am Figurative Ceramics, Art Gallery Western Australia, Perth & traveling, 89; The Nude, Perimeter Gallery, Chicago & Wustum Mus, Wis, 95. *Teaching:* Vis artist & lectr, numerous schs & institutions, 80-; instr ceramic sculpture, Parsons Sch Design, NY, 84-87 & Hunter Col, NY, 86-87; vis prof, Univ Hartford, 90 & RI Sch Design, 93, 94 & 97, Mass Col Art, 95 & 96. *Awards:* NY Found Arts Fel, 85 & 89; Virginia A Groot Found Grant, 91; Gottlieb Found Grant, 94. *Bibliog:* Gnossis Nos (auth), Judy Moonelis, Am Ceramics Mag, 5/86; Edward Sozanski, Rev, Philadelphia Enquirer, 2/21/92; Janet Koplos (auth), Judy Moonelis, Hillwood Art Mus, 94. *Mem:* Int Sculpture Ctr Am Craft Coun. *Media:* Clay, Mixed Media. *Dealer:* John Elder Gallery 529 West 20th St New York NY 10011. *Mailing Add:* 434 E 11th St Apt 3F New York NY 10009

MOONEY, MICHAEL J
PAINTER, ASSEMBLAGE ARTIST
b Albany, NY. *Study:* Empire State Col, Albany, BPS (arts), 80; State Univ NY, Albany, MA (painting), 82, MFA (painting), 83. *Work:* Center Galleries & State Univ, Albany; F D Rich Co, Stamford, Conn; State Univ NY, Albany; Paterson Mus, Paterson, NJ; Paco Das Artes, Sao Paulo; Museu Da Imagem Do Som, Sao Paulo. *Exhib:* East Village, NY, Galerie Knud Grothe, Copenhagen, Denmark, 83; Chicago Art Expo, Navy Pier, 84; Ruth Siegel Gallery, 83, 84, 86 & 91; solo exhibs, Sixth Sense Gallery, 85, Bridgewater Gallery, 86, EM Donahue Gallery, 86, 88, 89 & 93 & Landscape Antology, Grace Borgeniet Gallery, NY, 88; Grace Borgenicht Gallery (landscape anthology), 88; Albany Ctr Gallery, 94; Ctr Galleries, Albany, NY, 97; Schnectady Mus, 98; Rensselaer Co Coun Arts, Troy, NY. *Teaching:* Grad lectr painting, Col St Rose, Albany, NY, 92; instr drawing, State Univ NY Albany, 92. *Awards:* David Kroman Award, Discovery 78, Schenectady Art Group, 78; Albany Regional Painting Award, State Univ NY, Albany, Art Gallery, 81. *Bibliog:* Fred LeBrun (auth), Mooney at Center Gallery, Albany Times Union, 10/6/79; Peg Churchill-Wright (auth), Works Within Works, Schenectady Gazette, 10/11/79; James Lewis (auth), Art Forum, 12/89; William Jaeger (auth), Michael Mooney, How to Live in the World, Albany Times Union, 12/99; William Jaeger (auth), Michael Mooney, Life Reflections, Ctr Galleries, Albany, NY, 4/2000; Karen Bjornland (auth), Michael Mooney at Ctr Galleries, Schenectedy Gazette, 4/2000; Stacey Lauren (auth), Michael Mooney, Opposites Attract, Ctr Galleries, Metroland Magazine, 4/2000. *Media:* Oil. *Mailing Add:* 13 Belvidere Ave Albany NY 12203

MOONIE, LIANA
PAINTER, LECTURER
b Trieste, Italy. *Study:* Ist Magistrale G Carducci, Univ Trieste, BA(educ), 45; Art Student League, with Robert Brachman, 69; New York Univ; New Rochelle Coll, 79 (printmaking). *Work:* State Assembly, Albany, NY; Salomon Inc, NY; Reference Libr, Nat Mus Arts, Washington; Pepsico Inc; Credit Anstalt Bank, Verein, NY; Natl Assn Women Artists Coll, Jane Vorhees Zimmerli Art Mus, NJ; Palm Beach intl Airport, West Palm Beach, FL; Coral Springs Mus Art, Fla. *Exhib:* Silvermine Artists Guild, New Canaan, Conn, 79 & 90-94, 2011; Hudson River Mus, NY, 79; traveling exhib, USA, 85-89; traveling exhib, India, 89; The Hurlbutt Gallery, Greenwich, Conn, 90-96; Greenwich Arts Ctr, Greenwich, Conn, 91; Art of the Northeast, USA, 95-96, 2010; The Flinn Gallery, Greenwich, Conn, 97-2008, 2012; UMA Gallery, NY, 2004; Interchurch Ctr, NY, 2004; Coral Springs Mus Art, Coral Springs, Fla, 2006; G E World Hq, Fairfield, Conn, 2006; Faber Birren Color Award Show, Stamford, Conn, 2007; Art Place Gallery, Fairfield, Conn, 2009, 2011; Watermark Gallery, Bridgeport, Conn, 2010, 2012; Greenwich Pen Women, Schubert Libr, Bryan, Conn, 2012; Art Greenwich, Aboard the Searfair, Conn, 2012; PMW Gallery, Stamford, Conn, 2013; Retrospective, Bendhein Gallery, Greenwich, Cconn, Morris Mus, Morristown, NJ, 2014; Whistler House Mus Art, Lowell, Mass, 2014. *Pos:* Chair, Nat Asn Women Artists Collection, Jane Voorhees Zimmerli Art Mus, New Brunswick, NJ, 90-96 & 2003-2011. *Teaching:* Pvt instruction, 79-81. *Awards:* Quinns Award, Greenwich Coun Arts, 92; Mary B Hathaway Award, Hurlbutt Gallery, 93; President's Award, A Celebration of Conn Art, CosCob, Conn, 94; The Owl Award, Nat League of Am Pen Women, 97; The Fred Krause Award for an Abstract Painting, Flinn Gallery, Greenwich, Conn, 2000; Mez & Sid Noble Award, Greenwich Art Soc, 2005; Frances K Brooks Award, Greenwich Art Soc, 2007; Gold Medal Award Outstandig Serv to the Arts, Nat Asc Womens Artists, 2007; Gold Medal Award for Lifetime Achievement, Nat Asn Women Artists, 2012. *Mem:* Mamaroneck Artists Guild (pres, 76-78); Hudson River Contemp Artists (pres, 81-83); Nat Asn Women Artists (vpres, 85-86, pres, 87-89); Silvermine Artists Guild; Greenwich Art Soc (pres, 90-91, co-pres, 2007-08). *Media:* Watercolor, Oil. *Publ:* Contribr, article, Beaux Arts Mag, 74-76 & Philosophizing about art, 75. *Mailing Add:* 4 Lafayette Ct No PH Greenwich CT 06830-5320

MOORE, ALAN WILLARD
ART CRITIC, HISTORIAN
b Chicago, Ill, Oct 21, 1951. *Study:* Univ Calif, Riverside, BA, 74; City Univ NY Grad Ctr, PhD, 2000. *Pos:* Intern writer, Art Forum, 73-74; writer, Art-Rite, 74-75 & Art Net Mag; co-founder, ABC No Rio, 80-83; dir MWF Video Distribution, 86-; co-ed, Part Mag. *Teaching:* vis asst prof, Kennesan State Univ; Adj Lectr, Ramapo Col, City Col, Col Staten Island; grad teaching fel, Bronx Community Col; instr, Pratt Inst. *Awards:* John Revald Disertation Fel. *Mem:* Coll Art Asn. *Res:* History of Collaborative Projects, NY. *Publ:* Coauth (with Marc Miller), ABC No Rio Dinero: Story of a LES Art Gallery, NY, 83; ed, A Day in the Life: Tales from the Lower East, Semiotexte, 91; coauth (with James Cornwell), Local History: The Battle for Bohemia in the East Village, chap in: Alternative Art New York, 1965-1985, Univ Minn Press, 2002; auth, Political Economy as Subject & Form in Contemporary Art, Review of Radical Political Economics, Coll 36, No 4, fall 2004; auth, General Introduction to Collectivity in Modern Art, Journal of Aesthetics & Protest, 8/2003, Spanish transl, 2005; coauth (with Debra Wacks), Being There: The Tribeca Neighborhood of Franklin Furnace, The Drama Review, Vol 49, No 1, spring 2005. *Mailing Add:* 123 Scribner Ave Staten Island NY 10301

MOORE, ANNE F
MUSEUM DIRECTOR, EDUCATOR
b Jackson, Tenn, Jan 6, 1946. *Study:* Columbia Univ, BA, 69, MFA & MFAEd, 71; Hunter Coll, MA, 82; Cert in Mus Management, 93; Cert in Appraisal Studies, 2003. *Pos:* Lectr & res assoc, Kimbell Art Mus, 80-83; outreach dir, Dallas Art Mus, 86-88; cur ed & acad prog, Allen Art Mus, Oberlin Coll, 88-91, from actg dir to dir, 91-96; dir ctr for Book Arts, 2000; proj mgr, Peabody Essex Mus, 2000-2002; owner Ann Frances Moore Fine Art, Brooklyn, 2002-. *Teaching:* Lectr mus studies, Oberlin Coll, 88-95; lectr, NY Univ, 99. *Bibliog:* Art & Auction Mag, 8/06. *Mem:* Asn Art Mus Dirs (93-96); Coll Art Asn; Intermus Conserv Asn (vpres, 92-95); Appraisers Asn Am; Int Found Art Res; Century Asn (2007-). *Res:* Am portraits. *Publ:* Ed, Allen Memorial Art Museum Bull, 91-93 & AMAM Newsletter, 91-, Oberlin Coll. *Dealer:* Anne Frances Moore Fine Art

MOORE, BRIDGET
GALLERY DIRECTOR
b York, Maine, Aug 22, 1957. *Study:* Smith Col, Northampton, Mass. *Pos:* Co dir, Ledel Gallery, NY, 81-84; dir, Midtown Galleries, NY, 85-90 & Midtown-Payson Galleries, 90-95; Gallery owner/pres, DC Moore Gallery, NY, 95-. *Specialty:* Twentieth Century and Contemp Am art. *Publ:* The Reflective Image: Am Drawings 1910-1960, Midtown Galleries, 90. *Mailing Add:* DC Moore Gallery 535 W 22nds St 2nd Fl New York NY 10011

MOORE, FAY
PAINTER, ADMINISTRATOR
b Cambridge, Mass. *Study:* Henry Hensche Sch, Provincetown; Boston Mus Sch; Phillips Gallery Sch, Washington, DC; Bennington Coll, Vt, with Stephan Hirsch & Paul Feeley; Yale Grad Sch with Donald Oenslager. *Work:* NY Racing Asn; Nat Art Mus Sport, Indianapolis; Detroit Race Course, Mich; Univ Va, Charlottesville; Kentucky Derby Mus, Louisville; Georgetown Univ, Jacobs Coll; Univ Ky Fine Arts

Libr. *Comn:* Univ Va, Charlottesville, 67; Hockey Hall Fame, Can, 70; New York Giants, 71; seven murals, Kelso Rm, NY Racing Asn, 78; murals, Rockwell Rm, Three Rivers Stadium, Pittsburgh, 76. *Exhib:* Saratoga Mus Racing, NY, 65; Pittsburgh Plan Art, Pa, 69; Nat Arts Mus Sport, New York, 70; Mus Contemp, Madrid, Spain, 72; retrospective, Headley Whitney Mus, Ky, 90; Modern Masters, Ky Derby Mus, 92; Nat Arts Club, New York, 93 & 2001; Butler Inst Am Art, Ohio, 2001-2003; and others. *Teaching:* Instr, Univ Kansas City, Mo, 55-57, Carnegie-Mellon Univ, Pittsburgh, 57-59 & Yale Univ Grad Sch, New Haven, Conn, 59-60; workshops, Int Mus Horse, Lexington, Ky. *Awards:* Nat Arts Club Awards; Knickerbocker Artists Awards; Allied Artists Am Awards; Spirit Award, Pastel Soc Art. *Bibliog:* Creative painting with pastel, Katchen, Northlight Publ; The Best of Pastel, Rockport Publ, 96; L Price (auth), A Neo-Pointillist in Pastel, Am Artist Mag, 97; Arboreal Attitudes Mag, 2006; A Woman Artist in a Sporting World (exhib catolog), Int Mus of the Horse, 2009. *Mem:* Nat Soc Mural Painters; Nat Arts Club; Artists Fel (pres, emer); Nat Art Mus Sport (acquisitions); Allied Artists Am (vpres); Pastel Soc Am; Catherine Lorrilard Wolfe Art Club (bd dir); Pen & Brush; Am Acad Equinear (chmn bd). *Media:* Oil, Pastel. *Publ:* Equine Images, fall 90 & 97; The Artist's Mag, 11/90; Informart, 6/93; Am Artists, 12/97; Artists Mag, 7/99; Kentucky Derby Mag, 2006; Lexington Herald Leader, 3/2009; Lexington Courier J, 4/2009. *Dealer:* Heike Pickett Gallery 110 Morgan St Versailles KY; The Sporting Gallery Middleburg VA. *Mailing Add:* Nat Arts Club 15 Gramercy Park S New York NY 10003

MOORE, INA MAY
PAINTER, EDUCATOR
b Hayden, Ariz, Feb 20, 1920. *Study:* Univ Ariz, BA (educ, art & music); Ariz State Univ, MA (art educ). *Work:* First Interstate Bank, Valley Nat Bank, Ariz Bank & Thunderbird Bank, Phoenix, JP Morgan Chase Bank; First Fed Savings & Loan Asn, Yuma; Morgan Chase bank of Phoenix; pvt collections. *Exhib:* Nat League Am Pen Women, Salt Lake City, Utah, 71; Nat Watercolor Exhib, Ctr Performing Arts, Scottsdale, Ariz, 77; Southwest Watercolor Fedn Exhib, San Diego, 83; Kerr Ctr, Scottsdale, Ariz, 83; Southwest Fedn, Houston, Tex, 86; Univ S Dak; Invitational exhib in Taiwan. *Collection Arranged:* Bimson Coll, Valley Nat Bank, Thunderbird Bank, Western Savings and Loan. *Teaching:* Full-time instr art, Elem Pub Schs, 40-50; pvt classes, 50-64; instr watercolor, Phoenix Art Mus, 65-88, Phoenix Coll, 78-97; juror & watercolor workshops; instr art, Paradise Valley Community Coll, Phoenix, ret; master teacher, Phoenix Coll; retired instr, Phoenix Art Mus Coll, Paradise Valley Com Coll. *Awards:* Purchase Award, Empire Machinery Co, 77; Purchase Award, Thunderbird Bank, 79; Merit Award, Ariz Watercolor Exhib, 85; Gold Medal, Grumbacher Award, 86 & 88; Merit Award, Ariz Artists Guild, 86 & 89; and more. *Bibliog:* Phil and Marion Kovonick (authors), Encyclopedia of Women Artists of the American West, Univ Tex Press, Austin, Tex; Walter Bimson (auth), Arizona Artists. *Mem:* Ariz Watercolor Asn (pres, 66-68); Nat League Am Pen Women; Ariz Artist's Guild; Delta Kappa Gamma; Contemp Watercolor Asn (found). *Media:* Watercolor. *Specialty:* Landscapes, seascapes, & abstracts. *Interests:* Art, music, travel, & poetry. *Collection:* Herb Ossen, Doug Greenbowe, Robert Olivier. *Publ:* Illusr, Junior League Calendar, 86; Encyclopedia of Women Artists of the American West. *Dealer:* Kachina Gallery Taos NM. *Mailing Add:* 350 Eva St Apt 120 Phoenix AZ 85020

MOORE, JOHN J
PAINTER, EDUCATOR
b St Louis, Mo, Apr 25, 1941. *Study:* Washington Univ, Nat Found Arts & Humanities grant, Milliken foreign travel fel, BFA, 66; Yale Univ, MFA, 68. *Work:* Philadelphia Mus Art; Pa Acad Fine Arts, Philadelphia; Yale Univ Art Gallery, New Haven; Mus Fine Arts, Boston; Metrop Mus Art, NY. *Comn:* Lincoln Ctr, NY, 80; Fabric Workshop, Philadelphia, 81; Hancock Insurance, Boston, 85; Smith, Kline, French, Philadelphia, 86; Becton-Dickinson, NJ, 88. *Exhib:* Real, Really, Super Real, San Antonio Mus Art, Tex, 81; Contemp Am Realism Since 1960, Pa Acad Fine Arts, 82; Hirschl & Adler Mod, NY, 83, 86, 90, 94 & 2007; Am Realism: The Precise Image, Tokyo, Osaka, Yokohama, 86; Am Art Today: Night Paintings, Art Mus, Fla Inst Univ, 95. *Teaching:* Prof painting & drawing, Tyler Sch Art, Temple Univ, 68-88 & Sch Arts, Boston Univ, 88-99; artist-in-residence, Yale Summer Sch, 68 & 69; fac, Skowhegan Sch Painting & Sculpture, summers, 74, 80 & 84; vis prof painting, Univ Calif, Berkeley, 81-82; Gutman Prof Fine Arts, Univ Pa. *Awards:* Hassam Award, Am Acad Arts & Lett, 73 & 87; Vis Artist Fel Painting, Nat Endowment Arts, 82 & 92; Acad Award Painting, Am Acad Arts & Lett, 96. *Bibliog:* Carol Zemel (auth), Still Life and City View, Buscaglia-Castellani Art Gallery, 83; Laura Rath (auth), Uncommon Vistas, Boston Univ Art Gallery; Therese Dolan (auth), Inventing Reality: The Paintings of John Moore, Hudson Hills, 96. *Mem:* Univ Coun, Yale Univ 85-90; CIES (sr Fulbright comt, 89-92); Nat Acad Design. *Media:* Oil, Watercolor. *Dealer:* Hirschl & Adler Modern 21 E 70th St New York NY 10021; Locks Gallery 600 Washington Sq S Philadelphia PA 19106

MOORE, JOHN L
PAINTER, CURATOR
b Cleveland, Ohio, Feb 2, 1939. *Study:* Kent State Univ, BFA, 72, MA, 74. *Work:* Cleveland Mus Art; High Mus, Atlanta; New York Pub Libr; Montgomery Mus Fine Arts, Ala; New Jersey State Mus, Trenton; New York Pub Libr; Brooklyn Mus Art, NY; plus others. *Comn:* Ceiling Mural, Cleveland Pub Libr, Ohio, 96. *Exhib:* Solo exhibs, Miami Univ Art Mus, 90, Indianapolis Ctr Contemp Art, Herron Gallery, 90, High Mus Art, Ga Pac Ctr, 90, Cleveland Ctr Contemp Art, 90, M-13 Gallery, NY, 92, 94 & 96, Amalie A Wallace Gallery, Coll Old Westbury, 95, Montgomery Mus Fine Arts, 96; Slow Art: Painting in NY Now, Inst Contemp Art PS1, Long Island City, 92; Dream Singers, Story Tellers: An African-Am Presence, Fukui Fine Arts Mus, Japan, 92; Selections from the Collection, Brooklyn Mus, 94; Aspects of Abstraction, NJ State Mus, 96; Old Glory: The Am Flag in Contemp Art, Phoenix Art Mus, 96; After the Fall, Aspects of Abstract Painting Since 1970, Newhouse Ctr Contemp Art, Snug Harbor Cult Ctr, 97; Cleveland Collects Contemp Art, The Cleveland Mus Art, Ohio, 98; JCAL, Queens, NY, 2009. *Pos:* Asst cur dept educ, Cleveland Mus Art, 74-85; guest cur, Studio Mus Harlem, 86-87. *Teaching:* Adj asst prof, Queens Col, City Univ, 90; Adj prof, Parsons Sch Design, 92, La Guardia Community Col, 94-2004; vis prof, Rhode Island Sch Design, 92 &93, Univ Tex, Austin, 92; vis assoc prof, Skidmore Col, Saratoga Springs, 94-. *Awards:* Fel painting, Nat Endowment Arts, 87; fel painting, New York Found Arts, 89 & 94; Joan Mitchell Award, 99. *Bibliog:* Eleanor Heartney (auth), John L Moore: at M-13, Art in Am, 6/92; Marianne Doezema (auth), Painting Abstract, Mount Holyoke Univ, 96; Charlotta Kotiz (auth), John L Moore: Work of the Decade, Montgomery Mus Fine Art, 96. *Mem:* Art in Gen; Coll Art Asn. *Media:* Painting. *Publ:* Coauth, The Contemporary Landscape: Five Views, Waterworks Visual Arts Ctr, 89; auth, New York City Works, One Penn Plaza, 88; dir, Bill Hutson, Paintings 1978-1987, Studio Mus Harlem, 88; auth, The Passion Pit, Anna Marie Arnold, for the Cleveland Ctr for Contemporary Art Ohio Selections, Dialogue Art J, 5/86; New Color Abstraction, Dialogue Art J, 1/85. *Dealer:* Howard Scott Gallery 529 W 20th St New York NY 10001. *Mailing Add:* 3515 84th St Apt 3G Jackson Heights NY 11372

MOORE, MATTHEW
ENVIRONMENTAL SCULPTOR
b Wadell, Arizona, 1976. *Study:* Santa Clara Univ, Calif, BA, 1998; San Francisco State Univ, MFA (Sculpture), 2003. *Comn:* PEACH Award, St Luke's Health Initiative, Phoenix, 2002. *Exhib:* Solo exhibs include Univ S Miss Art Mus, Hattiesburg, 2006; group exhibs include Biennial Outdoor Sculpture Exhib, Triton Mus, Santa Clara, Calif, 2001; MFA Exhib, San Francisco State Univ Fine Art Gallery, 2003; Across the Desert, Raid Projs, Los Angeles, 2004; Images Against War, Galerie Lichtblick, Cologne, Germany, 2004; Contemp Forum Grants Awards Exhib, Phoenix Art Mus, 2006; Worlds Away, Walker Art Ctr, Minneapolis, 2008. *Awards:* Creative Capital Found Grant, 2008. *Mailing Add:* Lisa Sette Gallery 4142 North Marshall Way Scottsdale AZ 85251

MOORE, PAMELA A
PAINTER, PRINTMAKER
Study: San Francisco Art Inst, BFA. *Work:* Smithsonian Inst, Washington; Lincoln Ctr, Sanyo Corp, Pepsico Corp, NY; Canon Corp, NJ; Hofstra Mus; Am Inst Foreign Studies; Union League Club, NYC; Zimmerli Mus, Rutgers Univ, NJ; and other corp, pub & pvt collections. *Comn:* paintings as moveable set, Joyce Theater, Roz Newan & Dancers, NY, 85; 3' x 5' painting for fanfare, NY Philharmonic, 93; 18 paintings on film paper, Price Waterhouse, NY, 93; Am Inst For Studies, 99; Emcor Comn, 99; Thames Water, London, 2000; Am Inst Fgn Studies, 2000; United Airlines, 2001; John Wiley & Sons, 2002; Odyssey, 2002; Castel Hill, 2003; Time Warner Collection, 2005; pvt comn by Congressman Bill Pascrell, 2006; 3 paintings, Il Giglio Restaurant, NYC, 2006; permanent outdoor sculpture, Town of Montclair, NJ, 2007; and others. *Exhib:* New Talent, Castelli Graphics, NY, 85; solo exhibs, De Rotterdanse Schouburg, Rotterdam, The Neth, 85, Akad de Kunst, Berlin, Ger, 85, Gallerie Fenna de Vries, Rotterdam, The Neth, 87, Fay Gold Gallery, Atlanta, Ga, 92, Blue River Gallery, Jacksonville, Fla, 99, Walker/Kornbluth Gallery, 2000, Kathryn Markel Gallery, New York City, 03; Locus Gallery, St Louis, 99; Dillon Gallery, NY, 2000; White House Egg Display Representing NY State, 2001; Walker/Kornbluth Gallery, 03. *Pos:* manager, solo press shop, 80-85; owner, manager, Rhino Studios, 75-. *Teaching:* Queens Col, Printmaking Coun NJ, Pratt Graphic Ctr, Sch Queens Col, Printmaking Workshop, New York, Conn, Graphic Arts, Montclair Art Mus, Acad Art San Francisco & Viridian Print Studio. *Awards:* artist-in-residence, Oxbow Sch Art, 84 & Altos de Chavon Dominican Repub, Gulf & Western, 84; Dick Blick Arts Material Grant, 99; Artist Angel Grant, Vt Studio Ctr, 97; Pollock/Krasner Grant, 2006. *Media:* Acrylic, Oil; Miscellaneous Media; Copper. *Publ:* 8 Book Covers, Simon & Schuster, 99. *Dealer:* Kathryn Markel Gallery 520 W 20th St New York NY. *Mailing Add:* 67 Vestry St New York NY 10013

MOORE, ROBERT JAMES
PAINTER, PHOTOGRAPHER
b San Jose, Calif, July 24, 1922. *Study:* USAF Photo Sch, Lowry Field, Colo, grad; San Jose State Univ, BA; NY Inst Fine Arts, with Salmony, Schoenberger, Panofsky & Offner; Columbia Univ Teachers Col, MFA; Art Students League, with Brackman, Miller & Will Barnet. *Work:* NY Pub Libr Print Collection. *Comn:* Portrait, pvt comn by Ms Janet Zavatto. *Exhib:* Pa Acad Fine Arts, Philadelphia, 50; James D Phelan Awards Competition, San Francisco Art Mus, 51; 11 Yr Retrospective of Prizewinners, Village Art Ctr, Whitney Mus Am Art, NY, 54; New York City Ctr Gallery, 59; Audubon Artists, Nat Acad Design, NY, 62; One-man shows, Ruth Sherman Galleries, NY, 64 & Adele Bednarz Galleries, Los Angeles, 65; Berkshire Mus, Pittsfield, Mass, 66; Art Students League & Ford Found Show, NY, 75; and others. *Pos:* Owner, Robert J Moore Studio, New York. *Teaching:* Assoc prof art, Goddard Col, 54-57; instr art & photog, Battin High Sch, Elizabeth, NJ, 59-64; instr art, Julia Richman High Sch, New York, 64-90. *Awards:* Second Prize, Village Art Ctr 7th Ann Graphic Art Show, Village Art Ctr, New York, 52; Blue Ribbon, New Talent Show, Ruth Sherman Gallery, New York, 64; Berkshire Mus Award, 66. *Mem:* Artists Equity Asn of New York; life mem Art Students League; Visual Artists and Galleries Asn. *Media:* Oil, Graphics. *Res:* Underwater photog for painting subjects; underwater use of light & colors. *Interests:* Reading, museums, environmentalism, philanthropy, cuisine

MOORE, SABRA
ARTIST, CURATOR
b Texarkana, Tex, Jan 25, 1943. *Study:* Univ Tex, Austin, BA (cum laude), 64; Brooklyn Mus Art Sch, 66; Centre W African Studies Univ Birmingham, Eng, 67. *Work:* Mus Mod Art, Whitney Mus, Brooklyn Mus & Guggenheim Mus, New York; Sylvia Sleigh Coll, Rowan Univ, NJ. *Exhib:* Classified: Big Pages from the Heresies Collective, New Mus, New York, 85; Committed to Print, Mus Mod Art, New York, 88; Conections Project / Conexus, Mus de Arte Contemp, Sao Paulo, Brazil, 89; 2x2 Intersections, Kuntshalle Dominikanerkirche, Osnabreuck, Ger, 2002; Mind Over

Matter, Mus Fine Arts, Santa Fe, 2002; solo exhib, Out of the Woods, Harwood Mus Art, Taos, NMex, 2007. *Awards:* Fulbright Fel/Eng, 67; Helene Wurlitzer Found NMex, Artists Residency, 86 & 88; 2d Place, First Logan Biennal Nat Outdoor Sculpture, Utah State Univ, Logan. *Bibliog:* Deborah Wye (auth), Catalogue statement, Committed to Print, Mus Mod Art, New York, 88; Diane Armitage (auth), Sabra Moore - Place/Displace, The Mag, 3/97; Aline Brandauer (auth), art/techne, Fresco Fine Arts, Albuquerque, NM, 2004; Lucy Lippard (auth), Out of the Woods (exhib catalog), Hardwood Mus Art, 2007; and others. *Mem:* Women's Caucus for Art (pres, 80-82); Heresies Collective. *Media:* Mixed Media. *Publ:* Illusr, Petroglyphs: Ancient Language/Sacred Art, Clearlight Publ, Santa Fe, 98; On the Move: A Memior from the Women's Art Movement/NYC 1970-1992, New Village Press, NYC, 2016. *Mailing Add:* PO Box 96 Abiquiu NM 87510

MOORE, SCOTT MARTIN
PAINTER, INSTRUCTOR
b Los Angeles, Calif, Oct 13, 1949. *Study:* Calif State Univ, Long Beach, 67, 72 & 73; USMC, Hawaii, 70-72; John Pike Watercolor Sch, Woodstock, NY, 78. *Work:* Laguna Art Mus, Laguna Beach, Gibson, Dunn & Crutcher, Newport Beach, Rutaan & Tucker, Costa Mesa, Calif; Quaker Oats Co, Chicago. *Comn:* Four works oil & watercolor, Sedjwick James Insurance, 89-92. *Exhib:* Am Watercolor Soc Ann, Nat Acad, NY, 78, 80-84 & 86-87; Watercolor West, Riverside, Calif, 79-84 & 86-87; Nat Watercolor Soc, Los Angeles, 79-87; Allied Artists, Am Acad & Lett, NY, 80; Watercolor USA, 87. *Pos:* Illusr, USMC, Hawaii, 70-72; graphic designer, Scott Moore Studio, 73-78, painter, 78. *Teaching:* Instr transparent watercolor workshops, 76-92. *Awards:* First Awards, Watercolor West, 79 & 86; Walser S Greathouse Medal, 81 & Arjomari-Arches Paper Award, 86, Am Watercolor Soc. *Bibliog:* Julia P Chase (auth), Scott Moore: sheer color and light, Orange Co Illustrated, 8/79; Charles Dickens Phillips (auth), Gallery: Scott Moore, Westways Mag, 7/81; Jane Summer (auth), Familiar moments, Showcase Mag. *Mem:* Nat Watercolor Soc; Watercolor West; Am Watercolor Soc. *Media:* Transparent Watercolor, Oil. *Publ:* Auth, The drama of backlighting, The Artist's Mag, 12/84; Splash, American's Best Contemporary Watercolors, North Light Bks, 91. *Mailing Add:* 1435 Regatta Rd Laguna Beach CA 92651

MOORE, TODD SOMERS
PAINTER, EDUCATOR
b Oceanside, Calif, Nov 9, 1952. *Study:* Evergreen State Col, Olympia, Wash, BA, 75; RI Sch Design, MFA, 84. *Work:* Am Repub Insurance Co, Des Moines, Iowa; Hillhaven, Inc, Tacoma, Wash; Edwards & Angell, Boston, Mass; Princess House, Tavnton, Mass. *Comn:* Hist mural, RI State Coun Arts, E Providence, 84; mural, Princess House Corp, Taunton, Mass. *Exhib:* Wash Ann, Tacoma Art Mus, 77; Small Works, Wash Sq E Galleries, NY Univ, 80; Ann Exhib Am Art, Chautauqua Art Asn Galleries, 81 & 82; Solo exhib, Newport Art Mus, Newport, RI, 81; Nat Ann Show, Butler Inst Am Art, Youngstown, Ohio, 81 & 82; Untitled-without Theme (with catalog), Alternative Mus, NY, 82; The Real Thing, N Miami Mus, 85; Art of Northeast USA, Silvermine Galleries, New Cannan, Conn, 86; 1987: A Yr of the Arts, Newport Art Mus, RI, 87; two-man exhib, Wheeler Gallery, 91; Invitational Show, Bristol Art Mus, RI, 93; Todd Moore, 18 Views of Rumstick Point, White Gallery, Barrington, RI, 98; Somakatoligon, Fed Reserve Bank Gallery, Boston, 98; What's Really Real, Thoreau Gallery, Franklin Pierce Gallery, Rindge, NH, 99. *Pos:* actg dean, Div Found Studies, 2003. *Teaching:* Instr 2-D design & drawing, RI Sch Design, 84-93, assoc prof, 93-; curriculum coordr, Div Found Studies, 2000-04. *Awards:* 2-D Grant, RI State Coun of Arts, 79; Brown Mem Prize, Am Ann at Newport, Newport Art Mus, RI, 81; Juror's Spec Mention, Nat Ann Show, Butler Inst Am Art, 82. *Bibliog:* Bill van Siclien (auth), rev, Providence J, 7/88, 9/89, 3/93 & 4/93; Beth Gersh-Nesic (auth), Rev, Art New England, 12/91; Bill van Siclen (auth), rev, Providence 9/95, 9/97 & 7/98. *Mem:* RI Sch Design Faculty Asn (pres, 99-2003; treas, 2004-06). *Media:* Painting. *Mailing Add:* 991 Seapowet Ave Tiverton RI 02878

MOORE, WAYLAND D
PAINTER, PRINTMAKER
b Belton, SC, Sept 8, 1935. *Study:* Pvt art study, Belton, SC, 50-54; Ringling Coll Art & Design, Sarasota, Fla, cert, 54-57. *Work:* Headley Mus, Lexington, Ky; Nat Sports Hall Fame; corp & pvt collections. *Comn:* Ky Derby, Felicie, NY, 78; Maccabian Games of Israel, Horace-Richter Galleries, Old Jaffa, 79; medallion, 100th Anniversary Madison Sq Garden; 1984 & 1996 Olympics, Coca-Cola, USA, Atlanta, Ga, 84; Davis Cup, 98. *Exhib:* Solo exhibs, Studio 53, NY, 78, Quito, Ecuador, 78, Hermitage, La Braule, France, 80 & Gallerie Felicie, NY, 80; Cent Acad, Peking, China, 79; Tuscany One Man Show. *Collection Arranged:* Private Collection, Corp./Tennis Hall of Fame; Baseball Hall of Fame, US Olympic Hall of Fame, College, Etc. *Pos:* trustee, Ringling Coll Art & Design, Sarasota, Fla, formerly; mem visionary bd, Clemson U, Clemson, SC. *Teaching:* Instr art, Atlanta Fed Penitentiary, 70-76; instr art evening classes, Emory Univ, 83-2012; instr workshops, Greece, 2008, Jamaica, 2010. *Awards:* Pulitzer Prize nominee, Journalism, 67; Teaching Commendation, The White House, 74; Creativity award, Emory Univ. *Bibliog:* Brushstrokes of Poetry, 2005. *Mem:* Int Soc Artists; New York Soc Illusr. *Media:* Watercolor; Acrylic, Serigraphy. *Res:* Each Yr travel to Europe on Painting locations adn workshops. *Specialty:* Landscape o Figures. *Interests:* sailing, tennis, adverture poetry, tall tales Festival. *Publ:* Articles in The Olympian Mag, Peachtree, Sports Illus, Braves Yrbk, Southwest Mag, Atlanta Mag; S.C. Education TV. *Mailing Add:* 2124 Azalea Cir Decatur GA 30033

MOORE NICHOLSON, MYREEN
PAINTER, ART APPRAISER
b Norfolk, Va, June 2, 1940. *Study:* William & Mary Coll, AA, 60, Tidewater Community Coll, 95-2000; Old Dominion Univ, BA, 62; Chrysler Mus/Corcoran Gallery Art Sch, 64; Gibbes State Art Gallery, 68; Univ NC Chapel Hill, MS, 71; Mus Contemporary Art, 73; with Charles Sibley, Wm Reimann & Ray Goodbred; Old Dominion Univ, MA, 97 with Linda McGreevy & others; additional graduate work, 98-05. *Work:* Old Dominion Univ, Norfolk, Va; Gibbes State Art Gallery, Charleston, SC; City of Chesapeake, Va. *Comn:* Statues, Child Study Ctr, comn by Reuben Cooper, Dept Speech Chair, Norfolk, 67; portrait, Founder of Friends, Kennedy Ctr, comn by Victor Rosenbloom,; Statue Designs, St Mark's Church, comn by St Marks, 91; 70th Anniversary of Poetry Society (collage), Wren Bldg, comn by James McNally, 93; statue, Saint Bridget, Ore, 2005. *Exhib:* Int Platform Asn, 89-97; Artists of Va 1996 Juried Art Show, Peninsula Fine Arts Ctr; Tidewater Artists Miniature Show, 96, 98, 2007, 2009-2013; Hampton Arts Comn Bay Days Juried Art Show, 96, 97, & 2002; Suffolk Mus Invitational Artists & Writers Exhib, 96, 2011; Yorktown Virginia Heritage Show, 97 & 98; Trinity Church Stations of the Cross, Portsmouth Mus, 97; Hermitage Mus Found Mini Show, 98, 2007, 2009, & 2011; Nauticus Nat Maritime Ctr, 98, 2000; Norfolk (VA) Int Airport, 2001-2003, Renewal show, 2010, 2011; Portfolio Show, D'Art, 2011; Portfolio Show, Suffolk Mus, 2012; 15x15 Exhib with Andy Warhol Show, Mus Contemp Art, 2012; Better Block Art Exhib, 2013. *Collection Arranged:* Chrysler Mus Stud Art Show, 65; Charleston Pub Schs Permanent Print Collection, SC, 69; Original Art Collection, Norfolk Pub Libr Pub Lending, 72-75; W Ghent Arts Alliance Art & Literary Festival, 79; Life-Saving Mus Va Beach, 91; Crestar Bank, 91; Hermitage Mus, 92. *Pos:* Staff artist, William & Mary Coll, 58-61; hearing reporter & secy, City of Norfolk Fine Arts Comt, 64-65, asst to Ephraistic Art Poet, Pulitzer Winner Poetry, WD Snodgrass, 78-80; art librn & researcher, Norfolk Pub Libr, 70-90, dir model city libr program, 70-71; contribr & reviewer, Libr J, 73-76; ed, Poetry Soc Va, 90-93; pres, Tidewater Artists Alliance, 91-92, historian, 2011-2013; bd dir, Dockside Art Review, D'Art Ctr, 91-92; writer art, Mid Atlantic Antique Mag, 94-2001; dir, W Ghent Arts, 97-; Art Appraiser, 99-2013; Drawtoberfest Com, Va Mus Contemporary Art, 2012-2013. *Teaching:* Art teacher, Norfolk Pub Schs, 65-67; prof art, Palmer Jr Coll, Charleston, SC, 67-68, St. John's Island, SC, 68, W Ghent Arts Alliance, 78-83 & 98-; prof literature, Tex Central Coll, 97-2009, Moore-Nicholson Arts, 2011-. *Awards:* Nat Endowment Arts, 75; Tricentennial Alumni Award, William & Mary Coll, 93; Gov Cert, Voluntary Contrib Arts Va, 94; Color Graphics Award, 96; IPA, First Place Internationally, Printmaking and Graphics, 98. *Mem:* Poetry Soc of Va (vpres, edit of newsletter, 84-93), 84-; Irene Leache Soc, 91-2000; Va Writers Club, 95-; Tidewater Art Alliance (grants chmn, 90, pres, 91-92, & historian, 2011-2013), 2005-; Hampton Arts League, 2005-2011; Norfolk Drawing Group, 2008-; Norfolk Historical Soc, 2011, 2013; co-organizer, art comt, UN Peace Day, 2012, 2013. *Media:* All Media. *Res:* The Sullys and the Poes, Norfolk, Va; 400th Anniversary of Jamestown, Va; Alex B Jackson, First Afro-American Art graduate of Yale Univ, bio in progress. *Interests:* restoration of stone work, paintings. *Publ:* Anthologies, Poetry Soc of Virginia, 85, 93, 2003; Poets Domain series, Live Wire Press, 95-2008; Staff, Articles published in Mid Atlantic Antiques Mag, 94-2010; Maine Antique Digest, 2007-; Common Betrayals in Progress (autobiography with W.D. Snodgrass). *Dealer:* Moore-Nicholson Arts. *Mailing Add:* 1404 Gates Ave Norfolk VA 23507

MOORES, PETER
COLLECTOR
b Lancashire, England, April 9, 1932. *Study:* Student, Oxford Univ, 1954; Christ Church, Oxford Univ, MA, 1975. *Pos:* Dir, The Littlewoods Organization, Liverpool, England, 1957-93, chairman, 1977-80; director Singer & Friedlander, London, 1972-92. *Awards:* Decorated medaglia d'oro (Italy); Commander Brit Empire; Named One of Top 200 Collectors, ARTnews mag, 2004-09. *Collection:* 15th- to 20th-century European art; Chinese archaic bronzes; contemporary British art

MOOS, JULIE
PHOTOGRAPHER
b Ottawa, Canada, Nov 25, 1965. *Study:* McGill Univ, Montreal, BA, 1987; Sorbonne Univ, Paris, 1989; NY Univ, 1989-91; Int Ctr Photog, New York, 1991-92. *Work:* Mint Mus, Charlotte, NC; Birmingham Mus Art, Ala; Whitney Mus Am Art, New York. *Exhib:* Solo exhibs include Fredericks Freiser Gallry, New York, 2000, 2001, 2004, Birmingham Mus Art, Ala, 2002, Contemp Mus Art, Honolulu, 2002, Renaissance Soc, Univ Chicago, 2002, Mint Mus Art, Charlotte, NC, 2003, Franklin Art Works, Minneapolis, 2005, Fay Gold Gallery, Atlanta, 2005, Mus Contemp Art, Cleveland, 2007; group exhibs include Nubreed, Lincoln Ctr, New York, 1996; Group Show, Fay Gold Gallery, Atlanta, 2000; Collectors Choice, Exit Art, New York, 2000; Chelsea Rising, Contemp Art Ctr, New Orleans, 2001; Staging, Contemp Art Mus, St Louis, 2002; Whitney Biennial, Whitney Mus Am Art, New York, 2002, Visions from America, 2002; Int Ctr Photog, Newe York, 2003; Summerize/Summer Eyes, Jan Weiner Gallery, Kansas City, 2004; Illusions of Innocence, Frist Ctr Visual Arts, Nashville, 2004; Face & Figure: Portraits & Figure Studies in Contemp Photog, Westport Art Ctr, Conn, 2005; People, Jim Kempner Fine Art, New York, 2008. *Teaching:* Adj prof photog, Wichita State Univ, 1997-98. *Mailing Add:* Fredericks & Freiser 536 W 24th St New York NY 10011

MOOS, WALTER A
DEALER
b Karlsruhe, Ger, 1926. *Study:* Ecole Superieure Com, Geneva, Switz, BA; New Sch Social Res, with Paul Zucker & Meyer Shapiro. *Pos:* Dir, Gallery Moos Ltd; vpres, Arts Mag, 77, pres, 82-83. *Awards:* TIAF Award Distinction, 2002. *Bibliog:* Paul Duval (auth), Ken Danby, 74; Paul Duval (auth), Ken Danby: The New Decade, 84. *Mem:* Prof Art Dealers Asn Can (pres, 71-74). *Specialty:* Contemporary Canadian, European and American paintings, sculpture and graphics. *Mailing Add:* Gallery Moos Ltd 622 Richmond St W Toronto ON M5V 1Y9 Canada

MOQUIN, RICHARD ATTILIO
PAINTER, SCULPTOR
b San Francisco, Calif, July 1, 1934. *Study:* City Coll San Francisco, AA; San Francisco State Col, with Seymour Locks, BA & MA. *Work:* Oakland Mus, Calif; Saks Fifth Ave, NY; Trans Am Bldg, San Francisco, Calif; San Francisco Mus Art; Mayor's Office, City Hall, San Rafael, Calif. *Exhib:* Solo exhibs, sculpture, Meyer-Breir-Wise Gallery, San Francisco, 80, sculpture, Gallery Paule Anglim, San

Francisco, 84, sculpture & works on paper, Michel Dunev Gallery, San Francisco, 89 & 92, paintings, Select Art Gallery, Ariz, 97 & paintings, Ebert Gallery, Calif, 97; sculpture, Gallery Paule Anglim, San Francisco, 86; sculpture, James Calahan Gallery, Calif, 88; sculpture, Harleen-Allen Gallery, San Francisco, 95; paintings, Light and Spirit, Somar Gallery, San Francisco, 96; paintings, Omma gallery, Crete, Greece, 00 & 02; sculpture & paintings, Art Works gallery, San Rafall, Calif, 05. *Pos:* Vpres, Asn San Francisco Potters, 67-68. *Teaching:* Instr sculpture, City Col San Francisco, 69-. *Awards:* Purchase Awards, Sacramento State Fair, 68; M H de Young Mus, San Francisco, Calif, 66, 68 & 70; Clay and Glass, Oakland Mus, Calif, 74; sculpture, Coll Marin, Kentfield, Calif, 75. *Bibliog:* Thomas Albright (auth), Art in the San Francisco Bay Area; Les Krantz (auth), articles in Am Artists, Calif Art Rev & NY Art Rev; Art News Mag, 7/97. *Media:* Acrylics, Oil; Oil bars. *Dealer:* Art Smart Gallery San Francisco CA; Ebert Gallery San Francisco CA. *Mailing Add:* 255 Richards Blvd Sonoma CA 95476

MORALES, RODOLFO
PAINTER

b Oaxaca, Mex, 1925. *Study:* Nat Sch Fine Art, San Carlos, BFA, 49, study with Rufino Tamayo. *Work:* Inst Polytecnico & Escuela Prep, Mexico City; Mus City Ocatlan, Oaxaca, Mex; Rincon de los Bosques, Bosques de las Lomas, Mex. *Exhib:* State Palace Malaga, Spain, 73; Mus Mex Art, San Francisco, Calif, 78; Mexico: The Next Generation, San Antonio Mus, Tex, 85; solo exhib, Vorpal Gallery, NY, 85. *Teaching:* Instr art, Escuela Preparatoria No 5, 53-86. *Awards:* Medal, Oaxacan Culture House, Mexico, 86. *Bibliog:* Antonio Rodriguez (auth), Nostalgia accompanies solitude, Inst Politech Nat, Mex, 81. *Publ:* Auth, Rodolfo Morales (exhib catalog), Vorpal Gallery, New York & San Francisco, 88. *Mailing Add:* c/o Bond Latin Gallery 251 Post St Suite 610 San Francisco CA 94108

MORCOS, MAHER N
SCULPTOR, PAINTER

b Cairo, Egypt, Feb 23, 1946; US citizen. *Study:* Cairo Univ, BA (archit), 69; Leonardo de Vinci, Italy, 70. *Comn:* Bust Egyptian President Nasser, Ministry of Educ, Cairo, Egypt, 62; religious paintings, Heliopolis Cathedral, Cairo, Egypt, 64; mural, Valley Nat Bank, Scottsdale, Ariz, 84. *Exhib:* Charles Russell Show, Charles Russell Mus, Great Falls, Mont, 80 & 81; Am Inst Contemp Art, San Dimas, Calif, 80 & 81; Western Artists Am, Coliseum, Reno, Nev, 80 & 81; Western Heritage Show, Arapahoe Co, Littleton, Colo, 80 & 81; George Phippen Show, CofC, Prescott, Ariz, 80 & 81. *Awards:* Gold Medal, Death Valley Show, 80; Best of Show, Western Heritage Show, Arapahoe Co Asn, 81; Best of Show, Western Artists Am, City Reno, 81. *Bibliog:* William E Freckleton (auth), Guided by imagination, Southwest Art, 4/78; Scene, Tulsa Tribune, 78; Dick Spencer (auth), Western heritage, The Western Horseman, 80. *Media:* Bronze; Oil, Watercolor. *Mailing Add:* Eagle Art Gallery 1250 Prospect La Jolla CA 92037

MORENO, DAVID
PAINTER

b Los Angeles, Calif, 1957. *Study:* Univ Ariz, BFA, 1982; Calif Inst Arts, Valencia, 1984-85. *Exhib:* Solo exhibs, Feature Inc, New York, 1989, 1991, 1993, 1994, 1997, 1999, 2002, 2005 & 2006, Ctr Contemp Art, Chicago, Ill, 1990 & 1992, Univ Galleries, Ill State Univ, Normal, 1991, Neuberger Mus, Purchase Col, State Univ NY, Purchase, 1997; group exhibs, Dorothy, Ctr Contemp Art, Chicago, 1989; Round Trip (with catalog), Fernando Alcolea Gallery, New York & Barcelona, Spain, 1990; Ctr Contemp Art, Chicago, Ill, 1991; On Condition: Painting Between Abstraction and Representation (brochure), Gallery 400, Univ Ill, Chicago, 1992, Slice & Dice, 1994 & Word Perfect, 1998; Tattoo Collection, Galerie Jennifer Flay & URBI et ORBI, Paris, France, Daniel Buchholz, Cologne, Ger, Ctr Regional d'Art Contemporain, Nantes, France, Andrea Rosen Gallery, New York & Air de Paris, Nice, France, 1992; Cutting Bait (brochure), Randolph Street Gallery, Chicago, Ill, 1993; Art in the Age of Information (with catalog), 808 Penn Mod, Pittsburgh, Pa, 1993; Feature Inc, New York, 1994 & 1996, Strung Into the Appollonian Dream, 1996, AbFab, 1996, Paintings, 1998, Science, 1998, Drawers, 1998, Hairy Forearm's Self-Referral, 2000, Grok Terence McKenna Dead, 2000, Another, once again, many times more, 2001, The sun rises in the evening, 2005, Thoughts, 2007 & Packedsockdrawer, 2007; The Arabesque, PPOW, New York, 1994; Smells Like Vinyl, Roger Merians Gallery, New York, 1995; Acts of Obsession, Carla Stellweg Gallery, New York, 1996; Frankensteinian, Caren Golden Fine Art, New York, 1997; A Decade of Collecting: Selected Recent Acquisitions in Contemp Drawings (brochure), Mus Mod Art, New York, 1997, More Pieces to the Puzzle, 1998, Sight Gags: Grotesque, Caricature & Wit in Mod & Contemp Drawings (brochure), 1999, Modern Starts: The Raw & the Crooked, 2000, Transforming Chronologies, 2006; Wop: works on/off paper, ANP, Antwerp, Belgium, 1998; Normal Editions Workshop-A Print Retrospective, Elmhurst Art Mus, Ill, 1998; Drawing to an End, Anna Kustera Gallery, New York, 1998; Amused, Carrie Secrest Gallery, Chicago, 2001; Greater NY 2005, PS1 Contemp Art Ctr, NY, 2005; Looking Back, White Columns, New York, 2006; Recordings, Atlanta Contemp Art Ctr, 2007; Invitational Exhib Visual Arts, AAAL, New York, 2008. *Awards:* Louis Comfort Tiffany Award in Painting, Sculpture, Printmaking, Photography & Craft Media, 1997; Hassam, Speicher, Betts & Symons Purchase Award, AAAL, 2008. *Bibliog:* Tom Moody (auth), rev, Art papers, 11-12/96; Holland Cotter (auth), Ideas from the air: wrapped in paper, NY Times, 12/19/97; Ken Johnson (auth), Art in review, NY Times, 1/23/98

MORENON, ELISE
PAINTER, INSTRUCTOR

b Paris, France, June 26, 1939; US citizen. *Study:* Northwestern Univ, BS, 58-61; Sch Mus Fine Arts, Boston, 62 & 63; studied with Mario Cooper, Charles Reid & Edgar A Whitney, Yale Univ Grad Sch, 64 & 65. *Work:* Numerous pvt collections. *Comn:* Portrait, comn by A Nisula, NJ, 89; double portrait, comn by G Barrow, NY, 90; portrait, comn by L S Craig, NY, 92. *Exhib:* Am Watercolor Soc, Nat Acad, NY, 75, 77, 79 & 81; Audubon Artists, Nat Art Club, NY, 82 & 91 & Salmagundi Club, NY, 97-2011; Allied Artists Am, NY, 86-89, 97-2011; Two Artists-Natural Images, Fordham Univ, NY, 89; Watercolor USA, Springfield Art Mus, Mo, 91; Philadelphia Watercolor Club, Philip & Muriel Berman Mus Art, Collegeville, Pa, 92 & 94; Butler Inst Am Art, Youngstown, Ohio, 2001; Morris Mus, NJ, 2002-03; NJ Watercolor Soc, The Monmouth Mus, NJ, 2006, 2007, 2009, 2011. *Pos:* Scenic artist, designer, Berkshire Playhouse, Stockbridge, Mass, 62-64; display artist, Omega Watch Corp, New York, 66-86; lectr & juror, 78-. *Teaching:* Instr watercolor, Sch Visual Arts, New York, 78-84; instr, Teaneck Community Educ Ctr, NJ, 91- & Hyatt Classic Residence, NJ, 94-2011; Five Star Premier Residence, Teaneck, NJ, 2012-; Art Sch at Old Church, Demarest, NJ, 2013. *Awards:* Juror's Special Choice Award, Nat Arts Club, 85; Nicholas Reale Mem Award, NJ Watercolor Soc, 91 & Audubon Artists, 97; Winsor & Newton Award, Allied Artists Am, 97; Strathmore Award, Allied Artists Am, 2002; Kent Day Coes Award, Allied Artists Am, 2008; Forbes Mag Award, NJ Watercolor Soc, 2010; 1st Prize, drawing, Bergen County NJ, Ninth Ann, Juried Art Show, 2011; H Bailin award, Audubon Artists, 2011; 2nd Prize, Drawing, State of NJ, 2011. *Bibliog:* Beckwith (auth), Creative Watercolor, Rockport Publ, 95; Schlemm (ed), Watercolor Expressions, Rockport Publ, 99; Biographical Encylopedia of American Painters, Sculptors and Engravers of the US, Colonial to 2002, Dealers Choice Books, Inc. *Mem:* Am Watercolor Soc; Nat Asn Women Artists; Allied Artists Am; Philadelphia Water Color Club; Audubon Artists; NJ Watercolor Soc; Transparent Watercolor Soc Am; Garden State Watercolor Soc. *Media:* Watercolor. *Interests:* Photography. *Mailing Add:* 420 Fairview Ave Fort Lee NJ 07024

MORGAN, CLARENCE (EDWARD)
PAINTER, EDUCATOR

b Philadelphia, Pa, May 21, 1950. *Study:* Pa Acad Fine Arts, cert, 75; Sch Fine Arts, Univ Pa, MFA, 78; Temple Univ, summer 78. *Work:* Equitable Life Assurance Soc US, Washington, DC; Prudential Insurance Co Am, Jacksonville, Fla; Pa Acad Fine Arts, Philadelphia; Mem Union Gallery, Ariz State Univ, Tempe; General Mills Corp, Minneapolis, Minn. *Comn:* Large scale painting, comn by NC Gen Assembly, Raleigh, 83 & St Thomas Celebration Arts, Wilmington, 86, NC. *Exhib:* Seven Contemp Am Artists, Cleveland Mus Art, Ohio, 83; Portrait of the South, Palazzo Venezia, Rome, Italy, 84; Recent Works, Wake Forest Univ, Winston-Salem, NC, 84; Paradoxical Behavior, Hodges Taylor Gallery, Charlotte, NC, 85; Drawings & Paintings, Carleton Col, Northfield, Minn, 85; Southern Exposure, Alternative Mus, NY, 85; solo exhib, Harris Brown Gallery, Boston, Mass, 86. *Teaching:* Assoc prof painting & drawing, Sch Art, East Carolina Univ, 78-; artist-in-residence, Minneapolis Col Art & Design, 84-85. *Awards:* Fac Res Grant, East Carolina Univ, 79; Merit Award Painting, Fayetteville Mus Art, 82; Visual Arts Fel, NC Arts Coun, 82. *Bibliog:* Rubel Romero (auth), Universal language, Spectator, 84; Mason Riddle (auth), Midwest reviews, New Art Examiner, 84; Richard Maschal (auth), Abstractionist uses religious imagery, Charlotte Observer, 85. *Mem:* Coll Art Asn Am. *Dealer:* Elizabeth Harris-Harris Brown Gallery 476 Columbus Ave Boston MA 02118; Dot Hodges-Hodges Taylor Gallery 227 N Tryon St Charlotte NC 28202. *Mailing Add:* c/o Marita Gilliam Gallery 912 Williamson Dr Raleigh NC 27608

MORGAN, DAHLIA
MUSEUM DIRECTOR, EDUCATOR

Study: McGill Univ, BA, 58; Sir George Williams Univ, Can, 68-69; Univ Miami, Fla, dipl Coll teaching, art hist, 74. *Pos:* Dir, Art Mus, Fla Int Univ, 80-96, Art in State Bldg Prog, Miami, Fla, 84-96. *Teaching:* Lectr art hist, Fla Int Univ, 75-96, creator/moderator, Critics' Lect Series, 80-. *Awards:* Maxie Award, Miami Arts Exchange, 90; Excellence in Res Award, Fla Int Univ, 93. *Bibliog:* Michael Hayes (auth), Newsmakers: Dahlia Morgan, Miami Today, 12/7/89; Helen L Kohen (auth), Portraits, Miami Herald, 8/21/94; Sue Hearns (auth), Eyes on the Prizes, Miami Herald, 5/2/96. *Mem:* Fla Mus Dir Asn; Int Coun Mus; Fla Cult Action Alliance; Am Asn Mus; Asn Coll & Univ & Galleries. *Res:* American modern and contemporary art. *Mailing Add:* c/o Fla Int Univ Art Mus Univ Park PC 110 Miami FL 33199

MORGAN, JAMES L
PAINTER

b Aug 7, 1947. *Study:* Utah State Univ, BFA, 70. *Work:* Utah State Univ, Logan; Crecent Cardboard Co, Chicago; Leigh Yawkey Woodson Art Mus; Nat Wildlife Art Mus, Jackson, Wyo; Buffalo Bill Art Mus, Cody, Wyo; Mont Historical Mus, Helena, Mont. *Comn:* 36 Paintings, Texaco, Washington, Iowa, 83-85; Merril Lynch, Salt Lake City, Utah, 87. *Exhib:* Nat Acad Western Art, Oklahoma City, Okla; NW Rendezvous Group, Park City, Utah; Landscape and Closer Views, CM Russell Mus, Great Falls, Mont; Birds in Art, Leigh Yawkey Woodson Mus, 82-83 & 86-94; Soc Animal Artists Exhib, 86; Birds Art Nat Tour, 88-91 & 92-2004. *Collection Arranged:* Nat Mus Wildlife Art, Jackson Wyo; Buffalo Bill Art Mus, Cody, Wyo; Montana Hist Society, Helena, Mont. *Awards:* Red Smith Artists Choice Award, Nat Mus Wildlife Art, Jackson, Wyo; Artists Choice Award, Northwest Rendezvous Group, 93-94; Robert Lougheed Mem Award, Nat Acad Western Art, 94. *Bibliog:* Donald Hagerty (auth), Leading the West-100 Contemporary Artists, N Land Press; Modern Wildlife paintings, Yale Univ Press; Nicolas Hammond (auth), Modern Wildlife Painting, Yale Univ Press; Donna Poulton & Vern Swanson (auths), Painters of Utah's Canyons & Deserts, Gibbs Smith Publ. *Mem:* Soc Animal Artists; Northwest Rendezvous Group; Nat Acad Western Art. *Media:* Oil, Watercolor. *Specialty:* Representational Western and Wildlife. *Interests:* Fly fishing, bird watching. *Publ:* Cache Mag, Herald J, 85; Fishes of the Great Basin, Univ Nev Press, 86; Art of the West Mag, 92-96, 2009; Southwest Art Mag, 92, 2005; Wildlife Art News Mag, 11-12/94-2005; and others; Western Art Collector, 8/2011. *Dealer:* Trailside Galleries Jackson WY; J N Bartfield Gallery New York NY; Simpson Gallagher Gallery Cody WY; Gerald Peters Galleries Santa Fe NM; Claggett/Rey Gallery, Vail, Colo. *Mailing Add:* PO Box 331 Mendon UT 84325

MORGAN, ROBERT COOLIDGE
WRITER, PAINTER
b Boston, Mass, July 10, 1943. *Study:* Univ Redlands, BA, 64; Northeastern Univ, EdM, 68; Univ Mass, Amherst, MFA; 75; NY Univ, PhD, 78. *Work:* Mus Mod Art, NY; Clark Art Inst, Williamstown, Mass; NY Pub Libr; Chase Manhattan Bank Collection; Commodities Corp Collection, NJ; Mus Contemp Art, Chgo; Univ SC, Columbia; Univ Oldenburg, Ger; Mus Modern Art Libr, NY; Kaminsky Found, 2010; and many pvt collections. *Comn:* Painted Forms on Steel, Mayor's Off Cult Affairs, Boston, 72; Curved Curbs, Mass Coun on Arts, Boston, 74. *Exhib:* Interventions in Landscape, Hayden Gallery, Mass Inst Technol, Cambridge, Mass, 74; Performances: 4 Evenings, 4 Days, Whitney Mus Am Art, NY, 76; Erik Stark Gallery, 92; Daniel Newburg Gallery, 92; Galerie AB, Paris, 92; Construction in Process, Lodz, Poland, 93; Centro Espositivo della Rocca, Paolina, Italy, 94; Amilie Wallace Galery, State Univ NY Old Westbury, 2007; Wooster Art Space, New York, 2007; Bjorn Ressle Gallery, NY, 2009; Sideshow Gallery, Brooklyn, 2009; Sideshow gallery, Brooklyn, 2010; Lodz Biennial, 2010. *Pos:* Bd adv, Art Omi, appt, 92; Consult to several granting found in the visual arts. *Teaching:* prof emeritus, Rochester Inst Technol, NY, 81-2001; instr, Sch Visual Arts, Columbia Univ, NY, 90 & Barnard Col, 91-92; adj prof, Pratt Inst, 91-. *Awards:* Nat Endowment Humanities Fel, 80, 87 & 88; Arcala award Salamanca, 99; NEA Rockefeller Grant, 88; European Acad of Sciences and Arts, 2011. *Bibliog:* Vivian Raynor (auth) NY Times, 76, 77; David Craven (auth), article, Arts Mag, 9/83; Collins and Milazzo (coauth), article, New Observations, 87; Gary Nickard (auth), article, CEPA Quarterly, 87; Interview by Phong Bui (ed publ), Brooklyn Rail, Summer 2009; Denise Carvalho (auth), Art in Am, 2009; Robert Ayers (auth), ArtNews, 2010. *Mem:* Coll Art Asn Am; AICA (Art Critics); The Century Assn, NY. *Media:* Writing, Painting, Photography, Film, Installation. *Res:* Role of documentation in conceptual art; structural interactions, literal time and progressive sequence, often manifested in appropriation of swim images & TV images, recent photos of tondo paintings, art & criticism, critical theory; Role of Connoisseurship in contemp Chinese painting. *Interests:* Art Criticism, Theory, History, and Painting. *Publ:* After the Deluge: The Return of the Inner-Directed Artist, Arts, 3/2; Conceptual Art: An American Perspective, McFarland, 94; Art into Ideas: essays on conceptual arts, Cambridge Univ Press, 96; Between Modernism and Conceptual Art, McFarland, 97; auth The End of the Art World, Allworth Press, NYC 98; Gary Hill, ED, Johns Hopkins Univ Press, 2000; Bruce Nauman, Ed, Johns Hopkins Univ Press, 2002; Clement Greenberg, Ed, Univ of Minn Press, 2003; Vasarely, Geo, Braziller, 2004; Wild Dogs in Bali, NFS Press, Singapore, 2005; The Artist & Globalization, Municipal Gallery, Lodz, Poland, 2008; trans, The Artists at the Dawn of Globalization, Buenos Aires, Eduntref, 2012; Reflections on the Condition of Recent Chinese Art, Hebei Edn Publishers, Beijing, 2013. *Dealer:* John Davis Hudson New York; Rooster Gallery New York

MORGAN, ROBERTA MARIE
PAINTER, WRITER
b Baltimore, Md, Nov 24, 1953. *Study:* Md Inst Coll Art, BFA, 75, Univ Md, 91-92, Towson State Univ, 92. *Work:* City of Gaithersburg Coun Art, Md; Inst Notre Dame, Baltimore, Md. *Exhib:* Free State Three, Rockville Arts Place, Md, 93; Mamaroneck Artists Guild 36th Ann Exhib, Westbeth Gallery, NY, 94; 9th Ann Tallahassee Fla Nat Competition, Fine Arts Gallery & Mus Fla State Univ, 94; Art of Healing, E Campus Gallery, Valencia Community Col, Orlando, Fla, 95; Promising New Talent 1995-96, Mus Contemp Art, Washington, 96; Three Women Gallery Lumiere (with catalog), Savannah, Ga, 97; More Than Meets The Eye, Studio Gallery, Washington, DC, 98; Reflections of Humanity, Marlborough Gallery, Largo, Md; Brute Elegance, Mill River Gallery, Della, Md; Ancient Mother, Columbia Art Ctr, Columbia, Md. *Pos:* Gallery dir, Gaithersburg Coun Arts, 91-94, The Artists' Gallery, Columbia, Md, 95; co-cur, Watercolors of Belisario Contreras, 94; cur, Envelope, Rockville Arts Place & Visual Arts Exhib, Columbia Festival Arts, 2000. *Teaching:* Instr drawing & painting, Columbia Asn Ctr Arts, 94-. *Awards:* Coun Members Award, 75th Nat Exhib, George Walter Vincent Smith Art Mus, 94; Individual Artist Award, Md State Arts Coun, 95. *Bibliog:* Robin Z Goodstein (auth), Gaithersburg artist colors contemplation, Express Newspapers, 9/12/90; Mike Guiliano (auth), New at Slayton House, The Columbia Flyer, 1/23/92; George Howell (auth), Town meeting, Art Papers, 9-10/95; Marty Shooter (auth), The art of three women, Savanna News Press, 2/9/97; Marilyn Stevens (auth), Committment to a good co-op will reap rewards, Art Calendar, 6/97; Rima Shul Kind (auth), Roberta Morgan: more than meets the eye, Koan, 6/97; Phyllis Jacobs (auth), Envelope: Louis Roway, Jill Romanoke, Helga Thomson, Koan, 7/97; George Howell (auth), Wayne Edson Bryan: WEB/Roberta Morgan: more than meets the eye, Art Papers, 9/98; Included in Still Life in Oils edited by Theodora Philcox, published by Ava Publishing SA, this is a book about still life painting. *Media:* Oil. *Publ:* Auth, Creativity on display: Art center studios, 93 & Your local art critic, Art Calendar, 93; Elizabeth Friedman: Photographic explorations, Washington Review, 94; Separating the wheat from the chaff, 4/95 & Interview with Denee Barr: An emerging artist exhibits internationally (art calendar), 9/95; Do It On Your Desktop: Producing Your Own Color Catalog (art calendar), 11/97. *Dealer:* Sloane Jordan Gallery The Arboretum 10,000 Research Blvd Suite 257 Austin TX 78759. *Mailing Add:* Columbia Art Ctr and Gallery 61 Foreland Garth Columbia MD 21044

MORGAN, SUSAN
PAINTER, INSTRUCTOR
b Queens, NY, June 3, 1953. *Study:* Art Students League, New York, 73-77. *Exhib:* Int Multimedia Exhib, Univ Sao Paolo, Brazil, 79; Tree Guards, Foundations Gallery, 82 & The Arsenal, 85, NY; Cloudworks, Stuart Neill Gallery, NY, 82; Ann Exhib, Queens Mus, Flushing, NY, 83; Solo exhib, South-Dade Libr, Miami, 84, Silpakorn Univ, Bangkok, US Info Serv, Chiang Mai, Thailand, 90; Off the Wall, Kamikaze Gallery, NY, 86; Second Ann Women's Exhib, Bangkok, Thailand. *Collection Arranged:* Community Cultural Center Annual Exhibitions, Brookings, SDak, 80. *Pos:* Co-owner, Nobe Gallery, NY, 77-79; asst to Jeanne-Claude Christo, NY, 82-84; co-owner, The Five & Dime, NY, 84-86. *Teaching:* Vis lectr, Silpakorn Univ, Bangkok, 90, Chaing Mai Informal Group, 92, Thailand; vis artist, Chaing Mai Univ, 90. *Bibliog:* Helen L Kohen (auth), article, Miami Herald, 84; Artists in the city, by Jenny Dixon, WNYC radio broadcast, 84; Ban Suan mag & several Thai newspaper articles, 90. *Media:* Oil Paint, Oil Pastel. *Publ:* Coauth, Tree Guards, with Holly O'Grady, silk screen edition, 80, Morgan/O'Grady publ, 82; For a Lahu Girl (video), 89

MORGAN, WILLIAM
ART HISTORIAN, WRITER
b Princeton, NJ, June 13, 1944. *Study:* Dartmouth Coll, AB; Columbia Univ, MA & cert in restoration & preservation hist archit; Univ Del, PhD. *Work:* Portland Mus; Miami Univ; Univ Louisville. *Exhib:* JB Speed Mus, Louisville, Ky, 88. *Pos:* Chmn, Ky Hist Preservation Rev Bd, 75-90; archit critic, Courier-J, 75-80; bk rev ed, Landscape Archit Mag, 76-78; ed bd, Competitions, 90-; contrib ed, Art New Eng, 2000-2002. *Teaching:* Lectr art & archaeol, Princeton Univ, 71-74; asst prof fine arts, Allen R Hite Art Inst, Univ Louisville, 74-76, assoc prof, 76-81, prof, 81-, disting teaching prof, 95-99, vis prof, Roger Williams Univ, 99-2001, vis. prof, Wheaton Coll, 2002; vis prof, Brown Univ, 2008. *Awards:* Nat Collection Fine Arts Vis Res Fel, Smithsonian Inst, 71; Nat Endowment Humanities Res Fel, 84-85. *Media:* Photographer. *Res:* American art and architecture. *Publ:* Auth, Louisville - Architecture and the Urban Environment, Bauhan, 79; Portals: Photographs by William Morgan, Bauhan, 81; The Almighty Wall: Architecture of Henry Vaughan, Archit Hist Found, 83; Collegiate Gothic: Architecture Rhodes Coll, Mo, 89; Heikkinen & Komonen, Monacelli, 2000; American Country Churches, Abrams, 2004; Abrams Guide to American House Styles, Abrams, 2004; Cape Cod Cottage, Princeton Architectural Press, 2006; Yankee Modern, Princeton Architectural Press, 2009; Peter Rose Houses, Princeton Archit Press, 2010; Monadnock Summer: Arch Legacy of Dublin, NH, David R. Goding, 2011; A Simpler Way of Life: Old Farmhouses of New York & New England, Norfleet Press, 2013. *Mailing Add:* 24 Orchard Pl Providence RI 02906

MORGANSTERN, ANNE MCGEE
HISTORIAN, EDUCATOR
b Morgan, Ga, Feb 5, 1936. *Study:* Wesleyan Col, Ga, BFA, 58; Inst Fine Arts, NY Univ, MA, 61, PhD, 70. *Teaching:* Instr art hist, Vassar Col, Poughkeepsie, NY, 65-66; lectr art hist, Univ Wis, Milwaukee, 70-73; asst prof & prof, Ohio State Univ, 73-2004, prof emerita, currently. *Awards:* Kress Sr Fel, 82-83; Kress Found Grant, 97. *Bibliog:* Brendan Cassidy (auth), Gothic Tombs of Kinship, Art Book, Vol 8, No 2, 42-43, 2001; Julian Luxford (auth), Religion & the Arts, Vol 5, No 4, 529-531, 2001; Jacqueline Leclercq-Marx (auth), Revue belge d'archeologie et d'histoire de l'art, 71, 104-105, 2002. *Mem:* Medieval Acad Am; Coll Art Asn; Int Ctr medieval Art (domestic adv, 83-86); Société Française, d'Archéologie. *Res:* Gothic sculpture in north Europe; Flemish painting of the 15th century. *Publ:* The rest of Bosch's Ship of Fools, Art Bull, 84; The Bishop, the Lion & the Two-headed Dragon: The Burghersh Memorial in Lincoln Cathedral, Acts of the XXIVth International Congress of the History of Art, 96; Gothic Tombs of Kinship in France, the Low Countries and England, 2000; Art and Ceremony in Papal Avignon: A Prescription for the Tomb of Clement VI, Gesta, 2001; Liturgical and Honorific Implications of the Placement of Gothic Wall Tombs, Hortus Artium Medievalium (Journal of the Intl Center for Late Antiquity and Middle Ages), 2004; High Gothic Sculpture at Chartres Cathedral, the Tomb of the Count of Joigny, and the Master of the Warrior Saints, Penn State Univ Press, 2011. *Mailing Add:* 70 Webster Park Columbus OH 43214

MORGANSTERN, JAMES
HISTORIAN, EDUCATOR
b Pittsburgh, Pa, Oct 16, 1936. *Study:* Williams Coll, BA, 58; NY Univ, MA, 64, PhD, 73. *Pos:* Vis lectr, Univ Va, 1987. *Teaching:* Asst prof hist art, Univ Wis, Milwaukee, 70-73; asst prof, Ohio State Univ, Columbus, 73-80, assoc prof, 80-90, prof, 90-2008, emer, 2008-. *Awards:* Am Philos Soc Grant; Fulbright Research Award; World Monuments Fund & Samuel H Kress Found Grant. *Mem:* Coll Art Asn; Soc Archit Historians; Medieval Acad; Soc Franc d'Arch; Soc des Antiq de Normandie. *Res:* Architecture and archaeology; western medieval architecture. *Interests:* Notre Dame and Saint-Pierre de Jumieges. *Publ:* The Byzantine Church at Dereagzi and its Decoration, Ernst Wasmuth, 83; Working procedures in Byzantium: New evidence from southwestern Anatolia, Artistes, artisans et production artistique, Actes, II, Picard, 87; coauth, The fort at Dereagzi, and other material remains in its vicinity: From antiquity to the middle ages, Wasmuth, 93; coauth, Le Massif occidental de Notre-Dame de Jumieges: Recherches recentes, in Christian Spain, Avant-nefs et espaces d'accueil dans l'eglise entre le IVe et le XIIe siecle: CTHS, 2002; coauth, Jumieges eglise Notre Dame & Jumieges eglise Saint-Pierre, Les vestiges preromans, Congress Archeologiques de France, Soc Franc d'Arch, 2006. *Mailing Add:* Dept Hist Art Ohio State Univ Columbus OH 43210

MORGENLANDER, ELLA KRAMER
PAINTER, INSTRUCTOR
b Bronx, NY, Aug 7, 1931. *Study:* Brooklyn Col, 53; Brooklyn Mus Art Sch, with Reuben Tam, 60-70; New York Univ, 62; Barnes Found, Merion, Pa, 74-76; Art Students League, with Will Barnett, 78-79. *Exhib:* Ann Nat Asn Women Artists, Nat Acad Arts Gallery, NY, 71-81; Brooklyn Mus, NY, 76; Solo exhib, Nicholas Roerich Mus, NY, 76; Artists Depicting the Humanities, Henry St Settlement, NY, 82. *Teaching:* Instr art, St George's Pre-Sch NY, 62-67; instr, Ethical Culture Sch, Brooklyn, NY, 63-66; instr art, Bank St Sch Childhood Educ, 68-72. *Awards:* Adelle M Schiff Award, 73; Ziuta & Joseph James Akston Found, 88th Ann Nat Asn Women Artists; Lillian Cotton Mem Award, 90; Hon Mention Award, Nat Asn Women Artists, 92. *Mem:* Artists Equity Asn, NY; Nat Asn Women Artists; Contemp Artists New York. *Media:* Oil, Watercolor. *Dealer:* Brooklyn Mus Community Gallery File 188 Eastern Parkway Brooklyn NY. *Mailing Add:* 210 Park Pl Apt 2C Brooklyn NY 11238-4324

MORGIN, KRISTEN
CERAMIST
b Brunswick, Ga, 1968. *Study:* Calif State Univ, Hayward, BA; Alfred Univ Sch Ceramics, NY, MFA. *Exhib:* Solo exhibs include Viento y Agua Gallery, Long Beach, Calif, 2004, Marc Selwyn Fine Art, LA, 2006; group exhibs include Because the Earth is 1/3 Dirt, Art Mus Univ Colo, Boulder, 2004; Thing: New Sculpture from LA, Hammer Mus, LA, 2005; Trans-Ceramic Art, Word Ceramic Biennale, Icheon, Korea, 2005; Unmonumental: The Object in the 21st Century, New Mus Contemp Art, New York, 2008. *Teaching:* Asst prof ceramics, Calif State Univ, Long Beach. *Dealer:* Marc Selwyn Fine Art 6222 Wilshire Blvd Ste 101 Los Angeles CA 90048

MORIMOTO, HIROMITSU
PHOTOGRAPHER
b Yokohama, Japan, 1942. *Study:* St Joseph Col, 62; Calif State Univ, Long Beach, BA, 67; Art Students League, 67-68. *Work:* Baltimore Mus Art; Japan Found & Mus Mod Art, NY; Milwaukee Art Mus; Mus Fine Arts, Houston. *Exhib:* 20th Anniversary Show, Westbeth Gallery, NY, 90; XXI Sao Paulo Biennial (with catalog), Brazil, 91; Figureworks, Gomez Gallery, Baltimore, 95; Body Abstract, Korean Cult Serv, NY, 96; Diverse Visions//Photog Perspectives, Pittsburgh Ctr Arts, 97; solo exhibs, Nishimura Gallery, Tokyo, 89-93, Past Rays Photo Gallery, Yokohama, Japan, 94, Alternative Mus, NY, 95, Sarah Morthland Gallery, NY, 97 & Hiromitsu Morimoto-Vellum & Rice Paper, Tokyo, 98. *Awards:* Creative Artists Pub Serv Grant, NY, 75 & 79; Nat Endowment Arts Grant, 80; Minister of Educ Prize, 11th Int Biennial Prints, Tokyo, Japan, 80. *Bibliog:* Vince Aletti (auth), Voice choices, Village Voice, 3/29/94; Caran-Maries Zambo (auth), Arts displays offers diversity, Daily News, McKeesport, Pa, 5/8/97; Mary Thomas (auth), Photography exposed to new processes, Pittsburgh Post-Gazette, 6/21/97. *Mailing Add:* c/o Jayne H Baum Gallery 26 Grove St Suite 4C New York NY 10014

MORIMOTO, MASAO
SCULPTOR
b Okayama, Japan. *Study:* Sculpture Ctr Sch, NY; Art Students League of NY. *Exhib:* Hudson Valley Art Asn, Lyme Art Asn Gallery, Old Lyme, Conn, 2008; Park Ave Atrium, NY, Brookgreen Gardens, Pawleys Island, SC, 2009; Nat Sculpture Soc Ann Exhib, 2009; Audubon Artists, Salmagundi Club, NY, 2009; Am Artist Profl League, Salmagundi Club, NY, 2009; Allied Artists of Am, Nat Art Club, NY, 2009; Audubon Artists Online Ann Exhib, 2012. *Awards:* Elliot Liskin Meml award for Realistic Sculpture, Audubon Artists, 2001; Eleanor Gorman Meml award, Springfield Art League, 2004; Nessa Cohen Grant, Art Students League of NY, 2005; Agop Agopoff Meml award, Hudson Valley Art Asn, 2006; Alma Preede Meml award, Am Artists Profl League, 2006, Kathryn Thayer Hobson Meml award, 2007; Elliot Liskin Meml award, Allied Artists of Am, 2007; Marquis Whos Who in Am Art Reference award in Sculpture, Audubon Artists, New York, 2012. *Mem:* Audubon Artists; Allied Artists of Am; Hudson Valley Art Asn

MORIN, FRANCE
CURATOR
b Montreal, Que. *Study:* Montreal Univ, BA (art hist & film), 75. *Collection Arranged:* Canada-NY: From the Studios of Canadian Artists Living in NY, 84 & Icarus: The Vision of Angels, 86, 49th Parallel, Ctr Contemp Can Art, NY. *Pos:* Co-founder & co-ed, Parachute (comtepm art mag), 75-80; dir, Galerie France Morin, 80-83; dir & cur, 49th Parallel Ctr Contemp Can Art, 83-89; sr cur, New Mus Contemp Art, 89-95; independent cur, 95-. *Teaching:* Teacher art hist, grad prog, Concordia Univ, Montreal, 81-83. *Mailing Add:* One 5th Ave Apt 10A New York NY 10003

MORIN, JAMES CORCORAN
CARTOONIST, EDITOR
b Washington, DC, Jan 30, 1953. *Study:* Syracuse Univ Sch Art, BFA, 75. *Work:* Mus Cartoon Art, Boca Raton, Fla; Emerson Col, Boston, Mass; Ohio State Univ, Columbus. *Exhib:* Art Collectors Gallery, Coral Gables, Fla, 93; Morin of the Herald, Mus Cartoon Art, Boca Raton, Fla, 96. *Pos:* Ed cartoonist, Beaumont Enterprise & J, 76-77, Richmond Times Dispatch, 77-78 & Miami Herald, 78-. *Awards:* H L Mencken Award; Berruman Award, 96; Pulitzer Prize, 96. *Bibliog:* Dick Comer (auth), A baker's dozen questions for one of America's brightest young cartoonists, Cartoonist Profiles, 9/79; David Finkel (auth), Etching political, Miami Mag, 8/79; David Astor (auth), Great Year for Ed Cartoonist, Ed & Publ, 10/96. *Mem:* Asn Am Ed Cartoonists; Nat Cartoonists Soc. *Media:* All Media. *Publ:* Contribr, Best Editorial Cartoons of the Year, Pelican, 78 & 79; America's Political System, Random House, 79; Famous Cats, William Morrow, 82; auth, Jim Morin's Field Guide to Birds, William Morrow, 85; James Morin's Line of Fire, Fla Univ Press, 92. *Mailing Add:* El Nuevo Herald One Herald Plaza Miami FL 33132

MORIN, THOMAS EDWARD
SCULPTOR, EDUCATOR
b Malone, NY; Sept 22, 1934. *Study:* Mass Coll Art, BS (educ), 56; Cranbrook Acad Art, MFA, 57; Brown Univ, cert (basic metal), 66, cert (plastics technol), 67. *Work:* Richmond Mus Art, Va; Brown Univ, Providence, RI; Barn Gallery Assoc, Ogunquit, Maine; NY Univ, Oneonta. *Comn:* Cast aluminum high relief, Brown Univ, 64; bronze sculpture & bronze screen, Am Tube, 72. *Exhib:* Inst Contemp Art Invitational, Boston, 60; Whitney Mus Am Art Ann, NY, 61; 11 New Eng Sculptors, Wadsworth Atheneum, Hartford, Conn, 63; Contemp Box & Wall Sculpture Invitational, RI Sch Design Mus Art, 65; Univ Conn Mus Art, Storrs, 70. *Teaching:* Head dept sculpture, Silvermine Guild Artists Col Art, 58-60; assoc prof sculpture & head sculpture grad prog, RI Sch Design, 61-. *Awards:* First Prize & Best in Show, Silvermine Guild Artists, 60; First Prize, RI Art Festival, 63; First Prize, New Haven Art Festival, 66. *Mem:* Union Independent Cols Art; Am Foundrymens Soc. *Mailing Add:* 15015 Woods Edge Minnetonka MN 55345-2900

MORISHITA, JOYCE CHIZUKO
HISTORIAN, PAINTER
b Newell, Calif, 1944. *Study:* Northwestern Univ, Evanston, Ill, BA (painting), 64, MA (painting), 65, PhD (art hist), 79. *Work:* Michael Reese Hosp & Med Ctr, Chicago, Ill; Rockford Art Mus, Ill. *Comn:* Oil-vaporous nudes, Michael Reese Hosp & Med Ctr, 72. *Exhib:* Rockford & Vicinity, Ill, 1983, 1985-86 & 1994; Her Works, Art Ctr, Sound Bend, IN, 1989 & 1992; New Horizons in Art, Evanston, IL, 1990; Aldo Castillo Gallery, 1996; Womens Work, 1996, 2000, 2002, 2003; and others. *Collection Arranged:* Third World Art Exhib, Gov State Univ, 76 & 77; Women's Suffrage documents (over 100). *Pos:* Mem adv comt, Renovation of Chicago Pub Libr, 73; bd trustees, Third World Conf Found, Chicago, 82-. *Teaching:* Prof art, painting & art hist, Gov State Univ, University Park, Ill, 73-. *Awards:* Artists & Lectrs Grant, 74 & Craftsman in Residence Grant, 75, Nat Endowment Arts; Acquisition Prog Grant, 76, Artist Grant, 84, Ill Art Coun. *Mem:* Coll Art Asn Am; Chicago Artist Coalition; Turner Soc, London; Womens Caucus Art. *Media:* Oil, Mixed. *Res:* Study of J M W Turner at Petworth, 1802-1837. *Mailing Add:* 5000 S Eastend Ave Apt 6B Chicago IL 60615

MORISUE, GLENN TAKANORI
PAINTER, INSTRUCTOR
b San Francisco, Calif, Nov 22, 1940. *Study:* Art Inst Pittsburgh (Willis Shook Scholar), dipl(advertising illus), 63; Cleveland Inst Art, BA, 65. *Work:* Hansen Mfg Co, Cleveland, Ohio. *Exhib:* 34th & 41st Ann Midyear Shows, Butler Mus Am Art, Youngstown, Ohio, 69 & 77; Butler Mus Am Art, 97, 98 & 99; Cleveland Inst Art, 2000. *Pos:* Illusr & photo retoucher, various Cleveland com art studios, 65-79, graphic designer & art dir, 81-91; product designer & creative dir, Copper K Indust, Cleveland, Ohio, 91-95. *Teaching:* Prof life drawing & airbrush, Cooper Sch Art, Cleveland, Ohio, 79-80, dean educ, 80-81. *Awards:* City of Geneva, Ohio, Best of Show & First Place Painting, Geneva Grape Jamboree Art Exhib, 94; Friends of Andover Best of Show, Andover Libr Art Exhib, 95, 99; 1st Place Painting, Bay Crafters Art Ctr, Bay Village, Ohio, 99 & Eastern Counties Show, Lake Erie Col, Painesville, Ohio, 99; National Prize Winner, American Artist Drawing Magazine, Sept, 04; others. *Bibliog:* Designers, illustrators, photogr show - Cleveland, Commun Arts, Mag, 68. *Mem:* Meadville Coun Arts, Pa; Am Soc Portrait Artists; ANA Elect, Nat Acad, 2011. *Media:* Graphite, Oil. *Publ:* featured artist, American Artists Drawing Magazine, Sept, 04. *Dealer:* Tulip Tree Gallery Ashtabula OH; Glenn Morisue Internet World Wide Web; Kada gallery Erie PA; Lakeview gallery Saybrook OH. *Mailing Add:* 6201 1/2 Lake Rd W Ashtabula OH 44004

MOROLES, JESÚS BAUTISTA
SCULPTOR
b Corpus Christi, Tex, Sept 22, 1950. *Study:* El Centro Col, Dallas, AA, 1975; NTex State Univ, Denton, BFA, 1978; apprentice under Luis Jiménez, El Paso, Tex, 1978-79. *Work:* Albuquerque Mus, NMex; Mus Fine Arts, Santa Fe; Old Jail Art Ctr, Albany, Tex; Univ Houston, Tex; Mint Mus, Charlotte, NC; Dallas Mus Art, Tex; Nat Mus Am Art, Smithsonian, Washington, DC. *Comn:* Lapstrake, Tex Commerce Bank, Dallas, 1983; Inner Column Towers, Riata Develop, Houston, 1984; Zig Zag Inner Column, Siena Sq, Boulder, Colo, 1985; Interlocking, Nat Health Insurance Co, Dallas, 1986; Zig Zag Inner Column, IBM, Raleigh, NC, 1986. *Exhib:* One-person exhibs include Arthur Roger Gallery, New Orleans, 2000, 2002, 2004, 2007, LewAllen Contemp, Santa Fe, 2000, 2001, 2002, 2003, 2004, 2005, 2007, Barbara Davis Gallery, Houston, 2000, 2002, McClain Gallery, Houston, 2001, 2003, (Untitled) Gallery, Okla City, 2001, 2006, Dallas Mus Art, 2004; group exhibs include Group Sculpture Show, Wirtz Gallery, San Francisco, Calif, 1990; Escultura 1991, Expositum, Polanco, Mex, 1991; Adams-Middleton Gallery, Dallas, Tex, 1992; Carl Schlosberg Fine Art, Sherman Oaks, Calif, 1992; Arte Latino: Treasures from the Smithsonian Am Art Mus, traveling, 2000-07; Grand Opening, Art Ctr Corpus Christi, Tex, 2003; Art in the Garden, San Antonio Botanical Gardens, Tex, 2005, 2006. *Pos:* Bd dirs, Int Sculpture Ctr, Washington, 1988-97; bd trustees, Art Mus South Tex, Corpus Christi, 1993-96; bd commissioners, Nat Am Art Mus, Smithsonian Inst, Washington, 1996-. *Teaching:* Instr, Nat Mus Am Art Symposium, 1992; visual arts adv bd, Univ North Tex, Denton, 2001-. *Awards:* Visual Art Fel, Southeastern Ctr Contemp Art, Winston-Salem, NC, 1982; Matching Grant, Nat Endowment Arts, Birmingham Botanical Gardens, Ala, 1984; President's Citation Award, Univ North Tex, 1992, Martha Turner Award of Distinction, 2006; Am Inst Archits Award, 1995, Award of Merit, 1998; Artist Award, Multicultural Educ Ctr Arts, Houston, 1997; Colo chapter of Landscape Archits Award, 1999; Outstanding Citizen, Corpus Christi, Tex, 2004; Tex Medal of Arts Award, 2007; Nat Medal of Arts, 2008. *Bibliog:* Dorothy Chaplik (auth), review, Latin Am Art, fall 91; Joseph Cunniff (auth), review, Inside Lincoln Park, 6/24/91; Rafael Longorla (auth), A Conversation With Jesus Bautista Moroles, Cite Mag, spring 91. *Mem:* Tex Sculpture Asn, Houston. *Media:* Granite. *Publ:* Auth, Granite Sculpture, Meriden Gravure Co, Conn, 84. *Dealer:* McClain Gallery 2242 Richmond Ave Houston TX 77098; Untitled ArtSpace 1 NE 3rd Oklahoma City OK 73104. *Mailing Add:* 408 W 6th St Rockport TX 78382-4422

MOROSAN, RON
PAINTER, ASSEMBLAGE ARTIST
b Detroit, Mich, Mar 25, 1947. *Study:* Wayne State Univ, Mich, BFA, 71; Univ Iowa, Iowa City, MA & MFA, 73; Univ Mich, Ann Arbor, 74-75. *Work:* Univ Iowa Mus, Iowa City; Mus Contemp Art, Chicago; Detroit Inst Arts; The New Mus, New York; Martin Art Gallery, Muhlenburg Coll, Pa; NJ State Mus, Trenton; Mint Mus, Charlotte, NC; Mos Int, Japan. *Exhib:* Solo exhibs, Feigenson-Rosenstein Gallery, Detroit, 77 & 81, Robert Freidus Gallery, New York, 78 & Sheldon Ross Gallery, Birmingham, Mich, 90, Bemis Found, 93, Schloss Overhagen Gallery, Lippstadt, Ger, 94, New House Ctr Contemp Art, Staten Island, New York, 99, Andre Zarre Gallery, New York, 2000 & 2003; Deaocónotation, Connotation, Implication, Eisner Gallery, City Coll New York, 88; Snug Harbor Sculpture Festival, Staten Island, New York, 89; Art & Suitcase Will Travel, Gallery Gertrude Stein, New York City, 2000; Chánce of Meaning, Gallerie Schulgasse 18, Wiirzburg, Ger, 2001; Multi-Tasking, Islip Art Mus,

2005; Gallery Schulqasse 18, 2005; Case Studies, Katonah Art Mus, 2006; Head Up & Good Luck, Kunstwerk, Cologne, Germany, 2006; Andre Zarre Gallery, 2009; Loft Note Bene, Cadaques, Spain, 2010. *Teaching:* Vis lectr, Frostburg State Coll, Md, 77, Ill State Univ, Normal, 79 & Univ NC, Greensboro, 80; vis artist, Univ Nev, Reno, Univ Tex, Denton, Molloy Coll & Rockville Ctr, New York. *Awards:* Nat Endowment Arts Grant, 74; Grant in Sculpture, Louis Comfort Tiffany Found, 77; Ariana Found Grant, 83; Artists Fel Grant, 85; Residency: Bemis Found, Omaha, Nebr. *Bibliog:* New York Terminal Show, EVillage Eye, 83; Bill Zimmer (auth), Art & Suitcase Will Travel, NY Times, 97; George Tysh (auth), Alley Culture, Metro Times, Detroit, 2000. *Mem:* Coll Art Asn; Am Asn Mus; Am Asn Mus. *Dealer:* Gallery Gertrude Stein 56 W 57th St New York NY 10019. *Mailing Add:* 315 Eighth Ave Apt 16B New York NY 10001

MORPER, DANIEL
PAINTER, PRINTMAKER
b Ft Benning, Ga, Mar 26, 1944. *Study:* Univ Notre Dame, BA, 66; Sch Arts, Columbia Univ; Corcoran Sch Art, Washington, DC. *Work:* Cleveland Mus Art; Minneapolis Art Inst; Indianapolis Mus Art; Ft Wayne Mus Art; Shite Mus Art, Notre Dame. *Comn:* Tulsa Panorama, Facet Corp, Okla, 86; South Bend Aerial View, St Joseph Bank, Ind, 86; Washington DC Panorama (mural), Mobil Oil, Merrifield, Va, 90; Grand Canyon depiction, Texaco, White Plains, NY, 92. *Exhib:* 19th Area Exhib, Corcoran Gallery Art, Washington, DC, 74; one-man show, Shite Mus Notre Dame, 86; 1987 Biennial, NMex Mus Art, Santa Fe, NMex, 87; Home Again, Colombus Mus, Ga, 90. *Media:* Oil, Gouache; Etching. *Mailing Add:* c/o Robischon Gallery 1740 Wazee St Denver CO 80202

MORPHESIS, JIM (JAMES) GEORGE
PAINTER, EDUCATOR
b Philadelphia, Pa, Aug 26, 1948. *Study:* Tyler Sch Art, with Stephen Greene, with David Pease, BFA, 70; Calif Inst Arts, with Paul Brach, Miriam Schapiro & Allan Kaprow, MFA, 72. *Work:* Orange Co Mus Art; Phoenix Art Mus; Los Angeles Co Mus Art; San Francisco Mus Mod Art; Oakland Mus; plus others. *Comn:* The Fall of Icarus (mural), Loyola Sch Law, Los Angeles, 83-84; Painting, Broder-Kurland-Webb-Ufner Agency, Beverly Hills, 86; painting, Gannett co Inc, Washington, DC, 86; painting, John Wayne Airport, Costa Mesa, Calif, 90. *Exhib:* Los Angeles Artists, 76, Eight Artists, 76 & Young Talent Awards: 1963-1983, 83, Los Angeles Co Mus Art; solo exhibs, Tortue Gallery, Santa Monica, Calif, 83-84, 86-87, 90 & 92, Los Angeles Co Mus Art, Calif, 87, Deson/Saunders Gallery, Chicago, Ill, 87, 90 & 93, Littlejohn/Sternau Gallery, New York, 92, The Fate of Marsyas, Deep River, Los Angeles, Calif, 2001, Flora Lamson Hewlit Mus, Grad Theological Union, Berkeley, Calif, 2002, Cuts, Jan Baum Gallery, Los Angeles, Calif, 2005 & Da Vinci Art Gallery, Los Angeles City Coll, Calif, 2006; Concerning the Spiritual, San Francisco Art Inst, Time and Desire: Garboushian Gallery, Beverly Hills, Calif, 2012; Roses and Wounds, 2013; Flora LamsonHewlit Libr/Gallery, Graduate Theological Union, Berkeley, Calif, 2015; Jim Morphesis:Wounds of Existence, Pasadena Mus of Calif Art, Pasadena, Calif, 85; group exhib, Ancient Currents, Fisher Gallery, Univ Calif, Los Angeles, 86; Avant-Garde in the Eighties, Los Angeles Co Mus Art, Calif, 87; Abstract Expressionism & After, San Francisco Mus Mod Art, Calif, 87; Images of Death in Contemp Art, Haggerty Mus, Milwaukee, Wis, 90; Cruciformed: Images of the Cross Since 1980, Cleveland Ctr Contemp Art, Ohio, 92; Sanctuaries: Recovering the Holy in Contemp Art, Mus Contemp, Relig Art, St Louis, Mo, 93; Kardia, Tortue Gallery, Santa Monica, Calif, 94; Transformations: The Human Form in Diverse Contexts, Wignall Mus, Rancho Cucamonga, Calif, 94; Searching for the Spiritual, Hope Coll, Mich, 98; The One Chosen, Brauer Mus Art, Valparaiso, Ind, 2000; Surreal, Jan Baum Gal, Los Angeles, Calif, 2000; Modern Odysseys, Queens Mus, New York, 2000; invitational exhibs, Representing LA: Pictorial Currents in Southern Calif Art, Frye Mus, Seattle, Wash, Art Mus S Tex, Corpus Christi, Tex & Laguna Art Mus, Laguna Beach Calif, 2001, Fourth Florence Int Biennial Contemp Art, Fortezza da Basso, Florence, Italy, 2003, On the Walls: Murals, Armory Ctr Arts, Pasadena, Calif & Peace Tower 2006 & Whitney Mus Am Art Biennial Exhib, Day for Night, New York, 2006; A View from Within, Frederick R Weisman Mus, Malibu, Calif, 2007; Jim Morphesis: Anastasis, Biola Univ Art Gallery, La Mirada, Calif, 2008; Painting in Southern Calif: The 1980's Neo-Expressionism, Riverside Art Mus, Riverside, Calif, 2008; Psychedelic: Optical and Visionary Art since the 1960's, San Antonio Mus, Tex, 2010; Heads, Dolby Chadwick Gallery, San Francisco, Calif, 2011; La Raw: Abject Expressionism in Los Angeles 1945-1980, Pasadena Mus Calif Art, Pasadena, Calif, 2013; Overload, Garboushian Gallery, Beverly Hills, Calif; Letters from Los Angeles: Texts in So Calif Art, Jack Rutberg Fine Art, Los Angeles, Calif, 2014; Thresholds, MOCRA at 20 Part Two, The First Decade, Mus Contemporary Religious Art, Saint Louis Univ, St Louis, Mo. *Teaching:* Instr painting, Calif Inst Arts, Valencia, 75, Immaculate Heart Coll, 73-74, Los Angeles City Coll, 74-79, Otis Art Inst, 80-86, Claremont Grad Univ, 86-87, Art Inst Southern Calif, 96 & Pasadena City Coll, 97-. *Awards:* Nathan Margolis Mem Award Painting, Tyler Sch Art, 70; Louis Comfort Tiffany Found Grant Award, 85-86; Artist-in-residence, Claremont Grad Sch, Claremont, Calif, 87 & Fullerton Coll, Fullerton, Calif, 93; First Prize, Florence Int Biennial Contemp Art, 2003. *Bibliog:* Robert L Pincus (auth), Art as Artifact, Flash Art, summer 85; John Dillenberger (auth), Theology of Artistic Sensibilities, 86; Justin Spring (monogr), Jim Morphesis: Paintings, 91-92; Terrence Dempsey (auths), The Tragic Sense of Life: J Morphesis, Image, spring 94; John Williams (auth), Portraits of Passion, 99; Suzanne Muchnic (auth), Classical Kinship, Los Angeles Times, 2007; Peter Frank (auth), The 1980's Neo-Expressionism, Art Ltd Mag, Oct 2008; David S Rubin (auth), Psyche Delic: Optical and Visionary Art Since 1960, 2009; Peter Selz (auth), Heads, 2011; Michael Duncan (auth), LA Raw: Abject Expressionism in Los Angeles 1945-1980, 2012; Eve Wood (auth), Time and Desire, Art Ltd Mag, 4/2012. *Mem:* Coll Art Asn Am; Am Hellenic Inst. *Media:* Oil, Mixed Media. *Publ:* James Elkins (auth), On the Strange Case of Religion in Contemporary Art, Rutledge, New York, 2003; We'll Never Be Young Again, Tallfellow Press, Los Angeles, 2003; Gregory Wolfe (ed), Bearing the Mystery: Twenty Years of Image, WM B Berdmans Publ, UK; Peter Clothier (auth), Jim Morphesis: Wounds of Existence: Art Review, Huffington Post Art and Culture, February 24, 2015. *Dealer:* Littlejohn Contemp Gallery 41 E 57th St New York NY 10022; Garboushian Gallery 427 North Camden Dr Beverly Hill CA; Lawrence Asher Gallery 5820 Wilshire Blvd Los Angeles CA 90036. *Mailing Add:* PO Box 21306 Los Angeles CA 90021

MORREL, OWEN
SCULPTOR, PHOTOGRAPHER
b Amityville, NY, May 15, 1950. *Study:* Colgate Univ, 68; Skidmore Col, BA, 70; Cranbrook Col, 72. *Hon Degrees:* NEA, 1980; CAPS, 1981. *Work:* Centre Nat d'Art Pompidou Mus, Paris, France; Artpark/Nat Heritage Trust, Lewiston, NY; Madison Art Center, Wis; Prudential Bache Co, New York City, NY; First Nat Bank Chicago, Ill; Fifth Ave, Flatiron Dist, NY, 97; Saint Paul Western Sculpure Park, Minn, 98; New Mus Building, NY, 99; and many pvt collections. *Comn:* sculpture, Pub Art Fund, NY, 84; sculpture, Natural Heritage Trust, Lewiston, NY, 80; sculpture Dresdner Bank, NY; sculpture Sithe Energy Group, Oswego, NY, 96; sculpture BPM assoc, NY, 99. *Exhib:* Solo retrospective, Contemp Art Mus, Houston, 86, Madison Art Ctr, Wis, 88; solo exhibs, Walker Arts Center, Minneapolis, Minn, 88, Liz Galasso Fine Art, NY, 88, Jason McCoy, NY, 88, Philippe Staib Gallery, NY, 91; Phillippe Staib Gallery, New York, 94; Kapell Gallery, Greenport, New York, 2008; Galerie Ugo Ferranti, Rome, Italy, 2008. *Awards:* CAPS, NY State Coun Arts Grant, 79; Artists Fel, Nat Endowment Arts, Natural Heritage Trust, 80; CAPS, NY State Coun Arts Grant, 81. *Bibliog:* Michael McKinnon (auth), History of Western Art, London Visual Publ, 80; Tracking the marvelous, NY Times, 82; John Ash (auth) Morrel's Deleroius Structures, Art in Am, 91. *Media:* Steel, Aluminum. *Publ:* Public Art: A World's Eye View - Integrating Art into the Environment, ICO, 2008. *Mailing Add:* PO Box 182 Peconic NY 11958-0182

MORRELL, WAYNE (BEAM)
PAINTER
b Clementon, NJ, Dec 24, 1923. *Study:* Philadelphia Sch Indust Art; Drexel Inst-Famous Artist Sch. *Work:* Sloan Kettering Cancer Res Ctr, NY; Clark Mus, Carversville, Pa; Lahey/Clinic, Burlington, Mass. *Exhib:* Expos Intercontinentale, Monoco, France; Solo exhibs, Washington Co Mus, Hagerstown, 73, Bliech Gallery Carmel, Calif, 82 & Golden Web, Santa Fe, NMex; Grand Cent Gallery, NY; Mont Crest Gallery, Chattanoga, Tenn; Dassin Gallery, Los Angeles; Newman Gallery, Philadelphia; many others. *Pos:* Art dir, John Oldham Studios, Conn, 55-61; owner & dir, Wayne Morrell Gallery, currently; designer, Paris & Brussel-World Fairs, currently. *Awards:* Jane Peterson Prize, 69 & 74 & Coun Am Art Socs Award, 71, Allied Artist Am; Gold Medal, 70, Mariboe Award, 80 & Harriet-Mattson Award, 80, Rockport Art Asn. *Bibliog:* R Kolby (auth), A stand for nature, Am Artist, 3/72. *Mem:* Allied Artist Am; Springfield Acad Artist (coun, 60-61); Hudson Valley-Am Soc Veteran Artists; Rockport Art Asn. *Media:* Oil, Watercolor. *Publ:* Illusr, Readers Digest, 67; Yankee Magazine, 8/80. *Dealer:* Newman Galleries 1625 Walnut Philadelphia PA 19103. *Mailing Add:* One Squam Hollow Rockport MA 01966

MORRILL, MICHAEL LEE
PAINTER, EDUCATOR
b Springfield, Vt, Oct 23, 1951. *Study:* Alfred Univ, BFA, 73; Yale Univ, MFA, 75. *Work:* Carnegie Mus Art; Bayer Collection Contemp Art; Buchanan Ingersoll Prof Collection; Allda Corp; Mellon Financial Corp. *Comn:* Compass (site installation), Pittsburgh Int Airport, 93. *Exhib:* Solo exhibs, Siegfred Gallery, Ohio Univ, Athens, 80, Hewlett Gallery, Carnegie Mellon Univ, Pittsburgh, 81, Carnegie Mus Art Entrance Gallery (Forum Gallery), 82, Mattress Factory, 83, Jus de Pomme Gallery, NY, 85 & 86 & Concept Art Gallery, Pittsburgh, 88, 89, 91 & 94; Ten Americans, Carnegie Mus Art, 88; Pittsburgh in Chicago, Deson Saunders Gallery, Chicago, 90; Five Artists at the Airport: Insights into Pub Art, Wood St Gallery, Pittsburgh, 92; Degrees of Abstraction: Eight Pittsburgh Artists, Three Rivers Art Festival, Pittsburgh, 93; 25th Anniversary Exhib, Concept Art Gallery, Phila, 97; Allegheny Col, Meadville, Pa, 2000; Artists Image Resource, Phila, 2002; two-person show, Concept Art Gallery, Phila, 2000-01. *Teaching:* Assoc prof painting, Univ Pittsburgh, 76-. *Awards:* Ely Harwood Schless Mem Prize, Yale Univ, 75; Artists Fel, Pa Coun Arts, 81; Artist Residence Grant, Vermont Studio Ctr, Johnson, 96; Research Grant, Univ Phila, 2002. *Bibliog:* Kay Larson (auth), In brief, NY Mag, 11/86; Patrica Lowry (auth), Carnegie exhibit revives art of abstraction, Pittsburgh Press, 2/88; Mary Jean Kenton (auth), Lines, planes, colors & forms, new Art Examiner, 4/93. *Mem:* Coll Art Asn. *Publ:* Contribr, Mattress Factory: Installation & Performance 1982-1989, 91; Bayer Collection of Contemporary Art, Bayer Corp, 95; Mike May (auth), Artists Present, Pitts Mag, 2000; Kurt Shaw (auth), Artistic Reproduction, Phitts Tribune Rev, 2002. *Dealer:* Sam Berkovitz. *Mailing Add:* 1031 S Braddock Ave Pittsburgh PA 15218

MORRILL, ROWENA
ILLUSTRATOR
b 1944. *Publ:* Auth, The Fantastic Art of Rowena, Pocket Books, 83; auth, Imagine, France; auth, Imagination, Ger; auth, The Art of Rowena, Sterlig Publ Co, Inc, 2002. *Mailing Add:* 76 Lafayette Ave Coxsackie NY 12051

MORRIN, PETER PATRICK
ADMINISTRATOR, CRITIC
b St Louis, Mo, Oct 31, 1945. *Study:* Harvard Univ, AB, 68; Princeton Univ, MFA, 72. *Pos:* Dir, Vassar Col Art Gallery, 74-78; cur 20th century art, High Mus, 79-86; dir, Speed Art Mus, 86-2007; exec in residence, Univ Louisville, Ky, currently; dir, Ctr Arts & Cult Partnerships. *Teaching:* Instr art hist, Vassar Col, 74-78, Emory Univ, 80-86 & Univ Louisville, 87-. *Awards:* Nat Collection Fine Arts Res Rel, Smithsonian Inst, 73-74. *Bibliog:* The Advent of Modernism: Post-Impressionism & North American Art, 1986. *Mem:* Asn Art Mus Dirs (pres, 2003-04); Am Asn Mus. *Res:* Modern, American, contemporary & outsider art; Univ & mus relations; Hans Hofmann; contemp glass. *Publ:* Coauth (with Dr Eric M Zafran), Drawings from Georgia Collections: 19th and 20th Centuries (catalog), 81, 20th Century Paintings

from the Collection of the Museum of Modern Art: A Viewer's Guide (catalog), 82, Chase Manhattan: The First Ten Years of Collecting, 1959-1969 (catalog), 82, High Mus Art, Atlanta; Advent of Modernism: Post Impressionism and North American Art (catalog), High Mus, 86; Color Ignited: Glass 1962-2012 (catalog). *Mailing Add:* Dept Fine Arts Coll Art & Sciences Univ Louisville Louisville KY 40292

MORRIS, FLORENCE MARIE
DEALER
b Detroit, Mich, Apr 30, 1928. *Study:* Wayne State Univ, BS. *Pos:* Dir, Donald Morris Gallery, Detroit & New York, 58-. *Mem:* Art Dealers Asn Am; New Detroit (mem visual arts comt, 77-). *Specialty:* 20th century painting, sculpture and drawings; African sculpture. *Mailing Add:* 25915 Salem Rd Huntington Woods MI 48070

MORRIS, JACK AUSTIN, JR
MUSEUM DIRECTOR, ART DEALER
b Macon, Ga, Sept 29, 1939. *Study:* Univ SC, AB, with Edmund Yaghjian, Augusta Wittkowski & Catherine Rembert; Univ SC; Harvard Univ Inst Arts Admin. *Collection Arranged:* Arnold H Maremont Collection (20th Century Am & European Painting & Sculpture), 65; Ida Kohlmeyer (one-man exhib), 67; Jasper Johns Prints (with catalog), Harbor Town Mus, Hilton Head Island, SC, 71; Andrew Wyeth in Southern Collections, 78; Select Works by Andrew Wyeth: The Arthur and Holly Magill Collection, 79; Complete Serigraphs of Jasper Johns, 80; The John B Connally Collection, 88; The Robert Shelton Collection, 92; The Joan Bayer Collection, 2000; The John J McMullen Collection, 2003; The George Watford Coll, 2011. *Pos:* Curatorial assoc, Columbia Mus Art, 62-63, asst to dir, 63-65; exec dir, Greenville Co Mus Art, 65-80 & Greenville Co Art Asn, 75-80; mem exec bd, Metrop Arts Coun, 78-80; exec dir, Period Gallery West, 80-81; owner, Morris Fine Arts, 81-83; exec dir, Connally, Altermann & Morris Art Gallery, 83-87; co-owner, Altermann & Morris Galleries, Dallas & Houston, Tex, Santa Fe & Hilton Head Island, SC, 87-99; bd trustees, Mus Art Am West, Houston, 88; bd dir, Houston Art Dealers Asn, 90; owner, Morris & Whiteside Galleries, 99-; owner, Red Piano Art Gallery, 2002-; owner, Gallery at Palmetto Bluff, 2005-; founding partner: Scottsdale Art Auction, 2005; Charleston Art Auction, 2006; Licensed Auctioneer, Tex, 1985-2000; SC, 2000-. *Teaching:* Lectr, Kress Collection, Columbia Mus Art, SC, 62-65; instr drawing & painting, Richland Art Sch, Columbia, 64-65. *Mem:* Guild SC Artists (pres, 68); founder, SC Fedn Mus (vpres, 71-72, pres, 73-74); SC Arts Comn (chmn exec comt, 72-73); SC Arts Found (pres, 75-80); Houston Art Dealers Asn (vpres, 91); Arts Ctr Coastal Carolina (bd mem 2000-06, chmn 2005-06); and others. *Res:* Contemporary American art; Art of the American West; Southern paintings & sculpture. *Specialty:* 19th & 20th Century American Art; Western and wild life, sporting art. *Interests:* 19th & 20th century Am painting & sculpture. *Collection:* Contemp Am representational painting & sculpture. *Publ:* Auth, Contemporary Artists of South Carolina (catalog), 70; William M Halsey: Retrospective (catalog), 72; Western Collectors, 84-96; American Art Classic, 1986-2005; Texas Renaissance, 1989-2004; and others. *Dealer:* Morris Fine Arts. *Mailing Add:* 79 Baynard Cove Rd Hilton Head Island SC 29928

MORRIS, REBECCA
PAINTER
b Honolulu, 1969. *Study:* Smith Coll, Northampton, Mass, BA, 1991; Sch Art Inst Chicago, Post-Baccalaureate Studio Cert, 1992, MFA, 1994; Skowhegan Sch Painting & Sculpture, Maine, 1994. *Exhib:* Solo exhibs include Ten in One Gallery, New York, 2001, Shane Campbell Gallery, Oak Park, Ill, 2001, Santa Monica Mus Art, 2003, Susanne Vielmetter LA Projects, 2004, Renaissance Soc, Univ Chicago, 2005, Galerie Barbara Weiss, Berlin, 2006, Samson Projects, Boston, 2006, Karyn Lovegrove Gallery, LA, 2007; group exhibs include Post-Pop, Post-Pictures, Smart Mus Art, Univ Chicago, 1997; Cool Painting, Brian Gross Fine Art, San Francisco, 1998; Good Painting Makes You Want to Paint, POSTdowntown, LA, 1999; Sharing Sunsets, Mus Contemp Art, Tucson, Ariz, 2001; Sound, Video, Images & Objects, Donald Young Gallery, Chicago, 2001; Painting and Sculpture, Mark Moore Gallery, Santa Monica, 2004; Abstraktes, Galerie Barbara Weiss, Berlin, 2005; Figures in the Field, Mus Contemp Art, Chicago, 2006; Affinities: Painting in Abstraction, Hessel Art Mus, Annandale-on-Hudson, NY, 2007; Color Climax, James Graham & Sons, New York, 2008. *Awards:* Louis Comfort Tiffany Found Biennial Competition Artist Award, 1999; Guggenheim Fel, 2008. *Dealer:* Shane Campbell Gallery 1431 W Chicago Ave Chicago IL 60622; Galerie Barbara Weiss Zimmerstrasse 88-91 10117 Berlin Germany

MORRIS, SARA See Swetcharnik, Sara Morris

MORRIS, WENDY SUE
PAINTER
b Phoenix, Ariz, Feb 14, 1965. *Study:* Grossmont Jr Col, Assoc Arts, 1995; San Diego State Univ BA (magna cum laude), 1999). *Work:* Cedars Sinai Med Ctr, Beverly Hills, Calif. *Exhib:* Solo exhibs: Rib-Cage Series, Fischer Gallery, Palm Springs, Calif, 2005; Lung Series, Culver Plaza, Los Angeles, Calif, 2006; Group exhibs: Cerebral Candy, Infusion Gallery, Los Angeles, Calif, 2006; Group Show, Evidence Gallery, Los Angeles, Calif, 2007; Small Wonders III, Pharmaka Gallery, Los Angeles, Calif, 2007; Open Call LA (juried), Los Angeles Munic Art Gallery, Los Angeles, Calif, 2007. *Awards:* Kittredge Award, Splay Series, John Anson Kittredge, 2008. *Media:* Oil, Acrylic, Mixed Media. *Dealer:* Lev Moross Art Territory Int 964 N La Brea Los Angeles CA 90038

MORRISEY, MARENA GRANT
MUSEUM DIRECTOR
b Va. *Study:* Va Commonwealth Univ, BFA (interior design); Va Commonwealth Univ, MA (art hist); Fel, Colonial Williamsburg, Post Grad Studies. *Collection Arranged:* Japanese Art from the Mary and Jackson Burke Collection; Gold of el Dorado; Imperial Tombs of China; among many others. *Pos:* Cur educ, Orlando Mus of Art, Orlando, 1970-74, assist dir, 74-76, exec dir, 1976-. *Mem:* Asn Art Mus Dirs; Am Asn Mus. *Specialty:* vis art. *Mailing Add:* Orlando Mus Art 2416 N Mills Ave Orlando FL 32803

MORRISON, BOONE M
ARCHITECT, PHOTOGRAPHER
b Berkeley, Calif, Jan 28, 1941. *Study:* Stanford Univ, BA (archit), 62, BA (commun), 63; Yosemite Photog Workshops, with Ansel Adams, 71-73. *Work:* Honolulu Acad Art & Bishop Mus, Honolulu, Hawaii; State of Hawaii Collection; US Nat Park Serv; Nat Gallery Art, Washington, DC. *Comn:* Mural photographs, Kauai Mus, 71 & C Brewer & Co, 73; interior wall mural, State of Hawaii, Ka'u Hosp, 75. *Exhib:* Artists of Hawaii, 71-75; Mountains and the Shore, Honolulu Acad Traveling Exhib; Milolii, A Most Hawaiian Place Traveling Exhib, 75; Time on the Land Traveling Exhib, 76-77 & Am Photogrs and the Nat Parks, 81-83, Nat Park Serv. *Pos:* Owner-founder, The Foundry Gallery, Honolulu, 69-71; dir, Hawaii Photog Workshops, 71-; dir & founder, Volcano Art Ctr, Hawaii; pres & publ, Summit Press; principle & pres, Boone Morrison Archit, Inc, 88-; Fire Mountain Film, Producer, Pres. *Teaching:* Instr photog, Univ Hawaii, Manoa Campus, 69-71, instr archit, 70-72; instr photog, Hawaii Photog Workshops, 71-, State Hawaii Artists Schs, 74 & Kauai Community Col, 84; lectr, Univ Hawaii Ford Found, 80 & Art Dept, Univ Hawaii, Hilo, 82-84. *Awards:* Gold Medals For "Song of South Kona" San Francisco Int Film Festival, Houston Int Film Festival; Governor's Housing Commendation, 91; Preservation Honors Award, 93. *Bibliog:* Joan Murray (auth), Photography in Hawaii, Art Week, 73; Portfolio, 1979 Popular Photog Ann; The Photographers Eye (film), Hawaii, 80. *Mem:* Image Continuum Group; Am Inst Architects; Hist Hawaii Found; Nat Trust Hist Preserv. *Media:* Photography, Painting. *Publ:* Auth, Images of the Hula, Summit Press, 83; Song of South Kona (video), KHET Television & Hawaiian Air, 86; Legacy of Lia (video), 88; Mainstreet Hawaii (video), 88; articles, Hist Hawaii Mag, 93; columnist, Narrow Gauge Gazette mag, 95-; Sturgeous Sawmill, 2001; Video Caufornia Narrow Gauge, (video), 2003. *Mailing Add:* PO Box 131 Volcano HI 96785

MORRISON, EDITH BORAX
COLLAGE ARTIST, PAINTER
b New York, NY, July 14, 1926. *Study:* Studies at Woodstock Guild of Craftsmen, Woodstock, NY, 72; Empire State Coll, Long Island, NY, BA, 73; Long Island Univ, MA, 76; Studies at Silvermine Guild Art Sch, 86-. *Work:* Purdue Univ; Beth El Synagogue, Long Island, NY; Town of Oyster Bay, NY. *Exhib:* Solo Exhibs: Greenwich St Gallery, New York, Hillside Libr, New York & Picture This Gallery, Westport, Conn, 99; Silver Mine Art Guild, 6 & 9/2008, New Canaan Libr, 2009; Art in the Garden, invitational, Discovery Mus, Bridgeport, Conn, 99; Hecksher Mus, New York; Silvermine Art Guild, New Caanan, Conn; Kehler Liddell Gallery, New Haven, Conn, 2006; New Talent Competition Exhib, Fitchburg Art Museum, Mass, 2/17-6/1/2008; Kehler Liddell Gallery, 2008; Arts Coun of New House, 2009; Arts Coun New Haven, Conn, 2009; Kehler Liddell Gallery, New Haven, Conn, 2010-2014. *Teaching:* Guest lectr painting & sculpture, numerous clubs & orgns, 65-75; grad asst fine art, Long Island Univ, 75-76; pvt art tchr adult level, 76-85; art tchr, Floral Park High Sch, Long Island, NY. *Awards:* Award, Nat Competition, Purdue Univ; award, Nat Art League, Douglastown, NY; Purchase award, Biennial Competition, Purdue Univ, 69; 1st Prize, Ann Art Competition, Oyster Bay, NY, 60's; numerous awards, regional exhibs, 70-2002; Pres Award, Paint Clay Club, New Haven, Conn, 2008; Trustee Award, Art of the Northeast Silvermine, 2009. *Mem:* Silvermine Artists Guild; Arts Councili of Greater New Haven; Paint and Clay Club, New Haven. *Media:* Pen & Ink, Acrylic, Mixed Media, Drawings, Works on Paper. *Interests:* Antiques, tribal art & Alaskan artifacts. *Mailing Add:* 80 Cedar St Apt 217 Branford CT 06405

MORRISON, ROBERT CLIFTON
PAINTER, CALLIGRAPHER
b Billings, Mont, Aug 13, 1924. *Study:* Carleton Col, BA; Univ NMex, MA. *Work:* Harvard Univ Libr Print Collection, Cambridge; Ministry Art & Culture, Ghana; Rocky Mt Col, Billings; Int Coll Copenhagen, Denmark; Centre Medieval Studies, Oxford, Eng. *Comn:* Mosaic murals, Mont State Unemployment Comn, Helena, 61 & Lucerne Pub Schs Wyo; mural, Lockwood Pub Schs, Billings; Bicentennial mural, Yellowstone Co Courthouse, Billings; mural, Rocky Mountain Col, Billings. *Exhib:* Yellowstone Art Mus, 89; Pioneer Modernists of Mont Invitational, 90; CM Russell Mem Mus, 92. *Pos:* Ed, Rocky Mt Rev, 63-69; pres bd dir, Yellowstone Art Ctr, Billings, 64-65. *Teaching:* Dir art educ, Billings Pub Schs, 57-67; prof art, Rocky Mt Col, 67-90; artist-in-residence, Herning Folk Skole, Denmark, 83. *Awards:* Mont Artist-Teacher of Yr, Am Artists Prof League, 64; Best of Show Award, Landmarks Mont Exhib, 91. *Bibliog:* Montana Century, Falcon Press, 99; Writers Under the Rims, Parmly Libr Found Press, 2001. *Media:* Gouache, Oil. *Publ:* Translr & illusr, Maxims of LaRochefoucauld, 67. *Mailing Add:* 2815 Woody Dr Billings MT 59102

MORRISROE, JULIA MARIE
MUSEUM DIRECTOR, PAINTER
b Chicago, Ill, Sept 26, 1961. *Study:* Northern Ill Univ, Dekalb, BFA, 88; Univ Washington, Seattle, MFA, 90. *Work:* Appalachian State Univ, Charlotte Halpert Collection, NC; Cent Mich Univ, Mt Pleasant; WR Harper Col, Ill. *Exhib:* Halpert Biennial, Appalachian State Univ, 99, Saginaw Art Mus, 99; Fiber Art Int, 2002; one-women show, ACME Art Co, Ohio, 2002; traveling exhib, Comic Release: Negotiating a New Identity, Regina Miller Gallery & Carnegie Mellon Univ, 2003. *Collection Arranged:* Sari Khoury Retrospective (traveling exhib), 99; Home: A Reinterpretation, Ctrl Mich Univ, 99, Transformative Nature, 2000, Making a Mark, 2000, Natural Materials: Wood Fired Creamics, 2000, Subverting The Market: Art Work on the Web, 2001. *Pos:* pres, ARC Gallery, Chicago, Ill, 95-98; dir, Univ Art Gallery, Cent Mich Univ, 98-. *Teaching:* instr drawing/design, WR Harper Col, 91-98; instr curatorial practice Cent Mich Univ, 98-; instrnl asst prof, Ill State Univ, 2001-2002. *Awards:* Purchase Award, Halpert Biennial, 99; CMU Faculty Res Grant, 2000; Mich Coun for the Arts & Culture, 2000-01 & 2002-2003; Contemp Italian Art Faculty Res Grant, 2003. *Bibliog:* Chicago Tribune, 2001, Am Craft Mag, 2002, Fiber Art Mag, 2002, & Pittsburgh News, 2003. *Mem:* Coll Art Asn; Women's Caucus For Art. *Media:* Mixed. *Res:* Comtemp Art, Media Art and Curatorial Studies. *Specialty:*

Contemp Art. *Publ:* Wag, Wag, Wag (catalog essay), Univ Art Gallery, Central Mich Univ; Wood Sculpture, Encyclopedia of Sculpture, Fitzroy Publ; auth, review, Donald Sultan, New Art Examiner, 1-2/2002. *Mailing Add:* Cent Mich Univ Univ Art Gallery Wightman 132 Art Dept Mount Pleasant MI 48859

MORRISSEY, LEO
CONCEPTUAL ARTIST
b Philadelphia, Pa, Aug 22, 1958. *Study:* Marietta Col, Ohio; Univ Fla, BFA, 83; Mason Gross Sch Arts, Rutgers Univ, MFA, 85. *Work:* Flight 93 Nat Mem Archive, Nat Park Serv, Somerset, PA; Mus of Modern Art/Franklin Furnace Book Collection, NY; Taiwan Mus of Art, ROC, Taiwan, Republic of China; The Jane Voorhees Zimmerli Mus, New Brunswick, NJ; The Sharjah Art Mus, Sharjah, United Arab Emirates; Pilchuck Glass Sch Collection, Seattle, Wash; Boulder Mus of Contemp Art, A Sense of Place, Boulder, Colo; Brevard Mus of Art and Sci, Melbourne, Fla; Fulton Co Arts Council, Atlanta, GA; King Stephen Mus, Hungary; Glass Mus, Ebeltof, Denmark; Canadian Postal Mus, Ottawa, Can; The Noyes Mus, Educational Study Collection, Oceanville, NJ; The Ace Collection, Pvt Collection, NJ. *Exhib:* Jane Voorhees Zimmerli Art Mus, New Brunswick, 85; Experimental Art, Yamanashi Mus Art, Japan, 86; Sculpture Six, Bronx Mus Arts, NY, 86; New Yorkers in Spain, Togo Brunnes Gallery, Barcelona, 90; Gallery Vincent Bernat, Barcelona, Spain, 91; Z Gallery, NY, 91; Snapshot, Contemp Mus, Baltimore, Md, 2000; 6th Wexford Artist Books, The Workhouse Mus, Londonderry, Northern Ireland; The Non-informative Flyer Project, MH de Young Meml Mus, San Francisco, Calif, 99; The Sharjah Arts Mus, Sharjah, United Arab Emirates, 2000; plus others; Pierogi, Flat Files, Brooklyn, NY; Brent Sikkema Gallery, Postcards From the Edge, NY; Flight 93 Nat'l Memorial Design Competition, Somerset PA; Gallery Lelong, Visual AIDS Benefit, NY; Boulder Mus of Contemp Art, A Sense of Place, Boulder, Colo; Taiwan Mus of Art ROC11th Int Biennial Print and Drawing Exhib, Taiwan Republic of China; Monash Gallery of Art, Not Brick Chimmeys, Melbourne Australia; Exhib of Int Glass Art, Seattle WA; Gallery Lelong Postcards From The Edge, Visual AIDS Benefit, NY. *Collection Arranged:* Co-Curator w/Jackie Borsanyi, Book Art Show Scheduled for 2006, Brevard Mus of Art; in the eyes of the bewildered...(Things Printed), Brevard Mus of Art, 2005; Curator, Rutgers Sculpture, Rutgers Univ; Curator, Cuban Poster Show, Rutgers Univ. *Teaching:* teacher, Brevard Community Col, Melbourne, Fla; teacher, Indian River Community Col, Vero Beach, Fla. *Awards:* Pollock-Krasner Found Grant, 87. *Bibliog:* John Froonjian (auth), Noyes marks a year, 6/84 & Marjorie Donchey (auth), Morrissey self-portrait, 3/85, The Press, Atlantic City, NJ; Janson Kaufman, Watercolors and sculpture, Daily Tarqum, New Brunswick, NJ, 2/85; Art Smart, FLORIDA TODAY, Melbourne FL, August 30, 2002; Pilchuck Glass School, 24th Annual Auction, Catalog, Seattle, WA, 2002; This Glass has Class, FLORIDA TODAY, Melbourne, FL, May 28, 2003; Liberty Mus, Glass Now Auction, Catalog, 2004. Philadelphia, PA; Museletter, Brevard Mus of Art, Melbourne, FL, 2005; Mus Inside and Out, WMEL 920 AM, Radio Show Guest, 2005; American Art Collector, Book 4, Alcove Books, Berkeley, CA, 2005. *Mem:* Coll Art Asn; Community Coll Profs of Art and Art History. *Media:* All Media. *Publ:* Contribr, Books Build Bridges, Artist Bk, 86; The Search for Accidental Significance, Money for Food Press, 87. *Dealer:* Pierogi, Flat Files, Brooklyn, NY,; Catherine Person Gallery Seattle Wash

MORROW, TERRY
DRAFTSMAN, PRINTMAKER
b Austin, Tex, Oct 1, 1939. *Study:* Univ Tex, BFA; Univ Wis; Ind Univ, MS, study with Rudy Pozzatti. *Work:* Univ Tex, Austin; Tex Christian Univ, Ft Worth; Western Tex Col, Snyder; Odessa Col, Tex. *Exhib:* Appalachian Nat Drawing Competition, Boone, NC, 78 & 79; two-person exhibs, Sch Galleries, Houston Mus Fine Arts, 71 & Art Dept Teaching Gallery, Univ Tenn, Knoxville, 77; one-person exhib, Clara M Eagle Gallery, Price Doyle Fine Art Ctr, Murray State Univ, 73; and many others. *Pos:* Consult in litho printing, Tex Christian Univ, Ft Worth, 69, Western Tex Col, Snyder, 74 & San Angelo Col, Tex, 78; guest artist, ETex State Univ, Commerce, 79. *Teaching:* Instr painting & printmaking, Univ Pa, Philadelphia, 65-66; asst prof drawing & printmaking, Univ Chattanooga, Tenn, 67-68; assoc prof drawing, printmaking, Tex Tech Univ, Lubbock, 68-, prof art, currently; prof, ETex State Univ, 85-. *Awards:* Cash awards, 16th Ann Drawing and Small Sculpture exhib, 70 & Tri-State Art Exhib, 76; 12th Ann Del Mar Drawing & Small Sculpture, 78. *Media:* Pen and Ink; Intaglio. *Mailing Add:* Tex Tech Univ Dept Art Box 42081 Lubbock TX 79409-2081

MORSE, MARCIA ROBERTS
PRINTMAKER, WRITER
b Detroit, Mich, Mar 14, 1944. *Study:* Radcliffe Col, BA (cum laude), 66; Stanford Univ, MFA, 74; with S W Hayter, Misch Kohn, Adela Akers, Leonore Tawney, Walter Nottingham & Ed Rossbach. *Work:* Honolulu Acad Arts & Contemp Arts Ctr, Honolulu, Hawaii; Smithsonian Inst, Div Graphic Arts, Washington, DC; Int Paper Co, NY; Greenville Co Mus Art, SC. *Comn:* Ann gift print, Honolulu Printmakers, Hawaii, 77; prints, Hawaii State Found Culture & Arts, Honolulu, 78. *Exhib:* Collectors' Choice, Joslyn Art Mus, Omaha, Nebr, 68; New Am Graphics, Madison Art Ctr, Wis, 75; Solo exhib, Contemp Arts Ctr, Honolulu, Hawaii, 78; Textures, Contemp Artisans Gallery, San Francisco, Calif, 81; Nat Crafts, Greenville Co Mus Art, SC, 81; First Int Shoebox Sculpture, Univ Hawaii Art Gallery, Honolulu, 82. *Pos:* Freelance art writer, Artweek, 78-; art columnist, Honolulu Star Bulletin, Hawaii, 79-. *Teaching:* Instr printmaking, Univ Calif, Santa Cruz, 69-74; lectr printmaking & textiles, Univ Hawaii, 79-; instr papermaking, Honolulu Acad Arts, Hawaii, 80-. *Awards:* Craftsmen's Fel, Nat Endowment Arts, 81-82. *Mem:* Honolulu Printmakers (pres, 76-79, bd mem, 75-80); Hawaii Craftsmen (secy, 78); Surface Design Asn; Nat Soc Arts & Letters; Am Crafts Coun. *Media:* Handmade Paper. *Res:* Contemporary craft art; Japanese art both historical and contemporary. *Publ:* Illusr, Writing from the Inside, Addison-Wesley, 73; The Eight Rainbows of Umi, Topgallant Press, 76; auth, Nature distilled and distorted, 78 & auth, Language of materials, 81, Artweek; Filaments of the imagination, Fiberarts, 81. *Dealer:* The Source Gallery Folsom St San Francisco CA; Art Loft Honolulu HI. *Mailing Add:* Dept Humanities Honolulu Community Col 874 Dillingham Blvd Honolulu HI 96817

MORSE, MITCHELL IAN
DEALER, CONSULTANT
b Brooklyn, NY, Mar 10, 1926. *Study:* Himeji Univ, 45-46; City Coll New York, BBA, 47. *Pos:* Pres, Mann-Morse Graphics 68-69, Mitch Morse Gallery, Inc, 69-, M Morse Graphics, Inc, 69-91, Graphic Source I, 71-73; pres, Morse-Sun Art Assoc Inc, 72-75, Art Spectrum, 79-, China Spectrum Inc, 81-86, Art St Regis, 87-88; chief exec off, Morse Harris Art Group, Inc, presently; art consultant, 98-. *Awards:* Designer Official Seal, Village Lawrence, 67. *Specialty:* Artists agents; distributor painting, serigraphs on porcelain, original, limited S/N graphics. *Publ:* Auth, Graphics as an original art form, Designer, 8/73. *Mailing Add:* 9 Fox Hollow Rd Woodstock NY 12498

MORTENSEN, GORDON LOUIS
PRINTMAKER, PAINTER
b Arnegard, NDak, Apr 27, 1938. *Study:* Minneapolis Coll of Art & Design, BFA; Univ Minn. *Work:* Nat Mus Am Art, Washington, DC; Honolulu Acad Art; Philadelphia Mus Art; Walker Art Ctr, Minneapolis; Brooklyn (NY) Mus; also pvt collections; and others; Carnegie Inst, Pittsburgh, Pa; Tokyo Fuji Art Mus, Japan; Palace of the Legion of Honor, San Francisco, Calif. *Comn:* Green Giant Co, Cosgrove; Gov Karl Rolvag, Minn Hist Soc; membership print, Albany Print Club, NY, 1991; membership print, Rochester, NY Print Club, 2006. *Exhib:* Brooklyn Print Show, Brooklyn Mus, 76 & Eight West Coast Printmakers, 78; Plains Art Mus, Moorhead, Minn, 76 & 78; Boston Printmakers Nat Exhib, De Cordova Mus, 77, 79 & 83; Tokyo Cent Mus Art, Japan, 78; Ten West Coast Printmakers, RI Sch Design Mus; Rockford Int, Ill, 81; Passion & Process, Impressions from America's Master Printmakers, Louisville Visual Arts Asn, Ky, 2006; 60 Years of North American Prints, Boston Printmakers, 2007; and others. *Teaching:* Minn Art Mus, St Paul, Minn, Rochester Art Ctr, Minn & Minnetonka Art Ctr, Wayzaya, Minn. *Awards:* Juror's Award, Rockford Int, Ill, 81; Purchase Award, Boston Printmakers 35th Nat Print Exhib, 83; Donna Jenssen Award, 21st Nat Print & Drawing Exhib, Bradley Univ, Peoria, Ill, 87; plus others. *Bibliog:* Robert McDonald (auth), Four West Coast woodcut artists, Graphics, 8-9/79; Karen Haber (auth), Gordon Mortensen, Southwest Art, 11/86 & Am Artist, 4/88; Karen Haber (auth), Am Artist, 4/88; Kathy Freise (auth), NDak Horizons, spring 91; David Acton (auth), 60 Years of N Am Prints, 2007. *Mem:* Boston Printmakers; Philadelphia Print Club; Print Club of Albany; Los Angeles Printmaking Soc; Am Print Alliance; The Print Club of Rochester, NY. *Media:* Woodcut; Oil, Watercolor. *Dealer:* J Todd Galleries 572 Washington St Wellesley MA 02482; Concept Art Gallery 1031 S Braddock Ave Pittsburgh PA 15218; New Masters Gallery Carmel CA 93921; Davidson Galleries 313 Occidental Ave S Seattle WA 98104; Jane Hasler Gallery 2025 Hillyer Pl NW Wash DC; Amelie Art Gallery 797 E St 798 Art District; Jiu Xian Qiao Rd Beijing China. *Mailing Add:* 4153 Crest Rd Pebble Beach CA 93953

MORTON, ROBERT ALAN
EDITOR
b Jersey City, NJ, May 20, 1934. *Study:* Dartmouth Col, BA, 55. *Exhib:* Matthieu Ricard: The Compassionate Eye, 2005. *Pos:* Series ed, Time-Life Libr of Art, New York, 66-70; ed dir, New York Graphic Soc, Inc, 70-73; ed in chief, Harry N Abrams, Inc, 76-78, dir spec proj, 78-98; editor-in-chief, Aperture Found, 2002-03; Pres, Robert Morton Books Agency. *Teaching:* Western Conn State Col, 80-81; Int Ctr Photog, 82-83; Santa Fe Ctr for Photog, 2003-05; Photolucida, 2005 & 2007; Fotofest, Houston, Tex, 2006. *Awards:* Gold Medal, Soc of Illustrators, 98. *Res:* photography. *Publ:* Auth, Southern Antiques and Folk Art, Oxmoor House, 76; Mermaid and the Major, Abrams, 92; Leopold's Dream, Abrams, 93. *Mailing Add:* Box 16 Redding Ridge CT 06876

MOSCATT, PAUL N
PAINTER, INSTRUCTOR
b Brooklyn, NY, July 9, 1931. *Study:* Cooper Union Art Sch; Yale Univ Sch Fine Arts, BFA & MFA. *Work:* Univ Bridgeport, Conn; Yale Univ Art Gallery; Earlham Col, Richmond, Ind; Cincinnati Art Mus; Peale Mus, Baltimore, Md. *Comn:* Portrait, comn by Joseph Romano, 89; portrait, comn by Frank Toto, 89; portrait, comn by Fred Lazarus, 89; portrait, comn by Richard Kim Frank, 90; portrait, comn by S Reinholt; and others. *Exhib:* Solo exhibs, Portrait Drawings of the Am Indian, Md Inst Coll Art, 73, Interiors & Nudes, C Grimaldis Gallery, Baltimore, Md, 78, Heads, Faces & Portraits, Blue Mountain Gallery, NY, 90 & Studio Nudes, Blue Mountain Gallery, 92; Hassam Exhib, Am Acad Arts & Lett, 79; Pinchard Gallery, 99; Resurgam Gallery, Baltimore, 2000. *Teaching:* Instr painting & drawing, Univ Bridgeport, 62-64; instr painting & drawing, Art Acad Cincinnati, 64-66; prof painting & drawing, Md Inst Col Art, 67-, chmn, painting dept, 77-79, acting chmn, 90-92. *Awards:* Mellon Fac Enrichment Grant, 84; AICA Grant, 86; Md State Arts Coun Award, 99. *Mem:* Artists Equity Asn. *Media:* Oil, Acrylic. *Publ:* Bernard Chaet (auth), The Art of Drawing

MOSCH, DEBORAH CHERRY
EDUCATOR, PAINTER
b Sunbury, Pa, May 24, 1954. *Study:* Pa State Univ, BFA (painting), 77; Savannah Coll Art & Design, MFA (illus), 91. *Work:* Savannah Coll Art & Design Gallery, Ga. *Comn:* Mural, Miss Maggie's Morning Sch, Savannah, Ga, 92; mural, Garrison Elem Sch, Savannah, Ga, 93; cover, BellSouth Phonebook, Savannah, Ga. *Exhib:* Women's Works Exhib, Oglethorpe Ballroom, Savannah, Ga, 92; Traveling Exhib, South Gallery, Jacksonville, Fla, 93; Small Works Show, Exhibit A, Savannah Coll Art & Design, Ga; Savannah Coll Art & Design Fac Show, Bergen Hall Galleries, Ga, 98; Arts on the River, Ex Libris, Savannah, Ga, 98; Juries Alumni Show, Exlibris, 99; Small Works Exhib, Exhib A Gallery, 1999-2000; Mail Arts Exhibit, Lincoln Center, NY, 2000; Dog Days Exhibit, Atlanta, Ga, 2002; COD, Traveling Exhibit, 2003; Ga Music Hall of Fame Exhibit, 2003; Nancy's in ATL & Worthwhile in Charleston, 2004; Design House Exhibit & Artisan Connection, 2005; Mutations, Starland Gallery, Savannah, Ga, 2006. *Pos:* juror, Coastal Carolina Art Fair, 99-. *Teaching:* Prof foundations, Savannah Col Art & Design, 92-. *Bibliog:* Skirt Magazine, 9/2005. *Mem:* Found Art Theory & Educ; Ganoskin Orchid; Am Craft Coun. *Media:* Thread, Gouache. *Res:* Color theory

MOSEMAN, M L (MARK)
PAINTER, CURATOR
b Oakland, Nebr, Jan 23, USA, 1945. *Study:* Univ Nebr, BA, 69; Syracuse Univ, NY, MA, 72; Kans City Art Inst with M Monks, 78-89, pvt studio painting with Harry Fredman, 85 & with Phil Starke, 93; pvt sculpture instruc with Libby Ritter, Lincln Fox, 2009-2010. *Work:* Great Plains Art Mus, Univ Nebr, Lincoln; A.R. Mitchell Mus of Western Art, Trinidad, Colo; Sioux City Art Mus, Iowa; Homestead Nat Monument, Beatrice, Nebr; Sprint Corporate Art Collection, Kansas City, MO; Bone Creek Mus Agrarian Art, David City, Nebr; Mus Nebrk Art, Kearney, Nebr. *Comn:* painting, Northwestern Mem Hosp, Chicago, Ill, 97; painting, Coll of Agr, Univ of Nebr, 1998; painting, Overland Park Conv Center, Overland Park, Kans, 1999. *Exhib:* Pastel Masters Int Exhib, Saks Gallery, Denver, 95; Grand Nat Exhib, Salmagundi Club, NY, 96; Pastels only, Nat Arts Club, NY, 97; Art for the Parks Top 100 (touring exhib), USA Mus, Wyo, Mo, Utah, Mass, NC, 97-98; Membership Exhib, Albrecht-Kemper Mus, St Joseph, Mo, 98; Keepers of the Land, Birger Sandzen Mem Gallery, Lindsborg, Kans, 98; Realism Today, John Pence Gallery, San Francisco, Calif, 2000; Australian Am Int Pastel Exhib, The Hughes Gallery, Fullerton, Australia, 2002; Am Art in Miniature, Gilcrease Mus, Tulsa, Okla, 2002, 2004, 2006, 2007, 2008; Pastel Soc Am Exhib, Butler Inst Am Art, Youngstown, OH, 2003; Painting of My People, Dane Hansen Mus, Logan, KS, 2004; Solo Exhibit:Great Plains Art Mus (with catalog), Lincoln, NE, 2005; Bone Creek Mus Agrarian Art, David City, Nebr, 2008; Am Art Nat Invitational, A.R. Mitchell Mus, Trinadad, Colo, 2010; Homestead Nat Monument, Beatrice, Nebr, 2011. *Collection Arranged:* The Moseman Collection, Great Plains Art Mus, Lincoln, NE, 2005; At Bone Creek Mus of Agrarian Art: The Dale Nichols Collection, 2008; The Fortune Collection, 2009; The Mark & Carol Moseman Collection, 2009, The Luigi Lucioni Collection, 2012; Masters of Agrarian Art-1870-2010, 2012; Jean Terry-Upstate NY Farmstead, 2011 (exhibit/catalogue); Robert Lougheed-Fields of the Heart, 2012 (exhibit/catalogue); Remembering Dale Nichols-Transcending Regionalism, 2011 (exhibits/catalogue); other exhibits at Bone Creek Mus of Agrarian Art, David City Nebr from 2008-2012; Agrarian Spirit in the Homestead Era: Selections from the Moseman Coll, Homestead Nat Monument, Beatrice, Nebr, 2013-. *Pos:* Artist in residence, Living Hist Farms, Des Moines, Iowa, 97, Konza Prairie, Manhattan, Kans, 2000; founding bd mem, Bone Creek Art Mus, David City, Nebr; Chief cur, Bone Creek Mus Agrarian Art, David City, Nebr, 2008-2012. *Teaching:* Lectr archit design, Syracuse Univ, NY, 69-71; cur lectr, Bone Creek Mus Aqranan, 2008-2012. *Awards:* Pastel Soc Am Award, Allied Artists of Am, 11/95; Art for The Parks Top 100 Judges' Award Merit, Nat Park Acad Arts, 9/97; Am Artists Profl League Award, Hudson Valley Art Asn, 2000. *Bibliog:* Douglas Baughman (auth), Places in the Heartland, Am Artist, 12/98; Lewis Lehrman (auth) Master Painters of the World, International Artist, 2/99; Julie Osterman (auth) Artists to Watch, Southwest Art, 3/04. *Mem:* IAPS Master Circle; Sig Mem Pastel Soc of America; Sig Mem American Plains Artists; Master Pastelist, Mid America Pastel Soc. *Media:* Pastel, Mixed Media, Clay, Cast Metal. *Res:* Life and art of Dale Nichols; Masters of Agrarian Art from 1850-2010. *Specialty:* Agrarian Art. *Interests:* Donation of The Moseman Collection to the Great Plains Art Mus, Univ Nebr, Lincoln; Bone Creek Mus Agrarian Art, David City, Neb; guest cur, speaker, writer, juror and critic for art organizations and museums. *Collection:* Great Plains art; N Am Indian art; oriental art; arts & crafts pottery; Masters of Agrarian art: 1860-2010. *Publ:* contrib, Art for the Parks Top 100, Nat Park Acad, 97; The Best of Portrait Painting, N Light Bks, 98; Remembering Dale Nichols, Bone Creek Mus Agrarian Art, 2008; Robert Lougheed, Before Cowboys, Fields of the Heart, Bone Creek Mus Agrarian Art, 2012; Drawing & Sketching Secrets, Readers Digest Pub, 2012. *Dealer:* Am Art Resources 3260 Sul Ross Street Houston TX 77098; Streckton-Nelson Gallery 332 Poyntz Manhattan KS; The Guild 931 East Main Street Madison WI 53703; Moseman Studio/Gallery 1980 32nd Rd Brainard, NE 68632

MOSENA, DAVID
MUSEUM DIRECTOR
Study: Univ Tenn, BA, 69, MA, 71. *Pos:* dir rsch, Am Planning Asn, Chgo; mem staff, City of Chgo, 84-91, planning comn, 89-91, chief of staff, 91-92, aviation comn, 91-96; pres, Chgo Transit Authority, 96-97; pres, CEO Mus Sci and Industry, Chgo, 97-; mem visiting comn, physical sci div, Univ Chgo, 98-; chmn bd dirs, Univ Chgo Lab Schs; chmn comn, Chicagoland Landmarks; bd dirs, Exec Coun Metropolis 2020, After Sch Matters, Leadership Greater Chgo, SE Chgo Comn. *Mem:* Greater Chicagoland Chamber of Com; Econ Club Chgo. *Mailing Add:* Museum of Science and Industry 57th St and Lake Shore Dr Chicago IL 60637

MOSENTHAL, CHARLOTTE (DEMBO)
PAINTER, PRINTMAKER
b Cleveland, Ohio. *Study:* Case Western Reserve Univ, BA; Cleveland Inst Art, studied with Donald Stacy, Mus Mod Art; Gregorio Prestopino, New Sch, NY. *Work:* Exxon Inc, Florham Park, NJ. *Comn:* Poster Designs, Gallery 9, Chatham, NJ 82, 84 & 86. *Exhib:* Nat Asn Women Artists, 89-2005, Audubon Artists, NY, 89-94, Nat Soc Painters in Casein & Acrylic, 92-2003; Silvermine Guild Arts Ctr, New Canaan, Conn, 96; Gallaria Le Logge, Assisi, Italy, 96; Saginaw Art Mus, Mich, 98; Nat Acad Design, New York City, 2000; Smithsonian Inst, Washington, DC, 2000; Venezuelan, Consillate, New York City, 2001 & 2003. *Collection Arranged:* West Side Printmakers, Broadway Mall Gallery, NY, 89; Exxon, Inc, Florham Park, NJ. *Pos:* Ed, Newslett, Westside Arts Coalition, NY, 86-91; serials libr technician, Cooper-Hewitt Nat Design Mus, NY, 90-2003; chmn, printmaking jury, Nat Asn Women Artists, 93-95, historian, 97-98. *Awards:* Elaine & Jas Hewitt Mem Award, Audubon Artists, NY, 89; Best Show, Visual Individualists, NY, 89; First Prize Prints, Housatonic Art League, Conn, 90; S Magnet Knapp Award, Nat Asn Women Artists, 94. *Mem:* Nat Asn Women Artists; Nat Soc Painters in Casein & Acrylic; Washington Art Asn, Conn; NY Artists Equity Asn. *Media:* Acrylic, Canvas; Woodcut. *Mailing Add:* 230 E 15th St #2K New York NY 10003

MOSER, BARRY
GRAPHIC ARTIST, PRINTMAKER
b Chattanooga, Tenn, Oct 15, 1940. *Study:* Auburn Univ; Univ Tenn Chattanooga, with George Cress; also studied with Leonard Baskin & Jack Coughlin. *Work:* Brit Mus, London, Eng; Boston Athenaeum, Mass; Nat Gallery Art, Spec Collections, Washington, DC; Grolier Club, NY; Mus Fine Arts, Springfield, Mass; Newberry Libr, Chicago, Ill; Voices of Egypt, 2003; rep in permanent collections: Metrop Mus, British Mus, Harvard Univ, Princeton Univ, Libr. of Congress. *Comn:* principal works incl (illus) Alice in Wonderland, 1993 (Nat Book award for Design and illus, 1993) (publisher, illus) Moser-Caxton Bible, 1999. *Exhib:* Boston Printmakers, Waltham, Mass, 72; Solo exhibs, Berkshire Mus, Pittsfield, Mass, 73 & Boston Athenaeum, Mass, 76; Los Angeles Nat Print Show, Calif, 74; Libr Cong Nat Print Exhib, Washington, DC, 75-76; Hist Printed Books, San Francisco Pub Libr, Calif, 76; 4th Int Exhib Botanical Art, Hunt Inst, Carnegie-Mellon Univ, Pittsburgh, 77-78; R Michelson Galleries, Northhampton, Mass, 85-96. *Collection Arranged:* NY Pub Libr; Swarthmore Col, Pa; Harvard Univ, Cambridge, Mass; Univ Iowa, Ames (collection of illus bks); Smith Col, 76. *Teaching:* Head studio art, Williston Northampton Sch, Easthampton, Mass, 67-82 & RI Sch Design, 90-. *Awards:* Second Prize, Cape Cod Ann, 71; Award of Merit, New Hampshire Int, 74; Am Bk Award. *Bibliog:* Worcester Sunday Telegram, 11/86; American Traditions in Watercolor, Abbeville Press, 87; The Art of Seeing, Prentice-Hall, 88. *Mem:* Am Printing Hist Asn; Nat Acad (academician 1994-). *Media:* Ink; Wood. *Publ:* Contribr, The Tinderbox, Little, Brown, 90; The Guild Shakespeare, Doubleday Bk Club, 90; The Holy Bible, Oxford/Doubleday, 90; Appalachia, HBJ, 90; Messiah, HarperCollins (in Prep); and others; Illustrator: Appalachia, the Voices of Sleeping Birds, 1991 (Boston Globe-Horn Book award); And Still the Turtle Watched, 1991; Tales of Edgar Allan Poe, 1991; Ali Jadhu Storybook, 1992; Ariadne, Awake!, 1994; Call of the Wild, 1994; Cloud Eyes, 1994; Farm Summer 1942, 1994; Pilgrim's Progress, 1994; What You Know First, 1995; When Birds Could Talk and Bats Could Sing, 1996; Shiloh Season, 1996; Earthquack!, 2002. *Mailing Add:* c/o Cove Gallery Commercial St Box 482 Wellesley MA 02667

MOSER, JILL
PAINTER
Study: Brown Univ, BA, 78; Hunter Col, MFA, 81. *Work:* Mus Mod Art, New York; Metrop Mus Art, New York; Art Inst Chicago; Nat Mus Am Art, Washington, DC; Nat Gallery Art, Washington, DC; Mus Fine Arts, Houston, Tex; Yale Univ Art Gallery; Seattle Art Mus, Wash. *Exhib:* Solo exhibs include Drawings, Damon Brandt Gallery, NY City, 87, Paintings & Drawings, Black Greenberg Gallery, NY, 94, North Fork Drawings, Wynn Kramarsky, NY, 96, Topographies: Paintings, Danese Gallery, NY, 98, Inst Cultural Peruano Norteamericano, Lima, Peru, 99, Recent Work, Jan Maiden Fine Arts, Columbus, Ohio, 99, Works on Paper, Kate Ganz Gallery, NY, 2000, New Work, Kiang Gallery, Atlanta, Ga, 2001, Parings, osp gallery, Boston, 2004, Naming Game, Westby Gallery, Rowan Univ, 2005, Studio Caparrelli, London, 2005, Bentley Projects, Phoenix, Arix, 2006, Wade Wilson Art, Houston, Tex, 2007, 2009; group exhibs include Slow Art: Painting in NY Now, PS1, NY, 92; Black & White Drawings, The Mus Modern Art, NY, 93; Matter Matters, Proctor Art Ctr, Bard Col, NY, 94; Figurations Forward, Fine Arts Gallery, Univ RI, 96; After The Fall: Aspects of Abstract Painting Sicne 1970, Snug Harbor Cultural Ctr, NY, 97; Snapshot, Baltimore Mus Contemp Art, 2000; Painting Abstraction II, NY Studio Sch, 2001; Drawn From a Family: Contemp Works on Paper, Colby Coll Mus Art, Waterville, Maine, 2002; Define Line, Metaphor Contemp Arts, Brooklyn, NY, 2003; Masters of the Obvious, Hampden Gallery, Univ Mass, Amherst, 2004; New Prints, Int Print Ctr, NY, 2005; Opening Group Show, Wade Wilson Art, Houston, Tex, 2006; Action Precision, Lennon, Weinberg Inc, NY, 2006; Getting it 'right', Osp gallery, Boston, 2006; Au Courant, Bentley Projects, Phoenix, Ariz, 2006. *Pos:* Assoc dir, Materials for the Arts Program, NY City Dept Cultural Affairs, 81-91. *Teaching:* Adj prof, State Univ NY, New Paltz, 93, mentor, Empire State Col, 2003-06; lectr visual arts, Princeton Univ, 1994-2000; instr, Sch Visual Arts, NY City, 95, 2003-04; vis artist, NY Studio Sch, NY City, 89, Skidmore Col, NY, 92, State Univ NY, New Paltz, 93, Univ RI, 96-97 & 2002, Ohio State Univ, 99, Smith Col, 2000, Empire State Col, 2001-02, Princeton Univ, 2002, 2004, Univ Va, Charlottesville, 2005. *Awards:* Painting Fel, NY Found for the Arts, 92. *Dealer:* Wade Wilson Art 4411 Montrose Blvd #200B Houston TX 77006

MOSER, JOANN
CURATOR, HISTORIAN
b Chicago, Ill. *Study:* Smith Col, BA (art hist), 69; Univ Wis, Madison, MA (art hist), 72, PhD (art hist), 76. *Collection Arranged:* Atelier 17 (50 yr retrospective traveling exhib to five mus; auth, catalog), 77-78; Jean Metzinger in Retrospect, 85; Modernist Abstraction in Am Prints, 89; The Drawings of Joseph Stella, 90. *Pos:* Cur of collections, Univ Iowa Mus Art, 76-86, actg dir, 80-83; sr head cur graphic arts, Nat Mus Am Art, Washington, DC, 86-. *Awards:* Ford Fel, Dept Art Hist, Univ Wis, 71-73; Kress Fel, Nat Gallery Art, Washington, 75-76. *Mem:* Coll Art Asn; Print Coun Am; Am Asn Mus. *Res:* Prints and twentieth century art. *Publ:* Auth, The impact of Stanley William Hayter on post-war American art, Archives Am Art J, Vol 18, No 1; Jiri Anderle, 84; Visual Poetry: The Drawings of Joseph Stella, 88; Singular Impressions: The Monotype In America, 97; Singular Impressions: The Monotype in America, 97. *Mailing Add:* 5203 Benton Ave Bethesda MD 20814

MOSER, KENNA J
PAINTER
b Can, 1964. *Study:* Queens Univ, Kingston, Ont, BFA, 88. *Work:* San Jose Mus Art, Calif; Wash State Arts Comn, Tacoma; 3M Corp, Minneapolis, Minn; Walker Richer Quinn, Seattle; Bellevue Club, Wash. *Comn:* Wine Label Imagery Series, Benziger Winery, Calif, 96; Playing Card-Game of Chance, Perimeter Gallery, Chicago, 97; installation, Swedish Hosp, Seattle, 99. *Exhib:* Icons in Contemp Art, Calif Craft Mus, San Francisco, 93; In the Spirit of Nature, San Jose Mus Art, Calif, 94; From the Land, Tacoma Art Mus, Wash, 95; Concept in Form, Palo Alto Cult Ctr, Calif, 95;

Small Wonders, San Francisco Folk & Craft Mus, Calif, 96; drawings, Triton Mus Art, Santa Clara, Calif, 96; Series Series Series, Rockford Coll Art, Ill, 97; The Idea of the Sacred, Ctr Arts & Religion, Washington, DC, 98. *Awards:* Painting Fel, Arts Coun Santa Clara Co, 92 & Nat Endowment Arts, 94. *Bibliog:* Kathryn Shields & Chris Bruce (auth), Within Sight, Nat Endowment Arts, 95; Joe Shannon (auth), Kenna Moser at Linda Hodges, Art News, 98. *Media:* Beeswax, Oil. *Dealer:* Gallery A 300 W Superior Suite 100 Chicago IL 60610

MOSES, FORREST (LEE), JR
PAINTER, PRINTMAKER
b Danville, Va, May, 1934. *Study:* Washington & Lee Univ, BA, 56; Pratt Inst, 60-62. *Work:* Huntington Gallery, Univ Tex, Austin; Ill State Univ, Normal; Mus Fine Arts, Santa Fe, NMex; Citibank, New York; WR Grace & Co, Dallas; Mint Mus, Charlotte; Chicago Hilton, Ill; Roswell Mus, NMex. *Exhib:* Solo exhibs, Tibor de Nagy Gallery, 82 & 84, Marvin Seline Gallery, Austin, Tex, 85, Munson Gallery, 86-87, 89 & 92, Peregrine Press, Dallas, Tex, 86, Sheldon Mem Mus Gallery, Lincoln, Nebr, 86, Watson Gallery, Houston, Tex, 86 & Gumps Gallery, San Francisco, Calif, 89, Lew Allen Contemp, 2007; group exhibs, Contemp Landscape Painting, Okla Art Ctr, Oklahoma City, 75; Am Artists as Print Makers, 23rd Nat Print Exhib, Brooklyn Mus, New York, 83; Contemp Western Landscape, Mus Art Am West, Houston, Tex, 84; Egypt, Munson Gallery, Santa Fe, NMex, 85; James Fisher Gallery, Denver, Colo, 85; Monotypes, James Robischon Gallery, Denver, Colo, 85; Contemp Am Monotypes, Chrysler Mus, Norfolk, Va, 85. *Teaching:* Instr drawing, Pratt Inst, 61-62; instr drawing & watercolor, Univ Houston, 69. *Awards:* Selected Juror's Award & Mus Purchase, Mus NMex Biennial, 74. *Media:* Oil; Monotype. *Dealer:* Lewallen Contemporary 129 W Palace Ave Santa Fe NM 87501; 225 Canyon Rd Santa Fe NM 87501. *Mailing Add:* 837 El Caminito St Santa Fe NM 87501-2842

MOSES, JENNIFER
EDUCATOR, ADMINISTRATOR
Study: Tyler Sch of Art, Temple Univ, BFA, 1983; Indiana Univ, Bloomington, MFA (painting), 1987; studied at Bennington Col, Vermont, 1978-80, Temple Abroad, Rome, Italy, 1980-81, L'Academia D'arte, Roma, Italia, 1981. *Exhib:* Solo exhibitions include Precious Worlds, Pine Manor Col, Chestnut Hill, Mass, 1986, Clark Gallery, Lincoln, Mass, 1999, WaterMedia, Kingston Gallery, Boston, 2009, Spellbound, Roswell Mus of Art, NMex, 2011, Water Media, Kingston Gallery, Boston, 2012 and several others; Group exhibitions include Symbolism/Animals As Metaphor, Clark Gallery, Lincoln, Mass, 1985, Small Works Salon, Rike Center Gallery, univ Dayton, Ohio, 1991, Invitational Drawing Exhibition, Smith Col, Northampton, Mass, 1996, Boston Drawing Project, Inaugural Exhibition, Bernard Toale Gallery, Boston, 2002-, Group Exhibition, Naga Gallery, Boston, Mass, 2005, 2007, The Artist Revealed: 2010 Studio Faculty Exhibition, Univ NH, 2010, Still, Group Show, Kingston Gallery, 2011, Rice Polak Gallery, Provincetown, Mass, 2012 and several others. *Collection Arranged:* Collections include the Anderson Mus, Roswell, NMex, Decordova Mus, Lincoln, Mass, and Univ NH Mus, Durham. *Pos:* bd trustee Boston Visual Sch, 1994; illustrator for Hotwired, an online publication of the novel, As Francesca, San Francisco, 1995; mem bd, The Artist's Building, 300 Summer Street, Boston, 1996-99, 2009-10; co-coordinator, Fort Point Cultural Coalition's Public Art Series, Boston, 2001-02; staff mem working on ArtRescue, 2003; mem Fort Point Cultural Com Public Art Series III Review Panel, 2004; juror Fort Point Public Art Open Studios, 2008,; bd trustee Fort Point Cultural Coalition, 2008-10. *Teaching:* Asst prof, Southwest Missouri State Col, Springfield, Missouri, 1987-88; instructor, New England Sch of Art and Design, Boston, 1988-89; instructor, Massachusetts Col of Art, Boston, 1989-95; assoc prof art, Univ New Hampshire, 1995-, chair art and art history dept, currently. *Awards:* Recruitment Fellowship, Graduate Sch, Indiana Univ, 1985; Summer Faculty Fellowship, Univ NH Grad Sch, 1991; Faculty Fellowship, Univ NH, 1996; Roswell Artist in Residency Fellowship, 2011; Yaddo Artist Residency Fellowship, 2012; and several other grants. *Mailing Add:* 300 Summer St #43 Boston MA 02210

MOSLEY, JOSHUA
ANIMATOR
Study: St Louis Community Coll, AA (fine art), 1994; Sch Art Inst Chicago, BFA, 1996, MFA (art & technology), 1998. *Exhib:* Solo exhibs include Inst Contemp Art, Philadelphia, 2001, Donald Young Gallery, Chicago, 2002, 2004, 2007, Mus Gegenwartskunst, Basel, 2003, New Media Wall, Tufts Univ Art Gallery, 2005, Mus Mod Art, New York, 2007, Mod Art Ft Worth, 2008, Mus Contemp Art San Diego, 2008; group exhibs include New Media/New Faces/New Directions, Arthur Ross Gallery, Univ Pa, Philadelphia, 2000; Sound, Video, Film, Donald Young Gallery, Chicago, 2000, Drawings, 2003, Rodney Graham, Gary Hill, Joshua Mosley, 2003; Dual Identities, Philadelphia Art Alliance, 2002; Nuit Blanche/Nuit Vidéo, Paris, 2002; The Other Tradition: Alternative Representations & Eccentric Abstraction in Philadelphia 1967-2003, Rosenwald Wolf Gallery, Univ Arts, Philadelphia, 2003; Seriously Animated, Philadelphia Mus Art, 2003; Sesiones Animades, Mus Nat Ctr Art Reina Sofia, Madrid, 2005; Think with the Senses-Feel with the Mind: Art in the Present Tense, Venice Biennale, 2007. *Teaching:* Instr, Sch Art Inst Chicago, 1998-2000; assoc prof fine arts, Univ Pa Sch Design, Philadelphia, 2000-. *Awards:* A4 Arnhem Archit Animation Award, 2000; Pa Coun Arts Fel in Media Arts, 2001 & 2007; Louis Comfort Tiffany Found Award, 2003; Pew Fel Arts, 2005; Joseph H Hazen Rome Prize in Visual Arts, Am Acad Rome, 2006. *Dealer:* Donald Young Gallery 933 W Washington Blvd Chicago IL 60607. *Mailing Add:* UPenn Addams Hall 200 S 36th St Philadelphia PA 19104

MOSLEY, THADDEUS
SCULPTOR
b Pittsburgh, 1926. *Exhib:* Solo exhibs include Carnegie Mus Art, Pittsburgh, 1997 & Pittsburgh Ctr Arts, 2002; group exhibs include Ann Invitational Exhib Contemp Art, Nat Acad Mus, New York, 2008. *Pos:* Bd dirs, August Wilson Ctr African Am Cult. *Awards:* Artist of Yr Award, Pittsburgh Ctr Arts, 1978, Cult Award, 2000, Serv to the Arts Award, 2002; Gov's Award for Pa Artist of Yr, 1999. *Bibliog:* David Lewis (auth), Thaddeus Mosley: African-American Sculptor, Univ Pittsburgh Press, 1997. *Mem:* Pittsburgh Soc Sculptors; Soc Contemp Craft (bd dirs); Associated Artists Pittsburgh (bd dirs). *Media:* Wood. *Mailing Add:* 1112 Sherman Ave Pittsburgh PA 15212

MOSS, JOE (FRANCIS)
SCULPTOR, PAINTER
b Kincheloe, WVa, Jan 26, 1955. *Study:* WVa Univ, AB, 51, MA, 60. *Work:* Del Art Mus, Riverfront Develop Corp, Wilmington, Del; St Louis Art Mus, Mo; Sci & Cult Ctr, Charleston, WVa; Huntington Mus, WVa; and others. *Comn:* Sound Sculpture, Bloomsburg Coll, Pa, 72; Sound sculpture, Shepherd Coll, Shepherdstown, WVa, 78; Sound sculpture, Martin Fine Villa, Miami, Fla, 80; Sound sculpture, Cedar Crest Coll, Allentown, Pa, 80; Cross, Presbyterian Church, Morgantown, WVa; and others. *Exhib:* Members Exhib, Mus Mod Art, NY, 65; JB Speed Mus, Louisville, Ky, 77, Madison Square Park, NY, 80; Kunsthalle, Hamburg, Fed Repub Ger, 85; Monocle, Mass Inst Technol, 85 & 94; Boston Mus Sci, 87; Yeshiva Univ, NY, 88-89; and others. *Pos:* Fel, Ctr Advan Visual Studies, Mass Inst Technol, Cambridge, 73, 85 & 87-88. *Teaching:* Assoc prof art, WVa Univ, 60-70; vis prof, Univ Md, 67; prof sculpture, Univ Del, 70-98 & prof emer, 2001-. *Awards:* Prize for Environ Design, Three Rivers Arts Festival, Pittsburgh, 68; Sculpture Award, Appalachian Corridors Exhib, Charleston, WVa, 70; Fel, Nat Endowment Arts, 80-81. *Bibliog:* Alan Gerstle (auth), Joe Moss, Arts Mag; James Kelly (auth), The Sculptural Idea, Third Ed; Joe Moss, Sound Sculptor, CNN Sci Week, 88. *Media:* Metal, Miscellaneous Media; Oil, Acrylic. *Mailing Add:* 801 Valley Rd Newark DE 19711

MOSS, KAREN CANNER
PAINTER, EDUCATOR
b Boston, Mass, May 2, 1944. *Study:* RI Sch Design, BFA, 66; Tufts Univ, Boston Mus Sch, MFA, 74. *Work:* Boston Mus Fine Arts, Mass; Addison Gallery Am Art, Andover, Mass; Vassar Coll Art Gallery, Poughkeepsie, NY; Rose Art Mus, Brandeis Univ, Waltham, Mass; Bristol Community Col, Fall River, Mass. *Comn:* Outdoor mural, Mass Bay Transportation Authority, Boston, Mass, 77; ceramic tile mural, First Nat Bank Boston, 83. *Exhib:* Edinburgh Festival, Queens Col, Scotland, 74; Works on Paper, Fogg Mus, Harvard Univ, Cambridge, Mass, 74; Primitive Presence in the '70's, Vassar Col, Poughkeepsie, NY, 75; Boston Watercolor Today, Boston Mus Fine Arts, 76; Solo exhib, Addison Gallery Am Art, Andover, Mass, 76, Kathryn Markel Gallery, NY, 83; Contemp Issues: Works on Paper by Women (traveling), Los Angeles, Salt Lake City & Houston, 77; Prints & Drawings, Mus Mod Art, NY, 78; 12th ann drawing exhib; Images of the New World, Mus of Our Nat Heritage, Lexington, MA, 2000. *Pos:* Artist, trustee & rep, Boston Visual Artists Union, Inst Contemp Art, Boston, Mass, 71-73. *Teaching:* Instr drawing, Boston Mus Fine Arts Sch, 83. *Awards:* Blanche E Coleman Award, 72; First Prize for Watercolor, Silvermine Art Guild, 73; Finalist in State, Mass Arts & Humanities Found, 76-77; Bunting Finalist, 82. *Bibliog:* Wolf Kahn (auth), The subject matter in new realism, Am Artist, 11/79; Pam Allara (auth), Boston: shedding its inferiority complex, Art News, 11/79; Sarah McFadden (auth), Report from Boston, Art Am, 5/83. *Mem:* Boston Visual Artists Union. *Media:* Mixed Media Collage. *Publ:* New American Painting, Vol 26, 3/2000; Art New England, Apr/May 2001. *Mailing Add:* 14 Elm St Brookline MA 02445

MOSS, TOBEY C
ART DEALER, HISTORIAN
b Chicago, Ill, June 1, 1928. *Study:* Univ Ill, Champaign-Urbana; Univ Calif, Los Angeles, AA, 47. *Collection Arranged:* Helen Lundeberg Since 1970 (cur), Palm Springs Mus, 83; Colorforms (auth, catalog), Gallery-Security Pacific, 85; Helen Lundeberg, Sesnon Art Gallery, Univ Calif, Santa Cruz, 88; Nora Eccles Harrison Mus of Art; Peter Shire, Marks Allot Fountain, 2006. *Pos:* Dir, Tobey C Moss Gallery, Los Angeles, currently; consult to pvt, mus & corp collections. *Teaching:* instr, series: print connoisseurship. *Mem:* Coll Art Asn; Art Table; Women's Caucus Art; Los Angeles Co Mus Art Graphics Art Coun; Art Dealers Asn Calif; Int Fine Print Dealer Asn. *Res:* Modernist Californian artists working 1920-1960. *Specialty:* Modernism, Post-Surrealism, Hard-Edge; Lorser Feitelson, Helen Lundeberg, Peter Krasnow, Knud Merrild, Oskar Fischinger, S Macdonald Wright, Dorr Bothwell, Emerson Woelffer, Ynez Johnston, John McLaughlin, Palmer Schoppe, John Bernhardt, Gordon Wagner, Jean Charlot, William Dole, Jules Engel, David P Levine, Betye Saar, Peter Shire, George Herms & Lithography workshop of Lynton R Kistler. *Interests:* Tamarind lithography workshop. *Publ:* Auth, 2002 Gallery Catalog of Essays: Tobey C. Moss Gallery: Paintings, Sculptures; auth, Tobey C. Moss Gallery: Paper Passion, 2003; auth, California Gold, 2005; and others. *Mailing Add:* Tobey C Moss Gallery 7321 Beverly Blvd Los Angeles CA 90036-2534

MOSS-VREELAND, PATRICIA
PAINTER, DRAFTSMAN
b New York, NY, July 26, 1951. *Study:* Philadelphia Coll Art, BFA, 73; Tyler Sch Art, Philadelphia, 73. *Work:* Norton Mus Art, West Palm Beach, Fla; Chicago Art Inst; Beaver Co Arcadia Univ, Glenside, Pa; Atlantic Richfield Co, Los Angeles; Bell Tel Labs, NJ; Fed Reserve, Philadelphia, Pa; Philadelphia Mus Art, Pa; Arcadia Univ, Glenside, Pa. *Comn:* Numerous private portrait commissions; mural, Philadelphia Mus Art, 89; handpainted ceramic mural, pvt residence, 91; Holocaust Mus, Houston, Tex, 96; Art in Science XIV Univ City Science Center, Esther Klein Gallery, Phil, PA. *Exhib:* Solo-shows, Marian Locks Gallery, Philadelphia, 79, 83, 88, & 90 & Arronson Gallery, Univ Arts, Philadelphia, 93; Contemp Drawings (with catalog), Philadelphia Acad Fine Arts & Philadelphia Mus Art, 79; Made in Philadelphia III, Inst Contemp Art, Philadelphia, 80; Am Drawings: Black & White, Brooklyn Mus, 80; New Acquisitions, Philadelphia Mus Art, 86; Nat Group Invitational, Pindar Gallery, NY, 89; Contemp Women Artists Int Juried Exhib, Brussels, Belgium, 89; Julius Bloch Mem Exhib, Pertaining to Philadelphia, Philadelphia Mus Art, Pa, 92; Philadelphia Houston Exchange, Inst Contemp Art, Univ Pa; Memory Connections Matter (with

catalog), Ester Klein Gallery, Univ City Sci Ctr, Philadelphia, Pa, 2000; Solo show, Univ of St Thomas Frey Libr, St Paul, MN, 2004; Libro Curio, Nat Archives, Phila, Pa. *Collection Arranged:* Milwaukee Mus of Art Stephens Collections Little Rock, AR; Library of Congress, Wash, DC. *Awards:* Drucker Painting Award, Cheltenham Ann Painting Exhib, Pa, 77; Purchase Award, Ann Juried Exhib, Arcadia Univ, Pa, 86; Philadelphia Mus Art Award, Ann Juried Show, Cheltenham Art Ctr, 86; Spectrum Int Award in Design, 97; Honor Award in Design, Am Inst Architects. *Bibliog:* Articles, Philadelphia Inquirer, 75, 77, 86, 88 & 2000, Archit Mag, 96, Sculpture Mag, 96, Houston, Chronicle, 97, Baltimore Sun, 2000; On tour in Philadelphia, Am Artist, 80. *Mem:* Coll Art Asn. *Media:* Pencil, Oil, Mixed Media. *Mailing Add:* 2229 Bainbridge St Philadelphia PA 19146

MOSSER, CYNTHIA
PAINTER
Study: Whitman Col, BA (art hist), 92; Pratt Inst, Brooklyn, 96-98. *Exhib:* Solo exhibs include The Globe Coffeehouse & Bookstore, Prague, Czech Republic, 98, Studio Exhib, Prague, 99, Mazama Clubrooms Gallery, Portland, Ore, 99, Metrop Art Studio, Portland, 2001, Light Design Ctr, Portland, 2002, Marghitta Feldman Gallery, Portland, 2003, 2005, Washington State Univ, Vancouver, Washington, 2004, Augen Gallery, Portland, 2006; group exhibs include Urban Artists Guild Exhib, Metrop Art Studio, Portland, 2000, Generic Art Generic City, 2000; Open Walls Exhib, Portland Inst Contemp Art, 2000; Gender Symposium Exhib, Lewis and Clark Col, Portland, 2000; Lake Oswego Festival of Arts, Ore, 2001, 2002, 2003; Newberg Arts Festival, Ore, 2001; New Artists Exhib, Portland Art Mus Rental Sales Gallery, 2002, Fall Opening, 2002, Spring Opening, 2003; SARC Benefit Auction, Catlin Gabel Sch Cabell Theatre, Portland, 2002; Creative Arts Community Annual Show, Graystone Gallery, Portland, 2003; Faculty Show, Art Inst Portland, 2003, 2004, The Exquisite Corpse, 2004, Hard(ly) Soft Peep Show, 2007; Salem Salon Exhib, AN Bush Gallery, Salem, Ore, 2003; Mary Lou Zeek Gallery, Salem, 2003; Hungarian Multicultural Ctr, Art East Gallery, Hungary, 2003; Annual Sitka Art Invitational, World Forestry Ctr, Portland, 2003, 2004, 2005; Cascade Aids Project Benefit Auction, Portland, 2004, 2005, 2006; Art on the Vine, Ore Coll Art & Crafts, Portland, 2004, 2005; American Artists in Hungary, Vizivarosi Galeria, Budapest, 2004; Affair at the Jupiter Hotel, Portland, 2005; Signals from/about Central-Europe II, Ctrl European Cultural Inst, Budapest, 2006; Impulse, Nat Encaustic Show, Portland Art Ctr, 2006. *Teaching:* Found instr, Art Inst Portland, currently. *Awards:* Best of Show, Newberg Art Festival. *Mailing Add:* PO Box 80068 Portland OR 97280

MOSSET, OLIVIER
PAINTER
b Bern, Switzerland, 1944. *Work:* Eishalle Lerchenfeld, Farbkonzept & Bürogebäude der Raiffeisen-Gruppe, Fassade, St Gallen, Switzerland; Schweizerische Landesbibliotek, Bern, Switzerland; Swisscom, Neuchâtel, Switzerland; U-Bahn Toulouse, Station Minimes, France; Anyang Public Art Proj 2007, Pyeongchon Area, Anyang, Korea. *Exhib:* Solo exhibs include Galerie Rive Droite, Paris, 1968, 1969, Tony Shafrazi Gallery, New York, 1979, 1986, 1991, Galerie Marika Malacorda, Geneva, 1980, 1983, 1986, 1990, Galerie Susanna Kulli, Switzerland, 1984, 1986, 2004, New Mus Contemp Art, New York, 1985, Gilbert Brownstone & Cie, Paris, 1986, 1987, 1991, 1993, 1997, Ctr Art Contemp, Geneva, 1986, Venice Biennale, 1990, Galerie Tanit, Cologne, 1990, Mus Art Mod & Contemp, Geneva, 1994, 1995, 1996, Spencer Brownstone Gallery, New York, 1999, Charlotte Jackson Fine Art, Santa Fe, 2000, 2006, Le Spot, Studio d'Art Contemp, Le Havre, France, 2000, Sarah Cottier Gallery, Sydney, 2002, Galerie Incognito, Paris, 2005, Mus Beaux-Arts, École des Beaux-Arts, Rennes, France, 2007, Contemp Art Mus, St Louis, 2008; group exhibs include The Times Square Show, New York, 1981; Radical Painting, Williams Coll Mus Art, Williamstown, Mass, 1984; Paravision, Postmasters Gallery, New York, 1986, travelling to Margo Leavin Gallery, Los Angeles; From the Southern Cross: A View of World Art c 1940-1980, Sydney Biennial, 1988; Slow Art: Painting in New York Now, PS1 Mus, Long Island City, NY, 1992; Et tous ils changent le monde, Biennale d'Art Contemp, Lyon, France, 1993; Unbound: Possibilities in Painting, Hayward Gallery, London, 1994; Passions Privées, Mus d'Art Moderne de la Ville de Paris, 1995; Ne dites pas non!, Mus Art Mod & Contemp, Geneva, 1997, Multimetica, 2007; Dijon/leconsortium.coll, Ctr George Pompidou, Paris, 1998; Postmark: An Abstract Effect, SITE, Santa Fe, 1999; Ignition, Hazmat, Mus Contemp Art, Tucson, Ariz, 2001; From the Observatory, Paula Cooper Gallery, New York, 2002, Seven Grays, 2002; C'est arrivé demain, Biennale Lyon, 2003; Trésors Publics, Mus Nantes, France, 2004; Extreme Abstraction, Albright-Knox Gallery, Buffalo, NY, 2005; Whitney Biennial, Whitney Mus Am Art, New York, 2008. *Awards:* Caran d'Ache Prize, 1998. *Dealer:* Galerie Andrea Caratsch Waldmannstrasse 8 CH-8001 Zurich. *Mailing Add:* Galerie Andrea Caratsch Waldmannstr 8 Zurich CH-8001 Switzerland

MOSZYNSKI, ANDREW
PAINTER
b Eye, Suffolk, Eng. *Study:* Univ Nat de Buenos Aires, Argentina. *Work:* Metrop Mus Art, NY. *Exhib:* Solo exhibs, C Space, 80, J Walter Thompson Gallery, 83, Mission Gallery, 86, NY; Tweed Gallery, NJ, 82; Galeria Alberto Elia, Buenos Aires, Argentina, 83; PS1, Long Island City, NY, 84; Alternative Mus, NY, 85; Leonardo di Mauro Gallery, NY, 87. *Teaching:* Prof art & design, Fashion Inst of Technol, NY, 82-. *Awards:* Nat Endowment of Arts Grant, 85. *Bibliog:* Susana Torruella Leval (auth), Painting from under the volcano, Art News, 3/85; Elaine Louie (auth), Flat tops, NY Times, 4/90; John Howell White (auth), article, Artforum, 5/90. *Mailing Add:* 292 Lafayette St No 6E New York NY 10012

MOTTRAM, RONALD
ADMINISTRATOR, HISTORIAN
b Jersey City, NJ, Sept 27, 1940. *Study:* Rutgers Univ, BS, 63; New York Univ, MA, 73, PhD, 80. *Collection Arranged:* D W Griffith Centennial Exhib, Mus Mod Art, NY & Danish Film Mus, 75; New Acquisitions Show (Danish Cinema), Mus Mod Art, 78; North Light (accompanying film series), Brooklyn Mus, 82; The Mystic North (accompanying film series), Art Gallery Ontario, 84. *Teaching:* prof, film hist, Sarah Lawrence Col, 78-83; prof, Illinois State Univ Art Dept, 83-, chair dept art, 91-. *Awards:* George C Marshall fels (study of Danish film mus), 73 & 75; Louis B Mayer Film Hist Prog (study of early sound film), 74-75; Fulbright Scholar Prog (teaching on American studies), UK, 90-91. *Mem:* Nat Coun Arts Admins; Soc Cinema Studies; Fulbright Asn; Ill Higher Edn Art Asn. *Res:* Film history (early cinema with specialization in Danish silent film). *Publ:* Auth, Inner Landscapes: The Theater of Sam Shepard, Univ Missouri Press, 84; contribr, Schiavebianche allo specchio: le origini del cinema in Scandinavia, Edizioni Studio Tesi, 86; auth, The Danish Cinema Before Dreyer, Scarecrow, 88; auth, The great northern film company, Film History, 88; contrib, Questioning the Media: A Critical Introduction, Sage Publ, 90

MOULTON, SUSAN GENE
HISTORIAN, PAINTER
b Long Beach, Calif, June 7, 1944. *Study:* Univ Calif, Davis, study with Wayne Thiebaud, BA (art), 66; Univ Padua, Italy, 64-65; Acad, Venice, Italy, with Prof Balest, 64; Stanford Univ, MA (art hist; Carnegie Found Fel), 69, PhD (art hist), 77. *Comn:* Glenn Ellen Winery. *Teaching:* Prof Renaissance & mod art, Sonoma State Univ, 71-, chairperson dept art, 75-79 & 81-83. *Awards:* Nat Endowment Humanities, 76-78. *Bibliog:* Susan Moulton, Sojourn, Spring 98. *Mem:* Coll Art Asn; Women's Caucus Art; San Francisco Mus Soc; Nat Asn Schs Art & Design. *Media:* Mixed Media. *Res:* Sixteenth century Venetian painting, specifically Titian and the evolution of donor portraiture in Venice; 20th century American art, Aesthetics and Ecology; art of California; Neolithic Old Europe. *Publ:* Auth, Four From California, Edinburg, Scotland, 81; Works in Bronze; A Modern Survey, Sonoma State Univ, Calif, 85; Completing the Pictire: Native American, Mexican American, African American & Asian American Contributions to Twentieth Century American Art, Sonoma State Univ, Calif; Titan's Assunta as Hieros Gamos, From the Realm of the Ancestors, Kit, Manchester, Conn, 97; Venus envy, A Sexual Epistemology, Revision, winter, 98. *Mailing Add:* Dept Art Sonoma State Univ 1801 E Cotati Ave Rohnert Park CA 94928

MOUNT, MARSHALL WARD
EDUCATOR, ART HISTORIAN
b Jersey City, NJ, Dec 25, 1927. *Study:* Columbia Coll, AB, 48; Columbia Univ, MA, 52, PhD, 66. *Pos:* Leader art study tours to Mali, Cameroun, India, Explorer Tours, Montreal, 69-77; dir art hist prog, Finch Coll, San Marino, Italy, 73-75; cataloguer, Zim Collection of African Art, Children's Mus, Brooklyn, NY, 77 & 79; dir, L Kahan Gallery African Art, New York, 81-82. *Teaching:* Prof & chmn art hist dept, Finch Coll, New York, 58-75; vis prof, Univ Iowa, Iowa City, summer 70 & Parsons Sch of Design, New York, 70-72; vis assoc prof, Hunter Col, New York, 72-73; prof and chmn creative arts dept, Univ Benin, Nigeria, 77-80; adj asst prof art hist, Fashion Inst Technol, New York, 82-; vis asst prof, Rutgers Univ, 87-88; adj prof art hist, College Arts & Sciences, New York Univ, 2005-. *Awards:* Rockefeller Found Fel Rsch in Africa, 1961-62, 1968; Faculty Rsch award, Finch Coll, 65; FIT SUNY George Dorsch Faculty Rsch award, 2004-2005. *Mem:* Friends of African Art, Newark Mus. *Res:* Traditional and contemporary art of sub-Saharan Africa. *Publ:* Auth, African Art: The Years Since 1920, Ind Univ Press, 73, DaCapro Press, 89; African Art from New Jersey Collections, Montclair Art Mus, 83; A Cameroon World: Art & Artifacts from the Marshall & Caroline Mount Collection, Queensborough Community Coll Art Gallery, 2007. *Mailing Add:* 74 Sherman Pl Jersey City NJ 07307

MOVALLI, CHARLES JOSEPH
PAINTER, WRITER
b Gloucester, Mass, Aug 20, 1945. *Study:* Clark Univ, BA; Univ Conn, MA & PhD; spec study with Emile Gruppe, Roger Curtis, Zygmund Jankowski & Betty L Schlemm. *Work:* General Mills; High Voltage Engr; Hilton Hotel, Altamonte Springs; Exel Technol; Virginia Slims Collection; and others. *Exhib:* Rockport Art Assoc, 1979-; Guild of Boston Artists, 91,92; Judi Rutenberg Gallery, Boston, 95-2004; Old Lyme Art Assoc, 2002. *Collection Arranged:* Gloucester Historical Assoc. *Pos:* Contributing Ed, Am Artist, 1976-2004. *Awards:* Gold Medal, 82 & Silver Medal, 89, Rockport Art Asn; Gold Medal, Salmagundi Club, 85; Special Tribute, Hudson Valley Art Assoc, 2002. *Bibliog:* Numerous articles in American Artist Mag. *Mem:* Acad Artists; Guild of Boston Artists; Rockport Art Asn; N Shore Arts Asn. *Media:* Oil, Acrylic. *Res:* Contemporary and older painters working in Plein Air Tradition. *Publ:* Ed & coauth, Gruppe on Painting, 76; Brushwork, 77, Color in Outdoor Painting, 77 & Painting with Light, 78 & Art of Landscape Painting, 79, Watson-Guptill; auth, Croney on Watercolor, North Light, 82. *Mailing Add:* 237 Western Ave Gloucester MA 01930

MOWRY, ELIZABETH M
PAINTER, WRITER
b Kingston, NY, Mar 8, 1940. *Study:* Alliance Col, BA (magna cum laude), 61; Carnegie Inst, 72-74; State Univ NY, MA, 83. *Work:* Am Cancer Soc, Kingston, NY; Merrill Lynch, Albany, NY; Mgt Compensation Group NY; Woodstock Hist Soc Permanent Collection, NY. *Comn:* Children's ward large painting, Suburban Gen Hosp, Pittsburgh, Pa, 74; mural landscape, Intercounty Bank, New Paltz, NY, 85; painting series, 87 & descriptive paintings 10 states, 88-92, Key Corp, Cleveland, Ohio. *Exhib:* Solo exhib, Albany Inst Hist & Art, 86; Pastel Soc Am, Nat Arts Club, New York, 89-2000; Audubon Artists Am, Nat Arts Club, New York, 91; Allied Artists, Nat Arts Club, New York, 92; Knickerbocker Artists USA, Washington, 93. *Pos:* Sole Juror, Pastel Soc West Coast Nat Exhib, 98 & Pastel Soc NMex Nat Exhib, 98. *Teaching:* Instr painting & bd adv, Woodstock Sch Art, 87-. *Awards:* Pastel Soc Am, Landscape Award, Nat Arts Club, 89, 90 & 98; Excellence Award, Degas Pastel Soc, 91; Gold Medal Pastel & Most Innovative Use of Color, Knickerbocker Artists USA, 93; and others. *Bibliog:* Raymond J Steiner (auth), Profile: Elizabeth Mowry, Art Times, 4/86; John C Haviland (auth), Contemporary chronicle of HR, This Week NY, 6/86; Dennis Wepman (auth), Women's views of Woodstock, Artspeak, 11/87. *Mem:* Master pastelist Pastel Soc Am; Nat Asn Women Artists; Knickerbocker Artists

USA; distinguished pastelist Pastel Soc W Coast; Woodstock Artists Asn (bd dir, 84-87). *Media:* Pastel. *Publ:* contribr, Best Pastel, Rockport Publ, 96; auth, The Poetic Landscape, 2001; auth, The Pastelists' Year, 2001. *Dealer:* Fletcher Gallery Woodstock NY. *Mailing Add:* c/o Hardcastle Gallery 5714 Kennett Pike Wilmington DE 19807

MOXEY, PATRICIO KEITH FLEMING
ART HISTORIAN
b Buenos Aires, Arg, Jan 4, 1943; Brit & Arg citizen. *Study:* Univ Edinburgh, MA, 65; Univ Chicago, MA, 68, PhD, 74. *Teaching:* From instr to asst prof art hist, Tufts Univ, 71-74; from asst prof to assoc prof art hist, Univ Va, 74-86, prof, 86-, chmn art hist, 76-79 & actg chmn, 81-82; prof art hist, Barnard Col, 88-, chair art hist, 89-; prof art hist, Columbia Univ, 88-. *Awards:* Nat Endowment Humanities Fel, 78-79; sen fel, Ctr Advan Study Visual Arts, Nat Gallery Art, 80-81; Humboldt Found Fel, 82-83; scholar, J Paul Getty Ctr Hist Art & Humanities, 91 & 92. *Mem:* Coll Art Asn; Renaissance Soc; Hist Netherlandish Art; Sixteenth Century Soc. *Res:* Late medieval and Renaissance art in Northern Europe; critical theory & historiography. *Publ:* Auth, Peasants, Warriors & Wives, Popular Imagery in the Reformation, Chicago, 89; co-ed, Visual Theory: Painting & Interpretation, Polity, 91; the Practice of Theory, Cornell, 94; co-ed, Visual Culture: Images & Interpretations, Wesleyan/Univ Press New England, 94. *Mailing Add:* 39 Clarmont Ave New York NY 10027-6802

MOY, JAMES S
ADMINISTRATOR, EDUCATOR
Study: Univ Ill, Chicago, B (art), M (theater); Univ Ill, Urbana-Champaign, PhD (cultural studies). *Teaching:* Taught at Univ Tex Austin, Northwestern Univ, and Univ Oregon, formerly; chair, prof Dept Theater and Drama, Univ Wisconsin-Madison, formerly; dean Col of Fine Arts, Univ NMex, formerly, dean, prof, Sch of Creative Media, City Univ of Hong Kong, formerly; dean, prof art, Ontario Col of Art & Design, Toronto, formerly; provost, vpres academic affairs and research, Nova Scotia Col of Art & Design (NSCAD), formerly; Dean, Col of the Arts, Univ of South Florida, 2012-. *Mem:* International Council of Fine Arts Deans, Asn for Asian American Studies, Nat Asn of Schools of Theater, American Drama Soc and other professional affiliations. *Mailing Add:* College of The Arts University of South Florida 4202 E Fowler Ave FAH 110 Tampa FL 33620-7350

MOY, SEONG
PAINTER, PRINTMAKER
b Canton, China, Apr 12, 1921; US citizen. *Study:* St Paul Sch Art, with Cameron Booth, 36-40; Art Students League, with Vaclav Vytacil, 41-42; Hofmann Sch, with Hans Hofmann, 41-42; Atelier 17, New York, 48-50. *Work:* Mus Mod Art; Brooklyn Mus; Metrop Mus Art; Pa Acad Fine Arts; NY Pub Libr; plus others. *Comn:* Three ed, Int Graphic Arts Soc; NY Hilton Hotel; mural, Bd Educ, PS-131, NY. *Exhib:* Metrop Mus Art, 50; Whitney Mus Am Art, 50; Univ Ill, 51, 53 & 54; Carnegie Inst, 52 & 55; NY World's Fair, 64-65; plus many other solo & group exhibs. *Pos:* Dir, Seong Moy Sch Painting & Graphic Arts, Provincetown, Mass, summers 54-75. *Teaching:* Instr, Univ Minn, 51, Ind Univ, 52-53, Smith Col, 54-55, Univ Ark, 55, Vassar Col, 55, Cooper Union Art Sch, 57-70, Columbia Univ, 59-70 & Art Students League, 63-87; prof, City Col NY, 70-87. *Awards:* John Hay Whitney Found Grant, 50-51; Guggenheim Fel, 55-56; CAP, NY Arts Coun, 73-74; City Univ New York Research Found, 77-78. *Bibliog:* Saff & Sacilatto (auths), Printmaking--History and Process, Holt-Reinhart Winston Publ, 70. *Mem:* Art Students League; Am Fedn Arts; Artists Equity Asn; Coll Art Asn Am; Fedn Mod Painters & Sculptors. *Media:* All Media. *Publ:* Five American Printmakers (film), USIA, State Dept, Washington, DC, 57; Seong Moy-A Print Artist of Today (film), US Military Acad, Westpoint, NY, 70. *Mailing Add:* 100 La Salle St New York NY 10027-4703

MOYA, ROBERT
PAINTER, PRINTMAKER
b New York, NY, Oct 15, 1931. *Study:* Eastern NMex Univ, 51-53; Pratt Graphics Art Ctr, 60-62, USC with Harry Sternberg, 80-82. *Work:* Mus Fine Art, Ft Lauderdale, Fla; Rutgers Univ; Jane Voorhees Zimmerli Art Mus; Rutgers Univ, Printmaking Studios; Duke Univ, Schaefer House, Raleigh, NC; Museo de Arte Ponce, Mus Contemp Art, San Juan, PR; and others. *Comn:* Schaefer House, Duke Univ, comn by Mr & Mrs Norb Schaefer. *Exhib:* Solo exhib, Series-Large Scale Paintings, Pratt Inst, New York, 89; Muestra Nac, 94; Olympic Comt PR Invitational, 94-95; El Santo en el Arte Puertorriqueno: devocion imagen y transcendencia, 96; Computer Graphics, Mus Barrio, 96; Retrospective, From Island to Island (with catalog), Hui No' eau Arts Sch, HI; La Ciudad Infinita, 2000; Images of Our Hispanic Heritage, The Newark Pub Libr, NJ, 2001; Images of Our Hispanic Heritage, Newark Pub Libr, NJ, 2001 & 2006; Muestra Nacional, San Juan, PR, 2002; El Caballo, PR, 2007; Figuration, Museo de Arte de Puerto Rico, 2008; Coleccion Reyes Veray, Museo de Arte Contemporaneo de Puerto Rico, 2008. *Pos:* Founder & pres, Galeria Palomas, 78-88. *Teaching:* Artist-in-residence, computer generated studies, Univ PR, 89-; sem, Hui No' eau Arts Sch, HI, Spring, 98. *Bibliog:* E Ruiz de la Mata (auth), Roberto Moya Painter as Computer Whiz, 6/30/91; Sue Nash (auth), article, Island Currents; Retrospectiva de Roberto Moya en Hawaii, 6/10/98; La Ciudad Infinita, portfolio distributed to US & European Mus; and others. *Media:* Oil & Acrylic on canvas. *Dealer:* Galeria Palomas Sharon Cooper

MOYER, CARRIE
PAINTER, EDUCATOR
b Detroit, Mich. *Study:* Pratt Inst, BFA (painting), 1985; NY Inst Technol, MA (graphic design), 1990; Milton Avery Grad Sch Arts, Bard Coll, MFA (painting), 2001. *Exhib:* Becoming Visible: The Legacy of Stonewall, New York Pub Libr, 1994; In A Different Light, Univ Calif Art Mus, Berkeley, 1995; Mixing Messages: Graphic Design in Contemporary Culture, Cooper-Hewitt Nat Design Mus, 1996; The 21st Ann Nat/Int Studio Artists Exhib, PS1/Inst for Contemp Art, New York, 1997; Gender Trouble, Neuer Aachener Kunstverein, Aachen, Ger, 1999; The Color of Friendship, Shedhalle, Zürich, Switz, 2000; Stand Up Dick & Jane, Project Arts Centre, Dublin, Ireland, 2001; solo exhibs, Yerba Buena Ctr for the Arts, San Francisco, 2002, Diverseworks, Houston, 2004, Mary Baldwin Coll Hunt Gallery, Staunton, Va, 2007, Am Univ Mus, Washington DC, 2009; About Painting, Tang Teaching Mus, Skidmore Coll, Saratoga Springs, NY, 2004; Around About Abstraction, Weatherspoon Art Mus, Greensboro, NC, 2005; Beauty Is In the Streets, Mason Gross Sch Arts Gallery, Rutgers Univ, 2007; That Was Then...This Is Now, Mus Mod Art, New York, 2008. *Pos:* Artist-in-residence, Univ Tenn, Knoxville, 2001; vis artist, Cooper Union, New York, 2005. *Teaching:* Adj prof & instr, Art Inst Boston & Rutgers Univ, 2003-07, Queens Coll, Flushing, 2004-07, Pratt Inst, New York, 2005-07 ; asst prof painting, Tyler Sch Art, Pa, 2005 & RI Sch Design, 2007-. *Awards:* Creative Capital Found Grant, 2000; Ind Artist Grant, NY State Coun Arts, 2001; Elaine de Kooning Meml Fel, Bard Coll, 2001; Anonymous Was a Woman award, 2009; Joan Mitchell Found Grant, 2009. *Bibliog:* Robert Atkins (auth), Scene & Heard, Village Voice, 7/1994; David Joselit (auth), Exhibiting Gender, Art in Am, 1/1997; Holland Cotter (auth), Innovators Burst Onstage One (Ka-pow!) at a Time, NY Times, 11/10/2000; Cate McQuaid (auth), Revolution, Utopia and Other 60s Dreamscapes, Boston Globe, 1/26/2002; Dean Daderko (auth), A Mirrorball to Liberation, Gay City News, 2/1/2006. *Mem:* Coll Art Asn. *Mailing Add:* Rhode Island School of Design Dept Painting 2 College St Providence RI 02903-2784

MOYER, LINDA LEE
PAINTER, EDUCATOR
b Niles, Mich, Feb 11, 1942. *Study:* Occidental Col, Calif, 59-61; Univ Calif, Los Angeles, BA, 64; Calif State Univ, Long Beach, MA, 77, MFA, 80, Univ Calif, Irvine, student, 84. *Work:* 24 paintings, Home Savings of America, Los Angeles; Greensburg Deposit Bank, Ashland, Ky; Univ Calif, Irvine. *Comn:* 6 paintings, Nat Bank of La Jolla, Calif, 85; Robert Danlap, Rolling Hills, Calif, 88; Mr & Mrs Keith Kelly, Alexandria, Va, 92. *Exhib:* Solo exhibs, Calif Contemp Artists IV, Laguna Beach Mus Art, Calif, 82, Louis Newman Galleries, 86, 88 & 90, Cerritos Col, Norwalk, Calif, 86, Westmont Col, Santa Barbara, Calif, 92 & Maturango Mus, Ridgecrest, Calif, 96; Am Watercolor Soc, Nat Acad Galleries, NY, 82; The Church of Jesus Christ of Latterday Saints Mus Art & Hist, Salt Lake City, Utah, 88 & 91; Watercolor: Contemp Currents, Riverside Art Mus, Riverside Calif, 89; Watermarks, Mt San Antonio Col, Walnut, Calif, 96; and others. *Teaching:* Part-time instr painting & drawing, Calif State Univ, Long Beach, 81-86; part-time instr painting, Saddleback Col, Mission Viego, Calif, 86-88, Goldenwest Col, Huntington Beach, Calif, 90 & Fullerton Col, Calif, 90 & 94; Nat workshops, currently. *Awards:* Gold Medal, 82, Walter S Greathouse Medal, 88 Am Watercolor Soc, Watercolor West Award, 99; Gold Medal for Watercolor, Allied Artists Am, 82; 2nd Ann Int Exhib Award of Merit, Church Jesus Christ Latter-Day Saints Mus Church Hist & Art, 91; Best of Show Award, Utah Watercolor Soc, 2000. *Bibliog:* Splash 2, North Light Book Co, 92; Phil Metzger (auth), Enliven Your Paintings With Light, North Light Book Co, 93; Carole Katchen (auth), Make Your Watercolors Look Professional, North Light Bk Co, 95. *Mem:* Nat Watercolor Soc; Watercolor West; West Coast Watercolor Soc; Watercolor W (pres, 99-01); Utah Watercolor Soc. *Media:* Transparent Watercolor. *Interests:* music, reading. *Publ:* Auth, Building vibrant color--layer by layer, Artist's Mag, 5/85; contribr (with Valerie Shesko), Finding your center of interest, Artist's Mag, 4/86; Auth, Making Use of Symbolism, Am Artist, 8/97. *Dealer:* Phillips Gallery Salt Lake City UT; Louis Stern Galleries West Hollywood CA. *Mailing Add:* 553 E Jade Park Ln Draper UT 84020

MOYERS, WILLIAM
PAINTER, SCULPTOR
b Atlanta, Ga, Dec 11, 1916. *Study:* Adams State Col, major fine arts; Otis Art Inst. *Hon Degrees:* Adams State Col, PhD in Fine Arts, 1992. *Work:* Gilcrease Inst, Tulsa, Okla; Nat Cowboy Fame, Oklahoma City; Adams State Col; Albuquerque Mus; Sangre Cristo Arts Ctr, Pueblo, Colo; Cowboy Artists Am Mus, Kerrville, Tex. *Comn:* Wind & Rain (life size sculpture), Albuquerque Mus, NMex & Adams State Col; Cowboy Artists Am Mus, Kerrville, Tex. *Exhib:* Cowboy Artist of Am Shows, Cowboy Hall Fame & Phoenix Art Mus, since 68; Solo exhibs, Adams State Coll, Alamosa, Colo, 71 & Nat Cowboy Hall Fame, Oklahoma City, 73; Group exhibs, Mont Hist Soc, Helena, 72 & 73. *Awards:* Silver Medal sculpture, Cowboy Artists Am 1979 Exhib, Phoenix Art Mus, 79 & 80; Gold Medal-Sculpture, Cowboy Artists Am Exhib, 84; Silver Medal-Watercolor, Cowboy Artists Am Show, 89 & 91; and others. *Bibliog:* Ainsworth (auth), Cowboy in Art, World Publ, 68; Harmsen (auth), Western America, Northland, 71; Broder (auth), Bronzes of the American West, Abrams, 74. *Mem:* Cowboy Artists Am (vpres, 82-83, pres, 83-84 & 88-89). *Media:* Oil, Watercolor; Bronze. *Publ:* Illusr bks for nat publ, 45-62. *Dealer:* Taos Art Gallery Inc PO Box 1007 Taos NM 87571; Taos Gallery Scottsdale Ariz, 85251

MOZLEY, ANITA VENTURA
CURATOR, CRITIC
b Washington, DC, Aug 29, 1928. *Study:* Northwestern Univ, Evanston, Ill, BA (hon art); Art Students League, with Morris Kantor. *Exhib:* Maine Coast Artists, Landscapes, (invit), 89; Figurative Painting, Palo Alto Art League, 98; Fulton Street Gallery, NY. *Collection Arranged:* Ansel Adams: The Portfolios, Stanford Univ Mus Art, Calif, 72; Eadweard Muybridge: The Stanford Years, 1872-1882 (ed & co-auth, catalog), 72; Mrs Cameron's Photographs from the Life (auth, catalog), 74; Freshwater (producer), 74; Monsen Collection of Am Photography (auth, catalog), Seattle Art Mus, Wash, 76; Nadar: Portraits and Catacombs, from the coll of Samuel Wagstaff, 78; The Grand Tour: Mid-19th Century Photographs from the Leonard-Peil Collection, 79; Paintings by Joseph Raphael from San Francisco Coll (1869-1950), 80; Ansel Adams: Ski Experience, 83; Images of Hope and Despair: Robert Frank's Photographs, 85; Peter Stackpole, A photojournalist in Retrospect, 86. *Pos:* Reviewer, managing ed & West Coast corresp, Arts Mag, New York, 55-64; poster designer, Leo Castelli Gallery, New York, 55-62; film librn, Sextant, Inc, New York, 60-61; co-ed & publ, Scrap, a journal on the arts in NYC, 60-64; cur asst & ed, SEA Letter, San

Francisco Maritime Mus, 64-67; registr, Stanford Univ Mus Art, Calif, 70-78; cur photog, 71-86. *Teaching:* Hist photogr, Stanford Univ, spring 81. *Awards:* Faricy Art Award, Northwestern Univ, 49; Out-of-Town Scholar, Art Students League, 50; First Prize Palo Alto Art League, 98. *Bibliog:* Reviews (monogr), Arts Mag, Studio International, 55-63, Arts Mag, San Francisco, 64-67, Photograph, Image, Afterimage, Print Collector's Newsletter, 73-85. *Mem:* Phi Beta Kappa. *Media:* Gouache, Watercolor, Oil, Collage. *Res:* Nineteenth and twentieth century photographers, particularly the works of Eadweard Muybridge, Julia Margaret Cameron, Thomas Annan, Imogen Cunningham, Peter Stackpole & Lorie Novak. *Interests:* History, Science, Cooking. *Collection:* Esta Kramer Damariscotta ME, Regina Rosenzweig San Francisco CA. *Publ:* Contribr to several art publ, 72-85; auth introduction, Thomas Annan, Photographs of the Old Closes & Streets of Glasgow, 1868-1877, Dover, 77; auth, The Bridge Builders, Pomegranate, 84; The Stanfords and Photography, Mus Builders in the West, Stanford, 86; Leo Holub's Photographs of Artists in the Collection of Mr and Mrs H W Anderson, Vol I, Atherton, Calif, 89; Joel Leivick's Photographs of Carrara (exhib catalog), auth essay, Joe Deal's The Fault Zone, Stanford, 90; contribr, Catalogue of the Drawing Collection, Stanford Mus, 93; auth essay, Explorations and Excavations in Joseph Zirker, Translucent Transformations, Santa Clara, De Saisset Mus, 2004

MTHETHWA, ZWELETHU
PHOTOGRAPHER
b Durban, Kwazulu-Natal, South Africa, 1960 . *Study:* Michaelis Sch Fine Art, Univ Cape Town, South Africa, Diploma in Fine Arts, 1984, Advanced Diploma in Fine Arts, 1985; Rochester Inst Technol, Rochester, NY, MFA (Image Art), 1989. *Exhib:* Solo exhibs include Contemp Art, Paris, 2000, Mus Contemp Art, St Louis, 2002, Cleveland Mus, Cleveland, 2003, Jack Shainman Gallery, New York, 2004, 2006, Christine Koenig Galerie, Vienna, Austria, 2007, Contemporary Gladiators, Andrehn Schiptjenko, Stockholm, 2008, New Works, Jack Shainman Gallery, NY, 2009, iArt Gallery, Cape Town, South Africa, 2010, Is it our goal...? And Other Related Issues, Circa on Jellicoe, Johannesburg, South Africa, 2010, New Works, iArt Gallery, Cape Town, South Africa, 2011, John Hope Franklin Ctr, Duke Univ, Durham, NC, 2012, Baltimore Mus Art, Md, 2012; Group exhibs include Yesterday Begins Tomorrow: Ideals, Dreams & Contemp, Mus African Art, New York, 1998; Jack Shainman Gallery, New York, 2000, New Work, 2003; Mus Contemp Photography, Chicago, 2001; Common Ground: Discovering Community in 150 Years of Art, Selections from the Collection of Julia J Norrell, Corcoran Gallery, Washington, 2005; New Work/New Acquisitions, Mus Mod Art, New York, 2005; Defining Moments in Photograph from the MCA Collection, Mus Contemp Art, Chicago, 2007; Cross-Currents in Recent Video Installation: Water as Metaphor for Identity, Tufts Univ Art Gallery, Medford, Mass, 2008; Sordid and Sacred: The Beggars in Rembrandt's Etchings, Reynolds Gallery, Westmont Coll, Santa Barbara, Calif, 2009; Always Moving Forward: Contemporary African Photography from the Wedge Collection, Gallery 44, Houston, Tex, 2010; The Global Africa Project, Mus Art and Design, NY, 2010; Beyond Convention: Reimagining Human Rights in a Time of Change, Ford Found, NY, 2011; Are You a Hybrid, Mus Arts & Design, NY, 2011; La La La Human Steps: A Selection from the Collectrion of Museums Boijmans, Van Beuningen, Istanbul Mus Modern Art, 2012; Rise and Fall of Apartheid: Photography and the Bureaucracy of Everyday Life, Internat Ctr Photography, NY, 2012; Homebodies, Mus Contemporary Art, Chicago, 2013. *Mailing Add:* Jack Shainman Gallery 513 W 20th St New York NY 10011

MUCCIOLI, ANNA MARIA
PAINTER, SCULPTOR
b Detroit, Mich, Apr 23, 1922. *Study:* Soc Art & Crafts; with Sarkis Sarkisian, Charles Culver & Jay Holland. *Exhib:* Butler Inst Am Art, Youngstown, Ohio, 69; Birmingham Mus Arts, 74; La Galleria, Ital Am Cult Soc, Warren, Mich, 86; Retrospective Watercolors, Lawrence Inst Technol, Mich, 86; Muccioli Studio Gallery, Detroit, Mich, 87; Art Ctr, Mt Clemens, 91; 3rd Ann CCS-CAD Alum Exhib, Scarab Club, Detroit, Mich, 93; Fine Arts Assoc, Dearborn Col, Univ Mich, 95; Women Artists Henry Ford Cmty Collage Sisson Gallery, Dearborn, Mich, 99; 34th Ea Mich Int Art Exhib, Port Huron Mus, 2000. *Pos:* Owner, Muccioli Studio Gallery. *Awards:* Third Place, Scarab Club, 71, Hon Mention, Silver Medal Exhib, 76 & 79; Second Place, Ford Motor Co Art Exhib, 76, First Place, 77, & Second Place, 79; Pallet Guild Juror award, Spring Art Show, Livonia City Hall, 2003. *Bibliog:* Impresario Mag Art Leisaure, 11/74; Leaders & Achievers, Detroit News, 1/20/83; Am Artists: An Illustrated Survey of Leading Contemporary Americans, 85; NY Art Rev, 88. *Mem:* Founders Soc Detroit Inst Arts; Friends Mod Art; Arts Crafts Ctr Studies Alumni, Coll Art & Design, Detroit, Mich, 91. *Media:* Watercolor; Bronze, Stone. *Publ:* William T Noble (auth), The stockholder who told Henry how to build his new mustang, The Sunday News Mag, 9/73; Italian Tribune Paper, 1/98. *Mailing Add:* c/o Muccioli Studio Gallery 511 Beaubien Detroit MI 48226

MUCHNIC, SUZANNE
CRITIC, INSTRUCTOR
b Kearney, Nebr. *Study:* Scripps Coll, BA, 62; Claremont Grad Sch, MA, 63. *Pos:* Ed, Artweek, Los Angeles, 77-78, contrib ed, 78-80; art critic & staff writer, Los Angeles Times, 78-; Los Angeles correspondent, Art News, 93-2004. *Teaching:* Instr art hist, Los Angeles City Coll, 74-82; instr art criticism, Univ Southern Calif, 81 & Claremont Grad Sch, 83. *Awards:* Distinguished Alumna Award, Claremont Grad Sch, 82; Distinguished Alumna Award, Scripps Coll, 87; Donald Pflueger History Award, Historical Soc of Southern Calif, 2002. *Mem:* Int Asn Art Critics; Art Table; Coll Art Asn. *Res:* Contemporary art, Norton Simon Museum. *Publ:* Auth, exhibition catalogue essays on Tim Nordin, Martha Alf, Mark Lere, Paul Darrow, Aldo Casanova & Barbara Strassen; essay on art, World Book Encyl Year Book, 93, 94, 95; Odd Man In: Norton Simon and the Pursuit of Culture, Univ Calif Press, 98

MUDFORD, GRANT LEIGHTON
PHOTOGRAPHER
b Sydney, Australia, Mar 21, 1944. *Study:* Univ New South Wales, Australia, 63-64. *Work:* Mus Mod Art, NY; Int Mus Photog, George Eastman House, Rochester, NY; Victoria & Albert Mus; Australian Nat Gallery, Canberra; Nat Mus Am Art, Washington, DC; Mus Contemp Art, Los Angeles. *Comn:* Ten photog prints, Calif State Univ, Long Beach, 80 & CSR Ltd, Sydney, 81; Parliament House, Lewis comn, Canberra (under construct); Comprehensive Cancer Center Cedars-Sinai Medical Ctr, Los Angeles (under construction); Louis I Kahn: In The Realm Of Architecture, Moca, Los Angeles, 91. *Exhib:* The Land: 20th Century Landscape Photographs, Victoria & Albert Mus, 75-76; solo exhib, Hirshhorn Mus & Sculpture Garden, 79; Long Beach: A Photog Survey, Art Mus & Galleries, Calif State Univ, Long Beach, 80; Biennial Exhib, Whitney Mus Am Art, 81; Double Take: A Comparative Look at Photographs, Int Ctr Photog, NY, 81; Photog: A Sense of Order, Inst Contemp Art, Univ Pa, 81. *Teaching:* Instr, Art Ctr Sch Art & Design, Pasadena & Calif Inst Arts, Valencia. *Awards:* Nat Endowment Arts Photogr Fel, 80. *Bibliog:* Photographs by Grant Mudford, Interview Mag, 6/79; Celebrating the seldom-noticed, Los Angeles Times, 3/6/83; article, Artforum, summer 83; Available Light, Mus Contemp Art, Los Angeles; Grant Mudford (auth), catalogue, Gallery Min, 86; California Photographers; catalogue, Gallery Min, 86. *Dealer:* Rosamund Felsen Gallery 2525 Michigan Ave B4 Santa Monica CA 90404. *Mailing Add:* 2660 Dundee Pl Los Angeles CA 90027-1328

MUEHLEMANN, KATHY
PAINTER
b Feb 9, 1950. *Study:* State Univ NY, BFA, 79. *Work:* Ackland Art Mus, Univ NC, Chapel Hill; Cleveland Mus Art, Ohio; Contemp Mus, Honolulu, Hawaii; Calif Ctr Arts Mus, Escondido; Nelson-Atkins Mus Art, Kansas City, Mo; Milwaukee Art Mus, Wis; Mus Contemp Art, Miami, Fla; and others. *Exhib:* Solo exhibs, Oscarsson Siegeltuch Gallery, NY, 86, Lannan Mus (with catalog), Lake Worth, Fla, 88, Virginia Zabriskie Gallery, NY, 89, Contemp Mus Art, Honolulu, Hawaii, 91, Pamela Auchincloss Gallery, NY, 91 & 93-94, Nelson-Atkins Mus Art, Kansas City, Mo, 91 & Cedar Rapids Mus Art, Iowa, 94; Am exhib (with catalog), Am Acad Rome, Italy, 88; Nina Freudenhelm Gallery, Buffalo, NY, 90 & 93; Australian Print Workshop, Melbourne, 93; Jan Weiner Gallery, Kansas City, Mo, 93; Grey Art Gallery, NY Univ, 93; Fitchburg Art Mus, Mass, traveling, 93; Ackland Art Mus, Univ NC, Chapel Hill, traveling, 94; Maier Mus Art, Va, 95; The Hyde Collection Art Mus, NY, 98; and many others. *Teaching:* Assoc prof, Randolph Coll, Va. *Awards:* Prix De Rome, 87-88; Nat Endowment Arts Award, 88; Fel, John Simon Guggenheim, 94. *Bibliog:* John Yau (auth), rev, Art Forum, 3/92; Holland Cotter (auth), rev, NY Times, 9/17/93; Kim Levin (auth), rev, The Village Voice, 10/12/93; Paul Mattick (auth), rev, Art in Am, 1/94; Alicia Faxon (auth), rev, Art New Eng, 4-5/94; and many others. *Mem:* Fel Am Acad, Rome. *Media:* Oil. *Mailing Add:* 5024 Inglewood Dr Lynchburg VA 24503

MUELLER, LOUIS ALBERT
SCULPTOR, CRAFTSMAN
b Paterson, NJ, June 15, 1943. *Study:* Rochester Inst Technol, BFA, 69; RI Sch Design, MFA, 71. *Work:* RI Sch Design, Mus Art, Providence; Am Craft Mus, NY; Philadelphia Mus Art; Victoria & Albert Mus, London; Mus Fine Arts, Boston. *Comn:* Bronze sculpture, Philadelphia One Percent for Arts, 85; bronze medal, Philadelphia Mus Art, 85; three bronzes, Hyatt Hotel, Phoenix, 86; fences & gates, welded steel, Phoenix One Percent for Arts, 88; bronze & blown glass lighting, Port of Seattle, Wash, 91. *Exhib:* 1st Artist Soapbox Derby, San Francisco Mus Mod Art, 75; solo exhib, NDak Mus Art, Grand Forks, 82; Design in the Service of Tea, Cooper-Hewitt, Nat Design Mus, NY, 84; Poetry of the Physical, Am Craft Mus, NY, 86; Modern Jewelry, Philadelphia Mus Art, 86. *Collection Arranged:* The Virgin (auth, catalog), Int Jewelry Exhib, 91-92. *Teaching:* Lectr metal art, Calif Col Art & Crafts, 71-75; prof jewelry & metal, RI Sch Design, Providence, 77-; lectr, Sch Mus Fine Arts, Boston, 78-79; lectr casting, Wellesley Col, Mass, 78-80. *Awards:* Fel Design, NY Found Arts, 85; Fel Sculpture, RI Coun Arts, 90, Fel Design, 96. *Bibliog:* Peter Dormer (auth), The New Furniture, Thames & Hudson, 87; Otto Kunzli (auth), Providence, Art Aurea, 89; Ralph Turner (auth), New Time - New Thinking, Int Crafts Coun-London, 96. *Media:* Bronze Constructed; Fabricated Sterling & Karat Gold. *Dealer:* Franklin Parrasch 20 W 57th St New York NY 10019. *Mailing Add:* 508 Lloyd Ave Providence RI 02906

MUELLER, OP, (SISTER) GERARDINE
CALLIGRAPHER, STAINED GLASS ARTIST
b Newark, NJ, 1921. *Study:* Caldwell Coll, BA; Univ Notre Dame, MA & MFA, with A Lauck, W Otto of Berlin & Albinas Elskus; Inst Cult, Guadalajara, Mex; Fordham Univ; Columbia Univ. *Work:* Illumination, Newark Pub Libr; Caldwell Coll, NJ; Univ Notre Dame; Fordham Univ; Newark Libr, NJ; Retrospective mem Exhib 2010, Caldwell Coll. *Comn:* Wall mural, Dominican Sisters, Caldwell, NJ, 86; cloisonne enamel & wood tabernacle, windows, extended care facility, Newark, 87; stained glass stations, 89, life-size sculptures, 90 & 92, Dominican Sisters, Caldwell; 32 windows, Caldwell Coll Theatre, 93-98; 3 windows, Summit Mausoleum, 94; chapel walls, Sacred Heart Sch, Newark, 96; cd covers, ASI Records; engraved glass doors; 16 Windows, Care Facility, Caldwell, 2008; etched glass doors, Cloisonne Tabernacle, 2010. *Exhib:* Old Bergen Art Guild Tour, 79-86; N Am Calligraphers, Dallas, Tex, 74, Nat Miniature Art Soc, Fla, 75, 2001; Art by US Relig Women, Indianapolis, 81; Contemp Relig Art, Newark, 83-88; Barron Arts Ctr, Woodbridge, NJ, 86; Dominican 800th Univ Exhibits, Ohio, 2007. *Pos:* Mem, Archdiocese Comm Div Worship (art & archit), 74-2003; dir art & design, Liturgy Conv, 81; ed bd, Word on Worship, Newark Archdiocese, 95-2005. *Teaching:* Lectr lettering & crafts, Fordham Univ, 61; prof art, Caldwell Coll, 63-98, chmn art dept, 63-98, prof emer, 98. *Awards:* Nat Cath Educ Asn Award (glass), 86; Veritas Alumni Award, 91; Caldwell Coll Cup, 2002; Victoria C Egan Lettering Award, 71. *Bibliog:* Articles in The NY Times, 11/77, New Jersey Music & Arts 12/77, Today's Art, 1/81, Newark Advocate, 10/81, Newark Star-Ledger, 11/81 & 1/86, Jersey J, 5/86, Suburban Life, 4/86 & New Community, Newark, 5/87; Channel 5 News Report, 10/93; Sunday Star Ledger, 5/1/94. *Media:*

Stained Glass, Illumination. *Res:* Pre-Columbian Art. *Interests:* Lettering, Pre-Columbian Hist. *Publ:* Auth, Yearbook production, Photolith Mag, 61; Art in Latin America & Art in Indian Mission of US, Cath Youth Encycl, McGraw-Hill, 62; New mosaic evolvement, Cath Fine Arts Soc, 68; contribr, Stained Glass Quart, summer 78; 2 articles, Word on Worship, 93 & 95; Dominican News, 11/2000-2007. *Mailing Add:* 1 Ryerson Ave Caldwell NJ 07006

MUGAR, MARTIN GIENANDT
PAINTER
b Boston, Mass, Jan 23, 1949. *Study:* Yale Univ, with William Bailey & Bernard Chaet, BA (cum laude), 71, with Al Held & Lester Johnson, MFA, 74. *Work:* Mass Inst Technol Mus, Cambridge; Boston Pub Libr, Mass; Fuller Mus, Brockton, Mass; Weatherspoon Art Gallery, Univ NC, Greensboro; Tufts Univ Mus, Medford, Mass; Merrimack Coll, Mass; Simmons Coll, Mass; Danforth Mus, Framingham, Mass. *Exhib:* Solo exhibs, Mass Inst Technol, Cambridge, 87, Hood Mus, Dartmouth, Hanover, NH, 88 & Bowery Gallery, NY, 91 & Creiger-Dane Gallery, Boston, 98 & 2000, Merrimack Coll, 2005, New England School of Art & Design, 2006, Paul Mellon Art Center, Wallingford, Conn, 2007, Bowery Gallery, NY, 2008; Contemp Landscapes, Art Inst Boston, 91; Rising Tide Gallery, Provincetown, Mass, 93, 94 & 96; Bromfield Gallery, Boston, 93, 95, 2013; Visions of Order, Mercury Gallery, 95; New Eng, New Talent, Fitchburg Mus, 96; New Eng Triennial, Fuller Mus, Brockton, Mass, 99; Picture Perfect, New Eng Sch Design, 2000; Montserrat Coll Art Gallery, Wilderness of Sweets, 2001; Danforth Mus, Framingham, Mass, 2010-2011, Off the Wall, 2013; Int Show, Caelum Gallery, 2013. *Teaching:* Asst prof painting, Univ NC, Greensboro, 80-86, Univ NH, Durham, 86-87, Dartmouth Col, Hanover, NH, 87-88 & Art Inst Boston, 88-99; instr, Univ NH, 94-95. *Awards:* John Courtney Murray Fel, Yale Univ, 71. *Bibliog:* Gail Kelley (auth), article, Boston Globe, 10/19/97; Cate McQuaid (auth), Boston Globe, 6/15/2000, 1/26/2006, 2/13/2013; Charles Giuliano (auth), Arts Media, 6-7/2000; Dave Raymond (auth), Art New England, 6-7/2006; Rosanna Warren (auth), Provincetown Arts, 2007. *Media:* All. *Publ:* 100 Boston Artists 7/2013. *Dealer:* Bow Street Gallery 30 Plymouth St Cambridge MA 02138. *Mailing Add:* 314 Durham Point Rd Durham NH 03824

MUHL, ERICA
ADMINISTRATOR, EDUCATOR
Comn: as a composer works have been commissioned, performed, and broadcasted by Minnesota Opera, New World Symphony, Italy's Orchestra della RAI, Venezuela's Nat Philharmonic Orchestra, Orchestra of Saint Luke's, Arditti Quartet, Nat Public Radio, Mexican Nat TV and Radio and Radio-Televisione Italiana. *Pos:* Dir, Theory and Aural Skills Programs, Univ Southern Calif Thorton Sch of Music, 1991-1998, chair dept composition, 2006-2007, assoc. dean, 2009-2012, several committee memberships; interim dean, Univ Southern Calif Sch of Fine Arts, 2012-2013, dean, 2013-, founding exec dir, Lovine and Young Acad for Arts, Technology, and Business of Innovation, 2013-, prof fine arts and composition, 2013-; invited speaker in the field; featured on-camera expert, A&E Network's online version of Biography.com. *Awards:* several nat and internat fellowships and grants. *Mailing Add:* University of Southern California Roski School of Art & Design-Office of the Dean Watt Hall 104 University Park Campus Los Angeles CA 90089-0292

MUHLERT, CHRISTOPHER LAYTON
PAINTER, PHOTOGRAPHER
b Brooklyn, NY, Mar 24, 1933. *Study:* Case Western Reserve, BA, 64; Oberlin Col, MA, 66; Pratt Inst; Union Col; Cleveland Inst Art. *Work:* Cleveland Mus Art; Allen Mem Art Mus, Oberlin, Ohio; Phillip Morris Corp, Estate Joseph Hirshhorn, Washington, DC; Prudential Insurance Co, Merrillville, Ind; Brenton Bank of Cedar Rapids, Iowa; Alcon Lab, Ft Worth, Texas. *Exhib:* Black and White, Smithsonian Inst, 70-72; 19th Area Exhib, Corcoran Gallery Art, 74; two-person exhib, Barbara Fiedler Gallery, Washington, DC, 76; Solo exhibs, Davenport Munic Art Gallery, Iowa, 77, Barbara Fiedler Gallery, Washington, DC, 78, Carlin Gallery, Ft Worth, 83 & Graham Gallery, Houston, Tex, 84, Moudy Art Gallery, Texas Christian Univ, 87, William Campbell Contemp Art, 87-90 & Dutch Phillips & Co, 93-94. *Pos:* Preparator, Cleveland Mus Art, 60-64. *Teaching:* Instr design & painting, Oberlin Col, 66-68; instr found, Corcoran Sch Art, 70, asst prof drawing & design, 71-75. *Media:* Drawing, collage, photography. *Dealer:* William Campbell Contemporary Art Fort Worth TX. *Mailing Add:* 1108 Kay St Boalsburg PA 16827-1630

MUHLERT, JAN KEENE
MUSEUM DIRECTOR, HISTORIAN
b Oak Park, Ill, Oct 4, 1942. *Study:* Neuchatel Univ; Inst European Studies, Paris; Sorbonne, with Andre Chastel; Inst de Phonetique; Acad Grande Chaumiere, 1962-63; Albion Coll, BA, 1964; Oberlin Coll, with Ellen H Johnson & Wolfgang Stechow, MA, 1967. *Collection Arranged:* H Lyman Sayen (with catalog), Nat Collection Fine Arts, 1970, Romaine Brooks, Thief of Souls (with catalog), 1971 & William H Johnson 1901-1970 (with catalog), 1971; The Ninth Level: Funerary Art from Ancient Meso Am (with catalog), Mus of Art Univ Iowa, 78 & African Sculpture, The Stanley Collection (with catalog), 79; An American Sculptor, Seymour Lipton (with catalog), Palmer Mus Art, Pa State Univ, 99-2000; Celebrating 40 Years of Gifts: Work on Paper from the Permanent Collection, Palmer Mus Art, Penn State Univ, 2012. *Pos:* Asst cur collections, Allen Mem Art Mus, Oberlin Coll, 1966-68; asst cur contemp art, Nat Coll Fine Arts, 1968-73, assoc cur 20th century paintings & sculpture, 1974-75; dir, Mus Art, Univ Iowa, 1975-79, Amon Carter Mus, Ft Worth, Tex, 1980-95 & Palmer Mus Art, Pa State Univ, 1996-. *Teaching:* Mus studies, Pa State Univ, 1998-. *Awards:* Grant, Asn Art Mus Dir, 1979. *Mem:* Asn Art Mus Dir; Am Alliance Mus. *Res:* Charcoal drawings, 1900-1940; Arthur G Dove, 1880-1946. *Publ:* Coauth, Tribute to Mark Tobey (catalog), Nat Collection Fine Arts, 1974; contribr, Mauricio Lasansky, A Retrospective Exhibition, Univ Iowa, 1976; American Paintings Selections from the Amon Carter Mus, 1986; ed, proj mgr, An American Sculptor, Seymour Lipton, Palmer Mus Art, Pa State Univ, 1999; contribr, A Gift from the Heart, Am Art from the Collection of James and Barbara Palmer, Palmer Mus Art, Penn State Univ, 2013. *Mailing Add:* Pa State Univ Palmer Mus Art University Park PA 16802

MUIR, EMILY LANSINGH
PAINTER, SCULPTOR
b Chicago, Ill. *Study:* Art Students League, with Richard Lahey & Leo Lentelli; Univ Maine, LHD, 69. *Work:* Brooklyn Mus; Univ Maine; Margaret Chase Smith Libr. *Comn:* Designs & contracting of contemp summer & year round homes, mosaics & interior design, portraits and portrait busts for pvt owners. *Exhib:* Int Watercolor Soc; Maine Art Gallery; Univ Maine; Farnsworth Mus Art. *Pos:* Appointee, Nat Comn Fine Arts, 55-59. *Teaching:* Lectr art, Asn Am Cols, 50-60. *Awards:* Award in Archit, Maine Women in Arts; Maine Woman Yr, Westbrook Col; Mary A Vartman Award, UMO, Women in Arts, 94. *Bibliog:* Martin Dibner (auth), People of the Maine Coast, Doubleday; JR Wiggins (auth), article in Bangor Daily News; article in Maine Boats & Harbors, Island Inst; and others. *Mem:* Deer Isle Artists. *Media:* Oil, Mosaic; Clay, Wood. *Publ:* Auth, Small Potatoes, Scribner, 40. *Mailing Add:* Muir Studios PO Box 425 Blue Hill ME 04614-0425

MUIRHEAD, ROSS P
KINETIC ARTIST, PHOTOGRAPHER
b Vancouver, BC, June 20, 1956. *Study:* Emily Carr Inst Art & Design, dipl, 80; Univ BC, MFA, 89. *Exhib:* Solo exhib (contribr, catalog), Contemp Art Gallery, Vancouver, BC, 89; Un-Natural Traces: Contemp Art from Can (contribr, catalog), Barbican Art Gallery, London, Eng, 91; Working Truths/Powerful Fictions (contribr, catalog), MacKenzie Art Gallery, Regina, Sask, 91; Notions of Home (contribr, catalog), Edmonton Art Gallery, Alta, 92; Le Mois de la Photo a Montreal (contribr, catalog), Galerie Vox, Montreal, Que, 93; 69-94 Contemp Decades (contribr, catalog), Charles Scott Gallery, Vancouver, BC, 94. *Teaching:* Instr fine arts, Univ BC, 89. *Awards:* Proj Grant, Can Coun, 86 & B Grant, 91. *Media:* Photography

MULCAHY, KATHLEEN
GLASS ARTIST, SCULPTOR
b Newark, NJ, June 23, 1950. *Study:* Kean Coll NJ, Union, BA (art educ), 72; Alfred Univ, NY, MFA (glass sculpture), 74; Nat Endowment Arts Fel, 79; Individual Artist Fel, Pa Coun Arts, 81, 83 & 93; Lusk Meml Award Creative Artists, Fulbright Scholar, Italy, 84; Carnegie Mellon Univ Fac Res Grant, Italy & France, 86; Masterworks Fel, Creative Glass Ctr Am, Millville, NJ, 91. *Work:* Corning Mus Glass, NY; pvt collections, Westmoreland Co Mus Art, Pa; Carnegie Inst Mus Art, Pittsburgh; Am Craft Mus, NY; State Mus Pa, Harrisburg. *Comn:* Illuminated Glass Wall: Light Rail Transit, City Pittsburgh, 85, Donor Room, Rodef Shalom Congregation, 91 & Westinghouse Corp, Pittsburgh, 93; Centimark Corp, Wash, Pa, 96; Bayer Corp, 98; Pittsburgh Regional Alliance, 98; lobby installation, Pa Turnpike Comn Corp Hq, Harrisburg, Pa, 2001. *Exhib:* Corning Glass Ctr, 83, 87-88 & 93; one-person exhibs, Snyderman Gallery, Philadelphia, 86, Kimzey Miller Gallery, 91, Cleveland Ctr Contemp Art, 94, Kean Col, NJ, 95, Butters Gallery Ltd, Portland, Ore, 96 & Hodgell Gallery, Sarasota, Fla, 97; Crafts Today/USA traveling exhib, Am Crafts Coun, 89-92; Rosemont Col, Philadelphia, Pa, 99; Buy/By Women, Morgan Contemp Glass, Pittsburgh, 2000; Westmoreland Mus Art, Greensburg, Pa, 2000; and others. *Collection Arranged:* Am Craft Mus; Renwick Galleries; Bayer Corporation; Carnegie Mus of Art; Westmoreland Mus of Art; State Mus of Penn; Corning Mus of Glass and More; Mus of Am Glass at Wheaton Village. *Pos:* Vis artist, ArtPark, Lewiston, NY, 80; adv comt, Three Rivers Art Festival, Pittsburgh, 91-93; co-cur, In the Quest of Being, Three Rivers Art Festival Show, 93; artist-in-residence, Haystack Mt Sch Crafts, summer, 79 & 83, ArtPark, Lewiston, NY, summer, 80, Mid Atlantic Arts Fel, Studio Access to Glass, Corning, NY, 94 & Cité Int Arts, Paris, 97; artistic dir, Pittsburgh Glass Ctr, Pa, 1999-2002; co-founder, developer, Pittsburg Glass Ctr, Pa, 2001. *Teaching:* Head, glass prog, Bowling Green State Univ, Ohio, 75-76; dir & assoc prof art, glass sculpture prog, Carnegie-Mellon Univ, Pittsburgh, 76-89; lectr, Portcon Glass Conf, 82 & 83. *Awards:* Individual Artist Fel, Pa Coun Arts,, 93; artist-in-residence, Mid Atlantic Arts Fel, Corning, NY, 95 & Cite Int des Arts, Paris, 97; Heinz Endowment Arts Award, 96; Distinguished Alumnus in the Arts, Kean Univ, 2005; and others. *Bibliog:* Graham Shearing (auth), "Regional Focus" takes art to another juror, 8/11/96, "His & Hers & Ours" at treat in a loft, 9/27/96, Tribune Rev & The Westmoreland Museum of American Art Launches A Survey, 2/20/2000; Michael Krumrine (auth), Kathleen Mulcahy: Lawrence Gallery at Rosemont, Glass Mag, winter 99; Mary Thomas (auth), Historic, Modern Glassworks Sparkle in Show, 4/8/2000; Sculpture Reference, Sculpture Books Publ, 2004; and others. *Mem:* Glass Art Soc (bd dir, 86-89), NY; Am Crafts Coun; Chartiers Valley Arts Coun, (bd dir, 89-90 & bd advisors, 91-), Carnegie, Pa. *Media:* Glass, Sculpture; Mixed Media. *Publ:* Profile, Glass Studio Mag, 11/81; Profile, Glass Mag, 1/95; critique, Glass Mag, winter 99; Lucartha Kohler: Women working in Glass, Schiffer,2003; catalog, 20/20 Vision, Susanne Frantz, 2003; review, Glass Mag, 2004. *Dealer:* Butters Gallery 520 NW Davis Portland OR 97209; 336 4th Ave Pittsburgh PA 15222. *Mailing Add:* 260 Whittengale Rd Oakdale PA 15071

MULFINGER, JANE
EDUCATOR, ADMINISTRATOR, COLLECTOR
Study: Stanford Univ, BA (studio art), 1983; Royal Col of Art, London, MA (sculpture with distinction), 1989. *Exhib:* Endart Galerie, Berlin, 1987, Lost For Words, Flaxman Gallery, London, 1991, Boxer, Walsall Mus Art, England, 1995, Regrets, Franklin Furnace Archive, NY, 1995, Lightness, The Visual Arts Gallery, Wooster St, NY, 2000, Faculty Exhibition, Univ Art Mus, Santa Barbara, 2002, Exacting Minutia While History Repeats, Contemporary Arts Forum, Santa Barbara, 2004, Darkness and Lights, Armory Ctr of the Arts, Pasadena, 2007, Mobile Arts Lab II; Electronic Poetics, Casa de la Raza and Santa Barbara Mus Art, 2008, Sunset Most Popular II in Stardust Boogie Woogie, Art Lab Berlin, 2010, Sunset Most Popular I and Relative Speed of Masses I in Stardust Boogie Woogie, 2010 and several others. *Pos:* Resident artist, dept art, Univ NC, Chapel Hill, 1997. *Teaching:* Part-time lecturer, Chelsea Col Art and Design, London, 1992; workshop teacher, Southhampton City Arts, Southhampton Art Mus, 1993; lecturer, dept art studio, Univ Calif Santa Barbara, 1994-2001; lecturer, Col of Creative Studies & Dept Art Studio, Univ Calif Santa Barbara, 2001-2004; asst prof, art dept and Col of Creative Studies, Univ Calif Santa

Barbara, 2004-2006, assoc prof, 2006-2009, prof 3D spatial studies/sculpture, 2009-, art dept chair, 2011-. *Awards:* Unilever Sculpture award, London, 1988; Elephant Trust, London, 1989; OSARCA prize Old Students' Asn Royal Col of Art Soc, London, 1989; British Council Travel awards, 1993-1997; Creat, Play, Learn, Microsoft Research Grant, 2005. *Publ:* articles in both art magazines and nat newspapers including Flash Art (Italian version), Art and Design, Contemporary Visual Art, The Economist, The Times (London), The Guardian, La Stampa, Los Angeles Times and others. *Mailing Add:* University of California Santa Barbara Department of Art Building 534 Room 1316 Santa Barbara CA 93106-7120

MULHERN, MICHAEL
PAINTER
b Paisley, Scotland. *Study:* Newark Sch Fine & Indust Arts, Newark, NJ; Brooklyn Mus Sch, NY, 61-62; Sch of Visual Arts, New York. *Exhib:* One-person shows, Duane Street Gallery, 70, Adam Gimbel Gallery, 81, Exit Art Ringside Gallery, 85, Stephen Rosenberg Gallery, New York, 88, 90 & 93, Rosenberg & Kaufman Fine Art, NY, 95, 98, Salander-O'Reilly Galleries, NY, 2001; The Tenth Summer, Stephen Rosenberg Gallery, 93; The Inaugural Show, Painting Ctr, NY, 93; Presence & Absence (catalog), ES Vandam Gallery, NY, 93; Basic Marks: black & white paintings, Rosenberg & Kaufman Fine Art (auth catalog), 95; APC Galerie, Koln, Ger, 98; Salander O'Reilly Galleries, NY, 2001; Museo d'Arte Moderna, Gazoldo degli Ippoliti, Italy, 2002. *Awards:* Fel Grant, Nat Endowment Arts, 87; Painting Grant, Pollock-Krasner Found Inc, 89, 2000, Adolph & Esther Gottlieb Found, 2001. *Bibliog:* Peter Pinchbeck (auth), Incidence of Passage (exhib, catalog), 93; Alfred MacAdam (auth), Basic Marks, Art News, 3/95; Pepe Karmel (auth), Art in review, NY Times, 9/22/95; Maura Reilly (auth), Art in Am, 10/2001; Marid Naves (auth), The NY Observer, 1/2001; Karen Wikin (auth), Hudson Review, 2003. *Media:* Acrylic, Oil. *Dealer:* Salander-Oreilly, NY City; Spheris, Vt; Karolyn Sherwood, Des Moines

MULLEN, JAMES MARTIN
EDUCATOR, PRINTMAKER
b Altoona, Pa, May 14, 1935. *Study:* Pa State Univ, BA, 57, MA, 63. *Work:* NJ State Mus, Trenton; Portsmouth Va Mus; Everson Mus, Syracuse, NY; Pa State Univ, Univ Park; Pushkin Mus, USSR. *Exhib:* Am Drawings III, Portsmouth Arts Ctr, Va, 80; World Print III, San Francisco Mus Mod Art, 80; 5th Nat Print, Honolulu Acad Art, Hawaii, 80; Small Works, Wash Sq Gallery, NY Univ, 80; Silvermine Guild Prints, New Cannann, Conn, 80. *Pos:* Gallery dir, State Univ Col, Oneonta, NY, 76-. *Teaching:* Prof art, State Univ Col, Oneonta, NY, 63-. *Awards:* Chancellor's Award for Teaching Excellence, State Univ NY, 73; Chaning Hare Award, Soc Four Arts, Palm Beach, Fla. *Mem:* Soc Am Graphic Artist; Am Color Print Soc; Cooperstown Art Asn. *Media:* Watercolor. *Publ:* Auth, Subject matter, 66 & Student work, 69, Sch Arts Mag. *Dealer:* Miriam Perlman Inc Lake Point Tower Suite 1902 505 N Lakeshore Dr Chicago IL 60611

MULLEN, PHILIP EDWARD
PAINTER
b Akron, Ohio, Oct 10, 1942. *Study:* Univ Minn, BA; Univ NDak, MA; Ohio Univ, PhD. *Work:* Mckissick Mus; Sonje Mus, S Korea; Brooklyn Mus, New York. *Exhib:* 15 solo exhibs, David Findlay Galleries, New York; Biennial Contemp Am Art, Whitney Mus, New York; Smithsonian Inst Traveling Exhib. *Teaching:* Distinguished prof emer, Univ SC. *Bibliog:* Arts Mag, 2/76, 11/78, 3/82, 10/83 & 9/85; Art Voices S, 4/80; Art Am, 1/84; Artist's Mag, 4/85, 12/89, 5/90 & 6/91. *Media:* Acrylic. *Dealer:* Irene Morrah 206 Overbrook Rd Greenville SC 29607. *Mailing Add:* 5926 Marthas Glen Rd Columbia SC 29209

MULLER, JEROME KENNETH
ART DIRECTOR, PHOTOGRAPHER
b Amityville, NY, July 18, 1934. *Study:* NY Univ; Marquette Univ, BS; Layton Sch Art; Brandt Painting Workshop; Calif State Univ, Fullerton; Nat Univ, MA; Newport Psychoanalytic Inst. *Work:* Univ Calif, Irvine; Portland State Univ, Ore; Marquette Univ, Wis; plus others. *Exhib:* Gallery 2, Santa Ana, 71; Souk Gallery, Newport Beach, Calif, 72; Cannery Gallery, Newport Beach, Calif, 74; Mus Graphics Gallery, Costa Mesa, Calif, 92; South Coast Art Gallery, Costa Mesa & Bistango, Irvine, Calif, 94; White Gallery, Portland State Univ, Ore, 96; Univ Calif, Irvine, 97; Nat Tel & Commun, Irvine, Calif, 98; Robert Mondavi Wine & Food Ctr, Costa Mesa, Calif, 2000; Reflective Image Gallery, Santa Ana, Calif, 2007; Art Inst Calif, San Bernardino, Calif, 2010; The District Art Gallery, Tustin, Calif, 2012. *Collection Arranged:* Cartoon Show, Original Works by 100 Outstanding Am Cartoonists, Laguna Beach Mus Art, Calif, 72, Bowers Mus, Santa Ana, Calif, 76, EB Crocker Art Gallery, Sacramento, Calif, 77, Indianapolis Mus Art, Ind, 77, Tweed Mus Art, Duluth, Minn, 78, Everson Mus Art, Syracuse, NY, 78, Montgomery Mus Fine Arts, Ala, 78, South Bend Art Ctr, Ind, 79, Mem Art Gallery, Univ Rochester, 79, Neville Pub Mus, Wis, 79; Mickey Mouse: 1928-1978 (cur), Bowers Mus, 78; The Moving Image, art used in animated films, San Jose Mus Art, Calif, 80, Cooper-Hewitt Mus, NY, 81 & Nelson Gallery Art, Kansas City, 81, Mus of Sci & Industry, Chicago, 81; The Engravings of William Hogarth, Bowers Mus, 81; The Am Comic Strip, Univ Tex, Arlington, 81, Univ Chicago, 83, Wichita Art Mus, Kans, 84 & Monterey Peninsula Mus Art, Calif, 85, Wash State Capitol Mus, Olympia, 85. *Pos:* Photogr, New York, 53-56; ed & art dir, Orange Co Illus, 62-68, art ed, 70-79; dir, Mus Graphics, 79-; mng ed, Country Beautiful, Milwaukee, 60-62. *Teaching:* Instr photog, Lindenhurst High Sch, NY, 53-54; instr, The Cartoon & the Comic Strip in Am, Univ Calif, Irvine, 79; instr design, Orange Coast Coll, Costa Mesa, Calif, 97-2002. *Awards:* Two Silver Medals, 20th Ann Exhib of Advert & Ed Art in the West, Los Angeles Art Dir Club, 64; Award of Merit, Illustration West, Los Angeles Illusr Club, 72-74; Inkpot Award, San Diego Comic Conv, 80. *Bibliog:* Steven Parker (auth), Comics are collectible, Acquire Mag, 7/77; Paul Maynard (auth), Collecting Can Be a Funny Business, Orange Co Illus, 11/78; and others. *Mem:* Int Animated Film Soc; Art Mus Asn; Arts Orange Co; Laguna Art Mus; Orange Co Fine Arts. *Media:* Oil, Photography. *Res:* Developed presentations, Explorations in Color and Black & White Photogrpahy in NYC in 1950's. *Specialty:* Black & White Photog. *Interests:* 20th Century Am Painting. *Collection:* Cartoons, comic art and original animation art, exhibited in major museums throughout America. *Publ:* Auth, It's Rex Brandt, 10/73 & The comics: worth a second look, 11/73, SW Art; contribr, Mark Rothko, 74 & The Artist as Collector, 75, Newport Harbor Art Mus, Newport Beach, Calif, Mickey Mouse: 1928-1978, Bowers Mus, 78; Arts of Oceania, Shells of Oceania, Bowers Mus, 75; Publication Design & Production, 2000; Other Worlds: The Photography of Mike Glad, 2008. *Dealer:* Willem Photographic Monterey CA 93940; The District Art Gallery, Tustin, Calif 92782. *Mailing Add:* Box 11155 Costa Mesa CA 92627

MULLER, MAX PAUL
PAINTER, INSTRUCTOR
b Dover, NJ, Sept 26, 1935. *Study:* WVa Wesleyan, BA, 57; studied with Frank Webb, Valfred Thëlin & Fred Messersmith. *Comn:* Six paintings, comn by Dr Jack Corn, Sarasota, Fla, 89; two paintings, Handicapped Children's Ctr, Sarasota, 90. *Exhib:* Fla Watercolor Soc, Rollins Coll Mus, Winter Park, 89; Grand Nat Watercolor Exhib, Miss Mus Art, Jackson, 90; Am Artist Prof League, NY, 93; Inst Soc Marine Painters Exhib, Kings Point, NY, 94; solo show, Sarasota Visual Art Ctr, 94; and others. *Pos:* Pres, M P Muller Gallery, Sarasota, Fla, 89- & Art Uptown Gallery, Sarasota, 90-; mem bd dir & exhib chmn, Sarasota Art Asn, Fla, 90; exec dir, Sarasota Visual Art Ctr, 90-96. *Teaching:* Instr watercolor, Sarasota Art Asn, 90-91 & Leach Studios, Sarasota, Fla, 91-; instr, Ringling Sch Art, currently; instr workshop, Epcot Ctr, Disney World, 95 & 96 & Samos, Greece, 96. *Awards:* Award of Merit, Orange Co Arts Coun, 78; Grumbacher Silver Medal, Sarasota Art Asn, 89; Grumbacher Gold Medallion Award, Sarasota Art Asn. *Bibliog:* Joan Altabe (rev), article, Sarasota Herald Tribune, 89; Srotff (auth), Profile, Sarasota Mag, 90; article, Artists Fla Mag, Vol II, Mountain Productions Inc, 90. *Mem:* Am Watercolor Soc; Fla Watercolor Soc; Miami Watercolor Soc; Fla Artists Group; Int Soc Marine Painters; and others. *Media:* Watercolor, Oil. *Specialty:* Original art; contemporary American artists

MULLER, PRISCILLA ELKOW
ART HISTORIAN, CURATOR
b New York, NY, Feb 15, 1930. *Study:* Brooklyn Col, BA, 50; New York Univ, Inst Fine Arts, MA, 59, PhD, 63. *Collection Arranged:* Sorolla Paintings The Hispanic Soc Am, NY, 1988; Sorolla, An 80th Anniversary Exhib, NY, 1989; Ignacio Zuloaga in The Hispanic Soc Am, NY, 1991; Spain/Am, Circa 1840-1920, Small Oils by Am and Spanish Artists, NY, 1993; DeGoya a Zuloaga, La Pintura espanola de los siglos XIX y XX en The Hispanic Soc of Am, Madrid/Bilbao/Seville, 2000-01; L Dibujos españoles en la Hispanic Society of Am, del Siglo da Oro a Goya, 2006-2007. *Pos:* Asst cur, Hispanic Soc Am, 64-68, cur paintings & metalwork, 68-, cur mus, 70-, cur emer, 95-; consult, Time-Life Bks, 68-69, Tree Publ, 81-82; adv bd, Master Drawings, Archivo Espanol de Arte, Int Found for Art Res. *Teaching:* Lectr, Brooklyn Col, 66. *Awards:* Fel Nat Endowment Arts, 77; Real Acad de Ciencias, Bellas Letras y Nobles Artes de Cordoba; Real Acad de Bellas Artes de San Fernando, Madrid; and others. *Mem:* Am Soc Hispanic Art Hist Studies; Int Comt Fine Arts; Int Coun Mus; Soc Jewelry Historians; Int Found Art Res; and others. *Res:* Spanish and Hispanic fine arts, 15th-20th centuries. *Publ:* contribr, Francisco Goya's Portraits in Paintings, Prints and Drawings, Richmond, 72; auth, Jewels in Spain 1500-1800, New York, 72, Madrid, 2012; Goya's Black Paintings, Truth and Reason in Light and Liberty, New York, 84; and numerous articles in art-hist periodicals; De Goya a Zuloaga (exhib catalog), Madrid, 2000; L Dibujos españoles en la Hispanic Soc Am, del Siglo de Oro a Goya, Madrid, 2006 and Barcelona (catalan ed.), 2007. *Mailing Add:* Hispanic Soc Am Mus Broadway & 155th St New York NY 10032

MULLICAN, MATT
PERFORMANCE ARTIST, PAINTER, INSTALLATION SCULPTOR
b Santa Monica, Calif, 1951. *Study:* Calif Inst Arts, Valencia, BFA, 1974. *Work:* Whitney Mus Am Art, Mus Mod Art, New York; Mus Contemp Art, Los Angeles; Ludwig Mus, Cologne, Germany; Ctr George Pompidou, Paris. *Exhib:* Solo exhibs include Artists Space, New York, 1976, The Kitchen, New York, 1978, 1979, Mary Boone Gallery, New York, 1980, 1982, 1984, Inst Contemp Art, Boston, 1983, Ctr Art Contemp, Geneva, 1984, Everson Mus Art, New York, 1986, Mai 36 Galerie, Lucerne, Switzerland, 1988, Hirshhorn Mus & Sculpture Garden, Washington, 1989, Mus Mod Art, New York, 1989, Brooke Alexander Gallery, New York, 1991, 2000, Santa Barbara Mus Mod Art, Calif, 1992, Barbara Gladstone Gallery, New York, 1992, Daniel Blau, Munich, 1995, 1997, 2000, 2006, Mai 36 Galerie, Zurich, 1995, 2000, 2002, 2004, 2006, Bard Coll, Ctr Curatorial Studies, NY, 1997, Marian Goodman Gallery, Paris, 1998, Anton Kern Gallery, New York, 2002, 10th Biennial of the Moving Image, Ctr pour l'Image Contemp, Geneva, 2003, Tracy Williams Ltd, New York, 2004, 2006, 2011, Ludwig Mus, Cologne, 2005, Galerie George Kargl, Vienna, 2007, Whitney Mus Am Art, New York, 2008; two-person exhibs include In the Crack of Dawn (with Laurence Wiener), Mai 36 Galerie, Lucerne, 1991, PONG (with John Baldessari), Tracy Williams Ltd, New York, 2008; group exhibs include Made in India, Mus Mod Art, New York, 1985; Sacred Images in Secular Art, Whitney Mus Am Art, New York, 1986, Image World: Art & Media Culture, 1989, Whitney Biennial, 1989 & 2008; L'Epoque, la Mode, la Morale, la Passion, Ctr Georges Pompidou, Paris, 1987, 2007; Passions Privées, Mus d'Art Moderne de la Ville de Paris, 1995; ICONS: Magnets of Meaning, San Francisco Mus Mod Art, 1997; Heaven, PS1 Contemp Art Ctr, New York, 1997; Anticipation-Version 4, Ctr pour l'Image Contemp, Geneva, 1998; Traces of Science in Art, Royal Netherlands Acad Arts & Sciences, Amsterdam, 1998; Digital Printmaking Now, Brooklyn Mus Art, 2001; Ecstasy, In & About Altered States, Mus Contemp Art, Los Angeles, 2005; Looking Back, White Columns, New York, 2006; Gagosian Gallery, New York, 2007; The Puppet Show, Inst Contemp Art, Univ Pa, Philadelphia, 2008; PONG: John Baldessari/Matt Mullican, 2008, Tracy Williams Ltd, Anniversary Show, 2009, Ersatz Affiches, 2013; 55th Int Art Exhib Biennale, Venice, 2013. *Dealer:* Mai 36 Galerie Zürich Rämistrasse 37 CH-8001 Zürich Switzerland; Tracy Williams Ltd 313 W 4 St New York NY 10014. *Mailing Add:* 521 W 23rd St New York NY 10011

MULTHAUP, MERREL KEYES
PAINTER, SCULPTOR
b Cedar Rapids, Iowa, Sept 27, 1922. *Study:* State Univ Iowa, with Phillip Guston, 42-43; Carnegie Tech, Pittsburgh, 45-49; Summit Art Asn, with Joe Jones, 51; Rice Univ, 72. *Work:* Madonna, Hosp, Montclair, NJ; paintings incl in over 200 pvt collections in US & Europe. *Comn:* Elizabeth Savage (portrait), comm by Francis Savage, London, Eng, 65; Marilyn Joy (portrait), comn by Marilyn Joy, London, Eng, 66; Molly Bing (portrait), comn by John Bing, Houston, Tex, 72; Betty Hittinger (portrait), comn by William Hittinger, Summit, NJ 78; Nancy Soderberg (portrait), comn by Lars Soderberg, Nantucket, Mass; and many other portrait commissions. *Exhib:* 1st Prize Juried Nat, Hartford Atheneum Mus, Conn, 61; Stamford, Mus, Conn, 62; Bridgeport Mus, Conn, 63; Artist's Equity, Newark Mus, NJ, 79; Nat Asn Womens Artists Mem & traveling exhib, 96-99; Nat Asn Women Artists Mem Show, Atelier 14 Gallery, NY, 2000; plus many others incl seven solo shows. *Pos:* Bd mem & chmn statewide exhibs, Summit Art Ctr, NJ, 51-59; bd mem, Silvermine Guild, New Canaan, Conn, 60-64; bd mem & chmn statewide shows, Artists Equity, NJ, 76-83; chmn statewide shows, Assoc Artists, NJ, 86-92; artists adv coun, Hunterdon Art Ctr, Clinton, NJ, 89-92. *Teaching:* Instr oil painting, Summit Art Ctr, NJ, 56-59 & Livingston Night Sch Prog, 57-58; fac, Hunterdon Art Ctr, Clinton, NJ, 84-92. *Awards:* Winsor Newton Award, Acad Design, Nat Asn Women Artists, NY, 58, Dorothy Seligsson Mem Award, 80 & Charlotte Winston Mem Award, 89; and many other awards in Iowa, Pa, NJ, Conn & NY. *Bibliog:* Michael Lenson (auth), Realm of art, Newark News, NJ, many critiques from 54-59. *Mem:* Nat Asn Women Artists Inc (juror); Albuquerque United Artists, NMex; charter mem Nat Mus Women Arts, 82-2004; Silvermine Nat Portrait Group, New Canaan, Conn. *Media:* Oil, Acrylic. *Dealer:* Blankley Gallery 1700 Mountain Ave NW Albuquerque NM. *Mailing Add:* 1321 Stagecoach Rd SE Albuquerque NM 87123

MUNCE, JAMES CHARLES
PRINTMAKER, DRAFTSMAN
b Sioux Falls, SDak, Aug 24, 1938. *Study:* Minneapolis Sch Art, BFA, 66; Ind Univ, MFA, 71. *Work:* Brooklyn Mus, New York; Palace Legion Hon, San Francisco, Calif; Boston Printmakers, Mass; Univ Louisville, Ky; Mitsubishi Corp, Tokyo, Japan. *Exhib:* Los Angeles Printmakers 15th Biennial, 98; 43rd Exhib, Hunterdon Mus, NJ, 99; 75th Ann Int Competition, The Print Club, Philadelphia, Pa, 2001; Boston Printmakers, Paint Biennial, 2005; solo exhib, St Bonaventure, NY. *Teaching:* Instr prints, drawing, Univ Hawaii, Honolulu, 71-72; prof prints, drawing, Kans State Univ, Manhattan, 72-2003. *Awards:* Van Derlip Award, Minneapolis Sch Art, 66; Prints & Drawing Fel, Mid Am Arts Alliance, 84; Purchase Award, Boston Printmakers, 86; Chautauqua Inst Award, 92. *Bibliog:* Artists-A Kansas Collection, Rowley & Harper Artists Registry Inc. *Media:* Intaglio. *Dealer:* Strecker Gallery 332 Poyntz Manhattan KS 66502. *Mailing Add:* 1738 Fairchild Manhattan KS 66502

MUNDY, E JAMES
MUSEUM DIRECTOR, EDUCATOR
Study: Vassar Col, BA 74; Princeton Univ, MFA, 77, PhD, 80. *Collection Arranged:* The Draughtsman's Process, Milwaukee Art Mus, 86-87; Hidden Treasures, Milwaukee Art Mus, 87; Rookwood Pottery & the Arts, Milwaukee Art Mus, 87-88; Charting a New Frontier, Milwaukee Art Mus, 88; 1888: Frederick Layton & His World, Milwaukee Art Mus, 88; Renaissance & Baroque Bronzes, Milwaukee Art Mus, 89; Renaissance into Baroque, Milwaukee Art Mus & Nat Acad Design, 89-90; James Ensor Prints, Milwaukee Art Mus, 90. *Pos:* Chief cur, Milwaukee Art Mus, 86-91; dir, Frances Lehman Loeb Art Ctr, 91-. *Teaching:* Asst prof, Mt Holyoke Col, 79-85, assoc prof, 85-86; adj assoc prof, Univ Wis, Milwaukee, 87-91. *Publ:* Auth, Master Drawings Rediscovered, Mt Holyoke, 81; 1888: Frederick Layton and his world, Milwaukee Art Mus, 88; Renaissance into Baroque: Italian Master Drawings, Cambridge Univ Press, 89. *Mailing Add:* Vassar Col 124 Raymond Ave Box 23 Poughkeepsie NY 12601-6198

MUNHALL, EDGAR
CURATOR EMERITUS, EDUCATOR
b Mar 14, 1933. *Study:* Yale Univ, BA, 55, PhD, 59; New York Univ, MA, 57. *Pos:* Cur Emer, The Frick Collection, NY, 65-. *Teaching:* Instr art hist, Yale Univ, New Haven, Conn, 59-64, asst prof, 64-65; adj prof, Columbia Univ, 79 & 81-. *Awards:* Decorated Officer Ordre des Arts et des Lettres, 2001; Henry Allen Moe Prize, Frick Collection & NY State Hist Soc. *Interests:* 18th and 19th Century French Art. *Mailing Add:* 360 E 55th St Apt 5C New York NY 10022

MUNIOT, BARBARA KING
COLLECTOR
b New Orleans, La. *Study:* Sullins Col, Bristol, Va, art degree; Newcomb Col, spec study with Prof Franklin Adams. *Pos:* Asst dir, Orleans Gallery, 68-70, dir, 70-73; asst dir, Galerie Simonne Stern, 73-75, dir, 75-83. *Specialty:* Contemporary art. *Collection:* Paintings, drawings, prints, photographs & African art. *Mailing Add:* 5954 Laurel St New Orleans LA 70115-2140

MUNITZ, BARRY
ADMINISTRATOR, EDUCATOR
b Brooklyn, NY, July 26, 1941. *Study:* Brooklyn Col, BA, 63; Princeton Univ, NJ, MA, 65 & PhD, 68; Univ Notre Dame, Hon Dr Laws, 97; Hon Dr, Claremont Univ, Calif State Univ, Whittier Col. *Pos:* Chief Exec Officer & pres, trustee, J Paul Getty Trust, 98-2006; pres & Chief Operating Officer, Federated Develop Co, 82-91; vchmn, Maxxam Inc, LA, 82-91; acad vpres, Univ Ill Syst, 71-76; vpres, dean faculties, Cent campus Univ Houston, 76-77, chancellor, 77-82; chancellor, Calif State Univ system, Long Beach, Calif, 91-98; bd dir, KCET-TV, SLM Holdings, KB Home; trustee, Princeton Univ; chmn, Calif Gov Transition Team, formerly. *Teaching:* Asst prof dramatic arts & lit, Univ Calif, Berkeley, 66-68; fac humanities, San Franciso Art Inst, Calif, 69-70; staff associate, Carnegie Comn Higher Educ, 68-70; trustee prof, English Dept, Calif State Univ, LA, 2006-. *Awards:* Alumnus award, Bklyn Coll, 79; Alumni Pres medal, Univ Houston, 81; fellow, Am Acad Arts & Sci; Woodrow Wilson fellow; Phi Beta Kappa. *Mem:* Am Asn Mus; art mus vis com, Princeton Univ & Harvard Univ. *Publ:* Auth, The Assessment of Institutional Leadership. *Mailing Add:* English Dept Calif State Univ Engineering and Technology A604 5151 State University Dr Los Angeles CA 90032

MUNIZ, VIK
PHOTOGRAPHER
b Sao Paulo, Brazil, 1961. *Work:* Metrop Mus Art, Mus Mod Art, NY; Mus Fine Arts, Boston; San Francisco Mus Mod Art; Art Inst Chicago. *Comn:* Equivalents (photographs & sculptures), SEI Investments Corp, Oaks, Pa, 1998. *Exhib:* Solo exhibs include Rena Bransten Gallery, San Francisco, 1996, 1999, 2002, 2004 & 2006, Galeria Camargo Vilaca, Sao Paulo, Brazil, 1997, 2000 & 2001, Int Ctr Photog, NY, 1999, Mus Contemp Photog, Chicago, 1999, Renos Xippas Gallery, Paris, 1999, 2001, 2004 & 2006, Brent Sikkema Gallery, NY, 2000, 2002 & 2004, Frick Art & Hist Ctr, Pittsburgh, 2000, Whitney Mus Am Art, NY, 2001, Venice Biennial, 2001, Michael Hue Williams Fine Art, London, 2002, Fortes Vilaca Gallery, Sao Paulo Brazil, 2003, 2005 & 2007, Mus Art Contemp, Rome, 2003, Gallery Gan, Tokyo, 2003, Irish Mus Contemp Art, Dublin, 2004, Cardi Gallery, Milan, 2005, Konayagi Gallery, Tokyo, 2005, Miami Art Mus, 2006, Seattle Art Mus, 2006, Mus Contemp Art, San Diego, 2007; group exhibs include Multiples, Aldrich Mus Art, Ridgefield, Conn, 1992; The Photog Condition, San Francisco Mus Mod Art, 1995, Supernova, 2003, Between Art & Life, 2004; Panorama da Arte Contemp Brasileira, Mus Mod Art, Sao Paulo, 1995, Panorama de Arte Brasileira, 2003, Photog & Sculpture, 2004; Novas Aquisicoes, Mus Mod Art, Rio de Janeiro, Brazil, 1996; Recent Acquisitions, Metrop Mus Art, NY, 1996, Regarding War, 2003; New Photog 13, Mus Mod Art, NY, 1997, The Museum as Muse, 1999, Counter-Monuments & Memory, 2001, The Path of Resistance, 2001, Minimalism & After, 2001; New Faces, Art Inst Chicago, 1997, Defining Moments in Photog, 2007; Le Donné, le Fictif, Nat Photog Ctr, Paris, 1998, Bruit de fond, 2001; La Collection II, Found Cartier, Paris, 1998; 24th Internat Biennial, San Paulo, Brazil, 1998; Trace, Tate Gallery, Liverpool, Eng, 1999, Inverting the Map, 2005; Abracadabra, Tate Gallery, London, 1999; Landscape-Portrait, Michael Hue-Williams Fine Art, London, 2000, Last Supper, 2003; 46th Corcoran Biennial, Corcoran Gallery of Art, Washington, 2000, Both Sides of the Street, 2003; Biennial Exhib, Whitney Mus Am Art, NY, 2000, Visions from Am, 2002, What's New, 2002, Overhead/Underfoot, 2005; The Thread Unravelled, Mus del Barrio, NY, 2001, Retratos, 2004; Arte Latino, Galeria Fortes Vilaca, Sao Paulo, Brazil, 2001, A Nova Geometria, 2003, Hollywood Boulevard, 2006; Sean Kelly Gallery, NY, 2001, Hot Summer in the City, 2003; Brazil: Body & Soul, Solomon R Guggenheim Mus, NY, 2001, Moving Pictures, 2002; We Love Painting, Mus Contemp Art, Tokyo, 2002; Only Skin Deep, Internat Ctr Photog, NY, 2003; Surprise, Cardi Gallery, Milan, 2004, Home Sweet Home, 2004; Artist's Favorites: Act II, Inst Contemp Art, London, 2004; Nat Portrait Gallery, Smithsonian Inst, Washington, 2004; Fatamorgana, Haifa Mus Art, Israel, 2006; Timer: Intimacy, Milan Triennial, 2007. *Collection Arranged:* Making it Real, 1997; Beyond the Edges, Insider's Look at Early Photographs, Metrop Mus Art NY, 1998; Robert Mapplethorpe, Fortes Vilaca Gallery, Sao Paulo, Brazil, 2006. *Pos:* Ed, Blind Spot, Blind Spot Photog, 1993-; contribr, Parkett, Parkett Pub, currently. *Teaching:* Instr drawing for photog, Sch Visual Arts. *Awards:* Nat Artist Award, 2005. *Bibliog:* Andy Grundberg (auth), Sweet illusion, Art Forum, 9/97; Vince Aletti (auth), Organized confusion, Village Voice, 12/2/97; Vicki Goldberg (auth), It's a Leonardo? It's a Corot? Well, no, it's a chocolate syrup, NY Times, 12/25/98. *Dealer:* Sikkema Jenkins & Co 530 W 22nd St New York NY 10011; Galerie Xippas 108 rue Vieille du Temple 75003 Paris France; Galeria Fortes Vilaca Rue Fradique Coutinho 1500 05416-001 Sao Paulo Brazil T 55 11; Rena Bransten Gallery 77 Geary St San Francisco CA 94108; Elba Benitez Galeria San Lorenzo 11 28004 Madrid Spain. *Mailing Add:* 80 Hanson Pl Ste 703 Brooklyn NY 11217-1506

MUNK, LOREN JAMES
PAINTER, COLLAGE ARTIST
b Salt Lake City, Utah, Sept 9, 1951. *Study:* Idaho State Univ, 69-72; Univ Md, Ramstein Army Base, Ger, 73-75; Art Students League, 79. *Work:* Everson Mus, Syracuse, NY; Statue of Liberty Nat Monument; Chase Manhattan Bank, Sony Music Entertainment, Forbes Mag Collection, NY; Port Authority, NY & NJ; Mus City NY; Hood Mus Art, Dartmouth Col, Hanover, NH; numerous pvt colls including Vera List, NY, Dr & Mrs Donald Rubell, NY, Mrs Yitzhak Rabin, Jerusalem, Pierre Huber, Geneva, Tomas Wallin, Stockholm. *Comn:* Poster, Metrop Transit Authority, NY, 91-92; Montparnasse (wall mural), Mayors Office, Paris, 91-93; poster, C&C Vineyards, Bellville/Saone, France, 92; Litfass Design, Int Litfass Biennale, BMW, Munich, 92; mural, Independence Savings Bank, Brooklyn, NY, 95. *Exhib:* Solo shows, Galerie Svetlana & Hubner, Munich, 89, 90 & 92, Elisabeth Krief Galerie D'Art, Paris, 91 Andre Zarre Gallery, NY, 92 & 94 & in conjunction with BMW Introduction of 316i, Munich, 94, Amerikhaus, Munich, 95, Caesaria Gallery, Boca Raton, Fla, 96, Jeffrey Coploff Fine Art Ltd, NY, 97 & L'Antiquario, Sao Paulo, Brasil, 98, Am Contemp Art Gallery, Munich, Ger, 11/2000, 01, 02, MJ Wewerka Galerie, Berlin, Ger, 2002, Andre Zarre Gallery, NY, 2002, Mus Moderner Kunst, Passau, Ger, 2002; Prix de Peinture de Principal de Monaco, Monaco, Gallery Ruf, Munich, 92; Inaugural Exhib, J Claramunt Gallery, NY, 92; Through Thick & Thin, Andre Zarre Gallery, NY, 93; Blue, 450 Broadway Gallery, NY, 96; group shows, Summer Swelter, Gallery e49, NY, Basel Art Fair, Am Contemp Art Gallery, Munich; Mus City of NY, 99; Andre Zarre Gallery, NY, 2000; Am Contemp Art Gallery, Munich, Ger, 2000; many others. *Bibliog:* Robert Morgan (auth), Celebrating the American Vernacular (essay), 94; Hank Schlesinger (auth), Painting the town, Brooklyn Bridge, 12/95; Camila Viegas (auth), Cores vibrantes usadas por Munk establecem dialogo com o olhar, O Estado de S Paulo, 4/22/98; From the Mayors Doorstep, Halasz, Piri, 01/14/2003; New York Art Mag, 2002; Christopher Chambers (auth), Art Picks, Berliner Zeiturg, 9/21/2001. *Media:* Oil with Gold Leaf & Glass Tile. *Res:* Contemporary art. *Mailing Add:* 36 Tiffany Pl Brooklyn NY 11231

MUNO, RICHARD CARL
SCULPTOR, DIRECTOR
b Arapaho, Okla, July 2, 1939. *Study:* Okla State Univ Sch Tech Training, cert com art. *Work:* Diamond M Mus, Snyder, Tex. *Comn:* Sculpture of Cavalry Man and Horse, Winchester Firearms, Hartford, Conn, 68; Western Heritage Awards Wrangler Trophy, Nat Cowboy Hall Fame, Oklahoma City, 68; Sculpture of a Lawman, Colt Firearms, Hartford, 73; Sculpture of Cowboy Branding Calf, Oklahoma City CofC, 75; Lifesize Sculpture of Pioneer Man, Bicentennial Comn of Clinton, Okla, 75; Promenade (sq dancers), Oklahoma City Fairgrounds, 89; Memorial (figures & fountains), Edmond Post Off, Okla, 89; Young at Heart (Johnny Kelley figures), Boston Athletic Assoc, Newton, MA, 93. *Exhib:* Philbrook Mus Art Exhib, Tulsa, Okla, 67; Sci & Arts Found Exhib, Oklahoma City, 68; Oklahoma City Zoological Exhib, 68; Okla Mus Art Five State Salon, Oklahoma City, 71-72; Solon Borglum Mem Sculpture Exhib, Nat Cowboy Hall of Fame, Oklahoma City, 75. *Pos:* Preparator, Gilcrease Inst Am Hist & Art, Tulsa, 60-64; cur, Nat Cowboy Hall Fame, Oklahoma City, 65-69, art dir, 70-77, dep dir, 77-78, managing dir, 78-85; sculptor, 85-. *Awards:* Numerous ribbons in various art shows. *Bibliog:* Marcia Preston (auth), Orbit Mag, Okla Publ Co, 68; Dean Krakel (auth), End of the Trail, Okla Univ Press, 73. *Media:* Bronze, Wood. *Collection:* Nat Acad Western Art Ann Exhibs, 73-75. *Publ:* Contribr, Persimmon Hill Mag, 72-75. *Mailing Add:* 6300 E Danforth Edmond OK 73034

MUÑOZ, PALOMA
SCULPTOR
b Madrid, 1965. *Study:* Old Dominium Univ, BA, 78; Va Commonwealth Univ, MFA, 80. *Exhib:* Solo exhibs, PPOW, NYC, 94,96,98,2001, 2005, Moriarty Gallery, Madrid, 96, Alejandro Sales Gallery, Barcelona, 97, Espacio Caja Burgos, Spain, 99, Dis, Momenta, Brooklyn, 99, Loss of Experience, Santa Barbara Arts Forum, 2000, Travelers, Moriarty Gallery, Madrid, PPOW, NYC, 2003, Rhona Hoffman Gallery, Chicago, Museo de la Universidad de Alicante, Spain, 2004, The Fridgid Zone, Mario Mauroner Contemp Art Salzburg, 2004, Cold Front, PPOW Gallery, NYC, 2005; Group exhibs, Bienal del Mediterraneo, Barcelona, 86; El Jardin de las Sombras, Casa del Reloj, Madrid, 87; Talleres de Arte Actual, Circulo de Bellas Artes, Madrid, 89; Les Etoiles de la Peinture, AT Gallery, Paris, 90; The Body Human, Nohra Haime Gallery, NYC, 94; Revisiting the Landscape, Calif Center for Arts, Escondido, 95; The Subverted Object, Ubu Gallery, NY, 96; The Chalkboard Chronicles, TZArt & Co, NY, 97; No Small Feat: Investigations of the Shoe is Contemp Art, Rhona Hoffman Gallery, Chicago, 97; Memorial Book, Museo Pablo Gargallo, Zaragoza, Spain, 98; True West, PPOW, NYC, 99; Plastic Monuments, Centro Municipal de Exposiciones Subte, Montevideo, Uruguay; Animas!, The Rotunda Gallery, Brooklyn, 2001; Miami Art, PPOW Gallery, NYC, 2003-2004; Hot Summer in New York, Sean Kelly Gallery, NYC, 2003; MetroSpective at City Hall Park, Public Art Fund, NYC, 2003; The Art Show, PPOW Gallery, NYC, 2004; ARCO Galeria Moriarty, Madrid, 2004-2005; Arts for Transit Along the Way, UBS Gallery, NY, 2005; The Empire of Sighs, Numark Gallery, Wash DC, 2005; CIGE, China Int Gallery Expos, 2006; Art Brussels, MAM Mario Mauroner Contemp Art, Belgium, 2006; Bienal de Zamora, Claustro del Colegio Universitario, Zamora, Spain, 2006; Double Take, Schroeder Romero Gallery, NYC, 2006; Little Disasters, Mauroner RoomnumberOne, Vienna, 2006; installations include Changing Places, Metro Tech Center, Public Art Fund, Brooklyn, 1996, A Gathering, MTA's Arts for Transit Prog, NYC, 1997-2000, Forbidden Door, Bloomberg LP, Public Art fund, NY, 2001, Travelers, Grand Central Terminal, MTA Arts for Transit, NY, 2002-2003, Wilshire/Normandie Metro Rail Station, MTA Metro Art, LA, 2005, MetroSpective at City Hall Park, City Hall Park, NY,; A Gathering, MTA's Arts for Transit Prog, NYC, 1997-2000. *Awards:* Second prize, Festival de Video, Inst de la Mujer, Madrid, 90; Third Prize, Int Art contest, Paris, 90; Grant, Künstlerhaus Hamburg, Ministerio de Cultura, Spain, 90; Grant, Graphic Design, CETECAM, Comunidad Autonoma de Madrid, 92; Grants, Spanish Ministerio de Cultura, 94-96. *Bibliog:* Adolfo Castaño (auth), Las Otras Miradas, ABC, 12/1988; Elle, 2/1991; Choices, Village Voice, 10/1994; Poderoso caballero, Babelia (El Pais), 2/1995; Josephine Gear (auth), Changing Places, Review, 11/1996; Faultline, Journal of Art and Literature, Vol V, 11/1997; Christopher Chambers (auth), Picks, NY Arts, 3-4/1998; Paul Laster (auth), Brooklyn Spice, Artnet.com, 10/1999; Rob Wilson (auth), Walter Martín & Paloma Muñoz, Sculpture Magazine, Summer, 2001; Tomas Paredes, Walter Martín & Paloma Muñoz: Cuentos de Invierno, El Punto, 2/2003; A seasonal migration of cultural scope, The NY Times, 8/8/2003; McElheny succumbs to glass' seductiveness, Chicago Tribune, 2/27/2004; Walter Martín & Paloma Muñoz, The New Yorker, 2/2005; Reflecting on a cultural divide, The Washington Post, 10/6/2005; Amy Simon 9auth), Ars 06, Artforum, 4/2006; Rachel Somerstein (auth), The Weather Inside is Frightful, Artnews, 10/2006. *Media:* miscellaneous

MUNOZ, RIE
PAINTER, PRINTMAKER
b Los Angeles, Calif. *Study:* Washington & Lee Univ; Univ of Alaska; pvt lessons. *Work:* Alaska State Mus; Anchorage Hist & Fine Arts Mus; Gov Off, Alaska; Frye Mus, Seattle, Wash. *Comn:* Alaska Coun Churches Mural, Univ Alaska Libr, Fairbanks, 67; Reindeer Round-Up, Reindeer Serv Bur Indian Affairs, 68; Ethnic People of Alaska Mural, Alaska State Libr, Juneau, 69; ChilKat Dancers (mural), Juneau Int Airport; Alaskan Children at Play (mural), Harborview Elementary Sch, Juneau. *Exhib:* Charles & Emma Frye Mus, Seattle, Wash, 73, 75, 81, 86, 89 & 92; Contemp Art from Alaska, Smithsonian Inst, Washington, DC, 78; Alaska Art Tour, 88; Washington Art Tour, 89 & 92; Ore Art Tour, 88, 90 & 94. *Pos:* Political cartoonist, SE Alaska Empire, 52-67; cur exhib, Alaska State Mus, Juneau, 68-72. *Awards:* Outstanding Alaska Artist, Anchorage Fine Arts Mus Asn, 77. *Bibliog:* Article, Artist in Juneau captures Alaska, Alaska Log, 73; Rie Munoz Alaskan Artist, Alaska Northwest Publ Co, 84; Article, Rie Munoz, Alaska Mag, 94. *Media:* Water-Base Colors; Silkscreen and Stone Lithography. *Specialty:* Lithographic prints by Alaskan artists; etchings; engravings; tapestries; Soapstone sculpture; baskets and pottery. *Publ:* King Island Christmas, Greenwillow Books, 85; Runaway Mittens, Greenwillow Books, 88; Andy, Cambridge Univ Press, 88; Rie Munoz Artist in Alaska, pvt publ, 87; Rie Munoz Portrait of Alaska, pvt publ, 95. *Mailing Add:* c/o Rie Munoz Gallery 2101 N Jordan Ave Juneau AK 99801-8047

MUNRO, ELEANOR
WRITER, CRITIC
b Brooklyn, NY, Mar 28, 1928. *Study:* Smith Col, BA, 49; Columbia Univ, MA, 65; Sorbonne, Paris. *Pos:* Assoc ed, Art News, New York, 53-59; managing ed, Art News Ann, New York, 54-59. *Teaching:* Multiple vis-lectureships at Am Schs & Cols, 89-. *Awards:* Arts Prize, Cleveland, Ohio, 88; Woodrow Wilson Vis Fel, 89-; Medal, Smith Col, 94; Lifetime achievement award Women's Caucus for Art, 03. *Mem:* Am Asn Art Critics; Int Asn Art Critics; Authors Guild; PEN Am; Art Table. *Res:* American women artists; imagination and the creative process in the visual arts; pilgrimage in myth and art. *Publ:* Auth, Encyclop Art, Western Printing, 61; Originals: American Women Artists, Simon & Schuster, 79 & Touchstone Press, 82, enlarged edit, DA CAPO Press, 2000; On Glory Roads, A Pilgrim Book about Pilgrimages, Thames & Hudson, 87; Memoir of a Modernist's Daughter, Viking, 88; Art in America: Essays by contemp Soviet and Am writers, Univ Wash Press, 90; and auth of essays, articles & reviews in collections, national magazines & newspapers. *Mailing Add:* 176 E 71 St New York NY 10021

MUNRO, JANET ANDREA
PAINTER
b North Reading, Mass, Dec 8, 1949. *Study:* Self-taught artist. *Work:* The White House & Smithsonian Inst, Washington, DC; Am Mus, Bath, Eng; Jay Johnson Am Folk Heritage Gallery, NY; and others. *Exhib:* One-woman shows, Country Art Gallery, Locust Valley, NY, 80, Fowler Mills Galleries, Santa Monica, Calif, 80, Art World Gallery, Acton, Mass, 80-81 & America's Folk Heritage Gallery, NY, 81; Easter Egg Roll, White House, Washington, DC, 81; and others. *Bibliog:* Carolyn Norwood (auth), Mrs Munro paints for the White House, Islander Weekly, 81; Kevin Dean (auth), Mrs Munro, Art Voices, 11-12/81; Contemporary primitives, Colonial Homes Mag, 1-2/82. *Media:* Oil, Egg Tempera

MUNRO, JP
ARTIST
b Inglewood, Calif, 1975. *Exhib:* Ending is Better Than Mending, Sadie Coles HQ, London, 2002; Morbid Curiosity, I-20 Gallery, NY, 2002; Golden, Galerie Michael Jenssen, Cologne, 2003; Drawings, Metro Pictures Gallery, NY, 2003; 100 Artists See God, Inst Contemp Art, London, 2004; JP Munro, 2005; Contemp Art Ctr, Va, 2005; The Early Show, White Columns, NY, 2005; Whitney Biennial, Day for Night, Whitney Mus Am Art, 2006

MUNROE, VICTORIA
ART DEALER
Study: Radcliffe Col, BA (old master drawings), 1975. *Pos:* Dir, The Drawing Room, NYC, currently; pres, Victoria Munroe Fine Art, Boston, 2001-; bd mem, Citizen Schs and Tada Children's Theatre, NYC, currently; trustee, Beacon Acad, currently

MUNTADAS, ANTONIO
VIDEO ARTIST
b Barcelona, Spain, Sept 21, 1942. *Study:* Escuela Technica Superior des Ingenieros Industriales of Barcelona; Pratt Graphic Ctr, New York. *Work:* Guggenheim Mus, New York; Palais de Beaux-Arts, Brussels; Nat Gallery, Ottawa, Can; Galerije Contemp Art, Zagreb; Mus de Arte Contemp, Caracas. *Exhib:* Solo exhibs, Mus Mod Art, New York, 94, Atlanta Coll Art, Ga, 96, Mus de Arte Mod, Buenos Aires, Arg, 97 & 2000, Arad Mus, Arad, 98 & Ludwig Mus, Budapest, Hungary, 98, and others; Mus d'Histoire Geneva, Switz, 99; Mus Art Contemp, Montreal, Can, 2000; Mus d'Arte Mod, Rio de Janeiro, Brazil, 2000; Univ Art Mus, Berkeley, Calif, 2001. *Teaching:* Instr sems, Univ Calif, San Diego, Ecole des Beaux-Arts, Bordeaux, San Francisco Art Inst, Ecole Nat des Beaux-Arts, Paris & Univ San Paulo, Cooper Union, New York. *Awards:* Production Grant, Nat Endowment Arts, 91 & 95; Arts Electonica Prix for the File Room, 95; Premi Nac ce Arts Plastigues, Generalitat de Catalunya, 96. *Bibliog:* Susan Snodgrass (auth), Public domain, Muntadas and the file room, New Art Examiner, 10/94; Michael Tarantino (auth), Muntadas, Galerie de l'ancienne poste, Artforum, 2/95; Robert Atkins (auth), Art on line, Art in Am, 12/95. *Media:* Mixed Media, Multimedia. *Dealer:* Kent Gallery 67 Prince St New York NY 10012. *Mailing Add:* 395 Broadway Apt 5C New York NY 10013-3540

MUNZNER, ARIBERT
PAINTER, EDUCATOR
b Mannheim, Ger, Jan 9, 1930. *Study:* Syracuse Univ, BFA; Cranbrook Acad Art, MFA. *Exhib:* Nat & regional shows, 53-94. *Teaching:* Instr painting & design, Minneapolis Col Art & Design, 55-94, assoc prof painting, Div Fine Arts, 68-76, prof, 76-93, emer prof, 93-. *Mailing Add:* 3630 Phillips Pkwy Apt 605 Minneapolis MN 55426

MURAKAMI, TAKASHI
PAINTER, SCULPTOR, PRINTMAKER
b Tokyo, 1962. *Study:* Tokyo Nat Univ Fine Arts & Music, BFA, 86, MFA, 88, PhD, 93. *Exhib:* Solo exhibs include Aoi Gallery, Osaka, Japan, 94, 96 & 2005, Gallery Koto, Okayama, Japan, 94-97 & 99, Blum & Poe, Santa Monica, Calif, 97, 98, 2000, 2004 & 2008, Galerie Emmanuel Perrotin, Paris, 97, 2001, 2003 & 2006, Marianne Boesky Gallery, New York, 99, 2001 & 2003, PS1 Contemp Art Center, Long Island City, NY, 2000, Mus Fine Arts, Boston, 2001, Gagosian Gallery, New York, 2007, MURAKAMI, Mus Contemp Art, Los Angeles, 2007, traveling to Brooklyn Mus, Mus Mod Kunst, Frankfurt & Mus Guggenheim Bilbao, Spain; group exhibs include Transculture, Venice Biennial, 95, Pittura/Painting: Rauschenberg to Murakami, 1964-2003, 2003; People, Places, Things, Marianne Boesky Gallery, New York, 98,

2000; The Manga Age, Mus Contemp Art, Tokyo & Hiroshima City Mus Contemp Art, 98; New Modernism for a New Millennium, San Francisco Mus Mod Art, 99, The Darker Side of Playland, 2000, Supernova: Art of the 1990s from the Logan Collection, 2003; Carnegie Int, Carnegie Inst, Pittsburgh, 99; One Heart, One World, UN, New York, 2000; Let's Entertain, Walker Art Center, Minneapolis, 2000, traveling to Portland Art Mus, Oreg, Centre Georges Pompidou, Paris, Mus Rufino Tamayo, Mex City & St Lous Art Mus; Superflat, Los Angeles Mus Contemp Art, Walker Art Center, Minneapolis & Henry Art Gallery, Seattle, 2001; Public Offerings, Mus Contemp Art, Los Angeles, 2001; Out of the Box, Philadelphia Mus Art, 2002, Popular, Pop & Post-Pop, 2003; Drawing Now, Mus Mod Art, New York, 2002, Comic Abstraction, 2007; Pulp Art, Brooklyn Mus Art, 2003; On the Wall: Wallpaper & Tableau, RI Sch Design & Fabric Workshop & Mus, Philadelphia, 2003; Ecstasy: In & About Altered States, Mus Contemp Art, Los Angeles, 2005; Surprise, Surprise, Inst Contemp Arts, London, 2006; Jellyfish Eyes, Mus Contemp Art, Chicago, 2007; Kaikai Kiki Artists, Kaikai Kiki Gallery, Tokyo, 2008. *Pos:* Founder Kaikai Kiki LLC (formerly the Hiropon Factory, Japan, 95-, New York, 98-; founder & host, Gesai Art Fair, 2002-. *Teaching:* Vis prof, Univ Calif Los Angeles Sch Art & Archit, 98. *Awards:* Asian Cult Coun Fel, PS1 Internat Studio Program, 94-95; Spec Award, Japan Fashion Editor Club, 2003; Tag Heuer Bus Award, 2004; Japan Soc Imajiné Award, 2005; AICA USA Award for Best Thematic Mus Show, 2006; Heisei Educ Rookie of Yr Award, 2006. *Mem:* Hon mem Compagnons du Beaujolais. *Dealer:* Blum & Poe 2754 S La Cienega Blvd Los Angeles CA 90034; Galerie Emmanuel Perrotin 76 rue de Turenne 75003 Paris France. *Mailing Add:* Kaikai Kiki NY 5-17 46th Rd Long Island City NY 11101

MURANAKA, HIDEO
PAINTER, PRINTMAKER
b Mitaka-shi, Tokyo, Japan, Feb 4, 46, nat US, 1946. *Study:* Tokyo Nat Univ Fine Arts & Music, BFA, 70, MFA, 72, cert, 74. *Work:* Brooklyn Mus; Achenbach Found, Calif Palace Legion Hon; Yergeau-Musee Int d'Art, Can. *Exhib:* One Hundred New Acquisitions, Brooklyn Mus, 78; Pacific Coast States Collection From the Vice President's House, Nat Mus Am Art, 81; IEEE Centennial Art Contest, NY, 83; Am Drawing Biennial, Muscarelle Mus Art, 88; Grand Prix de France Int, Chapelle de la Sorbonne, Paris Mus, France, 90. *Teaching:* Instr sumie, Acad Art Col, San Francisco, 74-75 & 84; teacher sumie & calligraphy, Acad Muranaka, San Francisco, 76-79; San Francisco State Univ, 84, 88 & 91-. *Awards:* Second Prize, Mus Hosio, Capranica-Viterbo, Italy, 84, first prize, 88; Hon Mention, San Bernardino Co Mus, Redland, Calif, 85; VJ's Artist Award, Palm Springs Desert Mus, 95. *Bibliog:* Tom Kent (auth), Visuals, City, 5/14/75; Thomas Albright (auth), Art, San Francisco Chronicle, 5/14/75. *Media:* All. *Publ:* auth Art of Japanese Writing and Calligraphy, 1st Books Library, 2000. *Mailing Add:* 179 Oak St No W San Francisco CA 94102

MURASHIMA, KUMIKO
EDUCATOR, KATAZOME ARTIST
b Nishinomiya, Japan. *Study:* Women's Coll Fine Arts, Tokyo, BFA (fiber arts), 63; Serizawa Dyed Paper Inst, Tokyo, 63-67; Ind Univ, Bloomington, MFA (textiles), 70; Pasons Sch Design, New York, indust textile design cert, 91. *Work:* Evansville Mus Arts & Sci, Ind; Wills Eye Hosp, Philadelphia; Flour Corp Hq, Irvine, Calif; Hackensack Med Ctr, NJ; North Am Re-Insurance co, NY; Chubb Insurance Corp Hq, NJ; Caxton Commodities, Princeton, NJ; AT&T Telecommuns, NJ; Marck, Sharpe & Dorne, Penn; Time/Life Buiding, Canada; Century Broadcasting Co, Chicago; Metropolitan Design Properties, Ala; Citizens Nat Bank, NJ. *Comn:* Metrop design, Properties Inc, Birmingham, Ala, 74; mural (woven tapestry), Disneyland Hotel Conv Ctr, Anaheim, Calif, 75. *Exhib:* NJ State Mus, 78; Artists Equity Triennial Juried Exhib, Mus Philadelphia, Civic Ctr, 81; Oriental Influence in Contemp Am Crafts, The Craftman's Gallery, Scarsdale, NY, 81; Fairmount Inst, Philadelphia, 82; Henry Chauncey Conf Ctr, ETS, Princeton, NJ, 86; Art Alliance, Philadelphia, Pa; Stedman Art Gallery, Rutgers Univ, Camden, NJ, 2000; Jurors Award, Works on Paper Exhib, Perkins Ctr Arts, 2006; Solo exhibs: Villanova Univ Art Gallery, Pa, 06, Henry Chonncey Conf Ctr, ETS, Princeton, NJ, 09, Newark Mus, 2010, Southern NJ Art Redux, Hedmon Art Gallery, Rutgers Univ, 2010. *Pos:* Freelance fiber artist, Izumi Archit Design, Co, Tokyo, 65-67 & Saphier, Lerner, Schindler, Inc, Environetics, Chicago, Ill, 7-71. *Teaching:* Instr fiber art, Rowan Univ, NJ, 71-75, asst prof, 75-82, assoc prof, 82-2007. *Awards:* Purchase Award, Mid-States Crafts Show, Malcolm Koch Mus, 69; Mr & Mrs Paul Arnold Merit Award, Mid-States Crafts Show, 70; Dorothy Grafly Mem Award, Artists Equity Triennial Juried Exhib, Philadelphia Civic Ctr Mus, 81. *Bibliog:* Dona Meilach (auth), Art Fabric: Form/Design, Crown Publ, 77; Eva Balassa (auth), article, Fibre Arts, 1-2/79; Burton Wasserman (auth), article, Artcrafts Mag, 8-9/80. *Mem:* Am Fed Col/Univ Fac; Art Educ NJ; Nat Educ Asn; Surface Design Asn. *Media:* Tapestry Weaving, Japanese Paste-Resist Dyeing, Katazome. *Interests:* foreign and domestic travel, reading, walking, classical music. *Publ:* Contribr, Pamela Scheiman's American Crafts, Am Crafts Coun, 78; Courier Post, Gloucester Times, Philadelphia Inquirer & Philadelphia Bull; Katazome, Altamonte Press, 94. *Dealer:* Dumont-Landis Fine Arts New Brunswick NJ; Faviana-Olivie-Galleria Manhattan Beach CA. *Mailing Add:* 1430 Victory Ave Williamstown NJ 08094

MURCHIE, DONALD JOHN
WRITER, ARTIST
b Plainfield, NJ, Nov 23, 1943. *Study:* Univ Colo, BA; Dalhousie Univ, MLS. *Exhib:* Dalhousie Art Gallery, 82; Eye Level Gallery & Owens Art Gallery, 95. *Pos:* Libr dir, NS Col Art & Design, Halifax, 72-90; assoc curator, Art Gallery NS, 95. *Awards:* Fel Nat Gallery Can, 95-96. *Mem:* Art Libr Soc/NAm (mem exec bd, 75-78, chmn, 76). *Media:* Mixed. *Res:* Contemporary art; Canadian art history. *Publ:* Auth, A Quiet Evening, 79; Opening, Open, Closed, Eye Level Gallery, 80; An Invitation; or One-Way Ticket, 83; Seven, 96; Anaesthetic, 96. *Mailing Add:* 178-Pond Shore Rd Sackville NB E4L 1K8 Canada

MURDOCH, JOHN
MUSEUM DIRECTOR
Pos: Asst dir, collections Victoria and Albert Mus, London; dir, Courtauld Gallery, Univ London, 1993-2002, Huntington Art Collections, San Marino, Calif, 2002-. *Mailing Add:* Huntington Art Collections 1151 Oxford Rd Pasadena CA 91108

MURDOCK, GREG
PAINTER
b Saskatoon, Sask, Can, 1954. *Study:* Univ Sask, BFA, 77; Inst Allende, San Miguel De Allende, Mex, 77-78; Emily Carr Coll Art & Design, 79-81. *Work:* Osler-Hoskin, McMillan-Binch, Guaranty Trust, Midland-Doherty, Abols & Posthumous & Conwest Exploration Ltd, Toronto, Ont; Air Can & Maison Alcan Inc, Montreal, Que; Ring House Gallery, Edmonton, Alta; First City Trust, Vancouver, BC; Dept External Affairs, Ottawa; Microsoft Corp, Seattle; Disney Corp, Los Angeles; others. *Exhib:* Solo exhibs, 49th Parallel Ctr for Contemp Canadian Art (with catalog), NY, 85, Equinox Gallery, Vancouver, BC, 86, 88, 90, 92, 94 & 95 Tableaux (with catalog), 96, 98, 2000, Southern Alta Art Gallery, Lethbridge, 87, Olga Korper Gallery, Toronto, Ont, 87, 89, 91, 93, 96, 99, 2002, Littlejohn-Smith Gallery, NY, 87, Greg Murdock: On Paper, Kelowna Art Gallery, BC, 95 & Charles H Scott Gallery, Granville Island, Vancouver, BC, 95, Gail Harvey Gallery, Los Angeles, 97, 2001; Just a Taste of the Claridge Collection, Saidye Bronfman Centre, Montreal, Que, 92; A Taste of the Claridge Collection, Can Clay & Glass Gallery, Waterloo, Ont, 93; 64-94 Contemp Decades, Emily Carr Inst Art & Design, Vancouver, BC, 94; Hidden Values: Western Corporations Collect, Edmonton Art Gallery, Alta, 94. *Bibliog:* Elizabeth Godley (auth), review, Vancouver Sun, 9/14/88; Art Perry (auth), review, Province, Vancouver, 9/12/88; Monico Forestall (auth), review, Can Art Mag, spring 88. *Mailing Add:* c/o Olga Korper Gallery 17 Morrow Ave Toronto ON M6R 2H9 Canada

MURPHY, CATHERINE E
PAINTER
b Cambridge, Mass, Jan 22, 1946. *Study:* Skowhegan Sch Painting & Sculpture, with Elmar Bichoff, summer 66; Pratt Inst, BFA, 67. *Hon Degrees:* Pratt Inst, DFA, 2006. *Work:* Metrop Mus Art, Whitney Mus Art & Mus Mod Art, NY; Hirshhorn Mus & Sculpture Garden & Phillips Collection, Washington, DC; Chase Manhattan Bank, New York; Newark Mus; NJ Art Mus, Trenton; Va Mus Fine Arts, Richmond; Weatherspoon Art Gallery, Greensboro, NC. *Exhib:* Whitney Mus Am Art Ann, NY, 71 & 73; Am Acad Inst Arts & Lett, NY, 79, 87, 89, 90; Contemp Am Realism, Pa Acad Fine Arts, 81; Am Realism: Twentieth Century Drawings & Watercolors, San Francisco Mus Mod Art, 85; The Window in Twentieth Century Art, Neuberger Mus, Purchase, 86; Making Their Mark: Women Artists Move into the Mainstream, Cincinnati Art Mus, 89; solo exhibs, Lennon, Weinberg Gallery, NY, 89, 92, 95, 98, 2001-2002, 2005, Baumgartner Galleries, Washington, DC, 98, Tex Gallery, Houston, 2006 & Knoedler & Company, New York, 2008; NY Realism-Past & Present, Tampa Mus Art, 94; Catherine Murphy: Paintings 1990-1994, Greenville Co Mus, 94; Inspired by Nature, Neuberger Mus Art, Purchase, NY, 94; Reality Bites, Kemper Mus Contemp Art, Kansas City, 95; Biennial, Whitney Mus Am Art, 95; Still-Life: The Object in Am Art 1915-1995 - Selections from the Metrop Mus Art, Am Fed Arts, NY, 97-98; Apex Art Curatorial Prog, New York, 97; DC Moore Gallery, New York, 2000; Snug Harbor Cultural Ctr, 2000; Univ Arts Rosenwald Wolf Gallery, Philadelphia, 2000; Harvard Univ, Carpenter Ctr, Cambridge, 2002; This must be the place, Ctr Curatorial Studies, Bard Coll, 2005. *Teaching:* Sr critic, Yale Univ, 89-94. *Awards:* Purchase Award, Am Fedn Arts, 71; Nat Endowment Arts, 79 & 89; Guggenheim Fel, 82; Ingram Merrill Found Grant, 86; Art Award, Am Acad & Inst Arts & Letts, 90; Skowhegan Medal for Painting, Skowhegan Sch Painting & Sculpture, 2009. *Bibliog:* John Gruen (auth), Catherine Murphy: The rise of a cult figure, ARTnews, 12/78; Gerrit Henry (auth), The Figurative Field, Art in Am, 1/94; Francine Prose (auth), Catherine Murphy, BOMB, fall 95. *Mem:* Nat Acad (academician); Am Acad & Inst Arts & Letts. *Media:* Oil. *Dealer:* Lennon Weinberg Inc 560 Broadway Suite 308 New York NY 10012-3945. *Mailing Add:* c/o Lennon Weinberg Inc 514 W 25th St Apt 1 New York NY 10001-5585

MURPHY, DEBORAH
PAINTER, EDUCATOR
b North Platte, Nebr, June 5, 1950. *Study:* Kearney State Coll, BA, 72. *Work:* Univ Nebr, Omaha; Austin Peay State Univ, Clarksville, Tenn; Bradley Univ, Peoria, Ill; Great Plains Art Coll, Univ Nebr, Lincoln, Nebr; H and R Block, Kansas City, MO. *Comn:* Norfolk Veterans Home, Norfolk, Nebr, 2000; Hilton Hotel Convention Center, Omaha, NE, 2003. *Exhib:* Realism in Detail, Paramount Gallery, St. Cloud, Mn, 99; The Kreft Nat, Ann Arbor, Mich, 99; Group shows incl Nebr artists exhib, Ambassador Joseph Limprecht's residence, Tirana, Albania, 2000, Bemis Ctr for Contemporary Art, Omaha, Nebr, Annual Auction, 2009-2013; Art in Embassies Prog, US Dept State, 2000; represented in permanent collections Mus Nebr Art, Kearney, Omaha Airport Authority, Sioux City Art Ctr, Univ Nebraska Medical Ctr-Omaha and Kearney; Paper Trails, Art Haus, San Fran, Calif, 2003; Nat Juried Competition, First St Gallery, NY, 2009; Group show, Arthaus San Francisco, Calif, 2013. *Teaching:* Met Community Coll, Omaha, Nebr. *Awards:* Fel Award in Painting and Works on Paper, Mid-Am Arts Alliance/Nat Endowment for Arts, 94; Distinguished Achievement Fel Grant, Nebr Arts Coun, 98. *Bibliog:* Subtle Beauty, Nebraska Life Mag, 2005; Local Color, Lifestyle, Lincoln Mag, 2006; Gallery View, Omahas Lifestyle Mag, 2008. *Media:* Prismacolor, Acrylic, Graphite. *Dealer:* Kiechel Fine Art 1208 O St Lincoln NE 68508; Anderson O'Brien Fine Art 1108 Jackson St Omaha NE 68102. *Mailing Add:* 8945 N 56th Ave Circle Omaha NE 68152

MURPHY, DUDLEY C
EDUCATOR, GRAPHIC DESIGNER
b Danville, Ky, Apr 16, 1940. *Study:* Univ Tulsa, BA, 65, MA, 69; Univ Okla, MFA, 71. *Exhib:* Okla Art Ctr, Oklahoma City, 70; Contemp Int Landscape Sculpture, traveling, Mo Arts Coun, 72; Nelson Gallery Art, St Louis, Mo, 74; Joslyn Art Mus, Omaha, Nebr, 74; SDak Art Ctr, Brookings, 75; Pittsburg State Univ, Kans, 79; and

others. *Pos:* Design & layout artist, Litho Art Serv, Tulsa, Okla, 66-68; design & layout artist, Pub Relations Int Ltd, 68-69; owner & creative dir, Adworks, Springfield, Md, currently; ed, designer & publ, Nat Fishing Lure Collectors Mag, currently. *Teaching:* Instr design, SW Mo State Univ, Springfield, 69-70; cur educ, Springfield Art Mus, Mo, 71-78; assoc prof, Drury Col, Springfield, Mo, 78-. *Awards:* First Place, 80 & Merit Award, 82, Springfield Ad Club; Merit Awards, Springfield Ad Club, 89, 90 & 91. *Bibliog:* Edgar A Albin (auth), Dudley Murphy, Artcraft Mag, 80. *Mem:* Springfield Ad Club; Nat Coun Ceramic Arts. *Publ:* Auth, Straw, pvt publ, 71. *Mailing Add:* 1418 E Portland St Springfield MO 65804-1221

MURPHY, HASS
SCULPTOR, DRAFTSMAN
b Boston, Mass, Nov 1, 1950. *Study:* Pratt Inst. *Exhib:* Romantic Abstraction, Brandeis Univ, Waltham, Mass, 71; Works on Paper, Logic Transformations, Contemp Arts Gallery, NY, 74; Biennial Exhib, Whitney Mus Am Art, NY, 75; New Drawings, NY, Grapestake Gallery, San Francisco, 75; Spare, Cent Hall Gallery, NY, 75. *Bibliog:* Interview, Seven Painters, Artrite, spring 75; Judy Rifka & Willy Lenski (dirs), Ten Studios (film), Basel Art Fair, 75. *Media:* Steel, Limestone. *Dealer:* Nancy Lurie Gallery 1632 N La Salle Chicago IL 60614; Nancy Lurie Gallery 230 E Ohio St Chicago IL 60611. *Mailing Add:* 8 Locust Ridge Cold Spring NY 10516-1902

MURPHY, MARILYN L
PAINTER, EDUCATOR
b Tulsa, Okla, Sept 22, 1950. *Study:* Okla State Univ, BFA, 72; Univ Okla, MFA, 78. *Work:* State Univ NY, Potsdam; Boston Mus & Sch; Cheekwood Mus Art, Univ Wis, Parkside; Kemper Collection; Tenn State Mus; Benziger Estate Col Calif; Huntsville Mus Art; Siena Art Inst, Siena, Italy; First Bank, Tenn. *Comn:* Shelter (color drawing), Prudential, Chicago; graphite drawing, Carroll Corp-Citi Corp, Nashville; Night Theatre, WDCN-PBS TV, Nashville; color drawing, Third Nat Corp, Nashville; Home (graphite drawing), Tenn Humanities Comn, Nashville. *Exhib:* Nat Acad Design, NY, 96; Alexandria Mus Art, La, 98; Armory Arts Ctr, West Palm Beach, Fla, 2000; One-woman show Artemisia Gallery, Chicago, Ill, 2000; Mid Career Survey, First Ctr for the Visual Arts, Nashville, Tenn, 2004; Carl Hammer Gallery (solo show), Chicago, 2008; Two Person Exhibs, Huntsville Mus Art, Huntsville, Ala, 2011-12; Mus Contemp Art, Sydney, Australia, 2011; Masur Mus, Monroe, La, 2012; Nat Mus Contemp Art, Seoul, S Korea, 2012; Adler & Co Gallery, San Francisco, Calif, 2012, 2013; Solo show, Cumberland Gallery, Nashville, Tn, 2013. *Collection Arranged:* The Home Show, Tenn Arts Comn Invitational, 86; Dixie to Down Under, Perc Tucker Regional Gallery, Townsville, Australia & Sarratt Gallery, Vanderbilt, Univ, 92; All Kentucky Exhib, Capitol Arts Allicance, Bowling Green, Ky, 2009; 37th Ann BiState Competition, Meridan Mus Art, Miss, 2010. *Pos:* Drafter Geophysical Archit Drafting Rm, Oklahoma City, Okla, 74-76; geological drafter, John A Taylor Petrol Exploration, Oklahoma City, 76-77. *Teaching:* Instr drawing & prints, Univ Okla, Norman, 78-80; Prof painting & drawing, Vanderbilt Univ, 80-, chair Fine Arts, 97-99, 2005-2007. *Awards:* Fel, Southern Arts Fed, 90; Nat Painting Competition, Cheekwood Mus Art, Nashville, Tenn, 95; Spring Prize, Tulane Rev Art & Lit, La, 2004; Chancellors Award for Research, Vanderbilt Univ, 2004. *Bibliog:* article, Southern Quart, Univ Southern Miss, spring 91; The Democratic Print (CD-Rom catalog), Wright State Univ, 97; Lucy Lippard & Mark Scala (auth's), Suspended Animation: The work of Marilyn Murphy, 2004; New American Painting So Ed, 2006; Alimentum, 2009, 2010, 2011; Peter Baldaia (auth), Connections: Murphy & Trottman (catalog), 2011; International on Drawing Ann Manifest Gallery, 2011; Dorothy Joiner (auth), Marilyn Murphy & Bob Trotman (review), Art Papers, 5-6/2012; New American Paintings #106, So Ed, 2013. *Mem:* Sinking Creek Film Festival (vpres, bd dir, 87-97). *Media:* Drawing, Painting. *Dealer:* Cumberland Gallery Nashville TN; Carl Hammer Gallery Chicago IL; Adler & Co Gallery San Francisco Ca

MURPHY, MARY MARGUERITE
PAINTER, INSTRUCTOR
b Staten Island, NY, Mar 29, 1958. *Study:* Tyler Sch Art, Philadelphia, 76-78, MFA (painting), 1991; Barnard Col, BA (eng & writing), 1981; Va Ctr Creative Arts, 1985-86; NY Studio Sch, 1986-87; Skowhegan Sch Painting & Sculpture, Maine, 1990. *Work:* Ark Art Ctr; Brooklyn Mus, NY; Wilmington Trust, Los Angeles; Am Express, NY. *Exhib:* Solo exhibs include SPACES, Cleveland, Ohio, 1994, Larry Becker Contemp Art, Philadelphia, 1995, Fleisher Art Mem, Philadelphia, 1995, Schmidt/Dean Gallery, Pa, 1998, 1999, DFN Gallery, NY, 1999, Univ Alaska, 2002; group exhibs include Vibology, White Columns, NY, 1992; Beaver Col, Glenside, Pa, 1992, 1996, Painting Pictures; rendering the (photo) real, 1999; 14 at 55, 55 Mercer St, NY, 1994; Rhythm Bouquet, 558 Broome St, NY, 1994; Current Abstraction, Tyler Sch Art, Philadelphia, 1994; Flirting From a Distance, Del Ctr Contemp Art, Wilmington, 1997; Abstract Strategies, Philadelphia Art Alliance, Pa, 1997; Collector's Choice, NJ Ctr Visual Arts, Summit, 1998; Conceptual Abstraction, Univ of Arts, Phildelphia, 2000. *Teaching:* Instr, Fleisher Art Mem, Philadelphia, 1992-98, Tyler Sch Art, 1995; vis artist, Ohio State Univ, 1993 & 1997, Tyler Sch Art, 1994, Pa State Univ, 1997, Univ Alaska, 2002; instr artist, Inst Arts in Ed, Pa, 1994 & 1997; sr lectr, Univ Arts, Philadelphia, 1996-98 asst prof, 2000-; lectr, Wash Univ, Mo, 1998-99; and many other lectures throughout US. *Awards:* Skowhegan Sch Painting & Sculpture Fel, 1990; Nat Endowment Arts Fel, 1993-94; Fleisher Challenge Grant, Fleisher Art Mem, Philadelphia, 94; Indiv Fel Painting, Pa State Coun Arts, 1998; Venture Fund Grant, Univ Arts, 2002; Pa State Coun on Arts Grant, 2002. *Bibliog:* Robin Rice (auth), various articles in Philadelphia City Paper, 1992-97; Victoria Donohoe (auth), various articles in Philadelphia Inquirer, 1993-97; Edward Sozanski (auth), Making the Case for Abstraction as Natural, 11/4/94, Fleisher Art Memorial, 2/10/95, A Sampling of Abstraction From the Region, 1/98, Assesing Photography's Impact on Painting, 3/12/99 & Signaling Feeling with Deft Brushstrokes, 6/18/99; Liam Otten (auth), Campus Artists, Wash Univ Record, 2/25/99; Sid Sachs (auth), Conceptual Abstraction, Univ of Arts, 12/2000; and many others. *Mem:* Coll Art Asn; Tyler Alumni (bd, 1994-98). *Media:* Oil. *Publ:* Auth, various articles in The New Art Examiner, 1991-98; Drawing Rules (exhib catalog essay), 3/99

MURPHY, SUSAN AVIS
PAINTER, ART DEALER
b New London, Conn, Sept 18, 1950. *Study:* BS, Syracuse Univ, 72. *Work:* General Motors, US Gypsum, Int Harvester, Quaker Oats, Beatrice; FDIC; Mich Belle; Dataprompt. *Exhib:* Southern Watercolor Soc, 81-86, 90 & 93; Allied Artists Am, Nat Arts Club, NY, 81, 82 & 2009; Am Watercolor Soc, Nat Acad Design, NY, 82; Butler Inst Am Art Midyear Show, 82-88; Rocky Mountain Nat, Co, Adirondack Nat, 2010. *Pos:* owner, ARTouse Gallery and Studio Sch, 86-. *Teaching:* Instr watercolor, ARThouse Studio Sch, Sandy Spring, Md, 86-. *Awards:* Gold Medal, Baltimore Watercolor Soc Mid-Atlantic Exhib, 86; First Prize, Southern Watercolor Soc, 93. *Bibliog:* The Watercolor Page: Susan Murphy, Am Artist Mag, 3/86; Dream Studio, Am Artist Mag, 5/91. *Mem:* Baltimore Watercolor Soc. *Media:* Watercolor. *Specialty:* Watercolor, acrylics, oils & graphic arts. *Interests:* Portraiture, landscape & still life. *Publ:* Orange Marmalade, Falling Acorns Editions, 91; Carnations and Lace & Dear Diary, Front Line Graphics, 92. *Dealer:* ARThouse 17520 Doctor Bird Rd Sandy Springs MD 20860. *Mailing Add:* 17520 Dr Bird Rd Sandy Spring MD 20860

MURRAY, CATHERINE
SCULPTOR, EDUCATOR, ADMINISTRATOR
Study: Portland State Univ, BA (Sculpture with honors), 1982; Univ of Montana, MFA (Sculpture), 1987. *Exhib:* Solo exhibitions Univ Ctr Gallery, Univ Montana, 1985, Sykes Gallery, Millerville Univ, Pa, 1990, XYZ Gallery, Va, 1995, univ SC-Spartanburg, 2000-01 and others; two person or group exhibitions Mus of Eadt tex, Lufkin, Tex, 1988, Gallery 16, Great Falls, Montana, 1991, Armory Gallery, Va tech, 1995, William King Art Ctr, Abingdon, Va, 1997, Art and Design Department Faculty Show, Reese Mus, 2001, Avampato Discovery Mus, Charleston, West Va, 2005 and others. *Pos:* Artist in Residence, Montana Artists in Schools/Communities program, several short term residences at Missoula Mus of the Arts, and Fort Peck Reservation, 1987-89; long term artist in residence, Montana Artists in Schools/Communities program, Great Falls Public Schools, 1989-90; Artist in residence Ucross Found, 1993; artist in residence, Sitka Ctr for Art and Ecology, Otis, Oregon, 1994; artist residency, Scottish Sculpture Workshop, Lumsden, Scotland, 2004-; guest lecturer, juror and panelist in the field. *Teaching:* Teaching asst, sculpture and 3-D Found, univ Montana, 1984-86; instr Univ Montana, 1990; asst prof sculpture, 3-D Foundations, Art Appreciation, Millersville Univ, Pa, 1990-91; asst prof sculpture and 3-D Foundations, Univ Maine, 1992-93; vis asst prof, sculpture, design, and drawing, Vir Tech, 1994-95; asst prof sculpture and 3-D Design, East Tennessee State Univ, Johnson City, 1995-2000, assoc prof, sculpture, 3-D Design, 2000-, chair, Dept of Art and Design, currently. *Mailing Add:* Department of Art and Design 70708 Ball Hall East Tennessee State University37614 Johnson City TN 37614

MURRAY, FRANCES
PHOTOGRAPHER
b Drogheda, Ireland, Sept 17, 1947. *Study:* Self-taught. *Work:* Fine Arts Mus, Houston, Tex; Int Mus Photog at George Eastman House, Rochester, NY; Ctr for Creative Photog, Tucson, Ariz; Santa Barbara Mus Art, Calif; Okla Mus Art; Mus Photog Art, Belboa Park, San Diego, Calif; pvt collections include Laurence Miller, NY, Robert Taub, Mich, Mr & Mrs Woody Flowers, NY, Michael Stern, Tucson, Omar Claiborne, Tucson, Law Offices of Minnette Burges, Tucson, Desert Whale Jojoa Co Inc, Tucson, Presidio Grill, Tucson, John Richards, Tucson, Colistia Soble, Tucson, Marguerite & Sandy Mescel, Tucson, many others. *Exhib:* One-person exhibs, Univ Wis, Superior, 82, Etherton Gallery, Tucson, Ariz, 83, Neikrug Photographica Gallery, NY, 85, Univ Mo, St Louis, 87, Dinnerware Artists Coop Gallery, Tucson, Ariz, 89, Zeit Foto Gallery, Tokyo, Japan, 89, Temple Gallery/Etherton Stern, Tucson, Ariz, 92; Dinnerware Artists Coop Gallery, 85, 87, 89 & 90, Ctr for Creative Photog, Snell & Wilmer Collection, 90, New Acquisitions, Tucson, Ariz, 90, Tucson Mus Art/Fine Art for Fine Causes, 91; Etherton Stern Gallery, Tucson, 94; Luxarte Gallery, Canyon Rach, Tucson, 97; Etherton Gallery, Tucson, 96, 99; Dinnerware Contemp Gallery, Tucson, 99; Davis-Domingus Gallery, Tucson, 96; Mus Fine Arts, Houston, 93; Santa Barbara Mus Art, Calif, 89; and many others; Retrospective: Etherton Gallery, Tucson, Ariz, 2007. *Pos:* Freelance fine art photog. *Teaching:* lectr Saga Jr Col of Art, Kyoto, 88, Japan Photographic Col, Kyoto, 88, Internat House of Japan, Tokyo, 88, Ctr for Creative Photography, 90, Northlight Gallery, Ariz State Univ, 93. *Awards:* Nat Endowment Visual Artists, 86; Nat Endowment Arts US/Japan Exchange Fel, 87; Tucson Pima Arts Coun Visual Fel, 91. *Bibliog:* Photography for the Art Market, Watson Guphill Publ, 90. *Media:* Fine Art Photography. *Res:* Emphasizing intimate and surreal images. *Publ:* Psychologue: Photographs, 1977-2007. *Dealer:* Terry Etherton Tucson Ariz. *Mailing Add:* 301 E Fourth St Tucson AZ 85705

MURRAY, IAN STEWART
SCULPTOR, CONCEPTUAL ARTIST
b Pictou, NS, Nov 4, 1951. *Study:* NS Coll Art & Design, BFA (fine art), 72. *Work:* Art Gallery Ont; Can Coun Art Bank, Ottawa; Nat Gallery Can; Banff Ctr Walter Phillips Gallery; Art Metropole. *Comn:* Changing Channels (3 color monos), Projections: Positions-Point of View (audio/video collage) & NOVA BOETIA-Another World, Halifax, Dartmouth & Sackville Community TV Stas, NS, 76; Tutorial: Radio by Artists, Fine Arts Broadcast Serv, Toronto, Ont, 80; DIET: Television by Artists, Fine Arts Broadcast Serv, Toronto, Ont, 80; The Lunatic of One Idea, Public Access Videowall series, Mississauga, Ont, 88. *Exhib:* Record as Art, Royal Coll Art, London, 73; Audio Scene, Mod Art Galerie, Wein, Austria, 79; Books by Artists, 80-82; Biennale of Sydney, Australia, 82; Second Link, Banff Mus Art & traveling, 83; From Sea to Shining Sea, Power Plant, Toronto, 88; solo exhibs, Vancouver Art Gallery, 88, Definity Super, Thunder Bay, 89, White Water Gallery, NBay, Ont, 91, Macintosh Gallery, London, Ont, 93, Peterborough Art Gallery, 96 & Wynick Tuck Gallery, Toronto, 96 & 98; Art Gallery of Ontario, 99; Art Metropole, 2000, 2001, 2002, 2003; National Gallery of Canada, Ottawa, 2000; Univ Toronto, Blackwood Gallery, Edmonton Art Gallery, Edmonton Alberta, 2003, 2012;

Vancouver Art Gallery, 2012; Badischer Kunstverin, Baden-Baden, 2013. *Collection Arranged:* Attitudes Toward Photography (auth, catalog), Ann Leonowens Gallery, 72; Radio by Artists, 80. *Pos:* Bd govs planning & priority comt & chmn film/photog/video comt, Toronto Arts Coun, 86-92. *Teaching:* Instr, Media Arts Film & Video Courses & Film Tech Studies, Ryerson Polytech Inst, Toronto, 86-87. *Awards:* Can Coun Awards, 89; Medal Serv, City Toronto, 91; Ont Arts Coun Awards, 94; and others. *Bibliog:* Phillip Monk (auth), Television by artists, Can Forum, 81; Mary-Beth Laviolette (auth), Audio by artists, Vanguard Mag, 4/83; Jill Pollack (auth), Work rich in meaning, metaphor, Vancouver Courier, BC, 88. *Mem:* Artists Union; Can Artists Representation; Charles Street Video Soc (bd mem, 92-93); Toronto Arts Coun (bd dir, 86-92); Art Metropole (bd mem) 93-; Art Gallery Toronto (artist, life mem). *Media:* Multimedia; Collage. *Publ:* Auth, Twenty Waves in a Row, Straw Books, 71; Media Arts, Ontario Arts Council, 89; others. *Dealer:* V/Tapes Toronto Canada; Art Metropole Toronto Canada. *Mailing Add:* 10 Dora Ave Suite 807 Toronto ON M6H 4J2 Canada

MURRAY, JOAN
CRITIC, PHOTOGRAPHER
b Annapolis, Md, Mar 6, 1927. *Study:* Calif Coll Arts & Crafts, San Francisco Art Inst; Ruth Bernard Insight Studio; Univ Calif Exten; also studied with Wynn Bullock. *Work:* Int Mus Photog, Eastman House, Rochester, NY; San Francisco Mus Mod Art; Oakland Mus, Calif. *Exhib:* Male Nudes--One Man, Mind's Eye Gallery, Vancouver, BC, 73; 7 Visions, Heller Gallery, Berkeley, 89 & self portrait, 91; Children of Our Times, Steven Wirtz Gallery, San Francisco, 87; Joan Murray, Retrospective 1967-1992, Vision Gallery, San Francisco, 92; In Front of the Lens: Portraits of California Photographers, Oakland Mus, 96-97; A History of Women Photographers, NY Pub Libr, Smithsonian, Santa Barbara Mus & Akron Ohio Mus, 97-98; and others. *Pos:* Photog ed, Artweek, 69-; W Coast critic, Popular Photog, 75-77; contrib ed, Am Photogr, 78-81; consult, Photog Dept, Getty Mus, 86; mgr assoc, Art Studio, Univ Calif, 87-. *Teaching:* Instr photog, Univ Calif Exten, 70-82; instr photog, City Col San Francisco, 75-82; Friends of Photog Workshops, 90. *Awards:* Nat Endowment Arts Grant Art Criticism, 78. *Bibliog:* Naomi Rosenblatt (auth), A History of Women Photographers, Abbeyville Press, 94; Hisaki Kojima (ed), San Francisco Nude, Siskosa Publ, 95; Peter Palmquist (auth), Women In Photography, 96. *Mem:* Int Asn Art Critics; Soc Encouragement Contemp Art San Francisco Mus Art; San Francisco Mus Mod Art Foto Forum. *Dealer:* Vision Gallery 1155 Mission St San Francisco CA 94103. *Mailing Add:* 120 Blair Ave Piedmont CA 94611

MURRAY, JOHN MICHAEL
PAINTER
b Tampa, Fla, May 28, 1931. *Study:* Univ Tampa, BA, 63; Ohio Univ, MFA, 65. *Work:* Staten Island Mus, NY; Bundy Art Mus, Waitsfield, Vt; NS Coll Art, Halifax; NJ Mus. *Exhib:* Int Print Exhib, Crakow, 75; Langsam Gallery, Melbourne, Australia, 75; 19 Nat Print Exhib, Brooklyn Mus, 75; solo exhibs, Dorsky Gallery, NY, 72, Halifax, 72, Blue Parrot, NY, 74 & Am Ctr, Belgrade, 81. *Teaching:* Chmn dept fine arts, New York Inst Technol, 66-. *Awards:* First Prize in Painting, Fla State Ann, 63. *Mem:* Am Asn Univ Prof; Coll Art Teachers. *Publ:* Contribr, Art Work--No Commercial Value, Grossman, 72; Pratt Graphics Reprint, 74. *Dealer:* James Yu Gallery 393 W Broadway New York NY 10012. *Mailing Add:* 124 W Houston St No 4 New York NY 10012-2558

MURRAY, JUDITH
PAINTER
b New York, NY, 1941. *Study:* Pratt Inst, Brooklyn, New York, BFA, 62, MFA, 64; Acad Fine Arts, Madrid, Spain, 63. *Work:* Brooklyn Mus, NY Pub Libr & Chase Manhattan Bank, New York; Libr Cong; Nat Mus Am Art, Washington, DC; Mus Modern Art, New York; Brit Mus. *Comn:* Poster & print, Mostly Mozart Festival, Avery Fisher Hall, Lincoln Ctr, New York, 81 & 86; poster & print, Mozart Bicentennial, Lincoln Ctr, 91-92. *Exhib:* Print Exhib, Brooklyn Mus, New York, 62; Solo exhibs, The ClockTower, Inst Art & Urban Resources, New York, 78, Dallas Mus Fine Arts, 82, Bronx Mus Arts, 86, Schmidt Dean Gallery, Phila, 98, Ben Shahn Gallery, William Patterson Univ, Wayne, NJ, 99, Gibson Mus, SUNY at Potsdam, 2000, Mus Mod Art, Long Island City, NY, 2001, Sundaram Tagore Gallery, New York, 2003, Energies and Equations, 2004, Small Works, 2005 & Phases and Layers, 2006; 1979 Biennial Exhib, Whitney Mus Am Art, New York, 79; traveling exhibs, Art in Our Time, 80-82, A Living Tradition-Selections from Am Art Asn (Eur, Can, Near East), 86, Lines of Vision, Drawings by Contemp Women (US & Eur), 89-91; The Persistence of Abstraction, Noyes Mus, NJ, 94; Conde Gallery, New York; Int Invitational Paintings & Sculpture, Am Acad Arts & Letts, New York; Newhouse Ctr Contemp Art, New York, 97; two-person exhibs, Simon Gallery, Morristown, NJ, 99, 76 Varick St Gallery, New York, 99; group exhibs, Subliminal View, Trans Hudson Gallery, New York, 99, Slight of Hand, Cummings Art Center, New London, Conn, 99, Reconstructing Abstraction, The Mitchell Algus Gallery, New York, 2000, Painting Abstraction II, NY Studio Sch, 2001, Newhouse Ctr Contemp Art, 2003-2004, Am Acad Arts & Letters, 2005, Whitney Mus Am Art, 2006, East/West, Sundaram Tagore Gallery, New York, 2006, Surface Impressions, Islip Art Mus, East Islip, New York, 2007 & Continuum, In Celebration of the 70th Anniversary of the Am Abstract Artist, St Peter's Coll Art Gallery, Jersey City, NJ, 2007; Continuum, Sundaram Tagore Gallery, Beverly Hills, Calif, NY, 2009; New Paintings, Sundaram Tagore Gallery, NY, 2012; The Annual 2013: Nat Acad Mus, NY, 2013. *Teaching:* Artist-in-residence, USIA, Poland, 64-65; Long Island Univ, NY, 74-77; Princeton Univ, 94; lectr, New Arts Prog, Kutztown, Pa, 2003 & Nat Mus Women Arts, Washington, DC, 2006. *Awards:* Artist Fel Grant-Painting, Nat Endowment Arts, 83-84; Memorial fel John Simon Guggenheim Foundation, 2002-03; Acad Award Art, Am Acad Arts & Lett. *Bibliog:* Judy Collischan Van Wagner (auth), Judith Murray: Interview, Long Island Univ Catalog, 11/85; Gail Stavitsky (auth), Three aspects of abstraction, Arts Mag, 4/86; Duane & Sara Preble (ed), Artforms, 5th ed, 94; Andrew Long (auth), Openings in Art & Antiques, 4/98; Lilly Wei (auth), Review Art in Am, 11/98; Barry Schwabsky (auth), Abstract introspection in two distinct styles, NY Times, 10/99; James Carroll (interview), New Arts Alive: Judith Murray, 2001; Michael Amy, rev, Art in America, 134, 10/2003; Due Americani a Viterbo, Controvoce, 9/2005; Robert Ayers (auth), rev, Art News, 1/2005; Ken Johnson (auth), For a broad landscape an equality wide survey, Art Review, NY Times, E5, 5/31/2006; Denise Green (auth), New York New York, Art Monthly Australia #196, 2006-2007; Sandra Ban (auth), rev, Art News, 1/2007; Jonathan Goodman (auth), Revew of Exhibitions, Art in America, 3/2007. *Mem:* Am Abstract Artists; Nat Acad Mus Artist Fel Inc. *Media:* Oil. *Publ:* Richard Kalina (auth), Seeing into the abstract, catalogue, Sundaram Tagore Gallery, New York, 3/2003; James Carroll (auth), Conversation with Judith Murray, catalogue, 5/8/2001 & 10/14/2003; Albert Maysles & Mark Ledzian (co-dirs), Judith Murray: Phases and Layers, doc film, 2006; Alanna Heiss (auth), Judith Murray: Vibrato to Legato (monogr), Maupin Publ, 2006; David Cohen (auth), Open City, 2012. *Dealer:* Sundaram Tagore Gallery 547 W 27 St New York NY 10001; Sundaram Tagore Gallery Singapore; Sundaram Tagore Gallery Hong Kong. *Mailing Add:* 429 W Broadway New York NY 10012

MURRAY, REUBEN
ADMINISTRATOR
Study: Univ NMex, BFA (theatre), 85, Univ Phoenix, MA, 91. *Pos:* Exec dir, SArk Arts Ctr, El Dorado, 91-. *Mailing Add:* c/o Nan McDonald 3301 Louisiana St Pine Bluff AR 71601

MURRAY, RICHARD NEWTON
MUSEUM DIRECTOR, CURATOR
b Bartlesville, Okla, Aug 7, 1942. *Study:* San Jose State Univ, Calif, BA, 68; Univ Chicago, MA, 70. *Collection Arranged:* Art for Architecture: Washington DC 1895-1925 (auth, catalog), Nat Collection Fine Arts, Smithsonian Press, 75; Am as Art, 76; Elihu Vedder (auth, catalog), 78; Am Renaissance: 1876-1917 (auth, catalog), Brooklyn Mus, 79. *Pos:* Asst to dir, Nat Collection Fine Arts, Washington, DC, 76-79; dir, Birmingham Mus Art, Ala, 79-83 & Arch Am Art, Smithsonian Inst, 83-; cur, Nat Mus Am Art, Smithsonian Inst, 88-. *Publ:* Auth, Art of the American West, Birmingham Mus Art, 82; Murals of the American Renaissance, Influence on Am Art, 89; John Norton Mural Painter, In: John Norton, Ill Univ Press, 92; H Siddons Mowbray, Mural Painter; Murals in the Library of Congress. *Mailing Add:* 11300 Palisades Ct Kensington MD 20895

MURRAY, ROBERT (GRAY)
SCULPTOR, PAINTER
b Vancouver, BC, Mar 2, 1936. *Study:* Univ Sask Sch Art, 55-58; Mex, 59; Art Students League, New York, 60; Emma Lake Artist's Workshops. *Work:* Whitney Mus Am Art, Metrop Mus Art, NY; Walker Art Ctr, Minn; Everson Mus, Syracuse; Hirshhorn Mus, Washington; Chase Manhattan Collection, NY; Detroit Mus Fine Arts, Mich; Univ Toronto, Ont, Can; Del Art Mus; Art Gallery of Ont; Berkeley Mus; Joseph Hirshom Mus, Washington; Met Mus Art, NY; Nat Gallery of Canada, Ottawa; Whitney Mus Am Art, NY; Storm King Art Centre, Mountainville, NY; Grounds for Sculpture, Hamilton, NJ. *Comn:* Sculpture, Univ Mass, Amherst, 75; sculpture, Alaska Court Bldg, Juneau, 78; sculpture, Honeywell Inc, Minn, 79; sculpture, Univ Toronto, 83; sculpture, Can Nat Inst Blind, Toronto, 98; direct purchases as well as numerous commissions. *Exhib:* Nothing But Steel, The Lab, Cold Springs Harbor, LI, 87; The Opening Exhib, Nat Gallery Can, Ottawa, 88; Working Models & Other Sculpture, Del Art Mus, 90; Frank Martin Gallery, Muhlenberg Col, Allentown, 91; retrospective, Reading Pub Mus, Pa, 94; Solo-exhib, Andre Zarre Gallery, NY, 94, 95 & 96, Arno Maris Gallery, Westfield Col, Mass, 99, Moore Gallery, Toronto, Ont, Can, 99, Ericson Gallery, Philadelphia, 99, Art Gallery of Kelowna, BC, Can, 2000; The Factory as Studio, Nat Gallery Can, Ottawa, 99; Andre Zarre Gallery, NY, 2000; Appleton Mus, Ocala, Fla, 2000; Moore Gallery, Toronto, 2000; Barbara Edwards Contemp, Toronto, 2009; Sideshow Gallery, Williamsburg, NY, 2010. *Teaching:* Lectr, cols throughout US; instr, Sch Visual Arts, currently. *Awards:* Can Coun Bursary, 60 & Sr Grant, 69 & 83; Second Prize, X Sao Paulo Biennial, Brazil, 69; Nat Endowment Arts Grant, 69; Royal Archit Inst Can Allied Arts Medal, 77; Order of Canada, 2000. *Bibliog:* Krainin-Sage (auth), ArtIs (film), NY State Coun Arts, 71; Neil Marshall (auth), Robert Murray sculpture, Dayton Art Inst, 79; G Bellerby (auth), Robert Murray: Sculpture & Working Models, Art Gallery Greater Victoria, 83; Kim Rich (auth), Culture Shock (article), Anchorage Daily News, 10/9/88; Denise LeClerc, Barbara Rose (auth), Robert Murray, Factory as Studio, 99; Christine Finkelstein (auth), Robert Murray, 97, Grounds for Sculpture, Hamilton, NJ. *Media:* Steel, Aluminum. *Publ:* David Raskin (auth), Robert Murray: A Painter in Metal, Art in America, 9/99. *Dealer:* Moore Gallery 80 Spadina Toronto ON Can M5V 2J3; Winchester Galleries Victoria BC Can; Barbara Edwards Contemporary Inc 1069 Bathurst St Toronto ON M5R 3G8. *Mailing Add:* 345 Lamborntown Rd West Grove PA 19390

MURRELL, CARLTON D
PAINTER
b Bridgetown, Barbados, WI, July 17, 1945; nat US. *Study:* Art Student's League, 70; Pels Art Sch, 74. *Hon Degrees:* Stafford Univ, Hon BFA. *Work:* Ctr Art Cult Bedford-Styvesant, Brooklyn; Barbados Mus, Bridgetown; Howard Univ, Washington, DC; Barbados Cent Bank; Medgar Evers Col, Brooklyn, NY; Schomburg Libr & Carver Fed Bank, NY; Prentice Hall, Sch Div, NJ. *Comn:* Prentice Hall, Div Simon & Schuster. *Exhib:* West Indian Artist, Brooklyn Mus, 76; Caribbean Connection, Nat Afro Am Mus Cult Ctr, Ohio Hist Soc, 86. *Teaching:* Instr drawing & painting, Brooklyn Truth Ctr & Fort Greene Sr Citizen Ctr, 88-; Children's Aid Soc, 99-. *Awards:* Second Prize, Flushing Art League; Fulton Art Fair Award, 82 & 87; Goddard Enterprise Award, Barbados. *Bibliog:* David Shirey (auth), Realism stands out in show by blacks, New York Times, 81; Will Grant (auth), To a Bajan beat, Art Speak, 88; Jude Schwendenwien (auth), Appealing, informative West Indian-American art exhibit, Hartford Courant, 88. *Mem:* Brooklyn Watercolor Soc. *Media:* Oil, Watercolor. *Publ:* Am Biog Inst Int Register Of Profiles, Cambridge, Eng, 11/88. *Mailing Add:* 14447 77th Ave Flushing NY 11367

MURRILL, GWYNN
SCULPTOR
b Ann Arbor, Mich, June 15, 1942. *Study:* Univ Calif, Los Angeles, BA, 68, MA, 70, MFA, 72. *Work:* Bankers Life Co, Des Moines, Iowa; Bank Denver, Colo; Los Angeles Co Art Mus; Trans America, San Francisco, Calif; Security Pacific Bank, Los Angeles, Calif. *Comn:* Calif State Bldg, Los Angeles; Plaza Park Towers, Sacramento, Calif. *Exhib:* Los Angeles Eight, Painting & Sculpture, 76 & 20 Yrs of Talent Winners, Los Angeles Co Art Mus, Calif; Contemp Californians VIII, Laguna Beach Art Mus, Calif, 82; Wood Renditions, Security Pac Bank, Los Angeles, 84; Asher/Faure Gallery, Los Angeles, 87; John Berggruen Gallery, San Francisco; Gail Swerin Gallery, Ketchum, Idaho; and others. *Awards:* Prix Di Rome, Am Acad, Italy, 79; Nat Endowment Art Fel, 84 & Guggenheim Fel, 86. *Media:* All. *Dealer:* Asher Faure Gallery 612 N Almont Los Angeles CA 90069; John Berggruen Gallery San Francisco CA. *Mailing Add:* Patricia Faure Gallery 2525 Michigan Ave Suite B7 Santa Monica CA 90404

MURTIC, EDO
PAINTER, ENAMELIST
b Velika Pisanica, Croatia, 1921. *Study:* Sch Applied Arts; Acad Fine Arts, 43. *Work:* Mus Mod Art, NY; Tate Gallery, London, Gt Brit; Nat Mus, Prague, Czech Repub; Nat Gallery, Berlin, Ger; Mus Mod Art, Seoul, Korea. *Exhib:* Nat Gallery Mod Art, Rome, Italy, 56; Tate Gallery, London, Gt Brit, 61; Mus Arts & Crafts, Zagreb, Croatia, 63; Mus Mod Art, Belgrade, Yugoslavia, 64; Palazzo Reale, Milan, Italy, 71; Grand Palais, Paris, France, 71; Pompidou Ctr, Paris, France, 81; Mus Mod Art, Seoul, Korea, 88. *Bibliog:* Paule Gauthier (auth), Edo Murtic, 50; Gerhard Wurzer (auth), Edo Murtic (exhibit catalog), Gerhard Wurzer Gallery, 81; Tonko Marovic/Chromos (auth), Murtic, Multigraf, 86. *Media:* Oil, Pastel; Enamel

MUSCO, LYDIA
SCULPTOR
Study: Bennington Coll, BA, 2001; Boston Univ, MFA, 2007. *Work:* Mosan Mus, South Korea; Davidson Coll, NC; Vt Studio Ctr; Larvik Stone Quarry, Norway; Womble, Carlyle, Sandridge, and Rice, Atlanta, Ga. *Exhib:* Cortona Exhib, Lamar Dodd Sch Art, Atlanta, 2001; solo exhibs, Red Mill Gallery, Johnson, Vt, 2003-04, Commonwealth Gallery, Boston Univ, 2006, William H Van Every Gallery, Davidson Coll, NC, 2008-; Exposed! Outdoor Sculpture Show, Helen Day Art Ctr, Stowe, Vt, 2004; 8th Ann Outdoor Sculpture Show, North Bennington Art Park, Vt, 2005; Coll Art Asn Exhib, Mass Coll Art, Boston, 2006; Vis Arts Fac Exhib, Boston Univ Sch Visual Arts, 2007; Joan Mitchell MFA Grant Show, CUE Art Found, New York, 2008. *Awards:* Edward F Albee Residency Fel, Montauk, NY, 2007; Kahn Career Entry Award, 2007; Joan Mitchell Found Grant, 2007; Pollock-Krasner Found Grant, 2008

MUSGRAVE, SHIRLEY HUDSON
EDUCATOR, PHOTOGRAPHER
b Lexington, Ky, Nov 28, 1935. *Study:* Miss State Coll Women, BFA, 57; Colorado Springs Fine Arts Ctr, summer 56; Univ Kans, scholar, 57-58, MS, 63; Univ Ark, 64-65; Univ Iowa, 66-67; Fla State Univ, PhD (fel), 70. *Exhib:* One-artist photog exhib, Iowa City Civic Ctr, 65, Univ Ala-Huntsville, 72, Athens Col, Ala, 73 & Lambuth Col, Tenn, 74; Prof Women Artists of Fla, Lowe Art Mus, Miami, 76; Photograph, Huntsville Art League & Mus Asn Ann, Huntsville Art Mus, 79; and others. *Teaching:* Art supvr, Linwood Pub Schs, Kans, 58-60; assoc prof art educ, Memphis State Univ, 70-72 & Fla Int Univ; prof art educ & chairperson dept, Univ Ala, 78. *Awards:* Ark Artists Ann First Prize in Graphics, Little Rock Mus Fine Arts, 56; Fla Int Univ Found Grant, 76. *Mem:* Nat Art Educ Asn; Southeastern Coll Art Conf; Ala Alliance Arts Educ; Ala Art Educ Asn. *Publ:* Coauth, Experiences in the Arts, 77; coauth, Annotated sources for Afro-American arts and the ancestral African background, Art Teacher, spring 80

MUTU, WANGECHI
COLLAGE ARTIST, PAINTER
b Nairobi, Kenya, 1972. *Study:* United World Coll of the Atlantic, Wales, grad, 1991; Cooper Union, New York, BFA, 1996; Yale Univ, MFA, 2000. *Work:* Mus Mod Art, New York; Mus Contemp Art, Los Angeles; Saatchi Gallery, London; Whitney Mus Am Art, New York; Mus Contemp Art, Chicago. *Exhib:* Solo exhibs include Jamaica Center Arts & Learning, Queens, NY, 2003, Susanne Vilmetter Los Angeles Projects, 2003, 2005, 2008, Miami Art Mus, 2005, San Francisco Mus Mod Art, 2005, Salon 94, 2006, Sikkema Jenkins & Co, New York, 2006, Power House, Memphis, 2006, Site Santa Fe, 2006-07, Victoria Miro, London, 2007, PKM Gallery, Beijing, 2007; group exhibs include Out of the Box, Queens Mus, New York, 2001; Africaine, Studio Mus Harlem, New York, 2002, Figuratively, 2004, African Queen; Art Basel Miami Beach, 2002; Black President, New Mus, New York, traveled to Contemp Arts Center, Cincinnati, Yerba Buena Center Arts, San Francisco, Barbican Center, London, 2003; Open House, Brooklyn Mus Art, 2003, 2004; Only Skin Deep, Int Center Photog, New York, 2003; New, Susanne Vielmetter Los Angeles Projects, 2004, Cut, 2005; Pin-Up: Contemp Collage & Drawing, Tate Mod, London, 2004; Greater New York, PS1 Contemp Art Center, Long Island City, NY, 2005; Drawing from The Modern, Mus Mod Art, New York, 2005; Matisse & Beyond, San Francisco Mus Mod Art, 2005; After Cezanne, Mus Contemp Art Los Angeles, 2005; Th F-Word, Warhol Mus, Pittsburgh, 2006, Female Vocals, 2006; New African Art, Seattle Art Mus, 2006; Triumph of Painting, Saatchi Gallery, London, 2006; USA Today, Royal Acad Arts, London, 2006; Collage: The Unmonumental Picture, New Mus, New York, 2008. *Awards:* Richard Leakey Merit Award, 1994; MFA Fel, Yale Univ, 1998; Fannie B Pardee Fel, 2000; Jamaica Center Arts Fel, 2001; Joan Mitchell Found Grant, 2007; Louis Comfort Tiffany Found Grant, 2008; Artist of Yr, Deutsche Bank, 2010. *Media:* Miscellaneous Media. *Dealer:* Sikkema Jenkins & Co 530 W 22nd St New York NY 10011; Susanne Vielmetter Los Angeles Projects 5795 W Washington Blvd Culver City CA 90232. *Mailing Add:* 849 Lafayette Ave Brooklyn NY 11221-1901

MYATT, GREELY
SCULPTOR
b Aberdeen, Miss, Mar 17, 1952. *Study:* Delta State Univ, Cleveland, Miss, BFA, 75; Univ Miss, Oxford, MFA, 80. *Work:* Masur Mus Art, Monroe, La; Univ Miss, Oxford; Miss Mus Art & Miss Craftsmen's Guild, Jackson; Ringling Sch Art & Design, Sarasota, Fla; Franklin Furnace Archives, New York, NY. *Comn:* Wood sculpture, Triangle Cult Ctr, Yazoo City, Miss, 79; wood sculpture, Prudential Insurance, Memphis, Tenn, 80; on site installation, Arts Festival Atlanta, 83 & 86. *Exhib:* Solo exhibs, Southeastern Ctr Contemp Art, Winston-Salem, NC, 84 & Kansas City Artists' Coalition, Kansas City, Mo, 88; solo installations, ARC/Raw Space, Chicago, Ill, 87 & Memphis Ctr Contemp Art, Tenn, 88; window installation, Franklin Furnace, NY, 88; Galveston Art Ctr, Tex, 89; Robinson Willis Gallery, Nashville, Tenn, 89; Memphis State Univ, Tenn, 90. *Teaching:* Instr art, Itawamba Jr Col, Fulton, Miss, 80-85; asst prof art, Ark State Univ, Jonesboro, 85-88, assoc prof, 88-89; asst prof art, Memphis State Univ, Tenn, 89. *Awards:* Merit Awards, Miss Exhib, Miss Mus Art, Jackson, 78, Gertrude Herbert Mem Art Inst Competition, Augusta, Ga, 83 & Sept Competition, Alexandria Mus, La, 85; Individual Artist Grant, Art Space, New York, 88; Installation Grant, Alexander Mus Art, La, 89; Site Grant, Arts in the Park, Memphis, Tenn, 89. *Mem:* Int Sculpture Ctr. *Media:* Mixed. *Dealer:* Robinson Willis Gallery Nashville TN. *Mailing Add:* 416 S Main St Memphis TN 38103-4441

MYER, PETER LIVINGSTON
KINETIC ARTIST, PAINTER
b Ozone Park, NY, Sept 19, 1934. *Study:* Brigham Young Univ, BA, 56; Univ Utah, MFA, 59; summers with Harry Sternberg & Joseph Hirsch. *Work:* Springville Mus Art; Phoenix Art Mus, Ariz; Salt Lake City Art Ctr; Denver Art Mus; Las Vegas Art Mus; others; Nora Eccles Harrison Mus; Woodbury Art Gallery, UVSC. *Comn:* Sculpture, Mus Art, Brigham Young Univ. *Exhib:* Solo exhibs, Salt Lake Art Ctr, 80, Kimball Art Ctr, Park City, Utah, 85, Las Vegas Art Mus, 86, Brigham Young Univ Art Mus, 94, Nora Eccles Harrison Mus, Logan Utah 2000 & Bountiful Davis Art Ctr, 2002, Woodbury Art Gallery, UVSC, 2003; Light, Motion, Space, Walker Art Ctr, Minneapolis, 67; Some More Beginnings, Brooklyn Mus, 68; Art & Technology, High Mus Art, Atlanta, Ga, 69; Art of the 60's, Denver Art Mus, 70; Kinetic Light Show, Phoenix Art Mus, Ariz, 73; Utah Valley Sculptors Invitational Exhib, Springville Art Mus, 77; retrospective, Springville Art Mus, Utah, 79; AAPL Grand Nat Exhib, New York City, 2002; and others. *Teaching:* Assoc prof art & chmn dept, Univ Nev, Las Vegas, 62-72; art gallery dir, Brigham Young Univ, 72-78, prof art, 72-, studio area head, 92-95, prof emer. *Awards:* Alcuin Fel, 96-99; Best of Show, Pastel Soc Utah, Salt Lake City, 2000; Coll George J Morales Meml Award, Am Artist Profl League, NYC, 2002; The Newington Award-Best in Show 75th Grand National Exhibition AAPL- NYC-2003. *Bibliog:* Kranz (auth), Science and Technology and the Arts, Rheinhold, 74. *Mem:* Western Asn Art Mus; Am Asn Art Mus; Utah Mus Asn; Coll Art Asn; Am Artists Profl League. *Media:* Kinetic Light Art, Pastels. *Publ:* Art: Do It!, Kendall/Hunt, 96. *Dealer:* New Amsterdam Art Exchange-Park City, Utah; Tivoli Gallery, Salt Lake City, Utah. *Mailing Add:* 1425 Oak Cliff Dr Provo UT 84604-3706

MYERS, DOROTHY ROATZ
PAINTER, CRITIC
b Detroit, Mich, March 24, 1921. *Study:* Study with Yashuoe Kuniyoshi & Terrence Coyle; Antioch Coll, Corçoran Gallery Art Sch; Art Students League. *Work:* US Coast Guard Collection, Washington. *Comn:* Painting, Texas Rose, Hess Oil Corp; painting, Main Course, Seafood Leader. *Exhib:* Mini Print Int, Cadaques-Taller Galeria Fort, Barcelona, Spain, Salmagundi Mus, Hellenic Inst, Athens, Greece, Tangentl, Liechtenstein; Festival Int, Paris, 88, Osaka, Japan, 89; Phoebus II, Athens, Greece, 90; Cornel Med Ctr, 92; Brookdale Coll, 92; Ward-Nasse Gallery, 94; and others. *Pos:* Publicity, Montserrat Gallery. *Teaching:* Pvt critiques & art lecture progs. *Awards:* Diplome de Medaille d'Honneur Ligue d'Enseignement et Education Sociale, 87; Medialle Bronze Societe Academique d'education et d'encouragement (Paris) Arts, Sciences, Lettres, 88; Corresponding Academican, Accademia Internazionale Greci-Marino, Acad Off Knight, 2000. *Bibliog:* Anne Vanoli (auth), Roatz, La Cote des Arts, 10/84; feature article, Manhattan Arts Mag, 90. *Mem:* Life mem Art Students League; NY Artists' Equity; Salmagundi Club (dir, 88). *Media:* Oil, Watercolor; Monoprint. *Specialty:* contemp fine art. *Interests:* psychology. *Publ:* Freelance articles & reviews. *Dealer:* Ward-Nasse Gallery New York NY

MYERS, FRANCES J
PRINTMAKER
b Racine, Wis, Apr 16, 1938. *Study:* Univ Wis, BA, 59, MA 60, MFA, 65; San Francisco Art Inst. *Work:* Libr Cong & Nat Collection Fine Arts, Washington, DC; Victoria & Albert Mus, London; Metrop Mus Art, NY; Art Inst Chicago; Boston Mus Fine Arts; Brooklyn Mus. *Exhib:* 20th, 22nd & 24th Print Biennale, Brooklyn Mus, 76, 81 & 86; Perimeter Gallery, Chicago, 86, 88, 91, 93 & 97; Amerikahaus, Cologne, Ger, 91; Presswork: The Art of Women Printmakers, traveling exhib, Lang Communs Corp Collection; Portland Mus Art, Ore, 92; Duke Univ Mus Art, 94; Wis Acad Gallery, 97; and others. *Pos:* Cur, Printed by Women Exhib, Port Hist, Penn's Landing, Philadelphia, 83; cons Parsons Csh Art & Design, 2000. *Teaching:* Distinguished prof art, Mills Col, Oakland, Calif, 79; vis lectr, art dept, Univ Calif, Berkeley, 82; asst prof, Univ Wis, Madison, 86-88, assoc prof, 88-95, prof, 95-. *Awards:* Nat Endowment Arts Fel, 74 & 85; Wis Arts Bd Grant, 77-78; Romnes Fel, 91-92; Kellet Mid-Career Fel, 99-. *Mem:* Nat Acad. *Media:* Etching, Installations. *Dealer:* Perimeter Gallery Chicago IL. *Mailing Add:* 6641d Humanities Bldg Univ Wisc 455 N Park St Madison WI 53706

MYERS, JACK FREDRICK
PAINTER,
b Lima, Ohio, 1927. *Study:* Cleveland Art Inst, Ohio; Kent State Univ, MFA. *Work:* Butler Inst Am Art, Youngstown, Ohio. *Exhib:* May Show, Cleveland Mus of Art, 49-54, 76-81; Freedson Gallery, Lakewood, Ohio, 69; Mid-Year Show, Butler Inst of Am Art, Youngstown, Ohio, 76, 78, 79 & 82; Nat Print Competition, San Diego State

Univ, Calif, 80; Birke Art Gallery, Marshall Univ, Huntington, WVa, 81; Colorprint USA, Mus Tex Tech Univ, Lubbock, 83. *Pos:* Art dir, Premier Industrial Corp, 56-70. *Teaching:* Instr graphics & film, Cooper Sch Art, Cleveland, 70-80; prof art & dir commercial design, Univ Dayton, 82-87. *Awards:* First Prize (one minute animated film), ASIFA Festival, New York, 74; Purchase Prize, Mid-Year Show, Butler Inst of Am Art, 79; Special Mention, May Show, Cleveland Mus Art, 79 & 80; and others. *Media:* Oil, Various. *Publ:* The Language of Visual Art: Perception as a Basis for Design, Holt, Rinehart & Winston, 89; The Windy Side of Care & The Greatest Gift, Llumina Press, 2002. *Mailing Add:* 22269 Country Meadows Ln Strongsville OH 44149-2000

MYERS, MARTIN
SCULPTOR, PAINTER
b Syracuse, NY, April 21, 1951. *Study:* Va Commonwealth Univ, BFA, 73; Calif Coll Arts & Crafts, MFA, 74. *Work:* Oakland Mus; San Francisco Mus Mod Art; Univ Art Mus, Berkeley, Calif; Newport Harbor Art Mus. *Comn:* Sculpture, IBM, 85. *Exhib:* Virginia Artists--1973, Va Mus Fine Arts, 73; Cityscapes, Fine Arts Mus San Francisco, 77; 35th Biennial Contemp Painting, Corcoran Gallery Art, 77; A Sense of Scale, Oakland Mus, 77; Viewpoint/77--Options in Painting, Cranbrook Mus, 77-78; Sculpture in California, 1975-1980, San Diego Mus, 80; New Bay Area Painting & Sculpture, Calif State Univ, Northridge, 82 & San Francisco Art Inst, 83; Constructions: Between Sculpture and Architecture, Sculpture Ctr, NY, 88; Redding Mus, Calif, 90; Sandra Gering Gallery, NY, 96, 98, 99, 2000; Reynolds Gallery, Richmond, Va, 99. *Pos:* Founder & dir, Artist For Nuclear War. *Bibliog:* Judith Dunham (auth), Sculpture as painting as sculpture, Artweek, 77; Morris Yarowsky (auth), article, Art in Am, 79; Richard Armstrong (auth), catalog, Modernism, 81. *Media:* All Media; Acrylic, Oil. *Dealer:* Sandra Gering Gallery Newxonu Rd #2 Box 236 Jefferson NY 12093

MYERS, PHILIP HENRY
PAINTER
b Jersey City, NJ, Aug 16, 1922. *Study:* Art Students League, NY, studied with Reginald Marsh, 46-50, Robert Brackman, 50-52, Sidney Dickenson, 61-62. *Work:* Galleria de Bari, Bari, Italy; US Capitol, Washington, DC; Nat Inst Health, Bethesda, Md; Univ Miss Med Sch, State Col, Miss; Pollack Hosp, Jersey City, NJ. *Comn:* John McCormack portrait, Speaker of House, Washington DC, 65; Vpres Humphrey portrait, Toastmasters Int, Washington DC, 65; Sonny Jergensen portrait, Washington Redskins Football Team, Washington, DC, 66; Justice Thomas Stanton portrait, NJ Bar-John Stanton, Morristown, NJ, 67; Marchioness portrait, Marquis de Milfontes, Portugal, 77. *Exhib:* Salamagundi Club Nat Invitational, NY, 65; Southern Vermont Mus Nat Invitational, Manchester, 89; Schenectady Mus Nat Invitational, NY, 94. *Pos:* Partner, Portraits with Cortland Butterfield, New York City & Bucks Co, Pa, 59-76; resident artist, Werben Lang Gallery, NY, 63-65; resident artist, Legends Gallery, Saratoga Springs, NY, 96-98. *Awards:* NJ Performing Arts Prestige Award, Hudson Co Awards Comt, 76 & 77; Mulligan Award, Nat Juried Exhib, Southern Vt Mus & Art Ctr, 89; 1st Place Oil, Nat Juried Exhib, Atlantic City, NJ, 81. *Bibliog:* Washington Post, 3/65; Newark Star Ledger, Newark, NJ, 2/65; The Saratogian, 7/23/2000. *Mem:* Portrait Soc Am. *Media:* Oil. *Specialty:* 19th and 20th Century Am Art. *Dealer:* Legends 511 Broadway Saratoga Springs NY 12866; Saratoga Fine Art 15 Saddle Brook Dr Saratoga Springs NY 12866. *Mailing Add:* Philip Myers Fine Art 66 Meadowbrook Rd Saratoga Springs NY 12866

MYERS, RITA
VIDEO ARTIST
b Hammonton, NJ, Dec 10, 1947. *Study:* Douglass Col, Rutgers Univ, New Brunswick, NJ, BA, 69; Hunter Col, City Univ New York, MA, 74. *Exhib:* Video and Ritual, Mus Mod Art, NY, 84; Solo exhibs, The Allure of the Concentric, Whitney Mus, NY, 85, Rift/Rise, Mass Coll Art, Boston, 86, Alternative Mus, NY, 87, R H Love Mod, Chicago, 88, In The Drowning Pool, Long Beach Mus Art, Calif, 89, Berkshire Mus, Pittsfield, Mass, 90, Phantom Cities, Univ Gallery, Univ Mass, Amherst, 90, Carnegie Mus Art, Pittsburgh, Pa, 92 & Resurrection Body, Worldwide Video Ctr, The Hague, The Neth, 93; Am Landscape Video, Carnegie Mus Art, Pittsburgh, Pa, San Francisco Mus Mod Art, Calif, 88 & Newport Harbor Art Mus, Newport Beach, Calif, 89; Video-Sculptur Retrospektiv und Aktuell 1963-1989, Neuer Berliner Kunstverein, Berlin, 89 & Kolnischer Kunstverein, Koln, 89; Tenth Worldwide Video Festival, Kijkhuis, Hague, The Neth, 92; Video Int Festival, Sao Paulo, Rio de Janeiro, 94; ICI Benefit Exhib, 94; and other solo & group exhibs. *Pos:* Mem, New York State Coun Arts, 85-88 & New York City Film/Video Prog, Jerome Found, 88-90; film/video artists panel, MacDowell Colony, 90-93. *Teaching:* Var lectures & screenings, 76-92; adj prof video, Cooper Union, NY, 95-. *Awards:* Nat Endowment for Arts, Inter Arts Grant, 84, Media Arts Grant, 87 & Visual Artist's Fel, 76, 80 & 87; NY State Coun Arts, Media Production Grant, 83, 85, 91 & 98, Media Distribution Grant, 93; First Prize, 10th Worldwide Video Festival, Kijkhuis, The Hagoo, Neth, 92. *Bibliog:* Lee Sheridan (auth), Rev, Art New Eng, 2/91; Tina Wasserman (auth), Rev, New Art Examiner, 9/91; Marita Sturken (auth), The moving image in space: Public funding and the installation form, Set in Motion, NY State Coun Arts, 94. *Mem:* Coll Art Asn/Media Alliance. *Publ:* Auth, Directions/Questions: Approaching A Future Mythology, Illuminating Video; An Essential Guide to Video Art, Aperture with Bavc, 91

MYERS, ROBERT
MUSEUM DIRECTOR
Pos: Exec dir, Sangre de Cristo Arts Ctr, formerly; dir, Shanghai Theatre, 1988-1993; mgr, Norris Theatre for Performing Arts, Rolling Hills Estates; cultural servs dir, Torrance Cultural Arts Ctr; pres, Mus Latin Am Art, Long Beach, Calif, 2007-. *Mailing Add:* Museum of Latin American Art 628 Alamitos Ave Long Beach CA 90802

MYERS, TERRY R
CRITIC, CURATOR
b Ft Wayne, Ind, Jan 25, 1965. *Study:* Depauw Univ, Greencastle, Ind, BA, 87; City Univ New York Grad Ctr, New York, 88-91. *Collection Arranged:* Kay Rosen: lifelike, Mus Contemp Art and Otis Gallery, Los Angeles, 98; Robert Overby: Parallel, 1969-1978, UCLA Hammer Mus, Los Angeles, Calif, 2000. *Pos:* Libr asst, Mus Mod Art, New York, 87-90; catalogue coordr, Roy Lichtenstein Catalogue Raisonne, New York, 90-95; contrib ed, Artext, Los Angeles, Calif & New Art Examiner, Chicago, Ill; ed bd, Art Rev, London, Eng; contrib wrter, The Brooklyn Rail. *Teaching:* Vis instr art criticism, Pratt Inst, New York, 90-94; assoc prof, Otis Coll Art & Design, Los Angeles, 94-99; adj assoc prof, Art Ctr Coll Design, Pasadena, Calif, 95 & 99-2011; vis fac, Sch Art Inst Chicago, 2000-2007, assoc prof, 2007-; vis prof, Royal Coll Art, London, 2002-2004. *Mem:* Int Asn Art Critics; Coll Art Asn. *Res:* Criticism & chronicling of contemporary art & its context. *Publ:* Sunshine & Noir: Art in LA, 1960-1997, Louisiana Mus Modern Art, Humlebaek, Denmark, 97; Peter Doig Blizzard Seventy-Seven, Kunsthalle Kiel, Kunsthalle Nurnberg, Whitechapel Art Gallery, London, 98; Kay Rosen: Lifelike, Mus Contemp Art, Otis Gallery, Los Angeles, Calif, 98; Robert Overby: Parallel, 1969-1978, UCLA Hammer Mus, Los Angeles, Calif, 2000; Vitamin P: New Perspectives in Painting, Phaidon, London, 2002; Mary Heilmann: Save the Last Dance for Me, Afterall Bks, London, 2007; Dexter Dalwood, Zurich, 2010; Painting: Documents of Contemporary Arts (ed), The MIT Press, 2011. *Mailing Add:* 1021 S State St Apt 405 Chicago IL 60605

MYERS, VIRGINIA ANNE
PRINTMAKER, EDUCATOR
b Greencastle, Ind, 1927. *Study:* Corcoran Sch Art & George Washington Univ, Washington, DC, BA, 49 with Eugene Weisz, Richard Lahey & Jessalee Sickman; Calif Coll Arts & Crafts, MFA, 51 with Leon Goldin; Univ Ill, Champaign, printmaking with Lee Chesney 53-55; Univ Iowa, Iowa City, printmaking with Mauricio Lasansky 55-61; Atelier 17, Paris, printmaking with Stanley William Hayter, 61-62. *Work:* San Francisco Art Mus; Nelson-Atkins Mus, Kansas City, Kans; Toledo Mus Art, Ohio; Nat Collection Women's Art, Washington, DC; US State Dept; Des Moines Art Ctr, Iowa; Union League Club, Chicago; Herbert Johnson Mus, Cornell Coll, Ithaca, NY; Figge Mus Art, Davenport, Iowa; Fine Arts Coll, Cornell Univ, Ithaca, NY; Univ Iowa Mus Art, Iowa City, IA; Muscatine Mus Art, Ia; Culver Mus Art, Culver Acad, In. *Exhib:* One hundred and thirty solo exhibs, 53-2011; West '79/The Law Exhib, Minn Mus Art, St Paul; Seven Iowa Printmakers, Centro Internazionale della Graphica, Venice, Italy, 89-90; The Regilded Age, Newark Art Mus, NJ, 91; Ausstellung der Univ Iowa, Univ, Osnabruck, Ger, 2000; The Ghost Elm and Other Stories, 57 Drawings, Paintings & Prints, Univ Iowa Mus Art, 2006; 36 Prints & Drawings, State St Gallery, Chicago, Ill, 2009; A Time of Malfeasance, Figee Mus Art, Ia, Davenport, 2011. *Pos:* bd mem & treas, Elizabeth Found Visual Arts, NY; pres Iowa Foil Printer Corp. *Teaching:* Instr printmaking, Univ Iowa, Iowa City, 62-68, asst prof, 68-71, assoc prof, 71-80, prof, 81-. *Awards:* Fulbright Grant to Paris, 61; Develop Leave Award, Univ Iowa, 73, 78, 84, 89, 94-95 & 2000; Arts Endowment Grants, State Iowa Arts Coun & Nat Endowment Arts, 74, 82 & 85; Old Gold Summer Fel, Univ Iowa, 84 & 90; Major Arts & Humanities Initiative Award, 2006; Excellence in Teaching Printmaking Award, Southern Graphics Coun, 2009. *Bibliog:* William Benson (auth), Foil stamping as an art form, J Print World, spring, 93; Peter Alexander (auth), It all started as a Christmas card, Research, winter/spring, 98; Foil Stamping as a fine art, Hot Stamp News, spring, 98; Elaine Lindgren (auth), Foil imaging...a new art form, bk rev, J Print World, spring, 2002; Chris Mortenson (auth), Reflections: Foil Imaging: A New Art Form, The Little Village, spring 2011. *Mem:* Soc Gilders; Foil Stamping & Embossing Asn; Mid-Am Print Coun; Mid-Am Coll Art Asn; Iowa Foil Printer Corp (pres). *Media:* painting, drawing, printmaking, foil imaging. *Res:* Present, the definitive research & development to raise the craft of foil stamping, as pursued by the commercial printing industry, to the level of a fine art, 1986 thru 2013; Invention of the Iowa Foil Printer, US Patent 94, Underwriteres Listed, 97. *Interests:* reading; gardening; swimming. *Publ:* Auth & illusr, Owners Manual for the Iowa Foil Printer, Wenman Press, Iowa City, Iowa, 92; coauth & co-ed, Creating Original Prints with Hot Stamped Foil & the Iowa Foil Printer, Tenacre Print, Solon, Iowa, 93; auth, Foil stamping program at the univ of Iowa expands, J Print World, Meridith, NH, spring, 2000; Foil Imaging...A New Art Form, WDG Communications, Cedar Rapids, Iowa, 2001; Foil Imaging: The Original Editioned Prints, WDG Communications, Cedar Rapids, Iowa, 2006; Foil Imaging: The Original Editioned Prints Journal of the Print World, winter 2009; and others. *Mailing Add:* 4244 NE 210th St Solon IA 52333

MYFORD, JAMES C
SCULPTOR, EDUCATOR
b Brackenridge, Pa, Aug 9, 1940. *Study:* Edinboro Univ Pa, BS (art educ), 62; Ind Univ Pa, MEd (art educ), 66, MA (sculpture), 78. *Work:* Westmoreland Co Mus Art, Greensburg, Pa; Carnegie Libr, Pittsburgh, Pa. *Comn:* Outdoor aluminum sculptures, Aluminum Co Am, Pittsburgh, Pa, 75, First Nat Bank Pa, Erie, 78, Bloomsburg Univ, 80 & Manufacturing Data Systems Inc, Ann Arbor, Mich, 81; sculpture (stone & aluminum), City Pittsburgh, Pa, 83. *Exhib:* Assoc Artists Pittsburgh, Mus Art, Carnegie Inst, 70-83; 25th Ann Ball State Exhib, 79; Aluminum Sculpture, William Penn Mem Mus, Harrisburg, Pa, 79, Westmoreland Co Mus Art, Greensburg, Pa, 79 & Butler Inst Am Art, 83; Cast Aluminum Sculpture, Mus Art, Carnegie Inst, Pittsburgh, Pa, 80; Art Gallery Ont, 83; Sculptors Who Teach, Gov Mansion, Harrisburg, Pa, 83. *Teaching:* Assoc prof art, Slippery Rock Univ, 68-. *Awards:* Alcoa Award, Assoc Artist Pittsburgh, 78; Jurors Award, Pittsburgh Soc Sculptors, 80; Second Prize Sculpture, Great Lakes Art Exhib, 82. *Bibliog:* Richard Sutphen (producer), Preparation for Museum Show (videotape), 81; Marilyn Evert (auth), Discovering Pittsburgh's Sculpture, Univ Pittsburgh Press, 83. *Mem:* Int Sculpture Ctr; Pittsburgh Soc Sculptors (bd mem, 80-82); Asn Artists Pittsburgh. *Media:* Aluminum. *Mailing Add:* 320 Cranberry Rd Grove City PA 16127-4636

MYLAYNE, JEAN-LUC
PHOTOGRAPHER
b Marquise, France, 1946. *Exhib:* Lannan Found, Santa Fe, 2005, Glen Horowitz Bookseller, East Hampton, NY, 2006, Blaffer Gallery, Houston, 2007, Texas Gallery, Houston, 2007, Henry Art Gallery, Univ Washington, Seattle, 2008, Mus of Contemporary Art, Cleveland, 2008, Gladstone Gallery, NY, 2008, Centro Cultural Andratx, Mallorca, 2008, Musee d'art contemporain de Lyon, 2009, Camera Austria, Graz, 2009, 54th Int Art Exhib Biennale, Venice, 2011. *Mailing Add:* Gladstone Gallery 515 W 24th St New York NY 10011

MYRON, ROBERT
HISTORIAN
b Brooklyn, NY, Mar 15, 1928. *Study:* NY Univ, BA, 49, MA, 50; Ohio State Univ, PhD (fel), 53. *Teaching:* Prof art hist & art appraisal, Hofstra Univ, Hempstead, NY, 54-. *Awards:* Belgium-Am Found Awards, 53. *Mem:* Appraisers Asn Am. *Res:* Tribal arts; American-Asian and Western art. *Publ:* Auth, Prehistoric Art, 59 & Italian Renaissance, 61, Pitman; Mounds, Towns, Totems, 63 & Two Faces of Asia: India, China, 65, World; American Art, 2 vols, Crowell-Collier, 70. *Mailing Add:* 401 Garden Blvd Garden City NY 11530

N

NAAR, HARRY I
PAINTER, EDUCATOR
b New Brunswick, NJ. *Study:* Philadelphia Coll Art, BFA, 1968; Ind Univ, with Robert Bailey, James McGarrell, Robert Barnes, Marvin Lowe, Rudy Pozzatti, MFA, 1970; studied under French Painter Jean Helion, Paris, France, 1970-71; Printmaking Fel, Rutgers Univ Ctr Innovative Print & Paper. *Work:* Jane Voorhees Zimmerli Art Mus, Rutgers Univ; NJ State Mus, Trenton; Johnson & Johnson Corp, NJ; Bristol Myers Squibb Corp, Plainsboro, NJ; Am Coun on Edn, Washington; Morris Mus Art & Sci, Morristown, NJ; NJ State Mus, Trenton; Hunterdon Mus Art, Clinton, NJ; Montclair Art Mus, NJ; Newark Art Mus, NJ; Noyes Mus Art, Atlantic City, NJ; Jersey City Mus, NJ; Indiana Univ, Bloomington, Ind; Lyme Academy Col of Fine Arts, Lyme, Conn ; Rider Univ, Lawrenceville, NJ; Frances Loehman Loeb Art Mus, Vassar Coll, Poughkeepsie, NY; Western Carolina Univ, Callowhee, NC; plus others; Kean Univ, NJ; Lawrenceville Sch, NJ. *Exhib:* Nat Drawing Exhib, Corcoran Gallery Art, 1970 & High Mus Art, 1970; solo exhibs, Westby Art Gallery, Rowan Coll, 1994, Bowery Gallery, NY, 1995, Gallery S Orange, NJ, 1995, Lobby Gallery, NY, 1996 & Woodrow Wilson Sch, Princeton Univ, NJ, 1996, Bowery Gallery, NY, 2007; Beyond the Image, Rabbet Gallery, New Brunswick, NJ, 1996; Fields of Vision, Lobby Gallery, NY, 1996; Woodrow Wilson Sch, Princeton Univ, NJ, 1996; Arts Works Trenton, NJ, 1996; Hardcastle Gallery, Washington, DC, 1997; Rider Univ Art Gallery, Laurenceville, NJ, 1997; Bristol Myers Squibb, Princeton, NJ, 1998; New Jersey Landscapes, Rider Univ, NJ, 1999; Holman Hall Art Gallery, The Col of NJ, 2000; The Considine Gallery, Stuart Co Day Sch, Princeton, NJ, 2000; Les Malaut Art Gallery, Union, NJ, 1999; Sussex Co Col, Newton, NJ, 2000; Trenton City Mus, 2001, 2002; NJ State Mus, Trenton, 2001; Gallery South Orange, NJ, 2001; Blair Acad, Blairstown, NJ, 2001; Pringle Gallery, Princeton, NJ, 2002; Newark Mus, NJ, 2002; Mercer Co Community Col, Trenton, 2002; Acad Art Mus, Easton, Md, 2002; Bradley Univ, Prova, Ill, 2003; Eisenstranger, Howard Gallery, Univ Nebr, Lincoln, 2004; The Trenton City Mus, Trenton, NJ, 2004; Found for Hellenic Cult, NY, 2004; NJ State Mus, Trenton, NJ, 2005; A Sense of Place, Noyes Mus Art, Oceanville, NJ; Roman Gallery, Blair Acad, Blairstown, NJ; Coeman Book Exhib, Salon du River de Coeman, Coeman, Fr; Marsh Meditations, Monmouth Mus, Lancroft, NJ & Meadowlands Environ Center, Lyndhurst, NJ, 2007; Homer's Odyssey, Noyes Mus, Oceanville, NJ, 2008; The Artist's Eye, Paul Robeson Ctr, Princeton, NJ, 2008; Am Acad Arts and Letts Invitational, New York, 2009; 6 NJ Masters, Kean Univ, 2009; Honors & Awards Exhib, Am Acad Arts & Letts, NYC, 2009; Drawing Atlas, PA Coll Art & Design, Lohen Geduld Gallery, NY; Realism Unbound, Noyes Mus, Oceanville, NJ, 2009; Revision & Voices, The Brodsky Ctr, Rutgers Univ, NJ, 2010; Pine Barrons Rediscovered, Noyes Mus, Oceanville, NJ, 2010, Long Beach Island Found Gallery, 2011; Focus on Princeton, George Segal Gallery, Montclair State Univ, 2011; Dalet Gallery, Phila, Pa, 2012. *Collection Arranged:* Joan Wortis-A Textile Journey, Thoughask & Monopront Coll, 2000; Frederick Franck, Moments of Seeing, 2000; Marge Chavooshian, Drawings & Paintings From Here and Abroad, 2000; David Dewey-Past & Present, 2001; Leland Bell, Changing Phyths 1950's-1991, 2001; Michael Frechette, Malenel Life, 2002; Adolf Konrad, Moments of Vision, 2002; Michael Ramus, This & That, 2002; Altered Books: Spine Bonding Thrillers, 2003; Rosemarie Beck, Paintings, 2003; Louis Finklestein, Paintings, 1971-99; Judith K Brodsky, Memoir of an Assimilated Family, 2003; Joseph Fiore, 25 yrs Painting from Rock Fragments, 2004; Margaret Kennard Johnson, from Stone to Mesh, Sixty yrs, 2004; Diane Burko, Landscape: Paint/Pixel, 2005; Issac Witkin, Out of the Crucible: Images Born of Fire and Water, 2005; Aleksandr Manusov, The Tree of Life: Russian School Painting at the End of the Thirtieth Century, 2005; John Goodyear, The Elementary Series, 2005; James Kearns Continuities: Fifty Years, drawings & paintings, 2006; Thomas George, New Work, drawings & pastels, 2006; Alison Weld: The Figurative Impulse in Abstraction, 2006; Audrey Flack, Abstract Expressionist, 2007; W Carl Burger, NJ Landscapes, 2007; Peter Stroud Paintings: 1970-2007, 2007; Gary Saretzky, A Retrospective, 1972-2007; Bruce Rigby, Retrospective, 2008; Nancy Hagin: City/Country, Painting Watercolor from the Last 20 Years, 2008; Realism Unbound, Noyes Mus, NJ, 2009; Drawing Atlas, Penn Coll Art & Design & Loltin & Geduld Gallery, New York, 2009; Pine Barens Rediscovered, Noyes Mus, NJ, 2010; Revision & Voices, Brodsky Ctr, New Brunswick, NJ, 2010; Landscapes seen & Imagined, Maruente & James Hutchens Gallery, Lawrenceville Sch, NJ, 2010. *Pos:* Gallery dir, Rider Univ, Lawrenceville, NJ, 1989-. *Teaching:* Instr painting & drawing, Beaver Coll, Pa, 1975-78 & Rutgers Univ, 1978-80; assoc prof painting, drawing, printmaking & design, Rider Univ, Lawrenceville, NJ, 1980-93, prof fine arts, 1993-; vis artist, Philadelphia Coll Art, 1984; prof art, Rider Univ, 1993-. *Awards:* Summer Res Grant, Rider Col, 1982, 1988, 1999, 2001, 2010; Dorothy Malloy Mem Award, Trenton City Mus, 1992; Best in Show, Trenton City Mus, 2001 & 2002; Best in Show, Mercer County Artist Exhib, 2007; Printmaking Grant, Rutgers Univ Center for Innovative Print and Paper (Brodsky Center), 2005; Purchase Prize, Acad Arts and Letts, 2009; Hassam, Speicher, Betts & Synoms Award, Acad Arts and Letts; Frank N Elliott Distinguished Service award, 2009. *Bibliog:* Janet Purcell (auth), Bound to Open Eyes-State Museum Hosts Eyes on Trenton, The Times, NJ, 2/9/2001; Susan Van Dongen (auth), Sweptaway, The Times, Trenton, 10/4/2002; Nivcole Plett (auth), Line of Inquiry at Mercer County Community College, USI, Princeton, NJ, 12/1/2002; Jon Naar (auth), Photography Retrospective Exhibition 1958-2008, 2008; Rita Baragona & St Clair Sullivan (co-auths), A Marriage of Two Minds, 11/2008; Ellen K Levy (auth), Decoding Metaphors for the 21st Century, 3/2009; Judy K Brodsky (auth), Harry I Naar The Outside from Within: Envisioning Forest and Sea, Rider Univ, 2012. *Mem:* Col Art Asn Am. *Media:* Oil, Acrylic, Watercolor, Drawing. *Specialty:* Established and up and coming artists; Nat and Int works. *Publ:* auth, A Natural Thing, Jean Helion's Representational Paintings, Arts Mag, 4/1984; auth, Reginald Neal, Works from 1958-Present, NJ, State Mus, Trenton, NJ, 1989; auth, California Landscapes, Rider Col Art Gallery, NJ, 1991; auth, Lois Dodd, Views of Windows and Doors, Rider Col Art Gallery, 1992; auth, Louis Finkelstein, Paintings 71-99, Rider Univ Art Gallery, 1999; Howard Goklstein, A Painting Journ, Rider Coll Art, 2009; Grossman & Cajori, Forming the Figure, Rider Community Art Gallery, 2009; Paul Rickert, Industrial Visions, Rider COmmunity Art Gallery, 2010; Judith K Brodsky (auth), Memoir of an Assimilated Family, 2003.; Joseph Fiore (auth), 25 yrs Painting from Rock Fragments, 2004.; Margaret Kennard Johnson (auth), from Stone to Mesh, Sixty yrs, 2004.; Diane Burko (auth), Landscape: Paint/Pixel, 2005.; Issac Witkin (auth), Out of the Crucible: Images Born of Fire and Water, 2005.; Aleksandr Manusov (auth), The Tree of Life: Russian School Painting at the End of the Thirtieth Century, 2005.; John Goodyear (auth), The Elementary Series, 2005.; James Kearns Continuities: Fifty Years, drawings & paintings, 2006.; Thomas George, New Work, drawings & pastels, 2006.; Alison Weld (auth), The Figurative Impulse in Abstraction, 2006.; Audrey Flack (auth), Abstract Expressionist, 2007.; W Carl Burgervv(auth), NJ Landscapes, 2007.; Peter Stroud Paintings: 1970-2007, 2007.; Gary Saretzky (auth), A Retrospective, 1972-2007.; Bruce Rigby (auth), Retrospective, 2008.; Nancy Hagin (auth), City/Country, Painting Watercolor from the Last 20 Years, 2008; Joy Kreves: Translating Nature, 2010; Grace Graupe-Pillard: The Holocaust Massacre of the Innocents, 2010; Michael Graves Landscapes and Still-Lives, 2011; Jamie Greenfield, Bodies of Work, 2011; George Nike, The Upside Down Wind, 2011; John Suler: Photographic Psychology: Forces that Shape the Psyche, 2013; Joan Needham: Alterations, 2013; Geoffrey Dorfman: Eye and Mind, Painting & Monotype, 2013. *Mailing Add:* 4 Tracey Ct Lawrenceville NJ 08648

NADARAJAN, GUNALAN
CURATOR, EDUCATOR, ADMINISTRATOR
Study: Nat Univ of Singapore, Faculty of Arts and Social Sciences, undergraduate degree; Univ Warwick, UK, MFA (continental philosophy specializing in aesthetics), 1994; Nat Univ of Singapore, Master of Social Sciences (sociology/anthropology), 1997. *Pos:* artistic dir, ISEA, 2006-08; curator for Ambulations, Singapore, 1999, 180KG, Jogakarta, 2002, media_city, Seoul, 2002, Negotiating Spaces, Auckland, 2004, & DenseLocal, Mexico City, 2009; contributing curator for Documenta XI, Germany, 2002 and Singapore Biennale, 2006; served as a juror for several international exhibitions; artistic co-dir, Ogaki Biennale, Japan, 2006; artistic dir International Symposium on Electronic Art, Singapore, 2008; bd dirs Inter Soc for Electronic Art, adv bd Database of Virtual Art; co-principal investigator, National Science Foundation grant to establish a national Network for Science, Engineering, Art and Design. *Teaching:* Sr lecturer, dir studies of art theory and art history, Lasalle Col of the Arts, Singapore, 1996-2001, dean visual arts, 2001-03, founding dean research and creative industries, 2003-04; prof art, assoc dean for research and graduate studies, Pa State Univ, 2005-08; vice provost for research, Md Inst Col of Arts (MICA), Balt, Md, 2008-11, dean graduate studies, 2011-12; dean, prof, Sch Art & Design, U Mich, 2012-. *Mem:* Special Interest Group in Graphics and Interactive Technologies, Asn for Computing Machinery, Col Art Asn, Nat Coun of Univ Research Administrators, International Asn of Aesthetics, American Asn for the Advancement of Science; fellow Royal Soc Art. *Publ:* (auth) Ambulations, 2000 and Construction Site, 2004; (co-auth) Contemporary Art in Singapore, 2007; (co-ed) Place Studies in Art, Media, Science and Technology: Historical Investigations on the Sites and Migration of Knowledge, 2009 and The Handbook of Visual Culture, 2012; Over 100 book chapters, catalogue essays, academic articles and reviews. *Mailing Add:* University of Michigan School of Art & Design 2000 Bonisteel Blvd Ann Arbor MI 48109-2069

NADLER, ARNY
SCULPTOR
b Chicago, Ill, 1969. *Study:* Washington Univ, Sch Art, St Louis, BFA, 1991; Cranbrook Acad Art, Bloomfield Hills, Mich, MFA, 1994. *Exhib:* Solo exhibs include Rehabilitation Ctr, Kingswood Gallery, Bloomfield Hills, Mich, 1994, ARC Gallery Invitational 1, Chicago, 1995, Len G Everett Gallery, Monmouth Coll, Monmouth, Ill. 1998, Gallery 210, Univ Mo, St Louis, 2001, Bonsack Gallery, St Louis, 2001; Group exhibs include Enforced Proximity, Forum Gallery, Bloomfield Hills, Mich, 1992; Invitational Art Auction, Chicago Fine Arts Exchange, Chicago, 1994; A Sight For Sore Eyes, Ten In One Gallery, Chicago, 1995; Faculty Show, Evanston Art Ctr, Evanston, Ill, 1997; Aspects of Being, Hunt Gallery, Webster Univ, Webster Groves, Mo, 2000; Three Artists, Crowe T Brooks Gallery, St Louis, 2002; Sculptors 5, Innsbrook Resort & Conference Ctr, Innsbrook, Mo, 2002; Marshall Arts, Delta Axis, Memphis, 2003. *Teaching:* Asst Prof, Washington Univ St Louis. *Awards:* Carl Milles Scholar, Cranbrook Acad Art, Bloomfield Hills, Mich, 1993; Sam Fox Sch Creative Research Award, Washington Univ St Louis, 2007; George Sugarman Found Grant, 2007

NADOLSKI, STEPHANIE LUCILLE
PAINTER, PRINTMAKER
b Sacramento, Calif, Feb 21, 1945. *Study:* San Jose State Col, 62-68; Sch Art, Bellevue, Nebr, 72; with Edgar Whitney, Robert E Wood & Glen Bradshaw, 78-83. *Work:* Univ Miss Libr, Oxford; Tex Commerce Bank, Scurlock Towers, Arthur Anderson & Co & Mus Art Am West, Houston; Bowne Corp, Detroit Mich and Chicago Ill; Wausau Insurance Co, Wausau, Wis; Kane Co Courthouse, St Charles, Ill; Stora Corp, Schaumburg, Ill; Towne Bank, Portsmouth, VA. *Comn:* Painting & offset lithographs, LeClub Condominiums, Galveston, Tex, 84; Mixed media painting, ACA Corp, Streamwood, Ill, 89; Handcast Paper wall relief, S McAllister, Palatine, Ill, 89; Paper wall relief, Unique Coupon Corp, Lake Barrington Shores, Ill, 91; Abstr monoprints, three, comn by Mr & Mrs Dilworth, Kenilworth, Ill, 92; abstract monoprints, comn by Mr & Mrs Michael Murray, Barrington, Ill, 94; Relics, Mayan Monotype Assemblage, comn by Mrs. JoAnn Schirilo, W Chester, Pa, 2009. *Exhib:* Allied Artists Am 80th Ann Exhib, NY, 93; Solo exhibs: Gallery 18, Chesterton, Ind, 97; Claire E Smith Gallery, Barrington, Ill, 99; Chesapeake Ctr for the Creative Arts, Brooklyn, MD, 2002; Holley Gallery, Annapolis, MD, 2003; Acad Art Mus, Easton, MD, 2005; Artworks 2006, Annapolis Arts Alliance, 2006, Evolving Layers, Garden Gallery, Quiet Waters Park, Annapolis, Md, 2013, Nat Coll Society, Signature Mem Show, Mesa Contemporary Art Ctr, Mesa, Ariz, 2013, Views from the Other Shore, Tilghman Island, Md, 2013, BWS Signature Mem exhib, Black Rock Ctr Arts, Germantown, Md, 2013, Columbia Art Ctr, Columbia, Md, 2013; Gallery West, Alexandria, VA, 2002; The Art League, Alexandria, VA, 2002; Nat Landscape, MD fedn of Art, Annapolis, MD, 2003; Making Your Mark, Acad Art Mus, Easton, Md, 2003-2004; Md Fedn of Art, City Gallery, Baltimore, MD, 2004; Mid-Atlantic Regional Watercolor Exhib, Strathmore Hall, Rockville, Md, 2006; Water Works, Regional Exhib, Md Fed Art, Annapolis, Md; Md Printmakers, Glenview Mansion, Rockville, Md, 2007; Md Printmakers, Univ Md Eastern Shore, Salisbury, Md, 2007; Small Works, Md Fed Art Circle Gallery, 2007; Splash, Annapolis City Hall, 2007, 2008; Image & Imagination, St John's Col, Annapolis, Md, 2008, 2010, 2012; Working Artists Forum, Heron Point, Chestertown, Md, 2008, 2010; Open Juried Show, Kent Island Fedn Art, Stevensville, Md, 2008; Mid Atlantic Print Show, Pyramid Atlantic, Md, 2009; Adkins Arboretum Juried Ann Exhib, Md, 2009; Working Artists Forum, Md Hall for the Creative Arts, 2010; Women's Vision, Women's Art, Arundel Ctr, Annapolis, Md, 2010; Assemblage, Collage & Prints, Kent Island Fed Arts, Stevenville, Md, 2010; Group Retrospective, Quiet Waters Park, Annapolis, Md, 2010; Past, Present & Future, Kent Island Fed Art, Stevensville, Md, 2010; Working Artists Forum, Acad Art Mus, Easton, Md, 2011; Queen Annes County Arts Council, Centreville, Md, 2011; Art of the Book, Mitchell Gallery, St Johns Coll, Annapolis, Md, 2011; Annapolis Arts Alliance, Maritime Mus, Eastport, Md, 2012; Dorchester Ctr Arts, Cambridge, Md, 2012; Tidewater Inn, Lib Gallery, Easton, Md, 2012; Image and Imagination, Mitchell Gallery, St Johns Coll, Annapolis, Md, 2012. *Pos:* Dir, Archway Gallery Houston, 76-87; dir, Barrington Area Arts Coun, 87-89; adv bd, Barrington Area Arts Coun, 89-94; juror, Nat Miniature Exhib, Pa, 2005; juror, Regional Ann Exhib, Pa, 2006. *Teaching:* Instr watercolor, North Harris Co Col, 84-86; papermaking - mixed media monotypes, free lance workshops, 87-94; artist-in-residence, Virginia Lake Elem, Palatine, Ill, 90; Willow Grove Sch, Buffalo Grove, Ill, 93; instr experimental watermedia, Peninsula Art Sch, Fish Creek, Wis, 95, 96 & 98; artist in res, Chesterfield Co Public High Sch, Va, 2004; instr, Acad Art Mus (Monotypes & Beyond), Easton, Md, 2004-2005; Norfolk Pub Sch System, in serv teaching K-12, Art Teachers, Norfolk, Va, 2006; instr, Chestertown Art League, Monotype & Collage workshop, Chestertown, Md, 2007; instr, Queen Anne's Co Arts Coun, Monotype workshop Centerville, Md, 2007-2008; Monotype workship, Kent Island Fed Art, 2009; Collage workshop, Chestertown Arts League, 2009. *Awards:* 2nd Pl, Bel Air Art Festival Fine Art, MD, 2003; 3rd Place, Mixed Media, Mystic Outdoor Art Festival, Conn, 2004; 2nd Place, Mixed Media, Mystic Outdoor Art Festival, Conn, 2005; 3rd Place, Mixed Media, Mystic Outdoor Art Festival, Conn, 2006; 2nd place, Mixed media, Mystic Outdoor Art Festival, Conn, 2008; 2nd Place, Mixed Media, Mystic Outdoor Art Festival, 2011. *Bibliog:* Sandra Dybal (auth), Portrait of an Artist, Daily Herald Paddock Publs, 87 & Chicago Art Rev, 89; Jodie Jacobs (auth), Art on the road, Chicago, Tribune, 94; Leeland & Williams (auth), Creative Collage Tech, 94; Collage in All Dimensions, NCS, 2005; The Art of Layering, Making Connections, 2005; Wash Project for the Arts, Corcoran Artists Dir, 2005-2008, 2011. *Mem:* signature mem Soc Layerists Multi Media; Colored Pencil Soc Am; Nat Collage Soc; Baltimore Watercolor Soc; Md Printmakers; NAIA; Soc Layerists in Multi Media; Baltimore Watercolor Soc; Mem Pa Guild of Craftsman; Md Printmakers Muddy Creek Artists Guild, Md; Annapolis Art Alliance. *Media:* Watercolor, Acrylic; Monoprint, Handmade Paper, Collage. *Specialty:* Original contemp mixed media works on paper & Canvas. *Interests:* Mayan history, travel, golf & scuba diving. *Publ:* Coauth, Mixed Media Gallery, Crafts Report, 84 & Shuttle, Spindle & Dyepot, 84; auth, Paintings, monotypes & paper, Town Mag, 85; The Business Side of Art, 97; cover art, New Visions Calendar, 99; Am Art Collector, North East Edition, 2005. *Dealer:* Benfield Gallery 485 Jumpers Hole Rd Severna Park MD 21146. *Mailing Add:* 4785 Idlewilde Rd Shady Side MD 20764-9765

NAEGLE, MONTANA
PAINTER
b April 21, 1940. *Study:* Univ Wyo, BFA. *Work:* First Interstate Bank Ariz, Tucson; Miller & Blau, Casper, Wyo; Fred Dowd & Co, Casper, Wyo; Hines Indust, Albuquerque, NMex; Williams, Porter & Day, Casper, Wyo; and others. *Exhib:* NMex Inter, Clovis, 85; solo exhib, Wyo State Art Mus, Cheyenne, 79, Nicolaysen Art Mus, Casper, 79 & 84, Casper Coll Visual Art Ctr, 88; Watercolor USA, Springfield, Miss, 88; Univ NMex, Albuquerque, 88; Contemp Art in Cowboy State, Nicolaysen Mus, 9/88; and others. *Teaching:* Watercolor instr, Casper Col, Wyo, 83-84. *Bibliog:* Mary Carrol Nelson (auth), article, Southwest Art, 84; Montana Naegle-Report to Wyo, News Special, KTWO. *Media:* Watercolor. *Mailing Add:* 1540 Linda Vista Casper WY 82609

NAGAKURA, KENICHI
ARTIST
b Shizuoka, Japan, Oct 26, 1952. *Work:* Asian Art Mus, San Francisco, Calif; Clark Ctr for Japanese Art & Cult, Hanford, Calif; Mint Mus of Craft & Design, Charlotte, NC. *Exhib:* Bamboo Masterworks, Asian Soc, New York, 2000; Three Bwes of Bamboo: Fujinuma, Nagakura, Shono, Kansas City Jewish Mus, Overland Park, Kans, 2003; HIN: The Quiet Beauty of Japanese Art, Chicago Cult Ctr, Ill, 2006; Interwined:Contemp Baskets from the Sara & David Lieberman Collection, Ariz State Univ Art Mus, 2007, NM Mus Art, Santa Fe, NM, 2009; New Bamboo: Contemp Japanese Masters, the Japan Soc, New York, 2008; New Bamboo, The Clark Ctr for Japanese Art & Cult, Hanford, Calif, 2009. *Awards:* Winner, Cotsen Bamboo Prize, Lloyd E Cotsen, 2000. *Media:* Bamboo. *Publ:* Contemp Japanese Bamboo Arts, Art Media Resources, 99; HIN: The Quiet Beauty of Japanese Bamboo Art, Art Media Resources, 2006; Masters of Bamboo, Asian Art Mus, 2007; New Bamboo Contemp Masters, Japan Soc Inc, 2008. *Dealer:* Tai Gallery 1571 Canyon Rd Santa Fe NM 87501. *Mailing Add:* 1601 B Paseo de Peralta Santa Fe NM 87501

NAGANO, PAUL TATSUMI
PAINTER, PICTURE MAKER
b Honolulu, Hawaii, May 21, 1938. *Study:* Columbia Coll, BA, 60; Pa Acad Fine Arts, Philadelphia, 63-67. *Work:* Hawaii State Found of Cult & the Arts, Honolulu; William Rockhill Nelson Gallery, Kansas City, Mo; New Brit Mus Am Art, Conn; Boston Public Libr; Neka Mus, Bali. *Comn:* Lilac Sunday (watercolor), The Arnold Arboretum, Harvard Univ, 86; Sheraton Kauai Hotel, Hawaii, 90; mural, Campbell Estate, Hawaii, 93; The Tree (bronze sculpture) The Chapel, Hawaii Preparatory Acad, Waimea, 97; various portraits, 2008-2011; Rumah Komala, 2011. *Exhib:* Two Visions, Neka Mus, Ubud, Bali, 92; Nagano Variety Show, Somerville, Mass, 97; SymBALIst and Other BALI Views, Honolulu, 2000; Open Studio, Fenway Studios, 2001-2002 & 2004-2012; The SymBALIst Watercolors, Kupu-Kupu Gallery, Jakarta, Indonesia, 2002; Lotus Potpourri, Bibelot Gallery, Honolulu, Hawaii, 2003; Two decades: Nagano Watercolors of Bali, Jakarta, Indonesia, 2005; Nagano Works, Someing Aisa, Honolulu, 2006; Sister Islands: Bali, Hawaii, Baik Designs, Honolulu, 2008; Nagano on Bali: 25 Years, Bamboo Gallery, Ubud, Bali, 2009; Baik Designs, Honolulu; Ka'lkena, Kapiolani Community Col, Honolulu, 2011; Malam: Night in Bali, Bamboo Gallery, Ubud, Bali, 2014. *Pos:* Art dir, Pucker-Safrai Gallery, Boston, 67-89; trustee, Art Inst Boston, 93-98. *Awards:* First Prize Landscape with Figures, Popular Photog, 63; Grand prize, 16th Annual Shizuoka Friendship postcard Art Exhib, Honolulu, 2004. *Bibliog:* Nagano on Bali, 95. *Mem:* Fel Pa Acad Fine Arts. *Media:* Watercolor, Photography. *Interests:* opera, theatre, films. *Publ:* Contribr, Am Artist, 3/85; Watercolor Page, 5/78, 3/85. *Dealer:* Bamboo Gallery Ubud. *Mailing Add:* 1811 Palolo Ave Honolulu HI 96816

NAGANO, SHOZO
PAINTER
b Kanazawa, Japan. *Study:* Kanazawa Fine Arts Univ, Japan, AB, BD; Art Students League, with Julian Levi; Pratt Inst, NY. *Work:* Allentown Art Mus, Pa; Berkshire Mus, Pittsfield, Mass; Citicorp, NY; Hudson River Mus, Yonkers, NY; State Univ NY Albany. *Comn:* It is Finished (painting), comn by Richard Hirsch, cur James Michener Collection, 71; Arts of Asia, NY, 85. *Exhib:* Nat Inst Arts & Lett, 72; Brooklyn Mus, 75, 77 & 78; Solo exhib, Squibb Art Ctr, 76; Japan Today, 79; Sindin Gallery, 82; Newark Mus, 83; and others. *Teaching:* Instr painting, Seibu Gakuen, Tokyo, 60-65. *Bibliog:* Alvin Smith (auth), article in Art Int, 5/72; David Shirey (auth), articles in New York Times, 9/75 & 3/76; article, Arts Mag, 6/85. *Mem:* Japanese Artists Asn NY (pres, 75). *Media:* Acrylic on Shaped Canvas, Human Future Subject. *Publ:* New American Paintings, Open Studios Press, Boston, Mass, 4/94; Endzeit Stimmung, Dumont Taschenbucher, Cologne, Ger, 5/94. *Mailing Add:* 39 Race St Jim Thorpe PA 18229

NAGATANI, PATRICK A
ARTIST
b Chicago, Ill, Aug 19, 1945. *Study:* Calif State Univ, BA, 68; Univ Calif, Los Angeles, MFA, 80. *Work:* Baltimore Art Mus, Md; Denver Art Mus, Colo; Los Angeles Co Mus Art, Calif; Metrop Mus Art & Int Ctr Photog, NY; Mus Fine Arts, Houston, Tex; and others. *Comn:* Epoch (site specific photo mural permanent installation 9'x12'), MTA Hq, Gateway Ctr at Union Station, Los Angeles; and others. *Exhib:* Studio Work: Photographs by Ten Los Angeles Artists (with catalog), Los Angeles Co Mus Art, 82; Photog Fictions, Whitney Mus Am Art, 86; Arrangements for the Camera: A View of Contemp Photog, Baltimore Mus Art, 87; The Photog of Invention: Am Pictures of the 1980's (traveling), Smithsonian Inst, Mus Contemp Art, Chicago & Walker Art Ctr, 89; In Close Quarters: Am Landscape Photog Since 1968, Art Mus, Princeton Univ, 93; solo exhibs, James & Meryl Hearst Ctr Arts, Cedar Falls, Iowa, 93, State Univ NY, 93, Royal Photog Soc, Bath, Eng, 93, Stanford Univ Mus Art, 93, Salathe Gallery, Pitzer Col, 94, Calif Mus Photog, Univ Calif, Riverside, 94, Alexandria Mus, Lafayette, La, 95, Amarillo Mus Art, Tex, 96, Isla Ctr Arts, Univ Guam, Mangilao, 97, The Albuquerque Mus, NMex, 98, Univ Art Mus, Univ NMex, Albuquerque, 99, Ctr Creative Photog, Univ Ariz, Tucson, 2000, Univ Ky Art Mus, Lexington, 2001, Rochester Inst Technol, NY, 2002, Columbus Mus Uptown, Columbus, Ga, 2002, Yager Mus, Hartwick Col, Oneonta, NY, 2002, Reed Col, Portland, Oreg, 2003, Vt Ctr for Photog, Brattleboro, 2005, Olin Art Gallery, Kenyon Col, Gambier, Ohio, 2006, 516 ARTS, Albuquerque, NMex, 2007, Northlight Gallery, Ariz State Univ, Tempe, 2007, Lehigh Univ, Rauch Gallery, Bethlehem, Pa, 2009, Univ NMex Art Mus, 2010, Int Mus Surgical Sciences, Chicago, 2010 & others. *Collection Arranged:* The Ctr Creative Photography, Tucson, Ariz, 83-89. *Teaching:* Instr photog, Fairfax Community Adult Sch, 76-79, West Los Angeles Community Col, 80-83, Otis Art Inst, Parsons Sch Design, Los Angeles, 87; vis artist & instr, Art Inst Chicago, 83; artist residency, Calif Arts Coun, Los Angeles Theater Works, Juv Court & Community Schs, 86-87; asst prof art, Dept Art & Art Hist, Loyola Marymount Univ, 80-87; regents prof, Univ NMex, Albuquerque, 1987-2007, prof emeritus. *Awards:* Leopold Godowsky Jr Color Photog Award, 88; Kraszna-Krausz

Found Award, 92; Visual Arts Fel, Nat Endowment Arts, 92-93; Individual fel, Aaron Siskind Found, 98; Governor's Award for Excellence in the Arts, NMex, 2003; Eliot Porter Photog Fel Award, 2007; Honored Educator Award, 45th SAE Nat Conference, Denver, 2008. *Bibliog:* Great photographers of New Mexico-Showcase 1993, Santa Fe Reporter, 8/25/93-8/31/93; Patrick Nagatani (auth), We Must make this world worthy of its children, Ilford Photo Instr Newsletter, fall 93; Phillip A Greenberg (auth), Dreams die hard, Sierra, 11/93. *Mem:* AARP; Soc for Photog Educ. *Media:* Photography. Masking Tape. *Interests:* Black Jack. *Publ:* Auth, Nuclear Enchantment, Univ NMex Press, Albuquerque, NMex, 1991 & Desire for Magic: Patrick Nagatani 1978-2008; and others. *Dealer:* Volakis Gallery Napa CA; Andrew Smith Gallery Santa Fe NM; Scheinbaum & Russek Santa Fe NM. *Mailing Add:* 4255 Altura Vista Ln NE Albuquerque NM 87110

NAGIN, MARY D
PAINTER, EDUCATOR
b Amityville, NY, Dec 28, 1953. *Study:* State Univ Coll Plattsburgh, NY, BA, 75; Adelphi Univ, Garden City, NY, MA, 83, with Jeffrey R Webb. *Exhib:* Selections from the NDA, Hermitage Found Mus, Norfolk, Va, 88; Wichita Small Oil Competition, Wichita Art Asn, Kans, 88; Works on Paper Nat Exhib, Firehouse Gallery, NCC, Garden City, NY, 89; Allied Artists Ann, Nat Arts Club, NY, 90; Pastel Invitational, Mill Pond House STAC, St James, NY, 92; Solo Award Exhib, NY Pen & Brush Club, NY, 96; solo exhibs, East Meadow Libr, 98 & 2007; Pastel Soc America, Nat Arts Club, NY, 85, 86, 88-92, 94, 2010, & 2012. *Pos:* Exhib chmn, Nat Drawing Asn, 88-89; cur gallery, Nassau Community Col, 89-90; art comt, Salmagundi Club, 90; exhib chmn, pastel div, Pen & Brush Club, 92. *Teaching:* instr drawing & painting, Art League of Long Island, 83-; instr watercolor, St John's Univ, NY, 91; guest art instr, Mill Neck Manor Sch for the Deaf, 98; art instr, Owl 57 Gallery, Hewlett, NY, 99-2000; art instr, North Shore Montesson Sch, 2000-01; art instr, Harbor Country Day Sch, St James, 2004. *Awards:* Beatrice Vare Award, Ann Pastels Only, Pastel Soc Am, 90; Philip Isenberg Award, Ann Pastel Exhib, Pen & Brush, 92; Pen and Brush Merit Award, 98; Pen & Brush Solo Show Award, 95. *Bibliog:* Phyllis Braff (auth), Show mixes the unusual and the traditional, NY Times, 1/22/86; NF Karlins (auth), Pastels front & center, Westsider, New York, 9/92. *Mem:* Art League of Long Island (fac mem, 83); Pastel Soc Am, New York (mem, 88-); Pen & Brush, New York (mem, 88-2004); Salmagundi Club, New York (mem, 90-96). *Media:* Oil, Pastel. *Publ:* Tom Philbin (auth), The Everything Home Improvement Book, 97; Woman's Day Home Remodeling, Vol VIII, #4, 98; Tom Philbin (auth), The Irish 100, 99. *Mailing Add:* 280 Lowndes Ave Apt 307 Huntington Station NY 11746

NAGLE, RON
CERAMIST
b San Francisco, Calif, 1939. *Study:* San Francisco State Col, BFA, 61. *Work:* Everson Mus Art, Syracuse, NY; Oakland Mus, Calif; Philadelphia Mus Art; San Francisco Mus Mod Art; St Louis Mus Art; Berkeley Art Mus and Film Archive, Univ Calif; Corcoran Gallery of Art, Wash DC; Metropolitan Mus Art, NY; Stedelijk Mus, Amsterdam, Holland; Victoria and Albert Mus, London, England; Carnegie Mus Art, Pittsburgh, Pa; Detroit Inst Arts, Mich; Shigaraki Mus Contemporary Ceramic Art, Japan; George Gardiner Mus Ceramic Art, Can; Newark Mus, NJ; Nat Gallery Australia, Canberra. *Exhib:* Solo exhibs, Currents 4, St Louis Art Mus, Mo, 79, Charles Cowles Gallery, NY, 81, 83, 85 & 89, Quay Gallery, San Francisco, Calif, 82 & 84, Greenberg Gallery, St Louis, Mo, 82, Delahunty Gallery, Dallas, Tex, 83, Betsy Rosenfield Gallery, Chicago, Ill, 84, Ron Nagle: Big Work, Rena Bransten Gallery, San Francisco, Calif, 88, 99, 2005, 2009, 2011, Revolution Gallery, Ferndale, Mich, 2000, Garth Clark, NY, 2001, 2003, 2006, Frank Lloyd Gallery, Los Angeles, Calif, 2002, 2005, George Adams Gallery, 2008, 2011, Galerie Pierre Marie Giraud, Brussels, Belgium, 2008, 2012; Group exhibs, Clay Revisions: Plate, Cup, Vase, Seattle Art Mus, Wash, 87; Building with Clay, Hoffman Gallery, Oregon Sch Arts & Crafts, Portland, 90; Vessels: From Use to Symbol, Am Craft Mus, NY, 90; Garth Clark Gallery, Los Angeles, Calif, 90, 95 & 96; retrospective, Carnegie Mus, Pittsburgh, 93; Franklin Parrasch Gallery, NY, 2001; Franklin Parrasch, NY, 2004; Australian Nat Gallery, Canberra, Australia, 2005; Metropolitan Mus Art, NY, 2006; George Adams Gallery, NY, 2007; Inst Contemporary Art, Univ Pa, 2009; Blaffer Gallery, Art Mus Univ Houston, Tex, 2009; San Francisco Mus Modern Art, San Francisco, Calif, 2009; Stedelijk Mus, Hertogenbosch, The Netherlands, 2009; Am Acad Arts & Letts, NY, 2011; Xavier Hufkens, Brussels, Belgium, 2011; Salon 94, NY, 2011; Galerie Pierre Marie Giraud, Basel Switz, 2011; 55th Int Art Exhib Biennale, Venice, 2013. *Teaching:* instr, San Francisco Art Inst, 61-65, 76-78, Univ Calif, Berkeley, 62-73, Mills Coll, Oakland, 78-2010. *Awards:* Fel, Nat Endowment Arts, 74, 79, 86; Adaline Kent Award, 78; Mellon Grant, 81 & 83; Visual Artists Award, Flintridge Found, 98; Fac Res Grant, Mills Col, 99; Art award, Am Acad Arts and Letts, 2011; John Simon Guggenheim Meml Found Fel, 2012. *Dealer:* 7 rue de Praetere 1050 Brussels Belgium. *Mailing Add:* c/o Rena Bransten Gallery 77 Geary St San Francisco CA 94108

NAGY, REBECCA MARTIN
MUSEUM DIRECTOR, HISTORIAN
b Statesboro, Georgia, 1953. *Study:* Ga S Univ, BA, 1975; Univ NC, PhD, 1983. *Pos:* Sr Prog Coordr, NC Mus Art, Raleigh, 1985-94; assoc dir educ, NC Mus Art, Raleigh, 1994-2002; cur, NC Mus Art, Raleigh, 1997-2002; Ed, NC Mus Art Handbook Collections, 1998, Sepphoris in Galitee Crosscurrents Cult, 1998; bd dirs, Gallery Art & Design, NC S Univ, Raleigh, 1999-2000; dir, Harn Mus Art, Univ Fla, Gainesville, 2002-Present; bd mem arts coun, African Studies Asn, 2003-05; dir, Fla Art Mus Dir Asn, 2011-; trustee, Asn Art Mus Dirs, 2011-. *Teaching:* Instr Cleveland Mus Art, 1982-1985. *Awards:* Dist Alumna Award, Ga S Univ, 2004; Fel, Int Partnership among Mus Progs, Am Asn Mus, 1994; Fulbright-Hays Grant, US Dept Educ, 2000. *Mem:* S E Art Mus Dirs Consortium, Fla Art Mus Dirs Asn; Asn Art Mus Dirs, Gainesville Women's Forum, Rotary Club Gainesville. *Specialty:* African, Asian and mod & contemp art. *Publ:* co-auth, ed, Continuity and Change: Three Generations of Ethiopian Artists, 2007. *Mailing Add:* Samuel P Harn Mus Art PO Box 112700 Gainesville FL 32611

NAHAS, NABIL
PAINTER
b Beirut, Lebanon, 1949. *Study:* La State Univ, Baton Rouge, 1971; Yale Univ, MFA, 1973. *Comn:* Theatre set, Jennifer Muller Dance Co, 1988. *Exhib:* Solo exhibs incl Ohio State Univ, 1977, Robert Miller Gallery, NY, 1978, 1979, 1980, Holly Solomon Gallery, NY, 1987, 1988, Galerie Montenay, Paris, 1988, Baldwin Gallery, Aspen, Colo, 1994, Sperone Westwater, NY, 1997, 1999, 2005, 25th Bienal De Sao Paulo, 2002, J Johnson Gallery, Fla, 2002-03, Galerie Xippas, Paris, 2005; group exhibs incl Weatherspoon Art Gallery, 1977; Met Mus Art, NY, 1979; Basel Art Fair, 1979; Pratt Inst Gallery, NY, 1980; Studio Mus Harlem, NY, 1981; Queens Mus, NY, 1983; Holly Solomon Gallery, NY, 1988; Chicago Art Fair, 1988; Edward Thorp Gallery, NY, 1993; Brian Gross Gallery, San Francisco, 1994; Sperone Westwater, NY, 1996, 2001; Galerie Tanit, Munich, 1997; FIAC, Paris, 1997, 1998, 1999; Mus Guild Hall, NY, 1999-2000; Galerie Xippas, Paris, 2000; NY Studio Sch, NY, 2001; XXV Bienal de Sao Paulo, 2002; The Work Space, NY, 2002; represented in permanent collections Met Mus Art, NY, Vorhees Zimmerli Mus, Rutgers Univ, New Brunswick, NJ, FAE, Musee d'art moderne, Pully-Lausanne, Switzerland. *Awards:* Nat Endowment for Arts Fel Grant, 1980. *Media:* Acrylic. *Dealer:* Galerie Xippas 108 rue Vieille du Temple 75003 Paris France; Sperone Westwater 257 Bowery New York NY 10002. *Mailing Add:* c/o Sperone Westwater 257 Bowery New York NY 10002

NAKAZATO, HITOSHI
PAINTER, PRINTMAKER
b Tokyo, Japan, Mar 15, 1936. *Study:* Tama Coll Art, Tokyo, BFA (painting), 60, with Shosuke Oksawa; Univ Wis, MS (art, printmaking),64; Univ Pa, MFA (painting), with Piero Dorazio, 66. *Work:* Mus Mod Art, NY; Philadelphia Mus Art; Nat Mus Mod Art, Kyoto, Japan; Pa Acad Fine Arts, Philadelphia; Brooklyn Mus, NY. *Comn:* Mural, Furukawa Pavilion, Expo 70, Osaka, Japan. *Exhib:* Artists in Americas, Nat Mus Mod Art, Kyoto, 74; Three Hundred Yrs of Am Art, Philadelphia Mus, 76; Contemp Japanese Painting, Japan Art Festival 10th Anniversary, Tokyo, 77; Prints in Series: Idea into Image, Brooklyn Mus, NY, 77; One-man shows, Mercer Col, 78, West Chester Col, 79, Pa Acad Fine Arts, 79 Contemp Drawings: Philadelphia II, Philadelphia Mus Art, 79, One Eleven One, Tokyo Gallery, 89, Yaseido Gallery, Tokyo, 91, Gallery Kuranuki, Osaka, Japan, 92; Yokohama '92, First Int Contemp Art Fair, Japan, 92. *Teaching:* Asst prof painting, Tama Col Art, Tokyo, 68-71; asst prof printmaking, Grad Sch of Fine Arts, Univ of Pa, Philadelphia, 73-79, assoc prof, 79-. *Awards:* John D Rockefeller 3rd Grant, 66-67; Creative Artists Pub Serv Grant, 74-75. *Bibliog:* Joseph Love (auth), Tokyo Letter, Art Int, 3-12/71; Ruth Lehrer (auth), Three Hundred Years of American Art: Philadelphia, Philadelphia Mus, 76; Teruazu Suenage (auth), Art 78, Bijutsu Techo, 1/78. *Mem:* Am Color Print Soc. *Media:* Acrylic, Oil; All Media. *Mailing Add:* 361 W 36th St No 4A New York NY 10018-6408

NAKONECZNY, MICHAEL
PAINTER
b Detroit, Mich, Oct 30, 1952. *Study:* Cleveland State Univ, Ohio, BFA, 79; Univ Cincinnati, MFA, 81. *Work:* Progressive Corp, Cleveland; Cincinnati Bell; Mus N, Univ Alaska, Fairbanks, AK. *Comn:* Workbooks: Journal/Journeys, Columbia Col, Chicago Ctr for the Book & Paper Arts, Ill, 94. *Exhib:* 6 Artists Ohio/6 Artists Indiana, Cranbrook Acad Arts Mus, Bloomfield, Mich, 81; 39th Corcoran Biennial Exhibs Am Painting, Corcoran Gallery Art, Washington, DC, traveling, 85; solo exhibs, Zolla/Lieberman Gallery, Chicago, Ill, 86, 87, 90, 92 & 93, Eve Mannes Gallery, Atlanta, Ga, 91, Lew Allen Gallery, Santa Fe, NMex, 92 & 95, Cleveland Ctr Contemp Art, Ohio, 93, Evanston Art Ctr, Ill, 94, Purdue Univ, 95 & Columbia Col, Chicago, 96; AVA 7, Los Angeles Co Mus Art (with catalog), Calif, traveling, 87; USA Within Limits, Galleria De Arte, Sao Paulo, Brazil, 94; Tamarind into the Nineties (with catalog), Weatherspoon Art Gallery, Univ NC, Greensboro, traveling, 95; Witherspoon Art Gallery, Univ NC, 95; paintings, Horowitz-Lew Allen Gallery, Santa Fe, NMex, 96; and many others. *Teaching:* Artist-in-Residence, PS1, Long Island City, NY, 86, Bemis Found, Omaha, Nebr, 92; instr, Cuyahoga Community Coll, Cleveland, Ohio, 87, Cleveland Inst Art, 88; vis artist, Herron Sch Art, Ind Univ, 90, Kansas City Art Inst, Mo, 91, Tamarind Inst, Albuquerque, NMex, 92 & 95 & Mont State Univ, 97-98; assoc prof painting, Univ Alaska, Fairbanks, 2000-13. *Awards:* Fel, Awards in Visual Arts, 87; Individual Artist Fel, Ohio Arts Coun, 90; Fel, Arts Midwest, Nat Endowment Arts, 94-95; Fel, Ill Arts Coun, 95; Rasmunson Found Individual Fel, 2010. *Mem:* Chicago Artist Collection; Coll Art Asn. *Dealer:* Zolla Lieberman 325 W Huron Chicago IL

NAMA, GEORGE ALLEN
PRINTMAKER, SCULPTOR
b Pittsburgh, Pa, Feb 23, 1939. *Study:* Carnegie-Mellon Univ, BFA & MFA; Atelier 17, Paris, with Stanley William Hayter. *Work:* Philadelphia Mus Art; Smithsonian Inst, Libr Cong, Washington, DC; Brooklyn Mus; Butler Inst Am Art, Youngstown, Ohio; Carnegie Inst Mus Art; Biblioteque Nationale, Paris. *Comn:* Gulf Oil Co, Pittsburgh. *Exhib:* Original Prints, Calif Palace of Legion of Honor, San Francisco, 64; Pratt Graphic Art Ctr Serigraph Exhib, 65; Northwest Printmakers Int Exhib, 65-67; Contemp Am Prints, Gt Brit, 69-71; US Info Agency Exhibs, Japan Expo, 70; Nat Acad Design, 80-86. *Teaching:* Instr, Pratt Inst, 76-86, Sch Visual Arts, 79, The New Sch, 85-86 & Nat Acad Design, 80-86. *Awards:* David Berger Mem Prize, Mus Fine Arts, Boston, 67; Stuart M Egnal Prize, Philadelphia Print Club, 68; Stella Drabkin Mem Award, Am Color Print Soc, 71; Cannon Prize, Nat Acad Design, 85. *Bibliog:* Leonard Slatkes (auth), Printmakers on Exhibit, Art Scene, 68; Richard Shelton (auth), Journal of Return, Kayak, 69; S Hazo (auth), Poets & Prints, Artist Proof Mag, 71. *Mem:* Nat Acad. *Media:* Intaglio, Casting. *Publ:* Monuments, 71; Seascript, 71; Origin of Language, Nine Etchings, 79; Desert Water, 81; Grapes of Zeuxis, 87; and others. *Mailing Add:* Pratt Institute 144 W 14th St New York NY 10011

NANTANDY
PAINTER, MURALIST
b Abilene, Tex, Dec 22, 1927. *Study:* North Tex State U, 45-47, Tex Univ, 48; Otis Art Inst, 61; Univ Southern Calif, BFA, 64; Calif State Univ, Long Beach, MA, 67; studied sculpture, painting with Judy Chicago and Peter Plagens. *Work:* Newport Harbor Mus, Calif; Laguna Beach Mus Fine Arts, Calif; Vay Adam Mus, Vajay, Hungary. *Comn:* History of San Bernardino Co from 1810-1927 (mural), Calif State Architect's Office, San Bernardo, 78-80. *Exhib:* Solo Retrospective, Jocob Javits Federal Bldg, NY, 85, Artist League of Tex, 89, Survival Art, Westbeth Art Gallery, NY, 93, Lifetime Achievement Exhib, 2005; Art Camp Invitees, Vay Adam Mus, Hungary, 98; Group Show (10 paintings), Mark Timmerman Studio, NYC, 2001; Group Drawing Show, Westbeth Gallery, NYC, 2002; On Becoming a Woman, Westbeth Holiday Show, 2004. *Pos:* owner/operator, Tanar Art Gallery & Studio, Calif, 62-81. *Teaching:* instr art La Quinta High Sch, Calif, 64-71; instr art Mt San Antonio Col, Walnut, Calif, 75-77. *Awards:* Tex Watercolor Soc Joske's of Tex Award, 51; Prix De Paris Award Ligoa Duncan Gallery, NY, 58; Honorable Mention Award Orange Co Art Asn, 68. *Bibliog:* Diana Reed (auth), Nothing Flat About Her Painting, Orange Co Evening News, 5/17/70; Patty Kelly (auth), Redlands Featured in New State Mural, Daily Facts, 8/27/80. *Mem:* Nat Soc Mural Painters (sec 83-88, 1st vp 97-99, exhib coordr, 92); Westbeth Visual Arts (exhib coordr 92). *Media:* Watercolor. *Publ:* auth, photogr, The Week, 7-14, 2002. *Dealer:* Tanar Art Gallery & Studio 463 West St New York NY 10014. *Mailing Add:* 55 Bethune St New York NY 10014

NARANJO, MICHAEL ALFRED
SCULPTOR
b Santa Fe, NMex, Aug 28, 1944. *Study:* Wayland Coll, Plainview, Tex; Highland Univ. *Work:* Magee Womens Hosp, Pittsburgh, PA; Heard Mus, Phoenix, Ariz; Albuquerque Mus, NMex; Colorado Springs Fine Arts Ctr, Colo; Mus Fine Arts, NMex State Libr, Records & Arch, Santa Fe; Mercy Regional Med Ctr, Durango, Colo, 2006. *Comn:* The Dancer, six ft bronze, Albuquerque Mus; Justice, Pete V. Domineci, Federal Courthouse, Albuquerque, NMex, 94; Spirit Mother, Yale Park, Univ NMex, Albuquerque, NMex, 96; The Gift, Nonex State Libr, Records & Arch, Santa Fe, 98; Emergence, State Capitol, Santa Fe, NMex, 2001; All Things are Possible, City Albuquerque, NMex, 2005. *Exhib:* Eiteljorg Mus Am Indian & Western Art, 92; Albuquerque Mus, NMex, 94; New Art of the West, 6th Ann Eiteljorg Mus Biennial, Indianapolis, Ind, 98; Veterans Admin Cent Off, Washington, DC, 98; Pfizer Gallery, New York, 98-99; United States Embassy, London, Eng, 2001; Inner Visions, the Sculpture of Michael Naranjo, The Heard Mus, Phoenix, Ariz, 2000-2001; The Works of Michael Naranjo & RC Gorman, The Governor's Gallery, Santa Fe, NMex, 2004; permanent, Michael Narangjo - Touching Beauty, Atrium Gallery, Bataan Bldg, Santa Fe, NMex, 2006; Grounds for Sculpture, Hamilton, NJ, 2008. *Pos:* Bd mem, NMex Arts Comn, 71-73, NMex Very Spec Arts Festival, 83- & Access to Art, Mus Am Folk Art, 87; vis artist, Pojoaque High Sch, NMex, 96; educ, Found for Blind Children, Phoenix, Ariz, 2001; panelist, Am Asn Mus Ann Meeting, Dallas, Tex, 2002. *Awards:* Distinguished Achievement Award, Am Indian Resources Inst, 90; Clinton King Purchase Award, Mus Fine Arts, Santa Fe, NMex, 91; Outstanding Disabled Veteran of the Year, by the Disabled Am Veterans, 99; Santa Fe Rotary Found, Distinguished Artist of the Yr, NMex, 2004; Lifetime Achievement Award, Southwestern Asn Indian Arts, 2007; and others. *Bibliog:* Bob Dotson (auth), In Pursuit of the American Dream, publ by Atherum, 85; Bodywatching, CBS Special produced by New Screen Concepts, 88; Mary Carroll Nelson (auth), Artist of the Spirit, Arcus Publ, 94; Teri Degler (auth), The Fiery Muse: Creativity & the Spiritual Quest, Random House, Can, 96; David Kirby (auth), An Artist Vision, Mod Maturity Mag, 3/2000-4/2000; Jesse Brown & Daniel Paisner (auths), The Price of Their Blood, Bonus Bks, 2003; Touching Beauty, Am Stories with Bob Dotson (tv), The Today Show, NBC, 8/2006; Gussie Fauntleroy (auth), Sight Unseen, Southwest Art Mag, 8/2008; and others. *Media:* Bronze, Stone. *Publ:* Auth, Arizona highways, Ariz Dept Transportation, 5/86; Southwest Art Mag, 10/89; Colores, Pub Broadcast System doc, 92; Article, Santa Fean Mag, 8/98; Inner Vision: The Sculpture of Michael Naranjo, Two Little Girls Pub. *Dealer:* Nedra Matteucci Galleries Santa Fe NM. *Mailing Add:* PO Box 7576 Albuquerque NM 87194

NARDIN, MARIO
COLLECTOR, SCULPTOR
b Venice, Italy, Mar 17, 1940. *Study:* Acad Belle Arti, Venice, with Guido Manarin. *Work:* Hudson River Mus, Yonkers, NY; Fordham Univ; City of Santa Rosa, Calif; also in pvt collections. *Comn:* Actaeon Corp. *Exhib:* Solo exhibs, Fordham Univ, 69, Lesnick Gallery, 70, Sindin Galleries, 77, Village Gallery at Gallimafry, Croton-on-Hudson, NY, 78 & Soho Gallery-Herald Ctr, NY, 86; State Univ Plattsburgh, NY, 71; Sculpture in the Park, Loveland, Colo, 95; Garrison Art Ctr, 85, 86, 87, 89, 90; Meisner Gallery, Farmingdale, NY, 84; Howland Libr, Beacon, NY, 99; Garrison Art Ctr Benefit Exhib, Tallix, 2004; and others. *Pos:* Asst to Jacques Lipchitz, 64-71; asst mgr, Avent-Shaw Art Foundry, 64-75. *Awards:* New Rochelle Art Asn Award, 67; Greenburgh Arts & Cult Comt Award, 71 & 72; Mamaroneck Artist Guild Award, 73. *Bibliog:* Noel Frankman (auth), Nardin at the Hudson River Museum, Arts Mag, 3/72; Successo a Nuova York di uno scultore Veneziano, Gazzetino Venice, 72; David L Shirey (auth), Sculptor as master builder, New York Times, 3/78; Meg McConahey (auth), Sculptor Illuminates City Hall, The Press Democrat, 9/10/98. *Mem:* NY Artists Equity Asn. *Media:* Bronze; Stainless Steel. *Collection:* African art. *Mailing Add:* 184 Warburton Ave Hastings On Hudson NY 10706-3706

NARDONE, VINCENT JOSEPH
PAINTER, JUROR
b South Orange, NJ, Oct 19, 1937. *Study:* Newark Sch Fine and Indust Arts, NJ 55-56, Montclair State Col, NJ, BA, 61; Univ Southern Calif, Los Angeles, MFA, 66; Paris Am Acad Ecole De Beaux-Arts France, 78; Rosary Coll Grad Sch Art, Florence, Italy, 81, with Genieve Secord, Joseph Domareki, Isa Petrozzani, Mildred Taylor, Paul Harris & Arnauld D'Hauterives, John Grabach, James Carlin. *Work:* Newark Mus & Newark Pub Libr, NJ; Collection Int, Paris Am Acad, France; Duncan Mus, Paris; Relais et Chateaux Inn, Lake Saranac, NY; Bristol-Meyers/Squibb Gallery, Princeton, NJ; Seton Hall Univ, NJ; Neurological Regional Assocs, Mapleshade, NJ; Permanent Collection: Nat Mus of Fine Arts, Budapest, Hungary; The Noyes Art Mus, Oceanville, NJ, Kean Univ Mus, Union, NJ; Butler Inst Am Art, Youngstown, Ohio; Radtke Recruitment LLC, Sarasota, Fla; Embassy Circle Guest House, Wash DC. *Comn:* exterior stone carving, Music & Art Corp, NJ, 70; original litho insert, NJ Music & Arts Mag, 72; watercolor altarpiece, Christ the King Parish, Ploughe, Sardinia, 72; mural, NJ Transit Sta, Maplewood, 92; Embassy Circle Guest House, Washington, DC. *Exhib:* Solo exhibs: Ligoa Duncan Gallery, NY, 78; Luxembourg Mus, Paris, 78; Barron Arts Ctr, Woodbridge, NJ, 80; Il Centro Artistico, San Niccolo, Florence, Italy, 81; ITT Worldwide Commun Inc, NJ, 88; Robin Hutchins Gallery, Maplewood, NJ, 92-94; AT&T Corp, Basking Ridge, NJ, 93; Frederick Gallery, Allenhurst, NJ, 2006; Seoul Int Exhib Tour, Korea, 84-85; Audubon Artists Nat, 90-2015; La Watercolor Soc Int, New Orleans, 95; Soc Watercolor Artists Nat, Ft Worth, Tex, 95; Western Colo Watercolor Nat, Grand Junction, 95; Allied Artists of Am, 96-2015; Anchor and Palette Gallery, NJ, Jersey Five Group, 99; Atlantic City Art Center, NJ, 2001; The Morris Mus, NJ, The Art of Collecting Fine Art, 2002 & 2003; Ocean Co Artists Guild, NJ, 2003; Pastel Soc Am Int Juried Exhib, 2006; NJ State Juried Exhib, Artists Guild, Island Heights, NJ, 2006 & 2010; Group exhibs: Exposition Int d'Art de Mode, Pavillion du Val-de-Grace, Paris, 95; Ctr for Int Art & Cult Int Exhib, New York City, 2005, 2007; Taiwan Ctr, Flushing, NY Int Ann Pastels Juried Exhib, 2005-2011; Noyes Art Mus, 2006; Int Pastel Artists Invitation Exhib, Tapei, Taiwan, 2007, 2012; Allied Artists Am Invitational at Bennington Ctr Arts, Vt, 2007; Signature Artists Exhib, The Noyes Mus Art, NJ, 2007-2015; From Realism to Abstraction, Tycoon Galleries, Pt Pleasant, NJ, 2009; Monmouth Festival of the Arts, Tinton Falls, March 2009- 2013, Spring Lake Art Gallery, 2013, From Realism to Abstraction, 2013; MidYear Juried Show, Butler Inst Am Art, Ohio, 2011-2013; North America Pastel Artists Asn Invitational, Cultural Ctr Taipei, Flushing, NY, 2011-2015; Allied Artists Centennial Invitational, Canton Art Mus, Ohio, 2015. *Pos:* Illusr & art consult, NJ Music & Art Mag, 69-73; art collector, 70; art adminr, NJ State Coun Arts Grant, Essex Co, NJ, 73; art dir, NJ Transit Mural Project, Maplewood, 92; nat nominating consultant, Biog Encyl Am Painters, Sculptors and Engravers: Colonial to 2002; pres, Audubon Artists, NYC, 2007-; vpres, Allied Artists of America, NY, 2011, 2015; vpres, Manasquan River Group of Artists, NJ, 2012, 2013. *Teaching:* art specialist, South Orange/Maplewood Sch Dist, NJ, 61-89; instr painting adult sch, Maplewood, NJ, 66-70; adj art Prof, Seton Hall Univ, S Orange, NJ, 68-74; demo workshops, Monmouth Co, NJ, 96-2005. *Awards:* Raymond Duncan Medal, Prix de Paris, 79, Painting Award, Le Salon, Grand Palais, Paris, 78, Queen Fabiola, Prix Rubens Medal, Belg, 78; Medal of Artistic Merit, Rosary Col, Florence, Italy, 81; Silver Medallion, Int Arts Competition, Seoul, Korea, 84; Mid-Atlantic Regional Watercolor Award, Baltimore, 95; Louisa Melrose Gallery Painting Award, Frenchtown, NJ, 2002; Achievement Painting Award, Int Artists Invitational Exhib, NYC, 2008; Dick Blick Award Mixed Media, Audubon Artists, NYC, 2008; Seniors Award, Ocean Co Coll, NJ, 2011-2015; NJ State Finalist, 2013 & 2015. *Bibliog:* Francois Perche (auth), critique, La Revue Moderne des Arts, Paris, 78; Viaczeslav Zavaliszen, Art Critic/Novoye Russkoye Slovo, NY, 78; Dorothy Hall (auth), critique, Park East, NY, 11/78; Lou Pessolano (auth), Artist of the month, NJ Artform, 82; Beth Fand (auth), Major Auction Review News Record of S Orange, Maplewood 8/91; The Coast Star, Artist Rev, Monmouth Co, NJ, 2/2009; Rhoda Yanow (auth), Pastel Portrait (permanent collection), Butler Inst Am Art, Oh; Tova Navarra (auth), NJ Artists Through Time, 2015. *Mem:* Audubon Artists, NY (pres, 2013-2015); Allied Artists Am (vpres); Manasquan River Group Artists, NJ; Guild Creative Art, Shrewsbury, NJ; Salmagundi Art Club, NY (hon mem); Noyes Art Mus, NJ (signature artists mem); Belmar Arts Council, NJ. *Media:* Acrylics, Pastels, Watercolor, Mixed Media. *Publ:* Ecological Genesis (litho portfolio), Rubicon Graphics, NJ, 72; Contribr, Franklin & James Decade Review of Am Artists at Auction, 5/88 - 6/98; Davenports's Art Reference/Price Guide, 2010-2014; Art at Auction in America, Krex Press Publ Co, Silver Springs, Md, 91-95; Giclee Ltd Ed Print Series, Archive Print Inc, Allenwood, NJ, 2002-2003; contbr, Biographical Encyclopedia of American Painters, Sculptors, & Engravers: Colonial to 2002. *Dealer:* Spring Lake Art Gallery 1408 3rd Ave Spring Lake NJ 07762

NARKIEWICZ-LAINE, CHRISTIAN K
MUSEUM DIRECTOR, WRITER
b Colorodo Springs, Colo, Jun 3, 1952. *Study:* Université Strasbourg, Strasbourg, France, (archit), 70; Lake Forest Col, Lake Forest, Ill, (art hist), 75. *Hon Degrees:* Am Acad Rome, 80. *Exhib:* Art to Swatch, Pac Design Center, Los Angeles, Calif, 95; Wright in Chicago, Design Mus, London, Eng, 97; New Chicago Archit, Buenos Aires Biennale, Arg, 98; Children of Chernobyl, Thessaloniki Mus, Greece, 99; Nordic Visions, Cult Ctr of Cath Ch, Naxos Castle, Naxos, Greece. *Pos:* dir/pres, Chicago Athenaeum: Mus Archit and Design, Chicago and Schaumburg, Ill, 88-; dir/CEO, Eurpean Ctr Archit Art Design and Urban Studies, Dublin, Ireland, 2008-. *Teaching:* adj prof, Archit Ill Inst Technol, 86-89. *Awards:* Goldsmith Award, Indust Designers Soc Am, 93; Humanitarian Award, David K Hardin Generativity Trust, 97. *Publ:* auth, Distant Fires, 97, Baltic Hours, 99, Inspiration: Nature and Poet, 99 & Enemy of the People: Forty Belarusian Poets, 2001, Metrop Arts Press; Greenland, Metrop Arts Press, 2003. *Mailing Add:* Chicago Athenaeum 601 S Prospect St Galena IL 61036

NAROTZKY, NORMAN DAVID
PAINTER, PRINTMAKER
b Brooklyn, NY, Mar 14, 1928. *Study:* Brooklyn Col, BA (cum laude), 49; Art Students League, 45-49; Cooper Union, 52, BFA, 79; Atelier 17, Paris, 54-56; Kunstakademie, Munich, 56-57; New York Univ, Inst Fine Arts, 57-58; study with Moses Soyer, Ad Reinhardt, S W Hayter, Morris Kantor, Nicholas Marsicano, Howard Trafton, Charles Seide. *Work:* James A Michener Collection of 20th Century Am Painting, Univ Tex Art Mus, Austin; Philadelphia Mus Art; Mus Contemp Art, Madrid, Spain; Mills Coll Art Gallery, Oakland, Calif; Cincinnati Art Mus, Ohio; Columbia Univ Rare Book & Manuscripts Libr, NY; John Hay Libr, Brown Univ,

Providence, RI; Museu De L'Emporda, Figueres, Spain; Univ Iowa Libr, Iowa City; NY Public Libr, NY City; Museu de Montserrat, Spain. *Comn:* Mural, Banco de Guipuzcoa, San Sebastian, 63; ltd ed lithograph, Collectors Guild Ltd, 69 & Fine Arts 260, 72 & 76; ltd ed etchings, Galeria Fort, Barcelona, 75 & 83; Miquel Plana (ltd ed etching), Olot, 90. *Exhib:* VI Bienal Sao Paulo, Brazil, 61; Recent Painting USA: The Figure; Mus Mod Art, 62; Whitney Mus Am Art Ann, NY, 62; Arte Am y Espana, traveling Europe, 63-64; San Francisco Mus Art, 68; Grosse Kunstler Ausstellung, Haus der Kunst, Munich, 71; Fundacion Joan Miro, Barcelona, 84, 85 & 86; Bienal d'Art, Barcelona, 85 & 87; L'Informalisme a Catalunya, Barcelona, 90; 40 Yr Retrospective, Museu de L'emporda, Figueres, Spain, 94; Landscapes, Centre D'art Santa Monica, Barcelona, Spain, 99; 50 Year Retrospective Casino Art Gallery, Cadaques, Spain, 2007; Monserrat/Visions, Museu de Montserrat, Spain, 2011-12; and 56 solo exhibs. *Pos:* Staff, Collector's Guild Inc, 69-71 & Fine Arts 260, 71-80; dir art gallery, Cadaques, 73; dir painting workshop, Northern Mich Univ, summer 79. *Teaching:* Pvt studio, Cadaques, Spain, 59-69, Barcelona, 76-85; Northern Mich Univ, summer, 79. *Awards:* French Govt Fel, Paris, 55-56; Fulbright Fel, Ger, 56-57; Painting Grant, Generalitat de Catalunya, Spain, 83; Grand Prize, II Bienal d'Art, Barcelona, 87; Wooley Found Fel, Paris, 54-55. *Bibliog:* James A. Michener (auth), Iberia, Random House, NY, 68; Jose M, Moreno Galvan (auth), Spanish painting, the latest avant-garde, NY Graphic Soc, 69; Meilach & Ten Hoor (auth), Collage & Assemblage, Crown Publ, 73; Knigin & Zimiles, Contemporary Lithographic Workshop Around the World, Van Nostrand Reinhold, NY, 74; Joan Josep Tharrats, Cent Anys de Pintura A Cadaques, Edicions del Cotal, Barcelona, 81; Lourdes Cirlot (auth), La Pintura Informal en Cataluna, 1951-1970, Anthropos, 83; Jose Corredor-Matheos (auth), Historia de L'Art Catala, Ediciones 62, Barcelona, 96. *Mem:* Art Students League NY; Cercle Artistic de Sant Lluc, Barcelona; Associacio D'Artistes Visuals De Catalunya. *Media:* Acrylic, Oil; Etching, Lithography; Collage. *Publ:* Auth, Spain: a disenchantment with materia, 9-10/65, Conversation with Cuixart, 3/66 & The Venice Biennale: pease porridge in the pot nine days old, 9-10/66, Arts Mag; Ibiza--from art refuge to art center, Art Voices, fall 65; Form & communication in my art work, Leonardo Mag, 7/69; The Raven, A Limited Edition Artists Book of Poe's Poem with 9 original color etchings & one embossed relief, Barcelona, 93. *Dealer:* Galeria De La Riba Cadaques Spain

NASGAARD, ROALD
CURATOR, HISTORIAN
b Denmark, Oct 14, 1941; Can/US citizen. *Study:* Univ BC, BA, MA, 67; Can Coun Fels, 67-71; NY Univ Inst Fine Arts, PhD, 73. *Pos:* Cur contemp art, 75-78, chief cur & cur int contemp art, 78-, Art Gallery Ont; deputy dir and chief cur, 90-93; co-dir prog, Inst Mod & Contemp Art, Calgary, Alta, 95-00. *Teaching:* Asst prof art hist, Univ Guelph, Ont, 71-75; vis lectr, York Univ, Toronto, 76-78; vis lectr, Univ Toronto, 83-92; adj prof, Univ Toronto, 92-95; prof & chmn studio art, Fla State Univ, 95-2006, prof art history, 2006-2011. *Awards:* Can Coun PhD Fel, 67-68, 70-71; Rsch Fel Nt Gal Can, 02; Cornerstone Grant, Fla State Univ, 2006-07; COFRS Grant, Fla State Univ, 2008; CRC Planning Grant, Fla State Univ, 2011; Office of the Order of Canada, 2012; Queen Elizabeth II Diamond Jubilee Medal, 2013. *Mem:* Coll Art Asn; Univ Art Asn Can; Int Art Critics Asn (Canadian secy-gen, 76-78); Toronto Pub Art Comn, 86-88; Gershon Island Found (trustee, 91-). *Res:* Late 19th century to contemporary art. *Publ:* Auth, Structures for Behaviour, New Sculptures by Robert Morris, David Rabinowitch, Richard Serra and George Trakas, 78, Gary Neill Kennedy: Recent Works, 78, Yves Gaucher: Fifteen Year Perspective, 79 & 10 Canadian Artists in the 1970's, 80, Art Gallery Ont; The Mystic North: Symbolist Landscape Painting in Northern Europe and North America, 1890-1940, Art Gallery Ont, Univ Toronto Press, 84; Gerhard Richter: paintings, Thames & Hudson, London, Eng, 88; Individualtes: 14 contemporary Artists from France, 91 & Free Worlds: Metaphors and Realities in Contemporary Hungarian Art, 91, Art Gallery Ont, Toronto, 91; Concealing/Revealing, Voices from the Canadian Foothills, Mus Art, Fla State Univ, 97; Pleasures of Sight and States of Being: Radical Abstract Painting Since 1990, Mus Art, Fla State Univ, 01; Abstract Painting in Canada, Douglas & McIntyre, Vancouver, 2007; The Automatiste Revolution: Montreal 1941-1960, Douglas & McIntyre, Vancouver, 2009; The Plastichens and Beyond: Montreal 1955-1970, MNBAQ/Varley Art Gallery, 2013. *Mailing Add:* 701-70 Montclair Ave Toronto ON M5P1P7 Canada

NASH, ALYCE LOUISE (SANDY)
CONSULTANT
b Mattoon, Ill, 1915. *Study:* James Millikin Univ, Decatur, Ill, 35-36; Heatherleys Sch Fine Art, London, Eng, 47-48; Atelier Zadkine, with Ossip Zadkine, Paris, France, 48-49; Chelsea Coll Art, London Univ, with Henry Moore & Bernard Meadows, 49-51; Anglo-French Art Sch, London, 52. *Pos:* Exec secy, Edward MacDowell Assocs, 57-60; asst dir, Contemporaries Gallery, New York, 60-62; dir, Osgood Gallery, New York, 62-63 & Alice Nash Gallery, New York, 63-65; staff mem for exhibs & librn, Am Acad & Inst Art & Lett, New York, 65-72; assoc, Harmon Gallery, Naples, Fla, 78-84; dir, Friends Art Mus Gallery, Naples, Fla, 84-89; assoc cur & registrar, Philharmonic Ctr Arts, Naples, Fla, 89-, actg cur, 91-, cur, 92-2000; cur, Naples Mus Art, 2000-03. *Mem:* Fel Royal Soc Arts, Eng; Naples Art Asn (bd mem 78-); Naples Mus Art (life). *Specialty:* Contemporary American and European paintings and sculpture. *Publ:* Auth, Collectors Handbook, Harmon-Meek Gallery, 82

NASH, DAVID
SCULPTOR
b Eng, 1945. *Study:* Kingston Coll Art, BA (hons, fine art), 67; Chelsea Coll Art, 69. *Hon Degrees:* Kingston Univ, Hon Dr in Fine Art, 98. *Work:* Walker Art Ctr, Minneapolis, Minn; Metrop Mus Art, NY; Laumeier Sculpture Park, St Louis, Mo; Mus Contemp Art, Los Angeles; Contemp Mus, Honolulu, Hawaii; Guggenheim Mus, NY; Tate Gallery, London; Kröller-Müller, Neth; Mus Wales; Louisiana Mus, Denmark; Nat Mus Art, Wash. *Comn:* Sculpture, Grizedale Forest, Lake District, United Kingdom, 78; sculpture, Djerassi Found, Calif, 87; planted sculpture, General Mills, Minn, 94; sculpture, Nagoya City Mus, Japan, 94; sculpture, Towner Art Gallery, Eastbourne, United Kingdom, 96. *Exhib:* Otoineppu: Spirit of Three Seasons, Asahikawa Mus Art, Hokkaido, Japan, 94; Voyages and Vessels, Joslyn Art Mus, Omaha, Nebr, 94; Mes Enlla Del Bosc, Palaa De La Virreina, Barcelona, Spain, 95; Elements of Drawing, Leed City Art Gallery, Leeds, United Kingdom, 96; Line of Cut, Henry Moore Inst, Leeds, United Kingdom, 96; solo exhib, Mus Van Hendegasse Kunst, Antwerp, Belg, 96; Cincinnati Int Friendship Park, 2003; Making and Placing, Tate Gallery, 2004; Six Noon Columns, Nat Forest, Eng, 2006; Abbot Hall, Cumbria, Eng, 2009; Kunsthalle Mannheim, Germany, 2009; Yorkshire Sculpture Park, 2010; Royal Botanic Gardens, London, 2012. *Teaching:* vis prof, Univ Northumbria, UK, 98-; Master, masterclass, Atl Ctr Arts, Fla, 98 & masterclass, Northlands, Scotland, 2004. *Bibliog:* Marina Warner (auth), Forms into time, Acad ed; Julian Anderlis (auth) & Lund Humphries (coauth), The sculpture of David Nash; Graham Beal (auth) Voyages and Vessels, Joslyn Art Mus; Ian Barker (auth), David Nash: Pyramids Rise, Spheres Turn, and Cubes Stand Still, Annely Juda Fine Art, London, 2005; Nils Olsen (auth), David Nash: Trunks Thicken, Branches Lengthen, Roots Deepen, Galerie Scheffel, 2006; Norbert Lynton (auth), David Nash, Cameron & Hollis, 2007; David Nash at the Yorkshire Sculpture Park, 2010. *Mem:* Royal Academician. *Media:* Wood. *Res:* Environ based research. *Specialty:* constructivism and contemporary art. *Interests:* the environment. *Publ:* Mes enlla del bosc, 95; Wood Primer, The Sculpture of David Nash, 87; David Nash Skulpturen, 97; David Nash, Spirit of Three Seasons, Hokkaido Asahikawa Mus of Art, 94-95; David Nash, Charwel Goed, Ctr for Visual Arts, Cardiff, 2000; The Return of Art to Nature, Schettel Galerie, Germ, 2003; Making & Placing, Tate Gallery, London, 2004; David Nash, Thames and Hudson, 2008; David Nash at the Yorkshire Sculpture Park, 2010. *Dealer:* Annely Juda Fine Art, London; Cheryl Haines 49 Geary San Francisco CA; Gallerie Scheffel Bad Humburg UDG Ger; Galerie Lelong Paris Paris and Zürich; Alvaro Alcazar Madrid. *Mailing Add:* Capel Rhiw Blaenau Ffestiniog United Kingdom LL413NT Gwynedd

NASH, MARY
PAINTER, LECTURER
b Washington, DC, May 8, 1951. *Study:* George Washington Univ, BA, 73; Wash State Univ, Pullman, MFA, 76. *Work:* San Antonio Mus Mod Art, Tex; Mus Contemp Art, Chicago, Ill; Whitney Mus Am Art, Mus Mod Art, NY; Cleveland State Univ; J Paul Getty Trust, Calif; and others. *Comn:* Painting, Nat Hockey League, NY, 2000; painted sculpture, Birds I View, Public Art Proj, Prince George's Co, MD, 2003; sculpture, Raise the Roof, Public Art Proj, Prince George's Co, MD, 2005; The Cradle Project (sculpture), Albuquerque, NMex; sculpture, Museu Brasileiro da Escultura, Sao Paulo, Brazil, 2011. *Exhib:* Corcoran Gallery Art, Washington, DC, 92; Stetson Univ, 94 & 97; Univ Ill, Chicago, 94; Anchorage Mus, Alaska, 94-95 & 96-97; New Orleans Mus Art, La, 95; Alexandria Mus, La, 95; solo exhibs, Emerson Gallery, McLean, Va & Lincoln Ctr, Ft Collins, Colo, 97; Neighbors, Art Mus Ams, Washington, 98; Dialogues, Gallery Korea, NY, 99; The Art is in the Cards II, Lake Co Mus, Ill, 2001; Sun Bowl Art Exhib, Int Mus Art, El Paso, 2002. *Pos:* Guest lectr, Mus Art, Wash State Univ, 76-, Second St Gallery, Charlottesville, Va, 78-, Univ Ala, Tuscaloosa, 81-, Southeastern Women's Studies Asn Conf, Univ Va, Charlotteville, 83, Arlington Arts Ctr, Va, 85 & 86 & Johnson State Col, Vt, 95; artist-in-residence, alkyd painting, Va Mus Fine Arts, 84-85 & Stetson Univ, Deland, Fla, 97; guest cur, 2001 New Orleans Triennial, New Orleans Mus Art, 2001. *Teaching:* Guest lectr, Emerson Gallery, 97. *Awards:* MacDowell Colony Fel, 77; Honorable Mention, Southeastern Ctr Contemp Art, 79; Purchase Award, Wash State Arts Comn, Olympia, 82. *Bibliog:* Artists' book beat, Print Collector's Newsletter, 5-6/88; Dan Cameron (auth), New Orleans Triennial, 95; Gordon Lubold (auth), Vienna Times, 95. *Mem:* Fel MacDowell Colony; Coll Art Asn; Phi Kappa Phi Hon Soc; Visual Artists & Their Advocates. *Media:* Acrylic, Ink. *Interests:* Film, Interior Design, Travel. *Publ:* Auth, Skulls are Forever, Ichthys Bks, 86; Eye on Washington, Eye Wash, Washington, 92. *Dealer:* MN Works of Art. *Mailing Add:* 8536 Aponi Rd Vienna VA 22180

NASH, STEVEN ALAN
MUSEUM DIRECTOR, CURATOR, HISTORIAN
b Wadsworth, Ohio, Apr 8, 1944. *Study:* Dartmouth Col, BA; Stanford Univ, PhD (art history). *Pos:* Res cur, Albright-Knox Art Gallery, Buffalo, 1973-77, chief cur, 1977-80; asst dir & chief cur, Dallas Mus Fine Arts, 1980-88; assoc dir & chief cur, Fine Arts Mus San Francisco, 1988; dir, Nasher Sculpture Ctr, Dallas, Tex, 2001-2007; exec dir, Palm Springs Art Mus, Fla, 2007-. *Teaching:* Adj prof, State Univ NY, Buffalo, 1973-80. *Awards:* Mabel McCloud Lewis Found Fel, 1971; Fr Govt Res Grant, 1971; Prof Grant, Nat Endowment Arts, 1981. *Mem:* Archives Am Art (adv panel); Am Asn Mus. *Publ:* Auth, Ben Nicholson: Fifty Years of His Art, Buffalo Acad, 1978; Albright-Knox Collection (catalog), 1979; Naum Gabo: 60 Years of Constructivism, 1985; A Century of Modern Sculpture: The Nasher Collection (exhib catalog), Dallas Mus Art, 1987; 100 Years of Landscape Art in the Bay Area (exhib catalog), Fine Arts Mus San Francisco, 1995. *Mailing Add:* Palm Springs Art Museum 101 Museum Dr Palm Springs CA 92262

NASISSE, ANDY S
SCULPTOR, WRITER
b Pueblo, Colo, Nov 1, 1946. *Study:* Inst Allende, Mex, 69; Univ Colo, MFA, 73. *Work:* High Mus Art. *Comn:* Four Walls, City Atlanta, 81. *Exhib:* Southeast Ctr Contemp Arts Exhib, Winston-Salem, NC, 79; Ga Artists, High Mus, 79, 80 & 83; More than Land or Sky, Nat Mus Am Art, 82; Southern Fervor, Anderson Gallery, Richmond, Va, 83; Birmingham Mus Biennial, 83; New Epiphanies, Univ Colo Mus, 83; New Talent, Nexus Space, Atlanta, 83; solo exhib, La Mar Dodd Ctr, La Grange, Ga, 84. *Teaching:* Assoc prof, Univ Ga, Athens, 76-, gallery dir, 82-83. *Awards:* Nat Endowment Arts Grant, 79; Creative Res Award, Univ Ga, 82; Ga Coun Grant, 84. *Media:* Ceramic. *Res:* Folk art. *Dealer:* Fay Gold Gallery 3221 Cains Hill Pl Atlanta GA 30305

NATALE, MARIE
PAINTER, INSTRUCTOR
b Hammonton, NJ, Sept, 18, 1953. *Study:* Rowan Univ, BA, 75, MA, 79; studied with, Charles Reid, 2005-2010, Mel Stabin, 2006-2012. *Exhib:* NJWCS, Ridgewood Art Inst/Monmouth Mus, Ridgewood, Monmouth, 2005-2012; 89th Nat Watercolor Color Soc, Brea Civic & Cultural Ctr, Brea, Calif, 2009; 109th PWCS, Mus Art at Ursinus

Coll, Collegeville, Pa, 2009, 110th PWCS, Comm Arts Ctr, Wallingford, Pa, 2010; NJ Chapter, Am Artists Prof League, Riverfront Renaissance Ctr Arts, Milville, NJ, 2011; Signature Artists Exhib, Noyes Mus Art, Galloway, NJ, 2011-2012. *Teaching:* K-12 teacher art, Brigantine & Pleasantville Public Sch, NJ, 76-85; instr watercolor, Ocean City Art Ctr, 2004-; instr watercolor, pvt studio art ctrs in USA & abroad, 2004-; art instr watercolor, Gloucester Co Coll, 2008-2009. *Awards:* Magli-Gottesthal award, NJWCS, 2005, Best in Show, NJWCS, 2006, Award of Excellence, 2007; Watercolor award, Phila Watercolor Soc, PWCS, 2010; Award of Excellence, NJ State Exhib, 2010; Ida Wills & Clara Stroud award, Am Artist Prof League, NJ Chap, 2011. *Bibliog:* Featured Artist of the Month, Jersey Pride Found, Discover Jersey Arts, 2008; Jacqueline L Urgo (auth), Bathing in the Spotlight, Phila Inquirer, 7/10/2011; David Simpson (auth), EHT Artist Natale Brings a Little Italy Home, Hometown ed EHT & Hamilton Press, Atlantic City, 11/13/2011; Karen Fox (auth), Art and Artists at the Chalfonte, The Chalfonte/Exit Zero Pub, 2011. *Mem:* NJWCS; Noyes Mus Art (signature mem, 2009-); PWCS; Riverfront Renaissance Ctr Arts (signature mem, 2009); Plein Air Artists. *Media:* Watercolor. *Publ:* contbr, Art & Artists at the Chalfonte, Exit Zero Pub, 2011; Ocean City mag, Gone Native Communications, 2013; Splash 14 Light & Color Best of Watercolors, F & W Media Inc/North Light Books, 2013. *Dealer:* SOMA Gallery 31 Perry St Cape May NJ 08204; William Ris Gallery 9400 2nd Ave Stone Harbor NJ 08247

NATZMER VALENTINE, CHERYL
DEALER, HISTORIAN
b Detroit, Mich, May 14, 1947. *Study:* Mich State Univ, BA, 69, MA, 99. *Collection Arranged:* Zuniga, Drawings, Graphics & Sculpture, 78; Sebastian-Geometric Transformables, steel sculpture, 79; A Tribute to Rufino Tamayo, Recent Works, 79; Dibujos/Drawings, survey of Latin Am drawings, 79; The New World and the Beast, Animal Imagery in Latin Am Art, 79; Tamayo's Mexico, 80; The Imaginary Surface, paintings by Manuel Felguerez, 81; El Zodiaco--Sculpture by Sebastian Traveling Exhib, 82-83; Images From Dream Myth and the Subconscious, 88; Artists Choose Artists, 89; First Ann Muraling Festival, 90. *Pos:* Dir & pres, Gryphon Galleries, Ltd, Denver, 71-78; dir & bd dir, Rutherford Barnes Collection, Ltd, Denver, Colo, 78-; adv Mex art, Denver, 82-; cur, Centerspace, Lansing, Mich, 88-90. *Teaching:* instr socio-cult diversity, dept anthropology, Mich State Univ, 99-2000. *Mem:* Family Arts Network. *Res:* Creative Potential of Later Life. *Specialty:* Twentieth century Mexican and Latin American art; works of the Masters Tamayo and Cuevas. *Publ:* Co-producer, Columbian Art in the 80's (video). *Mailing Add:* 792 Knollwood Ct Saline MI 48176

NAUMAN, BRUCE
SCULPTOR, VIDEO ARTIST
b Ft Wayne, Ind, Dec 6, 1941. *Study:* Univ Wis, Madison, BS, 1964; Univ Calif, Davis, with William T Wiley, Robert Arneson, Frank Owen & Stephen Kaltenbach, MFA, 1966; San Francisco Art Inst, 1989. *Hon Degrees:* San Francisco Art Inst, DFA, 1989; California Inst Arts, ArtsD, 2000. *Work:* Whitney Mus, NY; Wallraf-Richartz-Mus, Cologne, Ger; Kunstverein, Aachen, Ger; Mus Mod Art, & Guggenheim Mus, NY; Los Angeles Co Mus Art, Calif; Fogg Art Mus, Cambridge, Mass; Australian Nat Gallery, Canberra, Australia; Art Inst Chicago; Hirshhorn Mus and Sculpture Garden, Wash; Tate Modern, London; Hamburger Bahnhof/Friedrich Christian Flick Collection, Berlin; and many others, including pvt collections. *Exhib:* Retrospective, Mus Nacional Centro de Arte Reina Sophia, Madrid, Walker Art Ctr, Minneapolis, Mus Contemp Art, Los Angeles, Smithsonian Inst, Mus Mod Art, NY, others, 1993-95; Solo exhibs, Nicholas Wilder Gallery, Los Angeles, 1966, Leo Castelli Gallery, NY, 1968 & 1981, Art in Progress, Munich, Ger, 1974, Minneapolis Inst Arts Coll Gallery, Minn, 1978, Hester van Royer Gallery, London, Eng, 1979, Carol Taylor Art, Dallas, Tex, 1983, Kunsthalle, Basel, Switz, 1986, Drawings 1965-1986, traveling exhib to Europe & US, 1986, Sperone Westwater Gallery, NY, 1988, Infrared Outtakes, Biennial Exhib, Whitney Mus Am Art, NY, 1991, Mus Boymans-van Beuningen, Rotterdam, The Neth, 1991, Fundacio Espai Poblenou, Barcelona, Spain, 1991-92, Use Me (Graphics, Multiples, Videos and Installations), Inst Contemp Arts, London, Eng, 1991-92, Neons, Anthony d'Offay Gallery, London, Eng, 1992 & Ydessa Hendeles Found, Toronto, Ont, Can, 1992, Walker Art Ctr, Minn, 1993-95, Falls, Pratfalls and Sleighs of Hand, Leo Castelli Gallery, NY, 1994, Hayward Gellery, London, 1997-99,Kunsthalle Wien Karisplatz, Vienna, 2000, Zwirner & Wirth, NY, 2001, Sperone Westwater, NY, 2002, 2008, Ludwig Mus, Cologne, Germany, 2003, PKM Gallery, Seoul, 2004, Tate Modern, London, 2004-2005, Tate Liverpool, 2006, Milwaukee Art Mus, 2006 Gemnni GEL, 2006, Univ Calif Berkeley Art Mus & Pacific Film Archive, 2007, Castello di Rivoli Museo d'Arte Contemporanea, Torino, Italy, 2007, Mencil Collection, Houston, Tex, 2008, Sperone Westwater, New York, 2010, Kunsthalle Manheim, Ger, 2011, Konrad Fischer Galerie Berlin, 2011, Donald Young Gallery, 2011, Gagosian Gallery, NY, 2012, Hauser & Worth, 2013; Group shows, Am Sculpture of the Sixties, Los Angeles Co Mus Art, Calif, 1967; Corcoran Gallery Art, Wash, DC, 1969; Anti-Illusion: Procedures/Materials, Whitney Mus Art, NY, 1969; Solomon R Guggenheim Mus, NY, 1969, 2004; Info, Mus Mod Art, NY, 1971; Art & Image in Recent Art, Art Inst Chicago, 1974; Mus Mod Art, NY, 1975, 1987 & 1988; Whitney Mus Am Art, NY, 1976, 1987 & 1988; Los Angeles Co Mus Art (also traveling), 1982; Fogg Art Mus, Cambridge, Mass; retrospective, Galerie Hummel, Vienna, Austria, 1991; Documenta IX, Kassel, Ger, 1992; Transform BildObjektSkulptur im 20, Jahrhundert, Kunsthalle Basel, Switz, 1992; Szenenwechsel, Mus Moderne Kunst, Frankfurt am Main, Ger, 1992; Re: Framing Cartoons, Wexner Ctr, Ohio State Univ, Columbus, Ohio, 1992; Both Art and Life: Gemini at 25, Newport Harbor Art Mus, Newport Beach, Calif, 1992; Contemp Art Mus, Houston, 1999; DIA Ctr for the Arts, New York, 2001; Donald Young Gallery, Chicago, 2002; Cleveland Mus of Art, 2003; SITE Santa Fe Fifth Int Biennial, 2004; Wexner Ctr for Arts, Columbus, Ohio, 2005; Mus Mod Art, New York, 2006; Venice Biennale, 2007, 2009; Summer Exhib, Sperone Westwater, NY, 2007, 2008, Drawings for Installations, 2008; Dead Shot Dan, Contemp Art Mus, St Louis, Missouri, 2009; 8th Gwangju Biennale 2010: Maninbo-10000 Lives, Gwangju Biennale Hall, Gwangju Mus Art, Folk Mus, 2010; Videosphere: A new Generation, Albright-Knox Art Gallery, Buffalo, NY, 2011, Wish You Were Here: The Buffalo Avant-Garde in the 1990s, 2012; Something Along Those Lines, Barbara and Steven Grossman Gallery, Sch Mus Fine Arts, Boston, 2012; An Accumulation of Information Taken from Here to There, Sperone Westwater, 2012; less like an object, more like the weather: Don't blame anyone, CCS Bard Hessel Mus, Annandale-on-Hudson, 2013; 55th Int Art Exhib Biennale, Venice, 2013; and many others. *Teaching:* Instr, San Francisco Art Inst, 1966-68; instr sculpture, Univ Calif, Irvine, 1970. *Awards:* Nat Endowment Grant, Washington, DC, 1968; Aspen Inst for Humanistic Studies Grant, Colo, 1970; Wolf Found Prize in Arts (Sculpture), 1993; Aldrich Prize, Aldrich Mus, Ridgefield, Conn, 1995; Golden Lion, Venice Biennale, 1999; Praemium Imperiale Prize for Visual Arts, Japan, 2004; Named Best Internat Artist, Beaux-Arts Mag, Paris, 2004; Golden Lion for the Best National Participation to the US, Venice Biennale, 2009; Named one of Contemporary Art's 100 Most Powerful Figures, ArtReview mag, 2009. *Bibliog:* Robert Pincus-Witten (auth), Bruce Nauman: Another kind of reasoning, Artforum, 2/1972; Brenda Richardson (auth), Bruce Nauman: Neons, Baltimore Mus Art, 1982; Peter Schieldahl (auth), Profoundly Practical Jokes, The Art of Bruce Nauman, Vanity Fair, 1983; many others. *Mem:* Fel Am Acad Arts & Scis; Akad der Künste, Berlin; Sagamore of the Wabash; Am Acad Arts and Letters; Nat Acad. *Publ:* Auth, Pictures of Sculptures in a Room, Davis, Calif, 1966; Clear Sky, San Francisco, 1968; Burning Small Fires, San Francisco, 1968; LA Air, Los Angeles, 1970; Body Works, Interfunktionen, Cologne, Ger, 9/1971. *Dealer:* Sperone Westwater New York NY. *Mailing Add:* c/o Sperone Westwater Gallery 257 Bowery New York NY 10002

NAUMANN, FRANCIS M
HISTORIAN, CURATOR
b Albany, NY, Apr 25, 1948. *Study:* State Univ NY, Buffalo, BA, 70; Sch Art Inst Chicago, MFA, 73; City Univ New York, PhD, 88. *Exhib:* Making Mischief: Dada Invades New York, Whitney Mus Am Art, 96-97; Beatrice Wood: A Centennial Tribute, Am Craft Mus, NY, 97; Man Ray: An American Surrealist Vision, Andre Emmerich Gallery, NY, 97 & Maria: The Surrealist Sculpture of Maria Martins, 98; Marcel Duchamps, The Art of Making Art in the Age of Mechanical Reproduction, 99, Art of Chess, 2009. *Pos:* Dir, Parsons Summer Prog Italy, 81-84. *Teaching:* Instr art hist, Art Inst Chicago, 72-73; adj prof, Queens Col, City Univ New York, 74-75; prof, Parsons Sch Design, 77-90. *Awards:* Nat Endowment Humanities Fel, 91-92; Best Show in a New York City Mus, Whitney Mus Am Art, Int Asn Art Critics, 96-97. *Mem:* Art Dealer's Asn Am. *Res:* Dada and surrealism in Europe and America. *Specialty:* Art of the Dada & Surrealist periods, & contemp art artists of related aesthetic sensibilities. *Publ:* co-ed, Marcel Duchamp: Artist of the Century, Mass Inst Technol Press, 89; New York Dada 1915-23, 94 & Marcel Duchamp: The Art of Making Art in the Age of Mechanical Reproduction, 99, Abrams; Making Mischief (exhib catalog), 97; Affectionately Marcel: The Selected Correspondence of Marcel Duchamp, Ludion, Ghent, 2000. *Mailing Add:* 1632 Hunterbrook Rd Yorktown Heights NY 10598

NAVA, JOHN
TAPESTRY ARTIST
b San Diego, Calif, 1947. *Study:* Univ Calif, Santa Barbara, BA, 69; Villa Schifanoia Grad Sch Fine Art, Florence, MFA, 73. *Exhib:* Solo shows incl Koplin Gallery, Los Angeles, 83, 85, 86, 87, 89, 92, Modernism, San Francisco, 84, Pamela Auchincloss Gallery, Santa Barbara, 85, Western Gallery, Western Wash Univ, 86, Univ Art Gallery, 86, Weingart Gallery, Occidental Coll, Los Angeles, 89, Wright Gallery, New York, 97, Van de Griff Gallery, Santa Fe, 99, Hendrik Pickery Zaal of Halls of Belfry tower, Grote Market, Bruges, Belgium, 2001, Studio Channel Islands Gallery, 2003, Ventura County Mus Hist and Art, 2003-2004, Sullivan Goss Gallery, Santa Barbara, 2006, Klaudia Marr Gallery, Santa Fe, 2007; group shows incl Ark Arts Ctr, Little Rock, 85; Portland Art Mus, Ore, 87; Henry Art Gallery, Univ Wash, Seattle, 88; Contemp Mus, Honolulu, 90; Nat Mus Am Art, Smithsonian Inst, 91; Fletcher Gallery, Santa Fe, 95, 95; Galleria Millan, Sao Paolo, Brazil, 95; Van de Griff Gallery, Santa Fe, 98, 2002; Wright Gallery, New York, 99; Jenkins Johnson Gallery, San Francisco, 2003, 2004, 2005, 2006, 2007; Klaudia Marr Gallery, Santa Fe, 2004, 2006; Sullivan Goss Gallery, Montecito, Calif, 2004, 2005, 2006; Bedford Gallery, Walnut Creek, Calif, 2005; Jose Druidis-Biada Art Gallery, 2006. *Mailing Add:* c/o Sullivan Goss Gallery 7 E Anapamu St Santa Barbara CA 93101

NAVARETTA, CYNTHIA
PUBLISHER, WRITER
b New York, NY. *Study:* Univ Wis; NY Univ; Columbia Univ, BA, 44, MA, 47. *Collection Arranged:* Women Choose Women (auth, catalog), Cult Ctr, NY, 73; Artists of Long Island (contribr, catalog), Guild Hall, East Hampton, NY, 79; Int Exhib Women Artists, Milan, Ital, 79; Int Festival Women Artists, Copenhagen, 80; A Lifetime of Art: Six Women of Distinction, Women's Caucus Art, NY, 82; Am Women in Art; Works on Paper Africa & Europe (auth, catalog), 85. *Pos:* dir corp archit, 50-86; Ed, Women Artists News & dir, Midmarch Arts Press, 75-; ed adv, Art Press, 80-86. *Teaching:* lectr, 76-82; lectr, ann humanities sem, 78-82. *Awards:* Nat Orgn Women, 80. *Mem:* Coalition of Women's Art Orgns (chmn, 77-78); Nat Women's Caucus for Art (bd mem, 74-98); Found for Community of Artists (bd mem, 75-89); Women Artists Filmmakers (bd mem, 78-88); Artists Talk on Art (bd mem, 76-); NY Dept Cultural Affairs (bd mem, 75-88); NYC Loft Board (bd mem 82-96). *Res:* Women artists; women's art groups; art and politics; Mid 20th Century Artists. *Specialty:* Women Artists. *Interests:* Art & literature. *Collection:* art books in libr collections. *Publ:* Auth, Guide to Women's Art Organizations, 79; ed, Voices: Three on Three on Three, Midmarch Arts Press, 80; contribr, An Encyclopedia of 20th Century N Am Artists, 82; auth, Women Artists of the World, 85; auth, Whole Arts Dir, 86; auth, Artists and their Cats, 90; auth & ed, Women Artists in the US, 90; auth, Artists Colonies, Retreats & Study Centers, 95 & 98 (rev ed); auth, How to Publish Your Own Book, 2001; Club Without Walls, 2007; and many articles in nat publ & ed of same (50 bks). *Mailing Add:* 300 Riverside Dr No 8A New York NY 10025

NAVARRO, EDUARDO
INSTALLATION SCULPTOR
b Argentina. *Study:* Workshop with Sergio Bazan, 2002-03; Program for the Visual Arts, CCRR-UBA, with Guillermo Kuitca, 2003-05; Skowhegan Sch Painting, 2006. *Exhib:* Solo exhibs include The POD Show, Art Palace, Austin, Tex, 2004; group exhibs include Currículum 0, Gallery Ruth Benzacar, Buenos Aires, 2002; Muestra Numero 2, Proyecto A Buenos Aires, 2002, Muestra N12, 2003, Piso Once, 2003; Das Adbesidade Vivemos, Brazilian Studies Ctr, Buenos Aires, 2003; Harrods, Open Studio, Buenos Aires, 2003; Mus Modern Art Carlos Merina, Guatemala, 2004; Cultural Space Renata Russo, Brazil, 2004; Tempranos Intereses Personales, Gallery Alberto Sendrós, Buenos Aires, 2004; Mus Sofía Imber, Venezuala, 2005; Santiago de Chile Mus Contemp Art, Chile, 2005; Panama Mus of the Canal Interoceanico, 2005; FOLK, Daniel Abate Gallery, Buenos Aires, 2005; MACRO Contemp Art Mus of Rosario, 2005; Mus Bellas Artes Castagnino, Rosario, 2006. *Mailing Add:* Art Palace 2109 Cesar Chavez Austin TX 78702

NAVES, MARIO
COLLAGE ARTIST, CRITIC
b Salt Lake City, 1961. *Study:* Univ Utah, Salt Lake City, BFA (cum laude), 1984; Pratt Inst, Brooklyn, MFA (with distinction), 1987. *Exhib:* Solo exhibs include Univ Utah, Salt Lake City, 1984, Long Island Univ, Brooklyn, 1989, Elizabeth Harris Gallery, 2001, 2003 & 2005; two-person exhib, Allyn Gallup Contemp Art, Sarasota, Fla, 2004; group exhibs include Utah, Salt Lake Art Ctr, Salt Lake City, 1985, Pete & Repeat, 1988; Small Works, Brooklyn Arts Coun, 1987; Artist in the Marketplace, Bronx Mus Arts, 1989, A Decade of the Marketplace, 1990; NY Selections 1995-96, Albright-Knox Art Gallery, Buffalo, 1995; Art for Kids' Sake, Thread Waxing Space, New York, 1999, 2000; Art for Kids' Sake, IS-20, New York, 2001, 2003; The Elements, NY Studio Sch, New York, 2002; Drawing Conclusions: Work by Artists-Critics, NY Arts, New York, 2003; Balancing Act, Abrons Arts Ctr, Henry St Settlement, New York, 2004; In Context: Collage + Abstraction, Pavel Zoubok Gallery, New York, 2007; Ann Invitational Exhib Contemp Am Art, Nat Acad, New York, 2008. *Pos:* Freelance art critic, 1989-; gallery critic, NY Observer, 1999; art critic, Slate, New York, 2004-. *Teaching:* Instr drawing, Sch Prof Studies, Pratt Inst, Brooklyn, 1989-95, vis prof fine arts, 2002-; lectr art history, NY Studio Sch, 1996-; instr drawing, Cooper Union, 1999-. *Awards:* Binney & Smith Liquitex Grant, 1987; Nat Endowment Arts Visual Artists Fel, 1989; ED Found Grant, 1994; George Sugarman Found Grant, 2003; John Pike Mem Award, Nat Acad, 2008. *Mailing Add:* c/o Elizabeth Harris Gallery 529 W 20th St New York NY 10011

NAVRAT, DEN(NIS) EDWARD
EDUCATOR, PAINTER
b Marion, Kans, May 15, 1942. *Study:* Kans State Univ, Manhattan, BA, 64; Wichita State Univ, Kans, MFA, 66; Univ Iowa, Iowa City, 69, with Virginia Myers; Photographer's Place, Derbyshire, Eng, 77, with Paul Hill & Ralph Gibson; Anderson Ranch Arts Ctr, Aspen, 83, with Catherine Reeve, Marilyn Sward, Bernie Vinzani, Katie McGregor and Terry Allen, Emma Lake, Sask, Can, 86, with Peter Bradley and John Link; Insel HombroiBh, Neuss, Ger, with Anatol Herzfeld, 96. *Work:* Mus of Fine Art, Houston, Tex; Atkinson Art Gallery, Metrop Bur of Sefton, Eng; Plains Art Mus, Moorhead, Minn; Sioux City Art Ctr, Iowa; NDak Heritage Ctr, Bismarck; Mus Der Stadt Ratingen, Ger; Mus der Stadt Ratingen, Ger, 99; Univ S Dakota; Univ N Dakota; Wichita State Univ; Univ Iowa. *Exhib:* Solo exhibs, Paper Press, Chicago, Ill, 91, Sud Dahcotah (with catalog), Univ Art Gallery, Vermillion, SDak, 96 & Imaging the Edge of Whirl, Den Navrat Retrospective, 1965-2005 (with catalog), Univ Art Galleries, Univ of SDak, 1/11-31/2005; Am Embassy, Dakar Senegal, Africa, 94-96; Great Outdoors Invitational Exhib, SDak Art Mus, Brookings, 94; 53rd Ann Exhib, Sioux City Art Ctr, Iowa, 95; Summer Arts XVIII Regional Exhib, Univ Art Gallery, Vermillion, SDak, 95; Imaging the Edge of Whirl, 2005. *Collection Arranged:* Catalog. *Pos:* Visual consult, ASAAUM, Minneapolis, 81; COMPAS Artist Group, St Paul, Minn, 82; visual consult, Arts Midwest, Minneapolis/Des Moines, Iowa, 88; artist-in-residence, Sioux City Art Center, Iowa, 2001-2002; visitation team leader, Nat Asn Schs Art & Design, 2002-2009 & consult, 2007-. *Teaching:* Instr, Inst of Logopedics, Wichita, Kans, 65-66; from instr to asst prof art, Dickinson State Univ, 66-71, assoc prof art & chmn art dept, 72-79, prof art, 79-89; Fulbright-Hays Exchange prof art, Southport Coll Art, Eng, 76-77; prof art & chmn, Univ SDak, 89-97; prof art & CFA Int Studies Coord, 97-2005, emer prof art, 2005. *Awards:* Grants for Creative Res, Paper Art, Off Res, Univ SDak, 92, 94, 2002; Purchase Award for Collection, Sioux City Art Ctr, Iowa, 93; Cash Award, 19th Biennial Nat Art Exhib, 2nd Crossing Art Ctr, Valley City, NDak, 95; Res Grant, Office of Rsch, USD, 97-99; Gov's Tech Awards, 2001 & 2002. *Bibliog:* Sally Prince Davis (auth), The Fine Artist's Guide to Showing and Selling Your Work, North Light Bks, Cincinnati, Ohio, 89; Catharine Reeve (auth), Darkroom Photog Mag, 12/90. *Mem:* Coll Art Asn; Fulbright Alumni Asn. *Media:* Mixed Media. *Res:* Internet website development of instructional materials; Handmade paper art at the Hummingbird mill/studio, Vermillion, SDak, 92-2005. *Specialty:* Paper art/landmade paper. *Interests:* Children, grandchildren, travel & golf. *Collection:* 20th Cenutry printmakers, Ceramists, Photographs. *Publ:* Auth, Images on Exchange, Mind's Eye Gallery, 78; illusr, Sud Dahcotah: Art on/of Paper, 96 & Imaging the Edge of Whirl, 2005, Univ Art Galleries, Vermillion, SDak. *Mailing Add:* 32191 Ponderosa Dr Burbank SD 57010-7004

NAVRATIL, AMY See Ciccone, Amy Navratil

NAVRATIL, GREG ALLAN
ARTIST
b Denver, Co, Oct 14, 1946. *Study:* Metrop State Coll, BFA, 73. *Work:* Parkersburg Art Center, WV; Pikes Peak Community Coll, Colo Springs; Rocky Mountain Nat Park Vis Center, Estes Park; Ouray Art Center, Colo; Kaiser Permanente, Lakewood, Colo. *Exhib:* The New West, Sangre de Cristo Fine Arts Center, Pueblo, Colo, 96; ANA 26, Holter Mus of Art, Helena, Mont, 97; Landscapes of the Wilderness, Univ Mont, Missoula, 96; Colo Landscapes, Lakewood Cult Center, Lakewood, Colo, 2000; Our Beautiful Heritage, Lakewood Heritage Mus, 2003-. *Awards:* Purchase Award, Am Realism, Parkersburg Art Center, 92; Top 100, Arts for the Parks, 97; Best of Show & Peoples Choice, Louisville Art Center, Colo, 98. *Media:* Acrylics. *Publ:* Jenny Phalzgraf (auth), Form from Abstraction, Artists Mag, 93; Gil Whiteley (auth), Greg Navratil, Colo Expression, 2001; Leigh Duncan (auth), Greg Navratil Cover Artist, Sunshine Artist, 2002; Greg Navratil: Balancing Representation and Abstraction, Skywest Mag, 5/6/2005. *Dealer:* William Havu Gallery 1040 Cherokee St Denver CO 80204; Peggy Rice Gallery 7060 West 135th St Overland Park KS 66223; Sumner & Dene 517 Central NW Albuquerque NM 87102. *Mailing Add:* PO Box 2346 Seaside OR 97138

NAWABI, KYMIA
PAINTER
b San Diego, Calif, 1980. *Study:* East Carolina Univ, BFA, 2003; Univ Fla, MFA, 2006. *Work:* The Drawing Ctr, New York. *Exhib:* 33rd Ann Toys Designed by Artists, Ark Arts Ctr, Little Rock, 2005; Open Studios, Lower Manhattan Cult Coun, New York, 2008; Queens Int Biennial, Queens Mus, New York, 2009; Tragic Sense of Life, Fine Arts Gallery, Westchester Cmty Coll, 2010; Paul Hartley Legacy, Greenville Mus Art, NC, 2010. *Pos:* Coord, Univ Gallery, Univ Fla, 2005-06; intern, Exit Art, New York, 2006-07; asst, Richard Mendoza, Chavez Studios, Los Angeles, 2008-09. *Teaching:* Instr, Ashcan Studio Art, New York, 2007-08. *Awards:* Women's Studio Workshop Fel, 2007; Lower Manhattan Cult Coun Grant, 2007, 2009; NY Found Arts Gregory Millard Fel, 2009

NAWARA, JIM
PAINTER, EDUCATOR
b Chicago, Ill, Jan 25, 1945. *Study:* Sch Art Inst Chicago, BFA, 67; Univ Ill, Champaign, MFA, 69. *Work:* Boston Mus Fine Arts; Detroit Inst Arts; Bradford City Art Gallery, Eng; Cleveland Mus Art; Nat Mus, Warsaw, Poland; Toledo Mus Art, Ohio; Butler Inst Am Art; and others. *Comn:* Screenprints, Western Mich Univ, Kalamazoo, 74; etchings, Mich Workshop Fine Prints, 75; wall drawing, Dept Recreation, 78; billboard, First Fed Savings, Detroit, 80. *Exhib:* Oakland Community Coll, Farmington Hills, Mich, 94; Mich Gallery, Detroit, 95; Cary Gallery, Rochester, Mich, 98; Knoxville Mus Art, Tenn, 2002; Wayne State Univ, Mich, 2002; Parkland Coll Champaign, Ill, 2003; Austin Peay State Univ, Clarksville, Tenn, 2005; solo exhib, Muskegon Mus Art, 2007-. *Pos:* Acting chmn, dept art & art hist, Wayne State Univ, 88-89. *Teaching:* Prof drawing & painting, Wayne State Univ, 69-. *Awards:* Purchase Awards, Butler Inst Am Art Mid yr, 72 & Mich Printmakers, Detroit Inst Arts, 77; Res Awards, Wayne State Univ, 77, 81, 84, 87-88 & 90-94; Creative Artists Grants, Mich Co Arts, 81, 85 & 89; Creative Res Grant, Wayne State Univ, 2005, 2009; Fac Develop Grant, Wayne State Univ, 2008; Pres's Res Enhancement Prog Grant, Wayne State Univ, 2009. *Bibliog:* Simon Zalkind (auth), 30 years of American printmaking, Arts Mag, 2/77; Elizabeth Glassman & Marilyn Symmes (coauth), Cliche Verre: Hand-Drawn, Light-Printed, A survey of the medium from 1839 to the present, Detroit Inst Arts, 80; Gottfried Jager (auth), Bildgebende Fotografie, Fotografik-Lichtgrafik-Lichtmalerei, Dumont Buchverlag Cologne, 88. *Mem:* AAUP/AFT. *Media:* Oil. *Res:* painting, natural & unnatural phenomena in landscape, painting materials and methods. *Publ:* auth, Chapter 15: About Painting, Remapping the Humanities: Identity, Community, Memory, (Post) Modernity, ed Mary Garrett, Heidi Gottfried & Sandra Vanburkleo, Wayne State Univ Press, Detroit, Mich, 2008. *Dealer:* Stewart and Stewart 5571 Wing Lake Rd Bloomfield Hills MI 48301. *Mailing Add:* 30585 Vernon Dr Beverly Hills MI 48025-4944

NAWARA, LUCILLE PROCTER
PAINTER
b Oklahoma City, Okla, June 26, 1941. *Study:* Smith Coll, with Leonard Baskin, BA, 62; Boston Univ, Sch Fine & Applied Arts, with Walter Murch & Arthur Polonsky, BFA, 67; Univ Ill, Champaign, MFA, 69. *Work:* Mich Coun Arts & Detroit Inst Arts, Detroit; Springfield Coll, Mass; Nat Endowment Arts, Washington, DC; Univ Mich Art Mus, Ann Arbor; Kalamazoo Art Inst; Detroit Inst Art; Butler Inst Am Art; Oklahoma Art Ctr; Krannest Art Mus; Ford Motor co; IBM. *Comn:* Sea Squirts (intaglio), Oxbow Portfolio, Mich Coun Arts, Detroit, 73; Prisms (intaglio), Women's Portfolio, Nat Educ Asn & Mich Workshop Fine Prints, Detroit, 76; mural, Broken Symmetries, Fraser High Sch, Mich Coun Arts, 86. *Exhib:* San Francisco Mus Art, 70; Mid-Yr Ann, Butler Inst Am Art, Youngstown, Ohio, 75; two-person exhibs, Pontiac Art Ctr, 87, Dennos Mus Ctr, Traverse City, Mich, 93 & Padziewski Gallery, Ford Community and Performing Arts Ctr, Dearborn, Mich, 2002; The Unseen Landscape, 7 Artists, Community Art Gallery, Wayne State Univ, Detroit, 91-92; Expressive Visions & Exquisite Images: Part Two, Mich Artists, Meadowbrook Gallery, Rochester, Mich, 92; group exhib, Water, Mich Gallery, Detroit, 95; Out of Solitude, Mich Gallery, Detroit, 96; Art & Technology: The Polk Competition, Birmingham, Bloomfield Art Asn, Mich, 98; At the Water's Edge, APE Ltd, Northampton, Mass, 2000; Rivers and other Bodies of Water, River Gallery, Chelsea, Mich, 2004; 75th Anniversary All Media Exhib, Detroit Artists Market; 60th Ann Exhib, Mich Watercolor Soc, 2007; Seven Painters, The Devos Art Mus, N Mich Univ, Marquette, Mich. *Pos:* Exhib coordr, Detroit Focus Gallery, 80; Artist-in-the-schs residency, Mich Coun Arts, Fraser Pub Schs, 83-86; dir, Nawara Gallery, Walled Lake, Mich, 86-88; co-pres bd, Detroit Focus Gallery, 91-92. *Teaching:* Asst prof drawing, Wayne State Univ, Detroit, 69-76; painting & design, Macomb Community Coll, Mt Clemens, Mich, 77-84; instr drawing, Henry Ford Community Coll, 82 & Ctr Creative Studies, 82-83; vis artist painting, Cranbook Acad Art, Bloomfield Hills, Mich, 92; instr, Birmingham, Bloomfield Art Ctr, Mich, 2004-05; instr watercolor, Coll for Creative Studies, Detroit, 2006-2007. *Awards:* Purchase Award Art & Tech, Birmingham Blomfield Art Asn, Mich, 98; Art in the Villages, Livonia Art Comn, Mich, 99; Our Town Community House, Birmingham, Mich, 2003. *Media:* Oil, Watercolor. *Interests:* Violin, gardening. *Mailing Add:* 30585 Vernon Dr Beverly Hills MI 48025-4944

NAWROCKI, DENNIS ALAN
EDUCATOR, CURATOR

b Grand Rapids, Mich, Dec 29, 1939. *Study:* Aquinas Coll, Grand Rapids, Mich, BA, 62; Wayne State Univ, Detroit, Mich, MA, 64, MA 81. *Collection Arranged:* Kick Out The Jams, Detroit Inst Arts, 80; Dada & Surrealism in Chicago, Mus Contemp Art, 84; Grounded: Sculpture on the Floor, Univ Mich Mus Art, 90; Robt Farber & Hannah Wilke, Ctr Galleries, Coll for Creative Studies, 93 & Liza Lou: A Beaded Installation, 96; Up from the Streets: The Duffy Warehouse Collection, Wayne State Univ, Detroit, 2001; Polemical Clay, Pewabic Pottery, Detroit, 2005; Menage a Detroit: Three Generations of Expressionist Art 1970-2012, N'Namdi Ctr Contemporary Art, Detroit, Mich, 2012. *Pos:* Cur educ, Detroit Inst Arts, 81-83 & Univ Mich Mus Art, Ann Arbor, 89-90; cur res & educ, Mus Contemp Art, Chicago, 83-88; dir, Ctr Galleries, Coll Creative Studies, Detroit, 90-98. *Teaching:* Prof art hist, Coll for Creative Studies, Detroit, 90-2010; adj instr, Chicago Art Inst, 90-2002; adj fac, Wayne State Univ, Detroit, 93-. *Mem:* Coll Art Assn. *Res:* 20th century modernism; post-modernism; contemporary art and architecture. *Publ:* Coauth, Art in Detroit Public Places, Wayne State Univ Press, 80, auth, rev ed, 99, 2nd rev ed, 2008; auth, Gilbert & George: "Parked" in Nature, Bull Detroit Inst Arts, 89; auth, Bill Viola: Intimations of Mortality, Bull Detroit Inst Arts, 2000; contribr, Three Decades of Contemporary Art, Cranbrook Art Mus, 2001; auth, Where's Detroit in the new Detroit Institute of the Arts, Detroit Stories, MOCAD, 2008; auth, The Lewiston Years: Kathryn Brackett Luchs and Michael Luchs, Center Galleries, Coll Creative Studies, Detroit, Mich, 2008; auth, Parallel Currents: Selections from the James Pearson Duffy Collection, Bull Detroit Inst Arts, 2011; contribr, Essay'd (online profiles of selected regional artists):http://essayd.org, 2014-

NAWROCKI, THOMAS DENNIS
PRINTMAKER, EDUCATOR

b Milwaukee, Wis, June 26, 1942. *Study:* Univ Wis-Milwaukee, BFA, 64, MA, 65, MFA, 67. *Work:* Univ Wis-Madison; Northern Ill Univ; Brand Libr Art Galleries, Glendale, Calif; Montgomery Mus Art, Ala; Miss Art Asn, Jackson; Dulin Gallery Art, Knoxville, Tenn; Hunterdon Art Ctr, NJ; Univ Miss, Oxford; Pratt Graphic Art Ctr, New York; Boston Printmakers. *Exhib:* Seattle Int Print Exhib, Seattle Art Mus, 68 & 71; Hawaii Nat Print Exhibs, Honolulu Acad Arts, 73, 75, 79, 82 & 84; World Print Competition, San Francisco Mus Mod Art, 77; Int Print Biennial, Krakow, Poland, 78, 80, 84, 86, 88, 91 & 94; Wesleyan Int Exhib, 80; Rockford Int, Ill, 81 & 82; Bradley Univ Nat Exhib, Peoria, Ill, 81, 85, 89 & 91; 57th Ann Int, Print Club, Philadelphia, 81 & 83; Soc Am Graphic Artists, NY, 88, 89, 91 & 93; Boston Printmakers, 90; Desert Treasures, Nat Print Exhib, Los Angeles Printmaking Soc, Tang Gallery, Ariz, 2002; Boston Printmakers N Am Int Print Biennial, Emmanuel Coll, Mass, 2005; Ink & Idea, Nat Print Exhib, Univ Judaism, Los Angeles, 2006; Continuum5(0), Peck Sch Arts, Univ Wis, Milwaukee, 2006; Fla Printmakers 15th Nat Print Competition, Dunedin Fine Arts Ctr, Fla, 2007; Miss Univ Women Art Fac Exhib, Meridian Mus Art, Miss, 2008; Mid Am Print Coun Salon, Morgan Art Papermaking Conservatory & Educ Found, Cleveland, 2009; Market Street Arts Festival, Columbus, Miss, 2010; Bridge: East Coast USA Meets East Coast Australia, 77th Exhib of Prints, Frye Gallery, Braidwood, New South Wales, Australia, 2010; 31st Ann Paper in Particular Nat Exhib, Columbia Coll, Mo, 2010; thINK, Print Exhib of the Boston Printmakers Zullo Gallery, Medfield, Belmont Gallery of Art, 2010. *Teaching:* Instr printmaking, Southwest Tex State Univ, 67-70; from asst prof printmaking & drawing to assoc prof, Miss Univ Women, 70-83, prof, 83-. *Awards:* Dixie Annual Print Competition Award, Montgomery Mus Art, 74; Purchase Award, Nat Print Competition, Edinboro State Col, Pa, 79; Okla Nat Print Award, Okla Art Ctr, 82; Purchase Award & Top Graphics Award, Nat Arts Festival, Tupelo, Miss, 83; Purchase Award, Dulin Nat Works on Paper Competition, Dulin Gallery Art, 85; Summer res grant, Miss Univ Women, 71-2010. *Mem:* Southern Graphics Coun; Los Angeles Printmaking Soc; Society of Am Graphic Artists, New York City; Fla Printmakers Soc; Graphic Arts Coun of New York; Kappa Pi (treas, mem exec bd); Boston Printmakers; Am Color Print Soc; The Print Ctr; Print Connoisseurs Soc, NY. *Media:* Printmaking, Fiber Arts. *Res:* Shaped dimensional digital prints. *Interests:* Design & construction of art deco objects. *Collection:* Pratt Graphic Art Ctr, New York, Soc Am Graphic Artists, New York, No Ill Univ, DeKalb, Mississippi Mus Art, Jackson, miss, Dulin Gallery of Art, Knoxville, Tenn, others. *Publ:* contrib, Artists proof, Vol VI, no 9-10, Pratt Graphic Art Ctr, New York, 67; 1st National Invitational Color-Blend Print Exhibition, Univ Miss Press, 78-80. *Mailing Add:* 147 Shane Cir Columbus MS 39702

NAYLON, BETSY ZIMMERMANN
PAINTER, MURALIST

b Buffalo, NY, Jan 27, 1934. *Study:* Rosary Hill Col, BA, 55; Daeman Col, 76; tutorial with William Paden, New York, 86. *Work:* Albright-Knox Members Gallery, Buffalo; Blue Cross of Western NY; NY State Univ Archives, Buffalo; Burchfiled- Penney, State Univ Buffalo, NY. *Comn:* Woodcut & drawing for play Men Should Weep, Studio Arena Theater, Buffalo, NY, 88; Integrated Waste Systems, 95; Milstones (5' x 11' acrylic mural), Niagara Falls Mem Hosp, 95; 35 sq ft mural, JNW Enterprises, Lewiston, NY, 97; Women Free (painting), Seneca Falls, NY, 98; 30 Sq Foot Triptych Mural for WTS, INC, Lewiston, NY; Burchfield-Penney Art Collection, Buffalo State College, 2008, 2012. *Exhib:* 38th Western NY Exhib, Albright-Knox Gallery, Buffalo, 80; Art of the Printmaker, Burchfield Art Ctr, State Univ NY, Buffalo, 81; Eight Am Artists, O'Keefe Ctr, Toronto, Can, 82; Nat All on Paper Exhib, AAO Galleries, Buffalo, NY, 84; Solo Exhibs: Postcards from Italy, EW Brydges Pub Libr, Niagara Falls, 84; Woodcuts & Drawings, Chautauqua Inst Art Gallery, NY, 84; Woodcut Prints & Woods, Capen Hall, State Univ NY, Buffalo, 86; Paintings & Wood Cut Prints (works, 30 poems), 94; Kenan Ctr, Lockport, NY, 12/89; Stella Niagara, 94-96; Nat League Am Pen Women, Inc, NY, 85-96; Buscaglia-Castellani Art Gallery, 85-90; Nat Asn Women Artists, Jacob K Javits Fed Bldg, NY, 86-96 & Soho, NY, 98; Nat Asn Women Artists Traveling Printmaking Show, Woodcut Print, 87-89; Response '87, Emerging Vision, Univ Wis Nat Art Exhib, 87; paintings & woodcut prints & drawings, PC Chelsea Art Gallery, Buffalo, NY, 88; Nat Asn Woman Artists Traveling Painting Show to India, 89; Int Juried Exhib, Lockport, NY, 97; Int Juried Fine Arts Exhib, Fla, 97; Castellani Art Gallery, Niagara Univ, 2005; ZGM Gallery, Buffalo, NY, 2012; Buffalo Soc Artists, 2012. *Teaching:* Instr drawing, Daeman Col, Buffalo, 69-70; instr drawing & painting, State Univ NY, Buffalo, 74-79; Art Park, Lewiston, NY, 76, instr figure drawing, Adult Educ, Niagara Univ, 81-83; monotypes & painting, Trinity Adult Educ, Buffalo, 90-91; Teaching Adults in my Studio, 80-2004. *Awards:* Painting Award, Niagara Frontier Watercolor Soc, 90 & First Prize, 94; NLAPW Biennial Nat Juried Art Exhib, Washington, 96; Grumbacher Gold Medal Award, Spring Show, 96. *Bibliog:* Kathleen M DeLaney (auth), Updraft Sweeps You Away, Niagara Gazette, 6/24/86; E Comerford (auth) Niagara Gazette, 12/30/88, 12/8/89; Grace Banks (auth & judge), Niagara Guild Show, Union Sun J, 4/7/97; LCTV Channel 21, Interviews on Monotype with Acrylic. *Mem:* Niagara Coun Arts (bd mem, 83-84); National Women's Caucus for Art; Albright-Knox Art Gallery; Nat Asn of Women Artists; Nat League of Am Pen Women; Buffalo Soc Artists. *Media:* Acrylic, Watercolor, Glass. *Interests:* Reading NY Times Arts & Leisure on Radio Weekly for the blind, 15 years. *Publ:* Special Editions, The Catalogue of Regional & Nat Art; Artistic Objective (article), Pen Women Nat Mag, 88; Related Possibilities (video, slides); Quadrant J, 9/90; ed, Les Krantz, NY Art Rev; Room of Our Own (artwork), NY State Univ, Buffalo. *Mailing Add:* 33 Gates Cirlce 6F Buffalo NY 14209

NAZARENKO, BONNIE COE
PAINTER

b San Jose, Calif, Oct 26, 1933. *Study:* San Jose State Col; Carmel Art Inst, under John Cunningham. *Work:* Mint Mus, Charlotte, NC. *Exhib:* Soc Animal Artists, Grand Cent Art Gallery, NY, 72, 74 & 75, Daytona Beach, Fla, 90, Mus Natural Hist, Cleveland, 91 & Tacoma, Wash, 93; Game Conservation Int, San Antonio, Tex, 80; Int Fish & Wildlife Expo, NY, 86; One Touch of Nature Gallery, Chicago, 95; Bennington Art Ctr; and others. *Awards:* Beaufort Art Festival Award, SC, 66; Mint Mus Purchase Award, 68. *Mem:* Soc Animal Artists; Am Artists Prof League. *Media:* Oil, Mixed Media. *Mailing Add:* 8314 Pocahontas St W Tampa FL 33615

N'COGNITA, VERNITA See Nemec, Vernita McClish

NEAL, ANN PARKER See Parker, Ann (Ann Parker Neal)

NEAL, (MINOR) AVON
WRITER, PUBLISHER

b Indiana, July 16, 1922. *Study:* Long Beach Col; Escuela Bellas Artes, Mex, with Siquieros, MFA. *Work:* Metrop Mus Art, NY; Libr Cong & Smithsonian Inst, Washington, DC; Abby Aldrich Rockefeller Mus Am Folk Art, Williamsburg, Va; Winterthur Mus, Wilmington, Del. *Comn:* 500 original rubbings, 70, 250 original rubbings, 71 & ed 350 original rubbings, 74, Am Heritage; ed 100 original rubbings, 70 & ed 70 original rubbings, 74, for Arton Assocs (all with Ann Parker); ed 100 original rubbings, Mead Art Gallery, Amherst Col, 76; ed 475 original rubbings, Sweetwater Editions, NY, 82. *Exhib:* New Eng Gravestone Rubbings, Mead Art Gallery, 76; Gravestone Art, William Benton Mus Art, Univ Conn, 76; Molas, Art of the Cuna Indians, Alternative Ctr Int Arts, NY, 76; and others. *Pos:* Founder & pres, Thistle Hill Press, 78-. *Awards:* Ford Found Grants, 62-63 & 63-64; Fiction writing fellow Mass Arts Found, 79; Harriette Merrifield Forbes Award, Asn Gravestone Studies, 84; Mass Arts Coun Award, 96. *Bibliog:* M J Gladstone (auth), New art from early American sculpture, Collector's Quart Report, 63 & Pedestrian art, Art in Am, 4/64; Stephen Chodorov (auth), Know Ye the Hour, Camera Three, CBS-TV, 11/68. *Mem:* The Artists Found, Mass Artists Fel Prog, 79; Am Antiquarium Soc. *Interests:* Stone rubbing and folk art. *Publ:* co-auth, Molas, Folk Art of the Cunas Indians, Barre, 77; auth, Scarecrows, Barre, 78; auth, Pigs & Eagles, Thistle Hill Press, ltd ed, 78; coauth, Early American Stone Sculpture, Sweetwater Editions, 82; auth, Los Ambulantes, the Itinerant Photographers of Guatemala, MIT Press, 82; auth, Hajj Paintings, Folk Art of the Great Pilgrimage, 95; auth, Die Kunst des Hadsch, 95; contribr to articles to profl jours. *Dealer:* Gallery of Graphic Arts 1603 York Ave New York NY 10028. *Mailing Add:* 126 School St North Brookfield MA 01535-1961

NEAL, FLORENCE ARTHUR
SCULPTOR, PAINTER

b Columbus, Ga, Nov 12, 1954. *Study:* Auburn Univ, BFA, 76; Hunter Col, 77. *Work:* New York City Pub Libr, Mus Mod Art, NY. *Comn:* Four Winds (outdoor wind sculpture), Art Omaha, Nebr, 90; Dance of Life (outdoor wind sculpture), Univ Ala, 93. *Exhib:* Niagara Falls & Fossil Fuels, Bronx Mus Arts, NY, 86; 8 Women Sculptors, Erie Art Mus, Pa, 86. *Pos:* Founder, Everglade Press, Brooklyn, NY, 85-; dir, Kentler Int Drawing Space, Brooklyn, NY, 90-. *Awards:* Mid-Atlantic Arts Consortium, Erie, Pa, 87; Pollock-Krasner Found, 90; NY State Coll Ceramics Alfred Univ Award, Prospect Park, 98. *Bibliog:* Voshiko Ebihara (auth), My art scene is a survival game, Brutus-Japan, 8/89; Kyle MacMillan (auth), Flaglike art gets feet wet, Omaha World-Herald, 11/5/90; Christine Stenstrom (auth), Florence Neal opens her studio, Brooklyn Woman, 7/94. *Mem:* Brooklyn Waterfront Artists Coalition. *Mailing Add:* 353 Van Brunt St Brooklyn NY 11231

NEAL, IRENE
PAINTER, SCULPTOR

b Greensburg, Pa, May 14, 1936. *Study:* Wilson Col, BA, 58; Sch Visual Arts, Rio de Janeiro, Cert, 76-77; Memphis State Univ, 79-80; Univ Bridgeport, 82-83; Triangle Art Workshop, (Sir Anthony Caro, organizer), Pine Plains, NY, 85. *Work:* Planetarium, Rio de Janerio, Brazil; Westmoreland Mus Art, Greensburg, Pa; Newport Harbor Art Mus, Calif; Hoover Inst, Stanford Univ, Calif; Columbia Univ, NY; Int Paper, NY; Ft Lauderdale Mus; Nat Galerie of Prague; Denver Ctr of Performing Arts; Nat Mus Women in Arts; Appleton Mus Art, Ocala, Fla; Edmonton Art Gal, Can; Population Inst, Capital Hill, Wash, DC; Flint Inst Arts, Mich; A.N.E.W. Found Arts, Ft Lauderdale, Fla; Nat Mus Women in the Arts, Wash, DC; New Britain Mus Amer Art; Fair, Capital Hill, Wash DC; The Federal Reserve Bank, Wash DC. *Exhib:* State Ten, NJ State Mus, Newark, 75; New Directions in Abstraction, Shippee Gallery, NY, 86;

State of the Artist, Aldrich Mus Contemp Art, Ridgefield, Conn, 87; Eight Winners Exhib, Stamford Mus, Conn, 89; Outside NY, Univ Alta, Can, 90; Galerie Gerald Piltzer, Paris, France, 96; Fine Art 2000 Gallery, Stamford, Conn, 96 & 97; York Col, Queens, NY, 97; Mus Contemp Art, Palm Beach, Fla, 97; The Griffis Art Ctr, New London, Conn, 97; Flint Inst Arts, Mich, 99; Mus Contemp Art, Denver, Colo, 2000; Hotel de Ville, Brussels, Belgium, 2000; 69th Regiment Armory, NY, 2001; Nat Gallery, Prague, Czech Republic, 2002; Cooper Classics Collections, New York City, 2001-02; The Durst Organization, New York City, 2002-03; Musee du Bas-Saint Laurant Riviere de Lupe, Que, Can, 2002-03; Scope NY, Stevenson Fine Art, New York City, 3/2003; About Paint, Westpoint, Conn; Roultra, Cork, Ireland; Lurie Gal, Miami & Boca Raton, Fla, 2005; Lurie Gal, Los Angeles, Calif, 2006; The Autumn Show, Tong Gallery, Beijing China, 2007; Group Exhibs: Gallery One, Old Saybrook, Conn, 2007; Acton Pub Libr, Old Saybrook, 2007; Saint Ann's Episcopal Church, Old Lyme, Conn, 2007; Huitai Art Center, Tianjin, China, 2007; Tong You Gallery, Beijing, China, 2007; Tianjin Museum, Tianjin, China, 2007; Florence Biennale, 2009; Art Basel Miami Beach, Miami, Fla, 2009; The US Artists Biennial, NY Arts Mag, Broadway Gallery, New York, 2010; Int Biennale Art, Nina Torres Gallery, Miami, Fla, 2010, Lumin Arte Design, Dallas, Tex, 2011, Adam White Gallery 101, Abstract, Ft. Lauderdale Art Expo, NY, Pier 94, NYC, 2011; Abstract Expressionism Then & Now, The Flint Inst Arts, 2012; The Huitai Art Ctr, 2012; Solo Exhib: Huitai Art Center, Tianjin, China, 2008, Art Basil Miami, New Art Ctr, 2012; Tianjin Port Mus, Tianjin Port Int Contemp Art Exhib, 2012; Lumin Arte Design, Dallas, Tex, 2012; Artifact Gallery, NY, 2013; Galerie Marcel Paquet, 2013. *Teaching:* Guest speaker, Col Santa Fe, Albuquerque, NMex, 94; Painting Workshops, Old Saybrook, Conn, 2008; lectr, Foosuner Art Mus, Melbourne, Fla, 2012. *Awards:* Special Mention of Honor, Brazilian Acad Arts & Letters, 77; Bronze Medal, Secy Brazilian Navy, 77; Tift award, Wilson Col, Chambersburg, Pa, 2003. *Bibliog:* Kenworth Moffett (auth), New New Painting, Nouvelles, Francaises, 92; William Zimmer (auth), A dozen new painters and a sculptor too, NY Times, 12/96; David Ebony (auth), article, Art Am, 4/97; Ken Carpenter (auth), With Honours in Prague, CA Art, Winter 2002; Jan H. Vitvar (auth), Barbansti malini 2 Ameriky dorazili do Prahy, Mlada Fronta Dnes, Prague, 4/18/2002; Jean Dumont (auth), Peinture: une voie nouvelle, New Painting Expositions Vie des Arts, Montreal; Bill Kort (auth), Beijing Art Review, 9/2007; Thunderhead (image p. 151), Open Studios Press; The Artist Showcase, Hamptons, pp 82, 83, 2012; John Austin (auth), Dynamic Space in the Work of Irene Neal (artifact catalog), 2013. *Mem:* Nat Mus Women Arts. *Media:* Acrylic on Canvas, Wood, Lexan, Paper; Miscellaneous Media. *Publ:* Contrib, Abstract Painting, (Vicky Perry, auth), Watson-Guptill, 2005; Art 11, Montreal, QB. *Dealer:* Kenworth W. Moffett Stamford CT; A.N.E.W. Foundation for the Arts Ft Lauderdale Fla; Art Gallery of Viera Fla; Kavachnina Contemporary Miami Fla; Lumin Arte Design Dallas Tx; Art 11 Montreal; Galerie Marcel Paquet Biarritz France; Artifact Gallery NY. *Mailing Add:* 260 Madrid Ct Merritt Island FL 32953

NEAL, MICHAEL SHANE
PAINTER, INSTRUCTOR

b Nashville, Tenn, Nov 23, 1968. *Study:* David Lipscomb Univ, BFA, 91; Santa Fe Inst Fine Arts, 94-95; Scottsdale Artist Sch; Everett Raymond Kinstler, 93-. *Work:* US Capitol, US Senate, Washington DC. *Comn:* Paul Nitze, former Secy the Navy, John Hopkins Univ, Sch Int Affairs, Washington DC, 2003; Sen Arthur Vandenberg (portrait), US Capitol, Washington DC, 2004; Marian McPartland (portrait), Nat Arts Club, NY; Whitney MacMillan (portrait), Cargill Corp, Minneapolis, Minn; The Architect of the Capitol Alan Huntman, US Capitol Hist Soc, Washington DC, 2004; Spencer Abraham, Secy Energy, Dept Energy, Washington DC, 2005; Justice Sandra Day O'Connor, Friends the Univ Ariz, Phoenix, Ariz, 2006. *Exhib:* Allied Artists of America, Nat Arts Club, New York, NY, 96-98, 2000 & 2004; Allied Artists Juried Exhib, Butler Mus Am Art, Youngstown, Ohio, 2000; Mentors & Proteges, Teaching the New Realism, Vose Gallery, Boston, Mass, 2004. *Collection Arranged:* Vanderbilt, Columbia, Johns Hopkins, Yale & Tulane Univs. *Teaching:* guest instr, Portraits, Acad Art Univ, San Francisco, Calif, 2006. *Awards:* Grand Prize, Portrait Soc America's Int Portrait Competition, 2001; Avalon Award for Creative Excellence, David Lipscomb Univ; Tara Fredrix Award, Audubon Artists Ann, 2004; Catharine Lorillard Wolfe Award, Nat Arts Club Ann, 2004; Artist's Mag Award of Excellence, Oil Painters of Am Nat Exhib, 2004. *Bibliog:* On the rise (article), Artist's Mag; Stephen Doherty (auth), The first 10 years, Am Artist, Mag, 2001; Jennifer King (auth), Commissioned portraiture, Fine Art Connoiseur, 2006; Sandra Carpenter (auth), Passing the torch, The Artist Mag, 2006. *Mem:* Nat Arts Club; Allied Artists of Am & Audubon Artists (full mem); Artist Fel of NY; Cumberland Soc of Painters; Portrait Soc of Am. *Media:* Oil on Canvas. *Mailing Add:* 4306 Lone Oak Rd Nashville TN 37215

NEALS, OTTO
SCULPTOR, PAINTER

b Lake City, SC, Dec 11, 1930. *Study:* Self-taught; studies at Brooklyn Mus Art Sch with Isaac Soyer; printmaking workshop, studies with Bob Blackburn, Robert DeLamonica & Krishna Reddy. *Work:* Ghana Nat Mus, Accra; Prime Minister Forbes Burnham, Guyana Statehouse; Columbia Mus, SC; Medgar Evers Coll; pvt collections of Randy Weston, Oprah Winfrey, George C Wolfe, David Dinkins, Willie Randolph, Hon John Lewis, Elombe Brath & Harry Belefonte; City Univ NY. *Comn:* Earl Graves Publ co; Prospect Park Alliance; Strivers Ctr Walk of Fame; Ezra Jack Keats Found; mural, Kings Co Hosp Ctr, 2001; portrait, Yale Univ Divinity Sch, 2003; Bronze awards for Woodie King's New Fed Theatre. *Exhib:* Resurrection, Studio Mus, New York, 71; Millenium, Philadelphia Mus Art, Pa, 73; Selections 73, Brooklyn Mus, 74; 14 Black Artists, Pratt Inst Gallery, Brooklyn, 76; Migrations, Museo De Arte Moderno, Cali, Colombia, S Am, 76 & Caracas, Venezuela, 77; Columbia Mus of Art, Columbia, SC, 89; Herbert F Johnson Art Mus, Ithaca, NY, 2000; Hampton Mus, Hampton, Va, 2002; St Joseph's Col, Brooklyn, NY, 2003; Brooklyn Mus, NY, 2004; MOCADA Mus, Brooklyn, NY, 2006; Nat Arts Club, NY, 2007; Bank of the Arts, New Bern, NC, 2009; Windsor Art Ctr, Conn, 2012. *Pos:* Former dir, Fulton Art Fair, Brooklyn, NY. *Teaching:* Instr etching, Bob Blackburn Printmaking Workshop. *Awards:* Award for Excellence in Design, New York City Arts Comn. *Bibliog:* Peter Bailey (auth), Ten Black artists depict Christ, Ebony Mag, 4/71; Diane Weathers (auth), Black artists taking care of business, NY Times, 8/19/73; Elton Fax (auth), Black Artists of the New Generation, Dodd/Mead & Co, 77. *Mem:* Nat Conf Artists; Fulton Art Fair; Dorsey Art Comt; Fed Modern Painters & Sculptors. *Media:* Wood, Stone, Oil, Watercolor. *Publ:* Illusr, African Heritage Cookbook, Macmillan, 71; The Adventures of Tony David & Marc, Exposition Press, 76; Am Visions Mag, 8-9/94; Sculpture Mag, 2/98; Current Biography, 3/2003; African Voices Mag, 2007; Best of Water Media Artists, 2009. *Dealer:* Dorsey's Gallery 553 Rogers Ave Brooklyn NY 11225. *Mailing Add:* 138 Sullivan Pl Brooklyn NY 11225

NECHIS, BARBARA
PAINTER, LECTURER

b Mt Vernon, NY, Sept 25, 1937. *Study:* Univ Rochester, BA, 58; Alfred Univ, MS, 59; Parsons Sch Design. *Work:* Butler Inst Am Art; Slater Mem Mus, Conn; Banco de Crefisul, Sao Paulo, Brazil; Citicorp, New York; Int Bus Machines, New York; Westinghouse. *Comn:* NY Graphic Soc; Napa Valley Heritage Fund. *Exhib:* Am Watercolor Soc Exhib, Nat Acad Design, New York, 70-2007; Mainstreams, Marietta Coll, Ohio; Nat Acad Design Ann; Hudson River Mus; Tweed Mus, Minn; Bard Coll, 2005; Contemporary Int Watermedia Tasters, 2007, 2010, 2012. *Pos:* dir, juror, demonstrator, Am Watercolor Soc, 85, 2006, 2007; juror, New Eng Watercolor Soc Nat Exhib, Boston, 2000, Nat Watercolor Soc Membership Exhib, Calif, 2000, Transparent Watercolor Soc of Am (TWSA) 2005, Watercolor West, 2006, juror, Nat Watercolor Soc, 2012. *Teaching:* Fac mem, Parsons Sch Design 80-92; lectr workshops, currently; guest lectr, Pratt Inst, 94-97 & Can Soc Painters Watercolor. *Awards:* Lena Newcastle Award, Am Watercolor Soc, 85. *Bibliog:* AVP Video, 88; Watercolor 93, fall 93; Splash II, North Light Bks, 93; Best of Watercolor (title page), Rockport Publ, 97. *Mem:* Am Watercolor Soc; Artists Equity. *Media:* Watercolor, Mixed. *Interests:* Photography, travel. *Publ:* Illusr, American Artists Group Reproduction, 73; auth, Watercolor, The Creative Experience, North Light/Van Nostrand Reinhold, 79; North Light Bks, 6/79-92; Watercolor From the Heart, Watson-Guptill Publ, 93; auth, Am Artist Mag, Watercolor Page, 11/2000; Invitational Exhibition of Contemporary Invitational Watermedia Masters, Jiangsu Watercolor Reserach Inst, 2007, 2010, 2012; DVD Creative Catalyst Productions, 2009, 2013. *Mailing Add:* 1085 Dunaweal Ln Calistoga CA 94515

NEEDLER, MABEL GLIDDEN See Howard, Linda

NEELY, ANNE
PAINTER

b 1946. *Study:* Colby-Sawyer Coll, New London, NH, AA, 1966; Old Dominion Univ, Norfolk, Va, 1970. *Exhib:* Solo exhibs include Pine Manor Coll Gallery, Mass, 79, Impressions Gallery, Boston, 81, 83, Victoria Munroe Gallery, NY, 86, 88, Fine Arts Gallery, Univ RI, 87, Alpha Gallery, Boston, 89, 92, 94, 97, 2001, 2003, Frick Gallery, Maine, 93, DeCordova Mus, Mass, 93, Nesto Gallery, Milton Acad, Mass, 95, Emmanuel Coll, Boston, 2000, Jenkins-Johnson Gallery, San Francisco, 2003, Lohin Geduld Gallery, NY, 2005, 2007, Catherine Hammond Gallery, Ireland, 2005; group exhibs include North Haven Gallery, Maine, 2003, 2004; New Art Ctr, Newton, Mass, 2003; Ballycastle, County Mayo, Ireland, 2004; Jenkins-Johnson Gallery, 2004; Courthouse Gallery, Ireland, 2004; Alpha Gallery, 2004, 2005, 2006; Lascano Gallery, Great Barrington, Mass, 2006; Ctr for Maine Contemp Art, Rockport, 2006. *Teaching:* Artist in residence, Earthwatch Expedition, 87. *Awards:* Blance E Coleman Award, Painting, Boston, 82; Klingenstein Grant, British Trust for Ornithology, Scotland, 87; Polaroid Grant, Artist Support Program, 20 x 24 Studio, NY, 95; Ballinglen Arts Found Fellowship Program, County Mayo, Ireland, 98, 2001, 2004

NEES, LAWRENCE
EDUCATOR, HISTORIAN

b Chicago, Ill, Aug 9, 1949. *Study:* Univ Chicago, BA, 70; Harvard Univ, MA, 73, PhD, 77. *Pos:* pres, Int Ctr Midieval Art. *Teaching:* Vis lectr, Univ Victoria, BC, 76-77; lectr, Univ Mass, Boston, 77-78; from asst to prof, Univ Del, Newark, 78-. *Awards:* Mellon fel, 1982-82; Samuel H Kress sr fel, Ctr for Advanced Study in Visual Arts, 86; John Simon Guggenheim Mem fel, 2000-01; Berlin Prize Fel, Am Acad Berlin, 2005; Fel, Nat Humanities Ctr, 2010-2011. *Mem:* Int Ctr Medieval Art (pres, 2011-); Byzantine Studies Asn; Medieval Acad Am; Coll Art Asn Am; Historians Islamic Art Asn; Italian Art Soc; Soc Antiquaries London (fel). *Res:* Medieval manuscript illumination; Carolingian art. *Publ:* From Justinian to Charlemagne, G K Hall, 85; The Gundohinus Gospels at Autun, Medieval Acad Am, 87; A Tainted Mantle Hercules & the Classical Tradition at the Carolingian Court, Univ Pa, 91; ed, Approaches to Early-Medieval Art, Medieval Acad Am, 98, 2002; Early Medieval Art, Oxford Univ Pres, 2002. *Mailing Add:* Dept Art Hist Univ Del Newark DE 19716

NEESON, H GAEL
COLLECTOR

Awards: Named one of Top 200 Collectors, ARTnews mag, 2009-13. *Collection:* Contemporary art. *Mailing Add:* 175 E Delaware Pl Chicago IL 60611

NEFF, JOHN A
PAINTER, DESIGNER

b Lebanon, Pa, May 5, 1926. *Study:* Whitney Sch Art, New Haven, Conn, cert; Paier Coll Art, Hamden, Conn, with Herbert Gute. *Work:* New Brit Mus Am Art, Gtr Hartford Arts Coun & Mus Art, Sci & Indust, Bridgeport, Conn; Mus Fine Arts, Springfield, Mass; First Nat Bank Boston. *Exhib:* Am Watercolor Soc, NY, 98; RI Watercolor Soc, Pawtucket, RI, 98; Conn Watercolor Soc, 2002; Mystic Int, Maritime Gallery, Mystic, Conn, 2002; Modern Marine Masters, Maritime Gallery, Mytic, Conn, 2003. *Pos:* Sr graphic designer, Muirson Label Co, North Haven, Conn, 50-71; owner, Crossmark Assocs, Wallingford, Conn, 72-87. *Teaching:* Watercolor, privately. *Awards:* Esther Fay Mem Award, Conn Watercolor Soc, 98; 1st Prize Findlay Award, RI Watercolor Soc; Berets Award, Reed Marine Exhibit, Stamford, Conn, 99. *Bibliog:* T F Potter (auth), A proxy visit, Meriden Rec-J, Conn, 69; John Bickford (auth)

Painting figures with impact, Artist's Mag, 5/97; Watercolor Expressions, Quarry Pub, 98. *Mem:* Am Watercolor Soc; Allied Artists Am; Conn Watercolor Soc (bd dir, 71-72); Whiskey Painters Am; Am Soc Marine Artists. *Media:* Transparent Watercolor. *Publ:* auth, Collected Best of Watercolor, Rockport Publs, 2002. *Mailing Add:* 17 Parkview Rd Wallingford CT 06492-3051

NEFF, JOHN HALLMARK
ART HISTORIAN, MUSEUM DIRECTOR
b Miami, Fla, Mar 28, 1944. *Study:* Wesleyan Univ, Middletown, Conn, BA, 66; Harvard Univ, MA, 68, PhD, 74. *Collection Arranged:* 180 Beacon Collection (auth, catalog), Boston, Mass, 67; Great Ideas Prog, Container Corp, 78-80; First Nat Bank Chicago, 84-97; Am Medical Asn, Chicago, 89-90; John D and Catherine T MacArthur Found, 91-95; Holleb & Coff, 96. *Pos:* David E Finley fel, Nat Gallery Art, Washington, DC, 69-72; asst cur, Sterling & Francine Clark Art Inst, Williamstown, Mass, 72-73; cur mod art, Detroit Inst Arts, 74-78; dir, Mus Contemp Art, Chicago, 78-83; mem, adv comt for exhibs, Am Fedn of the Arts, 81-; mem, Nat Adv Comt, Art in Pub Places, Dade Co, Fla, 82-90; dir, art prog-art adv, First Nat Bank Chicago, 83-97; mem adv comt, Art & Ideas Prog, Sch Art Inst Chicago, 85-; Mus d'Art Am, Giverny, France, 97-99; Terra Mus Am Art, Chicago, 97-2001. *Teaching:* Teaching fel 19th & 20th century art hist, Harvard Univ, 67-69; asst prof 19th & 20th century art, Williams Col, Williamstown, Mass, 72-74, vis lectr, grad prog, 73-74; Matisse seminar, Grad Sch, Sch Art Inst Chicago, 94; Anselm Kiefer Seminar, Anderson Arts Ranch, Snowmass, Colo, 97. *Bibliog:* Hilton Kramer (auth), Rediscovering the genius of Henri Matisse, New York Times, 7/27/75; Robert Pincus-Witten (auth), Detroit notes, Arts Mag, 78; Anselm Kiefer (auth), A 'Gnostic' Triptych, NC Mus Art Bulletin, 97. *Mem:* Arts Club, Chicago; AAMD (bd mem, 83-94); Coll Art Asn (bd dir, 96-2000); Renaissance Soc; Sculpture Chicago; ICOM. *Res:* Matisse scholar; Anselm Kiefer; public art, Kabbalistic imagery, corporate patronage. *Publ:* An Early Ceramic Triptych by Henri Matisse & Matisse's Forgotten Stained Glass Commission, The Burlington Mag, 12/72; Coauth, The Gott Impression of Pollaiuolo's Battle of Nudes, Nat Gallery of Art, Washington, DC, 73, Henri Matisse: Paper Cut-Outs, Abrams, 77; Some Thoughts on Barnett Newman, The Bulletin, Detroit Inst Arts, Spring, 78; Charles Simonds: Circles and Towers Growing, Mus Contemp Art, Chicago, 81; Contemporary Art from the Netherlands, Smithsonian Inst Traveling Exhib Service, 82; Anselm Kiefer, Bruch und Einung, Marian Goodman, New York, 87; contribr, Natural Light: Roger Ackling, Centre d'Art Contemp, Geneve, Switz, 91; Daring To Dream, Univ Chicago Press, 92; Hands On: Irwin and Abstract Expressionism (catalog essay), Mus Contemp Art, Los Angeles, 93; Kabbalistic Imagery in Negotiating Rapture, Mus Contemp Art, Chicago, 96

NEGROPONTE, GEORGE
PAINTER
b New York, NY, Feb 11, 1953. *Study:* Skowhegan Sch of Painting & Sculpture, 73; Yale Univ, BA, 75. *Work:* Chemical Bank, New York, NY; Bank of Am, San Francisco, Calif; Reader's Digest Asn, New York, NY; Metrop Mus Art, NY; Mus Art, Andros, Greece. *Comn:* Paintings, Olympia & York, 81 & TWA, 86, NY; IBM, NY. *Exhib:* Solo exhibs include Brooke Alexander Inc, NY, 81, 83 & 85, John Good Gallery, NY, 87-88, Real Art Inc, NY, 90 & Jason McCoy, 90-91, 95, 96 & 98, Jason McCoy, 03, Jason McCoy Inc, NY, 2007; group exhibs include New Drawing in Am, Mus Mod Art Ca'Pesaro, Venice, Italy, 83; An Int Survey of Painting & Sculpture, Mus Mod Art, NY, 84, 87 & 88; Recent Acquisitions, Metrop Mus Art, 89; Yale Collects Yale, Yale Univ Art Gallery, New Haven, Conn, 93; Contemp Artists in NY, Edobori Gallery, Osaka, Japan. *Pos:* Consult, Drawing Ctr, NY, 82-84; visual arts panelist, NY State Coun Arts, 85-89, appeals panel, co-chmn Drawing Ctr, NY, 98-; co-chmn, Drawing Ctr, 98-02, pres, 2002. *Teaching:* Instr, Studio Sch, NY, 90- & Parsons Sch Design, 96-99, Princeton, 99-2000. *Awards:* Individual Artists Award, NY State Coun Arts, 88. *Bibliog:* Charles Hagen (auth), Art Forum, 10/87; Robet Edelman (auth), Art Am, 1/89; Jed Perl (auth), New Criterion, 3/89. *Media:* Oil. *Dealer:* Jason McCoy Inc New York NY; Charles Cowles Gallery New York

NEHER, ROSS JAMES
PAINTER, WRITER
b Kingston, NY, June 5, 1949. *Study:* Art Students League with Henry Billings & Fletcher Martin, 64-67; Sch Fine Arts, Wash Univ, BFA, 71; Pratt Inst, NY, MFA, 75. *Work:* Brooklyn Mus, NY; Mint Mus, Charlotte, NC; Sidney Lewis, Richmond, Va; Commonwealth Co, Lincoln, Nebr; Binney & Smith, Easton, Pa; Chase Manhattan Bank & Chemical Bank, NY. *Exhib:* Recent Abstract Painting, State Univ NY, Brockport, 76; The New Spiritualism, Robert Hull Fleming Mus, Burlington, 81; GRP Exhib, Albright Knox, Buffalo, 82; Newcastle Salutes NY, Newcastle-upon-Tyne Gallery, Eng, 83; 2 Smart Art Too, 55 Mercer, NY, 85; New Work, NY, Harvard Univ, Cambridge, 85; The New Response, Contemp Painters of the Hudson River, Albany Inst Art, NY, 86. *Teaching:* Prof grad painting, Pratt Inst, 80-; adj assoc prof. *Awards:* Tiffany Award, Tiffany Found, 86; Cité Des Arts, Paris Residency, Wash Univ, 86. *Bibliog:* Adrian Goddard (auth), Ross Neher: Painting Behavior, Artforum, 12/79; April Kingsley (auth), The New Spiritualism, Oscarrson Hood, 81. *Media:* Oil, Canvas. *Publ:* Auth, Bathysiderodromophobia, The Fox, 76; Dennis Masback's Paintings, 78 & Mentalism Versus Painting, 79, Artforum; The Death of Perception, Issue No 1, 84 & The Legacy of Picasso, Issue No 2, 85; auth, Blindfolding the Muse, Prenom Press, 99; auth, Sforza, Prenom Press, 2008. *Dealer:* Howard Scott 72 Greene St New York NY 10012. *Mailing Add:* 545 Broadway New York NY 10012

NEIL, ERIK H
MUSEUM DIRECTOR
Study: Princeton Univ, BA (history); Harvard Univ, MA & PhD (history of art and architecture). *Pos:* Dir, Newcomb Art Gallery, Tulane Univ, formerly; exec dir, Heckscher Mus, Huntington, NY, formerly; dir, Acad Art Mus, Easton, Md, 2010-14; dir, Chrysler Mus Art, 2014-. *Teaching:* Adj prof history of art, Tulane Univ, formerly. *Mailing Add:* The Chrysler Museum of Art One Memorial Plaza Norfolk VA 23510

NEIL, J M
WRITER
b Boise, Idaho, June 2, 1937. *Study:* Yale Col, AB, 59; Univ Wis, MS, 63; Wash State Univ, PhD, 66. *Collection Arranged:* Will James: The Spirit of the Cowboy (ed, catalog), 85-86 & Historic Ranches of Wyoming (with catalog), 86 & traveling, Nicolaysen Art Mus, Casper, Wyo. *Pos:* Dir, Idaho Bicentennial Comn, Boise, 72-76 & Nicolaysen Art Mus, Casper, Wyo, 83-89; city conservator, Seattle, Wash, 78-81. *Teaching:* Asst assoc prof Am studies, Univ Hawaii, 67-72; vis lectr art hist, Univ Victoria, BC, 76-77. *Mem:* Wyo Coun Arts (bd mem, 85-89); Natrona Co Pub Libr (bd mem, 88-89); Boise City Hist Preserv Comn. *Res:* Primarily in the history of American environmental design--architecture, landscape design, urban planning and others. *Publ:* Auth, Toward a National Taste: America's Quest for Aesthetic Independence, Univ Press Hawaii, 75; Saints & Oddfellows: A Bicentennial Sampler of Idaho Architecture, Boise Gallery Art, 76; The impact of the Armory Show, S Atlantic Quart, 80; Paris or New York? The shaping of downtown Seattle, 1903-1914, Pac NW Quart, 84. *Mailing Add:* 300 S Straughan Ave Apt 402 Boise ID 83712

NEILSON, MARY ANN
PAINTER
b Springfield, Mass, May 16, 1952. *Study:* Syracuse Univ, BFA, 74; Art Students League, studies with Diana Kan & TJ Clark. *Work:* New York Health & Hosp Corp, NY; Carnegie Hall Offices, NY. *Comn:* Vanderbilt Univ Med Ctr. *Exhib:* Solo exhib, Staten Island Botanic Garden, NY, 92; Ann Am Artists Prof League, Salmagundi Club, NY, 92; Autumn Showing, Newark Mus, NJ, 94; Focus on Nature, NY State Mus, Albany, 94; Nicholas Davies Gallery, NY, 95; Nature Ctr, Westport, Conn; Vogel Gallery, Ridgefield, Conn, 2002; Brick Gallery, Essex, Conn; Westport Arts Center, 2011; Westport Lib, 2011. *Pos:* Sr graphic designer, Cosgrove Assocs, New York, 76-82. *Teaching:* Instr botanical illus, Brooklyn Botanic Garden, 90-96; pvt instr. *Mem:* Catharine Lorillard Wolfe Art Club; Westport Arts Center; Brooklyn Watercolor Soc (vpres, 91-94); Guild Natural Sci Illusr; Am Artist Prof League; Lyme Art Asn; Am Soc Botanical Artists . *Media:* Watercolor, Alkyd, Oil. *Publ:* Contribr, Graphics International (Switzerland) Graphis, 85, Splash 6, Best of Watercolor, 2001. *Mailing Add:* 5 Daybreak Lane Westport CT 06880

NEIMANAS, JOYCE
PHOTOGRAPHER
b Chicago, Ill, Jan 22, 1944. *Study:* Art Inst Chicago, MFA, 69. *Work:* Mus Contemp Art, Chicago, Ill; San Francisco Mus Mod Art, Calif; Art Inst Chicago; Mus Fine Art, Houston; Int Mus of Photog, George Eastman House, Rochester, NY. *Exhib:* Solo exhibs, Recent Work, Ctr Contemp Photog, Chicago, 79, Color Construction, Oakland Mus, Calif, 79, Ctr Creative Photog, Tucson, Ariz, 84, Collisions, Presentation House, Vancouver, BC, 88, Ctr Photog, Woodstock, NY, 89 & Legends of Powerless, Gallery 954, Chicago, 93; BIG Pictures by Contemp Photog, Mus Mod Art, NY, 83; Signs of the Times: Some Recurring Motifs in Twentieth-Century Photog, San Francisco Mus Mod Art, Calif, 85; traveling exhib, Photog and Art: Interactions Since 1946, Los Angeles Co Mus Art, 87; Recorded and Revealed, Art Inst Chicago, Ill, 87; Photog Ill, State Ill Ctr Art Gallery, Chicago, 89; Am Photog since 1920: From the Collection of the Ctr for Creative Photog, Tucson, Ariz, 91; Past, Present, Mus Fine Arts, Houston, Tex, 92; Three Decades of Midwestern Photog, Davenport Mus Art, Iowa, 92; The Mediated Image, Univ Art Mus, Univ NMex, Albuquerque, 93; Dog Show, Wood St Gallery, Chicago, 99; Am Perspectives: Photog from the Polaroid Collection, Tokyo Met Mus of Photog, Japan, 2000; Crossing the Line: Photog Reconsidered, Art Inst Chicago, 2000; and others. *Pos:* Chairperson, Photog Dept, Art Inst Chicago. *Teaching:* Prof photog, Art Inst Chicago, 77-. *Awards:* Visual Arts Fel, Nat Endowment Arts, 79, 83 & 90; Artist Grant, Ill Arts Coun, 87; Computer Grant, Apple Corp, 92; Chicago Women's Caucus for Art Honoree. *Bibliog:* Poppy Evans (auth), Fresh Ideas in Photoshop, N Light Bks, 98; Floris Neussus (auth), Photo Poche Series: Photograms, Nathan Publ, Paris, 98; J Luciana & J Watts (auths), The Art of Enhanced Photography, Beyond the Photographic Image, Rockport Publ, 99; T Barrett (auth), Criticizing Photographs: An Introduction to Understanding Images, Mayfield Publ, 2000. *Media:* Collage, Digital Images. *Mailing Add:* Mus of Contemp Photog Columbia Coll Chicago 600 S Michigan Ave Chicago IL 60605

NELLIS, JENNIFRED GENE
SCULPTOR
b Lincoln, Nebr. *Study:* Univ Nebr, Lincoln, BFA, 70; Univ Iowa, Iowa City, MA, 76, MFA, 77. *Work:* Masur Mus, Monroe, La; Fine Arts Gallery, Univ Minn, Morris; Sprague Art Gallery, Joliet Jr Col. *Exhib:* Dahl Fine Arts Ctr, Rapid City, SDak, 89; three-person exhib, WARM Gallery, Minneapolis, Minn, 89; Icons made in Minnesota, AIR Gallery, NY 89; WARM Kansas City Artists Coalition, 90; Artemisia Gallery, Chicago, 90; plus many other group & solo shows. *Teaching:* Assoc prof sculpture, drawing, basic studio & ceramics, Univ Minn, Morris, 78-86, assoc prof, 86-. *Awards:* Sculpture Award, 29th Ann Iowa Artists, 77; Purchase Award, Monroe Nat, 79; Second Prize Award, Pyramid Art Ctr, Rochester, NY, 84. *Bibliog:* Mellissa Stang (auth), New Art Examiner, 5/87; Norita Dittberner (auth) Warm Journal, Vol 8, No 2, 87; Nancy Cohen (auth), Warming Up, Vinyl Arts, 1/12/88. *Mem:* Women's Art Registry Minn; Coll Art Asn; Women's Caucus for Art. *Media:* Mixed Media. *Publ:* Auth, Geographies-Geologies, Milkweed Chronicle, winter 83; 1984 Calendar, Women in Art, 84. *Dealer:* Anderson & Anderson Gallery Minneapolis MN; Hamilton Frame & Gallery Independence MO. *Mailing Add:* 505 E 9th St Morris MN 56267-1027

NELSON, AIDA Z
PAINTER, WRITER
b New York, NY. *Study:* New York Univ, BA; Sorbonne, Paris; Art Students League. *Work:* Mus De San Miguel, Mex; Mus des Arts Decoratifs, Paris, france; Mus des Bellas Artes, Buenos Aires, Arg; Banff Ctr Arts, Can; Camac Center, France. *Exhib:* Contemp Group, Centre Culturel Am, Paris, 64; Salon de Jeune Peinture, Mus D'Art Moderne, Paris, 65 & Salon Interministeriel, 67; Art from 2 Americans, M Samtander

Gallery, NY, 93; Love & Kisses, MBM Gallery, NY, 94; Pintoras Modernas, Galeria Juan Levy, Mex, 96; Aphrodites Revenge, Mus de San Miguel, Mex, 96; Song of Songs, Banff Ctr for Arts, Alberta, Can, 2000. *Teaching:* instr, Col New Rochelle, NY, 85-87, Sch Visual Arts, New York, 87-90 & New York Univ, 90-93. *Awards:* Emerging Excellence, Mus D'Art Moderne, 65 & Cezanne, 67; Originality in Concept, Mus de San Miguel, 96. *Media:* Acrylic, Mixed Media. *Mailing Add:* 444 Central Park West New York NY 10025

NELSON, ARDINE
PHOTOGRAPHER
Study: Northern Ill Univ, DeKalb, BS (Art Educ), MA (Sculpture/Photog); Univ Iowa City, MFA (Photog). *Teaching:* Assoc prof, Dept Art, Ohio State Univ. *Awards:* Ohio Arts Coun Fel; Greater Columbus Arts Coun Fel, 1990; John Simon Guggenheim Mem Found Fel, 2008. *Mailing Add:* Ohio State University Dept Art Haskett Hall 303C 128 N Oval Mall Columbus OH 43210

NELSON, HAROLD B
DIRECTOR
b Providence, RI, May 14, 1947. *Study:* Bowdoin Col, AB, 69; Univ Del, MA, 72. *Collection Arranged:* Sounding the Depths: 150 Years of Am Seascape, Am Fedn of Arts, 90-91; California Focus: Selections From the Collection of the Long Beach Mus Art, 96; New Visions: Selina Trieff (auth, catalog), 96-97; In Ye Grandest Manner and After Ye Newest Fashion (auth, catalog), 2000; Conjunction: The Melba and Al Langman Collection (auth, catalog), 2000; Imps on a Bridge: Wedgwood Fairyland and Other Lustres, (auth, catalog), 2001; The Enamels of Annemarie Davidson (auth catalog), 2004; The Modernist Jewelry of Claire Falkenstein (auth catalog), 2004; Port Visions, photographs by Tom Raiva (auth catalog), 2004; For the People, Am Folk Art (auth catalog), 2004. *Pos:* Cur mus art & archaeology, Univ Mo, 77-79; registrar, Solomon R Guggenheim Mus, 79-83; chief admin for exhibs, Am Fedn Arts, 83-89; dir, Long Beach Mus Art, 89-. *Awards:* Fel, Smithsonian Research, Nat Mus Am Art, 76. *Mem:* Coll Art Asn; Am Asn Mus; Asn of Art Mus Dirs. *Res:* Ceramics, Decorative Arts. *Interests:* 20th Century Enamels. *Publ:* Auth, Sounding the Depths: 150 Years of American Seascape (catalog), Chronicle Books, 89. *Mailing Add:* Long Beach Mus Art 2300 E Ocean Blvd Long Beach CA 90803

NELSON, JAMES P
PAINTER
b Boston, Mass, 1949. *Study:* Carnegie-Mellon Univ, BFA, 71. *Work:* Carnegie Mus Art; PNC Bank; Western Pa Hosp; Bayer Corp; plus others. *Exhib:* Solo exhibs, Westmoreland Mus Art, Greensburgh, Pa, 80, Hewlett Gallery, Carnegie Mellon Univ, 81, Pittsburgh Plan Art, 84, Carson Street Gallery, Pittsburgh, 87, 90 & 93, Pittsburgh Ctr Arts, 88 & Chatham Coll Art Gallery, Pittsburgh, 94, The Univ Club Pittsburgh, 98; Ann Assoc Artists Pittsburgh, Carnegie Mus Art, Pittsburgh, 83-86, 88-89, 91-92 & 94-95; Pittsburgh in Chicago, Deson-Saunders Gallery, Chicago, 90; Pittsburgh X 7, Pittsburgh Ctr Arts, 93; Regional Focus, Pittsburgh Ctr Arts, 96; 42nd Chautauqua Nat, Chautauqua, NY, 99; Exquisite Surfaces, Concept Gallery, Pittsburgh, 2000, 2001 & 2002. *Teaching:* La Roche Col, Pittsburgh, Pa. *Awards:* Purchase Award & Juror's Award, Carnegie Mus Art, Pittsburgh, 87; Festival Award & Highlight Award, Three Rivers Arts Festival, Pittsburgh, 87; Nat Endowment Arts, 89; Painting Award 42nd Chautauqua Nat, Chautauqua, NY, 99. *Bibliog:* Cheryl Regan (auth), James P Nelson, Dialogue Mag, 36, 1-2/88; William Homisak (auth), Nelson's Pittsburgh: Moody City on the Mon, Tribune Rev, 4/21/89; Vicky Clark (auth), James P Nelson, 90; Murray Horne (auth) Pittsburgh X7 Catalogue, 93. *Mem:* Assoc Artists Pittsburgh. *Media:* Oil, Watercolor. *Dealer:* Concept Gallery Pittsburgh PA. *Mailing Add:* c/o Concept Art Gallery 1031 S Braddock Ave Pittsburgh PA 15218

NELSON, JANE GRAY
CURATOR
b Kankakee, Ill, Oct 10, 1928. *Study:* Univ Calif, Berkeley, MLS, 63, MA (classical archeol), 71. *Pos:* Librn, Fine Arts Mus, San Francisco, 71-89, asst cur, Dept Ancient Art, 74-76 & 89-. *Mem:* Am Inst Archeol; Soc Promotion Hellenic Studies; Brontë Soc; Jane Austen Soc; Calif Classical Asn. *Res:* Gnathia ware. *Publ:* Contribr, Three Centuries of French Art, 73, Claude Monet, 73, Africa, Ancient Mexican Art: The Loran Collection, 74, Two Early Hittite Theriomorphic Vessels of the Karum-Period, 82, Inside Wuthering Heights, 84 & Xylophones on Gnathia Vases, 86. *Mailing Add:* Calif Palace Legion of Honor 100 34th Ave San Francisco CA 94121

NELSON, JOAN
PAINTER
b Torrance, Calif, 1958. *Study:* Wash Univ, St Louis, Mo, BFA, 81; Brooklyn Mus Sch, Max Beckman Mem Scholar, 81-82. *Work:* Mus Mod Art, Solomon R Guggenheim Mus, NY; Los Angeles Co Mus Art; Hirshhorn Mus & Sculpture Garden, Nat Mus Women Arts, Washington; Mus Fine Arts, Boston; Toledo Mus Art. *Exhib:* Solo exhibs, Contemp Arts Mus, Houston, Tex, 88, Freedman Gallery, Albright Col, Reading, Pa, 91, Michael Kohn Gallery, 92, John Berggruen Gallery, San Francisco, 94 & Robert Miller Gallery, NY, 95; Currents 39, St Louis Arts Mus, 89; Biennial, Whitney Mus Am Art, NY, 89; Quotations, Aldrich Mus Art, Ridgefield, Conn, 92; 47th Ann Purchase Exhib, Am Acad Arts & Letts, NY, 95; The Small Painting, O'Hara Gallery, NY, 95-96; Changing Horizons: Landscape on the Eve of the Millennium, Katonah Mus, NY, 96; Cuenca Bienal of Painting, Ecuador, 96-97; Rediscovering the Landscape of the Americas (traveling), Gerald Peters Gallery, Santa Fe, NMex, 96-98. *Bibliog:* Michael Brenson (auth), Straightened landscapes of a post-modern era, NY Times, 1/13/89; Kay Larson (auth), Back to Nature, New York, 4/90; Michael Boodro (auth), Joan Nelson: Second Nature, Artnews, 9/90. *Media:* Oil, Wax on Wood. *Mailing Add:* c/o Robert Miller Gallery 526 W 26th St #10A New York NY 10001-5541

NELSON, JON ALLEN
CURATOR, HISTORIAN
b Omaha, Nebr, July 9, 1936. *Study:* Univ Nebr, Lincoln, BFA, 59; museology, Univ Minn. *Collection Arranged:* Etchings of J Alden Weir (auth, catalog), 67, Thomas Coleman, Printmaker (auth, catalog), 72 & Sigmund Abeles: The First Twenty Years (auth, catalog), 79, Sheldon Mem Art Gallery, Univ Nebr, Lincoln; Great Plains 1930-1939 (auth, catalog), Ctr in Greater Plains Studies, Univ Nebr, 85. *Pos:* Pres, Nebr Mus Conf, 73; cur, Ctr Great Plains Studies Art Collection, Univ Nebr, formerly. *Teaching:* Adj asst prof, dept art & art hist, Univ Nebr, Lincoln, 91-. *Publ:* Auth, Art of Printmaking, Univ Nebr, Lincoln, 66

NELSON, MARY CARROLL
WRITER, PAINTER
b Bryan, Tex, Apr 24, 1929. *Study:* Barnard Coll, BA (fine arts), 50, art hist with Julius Held & painting with Peppino Mangravite & Dong Kingman; Univ NMex, MA (art educ), 63, painting with Kenneth M Adams; art educ with Alexander Masley; grad studies art hist with John Tatschl, 69-70. *Exhib:* Art is for Healing, Tex, 92; Layering, NMex, 93; The Layered Perspective, Ark, 94; Artists of the Spirit (auth, catalog), Walton Arts Ctr, Fayetteville, Ark, 94; Celtic Connections, Mass, 98; Landscape Memory, Ariz, 2001; NMex Women in the Arts, Originals, Traces of the Journey, 2003; Masterworks, Miniatures, 2004; Art of Space, Rock, Paper, Scissors, Los Alamos, NMex, Connections, We Are All One, Celebración, Yes, Albuquerque, NMex 2006; Soul Shrines, Las Cruces, NMex, 2006; Exploring Multiple Dimensions, Albuquerque Mus, 2007; Illumination, Fort Myers, Fla, 2008; Masterworks, Miniatures, 2008; Beyond the I, Masterwork Miniatures, Albuquerque, NMex, 2009; BECA Int Exhib and New Art New Design, Albuquerque, NMex, 2011; Mining the Unconcious, Santa Fe, 2011; Treasures in Time, Albuquerque, 2011; Alchemists, Albuquerque, 2011; Unity, Albuquerque, 2011; Beneath the Surface, Socorro, NMex, 2011; Masterworks Miniatures, Albuquerque, 2012; NMex Enchants, Ashland, Ore, 2012; The Omega, The Alpha, Taos, NMex, 2012; Masterworks Miniatures, Albuquerque, NMex, 2013; Who is God? Olympia, Wash, 2013; Weynich Gallery, Albuquerque, 2013. *Pos:* Cur, Layering, An Art of Time & Space, Albuquerque Mus, 85, Shrines and Sacred Space, NMex, AC Fair, 88; judge, Masterworks Miniatures, Albuquerque, NMex, 2012, Encantada, 2013, Albuquerque. *Teaching:* Instr, Elem & Art in USA & Ger, 55-83. *Awards:* Honoree Magnifico, Albuquerque, 97; Bravo Award, Albuquerque, NMex, 2004; Achievement Award, Masterwork, 2005; Bardean Award, Masterwork, 2009; Local Treasure, 2013. *Bibliog:* Something about the author, Vol XXIII, 81; Creative Collage: Techniques, Leland Williams, North Light Bks, 94; Collage: A Dynamic Medium of Experimentation, Bromer, Watson-Guptill, 94; Ann B Hartley (ed), Bridging Time & Space, Markowitz Publ, 98; Mary Todd Beam (auth), Celebrate Your Creative Self, North Light Bks, 2001; The Art of Layering Making Connections, 2001; Visual Journeys, Art of the 21st Century, 2010; Art is Life, NMex Mag, 2011; Everything is Connected, abq Arts, 2011; A Journey of Expression, Albuquerque Jour, 2011. *Mem:* Soc Layerists Multi-Media (founder, 82, pres, 82-84, ed newslett 82-94, hon, 2002, life mem). *Media:* Mixed Media. *Res:* American, Native American & Southwest artists; the relationship of artists' philosophy, spirituality and their technique. *Specialty:* Spirituality. *Interests:* Holism, early child education. *Publ:* Coauth (with R Kelley), Ramon Kelley Paints Portraits, Figures, 77, Legendary Artists of Taos, 80 & auth, Masters of Western Art, 82, Watson-Guptill; auth, Connecting, The Art of Beth Ames Swartz, Northland Press, 84; A Vision of Silence, The Art of Dons Steider, Alta Luz Ltd, 96; coauth, Bridging Time & Space, Markowitz Pub, 98; The Art of Layering/Making Connections, 2004; Crop Circles, An Art of Our time, 2007; coedit, Visual Journeys, Art of the 21st Cent, 2010. *Dealer:* Weyrich Gallery, Albuquerque, NM. *Mailing Add:* 1408 Georgia NE Albuquerque NM 87110

NELSON, PAMELA HUDSON
ASSEMBLAGE ARTIST, SCULPTOR
b Oklahoma City, Okla, Mar 25, 1947. *Study:* Southern Methodist Univ, Dallas, Tex, BFA, 74. *Work:* MTV Collection, NY; Steak & Ale Collection, Dallas, Tex. *Comn:* Relief Animals, Dallas Zoo, Tex; Cotton Crown, Co Govt, Blytheville, Ark; Parkland Hosp, Dallas. *Exhib:* Tex Exhib, Nat Mus Women, Washington, DC, 88; Handmade in Texas, LTV Ctr, Dallas, Tex, 87; Tex Ann, Laguna Gloria Mus, Austin, 87. *Pos:* co-cur, Theatre Gallery, Dallas, 1985; workshops Dallas Mus Art, 1982, 85; created, produced award for Leadership Tex, 1993, Girls Club Am, Dallas, 1987, 89; superv, studio assts in mentor prog, 1988-91; juror DART Garland (Tex) Bus Transit Ct, 1992, Site Sculpture Competition, Municipal Ctr, Plano, Tex, 1993; Design Artist, Dallas Light Rail System. *Teaching:* Arlington Art Mus, Tex; pvt art tutor, 1987-93; Instr, Arlington Mus Art, 1991; guest lectr, Dallas Mus Art, 1993. *Awards:* Ron Gleason Award, Excellence 88, Tex Sculpture Asn, 88; Billboard Winner, Outdoor Art, Patrick Media Group, 88; Rec award Laguna Art Mus, 1982, Merit award Tex Christian Univ, 1984, Crystal award Dallas Cable Syst, 1985, Merit award Crescent Gallery, 1986, Merit award Alexandria Mus, 1987, Patrick Media Billboard award, 1988, Excellence '88 award Plz of Ams, 1988, Hon Mention award Longview Mus and Arts Ctr, 1990, Legend award, Dallas Visual Art Center, Merit award, Am Inst of Archits; named Artist-in-Residence, Connemara Conservancy, 1993. *Bibliog:* Judy Kelly (dir), Artseye (TV prog), KERA-Pub Television, Dallas, 87; Paul Nathan (auth), Texas Collects, Taylor Publ Co, 88; Sylvia Moore (auth), No Bluebonnets, No Yellow Roses, Midmarch Arts, 88. *Mem:* Tex Sculpture Asn. *Media:* Wood, Mixed Media. *Dealer:* Peregrine Gallery at the Crescent 2200 Cedar Springs Rd Dallas TX 75201. *Mailing Add:* 312 S Harwood Dallas TX 75201-5602

NELSON, R KENTON
PAINTER
b Los Angeles, Calif, 1954. *Study:* Calif State Univ, 1977-79; Otis Parsons Art Inst, 1979. *Exhib:* Solo exhibs, Mendenhall Gallery, Pasadena, Calif, 1993-97, 99 & 2005, Cerritos Coll, Calif, 96, Muckenthaler Cultural Arts Ctr, Fullerton, Calif, 97, Eleanor Ettinger Gallery, NY, 1997-2002 & 2004-2005, Davidson Gallery, Seattle, Washington, 98, Diane Nelson Fine Art, Laguna Beach, Calif, 1999-2000 & 2002, Van

de Griff Gallery, Santa Fe, NNex, 2000, DNFA Gallery, Pasadena, Calif, 2002, Sullivan Gross, Santa Barbara, 2003-2004, Scott White Contemp Art, La Jolla, Calif, 2003, Klaudia Marr Gallery, Santa Fe, 2004-2005, SCAPE Corona Del Mar, Calif, 2004, Ruzicska, Salzburg, Austria, 2005; Realism Knows No Bounds, Van de Griff Gallery, 1999-2003; Diane Nelson Fine Art, 99; American Figurative Painting, Albemarle Gallery, London, 99; Mendenhall Gallery, Pasadena, Calif, 2000; DNFA Gallery, Pasadena, 2000; Figure in American Art, Eleanor Ettinger, NY, 2001-2003 & 2005; An American Scene, Scott White Contemp Art, La Jolla, Calif, 2002; Sullivan Goss, Santa Barbara, Calif, 2002. *Teaching:* Instr, San Francisco Acad Art, formerly, Otis Parsons Art Inst, formerly. *Bibliog:* Norman Kolpas (auth), Perfect Worlds, Southwest Art, 3/2001; Teri Thomson Randall (auth), Glorifying the Utterly Ordinary, Pasatiempo, 12/2003; Josef Woodward (auth), Full Nelson Effect, ArtsScene, 12/2005. *Dealer:* Mendenhall Sobieski Gallery 40 Mills Pl Pasadena CA 91105; Ruzicska Faistauergasse 12 A5020 Salzburg Austria; Plus One Gallery 91 Pimlico Rd London SW1W 8PH; Klaudia Marr Gallery 668 Canyon Rd Santa Fe NM 87501; SCAPE 2859 E Coast Highway Corona del Mar CA 92625. *Mailing Add:* c/o Eleanor Ettinger Gallery 24 W 57th St Ste 609 New York NY 10019

NELSON, RICH
PAINTER, INSTRUCTOR
b Detroit, Mich, Aug 27, 1961. *Study:* Col Creative Studies (CCS), Detroit Mich, BFA, 1988; Studied with E Raymond Kinstler, NYC, Jeremy Lipking, Los Angeles; Post Degree Study: Wayne State Univ (Robert Wilbert, Tom Parish, Irina Nakhova), Masters Level classes, 1993. *Work:* Scarab Club, Detroit, Mich. *Comn:* Portrait, John Smale, comn by Chmn Gen Motors, Detroit Mich, 2002; Portrait, Jack Smith, comn by Chmn Gen Motors, 2003; Portrait, Hon M S Howard, comn by Fed Judge, Greenville, NC, 2006; Portrait, Leonard & Rose Herring, comn by former Chmn Lowes, Wilkesboro, NC, 2006; Portrait, Dr D Ralph Davison, Jr, comn by Dean Greensboro Day Sch, Greensboro, NC, 2006. *Exhib:* Solo Exhibs: Red Clover Gallery, Landrum, SC, 2006; Conn Gallery, Landrum, SC, 2007; People, Places & Things, Edward Dare Gallery, Charleston, SC, 2007; Portrait Soc Am, Tri-State Competition, Raleigh, NC, 2006; Oil Painters Am, Eastern Regional Exhib, Richmond, Va, 2006; 10th Ann Art of the Portrait, Portrait Soc Am, Philadelphia, Pa, 2008. *Teaching:* instr, Anatomy Figure Drawing, Ctr Creative Studies, Detroit, Mich, 1995-2002; Inst, Painting, Tryon Painters & Sculptors, Tryon, NC, 2004-; instr, various workshops, 2004-. *Awards:* Finalist, Int Artist Mag Competition, 2003; Cert of Merit, PSOA Ann Tri-State Competition, 2005; 2nd Place, Peoples Choice PSOA Tri-State Competition, 2006; Finalist, PSOA Children's Portrait Competition, 2007; Semi Finalist, Am Artist Mag 70th Anniversary Competition, 2007; 2nd Prize, Portrait Soc Am Outdoor Competition, 2008. *Bibliog:* Wendy Loomis (auth), Rich Nelson Recent Paintings, Tryon Daily Bull, 10/2007; M Stephen Doherty (auth), 15 Portrait Artists, Am Artist, 11/2007; Amanda Apostol (auth), Recent Works Showcase, PSOA, 5/2008. *Mem:* Portrait Soc Am; Oil Painters Am; Tryon Painters & Sculptors (bd mem, 2004-2007). *Media:* Oil, Charcoal. *Publ:* Auth, Painting the Outdoor Portrait, Am artist, 3/2008; auth, drawing the Charcoal Portrait, PSOA, 12/2008. *Dealer:* Haen Gallery 52 Biltmore Ave Asheville NC 28801; Edward Dare Gallery 31 Broad St #100 Charleston SC 29401; Linville Gallery 4004 Hwy 105 Banner Elk NC 28604. *Mailing Add:* 622 Hogback Rd Tryon NC 28782

NELSON, RON
MUSEUM DIRECTOR
Study: Pacific Lutheran Univ, Tacoma, Wash, BA (Fine Art). *Collection Arranged:* cur, Art Auction X, 2004, Art Auction XI, 2005. *Pos:* Graphic designer, illustrator, art consultant, formerly; cur, private art & antique collections, currently; interim exec dir, Long Beach Mus Art, 2006-2008, exec dir, 2008-. *Mem:* President, Long Beach Mus Art Found; United Cerebral Palsy Special Children's League. *Mailing Add:* Long Beach Museum of Art 2300 E Ocean Blvd Long Beach CA 90803

NELSON, SIGNE
PAINTER
b New London, Conn, Dec 3, 1937. *Study:* Univ Conn, BA, 59; Yale-Norfolk Summer Art Sch, 59; Univ NMex, MA, 60; Univ Ore, sem with Ad Reinhardt, 63. *Work:* Tacoma Art Mus, Wash; Roswell Mus & Art Ctr, NMex; SDak Art Mus; Plains Art Mus, Minn; Sheldon Mem Art Gallery, Lincoln, Nebr; Benton Mus Art, Storrs, Conn; Joslyn Art Mus, Omaha, Nebr; NDak Mus Art, Grand Forks; NMex Mus Art, Santa Fe, NY; and others. *Comn:* Landwave (mural), Five Seasons Ctr, Cedar Rapids, Iowa, 77-79; Dakotaloft (painted relief), Convention Ctr, Aberdeen, SDak. *Exhib:* Solo exhibs, Sheldon Mem Art Gallery, 72, Montgomery Mus Art, 77, Plains Mus Art, 89, Civic Fine Art Ctr (with catalog), Sioux Falls, SDak, 89, NDak Mus Art, 90 & Kans State Univ, 91; Vessels and Paper, Minneapolis Art Inst, 82; Art for a New Century, SDak Art Mus, 89; Midlands Invitational, Joslyn Art Mus, 90; retrospective (with catalog), SDak Art Mus, 95 & 98; Taos, Santa Fe and Albuquerque: The City Series, Cedar Rapids Art Mus, 98; Albuquerque Mus; Ctr Contemp Art, Santa Fe, 2004; Joslyn Art Mus, Omaha, Nebr; SDak Art Mus, 2005; Washington Pavilion Arts, Sioux Falls, SDak, 2005; Circles Gallery, Columbus, Ohio, 2007; Untitled Artspace, Okla City, 2008; William Siegal Gallery, Santa Fe, NM, 2007, 2008, 2009; Anderson/O'Brien Gallery, Omaha, Neb, 2009, 2010, 2012; Synesthesia, Albuquerque Art Mus, 2010; Xhibit 6, Preston Contemporary Art Ctr, Las Cruces, NMex, 2011. *Teaching:* Prof emer, Visual Arts Dept, SDak State Univ, 80-94. *Awards:* Fel Nat Endowment Arts 76 & Art Pub Places, 78-79; U-Cross Found, residency, 90; fel, NMex Experimental Glass Wkshp, 2012. *Bibliog:* Jan Vander Marck (auth), The chromatic waves of Signe Nelson, Artscanada, 71; Mosaic: Interview with Signe Stuart (TV film), SDPTV, 77 & 86; Romantic Materialism, Untitled Artspace Okla City, Okla, 2008. *Media:* Acrylic on Canvas and Paper Constructions. *Publ:* Patient process, Faulocner Gallery (catalog), 2001; The Mag, Signe Stuart, 2001; Insight Out (catalog), CCA, 2004; Synesthesia (catalog), Albuquerque Art Mus, 2010. *Dealer:* Anderson O'Brien Gallery Omaha NE; William Siegal Gallery Santa Fe NM. *Mailing Add:* 18 Gavilan Rd Santa Fe NM 87505

NEMEC, VERNITA MCCLISH
ARTIST, CURATOR
b Painesville, Ohio, 1942. *Study:* Ohio Univ, BFA; New York Univ, MA; Naropa Inst; Performance writing with Simone Forti; Butoh movement with Noboru Kamita, Eiko, Kim Ito, Akira Kasai, Atsushi Takenouchi, Ko Murobushi, Yumiko Yoshioka & others, Japan Soc & The Cave, Williamsburg, Bkly, NY. *Work:* Savaria Mus; Group Junij; Asian Am Arts Centre; Fairfax Hosp; Franklin Furnace; Mus Mod Art, NY; NY Arts Beijing Collection; Asian Am Mus, NY. *Comn:* Jersey City Mus, 1976. *Exhib:* Solo exhibs, Fiatal Muveszek Klubja, Budapest, 80, I Stood Without Moving, 10 on 8, 84, Private Places, Women's Bldg, Los Angeles & Franklin Furnace, NY, 85 & Surface Tensions, Experimental Intermedia Found, 86, South Eastern Mo State Univ Mus, 2001, Schacknow Mus, Plantation, Fla, 2006, Fountain St Gallery, Cape Girardeau, Mo, 2006; The Autumn of Her Descent (performance), AIR Gallery, 83, NY; Snug Harbor Cult Ctr, NY, 87; Casa del Lago, Mexico City, 88; Nat Inst Health, Washington, 95; Five Cities Project, Tokyo, Japan, 99; West Chester Community Col, 99; Gallery 128, NY, 2005; Vogelfrei G, Darmstadt, Ger, 2005; Monster Truck Gallery, Dublin, Ireland, 2007; Field Emerging Artists Residency, Dance Theater Workshop, 2010; The Black Dress, Savior Faire Soho 20 Gallery, 2012; The Trail of Sighs and Whispers, Hamburg Am Main, Ger, 2012; Theater for New City, 2013. *Collection Arranged:* The Stories Exhib (cur), Henry St Abrons Art Ctr, NY, 92; Recycling From Imagination Art from Detritus Metro (catalog), Portland, Ore, 94, Kansas City, Mo, 95, Pittsburgh, Pa, 96, New York, 97-2007; Art of Detritus, Traveling Show of Art from Recycled 1994 Materials & Trash. *Pos:* Exhib coordr, Mus, A Project for Living Artists, NY, 69-70; contrib ed, Womanart, NY, 76-77; co-dir, Whitney Counterweight, NY, 77-81; dir, Floating Performance, 86-; bd dir, Found New Ideas, 86-; pres & exec dir, Artists Talk on Art, 89-97; vpres, Heresies Collective Art & Politics, 92-96; cur, Art from Detritus, 94-; dir, Viridian Artists, 98-2006; bd dir, SOHO 20 Gallery, 2007-, dir Viridian Artists, 2010-. *Teaching:* Prof art, City Univ NY, 73-79; vis artist, Univ Calif, Santa Barbara, 83; Studios in a Sch, NY, 86-87; vis artist Rutgers Univ, new Brunswick, 96; vis artist Mich State Univ, 2000; vis artist, Central Wyo College, 2005; vis artist, South Eastern Mo Univ, 2006; vis artist, Burren Coll Art, Ireland, 2007. *Awards:* Exhib Grant, Artists Space, 79, 83, 85 & 86; Jerome Found Grant, 88; Kauffman Found, 1995; IACP Grant, The Field, NYC, 1997; Travel Grant, Performance Studies Int, Mainz, Gr; 7 Years of Living Art, Linda Montano, 2004-; Earthdance Residency, The Field, 2008; Puffin Found Grant, 2007; Movement Res, Monday Night Series, 2009; Residency, N Am Cultural Lab; Kickstarter, 2012. *Bibliog:* Michael Fressola (auth), Staten Island Advance, 7/31/87; Kathleen Beckett (auth), NY Times, 3/17/91; Budapest Daily Courier, 3/93; Norma Bourde & M Garrard (eds) The Power of Feminist Art, 94; Lucy Lippard (auth), The Pink Glass Swan, 95; Linda Montano (ed), Performance Artists Talking in the 80's, 2000; Ed McCormack (auth), Gallery & Studio, 2/2004 & 11/2004; Downtown Express, 5/2005; BJ Love (ed), Feminists Who Changed America 1963-1975, 2006; The Art of 9/11, The Nation, 9/23/2003; Reckloteca Arte, Mar 2007. *Mem:* Am Asn Mus; The Field; NOW; Nat Asn Women Artists. *Media:* Installation, performance, collage. *Res:* contemporary performance and feminist art. *Specialty:* contemporary art. *Interests:* Travel & photog. *Publ:* contribr, WomanArt, 76; Auth, Unmaled, pvt pub, 78; contribr, Re-View: Artists on art, Vered Lieb, 78; Tenth assembling, Richard Kostelanetz, 80; auth, Private Thoughts, Private Places, pvt publ, 84; The Red Pagoda, Modern Haiku Zasshi Zo, 88; Downtown Viewpoint, 94; plus others. *Mailing Add:* 361 Canal St New York NY 10013

NEMSER, CINDY
ART AND THEATRE CRITIC, WRITER
b Brooklyn, NY, Mar 26, 1937. *Study:* Brooklyn Coll, with Milton Brown, BA, 58, MA, 64; Inst Fine Arts, NY Univ, with Walter Friedlander, Charles Sterling & Donald Posner, MA (art hist). *Exhib:* In Her Own Image, Fleisher Art Mem, Phila Mus Art, 74; Women's Work, Civic Ctr, Philadelphia, 74; Women's Work: Homage to Feminist Art, Tabla Rasa Gallery, Brooklyn, NY, 2007. *Pos:* Curatorial intern, NY State Coun Arts, Mus Mod Art, 67; contrib ed, Arts Mag, 71-; ed, Feminist Art J, 72-77; theatre critic, NY Law J, 90-96, Our Town, 94-95, West Side Beat, 96, Town & Village, 96, City Search, 99. *Teaching:* Guest lectr, Pratt Inst, Md Inst, RI Univ, NY Univ, Queens Mus, Brooklyn Mus, Tabla Rasa Gallery, CAA, Krasner Inst, Artists Talk on Art, 2007, Women in the Arts, 2007. *Awards:* Art Critics Fel, Nat Endowment Arts, 76; Commencement Speaker, Minneapolis Coll Art, 77; semi-finalist, L Arnold Weisberger Playwriting Competition, New Dramatists, 90; Cert hon, Veteran Feminists of Am. *Bibliog:* Judy K Collischan Van Wagner (auth), Women Shaping Art, Praeger Special Studies, NY, 84. *Mem:* Founding mem Women in the Arts; Pen Am Ctr; Poets & Writers; Women's Cacus Art (adv bd mem, 75-78); Veteran Feminist Am; Art Table; Coll Art Asn, 2007-2008. *Res:* Position of women in the art world. *Interests:* Writing memoir about art world in 60's and 70's. *Publ:* Auth, Art Talk Conversations with 12 Women Artists, Scribners, 75; Eve's Delight, Pinnacle Books, 82; Ben Cunningham Monograph, 86; Art to Defy, Reveal and Heal, MS, Vol 3, 11 & 12, 12/92; auth, Art Talk Conversations with 15 Women Artists, HarperCollins, 95. *Mailing Add:* 41 Montgomery Pl Brooklyn NY 11215

NERBURN, KENT MICHAEL
SCULPTOR, CRITIC
b Minneapolis, Minn, July 3, 1946. *Study:* Univ Minn, BA, 68; Stanford Univ, 70; Grad Theological Union, PhD (with distinction), 80; training in wood technique, Marburg, WGer, 71; life drawing with Helmut Schmitt, 74-76; stone sculpture technique, Pietrasanta, Italy, 76; anatomy study with Herbert Shrebnik, Univ Calif, Berkeley, 76. *Work:* Greek Orthodox Diocese, San Francisco; Christ United Methodist Church, St Paul, Minn; Hiroshima Peace Mem Hall, Japan. *Comn:* Wood sculpture: pvt commissions, San Francisco, 74, Taylors Falls, Minn, 75 & Big Sur, Calif, 76; wood sculpture, Westminster Benedictine Abbey, Mission, BC, 80; bronze sculpture, New World Libr, San Rafael, Calif, 85; Humane Soc Hennepin Co, Minn, 91. *Exhib:* Spring Invitational Exhib, United Theological Seminary, New Brighton, Minn, 82; Religious Art, Lutheran Brotherhood Int Hq, Minneapolis, 83; Spiritual Forms, Hennepin Avenue Methodist Church, Minneapolis, 83; Religious Artifacts, Wesley

United Methodist Church, Minneapolis, 85; Elegy-an installation in memory of victims of the holocaust, Bemidji State Univ, Bemidji, Minn, 88. *Pos:* Visual Arts Critic, St Paul Pioneer Press & Dispatch, 86, 87; sculpture writer, Art Mag, 86, 87, 88; founder & visual arts critic, Northern Arts Reviewers, Bemidji, Minn, 88; art criticism specialist, Minn Discipline - Based Art Educ Consortium, Minneapolis, 88-. *Teaching:* Instr, Grad Theological Union, 77-79 & Minneapolis Inst Arts, 85 & 86; J Paul Getty Found lect art criticism, Robbinsdale Sch Dist, 87, 88; Minn Humanities Comn visiting prof in Humanities & visual arts, Bemidji State Univ, Minn, 88. *Bibliog:* Adelheid Fischer (auth), The art of Kent Nerburn, Minn Monthly, 5/83. *Mem:* Soc Art, Religion & Cult; Soc Values in Higher Educ. *Media:* Wood. *Publ:* Auth, The age of bronze, Arts Mag, 86; Tribal masks evoke spirits of culture & Artists focus on Minnesota, St Paul Pioneer Press, 86; Peerless Perfection Polykleitos' Doryphoros, Arts Mag, 87; Henry Moore's Warrior with Shield, Arts Mag, 88; numerous reviews, critical articles & commentaries, currently

NERDRUM, ODD
PAINTER
Study: Art Acad, Oslo; study with Joseph Beuys, Dusseldorf. *Work:* Nat Gallery & Riksgalleriet, Oslo; Walker Art Ctr, Minneapolis; Hessisches Landes Mus, Darmstadt, WGer; Norsk Kultarrad, Norway. *Exhib:* Solo exhibs, Kunstnerforbundet, Oslo, 64, 67, 70, 73, 76 & 80, Gallery Tanum, Norway, 77 & 83, Martina Hamilton Gallery, NY, 84-87, Del Art Mus, Wilmington, 85 & Germans Van Eck Gallery, NY, 86, Forum Gallery, Los Angeles, 2006; Group exhibs, The Classic Tradition in Painting and Sculpture, Aldrich Mus, Conn, 85; Neo-Neoclassicism, Edith Blum Inst, Bard Col, Annandale, NY, 86; Second Sight: Biennial IV, San Francisco Mus Mod Art, San Francisco, 86; The Here and Now, Greenville Co Mus, SC, 86; Morality Tales: Hist Painting in the 1980s, Grey Art Gallery, NY Univ, 87; Univ Art Mus, Long Beach, Calif, 88; Mus Contemp Art, Chicago, 88; Madison Art Ctr, Wis, 88; Edward Thorp Gallery, NY, 88; Nelson-Atkins Mus, Kansas City, 89; Forum Gallery, NY, 2007. *Bibliog:* Donald Kuspit (auth), Odd Nerdrum: The Aging of the Immediate, Arts Mag, 9/84; Eleanor Heartney (auth), Apocalyptic visions, arcadian dreams, Art News, 1/86; John Russell (auth), rev, in: New York Times, 5/16/86; Charles Jencks (auth), Postmodernism; and other art criticism. *Mailing Add:* Forum Gallery 730 5th Ave Ste 201 New York NY 10019

NERI, MANUEL
SCULPTOR
b Sanger, Calif, Apr 12, 1930. *Study:* San Francisco City Col, 49-50; Univ Calif, Calif Coll Arts & Crafts, 52-57; Calif Sch Fine Arts, 57-59. *Hon Degrees:* San Francisco Art Inst Hon Dr, 90; Calif Coll of Arts & Crafts Hon Dr, 92; Corcoran Sch Art Hon Dr Washington, DC, 95. *Work:* Oakland Mus, Calif; San Francisco Mus Mod Art; Nat Gallery Art; Seattle Art Mus; Fine Arts Mus, San Francisco; Memphis Brooks Mus, Tenn; Portland Art Mus, Portland OR; San Jose Mus of Art, San Jose, CA; Denver Art Mus; Honolulu Acad Arts; Hirshhorn Mus; Smithsonian Inst; Whitney Mus Am Art, New York. *Comn:* Marble sculpture, State Calif Gen Serv Admin, Bateson Bldg, Sacramento, 81-82, Fed Bldg, Portland, Ore, 88 & Iowa State Univ, Ames, Iowa, 2003. *Exhib:* Solo exhibs, The Corcoran Gallery Art, traveling exhib, Washington, DC, 96-98, Manuel Neri: Artists' Books, Fine Arts Mus San Francisco, 2003, Manuel Neri: The Figure in Relief Grounds for Sculpture, Hamilton, NJ, 2006-07, Hackett Freedman Gallery, San Francisco, 2007, Relief Sculptures, Portland Art Mus, Ore, 2007, Hackett/Mill, San Francisco, 2010 & 2014, Stanford Univ Libr, 2012; Group exhibs, include Twentieth Century Am Sculpture at the White House, The White House, Washington, DC, 94-95 & 99-2000; Beat Cult and the New Am, 1950-1965, Whitney Mus Am Art, NY, 95-96; Mus Moderner Kunst, Vienna, 97; Cantor Arts Ctr, Stanford Univ, 2004 & 2010; Seattle Art Mus, 2009. *Teaching:* Instr, Calif Sch Fine Arts, 59-64; prof art, Univ Calif, Davis, 64-90. *Awards:* Guggenheim Fel, 79; Nat Endowment Arts Fel, 80; Am Acad & Inst Arts & Lett Award, 82; award of merit in sculpture San Francisco Arts Comn, 1985; Distinguished Artist award, Orange Co Mus Art, Calif, 99; Lifetime Achievement Award, Int Sculpture Ctr, NY, 2006; Bay Area Treasure, San Francisco Mus Mod Art, 2008. *Bibliog:* Thomas Albright (auth), Manuel Neri, Bay Area Figurative Art, 89; Carolyn Jones (auth), Manuel Neri Plasters, Bay Area Figurative Art, 89; Jack Cowart (auth), Manuel Neri, Corcoran Gallery, Washington, DC, 95; Bruce Nixon (auth), Manuel Neri: Artists' Books, Fine Arts Mus of San Francisco, 2003; Bruce Nixon (auth), Manuel Neri: The Figure in Relief, Grounds for Sculpture, 2006; Bruce Nixon et al, Things that Dream, Contemporary Calligraphic Artists Books, Stanford Univ Libraries, 2012. *Mem:* Nat Acad. *Media:* Marble, Plaster, Bronze. *Dealer:* Riva Yares Gallery 3625 Bishop Ln Scottsdale AZ 95251; Hackett/Mill 201 Post St San Francisco CA 94108. *Mailing Add:* c/o 115 Stonegate Rd Portola Valley CA 94028

NES, ADI
PHOTOGRAPHER
b Kyriat Gat, Israel, 1966. *Study:* Bezalel Acad Art & Design, Jerusalem, Israel, BFA (Photography), 1992; Sivan Computer Sch, Tel Aviv, Israel, Multimedia & Programming, 1996-97. *Work:* Corcoran Gallery of Art, Wash DC; Israel Mus, Jerusalem; Tel Aviv Mus Art, Tel Aviv; Jewish Mus, NY; Mus Contemporary Art, San Diego; Montreal Mus Fine Arts, Canada. *Exhib:* Solo exhibs include Mus Contemp Art, San Diego, 2002, Mus Contemp Photography, Columbia Coll, Chicago, 2002, Jack Shainman Gallery, New York, 2003, 2004, Fine Arts Mus San Francisco, 2004, Wexner Ctr Art, Columbus, Ohio, 2008, Biblical Stories, Contemporary Jewish Mus, San Francisco, Calif, 2009, Masle Pulitika Gallery, Dubrovnik, Croatia, 2010, Nat Theatre, Zageb, Croatia, 2010, Deposition, Mus Croatian Acad Sci and Arts, Zagreb, Croatia, 2010, Instituto Nazionale per la Grafica, Rome, 2010, Museo Nazionale Alinari della Fotografia, Florence, 2011, Adi Nes, Koffler Ctr for the Arts, Toronto, 2012, The Village, Galerie Praz Delavallade, Paris, 2012, Sommer Contemporary Art, Tel-Aviv, 2012, Jack Shainman Gallery, NY, 2012; Group exhibs include Capturing Reality: 19 Israeli & Palestinian Photographers, Tenn Mus, 1998; After Rabin: New Art from Israel, Jewish Mus, New York, 1998, Collective Perspectives: New Acquisitions Celebrate the Centennial, 2004; Photography in Israel: A changing View, Photofest 2000, Margolis Gallery, Houston, 2001; 100 Year of Photography, Eretz Israel, Israel Mus, Jerusalem, Israel, 2001; Aspiration: Toward the Future in the Middle East, Riffe Gallery, Columbus, Ohio, 2001; Common Ground: Discovering Community in 150 Years of Art, Corcoran Gallery, Washington, 2005; Acting Out: Invented, Melodrama in Contemp Photography, Univ Iowa Mus Art, 2005; Chaim, Life, Israel through the Photographers' Lens, Laurie M Tisch Gallery, New York, 2005; Recent Acquisitions, Fine Arts Mus San Francisco, 2006; Art of Living: Contemp Photography & Video from the Israel Mus, Contemp Jewish Mus, San Francisco, 2006; In Between Places: New Art from Israel, Vivian Horan Gallery, New York, 2006; In Detail: From the Collection of Arnie Druck, Hairfa Mus Art, 2010; Daily Treasures, Hamidrasha Art Coll, Beit Berl Academic Coll, Kalmaniya, 2010; From the Collection/on Permanent View, Israel Mus, Jerusalem, 2010; Rendering, Instituto Nazionale per la Grafica, Rome, 2010; Teror, artists respond, Dershowitz Ctr Gallery, Industry City, Brooklyn, NY, 2011; Tel-Aviv-Jaffa, Academic Coll Tel Aviv Jaffa, 2011; Human Landscape, Artist House, Tel Aviv, 2011; Face of Cain: Representations of the Others in Contemporary Art in Isreal, Ben Gurion Univ the Negev, Israel, 2012; Windows to Reality, Isreali Homages to Italian Renaissance Art, Univ Israel, Raanan, 2012; Composed: Identity, Politics, and Sex, The Jewish Mus, NY, 2012; Neuberger Mus Art, Purchase Coll, State Univ NY, Purchase, NY, 2013. *Awards:* Sandra Jacobs' Anglo-Israeli Photographic award Project Scholarship, Dept Plastic Arts, Ministry of Culture, 93; Educ, Culture, & Sports Minister's prize for Artists in the Visual Arts, 99; Nathan Gottesdiener Found Israeli Art prize, Tel Aviv Mus Art, 2000; Constantiner prize for Photography, Tel Aviv Mus Art, 2003. *Mailing Add:* Jack Shainman Gallery 513 W 20th St New York NY 10011

NES, MARGARET ISABEL
PAINTER
b Paris, France, Sept 17, 1950; US citizen. *Work:* Univ Tex Law Sch, Austin, Tex; Mt Sinai Med Ctr, NY; Mountain Bell Telephone Co, Denver; Mary Cabot Enterprises, Taos, NMex. *Exhib:* Solo exhibs, White Crane Gallery, Taos, NMex, 80, Gallery Sigala, Taos, NMex, 81-82, Varient Gallery, Taos, NMex, 85, Kyle Belding Gallery, Denver, Colo, 87-88 & E S Lawrence Gallery, Taos, NMex, 88-91; Another Great Love Affair, Denver Art Mus, 86; Right to Write, Opening Scene Gallery, Taos, NMex, 93 & 94; Indiana Collects the West, Eiteljorg Mus, Indianapolis, 94; 3rd Generation Show, Taos Art Asn-Stables Art Ctr, NMex, 94; and others. *Teaching:* Instr art, San Felipe Children's Home, San Cristobal, NMex, 82-83. *Awards:* Best in Show, Spirit in Art, Taos Spring Arts, 85; Rembrandt Pastel Award, Md Pastel Soc Exhib, 89; Best of Show, Taos Invites Taos, 93. *Bibliog:* Sylvia Paine (auth), Secret lives of buildings, US Art Mag, 10/89; Simone Ellis (auth), Sante Fe Art, Random House, 93; Martha Longley (auth), Exploring the realm of the unknown, Focus Mag, 9/93. *Media:* Pastels, Monotype. *Dealer:* Edith Lambert Gallery Santa Fe NM; Collins-Pettit Gallery Taos NM. *Mailing Add:* c/o Michael McCormick Gallery 106-C Paseo del Puerto Norte Taos NM 87571

NESBITT, ILSE BUCHERT
PRINTMAKER, ILLUSTRATOR
b Frankfurt-Main, Ger, Sept 6, 1932. *Study:* Univ Frankfurt, 53-54; Art Acad Hamburg, 54-56, with Richard von Sichowsky, 57-59; Art Acad Berlin, 56-57. *Work:* Deutsche Staatsbibliothek, Leipzig, Ger; Klingspor Mus, Offenbach, Ger; Hunt Botanical Libr, Pittsburgh; Houghton Libr, Harvard Univ, Cambridge, Mass; Newberry Libr, Chicago; State & Univ Libr, Hamburg, Ger; and others. *Comn:* Woodblock prints, Redwood Libr, Salve Regina Univ, Newport, RI, 90 & 2002. *Exhib:* Int Book Exhib, Leipzig, Ger, 65 & 71; 20th Century Botanical Illust, Hunt Botanical Libr, Pittsburgh, Pa, 68-69; solo exhibs, Brown Univ Libr, Providence, 83, Rutgers Univ Libr, New Brunswick, NJ, 84, State & Univ Libr, Hamburg, Ger, 88, Galerie Wolf-Buetow, Oberursel, Ger, 91 & 95 & Brown Univ Libr, Providence, RI, 96 & 2006; NE Fine Arts Inst, Boston, Mass, 93; Reepschlagerhaus, Wedel, Ger, 98 & 2006; Newport Art Mus, 2007; Pacific Grove, Calif, 2008, 2010. *Pos:* Owner, designer, illusr & printer, Third & Elm Press, Newport, RI, 65-. *Teaching:* Asst, typography & book design, RI Sch Design, Providence, 60-65. *Awards:* Hon Mention, Int Book Exhib, Leipzig, Ger Democratic Repub, 65, Bronze Medal, 71; First Prize, Print, Newport Art Mus, RI, 83. *Bibliog:* Ronald Salter (auth), Ilse Buchert Nesbitt-eine deutsche Buchkuenstlerin in den USA, Illus, 63 & 97; William Flanagan (auth), The Third and Elm Press, Yankee Mag, 77; Walter Plata (auth), The Third and Elm Press, Philobiblon Quart, 85. *Mem:* Boston Soc Printers; Newport Art Asn & Mus. *Media:* Woodcut; Book Design. *Interests:* Gardening. *Publ:* Coauth & illusr, Weathercocks and Weathercreatures, 70, illusr, The Wren and the Bear, 71, coauth & illusr, Sandy's Newport, 75, ed & illusr, The Best Tailor in the World, 83, auth & illusr, My Garden, 88, Third & Elm Press; ed & illusr, Steigendes, Neigendes Leben, 2000; illusr, Captured Views, 2006. *Dealer:* The Third & Elm Press; Vamp & Tramp Booksellers LLC. *Mailing Add:* c/o Third & Elm Press 29 Elm St Newport RI 02840

NESSIM, BARBARA
PAINTER, COLLAGE ARTIST
b Bronx, NY, Mar 30, 1939. *Study:* Pratt Inst, BFA. *Work:* Smithsonian Inst, Wash; World Trade Ctr, NY; Libr Cong, Washington, DC; Victoria & Albert Mus, London; Norman Rockwell Mus Stockbridge, Mass. *Comn:* Digital paintings, 600 Wash St Bldg lobby, Centria Bldg lobby & 18 W 48th St Bldg, New York; Eventi Hotel, New York. *Exhib:* Solo exhibs, Ram 400, Colo State Univ, Ft Collins, Colo, 92, Ariz State Univ, Tempe, 93, Adams Landing Art Ctr, Cincinnati, Ohio, 94, Random Access Memories, Centro Colombo Americano, Bogota, Colombia, 95, Visual Solutions, Norman Rockwell Mus, Stockbridge, Mass, 99-, Black Truths/White Lies, Bitforms Gallery, Chelsea, New York, 2003-, Transitions, Sienna Gallery, Lenox, Mass, 2007 & The Model Project, 2009, The Model Proj, DFN Gallery, 2009, Chronicles of Beauty, Conde Nast, New York, 2010, Signs, Signals & Satin Dolls, Westfield, Mass, 2010, Barbara Nessim, Victoria and Albert Mus, 2013; group exhibs, Inaugural Show, Bitforms Gallery, Chelsea, NY, 2001, A Teachers Legacy, Babbage Art Gallery Univ Conn, 2002-2003 Int Women Designers Exhib, Seoul Arts Ctr, Korea, 2003 & The

Transparent Network, Somarts Gallery, 2004. *Teaching:* adj prof visual concepts, Sch Visual Arts, NY, 67-87, adj prof computer art, 87-92; adj prof, Pratt Inst, Brooklyn, NY, 74-84; chairperson illus dept, Parsons The New Sch for Design, NY, 92-2004, prof Visual Concepts, Painting & Drawing, 2004-2006. *Awards:* Siggraph Grant, 90. *Bibliog:* Elinor Craig (auth), Barbara Nessim, Macweek, 5/88; Carol Olsen Day (auth), The art of Barbara Nessim, PC Computing, 10/88. *Mem:* Nat Computer Graphics Asn (bd mem & treas, Arts Sect, 87-); Graphic Artists Guild (treas, 88-); Siggraph; Art Dirs Club; Soc Illustrators; AIGA. *Media:* Digital paintings & installation; Watercolor, Etching. *Interests:* Salsa Dancing. *Publ:* Auth, Barbara Nessim Sketchbook, pvt publ, 75; contribr, Living with Art, Alfred A Knopf, 87; Digital Visions, 87 & Varieties of Visual Experience, 87, Harry Abrams; Barbara Nessim: An Artful Life, Abrams Pub, 2013. *Dealer:* Sienna Gallery Lenox Ma; Sienna Patti Contemporary Lenox Ma; DFN Gallery NYC. *Mailing Add:* 1 Morton Sq Loft 6AW New York NY 10014

NESTOR, LULA B
PAINTER, ADMINISTRATOR

b Weirton, WVa. *Study:* WVa Univ, 55-56; West Liberty State Col, WVa, BAE; Eastern Mich Univ, MA (art), 73. *Work:* Pittsburgh Plate & Glass Co; Mt Lebonen Greek Orthodox Church, Pittsburgh; WVa Univ; Mich Educ Asn, State Collection Art; Ins Com & Galleries, Michalsons Gallery, Washington, DC. *Exhib:* Butler Inst Art, Butler Mus, Youngstown, Ohio, 73 & 75; Nat Soc Painter in Casien, Nat Gallery of Acad, NY, 76; Audubon Artist 35th Ann Exhib, Nat Acad Gallery, NY, 76; Nat Watercolor Soc 57th Ann, Calif State Univ, 77; solo exhibs, Univ Mich, 75, Univ WVa, Morgantown, 75, Constantine Grimaldis Gallery, 80 & 81 & Bowling Green State Univ, Ohio, 83; Univ Mich, 91. *Pos:* Dir, Hartland Regional Fine Arts Festival, 68-77; past pres & trustee mem, Hartland Art Show, Mich. *Teaching:* Instr, Richie Jr High Sch, Wheeling, WVa, 57-58, Elida High Sch, Elida, Ohio, 58-59 & South Lima Jr High Sch, Lima, Ohio, 60-62; art instr & dir art dept, Hartland High Sch, Mich, 68-81; instr adult educ classes, Hartland Consolidated Schs. *Awards:* First Place, Nat Pittsburgh Watercolor Aqueous Open Competition, 74 & 76; Int Artist in Watercolor Competition, London, 82; Award, Nat Watercolor Soc Ann, 82. *Mem:* Mich Watercolor Soc (mem bd); Midwest Watercolor Asn, Minn; Nat Watercolor Soc; Watercolor USA Honor Soc. *Media:* Watercolor; Casein. *Mailing Add:* 9865 Edward Dr Brighton MI 48116

NETTLER, LYDIA KANN
PAINTER

b New York, NY, Aug 20, 1947. *Study:* UCLA, BA, 68; Sch Social Work, MSW, 75; Univ Mass, Amherst, 76-78; Sch Mus Fine Arts, Boston, 78-79. *Work:* Sterling Drug Co, Philadelphia, Pa; Melcher Newman Collection; Meeropol Collection; Nigrosh Collection. *Comn:* paintings, Northampton Sch System, Mass, 97 & 98; mural, Hampshire City Long Term Care, Northampton, Mass, 99. *Exhib:* Drawing Show, Boston Ctr for Arts, 88, 89; solo exhibs, Hillyer Gallery, Smith Col, Northampton, Mass, 88, Sarah Doyle Gallery, Brown Univ, Providence, RI, 92 & Student Union Gallery, Univ Mass, Amherst, 97; River Passage, Springfield Mus Fine Arts, Mass, 91; On the Verge, Equis Gallery, Boston, 93; Collaboration, Albany Inst Art & Hist, 94; Art at City Hall, Northampton, Mass, 1997; Over the Edge Installation, Univ Mass, 1998; Break Away Installation, Northampton Center for the Arts, 2006; Oils, Oxbow Gallery, Northampton, Mass, 2006, 2007; Work in Progress, Oxbow Gallery, 2007; Circling, An Environ Installation, Towne Art Gallery, Wheelock Coll, Boston, 2008; 1st graft, Oxbow Gallery, Northampton, Mass, 2010; Oxbow Gallery, Northampton, Mass, 2012; Embedded Legacies Installation, Brandeis Univ, WSRC Gallery, 2012; The Art of Trees, Yale Univ, 2012; Montserrat Coll Art, Beverly, Mass, 2013. *Awards:* First prize, Women's Art Show, Mass, 77; Award, Greenfield Comn Coll Show, 87 & 89; Finalist, Amherst Pub Art Competition, 90; Finalist, Mass Cult Comn Artist Grant, 2000; Grant & residency, Vermont Studio Ctr, 2003; Artist Residency, Am Acad Rome, 2005; Artist residency, Julia & David White Artist Colony, 2008; Artist Residency, CAMAC, France, 2012. *Bibliog:* rev, Art New England, Boston Globe. *Media:* Oil, Charcoal. *Collection:* Private Collections. *Mailing Add:* 66 Washington Ave Northampton MA 01060

NETZER, NANCY
MUSEUM DIRECTOR, EDUCATOR

b Pittsburgh, Pa, Jul 25, 1951. *Study:* Harvard Univ, MA, 78, PhD, 86. *Hon Degrees:* Univ Ulster, N Ireland, LittD (hon), 2000. *Pos:* Asst cur, Mus Fine Arts, Boston, 82-90; prof fine arts, Boston Coll, 90-; dir, McMullen Mus Art, 90-; board advs, Int Ctr Medieval Art, New York, 90-94, dir, 95-, Fragmented Devotion, 2000, Secular/Sacred, 2006; dir, Mass Found for the Humanities, 2003-. *Mem:* Soc Antiquaries London; St Botolph club; CAA; ICMA; Medieval Acad. *Publ:* Auth, Medieval Objects in the Mus of Fine Arts, 86, Vol II, 91, Cultural Interplay in the Eighth Century, 94 & Memory and the Middle Ages, 95. *Mailing Add:* McMullen Mus Devlin Hall #423 140 Commonwealth Ave Chestnut Hill MA 02467-3800

NEUMAN, ROBERT S
PAINTER

b Kellogg, Idaho, Sept 9, 1926. *Study:* Calif Coll Arts & Crafts; Calif Sch Fine Arts, BAA, 50, MFA, 51; Univ Idaho, 44 & 46; studied with Max Beckman, Mills Coll, James Budd Dixon & Hassel Smith, San Francisco Sch Fine Arts, Willi Baumeister, Statliche der Akademie der Bildenden Kunste, Stuttgart, Ger. *Work:* San Francisco Mus Art; Boston Mus Fine Arts; Fogg Mus Art, Harvard Univ; Mus Mod Art, NY; Farnsworth Mus, Rockland, Maine; Carrier Mus Art, Manchester, NH; and many others. *Exhib:* San Francisco Mus Art, 50; Oakland Mus Art, 50; solo exhibs, Gumps Gallery, San Francisco, 51 & 52, Galleria del Cavallino, Venice, Italy, 60, Allan Stone Gallery, NY, 72, Wingspread Gallery, Northeast Harbor, Maine, 80, Eliza Spenser Gallery, Newton, Mass, 91 & Alhambra Paintings, Lahey Clinic North, Peabody, Mass, 94; De Cordova & Dana Mus, 60-65; New Eng Art Today, 63 & 65; Allan Stone Gallery, NY, 63; Mus Mod Art, 64; Pace Gallery, Boston, 65; Sunne Savage Gallery, Boston, 79; Allan Stone Gallery, NY, 2006; Abbe Mus, Bar Harbor, ME; Fogg Art Mus, Harvard Univ; Wheaton Coll, Norton, Mass, 2007; Paintings, Prints, and Drawings 1949-1959, Sunne Savage Gallery, Winchester, Mass, 2008; Inspiration Maine, Coll of the Atlantic, Bar Harbor, ME, 2009; Works on Paper, Redfield Gallery, Northeast Harbor, ME, 2011; Ship to Paradise, Hecksher Mus Art, Huntington, NY, 2012, Bater Coll Mus Art, Lewiston, Me, 2013. *Teaching:* Fac, San Francisco Sch Fine Arts, Calif Coll Arts & Crafts, 52, Harvard Univ, RI Sch Design & Brown Univ; instr, State Univ NY, New Paltz, 55-57, Mass Coll Art, Boston, 57- & Brown Univ, 61-63 & Carpenter Ctr Visual Arts, Harvard Univ, 63-72; prof art & chmn art dept, Keene State Coll, NH, 72-90; guest lectr, Simmons Coll, Boston, 65 & Univ Idaho, 69. *Awards:* Fulbright Grant, 53-54; Prize, San Francisco Mus Art; Guggenheim Fel, 56-57; Bender Grant-in-Aid, San Francisco Art Asn, 1952. *Media:* Oils, Watercolor, Lithographs, Etchings, Drawing. *Specialty:* 20th Century Am & European Art. *Publ:* Auth, Artists Book: Ship of Fools/Ship to Paradise, High Loft Press, Seal Harbor, Maine. *Dealer:* Allan Stone Gallery New York NY; Sunne Sauage Gallery Winchester MA. *Mailing Add:* 135 Cambridge St Winchester MA 01890

NEUMANN, HUBERT
COLLECTOR

b Chicago. *Study:* Univ Chicago. *Pos:* investor. *Awards:* Named on of Top 200 Collectors, ARTnews mag, 2009-11. *Collection:* Contemporary art, especially young artists

NEUSTEIN, JOSHUA
PAINTER, CONCEPTUAL ARTIST

b Danzig, Poland, Oct 16, 1940; US citizen. *Study:* City Coll New York, 57-61, BA, 61; Art Students League, 59-61; Pratt Inst, Brooklyn, NY, 60-63. *Work:* Mus Mod Art, Whitney Mus Am Art, NY; Jerusalem Mus of Israel; Tel Aviv Mus of Art, Israel; Louisiana Mus, Copenhagen, Denmark; Metropolitan Mus Art; Albright-Knox Art Gallery, Buffalo, NY. *Exhib:* Travel Art, Mus Mod Art, Oxford, Eng, 71; Documenta V, Kassel, Ger, 72; Photog in Art Camden Art Ctr, London, 72; Photog Triennale, Israel Mus, Jerusalem, 76; Solo exhib, Mus Art, Wocester, Mass, 75 & Neutein-Ten Yrs, Tel Aviv Mus, Israel; With Paper About Paper, Albright-Knox Gallery, Buffalo, 80; Henri Onstad Art Ctr (catalog), Norway, 81; and many other solo & group exhibs. *Awards:* Willem Sandberg Prize, Jerusalem, 74; Guggenheim Fel, 87. *Bibliog:* R Pincus-Witten (auth), Sons of Light, 9/75, Six propositions, 12/75 & Neustein papers, 10/77, Arts Mag; Steven Kasher (auth), The substance of paper, 3/78 & Seven Artists of Israel, summer 79, Artforum Mag; Joseph Masheck (auth), Nothing not nothing something, Artforum Mag, 11/79 & Marking & Disclosure, H Johnson Mus, 83; Donald Kuspit (auth), Art with a moral mission, Flash Art, 87; Robert Morgan (auth), Neustein, Flash Art, 88; Arthur C Danto (auth), Unnatural Wonders: Essays from the Gap Between Art and Life, Two Installations by Joshua Neustein, p. 303, 9/2007; Martin Jay (auth), Drawing in the Middle Voice: Joshua Neustein and the Search for Experience; and many others. *Media:* Environment, Photo. *Res:* Art criticism. *Dealer:* Mary Boone 420 W Broadway New York NY 10012; B Urdang 23 E 74th St New York NY 10021. *Mailing Add:* 7 Mercer St New York NY 10013-2548

NEVIA, JOSEPH SHEPPERD ROGERS
PAINTER

b Washington, DC. *Study:* Longfellow Sch with Theodora Kane and Berthold Schmutzart, 63; Greensboro Col, with Irene Cullis and Callie Braswell, BA, 67; Univ NC, Greensboro, with Will Insley, Peter Agostini, Walter Barker, Andrew Martin, Gilbert Carpenter & Stephen Antonagis, MFA, 69. *Work:* Maryland Collection, Univ Md. *Comn:* Mural, Bishop O'Connell Sch, Arlington, Va, 79; also pvt comns. *Exhib:* Artists of the 80's, Dallas, Tex, 85; Shelters '85, Zenith Gallery, Wash, DC, 85; The Art of Fantasy, Artspace, Raleigh, NC, 87; The Artful Chair, Target Gallery, Alexandria, Va, 90; Dream House, Peninsula Fine Arts Ctr, Newport News, Va, 90; Avien of Counter Vail, 2006; Crossing, Herden, Va, 2010; Window Display, DC City, 2010; Hyattsville Artist Alliance Showings, Brentwood Art Ctr, 2011; Emerging from Hyattsville, Lustin Ctr, 2011; Monkey Mural, Toni Ray Collection, Annapolis, 2011; Warmth, Three Oaks Ctr, Leonardtown, MD, 2011; WSSE Building, Laurel, Md, 2012; PGPCC, 2012; DC Art, HCAA 13, Hyatts, MD. *Pos:* Dir, Garfinckle's Art Gallery, Washington, DC, 72-74, Porcelaine Galleries, Baltimore, 74-75. *Teaching:* Instr art, Prince George Co Bd Educ, Upper Marlboro, Md, 69-70, Corcoran Sch Art & Col Inst Art, Columbia, Md, 70-71. *Bibliog:* Klim Caviness (auth), Renaissance and Joe Rogers, Alexandria Port Packet, Va, 84; Doris Miller (interviewer), Artist Nevia, Channel 10 Cable Station, Alexandria, Va, 84; Ann M Augherton (auth), Nevia's shadow boxes, Alexandria Gazette, Va, 84; Nevia's Historic Landover Home, Gazette News, 6/12/2008; Daniel Leaderman (auth), Hyattsville Spring Gazette, 3/2011. *Mem:* Hyattsville Artists Alliance. *Media:* Oil, Acrylic, Collage. *Dealer:* The Frame Factory 212 Dominion Rd Vienna VA; Picasso Gallery Wisc Ave DC; The Jail House Gallery, Milton, Del. *Mailing Add:* Beall's Pleasure PO Box 1268 Hyattsville MD 20785

NEWBEGIN, KATHERINE
PHOTOGRAPHER

b Portland, Ore, 1976. *Study:* Yale Univ, BA, 1999; Hunter Coll, CUNY, MFA, 2005. *Exhib:* Umgebung Flache Raum, Galerie Open, Berlin, 2006; Utopian Mirage, vassar Coll, New York, 2007; Art for AID, JCI Sotheby's, Amsterdam; Fractions of Sight, Rockland Ctr for the Arts, NY, 2009; Pin Auction, Pinakothek Mod Mus, Munich, 2009. *Awards:* Graf Travel Grant, Hunter Coll, 2004; Yaddo Artist Fel, 2008; DAAD Fel, Berlin, 2008; Louis Comfort Tiffany Found Grant, 2009

NEWBERG, DEBORAH
PAINTER, PRINTMAKER

b New York, NY, June 25, 1961. *Study:* Oberlin Coll, BA, 83; Univ NMex, 87. *Work:* State NMex Transportation Dept; Bernalillo Co Libr, Wyoming Br, Albuquerque, NMex; La Familia Clinic, Santa Fe, NMex. *Exhib:* SW 96 Biennial, Mus Fine Arts, Santa Fe, 96; solo exhib, Mus of the Southwest, Midland, Tex, 2000. *Teaching:* Adj faculty, Santa Fe Community Coll. *Awards:* Fuller Lodge Art Ctr Second Place Award, Que Pasa?, Art in NMex, 92. *Media:* Oil, Monotypes. *Mailing Add:* PO Box 33184 Santa Fe NM 87594

NEWCOMB, LYNN
SCULPTOR, PRINTMAKER
Work: Boston Pub Libr; Philadelphia Mus Art; Fogg Art Mus; New York Pub Libr; Zimmerli Art Mus. *Comn:* Accounting bldg, Univ Fla, Gainesville, 2003; Williston N rest area sculpture, State of Vt, 2004. *Exhib:* San Diego Art Inst, 1994; Hunterdon Art Ctr, 1995; The Graphic Proof: A Century of Print Collecting, Newark Pub Libr, NJ, 1997; solo exhibs, Wood Art Gallery, Vt Coll, 1997, Lyndon State Coll, Vt, 2001, ARt Union of Hungarian Lithographers & Etchers, 2006; Brattleboro Mus, Vt, 2003; Ten Vt Women, Fleming Mus, Burlington, 2003; Artist Resource Trust Fels, Simmons Coll, 2006; Asn Atelier de Gravure Bo Halbirk, Paris, 2007; Gallery Korea, Korean Cult Coun, New York, 2008. *Awards:* Purchase Award, Philadelphia Print Club, 1978; Pollock-Krasner Found Grant, 1992, 2008; Artist Develop Grant, Vt Arts Coun, 1993, 1996, 2000, 2006; New England Found for the Arts Grant, 1996. *Dealer:* K Caraccio Printmaking Studio 315 W 39th St Rm 505 New York NY 10018

NEWHOUSE, VICTORIA & SAMUEL I, JR
COLLECTOR
b 1928; Victoria: b Jan 27, 1938. *Pos:* Pub, Vogue mag, 1964; chmn, Condé Nast Publs Inc, New York, 1975-; chmn bd dir & chief exec officer, Advance Publs Inc, Staten Island, NY, 1979-. *Awards:* Named one of Top 200 Collectors, ARTnews mag, 2004-13; named one of Forbes' Richest Americans, 1999- & World's Richest People, 1999-; Henry J Fisher Award, Mag Pub Asn, 1985. *Collection:* Modern and contemporary art. *Mailing Add:* 950 Fingerboard Rd Staten Island NY 10305

NEWICK, CRAIG D
ARCHITECT
b Feb 14, 1960. *Study:* Lehigh Univ, Bethlehem, Pa, BA, 82; Yale Univ, New Haven, Conn, MArch, 87. *Comn:* Gallery Jazz, design for art gallery, New Haven, 85-86; interior renovation & exterior rehab, residence, 85-88; exhib display cabinet, Artspace, Inc, New Haven, 87; interior renovation & addition, residence, Florham Park, NJ, 88; Kroes Residence, 2000; Gallery & artists' studios, Eyebeam Atelier, NY, 2000; Harder & Co residence and video editing studio, 2002; Hamden Arts Commn Performance Space. *Exhib:* Home/Less: A Visual Dialogue, Artspace, New Haven, Conn, 92; The New Eng Holocaust Mem Competition: An Am Process, Gund Gallery Harvard Grad Sch Design, Cambridge, Mass, 92; Small Works Invitational, Artspace, New Haven, Conn, 93; The Visual Stage: Art in and Around the Theater, John Slade Ely House, 94; The African Burial Ground Memorial Competition, Munic Art Soc, NY, 94; Out of Bounds: Artists' Books, Creative Arts Workshop, New Haven, Conn, 94; and many others. *Pos:* Designer/draftsman, The Archit studio, Easton, Pa, 81 & 83-84 & 86; Centerbrook Architects, 86; Allan Dehar & Assoc, 88-90; partner, Lindroth & Newick, 88-; designer, Cesar Pelli & Assocs, 92; project archit, Tai Soo Kim Partners, 95-; prin, Newick Architects, 2001-. *Teaching:* Vis critic basic design, RI Sch Design, 88; vis critic archit design, Wesleyan Univ, 90-93; instr, drawing course in perspective, Creative Arts Workshop, New Haven, Conn, 91-92; vis critic archit design, Lehigh Univ, 93; vis critic, Yale, 2000-2011. *Awards:* New Eng Found Arts/Nat Endowment Arts, Fel in Sculpture, 93; Second Place, African Burial Ground Mem Competition, Munic Art Soc, NY, 94; First Prize, Out of Bounds, Artists' Books, 94; Hon Mention, Pub Space in the New Am City/Atlanta 1996 Design Competition, 94; Conn Comn Arts, Fel in Sculpture, 98; Design Award, AIA Conn, 2000, 2010, 2011; AIA Nat Award, 2006; Alice Washburn award, 2010. *Bibliog:* Annual Design Review, ID Int Design Mag, 7-8/90, 7-8/91 & 7-8/93; Reports, Storefront for Art & Archit, New York, summer, 91; AETNA Photography Series 4, catalog, 9/91. *Mem:* Am Inst Architects; Conn Soc Architects. *Mailing Add:* 219 Livingston St New Haven CT 06511-2209

NEWKIRK, KORI
ASSEMBLAGE ARTIST
b Bronx, NY, 1970. *Study:* Sch Art Inst Chicago, BFA, 1993; Univ Calif, Irvine, MFA, 1997. *Work:* The World and the Way Things Are, 2001; Glint, 2005. *Exhib:* Solo exhibs include BLOWOUT, Fine Arts Gallery, Univ Calif, Irvine, 1997, Higher Standard, Project Room, Rosamund Felsen Gallery, Santa Monica, Calif, 1998, Legacy, Deep River, LA, Calif, 1999, Midnight Son, Rosamund Felsen Gallery, Santa Monica, 1999, To See It All, Henry Art Gallery, Seattle, 2003, Bodybuilder & Sportsman Gallery, Chicago, 2004, Locust Projects, Miami, Fla, 2005, Art Gallery of Ontario, Toronto, Canada, 2005, The Project, New York, 2006, Studio Mus Harlem, New York, 2007, Pasadena Mus Calif Art, 2007; group exhibs include Custom Complex, Helen Lindhurst Gallery, Univ Southern Calif, 1995; Just a Taste, Fine Arts Gallery, Univ Calif, Irvine, 1996; Five Emerging Black Artists, Dan Bernier Gallery, Santa Monica, 1997; Black is a Verb! WORKS, San Jose, Calif, 1997; The Comestible Compost, Gallery 207 & Pavilion's, West Hollywood, Calif, 1998; Homeless in Los Angeles, The Mota Gallery, London, 1999; Frest Cut Afros, Watts Towers Arts Ctr, Los Angeles, 2000; Capital Art, Track 16 Gallery, Calif, 2001; Whippersnapper III, Vedanta Gallery, Chicago, 2001; Drive By, Reynolds Gallery, Richmond, Va, 2002; Loop, Gallery 400, Chicago, 2002; Hair Stories, Scottsdale Mus Contemp Art, Ariz; Only Skin Deep, Int Ctr Photography, NY, 2003; Great White, Ctr Curitorial Studies, Bard Col, NY, 2004; Eye of the Needle, Roberts & Tilton Gallery, Calif, 2004; Southern Exposure, Mus Contemp Art, San Diego, 2005; Biennial, Whitney Mus Am Art, NY, 2006; Dakar Biennial, Senegal, 2006; Black Alphabet, Zacheta Nat Gallery Art, Warsaw, 2006; Alien Nation, Inst Contemp Arts, London, 2006; Viewfinder, Henry Art Gallery, Seattle, 2007; Out of Nothing, 4 Walls, Austin, Tex, 2007; Material for the Making, Elizabeth Dee Gallery, New York, 2007. *Teaching:* Artist-in-residence, Skowhegan Sch Painting and Sculpture, Maine, 1997. *Awards:* William H Johnson Prize, 2004; Louis Comfort Tiffany Found Grant, 2008

NEWMAN, ELIZABETH H
SCULPTOR
Study: Mich State Univ, BFA, 78; Sch Art Inst Chicago, MFA, 84. *Exhib:* One-woman shows, Marianne Deson Gallery, Chicago, 86, Galerie Eric Franck, Geneva, Switz, 89, Galerie Lelong, NY, 92, 95 & 98, Inst Contemp Art, Boston, Mass, Mus Contemp Art, Chicago, Ill, 92, San Diego State Univ Art Gallery, 95, Elizabeth Leach Gallery, Portland, Ore, 96, Zolla Lieberman Gallery, Chicago, 97, Van Every Smith Galleries, Davidson, NC, 98 & Galerie Lelong, New York City, 99; Resonance, Gibson Art Gallery, State Univ NY, 95; Art in Chicago: 1945-1995, Mus Contemp Art, Chicago, 96; Food for Thought, Kohler Arts Ctr, Sheboygan, Wis, 96; No Small Feat: Investigations of the Shoe in Contemp Art, Rhona Hoffman Gallery, Chicago, 97; Roots and Reeds: The Amazing Grace of the Gullah People, Bertha & Karl Leubsdorf Gallery, Hunter Col, NY, 98; Domestic Pleasures, Galerie Lelong, NY, 99; Welcome, Wave Hill, Bronx, NY, 2000; Almost Warm and Fuzzy: Childhood and Contemp Art (traveling exhib), Des Moines Art Ctr, Iowa, 99, Tacoma Art Mus, Washington, 2000, Scottsdale Mus of Contemp Art, Ariz, 2000, PS 1 Contemp Art Ctr, Long Island City, NY, 2001, Fundacio la Ciaxa, Barcelona, Spain, 2001. *Awards:* Nat Endowment Arts, 88; Ill Art Coun, 86, 87 & 89. *Bibliog:* Roberta Smith (auth), Also of note, NY Times, 3/17/95; Martha McWilliams (auth), Object lessions, Washington City Paper, 8/11/95; Robert L Pincus (auth), Childhood regained, San Diego Tribune, 11/30/95

NEWMAN, JOHN
SCULPTOR, DRAFTSMAN
b Flushing, NY, May 31, 1952. *Study:* Independent Study Prog, Whitney Mus Am Art, 72; Oberlin Col, BA, 73; Sch Art, Yale Univ, MFA, 75. *Work:* Metrop Mus Art, Mus Modern Art, Whitney Mus Am Art, NY; Mus Fine Arts, Boston; Art Inst Chicago. *Comn:* Large scale sculpture-installation, City Univ New York, 77; large scale wall-relief, Northrop Industs, Los Angeles, 84; large scale outdoor sculpture, Dept Transportation, Washington, 84; large scale outdoor sculpture, Gen Mills Outdoor Sculpture Park, Minneapolis, 89; large scale outdoor sculpture, Storm King Art Ctr, Mountainville, NY, 89. *Exhib:* Sculpture: Inside/Outside, Walker Art Ctr, Minneapolis, 88; Four Americans: Aspects of Current Sculpture, Brooklyn Mus, 89; Art in place, Whitney Mus Am Art, NY, 89; The Unique Print: 70s into 80s, Mus Fine Arts, Boston, 90; Singular and Plural, Recent Accessions: Drawing and Prints 1945-1991, Mus Fine Arts, Houston, 92; solo exhib, Ft Wayne Mus Art, 93; New Acquisitions, NY Pub Libr, 94; Ideas and Objects: Selected Drawings and Sculptures from the Permanent Collection, Whitney Mus Am Art, 94. *Teaching:* Asst prof fine art, Grad Prog, Queens Col, City Univ New York, 80-82 & Sarah Lawrence Col, Bronxville, NY, 81-84; dir grad studies sculpture, Yale Sch Art, New Haven, 92-. *Awards:* Nat Endowment Arts Grant, 86; New York Found Arts Grant, 90; John S Guggenheim Found Fel, 92; Pollock-Krasner Found Grant, 2008; Joan Mitchell Found Grant, 2009; Louis Comfort Tiffany Found Grant, 2009. *Bibliog:* Nancy Princenthal (auth), Beyond the Zero: John Newman's Recent Prints, Drawings & Sculpture, Mt Kisco: Tyler Graphics, Ltd, 90; Holland Cotter (auth), John Newman, New York Times, 92; Klaus Kertess, Angela Fritz & Emily Kass (auths), John Newman: Sculpture and Works on Paper (exhib catalog), Ft Wayne Mus Art, 93. *Mem:* Coll Art Asn. *Media:* All Media. *Mailing Add:* 59 Franklin St New York NY 10013

NEWMAN, LAURA
PAINTER
Study: Cooper Union Sch Art, BFA, 1978; Calif Inst Arts, 1981; Nova Scotia Coll Art & Design Grad Prog, 1981. *Exhib:* Solo exhibs include Victoria Munroe Gallery, New York, 1987 & 1989, Tenri Gallery, New York, 1996, Vassar Coll, Poughkeepsie, NY, 2000, Bellwether Gallery, Brooklyn, 2002 & Randolph-Macon Coll, Ashland, Va, 2004; group exhibs include Am Acad & Inst Arts & Letters, 1992; Temporarily Possessed, New Mus, New York, 1995; Imaginary Beings, Exit Art, New York, 1995; Elizabeth Harris Gallery, New York, 1997; Current Undercurrent: Working in Brooklyn, Brooklyn Mus, 1998; Rutgers Univ, New Brunswick, NJ, 1999; All Drawing, Univ Arts, Philadelphia, 2002; Art on Paper, Weatherspoon Art Mus, Greensboro, NC, 2002; Celestial, The Workspace, New York, 2003; Galapagos Art Space, Brooklyn, 2004; Ann Invitational Exhib Contemp Am Art, Nat Acad Mus, New York, 2008. *Teaching:* Instr, Nova Scotia Coll Art & Design, Halifax, 1989-90; adj instr, Cooper Union, New York, 1990-92; asst prof, Yale Univ Sch Art, 1993-97 & Yale Univ Summer Sch at Norfolk, 1996 & 1997; adj asst prof, RI Sch Design, 1998; asst prof, Brown Univ, 1998-99; vis asst prof, State Univ NY, Purchase, 1998 & Pratt Inst, Brooklyn, 1999-2000; asst prof, Vassar Coll, Poughkeepsie, NY, 1998-2005. *Awards:* Rome Prize Fel, Am Acad in Rome, 1980; John Simon Guggenheim Fel, 1981; Rosenthal Found Award, Am Acad Arts & Letters, 1992; NY Found Arts Fel, 1996; Vassar Coll Res Round Award, 2001 & 2004

NEWMAN, LIBBY
PAINTER, PRINTMAKER
b Rockland, Del. *Study:* Univ Arts, BFA. *Work:* Philadelphia Mus Art; Israel Mus, Jerusalem; Mus Mod Art, Buenos Aires, Argentina; Nat Mus Women Arts, Washington, DC; Paper Mus, Tokyo, Japan; Nat Mus Belgrade; Tianjin Fine Art Coll, China; Indus Valley Sch Art & Arch, Karachi, Pakistan; US Info Agy, S Am; US Libr of Congress, DC; Alexandrina Libr, Egypt; King St Stephen Mus, Hungary; Contemp Mus Small Artists Books, Baku, Azerbaijan; and numerous other pub, pvt & corp collections. *Comn:* Univ Pa Law Sch; Buchanan and Ingersoll Law Office; Dorfman Med Office; Newman Cosmetic Surgery Ctr. *Exhib:* Nat Watercolor & Drawing Exhib, Pa Acad Fine Arts, 64; Eastern Cent Drawing Exhib, Philadelphia Mus Art, 65; solo exhibs, Mangel Gallery, Philadelphia, 70-2004 & Philadelphia Art Alliance, 81; Twenty-Five Pa Women Artists, Southern Alleghenies Mus Art, Loretto, Pa, 79; Am Colorprint Soc Exhib, 79; Gov Thornburgh's Inaugural Art Comt--Cur of Contemp Sculpture Exhib, 79; Syria, Demasus, Syria, Baltimore Mus Art; Woodmere Art Mus, 2003; Retrospective, Villanova Univ, 2008. *Pos:* Cur exhibs, Univ City Sci Ctr, 1975-2001; Cur, Richard Thornburgh, Pa. *Awards:* Best Picture of Year Award, Philadelphia Art Alliance, 65; National Print Award, Cheltenham Art Ctr, Pa, 70; Carl Zigrosser Award, Am Color Print Soc, 81; Distinguished Daughter of Pa, 92; Percy Owens Aeard, Pa Acad of Fine Arts, 95; The mayor's Citation for Artistic Merit, Mayor Ed Rendell, 95, Mayor John Street, 2001; Stella Drabkin Award, Am Color Print Soc, 2007. *Bibliog:* Victoria Donohoe (auth), article, Philadelphia Inquirer, 72; Sheila Reid (auth), exhib catalog, Mus de Grand Palais; Edward Sozanski, Philadelphia Inquirer, 97-99; Dr Burton Wasserman (auth), Art Matters, 2008; Robin

Rice (auth), City Paper, 2008. *Mem:* Artists Equity Asn (pres, Philadelphia Chap, 68-70, nat vpres, 71-75); Philadelphia Art Alliance; Am Color Print Soc; Philadelphia Watercolor Soc; and others. *Media:* Acrylic; Woodcut; Folding Screens. *Interests:* reading, opera, classical music, gardening. *Publ:* Auth, Obtaining art grants, Artists Equity Nat Newslett, 74; A City Sketched, a Guide to the Art & History of Philadelphia; R Buckminster Fuller Sketchbook, 81; Dr Burton Wasserman, Art Matters, 92, 97, 2001 & 2003. *Dealer:* Mangel Gallery 1714 Rittenhouse Sq Philadelphia PA 19103. *Mailing Add:* 2401 Pennsylvania Ave Apt 7B34 Philadelphia PA 19130-3029

NEWMAN, LOUIS
ART DEALER, COLLECTOR

b June 21, 1947; US citizen. *Study:* Ariz State Univ, BA, 1970; Univ Southern Calif, Los Angeles, MA, 1974. *Collection Arranged:* The Richard Zahn Collection. *Pos:* Art dealer & dir, David Findlay Jr Gallery; bd mem, Encompass New Opera Theater; adv bd, Lark Theater Co. *Bibliog:* Robert Metzger (auth), Louis Newman: Bringing Artists to Light, Antiques & the Arts Weekly, 4/2006, Joseph Jacobs (auth), Indian Space Painters, Arts & Antiques, 2/2007; Daniel Grant (auth), The Disappearing Catalog Essay, Am Artist, April 2009, Barrons Mag, 7/2009; Calvin Goodman (auth), Art Marketing Handbook, 2003; Calvin Goodman (auth), Nine Artists from the 9th Street Show, Antiques & the Arts Weekly, 7/2006; John Parks (auth) Inside the Mind of an Art Dealer, American Artist, 2/2011; V.L. Hendrickson (auth), East Side Migration Patterns, City Arts, 2/2011; John Parks (auth), Artists to Watch-Peter Brook, American Artist, 2011. *Mem:* Municipal Arts Soc; Ctr Contemp Opera (bd mem, 1997-2002); Nat Acad Design; NY Landmarks Conservancy (1996-); Fine Arts Fedn of NY city (bd mem, adv comt, 2000-); Encompass New Opera Theatre Bd (adv coun, 2001-); Century Asn (2007-); Hist Districts Coun, New York, 2000-; Art Dealers Asn Southern Calif, (bd mem 75-94). *Specialty:* Mid-twentieth century American paintings, prints, drawings & sculpture. *Publ:* Elie Nadelman: Selected Drawings, 1987; Kurt Schwitters: Collages and Other Works on Paper, 1988; Edward Hopper: Selected Drawings, 1985; Reginald Marsh: Selected Works on Paper, 1990; Thomas Hart Benton: Paintings and Drawings, 1990; essay, Robert Richenburg: The Richard Zahn Collection, Nat Arts Educ Found, 2006; auth, Robert Beauchamp: A Survey, 2008; Houghton Cranford Smith, 2009; auth, John Opper: The Late Paintings, 009; auth, Alcopley: A Survey, 2009; auth, Robert Richenburg: The Richard Zahn Collection, The Nat Arts Educ Found, 2006; auth, Nine Artists from the 9th Street Show, David Findlay Jr Fine Art, 2006; Apeaking Engagements: Louis & Calvin, Newman interviews Careers in Art Consult, Calvin Goodman, 2009, Turnaround is Fair Play, Louis Newman Interview Molly Barnes, 2006, A Conversation with Louis Newman, Molly Barnes Brown Bag Lunches, 2002, Art Dealers: How they Choose Artists, Artists talk on Art Panel Series, 2001, Seven Things Never to Say to an Art Dealer, Pratt Univ, 2001, Artists Talk on Art, Molly Barnes Lecture Series, 99; auth, David Aronson: Music of the Soul, 2011. *Mailing Add:* c/o David Findlay Jr Gallery 724 5th Ave 8th Fl New York NY 10019

NEWMAN, MARI ALICE MAE
PAINTER, SCULPTOR

b Esterville, Iowa. *Study:* Minneapolis Tech Col, 83-90; Minneapolis Community Col, 85-95; Minneapolis Center for Book Arts, 85-88; Minneapolis Coll Art and Design, 89; Univ Minn (archit), 91-94. *Work:* Minn Mus Art, St Paul; Minneapolis Inst Arts, Minn; New Columbus Mus Art, Ohio; LeRoy Neiman, NY; New Orleans Mus Art, La; Pensacola Mus Art, Fla; Very Special Arts Mus, Washington, DC; Milwaukee Mus Art; MOBA Mus Art; Tampa Mus Art, Fla; Mennello Mus, Orlando, Fla; Drake Univ; Capital One Financial Corp; Citi Bank; John Hancock Financial Svcs; Merril Lynch & co; Morgan Stanley; and numerous other corp collections; Moss Rehabilitation Hospital Art Collection, 2009. *Comn:* card designs, Anita Beck Cards, Minneapolis, 70-80, 98; train mobiles, Bruegger's Bagels, Minneapolis, 98; Alcoholics Anonymous 2000 (poster), Hazelden Found, Minneapolis, 2000; two extension murals, Dunn Brothers Inc, 02. *Exhib:* White Oak Gallery, Minneapolis, 88, 99, 2000-2003; Vaughan and Vaughan Gallery, Minneapolis, 89, 90, 92; Artlines, Minneapolis, 90-91, 93-95, 96-97, 99-2000; Sonia's Gallery, Minneapolis, 90, 92; No Name Gallery, Minneapolis, 92-94; Jack Wold Gallery, 92-96; Ice Box Gallery, Minneapolis, 99-2003; Gallery 360, 99-2004; Sister Kenny, Minneapolis, 2002-2004; The Art of Democracy: Tools of Persuasion, Minneapolis Inst Arts, Minn, 2004; Cotty Lowry Craffiti Series (Hackneyed Portraits, works by Mary Newman), 2006; Real Artists and Landscapes, NDak Mus Art, 2006; Lighthouse InSights, Calif, 2007; Art Ability 12th Nat Show, Bryn Mawr, Malvern, Pa, 2007; 7th Nat Acquisitions Exhib for Artists, View Point Gallery, Schenectady, NY, 2007. *Pos:* Designer & artist, Warren-Keith Stained Glass Studio, 86-89. *Awards:* Abbey Weed Gray Scholar, Minneapolis Coll of Art & Design, 89; Artist Recognition Grant, Jerome Foundation, 98; Best Minn Self-Taught Artists, City Pages, 2000; Sister Kenny Inst Int Juried Show, Best of the Show Award, 2001, First Place Award, 2002 & 2007, Snyder Calendar Award; Puffin Found Grant Award, 2002; First Place, APH In Sights, 2006; De'Via 2nd Place Award, Nashville, Tenn, 2006; First Place Sister Kenny 44th Ann Int Juried Show, 2007. *Bibliog:* Mark Engebretson (auth), Do Artist's Offensive Symbols Stir Hate on Reflection, Southwest Journal, 3/24/98; Michael Fallon (auth), The Outsiders, City Pages, Arts, 9/13/2000; Richard Chin (auth), Artists in Residence, St. Paul Pioneer Press, Express, 9/24/2000; Doug Grow (auth), Eyes of Beholder See No Art In Home, Artist's Neighbors Don't Lack For Opinions of Her House Work, 3/16/98; Full color with Mari Newman, Industry Mag #2, 9-10/2004; Mari Newman's Sculpture Garden - art or obstruction, Raw Vision #48, Autumn-Fall 2004; Are you an antlaw? Southwest Journal, 6/24/2004; Mary Abbe (auth), One of the Twin Cities most authentic and original artists, Minneapolis Star Tribune News, 5/30/2003; Art Spotlight, Gallery 360 Exhibit, Southwest J, 5/15-28/2003; New MOBA Artist Recognized, MOBA News, No 74, 3/2004; February Artists Gallery, Art & Antiques Mag, 2006; Kyle Radcliff (auth), House at End of the Rainbow, Raw Vision, No 59, Summer, 2007; Jonathin Kaminsy (auth), House Hunters, City Pages, 2007; Kyle Radclipp (auth), House at End of the Rainbow, Raw Vision 59, 2007; Kyle Radclipp (auth), House at End of the Rainbow, Raw Vision 59, 2007. *Mem:* Minn Soc Children's Book Writers & Illusr; Nat Sculpture Soc; Nat Asn Women Artists; Guild Metalsmiths Pastel Soc; Minn Wood Workers Guild; Nat Watercolor Soc; Am Watercolor Soc; Am Soc Contemp Artists; Am Society of Marine Artists; Nat Oil & Acrylic Painters Society; Pastel Society Am; Am Watercolor Society; Soc Animal Artists; Am Soc Botanical Artists; Nat Soc Mural Painters. *Media:* Tempera, crayon, found materials. *Publ:* Illusr, All Hearts with Bubbles, Raw Vision Mag, NY; Self Portrait of Polka Dot House, Readers Digest Inc, NY; Turkey of the Rainbow, Star Tribune, Minneapolis, Minn; West 81 Art & The Law, West Publ, St Paul, Minn, 81; Jambalaya Mag, Houghton Mifflin Co, 95; Raw Vision Mag, Raw Classics, England, 97; New Art Internat edition, 2001-, Book Art Press, NY, 2001; Art News Mag (summer), Artists Directory, NY, 2001; auth, Blue Horse, Artnews Mag, 3/2002; The Art of Mari Newman at Lava Lounge, Lyn-Lake Art Crawl, 2002; Sun in Costume, Artnews Mag (Summer), 2002; News council upholds two, denies one complaint by local artist against the Minnesota Daily, Minnesota News Council Public Hearing 151, 2007. *Dealer:* Christopher Park Gallery. *Mailing Add:* 5117 Penn Ave South Minneapolis MN 55419

NEWMAN, MARY ALICE MAE
PAINTER, SCULPTOR

b Esterville, Iowa. *Study:* Minneapolis Tech Col, cert upholstery, 85, cert cabinet making, 86, cert jewelry making, 88; Minneapolis Community Col, 84-90 & 95; Minneapolis Ctr Book Arts, 85-88; Minneapolis Col Art & Design, 89-90; Univ Minn, 91-94. *Work:* Minn Mus Art; pvt collection, Dorothy & Herbert Vogel, New York; Jonas Salk Inst, La Jolla, Calif; YMCA, Minneapolis; West Publ Co, Saint Paul, Minn. *Comn:* Card designs, Anita Beck Cards Inc, Minneapolis, 75-80. *Exhib:* Metamorphase One, Minn Mus Art, St Paul, 76; West Art & the Law, Minn Mus Am Art, St Paul, 82; Foot in the Door, Minneapolis Inst Art, 82; solo shows, Walker Art Ctr, Minneapolis, 89 & Minneapolis Inst Arts, 90; Sculptures by Mari & others, Hennipen Ctr Arts, Minneapolis, 96. *Awards:* Purchase Award, Minn Mus Art, 76; West Publ Co Honor Award, Minn Mus Art, 82; Abbey Weed Gray Scholar, Minneapolis Col Art & Design, 89. *Bibliog:* Doug Toft (auth), Where most people see junk - Mari Newman sees art, Southwest J, 91; Brad Zeller (auth), House of style, City Page, 96. *Mem:* Guild Metalsmiths, St Paul, Minn; Minn Woodcarvers Asn; Soc Minn Sculptors; Children's Book Illustrators Guild, Minn; Electronic Artists Group, Minn. *Media:* Acrylic; Wood, Ceramics. *Publ:* Illusr, Jambalaya, Houton Mifflin Div, 95. *Mailing Add:* c/o Newman Galleries 5117 Penn Ave S Minneapolis MN 55419

NEWMAN, RICHARD CHARLES
SCULPTOR, COLLAGE ARTIST

b North Tonawanda, NY, Dec 29, 1938. *Study:* Cleveland Inst Art, dipl painting, 60; Cranbrook Acad Art, BFA, 62; Cornell Univ, MFA, 64. *Work:* Addison Gallery Am Art, Phillips Acad, Andover, Mass; Middle Tenn State Univ, Murfreesboro; Herbert F Johnson Mus Art, Ithaca, NY; Univ Ore Mus Art, Eugene; Robert Lehman Art Ctr, Brooks Sch, N Andover, Mass. *Exhib:* Birth of Wisdom, St John's Col, Santa Fe, 2000; Icons and Altars, New Art Ctr of Newton, Newtonville, Mass, 2000 & 2001; Gallery of Contemp Art, Univ Colo, 2001; Landscape and Memory, Sedona Art Ctr, Ariz, 2002; New Bedford Art Mus, Mass, 2003; No AM SC Exhib Foothill Art Ctr, Golden, Colo, 2004; 38th LaGrange Nat Biennial, Lamar Dodd Art Ctr, LaGrange Coll GA, 2004; On the Edge, Peninsula Fine Art Ctr, Newport News, Va, 2005; A Couple of Artists, Acton Mem Libr, Mass, 2005; Digital art, Owen Smith Sheeman Gallery, Groton, Mass, 2006; Nat Collage Soc 21st Neal Butler Inst Am Art, Ohio, 2006; Digital Meditations, Rockport Ctr Arts, Tex, 2006; Icons & Altars, 2000-2009; The Cutting Edge, Coos Art Mus, Oregon, 2009; The Mythical State of Jefferson, Schneider Mus, S Ore Univ, 2010; A Couple of Artists, Hilltop Art Gallery, Ashland, Ore, 2011; Heads Up, Hilltop Art Gallery, Ashland, Ore, 2012; Timeless Meditations-Mandala & Patterns in Nature, Tuban Ctr Arts, Tubac, Ariz, 2012; Nat Collage Soc Exhib, Mesa Art Ctr, Ariz, 2012. *Pos:* Juror, Marblehead Art Asn, Mass, 78: Ann Spring Art Exhib, Newton Art Asn, Mass, 80, Boston Globe Scholastic Art Awards, State Finals, Mass, 87, 88 & 89; guest speaker, Artists on Art (lectr ser), Addison Gallery/Phillips Acad, Andover, Mass, 78, Artists Series, Boston Visual Artists Union, Mass, 80; panelist, T W MacKesey Seminar Ser, Coll Archit, Art & Planning, Cornell Univ, Ithaca, NY, 82; cur, Sculpture As Monument Exhib, Boston Visual Artists Union Gallery, Mass, 84, The Healing Experience, Soc Layerists, Bradford Col, 91 & Crossings Exhib, 94; keynote speaker, Reflection of Life & Death: The Arts and Thanatology Symp, Found Thanatology, New York, 89; speaker, Art and Healing Conf, New Harmony, Ind, 90, Affirming Wholeness Conf, San Antonio, Tex, 92 & Artists of the Spirit Symp, Walton Arts Ctr, Fayetteville, Ark, 94, numerous other confs; pres, Soc Layerist in Multi-Media, 86-2003; artist-in-residence, Merrimack Coll, N Andover, Mass, 2000. *Teaching:* Instr art, Univ Wash, Seattle, 64-65; asst, Sch Archit, Cornell Univ, 63-64; prof & chmn Creative Arts Div, Bradford Coll, 65-99, prof emer, 99-; adjunct prof, Merrimack Coll, N Andover, Mass, 2001-2009. *Awards:* Finalist in Sculpture, Mass Artists Found Grant, 77; Jubilee Celebration Showcase Artist for window proj, City Hartford, Conn, 86; Jane Walker Kopf Chair (art hist & theory), Bradford Coll, Mass, 92-98. *Bibliog:* Rochelle Newman & Donna M Fowler (auths), Space, Structure & Form, Pythagorean Press & Brown & Benchmark, 95; Nicholas Roukes (auth), Humor in Art, Davis Publ, Mass, 96; M C Nelson (auth), Bridging Time and Space, Markowitz Publ, 98; Rochelle Newman (auth) Malleable Matter/Stretchable Space, Pythagorean Press, Bradford, Mass, 2000; Arthur Williams (auth), The Sculpture Referernce, Sculpture Books, 2004; Mary T Beam (auth), Celebrating Your Creative Self, N Light Books, 2001; Nicholas Roeckes (auth), Artful Jesters, Ten Speed Press, 2003; Nita Heland (auth), The New Creative Artist, North Light Books, 2010. *Mem:* Soc of Layerists in Multi-Media, Albuquerque, NMex (pres, 86-2004); Boston Mus Fine Arts, Mass; Pythagorean Press, Bradford, Mass; New Eng Sculptors Asn. *Media:* Mixed Media. *Interests:* Photography. *Publ:* Contribr, Collage: Critical Views, Univ Mich Press, 89; Am Craft Mag, 8-9/90 & 4/91; Artists of the Spirit, Arcus Publ, 94; Humor in Art, Davis Publ, Worchester, Mass, 97; Artful Jesters, Ten Speed Press, 2004, by Nicholas Roukes; The Sculpture Reference, Sculpture Books Pub, by Arthur Williams, 2004; The New Creative Artist, Nita Leland, North Light Bks, 2006; and others. *Dealer:* Hilltop Gallery Ashland Ore

NEWMAN, WALTER ANDREWS, JR
ART DEALER, GALLERY DIRECTOR
b Philadelphia, Pa, May 16, 1930. *Collection Arranged:* Daniel Garber Mem Exhib, 65; Edward W Redfield, Retrospective Exhib, 68; Joe Brown, Bronzes, Retrospective Exhib, 87; John Fulton Folinsbee, Following His Own Course, 90; The Folinsbee Legacy, 2005. *Pos:* Pres, Newman Galleries, Philadelphia, Pa, 69-. *Specialty:* Early 20th century impressionists; Pennsylvania landscape school. *Dealer:* Newman Galleries, 1625 Walnut St, Philadelphia PA. *Mailing Add:* 1625 Walnut St Philadelphia PA 19103

NEWMAN-RICE, NANCY
PAINTER, CRITIC
b New York, NY, Mar 28, 1950. *Study:* Cornell Univ; Washington Univ, BFA, 72, MFA, 74. *Work:* Univ London, King's Coll; Univ Cardiff; St Louis Univ Mus Art; Laumeier Int Sculpture Park; Wash Univ Sch Med. *Comn:* Univ London, England; Univ Cardiff, Wales. *Exhib:* solo exhibs, Currents 2, St Louis Art Mus, 79 & Brentwood Gallery, St Louis, 85 & 86, Sazama/Braver Gallery, Chicago, 87, 89, Mus Gallery, Southeast Mo State Univ, Cape Girardeau, Mo, 93, Laumeier Int Sculpture Park, St Louis, Mo, 98, St Louis Univ Mus Art, Mo, 2007; Group exhibs, St Louis Artists, Cervantes Convention Ctr, St Louis, 78; Painting Invitational, Salisbury State Univ, Md, 79; Mississippi Corridor, Davenport Art Gallery, Iowa, 80; Works On-Of Paper, Bixby Gallery, Washington Univ, Landscapes 88 BZ Wagman, 80; Drawing & Sculpture, Ball State Univ, Ind, 76; A Mod Bestiary: Artists View the ANimal Kindgon, Charles A Wustum Mus Fine Arts, Racine, Wis, 2002; Flowart, Miami, 2007; St Louis Painters Invitational, Daum Mus Contemp Art, Sedalia, Mo, 007; Duane Reed Gallery, St Louis, 2009. *Pos:* Ed in chief, St Louis Seen, Newspaper for Visual Arts, 75-77; St Louis ed & critic, New Art Examiner, 78-; Critic, St Louis Post Dispatch. *Teaching:* Asst painting, Washington Univ, 72-74; assoc prof, Maryville Col, 74-2009, Whitaker Found Visitng Artist Prog, Maryville Univ, 2000-, dir Morton J May Found Gallery, 75-2005, dir studio art, 2008-2009, dir art & design prog, 2004-2008, prof emerita art; instr, St Louis Community Coll Forest Park, 74-75. *Awards:* Midwest Art Alliance-Nat Endowment Arts Grant; Nat Endowment Arts/MMA Fel Award, 86; Nomination for Award in Visual Art Fel, 88; Nomination Mo Biennial, 92. *Bibliog:* Sidra Stitch (auth), Nancy Rice & Yvette Woods, New Art Examiner, 79; Mary King (auth), Rice's floating lattice spheres, St Louis Post Dispatch, 80; P Desmer (auth), Nancy Rice's work dazzles, St Louis Post Dispatch; Herb Gralnick (auth), Nancy Rice, St Louis Globe Democrat; Betsy Goldman (auth), Nancy Rice, New Art Examiner; Carol Ferring Shepley (auth), Nancy Newman Rice Uses Middle Ages, her dream as springboard for creativity, St Louis Post Dispatch, Jan 2003; Teresa Callahan (auth), Muted Palette, Sharp Technique, West End Word, Mar 2005; David Bonetti (auth), Seascapes Show Rice's Pointilism Technique, St Louis Post Dispatch, Mar 2005. *Mem:* Coll Art Asn; Midwest Coll Art Asn; Women's Caucus for Art (bd dir, 76-77); Artspace. *Media:* Oil. *Publ:* auth, Fine Focus (essay), Fibert Arts Mag, Mar/April 85; Mary Giles, Am Craft Mag, 2003; auth, The Education of an Artist, Creative Outlook, 2007; auth, Art History, Our Heritage, Creative Outlook Mag, 2008; auth, Fragile Memories, the Origin of my Paintings, self published, 2008. *Dealer:* Sazama/Braver Gallery 361 West Superior Chicago IL 60610; BZ Wagman Gallery Galleris St Louis MO 63117; Duane Reed Gallery 4729 McPherson Ave St Louis Mo 63108. *Mailing Add:* 4545 Maryland Ave Saint Louis MO 63108

NEWMARK, MARILYN
SCULPTOR
b New York, NY, July 20, 1928. *Study:* Adelphi Coll; Alfred Univ; also with Paul Brown, Garden City, NY. *Work:* Nat Mus Racing, Saratoga, NY; Nat Art Mus Sport, Indianapolis; Am Saddle Horse Mus, Lexington, Ky; Int Mus Horse, Ky Horse Park, Lexington, Ky; Firestone; Phipps; Galbreath; DuPont III; Brookgreen Gardens, NC; and others. *Comn:* Bronzes of Majestic Light, comn by Ogden Phipps Jr, 76; Man o' War, Franklin Mint, 77; Affirmed, Thoroughbred Racing Asn, 78; Ruffian, 83 & Genuine Risk, 84, Int Mus Horse; Race Horse, Japan Racing Asn, Japan, 97; and others. *Exhib:* Nat Acad Design, NY, 71-72, 74-82, 86-95, 97, 99, 2001, 2003, 2005 & 2007; Int Mus Horse, Ky, 92-2002 & 2005-2007; Palazzo Mediceo di Seravezza, Italy, 94; Old Algonquin Mus, Can, 95; Fleisher Mus, Ariz, 99; Butler Inst Am Art, Ohio, 2001; Brookgreen Gardens, SC, 2002-2011; Wildlife Experience, Colo, 2002-2008. *Pos:* former Vpres (bd mem), Soc Animal Artists; former coun (recording secy), Nat Sculpture Soc; founder, Dir Sculpture, Am Acad Equine Art. *Awards:* Ellin P Speyer Award, Nat Acad Design, 74, 93 & 99; Gold Medal, Allied-Artist Am, 81 & 93; Leonard Meiselman Mem Award, Nat Sculpture Soc & Audubon Soc, 2003. *Bibliog:* Horsewoman & Artist Extraordinaire, Horse of Course, 77; She Wanted Horses, Equine Images, 92; Masters of American Sculpture, 93; Donald Martin Reynolds (auth), Unbridled passion, sculpture rev, summer, 2006. *Mem:* Nat Acad; Nat Sculpture Soc; Allied Artists Am; Soc Animal Artists; Pen & Brush; Am Acad Equine Art. *Media:* Bronze Cast, Clay. *Specialty:* Animal Art. *Publ:* Contribr, Equine Sculpture, A Mixed Medium, Morning Telegraph, 8/9/71; Equine Sculpture, Chronicle of the Horse, 9/10/71; Horse in sculpture, Am Horseman, 12/72; From the love of horses, Catasus, spring 89. *Dealer:* The Sportsman's Gallery 309 E Paces Ferry Rd Atlanta GA 30305. *Mailing Add:* 4 Central Dr Glen Head NY 11545-1106

NEWPORT, MARK
TAPESTRY ARTIST, DESIGNER
b Amsterdam, NY, 1964. *Study:* Kansas City Art Inst, BFA, 1986; Sch Art Inst Chicago, MFA, 1991. *Exhib:* Solo exhibs include Writer's Place, Kansas City, 1996, Lusty Lady Gallery, Seattle, 1997, Lyons Wier Gallery, Chicago, 1998, Greg Kucera Gallery, Seattle, 1999, 2000, 2004, Chicago Cult Ctr, 2004-05, Ariz State Univ Art Mus, Tempe, 2005, Lyons Wier Gallery, New York, 2005, San Diego State Univ Art Gallery, 2006; two-person exhibs with Jerry Bleem, Mus Textiles, Toronto, 1994, Maryville Univ, St Louis, 2001; group exhibs include Material Departures: Tradition & Change, Ill Art Gallery, Chicago, 1992; 20th Anniversary Exhib, Contemp Gallery Mus Textiles, Toronto, 1995; Celebrity: Figures of Worship, Fame, Fortune, Heroism & Infamy, Bumbershoot Festival Arts, Seattle, 1997; Game Show, Bellevue Art Mus, 1999-2000; Read All About It!, Greg Kucera Gallery, Seattle, 2001, A Selection of Recent Inventory Acquisitions, 2005; SuperHero, Galerie Edward Mitterand, Geneva, 2002; Comic Release: Negotiating Identity for a New Generation, traveling, 2003; Pins & Needles, John Michael Kohler Art Ctr, Sheboygan, Wis, 2003-04; Humor, Fiberscene, San Francisco, 2005. *Awards:* Juror's Award, Arrowmont Sch Arts & Crafts, Gatlinburg, Tenn, 1991; Faculty Develop Grant, Kansas City Art Inst, 1994; Grant-in-Aid, Bur Faculty Res, Western Wash Univ, 1997, 1999, 2000, Mini-Grant, 1998, Summer Res Grant, 2001; Katherine K Herberger Res Grant, Ariz State Univ, 2004-05; Creative Capital Visual Arts Grant, 2005; Career Advancement Grant, Ariz Comn Arts, 2005. *Mailing Add:* Cranbrook Academy of Art 39221 Woodward Ave Bloomfield Hills MI 48304

NEWSOM, BARBARA YLVISAKER
ADMINISTRATOR, WRITER
b Madison, Wis, July 14, 1926. *Study:* Bethany Lutheran Col, Mankato, Minn, AA; Univ Minn, BA; Hunter Col, MA. *Pos:* Pub affairs consult to 100th Anniversary Comt, Metrop Mus Art, New York, 67-70, consult to vdir for educ, 70-71; study dir, Coun Mus Educ, 71-73; proj dir, Coun Mus & Educ in Visual Arts, New York & Cleveland, Ohio, 73-78; staff assoc, Rockefeller Brothers Fund, 73-80, consult, 80-. *Mem:* Am Asn Mus (coun mem, 75-78). *Media:* Oil. *Res:* Art museum education and urban aesthetics. *Publ:* Auth, The museum as the city's aesthetic conscience, Metrop Mus Bull, 68; The Metropolitan Museum as an Educational Institution, 70; ed, The Art Museum as Educator, 78

NEWSOME, RASHAAD GERMAIN
VIDEO ARTIST, SCULPTOR
b New Orleans, La, Dec 19, 1979. *Study:* Tulane Univ, BA (art hist), 2001. *Work:* Mus Mod Art, New York; Brooklyn Mus, New York. *Comn:* FIVE 2010, Whiteny Mus Am Art, New York; Shade Compositions 2009, The Kitchen, New York; Shade Compositions 2010, PS1, New York. *Exhib:* Standards Ramis Barquet Gallery, Ramis Barquet Gallery, New York, 2009; Whitney Biennial, Whitney Mus Am Art, New York, 2010; Greater New York, PS 1, New York, 2010. *Awards:* Visual Arts Grant, Rema Hort Mann Found

NG, NATTY (YUEN LEE)
PAINTER, GRAPHIC DESIGNER
b Hong Kong, May 14, 1948; Can citizen. *Study:* Poly Tech Col, 67; Sir Robert Black Coll Educ, 68; Grantham Coll Educ, Hong Kong, 86, Kwantlan Col, Vancouver, Can, 91. *Comn:* oil on canvas painting, Can Brass Hardware, 2000; 2 oil & mixed media paintings, Intra Corp, Can, 2001; oil on canvas painting, Internat Language Sch Can, 99, 2002; 2 oil & mixed media paintings, Progressive Wireless Co, Can, 2004. *Exhib:* Project E '88, Hong Kong Art Show, Art Ctr, 88; Mind & Matter Festival of the Art, Mind & Matter Gallery, Vancouver, BC, Can, 91; Victoria Regional Art Show, BC, Can 91; Ninth Ann Art Exhib, Community Art Coun, Vancouver, BC, Can, 91; Images '92, Burnaby Arts Coun & Arts Coun New Westminster, Can, 92; one-person art show, We "B" Art Gallery Seattle, Wash, 92; The Grind Gallery, Vancouver, BC, Can, 93-94; Biennale Internat Dell 'Arte Contemporanea, 2005. *Pos:* Graphic designer, Imageworks, Port Coquitlam, BC, Can, 91-. *Teaching:* Art & design, Kwun Tong Govt Sec Sch, Hong Kong, 86-90. *Awards:* First Place Honors Oil Painting, All Cols & Univ Art Show, 86; and others; Hon Mention Image 92, Burnaby Arts Coun, Arts Coun of New Westminster, Can, 92. *Media:* Oil, Mixed Media. *Publ:* Preview of Visual Arts, Alberta, BC, Oreg and Wash, 93; Quinta Edizione - Biennale Internat. Dell 'Arte Contemporanea, 2005

NIARCHOS, PHILIP S
COLLECTOR
Study: Atlantic Coll; London Sch Economics. *Pos:* Bd dirs, Stavros Niarchos Found, Athens, Greece, 1996-. *Awards:* Named one of Top 200 Collectors, ARTnews mag, 2003-13. *Collection:* Old Masters; Impressionism; modern and contemporary art

NIBLETT, GARY LAWRENCE
PAINTER
b Carlsbad, NMex, Jan 9, 1943. *Study:* Art Instruction Inc, Minneapolis, Minn; Eastern NMex Univ, Portales; Art Ctr Coll Design, Los Angeles, Calif. *Work:* Nedra Matteucci, Fenn Gallery, Santa Fe, NMex; Claggett, Rey Gallery, Vail, Colo; Trailside Galleries, Scottsdale, Ariz & Jackson Hole, Wyo. *Comn:* Albuquerque Munic Airport, 88; Carlsbad Mus Fine Art, NMex, 88; Sunwest Bank Hist Collection, Santa Fe, NMex; NMex State Capitol Bldg; calendar artist, NMex Mag, 90; and others. *Exhib:* Grand Palais Paris, France, 75 & 76; Cowboy Artists Am, Phoenix Art Mus, Ariz, 77-91; Artists of Am, Colo Hist Mus, Denver, 82-91; Royal Watercolor Soc, London, 90-91; A New Mexico Tradition: Southwestern Realism, Taiwan Mus Art, Taichung, 91; and others. *Teaching:* Cowboy Artist Am Mus, 86 & 88. *Awards:* Silver Medals, Cowboy Artists Am Show, Phoenix Art Mus, 77, 82-83, 86 & Gold Medal, 91; Artist of Year, Tucson Festival Soc, 86 & Gold Medal, 2005; Hubbard Award Excellence, Hubbard Mus, Ruidoso, NMex, 90-91; Am Cowboy Cult Western Art Award, 2007; and others. *Bibliog:* Vicki Stavig (auth), Art of the West, 9-10/89; Mary Terrence McKay (auth), Gary Niblett: A New Look at the Old West, Actian Press, 90; Neirdra Jane Almjer (auth), A new look at the old west, Int Fine Art Collector, 8/91; Gussie Fauntleroy (auth), Southwest Art Mag (biog), 9/2007. *Mem:* Cowboy Artist Am; charter mem Santa Fe Watercolor Soc. *Media:* Oil. *Publ:* Cowboy Artist of Am, Desert Hawk Publ, El Paso, Tex, 88. *Mailing Add:* 308 Vistoso Pl Santa Fe NM 87501

NIBLOCK, PHILL
FILMMAKER, VIDEO ARTIST
b Anderson, Ind, Oct 2, 1933. *Study:* Ind Univ, BA, 56. *Work:* Carpenter Ctr Visual Arts, Harvard Univ. *Comn:* NY Found Artists, 87; New Works Prog, Mass Coun Arts, 88; Found Contemp Performance Arts, 94. *Exhib:* Cineprobe, Films and Music, Mus Mod Art, NY, 73; Sur, Wadsworth Atheneum, Hartford, Conn; Trabajando, Herbert F

Johnson Mus, Cornell Univ, 76; Carpenter Ctr Visual Arts, Harvard Univ; Inst Contemp Arts, London; Contemp Arts Forum, Santa Barbara, Calif; and others. *Pos:* Dir, Experimental Intermedia Found, New York, 70-. *Awards:* NY State Coun Arts Grant, Kirkland Art Ctr, 70, Exp Intermedia Found, 72-74; Nat Endowment Arts Pub Media Prog, 75-76; Guggenheim Fel; and others. *Bibliog:* Tom Johnson (auth), Music reviews, Village Voice, 72, 73 & 74; John Rockwell (auth), What's new, High Fidelity/Musical Am, 5/74; Abigail Nelson (auth), Who's Who in Film, Sight Lines, winter 74. *Mem:* Experimental Intermedia Found. *Mailing Add:* 224 Centre St New York NY 10013

NICE, DON
PAINTER
b Visalia, Calif, June 26, 1932. *Study:* Univ Southern Calif, BFA, 54; Yale Univ, MFA, 64. *Work:* Del Art Mus, Wilmington; Minneapolis Inst Art; Mus Mod Art & Whitney Mus Am Art, NY; Walker Art Ctr; Julius Bar Bank, Zurich, Switz; and many others. *Comn:* Wall murals, Nat Fine Arts Comn, Lake Placid, NY; Art in Archit Prog, Vets Admin, White River Junction, NY; participant bicentennial exhib, America, 76, US Dept Interior; Mostly Mozart Festival, 78 & 18th Ann Holiday Festival, Lincoln Ctr Posters, 88. *Exhib:* A Feast for the Eyes, Mus Mod Art, 84; The New Expressive Landscape, Sordoni Art Gallery, Wilkes Barre, Pa, 85; solo exhibs, John Berggruen Gallery, San Francisco, 89, Frederick Gallery, Washington, 89, Sun Valley Ctr Arts & Humanities, Idaho, 90, Images Gallery, Toledo, Ohio, 91, Albany Inst Art, NY, 92, Huntington Art Mus, WVa, 95 & Hudson River Mus, Yonkers, NY, 95; Common Objects, Pfizer Inc Loan, Art Adv Servs, Mus Mod Art, NY, 91; The Unique Print, Pace Prints, NY, 91; The Art of Advocacy, Aldrich Mus Contemp Art, Ridgefield, Conn, 91; On Rivers Edge, Hudson River Mus, Yonkers, NY, 95; solo exhib, Huntington Art Mus, WVa, 95. *Teaching:* Instr, Minneapolis Sch Art, 60-62; instr, Sch Visual Arts, New York, 63-, dean, 64-66; artist-in-residence, Dartmouth Col, New Hampshire, 82. *Awards:* Ford Found Purchase Award, 63. *Bibliog:* Todd Strasser (auth), interview, Ocular, fall 79; Suzanne Muchnic (auth), Really big show in Newport, Los Angeles Times, 80; Donald B Kuspit (auth), What's real in realism, Art in Am, 81. *Mem:* Nat Acad. *Dealer:* Babcock Galleries 724 5th Ave New York NY 10019. *Mailing Add:* Tandem Press Univ Wisc 201 S Dickinson St Madison WI 53703

NICHOLAS, DONNA LEE
CERAMIST, SCULPTOR
b South Pasadena, Calif, Mar 30, 1938. *Study:* Pomona Col, BA (cum laude), 59; apprentice with Hiroaki Morino, Kyoto, Japan, 60-62; Claremont Grad Sch & Univ Ctr, with Paul Soldner & MFA, 64-66. *Work:* Flint Inst Arts, Mich; Edinboro Univ, Pa; Lowe Gallery, Miami; Calif Polytechnic Univ; Plains Art Mus, Moorhead, Minn; St Petersburg Univ Art, Russia; Erie Art Mus. *Exhib:* Salt Glaze Ceramics, Mus Contemp Crafts, NY, 72; Object as Poet, Renwick Gallery, Smithsonian Inst, Washington, DC & Mus Contemp Crafts, NY, 76; Clay, Fiber, Metal, Women Artists, Bronx Mus, NY, 78; A Century of Ceramics in the US 1879-1979, Everson Mus, Syracuse, NY, 79; Solo exhib, Canton Art Inst, Canton, Ohio, 88; Fragile Blossoms, Enduring Earth, Everson Mus Art Syracuse, NY, 89; AC Delegates Exhib, Scottish Gallery, Edinburgh, Scotland, 90; and other solo & group exhibs. *Teaching:* Instr ceramics, Mott Community Col, Flint, 66-69; prof ceramics, Edinboro Univ, 69-96; vis artist-instr, Penland Sch Crafts, NC, 71, Scripps Col, 74 & Moore Col Art, Philadelphia, 75. *Awards:* Outstanding Educators Am Award, 75; Distinguished Teaching Chair, Commonwealth of Pa Teachers, 81. *Bibliog:* Susan Wechsler (auth), Low Fire Ceramics, Watson-Guptill, 81; Elsbeth Woody (auth), Handbuilding Ceramic Forms, Farrar Strauss & Giroux, 78; John Byrum (auth), New Art Examiner, 88; Richard Zakin (auth), Ceramics, Mastering the Craft, Chilton, 90. *Mem:* Am Craftsmen's Coun (Pa rep to Northeast Assembly, 75-78); Northwest Pa Artists Asn; Assoc Artists of Pittsburgh; Nat Coun Educ Ceramic Arts; Am Crafts Coun. *Media:* Clay. *Publ:* Auth, 27th Syracuse Nat, Craft Horizons, 12/72; Nat Coun on Educ for Ceramic Arts J, Vol 9, No 1, fall 88; Gai Jin, Studio Potter, 12/92; Japanese Women Ceramists-Part I, Studio Potter, 12/94. *Mailing Add:* 119 Valley View Dr Edinboro PA 16412-2316

NICHOLAS, THOMAS ANDREW
PAINTER, GALLERY OWNER
b Middletown, Conn, Sept 26, 1934. *Study:* Studied with Ernest Lohrmann, Meriden, Conn, 50-53; Sch Visual Arts, NY, scholar, 53-55. *Work:* Butler Inst Am Art, Youngstown, Ohio; Ga Mus, Athens; Farnesworth Mus, Rockland, Maine; Hispanic Soc Am, New York; Peabody Mus, Salem, Mass; Springfield Art Mus, Mo. *Comn:* Four ten-colored lithographs, Franklin Mint, 77; Peter A Juley & Son Coll, Nat Mus Am Art; 80 images, Smithsonian Inst, Wash DC. *Exhib:* Major exhibs, NY, New Eng, Wash & Calif, 62-2007; 200 Years of Water Color Painting in America, Metropolitan Mus Art, NYC, 67. *Teaching:* Instr, Famous Artists Schs, Westport, Conn, 58-61, summer workshops, Rockport, Mass, 62-65, etc, Jade Fon Watercolor Workshop, Carmel, Calif, 78-2000. *Awards:* Elizabeth T Greenshields Mem Found Grants, 61 & 62; Gold Medal Honor, Allied Artists Am, 68; Gold Medal Honor, Am Watercolor Soc, 69; recipient Gold medal of Hon New Eng Watercolor Soc, Boston, 85; Acad Artists Asn, 85; named Knickerbocker Honoree Artist of Yr, 89; recipient Grumbacher award watercolor, Acad Artists Asn, 90; Grumbacher Gold medal Gouache New Eng Watercolor Soc, 92; Gouache Transparent Watercolor, 95; 43 Medals of Honor 62-2007; Mary Bryan Mem award, Rockport Art Assn, 2011, Alden Bryan Mem award, 2011; Strisik Memorial Gold medal, Rockport Art Assn, Ma, 2012; Gold Medal, New England Watercolor Soc, Boston, Ma, 2013. *Bibliog:* Articles in Am Artist, 3/60 & 8/72; article in North Light Mag, fall 70; John L Cooley (auth), article in The Old Watercolor Soc, Eng, 71; plus others; Watercolor Landscape Techniques of 23 International Artists, Int Artists Publ Inc, Verdi, Nev, 2003. *Mem:* Nat Acad; Am Watercolor Soc; Allied Artists Am; New Eng Watercolor Soc; Boston Guild Artists (Grumbacher Gold medallion award watercolor 88, N Shore Arts Asn award oil 91); Rockport Art Asn (Gold medal, 66, 68, 76, 85, 96-97, 99 & 2002-2004, 2007, 2010), Silver medal, 88 & 94, Darrand award oil 92, Cirino award 1st prize Gouache 92, Clark Polupar award Gouache 92, Cooley award graphics 95, Clark Popular award Gouache 95, Cirino award Gouache 95, Davis Mem award watercolor 96, Mills Mem award Gouache 96); Hudson Valley Artists (Gold medal 74, 85 & 94, Huntington Mem award oil 95, Bohnert Mem award oil 96). *Media:* Oil, Watercolor. *Specialty:* Romanitic realism, impressionism. *Publ:* Auth, article, SW Art, 12/82; Creative Watercolor, Rockport Pub Inc, 95; A Gallery of Marine Art, Rockport Pub Inc, 98; American Art Collector, Premiere Issue, Oct 2005; contribr, Am Watercolor Soc (images & presentation), 2008. *Dealer:* Tom Nicholas Gallery 65 Main St Rockport MA 01966; Vermont Fine Art Stowe VT; Argosy Gallery Bar Harbor ME. *Mailing Add:* 7 Wildon Heights Rockport MA 01966

NICHOLS, EDWARD EDSON
PAINTER, EDUCATOR
b Chicago, Ill, Nov 6, 1929. *Study:* Univ Kans, BFA, 57, MFA, 59; Huntington Hartford Found, 60, 64. *Work:* Miss Art Asn, Jackson; Tex Instruments Collection, Dallas; McAllen Int Mus, Tex; Univ Tex-Pan Am, Edinburg. *Comn:* Painting, Hidalgo Co Hist Mus, 92. *Exhib:* Tenth Washington Area Show, Corcoran Gallery Am Art, 56; 22nd Ann, Butler Inst Am Art, 57; 154th Ann, Pa Acad Fine Arts, 59; Third Ann Delta Exhib, Ark Arts Ctr, Little Rock, 60; 23rd Am Drawing Biennial, Norfolk Mus Art, Va, 65; Art Mus STex Ann, Corpus Christi, 70; Tex Painting & Sculpture, Dallas Mus Fine Art, 71; TWS, 50th Ann Exhib, 99; Tex Watercolor Soc Travel Award Exhib, San Antonio, 80, 2002. *Teaching:* Assoc prof to full prof Art, Univ Tex Pan-Am, Edinburg, Tex, 65-99, retired, 99. *Awards:* Winsor Newton Award, Tex Watercolor Soc Exhib, 80, Patron's award, 2002; Del Mar Coll Drawing Award, Ann Nat Drawing Competition, 84; Juror's Choice Award, Tip o' Texas Exhib, 91. *Mem:* Tex Watercolor Soc. *Media:* Watercolor, Oil. *Publ:* Riversedge, Univ Tex Pan-Am, Edinburg, Tex, 92; Fifty Years of Excellence, Tex Watercolor Soc, 99. *Mailing Add:* 2018 Shary Rd Mission TX 78572

NICHOLS, FRANCIS N, II
PRINTMAKER, EDUCATOR
Study: Wichita State Univ, MFA; also with David Bernard & Robert Kiskadden. *Work:* Anderson Fine Art Ctr, Ind; Univ Miss; Wichita State Univ, Wichita Art Mus; Deines Cult Arts Ctr, Kans. *Exhib:* Kans 17th Ann Small Painting, Drawing & Print Exhib, 91; Print Types Consortium Exhib, Ind Univ, 91; Cimarron Nat Works on Paper, Okla State Univ, 91; 8th Ann Nat Works on Paper, Berkeley, Calif, 92; and others. *Teaching:* Fel, Wichita State Univ, 65-67; prof printmaking, Ft Hays State Univ, 67-. *Awards:* Merit & Purchase Award, Anderson Winter Show, Ind, 89; Best of Show, 15th Ann Prairie Art Exhib, Sterling, Kans, 89; First Place, Carrier Found Nat Competition, Belle Meade, NJ, 91. *Mem:* Kans Art Educ Asn; Print Consortium; Nat Educ Asn; Nat Art Educ Asn; Kans Art Educ Asn. *Media:* Intaglio, Lithography. *Dealer:* Rueben Saunders Gallery Wichita KS. *Mailing Add:* 1100 Amhurst Hays KS 67601

NICHOLS, MAXINE MCCLENDON See McClendon, Maxine Nichols

NICHOLS, WARD H
PAINTER
b Welch, WVa, July 5, 1930. *Study:* WVa Univ. *Work:* Integon Corp & R J Reynolds Co, Winston-Salem, NC; Gutenberg Mus, Mainz, Ger; Huntington Gallery Art, WVa; Springfield Mus Art, Mass; Lowes Corp, North Wilkesboro, NY; BankAmerica, Charlotte, NC; RJ Reynolds Tobacco Co, Winston Salem, NC; Wachovia, Winston-Salem; Daytona Speed Mus, Fla; Mus Tex Tech; Hickory Mus Art, Hickory, NC. *Comn:* Oil painting, Integon Corp, Winston Salem, NC, 75; oil painting, Printing Indust Carolina, Charlotte, NC, 81, 83 & 92; oil painting, NC State Beekeepers Asn, Raleigh, 82. *Exhib:* Allied Artist Exhib, Nat Acad Galleries, NY; El Paso Mus Art, Tex; Russell Centenary Exhib, Nottingham, Eng; NC Mus Art, Raleigh; Mainstreams, Fine Arts Ctr, Marietta Col, Ohio; Retrospective @ 80, 2010. *Pos:* Artist-in-residence, Univ Ind, Terre Haute, Ind, Greenbrier, White Sulphur Springs, WVa & W Liberty Col, West Liberty, WVa. *Teaching:* Guest lectr, many cols in eastern US. *Awards:* Grumbacher Award Merit, El Paso Mus Art, 70; Jurors Merit Award, Miss Mus Art, 71; PICA Award, Printing Indust Carolinas, 75-90. *Bibliog:* Article, Pace Mag, Piedmont Airlines, 78; article, Todays Art, 80; Invitation to a Country Walk (film), Assoc Images, 80; The Realism of Ward Nichols, American Trails, Lincoln, Neb; La Revue Moderne, Paris, France; Academia Italia Annual, Parma, Italy; Retrospective at 80, American Trails, TV Documentary Program, T0-day's Art. *Mem:* Wilkes Art Guild. *Media:* Oil. *Interests:* music, sports, racing. *Publ:* Contemp Graphic Artists, 87; New York Art Rev, 90; Dict Int Bio, 91; Country J, 2/92; The Biographical Dictionary of American Artists, Nat Artist Directory, Artists USA, Men of Achievement. *Dealer:* Blue Spiral Asheville NC. *Mailing Add:* 734 Beaumont Elm St Wilkesboro NC 28659

NICHOLSON, MYREEN MOORE See Moore Nicholson, Myreen

NICHOLSON, NATASHA
ASSEMBLAGE ARTIST, SCULPTOR
b St Louis, Mo, May 29, 1945. *Study:* Ringling Sch Art, 64-65. *Work:* Oakland Mus Art, Calif; Addison Gallery Am Art, Phillips Acad, Andover, Mass; Los Angeles Co Mus Art; Madison Art Ctr, Wis. *Comn:* Sculpture, Rayovac Corp, Madison, Wis, 86. *Exhib:* Solo exhibs, Addison Gallery Am Art, 74, Asher-Faure Gallery, Los Angeles, 81 & 83 & Perimeter Gallery, Chicago, 83; Collage and Assemblage in Southern Calif, Los Angeles Inst Contemp Art, 75; A Sense of Space, Oakland Mus Art, 77; Global Space Invasions, San Francisco Mus Mod Art, 78; Our Own Artists: Art in Orange Co, Newport Harbor Art Mus, 79; Tableau, Middendorf-Lane Gallery, Washington, DC, 80; Forgotten Dimension: A Survey of Small Sculpture in Calif Now, Fresno Art Ctr, traveling, 82; Chicago & Vicinity Exhib, Chicago Art Inst, 84; and others. *Collection Arranged:* The Other Things That Artists Make, San Francisco Mus Mod Art, 76; Useable Art, Decorative Arts, Quay Gallery, San Francisco, 77; Decorative Arts of Dane Co, Madison Art Ctr, Wis, 82. *Pos:* Dir, Natasha Nicholson/works of Art, Madison, Wis, 87-90. *Awards:* Individual Artist Grant, Nat

Endowment Arts, 77; Artists Fel, 83 & Proj Grant, 83, Wis Arts Bd. *Bibliog:* Alfred Frankenstein (auth), For the magical love of oddities, San Francisco Chronicle, 77; Melinda Wortz (auth), Los Angeles, Art News Mag, 12/79; Vivien Raynor (auth), Anxious interiors, NY Times, 9/85. *Media:* Mixed. *Mailing Add:* 1962 Atwood Ave PO Box 3493 Madison WI 53704

NICHOLSON, RONI
SCULPTOR
Study: Earlham Coll, Ind, BA, 1964; Columbia Univ, New York, 1977. *Work:* Var pvt collections. *Exhib:* X-Tream X-Teriors, Marcus Garvey Park, New York, 2000; solo exhibs, Lobby Gallery, Audubon, New York, 2001-07, DiSanti Plaza, Hartsdale, NY, 2001, 2004 & 2006, Montserrat Gallery, New York, 2001; Drawings, Isley Libr, Middlebury, Vt, 2001; German Accents, Selena Gallery, Long Island Univ, 2004; Design For Living, Islip Art Mus, NY, 2005; Red Is Everywhere, Rockland Art Ctr, West Nyack, NY, 2005-06; Line & Surface, Art League of Long Island, NY, 2007. *Awards:* Pollock-Krasner Found Grant, 2008

NICHOLSON, ROY WILLIAM
PAINTER, EDUCATOR
b Cambridge, Eng; US citizen, Mar 21, 1943. *Study:* Hornsey Coll Art, London, Eng, with John Hoyland, NDD, 65; Brooklyn Mus Sch Art, Max Beckmann Mem Scholar, 66; Vermont Col, Norwich Univ, MFA, 95. *Work:* Guild Hall Mus; State Univ Stony Brook; Heckscher Mus, Huntington, NY; Royal Coll Heralds & Abbot Hall Art Gallery Mus, Eng; Fed Reserve Bank Atlanta, Ga; Long Island Mus Am Art; Yale Univ Art Gallery, New Haven CT; The Parrish Art Mus, Water Mill, NY. *Comn:* Count Robin De Lanne-Mirrles (portrait), 64; Met Transportation Authority, Arts for Transit, 2 glass mosaics, 2002; Holder Properties, Post Meridian; Twilight in the Garden, Columbia, SC, 2004; Los Angeles MetroArt, Union Station, Goldline, 3 glass mosaics, 2006. *Exhib:* US Consulates, Brazil, 87; Katharina Rich Perlow Gallery, NY, 91; 18 Suffolk Artists, Univ Art Gallery, State Univ NY, Stonybrook, 95; 52 Weeks, Heckscher Mus, Huntington, NY, 98; Rathbone Gallery, Sage Col, Albany, NY, 99; Lizan Tops Gallery, East Hampton, NY, 2000; Dunedin Art Ctr, Fla, 2000; Gloamings, Avram Gallery, Southampton Col, NY, 2002; Telfair Mus Art, Savannah, Ga, 2007-2008; Spainierman Gallery, E Hampton, NY, 2005; Giordano Gallery, Dowling Gallery, New York, 2010; Stony Brook Univ Art Gallery, NY, 2011; The Four Seasons Restaurant, NY, 2012-2013. *Collection Arranged:* The Art of Claude Lorrain, Newcastle & London, 69; The Art of Paul Nash, Newcastle, 71; Alan Davie/David Hockney: Watercolors & Drawings, touring, 71; The Craftsman's Art, Victoria & Albert Mus, London, 73; Watercolor & Pencil Drawings by Paul Cezanne, Hayward Gallery, London & Newcastle, 73; many one person & group exhibs organized at Long Island Univ, Southampton Fine Arts Gallery, 86-93, including photography of Peristroika, 91 & Betty Parsons, 92. *Pos:* Asst dir, Brook Street Gallery, London, 66-68; visual arts officer, Northern Arts, Newcastle, Eng, 68-74; bd gov, Lancaster Col Art, Eng, 72-74; dir, art gallery, Long Island Univ Southampton Campus, 86-93. *Teaching:* Vis artist, State Univ NY, Stony Brook, 78-79; adj assoc prof art, Long Island Univ Southampton Campus, 81-86, asst prof art, 86-93 & assoc prof art 93-2001, prof art Emeritus, 2005; prof art, Victor d'Amico Art Inst, Easthampton, NY, 89-94. *Awards:* Max Beckmann Mem Scholar; LI Univ Trustees Award, Scholarly Achievement, 2000; Municipal Art Soc NY, MTA Masterworks award, 2003. *Bibliog:* several articles, reviews, New York Times between 83 & 2001; Ronald Pisano (auth), Long Island Landscape Painting, Vol II, Bulfinch Press, 1990; Marion Wolberg Weiss (auth), article, Country Mag, 95; Ariella Budick (auth), Article, Newsday, 98; Becker and Colacello (auths), Studios by The Sea Abrams, 2002; John Eston, Hampton Gardens; A 350 Year Legacy, New York, Rizzoli, 2004; Along the Way, MTA Arts for Transit, Monacelli Press, 2006. *Mem:* Guild Hall, East Hampton, NY; Parrish Art Mus, Water Mill, NY. *Media:* Oil, Acrylic; Lithography, Etching. *Interests:* Gardening. *Dealer:* Suzanne Randolph Fine Art 234 5th Ave Ste 303 New York NY 10001; Gallery North Setauket NY. *Mailing Add:* 760 E Hampton Tpke Sag Harbor NY 11963

NICK, GEORGE
PAINTER, EDUCATOR
b Rochester, NY, Mar 28, 1927. *Study:* Cleveland Inst Art, 1948-1951; Brooklyn Mus Art Sch, with Edwin Dickinson, 1951-52; Art Students League, New York, 1957-58; Yale Univ, BFA, MFA, 1961-63. *Work:* Hirshhorn Mus, Washington, DC; Boston Mus Fine Arts; Joslyn Art Mus, Omaha, Nebr; Rose Art Gallery, Brandeis Univ, Waltham, Mass; Metro Mus, NY; group exhibs: Corcoran Gallery, Mus Baltimore, Boston Mus Fine Arts; rep in permanent collections: Boston Mus Fine Arts, Metrop Mus Art, Folks Mus, Essen, Ger, Nat Mus, Johannesburg, Southern Africa, Hirshorn Mus and Sculpture Garden, Wash, John Updike, Bob Dylan, Governor Michael Dukakis. *Exhib:* Graham Gallery, New York, 1964; Carnegie Inst Art, Pittsburgh, Pa, 1964; Schoelkolpf Gallery, New York, 1965, 1967; Richard Gray Gallery, Chicago, 1968, 1969, 1972, 1974, 1977, 1982, 1989; Harcus Krakow Gallery, Boston, 1974, 1979, 1982, 1984, 1987; Tibor de Nagy Gallery, New York, 1977, 1978, 1979, 1982, 1984, 1985, 2005; Pa Acad Fine Arts, Philadelphia, 1981; Gross McCleaf Gallery, Philadelphia, 1984; Fischbach Gallery, New York, 1986, 1988, 1991, 1993, 1994, 1996, 1998, 2000, 2003; Coll Fine Art, Baltimore, 1989-90; Miyagi Mus Art, Japan, 1991-92; Levinson Kane Gallery, Boston, 1992; Mass Coll Art, Boston, 1993; Gallery NAGA, Boston, 1997, 2000, 2002, 2007; Tel Aviv Mus Art, Israel, 1999; Lemberg Gallery, Ferdale, Mich, 2007. *Teaching:* Assoc prof drawing, Carnegie-Mellon Inst, 1964-65, painting, Univ Pa, 1966-69, Mass Coll Art, Boston, 1969-1994; tchr, Md Inst Fine Art, Baltimore, 1965-66; fac, Hollins Univ, Va, 2000-01, NY Studio Sch currently. *Awards:* Mass Coun Arts Grant, 1974; Nat Endowment Arts Award, 1976; Am Acad Arts & Lett Award, 1976; Dept of Interior Bicentennial grant. *Mem:* Nat Acad. *Media:* Oil. *Dealer:* Lemberg Gallery 23241 Woodward Ave Ferndale MI 48220; Tibor de Nagy Gallery 724 Fifth Ave New York NY 10019. *Mailing Add:* c/o Concord Art Assn 37 Lexington Rd Concord MA 01742

NICK, LLOYD
MUSEUM DIRECTOR, PAINTER
b Rochester, NY, Mar 11, 1942. *Study:* Yale, Norfolk, with William Bailey, 65; Hunter Col, with Tony Smith, BFA, 66; Skowhegan Sch Painting & Sculpture, with Philip Pearlstein, 67; Univ Pa, with Neil Welliver, MFA, 68. *Work:* Princess Grace de Monaco; Baron & Baroness Guy de Rothschild, Monaco; AT&T, Bank South, Atlanta; Barclays Bank, Charlotte, NC & Eng. *Comn:* Four color lithograph print, Hurt Building's 50th Anniv, 86; Colored pencil drawing, Petainer Inc, Atlanta & Stockholm, Sweden, 87; Drawing for book, Your Fondest Dream, The Power of Creativity, 89. *Exhib:* Philadelphia Mus Art, Nicholas Roench Mus & Automation House, NY; Gallery Contemp Art, Philadelphia, Pa; Fayetteville Mus Art, NC; Gallerie Monte Carlo, Monaco; Gallery Mod Art, Fredericksburg, Va; and others. *Collection Arranged:* The Family Photographs of Claude Monet (auth, catalog), Oglethorpe Univ Mus, 86; Black Artists from South Africa (auth, catalog), Oglethorpe Univ Mus, 89; Four from Madrid: Contemp Spanish Realism Oglethorpe Univ Mus, 94; The Spirit & the Flesh: Contemp Am Realism, Oglethorpe Univ Mus, 95; The Mystical Artists of Tibet, Oglethorpe Univ Mus, 96. *Pos:* Art gallery dir, Oglethorpe Univ, Atlanta, Ga, 83-92, mus dir, 92-. *Teaching:* Chair & prof art, Am Col Monaco, Monte Carlo, 69-70; prof painting, Guilford Col, Greensboro, NC, 73-76; chair & prof painting & art cult, Oglethorpe Univ, Atlanta, 84-. *Awards:* Nat Endowment Humanities Grant, 74; Int artist-in-residence, Ljubljana, Slovenia, Yugoslavia, 77; Fac Develop grants, Guilford Col, 74 & Oglethorpe Univ, 90 & 94. *Bibliog:* Atlanta J/Constitution, Atlanta, 86; Aesthetics & Philosophy, Sofia, Bulgaria, 91; Interview, Bulgarian Nat Radio, 91. *Mem:* Am Asn Mus; Asn Coll & Univ Mus & Galleries; Ga Asn Mus & Galleries; panelist, Asian Art Conf, Int East-West Ctr, Atlanta, 98. *Media:* Oil. *Publ:* Ed, The Family Photographs of Claud Monet, 86, The Many Faces of Buddha, 86, Oglethorpe Univ; contribr & ed, Four from Madrid: Contemporary Spanish Realism, 94, The Spirit & the Flesh: Contemporary American Realism, 95, Oglethorpe Univ Mus; contribr, The Mystical Arts of Tibet, featuring the Personal Sacred Objects of the Dalai Lama, Longstreet Press, 96; and many others. *Mailing Add:* Oglethorpe Univ Mus 4484 Peachtree Rd NE Atlanta GA 30319

NICKEL, DOUGLAS ROBERT
CURATOR, CRITIC
b Williamsport, Pa, Apr 24, 1961. *Study:* Cornell Univ, BA, 83; Princeton Univ, MFA, 89, PhD, 95. *Collection Arranged:* Picturing Modernity, 94-; Nature/Culture, 94; The Photographic Condition, 95; Snap Shots: The Photography of Everyday Life, 1888-The Present (with catalog), 98; Carleton Watkins: The Art of Perception (with catalog),1999; Stranger Passing: Collected Portraits by Joel Sternfeld (with catalog), 2001; Dreaming in Pictures: The Photography of Lewis Carroll (with catalog), 2002. *Pos:* cur photog, San Francisco Mus Art. *Teaching:* Instr studio art & photog, Cornell Univ, 84; adj asst prof art hist, Univ Calif, Berkeley, 95; adj prof art history, Stanford U, 1999, 2002. *Mem:* Coll Art Asn. *Publ:* Auth, American photographs revisited, Am Art, spring 92; Nature's supernaturalism, Tamarind Papers, Univ NMex, 96; Francis Frith in Egypt and Palestine, Princeton Univ Press, 2003. *Mailing Add:* 151 Third St San Francisco CA 94103

NICKERSON, SCOTT A
PAINTER
Study: Sch Visual Arts, NY, BA, 96; Art Students League of NY, 2000-; studied with Nelson Shanks, Art Students League, NY. *Comn:* Friends of Akim. *Exhib:* solo exhib, Thompson Park Art Exhib, Lincroft, NJ, 98, Orchid Island Golf & Beach Club, Vero Beach, Fla, 98, JW Ross Sea Bright Libr, NJ, 98; Annual Scholarship Competition, Soc of Illustrators, NY, 96; Open State Juried Exhib, Am Artists Prof League, Toms River, NJ, 98; Nat Exhib, Acad Artists Asn, Springfield, Mass, 99; group exhib, Frederick Gallery, Allenhurst, NJ, 99, Cork Gallery, Avery Fisher Hall Lincoln Ctr, NY, 2000; Open Portrait Exhib, The Portrait Soc Átlanta, Ga, 2000; Juried Children's Portrait, The Portrait Soc Atlanta, Ga, 2001. *Pos:* Portrait artist, currently. *Teaching:* instr, figure drawing & oil painting, Guild of Creative Art, Shrewsbury, NJ, currently. *Awards:* Hon Mention, Monmouth Co Arts Coun, Lincroft, NJ, 98; Best Portfolio Award, Am Soc Portrait Artists, NY, 2000; People's Choice Award, Portrait Soc of Atlanta, Roswell, Ga, 2001. *Bibliog:* illustr, Artist's Mag, 12/97; article, NJ Savvy Living Mag, winter, 2000. *Mem:* Portrait Soc Am; Am Soc Classical Realism; Am Soc Portrait Artists, Montgomery, Ala; Guild Creative Art, Shrewsbury, NJ. *Media:* Oil & Pencil. *Mailing Add:* 56 Phoenix Ct Asbury Park NJ 07712

NICKSON, GRAHAM G
PAINTER, EDUCATOR
b Knowle Green, Lancashire, Eng, 1946. *Study:* Camberwell Sch Arts & Crafts, London, BA, 69; Royal Coll Art, London, MA, 72; Prix de Rome (scholarship) RS, 72-74; Yale Univ Sch Art, Harkness Fel, 1976. *Work:* Metrop Mus Art, NY; Neuburger Mus, Purchase, NY; Albright-Knox Gallery & Mus, Buffalo, NY; La Jolla Mus Contemp Art, Calif; William Benton Mus Art, Univ Conn; Rep in permanent collections Metrop Mus Art, NY City, Neuberger Mus, NY, La Jolla Mus Contemp Art, Calif, Israel Mus; exhibs incl Art Mus, Fla Inter, 1996. *Comn:* Painting, Skidmore Owings & Merrill, San Francisco, 85. *Exhib:* Solo exhibs include William Benton Mus, Storrs, Conn, 82, Northern Ctr Contemp Art, Sunderland, Eng, 88, Warwick Arts Ctr, Mead Mus, Eng, 89 & Weatherspoon Art Gallery, Univ NC, Greensboro, 91, Salander-O'Reilly Gallery, NY, 2007; group exhibs include 30 Painters: New Acquisitions, Metrop Mus Art, NY, 82; New Drawing in Am, Drawing Ctr, NY, 82; Motion-Arrested Motion, Chrysler Mus, Norfolk, Va, 87; London-Glasgow-NY, Metrop Mus Art, NY, 88; exhibs incl Terry Dintfass Gallery, NY, 1996, Lizan-Tops Gallery, E Hampton, NY, 1996, Nat Acad of Design, New York City, 1996, Ark Art Ctr, Little Rock, 1997; Represented in permanent collections Albright Knox Art Gallery, NY. *Pos:* Head, first-year diploma studies Byam Shaw Sch Art, London, 1974; Dean, NY Studio Sch Drawing Painting & Sculpture, 88-. *Teaching:* painting fac Rome Scholarships, British Sch, Rome, 1975; lectr, drawing Philadelphia Sch Art, 1980; fac New York Studio Sch, New York City, 1981-88. *Awards:* Harkness Fel,

Commonwealth Fund, 76; Howard Found Fel, Brown Univ, 80; Howard Found Fel in Fine Art, 80; Guggenheim Fel, 89; Ingram Merill Fel in Painting, 93. *Bibliog:* Jack Flam (auth), Graham Nickson: Drawing into color, William Benton Mus, 82; John Russell (auth), Painter of beach life, Nickson's Beaches, New York Times, 82; Andrew Forge/Jack Flam/Bob McDaniel (coauths), Graham Nickson paintings & drawings, Northern Ctr Contemp Art, 88. *Mem:* Nat Acad. *Media:* Oil, Acrylic. *Dealer:* Salander-O'Reilly Galleries Inc 20 E 79th St New York NY 10021. *Mailing Add:* NY Studio School Office of Dean 8 W 8th St New York NY 10011

NICOLL, JESSICA F
CURATOR
Study: Smith Coll, Northampton, Mass, Bachelors (Art Hist & Am Studies), 1983; Univ Del, Masters (Early Am Cult & Mus Studies). *Collection Arranged:* Meet Your Neighbors, Old Sturbridge Village, Mass, Changing Times Changing Lives. *Pos:* Guest Cur, Winterthur Mus, Winterthur, Del, 1985-86; cur exhibs, Old Sturbridge Village, Mass, 1986-92; cur Am art, Portland Mus Art, Ore, 1992-1995; chief cur, Portland Mus Art, Ore, 1995-2005; dir, Smith Coll Mus Art, Northampton, Mass, 2005-Present. *Mem:* New England Adv Comt Arch Am Art Smithsonian Inst. *Mailing Add:* Smith College Mus Art Northampton MA 01063

NICOSIA, NIC
PHOTOGRAPHER
b Dallas, Tex, 1951. *Study:* Univ N Tex, BS, 1974. *Work:* Guggenheim Mus; Mus Mod Art, New York; Whitney Mus Am Art; Los Angeles County Mus Art; San Francisco Mus Mod Art; Mus Contemp Art, Chicago; Dallas Mus Art; Houston Mus Fine Arts; High Mus, Atlanta; Walker Art Ctr. *Exhib:* Acts and Sex Acts, Gerald Peters Gallery, Dallas, 1977; Pleasures and Terrors of Domestic Comfort, Mus Mod Art, New York, 1991; solo exhibs, Pace/MacGill Gallery, New York, 1991, Richard Foncke Gallery, Belgium, 1992, Linda Cathcart Gallery, Santa Monica, 1993, Stephen Wirtz Gallery, San Francisco, 1998, Dallas Mus Art, Tex, 1999, Ulrich Mus Art, Wichita, 2002, Centro de Arte de Salamanca, Spain, 2003, Charles Cowles Gallery, New York, 2004, Sheldon Meml Art Gallery, Nebr, 2005, Bemis Ctr Contemp Art, Nebr, 2008; Visions of Hope and Despair, Mus Contemp Art, Chicago, 1995; Telling Stories, Jacksonville Art Mus, Jackson, 1996; Texas Wired, Contemp Art Ctr, Ft Worth, 1998; Whitney Biennale, New York, 2000; Domestic Disturbance, Salina Art Ctr, Kans, 2001; Ambiguous Beauty: Photography from the Collection, El Paso Mus Art, 2004; Long Exposures, Los Angeles County Mus Art, 2006. *Awards:* Louis Comfort Tiffany Found Grant, 1984; NEA Photog Fel, 1991; Tesuque Found Arts Fel Grant, 1998; Guggenheim Found Fel, 2010. *Bibliog:* Susie Kalil (auth), The Burbs, Houston Press, 11/1999; Michael Ennis (auth), Northern Exposure, Tex Monthly, 2/2000; Jeanne Claire Van Ryzin (auth), Like Real Life only different, Austin Am-Statesman, 1/11/2001; Sarah Kent (auth), The Mind is a Horse, Time Out London, 9/18/2002; Kate Hackman (auth), Seething in Suburbia, Kans City Star, 6/4/2004. *Dealer:* James Kelly Contemporary 1601 Paseo De Peralta Santa Fe NM 87501-3723

NIEDERER, CARL
PAINTER
b Portland, Ore, Mar 14, 1927. *Study:* Univ Ore, Eugene, with Jack Wilkinson, BS, 49; Atelier Fernand Leger, Paris, France, 51; New Sch, New York, with Alexi Brodovitch, 53. *Work:* Univ San Francisco Collection & City of San Francisco Collection, Calif; Univ Wyo Mus, Laramie; Peace Harbor Hosp, Florence, Ore. *Comn:* Bronze facia frieze, Bank Calif Hq, San Francisco, 63; polychrome ceiling stabile, Univ Calif, Berkeley, 74; enamel entryway panels, Pac Bell, San Francisco, Calif, 75; elevator door murals, Chevron, 75 & AT&T, 77, San Francisco, Calif. *Exhib:* Pac Int, Perc Tucker Gallery, Townsville, Australia, 82; Australian Observations, Nicolaysen Art Mus, Casper, Wyo, 82; Wyo Biennial, traveling exhib, Cheyenne, 86 & 88; Wyo Fel Show, 88; solo shows, Citicorp Plaza, Los Angeles, Calif, 91, Triad Gallery, Seal Rock, Ore, 96; and others. *Pos:* Prof emer, Univ Wyo, Laramie, 91. *Teaching:* Assoc prof design, Univ Ore, Eugene, 68-70; head dept painting, Univ Wyo, Laramie, 77-82, prof art & watercolor, 82-89. *Awards:* Purchase Award, San Francisco Arts Festival, 64; Second Prize, Laramie Art Guild Show, 86; Best of Show, Wyo Watercolor Soc Show, 87; Wyo Coun Arts Fel, 88. *Bibliog:* Francis H Hoover (auth), San Francisco Gallery Guide, 75. *Mem:* Laramie Art Guild; Wyo Watercolor Soc. *Media:* Miscellaneous Media, Watercolor

NIEDZIALEK, TERRY
SCULPTOR, ENVIRONMENTAL ARTIST
b July 10, 1956. *Study:* Univ Colo, Boulder, 78-80; NY Inst Technol, Old Westbury, NY, BFA, 81. *Work:* Galerie Alain Oudin, Paris; NY Inst Technol, Old Westbury; Galerie Il Diaframma, Milan, Italy; Italian Vogue; The Body Shop Int, United Kingdm; Queen Latifah Show, New York. *Exhib:* Long Island's Alternative Spaces, Islip Mus, NY, 85; Fashion & Surrealism, Fashion Inst, NY, 87 & Victoria & Albert Mus, London, 88; The Political Landscape, Hillwood Art Mus, Greenvale, NY, 90; Hair Sculpture & Its Roots, Lehigh Univ Mus, Bethlehem, Pa, 91; and others; Nature with a Twist, Albright Coll, Freedman Gallery, Reading, Pa, 2010; Small Work Invitational, New Arts Prog, Kutztown, Pa, 2010. *Teaching:* Fac sculpture, Pa Govs Sch Arts, Erie, 92. *Awards:* Nat Endowment Arts Grant, 88; Individual Artists Award, Pollock-Krasner, 89; Cross Disciplinary Award, Performance, Pa Counc Arts, 91. *Bibliog:* Julius Vitali (auth), Hair Sculpture, Domus, Italy, 85; Andrienne Redd (auth), Hair Sculpture & Its Roots, Lehigh Univ Mus, 91; Dan Friedman (auth), Terry Niedzialek Hair Sculpture, Fiber Arts, 91. *Media:* Miscellaneous Media. *Publ:* Illus, Italian Vogue, 86, Epoca, Mondadori, Italy, 86 & New look, Filipachi, France, 86; contribr, The Costume Maker's Art, Lark Bks, 92; Earth Journal, Buzzworm Bks, 92. *Mailing Add:* 107 Mill Hill Rd Woodstock NY 12498

NIELSEN, NINA I M
DEALER
b Riverdale, NY, Nov 5, 1940. *Study:* Bucknell Univ, BA, 62; Univ Vienna. *Pos:* Owner, Nielsen Gallery, Boston, currently; vis comt mem, Boston Mus Sch, 79-80. *Specialty:* Modern and contemporary paintings, drawings and sculpture. *Mailing Add:* c/o Nielsen Gallery 128 Eastbrook Rd Carlisle MA 01741-1755

NIEMANN, EDMUND E
PAINTER, SCULPTOR
b New York, NY. *Study:* Nat Acad Design; Art Students League. *Work:* Slater Mus, Norwich, Conn; Butler Inst Am Art, Youngstown, Ohio; Syracuse Univ Art Mus; Swarthmore Col. *Exhib:* Directions of Am Painting, Carnegie Inst, Pa, 41; Nat Acad Design Ann, 62-68; Pa Acad Fine Arts Watercolor & Drawing Ann, 64; Butler Inst Am Art Painting Nat, 68, 74, 77 & 80; Watercolor USA, 72. *Awards:* New Eng Ann Lyon Award, 77; Audubon Artist Ann Hirsch Mem Award, 78; Young-Hunter Mem Award, Allied Artists, 80; and others. *Mem:* Audubon Artists; Am Watercolor Soc; Allied Artists Am; Nat Soc Painters Acrylic & Casein. *Publ:* Contribr, Todays Art, 7/68 & 8/73; auth, Drawing with unusual tool, Am Artists, 1/70. *Mailing Add:* 327 Central Park W #47 New York NY 10025-7631

NIESE, HENRY ERNST
PAINTER, EDUCATOR
b Jersey City, NJ, Oct 11, 1924. *Study:* Cooper Union, cert, with Robert Gwathmey & Morris Kantor; Acad Grande Chaumiere, cert, with Othon Friesz; Columbia Univ, BFA, with Leo Manso, John Heliker & Meyer Schapiro. *Work:* Whitney Mus Am Art, NY; Corcoran Gallery, Washington; SAAMI, Washington; Filmkundliches Arkiv, Cologne, Ger; Chrysler Mus, Norfolk; and others. *Exhib:* Young Am, Whitney Mus Am Art, 62 & 40 Artists Under 40, 64; 4th Int Exp Film Festival, Brussels, Belg, 69; NY Avant Garde Festivals, 69-78; Six Nations Mus, NY & Corcoran Gallery, 76; Foundry Gallery, Washington, 80; Solo exhib: Gold Leaf Studio, Wash DC, 9-11/2011; also numerous on-site ceremonial structures and performances in New York City, Mass, Vt, Md & SDak, 78-; And others. *Collection Arranged:* Cur, Edward Corbett, Univ Md Art Gallery Essays by Gerald Nordland and Henry Niese (catalog/bk, color & B&W), 1979, and others. *Pos:* leader/participant, 36 Sundances, 1976-2011; Univ Hons Program, Univ Md Col Park (UMCP), 1982-1995; Dir, Traditional Wisdom Prog, Eagle Voice Ctr, Glenelg, Md, 93-2014; pres, Wisdom Keepers, Hot Springs, NC, Cherokee, Iroquois, Lakota Teachers, 1997-2011; Md Inst Coll Art, 2003-2014; guest lectr, Va Tech; consult, Native Am Lifelines, Baltimore, Md, 2006-2007; HUD-Off NA Progs (traditional knowledge presenter), Ariz, Colo, Alaska, 2002-2003. *Teaching:* Spec lectr grad humanities, NY Univ, 65-69; asst prof studio art, Ohio State Univ, 66-69; assoc prof studio art, Univ Md, 69-95; vis artist, Univ Calif, Santa Barbara, 75; guest fel, Yale Univ, 79-, guest speaker, Timothy Daright Coll, 1986. *Awards:* Pulitzer Found Traveling Fel, 55; Int Cinema Prize, Mus Arte Mod, Vitoria, Brasil, 69; Creative & Performing Arts Grant, Univ Md, 71 & 73; And others. *Bibliog:* essays by Carlos Williams, 57; essays by WM Kloss, 2011. *Mem:* Sioux Nation Sundance; Epidaurus Project, Bethesda US Naval Hospital. *Media:* Multimedia. *Interests:* Native American ceremonial structures, painting, pastel. *Publ:* auth, The Man Who Knew the Medicine: Bill Eagle-Feathers Teaching, Bear & Co, 2002; 6 color reproductions & interivew, Little Patuxent Review, 1/2009; The Medicine is Sacred, Zogosothia Books, 2014. *Dealer:* WM Adair Gold Leaf Studio

NIETO, JOHN W
PAINTER, SCULPTOR
b Denver, Colo, Aug 6, 1936. *Study:* Pan Am Univ, 55-56; Southern Methodist Univ, 57-59; Dallas Mus Fine Arts, 60. *Work:* Heard Mus, Phoenix, Ariz; Smithsonian Inst, Washington, DC; NMex Mus Fine Arts, Santa Fe; Wagner Corp Collection, Austin, Tex; Goldwaters Pvt Collection; The White House, Washington, DC; Marine Corp Mus. *Comn:* Murals, Lakewood State Bank, Dallas, 61; bronze bust of chmn of bd, Tex Power & Light, Dallas, 80; portrait of Barry Goldwater, Goldwaters, Phoenix, Ariz, 83; Plains Prayer (poster), comn by ABC. *Exhib:* 20th Century Am Indian Artist, Kimball Art Mus, Park City, Utah, 81; Am Indian Contemp Art, Smithsonian Inst, Washington, DC, 82; Night of the First Am, John F Kennedy Ctr, Washington, DC, 82; Salon d'Automne, Grand Palais, Paris, 82; solo exhibs, US Embassy, Barbados, 82 & Wheelwright Mus, Santa Fe, 86; Images of Ranchos de Taos Church, NMex Fine Arts Mus, Santa Fe, 83; Native Am Works, Pensacola Mus Art, Fla; The Art of the Native Am, Owensboro Mus Fine Art, Ky; Le Salon Des Nations A Paris, Centre Int D'Art Contemporain, 86. *Pos:* Bd dir, Wheelwright Mus, Santa Fe, NMex, 84. *Teaching:* Art, NTex State Univ, Denton, 64-65 & Southern Methodist Univ, Dallas, 74-75. *Awards:* Blue Ribbon Award, Arts & Crafts Show, Heard Mus, Phoenix, 81; Artist of Year, Santa Fean Mag, 82; Featured Artist, Festival Arts & Pageant of Masters, Laguna Beach, Calif; Feather Dancer Poster Piece, 65th Inter-Tribal Indian Ceremonial, Gallup, NMex, 86. *Bibliog:* Erica Benis (auth), John Nieto Artist, Voice Am, US Int Commun Agency, 81; Ms Goldman (auth), Artist in Santa Fe, Nat Pub Radio, Washington, DC, 82; William Carpenter (auth), Profile of John Nieto, Carpenter & Assoc, 83. *Media:* Oil, Watercolor; Clay. *Dealer:* J2 Cacciola Galleries 125 Wooster St New York NY. *Mailing Add:* c/o Ventana Fine Art 400 Canyond Rd Santa Fe NM 87501

NIGROSH, LEON ISAAC
CERAMIST, WRITER
b Cambridge, Mass, Aug 7, 1940. *Study:* Carnegie Inst Technol, 58-59; RI Sch Design, BFA, 63; Rochester Inst Technol, MFA, 65. *Comn:* Ceramic sculpture, Temple Shalom Emeth, Burlington, Mass, 83; porcelain wall panel, comn by Mr & Mrs Joseph Epstein, Carlsbad, Calif, 83; porcelain signature wall, Holden District Hosp, Barre, Mass, 84; porcelain mural, Worcester Historical Mus, Mass, 86; ceramic mural, JCC Springfield, Mass, 94. *Exhib:* Artworks, Worcester, Mass, 81; Mirage Collectables, Miami, Fla, 82; Ely Art Gallery, Westfield, Mass, 83; Benchmarks Gallery, Washington, DC, 84; Signature, Boston, 85, 93-96; Cambridge Gallery, Worcester, 88 & 91; Higgins Armory Mus, Worcester, Mass, 98; ARTS Worcester, 00-02. *Collection Arranged:* Bay State Clay, Fitchburg Art Mus, Mass, 93. *Pos:* Comnr, Worcester Cult Comn, 86-88. *Teaching:* Instr ceramics, Auburn Community Col, 64-65; instr ceramics & studio mgr, Greenwich House Pottery Sch, New York, 65-66; instr ceramics & head dept, Craft Ctr, Worcester, 67-78; vis prof, RI Col, 78-79; lectr art, Clark Univ, Worcester, Mass, 81-89; adj prof art, Quinsigamond Community Col, 99-. *Awards:* Mass Arts Lottery Coun Grant, 82, 84, 89, 92, 95 & 97; Third Prize, Arts Worcester, 85; Award for Sculptors, Higgins Armory Mus,

Worcester, 91; Artsworcester Biennial, 97; Artist Fel, Worcester, Cult Comn, 2004. *Bibliog:* Articles, Moment Mag, 84 & Worcester Mag, 85; Worcester Telegram and Gazette, 91. *Mem:* Arts Worcester; Am Crafts Coun; Nat Asn Educ in Ceramic Arts. *Media:* Ceramic. *Publ:* Auth, Claywork, 75 & Low Fire, 80, Davis; five articles in Sch Arts, 76-77; Claywork, second ed, 86; Sculpting Clay, 1991, Claywork, 3rd ed, 94, Art Critic-Worcester Phoenix, 93-2001; Art Critic, Worcester Mag, 2000-05; contri ed, Arts Medica, 2002. *Mailing Add:* 21 Bates St Northampton MA 01060-2354

NIKKAL, NANCY EGOL
COLLAGE ARTIST
b New York, NY, 1944. *Study:* Syracuse Univ Sch Fine Arts, 62-64; Hunter Col, City Univ New York, 73; Pratt Graphics, Manhattan, 80. *Work:* Exec offs, Sun Chemical, NY; exec offs, Dainippon Ink & Chemical, Tokyo, Japan; Kawamura, Mus Mod Art, Tokyo, Japan; exec offs, St Paul Reinsurance Mgt, NY; Cong Off, Cong Dioguard, Washington, DC. *Exhib:* 9th Small Works Exhib, Wash Sq Galleries, NY, 85; New Art USA, Isis Gallery, Long Island, NY, 86; Ann Exhibs, Bergen Mus Arts Sci, Paramus, NJ, 87 & 89; Metro Show, City Without Walls Gallery, Newark, NJ, 88; Other Realities, Jadite Gallery, NY, 88; solo exhib, William Carlos Williams Ctr Performing Arts, Rutherford, NJ, 88; Centennial Exhib, Jehangir Gallery, Bombay, India, 89. *Awards:* Fourth Prize, New Art USA, Isis Gallery, 86; Irwin Z Lowe Mem, Fed Plaza, Nat Asn Women Artists, NY, 88; Contemporary Art/Painting Award, Westbeth Galleries, Am Soc Contemp Artists, 90. *Bibliog:* Helen A Harrison (auth), Winners in a juried show whose novelty is in its concept, NY Times, 4/13/86; John Zeaman (auth) A clearer picture at Bergen Museum, Record, 1/3/88; Jerry Tallmer (auth), Art's sexism gets a good once-over, NY Post, 8/4/89. *Mem:* Am Soc Contemp Artists; NJ Women's Caucus Art; Nat Asn Women Artists (foreign exchange co-chmn, 88-89); Salute Women Arts (regional, pres, 90-92). *Media:* Collage, monoprint, mixed media. *Mailing Add:* Studio F1 50 Webster Ave New Rochelle NY 10801

NILSSON, GLADYS
PAINTER
b Chicago, Ill, May 6, 1940. *Study:* Art Inst Chicago, dipl, 1962. *Work:* Mus Mod Art, Whitney Mus Art, New York; Art Inst Chicago; Mus Mod Kunst, Vienna; Philadelphia Mus Art; Milwaukee Art Mus. *Exhib:* Solo shows incl Whitney Mus Am Art, 1973, Fleisher Gallery, Philadelphia, 1991 & 1993, Ovsey Gallery, Los Angeles, 1992 & 1993, Braunstein/Quay Gallery, San Francisco, 1991 & 1996, Kind Gallery, Chicago, 1994, John Natsoulas Gallery, Davis, Calif, Tarble Arts Ctr, Eastern Ill Univ, 2006, Jean Albano Gallery, Chicago, 2007, 09, Luise Ross Gallery, New York, 2008; group shows incl The Hairy Who, Dupont Ctr, Corcoran Gallery Art, 1969; Poetic Fantasy, San Francisco Mus Art, 1971; Chicago Imagist Art, Mus Contemp Art, Chicago, 1972; The Koffler Foundation Chicago Currents, Smithsonian Inst, 1979; Parallel Vision: Modern Artists and Outsider Art, Los Angeles Co Mus (traveling exhib), 1992-93; Nilsson & Nutt: Works on Paper, Staller Ctr Arts, State Univ NY, Stonybrook, 1996; Images De Femme, Galerie Bonnier, Geneva, 1996; Jean Albano Gallery, Chicago, 2005. *Bibliog:* Gladys Nilsson, John Natsoulas Press, 1994. *Media:* Watercolor. *Dealer:* Jean Albano Gallery 215 W Superior Chicago IL 60610; Tory Folliard Gallery 233 N Milwaukee St Milwaukee WI 53202. *Mailing Add:* 1035 Greenwood Ave Wilmette IL 60091

NILSSON, KATHERINE ELLEN
PAINTER
b Sept 12, 1966. *Study:* Conn Col, BA, 93. *Work:* US Trust Co, Essex, CT. *Exhib:* 21st Juried Show, Soc Watercolor Artists; 62nd Ann Juried Show, Conn Watercolor Soc; Art of New Eng, Old Lyme Art Asn, CT; 22nd Juried Show, Soc Watercolor Artists. *Awards:* Chairman's Award, Soc Watercolor Artists, 2002; Judges Award, Ann Artists Show, Essex Art Asn, 2001. *Mem:* Old Lyme Art Asn; Essex Art Asn. *Media:* Watercolor, Acrylic, Oil. *Mailing Add:* One Spring St PO Box 261 Chester CT 06412

NIMMER, DEAN
EDUCATOR, PAINTER
Work: Milwaukee Art Inst; DeCordova Mus; Mus Fine Arts Boston; NY Pub Libr; Peabody Essex Mus. *Pos:* Cons & vis artist, MIT, Harvard Univ, Yale Univ, Vanderbilt Univ, James Madison Univ & others. *Teaching:* Prof & chmn dept painting & printmaking, Mass Coll Art, 1970-2004, prof emer, 2004-; prof art, Holyoke Cmty Coll & Curtis Blake Day Sch, currently. *Awards:* Disting Teacher of Art award, Coll Art Asn, 2010. *Publ:* Auth, Art from Intuition: Overcoming Your Fears and Obstacles to Making Art, Watson-Guptill, 2008

NIND, JEAN
PAINTER, PRINTMAKER
b Miri, Sarawak, Borneo, June 17, 1930; Can citizen. *Study:* Chelsea Art Sch, London, Eng; Univ Sask, Can, studied with Otto Rogers & Eli Bornstein. *Work:* Sask Power Corp, Regina; Esso Can Ltd, Vancouver, BC; Trent Univ, Peterborough, Ont; Volvo Corp, Halifax, NS; Art Gallery Peterborough, Ont. *Comn:* Symphony (oil), comn by mem bd, Saskatoon Symphony, Sask, 64; five serigraphs (for presentation to guest speakers), Trent Univ, Peterborough, Ont, 69. *Exhib:* Kingston Spring Exhibs, Agnes Etherington Art Ctr, Ont, 69; one-person shows, Artspace, Ont, 75, 77, 78 & 88, Bau-xi Gallery, Toronto & Vancouver, 78 & 79 & Williamson House Gallery, Peterborough, Ont, 88 & 90; Art Gallery Peterborough, 81 & 89; Lindsey Gallery, Ont, 89; Magic Image Gallery, Pickering Village, On, 92; Russell Gallery, Lindsay, 93; and others. *Teaching:* Instr child art classes, Mendel Art Gallery, Saskatoon, Sask, 65-66; instr early childhood art, Sir Sandford Fleming Col, Peterborough, Ont, 69-71, painting instr art admin, 73-77. *Awards:* Merit Award, Ont Arts Coun, 74, 75, 89 & 90; Award Winner, Juried Show, The Lindsay Gallery, 87; Award Winner, Juried Show, Art Gallery Peterborough, 94. *Bibliog:* Harry Underwood (auth), Spirit in the Art of Jean Nind, Globe & Mail, Toronto, 76; Colin Macdoneld (ed), Dictionary of Canadian Artists, Vol 5, Can Paperbacks, Ottawa, 77; Hennie Wolff (auth), The index of Ontario artists, 77; Printworld Inc, Bala Cynwyd, Pa, 87; Marketa Newman (auth), Biographical Dictionary of Saskatchewan Artists, Women, 90. *Mem:* Art Gallery Peterborough (mem bd, 72-78); Artspace, Peterborough, Ont (mem steering comt, 75); Visual Arts Ont; Art Gallery Ont, Toronto. *Media:* Oil on Canvas; Serigraphy. *Dealer:* Russell Gallery Peterborough Ont

NIPPER, KELLY
PHOTOGRAPHER
b Edina, Minn, 1971. *Study:* Minneapolis Coll Art & Design, BFA, Minneapolis, Minn, 1993; Calif Inst Arts, Valencia, Calif, MFA, 1995. *Exhib:* Breath, The Soap Factory, Minneapolis, 1998; solo exhibs, Shoshana Wayne Gallery, Santa Monica, Calif, 1999, 2001, Anna Helwing Gallery, 2007, Contemp Arts Mus Houston, Tex, 2007, Performa07, New York, 2007; A Sport & A Pastime, Greene Naftali Gallery, New York, 2001; Passion for Art: The Disaronno Originale Photography Collection, Miami Art Mus, 2001; People See Paintings, Mus Contemp Art, Chicago, 2002; Untitled, Santa Barbara Contemp Arts Forum, CA, 2005; Exist Music, Grimm Rosenfeld Gallery, New York, 2007; Whitney Biennial, Whitney Mus Am Art, 2010. *Awards:* Alberta Prize for Visual Art, 2004; Louis Comfort Tiffany Found Grant, 2008. *Dealer:* Anna Helwing Gallery 2766 S La Cienega Blvd Los Angeles, CA 90034

NISSEN, CHRIS (JOHN CHRISTIAN NISSEN), III
PAINTER
b Patterson, NJ, May 25, 1949. *Study:* Univ Va, BA, 71; Pa Acad Fine Arts (Fel, 4 yr cert), 80. *Work:* Cleveland Mus Art; Va Mus Fine Art, Richmond; Pa Acad Fine Arts, CIGNA Mus & Art Collection, Woodmere Art Mus, Philadelphia. *Comn:* Large paintings, Northwestern Univ, Chicago, Ill, 99; painting, Coopers Lybrand Inc, Philadelphia, 88; painting, Firestone Country Club, Akron, Ohio, 91; painting, comn by E I Dupont de Nemours, Wilmington, Del, 93; painting, Manufacturers Hanover Trust, Wilmington, Del, 93. *Exhib:* The Art of Business, Del Art Mus, Wilmington, 86; 2nd Ann Nat Juried Show, First Street Gallery, NY, 89; Evening Skies, Noyes Mus, Oceanville, NJ, 89; Contemp Philadelphia Artists (with catalog), Philadelphia Art Mus, 90; Marcel DuChamps Mothers Potato Masher & Other Works of Art, Va Mus Fine Art, Richmond, 90; 91st Ann Exhib, Woodmere Mus Art, Philadelphia, 92; US Artists '98, Pa Acad Fine Arts, Philadelphia, 98. *Teaching:* Adj asst prof drawing & design, Temple Univ, Philadelphia, 88-95. *Awards:* Purchase prize, Pa Acad Fine Arts, 80-81; Gifunni Brothers Purchase Prize, Pastel Soc Am, 84. *Bibliog:* Victoria Donohoe (auth), The arts, Philadelphia Inquirer, 92; Atlas of Florida, Fla State Univ Press, 93. *Media:* Oil, Pastel. *Dealer:* Carspecken Scott Gallery 1707 N Lincoln St Wilmington DE 19806. *Mailing Add:* 67 E Mermaid Ln Philadelphia PA 19118

NISULA, LARRY
PAINTER, SCULPTOR
b Phoenix, Ariz, Oct 10, 1960. *Study:* Glendale Community Col, 83; self-taught painting. *Work:* Tavan Sch Masterpiece Collection, Phoenix; Nott Corp, Irving, Tex; Mus Northern Ariz, Flagstaff; Merchants Press, Poughkeepsie, NY; Ariz State Univ West. *Comn:* Abstract painting, comn by John Gibney Med Ctr, Scottsdale; sculpture, comn by Mr & Mrs Augustus Boss, Ramada Corp, Scottsdale; sculpture, comn by Glendale Community Col, Glendale, Ariz; paintings, Valley Nat Bank, Phoenix, Ariz; prints, Designology, Scottsdale, Ariz. *Exhib:* Solo exhibs, Phoenix Col, 85, Fagen-Peterson Fine Art, Scottsdale, Ariz, 87-98 & Glendale Community Coll Art Mus, Ariz, 92 & 95; Mars Gallery, Phoenix, Ariz, 86, 93 & 96; Bell-Ross Gallery, Memphis, Tenn, 87; Bristol Gallery, Denver, Colo, 95; West Valley Art Mus, 98-. *Awards:* Third Place Sculpture, Glendale Festival of Art, 82 & 84, First Place, 83. *Bibliog:* Barbara Cortright (auth), Profile Larry Nisula, Zone Mag, spring 91; Jesse Evans Gray (auth), Larry Nisula, From the Ashes, 2/93. *Mem:* Phoenix Blues Soc. *Media:* Acrylic; Ceramic. *Publ:* Barbara Cortright (auth), Profile Larry Nisula, Zone Mag, spring 91. *Dealer:* MARS Artspace 126 S Central Ave Phoenix AZ 85004; The Bell Gallery 6150 Poplar Ave Memphis TN 38119

NIX, NELLEKE
WRITER, VISUAL ARTIST
b Utrecht, Netherlands. *Study:* Royal Acad Visual Arts, MFA, 58, The Hague, Netherlands. *Hon Degrees:* Certificate Degree, Stanford Calif Prof Publ, 94. *Work:* Nat Mus Women in the Arts, Washington, DC; Mus of the Holocaust, Providence, RI; Victoria and Albert Mus, London; Allen Libr Univ Washington, Seattle; Coll Art and Design; Corcoran Mus, Wash DC. *Comn:* The Inadvertent Garden Mural, NY, 1999; Zones of Time Sand & Rain, Libr Tellows Nat Mus of Women in the Arts, Washington, 2000. *Exhib:* Book as Art XIV, Nat Mus Women in Arts, Washington, 02; Northwest Ann, Bellevue Art Mus, WA, 95; Dutch Contribution, Nordic Heritage Mus, Seattle, 94; Noble Maritime Coll, Staten Island, NY, 2005; The Book as Art, Nat Mus Women in the Arts, Washington, DC, 10/2006-2/2007; McMullen Mus, Boston, Mass, 2009; The Book as Art, selections from NMWA, DC, 2009, 2011; Misbehaving, traveling group exhib, Great Britain, 2014-15; Saint Augustine's Tower, group exhib in Great Britain, 2015. *Collection Arranged:* Chinchilla Right Sculpture (Ronald McDonald collection), Lisa Harris Gallery, Seattle; Zones of Time, Sand & Rain, Victoria & Albert Mus; 1940-1945 Remembered; Nat Mus Women in the Arts, Wash DC, Royal Child, Childrens Hosp Sculpture, Seattle, Wash, 82-; Zones of Time, Corcoran Gallery, 2011, Sand and Rain by Krystyna Wasserman, NMWA, Wash DC. *Pos:* Artist in Residence, Fairhaven Coll, Bellingham, WA, 74; Owner Nelleke Nix Studio, 75-. *Teaching:* Artist in Residence, Boyer Children's Clin, Seattle, 99; Head Art Dept, Bush Sch, Seattle, 69-72; Artist in Residence, Noble Maritime Mus, Staten Island, 2002. *Awards:* 2000 Libr Fel Grant Award, Nat Mus Women in Arts, 2000; Gold medal, Best of Show, Int Platform Asn, 89. *Bibliog:* Lee Goss (auth), Time is on her side, Eastside Week, 10/14/1992; Mary McCoy (auth), Women in the arts: recreating a medium to send their messages, The Washington Post, 12/24/1992; Barbara Brachti (auth), For the love of art, The Journal American, 2/1993; Ted Lindberg (auth), A Dutch contribution, Nordic News, 4/1994; Marjorie Hack (auth), Hauntingly good taste, Staten Island Advance, 10/26/1995; Krystyna Wasserman

(auth), Artists on the Road, Travel as Inspiration, The Nat Mus of Women in the Arts, 1997; Virginia Baron (ed), Woman Spirit Moving Towards Peace and Justice, War Resisters League, 1997; Painters put imagination first, The Seattle Times, 4/24/1997; The Magic of Remedios Varo, Brochure Annual Gala Nat Mus Women in the Arts, Spring 2000; The Book As Art, Nat Mus of Women in The Arts, Wash, DC, 2006; Robert Vianna (auth), Remembering 911, 2007; Staten Island Advance: Titanic An Exhibition of Contemporary Art Remembering the 100 Year Anniversary of the Disaster at the Noble at Snugharbor, Staten Island, NY, 2012. *Mem:* Nat Mus Women in Arts; Women in the Arts; Artist Trust; Mus Modern Art; Soho20 Gallery; Seattle Print Arts. *Media:* Mixed Media, Digital, Sculpture, Photography, Painting. *Res:* women's art cross culturally. *Specialty:* Women's Art, Relationships, Family & Friends, Frida Kahlo. *Interests:* Reading, travel, vis art collections, animals, preservation, canoeing, biking & hiking. *Collection:* Frida Kahlo & Friends; Women's Art. *Publ:* auth, Zones of Time, Sand & Rain, 94; 1940-45 Remembered: Golden Dogs of Autism, 2009; Mamacita Linda, translations by M Huber, 2006. *Dealer:* SOHO2O Brooklyn, NY

NIX, PATRICIA (LEA)
SCULPTOR, PAINTER

b US citizen. *Study:* NY Univ, BA; New Sch Soc Res, with Anthony Toney; Art Students League, with Vaclav Vytlacil. *Work:* Nat Mus Am Art, Smithsonian Inst, Washington, DC; Heckscher Mus, Huntington, NY; Univ Windsor, Can; Staten Island Mus, NY; Newport Harbor Mus, Calif; Credit Suisse, NY; San Antonio Mus Art; Santa Fe Mus Fine Art; Texa tech Mus. Lubbock, 2000; rep in numerous permanent collections, designer sets and costumes (ballets) Petrushka, Pulcinella, Jeu de Cartes, 2002; Hudson River Mus, Yonkers, NY. *Comn:* Sets & Costumes for 3 Stravinsky Ballets, Carolina Ballet. *Exhib:* Nat Acad Mus, NY, 77, 79, 81, 83, 85, 87, 89, 91, 92, 93, 95, 97 & 99; solo exhibs, NY Univ Contemp Arts Gallery, 80, Am Embassy, Nambia, 99, Slovenia, 99, Merrill Chase Gallery, Chicago, Ill, 99, Tex Tech Mus, 2000, San Angelo Mus Art, 2000, Evelyn Siegel Galleries, Ft Worth & Dallas, Tex, 2000, Hilligoos Gallery, Chicago, Ill, 2000, 2002; Dillon Gallery, NY, 94-97; Galerie Donguy, Paris, France, 94; Boxes, Fatoui-Cramer Gallery, 95; Magic & Mystery, Austin Mus Art, Tex, 95; Hilligoos Galleries, 2000-03; Norton Mus & Sculpture Garden, Palm Beach, Fla. *Collection Arranged:* Totem Aitar, St Peters Church, NYC, 2004; Gallerie Marie Claude Goinnard, Paris, France, 2005. *Awards:* Salzman Prize, Nat Arts Club Ann, 78 & 88 & 1st Prize, 86; First Prize Gold Medal City Paris, Fedn Internationale Culturelle Fe'Minine, 93. *Bibliog:* Patricia Nix, Dillon Press, 96; Icons & Altars, Dillon Press. *Mem:* Nat Acad. *Media:* Oil, Found Objects; Mixed. *Publ:* Cover illusr, The Family, Random House, 97; Readers Dig, 97; Meninger Found J. *Dealer:* Hilligoos Galleries Chicago IL 60611; Evelyn Siegel Gallery 3700 W 7th St Ft Worth TX 76107; Dillon Gallery New York NY

NOBLE, HELEN (HARPER)
PRINTMAKER, PAINTER

b Northville, Mich, Mar 27, 1922. *Study:* Wayne State Univ, 39-41; Western Reserve Univ, 42-43; Santa Barbara Art Inst, 70-72; Douglass Parshall, Nat Acad, 75. *Work:* Numerous pvt collections. *Exhib:* Small Works Nat 81, Rochester, NY; Second Nat Print Exhib, Springfield, Ill, 82; 24th Ann Exhib Prints & Drawings, Oklahoma City, 82; Third Women in Art Exhib, Springfield, Ill, 83; Arts Festival, Santa Barbara, Calif, 85; 40th Ann Nat Juried Print Competition, Clinton, NJ, 96; StoneMetal Press, San Antonio, Tex, 12/2005-1/2006. *Awards:* Eight Awards, Santa Barbara Art Asn, 71-79; Third Place, 41st Ann Miniature Art Soc, Washington, DC, 74; Hon Mention Seventh Annual Exhib Miniature Art Soc, NJ, 77. *Mem:* StoneMetal Press, San Antonio, Tex. *Media:* Watercolor, Woodcut, Color Printmaking. *Dealer:* Ward-Nasse Gallery 178 Prince St New York NY 10012. *Mailing Add:* 1702 Cliff Dr Santa Barbara CA 93109

NOBLE, KEVIN
PAINTER, PHOTOGRAPHER

b Brooklyn, NY, 1952. *Study:* State Univ Col, Buffalo, NY, BA, 75; State Univ NY, Buffalo, MFA, 78. *Work:* Burchfield-Penny Art Ctr & Albright-Knox Art Gallery, Buffalo, NY. *Exhib:* Solo exhibs, Artists' Space, NY & Cepa Gallery, Buffalo, 80, The Kitchen, NY, 81, White Columns, 86, Mednick Gallery, Philadelphia, 87, Frank Bernaducci Gallery, NY, 87 & Panopticon, Irish Art Ctr, NY, 91; A Decade of New Art, Artists' Space, NY, 84; Photo-Syntheseis, Frank Bernaducci Gallery, NY, 87; Belfast/Beirut, A Tale of Two Cities, Alternative Mus, NY, 89; Images of War, El Bohio, NY, 91; Bloody Sunday Show, Irish Arts Ctr, NY, 92; Cepa Gallery, Buffalo, NY, 99. *Awards:* Artists Fel, Nat Endowment Arts, 79 & 87. *Mailing Add:* 227 DeWitt Rd Olivebridge NY 12461-5223

NODA, MASAAKI
PAINTER, PRINTMAKER

b Hiroshima, Japan, Dec 19, 1949. *Study:* Osaka Univ Art, Japan, BFA, 72; Art Students League, NY, 80. *Work:* Brooklyn Mus; Albright Knox Mus, Buffalo, NY; Philadelphia Mus Art; Hofstra Mus, Hemstead, NY; Portland Art Mus, Ore. *Comn:* stained glass, Keihan Rail Road, Kyoto, Japan, 97; sculpture & monument, Shinichi Lions Club, Hiroshima, Japan, 2000. *Exhib:* Int Biennial of Graphic Art, Mus Mod Art, Ljubjana, Yugoslavia, 85, 89, 91 & 95; National Triennial Print Exhibition, Schenectady Mus, NY, 95; Int Print Triennial, Nat Mus, Cracow, Poland, 84 86, 88, 94 & 96; The Boston Printmakers, Duxbury Art Complex Mus, Boston, 97; Stockton National Exhibition, Haggin Mus, Calif, 98; Surface and Diversity, Housatonic Mus Art, Bridgeport, Conn, 98; 20th National Print, Schenectady Mus, NY, 98; White and Black, Fukoyama Mus Art, Hiroshima, Japan, 99. *Pos:* Printmaker & painter, self employed. *Teaching:* vis artist, Univ Pennsylvania, 83-89, New School, NYC, 94. *Awards:* First Award, 1st Internat Art Show, Ga Art Soc, 86; First Award, 16th Internat Dogwood Art Show, Atlanta, 89; Purchase Award, Audubon Artist, NY, 2000. *Bibliog:* Robert S Bianch (auth), Art-Phitheater, PT Efstathiou Fine Art, 94; Srdan Markovic (auth), Leskovac International Biennial, Gallery Sunre, 98; Pam Koob (auth), 30/30, Art Students League, 2000. *Mem:* Audubon Artist Inc (dir, 98); Soc Am Graphic Artist (coun, 96); Boston Printmakers; Print Club Albany; Graphic Art Coun NY. *Media:* Serigraphy, Silkscreen. *Publ:* auth, Masaaki Noda Works in New York 1980-91, Abe Publ Company, 91; auth, Abstract Expression, 94 & Twisted Circulation, 95, Les Cyclades; auth, Breeze From New York, PT Efstathiou Fine Art, 2000. *Dealer:* 12 East 86th St #609 New York, NY 10012. *Mailing Add:* 393 W Broadway Apt 5WM New York NY 10012

NODA, TAKAYO
COLLAGE ARTIST, PRINTMAKER

b Tokyo, Japan. *Study:* Gakushuin Univ, Tokyo, Japan; Art Students League, studied printmaking with Michael Ponce de Leon and Seong Moy, 79-83; Pvt Study with Leo Manso. *Work:* Honolulu Acad Arts, Hawaii; NJ State Coun Arts, Trenton; Hawaii State Found Cult & Arts; Jane Voorhees Zimmerli Art Mus, New Brunswick, NJ; Portland Art Mus, Ore; The Nat Arts Club, New York City; Art Students League, New York City; New Orleans Mus Art, La; MTA, New York City; Lotos Club, New York City. *Comn:* Subway Poster Proj, Metrop Transportation Authority, NY, 98; Subway station window design, Metrop Transportation Authority, NY, 2006; Art Card for Subway Train, Metropolitan Transportation Authority, 2010. *Exhib:* Group shows, Nat Print Exhib, Honolulu Acad Arts, Hawaii, 85; Wenniger Graphics, Boston, MA, 88; Nat Acad Design, NY, 90 & 96; Nat Asn Women Artists, Bergen Mus Art & Sci, NJ, 91; Portland Art Mus, Ore, 92; Mus Provincetown Art Asn, Provincetown, Mass, 93; Nat Asn Women Artists Collection, Rutgers, Zimmerli Art Mus, New Brunswick, NJ, 94; Alexandria Mus, La, 96; Newark Mus, NJ, 99; Interchurch Center, NY, 2007; Longview Mus Fine Art, Tex, 2007; UBS Gallery, NY, 2009; MTA Transit Mus, New York, 2010; FYRE Gallery, Australia, 2010; Zullo Gallery, Ctr Arts, Boston, 2010; Printmakers Mem Show, Mass, 2010; Interchurch Ctr, New York, 2010; Salmagundi Club, Audubon Artist Show, 2011; Huntsville Mus, Huntsville, Alabama, Boston Printmakers Mem Show, 2011; Worcester State Univ, Worcester, MA, Boston Printmakers Mem Show, 2012; Old Print Shop, NY, SAGA Mem Show, 2012; Solo shows, Interchurch Ctr, NY, 94 & 2007; Tiffany Windows, NY, 95; Port Washington Pub Libr, Port Washington, NY, 98; Donnell Libr, NY, 2003; Wolcott Libr, NY, 2003; Austin Pub Libr, Tex, 2003; Hartford Co Libr, Mo, 2003; Phoenix Pub Libr, Ariz, 2004; Zimmerli Art Mus, NJ, 2005, 2009; Donnell Libr, NY, 2006; Gallery Hakudoutei, Tokyo, Japan, 2013. *Awards:* Gold Medal for Graphics, Audubon Artists Exhib, 92; Nat Print Exhib Acquisition Award, Univ Hawaii, 94; Nat Arts Club Award for Graphics, Allied Artists Am, 2003; V Stukey Mem Award, 120th Ann Exhib, 2009; Silver Medal for Graphics, Audubon Artists Exhib, 2011. *Bibliog:* Geraldine E Rhoads (ed), It's all in a woman's day, Woman's Day Mag, Fawcett Publ, 3/70; Helen A Harrison (critic), Hard-Edged imagery but surprisingly sensuous, New York Times, 5/10/98; John Edward Peters (auth), Sweetly Lyrical & Deeply Engaging, Kirkus Review, 2003; Julie Cummins (auth), The Bright Images with details that Literally Pop Off the Background, Booklist, Am Library ASD, 2006; Hope Marie Cook (auth), The Bold Collage Artwork in Exceptional, Sch Library Journal, 2006; Christopher Healy (auth), The Breath Taking Art, Cookie Mag, 2006; Beautifying Brownsville with Stained Glass, NY Sun, 7/14/2008. *Mem:* Boston Printmakers; Soc Am Graphic Artists; Audubon Artists; Nat Asn Women Artists; Acad of Am Poets; Allied Artists of Am; Lotos Club; Artist Fel. *Media:* Graphics, Dimensional-Collage. *Publ:* contbr, At Grandmother's Table, Fairview Press, 2000; Dear World, Penguin Young Readers Group, 3/2003; Song of the Flowers, Penguin Young Readers Group, 4/2006. *Mailing Add:* Five Charles St New York NY 10014

NODIFF, JACK
PAINTER

b New York, NY, May 2, 1922. *Study:* New York Univ, BA, 45; Long Island Univ, BS, 51; Art Students League, 55; New York Dept Cult Affairs, artist cert, 87. *Exhib:* Solo exhibs, East Rockaway Libr, NY, 78 & 89, Village Gallery, Hewlett, NY, 80, Malverne Gallery, NY, 82, Welles Gallery, Lenox, Mass, 91, Becket Art Ctr, Mass, 97 & Hewlett-Woodmere Libr Downstairs Gallery, NY, 2000; group exhibs, Int Art Festival, East Rockaway, NY, 83, Salmagundi Club, NY, 83 & 87, Chung-Cheng Art Gallery, Queens, NY, 84, Shelter Rock Libr, Albertson, NY, 85, Freeport Mem Libr, NY, 86 & 87, Nassau Co Mus Fine Arts, Roslyn, NY, 86 & 94, Garden City Pub Libr, Garden City, NY, 86, Syosset Pub Libr, NY, 87, Sheffield Art League, Mass, 92, 93, 95 & 96, Chelsea Art Ctr, Muttontown, NY, 92, Owl Gallery, Woodmere, NY, 96, Becket Art Centre, Becket, Mass, 96; E Rockaway Libr, NY, 97-98; Nassau Co Mus, Roslyn, NY, 97-98; downstairs Gallery, Hewlett Wood Mere Pub Libr, Hewlett, NY 2000; Sheffield Art League, Mass, 97-2005. *Awards:* Grumbacher Silver Award, Freeport Mem Libr, 87; First Prize, Sheffield Art League, 96, 97 & 99; Merit Award, Nassau Co and LI Partnership Fine Art Exhib, 2001; Award, Housatonic Valley Art League, 2008-. *Bibliog:* Valley Stream, Malverne J, 82; Long Island Local News, 82; Nassau Herald, 83. *Mem:* Tri Co Artists; Housatonic Valley Art League (2006); Becket Art Ctr; Communities Art League (CAL). *Media:* Oil. *Publ:* Lynbrook, E Rockaway Herald, 11/8/2007

NODINE, JANE ALLEN
PAINTER, SCULPTOR

b Spartanburg, SC, Mar 14, 1954. *Study:* Western Carolina Univ, Cullowhee, 72-73; Univ SC, Columbia, BFA, 76, MFA, 79; Kent State Univ, 78. *Work:* Equitable Life, NY; Palmetto Bank & Trust, SC; two Stouffers Hotels, NC; Capital South Inc, SC; Buyers Communs Systems, Atlanta, Ga; SC State Collection. *Exhib:* Americas 2000: Works on Paper, Minot State Univ, ND, 93; The Wichita Nat, Wichita Ctr Arts, Kans, 93; Dakotas Int Exhib of Artwork on Paper, Univ SD, 94; Visual Voices; The Female, Univ WFla, Pensacola, 94; LaGrange Nat Biennial XVIII, LaGrange, Ga, 94; 28th Nat Drawing & Small Sculpture Show, Del Mar Col, Corpus Christi, Tex, 94; Traces, traveling exhib, 2002-04; and others. *Pos:* Gallery dir, Univ SC, Spartanburg, 94-95. *Teaching:* Instr, Greenville Mus, SC, 79-80, Presby Col, Clinton, SC, 80-, Wofford Col, Spartanburg, SC, 81 & 83 & Sacred Heart Col, Belmont, NC, 82-; Converse Col, Spartanburg, SC, 90-95; Dir Univ of SC Art Gallery; assoc prof art, Univ SC, Spartanburg. *Awards:* Individual Artist Fel, NEA/SECCA Southeast Seven IV, 80;

Artists Fel, SC Arts Comn, 81-82 & 90-91; Belle W Baruch Scholar, 2002-03. *Mem:* Coll Art Asn; Am Crafts Coun. *Media:* Metal, photo-based two and three dimensional work. *Dealer:* Mary Praytor Gallery 26 Main St Greenville SC; Hodges Talor, Charlotte, NC; Zone One, Asheville, NC. *Mailing Add:* 113 Rockwood Dr Spartanburg SC 29301-3822

NOE, JERRY LEE
SCULPTOR, EDUCATOR
b Harlan Co, Ky, Sept 27, 1940. *Study:* Univ Ky, BA; Art Inst Chicago, Ford Found Scholar, MFA. *Exhib:* Sculpture 70, Art Inst Chicago, 70; Forty Yrs Am Landscape, Gimpel-Wietzenhoffer Gallery, NY, 73; Nat Sculpture Traveling Exhib, 73-75; Contemp Reflections, 1973-74, Aldrich Mus Art, Ridgefield, Conn, 74; Southeast 7, Southeastern Ctr Contemp Art, Winston-Salem, NC, 77; Solo exhibs, Henri Gallery, 77 & Mercer Gallery, 77. *Teaching:* Sculptor, Young Artists Studio, Art Inst Chicago, 69-71; vis lectr sculpture, Wis State Univ, Whitewater, 70-71; assoc prof art, Univ NC, Chapel Hill, 71-. *Awards:* John Quincy Adams Traveling Fel, 71; First Place, 73 & Third Place, 75, Southern Asn Sculptors; Nat Endowment Arts Grant, 77; and others. *Bibliog:* B J Ott (auth), Artist builds bridge, Buffalo Courier Newspaper, 75; Fun & games at art park, New York Times Sunday Ed, 75; and others. *Mem:* Southern Asn Sculptors (mem bd dir, 74-75, conf chmn, 75, exhib chmn, 75); Coll Art Asn; Southeastern Coll Art Conf; Southeastern Ctr Contemp Art. *Media:* Neon, Mixed. *Publ:* Coauth, Neon--The Artist (film), Res Coun, Univ, NC, 75. *Dealer:* Henri Gallery 1500 21st St NW Washington DC 20036. *Mailing Add:* 2008 Ridgewood Rd Chapel Hill NC 27516-9310

NOEL, GEORGES
PAINTER, SCULPTOR
b Beziers, France, Dec 25, 1924. *Study:* Studied in France. *Work:* Albright-Knox Art Gallery, Buffalo, NY; Chase Manhattan Bank, NY; Aldrich Mus of Contemp Art, Ridgefield, Conn; Centre Nat d'Art, Contemporain, Paris; Mus Mod Art, NY; Schlumberger Co, Paris; Guggenheim Mus, NY; National Galerie, Berlin. *Comn:* Painting, Cité de la Musique, Paris. *Exhib:* Galerie Municipale d'Art Contemporain, Saint-Priest, Musee de Brou, Bourg en Bresse-Centre National des Arts Plastiques, Paris/NY, Arnold Herstand Co, 88 & 90; Galerie Nothelfer, Berlin, Ger, 89 & 92; Arnold Herstand Co, NY, 88 & 90; Denis Hotz Fine Art Ltd, London, 90; Lorenzelli Arte, Milan, Italy, 90; Galerie Sander, Darmstadt, Ger & Zurich, Switz, 91; Galerie Baumgarten, Freiburg, Ger, 91; Base Gallery, Tokyo, 91 & 92. *Teaching:* Instr, Minneapolis Sch Arts, 68-69. *Media:* Multi. *Dealer:* Arnold Herstand 24 W 57th St New York NY 10019. *Mailing Add:* Haim Chanin Fine Arts 121 W 19th St Apt 10B New York NY 10011-4135

NOEL, JEAN
SCULPTOR
b Montreal, Que, Can, 1940. *Study:* Assumption Col, Worcester, Mass, 60; Ecole des Beaux-Arts, Montreal, Que, 63. *Work:* Assumption Col, Worcester, Mass; Musee des Beaux-Arts, Montreal; Galerie Nationale du Can, Ottawa; Musee nat D'Art Moderne, Paris; Rose Art Mus, Waltham, Mass; and others. *Comn:* Nat Res Council, Ottawa, Setauroute Bldg, Guyancourt, France; Univ Montreal, Can. *Exhib:* Group; Musée de Toulon, France, 82; Art Bank, Can Coun, Montreal & Vancouver, 82; Photosequences, Art Gallery Peterborough, Ont, 83; Plastiques et Plasticiens, Musee de Martiques, Centre Georges Pompidou, Paris, 84; Galerie Pixi, Paris, 2006; Solo Exhibs: Musee de Martiques, 84; Musee de Rochechouart, France 85; Found Cartier, Paris, 85; Musee de Valence, France, 87; Galerie Michel Tetreault, Montreal, 85-88; Musee de Maubeuge, France, 91; Galerie Krief, Paris, 86, 89 & 94, Musee Joliette, Canada, 2002, Galerie Pixi, Paris, 2006, Gallery Pink, Montreal, 2008. *Teaching:* Instr, Parsons Sch Design, Paris, France, 82-88. *Media:* Wood, Fiberglass, Steel. *Interests:* Architecture, history, archaeology. *Dealer:* Pink Gallery Montreal Can; Gallery Pixi, Paris, Gallery Krief, Paris. *Mailing Add:* 5 Cite Griset Paris 75011 France

NOGUCHI, RIKA
PHOTOGRAPHER
b Saitama, Japan, 1971. *Study:* Nihon Univ, Coll Art, Japan, BFA (Photography), 1994. *Work:* Walker Art Ctr, Minneapolis; Benesse Art Site Naoshima, Japan; Hara Mus Contemp Art, Tokyo; Kiyosato Mus Photographic Arts, Japan; Marugame Genichiro-Inokuma Mus Contemp Art, Japan; Solomon R. Guggenheim Mus, New York; Takamatsu City Mus Art, Japan; Mus Contemp Art, Los Angeles; Nat Mus Mod Art, Tokyo; The Vangi Sculpture Garden Mus, Japan; 21st Century Mus Contemp Art, Japan. *Exhib:* Solo Exhibs include D'Amelio Terras, New York, 2001, 2003, 2005, Hara Mus Contemp Art, 2004, DAAD Gallery, Berlin, 2006; Group exhibs include Gel, D'Amelio Terras, New York, 1998; Sensitive, Printemps de Cahors, Cahors, France, 2000; Under Construction/Fantasia, East Mod Art Ctr, Beijing, China, 2002; Time After Time: Asia and Our Moment, Yerba Buena Ctr Arts, San Francisco, 2003; Brave New Worlds, Walker Art Ctr, Mineapolis, 2007; Life on Mars: Carnegie Int Exhib, Carnegie Mus Art, Pittsburgh, 2008

NOLAND, WILLIAM
SCULPTOR, PHOTOGRAPHER
b Washington, DC, May 13, 1954. *Study:* Hampshire Col, with Gary Hudson & Leonard Delonga, 72-74; Sarah Lawrence Col, with Lou Sgroi & Mary Miss, BA, 77. *Exhib:* Solo exhib, Va Polytechnic Inst Art Gallery, 81; New Works in Clay III, Everson Mus Art, 81; Sculpture Invitational, Tibor de Nagy Gallery, NY, 81; Contemp Art in Detroit Collections, Detroit Inst Arts, 82; Five Am Artists, Galeria Joan Prats, NY, 83; Am Cult Ctr, Taipei, Taiwan, 99; McAllen Int Mus, Tex, 2000. *Bibliog:* Gene Baro (auth), article, Art Int, 8-9/81; Jo Ann Lewis (auth), article, Washington Post, 11/5/81; Valentin Tatransky (auth), article, Arts, 1/84. *Media:* Metal

NOLD, CARL R
MUSEUM DIRECTOR, HISTORIAN
b Mineola, NY, Nov 26, 1955. *Study:* St John's Univ, Jamaica, NY, BA (hist), 77; Cooperstown Grad Prog, MA (mus studies), 82. *Pos:* Registr, NY State Hist Asn, Cooperstown, 78-80; dir, Gadsby's Tavern Mus, Alexandria, Va, 80-84, State Mus Pa, 84-91 & Mackinac State Hist Parks, 92-; bd mem & treas, Midwest Mus Conf, 98-2000; pres, Asn Midwest Mus, 2001-. *Teaching:* Lectr, Cooperstown Grad Prog, 78-80 & George Washington Univ, Washington, DC, 82-84. *Mem:* Am Asn Mus (chair coun regions, 2000); Am Asn State & Local Hist; Mid Atlantic Asn Mus (bd mem, 87-88); Cooperstown Grad Asn (bd mem, 85-88); Mich Mus Asn (bd mem, 95-98, 99-, bd sec, 99-2001). *Publ:* Auth, Co-op docents: Volunteer management, Hist News, Am Asn State & Local Hist, 84; coauth, Gadsby's Tavern Museum Interpretive Master Plan, Alexandria, Va, 85. *Mailing Add:* c/o Mackinac Island State Park Commission Box 30028 Lansing MI 48909-7528

NONAS, RICHARD
SCULPTOR
b New York, NY 1936. *Work:* Mus Contemp Art, Los Angeles, Calif; Mus Mod Art, NY; Moderna Museet,Stockholm, Sweden. *Exhib:* Solo exhibs, Ink, Zurich, Switz, 79, Oil & Steel Gallery, NY, 80, Hudson River Mus, Yonkers, NY, 81 & Univ Mass, Amherst, 82; Ace Gallery, Los Angeles, Calif, 93; Xibbos, Paris, 94; Gallery 1-5, Brussels, Belg, 94; Ace Gallery, Denmark, 95. *Bibliog:* Jonathan Crary (auth), Richard Nonas: Boundary works, Artforum, 4/78; Donald Kupsit (auth), rev, Art in Am, 3/81; Grace Glueck (auth), An art blackout in Poland, 1/24/82. *Publ:* Auth, Summer 1906, 73, My Life on the Floor, 75 & Lost in Spoleto, 76, Buffalo Press; Hotel, 80, Boiling Coffee, 80 & Goats Itch (sound tape), 82, Tanam Press; auth, Richard Nonari Sculpture 1970-1988, Ace Contemp Exhibits, 88. *Dealer:* Ace Contemporary Exhibitions 5514 Wilshire Blvd Los Angeles CA 90036. *Mailing Add:* 14 Harrison St New York NY 10013

NORDAN, ANTOINETTE SPANOS JOHNSON
CURATOR, CONSULTANT, HISTORIAN
b Birmingham, Ala, June 27, 1953. *Study:* Univ Ala, Birmingham, BA, 75; Vanderbilt Univ, MA, 85. *Work:* Digital Manipulation-Contemp Printmaking, 2000; Contemp computer Photography, 2000; 2 Views: Photographs by Dan Budnik and Paintings by Bernard Williams, 2001; Paintings by Mark Messersmith, 99; Works from the Paula Cooper Gallery, 98. *Collection Arranged:* Ed Willis Barnett: Photographs, 86; Vision of the West: The Art of Will Crawford (auth, catalog), Birmingham Mus Art, Ala, 86; Post-Industrial Steel Town (auth, catalog), 88; Birmingham/Hitachi: An Exhib of Contemp Birmingham Artists (auth, catalog), Hitachi, Japan, 89; Michael Ponce de Leon: Prints and Plates (auth, catalog), 90; Prints and Preparatory Drawings of Felix Vallotton (auth, catalog), 93; Ferrously Yours: Contemporary Cast Iron Art (intro & ed, catalog), 94; Hans Grohs, Prints, Painting & Watercolor, 97; A Collectors Eye, SB Barker Collections, 98; catalog, UpSouth, 99; Perspectives on HIV & Women, 99; Paintings by Mark Messersmith, 99; catalog, 2 Views-Photographs by Dan Budnick & Paintings by Bernard Williams, 2001. *Pos:* Ed, Visual Arts Gallery Papers, 80- & contribr, 85-, Univ Ala, Birmingham; instr art hist, 84-90; cur, Visual Arts Gallery, 85-01, admin dir, 9-01, cons 2001-. *Teaching:* Instr art hist, Univ Ala, Birmingham, 83-. *Awards:* ARLIS-SE Award, 94; Ferrously Yours: Contemp Cast Iron Art, 95. *Mem:* Coll Art Asn; Southeastern Coll Art Asn. *Res:* 19th and 20th Century drawing and illustration. *Publ:* Auth, Vision of the West: The Art of Will Crawford, Birmingham, 86; Birmingham/Hitachi: An Exhibition of Contemporary Birmingham Artists, Birmingham/Hitachi, Japan, 89; Ferrously Yours: Contemporary Cast Iron Art, 94; Felix Vallotton (auth), Prints and Preparatory Drawings, 93; Up South, 99. *Mailing Add:* 2907 Virginia Rd Birmingham AL 35223-1253

NORDIN, PHYLLIS E
SCULPTOR, PAINTER
b Chicago, Ill. *Study:* Beloit Coll & Wayne State Univ, 54-56; Univ Toledo, BS, 63, BA (cum laude), 74; Toledo Mus Art, grad, 74, Univ Toledo, MLS Grad Degree, 92. *Work:* Ronald McDonald House, Toledo, Ohio; Town Ctr Mall, Port Charlotte, Fla; Univ Toledo; Beloit Col, Wis; Lucas Co Main Libr & Lucas Co Courthouse, Toledo, Ohio; Ft Defiance Park, Defiance, Ohio. *Comn:* Playmates (bronze), Treasure Coast Mall, Stuart, Fla; Beloved Son (bronze), Christ Presby Church, Toledo; Time Out (bronze), Ore, Ohio Branch Libr; Discovery (bronze), Port Clinton, Ohio Libr; Spiritus (ferro-cement), Flower Hosp, Sylvania, Ohio; and others. *Exhib:* Ann Sculpture & Ceramic Show, Butler Inst Am Art, 68-78; Liturgical Arts Nat, McFall Gallery, Bowling Green State Univ, 81 & 83; Liturgical Art Guild Ohio Ann, Schumacher Gallery, Capital Univ, 81 & 83; Allied Artists Am Ann, Nat Acad Galleries, NY, 84; N Am Sculpture Exhib, Far Hills Gallery, Golden, Colo, 84; Salmagundi Club & Audubon Artists Ann Exhib, Nat Arts Club, NY, 87; and others. *Pos:* former trustee, Toledo Mod Art Group; bd mem, Toledo Arts Comn & Toledo Artist's Club. *Teaching:* Instr, Lourdes Col, Sylvania, Ohio, Univ Toledo; instr ceramics & sculpture, home studio. *Awards:* First Prize, 43rd Ann Nat Art Exhib, Cooperstown Art Asn, NY, 78; Alpha Award, Best of Show, Energy Art Nat Exhib, Foothills Art Ctr, Golden, Colo, 83; Named to Lyons Twp High Sch Hall of Fame, La Grange, Ill, 96; Silver Medal Hon, NJ Watercolor Soc, 2006. *Bibliog:* Louise Bruner (auth), Toledo, city of sculptures, Blade, 80; M Biedron (ed), On the Cover, Radio Listener, WGTE Pub Radio, 80; J Hayes (auth), Contemporary sculpture alive, Columbus Dispatch, 82. *Mem:* Nat Asn Women Artists; Ohio Designer Craftsmen; NW Ohio Watercolor Soc; Liturgical Art Guild Ohio; Athena Art Soc; Catharine Lorillard Wolfe Art Club. *Media:* Bronze, Welded Steel. *Publ:* Auth, Downtown churches house treasures, Accent Arts, 80; contribr, Centennial Mall's crowning jewel, Alumnus, Univ Toledo, 80; Auxiliary presents sculpture, Toledo Hosp News, 81; Gallerie Women Artists, 90; Liturgical Art Guild Ohio, newsletter, 92

NORDLAND, GERALD JOHN
GALLERY DIRECTOR, CRITIC
b Los Angeles, Calif, 1927. *Study:* Univ Southern Calif, AB & JD. *Collection Arranged:* Gaston Lachaise (with catalog), Los Angeles Co Mus Art & Whitney Mus Am Art, 63-64; Richard Diebenkorn Retrospective, 64, Josef Albers, 65, Washington Color Painters, 65, Washington Gallery Mod Art, Washington, DC; John Altoon, Julius Bissier (with Guggenheim Mus), Robert Natkin, Al Held, Fritz Glarner, Paul Jenkins, Frederick Sommer with Philadelphia Col of Art, Peter Voulkos Bronzes, San Francisco Mus Art; Gaston Lachaise Retrospective (with Cornell Univ; catalog), 74,

Alberto Burri (with Guggenheim Mus; catalog), 77, and others, Frederick S Wight Art Gallery, Univ Calif, Los Angeles; Richard DeVore 1972-1982, 83, Controversial Public Art (with catalog), 83, Milwaukee Art Mus. *Pos:* Dean, Chouinard Art Sch, Calif Inst Arts, 60-64; dir, Washington Gallery Mod Art, 64-66, San Francisco Mus Art, 66-72, Frederick S Wight Galleries, Univ Calif, Los Angeles, 73-77 & Milwaukee Art Mus, 77-85; art consult, Chicago, 86-. *Awards:* Lachaise Found Grant, 73; Guggenheim Found Fel, 85-86. *Res:* More than forty museum publications on twentieth century artists and movements, emphasizing American painting, sculpture and photography. *Publ:* Auth, Richard Diebenkorn / Graphics 1981-88, Yellowstone Art Center, 1989; In the Spirit of the Times, Nora Eccles Harrison Museum of Art, Utah State Univ., 2003; Emerson Woelffer, RedCat, Calif Inst Arts, 2003; Reuniting an Era: abstract expressionists of the 1950's, Rockford Art Mus, Ill, 2004; ed, Richard Diebenkorn, Rizzoli Int, 87 (2nd ed, 2001), Frank Lloyd Wright: In the Realm of Ideas, SIU Press, 88; Zhou Brothers, Chicago: East-West Ltd Ed, 94; Ynez Johnston, Grassfield Press, Univ Ohio, 96; Twentieth Century American Drawings, Ark Arts Ctr, Little Rock, Ark, 98; Jon Schueler: To The North (with Richard Ingleby), London Merrell, 2002; Emerson Woelffer: A Solo Flight Los Angeles, RedCat, 2003; Breaking the Mold, Okla City Art Mus, 2007; Richard Drebenkorn in New Mexico, Univ NMex Press, 2007; and others. *Mailing Add:* 645 W Sheridan Rd No 3FL-2 Chicago IL 60613-3316

NORDSTROM, ALISON DEVINE
ADMINISTRATOR, CURATOR

b Boston, Mass, Jan 17, 1950. *Study:* Boston Univ, BA; Univ Okla, MLS. *Work:* New Work Japan (sculpture), 87. *Collection Arranged:* Robert & Frances Flaherty (film & photographs; auth, catalog), 83; Pro Femina (photographs of women by women), 93; Nervous Landscapes (7 photogr; auth, catalog), 94; Colonial Photography of Somoa (auth, catalog), 94. *Pos:* Dir, Brattleboro Mus, Vt, 83-88; res assoc, Peabody Mus, Harvard Univ, 89-91; dir and sr cur, Southeast Mus Photog, Daytona Beach, Fla, 1991-2001. *Teaching:* Int Partnerships Among Museums Fellow, Australian Ctr for Photog, 1992; NEH Fellow at City Univ, NY, 1993; Ansel Adams Fellow, Ctr Creative Photog, Univ Ariz, 1998. *Awards:* Darrah Award, 89; Nat Endowment Humanities Fel, 91. *Mem:* Am Asn Mus; Fla Asn Mus (trustee, 90-91); Soc Photog Educ; Oracle; Vt Mus & Gallery Alliance (trustee, 88-90); Atlanta Photog Group. *Publ:* Auth, Early photography in Samoa, Hist Photog, 91; Imag(in)ing the Seminoles, SEMP, 93; Persistent images: photographs in ethnographic collections, Continuum, 93

NORELLI, MARTINA ROUDABUSH
CURATOR

b Washington, DC, Oct 2, 1942. *Study:* Mary Washington Col, Fredericksburg, Va, 60-62; George Washington Univ, DC, BA (art hist), 69, MA (museology), 72, PhD (art hist),99. *Collection Arranged:* Artist-Naturalists: Observations in the Am (auth, catalog), 72, Birds (auth, catalog), 80, An Am Perspective: Selections from the Bequest of Frank McClure (auth, catalog), 81, Werner Drewes, Sixty-five Years of Printmaking (auth, catalog), 84, Art, Design and the Modern Corporation (auth, catalog), 85, Symbols and Ceremonies: Pueblo Indian Watercolors, 86, Figure Prints: Washington Print Club 11th Biennial Members' Exhibition (auth, catalog), 86, Close Focus: Prints, Drawings, & Photographs, 87, Nat Mus Am Art, Smithsonian Inst, Washington; East Meets West: Chen Chi Watercolors (auth, catalog), Columbus Mus Art, Ga, 89; Naturally Drawn: Drawings from the Collection (auth, catalog), Leigh Yawkey Woodson Art Mus, Wausau, Wis, 92. *Pos:* Curatorial asst, Dimock Gallery, George Wash Univ, 68-69; secy, Dept Graphic Arts, Nat Mus Am Art, Smithsonian Inst, Washington, DC, 70-71, mus technician, 71-74, asst cur, 74-78, assoc cur, 78-91; independent cur, 91-. *Awards:* Serv Award, Leigh Yawkey Woodson Art Mus, Wausau, Wis, 86; David Lloyd Kreeger Prize in Art History, George Wash Univ, 88; Univ Fel, George Wash Univ, 88-92. *Mem:* Print Coun Am. *Res:* American prints and drawings; Estonian 19th & 20th art; Franz Marc German expressionism; Wildlife art. *Publ:* Auth, The Watercolors of Antoine-Louis Barye, Antione-Louise Barye, Corcoran Collection, Washington, 88; John James Audubon, John Woodhouse Audubon, Vincent Gifford Audubon, 92; Drawing on Nature, Geelong Art Gallery, Melbourne, Australia, 92; Thoughts on Smallness, essay in Natural Wonders: John & Alice Woodson Forester Miniature Collection, Leigh Yawkey Woodson Art Mus, Wausau, Wis, 93; Mark Catesby, William Clutz & Ford Crull, Werner Drewes, Eleanor Dickinson, Harald Eelma, Sirje Eelma, Onne Eelma, Kenneth Engblom, Oriole Farb Feshbach, Janet Fish, Susan Fishgold, SV, Allgemeines Kunstlerlerlexikon, Saur Verlag, Leipzig, 96-2006. *Mailing Add:* 11219 S Shore Rd Reston VA 20190

NORFLEET, BARBARA PUGH
CURATOR, EDUCATOR

b Lakewood, NJ. *Study:* Swarthmore, BA, 47; Harvard-Radcliffe, MA, 50 & PhD, 51. *Hon Degrees:* New Hampshire Inst of Art, 97; Swarthmore Coll, 2014. *Work:* Mus of Mod Art, NY; Mus Fine Arts, Boston; Corcoran Gallery Art; Whitney Mus Am Art; Houston Mus Fine Arts; San Francisco Mus of Modern Art. *Comn:* Writers & The American Photogr Scene, 99; The Landscape of the Cold War, 2007. *Exhib:* Boston Mus Fine Arts Arch, 83; Inst Contemp Art, Boston, 83 & 91; Mass Coll Art, Boston, 85; Mus Art, Eugene, Ore, 86; Int Ctr Photog, NY, 87 & 93; Philadelphia Mus Art, Philadelphia, 87; Mus Mod Art, NY, 87; George Eastman House, 89, 2007; Houston Mus Fine Arts, 93; Davis Mus, Wellesley Col, 96; Whitney Mus Am Art, 96; San Francisco Mus Mod Art, 96; St Louis Art Mus, 97; Traveling exhib, 97-98; DeCordova Mus, 2008, 2010; George Eastman House, 2012; Form, Perth, Australia, 2012; Gayhead Gallery, 2013; Hampshire Coll, 2014. *Collection Arranged:* The Photography Archive on the Photographic Social History of the US; The Social Question: Social Reform at the Turn of the Century, Harvard & Mus Mod Art, 73; Richard Misrach, 80; Joseph Kondelka, 90; Looking at Death, 93; When We Liked Ike, 2001; Carpenter Center Photog Collection, Fogg Art Mus, Harvard Univ, 2008. *Pos:* Cur, Harvard Univ, 72-2001, emerita currently; consult on art, numerous orgns, 73-; Assoc, Carpenter Center for the Visual Arts, Harvard Univ, Cambridge, 2001-2009. *Teaching:* Sr emer lectr photog, Harvard Univ, Cambridge, 70-96. *Awards:* Nat Endowment Arts, 75, 79; MA Artists Fel, 87; Nat Endowment Arts Fel, 82, 84; John Simon Guggenheim Fel, 84; MA Artists Fel in Photog, 82; Aaron Siskind award, 91. *Mem:* Coll Art Asn. *Media:* Photography. *Res:* Have compiled an archive of over 30,000 negatives and prints on the social history of the US from 1900-1970. *Specialty:* Photog social hist of Am. *Interests:* Am hist & photog. *Publ:* Wedding, Simon and Schuster, 79; The Champion Pig, 79 & Killing Time, Godine, 83; All the Right People, New York Graphic-Little Brown, 86; Manscape with Beasts, New York, Harry Abrams, 90; Looking At Death, Godine, 94; When We Liked Ike, Norton, 2001; Landscape of the Cold War, 2007; and others; Faith, Hope, and Charity, Forthcoming, Godivie, 2012; Archives and Archtypes: Photographs by Barbara Norfleet, Southeast Mus Photography. *Dealer:* Howard Yezerski. *Mailing Add:* One Bowdoin St Cambridge MA 02138

NORGARD, KAREN-SAM
SCULPTOR, EDUCATOR

b Plainfield, NJ, June 6, 1952. *Study:* Univ NC, Greensboro, BFA, 74; Univ Cincinnati, MFA, 76. *Work:* Ga Southwestern Univ, Americus; Savannah Coll Art & Design, Ga. *Comn:* Blue Moon Experience (collab series), 99, 20 Dresses in Celebration (paper relief constructs), 99, Provost Comn, Savannah Coll Art & Design, 99; Suspended Matters, Galerie Blue. *Exhib:* Ten Artists, Gallery in Cork St, London, Eng, 96; Arts on the River, City of Savannah, Ga, 97; Women at Work, Univ Wis-Whitewater, 97 & 98; 20 x 10, Fleischer Art-Philadelphia Mus, 98; Razzle Dazzle, Savannah Coll Art & Design, Atlanta, 2008; Women are Everywhere: Sunflower Fug, Jarden de Murier, Lacoste, France, 2009. *Pos:* Chair visual arts, Metrop Sch Arts, 93-94. *Teaching:* Prof, Savannah Col Art & Design, Ga, 94-99, 2008-; asst prof, Univ Wis, Whitewater, 99-2008. *Awards:* Chancellor's Award, Univ Wis-Whitewater, 98; Pres Fel, Savannah Coll Art & Design, 2008. *Mem:* Found Art Theory & Educ; Coalition Active Sculptors Teaching. *Media:* Mixed Media. *Dealer:* Peltz Gallery 1119 E Knapp St Milwaukee WI 53202-2828. *Mailing Add:* 916 Woodpecker rd Savannah GA 31410-1207

NORIEGA, CHON A
EDUCATOR, EDITOR

b Miami, 1961. *Pos:* Ed, Aztlan: J Chicano Studies, 1996-; series ed, A Ver: Revisioning Art Hist & the Chicano Archive; adj cur Chicano & Latin Am Art, LA County Mus Art. *Teaching:* Prof dept film, tv & digital media, UCLA, dir Chicano Studies Rsch Ctr, 2002-. *Awards:* named one of Top 100 Most Influential Hispanics, Hispanic Bus; Getty Postdoc Fel in Art Hist; Film/Video/Multimedia fel, Rockefeller Found; Ann C Rosenfield Distinguished Community Partnership Prize, 2005. *Mem:* Nat Asn Latino Ind Producers (co-founder, 1999-); Independent Television Svc, (bd dirs, 2001-2007); Ctr for Human Rights and Constitutional Law (bd chmn). *Publ:* Auth, Shot in America: Television, the State, and the Rise of Chicano Cinema, Minn, 2000; ed, Visible Nations: Latin American Cinema and Video, Minnesota, 2000 & I, Carmelita Tropicana: Performing Between Cultures, Beacon, 2000. *Mailing Add:* UCLA School of Theater Film and Television 102 E Melnitz Hall Box 951622 Los Angeles CA 90095

NORRIS, MERRY
CONSULTANT, CURATOR

b Rochester NY. *Study:* Univ Calif, Berkeley, AA; Univ Calif Los Angeles, 80. *Hon Degrees:* AIA; LA. *Work:* Cerritos Ctr Performing Arts, 93. *Comn:* BMC Software, Houston, 98; Los Angeles Ctr Studios, 99; Universal City Walk; Hollywood Athletic Club, 94; Del Mar Station, Pasadena, Calif, 2004; Wilshire Vermont, Los Angeles, Calif, 2007; Andaz West Hollywood Hyatt Hotel, Calif, 2008; William Morris Endeavor Agency, Beverly Hills, Calif, 2010; Los Angeles Police Dept Bldg; West Hollywood Libr, 2011. *Exhib:* Cool Dogs, Hot Digs, 94 & 96; Calif Grown: Kenny Scharf, 2004; Drive-By Shooting, April Greiman, 2006; Traffic, Benny Chan, 2009. *Collection Arranged:* Community Redevel Agy, Los Angeles, 81-87; Cedars- Sinai Comprehensive Cancer Ctr, 87; Gonda Neuroscience & Genetics Res Ctr, UCLA, 98; Ernst & Young LLP Hq, 99; Heller, Ehrman, White & McAuliffe, Los Angeles, 92. *Pos:* Founder & co-chmn Major Gifts Com, MOCA, 79-84; pres & vpres, Los Angeles Cult Affairs Comn, 84-90; vpres bus develop, Pacific Design Ctr, 95-96; exec dir, Gateway to LA, PBID, 97-2001. *Awards:* AIA/CC Pub Serv Award, 93; Hall of Fame award, Set Decorators Soc Am, 2007; AIA/LA Bldg Team of Yr, LAPD HQ, 2009; Design Advocate, AIA/LA Presidential Honoree, 2011. *Bibliog:* The Art Newsletter, 5/95; Los Angeles Times Mag, 7/30/96 & 10/18/93; Access Los Angeles, 91 & 93; cover story, House of Business, 11/2000; Los Angeles Times, Concrete Canvas, 7/10/04; House of Bus, Mark Stock Paintings, 2000; Homes Across Am, HG-TV, 98; Artful Lodger, Los Angeles Times Mag, 7/30/05; Mover/Shaker, Interior Design, 2008; Pasadena Mag (cover), May 2010. *Mem:* SCI-Arc (bd dir, 87-); AIA/LA (bd dir, 95-2010); AIA (Am Inst of Archit) Los Angeles Chap. *Collection:* Young and emerging artists. *Publ:* Auth, Daniel Weinberg, Galeries Mag, 12/89-1/90. *Mailing Add:* 1473 Oriole Dr Los Angeles CA 90069

NORRIS, WILLIAM A
COLLECTOR

b Turtle Creek, Pa, Aug 30, 1927. *Study:* Princeton Univ, BA, 51; Stanford Univ, JD, 54. *Collection:* Contemporary California paintings and sculpture. *Mailing Add:* Akin Gump Strauss Hauer & Feld LLP 2029 Century Park E Ste 2600 Los Angeles CA 90067

NORSTEN, TODD
ARTIST

Study: Yale Univ, Norfolk Prog, 1989; Minn Coll Art & Design, BFA, 1990. *Exhib:* Solo exhibs, Paintings & Drawings, Willmar Community Col, Minn, 1992; Vermillion Gallery, Minn, 1992; Montgomery Glasoe Fine Art, Minn, 1994; New Paintings, 1996; Paintings & Drawings, Jennifer Armetta Fine Art, Chicago, 1997; Sighting, Weinstein Gallery, Minn, 1998; Paintings, Stephen, Wirtz Gallery, San Francisco, 1999; Recent Paintings, Finesilver, San Antonio, 1999; TrueFalse, 2001; Allsomenone, High Point Center Printmaking, Minn, 2003; Happy Happy Happy,

Franklin ArtWorks, Minn, 2004; Treasures from the Upper Midwest, Cohan & Leslie, 2006; Safety Club, Midway Contemp Art, Minn, 2006; group exhibs, Marks & Lines, Montgomery Glasoe Fine Arts, 1993; Brown Whiskey Club, 1995; Composing a Collection, Walker Art Center, Minn, 1996; Vistor's Voices: Recomposing the Collection, 1996; Dialogues, 1997, 1998; Elizabeth Dee Gallery, NY, 1998; Five McKnight Artists, MCAD Gallery, Minn, 1999; Summer Show, Margaret Thatcher Gallery, NY, 2000; Uncanny Visions, Plains Art Mus, Fargo, 2004; Abstract Painting in Minnesota, Minn, Mus Am Art, 2005; Young Am, Arario Mus, Seoul, 2006; Whitney Biennial: Day for Night, Whitney Mus Am Art, NY, 2006. *Mailing Add:* c/o Cohan and Leslie 138 Tenth Ave New York NY 10011

NORTH, JUDY K RAFAEL
PAINTER
b Los Angeles, Calif, June 24, 1937. *Study:* Otis Art Inst, 55-58; San Francisco Art Inst, 58-59. *Work:* Los Angeles Co Mus, Security Pac Bank, Los Angeles; Mus Contemp Art, Chicago; Oakland Mus, Calif; Opera Plaza Restaurant, San Francisco, Calif; Boise Art Mus, Idaho; Madison Art Ctr, Wis. *Çomn:* Stained Glass, Northbrae Community Church, 59; stained glass, Holy Name Jesus Christ, 63; stained glass, Salvation Army, 72; Portrait of Dean of Law Sch, Stanford Univ, 77. *Exhib:* Pilchuck Fac Exhib, Seattle, Wash, 85; Am Realism, 20th Century Drawings & Watercolors, 85; Prichard Gallery, Idaho, 86; Monumental Image, Springfield, Mo, 86; solo shows, Contemp Arts Forum, Santa Barbara, Calif, 90, Lidija Grzac Gallery, San Anselmo, Calif, 90, Portland Community Col, Ore, 91, Calif Mus Art, Santa Rosa, 91, Gallery Stevenson Union S Ore State Col, Ashaldn, 92, Slanted Door, San Francisco, Calif, 95, Immortal-Eye Your Pet, San Francisco Mus Mod Art Gallery, Ft Mason, Calif, 96; Liberation By Seeing, Gold Ridge Sangha, Am Sch Japan Arts, Santa Rosa, Calif, 94; No More Scapegoats, Anne Frank and the World Today, Corte Madera, Calif, 95; East Meets West, Bolinas Mus, Calif, 95; Animal Portraits, 3Com Corp-Great Am Site, Santa Clara, Calif, 96; Animal Portraits in Executive Ctr, Hitatchi Data Systems, Los Altos, Calif, 96. *Pos:* Staff designer, Actors Workshop, 60-64 & Cummings Stained Glass Studio, 63-65; designer, Bennington Col, 66-69. *Teaching:* Instr theatre design & stained glass, Bennington Col, 66-69; instr theatre design, Actors Workshop, San Francisco, 60-64; instr, Univ Calif, Davis, 83-86, Acad Art, San Francisco, 85 & Pilchuck Glass Sch, 85-88. *Awards:* Marin Arts Coun Grant, San Rafael, Calif, 90. *Bibliog:* Joseph Woodard (auth), Iconography of sacred and profane, Artweek, 90; Thomas Garver (auth), Regarding Art: Artworks about art, 90; Wayman R Spence (auth), Celebration of life, The Art of Medicine, 94. *Media:* Watercolor; Mixed. *Dealer:* Marion Parmenteer San Francisco Mus Gallery Ft Mason San Francisco CA. *Mailing Add:* PO Box 425 San Geronimo CA 94963

NORTHRIDGE, MATTHEW
SCULPTOR, COLLAGE ARTIST
b Manchester, NH, 1974. *Study:* Boston Coll, BA (studio art), 1997; Sch Art Inst Chicago, MFA (painting & drawing), 1999; Skowhegan Sch Painting & Sculpture, 2000. *Exhib:* Solo exhibs include Gorney Bravin & Lee, New York, 2003, Irish Mus Mod Art, Dublin, 2005, Western Exhibs, Chicago, 2006, Kantor/Feuer Window, New York; group exhibs include Out of Site: Fictional Archit Spaces, New Mus Contemp Art, New York & Henry Art Gallery, Seattle, 2003; Open House: Working in Brooklyn, Brooklyn Mus Art, 2004; Things We Said We'd Never Do Again, Western Exhibs, Chicago, 2005; Odd Lots: Revisiting Gordon Matta Clark's Fake Estates, White Columns, New York & Queens Mus, 2005; X-Mass the Spot, Draiocht Arts Centre, Dublin, Ireland, 2006; Viewing MacDowell: Works by Recent MacDowell Colony Artists, Sharon Arts Center, Peterborough, NH, 2007; Ann Invitational Exhib Contemp Am Art, Nat Acad Mus, New York, 2008. *Awards:* MacDowell Colony Grant, 2003 & 2008; Pollock-Krasner Found Grant, 2005; Helen Foster Barnett Prize for Sculpture, Nat Acad, 2008

NORTON, MARY JOYCE
PAINTER, JEWELER
b Tampa, Fla. *Study:* Akron Univ; Ariz State Univ; color theory with Dorothy Fratt. *Work:* Honeywell Corp, Minneapolis, Minn; First Nat Bank, Phoenix; Houston Oil & Mineral Corp, Tex; IBM, Endicott, NY; Drexel, Burnham, Lambert, Scottsdale, Ariz. *Comn:* Gateway Hotel, Phoenix, 85. *Exhib:* Watercolor Biennial, Phoenix Art Mus, 70-72, Four-Corners Biennial, 71-73; 8 West Biennial, Colo Ctr Arts, 72-74; Southwestern Fine Arts Biennial, Mus NMex, 72-74; Joslyn Mus, Omaha, Nebr, 74; and others. *Awards:* Southwestern Purchase Prize, Yuma Fine Arts Ctr, 67 & 73; 19th Nat Sun Carnival Exhib, El Paso Mus Art, 77; Ariz Painting Nat Competition, Scottsdale Ctr Arts, Ariz, 77. *Bibliog:* Barbara Cortright (auth), Meet the circle, Phoenix Mag, 2/75 & The look of nature, the flow of paint, Artweek, 5/75; Rosemary Holusha (auth), Mary Joyce Norton, Art Voices S, 5-6/79. *Mem:* Nat Women's Caucus Art. *Media:* Acrylic; Mixed

NORTON, PAUL FOOTE
HISTORIAN, EDUCATOR
b Newton, Mass, Jan 23, 1917. *Study:* Oberlin Col, BA, 38; Princeton Univ, MFA, 47, PhD, 52. *Pos:* Mem, Amherst Hist Com, 1970-74, 2002-06 & Mass State Hist Comn, 80-83; asst nat dir, Census Stained Glass Am. *Teaching:* From asst prof to assoc prof hist art, Pa State Univ, University Park, 47-58; from assoc prof to prof hist art, Univ Mass, Amherst, 58-93, chmn art dept, 58-71, chmn art history, 82-85 & 89-93, emer prof, 93-. *Awards:* Fulbright Sr Res Fel, 53-54; Nat Endowment Humanities Sr Fel, 71-72; Fel, JN Brown Ctr Study Am Cult, 93-95; Rhode Island Com Humanities Grant, 95-96; Merit Award, Am Asn State and Local History, 2002. *Mem:* Soc Archit Historians (dir & ed jour, 59-64); Soc Archit Historians Gr Brit; Archeol Inst Am; Soc Preserv NEng Antiquities; Ctr Int Vitrail; Pioneer Am Soc; Victorian Soc; Mountain View Country Club; US Tennis Asn; others. *Res:* History of architecture; England and America in the 18th and 19th centuries; survey of stained glass windows in Mass & Vermont; architecture in Amherst. *Publ:* auth, Amherst: A Guide to its Architecture, 75; Latrobe, Jefferson and the National Capitol, 77; auth, articles in J Soc Archit Historians, Art Bull, Britannica Encycl Am Art, Stained Glass Quart & Encycl World Biog; ed, Jour Soc Archit Historians; The Mountain View Country Club: Centennial 1898-1998, 98; auth, Rhode Island Stained Glass, 2001. *Mailing Add:* 42 Chmura Rd Hadley MA 01035-9727

NORTON, PETER K
COLLECTOR, PATRON
b Aberdenne, Wash, Nov, 14, 1943. *Comn:* Trustee Mus Modern Art, New York City. *Pos:* Prog, Norton Utilities (sold bus to Symantec), formerly; trustee, Mus Mod Art, New York, currently. *Awards:* Named one of Top 200 Collectors, ARTnews mag, 2004-11. *Collection:* Contemporary art. *Publ:* Coauth (with David Wild), Peter Norton's Computing Fundamentals, 1995; coauth (with Arthur Griffith), Peter Norton's Complete Guide to Linux, 1999; coauth (with Scott Clark), Peter Norton's New Inside the PC, 2002; contribr, articles to prof jour. *Mailing Add:* 225 Arizona Apt 350 Santa Monica CA 90401-1244

NORTON-MOFFATT, LAURIE
MUSEUM DIRECTOR
Study: Conn Coll, BA, 1978; Mus Mgmt Inst, Univ Calif, Berkeley, 1987; Univ Mass, Amherst, MBA, 1998. *Pos:* Docent, Old Corner House, Stockbridge Hist Soc, Mass, 1977-78, researcher, asst to dir, 1978-81; cur, Norman Rockwell Mus at Old Corner House, Stockbridge, Mass, 1982-86, dir, CEO, 1986-. *Mem:* AAM; Asn Art Mus Dirs; New England Mus Asn; Mass Advocates for Arts, Sciences & Humanities. *Mailing Add:* Norman Rockwell Mus PO Box 308 Stockbridge MA 01262

NORWOOD, MALCOLM MARK
PAINTER, EDUCATOR
b Drew, Miss, Jan 21, 1928. *Study:* Miss Coll, BA & MEd; Univ Ala, MA; Univ Colo, painting with Mark Rothko. *Work:* Miss Mus Art, Jackson; Miss Collection, Trustmark Bank, Jackson; Miss Col; Belhaven Col; Jackson Country Club. *Comn:* Landscapes & watercolors, First Nat Bank, Cleveland, Miss, 1964 & 1966; Rosalie (painting), comn by Daughters Am Revolution for USS Miss, 1978; 5 Mile Run, comn by Gov's Coun on Physical Fitness, 1981; and others. *Exhib:* Southern Methodist Univ Invitational, Ft Worth, Tex, 1962; Washington Watercolor Asn, Smithsonian Inst, 1963; Contemp Southern Art Exhib, Weatherspoon Art Gallery, Univ NC, 1966; Artists Registry Exhib, Brooks Art Gallery, Memphis, Tenn, 1969; La State Art Comn, Baton Rouge, 1969. *Pos:* Bd dir, Miss Mus Art, Jackson; dir festival, Crosstie Arts Coun, 1970-75, pres 1979-80; mem bd dir, Miss Arts Comn, 1980-85. *Teaching:* Prof & chmn dept art, Delta State Univ, 1962-90, emer prof, 1990-. *Awards:* Painting Award, Holiday Inns Am Arts Festival, 1969; First Prize in Drawing, Edgewater Merchants Asn Ann, 1971; Miss Governors Award for Excellence in Arts, 1992. *Mem:* Miss Art Asn; Cross-Tie Arts Couns. *Media:* Watercolor, Oil. *Publ:* Auth, article in Jackson Daily News/Clarion Ledger, 1964; illusr, 1964 & cover, 1968, Delta Rev; coauth, The Art of Marie Hull, 1975; auth, Guide to the Roberts Library Art Collection, 1977; The Garrard Collection, 1994

NOTESTINE, DOROTHY J
INSTRUCTOR, PAINTER
b Udall, Kans, Dec 3, 1921. *Study:* Univ Houston, 62-63; study with John Pike, Zolten Szabo, Edgar Whitney and others, 76-85. *Exhib:* Ann Art Show, Hill Country Arts Found, Ingram, Tex, 77; Art of Dorothy/Tom Notestine, Univ Tex Sci Ctr, San Antonio, 79; Carrizo Art Inst Show, Ruidoso, NMex, 85 & 86; Artists of Tex, Dallas Creative Arts Bldg, 86; Art of Travel, Love Gallery, Int Airport, San Antonio, 88. *Collection Arranged:* Watercolors of the World (with catalog), Northside Bank, San Antonio, 76; Collection Int Known Artists (with catalog), Kerrville, Tex, 77. *Pos:* Co-ed, monthly pub, San Antonio Watercolor Group, 76-78; bd-mem, Coppini Acad Fine Arts, San Antonio, 80-82. *Teaching:* Instr watercolor, Carrizo Art Ctr, Ruidoso, NMex, 85-86, Artists of SW Cruise Art, 86, San Antonio Col, 70-86; art instr, SS Star Princess, cruising Mediterranean & Europe, 92 & SS Dawn Princess, cruising Mex Riviera, Panama Canal & Caribbean, 93. *Bibliog:* Pat Breedlove (auth), Artists of Texas, Mountain Productions Inc, 86; Carla Tam (auth), Carrizo Art Mag, 86; Skip Singleton (auth), Ruidoso Life Style, Sunrise Productions, 87. *Mem:* San Antonio Watercolor Group (co-founder); River Arts of San Antonio; Colonial Hills Watercolor Artist Asn. *Media:* Watercolor. *Publ:* Coauth, Oklahoma Artists of Distinction, Paint Spree Publ, 89; many articles in daily and monthly publ. *Mailing Add:* 642 Glamis Ave San Antonio TX 78223-1506

NOTKIN, RICHARD T
SCULPTOR, CERAMIST
b Chicago, Ill. *Study:* Kansas City Art Inst, with Dale Eldred & Ken Ferguson, BFA, 1970; Univ Calif, Davis, with Robert Arneson, MFA, 1973. *Work:* Stedelijk Mus, Amsterdam, Holland; Nat Collection Fine Arts, Smithsonian Inst, Washington DC; Los Angeles Co Mus Art; Victoria & Albert Mus, London, Eng; Met Mus Art, NY; and others. *Exhib:* One-man shows, Allan Frumkin Gallery, Chicago, 1975, Garth Clark Gallery, NY, 1988, 1989, 1991, 1993, 1995, 1997, 2000 & 2003, Seattle Art Mus (catalog), 1990, Everson Mus, 1991, Newark Mus, NJ, 1991, Crocker Art Mus, Sacramento, 1991, Margo Jacobsen Gallery, Portland, Oreg, 2001, Elizabeth Leach Gallery, Portland, Ore, 2006, Zolla/Lieberman Gallery, Chicago, 2010, Fla Holocaust Mus, St Petersburg, Fla, 2011, Belger Arts Center, Kansas City, Mo, 2011; group exhibs, Contemp Ceramics: Sells from the Met Mus Art, NY; Int Ceramics Exhib, Hovikodden Art Ctr, Oslo, Norway, 1990; Metamorphosis of Contemp Ceramics: The Int Exhib Contemp Ceramics, Shigaraki Ceramic Cult Park, Shigaraki, Japan, 1991; Color and Fire: Defining Moments in Studio Ceramics 1950-2000, Los Angeles Co Mus Art, 2000; Contemp Am Ceramics 1950-1999, Nat Mus of Modern Art, Kyoto, Japan, 2002. *Pos:* Artist-in-residence, Kohler Co, Wis, 1976, 1978; artist-in-residence, Archie Bray Found, Helena, Mont, 1981; guest artist, Shigaraki Ceramic Cult Park, Shigaraki, Japan, 2002; guest artist, Int Ceramic Reseach Ctr, Skaelskor, Denmark, 2005. *Teaching:* Vis asst prof sculpture & ceramics, Univ Utah, Salt Lake City, 1975;

acting chmn & vis lectr ceramics, Md Inst Col Art, Baltimore, 1977; vis artist/lectr, Ohio State Univ, 1982; vis artist, Found Dept, Kansas City Art Inst, 1984, 1995; vis artist, Bezalel Acad Art & Design, Jerusalem, Israel, 1990. *Awards:* Visual Arts Fel, Nat Endowment Arts, 1979, 1981 & 1988; Guggenheim Found Fel Sculpture, 1990; Louis Comfort Tiffany Found Fel, 1991; Jerry Metcalf Found Award, 2000 & 2006; Fel Am Crafts Coun, 2008; Meloy-Stevenson Award, Archie Bray Found, Helena, Mont, 2008; Hoi Fel/crafts & Traditional Arts, US Artists, 2008. *Bibliog:* Patricia Failing (auth), Richard Notkin: Conduits for Social Meaning, Am Craft, April/May, 1991; Glen R Brown (auth), Embodied Conscience: The Sculptures of Richard Notkin, Ceramics: Art & Perception, No 43 p 15-18, Sydney, Australia, 2001; Walter H Lokav, Postmodern Moralities, New Ceramics, p 8-13, Germany, Feb 2006. *Mem:* Nat Coun Educ Ceramic Arts; Am Crafts Coun; Archie Bray Found, Helena, Mont. *Media:* Ceramics, Mixed. *Dealer:* Zolla/Lieberman Gallery Chicago Ill. *Mailing Add:* PO Box 698 Helena MT 59624

NOTTEBOHM, ANDREAS
PAINTER
b Eisenach, Ger, Oct 13, 1944. *Study:* Acad Fine Arts, Munich, Ger, 65-68. *Work:* Nat Air & Space Mus, Smithsonian Inst; Bundestag Cong Ger, Bonn; Asn Friends House Arts, Munich Ger; NASA Art Col, Kennedy Space Ctr, Fla; Lily of Salzburg, Austria. *Exhib:* Ann Shows, Haus der Kunst, Munich, Ger, 66 & 67; Halley's Comet Commemorated, State of the Universe & Calling All Stars, Nat Air & Space Mus, Washington. *Media:* Acrylic on Aluminum. *Publ:* Auth, Astropoeticon, Jurhot, Munich, Ger, 79. *Dealer:* Weinstein Gallery Geary St San Francisco CA 94102. *Mailing Add:* 17496 7th St E Sonoma CA 95476-4727

NOURSE, MIKE
VIDEO ARTIST, INSTRUCTOR
Study: DePaul Univ, BA (comm), 1999; Sch Art Inst Chicago, MFA (visual comm), 2002. *Exhib:* Aurora Film Show, Austin, 2001; Select Media Festival 1, Chicago, 2002; San Francisco Independent Film Festival, Calif, 2003; Rapid Eye Festival, The Hague, Neth, 2004; Athens Int Film & Video Festival, 2005; Art of Games, St Xavior Univ, 2006; 101 Paintings, Co-Prosperity Sphere, Chicago, 2007; Outdated Polaroid Show, Country Club Gallery, 2008; solo exhib, City of Found Children, Salvage One, Chicago, 2009. *Pos:* Principal, Zero One Projects LLC, 2001-2006; co-founder, The Chicago Art Dept, 2004-; mgr studio programs, Marwen, Chicago, 2006-2009. *Teaching:* Teaching asst, DePaul Univ, 1999 & Sch Art Inst Chicago, 2000-2002; adj prof, DePaul Univ, 2002-2004. *Mailing Add:* Chicago Art Dept 1837 S Halsted Chicago IL 60608

NOVA, RES See Yarotsky, Lori

NOVINSKI, LYLE FRANK
PAINTER, EDUCATOR
b Montfort, Wis, June 23, 1932. *Study:* Univ Wis/Platteville, BA; Univ Wis, MS & MFA; Marquette Univ. *Hon Degrees:* Univ Wis, Platteville, Wis. *Work:* Univ Dallas; SMU; DMA. *Comn:* Major leather wall construct, Amarillo & Dallas, Tex, 77; Chapel of the Incarnation, Univ Dallas, 85; St Joseph Church, Moulton, Tex, 94; Major stained glass installations, St Rita, Dallas, 86 & St Joseph's, Arlington, Tex., 97; Perkins and Neuhoff Chapel appointments, Southern Methodist, Dallas, 99; Bronze Relief, Marquette Univ, Milwaukee, 2000; Sacred Heart Church, Spearman, Tex, 2000; Stained Glass Stations, Holy Family Christian Church, Coppell, Tex, 2006; Holy Spirit, Duncanville, Tex, 2012. *Exhib:* Tex Gen, 64 & 72; Okla Eight State Exhib, 68; Okla Invitational, 70; Ft Worth Art Ctr, 71; Nat Interfaith Conf on Relig & Archit, 75; Tex Wesleyan, 2002; CIVA, 2001; Dart Station, Public Art, 2012; Mosaic, Rome Chapel, Univ Dallas, 2013; First Presbyterian, Bonham, Tex, 2013. *Collection Arranged:* Korea Then and Now, 2004. *Pos:* emer prof, Univ Dallas; owner, Novinski Studio. *Teaching:* Prof art & Art Hist, Univ Dallas, 60-; fel, Dallas Inst Humanities & Cult, 80-. *Awards:* Purchase Award, Okla Eight State, 68; Top Award, Tex Gen, 72; Distinguished Alumni, Univ Wis Platteville, 95; Novinski Art Found Bldg, Univ Dallas, 2001. *Bibliog:* Articles, Christian Arts, 68, Liturgical Arts, 70 & Art Gallery, 71-72. *Mem:* Interfaith Forum Relig, Art & Archit; Coll Art Asn; CIVA; Kimball; Christians in Visual Arts. *Media:* Leather, Oil, Ceramic, Bronze, Stained Glass. *Res:* Liturgical Art and Design. *Specialty:* painting, stained glass. *Interests:* religious art, land design. *Publ:* Shaping Space; Reflected Knowing. *Dealer:* Valley House Gallery 6616 Spring Valley Rd Dallas TX 75240. *Mailing Add:* 1101 Owenwood Dr Irving TX 75061-5536

NOWYTSKI, SVIATOSLAV
FILMMAKER, PHOTOGRAPHER
b Oct 19, 34; Can & US citizen. *Study:* Pasadena Playhouse Coll Theatre Arts, BA (theatre), 58; Columbia Univ, MFA (motion pictures), 64. *Work:* Educ Film Libr Asn, NY; Libr Cong; Dept Tourism, Recreation & Cult Affairs, Govt Man; Fedn Asn Arts, Man; Ont Ministry Educ, Toronto. *Comn:* Reflections of the Past (film), Ukrainian Cult & Educ Ctr, Winnipeg, 74; Last of the Jacks (film), Minn Hist Soc, 76; Immortal Image (film), Filmart Prod, 78; Grass on the Roof (film), Underground Space Ctr, Univ Minn, 79; The Helm of Destiny (film), UNA, NJ, 81; Harvest of Despair (film), UCRDC, Can, 84; We're Not Robots, You Know (video), Synergenesis Corp, 88. *Exhib:* Sheep in Wood (film), Am Film Festival, NY, 71; Reflections of the Past (film), Can Film Awards, Niagara on the Lake, Ont, 75 & 11th Int Chicago Film Festival, Ill, 75; Pysanka: The Ukrainian Easter Egg (film), Chicago Int Film Festival, 76; 1 hr feature documentary for UCRDC (Toronto): Between Hitler and Stalin, Ukraine in WW II - The Untold Story (prodr/dir), narration by Jack Palance, 01. *Pos:* Ed, Ukrainian, Polish & Russian Sect, Cinema & TV Digest, 63-; ed, Filmart Prod, St Paul, Minn, 71-82; freelance prodr/dir Slavko Nowytski & Assocs, 82-93; internat TV broadcaster & video journalist Voice of America TV, Window on America weekly program on UT-1 nat TV network, Ukraine, 93-. *Awards:* Blue Ribbon Award for Sheep in Wood, Am Film Festival, 71; Gold Hugo for Pysanka: The Ukrainian Easter Egg, Chicago Int Film Festival, 76 & Silver Venus Medal, Virgin Islands Int Film Festival, 77; Bronze Medal for Immortal Image, Int Film & TV Festival, NY, 78. *Mem:* Minn Soc Fine Arts; Twin Cities Metrop Arts Alliance; Intermedia Arts. *Media:* Film; TV. *Interests:* Prodn of historical and cultural films & programs

NOYES, SANDY
PHOTOGRAPHER
b New York, NY, Dec 18, 1941. *Study:* Yale Univ, with Bud Leak, BA, 63; workshop with Paul Caponigro, 73 & Minor White, 74; New Sch Soc Res, with George Tice, 74. *Work:* Metrop Mus Art, NY; Bibliot Nat, Paris; Addison Gallery Am Art; High Mus Art; Amon Carter Mus, Ft Worth, Tex; Int Mus Photog at George Eastman House, Rochester, NY. *Exhib:* NJ State Mus, Trenton, 79; Contemp Platinotype, Rochester Inst Technol, NY, 79; Intervals, 22 Wooster St Gallery, NY, 82; Nikon House, NY, 84; Albany Inst Hist & Art, 89. *Teaching:* Instr, Int Ctr Photog, New York, 76-81. *Awards:* Proj Grant (co-recipient), Seven Photogrs, Del Valley, Nat Endowment Arts, 77; Ossabaw Island Proj Fel, Ga, 79; Creative Artists Prog Serv Grant, NY, 83. *Mem:* Albany/Schenectady League Arts; Soc Indust Archeol. *Mailing Add:* Sandy Noyes Photography 745 Dugway Rd Chatham NY 12037-2214

NOZKOWSKI, THOMAS
PAINTER
b Teaneck, NJ, 1944. *Study:* Cooper Union, BFA, 1967. *Exhib:* Solo exhibs include Max Protetch Gallery, NY City, 90, 91, 93, 95, 97, 2000, 2001, 2003, 2006, Ludwig Museum, Koblenz, 2007; group exhibs include From Earth to Archetype, Ledisflam Gallery, NY, 90, Michael Berger Gallery, Pitts, 2003; 10 Abstract Painters, Baumgartner Galleries, Washington, 91; Shades of Difference, Sandra Gering Gallery, NY City, 92; Return of the Cadavre Exquis, The Drawing Ctr, NY City, 93; A Hundred Hearts, The Contemp, NY City, 94; Re-Picturing Abstraction, 1708 Gallery, Richmond, Va, 95; New Narrative Abstraction, Brooklyn Col, 96; Purely Painting, Elizabeth Harris Gallery, NY City, 97; Pertaining to Painting, Contemp Arts Mus, Houston, 2002; Nat Acad Mus, NY City, 2006; Venice Biennale, 2007; represented in public collections of Whitney Mus Am Art, NY City, San Francisco Mus Modern Art, Orlando Mus Art, Fla, Mus Modern Art, NY City, Metrop Mus Art, Hirshhorn Mus and Sculpture Garden, Washington, DC, High Mus Art, Atlanta, Corcoran Gallery Art, Washington, DC, Brooklyn Mus Art. *Teaching:* Assoc prof Mason Gross Sch Arts, Rutgers Univ, NJ, 2000, prof painting, currently. *Awards:* Purchase Prize, Am Acad Arts and Letters, 98, 99; Am Acad Arts and Letters Award in Painting, 99; Individual Artist Grant, Nat Endowment Arts, 84; NY State Creative Artists Public Serv Grant, 85; NY State Found Arts Fellowship, 89; John Simon Guggeheim Memorial Found Fellowship, 93; Award of Merit Painting Medal, Am Acad Arts and Letters, 2006. *Mem:* Nat Acad Design; Am Acad Arts & Letts. *Dealer:* Harlan and Weaver 83 Canal St New York NY 10001. *Mailing Add:* Mason Gross Sch of Arts 33 Livingston Ave New Brunswick NJ 08901

NUCHI, NATAN
PAINTER, PRINTMAKER
b Nahalal, Israel, Feb 8, 1951; US & Israeli citizen. *Study:* Self educated. *Work:* Jewish Mus, NY; Mus RI Sch Design; Nat Jewish Mus, Washington; Haifa Munic Mus Mod Art, Israel; Israel Mus, Jerusalem; Metropolitan Mus Art, NY; NY Public Libr; Queens Mus, NY; New Orleans Mus Art; Rhode Island Sch Design Mus. *Exhib:* Solo exhibs, Haifa Mus Mod Art, Israel, 93, Nat Jewish Mus, Washington, 95 & Digital Drawings, Ramat Gan Mus Israeli Art, 97; Acquisitions, RI Sch Design, Providence, 94; After Auschwitz: Responses to the Holocaust in Contemp Art, Royal Festival Hall, London, Manchester City Art Gallery, United Kingdom, 95-96; Windows: Seven Subjects in Contemp Art, Israel Mus, Jerusalem, 96. *Bibliog:* Donald Kuspit (auth), The Abandoned Nude, Klarfeld Perry, 92; Gerrit Henry (auth), Review one-man show, Art in Am, 93; Matthew Baigell (auth), The Persistence of Holocaust Imagery in American Art, Minn Art Mus, 95 & Jewish American Artists and the Holocaust, Rutgers Univ Press, 97. *Mailing Add:* 5 E 3rd St New York NY 10003

NUGENT, BOB L
PAINTER, PRINTMAKER
b Santa Monica, Calif, Aug 15, 1947. *Study:* Coll Creative Studies, Univ Calif, BA, 69; Univ Calif, Santa Barbara, MFA, 71. *Work:* Bank Am Headquarters, San Francisco, Calif; Washington State Art in Public Places, Spokane; Indianapolis Mus Art, Ind; Ariz State Univ, Tempe; Brooklyn Mus, NY; Oakland Mus Art; Philadelphia Mus Art; Mus Art Sao Paulo; Mus Contemp Art, Rio de Janeiro; Triton Mus Art, Santa Clara, Calif. *Comn:* Hyatt Hotel, Phoenix, Ariz, 99; Westin Hotel, Indianapolis, Ind, 99; Mirage Hotel, Las Vegas, Nev, 2008 ; Atlantis Hotel, Dubai, Saude Arabia, 2008. *Exhib:* Solo exhibs, Antiscope, Brussels, Belgium, 79, Kathryn Markel Fine Arts, NY, 80, Los Angeles Munic Art Gallery, Calif, 80 & Tucson Mus Art, Ariz, 81, Dan Galleria, Sao Paulo, Brazil, 99, Robert Kidd Gallery, Birmingham, Mich, 2000, Triton Mus, Santa Clara, Calif, 2007 Perimeter Gallery, Chicago, Ill, 2008, Herrit Mus, Twin Falls, Idaho, 2008, Carnegie Art Mus, Oxnard, Calif, 2009, Inst Tomie Ohtake, São Paolo, Brazil, 2009; Paper Art, Smithsonian Inst, Washington DC, 80; Painting & Sculpture Today, Indianapolis Mus Art, Ind, 80. *Collection Arranged:* California Collage (auth, catalog), 81; California Clay (auth, catalog), 81; Sculpture 82 (auth, catalog); Chicago Abstract Painting (auth, catalog). *Teaching:* Prof art painting, Pepperdine Univ, Calif, 73; prof art painting, Col Siskiyavs, Calif, 73-81; prof art, Sonoma State Univ, Rohnert Park, Calif, 81-2005; prof emeritus, Sonoma State Univ, 2005. *Awards:* Tiffany Fellowship, 77; Individual Artists Fel, Nat Endowment Arts, 79; Fulbright Travel Grant to Brazil, 86; Fel, Calif Arts Coun Artist, 90; Gourmand Award, 2006. *Media:* Mixed. *Res:* Flora of Amazon River and Basin, Matto Grosso, Brazil, 1984-2008. *Publ:* Contribr, Paper Art, E B Crocker Art Mus, 80; auth, Imagery Art for Wine, Wine Appreciation Guild, San Francisco, Calif, 2005; Bob Nugent, Painting & Drawing, Triton Mus, Abandoned Press Publ Inc, 2006. *Dealer:* Elins Eagle Smith San Francisco CA; Cumberland Gallery Nashville TN; Sandy Erickson Fine Art Healdsburg Calif; Dan Gallery Sao Paolo Brazil; Perimeter Gallery Chicago Ill; Kathryn Markel NY; Susan Street Fine Art San Diego CA; Fresh Paint Los Angeles CA. *Mailing Add:* 5115 Middlebrook Ct Santa Rosa CA 95404-1959

NUNES, GRAFTON J
ADMINISTRATOR
Study: Col of Holy Cross, BA (English and religion); Columbia Univ, MFA (film, history, theory, and criticism), MPhil (theater history and film studies). *Pos:* Assoc dean, Sch of Arts, Columbia Univ, formerly; founding dean, Sch of Arts, Emerson Univ, Boston, formerly; pres & CEO, Cleveland Inst Art, 2010-. *Mailing Add:* Cleveland Institute of Art Office of President 11141 E Boulevard Cleveland OH 44106

NUNN, ANCEL E
PAINTER, PRINTMAKER
b Seymour, Tex, Apr 27, 1928. *Work:* Univ Tex, Austin; Tyler Mus Art, Tex; Tex A&M Univ, Coll Station; Baylor Univ, Fine Arts Ctr, Waco, Tex; E Tex Mus, Lufkin. *Exhib:* Fire, Contemp Arts Mus, Houston, 79; Making of a Lithograph, Mus E Tex, Lufkin, 83; Carousel Fantasia, Mich State Univ Mus, E Lansing, 86; The McDonald Collection, Mus Abilene, Tex, 92. *Bibliog:* Bob Bowman (auth), The Best of East Texas, Lufkin Printing Co, 79; Smithsonian, Texas Project, Archives Am Art J, 84. *Media:* Acrylic; Pencil. *Mailing Add:* 1106 S Shepherd Dr Houston TX 77019-3610

NUNNELLEY, ROBERT B
PAINTER
b Birmingham, Ala, Sept 5, 1929. *Study:* Univ Ark, BA (art), 51, with David Smith, MFA (painting), 56; Boston Mus Sch, with Karl Zerbe & David Aronson, 51-52; Colo Springs Fine Arts Ctr, with Robert Motherwell, 54. *Work:* Meml Sloan-Kettering Cancer Ctr; and many pvt collections. *Exhib:* Solo exhibs, Hudson River Mus, Yonkers, 67 & Schenectady Mus, NY, 79, Rensselaer Co Coun Arts, NY, 80, Fairleigh Dickinson Univ, Madison, 82, Besides Myself Gallery, Arlington, 83 & 88, Univ Coll Gallery, Jeaneck, 94 & Blue Mountain Gallery, NY, 97, Gallery 668, Battenville, NY, 2000, 2003, 2004, 2007 & 2009; Focus on the Arts, Bergen Community Mus, Paramus, NJ, 82; Nat Competition 2 Dimensional Work, Bowery Gallery, NY, 91; Nat Drawing, Newark Mus, Trenton State Col, NJ, 92; The Contemp Am Landscape, Yale Univ Art Gallery & Erector Square Gallery, New Haven, Conn, 92; Works on Paper, Fairleigh Dickinson Univ Coll Gallery, Teaneck, San Jacinto Coll S, Houston & The Drawing Ctr, NY, 93; EZ Studios, NY. *Pos:* Dir, Maples Gallery, Fairleigh Dickinson Univ, Teaneck, NJ, 82-87. *Teaching:* Prof painting-drawing-design. *Awards:* Purchase Award, Mid-Am Coll Art Asn, 55; Research Grant, Fairleigh Dickinson Univ, 67 & 77; Prize, Nat Competition Works on Paper, San Jacinto Coll South, 93. *Mem:* Nat Asn Sch of Art & Design; Coll Art Asn. *Media:* Oil. *Specialty:* Still Life and Landscape. *Interests:* Reading, 18th Century Am Furniture. *Publ:* Rev, Arts News, 3/57 & 10/59; France-Amerique, 10/59; Arts Mag, 9/59 & 1/68. *Dealer:* Veronique Chopin de La Bruyere Greenwich NY 12834. *Mailing Add:* 2850 State Route 29 Greenwich NY 12834

NUSS, JOANNE RUTH
SCULPTOR, PAINTER
b Great Bend, Kans, May 2, 1951. *Study:* Valparaiso Univ, Ind, 69-71; Studied Univ Kans, 72-73, Univ Copenhagen, Denmark, 74; Ft Hays State Univ, Kans, BA, 75; studied with The Henry Moore Found, 80; Santa Fe Inst Fine Arts, M, 91; special study with world renowned sculptor Beverly Pepper. *Work:* The Am Legation Mus, Tangiers, Morocco; The Univ Gallery, Ft Hays State Univ, Kans; The Lawrence Arnott Art Gallery, Tangiers, Moroco; The Royal Train, King Hassan of Morocco, Rabat; The Royal Palace, The Prince of Borneo, Brunei; many other pvt collections in the US, Europe, Morocco & Malaysia, 84-. *Comn:* bronze sculpture, Sherman Dreiszun Develop, Inc, Overland Oark, Kans, 83; bronze sculpture, The Royal Palace, Brunei, 85; painting, Mimoun Mokhtar, Morocco, 88-90; Tangiers, Morocco Leading Archit, 84. *Exhib:* Mid-West Regional Artist, Spiva Art Ctr, Joplin, Mo, 81; North Am Sculpture Show, Art Ctr Gallery, Golden, Colo, 84; Joanne Nuss: Bronze Sculptures, Univ Gallery Ft Hays State Univ, Kan, 85, Agora Gallery, NY, 2001; Joanne Nuss: Sculpture in Bronze, Inma Gallery, Saudi Arabia, 94; Gallery Artists, Shidoni Gallery, Tesuque, NMex, 99, 2000; Influences, The Birger Sandzen Meml Gallery, Kans, 2000; Attleboro Mus, Attleboro, Mass, 2002; Laboratorio del Galileo restaurant, DC, 2002; Jeanette Hare Art Gallery, West Palm Beach, Fla, 2002; 12th Ann Benefit Auction, Attleboro Mus, Mass, 2002; Amsterdam-Whitney Int Fine Art Inc, NY, 2003; 114th Ann Exhib, Nat Asn Women Artists, Fifth Ave Gallery, NY, 2003; Attleboro Mus, Mass, 2003; Baker Arts Ctr, 7th Nat Juried Art Exhib, 2004; Carolina Exhibs, McDowell Arts and Crafts Asn; Shelby Arts, Ashe Co Arts, 2004-05; Ann All Media Int Juried Online Exhib, Upstream People Gallery, Omaha, 2005-06; Personal Landscapes (juried), Longview Mus Fine Arts, Longview, Tex, 2007; 123rd Ann Exhib, Nat Asn Women Artists, Inc, Sylvia Wald & Po Kim Art Gallery, NY, 2012. *Collection Arranged:* bronze sculptures in numerous pvt and univ collections int and nat. *Teaching:* instr drawing, Nelson-Atkins Mus, Kansas City, Mo, 79-81; lectr, instr Brookside Elem Sch, 81-82; lectr, Barton County Community Col, Great Bend, Kans, 84; lectr, Nelson-Atkins Mus, Kansas City, Mo, 84. *Awards:* 3-D Work Award, Kans Artist Craftsmen Asn, Wichita, Kans, 83; Artist in Residence Grant, The Helene Wurlitzer Found, Taos, NM, 84 & 90; Purchase Award, Kans Profl Artists Collection, Ft Hays, 85; First Place, cash award, Univ Northern Iowa, Cedar Falls, Iowa, 2001; Women Achievement Award, Am Biog Inst, Raleigh, NC, 2006; Distinguished Serv to Human Kind Award, Int Biog Center, Cambridge, Eng, 2007; Lifetime Achievement Award, Int Biog Center, Cambridge, Eng, 2007; Pres's Citation Recognition of Excellence, Am Biog Inst, Raleigh, NC, 2007; 21st Century Visionary Award, American Biographical Inst, Raleigh, NC, 2011; Diamond Award for Outstanding Achievement, Humanitarian Contribution, Remington Registries of Outstanding Professionals, 2009-2010, 2013. *Bibliog:* Jennifer Schartz (auth), Bronze Work Shown First In Hometown, Great Bend Tribune, Kans, 4/4/80; Rick Dunway (auth), Artists Gets Her Chance With Borneo Commission, The Hutchinson News, Kans, 3/25/85; Alexander McCormick (auth), Joanne Nuss, ArtisSpectrum Magazine, Agora Gallery, New York, Vol 8, 2001. *Mem:* Nat Asn Women Artists; Nat Sculpture Soc; Internat Sculpture Ctr; Nat Mus Women in Arts. *Media:* Bronze, Stone. *Interests:* Working with other artists, creating a sculpture garden. *Publ:* Louisa Abernathy (auth), Kansas City's Single Professionals: Woman and Men, Sher, Jones, Shear & Assocs, 81; Glenn B Optiz (auth), Dictionary of American Sculptors 18th Century to the Present, Apollo Book, 84; Philip Martin (auth), Artists Working in Morocco/BBC Radio Network, London, 86. *Dealer:* The Lawrence-Arnott Art Gallery, Tangiers & Marrakech, Morocco. *Mailing Add:* 4843 Camelot W Great Bend KS 67530

NUTT, CRAIG
CRAFTSMAN, SCULPTOR
b Belmond, Iowa, Apr 13, 1950. *Study:* Univ Ala, BA, 72. *Work:* Birmingham Mus Art; Mobile Mus Art; High Mus Art; Huntsville Mus Art; Hawaii State Found Cult & Arts; Renwick Gallery, Smithsonian's Am Art Mus; Tenn State Mus; Columbus Mus, GA. *Comn:* Many comns for pvt collections; sculpture, Schering-Plough Corp, 93; sculpture, Birmingham Int Airport, 93; Hartsfield Atlanta Int Airport. *Exhib:* Solo exhibs, Dinosaurs & Flying Vegetables, Kentuck Mus, Northport, Ala, 87, Huntsville Mus Art, 89, Meredith Gallery, Baltimore, 93, Southeastern La Univ, Hammond, 94 & 95 & Univ N Ala Art Gallery, Florence, 97; Red Clay Survey, Huntsville Mus Art, 88; Nat Objects Invitational, Ark Arts Ctr, Little Rock, 89; Focus: Four Alabama Artists, Birmingham Mus Art, 90; Signs of Support: Furniture Forms in Contemp Am Art, Kohler Arts Ctr, Sheboygan, Wis, 90; Contemp Works in Wood, Southern Style, Huntsville Mus Art, 90; Artists, Archits & Designers: Furniture of our Century High Mus Art, Atlanta, Ga, 92; Seeds of Change, Smithsonian Inst, 91; Contemp Crafts: The National Scene, Ky Art & Craft Found, 93; Please be Seated: Masters of the Art of Seating, Flagler Mus, Palm Beach, Fla, 95; Alabama Impact, Mobile Mus Art & Huntsville Mus Art, 95; On the Surface: The Spirit Revealed, Am Craft Coun SE Region Conf, Louisville, Ky, 96; Craig Nutt: Furniture With a Flair, Huntsville, Ala, 97; By Heart and Hand: Collecting Southern Decorative Arts, Art Mus WVa, Roanoke, 98; Craig Nutt: Furniture & Sculpture, Joan Derryberry Art Gallery, Tenn Tech Univ, Cookeville, Tenn, 99; Studio Furniture: A Fine Art Invitational, Memphis, Coll Art, Tenn, 2000; Objects for Use: Handmade by Design, Am Craft Mus, New York City, 2002; Studio Art Furniture Invitational, Ark Art Ctr, Little Rock, 2002; Southeastern Craft Innovations, Knoxville Mus Art, Tenn, 2002; Materials & Contemp Illusions: Innovations in Lathe Turning, Brookfield Craft Ctr, Conn, 2002; Wood Turning Ctr, 2001; Yale Univ Art Gallery, 2001, 02; Minneapolis Institute Art, 2001; Renwick Gallery, 2001; Retrospective: Craig Nutt: Certified Organic, Mobile Mus Art, Ala, 2008; Traditions/Innovation: American Masterpieces of Southern Craft and Traditional Art, Southern Arts Fed, Multiple Venues, 2008-13; Alabama Masters, Julie Collins Smith Mus Fine Art, Ala, 2007; Cornography, Soc Contemp Craft, Pittsburgh, Pa, 2009-2010; Craig Nutt: Wood Transformed, Leigh Yawkey Woodson Mus Art, Wausau, Wis, 2009. *Pos:* Artist-in-residence, Appalachian Ctr Crafts, Smithville, Tenn, 97-98; artist lectr, Univ N Ala, Florence, 97; bd trustees, Furniture Soc, 97-, chmn, Web Site Comt 96- & Steering Comt, 96-97, fin coord, 99; interim exec dir, Tenn Asn Craft Artists, 2006; dir prog, Craft Emergency Relief Fund, 2006-. *Teaching:* Guest lectr, SUNY, NY, 2000. *Awards:* Gov Art Award, Ala State Coun Arts, 85, fel, 88 & 95; Nat Endowment Arts Fel, 89; Tenn State Arts Com Fel, 98; Alumnus Arts Award, Univ Ala, 97. *Bibliog:* Craig Nutt (auth), article in Am Craft, 87 & From furniture to flying vegetables, Southern Accents Mag, 88; Craig Nutt: Combining Humor and a Bit of Cayenne, Fine Woodworking, 91; Southern Ohio Mus, Portsmouth (review), Am Craft, 12/05-1/06; Studio Furniture of the Renwick Gallery, Oscar P Fitzgerald, Fox Chapel, 2008; Art of Tenn, Frist Ctr Visual Arts, 2003; auth & juror, 500 Chairs, Lark Boosk, 2008; New Masters of the Wooden Box, Oscar P Fitzgerald, Fox Chapel, 2009. *Mem:* Ala Crafts Coun (trustee, 80-86); Am Craft Coun, SE Region (bd dir, 82-89); Furniture Soc (founding bd mem). *Media:* Wood. *Publ:* Auth, Lathe turned, woodturners gather at Arrowmont, Am Craft, 86; A partnership, The Guild, 87; Ed, Spotlight 88, SE/SW Crafts Exhib Catalog, Am Craft Coun, SE Region, 88; Turners in Texas, Am Craft, 91; auth, Craft and ethics, Am Craft, 94, Keyboard Instruments by Anden Houben, 98; auth, Vegetable Bebop & Tut Uncommon, in: Penland Book of Woodworking, Lark Books, 2006. *Mailing Add:* 1305 Kingston Springs Rd Kingston Springs TN 37082-9282

NUTT, JIM
PAINTER, DRAFTSMAN
b Pittsfield, Mass. *Study:* Wash Univ, St Louis, 1958-59; Art Inst Chicgo, with Whitney Halstead & Dominic DiMeo, dipl, 1965. *Work:* Whitney Mus Am Art, Mus Mod Art, Metrop Mus Art, NY; Mus Contemp Art, Chicago; Mus Mod Kunst, Vienna; High Mus, Atlanta, Ga; Philadelphia Mus Art; Scottish Nat Mus, Glasgow; Hirshhorn Gallery/Mus, Washington, DC; Mem Art Gallery, Univ Rochester, NY. *Exhib:* Am Exhib, Art Inst Chicago, 1972 & 1976; solo exhibs, Phyllis Kind Gallery, Chicago, 1982, 1985 & 991, Phyllis Kind Gallery, NY, 1980, 1984, 1988, 1991, Galerie Bonnier, Geneva, Switz, 1992, Mus Contemp Art, Chicago, 1999 & Nolan Eckman Gallery, NY, 1999, Nolan/Eckman Gallery, NY, 2003; 39th Biennial Exhib Contemp Am Painting, Corcoran Gallery Art, 1985; Word As Image: Am Art 1960-1990, Milwaukee Art Mus(solo), Wis & traveling to Oklahoma City Art Mus & Houston, 1990-91; Parallel Visions: Modern Artists & Outsider Art, Los Angeles Co Mus Art traveling to Madrid & Tokyo, 1992-93; From America's Studio: Twelve Contemp Masters, Art Inst Chicago, 1992; traveling exhib, Milwaukee Art Ctr, Henry Art Gallery, Seattle, Mus Am Art, Washington & Contemp Art Ctr, Cincinnati, 1994-95; Printmaking in Am, Collaborative Prints & Presses 1960-1990 (traveling), incl Mus Fine Arts Houston, 1995-96; Am Acad Invitational Exhib Painting & Sculpture, NY, 1996; Second Sight: Printmaking in Chicago 1935-1995, Northwestern Univ, 1996; Art in Chicago 1945-1995, Mus Contemp Art, Chicago, 1996; solo exhibs, Mus Contemp Art, Chicago, Ill & Nolan Eckman Gallery, NY, 1999; 117th Ann, Nat Acad of Design, NY, 2002; Am Acad Arts and Letts Invitational, New York, 2009. *Teaching:* Assoc prof painting & drawing, Calif State Univ, Sacramento, 1968-75; adj assoc prof, Sch Art Inst Chicago, 1990-. *Awards:* Nat Endowment Arts Grant, 1989; Acuff Chair Excellence, Austin Peay State Univ, Clarksville, Tenn, 1994; Acad Award in Art, 1996, Purchase Prize, 2009, Am Acad Arts & Letts, New York. *Bibliog:* Russell Bowman (auth), Jim Nutt (exhib catalog), Rotterdam Kunststichting Lijnbaan Centrum, 1980; John Yau (auth), Jim Nutt: Recent Works, Mayor Gallery, London, Eng; Russell Bowman, Linda Hartigan & Robert Storr (auths), Jim Nutt (exhib catalog), Milwaukee Art Mus, 1994. *Dealer:* Nolan/Eckman Gallery 560 Broadway New York NY. *Mailing Add:* 1035 Greenwood Ave Wilmette IL 60091

NUTZLE, FUTZIE (BRUCE) JOHN KLEINSMITH
CARTOONIST, PAINTER
b Lakewood, Ohio, Feb 21, 1942. *Study:* Self-taught. *Work:* Mus Mod Art, NY; San Francisco Mus Mod Art; Oakland Mus, Calif; Santa Cruz City Mus, Calif; Whitney Mus Am Art, NY. *Comn:* ITT, 79. *Exhib:* New York Corresp Art, Whitney Mus, NY, 70; Empty Canoes, Lithographs, San Francisco Mus Mod Art, 72; Opening, Santa Cruz Artists' Mus Proj, 73; Twin Rocker Paper Exhib, Indianapolis Mus Art, Ind, 75; Laica, Los Angeles, 78; Solo exhib, Santa Barbara Mus Art, 80; Univ Coll Santa Cruz, Retrospective, 90; Prague Eco-Fair, 91; Fresno Art Mus, 2010; Motiv, 2010; Cabrillo Coll, 2011; Mus Art & History, Santa Cruz, 2011-2012; Blitzer, 2012, 2013; Carl Cherry/Carmel Art Ctr, 2014. *Pos:* owner, Ano Né Gallery. *Awards:* Jounalism award, Rolling Stone Profile, 7/1/81; Gail Rich award, 2013. *Bibliog:* My art belongs to Dada, Esquire Mag, 8/74; feature article, Quest, 6/79; Stephen Kessler (auth), Nutzle Enigma, The Tolstoy of the Zulus, 2011. *Mem:* Masonic Lodge; Tex Lodge 46. *Media:* Pen and Ink, Wash on Paper, Oil on Canvas. *Specialty:* Futzie Nutzle Originals. *Interests:* jazz. *Publ:* Contribr, Ohio State Sundial, 61-63, Balloon Newspaper, 68-74, New York Correspondence School, 68-74 (in numbers: artists periodicals since 55, Andrew Roth, New York, 2009), Rolling Stone, 75-80, Quarry West, 77 & San Francisco Bay Guardian, 81-83, 86-98, Boston Real Paper, 80's; Japan Times, 85-95; auth, Modern Loafer (cartoons & drawings) Thames & Hudson, Inc, 81; Futzie Nutzle, Jazz Press, 83; Run the World: 50 cents, Chronicle Bks, 91; Bob Brozman, Devil's Slide, Rounder Records; Twenty-Fifth Int Salon of Cartoons, 88; SKRT, Prague, 91; Int Pavilion of Humour, Man and His World, Montreal, Can; Santa Cruz Independent Weeklies, Good Times, Leviathan, Metro, Independent, Sundaz, Weekley, 68-; Contribr, The Bugle, Redwood Coast Review; Making Wet; Vivace 4; The Crows a Blinken, 2014. *Dealer:* Fools Gold 34A Polk St San Juan Bautista CA 95045; Winfield Gallery PO Box 7393 Carmel CA 93921; Ano Né Gallery PO 1261 San Juan Bautista Ca 95045. *Mailing Add:* PO Box 1083 San Juan Bautista CA 95045

NYDORF, ROY HERMAN
PAINTER, PRINTMAKER
b Port Washington, NY, Oct 1, 1952. *Study:* Art Students League, New York, 69; State Univ NY, Brockport, with Robert Marx, BA, 74; Yale Univ Sch Art, with Peterdi, Bailey & Johnson, MFA, 76; Arrowmont Sch Crafts, with Hunt Clark, Tenn, 2009. *Work:* Hirshhorn Mus & Sculpture Garden & Smithsonian Am Art Mus, Washington, DC; Honolulu Acad Art, Hawaii; Weatherspoon Art Mus, Greensboro, NC; Yale Art Gallery, New Haven, Conn; Nelson Atkins Mus Art, Kansas City, Mo; Huntsville Mus Art, Ala; Georgetown Univ, Washington, DC; Ark State Univ, Ark; Coll Santa Fe, NMex; Duke Univ Med Ctr, NC; Mus Tex Tech Univ, Tex; Univ Hi-Hilo. *Comn:* Wall mural, comn by Garret Trudeau, New Haven, Conn, 77; pres portrait, Guilford Coll, Greensboro, NC, 81 & 96; etchings, NC Nat Bank, Charlotte, 87; etchings, United Arts Coun Greensboro, NC, 87. *Exhib:* 27th Bradley Nat Print & Drawing Exhib, Bradley Univ, Peoria, Ill, 98; Red Clay Survey: Biennial Exhib of Contemp Southern Art, Huntsville Mus Art, Ala, 98; About Memory: A Selection of 20th Century Portraits, Ball State Univ Mus, Muncie, Ind, 97; Pablo Picasso: Homage to a Modern Icon, Fraser Gallery, Washington, DC, 98; Painted Realms, Christel De Haan Fine Arts Ctr, Univ Indianapolis, Ind, 99; Monothon, SITE Santa Fe, 2001; Lean on Me, Wharton Eshrick Mus, Pa, 2001; Celebrating the Legacy of Romare Bearden, Mint Mus of Art, Charlotte, NC, 2002; Roy Nydorf & Turner McGehee, Haydon Gallery, Lincoln, Nebr, 2002; Art on Paper, Maryland Federation of Art, Annapolis, Md, 2004; solo exhib, Gallery 55, Natick, Mass, 2005, 20th Parkside Nat Small Print Exhib, Kenosha, Wis, 2007, Int Group Exhib, Tsingzhou Mus, Beijing, China, 2007, Printed: Contemp Prints & Books by NC Artists, Green Hill Ctr, Greensboro, NC, 2008, S Elm Gallery, Greensboro, NC, 2008; Giovanili Pulsioni, Cetrona, Italy, 2008; The Print Fantastic, Theatre Art Gallery, High Point, NC, 2009; Solo exhib, Hawthorne Gallery, Winston-Salem, 2009; Art in Embassies Program, Kampala, Uganda, Art of Paper, Weatherspoon Art Mus, Greensboro, NC, 2010; Roy Nydorf, Four Decades, Green Hill Ctr, Greensboro, NC, 2012; American Art Today: Figures, The Bascom, Highlands, NC, 2013. *Teaching:* Instr design, Univ New Haven, Conn, 77; asst prof art & art hist, Guilford Coll, Greensboro, NC, 78-86, assoc prof, 86-96, prof, 96-, chmn, Art Dept, 83-85, 88-91, 96-99, & 05-08; prof art, Univ GA, study abroad program, Cortona, Italy, 2008. *Awards:* Robert Donaldson Award for drawing, Govs Bus Coun Arts & Humanities, Raleigh, NC, 95; Purchase Award, Delta Nat Small Print Exhib, 96; ARText 98 Best in Show, Asn Artists Winston-Salem, NC, 98; and others. *Bibliog:* Tom Patterson (auth), South Passion for Racing Gets Artistic, Atlanta J Constitution, 9/6/99; Lisa Skeen (auth), Roy Nydorf, Living the Art, Northwest Observer, 11/16/2001; Cathy Gant-Hill (auth), Paperwork, Greensboro News & Record, 11/22/2002; Bill Fick and Beth Grabowski (auths), Printmaking: The Complete Guide to Processes and Techniques, Lawrence King Publishing, 2009; Christopher Benfey (auth), Red Brick, White Clay, and Black Mountain, Penguin Press, 2011; E Carpenter and C Benfey (auths), Roy Nydorf: Four Decades, Green Hill Ctr, 2012; Dawn Kane (auth), Roy Nydorf: Reflections on 40 years of Creating Art, Greensboro News & Record, 2012; Art Ala Carte: A Fusion of Art, Wine, and Food, US Airways Mag, 2012. *Mem:* Southeastern Ctr Contemp Art; Green Hill Ctr NC Art; Southern Graphics Coun. *Media:* Wood, Gouache; Etching, Monotype. *Mailing Add:* 1815 Oak Ridge Rd Oak Ridge NC 27310

NYERGES, ALEXANDER LEE
MUSEUM DIRECTOR, HISTORIAN
b Feb 27, 1957. *Study:* George Washington Univ, BA (Am studies & anthrop), 1979, MA (mus studies), 1981. *Exhib:* In Praise of Nature, (auth, catalog) 1999; Edward Weston: A Photogrs Love of Life (auth, catalog), 2004. *Collection Arranged:* Southeastern Watercolorist I-III (auth, catalogs), 1983-85 & Piranesi: 18th Century Etchings (ed, catalog), 1984, DeLand Mus Art, Fla; Collector's Choice 1985 & French and Am Impressionism 1855-1912, 1985 & The Am Landscape 1850-1910, 1986, Miss Mus Art, Jackson; Norman Rockwell: The Great Am Storyteller, 1988. *Pos:* Exec dir, Deland Mus Art, Fla, 81-85 & Miss Mus Art, Jackson, 1985-92; southeast regional rep, non-print media comt, Am Asn Mus, 83-85, legislative comt, 1986-; dir & chief exec off, Dayton Art Inst, Ohio, 1992-2006; dir, Virginia Mus Fine Art, 2006-. *Awards:* Phi Beta Kappa, 1979. *Mem:* Miss Inst Arts & Letts (bd trustee); Southeast Mus Conf (bd trustee); Art Mus Asn Am (regional rep); Am Asn Mus (accreditation field reviewer); Asn Am Govt Affairs Comt; Asn Art Mus Dirs (bd trustees, 2007-, mentoring task force); FRAME (exec comt); Forum Club Richmond Va; Asian Am Soc Central Va (advisory bd mem); Armory Steering Comt, Black History Cultural Mus, Richmond, Va; Mayor's Real Estate Task Roundtable; Mayors Tourism Comn. *Res:* South American, Pre-Columbian art; photography; American & European 20th century photography. *Publ:* The Ages of Mexico (exhib catalog), DeLand Mus Art, No 4, 1983; auth, In Praise of Nature: Ansel Adams and Photogrs of the Am West (catalog), 1999; Edward Weston, Pre Columbian Treasures, 2003 & A Photogrs Love of Life, 2004. *Mailing Add:* Virginia Mus Fine Arts 200 N Boulevard Richmond VA 23220

NYMAN, GEORGIANNA BEATRICE
PAINTER
b Arlington, Mass, June 11, 1930. *Study:* Boston Mus Fine Arts Sch, study with David Aronson & Karl Zerbe, dipl, 52, cert, 54; Longy Sch Mus, 65-75; McClosky Voice Inst, 75-81; Boston Acad Mus, with Richard Conrad, 91-95. *Work:* Rose Art Mus, Brandeis Univ, Waltham, Mass; New Eng Sch Law, Boston, Mass; Sch Med, Univ Pittsburgh; Milton Acad, Mass; US Supreme Court; State House, RI; Thomas Jefferson Sch Med, Phila, Pa. *Comn:* Portrait, Justice Sandra Day O'Connor, New Eng Sch Law, 91; portrait, Justice Harry Blackmunn, New Eng Sch Law, 93; portrait, Justice Clarence Thomas, New Eng Sch Law, 96; portrait, Gov Lincoln Almond, RI, 2003; portrait, Justice Anthony B Kennedy, New Eng Sch Law, 2005; portrait, Justice Antonin Scalia, New Eng Sch Law, 2006; portrait, Orit Gadiesh, chmn Bain & Co, Boston, Mass, 2008; portrait, Justice Ruth Bader Ginsburg, 2009. *Exhib:* Boston Arts Festival And Juried Exhibs, 54 & 61; Shore Studio Galleries, Boston, 63; Group Show, Lee Nordness Galleries, NY, 65; Nat Acad Design, NY, 90; solo exhib, Nancy Lincoln Gallery, Chestnut Hill, Mass, 90; group show, Alter & Gil Galleries, Beverly Hills, Calif, 99; Ogunquit Mus, Maine, 2011. *Teaching:* Instr drawing & painting, Boston Ctr Adult Educ, 52-54; instr painting, Boston Univ Sch Continuing Educ, 58-59. *Awards:* Boit Prize, Boston Mus Sch, 51; Kate Morse Prize, Boston Mus Fine Arts, 53; Cert Merit, Nat Acad Design, NY, 92; Medal for Excellence, awarded by Adjutant Gen of RI, 2003. *Bibliog:* Darlene Arden (dir), Creatively Speaking (film). *Mem:* Boston Acad Music; life mem Women's Indust Inst; Mass Soc & May Flower Descendants; Currier Vocal Quartet. *Media:* Pastel, Oil. *Interests:* music & vocal recitals. *Publ:* Contribr, Native Island (Gerta Kennedy), Houghton-Mifflin, 56; Art of Karl Zerbe (film), 88. *Dealer:* Pucker Gallery 171 Newbury St Boston MA 02116. *Mailing Add:* 137 Brimstone Ln Sudbury MA 01776

NYREN, EDWARD A
PAINTER
b Boston, Mass. *Study:* Boston Mus Fine Arts Sch; Art Students League; Frank Reilly Sch, NY. *Work:* Reader's Digest Asn Inc, NY; Lynden Air Freight, Seattle; Key Bank, Seattle; Rainier Bank, Seattle; Shawmut Bank, Boston; Raymond James Financial, Inc, St Petersburg, Fla; Coll Marine Sci, Univ S Fla, St Petersburg, Fla. *Exhib:* NJ Watercolor Soc, Morris Mus Arts & Sci, 70; Conn Watercolor Soc, Wadsworth Atheneum, 72; Grand Nat, Am Artists Prof League, 73, 79, 80, & 81; one-man show, Newport Art Mus, RI, 81; Major Fla Artists Show, Foster-Harmon Galleries Am Art, Sarasota, Fla, 90; Art Encounter State Competition, Naples Art Asn, Fla, 90; Fla Artists Group, Mus Arts & Sci, Daytona, Fla, 94; Uncommon Ground, Pinellas Co Art Coun, Fla, 99; Nat Park Acad Arts, 2001; Tex Nat, Stephen F Austin State Univ, Nacogdoches, Tex, 2007; 9th Ann Exhib, VMRC Art Exhib, Harrisonburg, Va, 2012. *Awards:* Second Prize, Newport, RI, Outdoor Art Festival, 80s; First Prize, Magnolia Outdoor Art Festival, Seattle, Wash, 80s; First Prize, Art Asn, Newport, RI, 80s; Second Prize (aquamedia), Art Encounter State Competition, Naples, Fla, 90; Best in Category (pastel), Sarasota Visual Arts Asn, Fla, 96; Purchase Award, Univ South Fla, 2001; Top 200, Nat Park Acad Arts, 2001; Finalist in Landscape category, The Artist's Mag, 27th Ann Art Competition; Second Prize, Flora and Fauna Exhib Comp, Venice Fla Art Center, 2010. *Bibliog:* Edward J Sozanski (auth), Masculine hand led by mind with vision, Providence J, 81; Chuck Twardy (auth), Nyren's pastels, richly done and highly appealing, Orlando Sentinel, 12/16/90; Mary Ann Marger (auth), Art by Mellow Masters, St Petersburg Times, 9/30/94; and others. *Mem:* Salmagundi Club. *Media:* Pastel, Watercolor. *Mailing Add:* PO Box 22784 Saint Petersburg FL 33742-2784

O

OAKES, JOHN WARREN
EDUCATOR, PAINTER
b Bowling Green, Ky, Feb 26, 1941. *Study:* Art Instr Sch Minneapolis; Art Students League, New York, Albert Dorne Scholar; Western Area Voc Sch; Western Ky Univ, AB, 64; Univ Iowa, MA, 66, MFA, 73; Harvard Univ, cert arts admin, 75. *Work:* Numerous works in pub and pvt collections in Ala, Calif, Colo, Fla, Ga, Ind, Iowa, Ill, Ky, Mass, ME, Md, Mich, Miss, Nev, NJ, NY, NH, SDak, Tenn, Tex, Va, Wash, Argentina, England, Ireland, Japan, Romania, Belgium, Australia, Brazil, Canada, Germany, Turkey, Czechoslovakia, Italy, Netherlands, Norway, Poland, Spain, West Indies. *Exhib:* Forty solo exhibs. *Pos:* Gallery dir, Western Ky Univ Gallery, 66-85, staff asst, off dean, Potter Coll Arts & Humanities, 73-75, asst dean admin, 75-85. *Teaching:* Instr art, Western Ky Univ, 66-71, asst prof art, 71-76, assoc prof art, 76-87, prof art, 87-. *Bibliog:* Joseph G Rosa (auth), The West of Wild Bill Hickok, Daily News 6/82 & Univ Okla Press, 83. *Mem:* Ky Arts Admin (pres, 82-83); Ky Citizens for Arts; Southern Ky Photog Soc (pres, 86-89); Kappa Pi. *Media:* Painting, Computer Graphics. *Res:* Influences of Pablo Picasso's work that have been overlooked; minimum aperture photography; The Role of Gender in art production and criticism. *Publ:* Auth, Camera Blending, Instant Projects, Polaroid Corp Publ, 86; Photography

Using Pinhole Cameras, Univ Press of Am, 86; Action Amiga: Computer Graphics, Animation and Video Production, Univ Press of Am, 88; Art by Computer, Acorn Press, 90; contribr, Electronic Art Lab Manual, Acorn Press, 98; Kentucky Women Artists 1850-1970 pub in Arts Across Kentucky, 2001; Catalog Contribr Kentucky Women artists 1850-1970 Owensboro Art Mus KY 2002; auth, The Servicemen's Readjustment Act of 1944: How it Affected the Education of Women Artists, Int Jour Vis Culture & Gender, 2006. *Dealer:* Capitol Arts Ctr Main St Bowling Green KY 42101; 916 State St Bowling Green KY 42101. *Mailing Add:* 1315 Lois Ln Bowling Green KY 42104-4673

O'BANION, NANCE
ASSEMBLAGE ARTIST
b Oakland, Calif, June 7, 1949. *Study:* Univ Calif, Berkeley, BA, 71, MA, 73. *Work:* Seattle Art Mus; Mus Arts Decoratifs Ville Lausanne, Switz; Am Craft Mus, NY; London Inst, Victoria & Albert Mus, London, Eng; Cleveland Art Mus; Bellerive Mus, Zurich, Switzerland; Co of Los Angeles; Getty Mus, Los Angeles; Ghent Mus, Belgium; Haderslev Mus, Jutland, Denmark; Harvard Univ, Cambridge, Mass; Kaho-Machi Mus, Kyushu, Japan; Mills Col, Oakland, Calif; RI Sch Design, Providence; San Francisco Mus; Univ Alta, Edmonton, Can; Univ Ga Art Mus, Athens; Univ Wis, Madison; Victoria & Albert Mus, London; Va Commonwealth Univ; Yale Univ, New Haven. *Comn:* Large wall construction (paper & bamboo), Sheraton Hotel, Tokyo, Japan, 87; painting (paper & bamboo), Bishop Ranch, Calif, 87; construction (paper & bamboo), Cranston Securities; well construction, pair (paper & bamboo), Ballston, Va, 88. *Exhib:* Solo exhibs, Kauffman Galleries, Houston, 83, Hestkobgaard-Birkerod, Denmark, 84, BZ Wagman Gallery, St Louis, 84, Allrich Gallery, 80-85, 87-88 & 91, Monterey Art Mus, Calif, 89, Day Dreams for the Heart, Oakland Mus, Calif, 98, Breaking the Sorface: Telling Stories, JFK Univ Art Gallery, Berkeley, Calif, 2001; Mythical Figures & Fantastic Facades: O'Banion and Winter, San Francisco Folk & Craft Mus, 91; Eleven at 1111, Oakland Mus, Calif, 91; Works on Paper: The Craft Artist as Draftsman, Renwick Gallery Nat Mus Am Art, Washington, DC, 92; Craft Today USA, Zappeion Mus, Athens, Greece, 92; Self-Portraits in Black and White, Edith Caldwell Gallery, San Francisco, 93; Contemp Crafts and the Saxe Collection, Newport Harbor Mus, Calif, 94; The Chair, Oakland Mus, Calif, 96; Re-Incarnation, Oakland Mus, Calif, 96; The Paper Path, Haderslev Mus, Jutland, Denmark, 96; Fiberarts, Cult Centrum Mus, St Truiden, Belg, 96; 25 Yrs of Book Arts at CCAC, San Francisco Ctr for Book, 97; Out West: The Artist's Book in Calif, Ctr for Book Arts, New York City, 98; Hypnoponia, Int Asn for Study of Drams, Univ Calif Art Gallery, Santa Cruz, 99; Making Change, Jewish Art Mus, San Francisco, 99; Book as Object as Book, Fla Atlantic Univ Art Mus, Miami, 2000; Reading the Cards, San Francisco Ctr for the Book, 2001. *Teaching:* Instr, Univ Calif, Davis, 72-79; assoc prof textiles, Calif Col Arts & Crafts, 74-84, prof printmaking, 74--; vis artist & lectr, Hestkobgaard-Birkerod, Denmark & Carnegie Mellon Inst, Pittsburgh, Pa, 84, Chicago Art Inst, 87, San Francisco Craft Folk Art Mus & San Luis Obispo Art Asn, 89 & many others. *Awards:* Arthur Jacobsen Mem Award for Excellence in Arts, 75; Vis Art Fel, Nat Endowment Arts, 82-83 & 88-89; Juror, Calif Arts Coun Fel, 90. *Bibliog:* Charles Talley (auth), Nance O'Banion: Lines of energy, Artweek, 11/15/88; Robert Atkins (auth), Artspeak: A Guide to Contemporary Ideas, Movements and Buzzwords, Abbeville Press, New York, 69; Claire Campbell Park (auth), Finding the Link Between Fiber and Mixed Media: Nance O'Banion, Fiber Arts, summer 91. *Media:* Handmade Paper and Bamboo. *Publ:* Contribr, Contemporary American Craft Art: A Collector's Guide, Peregrine Bks, 88; auth, Cosmetic Science: Pop-up Icons and Idioms, Flying Fish Press, 90; auth, Design for Utopia, Coll Environ Design Alumni Newsletter, Univ Calif, Berkeley, 92; Correspondence Course, Flying Fish Press, 93; Commentary: Intersections of Thought, Fiberarts, Vol 21, No 1, summer 94; Magic Door, Permanent Press, 95; Collaborator, Two-Sided Ricochet: Angelita Surmon and Nancy O'Banion, Southwest Craft Ctr, San Antonio, 90, Handwriting: Thomas Wojak and Nance O'Banion, Calif Craft Mus, San Francisco, 93, Lines of Correspondence: Angelita Surmon and Nance O'Banion, Hoffman Gallery, Oreg Sch Arts & Crafts, Portland, 94. *Mailing Add:* 5756 Ivanhoe Rd Oakland CA 94618

O'BEIL, HEDY
PAINTER, WRITER
b New York, NY. *Study:* Art Students League, 53; Brooklyn Mus Art Sch, 58 & 59; Skowhegan Sch Art, 59; Empire State Col, State Univ NY, BS, 77; Goddard Col, MFA, 79. *Work:* Libr Cong; Dr G Alsip, Dr E Preston & Mr & Mrs Pravda, Susan Wolf; Savannah Coll Art & Design, Birmingham Coll; Art for Public Sch; Smithsonian Inst Graphics; and other pvt collections. *Exhib:* One-person exhibs: Hofstra Univ Gallery, 65; Firehouse Gallery, Nassau Community Coll, 68; Oswego Univ Gallery, 69; Guild Hall, Easthampton, NY, 70; Heckscher Mus, Huntington, NY, 72; Islip Mus, 74; Landmark Gallery, 79; Barbara Ingber Gallery, 83; Sunnen Gallery, 92; La Mama Gallery, NY, 2002; The Westbeth Gallery, NY, 2007; Elayne Benson Gallery, Bridghamton, 96; Katharina Perlowr Gallery, 98, 2007; New York City Andre Zarre Gallery, 01; New York City Studio 18 Gallery, 03; Westbeth Art Gallery, 2004, 2009; Art League of Long Island, 2005; Siren Song Gallery, 2008; Grand Gestures, Broome St Gallery, 2009; Diverse Interludes, Andre Zarre Gallery, 2009; Westbeth, 2012; Gallery 307, 2011, 2012; Carter Burden Gallery, 2013. *Collection Arranged:* The Symbolic View, Soho 20 Gallery, 82; Revelations, Pleiades Gallery, 84; Costumes, Masks & Disguises, The Clocktower Gallery, 86, Painting-Yes, 98 & The Gesture & The Brush, 99; NYC Broome St Gallery, Abstraction-5, 1993; Grand Gestures, The Broome St Gallery, 2009. *Pos:* Critic, Arts Mag, 76-86, Manhattan Arts Mag, 89-, West Side Beat, 96 & 97, The Proof, 95-. *Teaching:* Instr art, Nassau Community Col, 74; lectr, Art Ctr Northern NJ, 76-; lectr art hist, 92nd St Y, NY, 81-82. *Awards:* Fel, Cummington Community Arts, 80, YADDO, 84, Printmaking Workshop, 92; Pollock-Krasner Found, 2008; Am Inst Arts & Letters, 2008, 2011; Paul Reger Found, 2007; Fel, The Print Making Wkshp, 88; fel, Workshop Cummington Community of the Arts, 83. *Bibliog:* William Zimmer (auth), article, Soho News, 79; Elaine Wechsler (auth), article, Arts Mag, 83; Jennifer Dunning (auth), article, New York Times, 86; Diana Roberts (auth), Manhattan Arts, 90; Artspeak, 90; and others; Ed McCormack (ed), Gallery & Studio mag, 2007, 2008, 2011. *Mem:* Am Inst Critics Asn; Artists Equity; Am Soc Contemp Artists. *Media:* Acrylic, Ink, Charcoal. *Res:* Classical and modern art history with emphasis on surrealism; Minoan History. *Specialty:* Abstract painting. *Interests:* Music, piano, guitar. *Publ:* NY Times; Newsday; Long Island Press; Soho News; Studio & Gallery; Arts Mag; Gallery Guide, The Villager. *Dealer:* Carter Burden Gallery NY. *Mailing Add:* 463 West St Apt 1103A New York NY 10014

OBERING, MARY M
PAINTER
b Apr 3, 1937. *Study:* Hollins Col, Va, BA, 58; Radcliffe Col, Boston, 59; Univ Denver, MFA, 71. *Work:* Aldrich Mus Contemp Art, Ridgefield, Conn; Museo de Arte Costariccense, San Jose, Costa Rica; Wadsworth Atheneum, Hartford, Conn; Detroit Inst Art; Mus Fine Arts, Boston; Whitney Mus, New York. *Comn:* Painting, Norfolk & Southern Corp, Roanoke, Va, 94. *Exhib:* Whitney Mus Am Art Biennial, New York, 75; solo exhibs, Ben Shahn Galleries, Wayne, NJ, 81 & Museo de Arte, San Jose, 88; Am Abstr Artists, Ulrich Mus, Wichita, 92; Abstraction, Mus Fine Arts, Boston, 95; Tribute to Julian Pretto, Wadsworth Atheneum, Hartford, Conn, 96; Painting, Mus de Arte Costaricense, Costa Rica. *Teaching:* Fel basic design & art hist, Univ Denver, 70-71; spec sem egg tempera & gold leaf, Princeton Univ, 94. *Mem:* Am Abstr Artists. *Media:* Egg Tempera, Gold Leaf. *Dealer:* Little John Contemp 41 E 57th St New York NY 10028. *Mailing Add:* 69 Wooster St New York NY 10012

OBLER, GERI
PRINTMAKER, COLLAGE ARTIST
b New York, NY, May 1, 1942. *Study:* Pratt Inst, with Richard Lindner & Fritz Bultman, BFA, 63; Hunter Col, with Ron Gorchov, MA, 66; Columbia Univ, with Peter Golfinopolis, EdD (fine arts & fine arts educ), 74. *Work:* Berkshire Mus, Pittsfield, Mass; Univ Wyo Art Mus, Laramie; US Embassy, Nairobi, Kenya; Conf Bd, Scottish Develop Agency, NY. *Exhib:* Nat Asn Women Artists, NY Dept Cult Affairs, 81 & Traveling Graphics Exhib, 92; 67th Hudson River Mus Ann, Yonkers, NY, 82; Jesse Besser Mus, Alpena, Mich, 83; Pratt Graphics Ctr Ann, NY, 83; Hunterdon 27th Nat Print Exhib, Wallingford Art Ctr, Pa, 83; Sarah Lawrence Col, Bronxville, NY, 92; and others. *Bibliog:* Malcolm Preston (auth), Three printmakers on display, Newsday, 6/18/79; Helen Harrison (auth), Many shades of white, New York Times, 1/11/81; Jeanne Paris (auth), A showing of Long Island's best graphics, Newsday, 10/6/81; Phyllis Braff (auth), Bending Paper into a Complex Modern Medium, New York Times, 3/16/86. *Mem:* Nat Asn Women Artists; Philadelphia Print Club; Graphic Eye Artists (pres, 78-80, bd dir, 81). *Dealer:* Henry Howels Gallery 164 Thompson St New York, NY 10012. *Mailing Add:* 26 Brokaw Ln Great Neck NY 11023

OBRANT, SUSAN ELIZABETH
PAINTER, FIBER ARTIST
b Phildaelphia, Pa, Aug 24, 1946. *Study:* State Univ NY, Buffalo, 66; Parsons Sch Design, 68; Spec studies in Louvre, Paris, 83. *Work:* Palace Mus, Malta; Mus Mod Art, Caracus, Venezula; The Hapsburg Found, Vienna; Knights of the Teutonic Order, New York. *Comn:* Oil on canvas, The Hackley Sch, Tarrytown, NY, 95; oil on canvas, The Dominican Sisters, Ossining, NY, 96; oil on canvas, Portrait of Whitney Peter Thomas Ciccone; portrait, Charles Langone; Double Portrait, William Racolin & Alison Williams. *Exhib:* Hudson River Mus, New York, 76; Hammond Mus, New York, 97; Invitational Exhib, Nat Arts Club, Pastel Soc Am, New York, 76; Mcnay Inst, Tex, 97; World Futurists Soc, New York, 86; Columbia Univ, New York, 87; Santa Fe Weaving Gallery, 2004; Katona Mus, New York, 2004; Grammercy Park Armory, New York, 2007; Jane Wilson, Marquis Art Salon, Trunk Show, Soho, NY; Gilles Larrain Studio, 2011; Javits Ctr, Art Fair NYC, 2012; Daisy Jopling, Couture Crochet Attire; The Vinny Vella Show, Fine Art & Runway Fashion Show with Models of my Crochet Couture, 2013; Brooklyn Mus Art, 2013; Serious Art Discussion I, Javits Art Installation, 2013; The Amsterdam Whitney Gallery, Chelsea, NY, 2014; Gallery Obrant Popup Sommer, 2014; Gallery 66, Serious Art Discussion II, 2014. *Pos:* Artist-in-residence, Eastview Tech Ctr, 96-99 & Pace Univ Law Sch, 97; judge, Soc Illusr, New York, 73. *Teaching:* Instr, Sch Visual Arts, New York, 74; lectr, Syracuse Univ, NY, 2002. *Awards:* Grammy Nomination, Through A Looking Glass, Nat Acad Recording Arts & Scis, 71; Award of Excellence, Melanie, Soc Illusr, New York, 72. *Bibliog:* Lynn Roessle (auth), Visions & Voices, Half Moon Press, 97; Teresa Lawrence (auth), Cyberspace Maelstrom, Curio Mag, 98; 944 Mag, 12/2006 & 12/2008; Westchester Mag, 2/2007, 2/2008 & 12/2008; West Chester Mag, 2010. *Mem:* Westchester Arts Coun; Ossining Arts Coun; World Found for Original Human Develop (adv bd); Perkskill Arts Alliance. *Media:* Oil, Pastel; Pen & Ink, Watercolor, Crochet. *Publ:* Visions and Voices of Westchester, London, 97; Journeys I: The Southwest, London, 98; A Visual Suite, London, 2002; Belle Armoire, 9/10/2008; Art Acquisitor Mag, 2014. *Dealer:* Julian Von Heisermann 1150 Fifth Ave New York NY 10028; Rothie Tucker 511 W 25th St NY 10001. *Mailing Add:* 341 Furnace Dock Rd #8 Cortlandt Manor NY 10567

O'BRIEN, BARBARA
MUSEUM DIRECTOR
Study: attended, Univ Kans; RI Sch Design, MFA. *Collection Arranged:* has curated nearly 50 exhibs. *Pos:* gallery dir, Monserrat Coll Art, Beverly, Mass, 90-2001; regional reviews coordr, Art New England Mag, 2002-2006, ed in chief, 2003-2006; public art consultant, City of Boston, 2004-2005; various positions, Simmons Coll, 2006-2008; cur, Kemper Mus Contemp Art, 2009, chief cur, dir exhibs, 2009-2012, dir, 2012-. *Awards:* Nat Alumni award, RI Sch Design, 2006. *Mem:* ArtTable; Int Asn Art Critics; Coll Art Asn; Am Asn Museums. *Mailing Add:* Kemper Museum of Contemporary Art 4420 Warwick Blvd Kansas City MO 64111

O'BRIEN, KEVIN JAMES
MUSEUM DIRECTOR
b St Cloud, Minn, 1954. *Study:* Univ Notre Dame, BFA, 1977; Tulane Univ, MFA, 1979. *Pos:* Dir, Community Ctr for Arts, Michigan City, Ind, 1981-1985; dir, South Ohio Mus & Cultural Ctr, Ohio Arts Coun, 1985-1988; Pensacola Mus Art, Arts Coun, 1988-1991; Everhart Mus, Scranton, Pa, 1991; Pa Coun Arts, 1994; exec dir, Key West Art & Hist Soc, 1995-2000; dir, Tippecanoe County Hist Asn, Lafayette, Ky; dir, Mus Art & Craft, Louisville, Ky, 2006-. *Mailing Add:* Museum of Art and Craft 715 West Main St Louisville KY 40202

OBRINGER, PATRICIA MARY
SCULPTOR, MURALIST
b Fort Wayne, Ind Jan 28, 1948. *Study:* Temple Univ, BS (cum laude), 1974; Ind Univ, MS, 1977; Ind Univ, studied with Karl Martz (ceramics), MS, 1977. *Work:* Woodstock Artist Guild Gallery, Woodstock, NY; Terrance Depietro Gallery, Palenville, NY. *Comn:* 50 one of a kind sculptural vessels, Campbell Taggart Inc, Dallas, Tex, 1979; Three Faces (tile relief mural), Hollywood Mem Gardens, Union, NJ, 1981; Windows to Innerspace (tiles relief mural), Durst Orgn, NYC, 1982-1983; Coming to American (painted mural), Great Location Group, Time Sq, NYC, 1986; Commemorative Medallion, Dave Brubeck Orgn, Dansbury, Conn, 2000. *Exhib:* Group Exhib, Schenectady Art Mus, Schenectady, NY 1981; Christian's D'Cota Design Center (serving pieces exhib), Dania, Fla, 1999; Bol Art Custom Tiles, D'Cota Design Center (relief tile exhib), Dania, Fla, 1999; Am Soc Interior Designers, ASID (website featured artists), 2007; Audubon Artists 65th Ann Exhib (Marquis Award), 2007; 100% Pure Fla Exhib, Fifth Ave Art Gallery, Melbourne, 2010; Fla Purchase Grustaceaon and Mollusk Globe, Robert Bigge, Ft. Lauderdale, 2010. *Pos:* Artist-in-residence, Zen Mountain Monastery, Mt Tremper, NY, 1985. *Teaching:* ITT Tech Inst, Art Appreciation, St Rose, Louisianna, 2012-. *Awards:* Ester & Adolph Gottlieb Found Grant, New York, 95; Marquis Award, Audubon Artist 65th Ann, Salmagundi Art Club, 2007. *Bibliog:* Spider Barbour (auth), Arts Obringer's Wall, Woodstock Times, 7/1987; Dakota Lane (auth), Work Locally, Sculpt Globally, Woodstock Times, 11/1994; Jorge Arrango (auth), Music of the Spheres, Hudson Valley Mag, 6/1995; Draeger Martinez (auth), Historic Depot Back in Business as Museum, Herald, 6/15/2003. *Mem:* Nat Mus Women in the Arts. *Media:* Clay, Sculpture

OBUCK, JOHN FRANCIS
PAINTER
b Detroit, Mich, Aug 20, 1946. *Study:* Wayne State Univ, BFA, 68; Sch of Art Inst Chicago, MFA, 72. *Work:* Mus Contemp Art, Chicago; Cincinnati Mus Art; Chase Manhattan Bank. *Exhib:* Chicago and Vicinity Show, Art Inst Chicago, 80; Solo Exhibs: Delahunty Gallery, Dallas, 82, Barbara Gladstone Gallery, NY, 82, Young/Hoffman Gallery, Chicago, 83, Hanes Art Ctr, Univ NC Chapel Hill, 87, Am Acad, Rome, Italy, 89, Feigenson/Preston Gallery, Birmingham, Ala, 90 & 92 & Jack Hanley Gallery, San Francisco, 91, OHT Gallery, Boston, Mass, 2004 & 06; New Abstraction, Milwaukee Art Ctr, 85; The Persistence of Abstraction, Edwin A Ulrich Mus, Wichita State Univ, Kans, 92; Basic Marks: Black & White Paintings, Rosenberg/Kaufman Fine Art, NY, 95; 60th Anniversary Exhib, Westbeth Gallery, NY, 96; Affinities: Contemp & Historic Art, Snyder Fine Art, NY, 96; Thing, Deven Golden Fine Art Ltd, NY, 96; Mus Contemp Art, Chicago; Cinn Art Mus; Herbert F Johnson Mus Art, Cornell Univ, Ithaca, NY; Harry Ranson Ctr, Univ Tex; OHT Gallery, Boston, Mass, 2009. *Teaching:* Instr, Univ NC, 87; Univ Tex, Austin, 87, 90-91; Tyler Sch Art, Philadelphia, 92; Princeton Univ, NJ, 92-93, 94-97; Harvard Univ, 2003; Ariz State Univ, Tempe, Ariz (current). *Awards:* NY State Coun on the Arts, 88; Rome Prize Fel Painting, 88-89; Pollock-Krasner Grant, 92 & 2007. *Bibliog:* Judith Kirshner (auth), rev, Art Forum, 83; Grace Glueck (auth), NY Times, 11/16/84; Kim Levin (auth), rev, Village Voice, 85. *Mem:* Am Abstract Artists; fel Am Acad Rome. *Media:* Oil Paint, Watercolor. *Dealer:* Feigenson-Preston Gallery 796 N Woodward Birmingham MI; Jack Hanley Gallery, 2610 Jackson St, San Francisco, CA; OH&T Gallery 450 Harrison Ave Boston MA 02118. *Mailing Add:* 20 Murray St #5S New York NY 10007

OCAMPO, MANUEL
PAINTER
b Quezon City, Philippines, 1965. *Study:* student, Univ Philippines, Quezon City, 84; student, Calif State Univ, 85. *Work:* Heridas de la Lengua. *Exhib:* Solo exhibs: Corcoran Biennial, 1993, Kwangju Biennial, 1997, Biennale d'art Contemporain de Lyon, 2000, Berlin Biennale, 2001, Venice Biennale, 2001, Seville Biennale, 2004, Casa Asia, Barcelona, 2005, New Works, LAC, Lieu d'Art Contemporain, Sigean, France, 2005, Bastards of Misrepresentation, Casa Asia, Barcelona, Spain, 2005, The Holocaustic Spackle in the Murals of the Quixotic Inseminators, Lizabeth Oliveria Gallery, Los Angeles, 2005, Mumu Territorium, ArtCenter Megamall, Mandaluyong, Metro Manila, Philippines, 2005, Down with Reality, Galerie Jesco von Puttkamer, Berlin, Germany, En El Cielo No Hay Cerveza sin Alcohol (with Curro Gonzalez), Galeria adhoc, Vigo, Spain, 2006, Guided by Sausage, Nosbaum & Reding, Art Contemporain, Luxembourg, 2007; Group exhibs, Seville Biennale, 2004 Casa Asia, Barcelona, 2005; Lieu d'Art Contemporain, Sigean, France, 2005; MOCA, Los Angeles, 1992; Asia Soc, New York, 1994; Setagaya Art Mus, Tokyo, 1997; Aldrich Mus Art, 1998; LA Co Mus Art, 2000; Schirn Kunsthalle, Frankfurt, 2009. *Collection Arranged:* Pvt collections. *Teaching:* instr, Univ Calif Berkeley, 1999; instr, Calif Coll Arts, San Francisco, 2004. *Awards:* Rome Prize, Am Acad, 1995, award, Nat Endowment for the Arts, 1996, Pollock-Krasner Found, 1995. *Bibliog:* Virgin Destroyer: Manuel Ocampo, Hardy Marks Publ, Honolulu, 1994; Heridas de la Lengua, Smart Art Press, Santa Monica, 1997; Hacer Pintura es Hacer Patria, Galeria OMR, Mexico City, 1997; Yo Tambien Soy Pintura, Museo Extremeno e Iberoamericano de Arte Contemporaneo (MEIAC), Badajoz, Spain, 1998; The Inversion of the Ideal: Navigating the Landscape of Intestinal Muck, Swastikating Between Love and Hate, Galeria Soledad Lorenzo, Madrid, 1999; The Nature of Culture, Manuel Ocampo/Gaston Damag, Interventions in the Monasterio de la Cartuja de Santa Maria de las Cuevas, Centro Andaluz de Arte Contemporaneo, Seville, 1999; Vitamin P, New Perspectives in Painting, Phaidon, London, New York, 2002; Art Now, 137 Artists at the Rise of the New Millenium, Taschen, Cologne, 2002; Manuel Ocampo, Bastards of Misrepresentation, Edition Casia Asia, Barcelona, 2005. *Media:* Acrylic, Oil. *Specialty:* Social and Political themes. *Dealer:* Galerie Baerbel Graesslin, Frankfurt; Galeria Tomas March, Valencia, Spain; Galerie Nathalie Obadia, Paris, Brussels; Galerie Nosbaum Reding, Luxembourg; Ad Hoc Galeria, Vigo, Spain; Pablo Gallery, Taguig City, Philippines; Finale Gallery, Makati City, Philippines; Mag: net Gallery, Quezon City, Philippines. *Mailing Add:* 4600 Jessica Dr Los Angeles CA 90065

OCEPEK, LOU (LOUIS) DAVID
PRINTMAKER, PAINTER
b Detroit, Mich, Aug 27, 1942. *Study:* Wayne State Univ, BFA, 64; Univ Iowa, Iowa City, with Lasansky, MA, 67. *Work:* Portland Art Mus, Ore; Portland State Univ, Ore; San Diego State Univ; State Univ NY, Oswego; Western Mich Univ, Kalamazoo. *Comn:* Paintings, Metrop Arts Comn, Portland, Ore, 78 & Art Advocates Inc, Portland, Ore, 78; prints, Clairmont Hotel Collection, Berkeley, 78, Seattle Arts Comn, 80 & Wash Arts Comn, Olympia, 81. *Exhib:* Northwest Printmakers Int, Seattle Art Mus, 70; Testimony to a Process, 74 & Constructions, Drawings and Prints, 76, Portland Art Mus; 12 Northwest Artists, 77 & A Directors Choice, 81, Portland Ctr Visual Arts, 81. *Teaching:* Prof design & printmaking, Portland State Univ, 71-83; prof design & illus, Mont State Univ, Bozeman, 83-; instr graphic & art design, NMex State Univ. *Awards:* Purchase Awards, The Artist Teacher Today, State Univ NY, 68, San Diego State Print Exhib, 69 & Multiples USA, Western Mich Univ, 70. *Bibliog:* David Stewart (producer), Lou Ocepek, artist, teacher, eckist, ECK World News, 78. *Mem:* Northwest Print Coun (bd dir, 83). *Media:* Silkscreen; Gouache, Acrylic. *Mailing Add:* 1761 Pomona Dr Las Cruces NM 88011-4919

OCHOA, RUBEN
SCULPTOR, ENVIRONMENTAL SCULPTOR
b Oceanside, Calif, 1974. *Study:* Parsons Sch Art & Design, New York, 1996; Otis Coll Art & Design, Los Angeles, BA, 1997; Univ Calif, Irvine, MFA, 2003. *Work:* Albright Knox Art Gallery, Buffalo, NY. *Exhib:* Solo exhibs include Vox Alta Projects, San Diego, 2004, Lizabeth Oliveria Gallery, Los Angeles, 2006, LAXART, 2006, Hallwalls Contemp Art Ctr, Buffalo, NY, 2007, Susanne Vielmetter Los Angeles Projects, 2007, Susanne Vielmetter Berlin Projects, 2008; two person exhibs with Marco Rios include Rigor Motors, Laguna Art Mus, Calif, 2004, Embryonic Loop, LAXART, 2006, & Storage, 4-F Gallery, Los Angeles, 2006; other two person exhibs include (with Peter Tavera) Caltransposed, Gallery 727, Los Angeles, 2005, (with Mark Bradford) Art Swap, Los Angeles County Mus Art, 2007-08; group exhibs include Better Look Twice, Pasadena City Coll Art Gallery, 2002; Calif Biennial, Orange County Mus Art, Newport Beach, Calif, 2004; 25 Bold Moves, Campari Emerging Artists Exhib, Los Angeles, 2006; The Newstand Project, Los Angeles, 2006; Phantom Sightings, Los Angeles County Mus Art, 2008; Whitney Biennial, Whitney Mus Am Art, New York, 2008. *Awards:* Univ Calif Instnl Res Award, 2002; Durfee Found Grant, 2004; Emerging Artist Fel, Calif Community Found, 2004; Visual Arts Grant, Creative Capital Found, 2005; Media Arts Fel, Rockefeller Found, 2006; John Simon Guggenheim Mem Found Fel, 2008. *Bibliog:* Mexican Artists, Books LLC, Memphis, Tenn, 2010

OCKENGA, STARR
PHOTOGRAPHER, EDUCATOR
b Boston, Mass. *Study:* Wheaton Col, Ill, BA, 1960; RI Sch Design, with Harry Callahan & Aaron Siskind, MFA, 1974. *Work:* Sheldon Art Gallery, Univ Nebr; Bibliot Nat, Paris; Mus Mod Art, NY; Addison Gallery of Am Art, Andover, Mass; Albert O Kuhn Gallery, Univ Md; Polaroid Collection, Cambridge, Mass; Univ Md, Baltimore. *Exhib:* Univ Bridgeport, Conn, 1983; Ga State Univ, Atlanta, 1983; Currents, Inst Contemp Art, Boston & Baskerville & Watson, NY, 1984; Boston Now, Inst Contemp Art, Boston & Contemp Arts Ctr, New Orleans, 1985; Catskill Ctr Photog, Woodstock, NY, 1986; Albert O Kuhn Gallery, Univ Md, 1987; The Ark in the Attic, Children's Mus Boston, Mass, 1987; Starr Ockenga, Film in the Cities, St Paul, Minn, 1987; Mothers & Daughters, Aperature Found, NY, 1987; Photog: A Child's World, Michael Shapiro Gallery, San Francisco, Calif, 1988; Am Color, Slatell Art Gallery, Los Cruces, NMex, 1988; Photog in Boston: 1955-1985, Lincoln, Mass, 2001. *Pos:* Pres, Stone Wall Studio, Inc, currently. *Teaching:* Dir, Creative Photog Lab, & assoc prof photog, Mass Inst Technol, 1976-82; vis prof, Bennington Col, 1984. *Awards:* Nat Endowment Arts Photog Fel, 1981; Mass Artist Photog Fel, 1983; Am Horticultural Soc Book Award, 1999; Garden Writers of Am Best Book Award, 2003, Silver Award of Achievement for Photog/Electronic Media, 2006. *Bibliog:* Parish Dobson (auth), Views, PRC Boston, Vol 2 & 3, 1981; article, Mass Rev, Vol XXIV, No 1; Kelly Wise (auth), Boston Globe review, 2/27/84; John Dorsey (auth), Baltimore Sun review, 3/9/87; Steve Purchase (auth), Baltimore Sun review, 3/26/87. *Media:* Polaroid & Fresson Prints. *Publ:* Auth, The Ark in the Attic, Godine, 1987; World of Wonders, Houghton Miffin, 1988; coauth, A World of Wonders, A Trip Thru Numbers, 1989 & Then & Now, a Book of Days, 1990, Houghton & Mifflin; On Women and Friendship, Stewart, Tabori and Chang, 1993; Earth on Her Hands: The American Woman in Her Garden, Clarkson Potter Publ, 1998; Eden on Their Minds: American Gardeners with Bold Visions, Clarkson Potter Publ, 2001; Amaryllis, Clarkson Potter Publ, 2002. *Dealer:* Tria: The Suchman-Mart-Metheny Gallery 547 West 27th Street New York NY 10001. *Mailing Add:* c/o Bargara Hogenson Barbara Hogenson Agency 165 W End Ave Ste 19C New York NY 10023

O'CONNELL, ANN BROWN
PRINTMAKER, COLLECTOR
b Worcester, Mass, June 3, 1931. *Study:* Bradford Col, AA; Boston Univ Exten; George Mason Univ, BA (art hist); Sumi-e with Evalyn Aaron, Port Washington, NY; Chinese brush painting with Audrey Nossal, Potomac, Md; also with Roddy McLean, Annandale, Va; etching, monotype, watercolor, Art League Sch, Alexandria, Va;

monotype with Joyce Zavorskas & Beverly Edwards, Cape Cod, Mass. *Exhib:* Sixth Ann Exhib, Bank of Tokyo Trust Co, NY, 69; 7th Ann Exhib, Nippon Club, NY, 70; Am Inst Architects, 79 & 80; Open Ann Art Exhib Anthenaecen, Mid-Atlantic Region, 92 & 94; Art League Juried Exhibs, 92, 93 & 94; juried exhibs, Cape Cod Art Asn, 95-98, 99, 2000 & 2001-03; and others. *Awards:* First Prize Mixed Media Graphics, Cape Cod Art Asn, 95, 96 & 97, Jurors Award, 98. *Mem:* Sumi-e Soc Am, Inc (mem secy, 71-73, founder, Wash Chap, 72, nat vpres, 72-73, nat pres, 74-78); Cape Cod Art Asn; Creative Arts Ctr; Printmakers Cape Cod & Monotype Guild, New Eng; Bd mem, Cape Cod Mus Art. *Media:* Monotype. *Specialty:* Eclectic collection. *Collection:* Print collection specializing in early 20th century American printmakers; 19th and early 20th American and European paintings. *Publ:* Coauth (with Brian O'Connell), Volunteers in Action, Found Press, New York, 89. *Dealer:* Fresh Paint Gallery 169 Route 6A Yarmouth Port MA 02675. *Mailing Add:* 50 Chase St Chatham MA 02633

O'CONNELL, DANIEL MOYLAN
MURALIST, ADMINISTRATOR

b Springfield, Mass, Aug 24, 1949. *Study:* Univ Iowa, Iowa City, BFA, 72, MA, 75. *Work:* Berkshire, Pittsfield, Mass; Univ Iowa; Air Gold, NY; City of Pittsfield, Mass; Canyon Ranch of Berkshires, Lenox, Mass. *Comn:* Mural, Nichols Brothers Inc, 87; Vietnam Vets Mem Mural, 90 & 91; mural, Capitol Theatre, Pittsfield, Mass, 92-93; Dedicated to Those Who Serve, firefighters mural, 96; mural, To Serve and Protect-Together, Pittsfield Police Dept, Mass, 98; Transitions, Pittsfield Boys & Girls Club 100th Anniversary, Mass, 02; Intermodel Transportation Ctr mural, Pittsfield, Mass, 03-. *Exhib:* Abstract Landscapes, Berkshire Artisans, Pittsfield, Mass, 76; Berkshire Art Asn Exhib, Berkshire Mus, Pittsfield, 80 & 81; Artists Living in the Berkshires, Clark Whitney Gallery, Lenox, Mass, 86; Collection of Mort Cooperaman, The Studio, 96. *Pos:* Comnr Cult Affairs, Pittsfield, Mass, 76-; regional consult, Nat Endowment Arts, 80-82. *Teaching:* Prof watercolor, Berkshire Artisans, 78-80, 81-, mural painting 86-. *Awards:* Gov's Award, Design in Mass, 82; Arts Inter-Arts Grant, Nat Endowment, 85; Nat Endowment Arts Int Exchange Grant, 96. *Bibliog:* Rosalyn Wilder (auth), Arts and Older Americans, Harcourt Press, 82; Vietnam Muralist, Am Vet, 12/91. *Mem:* Consortium of Local Arts Agencies in Mass; Berkshire Arts Alliance; Nat Alliance Local Arts Agencies; Lichtenstein Found Music & Art (assoc dir, 82-88); Pittsfield Cult Comn (assoc dir, 85-86, comnr 87-, chair, 98-); Pittsfield Cult Coun. *Dealer:* Diane Marchal Fine Art, Telluride, Colo. *Mailing Add:* Berkshire Artisans/Lichtenstein Ctr Arts 28 Renne Ave Pittsfield MA 01201

O'CONNELL, GEORGE D
PRINTMAKER, EDUCATOR

b Madison, Wis, Oct 16, 1926. *Study:* Univ Wis, BS, 50, MS, 51; Ohio State Univ; Rijksakademie Van Beeldende Kunsten, Amsterdam, Netherlands, Fulbright fel, 59-60. *Work:* Smithsonian Inst, Washington, DC; Libr Cong, Washington, DC; Gemeentemuseum Van Schone Kunsten, The Hague, Neth; Brit Mus, London, Eng; Archives of Am Art. *Comn:* Volunteer artist prog, Dept Hist Army, 71; presentation print ed, Rochester Print Club, 83. *Exhib:* Am Embassy, Dublin, Ireland; Baltimore Mus; John & Mabel Ringling Mus Art; Contemp Am Graphic Art, Corcoran Gallery Art, Washington, DC; US Info Agency Traveling Exhib Contemp Prints; Miriam Perlman Gallery, Chicago, 84; one man show, The Jazz Series, Oswego Art Guild, NY, 88; Retrospective (auth, catalog), All that Jazz, 54-92, SUNY Oswego, Tyler Gallery, NY, 92; Birch head Center, Buffalo, NY, 2011. *Pos:* Dir, Master Printer, Grey Heron Press, Oswego, NY. *Teaching:* Assoc prof printmaking, Univ Md, 61-68; prof printmaking, State Univ New York Col, Oswego, 69-91, prof emer, 91-; vis artist, Tamarind Inst, Univ NMex, 79. *Awards:* Creative Art Award, State Univ NY, Oswego, 86; Soc Am Graphic Artists Award, 89; Juror's Commendation, Boston Printmakers, Mem Exhib, 92. *Mem:* Boston Printmakers; Soc Am Graphic Artists; Int Soc Graphic Artists. *Media:* Etching, Lithography, Mezzotint, Woodcut. *Dealer:* Oxford Gallery 267 Oxford St Rochester NY. *Mailing Add:* 14 Baylis St Oswego NY 13126

O'CONNELL, KENNETH ROBERT
FILMMAKER, ADMINISTRATOR

b Ogden, Utah, Jan 22, 1945. *Study:* Univ Ore, BS, 66, MFA, 72. *Work:* Sinking Creek Film Collection, Nashville; Univ Ore Film Libr, Eugene; Uncross Found Collection, Wyo; Northwest Film Study Ctr, Portland; Charles Samu Int Prod, NY; Int Animation Libr, Tokyo, Japan. *Exhib:* USA Film Festival, Cult Ctr Hall, Dallas, 80; Athens Int Festival, Univ Theater, Athens, Ohio, 81; Hong Kong Film Festival, Exhib Hall, Hong Kong, 81; Ore Biennial, Portland Art Mus, 83 & 87; NY Film Festival Exposition, Metrop Mus Art, NY, 85; Bumbershoot '85, Seattle Art Comn, 85; Hiroshima '85, Peace Park, Japan, 85; Zagreb '86 World Animation Festival, Yugoslavia, 86; Stuttgart '90 Animation Festival, Int Festival of Children's Films, Chicago, 90; Medicine Wheel Animation Festival, Groton, Mass; Univ Ore Mus of Art, 99; Portland State Univ Gallery, 2000. *Collection Arranged:* Computers in the Creative Process (traveling exhib), Univ Ore Mus Art, 86-89; Computers in the Creative Process II, 89-91; Jack Wilkinson; Artist, Philosopher 1914-1973, Univ Ore Mus Art, 90. *Pos:* Co-dir, Comput Graphics Conf, Univ Ore, Eugene, 81-82; steering comt mem, Pac NW Comput Graphics Conf, Eugene, Ore, 82-90; Electronic Theather Comt, ACM/SIGGRAPH, Chicago, Ill; dir Internat Media Design Lab. *Teaching:* Prof film & visual thinking, Univ Ore, Eugene, 78-83, assoc prof comput art & head dept, 83-; adj prof slides & film, Goddard Col, Vt, 80-81. *Awards:* Cash Award, Ann Arbor Film Festival, 80; Third Place, USA Film Festival, 80; Selection Award, New York Film Expos, 85; First Place, Eugene Celebration Film & Video Festival. *Bibliog:* Cathy Goethals (auth), Painting at the Speed of Thought, Venture, 84. *Mem:* Coll Art Asn; Found Art, Theory & Educ; Soc Animation Studies (SAS); Assoc Computer Machinery (ACM-SIGGRAPH). *Media:* Computer Graphics, Drawing. *Publ:* Auth various articles in Sch Arts Mag, 84-90; ed Jack Wilkinson: Artist/Philosopher, 89. *Dealer:* Film Distributor: Picture Start 221 E Cullerton 6th Fl Chicago IL 60616; Chicago Filmmakers 1229 W Belmont Chicago IL 60657; Internat Film Libr Tokyo Japan. *Mailing Add:* Univ Ore 220 W 23rd Ave D Eugene OR 97405-2856

O'CONNOR, FRANCIS VALENTINE
HISTORIAN, CONSULTANT

b Brooklyn, NY, Feb 14, 1937. *Study:* Manhattan Col, New York, BA, 59; Johns Hopkins Univ, MA, 60, PhD (art hist), 65. *Pos:* Sr vis res assoc, Nat Collection of Fine Arts, Smithsonian Inst, Washington, DC, 70-72; ed & publ, Fed Art Patronage Notes, 74-86; dir, Raphael Res Enterprises, 79-2008; editor, publ, O'Connor's Page. *Teaching:* Lectr art hist, Univ Md, 64-66, asst prof, 66-70; Robert Sterling Clark, vis prof art hist, Williams Col, 90; vis prof art hist, George Washington Univ, 93. *Awards:* Grant, Nat Endowment Arts, 67-68; Independent Scholars Fel, Nat Endowment Humanities, 87-88; Rockefeller Resident Fel, Inst Med Humanities, Univ Tex, Med Br, Galveston, 91; Fel, Nat Humanities Ctr, 94-95. *Mem:* Soc for the Arts, Relig & Contemp Cult (mem bd, 74-80); Coll Art Asn; Founder Asn Independent Hist Art (pres, 83-87). *Res:* Twentieth century American art; New Deal Art Projects; abstract expressionism; projected history of American mural; psychodymanics of creativity. *Publ:* Auth, Jackson Pollock, New York: The Mus Modern Art, NY, 67; ed, Art for the Millions, The New York Graphic Soc Ltd, Greenwich, CT, 73; co-ed & co-auth, Jackson Pollock: A Catalogue Raissone of Paintings, Drawings and Other Works, Yale Univ Press, New Haven, 78; auth, Charles Seliger: Redefining Abstract Expressionism, Hudson Hills Press, New York, NY, 2003; auth, Mural in America: Wall Painting from Prehistory to the Present, www.muralinamerica.com (website), 2010. *Mailing Add:* 250 E 73rd St 11C New York NY 10021-4310

O'CONNOR, JOHN ARTHUR
PAINTER, CONSULTANT

b Twin Falls, Idaho, Jan 23, 1940. *Study:* Univ Calif, Davis, AB (with hon & scholar), 61, with Wayne Thiebaud & William T Wiley, MAA, 63; San Francisco Art Inst (scholar), with James Weeks, 61. *Work:* Ringling Mus Art, Sarasota, Fla; State Calif Collection, Sacramento; Kemper Gallery, Kansas City Art Inst, Mo; IBM Corp; Cornell Fine Arts Mus, Rollins Coll, Winter Park, Fla. *Comn:* Carr Van Anda Award for NY Times, Ohio Univ, 68; triptych, comn by Mr & Mrs George Varian, Palo Alto, Calif, 71. *Exhib:* Reality of Illusion, Denver Art Mus & traveling; Ann Exhib Am Painting, 82 & Mainstream Am: The Collection of Phil Desind, 87, Butler Inst Am Art, Youngstown, Ohio; 52nd Ann Nat Exhib Contemp Paintings, Soc Four Arts, Palm Beach, Fla, 90; 1991 Cheekwood Nat Painting Exhib, Nashville, Tenn, 91; Art Cult Technol at Rio, Summer Olympic Games, Atlanta, Ga, 96; Int Sculpture Garden & Park, Chelsea Pier, New York, 96; retrospective exhib, Cornel Fine Arts Mus, Winter Park, Fla, 98; Univ Fla Ctr Atrs, 2000; Retrospective Exhib, Pensacola Mus of art, Univ WFla, 2003; The Art Gallery, Univ of Fla, 2005; Thomas Ctr Main Gallery, 2005; Real illusions, John O'Connor's Blackboards & their Origins, Thomas Ctr main Gallery, Gainesville, Schmidt Ctr Gallery, Fla Atlantic Univ, Boca Raton, 99, Kendall Campus Art Gallery, Miami Dade Community Coll, 2000; 33rd Int Festival of Painting, Chateau Mus, Mediterranean Mus Contemp Art, Cagnes-Sur-Mer, France, 2001; Liquid Muse, Painting from the St Johns Region, Thomas Ctr Main Gallery, Gainesville, Alexander Brest Gallery, Jacksonville univ, Tallahassee Mus, Fla, Mus Fla Art, Deland, 2008-2009; Region 4: Transformation Through Imagination, Thomas Ctr Main Gallery, Gainesville, Fla, 2012; Tallahassee Mus, Tallahassee, Fla, 2012; John A O'Connor: A Retrospective in Four Parts, Thrasher - Horne Ctr for the Arts, Orange Park, Fla, 2012. *Collection Arranged:* August L & Tommie Freundlich Collection, Harn Mus Art, Gainesville, Fla, 2011. *Pos:* Dir, Art Gallery, Univ Calif, Davis, 62-63, Art Gallery, Ohio Univ, 67-68 & Appalachian Ctr Crafts, Smithville, Tenn, 81-82; sr investr, Ctr Creative & Optimal Design, Univ Fla, 72-2005, dir dept art gallery, 79-80, dir, MBA degree prog arts admin, 91-2005; artist-in-residence, Coll Creative Studies, Univ Calif, Santa Barbara, 74; fac prog consult, Bd Regents, State Univ System, Fla, 83-95; exec dir, Fla Higher Educ Arts Network, 85-2005; dir, Ctr Arts & Pub Policy, Univ, Fla, 88-2005. *Teaching:* Inst painting & drawing, Univ Calif, Santa Barbara, 63-64 & Ohio Univ, 65-69; asst prof art, Univ Fla, 69-75, assoc prof, 75-85, prof, 85-2005. *Awards:* State of Fla Individual Artist's Fel, 91-92 & 2003; Southern Arts Fedn, Nat Endowment Arts Regional Fel, 92-93; Lifetime Achievement Award, Fla Higher Educ Arts Network, 2005. *Bibliog:* Peter Frank (auth), John O'Connor, How you see it, How you don't, Conceptual Realism, 68-2003, Pensacola Mus of Art & Univ of FL, 2003-2005; Richard Vine (auth), The Truth of Illusion, Conceptual Realism, 68-2003; Pensacola Mus Art & Univ Fla, 2003-2005; Bill Zimmer (auth), John O'Connor Retrospective, Conceptual Realism, 68-2003, Univ Fla Art Gallery & Thomas Ctr Main Gallery, Gainesville, 2005. *Mem:* Fla Cult Alliance; Fla Higher Educ Arts Network (exec dir, 85-2005); Harn Mus Art, Gainesville, Fla. *Media:* Acrylic, Mixed Media. *Publ:* Ed, Graphics 1968-Ultimate Concerns, 68; coauth, Unbottle Your Creative Ideas-A Cooperative Venture of Engineering and Art, 72; contribr, A Pictorial History of the World, 75; Florida Arts Celebration and the Art in Public Places Initiative, Int Conf Sculpture, Dublin, Ireland, 89; auth, The public art process in Gainesville: a case history, J Arts Mgt, Law & Soc, fall 92. *Dealer:* Art4business Inc 161 Leverington Ave, Phila, PA 19127. *Mailing Add:* P O Box 14652 Gainesville FL 32604

O'CONNOR, JOHN JEROME
PAINTER

Study: Westfield State Coll, Mass, BA (Graphic Design), 1995; Pratt Inst, Brooklyn, NY, MFA, 2000, Master of Theory, Criticism & Hist of Art, 2000; Skowhegan Sch Painting & Sculpture, Skowhegan, Maine, 2000. *Exhib:* Solo exhibs include Jasper Rand Mus, Westfield, Mass, 1997, Pratt Inst, Brooklyn, NY, 1999, Pierogi, Brooklyn, NY, 2002, 2005, 2008; group exhibs include Cooperstown Art Assoc, NY, 1998; Showcase 2000, Hammerstein Ballroom, New York, 2000; New Drawing 2002, Coll New Jersey, Ewing, 2002; Altoids Curiously Strong Collection, New Mus Contemp Art, New York, 2003; Andy Warhol Mus, Pittsburgh, 2004; Greater New York, PS1 & Mus Mod Art, Queens, NY, 2005; Flatfiling, Artnews Projs, Berlin, 2007; Analogous Logic, Brooklyn Fire Proof, NY, 2007; Psychadelic, San Antonio Mus Art, 2008. *Teaching:* Adjunct Prof, Princeton Univ, NJ, Present. *Awards:* Pollock-Krasner Found Grant, 2007. *Dealer:* Pierogi 177 N 9th St Brooklyn NY 11211. *Mailing Add:* 2050 Hazen St East Elmhurst NY 11370-1114

O'CONNOR, STANLEY JAMES
HISTORIAN, EDUCATOR
b 1926. *Study:* Cornell Univ, BA, 51, PhD, 64; Univ Va, MA, 54. *Pos:* Chair Dept Asian Studies, Cornell Univ, 66-70, chair Dept Art History, 71-76, Dir, Southeast Asia Program, 79-84; bd, Studies in SE Asia; editorial, Wells Coll Book Art & Ctr. *Teaching:* Prof art hist, Cornell Univ, 64-. *Awards:* Fellow, Explorers Club. *Mem:* Asn Asian Studies (SE Asia Coun, 78-81); Malaysian Br, Royal Asiatic Soc; Am Comt South Asian Art; Siam Soc. *Res:* Early trade of Southeast Asia; Buddhist and Hindu art. *Publ:* Coauth, Excavations of the Prehistoric Iron Industry in West Borneo, 69; Gold and Megalithic Activity in West Borneo, 70; auth, Hindu Gods of Peninsular Siam, Artibus Asiae, 72; contribr, Buddhist Votive Tablest & Caves in Peninsular Siam, Nat Mus Bangkok, 74; Iron working as spiritual inquiry in Indonesia, Hist of Relig, 75; Tambralinga and the Khmer Empire, Siam Soc J, 75; coauth, Dyer's Art, Weaver's Hand: Textiles from the Indonesian Archipelago, 85; Critics, Connoisseurs in the Southeast Asian Rainforest, Asian Art and Culture, 91; Humane Literacy and Southeast Asian Art, Jour of SE Asian Studies, 95; Tuyeres and the Scale of the Santubong Iron Industry, Living a Life in Accordance with Dhamma, Bangkok, 97. *Mailing Add:* 617 Highland Rd Ithaca NY 14850-1411

O'CONNOR, THOM
PRINTMAKER
b Detroit, Mich, June 26, 1937. *Study:* Fla State Univ, BA; Cranbrook Acad Art, MFA; Tamarind Printery Fel, 64; State Univ NY Res Found Fel, 65 & 72. *Work:* Mus Mod Art, Whitney Mus Am Art, NY; Brooklyn Mus; Philadelphia Mus Art; Pushkin Mus, Moscow; Hermitage, St Petersburg; Nat Collection of Fine Arts, Washington, DC; Smithsonian Instn, Washington, DC; Baltimore Mus Art; Boston Pub Libr; San Diego Art Mus; Santa Barbara Art Mus, Calif; NY Pub Libr; Rochester Meml Mus, NY. *Comn:* Witches of Salem (suite), State Coun Arts, NY, 72. *Exhib:* solo exhibs, Am Ctr, Belgrade, Yugoslavia, 80, Univ Art Mus, Univ Albany, 82, 99, Kalundborg Art Ctr, Denmark, 83, Gallery Strindberg, Helsinki, Finland, 84, Mus Mod Art, Belgrade, Yugoslavia, 87, Taidegraphik, Helsinki, Finland, 87, 90, Sarajevo Acad Gallery, 88, Albany Ctr Galleries, NY, 91, Haenah-Kent Gallery, NY, 92, 93, Raleigh Contemp Gallery, NC, 98, WDO Gallery, Charlotte, NC, 98, Mus Art Espirito Santo, Vitoria, Brazil, 2000; group exhibs, Detroit Print Symposium, Cranbrook Acad Art, Bloomfield Hills, Mich, 80; Int Biennial, Ljubljana, Yugoslavia, 85, 86; Joensuu Mus, Finland, 95; Ark State Univ, Fayetteville, 96; Richmond Art Ctr, Calif, 96; Union Col, Schenectady, NY, 99; Wexford Art Ctr, Ireland, 2001; Rice Gallery, Albany Inst Hist & Art, NY, 2002; Lessedra World Art Print Ann, Sofia, Bulgaria, 2003, 04; Boston Printmakers, 2005; Mus Contemp Art, Liege, Belgium, 2005; and many others. *Teaching:* Prof lithography, Univ Albany, 62-; vis artist, Swedish Acad Fine Arts, 78 & Cranbrook Acad Art, 81. *Awards:* Rissanen Prize, Kuopio, Finland, 83; Fulbright Award, Yugoslavia; Nat Endowment Arts Grant. *Publ:* auth, Wizards, Cabalists, Mystics and Magicians, 66; auth, Witches of Salem, 72; auth, Daydreams, 83; auth, Dreams of Kuopio, 84; auth, Night Dreams, 85. *Dealer:* Hanna-Kent Gallery, New York NY. *Mailing Add:* Moss Rd Voorheesville NY 12186

O'CONNOR-MYER, ROSE ANN
ART DEALER, LECTURER
b New York City, NY, Nov 14, 1960. *Study:* SUNY at Buffalo, Buffalo, NY, BA, 82; NY Univ, New York City, NY, 94. *Collection Arranged:* Charles Hoffbauer (1875-1957), Comenos Fine Arts, 87; Paintings of Trav Niedlinger, Moonstruck, 2000; Mid Century Masters, Moonstruck, 2001; New Yorker Cartoonist: Barbara Shermund, Corner Joint, 2002; A NJ Artist: Alex Cotler, Fredrick Gallery, 2005; and others. *Pos:* Dir, Comenos Fine Arts, Boston, Mass, 82-93; Pres, Art Research Assocs, Allenhurst, NJ, 93-. *Teaching:* Identifying Fine Art Prints, Cambridge Ctr for Adult Educ, 88-90. *Mem:* Appraiser Asn Am. *Specialty:* Am & Europ 18th, 19th, & early 20th century paintings, drawings, sculptures & prints. *Mailing Add:* 44 Ocean Ave Allenhurst NJ 07711

OCVIRK, OTTO G
SCULPTOR, PRINTMAKER
b Detroit, Mich, Nov 13, 1922. *Study:* State Univ Iowa, BFA & MFA. *Work:* Dayton Art Inst, Ohio; Detroit Inst Art; Dayton Co, Minneapolis. *Comn:* Sculpture, Bowling State Univ, 69. *Exhib:* Walker Art Ctr, Minneapolis, 47-49; Brooklyn Nat Print, New York, 49; Northwest Printmakers, Seattle, Wash, 49; San Francisco Ann Print & Drawing, 49-50; Libr Cong Nat Print Show, Washington, DC, 50. *Teaching:* Prof emer art, Bowling Green State Univ, 50-85. *Awards:* Sculpture Exhib, Walker Art Ctr, Minneapolis, 47; Mich Artist Exhib, Hal H Smith, Detroit, 50; Broadcast Media Award, WBGU-TV, 19th Ann Broadcasters, San Francisco. *Media:* Stone; Intaglio. *Publ:* Coauth, Art Fundamentals, Theory and Practice, Brown, 60, 68, 75, 81, 85, 90, 94, 97, 2001 & 2005

ODA, MAYUMI
PAINTER, PRINTMAKER
b Tokyo, Japan, June 2, 1941. *Study:* Tokyo Univ Fine Art, BA, 66. *Work:* Mus Mod Art, NY; Mus Fine Arts, Boston; Libr Cong, Washington, DC; Honolulu Acad Art; Cincinnati Art Mus; Cleveland Mus; Portland Art Mus. *Comn:* Poster, Rainbow Art Found, NY, 77; Goddess of Hawaii, East West Ctr, Honolulu, 85; poster, Hawaiian Int Film Festival, Honolulu, 85. *Exhib:* 22nd Nat Exhib Prints, Libr Cong, Washington, DC, 71; solo exhibs, Goddesses: Visions of Women, Univ Hawaii, Honolulu, Tucson Art Mus, Ariz, 82 & Expression of Yin, Mills Col, Oakland, Calif, 86; retrospective, East West Ctr, Honolulu, 85; Honolulu Acad Art 87; Cathedral St John the Divine, NY; Centro Int della Grafica, Venice, Italy, 90; and others. *Teaching:* Artist-in-residence, Inst Cult & Communication, East West Ctr, Honolulu, 85-86. *Awards:* Lindisfarne Fel. *Bibliog:* Martha Gressing (producer), Women Artists, KQED-TV, San Francisco, 78; Mary & Norman Tolman (auths), People who make Japanese prints, Sobunsha, 83; Pauline Sugino (auth), Goddesses, vision of women, Bridge Mag, 84; Connecting Conversations, Eucalyptus Press; Women's Culture, Bettina Aptheker Gallerie, 88; Mary Ann Lutzker (auth), Goddess Banners, Orientation, 2/90. *Media:* Acrylic; Silkscreen, Etching. *Publ:* Collabr, Goddesses, Lancaster Miller, 84; Song of Vegetables, Koguma Sha, Tokyo, 86; Goddesses, Volcano Press, 88; Happy Veggies, Parallex Press, 88; Random Kindness and Senseless Acts of Beauty, Volcano Press, 93. *Dealer:* The Tolman Collection New York; Ren Brown Collection CA. *Mailing Add:* 1795 Shoreline Hwy Sausalito CA 94965-9724

ODATE, TOSHIO
CONCEPTUAL ARTIST, EDUCATOR
b Tokyo, Japan, July 9, 1930. *Study:* Art Workshop, Tokyo, 50-54; Nat Chiba Univ, 57-58. *Work:* Rochester Mem Art Gallery, NY; Bundy Art Gallery, Waitsfield, Vt; Great Southwest Atlanta Corp, Atlanta, Ga; Mus Wis; Hirshhorn Mus, Washington; The Norton Gallery Art, W Palm Beach, Fla; and others. *Exhib:* Waning Moos and Rising Sun--Japanese Artists, Houston Mus Art, Tex, 59; Joseph H Hirshhorn Collection, Solomon R Guggenheim Mus, NY, 63; The Artists Reality, New Sch Social Res, NY, 64; Whitney Mus Am Art Sculpture Ann, 65-66; Attitudes, Brooklyn Mus, 70; Md Inst Coll Art, Baltimore, Md, 87; Brattleboro Mus, 89; Matters of the Heart, Mattatuck Mus, 92; Symbols, Myths & Dreams, Glass Mountain Gallery, Bantam, Conn, 99; 25 Yrs Fine Craftsmanship, The Silo, New Milford, Conn, 2001; 50th Anniversary Show, Washington Art Assoc, Washington, Conn, 2002; and many others. *Teaching:* Instr sculpture, Brooklyn Mus Art Sch, 63-79; assoc prof sculpture, Pratt Inst, 68-2004; vis prof advan sculpture, Cooper Union, 76, prof sculpture, 77-78; instr, Brookfield Craft Ctr, Conn, 78-; vis prof upper level sculpture, Coll at Purchase, NY, 83, 85-88; guest lectr, Denver Mus Art, 67, Univ Wis, Wausau, 68 & Univ Ky, 69, Cooper Union, 72, Cooper-Hewitt Mus, 77, Harvard Univ, 88, Yale Univ Art Gallery, 89, Carnegie-Mellon Univ, 95-96 and many others. *Media:* Mix. *Publ:* Contribr, Modern sculpture from the Joseph H Hirshhorn Collection, 62; Modern American sculpture, 67; auth, Japanese Woodworking Tools Their Tradition, Spirit & Use, 84; Asian Art-Soul of the Tool, Arthur M Sackler Gallery, Smithsonian Inst, Oxford Univ Press, 91; Am Woodworker, 1/91, 10/92, 9-10/93, 2/95 & 10/95; Outils Japonais: Tradition, Esprit et Usages, Editions H Vial, Dourdan, France, 2004; and others. *Mailing Add:* 63 Pomperaug Rd Woodbury CT 06798-3714

O'DELL, ERIN (ANNE)
PAINTER, DESIGNER
b Phoenix, Ariz, Dec 7, 1938. *Study:* Moore Coll Art, BFA (textile design); Ariz State Univ; with John Pike in Mex, Jamaica, Ireland, Italy & Guatemala. *Work:* Ariz Bank, Phoenix; Colo Nat Bank, Colorado Springs; First Nat Bank, Mesa, Ariz; Valley Nat Bank, Scottsdale & Mesa, Ariz. *Exhib:* Two Flags Festival Arts, Douglas, Ariz, 73-79; Laramie Nat Miniature Show, 78 & 79; Ariz State Fair, 81; La Galeria Group Show, Casa Grande, 85; solo exhibs, Scottsdale Methodist Church, Ariz, 86 & Phoenix Women's Club, 88; and others. *Pos:* Designer, Henry Cantor, Inc, Philadelphia, Pa, 61-64; freelance designer, C A Reed Co, Williamsport, Pa & Beach Prod, Kalamazoo, Mich, 64-75; artist, Modern Color Printing, Mesa, 69-74. *Teaching:* Instr hist textiles, Moore Coll Art, 63-65. *Awards:* Mesa Artist of the Year, Mesa Art League, 73 & 79; Watercolor Award, Douglas Art Asn, 73; Artist of the Year, Ariz Saguaro Artists League, 77. *Mem:* Southwestern Watercolor Soc; Scottsdale Artists League; Midwest Watercolor Soc; Ariz Artists Guild; Watercolor West. *Media:* Watercolor

ODITA, ODILI DONALD
PAINTER
b Enugu, Nigeria, 1966. *Study:* Ohio State Univ, BFA, 1988; Bennington Coll, Vt, MFA, 1990. *Work:* Birmingham Mus Art, Ala; Hirshhorn Mus & Sculpture Garden, Washington; Miami Art Mus; Philadelphia Mus Art; Studio Mus Harlem, New York; Ulrich Mus, Wichita State Univ, Kans. *Exhib:* Solo exhibs include Florence Lynch Gallery, New York, 1999, 2001, 2004, Miami Art Mus, 2002, Galerie Schuster, Frankfurt, Germany, 2002, 2004, Haunch of Venison, 2004, Jack Shainman Gallery, New York, 2006, 2010, 2013, Contemporary Art Ctr, Cincinnati, 2007, Studio Mus Harlem, New York, 2007, Michael Stevenson Gallery, Cape Town, South Africa, 2008, 2012; Art Under 30, Nat Acad Design, New York, 1993; Split-Level, Art In General, New York, 1995, Crossing Lines, 1998; Ideoscape, Boston Ctr Arts, 1999; Material & Matter, Studio Mus Harlem, New York, 2001, Collection in Context, 2002; Against the Wall: Painting Against the Grid, Surface & Frame, Inst Contemp Art, Philadelphia, 2001; After Matisse & Picasso, PS1 Contemp Art Ctr, New York, 2003; Black President, New Mus Contemp Art, New York, Yerba Buena Ctr Arts, San Francisco, Barbican Art Galleries, London & Contemp Arts Ctr, Cincinnati, 2003; DAK'ART 2004, Dakar Biennale Contemp African Art, 2004; Tapping Currents: Contemp African Art & the Diaspora, Nelson-Atkins Mus Art, Kansas City, 2007; Think With the Senses, Feel With the Mind, Venice Biennale, 2007; Third Space, Inst Contemporary Art, Phila, 2008-2009; Television, Ulrich Project Series, Ulrich Mus Art, Wichita, Kans, 2010; Perspectives 169: Odili Donald Odita, Contemporary Arts Mus, Houston, 2010; Karmic Abstraction, Bridgette Mayer Gallery, Phila, 2011; The Bearden Project, Studio Mus in Harlem, NY, 2012; Magical Visions, Univ Mus, Univ Del, Newark, 2012; African Abstraction Michael Stevenson Gallery, Art Basel, Switz, 2012; Never Underestimate a Monochrome, Univ Iowa Mus Art, 2012-2013; North by Northwest, Marginal Utility, Phila, 2013; Sound Vision: Contemporary Art from the Collection, Nasher Mus Art at Duke Univ, Durham, NC, 2014. *Awards:* Penny McCall Found Grant, 1994; ArtsLink Collag Projects Award, 2000; Joan Mitchell Found Grant, 2001; Thami Mnyele Residency Found Grant, 2004; Louis Comfort Tiffany Found Grant, Biennial Award, 2007. *Bibliog:* Brandon K Rudd and Gregory Nosan (auths) Painting: From the Collection of the Sheldon Mus Art, Lincoln and London: Univ Nebr Press, pp 248-249, 2014. *Dealer:* Michael Stevenson Gallery Buchanan Bldg 160 Sir Lowry Rd Woodstock 7925 Cape Town South Africa. *Mailing Add:* c/o Jack Shainman Gallery 513 W 20th St New York NY 10011

OERI, MAJA
COLLECTOR
b Switz. *Pos:* Pres, Emanuel Hoffman Found, Basel, currently; founder, Laurenz Found, Basel, 1999-, The Schaulager, Basel, 2003-; trustee, Mus Mod Art, New York, currently; advisory bd, Tate Modern. *Awards:* Named one of Top 200 Art Collectors, ARTnews mag, 2003-12. *Collection:* Modern and contemporary art. *Mailing Add:* Schaulager Ruchfeldstrasse 19 Munchenstein/Basel CH-4142 Switzerland

OETTINGER, MARION, JR
CURATOR
Study: Univ of the Americas, Mex, BA (anthrop); Univ NC-Chapel Hill, PhD (anthrop). *Collection Arranged:* Project dir & co-cur, Retratos: 2,000 Years of Latin American Portraits, 2004. *Pos:* Cur Folk Art & Latin Am Art, San Antonio Mus Art, 1985-93, sr cur & cur Latin Am Art, 1994-, interim dir, 2004-05, Betty & Bob Kelso dir, 2005-2011,. *Awards:* Res Grant, Nat Geographic Soc, Am Philos Soc, Nat Endowment for the Arts, Nat Endowment for the Humanities & Nat Sci Found; Fulbright Sr Res Fel, 1979; Imagineering Award, Mind Sci Found, 1992. *Publ:* Auth, Folk Treasures of Mexico: The Nelson A. Rockefeller Collection, Harry N Abrams, 1990; The Folk Art of Latin America: Visiones del Pueblo, Dutton, 1992; The Folk Art of Spain and the Americas: El Alma del Pueblo, Abbeyville, 1997. *Mailing Add:* San Antonio Mus Art 200 West Jones Ave San Antonio TX 78215

OGINZ, RICHARD
SCULPTOR, DRAFTSMAN
b Philadelphia, Pa, Feb 7, 1944. *Study:* Tyler Sch Art, Temple Univ, BFA, 66; Univ Wis-Madison, MA, MFA, 68. *Work:* Los Angeles Co Mus Art; Arts Coun Gt Brit, London; Bradford Mus, Yorkshire; Leeds City Art Mus, Madison, Wis; Madison Art Mus, Wis. *Comn:* Elevator Doors lobby, Junipero Serra State Office Bldg, Los Angeles, Calif, 98. *Exhib:* Artists Chairs, Santa Monica Mus Art, Calif, 95; Drawn From Los Angeles, Armory Ctr Arts, Pasadena, Calif, 96; Containers, Los Angeles Co Mus Art, 96; Grins: Humor and Whimsy in Contemp Art, Millard Sheet Gallery, Los Angeles Co Fair, Pomona, Calif, 97; Mechanical Wonders, Craft & Folk Art Mus, Los Angeles, 2001; Sculptors Draw Art Gallery, Glendale Community Col, Calif, 2001; Raw Draw, Pasadena City Coll Art Gallery, Calif, 2002; Solo exhibs, Recent Sculpture, Glendale Community Col, Calif, 92, Ruth Bachofner Gallery, Santa Monica, Calif, 91 & 93, Worlds-Bodies-Machines, Sam Francis Gallery, Crossroads Sch, Santa Monica, Calif, 95, Richard Oginz, Drawing from a Sculptor's View, Los Angeles Co Mus Art, Calif, 97, New Work: Gallery of Functional Art, Santa Monica, Calif, 99, Richard Oginz, Jan Baum Gallery, Calif, 2001; New Work Gallery of Functional Art, Santa Monica, Calif, 2005. *Pos:* bd dir, Los Angeles Contemp Exhibs (LACE), 1983-1987. *Teaching:* Principal lectr sculpture, Middlesex Polytech, London, 74-76; sculpture fac, Otis Art Inst, Los Angeles, 76-95; Pierce Community Col, 2002-04; Glendale Community Col, 2003; UCLA World Arts and Cultures, 2005-06. *Awards:* Ford Found Grant, 78-79; Young Talent Award, Los Angeles Co Mus Art, Calif, 79; Nat Endowment Arts Visual Artists Forum Grant Figurative Sculp, Otis Arts Inst, Calif, 84; Gregory Fel, Leeds (Eng) Univ, 1971-1973. *Bibliog:* Pamela Hammond (auth), Narratives of isolation, Artweek, 11/10/84; Peter Plagens (auth), Bee-Bop Da Reebok in LA, Art in Am, 4/85; Peter Clothier (auth), Richard Oginz Sculpture, Art News, 5/91. *Media:* Mixed. *Publ:* Illusr, Drawing A contemporary Approach, Holt Rhinehart & Winston, 87; Joseph Campbell, Maurice Tuchman (auths), Masquerade, Chronicle Books, 1993; Budd & Arloa Goldston (auths), Watts Towers, The Getty Conservation Inst, 1997; Barbara Tober (auth), Object Lessons, Guild Inc, 2001

O'GORMAN, JAMES FRANCIS
LECTURER, WRITER
b St Louis, Mo, Sept 19, 1933. *Study:* Washington Univ, Mo, BA (arch); Univ Ill, Urbana, MA (arch); Harvard Univ, MA, PhD. *Teaching:* Grace Slack McNeil Prof Emeritus of Hist of Am Art, Wellesley Col, 75-2004 (Emer 2004). *Awards:* Franklin Rsch grant, Am Philosophical Society, 83, 90, 2011, 2013; NEH fel, 88-89 & 96; Mellon Foundation Fellow, 2005-06; Henry-Russell Hitchcock Book award, Victorian Soc Am, 97, 2010; Ann Book Prize, Hist New England, 98, 2008; Distinguished Alum Award, Sch Archit, Wash Univ, 94. *Mem:* Soc Archit Historians (pres, 70-72, fel 2007); Coll Art Asn; life fel Philadelphia Athenaeum; Am Antiquarian Soc; Maine Historic Preserve Com, (chmn, 2006-11). *Res:* American art and architecture. *Publ:* Auth, The Architecture of the Monastic Library in Italy, New York Univ Press, 72; coauth, The Architecture of Frank Furness, Philadelphia Mus of Art, 73; auth, H H Richardson and His Office: Selected Drawings, Harvard Col, 74; This Other Gloucester, pvt publ, 76; H H Richardson, Architectural Forms for an American Society, Univ Chicago Press, 87; Three American Architects: Richardson, Sullivan and Wright, 1865-1915, Univ Chicago Press, 91; Living Architecture: A Biography of H.H. Richardson, Simon and Schuster, 97; ABC of Architecture, Univ Pennsylvania Press, 98; Accomplished in All Departments of Art: Hammatt Billings of Boston, Univ Mass Press, 98; Connecticut Valley Vernacular, Univ Pennsylvania Press, 2002; coauth, The Maine Perspective: Architectural Drawings, 1800-1980, Portland Mus Art, 2006; Henry Austin: In Every Variety of Architectural Style, Wesleyan Univ Press, 2008; ed, Drawing Toward Home: Designs for Domestic Archit from Hist New England, 2010; ed, Hill-Stead: The Country Place of Theodate Pope Riddle, 2010; coauth, Gervase Wheeler, 2011. *Mailing Add:* 6 Stoneledge Dr Portland ME 04102

O'GRADY, LORRAINE
PHOTOGRAPHER, VIDEO ARTIST
b Boston, Mass, 1934. *Work:* Davis Mus & Cult Ctr, Mass; Wadsworth Atheneum, Conn; Peter Norton Family Found, Calif. *Exhib:* Exquisite Corpses, Drawing Ctr, New York, 1993; A Range of Views: New Bunting Fellows in the Visual Arts, Bunting Inst, Harvard Univ, 1995; New Histories, Inst Contemp Art, Boston, Mass, 1996; Identity Crisis: Self Portraiture at the End of the Century, Milwaukee Art Mus, 1997; Whitney Biennial, Whitney Mus Am Art, New York, 2010. *Mailing Add:* 155 Bank St Apt A-625 New York NY 10014

O'HAGAN, DESMOND BRIAN
PAINTER
b Wiesbaden, Ger; US citizen/Irish citizen. *Study:* Univ NMex 77-79; Colo Inst Art, AA, 82. *Work:* Denver Pub Libr Art Collection, Colo; City of Loveland, Colo; and many pvt corp collections. *Exhib:* Pastel Soc Am Show, NY, 87,88, 97 & 98, 99; Artists of the West Exhib, Pioneers Mus, Colorado Springs, 93; Artists of Am Exhib, Colo Hist Mus, Denver, 96-98; Pastel Soc Am China Exhib, Xian, China, 97; Galleria Prov, Tokyo, Japan, 98; Int Asn Pastel Soc Exhib, Albuquerque, 99; solo show, ES Lawrence Gallery, Aspen, Colo, 2005. *Pos:* master pastelist, Pastel Soc Am Asn. *Teaching:* workshop instr, various art socs and schs. *Awards:* George Innes, Jr Mem Award for a pastel, Salmagundi Club, 96; Conn Pastel Soc Asn Show Award, 9/97; Mrs Pearl Kalikow Award, Pastel Soc Asn Show, 9/98; Prix'd Pastel Award, Best of Show Int, Asn Pastel Soc, 99; Hudson Valley Art Asn Award, PSA Open Show, 99. *Bibliog:* M Stephen Doherty (auth), Stirring the viewer's imagination, Am Artist Mag, 12/89; Desmond O'Hagan, United Airlines Hemispheres Mag, 1/96; Gekkan Bijyutsu Art Mag, Japan, 5/98. *Mem:* Pastel Soc Am; Pastel Soc Colo Asn; Int Asn Pastel Soc (masters circle). *Media:* Pastels, Oils. *Specialty:* Contemporary Representational. *Interests:* The Study of Light on the Urban Landscape. *Publ:* auth, Light on the subject, Artists & Illusrs Mag, 10/98; A sense of place, Artist's Mag, 9/01; Desmond O'Hagan, Pastel J, 5/03; Contrasting Color, Contrasting Mediums, Int Artist Mag, 2/01. *Dealer:* ES Lawrence Gallery 516 East Hyman Aspen CO 81611; Saks Galleries 3019 E 2 Av Denver CO 80206; The Gallery 329 Primrose Rd Burlingame CA 94010. *Mailing Add:* 2882 S Adam St Denver CO 80210

O'HARROW, SEAN
MUSEUM DIRECTOR
b Hawaii. *Study:* Harvard Univ, BA (Art History); Cambridge Univ, PhD (Architecture History). *Pos:* Develop dir, St Catharine's Coll, Univ Cambridge, England, formerly; exec dir, Figge Art Mus, 2007-. *Mailing Add:* Figge Art Museum 225 West 2nd Street Davenport IA 52801

OHE, KATIE
SCULPTOR, INSTRUCTOR
b Peers, Alta, Can, Feb 18, 1937. *Study:* Alta Coll Art, dipl (fine arts); Montreal Sch Art & Design, with Dr Lismer; Sculpture Ctr, New York, with Sahl Swarz & Dorothy Denslow, Fonderia Fabris, Verona, Italy. *Hon Degrees:* Univ Calgary, LLD, 01. *Work:* Can Coun Art Banks, Ottawa, Ont Alta Art Found, Edmonton; Visual Arts, Cult Activities, Edmonton; Shell Can Art Collection, Calgary; Alta Coll of Art; Glenbow Mus, Calgary, Alberta, Can; Kahanoff Found, Calgary, 2012. *Comn:* chromed steel sculpture, Univ Calgary, 67 & 75; cast stone sculpture relief, Fed Western Regional Bldg, Calgary, 67; bronze sculpture, Sch Bd, City of Calgary, 75; Esso: Imperial Oil, Res Ctr, Calgary, 90; Univ Calgary, 96; Alberta Coll Art & Design, 2001. *Exhib:* Sculpture Ctr, NY, 62-70; Brit Int Print Show, London, Eng, 71; Venice Biennial, Italy, 72; Alta Art Found Traveling Exhib, Can House Gallery, London, Brussels, Paris & NY, 75-76; Changes: 11 Artists Working on the Prairies Traveling Exhib, 75-76; retrospectives, Alta Coll Art, Calgary, 91, Edmonton Art Gallery, 97-98 & Nickle Art Mus, Univ Calgary, 96; solo exhibs, Glenbow Mus, Calgary; and many other group exhibs in Gdansk, Poland, Porto, Portugal, Tinos, Greece, Amsterdam, Holland. *Collection Arranged:* Edmonton Art Gallery, Glentow, Calgary, Alberta, Can. *Pos:* cur, Triangle Gallery Visual Arts. *Teaching:* Instr sculpture, Mt Royal Col, Calgary, 70-, Alta Col Art, Calgary, 70-03 & Univ Calgary, 79, Calgary Allied Art Ctr. *Awards:* Nat Gallery Study Grant, 58; Can Coun Grants, New York, 63, Europe, 68 & Verona, Italy, 74; Allied Arts Award Medal, Royal Archt Inst of Can, 84; ACAD Award of Excellence. *Bibliog:* Clement Greenburg (auth), View of art on the prairies, Can Art, 63; Anita Aarons (auth), Allied Art Catalogue, Vol 2, Arts and Architecture, Royal Archit Inst Can, 68; Barb Kwasney (auth), Canadian Golden West, Western Artist, spring 76; Canadian Art, Winter, 2009. *Mem:* Royal Can Acad Arts; Alta Soc Artists. *Media:* Multimedia, Metal. *Publ:* Canadian Art; Encyclopedia of Twentieth Century North Am Women Artists; Alberta Art Chronicle. *Mailing Add:* 244034 Horizon View Rd Calgary AB T303M5 Canada

OHNO, MITSUGI
GLASSBLOWER
b Tochigi, Japan, June 28, 1926; US citizen. *Work:* US Capitol replica, Smithsonian Inst, Washington; Independence Hall, White House, 72; US Capitol, 75; Anderson Hall, Kans State Univ, 77; Dwight D Eisenhower Libr; Chemistry Bldg, Tokyo Univ, Japan; Royal carriage & harp replica (given to Crown Prince of Japan), 87. *Comn:* Ohno Klein Bottle, Smithsonian Inst, Washington, 75, given to Emperor of Japan, 79; Nikko Toshogu Shrine, 86 & 88, Tochigi Prefecture, Japan; Nippon-Maru, given to Emperor of Japan, 94. *Exhib:* Smithsonian Inst, 75; Tochigi Mus, Japan, 88; Hyogo History Mus, Japan, 93; Imperial Palace, Japan, 94; Aircraft Carrier USS Nimitz, Battleship USS Mo & USS Constitution (Old Ironsides), Kans State Univ, 96; HMS Victory, Kans State Univ, 98. *Pos:* Sr master sci glassblower, Kans State Univ, retired. *Teaching:* Prof, Scientific Glassblow, 94; adj prof, Kans State Univ, 94. *Awards:* Yoshikawa-Eiji Prize for Cult Merit, Tokyo, Japan, 79; Walter E Morrison Award, Kans State Univ, 79; University Medallion of Excellence, Kans State Univ, 98. *Media:* Glass. *Publ:* The Life of Japanese Man living in Kansas; Japan (A man captivated by glass), 90. *Mailing Add:* 2808 Nevada St Manhattan KS 66502

OJI, HELEN SHIZUKO
PAINTER
b Sacramento, Calif, Aug 27, 1950. *Study:* Yuba Col, Marysville, Calif, AA, 70; Calif State Univ, Sacramento, BA (art), 72, MA (art), 75. *Work:* Jacksonville Art Mus, Fla; Mus S Tex, Corpus Christi; Gen Elec Corp, Fairfield, Conn; Mus Mod Art, NY; Jane Voorhees Zimmerli Art Mus, Rutgers State Univ, New Brunswick, NJ. *Comn:* Calendar-poster, Asian Cinevision, NY, 84; Monoprint etching, The Jane Voorhees Zimmerli Art Mus, New Brunswick, 85. *Exhib:* Solo exhibs, Fine Arts Ctr/Wake Forest Univ, Winston-Salem, NC, 80, Monique Knowlton Gallery, NY, 81 & 82, Nelson Gallery, Univ Calif, Davis, 82, Real Art Ways, Hartford, Conn, 84 & Intar

Gallery, NY, 86; Mus Mod Art, NY, 81 & 88; Corcoran Gallery Art, Washington (traveling), 93; Zimmerli Art Mus, NJ, 96; A Woman's Place, Monmouth Mus, Randolph, NJ, 96; Would You Mind Repeating That Again?, Broadway Gallery, NY, 96; If the Shoe Fits, FAO Gallery, NY, 96; plus many others. *Pos:* Panelist, NY Found Arts, 86-87, Mass Artists Fel Prog, 87, NY State Coun Arts, 89-91 & New Langton Arts, 90; guest panelist, Soho 20 Gallery, WCA, NY, 88, Chinatown Hist Proj, NY, 88 & Prowess Interarts Inc, NY, 92. *Teaching:* Instr beginning painting & printmaking, Yuba Col, Marysville, Calif, 76; guest lectr, Women's Caucus Arts, NY, 81, Asian Am Art Ctr, NY, 85, Parsons Sch Design, NY, 89 & Alternative Mus, NY, 92; instr visual art workshop, Hospital Audiences Inc, 87-89 & Bergen St Residence, Brooklyn, NY, 92-; guest artist Penn State Univ, 92, State Univ NY, New Paltz, 93 & Columbia Univ, 94; substitute instr art dept, St Ann's Sch, Collegiate Sch, grades K-12, 96; adj instr, Fashion Inst Technol, NY, 96-. *Awards:* Ariana Found Arts Inc Mixed Media Grant, 84; Artists Space Mat Grant, New York, 86; Vis Artist Fel, Brandywine Workshop, Philadelphia, 95. *Bibliog:* Arlene Raven & Cassandra L Langer (auths), positions, NYFAI, New York, 89; The Return of the Cadavre Exquis (exhib catalog), Drawing Ctr, 94; Alice Yang (auth), Haenah-Kent, Asian Art News, 3/94. *Media:* Painting. *Mailing Add:* 360 W 36th St Apt 5NW New York NY 10018

OKALA, CHINEDU
PAINTER, SCULPTOR, ADMINISTRATOR
Study: Howard Univ, MFA (Painting, Sculpture), 1991. *Pos:* Owner, creative strategist, master painter and sculptor, Strokes Agency, Chesapeake, Va, 1994-. *Teaching:* Prof Art, Norfolk State Univ, currently, chmn dept art, 2004-06, currently. *Mailing Add:* Norfolk State University Hamm Fine Arts Building Room 112 700 Park Ave Norfolk VA 23504

OKAMURA, ARTHUR
PAINTER
b Long Beach, Calif, Feb 24, 1932. *Study:* Art Inst Chicago (scholar), 50-54; Univ Chicago, 51 & 53; Yale Univ Summer Art Sem, 54; Edward L Ryerson Travel Fel, 54; Univ Chicago, 57. *Work:* Corcoran Gallery Art, Washington, DC; Nat Collection Fine Arts, Smithsonian Inst; Nat Inst Arts & Lett; Hirshhorn Mus, Washington, DC; San Francisco Mus Art, Calif; and others. *Exhib:* Painters Behind Painters, Calif Palace Legion Honor, San Francisco, 67; Solo exhibs, San Francisco Mus Art, 68, Calif Coll Arts & Crafts, 72, Southern Idaho Coll, 72, Kent State Univ, Ohio, 73 & Honolulu Acad Arts, 73; Takashima 1970 Expos, Osaka, Tokyo, Japan, 70; Asian Artists, Oakland Mus, 71; and others. *Pos:* Dir, San Francisco Studio Art, 58. *Teaching:* Instr, Cent YMCA Col, Chicago & Evanston Art Ctr, Ill, 56-57, Art Inst Chicago, N Shore Art League, Winnetka, Ill & Acad Art, San Francisco, 57, Saugatuck Summer Art Sch, Mich, 59 & 62; prof, Calif Col Arts & Crafts, 58-59 & 66-97; guest lectr, Univ Utah, 64 & 75. *Awards:* Schwabacher-Frey Award, 79th Ann, San Francisco Mus, 60; Neysa McMein Purchase Award, Whitney Mus Am Art, 60; Purchase Award, Nat Soc Arts & Lett; plus many others. *Bibliog:* Lee Nordness (ed), Art: USA: Now, C J Bucher, 62; Art Trek Watercolor Workshop, Univ Calif, 89 & 92. *Mem:* Am Fedn Arts. *Dealer:* Ruth Braunstein Gallery 254 Sutter St San Francisco CA 94108. *Mailing Add:* 210 Kale St Bolinas CA 94924

O'KEEFE, MICHAEL
ADMINISTRATOR
b Mc Cloud, Minn. *Study:* Marquette Univ, BS in Physics, Mathematics & Philos; Univ Pittsburgh, MS in Nuclear Physics & Mathematics; Hamline Univ, LittD (hon). *Pos:* Pres, Consortium for Advan of Pvt Higher Educ, Wash, 83-89; exec vpres & Chief Exec Officer, McKnight Found, Minneapolis; asst secy, Fed Dept Health, Educ & Welfare; pres, Minneapolis Col Art & Design, 2002-; human serv comnr State of Minn, 99-2002. *Mailing Add:* Minneapolis Col Art & Design Off of Pres 2501 Stevens Ave S Minneapolis MN 55404

OKOSHI, E SUMIYE
PAINTER, COLLAGE ARTIST
b Seattle, Wash. *Study:* St Margaret & Futaba Coll, Tokyo; Seattle Univ, with Fay Chang & Nicholas Damascus; Henry Frye Mus Sch & New Sch Workshop, with Jacob Laurence. *Work:* Zimmerli Art Mus, Rutgers Univ, NJ; Hammond Mus, North Salem, NY; Palace Hotel, Guam Island; Ikue Gakuen, Japanese Children Sch, NJ; Nagoya Bank New York; plus many others. *Exhib:* Metrop Mus Art, New York, 77; Newark Mus, NJ, 83; Bergen Mus Art & Sci, NJ, 83; Nat Acad Sci, Washington, DC; Port Washington Pub Libr; Viridian Gallery, New York; Hammond Mus, New York; and others. *Awards:* Belle Cramer Mem Award; Ziuta & Akston Found Award; Bertha P Greenblatt Mem Award for abstract painting, 2000. *Bibliog:* Articles in Wash Post, NY Times & OCS News, NY; Gerald Brommer (auth), Collage Techniques. *Mem:* Nat Asn Women Artists. *Media:* Acrylic; Etching. *Publ:* Contribr, Int Economy Mag, Yomiuri News, Manhattan Art & NY Times

OKUHARA, TETSU
PHOTOGRAPHER, CONCEPTUAL ARTIST
b Los Angeles, Calif, 1940. *Study:* Univ Chicago, 58-61; Cooper Union, New York, 70. *Work:* Los Angeles Co Mus of Art; Hasselblad Collection, Sweden; Mus Mod Art, NY; Tokyo Metrop Mus Photog, Japan; Metro Mus Art, New York; Art Inst Chgo; San Francisco Mus Modern Art; Minn Inst Art. *Comn:* B&W photo Tryptch, Greater Hartford Comm Coll, Conn, 82; Photographic mural, Automated Data Processing, Chicago, 88. *Exhib:* Mirrors & Windows, Mus Mod Art, NY, 78; Big Pictures, Mus Mod Art, NY, 84; Chicago Art Inst Ill, 91-92; Los Angeles Co Mus, 2002; San Francisco Mus Art, 2003; Tokyo Metro Mus Photography, 2005. *Awards:* Guggenheim Found, 75; NY Found for Arts, NY State, 1988, 2000; Nat Endowment Arts, 88-89; James D Phelan Award, Nat Endowment Arts, 94. *Bibliog:* Marjorie Bevlin (auth), Design Through Discovery, HR&W, 77; Ralph Gibson (auth), Contact: Theory, Lustrum Press, 80; Article in Contact Sheet, 90, Light Work, 97, Christies Mag, 99. *Publ:* New York Mag, 88; 100 Nudes, Sun Mag, Tokyo, Japan, 91; Intuitive Eye, Chicago Art Inst, 92; Artist Space, New York, 99; History of Phtographics, Tokyo Met, 2005. *Dealer:* Steven Kasher Gallery New York NY. *Mailing Add:* 202 E 42nd St New York NY 10017

OKUMURA, LYDIA
PAINTER, SCULPTOR
b Sao Paulo, Brazil. *Study:* Fac Plastic Arts, Armando Alvares Penteado Found, Sao Paulo, Brazil, BFA, 73; Pratt Graphics Ctr, New York, 74-77. *Work:* Hara Mus Contemp Art, Tokyo; Pinacotheca of State & Mus Contemp Art, Sao Paulo, Brazil; Mus Mod Art, Bogota, Colombia; Mus Belas Artes, Caracas, Venezuela; Mus Modern Art, Sao Paulo, Brazil; Itamaraty Palace, Ministry of For Affairs, Brazil; Mario de Andrade Pub Libr, Sao Paulo; Metrop Mus Art, New York; Museu de Arte do Parlamento de Sao Paulo; Mus Solidariedad, Chile; Akron Mus Art, Ohio; Hyogo Prefectural Mus Art, Kobe, Japan; Ctr Cultr, Sao Paolo, Brazil; Mus Brazilian Art, Sao Paolo. *Comn:* Painting, IBM, Atlanta, 81; Atlantic Capital Corp, NY, 81. *Exhib:* Solo exhibs in Sao Paulo, Tokyo, Osaka, NY & Ottawa, 68-2004, Int Biennial 77, 79, 83; Metrop Mus Mod Art, New York, 78; Biennial Art, Medellin, Colombia, 81; Nat Mus Osaka, Japan, 81; Hara Mus Contemp Art, Tokyo, 85; Mus Mod Art, Sao Paulo, 84; Hyogo Prefecture Mus Art, Kobe, Japan; Coleçã de Arte da Cidade de São Paulo/Centro Cultural São Paulo; Akrom Mus Art, Ohio. *Awards:* Int Biennial Sao Paulo Prize, 73, 77; Creative Artists Pub Serv Prog Graphic Grant, 78; Japan Found Fel, 79; Norway Graphic Biennial, 80. *Bibliog:* Ellen Schwartz (auth) Nobe Gallery (catalog), NY, 78; Isla Leal Ferreira (auth), Mus Modern Art (catalog), Sao Paolo, 4/84; I L Brandao (catalog), Galeria Sao Paulo, Brazil, 4/84; A Amaral (auth), Today's Art of Brazil (catalog), Hara Mus Contemp Art, Tokyo, Japan, 11/85; William Zimmer (auth), NY Times, 90; Joao Spinelli (exhib catalog), Galeria Deco, Sao Paulo, 2004; Paolo Herkenhoff (auth) Lacos do Olhar Roteiros entre o Brasile o Japao, Instituto Temie Ohtake, 2009; Isobel Whitelegg (auth), The Forgotten History of the Bienal de Sao Paolo during the 70s, Afterall, pp 107-111, 2009; Hans Ulrich Obrist (auth), Uma Breve Historia da Curadoria, pp 194, BEI, Sao Paolo, 7/2010; Maria Pontes (auth) Adelaide do Nascimento, Documentation in the Artistic Practices of the Sao Paulo based Groups Arte/Acao and 3NO53, Extra Disciplinary Spaces and De-Disciplinizing Moments (In and Out of the 30th Bienal de Sao Paolo), pp 471-488, OEI #60-61, Sweden, 2013. *Media:* Acrylic, Oil, Installations, Mixed Techniques. *Publ:* Coauth, Fujieda, Akio Dialogue with the contemporary, Mizue Mag, No 904, Tokyo, 80; Ignacio de Loyola Brandao (catalog), Galeria Sao Paolo, 84; Aracy Amaral, Today's Art of Brazil (catalog), The Hara Mus, Tokyo, 95; John Mendelson (exhib catalog), Pinacoteca, Sao Paulo, Brazil, 9/95; Hariu Ichiro, Kanazawa Takeshi (catalog), Kate Art Gallery, Sao Paulo, 91. *Dealer:* Broadway 1602 Gallery NY; Jaqueline Martins Gallery Sao Paolo Brazil. *Mailing Add:* 32 Union Square E 513 New York NY 10003

OKUN, JENNY
PHOTOGRAPHER
b NJ, Oct 3, 1953. *Study:* Wimbledon Sch Art, London, found degree, 71; Chelsea Sch Art, London, BA & MA, 75; Slade Sch Art, London, postgrad degree, 77. *Work:* Victoria & Albert Mus, London; Brooklyn Mus; Herbert F Johnson Mus, Cornell, NY; Morgan Stanley; Hewlett Packard. *Comn:* 18 60″ photographs, Baker & Daniels, Indianapolis, 89; 6 x 120″ photographs, Bournemouth, Gen Hosp, England, 89; 8 x 80″ photographs, JP Morgan, London, 91; 78 CD covers, Decca Records/London Records, 93. *Exhib:* Solo exhibs: Craig Krull Gallery, Santa Monica, Numark Gallery, Washington, Claudia Carr Gallery, NYC, Il Millione, Milan, Rhonda Hoffman Gallery, Chicago, Bertha Urdang Gallery, NYC, RIBA Gallery, London, Kashya Hildebrand, NYC, Geneva, Zabriskie Gallerie, Paris, Institute of Contemporary Arts, London; Film/London, Nat Film Theatre, London, 84; Dining Room, Albright Knox Mus, 89; 25 Yrs of British Avant Garde Film, Tate Gallery, London, 91; LA Current: UCLA Armand Hammer, 96. *Teaching:* Teacher found art/painting, Cent Sch Art, London, 77-80, Chelsea Sch Art, London, 80-84. *Bibliog:* Max Wykes-Joyce (auth), Jenny Okun Galerie Zabriskie, Herald Tribune, 3/80, Arts/Leisure, 3/85; Charles Knevitt (auth) Building Images on Negatives, London Times, 2/85; Summer 1992 reviews, Art News, 92; William Packer (auth), The art of wrapping up, Financial Times, London, 3/95; Vikki Goldberg (coauth) & Robert Silberman (coauth), American Photography: A Century of Images; Henry T. Hopkins (coauth) & Michael Webb (coauth), Variations: The Architecture Photographs of Jenny Okun; Garrett White (auth) Nash Editions: Photography and the Art of Digital Printing. *Publ:* contribr, The Full Body Project: Photographs by Leonard Nimoy; auth, The Blackburn House, Hampstead, BBC2, 10/89. *Dealer:* Craig Krull Gallery Bergamont Sta 2525 Michigan Ave Bldg B Santa Monica CA 90404

OLBRICHT, THOMAS
COLLECTOR
Pos: Doctor and chemist. *Awards:* Named one of Top 200 Collectors, ARTnews mag, 2009-12. *Collection:* Modern and contemporary art

OLDENBURG, CLAES THURE
SCULPTOR
b Stockholm, Sweden, Jan 28, 1929. *Study:* Yale Univ, BA, 51; Art Inst Chicago, 52-54; studied Oberlin Coll, 70, Art Inst Chicago, 79, Bard Coll, 95, Royal Coll Art, London, 96, with Coosje van Bruggen, Nova Scotia Coll Art and Design, 2005. *Work:* Albright-Knox Art Gallery, Buffalo; Mus Mod Art, Whitney Mus Am Art, Guggenheim Mus, NY; Art Gallery Ont, Toronto; Art Inst Chicago; Walker Art Ctr; Centre Georges Pompidou, Paris; Hirshhorn Gallery & Sculpture Garden, Washington, DC; Mus Contemp Art, Los Angeles; Nelson-Atkins Mus Art, Kansas City, Mo; Tate Gallery, London; plus many others. *Comn:* Clothespin, Center Sq, Philadelphia; column, HW Social Security Ctr, Chicago; stake, Dallas Mus Art; sculptor, Parc de la Villette, Paris; Piazzale Cadorna, Milan; and others. *Exhib:* Solo exhibs, Reuben Gallery, NY, 60, Green Gallery, NY, 62, Sidney Janis Gallery, NY, 64-70, Galerie Ileana Sonnabend, Paris, 64, Robert Fraser Gallery, London, 66, Moderna Mus, Stockholm, 66, 77, Mus Contemp Art, Chicago, 66, 77, Irving Blum Gallery, Los Angeles, 68, Mus Modern Art, NY, 69, Stedelijk Mus, Amsterdam, 70, 77, Tate Gallery, London, 70, Pasadena Art Mus, 71, Nelson-Atkins Mus, Kansas City, 72, Art Inst Chicago, 73, Leo Castelli Gallery, NY, 74, 76, 80, 90, Margo Leavin Gallery, Los Angeles, 75, 76, 78, 88, 89, Centre Georges Pompidou, Paris, 77, Rijksmus Kroller-Muller, Ontario, 79, Mus Ludwig, Cologne, 79, Wave Hill, Bronx, NY, 84,

Guggenheim Mus, New York, 86 & 95, Mus Haus Esters Krefeld, Ger, 87, Kunstmus Basel, 92, Kunst-und Ausstellungshalle der Ger, Bonn, 96; group exhibs include Metrop Mus Art, NY, 69; retrospective, Mus Mod Art, NY, 69, Pasadena Art Mus, Calif, 71, Walker Art Ctr, 75 & Kunsthalle, Tubingen, WGer, 75; Los Angeles Co Mus Art, 71; Seattle Art Mus, Wash, 73; Am Pop Art, Whitney Mus Am Art, 74; Mus Mod Art, NY, 87, 88, 90, 91; Whitney Mus Am Art, 88; The Art of Assemblage, Locks Gallery, Philadelphia, 94; Aldrich Mus Contemp Art, 94; Marian Goodman Gallery, NY, 94; Drawing on Sculpture, Cohen Gallery, NY, 94; White Works, Pace Wildenstein, NY, 94; Worlds in a Box (traveling), City Art Centre, Edinburgh, 94-95; Museo Correr, Venice, 99; Museu Serralves, Porto, Portugal, 2001; Wexner Ctr for Arts, Columbus, Ohio, 2002; Paula Cooper Gallery, NY City, 2002; Gerhard Wurzer Gallery, Houston, 2002; Int Sculpture Ctr, 2002; Dunn and Brown Contemp, Dallas, 2004; Craig F Starr Assocs, NY, 2006; Castello di Rivoli Mus Contemp Art, Rivoli-Turin, 2007. *Awards:* Sculpture award, Art Inst Chicago, 76; Wilhelm-Lehmbruck Prize for Sculpture, Duisburg, Ger, 81; Creative Arts Award for Lifetime Artistic Achievement, Brandeis Univ, 93; Lifetime Achievement Award in Contemp Sculpture, Int Sculpture Ctr, Washington, 94; Rolf Shock Prize, Stockholm, Sweden, 95. *Mem:* Am Acad Inst Arts & Lett; Am Acad Arts & Sci; Nat Acad. *Publ:* Auth, Notes in Hand, Dutton & Petersburg, 1971; Object into monument, Pasadena Art Mus, 1971; Raw Notes, Nova Scotia Coll Art & Design Press, 1973; coauth (with Coosje van Bruggen), Sketches and Blottings Toward the European Desk Top, Milan and Turin: Galleria Christian Stein; and Florence: Hopeful Monster, 1990; Multiples in Retrospect, Pizzoli Int, 1990; and others. *Dealer:* PaceWildenstein 32 E 57th St New York NY 10022; Paula Cooper Gallery 534 W 21st St NY City NY 10011. *Mailing Add:* Pace Wildenstein Gallery 32 E 57th St New York NY 10022

OLDENBURG, RICHARD ERIK
MUSEUM DIRECTOR
b Stockholm, Sweden, Sept 21, 1933; US citizen. *Study:* Harvard Col, AB, 54. *Pos:* Dir publ, Mus Mod Art, New York, 69-72, dir mus, 72-94, dir emer, 95-; chmn, Int Comt Mus Collections Mod Art, Int Coun Mus, 83-86, exec bd; chmn, Sotheby's North & South Am, 95-. *Awards:* Order of North Star, Sweden; Order of Isabel la Catolica, Spain; Order of Arts & Lett & Chevalier of Legion d'honneur, France. *Mem:* Asn Art Mus Dirs (1st vpres, 86-87, pres, 87-88). *Mailing Add:* 11 W 53rd St New York NY 10019

OLDMAN, TERRY L
MUSEUM DIRECTOR
Study: Univ Kans, BS; Univ Kans, MA (art mus educ); Univ Hawaii, MS (bus admin). *Pos:* Interim assist dir, Spencer Mus, Lawrence, Kans; dir/cur educ Mus Art, Tallahassee; dir Albrecht-Kemper Mus Art, St Joseph, Mo, 99-. *Awards:* Decorated Distinguished Flying Cross, Bronze Star, Aerial Achievement Medal. *Mailing Add:* Albrecht-Kemper Mus Art 2818 Frederick Ave Saint Joseph MO 64506

OLEA, HECTOR
CURATOR
b Mexico City, 1945. *Study:* Univ Texas, Austin, PhD (comparative lit), 92; ENA/UNAM (archit), Mex 69; FAU/USP, MA (archit), Brazil, 77. *Exhib:* with Dorothea Strauss, Dimensionen, Konstructiver Kunst, in Brasilien: Die Sammlung, Adolpho Leirner, Haus Konstruktiv, Zurich, Switzerland, 2009. *Collection Arranged:* The Adolpho Leirner Collection of Brazilian Constructive Art, MFAH, 2007. *Pos:* Independent cur, writer, translator; co-cur (with Mari Carmen Ramirez), Inverted Utopias: Avant-Garde Arts in Latin America, 2004. *Awards:* Award for Best Thematic Mus Show Nationally, Int Asn Art Critics/USA, 2005; First Prize, Scholarly Journals, Am Asn Mus, 2007; 50 Best Designed Books, Am Inst Graphic Arts, 2000. *Res:* editor of the Int Ctr Arts of the Am/ Documents of the 20th century Latin Am & Latino Art, A digital archive & Publ Proj at the MFAH. *Publ:* Coauth (with Mari Carmen Ramirez), Inverted Utopias: Avant-Garde Arts in Latin America, 2004; co-ed (with Mari Carmen Ramirez), Versions and Inversions: ICAA #3, Houston/London, MFAH/YUP, 2006; auth & co-designer (with Henk Van Assen), Tenoche Me Ronda, Austin, Whichever Press, 99; ed, Poly/Graphic San Juan Triennial: Latin America & the Caribbean & Harbingers of Expansion in Latin American Printing, Santiago, Chile, Ocholibros, Bilingual eds by ICP, 2004; ed (with Mari Carmen Ramirez), Building on a Construct: The Adolpho Leirner Collection, Mus Fine Arts, Houston, Yale Univ Press, London, 2009; ed (with Mari Carmen Ramirez), Cruz-Diez: Color in Space & Time, Yale Univ Press, London, Mus Fine Arts, Houston, 2011

O'LEARY, DANIEL
ADMINISTRATOR
Study: Princeton Univ, PhD (art hist); Univ Mich, MBA (mktg & mgt). *Pos:* Exec dir, Artrain, Ann Arbor, Mich, formerly; asst dir, Minn Inst Arts, 1988-93; dir, Portland Mus Art, Maine, 1993-2008, dir Winslow Homer Studio proj, 2008-. *Mailing Add:* Portland Mus Art 7 Congress Square Portland ME 04101

O'LEARY, HELEN
PAINTER, EDUCATOR
b County Wexford, Ireland, 1961. *Study:* Sch Art Inst Chicago, BFA, 1987, MFA, 1989. *Exhib:* Randolph St Gallery, Chicago, 1989; solo exhibs, Zolla/Lieberman Gallery, Chicago, 1990-91 & 93, Kerlin Gallery, Dublin, Ireland, 1995, Michael Gold Gallery, New York, 1997-98 & 2000, Limberick City Gallery, Ireland, 2000; Rezac Gallery, Chicago, 1991; Saint Xavier Coll, Chicago, 1992; Rockford Mus Art, Ill, 1993; Zollar Gallery, Univ Park, Pa, 1995; Kerlin Gallery, Dublin, Ireland, 1996; Michael Gold Gallery, New Yrok, 1997; Nat Inst Art, Manchester, NH, 1999; Ostende Munic Mus, Belgium, 2000; Island Arts Centre, Lisburn, UK, 2001; Mus Contemp Art, Denver, 2002; Abnext, Southbend Regional Mus Art, Ind, 2003. *Teaching:* prof, Pa State Univ, 1991, 1993-2000, assoc prof, 2002-. *Awards:* Pollock-Krasner Award, 1989 & 1996; Joan Mitchell Found Award, 1999; Guggenheim Found Fel, 2010. *Bibliog:* Alan Artner (auth), Sensitive Debut, Chicago Tribune, 8/23/1990; Brian Fallon (auth), An Abstract Expressionist, Irish Times, 12/21/1995; Regina Hackett (auth), Panning for Art Gold Yields Nuggets at Fair, Seattle Post-Intelligencer, 2/21/1997. *Mailing Add:* Penn State Univ School Visual Arts 109 Arts Cottage State College PA 16802

OLENICK, DAVID CHARLES
ADMINISTRATOR, DEALER
b Rockville Centre, NY, Apr 21, 1947. *Study:* NY Univ; Hofstra Univ; New Sch Social Res; State Univ NY. *Pos:* Co-dir, Mansight Educ, Full Circle Assocs, 68-69; owner & dir, Park Gallery, Brooklyn, 69-71; ed consult & field prog coordr, Proj Am Develop, US AID State Dept, 69-70; asst dir, Brooklyn Mus Art Sch, 74-77, admin head, 77-81, adminr educ & prog develop, 78-81; gallery dir, Adam L Gimbel Gallery, New York, 81-83; cur contemp art, Saks Fifth Ave, New York, 81-83; owner & dir, David Olenick Fine Art, New York, 85-. *Specialty:* Contemporary paintings and sculpture; tribal art; Asian art. *Mailing Add:* 120 Park Pl Brooklyn NY 11217

OLIN, FERRIS
HISTORIAN, CURATOR
b 1948. *Study:* Douglass Col, BA, 1970; Rutgers Univ, MLS, 1972, MA, 1975, PhD, 1998. *Work:* Hopewell Mus, NJ. *Collection Arranged:* Architecture of New Brunswick and its Environs, 1979; Women in the Community, series exhibs, 1982; Artists Books: From the Traditional to the Avant-Garde, 1982; Women's Spheres (co-ed, catalog), 1983; Baroness Hyde de Neuville, Sketches of Am, 1807-22, 1983; Representative Works and Focused Fragments, 1984; Past and Promise: Lives of New Jersey Women, 1990; Mary H Dana Women Artists Series, 1994-; 25 Years of Feminism, 25 Years of Women's Art, 1996; How Am Women Invented Postmodernism, 1970-75, 2005-07; Eccentric Bodies, 2007; Passage to New Jersey: Women Artists of the South Asian Diaspora in Our Midst, 2008; Declaration of Independence: 50 Yeas of Art by Faith Ringgold, 2009; The Last Frontier: Contemporary African Artists Use their Artistic Voices to Mobilize their Communications, 2010; Feminist Masked Avengers: Guerilla Girls, 2010; Recent Pages from an Ancient Past: Audrey Flack, 2012; Fertile Crescent: Gender, Art, and Society, 2012. *Pos:* Dir, Rutgers Art Libr, 1976-85; res-consult, New York Feminist Art Inst, 1977-78; bk reviewer, Leonardo, 1977-82; ed prof lit column, Art Libr Soc NAm Newslett, 1980-84; exec officer, Inst Res on Women, Rutgers & Laurie NJ Chair in Women's Studies, 1985-94; Librn, Douglass Col Libr, 1994-; cur, Mary H Dana Women Artists Series, 1994- & Women's Arch, 1994; founding head, Margery Somers Foster Ctr, 2000-2008; founding dir, Inst Women & Art, Rutgers University, 2005-2012; ed bd, Visual Rescources, 2007-; Bd, Jersey City Mus, 2009-11, Neighborhood Narratives Proj, 2008-, Feminist Therorists Proj, 2008-, Coll Art Asn, 2004-2007. *Teaching:* Dir & art librn, Rutgers Univ, New Brunswick, 1976-85, dir, Inst for Women and Art, full prof, 2005-2012. *Awards:* Art to Life Award, 2008; Alice Paul Equity Award, 2008; Coll Art Assoc Comitee on Women & Art Ann Recognition Award, 2007; Lifetime Achievement Award, Women's Caucus for Art, 2012. *Mem:* Womens Caucus for Art; Coll Art Asn; Art Table. *Res:* Contributions of women artists to art history; regional history and material culture; 20th century American woman art collectors. *Specialty:* Emerging & established contemp women artists, worldwide. *Interests:* 19th, 20th, 21st Century Europ & Am art & archit; women's art history; Cult Hist. *Publ:* Contrib, Dictionary of Women Artists Born Before 1900, GK Hall, 1985; coauth, Making Their Mark: Women Artists, 1970-85, 1989; auth & co-ed, The New Jersey Project: Integrating the New Scholarship on Gender, 1986-90, 1990; Past and Promise: Lives of New Jersey Women, 1989 & 1996; 25 Years of Feminism, 25 Years of Women's Art, 1996; Dana Women's Art Series Catalogs, 1994-; Eccentric Bodies, 2007; Feminist Masked Avengers: Guerilla Girls, 2011; Recent Pages from an Ancient Past: Audrey Flack, 2012; Fertile Cresent: Gender, Art, and Society, 2012; coauth, Holly Trostle Brigham:Dis/Guise, NJ Inst Women and Art, New Brunswick, NJ, 2013. *Mailing Add:* 59 Governors Lane Princeton NJ 08540

OLIN, LAURIE DEWAR
ARCHITECT, EDUCATOR
Study: Univ Washington, Seattle, BArch, 1961. *Work:* Los Angeles Co Mus Art, 1987, Toledo Mus Art, 1995. *Comn:* Prin works incl ARCO Hdqs, Newtown Sq, Pa, 1976, Johnson & Johnson Hdqs, Denver, 1977, Canary Wharf, London, 1985, Vila Olimpica, Barcelona, Spain, 1991, Independence Nat Historic Park, Philadelphia, 1997, Beringer Vineyard and Chateau St Jean Winery, Calif, 1998, site design, Washington Monument, 2002. *Exhib:* Nat Gallery Sculpture Garden, Washington, DC, 1993. *Pos:* chr, landscape archit dept, grad sch design Harvard Univ, 82-86; prin, Hanna/Olin Ltd landscape archits, Philadelphia, 76-96; founding partner, principal, Olin Partnership, Philadelphia, 96-. *Teaching:* Lectr, to practice prof landscape archit, regional planning Univ Pa, 76-. *Awards:* Recipient Rome Prize in Landscape Architecture, 72, Bradford Williams medal for writing on landscape archit, 91, National Medal of Arts National Endowment for the Arts, 2012, Thomas Jefferson medal in Architecture, 2013. *Mem:* Fel, Am Acad Arts & Letters (award, 98), Am Acad Arts & Sciences, Am Soc Landscape Archits (medal, 2011); Am Inst Archits (hon) (Design medal, 2005); Nat Acad. *Mailing Add:* Olin Partnership Public Ledger Bldg 150 S Independence Mall W Ste 1123 Philadelphia PA 19106

OLITSKI, EVE
PAINTER
Exhib: Solo exhibs include Greater Hartford Welcome Ctr, Hartford, Conn, 2007; group exhibs include 18th Ann Open Studio Weekend, Gallery 11 Whitney, Hartford, Conn, 2008; Espressivo Art Exhib, West Hartford, Conn, 2008; 183rd Ann: Invitational Exhib Contemp Am Art, Nat Acad Mus, New York, 2008. *Mailing Add:* PO Box 440 Marlboro VT 05344

OLIVER, BOBBIE
PAINTER
b Canada, June 17, 1949. *Study:* Ctr Creative Studies, Detroit, 66-68; St Albans Sch Art, Eng, 68. *Work:* Robert McLaughlin Gallery, Oshawa, Can; Nuffield Found, Eng; Can Coun Art Bank, Can; Glenbow Mus, Alta, Can; pvt collections. *Exhib:* Solo Exhibs: Wolfe Gallery, 85; Olga Korper Gallery, Toronto, 86-88, 88, 91, 94, 96, 99, 2003, 2006, 2010, 2013; Lenore Gray Gallery, Providence, RI, 95 & 98; Univ Waterloo, Can, 99; Thompson Gallery, Owen Sound, Can, 99; Nature Morte Gallery, India, 99; West Space, NY, 2002; Olga Korper, 2003 & 2006; Jancar Gallery, LA, 2007; Art Gallery Ont, Toronto, 78. *Teaching:* Prof, RI Sch Design, Princeton Univ, Sch Visual Arts, New York & Banff Sch Fine Arts, Can; chair, painting dept, RI Sch Design, 2006, 2007. *Awards:* Ont Arts Coun Grant, 80; Pollock-Krasner Grant, 86; Can Coun Arts Grants, 80, 83, 85 & 96; and others. *Bibliog:* J Zinsser (auth), Bobbie Oliver at Wolff, East Village Eye, 5/85; John Bentley Mays (auth), Invoking a sense of place, Globe & Mail, 3/89; John Kissick (auth), A tale of two painters, Can Art; James Campbell (auth), Nameless Waters, 99; Ken Johnson (auth), NY Times, 99. *Media:* Acrylic. *Dealer:* Olga Korper Gallery Toronto Canada. *Mailing Add:* 140 W Broadway New York NY 10013

OLIVER, JULIE FORD
PAINTER, INSTRUCTOR
b Manchester, Eng, Nov 23, 1942; US citizen. *Study:* Manchester Sch Art, Eng, 57-60; Art Students League, Denver, Colo, 85-89. *Work:* Pronof Mus Art, Juarez, Mex; Int Mus Art, El Paso, Tex; Americana Mus, El Paso, Tex; Federal Courthouse, Las Cruces, NMex. *Comn:* Children's Ward, Thomason Hosp, El Paso, Tex, 98; 4 oil paintings, Univ Medical, El Paso, Tex, 2011. *Exhib:* solo exhib, Americana Mus, El Paso, Tex, 97, Charmizal Nat Mem, El Paso, Tex, 2003; Exchange, Pronof Mus Cuidad Juarez, Chihuahua Mex, 98; Divas, Charmizal Nat Mem, El Paso, Tex, 2000; Desert Echo, Women's Mus Dallas, Tex, 2001; Border Artists, Mus Fine Art & Cult, Las Cruces, NMex, 2002; Curators Invitational, Int Mus Art, El Paso, Tex, 2004; Along the Rio Grande, Mus Dept Interior, Washington DC, 2005; The Cycle of Life, Brannigan Cult Ctr, Las Cruces, NMex, 2009. *Pos:* illusr & graphic design, Banker & Bris Bois, Grand Rapids, Mich, 85-90; illusr, E & J Distributing, Las Cruces, NMex, 90-97. *Teaching:* teacher, painting, Monday Studio, Las Cruces, NMex, 2004-06; Artist's Guild Southern, NMex, 2006-2011. *Bibliog:* Jaquelyn Stroud Sniper (auth), Desert Echo, Women's Mus: An Inst for the Future in Association with the Smithsonian Institution, 2001; Nita Leland (auth), New Creative Artist, North Light, 2006; Nita Leland (auth), Confident Color, North Light, 2008. *Mem:* Art Asn Las Cruces; Artist Guild Southern NMex; Art Studio Las Cruces. *Media:* Oil, Egg Tempera. *Publ:* contribr, Desert Echo, Woman's Mus, Dallas, 2000; contribr, The New Creative Artist, N Light, 2006; Artist Mag, 2008; Confident Color, N Light, 2008. *Dealer:* Joseph Bender Art & Antiques 100 Executive Center Blvd El Paso TX 79902; M Phillips Fine Art Gallery 221 N Main St Las Cruces NMex 88001. *Mailing Add:* 1590 Imperial Ridge Las Cruces NM 88011

OLIVER, MARVIN E
CRAFTSMAN
b Seattle, Wash, 1956. *Study:* San Francisco State Univ, BA, 70; Univ Wash, MFA, 73. *Comn:* Bronze, glass & concrete sculpture, Spirit of Washington, 92; 40 ft bronze sculpture, Spirit of Our Youth, 92-93; River of Life, South Puget Sound Col, Olympia, Wash, 93; Red Wolf, Cedarcrest High Sch, Duvall/Carnation, 94; Arctic Lights (steel & glass sculpture), Arctic Light Elem Sch, Fairbanks, Alaska, 94. *Exhib:* Salmon: Ritual & Resource, Stonington Gallery, Seattle, 92; From the Woods, Bellevue Art Mus, Wash, 92; Unending Journey: A Selection of Contemp Native Am Crafts, Sch Visual Arts Mus, NY, 92; Traditional & Contemp Trends in Native Arts, Western Gallery, Western Wash Univ, Bellingham, 93; Signals in Sculpture, Inst Am Indian Arts Mus, Santa Fe, NMex, 93; and many others. *Pos:* Bd pres, Inst Am Indian Arts, 83-87; artists, Elders Forum, 86; comt mem, Wash State Centennial, 89; instr, Pratt Fine Arts Ctr, 91; lectr, Seattle Art Mus, 92. *Teaching:* Assoc prof, Univ Wash. *Awards:* Nat Endowment Arts, 88; Fel Glass Casting, Pratt Fine Arts Ctr, 90; Artists Guest Hosts' Honor, Northwest Visionaries, Seattle Art Mus, 94. *Bibliog:* Ten Artists From Washington State (film), Tacoma Art Mus, Wash, 90; Mayumi Nakazawa (auth), Native American arts, Elle Deco, Japan Mag, No 3, winter 91; Robin K Wright (auth), A Time of Gathering: Native Heritage in Washington State, Burke Mus, Univ Wash Press, Seattle, 91. *Mem:* Asn Nat Humanities Fac, 78-88; pres, Inst Am Indian Arts, 84-86. *Publ:* Illusr, cover & book, Shamans & Kushtakas, Mary Beck, 91; Potlatch, Mary Beck, 93; front cover, Wash State Treasurer's Report, 94; Reaching Home, Fobes, Jay & Matsen. *Mailing Add:* Univ Wash Am Indian Studies Ctr Box 354305 Seattle WA 98195

OLIVER, SANDRA (SANDI)
ART DEALER, PAINTER
b Bronxville, NY, Apr 2, 1941. *Study:* Marymount Coll, Tarrytown, BA, BFA, 63. *Hon Degrees:* New England Fine Arts. *Work:* Hammer Mus Gallery, Conn; Lilco Gallery, Long Island; McKlean-Grove Mus, Greenwich. *Comn:* Productions & prom, ABC & NBC TV, 80; USA space production, United Tech-Norden, 80; St Mary's, 98. *Exhib:* Westport Merchants Show, Conn, 78, 86, 87 & 92-2001; Waveny Barn Mus, New Canaan, 85, 86 & 87; Westport Art Ctr Mus, 86 & 87; Wilton Historical, Soc Am Craftsmanship Show, Conn, 91 & 92; Westport Art Ctr, 2007-2008. *Collection Arranged:* Paul A Williams, Am Impressions, Greenwich, Conn, 97 & Georgetown, Conn, 2007. *Pos:* Commercial artist rep, Sandi Oliver Inc, Weston, 79-84; pres, Sandi Oliver Fine Art Inc, 82-; dir, Sandi Oliver, 91-. *Teaching:* Art & art hist teacher, New York City Sch System, 63-65 & Westchester Diocese Cath Sch, 64-67. *Awards:* First Prize, Christmas Show, Pelham Chamber of Com, 60; Revlon Bravo Award, Revlon Corp, 80; First Prize, Casa D'Oliver Garden Show, Conn, 91. *Bibliog:* Contribr, Vision of flowers (article), Your Family, 3/90. *Mem:* NEAA; AAA Inc; AFA. *Media:* Oil. *Specialty:* American impressionist painting & sculpture. *Interests:* Walking, raising dogs, collecting antiques. *Collection:* Antique Impressionist art, American & European, 20th century Impressionism. *Publ:* Auth, American Impressionist Paul Alan Williams His Garden & His Oil Paintings, 91, 92 & 93. *Mailing Add:* Sandi Oliver Fine Art PO Box 1203 Weston CT 06883-0203

OLIVERE, RAYMOND
PAINTER, ILLUSTRATOR
b Wilmington, Del. *Study:* Wilmington Acad Art, studied with NC Wyeth & Frank Schoonover; Art Student League NY, with Ivan Olinsky. *Work:* NY Co Lawyers Asn, New York; Lasell Coll, Newton Mass; Pernod Ricard Inc, Lewisburg, Ky. *Comn:* Illus, approx 250 book covers, Harlequin, Bantan, Dell, Jove, Ace & Signet, 79-94. *Exhib:* Nat Acad Ann, Nat Acad Art, New York, 73; Provincetown Art Asn Show, Provincetown Art Mus, Mass, 74; Allied Artist Ann, Nat Arts Club, New York, 2000-2003; 67th Midyear Exhib, Butler Mus Am Art, Butler Inst, Youngstown, Ohio, 2003; Audubon Artists Ann, Salmagundi Club, New York, 2004-2005. *Pos:* Portrait artist (professional, official & personal), illusr, ad agencies, New York; painter book covers, Harlequin, Bantom, Dell, Jove, Ace & Signet, 79-94. *Awards:* First Prize & Cover winner, North Light Mag, 2001; Finalist & Certificate of Merit winner, Am Soc Portrait Artists, 2002; Tara Fredix Artist Award, Audubon Artists Show, Tara Fredix Co, 2005. *Bibliog:* Libby Fellerhoff (auth), North Light Mag, Artists Mag, 2001-2003. *Mem:* Allied Artists Am; Audubon Artists (corresp secy, 2001-); Soc Illusrs; Portrait Soc Am. *Media:* Acrylic, Oil, Portrait. *Dealer:* Kathryn Wakefield 1435 Lexington Ave NY 10128. *Mailing Add:* 1530 Locust St Apt 13C Philadelphia PA 19102

OLIVIER, KARYN
SCULPTOR
b Port of Spain, Trinidad & Tobago. *Study:* Dartmouth Coll, BA, 1989; Univ Arts, Pa, Post-Baccalaureate Prog, 1999; Cranbrook Acad Art, Michigan, MFA, 2001. *Work:* Mus Fine Arts, Houston, Tex; Studio Mus Harlem, New York. *Exhib:* Solo exhibs include Proj Row Houses, Houston, 2002, 2004, Dunn & Brown Contemp, Dallas, 2005, Women & Their Work Gallery, Austin, 2005, Mattress Factory, Pittsburgh, 2006, Laumeier Sculpture Park, St Louis, 2007; Two-person exhibs include Cranbrook Art Mus, Mich, 2000, Nave Mus, Victoria, Tex, 2003; Group exhibs include Emerging Artists Fel Exhib, Socrates Sculpture Park, Long Island City, New York, 2004; Greater New York, PS 1 Contemp Art Ctr, Queens, New York, 2005; Double Consciousness: Black Conceptual Art since 1970, Contemp Arts Mus, Houston, 2005; Making Do, Yale Sch Art Gallery, Conn, 2006; Quid Pro Quo, Studio Mus Harlem, New York, 2006; Trace, Whitney Mus Am Art, New York, 2006; Inbound: Houseton, Tex; Learning by Doing, Mus Fine Arts, Houston, 2008; Gwangju Biennial, Gwangju, Korea, 2008; Colleted, The Studio Mus Harlem, New York, 2009; 30 Seconds off an Inch, Studio Mus Harlem, 2009; Rockstone & Bootheel: COntemp West Indian Art, Real Art Ways, Hartford, Conn, 2009. *Teaching:* Assis prof sculpture, Tyler Sch Art, Temple Univ, Pa. *Awards:* Camille Hanks Cosby Fel, Skowhegan Sch Painting & Sculpture, 2000; Richard & Jean Coyne Family Found Award, World Studio Found, 2000; Eliza Prize, Glassell Sch Art, Mus Fine Arts, Houston, 2002, 2003; Louis Comfort Tiffany Found Biennial Award, 2003; Emerging Artists Fel, Socrates Sculpture Park, Long Island City, New York, 2004; Creative Capital Found, 2005; Joan Mitchell Found Grant, 2007; John Simon Guggenheim Found Fel, 2007; Art Matters Grant, 2007. *Bibliog:* Claire Tancons (auth), Carnival & the Artistic Contract, nka Journ Contemp African Art, Winter, 2009; Nicholas Laughlin (auth), Hungry for Words, Caribbean Rev Books, 2010. *Mailing Add:* Dunn & Brown Contemporary 5020 Tracy St Dallas TX 75205

OLLMAN, ARTHUR L
PHOTOGRAPHER, MUSEUM DIRECTOR
b Milwaukee, Wis, Mar 6, 1947. *Study:* Univ Wis-Madison, BA, 69; Visual Studies Workshop, Rochester, 72; San Francisco Art Inst, 74; Lone Mountain Col, MFA, 77. *Work:* Mus Mod Art, NY; Bibliot Nat, Centre Georges Pompidou, Mus Nat d'Art, Paris, France; Mus Mod Art, San Francisco; Mus Fine Arts, Houston; Tokyo Inst Polytech. *Exhib:* Mirrors & Windows, Mus Mod Art, NY, 78; Grapestake Gallery, San Francisco, 79; Beyond Color, San Francisco Mus Mod Art, 80; Biennial, Whitney Mus, NY, 81; Solo exhibs, Contemp Art Ctr, New Orleans, 80, Photog Gallery, NY, 81; Centre Georges Pompidou, Mus Nat d'Art, Paris, France; Tower of David Mus, Jerusalem, 96. *Collection Arranged:* Oversaw Building of 9,000 item Collection, Mus photog Art, San Diego, CA. *Pos:* Dir, Mus Photog Arts, San Diego, 83-. *Awards:* Special Proj Award, Calif Arts Coun, 77; Nat Endowment Arts Fel, 79. *Bibliog:* Charles Whitin (auth), Arthur Ollman, Am Photog Image Nation, 11/78; Arnaud Claass (auth), Arthur Ollman, Zoom/Publicness, 6/79; Arthur Ollman, Time-Life Photog Yr, 79. *Mem:* Am Asn Mus; Oracle. *Media:* Photography; Writing. *Publ:* Other Images, Other Realities, Rice Univ Press, 89; Revelaciones, Art of Manuel Alvarez Bravo, Mus Photog Arts, 90; Persona, Mus Photog Arts, 92; Seduced By Life: The Art of Lou Stoumen, Mus Photog Arts, 93; Points of Entry: A Nation of Strangers, Mus Photog Arts, 95; The Model Wife: 1999, Bullfinch Press; First Photographs: The Art of Wm Henry Fox Talbot, 2004, Mus of Photog Arts. *Mailing Add:* 4310 Goldfinch St San Diego CA 92103

OLSEN, DIANE C
PAINTER, WRITER
b Muskegon, Mich, Dec 12, 1950. *Study:* Hope Coll, BA (summa cum laude), 91; Western Mich Univ, MA, 94. *Work:* Tulip Expression, Holland Community Hosp, Holland, Mich. *Comn:* Horse portraits, pvt collections. *Exhib:* Solo exhibs, A Variety of Work, Gallery Upstairs, Grand Haven, 95, Israel: Art of the Journey, 96; Trinity Presbyterian Church, Denton, Tex, 97; Children At Play, Moynihan Gallery, Holland, 97, Art of the Journey II, 97; Trunk Show, El Presidio Gallery, Tucson, 2003; Michigan Avenue Cafe, Holland, 2004; Group exhibs, Am Artists Professional League, NY, 2002; Annual Nat Exchange Oil Painters of Am, Taos, NMex, 2003; Annual Open Exhib, Allied Artists of Am, 2004; Six Person Show, El Presidio Gallery, Tucson, 2005, Miniatures in the Mountains, 2005, Christmas Show, 2005; Biennale Int Dell'Arte Contemp, Florence, Italy, 2005; Oil Changes, Gallery Uptown,

2005, From Ghost Ranch to Grand Haven, 2006; Faith, Artiques, 2006; Catherine Lorillard Wolfe, Nat Arts Club, NY, 2006; Small Works NA, Greenwhich Workshop Gallery, 2008; Am Women Artists, Scottdale, Ariz, 2008; Button Gallery, Douglas, Mich, 2008; Celebration of Fine Art, Scottsdale, Ariz, 2008, 2009, 2010; Nomadas Del Arte, Dallas, Tex, 2009; Gallery Uptown Anniv Show, 2013; Artwalk Grand Haven, 2013. *Pos:* life coach, artist, Am Asn Christian Counselors, 2010, Grand Haven Chamber of Commerce. *Teaching:* Plein Air Watercolor, Plein Air Oil, 2006-2009; Instr pvt lessons, Saugatuck Center for the Arts, Mich, 2008-2009; mountain Artists Asn, Yuma, Ariz, 2009; Mountain Artists Guild, 2011-2012; Color Your World, A Dream Shop for Creativity, Phoenix, Scottsdale, 2011-2012; Animal Portraits, 2011-2012; Painting Your Journey, 2013. *Awards:* Merchant's Award, Lakeland Painters Members Exhib, 96; Merit Award, Ariz Watercolor Asn Fall Membership Exhib, 97; Merchant's Award, Northern Ariz Watercolor Asn, 99 & Dianne Parssinen Memorial Award, 2001. *Bibliog:* The Best Kept Secret of Plein Air Painters, Int Artists Mag, April 2004; Contemp Art Still on the Easel, Am Art Collector Mag, April 2006. *Mem:* Oil Painters Am; Tucson Plein Air Painters Soc; Allied Artists Am; Am Women Artists. *Media:* Oil, Acrylic, Watercolor. *Interests:* Teaching horseback riding, swimming, walking, reading, life coaching. *Publ:* Contrib, The Best of Watercolor, Rockport Publ, 95; contrib, A Passion for Landscape, Artists Mag, May 2004; contrib, How Did You Paint That? 100 Ways to Paint the Landscape, Int Artist Mag, 2004; contrib, How Did You Paint That? 100 Ways to Paint Flowers and Gardens, Int Artist Mag, 2004; contrib, Am Art Collector Mag, Int Artist Mag, 2006; An Honorable Journey of Healing, 2012; An Honorable Journey of Healing, A Workbook for Women, 2012; A Daily Journey for Women of Honor, A Writing Journal, 2012. *Mailing Add:* 14799 Shadowood Ct #201 Grand Haven MI 49417

OLSEN, RUNE
SCULPTOR
b Stord, Norway. *Study:* Coventry Univ, UK, BA, 1996; Goldsmith Coll, London, MFA, 1999. *Exhib:* Solo exhibs, Bronx Mus Arts, New York, 2001, Islip Art Mus, 2002, Mus Sex, New York, 2008, Hanes Gallery, Wake Forest Univ, 2010; Homomuseum, Exit Art, New York, 2005; Archival to Contemporary: Six Decades of the Sculptors Guild, Hillwood Art Mus, New York, 2006; Keeping it Real, Western Mich Univ, 2007; The Exquisite Line, Sherman Gallery, Boston Univ, 2008; Back to the Drawing Board, Arin Contemp Art, Laguna Beach, 2009. *Teaching:* Mgr printmaking dept, Nat Coll Art & Design, Norway, 1996-98; instr, Cooper Union, New York, 2007-09, John Jay Coll Criminal Justice, New York, 2008. *Awards:* Creative Capital Grant, 2003; NJ State Coun Arts Fel, 2005; NY Found Arts Fel, 2009. *Bibliog:* Brandon Keim (auth), Animals Get Freaky at Museum of Sex, Wired, 7/24/2008; Francine Koslow Miller (auth), Revising Natural and Sculptural History, Sculpture Mag, 1/2009; Cate McQuaid (auth), Man vs Measures of Masculinity, The Boston Globe, 5/9/2010

OLSEN BERGMAN, CIEL (CHERYL) BOWERS
PAINTER, ENVIRONMENTAL ARTIST
b Berkeley, Calif, Sept 11, 1938. *Study:* San Francisco Art Inst, MFA (with honors); Univ Calif, Berkeley with Fred Martin, Bob Hudson, Peter Voulkos, Harold Paris & Peter Plagens. *Work:* New Port Harbor Art Mus; Arts Coun Gt Brit; Oakland Mus; San Francisco Mus Mod Art; Metrop Mus Art, NY. *Comn:* Painting Solar Screen, Gildea Ctr, 87; Paseo Nuevo (136 Ceramic Form), Gildea Ctr, 90. *Exhib:* Women From Permanent Collection, Univ Mus, Berkeley, 73; Biennial, Whitney Mus Am Art, NY, 75; San Francisco Mus Art, 75; 18 Bay Area Artists, Los Angeles Inst Contemp Art, 76; New Work, Oakland Mus, 76; Hamilton Gallery Contemp Art, NY, 79; Ruth Schaffner Gallery, Los Angeles, 79; Ian Birksted, London; Fresh Paint--15 Calif Artists (auth, catalog), San Francisco Mus Mod Art, 82; Revelations, The Transformative Impulse in Recent Art, Aspen Art Mus, (catalog), 89; Flora: Contemp Artists & The World Of Flowers, traveling exhib (catalog), 95; Ciel Bergman: Before New Mexico, After California, Richard L Nelson Gallery & Fine Arts Col, Univ Calif, Davis, 98; Antidote, Linda Durham Contemp Art, NMex, 2000; The Last Sunset of the 20th Century, RB Steveson Gallery, Calif, 2000; The Alchemy of Devotion, RB Steveson Gallery, San Diego, 2002. *Teaching:* Lectr painting, Calif State Univ, Hayward, 75; vis lectr painting, Univ Calif, Berkeley, 75-79; assoc prof painting & drawing, Univ Calif, Santa Barbara, 79, prof 80-94, emer prof, 94. *Awards:* Tamarind Lithographic Inst Fel, 72; SECA Award, Soc Creative Arts, San Francisco, 75; Louis Comfort Tiffany Award, 80. *Bibliog:* Sylvia Moore (auth), Yesterday & Tomorrow Calif Woman Artists; Dr Elinor Gaddon (auth), The Once & Future Goddess; Suzi Gablik (auth), The Reenchantment of Art, 91; Sandy Ballatore (auth), Ciel Bergman Reconnecting Art, Crosswinds, 9/93. *Mem:* Santa Barbara Contemp Art & Art Forum, New Mus, NY. *Media:* Oil, Watercolor Sculpture. *Dealer:* Laura Carpenter Fine Art 309 Read St Santa Fe NM 87501. *Mailing Add:* PO Box 95 Coyote NM 87012

OLSHAN, BERNARD
PAINTER, PRINTMAKER
b New York, NY, Jan 31, 1921. *Study:* Am Artists Sch, NY, 37-40; Ozenfant Sch Fine Arts, NY, 47; Acad de la Grande Chaumiere, Paris, 48-51. *Work:* Emily Lowe Mus, Coral Gables, Fla; New York City Community Coll & Health & Hosp Corp, NY; Nat Acad Design, NY; Emily Lowe Gallery, Coral Gables, Fla; Health & Hosp Corp NY. *Comn:* Mural, Theodore Roosevelt High Sch & WPA, NY, 39-40. *Exhib:* Camp Maxey Art Exhib, Dallas Mus Fine Arts, 43; Whitney Mus Am Art, NY, 48; Art USA, Madison Sq Garden, NY, 58; 144th Ann Exhib, Nat Acad Design, NY, 69; Hudson River Mus, NY, 71; Seven Bronx Artists, Herbert H Lehman Col, NY, 74; GCCA Mountain Top Gallery, Windham, Vt, 84; Bronx Mus Arts, 86; Lehman Coll Art Gallery, 86; Solo exhibs, Greenberg Pub Libr, NY, 96, Bronx Mus of the Arts, 91-92, Grace Gallery, NY, 89, others; Nardin Gallery, Somers, NY, 97; Beatrice Conde Gallery, NY, 2000. *Pos:* Chmn visual arts comt, Amalgamated Houses, NY, 80-; cultural arts dir, Mosholu Montefiore YM-YWHA, NY. *Teaching:* Instr, Crafts Students League, 53 & New York City Community Col, 65-69; teacher & dir, Cult Arts Dept, Mosholu-Montefiore Community Ctr, NY, 66-79; instr, Nat Acad Design Sch Fine Arts, 98. *Awards:* Inter-city Mural Award, Theodore Roosevelt High Sch & Works Progress Admin, 39-40; Emily Lowe Award 1st Prize, 2nd Ann, 50; Ralph Mayer Mem Award, 84, 87; Andrew Carnegie Award, Nat Acad Design, 99. *Bibliog:* Dr Lawrence J Hatterer (auth), The Artist in Society, Grove Press, New York, 65; Barry Schwartz (auth), The New Humanism in Time of Change, Prager Publ, 74; articles in New York Times, Art News, Herald Tribune, Art Digest & others; Riverdale Press. *Mem:* New York Artists Equity Asn; Am Soc Contemp Artists (treas); Bronx Soc Sci & Lett; Nat Acad; Fedn of Modern Painters & Sculptors. *Media:* Oil, Watercolor, Pastel, Pen & Ink, Etching. *Mailing Add:* Nat Acad Sch 5 E 89th St New York NY 10128

OLSON, BETTYE JOHNSON
PAINTER, EDUCATOR, LECTURER
b Minneapolis, Minn, Jan 16, 1923. *Study:* Univ Minn, BS (art educ), 45, MEd, 49; Univ NMex, Taos, summer 46; Cranbrook Acad Art, summer, Mich, 48; Sante Fe, NMex Workshop, 2000. *Work:* Vaxjo, Sweden; Pillsbury World Hq, Minneapolis; Augsburg Coll; Luther Coll, Decorah, Iowa; Luther Seminary, St Paul; 3 M, Minn Mining & Manufacturing; Thrivent Co; Kuopio, Finland; Minn Mus Am Art; Minn Hist Soc; Boyton Health Svcs; Wiesman Mus; St Catherine's Univ; St Olaf Coll, Northfield, Mn; Luther Coll. *Comn:* Radisson Hotel, Fla, 83; Alter hanging, Gloria Des Lutheran Church, St Paul, 2013. *Exhib:* 56 solo exhibs including St Olaf Coll, 77, Augsburg Coll, 79, Luther Coll, Decorah, Iowa, 80, Am Swedish Inst, Minneapolis & Smaland Mus, Vaxjo, Sweden, 82, Westlake Gallery, Minn, 64-82, Thrivent Co, 83, Berge Gallery, Stillwater, 95 & 2001, Augsburg Coll, Minneapolis, 96, Luther Seminary, St Paul, 98, Johnson Heritage Gallery, Grand Marais, 2002, St Catherine Univ Retrospective, 2006, Hennepin History Mus, 2012; Women's Club of Minneapolis, 2011; Juried Group shows, Walker Art Ctr Biennial, 47 & Minneapolis Art Inst Biennial, 47; Metamorphose One, Minn Mus Am Art, 76; Mid Yr Show Ann, Butler Inst Am Art, Youngtstown, 77; Watercolor USA, Springfield, Mo, 77; Minn Artists Selected for Kuopio Invitational, Finland, Univ Minn Gallery, 81; Artists, Looking Back, Minn Mus Am Art, 88; Macalester, Modena, Italy, 89, Mentor-Protegee show, Macalester Coll, 92, Univ Minn, Nash Gallery, 94; Hill House Swed Am Artists, 96; Hill House Gardens, 98; Sosin Gallery, 2002; 8 Women Bldg, St Paul, 2009. *Pos:* Art fac, Univ Minn, 47-49, Concordia Univ, 75-79, 83-84, Summer School, 83-88, Augsburg Coll, 88-89; judge, Univ Minn Student Show, 56, Minn Watercolor Soc, 88, Minn State Fair Exhib, 2000; Warm Gallery, Minneapolis Mentor Prog, 91-94; dir, Coll of Third Age Augsburg Coll, 92-98. *Teaching:* Instr, Summit Sch Girls, 45-47 & Univ Minn, 47-49; artist-in-residence, Holden Village Lutheran Retreat Ctr, Chelan, Wash, 67-79, 86-88, 89-90 & 94; instr painting & design, Concordia Univ, St Paul, 75-78, 83-84; instr, Augsburg Summer Sch, 83-88; instr painting & printmaking, Augsburg Coll, Minneapolis, 88-89; Grunewald Guild, Wash, 90; mentor proj, Women's Art Registry of Minn, 1991-94, bd mem, elder Learning Inst, Univ Minn, 2001-2003; fac, 2000-2006; Augsburg Coll Third Age, lectr 85-2012, arts lectr, 2013. *Awards:* Merit Award, Twin City Show, Minn Mus Art, 61; 3rd Prize, Merit Award, Minn State Fair, 76 & 77-93; Grand Prize, Purchase Award, Northern Lights Show, White Bear Arts Coun, Lakewood Coll, 77; Am Asn Univ Women Arts Award, St Paul, 85; Best of Show, St Matthews Community Show, 2004; Greatest Generation Artist, Minn Hist Soc, 2010. *Bibliog:* Two Women Artists Sweden (video interview), Video Team Westover, 93-94; Brochure, Augsburg Coll, 96; St Catherine Univ Brochure, 2006. *Mem:* Delta Phi Delta (pres, 46); Artists Equity Asn (secy, 74); Women's Art Caucus; Women's Art Registry Minn (bd 92-94). *Media:* Watercolor, Acrylic, Monotype. *Specialty:* watercolor themes. *Interests:* Theater, lectures, books, travel, family & friends. *Publ:* Great River Review, JC Press, 80-83; Crisp Pine, Poetry Sketches, AAUW Press, St Paul, 90; Creativity in Aging Art (video), Minn Arts, 94; Minnesota Artists (video), 95 & 96; Retrospective brochure, Augsburg Coll, 96; Insights, Osher Life Long Learning Inst, Univ Minn, 2005; Persistence of Vision (brochure), St Catherine Univ, 2006; Metro Mag, 11/2006; Bugle Newspaper, St Paul, Nov 97; St Paul Pioneer Press, (article), 77. *Mailing Add:* 1721 Fulham St Unit H Saint Paul MN 55113-5152

OLSON, CHARLES
PAINTER, INSTRUCTOR
Study: Ind Univ Pa, BS, 74, MA, 76; Tyler Sch Art, Temple Univ, 81. *Work:* Carnegie Inst Mus Art, Pittsburgh, Pa; Osaka Mus Mod Art, Japan; Charleston Mus Art, WVa; Gallery Liilebonne, Nancy, France; S Allegheny Mus Art, Loretto, Pa. *Exhib:* Springfield Nat Exhib, Mass, 82; Seven New Artists, Carnegie Mus Art, Pittsburgh, Pa, 84; Artist Educator Exhib, 84, William Penn Mus, Harrisburg, Pa & Art of the State, 89; Invitational Exhib, Del Mus Art, Wilmington, 90; Winterlude Invitational, W Moreland Mus, Greensburg, Pa, 93; Am Abstraction, Alleghenies Mus, Loretto, Pa, 94; Pittsburgh Ctr Arts Biennial, Pa, 98. *Teaching:* Assoc prof art & chmn fine arts dept, St Francis Col, Loretto, Pa, 76-. *Bibliog:* Rachel Youeng (auth), Naturalized depth, Cover Mag, NY, 96; Graham Shearing (auth), Abstract Olson rooted in real, Tribune Rev, Pa, 96; Mary Thomas (auth), Olson & work paints enticing landscape of Shaker experience, Pittsburgh Post Gazette, 97. *Media:* Acrylic on Canvas & Paper. *Dealer:* Denise Bibro Fine Art 529 W 20th 4th Flr New York NY 10011. *Mailing Add:* 427 S 7th St Indiana PA 15701

OLSON, DOUGLAS JOHN
EDUCATOR, COLLECTOR
b Wausau, Wis, Aug 26, 1934. *Study:* Layton Sch Art, BFA; Univ Cincinnati, MFA. *Work:* Montgomery Mus Fine Arts, Ala; Pope & Quint Corp; Gallery S; First Nat Bank Ala; South Central Bell, Birmingham, Ala; and others. *Exhib:* Solo exhibs, Southeastern Ark Univ, Magnolia, 99, Kans Wesleyan Univ, Salina, 2000, Quincy Univ, Ill, 2001; Emeritus Faculty Exhib, Auburn Univ, 2003; Glacial Rocks Exhib, Cedar Grove, Wis, 2005, Plymouth, Wis, 2006 & Port Washington, Wis, 2007, Random Lake, Wis, 2008, Grafton, Wis, 2009; Mead Pub Libr, Sheyboygan, Wis, 2010; Oostburg Pub Libr, Oostburg, Wis, 2011; Zablocki Lib, Milwaukee, Wis, 2012; Sheboygan Falls Meml Libr, Sheboygan Falls, Wisc, 2013; Oscar Grady Public Libr, Saukville, Wisc, 2014. *Teaching:* Instr drawing, Univ Cincinnati, 67-68; prof drawing, design & photog, Auburn Univ, 68-2003. *Awards:* Best of Show, LaGrange Nat X,

Chattahoochee Valley Art Gallery, 85; Res Awards, Auburn Univ, 85-2000, Photog, 99; 1st Place, Tenn Valley Art Ctr, 99; and others. *Media:* Wisconsin Glacial Rocks; Electronic Imaging. *Publ:* The Civil War News (3 photos & captions), Tunbridge, Vt, 12/97 & 12/98, (5 photos & article), 6/99 & (3 photos & article), 2-3/2000; many others. *Mailing Add:* 302 E Thach Ave Auburn AL 36830

OLSON, GENE RUSSELL
SCULPTOR, TAPESTRY ARTIST
b Lake City, Minn, Mar 1, 1949. *Study:* Univ Minn, 67-72. *Work:* Pac Gas & Elec, San Francisco, Calif; Univ Wis, River Falls, Anodized Aluminum, Univ Wis, River Falls, 88-89. *Comn:* Steel Painted Welded Kinetic, Children's Mus, Minneapolis, Minn, 83; Cast Bronze, City of Minneapolis, Minn, 85 & Minneapolis Pub Libr, 87; Woven Bronze & Copper, Jostens Inc, Minneapolis, 86; Anodized Aluminum, Univ Wis, River Falls, 88-89; Woven Copper wall relief, Fountains Country Club, Lake Worth, Fla, 90; Bronze & Slate Fountain, River Falls Area Hosp, Wis, 94. *Exhib:* A Feast of Function, Gallery Functional Art, Santa Monica, Calif, 88; Adventures in the Art Zone, Minn Mus Art, St Paul, 95-96; Artists who Collaborate with Architects, Phipps Art Ctr, Hudson, Wis, 96. *Awards:* Second Honor, 74th Fine Arts Show, Minn State Fair, 85; Cover Background Artist, The Guild, Kraus Sikes, 88; 1st Peer Award & Artist's Choice Award, Minn Fiber/Metal, 93. *Bibliog:* Robert T Smith (auth), column, Minneapolis Start Tribune, 81; Gary Gillson, TV review interview, KTCA Channel 2, Minneapolis/St Paul, 83. *Mem:* Int Sculpture Ctr. *Media:* Bronze. *Mailing Add:* c/o The Mettle Works 8600 NE Odean Elk River MN 55330-7167

OLSON, LINDA A
SCULPTOR, EDUCATOR
b Harvey, NDak, Aug 14, 1956. *Study:* Minot State Univ, NDak, BS (cum laude, Gertrude M Eck Scholar), 84; Univ Mont, Missoula, MA (ceramic sculpture, magna cum laude), 87; Univ NDak, Grand Forks, MFA (ceramic sculpture, magna cum laude, NDak Bd Higher Educ Scholar, Grad Res Grant & Ethel, Harriet & Stella Haugan Art Scholar), 90. *Work:* Univ NDak, Grand Forks; Minot State Univ, NDak; Bemidji State Univ; plus many pvt collections. *Comn:* Archaeol recs, Bur Land Mgt, Billings Resource Area, Mont, 92; archaeol recs, Bur Land Mgt, Worland, Wyo, 92; illustrations, Indian Cultures on the Great Plains, AD 500-1500: Prehistory to History, Karl H Schlesier (ed), 93; cover art, University 101: An Orientation Textbook for Freshman Students, Midcontinent Inst, Minot State Univ, NDak, 93; cover illus, Connections Mag, Develop Asn, Minot State Univ, 93. *Exhib:* Midwestern Invitational, Rourke Gallery, Moorhead, Minn, 89, 90, 93, 94 & 96; Tribal & Western Art of the Great Plains, Oscar Howe Art Ctr, 95; Minot State Univ Fac Biennial Exhib, Hartnett Hall Gallery, Minot State Univ, 96; North Am Rock Art, Minds Eye Gallery, 96, James Mem Preserv Soc, 96, Bismarck Art Gallery, 97 & Jamestown Art Ctr, 98; Womens Self Images, Tallery Gallery, 96, Libr Gallery, Minot State Univ, 97; Pekin Juried Art Competition, Pekin Art Center, Pekin, NDak, 2002, 2005, 2007; Figurative Works, 62 Doors, Minot, NDak, 2006; Celebrating Explorers, NDak Mus Art, Grand Forks, NDak, 2007; Women in the Picture, Northwest Art Center, Minot, NDak, 2007. *Pos:* Gallery asst, Hartnett Hall Gallery, Minot State Univ, NDak, 80-83; rock art recording artist, proj mgr & instr, 89-; dir, NW Art Ctr, Minot State Univ, 91-; NDak Art Gallery Asn, 94-. *Teaching:* Art asst, Minot State Univ, 80-84, instr art dept, 90-95, asst prof, 95-; grad teaching asst, Univ NDak, formerly. *Awards:* Grants, NDak Coun Arts, 93-96; Artworks Fund Grant, NW Art Ctr, 95; Woman of Distinction Nominee, YWCA, 95. *Bibliog:* Rock Artist Brings Work to Hazen Kids, Hazen Star, 11/3/94; Artist Encourages Kids to Create, Hazen Star, 11/17/94; Capturing the Native Image, Resident artist teaches children/adults, Foster Co Independent, 3/20/95. *Mem:* Minot Area Coun Arts; Minot Art Gallery (vpres, 92-94 & comt chair, 93, 95 & 96); Minot Art Asn; NDak Coun Arts; NDak Art Galleries Asn (pres, 92-94). *Media:* Ceramic. *Res:* North American rock art; archaeological recording. *Publ:* Auth, Secondhand Storytellers, Mont Writing Proj, 86; Rock Art Study Yields New Evidence of Bear Ceromonialism, Am Rock Artist Asn, 5/91; Ideas for drawing development, Ideas: Mid Continent Inst Newsletter, 10/93. *Mailing Add:* 412 Nineteenth Ave SW Minot ND 58701-6420

OLSON, MAXINE
PAINTER, INSTRUCTOR
b Kingsburg, Calif, June 29, 1931. *Study:* Otis Art Inst, Los Angeles, Calif, 71 & 72; Inst Allende, San Miguel, Mex, 73; Calif State Univ, Fresno, BA (summa cum laude), 73, Calif State Univ, Fresno, MA (with distinction), 75; Univ Calif, Santa Barbara; Bennington Coll, Vt, 97. *Work:* Mural Design Friends Libr, Kingsburg San Francisco Mus Mod Art/Artist Gallery, 2002; Lost in Translation, Fresno Art Mus, 2006; Fed Land Bank, Hanford, Calif; and others. *Comn:* Mural painting, Fresno Arts Mus, Fresno, Calif, 93-94; Cross Church (mural), Fresno, Calif; Calif Dept FIsh and Game, Fresno, 2002; 12 Portraits of Farmers for the Fed Land Bank, Hanford, Calif, 2002; Friends of the Libr Mural Design, 2003; Kingsburg Rotary Club Centennial Mural Design, 2009. *Exhib:* About Women, Orange Co Ctr Contemp Art, 82; Symposium on Portuguese Traditions, Univ Calif, Los Angeles, 85; Fresno Arts Mus, 85; Am Realism, William Sawyer Gallery, San Francisco, Calif, 85; Palazzo Vagnotti, Cortona, Italy, 87; Nexus Contemp Gallery, Atlanta, Ga, 88 & 90; Church of San Stae, Venice, Italy, 89; Archival Gallery, Sacramento, Calif, 93; Seybold, San Francisco, Calif, 98; Artist's Gallery, San Francisco Mus Mod Art, 2001; The Great S Patterson Bldy, Fresno, Calif, 2005; Chait Galleries, Iowa City, Iowa, 2005; Lost in Translation, Fresno Art Mus, 2006 & Univ Calgary, Can, 2007; UMAR: Nas Asas De Iqualdade/Religiosidade No Feminino, The Cult Ctr, San Miguel, Azores, May 2007; Peninsula Mus Art, Belmont, Calif, 2007; Spectrum Gallery, Fresno, Calif, 2008; The Great 8, Patterson Bldg, Fresno, Calif, 2004; Centralism, Gallery 25, Fresno, Calif 2009; Int Mus of Women, San Francisco, 2009; Boston Pub Libr, 2009; Artik, San Jose, 2013. *Teaching:* Instr, Calif State Univ, 76-85; asst prof painting & drawing, Univ Ga, Athens, 86-89; asst prof, Univ Ga Studies Abroad Prog, Cortona, Italy, 86-87 & 93; Inst Allende, San Miguel de Allende, Mex, 73; UCLA ArtsReach Prog, Corcoran State Prison, 96. *Awards:* Phi Kappa Phi, 75; Harold J Cleveland Mem Awar,d 20th Nat Jury Show, Chautauqua, NY, 77; IDN Design Awards, Wanchai, Hong Kong, 97-98. *Bibliog:* David Hale (auth), Art in California Awards, The Fresno Bee; Ageing The Process: The Perception (catalog), Forum Gallery, Jamestown, New York, 90; Susan R. Ressler (auth), Women Artists of the American West, Mc Farland & Company, 2003; Rosa Maria Neves Simes (auth), Women in the Azores and Immigrant Communities (A Mulher Nos Acores E Nas Communidades), Universidade dos Azores, San Miguel, Azores; Fala de Lost in Translation, Acoriano Oriental, Azores June 2007; and others. *Mem:* Fresno Art Mus; Nat Women's Mus Art, Washington, DC; Int Mus Women, San Francisco, Calif; Coll Art Asn; Phi Kappa Phi. *Media:* Oil, Pencil; Computer Art. *Publ:* Art in Calif, 12/92; Computer Artist Mag, 10/94; book cover, Al Graves (auth), Immigrants in Agriculture, the Portuguese, 2004; book cover, Glaube & Geschlecht, Herausgegeenk Von Ruth Albrecht, A Buhler-Dietrich, & F Strzelczyk, Bohlau, Cologne, Germany, 2006. *Dealer:* Spectrum Gallery Fresno CA. *Mailing Add:* 1555 Lincoln St Kingsburg CA 93631

OLSON, RICHARD W
PAINTER, EDUCATOR
b Rockford, Ill. *Study:* Univ Wis, Madison, BS & with R Knipschild, Leo Steppat & Italo Scanga, 60, MS (studio art-painting & graphics) 61 & MFA with Warrington Colescott, 62. *Work:* Mus Contemp Art, Chicago; Nat Gallery; Albright-Knox Gallery; Walker Art Ctr; Mus Mod Art, NY; and others. *Exhib:* 25th Print Nat, Intaglio, Nat Collection Fine Arts Div, Smithsonian Inst, Washington, 64; Book as Object, Visual Studies Workshop, 79; Artists Books Permanent Collection, 82 & Artists Books & Recordings, 85, Mus Contemp Art, Chicago; Less is More, Pratt Manhattan Ctr, NY, 83; Artifacts at the End of a Decade, Franklin Furnace, NY, 83; Artists Books, Univ Ore, Eugene, 88; Arts of the Book, Philadelphia Coll Art & Design, 88; Retrospective, Wright Mus, Beloit, Wis. *Teaching:* From asst prof to assoc prof, Beloit Col, Wis, 63-77, chmn dept art, 69-76, 80-82, 84-85, 87-88, 96-99, prof art drawing, printmaking, painting, 77-. *Awards:* Gimbels Award, Wis Painters & Sculptors, Gimbels-Milwaukee, 62; Gimbels-Schusters Award, Wis Salon Art, Gimbels-Schusters, 68; Cullister Awards, 78-85; Hewlitt Mellon Award, 83; Wis Artists Biennal Cash Award, 87; Cullister Grant, 86-99. *Bibliog:* Books in an expanded context, Artweek, 7/81; Fluxus and friends, Milwaukee J, 11/84. *Publ:* Illusr covers, Beloit Poetry J, 64 & 69; Artifacts at the End Decade, Watson & Heubner, 81. *Dealer:* Printed Matter 77 Wooster St New York NY 10013. *Mailing Add:* Dept Art Beloit Col 700 Col St Beloit WI 53511

OLSON, RICK
PAINTER
b Mayville, NDak, Mar 15, 1950. *Study:* Moorhead State Univ, Minn, 68-72. *Work:* Mus Art, Ft Lauderdale, Fla; Minneapolis Inst Arts, Minn; Canton Art Inst, Canton, Ohio; Nat Portrait Gallery, Smithsonian Inst, Washington; Butler Inst Am Art, Youngstown, Ohio. *Comn:* Five portraits, Joseph H Hirshhorn, Washington, 79; 1st pres Patty Berg (portrait), Ladies Prof Golf Asn, Fla, 98. *Media:* Pastels, Oil On Canvas. *Mailing Add:* 32929 135th St Dalton MN 56324

OLSON, ROBERTA JEANNE MARIE
HISTORIAN, CURATOR
b Shawano, Wis, June 1, 1947. *Study:* St Olaf Coll, BA, 69; Univ Iowa, MA, 71; Princeton Univ, MFA, 73, PhD, 76. *Collection Arranged:* Forty Drawings: Graphic Gaudier-Brzeska, Art Mus, Princeton, Univ, 74; An Album, Italian 19th Century Drawings & Watercolors (auth, catalog), Shepherd Gallery, New York, 76; Sixty Italian 19th Century Drawings (auth, catalog), San Jose Art Mus, 76; Italian Drawings 1780-1890 (auth, catalog), (traveling), Nat Gallery Art, Washington, DC, 80-81; Disegni di Tommaso Minardi (auth, catalog), Galleria Nazionale d'Arte Moderna, Rome, 82-83; Fire & Ice: A History of Comets in Art (auth, catalog), Nat Air & Space Mus-Smithsonian Inst, 85-86; Thomas Jefferson Bryan Gallery: Changing Attributions, NY Hist Soc, 90; Ottocento: Romanticism and Revolution in Nineteenth Century Italian Painting, (traveling) Walters Art Gallery, Baltimore, 92-93; The Art of Drawing: Selections from The Wheaton Coll Collection (auth, catalog), Watson Gallery, Norton, Mass, 97; Manhattan Unfurled, NY Hist Soc, 2002; Building on the Flatiron: The Centenary of a NYC Icon, 1902-2002, NY Hist Soc, 2002; Seat of Empire: Napolean's Armchair from Malmaison to Manhattan, NY Hist Soc 2003; Petropolis: A Social Hist of Urban Animal Companions, NY Hist Soc, 2003; Birds of Central Park: Audubon's Watercolors, NY Hist Soc, 2004; Audubon's Aviary, NY Hist Soc, 2005-2006; The Hudson River Sch at the NY Hist Soc: Nature and the Am Vision, NY Hist Soc, 2005; Audubon's Aviary: Natural Selection, NY Hist Soc, 2007, Audubon's Aviary: Endangered Species, 2008; New York: Six Centuries of Drawings and Watercolors at the New York Hist Soc, New York Hist Soc, 2008; Audubon's Aviary: Somethings Old, Something Borrowed, but Most Things New, NY Historical Soc, 2009; Audubon's Aviary: The Early Birds (Part I of the Complete Flock), NY Historical Soc, 2013; Audubon's Aviary: Parts Unknown (Part II of the Complete Flock), NY Historical Soc, 2014; Audubon's Aviary: The Final Flight (Part III of the Complete Flock), NY Historical Soc, 2015; Picasso's Le Tricorne, NY Historical Soc, 2015-16. *Pos:* Contrib ed, Arts Mag, 73-75; guest cur, Art Mus Princeton Univ, 74 & Nat Gallery Art, 80; art news ed, Soho Weekly News, 76-78; bd dir, The Drawing Soc, 84-94; consult, Smithsonian Inst, 84-86; The NY Hist Soc, cur, drawings, 90-; mem vis comt Drawings & Prints Dept, Metrop Mus Art, New York, 93-, vis comt paper conservation, 2004-2007; mem, Vis comt Drawings Dept, Morgan Libr and Mus, NY, 2012-. *Teaching:* From instr to prof art hist, Wheaton Coll, 75-2000, chmn, Art Dept, 87-89, 92-93 & 97-98, Howard Meneely chair, 90-92 & Mary L Heuser fac chair arts, 97-2000. *Awards:* Fel, Whiting Found for Humanities, 74-75, NEH 82-83; Phi Beta Kappa, 82-87; Am Philos Soc Grant, 89; Am Coun Learned Soc Grant, 90-91; Sr Res Grant, Getty Found, 94-95; Samuel H Kress Fel, 73-74 & 2001-02; Getty Grantee, NY Hist Soc, 2003-05 & 2007; Outstanding Permanent Collections Catalog, Asn Art Mus Cur, 2008, 2012; Henry Allen Moe Prize for Catalogs of Distinction in the Arts, NY State Historical Assn, 2013. *Mem:* Coll Art Asn Am; Drawing Soc (bd dir, 84-94); Halleys Comet Soc (bd adv, 86-); Italian Art Soc; Asn Univ Pros Italian; Ren Soc Am; Phi Beta Kappa (pres, Kappa Chapt 80-82 & 87-88); Art Table, 2003; Asn Art Mus (cur, 2008-). *Res:* Italian renaissance; 19th century Italian painting, sculpture and

drawings; American and European drawings; aimed at illuminating cultural backgrounds and interconnections across disciplines; astronomical images in art. *Publ:* Contribr, var mags, 73-; Giotto's Portrait of Halley's Comet, Scientific Am, 75; Italian Drawing, 1780-1890 (catalog), 80; Fire & Ice: A History of Comets in Art, Walker & Smithsonian Inst, 85; Italian Renaissance Sculpture, Thames & Hudson, 92; Ottocento: Romanticism & Revolution in the 19th Century Italian Painting, AFA & Centro Di, 93; An Old Mystery Solved: The 1487 Payment Document to Botticelli for a Tondo, Mitteilungen des Kunsthistorichen Inst Florenz, 95; Fire in the Sky: Comets and Meteors, the Decisive Centuries, Brit Art & Sci, Cambridge Univ Press, 98; The Florentine Tondo, Oxford Univ Press, 2000; Seat of Empire, NY Hist Soc, 2002; One of the Best-Kept Secrets: The Collection of the New York Historical Society, Master Drawings, 2004; John Singer Sargent & James Carroll Beckwith, Americans in Paris: A Trove of their Unpublished Drawings, Master Drawings, 2005; The Biography of the Object in Medieval and Renaissance Art, Blackwell Publ, 2006; The Discovery of a Cache of Over 200 Sixteenth-Century Avian Watercolors: A Missing Chapter in the History of Ornithological Illustration, Master Drawings, 2007; St Benedict Sees the Light: Asam's Solar Eclipses as Metaphor, Religion and the Arts, 2007; John James Audubon: Artist, Naturalist and Adventurer, in Great Natural Historians, 2007; Drawn by New York: Six Centuries of Watercolors and Drawings at the New York Historical Society, NY Hist Soc & D Giles Ltd, 2008; George Harvey's Anglo- American Atmospheric Landscapes, Mag Antiques, 2008; entries in Dutch New York Between East & West: The World of Margrieta van Varick, 2009; Are Two Really Better than one? The collaboration of Franz Kaiserman, and Bartolomeo Pinelli, Master Drawings, 2010; A Magnificent Obsession: Durand's Trees as Spiritual Sentinels of Nature, in Am Landscapes of Asher B Durand (1796-1886), Fundacin Juan March, 2010; New Methods for Studying Serialization in the Workshop of Andrea della Robbia: Technical Study and Analysis, Dix ans d'études, 2011; Audubons Aviary: The Original Watercolors for The Birds of America, NY Historical Soc and Rizzoli/Skira, 2012; Audubon's Early Birds, Master Drawings, 2012; Identifying Felice Giani's double portrait with Michael Kock and the friendship portrait in late Settecento Rome, Mittheilungen des Kunsthistorisches Institut, 2012; Drawings at the Armory: The Currency of Change and Moderism, in the Armory Show at 100: Modernism and Revolution, NY Historical Soc and D Giles Ltd, 2013; Art of the Eclipse, in Nature, 2014; The Comets of Caroline Herschel, Sleuth of the Skies at Slough, in Culture and Cosmos (proceedings of the conference INSAP VII), 2014; Making It Modern: The Folk Art Collection of Elie and Viola Nadelam, NY Historical Soc and D Giles Ltd, 2015. *Mailing Add:* 1220 Park Ave 3C New York NY 10128-1733

OLYNYK, PATRICIA J
PAINTER, EDUCATOR
b Regina, Saskatachewan, Can, Oct 4, 1961. *Study:* Alberta Coll of Art and Design, Can, 79-83; Calif Coll of Arts and Crafts, MFA, 85-88; Osaka Nat Univ of Foriegn Studies, 89; Kyoto Seika Univ, Kyoto, Japan, 90-93. *Work:* East Tenn State Univ, Johnson City; Athabasca Univ, Calgary, Alberta, Can; Can Western Nat Gas, Calgary, Alberta, Can; Fogg Mus, Harvard Univ; Life Sci Inst, Univ Mich; Am Council on Educ, Washington, DC. *Comn:* Hewlett Packard Corp Hq, Palo Alto, Calif; Fairmont Moter, Dallas, Tex; Schultz Law Offices, Sacramento, Calif, 2000. *Exhib:* Los Angeles Int Biennial Invitational, Toby Moss Gallery, Calif, 95; Paper in the Millennium, RC Williams Am Mus Papermaking, Atlanta, Ga, 2000; Int Artists Book Triennial, Gallery Iarkai, Vilhus, Lithuania and Galerie 5020, Salzberg, Austria, 2000; Paper Road, Mused Del Croso, Rome, Italy, 2001; Print Nat, Brooklyn Mus, NY, 2001; Gallerie Grafica Tokyo, Japan, 2002; North Am Print Biennial, Gallery 808, Boston, Mass, 2003; solo show, Transfigurations/Transmutations, Art Life, Mistuhashi, Kyoto, Japan, 2003; solo show, Material Shadows, Ufer! Gallery, Kyoto, Japan, 2003; group show, Transitions Int, Trends in Contemp Printmaking, Int Gallery Contemp Art, Anchorage, AK; group show, Sculpture Prints, Print Ctr, Philadelphia, PA, 2003; group show, 2003 Contemp Art Festival Exhib, Saitama Modern Art Mus, Saitama, Japan, 2003; group juried show, Lessedra 3rd World Art Print Ann, Nat Palace of Cult, Sofia, Bulgaria; solo show, Nat Acad Sciences, Washington, DC, 2006; solo show, Life Sciences Inst, Univ Mich, 2006. *Pos:* adminr, Headland's Ctr for Arts, Sausalito, Calif, 87-89; coordr internships, Calif Col Arts & Crafts, San Francisco; vis scholar, Kyoto Seika Univ, Kyoto, Japan, 90-93; dir Grad Sch Art, Washington Univ, St Louis, 2007-; prof art (Florence & Frank Bush), Washington Univ, St Louis, 2007-. *Teaching:* instr dept printmaking, Seika Univ, 91-93; asst prof, Univ Neb, 99; dir of Stamps Disting Visitors Prog; asst prof, Univ Mich, 99-2005; assoc prof & res assoc prof, Sch Art & Design, Univ Mich, 2005-07. *Awards:* Purchase Award, East Tenn State Univ, 89; Rakuyo Exhibition Prize Award, Mus of Kyoto, 92, 93; Juror's Award, Works on Paper Nat Juried Exhib, 99; North Am Print Biennial Award, 2003; First Prize Award, Lessedra 3rd World Art Print Ann, Intl Juried Show, 2004. *Bibliog:* Akira Kurosaki (auth), New directions in print, Hangwa Geijutsu, 93; Michael Anderson (auth), Shinpei Sakakura, Akira Nagasawa & Patricia Olynyk, Art Issues, 95; Glenn Kurtz (auth), The art of digital technology, Artweek, 98; John Carlos Cantu (auth), Olynyk's Sticks, Pods, Bones, Ann Arbor News, 11/2000; Jeanette Wenig Drake (auth), Dialogue, 2001; Mariane Rzepka (auth), Printmaking Merges Art & Science, Ann Arbor News, Sept 2, 2004. *Mem:* Am Print Alliance; Southern Graphics Coun; Mid Am Print Coun; Coll Art Asn; Women's Caucus for the Arts; Boston Printmakers; Inter Soc for Electronic Arts; Art & Science Collaborations Inc. *Media:* Installation, Sculpture, Sound, Mixed Media. *Specialty:* Modern and Contemp. *Interests:* Art and Sci. *Publ:* ROC Internat Print Biennial (exhib catalog), 85; Stonemetal Press (exhib catalog), 2000; Mid Am Print Coun (exhib catalog), 2000; Paper Road (exhib catalog), 2000; Transfigurations, 2002; American Print Alliance, 2002. *Dealer:* Michael Himovitz Gallery 1616 Del Pasi Blvd Ste 3 Sacramento CA 95815. *Mailing Add:* c/o Bruno David Gallery 3721 Washington Blvd Saint Louis MO 63108

OMAR, MARGIT
PAINTER, EDUCATOR
b Berlin, Ger, May 17, 1941; US citizen. *Study:* Univ Colo, Boulder, MFA, 71. *Work:* Los Angeles Co Mus Art, Mus Contemp Art & Polygram Pictures, Los Angeles; Atlantic Richfield Co, Denver; Turtle Creek Mansion, Dallas; and others. *Comn:* Aerojet Gen, La Jolla, Calif, 82; Robinson's, Newport Beach & Santa Monica, Calif, 82. *Exhib:* New Abstract Painting in Los Angeles, Los Angeles Co Mus Art, 76; solo exhibs, Janus Gallery, Venice, Calif, 77, 78, 80, 82 & 84, Univ Southern Calif, Los Angeles, 86 & Calif State Univ, Long Beach, 87; Fresh Paint, San Francisco Mus Mod Art, 82; Drawings by Painters, Oakland Mus Art, 83; Young Talent Awards 1963-1983, Los Angeles Co Mus Art, 83. *Teaching:* Assoc prof graduate studies & painting, Univ Southern Calif, Los Angeles, 73-. *Awards:* Young Talent Award, Los Angeles Co Mus Art & Contemp Art Coun, 77; Individual Artists' Grant, Nat Endowment Arts, 80. *Bibliog:* Susan C Larsen (auth), Margit Omar's California Suite, Arts Mag, 9/78; Water Gabrielson (auth), Pasadena pluralism: The painting Seventies, Art Am, 5/81; Ruth Weisberg (auth), Margit Omar at Janus, Images & Issues, 10/82. *Mem:* Los Angeles Contemp Exhibs. *Media:* Acrylic; Mixed Media. *Mailing Add:* Univ Southern Calif School of Fine Arts Watt Hall 104 Los Angeles CA 90089

ONDISH, ANDREA
PRINTMAKER, EDUCATOR
b Scranton, Pa, Apr 29, 1960. *Study:* Marywood Univ, BFA, 85; Eastern Ill Univ, MA, 86; Ind State Univ, MFA, 92. *Work:* Minnetrista Cult Center, Muncie, Ind; Ind Hist Soc, Indpls; Ind State Univ, Terre Haute, Ind; Acad Fine Arts & Design, Bratislava, Slovakia; Univ Manitoba, Winnipeg, Man, Can; Julian Ctr, Indpls. *Exhib:* Contract on Am, Artemesia Gallery, Chicago, 95; Isn't It a Pretty World, ARC Gallery, Chicago, 95; Conflict/Resolution, Woman Made Gallery, Chicago, 99; Pressing Forward, Hoosier Salon Gallery, Indianapolis, 2001; INdiana and Beginnings, Ind Hist Soc, Indianapolis, 2001; INjoy, Ind Univ-Kokomo Art Gallery, Kokomo, Ind, 2002; Beginnings, Muncie Art Ctr, Zionsville, Ind, 2003; INtouch and INdigenous, Indianapolis Art Ctr, Ind, 2004; Gordy Fine Art Gallery, Muncie, Ind, 2005; Indianapolis Art Center, Ind, 2007; Space Studio, Midland, Mich, 2007-2008; From Our Prospective Nat Womens' Art Exhib, Oakland Comm Coll, Farmington Hills, Mich, 2007; INspire and mINetrista, Cortona Art Gallery, Ashford Univ, Clinton, IA, 2008; Paradigms, Buckham Gallery, Flint, Mich, 2009; IN Irvington, Bona Thompson Memorial Ctr, Indianapolis, In, 2010; Andrea Ondish: Recent Works, Studio 23, Bay City, Mich, 2011; Flora Kirsch Beck Gallery, Alma Coll, Alma, Mich, 2012. *Pos:* Preparator permanent collection, Ind State Univ, 89-92; prog & exhibs coord, Swope Art Mus, Terre Haute, Ind, 97-2001; cur educ, interim dir, Marshall Fredericks Sculpture Mus, Univ Ctr, Mich, 2001-. *Teaching:* Instr, screenprinting, Indianapolis Art Ctr, 98; adj instr, art appreciation, Saginaw Valley State Univ, 2002-, adj lectr, 2003-, adj faculty printmaking, 2005-. *Bibliog:* Regina Grady Schieffer (auth), Fresh Targets, Spectrum Weekly, Little Rock, Ark, 11/91; Patty Poremba (auth), 50th Wabash Valley exhibit at Swope..., Indiana Statesman, 3/18/94; Roger Green (auth), Exhibit of comics is ambitious..., The Grand Rapids Press, 1/2/96; Josef Woodard (auth), Making an Impression, LA Times, Calif, 99; Lawton Exhibit Shows Artists Who Work Behind the Scenes, Univ Wis, Green Bay Inside Mag, Wis, 2000; Technology, Astroturf, and Roadkill: Contemporary Art on Display at Allegheny College, Allegheny News, Meadville, Pa, 2001; Pati LaLonde (auth), Work of Female Artists Highlighted in Bay City, Bay City Times, Mich, 2010. *Mem:* INprint (founding mem); Mid-Am Print Coun; Am Print Alliance; Coll Art Asn. *Media:* All Media. *Mailing Add:* PO Box 5146 Saginaw MI 48603

O'NEAL, ROLAND LENARD
ILLUSTRATOR, PAINTER
b Meridian, Miss, Feb 1, 1948. *Study:* Meridian Mus Art, Miss, 68; Jackson State Univ, BS (art educ), 72, studied with Hale Woodruff, New York, 76. *Work:* Wyo Univ Art Mus, Laramie; Idaho Univ Art Mus, Moscow; Sch Archit, Univ Southern Calif; Family Serv Ctr, W A Reed Jr Vocational & Tech Bldg, Meridian Community Coll, Meridian, Miss; Retired Sr Vol Prog, Meridian; Belhaven Coll, Jackson, Miss; Family Service Ctr, Meridian Naval Air Sta; Meridian Lauderdale Co Pub Libr; Meridian City Hall; W A Reed Jr Vocational & Tech Bldg, Meridian Community Coll, Miss. *Exhib:* Ball State Univ Drawing & Sculpture Exhib, 74; Colo Print & Drawing Exhib, Sch Art, Univ Colo, Boulder, 75; Wind River Nat, Wind River Artist Guild, Ladner, Wyo, 76; Meridian Pub Libr, 77. *Teaching:* Miss Action For Progress Volunteer Arts and Crafts, 69-79; substitute teacher art educ, Meridian Pub Schs, Miss, 72-79. *Mem:* Wind River Valley Artist Guild; Athenian Art Club, Jackson State Univ. *Media:* Pencil, Charcoal; Watercolor, Mixed Media

O'NEIL, ROBYN
PAINTER
b Omaha, 1977. *Study:* Kings Coll London, 97; Tex A & M - Com, BFA, 2000; Univ Ill, 2000-01. *Exhib:* Solo exhibs: These Are Pictures of Boats & Dinosaurs, Angstrom Gallery, Dallas, 2002; Even If It Shall Break Them: Prelude to a Solid Hope for Something Better, Clementine Gallery, NY, 2003; New Works, ArtPace, San Antonio, 2003; Bodybuilder & Sportsman, Chicago, 2004; Clementine Gallery, NY, 2005, 2007; Group exhibs: Bad Touch, Ukrainian Inst Modern Art, Chicago, 2002; Drawn II, Barry Whistler Gallery, Dallas, 2002; Summer Drawings, Mixture Gallery, Dallas, 2002; Super Nature, Inman Gallery, Houston, 2002; The Co We Keep, 2003; Come Forward, Dallas Mus Art, 2003; Am Dream, Ronald Feldman Fine Arts, NY, 2003; Whim?, Angstrom Gallery, Dallas, 2003; Young Am, Galerie Hof & Huyser, Amsterdam, The Neth, 2004; The Drawn Page, Aldrich Mus Contemp Art, Ridgefield, Conn, 2004; It's a Wonderful Life: Psychodrama in Contemp Painting, Spaces, Cleveland, 2004; Whitney Biennial, Whitney Mus Am Art, 2004. *Awards:* Artadia Grant, Fund Art & Dialogue, NY, 2003; Tex Int Artist in Residence, ArtPace Found Contemp Art, San Antonio, 2003. *Dealer:* Dunn and Brown Contemporary 5020 Tracy St Dallas TX 75205; Galerie Praz-Delavallade 28 rue Louise Weiss 75013 Paris France

ONO, YOKO
CONCEPTUAL ARTIST
b Tokyo, Japan, Feb 18, 1933; US citizen; arrived in Calif, 1935. *Study:* Peers' Sch, Gakushuin Univ, Tokyo; Sarah Lawrence Coll, New York; Harvard Univ, Cambridge, Mass. *Hon Degrees:* Art Inst Chicago, PhD (hon), 1997; Liverpool Univ, PhD (hon), 2001; Bard Coll, PhD (hon), 2002. *Exhib:* Solo exhibs, Alchemical Wedding, Albert

Hall London, 1967, Evening with Yoko Ono, Birmingham, 1968, Event, Univ Wales, 1969, & Everson Mus, Syracuse, NY, 1971, Objects, Films, Whitney Mus Am Art, 1989, A Piece of Sky, Galleria Stefania Miscetti, Rome, 1993, Endangered Species, Wacoal Art Ctr/Spiral Garden, Tokyo, 1993, Fluxus, Royal Festival Hall, South Bank Centre, London, 1997, Have You Seen the Horizon Lately? Mus Mod Art, Oxford, 1997, Open Window, Umm El-Fahem, Israel, 2000, Yes Yoko Ono, Japan Soc, 2001, My Mommy Was Beautiful, Shoshana Wayne Gallery, Santa Monica, 2002, Yoko Ono Women's Room, Mus d'Art Moderne de la Ville de Paris, 2003, Odyssey of a Cockroach, Inst Contemp Arts, London, 2004, Heal, 2006, Imagine Peace, 2007, Yoko Ono, Gemalde/Paintings, 2008, Yoko Ono: Add Colour, 2012, Yoko Ono: Moment, Moderna Museet, Stockholm, 2012, Yoko Ono: SMILE, Serpentine Gallery, London, 2012; Fluxshoe, Sch Art, Falmouth, Cornwall, Eng, 1972, Venice Biennale, 2009; Liverpool Biennial Contemp Art, 2004; Techniques of the Visible, Shanghai 5 Biennial, 2004; Do You Believe in Reality? Taipei Biennial, 2004; At the Mercy of Others: The Politics of Care, Whitney Mus Am Art, 2005; Experiencing Duration, Biennale de Lyon, 2005; Looking at Words, Andrea Rosen Gallery, NY, 2005; To the Human Furture, Flight from the Dark Side, Art Tower, Mito ATM, Mito; The Expanded Eye, Kunsthaus, Zurich, 2006; 53rd Int Venice Biennial, Venice, Italy, 2009; Dublin Biennial, 2012; Innocence and Experience, Tate Liverpool, 2012; XV Women Biennale: Violence, PAC Mus, Ferrara, Italy, 2012. *Pos:* Established the Lennon Ono Grant for Peace in 2002 given to artist living in regions of conflict.; named Global Autism Ambassador, Autism Speaks Orgn, 2010-. *Awards:* Helen Caldicott Leadership Award, 1987; Showhegan Award, 2002; Lifespire Award, 2002; MOCA Award, 2003; Lifetime Achievement Award, Japan Soc NY, 2005; CAA Award for Disting Body of Work, 2008; Golden Lions for Lifetime Achievement, Venice Biennale, 2009; 8th Hiroshima Art prize, 2011; Oskar Kokoshka prize, Univ Applied Arts Vienna, 2012. *Bibliog:* P Devlin (auth), Yoko Ono, Vogue, New York, 12/1971; Michael Benedikt (auth), Yoko notes, Art & Artists, London, 1/1972; E Wasserman (auth), This is not here: Yoko Ono at Syracuse, Artforum, New York, 1/1972. *Publ:* Auth, Six Film Scripts, Tokyo, 1964; Thirteen Film Score Scores, London, 1967; John & Yoko Calendar, New York, 1970; Grapefruit, London, 1970 & A Hole to See the Sky Through, New York, 1971 Just Me! (Tada No Atashi), 1986, Sometime in New York City, 1995, Acorns, 1996

ONOFRIO, JUDY
SCULPTOR
b New London, Conn, 1939. *Study:* Sullins Coll, Bristol, Va. *Exhib:* Solo shows incl NDak Mus Art, Grand Forks, 1993, Minneapolis Inst Art, 1993, Laumeier Sculpture Park and Mus, St Louis, 1995, Thomas Barry Fine Arts, Minneapolis, 1995, 2004, Leedy Voulkos Gallery, Kans City, 1995, Sherry Leedy Contemp Art, 2004, Rochester Art Ctr, 2005, Ark Arts Ctr, 2005, Daum Mus Contemp Art, 2005; group shows incl Boise Art Mus, 1998; Phipps Ctr for Arts, Hudson, Wis, 1998; Mus Art and Design, Helsinki, Finland, 1998; Leedy Voulkos Gallery, Kans City, 1999; Lowe Art Mus, Coral Gables, Fla, 1999; Am Craft Mus, New York, 1999; DESIGNyard, Dublin, Ireland, 1999; Frederick R Weisman Art Mus, Minneapolis, 1999, 2001; Northern Clay Ctr, Minneapolis, 2002; Gallery Hertz, Louisville, Ky, 2002; Duane Reed Gallery, 2003; Sherry Leedy Contemp Art, 2003, 2004; Tory Folliard Gallery, Milwaukee, 2004; Thomas Barry Fine Art, 2004; Gold Treasury Mus, Melbourne, Australia, 2004. *Pos:* Dir Rochester Art Ctr, Minn, 1960-70, prog dir, Total Arts Day Camp, 1960-98, exhib/edn cons, 1970-95. *Teaching:* Prog dir, Minneapolis Coll Art and Design, 1978; instr, Rochester Cmty Coll, 1986. *Awards:* Minn State Arts Bd Fel Grant, 1978, Career Opportunity Grant, 1993; YMCA Women in Achievement Award, 1983; Arts Midwest/Nat Regional Fel Grant, 1993-1995; McKnight Found Fel in Visual Arts, 1994-95; Bush Artist Fel, 1998-99; Lifetime Achievement Award, Rochester Art Ctr, 2000; Lifetime Achievement Award, Minn Crafts Coun, 2001; Distinguished Artist Award, McKnight Found, 2005. *Bibliog:* H Ellion (auth), Minneapolis Institute of Arts, 5/1993; Laurel Reuter (auth), Judyland: The Art of Judy Onofrio, NDak Mus Art, 1993; R Silberman (auth), The Stuff of Art, American Craft, Summer/1996. *Mem:* Minn Crafts Coun; Southeastern Minn Arts Coun; Minn Inst Arts. *Media:* Miscellaneous Media. *Publ:* Judyland, Star Tribune, 1993. *Dealer:* Sherry Leedy Contemp Art 2004 Baltimore Ave Kansas City MO 64108; Tory Folliard Gallery 233 N Milwaukee St Milwaukee WI 53202; Thomas Barry Fine Arts 110 N 5th St Minneapolis MN 55403. *Mailing Add:* 1105 10 St SW Rochester MN 55902

ONORATO, RONALD JOSEPH
HISTORIAN, EDUCATOR
b Jersey City, NJ, Jan 26, 1949. *Study:* Rutgers Col, AB, 70; Brown Univ, MA, 73, PhD (Kress Found Grant), 77. *Collection Arranged:* Labyrinths, 75; Watson Gallery, Wheaton Col, 75-77; Mary Miss Interior Works, 82; Sailing Design Today, 86; Vito Acconci Domestic Trapping, 87; The Art of Douglas Huebler, 88; J D Johnston, Archit Drawings, 1995. *Pos:* Asst cur, NY Cult Ctr, 73-74; dir exhib, Univ RI, 77-82; sr cur, La Jolla Mus Contemp Art, 85-88; trustee, Newport Hist Soc, 92- & Newport Art Mus, 92-; bd mem, RI Comt Humanities, 93; pres, Pettaquamscutt Hist Soc, 2004-2008. *Teaching:* Vis lectr art hist, Wheaton Col, 75-77; chmn & prof, Univ RI, 77-; adj prof criticism & art hist, RI Sch Design, 1981-1999. *Awards:* Nat Endowment Humanities Grant, 83; Nat Endowment Arts Exhib Grants, 86 & 87; Grants, Champlin Found, 92, CLG, 95-96 & Prince Found, 97; SIMSMC, MIT, 2003; Am Inst Architect (hon mem, 2008); Swan Point Survey grant, 2013. *Mem:* RI Hist Preserv Comn; Nat Regist Rev Board; Am Inst Architects. *Res:* Nineteenth century American art, and architecture; public sculpture. *Publ:* Auth, Douglas Huebler, 88; Richard Fleischner's St Louis Project (catalog), 90; Selections: Permanent Collection, San Diego Mus Contemp Art, 90; Blurring the Boundaries, 25 Years of Installation Art, 96; Outdoor Sculpture of Rhode Island, 98; Buildings of Rhode Island, 2004; AIA Guide to Newport, 2007; Architecture and Drawing: The Newport Career of John Dixon Johnston, 2008; Peabody and Stearns, Residential Resort Architecture, 2011; Horace Trumbauer, Newport, 2012; Ogden Codman in Newport, 2013. *Mailing Add:* Dept Art & Art Hist Univ RI Upper College & Bills Rd Kingston RI 02881-0820

OPIE, JOHN MART
PAINTER
b Sandusky, Ohio, Dec 10, 1936. *Study:* Kent State Univ, BFA, MA. *Work:* Allentown Art Mus, Pa; Akron Art Inst, Ohio; Fordham Univ, NY; New Orleans Art Mus, La; St Lawrence Univ, NY; Michener Mus Art. *Exhib:* Solo exhibs, New Orleans Art Mus, 68, Galerie Simonne Stern, New Orleans, 69, 70, 72, 75, 80 & 83, Bowery Gallery, NY, 73, 76 & 79 & Allentown Art Mus, Pa, 84; The More Gallery Inc, Philadelphia, 81, 82, 87-89; Award Winning Artists, Witte Mem Mus, San Antonio, Tex; Art Now, Philadelphia Mus Art, 90; East Stoudsburgh Univ, PA, 2003. *Teaching:* Instr painting, Pasadena City Col, Calif, 63-65; assoc prof painting, La State Univ, Baton Rouge, 65-70. *Awards:* Natl Endowent for the Arts, 67, 89; Nat Endowment Arts Award, 67; Best of Show, 21st Ann Juried Exhib, State Mus Pa, 88. *Bibliog:* Leonard Edmondson (auth), Etching, Van Nostrand Reinhold, 73. *Media:* Acrylic and Oil on Panel. *Mailing Add:* 1765 State Rd Quakertown PA 18951-3338

OPPENHEIMER, SARA
INSTALLATION SCULPTOR
b Austin, Tex, 1972. *Study:* Brown Univ, BA, 1995; Yale Univ, MFA, 1999. *Exhib:* Transposed: Analogs of Built Space, Sculpture Ctr, Queens, 2000; Storage and Retrieval, Midway Contemp Art, St Paul, Minn, 2002; solo exhibs, Drawing Ctr, New York, 2002, Queens Mus Art, New York, 2003, Youkobo Art Space, Tokyo, 2004, St Louis Art Mus, 2008, Art Basel, Switz, 2009; Odd Lots, White Columns, New York, 2005; Invitational Exhib, Am Acad Arts & Letts, New York, 2007; Automatic Cities: The Architectural Imaginary in Contemporary Art, Mus Contemp Art, San Diego, 2009. *Bibliog:* Michael Kimmelman (auth), Inspiration from Real Estate Rejects, NY Times, 9/9/2005; Nancy Princenthal (auth), Sarah Oppenheimer at P.P.O.W., Art in Am, 11/2006; Meredith Hull (auth), New Installations at Annely Juda Fine Art, The Architects' J, 9/2009

ORBEGOSO, ANA DE
PHOTOGRAPHER
b Peru. *Study:* Fine Art Decorating, Art Restoration, New York, 1986-88; Art Students' League, New York, Drawing & Painting, 1986; NY Univ, Cinematography, 1987-88; Pratt Inst, New York, Photog, 1989; Int Ctr Photog, New York, 1991-93. *Exhib:* Solo exhibs include Galerìa 715, Lima, Peru, 1989, Artists in Residence Gallery, New York, 1993, Tallerìa Cult Space, Mèxico, 1996; group exhibs include Peruvian Colloquy Photog, Peru, 1989; 3 Documents, Dècadas de Photog, Perù, 1997; Cult Ctr Britànico, Lima, Peru, 2000; SalÓn of Lima, Rìmac House, Lima, Peru, 2000; Amnistìa the Int, Inst Cult Peruano N Am, Lima, Peru, 2000; It files, Galerìa Obsidian, Peru, 2001. *Awards:* New York Found Arts Fel, 2008. *Mailing Add:* En Foco Inc 1738 Hone Ave Bronx NY 10461

ORDUNO, ROBERT DANIEL
PAINTER, SCULPTOR
b Ventura, Calif, Sept 5, 1933. *Study:* Los Angeles Art Ctr, 60. *Work:* Charlie Russell Mus, Buffalo Bill Hist Ctr, Cody, Wyo; Red Cloud Indian Sch, The Heritage Ctr Inc, Pine Ridge, SDak. *Comn:* Lewis & Clark, mural, City of Great Falls, Mont, 83. *Exhib:* Colo Indian Market, Denver, 87; Mont Indian Nations Art Rendezvous, Gov's Residence, Helena, 87; The New West, Buffalo Bill Hist Ctr, Cody, Wyo, 90; Life Death Rebirth, Paris Gibson Sq Mus Art, Great Falls, Mont, 93; and others. *Teaching:* Lectr native Am Indian art, Australian Asn Adult & Community Educ, Coun Adult Educ, Australia, 93. *Awards:* Best in Show, First Place Contemporary Divsion, Buffalo Bill Historical Ctr, 87; 5th Ann Native Am Art exhib, artists choice, best painting, merit award, Great Falls, Mont, 87; Special Merit Award, 7th Ann Native Am Art Exhib, 89; Jurors Choice & Best Show Award, 11th Ann Native Am Art Exhib, 93. *Bibliog:* Featured Artist & Cover Image, InformArt Mag, 7-8/94; Native America calling (interview), KUNM Radio, 1/16/96; Trophies of honor, art chronicles of indigenous peoples, Fineart Online, 8/96. *Mem:* Nat Serv Orgn Native Arts. *Media:* Oil on linen. *Res:* life, liberty, the pursuit of happiness. *Interests:* health and longevity, skiing. *Collection:* John Nieto, Suzanne Wiggin, Toby, Jamie Chase. *Publ:* Southwest Art Mag, 6/90; Shamons Drum. Int Fine Art Collector, 2/92; Inform Art Mag, 7-8/94; cover artist, Indian Gaming Mag, Jan 2000, Apr 2003, 2004, July 2005, Apr 2007, Mar 2009, Mar 2010, Mar 2012. *Dealer:* Brad Smith Gallery Santa Fe NMex. *Mailing Add:* 87 Old San Marcos Trl Santa Fe NM 87508

ORELLANA, FERNANDO
SCULPTOR
Study: Sch Art Inst Chicago, BFA, 1998; Ohio State Univ, MFA, 2004. *Work:* Western Mich Univ; Ohio State Univ. *Exhib:* Solo exhibs, Moberly Area Community Coll, 2002, NOVA Project Space, Chicago, 2005, Tang Teaching Mus, Skidmore Coll, 2007, Shelnutt Gallery, Rensselare Polytechnic Inst, Troy, NY, 2009; Observation, Columbus Mus Art, Ohio, 2004; Babes in Toyland, Ohio State Univ, 2005; High Voltage Fields, Schenectady Mus, NY, 2006 ; Art and Science XXIV: Artbots, Klein Art Gallery, Philadelphia, 2007; Unintended Uses, NEXUS Found, Philadelphia, 2009. *Pos:* Art dir, (ART)N Laboratory, 1998-2002; artist-in-residence, Moberly Area Community Coll, 2001-02; project asst, Ann Hamilton Studio, 2004-05. *Teaching:* Asst prof, Union Coll, 2005-. *Awards:* New York Found Arts Fel, 2009. *Bibliog:* Mark Robarge (auth), Robot Camp combines technology, art, The Gazette, 6/2007; Eleanor Heartney, Mind Matter, Art in Am, 4/2008; Ann Landi (auth), Brain Wave, ARTnews Mag, 6/2009

ORENSTEIN, GLORIA FEMAN
EDUCATOR, HISTORIAN
b New York, NY, Mar 8, 1938. *Study:* Brandeis Univ, BA (romance lang & lit), 59; Radcliffe Col, MA (Slavic lang & lit), 61; NY Univ (Danforth Grad Fel for Women), 66-71, PhD (comp lit), 71. *Pos:* Contrib ed, Womanart, Chrysalis Mag & Feminist Art J; co-founder, The Woman's Salon; dir, cult prog for hon students & fac-in-residence, Pac Apartments, Univ Southern Calif, 81-85; coord & dir, UN End of Decade Conf on

Women, Nairobi, 85; Contr Ed, FemSpec; Coordr Reberon Festivities America, Salute to Women Artists. *Teaching:* Lectr women of surrealism, Cornell Univ, 73, Pa State Univ, 74, Inst 20th Century Studies, Univ Wis, 75, Sheridan Col, 75 & Artists Space, New York, 75; asst prof women in contemp arts, Douglass Col, 74-, asst prof Eng, 75-, chairperson women's studies prog, 76-78; dir, Rutgers Jr Yr in France, 78-79; assoc prof comparative lit & prog for study of women & men in soc, Univ Southern Calif, Los Angeles, 81-82. *Bibliog:* Article in Female Artists: Past & Present, Women's Hist Res Ctr, 74; coordr panel, Women Artists: Preparing for Changing our Future, Centre Cult Am, Paris, 79; articles in: WomanArt, Feminist Art J, Fireweed, Chry Salis, Heresies, The Power of Feminist Art. *Mem:* Mod Lang Asn; Jewish Women Fac Group; Nat Women's Studies Asn; Int Comparative Lit Asn; Int Asn Study Dada & Surrealism; Veteran Feminists of America. *Res:* Surrealism; women's art history; women in the arts; re-emergence of the goddess in contemporary art and literature. *Specialty:* Ecofeminists Art, Shamanism & the Arts, Jewish Women Artists. *Publ:* Auth, A renaissance of goddess-culture art, Fireweed: A Woman's Lit & Cult J, No 1, 78; coauth (with Miriam Brumer), Americans in Paris revisited, Women Artists News, 79; The goddess in art by contemporary women, Women's Resource & Res Ctr, London, Eng, 79; Reclaiming the great mother: A feminist journey to madness and back in search of a goddess heritage, Symposium, spring 82; Towards a bifocal vision in surrealist aesthetics, Trivia, fall 83; A World in words, in: Women Artists of the World, Midmarch Arts, NY, 85; The Theatre of the Marvelous: Surrealism & the Contemporary Stage, NYU Press, 75; The Re-Flowering of the Goddess, Perganon Press, Athene Series, 90; Re-Weaving the Word: The Emergence of Eco-Feminsim, Sierra Club Books, 90. *Mailing Add:* Dept Comp Lit & Sociology Univ Southern Calif Univ Park Los Angeles CA 90089

ORENTLICHER, JOHN
VIDEO ARTIST, SCULPTOR

b Roanoke, Va, June 7, 1943. *Study:* Goddard Col, BA, 68; Art Inst Chicago, MFA, 70. *Work:* Everson Mus, Syracuse, NY; Video Collection, Long Beach Mus, Calif; V-tapes, Toronto, Ont; Montevideo, Amsterdam; London Video Arts, London; Nat Gallery Art, Ottawa. *Exhib:* Outrageous Film, Whitney Mus Am Art, NY, 74; one person exhibs, Art Metropole, Toronto, 82, Ctr Art Tapes, Halifax, NS & Hallwalls (video), Buffalo, NY, 82 Festival AFI, Los Angeles, 88; Dutch Film Mus, Amsterdam, The Neth; Bienal de Video Santiago, Chile, 94; Worldwide Video Festival, Amsterdam, The Neth, 97; Ovni 2000, Barcelona, Spain; De Sendungen Zum, Int Media Competition, 2000; Athens Int Film Video Festival, 2000; and others; Paris/Berlin Recontres. *Pos:* Peace Corps, Chile, 64-66; bd trustees, Synapse Video, Syracuse, NY, 78-81. *Teaching:* Prof video, Col Visual & Performing Arts, Syracuse Univ, 76-81, chmn dept experimental studios, 81-85, chmn art media studies, 83-85 & 87-89; Fulbright lectr video, Bogota, Colombia, 85 & Santiago, Chile; chmn, Art Media Studies, 81-85 & 87-89, chair, 98-2004, chair dept transmedia, 2004-2008. *Awards:* Nat Endowment Arts, 76; Fulbright, 85 & 94; Rockefeller, 88. *Bibliog:* Sherry Chayat (auth), America on video, Syracuse Herald Am, 9/4/88; Vidiesta John Orentlicher El Mecurio, 9/18/93; Kathy High (auth), Felix, vol 2 no 2, 1999; and others. *Mem:* Media Alliance, NY; Am Independent Video Film Univ Asn; Fulbright Asn. *Media:* Video. *Res:* Video documentary. *Specialty:* V-Tape, Toronto. *Dealer:* V-Tape Toronto; The Kitchen New York NY. *Mailing Add:* Dept Transmedia Syracuse Univ 102 Shaffer Syracuse NY 13244

ORLAINETA, EDGAR
SCULPTOR

b Mexico City, 1972. *Study:* La Esmeralda, Escuela Nacional de Pintura, Escultara & Grabado, BFA (Painting), 1998; Pratt Inst, Brooklyn, MFA (Sculpture), 2004. *Work:* Hirshhorn Mus & Sculpture Garden, Washington. *Exhib:* Solo exhibs include Art Deposit, Mex City, 1996, 1999, Galería Arte Mexicano, Mex City, 1999, 2002, 2005, 2007, Cuchifritos Art Gallery, New York, 2003, Stueben East Gallery, Pratt Inst, Brooklyn, 2004, Jet Gallery, Berlin, 2006, Sara Meltzer Gallery, New York, 2007; group exhibs include Instalaciones Para Sitio Especificio, Galería Arte Mexicano, 1999, Promo, 2000, Los Retratos de Dorian Gray, 2005, Under My Skin, 2005, Une Promesse de Malheur, 2005; Peppermint, Curiously Strong, Smack Mellon Studios, Brooklyn, 2001; Centro Nacional de las Artes, Mex City, 2003; Metastasize, Bronx River Art Ctr, Bronx, NY, 2003, Mex Video Extravaganza, 2003; Anónimo, Momenta Art Gallery, Brooklyn, 2003; Plant, Williamsburg Art & Hist Ctr, Brooklyn, NY, 2004; Denial is a River, Sculpture Ctr, Long Island City, NY, 2006; Introductions, Sara Meltzer Gallery, New York, 2007, Ceci n'est pas..., 2007; Currents: Recent Acquisitions, Hirshhorn Mus & Sculpture Garden, Washington, 2007. *Mailing Add:* c/o Sara Meltzer Gallery 73 Worth St Apt 5B New York NY 10013

ORLAND, TED N
PHOTOGRAPHER, WRITER

b San Francisco, Calif. *Study:* Univ Southern Calif, BS (industrial design), 63; San Francisco State Univ, Calif, MA (interdisciplinary arts), 74. *Work:* Corcoran Gallery Art, Washington, DC; San Francisco Mus Mod Art, Calif; Amon Carter Mus, Tex; Boston Mus Fine Art, Mass; Univ Ariz Ctr Creative Photog, Tucson. *Exhib:* New Acquisitions, Corcoran Gallery Art, Washington, DC, 81; Am Photog & Nat Parks, national tour, 81-83; Univ Ore Art Mus, Eugene, 82; Monterey Art Mus, Calif, 86; Nat Mus Mod Art, Kyoto, Japan, 87; Crocker Art Mus, Sacramento, Calif, 90; Fresno Metrop Mus, Fresno, Calif, 93; Ansel Adams Gallery, Yosemite, Calif, 94. *Pos:* Apprentice, Saul Marks, Los Angeles, Calif, 62-63; asst, Charles Eames, Venice, Calif, 68-71; asst, Ansel Adams, Carmel, Calif, 72-75; ed, Image Continuum Press, 74-. *Teaching:* Asst prof & dir undergrad and grad prog, Univ Ore, 81-84; dir, Ansel Adam's Gallery Photog Workshops, 84-86; resident fac, Maine Photog Workshops, 85-90; Roy Acuff Chair of Excellence in the Creative Arts, Austin Peay State Univ, Tenn, 89. *Awards:* Artist-in-residency, Volcanoes Nat Park, Volcano Arts Ctr, Hawaii, 76; Individual Artist's Fel, Ore Arts Comn, 82; Artist-in-residency, Yosemite Nat Park, 2000. *Bibliog:* Joel Pickford (auth), Ansel Adams & Ted Orland: A critical comparison, Image Continuum J, 79; David Robertson (auth), The Art & Literature of Yosemite, Yosemite Nat Hist Asn, 82. *Mem:* Ctr Photog Art, Carmel, Calif. *Media:* Hand-colored Silverbase Prints, Electronic Imaging. *Publ:* Illusr, Yosemite Reflections, Flying Spur Press, 77; auth, T Orland's Compendium of Photographic Truths, Image Continuum Press, 81; Man and Yosemite: A Photographer's View of the Early Years, Image Continuum Press, 85; Scenes of Wonder & Curiosity: The Photographs and Writings of Ted Orland, David R Godine Publ, 88; coauth, Art & Fear: Observations on the Perils (and Rewards) of Artmaking, Capra Pub, 94. *Dealer:* Ansel Adams Gallery PO Box 455 Yosemite CA 95389. *Mailing Add:* 1017 Seabright Ave Santa Cruz CA 95062

ORLYK, HARRY V
PAINTER

b Troy, NY, Jan 8, 1947. *Study:* New York State Univ Col, New Paltz, BS, 70; Univ Nebr, Lincoln, MFA, 74. *Work:* Springfield Mo Art Mus; Albany Inst Hist & Art, NY; Sheldon Art Mus, Lincoln, Nebr. *Exhib:* Candidates for Art Awards, Am Acad & Inst Arts & Lett, NY, 87; Contemp Landscape Photographs & Paintings, Mem Art Gallery, Univ Rochester, 88; Artists of the Mohawk-Hudson Regional Invitational, Ctr Galleries, Albany, NY, 90; Truth & Beauty, Loyola Marymount Univ, Los Angeles, Calif, 92; Under the Influence, Tatistchiff, Santa Monica, Calif, 92; Venable/Neslage Gallery, Washington, DC, 92. *Awards:* L A Sawyer, Mohawk-Hudson Regional, 89; Purchase Award, Albany Inst Hist & art, 89,92. *Bibliog:* Thomas Bolt (auth), Harry Orlyk, Arts Mag, 11/86; Margaret Mathews Berenson (auth), Am Artist, 7/87; Timothy Cahill (auth), Working the Land, Metroland, 12/88. *Dealer:* Tatistcheff 50 W St New York NY 10019. *Mailing Add:* Blind Buck Rd Salem NY 12865

ORNSTEIN, JUDITH
PAINTER

b Newark, NJ, May 4, 1951. *Study:* Wimbledon Sch Art, Eng, 70-71, Philadelphia Coll Art, BFA, 73, Yale Univ, MFA, 75. *Work:* Albright Knox Mus, Buffalo, NY; Cooper Hewitt Mus, NY; Vassar Coll Mus, Poughkeepsie, NY. *Exhib:* One-person shows, Willard Gallery, NY, 77, 79, Cirruss Gallery, Los Angeles, 83, V Levy Fine Arts, NY, 84. *Awards:* Nat Endowment Arts Fel; CAPS award; Tiffany Found grant; Ford Found grant. *Mem:* Yale Alumni Assn. *Collection:* numerous pvt collections. *Mailing Add:* 28 Tiffany Pl Brooklyn NY 11231-2917

ORR, JOSEPH CHARLES
PAINTER

b Tokyo, Japan, Oct 31, 1949; US citizen. *Study:* With Anthony Allison, 71; Univ Mo, Columbia, with Frank Stack, 77-78. *Work:* State Mo Hist Soc, Columbia; Nat Collegiate Athletic Asn, Kansas City, Mo; Osage Co Hist Soc, Linn, Mo; Dunnegan Mus Art, Bolivar, Mo; Fed Reserve Bank, Kansas City, Mo. *Comn:* Paintings, Community Fed Savings, Mexico, Mo, 80 & Mercantile Bank, Eldon, Mo, 81; centennial painting, City Eldon, Mo, 82. *Exhib:* Arts for Parks Top 100, Jackson Hole, Wyo, 90, 93, 94, 2002, 2003 & 2006; Miniatures, Albuquerque Mus, NMex, 94 & 98; Am Art in Miniature, Gilcrease Mus, Tulsa, Okla, 94, 99-2001, 2004 & 2006; Akron Soc Artists, Ohio, 96; Ashby-Hodge Gallery Am Art, Fayette, Mo, 97; Margaret Harwell Art Mus, Poplar Bluff, Mo, 99 & 2006; Birger Sandzén Mem Gallery, Lindsborg, Kans, 2009; and others. *Awards:* First Prize, Nat Wildlife Collectors Soc Ann Exhib, Minneapolis, Minn, 84; Winsor & Newton Award, 14th Salmagundi Club Exhib, NY, 91; Arts for Parks Top 100 Hist Art Award, Jackson, Wyo, 93. *Bibliog:* Rita Mathews-Orr (auth), My husband the artist, Mo Life, 75; Hope Mathews (auth), Rural scenes with an Ozark Flavor, Midwest Art, 10/84; Franz Brown (auth), Joseph Orr, Southwest Art, 4/97; Nancy Gillespie (auth), Wonderful Wanderlust, Art of the West, 2003; Stephen Doherty (auth), Joseph Orr, Workshop Magazine, 2005. *Mem:* Nat Soc Painters Casein & Acrylic; co-founder, Nat Oil & Acrylic Painters' Soc, Osage Beach, Mo. *Media:* Acrylic on Masonite & Canvas, Watercolor. *Publ:* Auth, Painting in acrylic, Am Artist, 3/86; auth, Lighting your way to stronger landscapes, The Artists, 1/96; Acrylic Painting Techniques, 95, Northlight Artists Guide to Materials & Techniques, 96 & Acrylic Painting, Styles and Techniques, 97, North Light Bks. *Dealer:* Morris & Whiteside Galleries, 807 Wm Hilton Pkwy, Hilton Head, SC 29928; American Legacy Gallery, 5911 Main St, Kansas City, MO 64113. *Mailing Add:* 1405 Hwy KK Osage Beach MO 65065

ORR, LEAH
SCULPTOR

b Hammond, Ind, Aug 16, 1937. *Study:* John Herron Sch Art, Indpls/ St Mary of the Woods, Ind, BS (educ), 61; St Mary of the Woods, Ind, BS (art), 69; Ind Univ, Bloomington, MS (art), 72. *Comn:* wirework, Ameritech, Indianapolis, Ind, 88; wirework, Am Red Cross, Indianapolis, Ind, 91; wirework, Kendrick Mem Hosp, Mooresville, Ind, 93; wirework, Health pointe, Jasper, Ind, 96; wirework, Horizon Bank, Mich, Ind, 97. *Exhib:* 68th & 69th Ann Ind Artists Show, Indianapolis, 81 & 83; Bonnie Stahlecker and Leah Orr: The Creative Process, Indianapolis Artsgarden, 2000. *Pos:* asst cur, Indianapolis Mus Art, 73-76. *Teaching:* private lessons throughout Ind, 57-73; summer sch, St Mary of the Woods, 61-63. *Awards:* First Place Sculpture, Am States, 94; Creative Renewal Fel Arts Coun of Indianapolis. *Bibliog:* Pat Pickett (auth), Capture the vision, The Indianapolis Register, 93; Leah Orr (auth), Am states exhib, Fiberaris Mag, 95. *Media:* Wireworks, Miscellaneous Media. *Mailing Add:* 926 Alabama St Indianapolis IN 46202-3319

ORR-CAHALL, ANONA CHRISTINA
MUSEUM DIRECTOR, CURATOR

b Wilkes-Barre, Pa, Jun 12, 1947. *Study:* Mt Holyoke Col, BA; Oxford Univ; Ecole du Louvre; Yale Univ, MA, MPhil, PhD. *Collection Arranged:* Am Drawing 1970-1973, Yale Univ Art Gallery, 1973; Addison Mizner Architect of Dreams and Realities, Norton Gallery Art, 1977; Charles Griffin Farr: A Retrospective, 1984 & Gordon Cook: A Restrospective, 1987, Oakland Mus. *Pos:* Chief cur art, Oakland Mus, formerly; dir art div & chief cur, Oakland Mus, Calif, 1981-88; dir & CEO, Corcoran Gallery Art, Wash, 1988-90; dir, Norton Mus Art, West Palm Beach, Fla, 1990-2010; dir & CEO, Experience Music Project, Science Fiction Mus & Hall Fame, Seattle, 2010. *Teaching:* Asst prof art hist & mus studies, Calif Polytech State Univ, San Luis

Obispo, 1978-81, distinguished pro, 1981. *Res:* California art 1925-present. *Publ:* Auth: Addison Mizner: Architect of Dreams and Realities, 1974, 2d printing, 1993, Gordon Cook, 1987, Claude Monet: Am Impression, 1993; editor: The Art of Calif, 1984, The Am Collection at the Norton Mus of Art, 1995. *Mailing Add:* Norton Mus Art 1451 S Olive Ave West Palm Beach FL 33401

ORRELL, MICHAEL JAMES
GRAPHIC ARTIST
b San Diego, Calif, Nov 26, 1956. *Study:* Platt Coll (graphic design), 84-86. *Pos:* Computer artist, Am Film Technol, San Diego, Calif, 86-88; Layout artist, Wesco Models, San Diego, Calif, 88-90; Account exec, Smoothreads Custom T-Shirts, San Diego, Calif, 90-91; Property maintenance, Co of San Diego, Calif, currently; Webmaster, a popular reserach website about UFOs. *Awards:* Achieved numerous front page features, radio interviews & TV spots; first human to unravel the Nazca Lines in Peru by proving how, why, and who made them; discovered a lost sacred pattern in an UFO photo that linked UFOs to each other as well as ancient artifacts, crop circles, & the Nazca Lines in Peru; Photographic Award, San Diego Competition & Exhibition, 1990. *Bibliog:* Actor in 10 major motion pictures

ORTEGA, TONY (ANTHONY) DAVID
PAINTER, PRINTMAKER
b Santa Fe, NMex, Feb 24, 1958. *Study:* Univ Colo, BA, 80; Rocky Mountain Sch Art, AA, 82; Univ Colo, MFA, 95. *Work:* Denver Art Mus; Museo Estudio Diego Rivera, Mexico City; Los Angeles Co Art Mus; Mus del Barrio, NY; Laguna Art Mus, Calif. *Comn:* Mosaic mural, City & Co of Denver, Colo. *Exhib:* Los Three, Millicent Roger Mus, Taos, NMex, 92; First Sighting: Recent, Modern & Contemp Aquisitions, Denver Art Mus, Colo, 93; Chicano Expression, Musee du Nouveau Monde, La Rochelle, France, 95; Pasion por Frida, Centro Cult Neco Leta, Buenos Aires, 96; The View from Denver, Mus Mod Art, Vienna, Austria, 97; Prints from Self-Help Graphics, Los Angeles Co Mus Art, Calif, 97; Paraiso, Mus Nacional de Bellas Artes, Santiago, Chile, 98; La Guadalupana, Tacoma Art Mus, Wash, 98. *Awards:* Alliance Contemp Art Award, Denver Art Mus, 91; 1998 Artist Fel, Colo Coun Arts, 98; Mayor's Award for Excellence in the Arts, City & Co of Denver, 98. *Bibliog:* Carol Ketchum (auth), Painting in two stages, Artist Mag, 12/86; Carol Dickerson (auth), Tony Ortega, Southwest Art, 7/89. *Media:* Pastel, Acrylic. *Publ:* Illusr, A Migrant Child's Dream, CU Boulder, 93; coauth, Focus, 94; with Donald J Hagerty, Leading the West: 100 contemporary Painters & Sculptors, Northland Publ, 97; illusr, Days of the Dead: Aztec Adventures of Chalo, Vato & Paro, CU Boulder, 98. *Dealer:* William Haku Gallery 1040 Cherokee St Denver CO 80204. *Mailing Add:* 3650 Eliot Denver CO 80211

ORTH, MAGGIE
ARTIST
b Columbus, Ohio, 1964. *Study:* Rhode Island Sch Design, BFA, 1986; Mass Inst Tech, Ctr Advan Visual Studies, Cambridge, Mass, MS(Visual Studies), 1993, PhD(Media Arts & Sciences), 2001. *Comn:* Ontario Science Ctr, Canada, 2006. *Exhib:* exhibs include Musical Jacket, Science Mus, United Kingdom, 1999; Embroidered Musical Instruments, Mus Science, Boston, 2001; Dynamic Double Weave, Space Between, Australia, 2004; Fuzzy Light Wall, Leaping Lines, Cooper-Hewitt Nat Design Mus, New York, 2005; Firefly Dress, Tufts Univ Gallery, Medford, Mass, 2005-08; Almost Square, Tufted Dimmers, San Francisco Mus Craft & Design, 2006; Pom Pom Dimmer, Gallery Artists Studio Proj, Brookline, Mass, 2006; Firefly Dress, Krannert Art Mus, Univ Ill, Urbana-Champaign, Ill, 2006. *Awards:* US Artists Fel, 2007

ORTIZ, GEORGE
COLLECTOR
b 1928. *Awards:* Named one of Top 200 Collectors, ARTnews mag, 2004-09. *Collection:* Antiquities; tribal art; 15th-century Italian art; 18th-century European art. *Mailing Add:* Chougny Fontaine Vandoeuvres CH 1253 Switzerland

ORTIZ, RAPHAEL MONTANEZ
CONCEPTUAL ARTIST, EDUCATOR
b New York, NY, Jan 30, 1934. *Study:* Brooklyn Mus Art Sch; Art Students League; Pratt Inst, BS & MFA; Columbia Univ, EdD, 82. *Work:* Whitney Mus Am Art, Finch Mus, Mus Mod Art, NY & Museo del Barrio, NY; Syracuse Mus Contemp Art, NY,; Ludwig Mus, Cologne, Ger; Mus Mod Art, Brussels, Belg; Friedricheshof Mus, Zurndorf, Austria; and many others. *Exhib:* Traveling Assemblage Exhib, Mus Mod Art, NY, 63; Young Am Exhib, Whitney Mus Am Art, NY, 65; retrospective, sculpture, performance, computer-laser-video, Museo del Barrio, NY, 88; Computer-Laser-Video, Selected Works, Berlin Video & Film Festival, Ger, 91; performance, Rites of Spring, Alternative Mus, Soho, NY, 92; exhib, Artists of Conscience, Alternative Mus, Soho, NY, 92; performance, Ritual and Installation, Kunst, Vienna, Austria, 92; performance, Utilizing Video Conference Syst Between Kôln & Kassel Ger, Documenta, Electronic Cafe, 92; plus numerous solo & group exhibs & performances. *Pos:* Founder, dir & cur, Museo del Barrio, NY, 69-; comt mem, Ghetto Arts Panel, NY State Coun Arts, 70-71; vchmn, Planning Corp Arts, NY, 71; chmn bd, Fondo Del Sol, Washington, DC, 79-81; founder & pres, Mus Computer Art, NJ, 84. *Teaching:* Full prof visual arts, grad & undergrad fac, Mason Gross Sch Arts, Rutgers Univ, 72-. *Awards:* John Hay Whitney Fel Grant, 65; Nat Endowment Arts Grant, 72; NJ Coun Arts, 87. *Bibliog:* Dr Kristine Stiles (auth), Work discussed in Out of Control, ARS Electronea, Duke Univ, 91; Dr Kristine Stiles (auth), Survival ethos and destruction art (discourse), J Theoretical Studies Media & Culture, Duke Univ, spring 92. *Mem:* Coll Art Asn of Am; Mus Computer Art (founder & pres, 84); Hispanic Asn Higher Educ, NJ; Asn Res & Enlightenment. *Media:* Mixed Media, Technology. *Publ:* Auth, Disassemblage, Art & Artists, 66; ed & auth, Ritual theatre, Aspen Mag, 69; auth, Culture and the people, Art in Am, 71; Towards an Authenticating Art, Univ Mich, Dissertation Serv, Ann Arbor, 82. *Mailing Add:* Rutgers Univ Visual Arts Dept PO Box 5062 New Brunswick NJ 08903-5062

ORTIZ, VIRGIL
CERAMIST, DESIGNER
Exhib: Solo exhibs include Heard Mus, New York, 2004, Garth Clark, New York, 2004, Indian Market Show, Ursa Gallery, Santa Fe, 2008; group exhibs include Who Stole the Teepee?, Nat Mus Am Indian, Smithsonian Inst, Washington, 2000. *Awards:* US Artists Target Fel, Crafts & Traditional Arts, 2007. *Dealer:* King Galleries of Scottsdale 7100 Main St #1 Scottsdale AZ 85251. *Mailing Add:* King Galleries of Scottsdale 7100 Main St #1 Scottsdale AZ 85251

ORTLIP, PAUL DANIEL
PAINTER
b Englewood, NJ, May 21, 1926. *Study:* Houghton Acad; Art Students League; with Louis Bouche, 47, Reginald Marsh, 48, Robert Brackman & Edwin Dickinson, 49; Acad Grande Chaumiere, 50; Houghton Coll, Hon DFA, 88. *Work:* US Navy Art Collection, Pentagon, Washington, DC; Air & Space Mus, Smithsonian Inst, Washington, DC; Am Coll Clin Pharmacology, NY Acad of Med, New York; Hist Mural, Visitors Ctr Palisades Interstate Park, Ft Lee, NJ; Bush Presidential Libr Coll Sta, Tex. *Comn:* Mem portrait of JFK, Fairleigh Dickinson Univ Libr, 64; Gemini 5 Astronauts, 65, Vietnam (painting), 67, Apollo 12 Astronauts, 69 & Apollo 17 Astronauts, 72, Off Info, USN; and others. *Exhib:* Salon L'Art Libre Ann, Paris, France, 50; Allied Artists Am Ann, 60-71; Collection of Fine Arts, Smithsonian Inst, Wash, DC; Galerie Vallombreuse, Biarritz, France, 74; La Galerie Mouffe, Paris, 75; James Hunt Barker Galleries, NY, Palm Beach & Nantucket, 83; retrospective, Houghton Col, NY, 01. *Pos:* Off US Navy artist, Off Info, Washington, DC, 63-; art cur, Fairleigh Dickinson Univ, 67-70. *Teaching:* Instr painting, Montclair Acad, NJ, 57-58; artist-in-residence, Fairleigh Dickinson Univ, 57-67; instr painting, Montclair Mus, 58-59 & 76-80. *Awards:* First Prize, US Armed Forces Exhib, Far East, 46; First Prize, Am Artist Prof League, State Exhib, NJ Chap, 60; Outstanding Achievement Award, Oil Painting, USN, 68; Artist of Year Award, Hudson Artists, Jersey City Mus, NJ, 70. *Bibliog:* Marg Dulac (auth), Odyssey of an artist, NJ Mus & Arts, 5/71; Luc Elysee Serraf (auth), Paul Ortlip, Artiste American, La Cote des Arts, cover, Marseil, France; M Stephen Doherty (auth), Paul Ortlip, His Heritage and His Art, Phoenix Publ, 83. *Mem:* Life mem Art Students League NY; Allied Artists Am; Salmagundi Club; Nat Soc Mural Painters; Artists Fel Inc; Portrait Soc Am. *Media:* Mixed. *Interests:* Travel, classical music. *Dealer:* Four Generations Art Gallery 517 SR PO Box 4150 Vineyard Haven MA 02568

ORZE, JOSEPH JOHN
ADMINISTRATOR, SCULPTOR
b Exeter, Pa, Dec 11, 1932. *Study:* Syracuse Univ, BFA (magna cum laude), 55, MS, 56; George Peabody Col, EdD, 70. *Work:* Munson, Williams, Proctor Inst, Utica, NY; Sch Benedictine Fathers, Rome, Italy; Mass Maritime Acad, Buzzards Bay. *Exhib:* Solo & Two-person exhibs, J B Speed Art Mus, Louisville, Ky, 65, Dana Arts Ctr, Colgate Univ, Hamilton, NY, 69; Brooks Mem Gallery, Memphis; Hunter Gallery, Univ Chattanooga; Syracuse Univ, NY; Conn Acad Fine Arts, Wadsworth Atheneum, Hartford; Everson Mus Fine Art, Syracuse; and others. *Pos:* Vpres & dir, Southern Asn Sculptors, 64-66; chmn, Conn Col Coun Arts, 67-69; vpres & dir, Marion Art Ctr, Mass, 73-75; dir & treas, Pub Art Proj, Inc, New Bedford, Mass, 74-. *Teaching:* Instr art & educ, Syracuse Univ, 56-59; assoc prof sculpture & art educ, State Univ NY Col New Paltz, 59-61; assoc prof art & head dept, Middle Tenn State Univ, 61-66; prof art & chmn dept, Southern Conn State Col, 66-69; dean, Col Fine & Applied Arts, Southeastern Mass Univ, 69-75; pres, Worcester State Col, 75-, Northwestern La State Univ, currently. *Awards:* Purchase Award for Sculpture, Munson, Williams, Proctor Inst, 58; R A Rathbone Best in Show Award, New Haven Print & Clay Club, 66; First Prize in Sculpture, New Eng Arts Festival, Waterbury, Conn, 67 & 68. *Mem:* Coll Art Asn; Nat Art Educ Asn. *Publ:* Auth, Understanding children's art, Instr Mag, 5/64; Enigma of modern art, Peabody Reflector, 5/66; Role of the Fine Arts in the University, Middle Tenn State Univ, 69; Visual arts in higher education, Mass Art Educ Asn, 70; co-auth, Art From Scrap, Davis, 2nd ed, 73. *Mailing Add:* 921 Cypress Way Boca Raton FL 33486

OSBORN, KEVIN RUSSELL
BOOK ARTIST, PRINTMAKER
b Boston, Mass, July 3, 1951. *Study:* Ecole Nat Arts Decoratifs, Nice, France, 71-72; Univ Vt, Burlington, BA (cum laude), 73; Visual Studies Workshop, State Univ NY, Buffalo, MFA, 77. *Work:* Mus Mod Art, NY; Mus Nat Art Mod, Paris; Whitney Mus; Art Inst Chicago; DeYoung Mus, San Francisco. *Comn:* Parallel (artist book), Ga State Arts Coun, Atlanta, 80. *Exhib:* Words and Images, Philadelphia Art Alliance, 80; solo exhib, Washington Proj Arts, 80; Ex Libris, Traction Gallery, Los Angeles, 81; Re/pages, New Eng Found Arts Touring Exhib, 81-82; Cent Livres d'Ailleurs, Ed Jean-Michel Pl, Paris, 82; 12th Biennale Paris, Mus Mod Art, Paris, 82. *Pos:* Dir, Bookworks Prog, Writer's Ctr, Bethesda, Md, 77-. *Teaching:* Instr workshops, Calif Col Arts & Crafts, 80, Va Commonwealth Univ, 83 & State Univ NY, Purchase, 83. *Awards:* Grant Vector Rev (artist book), Found Todays Art, 83; Va Mus Fel, 83; Nat Endowment Arts Fel, 84. *Bibliog:* Clive Phillpot (auth), Real lush, Artforum, 5/82; Paul Zelevansky (auth), Visual literature, Am Book Rev, spring 83; Nancy Solomon (auth), The layered look, Afterimage, summer 83. *Media:* Artists Books; Experimental Offset. *Mailing Add:* 3411 15th St N Arlington VA 22201-4911

OSBORNE, CYNTHIA A
PRINTMAKER, EDUCATOR
b New Milford, Conn, Dec 13, 1947. *Study:* Conn Col, New London, BA, 69; Univ Wis-Madison, MFA, 73. *Work:* Bradley Univ, Peoria, Ill; Davidson Col, NC; Security Pac Nat Banks, Calif; State Univ NY Buffalo; US Info Agency, Selected US Embassies. *Exhib:* Miami Graphics Biennial, Metrop Mus, Fla, 76 & 80; Current Directions in Southern Calif Art, Los Angeles Inst Contemp Art, 77 & 78; Nat Print Exhib, Soc Am Graphic Artists, NY, 77 & 79; Drawings & Prints, Space, Los Angeles, 79; Paper in Particular, Columbia Col, Mo, 80; and many others. *Pos:* Vis artist, Nat Print Symp, Cranbrook Acad Art, Detroit, spring 80. *Teaching:* Assoc prof

printmaking, Calif State Univ, Long Beach, 75-82, assoc prof art, currently; lectr printmaking, Otis Art Inst, Los Angeles, 77. *Awards:* Purchase Awards, Griffin Press Co, Oakland, Calif, 75 & Los Angeles Printmakers Nat Exhib, Graphic Chemical, Chicago, 77. *Mem:* Los Angeles Printmaking Soc (bd mem, 77); Soc Am Graphic Artists; World Print Coun, San Francisco. *Media:* Printmaking; Lithography. *Mailing Add:* Dept Art Calif State & Long Beach 1250 Bellflower Long Beach CA 90840

OSBORNE, FREDERICK S
EDUCATOR, ADMINISTRATOR
b Philadelphia, Pa, Sept 10, 1940. *Study:* Tyler Sch Fine Arts, Temple Univ, BFA, 63; Yale Univ, MFA, 65. *Exhib:* Woodmere Gallery, 59, 60 & 63; Makler Gallery, 61-62; Haverford Col, 62; Pa Acad Fine Arts, 62; Smith Col, 66; Temple Univ, 76; Girard Bank, 84. *Pos:* Dir continuing educ, Philadelphia Col Art, 77-85; co-founder, co-dir & trustee, Vt Studio Ctr, Johnson, 83-89; dean & dir, Pa Acad Fine Arts, Philadelphia, 85-; consult, Inst Int Educ, New York, 84; Jury, Korean War Vet Mem, Washington, DC, 89; vpres external & alumni affair, dir edn program Violette de Magia Trust, 99-. *Teaching:* Univ of the Arts, Philadelphia, 76-85 & Pa Acad Fine Arts, Philadelphia, 91-; From instr sculpture to asst prof, Grad Sch Fine Arts, Univ Pa, 66-77; lectr, Smith Col, 66 & Univ Maine, 80; lectr, Violette de Magia Trust, Barnes Found. *Mem:* Nat Asn Schs Art & Design (bd dir, 89-96); Asn Independent Cols Art & Design (trustee, 91-95); Coll Art Asn; Am Coun Arts. *Publ:* Auth, The Classical Education of an Artist: Another View from a Contemporary Window, Art J/Coll Art Asn, 94. *Mailing Add:* Pa Acad Fine Arts 118 N Broad St Philadelphia PA 19102

OSBORNE, JOHN PHILLIP
PAINTER, INSTRUCTOR
b Paterson, NJ, July 9, 1951. *Study:* Pratt Inst, cum laude BFA (art educ & environ design), 73. *Work:* NY Life; Union Labor Life, Washington, DC; Metrop Life & Int Telephone & Telegraph Hq, NY; First Common Wealth Saving Bank, Washington, DC. *Comn:* 4 Landscapes of each season, comn by pvt collector, Kinnelon, NJ, 85-86; Portrait, comn by pvt collector, Saddle River, NJ 92. *Exhib:* solo exhibs, Union League Club, NY, 97, John Pence Gallery, San Francisco, 2003, Coleman Fine Art, Charleston, SC, 2004; Group exhibs, Invitational Exhib, US Embassy, Moscow, 91-93, Harare, Zimbabwe, 92-94, Jarkarta, Indonesia, 93-95, Columbia, South Am, 94-96 & Reykjavik, Iceland, 99-2000; Invitational Exhib, pvt gallery, Taiwan, 92; Bergen Mus Art & Sci, NJ, 96; Invitational Exhib, Nat Arts Club, NY, 88; Nat Park Acad Arts, USA Tour, 98; The Legacy of Frank Vincent Du Mond, Belmont Univ, Nashville, Tenn, 2002; Eleanor Ettinger Gallery 97-2007. *Pos:* Illustr, Rudolph, Russell & Fluery Assoc, New York, 72; art restorer & conserv of oil paintings, Frank Moratz, Wyckoff, NJ, 79-84; gallery partner, Albert, Schlenz & Osborne Studio-Gallery, Midland Park, NJ, 81; pres & owner, Artists on Location-J P Osborne, Inc, Ringwood, NJ, 85-. *Teaching:* Dir oil painting, Artists on Location-J P Osborne Inc, Ringwood, NJ, 85-; sr instr oil painting, Ridgewood Art Inst, NJ, 86-; instr, Plein-air workshop, Nantucket, Mass, 89-2012; instr oil painting, Hilton Head Art League, SC, 94. *Awards:* Gold Medal Honor, Hudson Valley Art Asn, 86; Nat Achievement Award, Teacher Oil Painting, Am Artist Mag, 92; Inaugural Inductee, Masterdon Artists Soc, Bergen Mus Art & Sci, 97. *Bibliog:* Art on tour, NJ Monthly, 92; Review of one man show at Mongerson-Wunderlich, ARTnews, 94. *Mem:* Ridgewood Art Inst (trustee, 87-); Am Artists Prof League; Allied Artists Am; Hudson Valley Art Asn (trustee, 93-99); Knickerbocker Artists, NY; Kent Art Asn (life mem). *Media:* Oil. *Interests:* Classical music & gardening. *Publ:* Auth, Romancing the Light, Am Artist, 91; Critical Initial Lay-In, Palette Talk, Grumbacher, 91; The Joy of Painting Large, Am Artist, 95; American Artist Summer Workshop, 2006; Cover & feature article, Highlights, Am Artist, 2009. *Dealer:* The John Pence Gallery 750 Post St San Francisco CA 94109; The Gallery at Four India St Nantucket MA 02554; JM Stringer Gallery of Fine Art 21 Claremont Rd Bernardsville, NJ 07924; The Admiralty Gallery 3315 Ocean Dr Vero Beach FL 32963; Cooley Gallery Inc 25 Lyme St Old Lyme Ct 06371. *Mailing Add:* 325 Lakeview Ave Ringwood NJ 07456

OSBY, LARISSA GEISS
PAINTER
b Artemowsk, Russia, June 7, 1928; US citizen. *Study:* Lyceum & Univ Goettingen, Ger; Univ Munich; Acad Fine Arts, Munich, Ger. *Work:* Carnegie Inst, Pittsburgh; Alcoa Collection; US Steel Collection; Westinghouse Elec Co Collection; plus others. *Comn:* Am for Democratic Action, 69; Koppers Co & First Fed Savings & Loan Asn, Pittsburgh, 72; United Steelworkers of Am, 73; Nat Steel Corp, 77. *Exhib:* Mid-Yr Nat, Butler Inst Am Art, Youngstown, Ohio, 58, 59 & 79; Guest of Hon Exhib, Birmingham Arts Festival, Mich, 61; Drawings USA, St Paul Art Ctr, Minn, 63; Chautaugua Art Ctr Ann, NY, 64; Walker Art Ctr Biennial, Minneapolis, 66; Solo exhibs, Carnegie Inst Mus Art, 72 & Pa State Unit, New Kensington, 73; Am Artists in France, Palais des Congres, Paris, 75-76; Solo exhib, Pittsburgh Ctr Arts, 83-; Dunfermline, Scotland, 84; Women in Art, Youngstown, Ohio, 95-96; Art in SW Pennsylvania, Westmoreland Co Mus Art, Greensburg, Pa, 96. *Teaching:* Instr art, Pittsburgh High Sch Creative & Performing Arts & Pittsburgh Ctr Arts. *Awards:* Jury Award of Distinction, Mainstreams Int, 68 & Assoc Artists Pittsburgh Ann, 58-59, 60-61 & 69; Pittsburgh Artist of the Year, 83; and others. *Mem:* Asn Artists Pittsburgh. *Media:* Oil, Collage. *Mailing Add:* 2665 Hunters Point Dr Wexford PA 15090

OSHIRO, KAZ
INSTALLATION SCULPTOR
b Okinawa, Japan, 1967. *Study:* Calif State Univ, Los Angeles, BA, 1998, MFA, 2002. *Exhib:* Solo exhibs include Luckman Gallery, Calif State Univ, 2002, Rosamund Felson Gallery, Santa Barbara, Calif, 2002, 2004, 2006, Steven Wolf Gallery, San Francisco, 2006, Las Vegas Art Mus, 2007, Yvon Lambert, New York, 2007; Group exhibs include A Proper Aesthetics of the War, Gallery Zero One, Los Angeles, 2001; I'm In This Show, Fifty Bucks Gallery, Los Angeles, 2001; LA, CA, Newspace, Los Angeles, 2001; Raw Soup, Gallery 207, Los Angeles, 2001; 2003 Summer Prog, Apex Art, New York, 2003; Rock, Mark Moore Gallery, Los Angeles, 2004; Giggles, Angstrom Gallery, Dallas, 2004; Things: New Sculpture From Los Angeles, UCLA Hammer Mus, Los Angeles, 2005; One Way Or Another: Asian Am Art Now, Asia Soc & Mus, New York, 2006; Beneath the Underdog, Gagosian Gallery, New York, 2007; Sculptors' Drawings: Ideas, Studies, Sketches, Proposals, & More, Angles Gallery, Santa Monica, 2007; Humour Us, Los Angeles Munic Art Gallery, Los Angeles, 2007. *Awards:* Louis Comfort Tiffany Found Grants, 2008. *Dealer:* Rosamund Felsen Gallery Bergamot Sta B4 2525 Michigan Ave Santa Barbara CA 90404

OSHITA, KAZUMA
SCULPTOR
b Hiroshima, Japan, Oct 17, 1949. *Study:* Nat Tokyo Univ Arts Grad Sch, 74. *Work:* Am Express Co, NY; J B Speed Mus, Louisville, Ky. *Comn:* Forbes Mag, NY, 88; Hiroshima Univ Libr, Japan, 93; Biwako Hotel, Kyoto, Japan, 98; IS 125, NY. *Exhib:* Solo exhibs, Kanuma Gallery, Tokyo, 76, Alexander F Milliken Inc, NY, 83, 87 & 90, Hokin Kaufman Gallery, Chicago, 89 & 92, Hiro Chikashige Gallery, Okayama, 92, Suzukawa Gallery, Hiroshima, 92 7 96, Ryoko Art Corp, Kyoto, 92 & Yamamoto-Tarpin Gallery, Kyoto, 93, Arden Gallery, Boston, 94, Suzukawa Gallery, Hiroshima, Japan, 96, Humanite Gallery, Nagoya, Japan, 97; Arden Gallery, Boston, 88, 93-95; Fall Exhibition-Gallery Artists, Alexander F Milliken Inc, 88; On Paper, Hokin Kaufman Gallery, Chicago, 90; Metal Work and Sculpture, Gallery Art, Univ Northern Iowa, Cedar Rapids, 93; Art in Metal, Hamanite Gallery, Nagoya, 97; Int Art Fair NiCAF, Toyko, 97; two-person show, Ryoko Art Corp, 97; New Works by Contemp Artists and Selections from Our Archives, Gerald Peters Gallery, Santa Fe, 98; Pub collections: Am Express, New York City, Forbes Mag, New York City, The Speed Mus, Louisville, Hiroshima (Japan) Univ Libr. *Awards:* Salon de Printemps Prize, Nat Tokyo Univ Arts, 72; Fel, Nat Endowment Arts, 86-87. *Bibliog:* Therise Lichtenstein (auth), article, Arts Mag, 1/84; Lynn Nesmith (auth), The arts-metal fragments of reality, Archit, 11/84; Christiana DePaul (auth), Kazuma Oshita: The Art of Metal Hammering, Metalsmith, Spring 88. *Media:* Hammered Metal. *Dealer:* Arden Gallery 129 Newbury St Boston MA 02116; Gerald Peters Gallery 1011 Paseo De Peralt Santa Fe NM 87501. *Mailing Add:* 511 S Mountain Rd Gardiner NY 12525-5030

O'SICKEY, JOSEPH BENJAMIN
PAINTER, EDUCATOR
b Detroit, Mich, Nov 9, 1918. *Study:* Cleveland Sch Art, with Paul Travis, Henry G Keller, Carl Gaertner, Frank N Wilcox & Hoyt L Sherman, cert. *Work:* Cleveland Mus Art; Cleveland Arts Asn; Canton Art Inst, Ohio; Westmoreland Art Mus; Butler Inst Am Art, Youngstown, Ohio. *Exhib:* Two-person show, Butler Inst Am Art; Pa Acad Fine Art, Philadelphia; solo exhibs, Akron Art Inst, Canton Art Inst, Butler Inst Am Art, Youngstown, Ohio, seven shows, Jacques Seligman Galleries, NY, 64-78, Cleveland Inst Art, 82, Kennedy Galleries, NY, 88, 91 & 94 & Philharmonic Ctr Arts, 90; and others. *Pos:* Art dir & graphic designer, pvt co, 49-64. *Teaching:* Instr art, Ohio State Univ, 46-47 & Akron Art Inst, 49-52; lectr art, Case Western Reserve Univ, 56-64; prof art, Kent State Univ, 64-88, coordr painting & sculpture, 68-73; retired. *Awards:* Cleveland Arts Cash Prize for Outstanding Achievement in the Arts, 74; Medal, Cash Award & Purchase Award, Butler Inst Am Art, Ohio, 74; First Prize Cash Awards, All-Ohio Exhibs, 74 & 77 & Best in Show Cash Prize, 74; Purchase Award, Am Acad and Inst Art and Letters, 11/88. *Media:* Oil, Watercolor. *Mailing Add:* 7308 SR 43 Kent OH 44240

OSTENDARP, CARL
PAINTER
b Amherst, Mass, Nov 15, 1961. *Study:* Boston Univ, BA, 83; Yale Univ, MFA, 96. *Work:* Whitney Mus Am Art; Wadsworth Atheneum; Art Inst, Chicago; Fogg Art Mus, Harvard Univ; Mus Moderne Kunst, Frankfurt, Germ; Mus Contemp Art, Los Angeles; San Francisco Mus Mod Art; Risd Mus Art; Herbert F Johnson Mus Art. *Exhib:* Jay Gorney Mod Art, New York, 93, 95; Altered States-USA Art of 90's, Forum Contemp Art, St Louis, Mo, 95; Pittura-Immedia, Landesmuseum Joanneum, Guaz, Austria, 95; Galerie Rolf Ricke, 95, 98, 2002, Koln, Germany; Transformal, Weiner Secession, Vienna, 96; Elizabeth Dee Gallery, New York, 2001, 2003, 2004, 2007; Carl Ostendarp 189 Drawings, Aldrich Mus Contemp Art, Ridgefield, Conn, 2003; All Tomorrow's Parties, Mus Mod Kunst, Frankfurt, Ger, 2007; Mural: Works on Paper, Peter Ludwig Mus, Koln, Ger, 2007; Pulled Up, Risd Mus Art, Providence, RI, 2009; Fat Cakes/Myopic Void, Herbert F Johnson Mus of Art, Ithaca, NY; Some Noises, Galerie Schmidt Maczollek, Cologne, Ger; solo exhib, Blanks at Elizabeth Dee, NYC, 2014; group exhib, Everything Falls Faster that an Anvil, Pace Gallery, London. *Teaching:* Adj prof painting, NY Univ, 92-96; instr drawing, Sch Visual Arts, NY, 94-95, Tyler Sch Art, Temple Univ, Philadelphia, 97, Rutgers State Univ, NJ, 98; asst vis prof, Cornell Univ, 2000-2012, assoc prof, currently. *Bibliog:* Anthony Ianacci (auth), Ostendarp/Weinstein, Studio Citta-Verona, 96; John Waters & Bruce Hainley (co-auths), Art-A Sex Book, New York, Thames & Hudson, 2003; Udo Kittelmann & Klaus Görner (co-auths), What's New Pussycat? Recent Acquisitions 2002-2005, Museum Modern Kunst, Frankfurt, Ger, 2006; Christine Meye-Stoll (auth), Sammmlung Rolf Ricke, Hatje Cantz, 2008; Carl Ostendarp The Essay, Katy Siegel (auth) Grafische Sammlung Mus Ludwig. *Specialty:* Contemporary art. *Dealer:* Elizabeth Dee Gallery New York NY; Galerie Schmidt Maczollek Koln Ger; Carroll & Sons Boston MA

OSTERBURG, LOTHAR
PRINTMAKER, EDUCATOR
b Braunschweig, Ger, 1961. *Study:* Hochschule fur Bildende Kunste, 1987 & 1990; San Francisco State Univ, 1989. *Work:* Art Inst Chicago; Fine Arts Mus Houston; Jersey City Mus; Libr Congress; NY Pub Libr; Palmer Mus, Pa State Univ. *Exhib:* Solo exhibs, Student Union Gallery, San Francisco State Univ, 1988, Hatley Martin Gallery, San Francisco, 1990, Show N Tell Gallery, San Francisco, 1992, Gallery APJ, Japan, 1993, Takara Gallery, Houston, 1996 & 1998, Asyl Gallery, New York, 1998, Wendy Cooper Gallery, Wis, 1999, Saint Cloud State Univ, Minn, 2000, Haverford Coll, Pa, 2002, Zoller Gallery, Pa State Univ, 2003, Highpoint Ctr for Printmaking, Minn, 2006, Lesley Heller Gallery, NY, 2009, Woodstock Center for Photog, 2010,

Instituto Cultural Peruano North Americano, Lima, Peru, 2010, Moelle Fine Art, Berlin, Germany, 2011; Group exhibs, Line and Form, Hatley Martin Gallery, San Francisco, 1989; Under Surface, Gallery 128, New York, 1994; Get In Here (Again), Traywick Gallery, Berkeley, 1997; Contemporary Photogravure, Kala Art Inst, Berkeley, 2001; New Prints Fall, Int Print Ctr, New York, 2007; Contemporary Prints, Chaupauqua Inst Strohl Art Ctr, NY, 2008; Am Acad Arts & Letts Invitational, New York, 2010. *Pos:* Printer lithography & etching, Studio Druckgrafick, Ger, 1985-87; printer & asst lithographer, De Soto Workshop, San Francisco, 1987-89; master printer, Crown Point Press, San Francisco, 1989-93; artist-in-residence, MacDowell Colony, Peterborough, NH, 1996-97, Liguria Study Ctr Bogliasco Found, 1998, Va Ctr Creative Arts, 1999. *Teaching:* Asst instr lithography, Hochschule fur Bildende Kunste, Ger, 1984-87; vis prof, Lacoste Sch Arts, France, 1999-2000; adj prof printmaking, Columbia Univ, New York, 2000-2002, Cooper Union, New York, 2002-, Pratt, Brooklyn, 2006; vis asst prof, Bard Coll, 1998-. *Awards:* NY Found Arts Fel, 2003 & 2009; AEV Found Grant, 2009; Bard Coll Res Grant, 2010; Guggenheim Found Fel, 2010; Art award, Am Acad Arts & Letts, 2010. *Bibliog:* Rochelle Feinstein (auth), Rethinking Genres in Contemporary Photography: Artifacture, Art On Paper, 1-2/1999; Blair Tindall (auth), Old technique, new twist, Contra Costa Times, 2/19/2001; Kelvin Lynch (auth), Visions of Energy and Hope, The Capital Times, 5/9/2002; Maggie Anderson (auth), Reinventing Photography, with Memory, The Daily Iowan, 3/8/2007. *Mailing Add:* 232 3rd St Bldg B #303 Brooklyn NY 11215

OSTERMAN, WILLIAM T
PHOTOGRAPHER, EDUCATOR
Study: Ohio Univ, BFA; Univ Ore, MFA, 1981. *Pos:* Cur photog, Univ Ore Mus Art, formerly; printing asst, Ansel Adams. *Teaching:* Assoc prof photog & chmn Photog Dept, Rochester Inst Technology, 1984-; instr, Ansel Adams Workshop, Yosemite Nat Park. *Awards:* Fulbright Grant, 2010. *Mailing Add:* 55 Lomb Memorial Dr Rochester NY 14623-5603

OSTERMILLER, DAN
SCULPTOR
b Cheyenne, Wyo, 1956. *Comn:* Fuente de Los Osos, Quail Run, Santa Fe, NewM; Fleischer Mus, Scottsdale, Ariz; Trammel Crow, Chicago, Ill; Wyoming State Capital, Cheyenne, Wyo; Brookgreen Gardens, Murrells Inlet, SC; Dupont Corp. *Pos:* pres, National Sculpture Soc, New York, 2005-. *Mem:* Soc Animal Artists; Allied Artists of Am; Fel Nat Sculpture Soc. *Dealer:* Nedra Matteucci Gallery and Medra Matteucci Fine Art Gallery Santa Fe NewM; Claggett-Rey Gallery Vail Colo; Spanierman Gallery New York NY. *Mailing Add:* 100 W First St Loveland CO 80537

OSTIGUY, JEAN-RENE
PAINTER, ART HISTORIAN
b Marieville, PQ, Aug 14, 1925. *Study:* Univ Montreal, BA; Ecole des Beaux-Arts, Montreal; Sch Art & Design, Montreal, dipl. *Work:* Carleton Univ, Ottawa; Ottawa Univ. *Exhib:* Montreal Spring Exhib, 51 & 52. *Collection Arranged:* Leon Bellefleur, 68, Adrien Hebert, 71 & Ozias Leduc, 74, Nat Gallery Can. *Pos:* Cur Can art, Nat Gallery Can, 64-85, res cur, 86; cur, Nat Bank Can, 87-90. *Teaching:* Prof, Ecole des Beaux-Arts, Montreal, 53-55; prof Can art, Ottawa Univ, 66-71; vis prof Can art, Laval Univ, 71-72. *Awards:* Chriss Award, 62. *Mem:* Can Mus Asn (councillor, 63-65); Int Comt Mus. *Res:* Nineteenth and early twentieth century Canadian art. *Publ:* Auth, Un siècle de peinture canadienne (1870-1970), Les Presses de l'Université Laval, 1971; Peinture et Sculpture Quebecoises/Structures et Points Forts 1676-1995. *Mailing Add:* 250 Blvd St-Raymond Apt 4051 Gatineau PQ J9AOB1 Canada

OSTROM, GLADYS SNELL
WRITER, EDUCATOR
b Schenectady, NY, Nov 1, 1935. *Study:* Famous Writers School,Westport, Conn, cert, 70, 79; Beacon Col, Washington, MA, 83; Nat Inst Expressive Therapy, Hon PhD, 92; Summit Univ La, Hon PhD, 94. *Work:* Arts-In-Education Showcase, Albany/Schenectady League of Art, Glenville, NY; Ecosynthesis, Yale Univ Conf Ctr. *Comn:* Irene Balas: Portrait Painter, Nat Asn Creative Child & Adult, Toronto, 77; Imagery and Intuition, Am Imagery Asn, NY, 81; Imagery and Magic Island, Am Asn Art Therapy, Cambridge, Mass, 82; Ecosynthesis, Am Imagery Inst, Toronto, Can, 87; Ecosynthesis, Nat Asn Creative Child & Adult, Terrytown, NY, 87. *Exhib:* Creative Artistic Training, Univ Utah, Salt Lake City, 89; Creative Artistic Training, Fort Mason Conf Ctr, Fort Mason, Calif, 91. *Pos:* Vpres, Zonta Club Schenectady, 83-. *Teaching:* Fac, Creative Artistic Training, Nat Inst Expressive Therapy, 92-; provost, Summit Univ La, 94-; part-time fac, Empire State Col, State Univ NY, 94-, Argosy Univ, Salt Lake City, 2013. *Awards:* Key Award, Am Biog Inst, 95; Order Int Ambassador, 20th Century Award for Achievement, Int Biog Ctr, 96. *Mem:* Nat Asn Creative Children & Adults (exec secy & vpres, 74-); Nat Sch Art & Design; Am Inst Graphic Artists; Int Platform Asn. *Res:* Self-realization training for artists & writers using imagery, music & realization. *Interests:* writing, art, music, real estate. *Publ:* Auth, Ecosynthesis: Creative parenting, Mensa 28 Res J, 90; Creative Artistic Training, Vantage Press, 95; ed, Marcel Vogel Workbook, CATCO Publ, 96; auth, Leggys in Letter-Land, 97; Leggys in Number-Land, Open Door Publishers, Malta, NY, 2011. *Mailing Add:* c/o Creative Artistic Training 2887 Shaw Rd Middle Grove NY 12850

OSTROW, SAUL
CRITIC, EDUCATOR
Study: Sch Visual Arts, BFA; Univ Mass, MFA. *Pos:* Dir, Ctr for Visual Art & Cult, Univ Conn, Storrs; ed, Critical Voices in Art, Theory and Cult; art ed, Bomb Mag; co-ed, Lusitania Press, 1996-2004. *Teaching:* Dean, Dept Visual Arts & Technol, Cleveland Inst Art, 2003-, assoc prof painting, currently; former instr, Pratt Inst, Syracuse Univ, Sch Visual Arts

OSTROW, STEPHEN EDWARD
ADMINISTRATOR, CURATOR
b New York, NY, May 7, 1932. *Study:* Oberlin Col, BA, 54; NY Univ Inst Fine Arts, MA, 59, PhD, 66. *Collection Arranged:* Baroque Painting: Italy and Her Influence (with catalog), 68; Visions and Revisions (with catalog), 68; Raid the Icebox I, with Andy Warhol, (with catalog), 69-70. *Pos:* Cur collections, Herron Mus Art, 66-67; chief cur, Mus Art, RI Sch Design, 67-71, dir, 71-78; dean Sch Fine Arts, Univ Southern Calif, 78-, dir mus studies prog, 79-82; exec dir, Portland Art Asn, 82-84; chief, Prints & Photog div, Libr Congress, 84-97; guest cur, Nat Gallery Art, Washington, DC, 99-2007. *Teaching:* asst prof art hist, Univ Mo-Columbia, 62-66; vis lectr art hist, Brown Univ, 70, 71, 74, 76 & 77; prof art hist, Univ Southern Calif, 78-82. *Awards:* Stephen E Ostrow Distinguished Visitor Prog, Reed Col, Portland, endowed by Sue Cooley and Betty Gray, 96. *Mem:* Print Coun Am (exec bd, 86-89). *Publ:* Auth, Annibale Carracci and the Jason frescoes: Toward an internal chronology, Art Bull, 64; Diana or Bacchus in the Palazzo Riario, Marsyas, 65; A drawing by Annibale Carracci for the Jason frescoes and the S Gregorio baptism, Master Drawings, 70; prefaces and introductions, In: The Selection Series & Classical Collection (10 catalogs), Mus Art RI Sch Design, 72-77; Digitizing Historical Pictorial Collections for the Internet, CLIR, 98

O'SULLIVAN, DANIEL JOSEPH
PAINTER
b Brooklyn, NY, Aug 18, 1940. *Study:* Fordham Col; Brooklyn Mus Art Sch; Pratt Graphics Ctr. *Work:* Commerce Trust Co, Kansas City, Mo; Wichita Art Mus; Mus of Albuquerque, NMex; also in pvt collections of Hirshhorn, Neuberger & West; Tobin Collection, San Antonio, Tex. *Comn:* Portraits, Brooklyn Bar Asn & Pace Univ, Adelphi Univ & Cox Enterprises. *Exhib:* US Dept State Art in Embassies Prog, Korea, 75; Am Acad Arts & Lett, NY, 75 & 76; solo exhibs, Kraushaar Galleries, NY, 75 & 79, 82 & 86; Food, Bronx Mus Art, NY, 87; Narrative Art, Fla Int Univ, Miami, 88; Newspapers, Amherst Coll Mus, 88, Art & Law, 90, David Adamson, Washington, 93; Hampton Sq Gallery, W Hampton Beach, NY, 94; Krasdale Galleries, White Plains, NY, 95; Heckscher Mus, Huntington, NY, 97. *Awards:* Purchase Award, Am Acad Arts & Lett, New York, 76; Art & Law Purchase Award, West Publ Co, 90. *Media:* Oil, Acrylic. *Mailing Add:* c/o Kraushaar Galleries 15 E 71st St #2b New York NY 10021

O'SULLIVAN, JUDITH ROBERTA
MUSEUM DIRECTOR, PAINTER, WRITER
b Pittsburgh, Pa, Jan 6, 1942. *Study:* Carlow Coll, BA, 63; Univ Md, MA, 67, PhD, 76, Georgetown Univ, JD, 96. *Pos:* Ed, Am Film Inst, 74-77; assoc prog coordr, Smithsonian Assocs, 77-78, dir develop Nat Arch, 78-79; exec dir, Md State Humanities Coun, 79-84 & Ctr for Bk in Libr of Cong, 81-82; deputy asst dir, Smithsonian Inst, Nat Mus Am Art, 84-89; pres & Chief Exec Officer, Mus Stony Brook, NY, 89-92; Trial attorney, US Dept Justice, 96-. *Teaching:* Smithsonian Assocs For Studies, Trinity Coll & Univ Md. *Mem:* Am Asn Mus; Mid Atlantic Mus Conf; Smithsonian Women's Coun (chair, 88-89); Asn Art Mus Dirs; Mystery Writers of America's Sisters in Crime. *Media:* Landscape Painting. *Interests:* southwestern landscape painting. *Publ:* Auth, The Art of the Comic Strip, 71 & Workers and Allies, 75, Smithsonian; ed, Am Film Inst Catalog, R R Bowker, 76; coauth, The Complete Prints of Leonard Baskin, 84 & auth, The Great American Comic Strip, 90, Little Brown; Suicide in Sea Isle City, 2006, Death and the Jersey Devil, 2007, A Drop of Deadly Ink, Deadly Ink Press, 2008; Death & the Jersey Devil, 2009; Destination: Hell, 2010; A Connecticut Cowboy at King Arthur's Clambake, 2011

OTANI, JUNE
ILLUSTRATOR, PRINTMAKER
b Santa Paula, Calif, July 7, 1934. *Study:* Pasadena City Col, Calif, AA, 54; Art Ctr Coll Des, BFA, 56; Pratt Graphic Ctr, 76-85. *Exhib:* Solo exhib, Palisades Gallery of Hudson River Mus, Yonkers, NY, 87. *Awards:* Printmaking Award, Gallery at Hastings-on-Hudson, 78; Mamaroneck Artist Guild Award, ann show, 80; Dr & Mrs I C Gaynor Award, Nat Asn Women Artists, ann show, 87. *Mem:* Nat Asn Women Artists; Silvermine Guild. *Media:* Etching, Oils. *Publ:* Illusr, The Poodle Who Barked at the Wind, 87, Ten Potatoes in a Pot, 90 & Oh Snow, 91, HarperCollins; Peach Boy, Bantam, 92; If You Lived in Colonial Times, Scholastic, 92

OTERO-PAILOS, JORGE
ARCHITECT, HISTORIAN
Study: Cornell Univ, BArch, 1994, MArch, 1995; MIT, PhD, 2002. *Exhib:* 53rd Int Venice Biennial, Venice, Italy, 2009. *Pos:* Founder & ed, Future Anterior J. *Teaching:* Asst prof archit, New Sch Archit, Polytechnic Univ Puerto Rico, formerly; Asst prof, Grad Sch Archit, Planning & Preservation, Columbia Univ, currently. *Awards:* Opler Fel, Soc Archit Historians, 2007; Practice of Conservation Grant, Samuel H Kress Foudn, 2008; Individual Grant, Graham Found for Advanced Studies in the Fine Arts, 2009. *Mem:* DoCoMoMo US (vpres). *Publ:* Auth, Architecture's Historical Turn: Phenomenology and the Rise of the Postmodern, Univ Minn Press, 2010; contribr, Artforum, Archit Record, AA Files, J of the Soc Archit Historians, J of Archit Educ, Postmodern Cult, Byggekunst, Il Progetto, Il Giornale Dell'Architettura, Archivos de Arquitectura Antillana. *Mailing Add:* Columbia University Graduate School of Architecture 1172 Amsterdam Ave New York NY 10027

O'TOOLE, JUDITH HANSEN
MUSEUM DIRECTOR, WRITER
b Minneapolis, Minn, Sept 24, 1953. *Study:* Univ Minn, BA (art hist), 75; Pa State Univ, MA (art hist), 80; Mus Mgt Inst, Boulder, Colo, 89. *Collection Arranged:* Pennsylvania Prints (auth, catalog), Mus Art, Pa State Univ, 80; Carl Sprinchorn: Realist Impulse & Romantic Vision (auth, catalog), Sordoni Art Gallery, Wilkes Col, 83; George Luks: An Am Artist (auth, catalog), Sordoni Art Gallery, Wilkes Col, 87; Valley of Work: Scenes of Industry in Western Pennsylvania, Westmoreland Mus Am Art, 93; George Luks-Expressionist Master of Color: Watercolors Rediscovered (auth,

catalog), Canton Mus Art, 95. *Pos:* Dir, Sordoni Art Gallery, Wilkes Univ, 82-93; dir & chief exec officer, Westmoreland Mus Am Art, 93-. *Teaching:* Assoc prof, Art Dept, Wilkes Univ, 90. *Mem:* Am Asn Mus; Asn Coll & Univ Art Mus; Asn Historians Am Art; Coll Art Asn; Middle Atlantic Asn Mus. *Publ:* Auth, Severin Roesen (catalog), Bucknell Univ Press/Assoc Univ Presses, 92; contribr, Essay George Luks (catalog), Mus Fine Art, St Petersburg, Fla, 94; George Luks-expressionist master of color: the watercolor rediscovered, Canton Mus Art, 95; A collaboration in limbo, In:Institutional Trauma, Am Asn Mus, spring 95; Valley of work: scenes of industry in western Pennsylvania, Am Art Rev, 3/96. *Mailing Add:* Westmorel Mus Art 221 N Main St Greensburg PA 15601

OTT, WENDELL LORENZ
MUSEUM DIRECTOR, PAINTER

b McCloud, Calif, Sept 17, 1942. *Study:* San Francisco Art Inst, 60-61; Trinity Univ, San Antonio, Tex, BA, 68; Univ Ariz, Tucson, MFA, 70. *Work:* Witte Mem Mus, San Antonio, Tex. *Exhib:* Tex Painting & Sculpture, Dallas Mus Fine Arts, 66; 11th Ariz Ann, Phoenix Art Mus, 69; Yuma Fine Arts Asn, Ariz, 69; Juarez Mus Art, Mex, 73; Solo exhibs, George Walter Vincent Smith Art Mus, Springfield, Mass, 73 & Eastern NMex Univ, Portales, 74. *Pos:* Dir, Roswell Mus & Art Ctr, NMex, 70-86; dir, Tacoma Art Mus, Wash, 87-92; pres, Wash Art Consortium, 89-90; pres, Mus Southwest, 92-94; pres, Tyler Mus Art, 95-. *Teaching:* Instr painting, NMex Mil Inst, Roswell, 74-80. *Awards:* Onerdonk Award, Witte Mem Mus Ann, 68; Purchase Award, 11th Ariz Ann, Phoenix Art Mus, 69; Nat Mus Act Travel Grant, 73. *Mem:* Am Asn Mus; NMex Asn Mus (chmn, 73-75). *Media:* Oil. *Mailing Add:* Tyler Mus of Art 1300 S Mahon Tyler TX 75701

OTTERNESS, TOM
SCULPTOR

b Wichita, Kans, June 21, 1952. *Study:* Art Students League, New York, 70; Independent Study Prog, Whitney Mus Am Art, 77. *Work:* Brooklyn Mus; Whitney Mus Am Art, Mus Mod Art & Solomon R Guggenheim Mus, NY; Israel Mus, Jerusalem. *Comn:* The Real World, Battery Park City Authority, NY, 92; Die Uberfrau, Munster State Libr, Ger, 93; Eli Broad Family Found, Santa Monica, Calif, 95; Dreamers Awake, Wichita Art Mus, Kans, 95; The Music Lesson, Music Bldg, Univ NC, Greensboro, NC Arts Coun, 99. *Exhib:* New Art at the Tate Gallery, London, 83; An Int Survey of Recent Painting & Sculpture, Mus Mod Art, NY, 84; The Human Condition: Biennial III, San Francisco Mus Mod Art, 84; Biennial Exhib, Whitney Mus Am Art, 85; The Classic Tradition in Recent Painting & Sculpture, Aldrich Mus Contemp Art, Conn, 85; Working in Brooklyn, Brooklyn Mus, 85; Spectrum: The Generic Figure, Corcoran Gallery Art, Washington, 86; solo shows, Mus Mod Art, NY, 87, 90, IVAM Centre Julio Gonzalez, Valencia, Spain, 91, Portikus/Senckenbergmuseum, Frankfurt am Main, 91, Haags Gemeentemuseum, The Hague, The Neth, 91, Carnegie Mus Art, Pittsburgh, 93, Wichita Art Mus, Kans, 95 & Galeria Marlboro, Madrid, Spain, 99; Sounding the Depths, 150 Yrs of Am Seascape, Butler Inst Am Art, 89; Allegories of Modernism, Mus Mod Art, NY, 92; The Elusive Object: Selections from the Permanent Collection, Whitney Mus Am Art, 93; Eleventh Biennial Benefit, San Francisco Mus Mod Art, 94; Marlborough Gallery, NY, 95-96; Imaginary Beings, Exit Art, NY, 95-96; The Gun, Icon of the Twentieth Century, Ubu Gallery, NY, 96; A Century of Am Drawing from the Collection, Mus Mod Art, NY, 96; Contemp Sculpture: The Figurative Tradition, Woodson Art Mus, Wasau, Wis, 97; Alternating Currents: Am Art in the Age of Technology, San Jose Mus Art, Calif, 97-98; Pop Surrealism, Aldrich Mus Contemp Art, Ridgefield, Conn, 98; An Exhibition for Children, 242, NY, 98; Free Money and Other Fairy Tales, See No Evil, Marlborough Gallery, NY, 2002; What the Hay, Utica, Mont, 2002; Free Money on Park Avenue, NY, 2003; Bombeater, Skoto Gallery, NY, 2003; Navy Pier Walk 2002, the Chicago Int Sculpture Exhib, Ill, 2002. *Bibliog:* Tony Kushner (auth), Four artists on dreams: Egos and the learning process, NY Times, 5/26/96; Holland Cotter (auth), Sculpture that basks in summer sunlight and air, NY Times, 8/9/96; Jill Kopelman (auth), Tom's treat, Interview, 8/96. *Mem:* Nat Acad. *Mailing Add:* c/o Marlborough Gallery Inc 40 W 57th St New York NY 10019

OTTMANN, KLAUS
CURATOR, CRITIC

b Nuremberg, Ger, 1954. *Study:* Free Univ Berlin, Ger, MA (philos, art hist), 80. *Pos:* Ed, J Contemp Art, 90-; cur, Am Fedn Arts, New York, currently. *Mem:* Am Asn Mus; Int Asn Art Critics. *Res:* Twentieth century art. *Publ:* Auth, Painting in the age of anxiety, Flash Art Mag, 84; The re-invention of painting, Arts Mag, 89; The new spiritual, Arts, 90; L'activite fractale, Art Press, Paris, 90; Heidegger, Bevys & the consequences, Flash Art, 10/90. *Mailing Add:* c/o Ezra & Cecile Zilkha Gallery Center for the Arts Wesleyan Univ Middletown CT 06459-0442

OUTLAND, WENDY HELEN
CONSULTANT, JUROR

b St Petersburg, Fla, Jan 9, 1953. *Study:* Ringling Coll Art & Design, Cert, 79, BFA, 84. *Collection Arranged:* Images of the Everglades, Gov off, Tallahassee & traveling, 86; Maggie Davis, 87, The Ten: Women in Art, 88, Akiko Sugiyama, 89, selected exhibs from Capitol Complex Exhib Prog, Tallahassee; The Three Graces: Janet Mauney, Dawn McMillan & Yvonne Tucker, 90. *Pos:* Cur asst & asst registr, Ringling Mus Art, Sarasota, Fla, 81-85; arts adminstr, Fla Arts Coun, Tallahassee, 85-91; gallery mgr Blue Spiral 1, Asheville, NC, 91-2003; pres, Who Knows Art, cons Visual Artists & Arts Org, 2004-. *Awards:* Fla dept of State Service Award, 89. *Mem:* Am for the Arts; Am Craft Coun. *Interests:* Contemporary art, fine craft & public art. *Publ:* Asst Ed, Ringling MoA Jour, Ringling Mus Art, 82; contribr, Art museums of the world, Greenwood Press, 87; Mus Fine Arts, St Petersburg, Fla, Figures from Life: Porcelain Sculpture from Met Mus Art c 1740-1780, 92; ed, Blue Spiral 1, Rbt Johnson: The Nature Conservancy Series, 99. *Mailing Add:* PO Box 1382 Asheville NC 28802

OUTTERBRIDGE, JOHN WILFRED
SCULPTOR, ADMINISTRATOR

b Greenville, NC, Mar 12, 1933. *Study:* Agr & Tech Univ, Greensboro, NC; Am Art Acad, Chicago, with Vernon Stakey; Otis Coll Art & Design, Calif, hon, DFA, 94. *Work:* Oakland Mus, Mills Col, Oakland, Calif; Calif State Col, San Jose; Compton Community Col, Calif; Watts Health Found, Univ Southern Calif, Los Angeles; Calif African Mus Art, Los Angeles; Co Art Mus, Los Angeles. *Comn:* Mural collages (mixed-media), Communicative Arts Acad, Compton, 70; Ethnic Heritage Doll Ser (five units), Studio Watts Endowment Fund, 77; CHG Architec Bldg, Old Town, Pasadena, 91; The Avalon/Imperial Green Station Plaza, Los Angeles, 94; El Central Cult Onsite Collaboration & Sculpture, Tijuana, Mex, 94; Staples Ctr Grounds, Los Angeles, 98. *Exhib:* Solo exhibs, Outterbridge, Brockman Gallery, Los Angeles, Calif, 71, 82; Watts Tower Art Ctr, Los Angeles, Calif, 88, 96; John Outerbridge: Sculptor of Opposition, Rancho Santiago Coll Art Gallery, Santa Ana, Calif, 92; John Outterbridge: A Retrospective, Calif Afro-American Mus, Los Angeles, Calif, 93; John Outterbridge: Mobilization of the Spirit, El Camino Coll Art Gallery, Torrance, Calif, 97; Tilton Gallery, NY, 2009, 2012; The Rag Factory, Los Angeles, Calif, 2011; Group exhibs, Ten from Los Angeles, Seattle Art Mus, Wash, 66; Black Artists Exhib, Inglewood Public Libr, Calif, 68; Dimensions in Black, La Jolla Mus Art, Calif, 70; Five Black Artists: Benny, Bernie, Betye, Noah, and John, Lang Art Gallery, Scripps Coll, Claremont, Calif, 71; Black Art: The Black Experience, Occidental Coll, Los Angeles, Calif, 71; Los Angeles 1972: A Panorama of Black Artists, Los Angeles Co Mus Art, Calif, 72; Renshaw Gallery, Linfield Coll, Ore, 73; The Black Image: West Coast 74, EB Crocker Art Gallery, Sacramento, Calif, 74; West Coast Black Artists, Union Gallery, Cal PLy Univ, Pomona, Calif, 75; A Tribute to Martin Luther King, Jr, Los Angeles Municipal Arts Gallery, Barnsdall Park, Calif, 76; Festival in Black Otis Art Exhib, Otis Art Inst, Calif, 77; Tanner Gallery, Calif, 78; William Grant Still Community Art Ctr, Calif, 790; African American Artists of NC, Raleigh, 80; Black Doll Exhib, William Grant Still Community Arts Ctr, Calif, 81; Other Gods, Containers of Belief, Everson Mus Art, Syracuse, NY, 86; 40 Yrs of Calif Assemblage, Wight Art Gallery, Univ Calif, 89; Long Beach Mus Art, Calif, 90; Dolls in Contemporary Art, Patrick and Beatrice Haggerty Mus Art, Wisc, 93; ARTCORE, Los Angeles, Calif, 94; ALTARS, Armory Ctr Arts, Pasadena, Calif, 95; African Influence/Contemporary Artists, Nat Civil Rights Mus, Memphis, Temn, 96; The Right to Assemble, Fine Arts Gallery, Calif State Univ, 2000; Renaissance, Dignity, and Pride: African American Artists in LA, Univ Calif, 2004; LA Obeject & David Hammons Body Prints, Tilton Gallery, NY, 2006, 2007, 2011; 30 Seconds off an Inch, The Studio Mus Harlem, NY, 2009; At Home/Not at Home: Works from the Collection of Rebecca and Marin Eisenberg, Ctr Curatorial Studies and Art in Contemporary Culture, Bard Coll, NY, 2010; In Context, Roberts & Tilton, Calif, 2011; Now Dig This! Art and Black Los Angeles 1960-1980, PS 1 MoMA NY, 2012; John Outterbridge: Rag Factory II, Studio Mus Harlem, NY, 2012; 55th Int Art Exhib Biennale, Venice, 2013. *Pos:* Painter/designer, Art Craft, Div Traid Corp, Burbank, 64-68; artistic dir, Communicative Arts Acad, Compton, 69-75, mem bd dir, presently; dir, Watts Towers Arts Ctr, Cult Affairs Dept, Los Angeles, 75-92; US Rep, Sao Paulo Biennial, Brazil, 94, Johannesburg, 1st Biennial, South Africa, 94; Flint Ridge Found Adv Panel, 98-99. *Teaching:* Instr assemblage & sculpture, Pasadena Art Mus, 67-70; lectr art hist, Calif State Col, Dominguez Hills, 67-71; Univ Calif, Irvine, Claremont Col, Calif, Dillart Univ, New Orleans, 2001. *Awards:* Nat Conf Art Educators award, 87; Fullbright fellow, Nat Conf Maori Artists, New England, 88; HR Hyde Visiting Artist fellowship, Memphis Inst Arts, Memphis, Tenn, 94; Nat Endowment Arts fellowship, 94; J Paul Getty fellowship, 94; Artists Legacy Found award, 2010; US Artists fellowship, 2011; Calif African American Mus Lifetime Achievement award, 2012. *Bibliog:* article, Wilson Libr Bull, 4/69; Elton C Fax (auth), Black Artists of the New Generation, Dodd, Mead & Co, 77; interview, Am Oral History, Univ Calif, Los Angeles, 93; Steven Harris, D Burke (ed) Architecture of the Everyday, Princeton Archit Press & Yale Publ on Archit, 98; Barbara Isenberg (auth) State of the Arts, Wm Morrow, Harper Collins Publ, 2001; catalog, Made in California, 1900-2000, 2001; and others. *Mem:* Calif Confedn of Arts, Los Angeles; Advocates for the Arts; Mus African Am Art; Nat Conf Artists, Va Commonwealth Univ. *Media:* Welded Metal, Wood. *Publ:* Letters Documents, American Archives, Huntington Library, Smithsonian Inst, San Marino, Calif, 94; catalog, 22nd Biennale, Sao Paulo, 94; catalog, 1st Bienale Under New Adminstrn, South Africa, 94; and others. *Mailing Add:* Tilton Gallery 8 East 76th St New York NY 10021

OVERLAND, CARLTON EDWARD
CURATOR, HISTORIAN

b Stoughton, Wis, Feb 28, 1942. *Study:* St Olaf Col, BA; Univ Wis-Madison, MA. *Collection Arranged:* 20th Century Graphics: The Hollaender Collection, 74. *Pos:* Cur prints & drawings, Elvehjem Art Ctr, Madison, Wis, 72-77, cur collections, from 77. *Teaching:* Instr art hist, Univ Northern Iowa, Cedar Falls, 68-70. *Mem:* Am Asn Mus

OVITZ, JUDY & MICHAEL S
COLLECTOR, PATRON

b Dec, 14, 1946. *Study:* Univ Calif, Los Angeles, 1968. *Comn:* Trustee Mus Modern Art, New York City; bd governors Cedars-Sinai Hosp, Los Angeles; mem exec adv bd Pediatric AIDS Found; bd dir, DARE Am; nat bd adv, Children's Scholarship Fund. *Pos:* Co-founder & chmn, Creative Artists Agency, Los Angeles, 1975-95; pres, Walt Disney co, Burbank, Calif, 1995-97; trustee, Mus Mod Art, New York; bd dirs, Calif Inst Arts, Sundance Inst, Livent, Inc, Gulfstream Aeronautical Corp, J Crew Group, Inc, Opsware, Inc & Yankee Candle Corp; chmn exec bd dir, UCLA Hosp and Med Ctr; bd adv, Sch Theater, Film and TV UCLA; principal, Artists Mgt Group, 1998-2002; owner & principal, CKE Associates, Beverly Hills, 1998-. *Awards:* Named one of Top 200 Collectors, ARTnews mag, 2004-13. *Mem:* Council Foreign Relations, Zeta Beta Tau. *Collection:* Contemporary art; Ming furniture; modern painting; African art. *Publ:* Exec prodr (films), Gangs of New York, 2002 & Timeline, 2003

OWEN, FRANK (FRANKLIN) CHARLES
PAINTER
b Kalispell, Mont, May 13, 1939. *Study:* Antioch Col; Calif State Univ Sacramento; Univ Calif, Davis, BA & MA. *Work:* Corcoran Gallery of Art, Washington, DC; Albright-Knox Art Gallery, Buffalo, NY; St Louis Art Mus, Mo; Des Moines Art Ctr, Iowa; Madison Art Ctr, Wis; plus others. *Exhib:* 32nd Corcoran Biennial, Washington, DC, 71; Madison Art Ctr Exhib, 73; 15th Nat Exhib of Contemp Am Painting & Sculpture, Univ Ill, 74; 71st Ann Exhib, Art Inst Chicago, 74; Soho in Berlin, Berlin Kunstmuseum, WGer, 76; Solo exhibs, Leo Castelli Gallery, 72, 75 & Sable-Castelli Gallery, Toronto, 77. *Teaching:* Instr painting, Calif State Univ, Sacramento, 67-68; instr fine arts, Sch Visual Arts, New York, 70-. *Bibliog:* Peter Schedjahl (auth), Six painters of the 70s, Ackland Art Ctr, NC, 73; Douglas Davis (auth), Painter's painters, Newsweek, 5/13/74. *Mailing Add:* Atea Ring Gallery Sam Spears Rd Westport NY 12993

OWENS, GWENDOLYN JANE
ADMINISTRATOR, CURATOR
b Baltimore, Md, July 8, 1954. *Study:* Tufts Univ, BA, 76; Williams Col, MA, 79. *Collection Arranged:* Watercolors by Maurice Prendergast from New England Collections (auth, catalog), 78 & Master Drawings from the Collection of Ingrid and Julius Held (co-auth, catalog), 79, The Dr and Mrs Milton Lurie Kramer Collection (auth, catalog), 81; Golden Day, Silver Night, Perceptions of Nature in Am Art, 1850-1910 (coauth, catalog), 82; The Watercolors of David Milne (auth catalog), 84; Nature Transcribed: The Landscapes and Still Lifes of David Johnson, 1827-1908 (auth, catalog), 88; Viewing Olmsted (proj dir) 96; Departure for Katsura (proj dir) 98; Between Observation & Intervention: The Painted Photographs of Melvin Charney (cur, atuh, catalog), 2008. *Pos:* Ed asst, Am Asn Mus, Washington, DC, 76-77; registr, Williams Col Mus Art, Mass, 78-79; asst cur, Herbert F Johnson Mus, Cornell Univ, Ithaca, NY, 79-81, assoc cur, 81-85, cur, 85-86; Prendergast Fel, Williams Col Mus Art, 86-88; dir, The Art Gallery, Univ Md, 88-91; affiliated fac, 88-91; asst dir, Can Ctr Archit, Montreal, 91-2003; Consulting Cur, Canadian Ctr for Archit, Montreal, 2003-. *Teaching:* Affiliated fac, Univ Md, dept art hist, 88-91; John Abbott Coll, 2007. *Mem:* Coll Art Asn; Am Asn of Mus; Am Studies Asn; Can Mus Asn; Soc Archit Historians. *Res:* 19th and 20th century American art and architecture. *Publ:* Contribr, Pioneers in American Museums: Bryson Burroughs, Mus News, 79; H Siddons Mowbray, Easel Painter, Art & Antiques, 80; Alive, Well and Prospering, Cooperative Conservation Centers Come of Age, Mus New, 82; coauth, Maurice & Charles Prendergast; A Catalogue Raisonne, Prestel, 90; contribr, Painters of a New Century: The Eight, Milwaukee Art Mus, 91; American Women Modernists The Legacy of Robert Henri, 2005; coauth, Painting Lake George, Syracuse Univ Press, 2005; contribr, Gordon Matta-Clark: You Are the Measure, Whitney Mus, 2007. *Mailing Add:* 418 Mt Stephen Westmount PQ H3Y 2X6 Canada

OWENS, RACHEL
SCULPTOR
b Atlanta, Ga. *Study:* Univ Kans, Lawrence, BA, 1995; Sch Art Inst Chicago, MFA, 1999. *Exhib:* Madrid, Madrid Theater, Kans City, 1998; House, Wicker Park, Chicago, 1999; Parallel Sensations, Willimasburg Art & Hist Ctr, Brooklyn, 2002; Fear of Flight, Sara Nightingale Gallery, New York, 2003; Postcards from the Edge, Brent Sikkema Gallery, New York, 2004; Empathetic, Temple Univ Gallery, Philadelphia, 2006; Nineteen Eighty Four, Austrian Cult Forum, New York, 2010. *Awards:* Hollander Family Found Award, 1994; GK Baum Travel Grant, 2002; Emerging Artist Fel, Socrates Sculpture Park, 2007; Artist Grant, Harpo Found, 2007; Pollock-Krasner Found Grant, 2008. *Bibliog:* Alice Thorson (auth), Figuring the Body, Kans City Star, 11/17/1997; Helen A Harrison (auth), Fear of Flying, NY Times, 11/2/2003; Kim Levin (auth), Critic's Pick: Some Exhaust, New Yorker, 9/6/2004; Roberta Fallon (auth), Feel the Pain, Philadelphia Weekly, 11/5/2006; Rachel Wolff (auth), See Here Now, New York Mag, 10/12/2009. *Mailing Add:* c/o ZieherSmith Inc 516 W 20th St New York NY 10011

OWENS, TENNYS BOWERS
DEALER
b Washington, NC, June 25, 1940. *Study:* St Mary's Jr Col, Raleigh, NC; Univ NC. *Pos:* Pres & owner, Artique Ltd, 71-. *Specialty:* General art merchandise, prints, paintings, sculpture and pottery, traditional and contemporary. *Mailing Add:* c/o Artique Ltd 314 G St Anchorage AK 99501

OWENS, WALLACE, JR
PAINTER, SCULPTOR
b Muskogee, Okla. *Study:* Langston Univ, BA (art educ), 59; Cent State Univ, Edmond, Okla, Masters (teaching), 65; Inst Allende, San Miguel de Allende, Mex, MFA (painting), 66; Doctorial Studies, N Tex State Univ, 70-71. *Work:* Okla State Permanent Collection, Oklahoma City; Gainesville Col, Ga; Okla Univ. *Comn:* 20 ft tall metal sculpture, from Langston Univ to the Universe, Langston Univ. *Exhib:* Cent State Univ, Edmond, 65; Univ Okla, Norman, 69; Retrospective Show, Kirkpatrick Ctr, Oklahoma City, 2003. *Pos:* Dir, Owens Arts Place Mus (Fine Arts Mus), Guttrie, Okla. *Teaching:* Dept chmn visual arts, Langston Univ, Okla, 66-80; dept art, Edmond, Okla, 80-87; retired. *Awards:* Fulbright Scholar Italy, Univ Rome, 70; Study Tour Award, African Am Inst, New York, 74. *Mem:* Okla Art Ed Asn; Nat Conf Artist (charter mem, 60). *Media:* Acrylic, Metal. *Collection:* Contemporary paintings in acrylic and oil; fine prints in lithography woodcuts and etching; concentrating on metal sculpture. *Publ:* Status of Art Education in State of Oklahoma, 68. *Mailing Add:* 3374 Sunny Acres Ln Guthrie OK 73044

OWSLEY, DAVID THOMAS
CONSULTANT
b Dallas, Tex, Aug 20, 1929. *Study:* Harvard Coll, AB, 51; Inst Fine Arts, NY Univ, MFA, 64. *Hon Degrees:* Ball State Univ, Muncie, Ind, LHD, 2005. *Work:* Ball State; Dallas Mus Art. *Collection Arranged:* Carnegie Inst Mus Art; Ailsa Mellon Bruce Collection Decorative Arts; Hovey Collection Islamic & Chinese Art; Reeves Collection, Dallas Mus Art. *Pos:* Fel, Am Wing, Metrop Mus Art; asst cur decorative arts & sculpture, Mus Fine Arts, Boston; visitor, Victoria & Albert Mus, London, Eng; cur antiquities, Oriental & decorative arts, Carnegie Inst Mus Art. *Teaching:* Decorative arts, Univ Pittsburgh Ext. *Awards:* Cert Appreciation, Am Soc Appraisers, 83; Westmoreland Soc Medal; Pres Medal, Ball State Univ. *Mem:* Knickerbocker Club. *Collection:* Indian & SE Asia, old master paintings, sculpture. *Publ:* articles for Mellon Bruce Collection; Auth, article, Antiques, 12/72 & 4/73 & Apollo, 8/73; Connoisseur, 73; coauth, Wendy and Emery Reves Collection (exhib catalog), Dallas Mus Art, 85. *Mailing Add:* 116 E 68th St New York NY 10065

OXBOROUGH, PAUL G
PAINTER
b Minn, 1965. *Study:* Attended Minneapolis Coll Art and Design; four year apprenticeship in the French academic tradition at Alelier Leseuer. *Exhib:* Solo exhibs, Gallery 3916, Minneapolis, Minn, 95, 96, 97; Eleanor Ettinger Gallery, NY City, 2000, 2001, 2003, 2004, 2006; Albemarle Gallery, London, Eng, 2005; Group exhibs, Am Soc Portrait Artists, Montgomery, Ala, 97; New Masters of Realism, Eleanor Ettinger, NY City, 99, Summer Salon, 99, 2000, 2001, 2002, 2003, 2004, The Figure in Am Art, 99, 2001, 2003, 2004, 2006, Winter Salon, 2002, Int Winter Salon, 2005; Am Figurative Art, Ablemarle Gallery, London, 99; Audubon Artists 59th Ann Exhib, Salmagundi Club, NY City, 2001; Nat Portrait Gallery, London, Eng, 2003. *Awards:* Award of Excellence, Communication Arts Mag, 94, 97; Guilia Palerma Award, Audubon Artists, 2001; BP Portrait Award, Nat Portrait Gallery, London, 2005. *Dealer:* Albemarle Gallery 49 Albemarle St London W1S 4JR. *Mailing Add:* c/o Eleanor Ettinger Gallery 24 W 57th St Ste 609 New York NY 10019

OXMAN, KATJA
PRINTMAKER
b Munich, Ger; US citizen. *Study:* Pa Acad Fine Arts, Philadelphia, cert, 65; Acad Munich, 65-66; Royal Coll Art, London, Eng, cert, 67. *Hon Degrees:* Univ Md. *Work:* Muskegon Mus Art, Mi; Philadelphia Mus; Smithsonian Inst, US State Dept, Washington, DC; Pa Acad Fine Arts; Southern Alleghenies Mus Art; Art Complex Mus, Duxbury, Mass; Accad Art Mus, Easton, Md; Nat Mus Women in the Arts, DC; Boston Mus Fine Arts; Worcester Art Mus; Smithsonian Mus of Am Art; Detroit Art Mus; Univ Md Univ Col; Wright State Univ Art Mus; Hobart and William Smith Col Art Mus; Smith Coll Art Mus; Mount Holyoke Col Art Mus. *Exhib:* Solo exhibs: Jane Haslem Gallery, Washington, DC, 81; 2006; Assoc Artists, NY & Philadelphia, 83; The Print Club, 86; David Adamson Gallery, 87; 89; 93; Marcus Gordon, Pittsburgh, Pa, 89; Randal Beck Gallery, Boston, Mass, 89; 90; 94; Locus Gallery, St Louis, Mo, 95; Hollins Coll, Roanoke, Va, 97; Esmay Fine Arts, Rochester, 97; 2000; Chautaugua Inst, NY, 2005; Steven Scott Gallery, Owings Hills, Md, 2006; Rosemont Coll, Pa, 2007; Wenniger Gallery, Rockport, Maine, 2007, 2008, Jane Haslem, 2012; Steven Scott Gallery, Baltimore, MD, 91-2002; Women in Print: Prints from 3M by Contemp Women Printmakers Traveling Exhib (with catalog), 95-; Nat Acad Mus, New York, 96, 98, 2000 & 2002; Susan Conway Gallery, DC, 99-2000; Nat Mus Women Arts, DC, 2000; MidAmerican Print Coun Conf, Univ Dallas, 2002; Am Realist, Portmouth Mus Fine Arts, Portsmouth, NH, 2009; The Painterly Image, Steven Scott Gallery, Baltimore, Md, 2009, As Far as the Eye Can See, 2009; Portsmouth Mus Fine Arts, NH, 2009; WM Baczek Fine Arts, N Hampton, Mass, 2010; Group exhib: The Contemporary Printmaker, Chautauqua Inst, NY, 6/2011. *Teaching:* Adj prof printmaking, Am Univ, 76-85; vis lectr, Univ Mass, 75; vis critic, Pa Acad Fine Art, Philadelphia, 96-2000. *Awards:* Purchase Prize, Bradley Univ, Peoria, Ill, 95; Awards in the Visual Arts, Md State Arts Coun, 2000; Purchase Prize, 28th Annual Bradley Nat Print Exhib, Bradley Univ, Peoria K, Ill, 2001. *Bibliog:* Ann Evry (dir), Art Strokes, Blue Cow Productions, Sandy Spring, Md, 94; Carol Ferring Shepley (auth), Works in mixed media and works on paper, Get Out Corresp, St Louis, Mo, 6/95; Ferdinand Protzman (auth), Galleries, Wash Post, 7/6/96; Lynne E Moss (auth), Daily life in still life, Am Artist, 5/98; plus others. *Mem:* Boston Printmakers; Print Club of Philadelphia. *Media:* Etching, Aquatint. *Dealer:* Station Gallery Greenville DE; Steven Scott Gallery Owings Mills MD; WM Baczek North Hampton MA; The Print Center Philadelphia PA; Esmay Fine Art Rochester NY; Stewart & Stewart Bloomfield Hills MI ; Jane Haslem Gallery Washington DC

OXMAN, MARK
SCULPTOR, EDUCATOR
b New York, NY, Mar 9, 1940. *Study:* Adelphi Univ, Long Island, NY, 58-61; Pa Acad Fine Arts, Philadelphia, 61-65; Showhegan Sch, summer 65; City & Guilds London, 65; Art Sch, London, 67. *Comn:* Large sculpture relief, Bellmore Mem Libr, Long Island, NY, 73; large sculpture relief, Queens Plaza Complex, NY, 76; portrait bust of Dr. John Varrano, 2011; portrait bust of Elizabeth Joy Roe, 2012; portrait, Werner Brandes, 2013; portrait, Bust of Mrs Betsy Johnson, 2014. *Exhib:* Solo exhibs, Wash Co Mus Fine Arts, Hagerstown, Md, 88, Fountains & Figures, Am Univ, 90, Western Md Col, 92, Arts Alive, Montgomery, Md, 93, West Chester Univ, Penn, 94, Watkins Collection, Wash, DC, 98 & Hobart & William Smith Col, Geneva, NY, 99, Wash & Jefferson Col, 2000, Harmony Hall Gallery, Ft Wash, Md, 2001, Notre Dame Univ, 2002, Thiel Col, Pa, 2003, The Gallery at Quiet Waters, Annapolis, Md, 2004, Marlboro Col, Vt, 2004, Rosemont Col, Pa, 2005, Southern Md Col, La Plata, Md, 2005, Amherst Coll, Mass, 2010, The Decimation of Professor Richard Fink, Amherst Coll, Mass, 9/2010; 21st Area Show Sculpture, Corcoran Mus, Wash, 78; Sculpture On & Off the Wall, A Salon Ltd, Wash, 95; Washington Figurative Sculptors, Md Sch Art & Design, 95; 16 Sculptors, Watkins Gallery, Wash, 95; Artist to Artist, Art Barn, Wash, 95; Katzen Mus, Wash DC, 2006. *Pos:* Dean students, Skowhecan Sch, 69 & 72. *Teaching:* Lectr art, Haverford Col, Pa, 67-70; asst prof art, Amherst Col, Mass, 70-76; assoc prof sculpture, Am Univ, Washington, DC, 76-94, prof, 94-. *Awards:* Travel Res Grant, Amherst Col, 75; Mellon Fac Develop Grant, Am Univ, 80 & Curric Develop Award, 88; CAS Course Release, 93 & 94. *Media:* Bronze, Plastic

OYUELA, RAUL M
MUSEUM DIRECTOR, CURATOR
b Buenos Aires, Argentina, Nov 7, 1935. *Study:* Univ Buenos Aires, PhD, 59; Fedn Int D'Art Photographique, AFIAP, 72. *Work:* Fla Mus Hispanic & Latin Am Art, Miami; San Francisco Mus Contemp Hispanic Art, Calif. *Collection Arranged:* Orlando Agudelo Botero, One Woman Show, 93; From Africa to Cuba, 34 Artists, 96; Women in the Arts, 52 Women Artists, 96; Hispanic Heritage in Am, 29 Artists, 96; Romero Britto, One Woman Show, 96. *Pos:* Dir, Mediterranean Art Ctr, Barcelona, 85-88, San Francisco Mus Hispanic Art, 88-90, dir & pres, Fla Mus Hisp Art, Miami, 91-96; dir, Fla Mus Hispanic & Latin Am Art, currently. *Teaching:* Prof photog, Argentine Fedn Photog, 74-76. *Awards:* Gold Medal, Sao Paulo Biennial, 64; Bronze Medal, Govern of Romania, 64; Gold Medal, Kaiser Corp, 66. *Mem:* Int Coun Mus; Am Asn Mus. *Res:* Latin American and Spanish Art. *Publ:* Auth, Street Sculptures in Chicago, Batik, 89; Tibet: The Forgotten Land, Bohemia News, 89; Los Falsos (The Flakes), La Bohemia, 94. *Mailing Add:* c/o Museum of the Americas Ste 104 2500 NW 79th Ave Doral FL 33122-1071

OZONOFF, IDA
PAINTER, COLLAGE ARTIST
b La Crosse, Wis, July 27, 1904. *Study:* State Teachers Col, Milwaukee, grad, 24; Milwaukee Downer Col, 58 & 59; Univ Wis-Milwaukee, 60-64 & 69-70. *Work:* Print Div, Smithsonian Inst, Washington, DC; Milwaukee Pub Schs; Univ Wis, Fond du Lac Campus; Abilene Fine Arts Mus, Tex; Carleton Col, Northfield, Minn. *Exhib:* Nat Acad Design Exhib, NY, 68 & 69; Allied Artists Am Exhib, NY, 70; West Bend Gallery Fine Arts, Wis, 76 & 77; Univ Wis Alumni Exhib, 78; Kohler Art Ctr, Sheboygan, Wis, 88-90. *Awards:* Purchase Award, Western Publ, 66; Benjamin Altman First Prize, Nat Acad Design, 68; Carleton Coll Purchase Award, Charles E Merrill Trust Fund, 75. *Bibliog:* Gerald F Brommer (auth), The Art of Collage, 78; Wis Acad Rev (spec ed), Wis Painters & Printmakers, 3/83; and others. *Mem:* Wis Arts Coun. *Media:* Acrylic, Oil. *Dealer:* Bradley Galleries 2639 N Downer Milwaukee WI 53211

OZUBKO, CHRISTOPHER
EDUCATOR, GRAPHIC ARTIST
Study: Univ Alberta, Edmonton, BFA, 1977; Cranbrook Acad Art, MFA (design), 1981. *Teaching:* Prof design, Univ Wash, 1981-, dir, Sch of Art, 1996-, Alison and Glen Milliman ednowed chair art, currently. *Awards:* AIGA fellow, 2002. *Mem:* Asn Typographique Internationale; Am Inst of Graphic Arts. *Mailing Add:* University of Washington School of Art Box 353440 Seattle WA 98195-3440

P

PACE, JAMES ROBERT
COLLAGE ARTIST, PRINTMAKER
b Tahlequah, Okla, Feb 19, 1958. *Study:* Univ Okla, BFA, 81; Ariz State Univ, MFA, 84. *Work:* Fogg Art Mus, Harvard Univ; Nelson-Atkins Mus Art; Scottsdale Mus Contemp Art; Okla State Art Collection; St John's Mus Fine Art; many others. *Exhib:* 13 Parkside Nat Print Exhib; The Song of Images, New Delhi, India; Centerfold, Leslie Powell Found Gallery; Snapshot (int); Another View: Selected Works from Contemp Am Printmakers; many others. *Teaching:* Grad asst drawing, Ariz State Univ, Tempe, 82-83; art instr drawing & design, S Mt Community Col, Phoenix, Ariz, 85; assoc prof drawing & printmaking, Univ Tex, Tyler, 85-, prof art, Oge prof, 98-. *Awards:* HL Gully Res Award, Ariz State Univ, 84; Juror's Choice Award, New Art: Painting from NY, Calif & Tex; Nat Endowment Arts, 92; and many others. *Mem:* Coll Art Asn. *Media:* Mixed; Drawing, Collage. *Publ:* Beyond Ourselves, X-Press, 96. *Mailing Add:* 14688 County Rd 2337 Tyler TX 75707

PACHNER, WILLIAM
PAINTER
b Brtnice, Czech, Apr 7, 1915; US citizen. *Study:* Acad Arts & Crafts, Vienna, Austria; Univ Tampa, DFA AC, 81. *Work:* Whitney Mus Am Art, New York; Butler Inst Am Art, Youngstown, Ohio; Ft Worth Art Ctr, Tex; Hirshorn Mus, Washington, DC; Delgado Mus, New Orleans; Detroit Inst Am Art; Ein-Herod Mus, Israel; Gulf Coast Mus Art, Largo, Fla; Holocaust Mus, St Petersburg, Fla; pvt collections, Lee A Ault & Walter P Chrysler; and others. *Exhib:* Carnegie Inst Int, Pittsburgh; Whitney Mus Am Art Ann; Corcoran Gallery Art Biennial, Washington, DC; Pa Acad Fine Arts, Philadelphia; US Fine Arts Pavilion, NY World's Fair, 65; Gallery Mod Art, New York, 69; Univ Tampa, 81; Detroit Inst Fine Arts; solo exhibs, Pachner Landscapes (with catalog), Mus Fine Arts, St Petersburg, Fla, 83 & more than 12 solo exhibs in New York; Affirmations--1936-1986, 50 yr retrospective (with catalog), Tampa Mus Art, Fla, 86; black & white drawings, Univ S Fla, 86 & Art Ctr, St Petersburg, Fla, 87; retrospective, Holocaust Mus, St Petersburg, 2005. *Teaching:* Instr painting & drawing, Art Students League, 69-70. *Awards:* Am Acad Arts & Lett Award, 49; Ford Found Awards, 59-64; Guggenheim Fel, 60. *Bibliog:* Kenneth Donahue (auth), William Pachner, NY, The Am Fed Arts, 59; Robert Martin (auth), Pachner Landscapes, Mus Fine Arts, St. Petersburg, Fla, 2/87; Lennie Bennett (auth), Season in the Sun, St. Petersburg Times, 5/16/2004. *Media:* Oil, Watercolor, Collage. *Dealer:* Brad Cooper Gallery 1712 E 7th Ave Tampa FL 33605. *Mailing Add:* c/o Brad Cooper Gallery 1714 E 7th Ave Tampa FL 33605

PACHTER, CHARLES
PAINTER, PRINTMAKER
b Toronto, Ont, Dec 30, 1942. *Study:* Sorbonne, Paris, dipl de L'ESPFE, 63; Univ Toronto, BA, 64; Cranbrook Acad Art, Mich, MFA, 66. *Work:* Nat Libr, Ottawa; Art Gallery Ont, Toronto; Mus d'Art Contemporain, Montreal; Can Embassy, Washington, DC; Centre d'Art Présence Van Gogh, St Rémy de Provence, France. *Comn:* To All In Tents (35th anniversary painting & commemorative poster), Stratford Shakespearean Festival, Stratford, Ont; Hockey Knights in Canada (subway mural), Toronto Transit Comn, 85. *Exhib:* Solo retrospectives, Centre d'Art Présence Van Gogh, St Rémy de Provence, France, 91 & Haus an der Redoute Bonn, Ger, 92; Esler/Pachter ESP, Nat Gallery Can, Ottawa; Color Prints of the Americas, NJ State Mus; Int Print Biennale, Mus Mod Art, Tokyo; Vestiges of Empire, Camden Centre, London; solo exhib, Royal Ont Mus, Toronto, 94. *Bibliog:* Charles Pachter (monogr), B Welsh-Ovcharov, McClelland & Stewart, Toronto; 30/50 Pachter (film), Nat Film Bd Can; Private Presses, Can Encyl, Hurtig, page 1488. *Publ:* Auth & illusr, The Queen of Canada Colouring Book, Anansi, Toronto, 76; illusr, J Susanna Moodie, Margaret Atwood, 80; illusr & contribr, Soho Square III, pages 89-90, Bloomsbury Publ, London, 90; illusr, How We Are Governed, Harcourt-Brace, Toronto, 94

PACHTER, MARC
MUSEUM DIRECTOR
Study: Univ Calif Berkeley, B summa cum laude; Harvard Univ, postgrad. *Pos:* chief historian, Smithsonian's Nat Portrait Gallery, 74-90, asst dir, 74-90, deputy asst secy external affairs, 90-94; dir Nat Portrait Gallery, 2000-2007; acting dir, Smithsonian's Nat Mus Am History, 2001-2002; former counselor to secy, Smithsonian Inst, 95-2000; dir, Smithsonians Nat Mus Am History, 2011-2012. *Awards:* Woodrow Wilson Fel, Harvard Univ. *Publ:* commentator, CBS, Voice of Am, C-SPAN; auth, editor, Abroad in America: Visitors to the New Nation, Champions of American Sport; Documentary History of the Supreme Court; Telling Lives: The Biographer's Art; A Gallery of Presidents. *Mailing Add:* National American History Museum Directors Office PO Box 37012 Washington DC 20013

PACKARD, SALLY
EDUCATOR, ADMINISTRATOR
Study: Texas Christian Univ, MFA. *Exhib:* Exhibited installations and sculptures throughout Texas, as well as, Sweden, Poland, and England. *Pos:* Worked for companies such as Metropolitan Opera, Santa Fe Opera, Minnesota Ballet, Atlanta Ballet, Guthrie Theater, Jim Henson Co, and Juilliard Sch of Music, formerly. *Teaching:* with Univ of North Texas, Col of Visual Arts + Design, 1999-2008, co-coordinator Core Program;chair Department of Visual Arts, Sage Col, Albany, NY, 2008-11; dir, Col of Fine Arts, Sch of Art, Texas Christian Univ, 2011-. *Mailing Add:* Texas Christian University School of Art TCU Box 298000 Fort Worth TX 76129

PADOVANO, ANTHONY JOHN
SCULPTOR, DRAFTSMAN
b Brooklyn, NY, July 19, 1933. *Study:* Carnegie Inst Technol; Pratt Inst; Columbia Univ, with Oronzio Maldarelli; Hunter Col, MA, 80. *Work:* Whitney Mus Am Art; Nat Collection Fine Arts, Washington, DC; Univ Ill; John Herron Art Inst; Storm King Art Ctr, NY; Holycroft Found. *Comn:* Sculpture In The Park, Parks Dept, NY, 68; design, NY State Art Awards, NY State Coun Arts, 69; sculpture, World Trade Ctr, Port Authority NY & NJ, 70; three arcs, donated by Trammel & Crow Co for City of Dallas, 72; sculpture, Nebr Bicentennial Sculpture Corp, 76. *Exhib:* 3rd Mostra Arte Figurative Int, Rome, Italy, 61; Young Am, Whitney Mus Am Art, 65; Am Sculpture, Mus Mod Art, 66; Am Express Pavilion, NY World's Fair, 66; Inauguration of Nat Collection Fine Arts, Washington, DC, 67; Sculpture Mile, 98-. *Pos:* Adv mem, NJ State Coun Arts, 65-67. *Teaching:* Asst prof sculpture, Columbia Univ, Univ Conn, 72 & Kingsborough Community Col, 83; adj asst prof sculpture, Queens Col, City Univ NY, 72; instr, Dept Art, Art Students League, NY; assoc prof, Kingsborough Community Col, 83-2001, full prof, 2001-. *Awards:* Guggenheim Found Fel, 64; Ford Found Purchase Award, 66; Inst Arts & Lett Award, 76; Prix de Rome, 60 & 61; Marquis Who's Who in American Art References award in Sculpture, Audubon Artists, 2014. *Bibliog:* Young talent, Art Am, 65; James Mellow (auth), article in New York Times Sun Rev, 4/70. *Mem:* Sculptors Guild (vpres, 68-69); Silvermine Guild Artists; Nat Acad. *Media:* Metal, Stone. *Publ:* Auth, Process of Sculpture, Doubleday Co, 81. *Dealer:* Vorpal Gallery 411 W Broadway New York NY 10012

PADULA, FRED DAVID
FILMMAKER, PHOTOGRAPHER
b Santa Barbara, Calif, Oct 25, 1937. *Study:* Univ Calif, Santa Barbara; Calif State Univ, San Francisco, BA (music), with Jack Welpott, Don Worth & Wynn Bullock, MA (art). *Work:* George Eastman House, Rochester, NY; San Francisco Mus Art; Oakland Mus Art; Kalamazoo Art Ctr, Mich; Crocker Mus Art, Sacramento, Calif; and many pvt collections. *Comn:* Children's Letters to God (film), Lee Mendelson, San Francisco, 68; Navaho (film), Pub Broadcast Lab, KQED-TV, San Francisco, 68; S F Mix (film), Ford Found, 70; film, Am Film Inst. *Exhib:* 30 Photographers Nat Exhib, Buffalo, NY, 64; solo exhibs, San Francisco Mus, 64, George Eastman House, 68 & DeYoung Mus, San Francisco, 69; Mus Mod Art, NY, 67; completion & premiere showing of El Capitan (film), San Francisco Mus of Mod Art, 78; and others. *Pos:* Mem Selection comt, US Art in the Embassies, 68; mem bd dir, Canyon Cinema Coop, 71-. *Teaching:* Lectr photo & film making, San Francisco State Univ, 63- & Univ Calif, San Francisco, 66-71; resident artist, Univ Minn, Minneapolis, 70. *Awards:* Awards for film El Capitan: Grand Prize, Banff Festival Mountain Films, Can, 79, Gold Medal, Festival Int Film Alpin, Les Diablertets, Switz, 79 & Silver Medal, Int Bergfilm Munchen, Munich, Ger, 79; and others. *Bibliog:* Callenbach (auth), Ephesus, Film Quart, Univ Calif, winter 66-67; Winston (auth), American film maker, Melbourne Art Rev, fall 68; Hoffmann (auth), Ephesus, Weg Zum Nachbarn, Oberhausen, Ger, 68. *Dealer:* Canyon Cinema Coop San Francisco, CA. *Mailing Add:* PO Box 254 Mill Valley CA 94941

PAGANI, CATHERINE
EDUCATOR, ADMINISTRATOR
Study: Univ Toronto, PhD, 1993. *Pos:* Worked at Royal Ontario Mus, Toronto, Nat Mus of History, Taipei, Taiwan; invited lecturer in the field. *Teaching:* Mem of dept of art, Univ Alabama, 1993-, Prof Asian art history, currently, chair, 2008-. *Mem:* Nat Council of Arts Administrators. *Publ:* auth, Eastern Magnificence and European

Ingenuity:Clocks of Late Imperial China, 2001; co-auth with R.W.L. Guisso, The First Emperor of China; work has appeared in Arts of Asia, Apollo, Burlington Magazine, and Arts Asiatiques. *Mailing Add:* Department of Art and Art History The University of Alabama 103 Garland Hall Box 870270 Tuscaloosa AL 35487-0270

PAGE, JEAN JEPSON
COLLECTOR, HISTORIAN
b Minneapolis, Minn, Aug 22, 1924. *Study:* With Walter S Baum; Minneapolis Inst Arts; San Francisco Inst; Smith Col, BA, 46. *Pos:* Comnr, Dist Columbia Comn Arts & Humanities, 76-80; dir, Am Painting Info Serv; Am painting appraiser. *Res:* American painting, particularly 19th century; political aspects of art patronage; Frank Mayer. *Collection:* American paintings. *Publ:* Auth, Francis Blackwell Mayer, Antiques, 2/76; Frank Blackwell Mayer: Painter of the Minnesota Indian, Minn Hist, 78; Notes on the contributions of Francis Blackwell Mayer and his family to the cultural history of Maryland, Md Hist Mag, 81; James McNeill Whistler, Baltimorean, and The White Girl, Md Hist Mag, 89

PAGEL, DAVID
EDUCATOR, CRITIC
Study: Stanford Univ, BA (modern thought and lit), 1985; Harvard Univ, MA (art history), 1987. *Pos:* Contribr, art critic, Los Angeles Times, 1997-; assoc prof, chair, Art Dept, Claremont Grad Univ, Calif, currently. *Awards:* Andrew W Mellon Fellowship in Contemporary Art Criticism, 1990; Macgeorge Fellow, Univ Melbourne, 2002. *Mailing Add:* Claremont Graduate University Art Department 251 E 10th St Claremont CA 91711

PAGLEN, TREVOR
PHOTOGRAPHER
Study: Univ Calif Berkeley, BA, PhD; Sch Art Inst, Chicago, MFA. *Exhib:* 1926 Gallery, Chicago, 2000; Betty Rymer Gallery, Chicago, 2001; solo exhibs, Salina Art Ctr, Kans, 2001, Deadtech, Chicago, 2001, Calif Col Arts and Crafts, San Francisco, 2002, The LAB, 2005, Bellwether, New York, 2006 & 2009, Berkeley Art Mus, 2008, Galerie Thomas Zander, Koln, Germany & Altman Siegel Gallery, 2009; Mus Contemp Art, Chicago, 2002; 16 Beaver Space, New York, 2003; Mills Col Art Mus, Oakland, 2003; Philadelphia Inst Contemp Art, 2004; Gallery 400, Chicago, 2004; Diverse Works, Houston, 2005; Mass Mus Contemp Art, North Adams, 2006; Heather Marx Gallery, San Francisco, 2007; Taipei Biennial, 2008; Artists Space, New York, 2008; New Sch, New York, 2008; Neuberger Mus Art, SUNY Purchase, 2008; TANAS - Space for Contemp Turkish Art, Berlin, 2009; Schneider Mus Art, Southern Oreg Univ, Ashland, 2009; Havana Biennial, 2009; Int Istanbul Biennial, Turkey, 2009. *Awards:* Art Matters Found Grant, 2008. *Publ:* Coauth (with AC Thompson), Torture Taxi: On the Trail of the CIA's Rendition Flights, Melville House, 2006; auth, I Could Tell You but Then You Would Have to Be Destroyed by Me: Emblems from the Pentagons Black World, Melville House Publishing, 2007 & Blank Spots on the Map: The Dark Geography of the Pentagon's Secret World, Penguin Publishers, 2009

PAIGE, WAYNE LEO
PAINTER, DRAFTSMAN
b Chicago, Ill, Mar 5, 1944. *Study:* Univ Ill, Urbana, BFA, 68; George Washington Univ, MFA, 71. *Work:* George Washington Univ; Western Mich Univ; Danville Mus Art & Hist, Va; American Univ, Wash DC. *Exhib:* Solo exhibs, Gallery K, Washington, DC, 78, 82, 84, 88, 91, 93 & 95, 2003, Washington Co Mus, Hagerstown, Md, 85, Zaks Gallery, Chicago, 85, 91, 2004, Western Mich Univ, 90, Danville Mus Art & Hist, 91, Md Coll Art & Design, Silver Spring, Md, 98, Middle Street Gallery, Wash, Va, 2004, 2006, 2008, 2010, 2014, Phoenix Gallery, NY, 2012; Works on Paper, Corcoran Gallery, Washington, DC, 80; group exhibs, Southern Fervor, Anderson Art Gallery, Richmond, Va, 83, Katzen Arts Ctr, Am Univ, Washington, DC, 2006; Emergency, Md Art Place, Baltimore, 83 & Arlington Arts Ctr, Va, 94; Lord Fairfax Community Coll, 2008; Wash Art Matters; Am Univ Mus; Elisabeth French Coll; Western Mich Univ; Gudelsky Coll; Radio One; George Washington Univ; Prudential Insurance Co Am. *Teaching:* Instr drafting, Eastern High Sch, Washington, DC, Md Drafting Inst, 72-95; Md Drafting Inst, 79-89; chair, Art Dept, Middleburg Acad, Middleburg, Va, currently; assoc prof art, Lord Fairfax Community Coll, Warrenton, Va, 2007. *Awards:* Cecille Hunt Award, George Washington Alumni Competition, 88; Va Comn on the Arts (print & drawing category), 89; NEA Funded Grant, Sch Art Inst Chicago, Teachers Inst Contemp Art, 2002. *Bibliog:* Jo Ann Lewis (auth), Galleries: Paintings by Wayne Paige, Washington Post, 2/13/82; Judith Cox (auth), East Coast Review: Wayne Paige, New Art Examiner, 4/82; Miller Leonore (auth), Wayne Paige Drawings Gallery K, Washington Rev, 88; Maggie Wolf Peterson (auth), Works in Progress Wayne Paige, Elan Mag, 11/2006. *Media:* Miscellaneous. *Dealer:* Middle Street Gallery PO Box 341 Washington VA 22747. *Mailing Add;* 5406 Connecticut Ave NW #506 Washington DC 20015

PAIKOWSKY, SANDRA R
CURATOR, HISTORIAN
b St John, NB, Can, Dec 29, 1945. *Study:* Sir George Williams Univ, BA (art hist), 67; Univ Toronto, MA (art hist), 70. *Collection Arranged:* Eric Fischl: Painting (auth, catalog), 83, The Non-Figurative Artist's Association of Montreal (auth, catalog), 83, Goodridge Roberts: The Figure Works (auth, catalog), 84, Betty Goodwin: Passage (auth, catalog), 86, Ron Shuebrook: Recent Work (auth, catalog), 86, David Craven: Recent Work (auth, catalog), 86, Concordia Art Gallery, Montreal, Que; Rita Letendre: The Montreal Years (auth, catalog), 89. *Pos:* Cur, Concordia Univ Art Gallery, Montreal, Que, 81-. *Teaching:* Assoc prof art hist, Concordia Univ, 69-. *Publ:* Publ & co ed, The Journal of Canadian Art History, Owl's Head Press, 76. *Mailing Add:* Concordia Univ Art Gallery 1455 W de Maisonneuve Blvd W-VA432 Montreal PQ H3G 1M8 Canada

PAILOS, JORGE OTERO
ARCHITECT
b Madrid, 1971. *Exhib:* Archit includes: Horizon House, 1993, Villa Quiles-Mariani, 1997, Manes Loft and Painting Studio, 2002, Nurun Interactive Agency, 2003, Marin Penthouse, 2003, Flat-Rate Moving Company, 2003, Boutique Eco-Hotel Lake Dos Bocas, 2007, KNEW Buildings, 2008, AD2116, 2008; Art includes: En la Republica, 1996, Afternoon in NY, 1999, Wedding, 2000,, Up in Smoke, 2004, Lipstick, 2004, The Ethics of Dust: Alumix, Bolzano, 2008; group exhibs Venice Biennale, Italy, 2009. *Teaching:* Teacher, Columbia Univ Grad Sch Archit. *Awards:* Finalist, Koizumi Internat Lighting Design Competition, Japan, 1992; E.A. Seipp Design award, Cornell Univ, 1992; R.H. Shreve award for best Masters thesis in urban design, Cornell Univ, 1995; NY State Council in the Arts, Archit Planning and Design Program, Independent Project award, 2003; Soc Architectural Historians, Opler Fellowship for Emerging Scholars, 2007. *Publ:* auth, The Ethics of Dust, Spain on Spain: Debates on Contemporary Architecture, 2009. *Mailing Add:* 40 W 72nd St Apt 111 New York NY 10023

PAINE, ROXY
SCULPTOR, CONCEPTUAL ARTIST
b New York. *Study:* Pratt Inst; Coll Santa Fe. *Work:* New Sch Social Res, NY. *Exhib:* Solo exhibs, Herron Test Site, NY, 1992, Ronal Feldman Fine Arts, NY, 1995, Rose Art Mus, Waltham, Mass, 2002, James Cohan Gallery, New York, 2006, 2010, Portland Mus Art, 2006, Madison Sq Park, New York, 2007 & Met Mus Art, New York, 2009; The Nature of the Machine, Chicago Cult Ctr, Ill, 1993; Out of Town, Krannert Art Mus, Champaign, Ill, 1993; Human/Nature, New Mus Contemp Art, NY, 1995; Inside, Calif Ctr Arts Mus, Escondido, 1996; New York Gallery, 2005, 2007 & 2009; Am Acad Arts and Letts Invitational, New York, 2009. *Bibliog:* Jonathan Fineberg (auth), Art Since 1940, Prentice-Hall, 1995; Elizabeth Hess (auth), Cross hatching, Village Voice, 5/16/1995; Eleanor Heartney (auth), Roxy Paine at R Feldman, Art in Am, 11/1995. *Media:* Stainless Steel. *Dealer:* James Cohan Gallery 533 W 26th New York NY 10001

PAISNER, CLAIRE
PAINTER
b Boston, Mass. *Study:* Cornell Univ, BA; Harvard Univ, MA. *Work:* Figurative painting, Queens Public Libr. *Exhib:* Various juried Exhib, New York City. *Awards:* Pastel Soc Am Award, (PSA); Alliance Queens Artists Award; Nat Art League, The Salmagundi Club. *Bibliog:* Best of Pastel 2, Rockport Publ, 98; L'Art du Pastel, France, 2005. *Mem:* Pastel Soc Am (PSA), (sig mem, bd mem, 2001-2011). *Media:* Pastel. *Interests:* New York City scapes. *Publ:* Ed, Exhibition Catalog and Pastelagram, Pastel Soc Am, 2001-2011. *Dealer:* J Lippmann Fine Arts Gallery 8 N Dutcher St Irvington on Hudson NY 10533

PAL, PRATAPADITYA
CURATOR, ART HISTORIAN
b Sylhet, Bangladesh, Sept 1, 1935. *Study:* Delhi Univ, BA (hons), 56; Calcutta Univ, MA, 58, DPhil, 62; Cambridge Univ, PhD, 65. *Collection Arranged:* The Sensuous Line (with catalog), 76; The Sensuous Immortals (with catalog), 77; The Divine Presence (with catalog), 78; The Classical Tradition in Rajput Painting (with catalog), 78; The Ideal Image (with catalog), 78; Elephants and Ivories (catalog), 81; Light of Asia (with catalog), 84; From Merchants to Emperors (with catalog), 86; Romance of the Taj Mahal (with catalog), 89; Art of the Himalayas (with catalog), 91; The Peaceful Liberators (with catalog), 94; A Collecting Odyssey (with Catalog), 1997; Tibet Change and Tradition (with catalog) 97; Desire & Devotion (with catalog), 2001; Himalayas: An Aesthetic Adventure (with catalog), 2003; Painted Poems (with catalog), 2004; Durga: Avenging Goddess, Nurturing Mother (with catalog), 2005; Kashmir: The Artistic Heritage (with catalog), 2007; Ocean of Wisdom Embodiment of Compassion (with catalog), 2008; EO Hoppe's Santiniketan and EO Hoppe's Bombay, 2010; Elegant Image, 2011. *Pos:* Sr res assoc, Am Acad Benares, 66-67; keeper of Indian collections, Mus Fine Arts, Boston, 67-69; cur Indian & Southeast Asian art, Los Angeles Co Mus Art, 70-95; ed MARG publ, Mumbai, 93-2012; Fel for Research, Norton Simon Mus, Pasadena, Calif, 96-2005; vis cur, Art Institute, Chicago, Ill, 97-2003. *Teaching:* Lectr Indian art, Harvard Univ, 68-69; lectr Nepali art, Univ Calif, Los Angeles, 70; adj prof Southeast Asian art, Univ Southern Calif, 70-89; fac, Univ Calif, Irvine, 92-94; instr, courses on hist of Indian, Himalayan, Souteast Asian & Islamic Arts. *Awards:* Commonwealth Scholar, 62-65; Most Distinguished Indian (fine arts award), Fed Indian Asn NAm, 80; BC Law Gold Medal, 93; Getty Scholar 95-96; RP Chanda Gold Medal, Asiatic Soc, Calcutta, India, 2003; Padma Shri Award, Govt India, 2009. *Mem:* Hon fel Bombay Asiatic Soc; Am Comt South Asian Art; Asia Soc, Calcutta; Pac-Asia Mus, Pasadena, Calif; Santa Barbara Mus Art; Rubin Mus Art, NY; Fowler Mus, UCLA, Calif; Asian Art Mus, San Francisco. *Res:* Arts, archit and cult hist of India, Islamic countries, Nepal, Tibet & Southeast Asia. *Interests:* Traveling, music, reading & photog. *Publ:* Divine Images Human Visions, 97; auth, Catalogue of the Indian Coll, LACMA, Vol I, Sculpture, 86, Vol II, Sculpture, 88; Indian Painting (Vol III), 93; auth, Asian Art at the Norton Simon Mus (3 vols), 2003-04; Himalayas An Aesthetic Adventure, 2003; Kashmir: The Artistic Heritage, 2004; Sindh: Past Glory Present Nostalgia, 2008; Goddess Durga: The Power & the Glory, 2009; Something Old Somthing New, Tagore, 2011; The Elegant Image, 2011. *Mailing Add:* 10582 Cheviot Dr Los Angeles CA 90036

PALADINO, PAUL
PHOTOGRAPHER, EDUCATOR
b Boston, Mass, 64. *Study:* Fla Atlantic Univ, Boca Rotan, Fla, BFA, 86, MFA, 88, PhD, 94. *Hon Degrees:* Hon doctorate, 99. *Work:* MoMA; Ames Mus; Cherry Valley Mus. *Exhib:* Seasonal Photos, Suffolk Mus Art, Va, 2010, Photographs of Love, 2012. *Pos:* portrait photogr, Siliane Photog; wedding specialist, Longview Weddings; on-site photogr, Kings Mills; wedding photogr, Meriks Wedding Photog, family photgr. *Teaching:* adj prof, photog, Univ SC; vol photog, Sch Dist; art therapy instr, Meriks

Hosp. *Mem:* Photog Guild; Soc Prof Photog; San Francisco Art Soc; Monterrey Artists Photog Asn (vpres 2015-). *Media:* Portrait. *Res:* Longfellow. *Collection:* 18th Century Poetry. *Publ:* auth, The Color of Life, Meriks, 2012; auth, Photography of Emotion, 2013; auth, Capture the Moment, 2014; auth, The Look of Love, 2016

PALAIA, FRANC (DOMINIC)
PHOTOGRAPHER, MURALIST
b New Rochelle, NY, Sept 18, 1949. *Study:* Newark State Col, Union, NJ, BA (fine arts), 71; Univ Cincinnati, Ohio, MFA (scholar, teaching asst), 73. *Work:* Newark Mus, NJ; Stedelijk Mus, Holland; McDonald Corp; Smithsonian, Washington, DC; Polaroid Corp; and others. *Comn:* Painting, comn by Richard Ekstract, NY. *Exhib:* Alternative Mus, NY, 81; Fashion Moda, NY, 84; Metrop Mus Art, NY, 84; New Mus, NY, 85; Hal Bromm Gallery, NY, 85; Sidney Janis Gallery, NY, 88; Morris Mus, 95; Exit Art, 96; and others. *Teaching:* Instr art hist, Essex Co Col, Newark, NJ, 76-77; instr sculpture, Upsala Col, East Orange, NJ, 76; instr painting, Kean Col, NJ, 78-82. *Awards:* Grant, Louis Tiffany Found, New York, NY, 84; Rome Prize (Painting), Am Acad in Rome, Italy, 85; Sponsorships, Polaroid Corp, Boston, Mass, 86 & 87. *Bibliog:* Peter Frank (auth), article, Village Voice, 78; John Caldwell (auth), review, New York Sunday Times, 81; Precious, Grey Art Gallery, Art in Am, 85. *Media:* All. *Publ:* Contribr, Art Am, Appearances Mag, Umbrella Mag, NJ, Monthly Mag, 83, New Look Mag, 85 & Street Art, Dial Press, 85; Great Walls of China, Eastview Eds, 74. *Mailing Add:* 371 Fourth St Jersey City NJ 07302

PALAU, MARTA
ENVIRONMENTAL ARTIST, SCULPTOR
b Albesa, Lerida, Spain, July 17, 1934; Mexican citizen. *Study:* La Esmeralda, Inst Nat Bellas Artes, Mex; San Diego State Univ, Calif; Grau Garriga's Atelier, Barcelona, Spain. *Work:* Secretaria Relaciones Exteriores, Mexico City; Mus Mod Art, Mexico City; Mus Mod Art Latin America, Washington; Tamayo Mus, Mexico City; Mus Mod Art, Univ Sao Paulo, Brazil; Mus Contemp Art, La Jolla, Calif; Fisher Gallery, Univ S Calif, Los Angeles; Mus de Arte Contemporaneo, Mexico City. *Comn:* Purépecha, Metal Sculpture 18 meters, Morelia, Michoacan, 85; 19 Biennial of Sao Paulo, Brazil, Recinto de Chamanes installation, 87; Aztlan, Exterior Mural, MAM Mexico City, 88; Art Museum of the Americas, Naualli Circulo de Sal, installation, Washington, 90; Genova 92, Naualli Centinelas, installation, Genova, Italy, 92. *Exhib:* Americas-Japan, MAM, Tokyo, Japan and MAM Kyoto-Japan, 77; 8th Int Biennial of Tapestry, Laussana, Suiza, 77; Mus de Arte Mod, Mexico City, 78, Sala Nac, Palacio de Bellas Artes, Mexico City, 85, Fisher Gallery, installation, Los Angeles, Calif, 91 & Galeria de Arte Mexicano, Mexico City, 93; Mücsarnok Palace of Exhibitios Kunsthalle, Budapest, Hungary, 92; Naualli-Centinelas, Nexus Contemp Art Ctr, Atlanta, Ga, 93; and others. *Teaching:* Artist-in-residence, Casa Americas & Inst Superior de Arte, Havana, Cuba. *Awards:* Installation Award, Second Biennial, Havana, Cuba, 86; Burgerpreis, 5th Triennial, Fellbach, Ger, 92; Artistic Creator, Conacult Fel, Mexico City, 93. *Bibliog:* Juan Acha (auth), Fiber Works, Americas-Japan, Mus Mod Art, Kyoto, Japan, 78; Rita Eder (auth), Marta Palau, La Intuicion in y la Tecnica, CEGM, 85; Margaret Sayers Peden (auth), Out of the Volcano, Smithsonian Inst Press, 91. *Publ:* Auth, Lo Mas Antiguo y Lo Mas Moderno en el Arte de Marta Palau, Antonio Rodriguez, 73; co-auth, numerous essays. *Dealer:* Galeria Juan Martin Dickens 33 B Polanco 11560 DF; Kunsthaus Santa Fe San Miguel de Allende Guanajuato Mexico. *Mailing Add:* Galileo 16-6 Mexico DF 11560 Mexico

PALAZZOLO, CARL
PAINTER
b Torrington, Conn, 1945. *Study:* Boston Mus Sch, 65-69; Tufts Univ Mus Sch Prog, 66-68; Boston Mus Sch (independent grad prog), 69-70. *Exhib:* Whitney Mus Am Art, 75; Inst Contemp Art, Boston, 75; Mus Fine Arts, Boston, 85 (two exhibs); solo exhibs, Bette Stoler Gallery, 86, Harcus Gallery, Boston, 88, Lennon, Weinberg Inc, NY, 90 (with catalog) & 92, Marguerite Oestreicher Fine Arts, New Orleans, 91 & 93, Thomas Babeor Gallery, La Jolla, Calif, 92 & Carl Palazzolo: Private Viewing, AN Exhibition of Recent Watercolors, Miller Block Gallery, Boston, MA, 99 & Recent Work, Rebecca Ibel Gallery, Columbus, Ohio, 99& Recent Work, Robert Bowman Ltd, London, Eng, 2001; Truth Be Told: It's All about Love, Lennon, Weinberg Inc, NY, 94; Novices Collect: Selections from the Sam & May Gruber Collection, Currier Gallery Art, Manchester, NH, 94; Works on Paper, Allez les Filles, St Louis, 94; Lennon, Weinberg Inc, NY, 95; group exhibs, Drawing Rooms: Carl Palazzolo, Denyse Thomasos, Robin Hill, NY, Lennon, Weinberg, Inc, 2000, Reflection, Rebecca Ibsl Gallery, Columbus, Ohio, Underfoot, Dan Galeria, Sao Paulo, 2001; Retrospective (with catalog), Weinberg, Inc, 90; retrospective, Miane Coast Artists, 92. *Teaching:* Dean, Boston Music Sch, 92-; instr advanced painting seminar, Sch of Boston Mus of Fine Arts, 96; vis lectr slide presentation, Boston Col, 96; vis lectr slide pesentation, Bates Col, 99. *Awards:* Bicentennial Traveling Exhib Grant, Mass Coun Arts, 75; Clarissa Bartlett Traveling Scholar Alumni Award, Sch Boston Mus Fine Arts, 85; Nat Endowment Arts & Humanities, 87; Grant, Nat Endowment for the Arts and Humanities, 87. *Bibliog:* Robert L Pincus (auth), Visual arts: Critics choice, San Diego Union-Tribune, 3/12/92; Jonathan Saville (auth), Hovering at the edge of meaning, San Diego's Weekly Reader, 2/20/92; George Melrod (auth), Openings: Carl Palazzolo, Art & Antiques, 11/94. *Publ:* Carl Palazzolo at Lennon, Weinberg, Art in America, 11/90; About town: art, The New Yorker, 6/4/90. *Dealer:* Lennon-Weinberg Gallery 560 Broadway Ste 308 New York NY 10012-3945. *Mailing Add:* 35 Two-Dog Ln Georgetown ME 04548

PALERMO, JOSEPH
PAINTER, SCULPTOR
b Pittsburgh, Pa. *Study:* Ecole des Beaux Arts, Paris, cert des arts, 64; Univ Complutense de Madrid, dipl de coupletacion, 78. *Work:* USAF Mus, Dayton, Ohio; Air and Space Mus, Washington, DC; Sumter Co Historical Soc, SC; Libr Cong, Washington, DC; Banco Hispano Americano, Madrid, Spain; S Nev Mus Fine Art; Asto Mus Fine Art, Los Angeles; Bellas Artes, Barcelona, Spain; 37 Public Collections. *Comn:* 20 foot stainless steel sculpture, Banco Hispano Americano, Madrid, Spain, 76; 18 foot stainless steel sculpture, Ameribank, Madrid, Spain, 76; 20x30 foot oil mural, Massaro Corp, Pittsburgh, Pa, 94; 12 foot stainless steel sculpture, McCarran Corp Plaza, Las Vegas, Nev, 99; 20 foot stainless steel sculpture, DAVRIC Corp, Henderson, Nev, 2000; Clark Co Parks and Recreation, Nev; Simon Morgage Co, Calif; Alcoa Aluminum; Trans World Airlines; Xerox Corp, New York; Price Waterhouse; Neonopolis, Las Vegas, Nev; Nev Arts Advocates, Las Vegas, Nev. *Exhib:* 34th Biennial Contemp Am Painting, Corcoran, Washington, DC, 75; Sixto Exposition de Arte, Galleria de Arta Int, Madrid, Spain, 76; Biennial, Ministrario de cultura Espagna, Samora, Spain, 76; Secundo, Exposition National de Arte Contemporaneo, Madrid, Spain, 76; Biennial, Musei Espanole de Arte Contemporaneo, Madrid, Spain, 77; Assoc Artists, Carnegie Mus, Pittsburgh, Pa, 90; Annual Juried, Pittsburgh Ctr Arts, 92; Annual Juried, Assoc Artists Pittsburgh, 93; Retrospective Las Vegas Art Mus, 2005; solo exhib, New Art Ctr, NY, 2008; Southern Nev Mus Fine Art, 2009; Rainforest Art Found Gallery, Long Island City, 2010; S Nevada Mus Art, Las Vegas, 2011; Rainforest Art Found Gallery, Long Island City, 2011; Allure Modern and Contemp Art Gallery, Las Vegas, 2012; Mark Rowland Contemp Las Vegas, 2012. *Pos:* Exec dir, Las Vegas Art Mus, 97-2004; consult exec dir, S Nev Mus Fine Art, 2005-; appointee bd mem, Nev Arts Coun, 2007. *Awards:* Secunda Medalla, Bellas Artes, Musei Epsanole, 77; Medalla de Oro, Biennial de Artistas plasticos, Samora, 77; Spain ARTV Award, 2003; 2 ARTV Awards, Artist of the Year and Printmaking 2005. *Bibliog:* Emilio Delgado Espenosa (auth), Escultures, Esculture de Madrid, 75; Antonio Vivas (auth), Ceramica, Nuavo, Ceramica Espagna, 85; James Mann (auth), International Dictionary of Modern & Contemporary Art, 99-2000, rev ed, 2001-2002. *Mem:* Las Vegas Art Mus (pres 96-97); Contemp Arts Collective; Desert Sculptors; Asn Artistsas Plasticos Madrid; Henderson Art Asn (co-founder); Southern Nev Ctr Arts (co-founder). *Media:* Oil, Acrylic, Steel, Clay, Stainless. *Interests:* The direction of art & artist for the 21st century & art beyond post-modernism. *Collection:* more than 300 pvt collections. *Publ:* Art Scene, Pittsburgh Post Gazette, 93; Viva Las Vegas, Creative Loafing, Arts Around the World, Dr James Mann, 96; Internet Gambling Report and II Cover & Bio, Anthoy Cabot, 97-98; International Dictionary of Modern & Contemporary Art, Casaeditrice Alba, 99, rev ed, 2000-2002; Distinguished Men of Nev, Distingsuished Publ Co, 2000-; Las Vegas Review J, Ken White, 2005; VIP Mag, Audrey Roberts, Las Vegas, 2006; John Austin, NY, Art Review, 2008. *Dealer:* Timeless Treasures 982 American Pacific Ste 204 Henderson NV; Southbank Galleries Pittsburgh PA 15203; Gallery P Las Vegas NV 89102; Seyhoun Gallery Los Angeles 9007 Melrose Ave W Hollywood CA 90069; New Art Ctr 580 8th Ave 5th Fl New York NY 10018; Allure Fine Art Gallery Las Vegas NV; Rainforest Gallery Long Island City NY; Mark Rowland Contemporary Las Vegas NV 89101. *Mailing Add:* 4572 New Dupell Way Las Vegas NV 89147

PALEVITZ, ROBERT
PAINTER, DRAFTSMAN
b Brooklyn, NY. *Study:* School of Visual Arts, cert, 1955-58; Art Students League, 1982-93. *Work:* Nat Arts Club. *Comn:* Pvt collections nationwide. *Exhib:* Calif Art Club Exhib, Ebell Club, Los Angeles, 97; The Figure in Am Art, Eleanor Ettinger Gallery, NY, 99; NY Soc Portrait Artists, Salmagundi Club, NY, 2002; Greenhouse Galery Salon Int, San Antonio, TX, 2002; Allied Artists of Amer, Nat Arts Club, New York, (89th Juried) 2002, (92nd Juried) 2006, (94th Juried) 2007; Audubon Artists, Salmagundi Club, NY, 2003 & 2004; Allied Artists of Am, Nat Arts Club, New York, 2009, 2010 & 2011; The Butter Inst of Am Art, Youngstown, Ohio, 2011; Les Pastellistes de France, Feytiat, France, 2013. *Teaching:* Instr still life painting, The Art Students League, New York, June-Aug 2004; instr figure drawing, Univ NC Willmington (UnCW), Spring 2006; Pvt teaching, concepts of composition space & air, currently; workshop, portrait with pastel, Pastel Soc Am, New York, 2012. *Awards:* First Place Blue Ribbon for Still Life, Calif Art Club Exhib, Ebell Club, Los Angeles, 97; Grumbacher Gold Medal, Allied Artists, 2001; NY Pastel Award, Audubon Artists, 2001; Paul Puzinas Mem Award, Allied Artists, 2002; Gene Magazzini Award, Allied Artists, 2003; American Artists Prof League, Audubon Artists, 2003; Gary Erbe Award, Allied Artists, 2007; Jack Richeson and Co Award for Pastel Portrait, Pastel Soc Am, 2011. *Bibliog:* Anne Hevener (auth), Robert Palevitz, The Pastel Journal, 10/2006; Debra Secor (auth), Robert Palevitz, The Pastel Journal, 2012. *Mem:* Allied Artists of Am (corresp secy, 2007); Audubon Artists Soc; Portrait Soc of Am; life mem Art Students League; signature mem Pastel Soc of Am. *Media:* Oil, Soft Pastel, Charcoal. *Specialty:* Representational Still Life Compositions in Oil. *Publ:* Coauth (with Richard Frederick), Robert Palevitz: A Portfolio of Painting & Drawings, New Concept Press, 2005; auth, Drawings of the Nude in Todays Culture, The Artists Mag, 6/2006; auth, Art of Body Movement, Pastel Journal Mag, 2012. *Dealer:* The Sylvan Gallery 171 King St Charleston SC 29401; Beardsley Gallery 196 Danbury Road Wilton CT 06897. *Mailing Add:* 333 E 30th St Apt 4P New York NY 10016

PALEY, ALBERT RAYMOND
GOLDSMITH, DESIGNER
b Philadelphia, Pa, Mar 28, 1944. *Study:* Tyler Sch Art, Temple Univ, BFA, 66, with Stanley Lechtzin, goldsmithing, MFA, 69; Univ Rochester, Hon Dr, 89. *Work:* Metrop Mus Art, NY; British Mus Art; Philadelphia Mus Art; Smithsonian Inst, Renwick Gallery, Washington, DC; Victoria & Albert Mus, London. *Comn:* Wrought iron portal gates, Renwick Gallery, Smithsonian Inst, Washington, DC, 74; Stairway sculptures & door pulls, Wortham Theatre Ctr, Houston, Tex, 87; Sculpture, Adobe Systems, Inc, San Jose, Calif, 98; Sculpture, Bausch & Lomb Corp, Rochester, NY, 96; Sculpture, Fed Bldg, Asheville, NC, 95. *Exhib:* Art to Art, Paley, Dine, Statom, Toldeo Mus Art, Ohio, 96; Age of Steel: Recent Sculpture, Brigham Young Univ, Provo, Utah, 96; Sculpture, San Antonio Art Inst, Tex, 93; Sculpture, Samuel P Harn Mus Art, Univ Fla, Gainesville, 92; Nat Mus Wales, Cardiff, 89; Towards a New Iron Age, Victoria & Albert Mus, London, 93; Zonju Int Biennial, Comju City, Korea, 99; Carl Solway Gallery, Cincinnati, 2007. *Pos:* pres, founder, Paley Studios Limited, Rochester, NY, 72. *Teaching:* prof, State Univ NY Col, Brockport, 72-84; prof & artist-in-residence,

Sch Am Craftsmen, Rochester Inst, 84-. *Awards:* Master of New Medium Award, Smithsonian Inst, 97; Lifetime Achievement Award, Am Inst Archit, 95; Citation Distinguished Svc in Visual Arts Award, Nat Asn Schs Art & Design, 95. *Bibliog:* Edward Lucie-Smith (auth), The Art of Albert Paley, 96. *Mem:* Internat Sculpture Ctr. *Media:* Forged and Fabricated Mild Steel. *Mailing Add:* Paley Studios Ltd 1677 Lyell Ave #A Rochester NY 14606

PALKO KOLOSVARY, PAUL
COLLAGE ARTIST, PRINTMAKER
b Bekescsaba, Hungary; US citizen. *Study:* Atelier Art Sch, Budapest, dipl, 40; Acad Fine Art, Budapest, dipl, 52. *Work:* Mus Fine Arts, Budapest, Hungary; Norton Simon Corp, Fullerton, Calif; Downey Mus Art, Calif; Huntsville Mus Art, Ala; Tex Tech Univ, Lubbock. *Exhib:* Retrospective, Huntsville Mus Art, Ala, 80; Recent Am Works on Paper, Smithsonian Inst, 85-87; 4 Contemp Printmakers, Downey Mus Art, Calif, 88; juried, Royal West Eng Acad, Bristol, Eng, 89; invitational, Salford Mus, Salford, Eng, 89; Int Survey, Stamford Mus, Conn, 90. *Awards:* Nat Munkacjy Prize, Mucsatlnok, Budapest, 52; Int Art Contest Gold Medal, Los Angeles, 84; Art Quest Nat 1st Prize, Boston/Los Angeles, 87. *Bibliog:* Michael Preble (auth), Paul & Eva Kolosvary, Walnut Col, 75. *Mailing Add:* 30211 Via Rivera Rancho Palos Verdes CA 90274

PALLADINO-CRAIG, ALLYS
DIRECTOR, CURATOR
b Pontiac, Mich, Mar 23, 1947. *Study:* Fla State Univ, BA, 67, MFA, 78, PhD, 96; Univ Toronto, 68-69; Univ Va, 75-76. *Pos:* Dir contemp art, Four Arts Ctr, Tallahassee, 79-82; ed, Athanor, Fla State Univ, Ann J Art Hist, 80-; dir, Fla State Univ Mus Fine Arts, Tallahassee, 82-; ed-in-chief, Fla State Univ, Mus Fine Arts Press, currently. *Teaching:* Mus Practices and studio. *Awards:* Individual Artist Fel, Fla Arts Coun, 79; and over 100 grants for Fla State Univ, Mus Fine Arts. *Mem:* FAMDA; FAM; Am Alliance Mus; AAMG. *Publ:* contrib ed, Chroma, Fla State Univ Mus Fine Arts, 94; contrib ed, Body Language, Fla State Univ Mus Fine Arts, 96; auth, Mark Messersmith: new mythologies, Fla Gulf Coast Art Ctr, 96; Alexa Kleinbard (auth), Talking Leaves, Gulf Coast Mus Art, 99; Jake Fernadez (auth), Ethereal Journeyman, Ft Lauderdale Mus Art, 2000; Jim Roche (auth), Sense of Place, Gulf Coast Mus Art, Largo, Fla, 2003; contrib ed, Terrestrial Forces, Fla State Univ, Mus Fine Arts, 2004; contrib ed, High Roads & Low Roads, 2006; Fla State Univ, Mus Fine Arts; contrib ed, Jim Roche: Glory Roads, 2011; contrib ed, Gabrielle Wu Lee: Retrospective, 2013. *Mailing Add:* 1410 Grape St Tallahassee FL 32303

PALMER, KATE (KATHARINE) A
PAINTER
b Oklahoma City, Okla, July 28, 1948. *Study:* Okla City Univ, BA (Eng lit), 70, BA (art), 74; Studio classes with Richard Goetz, 79-81, David A Leffel, 83-84; Workshops with William Reese, 88, Mark Daily, 90, Michael Lynch, 97-98. *Exhib:* Wichita Ctr Arts, Kans, 96; Butler Inst Am Art, 97; Allied Artists Am at the Butler, Butler Inst Am Art, 2000; Am Women Artists, The Cloisters, Sorrento, Italy, 2000; Am Artists Prof League Grant Int, Salmagundi Club, NY, 2000; Oil Painters Am Nat, Gallery Americana, Carmel, Calif, 2000; Allied Artists Am Ann, Nat Arts Club, NY, 2000; among others. *Pos:* cons art restoration, Mabee-Gerrer Mus, Shawnee, Okla, 85-86; workshop asst, Albert Handell, 94-95. *Awards:* Alfred C Crimi Mem Award, Audubon Artists, 97; Gamblin Artists Colors Award Excellence, Oil Painters Am, 97; First Prize Medal of Honor, Catharine Lorillard Art Club, 98; Frank C Wright Best in Show Medal, Am Artists Prof League, 2000; Jack Richeson First Prize Best Artist Products Award, Salmagundi Club, 2000; Grumbacher Gold Medal, Allied Artists Am 87th Ann, 2000. *Bibliog:* Christina Adams (auth), Oil Painters of America, Southwest Art, 5/98; Jim Lynch (auth), Making the Landscape Your Own: Kate Palmer, Am Artist Mag, 11/99; Gussie Fauntleroy (auth), Women in the Arts, Southwest Art, 6/2000. *Mem:* Allied Artists Am Inc; Am Women Artists (chair exec bd); Audubon Artists; Catharine Lorillard Wolfe Art Club; Salmagundi Club. *Media:* Oil, Pastel. *Dealer:* Joe Wade Fine Arts 102 E Water St Santa Fe NM 87501; Dragonfly Gallery Chapel Sq Avon CO 81620. *Mailing Add:* 103 Vista Redonda Santa Fe NM 87506

PALMER, LAURA HIGGINS
ARTIST
b Kansas City, Mo, Mar 16, 1955. *Study:* Corcoran School Art; Cornell Univ, with Freidel Dzubas, BFA, 75; George Washington Univ, History of Art, MA, 78; Inst Doc Studies Visual Arts. *Work:* Md Artists Col, Univ Md, College Park, Md, 85-2005; Cecil Coll, Md. *Comn:* Dianne Hunt Dance Ensemble, Takoma Park, 80-81; Numerous props, sets, etc, Ballet Theatre Maryland, Annapolis, MD, 85-2005. *Exhib:* Three Rivers Arts Festival, Carnegie Mus Art, Pittsburgh, Pa; Area 86, Hirshhorn Mus, Washington, DC; New Artists, Madison Square Garden, NY. *Pos:* Coll mgr asst, Smithsonian Nat Mus Am Hist, 78-80; Slide Librn, Howard Univ Sch of Art, 80-82. *Teaching:* Instr, Drawing & Painting, Mt Holyoke Coll, 78; Instr, Drawing, Painting Design, Md Hall, Annapolis, MD, 86-94. *Awards:* Faculty scholarship, George Washington Univ, 77-7; Md Fedn Art, 85; painters choice, Wall to Wall. *Bibliog:* The Art of Dance, Baltimore Sun Newspaper, 4/5/91; Mike Driscoll (auth), Impressions of Ballet, Capitol, Annapolis, 92; Artist in Step with Dance, Washington Post, 4/8/2004. *Mem:* Coll Art Asn; Ballet Theatre Md Bd of Trustees, secy, 2002-2003; Cult Arts Found of Anne Arundel Co. *Media:* Brush & Ink, Oil. *Interests:* dance. *Collection:* Sheppherd Pratt. *Publ:* Dance this Notebook, 2012

PALMER, MARILLA
PAINTER, SCULPTOR
b 1956. *Study:* Alfred Univ, NY; Philadelphia Coll Art, Pa, BFA, 77. *Exhib:* Solo exhibs, Christopher Grimes, Santa Monica Calif, 94, Deven Golden Fine Art, New York, 97, PPOW Project Room, New York, 98, Backyard Paradise, Peirogi Gallery, Brooklyn, 2002, Optimism Reigns and Rains, 2005, Rovert V Fullerton Art Mus, Calif State Univ, 2002, Fringe Benefit Exhib, 2002; group exhibs include The Neurotic Art Show, Artists Space, New York, 92; America Europa Evento a 360, Pino Molica Gallery, Rome, 92; Fear of Painting, Arthur Roger Gallery, New York, 92; Barbara Braathen Gallery, New York, 92; Libidinal Painting, White Columns Gallery, 93, WhiteColumns Benefit, 97 & 2000; ...figure out..., Trial BALLOON, New York, 93; Arabesque, PPOW, New York, 94; That Obscure Object of Desire, Four Walls, Brooklyn, 94; Artychoke, Flamingo East, 94; Dyad, Peirogi 2000, New York, 94; Nature, Arena, Brooklyn, 95; Curt Marcus Gallery, New York, 95; Bloom, Christinerose Gallery, New York, 95; Vulnerability, Dahn Gallery, New York, 95; Les Levine Collection, New Acquisitions, Freedman Gallery, Redding, Pa, 96; Bronwyn Keenan Gallery, New York, 96; Landscape as Abstraction, James Graham & Sons, New York, 97; Pierogi 2000 Flatfiles, Gasworks, London, 97; Current Undercurrents, Brooklyn Mus, 97; Just what do you think you're doing Dave?, Williamsburg Art & Hist Soc, Brooklyn, 97; Stellar Spectra, Mary Barone Gallery, New York, 97; Affirm Identity, Kingsboro Coll Gallery, Brooklyn, 98; The Idea Made Physical, Calif State Univ Fullerton, 98; Ten from Brooklyn, 2nd St Gallery, Charlottesville, Va, 98; Gallery Artists, Deven Golden Fine Art, New York, 98; Eye Candy, 2000; Pierogi 2000 Flatfiles, Yerba Buena, San Francisco, 2000; Haulin A in LA, Post Gallery, LA, 2000; Mininal to Excess, Bucheon Gallery, San Francisco, 2002; The Brooklyn Rail Presents Selection 1, Wythe Studio, Brooklyn, 2002; NextNext Visual Art, Brooklyn Accad Music, 2002; Flicker, Jeffrey Coploff Gallery, New York, 2003; Tasty Buds, Work Space, New York, 2003; Look Up!, NY Accad Sci, 2003; New Work, NY-NMex, Carlsgad Mus & Art Center, 2003; Vacation Nation, Pierogi Gallery, Brooklyn, 2004; Critics Select, Shore Inst Contemp Arts, Long Beach, NJ, 2005. *Media:* Miscellaneous Media. *Mailing Add:* 704 Humboldt St Brooklyn NY 11222-3505

PALMER, MEREDITH ANN
ART DEALER
b Los Angeles, Calif, July 7, 1951. *Study:* Radcliffe Col, Harvard Univ, with Rudolf Arnheim, BA, 73; Harvard Bus Sch, Owner/Pres Prog, 84. *Collection Arranged:* Chinese Archeol Exhib, US Dept State, 74-75; US Info Agency (overseas exhibs), Print Publishing in Am, 79-80, Sam Francis: Works on Paper, 80-81, Am Paintings from the Boston Mus Fine Arts in China, 81 & The New Am Realism 1960-80, 82; Shoichi Ida, 86 & 89; Figurative European Moderns, 87; Bunka-Viewing: Sculptors & Their Drawings from Japan (auth, catalog), 90; George Peck: Composite Pictures, 94-95. *Pos:* Foreign serv reserve officer (art specialist), US Dept State, 73-76 & US Info Agency, 76-82; dir & partner, Herbert Palmer Gallery, Los Angeles, Calif, 82-91; pres, Meredith Palmer Gallery Ltd, New York, 91-. *Awards:* Grant, Nat Endowment Arts, 73. *Bibliog:* Susan Bidel (auth), Like Father, Like Daughter, Success: The Next Generation, Angeles Mag, 6/91. *Mem:* Am Asn Mus; Coll Art Asn; Art Table, Inc; Curators Coun; Mus Contemp Art Los Angeles; and others; Mus Mod Art, New York; Archit and Design Cir. *Res:* Influence of traditional Asian arts on contemporary American and European art; Legislation and issues concerning illicit trafficking in cultural properties; cross-cultural exchange and public diplomacy. *Specialty:* 20th century Modern masters and Contemporary art, painting, sculpture and drawings, includes American, European and emerging Asian artists. *Publ:* Auth, The Plundered Past, J Int Law, 4/74; China Premiers Art, US Dept State Exchange Mag, spring 75; Monet to Matisse Exhibition: A look at its positive elements, Los Angeles Times, 8/26/91. *Mailing Add:* 40 E 94th St 22D New York NY 10128-0375

PALMGREN, DONALD GENE
PAINTER, PHOTOGRAPHER
b Moline, Ill, Nov 22, 1938. *Study:* Augustana Col, BA; Lutheran Sch Theol, Chicago, MDiv; Detroit Soc Arts & Crafts; Cranbrook Acad Art, with George Ortman, MFA. *Work:* St John's Univ; Anoka-Ramsey Col; Gustavus Adolphus Col; 3 M Corp. *Exhib:* Drawings USA, 73; Appalachian Nat Drawing Competition, Appalachian State Univ, Boone, NC, 77; Rutgers Nat Drawing, 79; Talent at Allan Stone Gallery, NY, 89; Hamline Univ, 89; Mankato State Univ, 89; plus many others. *Teaching:* Vis asst prof drawing & design, Murray State Univ, 72; assoc prof drawing & photog, Gustavus Adolphus Col, 72-. *Awards:* Res grants, Gustavus Adolphus Col, 73, 75 & 76. *Media:* Charcoal, Pastel Oil; Black & White Film. *Publ:* Auth, Space Upon Space: The Liberal Connection, Art and Academe, spring 89. *Dealer:* Jane Haslem Gallery Washington DC; Groveland Gallery Minneapolis MN. *Mailing Add:* 566 State St Apt C Saint Paul MN 55107-3091

PALOMBO, LISA
PAINTER
b Providence, RI, Mar 1, 1965. *Study:* RI Sch of Design, BFA, 87. *Work:* MD Anderson Hosp, Houston; Cenavra Bank, Rocky Mount, NC; Hilton Garden Inn, Washington, DC. *Exhib:* Oil Painters of Am Regional Exhib, Brazier Fine Art, Richmond, Va, 02; Hudson Valley Art Asn, Found of Art, Hasting on the Hudson, NY, 02; Pen & Brush Regional Open Exhib, NY, 2003; Best of Am, The Nat Oil & Acrylic Painter's Soc Ann, Nat Exhib, Bolivar, MO, 2004; Conn Acad Fine Arts Ann Exhib, Mystic, Conn, 2004; Schaknow Mus Fine Arts, Plantation, Fla, 2006; Audubon Artists, NY, 2011. *Pos:* owner, Lisa Palombo Studios. *Awards:* Award of Merit, Am Artist Prof League, 02; Showcase Award Winner, Manhattan Arts Internat Competition, 96; Finalist, Artist Mag Ann Art Competition, 02. *Mem:* Oil Painter of Am; Am Artists Prof League; Am Impressionist Soc. *Media:* Oil. *Publ:* Best of Oil Pianting, Rockport Pub, 96; Exploring Color, NorthLight Books, 98; Best in Am Oil Artists Vol II, Kennedy Publ. *Mailing Add:* c/o Palombo Studios 55 Mountain Ave Caldwell NJ 07006

PALUMBO, JACQUES
PAINTER, SCULPTOR
b Philippeville, Algeria, Sept 16, 1939; Can citizen. *Study:* Sch Fine Arts, Algiers, Algeria, BA, 60; Sch Fine Arts, Paris, France, MA, 65; Educ Technols Univ Montreal, PhD, 87. *Work:* Mus Contemp Art, Mus Fine Arts, Montreal, Que; Nat Gallery, Ottawa, Ont; Sincron Cult Ctr, Brescia, Italy; Found IDC, Zoetermeer, Neth. *Comn:* Monumental sculpture, City Hall, Trois-Rivieres, 92. *Exhib:* Konkret Acht, Kunsthaus, Nuremberg, 88; Systematic & Constructive Art, Villa de Madrid, Spain,

88; Europa 90, Sincron Cult Ctr, Brescia, Italy, 90; De L'Abstraction Geometrique, Mus Fine Arts, Montreal, 91; Propos D'Art Contemp, Mus Contemp Art, Montreal, 91; and others. *Bibliog:* Peter Perrin (auth), Icon and Numbers, Arts Can, 78; Gianguido Fucito (auth), Dualita, catalogue, 89; Leo Rosshandler (auth), Vers un Art Exact, Vie Des Arts, 90. *Mem:* Soc des Artistes Profs du Que, Montreal, 71; Conseil de la Peinture, Montreal, 91. *Media:* Acrylic, Oil; Metal, Cast. *Dealer:* Galerie Bervard, 90 rue Laurier Ouest, Montreal, Quebec, Canada, H2T 2N4. *Mailing Add:* 467 Ave Wiseman Montreal PQ H2V 3J9 Canada

PANAS, LYDIA
PHOTOGRAPHER
b Philadelphia, Pa. *Study:* Boston Coll, BA, 80; Sch Visual Arts, BFA, 84; New York Univ, Int Ctr of Photography, MA, 89; Special study, Whitney Mus Independent Study Fel, 85-86. *Work:* Mus Fine Arts, Houston, Tex; Allentown Art Mus, Allentown, Pa; Lehigh Univ, Bethlehem, Pa; Zendai Mus Mod Art, Shanghai, China; Muhlenberg Coll, Allentown, Pa; Brooklyn Mus, New York. *Exhib:* Solo exhib, Chocolate, Hair, & Lint, Univ Arts, Philadelphia, Pa, 2004, The Mark of Abel, Foley Gallery, New York, 2010; Group exhibs, Humanscape, Seoul Int Photography Festival, Korea, 2008; A Starting Point: Intrude 366-Dynamics of Change & Growth, Zendai, Mus of Mod Art, Shanghai, China, 2009; Crossing Lines, Dela Ctr Contemp Arts, Wilmington, Dela, 2009; 17th Ann Contemp Art Exhib, Korean Cult Ctr, Los Angeles, Calif, 2009; Mirror, Mirror: Contemp Portraits & Fugitive Self, Brigham Young Univ, Provo, Utah, 2009; All my Lovin, Berlin, Germany, 2010; Human Nature, SIPF, Singapore, 2010. *Teaching:* adj prof, Muhlenberg Coll, 91-99; adj instr photography, Kutztown Univ, 93-94; adj instr, Lafayette Coll, 2001-2002; fac, Maine Photographic Workshops, Rockport, Maine, 2000-2005; artist & instr, Vt Coll, MFA Visual Arts Prog, 2006-; adj instr, Baum Sch Art, Lehigh Carbon Community Coll, Allentown, Pa, 96-. *Awards:* Cur's Distinction, Houston Ctr Arts, 25th Ann Mem Exhib, Houston, Tex, 2008; 1st Place, TPS 16, Nat Competition, Tex Phtographic Soc, San Antonio, Tex, 2007; Top 50, Critical Mass, Photolucida, 2007-2008; 1st Place: Singular Image, Publisher's Choice Award, Center, Santa Fe, 2009; 2nd Prize, Korean Cult Ctr, Mus Contemp Art, Los Angeles, 2009; 3rd Place, Soho Nat Competition, Soho Photo, New York, 2009. *Mem:* Soc for Photographic Educ; Houston Ctr for Photography, Tex; Ctr for Photography Woodstock, NY; Tex Photographic Soc, San Antonio, Tex; Silver Eye Ctr for Photography, Pittsburgh, Pa. *Dealer:* Foley Gallery 547 W 27th 5th Fl New York NY 10001; Wallspace Pioneer Building 600 1st Ave Suite 322 Seattle Wash 98104; Maja Kaszkur Yours Gallery Warsaw Poland

PANCZENKO, RUSSELL
MUSEUM DIRECTOR
b Frille, Ger, Mar 23, 1947. *Study:* Fairfield Univ, BA, 1969; Universita degli Studi di Firenze, Italy, Dottore in Lettere, 1979. *Pos:* Asst dir, Williams Col Mus Art, 1980-84; dir, Elvehjem Mus Art, Univ Wis, Madison, 1984-. *Teaching:* Mus studies & connoisseurship. *Awards:* Mus Fel, Nat Endowment Arts. *Mem:* Asn Art Mus Dirs; Am Asn Mus; Coll Art Asn; Int Coun Mus; Wis Fedn Mus. *Res:* Early Italian Renaissance; late 19th Century and 20th Century Art. *Publ:* Auth, Gentile da Fabriano and classical antiquity, 1980 & Umanesimo di Gentile da Fabriano, 1983, Artibus et Historiae; Florence in Italian Paintings, 1850-1910, Clark Inst, Williamstown, Mass, 1982; Richard Artschwager: PUBLIC/public (exhib catalog), 1991. *Mailing Add:* Chazen Museum of Art 800 University Avenue Madison WI 53706

PANDOZY, RAFFAELE MARTINI
CONCEPTUAL ARTIST, LECTURER
b Rome, 1937. *Study:* Acad Belle Arti Roma, 63; Univ Dallas, Tex, MA (sculpture), 74; New York Univ, NY, PhD, 85. *Work:* Dallas Mus Fine Arts, Tex; Ft Worth Mus Mod Art, Tex; San Francisco Mus Art, Calif. *Comn:* Pubsculpture, Eastfield Col, Dallas, Tex; indoor sculpture, Univ Tex, Dallas. *Exhib:* Tarrant Co Exhib, Ft Worth Mus, Tex, 72; Dallas Artist, Dallas Mus Fine Arts, Tex, 75; Twelve Texas, Mus Contemp Art, Houston, Tex, 76; 25 Contemps, Ft Worth Mus, Tex, 76; Texas Art, Univ Tex Campus, Dallas, 78; Dallas-San Francisco Exchange, San Francisco Mus Art, Calif, 78; Epigraphs, Hunter Coll Gallery, NY, 80; Earth & the Environment, DCAM, Dallas, 94. *Awards:* Campbell Found Award for Sculpture, 75; First Place Award, Dallas City Hall, 78. *Bibliog:* Janet Kunter (auth), The art of hole making, Art News, 76; Janet Kunter (auth), Phenomenology, Dallas Morning News, 81. *Mem:* Coll Art Asn; Nat Art Educ Asn; Nat Comt Hist Art; Am Soc Aesthetics; Int Asn Philos & Lit. *Media:* Earth Pigment. *Publ:* Of Arteology, Artimes Ed. *Dealer:* Art for the 90's 65 S 11th St Brooklyn NY 11211

PANTELL, RICHARD KEITH
PAINTER, PRINTMAKER
b Bronx, NY, May 2, 1951. *Study:* Univ Bridgeport, Conn, 69-71; Art Students League, with David Leffel, Frank Mason & Earl Mayan, 74-75. *Work:* Butler Inst Am Art, Youngstown, Ohio; Wichita Art Mus, Kans; New York Pub Libr; Jewish Mus, Stokholm, Sweden; British Mus, London. *Comn:* Mural Saugerties Timescape, Saugerties Cent Schs, NY, 93. *Exhib:* Butler Inst Am Art, 81-83, 2001, 2003; Nat Acad, 82, 88, 90, 2000; Ann Allied Artists Exhib, Nat Arts Club, NY, 83-2013; Bernard & S Dean Levy Gallery, NY, 84; Soc Am Graphic Artists, NY, 86-2005; Limner Gallery, NY, 92; Old Print Shop, NY, 86-2010, 94, 2002 & 2007; Saginaw Valley State Univ, Mich, 94; NY Transit Mus, 96, 2003; Zimmerli Art Mus, Rutgers Univ, 98, 2004; Mus City New York, 2002; solo exhibs, Belskie Mus Art & Sci, NJ, 2008, Wagner Coll, 2008; and others. *Teaching:* Instr painting & drawing, Continuing Educ, Univ Uppsala, Sweden, 76-77 & Woodstock Sch Art, NY, 79-93; instr printmaking, State Univ NY, Coll New Paltz, 89-91 & Art Students League, NY, 96-. *Awards:* Hallgarten First Prize, Nat Acad, 82; NY State Found Grant, 92; Gold Medal Hon Painting, Allied Artists Am, 2003. *Bibliog:* Palmer Paroner (auth), The art of Richard Pantell, 7/23/81 & A transplanted New Yorker, 7/7/83, Artspeak; Tram Combs (auth), Pantell's luminous urbanities, Woodstock Times, 7/21/83; Fridolph Johnson (auth), Richard Pantell, Am Artist, 2/87. *Mem:* Allied Artists Am; Art Students League, NY; Woodstock Artists Asn (bd dir, 79-80 & 82-83); Soc Am Graphic Artists (coun mem, 89-94); Audubon Artists. *Media:* Oil; Etching. *Dealer:* Old Print Shop 150 Lexington Ave New York NY; Bearsville Graphics Fine Art Gallery 68 Tinker St Woodstock NY 12409. *Mailing Add:* PO Box 550 Bearsville NY 12409

PANZERA, ANTHONY
ARTIST
Study: State Univ NY, New Paltz, BS; Southern Ill Univ, Carbondale, MFA. *Work:* Ariz State Univ Mart Mus, Tempe, NJ State Mus, Trenton, Jane Voorhees Zimmerly Art Mus, New Brunswick, NJ. *Exhib:* Solo exhibs, Bates Col, Lewiston, Maine, Marsh Art Gallery, Richmond, Va, Colgate Univ Art Gallery, Hamilton, NY; Group exhibs, Nat Acad Ann, Century Assoc, Leubsdorf Gallery, Laurel Tracy Gallery, Red Bank, NJ, Robert Wilson Gallery, Nantucket, Rep in permanent collections Bristol-Myers Squibb Collection, Princeton. *Pos:* Mem Abbey Mural Comt Nat Acad. *Teaching:* Teacher, fine arts, Hunter Col, City Univ of NY, 68-, Brooklyn Col, New York Acad of Art; co-dir, Art in Florence/Rome Summer prog; fresco instr, RI Sch of Design; now fac Nat Acad, New York City. *Publ:* contribr articles on art hist to Art World Mag. *Mailing Add:* Hunter Coll Dept Art N Bldg 11th Fl 695 Park Ave New York NY 10021

PAONE, PETER
PAINTER, PRINTMAKER
b Philadelphia, Pa, Oct 2, 1936. *Study:* Philadelphia Coll Art, BFA, 58. *Work:* Libr Cong; Philadelphia Mus Art; Mus Mod Art; Art Inst Chicago; Victoria & Albert Mus, London, Eng; Nat Portrait Gallery, Wash, DC; Jersey City Mus Art; Okla Mus Art; Nat Academy of Design; and others. *Exhib:* Brooklyn Mus, 62 & 64; Butler Inst Am Art, 65; Forum Gallery NY; Otis Art Inst, Los Angeles, 64 & 66; Kennedy Galleries, 70-74; Solo exhibs, Contemp Art Mus, Houston, 76, Roswell Mus, NMex, 77 & Hooks-Epstein Galleries, Houston, 78-88; Pa Acad Fine Arts, 83; Merlin Verlact, Ger, 97-98; 12 Anonymous Poets, Nat Acad Design Mus; and many others. *Teaching:* Instr, Philadelphia Col Art, 59 & Pratt Inst, 59-66; instr art hist, Positano Art Sch, Italy, 61; prof drawing & chmn graphics dept, Pa Acad Fine Arts, 78-. *Awards:* Guggenheim Fel, 65-66; Tiffany Grant, 65-67; Print Club Award of Merit, Philadelphia, 83; MidAtlantic Grant, 98; and others. *Bibliog:* Selden Rodman (auth), The Insiders, La State Univ, 60. *Mem:* Soc Am Graphic Artists; Nat Acad. *Media:* All. *Res:* Bernarda Bryson Shahn. *Publ:* Auth & illusr, Paone's Zoo, 61, Five Insane Dolls, 66 & My Father, 68; auth, Kachina--Paone, 76; and others. *Mailing Add:* 1027 Westview St Philadelphia PA 19119

PAPAGEORGE, TOD
PHOTOGRAPHER
b Portsmouth, NH, Aug 1, 1940. *Study:* Univ NH, BA. *Hon Degrees:* Yale Univ, Hon MA. *Work:* Mus Mod Art, Seagrams Inc, NY; Art Inst Chicago; Bibliot Nat, Paris; Boston Mus Fine Arts; Dallas Mus Fine Art. *Comn:* The American Courthouse Bicentennial Doc, Seagrams, Inc, 75; American Images, AT&T, 78; The Acropolis, Warner Commun Inc, 83. *Exhib:* Recent Acquisitions, Mus Mod Art, 71, 73, 74 & 79, Pub Landscapes, 74 & Mean Streets, 91; 14 Am Photogr, Baltimore Mus Art, 75; Mirrors & Windows, Mus Mod Art, 78; Solo exhibs, Art Inst Chicago, 78, Galerie Zibriskie, Paris, 80, Daniel Wolf Gallery, NY, 81 & 85, Akron Art Mus, 81, Galerie Lange-Irschl, Munich, WGer, 81, Sheldon Mem Art Gallery, Lincoln, Nebr, 81 & Franklin Parrasch Gallery, NY, 91; California Dreaming, Franklin Parrasch Gallery, NY, 92; Summer Pastimes, Joseph Seagrams & Sons, NY, 92; Art in the Machine Age, Worcester Art Mus, Mass, 94; Varied Viewpoints, Seagram Gallery, NY, 95; The Permanent Collection, Mus Mod Art, NY, 95; DeCordova Mus, Lincoln, Mass, 96. *Teaching:* prof photography and dir grad study, Yale Sch Art, 79-; teacher Parson Sch, 69-72, Pratt Inst, Cooper Union, 71-74; instr Queens Coll, 72-74, MIT, 75, Harvard, 76, Yale Sch Art, 78-. *Awards:* Guggenheim Found Fel Photog, 70 & 77; Nat Endowment Arts Fel Photog, 73 & 75. *Bibliog:* Leo Rubinfien (auth), Love-hate relations, Artforum, summer 78; Ben Lifson (auth), Clothed in possibilities, Village Voice, 12/12/79; Maren Stange (auth), Tod Papageorge, In: Contemporary Photographers, St Martin's Press, 82. *Publ:* Contribr, articles, Aperture, Vol 19, No 1 & No 85, 81; auth & ed, Public Relations, The Photographs of Garry Winogrand, Mus Mod Art, 77; auth, Walker Evans and Robert Frank: An Essay on Influence (catalog), Yale Art Gallery, 81; auth, What We Brought, The Photographs of Robert Adams, Yale Art Gallery, 2002; and others. *Mailing Add:* 122 Cottage St New Haven CT 06511-5652

PAPE, SKY
PAINTER
b Canada. *Study:* Attended Queens Univ, Canada, 81-82; Parson Sch Design, NY, 82-83; Art Students League, NY, studied with Richard Pousette-Dart, Bruce Dorfman, Knox Martin, 83-85. *Work:* Mus Mod Art; Solomon R Guggenheim Mus; Brooklyn Mus Art; Nat Mus Women Arts; Art Gallery Ontario. *Exhib:* Solo exhibs include Two Worlds Away, Lawrence Gallery, NY, 90; Odd and Normal Scenes, Ward-Lawrence Gallery, NY, 91, Recent Paintings, 92; Peripheral Visions, Prezant Gallery, Bronx, NY, 94; Terra Incognita, Treasure Room Gallery, NY, 95; Mortal Touchstones, Shenandoah Valley Fine Art Ctr, Va, 97; Inklings: Drawings, June Kelly Gallery, NY, 99; Silver Lining: Graphite Drawings, 2001, Behind the Seen: Saturated Ink Drawings, 2003, Drawing Breath, 2006; Drawing Breath: New Work on Paper, d e n contemp art, Los Angeles, 2006, Water Work: Surface Tension, 2010; Lake George Art Project, Courthouse Gallery, NY, 2004; Drawing Breath, Tompkins Gallery, Cedarcrest Coll, Allentown, Pa, 2007; Ink Scissors Paper, River Stone Arts, Haverstraw, New York, 2007; group exhibs include Emerging Artists, Harper Gallery, NY, 95; Hiroshima: From Me to You, Fukuya Art Gallery, Japan, 95; Women/Violence: Testimony & Empathy, State Univ NY, New Paltz, 96; Heckscher Mus Art, Huntington, NY, 96; Cross Currents: Biennial Exhib Contemp Art, Walter Anderson Mus Art, Ocean Springs, Miss, 97; Small Works, NY Univ, 98; Priva B Gross Int Works on/of Paper City NY, Queensborough Coll, New York, 98; From Hairbread to Wishing Machines,

Art Gallery Ontario, Canada, 99; The Collector's Show, Ark Art Ctr, 2000; Women and Books: Uncovered, Converse Col, SC, 2001; Drawing Nat Montmoery Coll, Rockville, Md, 2001; Memory and Metaphor, Seton Hall Univ, NJ, 2002; Cycles, Patterns, Intervals, Fredericksburg Ctr Creative Arts, Va, 2003; Now: Here: This, Studio Gallery 88, NY, 2005; Drawing National, Montgomery Col, Md, 2005; Span, Collaborative Concepts, Beacon, NY, 2005; Pulp Friction: New Takes on Paper, Betty Barker Gallery, New Canaan, Conn, 2005; Holiday Group Show, George Billis Gallery, Los Angeles, 2005; cARTalog, Univ Iowa Libraries, Iowa City, 2006; Visions: Selection from the James T Dyke Collection of Contemp Drawings, Naples Mus Art, Fla, Ark Art Ctr, 2007; Art on Paper, Weatherspoon Art Mus, Greensboro, NC, 2008; Timeless: The Art of Drawing, Morris Mus, Morristown, NJ, 2008. *Awards:* Pollock-Krasner Found Fel, 98; Can Coun Arts, Midcareer Fel, 2001; Rockefeller Found, residency fel, Bellagio Ctr, Italy, 2010. *Bibliog:* Paul Garner (auth), Peer Reveiws: The Best of 1997, Artnews, vol 97, 98; Pamela A Popeson (auth), Illuminated Brush Strokes, NYArts, Mar/April 2004, Ink Scissors Paper, July 2007. *Media:* Drawing, Works on Paper. *Dealer:* June Kelly Gallery 166 Mercer St Fl 3 New York NY 10012; d.e.n. Contemp Art Pacific Design Ctr 8687 Melrose Ave b275-2nd Fl West Hollywood CA 90069. *Mailing Add:* 91 Payson Ave #1C New York NY 10034

PAPIER, MAURICE ANTHONY
EDUCATOR, PAINTER
b Ft Wayne, Ind, Apr 14, 1940. *Study:* Ball State Univ, Muncie, Ind, BS, 63; St Francis Col, Ft Wayne, Ind, MS, 67; Bowling Green State Univ, Ohio, MA, 78. *Work:* Lincoln Life Insurance Co; Gen Tele Co; First Nat Bank; North Am Van Lines; Warner Commun, NY. *Exhib:* Ball State Drawing & Small Sculpture, Ball State Univ, Muncie, Ind, 68; Northwestern Indiana Artists, Hammond Mus, Ind, 76; Paper Chase, Artlink Gallery, Ft Wayne, Ind, 83; Tri-Kappa Regional Artists, Ft Wayne Mus Art, Ind, 83; Rental Gallery, Ft Wayne Mus Art, Ind, 83. *Teaching:* Instr art, Ft Wayne Community Sch, 63-72; dept head art, St Francis Col, 72-. *Awards:* Third Prize Sculpture, Van Wert Regional, 70; Tri-Kappa Regional Artists Exhib, several awards; Outstanding Professor of Year, St Francis Col, 92. *Mem:* Artlink Alternative Artists' Space (panel mem); Mayor's comt Pub Art Works; Coll Art Asn. *Media:* Acrylic, Collage. *Dealer:* Sharon Eisbart 3601 N Washington Rd Ft Wayne IN 46808. *Mailing Add:* Dept Art St Francis Col 2701 Spring St Fort Wayne IN 46808

PAPO, ISO
PAINTER
b Sarajevo, Bosnia, May 2, 1925; US citizen. *Study:* Polytech Milan; Brera Acad Fine Arts, Milan, Italy, grad, 51; Boston Mus Sch; also with Carlo Carra. *Work:* Boston Pub Libr; Danforth Mus Art, Framingham, Mass. *Comn:* Paintings for films & posters, United Church of Christ, 64-65. *Exhib:* Inst Contemp Art, Boston, 68; solo exhibs, Boston Athenaeum, 73 & Boston Psychoanal Soc & Inst, 75 & 86; Boston Visual Artists Union, 78; Helen Bumpus Gallery, Duxbury, 80 & 94; Hess Gallery, 86, 88, 91, 95, 98 & 2008; Allon Gallery, Brookline, 90; Art of Corea, Ellsworth, 95; Wiggins Gallery, Boston Pub Libr, 2000; Danforth Mus, 2001; St Botolph Club, Boston, Mass, 2009; and others; Thayer Acad Gallery, 2012. *Teaching:* Instr art, Kirkland House & Quincy House, Harvard Univ, 64-69; assoc prof painting, Boston Univ, 67-75; assoc prof & chmn, Arts and Commun Div, Pine Manor Coll, 68-89, prof emer, currently. *Awards:* Nat Scholastic Competition First Prize, Govt Italy, 50; Camargo Found Fel, 86. *Mem:* Boston Visual Artists Union. *Media:* Watercolor, Oil, Pen, Ink, Pastel. *Publ:* Illusr, The Art of Responsive Drawing & Figure Drawing, Prentice-Hall; Artistic Anatomy and Figure Drawing, Van Nostrand Reinhold; Catalogue of Boston Public Library's Collection. *Mailing Add:* 212 Aspinwall Ave Brookline MA 02446

PAPPAJOHN, JOHN & MARY
COLLECTORS, PATRONS
b July 31, 1928 and Oct 6, 1933. *Study:* John: Univ Iowa, BSc, 1952; Mary: Univ Minn, BS, 1955; John: Iowa State Univ, LHD, 2007; John: Grand View Coll, LHD, 2008; Univ Iowa, LHD, 2010. *Work:* Nat Gallery Art; Walker Art Mus; Des Moines Art Ctr; Mae Nider Mus, Mason City. *Comn:* Debra Butterfield, Ancient Forest, 2009. *Pos:* Owner, pres, and founder, Guardsman Life Investors, Inc, & Guardsman Life Insurance co, Des Moines, 1962-69; pres, Equity Dynamics Inc, Des Moines, 1969-, Pappajohn Capital Resources, Inc, Des Moines, 1969-; dir in over 40 companies. *Awards:* Spec Achievement Award Big Brothers, 1972; Big Brother of Yr Award, 1974; Oscar D Schmidt Iowa Bus Leadership Award, Univ Iowa Coll Bus, 1993; Horatio Alger Award, Horatio Alger Asn, 1995; Brotherhood Award, Iowa Region Nat Conference of Christians and Jews, 1997; Beta Gamma Sigma Medallion for Entrepreneur of Yr, 1997; Hellenic Heritage Achievement Award, 1997; Meredith Willson Heritage Award; 1998, Ellis Island Medal of Honor, 2000; Greek Orthodox Archon award, 2000; Finkbine award, Univ Iowa Bus Sch, 2004; named Iowa Bus Leader of Yr, 1993; named to Iowa Hall of Fame, 1996, Central Iowa Bus Hall of Achievement, 1999; named one of Top 200 Collectors, ARTnews mag, 1998-2011; Named one of Top 200 Collectors, ARTnews mag, 2004-2013. *Mem:* Nat Gallery Art, Washington, DC (collector's comt & trustee's coun); Whitney Mus Am Art (nat comt); John F Kennedy Ctr Performing Arts (nat comt); Mem Univ Iowa Alumni Asn (pres' club), hon trustee, Des Moines Club, Embassy Club, Univ Club, Order AHEPA, Masons, Shriners, Phi Gamma Delta; Hirshorn Mus (dir); Walker Art Mus (dir); Univ Iowa Found Bd. *Interests:* Art philanthopy in sculpture park, Des Moine. *Collection:* Modern and contemporary art. *Mailing Add:* 2166 Financial Ctr Des Moines IA 50309

PAPPAS, GEORGE
PAINTER
b Boston, Mass, Jan 25, 1929. *Study:* Mass Coll Art, BS, 52; Harvard Univ, MA, 53; Mass Inst Technol, with Gyorgy Kepes, 52-53; Pa State Univ, PhD (educ), 57. *Work:* De Cordova Mus, Lincoln, Mass; St Paul Gallery Art, Minn; Tampa Bay Art Ctr, Fla; Pa State Univ, Univ Park; Nat Gallery Art, Washington, DC; First Fla Bank, Tampa; McDonald Corp, Chicago, Ill; Neiman Marcus, Dallas; Des Moines Mus Art, Des Moines, Iowa; Knoll Assoc, Boston, Mass; Ringling Mus, Sarasota, Fla. *Exhib:* Corcoran Biennial, Washington, DC; De Cordova Mus Art, Lincoln, Mass; Ringling Mus Art, Sarasota, Fla; Detroit Inst Art, Mich; Boston Mus Fine Arts, Mass; Kanegis Gallery, Boston; Nordness Gallery, New York; Stein Gallery, Tampa, Fla; Fla Gulf Coast Art Ctr; Univ S Fla Mus. *Teaching:* Prof painting & art educ, Pa State Univ, 55-56; chmn dept art, Univ S Fla, 66-83, prof art, 66-93, chair & prof emer, 93-. *Awards:* Purchase Awards, Drawing USA, St Paul Gallery Art, Chautaqua Nat, Chautaqua Art Asn & Tampa Bay Art Ctr, Fla; Indiv Artists Grants, Fla, 83 & 96. *Mem:* Coll Art Asn; Nat Conf Art Adminr; Nat Art Educ Asn; Sarasota Arts Coun. *Media:* Oil. *Res:* Painting with artificial light, 71; Tracing the Odyssey in Greece & Turkey, 90; Study of William Turner landscapes, London, 91; Greek archeological sites, 93. *Specialty:* contemporary art. *Collection:* Contemporary prints: works by Barnett Newman, James Rosenquist, Philip Perlistein, Ed Ruscha, Ed Paschke & others. *Publ:* Coauth, Design, It's Form and Function, Pa State Univ, 65; Concepts in Art & Education, Macmillan, 70. *Dealer:* Clayton Galleries Tampa FL; Allen Gallup Contemporary Art, Sarasota FL; Arts on Douglas New Smyrna FL. *Mailing Add:* 924 Indian Beach Dr Sarasota FL 32168

PAPPAS-PARKS, KATHERINE
PAINTER
b Detroit, Mich, June, 1, 1942. *Study:* Wayne State Univ, BFA, 65, MA, 72. *Work:* Koehnline Mus, Des Plaines, Ill; Mus Tex Tech univ, Lubbock, Tex; Augusta-Richmond Mus, Ga; Ottawa Co Mus, Minneapolis; Harry S Truman Coll Collection, Chicago, Ill. *Comn:* images of doctors and students at work, Chicago Coll Osteopathic Med, 75. *Exhib:* New Horizons in Art, Chicago Cult Art Ctr, Chicago, Ill, 84; New Horizons in Art/Vehicles, Northwestern Univ, Evanston, Ill, 87; Evanston & Vincinity Exhib, Evanston Art Ctr, Evanston, Ill, 94. *Collection Arranged:* cur, Raw Space, ARC Gallery, 82, 83; cur, Take a Peek, ARC Gallery, 83; cur, Art Expo Chicago, Int Exhib, 96-. *Teaching:* adj prof, Harry Truman Coll, Chicago, 89-93, Oakton Community Coll, Des Plaines, Ill, 80-98, Portland State Univ, Oregon, 99-2000. *Awards:* Proj Completion Grant, ARC Gallery, Ill Arts Coun, 81; Purchase Award, Kemper Group, 87; Purchase Award, Harry S Truman Coll, Ill Percent Arts, 90. *Bibliog:* Joan Boatwright (auth), Visionary Landscapes, The Argus/Oregonian, 2004; Dk Row (auth), Hot Sheet-Best Bets, The Oregonian, 2004; Andie De Luca (auth), At the Edge of the Sky, Port Art, News & Rev, 2005; Jonathan Goodman, If the Plants Don't Make It, How Will We? Walter Wickiser Gallery, 2006; Valerie Gladstone (auth), Flying Through Moments, Feeling the Earth Turn, Walter Wickiser Gallery, 2010. *Mem:* European & Am Art Coun, Portland Art Mus; Contemp & Mod Arts Coun, Portland Art Mus. *Media:* Oil. *Publ:* contribr, The New Photography, Prentice Hall, 84; Visionary Landscapes, The Argus, 2004; Art the Edge of the Sky, Port, 2005; illustr, If the Plants Don't Make It, how Will We? catalog, Walter Wickiser Gallery, 2007; illustr, Flying Through Moments, Feeling the Earth Turn, catalog, Walter Wickiser Gallery, 2010. *Dealer:* Walter Wickiser Gallery Inc 210 11th Ave Suite 303 New York NY 10001; Iliana Schoinas 12180 NW Sunnindale Dr Portland OR 97229

PARAVANO, DINO
PAINTER
b Rome, Italy, Nov 9, 1935. *Study:* Johannesburg Art Col, S Africa, 1954-1955. *Work:* Leigh Yawkey Woodson Art Mus, Wausau, Wis; The Wildlife Experience, Parker, Colo; Hiram Blauvelt Art Mus, Oradell, NJ; Bennington Ctr Arts, Bennington, Vt. *Comn:* Paintings of Nat Parks, S African Prks Bd, Pretoria, Johannesburg, 1983. *Exhib:* Birds in Art, Leigh Yawkey Woodson Art, Wausau, Wis, 1985-2006; Birds in Art, Beijing Mus Nat His, Beijing, China, 1986; Art and the Animal, Old Algonquin Mus, Algonquin, Ont, 1995; Visions of the Veld, Nat Mus Wildlife Art, Jackson, Wyo, 1996; Art & the Animal Kingdom, Bennington Ctr Arts, Bennington, Vt, 1996-2006; Feline Fine Art of Cats, Arts & Sci Ctr S Ark, Pine Bluff, Ark, 2002; American Art in Miniature, Gilcrease Mus, Tulsa, Okla, 2005. *Awards:* Award of Excellence, Art & the Animal, Soc Animal Artists, 1990; Master Wildlife Artist, Birds in Art, Leigh Yawkey Woodson Art Mus, 1993; First Place Winner, Pastel 100 Competition, Pastel J, 2005. *Bibliog:* Ruth Summer (auth), Painting Wildlife & Wild Scenes, Pastel J, 2000; Devon Jackson (auth), Out of Africa, Southwest Art, 2005; Michael Scott-Blair (auth), A Virtuoso in Light Shadows, Wildlife Art, 2005. *Mem:* Soc Animal Artist (signature mem 1979-2006); Pastel Soc Am (signature mem 1992-2006); Oil Painters Am (2004-2006). *Media:* Pastel, Acrylic, Oil, Miscellaneous Media. *Publ:* Illusr, Last Horizons, St Martins Press, 1989; Contribr, African Wildlife in Art, Clive Holloway Books, 1991; Illusr, Hunting in Botswana, Safari Press, 1994; Contribr, Drawing and Painting Animals, Watson Guptill, 1998; Contribr, Best of Wildlife 2, North Light Books, 1999. *Mailing Add:* 9030 E Chof Ovi Dr Tucson AZ 85749

PARDEE, HEARNE
EDUCATOR, PAINTER
Study: Yale Univ, BA, 1969; New York Studio Sch, attended, 1969-73; Columbia Univ, MFA, 1975. *Work:* Franklin Boulevard Urban Plein Air Project, 2009. *Exhib:* Solo exhib, Bowery Gallery, New York City, 1982, 1985, 1986, 1989, 1992, 1995, 1998, 2000, 2004, 2006, 2010, John Natsoula Gallery, Davis, 2003, Weigand Gallery, Belmont, 2007, Univ Art Gallery, Calif State Univ, 2011; group exhibitions Small Works, Washington Square East Gallery, NY, 1980, Artists Who Teach in Maine, Maine Coast Artists, Rockport, 1987, Perceptual Drawings, Wright State Univ, Dayton, 1999, Drawing Conclusions: Work by Artist-Critics, NY Arts Ctr, 2003, The Continuous Mark, Forty Years of the NY Studio Sch, NY Studio Sch Gallery, 2004, Nine at Gaia, Gaia Arts Ctr, Berkeley, Calif, 2006, Surface and Substance: Works on Paper, San Francisco Studio Sch, 2008, Geomorph: New Currents in Geometric and Piomorphic Abstraction, Pence Gallery, Davis, Calif, 2009. *Teaching:* Prof painting, Univ Calif, Berkeley, 2000-, chair Art Studio Dept, currently. *Mailing Add:* University of California, Davis Department of Art and Art History One Shields Ave Davis CA 95616

PARDEE, WILLIAM HEARNE
PAINTER, EDUCATOR
b Pittsburgh, Pa, Aug 25, 1946. *Study:* Yale Univ, with Sewell Sillman, BA, 69; New York Studio Sch, with Philip Guston, George McNeil & Leland Bell, 69-73; Columbia Univ, with Meyer Schapiro, MFA, 75. *Work:* Maine Savings Bank; Blue Cross/Blue Shield of Maine; Yosemite Mus. *Exhib:* Bowery Gallery, 85, 86, 89, 92 & 95; Jersey City Mus, NJ, 86; Maine Coast Artists, Rockport, 87; Bowery Gallery, 89, 92, 95 & 98; Congress Square Gallery, Maine, 92; and others. *Collection Arranged:* Linens, Wall-Clothing and Straw Sculpture, sculptures by Maureen Connor, 82; Aspects of Abstraction, sculpture by Deborah de Moulpied, Gerald DiGiusto & Lawrence Fane, 83; Landscape and Abstract Art: A Continuing Dialogue, 85, Inner Images, 86 & Clear Perceptions, 88, Colby Mus Art, Maine; Meyer Schapiro's Semiotics of Painting, NY Studio Sch, 89; Joan Mitchell, Maier Mus Art, Lynchburg, Va; Reinterpreting Landscape, Maier Mus Art, 96. *Pos:* Consult contemp art, Colby Col Mus Art, Maine, 82-88; asst prof painting & design, Colby Col, Maine, 82-90; adj cur, Maier Mus Art. *Teaching:* Vis asst prof, Col William & Mary, 83; asst prof painting & design, Colby Col, Maine, 82-90; painting & drawing, Univ Va, 92, Rice Univ, 97-98 & Univ Conn, 98-99. *Awards:* Residency, Djerassi Found, 86, Yosemite Nat Park, 93. *Bibliog:* Gerrit Henry (auth), Hearne Pardee, Artnews, 12/92; Jonathan Goodman (auth), Hearne Pardee, Artnews, 4/95; Valerie Gladstone (auth), Hearne Pardee, Artnews, 6/98. *Mem:* Coll Art Asn Am. *Media:* Oil, Collage. *Publ:* Auth, Proust's visual imagery, Yale French Studies, 65; A reading of Marsden Hartley, 83, Six painters at the Hudson River Museum, 83, Landscape and the language of abstraction, 9/85, Inner Images, 11/86 & Peter Campus, 11/88, Arts Mag; short reviews, Artnews, 87-94. *Dealer:* Bowery Gallery 121 Wooster St New York NY 10012. *Mailing Add:* 2855 Mallorca Ln Davis CA 95616-6579

PARFENOFF, MICHAEL S
EDUCATOR, LITHOGRAPHER
b Gary, Ind, Aug 8, 1926. *Study:* Art Inst Chicago, with Boris Anisfeld & Max Kahn, BFA & MFA. *Exhib:* Print Exhib, Libr Cong, Washington, DC; Momentum, Art Inst Chicago; Philadelphia Print Club. *Pos:* Pres, Blackhawk Mountain Sch Art, 63-. *Teaching:* Instr lithography, Art Inst Chicago, 58-65; prof art, Chicago City Col, 58-. *Mem:* Am Asn Univ Prof; Ill Art Educators. *Media:* Stone. *Mailing Add:* 453 W Roslyn Pl Chicago IL 60614-2712

PARISI, MARTHA
GRAPHIC ARTIST, PRINTMAKER
b July 29, 1946. *Study:* Sir Wilfred Laurier Univ, BA, 68; Univ Toronto, MED, 69, specialist, 78. *Work:* NY Mus, Albany. *Comn:* Drawing, Northeastern Wildlife Expo, Albany, 88; cover design, Saugerties Cent Schs, NY, 90; cover design, Smithsonian, Nat Zoological Park, Washington, 91; portrait, Marc Curtrone, Jupiter, Fla, 96. *Exhib:* The Arts, Schenectady Mus, NY, 86; The Arts, NY State Mus, Albany, 87; Northeastern Wildlife Expo, NY State Mus, Albany, 87; solo exhibs, Stedman Gallery, Colonie, NY, 87, Town Hall, Saugerties, NY, 90, Sundancer Gallery, Cocoa Village, Fla, 96; group exhibs, Amrita Gallery, Poughkeepsie, NY, 95, Signature Gallery, San Diego, Calif, 95. *Pos:* Owner, Nature Art Gallery, 87-. *Awards:* Art in DC Award, Ulster Arts Alliance, 96; Best of Show, Art League, 95; First Place: Drawing, Mandarin Arts Coun, 96. *Bibliog:* Kevin Geoghan (auth), A festival of art, ESCA, Chemung Valley, 8/22/92; James G Shine (auth), Art beat, Daily Freeman, 10/28/94; Tribute to Women, YWCA Arts Coun, 95. *Mem:* Southern Utah Art Ctr; Nat Mus Am Indian; Empire State Crafts Alliance. *Media:* Drawing, Pencil; Printmaking. *Publ:* Illusr, International Cheetah Studbook, Smithsonian Inst, 91. *Mailing Add:* PO Box 1798 Jamestown TN 38556-1798

PARK, LEE
PAINTER
b Seoul, Korea, Oct 25, 1938; US citizen. *Study:* Fla State Christian Univ, MA, 86. *Work:* Bridgeport Univ, New York; YWCA HQ, Los Angeles; Los Angeles City Councilman 10th Dist Off, Los Angeles; Christian Children's Fund Inc, Beverly Hills, Calif. *Exhib:* Pacific Asia Mus, Pasadena, Calif, 86; Asia Art Exhib, Metro Politan Mus Art, Seoul, Korea, 93; Musee d'Art Moderne de la Commanderie d'Unet, Paris, France, 94; Biennale Int de Paris, City Hall Paris, France, 94; Art Addiction Int, Stockholm, Sweden, 97; Prima Biennale Int di Art Contemporanea, Perugia, Italy, 98; World Peace Art Exhib, Saejong Ctr, Seoul, Korea, 99; 50th Commemoration Nat Found China, Beijing, 99. *Teaching:* Instr oriental art, K-A Art Inst, Los Angeles, 93. *Awards:* Bronze Discovery Award, Art Calif Mag, 93; Gold Medal, Art Addiction, 97; Art Addiction Int Prize, Organizing Comt, Stockholm, 97. *Mem:* World Artist Asn; Korea Modern Art Asn; Asia Art Invitational Asn; Korea-Japan Art Exchanging Asn; Art 2000 Inst. *Media:* All media. *Publ:* Contribr, Art of Calif Mag, Artweek Mag, Art Exposure, Art Diary, Encyl Living Artists Mag, Int Encyl Dictionary Mod & Contemp Art, Ferrara, Italy; The Mag (VERGIL) for World Art & Cult, Seoul, Korea. *Dealer:* Simon Kim Gallery 8643 Wilshire Blvd Beverly Hills CA 90211. *Mailing Add:* 1935 S La Salle Ave Ste 31 Los Angeles CA 90018

PARK, SOO SUNNY
SCULPTOR
b Seoul, Korea. *Study:* Columbus Coll Art & Design, Ohio, BFA (painting & sculpture); Cranbrook Acad Art, Bloomfield Hills, Mich, MFA (sculpture); Skowhegan Sch Painting & Sculpture, 2000. *Exhib:* Solo exhibs include Contemp Art Mus St Louis & Laumeier Sculpture Park, St Louis, 2004; group exhibs include Exposure IV, The Space In-Between, Park Ave Gallery, Mo; The Distance Between Us, Dupreau Gallery, Chicago; Skowhegan Alumni, Knoedler Gallery, New York; Sheldon Art Galleries, St Louis; Ann Invitational Exhib Contemp Am Art, Nat Acad Mus, New York, 2008. *Teaching:* Lectr, Washington Univ, St Louis, formerly; asst prof studio art, Dartmouth Coll, currently. *Awards:* Joan Mitchell MFA Grant; Grand Prize, 19th Ann Mich Fine Arts Competition; Best of 2001, Sculptor of St Louis, River Front Times, 2001; Helen Foster Barnett Prize, Nat Acad, 2008. *Mailing Add:* Studio Art Dept Dartmouth Coll Hinman Box 6081 Hanover NH 03755

PARKER, ANN (ANN PARKER NEAL)
PHOTOGRAPHER, WRITER
b London, Eng, Mar 6, 1934; US citizen. *Study:* RI Sch of Design; Yale Univ, BFA. *Work:* Metrop Mus Art, NY; Smithsonian Inst, Washington, DC; Mus Mod Art, NY; Boston Pub Libr, Mass; Ctr Creative Photog, Tucson, Ariz. *Comn:* Arton Assoc, 70 & 74; Mead Art Gallery, Amherst, Mass, 76; Sweetwater Eds, 82; Thistle Hill Press, 83-85. *Exhib:* Solo exhibs, Nat Mus Art, La Paz, Bolivia, 85, Princeton Univ Libr, NJ, 86, Inst Dominicano de Cultura Hispanica, Santo Dominican Republic, 87, Maxwell Mus, Univ NMex, Albuquerque, 88. *Awards:* Ford Found Grant in Arts & Humanities, 62-64; First Prize in Photog, Americana Bicentennial Photog Contest, 76 & Mass Open, 77. *Bibliog:* Stephen Chodorov (producer), Know Ye the Hour, Camera Three, CBS-TV, 11/68; Vicki Goldberg (auth), Am Photogr, 1/83; Lois Parkinson Zamora (auth), Spot, Houston Ctr Photog, fall 89. *Mem:* Friends of Photog; Photog Resource Ctr, Boston Mass; Asn Gravestone Studies. *Media:* Cibachrome, Silver Prints; Non Fiction. *Publ:* Photogr, Ephemeral Folk Figures, Clarkson Potter, New York, 69; Molas Folk Art of the Cuna Indians, Barre Publ, New York, 77; Scarecrows, Barre Publ, New York, 78; Early American Stone Sculpture, Sweetwater Eds; Los Ambulantes, the itinerant photographers of Guatemala, Mass Inst Technol, Cambridge, Mass, 82; coauth, Folk Art of the Great Pilgrimage, Smithsonian, 95. *Dealer:* Gallery of Graphic Arts 1603 York Ave New York NY 10028. *Mailing Add:* 126 School St North Brookfield MA 01535-1961

PARKER, GERTRUD VALERIE
SCULPTOR
b Vienna, Austria; US citizen. *Study:* Univ Calif, Berkeley, BA (political sci); San Francisco State with Alexander Nepote, Pac Basin Sch Textiles with Lillian Elliott. *Work:* NY Times Offices, NY; Oakland Mus, Oakland, Calif; Smithsonian Archives, Washington; Prefecture of Gunma Gun, Japan. *Exhib:* Innerskins/Outerskins Gut & Fishskins, Anchorage Mus, State Mus Juneau & Univ Alaska Mus, Fairbanks, Alaska, 88; Mixing It Up, Coos Art Mus, Ore, 88; solo exhibs, Art Exhib Galleries, Manu Co Civic Ctr, San Rafael, Calif, 88 & San Francisco Craft & Folk Art Mus, 93, Galerie Haasner, Wiesbaden, Ger, 2000 & 2006, Vernissage & Kolloquium, Bundes Inst, St Wolfgang, Austria, 2000, Spertus Mus, Chicago, 2000, San Jose Mus Art, 2001, Richmond Art Ctr, 2002, Dominican Univ, San Rafael, Calif, 2003 & 2009-10, Joe Kish, San Francisco, 2005, Klagenfurt, Austria, 2006, Art Santa Fe Int Biennale, NMex, 2007. *Pos:* Co-founder & chmn bd, San Francisco Craft & Folk Art Mus, Calif, 82-89. *Awards:* Cert Excellence Outstanding Archit Fiber, Int Art Competition, New York, 88; Discovery Award-Bronze Medal, Art Calif Mag, 92; Richard A Florsheim Art Fund Grant, San Francisco Craft & Folk Art Mus Solo Show, 93; Gold Medal Iser Int Exhib, Stockholm, Sweden, 97; Ornament for the White House Tree, Washington, 98. *Bibliog:* Wayne Freedman (producer), Inside Art, KRON-TV, 88; Doromay Keasbey (auth), Sheer Delight-Handwoven Transparencies, Stella Publ House, 90; Jeanna Haney (auth), Gertrude Parker-Metamorphosing a humble material, Fiber Arts, 91; Gertrud Parker: Sheer Artistry, Woman's Art Jour, 99; Toyamura Int Sculpture Biennal, Japan (catalog), 99; The Biennale Shoebox Show, Univ Hawaii, (catalog) ArtWeek, 2000; Peter Selz (auth), Visceral Sculpture of Gertrud Parker, Richmond Art Ctr, 2002. *Mem:* Marin Arts Coun (bd dir, 83); Marin Soc Artists; Pacific Rim Sculptors Group. *Media:* Metal, Gutskin. *Dealer:* B Haasner Gallery Wiesbaden Germany; Heiderose Hildebrand Klagenfurt Austria. *Mailing Add:* 2 Tara Hill Rd Tiburon CA 94920-1523

PARKER, JAMES VARNER
DESIGNER
b Senath, Mo, June 27, 1925. *Study:* Phoenix Community Coll, AA; Ariz State Univ, BFA & MA. *Work:* Southeast State Teachers Coll; City of Phoenix Civic Art Collection; Malaysian Embassy, Washington, DC; Scottsdale Art Collection; pvt collection Pres Ronald Reagan. *Comn:* Carl Hayden High Sch Student Body, Phoenix, 60; Greater Ariz Savings Bank, Tucson; Heard Mus; Cape Girardeau Pub Libr. *Exhib:* Tucson Art Ctr, 66; Phoenix Art Mus, 66; Stanford Res Inst, Palo Alto, Calif, 66; Yuma Art Asn, Ariz, 70; plus others. *Collection Arranged:* Indian Art Collection, 68 & 72; African Art, Heard Mus, 6/72 & 9/72; Indian Art of the Americas; Missouri Mills, 77; Beckwith Collection, 77; William Faulkner, 80. *Pos:* Cur educ, Heard Mus, 58-68, illusr, 58 & 71 & cur art, 68-75; mus dir, Southeast Mo State Univ Mus, 74-90; consult adminr, Phoenix Mus Hist, 75-77; retired. *Teaching:* Instr art, Phoenix Coll, 68-70; instr art, Glendale Community Coll, 71-72; instr, Southeast Mo State Univ, 76-90. *Awards:* Nat Vet Award, Santa Monica Recreation Dept, 53; O'Brien Art Award, Ariz State Fair, 60; UNICEF Award, 68. *Bibliog:* Design-Crafts-Education (film), KAET TV, Ariz State Univ, 60. *Mem:* Ariz Watercolor Asn (founder & pres, 59); Ariz Art Asn (pres & secy, 60); Nat Art Educ Asn; Am Mus Asn. *Publ:* Illusr, The Story of Navaho Weaving, 61; Pima Basketry, 65; The Dennis Collection, Egyptian Antiquities, 79; The Art of Collage, 79. *Mailing Add:* 445 Marie Cape Girardeau MO 63701

PARKER, JUNE
PAINTER
b Bryn Mawr, Pa, June 30, 1928. *Study:* Student Shelly Fink (drawing), 70; student Charles Movalli, 91; student Constance Flavell Pratt, 95; student Frank Federico, 2000-02. *Comn:* numerous comns for portraits, pvt homes, and landmarks. *Exhib:* Berkshire Art Asn Juried Exhbn, Berkshire Mus of Art, Pittsfield, Mass, 70; Pittsfield Art Asn Juried Exhbn, Berkshire Mus, 88; NB Juried Members Show, New Britain Mus of Am Art, New Britain, Conn, 2000-2002; Renaissance in Pastel, Slater Mem Mus, Norwich, Conn, 2002-2006. *Collection Arranged:* Fox Valley Corp, Appleton, Wis; Berkshire Bank, Pittsfield, Mass; Canaan Nat Bank, Egremont, Mass; Wyantenuck Co Club, Gt Barrington, Mass. *Pos:* Chair, Egremont Arts Lottery, Cult Coun, Mass, 88-91. *Teaching:* Instr pastels, Art Sch of the Berkshires, 2003-2011; instr workshops, Norman Rockwell Mus, Sheffield Art League, Becket Art Center. *Awards:* Dianne Bernhard Silver Medal, Hudson Valley Art Asn, Hastings-on-Hudson, NY, 2001; Award for Excellence, Renaissance in Pastel, Conn Pastel Soc, 2001; Honor Award-Pastel, Acad Artists Asn, Springfield, Mass, 1993; Best of Show Awards

Sheffield Art League, Mass, 1992, 2000, 2001; and many others; john T Mott Award for marine painting, President's Show, Kent Art Asn, 2010. *Mem:* Acad Artist Asn; Hudson Valley Art Asn; Conn Pastel Soc; Kent Art Asn (Conn); Housatonic Valley Art League. *Media:* Pastel. *Interests:* Walking, traveling, family, music, theater & art. *Publ:* contribr, Portraits of an Artist, Berkshire Eagle, 7/75; Profile June Parker Artists, Berkshire Courier, 3/79; contribr-illus, cover art, Only in Berkshires, Berkshire Courier, 85; contribr, June Parker Artists in Many Media, Berkshire Media Group Publ, 9/85; illus, Artwork for Cancer Control Journal, Moffett Cancer Ctr at Univ S Fla, 3/2003-2004; contribr, Art & the River (bk), Sheffield Art League, 2004. *Dealer:* Gallery on the Green S Egremont MA 01258

PARKER, MARY JANE
SCULPTOR, PAINTER
b New Orleans, Louisiana, 1955. *Study:* La State Univ, Baton Rouge, BFA, 1977; Ill State Univ, Normal, MA, 1979, MFA, 1980. *Work:* New Orleans Mus Art; Ctr Book Arts, New York. *Exhib:* Solo exhibs inlcude Bienville Gallery, New Orleans, 1988, 1990, Gallery Arts Exchange, Atlanta, 1993, 1708 Gallery, Richmond, Va, 1999, Contemp Arts Ctr, New Orleans, 2000, Baton Rouge Gallery, 2000, Arthur Roger Gallery, New Orleans, 2002, 2005, R&F Gallery, Kingston, NY, 2008; Group exhibs include Women About Men/Men About Women, Acad Gallery, New Orleans, 1986; New Orleans Noir, Zeitgeist Alternative Arts Ctr, New Orleans, 1997; New Orleans Ctr Creative Arts, 2000; Hot Glass Cool Glass, La State Univ Union Gallery, Baton Rouge, 2004; State of La Glass, River Oaks Art Ctr, Alexandria, La, 2004; Sculptors on Paper, Carroll Gallery, Tulane Univ, New Orleans, 2004; Am Relief Printing Today, Univ Place Art Ctr, Lincoln, Nebr, 2004; Louisiana in Print, Collins C Diboll Art Gallery, Loyola Univ, New Orleans, 2005; Women With Guns, Isaac Delgado Fine Arts Gallery, New Orleans, 2006; Red Herring Portfolio Exhib, Ctr Book Arts, New York, 2007; Close Up, Kathryn Markel Fine Arts, New York, 2008. *Awards:* Pollock-Krasner Found Grant, 2007. *Dealer:* Arthur Roger Gallery 432 Julia St New Orleans LA 70130

PARKER, NANCY WINSLOW
ILLUSTRATOR, WRITER
b Maplewood, NJ, Oct 18, 1930. *Study:* Mills Coll, Calif, BA, 52; Art Students League & Sch Visual Arts, New York. *Work:* Rutgers Univ, The Zimmerli Art Mus; Univ S Mississippi, De Grummond Coll; Univ Minnesota, The Kerlan Coll. *Exhib:* Audubon Artists 29th Ann Exhib, New York, 71; Webb & Parsons, Bedford Village, NY, 76; Master-Eagle Gallery, New York, 80, 83, 85 & 87; Webb & Parsons, New Canaan, Conn, 83; Jane Vorhees Zimmerli Art Mus, Rutgers Univ, NJ, 86; Bay Head Hist Soc Mus, NJ, 2004. *Pos:* Art dir, Appleton, Century, Crofts, New York, 68-70; graphic designer, Holt Rinehart & Winston, New York, 70-72. *Awards:* Christopher Award, 76 & 81; AIGA Book Show, 76 & 81; My Mom Travels A Lot, NY Times Ten Best Illustrated Bks, 81. *Mem:* Authors Guild. *Media:* Watercolor, Wood. *Publ:* The President's Cabinet (rev), Harper Collins, 91; Barbara Frietchie (Whittier), 92, Working Frog, 92, The Dress I'll Wear to the Party (Neitzel), 92 & Sheridan's Ride (Read), 93, Greenwillow; Money, Money, Money: The Meaning of the Art and Symbols on United States Paper Currency, Harper/Collins, 95; Locks, Crocs and Skeeters: The Story of the Panama Canal, Greenwillow, 96; Land Ho! Fifty Glorious Years in The Age of Exploration with 12 Important Explorers, Harper Collins, 2001; Organs: How they work, fall apart, and can be Replaced, Greenwillow, 2009; The St James Book of ABC, the Rector, Churchwardens, Vestrymen of St. James Church, NY, 2011. *Dealer:* Webb & Parsons Burlington Vt. *Mailing Add:* 51 E 74th St New York NY 10021

PARKER, OLIVIA
PHOTOGRAPHER
b Boston, Mass, June 10, 1941. *Study:* Wellesley Col, BA, 63. *Work:* Victoria & Albert Mus, London; Boston Mus Fine Arts; Mus Mod Art, NY; Art Inst Chicago; Int Mus Photog, Eastman House, Rochester; and others. *Comn:* Photographic Resource Ctr, Boston, 81. *Exhib:* 14 New Eng Photogr, Boston Mus Fine Arts, 78; Loans to the Collection, Art Inst Chicago, 78; One of a Kind Traveling Exhib, Mus Fine Arts, Houston; 20 x 24, Light Gallery, NY, 79; one-person shows, Friends Photog, Carmel, Calif, 79 & 81, Eastman House, Rochester, 81, Mus Art, Univ Ore, 82, Catskill Ctr Photog, Woodstock, 82 & Art Inst Chicago, 82; and others. *Awards:* Artists Found fel, 78; Cert of Excellence, Am Inst of Graphic Arts Bk Show, 79; Ferguson Grant, 81. *Bibliog:* Owen Edwards (auth), The clear Yankee eye, Saturday Rev, 79; Vicki Goldberg (auth), Signs of (still) life, Am Photogr, 79; David Featherstone (auth), Olivia Parker, Mod Photog, 80. *Mem:* Soc for Photog Educ; Friends Photog. *Media:* Photography. *Publ:* Auth, Signs of Life, 78 & contribr, One of a Kind, 79, David Godine; contribr, Darkroom Dynamics, Curtin & London, 79; auth, Under the Looking Glass, New York Graphic Soc, 83. *Mailing Add:* 3901 Elm St Sacramento CA 95838-3614

PARKER, ROBERT ANDREW
PAINTER
b Norfolk, Va, May 14, 1927. *Study:* Art Inst Chicago, BAE, 52; Skowhegan Sch Painting & Sculpture; Atelier 17, New York, 52-53. *Work:* Los Angeles Co Mus; Metrop Mus Art; Morgan Libr, NY; Mus Mod Art; Whitney Mus Am Art; plus others. *Comn:* Designer sets, William Shuman Opera, Mus Mod Art, 61. *Exhib:* Brooklyn Mus, 55; Mus Mod Art, 57; Laon Mus, Aisne, France, 56; New Sch Social Res, 65; Sch Visual Arts, NY, 65; and many others. *Teaching:* Instr, Parson Sch Design, 80-85, RI Sch Design, 84 & Pratt Inst, Brooklyn, NY, 85. *Awards:* Rosenthal Found Grant, Nat Inst Arts & Lett, 62; Tamarind Lithography Workshop Fel, 67; Guggenheim Fel, 69-70; plus others. *Mem:* Nat Acad. *Media:* Watercolor, Etching. *Publ:* Illusr, hand-colored ltd ed poems, Mus Mod Art, 62; illusr poetry, The days of Wilfred Owen (film), 66. *Dealer:* Doris Longdale 231 E 60th New York NY 10022. *Mailing Add:* c/o Flinn Gallery Greenwich Libr 101 W Putnam Ave Greenwich CT 06830

PARKER, RON
EDUCATOR, ADMINISTRATOR
Study: Studied Typography and Bookbinding, London Col of Printing. *Pos:* Postgraduate position, Univ Tex, Austin, formerly; design practice in scholarly publishing, Univ Texas Press; magazine and book design, Texas Monthly; worked in corporate identity design and implementation for companies in the UK and Europe; with Louisiana State Univ Press, Baton Rouge; founder DSI/LA, 1984-1995. *Teaching:* Instructor, Sch of Art, Louisiana State Univ, 1981-1995, joined graphic design faculty, 1995, assoc prof, dir, School of Art, currently; mem founding group, Louisiana Avatar (Arts, Visualizatin, Advanced Technolgies and Research, Louisiana State Univ, collaborated with colleagues to establish the Graphic Design Student Office, 1998. *Mailing Add:* College of Art & Design 123 Art Building Louisiana State University Baton Rouge LA 70803

PARKER, SAMUEL MURRAY
PAINTER
b Madison, Wis, Aug 6, 1936. *Study:* Wis State Univ, Eau Claire, BA (art), 63; Univ Wis, MS (painting & drawing, 64, MFA (painting), 65. *Work:* Springfield Mus; Playboy Club; Laura Musser Mus, Muscatine, Iowa; Container Corp Am. *Comn:* Serigraphy, Ill Print Comn, Ill Arts Coun, 73. *Exhib:* Univ Pac Nat Small Painting Show, 71; 3rd Nat Drawing Show, Oshkosh, Wis, 71; New Talent: Midwest USA, Gallery 1640, Montreal, Que, 72; Dong a Ibo Korean Int Print Show, Seoul, 72; Nat Print Invitational, Artists Contemp Gallery, Sacramento, Calif, 73. *Teaching:* Assoc prof painting & drawing, Western Ill Univ, 65-78, prof, 78-. *Awards:* First Prize for Painting, Ill State Fair Show, 72, 25th Ill Invitational, Ill State Mus, 72 & Laura Musser Mus, 73. *Media:* Acrylic Polymer. *Mailing Add:* 216 E Jefferson St Macomb IL 61455-2204

PARKER, WILMA
PAINTER
b Springfield, Mass, 1941. *Study:* RI Sch Design, BFA, 63; Art Inst Chicago, MFA, 66. *Work:* Nat Mus Naval Aviation, Pensacola, Fla; Palm Springs Desert Mus, Calif; Laguna Gloria Mus Austin, Tex; Mesa Southwest Mus, Mesa, Ariz; Yergeau Musee d'Art Int, Montreal, Can; De Saisset Mus, Santa Clara, Calif; Mus Fine Arts, Springfield, Mass; Nat Air and Space Mus, Washington, DC; Springfield Pub Libr, Aston Collection of Wood Engravings, Mass; The Marquis of Bath, Longleat House, Eng; Embassy of US, Kazakstan, Lesotho, Bangladesh; USS Hornet; Alameda IBM Corp; Naval War Coll, Newport, Fla; and many others; Household Cavalry Mus; Naval War Coll; Newport, RI; Mus Gulf Coast. *Comn:* IBM, Tucson, 81; IBM, Poughkeepsie, NY, 85; Sonora Cafe, Los Angeles, 86; Presidential Suite, Fairmont Hotel, Calif, 88; Launch of the Springfield, US Navy, 92; Legacy Painting, Officers Club, Alameda, Calif; US Coast Guard; US Navy. *Exhib:* Amsterdam Whitney Gallery, New York; Salmagundi Club, New York; Lyman Allyn Mus, New London, 92; Nautilus Mus, Groton, Conn, 92; Am Soc Marine Artists, Frye Art Mus, Seattle, 97; Rotunda, House Rep, Washington, DC, 97; Cummer Art Mus, Jacksonville, Fla, 97; Int Soc Marine Artists, Camden, Maine, 98; Arnold Gallery, Newport, RI, 98; and others. *Pos:* Painter & principal, currently; docent, San Francisco Mus Mod Art; trustee, RI Sch Design; Parker Fine Art, 2006-2014; Restroom Cultural Park; Soma Gallery; Commonwealth Club. *Teaching:* Dean, Clara St Studio Sch, currently. *Awards:* COGAP Award, Salmagundi Club, New York, 94. *Bibliog:* Art Talk, Scottsdale, Ariz, 10/89; Calif Art Rev, 91; Am Artists, Am Ref Publ Group, 91. *Mem:* COGAP; Salmagundi Club, New York; Am Soc Marine Artists. *Media:* Oil on Canvas, Acrylic, Mixed Media Collage. *Res:* Watercolors of John Parker English, Parker/Ball silver reissues. *Specialty:* marine paintings, horseguards, blues & royals. *Interests:* Art history, Architecture, Blues and Royals, Horseguards, US Navy, US Coast Guard. *Publ:* Auth, Wilma Parker, An Interchange of Life, SW Art Mag, 81; Mono No Sono, SF Tea Poetics Soc, 91; A Gallery of Marine Art, Rockport Pub. *Dealer:* Parker Fine Art Clara St San Francisco Calif. *Mailing Add:* 222 Clara St San Francisco CA 94107

PARKERSON, JOHN E
ART DEALER, GALLERY DIRECTOR
Study: Rice Univ, BA, 60; Univ Va, MA (art hist), 70. *Pos:* vpres, Sotheby's USA, 70-80; head painting dept, Sotheby's Los Angeles, 76-80. *Mem:* cert mem Appraisers Asn Am, Inc (76-); Cult Arts Coun Houston (vpres, 95-). *Specialty:* 19th & 20th century American and European art. *Mailing Add:* Parkerson Gallery 3510 Lake St Houston TX 77098

PARKS, ADDISON
PAINTER, SCULPTOR
b Shaker Heights, Ohio, 1953. *Study:* Skidmore Coll, 1972-74; Brown Univ, 1974-75; RI Sch Design, BFA, 1976. *Work:* PS1 / Mus Mod Art, New York; Univ Conn; numerous pvt collections. *Exhib:* Solo exhibs, Anyart Contemp Art Ctr, Providence, 1977, RI Sch Design, Woods-Gerry Gallery, 1978, PS1 Inst Art & Urban Resources, New York, 1980, Andrew Crispo Gallery, New York, 1982, XOX Gallery, Providence, 1989, Creiger-Dane Gallery, Boston, 1998 & 2000, Bow Street Gallery, 2007-2009; Seven Americans, Joan Washburn Gallery, New York, 1982; Andrew Crispo Gallery, New York, 1983; Vivita Gallery, Florence, Italy, 1984; Brouhaha Gallery, Providence, 1986; Valentine Show, Helander Gallery, New York, 1991; Charles Sq, Cambridge, 1992; Severed Ear: The Poetry of Abstraction, Creiger-Dane Gallery, 1999; In the Spirit of Landscape v, Nielsen Gallery, 2000; Water, DNA Gallery, Provincetown, 2004; Bedtime Stories, Flying Space Gallery, Sag Harbor, 2005; Salon Show, Harvard Sq, Bow Street Gallery, 2006. *Pos:* Cur, NY State Arts Coun, 1988, Nielsen Gallery, Boston, 1993 & Bernard Toale Gallery, Boston, 1995; writer & critic, The Christian Sci Monitor, 1990-94; broadcast designer, The Christian Science Publ Soc, 1990-93 & Loconte/Goldman Design, 1993; publ & ed, ArtDeal, 1995. *Teaching:* Instr, RI Sch Design, 1977-78, 1987, 1991 & 1996 & The Putney Sch, 1982-83; guest lectr & critic, Mus Sch, Boston, 1986 & 1995 & Brown Univ, 1986-1989 & 1994; instr, gallery dir

& cur, New England Sch Art & Design, Suffolk Univ, 1993-95. *Awards:* Larkin Meml Art Prize; Bradley Arts Prize. *Bibliog:* Jon Friedman (auth), ARTS Mag, New York, 11/1982; Bill Van Siclen (auth), The Providence J, 5/1989; Nancy Stapen (auth), Color Amid Winter's Gray, The Boston Globe. 2/1994. *Mailing Add:* Box 6083 Lincoln MA 01773

PARKS, CARRIE ANNE
SCULPTOR, EDUCATOR
b Chattanooga, Tenn, Jun 9, 1955. *Study:* Wesleyan Col, BFA, 76; apprentice to Takeo Sudo, Mashiko, Japan, 77-78; Va Commonwealth Univ, Richmond, MFA, 81. *Work:* Clemson Univ, Clemson, SC; Rutgers Univ, Camden, NJ; Auburn Univ, Ala; Austin Peay State Univ, Clarksville, Tenn; Saginaw Valley State Univ, University Center, Mich. *Comn:* Ceramic tile murals, Alma Col, Alma, Mich, 87 & 90; Pine Ave Sch, Alma, Mich, 97. *Exhib:* Form from Fragment: Four Contemp Tilemakers, SW Crafts Ctr, San Antonio, Tex, 97; NCECA Clay Nat RJ Stevenson Gallery, San Diego, Calif, 2003; Spaces: Interior & Exterior, The Clay Studio, Philadelphia, 2000; Am Mus Ceramic Art, Pomona, Calif, 2005; 4th Cheongju Int Craft Comp, Cheongju Crafts Hall, Cheongju, Korea, 2005; Domesticizing: Interior and Exterior Relations, Pottery, Detroit, Mich, 2007. *Teaching:* Adj fac ceramics, Va Commonwealth Univ, Richmond, Va, 81; prof art, Alma Col, Mich, 82. *Awards:* Second Place, Lill Street Gallery, 91; First Place, Wichita Falls Mus, 91; Regional Visual Arts Fel Award, Arts Midwest/Nat Endowment Arts, 93-94; Award of Excellence, Rosewood Gallery, 2002; Special Citations Award, Cheongju Arts Hall, Korea, 2005. *Bibliog:* Frank Giorgini (auth), Handmade Tiles, Lark Bks, 94; Kathy Triplett (auth), Handbuilt Ceramics, Lark Bks, 97; Peter King (auth), Architectural Ceramics for the Studio Potter, Lark Bks, 1999; Lynn Peters (auth), Surface Decoration for Low Fire Ceramics, Lark Bks, 1999; Chris Rich (auth), The Ceramic Design Book, Lark Bks, 1998; Peter King (auth), Architectural Ceramics for the Studio Potter, Lark Books, Fall, 1999; Angelica Pozo (auth), The Penland Book of Ceramics, Lark Books, Spring, 2003; Dona Z Meilach (auth), Teapots: Makers and Collectors, Schiffer Publ, 2005; Angelica Pozo (auth), 500 Tiles, Lark Books, 2008. *Mem:* Nat Coun Educ Ceramic Arts; Am Crafts Coun; Mich Potters Asn; Tile Heritage Found. *Media:* Clay, Pencil. *Interests:* Figurative sculpture, tiles, teapots. *Dealer:* Ariana Gallery 119 S Main St Royal Oak MI 48067; A Houberbocken Cudany Wisc. *Mailing Add:* 1007 Falkirk Rd Alma MI 48801-1438

PARLIN, JAMES
SCULPTOR, EDUCATOR
b Brooklyn, NY, 1954. *Study:* Univ Pa, Philadelphia, Ba (in Religious Thoughts), 1976, MFA (in Sculpture), 1981. *Exhib:* Solo exhib include: Sloan Fine Arts Ctr & Gallery, Lock Haven Univ, Pa, solo exhib, 2008, Little Gallery, Bowling Green Univ, Firelands Col, Ohio, 2009, Northwest Art Ctr, Minot State Univ, ND, 2010,; Group exhib include: Schmidt Dean Gallery, 2007, 2012, 2013; Nat juried exhib include: Cade Fine Arts Ctr Gallery, Arnold, Md, The Aktuell, 2008, Strohl Art Ctr, Chautauqua Inst, NY, 51st Chautauqua Nat Exhib of American Art, 2008, Fine Arts Gallery, Valosta State Univ, Georgia, Valdosta Nat 2009, K Space Contemporary Corpus Christi, Texas, The Third Coast Nat, 2010, Visual Art Soc Texas, Denton, 42nd Annual Exhib, 2011, Chico Art Ctr, Calif, All Media 2012, Galesburg Civic Art Ctr, Illinois, Galex 47, 2013, Northwest Art Ctr, Minot State Univ, America 2000: Best of the Best Invitational, 2013 and others. *Teaching:* Adj asst prof drawing and various three-dimensional studies, Drexel Univ, Philadelphia, 1988-1992; asst prof, 1992-97, Edinboro Univ of Pennsylvania, assoc prof, 1997-2003, prof, 2003-, chair art department, sculpture, foundations, 2008-. *Dealer:* Schmidt Dean Gallery, Philadelphia, Pa, 1989-. *Mailing Add:* 12420 Treaty Court Edinboro PA 16412

PARMENTER, SUSAN ELIZABETH
PAINTER, ILLUSTRATOR
b Mass. *Study:* Mass Coll Art; Painting the Landscape with John C Traynor, Swanzey, NH, 2003; Int painting sessions (Putney Painter & Friends), with Richard Schmid & Nancy Guzik, 2004-2006. *Comn:* Endangered Species (mural), 5th grade elementary class with Mr Goyette, Sunapee, NH, 1993; BF6 (mural), Sunapee Cent Sch Libr, Sunapee, NH, 1994. *Exhib:* Acad Artists Assoc, Nat Juried Exhibs, Springfield, Mass, 2004-2005; Pastel Painters Soc Cape Cod, Nat Juried Shows, 2004-2007; Oct Festival Art, Village Arts Putney, Putney, Vt, 2005; Seven by Seven, Int show, Red Roof Gallery, Enfield, NH, 2006; Putney Painters & Friends, Vermont Visions, Susan Powell Fine Art, Madison, Conn, 2006; Pastel Soc Am, Nat Open Juried Competitions, New York, NY, 2006, 2007; Pastel Soc NH, 1st Juried New Eng Show, Enfield, NH, 2007; Solo Exhib, An Artist's View, Red Roof Gallery, Enfield, NH, 2007. *Pos:* Graphic Designer, Illus, Artisans Workshop, New London, NH, 1983-2003. *Teaching:* Pvt instr, drawing & painting, Sunapee, NH, 1990-1991. *Awards:* Canson Pastel Award, Acad Artists Asn Canson, Springfield, Mass, 4/2004; Dakota Pastel Award (Heron), Dakota Pastels, 8/2006; Hon Mention (Green Apples), Pastel Soc NH Mem Show, 2006; Hon Mention (Heron), Pastel Soc NH Open Juried NE Show, Terry Ludwig Pastels, 2007; Daler Rowney Award, Daler Rowney Pastels, 8/2007; Air Float Systems Award (Woman with Parasol), Pastel Soc Am 35th Open, Bryan White Air Float Systems Inc, 9/2007. *Bibliog:* Jane White (auth), Of Mice and Dreams, Soo Nipi Mag, Ron Garceau, 8/1999; Artisan's Workshop, Cover Art (Downhill Mouse), Soo Nipi Mag, Ron Garceau, winter 2002. *Media:* Oils, Pastel. *Publ:* Auth (illus), Peter Christian's Favorites, Enterprising Edibles, 1987. *Dealer:* Red Roof Gallery 11 High St Enfield NH 03748; Susan Powell Fine Art 679 Boston Post Rd Madison CT 06443; Woodsum Art Gallery 25 E Main St Wainer NH 03278; Village Arts of Putney at Putney Inn 114 Westminster Rd Putney VT 05346. *Mailing Add:* 20 Ridgewood Rd Sunapee NH 03782

PARNESS, CHARLES
PAINTER
b Staten Island, New York, Jan 1, 1945. *Study:* Parsons Sch Design, 65; New York Univ, Sch Educ, BS, 66; Pratt Inst Grad Sch, MFA, 69. *Work:* Oakleigh Collection, Pleasantuxle, NY; Reader's Dig, Westchester, NY; Butler Inst, Youngstown, Ohio; Ruhrwest Mus, Wis; Reader's Digest, NY; Philadelphia Mus Art. *Exhib:* Solo exhibs, GW Einstein Gallery, NY, 94, Univ Wis Art Mus, Milwaukee, 94, Rockport Art Mus, Ill, 95, Vt Wax Works & Mus Store, Manchester, 95, Hebrew Home Aged Riverdale, Bronx, NY, 96 & Rahr-West Mus, Manitowoc, Wis, 97 & Krasdale Gallery, White Plains, NY, 98, Anne Dean Terk Fine Art Center, Kilgore Coll, Kilgore, Tex, 2002, Lewallen Contemp Gallery, Santa Fe, NMex, 2004; Positive ID, Southern Alleghenies Mus, Lovetto, Pa, 89; Marian Graves Mugar Art Gallery, Colby-Sawyer Coll, NH, 96; Self Relevation: Artist Confrontation, George Sherman Union Gallery, Boston Univ, 98; MB Mod Gallery, NY, 99; Weil Gallery, Tex A&M Univ, Corpus Christi, 2001; Recent Am Portraits; Fischbach Gallery, 2000; Am Acad Arts & Letters, 2001; Nat Acad Art Design; Nat Biennial Watercolor Invitational, Parkland Art Gallery, Champaigne, Ill, 2005; Artful Jesters, The Painting Ctr, NY, 2006; Korn Gallery, Dorothy Young Ctr for Arts, Drew Univ, Madison, NJ, 2008; I Am What I Am, Visual Art Gallery, SUNY, Adirondack, NY, 2010; Hunt & Chase, Salomon Contemporary, East Hampton, NY, 2010. *Teaching:* Vis artist painting, Marie Walsh Sharpe Found, 89-2008; Vt Studio Sch, 91, 93, 2002 & 2006. *Awards:* Vis Artist Fel, Brandywine Workshop, Philadelphia, Pa, 88; Carnegy Award, Nat Acad, 2002; Purchase Award, Am Acad, 2001; Harry Watrous Prize for Painting, Nat Acad Invitational Exhib Contemp Art Awards, 2010 . *Bibliog:* Sasha Brodsky (auth), rev, Villager, 3/16/94; Grace Gleuck (auth), rev, NY Observer, 3/21/94; Edmund Lietes (auth), rev, Cover Mag, 5/94; Nicholas Roukes (auth), Artful Jesters, Ten Speed Press; & many others. *Mem:* Rocky Mt Elk Found. *Media:* Mixed Media, Watercolor, Oil. *Mailing Add:* 68 Greene St New York NY 10012

PARRA, CARMEN
PAINTER, PRINTMAKER
b Mexico City, Mex, Nov 12, 1944. *Study:* Escuela Nac Antropologia e Hist, Mexico City, BA, 64; Acad Belles Artes, Rome, BFA, 67; Esmeralda, 67; Royal Coll Art, London, 70. *Work:* Mus de Arte Mod, Mexico City; Univ Nac Autonoma Mex. *Comn:* XIV Anniversary of Tabamex Libr, 84-; Mural Libr of Justice Dept, Mexico City. *Exhib:* Decima Bienal Paris, Mus D'Art Mod, France, 77; Las Ventanas, Mus Art Mod, Mexico City, 79; Mexico de Manana, Mus Bibliot Pape, Monetove, Coahuila, 79; La Creacion Femenina, Kunstler Haus Bethanien, Berlin, 80; Musica y Angeles, Metrop Cathedral Mex, Mexico City, 83; La Catedral de Mexico, Temps Captif, Orangerie in the Sully Hotel, Paris, France; Hojas Transfiguradas, Palacio de Minieria of the Nat Univ Mex, Mexico City, 86; Eternidad de lo Efimero, Mus de Arte Mod, Mexico City, 87; Museo Nacional de la Estampa, 91. *Pos:* Stage & wardrobe designer; film art dir, Frida, Naturaleza Viva, 88. *Awards:* Fiesta Primavera Otono, Mexico City, 81. *Bibliog:* Imagenes (Videotape) Carton y Papel de Mex, 82; La Mujer Mex en el Arte, ed Bacreser, 87. *Mem:* Soc Amigos del Centro Hist de la Ciudad de Mexico; Soc Amigos de la Catedral Metropolitana. *Media:* Acrylic, Oil; Lithography. *Publ:* Illusr, La Grafostatica u Oda a Eiffel, Talleres Graficos Nacion, 78; Tiempo Cautivo, La Cathedral de Mexico, Ed Arvil, 80; De la Pluma al Angel, Ed Nayaqui, 83; Templo Mayor, Ed Multiarte, 83; La Eternidad to lo Efimero, Miquel Angel Porrua, 83; Via Crucis, Multiarte, 91. *Dealer:* Lourdes Chumacero Gallery Estocolmo 34 Mexico DF Mex 06600; Sloane Arcotta Gallery. *Mailing Add:* Primera Cerrada de Galeana 13 San Angel Mexico DF 01000 Mexico

PARRENO, PHILIPPE
VIDEO ARTIST
b Oran, Algeria, 1964. *Study:* Inst Hautes Etudes en arts plastiques, Palais de Tokyo, Paris, 1989; Ecole Beaux-Arts, Grenoble, 1983-88. *Work:* Guggenheim Mus, New York; Mus d'Art Moderne de la Ville de Paris; Ctr Pompidou, Paris; Walker Art Ctr, Minneapolis. *Exhib:* Solo exhibs, Ctr Georges Pompidou, Paris, 1994, Air de Paris, Paris, 1994, 1997, 2001, 2005, 2007, Mus Art Mod, Paris, 1998, 2002, San Francisco Art Inst, 2000, Contemp Arts Ctr, Cincinnati, 2001, Friedrich Petzel Gallery, 2001, 2003, 2005, 2006, 2007, 2008, Inst Contemp Arts, London, 2001, Art Basel Miami Beach, 2002, Sky of the Seven Colors, Ctr for Contemporary Art, Kitakyushu, Japan, 2003, Atlas of Clouds, Brian Butler/1301PE, Los Angeles, 2005, Interior Cartoons, Ester Schipper, Berlin, 2006, Kunsthalle Zurich, 2006, Haunch of Venison, London, 2007, Walker Art Ctr, Minneapolis, 2008, Irish Mus Modern Art, Dublin, 2008, 2009, Serpentine Gallery, London, 2009, Kunsthalle Zurich, 2009; Int Art Exhib Biennale, Venice, Italy, 1993, 1995, 1998, 2003, 2007, 2009, 2011; Passions privees, Mus Art Mod, Paris, 1995; Let's Entertain, Walker Art Ctr, Minneapolis, Portland Art Mus, Ctr Georges Pompidou, Mus Rufino Tamayo & Miami Art Mus, 2000; Au-dela du spectacle, Ctr Georges Pompidou, Paris, 2000, Airs de Paris, 2007; Animations, PS 1 Contemp Art Ctr, Long Island City, NY, 2001; No Ghost Just a Shell, San Francisco Mus Mod Art, 2002; Light x Eight: The Hanukkah Proj, Jewish Mus, New York, 2002; Sodium Dreams, Bard Coll, NY, 2003; The Big Nothing, Inst Contemp Art, Philadelphia, 2004; Establishing Shot, Artists Space, New York, 2004; Artists's Favorites, Inst Contemp Art, London, 2004; Shadowland, Walker Art Ctr, Minneapolis, 2005; Universal Experience: Art, Life & the Tourists's Eye, Mus Contemp Art, Chicago, 2005; Tate Triennial, Tate Britain, London, 2006; Again for Tomorrow, Royal Coll Art, London, 2006; Learn to Read, Tate Mod, London, 2007; Words Fail Me, Mus Contemp Art Detroit, 2007; The Puppet Show, Inst Contemp Art, Philadelphia, 2008. *Collection Arranged:* Tate Modern, London, Mus Modern Art, NY, Walker Art Ctr, Minn, Centre Georges Pompidou, Paris, CIRVA, Marseille, and several others. *Mailing Add:* Friedrich Petzel Gallery 535 W 22nd St New York NY 10011

PARRIS, NINA GUMPERT
EDUCATOR, PHOTOGRAPHER
b Berlin, Ger, Sept 11, 1927; US citizen. *Study:* Bryn Mawr Col, BA (art hist); Woodrow Wilson Fel, 68; Univ Pa, MA (art hist), 69, PhD (art hist), 79. *Work:* Robert Hull Fleming Mus. *Exhib:* Cameo Gallery, Univ Vt, Columbia, SC; St Michael's Col, Vt; Colburn Gallery, UVM; Burlington Col; Wood Gallery, Montpellier, VT. *Collection Arranged:* Prints & Paintings in Permanent Collection (auth, catalog), Robert Hull Fleming Mus, 71; The South Carolina Collection of the Columbia Mus Art, 76. *Pos:* Cur, Robert Hall Fleming Mus, Univ Vt, 71-79; chief cur, Columbia Mus Art, 79-90; fac 92-2005. *Teaching:* Lectr art hist, Philadelphia Col Art, 70-71,

Univ Vt, 71-80; lectr mus studies, Univ SC, Columbia, 80-90; fac, MFA Visual Arts, Vt Col, 92-2005; lectr, Burlington Coll, 1990-2012. *Awards:* Woodrow Wilson Fel, 68. *Mem:* Am Asn Mus; Coll Art Asn; Soc for Photog Educ. *Media:* Photography. *Res:* Late 19th and 20th century art including contemporary art. *Publ:* Prints & Paintings the Collection of the Robert Hull Fleming Mus, 76; Auth, Van de Velde, Obrist, Hoelzel: The Basic Course at the Bauhaus, McMaster Colloquium, 81; The South Carolina Collection, Columbia Mus Art, 86; Retrospective exhib catalogue (with Celia Oliver), Essay for Exhib of Am Art of the 20th Century, Robert Hull Fleming Mus, 94; Outside Employment by Museum Staff & Thoughts on Personal Collecting, Legal Problems of Museum Administration, the Smithsonian Inst with the Coop of the Am Asn of Mus, 84; Biweekly columns for the State Newspaper, Columbia, SC, 85-88; Essay in catalogue, 100 Artists-100 Years, SC State Mus, Columbia, SC, 99; ed & production, Art & Artists ofthe South: the Robert P Coggins Collection, Univ SC Press, 84; Catalogue of the SC Collection of the Columbia Mus Art, 86; and many exhib catalogues. *Mailing Add:* 14 E Village Drive Burlington VT 05401-3471

PARRISH, DAVID BUCHANAN
PAINTER
b Birmingham, Ala, Jun 19, 1939. *Study:* Washington & Lee Univ, Lexington, Va, 57-58; Univ Ala, with Melville Price & Richard Brough, BFA, 61. *Work:* Wadsworth Atheneum, Hartford, Conn; Birmingham Mus Art, Ala; Everson Mus Art, Syracuse, NY; Montgomery Mus Fine Arts, Ala; Tenn Art League, Nashville; Rose Art Ctr, Braindeis Univ, Waltham, Mass; Huntsville Mus Art, Ala. *Exhib:* Southeastern Ann Exhib, High Mus Art, 63, 67-69; Ann Jury Exhib, Birmingham Mus Art, Ala, 63-71; Butler Inst Am Art, 69; 15th Ann Mid-South Exhib, Brooks Mem Art Gallery, 70; Solo exhib, Galerie Andre Francois Petit, Paris, 73, Sidney Janis Gallery, 75, Huntsville Mus Art, Ala, 77 & 81, Nancy Hoffman Gallery, NY, 81, Greenville Co Mus Art, NY, 90-95, Louis K Meisel Gallery, NY, 90-95 & 2003 & Westpac Gallery, Victorian Arts Ctr, Melbourne, Australia, 96; New/Photo Realism, Wadsworth Atheneum, Hartford, Conn, 74; Super Realism, Baltimore Mus Art, Md, 75; Some Faces, Louis K Meisel Gallery, NY, 92; Am Realism: The Urban Scene, Selections from the Glenn C Janss Collection Traveling Exhib, Redding Mus & Art Ctr, 93-94; The Detailed Image: Realism Here and Abroad, Harcourts Contemp, San Francisco, 86; Photorealists, Savannah Coll Art & Design, Ga, 97; The Photorealists, Ctr for Arts, Holmes Gallery, Vero Beach, Fla, 2000; This is Am, Aarhus Kunstmuseum, Copenhagen, Denmark, 2001. *Awards:* Award of Merit, 23rd Southeastern Ann Exhib, High Mus, Atlanta, 68; Top Award, 61st Ann Exhib, Birmingham Mus Art, 69; Top Award, Mid-South Ann, Brooks Mem Art Gallery, 70. *Bibliog:* John L Ward (auth), American Realist Painting 1945-1980, UMI Res Press, 86; Ann Marie Martin (auth), The World of David Parrish-Huntsville artist transforms ordinary items into vibrant images, Huntsville Times, 5/10/89; Stephanie Hanor (auth), Review of Photorealism since 1980, Tulanian, New Orleans, 93. *Media:* Oil. *Publ:* Ed, The South: A Treasury of Art & Literature, Lisa Howorth, Hugh Lauter Levin Assocs, New York, 93; The Fine Art Index, Vol I, Int Art Reference, Chicago, 94; New art in an old city/2 (essay), Edward Lucie-Smith, Virlane Found & K&B Corp Collections, New Orleans, 94. *Dealer:* Louis K Meisel New York NY 10012. *Mailing Add:* 700 Cleermont Dr SE Huntsville AL 35801-1842

PARRY, ELLWOOD COMLY, III
HISTORIAN
b Abington, Pa, Aug 9, 1941. *Study:* Harvard Univ, AB, 64; Univ Calif, Los Angeles, MA, 66; Yale Univ, PhD, 70. *Teaching:* Asst prof, Dept Art Hist & Archaeol, Columbia Univ, 69-75; assoc prof, Sch Art & Art Hist, Univ Iowa, 76-81; prof, Dept Art, Univ Ariz, Tucson, 81-. *Awards:* Nat Endowment Humanities Fel, 75-76; Huntington Libr Fel, 88. *Mem:* Coll Art Asn; Asn Historians Am Art. *Res:* Iconography of American art and the interaction between 19th-century painting, the popular arts, photography, and science. *Publ:* Auth, The Image of the Indian and the Black Man in American Art, 1590-1900, George Braziller, 74; coauth, Reflections of 1776: The Colonies Revisited, Viking Studio, 74; auth, Thomas Eakins's "Naked Series" reconsidered: another look at the standing nude photographs made for the use of Eakins's students, Am Art Journal, vol 20, no 2, 88; The Art of Thomas Cole: Ambition and Imagination, Univ Del Press, 88; Cooper, Cole and The Last of the Mohicans, Papers in Art History, Art and the Native American: Perceptions, Reality and Influences, Vol X, Pa State Univ, 2001. *Mailing Add:* Univ Ariz Dept Art Tucson AZ 85721

PARRY, EUGENIA
WRITER
b July 28, 1940; US citizen. *Study:* Univ Mich, with Marvin Eisenberg, BA, 61; Harvard Univ, with Agnes Mongan & Jacob Rosenberg, MA, 63, PhD, 71. *Teaching:* Prof art hist, Wellesley Col, Mass, 68-86 & Univ NMex, Albuquerque, 87-94; prof art hist & Photog, Univ NMex, Albuguerque, NMex. *Awards:* Guggenheim Fel, 74; Decorated Chevalier des Palmes Academiques, Fr Gov, 87; Award in lit, Nat Endowment Arts, 93. *Res:* Graphic arts of the 19th century; monotypes of Edgar Degas; early artistic photographers in France, the Calotypists; contemporary photographers. *Publ:* Coauth, The Art of French Calotype, Princeton Univ Press, 83; auth, The Art of a Collector: Henri Le Secq Photographer, Musee des Arts & Decoratifs & Flammarion, 86; The Photography of Gustave LeGray, Univ Chicago Press, 88; contribr, Nuclear Enchantment, Photographs of Patrick Nagatani, Univ NMex Press, 91; Joel Peter Witkin, Centre Nat de la Photog, Paris, 91; and others. *Mailing Add:* PO Box 864 Cerrillos NM 87010-0864

PARRY, PAMELA JEFFCOTT
LIBRARIAN, ADMINISTRATOR
b New York, NY, Mar 6, 1948. *Study:* Univ Ariz, BA, 69; Columbia Univ, MA (art hist & archaeol), 72, MLS, 73. *Pos:* Asst fine arts librn, Columbia Univ, NY, 72-76; ed, Art Reference Collection, 78-82 & Art Doc, 82, 85-86; ed, Art Libr Soc NAm, 78-81, exec secy, 80-83, exec dir 83-93; librn, Int Dada Arch, Univ Iowa, 79-81. *Mem:* Art Libr Soc Nam; Tucson Mus Art Contemp Art Soc. *Publ:* Contribr, From Realism to Symbolism: Whistler and His World, Columbia Univ/Philadelphia Mus Art, 71; auth, Contemporary Art and Artists, 78, Photography Index, 79 & Print Index, 83, Greenwood Press. *Mailing Add:* 3846 N Adobe Garden Loop Tucson AZ 85716-1148

PARSONS, CYNTHIA MASSEY
PAINTER, WRITER
b Birmingham, Ala, Oct 29, 1946. *Study:* Fla State Univ, Tallahassee, with William Walmsley (lithography) & Arthur Deshaies (etching), BA, 68. *Work:* Frederick Co Judicial Ctr, Winchester, Va; William B Bunker Bldg, Redstone Arsenal, Ala; US Olympic Mus, Phoenix, Ariz; Florence Conf Ctr, Ala; Huntsville Mus Art, Ala. *Comn:* President James Davis (painting), Shenandoah Coll Conserv, Winchester, Va, 90; Montage of Huntsville, Madison Co Chamber Com, Ala, 96; Pope John Paul II (painting), Archdiocese of NY, 98; Gen Hamilton H Howze (painting), Aviation-Bunker Bldg, Redstone Arsenal, Ala; Sen Howell Heflin (painting), Howel T Heflin Complex, Redstone Arsenal, Ala, 98. *Exhib:* Birmingham Mus Art Ann Exhib, Ala, 68; Ala Contemp Women Artists Exhib, Ala State Coun Arts, Montgomery, 93; Printworks: Images & Words Tell a Story, Mus ETex, Lufkin, 95; solo exhib, Kennedy-Douglas Art Ctr, Florence, Ala, 95; 18th Ann Mini Works Exhib, Jacksonville State Univ, Ala, 96; Watercolor Soc Ala Exhib, Birmingham Pub Libr, 96; New Works: Opulence & Frivolity Invitational, Loft Gallery, Huntsville, Ala, 98; Billboard, Mass Mus Contemp Art, North Adams, 99. *Awards:* Ala Outdoor Billboard Prog Grant, Ala State Coun Arts, 93; Proclamation of Recognition of Artistic Contrib, State of Ala Legislature, 97. *Bibliog:* Kathy Holland (auth), Taking Art to the Streets, Ala Arts Mag, Vol III, No 1, Ala State Coun Arts, spring 94; Melissa Ford Thornton (auth), Art for Sake, Hometown Press Mag, Vol 8, No 1, Hometown Press, spring 94; Charles Groover (auth), Artist 2 Artist, Ala Art Monthly, Vol I, Issue 10, Agnes, 4/95. *Mem:* Watercolor Soc Ala (publicity chmn, 95-96); Nat League Am Pen Women; Nat Artist Slide Registry, Washington, DC. *Media:* Oil, Watercolor; Mixed Media. *Res:* Leonardo da Vinci love letters. *Publ:* Illusr, Stars of Alabama-Official Commemorative Poster of Alabama, 175 Years of Statehood, Ala Bureau Tourism & Travel, 94; Pride Runs Deep-Official Coach Gene Stallings, '96 Iron Bowl Poster, 96 & auth/illusr, Impressions-Men's Summer Soccer '96, 96, ArtSouth Enterprises; contribr, Annual Maple Hill cemetery walking tour, Hist Huntsville Quart, Huntsville Hist Found Inc, spring 98; illusr, The unsung heroine & glutenous gofer, Right Road Mag, Vol I, Right Road Ministry, 11/98. *Dealer:* The Loft 1201 Meridian St N Huntsville AL 35801. *Mailing Add:* Carlisle Gallery 601 Pratt Ave Huntsville AL 35801

PARSONS, MERRIBELL MADDUX
MUSEUM DIRECTOR, CURATOR
b San Antonio, Tex. *Study:* Newcomb Coll, BFA; Ecole du Louvre, cert; Inst Fine Arts, NY Univ, MA; Metrop Mus & Inst Fine Arts, dipl (mus training). *Collection Arranged:* Permanent collection, Minneapolis Inst Arts, 72-74, Metropolitan Museum's Uris Ctr for Educ, 84-86; permanent collection, Columbus Mus Art and renovation of historic site for major exhib from China 88-90, San Antonio Mus. Arts European Art collection, 2015-16; developed Mus Shenadoah Valley, Va, 94-98; Villa Finale, a Nat Trust for Historic Preservation House, San Antonio, Tex, 2008-. *Pos:* Bell mem cur decorative arts, Minn Inst Arts, 69-74, chief cur & cur sculpture & decorative arts, Minn Inst Arts, 74-79; chmn & curatorial liaison for educ, Metrop Mus Art, 79-80, vice dir, 80-87; dir, Columbus Mus Art, 87-94; acting dir & consult, Glass-Glen Burnie Found to develop Mus of Shenandoah Valley, 94-98; pres, Parsons & Assocs, consult to mus, 98-; researcher, Villa Finale, Nat Trust for Historic Preservation, San Antonio, Tex, 2008; curator European Art, San Antonio Mus Art, Tex, 2013-. *Teaching:* adj prof, Univ Minn, 74-79; Adj prof, Inst Fine Arts, NY Univ, 80-87, Ohio State Univ, 87-93. *Awards:* Longhi Fel; Ford Found Fel; Nat Endowment Arts Fel; Distinguished Leadership, Columbus Council, 90. *Mem:* Am Asn Mus; Asn Art Mus Dirs; Nat Trust for Hist Preservation. *Res:* European sculpture, 1600-1900, decorative arts 1600-1900. *Publ:* Auth, Sculpture in the David Daniels collection, Minn Inst Arts Bull, 69-74. *Mailing Add:* 486 E Olmos Dr San Antonio TX 78212

PARSONS, RICHARD DEAN
PATRON
b NY City, Apr, 4, 1948. *Study:* Univ Hawaii, 68; Univ Ala Law Sch, JD, 71. *Hon Degrees:* Adelphi Univer, LLD, 90; Medgar Evers Col, NY City, LLD, 91; Univ Hawaii, LHD, 2003. *Pos:* gen counsel, assoc dir, domestic coun White House, 75-77; partner, Patterson Belknap Webb & Tyler, New York City, 79-88; pres, Chief Operating Officer, Dime Savings Bank NY, 88-90, chmn, Chief Exec Officer, 90-94; dir, Time Warner, 91-, pres, 95-99, Chief Exec Officer, Time Warner Inc, 2002-, chmn, 2003-; co-Chief Operating Officer, AOL Time Warner, Inc, 99-2002; Mus Modern Art, Howard Univ; Met Mus Art. *Awards:* Recipient Distinguished Alumnus Award, Univ Hawaii, 2003. *Mem:* Apollo Theatre Found (chmn, currently); Pres Drug Task Force; Wildcat Serv Orgn, New York City Econ Develop Corp (chmn, currently); NY Zoological Soc (bd dir, currently); Howard Univ, Metrop Mus Art (trustee, currently). *Collection:* Owns winery in Tuscany, Italy

PARTEGAS, ESTER
INSTALLATION SCULPTOR
b Barcelona, 1972. *Study:* Eina Sch Art & Design, Barcelona, 1990-92; Univ Barcelona, MFA (sculpture), 1996; Hochschule der Kunste, Berlin, 1996-98. *Exhib:* Solo exhibs include La Capella, Barcelona, 1996, DFN Gallery Proj Room, New York, 1998, De Chiara/Stewart Gallery, New York, 2000, 2001, Galeria Helga de Alvear, Madrid, 2003, 2005, 2008, Rice Univ Art Gallery, Houston, 2003, Hallwalls, Buffalo, 2003, Proj Spaces at Art Chicago, 2004, Foxy Prodn, New York, 2004, 2006, Salina Art Ctr, 2004, Christopher Grimes Gallery, Santa Monica, 2006, 2007, Reina Sofia, Madrid, 2007, Alrich Mus Contemp Art, Conn, 2008; group exhibs include Anywhere But Here, Artists' Space, New York, 2000; The Good, the Bad & the Ugly: A Spaghetti Western, Mus Contemp Art, Denver, 2001; Paper, Aldrich Mus Contemp

Art, Conn, 2001; Outer City, Inner Space, Whitney Mus Am Art at Altria, New York, 2002; Street Level, Ctr Curatorial Studies Mus, Bard Coll, NY, 2003; Harlem Postcards, Studio Mus in Harlem, 2003; The Paper Sculpture Show, Sculpture Ctr, Long Island City, NY, 2003, Nake it Now: Sculpture in NY, 2005; Long Term Installations, PS1 Contemp Art Ctr, Long Island City, 2004; Art on Paper, Weatherspoon Art Mus, Univ NC, Greensboro, 2006. *Collection Arranged:* SoftCell, Foxy Prodn, Brooklyn, NY, 2003. *Awards:* Joan Mitchell Found Grant, 2004. *Dealer:* Galeria Helga de Alvear Dr Fourquet 12 Madrid 28012 Spain; Nogueras Blanchard Xucla 7 Barcelona 08001 Spain; Christopher Grimes Gallery 916 Colorado Avenue Santa Monica CA 90401. *Mailing Add:* c/o Foxy Prodn 623 W 27th St New York NY 10001

PARTON, RALF
SCULPTOR, EDUCATOR
b New York, NY, July 2, 1932. *Study:* Albright Art Sch, Buffalo, dipl, 53; NY Univ Col, Buffalo, BS (art educ), 54; Columbia Univ, MA (art), 55. *Work:* Civic Ctr, Turlock, Calif; City Hall, Turlock, Calif; Northwestern Mich Coll Gallery, Traverse City, Mich; Our Lady of Fatima, Modesto, Calif. *Comn:* Tree of Life (steel sculpture), Beth Shalom Synagogue, Modesto, Calif, 79; and many pvt commissions. *Exhib:* Solo exhibs, Galerie de la Maison des Beaux-Arts, Paris, 82, Artists Forum, Los Angeles, Calif, 85; San Francisco Mus Art, San Francisco, Calif, 72; Art Fac Exhib, Calif State Coll Stanislaus, Turlock, Calif, 73; Calif State Coll Stanislaus Art Fac Exhib, Univ of Pac, Calif, 76; McKissick Mus, Columbia, SC, 88. *Pos:* Dir, Art tours around the world, 90-; tour dir, Art Tours Around the World, 94-. *Teaching:* Chmn dept painting & sculpture, Northwestern Mich Col, 58-62; prof sculpture, Calif State Univ, Stanislaus, 63-96, chmn dept art, 63-70, prof emer, 96-. *Awards:* Horohoe Prize Originality Sculpture, Sisti Gallery, Buffalo, NY, 57; Reynolds Prize Sculpture, Stockton Art Show, Calif, 66. *Bibliog:* David Otth (auth), Monoliths to miniatures, Toy Train Operating Soc Bulletin, Vol 2, No 2; Dr H Werness (auth), Calif Landscapes, catalog, 86; Dictionary of Am Sculptors, 87. *Mem:* Diablo Reg Art Asn; Rossmoor Art Asn (bd trustees). *Media:* Bronze, Vacuum Formed Styrene. *Publ:* Auth, Art lovers tour, Artsline, 1/93; A Professorial Trip, Contra Costa Times, 1/2/94; Mask Making, Rossmoor News, 1/18/95; auth, Parton's Art Tours, Artsline, 11-12/2000, Rossmoor News, 11/15/2000 & Contra Costa Times, 3/11/2000. *Mailing Add:* 1122 Skycrest Dr No 8 Walnut Creek CA 94595

PARTRIDGE, DAVID GERRY
PAINTER, SCULPTOR
b Akron, Ohio, Oct 5, 1919; Can citizen. *Study:* Univ Toronto, BA; Queen's Univ, Kingston, Ont; Art Students League; Slade Sch, London; Atelier 17, Paris, with WS Hayter. *Hon Degrees:* DSLitt, Order of Can. *Work:* Tate Gallery, London; Nat Gallery Can, Ottawa; Libr Cong, Washington; Art Gallery Ont, Toronto; Gallery NSW, Sydney, Australia. *Comn:* Nail murals, York Univ, Toronto, 70, Westminster Cathedral, London, 71 & foyer, Toronto City Hall, 77, Bell Trinity, Toronto, 83 & Can Capital Cong Ctr, Ottawa, 83; and others. *Exhib:* Montreal Mus Fine Arts Spring Show, 62; Art of the Americas & Spain, Madrid & Barcelona, 63; Carnegie Int, Pittsburgh, 65; Sculpture '67, Toronto; Art Gallery Windsor, 79; Circa 1996, Toronto, 96. *Teaching:* Art master, Ridley Col, St Catharines, Ont, 46-56; instr art, Queens Univ, Ont, summers 56-60 & Ont Col Art, 74-75. *Awards:* Brit Coun Scholar to Slade Sch, 50-51; Sculpture Prize & Purchase Award, Montreal Mus Fine Arts, 62. *Bibliog:* Kenneth Coutts-Smith (auth), David Partridge, Quadrum, 65; Jim Tiley (auth), Vanguard Vol 2, No 3, David Partridge, Art in Archit, Visual Arts, Ont, 82; Modern Mosaic Techniques/Lovoos Paramoore, David Partridge, Nail Mosaics, Watson Guptill. *Mem:* Fel Royal Soc Arts; Royal Can Acad. *Media:* Acrylic on Canvas; Wood, Nails. *Dealer:* Moore Gallery Ltd 80 Spadina Ave Suite 404 Toronto M5V 2J3 ON Canada; The Russell Gallery Peterborough Ont Canada. *Mailing Add:* 77 Seaton St Toronto ON M5A 2T2 Canada

PARTRIDGE, LOREN WAYNE
EDUCATOR, HISTORIAN
b Raton, New Mex, Apr 11, 1936. *Study:* Yale Univ, Ba in Eng Lit, 58; Univ Buenos Aires, Cert in Latin Am Lit, 59; US Army Language Sch, Monterey, Calif, Diploma in Russian, 61; Harvard Univ, MA in Fine Arts, 65; Harvard Univ, PhD in Fine Arts, 69. *Pos:* Reviewer Art Bull, 72, 78, 80 & 83, Renaissance Quarterly, 84, 87, 90 & 99, Design Book Rev, 87, Master Drawings, 87, Am Hist Rev, 93 & Apollo, 96; chmn, dept hist of art, 78-87 & 90-93; chmn dept art practice, 2004-2008. *Teaching:* Fel Harvard Univ, Cambridge, Mass, 64-66; lectr, Univ Calif, Berkeley, 68, acting asst prof, 69-70, asst prof, 70-76, assc prof, 76-80, prof, 80-; resident, in art hist Am Acad in Rome, 85. *Awards:* Scholar Yale Univ, 55-58; Fulbright fel, 58-59 & 75; Harvard Univ, 64-66; Am Acad in Rome fel, 66-68; grantee Kress Found, 68-69 & 71-72; Univ Calif, 72, 77, 82, 85, 93-94, 99-2000 & 2003-2004; Kress fel Inst for Advanced Studies, 74-75; Guggenheim fel, 81-92; Getty sr res grantee, 88-89. *Publ:* Auth, John Galen Howard and the Berkeley Campus, Beaux-Arts Archit in the Athens of the West, 78; Arts of Power: Three Halls of State in Italy 1300-1600, 92; The Art of Renaissance Rome, 1400-1600, 96; Michelangelo: Michelangelo Last Judgment: A Glorious Restoration, 97; contribr auth, Encycl of Italian Renaissance, 81, Int Dict Art and Artists, 90 & Dict of Art, 94; coauth (with Randolph Starn), Caprarola, Palazzo Farnese, 88 & A Renaissance Likeness: Art and Culture in Raphael's Julius II, 80; contribr articles to prof J. *Mailing Add:* U Calif Dept Hist of Art 6020 416 Doe Library Berkeley CA 94720-6020

PAS, GERARD PETER
PAINTER, SCULPTOR
b Valkenswaard, North Brabant, Neth; Can citizen. *Study:* H B Beal Tech Sch, London, Can, Spec Art, 73-74; assisted artist-inventor Murray Favro in Art Fabrication, independent study, 74; L'Abri, Eck En Wiel, Neth, independent study, 75-81. *Work:* De Appel, Amsterdam, Neth; Middelburg Archieven, Rotterdam, Neth; McIntosh Gallery, Univ Western Ont, London, Can; Ont Arts Coun, Toronto, Can; London Regional Art Gallery, Can. *Comn:* The Public Crutch in the Private House, Filmworks Inc, London, Can, 87. *Exhib:* This Is Information, Gallery T'Venster, Rotterdam, The Neth, 80; Solo shows, Päs Plus-Päs Moins, Walter Phillip Gallery, Banff Ctr Arts, Can, 88 & Red-Blue Works, Mercer Union Ctr Contemp Arts, Toronto, 89; Hommage-Demontage, group show, Neve Galerie-Sammlung Ludwig, Aachen, Ger, 88-89; Hommage-Demontage, traveling exhib, Wilheim Hack Mus, Ludwigs Hafen, Ger, 88-89 & Mus Moderner Kunst, Vienna, Austria, 88-89; The Place of Work, traveling exhib, Royal Archit Inst Can, Winnipeg, 89-90. *Pos:* Mem bd dir, Forest City Art Gallery, London, Can, 75-79 & Embassy Cult House, London, Can, 89-91; writer & critic, Art Zien Mag, Amsterdam, Neth, 78-79. *Teaching:* Lectr performance art, Academisch Kunst Institute, Enschede, Neth, 79; instr drawing figure, London Regional Art Gallery, Can, 86-88; prof drawing & painting, Redeemer Col, Ancaster, Can, 89-. *Awards:* Travel Award, Ministry Cult Neth, 79; B Grant Award, Can Coun, 90; Proj Grant, Ont Arts Coun, 79. *Bibliog:* Dr Uli Bohnen (auth), Pas: Less & More-More of Less, McIntosh Gallery, V W O, Can, 87; Linda Genereux (auth), Toronto-Gerard Pas, Art Forum, New York, 89; Dr Graham Birtwistle (auth), Pas: The Modular Ambulant, Ctr Art Gallery-Calvin Col, 91. *Media:* Mixed. *Publ:* Contribr, L'Arte Di Gerard P Päs, Domus Mag, 88; The Living Meridian, Visual Aids London Life/AIDS Comt, 88; Typographie, Rotis Inst, Druckhaus Mack, 88; A Re-invented Object, Can Art, 90; Untitled Legs, Banner Publ, 91. *Mailing Add:* 631 Wallace St London ON N5Y 3R8 Canada

PASCHALL, JO ANNE
PRINTMAKER, LIBRARIAN
b Murray, Ky, Mar 9, 1949. *Study:* Memphis State Univ, BFA, 71; Univ GA, MFA, 74; Art Studies Abroad, Cortona, Italy, Dodd-Carnegie scholar, 73-74; Univ Ala, 76-77; Atlanta Univ, MLS, 81. *Work:* Huntsville Mus Art, Ala; Memphis State Univ Collection; Univ Ga Collection. *Exhib:* Eleven Printmakers, Southeastern Ctr Contemp Art, Winston-Salem, NC; Invitational Exhib, Atlanta Artworkers Coalition Gallery, Ga; Invitational Print Exhib, Huntsville Mus Art, Ala; one-person exhib, Memorabilia, Univ Ala Gallery, Huntsville; Inst Prof Femminnile di Stato Gino Severini, da Cortona, Italy. *Pos:* Grad asst printmaking, Univ Ga Art Dept, 73-74; intern, Art for Exceptional Children, Ga Retardation Ctr, 77; cur, Visual Collections, Atlanta Col Art Libr, 78-79, head librn, 79-86; orgn consult, High Mus Art, 83-85; asst dir, Nexus Press, 86-93, dir, 93-. *Teaching:* Assoc instr printmaking, Art Studies Abroad, Cortona, Italy, 74; div head printmaking dept, Univ Ala, Huntsville, 75-77 & Atlanta Col Art, 80-85. *Awards:* Third Place, painting, Tenn All-Artists Exhib, Nashville, 71; Special Purchase Award, Inst Prof Femminnile di Stato Gino Severini da Cortona, Italy, 74. *Mem:* Art Libr Soc NAm; Anarchist Librns Group Am. *Media:* All Media. *Interests:* 20th century; contemporary issues; artists books and publications, bookworks; developed the Atlanta Coll Art artists books collection. *Publ:* Contribr, Macmillan Encycl Archits, Macmillan Publ Co, 82. *Dealer:* Heath Gallery 416 E Paces Ferry Atlanta GA 30305. *Mailing Add:* 733 Sherwood Rd Atlanta GA 30324-5279

PASCUAL, MARLO
PHOTOGRAPHER, SCULPTOR
Study: Univ Tenn, BA (Photography), 1994; Tyler Sch Art, Philadelphia, MFA (Photography), 2007. *Exhib:* Exhibs include MFA show, Univ New Orleans, 2005; VA4398UV, Memphis, 2006; Constructions: Selected Works by Second Year MFA Students, New York, 2007 ; Powers of Ten, Philadelphia, 2007; White Columns, 2008; Crop Rotation, Marianne Boesky Gallery, New York, 2008. *Mailing Add:* c/o Marianne Boesky Gallery 509 W 24th St New York NY 10011

PASKEWITZ, BILL, JR
PAINTER, EDUCATOR
b Brooklyn, NY, Aug 5, 1953. *Study:* Cooper Union, with Deborah Remington, BFA, 75; Queens Coll, City Univ, New York, with Louis Finkelstein, MFA, 78. *Work:* KUB Res, Irvine, Calif; Armorall Inc, Los Angeles; also pvt collections of Mr & Mrs Herbert Brownell, Laguna Beach, Calif, Mr James Rush, New York, Dr & Mrs Michael Moses, Newport Beach, Mr Jules Marine, Newport Beach, Calif, Mr R Altmann, New York & Barbara Cavaliere, New York, Barbara Dismas, Roslyn Heights, NY, the Dillard Family, Palm Springs, Calif, Carol Heart, Pleasanton, Calif, Victor Herstein, Val Verde, Calif, Gina Kaiper, Pleasanton, Calif, Pam Luster, Livermore, Calif, Sylvia Rodriguez, San Francisco, Calif, Michael Rose, Darien, Conn, the Yontz Family, Indian Wells, Calif, and more. *Comn:* Mural, comn by Henry Seger Strom, Costa Mesa, Calif, 86. *Exhib:* Solo exhibs, Contemp Art Gallery, New York, 72, Jacques Seligmann, New York, 78, West Coast Gallery, Newport, Calif, 80, James Turcotte Gallery, Los Angeles, 84, Orange Coast Coll, Costa Mesa, Calif, 87 & Merging One Gallery, Santa Monica, 96; NY Painters, Columbus Mus Art, Ohio, 78; Art in Orange Co, Newport Harbor, Newport Beach, Calif, 79; Triton Mus Art, Santa Clara, Calif, 98, 2000, 2007, 2008. *Pos:* Dir, Art Squad, Bayside, NY, 73-75. *Teaching:* Instr printmaking, Newport Harbor Art Mus, 79-81; instr painting, Irvine Valley Coll, Irvine, Calif, 79-; adj lectr fine arts, Golden West Coll, Huntington Beach, 80-; Visual Arts Dept coordr & instr painting, drawing, art hist & art appreciation, Las Positas Coll, Livermore, Calif, currently. *Awards:* Harvey Medal, 71, Sch Art League; Gold Metal Scholastic Award, Printmaking, 72; Anna E Meltzer Soc Award for Creativity in Painting, 75. *Bibliog:* Barbara Cavaliere (auth), Newcomers, 9/77 & Bill Paskewitz, 9/78, Arts Mag; Ralph Bond (auth), Texture image diversity, Artweek, 81. *Mem:* Coll Art Asn Am. *Media:* Watercolor, Pastel, Oil. *Specialty:* Watercolor, oil. *Interests:* Inspiring through brushstrokes. *Publ:* Auth, Art connections, Orange Co Arts Comn, 74; Art in Orange County, Newport Harbor Art Mus, 79; Carving out an artistic lifestyle, Branding Iron, 4/12/84; The why and how of making your own pastels, Inksmith, 9/85. *Dealer:* www.bpaskewitz.com; Figurehead Gallery Livermore Ca. *Mailing Add:* 115 Hillside Rd Antioch CA 94509

PASQUARELLI, GREGG ANDREW
ARCHITECT
Study: Villanova Univ, BS; Columbia Univ, MArch (design), 1994. *Work:* Mus Mod Art. *Pos:* designer, project mgr, site architect, Greg Lynn FORM; co-founder, SHoP Architects, NY, 1997-; Young Leader's Fel, Nat Com on US-China Relations. *Teaching:* adj asst prof archit, Columbia Univ Grad Sch Archit, 1996-2003; Shure prof archit, Univ Va, 2003; Louis I Kahn vis asst prof, Yale Univ; Saarinen prof archit, Yale Univ, 2006. *Awards:* Nat Design Award for Archit Design (for SHoP), Cooper Hewitt Nat Design Mus, 2009; Chicago Athenaeum Am Archit Awards (for SHoP), AIA New York City and state chapters. *Bibliog:* Out of Practice (monogr), The Monacelli Press, 2012. *Mem:* Nat Acad; Archit League of NY (bd dirs). *Mailing Add:* c/o SHoP Architects 11 Park Pl New York NY 10007

PASQUINE, RUTH
ARTIST, HISTORIAN
b Newark, NJ, Jan 21, 1948. *Study:* Franconia Col, BA, 70; Clark Art Inst, MA, 81; Grad Ctr, City Univ NY, PhD, 2000. *Pos:* Res asst, Nat Acad Design, New York, 86-89; cur educ, Norton Art Gallery, West Palm Beach, 89-91; cur collections, Ark Arts Ctr Little Rock, 91-97. *Teaching:* lectr visual arts, Pulaski Tech Col, 2000; asst prof, gallery dir, Univ Ark, Pine Bluff, 2001-03, Univ Cent Ark, 03-04. *Res:* American art, 20th century, Tibetan art. *Publ:* Poetry in Drawing & Hollis Sigler, Ark Arts Ctr, Little Rock, 96; Emil Bisttram 1895-1976, American Painter, vo2, Lambert Acad Publ, 2010. *Mailing Add:* 1850 S Gaines St Little Rock AR 72206

PASSANTINO, GEORGE CHRISTOPHER
PAINTER, INSTRUCTOR
b New York, NY. *Study:* Art Students League, 48-53. *Work:* Adelphi Univ, Garden City, NY; Metrop Opera Guild, NY; and many others. *Comn:* comn by Hanes Family, Rockefeller, Roosevelt. *Exhib:* Conn Acad Fine Arts, Wadsworth Antheneum, Hartford, 75-76; Audubon Artists, Nat Acad, NY, 76; 49th Ann Exhib, Hudson Valley Art Asn, White Plains, NY, 77; Silvermine Guild, New Canaan, Conn; Stamford Mus, Stamford, Conn; solo exhib, Idyllic Impressions, Southport Harbor Gallery, Conn, 2003. *Teaching:* Instr drawing, painting & compos, Famous Artists Sch, Westport, Conn, 57-63, supervisor, 63-74; instr, Univ Bridgeport, Conn, 74-75; instr drawing & painting, Art Students League, 78-; instr, landscape workshops, New York, 91, France, 93 & Vero Beach, Fl; instr, portrait & landscape, Silvermine Guild, New Canaan, Conn, 95 & Valdes, Santa Fe, NMex. *Awards:* Charles Noel Flagg Mem Prize, Conn Acad Fine Arts, 76. *Mem:* Life mem Art Students League; Allied Artists Am. *Media:* Oil, Watercolor. *Publ:* Coauth, Six artists paint a portrait, Northlight, 74; The Portrait and Figure Painting Book, Watson-Guptill, 79. *Dealer:* Portraits Inc 985 Park Ave New York NY 10022; Portrait Brokers of America 36B Church St Birmingham AL. *Mailing Add:* 484A Commanache Ln Stratford CT 06614-8261

PASSUNTINO, PETER ZACCARIA
PAINTER, PRINTMAKER
b Chicago, Ill, Feb 18, 1936. *Study:* Art Inst Chicago, scholar, 54-58; Oxbow Sch Painting, Mich, summer 58; Inst Art Archeol, Paris, 63-65. *Work:* Walter P Chrysler Mus; Hirshhorn Mus, Washington, DC; Norfolk Mus, Va; Titan Steel Corp; Provincetown Art Asn & Mus; also pvt collections of Joseph H Hirshborn, Walter P Chrysler, Henry Geldzahler and others. *Exhib:* Art Inst Chicago, Ill, 57; Corcoran Gallery Art, Washington, DC, 74; solo exhibs, The White Room, Belg, 81, Yvonne Seguy Gallery, NY, 82 & 84, Fordham Univ at Lincoln Ctr, NY, 86, Terne Gallery, NY, 86, Pike St Art Ctr, Pt Jervis, NY, 91, Lakin Jones Gallery, Omaha, Nebr, 96 & Nat Arts Club, NY, 99; AIR Invitational Exhib, NY, 83-84; Trisolini Gallery, Ohio Univ, Athens, 84; Expressionism an Am Beginning, Provincetown Art Asn & Mus, RI, 85; Kisker Gallery, Scottsdale, Ariz, 86; Daedal Fine Arts, Fallstown, Md, 88; Frankel Estate, Mus Contemp Art, Chicago, Ill, 88; Arts Club of NY, 99; Broome St Gallery, NY, 99. *Pos:* Chmn, Momentum, Chicago, 57-58. *Teaching:* Instr, Rutgers-Livingston Col, Bayonne Jewish Community Ctr, NJ & Greenwich Art Soc, Conn. *Awards:* Fulbright Fel, 63-64; Guggenheim Fel in Graphics, 71; Nat Endowment Arts Grant, 83. *Bibliog:* Articles in Art News, summer 76 & 9/84, Art in America, 5/75 & 9/84, Soho News, 4/76 & 3/79, Arts Mag, 3/76 & 6/76

PASTERNAK, ANNE
ADMINSTRATOR, CURATOR
Study: Univ Mass, BA (art hist); Hunter Coll, MA (art hist). *Pos:* Dir, Stux Galleries, Boston, formerly; cur, Real Art Ways, Hartford, formerly; pres & artistic dir, Creative Time, 1994-. *Mailing Add:* c/o Creative Time 59 East 4th Street 6E New York NY 10003

PASTINE, RUTH
PAINTER, LECTURER
b New York, NY, Dec 10, 1964. *Study:* SUNY Coll Purchase, 82-84; Cooper Union for Advan Sci & Art, BFA, 87; The Rietveld Akademie, Amsterdam, 87-88; Hunter Col, City Univ of NY, MFA, 93. *Exhib:* Group Exhib, Metrop Mus Art, NY, 82; Nat Arts Club Ann Exhib, NY, 87; East Meets West, Claremont Grad Univ, Calif, 96; Presentational Painting II, Bertha & Karl Leubsdorf Art Gallery, NY, 97; Current Expressions in Contemp Art, TIAA/CREF, NY, 97; Sudden Incandescence, Bemis Ctr for Contemp Arts, Omaha, Nebr, 99; Abstraction & Immenence, Hunter Coll Times Sq Gallery, NY, 2001; Monochrome/Monochrome?, Florence Lynch Gallery, NY, 2001; Solo exhibs, Arc Paintings, Houghton Gallery, Cooper Union, NY, 87, Diffusion Paintings, Times Square Gallery, Claremont, Calif, Ray Paintings: Blue-Orange-Violet, Brian Gross Fine Art, San Francisco, 98, New Paintings, Quint Contemp Art, La Jolla, Calif, Numinous Duochrome, Yellow Magenta-Violet Paintings, Bentley Gallery, Scottsdale, Ariz. *Teaching:* asst prof painting, Hunter Col, New York, 92-93; guest artist & lect, Dept Art, UCLA, Los Angeles, 4/96; vis prof, Ariz State Univ, Phoenix, 11/97. *Awards:* Alexander Medal, Metrop Mus Art Hon Awards, 82; Grumbacher Artist Award, 86; Elizabet Found for Arts Grant, 99. *Bibliog:* Robert L Pincus (auth), Color Guard: Ruth Pastine Revels in the Art, San Diego Union Tribune, 4/1/99; Kenneth Baker (auth), Paintings Colored by Illusion, San Francisco Chronicle, 8/12/2000; Ken Johnson (auth), Ruth Pastine, NY Times, 10/6/2000; Ken Johnson (auth), Abstraction and Immanence, Hunter Col, Times Square Gallery, NY Times, 3/23/2001. *Media:* Oil. *Dealer:* Margaret Thatcher Projects 529 W 20 St New York NY 10011; Haines Gallery 49 Geary St San Francisco CA 94108. *Mailing Add:* 11225 Creek Rd Ojai CA 93023

PATCHEN, JEFFREY H
MUSEUM DIRECTOR
b Syracuse, NY, April 28, 1954. *Study:* Ithaca Coll, Mus B, 76, MusM, 81; Ind Univ, DME, 86. *Pos:* state music/arts supr, Ind Dept Educ, Indianapolis; sr program officer, Getty Educ Inst for the Arts, La, 96-99; pres, CEO, Childrens' Mus Indianapolis, Ind, 99-. *Teaching:* asn instr, Ind U, Bloomington, 82-84; prof music educ, Lyndhurst chair of excellence in arts educ, Univ Tenn, Chattanooga. *Mem:* Asn Children's Museums; Nat Network for Educ Develop; Nat Coun State Suprs; Music Educators Nat Conf; Ind Music Educators Asn; Nat Art Educators Asn; Art Edn Asn of Ind. *Mailing Add:* Childrens Museum Indianapolis PO Box 3000 Indianapolis IN 46208

PATERNOSTO, CESAR PEDRO
PAINTER, SCULPTOR
b La Plata, Buenos Aires, Arg, Nov 29, 1931; US citizen. *Study:* Nat Univ La Plata, Sch Fine Arts, 57-59, Inst Philos, 61. *Work:* Mus Mod Art, NY; Nat Fine Arts Mus, Buenos Aires; Albright-Knox Gallery, Buffalo; Hirshhorn Mus, Washington; and others. *Exhib:* The 1960's, Mus Mod Art, NY, 67; Solo exhibs, Dusseldorf, WGer, 72, NY, 73, Paris, 74 & Tokyo, 82; Painting Since WWII, Guggenheim Mus, NY, 87; Am, Bride of the Sun, Royal Fine Arts Mus, Antwerp, Belg, 92; Lat Am Artists of Twentieth Century, Mus Mod Art, NY, 93; and others. *Awards:* Guggenheim Fel Painting, 72; Pollock-Krasner Found Grant, 90; Gottlieb Found Grant, 91. *Bibliog:* Sam Hunter (auth), The Cordoba biennial, Art Am, 4/67; Lucy R Lippard, Overlay, 83; Barbara Braun (auth), Pre-Coll Art in Post-Coll World, Abrams, 93. *Media:* Acrylic & Oil on Canvas; Cast Cement, Wood. *Publ:* Auth, Piedra Abstracta, Mexico-Buenos Aires, 89; English translat, The Stone and The Thread, Univ Tex Press, 96. *Mailing Add:* 135 Hudson St New York NY 10013

PATERSON, ANTHONY R
SCULPTOR, EDUCATOR
b Albany, NY, Dec 17, 1934. *Study:* Sch of Mus Fine Arts, Boston, dipl & grad dipl; study with Harold Tovish, Ernest Morenon, Peter Abate; La Grande Chaumiere Sch Drawing, Paris; Mass Inst Technol, welding; Univ Guadalajara, Mex. *Work:* Rose Art Mus, Brandeis Univ, Waltham, Mass; Univ Art Gallery, Univ Pittsburgh, Pa; San Bernardino Fine Arts Mus, Calif; Eastman Sch of Music, Rochester, NY; Juliard School of Music, New York. *Comn:* Portrait of Seymour H Knox (bronze torso), comn by Buffalo Found, 78-79; life-size portrait of Charles Darwin, Centennial Conf on Darwin, 82; portrait of composer Samuel Adler, 94; Univ Rochester, Rochester, NY; Phillipe Elliot, Univ Buffalo, Buffalo, NY; Gregory Jarius, Astronaut, Univ Buffalo 93. *Exhib:* N Am Sculpture Exhib, Denver, Colo, 86, 88 & 90; Dimensions 88-3D Art Show, Lenexa Ann Nat, Kans, 86, 88 & 90; 63rd Ann Nat Exhib, Nat Acad Design, New York, 88; solo exhib, Andrews Gallery, William & Mary Coll, Williamsburg, Va, 88; Metal Media, Sawtooth Ctr Visual Arts, Winston-Salem, NC, 90; The Am Way, Mobile Mus of Art Invitational Exhib, 2002-04; 40 Yr Retrospective, Ctr for Inquiry Int; and others. *Pos:* Restorer, 68-2003. *Teaching:* Instr sculpture, Sch Mus Fine Arts, Boston, 62-65 & Mt Ida Jr Coll, Newton, Mass, 64-68; assoc prof sculpture & head of sculpture, State Univ NY, Buffalo, 68-2003; dir, Casting Inst, Univ Buffalo, 2003; prof emer, 2003-. *Awards:* Festival Award, Three Rivers Art Nat Festival, 89 & 90; Elliot Lisken Award for Sculpture, Audubon Artists Nat Soc, 89; Acad Artist Asn Nat Award, Springfield, Mass, 90. *Bibliog:* Colin Dabrowski (auth), Return to Form, Buffalo News, Gusto March, 2008. *Mem:* Artists Comt, Buffalo; Nat Sculpture Soc, New York; Int Sculpture Soc, Washington, DC; N Am Sculpture Soc, Denver, Colo. *Media:* Metal, Cast. *Res:* Connections: A study of the interrelatedness of Native American art and architecture of the North American continent, 98. *Interests:* Restoration, photography, archaeology. *Publ:* Auth, Portrait Sculpture: Contemporary Points of View, Univ Buffalo publ, 83. *Dealer:* Gallery Int Ctr Inquiry Amherst NY. *Mailing Add:* 530 Norwood Ave Buffalo NY 14222-1319

PATHA, CAMILLE
PAINTER
b Seattle, Washington. *Study:* Univ Washington, Seattle, BA; Ariz State Univ, MFA. *Comn:* Thirteen Coins Restaurant, 92; Highline Hosp Emergency Waiting Room, 94. *Exhib:* Solo exhibs include Gordon Woodside Gallery, Seattle, 73, 75, 77, 78, 80, 81 & 83; Foster/White Gallery, 85, 88, 89, 95, White Bird Gallery, Cannon Beach, Ore, 2004, Davidson Contemp, Seattle, 2006; group exhibs include Women in Art Survivors, Henry Art Gallery, Seattle, 72; White Whale Gallery, Gig Harbor, Washington, 73; Pacific Northwest Arts and Crafts Fair, Bellevue, Washington, 75; Bicentennial Invitation, Charles M Russell Mus, Great Falls, Mont, 75; Anacortes Art Gallery, Washington, 76; Northwest Women in Art, Calyx Int, Portland, 82; Foster/White Gallery at Frederick & Nelson, Seattle, 84; Bumberbiennale Seattle Painting, 1925-1985, 85. *Bibliog:* Matthew Kangas (auth), (forward by Judy Chicago), Camille Patha: Geography of Desire, 2006. *Media:* Miscellaneous Media. *Mailing Add:* Davidson Galleries c/o Sam Davidson 313 Occidental Ave South Seattle WA 98104

PATNODE, J SCOTT
EDUCATOR, MUSEUM DIRECTOR
b Seattle, Wash, Oct 19, 1945. *Study:* Gonzaga Univ, AB, 68; Pratt Inst, fel, 68, MFA, 70; also with George McNeil, Walter Rogalski & Clare Romano. *Work:* Cheney Cowles Mem Mus, Spokane; Kalamazoo Inst Arts, Mich; Evergreen State Col, Olympia, Wash; Pac Nat Bank of Wash, Seattle; Honolulu Acad Art, Hawaii. *Exhib:* Hawaii Nat Print Exhib, Honolulu Acad Art, 71 & 73; CCAC World Print

Competition, San Francisco Art Mus, 73; New Generation Drawings Exhib, circulated by Western Asn Art Mus, 73-75; 59th Ann Exhib Northwest Artists, Seattle Art Mus, 74; Gov Invitational, 78; Northwest Juried Art, 83; Cheney Cowles Mem Mus, Spokane, Wash, 83. *Pos:* Dir, Ad Art Gallery, Gonzaga Univ, 71-94, Jundt Art Mus, 95-. *Teaching:* Prof art, Gonzaga Univ, 70-, chmn dept art, 79-82. *Awards:* Print Purchase Award, Honolulu Acad Art, 71; Fremont Lane South Award for Painting, Spokane Art Mus, 72. *Mem:* Am Asn Mus. *Mailing Add:* Jundt Art Mus Gonzaga Univ E 502 Boone Ave Spokane WA 99258-0001

PATNODE, MARK WILLIAM
PAINTER, DESIGNER
b Ilion, NY, Apr 29, 1956. *Study:* State Univ New York, Purchase, BFA, 78. *Work:* New London Harbor, Julia "Susette Kelo's House"; Mitchell Coll, New London, Conn; Chelsea Groton Bank; Radek Assocs; Babson Capital; Smithsonian Mus; Smolian Art Mus, Bulgaria; Alexey Von Schlippe Gallery; I Park Artists Enclave. *Comn:* charter oak painting for 375th anniversary, comn by State of Conn Arts Div & Governors Office, Governor's Conservency, 2010. *Exhib:* Neuberger Mus, 78, Lyman Allyn Art Mus, New London, Conn, 89, Artist Sees New London, 91; Conn Open, Real Art Ways, Hartford, Conn, 95; 4 Faber Birren Nat Color Award Show, Stamford Art Asn, Conn, 95 & 2008, New London Art Soc, 99; Latin Views, Conn, 2006, 2012; 69th Ann Conn Art Exhib, Slater Memorial Mus, 2013. *Pos:* Int artist residence, mem Am, Bulgarian American Creative Society; residencies to VT Studio Ctr; CCT Arts in Public Spaces Prog, Sen Joseph Lieberman's Office, Washington, DC, 2006-2008; Conn state rep (selected by Sen Lieberman), ann White House ornament design, 2008. *Teaching:* Master teaching artist, Conn Div Arts; adj prof, painting on the beach, Mitchell Coll; instr visual arts, Cape Verde Ctr Creative Youth, Capital Region Educ Coun & Greater Hartford Acad Arts. *Awards:* Urban Artists Initiative Fel Grantee; Three hon mentions MAC; Conn Comn Cult & Tourism Award; Essex Art Assn award, 2010; Best in Show, 69th Ann Conn Artists Exhib, 2013. *Bibliog:* United States Submarines, Hugh Lauter Levin, 2002. *Mem:* Salmagundi Club (elected mem); Mystic Art Asn (elected assoc); Lyme Art Asn (assoc); Norwich Arts Coun (elected); Bulgarian American Creative Soc; Purchase Col Alumni Assoc (exec bd dir); Rotary Int (New London Bd Dirs); Hygienic Gallery Prog Comt. *Media:* Oil, Watercolor, Drawing, Pastel. *Interests:* Weight training, skiing. *Collection:* Julia "Susette Kelo's House". *Publ:* Auth, Art Folio; Am Artist Mag; Studio Visit Mag, 2012; Int Contemp Artists, 2012. *Dealer:* www.artid.com. *Mailing Add:* 33 Granite St New London CT 06320-5944

PATRICK, ALAN K
CERAMIST, PAINTER
b Richmond, Ind, June 16, 1942. *Study:* Ball State Univ, with Byron Temple, BS, 64, MA, 66. *Work:* Ball State Univ Art Gallery; Earlham Coll & Richmond Art Mus, Ind; Minnetrista Cul Ctr, Muncie, Ind; City of Muncie, Ind; McGraw Hill Publ, New York; Driehaus Capital Mgt, Chicago, Ill; First Merchants Corp, Muncie, Ind; Richmond Art Mus, Richmond, Ind. *Comn:* Painting, Minnetrista Cult Ctr, Muncie, Ind, 96; painting, Alltrista Corp, Muncie, Ind, 97. *Exhib:* Hoosier Salon, Indianapolis, 90-2009; Ind Artist Club Juried Exhib, Indianapolis, 92-2009; The Bethel Pike Pottery: The First Thirty Yrs, Minnetrista Cult Ctr, 96; Eds Ltd Gallery, Indianapolis, 96; Richmond Art Mus, Ind, 98-2005. *Awards:* Best of Show, Hoosier Salon, Indianapolis, Ind, 91-; Best of Show, Minnetrista Regional Exhib, Muncie, Ind, 92-; Best Landscape, Hoosier Salon, Indianapolis, Ind, 92-; Best of Show, Ind Artists Club, Indianapolis Mus Art, 2000. *Bibliog:* Kathleen R Postle (auth), Bethel Pike Pottery, Spinning Wheel, 6/79; Gerry Williams (auth), Conversations with Indiana Potters, Studio Potter 19:2, 6/91; Ned H Griner (auth), The Bethel Pike Pottery, the First Thirty Years, Minnetrista Cult Found Inc, Muncie, Ind, 96. *Mem:* Hoosier Salon; Ind Heritage Arts; Ind Artists Club. *Media:* Stoneware, Porcelain; Oil. *Dealer:* Gordy Fine Arts Muncie IN; Patrick Gallery Albany IN; Corporate Artworks Schaumberg IL; Steeple Gallery St John IN. *Mailing Add:* 5809 E Pottery Rd Albany IN 47320

PATRICK, DARRYL L
HISTORIAN
b Havre, Mont, Oct 5, 1936. *Study:* Northern Mont Col, BS, 62; Univ Wash, MA, 70; N Tex State Univ, PhD, 78. *Teaching:* Instr art hist, Factory of Visual Arts, Seattle, Wash, 69-71; Assoc prof, Sam Houston State Univ, Huntsville, Tex, 71-79, dir dept art, 78-84, asst prof, 79-80 & prof, 91-. *Mem:* Coll Art Asn. *Res:* Late 19th century Europe, 19th and 20th century American art. *Mailing Add:* Sam Houston State Univ Dept Art Huntsville TX 77340

PATRICK, GENIE HUDSON
PAINTER, INSTRUCTOR
b Fayetteville, Ark, Nov 25, 1938. *Study:* Miss State Coll Women, 56-58; Univ Ga, BFA, 60; Univ Ill, Urbana-Champaign, 60-61; Univ Colo, MA, 62. *Exhib:* Walker Ann, Minneapolis, 66; Mid-Miss Invitational, Davenport Munic Art Gallery, 79; two-man exhib, Drawing & Painting, Coe Coll Galleries, Cedar Rapids, Iowa, 71, Laura Musser Mus, Muscatine, Iowa, 72 & 77, Fine Art Ctr, Univ Mo-Columbia, 75 & Myers Fine Art Gallery, State Univ NY, Plattsburgh, 76; and others. *Pos:* Fel-in-Residence, Huntington Hartford Found, Pacific Palisades, Calif, summer 64. *Teaching:* Instr art, Northeast Miss Jr Col, Booneville, 62-64; instr art, Radford Col, Va, 64-65; instr children's art classes, Cedar Rapids Art Ctr, Iowa, 65-70; instr drawing & painting, Univ Iowa Exten, 74-, instr drawing, Sch Art & Art Hist, Univ Iowa, Iowa City, 74 & 80. *Media:* Oil, Drawing. *Mailing Add:* 1190 E Court St Iowa City IA 52240-3232

PATRICK, JOSEPH ALEXANDER
PAINTER, EDUCATOR
b Chester, SC, Feb 10, 1938. *Study:* Univ Ga, BFA, 60; Univ Colo, Boulder, MFA, 62. *Work:* Keokuk Art Asn, Iowa; Luther Col, Iowa; SDak Mem Art Ctr, Brookings; Laura Musser Mus, Muscatine, Iowa; Univ Mo Alumni Collection, Columbia. *Exhib:* Solo exhibs, Augustana Coll, SDak, 72, Univ Iowa Mus Art, 73, Iowa State Univ Design Ctr, Ames, 74, Kans State Univ, Manhattan, 75, Northwest Mo State Univ, Maryville, 77 & Friends Gallery, Minneapolis Inst Arts, Minn, 77; and others. *Pos:* Mus asst, Univ Ga Mus Art, Athens, 58-60. *Teaching:* Asst art, Univ Colo, Boulder, 60-62, instr drawing & painting, 61-62; instr & head dept, Northeast Miss Jr Col, Booneville, 62-64; instr, Radford Col, 64-65; instr, Univ Iowa, 65-68, asst prof drawing & painting, 68-71, assoc prof drawing, 71, head dept drawing, 79-. *Awards:* Residence Fel, Huntington Hartford Found, 64; Summer Fac Fel, 69 & Fac Grants, 73, 77 & 78-79, Univ Iowa Found. *Mem:* Mid-Am Art Asn; Coll Art Asn Am. *Media:* Oil, Watercolor. *Mailing Add:* 1190 E Court St Iowa City IA 52240-3232

PATTERSON, CLAYTON IAN
SCULPTOR, VIDEO ARTIST
b Calgary, Alta, Oct 9, 1948. *Study:* Univ Alta, BEd, 73; Nova Scotia Coll Art, BFA, 77. *Work:* Brooklyn Mus, NY; New York Pub Libr; Libr Cong, Washington; Rutgers Mus, New Brunswick, NJ; Flint Mus, Mich; Matt Dillon, also pvt collections of Mick Jagger & Jack Nicholson. *Exhib:* Sacred Artifacts and Objects of Devotion, Alternative Mus, NY, 82; Works on Paper, NC Mus, Greenville, 84; Australian Invitational Traveling Print Show, 84-85; Works on Paper, Bronx Mus, 85; Tiffany Collection, Brooklyn Mus, 85; Beauty and the Beast, Pratt Inst, NY, 85; Am Collections Pvt & Publ, Brooklyn Mus, 86; Rock and Roll Hall of Fame Archives, 95; and others. *Teaching:* Instr art, Alta Col Art, 78. *Awards:* Justice Orgn Award, 92; Manhattan Cable Access Awards, 92; Manhattan Neighborhood Network Proj Grant, 95; and others. *Bibliog:* Richard Merkin (auth), The discreet charm of the baseball cap, Gentleman's Quart, 89; Mark Rose (auth), Top hat, New York Press, 91; Richard Kostelanetz (auth), Dictionary of the Avant-Gardes, A Cappella Books, 93. *Mem:* Tattoo Soc New York (pres). *Media:* All. *Publ:* Lower East Side, New York (video), 87-88; Tompkin Square Park Police Riot (video), 88. *Dealer:* Arborite Art 161 Essex St New York NY 10002-1507

PATTERSON, CURTIS RAY
SCULPTOR, INSTRUCTOR
b Shreveport, La, Nov 11, 1944. *Study:* Grambling State Univ, BS, 67; Ga State Univ, MVA, 75. *Comn:* mild steel, Atlanta Rapid Transit Authority, 78; David Franklin Assoc, Atlanta, 89; Roy Wilkins Bond, St Paul, Minn, 92; Rapid Transit, Cleveland, Ohio, 94; Hartsfield Int Airport, Atlanta, Ga, 99. *Exhib:* Thirty-five Artists in the SE (contribr, catalog), High Mus Art, Atlanta, Ga, 76; 35 Artists in the SE Traveling Show, 77-78; Festival of Arts & Cult, Lagos, Nigeria, 77; Fourteen Sculptors, High Mus Art, Atlanta, 77; Nexus Contemp Art Ctr, Atlanta, Ga, 93; Middle Tenn State Univ, 94; Spaces Gallery, Cleveland, Ohio, 96. *Pos:* Vpres, Thirteen Minus One, 76-77. *Teaching:* Teacher sculpture & pottery, Therrell High Sch, Atlanta, 70-76; instr sculpture, Atlanta Col of Art, 76-. *Awards:* City Atlanta Bur Cult Affairs Award, 93; Fulton Co Arts Coun Award, Atlanta, 93; Nat Endowment Arts, 94-95. *Mem:* Black Artist of Atlanta; Thirteen Minus One. *Media:* Metal, Clay. *Mailing Add:* 1091 Flamingo Dr SW Atlanta GA 30311

PATTERSON, DANE
PRINTMAKER, COLLAGE ARTIST
b Columbus, Ind, 1978. *Study:* Herron Sch Art, Ind, BA, 2002; Sch Visual Arts, New York, MFA, 2005. *Exhib:* Emerging: NYC, Pool Art Ctr, Drury Univ, Mo, 2004; Representing the Self, Spencertown Acad Arts Ctr, NY, 2006; Timeless: An Exhib of Drawings, Morris Mus, NJ, 2008; 5th Ann Int Juried Exhib, Shore Inst Contemp Arts, Long Branch, NJ, 2008. *Awards:* NY Found Arts Fel, 2009. *Mailing Add:* c/o Proposition Gallery 2 Extra Pl New York NY 10003

PATTERSON, PATRICIA
FILM CRITIC, PAINTER
b Jersey City, NJ, Mar 17, 1941. *Study:* Parson's Sch of Design, grad cert. *Exhib:* Houston Mus Contemp Art, Tex, 77; La Jolla Mus Contemp Arts, Calif, 78; Inst for Art & Urban Resources, PS1, NY, 78; Cleveland Mus Art, Ohio, 78; Fine Arts Gallery, Univ Calif, Irvine, 78; and others. *Pos:* Contrib writer, Film Comment Mag, New York, 75-. *Teaching:* Asst prof painting, drawing & art criticism, Univ Calif, San Diego, 76-. *Media:* Casein, Enamel; Watercolor. *Publ:* Coauth, Werner Herzog, The cinema of Fata Morgana, 75 & The new breed of filmmakers: A multiplication of myths, 75, City Mag; auth, Fassbinder, 75 & coauth, Gun crazy--Part II, 76 & Beyond the new wave: I (Kitchen without Kitsch), 77, Film Comment; auth, Aran kitchen, aran sweaters, Heresies, 78. *Dealer:* Ellie Blankfort Gallery 2341 Ronda Vista Dr Los Angeles CA 90027. *Mailing Add:* 467 La Costa Encinitas CA 92024

PATTERSON, SHIRLEY ABBOTT
PAINTER, INSTRUCTOR
b Buffalo, NY, Dec 13, 1923. *Study:* Albright Sch Fine Art, Buffalo, NY, dipl, 44; New York State Univ, Buffalo, BS (art educ), 45. *Work:* E I Dupont deNemours & Co, Del Trust Co, Sun Oil Co & Blue Cross-Blue Shield, Wilmington, Del; Widener Coll Mus, Chester, Pa; State Del Div Libr, Dover. *Exhib:* Regional Art Echib, Univ Del, Newark, 75-77, 79 & 81; Regional Art Exhib, Del Art Mus, Wilmington, 75, 78-79 & 81; Am Watercolor Soc, Nat Acad Galleries, NY, 79; Pa Soc Watercolor Painters, Harrisburg, 79 & 85; Ky Watercolor Soc, Louisville Water Tower Mus, 80-81; Mattatuck Mus, Waterbury, Conn, 90, 91; Conn Women Artists, New Haven, Conn, 91; solo exhib, S Windsor Pub Libr, 91. *Collection Arranged:* Mid-Atlantic Regional Exhib Collage, Univ Del, 79; Charter Oak Temple Annual Exhib, Hartford, Conn, 91. *Pos:* Juror, Delaware Camera Club, 86, 87, 88; Radio Talks, WXDR, 86, 87, 88; WDEL, 76, 79, 81. *Teaching:* Instr art, Griffith Inst Cent Sch, Springville, NY, 45-46; critic instr art, Kenmore Pub Sch, NY, 46-49; instr art, privately, 58-70. *Awards:* Artist of the Year, Hotel DuPont, Wilmington Christmas Comt, 76; First Prize, Del State Biennial, Nat League Am Pen Women, 77, 79, 81, 83 & 85. *Bibliog:* Lise Monty (auth), feature in Sunday News J, 4/8/79; article in Artists register, Del Artline, 7/79; Delaware Artists Series (slides), Univ Del, 83, 86. *Mem:* Nat League Am Pen Women, Diamond State Branch (pres, 78-80); Studio Group Inc, Wilmington, Del (pres, 78-80); Pa Watercolor Soc; Ky Watercolor Soc. *Media:* Watercolor, Mixed Media. *Mailing Add:* 15 Wedgewood Ln South Windsor CT 06074

PATTI, TOM
SCULPTOR
b Pittsfield, Mass, 1943. *Study:* Pratt Inst Sch Art & Design, BID, 67, Grad Sch Art & Design, MID, 69; New Sch Social Res, with Rudolph Arheim, 69. *Work:* Metrop Mus Art & Mus Mod Art, NY; Toledo Mus Art, Ohio; Kunstmuseum Dusseldorf, WGer; Victoria & Albert Mus, London. *Comn:* Plastics Technol Ctr, Gen Elec Plastics Genic Doron Divider (atrium), 84; Gen Elec Co, Plastics Group Awards Comn, 86. *Exhib:* Art & Relig, Vatican Mus, Rome; Mex-NAm Cult Inst, Mexico City, 82; Recent Acquisitions: Archit & Design, Mus Mod Art, NY, 79; New Glass: A Worldwide Survey, Corning Mus Glass, 79. *Awards:* Nat Endowment Arts, 79; 1st Prize, Glaskunst 81, Kassel, WGer. *Media:* Glass. *Publ:* Auth, articles, Neues Glas, 3/81 & Art News, summer 81. *Dealer:* Ute Stebich Gallery 69 Church St Lenox MA 01240. *Mailing Add:* Tom Patti Studios 10 Federico Dr Pittsfield MA 01201

PATTON, ANDY (ANDREW) JOHN
PAINTER
b Winnipeg, Man, Feb 25, 1952. *Study:* Univ Man, BA, 72. *Work:* Nat Gallery Can, Ottawa; Art Gallery Ont, Toronto; Univ Lethbridge, Alta. *Exhib:* Fifth Biennial Sydney (with catalog), Art Gallery New SWales, Australia, 84; Toronto Painting 84 (with catalog) & Art Gallery Ont, 85, Toronto; Fire & Ice (with catalog), Gallery Walcheturm, Zurich, 85; Late Capitalism (with catalog), Harbourfront, Toronto, 85; Allegorical Image (with catalog), Agnes Etherington Arts Ctr, Kingston, Ont, 85; Songs of Experience (with catalog), Nat Gallery Can, Ottawa, 86; Day After Day: A Wall Painting, Winnipeg Art Gallery, Winnipeg, 92; The Whole Light of the Sky, Oboro, Montreal, 94; and others. *Teaching:* Painting instr, Univ Western Ont, London, 95-. *Awards:* Canada Coun B Grants, 84 & 85. *Bibliog:* David Craven, (auth), Toronto, Bomb Mag, NY, Spring, 88; Myron Turner (auth), The Indescribable Blueness of Being, Border Crossings, Winnipeg, spring 93. *Mem:* YYZ Artists Outlet (bd mem, 82-); Independent Artists Union. *Media:* Oil on Canvas, Oil on Linen. *Publ:* Auth, Poems and Quotations, Four Humours Press, 75; The Real Glasses I Wear, A Space, Toronto, 81; Civil space, Parachute Mag, Montreal, 83; Buchloh's history, C Mag, Toronto, 85; coauth, The Interpretation of Architecture (exhib catalog), YYZ, Toronto, 86; Sorrow at the End of the Canal, Stride Gallery (exhib catalogue), 90; No Communication between the living and the dead (in Wanda Koop, exhib cat), Southern Alberta Art Gallery, Lethbridge, 92; Introduction to the Introduction to Wang Wei, Brick Books, 2000. *Mailing Add:* 243 Macdonell Ave Unit 2 Toronto ON M6R 2A9 Canada

PATTON, KAREN ANN
PAINTER
b New York, NY, Oct 27, 1937. *Study:* Studied with Wolf Kahn, Nat Acad Art, New York, 2000, Polly Hammett, AWS, Skip Lawrence, AWS, Glen Bradshaw, AWS, 99. *Work:* Watercolor Olympus Corp Am; oil, Baptist Med Ctr So; Fla Hosp, Memorial Med Ctr. *Comn:* Watercolor, Am Automobile Asn, Garden City, NY, 85. *Exhib:* HTAL Open Juried Show, Heckscher Mus, Huntington, NY, 81 & 85; Nassau Co Mus Fine Arts, Roslyn, NY, 88; 57th Treasury Gallery, St Augustine Art Asn, 2003; Atlantic Ctr Art, Harris House, New Smyrna Beach, Fla; Ormond Beach, Fla, 2004; Ormond Mem Mus & Gardens, Ormond Beach, Fla, 2006; Casements, Ormond Beach, Fla, 2006, 2010, 2012; Rare Room Gallery, Peabody Auditorium, Daytona Beach, 2012. *Pos:* Art judge, juror & teacher, Plantation Bay, Ormond Beach, Fla. *Awards:* Award of Excellence, Malverne Artists of Long Island, 83 & Art League Nassau Co, 85; Grumbacher Silver Medal, Tri-Co, 88; Best of Show, Artists Workshop, New Smyrna Beach, Fla; Award of Merit, Island Art, St Augustine, Fla, 2006; Distinguished Artist Award, Daytona Beach Art League, 2007; Achievement Award, Art League of Daytona, 2009. *Bibliog:* Malcolm Preston (auth), articles in Newsday, 83 & 85; Laura Stewart (auth), News J, 2003. *Mem:* Plein Aire Painters; Daytona Beach Art League; Plein Air Fla. *Media:* Watercolor, Pastel, Oil. *Interests:* Plein air painting. *Publ:* The Best of Flower Painting, 12/96, North Light Publ; Florals by Karen Ann, Landmark Calendars, 93. *Dealer:* Metropolitan Gallery Ormond Beach Fla; Fogle Fine Art Jacksonville FLa. *Mailing Add:* 91 Bridgewater Ln Ormond Beach FL 32174

PATTON, SHARON FRANCES
MUSEUM DIRECTOR, ART HISTORIAN
b Chicago, Ill. *Study:* Roosevelt Univ, BA (studio art) with Don Baum, 1966; Univ Ill, Urbana, MA, 1969; Northwestern Univ, (African art) with Frank Willett & Ivor Wilks, PhD (art hist), 1980. *Work:* Print, Black Am Art Collection, Johnson Publ Co, Chicago. *Exhib:* Contemp Afro-Am Artists, Lake Forest Coll, 1972; Traditional Forms & Modern Africa: W African Art at the Univ MD, Coll Park (auth, catalog), 1983; E-W Contemp Am Art, Calif Afro-Am Mus Los Angeles (auth Catalog), 1984; The Decade Show Studio Mus New Mus Contemp Art, 1990; Home: Contemp Urban Images by Black Photogrs, Studio Mus in Harlem, NY, 1990; Memory & Metaphor, Art of Romare Bearden (traveling exhib) The Studio Mus in Harlem, 1991; African Art: A Celebration, Univ Mich Mus Art, 1993; Ralph T Coe Collection of African Art; Treasures, Allen Art Mus, 2002; Nat Mus African Art, 2004. *Collection Arranged:* Contemporary Afro-Am Artists, Lake Forest Col, 1972; Traditional Forms & Modern Africa: West African Art at the Univ Md, College Park (auth, catalog), 1983; East-West Contemp Am Art, Calif Afro-Am Mus, Los Angeles (auth catalogue), 1984; The Decade Show, Studio Mus New Mus Contemp Art, 1990; Home: Contemp Urban Images by Black Photographers, Studio Mus in Harlem, NY, 1990; Memory & Metaphor, Art of Romare Bearden, (traveling exhib) The Studio Mus in Harlem, 1991; African Art: A Celebration, Univ Mich Mus Art, 1993. *Pos:* Mem Collections Comt, Baltimore Mus of Art, 1983, 1984; dir, The Art Galleries, Montclair State Univ, 1986-87; chief cur, The Studio Mus in Harlem, NY, 1988-91; John GW Cowels dir, Allen Mem Art Mus Oberlin Col, Ohio, 1998-2003; dir, Ctr for Afroamerican and African Studies, 1996-98; mem adv bd, Nat Mus African Art, Washington, 2000-08, dir, 2003-08; African Am Advisory Committee, Cleveland Mus of Art, 2001-2003. *Teaching:* Instr, Mankato State, Minn, 68-70 & Lake Forest Col, Ill, 1971-72; asst prof art hist, Va Commonwealth Univ, Richmond, 1972-73; instr, African-Amm & African art, Univ Houston, 1976-79; asst prof, African art hist, Univ Md, Col Park, 1979-85; assoc prof art hist, Univ Mich, Ann Arbor, 1991-98; prof art Oberlin Col, 1998-2000. *Awards:* FAC Research Fel Smithsonian, 1985; Outstanding Academic Book African Art Award, Choice Mag, 1998. *Mem:* African Studies Asn; Arts Coun African Studies Asn; Nat Conf Artists; charter mem African & African-Am Hist Soc; Art Table; Leadership Cleveland, 2000; Asn Art Mus Dirs. *Res:* Sub-Saharan West Africa, especially Asante; African art as Political & Prestige emblem; antebellum Louisiana African-American art; Contemporary African American Art. *Publ:* auth, Asante umbrella, African Arts, 1984; Vincent D Smith, Riding on a Blue Note, Louis Abrons Art Ctr, 1990; auth, Andebellum Louisiana artisans, Int Rev African Am Art, 1995; Sharon Patton (auth), Home: Contemp Urban Images by Black Photogr, Studio Mus, 1990; Sharon Patton (auth), Memory & Metaphor, Art of Romare Beardon, Oxford Press, 1991; Sharon Patton (auth) African Am Art, Oxford Univ Press, 1998; Treasures, 2004; Romare Bearden, Narrations, Neuberger Mus, 2002; Emma Amos, Art Matters, NICA Journal of Contemp Art, 2002. *Mailing Add:* Nat Mus African Art Smithsonian Instn MRC 708 PO Box 37012 Washington DC 20013-7012

PATTON, TOM
PHOTOGRAPHER, CURATOR
b Sacramento, Calif, May 17, 1954. *Study:* San Francisco Art Inst, BFA, 76; Univ NMex, MA, 77, MFA, 82. *Work:* San Francisco Mus Mod Art; Australian Nat Gallery, Canberra; St Louis Art Mus; Oakland Mus, Calif; Art Mus, Univ NMex, Albuquerque; and others. *Exhib:* Recent Acquisitions, San Francisco Mus Mod Art, 79; Highlights: Aspects of the Collection, Mus Photog Art, San Diego, 85; The Isolation & Intrusion Series, Developed Image, Adelaide, Australia, 85; New Landscapes (auth, catalog), Tasmanian Sch Art & Australian Ctr Photog, Hobart, Sydney, Australia, 85; Night Light: A survey of 20th century night photog (traveling exhib), Nelson-Atkins Mus Art, Kansas City, Evansville Mus Art, Ind, Lowe Art Mus, Coral Gables, Fla, 89; Kansas City Art Inst, 94; Technol Cult, Erie Art Mus, 98; Feed, San Francisco Camerawork Gallery, 98; Snapshot, Contemp Mus, Baltimore, Md, 2000. *Collection Arranged:* New Views: Landscape Photographs From Two Continents, Univ Mo, St Louis, 86. *Teaching:* Instr photog, Skidmore Col, Saratoga Springs, NY, 82-83; prof photog, Univ Mo, St Louis, 83-, dept chair, dir, Gallery 210, 84-86; vis lectr, Univ Tasmania, Australia, 85. *Awards:* Visual Artists Fel, Nat Endowment Arts, 90-91. *Bibliog:* James Jacobs (auth), Prelude 1976, Artweek Mag, 1/31/76; Joan Murray (auth), Books: The individual and history receive recognition, Artweek, 9/15/79; Michael Costello (auth), Space invaders, Afterimage (visual studies workshop), Rochester, NY, 4/9/80. *Mem:* Soc Photog Educ. *Media:* Digital Imaging. *Mailing Add:* Art Dept Univ Mo 8001 Natural Bridge Rd Saint Louis MO 63121

PAUL, ART(HUR)
DESIGNER, PAINTER
b Chicago, Ill, Jan 18, 1925. *Study:* Art Inst Chicago, 41-43; Inst Design, Chicago, 46-50. *Comn:* Playboy Mag. *Exhib:* Traveling exhibs, Beyond Illus-the Art of Playboy, Royal Coll Art, London, 71 & The Art of Playboy-the First 25 Yrs, Chicago Cult Ctr, 78; Kunstverein Munchen, Munich, Fed Repub Ger, 72; mus des Art Decoratifs, Lausanne, Switz, 72; Lowe Mus Art, Coral Gables, Fla, 73; Munic Art Gallery, Los Angeles, 74; NY Cult Ctr, 74; Columbia Coll, 81; Bowling Green Univ, 88; Chicago Art Inst, Betty Rymer Gallery, 92; solo exhibs, Chicago Cult Ctr, 97-98 & Parkland Coll, Ill, 98; group exhibs, The Manuscript Illuminated, Columbia Coll, Chicago, Ctr Book & Paper Arts, 2001 & NY Art Directors Club Mus, 2002. *Pos:* Self-employed freelance designer, 50-53; art dir, Playboy Mag, 53-82, vpres corp art & graphics dir, Playboy Enterprises Inc, 78-82. *Teaching:* Guest lectr mag design & illus, Art Inst Chicago, 78, Syracuse Univ, NY, 79, summer designers course, 83 & hon instr, Tokyo Design Sch, Japan, 81, Art Ctr, Pasadena, 86 & Univ Ill, Chicago, 87. *Awards:* Trademark, Soc Typographic Arts, 64; Gold Medal, City Milan, Italy, 72; Polycube Award, Art Dirs Club Philadelphia, 75; Gold Medal, Poster Design, NY Acad Club, 80; IIT Alumni Assoc Professional Achievement Award, 83; Art Directors Hall Fame, 86; The Soc Publ Designers Herb Lubalin Award for Lifetime Achievement, 2006; Gov Appointment Charter Trustee to Ill Summer Sch the Arts, 6 yr term, Post Playboy. *Bibliog:* Sarah Bodine (auth), Contemporary Designers, 90; Mark Hawkins-Dady (auth), Contemporary Master Work, 91; Koichiro Inagaki (auth), Visual Identity in Chicago, 91; Aomando Milani (auth), A Double Life of 80 Agi Designers (Creativity and Sense of Humor), 96; The Art of Playboy, Print Mag, Jan-Feb/2000; Art Paul, Graphics Mag, 9-10/2004. *Mem:* Alliance Graphique Int; Mus Contemp Art (bd trustees, 71-86); Am Ctr Design; NY Art Dir Club; elected fel Chicago Chap AIGA. *Media:* Acrylic, Mixed. *Interests:* Prismacolor. *Publ:* The high art of low art, Print Mag, 72; The world of work: An artists-design view, In: Nat Art Educ Asn Career Educ Handbook, Purdue Univ; Vision, Art Paul, Japan Publ, 81; The Art of Playboy, Alfred Van Dermark Publ, 85; 1950s-60s Transition of Modern Typography Europe & America, 96; Sex Appeal: The Art of Allure in Graphic and Advertising Design (ed, Steven Heller), 2000; auth, Graphics # 353, 2005. *Mailing Add:* 175 E Delaware Pl Chicago IL 60611

PAUL, KEN (HUGH)
PRINTMAKER, PAINTER
b Ogden, Utah, Apr 24, 1938. *Study:* Univ Utah, 58-59; Univ Wyo, BA (with honors), 61, MA, 65. *Work:* Art Gallery SAustralia, Adelaide; Univ Ore Mus of Art, Eugene; Portland Art Mus, Ore; Cheney Cowles Mus, Spokane, Wash. *Comn:* Translucent painting, Adelaide Arts Festival, 67; ceiling panel restoration, Sacred Heart Chapel, Geelong, Australia; Directors' Print Portfoloio, Northwest Print Coun, Ore, 92. *Exhib:* First Springfield Coll Nat Print Exhib, Mass, 65; Denver Art Mus Nat Show, 65; Calif Soc Printmakers Ann, Richmond, 71; Seattle Print Int, 71; Ore Artists Ann, Portland, 72-73 & 75; Solo exhib, Cheney Cowles Mus, Spokane, 79; Univ Ore Mus Art, Eugene, 81; Ore State Univ, Corvallis, 94. *Teaching:* Lectr art, Gordon Inst Technol, Geelong, 66-67; lectr printmaking, SAustralian Sch Art, Adelaide, 67-69; assoc prof printmaking, Univ Ore, 70-; vis instr, M I Kerns Art Ctr, Eugene, Ore, summer 71; vis instr, Pac Northwest Graphics Workshop, Cheshire, Ore, 74; vis assoc prof, Univ

Calgary, Alta, 89. *Awards:* Prize for Painting, Ore Coll Educ, Monmouth, 72; Graduate Sch Summer Res Grant, Univ Ore, 73 & 83; Purchase Award, Printmakers Ore, 75. *Mem:* NW Print Coun (bd/secy, 82-). *Media:* All Print Media; Oil, Acrylic. *Mailing Add:* 3837 Potter St Eugene OR 97405

PAUL, RICK W
SCULPTOR
b 1945. *Study:* Univ Fla, Gainesville, BFA, 67; Pa State Univ, Univ Park, MFA, 69. *Work:* McDonalds Corp, Chicago, Ill; Blakley Corp, Ind State Mus, Young & Laramore, Mansur Develop Corp & Indianapolis Art League, Ind; Univ NDak, Grand Fork; Miami Univ, Oxford, Ohio; Owensboro Mus Fine Art, Ky; plus numerous others in pvt collections. *Exhib:* Ohio & Indiana Artists & Viewpoints 1980, Cranbrook Acad Art, Detroit, Mich, 81; solo exhibs, Huntsville Mus Art, Ala, 87, Ft Wayne Mus Art, Ind, 89, Shepherd Col, Shepherdstown, WVa, 89, Portland Sch Art, Orem 89, Patrick King Contemp Art, Indianapolis, Ind, 91, Gallery uno, Univ Nebr, Omaha, 94, Artlink, Ft Wayne, Ind, 94, Albion Col, Mich, 98, Purdue Univ, Lafayette, Ind, 99; Computer Artists Invitational, Augusta Col, Ga, 88; Ann Marie LeBlanc and Rick Paul, Eastern Ky Univ, Richmond, Ky, 89; Curator's Choice, Northern Ind Arts Asn, Munster, 89; Sculpture Invitational, Greater Lafayette Mus Art, Ind, 91; Group Exhib, Wabash Col, Crawfordsville, Ind, 94; plus many others. *Pos:* Vis artist & speaker at numerous Univs & orgns, 81-89. *Teaching:* Asst prof art, Eastern Ky Univ, Richmond, 69-74; assoc prof art & design, Purdue Univ, W Lafayette, Ind, 74-; co-instr, Univ Mich, Ann Arbor, 86; computer workshop, Huntsville Mus Art, Ala, 87; lectr, Univ Mass & Augusta Col, Ga, 88; computer graphics workshop, Wabash Col, Ind, 94. *Awards:* Individual Artist Fel, Ind Arts Coun, 87; Master Fel Sculpture, Nat Endowment Arts, 90; Creative Endeavors Fel, Purdue Univ, 97. *Bibliog:* Stephen Sylvester (auth), Dialogue, Columbus, Ohio, 87; Sharon L Calhoon (auth), New Art Examiner, Chicago, Ill, 90; Carl Brentengani (auth), Dialogue, Columbus, Ohio, 94; plus many others. *Dealer:* Patrick King Contemp Art Inc 427 Massachusetts Ave Indianapolis IN 46220-1610. *Mailing Add:* Purdue U Div Arts & Science 701 W Stadium Ave Purdue University IN 47907-2045

PAUL, WILLIAM D, JR
PAINTER, COLLECTOR
b Wadley, Ga, Sept 26, 1934. *Study:* Atlanta Coll of Art, BFA; Univ Ga, AB & MFA; Emory Univ; Ga State Col; Univ Rome, Italy. *Work:* Hallmark Cards, Kansas City, Mo; Little Rock Art Ctr, Ark; Univ Ga, Ga Mus Art, Athens; Kinsey Inst, Univ Ind; Calif State Univ, Northridge; and others. *Exhib:* Va Intermont Col, Bristol; Birmingham Ann, Ala; Corcoran Gallery Art, Washington, DC; Art of Two Cities, Nat Traveling Exhib, Am Fedn Arts; USA-Volti del Sud, Palazzo Venezia, Rome, Italy; solo shows, Gasperi Gallery, New Orleans, La, 93 & Contemp Arts Ctr, New Orleans, La, 94; and many others. *Collection Arranged:* Sixty small original exhibs, Charlotte Crosby Kemper Gallery, Kansas City Art Inst, 61-65; Art of Two Cities, Am Fedn Arts Traveling Exhib, 65; The Visual Assault, 67, Drawings by Richard Diebenkorn, Selections: The Downtown Gallery, Drawing and Watercolors by Raphael Soyer, Recent Collages by Samuel Adler, 20th Anniversary Exhibition & Art of Ancient Peru, The Paul Clifford Collection, Ga Mus Art; Am Painting: the 1940's, 68; Am Painting, the 1950's, 68; Am Painting: the 1960's, 69; Philip Pearlstein, Retrospective Exhibition (auth, catalog), 70; Alice Neel, Retrospective Exhib (auth, catalog), 75; and many others. *Pos:* Dir exhibs & cur study collections, Kansas City Art Inst, 61-65; cur, Ga Mus Art, 67-69; dir, Ga Mus Art, 69-80. *Teaching:* Instr art & art hist, Kansas City Art Inst, 59-64; asst prof, Univ Ga, 65-69, assoc prof, 69-97, prof, 97-; prof, Gen Sandy Beaver, 2000-03; prof emeritus, 2002-. *Awards:* Macy's Ann, Kansas City, 59, 61, 63 & 64; Atlanta Paper Co Ann, 61; Hallmark Award, Mid-Am Ann, 62; Outstanding Undergrad Mentor Award, Univ of Ga; and others. *Bibliog:* Michael McLeod (auth), Portrait of a daring artist, The Orlando Sentinel, 6/16/91; Peek Photographs from the Kinsey Institute, Arena Editions, 2000; and others. *Mem:* Am Fedn Arts (trustee, 69-80); Coll Art Asn; Southeastern Mus Conf; Am Asn Mus; Arts Festival Atlanta (vpres, 82-85); Ga Native plant Soc, 2002-; Ga Botanic Soc, 2002-. *Media:* Collage, Installation; Painting. *Res:* Gender identity issues in visual arts. *Specialty:* Paintings, Pottery. *Interests:* constitutional rights, censorship, ecosystem protection. *Collection:* Am Art Pottery, 1900-1960; The Life and Work of Stoin M Stoin. *Publ:* Auth foreword, Alice Neel, Harry N Abrams, 83; auth, Pottery for the People, Jour Am Art Pottery Asn, fall 2011, Vol 27, No 4; and others. *Dealer:* Independent Gallery 4900 Barnett Shoals Rd Athens GA 30605. *Mailing Add:* 150 Bar H Ct Athens GA 30605

PAULOS, DANIEL THOMAS
PRINTMAKER, WRITER
b Sioux City, Iowa, Dec 16, 1949. *Study:* Studied paper-cutting under Sister Mary Jean Dorcy; studied iconography under Robert Lentz; studied oil painting under Grieg Chapian; studied calligraphy under Sister M DeLourdes Bragg. *Work:* La Salle Univ Fine Art Mus, Philadelphia, Pa; Billy Graham Sacred Art Mus, Wheaton, Ill; Biblical Arts Mus, Dallas, Tex; Libr Contemp Art, Vatican. *Comn:* Profile-portrait, Cardinal Cooke Guild, 87; paper-cuts illustrating book, He's Put The Whole World in Her Hands; paper cut, Santa Maria de la Paz Church, Santa Fe, NMex, 92; granite etched designs, St Mary's Prayer Garden, Pueblo, Colo, 93. *Exhib:* Butler Inst Am Art, Youngstown, Ohio; Biblical Arts Mus, Dallas, Tex; Villanova Univ Fine Arts Gallery; Marian Libr, Dayton, Ohio; Billy Graham Sacred Arts Mus, Wheaton, Ill; Paul VI Inst Arts, Washington; El Santuario De Guadlupe, Santa Fe; Visions Gallery, Albany, NY. *Pos:* Dir, St Bernadette Inst Sacred Art. *Awards:* AURA Ann Arts Award, 91; First Place Journalism Award for Best Cover, 93; Juror's Award, Fontbonne Fine Arts Gallery, 96. *Bibliog:* Raymond Carrillo & Daniel Kopald (dirs), A Seeing Heart, 92; Bernadette, 97; Guadalupita, 98. *Mem:* Cath Artists Am; Cath Fine Arts Soc; Asn Uniting Relig & Art; Christians Visual Arts; Escribiente-Calligraphy Soc NMex. *Publ:* Contribr, Spring Comes to the Hill Country, Roman, Inc, 84; He's Put The Whole World In Her Hands, Roman, Inc, 89, Ignatious Press, 93; A Living Love Hurts, Don Bosco Press, Tokyo, Japan, 90; Dio Ha Posto Il Mondo Intero Nelle Mani Di Maria, Vatican Press, 92; Behold The Women, St Bernadette Inst, 97. *Mailing Add:* c/o St Bernadette Inst Sacred Art PO Box 8249 Albuquerque NM 87198-8249

PAULSEN, BRIAN OLIVER
PAINTER, PRINTMAKER
b Seattle, Wash, Mar 29, 1941. *Study:* Univ Wash, BA, 63; Wash State Univ, MFA, 66. *Work:* Western Ill Univ; S S Kresge Inc, Detroit, Mich; Wesleyan Univ, Lincoln, Nebr; Kemper Insurance Co, Ill; Sioux City Art Ctr, Iowa; and others. *Comn:* 3 Wall murals, Nat Endowment Arts, 77. *Exhib:* San Francisco Art Int Centennial Exhib, San Francisco Mus Art, 70; Extraordinary Realities, Whitney Mus Am Art, NY, 73; Smithsonian Traveling Drawing Exhib, 79-80; Solo Exhibs: Rochester Art Ctr, Minn, 80; NP Mus Art, 2007; New Am Graphics 82-83, Butler Inst Am Art, 82; Shelby, NC, 87; Colorprint USA, 88; Springfield Art Mus, Mo, 91; Washington-Jefferson, Pa, 94; Baylor Univ, 98. *Collection Arranged:* Prints: Ruscha, Grooms, Abeles, Shimomura. *Teaching:* Asst prof printmaking & drawing, Calif State Univ, Chico, 66-71; Asst prof painting & drawing, Univ Calgary, 71-73; Prof, Univ NDak, 73-2007 (Retired). *Awards:* Purchase Awards, Lagrange, Ga, 78, Owensboro Mus, Ky, 79 & Masur Mus, La, 79; Watercolor USA, 77, 80-85; Nat Endowment Arts Fel, 81-82; SWTSU San Marcos, 85; Print Club, 85; Hoyt Inst, 87. *Bibliog:* Article, Art Express Mag, 1-2/82; Article in Am Artist, 10/86. *Mem:* Nat Acad. *Media:* Watercolor; Engraving. *Publ:* Auth, Watercolor, 94. *Mailing Add:* 320 N 16th St Grand Forks ND 58203

PAVLOVA, MARINA
DIRECTOR, EDUCATOR
b Gottingen, WGer, Sept 29, 1952; US citizen. *Study:* Rutgers Univ; Broward Community Col; Fla Atlantic Univ, BFA, 83; Univ Miami (scholar); MS, Fla Int Univ, Miami, 92. *Work:* Mus Discovery and Sci, Ft Lauderdale, Fla; and other pvt collections. *Exhib:* Andrews Ave Gallery, 94; BAG Gallery, Fort Lauderdale, Fla, 85-90. *Collection Arranged:* Ann Exhib (with catalog), 85-90; Human Image Exhib, 85-90; Membership Exhib (with catalog), 85-90; Riverwalk Art Festival (with catalog), 87-90; Salon des Refuse (with catalog), 87-90. *Pos:* Exec dir, Broward Art Guild, Ft Lauderdale, Fla, 85; community adv bd, WXEL; pres, Fla Asn Nonprofit Organizations Inc, currently; asst exec dir, Miami-Dade Co League of Cities; ed bd, ASPM Pub. *Teaching:* Artist-in-residence weaving, Discovery Ctr Mus, 78-86, Univ Miami, 86-87, Broward Community Col, 90-93, 2000-, Fla Int Univ, 92-2000. *Awards:* Moretti Award, Community Achievement Comt, 88 & 89; Outstanding Community Service, Junior League, Ft Lauderdale, 88. *Mem:* Broward Co Teachers Art Guild; Women's Caucus Art; Coalition Women's Art Orgn (vpres corresp S states, 91-93); Nat Coun Nonprofit Asn (dir, 98, ind sector Washington DC). *Media:* Mixed Media

PAYNE GOODWIN, LOUIS (DOC)
CARTOONIST, PAINTER
b Flintville, Tenn, Oct 9, 1922. *Study:* Ark Polytech Col, 41-42; Univ Chattanooga, BA, 48; Ohio State Univ, 74. *Pos:* Advert & ed cartoonist, Dispatch Printing Co, Columbus, 52-62; ed cartoonist, Columbus Eve Dispatch, 62-87. *Awards:* Cartoon Award, Freedoms Found, 62-69, 71, 73 & 79; Cartoonists Award, Hwy Safety Found, 66. *Mailing Add:* 5158 Woodside Dr Columbus OH 43229-5128

PAYSON, JOHN WHITNEY
ART DEALER, COLLECTOR
b New York, NY, Aug 7, 1940. *Study:* Pepperdine Univ, BA, 66. *Pos:* Founder, Joan Whitney Payson Gallery Art, Westbrook Col, Portland, Maine; bd trustees, Skowhegan Sch Painting & Sculpture, currently; mem, bd trustees, St Gaudens Mem, Cornish, NH, currently; pres, Payson Enterprises, Inc; pres, Hobe Sound Galleries & Hobe Sound Galleries, North; pres, Midtown Galleries, Inc; bd mem, Spoleto, 87. *Awards:* Maine Patrons Award, Skowhegan Sch Painting & Sculpture, 77. *Bibliog:* David Patillo (auth), The real Hobe Sound, Palm Beach Life Mag, 7/86. *Mem:* Martin Co Coun Arts (mem, adv bd); fel Portland Mus Art; Salmagundi Club, NY; Barn Gallery Assocs; Penobscot Marine Mus. *Specialty:* Contemporary American art. *Publ:* Auth, forward to catalog, Expressions from Maine, 76; forward to catalog, From Goya to Wyeth, The Joan Whitney Payson Collection, 80; forward to catalog, Bernard Langlais, The Middle Years, 86; forward to catalog of the permanent collection, Joan Whitney Payson Gallery Art, Westbrook Col, Portland, Maine. *Mailing Add:* Midtown Payson Galleries Exec Offices 11870 SE Dixie Hwy Hobe Sound FL 33455

PAYTON, CYDNEY M
MUSEUM DIRECTOR, CURATOR
Pos: Asst, K Phillips Gallery, 1984; owner, Cydney Payton Artfolio, 1985-90; co-owner, Payton-Rule Gallery, 1990-92; dir, Boulder Mus Contemp Art, Colo 1992-2000; dir, cur, Mus Contemp Art/Denver, 2001-08. *Mailing Add:* Mus Contemp Art/Denver 1840 15th St Unit D Denver CO 80202

PAZ, BERNARDO
COLLECTOR
Pos: In the mining bus. *Awards:* Named one of Top 200 Collectors, ARTnews mag, 2004-13. *Collection:* Contemporary art. *Mailing Add:* Instituto Horizontes Salas 304-305 Rua da Bahia 1598 Belo Horizonte MG 30160-011 Brazil

PEACE, BERNIE KINZEL
PRINTMAKER, COLLAGE ARTIST
b Williamsburg, Ky, Oct 20, 1933. *Study:* Berea Col, AB (art), 54; Ind Univ, MFA (painting), 57. *Work:* Fed Reserve Bank, Richmond, Va; Ind Univ; WVa Univ; State WVa, Charleston; Wash & Jefferson Col; and others. *Comn:* Painting, WVa Arts & Humanities Coun, Charleston, 72. *Exhib:* Retrospective (catalog essays) Charleston Art Mus, WVa, 78, Delf Norona Mus, WVa, 80 & (catalog essays), Liberty State Col, 95; 12th Nat Painting Show, Wash & Jefferson Col, Pa, 80; 14th Ann Nat, Marietta Col, Ohio, 81; W&J Nat Painting Show, 87 & 91; Erie Art Mus, Erie, PA; solo exhibs, Northeast Mo State Univ, Kirksville, 87, WVa Juried Exhib 87, 89, Oak Ridge Mus Fine Art, Tenn, 88, Art Store Gallery, Charleston, WVa, 92, Ohio Univ Ea Campus, St Clairsville, Ohio, 99; and others. *Teaching:* Prof drawing & painting, West Liberty

State Col, 60-95, emer prof art, 95. *Awards:* Grumbacher Medal Merit, 89, 92; Best Show, Bethany Col, Fall, 91; Grumbacher Gold Medallion, Wash & Jefferson Coll Nat Painting Show, 95; Disting Alumnus Award Berea Col, Berea, KY, 98; plus others. *Mem:* Wheeling Area Photog Club; Allied Artists WVa; WVa Art & Craft Guild. *Media:* Woodcuts, Photo Collage. *Dealer:* The Art Store Charleston WVa; The Silver Eye Center for Photography Pittsburgh PA. *Mailing Add:* 1214 Washington Farms Wheeling WV 26003

PEACOCK, CLIFFTON
PAINTER
b Chicago, Ill, Oct 21, 1953. *Study:* Boston Sch Fine Arts, Boston Univ, BFA, 75, MFA, 77, with Philip Guston. *Work:* Mus Fine Arts, Boston; Hood Mus, Dartmouth Col, Dartmouth, NH; Carnegie-Mellon Univ Art Gallery, Pittsburgh, Pa; Rose Art Mus, Brandeis Univ, Waltham, Mass; Mass Inst Technol, Cambridge; Decordova Mus, Lincoln, Mass; Greenville County Mus Art, SC; Weatherspoon Art Mus, Greensboro, NC. *Exhib:* Boston Now: Figuration, Inst Contemp Art, Boston, 82, 83; solo exhibs, Thomas Segal Gallery, Boston, 83, 86 & 90, Germans Van Eck, NY, 89 & 90, Jan Baum Gallery, Los Angeles, 91, William Halsey Gallery, Coll Charleston, SC, 91 & 2003, Greenville Co Mus Art, SC, 91 & 93, Southeastern Ctr Contemp Art, NC, 92, Germans van Eck Gallery, NY, 93; Boston Collects, Mus Fine Arts, Boston, 86; Awards in the Visual Arts, Los Angeles Co Mus Art, 88; AVA 7, Va Mus Fine Arts, Richmond, 89; Nuclear Solstice, Boston Ctr Arts, 91; Germans Van Eck Gallery, 91 & 92; Thomas Segal Gallery, Boston, 91 & 92; Drawing Ctr, NY, 92; SC State Mus, Columbia, SC, 1998; DeCordova Mus, Lincoln, Mass, 2000; City Gallery, Charleston, SC, 2003; and others. *Pos:* Vis artist painting & drawing, Monserrat Col Art, Beverly, Mass, 85 & 87. *Teaching:* Instr painting & drawing, Boston Mus Sch Arts, Mass, 88-91; prof, Dept Art, Col Charleston, 91-93, prof, 93-. *Awards:* Nat Endowment Arts Grant, 81, 83 & 87; Louis Comfort Tiffany Grant, 89; Rome Prize Fel, Am Acad Rome, 93; SC Arts Commission Artist Fel, 1999; John Simon Guggenheim Fel, 2007; Adolph and Esther Gottlieb Foundation Fel, 2007. *Bibliog:* David Hornung (auth), Artnews, 12/90; Richard Kalina (auth), Art in Am, 12/90; Ingrid Shaffner (auth), Arts, 12/90; William Wilson (auth), Los Angeles Times, 6/88; Michael Kimmelman (auth), The New York Times, 2/89; Charles Hagen (auth), Artforum, 12/91. *Mailing Add:* c/o Art Dept Col Charleston 66 George St Charleston SC 29424

PEARLMAN, GEORGE L
CERAMIST
b Brooklyn, NY, Oct 06, 1961. *Study:* Syracuse Univ, BS, 83; NY Sch Visual Arts, 84; Pa State Univ, MFA, 94. *Exhib:* Solo exhibs, The Clay Studio, Philadelphia, 88, 91; Fletcher Challenge, Auckland Center, New Zealand, 94; Monarch Clay Nat, Kennedy-Douglas Center, Ala, 97; Eleven Me Arts Comn Fel, Univ Me Farmington, 2002; Pearlan Current Work, St George Pottery, ME, 2002; St George Pottery, 05; La Coste Gallery, Mass, 05; Firehouse Gallery, Maine, 05. *Pos:* artist-in-residence, The Clay Studio, Philadelphia, 88-92; artist-in-residence, Watershed Ctr for Ceramic Art, Me, 94-96; owner, St George Pottery, Me, 99-. *Teaching:* adj instr ceramics, Pa State Univ, 92-94; adj instr, Univ Me, 96; head of ceramics, Hope Coll, Holland, Mich, 97-98. *Awards:* Artist Fel 2002, Me Coun Arts, 2002; McKnight Fel, 3M Corp, 2002; Good Idea grant, Maine Coun Arts, 05. *Mem:* Center fro Me Contemp Art; ACC; Nat Coun Educ Ceramic Art. *Media:* Ceramics, Porcelain. *Specialty:* ceramics. *Dealer:* St George Pottery 1012 River Rd St George ME 04860. *Mailing Add:* St George 1012 River Rd Saint George ME 04860

PEARLMAN, MIA
SCULPTOR
Study: Cornell Univ, BFA, 1996. *Exhib:* Tributary, AIR Gallery, New York, 2001; Lucky Draw, Sculpture Ctr, Long Island City, 2003; solo exhibs, Ten Tents Gallery, Beacon, NY, 2006, Centre for Recent Drawing, London, 2008, Septieme Etage, Geneva, Switz, 2008, Montgomery Mus Fine Arts, Ala, 2009, Plaatsmaken, Arnhem, Neth, 2010; Drawing the Line, Mills Gallery, Boston Ctr for the Arts, 2007; Site Specifics '08, Islip Art Mus, NY, 2008; Cutters, Hunter Coll, New York, 2009; Paper Jam 2, Neuberger Mus Art, Purchase, NY, 2010. *Pos:* Artist-in-residence, Vt Studio Ctr, 2001 & 2008, Lower East Side Printshop, New York, 2001, Byrdcliffe Arts Colony, NY, 2003 & 2008, Proyecto'Ace, Buenos Aires, 2009, Plaatsmaken, Neth, 2010. *Awards:* Pollock-Krasner Found Grant, 2008; UrbanGlass Vis Artist Fel, 2009. *Bibliog:* Cate McQuaid (auth), Drawing Show Works Around Edges, Boston Globe, 12/20/2007; Jennifer Cardenas (auth), Agenda: Paper, South China Morning Post, Hong Kong, 6/6/2008; Karen Rosenberg (auth), Move Over, Humble Doily: Paper Does a Star Turn, NY Times, 10/20/2009

PEARLSTEIN, ALIX
VIDEO ARTIST
b New York, NY, 1962. *Study:* Cornell Univ, BS, 83; SUNY Purchase, MFA, 88. *Work:* Commodities Corp, Princeton, NJ. *Exhib:* Solo exhibs, White Columns, NY, 88, Laurie Rubin Gallery, NY, 90, Tom Solomon's Garage, Los Angeles, 91, Elizabeth Koury Gallery, Project Room, NY, 92, Postmasters Gallery, NY, 92, 94, 96 & 99 & Johan Jonker Galerie, Video Room Project, Amsterdam, 93; Blast 4: Bioinformatica, Sandra Gering Gallery, NY, 94; Use Your Allusion: Recent Video Art, Mus Contemp Art, Chicago, 94; Simply Made in Am, Aldrich Mus, Conn & Contemp Arts Ctr, Cincinnati, Ohio, 94; Lauren Whittles Gallery, NY, 95; Postmasters Gallery, NY, 96; Up Close and Personal, Philadelphia Mus Art, Pa, 98; Yound and Restless, Mus Mod Art, NY, 98; Video Lisboa 99, Lisbon, 99; In Video Festival, Milan, Italy, 99; TransMediale Festival, Berlin, Ger, 99; Galleria Marabini, Bologna, 99; and many others. *Teaching:* Instr, State Univ NY, Purchase, 87, Rockland Community Col, 90-91, Brooklyn Col, NY, 91, Sch Visual Arts, NY, 91-93, 94 PSI, Youth Arts Prog, NY, 93-94, Cornell Univ, 93 & NY Univ, 93; guest lectr, Montclair State Col, NJ, 91, Parsons Sch Design, 99, Rugers Univ, 99 & Tyler Sch Art, 99; vis artist, NY Univ, 94. *Awards:* Nat Endowment Arts, 89; Fel, Edward F Albee Found, 92; Art Matters Inc Fel, 96. *Bibliog:* Kim Levin (auth), Art/Choices, Alix Pearlstein at Postmasters, Village Voice, 5/3/94; Claire McConaughty (auth), SIB, Pretty Decorating, 9/94; Working Conditions: A Forum on Art & Everyday Life, Meaning, no 16, fall 94; and many others. *Dealer:* Postmasters Gallery 459 W 19th St New York NY

PEARLSTEIN, PHILIP
PAINTER, EDUCATOR
b Pittsburgh, Pa, May 24, 1924. *Study:* Carnegie Inst, with Sam Rosenberg, Robert Lepper & Balcomb Greene, BFA, 1949; Inst Fine Arts, New York Univ, MA, 1955. *Hon Degrees:* Carnegie Mellon Univ, hon doctorate, 1983; Brooklyn Coll, hon doctorate, 1996; Ctr for Creative Studies & Coll Art & Design, Detroit, hon doctorate, 2000; NY Acad Arts, hon doctorate, 2001. *Work:* Boston Mus Fine Arts; Metrop Mus Art, Whitney Mus Am Art & Mus Mod Art, NY; Corcoran Gallery Art, Hirshhorn Mus & Sculpture Garden, Washington; Philadelphia Mus Art; Art Inst Chicago; also in pvt collections. *Exhib:* Solo exhibs, Weatherspoon Art Gallery, Univ NC, Greensboro, 1981, Philip Peralstein: A Retrospective, 83-84, Brooklyn Mus, NY, 1989, Butler Inst Am Art, 1992, Honolulu Acad Art, 1994, Springfield Art Mus, Mo, 1995, Robert Miller Gallery, NY, 1986, 1995, 1996, 1997, 2001, Associazione d'Arte e Cultura, Rome, 1997-1998, Galerie Daniel Templon, Paris, 1998, 2007, Galerie Charlotte Moser, Geneva, 1999, Univ Haifa, Israel, 2002, Galerie Fahnemann, Berlin, 2003, Galerie Haas, Berlin & Zurich, 2004, Frye Art Mus, Seattle, 2005, Tween Mus Art, Univ Minn, 2006-2008, Betty Cuningham Gallery, NY, 2005, 2007, 2008, 2010, Galerie HaasL Fuchs, Berlin, Germany, 2008, Victoria Miro Gallery, London, 2008, Montclair Art Mus, NJ, 2008-2009; Group exhibs, Ann Exhib, Whitney Mus Am Art, 1955-56, 1956-57, 1958-59, 1962-63, 1967-68 & 1969-70, Recent Acquisitions, 1958 & 1970, Biennial Exhibs, 1973, 1979 & 1991, Am Drawings, 1973, New Portraits, 1974, Nothing but Nudes, 1977, American Prints: Process and Proofs, 1981-82, The Am Century: Art & Culture 1950-2000, 1999-2000; Biennial Exhib, Corcoran Gallery Art, Washington, 1967, 1971, 1975, Am 1976 (traveling), 1976, The Human Form, Contemp Am Figure Drawing and the Academic Tradition, 1980, The 45th Biennial, 1998; Return to the Figure, Pa Acad Fine Arts, Philadelphia, 1971-72, Eight Contemp Realists, 1977, Contemp Am Realism since 1960 (traveling), 1982, Perspectives on Contemp Am Realism, 1983; Hayden Gallery, Mass Inst Technol, 1971; Seventy-First Am Exhib, Art Inst Chicago, 1974, Seventy-Second Am Exhib, 1975, Contemp Am Realist Drawings, 1999-2000; Twelve Am Painters, Va Mus Fine Arts, Richmond, 1974; Am Drawing in Black and White, Brooklyn Mus, NY, 1980-81; New Dimensions in Drawing, Aldrich Mus, Ridgefield, Conn, 1981; 45th Ann Nat Painting Exhib, Butler Inst Am Art, 1981; Homo Sapiens: The Many Images, Aldrich Mus Contemp Art, 1982; Viewpoint: Painting and the Third Dimension, Cranbrook Acad Art Mus, 1986-87, Three Decades of Contemp Art, 2001-02; From the Model, Whitney Mus Am Art at Philip Morris, NY, 1989; The Body Human, Nohra Haime Gallery, NY, 1994; NY Realism Past and Present (traveling), Odakyu Mus, Tokyo, 1994-95; Embody, Proctor Art Ctr, Bard Col, 1994; Am Art Today: Night Paintings, Art Mus, Fla Int Univ, Miami, 1995; 171st Ann Exhib, Nat Acad Design, NY (traveling), 1996; The Contemp City, DC Moore Gallery, NY, 1999, Self-Made Men, 2001; Portraits & Figures, Carl Schlosberg Fine Arts, Sherman Oaks, Calif, 2000; Festa di compleanno, Il Polittico, Rome, 2001, Cento, 2004; The Great Am Nude, Bruce Mus, Greenwich, Conn, 2002; Nudo, Galleria Forni, Bologna, 2004; Picasso to Pop, Phoenix Art Mus, Ariz, 2004-05; Disegno, The 108th Ann Exhib, Nat Acad, NY, 2005; 182nd Ann Exhib Contemp Am Art, Nat Acad Mus, NY, 2007; plus many others. *Pos:* Vis critic, Yale Univ, 1962-63; artist-in-residence, Am Acad Rome, 1982. *Teaching:* Instr, Pratt Inst, 1959-63; from asst prof to prof art, Brooklyn Col, 1963-88, distinguished prof art emer, 1988-. *Awards:* Fulbright Fel to Italy, 1956-59; Nat Endowment Arts Fel, 1968; Guggenheim Fel, 1969; Disting Achievement Award, Carnegie Mellon Univ, 1986; Nat Acad Design Award, 1996; Nat Coun Arts Admins Visual Artist Award, 1998; Disting Alumni Award, NY Univ, 2001; Benjamin West Clinedinst Mem Medal, Artists Fellowship, Inc, 2004; Adolph & Clara Obrig Prize, Nat Acad, 2005; Artist of the Year, Am Friedns of the Tel Aviv Mus Art, New York, 2010; Scholastic Distinguished Alum Achievement Award, New York, 2008; Lifetime Achievement Award, Nat Acad, New York, 2008. *Bibliog:* Jerome Viola (auth), The Paintings and Teachings of Philip Pearlstein, Watson & Guptill, 1982; Mark Strand (ed), Art of the Real: Nine American Figurative Painters, Clarkson N Potter, Inc, 1983; Russell Bowman (auth), Philip Pearlstein: The Complete Paintings, Alpine Fine Arts Collection, 1983; Philip Pearlstein draws the artist's model, Interactive laserbeam videodisc or videocassette, Interactive Media Corp, New York, 1985; John Perreault (auth), Philip Pearlstein Drawings and Watercolors, Harry N Abrams Inc, 1988. *Mem:* Amer Acad Arts and Letters (pres 2003-06), Nat Acad. *Media:* Oil, water color, graphics. *Publ:* Auth, Figure paintings are not made in heaven, Art News, 1962; Whose painting is it anyway? Arts Yrbk 7, 1964; A Concept of New Realism: Real, Really Real, Superreal, San Antonio Mus Asn, 1981; When paintings were made in heaven, Art in Am, 2/82. *Dealer:* Betty Cunningham Gallery, 541 W 25th Street, New York, NY, 10001

PEARMAN, SARA JANE
HISTORIAN, LIBRARIAN
b Dallas, Tex, Sept 6, 1940. *Study:* Univ Wichita, BAE; Univ Kans, MA (art hist); Case-Western Reserve Univ, PhD (art hist). *Collection Arranged:* Glass Collection of the University of Kansas (auth, catalog); The Fine Art of Graphic Design, 85 & The Fine Art of Graphic Design (auth, catalog), 86, Beck Fine Arts Ctr, Cleveland Mus Art. *Pos:* Image librarian, Cleveland Mus Art, 80-2005; Bk reviewer, Art Documentation & Visual Resources, 85. *Teaching:* Instr art hist, Kearney State Col, 64-66; lectr, Akron State Univ, 68-2005, Cleveland State Univ, 77-2005 & Kent State Univ; adj asst prof, Kent State Univ, retired. *Mem:* Coll Art Asn; Midwest Art Hist Asn; Cleveland Medieval Soc; Art Libr Soc NAm; Mid-Am Coll Art Asn; Visual Resources Asn; Hist Netherlandish Art. *Media:* Jewelry. *Res:* Iconography of all periods; Late Medieval and northern Renaissance wood sculpture; slide classification systems and visual resources; history of graphic design. *Interests:* Beaded Jewelry. *Publ:* Auth, Mirror of Art, Ralph, Vol 4, 77; Otto Dix, A Self Portrait (exhib catalog), Univ Kans; A Netherlandish Saint Andrew from Cleves, Bull Cleveland Mus Art,

12/80; auth, MacMillan Dictionary of Art Essays on Weepers, Jane de Marville, Claus Sluter, London, Eng, 97; auth, From Lantern Slides to Slide Libraries to Image Collections: The View from the Cleveland Museum of Art in Art Museums Libraries and Librarianship; co-auth with Walter C Leedy, Eric Mendelsohn's Park Synagogue, Kent State Univ Press, 2011. *Dealer:* Venerable Bead Jewelry. *Mailing Add:* 4242 Colony Rd South Euclid OH 44121

PEARSON, ANTHONY
SCULPTOR
b Los Angeles, Calif, 1969. *Study:* Calif Coll Arts, Oakland, BFA, 1996; UCLA, MFA, 1999. *Exhib:* Transfiction I, Charim Klocker Gallery, Vienna, Austria, 1996; Bloodlines, Roberts & Tilton Gallery, Los Angeles, 1999; solo exhibs, Shane Campbell Gallery, 2003, David Kordansky Gallery, Los Angeles, 2007, Midway Contemp Art (with catalog), Minn, 2008, Marianne Boesky Gallery, New York, 2009; Brown Constructions, Lemon Sky Projects, 2004; The Disillusion of Illusion, Paul Mesaros Gallery, WVa Univ, 2005; Modern Primitivism, Shane Campbell Gallery, Chicago, 2006; Mus Contemp Art Detroit, 2007; Photography as Sculpture (with catalog), Calif Mus Photog, Riverside, 2008; A Twilight Art, Harris Lieberman, New York, 2009. *Bibliog:* Allan Artner (auth), rev, Chicago Tribune, 12/13/2003; Anthony Elms (auth), Modern Primitivism, Time Out Chicago, Issue 88, 11/2/2006; Holland Cotter (auth), Art in Review: Aspects, Forms, and Figures, NY Times, 3/2/2007; Christopher Bedford (auth), Catherine Opie, Issue 14, 189, Frieze, 9/2008; Martha Schwendener (auth), Paul Graham and Harris Lieberman's A Twilight Art Confront the Future, The Village Voice, 2/17/2009. *Mailing Add:* c/o David Kordansky Gallery 3143 S La Cienega Blvd Unit A Los Angeles CA 90016

PEARSON, BRUCE
PAINTER
Exhib: Out of Town, Krannert Art Mus, Univ Ill, Urbana-Champaign, 92; Working: 4 Walls in Munich, Munich Kunstverein, Ger, 94; Faux, Ronald Feldman Fine Arts, NY, 94; NY State Biennial, Albany Mus, 96; Redefinitions, A View from Brooklyn, Calif State Univ, Fullerton, 97; Current Undercurrent: Working in Brooklyn, Brooklyn Mus, 97; Project 63 (with catalog), Mus Mod Art, NY, 98; Wild, Exit Art, NY, 98; Univ Galleries, Ill State Univ, Normal, 99; Shaheen Mod and Contemp Art, 00; Robert V Fullerton Art Mus, Calif State Univ, 01; Palm Beach Inst Contemp Art, Lake Worth, Fla, 01; Rose Art Mus, Brandeis Univ, 01; Locks Gallery, Philadelphia, 02; Times Sq Gallery, Hunter Col, New York City, 03; Schroeder Romero, Brooklyn, NY, 03; solo exhib, Peirogi 2000, NY, 98, Ronald Feldman Fine Arts, NY, 99, 01. *Collection Arranged:* Karl Ernst Haus Mus, Hagen, Ger; Mus Mod Art; Rose Art Mus, Brandeis Univ; Sprint Corp; Whitney Mus Am Art. *Awards:* Biennial Competition Award, Louis Comfort Tiffany Found, 97; Residency Prog for Advanced Vis Arts, Skowhegan Sch Painting & Sculpture, 2001; Basil H Alkazzi Award for Excellence in Painting, 2010. *Bibliog:* Museum of Modern Art, The New Yorker, 6/15/98; David Clarkson (auth), When words fail: the psychedelic solution of Bruce Pearson, BOMB, winter 98; Donna Desrochers (auth), The Alchemies of the Sixties' and Bruce Pearson at the Rose, 9/99; Andras Szanto (auth), A Business Built on the Hard-to-Sell, NY Times, AR 35, 37, 10/6/2002. *Mailing Add:* c/o Ronald Feldman Fine Arts 31 Mercer St New York NY 10013

PEARSON, JAMES EUGENE
INSTRUCTOR, SCULPTOR
b Woodstock, Ill, Dec 12, 1939. *Study:* Northern Ill Univ, BS (educ), 61, MS (educ), MFA, 64; Tyler Sch Art, Temple Univ; Ithaca Col. *Work:* Northern Ill Univ, DeKalb; Palais des Beaux Arts, Charleroi, Belg; Taft Field Campus, Northern Ill Univ, Ore; Dixon State Sch, Ill; Sch Dist 15, McHenry, Ill; Muscarelle Mus Art, Coll William & Mary, Va. *Comn:* Lorado Taft, Taft Field Campus, Northern Ill Univ, 67; Vicki Unis, Sarasota, Fla, 69; Mae Stinespring, Harry Stinespring, McHenry, Ill, 69; portraits in oils of Mr & Mrs Francis Hightower, comn by Mrs Nancy Langdon, Woodstock, Ill, 71; Civil War Monument, Greenwood Cemetery, Ill, 77; AG Edwards & Sons, Murals, Woodstock, Ill, 88. *Exhib:* 21st Am Drawing Biennial, Norfolk Mus Arts & Sci, Va, 65; 54th Ann Exhib, Art Asn Newport, RI, 65; 2 eme Salon Int de Charleroi, Palais des Beaux Arts, Belg, 69; 5th Int Grand Prix Painting & Etching, Palais de la Scala, Monte Carlo, Monaco, 69; Solo exhib, sculpture, Mitchell Art Mus, Mt Vernon, Ill, 75. *Pos:* Editorial cartoonist, The Woodstock Independent, 1994-. *Teaching:* Instr art, Woodstock High Sch, Ill, 61-94; instr art, McHenry Co Col, Crystal Lake, Ill, 62-78. *Awards:* Best of Show Award, William Boyd Andrews, 61; Purchase Prize, Mr & Mrs Allen Leibsohn, 63; Mary E Just Art Award, Waukegan News-Sun, 69; First Prize, Ill Press Asn, 98, 01 Northern Ill Press Asn, 96, 97, 98 & 02; Recognized by Nat Newspapers Asn 98 & 99. *Bibliog:* F Tramier (auth), James E Pearson, La Rev Mod, 65; Sally Wagner (auth), Volume tells McHenry history, Chicago Tribune, 69. *Mem:* Coll Art Asn Am; Ill Art Educ Asn; Ill Craftsmen's Coun; Am Fedn Arts; Centro Studi E Scambi Internazionali, Rome. *Publ:* Illusr, McHenry County 1832-1968, 68; auth, A dream never realized, 69 & Eagle's nest colony, 70, Outdoor Ill; Perspective: outdoor education from an artists point of view, J Outdoor Educ, 71; illusr, The rectangle, 72. *Mailing Add:* 5117 Barnard Mill Rd Ringwood IL 60072

PEARSON, JOHN
PAINTER, EDUCATOR
b Boroughbridge, Yorkshire, Eng, Jan 31, 1940. *Study:* Harrogate Coll Art, Yorkshire, nat dipl design, 60; Royal Acad Schs, London, cert, 63; Northern Ill Univ, MFA, 66. *Work:* Mus Mod Art, NY; Bochumer Mus, Stuttgart, WGer; Pasadena Mus Fine Art, Calif; Kleye Collection, Doertmund, WGer; Kunstverien, Hanover, WGer; Art Inst Chicago; Cleveland Mus Art. *Exhib:* Am Drawing 1963-73, Whitney Mus Am Art, NY; solo exhibs, Gray Gallery, Chicago, 67, 68 & 82, Paley & Lowe Gallery, 71, Fischbach Gallery, 74 & 76, NY & Akron Art Mus, 83, Here Here Gallery, Cleveland, Ohio, 2003, PMC Gallery, Tokyo Japan, 2004, INGENUITY, Cleveland, Ohio, 2006, 1point618 Gallery, Cleveland, Ohio, 2007, 2009, 2011. *Teaching:* Instr painting, Univ NMex, 66-68; assoc prof painting & head dept, NS Col Art & Design, Halifax, 68-70; int artist-in-residence, Cleveland Inst Art, Ohio, 70-72; prof art & chmn dept art, Oberlin Col, 72-. *Awards:* Can Coun Grant, 70; Cleveland Arts Prize, 75; Nat Endowment Arts, 76; Nord Family Found Award, 89; Phillips Found Award, 91; Japan Studies Research Award, Earlham Lou, 97, 2003. *Bibliog:* Jock Wittet (auth), Editorial, Studio Int, 3/68; Harry Borden (auth), John Pearson, Artforum, 2/72; James R Mellon (auth), article, New York Times, 2/3/75; Edward Henning (auth), The art of John Pearson: An analogy of works of art & general systems, Art Int, 4-5/77. *Media:* Painting. *Interests:* Collecting antique toys. *Publ:* Contribr, Art: The measure of man, Directions 66/67; article in Mus Educ J, 66. *Dealer:* Robert Mascke: 1 Point 618 Gallery, Cleveland. *Mailing Add:* 35 E College St Oberlin OH 44074-1612

PEART, JERRY LINN
SCULPTOR
b Winslow, Ariz, Feb 26, 1948. *Study:* Ariz State Univ, BFA (sculpture); Southern Ill Univ, Carbondale, MFA (sculpture). *Work:* Mus Contemp Art, Chicago; Palm Springs Desert Mus, Calif; Ill State Mus, Springfield; Mus NMex, Santa Fe; Univ Ariz Mus, Tucson. *Comn:* Sculpture, Hyatt Regency Peachtree Ctr, Atlanta, 90; sculpture, Boulevard Towers, Michigan Ave, Chicago, Ill, 86; sculpture, The Promontory, Rancho Barnardo, Calif, 90; sculpture, Carill on Building, Hesta Corp, Charlotte, NC, 91; sculpture, Bradley Univ, Peoria, Ill, 94. *Exhib:* Art in Chicago, 1945-95, Mus Contemp Art, Chicago; Solo exhibs, Richard Gray Gallery, Chicago, 88 & 92, Jean Art Ctr, Seoul, 95; Group exhib, Coast to Coast to Coast, Marquis-Taplin Gallery, Miami, Fla, 93. *Teaching:* Vis prof sculpture, Ariz State Univ, spring, 84. *Awards:* Jeannette Sacks Art Achievement Medal, Ariz State Univ, 70; First Chicago Art Awards for Best Body of Work Over the Yr, Chicago Art Asn, 76-77. *Mem:* Sculpture Chicago (comt mem, 85-); City of Chicago, Percent for Art (mem pub art comt, 86-90). *Dealer:* Richard Gray Gallery 620 N Michigan Chicago IL 60611. *Mailing Add:* 1544 N Sedgwick St Chicago IL 60610-1223

PEASE, DAVID G
ADMINISTRATOR, PAINTER
b Bloomington, Ill, June 2, 1932. *Study:* Univ Wis, Madison, BS, 54, MS, 55, MFA, 58. *Hon Degrees:* MAH Yale Univ, 83. *Work:* Whitney Mus Am Art, NY; Philadelphia Mus Art; Pa Acad Fine Arts, Philadelphia; Power Gallery, Univ Sydney, Australia; Des Moines Art Ctr, Iowa; Yale Univ Art Gallery. *Exhib:* Carnegie Int Exhib Painting & Sculpture, Carnegie Inst, Pittsburgh, 61; Corcoran Biennial Painting, Corcoran Gallery Art, Washington, 61 & 63; Whitney Ann Exhib Painting, Whitney Mus Am Art, NY, 63; Nat Drawing Exhib, San Francisco Mus Art, Calif, 69; Drawings USA, Minn Mus Art, St Paul, 71, 73 & 75. *Pos:* Dean, Tyler Sch Art, Temple Univ, 77-83; dean, Sch Art, Yale Univ, 83-96. *Teaching:* Prof painting dept painting & sculpture, Tyler Sch Art, Temple Univ, 60-83; prof painting, Yale Univ, 83-2000. *Awards:* William A Clark Award, Corcoran Gallery Art, 63; Guggenheim Fel, 65-66; Childe Hassam Fund Purchase Award, Am Acad Arts & Lett, 70. *Mem:* Coll Art Asn Am; Nat Coun Arts Adminr (bd dir, 88-2007); Nat Asn Sch Art & Design; Alliance Independent Cols Art (bd dir, 88-95); Louis Comfort Tiffany Found (bd trustees, 88-); Lyme Acad Coll Fine Arts (bd trustees, 96-2007. *Media:* Acrylic, Gouache. *Mailing Add:* 95 Thankful Stowe Rd Guilford CT 06437-2529

PECCHENINO, J RONALD
PAINTER, EDUCATOR
b Murphy, Calif, Apr 3, 1932. *Study:* Coll Pac, BA, 56; Calif Coll Arts & Crafts, MFA, 69. *Work:* Univ Calif, Chico; Univ Pac; Crocker Art Gallery. *Comn:* Acrylic lacquer paintings, Hilton Hotel, Stockton, Calif, 81; Sheraton Hotel, Boston, 83; Cruise Ships, MS Skyward, 85 & Song of Norway, 86. *Exhib:* Third Ann Art Invitational, Pleasant Hill, Calif, 69; Northern Calif Arts Exhib, Crocker Mus Art, Sacramento, 72; solo exhib, Lyon Art Gallery, San Francisco, 79 & 81. *Pos:* Mem, Art Adv Panel, Calif State Comn, 71-80. *Teaching:* Instr art, Manteca Unified Sch Dist, Calif, 56-70; prof painting, Univ Pac, 70-, chmn art, 83-. *Awards:* Purchase Awards, Lodi Ann Exhib, M Neufield & Sons, 68, Third Ann Art Invitational, City Pleasant Hill, 69 & Northern Calif Arts Exhib, Crocker Art Gallery, 72. *Media:* Acrylic Lacquer, Air Brush. *Dealer:* Contract Art Inc Falls River Offices PO Box 520 Essex CT 06426. *Mailing Add:* Dept Art Univ of the Pacific 3601 Pacific Ave Stockton CA 95211

PECH, ARLETA
PAINTER, INSTRUCTOR
b Princeton, IL, July 30, 1950. *Work:* Petro Lewis Inc, Denver, Colo; Greeley Nat Bank, Greeley, Colo. *Exhib:* Solo exhibs, Cardinal Art Gallery, 99, 2001, 2003, Gallery One, Mentor, Ohio, 2000, 2002, 2004, 2005, Germanton Art Gallery, 2001, 2003, Mary Mine Fine Art, Charleston, NC, Picture This Gallery, Germantown, NC, Maxims Fine Art, Greeley, Colo; Realism Today (invitational), John Pence Gallery, San Francisco, Calif, 2000; Birds in Art (traveling), Woodson Art Mus, Wasau, Wis, 2004, 2005; Best of Realism (invitational), Winstanley-Roark, Cape Cod, Mass, 2006; Int Guild of Realism Guild Exhib, Manitou Galleries, Santa Fe, NMex, 2006, 2008, 2009, 2010, 2011; The New Reality: The Frontier of Realism in the 21st Century, Smith Kramer Mus, 2007; Rocky Mt Nat Watermedia Exhib, Golden, Colo; Int Realism Guild Exhib, 2007, 2009, 2010; Birds in Art, Leeyaky Woodson Art Mus, 2004-2005; Oil Painters of Am, Western Regional, 2010; ARC Salon, 2012; Salon Int, 2013. *Teaching:* Instr (artist) watercolor, Foothills Art Center, Golden, Colo, 80-2005; instr (artist), Vancouver Art Acad, 98-2004 & The Rankin Art Center, Columbus, Ga, 2006; instr, Abend Art Gallery, Denver, Colo, 2010-. *Bibliog:* Painting Fresh Florals in Watercolor, 98; Radiant Oils, 2010. *Mem:* Int Realism Guild; Rocky Mountain Nat Watermedia Soc; Oil Painters of Am. *Media:* Oil. *Interests:* Realism with attention on oil color with glazes. *Publ:* Coauth, Keys to Commanding Light, Artist Mag, 95; coauth, Using Glazes to Paint Dramatic Watercolors, Artist Mag, 2000; Fixing 4 Common Floral Problems, Australian Artist, 2000; auth, Arleta Pech & Jane Jones, Friends Who Paint Flowers, InformArt Mag, 2002; Harnessing the Power of Light, Int artist Mag, 2004; The Airbrush Alternative, Artist Mag; Realism Today, Am Artist; A Sense of Wonder, Am Art Collecotr, 2010; Reality Check, Am Art Collector, 2010. *Dealer:* Abend Gallery 2260 E Colfax Denver CO. *Mailing Add:* 6024 Pierson St Arvada CO 80004

PECK, JOHN See Banning, Jack, Jr

PECK, JUDITH
SCULPTOR, WRITER
b New York, NY, Dec 31, 1930. *Study:* Adelphi Coll, BA; Art Students League; Sculpture Ctr, New York; Columbia Univ, MA & EdM; New York Univ, EdD. *Work:* Yale Univ; Ghetto Fighters Mus, Acco, Israel; Teaneck Pub Libr, NJ; West Palm Beach Libr, Fla; Citizens for Pub Art, Ridgewood, NJ; Ramapo Coll NJ, Mahwah, NJ; 80 public and private collections. *Comn:* Monuments, Temple Beth El, Spring Valley, NY, 71, James Richard Elster Mem Courtyard, Tenafly High Sch, NJ, 72 & Temple Oheb Sholom, Baltimore, Md, 75; Annual Partners Award Sculpture, Art Coun Rockland, 83-85; Rockland Ctr Holocaust Studies, Spring Valley, NY, 88; North Shore Synagogue, Syosset, NY, 92; Teaneck Centennial, NJ, 95; bronze sculpture, West Palm Beach Public Lib; bronze sculpture, Teaneck Public Lib, NJ; Fiberglass Sculpture, Temple Bethel, Spring Valley, NY; bronze sculpture, Ridgewood Train Station, NJ. *Exhib:* Solo exhibs, Unicorn Gallery, NY, 75 & 76, NJ State Mus, Trenton, 78, Reyn Gallery, NY, 81-83, Coll Misericordia, Dallas, Pa, 85 & Lincoln Ctr Campus, Fordham Univ, NY, 90 & 2000, Dag Hammarskjold Plz, New York City, 2001-2002; Blue Hill Cult Ctr, Pearl River, NY, 84-85; Edward Hopper House, Nyack, NY, 84; Montclair State Col, 92; Adelphi Univ, 92; Int Biennial Art, Malta, 95; Bergen Mus Art & Sci, 2005; Mount Beacon Fine Art, Beacon, NY, 2009; Wit and Whims, Stamford Downtown, 2011; Pomona Cultural Ctr, NY, 2013; Ramapo Coll, NJ, 2014. *Teaching:* Prof art, Ramapo Coll, NJ, 71-present; Rutgers Grad Sch Educ, 94. *Awards:* Grants, Art on the Outside, NJ Dept Higher Educ, Title I, 75, 76 & 77; Distinguished Serv Award, Rockland Co Legislature, 88. *Mem:* Int Sculpture Soc; Am Art Therapy Asn; Authors Guild. *Media:* Bronze, Fiberglass, Wood. *Res:* art as therapy in jails/mental health facilities. *Collection:* over 80 private collections. *Publ:* Auth, Leap to the Sun: Learning through Dynamic Play, Prentice-Hall, 79; Sculpture as Experience: Working with Clay, Wire, Wax, Plaster, Foil and Found Objects, Chilton Publ, 89; Art & Interaction, Ramapo Coll, 90; Smart Starts in the Arts, Imagination Arts Publ, 2003; Art Activities for Mind & Imagination, Imagination Arts Pub, 2004; Artistic Crafts, Imagination Arts Publications, Mahwah, NJ, 2004; Sculpture as Experience, Krause Publ, 2nd ed, Iola, Wis, 2007; Seeing in the Dark, Arielle's Story (novel), Wasteland Press, 2012; Art & Social Interaction, Linus Publications. *Mailing Add:* 57 Thunderhead Pl Mahwah NJ 07430

PECK, LEE BARNES
JEWELER, EDUCATOR
b Battle Creek, Mich, Sept 21, 1942. *Study:* Kellogg Community Col, AA, 63; Western Mich Univ, BS (art educ), 65; Univ Wis, MFA (art metal), 69. *Work:* Johnson Wax Co. *Exhib:* The Goldsmith, Renwick Gallery, Smithsonian Inst, Washington, DC, 74; Am Goldsmiths Now, Washington Univ, St Louis, 78; Sangree De Cristo Art Ctr, Pueblo, Colo, 78; Northeast Mo State Univ, Kirksville, 78; Visual Arts Ctr Alaska, Anchorage, 78; Solo exhib, Mich Tech Univ, Houghton, 78; Objects 79, Western Colo Arts, 79; and many others. *Teaching:* Assoc prof jewelry & metalwork, Northern Ill Univ, 70-82, prof art, currently, Distinguished Research Prof, 1998-2002; lectr in jewelry, Rosary Col, 72-. *Awards:* Lakefront Festival Art Prize, Milwaukee Art Ctr, 75; The Metalsmith Award, Phoenix Art Mus, Ariz, 77; First Prize in Metal, Cooperstown Art Asn, NY, 77. *Mem:* Am Crafts Coun (Ill rep, 72-74); Wis Designer Craftsman; Soc NAm Goldsmiths. *Media:* Precious Metals. *Publ:* Auth & illusr, Jewelry Making, Vol 3, In: Illustrated Libr of Arts & Crafts, 74

PECK, WILLIAM HENRY
HISTORIAN, EDUCATOR
b Savannah, Ga, Oct 2, 1932. *Study:* Ohio State Univ, 50-53; Wayne State Univ, BFA, 60, MA, 61. *Collection Arranged:* Mummy Portraits from Roman Egypt (with catalog), 67, Detroit Collects: Antiquities, 73 & Akhenáten & Nefertiti, 73-74; Cleopatra's Egypt, 89; Splendors of Ancient Egypt, 97; plus many others. *Pos:* Jr cur educ, Detroit Inst Arts, 60-62, asst cur educ, 62-64, assoc cur, 64-68, cur ancient art, 68-2004, sr cur, 88-2004; mem, Brooklyn Mus Theban Exped, 78-, assoc field dir, 80-2010; guest cur, Ark Art Ctr, Little Rock, 2008-2009. *Teaching:* Lectr art hist, Cranbrook Acad Art, 63-65; adj prof art hist, Wayne State Univ, 66-; vis lectr classics, Univ Mich, 70 & lectr art history, 2005-; lectr Coll for Creative Studies, 2004, hist, Univ Windsor, Ont, 2006. *Awards:* Travel Grant, Ford Motor Co, Eng, 62, Am Res Ctr Egypt Fel, 71 & Smithsonian Inst, 75; Arts Achievement Award, Dept Art & Art Hist, Wayne State Univ. *Mem:* Soc Study Egyptian Antiques; fel Am Res Ctr Egypt; Cranbrook Acad Art (mem bd gov, 74-85); Archaeol Inst Am; Int Asn Egyptologists; Oriental Inst, Univ Chicago; Asn Study of Travel in Egypt and Near East. *Res:* Currently writing book on true art of ancient Egypt. *Interests:* Oragami, early music, TE Lawrence, Silent Filming. *Publ:* Drawings From Ancient Egypt, Thames & Hudson, 78, German transl, 79, French transl, 80, Arabic transl, 87; The constant lure, chapter In: Ancient Egypt: Discovering its splendors, Nat Geographic, 78; The Detroit Institute of Arts: A Brief History, 91; Splendors of Ancient Egypt, 97; Egypt in Toledo (book), Toledo Mus Art, 2011; Many articles, bk revs and contribs to cncyclopedias; The Material World of Ancient Egypt (book), 2013. *Mailing Add:* 1901 Orleans Detroit MI 48207

PECKHAM, NICHOLAS
ARCHITECT, EDUCATOR
b Teaneck, NJ, Apr 11, 1940. *Study:* US Merchant Marine Acad, BS, 62; Univ Calif, Berkeley, 63; Univ Pa, BArch, 67, MArch, 73, with Louis Kahn, PhD cand with R Buckminster Fuller. *Pos:* Pres, Peckham & Wright Architects, Columbia. *Teaching:* Prof design, Stephens Col, Columbia, 75-. *Awards:* Cycle-4 Solar Award & Passive Cycle Award, Dept Housing & Urban Develop; Com Solar Award, Dept Energy. *Mem:* Construct Specifications Inst; Am Inst Architects; Int Solar Energy Soc. *Res:* Optimization in architecture. *Publ:* Auth, Evolution in architecture, Pass-Age, summer 75. *Mailing Add:* 3151 W Rte K Columbia MO 65203-9613

PEDEN WESLEY, DONALEE
PAINTER
b Syracuse, NY, Apr 1, 1952. *Study:* Syracuse Univ, BFA, 76, MFA, 92. *Work:* Everson Mus, Syracuse, NY; Munson-Williams-Proctor Mus, Utica, NY. *Exhib:* Solo exhibs, Munson-Williams-Proctor Inst, Utica, NY, 86, Gertrude Thomas Chapman Art Gallery, Cazenovia Col, NY, 86 & 87, Colgate Univ, Hamilton, NY, 88 & Tyler Art Gallery, Oswego, NY, 90, The Drawing Room, Schaffer Art Bldg, Syracuse, NY, 2006, Made in NY, Schweinfurth Art Center, 2006; New Visions Gallery, Ithaca, NY, 88; group shows, NY Women Artists, NY State Mus, Albany, 89-90, Burchfield Art Ctr, Buffalo, NY, 90, Ariel Gallery, NY, 90, Syracuse State, 90, Gertrude Thomas Chapman Art Gallery, Cazenovia Col, NY, 90-91, Colgate Univ, Hamilton, NY, 91 & Cooperstown Art Asn, NY, 95, SUNY, Oswego, Sydney Coll Gallery, Sydney Coll of the Arts, Kozelle, Australia, Contemp Realism III Gallery Alexy, Philadelphia, Pa, 25th Anniversary Exhib, ARC Gallery, Chicago, Ill, Four Artists Drawing, Kirkland Arts Ctr, Clinton, NY, State Univ Plaza, Albany, NY; Derecci Gallery, Edgewood Col, Madison, Wis, 93; Rome Art Ctr, NY, 96; ARC Gallery, Chicago, Ill, 98-99; Drawing Lives, Invitational Show, Emily & Lowe Mus, 2005; Delevan Art Ctr, Group Show, 2004, 10 from OCC, 2004; Fac Show, Syracuse Univ, 2004; Fac Show, Syracuse Univ & OCC, NY, 2004-2006; Biennial Rochester Mem Art Gallery, 2006. *Teaching:* Instr watercolor & figure drawing, Syracuse Univ, 83-, material & techniques, 89, 90 & 91; instr drawing, Cazenovia Col, 86-87, Hamilton Col, 89 & Univ Madison, Wisc, 93; instr drawing I & figure drawing, Syracuse Univ, NY; vis artist, Oswego, NY-SUNY, 96; asst prof, SUNY, Oswego; Onondaga Community College, 2003-; instr figure & drawing watercolor, Syracuse Univ, NY, 2003-2006. *Awards:* New York Found Arts Fel, Drawing, 86; Nat Endowment Arts Grant, Drawing, 87; Jacob Javits Fel, 90; Best of Show, Anderson Arts Ctr, Kenosha, Wis, 95. *Bibliog:* Arthur Williams (auth), The Sculpture Reference Illustrated, 2004. *Dealer:* Delavan Art Gallery, Syracuse, NY. *Mailing Add:* 8225 Vicksburg Pl Baldwinsville NY 13027-8303

PEDERSEN, CAROLYN H
PAINTER, COLLAGE ARTIST
b Dec 12, 1942; US citizen. *Study:* Syracuse Univ, BS, 64; Rockland Ctr for Arts, W Nyack, NY, studied printmaking with Roberta De Lamonica, 86-91, studied watercolor with Edgar A Whitney; painting and collage with Bruce Dorfman, 90. *Work:* Art Pub Places, Rockland Co, New City, NY; Gallery Mus Hebrew Home for Aged, Riverdale, NY; G C Hanford Mfg Co, Syracuse, NY; Pub Serv Elect & Gas, NJ; Katz Commun, San Francisco, Calif. *Exhib:* Watercolor USA, Springfield Mus, Mo, 85; Am Watercolor Soc, Salmagundi Club, NY, 84; Nat Watercolor Soc, Los Angeles, Calif, 84, 85, 87; Audubon Artists Ann, Nat Arts Club, NY, 85, 86, 88. *Pos:* Pres, Art Craft Asn Rockland Co, NY, 79-80; mem chmn, Northeast Watercolor Soc, NY, 87-89; exhib comt mem, Rockland Ctr Arts, NY, 88-91; asst treas, Catharine Lorillard Wolfe Arts Club, 90-92; founding mem, Piermont Fine Arts Gallery, NY, 93. *Teaching:* Instr watercolor (workshops & demonstrations) Rockland Ctr Arts, West Nyack, NY, 85-91, int workshops; adj prof, Col New Rochelle, NY & Seton Hall Univ, 96-99. *Awards:* Am Watercolor Soc Traveling Award, 84; travel award, Ky Watercolor Soc, Aqueous 86, 86. *Bibliog:* Adam Pfeffer (auth), On the arts, Spotlight Mag, 2/88. *Mem:* Nat Watercolor Soc; Nat Asn Women Artists; Audubon Artists; Catharine Lorillard Wolfe Arts Club; Transparent Watercolor Soc Am. *Media:* Watermedia, Collage. *Publ:* Auth, Splash, America's Best Contemporary Watercolors, 90 & Splash 6, 2000, Northlight; Best of Watercolor, watercolor book, 95 & Floral Inspirations, 97, Rockport Publ; The Artistic Touch 3, Creative Press, 98. *Dealer:* Johnsons of Madrid Galleries Madrid NM. *Mailing Add:* PO Box 99 Cerrillos NM 87010

PEDERSON, MITZI
INSTALLATION SCULPTOR
b Suart, Fla, 1976. *Study:* L'Ecole Nationale Superieure Des Beaux-Arts, Paris, 1998; Carnegie Mellon Univ, BFA(Printing, Painting & Drawing), 1999; Calif Coll Arts, MFA, 2004. *Work:* Hammer Mus, Los Angeles; San Francisco Mus Mod Art. *Exhib:* Solo exhibs include Ratio 3, San Francisco, 2005, 2007, White Columns, New York, 2006, Duchess, Chicago, 2006, Nicole Klagsbrun Gallery, New York, 2007, Hammer Mus, Los Angeles, 2008; Group exhibs include Color Wheel Oblivion, Marella Arte Contemporanea, Milan, Italy, 2004; Gazing Upwards, Adobe Books, San Francisco, 2004; Snap, Crackle, Pop, PlaySpace Gallery, Calif Coll Arts, San Francisco, 2006; Louis Morris, Atlanta Contemp Art Ctr, Ga, 2006; Power, Foxy Production, New York, 2008; Update, White Columns, New York, 2008; Whitney Biennial, Whitney Mus Am Art, New York, 2008. *Awards:* SECA Art Award, San Francisco Mus Mod Art, 2006. *Mailing Add:* Ratio 3 2831A Mission St San Francisco CA 94110

PEDERSON-KRAG, GILLIAN
PAINTER
Study: RI Sch Design, BFA; Cornell Univ, MFA, 1963. *Work:* Everson Mus; MH de Young Mus; Zimmerli Art Mus. *Pos:* Vis critic, Univ Iowa, Univ Ind, Univ Boston, and Vassar Coll; artist-in-residence, Hollins Univ, 2004. *Teaching:* Instr, Cornell Univ, Dartmouth Coll, and Queens Coll, formerly. *Awards:* Pollock-Krasner Found Grant, 2008. *Dealer:* Hackett-Freedman Gallery 250 Sutter St Ste 400 San Francisco CA 94108

PEEPLES-BRIGHT, MAIJA GEGERIS ZACK WOOF
PAINTER
b Riga, Latvia, Nov 21, 1942. *Study:* Univ Calif, Davis, BA, 64, MA, 65; also with William T Wiley, Robert Arneson & Wayne Thiebaud. *Work:* Crocker Art Mus, Sacramento, Calif; La Jolla Mus Art, Calif; Matthews Art Ctr, Tempe, Ariz; San Francisco Mus Art; Norman MacKenzie Art Gallery, Regina, Sask. *Comn:* Beast rainbow painting, City San Francisco, Civic Ctr, 67; rainbow house, pvt party, San Francisco, 67-68; ceiling murals, Rainbow House, San Francisco, 67-68; crocheted, woven & sewn beast curtains, Univ Calif Art Bldg, Davis, 71; Sun of Alion, Fiberglass Sculpture for pride of Sacramento, 2004; Univ Calif Davis Med Ctr, 2012. *Exhib:* San Francisco Art Mus, 73-75; Rainbow Show, De Young Mus, San Francisco, 74-75; solo exhibs, Iris Upon a Star, J'Nette Gardens, Oakland, Calif, 87-88, Maija's

Flowers, Candy Store Gallery, Folsom, Calif, 90, Life Is Just a Bowl of Terriers, Nev Mus Art, Reno, 91 & Paintings & Ceramics, Solomon/Dubnick Gallery, Sacramento, Calif, 95; All Creatures Great & Small, Natsoulas Gallery, Davis, Calif, 92; My Plezoores, Anya Horvath Gallery, Sacramento, Calif, 93 & 94; Small Wonders, I Wolk Gallery, St Helena, Calif, 93-94; Form and Fire, 2000; Regina Clay Worlds In the Making, MacKenzie Gallery, 2006; Woof's Heroes, Explodinghead Gallery, Sacramento, Calif, 2005; Laughing Owl the Way, Canadian Clay & Glass Gallery, Waterloo, Ontario, 2006; retrospective, Hog Hotel Down at the End of Lonely Street, Sacramento Municipal Utility Dist Gallery, Sacramento, Calif, 2007; Big Names Small Art, Cal-Expo, 2008; From Fire to Figura, Solomon Dubnick Gallery, Sacramento, Calif, 2009; Maija's Favorites, Solomon Dubnick Gallery, 2010; Plates and Tote MS Show, Roseville Blueline Gallery, Roseville, Calif, 2011; Maija's Hunting Tigers, Archival Gallery, 2012; Maija's World of Woof, Blue Line Gallery, Roseville, Calif, 2012; Her Crazy Critters, Pence Gallery, Davis, Calif, 2013; Crocker Art Mus, Sacramento, Calif. *Collection Arranged:* The Nut Show, for Kaiser-Aetna, Tahoe Verdes, Calif, 72. *Teaching:* Instr art, Laney Coll, Oakland, 68-69, Univ Calif, Davis, 71-72 & Sierra Coll, Rocklin, Calif, 71-73; painting workshop, Sierra Oaks Sch, Sacramento, Calif, 93; lectr, Crocker-Kinsley Group, Fall 2009. *Awards:* Award, Ceramics Excellence, Calif State Fair, 74. *Bibliog:* Ellen Schlesinger (auth), As Fate would have it, Peeples is an artist, Sacramento Bee, 7/4/82; Ronnie Cohen (auth), Maija's Zoo, Neighbors Mag, 2/84; Rachel Savage (auth), Always Merry and Bright, Inside the City Mag, 9/2005; Dawn Blunk (auth), At the Heart fo the Art, Sacramento Mag, 4/2004; Diane Chin Lui (auth), Colorfully Chaotic Managarie, Davis Enterprise; LeeAnn Dickson (auth), Fantastically Funky, Style Mag, 2012. *Media:* Multi. *Dealer:* Archival Gallery 3223 Folsom Blvd Sacramento Ca 95816. *Mailing Add:* 2845 Midas Ct Rocklin CA 95677

PEIPERL, ADAM
VIDEO ARTIST, KINETIC SCULPTOR
b Sosnowiec, Poland, June 4, 1935; US citizen. *Study:* George Washington Univ, BS, 57; Pa State Univ, 57-59. *Work:* Nat Mus Am Hist, Hirshhorn Mus & John F Kennedy Ctr Performing Arts, Washington, DC; Pa Acad Fine Arts, Philadelphia; Boijmans Van Beuningen Mus, Rotterdam, Holland; Gift of sculpture Tenderness 1969, Walker Art Center, 2015. *Comn:* Video shorts, WETA TV Channel 26, Washington, DC, 84; dance collab with Maida Withers, Lincoln Ctr Out-of-Doors, 96; dance collab with Denise Vale, Univ Okla, 2003; video collab with Eric Bridenbaker, Tunnel of Rays, 8/2011. *Exhib:* Corcoran Gallery Art, 68; solo exhibs, Baltimore Mus Art, 69, Pa Acad Fine Arts, 69, Nat Mus Am Hist, 72-73 & Philadelphia Art Alliance, 78; Kent State Univ, 69; Mem Art Gallery, Univ Rochester, 78; group exhib, Nat Mus Am Art, 81; Art of the Sixties, Fred Jones Jr Mus Art, Univ Okla, 2002; Radicals and Conservatives: Abstraction 1945 to Present; Pa Acad Fine Arts, 2004; Refract, Reflect, Project: Light Works from the Collection, Hirshhorn Mus & Sculpture Garden, Washington, DC, 2007. *Awards:* Int Platform Asn Art Show Silver Medal, 83, Gold Medal, 84. *Bibliog:* Frank Getlein (auth), He defied tradition and made it work, Sun Star, 7/21/68; Diane Chichura & Thelma Stevens (auths), Super Sculpture, Van Nostrand-Reinhold, 74; Victoria Donohoe (auth), Kinetic art lives on, Philadelphia Inquirer, 10/27/78; George Washington Univ Mag, spring 92 & winter 2002. *Media:* Polarized Light and Video. *Publ:* Image, Time/Life Book-of-the-Month Club, 95-96; Europeana Web Portal, 2013. *Mailing Add:* 1135 Loxford Terr Silver Spring MD 20901

PEKAR, RONALD WALTER
PAINTER, SCULPTOR
b Cleveland, Ohio, Oct 9, 1942. *Study:* Cleveland Inst Art; Wash Univ, BFA, fel, 66-67, MFA. *Work:* Memphis Brooks Mus Art; Mississippi Mus Art; Carroll Reece Mus, Tenn; Cheekwood Mus Art, Tenn; St Jude Children's Res Hosp; painting series, Federal Express Corp; represented in more than 200 corporate and mus collections worldwide. *Comn:* Mural series, Memphis Convention Ctr Complex; sculptural environments, Holiday Inns, Inc (nationwide); illuminated painting, Gen Pub Utilities, Pa; two 3-story illuminated sculptures, Lemoyne-Owen Col. *Exhib:* Solo shows: Memphis Brooks Mus, Miss Mus Art, Rhodes Col, Univ Tenn, Memphis Coll Art & Ark State Univ; 10 in Tennessee, Statewide-Traveling Bicentennial Exhib; Mid South Artists Traveling Exhib; Memphis Pink Palace Mus Commemorative Painting; Spirit of the River (audio-visual environment), Memphis Brooks Mus, 77-81. *Pos:* Found div chair, Memphis Col Art, currently; lectr & critic, Univ Tenn, ETex State Univ, Ark State Univ; former cons The Walt Disney Co, Worldwide. *Teaching:* Prof, 2-D and 3-D design, drawing and painting, Otis Col Art and Design & Calif State Univ, Northridge. *Awards:* Cult Contribution Award, State of Tenn; Tenn Valley Authority Monumental Sculpture Award. *Bibliog:* Man of steel and crayon, Mid South Mag Commercial Appeal; profile, Memphis Mag. *Mem:* Calif Art Club. *Media:* Acrylic, Oil; All, Bronze, Steel. *Publ:* Illusr, Air poster, Memphis Acad Arts, 69; illusr rec label, Ardent Rec, 72; ed & illusr, Homage to the Land and Sky, 73; illusr rec label, Privilege Rec, 74. *Dealer:* Tirage Gallery 1 West California Blvd Pasadena CA 91105. *Mailing Add:* 1426 Highland Ave Glendale CA 91202

PEKARSKY, MEL(VIN) HIRSCH
PAINTER, EDUCATOR
b Chicago, Ill, Sept 18, 1934. *Study:* Art Inst Chicago; Northwestern Univ, BA, MA. *Work:* Corcoran Gallery Art, Washington, DC; Minneapolis Inst Arts; Cleveland Mus Art; Weatherspoon Mus, Univ NC; Fogg Mus Art, Harvard Univ; Yale Univ Art Mus; Indianapolis Mus Art; Nev Mus Art; Roswell, NMex, Mus Art; Notre Dame Univ Art Mus; Zimmerli Mus, Rutgers Univ; Environ Protection Agency, DC; Block Mus, Northwestern Univ, Evanston, Ill; Simons Ctr Geometry & Physics, Stonybook Univ, Long Island, NY. *Comn:* Exterior mural, City Walls Inc: Kaplan Fund, 70; exterior mural, Nat Endowment Arts, 72; exterior mural, US Dept Housing & Urban Develop, 74; Corporate collections include AT & T, Am Express, Bank of Am, General Mills, Heublein, Marsh & McClennan, St Paul Companies, Standard Oil, Westinghouse, and many other corp & pvt collections. *Exhib:* New Editions 74-75 & NY Cult Ctr, 75; Drawings by Seven Am Artists, Cleveland Mus, 78; Musées Royeaux de Beaux-Arts de Belgique, 78; The Am Landscape: Recent Developments, Whitney Mus Am Art, NY, 81; Kuznetsky-Most Gallery, Moscow, 89; Selected Am Drawings, Noyes Mus Art, NJ, 96; New Acquisitions, The Fogg Mus of Art, Harvard Univ, 2000 & 2006; Nielsen Gallery, Boston, 2001-2004; Am Acad Arts and Letters, 2001; Nat Acad Design, 2001 & 2008; Albright Knox Gallery, Buffalo, NY, 2002-2003; Solo Exhibs: G W Einstein, New York, 75, 77-78, 80-81, 84, 86, 88, 91 & 95, Gallery 112 Greene St, New York, 80, Butler Inst Am Art, 90 & Mus Stony Brook, NY, 93, Nev Mus Art, 2001, Nielsen Gallery, Boston, 2002-2003; Etudes: Paintings, Drawings, & Prints, Van Deb Ed, NY, 3-5/2007; Gallery North, Setauket, NY, 2009; Anthony Giordano Gallery, Dowling Col, Long Island, NY, 2009; Stony Brook Univ, Univ Art Gallery, Retrospective 74-2009; Patchogue Arts Biennial, Briarcliffe, Coll, NY, 2011; Art Sites, Riverhead, NY, 2011; Black and White, Van Deb Editions, NY, 2013; Elementary, Gallery North, 2013. *Collection Arranged:* Cur, Reuben Kadish, Julius Tobias, Gladys Nilsson, Jim Nutt & Lucio Pozzi. *Pos:* Founding mem & mem bd, City Walls, Inc, 69-75, vpres, 70-75; bd dir, Reuben Kadish Found Arts, currently; adv bd, Gallery North, 2001-2011. *Teaching:* From asst to assoc dean art, Sch Visual Arts, New York, 67-69; fac, New York Univ Grad Sch Art, 70-71; prof art, State Univ NY, Stony Brook, 75-, chmn, 76-78 & 84-89, dir studio progs, 75-2003, dir, MFA Prog, 89-2003, chm, 2005-2007, prof emeritus & vist prof, 2009-. *Awards:* Grants, NY State Coun Arts, Nat Endowment for Arts, Kaplan Fund, Bernhard Found, US Dept Housing & Urban Devel. *Bibliog:* Donald Kuspit (auth), Mel Pekarsky, catalog, 10/84 & Pekarsky's Desert Tundra, catalog, 10/88; Robert G Edelman (auth), The Transformative Vision: Contemporary Am Landscape Painting, Pittsburgh Carnegie Mus, 89; John Driscoll & Arnold Skolnick (auths), The Artist and the American Landscape, San Francisco, 98; Blooming Desert, Mel Pekarsky's Inscapes, 2010. *Mem:* Coll Art Asn; Pub Art Fund; Many environmental organizations. *Media:* Oil, Mixed Media. *Res:* Painting, drawing, theory, public art. *Specialty:* paintings & drawings. *Interests:* Environmental issues. *Publ:* Illusr, The Curious Cow, 60, Little Quack, 61, The Three Goats, 63 & The Little Red Hen, 63, Follett; Handbook of Gestures, Mouton, The Hague, 72; Various print editions in etching, silk screen, and lithography. *Dealer:* GW Einstein Co Inc NY; Gallery North Setauket Long Island NY. *Mailing Add:* Box 1575 Stony Brook NY 11790

PÉLADEAU, MARIUS BEAUDOIN
WRITER, MUSEUM DIRECTOR
b Boston, Mass, Jan 27, 1935. *Study:* St Michael's Col, Winooski Park, Vt, BA (cum laude), 56; Boston Univ, Mass, MS, 57; Georgetown Univ, Washington, DC, MA (fel), 61. *Pos:* Dir, Maine League of Hist Soc & Mus, 72-76; dir, William A Farnsworth Libr & Art Mus, 76-87, consult & writer, 87-, dir emiritus, 2008; managing dir, The Theater, Monmouth, ME, 88; cur, LC Bates Mus, 93-2001. *Teaching:* guest lectr, Univ Maine and other art and hist orgn. *Mem:* VT Hist Soc, Co of Military Hist (fellow). *Media:* Print media. *Res:* American art and the decorative arts; 18th, 19th, and 20th century American Art, folk art & decorative arts. *Interests:* Am art, hist, & cult. *Publ:* Auth, The Verse of Royall Tyler, Univ Press Va, 1968; The Prose of Royall Tyler, Vt Hist Soc, 72; Adventures in Maine History, Maine League of Historical Socs, 76; auth, Chansonetta: The Photographs of Chansonetta Stanley Emmons, 1858-1937, Morgan & Morgan, 77; Charles Daniel Hubbard: American Impressionist, 1876-1951, LC Bates Mus, 96; John Francis Sprague: Chronicles of Maine History, LC Bates Mus, 1998; Looking at Katahdin: Maine Artists' Inspiration, LC Bates Mus, 99; Uncommon Treasures Folk Art at the Farnsworth, Farnsworth Art Mus, 2008. *Mailing Add:* 158 Thorp Shores Rd Readfield ME 04355

PELL, RICHARD
VIDEO ARTIST, EDUCATOR
Study: Carnegie Mellon Univ, BS; Rensselaer Polytechnic Inst, MS. *Exhib:* Zentrum fur Kunst und Medientechnologie, Karlsruhe, Ger; Mus Contemp Art, Mass; Contemp Arts Ctr, Cincinnati; Australian Ctr for the Moving Image, Melbourne; Aldrich Mus Contemp Art, Ridgefield, Conn; Nat Ctr for Contemp Arts, Russia; Israeli Ctr for Digital Art. *Pos:* Founding mem, Inst for Applied Autonomy; asst prof, Univ Mich Sch Art & Design, Rensselaer Polytechnic Inst & Carnegie Mellon Univ Sch Art; dir & founder, Ctr for PostNatural Hist. *Awards:* Best Mich Dir Award, Ann Arbor Film Festival, 2005; 1st Prize, Iowa Int Documentary Film Festival; New Media Fel, Rockefeller Found, 2007; New Media Art Fel, Rhizome, New Mus Contemp Art; Grant for Emerging Fields, Creative Capital Found, 2009. *Publ:* Dir, Don't Call Me Crazy On the 4th of July (documentary), 2005. *Mailing Add:* Carnegie Mellon Univ School of Art 500 Forbes Ave CFA 407 Pittsburgh PA 15213-3890

PELLETTIERI, MICHAEL JOSEPH
PRINTMAKER, PAINTER
b New York, NY, Nov 25, 1943. *Study:* The New School, 62; Art Students League New York, with Robert B Hale, Edwin Dickinson, Harry Sternberg & Joseph Hirsch, 63-66; City Coll New York, BA, 65; City Univ New York, MA, 69. *Work:* De Cordova Mus, Lincoln, Mass; Taz Gallery & Co, Boston; Newark Art Libr, NJ; Ben Goldstein Collection, NY; Columbia Mus Art, SC; NY Pub Libr; Libr Congress; Dave and Reba Williams Collection; NDak Univ; Art Students League of NY; Franz Grierhass Collection; Wallace Found; Amity Arts Found; NY Hist Soc; and others. *Exhib:* Boston Printmakers 32nd Nat, DeCordova Mus, Lincoln, Mass, 79; Hunterdon Art Ctr 23rd & 25th, Newark Art Libr, NJ, 79 & 81; Nat Acad & Inst Arts & Letts, 80; Charlotte Printmakers, NC, 81; Columbia Univ, NY, 87, 93; Landmark Gallery, Kingston, NY, 88; New Renaissance Gallery, NY, 91; City Views Decordova Mus, Lincoln, Mass, 98; Seaton Hall Univ, Ital Am Printmakers, NJ, 01; Up on the Roof, NY Hist Soc, 01; NY Etchers Soc Inaugural Exhib, 2000; Old Print Shop, NY, 01; A Message from NY, The Sky Gallery, Umeda Sky Building, Osaka, Japan, 02; NY Soc of Etchers, Mus of City of NY, 02; PaineWebber Galleries, A Century on Paper, Prints by Art Students League Artists, 125th Anniversary, 02; Retrospective, Paintings and Prints, Art Students League of NY, 02; Durst Gallery, A Message from NY, 03; Gallery of Graphic Art, Printmaking A to Z, NY, 03; Old Print Shop, Prints and Watercolors, NY, 2004; NY Hist Soc, Impressions of NY, 2004; NY Hist Soc, Around Town Underground, From the Coll of Dave and Reba Williams, NY, 2004; Boston Printmakers, Nat Exhib, 2005; Butler Mid Year Painting Exhib, Youngstown, Ohio,

2005; New Visual Treasures, Newark Art Libr, Newark, NJ, 2005; Contemp Printmakers Old Print Shop, 2007; Peoples Readings (selections from the collection of Donald & Patricia Oresman), Spartanburg Art Mus & Burroughs Chapin Art Mus, 2008; K.B. Gallery, NY, 2008; The Art of Democracy, NY Soc Etchers, 2009; The Old Print Shop, Contemporary Printmakers, NY, 2009, 2011, Saga Printmakers, 2012, Red, The Old Print Gallery, 2013. *Collection Arranged:* Exhibition advisor, A Century on Paper, Prints by Art Students League Artists, 125th anniversary exhib, PaineWebber Galleries, 02; coord, Twenty-first-Century Print Portfolio, Commemorative Print Portfolio Celebrating 125th Anniversary of the Art Students League of NY, 02; juror, Inaugural Exhib of NY Etchers Soc Exhib, 2000; coord, Portfolio 2000, The Graphics Workshop of the Art Students League, 2000. *Teaching:* Instr lithography, Art Students League New York, 77-79, instr graphics, 79-, instr intaglio, Summit Art Ctr, 82-88; instr printmaking, Columbia Univ, Teachers Col, 87-2005. *Awards:* Mitchell Fund Award, 86; Mac Dowell Colony Fel, 88; Purchase Prize, Nat Works Paper, Univ Miss, 91; and others; Ben and Beatrice Goldstein Found Award, 91; Robert Conover Mem Award, 2000; Burr Miller Award for litography, SAGA, 02. *Bibliog:* Garry Simpson (auth), Currier & Ives (film for television), Univ Vt, 76; In Honor of low tech printmaking, The Record, NJ, 2002; Portfolio, Old Print Shop, 20th Century Prints, 95. *Mem:* Artist Equity NY; Art Students League NY (bd control, 65, treas, 66-67); Audubon Artists (dir graphics 82-84, vp 1985); Boston Printmakers. *Media:* Intaglio, Lithography, Oil, Watercolor. *Specialty:* American Prints. *Publ:* Contribr, Print Review Ten, Pratt Graphic Art Ctr, 79; Linea, What Are the Greatest Obstacles to Developing as an Artist, 1998; New York Society of Etchers, Harry Stenberg, A Life Celebrated, 2000; Auth, A Retrospective, Michael Pellettieri, 2002; New York Soc Etchers, Catalogue Forward, Inaugural Exhib, 2002; Linea, Interview with Will Barnet on the Life of Bob Blackburn, 2004; auth, Will Barnet's Catalogue Raisonne, 1931-2005, An Artist's Journey, An Artists View; The Print Club of New York Newsletter, 2009. *Dealer:* The Old Print Shop 150 Lexington Ave New York NY 10016; Gallery of Graphic Art 1610 York Ave New York NY 10028. *Mailing Add:* 3334 Crescent St #9A Astoria NY 11106

PELS, MARSHA
ARTIST
b Brooklyn, NY, Dec 24, 1950. *Study:* RI Sch Design, BFA (painting), 72; Syracuse Univ, MFA (sculpture), 74. *Work:* United Jewish Appeal, New York; Grounds for Sculpture, Hamilton, NJ; Robinson Trelliss, Los Angeles. *Exhib:* Solo shows incl Oscarsson Hood Gallery, New York, 81, 84, 86, Dana Arts Ctr, Lancaster, Pa, 84, 87, Rotunda Gallery, Brooklyn, 90, Sculpture Ctr, New York, 95, Momenta Art, Brooklyn, 96, Schroeder Romero Gallery, Brooklyn, 2001, 2004, Irish Mus Mod Art, Dublin, 2004; group shows incl Krasner Gallery, New York, 74; Nielson Gallery, Boston, 80; Oscarsson Hood Gallery, New York, 81-82, 83; Academia Americana, Rome, Italy, 85; Aldrich Mus Contemp Art, 86; Kouros Gallery, New York, 92; Grounds For Sculpture, Hamilton, NJ, 93; Ronald Feldman Fine Arts, New York, 95; Chelsea Market, New York, 96; Connemara Sculpture Park, Plano, Tex, 99; Wythe Studio, Brooklyn, 2002; Rotunda Gallery, Brooklyn, 2002; Schroeder Romero Gallery, Brooklyn, 2003. *Collection Arranged:* Thomas Olbrieht Stifting, Berlin, Germany. *Teaching:* Assoc prof fine art, Coll Creative Studies, Detroit, Mich; Pratt Inst, Darthmouth Coll, RI Sch Design, Tyler Sch Art, Bennington Coll, SuNY Purchase. *Awards:* Prix de Rome, Fulbright Scholar, Pollack-Krasner. *Bibliog:* Art in Am, Art News, New York Times. *Mem:* CAA; Allmni Prix de Rome; Fulbright Asn. *Media:* Contemporary, Cutting Edge Work. *Publ:* Socrates Sculture Park, Anthology of Art, Women Sculptors of the 90's. *Dealer:* Schroeder-Romero Gallery 637 W 27th St Brooklyn NY 10001. *Mailing Add:* 99 Commercial St Brooklyn NY 11222

PELUSO, MARTA E
PHOTOGRAPHER, ART INSTRUCTOR
b New Brighton, Pa, Apr 30, 1951. *Study:* Allegheny Col, Meadville, Pa, BA, 73; Panopticon Photo Workshop with Garry Winogrand, Greece, 77; Univ Calif, Davis, MFA, 82. *Work:* Univ Calif, Davis/Nelson Gallery; Mercyhurst Coll Libr, Erie, Pa. *Exhib:* Solo exhib, Photographs, Pittsburgh Filmmakers Gallery, Pa, 81; The Guiding Light, Eye Gallery, San Francisco, Calif, 90 & Santa Barbara Contemp Arts Forum, Calif, 91; Scarred Texts/Sacred Territories, Scarlet Palette, Cambria, Calif, 92; Memorie, Arternatives, San Luis Obispo, Calif, 95. *Pos:* Photograph proj coord, Ethnic Impressions, Erie, Pa, 75-79; Gallery dir, Cuesta Col, San Luis Obispo, Calif, 86-2001; exec dir, ARTS Obispo, San Luis Obispo, Calif, 2006-2011. *Teaching:* Lectr photog, Cal Polytech State Univ, San Luis Obispo, 83-87; instr studio art, Cuesta Col, San Luis Obispo, Calif, 86-. *Bibliog:* Les Krantz (auth), California art review, Am References, 89. *Mem:* Soc Photog Educ (W Region chmn, 89); San Luis Obispo Co Arts Coun (bd mem, 90-93). *Media:* Photography, Assemblage. *Publ:* Marta Peluso's quest for the best, The Tribune, San Luis Obispo, 10/31/99; Art Rag, San Luis Obispo, Calif, 11/99 & fall 2000; Iris, Univ Va, Charlottesville, winter/spring 99; Rethinking the Natural (catalog) Austin Mus Art at Laguna Gloria, Austin, Tex, 95. *Mailing Add:* 557 Stoneridge Dr San Luis Obispo CA 93401-5671

PENA, AMADO MAURILIO, JR
PAINTER, ILLUSTRATOR
b Laredo, Tex, Oct 1, 1943. *Study:* Tex A&I Univ, BA(art), 65, MA (art & educ), 71. *Work:* Tex A&I Univ; Inter-Am Develop Bank, Washington; Univ Tex, Austin; Juarez-Lincoln Univ, Austin; Los Pinos, Pres Palace, Mexico; and others. *Comn:* Mural, Laredo Independent Sch Dist, Serv Ctr, 70; mural, City Hall, Crystal City, 72; painting, City Coun Crystal City, 72; centennial poster, Univ Tex, Austin, 83; Amarille Art Ctr, Tex, 83; and others. *Exhib:* Chicago Art Exhib, Nat Lulac Conf, Washington, 73 & Univ Tex Student Ctr, 74; Chicano Artists of the Southwest, Inst Mex Cult, San Antonio, 75; Solo retrospectives, Mus Nuevo Santander, Laredo, Tex, 83 & Laguna Gloria Art Mus, Austin, Tex, 83; and others. *Teaching:* Teacher art, Laredo Independent Sch Dist, 65-70, Crystal City Independent Sch Dist, 72-74, LC Anderson High Sch, Austin, 74-80 & Idyllwild Sch of Art, 88; artist-in-residence, instr Austin Community Coll, 90-92, Laredo Community Col, 97; founder, artist-in-residence, Studio Art Prog at Alexander High Sch, Laredo, 94-. *Awards:* Best of Show Award, First Place Award Painting & People's Choice Award, Southwest Arts Festival, Indio, Calif, 2000; First Place Award Painting, Bayou City Arts Festival, Houston, 2000; First Place Award Painting & First Place award Printmaking, Castle Rock Arts Festival, Colo. *Bibliog:* Amado M Pena to speak at graduation ceremony, The PAN AMERICAN, 97; Noted artist likes Alton enough to come back, The Telegraph, 97; Pena conversation starts Speaker Series, Laredo Morning Times, 97. *Mem:* Laredo Art Asn (pres, 68-69); Austin Art Teachers Asn (treas, 74-75). *Media:* Serigraphy; Watercolor. *Publ:* Contribr & auth, Chicano Art of the Southwest, Chicano Slide Collection, 73; contribr, Tejidos, Magazin & Calendario Chicano; illusr, Cuenots, 75. *Dealer:* El Taller Gallery 723 E Sixth St Austin TX 78701; Gallery Mack Seattle WA. *Mailing Add:* Pena Studio & Gallery 23A County Rd 117 S Santa Fe NM 87506

PENA, DAVID BEYNON
PAINTER, PORTRAIT ARTIST
b New York, NY, Dec 21, 1958. *Study:* Pratt Inst; Art Students League; Nat Acad Design; Santa Fe Inst Fine Art (master artist prog). *Work:* Newark Mus, NJ; Insurance Hall Fame, New York; Pfizer Pharmaceuticals Inc, New York; Sydney Univ Med Sch, Sydney, Australia; The Players Club, New York; Salmagundi Club, NY. *Comn:* Portrait, comn by Sen Howell Heflin, Tuscumbia, Ala, 94; portrait, Margery Edwards, comn by Dr KDG Edwards, New York, 90; portrait, Coster Family, comn by Tom Coster, NJ, 2000; portrait, Sir Edwin Manton (sr adv), AIG, NY, 2002; portrait, Fitzmaurice Family, comn by Rorbert Fitzmaurice, New York, 2005; portrait, Victor Kovner Esq, comn by Davis Wright Tremain, New York, 2006; portrait, Stanley F Druckenmiller, NY, Joshua Logan, Marty Riesman; portrait, Harold Prince, Players Club; portrait, Betty Comdon & Adolph Green. *Exhib:* Soc Illusr 29th Ann, Mus Am Illus, New York, 87; 163rd & 165th Ann Exhib, Nat Acad Design, 88; 63rd Ann Midyear Exhib, Butler Inst Am Art, Ohio, 99; 59th Ann, Audubon Artists Inc, 9/17-10/5, 2001; Solo Exhib: Union League Club, New York, 2003; Keyes Gallery, Springfield, Mo, 2005; Visual Art Ctr, NJ, 2008; 92 Ann Exhib, Allied Artists Am, New York, 2005; Bennington Ctr Arts Invitational, Vermont, 2007; Nat Arm Mus Sports, Indianapolis, Ind. *Pos:* Fac, Visual Art Ctr, NJ; Lett ed in chief, Artist Fel News. *Teaching:* Instr, portrait painting, Montclair Mus, 87-90; instr, figure painting, Visual Arts Ctr NJ, 2005- & Nat Acad Sch Fine Art, 2006. *Awards:* Benjamin Altman Prize, 163rd Nat Acad Design, 88; Elizabeth Greenshields Award, Greensheilds Found, 89; Cert Recognition, US Coast Guard COGAP Ann Dept Transportation, 98; Gold Medal of Honor, Allied Artists 89th Ann, 2002. *Bibliog:* John Russell (auth), Juried show highlights, NY Times, 4/29/88; Danille Gallo (auth), portfolio, Penthouse Letters, 11/88; M Stephen Doherty (auth), Portraits without formulas, 10/2002 & Portrait highlights, 4/2007, Am Artist; Casper Grathwohl (auth), Life lessons, NY Times, 8/18/2006; Allison Malafronte (auth), Times Personalities Captured by Contemporary Portraitists, Am Artist Mag; Sacha Jenkins & David Villorent (coauths), Secret Drawings of Graffiti Writers, Piece Bk; John Ponce (auth), Three Artists Draw in Pen & Ink, Am Artist Mag, fall 2008; Sheila Smith (auth), Artist David Beynon Pena Paints: Shepherd Randy Phillips, Lambs Script, spring/summer 2009. *Mem:* Hon life mem, Audubon Artists Inc (pres, 99-2005); Nat Arts Club; Artists Fel Inc (trustee, 99-); Allied Artists Am; life mem, The Players, Guest Signing Privileges; hon mem, The Salmagundi Club (99-2003); Nat Soc Mural Painters (treas, 99-2005). *Media:* Oil, Watercolor; All Media. *Specialty:* Am Impressionist, Portraiture, Landscape & Marine Paintings. *Interests:* Tennis, Squash, Sailing. *Publ:* Illusr, American Artists Materials, Kaltan Soundview Press, 85 & Illustrators 29, Madison Sq Press, 87; contribr, NY Insites Guide, Insites Guides, 95. *Dealer:* NY Art World; Portraits Inc 7 W 51st St New York NY 10019; Brazier Fine Art 3401 W Cary St Richmond VA 23221; Keyes Gallery 229 S Market Ave Sprinfield MO 65806. *Mailing Add:* 32 Union Sq E 1213 New York NY 10003

PENCE, JOHN GERALD
DEALER, PATRON
b Ft Wayne, Ind, Feb 8, 1936. *Study:* Wabash Col, BA, 58; Am Univ, MA, 63. *Collection Arranged:* Douglas Fenn Wilson, Worcester Mus, Dartmouth Col, Janus Gallery, Santa Fe, San Francisco Mus, Hibernia Bank, San Francisco & Deloitee, Haskins & Sells, NY; Michael Bergt, Pence Gallery, San Francisco & San Francisco Mus; Frank Mason, Clorox Co & Pence Gallery, San Francisco; Robert Maione, Pence Gallery, San Francisco, Clorox Co, Standard Oil of Calif, Hering & Assoc, Portland & Allen-Pacific Co, San Francisco; Gillian Wiles, Pence Gallery, San Francisco & URS Corp, Dallas; Donald Davis, Cellocon Inc, San Francisco, Deloitee, Haskins, Sells, NY & James Malott Architects; Will Wilson, Buckeye Petroleum, NJ & Butler Inst Am Art; McKenzie Family Found, Conn. *Teaching:* Instr, US Naval Acad, Annapolis, Md. *Mem:* San Francisco Art Dealers Asn (pres, 61-63). *Interests:* American contemporary realists--advance support prior to initial presentations. *Publ:* Auth, Will Wilson, Am Artist Mag, 5/83. *Mailing Add:* Pence Gallery 750 Post St San Francisco CA 94109

PENDERGRAFT, NORMAN ELVEIS
MUSEUM DIRECTOR, HISTORIAN
b Durham, NC, Mar 4, 1934. *Study:* Univ NC, Chapel Hill; Conservatorio di Musica G Rossini, Pesaro, Italy, with Maestra Raggi-Valentini; Ohio Univ, Athens; Mus Mgt Inst, Univ Calif, Berkeley; Nat Endowment Humanities Sem, Rome, Italy. *Pos:* dir art mus, NC Cent Univ, Durham, 76-96, emer; art consult, 96-. *Teaching:* Prof art hist, NC Cent Univ, Durham, 66-96, emer. *Awards:* Outstanding contrib to Art Educ Award, NC Art Educ Asn, 84; Prof Serv Award, NC Mus Coun, 95. *Bibliog:* OM Foushee (auth), Art in North Carolina: Episodes & Developments, Chapel Hill, NC, 72; LM Igoe (auth), 250 yrs of Afro-American Art: An Annotated Bibliography, RR Bowker, 81. *Mem:* Am Asn Mus; Southeastern Mus Coun; Coll Art Asn; Am Asn Univ Prof; NC Mus Coun. *Res:* Italian Renaissance, Afro-American and American art. *Specialty:* Afro-American Art. *Publ:* Auth, Heralds of Life: Artis, Bearden & Burke, 77 & Duncanson: A British American Connection, 84 & Geoffrey Holder: Painter, 86, & Gullah Life Reflections, 88, NC Cent Univ Art Mus; Joy of Living: Romare Beardons Late Work, NC Cent Univ Art Mus, 94; Artistic Legacy: Collection of Art from CIAA schools, Diggs Gallery, Winston-Salem State Univ, NC, 94; A Gift of Art, Herald Sun, Durham, NC, 98. *Mailing Add:* 807 W Trinity Ave Apt 258 Durham NC 27701

PENDERGRASS, CHRISTINE C
CERAMIST, SCULPTOR
b Detroit, Mich, Jan 5, 1952. *Study:* Stanford Univ, BA (studio art), 73. *Work:* State Art Collection, Dept Motor Vehicles, Salem Ore; State Art Collection, Badger Rd Sch & 2 Rivers Sch, Fairbanks, Alaska; Municipal Art Collection, Lynnwood, Wash; Dept Ecology Hq, Lacey, Wash. *Comn:* 4 ceramic wall sculptures, Mid-Columbia Med Ctr, The Dalles, Ore, 93 & 96; 4 ceramic wall sculptures, Mass Gen Hosp, Boston, 94; 2 ceramic wall sculptures, Wells Fargo Bank, Portland, Ore, 95; 3 ceramic wall sculptures, St Charles Med Ctr, Bend, Ore, 95; 2 outdoor artworks, Downtown Eugene Inc, Ore, 2002-2003. *Exhib:* Solo exhibs, Stanford Univ, 92, Reno City Hall Gallery, Nev, 93, Russell Senate Bldg, Washington, DC, 95, Chico Art Ctr, Calif, 96 & Sun Cities Mus Art, Ariz, 97; two-person exhib, Walters Cult Arts Ctr, Hillsboro, Ore, 2008. *Teaching:* Pvt tchr. *Awards:* Grant, Ludwig Vogelstein Found, New York, 84; Artist Award, Earthwatch, Watertown, Mass, 94; Internet Art Connection Award, 94. *Bibliog:* Danielle C Malka (auth), Merged realities-artists & scientists borrow from one another, Ariz Daily Star, 95; Larry Savadove (auth), Function follows form in found show, Sandpaper, Loveladies, NJ, 98; Morley Young (auth), A Sense of Humor, and Beauty, The Ruralite, 2004; Carmen Morgan (auth), An Interview with an Artist, Upwellings, Newport, Ore, 2009. *Media:* Ceramics. *Publ:* Auth, Ceramics Monthly Mag, 86, 90 & 93; Fans-The Bulletin of the Fan Circle Int, London, 90; contribr, Art Calendar-The Bus Mag for Visual Artists, 94; auth, Ceramics in Healthcare, Fine Art Ceramics, Welches, Ore, 2002; contribr, The Hastings Ctr Report, Garrison, NY, 2004; Body of Art, Willoughby & Baltic Fine Arts, Cambridge, Mass, 2006; contribr, The Alchemist, Corvallis, Ore, 2009. *Dealer:* Art Factors 7035 SW Macadam Portland OR. *Mailing Add:* 92130 Sharewater Ln Cheshire OR 97419-9704

PENKOFF, RONALD PETER
EDUCATOR, PAINTER
b Toledo, Ohio, May 18, 1932. *Study:* Bowling Green State Univ, BFA, 54; Ohio State Univ, MA, 56; Stanley William Hayter's Atelier 17, Paris, 65-66; Univ Kans, 80 & 81. *Work:* Libr Cong, Washington; Columbus Gallery Art, Ohio; Munson-Williams-Proctor Inst, Utica, NY; Montclair Mus, NJ; Ball State Art Gallery, Muncie, Ind. *Comn:* Frank Lloyd Wright-Wyoming Valley (paintings), VW Col, 94-98. *Exhib:* Pennell Int Exhib Prints, Libr Cong, Washington, 55-57; Notre Dame Mus, 70; Skylight Gallery, 73; Madison Art Ctr, 75; Alvehjem Mus, 77 & 83; Milwaukee Art Mus, 78; Crossman Gallery, Univ Wis, Whitewater, 90. *Teaching:* Asst prof art, State Univ NY, Oneonta, 56-59; asst prof, Ball State Univ, 59-67; vis prof, Bath Acad Art, Corsham, Eng, summer 66; prof, Univ Wis, Waukesha, 67-87, Richland Ctr, 87-98, chmn, Ctr Syst Art Dept, 70-89 & 95-98, prof emer. *Awards:* Munson-Williams-Proctor Inst Award, Cent NY Artists, 58-59; First Award Painting, Eastern Ind Artists, 64; Nat Endowment Humanities Grant, 78. *Bibliog:* W Fabricki (auth), Prints and drawings of Ronald Penkoff, Quartet, 63; ME Young (auth), Profile, Wis Acad Rev, 69; Donald Key (auth), Color printing is an elusive endeavor, Milwaukee J, 71. *Mem:* Coll Art Asn. *Media:* Intaglio, Painting. *Res:* Visual phenomena. *Interests:* Japanese woodblock; visual cognition. *Publ:* Auth, The eye and the object, Forum, 62; Roots of the Ukiyo-E, 65; Sign, Signal, Symbol, 70; The Japanese Print & the Grounding of Frank Lloyd Wrights' Architecture, 90; The Woodblock Prints of Andrea Rich, 2006. *Dealer:* Red Door Gallery Richland Ctr WI 53581. *Mailing Add:* 420 E Court Richland Center WI 53581

PENN, GELAH
SCULPTOR, INSTALLATION ARTIST
b Beaver Falls, PA, May 11, 1951. *Study:* Brandeis Univ, 69; San Francisco Art Inst, BFA, 73; Studied with Dore Ashton, New School, 90. *Work:* Columbus Mus, Ga; Chase Manhattan Bank, NY; Fox, Rothchild, LLP, Philadelphia, Pa; NV/da Architects, NY. *Exhib:* The Narrow Margin, Rowan Univ Art Gallery, Glassboro, NJ, 2008; Clash By Night, Real Art Ways, Hartford, Conn, 2009; Drawing Itself: A Survey of Contemporary Practices, Brattleboro Mus, Brattleboro, Vt, 2009; Degrees of Density, Columbus Mus, Columbus, Ga, 2010; Nat Acad Mus, NY, 2012. *Pos:* admin assoc, Dia Art Found, 80-82 . *Teaching:* lectr, Lehman Coll, 2007-2008; lectr, Univ Conn, 2010; lectr, SUNY Purchase, 2010; adj lectr, SUNY New Paltz, 2012. *Awards:* MacDowell Colony, 89; Saatchi Online Mag Critics' Award, Saatchi Online Mag, 2006; Sharpe Found Space Program, Marie Walsh Sharpe Found, 2010-11. *Bibliog:* Leigh Anne Miller (auth), Gelah Penn at Kentler, Art in America, 10/2006; Peter Frank (auth), Gelah Penn: Drawinstallations (essay), Rowan Univ, 1/2008; Benjamin Genocchio (auth), Drawings Set Apart in a World of Lines, New York Times, 3/2008; Patricia Rosoff (auth), Gelah Penn: Surface Tensions, Sculpture Mag, 11/2010. *Media:* Installation

PENNEY, CHARLES RAND
COLLECTOR, PATRON
b Buffalo, NY, July 26, 1923. *Study:* Yale Univ, BA; Univ Va, LLB & JD. *Hon Degrees:* Hon Dr Fine Arts, SUNY, Buffalo, 95; Hon Dr Fine Arts, Niagra Univ, 2006. *Collection Arranged:* Prints from the Charles Rand Penney Found, traveling NY & Tex, 64-75; Selections from the Charles R Penney Collection, Lakeview Gallery, NY, 70; Prints From the Charles Rand Penney Foundation, Niagara Co Community Coll Mus, 71 & 77; Staffordshire Pottery Portrait Figures, Niagara Co Hist Soc, 72; 44 Charles Burchfield Drawings & two paintings, Charles Burchfield Ctr, Buffalo, 73; Decade, Graphics in the Sixties, 74; NY State Photographers, 74; Victorian Staffordshire Figurines, Carborundum Mus of Ceramics, Niagara Falls, 74 & Columbus Gallery of Fine Arts, Ohio, 76; Charles Burchfield: The Charles Rand Penney Collection, traveling throughout US, 78-81; The Graphic Art of Emil Ganso, Univ Iowa Mus Art, 79; The Charles Rand Penney Collection: Twentieth Century Art, traveling throughout US, 83-88; The Charles Rand Penney Collection of Western NY Art, Burchfield Art Ctr, 92-93; The Charles Rand Penney Collection of Works by Charles E Burchfield, Burchfield-Penney Art Ctr, Buffalo State Coll, 94; The Charles Rand Penney Collection of Works by Roycroft Artists, Burchfield-Penney Art Ctr, Buffalo State Coll, 94; The Charles Rand Penney Craft Art Collection, Burchfield-Penney Art Ctr, Buffalo State Coll, 94; Selections from the Charles Rand Penney Collection of Prints of Niagara Falls, Mediatheque Municipale Jean Levy, Lille, France, 2002; Selections from the Charles Rand Penney Collection of Prints of Niagara Falls, Centre Culturel Mousckonnois Mouscron, Belgium, 2003. *Awards:* Distinguished Service to Culture Award, State Univ NY Coll Potsdam, 83; President's Distinguished Serv Award, Buffalo State Coll, 91. *Mem:* Am Ceramic Circle; hon life mem Rochester Art Club; hon trustee Buffalo Soc Artist; and many others. *Collection:* International contemporary art; works of Charles E Burchfield; Western New York artists; Spanish-American Santos and Retablos; Victorian Staffordshire pottery portrait figures; American textiles; American antique pressed glass; international primitive art; US World's Fairs & Expositions; Tiffany Collection; Mr Planter's Peanut Collection; African Art Collection; New Guinea Art Collection; Western New York Art Collection; Haitian Art Collection; Eskimo Art Collection. *Mailing Add:* c/o Burchfield-Penney Art Ctr Buffalo State Col 1300 Elmwood Ave Buffalo NY 14222

PENNEY, JACQUELINE
PAINTER, INSTRUCTOR
b Roslyn, NY, Mar 26, 1930. *Study:* Phoenix Sch Design, New York, 48; Black Mountain Col, 49; Inst Design, Chicago, 50, with Tom Hill, Carl Molno, Charles Reid, Frank Webb, Robert E Wood & Christopher Schink. *Work:* Port Authority, World Trade Ctr, NY; Stony Brook Sch, NY; Eastern Long Island Hosp, Greenport, NY; Unitarian Universalist Church, Oak Park, Ill; Jane Voorhees Zimmerli Art Mus, Rutgers State Univ, NJ. *Comn:* Cutchogue Pub Libr, Cutchogue, NY. *Exhib:* White Containers, Guild Hall Mus, East Hampton, NY, 86; What Comes After Winter, Audubon Artists Juried Exhib, 86; Nat Asn Women Artists Traveling Show, 88, 89 & 96; Monhegan Backyard, San Diego WC So Int, 89; Dancing in the Light, Salmagundi Club, NY, 92. *Teaching:* Art workshops acrylic & watercolor, 77-. *Awards:* ER Langer-Seligson Mem Award, Nat Asn Women Artists, 89; First Prize Best Landscape, Artist's Mag; Landscape Award, Mid-Atlantic Regional Watercolor Exhib, 90; William Meyerowitz Mem Prize, Nat Asn Women Artists, 86. *Bibliog:* Paul Demery (auth), An artist dreams in Cutchogue, Long Island Traveler-Watchman, 3/17/83; Marion Wolberg Weiss (auth), Downtown Cutchogue (cover), Honoring the Artist of East End, 10/9/92; 1998 National Competition, Artist's Mag, 12/98; Linda S. Price (Auth), Get the most out of painting abroad, Watercolor Mag, 99; M Stephen Doherty, Special report: 16 artists that paint together in Colorado, spring, 2000. *Mem:* Artist Equity New York; Nat Asn Women Artists; Salmagundi Club, New York, 92; Nat Asn Am Penwomen, 92. *Media:* Acrylic, Watercolor. *Specialty:* teaching and display of my art work. *Interests:* Computer graphics, photography. *Publ:* Auth, Painting Watercolor Greeting Cards, North Light Books; A painting in progress--from far to near, Palette Talk Mag, 92; Still lifes that wont stay still, Am Hist Mag, 12/92; Discover the Joy of Painting with Acrylics, North Light Books, 2001; co-auth, The Artful Journal, A Spiritual Quest, 2002; auth, Painting Charming Seaside Scenes, 2008; Me Painting Me a Memoir, 2012. *Dealer:* Penney Art Gallery & Studio 270 North St Cutchogue, NY 11935. *Mailing Add:* 270 North St Cutchogue NY 11935

PENNINGTON, CLAUDIA
MUSEUM DIRECTOR
Pos: Dir, Key West Mus Art & Hist, Fla, 2000-. *Mailing Add:* Key West Mus Art & Hist 281 Front St Key West FL 33040

PENNINGTON, ESTILL CURTIS
HISTORIAN, CURATOR
b Paris, Ky, Oct 3, 1950. *Study:* Univ Ky, BA, 72; Univ Ga; George Washington Univ. *Collection Arranged:* A New Quarter: Contemporary New Orleans Artists, 83; Birney Imes III: An exhib of photographs, 84; Storytime: Art as Episode, 85; William Edward West (1788-1857): Kentucky Painter (auth, catalog), 85; Reveries & Mississippi Memories, 86; A Southern Collection, Morris Mus Art, 92, Will Henry Stevens, An Eye Transformed, A Hand Transforming, 93, Gracious Plenty, Am Still Life Art in Southern Collections, 95, Echoes and Late Shadows, The Larger World of Southern Impressionism, 96, Frontier Sublime: Alaskan Art from the Juneau Empire Collection, 97. *Pos:* Guest cur & asst registrar, Nat Portrait Gallery, 77-78; art historian, Archives Am Art, 78-83; mus dir, Lauren Rogers Mus Art, Laurel, Miss, 83-87; cur, Ogden Collection, New Orleans, 87-88 & Morris Mus Art, 89-. *Awards:* Fel Royal Soc Arts. *Mem:* Miss Inst Arts & Letts (pres, 85-); Am Asn Mus; Victorian Soc Am. *Res:* American painting and portraiture. *Publ:* Auth, Joseph Cornell: Dimestore Connoisseur, 83 & Painting Lord Byron: An Account of William Edward West, 84, Archives Am Art J; The Climate of Taste in the Old South, Southern Quart, 85; collabr, The South on Paper: Line, Color & Light, Robert Hicklin, Inc, 85

PENNINGTON, JULIANA
DESIGNER, GRAPHIC ARTIST
Study: Foothill Coll, AA (fine arts), 71; Humboldt State Univ, BA (fine arts, printmaking), 74; CCA Calif Coll Arts & Crafts, 86-87; paper and bk intensive with Nance O'Banion, 97; paper, print, and book intensive, Fabriano, Italy, 2013, with Lynn Sures, San Francisco Ctr for Book, 2000-15. *Work:* Randall Mus & City San Francisco, Calif. *Comn:* Beyond Recycling, Norcal Waste Systems Inc, San Francisco, Calif, 95; cast paper sculpture, San Francisco Recycling Prog, Calif, 95. *Exhib:* Palo Alto Cult Ctr, Calif, 94; Reduce, Reuse, Recycle, San Francisco Int Airport, Calif, 95; Recycling: Preserving Natural Resources and Building a Sustainable Society, San Francisco War Mem Bldg & One Market Plaza, San Francisco, Calif, 95-97; Friends of Dard Hunter Paper Conf, Sonoma, Calif, 98, Chicago, Ill, 99; Wayne Thieband, Legion of Hon, 2000; Art Deco 1910-1939, 2003; Monet in Normandy, 2006; Annie Leibovitz, 2007; Chihuly at the de Young, 2008; Houghton Hall, 2014; Masterpieces from the Mus d'Orsay, deYoung, 2010-2011; Masters of Venice, 2011-2012; The Cult of Beauty, Legion of Hon, 2012; Man Ray I Lee Miller, 2012; Nureyev: A Life in Dance, deYoung, 2012; Girl with a Pearl Earring: Dutch Paintings from the Mauritshuls, deYoung, 2013. *Collection Arranged:* Guest cur, Recology Artist-in-Residence prog, San Francisco, Calif, 94-97; San Francisco Int Airport Comn, Calif, 95; Earth Options 90, Fort Mason Ctr, San Francisco, Calif, 90. *Pos:*

Graphic Designer, de Young Mus/Fine Arts Mus San Francisco, 97-99, Senior Graphic Designer, 2000-2007; Lead Exhib Graphic Designer, 2007-2015. *Teaching:* Instr papermaking & book arts, Randall Mus, San Francisco, Calif, 93-2001; instr, papermaking & printmaking, Kala Inst, Berkeley, Calif, 96-98; guest lectr, Univ Calif, Berkeley Coll Environ Design, 2000; artist bk studio, Legion of Honor Mus, 2001; instr, art, papermaking, Waldorf High Sch, San Francisco, Calif, 2004-05; guest lectr papermaking, Acad Art Univ, 2004-2007. *Awards:* Design Award, Am Planning Asn, Planning & Law Div, Logo Design Competition, 88; Nat Communs Merit Award, Am Soc Landscape Architects, Ann Awards, 97; Am Planning Asn Nat Pub Edn Award, 98; Design award, Pulp Fashion Inst, 2011. *Bibliog:* Communications, Landscape Archit Mag, 11/90 & 11/97; Robert Reed (auth), Recycling: Pictures & story, Recycle Today, 10/96; Marcia McNally (auth), Activist of the month, Urban Ecology, 11/96. *Mem:* Am Inst Graphic Arts (environ comt, 94-97, mem comt, 2011-); Textile Arts Council, Fine Arts Mus San Francisco, (mem bd, 2015); Friends Dard Hunter Papermaking Mus. *Media:* Papermaking, Printmaking; Installations. *Publ:* Auth, About Handmade Paper, Randall Mus, 94; designer, Palo Alto Comprehensive Plan, 1996-2010; Blueprint for a Sustainable Bay Area, Urban Ecology, 96; exhib pub, Fine Arts Mus San Francisco, 97-2015; San Francisco Opera Guild 75th Anniversary Commerative, 2014. *Mailing Add:* 546 Shotwell St San Francisco CA 94110

PENNINGTON, SALLY
PAINTER
b Seattle, Wash, 1953. *Study:* Mills Col, MFA (painting), 83. *Exhib:* Pro Arts Ann, Oakland, 85; Introduction Show, Triangle Gallery, San Francisco, 86; Connected by Nature, Pro Arts, Oakland, 86; Gallery Artists, Triangle Gallery, 86; Six East Bay Artists, Mills Coll Art Gallery, Oakland, Calif, 89. *Teaching:* Instr, Diablo Valley Col, Calif, 83-87; Edmonds Community Col, Wash, currently. *Awards:* Catherine Morgan Trefethen Fel in Art, 82; Visual Artists Fel Grant, Nat Endowment Arts, 87. *Dealer:* Triangle Gallery 95 Minna St San Francisco CA 94105. *Mailing Add:* 23216 SE 31st St Issaquah WA 98029

PENNY, DONALD CHARLES
CRAFTSMAN, SCULPTOR
b Atlanta, Ga, Oct 5, 1935. *Study:* Ga Tech, 57-58; Ga State Univ, with Joe Perrin & Joe Almyda, BBA, 61; Fla State Univ, with Karl Zerbe & Ralph Hurst, MS, 63; Penland Sch, studies with Cynthia Bringle, 66. *Work:* Metrop Mus Art, Miami; Ahmadu Bello Univ, Zaria, Nigeria; Macon Mus Arts & Sci, Ga; Valdosta State Univ, Ga; Renwick Gallery, Washington. *Comn:* Ga Coun Arts & Humanities, Valdosta, 81-82; Emory Univ, Atlanta, Ga, 81-82; and others. *Exhib:* Mint Mus Art, Charlotte, NC, 67, 69 & 70; Smithsonian Inst, Washington, 70; solo exhibs, Metrop Mus & Art Ctr, Miami, Fla, 70, Brenau Coll, Gainesville, Ga, 89, Fla Landscape, Loundes/Valdosta (Ga) Arts Coun, 97; Greenville Co Mus, SC, 74; Furman Univ-R J Reynolds, Winston-Salem, NC, 77; Mus Arts & Sci, Macon, Ga, 82 & 89; Fla Sch Art, 89; Broward Community Coll, 92; Lowndes/Valdosta Arts Coun, 2000; Mus Contemp Art, Atlanta, 2003; BascomLouiseGallery, Highlands, NC, 2003; Remains to be Seen, Bluespiral, Ashville NC, 2011. *Pos:* owner, Little River Studio. *Teaching:* Instr, Palm Beach Jr Coll, West Palm Beach, Fla, 61-63; prof art, Valdosta State Univ, Ga, 63-91; sr lectr, Ahmadu Bello Univ, Zaria, Nigeria, 72-73; prof emer art, Valdosta State Univ, Ga, 92. *Awards:* Best Show, Columbus Mus Arts & Crafts, Ga, 69; First Prize, St Augustine Festival, Fla, 70; Purchase Award, High Mus Art, Atlanta, Ga, 71; Purchase Award, Macon Mus Arts & Sci; Award Sculpture, Gala 2000, Gainesville, Ga. *Bibliog:* Barclay F Gordon (auth), Record houses: 1978, Archit Record Mag, 5/78; The connection, Atlanta Impressions Mag, summer 81; Alexandra Mettler (auth), Emory's Cannon Chapel: Master touches, Atlanta Mag, 12/81; American Craft, June/July, 2002; Valdosta Daily Times, June 9, 2002; 500 Vases, Lark Books, Oct 2010. *Mem:* Am Crafts Coun (trustee emer); Ga Designer Craftsman (vpres, 68); Nat Coun Educ Ceramic Arts; Lowndes/Valdosta Arts Comn; Southern Art League. *Media:* Clay. *Publ:* Auth, Nigerian Crafts, Nat Coun Educ Communication Arts. *Dealer:* Signature Shop Atlanta GA; Classic Art & Frame Valdosta GA; Blue Spiral 1 Asheville NC. *Mailing Add:* Little River Studio 8601 Morven Rd Hahira GA 31632

PENSATO, JOYCE
PAINTER
b Brooklyn, NY. *Study:* NY Studio Sch. *Work:* City of Paris, France; FRAC des Pays de la Loire, France; Hammer Mus, Los Angeles, Calif; Mus Modern Art, NY; Mus Modern Art, Calif; Speed Mus Art, Louisville, KY; St Louis Art Mus, St Louis, MO. *Comn:* Cooper Sq Hotel Public Art Wall, comn by Art Prodn Fund, 2009. *Exhib:* Solo exhibs, Hotel Bouhier de Savigny, Fondation Art & Societe, Dijon, Fr, 1994, Galerie Domi Nostrae, Lyon, France, 1994, Galerie Anne de Villepoix, Paris, France, 1994, 1996, 1998, 2000, 2010, Max Protetch Gallery, NY, 1995, Drawings, 1996, DiverseWorks, Houston, Tex, 1997, Windows Gallery, Brussels, Belgium, 2001, Elga Wimmer Gallery, NY, 2003, Isabella Brancolini Contemporary Art, Florence, Italy, 2004, This Must Be the Place, Parker's Box, NY, The Eraser, Friedrich Petzel Gallery, NY, 2007, Friedrich Petzel Gallery, 2008, Batman Returns, 2012, Capitain Petzel, Berlin, Ger, 2009, Hotel, London, 2011, You Gotta Do What You Gotta Do, Corbett vs Dempsey, Chgo, Batman Santa Monica Mus Art, 2013; Group exhibs, Selected Drawings, Jersey City Mus, Jersey City, NJ, 20th Anniv Retrospective Exhib, NY Studio Sch Gallery, NY, 1985, The Potent Image, The Morris Mus, Morristown, NJ, 1986, Drawn Out, Kansas City Art Inst, Kansas City, MO, 1987, Contemporary Syntax: Surface and Atmosphere, Robeson Ctr Gallery, Rutgers Univ, Newark, NJ, 1988, Re: Framing Cartoons, Loughelton Gallery, NY, 1990, Steve Wolfe: Painting and Sculpture, John Berggruen Gallery, San Francisco, Calif, 1992, A Discourse on the Emotions, Galerie Volker Diehl, Berlin, Ger, 1993, Redefining the Pop Icon in the Nineties, Pamela Auchincloss Gallery, NY, 1994, Raw, Postmasters Gallery, NY, 1995, On/In/Through, Morris Healy, NY, 1996, N'Ayons Rien Si Souvent En La Tete Que La Mort, Galerie Domi Nostrae, Lyon, France, 1997, Presumed Innocence, Anderson Gallery, Va Commonwealth Univ, Richmond, Va, 1998, Through the Looking Glass: Visions of Childhood, Newhouse Ctr Contemporary Art, 1999, Triangle, Marseille, France, 2000, Parker's Box, NY, 2002, 2005, 2006, 2010, Superbia, Coultry Gardens, Ballyum, Ireland, 2003, Mickey dans tous ces etats, Hotel Dassault-Artcurial, Paris, France, 2006, Alice Mahler: Drawings and an Object/Joyce Pensato: Recent Drawings, Schmidt Contemporary Art, MO, 2007, Black, G Fine Art, Wash DC, 2008, DARE, Galerie Conradi, Hamberg, Ger, 2009, In There, Out Here, Leo Koenig, Inc, NY, 2010, Focus Lodz Biennale, Poland, 2010, Dirt Dont Hurt, Jolie Laide Gallery, Phila, 2011, December, Mitchell-Innes & Nash, NY, 2011, Renwick Gallery, NY, 2012, Upsodown, New Art Ctr, Mass, 2013. *Awards:* Mid-Atlantic Arts Found, 1992; NY Found Arts, 1995; Guggenheim fellow, 1996; Pollock-Krasner Found award, 1997; Anonymous Was a Woman award, 2010; Award of Merit Medal of Painting, American Acad of Arts & Letts, 2012; Robert De Niro Sr prize, 2013. *Mailing Add:* Petzel Gallery 456 W 18th St New York NY 10011

PENTAK, STEPHEN
PAINTER, EDUCATOR
b Denver, Colo, Aug 24, 1951. *Study:* Union Col, NY, BA, 73; Tyler Sch Art, MFA, 78. *Work:* Schenectady Mus, NY; Free Libr Philadelphia; Columbus Mus Art; Wexner Ctr, Columbus. *Comn:* State Auto Insurance, Columbus; Thomson Electronics, Columbus. *Exhib:* Selected Works, Sutton Place, London, 82 & Gallerie D'Arte Mod Ca'Pesaro, Venice, 83; solo exhib, Jan Cicero Gallery, Chicago, 83 & Noel Butcher Gallery, Philadelphia, 83, Univ Akron, 87, J Rosenthal, Chicago, Wexner Ctr Arts, Columbus, 92, Toni Birckhead, Cincinnati, Linda Schwartz, Lexington, Ky, 97, Bonfoey, Cleveland, Ohio, 98 & Marie Park, Dallas, Tex, 98; Landscape Anthology, Grace Borgenicht Gallery, NY, 88; Ohio Selections IX, Cleveland Ctr Contemp Arts, 90; Rivers Revisited, Linda Schwartz Gallery, Cincinnati, 99; Common Ground, The Artist House, Jerusalem, Israel, 2000; Gibsone Jessop, Toronto, 2008; Keny Galleries, Columos, US, 2008; Kathryn Markel, New York, NY, 2009. *Collection Arranged:* Four Landscape Painters, Concept Art, Pittsburgh, 97; Back to Reality, Riffe Gallery, Columbus, 98. *Teaching:* Vis asst prof, Art Inst Chicago, 81-82; prof, Ohio State Univ, Columbus, 83-2006, prof emer. *Awards:* Ohio Arts Coun Individual Artists Fel, 85, 89 & 97. *Bibliog:* Lorraine Padden (auth), Columbus Art, 1/92; K Rouda (auth), Article, Columbus Monthly, 9/94; Sally Vallongo (auth), rev, ARTnews, 3/95. *Media:* Oil on Panel & Paper. *Publ:* Auth, Gregory Amenoff's new pictures, 81 & Daryl Hughto, 81, Arts Mag; Color Basics with Richard Roth, Wadsworth/Lengage, 2002; coauth, Design Basics (with David Lauer), Wadsworth/Lengage, 2008. *Dealer:* Concept Art Pittsburgh; Kathryn Markey Fine Arts NY; Susan Street Fine Art San Diego; Marie Park Dallas. *Mailing Add:* 1242 Garfield Rd Stephentown NY 12168

PENTELOVITCH, ROBERT ALAN
PAINTER
b Minneapolis, Minn, Oct 13, 1955. *Study:* Minneapolis Coll Art & Design, BFA, 78; San Francisco Art Inst, MFA, 80. *Work:* Walker Art Ctr & Regis Corp, Minneapolis, Minn; Chicago Inst Arts; Martin Marietta Corp, NY; Maslon, Kaplan, Borman & Brand, Minneapolis; Robin Farkas, NY; Gen Electric Group, NY. *Exhib:* Solo exhibs, Trumbull Art Guild, Warren, Ohio, 85 & Arras Gallery, NY, 86; Zumbach Gallery, NY, 88 & 89; Greenleaf Gallery, Nags Head, NC, 92-94; Animal Imagery, Juried, Madison, NJ, 92; Alaska Mus Hist & Art, 93; Nabisco Gallery, NJ, 2002; Cooper Classics Collection, NY, 2003; and others. *Awards:* First Place, Minneapolis Coll Art & Design, 77; Award of Excellence, Concours Auto Art, Oakland Univ, Troy, Mich, 85; Fel, John Simon Guggenheim Mem Found, 91. *Mem:* Artists Equity Asn. *Media:* Acrylic. *Publ:* Contribr, Edsel Owners News, 79 & 80, & Automotive Showcase, 1/82. *Dealer:* Cooper Classic Collections 137 Perry St New York NY. *Mailing Add:* 340 W 55th St Apt 2D New York NY 10019

PENTZ, DONALD ROBERT
PAINTER, PRINTMAKER
b Bridgewater, NS, Sept 18, 1940. *Study:* Mt Allison Univ, Sackville, NB, BFA, 66; Univ Regina, Sask, MFA, 79; Banff Sch Fine Art, Alta, 79. *Work:* Art Gallery NS, NS Art Bank, Halifax; Can Coun Art Bank, Ottawa; Imperial Oil, Calgary, Alta; Osaka Found Culture, Japan. *Comn:* Selected Birds, Parks Can, Newfoundland, 82. *Exhib:* Young Artists of the Prairies, Walter Phillips Gallery, Banff, Alta, 79; Force Field Series, Art Gallery NS, Halifax, 79; RCA Centennial Exhib, CNE Bldg, Toronto, 80; Emerging Canadian Artists, Muttart Gallery, Calgary, Alta, 81; Atlantic Artists, Shell Can, Calgary, Alta, 81; Studio 21, Halifax, 91; Kejimkujik Nat Park, NS, 99; Southern Vt Arts Ctr, Manchester, Vt, 2000; Trinity Galleries, NB, 2001. *Teaching:* Instr art, privately, 70-2002, Univ Regina, Sask, 77-79 & Mt St Vincent Univ, Halifax, NS, 80. *Awards:* Prof Artists Award, 75 & NS Talent Trust, 78, NS Govt; Can Coun Grant, 80; NS Arts Grant, 2002. *Bibliog:* Janet Smith (producer), D Pentz--Wildlife Artist, CBC-TV, 83; Arts Atlantic, 88; # 37 Arts Atlantic, 90; # 42 Arts Atlantic, 92; NS Visual Arts News, 2000. *Mem:* Visual Arts NS; Royal Can Acad; Can Soc Painters in Watercolour. *Media:* Acrylic, Oil, Watercolor. *Specialty:* Trinity Gallery,. NB: Realism; Fog Forest Gallery, NB: Realism; Studio 21, NS: Abstract. *Dealer:* Studio 21 5435 Spring Garden Rd Halifax NS Can B3J 1G1; Trinity Galleries 128 German St St John NB Can E2L 2E7; Fog Forest Gallery 14 Bridge St Sackville NB Can E4L 3N5; Peer Gallery 167 Lincoln St Lunenburg NS Can. *Mailing Add:* RR1 Pleasantville Lunenburg NS B0R 1G0 Canada

PEPE, SHEILA
TEXTILE ARTIST, EDUCATOR
b Morristown, NJ. *Study:* Albertus Magnus Coll, New Haven, BA, 1981; Mass Coll Art, BFA, 1983; Sch Mus Fine Arts Tufts Univ, Boston, MFA, 1995. *Work:* Jersey City Mus; Rose Art Mus, Brandeis Univ, Waltham; Simmonds Coll, Boston; Fogg Art Mus, Harvard Univ; List Visual Art Ctr, MIT, Cambridge. *Exhib:* Solo exhibs, Trustman Gallery, Simmons Coll, 1996, Judy Ann Goldman Fine Art, Boston, 1997, Boston Ctr for Arts, 1999, Zikha Gallery, Wesleyan Univ, 2000, Weatherspoon Art Mus, Univ NC, 2002, Visual Arts Ctr Richmond, Va, 2003, Palm Beach Inst Contemp Art, 2004, Univ Calif, Santa Cruz, 2005; Fuzzy Logic, Inst Contemp Art, Boston, 1996; Works on Paper, Weatherspoon Art Gallery, Greebsboro, 1998; Greater New York, PS1 Contemp Art Gallery, Long Island City, 2000; The Photogenic:

Photography Through Its Metaphors in Contemporary Art, Inst Contemp Art, Philadelphia, 2002; Decelerate, Kempner Mus Contemp Art, Kans, 2005; The Collection, Fog Art Mus, Cambridge, 2006. *Pos:* Asst chmn fine arts, Pratt Inst, Brooklyn, NY, currently. *Awards:* Nat Ann Award, Provincetown Art Asn, 1997; Louis Comfort Tiffany Found Grant, 2001; Profl Develop Grant, RI Sch Design, 2004; Joan Mitchell Found Grant, 2010. *Mailing Add:* Pratt Inst 200 Willoughby Ave Brooklyn NY 11205

PEPICH, BRUCE WALTER W
MUSEUM DIRECTOR, CURATOR
b Elmhurst, Ill, June 5, 1952. *Study:* Northern Ill Univ, De Kalb, BA (art hist), 74. *Collection Arranged:* Lee Weiss: 25 Years in Wisconsin, 87 & Wis Craft Masters, 88; For the Birds: Artists Examine Aviary Abodes, 90; Artists and the Am Yard: Lawn Gnomes, Pink Flamingoes and Bathtub Grottos, 91; Craft: The Discerning Eye, 91; Walter Samuel Hamady: Handmade Books, Collages and Sculptures, 91; Watercolor Wisconsin: Celebrating 25 Years, 91; Just Plane Screwy: Metaphysical and Metaphorical Tools by Artists, 92; Pets: Artists and an Am Obsession, 93, From Our Vault to the Studio: Am Crafts Artists and the Collection, 93, JoAnna Poehlmann: Books, Sculptures and Works on Paper, 1964-1994, 94, The Aesthetics of Athletics: Artists View Games, Sports and Exercise, 94, The Object Redux: Re-Used, Re-Newed and Re-Invested, 94, Wustum Mus Fine Arts, Racine, Wis. *Pos:* Cur, Univ Art Collection, Northern Ill Univ, 71-74; writer & contribr, Art Gallery Int Mag, 88-90; dir, Racine Art Museum, 2003-. *Awards:* Endowment Arts Avan Program, Overview Panel, 6/92. *Mem:* Am Craft Coun; Am Asn Mus; Contemp Glass Ctr Am, Millville, NJ (bd trustees, 94-); Textile Art Ctr, Chicago, Ill (adv bd, 94-); Friends Fiber Int (prof adv comt, 93-). *Publ:* Auth, Chicago New Art Forms Brings Spotlight to Craft, The Crafts Report, 12/90; Walter Hamady, with essays by Buzz Spector & Tom Olson, Wustum Mus, 3/91; The Art of Lee Weiss: Poetry in the Natural Landscape, Wis Acad Review, Fall, 94. *Mailing Add:* Racine Art Museum PO Box 187 Racine WI 53401

PEPPARD, BLAYLOCK A
PAINTER
b Burlington, Vt, Dec 28, 1952. *Study:* St Lawrence Univ, Canton, NY, BA (art honors), 75; Maryland Inst Coll Art, Hoffberger Sch Painting, study with Grace Hardigan, Sal Scarpitta & Robert Moskowicz, MFA, 79. *Work:* Lewis & Clarke Mus, Portland, Ore; St Lawrence Univ, Canton, NY; Hagstromer Col, Stockholm, Sweden; Best Products, Ashland, Va; Berger Col, NY. *Exhib:* Pace Gallery, Philadelphia, 80; Art Fair, Stockholm Mus, Sweden, 81; solo shows, Concord Gallery, NY, 82 & 83; Everson Biennial, Everson Mus, Syracuse, NY, 84; Art Quest, Sharadin Mus, Kutztown Univ, Pa, 86; Proj Studio Installation, PS1, Long Island City, NY, 86; St Lawrence Univ, 98. *Pos:* Tech Etching, Parker Etching Studio, New York, 83-84; installation technician, Queens Mus, Flushing, NY, 83-85; Exhibs coordr, Jewish Mus, New York, 85-86. *Teaching:* Painting instr, New York Univ, 82-83; vis lectr, St Lawrence Univ, Canton, NY, 83. *Awards:* Painting Fel, Nat Endowment Arts, 90. *Bibliog:* Sylvia Falcon (auth), Blaylock Pepperd, Arts Mag, 83; Katherine Howe (auth), Blaylock Pepperd, Images & Issues Mag, 83; Art Quest '86, Film/Artquest/Slabey, 86. *Mem:* Coll Art Asn; Orgn Independent Artists. *Media:* Oil, Beeswax

PEPPARD, JACQUELINE JEAN
PAINTER, INSTRUCTOR
b Calif, Feb, 12, 1954. *Study:* Univ Colo, studied fine art, 76-78; Colo Inst Art, AA, 81; studied with Frank Web, 82. *Work:* Telluride Coun Arts & Humanities Gallery, Bank Telluride & Mountain Village Metro Dist Offices, Telluride, Colo. *Comn:* Posters, Telluride Jazz Festival, Telluride, Colo, 87 & 88; poster, San Miguel River Coalition, Telluride, Colo, 94. *Exhib:* Watercolor West 20th Ann, Riverside Art Mus, Riverside, Calif, 88; 89th Ann Watercolor Exhib, Nat Arts Club, NY, 88; Watercolor West 21st Ann, San Bernardino Co Mus, Redlands, Calif, 89; Western Fedn Watercolor Soc 15th Ann, El Cajon Arts Ctr, El Cajon, Calif, 90; Colo Watercolor Soc State Exhib, Denver Hist Mus, 94. *Teaching:* Teacher watercolor landscape, AHA Sch Art, Telluride, Colo, 94-. *Awards:* Brush & Palette Club First Place Watercolor Landscapes, 39th Ann Nat Exhib, 86; Grant, Telluride Coun Arts & Humanities, 89; Second Place, NMex Watercolor Soc Nat, 90. *Bibliog:* Dinah B Witchel (auth), Colors of the Southwest, Snow Country Mag, 1/90; Art Goodtimes (auth), For art's sake, Telluride Mag, winter 90; M Stephen Doherty (auth), 5 ways to strengthen your landscapes, Watercolor 91/Am Artist Mag, spring 91. *Mem:* Signature mem Watercolor West; signature mem Nat Watercolor Soc. *Media:* Transparent Watercolor on Paper. *Publ:* Auth, True tones/Jacqueline Peppard colors the world her way, Southwest Art Mag, 8/94; contribr, Splash III/105 of America's Best Contemporary Watercolorists; auth, A Place of a Different Color, Watercolor Magic Mag, winter 98. *Dealer:* Antonia Clark Toh-Atin Gallery 145 W 9th St Durango CO 81301

PEPPER, BEVERLY
SCULPTOR, PAINTER
b Brooklyn, NY, Dec 20, 1922. *Study:* Pratt Inst; Art Students League; Studied with Fernand Leger & Andre L'hote. *Hon Degrees:* Pratt Inst, D (fine arts), 82; Md Inst, D (fine arts), 83. *Work:* Albright-Knox Art Gallery, Buffalo, NY; Mass Inst Technol, Boston; Fogg Art Mus, Cambridge, Mass; Walker Art Ctr, Minneapolis; Metrop Mus Art, NY; Whitney Mus Am Art, NY. *Comn:* Jerusalem Ritual sculptures, Jerusalem Found, Israel, 94; Todi columns, Venice, Italy, 95; Sentinels of Justice columns, Kansas City Fed Bldg, Mo, 97; Sacramento Stele sculptures, Calif Environ Protection Agency, Sacramento, 2000; Split Ritual, Nat Arboretum Friendship Garden, Washington, 1992; Panel Screen, Societe des Amis du National d'Art Moderne, Centre Georges Pompadou, 1992; Palingenesis, Credit Suisse, Zurich, Switzerland, 1992-94; Split Ritual II, Grounds for Sculpture, Hamilton, NJ, 96; Manhattan Sentinels, Federal Plaza, NY, 93-95; New Central Libr Project, Minneapolis,. *Exhib:* San Francisco Mus Mod Art, 76; Seattle Mus Contemp Art, 77; Earthworks & Land Reclamation, Seattle Mus, 79; Nat Collection Arts, Smithsonian Inst, Washington, DC, 80; Laumeier Int Sculpture Park, St Louis, 82; solo exhibs, Charles Cowles Gallery, NY, 90, 94, 97 & 98, Metrop Mus Art, NY, 91, Contemp Sculpture Center, Japan, 91; Cleopatra's Wedge, Battery Park, Pub Art Fund, NY, 93; Ternana Altar II, White House Exhib II, Washington, DC, 95; Teatro Celle in Context, Pistoia, Italy, 98; Retrospective, Albright-Knox Art Gallery, Buffalo, NY, 1970, Brooklyn Mus, NY, 1987, Ctr for Fine Arts, Miami, Fla, 1987, Forte Belvedere, Firenza, Italy, 1998, Palais Royal, Paris, France, 99, Marlborough Gallery, NY, 99, 2001, 03, Casal Solleric, Majorca, Spain, 2004. *Pos:* Artist-in-residence, Southeastern Ctr Contemp Arts, 81, Am Acad, Rome, 86 & Sante Fe Inst Fine Arts, 91, 93 & 94. *Awards:* Nat Endowment Arts Grant, 75 & 79; Hon Award, Nat Women's Caucus, Queens Mus Art, 94; Alexander Calder Prize, 99; Allied Arts and Craftsmanship Award, Am Inst Architects, 99; Preparatory Vision award, Xavier Col, 1999; Legends award in Sculpture, Pratt Institute, 2003. *Bibliog:* Vittorio Armentano (auth), B P Making Sculpture (film), G Ungaretti, narrator, 70; Amphisculpture (film), Barbara Rose & Beverly Pepper, narrators, 77; Rosalind Krauss (auth), Beverly Pepper-Sculpture in Place, Abbeville Press, 86; Suzaan Boettger (auth), Endless columns: the quest for infinite extension, Sculpture, 1-2/94; William Zimmer (auth), Sculptures and abstract expressionist prints in close harmony, NY Times, 4/3/94; Robert Hobbs (auth), Beverly Pepper: In the Querenia, Sculpture, Nov-Dec, 1994; Abby Remer (auth), Pioneering Spirits, The Lives and Times of Remarkable Women Artists in Western History, Davis Publs, 97; Barbara Rose (auth), Beverly Pepper: Three Site-Specific Sculptures, Spacemaker Press, 98; Tim Engle (auth), Sky high, Kansas City Star, 9/20/98; Anne Barclaw Morgan (auth), Memory, Monuments, Mystery and Iron: An Interview with Beverly Pepper, Sculpture, 4/98; Robert Hobbs (auth), Beverly Pepper at the Fattoria di Celle, Gori Collection, Societa Editrice Umberto Allemandi & Co, Italy, 98; Carlo Bertelli (auth), Beverly Pepper at Forte Belvedere, Trent Anni Di Scultura, Electa, Milano, 98; Maria Lluisa Borras (auth), Beverly Pepper: Una Poetica de L'Espai, Ajuntament de Palma, Casal Solleric, Spain, 2004. *Media:* Cast Iron, Earthwork, Stone, Bronze. *Specialty:* Sculptue. *Publ:* Art Fundamentals: Theory and Practice, McGraw Hill Higher Education, New York, 2002; Launching the Imagination: A Comprehensive Guide to Basic Design, McGraw Hill Higher Education, New York, 2002; Sculpture in Place, Western Wash Univ, Bellingham, 2002. *Dealer:* Marlborough Gallery 40 W 57th St New York NY 10011. *Mailing Add:* Marborough Gallery 40 W 57th St New York NY 10011

PERCY, ANN BUCHANAN
CURATOR, HISTORIAN
b Lynchburg, Va, Nov 13, 1940. *Study:* Sweet Briar Col, BA, 62; Pa State Univ, MA, 65; Courtauld Inst Art, Univ London, PhD, 74. *Collection Arranged:* Giovanni Benedetto Castiglione: Master Draughtsman of the Italian Baroque (auth, catalog), Philadelphia Mus Art, 71; A Scholar Collects: Selections from the Anthony Morris Clark Bequest (co-ed, catalog), Philadelphia Mus Art, 80; New Art on Paper 1 and 2 (coauth, catalog), Philadelphia Mus Art, 88, 96; Francesco Clemente: Three Worlds (coauth, catalog), Philadelphia Mus Art, 90; Art in Rome in the Eighteenth Century (coauth, catalog), Philadelphia Mus Art, 2000, Mus Fine Art Houston, 2000. *Pos:* Art hist ed, Pa State Univ Press, 69-72; asst cur drawings, Philadelphia Mus Art, 72-74, assoc cur drawings, 74-84, acting cur drawings, 81-84, cur, 84-. *Awards:* Fulbright-Hays Scholar, 64-65; Chester Dale Fel, 68-69; Vis Scholar, J Paul Getty Mus, 87. *Mem:* Print Coun Am. *Res:* Seventeenth and eighteenth century Italian drawings; contemporary drawings. *Publ:* Auth, Castiglione's chronology: Some documentary notes, Burlington Mag, 67; coauth, Philadelphia: Three Centuries of American Art, Philadelphia Mus Art, 76; Bernardo Cavallino of Naples, 1616-1656; catalogs, Cleveland Mus Art, Kimbell Art Mus, Ft Worth & Museo Pignatelli Cortes, Naples, 84-85; Ital Master Drawings, Philadelphia Mus Art, Pa, 2004; James Castle: A Retrospective, Philadelphia Mus Art, Pa, 2008. *Mailing Add:* Philadelphia Mus Art PO Box 7646 Philadelphia PA 19101

PERELMAN, ISAAC
GALLERY DIRECTOR
b Buenos Aires, 1964. *Study:* Found Higher Studies in Commerical Sci, BA (in advertising), Buenos Aires. *Pos:* Mgr studio svcs, I Magnin Co, Beverly Hills, Calif, 1990-93; comm dir SAm, Leger SA, Beunos Aires, Argentina, 1993-96; dir comm, mktg & image studio, D&P Assocs, Buenos Aires, Aregentina, 1996-99; co-dir & co-founder, Dot Fiftyone Gallery, 2003-. *Mem:* Mada Miaami Art Dealers Asn (pres). *Specialty:* Dot Fifty One Gallery

PERELMAN, JEFFREY E
COLLECTOR
Study: Univ Ill, BA (with hon); Ill Inst Tech, Chicago-Kent Coll Law, JD. *Pos:* Former owner & mgr, Commodities Brokerage Firm; with Sterling Real Estate Partners, Chicago, 1996-, now principal. *Awards:* Named one of Top 200 Art Collectors, ARTnews mag, 2006-13. *Collection:* Postwar and contemporary art. *Mailing Add:* Sterling Real Estate Partners 401 N Michigan Ave Chicago IL 60611

PERELMAN, MARSHA REINES
COLLECTOR
Pos: Co-founder & vpres, Clearfield Energy, Inc, 1983-90; co-founder & pres, Clearfield Ohio Holdings, Inc, 1983-90; founder & chief exec officer, Woodforde Mgmt Inc, 1993-; dir, Penn Va Resource, LLP. *Awards:* Named one of Top 200 Collectors, ARTnews mag, 2009-12. *Collection:* Postwar and contemporary art

PERELMAN, RONALD OWEN
COLLECTOR
b Greensboro, NC, 1943. *Study:* Univ Pa, BA, 64; Wharton Sch Fin, MBA, 66. *Pos:* With, Belmont Industries Inc, 66-78; chmn, chief exec off, MacAndrews & Forbes Group Inc (subsidiary), New York City, 78-; chmn, chief exec off, dir, MacAndrews & Forbes Holdings Inc, Wilmington, Del, 83-; chmn, chief exec off, dir, Revlon Group Inc (subsidiary MacAndrews & Forbes Group Inc), 85-, Revlon Inc (subsidiary), New York City, 85-; chmn, Nat Health Laboratories Inc, La Jolla, Calif, 85-, Andrews

Group Inc, La Jolla, 85-; pres bd of trustees, Solomon R Guggenheim Mus, 95-. *Awards:* Achievements; being named one of World's Richest People by Forbes in 99, 2000-2004; Named one of Top 200 Collectors, ARTnews Mag, 2004. *Collection:* Contemporary art. *Mailing Add:* Revlon Group Inc 237 Park Ave New York NY 10017

PERESS, GILLES
PHOTOGRAPHER
b Neuilly-sur-Seine, France, Dec 29, 1946. *Study:* Inst d'Etudes Politiques, dipl, 68; Univ Vincennes, dipl, 71. *Work:* Art Inst Chicago; Mus Fine Arts, Houston; Minneapolis Inst Art; Mus Mod Art & Metrop Mus Art, NY; Arts Coun-Great Britain, Bibliotheque Nationale, Paris; First Bank, Minn. *Comn:* Double Diary of the Twin Cities, First Banks Minnesota, Minneapolis, 86. *Exhib:* Photo Politic, PS 1/Inst Art & Urban Resources, NY, 80; Paris: Magnum, Palais du Luxembourg, Paris & traveling, 81; Photographie Français d'Aujourd'hui, Mus d'Art Mod, Paris, & traveling, 84; Telex: Iran, PS 1/Inst Art & Urban Resources, NY, 84; Magnum: Concert, Mus d'Art, Fribourg, Switz, 85; The Indelible Image, Corcoran Gallery, Washington, DC & traveling, 85; On the Line: New Color Photojournalism, Walker Art Inst, Minneapolis & traveling, 86; Power in the Blood: The North of Ireland, Art Inst of Chicago, 92; solo exhib, Palais de Tokyo, Paris, 93; Sex and Crime, The Silence, silver print installation: Sprengel Mus, Hannover, Ger, 96; Bosnia: Avant/Apres Guerre, digital print installation: Parc de la Villette, Paris, France, 98; and many others. *Pos:* Exec, Magnum Photos, Inc, currently. *Teaching:* Lectr photog, Int Ctr Photog, NY, 80-86, RI Sch Design, 82, Harvard Univ, 86-87. *Awards:* Nat Endowment Arts Grants, 79 & 84; Art Director's Club Award, NY Times, 97; Northampton Film Festival Award, Eye Witness Photo & Journalistic Impact, 98; Achievement in Photojournalism Award, Lucie Found, 2009. *Bibliog:* Charles Hanson (auth), Iran: Another view, Afterimage, fall 82; Michel Maingois (auth), L'Iran de Peress, Photo Mag, Paris, 5/8/84; Pete Hamill (auth), Prey for the dead, Am Photog, 8/84. *Mem:* Am Soc Mag Photogrs (vpres, 84-85, pres, 86-). *Publ:* Telex: Iran, Aperture/Contrejour, 84; contribr, Identities, Exposition Palais du Tokyo, Paris (exhib catalog), Editions du Chene, 85; Men's Lives, Random House, 86; auth, An Eye for an Eye: Northern Ireland 1970-1986, Aperture, 87; Power in the Blood: The North of Ireland, Jonathan Cape, Eng, Parkett, Zurich, 93. *Mailing Add:* 76 Lafayette Ave Brooklyn NY 11217

PEREZ, ENOC
PAINTER, PRINTMAKER
b San Juan, Puerto Rico, Nov 20, 67. *Study:* Pratt Inst, Brooklyn, NY, BFA, 90; Hunter Coll, NY, MFA, 92. *Work:* Mus Contemp Art, San Juan; Metropolitan Mus Art, NY; Mus Contemp Art, North Miami, Fla. *Comn:* lever house paintings, Lever House Art Coll, NY; casa malaparte, Maramotti Coll, Reggio Emilia, Italy. *Exhib:* Dear Painter, Paint Me, Center Pompidou, Paris, Schirn Kunsthalle, Frankfurt, 2002-3; The Undiscovered Country, Hammer Mus, Los Angeles, Calif, 2004-5. *Bibliog:* David Coggins (auth), Enoc Perez, Interview Mag, 12/2008; Hilarie M. Sheets (auth), Enoc Perez at Mitchell-Innes & Nash, Art Critical, 9/2009; Barbara Pollack (auth) Enoc Perez-Review, Time Out New York, 9/2009; Brandon Johnson (auth), Interview: Enoc Perez, Zing Mag, 5/2010; Alexander Wolf (auth), The Rule Breaker, Modern Painters, 2010. *Media:* Acrylic, Oil. *Publ:* auth, Caribe Club, Snoeck, 2005; auth, Tender, Snoeck, 2008. *Dealer:* Acquavella Galleries 18 East 79th St New York NY 10075; Faggionato Fine Art 49 Albermarle St 1st Fl London UK W1S4JR; Galerie Nathalie Obadia 3 Rue Cloitre St Merri Paris France 75004. *Mailing Add:* 10 Park Ave Apt 10C New York NY 10016

PEREZ, RICK
PAINTER
Study: Sch Vis Arts, Manhattan, NY, BFA; cert in painting, Art Students League of NY. *Exhib:* Group Shows: Faces in the Studio, Crosby Painting Studio, Soho, NY, 2005; Highland Lakes Ann Professional Art Show, Highland Lakes, NJ, 2006; Plein Air Landscapes Exhib, SCA&HC Gallery, Newton, NJ, 2007; My Favorite Subject, Salmagundi Club, NY, 2008 and many others; Exhibs: Rick Perez-Paintings & Drawings (one-person show), Boricua Col, NY, 2007; Bula's Restaurant & Jazz Club, Newton, NJ, 2008; Rick Perez: Artist of Month (Solo featured artist)-Artists at the Mill Gallery, Lafayette, NJ, 2009; 50th Ann Profl Art Show, Main Clubhouse, Highland Lakes, NJ, 2009; Blessed Kateri Church Wine Tasting & Art Show, Community Ctr, Sparta, NJ, 2010; Fitness Results, Inc 20th Year Ann Celebration and Art Show, NY, 2010; Hudson Valley Art Asn 81st Ann Exhib (juried), Old Lyme Acad, Conn, 2013; Art Student League Holiday Show and Sale, 2012, 2013, 2014; Annual Concours, Art Students League, NY, 2012, 2013, 2014, 2015; Salmagundi Spring Auctions, NY, 2015 and many others. *Collection Arranged:* many public, private and corporate collections. *Teaching:* Arts Students Leaguw, studied under master painters Gregg Kreutz, Tom Torak, MaryBeth McKenzie and Dan Gheno; class monitor in all of the classes; teaching asst for Gregg Kreutz painting class. *Awards:* Audubon Artists, 69th Ann Nat Exhib, Ellias and Lillian Newman Memorial award for Seated Nude, 2010; several Art Students League Concours Blue Dot awards, 2010, 2013, 2014; several Art Students League Concours Red Dot awards, 2011, 2012, 2013, & 2014; Am Artists Professional League, 83rd Grand Nat Exhib, Col George J Morales Memorial Award for Portait of Cathy, 2011; Am Artists Professional League, 84th Grand Nat Exhib, Frank C Wright Medal fo Honor for Tibetan Man, 2012; Hudson Valley Art Asn 81st An Exhib Mrs John Newington award for Excellence for Women in Blue Robe, 2013; Audubon Artists 72nd Grand Nat Exhib Marquis Who's Who in American Art award for Oils for Memories of Old Shanghai, 2014; and many others. *Mem:* Audubon Artists Soc, NY; Am Artists Profl League, NY; Hudson Valley Artists Asn, NY. *Media:* Oil. *Dealer:* Gallery35, 40 E 35 St, NYC; Salmagundi Club, NY; Art Students Leqgue of NY; (virtual) Saatchi Gallery; Virtual Art Space. *Mailing Add:* 35 Park Ave Apt 6F New York NY 10016

PEREZ, VINCENT
PAINTER, ILLUSTRATOR
b Jersey City, NJ, July 17, 1938. *Study:* Pratt Inst, BFA; Univ Am, Mex; Calif Coll Arts & Crafts, MFA. *Work:* Mus Art, Calif Palace Legion Hon, San Francisco; Oakland Art Mus, Calif; Playboy Enterprises, Chicago; Time Inc, NY; and many others. *Comn:* Mural, Arleigh Gallery, San Francisco, 69; portrait of State Supreme Court Judge Peters, comn by Clerks of Supreme Court for Univ Calif, Berkeley Law Sch, 74; woodcuts, Civic Arts Asn, Walnut Creek, Calif, 74. *Exhib:* Solo exhibs, Calif Coll Arts & Crafts, 77 & Hoover Gallery, 80; 12 Artists, Calif Coll Arts & Crafts, 78; Human Form, Walnut Creek Col, 78; Palo Alto Cult Ctr, 80; Ctr Visual Arts, 86. *Teaching:* Prof drawing & anat for artists, Calif Col Arts & Crafts, 66-. *Awards:* Union Independent Coll Art Res Grant, 70; Best of Show, Tech Writers Convention, Los Angeles, 72; Gold Medal, Acad Italy, 80; Gertrude B Murphy Award, 84. *Bibliog:* Fred Martin (auth), San Francisco letter, Art Int, 66; Cecille McCann (auth), Vincent Perez, FMb Fine Arts, 69; Palmer French (auth), San Francisco artists, Artforum, 69. *Mem:* Bohemian Club; San Francisco Soc Illusrs; Union Independent Coll Art. *Media:* Mixed. *Publ:* Illusr cover, Time Mag, 69; illusr, Art & Tools, 72; Archives of Institutional Change Humanizing Technology, 73; Psychol Today, 73; Playboy, 74. *Mailing Add:* Fine Arts Calif Col Arts & Crafts 5212 Broadway Oakland CA 94618-3941

PEREZ-ZAPATA, GUILLOUME
PAINTER, PUBLISHER
b Medellin, Colombia, July 2, 1957. *Study:* Belles Artes Inst, MA, 81. *Work:* Biblioteca Publica Piloto, Medellin, Colombia. *Comn:* Yuldama historical, Yuldama Hotel, Santa Marta, Colombia, 82; Ceipa Univ, Ceipa University, Medellin Colombia, 85. *Exhib:* Miniature Show, Albuquerque Mus, Albuquerque, NMex, 2000-2006; Biennale Internationale 3rd, Fortazzo De Vasso, Florence, Italy, 2003; Contemp Hispanic Market, Museo Cultural de Santa Fe, Santa Fe, NMex, 2005. *Teaching:* Sculpture, Bronze, Guilloume Studio Sandia Park, 2005-2006. *Awards:* First Pier 62-63 (painting), Latinoamerican Artist, Isis on First, Seattle, Wash, 2002; Latinoamerica (Can) 2nd Latinoamerican (Toranto), Fundarte, 2005; Industry Award, Sculptural Pursuit, The Complete Sculpture, 2006. *Bibliog:* Featured in Sculpture Magazine. *Mem:* Santa Fe Soc of Artist, 93-2006; NMex Art League, 95; Sonoran Art League, Ariz, 98. *Media:* Oil, Bronze Sculpture. *Publ:* Sculptures & Paintings, Guilloume, 2003. *Dealer:* Naked Horse Gallery 4151 N Marshall Way Suite B Scottsdale AZ. *Mailing Add:* 16 Dinos Rd Sandia Park NM 87047

PEREZNIETO, FERNANDO
PAINTER, SCULPTOR
b Mex, Aug 12, 1938. *Study:* Univ Nat Autonoma Mex, Architect, 62; studied etching, Villa Schifandia, Florence, Italy, 77. *Work:* Mus de la Ciudad de Mex, Mus Nac de la Estampa, Fomento Cult Banamex, Mexico City; Inst de Cult de Tabasco, Villahermosa, Tab; Bellas Artes, San Miguel, Mex. *Comn:* Quijote's Sculpture, Black Marbel, Mus Del Quijote Guanajuato, Mex; I Offer You My Heart Sculpture, White Marbel, City of Villahermosa, Tabasco, Mex. *Exhib:* 650 Anniversary of the City, Mexico City Mus, 75; Memories & Inventions, Univ Calif, Los Angeles, 80; L'Amour Pur La Musique, Municipal Mus, Castres, France, 81; Oniric Memories, Canning House, London, 87; Musica y Acompanamiento, Mus Nac de la Estampa, Mexico City, 94. *Pos:* archit. *Awards:* Premo Naz Pitura, Comune di Lampedusa, Italy, 84; Premio Ocho Columnas de Oro, Mex, 96; Premio Juchiman de Plata, Tabasco, Mex, 96. *Bibliog:* Gloria Cosi (auth), Pereznieto - Cento maghi unacitta, Eco D'Arte Moderna, 3-4/84; Thoughts on the work of FP, Castello Mediceo, Italy, 89; Alain Rener (auth), Pereznieto, L'art en mediterrnee, Montecarlo Cote D'Azur, 11/91. *Media:* All Media. *Publ:* Auth, Images of the Consciousness, Ed Unam, 80; Story of a Spell, Il Candelaio - Frenze, 82; Divertimento Erotico, Formal, 87; The Magic World of Fernando Pereznieto, Fund Tabasco, 94; Pereznieto - Sculpture, Ed Themis, 94. *Dealer:* Galerie D'Art Fernando Pereznieto 17 Ave Auber, Nice, 06000, France; Galeria Estela Shapiro Victor Hugo 72 Mex 11590. *Mailing Add:* Colina 47 Lomas De Bezares DF 11910 Mexico

PERGOLA, LINNEA
PAINTER, PRINTMAKER
b Los Angeles, Calif, Sept 23, 1953. *Study:* Univ Northridge, Los Angeles, BA, 76. *Exhib:* Ambassador Gallery, NY; Mus Flying, Los Angeles; Fine Art Mus, Long Island, NY; Martin Lawrence Galleries, Los Angeles, Chicago, & NY; Roberts Gallery, Scottsdale, Ariz. *Publ:* Illusr, I create a world-it's mine to enter, and share, SunStorm Fine Art, 95. *Mailing Add:* c/o Pierside Gallery 37 Vernon Newport Beach CA 92657

PERHACS, LES
SCULPTOR, INDUSTRIAL DESIGNER
b Studio City, Calif, Oct 5, 1940. *Study:* Chouinard Art Inst, 58; Pratt Art Inst, studied with David Smith, Salvador Dali & Willem Dekooning, 59-60; Art Ctr Sch Design, Los Angeles, Calif, 58; Sch Archit & Design, Univ Southern Calif, 61-62; Wildlife Studies, US Dept Interior, 67-79. *Work:* Frye Art Mus, Seattle, Wash; Whatcom Mus, Bellingham, Wash; State Capitol Mus, Olympia, Wash. *Comn:* People's Nat Bank, Lynden, Wash, 79; First City Nat Bank, Houston, Tex, 80; US Bank, Seattle, Wash, 83; Paragon Ranch Ltd, Denver, Colo, 90; San Diego Int Airport, Calif, 98; City of Leidschendam, Voorburg, The Neth, 2007; and others. *Exhib:* Group exhib, Royal Ont Mus, Can, 75; McNay Art Inst/Mus, San Antonio, Tex, 78; State Capitol Mus, Olympia, Wash, 79; Wildlife Sculptures, Frye Art Mus, Seattle, Wash, 80; Artists of Am, State Hist Mus, Denver, Colo, 81-86, 90, 95-96 & 2000; 30th Ann Group Show, Total Arts Gallery, Taos, NMex, 99; Beyond the Surface 2, Fallbrook Art Ctr, Calif, 2003; Construction & Metaphor, Univ Judaism, Bel Air, Calif, 2006; Chaos, Fallbrook Art Ctr, Calif, 2006; Oceanside Mus Art, Calif, 2009, 2010; Reflective Nature, Gerald Peters Gallery, Santa Fe, NMex, 2012. *Teaching:* Guest lectr indust design, Univ Calif, Los Angeles, 68. *Awards:* Nat Alcoa Indust Design Award, Alcoa Aluminum, 62. *Bibliog:* Mary Balcomb (auth), Stylized interpretations, Southwest Art, 3/80 &

Beyond accurate representation, Am Artist, 4/91; Judy Hughes (auth), Using art as a language, Wildlife Art News, 11/92. *Mem:* Nat Sculpture Soc. *Media:* Stone, Bronze, Steel. *Publ:* Contribr, Les Perhacs, Sculptor, Putnam Macdaniel/Mary Balcomb, 78; auth, An artist's perspective, Wildlife Art News, 11/92. *Dealer:* Perhacs Studio Fallbrook CA; Gerald Peters Gallery Santa Fe NMex. *Mailing Add:* 2540 Wilt Rd Fallbrook CA 92028

PERKINSON, ROY L
CONSERVATOR, HISTORIAN
Study: Atelier Chapman Kelly, Dallas, Tex, 60-61; MIT, Cambridge, Mass, BA, 63, post grad studies, 64-65; Sch Mus Fine Arts, Boston, 64-69; Boston Univ, MA (art hist), 67; apprentice to FW Dolloff, Conservator Prints & Drawings, Mus Fine Arts, Boston, 67-70. *Hon Degrees:* Lorenzo Award, Prof Picture Framers' Asn, 1979; Nat Endowment for the Arts, 1994; Sheldon and Caroline Keck Award, 1999. *Pos:* Asst Conservator prints & drawings, Mus Fine Arts, Boston, 67-71, assoc conservator, 71-73, conservator, 76-; conservator prints & drawings, Fine Arts Mus San Francisco, 73-76; designer, Western Regional Paper Conserv Lab, Fine Arts Mus San Francisco, 73; vis comt, Int Mus Photog, George Eastman House, Rochester, NY, 79-82; acad rev comt mem, Winterthur Grad Prog in Conserv & Early Am Studies, 86-94; conserv assessment comt, Mus Fine Arts, Boston, 90-91, ethics code comt, 94-95, conserv comt, 94-, head paper conserv, 98-. *Teaching:* Various lectures & workshops, 74-99; guest lectr, J Paul Getty Mus, Malibu, Calif, 4/94 & Nat Gallery Am Art, Washington, 10/95. *Awards:* Lorenzo Award, Prof Picture Framers' Asn, 79; Res grant for paper hist, Dir Mus Fine Arts, Boston, 93; Prof Develop Award, Nat Endowment Arts, 94. *Mem:* Fel, Am Inst Conserv; Fel, Int Inst Conserv; Nat Conserv Adv Coun; Nat Inst Conserv; Print Coun Am. *Publ:* Auth, Conserving works of art on paper, Mus News, Am Asn Mus, Washington, 77; coauth, Questions concerning the design of paper pulp for repairing art on paper, In: Preservation of Paper and Textiles of Historic and Artistic Value, Am Chemical Soc, Washington, 77; contribr, Mary Cassatt: The Color Prints,Abrams, New York, 89; auth, Notes on media and papers, In: Awash in Color: Homer, Sargent and the Great American Watercolor, Mus Fine Arts, Boston, Bulfinch Press, Little, Brown & Co, Boston, 93; coauth, Printmaking terminology, In: Emil Nolde: The Painter's Prints, Mus Fine Arts, Boston, 95; coauth, Les papiers bleus: identification de colorants, 96. *Mailing Add:* 365 Weston Rd Wellesley MA 02181

PERLESS, ROBERT
SCULPTOR
b New York, NY, Apr 23, 1938. *Study:* Univ Miami, Coral Gables, Fla. *Work:* Aldrich Mus Contemp Art, Ridgefield, Conn; Okla Art Ctr, Oklahoma City; Phoenix Art Mus, Ariz; Whitney Mus Am Art, NY; Boca Raton Mus Art, Boca Raton, Fla; Chrysler Mus, Norfolk, Va; Stamford Mus, Stamford, Conn; William Benton Mus Art, Storrs, Conn. *Comn:* Lake Forest Mall, Gaithersburg, Md, 78; Public Park, Port Chester, NY, 87; Bard Col, Annandale on Hudson, NY, 87; Space Ctr, Tysons Corners, Va, 88; Univ Northern Iowa, Cedar Falls, 90; City Ctr, Palm Desert, Calif, 92; Xerox Int Hq, McLean, Va, 93; 555 Madison Ave, NY, 94; Univ Conn, Storrs, 95; Bristol-Myers Squibb, New Brunswick, 96; Rusk Inst, NY, 98; Syracuse Hancock Int Airport, Syracuse, NY, 99; Miami Univ, Oxford, Ohio, 99; Salt Lake Comm Col, Salt Lake City, Utah, 2000; City of Corpus Christi, Tex, 2002; USVC, Heber City, Utah, 2004; Conn Comn on Cult & Tourism, Howell Cheney Tech High Sch, Manchester, Conn, 2008; Bucknell Univ, Lewisburgh, PA. *Exhib:* solo exhibs, Bodley Gallery, New York, 68, Bernard Danenberg Gallery, New York, 72, Bonino Gallery, New York, 76, Flinn Gallery, Greenwich, Conn, 2006; Recent Acquisitions, Whitney Mus Art, NY, 70; Forum Gallery, New York, 75; Recent Sculpture, Taft Mus, Cincinnati, Ohio, 80; group shows, Aldrich Mus Contemp Art, Ridgefield, Conn, 87, 94, 97, 98 & Stamford Mus Art, Conn, 88; Conn Biennial, Art New Eng (with catalog), Bruce Mus, Greenwich, Conn, 89; Andre Emmerich Top Gallant Farm, Pawling, NY, 91, 92, 93, 94, 95 & 96; Environmental Sculptures, Kukje Gallery, Seoul, Korea, 95; 12X12X12, Greenwich Art Soc, 2000; Space 2001, Bruce Museum, Greenwich, Conn, 2001; Sculpture Now, Stockbridge, Mass, 2003; Art Omi Int Arts Ctr, Omi, NY, 2004; Sculpture in the Park, White Plains, NY, 2006; In-Site, Governor's Island, NY, 2008. *Bibliog:* Structural drama for a New Canaan poolhouse, Archit Dig, 8/89; Art in public high places, Palm Desert Sun, 8/91; Somewhere over the rainbow, Hartford Courant, 8/16/95; Greenwich Time, Artist's Energy Reflected in Work, 97; From Greenwich with Light, Fairfield Co Times, 97; New York Times, What 72 Artists Figured Out About Boxes 1 by 1 by 1, 2000; Art at Transit Sites, Sculpture Magazine, 2000; Aerodynamic Abstract Art, Greenwich Times, 7/9/2001; Corpus Christi Caller Times, Onion's Belt Shows City's Coastal History, 2001; Stamford Advocate & Greenwich Times, Towering Controversy, Stamford Advocate & Greenwich Times, 2002; Recent Projects, Public Art Review, Spring/Summer 2002 & 05; For Art's Sake, New York Daily News, 9/24/06; Over the Rainbow with Greenwich's Perless, Greenwich Citizen, 9/29/06; Cosmic Conversations, Greenwich Mag, 9/06; Catching A Dream in Midair, ashlar.com; 150 Feet of Luminous Rainbows, courant.com. *Mem:* ISC, Sculptor's Guild. *Media:* Aluminum, Stainless Steel; Prisms; Holographic Material. *Mailing Add:* 37 Langhorne Ln Greenwich CT 06831-2611

PERLIN, RUTH RUDOLPH
EDUCATOR, ART HISTORIAN
b Washington, DC. *Study:* Wellesley Col, BA, 57; Metrop Mus Art, Inst Fine Arts, 61-62; New York Univ Inst Fine Arts, MA, 63. *Pos:* cur, ext prog, Nat Gallery Art, 1974-1980; deputy dir Educ Div Nat Gallery Art/Hd Dept Educ Res, 1980-2001; officer bd, Mus Educ Roundtable, 78-81; contrib ed, Sch Arts Mag, 78-82; proj dir, laserdisc, 83 & producer, digital image base/laserdisc, Am Art, Nat Gallery Art, Wash, 93, dir Euro Art, 2000; dir, Educ Tech, The Phillips Collection, 2001-06; spl asst to dir, Interpretation and Technological Initiatives, The Phillips Collection, Wash, 2001-06; assoc dir, Center for Study Mod Art, Phillips Collection, 2006-; bd trustees GWU/Textile Mus, 2013. *Teaching:* Head docent training art hist, Baltimore Mus Art, 65-69, lectr, 70-72; instr art hist, Towson State Col, Md, 67-69; adj prof, art hist & mus studies, Univ Ill, 2006-08. *Awards:* Cine Golden Eagle, 83-86 & 88-90; Mus Educator of Yr, Mus Div, Nat Art Educ Asn Eastern Region, 93; MUSE Awards, AAM, 2003 & 2006; Nat Art Mus Educator of the Yr (NAEA), 2006. *Mem:* Art Table, 90-; Am Asn Mus (vchair, 96-98, chair media and tech standing prof com, 98-2000, bd media and tech standing prof com, 2000-, coun of SPCS, 98-2000); Nat Art Educ Asn, Mus Educ Div (eastern region dir, 95-97); Non Print Mats (comn, 96-2003). *Res:* Collections, exhibitions of The Phillips Collection; 19th & 20th century painting; 19th & 20th century American art; Museum studies. *Specialty:* 19th & 20th century European and American Art. *Publ:* coauth, A video disc resource for interdisciplinary learning, Art Educ, Vol 48, No 3, 17-24, 5/95; Worlds of meaning, Art Educ, Vol 51, No 5, 25-28 & 45-48, 9/98; prodr, dir European Art from the Nat Gallery of Art (digital imagebase/laserdisc & videocassette), 2000; prodr, dir, writer Jacob Lawrence: Over the Line (interactive web pgm), 2001, prodr Jacob Lawrence CD-ROM, The Phillips Collection, 2002; prodr, Am Art at Phillips Collection (interactive web program), 2005. *Mailing Add:* c/o The Phillips Collection 1600 21st St NW Washington DC 20009-1090

PERLIS, DON
PAINTER
b New York City, Jul 29, 1941. *Study:* Art Students League, 61; Sch Visual Arts, NY City, 65; Skowhegan Sch, 65. *Work:* exhib in group shows Whitney Mus, NY City; Corcoran, Washington, DC; Minneapolis Mus Art; Nat Acad, New York. *Exhib:* Solo exhib, Sindin Gallery, New York City, 94-95; Walter Wickiser Gallery, New York City, 96-97; Claudia Carr Gallery, New York City, 99; Graham Gallery, 71, 75, Sindin Galleries, 93, 95, Charas-Elbohio, 93; Solo exhibs, Denise Bibro Gallery, 2001-2005; Narrative Reborn, Lancaster Mus Art, 2011. *Bibliog:* Donald Kuspit (auth), New Old Masters; Catalog of Stanley Grand, Lancaster Mus, 2011. *Mem:* Nat Acad; Nat Arts Club. *Media:* Oil on Canvas. *Publ:* Doc film on artist produced by Time Capsule Films, 1993; auth, (monogr) Allegories of Love, 1995

PERLMAN, BENNARD B
PAINTER, WRITER
b Baltimore, Md, June 19, 1928. *Study:* Carnegie-Mellon Univ, BFA, 49; Univ Pittsburgh, MA, 50. *Work:* Peale Mus & Baltimore Mus Art, Baltimore, Md; Univ Ariz, Tucson; Univ Md, College Park; Fed Reserve Bank, Balt; Am Airlines, Dallas; Joseph Pennell Collection, Libr of Congress, DC. *Comn:* Murals, 66 & History of Gardenville (oil), Patterson Park Ice Skating rink (enamel) Baltimore, Johns Hopkins Hosp (photographs), Baltimore, 80. *Exhib:* Baltimore Mus Art; Corcoran Gallery Art, Washington, DC; Carnegie Mus, Pittsburgh; Pa Acad Fine Arts, Philadelphia; IFA Galleries, Wash; Vanderlitz Gallery, Boston & Provincetown; Art Inst Chicago; and 78 solo exhibs. *Pos:* Art critic, The Daily Record, Baltimore, 84-92, Maryland Maturity, 92-93, S Fla Times, 99-2004; contribr, The Balt Sun, 48-, NY Times, 87-, Art & Antiques, 87-, ARTnews, Art in Am, Am Artists. *Teaching:* Prof & chmn dept art, Community Coll Baltimore, 54-86; vis lectr, Oxford Univ, Eng, 75 & Dartmouth Coll, 81; prof, Loyola Coll, Baltimore, 75-86 & Goucher Coll, 83-86. *Awards:* Freeland Art Award, Md Artists Exhib, Baltimore Mus Art; First Prize & Mus Purchase, Peale Mus Ann; First prize & Purchase, Easton Md Acad Art Mus. *Bibliog:* Md Pub Television, 2005. *Mem:* Artists Equity Asn (nat vpres, 69-71 & 77-79); Baltimore Mus Art Artists Comt (chmn, 59-61 & 69-70); Greater Baltimore Arts Coun (pres, 64-66); Coll Art Asn; Asn Historians Am Art. *Media:* Oils, Ink. *Res:* Photography's relationship to art: from imitation to inspiration; Andy Warhol (Pittsburgh Yrs, 28-49). *Interests:* Late 19th- Early 20th Cen Am Art. *Publ:* Auth, Arthur B Davies: Drawings and Watercolors (exhib catalog), Baltimore Mus Art, 87; Robert Henri: His Life and Art, Dover, 91; ed, Revolutionaries of Realism: The Letters of John Sloan and Robert Henri, Princeton Univ Press, 97; The Lives, Loves and Art of Arthur B Davies, State Univ NY Press, 98; ed, American Artists, Authors and Collectors: The Walter Pach Letters 1906-1958, State Univ NY Press, 2002

PERLMAN, HIRSCH
PAINTER
b Feb 7, 1960. *Study:* Yale Univ, BA, 82. *Exhib:* Solo exhibs, Cable, NY, 87, Galerie Claire Burrus, Paris, France, 88, 91 & 93, Shodhalle, Zurich, Switz, 90, Galerie Hufkens, Brussels, Belg, 90, Monika Sputh Galerie, Koln, Ger, 91, 94 & 97, Interim Art, London, Eng, 91, Feature, NY, 92 & Donald Young Gallery, Seattle, Wash, 93, Blum & Poe, Santa Monica, Calif, 2001, Donald Young Gallery, Chicago, Ill, 2002, Blum & Poe, Los Angeles, Calif, 2004, Gallery Min Min, Tokyo, Japan, 2005, Gimpel Fils, London, 2005, Saint-Gaudens Memorial Picture Gallery, Cornsh, NH, 2006, Drammens Mus, Drammens, Norway, 2006, Blum & Poe, Los Angeles, Calif, 2007, Gallery Nieves Fernandex, Madrid, Spain, 2007, Gallery Min Min, Tokyo, Japan, 2007, Robert Miller Gallery, NY, 2007; Whitney Mus Am Art, NY, 89; After and Before, Renaissance Soc, Chicago, 94; Radical Scavenger(s): the Conceptual Vernacular in Am Art (catalog), Mus Contemp Art, Chicago, 94; When Attitudes Become Form: Selections From a Contemp NJ Collection, Montclair Mus, NJ, 94; Notational Photog, Metro Pictures & Petzel Borgmann Gallery, NY, 94; Temporary Translation(s), Deichtorhallen, Hamburg, Ger, 94; Passions Privees, ARC, Paris, France, 95; Art in Chicago 1945-1995 (with catalog), Mus Contemp Art, Chicago, 96; Fake Ecstasy With Me, Mus Contemp Art, Chicago, 97; Next, Blum & Poe, Santa Monica, Calif, 97; Hello Mr Soul, Gallery 400, Univ Ill Circle, Chicago, 99; No Harm in Looking, Mus of Contemp Art, Chicago, Ill, 2001, (Tele)visions, Kunstyhalle, Vienna, Switz, 2001; Whitney Biennial, Whitney Mus Am Art, NY, 2002; Extreme Existence, Pratt Manhattan Gallery, NY, 2002; LA on My Mind, Mus Contemp Art, LA, 2002; Zones, Art Gallery Hamilton, Ontario, Canada, 2003; Outlook: Int Art Exhibition, Athens, Greece, 2003; 100 Artists See God (traveling); Premiere, A Gavlak Projects Production, NY, 2003; The Center is Anywhere, MCA, Chgo Ill, 2004; Dark Places, Santa Monica Mus Art, 2005; Sixteen Tons, UCLA Dept Art Faculty, Broad Art Ctr, 2006; Mus Fine Arts, Tallahassee, Fla, 2007; Amateurs, Wattis Inst, San Francisco, Calif, 2008; Nine Lives: Visionary Artists in L.A., Hammar Mus, Los Angeles, 2009; Selections from the Hammer Contemporary Collection, Hammer Mus, Los Angeles, 2010; Wicked Little Critter, Kristi Engle Gallery, Los Angeles, 2011; and many others. *Teaching:* Assoc prof sculpture, UCLA, currently; chair art

dept, UCLA, currently. *Awards:* Nat Endowment Arts, 89 & 91; Louis Comfort Tiffany Found Grant, 91. *Bibliog:* Fred Camper (auth), Minute art, Chicago Reader, 3/25/94; Laurie Palmer (auth), Repeat after me, Frieze, 7/94; Regina Hackett (auth), review, Seattle Post-Intelligencer, 11/25/94. *Publ:* Contribr, Artists Writings: Twice-Told Tales, Art J, fall 89; auth, Contingency, Iron & Solidarity, Artforum, 12/89; coauth (with Jeanne Dunning), Introduction to the Relationship Between Art & Pervision, DU, 6/91; coauth (with Jeanne Dunning), Getting to Know the Law or Make Things Mean What I Want Them to Mean or A Collection of Quotes I Like, Dirty Data (catalog), Ludwig Mus, Aachen, Ger; auth, Exhibit Z 1 (Judicial), Framework, vol 5, issued 2 & 3, 92. *Dealer:* Donald Young Gallery 933 W Washington Blvd Chicago IL 60607. *Mailing Add:* UCLA Dept Art 1100 Kinross Ave Ste 245 Los Angeles CA 90095

PERLMAN, JOEL LEONARD
SCULPTOR, INSTRUCTOR
b New York, NY, 1943. *Study:* Cornell Univ, BFA, 65; Cent Sch Art & Design, London; Univ Calif, Berkeley, MA, 68. *Work:* Whitney Mus Am Art; Los Angeles Co Mus; Hirshhorn Mus & Sculpture Garden; Metrop Mus Art, New York. *Comn:* Night Traveler (outdoor sculpture), Storm King Art Ctr, 77; Tenneco World Hq, Greenwich, Conn, 96; Kane Sports Ctr, Cornell Univ, 96; ABN Amro Plaza, Chicago, Ill, 2004; Hebrew Home at Riverdale, New York, 2005. *Exhib:* Andre Emmerick Gallery, NY, 73, 76, 80, 82, 85, 87, 90, 92; Whitney Mus Am Art Biennial, 73; Contemp Reflections, Aldrich Mus Contemp Art, 73; Roy Boyd Gallery, Chicago & Los Angeles, 78, 80-81, 83, 86, 88 & 96; Eve Mannes, Atlanta, 93; Retrospective (with catalog), Glen Horowitz Gallery, East Hampton, 96, 2013; Century Asn, New York, 96; Roy Boyd, Chicago, Ill, 96; Kouros Gallery, New York, 2000, 2002, 2004, 2007, 2010, 2012; Roy Boyd, Chicago, 2003, 2005, & 2008; Guild Hall Mus, East Hampton, NY, 2013; Loretta Howard Gallery, NY, 2014. *Teaching:* Instr sculpture, Sch Visual Arts, 73-. *Awards:* Nat Endowment Arts Grant, 79; Reynolds Aluminum Award, 87; Special Prize, Fujisankei Biennale, Japan, 95; Fel Guggenheim Found, 74; Pollack-Krasner Grant, 2012. *Bibliog:* Barbara Pollack (catalog), 2000; Jason Andrew (catalog), 2000; Peter Barton (interview), 2000; Jonathan Goodman, review Art in Am, 2002; Philip F. Palmedo (monograph), Joel Perlman, A Sculptor's Journey, Abbeville Press, 2006. *Mem:* Century Asn New York. *Media:* Welded Steel, Cast Bronze, Aluminum. *Specialty:* Post War Am Abstraction. *Interests:* Motorcycles, sports, dogs. *Publ:* Joel Perlman, New Sculpture 97-2000; Douglas Maxwell, article Sculpture Mag, 2002. *Dealer:* Loretta Howard Gallery NY; Roy Boyd Gallery Chicago; Lewallen Gallery, Santa Fe. *Mailing Add:* 250 W Broadway New York NY 10013-2431

PERLMAN, JUSTIN
SCULPTOR
b Aug 28, 1974. *Study:* Hampshire Coll (fine art & anthropology), 92-94; Studied with Lourie Goulet & Gary Lawrence Sussman, Art Students League, New york, 95-98; independent study, with Nathaniel Kaz & Gina Lombardi, 98-99; apprenticeship, Coopermill Bronze Works, Zanesville, Ohio, 99-2000. *Work:* Greenwich Arts Council; Conn Governors Res, Hartford, Conn; Ives Concert Park, Danbury, Conn; Ridgegield Guild Artists; Sculpture Park at the Governor's Residence, Hartford, Conn; Ridgefield Conservatory of Dance, Conn; Grace Avenue Park, Great Neck, Long Island; David L Lawrence Convention Ctr, Pittsburgh, Pa. *Comn:* Sculptural relief collab with Stephen O'Hearn, David L Lawrence Convention Ctr, Pittsburgh, Pa, 2003; Mem for Harry Perlman, Grace Ave Park, Great Neck, Long Island, 2006. *Exhib:* Solo exhibs, Slaughterhouse Gallery, Pittsburgh, Pa, 2003, Melrose Castle, Casanova, Va, 2007, Seti Gallery, Kent, Conn, 2012; Group exhibs, Aliquippa Art Alliance Exhib, Pa, 2000; 91st Ann Exhib, Assoc Artists of Pittsburgh, Pa, 2001; Off the Wall, Europe Art Gallery, Pittsburgh, Pa, 2002; 1st Ann group exhib, Slaughterhousegallery, 2002; Collector's exhib, Pittsburgh, Pa, 2004; Show for a Show, Artwell Gallery, Torrington, Conn, 2008; Suburban Artists Block Island Sculpture Show, Block Island, RI, 2008; Ann Open Art Competition, Artwell Gallery, Torrington, Conn, 2008; Sculpture Mile Exhib, Madison, Conn, 2008; Sherman Art Show, Sherman, Conn, 2008; Group Exhib with Ella Knox, Silo Gallery, Hunt Hill Farm, Nwe Milford, Conn, 2009; Audubon Artists Inc, Ann Exhib, 2009, 2010, 2011; Ridgefield Guild of Artists Group Exhib, Conn, 2011, 2012; Sculpturefest 2012, Peter Lawrence Gallery, Gaylordsville, Conn, 2012; Sculpture at Wildcliff, Wildcliff Manor, New Rochelle, NY, 2012; Sculpture Mile Exhib, Madison, Conn, 2012, 2013; Art at the Bartlett Arboretum, Stamford, Conn, 2012; Living on the Grid, Watershed Gallery, Ridgefield, Conn, 2013; The Women, Ridgefield Guild of Artists, Conn, Re-imagined, 2014, members exhib, 2014; Art to the Avenue, Greenwich, Conn, 2014. *Pos:* Artisan, Coopermill Bronze Works, Zanesville, Ohio, 99-2001; intern fel, Art Students league, New York, 2004-2005; tech instr, Art Students League, New York Vytlacil Sch, 2005-2006; independent artisan for Anthony Padovano, 2006-. *Awards:* Red Dot Winnter, Art Students League, New York, 98; winner, Show for a Show, Artwell Gallery, Torrington, Conn, 2008; winner, Jeffrey C Nicholas Silver Award, Artwell Gallery, 2008; winner, Gold Medal of Hon, Audubon Artists Ann Juried Exhib, 2009; Marquis Who's Who in Am Art References Award in sculpture, Audubon Artists, New York, 2010. *Bibliog:* Pulp mag, Nov 2003; Ann catalog of the Madison sculpture Mile, 2008; 9 catalog of the Madison sculpture Mile, Madison, Conn, 2008-2009; Jamie Ferris, A Sculptors Narrative, Housatonic Times, 4/10/2009; John Pirro (auth), Sherman Sculptor Makes His Mark, Danbury Newstimes, 1/24/2010; Susan Dunne (auth), Field Days, Catalog of the 1st Sculpture Park at the Governors Residence, Hartford, Conn, 6/19/2013; Jennifer Mathy (auth), Justin Perlman May be the Busiest Sculptor in CT, Ridgefield Hamlet Hub, 4/9/2013; Kristen Zimmer (auth), The Arts the Thing, Serendipity Mag, 2014. *Media:* Bronze, Marble, Copper, Wood, Steel, Handmade Paper, Encaustic. *Specialty:* Contemporary Art. *Interests:* Fine Art, Dance, Music, History, Astronomy, Physics, Poetry. *Dealer:* Watershed Gallery Ridgefield CT

PERLMUTTER, LINDA M
PAINTER, INSTRUCTOR
b New York, NY, Mar 1, 1943. *Study:* Hunter Coll, BA, 63, MA, 67; China Inst, Calligraphy, New York, 69; Art Student's League, with Mario Cooper, 71-81. *Work:* Gabelli Funds Inc, Rye, NY; Powell Duffryn Inc, Bayonne, NJ; Yonkers Bd Educ, NY; Blue Cross Blue Shield Md, Baltimore; Ernst & Young, Stamford, Conn. *Comn:* Marriott Corp, comn by Baird Eaton, Tarrytown, NY, 85. *Exhib:* Filth, Hudson River Mus, Yonkers, NY, 71; Beaux Arts, State Univ NY, Purchase, 78; Nat Asn Women Arts Traveling Exhib, Sarah Lawrence Coll, Bronxville, NY, 85, Jesse Besser Mus, Alpena, Mich, 86, Schenectady Mus, NY, 86 & Adelphi Univ Mus, Garden City, NJ, 87; River Gallery, Irvington, NY, 90, 92, 94, 97 & 2000. *Pos:* Art supervisor, New York Bd Educ, 68-69; art dir, N Tarrytown Art in the Park, 86-90; pres, Odyssey Art Ctrs, 95-. *Teaching:* Instr fine arts, New York Bd Educ, 66-69; instr, Creative Use Art Media, State Univ NY, 69 & Odyssey Art Ctrs, 75-present. *Awards:* Best in Show, Ossining Women's Club, 78; Ada Cecere Mem Award, Nat Asn Women Artists Ann, 89. *Bibliog:* Harriett Edelson (auth), Genius Culled from Natural Phenomena, Gannett, 77; Helene Brooks (auth), A singular woman, McCall's Mag, 79; Phyllis Riffel (auth), Organization and Creativity Makes Artists' Life Productive, 83; Valerie Bohigian (auth), Lady-Bucks, Dodd Mead & Co, 87. *Mem:* Nat Asn Women Artists (bd mem, 82-95); Sleepy Hollow Arts Coun. *Media:* Watercolor, Acrylic. *Specialty:* Watercolors, oils, pastels. *Interests:* Travel, boating & gardening. *Publ:* H George Caspari Inc as notecards, Posters, 78-. *Mailing Add:* 470 Bellwood Ave Sleepy Hollow NY 10591

PERLMUTTER, MERLE
PRINTMAKER
b London, Eng, Apr 16, 1936; US citizen. *Study:* Art Students League, with Ethel Katz; Pratt Inst, Brooklyn, NY; Ruth Leaf Graphic Workshop, Douglaston, NY. *Work:* Portland Mus Art, Wash; Musee de Petit Format, Couvin, Belgium; New York City Pub Libr, 42nd St Branch Print Collection; Housatonic Mus Art, Bridgeport, Conn; Newark Pub Libr, NJ. *Exhib:* Eleven one-person shows, Soc Am Graphic Artists, Taiwan, China, 84, Silvermine Gallery, Conn, 85, Ariz State Univ, Phoenix, 85, Katonah Gallery, NY, 86, Hudson River Mus, 88 & QCC Gallery, Queens Community Col, New York City; Boston Printmakers Nat Competition, Mass, 74, 76, 79, 80 & 83; Pratt Int Miniature Graphics Exhib, 75, 77, 81, 83, 85 & 87; Premio Int Biella Por L'Incisione, Italy, 76 & 80; Miami Int Biennial, Metrop Mus & Art Ctr, Fla, 77 & 80; Martha Jackson Gallery, NY, 79; NY State Mus, Albany, 81; Third & Fourth Int Biennial, 87-89; Taipei Fine Arts Mus, Taiwan, China; Tucson Mus Art, Ariz; Biennial graphic Art, Mus Mod Art, Ljublyana, Yugoslovia; Mus Mod Art, Wakayama, Japan, 88; Rufino Tamayo Mus, Chapultepec, Mex; Noyes Mus, NJ, 90. *Teaching:* Instr etching & printmaking, Ruth Leaf Graphic workshop, Douglaston, NY, 76-; guest printmaker prints & techniques, Grey Art Gallery & Study Ctr, NY Univ, 76. *Awards:* Two Gold Medals & Silver Medal, Audubon Artist Nat Competition, NY, 75, 77, 80, 84 & 88; Creative Artist Pub Serv Prog Fel, 76; Soc Am Graphic Artists Award, 78, 80, 90, 91 & 97; and many others. *Bibliog:* Ruth Leaf (auth), Intaglio Printmaking Techniques, Watson-Guptill, 77; Jacquline Brody (auth), Prints Published, Print Collectors News Lett, 9-10/78; Phyllis Braff (auth), articles, New York Times, 11/4/84 & 9/15/85; Carol Wax Abrams (auth), The Mezzotint, 90. *Mem:* Boston Printmakers, Mass; Audubon Artists; Soc Am Graphic Artists. *Media:* Intaglio, Etching. *Mailing Add:* 20 Cherry Ave New Rochelle NY 10801-5304

PERLOFF, MARJORIE G
CRITIC, HISTORIAN
b Vienna, Austria, Sept 28, 1931; US citizen. *Study:* Barnard Col, AB, 53; Catholic Univ, MA, 56, PhD, 65. *Teaching:* Prof English, comparative literature & art literature, Univ Southern Calif, 77-86, Stanford Univ, 86-; Sadie D Padek chair humanities, 91-. *Res:* Modern and postmodern poetry and painting; artists books; intermedia. *Publ:* Auth, The Dance of the Intellect, Cambridge Univ Press, 85; The Futurist Moment, Univ Chicago Press, 86; Poetic License, Studies in Modernist & Postmodernist Lyric, Northwestern, 90; Radical Artifice, 92; Wittgenden's Ladder, 96; and others. *Mailing Add:* 1467 Amalfi Dr Pacific Palisades CA 90272

PERLOW, KATHARINA RICH
DEALER, GALLERY DIRECTOR
b Vienna, Austria; US citizen. *Study:* Hunter Coll (art hist), 75-77. *Pos:* Dir, Jack Gallery, New York, formerly; partner, A M Sachs Art Gallery, 83-85; pres & dir emeritus, Katharina Rich Perlow Gallery, New York, 84; juror, Temple Univ, Alumni Exhib, Philadelphia; juror, Schoharie Art Ctr, Cobleshill, NY; private dealer, Katharina Rich Perlow Fine Arts, currently. *Teaching:* lectr, Art & Business, New York Univ, currently. *Bibliog:* Cover, Profile of a Galerist, 11/1991; Talk TV Show, Lynn Graham's Transetters, 9/29, 10/6/2001. *Mem:* Mus Mod Art, NY; Metrop Mus Art, NY; Whitney Mus Am Art; Guggenheim Mus Art; Norman Rockwell Mus; Berkshire Mus; Soc Illusr; Mus City of NY; Jewish Mus. *Media:* Painting, Sculpture photography. *Specialty:* Artists exhibited: Mary Abbott, Milton Avery, Sally Michel Avery, Donald Baechler, Norman Blum, James Brooks, Byron Browne, Alexander Calder, Giorgio Cavallon, William Clutz, Friedel Dzubas, Tom Ferrara, John Ferren, Sam Francis, Helen Frankenthaler, Gertrude Greene, Balcomb Green, John Grillo, Michele Harvey, Jean Helion, Ian Hornak, Brian Yoshimi Isobe, William King, Irving Kriesberg, Robert Kushner, George McNeil, Fred Mitchell, Robert Motherwell, Craig McPherson, Robert Natkin, Joe Naujokas, Kenzo Okada, Stephen Pace, Ray Parker, Milton Resnick, Jay Rosenblum, Jon Schueler, Richard Segelman, Brian Shure, Donald Sultan, Yvonne Thomas, Abraham Walkowitz, Abigail Varela; abstract expressionism & contemp art. *Interests:* Art, music, books. *Collection:* Ecclectic private collection of our gallery, artists and secondary market. *Mailing Add:* Katharina Rich Perlow Fine Arts 40 East 84th St New York NY 10028

PERRONE, JEFF
CERAMIST
b Atwater, Calif, 1953. *Study:* Univ Calif, Berkeley, BA (linguistics), 73. *Exhib:* Solo exhibs, Charles Cowles Gallery, NY, 87, 89, Thomas Tavelli Gallery, Aspen, 88, Sperone Westwater Gallery, NY, 91, Thomas Solomon Garage, Los Angeles, 92, Sybaris Gallery, Royal Oak, Mich, 93, Cavin Morris Gallery, NY, 94, Holly Solomon Gallery, NY, 97, Gallery Camino Real, Boca Raton, Fla, 98, Cheim and Read, NY, 2003; group exhibs, Sybaris Gallery, Detroit, 89, Cup: As a Metaphor, 91; Nancy Margolis Gallery, Portland, Maine, 90; Recent Acquisitions, Pacific Enterprises, Los Angeles, 91; Recent Acquisitions, Am Craft Mus, NY, 92; Plant Body, Cavin Morris Gallery, NY, 93, Animal Body, 93; Diversity, 24 Hour Gallery, NY, 94; Painting After Nature, Ctr Contemp Art, North Miami, 94; Think Pink, La MaMa Galleria, NY, 98; Opulent, Cheim & Read, NY, 2000; Allan Chasanoff Ceramic Collection, Mint Mus, Charlotte, NC, 2000. *Teaching:* Instr, Sch Visual Arts, NY, 77-83, Univ Tex, San Antonio, 84 & Brown Univ, Providence, RI, 86. *Awards:* Nat Endowment Arts Grant, 78; NY Found Arts Grant, 89; Louis Comfort Tiffany Found Grant, 91. *Bibliog:* J Kozloff (auth), Like a dense curry with coconut milk, Am Ceramics, 5/4/87. *Mailing Add:* c/o Cheim & Read 547 W 25th St New York NY 10001

PERRONI, CAROL
COLLAGE ARTIST, PAINTER
b Boston, Mass, July 28, 1952. *Study:* Boston Mus Sch, Mass, 70-71; Bennington Col, BA, 76; Skowhegan Sch Painting & Sculpture, 78; Hunter Col, NY, MFA, 83. *Work:* RI Hosp, Providence. *Exhib:* Solo exhibs, Boston City Hall, 78, Hunter Coll Gallery, Ny, 83 AS220, Hera Gallery, Wakefield, RI, 95 & 98, Providence RI, 96 & Community Coll RI, Lincoln Campus Gallery, 96; Gallery X, Fed Reserve Bank Boston Gallery, 96; Fall Painting Show, Sarah Doyle Gallery, Brown Univ, Providence, RI, 96; Ann Holiday Art Bazaar, Art Adv/Boston, Quincy, Mass, 96; Illusions of the Millennium, Renaissance Gallery, Fall River, Mass, 98. *Pos:* Studio asst for Isaac Wilkin, Bennington, Vt, 73-74, Mel Bochner, New York, 79 & Lee Krasner, E Hampton, 80; libr asst, Simmons Col Libr, 77-78; bookkeeper, Int House, New York, 79-80; res asst, Art News Mag, New York, 81; tech asst, Avery Archit & Fine Arts Libr, New York, 81-83; intern, Greenspace Gallery, New York, 82-83; librarian/researcher, Kennedy Galleries Inc, New York, 84-86; prog specialist/art teacher, Swinging Sixties Sr Citizen Ctr, Brooklyn, NY, 86-87; Arts in Educ Prog, RI, 93-96. *Awards:* Grant, Flintridge Found, 93. *Bibliog:* Bill Van Siclen (auth), Taking a fresh approach to ancient themes, Providence J, Providence, RI, 8/96; Alicia Craig Faxon (auth), Gallery Night/Providence, Art New Eng, Brighton, Mass, 12/96-1/97; Juliet Pennington (auth), Artist strives for a three-dimensional look, Sun Chronicle, Attleboro, Mass, 6/97. *Mem:* Hera Educ Found (bd dir, 94). *Media:* Oil, Acrylic; Collage. *Publ:* Auth of biographies of 35 Am Artists, Aspects of America: The Land & the People 1810-1930 (with catalog), Kennedy Galleries, New York, 5/85. *Dealer:* Art Advisory Boston 1245 Hancock St Suite 26 Quincy MA 02169. *Mailing Add:* 154 Lancaster St Providence RI 02906

PERROTTI, BARBARA
PAINTER, INSTRUCTOR
b Akron, Ohio. *Study:* Paier Sch Art, New Haven, Conn; Madison Sch Art, Robert Brackman, Conn; Burt Silverman, Cinnaminson, NJ; with Greg Kreutz, Maitland, Fla; Lois Griffiel, Willow Wisp Farm Studio, Fairview, NC. *Work:* Doan Col, Rall Gallery, Crete, Nebr; Mus Arts & Sci, Daytona Beach, Fla; St. Joe Corp, Port St Joe, Fla; Halifax Health Med Ctr, Daytona Beach, Fla; Fla Hosp Mem Medical Center, Ormond Beach, Fla. *Comn:* Kent Cottage (mural), Stuart Treatment Ctr, Daytona Beach, Fla, 86; mural, Family Study Ctr, Ormond Beach, Fla, 87; oil painting, Walt Disney-Epcot, 92; portrait of Chapman S Root, Mus Arts & Sci, Daytona Beach, Fla, 93; Portrait-Cold War Soldier Nat Inf Mus, Fort Benning, GA. *Exhib:* solo show, Poetry in Pose, Casements Cult Ctr, Ormond, Fla, 90, Inspirations, Cult Art Ctr, Valdosta, Ga, 94, Romancing the Landscape, Ctr for the Arts, Val Dosta, Ga, Church Alley Gallery, Easton, Md, 2009, Invitational on the Road of Good & Evil, Mus Fla Art; Two Women/Two Painters, Ormond Art Mus, Ormond Fla, 93; Small Works Show, Mill Gallery, Taos, NMex, 2005; Group Invitational, Fla on my mind, Sm Trust, 2004, Matheson Mus, A Painted History of Alachua county, 2006; Epcot Int Garden Festival, 2004-2011; Plein Air Easton, Md, 2007; World tour of Contemp Landscape Artists, Karpaeles Mus, Newburg, NY, St Augustine Gallery, St Augustine, Fla, Cult Arts Ctrm Estes Park, Colo, Link Gallery, Wis, Old Sc House, Vancouver, Can, Terrace Gallery, Orlando, Fla, 2008-2009; Orlando Mus Art, Fla, 2010, 2011; Polasek Mus, WinterPark Plein Air, Winter Park, Fla, 2012; Art in the Chamber, Orange Co, Orlando Fla, 2012. *Pos:* Guest Cur, Casements Cult Ctr; E Coast Plain Air-Shows, 2004-2010; coordr, Emmous Cottage Gallery Cooperative, 2007. *Teaching:* Instr oil portrait workshops, New Smyrna Beach, Fla, 94, Cult Art Ctr, Valdosta, Ga, 94 & Casements Cult Ctr, Ormond, Fla, 94; Instr oil painting, Art League, Daytona Beach, 79-2011; John C Campbell Folk Sch, Inst Oil & Pastel, Brasstown, NC, 2004-2011; Inst Child Plein Air-Ctr for the Arts, New Smylna Beach, FL, 2004; instr, workshops, Fla, 2008, Cedar Key Art Ctr, Fla, 2011; Inst John Campbell Folk Sch, Inter-generational program, 2012. *Awards:* various awards, Art League of Daytona, 2006-2012. *Bibliog:* Patricia Sporer (auth), Up Close & Natural, Orlando Sentinel, 2002; Laura Stewart (auth), Plein Air Artist Talks of Life, Painting, Daytona Beach News Jour, 2006; Steve Schwartz (auth), Celebrating Food of the Gods, Citrus Gallery Exhib, 5/2009. *Mem:* Int Plein Air Painters; Landscape Artists Int; Art League Daytona; Mus Arts & Sci Daytona; Albin Polasek Mus Winter Park, Fla; Orlando Mus Art, Orlando, Fla. *Media:* Oil, Acrylic & Pastel. *Specialty:* Fine Art & Framing. *Dealer:* Art Union 214 N Union Ave Harre de Grace MD; Clay Gallery 302 S Riverside Dr New Smyrna Beach Fla. *Mailing Add:* 1411 N Beach St Ormond Beach FL 32174-3401

PERROTTI-YOUNGER, ROBBIE L
PAINTER
b July 27, 56. *Work:* Painted Garden Gallery, Smithfield, VA; Suffolk Art Gallery, Suffolk, VA. *Comn:* portrait, Charles Blount, Ron Stauffer; furniture, Kentlaurie Esser. *Exhib:* Solo exhib: Trellis, Colonial Williamsburg, Va, 2004. *Collection Arranged:* Kathy Ferebee, Vice Pres to Towne Bank, Norfolk, Va; Drs Henry & Christina Prillaman, Newport News, Va; Peb Lockwood, Int Antique Dealer, Zuni, Va. *Awards:* Hon Mention, Collage Arts, 96. *Bibliog:* Paula R. Jones (auth), For Art's Sake, Smithfield Times, 6/2003; Breslow Partners (auth), An Artist in Bloom, Trellis Newletter, Colonial Williamburg, 2004; Melissa Watkins Starr (auth), Painted Dreams, Hampton Roads Mag, 6/2004, Inspired Creation, Victoria Mag, 1/2010; Phyllis Johnson (auth), Divine Impressions, Flourish Mag, 6/2011; cover, Flourish Mag, 2011. *Mem:* Am Impressionist Soc. *Media:* Acrylic

PERRY, DONALD DEAN
PAINTER, EDUCATOR
b Hutchinson, Kans, Sept 29, 1939. *Study:* Pittsburg State Univ, BFA, 62; Kans State Univ, MS, 67; Univ Wis-Madison, MFA, 67. *Work:* IBM Corp, United Telecommun Systems Inc, AT&T Corp, Kansas City, Mo; Software AG NAm, Chicago. *Comn:* Wildlife Panorama, Marshfield Libr, Wis, 70; sculpture installation, Security Benefit Building, Topeka, Kans. *Exhib:* Nat Print Exhib, State Univ NY, Potsdam, 67; Miami Graphics Biennial Int, Metrop Mus, Fla, 74; Nat Print & Drawing Exhib, Univ NDak, Minot, 76; Ann Printmaking West, Logan, Utah, 78; Ann Nat Drawing & Small Sculpture Show, Ball State Univ, Ind, 80; Telec III Int Exhib, Art Res Ctr, Kansas, City, Mo, 85; Abstract Paper (three-person exhib), Batz-Lawrence Gallery, Kansas City, 86; Hypergraphics Int VIII Exhib, Bannister Gallery, RI Col, Providence, 87; Dakotas 100 Int Works on Paper Exhib, Dickinson State Univ, NDak & Univ SDak, Vermillion, 88; Ann Faculty Art Exhib, Norman R Eppink Art Gallery, Emporia State Univ, Kans, 93-98; Kansas Abstract Artists Exhib, Cafe Gallery, Wichita Art Mus, Kans, 94; Constructions, Dykes Libr Art Gallery, Univ Kans Med Sch, 95; Prismacolor and Acrylic Works on paper, Emporia Arts Coun, Kans, 97; 29th Ann Smoky Hill Art Exhib, Hays Arts Ctr, Kans, 98; US Printmakers, Franco-Am Inst, Rennes, France, 2000; 12th Ann Nat Art Competition, Univ Art Gallery, Truman State Univ, Kirksville, Mo, 2000; Forty-Fifth Ann Nat Print Exhib, Hunterdon Mus Art, Clifton, NJ, 2001; Fourteenth Parkside Nat Small Print Exhbit, Communications Arts Gallery, Univ Wis-Parkside, Kenosha, 2001; Dirty Dozen Plus One, City Arts Gallery, Wichita, 2002; Print Jumble, Art and Design Gallery, Univ Kan, 2002; Sixteenth Parkside Nat Small Print Exhib, Communication Arts Gallery, Univ Wis-Parkside, Kenosha, 2003; and others. *Pos:* Mem bd dir, Community Arts Inc, Emporia, 73-74; dir, Univ Art Galleries, Emporia State Univ, 79-2001, chair art dept, 77-84, 92-2000. *Teaching:* Instr drawing & printmaking, Univ Wis, Marshfield, 67-72; prof art, Emporia State Univ, Kans, 72-, chmn art dept, 77- 84, 99-2000. *Awards:* Purchase Award, Miami Graphics Biennial, 74; Art Enhancer award, Kan Art Edu Asn, 92. *Mem:* Emporia Arts Coun, Kans. *Media:* Screenprint; Acrylic. *Mailing Add:* 1636 Dover Rd Emporia KS 66801

PERRY, EDWARD (TED) SAMUEL
ADMINISTRATOR, PROFESSOR
b New Orleans, La, 1937. *Study:* Baylor Univ, BA, 61; Univ Iowa, MA, 66, PhD, 68. *Pos:* Dir film dept, Mus Mod Arts, New York, 75-78; chair, Salzburg Seminar on Film, 94. *Teaching:* Prof cinema & chmn dept, Univ Iowa, Univ Tex & NY Univ, 69-75; Luce vis prof cinema, Harvard Univ, spring 75; chmn, Arts Div, Middlebury Coll, 78-97; Am Film Inst Ctr Advanced Film Study, 81-87; Fletcher prof arts, dir arts, Middlebury Coll, 97-. *Mem:* Soc Cinema Studies; Speech Commun Asn (mem res bd, 74-). *Publ:* You Are What You Look At, Film Cult, No 76, 92; Il mestiere di vivere, il mestiere di vivere, Arion, spring & fall 92-93; How Can One Sell the Air? The Book Publ Co, 93; A Secret Place, With A View in American Identities, ed by Robert Pack & Jay Parini, Univ Press New Eng, 94; William Arrowsmith (auth), Antonioni: Poet of Images, Oxford Univ Press, 94; My Reel Story, Univ Press New Eng, 2000; Buky Schwartz: The Seeing I, Acad, Chicago, 2004; ed, The Impulse to Preserve, New York, Harvard Univ Press, 2006; Masterpieces of Modernist Cinema, Ind Univ Press, 2006; Impersonation of the True Self, Psychoanalytic Review, No. 6, Vol 94, 2007. *Mailing Add:* 49 S St Middlebury VT 05753

PERRY, FRANK
SCULPTOR
b Vancouver, BC, Jan 15, 1923. *Study:* Univ BC, BA, 49; Cent Sch Arts & Crafts, London, Eng; Regent Poly, Chelsea Sch Art, London. *Work:* Granite carving, Vancouver Art Gallery, BC, 98; Vancouver Art Gallery; Univ BC Sch Archit; Art Gallery Greater Victoria, BC; Univ Victoria; London Art Gallery, Ont. *Comn:* Bronze fountain, Crescent Apts, West Vancouver, 61; cor-ten welded, Fed Govt Bldg, Victoria, 66; bronze cast, Playhouse Theatre, Vancouver, 67 & BC Govt for Prov Bldgs, 73. *Exhib:* Montreal Mus Fine Arts, 58; Winnipeg Show, 58; BC Centennial Outdoor Show, 58; BC Centennial Outdoor Sculpture Show, 67; Burnaby Art Gallery, 77. *Pos:* Pres, Northwest Inst Sculpture, 59-60. *Awards:* First Prizes, Montreal Mus Fine Arts, Winnipeg Show & BC Centennial Outdoor Show, 68; Grand Prize, BC Centennial Outdoor Sculpture Show, 67; Rothman Award, 67. *Mem:* Sculptor's Soc Can; Sculptor's Soc BC; Royal Can Acad Art. *Media:* Bronze, Welded Steel. *Mailing Add:* 137 W 17th St No 402 North Vancouver BC V7M 1V5 Canada

PERRY, GREGORY J
MUSEUM DIRECTOR
Study: Univ Ill, Urbana-Champaign, BA, 1982; DePaul Univ, JD, 1990; Sch of Art Inst Chicago, MA in modern art hist, theory and criticism, 2003. *Pos:* Assoc Robert W Smith & Assocs, Ill, Hillside, and Fein and Seeskin; assoc dir devel, spec projects Art Inst Chicago; assoc dir, Jane Voorhees Zimmerli Art Mus, Rutgers Univ, NJ, 2000-02, acting dir, 2002, dir, 2003-2008; dir, Allentown Art Mus, Allentown, Pa, 2008-. *Mailing Add:* Allentown Art Museum 31 North 5th Street Allentown PA 18101

PERRY, KATHRYN POWERS
PAINTER, GRAPHIC ARTIST
b Chico, Calif, Mar 13, 1948. *Study:* Stanford Univ, 68; Concordia Col, BA, 70: Art Students League, Studies with Will Barnet, Knox Martin, Gregory d'Alessio & Robert B Hale, 71-74; Emily Ferrier-Spear Scholar, 73-74; Sch Visual Arts, 78-79. *Comn:* var small works, 2002-2006. *Exhib:* Solo exhibs, Orpheus Gallery, NYC, 74, Aames Gallery, NYC, 76, Berg Art Ctr, Concordia Coll, Moorhead, MN, 77, Lopez Public Libr, Lopez, Wash, 2014; Group exhibs, Aames Gallery, NY, 76, American Drawings, Portsmouth, Va, 76, Arte Fiera, Bologna, Italy, 78, Marietta Nat, Ohio, 79, Post Card Size, PS1, NYC,79, Ligoa Duncan Gallery, NY, 79, C Running Gallery, Concordia, Moorhead, MN, 87. *Pos:* Art dir, Metrop Opera Guild, New York, 83-89. *Awards:* ECHO Leader Award for Educational Brochure Design, 86. *Bibliog:* Review of four Concordia College artists, Fargo Forum, 5/70; Rob Edelman (auth), Three Brooklyn artists probe their role in society, Courier-Life, 7/74; New York Challenges Artists, Concordia, winter 78; A sketch in time, Skagit Valley Herald, 2005-2006. *Mem:* Life mem Art Students' League; charter mem Nat Mus Women Arts. *Media:* Pastel, mixed media. *Mailing Add:* PO Box 373 Lopez WA 98261

PERRY, LINCOLN FREDERICK
PAINTER, SCULPTOR
b New York, NY, May 28, 1949. *Study:* Columbia Univ, BA, 71; Queens Col, MFA, 75. *Work:* Bayly Mus, Charlottesville. *Comn:* Work & Leisure (murals), John Hancock, Inc, Boston, 84; triptych, Solomon Brothers, NY, 86; MetLife (murals) St Louis, Mo, 88; Mural for 1700 Pennsylvania Ave, Washington, 90. *Exhib:* Tatistcheff Gallery, NY, 80, 82, 84, 86, 88 & 90; Contemp Realism, NY Coun Arts Mus, NY, 82; Bodies and Souls, Artists Choice Mus, NY, 83; New Talent-NY, Sioux City Art Mus, 84. *Teaching:* Asst prof painting & drawing, Univ NH, Durham, 75-80, Univ Ark Fayetteville, 83-84 & Univ Va, 85. *Awards:* Nat Endowment Arts Grant, 84. *Bibliog:* James Cooper (auth), rev, News World, 81 & 82; Eunice Agar (auth), Lincoln Perry, Am Artist, 84; Liebemann Butler (auth), intro to catalog, Sioux City Art, 84. *Media:* Oil, Terra Cotta

PERRY, REGENIA ALFREDA
HISTORIAN
b Virgilina, Va, Mar 30, 1941. *Study:* Va State Col, BS, 61; Case Western Reserve Univ, MA (Va Mus Fine Arts Out of State Fel), 62; Univ Pa, 63-64, PhD (art hist), 66; Yale Univ, 70-71. *Pos:* Spec res asst, Cleveland Mus Art, 64-65; vis scholar, Piedmont Univ Ctr, Winston-Salem, 71-72. *Teaching:* Asst prof art hist, Howard Univ, 65-66; asst prof art hist, Ind State Univ, Terre Haute, 66-67; prof art hist, Va Commonwealth Univ, 67-90, emer prof, 90-. *Awards:* Danforth Found Post-Doctoral Fel, 70-71. *Mem:* Coll Art Asn Am; Am Asn Mus; Soc Archit Historians; Am Asn Univ Prof. *Publ:* Auth, James Van Derzee--Photographer, 73; Free Within Ourselves: African American Artists in the Collection of the National Museum of American Art, 92; Harriet Powers's Bible Quilts, Rizzoli, NY, 94. *Mailing Add:* 3404 Moss Side Ave Richmond VA 23222-1826

PERSHAN, MARION
PAINTER, LECTURER
b New York, NY. *Study:* Hunter Coll, with William Starkweather, BA, 38; Pratt Inst, 40, Nat Acad Fine Arts, with Louis Bouche, 53; Art Students League, with Edwin Dickinson & Frank Mason, 54; watercolor with Edgar Whitney. *Work:* Dow Chemical Corp, Midland, Mich; Cardiology Assoc, Westport, Conn; Capital M, NY, Fla. *Comn:* watercolor, comn by Dr Ralph Kirmaer, 92; watercolor, comn by Dr Robert Moskowitz, 93; watercolor, comn by Dr Lawrence Kaplan, 98; watercolor, comn by Joseph Jensen, 98; Capital M, NY; and others. *Exhib:* Catharine Lorillard Wolfe Arts Club, Nat Arts Club, NY, 76-83 & 90; Salmagundi Club, NY, 81; 157th Ann, 82 & 159th Ann, 84, Nat Acad Design, NY; Knickerbocker Artists, 85-87; Madison Sq Garden, NY, 86; Lincoln Ctr, NY, 87, 89; Nature Ctr Westport, Conn, 90-95; Art Expo, Fla, 97-2007; Grand Cent Art Gallery, NY, 2005; Boca Hotel & Club, Fla, 2005; CVE Art Expo, 2005-09; Libr, Wilton, Conn, 2008; Kerschner Gallery; Wilton Libr Summer Show. *Collection Arranged:* Brooklyn Comes to the Met, Metrop Mus of Art, 76 & 77; Long Island Univ, 88; Brooklyn Mus, 90. *Pos:* Art dir, Camp Roselake, Honesdale, Pa, 54-55 & Camp Racquette Lake, NY, 57; juror, Nat Shows Catherine Lorillerd Wolfe Art Club, NY 85-89. *Teaching:* Instr & coordr art, New York City Pub Sch, 60-77. *Awards:* Gold Medal of Honor, Catharine Lorillard Wolfe Club, Inc, 79 & Silver Medallion, 82; Best in Show, Nat Arts Club, 82; Second Prize Watercolor, Knickerbocker Artists, 82 & Gold Medal, 85; Cynthia Goodgal Mem Award, 83; Top Award Watercolor, Hudson Valley Art Asn, 87; Best in Show, CVE Art Expo, 2009, 2010, First Prize, 2005-08. *Bibliog:* Walter Cruickshank (auth), Art Rev, Flatbush Life, 5/8/71; Les Krantz (auth), Am Artists. *Mem:* Catharine Lorillard Wolfe Art Club Inc; Knickerbocker Artists; Hudson Valley Art Asn; Asn Am Watercolor Soc; Salmagundi Club; Nat Arts Club. *Media:* Watercolor and Oils. *Res:* language art in the art curriculum. *Interests:* Visual art enjoyment; exhibiting & selling. *Collection:* Large collection, large & smaller watercolor paintings in variety of subjects in contemp realism, impressionism. *Publ:* Auth, Language Arts in the Art Curriculum, Fac News Asn, 4/72; illusr cover design, Career Opportunities Exposition, Am Educ Asn, 10/73. *Dealer:* Grand Central Art Galleries New York NY; Geary Gallery Darien CT. *Mailing Add:* 209-25 18th Ave Bayside New York NY 11360

PERSKY, ROBERT S
WRITER, PUBLISHER
b Jersey City, NY, Jan 5, 1930. *Study:* NY Univ, 49; Harvard Law Sch, JD, 52. *Pos:* Ed, The Photograph Collector, 80-96; publ, The Consultant Press Ltd. *Mem:* Am Photog Hist Soc. *Publ:* Auth, The Artist's Guide to Getting & Having a Successful Exhibition, Consul Press; ed & publ, The Photographic Art Market, Vol III-XIII; Guide to Tax Benefits: For Collectors, Dealers & Investors, third ed, Consultant Press, 91. *Mailing Add:* c/o The Photograph Collector 163 Amsterdam Ave New York NY 10023

PERUO, MARSHA
PAINTER, PRINTMAKER
b Brooklyn, N Y. *Study:* Queens Col, BA, 71; Pratt Inst, MFA, 80. *Exhib:* Miniature Painters, Sculptors & Gravers Soc Washington 58th Ann Int Exhib, DC, 91; Am Soc Contemp Artists Ann Exhib, Broome St Gallery, NY, 92; Am Soc Contemp Artists 75th Anniversary Exhib, Broome Street Gallery, NY, 93; Am Soc Contemp Artists Exhib Paintings, Graphics, Sculptures, Lever House, NY, 94; Miniature Art Soc Fla 21st Ann Int Show, Belleview-Mido Resort Hotel, Clearwater, Fla, 96; Nat Collage Soc 13th Ann Exhib, Stocker Ctr Gallery, Lorain Co Comm Col, Elyria, Ohio, 97. *Awards:* Dorothy Fiegen Mem Award for Graphics, 62nd Ann, Am Soc Contemp Artists, 80. *Mem:* Am Soc Contemp Artists (awards chmn, 80-81, corresp secy, 81-83, dir, 83-85, 1st vpres, 85-87); NY Artists Equity Asn. *Media:* Mixed Media. *Mailing Add:* 55 W 14th St New York NY 10011

PESANTI, HEATHER
CURATOR
Study: Univ Pa, Grad, 1997; Univ Oxford, Eng, MA (cult anthrop); NY Univ Inst Fine Arts, MA (mod/contemp art hist). *Collection Arranged:* Carnegie Int, 2008. *Pos:* With Mus Mod Art, New York, Jeanne Collins & Assocs, formerly; curatorial fellow, Mus Contemp Art, Chicago, formerly; asst cur contemp art, Carnegie Mus Art, Pittsburgh, 2005-08; mem, Cult Dist Design Com, Pittsburgh, formerly; cur, Albright-Knox Art Gallery, Buffalo, NY, 2008-. *Awards:* Marjorie Susman Curatorial Fel, 2005. *Mailing Add:* Albright-Knox Art Gallery 1285 Elmwood Ave Buffalo NY 14222-1096

PESNER, CAROLE MANISHIN
ART DEALER
b Boston, Mass, Aug 5, 1937. *Study:* Ecole du Louvre, Inst d'Art et d'Archit, Paris, 58; Smith Col, Northampton, Mass, BA, 59. *Pos:* Pres, Kraushaar Galleries, New York, currently. *Mem:* Art Dealers Asn Am Inc; Int Fine Print Dealers Asn. *Specialty:* 20th century and contemporary American art. *Publ:* Auth & coauth, Kraushaar Gallery Publ & Catalogs. *Mailing Add:* Kraushaar Galleries 74 E 79th St New York NY 10075

PETER, FRIEDRICH GUNTHER
PAINTER, CALLIGRAPHER, GRAPHIC DESIGNER
b Dresden, Ger, Feb 23, 1933. *Study:* Hochschule fuer Bildende Kuenste, WBerlin, Ger, 50-56; Meisterschueler Dipl in lettering & graphic design, 56-57. *Work:* Mural, Trinity Western Univ, Langley, BC; Calligraphy, Klingspor Mus, Offenbach, Germ; Postage Stamp designs, Nat Archives, Can; Lettering Painting, Regent Col, Univ BC, 2007; Coast Art Trust Collection, Maltwood Gallery, Univ Victoria, BC, 2009-. *Comn:* Murals, 90 ft for World Coun Churches 6th Assembly, 83, City of Vancouver Street Banners, 95; postage stamp designs, Can Post, Govt Can, for Can Nat Anthem, 80, Can Constitution, 82, Terry Fox, 82, Multiculturalism, 90; 100 dollar gold coin, 82 & 20 dollar silver Olympics coin, 88, One dollar special issue coin, 93, Royal Can Mint; four 50-cent proof coins, Can Sports Series, 98; Commemorative Silver Dollar, 50 yrs Can Coun Arts, Royal Can Mint, 2007; and others. *Exhib:* Solo exhibs, Following Higher Orders, Gulf War Drawings at Gallery Alpha and Lookout Gallery, UBC, Vancouver, BC, 91; Lookout Gallery, Regent Col, Univ BC, 89, 92, 99, 2001, 2006, 2008, 2009, 2012; Scripture Paintings, Seymour Art Gallery, N Vancouver, BC, 2002; Ferry Bldg Gallery, West Vancouver, BC, 94; Invitational exhib calligraphy (traveling), Christians Visual Arts, 97; The Art of the Coin, Royal Canadian Mint Roy Thompson Hall, Toronto, Ontario, 92; Celebrate Me, Scripture Paintings & Calligraphy Lookout Gallery, Regent Coll, UBC, 2009; Alphabet of Healing, Scripture Calligraphy Lookout Gallery, Regent Coll, UBC, 2012; Traveling, Scribes of Hope II, CIVA 2013; Bible Illustrations, Digital Art, Lookout Gallery, Regent Coll, UBC, 2013; Bible Illustrations, Digital Art Lookout Gallery, UBC, 2013. *Collection Arranged:* 26 Letters (traveling exhib), Fine Arts Gallery, Univ BC, Vancouver. *Pos:* Educator, Regional rep & found Mem, Graphic Designers, Can, 58; Postage Stamp Design Sub-Comt, Postage Stamp Adv Comt, Can Post, Fed Govt Can, 82-85. *Teaching:* Instr graphic design, Vancouver Sch Art, BC, 59-78, chmn dept, 76; instr graphic design, Emily Carr Col Art & Design, Vancouver, BC, 76-94, Emily Carr Inst Art & Design, 94-98; fac, Int Calligraphy Conference, Chicago, 2008. *Awards:* Nat Competition, Royal Can Mint, 81, 82, 88 & 92; winner typeface design competitions, Vivaldi Internat Typeface Corp, NY, 66, Magnificat, Letraset Internat, London, Sanbika, First Prize in Latin Category, 87, Shinko, 90, Peter Roman, Morisawa Corp, Osaka, Japan, 93; Nat Competition, Off Sports Medal (gold, silver, Bronze), XV Olympic Winter Games, Calgary, 1988. *Bibliog:* Natl Archives, Canada; 26 Extraordinary Canadians, CFMT Intl, Rogers TV Studio C, 2002; Canada at the Millennium, Can Heirloom Series, 2000. *Mem:* Royal Can Acad; Graphic Designers Can (fell); CIVA (Christians Visual Arts). *Media:* painting, calligraphy, lettering, drawing, digital art. *Specialty:* Painting, acrylic, watercolors, graphic. *Interests:* Visual Arts, Painting. *Publ:* illusr, Der Turm, Ulrich Schaffer (auth), Oncken, Ger, 79; Wenn Mauern fallen, U Schaffer (auth), Kreuz Verlag (publ), Ger, 90; Talking with Friedrich Peter (illus interview) Graphic Design Journs, Graphic Designers of Can, 2001; Child of God you are growing up, D Johnson, Vancouver, BC, 2007. *Dealer:* Bel Art Gallery Inc 2171 Deep Cove Rd North Vancouver BC Canada V7G1S8. *Mailing Add:* 193 E St James Rd North Vancouver BC V7N 1L1 Canada

PETERS, ANDREA JEAN
PAINTER
b Boston, Mass, Dec 27, 1947. *Study:* Vesper George Sch Art, Boston, 65-66; Mass Coll Art, Boston, 66-68; Roger Curtis, Gloucester, 78-83. *Work:* Warner & Stackpole, Boston; MBNA Am; Axelrod Enterprises, Tex; Voltaix Corp, NJ; Russell Reynolds Assocs, Boston, Mass; AUSAM Int; Farnsworth Art Mus, Rockland, Maine. *Exhib:* 17th Nat Works on Paper, Harnett Hall Gallery, Minot State, NDak; Bates Coll Mus Art, Lewiston, Maine, 98; Notations of Color: oil sketching in Maine; 8th Int Exhib, Am Intercontinental Univ, Atlanta, 98; USArtists, Pa Acad Fine Arts, Pa, 2000. *Awards:* Daniel B Hoye Mem Award, Hoyt Nat, 86; Pearl Paint Award, 15th Ann Pastel Soc Am, 87; J Giffuni Scher Award, 16th Ann Pastel Soc Am, 88; and others.

Bibliog: Miles Unger (auth), Art Review, Boston Sunday Globe, 9/90; Charlotte Floyd (auth), Artist Portrait, The Minuteman Chronicle, 9/90; Philip Isaacson (auth), Art Review, Maine Sunday Telegram, 6/97 & 7/2004; Carl Little (auth), The Art of Maine in Winter, Downeast Bks, 2002; Edgar Allen Beem (auth), The Blue Snows of the East Boothbay, Down East Mag, 2010; Genetta McLean (auth), Am Coastal Art, The Collection of Charles J and Irene Hamm, 2011. *Mem:* Am Artists Prof League, New York; Pastel Soc Am, New York (master pastelist); North Shore Arts Asn, Mass; Copley Soc Boston, Mass (copley artist); Maine Coast Artists. *Media:* Oil, Pastel. *Dealer:* Gleason Fine Art Boothbay Harbor and Portland ME

PETERS, DIANE (PECK)
PAINTER, MURALIST
b Corpus Christi, Tex, May 14, 1940. *Study:* Univ Okla with Milford Zornes, 75; Master class with Chen Chi, 76, Master Classes in Watercolor, with Edward Betts, 78 & 84; La Tech Univ, with Douglas Walton, 78; Del Mar Coll, with Joseph Cain; El Cobano Coll, Mex Art. *Work:* Corpus Christi Mus, Tex; McAllen State Bank, McAllen, Tex; Incarnate Word Convents, Corpus Christi, Tex, Lyon, France, Nairobi, Kenya, Tanzania, Mex, Cleveland, Ohio, Victoria, San Antonio & Houston, Tex; mural, Incarnate Word Sisters, 75th Jubilee, Kenya, Africa & Corpus Christi, Tex; mural, Incarnate Word Sisters, 25th Jubilee, Nakuru, Kenya; murals, Incarnate Word Sisters, Regional Chapel & Bardello Mission. *Comn:* Seascape mural, Dr William Roof; Lake wildlife mural, John Peters Mem, 86; In The Beginning Was The Word (Incarnate Word Missions in Africa) 96 & And The Word Was Made Flesh (mural), Order Incarnate Word, Corpus Christi, Tex, 95; The Baptism of Jeanne Chezard De Matel, France, 97; Series of the Tribes of Kenya, 97; Ascension, Chapel of Archbishop Peter Kairo, Kenya; mural, Tribal Peace Below Mt Kenya and Dwells Among Us, Incarnate Word Sisters Regional House, Nairobi, Kenya, 2006. *Exhib:* 39th Watercolor Soc Ala Ann Nat Competition, Birmingham Mus Art, Ala; Allied Artists Am 65th Ann Exhib, Nat Acad Galleries, NY; Salmagundi Club 2nd & 3rd Ann Non-mem Exhib, Salmagundi Galleries, NY; Southwestern Watercolor Soc Ann Membership Exhib, Dallas; Tex Watercolor Soc Exhib, 84; traveling exhib, mural Venerable Jeanne Chezard De Matel, Incarnate Word Convent, Tex, France, Kenya, 96, Incarnate Word Int Reunion, Ohio, 96; Africa A Painted Diary, Art Ctr Corpus Christi, 2005; World Trade Ctr Exhib, Allied Artists Nat Arts Club, New York; Raymond Duncan Gallery, Paris; Kottler Gallery, New York; Ownesboro Mus Fine Art; Birmingham Mus Art, Columbus Mus Arts & Sci; Mc Nay Inst. *Pos:* stained glass artist, Olszewski Stained Glass co, 69-73. *Awards:* La Tech Univ, 73; Purchase Award, Tex Watercolor Soc, 84; Best of Show Award, Art Community Ctr Exhib, 89 & 98; Brownsville Int Art Exhib, 91-93. *Bibliog:* Lee Dodds (auth), Tonkaland a winner, Corpus Christi Times, 6/79; Spotlight Ed (auth), Local artist has show in New York, Corpus Christi Times, 12/79; Local Artist Honored, Corpus Christi Caller Times, 5/90. *Mem:* Corpus Christi Art Ctr. *Media:* Watercolor, Acrylic; Aqua Media. *Interests:* Sailing, opera. *Collection:* Pokot tribe series & Masai tribe paintings. *Publ:* Illusr, cover, Star to Star, 1/72; cover, Giving (catalog), 85; cover, The Cooking Habit, 87; paintings featured, The Artist Mag, 5/88; paintings featured, The New Spirit of Watercolor, North Light Bks, 4/89. *Dealer:* Diane Peters Art Studio

PETERS, JIM (JAMES) STEPHEN
PAINTER, SCULPTOR
b Syracuse, NY, Aug 3, 1945. *Study:* US Naval Acad, Annapolis, Md, BS, 67; Mass Inst Technol, Cambridge, Atomic Energy Comn fel, 67-69, MS, 69; Md Inst, Coll Art, MFA, 77. *Work:* Flint Inst Art, Mich; Cent Cult Art Contemp, Mex City; Provincetown Art Asn & Mus, Mass; Ctr Fine Arts, Vero Beach, Fla; William Benton Mus, Univ Conn, Storrs. *Exhib:* Exxon Invitational, Solomon R Guggenheim Mus, 85; Fables and Fantasies, Duke Univ Mus Art, Durham, NC, 89; Am Art Today, Fla Int Univ, Miami, 89; The Art Show, 7th Regiment Armory, NY, 89; I, Myself and Me, Midtown Payson Gallery, NY, 92; Solo exhib, Age of Drawing: An Int Scene CDS Gallery, NY, 98, Collection of Provincetown Art Asn & Mus, Nat Art Club, NY, 2000, Redo China, Ethan Cohen Fine Arts, NY, 03, Cape Mus Art, Dennis, Mass, 04. *Pos:* Chmn, visual comt, Fine Arts Work Ctr, 85-89, 94- & fel, 82-84, Provincetown, Mass. *Teaching:* Artist-in-res, Hartwick Col, Oneonta, NY, 90-94. *Awards:* Fel & cash painting grant, Mass Artist Found, 85 & 88; Adolph & Esther Gottlieb Individual Artists Grant, 99; Mass Artist Grant, 2002. *Bibliog:* Lisa Denison (auth), New Horizons in American Art (exhib catalog), Solomon R Guggenheim Mus Found, 85; Vasari Diary (auth), Obsessed with women, Art News, 5/91; Ann Wilson Lloyd (auth), Jim Peters, Art Am, 10/91; Grace Giveck (auth), Art in Review, NY Times, 10/15/99; Cate McQuaid (auth), Shedding Light on the Tensions of Initamcy, Boston Globe, 8/30/02. *Media:* Oil, Mixed on Canvas; Wood Constructions & Wax. *Dealer:* CDS Gallery 76 E 79th St New York NY 10021. *Mailing Add:* PO Box 1171 Truro MA 02666-1171

PETERS, JOHN D
PAINTER, SCULPTOR
b Dover, NH, Jan 23, 1948. *Study:* Univ NH, BA, 71; Univ Toledo, JD, 75; Coll Creative Studies, Detroit. *Hon Degrees:* fellow in the arts, Univ NH. *Work:* Ferry St Inns Collection, Detroit; Danish Consulate, Detroit; Arab Am Nat Mus, Dearborn, Mich. *Comn:* Triptych Spring, Summer, Fall, Motor City Ventures, Detroit, 91. *Exhib:* Solo-exhib, Peters Circus, Dolan Ctr for the Arts, 2001; Solo-exhib, Eye Poppers, Ambleside Galleries, Grosse Point, MI, 02; Flowers, Fruit & Wheatfields, The Cascades, Telluride, CO, 02; group exhib, Amsterdam-Whitney Gallery, Chelsea, NY, 2004; Scarab Club group exhibs, 2005-06; Biddle Gallery, Wyandotte, Mich, 2007; Scarab Club group shows, Detroit, 2008, 2009, 2010, 2011, 2012; Show at Amsterdam, Whitney Gallery, 2013. *Collection Arranged:* Charfoos & Christensen PC; Inns on Ferry St; Univ NH Gallery, 70-71. *Pos:* Assoc prof, Wayne State Univ, 1978-. *Teaching:* Instr, Univ Toledo, Ohio, 72-73. *Awards:* 1st Place, NH Dept of Forrestry, 67; Winner Global Competition, Amsterdam-Whitney Gallery, Chelsea, NY, 2003. *Mem:* Oil Painters of Am; Allied Artists Am; Scarab Club. *Media:* Oil on canvas. *Res:* Painting techniques in the 1600s and 1700s. *Specialty:* Contemp Am Art (paintings, sculpture & photog). *Interests:* Archeology, world hist & antiquities. *Collection:* Heland, Va, Mandt, NY, Gross & Miller, Fla, Christensen, French, Charfoos, Trojanowski, Harbut & Baas, Mich, Mandt, Calif & Jacunski, NH. *Publ:* The Hand Painted Photographs of Charles Henry Sawyer, Treasure Press, 2002; Classic Hand Painted Photographs Are Fine Art, Antiques & Auction News, 2002; New Art Int, 84-85, 2006-2007; Motor City Rock and Roll: The 1960s and 1970s, Arcadia Press, 2008. *Dealer:* Juris Galleries, 5510 Woodward Ave, Detroit, MI 48202; Amsterdam Whitney Gallery 511 W 25th St New York NY 10001. *Mailing Add:* 5510 Woodward Ave Detroit MI 48202

PETERS, LARRY DEAN
CERAMIST, COLLAGE ARTIST
b Manhattan, Kans, July 15, 1938. *Study:* Washburn Univ, BFA, 62; Southern Ill Univ, with Nicholas Vergette, MFA, 65. *Work:* Afghanistan Embassy, Kabul; Singapore Embassy: art in eth Embassy Prog, Temp Loans, Union Pacific Corp; Mulvane Art Mus, Washburn Univ; Wichita Ctr for the Arts; Athens, Greece Embassy, Art in the Embassy Prog (temp loan), 2006-; Topeka Shawnee County Public Libr; Alice C. Sabatini Gallery (permanent collections); Emprise Bank Collection, Wichita, Kans. *Exhib:* 16th Mid-Am Exhib, William Rockhill Nelson Gallery, Kansas City, Mo, 66; North Coast Coll Soc Ann Exhib, Ohio, 86; Highland Community Col, 96; Wichita Ctr Arts, Kans, 98; Pittsburgh State Univ, 2000; McPherson Col, 2001; Strecker-Nelson Gallery, Manhattan, Kans, 2002 & 2006; Birger Sandzen Mem Gallery, 2006; Topeka Competition, The Alice C Sabatini Gallery, Topeka Shawnee Co Pub Libr, 2007; Bergan Gallery, Salina, Kans, 2007; Solo Exhib: Collective Gallery, Topeka, Kans, 2007; Strecker-Nelson Gallery, Manhatten, Kans, 1/2009; Hutchinson Art Ctr, Hutchinson, Kans, 2009; Kans Masters Invitational, Strecker/Nelson Gallery, Manhattan, Kans, 2009; Juried Exhib, Kansas Artist Craftsman Asn, Ft Hays State Univ, Kansas, 2009; two person exhib with Barbara Waterman Peters, Alice C Sabatini Gallery, Topeka Shawnee Co Pub Libr, 2010; Kans Masters, 2011; Material Mastery, Kans Artists Craftsman, 2012; 299th Month of Fine Crafts, Collective Gallery, Topeka, Kans, 2012, Collective At 25, 2012; Topeka Competition, Alice C. Sabatini Gallery of the Topeka and Shawnee Public Library, 2015; Strecker Nelson Gallery, Partners exhib, Manhattan, Kansas, 2015. *Collection Arranged:* Hard Mud: 30 Contemporary Works of Ceramics from the Permanent Collection of the Topeka & Shawnee Coun Pub Libr, Nat Ceramic Educ Conf, Kansas City, Mo, 89; Timock-Babu-Ferguson-Leedy-Pinnell, Kansas City Art Inst Ceramic Fac, 93; Topeka Competition 20, 96; Topeka Competition 22, Mulvane Art Mus, Washburn Univ, Topeka, 2001; Mid-West Contemp Clays, Cedar Rapids Mus Art, Iowa; Hard Mud II: 90 Contemp Works in Clay from the Permanent Collections of the Topeka & Shawnee Co Pub Libr. *Pos:* Readers adv, Dept Fine Arts, Topeka & Shawnee Coun Pub Libr, 65-73, gallery dir, Gallery Fine Arts, 73-; Gallery Dir Emer, Alice C Sabatini Gallery, Shawnee County Pub Libr, 2003-. *Teaching:* Instr pottery, Washburn Univ Topeka, Kans, 69-70. *Awards:* John C Ritchie Alum Award, Wash Univ, 2009; Washburn Univ Alum Fel, 2003. *Mem:* Kans Artist Craftsmen Asn (pres, 2005-2007). *Media:* Ceramic, Mixed Media. *Collection:* Ceramics and Regional Painting and Prints. *Dealer:* Collective Gallery Topeka Kans; Strecker/Nelson Gallery 406 1/2 Ave Manhattan KS 66502-6039. *Mailing Add:* 2223 SW Knollwood Dr Topeka KS 66611-1623

PETERSEN, FRANKLIN G
PAINTER
b Staten Island, NY, July 19, 1940. *Study:* Art Students League, 69-73. *Comn:* Portraits, Admiral A B Durek, US Navy, Washington, DC, former Gov Malcom Wilson, NY, former Atty Gen Louis J Lefkowitz, NY, Fed Judge Irving R Kaufman & Very Rev James Fewhagen, pres, General Theological Seminary NY for Allin Collection, Fordham Law Sch, NY; Commodore George Hinman, NY Yacht Club. *Exhib:* Salmagundi Club, NY, 72-78; Nat Arts Club, NY, 73-76; Staten Island Mus Ann, 74-75; Allied Artists, Nat Acad, NY, 74-75; Pentagon Exhib, Washington, DC, 75; Nacal Artists Exhib, US Navy War Mus, Washington, DC, 75; NY Press Club, 78; and others. *Awards:* Greenshields Found Grant, 73; Stacey Mem Grant, 74; Pouch Award, Staten Island Mus, 75. *Mem:* Life mem Art Students League (secy, 72). *Media:* Oil. *Dealer:* Portraits Inc 985 Park Ave New York NY 10028; Portraits Brokers 36 B Church St Birmingham AL 35213. *Mailing Add:* 8178 Deerbrook Cir Sarasota FL 34238-4375

PETERSEN, ROLAND CONRAD
PAINTER, PRINTMAKER
b Endelave, Denmark, Mar 31, 1926; US citizen. *Study:* Univ Calif, Berkeley, AB, 49 & MA, 50; San Francisco Art Inst, 51; Calif Coll Arts & Crafts, summer 54; Atelier 17, Paris, with Stanley W Hayter, 50, 63 & 70; Islington Studio, London, 77; The Print Workshop, London, 80. *Work:* Mus Mod Art & Whitney Mus Am Art, New York; Philadelphia Mus Art, Pa; Nat Collection Fine Arts, Washington, DC; Univ Reading, Eng; San Francisco Mus Mod Art; Hirshhorn Mus & Sculpture Garden, Washington, DC; M.H. de Young Mem Mus, San Francisco, Calif; Oakland Mus, Calif; Mus Contemp Art, San Diego, Calif; Va Museum Fine Art, Richmond, Va; Santa Barbara Art Mus, Calif; San Jose Mus Art, Calif; Montery Art Mus, Calif. *Comn:* Dams of the West (portfolio of 25 color prints), US Dept Interior, Bur Reclamation, Washington, DC, 70. *Exhib:* Carnegie Inst Int, Pittsburgh, 64; 25th Ann Exhib Contemp Art, Art Inst Chicago, 65; Solo exhibs, Staempfli Gallery, NY, 63, 65 & 67, Phoenix Art Mus, Ariz, 72, Santa Barbara Mus, Calif, 73, Rorick Gallery, San Francisco, 81-85, Roland Petersen: Recent Works, Maxwell Galleries, San Francisco, 95, Endelave Mus, Endelave, Denmark (traveling), 98, Roland Petersen: Recent Works, John Natsoulos Gallery, Davis, Calif, 98 & 2001, Roland Petersen: Early Paintings 1958-1969, Hackett-Freedman Gallery, San Francisco, 2002 & Roland Petersen: Works from the 1950s & 1960s, Hackett-Freedman Gallery, 2004; Vanderwoude/Tananbaum Gallery, NY, 87-89; Harcourts Gallery, San Francisco, 89-91; John Natsoulas Gallery, Davis, Calif, 98-2000; Hackett-Freedman Gallery, San Francisco, Calif, 2002-04, (with catalog) 2008; Monterey Mus Art, Calif, 2010; Bakerfield Mus, Calif, 2013; Fouts Gallery, Sacramento, Calif, 2013. *Pos:* Mem educ process, Coll Lett & Sci, Univ Calif, Davis, 65, mem exec comt, 65-66, prof emer 1991-. *Teaching:* Instr art hist,

Wash State Univ, 52-56; prof painting & printmaking, Univ Calif, Davis, 56-91; instr printmaking, Univ Calif, Berkeley, 65. *Awards:* Guggenheim Award, 63; Fulbright Award, 70. *Bibliog:* Carolyn Strickler (auth), Return of the Figure, Los Angeles Examiner, 61.; Max Kozloff (auth), Art Int Nat, 62.; Brian O'Doherty (auth), NY Times, 63.; John Gruen, NY Herald Tribune, 65.; Stewart Preston (auth), Review, NY Times, 65.; Victoria Dalkey (auth), Petersen Retrospective, Sacremento Bee, 78.; Andree Marchal-Workman (auth), article, Artweek, 81; Kenneth Baker (auth), article, San Francisco Chronicle, 89; Bruce Nixon (auth), Art of Calif, 91; Paul Karlstrom (auth), Book Forward, Hackett Freedman Gallery, 2002; Douglas, Bullis (auth), 100 Artists of the West Coast, Schiffer Publ, Atglen, Pa, 2003; Catalog Forward, Bruce Guenther, Hackett-Freedman Gallery, 2004; Catalog Forward, Susan Landaner, Hackett-Freedman Gallery, 2008; Marcelle Polednik (auth), Monterey Mus Art, 2010; Victoria Dalkey (auth), article, Sacramento Bee, 2013; Catalog Forward, Tim White, Fouts Gallery, 2013. *Media:* Acrylic, Oil. *Res:* Intaglio printing. *Specialty:* Contemporary and Modern Art. *Interests:* Nature. *Publ:* Catalogs, Harcourts Gallery, 89, 91 & 93, Maxwell Gallery, 95 & Hackett-Freedman Gallery, 2002-2004, 2008. *Dealer:* Winfield Gallery Carmel CA 93921; Fouts Gallery Sacramento CA. *Mailing Add:* 1148 Crespi Dr Pacifica CA 94044

PETERSON, BEN
DRAFTSMAN
b Hawthorne, Nev, 1977. *Study:* Calif Coll Arts, BFA (painting), 2004. *Work:* Whitney Mus Am Art; Pa Acad Fine Arts; Indianapolis Mus Art; Bayer Collection Contemp Art, Pittsburgh; DESTE Found for Contemp Art, Greece. *Exhib:* Solo exhibs, Door 7 Gallery, Oakland, 2002, Allston Skirt Gallery, Boston, 2003, Radio 3, San Francisco, 2004, 2006, & 2009, G Fine Art, Washington DC, 2005, Mary Goldman Gallery, Los Angeles, 2006; Visual Alchemy-Phase 2, Oakland Art Gallery, 2003; Color Wheel Oblivion, Marella Arte Contemporanea, Milan, Italy, 2004; Sprawl, Haley Martin Gallery, San Franciso, 2005; Panic Room, DESTE Found Centre for Contemp Art, Athens, Greece, 2006; Locally Localized Gravity, Inst Contemp Art, Univ Pa, 2007; Future Tense: Reshaping the Landscape, Neuberger Mus Art, Purchase Coll, NY, 2008. *Awards:* Pew Ctr for Arts Fel, 2009. *Bibliog:* Cate McQuaid (auth), Artist's metaphors..., Boston Globe, 1/17/2003; Abraham Orden (auth), Aperto San Francisco, Flash Art, Vol 38, No 243, 71-72, 9/2005; Hiya Swanhyuser (auth), Drawing Your Attention, San Francisco Weekly, Vol 25, No 9, 3/29-4/4/2006; David Pagel (auth), The instability of American Culture, Los Angeles Times, 5/12/2006

PETERSON, DOROTHY (HAWKINS)
PAINTER, EDUCATOR
b Albuquerque, NMex, Mar 14, 1932. *Study:* Univ NMex, Albuquerque, BSEd, 53; Dallas Mus Sch, studied painting with Otis Dozier, 63-64; Univ Tex, Permian Basin, Odessa, MA, 79. *Work:* First Nat Bank Chicago Collection, Ill; Eastern NMex Univ, Roswell; Immaculata Hosp, Westlock, Alta, Can; Mus Southwest, Midland; Odessa Coll, Tex. *Comn:* Libr Windows, Jal, NMex Jr High Sch; murals, Tarahumara Sch, Creel, Chi, Mex; catalog cover, ENM Univ, Roswell, 94-96. *Exhib:* Solo exhibs, Carlsbad Mus, NMex, 85, Mus Southwest, Midland, Tex, 85 & Thompson Gallery, Univ NMex, Albuquerque, 86; Eastern NMex Univ, Portales, 88; Centennial Gallery, Univ NMex, 89; Art Inst Permian Basin, Odessa, Tex, 94; Faculty Gallery, Roswell, NMex Mus, 2012; Roswell Mus, NMex, 2013. *Pos:* Comnr, NMex Arts Comn, Santa Fe, 83-96; artist rep, NMex Arts & Crafts Fair, Albuquerque, 84-86. *Teaching:* Instr painting, Midland Coll, Tex, 71-75, Roswell Mus, 81-; prof art hist, Eastern NMex Univ, Roswell, 89-2000; painting instr, NMex Military Inst, Roswell, 92, 94. *Awards:* Tricentennial Award, Masterworks, 2004; Third Place Award, Tex Watercolor Soc, 2005; First Place Award, Watercolors Masterworks, 2005. *Bibliog:* NMex Mag, 5/89& 2/2006. *Mem:* NMex Watercolor Soc; Nat Watercolor Soc, Signature Mem, 2001; Tex Watercolor Soc, Signature Mem, 2006; Tex Soc Watercolorists; Soc Layerists in Multimedia. *Media:* Oil, Watercolor. *Specialty:* Landscape, Figure. *Interests:* Travel, art hist, Spanish. *Publ:* Savoring the Southwest, RSG Pub, 83 & 98; Artists of NMex, Mtn Pub, 89 & 93. *Dealer:* The Gallery 107 E 5th Roswell NM 88201. *Mailing Add:* PO Box 915 Roswell NM 88202

PETERSON, GWEN ENTZ
PRINTMAKER, GRAPHIC ARTIST
b Newton, Kans, Mar 8, 1938. *Study:* Northern Colo Univ, BFA, 59; Goshen Coll, Florence, Italy, 77; Univ NMex, 77-79. *Work:* Golden Collection, Eastern NMex Univ; AT&T; Albuquerque Nat Bank; Miller Libr, McPherson Coll; Jonson Collection. *Comn:* Frame Work, Wright Edge Advert Agency. *Exhib:* Solo exhibs, Jonson Gallery, Univ NMex, 75, 77, 79 & 81 & McPherson Coll, Kans, 2003; retrospective, Thompson Gallery, Univ NMex, 84; Johnson's Gallery, Madrid, NMex, 2001. *Pos:* Independent artist, currently. *Teaching:* Instr pub sch, Colby, Kans, 59-61, Denver, Colo, 61-62 & Lake Bluff, Ill, 65-66. *Awards:* Poster Award, NMex Arts & Crafts Fair, 82; Purchase Award, Art in Pub Places, Fairbanks, Alaska, 86; Banner Design Award, Nat Presbyn Mariners, 97. *Bibliog:* Jean Blackmon (auth), Gwen Peterson, Southwest Profile, 9-10/84. *Media:* Serigraphy. *Interests:* Hiking. *Dealer:* Johnsons of Madrid Gallery Madrid NM. *Mailing Add:* 3717 General Patch NE Albuquerque NM 87111

PETERSON, LARRY D
PAINTER, EDUCATOR
b Holdrege, Nebr, Jan 1, 1935. *Study:* Kearney State Col, BA, 58; Northern Colo Univ, MA, 62; Univ Kans, EdD, 75. *Work:* Univ Minn; US Nat Bank, Omaha; Univ Nebr, Kearney; Nebr Art Collection; 585 works in pvt collections; Sheldon Art Mus, Lincoln, Nebr. *Comn:* Acrylic & oil paintings, First Methodist Church, Kearney; watercolor paintings, Kearney state Bank, 80. *Exhib:* Coll St Mary, Omaha, 80; Landworthy Watercolor Exhib, Seward, 85-91; Six-State Competitive, McCook Col, 88-91; Nebr Art Mus, 89 & 2005-07; Nebr Art Educators Exhib, Nebr Wesleyan Univ, Lincoln, 90-94; Fred Wells, Twelve-State Exhib, Nebr Wesleyan Univ, Lincoln, 91 & 93. *Pos:* Dir, Mus Nebr Art & Kearney Artists Guild; dir, Kearney Area Arts Council. *Teaching:* Instr art, North Platte Pub Schs, 58-65; North Platte Col, 66-67; prof art, Univ Nebr, Kearney, 67-2000; grad asst, Univ Kans, Lawrence, 70-71. *Awards:* Gold Medal Award, Calvatone, Italy, 86-88; Pratt-Heins Award, Kearney State Col, 87; Gov Ben Nelson's Award & One of Am Best, Art In Park, Kearney, 94; 30 Years Serv Award, Asn Nebr Art Club, Lincoln, 94; Art & Entertainment Person of Yr, Kearney Daily Hub, 2002. *Bibliog:* Nancy Kalis (auth), article, Art Rev, 68; Reva Remy (auth), one-man rev in Rev Mod Art, Paris, 68 & 72; Tom Norwood (auth), Contemporary Nebraska Art and Artists, Univ Nebr, 78; Nebraska Art Asn, Sheldon Art Mus, Lincoln, 88; Neb Decoy Makers, Nat Decoy Mag, May/June 2010. *Mem:* Nat Art Educ Asn (nat comt, 83-84); Nebr Art Teachers Asn (past pres); Asn Nebr Art Clubs (past pres); Kappa Pi (past pres, Beta Beta Chap). *Media:* Watercolor, Acrylic, Oil. *Interests:* gardening. *Collection:* folk art, Nebraska duck decoys. *Publ:* Coauth, John Lundgren, His Geese Were Made For Hunting, Decoy Mag, Natl Publ, 9/92; John Lundgren, Decoy Maker, Mag, Nebraskaland State Publ, 11/93; Cy Blacks Counterfeit Canadas, article, 11/95; contrib ed, Paper decoys, Nebraskaland State Publ, 10/96; Decoy Mag, article, 5/96; Nebraska Decoy Makers, Nebraskaland, 4/2008. *Dealer:* Mus Nebr Art 2401 Central Ave Kearney NE 68847. *Mailing Add:* Studio 44 4 Seminole Ln Kearney NE 68847

PETERSON, ROBYN G
CURATOR, DIRECTOR
b San Francisco, Calif. *Study:* UCLA, BA, 1979; Univ Wis - Madison, MA, 1982, PhD, 1987. *Collection Arranged:* Brilliance In Glass; Lost Wax Glass Sculpture of Frederick, 1993; Finding New Worlds; Am Frontier Photography (with catalog), Rockwell Mus, 1993, Edward Borein (with catalog), 1997 & Warp & Weft; Navajo Weaving (with catalog), 1997; Fabric of Life; Photographs of John Smart, 1994; Transforming Trash; Bay Area Fiber Art auth, catalog), Turtle Bay Mus, 2000; Richard Wilson: Paintings from the Nineties, Turtle Bay Mus., 2000; Putting the Pieces Together: Contemporary Quilts by Californians, 2000; Ansel Adams: Masterworks, 2002; Inspired Obsessions: Redding Collectors, 2002; The Earth is Singing: The Art of Frank LaPena, 2003; Second Nature:The Art of Michael Haykin, 2006; Sudden & Solitary, Mount Shasta & its Artistic Legacy, 1841-2008, 2008; Eye for an Eye: Photographs of Modern Artists, 2010; Insomnia: Works by Michael Zansky, 2013. *Pos:* cur collections, Rockwell Mus, Corning, NY, 1988-99; dir exhibs & progs, Turtle Bay Mus, Redding Calif, 1999-2006; dir, Yellowstone Art Mus, 2006-. *Mem:* AAM; CAA; AHAA. *Res:* 19th & 20th Century American Art; Ecological Art. *Mailing Add:* Yellowstone Art Museum 401 North 27th St Billings MT 59101

PETHEO, BELA FRANCIS
PAINTER, PRINTMAKER
b Budapest, Hungary, May 14, 1934; US citizen. *Study:* Univ Budapest, MA, 56; Acad Fine Arts, Vienna, with A P Guetersloh, 57-59; Univ Vienna, 58-69; Univ Chicago, MFA, 63. *Work:* Hungarian State Mus Fine Arts, Hungarian Nat Gallery, Budapest; Kunstmus, Bern, Switz; Boston Public Libr; Tweed Mus, Duluth, Minn; Plains Art Mus, Fargo, NDak; Minn Mus Art, St Paul; Univ Northern Iowa, Cedar Falls, Iowa; Reba and Dave Williams Collection, Nat Gallery Art, Washington, DC. *Comn:* Kindliche Untugenden (mural), Asn Austrian Boyscouts, Vienna, 58; The History of Handwriting (exhib panel), comn by Noble & Noble Publ for Hall of Educ, NY World's Fair, 64; Summer Day at The Quarry, Holiday Inn, St Cloud MN, 2004; The Wedding at Cana (mural), St. Agnes Church, Walker, Minn; The Japanese Garden, SCSU St Cloud, Minn; and others. *Exhib:* Hamline Univ, 66; Coffman Gallery, Univ Minn, 68; Moorhead State Univ, 69; Biennale Wis Printmakers, 71; Duluth: A Painterly Essay, Tweed Mus Art, Minn, 75; B P Themes: 1953-1983, CSB Gallery, St Joseph, Minn, 83; and others. *Teaching:* Instr art, Univ Northern Iowa, 64-66; assoc prof art & artist-in-residence, St John's Univ, 66-80, prof, 80-97, prof emer, 97-. *Awards:* Purchase Award, Pillsbury Invitational, 81; Burlington-Northern Fac Excellence Award, 92; Camargo Found Fel, Cassis, France, fall 94; and others. *Bibliog:* J Gray Sweeney (auth), Bela Petheo: Painter of the Center in an Age of Extremes (monogr), St John's Univ Publ, 85; Arts Salutes Bela Petheo, Arts, Minneapolis, 12/87; Bela Petheo, Works Between 1985-2000, A Retrospective (catalog), 2001; 50+ Drawings by Bela Petheo, Bloomington Art Ctr, Bloomington, Minn, 2008. *Mem:* Rotary Internat (hon). *Media:* Oil, Acrylics; Lithography. *Res:* German Expressionism, litho techniques. *Interests:* Art history, psychology of art. *Publ:* The college art gallery, Art J, summer 71; Lithography: an introduction, traveling exhib, 78; Kokoschka Remembered, Arts(Minneapolis), 12/87; Mission and Commissions: Oskar Kokoschka in Minnesota, 1949-1957 (monogr), SJU Press, 91; The Dimensions of Agreement: Arnheim & the Painter, J Aesthetic Educ, winter 93; plus others. *Dealer:* Groveland Gallery 25 Groveland Terrace Minneapolis MN 55403; Carver Beard Art Galleries 2817 Hennepin Ave S Minneapolis MN 55408. *Mailing Add:* 400 NE Riverside Dr Saint Cloud MN 56304

PETHICK, JERRY THOMAS BERN
SCULPTOR, ASSEMBLAGE ARTIST
b London, Ont, Sept 22, 1935. *Study:* Chelsea Polytechnic London, Gt Brit, Dipl Art, 60; Royal Coll Art, London, Gt Brit, ARCA (sculpture), 64. *Work:* Art Gallery Ont, Toronto; Seattle Arts Comn; Vancouver Art Gallery; Biblioteque Nat, Paris. *Comn:* Vowe Land Piece, Mr & Mrs H Peake, Sussex, 68; padded wall (junkie), Methadone Centre, San Francisco, 72; turret installation, Mr & Mrs D DeVost, Hornby Island, BC, 84; outdoor installation, Toronto Sculpture Garden, 92. *Exhib:* Trales Discovery, Vancouver Art Gallery, 84; Can Biennial, Nat Gallery Can, Ottawa, 89; Material Space, S Alta Art Gallery, Lethbridge, 91; solo exhibs, Ctr Int D'Art Contemairaine, Montreal, 92, The Power Plant, Toronto, 92; Notion of Nothing, Stadt Gaerie, Saarbruchen, Ger, 94. *Pos:* Pres, Young Common Wealth Artists (UK), 59-61; co-founder & instr, Sch Holography, San Francisco, 70-73. *Teaching:* Instr sculpture, San Francisco Art Inst, 69-70 & Emily Carr Inst Art & Design, 85-86. *Awards:* Grant, 84-90 & Media Arts Grant, Can Coun, 92. *Bibliog:* Billy Little (auth), Voluminous luminosity, Capilano Review, 89; Barbara Fischer (auth), The Sequin Veil, Texts Winter 9, 92; Mathew Kangas (auth), Material Space (exhib catalog), Lethbridge, 92. *Mem:* Art Gallery Ont, Toronto; Chelsea Arts Club, London; Western Front, Vancouver; Can Indian Artcrafts, Montreal. *Media:* Mixed, Photo. *Publ:* Contribr,

Holography Book, Avon, 80; auth, Lae Dot, Press Gang, 86; contribr, Virtual Sem on the Bioapparatus, Banff Centre, 91; Research & Reverie, Presentation House, 94. *Dealer:* Catriona Jeffries Gallery 3149 Granville St Vancouver BC V6H 3K1 Canada. *Mailing Add:* 1210 Savoie Rd Hornby Island BC V0R 1Z0 Canada

PETLIN, IRVING
PAINTER
b Chicago, Ill, Dec 17, 1934. *Study:* Art Inst of Chicago, BFA, 52-56; Yale Univ, MFA, with Josef Albers, 59. *Work:* Art Inst Chicago; Jewish Mus, NY; Mus Mod Art, NY & Whitney Mus Am Art, NY; Metrop Mus, NY; Hirshhorn Mus, Wash; Ark Art Ctr, Little Rock; Centre Georges Pompidou, Paris; Des Moines Art Ctr, Iowa; First Nat Bank Chicago; Hood Mus of Art, Dartmouth Coll, Hanover, NH; Mus Contemp Art, Chicago, Ill; Los Angeles Co Mus; San Francisco Mus Contemp Art; de Young Mus, San Francisco; Pa Acad Art, Philadelphia. *Exhib:* Art Inst of Chicago, 53, 56 & 72; Mus d'Art Mod, Paris, 61-66; Chicago Imagist Art, Mus Contemp Art, Chicago, 72; Whitney Mus Am Art, NY, 73; Retrospective, Palais des Beaux-Arts, Brussels, Belg, 65; Neuberger Mus, State Univ NY Col, Purchase, 78; Arts Club Chicago, 78; Wiessewald, Kent Fine Art, NY, 86; 25 yr Retrospective Pastels, Kent Fine Art, NY, 88; The World of Bruno Schulze, Krugier, Geneva, 92 & 97; Jan Krugier Gallery, NY, 98; Contini Gallery, Venice, Italy, 98; Solo exhibs, Irving Petlin Memoire du voyage, voyage de la memoire, Galerie Thessa Herald, Paris, 99, Basel 2000, Krugier-Ditesheim Art Contemporain, Switz, 2000 & Irving Petlin, Galleria Tega, Milano, Italy, 2001; Group exhibs, Light into Darkness, Kent Gallery, NY, 96, Leon Golub, RB Kitaj, Irving Petlin, Kent Gallery, NY, 97 & Chicago Loop: Imagist Art 1949-1979, Whitney Mus of Am Art, Stanford, CT, 2000; Jan Krugier Gallery, The World of Paul Celan, Geneva, 2003; Galerie Jan Krugier, Basel Int, 2001-2004; and others. *Teaching:* Vis artist, Univ Calif, Los Angeles, 63-66; artist-in-residence, Dartmouth Col, fall 83; vis prof, Cooper Union, New York, 77-89 & Pa Acad Grad Prog, 90-96. *Awards:* Ryerson Fel, 56; Copley Found Grant, 61; Guggenheim Found Fel, 71. *Bibliog:* Michel Butor (auth), Spiral, 65; RB Kitaj (auth), Irving Petlin: Rubbings, 78; Edward Fry (auth), Irving Petlin: Kent, 87. *Mem:* Century Club, NY; Nat Acad. *Media:* Oil on Canvas; Pastel on Paper. *Publ:* Coauth (with M Palmer), A Song for Sarah; Auth, Irving Petlin: 25 Yrs of Pastels, Paul Cummings, 88; Arte Americana e arte europea a NY ed oltre: 41 east 57th St, Terzocchio, 3/89; Coauth (with Michael Brenson), Irving Petlin, New York Times, 1/6/89; coauth (with Wroblewska and Zielinski), Irving Petlin: Bruno Schulz's World, Varsovie: Galeria Kordegarda (catalogue), 93; Paul Cummings (auth), Irving Petlin the Patels, NY, 88; (auth), The world of Edmond Jabes. *Dealer:* Kent Fine Art 67 Prince New York NY 10012; Krugier-Ditesheim 29-31 Grand-Rue Geneve 1204

PETRACCA, ANTONIO
PAINTER, PHOTOGRAPHER
b Rochester, NY, June 6, 1945. *Study:* Rochester Inst Tech Sch Art, BFA, 67, MFA, 69. *Work:* Mem Art Gallery, Rochester, NY; George Eastman House, Int Mus Photog, Rochester; Albright-Knox Mus, Buffalo, NY; NY Hist Soc; Mus City New York; Nat Sept 11 Mem & Mus, New York. *Comn:* Patrons Print (award), Mem Art Gallery, Rochester, NY, 78; Subway mural, Metrop Transit Authority Arts for Transit, NY, 92; Putt Modernism, Hole No 6, Artists Space, NY, 93. *Exhib:* Altered Landscape, Albany Inst Hist & Art, NY, 90; NY State Art Exhib, Herbert Johnson Mus, Cornell Univ, NY, 91; Isn't It Romantic?, Art Initiatives, NY, 94; solo exhibs, Kim Foster Gallery, New York, 95-97, 99-2000, 2002, 2007, 2009, & 2011, Galerie Bhak, Seoul Korea, 99, Oxford Gallery, Rochester, NY, 95, 99 & 2003 & SUNY, Oswego, NY, 99, The City, Lehman Coll Art Gallery, New York, 2005, Imagining Landscape, Hunterdon Mus, NJ, 2006, Italian-Am Mus, 2006, Urban/Suburban, Islip Art Mus, 2012; Mem Gallery Selections, Albright-Knox Mus, Buffalo, NY, 96 & 97; 4 Artists From NY, Galerie Bhak, Seoul, Korea, 97; Psychological Realism, Castle Gallery, Coll New Rochelle, NY, 98; Fanelli Show, OK Harris Gallery, New York, 98; Elbow Room, Kim Foster Gallery, Turner, NY, 2000; Inst of Hist & Art, NY, 2002; Flowers East, London, Eng, 2002; US Embassy, US State Dept, Art in Embassies Prog, Caracas, Venezuela, 2004-2005; Garibaldi Meucci Mus, 2007; Nature Calls, Shore Inst Contemp Arts, 2010. *Collection Arranged:* Performance Art, New Music, Nyack Center for Arts, Nyack, NY, 88. *Pos:* Dir & chief cur, Pyramid Art Ctr, Rochester, NY, 77-87; dir performing arts, Monroe Community Col, Rochester, NY, 88-89. *Teaching:* Adj instr painting, Rochester Inst Tech, NY, 82-83; Instr painting, Allofus Art Workshop, Rochester, NY, 71-77. *Awards:* Art Matters Inc Grant, 92; Best of Show, Casa Italiana, Nazereth Col, 92. *Bibliog:* Putt Modernism (TV doc), CBS Sunday Morning, 11/14/93; William Zimmer (auth), Definitive Decade Show, NY Times, 10/30/94; Margaret Mooreman (auth), Review of Exhibition, Art News, 10/97; Ken Johnson (auth), Review of Exhibition, NY Times, 9/13/02; Melissa Kuntz (auth), Review of Exhibition, Art in America Mag; Jonathan Goodman (auth), Overlay: Antonio Petracca at Kim Foster Gallery, 6/2009. *Media:* Oil on wood constructions. *Dealer:* Kim Foster Gallery 529 W 20th St New York NY 10011; Oxford Gallery 267 Oxford St Rochester NY 14607. *Mailing Add:* 552 Broadway 4th Fl New York NY 10012

PETRIE, SYLVIA SPENCER
PRINTMAKER, PAINTER
b Wooster, Ohio, June 15, 1931. *Study:* Coll Wooster, BA; State Univ Iowa, with Mauricio Lasansky & Eugene Ludens; Univ RI. *Work:* Art Ctr Mus, Wooster Coll; Hasbro Children's Hosp, Providence, RI; RI Hosp, Providence, RI; Providence Pub Libr; Boston Pub Libr; Newport Art Mus, RI. *Exhib:* Soc Am Graphic Artists 63rd Nat Print Exhib, NY; Springfield Art Mus, Mo, 90; solo exhib, Vet Mem Auditorium, Providence, RI, 94-95; By Virtue of Excellence, Bell Gallery, Brown Univ, Providence, RI, 95; Hunterdon 40th Nat Juried Print Exhib, Clinton, NJ, 96; Albrecht-Kemper Mus Art, St Joseph, Mo, 2000. *Pos:* Vis artist, Title III Prog, Coventry Elem Schs, RI, 75-77. *Awards:* Netta Strain Scott Prize Art, Wooster Coll, 53; First Prize & Purchase Award, Fantle's, 56; Awards, open juried exhibs, Providence Art Club, 90, 91, 97; First Prize, South Co Art Asn Open Juried Art Ann, 93 & 94; and many others. *Bibliog:* Elizabeth Findley (auth), Petrie prints and pastels depend on point of view, Eve Bull, Providence, 10/15/77; Edward Sozanski (auth), Print forms offer intriguing tones, Providence Sunday J, 10/15/78; Arline Fleming (auth), Variety of Interest Reflected in Work of Peace Dale Artist, Providence Jr Bull, 3/4/87. *Mem:* Print Consortium, Kansas City, Mo; Nineteen on Paper, Providence, RI; South Co Art Asn. *Media:* Intaglio, Collagraph; Oil, Pastel, Monotype. *Publ:* Illusr, From under the Hill of Night, Vanderbilt Univ, 69; The Idol, 73 & Time Songs, 79, Biscuit City Press; cover illustration, Paul Petrie-The Collected Poems, Antrim House, 2014. *Dealer:* David Charles Gallery 263 S Main St Providence RI 02903. *Mailing Add:* 200 Dendron Rd Peace Dale RI 02879

PETRO, JOE, III
PRINTMAKER, PAINTER
b Lexington, Ky, May 3, 1956. *Study:* Univ Tenn, 74-79. *Work:* Jimmy Carter Pres Libr, Atlanta, Ga; Am Acad Arts & Lett, NY; Ind Art Ctr, Indianapolis; Univ Ky Art Mus, Lexington. *Comn:* Sculpture TV, State Ky, Lexington, 92; silkscreen ed & poster, David Suzuki Found, Vancouver, Can, 93; silkscreen ed in collab with Ralph Steadman, 94; silkscreen ed & poster, Greenpeace, Canada, 94, 96 & 99; silkscreen ed in collab with Jonathen Winters, 97-99; silkscreen ed in collab with Ken Kesey, 97-99; Poster in collab with Barnum Mus, Bridgeport, Conn, 98-99. *Exhib:* Liberty Gallery, Louiseville, Ky, 89; Artists Attic, Lexington, Ky, 98. *Awards:* Cert Merit, Graphic Arts Awards Competition, Heidelberg, USA, 91, 92, 93, 94, 96 & 97. *Bibliog:* Craig Latscha (auth), Joe Petro III: A Printmaker of Many Interests, Screenprinting, 80, 107-111, 12/90; Terry Pope Freas (auth), Absolute Statehead, Young Am Artists gain Nat recognition, Sunstorm, Vol 18, pp 28-31, 93. *Media:* Silkscreen. *Dealer:* John Cavaliero Fine Arts 229 E 42nd St New York NY 10017

PETRULIS, ALAN JOSEPH
PRINTMAKER, PHOTOGRAPHER
b Queens, NY, June 20, 1954. *Study:* Queens Col, BA, 1977; Md Inst Coll Art, MFA, 1979. *Work:* Brooklyn Mus, Brooklyn, NY; Mus City NY, NY; NY Transit Mus, NY; NY Hist Soc, NY; Boston Athenaeum. *Exhib:* The Highland Set, Mus Hudson Highlands, Cornwall, NY, 1989; Hudson Valley Photography, Hudson River Mus, Yonkers, NY, 1995; New York by New Yorkers, Mus City of NY, NY, 2002; Transit Views, NY Transit Mus, NY, 2003; Impressions of NY, NY Hist Soc, NY, 2004; Tide Lines, Noble Maritime Collection, Staten Island, NY, 2006. *Pos:* Dir, First Street Gallery, NY, 1983-1989. *Awards:* Cannon Prize, 159th Exhib, Nat Acad Design, 1984; Ralph Fabri Prize, 161st Exhib, Nat Acad Design, 1986; Adriana Brina Award, Pastel Soc Ann, Pastel Soc Am, 1986. *Bibliog:* Madaline Rogers (auth), Only in New York /Local Color, Daily News Mag, 1985; Jerry Morgan, His Brush Captures the Outer Boroughs, News Day, 1985. *Mem:* Soc Am Graphic Artists; NY Etchers Soc. *Media:* Etching. *Publ:* Contribr, Art & the Law (bk), West Publ, 1996; contribr, Impressions of New York (bk), Princeton Archit Press, 2005. *Dealer:* Old Print Shop 150 Lexington Ave New York NY 10016. *Mailing Add:* 164-11 Underhill Ave Flushing NY 11365

PETTERSON, MARGO
PAINTER
b Los Angeles, Calif, Jan 12, 1944. *Study:* San Bernardino Valley Col, AA, 81. *Work:* CM Russell Mus, Great Falls, Mont; Holy Cross Hosp, Cleveland, Ohio; High Desert Cult Art Inst, Victorville, Calif. *Comn:* Collections of Wayne & Ann Miller, Myron Achenbach & Mr & Mrs Wm Tamietti. *Exhib:* Gold Medal Exhib, Calif Art Club, 95-97; Calgary Stampede, Can, 96-2005; Am Art in Miniature, Gilcrease Mus, Tulsa, OK, 1998-2006; Draft Horse Classic, Grass Valley, Calif, 2000-2006; Am Acad Equine Art, Lexington, KY, 2002 & 2004. *Awards:* 2nd Place, Calif State Fair, 2002; Best of Show, Snake River Showcase, Snake River Art Guild, 1995; Best of Show, Draft Horse Classic, 2004; Best of Show, Western States Horse Expo, 2006. *Mem:* Calif Art Club; Oil Painters of America; Women Artists of the West. *Media:* Oil, Pastel. *Interests:* The human figure; Equine paintings in the Western style. *Publ:* Sarah H Crampton, Romantic Sesibliity of Margo Petterson, Equine Visions Mag, 2002; Elizabeth Stevens, Romancing the Old West, Big, Bear Life & Grizzly, 2000. *Dealer:* Ken McDonald, 6834 Granola Las Vegas NV 89103. *Mailing Add:* 165 Pinon Place Coleville CA 96107-9400

PETTIBON, RAYMOND
VIDEO ARTIST
b Tucson, Ariz, June 16, 1957. *Study:* Univ Calif, Los Angeles, BA, 77. *Exhib:* Heart, Mind, Body & Soul, Whitney Mus Am Art, NY, 97-98 & Hindsight: 56 Recent Acquisitions, 98-99; Double Trouble: The Patchett Collection, Mus Contemp Art, San Diego, 98; Sea Change, Parrish Art Mus, Southampton, NY, 98; LA Current: Looking at the Light: 3 Generations of Los Angeles Artists, Armand Hammer Mus Art & Cult Ctr, Univ Calif, Los Angeles, 99; Life Lessons: How Art Can Change Your Life, The Judy and Stuart Spence Collection, Laguna Art Mus, 99; It's Only Rock and Roll Currents in Contemp Art, Austin Mus Art, 99; Solo exhibs, The Drawing Ctr, New York City, 99, Philadelphia Mus of Art, 99, Mus of Contemp Art, Los Angeles, 99, Galerie Meyer Kainer, Vienna, 99, Sadie Coles HQ, London, 2000, David Zwirner Gallery, New York City, 2000, Hauser +Wirth, Zurich, Switzerland, 2000, Regen Projects, Los Angeles, 2000, Contemp Fine Arts, Berlin, 2000, MAK, Vienna, 2000 & 2001, David Zwirner Gallery, 2000, Mus of Art, Calif, 2000, The Whitechapel, London, 2000 & Plots Laid Thick, MACBA, Barcelona, Spain, 2002; LA-ex, Mus Villa Stuck & Marstall, Munich, Ger, 2000; Am Art, Galerie Fudolfinum, Munich, 2001; Das Gute Leben, Galerie Gebr, Lehmann, Dresden, Ger, 2001; Sammlung Hauser und Wirth Part 2-Alternating Current, Sammlung Hauser & Wirth, 2001; Location Drawing, Lawing Gallery, Houston, 2001; Drawing Exhib, Lawing Gallery, Houston, 2001; Group exhibs, Ten Yrs, Galerie Hauser & Wirth, Zurich, Switz, 2002, Colorblind: Works in Black and White, Ikon Ltd/Kay Richards Contemp Art, Santa Monica, Calif, 2002, 2004, Permanent Collection Galleries, Post-1945 Art, Dallas Mus of Art, Dallas, Tex, 2002. *Awards:* Recipient Awards Painting, Sculpture, Printmaking, Photog, & Craft Media, Louis Comfort Tiffany Found, 1991, Wolfgang-Hahn-Prize, Ludwig Mus, Cologne, Ger, 2001, Busksbaum Award, Whitney Mus Am Art, 2004; Oskar Kokoschka Prize, Austrian Govt, 2010. *Mailing Add:* David Zwirner Gallery 525 W 19th St New York NY 10011-2808

PETTIBONE, JOHN WOLCOTT
CURATOR, ADMINISTRATOR

b Springfield, Ohio, Jan 30, 1942. *Study:* Wittenberg Univ, 62-63; Cleveland Inst Art, 63-65, Ford grant, 64. *Work:* Am Red Cross, Washington, DC; Town of Rockport, Mass. *Exhib:* Rockport Art Asn, 71-83; Am Fortnight Exhibition, Hong Kong, 73. *Pos:* Dir marketing, Hammond Castle Mus, Gloucester, Mass, 83-85, cur, 85-90, exec dir/cur, 90-; instr drawing, Rockport Pub Schs, 73-78, Endicott Col, 85; registrar, Higgins Armory Mus, Worcester, Mass, 78-83. *Teaching:* Instr drawing, Lakewood Pub Schs, Ohio, 59, Springfield Art Asn, Ohio, 61-63, Rockport Pub Schs, 73-78 & Endicott Col, 85-86. *Mem:* Rockport Art Asn; Arms & Armour Soc, London; Japanese Sword Soc USA. *Media:* Conte Crayon, Silverpoint. *Dealer:* Rockport Art Asn 12 Main St Rockport MA 01966. *Mailing Add:* 509 Washington St Gloucester MA 01930-1749

PEVEN, MICHAEL DAVID
PHOTOGRAPHER, EDUCATOR

b Chicago, Ill, Apr 12, 1949. *Study:* Univ Ill, Chicago, AB, 71; Sch Art Inst Chicago, MFA, 77. *Work:* Ctr Creative Photog, Tucson; Humanities Res Ctr, Austin; Mus Contemp Art, Chicago; Mus Mod Art, New York; Nat Gallery Art, Ottawa, Ont, Can. *Exhib:* Alternative Image II, Kohler Art Ctr, Sheboygan, 84; Offset: Survey of Artists Books (with catalog), Hera Found, Wakefield, RI, 84; one-man shows, Art Arts Ctr, Little Rock, 85, Amarillo Mus Art, 94, Daum Mus Contemp Art, Sedalia, No, 2003, Art Ctr of Ozark, 2004, Univ Mus, Southern Ill Univ, Carbondale, Ill, 2005; Photog Book Art in the United States, 91, travel, 94; Camera Obscura, Obscura Camera, Rymer Gallery Saic, Chicago, Ill, 94; Exploring Sight: Young Photographers of the 70's, Amon Carter Mus, Ft Worth, Tex, 2006; Silent Scream: Political and Social Comment in Books by Artists, Rare Books Lib, Monash Univ, Melbourne, Australia, 2011. *Teaching:* Prof art, Univ Ark, Fayetteville, 77-. *Awards:* Artists Fel, 82 & Photographers Fel, 83, Mid-Am Art Alliance; Photographers Fel, Ark Art Coun, 86 & 90; Master Teaching Award, Fulbright Col, 92; Honored Educator, Soc for Photographic Education, South Central Region. *Bibliog:* T Brown & E Partnow (auths), McMillian Biographical Encyclopedia of Photographic Artists and Innovators, 83. *Mem:* Soc for Photog Educ. *Media:* Photography, Book Arts. *Publ:* Auth, Snatches--or Man Made Wonders, Verb: Print, 79; Prophesy Panorama, 82, The Marriage of Heaven & Hell, Part 1, 86 Global Family, 90, Primitive Press; Cradle of Civilization, Primitive Press, 93; Slugs and Roses, Primitive Press, 2001; auth, Drive by Shootings, Primitive Press, 2004; Open...Heart Surgery, Primitive Press, 2006; Bird's Bar Mitzvah, Primitive Press, 2014. *Dealer:* Vamp & Tramp Booksellers LLC 1951 Hoover Ct Ste 105 Birmingham AL 35226; Printed Matter 195 10th Ave New York NY 10011; Abecedacian Gallery 910 Santa Fe #101 Denver CO 80204; 23 Sandy Gallery 623 NE 23rd Ave Portland OR 97232. *Mailing Add:* 514 N Mission Blvd Fayetteville AR 72701-3519

PEYTON, ELIZABETH JOY
WRITER, PAINTER

b Danbury, Conn, Dec 20, 1965. *Study:* Sch Visual Arts, NY City, BA, 87. *Work:* Mus Modern Art, 1998, Examining Pictures, Mus Contemp Art, Chicago, 1999, Whitney Biennial, Whitney Mus Am Art, 2004. *Exhib:* Solo shows incl Gavin Brown's enterprise, New York, 95, 96, 97, 99, 2000, 2002, 2004, neuger/riemschneider, Berlin, 96, 99, 2003, 2006, St Louis Art Mus, 97, Galerie Daniel Buchholz, Koln, Ger, 97, Side 2 Gallery, Tokyo, 97, Regen Projects, Los Angeles, 97, 99, 2003, 2007, Mus fur Gegenwartskunst, Basel, 98, Sadie Coles HQ, London, 98, 2000, 2002, 2005, Seattle Art Mus, 98, Deichtorhallen Hamburg, Ger, 2001; group shows incl Art of Four Decades 1958-1998, San Francisco, Remix: Contemp art & pop, Tate Liverpool, 2002, Cher peintre- Peintures figuratives despuis l'ultime Picabia, Centre Pompidou, Paris, 2002, Inaugural Exhib, Regen Project, Los Angeles, 2003, New Paintings, 2003, Edition Speciale, Galerier Suzanner Tarasieve, Paris, 2003, Aldrich Contemp Art Mus, Ridgefield, Conn, 2006. *Awards:* Larry Aldrich Found Award, 2006. *Publ:* Auth: Live Forever, 1997, Craig, 1998. *Mailing Add:* c/o Regen Projects 6750 Santa Monica Blvd Los Angeles CA 90038

PEZZUTTI, SANTO C
PAINTER, SCULPTOR

b Fontanafredda, Italy. *Study:* Art Students League, New York; Newark Sch Fine and Indust Arts; student of John Grabach. *Work:* Var pvt collections, Mont, S Africa & Argentina; Silver Palate, New York. *Comn:* South Africa Platinum Mines, Ltd; Brookdale Coll, NJ. *Exhib:* Nat Acad Design, New York; Monmouth Mus; Newark Mus; solo exhibs, Phoenix Gallery, New York, Carrimore Gallery, New York, Monmouth Univ, NJ & Emory Univ, Atlanta, Ga; Brookdale Coll, NJ. *Pos:* Exec art dir, Dancer Fitzgerald Advert Agency, Madison Ave, New York. *Teaching:* instr, Summit Art Ctr, NJ, Guild Creative Art & Bloomfield Art League; workshops instr, Ocean Co Art Guild. *Awards:* 1st Prizes: Monmouth Mus, Guild Creative Art & Monmouth Arts Coun; Silver Medal, NJWCS. *Mem:* NJ Watercolor Soc; Art Dir Club, New York. *Media:* Oil, Acrylic. *Interests:* People and marine subjects. *Collection:* Rober Harris; Dale Barney, Peter Dray. *Publ:* Illusr, The Best of Watercolor, NY Illusr Club, Soc Illusr Ann. *Dealer:* Anchor & Palette Gallery; Beacon Art Short Wave Gallery 9412 2nd Ave Stone Arbor NJ 08247. *Mailing Add:* 50 Conover Ln Red Bank NJ 07701

PFAFF, JUDY
SCULPTOR, EDUCATOR

b London, Eng, 1946. *Study:* Washington Univ, St Louis, BFA, 1971; Yale Univ, MFA, 1973. *Work:* Whitney Mus & Mus Mod Art, NY; Albright Knox Mus, Buffalo, NY; Brooklyn Mus, NY; High Mus, Atlanta. *Comn:* Special installation, Wacoal Ctr, Tokyo, Japan, 1985 & Spokane, Wash; site specific comn, GTE, Irving, Tex, 1991; Pa Convention Ctr, Philadelphia, 1994. *Exhib:* Whitney Biennial, Dragon Group, Whitney Mus Am Art, Columbus, Ohio, 1975; Rorschach, Ringling Mus, Sarasota, Fla, 1981; Solo exhibs, Rock-Paper-Scissors, Albright Knox Mus, Buffalo, NY, 1982, Holly Solomon Gallery, New York, 1983, Daniel Weinberg Gallery, Los Angeles, 1984, Hudson River Mus, 1985, John Weber Gallery, 1986, Whitney Mus Am Art, 1987, Carnegie Mellon Univ Art Gallery, 1988, Cleveland Ctr Contemp Arts, 1990, Susanne Hilberry Gallery, 1991, 1999, Nancy Drysdale Gallery, Wash, DC, 1993, Columbus Mus Art, 1994, Saint-Gaudens National Historic Site, Cornish, NH, 1997, Bellas Artes, Santa Fe, NMex, 1998, Flanders Gallery, Minneapolis, 2001, Sarah Moody Gallery Art, Tuscaloosa, Ala, 2002, Carl Solway Gallery, Cincinnati, 2004, Lemberg Gallery, Ferndale, Mich, 2005, Buckets of Rain, Ameringer Yohe Fine Art, NY City, 2006, Samuel Dorsky Mus Art, 2007; Int Survey of Recent Painting & Sculpture, Mus of Modern Art, NY, 1984; An Am Renaissance, Painting & Sculpture since 1940, Mus of Art, Ft Lauderdale, Fla, 1985; Recent Acquisitions, Whitney Mus, NY, 1986; Landscape as Metaphor, Denver Art Mus & Columbus Mus Art 1994 & 1995; Am Acad Arts & Letters Invitational Exhib NY, 1994; Recent Drawings, Andre Emmerich Gallery, NY, 1994; Rose Art Mus, Brandeis Univ, Waltham, Mass, 1995; DC Moore Gallery, New York, 2000; Elizabeth Leach Gallery, Portland, Ore, 2001; Am Acad Arts and Letters, 2002; William Traver Gallery, Seattle, 2003; Milwaukee Art Mus, 2004; Pavel Zoubok Gallery, New York, 2005; Sussane Hilberry Gallery, Detroit, 2006; Robischon Gallery, Denver, 2007; Mus Mod Art, New York, 2011. *Pos:* co-chair, Undergrad Dept Art, Bard Col. *Teaching:* instr sculpture, Yale Univ & Skowhegan Sch of Painting, formerly; prof Visual Arts, Columbia Univ, 1992-94 & Bard Col, 1995-. *Awards:* Creative Artists Pub Serv, 1976; Nat Endowment for the Arts Fel, 1979 & 1986; Guggenheim Fel, 1983; Bessie Award, 1984; Award of Merit Gold Medal for Sculpture, Am Acad Arts and Letts, 2002; MacArthur Fel, 2004; Barnett and Annalee Newman Found Fel, 2006; US Artists Rasmuson Fel, 2009. *Bibliog:* Wade Saunders (auth), Talking Objects, interviews with 10 younger sculptors, Art in Am, 10/1985; John Russel (auth), Bright young talents: 6 artists with a future, New York Times, 5/16/1986; Jerry Salz (auth), What's an artist's artist?, Art & Auction, 1993. *Mem:* Am Acad Arts and Letters. *Media:* All. *Dealer:* Ameringer & Yohe Fine Art 20 W 57th St New York NY 10019; Robischon Gallery 1740 Wazee St Denver CO 80202; Elena Zang Gallery 3671 Rte 212 Shady NY 12409; Bellas Artes Gallery 653 Canyon Rd Santa Fe NM 87501; Sears-Peyton Gallery 210 11th Ave Ste 802 New York NY 10001; William Traver Gallery 110 Union St Seattle WA 98101; Bard Col PO Box 5000 Annandale-on-Hudson NY 12504; Elvehjem Mus Art Univ Wis Madison. *Mailing Add:* Bard Col PO Box 5000 Red Hook NY 12504-5000

PFAFFMAN, WILLIAM SCOTT
SCULPTOR, DRAFTSMAN

b Albany, Ga, July 10, 1954. *Study:* Auburn Univ, BFA, 76; Hunter Coll, City Univ, NY, MA, 78. *Work:* John F Kennedy High Sch, Bronx, New York; Dept of Parks, Brooklyn, NY; Lookout Sculpture Park, Pa. *Comn:* Artpark Proj Comn, Natural Heritage Trust, Lewiston, NY, 84; Sculpture Chicago, Burnham Park Planning Bd, Chicago, Ill, 85; sculpture, NY State Coun Arts, Bronx, NY, 87; Brooklyn Bears Greenthumb Project, NY Dept Gen Serv, 88; Mus in the Schs I.S.49, Brooklyn, NY, 99. *Exhib:* Am Pantheon, City Univ NY Grad Ctr, 82 & Art on the Beach, Battery Park City, NY, 82; Spec Proj Exhib, Proj Studios One, Queens, NY, 83. *Pos:* Artist-in-residence, Athena Found; dir, Scott Pfaffman Gallery, NY; co-founder, Kentler International Drawing Space, KIDS. *Teaching:* Drawing instr, PS6, New York City, 2004; Berkeley Coll, New York, 2007-. *Awards:* Annual Award, Am Acad Arts & Lett, 85; Artist Fel, Pollack-Krasner Found, 86. *Bibliog:* Martignioni (auth), Socrates Sculpture Park, Athena Found, 86; Allen Rokach (auth), article, Sculpture Mag, Int Sculpture (tr, 87). *Mem:* Brooklyn Waterfront Artists Coalition (vpres); Found Community of Artists; Am Coun Arts. *Media:* Sculpture. *Res:* Buckminster Fuller. *Specialty:* Photog. *Publ:* Auth, Five years of outdoor sculpture, Brooklyn Waterfront Artists Coalition, 87. *Dealer:* Scott Pfaffman Gallery 35 E 1st St New York NY 10003. *Mailing Add:* 360 Van Brunt St Brooklyn NY 11231

PHARIS, MARK
CERAMIST

b Minneapolis, Minn, 1947. *Study:* Univ Minn, BFA, 71 with Warren Mackenzie and Curt Hoard. *Work:* Victoria & Albert Mus, London, Eng; Univ Colo; Univ Wis, River Falls; State Coll Ceramics, NY; also pvt collections of Robert Pfannebecker, Joan Mannheimer, Daniel & Caroline Anderson, Dr & Mrs Edward Okun, Betty & George Woodman and many others. *Exhib:* Solo exhib, Hadler Rodriguez, NY, Pro Art, St Louis, 87, 89 & 92, Garth Clark Gallery, NY, 87, 89 & 94; Rhode Island Sch Design, Providence, RI; Marion Art Ctr, Lancaster, Pa; Minneapolis Art Inst, Minn; Victoria & Albert Mus, London, Eng; Univ Minn, St Paul. *Teaching:* Assoc prof, Art Dept, Univ Minn, currently. *Awards:* Fel, Nat Endowment Arts, 86; Two Nat Endowment Grants for Individual Craftsmen; Minn State Art Coun Grant. *Media:* Clay. *Mailing Add:* c/o University of Minnesota Art Department 405 21st Ave S Minneapolis MN 55455

PHELAN, AMY
COLLECTOR

b Dallas. *Study:* Southerm Methodist Univ, BA. *Pos:* Managing dir marketing and bus develop, Blythe-Nelson; trustee, Art-Pace San Antonio & Guggenheim Mus, 2007-; mem bd dirs, NY Jr League; mem, Mus Mod Art Contemp Art Coun, Tate Am Acquisitions Comt, Aspen Art Mus Nat Coun & Whitney Mus Nat Coun; co-chair, Art Crush, Aspen Art Mus & 2007 Fall Gala, Whitney Mus Am Art. *Awards:* Named one of Top 200 Collectors, ARTnews mag, 2009, 2012, & 2013. *Collection:* Contemporary art. *Mailing Add:* Solomon R Guggenheim Mus 1071 Fifth Ave New York NY 10128

PHELAN, ANDREW L
EDUCATOR, WRITER

b Bryn Mawr, Pa, May 8, 1943. *Study:* Pratt Inst, BS, 65, MFA, 69; New York Univ, PhD, 86. *Exhib:* Solo exhib, Snug Harbor Cult Ctr, Staten Island, New York, 80. *Collection Arranged:* RB Sprague, 10-12/2001, Fritz Scholder, Recent Works, 5-9/2002 & Jim Waid, Recent Works, 10-12/2002, Fred Jones Jr Mus Art, Norman, Okla; Elias Rivera, The Other Side of the Street, 10/2003-1/2004 & John Fincher, Boughs Branches and Limbs, 10-11/2004, Oklahoma City Mus Art; Wilson Hurley's Campaign, Painting the Murals, Nat Cowboy & Western Heritage Mus, Fred Jones Jr Mus Art, 10-11/2005; Nelson Shanks, In the Classic Tradition, Fred Jones Jr Mus Art,

Norman, Okla, 2-3/2006; Koji Keda, Artist of Iconoclastic Contemporary Hanko, Lightwell Gallery, Univ Okla, 9-10/2005; 60 Yrs of Printmaking, Lightwell Gallery, Univ Okla, 2007. *Pos:* Consult & adv, Yugen Kashia Gregg Int, Tokyo, Japan, 90-92. *Teaching:* Dean acad affairs, assoc dean to dean art & design, chair art educ, Pratt Inst, Brooklyn, New York, 72-90; dir & prof, Sch Art, Univ Okla, 92-2006; dir, arts mgt progs & coordr int prog arts, Weitzenhoffer Family Coll Fine Arts, Univ Okla, 2006-2009, prof art & dir emer, Sch Art. *Mem:* Nat Asn Sch Art & Design; Coll Art Asn. *Res:* Technology and the arts; history of innovation in the artists education or training. *Publ:* Auth, The Bauhaus & studio art education, 81 & The impact of technology & post modern art, 84, Art Educ; The Albers Project - A model for multimedia courseware, Tech Horizons Ed, 88; 50 years at the Sch for Am Craftsmen, 2/95, Rowantrees Pottery, 2/98 & Western Waves in Oklahoma, 11/2004, Ceramics Monthly; Studio Art Educ Today, The impact of digital media & technology, Int J Arts Educ, 7/2006; auth, Paul Moore & His Sculpture Studio, a successful management case, Sculpture Mag, China, 12/6/2008; auth, Sculpture Education in the US, Sculpture Mag, China, 2/1/2009; auth, The Ontology of Sculpture, China Sculpture Mag, 2/2014; auth, El río sin tacto, Quail Creek ed, 2008; auth, Uncommonly Good, Quail Creek Ed, 2009; auth, Following the Brick Path, the Story of Rowantrees Pottery, Quail Creek Ed, 2010; ed, Two in Tuscany with a Donkey, Adelaide Pearson, Quail Creek Ed, 2011; auth, Becoming the Village Potter, The Life of Linn L Phelan, Quail Creek Ed, 2012; auth, Doors and Passageways in Eisenstadt, Quail Creek Ed, 2013; auth, On the Road, Into the Woods, In the Garden, and Within the House, Quail Creek Ed, 2015. *Mailing Add:* 1811 Quail Creek Dr Norman OK 73026-0944

PHELAN, ELLEN DENISE
PAINTER
b Detroit, Mich, Nov 3, 1943. *Study:* Wayne State Univ, BFA, 69, MA, 71, MFA, 73. *Work:* Detroit Inst Arts; Mus Mod Art, NY; Whitney Mus Am Art; Walker Art Ctr; Brooklyn Mus; High Mus of Art; Metrop Mus Art, NY; Fogg Mus, Harvard Univ; Smith Coll Mus; Baltimore Mus; Mass Inst Technol; Allen Mem Art Mus, Oberlin Col; Hood Mus Art, Dartmouth Col. *Exhib:* New Art for the New Year, Mus Mod Art, NY, 78; Drawings, Albright-Knox Art Gallery, Buffalo, NY, 79; Am Abstraction Now, Inst Contemp Art, Va Mus, Richmond, 82; Out of Square, Cranbrook Acad Art, Bloomingfield Hills, Mich, 84; The New Romantic Landscape, Whitney Mus Am Art, Stamford, Conn, 87; Recent Drawings, Whitney Mus Am Art, NY, 88; Contemp Environment, Mus Mod Art, 89; The 80's in Review: Selections from the Permanent Collection, Whitney Mus Am Art, Fairfield Co, Conn, 89; Drawings of the Eighties from the Collection of the Mus Mod Art, NY, 89; solo exhibs, Asher/Faure, Los Angeles, 89, 92 & 94, Baltimore Mus Art, 89, Susanne Hilberry Gallery, Birmingham, Mich, 90, Barbara Toll Fine Arts, NY, 84-94, Member's Gallery, Albright-Knox Art Gallery, Buffalo, NY, 91 & Univ Art Gallery, Univ Mass, Amherst, 92, traveling, 93, Patricia Faure Gallery, Santa Monica, Calif, 94 & 99, Donna Beam Gallery of Art, Univ Nev, Las Vegas, 98; Cincinnati Art Mus, 94; Am Acad of Arts and Letters, 95; Open Ends (1960-2000): Innocence and Experience, 2000; Bouquet: Art of Flowers, Conn Graphic Arts Ctr, Norwalk, 2002; Site and Insight: An Assenblage of Artists, Agnes Gund, MoMA, NY, 2003; Images of Time and Place: Contemporary Views of Landscape, Lehman Coll Art Gallery, Bronx, NY, 2004; Not for Sale, MoMA, NY, 2007; Time and Place: Art of Detroit's Corridor from the Wayne State Univ Coll, Elaine L Jacobs Gallery, Wayne State Univ, Detroit, Mich, 2009; Detroit, Kunsthall Wien, Vienna, Austria, 2010; Menage a Detroit: Three Generations of Expressionist Art in Detroit, 1970-2012, N'Namdi Ctr Contemporary Art, Detroit, Mich, 2012. *Teaching:* Instr painting, Calif Inst Arts, 78-79 & 83; instr painting & drawing, Sch Visual Arts, 81-83; instr, Bard Col, 81-94, Calif Inst Arts, 83; prof studio art, Harvard Univ, 95-, dir Carpenter Ctr for the Visual Arts, 96-, chair dept visual and environmental studies, 99-2001. *Awards:* Nat Endowment Arts Grant, 78-79; Arts Achievement Award, Wayne State Univ, 88; Academy Award, Am Acad Arts & Lett, 94; NY Times Fel, Am Acad in Rome, 99; Award of Merit, Archives Am Art medal, Smithsonian Inst, 2009. *Bibliog:* Francine Hunter McGivern (auth), Excerpts from an interview with Ellen Phelan, NY Arts, 12/99; Barry Schwabsky (auth), Ellen Phelan-Senior & Shopmaker Gallery, ArtForum, 5/2000; Lill Wei (auth), Art in America, July, 2002; Patterson Sims (auth), Resurrecting Nature: Five Contemporary Artists in Dialogue with the Natural World, Orion, pp 36-25, 2004; Donald Kuspit (auth), The Power and the Irony of the Blue, Art New England, pp 13, 55, 2005; Linda Yablonsky (auth), Scene and Herd: Happy Returns, Artforum.com, 2006; Nick Sousanis (auth), Ellen Phelan-the Scent of Memory, Susanne Hilberry Gallery, The Detroiter, 2006; Gail Gregg (auth), I Will Never Look at Painting the Same Way Again, Art News, pp 166-169, 2006; Phong Bui (auth), In Conversation, Ellen Phelan with Phong Bui, Brooklyn Rail, 2009; Rex Auchincloss (auth), Ellen Phelan, Landscapes and Still Lifes: A Selection, Brooklyn Rail, 2011; Nancy Princenthal (auth), Ellen Phelan, Gasser, & Grunert, Art in America, 2012; Phong Bui (auth), Ellen Phelan: Encyclopedia of Drawing, 1964-2012, Brooklyn Rail, 2012. *Media:* Oil, Gouache. *Dealer:* Senior & Shopmaker 210 Eleventh Ave New York NY; Tex Gallery 2012 Peden St Houston TX. *Mailing Add:* 130 E 67th St New York NY 10065

PHELAN, WYNNE
CONSERVATOR
Study: NYU Inst Fine Arts, MA (art hist), 1971. *Pos:* Intern, Metrop Mus Art; conserv dept, Mus Mod Art, 1970-1974; pvt practice conservator, 1974-1982; conservator, Menil Collection, 1982-1996; dir conserv dept, Houston Mus Fine Arts, 1996-, works on paper conservator & dir Art Conserv Database, currently. *Mailing Add:* 5601 Main St Houston TX 77005-1823

PHELPS DE CISNEROS, PATRICIA
COLLECTOR
Pos: founding pres, Fundación Cisneros; co-founder, chair, Colección Cisneros; trustee, Mus Mod Art, New York. *Awards:* Named one of Top 200 Collectors (with husband Gustavo A Cisneros), ARTnews, 2004-08; Gold Medal, Americas Soc, 2008; Gertrude Vanderbilt Whitney Award for Outstanding Patronage, Skowhegan Awards, 2008. *Mem:* Americas Soc (dir). *Collection:* Modern and contemporary Latin American, European, and American art; 17th-to-20th-century Latin American landscapes; Amazonian ethnographic objects. *Mailing Add:* Fundación Cisneros Quinta Centro Mozarteum Caracas Venezuela 1050

PHEOBUS, ALYSSA
PRINTMAKER
b Frederick, Md, 1982. *Study:* Yale Univ, Conn, BA, 2004; Columbia Univ, New York, MFA, 2008. *Exhib:* The New Academy, Robert Lehman Art Ctr, North Andover, Mass, 2008; Lost in Your Eyes, LeRoy Neiman Gallery, Columbia Univ, 2008; The Open, Deitch Projects, Long Island City, 2009; Art Nova, Art Basel Miami, Fla, 2010. *Awards:* Ellen Battell Stoeckel Fel, 2003; Richard B Sewall Prize, 2004; Andrew Fisher Fel, 2007; NY Found Arts Fel, 2009. *Bibliog:* Anne Doran (auth), The Practice of Joy Before Death; It just would not be a party without you, Time Out New York, 4/2009; Karen Rosenberg (auth), Yes, There Still is Avant-Garde Art in Soho, NY Times, 12/4/2009; JJ Charlesworth (auth), Edel Assanti/Jack Bell Gallery/Holster Projects, Time Out London, 2010. *Dealer:* Tracey Williams Ltd 521 W 23rd St 2nd Fl New York NY 10011

PHILBIN, ANN
MUSEUM DIRECTOR
b Boston, Mass, Mar 21, 1952. *Study:* Univ NH, BA in Art Hist, BFA in Painting, 1976; NYU, MA in mus studies/arts admin, 1982. *Collection Arranged:* Wolfgang Tillmans, 2006; Société Anonyme: Modernism for America, 2006; Francis Alÿs: Politics of Rehearsal, 2007; Eden's Edge: Fifteen LA Artists, 2007; Vija Celmins: A Drawings Retrospective, 2007; Between Earth and Heaven: The Architecture of John Lautner, 2008; Kara Walker: My Complement, My Enemy, My Oppressor, My Love, 2008. *Pos:* Res, Frick Art Reference Libr, New York City, 1977-79; asst to dir, prog coordr, Artists Space, 1979-80; asst cur coordr, The New Mus, 1980-81; cur, Ian Woodner Family Collection, 1981-83; asst dir, Grace Borgenicht Gallery, 1983-85; dir, Curt Marcus Gallery, 1985-88; account dir, Art Against AIDS Livet Reichard Inc, 1988-90; dir, The Drawing Ctr, 1990-1999, UCLA Hammer Mus Los Angeles, 1999-. *Awards:* Best Show of Underknown or Emerging Artist Award for Lee Mullican: Selected Drawings 1945-1980, Int Asn Art Critics, 1999 & 2000; Recipient Best Monographic Mus Show Nationally Award for exhib Lee Bontecou: A Retrospective, Inter Asn Art Critics/USA, 2004; Best Thematic Mus Show, THING: New Sculpture from Los Angeles, Inter Asn Art Critics, 2005. *Mem:* Asn Art Mus Dirs; The Andy Warhol Found for Visual Arts, NY (bd dir); Am Center Found (bd dir). *Mailing Add:* Univ of Calif UCLA Hammer Museum 10899 Wilshire Blvd Los Angeles CA 90024

PHILLIPS, ALICE JANE
PAINTER
b New York, NY, Aug 30, 1947. *Study:* NY Univ, with Chuck Close & John Opper, BS, 70, MA, 72. *Work:* Aldrich Mus Contemp Art, Conn; Mus City New York, Brooklyn Mus, Chase Manhattan Bank; Flossie Martin Mus, Va. *Exhib:* Works on Paper--Women Artists, Brooklyn Mus, 75; Contemp Reflections, Aldrich Mus, Conn, 77; Fifteen New Talents, Aldrich Mus, Conn, 79; Paperworks 80, Hudson River Mus, Yonkers, NY, 80; Solo exhib, David Findlay Galleries, NY, 82, van Straaten Gallery, Chicago, 83, Dubins Gallery, Los Angeles, 83, 84, 86 & 88 & Gallery 500, Elkins Park, Pa, 88, 91 & 95; Printed By Women, Port of Hist Mus, Philadelphia, Pa, 83; Art of the 1970s & 1980s, Aldrich Mus, Conn, 85; Am Art: Am Women, Stamford Mus, Conn, 85; Natural Image, Stamford Mus, Conn, 89; Salute to Women, Nat Mus Women Arts, Washington, 91; Group Exhibs: State Univ NY, Stonybrook, 94; Alice Phillips & Raymond Tomasso, Gallery 500, Philadelphia, 95; Pulse Points, Harvard Univ, Cambridge, Mass, 96; Generations, AIR Gallery, NY, 97; The Square Show, Ceres Gallery, NY, 01; group exhib, Pace Univ Gallery, NY, 03; Broome St Gallery, 2006. *Teaching:* Adj asst prof art & drawing, NY Univ, 81-82. *Bibliog:* Mary Vaughn (auth), article in Arts Mag, 1/82; Grace Glueck (auth), article in NY Times, 1/27/84; Mila Andre (auth), article in NY Daily News, 8/5/94. *Mem:* Women in Arts Found (exec coordr, 78-80, secy, 80-82); Women's Caucus Art (exec bd, 94-2000). *Media:* Acrylic, Pastel. *Dealer:* Gallery 500 Church & Old York Rds Elkins Park PA 19117. *Mailing Add:* 415 E 85th St #11CD New York NY 10028-6355

PHILLIPS, BERTRAND D
PAINTER, PHOTOGRAPHER
b Chicago, Ill, Nov 19, 1938. *Study:* Art Inst Chicago, with Paul Wieghardt & Leroy Neiman, BFA; Northwestern Univ, MFA. *Work:* Governors State Univ, Park Forest South, Ill; David & Alfred Smart Gallery, Univ Chicago, Ill; Du Sable Mus African Am Hist, Chicago; Art Inst Chicago; Erie Art Ctr, Pa; and others. *Exhib:* Art Inst Chicago, 78-80; Ill State Mus, 78 & 80; Nat Mus Haitian Art, 79-80; Cult Ctr Guyana, 79-80; NAME Gallery, Chicago, 81; Mid-Am Biennial Nat Exhib, Owensboro Mus Fine Arts, Ky, 82; and many others. *Teaching:* Instr drawing & painting, Elmhurst Col, 70-72; asst prof drawing & painting, Northwestern Univ, 72-79; vis artist, Sch Art Inst Chicago, 81-. *Awards:* George D Brown Foreign Traveling Fel, Art Inst Chicago, 61; Governor's Purchase Award, State Ill. *Bibliog:* Elton Fax (auth), Black Artists of the New Generation, Dodd Mead & Co, 77; and others. *Media:* Oils, Acrylic. *Mailing Add:* 6617 S Perry Ave Chicago IL 60621-3806

PHILLIPS, CHRISTOPHER
CURATOR, HISTORIAN
Collection Arranged: Atta Kim: On-Air; Between Past and Future: New Photography and Video from China (with catalog), 2004; The Rise of the Picture Press; The Metropolis and the Art of the Twenties; Heavy Light: Recent Photography and Video from Japan. *Pos:* Sr ed, Art in Am; cur, Int Ctr Photog, 2000-. *Teaching:* Instr, curatorial studies program, Columbia Univ. *Mem:* UBS Art Collection Bd. *Publ:* Auth, Steichen at War, 1981; coauth (with Maria Morris Hambourg), The New Vision: Photography Between the World Wars, 1989; auth, Photography in the Modern Era: Documents and Critial Writings, 1989

PHILLIPS, ELLEN T
SCULPTOR, ASSEMBLAGE ARTIST
Study: San Diego State Univ, MFA, 85. *Work:* Downey Mus Art, Calif; Alexandria Mus Art, La; Nat Handicraft Mus India, New Delhi; Hoyt Inst Fine Arts, New Castle, Pa; and over 75 pvt collections; solo exhib, Chadron State Coll, 99. *Comn:* Ceramic tile & bronze participation wall, Children's Hosp, San Diego, (collab), 93; polychrome wood relief, Malabar Libr, Los Angeles Cult Affairs Dept, (collab), 93-96; hist benches in photoetched granite & concrete, decorative fencing, pillars, Dairy Mart Rd & Bridge Proj, City of San Diego, 95-2000; 17 abstract metal bird forms, Washington St, City San Diego, Mission Hills Asn (collab), 95-2000; tile, concrete, steel animal form & fountain, Oncology Gardens, Children's Hosp San Diego, (collab), 98-99. *Exhib:* Solo exhibs, Athenaeum Music & Arts Libr, La Jolla, Calif, 91, Miracosta Col, Oceanside, Calif, 91, Southwestern Col, Chula Vista, Calif, 92, Univ Pacific Art Gallery, Stockton, Calif, 92, Minot State Univ, NDak, 94, McHenry Co Coll Gallery, 95 & Hyde Gallery, Grossmont Col; Girllila Art Invitational, Simay Space, San Diego, 2002; Little by Little, Mus Photographic Arts, San Diego, 2002; 4th Ann Nat, Kaufman Gallery, Shippensburg Univ, Pa, 2003; An Open Book, Gallery West, Cuyahoga Community Col,Cleveland, 2004; Low Altitude/High Altitude, Gallery Contemp Art, Univ Colo, Colorado Springs, 2004; Artists Architects: Modeling Our World, Southwestern Coll Art Gallery, Chula Vista, Calif, 2005; Nat Women's Exhib, Impact Artists Gallery, Buffalo, NY, 2007; and others. *Pos:* Show comt, Calif Fibers, 85-; bd mem, COVA, 87-91, Allied Craftsmen, 87-92 & SDMA Artist Guild, 88-92; design team, Indian School Road/Canal Bank Proj, City of Phoenix, Ariz, 91-92. *Teaching:* Instr 2- & 3-D design crafts, San Diego State Univ, 82-89; instr 3-D design crafts, Mesa Col, San Diego, 88-93; instr 3-D design, Grossmont Col, 95. *Awards:* Best Concrete Bridge Award, Am Concrete Inst, 2000, Am Pub Works Asn, 2000; Putnam Award, League of Calif Cities, 2001. *Bibliog:* D Gage (auth), Ellen Phillips: Going Public, Fiber Arts, 1-2/93; Discovery Award-Gold Winners, Art in Calif, 1/93; The Children's Wall, Sculpture Mag, 9-10/93. *Mem:* Calif Fibers; Allied Craftsmen; SDMA Artist Guild. *Media:* All Media. *Publ:* Auth, Line up, Carolyn Price Dyer, 2-3/88; ISTL/WAC Newslett, San Diego State Univ, spring 89. *Mailing Add:* 9463 Mesa Vista La Mesa CA 91941

PHILLIPS, GIFFORD
COLLECTOR, WRITER
b Washington, DC, June 30, 1918. *Study:* Stanford Univ, 1936-38; Yale Univ, BA, 1942. *Pos:* Partner, Pardee-Phillips, Los Angeles, formerly. *Mem:* Trustee Mus Mod Art, NY; trustee Phillips Collection, Washington, DC; trustee Rothko Found, NY; trustee Pasadena Art Mus (pres, 73-74, secy-treas, 75-76); Mus Mod Art Int Coun (bd dir); Los Angeles Co Mus Art Contemp Art Coun. *Collection:* Contemporary American painting and sculpture. *Publ:* Auth, Arts in a Democratic Society, 1966; auth, articles, Art News, Artforum & Art Am

PHILLIPS, HARRIET E
ILLUSTRATOR, BOOKMAKER, COLLAGIST, PAINTER
b New York, NY. *Study:* Hunter Col, BA, 51, Art Students League, NY, studied under Frank J Reilly, Coll Physicians & Surgeons, Columbia Univ, NY, with Alfred Feinberg, courses & workshops at Ctr Bk Arts, NY, Womens Studio Workshop, Rosendale, NY & Fashion Inst Technol, NY. *Exhib:* Okla Mus Natural Hist, Norman, 93; Oshkosh Pub Mus, Wis, 93; Houston Mus Natural Sci, 93; RW Norton Art Gallery, Shreveport, La, 93; Art & the Animal, Bennington Ctr Arts, Vt, 94; Nat Tour, Soc Animal Artists, 94-95, Disney's Animal Kingdom Park Ann Show, 98; Soc Animal Artists Ann Show, Witte Mus, San Antonio, 96; Nat Asn Women Artists Regional Invitational, Unison Arts & Learning Ctr, 98; Nat Asn Women Artists Show, Hutchinson Gallery, CW Post Col, 98; solo show, Unitarian Church, Rock Tavern, NY; group shows, Hiram Blauvelt Mus, Oradell, NJ, John Wehle Gallery of Sporting Art, Mumford, NY, Garrison Art Ctr of Sarasota, Sarasota, Fla, Banana Factory, Bethlehem, PA, Woodstock Artist Asn, Woodstock, NY, Haworth Libr Gallery, Haworth, NJ, Nat Asn Women Artists, NY; Bennington Art Center, Bennington, Vt. *Pos:* Med Art Service, 59-; Owner, Med Art Serv, 59-95; Owner, the HEP Press, 94-. *Teaching:* Instr med illus, Col Physicians & Surgeons, Columbia Univ, 66-68; instr air brush, BOCES, Orange City, NY, 90-. *Awards:* Paper Grant, 86 & 91; Puffin Grant, Puffin Found, 94; Stelly Sterling Mem Award, Nat Asn Women Artists, 95; Hon Mention, spring 2007 Woodstock Artists Asn & mus. *Mem:* Life mem Art Students League; Nat Asn Women Artists (rec secy, exhib comt); Soc Animal Artists (rec secy, exec bd, 90-); Women Studio Workshop, Rosendale, NY; and others; Woodstock Artist Asn Mus, Woodstock, NY. *Media:* Collage, Acrylic. *Publ:* illusr & coauth, Understanding the Human Form, Avery Publ Group, 81; illusr, Adrenal Disorders, Thieme Med Publ, 89; ed & illusr, Black Dirt, pvt publ, 91; auth & illusr, ABC Mammals, Internet publ, 2005; auth & illusr, Animals in Black & White, Internet publ, 2005; Donald Richard Miller, Catalogue 2003, The Hep Press. *Mailing Add:* 620 Georgetown Cir Fayetteville NC 28314

PHILLIPS, JAMES M
MUSEUM DIRECTOR, COLLECTOR
b Philadelphia, Pa, July 18, 1946. *Study:* Glassboro State Col, BA, 75. *Work:* Antietam Nat Mus, Sharpsburg, Md; and others. *Comn:* Sculpture-medallion, Spec Forces Regiment, 91. *Exhib:* Washington Co Mus Fine Arts, 86. *Pos:* Dir, Antietam Nat Mus, 68-; Bladesmiths Soc, 86-; bd dir, Am Mus Comt, 92. *Teaching:* Lectr, Univ Wyo, 83; Armed Forces Inst Pathology, 88; OP Gator, 88. *Awards:* Best of Show Award, Connie Kalitta Service Inc, 85. *Mem:* Co of Military Historians; Am Bladesmiths' Soc; Asn Former Intelligence Officers; Spec Forces Asn. *Res:* Clandestine weapons and equipment, subminiature cameras-photo devices, US elite Forces. *Collection:* Artifacts of soldiers who fought in the Civil War through the Viet Nam Wars; uniforms, weapons, photographs, paintings, documents and writings of participants; espionage and intelligence literature and related material. *Publ:* Auth, Stand in the Door, 88; coauth, Bowie Knives, 92; contribr, The Microcol, 92; Subminature Photography, 92; OSS Weapons, 94; and others. *Mailing Add:* PO Box 168 Williamstown NJ 08094

PHILLIPS, LISA
MUSEUM DIRECTOR, CURATOR
Study: Middlebury Coll, BA (art hist), 1971-75; City Univ New York Grad Ctr, doctoral prog (art hist), 1975-80. *Collection Arranged:* Cindy Sherman, Whitney Mus Am Art, 1987, Frederick Kiesler, 1989, Richard Prince, 1992, Terry Winters, 1992, Beat Culture & the New America, 1995, Biennial exhib, 1997, The American Century, 1999. *Pos:* Helena Rubinstein fel, Whitney Mus Am Art, New York, 1976, sr fel, 1977, mgr downtown branch, 1977-80, assoc cur branch museums, 1980-93, assoc cur, 1985-88, cur, 1988-98; asst dir exhibs, Philadelphia Coll Art, 1977; bd dirs, White Columns, New York, 1980-84, Lower Manhattan Cult Coun, 1982-88; advisory bd, Fabric Workshop, 1985, Gallery Asn NY State, 1985-90, LACE, 1998-, Frederick Kiesler Found, 1999-; dir, New Mus Contemp Art, New York, 1999-2007, Toby Devan Lewis dir, 2007-. *Awards:* Crain's 100 Most Influential Women in NYC Business, 2007. *Mailing Add:* 235 Bowery New York NY 10002-1218

PHILLIPS, MICHAEL
PAINTER, SCULPTOR
b New York, NY, Feb 22, 1937. *Study:* Inst Fine Arts, New York, with HW Janson & Robert Goldwater, MA, 62. *Work:* Inst Contemp Art, Boston; Sonesta Hotels; Rose Art Mus, Brandeis Univ, Mass; Bowdoin Coll Art Mus, New Brunswick, Maine. *Comn:* Mural, Inst Contemp Art, Boston, 70; sculpture, City of Boston, 70; painting, Sonesta Hotel, New Orleans, 83. *Exhib:* Solo exhib, Inst Contemp Art, Boston, 70, Frank Marino Gallery, New York, 82 & Univ Va, Charlottesville, Va, 96; 12 Americans, Mus Mod Art, Buenos Aires, Argentina, 87-88; Recent Guggenheim Paintings, IPA, Boston, Mass, 90 & 92; Abstraction Per Se, Pratt Inst, New York, 92; Artists Space Anniversary Exhib, New York, 94; Voices, IPA, Boston, Mass, 94; The Power of Abstraction, 8th Floor Gallery, New York, 97; SC Centennial, SC State Mus, 2000; and others. *Teaching:* Vis artist painting, Univ SC, Columbia, 81; prof painting, Coll Charleston, SC, 84-; vis artist, Am Acad Rome, 87 & 94 & Cardiff Coll Art, Wales, 88-89. *Awards:* Nat Endowment Arts Grant Painting, 80-81; (Caps) New York Fel in painting, 80; Painting Grant, SC Arts Comm, 85-86; Guggenheim fel, 89-90. *Bibliog:* Mary Sherman (auth), Three galleries invite closer look, Boston Globe, 5/30/90; Cate McQuaid (auth), Light shows, Southend News, Boston, Mass, 5/10/90; Nancy Stapen (auth), Michael Phillips, Boston Globe, 1/27/94. *Mem:* Coll Art Asn. *Media:* All. *Interests:* Philos & cosmology. *Publ:* Auth, New Options in Painterly Abstraction, OIA, New York, 79; Painting Self Evident: Evolutions in Abstraction, Gibbes Mus, Charleston, SC, 92; Phoebe Helman Mem Exhib (catalog), 95; Reconsidering Modernism, Line, 2004; auth, The Radical Meaning of Non-Determinism (online). *Dealer:* Joan Sonnabend/Obelisk Gallery Boston MA 02108. *Mailing Add:* Charleston College Art Dept Charleston SC 29424

PHILLIPS, ROBERT J
FILMMAKER, PHOTOGRAPHER
b Montclair, NJ, Feb 28, 1946. *Study:* Jersey City State Coll, BA (art educ), 68: New York Univ Grad Sch Arts, MFA (photog, film & TV), 72; Found for Mind Res, Pomona NY, creative actualization with Dr Jean Houston, Res & Teaching Assoc, 75-l Fairleigh Dickinson Univ, EdD, 88. *Exhib:* Faculty Show, Caldwell Coll, 86 & 90. *Pos:* Designer of high sch film educ prog, identified as exemplary model curriculum site by Am Film Inst, DC, 68-70; coordr, Film Festival, 19th Congress Int Soc for Educ Through Art, 69; asst proj dir, NJ State Coun on Arts, Inner City Arts Proj, Hoboken, NJ, 70; proj dir, Summer Arts Workshop for Mentally Handicapped, Title VI grant, East Orange, NJ, 71; chmn, Comt for Creative Actualization, New Ways of Being Inst Conf, Minneapolis, Dallas, Los Angeles & NJ, 78-79. *Teaching:* Instr art, Photog & film, Woodbridge Sr High Sch, NJ; educator-at-large, master classes & teacher-in-service training in creative actualization, camera arts & fine arts, schs, communities & cols throughout the east, 72-; adj instr, creative actualization & camera arts, Caldwell Col, NJ, 72-; art dir/designer, creative dir & dir mktg communications, WLMW & Assocs, Bozell Inc, FDS/Merrill Lynch. *Awards:* Bronze Phoenix Award for outstanding creative achievement in filmmaking, Atlanta Int Film Festival, Ga, 74; Award for Outstanding Achievement in film direction, in graphic design, Int Creativity Ann, Art Direction Mag, 74; Cert Excellence, filmmaking, NJ Art Dir's Club, 75; plus others. *Media:* Video Tape, Multi Media. *Publ:* Filmmaker & photog, Qualify (film), Net Channel 13, New York, 71; Choice Not Chance (film), 74 & Daydreams and Indecision, 79, NJ State Dept Educ; Asbury Park--A Renaissance, Asbury Park Dept Community Affairs, 79; Art and Multi-Sensory Learning (filmstrip), Educ Frontiers Assocs, 80-90. *Mailing Add:* 6 Linda Lane Edison NJ 08820

PHILLIPS, TONY
PAINTER, DRAFTSMAN
b Miami Beach, Fla, Sept 16, 1937. *Study:* Trinity Col, Hartford, BA (cum laude), 60; Sch Art, Yale Univ, BFA, 62, MFA, 63. *Work:* Art Inst Chicago; Mus Contemp Art, Chicago. *Exhib:* Art Inst Chicago, 73, 85, 87 & 89-90; Indianapolis Mus Art, 82; solo exhibs, Marianne Deson Gallery, Chicago, 82 & 86, Hyde Park Art Ctr, Chicago, 93 & Lyons-Wier Gallery, Chicago, 93 & 95, Gescheidle Gallery, Chicago, 2003; Mus Contemp Art, 83; Reveries, Ford Ctr Fine Arts, Knox Col, Galesburg, Ill, 96; Dogs! Mus of Contemp Art, Chicago (and traveling), 83; Lyonswier Gallery, 2000; Printworks, Chicago, 2000, 2006, 2009, 2011, 2013; Couples Discourse, Palmer Mus Art, Penn State Univ, 2006; Judith Raphael & Tony Phillips, Gallery of Ind Univ NW Gary, 2003; The 179th Ann Invitational, Nat Acad Mus, NY, 2004; Exquisite Snake, Mary & Leigh Block Mus Art, 2007; Not Just Another Pretty Face, Hyde Park Art Ctr, Chicago, 2008; Weather, Islip Art Mus, Islip, NY, 2009; Chicago Artists, Studios at Key West, Fla, 2010; Book covers, Printworks, Chicago, 2010; Research House for Asian Art, 2013; Two person show with Judith Raphael, Riverside Art Center, Riverside, Ill, 2016; participant in Surrealism: The Conjured Life, Mus of Contemporary Art, Chgo, Ill, 2015-2016. *Pos:* Prof Emer, Dept of Painting & Drawing, Sch of Art Inst of Chicago, currently. *Teaching:* Instr painting & design, Palo Alto Art Ctr, Calif, 65 & Sch Visual Arts, NY, 65-68; artist-in-residence, Univ Pa, Philadelphia, 68-69; prof & chmn dept painting & drawing, Art Inst Chicago, 69-2001, prof emeritus, 2002-; vis artist & lectr, var univs & art schs, 71-96. *Awards:*

Ann Arbor (super 8) 76; Prizes for films at Toronto Film Festival in 76 (super 8); Fel, Nat Endowment for the Arts, 78 & 85; Fel, Ill Arts Coun, 84, 88 & 90; Milton & Sally Avery Fel, McDowell Colony, NH, 94; Fel, YADDO, 88,89, 90, 94, 98; Va Ctr Creative Arts, 87, 88, 89; Djerassi Found 87, 2002. *Bibliog:* Robert Berlind (auth), rev, Art in Am, 7/86; Jasmes Yood (auth), essay, Spirited Visions, Univ Ill Press, 91; Alan Artner (auth), rev, Chicago Tribune, 4/2/93; also reviews 5/2/85 & 1/24/2003. *Media:* Oil, Pastel, Film. *Res:* Psychological Narrative. *Specialty:* Contemp Art. *Interests:* Ornithology. *Collection:* Art Inst of Chicago; Mus of Contemp Art. *Publ:* Auth, Joseph Beuys at the Art Institute, Quart Mag Art Inst Chicago, spring 74; Leon Golub: Portraits of political power, New Art Examiner, 1/78; Essay on Drawing, Whitewalls, spring 86. *Mailing Add:* 807 W 16th St Chicago IL 60608

PHILLIS, MARILYN HUGHEY
PAINTER, INSTRUCTOR

b Kent, Ohio, Feb 1, 1927. *Study:* Ohio State Univ, BS, 49; Toledo Mus Art Sch Design, 61; studied with Fred Leach, Jeanne Dobie, Edward Betts & Glenn Bradshaw. *Work:* Springfield Mus Art, Springfield, Ohio; EF McDonald co, Gem Savings, Dayton; Rolls Royce Ltd, Palmyra, NY; Neumann Indust, Cleveland; Dean Witter Reynolds Inc, Jackson, Miss; Holiday Inns, Memphis, Tenn; Online Computer Libr Ctr, Dublin, Ohio; Ohio Univ, Lancaster; Ohio Univ, Eastern; Heritage Hall Mus, Talladega, Ala; Monroe Community Coll, Mich; WVa Northern Community Coll; Univ Charleston, WVa. *Comn:* Harpslchord decorative design, comn by Rosalyn Schneider, 84; abstr painting, Dr & Mrs Eugene Schmiedl, 88. *Exhib:* Am Watercolor Soc, Nat Acad Gallery, New York & traveling, 1974, 1976, 1978-79, 1982, 1989, 1991, 1995-97, 2002, 2008, & 2012; Nat Watercolor Soc, Laguna Beach Mus & Palm Springs Mus, Calif, 74, 80, 83, 89, 96 & 2001; Watermedia Exhib, Springfield Art Mus, Ohio, 81 & 83; Ohio Northern Univ, 84; Davis & Elkins Univ, Elkins, WVa, 86; Zanesville Art Ctr, Ohio, 87; Watercolor Exhib, Nat Taiwan Art Educ Inst, Taipei, 94; Cheekwood Mus, Botanical Ctr, Nashville, Tenn, 95; New York City Lincoln Ctr, 2004; Strathmore Hall, Md, 2004; Idaho Falls Art Ctr, North Ariz Univ; US Northern Dist Fed Court House, WVa; Nanjing Research Inst Libr, Nanjing, China, 2010, 2012. *Pos:* Illusr, Western Reserve Mag, 1974-1978, co-ord, 1993, 1995, 1997, 1999, 2002 2007, 2010; seminar, Stretching Boundaries for Creative People Int; editor, Am Watercolor Soc, Int Newsletter, 98-2013. *Teaching:* Instr art, Edison State Community Coll, 1976; instr watercolor, Springfield Art Ctr, Ohio, 1976-84; guest lectr and instructor painting throughout US; juror nat painting and all media exhibs, 1978-2013. *Awards:* 1st award, Watercolor West, 90; Ohio Watercolor Soc Gold Medal, 93; Named Master Artist Mixed Media, Am Arts Mag, 96; William Church Osborne Award Am Watercolor Soc, 98; Inductee Hall of Fame Fine Arts Category, Kent, Ohio, 2000; Inductee Hall of Fame Cult Arts Category, Wheeling, WVa, 2000; 2nd award, Southern Watercolor Soc, 2001; Ohio Watercolor Soc, Gold medal, 2003, North Coast Award, 2004; Achievement award, Ohio Watercolor Soc, 2012; Lifetime Achievement award, Watercolor Soc, Ohio, 2012. *Bibliog:* Mike Ward (auth), The New Spirit of Watercolor, North Light, 89; Nita Leland (auth), The Creative Artist, North Light, 90; Gerald Brommer (auth), Understanding Transparent Watercolor, Davis Publ, 93; Vicki Lord (auth), Painting Acrylics, North Light, 96; Mary Todd Beam (auth), Celebrating Your Creative Self, F&W Publ, 2001; Maxine Masterfield (auth), Painting the Spirit of Nature, Watson-Guptill, 84. *Mem:* Am Watercolor Soc (bd dir, 1991-93, newsletter ed, 93-2013, mem jury selection); Allied Artists Am; Watercolor West; Ohio Watercolor Soc (rec secy, 1979-82, vpres, 1982-89 & pres, 1990-96); Soc Layerists Multimedia (vpres, 1988-93); Nat Watercolor Soc (chair jury selection 2001); Southern Watercolor Soc (pres), 97-98. *Media:* Watermedia, Collage. *Res:* Architectural research of historic homes, Piqua, Ohio; Exploring art as bridge between art and science; Int Soc Sci & Energy Medicine. *Interests:* psychology, history, geneology, music, art, history, and nature. *Publ:* Illusr, Historic Piqua: An Architectural Survey, Piqua Br, Am Asn Univ Women, 76; auth, Painting from the imagination, Artists Mag, 1/85; Watermedia techniques for releasing the creative spirit, Watson Guptill Pub, 92; Painting from the inner spirit, Watercolor Magic, 6/96; Learning from the Art Masters, Am Art Publ, 6/96; auth, Alchemy of a Creative Idea in: Bridging Time and Space, Maskowitz Publ, 98, Quiet your inner critic, Artist Mag, 4/2003 & Art and Healing, Watercolor Mag, spring 2003; The Artist Mag, Art Clinic, 6/2004; Watercolor Magic Mag, Studio Staples, 4/2005. *Dealer:* Art Works Around Town 2200 Market St Wheeling WV 26003. *Mailing Add:* 124 Pine Ave Saint Clairsville OH 43950

PHILLPOT, CLIVE JAMES
WRITER, CURATOR

b Thornton Heath, Eng, June 26, 1938. *Study:* Polytech of N London, ALA, 67; Univ London, Dipl HA (with distinction), 74; Fel Lib Asn UK, 90. *Collection Arranged:* The Art Press (auth, catalog), Victoria & Albert Mus, London, 76 & Art Gallery of Ontario, Toronto, 79; Fluxus: Selections from the Silverman Collection (auth, catalog), Mus Mod Art, NY, 88; Artist/Author: Contemporary Artists' Books (auth, catalog), US Tour, 98-99; Live in Your Head (auth, catalog), Whitechapel Art Gallery, London & Museu do Chiado, Lisbon, 2000 & 2001; Outside of a Dog (auth, catalog), Baltic, Gateshead, 2003-2004; Voids: A Retrospective (auth, catalog), Ctr Pompidou, 2009. *Pos:* Librn, Chelsea Sch Art, London, 70-77; dir libr, Mus Mod Art, New York, 77-94; freelance writer, cur; honorary fellow, Univ Arts London, 2013. *Mem:* Art Libr Soc N Am (pres, 89-90); Int Asn Art Critics. *Res:* Word & Image; marginal art, Ray Johnson, artists books & mags. *Interests:* Contemporary art. *Publ:* Britain at the Venice Biennale 1895-1995, British Coun, 95; Ed Ruscha Editions 1959-99, Walker Art Ctr, 99; Artist/Author: Contemporary Artists' Books, AFA, 98; Michael Porter: Gwavas Lake, Tate, 2001; Outside of a Dog, Baltic, 2003; Ray Johnson on Flop Art, Fermley Press, 2008; Nobody Nose, Amsterdam, 2011; Booktrek: Selected Essays on Artists Books, 1972-2010, JRP/Ringier, 2013. *Mailing Add:* 3 Pevensey Ave London United Kingdom N11 2RB

PHOENIX, KAOLA ALLEN
COLLAGE ARTIST, PAINTER

b Cincinnati, Ohio, June 16, 1952. *Study:* Univ NC, Chapel Hill, BA (art), 74. *Work:* R J Reynolds, Winston-Salem, NC; NCNB, Charlotte, NC; Duke Med Ctr, Durham, NC; Chapel Hill Children's Clinic, Chapel Hill, NC. *Exhib:* Forty-eighth Southeastern Competition for Drawing, Photog & Printmaking, Southeastern Ctr Contemp Art, 80; Charlotte Juried Exhib, Spirit Sq Galleries, NC, 81; Ensemble: Collage & Assemblage, Green Hill Art Ctr, Greensboro, NC, 82; Southeastern Graphics, Mint Mus Art, 82; Collage: Southeast, Southeastern Ctr Contemp Art & traveling with Southern Arts Fedn, 82-83; Xerox Show, Southeastern Ctr Contemp Art, 84; Women Printmakers of the Southeast, McKissick Mus, Columbia, SC, 84; The Artist's Self, Southeastern Ctr Contemp Art & traveling with Southern Arts Fedn, 85-86. *Awards:* Juror's Merit Award, Charlotte Exhib, 81; Best in Show Purchase Award, Southeastern Graphics Invitational, NC Nat Bank, 82; Grant, funded by Nat Endowment Asn & Feminist Am Art Inst, Visual Artists' Exchange in collaboration, 83. *Bibliog:* Allen, Irwin, Holsenbeck & Foster (producers), Birth Days: A Collaborative Room Installation (videotape), 82. *Media:* Miscellaneous

PIASECKI, JANE B
ADMINISTRATOR

b Brooklyn, NY, Jan 21, 1953. *Study:* Brooklyn Mus Art Sch, 72-75; City Univ New York-Coll Staten Island, AS (liberal arts), 78, BS(econ, 82; City Univ New York-Baruch Col, MBA, 85. *Pos:* Accounting asst, Brooklyn Botanic Gardens, 73-76; asst mgr finance & personnel, Brooklyn Mus, 76-80; bus & personnel mgr, NY Hall Sci, 80-85; assoc dir, Newport Harbor Art Mus, 85-93; assoc dir, Inst of Am Indian Arts Mus, 93-95; vpres, finance and Chief Financial Officer, Nat Hist Mus, Calif, 96-. *Teaching:* Calif State Univ, Fullerton, 99. *Mem:* Art Pub Places (comt, 88-92); Int Coun Mus (mgt comt, 92-92); Am Asn Mus, Mus Mgt Comt, (chmn, 2000-04); Calif Asn Mus (treas, 92-93). *Publ:* Int Coun of Mus Newsletter, 2002. *Mailing Add:* c/o Nat Hist Mus Los Angeles Co 900 Exposition Blvd Los Angeles CA 90007

PIATEK, FRANCIS JOHN
PAINTER, EDUCATOR

b Chicago, Ill, Dec 9, 1944. *Study:* Sch Art Inst Chicago, BFA & MFA. *Work:* Art Inst Chicago; Ill State Mus; First Nat Bank Chicago; Kemper Insurance Bong Warren Corp; John D & Catherine T MacArthur Found. *Comn:* Mural, Main State Bank Chicago, 72. *Exhib:* Whitney Mus Am Art Ann Exhib Contemp Am Painting, 68; Solo exhibs, Hyde Park Art Ctr, 69, Phyllis Kind Gallery, 72, NAME Gallery, Chicago, 75 & Roy Boyd Gallery, 84-87; Chicago Art Inst; Surfaces, 2 Decades of painting in Chicago Terra Mus Am Art, 87; Art in Chicago 1945-1995, Mus Contemp Art. *Teaching:* Instr painting, Art Inst Chicago; instr painting, Wash Univ, St Louis. *Awards:* Art Inst Traveling Fel, Francis Ryerson, 67; Pauline Potter Palmer Award, 68 & John G Curtis Prize, 69, Chicago & Vicinity Shows; Nat Endowment Arts, Visual Arts Fel, 85. *Bibliog:* Franz Schulze (auth), Frantastic Images: Chicago Art since 1945, Follett Publ Co, 72; Franz Schulze (auth), Artists the Critics Are Watching Art News, 5/81; Mary Mathews Gedo (auth), Abstraction As Metaphor: The Evocative Imagery of William Conger, Miyoko Ito, Richard Loving & Frank Piatek, Arts Mag, 10/82. *Media:* Painting, Multi Media. *Mailing Add:* 3925 N Troy St Chicago IL 60618-3407

PIBAL, ANN
PAINTER

Study: St Olaf Coll, Northfield, Minn, BA, 1991; Univ Iowa, BFA (painting), 1995. *Exhib:* Solo exhibs include Pierogi Gallery, Brooklyn, 2004, Jessica Murray Projects, New York, 2005, Schmidt Contemp, St Louis, 2008, Max Protetch Gallery, New York, 2008; group exhibs include About Painting, Tang Teaching Mus & Art Gallery, Skidmore Coll, Saratoga Springs, NY, 2004; Greater New York, PS 1 Contemp Art Ctr, New York, 2005, The Painted World, 2005; 10x Abstraction, Jessica Murray Projects, New York, 2005; The Place, Bernard Toale Gallery, Boston, 2006; An Ongoing Low-Grade Mystery, Paula Cooper Gallery, New York, 2007; Invitational Exhib Visual Arts, AAAL, New York, 2007; Geometric Abstraction, McKenzie Fine Art, New York, 2008. *Pos:* Artist-in-residence, UCROSS Found, 1998, MacDowell Colony, 2001, Cité Int Arts, Paris, 2002, Yaddo, 2004. *Teaching:* Instr, Sch Art & Design at Alfred, 1995-98, Bennington Coll, Vt, 1998-. *Awards:* Saltonstall Found Grant, 1998; NY Found Arts Fel, Painting, 2006; Pollock-Krasner Found Grant, 2006; Purchase Award, AAAL, 2007; Louis Comfort Tiffany Found Grant, 2009. *Dealer:* Jessica Murray Projects 150 11th Ave New York NY 10011. *Mailing Add:* 129 Hawks Ave North Bennington VT 05257-9202

PICCIANO, LANA
PAINTER

b Evanston, Ill. *Study:* Bloomfield Col, BA, 69; Art Students League, with Vaclav Vytlacil, scholar, 70-72 & with Theodoras Stamos, scholar, 71-72; Provincetown Workshop, with Leo Manso & Victor Candell, 74; Art Students League, Full Schol. *Work:* Int Monetary Fund, Washington; Bell Laboratories, Holmdel & Parsippany, NJ; Integrated Resources, Inc, NY; Wertheim Schroder & Co, Equitable Ctr, NY; Morrison & Foerester, NY. *Comn:* Painting, Bell Laboratories, Holmdel, NJ, 80; painting, Lutz and Carr, NY, 87; painting, Jad Corp of Am Coll Point, NY, 89; painting, comn by Mr & Mrs Martin Gottlieb, Boca Raton, Fla, 89. *Exhib:* Shirley Scott Gallery, Southampton, NY, 87-91; Contemp Artists, Islip Art Mus, East Islip, NY, 88; 100 Yrs/100 Works, Women Artists Today Salute Their Centennial, Islip Art Mus, East Islip, NY, 89, Fine Arts Mus of South Mobile, Ala, 89 & Chattanooga Regional Hist Mus, Tenn, 89; The New Romanticism, 8th Plaiedes Gallery, NY, 90; Works Gallery, NY, 1991-2007, 2012; Sultan Gallery, Bonita Springs, Fla, 2012; Arts for Act, Fort Myers, Fla, 2012. *Awards:* Ford Found Grant for Study; Christian Bucheit scholar; Art Students League scholar. *Bibliog:* First Place in Oils, Framingham Ann Competition, 74; Best in DC Slide Registry & Best of DC Artists, D Christensen, 82. *Mem:* Artists Equity NJ (pub relations dir, 79-81); Nat Asn Women Artists (financial relations dir,

86-88); Artist Equity NY. *Media:* Oil, Mixed Media, Giclee. *Res:* Monoprints. *Specialty:* Works Gallery 2350 Madison Ave NYC. *Interests:* Kriya Yoga, Tennis, Reading, Theatre, Bullet. *Publ:* Auth, An Illustrated Survey of Leading Contemporaries, Am Artists, 90; New York Art Review, Les Krantz, 90. *Mailing Add:* 14271 Reflection Lakes Dr Fort Myers FL 33907

PICCILLO, JOSEPH
PAINTER
b Buffalo, NY, Jan 9, 1941. *Study:* State Univ NY Coll Buffalo, MFA, 64, fel, 68, 69 & 72. *Work:* Mus Mod Art, NY; Brooklyn Mus; Art Inst Chicago; Butler Inst Am Art, Youngstown, Ohio; Minn Mus Art, Minneapolis; Metrop Mus, NY. *Comn:* Steuben Glass Commission, The Steed, 2008. *Exhib:* Solo exhibs include Monique Knowlton, NY, 84 & 96, Betsy Rosenfield, Chicago, 80, 85, 86, 88, 91 & 94, Elliot Smith Gallery, St Louis, Mo, 86 & 88, 94, Barbara Fendrick Gallery, NY, 88, Brendan Walter Gallery, Los Angeles, Calif, 90 & 92, Perimeter, Chicago, 97, 99, 2002, & 06, Chase Gallery, Boston, 99, 2000, 2003, 2007, 2010, Robert Kidd Gallery, Birmingham, 99 & 2002, R Duane Reed Gallery, St Louis, 2003, Gallery Camino Real, Boca Raon, Fla, 2003, Robert Kiss Gallery, 2006, George Billis Gallery, Los ANgeles, New York, 2008, Perimeter Gallery, Chicago, 2009, Elaine Baker Gallery, Boca Raton, Fla, 2009, Ichase Young Gallery, Boston, 2010, R. Duane Reed Gallery, St. Louis, 2010; group exhibs includ Smithsonian Inst Traveling Drawing Exhib, 71; Monique Knowlton Gallery, 80, 81 & 83; Betsy Rosenfield Gallery, 80, 83; Chase Gallery, Mass, 2000; Horse Tales, Am Images & Icons, Katonah Mus Art, 2001; New York Collects Buffalo State, Burchfield Penney Art Ctr, Buffalo, NY, 2004; Loveland Mus, Colo, 2011. *Pos:* Consult, NY State Coun Arts, 75-77. *Teaching:* Prof art, State Univ NY Col Buffalo, 67-. *Awards:* Childe Hassam Purchase Award, Am Acad Arts & Lett, 68; Nat Endowment for Arts fel, 79. *Bibliog:* Diane Cochrane (auth), J Piccillo's game structures, Am Artist, 12/73; Margaret Hawkins (auth), Joseph Piccillo, review, Chicago Sun Times, 2006. *Publ:* Illusr (covers), Poverty in America, 5/17/68 & Black vs Jew-A tragic confrontation, 1/31/69, Time Mag; contribr (cover), Art Gallery Int, 90. *Mailing Add:* 812 Elmwood Ave Buffalo NY 14222

PICCIRILLO, ALEXANDER C
PAINTER, INSTRUCTOR
b Brooklyn, NY, Jun 27, 1952. *Study:* Brooklyn Mus Art Sch - 1968-70; Special studies with Burton Silverman - 1972-75; Sch of Visual Arts, BFA, 1974. *Comn:* mem pastel, Bd Educ, Nutley, NJ, 1989. *Exhib:* Ann Exhib, The Nat Acad of Design, New York, 1975; Ann Exhib, Pastel Soc Am, New York, 1985-; Art Achievement Awards, Artist's Soc Int, San Francisco, 1986; Int Juried Show, Bergen Mus, Bergen Co, NJ, 1991-92; Int Juried Show, New England Fine Arts Inst, Boston, 1993; Int Juried Show, Patterson Mus, NJ, 1994; Master Pastelist Exhib, Hammond Mus, N Salem, NY, 1995; Int Juried Show, NJ Ctr Visual Arts, Summit, 1996. *Teaching:* Instr genre painting & drawing, Yard Sch Art Montclair Art Mus, NJ, 1983-; instr representational painting & drawing, NJ Ctr Visual Arts, Summit, 2001-06; instr painting & drawing all media, Livingston Art Asn, NJ, 2001-. *Awards:* Columbus Citizens, 1987 & Beatrice Camer, 1988, Ann Exhib, Pastel Soc of Am; Best in Show, Am Artist Prof League, NJ, 1989. *Bibliog:* John Zeaman (auth), Every lawn a king every man isolated, Bergen Record, 5/91; Patricia C. Turner (auth), Art in the ring, NJ Star Ledger, 7/92; William Zimmer, How a curator turns into a judge, NY Times, 4/96. *Mem:* Elected mem Pastel Soc Am, 1985; Yard School of Art Bd Trustees (faculty liaison) 1985-1994; elected master pastelist, Pastel Soc Am, 1987; elected mem Degas Pastel Soc, 1988; elected mem Art Ctr of NJ, 1989. *Media:* All Media. *Publ:* Contribr, The Art of Pastel Portraiture, Watson-Guptill, 1996; contribr, The Best of Oil Painting, Quarry, 1996; contribr, Portrait Inspirations, Rockport, 1997; contribr, The Best of Pastel I & II, Quarry, 1998 & 2000; contribr, The Best of Sketching & Drawing, Quarry, 1999. *Dealer:* Gallery 214 214 Glenridge Ave Montclair NJ 07042. *Mailing Add:* 26 Vine St Nutley NJ 07110-2636

PICCOLO, RICHARD
PAINTER
b Hartford, Conn, Sept 17, 1943. *Study:* Pratt Inst, 66; Art Students League, 67; Brooklyn Col, MFA, 68. *Work:* Crown Am Corp, Johnstown, Pa; Grosvenor Int, Sacramento, Calif; also pvt collections of Lillian Cole, Sherman Oaks, Calif, Mr & Mrs Robert Emery, San Francisco, Graham Gund, Boston, Robert Gutterman, San Francisco, Dr & Mrs Joseph Jennings, San Francisco and others. *Comn:* Mural, Crown Am Corp, Johnstown, Pa, 89; mural, Lobby Park Plaza Tower, Grosvenor Int, Sacramento, 91-94; Aer, Ignis, Terra, Aqua (mural), US Bank Plaza, Sacramento, Calif, 91-94. *Exhib:* Solo exhibs, Robert Schoelkopf Gallery, NY, 75, 79, 83 & 89, Suffolk Community Col, Long Island, 76, Am Acad, Rome, Italy, 77, Galleria Temple, Rome, Italy, 79, Galleria il Gabbiano, Rome, Italy, 85 & Contemp Realist Gallery, San Francisco, 89 & 95; The Ital Tradition in Contemp Am Landscape Painting (with catalog), Gibbes Mus Art, Charleston, SC with Spoleto Exhib, 90; Figure, Contemp Realist Gallery, Calif, 90; Paintings from Contemp Realist Gallery, NY Acad Art, 91-92; New Am Figure Painting, Contemp Realist Gallery, San Francisco, 92; Drawings by Am Artists, Contemp Realist Gallery, San Francisco, 93; Homage to the First 100 Yrs of Cinema, Il Gabbiano Gallery, Rome, Italy, 96; Still Lifes, Contemp Realist Gallery, San Francisco, Calif, 96; Re-presenting Representation III (with catalog), Arnot Art Mus, Elmira, NY, 97; 10th Ann Exhib, Hackett-Freedman Gallery, San Francisco, 97; Artists Who Look Back: Spirituality in Contemp Art (with catalog), Museo Italo Americano, San Francisco, Calif, 98. *Teaching:* Instr, Pratt Inst, New York, 66-68, Pratt Inst, Tyler Sch Art, Rome, Italy, 69-95 & Univ Notre Dame, Rome Prog, 84-95; dir, Pratt Inst, Rome Prog, 80-95. *Awards:* EA Abbey mem Scholar, 73-75; Nat Endowment Arts Grant, 89. *Bibliog:* Alfred Kay (auth), Grand Canvas, Sacramento Bee, 4/92; Thomas Bolt (auth), New American Figure Painting, Contemp Realist Gallery, San Francisco, 92; Richard Piccolo (exhib catalog), Contemporary Realist Gallery, San Francisco, 95; Elizabeth Helman Minchilli (auth), Homage to the First 100 Years of Cinema, Artnews, 96; and others

PICKER, SEBASTIÁN
PAINTER
Exhib: Gallery 355, Boston, 1976-77, 1980; Ctr Culturel de Villeparisis, Paris, 1978; Kunstamt Kreutzberg, Berlin, 1979; Galería Skandia, Bogotá, Colombia, 1979; Galeria D'Art Mestral, L'Escala, Spain, 1983; Cleveland Mus Contemp Art, 1986; Mass Coll Art, Boston, 1987; The Space, 1987, 1991; Bunker Hill Community Col, Boston, 1988; Optica Gallery, Montreal, 1990; Artists Found, Boston, 1990; Red Mesa, Gallip, NMex, 1993; Arden Gallery, Boston, 1995, 1997, 2000, 2002, 2004, 2005; Meredith Kelly, Santa Fe, 1996, 1997; Brewster Arts, NY, 1998; Art Miami, 1999, 2000; Turner Carroll Gallery, Santa Fe, 1999-2000; Museo de Arrte Contemporáneo, Jorge Chávez Carrillo, Colima, Mex, 2007; represented in permanent collections Fundació Vila Casas, Barcelona, Mus Lating Am Art, Longbeach, Calif, El Museo Cult de Santa Fe, Albuquerque Mus. *Awards:* Barcelona Sister City Tavel Grant, Boston, 1984; First Prize, Macworld Art Contest, 1985; Mass Coun on Arts and Humanities Grant, 1988; Mass Artist Fellowship Prog, 1991. *Mailing Add:* c/o Arden Gallery 129 Newbury St Boston MA 02116

PICKETT, JANET TAYLOR
ARTIST
b Ann Arbor, MI Aug 13, 1948. *Study:* Univ Mich, Sch of Art, BFA, 1970; Univ Mich, Rackham Sch Grad, MFA, 1972; Textile Design, Fashion Inst Technol, 1979; Graphic Art, Parsons Sch of Design, NY, 1980; Studied with Sam Gilliam, Vermont Studio Sch,. *Work:* Studion Mus of Harlem; Newark Public Libr; Univ Mich Sch of Social Work; Schomburg Center NYC; Found Valpariso, Mojacar, Spain. *Comn:* Hands on Healing (mural), Univ of Medicine & Dentistry, 1986-98; eight works of art commissioned by The Washington State Art Commission for Our Art-Our Selves: Art as Autobiography, 1990; banners depicting joy in movement (canvas), UMDNJ Sch of Osteopathic Medicine, Stanhope, NJ; 10 48x60 canvas flags, Johnson & Johnson, Research Facility, Princeton, NJ; outdoor mosaic project, New Community Corp of Newark; outdoor sculpture & mosaic project, Rutgers Univ, Camden Campus. *Exhib:* Art As Autobiography, Bellevue Art Mus, Bellevue, Washington, 1990; Book of Embraces, Jersey City Mus, Jersey City, NJ, 1996; More than One Way Home, Montclair Art Mus, Montclair, NJ, 1997; Religion in the 21st Century, Newark Mus of Art, 2003; Icons, Symbols & Alters, Noyes Mus, Oceanville, NJ, 2004. *Teaching:* Prof art, Essex Co Col, Newark, NJ, 1973-2004; adj prof, Bloomfield Col, Bloomfield, NJ,. *Awards:* Glass Blowing Fel, Pilchuck Sch, 1998; Found Valpariso, Mojacar, Almeria, Spain, 2001; MidAtlantic Arts Found, Commissioned Garden Sculpture, Rutgers Univ, Camden, 2002. *Bibliog:* Phil Lane & John Givens (coauths), Working Title (documentary), 2006. *Mem:* Montclair Art Mus (bd of trustees, 2006); Studio Montclair. *Media:* Mixed Media, Works on Paper. *Publ:* Gumbo YaYa, African American Women Artists; More Than One Way Home, exhib catalog, Monclair Mus, 1997. *Dealer:* Tarin Fuller Fine Arts, Newark NJ. *Mailing Add:* 50 Pine St # 205 Montclair NJ 07042

PICOT, PIERRE
PAINTER
b Tours, France, Jan 11, 1948. *Study:* Calif State Univ, Northridge, 66-69; Univ Calif, BFA, 70; Calif Inst Art, MFA (design), 73. *Work:* Los Angeles Co Mus Art, Calif; Security Pac Bank, Los Angeles, Calif; Patrick J Lannan Found, Los Angeles, Calif; Yale Sch Art Mus, New Haven, Conn; City of Rennes Munic Collection, France. *Exhib:* Solo exhibs, Jan Baum Gallery, Los Angeles, Calif, 81, 82 & 85, Richard L Nelson Gallery, Univ Calif, Davis, 83, Guggenheim Gallery, Chapman Univ, Orange, Calif, 92, La Criée Munic Gallery, Rennes, France, 94, Inst Franco-Am, Rennes, France, 96 & New Image Art, Los Angeles, Calif, 98; Directions '83, Hirshhorn Mus, Washington, DC, 83; Sunshine & Shadow, Recent Painting in Southern Calif, Univ Southern Calif, Fisher Gallery, 85; Miracles & Mysteries, Calif State Univ, Dominguez Hills, 86; Downey Mus Art, Calif, 89; Variations, Cal Arts Painting, R Bachofner Gallery, Santa Monica, Calif, 90; Domestic Setting, Susan Landau Gallery, Los Angeles, Calif, 93; Galerie du Placard, St Briac, France, 96; Sala Exposiciones Exoma, Cuenca, Spain, 97; Enghien-les-Bains, France, 2000; Works on Paper, Armory Center for the Arts, Pasadena, Calif, 2006. *Pos:* Publ & designer, Art in Los Angeles Mag, 87-91; contrib critic, Artweek Mag, 88-90, Visions Mag, Los Angeles, 91-94, New Art Examiner, 91-94; contrib ed, Artweek, 87-91, New Art Examiner, 91-92, Visions, 91-93 & Prism, 95; Vis lectr, Otis Art Inst Grad Sch, Los Angeles, Calif. *Teaching:* vis artist, Claremont Grad Sch, Calif, 81 & 83; vis artist, lectr, Calif State Univ, Fullerton, 82; Instr fine arts, Art Ctr, Pasadena, Calif, 83-; vis lectr, Univ Southern Calif, Los Angeles, 83-85 & Otis/Parsons, Los Angeles, Calif, 86-87. *Awards:* Art Fel, Nat Endowment Arts, 87; Award of Excellence, Art Dirs Club Houston; Silver Award of Excellence, Univ & Coll Designers Asn, 88. *Bibliog:* William Wilson (auth), LA Times, 80; Suzanne Muchnic (auth), LA Times, 12/11/81; Louis Fox (auth), Artweek, 12/81; Susan Larsen (auth), Artforum, 3/83; Betty Brown (auth), Arts Mag, 2/83; Christopher French (auth), Artweek, 12/3/83; Kristine MacKenna (auth), LA Times, 7/5/85; Joan Hugo (auth), LA Weekly, 7/25/85. *Publ:* Auth, The Archipelago of time: Charles Garabedian, Los Angeles Louver Gallery, Venice, Calif, 96; Sexy, Sensual Abstraction in California, 1950s-1990s, Armory Center Arts, Pasadena, Calif, 96. *Mailing Add:* 3516 Crestmont Ave Los Angeles CA 90026

PIEHL, WALTER JASON, JR
PAINTER, EDUCATOR
b Marion, NDak, Aug 1, 1942. *Study:* Concordia Col, BA, 64; Univ NDak, MA, 66; Univ Minn, 69. *Work:* Pillsbury Co, St Paul, Minn; Fed Reserve Bank Minneapolis; NDak Governor's Collection, Bismarck; Plains Art Mus, Moorhead, NDak. *Comn:* Mosaic mural, Devils Lake Sioux Tribe, NDak, 71; Univ NDak Mobile Art Gallery Graphic, Art Gallery Asn, NDak statewide tour, 79. *Exhib:* 19th Ann Drawing, Ball State Mus, Muncie, Ind, 73; Ann Images, Anoka Ramsey Coll Gallery, Minn, 73; Midwestern Graphics, Tulsa City Libr Mus, Okla, 74; 15th Ann Nat Graphics, Okla Art Ctr, Oklahoma City, 74; Solo exhibs, Dynamics of Rodeo & Landscape, Univ Art Galleries, Grand Forks, NDak, 75 & 81 & Rodeo Imagery, Plains Art Mus, Moorhead,

Minn, 66, 69, 70 & 76. *Collection Arranged:* Great Plains Traveling Exhib, 70-71; Northwest Biennial Invitation (auth, catalog), 71; Artrain (traveled), 75; Dakota Made, Mobile Gallery, 79; Nat Watercolor Invitation (auth, catalog), 79-80. *Teaching:* Instr art, Valley City State Col, NDak, 67-68; from asst prof to assoc prof art, Minot State Col, NDak, 69-. *Awards:* Purchase Awards, Nat Graphics, Univ NDak, 72 & Northwestern Bak Corp, 74 & Drawing USA, Minn Mus Art, 73. *Bibliog:* Nancy Edmonds Hanson (auth), Contemporary artists of the west, NDak Horizons, 75; article, Art Voices South, 81. *Mem:* NDak Art Gallery Asn (vpres, 79-80); NDak Coun on Arts. *Media:* Mixed. *Dealer:* Wildine Gallery 903 Rio Grande Blvd NW Albuquerque NM 87104. *Mailing Add:* 11000 86th St SE Minot ND 58701-2457

PIENE, CHLOE
DRAFTSMAN, VIDEO ARTIST
b 1972. *Study:* Columbia Univ, New York City, BA, 93; Goldsmiths College, United Kingdom, MFA, 97. *Work:* Mus Mod Art, NY; Whitney Mus Am Art, NY; Walker Art Ctr, Minneapolis; San Francisco Mus Mod Art, San Francisco; FNAC, France; FRAC, France; Sammlung Hoffman, Berlin; Ctr Nat D'Art et de Cult George Pompidou, Paris. *Exhib:* Me & More, Kunst Mus, Luzerne, 2003, Whitney Biennial, Whitney Mus Am Art, NY, 2004, Spirit, Galerie Nathalie Obadia, Paris, 2004, Videorome II, Bates College Mus Art, 2004, Boys Will Be Boys?, Mus Contemp Art, Denver, 2005

PIERCE, ANN TRUCKSESS
PAINTER, EDUCATOR
b Boulder, Colo, Aug 28, 1931. *Study:* Univ Colo, Boulder, BFA, 53, MFA, 55; Yale Univ summer sch, fel, 53; study with Bernard Chaet, Gabor Peterdi, Jimmy Ernst, N Marsicano; workshops with Harold Gretzner, Robert E Wood, Morris Shubin, Jade Fon, George Post, Tom Hill, Tom Nicholas, Millard Sheets, Glenn Bradshaw, Jane Burnham, William B Lawrence & George Gibson. *Work:* Tri-Counties Bank, Mangrove; Pillsbury Branches, Chico, Calif; Yale Univ, New Haven, Conn; Forum Gallery, NY; Calif State Univ, Chico; Univ Colo, Boulder; Mus Northern Calif Art. *Comn:* Oil painting, Colo State Univ, Fort Collins. *Exhib:* Rocky Mt Nat Watermedia Exhib, Foothills Art Ctr, Golden, Colo, 74, 77-79, 81-83, 85 & 88-89; San Diego Watercolor Soc Nat, Cent Fed Tower Plaza Gallery, 76-78 & 80-84; Scottsdale Watercolor Biennial, Scottsdale Ctr Arts, Ariz, 78 & 80; Ann Exhib Watercolor Soc Ala, Birmingham Mus Art, 78 & 79; Watercolor West, Riverside Art Ctr, Calif, 79, 81-83 & 87-88; Nat Watercolor Soc, Desert Mus, Palm Springs, Calif, 79-81 & traveling exhib, 79-80, 82 & 88; Watercolor USA, 80 & 88; Watercolor Now, Springfield Art Mus, 87 & 89-90; Aqueous '87, Owensboro Mus Fine Art, Ky, 87; New Visions Cult & Agr, Marshfield Clurie, Wis, 96; Watercolor West 29th Ann, Riverside Art Mus, Calif, 97; Nat Watercolor Okla, Kirkpatrick Gallery, Okla City, 98; Solo Exhib: Trinity Gallery, CSUC, Chico, 2009, Avenue 9 Gallery, Chico, Calif, 2010, Orland Art Ctr, Calif, 2011. *Teaching:* Grad asst drawing & watercolor, Univ Colo, Boulder, 53-54, instr, summers, 59 & 62; prof drawing & watercolor, Calif State Univ, Chico, 64-95, chmn art dept, 80-83, numerous workshops, Calif & Nev, 90-2012. *Awards:* Springfield Art Mus Award, Watercolor USA, 80; Purchase Awards, Joyce Media, Nat Watercolor Soc, 80 & Hutchings, Watercolor West, 81; First & Second Prize, Calif State Fair, 82; Award of Excellence & Purchase Award, Lodi Ann, 83; Watercolor USA Hon Soc Millennium Bk, 2004. *Bibliog:* Watercolor 89, Am Artist Mag Publ, 89; Greg Albert (auth), Splash, North Light Bks, 91; The Best of Watercolor, Rockport Publ, 95. *Mem:* Nat Watercolor Soc; West Coast Watercolor Soc; Watercolor West; Rocky Mountain Nat Watermedia Soc; Nat Asn Women Artists; Watercolor USA. *Media:* Watermedia. *Dealer:* Avenue 9 Gallery 180 E 9th Ave Chico CA 95926. *Mailing Add:* 819 Shepard Ln Chico CA 95926-2941

PIERCE, CHARLES ELIOT, JR
ADMINISTRATOR, DIRECTOR
b Springfield, Mass, Dec 25, 1941. *Study:* Harvard Col, BA, 64; Harvard Univ, PhD, 70. *Pos:* Dir, Pierpont Morgan Libr, NY, 1987-

PIERCE, CONSTANCE LAUNDON
PRINTMAKER, PAINTER
b Cleveland, Ohio, May 24, 1946. *Study:* Cleveland Inst Art, BFA, 73; Coll Art, Md Inst, Baltimore, MFA (Hoffberger fel), 75. *Work:* Nat Mus Women in Arts, Washington, DC; Smithsonian Arch of Am Art, Washington, DC; Nat Gallery Art Rare Book Libr, Washington, DC; Yale Ctr British Art Sketchbook Arch, Conn; Yale Art Book Collection, Conn; Georgetown Univ Special Collections, Washington, DC; Henry Luce III Ctr Arts, Washington, DC; Nat Inst Health Art Collection, Washington, DC; Massillon Art Mus, Ohio; Int Marion Research Inst, Ohio. *Exhib:* Solo exhibs,Wasmer Gallery, Ursuline Coll, Ohio, 89, Ekklesia Gallery, Murray Hill Art Dist, Ohio, 90, Wash Printmaker's Gallery, Dupont Circle Gallery Dist, Washington, DC, 93, Dadian Gallery, Washington, DC, 93, Gallery 475 Riverside, NY, 94, Newman Gallery, Capitol Hill Arts Dist, Washington, DC, 95, Yale Univ Divinity Libr, Conn, 98, Regina Quick Arts Ctr, NY, 2003, Henry Luce III Ctr Arts & Religion, Washington, DC, 2005, Houghton Coll Fine Arts Ctr, NY, 2006, Yale Univ, Divinity Libr, Conn, 2007, Yale Univ, Divinity Libr, Conn, 2009, Notre Dame Coll, Ohio, 2010, Harlan Gallery, Seton Hill Univ, Pa, 2010, Regina Quick Arts Ctr, NY, 2011; group exhibs, Edinburgh Painting Int, Scotland, 74, Camden Arts Ctr, London, 77, Allentown Art Mus, Pa, 77, Cleveland Art Mus, 83, Corcoran Hemicycle Gallery, Washington, DC, 94, Nat Mus Women in the Arts, Washington, DC, 94, Sarah Moody Gallery, Ala, 95, NIH Mugnuson Gallery, Md, 96, Jackson Art Mus, Miss, 97, 11th Miniature Print Int, NY, 98, Greenwich Arts Ctr, Conn, 2000; Macy Gallery, Columbia Univ, NY, 2000, Fairchild Gallery, Georgetown Univ, Washington, DC, 2000, Henry Luce III Ctr Arts, Washington, DC, 2001, Foundry Gallery, Washington, DC, 2004, Easton Acad Arts, Md, 2004, Glenview Mansion Gallery, Md, 2005, Artist's Sketchbooks, Nat Mus Women in Arts, Washington, DC, 2007; Nat Juried Exhib, Wash Theological Consortium, DC, 2007; Toyota Mus Art, Aichi, Japan, 2010; Mus Art, Toyota City, Aichi, Japan, 2010, 2011, 2012. *Collection Arranged:* Nat Mus Women in the Arts (DC); Smithsonian Archives of Am Art, (DC); Nat Gallery Art Rare Bk Libr (DC); Yale Ctr British Art Sketchbook Archives (CT); Yale Art of Book Collection (CT); Georgetown Univ. Special Col (DC); Henry Luce III Center for Arts (DC); Nat Inst of Health Art Coll (DC); Massillon Art Mus (OH); Int Marion Research Inst (OH). *Pos:* Artist-in-residence, Henry Luce III Ctr Arts & Religion, Washington, DC, 90-93; artist-in-residence, Millsaps Coll, Miss, 94-97; divinity res fel, Yale Univ, Conn, 97-2000. *Teaching:* Bowling Green Univ, Ohio, 75-76; Lafayette Coll, Pa, 77-80; Penland Sch, NC, 95; instr arts & sci, Cleveland State Univ, Ohio, 2000-2001; Nat Summer Prog, Cleveland Inst Art, Ohio, 2001; Smithsonian Inst Campus on the Mall, Washington, DC, 2002; Art Therapy Summer Prog, Ursuline College, Ohio, 2002-2006; assoc prof, St Bonaventure Univ, NY, 2002-present. *Awards:* Catholic Univ Am, Maji Endowment Award, 90-93; Journey Proj Awards, Lilly Endowment, 2003-04 & 2006-07; Martine & Keenan Awards, St Bonaventure Univ, 2003-2009; Leo E Keenan Fac Recognition Award, 2007; Fac Summer REsearch Award, 2007. *Bibliog:* Richard Freis (auth), IMAGE: J of Arts & Religion, #13; Mary McCoy & Janet Wilson (auths), The Wash Post; Douglas Utter (auth), Chicago's New Art Examiner; Lu Ann Bishop (auth), Yale Bull; William Zimmer (auth), Sunday NY Times; Carolyn Wyman (auth), The New Haven Register; Stephen Young (auth), Number: Independent Quarterly; Michelle Leslie (auth), The Cleveland Plain Dealer Sunday Feature; and many others. *Mem:* Coll Art Asn; Md Printmakers Asn; Southern Graphic Coun; Wash Print Club; Asn Integrative Studies; Soc Arts & Healthcare; Am Art Therapy Asn; Christians in the Visual Arts. *Media:* Painting, Monotype, Works on Paper, Sketchbooks, Imaging Journals, Illustrated Journals. *Publ:* Article, Opus Cordis, Art Inspiring Transmutations of Life, Analecta Husserliana, 2010. *Mailing Add:* PO Box 144 Olean NY 14760

PIERCE, DANNY P
SCULPTOR, PAINTER
b Woodlake, Calif, 1920. *Study:* Art Ctr Sch, Los Angeles, 1939; Chouinard Art Inst, Los Angeles, 1940-41; Am Art Sch, NY City, 1947-48, studied with William Gropper, Jack Levine, Raphael Soyer; Brooklyn Mus Art Sch, 1950-53, studied with Max Beckmann, Ben Shahn, Gabor Peterdi. *Work:* Mus Mod Art, NY; Nat Libr, Paris; Nat Mus Sweden, Stockholm; Huntington Libr, San Marino, Calif. *Comn:* Eskimo scene panels, 62, abstract design in concrete for cafeteria bldg, 63, Univ Alaska; Logging (diorama), White River Hist Soc Mus; 3 murals, Kent, Wash. *Exhib:* Traveling Exhib Prints, Europe, Eurasia, 59-62; Northwest Printmakers Int, Seattle Art Mus, 68; Washington Art, Worlds Fair, Osaka, Japan, 70; Edge of the Sea, Bradley Gallery, Milwaukee, 73, 75, 77, 79 & 81; Solo exhibs, Small Bronzes, 74 & Oostduinkerke, Belgium, 80; Retrospective exhib, City Hall, Kent, WA, 2010. *Pos:* Artist, novelty manufacturing company, 1941-42; founder, Red Door Studio, Kent, Washington, 1959. *Teaching:* Instr, Burnley Sch for Professional Art, 1953; instr art dept, Seattle Univ, 1953; artist-in-residence, Univ Alaska, 1959-63; asst prof art dept, Univ Wisconsin, Milwaukee, 1966, prof emeritus, 1985. *Awards:* Green Memorial Award for Best Oil, Conn Acad Art, 1949; Purchase Award, Libr Cong, 1952, 1953 & 1958; Northwest Printmakers International Award, Seattle Art Mus, 1968. *Media:* All. *Publ:* Auth & illusr, Little No Name, 1959, Cattle Drive '76, 1976, Shepherdess of Monument Valley, 1979, Man, Horse, Sea, 1980, Sea Wreck, 1981 & Birds, 1981; Golden Seas, Horse Logging; Sugaring Fever, 1989; Irish Vignettes, 92. *Dealer:* Jube Gallery 243 First Ave Kent WA. *Mailing Add:* Red Door Studio 404 Summit Ave N Kent WA 98030

PIERCE, DIANE JEAN
PAINTER, ILLUSTRATOR
b Evanston, Ill, Apr 9, 1952. *Study:* Univ Utah, 70-76. *Work:* Springville Mus Fine Arts, Utah; Nat Girl Scout Coun Am, Utah; Prof Figure Skaters Hq, Sun Valley, Idaho. *Comn:* Portraits, comn by James Montgomery, Salt Lake City, 91-92; portrait, comn by Sen Blaze Warton, Salt Lake City, 94-95; portrait, comn by John & Jane McCoy. *Exhib:* Springville Nat Salon, Springville Mus Fine Arts, Utah, 85; Univ Utah, Springville Mus Fine Arts, Utah, 87; Nat Asn Women Artists, NY, 87; Park City Open, Kimbal Art Ctr, 89, 90 & 93; 100 Yrs 100 Women traveling exhib, Nat Ash Women, NY, 89-91; Out of the Land, Springville Mus Fine Arts, Utah, 92. *Pos:* Artist & cur, Devereaux Mansion, 84-87; artist, New Dimensions Gallery, 94-. *Awards:* Artists Fel Inc, NY, 93; Merit Award, Springville Mus, 95; and others. *Bibliog:* Charlotte Romney Howe (auth), Artists who to kids, minor masterpiece, Parent Express, 9/88; Richard Christensen (auth), Business booms at art galleries, Desert News, 12/9/90; Vern Swanson (auth), Utah Artists, 91. *Mem:* Nat Asn Women Artists, NY; Salt Lake Art Ctr, Utah. *Media:* Oil, Pastel. *Publ:* Auth, Women Artists of Utah, Springville Mus Fine Art, 84; Utah Women Artists, Utah Div Am Asn Univ Women, 89; Out of the Land: Utah Women, Springville Mus, 92. *Dealer:* 1323 S 6th East. *Mailing Add:* 160 W 200 St Redmond UT 84652

PIERCE, PATRICIA JOBE
ART DEALER, HISTORIAN
b Seattle, Wash, May 18, 1943. *Study:* Univ Conn, 64; Boston Univ Sch Fine & Appl Arts, BFA, 65, Harvard Univ, 89-90. *Comn:* Camden Hist Soc, 1967, 71; El Paso Art Mus, Tex, 1972; William Penn Mem Art Mus, Pa, 1976; Schenectady Mus, NY, 1982; Art video, comn by Finlay Holiday Film Corp, 90; Republican Conv Art, Houston, 92. *Exhib:* Design Ctr, Boston, 92; Bridgewater State Col, Anderson Gallery, Mass, 92, 96, 98; Daniel Reni, Boston, 92; Gallery, Nantucket, 92-96; Pino (documentary), 2007; Pierce Galleries, Nantucket, Mass, 1999-2011; The Super-Realism of Zhen-Huan Lu, 2011; The Marine Paintings of Richard Loud, 2011. *Pos:* Pres, Pierce Galleries, Inc, Nantucket & Hingham, Mass, 68-; owner, Pierce Galleries Publ Co, 80-; exclusive agent, Joseph McGurl, Zhen-Huan Lu, Geoffrey Smith, F E Green, Richard Lowe, Samuel Rose, Rep of the art estate of W S Barrett (1854-1927); Chauncy F Ryder, N A Marguerite S Pearson, J W S Cox, Louise Woodroofe, Martin Kaelin, Anne Carleton; prof mgr, World Champion Tae Kwon Do Martial Artists, 82-; prof art appraiser, 2010 certified USPAP Appraisers Asn Am, NY, 74-; dir, Apollo-Pierce Galleries, Palm Beach, Fla, 2004-2006; writer, art column, Fine Art Connoisseur Mag, 2006-2007. *Teaching:* Tae Kwon Do. *Awards:* Golden Poet Award, Calif, 88, 89 & 90; Citation for Patriotism & Coverage, Pres Bush's Task Force, 89; Presidential Comn, Washington, DC, 92; and others. *Bibliog:* Who's Who in Am

Women, 99-2000; Outstanding Writers of the 20th Century, 2000; Patricia Jobe Pierce, Bostoria 67, 3/31/95; Stalking the Edge with Pat Pierce, Higham Times, 4/14/95; The Fine Art of Investing in Art, Newsmax, Dec 2007. *Mem:* Patron Brockton Art Ctr; Nat Writer's Club; Nat Writer's Union; Int Platform Asn; Presidential Task Force, 92-94 & 96; Appraisers Asn Am, 74-; Mus Fine Art Boston; Asn Hist Am Art, 2006-; Am Film Inst: Nantucket Hist Asn; Appraisers Asn Am, (cert mem 74-2011). *Res:* J A M Whistler, Elvis Presley, bluesman B B King, Stevie Ray Vaughn & Aerosmith; Cape Ann painters; surrealism; The Ten Am Painters. *Specialty:* Am paintings from Hudson River Sch through 1940 Modernism. *Interests:* Art hist, civil rights. *Collection:* Nineteenth century American & French impressionists, William S Barrett, Jane Peterson, E C Tarbell, J J Enneking, William Glackens, Everett Shinn, E H Potthast & J A M Whistler, realism, Pino de Angelico, Zhen-Huan Lu, sculpture by Kahlil Gibran; Claude Monet, Childe Hassam, F C Frieske, Richard Miller, Maurice Prendergast; Compiling catalogue raisonnés on Edmund T Tarbell, WS Barrett, CF Ryder, JJ Enneking. *Publ:* John Joseph Enneking, 1972, The Ten American Painters, Rumford Press, 1976; The Watercolored World of J W S Cox, 81; The Prophetic Odessey of Richard Earl Thompson, Am Impressionist, 82; auth, Introduction, Jane Peterson, Am Artist, 1982; The Master's Touch, 90; The Ultimate Elvis, Simon & Schuster, 94; Edmund C Tarbell and the Boston School, 1980; Love, Fine Art Pub, NY, 2000; Robert Hamada, Master Carver, Kauai Mus, Hawaii, 2001; Henry Wo-Yue Kee (intro), Art Collecting and Investing, 2003; Endnote, Pino Contemporary Realism, 2003; auth, Introduction-Pino DeAngelico, 2005; Edward Henry Potthast: More than One Man, 2006; auth, Richard Loud-Coastal Reflections, 2011. *Dealer:* Marco Apollo Pierce, Patricia Jobe Pierce. *Mailing Add:* c/o Pierce Galleries Inc 721 Main St Rte 228 Hingham MA 02043

PIERSON, JACK
ARTIST
b Plymouth, Mass, 1960. *Study:* Mass Coll Art, BFA, Boston. *Work:* Whitney Mus Am Art, NY, 1994, 1995, 2004; Mus Contemp Art, Chicago, 1995; Defining the Nineties, Mus Contemp Art, Miami, 1996. *Exhib:* Solo exhibs, Simon Watson, NY, 1990, Pat Hearn Gallery, NY, 1991, Richerd Kuhlenschmidt Gallery, Los Angeles, 1991, 1992, Tom Cugliani Gallery, NY, 1992, White Columns, NY, 1992, Jack Hanley Gallery, San Francisco, 1993, Regen Projects, Los Angeles, 1994, Edward Hopper & Jack Pierson: Am Dreaming, Luhring Augustine Gallery, NY, 1994, 1996, Fine Arts Work Ctr, Provincetown, Mass, 1994, Tex, Gallery, Houston, 1995, Parco Gallery, Tokyo, 1995, White Cube, London, 1996, Galerie Philippe Rizzo, Paris, 1996, Taka Ishii Gallery, Tokyo, 1995, 2001, Pay Me In Coke, 1998, An Artificial Night, Ginza Art Space, Tokyo, 1998, Cheim & Read, NY, 2000, 2003, 2006, Regrets, Mus Contemp Art, Miami, 2002, Truth, Galerie Aurel Scheibler, Cologne, Germany, 2002, 2003, Albert Merola Gallery, Provincetown, 2004, Danziger Projects, NY, 2005, Galerie Thaddeaus Ropac, Paris, France, 2006, Regen Projects, Los Angeles, 2007, Sabine Knust, Munich, 2007, Centre d'Art Santa Monica, Barcelona, 2007; group exhibs, The Moderns, Feature, NY, 1995; Defining the Nineties, Mus Contemp Art, Miami, 1996; Urgence, Mus d'Art Contemp de Bordeaux, France, 96; Art at the End of the 20th Century, Whitney Mus Am Art, 97, A Way With Words, 2001, Whitney Biennial, 2004, Uncontained, 2007; Early Works, Regen Projects, 98; Small Paintings, Cheim & Read, NY, 98, I am the Walrus, 2004; Times Squared, Keith De Lellis Gallery, NY, 99; Waxing Space, NY, 99; A Place Called Lonely, Greene Naftali, NY, 99; On Language, Sean Kelly Gallery, NY, 2000; Signs of the Times, H&R Art Space, Kansas City, Mo, 2001; Electric Dreams, The Barbican, London, 2002; Imaging the Abstract, Feigen Contemp, NY, 2003; Double Check, The Gallery of Contemp Art, Slovenia, 2004; Getting Emotional, Inst Contemp Art, Boston, 2005; Male Desire Two, Mary Ryan Gallery, 2005; Looking at Words, Andrea Rosen Gallery, NY, 2005; Seeing the Light, Carl Solway Gallery, Cincinnati, Ohio, 2006; Survivor, Bortolami Dayan, NY, 2006; Cheekwood Mus of Art, Nashville, Tenn, 2007. *Teaching:* Visiting artist, lectr, Cal Arts, Univ Arts, Philadelphia, Univ Miami, Calif, CAPC, Bordeaux, France, MoCa Miami, Calif, Univ Tex, Austin, Art Ctr, Pasadena, Mus Fine Arts, Boston, Yale Univ, Fine Arts Work Ctr, Provincetown, Mass. *Mailing Add:* c/o Cheim & Read Gallery 547 W 25th St New York NY 10001

PIET, JOHN FRANCES
SCULPTOR, INSTRUCTOR
b Detroit, Mich, Feb 23, 1946. *Study:* Detroit Soc Arts & Crafts, BFA, 73; Wayne State Univ, MFA, 75. *Comn:* Detroit Bank & Trust, Mich, 72; Pingree City Park, Detroit, Mich, 73; Grand Circus Park, Mich Coun Arts, 75; sculpture, KMart Courtyard, KMart Int, Troy, Mich, 79; Oakland Univ, Rochester, Mich, 81. *Exhib:* Tradition & Invention, Kresge Art Gallery, Mich State Univ, East Lansing, Mich, 77; Kick Out the Jams, Detroit Inst Arts, 80 & Mus Contemp Art, Chicago, 81; Detroit Artists, Cranbrook Acad Art, West Bloomfield, Mich, 80; Meadowbrook Invitational, Oakland Univ, Rochester, Mich, 81; and others. *Awards:* Nat Endowment Arts Grant, Oakland Univ Festival, 81. *Bibliog:* Robert Pincus-Witten (auth), Islands in the blight, Arts Mag, 1/78; Mary S Smyka (auth), Dreams in steel, Detroit Monthly Mag, 80; Dennis A Nawrocki (auth), Art in Detroit public places, Wayne State Press, 80. *Media:* Steel. *Dealer:* Cantor-Lemberg Gallery 538 N Woodward Ave Birmingham MI 48010. *Mailing Add:* 25501 Edgemont Dr Southfield MI 48034-2201

PIETRZAK, TED
DIRECTOR
b 1942, Kitchener, Ontario Canada. *Study:* Univ Guelph, BA, 1976. *Pos:* Asst to dir, Art Gallery Hamilton, Ont, 1976-1981, exec dir, 1992-1998; exec dir, Burlington Cult Ctr, Ont, 1981-1991; chmn, Bay Area Arts Collective, 1989-1991; dir, Burchfield-Penney Art Ctr, Buffalo, 1998-. *Teaching:* Instr leadership & commun, Sch Admin, Humber Col, 1990-1991. *Awards:* Exhib Assistance Grants, Ont Arts Coun, 1978; William T Wyle Award Arts Admin, Banff Sch Business, 1985. *Mem:* Can Art Mus Dir Orgn (treas, 1990-95); Ont Asn Art Galleries (pres, 1984-85). *Publ:* Contribr, Administration and Financial Planning, The Gallery Handbook, Ont Asn Art Galleries, 1979; A reason for collecting, Fusion Mag, 1985. *Mailing Add:* Burchfield-Penney Art Center Buffalo State College 1300 Elmwood Avenue Buffalo NY 14222

PIJANOWSKI, EUGENE M
EDUCATOR, CRAFTSMAN
b Detroit, Mich, Oct 5, 1938. *Study:* Wayne State Univ, BFA, 65, MA, 67; Cranbrook Acad Art, Bloomfield Hills, Mich, MFA, 69; Tokyo Univ Art, 69-71. *Work:* The Art Gallery of Western Australia, Perth; Nat Mus Mod Art, Kyoto; Nat Mus Art; Smithsonian Inst, Washington, DC; Detroit Inst Art; Am Crafts Mus, NY. *Exhib:* Contemp Metalcraft, Seoul, Korea, 88; Fourth Int Non Arts Forays Exposition, Navy Pier, Chicago, 88, 89, & 90; Crafts Today-USA traveling exhib (15 countries), 89-93; Sculptural Concerns: Contemp Am Metalworking, Contemp Arts Ctr, Cincinnati & Ft Wayne Mus, 93-94; Int Jewelry Biennele, Kunsthal, Rotterdam, 93; Sculptural Concerns, 93-96. *Pos:* Assoc dean & prof, Sch Art, Univ Mich, Ann Arbor, currently. *Teaching:* Instr metalwork, jewelry & crafts design, San Diego State Univ, Calif, 72-73; lectr Japanese metalworking, over 88 workshops throughout the US, Europe, Japan and Australia; assoc prof metalwork, jewelry & three-dimensional design, Purdue Univ, West Lafayette, 73-81; prof, Sch Art, Univ Mich, Ann Arbor, 81-. *Awards:* Fulbright Fel, Vienna Inst Appl Arts, Austria, 85; Herbert Hofman Prize Schmuck gene, 87; Best of Show, The Wichita Nat, 87. *Bibliog:* Mokume-Gane (film), Oberon Films, 81; Sculptural Concerns (video-one of 5 artists interviewed), 93. *Mem:* Distinguished mem, Soc NAm Goldsmiths. *Media:* Non-ferrous Metals. *Publ:* Contribr to 30 books on metalwork, 73-94; coauth, 15 articles on Lamination of nonferrous metals by diffusion: Adaptations of the traditional Japanese technique of Mokume-Gane, Goldsmiths J, 77; Mokume-Gane, Craft Horizons, 78; Chong Hap design: Korea, Goldschneide Zeitung, 81; Refractory metals, Jewel, Japan, 82; Update II: Mokume-Gane, Metalsmith, 83. *Mailing Add:* Univ Mich Sch Art Ann Arbor MI 48109

PIJOAN, IRENE MARIA ELIZABETH
PAINTER, INSTRUCTOR
b Laursanne, Switzerland, Nov 12, 1953; US citizen. *Study:* Univ Calif, Davis, MFA, 80. *Hon Degrees:* Artist grant, NEA, 1982 & Art Matters, 1996; Artist in Residence, Calif State Univ, 1998. *Work:* Guggenheim Mus, NY; Oakland Mus, Calif; Univ Art Mus, Univ Calif, Berkeley; Roswell Mus & Art, NMex; Santa Clara Pub Libr, Calif. *Comn:* theatrical set, Lines Ballet Co, San Francisco, 98; metal works, Harborview Res Ctr, Seattle, 99-2000; painting, Highland Hosp, Oakland, Calif, 2000-01. *Exhib:* Solo exhibs, Roswell Mus & Art Ctr, 82, DeSaisset Mus, 84; New Horizons in Am Art, Guggenheim Mus, 85; 42nd Bicennial of Am, Corcoran Gallery, 91; From the Studio, Oakland Mus, 92; Rena Brawlen Gallery, San Francisco, 98; Art at the Millennium, Univ Mus, Berkeley, 98; solo retrospective, Dean Lesher Ctr for the Arts, Bedford Col, Walnut Creek, Calif, 2001. *Teaching:* assoc prof, San Francisco Art Inst, 83-. *Awards:* Nat Endowment for the Arts Grant, 82; Art Matters Grant, 96; Artist in Residence Calif State Univ, 98. *Bibliog:* New Horizons at Guggenheim, NY Times, 85; Local painter's canvases really add up, San Francisco, 90; Abstract and personal, Washington Post, 91; Artweek focus: Irene Pijoan, Artweek, 91. *Media:* Paper, Aluminum, Paint. *Dealer:* Rena Bransten Gallery 77 Geary St San Francisco Ca 94108

PIKE, JOYCE LEE
PAINTER, WRITER
b San Fernando, Calif, July 25, 1929. *Study:* Sergei Bongart Sch Art, 1955-57; Los Angeles Valley Col, 1958-62; Art League Los Angeles, 1960-63. *Work:* Fort Hays State Univ, Kans; Brandes Art Inst, Northridge, Calif; Scottsdale Artists Sch, Ariz; Arnot Art Mus, Elmira, NY; Beijing Mus, China. *Comn:* Pico Adobe San Fernando Hist Soc, Calif, 1972; Ralph Liebman, Los Angeles, Calif, 1982; A J Diani Corp, Santa Maria, Calif, 1983; USAF, 1992. *Exhib:* One person shows, Brand Libr, Glendale Calif, 1973, Eng Gallery, Beverly Hills, Calif, 1984 & Americana Gallery Carmel by the Sea, Calif, 1985; Artists of Am, 1990-94; Am Artists Prof League, 1990; Arnot Mus, 1992; Mus Art, Elmira, NY; Mus Art, Palm Springs, Calif; Lindsey Gallery, Carmel by the Sea, Calif; Red Door Art Gallery, Morro Bay, Calif; Brand Galleria, Glendale, Calif; Miller Gallery, Cincinnati; Bowers Mus, Santa Ana, Calif. *Pos:* Vpres, San Fernando Valley Art Club, Calif, 1968-72; dir, Pikes School Workshops, Pacific Grove, Calif, 1972-88; consult, Art Video Prod, 1983-88. *Teaching:* Instr Fine Arts, Art League Los Angeles, Calif 1957-88, Art Students League, Northridge, Calif, 1978-88 & Scottsdale Artists Sch, Ariz, 1987-2003; instr editing, Los Angeles Valley Col, Calif 1961-78. *Awards:* Spec Merit Award, Artists of the Southwest, Southern Calif Arts Coun, 1970 & Oil Painters Am, 2001-03; Best of Show, Catalina Festival of Arts, Calif, 1972; Best of Show, Pasadena Festival of Arts, Calif, 1981; Am Artists Prof League Award for Floral, 1992. *Mem:* Emer mem Woman Artists Am West; Am Inst Fine Arts; Calif Coun Arts; San Gabriel Fine Arts Inc; Calif Art Club; fel Am Artist Prof League NY; master signature mem Oil Painters Am. *Media:* Oils. *Res:* Reference art material. *Publ:* Auth & illusr, Painting Floral Still Lifes, Northlight Publ Co, 1983; auth, Oil Painting, A Direct Approach, 1988-90 & Painting Flowers with Joyce Pike, 1992, Writers Digest. *Mailing Add:* c/o Oil Painters of Am PO Box 2488 Crystal Lake IL 60039

PILDES, SARA
PAINTER, COLLAGE ARTIST
b New York, NY. *Study:* Pratt Inst; Coll City of NY, with Doris Cross; Brooklyn Mus with Harold Baumbach. *Work:* Doane Coll Mus, Crete, Nebr. *Exhib:* Stuhr Mus, Grand Island, Nebr; Governor's Mansion, Lincoln, Nebr; Raymond Duncan Gallery, Paris, France; Galerie Int, NY; Loeb Ctr, NY Univ; and others. *Pos:* treas, Metrop Painters & Sculptors, 82-. *Mem:* Nat Asn Women Artists; Artists Equity; Metrop Painters & Sculptors; Burr Artists. *Media:* Acrylic

PILE, JAMES
PAINTER
b Pueblo, Colo, Nov 7, 1943. *Study:* Univ Nebr, BFA, 65, MFA (Woods Fel), 71. *Hon Degrees:* Univ de Sonora, Hermosillo, Mexico, hon diploma, 72. *Work:* Sioux City Art Ctr, Iowa; Krasdale Foods Inc, Bronx, New York; Kalicow Corp, New York; Phoenix Art Mus, Ariz; Univ de Guadalajara, Guadalajara, Jal, Mexico. *Exhib:* Solo

exhibs, PM & Stein Gallery, 82, Bernice Steinbaum Gallery, New York, 84, 86 & 89, Udinotti Gallery, Scottsdale, Ariz, 2001 & 2003 & Univ de Guadalajara, Guadalajara Jal, Mexico, 2000; Time Out-Sports & Leisure in Am, Tampa Mus, Fla, 83; Cowboys & Indians-Common Ground, Boca Raton Mus & Lock Haven Art Ctr, Orlando, Fla, 85; The City Observed-Point of View, Bronx Mus Arts, New York, 86; Annual Hassam & Speicher Purchase Exhib, Am Acad Arts & Lett, New York, 87-88; West Art & the Law, St Paul, Minn, 88-89 & 93. *Teaching:* Prof painting & drawing, Ariz State Univ, Tempe, 71-2006, prof emer, 2006. *Awards:* Visual Artists Fel, Nat Endowment Arts, 87. *Bibliog:* Peter Schwepker (auth), Summer's scattered rewards, Artspeak, Vol III, No 25, 6/24/82; Donald Locke (auth), Jim Pile: New icons for the southwest, Artspace, spring 82; Renee Phillips (auth), James Pile at Bernice Steinbaum, Manhattan Arts & Entertainment, 84. *Media:* Painting, Collage. *Dealer:* Udinotti Gallery Scottsdale AZ

PILGRIM, DIANNE HAUSERMAN
MUSEUM DIRECTOR, HISTORIAN
b Cleveland, Ohio, July 8, 1941. *Study:* Pa State Univ, Univ Park, BA (art hist), 63; New York Univ, Inst Fine Arts, MA, 65; City Univ New York Grad Ctr, 71. *Hon Degrees:* Amherst Coll, LHD, 91; Pratt Inst, Parsons Sch Design, Hon Dr, 2000. *Collection Arranged:* Am Impressionist and Realist Paintings and Drawings from the Collection of Mr & Mrs Raymond J Horowitz (auth, catalog), Metrop Mus Art, NY, 73; co-cur, Am Renaissance 1876-1917 (auth, catalog), traveling, Brooklyn Mus, Nat Collection Fine Arts, DC, Fine Arts Mus San Francisco, Denver Art Mus, 79-80; Renovation of 21 Period Rooms at the Brooklyn Mus, 80-84; co-cur, The Machine in Am 1918-1941 (auth, catalog), Brooklyn Mus, Mus Art Carnegie Inst, Pittsburgh, Los Angeles Co Art Mus & High Mus, Atlanta; MMA-Semesler in Am 1965, Dec Arts, 24 yrs, Chester Dale Fel. *Pos:* Asst to dir, Pyramid Galleries, Ltd, DC, 69-71; researcher, Metrop Mus Art, New York, spring, 71 & res consult, 72-73; asst to dir, Finch Coll Mus Art, New York, summer, 71; chmn, Decorative Arts, Brooklyn Mus, 73-88; dir, Cooper-Hewitt Mus, 88-, dir emer, currently. *Teaching:* Adj asst prof museological problems: the period rooms, Columbia Univ Sch Archit & Planning, 76-78. *Awards:* Chester Dale Fel, Metrop Mus Art, 66-68; Alumni Achievement Award, Pa State Univ, 90; Achievement Arts Award, Music & Arts Ctr for the Handicapped of Conn, 92. *Mem:* Decorative Arts Soc; Soc Archit Hist; Friends of Clermont; Victorian Soc in Am; Historic House Trust Conservancy (adv bd); Gracie Mansion Bd; Nat Multiple Sclerosis Soc (bd mem, 11 yrs). *Res:* American 19th and 20th century decorative arts and paintings. *Publ:* Auth, Alexander Roux, his plain and artistic furniture, 2/68 & Reopening of the period rooms at the Brooklyn Museum, 10/84, Antiques; Inherited from the past: the American period room, 5/78 & The revival of pastels in nineteenth century America: the Society of Painters in Pastel, l0/78, Am Art J; Eighteenth century American interiors, Apollo, 4/82; The American Renaissance 1876-1914, 79 & The Machine Age in America 1918-1941, 85, Brooklyn Mus, NY. *Mailing Add:* 295 Central Park W 17 D New York NY 10024-3008

PILOCO, RICHARD
PAINTER
b NY, 1964. *Study:* Sch Visual Arts, BFA; NY Acad Figurative Art; Art Students League. *Exhib:* Solo exhibs include Eleanor Ettinger Gallery, 2004, 2006; group exhibs includes Soc of Illustrators, 89; Gallery on 2nd, NY, 97, 98; Grand Nat Exhib, Am Artists Professional League, 99; Trompe l'Oeil Exhib, John Pence Gallery, San Francisco, 99, Scapes, 2000; Landscape: Urban and Rural, Eleanor Ettinger Gallery, NY, 99, Int Summer Salon, 99, 2000, 2003, 2006, Figure in American Art, 2001, 2002, 2003, 2004, 2005, 2006, 2007, Winter Salon, 2002, 2007, Autumn Salon, 2005, European Views, 2006; The Paint Group, Hirschl & Adler Gallery, NY, 99, Winter Landscape Show, 2000; NY Realists, ARC Gallery, Scottsdale, Ariz, 2000; The Dealer's Choice Award, Grenning Gallery, Sag Harbor, NY, 2000, 2002; Diane Nelson Fine Arts, Pasadena, Calif, 2001; The Forbes Galleries, NY, 2003; Albemarle Gallery, London, 2003; New York Realists, Century Gallery, Alexandria, Va, 2004. *Teaching:* Mentor, Fashion Inst Technology, NY, formerly; painting instr, Water Street Atelier, NY, 97-98. *Mailing Add:* c/o Eleanor Ettinger Gallery 24 W 57th St Ste 609 New York NY 10019

PINARDI, ENRICO VITTORIO
SCULPTOR, PAINTER
b Cambridge, Mass, Feb 11, 1934. *Study:* Apprentice with Pelligrini & Cascieri, five yrs; Boston Archit Ctr; Sch Mus Fine Arts, Boston; Mass Coll Art, BS (educ); RI Sch Design, MFA. *Work:* Worcester Art Mus, De Cordova Mus, Lincoln & Boston Inst Contemp Art, Mass; Chase Manhattan Bank, NY; Marmonac, San Ambogio Yalp, Verona, Italy; Rose Art Mus, Brandeis Univ, Waltham, Mass; Boston Pub Libr, Mass. *Exhib:* New Eng Art Part IV Sculpture, 64 & Surrealism, 70, De Cordova Mus; painting, sculpture, Pucker Gallery, Boston, Mass, 80, 88, 97 & 2002; sculpture, Vorpal Gallery, New York, 91; paintings & sculpture, Tufts Univ, 2004; Pucker Gallery, 2011. *Teaching:* Instr sculpture, Worcester Art Mus Sch, 63-67; prof, RI Coll, formerly, emer prof, currently. *Media:* Wood. *Dealer:* Pucker Gallery 171 Newbury Boston MA 02116. *Mailing Add:* 87 Child St Hyde Park MA 02136-1732

PINAULT, FRANÇOIS-HENRI
COLLECTOR
b Rennes, France, May 28, 1962. *Study:* Ecole des Hautes Etudes Commerciales (HEC), Grad, 1985. *Pos:* Internal sales to mgr procurement Pinault-Printemps-Redoute SA (now known as PPR SA), 1987-89; gen mgr, France Bois Industries, 1989-90; chmn & chief exec officer, Pinault Dist, 91-97, CFAO (Compagnie Française de l'Afrique Occidentale), 1993-97 & Fnac Group, 1997-2001; co-mgr, Financière Pinault, 2001-03; chmn, Artémis Paris, 2003-; bd dirs, Gucci Group, 1999- & supervisory bd mem, 2001-; chmn bd, PPR SA, Paris, 2005- & chief exec officer, 2005-; bd dirs, Financière Pinault Pinault-Printemps-Redoute SA (now known as PPR SA), Finaref, Fnac SA, Rexel, Soft Computing & TV Breizh; managing bd mem, Château Latour; supervisory bd chmn, PPR Interactive; permanent rep, Artémis, Conforma Holding, GuilbertFinacière Pinault & Bouygues. *Awards:* Named one of Top 200 Collectors, ARTnews mag, 2004-13. *Collection:* Contemporary art. *Mailing Add:* PPR SA 10 Ave Hoche Paris France

PINCHUK, VICTOR
COLLECTOR
b Kiev, Ukraine, Dec 14, 1960. *Study:* Dnipropetrovsk Metallurgy Inst, Ukraine, Grad (metal forming, with honors), 1983, PhD (engineering), 1987. *Pos:* Founder, Interpipe Group, Ukraine, 1990-2006, pres & chmn, 1997-98; mem, Ukrainian Parliament, 1998-, chmn bus & investment policy & economic policy subcomts, formerly; founder, EastOne co, Ukraine, 2006- & Victor Pinchuk Found, 2006-. *Awards:* Named one of World's Richest People, Forbes mag, 2005-; named one of Top 200 Collectors, ARTnews mag, 2008-13; 100 List: World's Most Influential People, TIME mag, 2010. *Collection:* Contemporary art. *Mailing Add:* Victor Pinchuk Foundation 2 Mechnikova Str Kiev 01601 Ukraine

PINCKNEY, STANLEY
PAINTER, TAPESTRY ARTIST
b Boston, Mass, Sept 30, 1940. *Study:* Famous Artist Sch, Westport, Conn, 57-61; Mus Sch Fine Arts, Boston, Mass, 67. *Work:* Nat Ctr African-Am Art, Roxbury, Mass; Mus Dynamique, Dakar, Senegal, W Africa; Palace de l'Pres, Dakar. *Comn:* Tapestry, Mus Sch Fine Arts, Boston, 75. *Exhib:* A Century of the Mus Sch, Boston Mus Fine Arts, 77; African-Am Master Artists-in-Residency Prog Exhib, Dodge Libr Gallery, Northwestern Univ, 78 & Univ Lowell, 79; Recent Tapestries, Mus Sch Fine Arts Gallery & Boston Mus Fine Arts, 78; Resist-Dyed Tapestries, Stanley McCormick Gallery, Boston Archit Ctr, 79; Traveling Scholarship Exhib, Mus Fine Arts, Boston, 81; Object of the Month, Mus Fine Arts, Boston, 84; Art in Craft Media, Newton Arts Ctr, Newtonville, Mass, 88; and others. *Collection Arranged:* Twelve Black Artists, Rose Art Mus, Brandeis Univ, 69; Osubamba (auth, catalog), Boston Ctr for the Arts, 76 & Cyclorama Gallery, Boston, 76; A Century of the Mus School (auth, catalog), Boston Mus Fine Arts, 77. *Teaching:* Instr African & traditional arts, Mus Sch Fine Art, Boston, 72-. *Awards:* 19th Albert H Whitin Fel, Boston Mus Fine Arts, 69; Ford Found Fac Enrichment-Artist Grant, Mus Sch Fine Art, 78; Blance E Colman Fel, 78; Mellon Found, Fac Enrichment Grant, Mus Sch Fine Arts, 87; and others. *Media:* Watercolor. *Publ:* Beyond Tradition (exhib catalogue), New England Fiber Collective, 83; auth, article, Am Crafts Mag, 86. *Mailing Add:* Dept African Arts 230 Fenway Boston MA 02115

PINCUS, LAURIE JANE
PAINTER, SCULPTOR
b New York, NY, Dec 14, 1951. *Study:* Bard Col, with Murray Reich, Matt Phillips; Sarah Lawrence Col, with Richard Povsette-Darte, BA, 75; Pacifica Grad Inst, MA, 94. *Work:* Los Angeles Co Mus Art; Univ Calif Los Angeles; LA Foret Mus, Tokyo; Norton Family Collection; Los Angeles Woman's Clinic. *Comn:* Tom & Betty (sculpture), Takashimaya Dept Store, Osaka, Japan, 85-90; spec art proj, Fuji Television, Tokyo, Japan, 90, Hollywood Roosevelt Hotel, Hollywood, Calif. *Exhib:* Calif Contemp Artists, Laguna Art Mus, Calif, 87; Guest Artist, Orange Co Ctr Continuing Art, Santa Ana, Calif, 89; 10 Yr Survey Show, LaBand Art Gallery, Loyola Marymount Univ, Los Angeles, 89; Am Pop Cult Today III, LA Foret Mus, Tokyo, Japan, 89; External Fantasies, Internal Realities, Security Pac Corp, Gallery at Plaza, Los Angeles, 91; Three From LA, Pima Community Col, Tucson, Ariz, 90; The Dream - A Performance, Cas de Maria church, Santa Barbara, Calif, 92; Am Studio at World Design Center, Gifu, Japan, 2000; Group Shows, NTT Japan, Calendar Projects by World-Famous Artists, 97, Obsessions, UCSB Women's Ctr Gallery, Santa Barbara, Calif, 97, Laguna Art Mus, Calif, 97, Angels Over Gifu, World Design Gallery, Japan, 2002; and others. *Pos:* artist-in-residence, World Design Ctr, Gifu, Japan, 2000. *Teaching:* West Side Arts Ctr, Junior Arts Ctr & Los Angeles Children's Mus; Santa Barbara's Children's Creative Projects, Carpinteria Sch Dist, Calif. *Bibliog:* Marva Marrow (auth), Inside The LA Artist, Penegrine Smith Books, 88; Betty Brown (auth), Exposures: Women & Their Art, New Sage Press, 89; Kei Nagashima (auth), America Pop Culture Today, Vol 3, Seibundo Shinkosha, 90. *Mem:* Westside Arts Ctr, Santa Monica (bd dir, currently); Friends Jr Arts Ctr, Los Angeles (bd dir & Joanna Cotsen fel comt); Artists Equity; Calif Arts Standards Comt; Soc Writers & Illus of Childrens Books. *Media:* Mixed Media, Paper, Acrylic; Wood. *Dealer:* USSO Toyko Japan; Takum Studio Gifucity Japan. *Mailing Add:* 629 Miramonte Dr Santa Barbara CA 93109

PINCUS-WITTEN, ROBERT A
EDUCATOR, WRITER
b New York, NY, Apr 5, 1935. *Study:* Cooper Union, Emil Schweinburg Grant, 56; Univ Chicago, MA (dept fel), 60, PhD (dept fel), 68; Univ Paris, Sorbonne, exchange fel, 63-64. *Pos:* Assoc ed, Arts Mag, 63-90; ed, Artforum Mag, 66-76; dir, Gagosian Gallery, New York, 90-96, dir exhib, C & M Arts, NY, 96-; dir exhibitions, L&M Arts, 2004-2006; Contrib Ed, Artforum, 2008. *Teaching:* Emer prof art hist, Queens Col & Grad Ctr, City Univ New York. *Mem:* Coll Art Asn (life mem). *Res:* Symbolism; the history of contemporary art and photography. *Specialty:* Abstract expressionism; 20th Century Masters. *Publ:* Auth, Occult Symbolism in France, Josephin Peladan and the Salons de la Rose-Croix, Garland Press, 76; Post-Minimalism, Art of the Decade, 77 & Entries (Maximalism), Art at the Turn of the Decade, 83, Out of London Press; Eye To Eye, Twenty Years of Art Criticism, UMI Res Press, 84; and others. *Dealer:* Twentieth Century and Modern Masters. *Mailing Add:* L & M Art 45 E 78th St New York NY 10021

PINDELL, HOWARDENA DOREEN
PAINTER, EDUCATOR
b Philadelphia, Pa, Apr 14, 1943. *Study:* Boston Univ Sch Fine & Applied Arts, BFA, 65; Cumminton Sch Arts, 63; Sch Art & Archit, Yale Univ, MFA, 67 Mass Coll Art, Hon Dr, 97. *Hon Degrees:* Hon Dr Mass Coll Art, Hon Dr, 97, Parsons Sch of Design and New School Univ, 99. *Work:* Mus Contemp Art, Chicago; Fogg Art Mus, Harvard Univ; Whitney Mus Am Art, Mus Mod Art, Metrop Mus Art, NY; Philadelphia Mus Art; Chase Manhattan Bank, NY & Tokyo; High Mus, Atlanta; Toledo Art Mus; NY Pub Libr; Detroit Inst of the Arts. *Comn:* Comn by IBM, 85; comn by GSA, 87; Metrop Mus Art, 91; Lehman Col, Bronx, NY, 93; Phoenix Int Airport, 96. *Exhib:*

Solo shows incl George N'Namdi Gallery, Birmingham, Mich, 95, Arting Gallery, Cologne, Ger, 95, Bethel Coll Art Gallery, St Paul, Minn, 96, Charter Oak Cult Ctr, Hartford, Conn, 96, N'Namdi Gallery, Chicago, 96, Kane Col, NJ, 97 & Suffolk Community Col, NY, 97; group shows incl Mus Mod Art, NY, 71, 76, 85, 89 & 96; Fogg Art Mus, Harvard Univ, 73; Mus Mod Art, Paris, 75; Inst Contemp Art, Boston, 77; Oakland Mus, 77, 81 & 92; Stadtische Kunsthalle Dusseldorf, Ger, 77; Los Angeles Co Mus Art, 78; New Orleans Mus Art, 78 & 89; Wadsworth Atheneum, 78 & 89; Nat Gallery Art, Washington, 78 & 92; Kunstmus Bern, Switz, 79; Metrop Mus Art, NY, 79 & 82; Everson Mus Art, 81; Va Mus Fine Arts, 87; Mus Fine Arts, Houston, 87; Baltimore Mus Art, 87; Philadelphia Mus Art, 88, 90, 93 & 94; Denver Art Mus, 89; Brooklyn Mus, 89 (2 exhibs), 90; Albright-Knox Art Gallery, 92 & 93; Mus Fine Arts, Boston, 92; Inst Contemp Art, Boston, 93; High Mus Art, 93; retrospective (traveling), 94; Bearing Witness: African Am Women Artists, traveling to Minn Mus Am Art & Edwin A Ulrich Mus Art, among others, 96; At the Foreground of Paths, Skoto Gallery, NY, 96; Religion: Through Brown Eyes, Minority Arts Coun, Philadelphia, 96; A Slave Ship Speaks: The Wreck of the Henrietta Marie, Spirit Sq Ctr Arts & Educ, Charlotte, NC, 96; The Thurlow Tibbs Collection, Corcoran Mus Art, 96; Witness to our Time: Hocardena Pindell, Heckscher Mus, Huntington, NY, 99. *Collection Arranged:* The War Show, Ann McCoy, 83; Michael Singer: Ritual Series, Retellings, 87; Poetic License, 90; Liliana Porter, Staller Fine Arts Ctr, Art Gallery, State Univ NY, Stony Brook, 98; Staller Fine Arts Ctr, Art Gallery, State Univ NY, Stony Brook. *Pos:* Exhib asst, Mus Mod Art, New York, 67-69, cur asst, 69-71 & asst cur, prints & illus books, 71-77, assoc cur, 77-79. *Teaching:* Assoc prof, State Univ NY, Stony Brook, 79-84, prof, 84-, dir MFA program, currently; vis artist fac, Skowhegan Sch Painting & Sculpture, Maine, summer 80 & Vt Studio Sch, Johnson, summer 85; vis prof art, Yale Univ, New Haven, Conn, 95-99. *Awards:* Nat Endowment Arts (painting), 72-73 & 83-84; Guggenheim Fel Painting, 87-88; Coll Art Asn Artist Award for Distinguished Body of Work, 90; Artist Award Studio Mus in Harlem, 94; Joan Mitchell Painting Award, 94; Artist Award for Disting Svc to the Profession, Women's Art Caucus, 98. *Bibliog:* Nancy Heller (auth), Women Artists, An Illustrated History, Ableville Press, New York, 91; Clarence White (auth), Howardena Pindell, Art Papers, 7-8/91; Charles Hagen (auth), Who's on first?, NY Times, 8/2/91. *Mem:* Coll Art Asn; Int Art Critics Asn. *Media:* Acrylic on Canvas. *Publ:* Auth, California Prints, Arts Mag, New York, 5/72; Ed Ruscha: Words, Print Collectors Newslett, 1/73; Robert Rauschenberg: Link, Mus Mod Art, 10/75; Alan Shields: Tales of Brave Ulysses, 1/75 & Artists' Periodicals: Alternative Space, 9/77, Print Collector's Newslett; Covenant of Silence: Defacto Censorship, 10/90 & 11/90; New Art Examiner, 3rd text, 9/90; The Heart of the Matter: The Writings and Art of Howardena Pindell, Midmarch Arts Press, New York, 97. *Mailing Add:* State Univ NY Dept Art Stony Brook NY 11794-5400

PINKEL, SHEILA MAE
PHOTOGRAPHER, COMPUTER GRAPHICS
b Newport News, Va, Aug 21, 1941. *Study:* Univ Calif, Berkeley, BA, 63, MFA, 77; Univ Calif, Los Angeles, with Robert Heinecken. *Work:* Walker Art Ctr, Minn; MOCA, Los Angeles Co Mus, Calif; Ctr Creative Photog, Tucson; MOMA & Int Mus Photog, George Eastman House, NY; Seattle Mus Art; San Francisco Mus Mod Art; Calif Mus Photog. *Comn:* Cyanotype mural, Park La Brea Towers, Los Angeles, 76; Mural, Sherman Oaks Libr, 03; Gate, Green Meadows Park, Los Angeles, 04. *Exhib:* Light from Illumination to Pure Radiance, San Francisco Mus Mod Art, 85; Art in Environment, San Francisco Mus Arts & Crafts, 93; exhibs, Prague, Czech, 93; Reinventing Documentary, Purdue Univ, 94; Reinventing Emblems, Yale Univ, 95; Contemp Photog; The California Focus, Univ Calif, Los Angeles & Armond Hammer Mus Art, 95; Platt Gallery, Univ Judaism, Los Angeles, 96; San Francisco Camera Work Gallery, 97, Calif Mus Photog, 98, Salapacorn Univ, Thailand, 2000; 2nd Annual Art Biennial, Buenos Aires, Argentina, 2002; Hanoi Univ Art, Vietnam, 2004; Lanitis Found, Cyprus, 2006; Nat Ctr Contemp Art, Ekaterinburg, Russia, 2009. *Collection Arranged:* Multicultural Focus (auth, catalog), Cross Cultural Photog Exhib. *Pos:* int ed, Leonardo mag. *Teaching:* Prof photog, Univ Calif Exten, Los Angeles, 76-83, Otis Parsons Art Inst, 81-83, Sch Art Inst Chicago, 83, Calif Inst Arts, 84-86 & Pomona Col, 86-; Friends of Photo Workshops, 87 & 88; Visual Studies Workshops, 93. *Awards:* Artist Grants, Nat Endowment for the Arts, 79, 82; Sloan Found Grant, 88; Artist of the Year, City Santa Monica, 88; Visual Studies Workshop Book Publ Award, 93; Hammer Award, Ctr for The Study Political Graphics, 95. *Bibliog:* Sylvia Moore (auth), Yesterday and Tomorrow: Collection Women Artists, Midmarch Press, NY, 89; Paul Von Bauer (auth), Other Voices, Other Visions, 95; Bethann Kevlis (auth), Naked To The Bone, 97. *Mem:* Los Angeles Ctr Photog Studies (vpres, 78-83); Soc Photog Educ (nat bd mem, 86-90); Coll Art Asn. *Media:* Photography, Xerography, Xeroradiography, Computer Graphics. *Publ:* coauth, Kou Changs Story, 93; Guest ed, Art & Social Issues, vol 5, Leonardo, 93. *Mailing Add:* 210 N Ave 66 Los Angeles CA 90042-2927

PINKNEY, JERRY
ILLUSTRATOR
b Philadelphia, Pa, Dec 22, 1939. *Study:* Philadelphia Mus Coll Art, 58-60. *Work:* Mus Am Illus, NY; H C Taylor Art Gallery, NC A & T State Univ; Miami-Dade Pub Libr; Afro-Am Hist & Cult Mus, Philadelphia; Air & Space Mus, Washington, DC. *Comn:* 10 US Postal Stamps, US Postal Serv, Washington, DC, 77-86; limited edition poster, Negro Ensemble, NY, 82; limited edition books, Franklin Libr, NY; NASA Art Team (painting), NASA, 82; Cover & interior illus, Nat Geog Mag, Washington, DC, 84. *Exhib:* Through Am Eyes; Moscow Int Bk Fair, USSR, 89; Biennale Illustrations, Bratislava, Czechoslovakia, 89; Soc Illustrators, 86-90; solo exhibs, Schomburg Ctr for Res, NY, 90. *Pos:* Mem, comts at US Postal Serv, Washington, DC, 82-. *Teaching:* Vis critic illus, RI Sch Design, 69-70, adj prof, 70-71; assoc prof illus, Pratt Inst, Brooklyn, NY, 86-; Distinguished vis prof, Univ Del, Newark, 86-87, assoc prof, 88-92. *Awards:* Randolph Caldecott Medal of Hon (bk), Mirandy and Brother Wind, 89; Coretta Scott King Award (bk), Mirandy and Brother Wind, 89; Award, Libr of Congress Books for Children (bk), More Tales of Uncle Remus, 89; award, The Year's Best Illustrated Book for Children, New York Times, 89; award, The Year's Twelve Outstanding Works for Children, Time Mag, 89; First Place, New York Bk Show; Randolph Caldecott Medal of Hon (bk), The Talking Eggs. *Bibliog:* Donald Stermer (auth), Jerry Pinkney, Communication Art Mag, 5-6/75; Nick Meglin (auth), The strength of weakness, Am Artist Mag, 1/82; Jerry Pinkney, Idea Mag, Japan, 82. *Mem:* Soc Illusrs. *Media:* Watercolor. *Publ:* Illusr, The Tales of Uncle Remus, 88; More Tales of Uncle Remus, 89; Home Place, Macmillan, 90; Further Tales of Uncle Remus, 90; Pretend You're Cat, 90. *Mailing Add:* 41 Furnace Dock Rd Croton On Hudson NY 10520-1406

PINNELL, PETER J
CERAMIST, ADMISTRATOR
Study: Columbia Col, Missouri, BA (music), 1976; NY State Col of Ceramics, Alfred Univ, BFA, 1980; Univ Colo, Boulder, MFA, 1982. *Exhib:* Work exhibited throughout the US and a variety of venues abroad (China, Japan, Korea, Taiwan, Australia, New Zealand, The Netherlands, Germany and South Africa); ceramics vis artist exhibition, Lorton Arts Found, 2011, Gallery W-16, 2011, Workhouse Arts Center, 2011. *Teaching:* with Univ Nebraska, Lincoln, 1995-, chair, Dept of Art and Art History, currently, prof of art, currently. *Publ:* columnist, As Far As I Know, Clay Times Magazine. *Mailing Add:* Department of Art and Art History University of Nebraska Richards Hall 120 Lincoln NE 68588-0114

PINSKER, ESSIE
SCULPTOR
b New York, 1918. *Study:* Brooklyn Col, BA; Art Students League, New York Univ NY (with Vincent Glinsky); Mus Mod Art; New Sch Soc Res (with Leo Manso); Cambridge Univ, Eng; Oxford Univ, Eng. *Comn:* marble sculpture, Marriott Hotels, USA, Minneapolis, Minn, 88; Bronze Sculpture RD SCINTO/Enterprise Corp, 88; bronze sculpture, Granard Comm Ltd, 89; painted steel sculpture, Tauck Tours, Westport, Conn, 90; steel sculpture, Queensboro Steel, Wilmington, NC; aluminum sculpture, City of Brea, Calif; bronze sculplture, KOCE PBS-TV, Orange Co, Calif, 2000; bronze sculpture, Ctr for Universal Truth, San Juan Capistrano, Calif; bronze sculpture, Anne Frank in the World, Calif; many others. *Exhib:* solo exhibs, Lifetime Retrospective (with catalog), Las Vegas Art Mus, Nev, 97, Vorpal Gallery, NY, Bodley Gallery, NY, Ross Watkins Gallery, Palm Desert, Calif, Left Bank Gallery, Dove Canyon, Calif; group exhibs, Lever Bros, NY, 81; Arco Int Art Fair, Madrid, Spain, 88; Galleri Atrium, Stockholm, Sweden; Sandra Higgins Fine Arts, London, Eng; Gallerie Ilse Lommel, Leverkusen, Ger; Feingarten Galleries, Los Angeles, Calif; many others. *Collection Arranged:* Permanent Mus Collections: Portland Art Mus Portland, OR; Nat Portrait Gallery, Smithsonian Inst; City of Peace, Rondine, Italy; Everson Mus, Syracuse, NY; Las Vegas Art Mus; Aldrich Mus Contemp Art, Ridgefield, Conn; War Mem, Yehud, Israel; Okla Art Ctr; Minn Mus Art; Mus Arts & Scis, Daytona Beach, Fla; Mus Mod Art, Warsaw, Poland; Orange Co Mus Art, Newport Beach, Calif; UCLA Med Ctr; Ctr for the Arts, Vero Beach, Fla; Vassar Mus, Poughkeepsie, NY; Fordham Univ at Lincoln Ctr; Rutgers Camden Collection of Art, NJ; Pace Univ, NY; Hinkhouse Collection, Eureka Col, Ill; NECCA Mus, Brooklyn, Conn; New Sch for Social Rsch, NYC. *Awards:* Sculpture Award, Knickerbocker Artists 24th Ann Exhib, 74; Sculpture Award, Metrop Life Ann Exhib; Lumiere Award, Ctr for Universal Truth, San Juan Capistrano, Calif; Anne Frank to Steven Spielberg for the film Schindler's List, Humanitarian Award. *Bibliog:* Benjamin Epstein (auth), Sculptor Fashions a Return to Form, Los Angeles Times, 98; Sean Simon (auth), Essie Pinsker, A Major Sculpture Retrospective, Artspeak, 97; Laurie Mendenhall (auth, brochure), Essie Pinsker: A Profile, Las Vegas Art Mus, 97; David Mann (auth, brochure), Essie Pinsker, Stones & Steel, Bodley Gallery, NYC, 81; Vorpal, David Shapiro Art Critic, The Art of Essie Pinsker; Las Vegas Art Mus James Mann curator, Essis Pinsker and Sculptor Today. *Mem:* Artists Equity, New York. *Media:* Stone, Metal

PINZARRONE, PAUL
GRAPHIC ARTIST, PAINTER
b Mich, 1951. *Study:* Univ Ill, BFA (painting), 73. *Work:* Butler Inst Am Art, Youngstown, Ohio; Ill State Mus, Springfield; Kemper Insurance, St Xavier Coll & Union League, Chicago. *Exhib:* New Horizons in Art, Chicago, 75, 76 & 80; 28th Ill Exhib, Springfield, 75; 39th & 40th Midyear Exhibs, Butler Inst, 75 & 76; Mainstreams 75-, Marietta Int, Ohio, 75; solo exhibs, Joy Horwich Gallery, Chicago, Ill, 76, 77, 80 & 83, Rockford Arts Coun, 88, Rockford Arts Coun, 89 & Univ Wis, 90, Kortman Gallery, Rockford, Ill, 2005; Rockford Midwestern Biennial, 2008. *Teaching:* Instr art, Rock Valley Coll, Rockford, Ill, 75-76 & 78, Rockford Coll, 76; guest lectr, Univ Miami, 77, Gloria Luria Gallery, Miami, 77, Regent Art Asn, 78, St Xavier Coll, Chicago, 80 & Highland Col, 81. *Awards:* First Prize, New Orleans Int, 75; First Prize, Ill State Fair Prof, 75; First Prize, Art Inst Juried, Chicago, 84. *Bibliog:* Article, New Art Examiner, Chicago, 12/80; Carrie Rebora & Laura Cottingham (auths), article in The Chicago Art Review, 81. *Media:* Airbrush, Digital Media. *Dealer:* www.pinzarrone.com; 4 Art Gallery Chicago Il; 4Artinc.com; State of the Art Gallery Rockford Ill

PIPER, ADRIAN MARGARET SMITH
CONCEPTUAL ARTIST, WRITER
b New York, Sept 20, 1948. *Study:* Sch Visual Arts, AA (fine art), 69; City Coll New York, BA(philos), 74; Harvard Univ, Cambridge, Mass, MA(philos), 77 & PhD(philos), 81. *Hon Degrees:* Calif Inst Arts, Valencia, 1992; Mass Coll Art, DA. *Work:* Art Inst Chicago; Baltimore Mus Art; Brooklyn Mus; Metrop Mus Art; High Mus Art, Atlanta; Denver Art Mus; Kunstverein München; Mus Mod Art, NY; Mus Contemp Art, Chicago; Whitney Mus Am Art; and others. *Exhib:* Solo exhibs incl Wadsworth Atheneum, 80, Whitney Mus Am Art, 90, Adrian Piper: A Retrospective, 99-2001: Adrian Piper Seit 1965, 2000-2001, Thomas Erben Gallery, 2000-2001, Adrian Piper Over the Edge, Emi Fontana Gallery, Milan, 2002, 2003-04, Lamoca, General Found, 2002-2003, Index, Swedish Contemp Art Found, 2005, CPH Kunsthal, Copenhagen, 2006, Smart Mus Art, Chicago, 2006; group exhibs incl 557,087, Seattle Art Mus (traveling), 69; Information, Mus Mod Art, NY, 70; Paris

Biennale, Mus Art Mod, Paris, 71 & 77; Commitment to Print, Mus Mod Art, NY, 88; Signs, Art Gallery Ont, Toronto, 88; L'Art Conceptuel: Une Perspective, Mus Art Mod, Paris, 90; The Art of Advocacy, Aldrich Mus Contemp Art, Ridgefield, Conn; Visions/Revisions, Denver Art Mus, 91; What it's Like, What it is, No 3, Dislocations, Mus Mod Art, NY, 91; Open Mind: The LeWitt Collection, Wadsworth Atheneum, Hartford, 91; The Theater of Black Refusal: Black Art & Mainstream Criticism, Univ Calif Fine Arts Gallery, Irvine, 93; L'Hiver de l'Amour, Mus Art Mod, Paris, 94; Thirty Years, Aldridge Mus Contemp Art, Ridgefield, Conn, 94; Mappings, Mus Mod Art, NY, 94; Black Male: Representations of Masculinity in Contemp Am Art, Whitney Mus Am Art, 95; Options 2: Selections from the Modern & Contemp Permanent Collection, Denver Art Mus, 95; It's Not a Picture, Galleria Emi Fontana, Milan, 95; Cornered, Paula Cooper Gallery, NY, 95; Art with Conscience, Newark Art Mus, NJ, 96; Now Here, La Mus Mod Art, Humlebaek, Denmark, 96; Reconsidering the Object of Art: 1965-1975, Mus Contemp Art, Los Angeles, 96; Thinking Print: Books to Billboards 1980-95, Mus Mod Art, NY, 96; Hidden in Plain Sight: Illusion in Art from Jasper Johns to Virtual Reality, Los Angeles Co Mus Art, 97; Devant l'histoire, Centre Georges Pompidou, Paris, 97; retrospective, Lamoca, 2000, New Mus, NY, 2000-2001; The Color Wheel Series, Paula Cooper Gallery, 2000; Whitney Mus Art, 1999-2000, 2004; Bronx Museum Arts, 2001-2002; Kulturhuset, Stockholm, Sweden, 2003; Tate Mod Mus, London, 2005; Andrea Rosen Gallery, 2005-2006; Elizabeth Dee Gallery, New York, 2006; Mus Contemp Art, Los Angeles, 2007; Centre d'art Contemporain, 2007. *Teaching:* Prof Philos, Wellesley Coll, Mass, Harvard Univ, Stanford Univ, Univ Mich, Georgetown & Univ Calif, San Diego. *Awards:* Visual Artists' Fel, Nat Endowment Arts, 79 & 82, Artists Forums Grant, 87; Guggenheim Memorial Found Fel, 89; Skowhegan Medal, 95; Distinguished Body of Work, Coll Art Asn, 2012. *Bibliog:* David Joselit (auth), Object lessons, Art in Am 84, 2/96; Gary Kornblau (auth), 1965-75: Reconsidering the object of art, Art Issues, 2/96; Museum of Contemporary Art at the temporary contemporary, The Print Collector's Newsletter, 2/96. *Media:* Installation, Video; Photo Text. *Publ:* Auth, Decide Who You Are, Reframings: New American Feminist Photographers, Temple Univ Press, Philadelphia, 95; Mortal Remains, Intermedia Arts, Minn, 96; Withdrawal clarified, Art in Am 84, 3/96; Dickinson's charm, NY Review Bks XLIII, 10/3/96; Out of Order, Out of Sight, MIT Press, 96. *Dealer:* Paula Cooper Gallery 534 W 21st St New York NY 10011; Robert Del Principe. *Mailing Add:* Adrian Piper Research Archive Postfach 54 02 04 Berlin 02135 D-10042 Germany

PIRKL, JAMES JOSEPH
EDUCATOR, DESIGNER, PAINTER
b Nyack, NY, Dec 27, 1930. *Study:* Pratt Inst, cert adv design, 51 & BID, 58; Wayne State Univ; Syracuse Univ, 81. *Hon Degrees:* Univ Monterrey, Hon diploma, Mexico, 81. *Exhib:* Syracuse Univ Fac Show, 65-91; The Future Is In Our Hands, Domus Acad, Tokyo, 96. *Pos:* Jr designer, General Motors Design staff, 58-59, designer, 59-60, sr designer, 61-64 & asst chief designer, 64-65; principal, James Joseph Pirkl/Transgenerational Design, NMex, 93-; adv, Universal Kitchen proj, RI Sch Design, 97-98; exec dir, Transgenerational Design Matters, Albuquerque, NMex, 2005-. *Teaching:* Instr, Ctr for Creative Studies, Detroit, Mich, 63-65; asst prof indust design, dept of design, Syracuse Univ, 65-68, assoc prof, 69-73, prof, 74-92, prof in charge, Indust Design Prog, 79-85, chmn, dept of design, 85-92, emer prof, 93-. *Awards:* Fel, Indust Designers Soc Am, 85; Sr Res Fel, ALL Univ Gerontology Ctr, Syracuse Univ, 90; Gold Indust Design Excellence Award, Indust Designers Soc Am & Bus Week Mag, 94; Educ award, Indust Designers Soc Am, 2001. *Bibliog:* Designing for the Elderly, Int Coun Soc Indust Design (interview), Nordmore LOKALTV, Kristionsund, Norway, 10/89; Talk of the Nation (invited guest), Nat Pub Radio, 98; This Bold House (article), AARP The Magazine, 9-10/2003. *Mem:* Indust Designers Soc Am (chmn cent NY chap, 77-79, vpres, mid-east region, 80-82, dir, 86-88, life); Human Factors Soc (life); Nat Asn of Sch of Art & Design; Author's Guild. *Media:* Oil, Pen and Ink, Computer Graphics. *Res:* Transgenerational Design: Making products & environments compatible with those physical & sensory impairments associated with human aging, which limit independence & accommodate the widest range of ages & abilities. *Specialty:* Special Collections Research Ctr. *Interests:* Promoting the concept of transgenerational design through educ, writing & consulting. *Collection:* James J Pirkl Papers, Syracuse Univ Lib. *Publ:* Coauth, Guidelines and Strategies for Designing Transgenerational Products, Copley, 88; many articles in mag, 88-97; Transgenerational Design: Products for an Aging Population, John Wiley & Sons, 94. *Mailing Add:* 2007 Quail Run Drive NE Albuquerque NM 87122

PIRNAT-DRESSLER, NIA
PAINTER, ADMINISTRATOR
Study: Univ Ill, Champaign, BFA; Ill State Univ (ceramics & watercolor). *Exhib:* Solo exhibs include BroMenn Med Ctr, Ill, 2002. *Pos:* Commercial artist, formerly; photographer's stylist, formerly; freelance graphics designer & commercial artist. *Teaching:* Artist-in-residence, Freight House Gallery, El Paso, Ill; teacher, Bloomington Parks & Recreation. *Mem:* Midwest Watercolor Soc (vpres, 2003-05 pres, 2005-). *Media:* Watercolor. *Mailing Add:* Transparent Watercolor Soc Am Box 111 738 E Dundee Rd Palatine IL 60074

PISANI, JOSEPH
MURALIST, PAINTER
b New Rochelle, NY, Oct 1, 1938. *Study:* San Francisco Art Inst; Calif Coll Arts & Crafts, with George Post, Richard Diebenkorn, Nathan Oliveira & Ralph Borge, BFA. *Work:* Dept of Defense & Hq Dept of Army, The Pentagon, Arlington, Va; The White House, Wash, DC; US Army Collection; US Air Force Collection; Royal Embassy of Saudi Arabia; plus others. *Comn:* Mondavi Tomb, Caesar Mondavi Family, St Helina, Calif, 62; General Marshall Mem Corridor, comn by Secy of the Army, Pentagon, 75; Army Bicentennial Murals, comn by Secy of Defense, 75-76; Gen Pershing mural, comn by Gen Yerks, Ft Myer, Va, 77-78; Gen MacArthur Mem, 81, Anzus Mem Corridor, 82, Military Womens Corridor, 83, Eisenhower Corridor, 85, Military Intelligence Corridor, 86 & Gen Mark Clark Display, 86, comn by Secy of Defense Weinberger, Pentagon, 90, Portrait Comn King Fahd, Saudi Arabia. *Exhib:* Army Wide Art Exhib, Pentagon, 63, 65; Corcoran Washington Area Show, 69; Artist Equity Group Shows, Washington, DC, 72 & 73; Va Beach Art Shows, 73 & 75. *Pos:* Chief graphic arts, Chief of Staff (Personnel), Pentagon, 67-73; graphic designer, Dept of Defense, 73-75; art dir, US Army Hq, 75-88; dir, Art Gallery 101-Ltd. *Awards:* Outstanding Achievement in Art, Bank of Am, 61; Scholar to Study Fine Arts, Scholastic Mag, 62; First Prize for Painting, Art League Va, 70; Third Prize for NCR Jesus, 99; and many other awards. *Bibliog:* Article, Art Voices/South, 5-6/78. *Mem:* Portrait Soc Am. *Media:* Mixed; Watercolor. *Res:* Analyzing old oil paintings with infared digital photography & photoshop. *Specialty:* conservation, research, training. *Interests:* Photography, painting. *Publ:* Illusr, Army Weapon Systems Covers, 80 & 81; Yorktown 1781-1981 Poster, 81; The Many Faces of Christ, Washington Post; Catholic Studies, Melbourne, Australia, 2006; The Many Faces of Christ. *Dealer:* Art Gallery 101 10640 Main St Fairfax VA 22030. *Mailing Add:* 2658 Quincy Adams Dr Herndon VA 22071

PISKOTI, JAMES
PRINTMAKER, PAINTER
b Logan, WVa, July 5, 1944. *Study:* Univ Mich, Ann Arbor, BS (design), 67; Yale Univ, MFA, 69. *Work:* Detroit Inst Arts; Bradley Univ; City of Stockton, Calif; Minot State Col; Calif State Univ, Stanislaus; Crocker Art Mus; Tex Tech Univ Mus, Lubbock, Tex. *Exhib:* Rutgers Nat 96 Works on Paper, Rutgers Univ Campus, Camden, NJ, 96; Pacific Prints - 8th Biennial Print Competition & Exhib, Pac Art League, Palo Alto, 96; Stockton Nat Print & Drawing Exhib, Haggin Mus, 96; 70th Crocker-Kingsley Juried Exhib, Crocker Mus, Sacramento, 96, 72nd Exhib, 2000; Int Print Triennial 97 Cracow, Poland & other countries, 97; Spirit of Handmade Prints, Triton Mus Art, 2001; Earth Matters, Creative Arts Ctr, Burbank, Calif, 2002; Valley View, Univ Gallery, Calif State Univ, Satanislaus, Turlock, Calif, 2004; Jim Piskoti: Works in Motion, Pence Gallery, Davis, Calif, 2006; Eccentric Imagery, Blue Line Gallery, Roseville, Calif, 2009; Bird Houses, Gregory Kondos Gallery, Sacramento City Coll, Calif, 2010; Plates, Totems, and Tea Pots, Blue Line Gallery, Roseville, Calif, 2012. *Teaching:* Lab asst Intaglio Printmaking Studio, Univ Mich, 65-67; teaching asst printmaking, Yale Univ, 68-69; vis lectr printmaking, Southern Conn State Col, spring 69; prof fine art, Calif State Univ Stanislaus, Turlick, 69-. *Awards:* Award of Excellence, Calif State Fair, 1987, Sacramento, 87; Cash Merit Award, Univ Mus, Miss, 1/90-3/90; Pac Art League Serigraphy Award & Timothy Duran Purchase Award, Pac Art League, Palo Alto, Calif, 5/90-6/90. *Bibliog:* Peter Fierz (auth), Young American Painter, Der Kunst, 69; Gabor Peterdi (auth), Four prints, Eye-Mag of Yale Arts Asn, 69. *Mem:* Calif Soc Printmakers; Los Angeles Printmaking Soc. *Media:* Acrylics; Color Intaglio. *Mailing Add:* 11 River Garden Ct Sacramento CA 95831

PISTOLETTO, MICHELANGELO
PAINTER, SCULPTOR
b Biella, Italy, 1933. *Hon Degrees:* Univ Turn, LHD, 2004. *Work:* Mus Mod Art, New York; Guggenheim Mus, New York; Museo Reina Sophia, Madrid; Hirshhorn Mus & Sculpture Garden; Tate Modern, London. *Exhib:* Solo exhibs, Walker Art Ctr, Minneapolis, 1966, Palais des Beaux Arts, Brussels, 1967, Boymans van Beuningen Mus, Rotterdam, 1969, Kestner Gesellschaft, Hannover, 1973, Nationalgalerie, Berlin, 1978, Rice Demenil Mus, Houston, 1979, Palacio de Cristal, Madrid, 1983, PS1 Contemp Art Ctr, New York, 1988, Galleria Nazionale d'Arte Moderna, Rome, 1990, Museet for Samditkunst, Oslo, 1991, Nat Mus Contemp Art, Seoul, 1994, Contemp Mus Bosnia, Sarajevo, 2001, and more; Venice Biennale, Venice, Italy, 1966, 1968, 1976, 1978, 1984, 1986, 1993, 1995, 2003, 2005, 2009; Modern Means: Continuity and Change in Art from 1880 to the Present, Mori Art Mus, Tokyo, 2003; Arte Povera, Toyota Munic Mus Art, 2004; Photo and Phantasy, Frederick R Weisman Art Found, 2006; Italian Mentalscapes. A Journey through Italian Contemporary Art, Tel Aviv Mus, 2007. *Awards:* Golden Lion Lifelong Achievement award, Venice Biennale, 2003; Wolf Found Prize in Arts, Jerusalem, 2007

PITCHER, JOHN CHARLES
PAINTER
b Kalamazoo, Mich, Aug 6, 1949. *Study:* Self taught. *Work:* Anchorage Mus Hist & Art, Alaska; Nat Wildlife Fedn, Washington, DC; Univ Alaska Mus; Leigh Yawkey Woodson Art Mus, Wausau, Wis; Juneau Empire, Alaska. *Exhib:* British Mus Nat Hist, London, 82; Alaska's Artists in Washington, DC, Capitol Rotunda Rm, 83; Alaska State Mus, 84-85; Beijing Natural Hist Mus, China, 86; Original Art Showcase, Can, 89-94; Southeastern Wildlife Expo, Charleston, SC, 94. *Teaching:* Leads workshops & gives slide/lectures on drawing & painting wildlife. *Awards:* First Place, Nat Exhib Wildlife Art, Anchorage Audubon Soc, 83; one of the featured artists, First Ann Pac Rim Wildlife Art Show, 88, 91-92; Keynote speaker, workshop presenter Alaska Loon Festival, Anchorage, 90. *Bibliog:* Elaine Rhode (auth), John Pitcher: In perspective with nature, Alaska J, autumn 79; Sandy Preston (auth), John Pitcher, perfect squares, Midwest Art (Now US Art), 88; Patricia Black Bailey (auth), John C Pitcher, Southwest Art, 3/92. *Mem:* Soc Animal Artists Inc. *Media:* Watercolor; Oil, Acrylic. *Publ:* Illusr, A Guide to the Birds of Alaska, Alaska NW Publ Co, 80; contribr-illusr, bird sect rev, World Bk Encycl, 81; illusr, Field Guide Birds of NAm, Nat Geographic Soc, 83; Birds of the Seward Peninsula, Alaska, brina Kessel, Univ Alaska Press, 89. *Mailing Add:* RR 1 Box 138 Dorset VT 05251

PITMAN, BONNIE
MUSEUM DIRECTOR
b Stanford, Conn. *Study:* Sweet Briar Coll, Va, BA (art hist); Tulane Univ, New Orleans, MA (art hist). *Pos:* Cur, educ, & admin positions, Univ Calif Berkeley Art Mus, formerly; dep dir, Seattle Art Mus & New Orleans Mus Art, formerly; acting dir, Winnipeg Art Gallery, formerly; exec dir, Bay Area Discovery Mus, formerly; dep dir, Dallas Mus Art, 2000-2008, Eugene McDermott dir, 2008-2011, consultant, 2011-; consult, Nat Endowment Arts. *Mailing Add:* Dallas Museum of Art 1717 North Harwood Dallas TX 75201

PITRE, GERMAN
PAINTER, SCULPTOR
b Buffalo, New York. *Study:* Art Student's League, New York, 1977; Printmaker's Workshop, New York, 1978. *Work:* Jersey City Mus, NJ; Montclair Art Mus, NJ; Newark Pub Libr, NJ; NJ State Mus, Trenton, NJ; Zimmerli Art Mus, New Brunswick, NJ. *Comn:* Allesandria Gallery, New York; Howard Scott Gallery, New York. *Exhib:* Solo exhibs include City Without Walls, Newark, NJ 1984, Artists Space, Newark, NJ 2002, Rupert Ravens Contemp, Newark, NJ 2008; Group exhibs include Small Works, Grey Art Gallery, NYU, 1980; Gallery Artists, Asage Art Gallery, New York, 1980, Visual Experiment, 1981; NJ Arts Annual, Jersey City Mus, 2002; New Works, Gale-Martin Fine Art, New York, 2002, Summer Exhib, 2003; Generations, Art in the Atrium, Inc, Morristown, NJ 2003; Touch + Feel: Messin With the High and Low, Red Saw Gallery, Newark, NJ, 2006; Emerge 7 Exhib, Aljira Gallery, Newark, NJ, 2006; Singularity in the Communal Tide, Gallery Pierro, S Orange, NJ 2007; Benny's Bungalow, Shore Inst Contemp Art, Long Branch, NJ 2008. *Awards:* NJ Print & Paper Fel, Rutgers Ctr Innovative Print & Paper, Rutgers Univ, New Brunswick, NJ 2005; Joan Mitchell Found Grant, 2007. *Mailing Add:* PO Box 20003 Newark NJ 07101

PITTS, RICHARD G
PAINTER, PRINTMAKER
b Ft Monmouth, NJ, Oct 15, 1940. *Study:* Newark Sch Fine Arts, 61; Pratt Inst, BFA, 68; New York Studio Sch, Paris, 72. *Work:* Anot Mus Art, Elmira, NY; General Electric Co, NY; Port Authority of New York; Continental Insurance Co, New Brunswick, NJ; Univ Va Mus, Charlottesville, Va; Univ SC; Askville Art Mus; Coos Art Mus; Reading Public Mus. *Comn:* Mural, Chelsea Health & Fitness, 91-92. *Exhib:* Solo exhib, David Findlay Jr, 83 & 85, Randolf Manchon, Ashland, Va, 84, Rutherin Gallery, Columbus, Ohio, 85, Deutche Bank Gallery NY, 93 & Caesarea Gallery, Boca Raton, Fla, 94; Contemp Images, Mendik Gallery, NY, 86; First Street Gallery Invitational, 86; Shirley Goodman Resource Ctr, FIT Galleries, 87; Cedar Art Ctr, Corning, NY, 92; Mus at FIT, NY, 99; and others. *Pos:* Chmn, Artist Bd, Artist Choice Mus, currently. *Teaching:* Assoc prof painting, Kansas City Art Inst, 70-73; prof fine arts, Fashion Inst Technol, 73-. *Bibliog:* Judd Tully (auth), Richard Pitts One Man Show, Arts Mag, 2/85; Jacqueline Hall (auth), Landscapes, Columbus Dispatch, 5/85; Animal Life at One Penn Plaza, Art World, 11/87; David Matlock (auth), Nature and Art, Art World, 4/88; Abigail Wender (auth), Paintings by Richard Pitts, Diversion Mag, 8/88. *Media:* Oil on Canvas. *Dealer:* David Findlay Jr Inc 41 E 57 St New York NY 10022; Carola Van der Houten 390 West End New York NY 10024. *Mailing Add:* 233 W 18th St New York NY 10011-4500

PITYNSKI, ANDRZEJ P
SCULPTOR
b Ulanow, Poland, Mar 15, 1947; US citizen. *Study:* Acad Fine Arts in Cracow, Poland, MFA (sculpture), 74; Art Students League, New York, 75. *Work:* Portrait bust M Curie (bronze on granite, 7'), Bayonne, NJ; Sculpture Partisans (aluminum, 3'), Polish Am Mus, Port Washington, NY. *Comn:* Ignacy Paderewski, 12' Cracow, Poland 73; Avenger (bronze on granite, 36'), Polish-Am Veterans US, Doylestown, PA, 87; Pope John Paul II (10' bronze granite), Ulanow, 1989; Katyn-1940 (bronze on granite, 38'), Katyn Mem Fund, Comt Jersey City, 91; Pope John Paul II (bronze on granite, 12'), Polish Am Cong, NY, 91; Blue Army Monument (bronze on granite, 48), Polish Am Veterans, Warsaw, 98; Flame of Freedom (60' gilded bronze on granite), Baltimore, Md, 2000; Sarmatian-Spirit of Freedom (70' steel figure), Hamilton, NJ, 2001; Gen Kosciuszko (14' bronze on granite), St Petersburg, Fla, 2002; Count Juliusz Tarnowski (10' bronze on granite), Tarnobrzeg, Poland, 2003; and others. *Exhib:* Allied Artists Am, Nat Art Club, NY, 94; Nat Sculpture Soc, Am Tower, NY, 95; retrospective, Polish Army Mus, Warsaw, Poland, 95 & 96; Contemp Artist's Guild, Broom Street Gallery, Soho, NY, 96; Audubon Artists, Fed Hall, NY, 96; and others. *Pos:* Asst to sculptor Alexander Ettl, Sculpture House, NY 75-79; supv modeling, enlarging, resins & moldmakings, Johnson Atelier Tech Inst Sculpture, Mercerville, NJ 79-. *Teaching:* Instr Sculpture, Rider Univ, Lawrenceville, NJ, 1992-1997; instr, Rutgers Univ, New Brunswick, NJ, 1997-2002. *Awards:* Silver Medal Honor, 72nd Ann Exhib, Allied Artists Am, NY, 85; Allied Artist's Am Mem & Asn Award, 81st Ann Exhib, NY, 94; Gold Medal Honor, 54th Ann Exhib, Audubon Artist's Soc, NY, 96, Silver Medal, 55th Ann Exhib, 97 & 56th Ann Exhib, 98. *Bibliog:* Donald M Reynolds (auth), Masters of American Sculpture, Abbeville Press, 94; Mirek Kin (producer), Avenger (20 min film), Polish, TV, 95; Irena Grzesiuk-Olszewska (auth), Polish Monuments from 1945-1995, Warsaw, Poland, 95. *Mem:* Contemp Artists Guild, NY; Audubon Artists, NY; Allied Artists Am, NY; fel mem Nat Sculpture Soc, NY; Am Medallic Sculpture Asn, NY. *Media:* Metal Cast-Bronze, Aluminum. *Mailing Add:* 90 Dupont St Brooklyn NY 11222

PIWINSKI, CARL B
ARTIST
b Lexington, Ky, Mar 25, 1958. *Study:* Univ Ky, BA (art studio), 1992. *Work:* Smithsonian, Washington, DC; pvt collection, Chuck & Jan Rosenak. *Exhib:* Carl Piwinski and Jim Shambho Drawing and Sculpture, Lexington Arts and Cult Coun, Lexington, Ky, 93. *Interests:* New media illustration, video, performance, environ, artist book, functional/nonfunctional art neon craft, art furniture in installation. *Publ:* Chuck & Jan Rosenak (auths), Contemporary Folkart: A Collectors Guide, Abbeville, 96. *Mailing Add:* 3272 Saxon Dr Lexington KY 40503-3429

PIZZAT, JOSEPH
EDUCATOR, COLLAGE ARTIST
b 1926. *Study:* Kalamazoo Col, Mich, BA, 49, MA, 50; Columbia Univ Teachers Col, New York, EdD, 55; vis scholar, Pa State Univ, 59 Pratt Inst, New York, 61. *Comn:* Stations of the Cross, Mercyhurst Col, Erie, Pa, 94. *Exhib:* Solo exhibs, Tapings 1975, Ivy Sch Prof Art, Pittsburgh, PA, 76, Spirituality & Religionty in Am, Albuquerque, 1997, Words-Image-Faith, Srehcen Gallery, Erie, Pa, 1997, Visions Gallery, Alrich, NY, 1998, Totally Digital, Invitational, Colo, 1999, Gicrube!, Johnson-Homrick House Mus, Ohio, 2002; Nat Christian Fine arts Exhib, San Juan Col, Farmington, NMex, 97, 98 & 99; Mary & The Arts (traveling exhib) Mariological Soc Am, Ohio, 98-99; Works of Faith, Portland, Oreg, 99, 2000, 2001, 2002; Appalachian Corridors Exhib, Charleston WVa, 2003. *Collection Arranged:* Pizzat Art Loan Collection, Northwest Renna Region, 1995-. *Teaching:* Prof art & chmn art prog, SW Minn State Col, Marshall, 67-71; prof art, Mercyhurst Col, Erie, Pa, 71-, chmn, creative arts div, 71-78, prof emeritus, 99-. *Awards:* Outstanding Educator Am Award, Southwest Minneapolis, 70 & Mercyhurst Coll, 75; Outstanding Art Educator Award, Pa Art Educ Asn, 81. *Mem:* US Prof Tennis Asn; Pa Art Educ Asn; Nat Art Educ Asn; Northwest Renna Artists Asn. *Media:* Pressure Sensitive, Self-Adhesives. *Res:* Pressure sensitive art, a visual-tactile art system using self-adhesive & pressure sensitive materials as primary art media. *Interests:* playing professional tennis; teaching. *Publ:* I'm a right brained person, why me God?, Nat Art Educ Asn Art Educ J, 79; The Book, A Learning Experience, 86 what!, 6/90, Kites: An art flight of fantasy, 10/91, Presenting Pres/sent Art, 10/92, Arts & Activities; What's Up? Art's Up-that's what!, 6/90, Kites: An art flight of fantasy, 10/91, Presenting Pres/sent Art, 10/92, Art & Activities; The Spiritual Dimensions in Child Development, The Pa Art Educ, fall 98; An Open Letter to Pope John Paul, Ministry & Literacy, 11/2000

PIZZUTI, RONALD A
COLLECTOR
Study: Kent State Univ, BS, 1962. *Pos:* Chmn & chief exec officer, Pizzuti Cos, Columbus, Ohio, 1976-; fac comn, Ohio Arts & Sports, currently; bd trustees, Kenyon Coll, currently; bd dir, Kent State Found, currently; chair bd trustees, Kent State Univ. *Awards:* recipient Shining Stars of Seminole Co, Lifetime Achievement award, 2002; named one of Top 200 Collectors, ARTnews mag, 2003-13. *Mem:* Columbus CofC (exec comt, currently). *Collection:* Modern and contemporary art. *Mailing Add:* Pizzuti Companies Ste 800 2 Miranova Pl Columbus OH 43215

PLACE, BRADLEY EUGENE
EDUCATOR, GRAPHIC ARTIST
b Rule, Tex, Nov 4, 1920. *Study:* Tex A&M Univ, 38-40; NTex Univ, with Carlos Merida & Ivan Johnson, BS, 42. *Pos:* Mem visual arts adv panel, Okla Arts & Humanities Coun, 72-; mem selection comt, Art for Pub Places, Tulsa, 75-. *Teaching:* From asst prof to prof lettering & typography, Univ Tulsa, 47-86, chmn dept art, 64-86, emer prof art, 86. *Awards:* Brad Trust Scholar, 73. *Bibliog:* Jenk Jones, Jr (auth), Honor roll for May, Tulsa Tribune, 71; Connie Cronley (auth), Profile of a teacher of artists, Tulsa, 6/14/73; Myrna Smart (auth), Dilemma of penal reform, Arts & Humanities Coun Tulsa & KTEW-TV, 5/74. *Mem:* Tulsa Advert Fedn; Tulsa Art Dir Club (exec bd, 70-75, 77 & 81-, pres, 74-75); Tulsa Arts & Humanities (mem bd, Chmn Mayor's Arts Comn, 77). *Mailing Add:* 2156 S Fulton Pl Tulsa OK 74114-2250

PLAGENS, PETER
PAINTER, CRITIC
b Dayton, Ohio, Mar 1, 1941. *Study:* Univ Southern Calif, BFA, 62; Syracuse Univ, MFA, 64. *Work:* Baltimore Mus Art; Albright-Knox Gallery, Buffalo, NY; Hirshhorn Mus, Washington, DC; Santa Fe Mus Art, NMex; Tawaraya, Kyoto; Denver Art Mus, Colo; Harris Bank, Chigago, Ill; InterMetro Industries Corp, Wilkes Barre, Pa; Irvine Co, Calif; Miami-Dade Community Coll, Fla; Mus Contemporary Art San Diego, La Jolla, Calif; Mus Fine Arts, Santa Fe, NMex; Owens-Cornign Fiberglas, Toledo, Oh; Power Gallery, Univ Sydney, Australia; Prudential Insurance Co America, Newark, NJ; Technimetrics, NY. *Exhib:* Solo exhibs, Univ Art Mus, Calif State Univ, Long Beach, 85, Jan Cicero Gallery, Chicago, Ill, 85 & 98, Nancy Hoffman Gallery, NY, 87, 90, 92, 96 & 97, Jan Baum Gallery, Los Angeles, 88, Akron Art Mus, Ohio, 96, Jan Cicero Gallery, Chicago, 98, Nancy Hoffman Gallery, NYC, 99, 01, Las Vegas Art Mus, 00-01, The Gallery, Fine Arts Hall, Columbus State Univ, Ga, 2002, Fisher Gallery, 2004-2005, Middlebury Coll Mus Art, Middlebury, Va, 2005, Investigators Soon Learned or Paintings on Wood + 3 Drawings of My Father, Warschaw Gallery, San Pedro, Calif, 2006, I Don't Give a Damn/Every Moment Counts, Nancy Hoffman Gallery, NY, 2011; Primarily Paint, Mus Contemp Art San Diego, La Jolla, Calif, 97; Nancy Hoffman: A Perspective on Art, Flanders Contemp Art, Minneapolis, Minn, 97; 25 Yrs, Nancy Hoffman Gallery, NY, 98; small scale LARGE SCALE, Nancy Hoffman Gallery, NY, 98, From Diptychs to Polyptychs, 98, Gateways, 99-2000, I Love New York, 2001, Summer, 2002, Celebrating 30 Years, 2003, Summertime, 2004, Drawing Line, 2006, Circles, 2006, Images and Words, 2007, Flying the Coop, 2007; Ark Art Ctr, Little Rock, 2002, 2005-2006, 2010-11; On Paper: The Lincoln Ctr/List Collection, UBS Art Gallery, NY, 2008; At the Edge, Portsmouth Mus Art, New Hamphire, 2010; Painting with Paint, Charlotte and Philip Hanes Art Gallery, Wake Forest Univ, Winston-Salem, NC, 2010. *Pos:* Designer, Barth & Dreyfuss Inc, Los Angeles, 64-65; cur, Long Beach Mus Art, Calif, 65-66; ed comt, J Los Angeles Inst Contemp Art, 74-75; contrib ed, Artforum, 66-76; chmn bd dir, Los Angeles Inst Contemp Art, 77-79; art critic, Newsweek Mag, 89-2003. *Teaching:* Instr, Univ Tex, Austin, 66-69; assoc prof art, Calif State Univ, Northridge, 69-78, Univ Southern Calif, 78-80; chmn, dept art, Univ NC at Chapel Hill, 80-83, prof, 80-84; prof, Hofstra Univ, Hempstead, NY, 1985-. *Awards:* John Simon Guggenheim Fel in Painting, 72-73; Nat Endowment Arts, Grant in Art Criticism, 73-74, Fel in Painting, 77-78; Sr Fel, Nat Arts Journalism Prog, Columbia Univ, 98. *Bibliog:* Holland Cotter (auth), Peter Plagens at Nancy Hoffman, Art in Am, 9/90; MA Greenstain (auth), Whitewash, Artweek, 2/6/92; Herne Pardee (auth), Peter Plagens, Artnews, Summer 92. *Publ:* Auth, Ecology of evil, 12/72, Peter and the pressure cooker, 6/74 & None dare call it BoHo, 9/75, Artforum; Sunshine Muse: Contemporary Art on the West Coast, Praeger Publ, 74; Moonlight Blues: An Artist's Art Criticism, UMI Research Press, 86; The Art Critic, 2013. *Dealer:* Jan Cicero Gallery Chicago IL. *Mailing Add:* c/o Nancy Hoffman Gallery 520 W 27th St Ste 301 New York NY 10001-5548

PLANKEY, ELLEN J
PAINTER
b Pittsfield, Mass. *Study:* Wm Schultz Schl of Art, Lenox, Mass - 1962-86; Eliot McMurrough Sch of Art study under Chas Reid, Robert E Wood, Haywood Veaf, Indialantic, Fla, 1964-66. *Hon Degrees:* Pastel Soc of Am, Master Pastellist. *Work:* Mint Mus Art, Charlotte, NC; Vero Beach Mus Art, Fla; City of Indialantic, Fla;

Alabama Power Co, Birmingham; Peoples National Bank, Naples, Fla. *Exhib:* Solo retrospective, Mint Mus Art, Charlotte, NC, 1978; solo exhibs, Fla Southern Col, Lakeland, 1979 & Brevard Art Ctr & Mus, Melbourne, Fla, 1983; Rocky Mountain Nat, Foot Hills Art Ctr, Golden, Colo, 1994; Fla Watercolor Soc, Fla Art Mus, Sarasota, 1995. *Teaching:* instr art, Studio, Melbourne, Fla, 1968-80; instr art, workshops in Fla, 1980-1986. *Awards:* First Prize, Rocky Mountain Nat, Intermedia Exhib, 1994; Best of Show, Pastel Soc of Am, 1976; Best of Show, Fla Watercolor Soc, 1995. *Bibliog:* J. Phyllis Hattan (auth), Plankey: The Search for the Light, Arts & Expressions, July & Aug 1984; Carole Surface (auth), Artist Brushes Love & Light, Orlando Sentinel, 7/1987; Bebe Raugel (auth), Artist Winning Watercolor of 1995, Artists Mag, 9/1995. *Mem:* Pastel Soc of Am, Nat Arts Club, New York City, 1963-; Arts Students Guild of Brevard (pres 1983); life charter mem Fla Watercolor Soc (pres 1983). *Media:* Acrylic, Oil, Pastel, Watercolor. *Mailing Add:* 2255 Abalone Ave Indialantic FL 32903

PLASTER, ALICE MARIE
PAINTER, INSTRUCTOR

b Hickory, NC. *Study:* Md Inst, Coll Art, BFA, 77. *Work:* George Wash House Mus, Bladensburg, Md; Nat Automotive Hist Collection Art, Detroit. *Comn:* Mural, Md Nat Capital Park & Planning Comn, Riverdale, 79. *Exhib:* Urban Landscapes, 3rd Ann Juried Visual Arts Exhib, Strathmore, Hall Arts Ctr, Rockville, Md, 88; Mansion Art Gallery, Rockville, 91; Ballasai Gallery, Laurel, Md, 91; Venable Neslage Galleries, Washington, 91; George Meany Ctr Labor Studies Gallery, Silver Spring, 94; National Automotive History Collection Campaign 100 Exhibit, Detroit, Mich, 96; Discovery Galleries, Ltd, Bethesda, Md, 96-; Open Exhib, Nat Mus Women Arts, Bell Atlantic Gallery, Ernst Community Cult Ctr, Northern Va Community Col, 97-99, 2002-2004; Art Expo, NY, 98; Art in Embassies Prog, US Dept State Embassy USA, Stockholm, Sweden, 2007. *Pos:* Graphic artist, Prince George's Co Mem Libr System, Hyattsville, Md, 80-. *Teaching:* Instr painting, Md Nat Capital Park & Planning Comn Montpelier Cult Arts Ctr, 86-. *Awards:* Cash Award, Nat Soc Arts & Letters, 73; 1st Prize Award, Oil, Open Exhib, Juror J Carter Brown, Dir Emer, Nat Gallery Art, Annadale, VA, 93, *Bibliog:* The Prince Georgian, (Publ Cover Artist), Wash Post, 6/17/88; Concours d'Elegance, British Car Day (video), Visual Edge Productions, Potomac, 92; Automobile Artist-Jaguars Across America (video), British Cars Across America Series, No 4, Brit Car Films, London, Eng, 98. *Mem:* Arts Council Fairfax Co, VA; Walters Art Mus, Baltimore, MD. *Media:* Oil, Pencil. *Publ:* The Prince Georgian (cover), Wash Post, 6/17/88; illusr, Writer's Choice, Ligature, Inc, 93; Old Cars Weekly (cover), Krause Publs Inc, Vol 23, No 2, 1/13/94 & Vol 23, No 5, 4/21/94

PLATOW, RAPHAELA
MUSEUM DIRECTOR, CURATOR

b Munich. *Study:* Albert-Ludwig Univ, Freiburg, Germany, BA (Art History); Humboldt Univ, Berlin, MA (Bus Admin, Art History). *Pos:* Staff member, Venice Biennale, 1999; Int cur, Contemp Art Mus, Raleigh, NC, formerly; cur, Rose Art Mus, Brandeis Univ, Mass, 2002-2006, interim dir, 2005, chief cur, 2006-2007; dir, chief cur, Contemp Art Ctr, Cincinnati, 2007-. *Mailing Add:* Contemporary Art Center 44 E 6th St Cincinnati OH 45202

PLATT, MELVIN
ADMINISTRATOR

Study: Univ Cincinnati Col-Conservatory of Music, B (music educ) and M (musicology); Univ Michigan, PhD (music educ). *Teaching:* Instrumental/choral music teacher, Armada Michigan Schools, formerly; teacher Catholic Univ of American, 1968-72, Kent State Univ, 1972-77; coordinator graduate studies in music, Univ Oklahoma, 1977-91; dir Sch of Music, Univ of Missouri, 1991-2008, chair Dept of Art, teaching a course in orchestral masterpieces for non-music majors, 2008-. *Awards:* Outstanding Music Educator, Oklahoma Secondary Sch Activites Asn, 1990; Governor's Arts and Education award for Exceptional Service to Music Educ in Oklahoma, 1990. *Mem:* Oklahoma Music Educators (vpres and pres, formerly); Missouri Asn of Departments and Schools of Music (pres 1996-98, 2006-08). *Mailing Add:* A126 Fine Arts Building University of Missouri Columbia MO 65211-6090

PLATTNER, PHYLLIS
PAINTER

b New York, NY, Apr 25, 1940. *Study:* Bennington Col, BA, 60; Brooklyn Mus Sch, 59; Claremont Grad Sch, Calif, MFA, 62. *Work:* St Louis Art Mus; Springfield Art Mus, Mo; The Kemper Group, Chicago; Xerox Corp, Stamford, Conn. *Comn:* Three-panel watercolor, Coinco, St Louis, 84; five-panel curved watercolor, IBM Bus Machines, Rochester, Minn, 85. *Exhib:* New Acquisitions, St Louis Art Mus, 83; Solo exhibs, BZ Wagman Gallery, St Louis, 85 & 86, Fendrick Gallery, Washington, 86 & 89, Esther Saks Gallery, Chicago, Ill, 87 Locus, St Louis, Mo, 89, Steven Scott Gallery, Baltimore, Md, 89 Brody's Gallery, Washington, 91-92 & Elliot Smith Gallery, St Louis, Mo, 92; Contemp Works on Paper, Frumkin & Struve Gallery, Chicago, 85; Watercolor USA: The Monumental Image, Springfield Art Mus, 86; and other solo exhibs. *Teaching:* Vis assoc prof painting, Washington Univ, St Louis, 81-85 & 91-93, vis assoc prof watercolor, 85-87; instr, Md Inst Col Art, Baltimore, Md, 87-. *Awards:* Mayor's Award for the Arts, St Louis, 84; Mid-Atlantic States Nat Endowment Arts, 88. *Bibliog:* Robert Duffy (auth), It's a jungle in there, St Louis Post Dispatch, 84; Betsy Goldman (auth), Phyllis Plattner, Am Artist Mag, 85. *Media:* Oil, Watercolor; Oil Pastels. *Dealer:* R Duane Reed Gallery 1 N Taylor St Louis MO 63141; Elliot Smith Gallery 4727 McPherson Ave St Louis MO 63108. *Mailing Add:* 6204 Redwing Rd Bethesda MD 20817

PLATZKER, DAVID
BOOK DEALER, CURATOR

Study: St Lawrence Univ, BA, 87; student, St Lawrence Univ, London, 86-87. *Collection Arranged:* Claes Oldenburg/John Baldessari, Brush Art Gallery, Canton, NY, 92; Claes Oldenburg: Multiples 1964-1990, various cities, 92-97; Claes Oldenburg: Books and Ephemera, 1960-1994, Glen Horowitz Bookseller, East Hampton, NY, 94, Printed Matter, Inc, NY, 94; Claes Oldenburg: The Geometric Mouse, Susan Inglett Gallery, NY, 94-95; Donald Judd: Drawings, Susan Inglett Gallery, NY, 96; Books by Edward Ruscha, Printed Matter, Inc, NY, 96; Claes Oldenburg: Printed Stuff (with Richard H Axsom), Madison (Wis) Art Ctr, 97, Columbus (Ohio) Mus Art, 98, Detroit (Mich) Inst Art, 98; Some More Books by Dieter Roth, Printed Matter, NY, 97; The Information Age: Baldessari, Barry, Huebler, Weiner, 1969-1971, Susan Inglett Gallery, NY, 98; Hard Pressed: 600 Years of Prints and Process (with Elizabeth Wyckoff), AXA Gallery, NY, 2001; Documenta 5, Specific Object, 2007; Art & Project, Specific Object, 2007; Bruce Nauma: Studies for Holograms 1970, 2008; St Raymond Pattibon, 2008. *Pos:* Vpres, exec bd dir, Printed Matter Inc, 92-98, dir exhib, 94-97, dir, 98-2004; cur, Claes Oldenburg and Cossje van Bruggen, 89-98; independent cur, 98-; pres, Specific Object, 2002-; host, Recorded Matter, WPS1 Art Radio, 2003-; proj dir, Art Spaces Archives Proj, 2004-2008. *Awards:* Wittenborn Mem Bk Award, ARLS, 97; Mus Publ Award, Am Asn Mus, 98. *Res:* Pop art; conceptual art; artists' publications. *Specialty:* Artists' books & editions. *Interests:* Conceptual arts, minimal arts, pop art. *Publ:* Contribr, John Baldessari, Rizzoli, 89; Claes Oldenburg: An Anthology, Guggenheim Mus, New York, 95; co-auth, Printed Stuff: Prints by Claes Oldenburg, Hudson Hills Press, 97; Hard Pressed: 600 Years of Prints and Process, Hudson Hills Press, 2000. *Dealer:* Specific Object. *Mailing Add:* Specific Object 601 W 26th St M285 New York NY 10001

PLEAR, SCOTT
PAINTER

b Vancouver, BC, Mar 26, 1952. *Study:* Univ BC, BFA, 76; Univ Sask, with Emma Lake, 77, 80, 84-85 & 88; Triangle Artists Workshop, Pine Plains, NY, 82. *Work:* Edmonton Art Gallery, Alta; The Art Bank; Burnaby Art Gallery, BC; Art Gallery Greater Victoria, BC; Surrey Art Gallery, BC. *Comn:* Mural painting commission, British Columbia Investment Management Corp, Livingston Place, Calgary, Alberta, 2008 & 2011; mural painting, British Columbia Investment Management Corp & SITQ, Montreal, 2010. *Exhib:* solo exhibs, Scott Plear: Recent Paintings, Edmonton Art Gallery, Alta, Grand Forks Art Gallery, BC, Burnaby Art Gallery, 87, BC House, London, Eng, 95, Vanderleelie Gallery, Edmonton, Alta, 97 & Swift Current, Nat Exhib Ctr, Sask, 98, Core Samples, Agnes Bugera Gallery, Edmonton, Alta, Core Quest, Darrell Bell Gallery, Saskatoon, Sask, 2009, Remote Viewing, SOPA Fine Arts, Kelowna, BC, 2009; The Current Generation, Edmonton Art Gallery, 83; North of the Border, Whatcom Mus Hist & Art, Bellingham, Wash, 90; My Own Space, Edmonton Art Gallery, Alta, 93; Driven to Abstraction, Surrey Art Gallery, BC, 93; Ten Painting Yrs (with catalog), Grand Forks Art Gallery, BC, 94; Harlech Biennale, Wales, 96; three-person exhib, Grand Forks Art Gallery, Grand Forks, BC, 99; Spiritus Forma, Grand Forks Art Gallery, Grand Forks, BC, 2001; Jerusalem, Jewish Community Ctr, Vancouver, BC, 2002; Harbingers, HSBC Bank Atrium, Vancouver, BC, 2003; Full Fathom, Petley Jones Gallery, Vancouver, BC, 2003; With Flying Colours, Fran Willis Gallery, Victoria, BC, 2005; Banners & Standards, Petley Jones Gallery, Vancouver, BC, 2005; Agnes Burgera Gallery, Edmonton, Alta, 2006; Aurora Flow, Petley Jones Gallery, Vancouver, BC, 2007; APT Gallery, Deptford, London, 2007; Core Samples, Agnes Bugera Gallery, Edmonton, Alta, 2008; Core Quest, Darrell Bell Gallery, Saskatoon, Sask, 2009; Remote Viewing, SOPA Fine Arts, Kelowna, BC, 2009; Bounty: A Case of Preposterous Optimism, Morely College Gallery, London, 2010; Color Salute, SOPA Fine Arts, BC, 2010; Core Theory, Agnes Bugera Gallery, Edmonton, 2011; Criss-Cross, SOPA Fine Arts, BC, 2011; Coarse Too Tender, Darrell Bell Gallery, Saskatoon, Saskatchewan, 2012; Summer Tributes, SOPA Fine Arts, BC, 2012; Skins and Hides, Bugera Matheson Gallery, Edmonton, Alberta, 2013. *Pos:* Guest artist, Mbile Int Artists' Workshop, Zambia, 93; with Sask Invitational Artist's Workshop, Emma Lake, Sask, 2000. *Teaching:* Instr, Univ BC, 78-79; asst prof, Univ Alta, 83; fac mem, 86-, Langara Coll, dept chmn, 92-94, div chmn, 94-2001. *Awards:* Special Univ Prize, 77; Head of Grad Class in Fine Arts, 77; Univ of BC, 77; Education Leave, Langara Coll, 2001, 2007, 2013. *Bibliog:* Roger H Boulet (auth), Scott Plear, Recent Paintings, The Edmonton Art Gallery, 87; Robert Amos (auth), Victoria Times Colonist, 92; Gilbert Bouchard (auth), Edmonton J, 2006. *Mem:* Royal Canadian Acad Arts. *Media:* Acrylic. *Publ:* Mythos, 2003; Harbingers, 2003; Full Fathom, 2004; With Flying Colours, 2005; Banners & Standards, 2005; Coarse Too Tender, 2012; Skins and Hides, 2013. *Dealer:* Agnes Bugera Gallery 12310 Jasper Ave Edmonton AB Canada; Darrell Bell Gallery 317-220 3rd Avenue South Saskatoon Sakatchewan Canada S7K1M1; Galerie MX 333 Avenue Viger Quest Montreal Canada H2Z0A1; Gevik Gallery 12 Hazelton Ave Toronto Ontario Canada M5R2E2; SOPA Fine Arts 2934 S Pandosy St Kelowna BC VIY IV9; PAIA Contemporary Gallery 83B Hana Hwy Paia Hi. *Mailing Add:* 106-237 E 4th Ave Vancouver BC V5T 4R4 Canada

PLETKA, PAUL
PAINTER, PRINTMAKER

b San Diego, Calif, 1946. *Study:* Ariz State Univ, Tempe; Colo State Univ, Ft Collins. *Work:* San Antonio Mus Art, Tex; Milwaukee Fine Arts Ctr, Wis; St Louis Art Mus, Mo; Minneapolis Inst Art, Minn; Phoenix Art Mus, Ariz; and others. *Comn:* Ghost Dancer (lithograph), Phoenix Art Mus, Ariz, 77; Those Living at the Sunrise (lithograph), Heard Mus, Phoenix, Ariz, 79; Papageno (poster), St Louis Opera Theater, Mo, 80. *Exhib:* Four Corners Biennial, Phoenix Art Mus, Ariz, 77; Solo exhib, El Paso Mus Art, Tex, 78; A Sense of Space, Univ NMex Art Mus, 79; Eiteljorg Collection, Indianapolis Mus Art, 79; Here and Now, Albuquerque Art Mus, NMex, 80. *Awards:* Certificate of Excellence, Chicago, 76; Nat Watercolor Soc Award, Watercolor USA, 77. *Bibliog:* Edna Gundersen (auth), Pletka bares Indian souls on canvas, El Paso Times, 5/13/78; Ed Montini (auth), Unmasking a dedicated artist, The Ariz Republic, 3/22/81; Edna Gundersori (auth), Pletka, Northland Press, 83. *Media:* Acrylic, Watercolor. *Mailing Add:* PO Box 34095 Santa Fe NM 87594-4095

PLETSCHER, JOSEPHINE MARIE
LIBRARIAN, PRINTMAKER

b Muscatine, Iowa. *Study:* Immaculate Heart Coll, BA, 62, MA, 64; Univ Calif, Los Angeles, Santa Monica Coll, Calif. *Comn:* Feel Free (poster), Wilson Libr Bull, Bronx, New York, 69. *Exhib:* Iowa Artists 4th Ann Exhib, Des Moines Art Ctr, 52 & 11th Ann Iowa Artists Exhib, 59; Calif State Fair, Sacramento, 62; McKenzie Gallery, Los Angeles, Calif, 68; City of Pasadena, Fgn Cities Affiliation Travel Exhib, Japan, Ger, 72-73; Hillcrest Festival Fine Arts, Whittier Calif, 96; Gallery, Calabasa, Calif, 97; Atria Bell Ct Gardens, Tucson, Ariz, 2009. *Collection Arranged:* Mexican Festival--Arts and Crafts, Pasadena Pub Libr, 72. *Pos:* Fine arts coordr, Pasadena Pub Libr, Pasadena, 64-82; reference librn, Rio Hondo Coll Libr, Whittier, Calif, 83-96 & Santa Monica Comm Coll, Libr, Calif, 95-06. *Awards:* Watercolor Hon Award, Des Moines Art Ctr, 59 & State Calif, 62; Recognition Award, Pasadena Pub Libr, 68. *Bibliog:* Larry Palmer (auth), Local art and artists, Pasadena Star News, 7/13/69; Jack Birkinshaw (auth), Joy of children painting is captured on librarian's film, Los Angeles Times, 9/4/69; Arthur Plotnik (auth), This is a library feel free, Wilson Libr Bull, 11/69. *Mem:* Art Libr Soc N Am; Hollywood Art Coun; Los Angeles Co Mus Art; Friends Corita Art Ctr; and others. *Media:* Serigraphy. *Interests:* Architecture, graphics, printmaking and rare art objects. *Collection:* Corita Kent original prints with archives. *Publ:* Illusr, Immaculate Heart College--Announcement of Courses, Immaculate Heart Coll, 63-64; illusr & contribr, Painting from the heart, Business: Pasadena CofC, 5/69; illusr, Learning By Heart, Bantan, 92; illusr & contribr, Primary Colors (film), 91; contribr, Clifford Coffin, Stewart, Tabor & Chang, 97; illusr & contribr, Life Stories of Artist Corita Kent, Loste, 2000; auth & illusr, The Little Doves, 2010. *Mailing Add:* 5660 N Kolb Rd Apt 209 Tucson AZ 85750

PLEVIN, GLORIA ROSENTHAL
PAINTER, PRINTMAKER

b Pittsburgh, Pa, July 25, 1934. *Study:* Ohio Univ, AA, 54; Cooper Sch Art, 74; Cleveland Inst Art, 75-85. *Work:* Cleveland Mus Art; Butler Inst Am Art, Youngstown, Ohio; Jewish Community Ctr, Cleveland, Ohio; Univ Hosps of Cleveland, Ohio; Temple Emanuel, Cleveland, Ohio; BF Goodrich Corp Hdqtrs, Charlotte, NC; Cleveland Clinic; Cleveland Marshall Coll of Law, Cleveland State Univ; plus others. *Comn:* Rabbi Alan Green Portrait, Temple Emanuel, Solon, Ohio, 78; bridal canopy, Temple Emanuel, Solon, Ohio, 84; Amish Fields (monoprint tryptich), University Hosp, Cleveland, 93; Univ Print Club, Etching Edit, 2000. *Exhib:* Chautauqua Nat, Chautauqua Art Asn Galleries, NY, 73-75; Mid-Year Show, Butler Inst Am Art, Youngstown, Ohio, 74; Women Artists Look at Men, Beck Ctr, Lakewood, Oh, 81; Access Ann, Adams Mem Gallery, Dunkirk, NY, 87; Am Drawing Biennial, Muscarelle Mus Art, Williamsburg, Va, 88; Interiors, Mansfield Art Ctr, Ohio, 90; Chautauqua Vistas, solo, Butler Inst Am Art, Salem, Ohio, 93; Print Collection of J Marlin Casker, Prendergast Gallery, Jamestown, NY, 98; Artists Archives, 2002; Dead Horse Gallery, 2001; Many Faces of Cleveland, Cleveland Artists Foundation, 2002; Ohio Print Biennial, 1999-2001; Kelly Randall Gallery, 2002; Parallel Lives, Gloria Plevin & Bonnie Dolin, Ursuline Coll Women's Invitational, 2004; Art of Gloria A Plevin, Kendal of Oberlin, Oberlin, Ohio, 2006; The View From Here, CCVA Logan Gallery, Chautauqua, NY, 2007; Gloria Plevin/Prints, Zygote Press Inc, Cleveland, Ohio, 2008; Gloria Plevin: Botanicals of Flowers, Roger Troy Peterson Inst, Jamestown, NY, 2011; Favorite Flowers, Cleveland Botanical Garden, Cleveland, Ohio, 2011; Portraits in Nature, West Virginia Univ, 2012; Hidden Treasures, The Verne Coll, Cleveland, Oh, 2013. *Pos:* Owner & dir, Gloria Plevin Gallery, Chautauqua, NY, 85-2002. *Awards:* Helen Logan Award, Chautauqua Nat, 73; Purchase Award, 85, Best Show, 89, Jewish Community Ctr Ann; Gov's Award, Ohio Arts Coun, 99. *Bibliog:* Dick Wooten (auth), The Cleveland connection, Salem News, 10/7/93; Helen Cullinan (auth), Plevin Displays a New Love, Cleveland Plain Dealer, 95; Lois Wiley (auth), Art on common ground, Erie Times, 8/16/96; Oral History Interview, Artists Archives, 2002; Fresh Ink (interview), Zygote Press, spring/summer 2002; Steven Litt (auth), Cleve Plain Dealer, Parallel Lives, 2004; Steven Litt (auth), 1 World 3 Views, Cleve Plain Dealer, 12/29/2005; Robert W Plyler (auth), Botanical Beauty, Post Jour, Jamestown, NY, 8/20/2011. *Mem:* New Orgn Visual Arts (pres, 82-84); Womens Mus Arts; Cleveland Artists Found; Cleveland Print Club; Artists Archives of Western Reserve. *Media:* Acrylics; Pastels, Watercolors, Monoprints. *Interests:* Gardening, reading, art & artists, films. *Publ:* Portfolio 83 (Paula L Grooms, dir/coordr), New Orgn Visual Arts, 93; The Art of Gloria Plevin (monogr), Ohio Artists Now, 98; Herb Ascherman (auth), The Artists Project, 2002. *Dealer:* The Verne Collection 2207 Murray Hill Rd Cleveland OH 44106. *Mailing Add:* 13901 Shaker Blvd Suite 1A Cleveland OH 44120

PLIESSNIG, MATTHIAS
DESIGNER, SCULPTOR

b New Orleans, La, 1978. *Study:* RI Sch Design, BFA, 2003; Univ Wis, Madison, MA, 2005, MFA, 2008. *Work:* Mus Art & Design, New York. *Exhib:* Solo exhibs, Worcester Ctr for the Crafts, Mass, 2002, Meredith Gallery, Baltimore, 2003, Red Gallery, Savannah Coll Art & Design, Ga, 2004, Silo Project Space, Wis, 2007, Wexler Gallery, Philadelphia, 2008. *Pos:* Vis artist, San Diego State Univ, 2007, Calif Coll Art, 2007, Univ Arts, Philadelphia, 2009, RI Sch Design, 2009. *Awards:* Joan Mitchell Found Grant, 2008; Best of Yr Award, Interior Design Mag, 2008; Louis Comfort Tiffany Found Grant, 2009

PLOCHMANN, CAROLYN GASSAN
PAINTER, GRAPHIC ARTIST

b Toledo, Ohio, May 4, 1926. *Study:* Toledo Mus Art Sch Design, 43-47; Univ Toledo, BA, 47; State Univ Iowa, MFA, 49; with Alfeo Faggi, 50; Southern Ill Univ, 51-52. *Work:* Evansville Mus Arts & Sci, Ind; Knoxville Mus Art, Tenn; Butler Inst Am Art, Youngstown, Ohio; Univ Chicago Librs Collection; West Collection, St Paul, Minn; Ill State Mus, Springfield, Ill. *Comn:* mural, North Side Old Nat Bank, Evansville, Ind. *Exhib:* Evansville Mus Arts & Sci, 62, 68 & 79; solo exhibs, Witte Mus, San Antonio, Tex, 68, Toledo Mus Art, 65 & Kennedy Galleries, NY, 73, 81, 83, 87, 89, 92, 94, 95 & 98; 164th Prints & Drawings Ann, Pa Acad Fine Arts, Philadelphia, 69; Knoxville Mus Art, Tenn, 91; Purch Exhib, 45th & 48th Ann Am Acad Arts & Letts, 93; Kutztown Univ, 96; Ill State Mus, 2002, 2007. *Collection Arranged:* Carolyn Plochmann: Between Two Worlds, Ill State Mus, 2002; Carolyn Plochmann's Gift, Ill State Mus, 2007. *Teaching:* Supervisor art, Southern Illinois Univ Training Sch, 49-50. *Awards:* George W Stevens Fel, Toledo Mus Art, 47-49; Tupperware Art Fund First Award, 53; Emily Lowe Found Competition Award, 58; First Award, Art and the Law, West Collection, 85. *Bibliog:* Selden Rodman (auth), Geniuses and other Eccentrics, Green Tree Press, San Francisco, 97; Michael Kammen (auth), The Creative and Enigmatic Imagery of Carolyn Gassan Plochmann, Kennedy Catalogue, 98; Matthew F Daub (auth), A Charmed Vision: The Art of Carolyn Plochmann, Evansville Ind Mus Arts & Sci, 90; and others. *Media:* Oil, Acrylic; Graphics. *Publ:* Auth, University Portrait: Nine Paintings by Carolyn Gassan Plochmann, Southern Ill Univ Press, 59; auth, Introductory Statement, Kennedy Galleries One-man show (catalog), 92; and others. *Dealer:* Kennedy Galleries 730 Fifth Ave New York NY 10019. *Mailing Add:* PO Box 592 Carbondale IL 62903-0592

PLOSSU, BERNARD
PHOTOGRAPHER

b Dalat, SVietnam, Feb 26, 1945. *Work:* Bibliotheque Nat, Paris; Amon Carter Mus, Ft Worth, Tex; George Eastman House, Rochester, NY; Ctr Creative Photography, Tucson, Ariz; Niepce Mus, Chalon, France; Mus Fine Arts, Santa Fe, NMex; Albuquerque Mus, NMex. *Exhib:* Plossu by Atelier Fresson, Eaton-Shoen Gallery, San Francisco, 82; solo exhib, Etherton Gallery, Tucson, Ariz, 82; The Spirit of Traveling, Arles Photo Fest, Arles, France, 82; In Place, Albuquerque Mus, NMex, 82; two-person show, Hoshour Gallery, Albuquerque, NMex, 83; The Mexican Voyage, Eaton-Schoen Gallery, San Francisco, 84. *Teaching:* Photography workshops, Okla Summer Arts Inst, 83. *Bibliog:* Gilles Mora (auth), La rupture creatrice du Voyage Mexicain, Cahiers Photo, 81; L Sherman & S Parks (auths), I photograph the weather, Artlines, 81; M Foley (auth), Bernard Plossu, Artspace, 81; Gilles Mora (auth), Bernard Plossu, Camera, 86. *Publ:* Photogr, Surbanalism, Chene, France, 72; Go West, Chene, France, 72; Le Voyage Mexicain, Contrejour, France, 79; Egypte, Photoeil, France, 79; New Mexico Revisited, Univ NMex Press, 83. *Mailing Add:* c/o Galerie Michele Chinette 24 Rue Beabourg Paris 75003 France

PLOTEK, LEOPOLD
PAINTER

b Moscow, USSR, 1948. *Study:* McGill Univ, Montreal; Sir George Williams Univ, Montreal, BFA, 70; study with Roy Kioyooka & Yves Gaucher; Slade Sch Art, London, Eng, study with William Townsend, 70-71. *Work:* Montreal Mus Fine Arts; Mus d'Art Contemporain; Concordia Univ; Can Coun Artbank; Alcan Aluminum; others. *Exhib:* 49th Parallel, NY, 89; Univ Que, Montreal, 92; Cenacle, 7 Montreal Painters, 93; Hidden Values, McMichael Can Collection, Kleinburg, 94; Artcité: quand Montréal devient Musée, Mus Contemp Art, Montreal, 2001; Leonard & Bina Ellen Gallery, Montreal, 2002; Solo exhibs, Vehicule Art, Montreal, 72 & 74, Weissman Gallery, Concordia, Que, 75, Galerie Optica, Montreal, 76, Galerie Yajima, Montreal, 79, 81 & 83, Olga Korper Gallery, Toronto, 84, 86, 88, 90, 93, 95, 97, 2002, Concordia Art Gallery, Concordia Univ, Montreal, 90 & Saidye Bronfman Ctr, Montreal, 92, Galerie Eric Devlin, Montreal, 2002. *Awards:* Alfred Pinsky Medal in Fine Arts; Four Can Coun Arts Coun; two travel grants to Italy

PLOTKIN, LINDA
PAINTER, PRINTMAKER

b Milwaukee, Wis, Dec 21, 1938. *Study:* Univ Wis, Milwaukee, BA, 61; Pratt Inst, Brooklyn, NY, MFA, 62. *Work:* Metrop Mus Art & Mus Mod Art, NY; Bibliotheque Nationale, Paris, France; Libr Cong, Washington, DC; Brooklyn Mus, NY. *Exhib:* 30 Yrs of Am Printmaking, Brooklyn Mus, NY, 76; 10th Ann Tokyo Int Print Biennial, Tokyo, Japan, 77; 30 Am Printmakers, Ohio State Univ, Columbus, 81; Int Print Exhib, Taipei Mus, Taiwan, 84; Va Mus Print Invitational, Va Mus Art, Richmond, 86. *Teaching:* Asst prof art, Pa State Univ, State Col Pa, 62-77; artist-in-residence, St Mary's Col, Notre Dame, Ind, 85; State Univ NY, Purchase, 86-. *Awards:* MacDowell Fel, 76, 78 & 79; Ossabaw Island Fel, 78; Camargo Found Fel, 81. *Bibliog:* Judd Tully (auth), Linda Plotkin, Arts Mag, 5/19/84; James Watrous (auth), A Century of American Printmaking, 84. *Mem:* Soc Am Graphic Artists (bd mem, 83-); Int Graphic Artists Found; Artists Equity. *Publ:* Contribr, In Praise of Women Artists (calendar), Bo-Tree Prods, 85. *Dealer:* G W Einstein Inc 591 Broadway New York NY. *Mailing Add:* 55 Perry St No 3A New York NY 10014-3218

PLOTNICK, ELIZABETH & HARVEY BARRY
COLLECTORS

b Detroit, Mich, Aug 5, 1941. *Study:* Univ Chicago, BA, 1963. *Pos:* Ed, Contemp Books, Inc, Chicago, 1964-66, pres pub, 1966-94; chief exec officer, Molecular Electronics Corp, Chicago, 2000-01, Paradigm Holdings, Inc, Chicago, 1994-. *Awards:* Names one of Top 200 Collectors, ARTnews mag, 2005-11. *Mem:* Univ Chicago (trustee, 1994-); Argonne Nat Laboratory (bd gov, 2001); Chicago Acad Scis (bd dirs, currently). *Collection:* Old Master prints; Islamic ceramics

PLOTT, PAULA PLOTT AMOS
PAINTER, SCULPTOR

b Wichita, Kans, Sept 22, 1946. *Study:* Wichita State Univ, BFA (cum laude), 68; Univ Ore, MFA (summa cum laude), 70. *Work:* Wichita Art Mus, Kans. *Comn:* Carved reception desk & 12 paintings, J P Weigand & Sons Real Estate, Wichita, 76-77; Day in the Life of an Aztec (paintings), Taco Tico, Inc, 78-84; Symphony Calendar, Wichita Symphony, 79-80; panel designs, Trinity Methodist Church, Hutchinson, Kans, 80-81; Herbal Calendar, 87 & Wildflowers Calendar, 88, 89, 90 & 91 Wildlife Fedn; Lipton Herbal Tea Calendar, 89 & 90, Commemorative Cup, 90, Lipton Tea Co; Wichita Art Mus Commemorative Christmas Ornament, 89. *Exhib:* Solo exhibs, Mus Fine Art, Los Gatos, 75, Wichita Gallery Fine Art, 78, Wichita Art Asn, 82 & Birger Sandzen Gallery Art, 83; Kansas Watercolor Tri State Show, 81, Seasons Greetings Invitational, 81, Facets in Wood, 84, Woods Worthy Christmas, 85, Wichita Art Mus;

Plott Toy Shop, 86, 87, 88, 89 & 90. *Collection Arranged:* Historic Cowtown, Religion in 1863, 82-83. *Pos:* Designer & graphic coordr, US Govt, Stuttgart, WGer, 71-73; tech adv, Chabot Galleries, 75-76; lectr religious symbolism, Methodist Church, 79-82; League artist pub relations, Jr League Wichita, 84-86; artist, Propellor Mag, currently. *Teaching:* Guest lectr Western art, Kurisini Inst Int, Dar Es Salaam, Tanzania, 67; teaching asst painting, Univ Ore, Eugene, 69-70. *Awards:* First Place & Grand Prize, Religion Art Festival, Congregational Church, 82. *Bibliog:* E O'Hara (auth), A woman for all seasons: Religious symbolism, The Wichitan City Mag, 82; Wonder of wood, Colonial Homes, 12/88. *Mem:* Wichita Artists Guild; Kans Watercolor Soc; Nat League Am Pen Women (treas, 85-86). *Media:* Watercolor; Woodcarving, Relief. *Publ:* Illusr, Diagnostic & therapeutic implications of schizophrenic Art, J Arts & Psychotherapy, 84; Country Wildlife, Hammond Publ, 85; auth, Seasons of Inspiration, 86 & Paula Plott's Herbal, 87, Hammond Publ; Wild Flowers, 89, 90 & 91. *Dealer:* Wichita Gallery Fine Arts 4th Financial Ctr Wichita KS 67201. *Mailing Add:* 350 S Fountain St Wichita KS 67218

PLOUS, PHYLLIS
CURATOR
b Green Bay, Wis, 1925. *Study:* Univ Wis, with Oskar von Hagen & James Watrous, BA, 47; Univ Coll London; Univ Calif, Santa Barbara. *Collection Arranged:* Ralph A Blakelock retrospective & tour (coauth, catalog); Charles Demuth retrospective & tour (coauth, catalog); 19 Sculptors of the 40's; Sculptors in the 50's, catalog & tour; Sculptural Perspectives in the 70's catalog; Richard Diebenkorn, Intaglio Prints 1961-1978, catalog; Dark/Light: Extensions of Photography, catalog and tour; New York, Report on a Phenomenon, catalog; Terry Winters, Painting & Drawings, catalog & tour; Abstract Options, (coauth, catalog), tour; Knowledge (coauth, catalog), tour; Carroll Dunham (catalog), Paintings & Drawings, 96. *Pos:* Asst to dir, Santa Barbara Mus Art, 54-56; asst to dir, Univ Art Mus, Univ Calif, Santa Barbara, 63-72, cur, 72-92. *Awards:* Nat Endowment Arts Fel, Mus Professionals, 80. *Mem:* Am Asn Art Mus; Coll Art Asn Am; Southern Calif Art Writers Asn; Int Coun Mus. *Mailing Add:* 33219 SE 15th St Washougal WA 98671-6814

PLOWDEN, DAVID
PHOTOGRAPHER, WRITER
b Boston, Mass, Oct 9, 1932. *Study:* Yale Univ, BA, 55; pvt study with Minor White, Nathan Lyons, 59-60. *Work:* George Eastman House, Rochester; Albright-Knox Gallery, Buffalo; Mus Contemp Photog, Chicago; The Baly Mus, Univ Va, Charlotteville; Albin O Kuhn Libr, Univ Md; The Beinecke Rare Book and Manuscript Libr, Yale Univ, New Haven, Conn; Ctr Creative Photog, Tucson, Ariz. *Comn:* Design resources photog study, Dept Transportation, Washington, DC, 66; Bridges of NAm, photog study, Smithsonian Inst, Washington, DC, 69-72; Railroad men, photog study, Smithsonian Inst, Washington, DC, 76; Chicago industry, photog study, Chicago Hist Soc, 80-85; State Hist Soc Iowa, 87; Iowa Humanities Bd & Nat Endowment Humanities, 87-88. *Exhib:* Photog in the Fine Arts V, Metrop Mus Art, NY, 67; solo exhibs, Smithsonian Inst, 71, 75, 76 & 89, Chicago Hist Soc, 85, Kunst Mus, Luzern, Switz, 87, Iowa State Mus, 88, Mid-Am Arts Alliance, Exhibs USA, 90-93, Kathleen Ewing Gallery, Washington, DC, 94 & Univ Miami, 96; The River, Walker Art Ctr, Minneapolis, Minn, 76-77; Industrial Sites, Whitney Mus, NY, 79; Chicago: The Architectural City, Art Inst Chicago, 83; An Open Land: Photographs of the Midwest 1852-1982, Art Inst Chicago, 83 & traveling, 83-86; Road & Roadside, Ill State Univ, 87 & Art Inst Chicago, 87; Trains, Boats & Planes, Witkin Gallery, NY, 88; The Photographer & the Railroad, Univ Louisville, 89; Three Decades of Midwest Photog, Davenport Mus Art, Iowa, 92; Plain Pictures: Images of the Am Prairie, Univ Iowa Mus Art, 96 & traveling, 97; When Aaron met Harry: Chicago Photog 1948-1971, Mus Contemp Photog, Chicago, 96 & 98; Beinecke Rare Book and Manuscript Libr, Yale Univ, 97; Baly Mus, Univ Va, Charlottesville, 97; Albright-Knox Gallery, Buffalo, 97-98; Albin O Kuhn Libr & Gallery, Baltimore, 98; Tatar/Alexander Gallery, Toronto, 99; Passages: A Forty Yr Retrospective, Laurence Miller Gallery, NY, 2000; Peter Fetterman Gallery, Santa Monica, Calif, 2000; Chicago Cult Ctr, 2003; Catherin Edelman Gallery, Chicago, 2007; Lawrence Miller Gallery, NY, 2008; The Frege Art Mus, Davenport, Ia; The Burchfield Penney, Art Ctr, Buffalo, NY; The Grohman Mus, Milwaukee, Wisc, 2012; Traveling shows, Requiem for Steam, 2010, David Plowden's Iowas, 2011, David Plowden's Iowa, Humanities, 2011. *Pos:* Photogr & writer, 62-. *Teaching:* Assoc prof design, Inst Design, Ill Inst Technol, Chicago, 78-84; lectr, Univ Iowa, Iowa City, 85-88; vis prof, Grand Valley State Univ, Allendale, Mich, 88-89 & 91-2007; artist-in-residence, Univ Baltimore, Inst for Publ Design, 90-91. *Awards:* Guggenheim Found Fel, 68; Wilson Hicks Award, Univ Miami, 77; Seymour & Knox Found, 87; Hon Imagemaker, Soc Photog Educ, Mideast Region, 2002. *Bibliog:* David McCullough (auth), Brave Companions, 92. *Mem:* Am Soc Media Photogr. *Publ:* Auth, An American Chronology, Viking, 82; A Time of Trains, Norton, 87; A Sense of Place, Norton, 88; End of an Era: The Last of the Great Lakes Steamboats, Norton, 92; Small Town America, Abrams, 94; Imprints the Photographs of David Plowden, Bulfinch, 97; Bridges: The Spans of North America, Norton, 2002; David Plowden: The American Barn, Norton, 2003; A Handful of Dust: Photographs of Disappearing America, Norton, 2006; Vanishing Point: Fifty Years of Photography, Norton, 2007. *Dealer:* Catherine Edelman Gallery 300 W Superior St Chicago IL 60610. *Mailing Add:* 609 Cherry St Winnetka IL 60093

PLUMB, JAMES DOUGLAS
PAINTER, EDUCATOR
b New Haven, Conn, Dec 20, 1941. *Study:* Univ Va; Philadelphia Coll Art, BFA. *Work:* Acad Arts, Easton, Md. *Exhib:* Ann Md Show, Acad Arts, Easton, Md, 74, 78, 79 & 81; Art Asn Newport Ann Show, RI, 75; Conn Acad Arts Ann Show, Wadsworth Atheneum, 75; Five From the Eastern Shore, 76 & Md Biennial, 78, Baltimore Mus Art. *Collection Arranged:* Collection of the Academy of the Arts, 175 Works (auth, catalog), 79; College Show (auth, catalog), Contemporary Maryland Photographers (auth, catalog), 79; Eight Artists' Invitational Shows (auth, catalog), 79; Contemporary Works on Paper, 80. *Pos:* Cur, Acad Arts, Easton, Md, formerly. *Teaching:* Instr painting & drawing, Acad Arts, Easton, MD, 71-76; lectr art hist, State Extension Home Economics & Improvement, Univ Md, 73-76, assoc prof, Chesapeake Col, 90-. *Awards:* Acad Arts Ann Show Awards, 74, 78 & 80; Best in Show, Easton Lions' Club Show, 75. *Media:* Oil on Canvas, Pencil on Paper. *Dealer:* David Adamson Gallery 406 7th St NW Washington DC 20004. *Mailing Add:* PO Box 1088 Easton MD 21601

PLUMMER, CARLTON B
PAINTER, ART EDUCATOR
b Brunswick, Maine, 1929. *Study:* Vesper George Sch Art, dipl, 48-51; Mass Coll Art, BS, 55-58; Boston Univ, MFA, 61-64. *Work:* Mus Military Art, Washington, DC; Whisler House Mus, Lowell, Mass; Mus Fine Arts, Springfield, Mass; Lighthouse Art Ctr & Mus; Tequesta, Fla, Miniature Artists Am, Clearwater, Fla. *Comn:* Faces of America, Old Forge, NY. *Exhib:* Mus Fine Arts, Boston; Royal Acad of Miniatures, London, Eng; Int Show, Nagano City, Japan; Miniature Art, Summer Olympics, Sydney, Australia; 20 New England Artists, Wenham Mus, Mass; 40 New England Watercolorists, Decordova Mus, Lincoln, Mass; Maine Artists, Bowdoin Colle, Maine; Nat Acad Design, New York. *Collection Arranged:* 50 yr Retrospective, Plummer Gallery, 2012. *Pos:* Free-lance illusr, own pvt studio, Summerville, Mass, 53-58; art coodr, Chelmsford Sch System, Mass, 58-64; instr watercolor, own pvt workshop studio East, Boothbay, Maine, 78-; vpres, New Eng Watercolor Soc, 79-82, pres, 82-84; owner, Plummer Gallery, 63-2013. *Teaching:* Prof art, drawing & painting, Univ Mass, 64-86; nat and int workshops, 75-; watercolor workshops in Boothbay, Maine, throughout US & Abroad, 78; Prof Emeritus, Univ Mass Lowell. *Awards:* Wash Sch Award, Am Watercolor Soc Ann, 79; Gold Medal Hon, Am Artists Prof League, 83; Gold Medal Hon, Allied Artists Am, 96; Gold Medal Hon, Salmagundi Club, 98. *Bibliog:* Watercolor Demo (film), DVD on miniatorism, Chelmsford Cable TV, 86. *Mem:* Am Watercolor Soc; Allied Artists Am; Guild Boston Artists; Rocky Mountain Nat Watermedia Soc; New Eng Watercolor Soc; Miniature Artists Am; Northeast Watercolor Soc; Soc Casein & Acrylic Painters. *Media:* Watercolor, Acrylics, Gouachem Oil. *Interests:* Tennis, hiking, gardening, rockwall building, travel. *Publ:* Auth, Using diagonal compositions in watercolor, 82 & Capturing the essence of a scene, 84, Am Artist; Exploring Watercolor, Northlight Publ, 85; Best of Watercolor III, Northlight Publ, 93; The Transparent Watercolor Wheel, Watson/Guptil Publ, 94; Best of Watercolor I, Northlight Publ, 94; auth, Create Dramatic Coastal Scenes in Watercolor, Int Artists, Melbourne, Australia. *Dealer:* Guild of Boston Artists Newbury St Boston MA; Wisc Bay Gallery Wiscasset ME; Virginia Barrett Greenwich CT; Forest Gallery Portland Me. *Mailing Add:* Plummer Gallery 154 King Phillips Trail East Boothbay ME 04544

PLUMMER, ELLEN
MUSEUM DIRECTOR
Study: Mt Holyoke, BA; Univ Mich, MA, PhD. *Pos:* Exec Dir, Artrain, Inc, 1989-90; asst Dir, Prog, U Mich Mus Art, 1990-96; prog Adminstr, Toledo Mus Art, 1996-99, head edn, 1999-2002; exec dir Ark Arts Ctr, Little Rock, 2002-. *Mailing Add:* Arkansas Arts Center PO Box 2137 Little Rock AR 72203

POCHMANN, VIRGINIA
PAINTER, DRAFTSMAN
b Starkville, Miss, Mar 13, 1938. *Study:* Univ Wis, Madison, BS, 59; Am Acad Art, Chicago, Ill, 66-68; De Burgos Sch Art, Washington, DC, 68-70. *Work:* City of Sunnyvale Permanent Collection. *Exhib:* Am Watercolor Soc Ann, New York, 82; Rocky Mt Nat Watermedia Exhib, Golden, Colo, 82, 84 & 86; Watercolor USA, Springfield Art Mus, Mo, 83; 15th Ann Watercolor West, Harrison Mus Art, Logan, Utah, 83; Watercolor West Ann, Riverside, Calif, 83, 85 & 86; West Coast Watercolor Soc, Monterey Peninsula Mus Art, Calif, 84; San Diego Watercolor Soc Int Exhib, Calif, 84; one-person shows, Fireside Gallery, Carmel, Calif, 84 & 85; 65th Ann, Nat Watercolor Soc, Brea, Calif, 85; Bernard Galleries, Walnut Creek, Calif, 88; Foliage and Flowers, Sunnyvale, Calif, 88. *Pos:* Retired. *Awards:* Purchase Award, La Watercolor Soc Exhib, Pontchartrain Clinic, 85; Cash Award, WTex Watercolor Soc Nat Exhib, Mus Tex Tech, 85; First Award, Northern Calif Watercolor Competition, Pacific Art League, Palo Alto, 85. *Mem:* Nat Watercolor Soc; Artists Equity; WCoast Watercolor Soc (treas, 84-85). *Media:* Watercolor, Pen, Ink. *Publ:* Contribr, Gerald Brommer, Watercolor & Collage Workshop, Watson-Guptill, 86; Contemp Women Artists, (calendar), Pomegranate Publ Co, Petaluma, Calif, 89; Contribr, Exploring Painting, Davis Publ Co, 87; contribr Understanding Transparent Watercolor, Brommer, Davis Pub Co, 93; contribr Splash 2, Watercolor Breakthroughs, North Light, 93; and others. *Mailing Add:* 235 Oak Rd Alamo CA 94507

PODUSKA, T F
LECTURER, PAINTER
b Cedar Falls, Iowa, Dec 6, 1925. *Study:* Univ Northern Iowa, BA (art educ). *Work:* Denver Art Mus, Contemp Collection; Atlantic Richfield Corp; Amoco; Int Bus Machines; Exeter; and others. *Exhib:* Colo Womens Col, 79; Aspen Inst, 79; Univ Wyo, 80; Watercolor USA, Springfield, Mo, 80; Carson-Sapiro Gallery, Denver, 82; and others. *Pos:* Lectr, consult & proj asst, Colo Coun Arts & Humanities, 73. *Teaching:* Bus skills workshops, 75. *Awards:* Colo Governor's Award for Arts & Humanities, 77; Merit Award, Nat Acad of Design, 77. *Mem:* Alliance Contemp Art; Asian Art Asn. *Media:* Water Media, Paper. *Publ:* Coauth, Insuring the artist's work, Am Artist Bus Lett, suppl, 74; Business Practices for Artists, Artists Equity Asn, 75. *Dealer:* Melinda Percell Inc Denver CO. *Mailing Add:* 10233 W Powers Ave Littleton CO 80127-1814

POEHLMANN, JOANNA
ILLUSTRATOR, PRINTMAKER
b Milwaukee, Wis, Sept 5, 1932. *Study:* Layton Sch Art, four-year dipl, 54; Kansas City Art Inst, 55; Marquette Univ, 58; Univ Wis, Milwaukee, 65 & 85. *Work:* Milwaukee Art Mus; Victoria & Albert Mus, London; Ruth & Marvin Sackner Archive Concrete & Visual Poetry, Miami Beach, Fla; Int Print Biennial, Embragel, Cabo Frio, Brazil; New York Pub Libr, NY; Mus Kunsthandwerk, Frankfurt, Ger;

Istvan Kiraly Muzeum-Szekasfechevar, Budapest, Hungary; and others. *Comn:* Animal note cards, Recycled Paper Co, Chicago, 81-83; Ed of Hand Colored Lithograph, Quad/Graphics Inc, Pewaukee, Wis, 87 & 93; Poster Design, Charles Allis Art Mus, Milwaukee, 88; 50th Anniversary card design, Wustum Mus Art, Racine, Wis, 91; Artist Book Retirement Gift, Midwest Express Airlines, Milwaukee, Wis. *Exhib:* Retrospective, Drawings, Collages, Mindscapes, Milwaukee Art Mus, 66; Wisconsin Directions I & II, Milwaukee Art Mus, 75 & 78; Works on Paper, Art Inst Chicago, 78; Prints, Multiples, Art Inst Chicago, 81 & Nat Mus Am Art, 82; 10 Yr Retrospective 1964-1994, Wustum Mus Fine Arts, Racine, Wis, Charles Allis Art Mus, Milwaukee, Wis, 91; Verbal Text/Non-Verbal Context: Handmade Books, Milwaukee Art Mus, 92; Cross Section World Financial Ctr, NY, 92; Artists Books in the USA, Galerie Druck & Buch, Tübingen, Ger; Retrospective, Wis Acad Art, Sci & Lett, 92; Book Arts in the USA, Ctr Bk Arts, NY, 90 (Touring Africa through 92); Milwaukee Art Mus, 2008; Wis Lutheran Coll, 2008; Racine Art Mus, 2010. *Teaching:* Assoc lectr, Univ Wis, Milwaukee. *Awards:* Purchase Awards, 20th Bradley Nat Print & Drawings Exhib, Bradley Univ, Peoria, Ill, 85, 22nd Nat Works on Paper Biennial, Univ of Del, Newark, 86, 10th Print Nat, Univ Dallas, Irving, Tex, 88 & Univ NDak Print & Drawing Ann, Grand Forks, 88; Milwaukee Co Individual Art Fel, 93; Arts/Midwest Regional Visual Artist Fel, Nat Endowment Arts, 94-95; Outstanding Artist of the Year, Milwaukee City Arts Bd, 2005; Hon Educators award, Delta Kappa Gamma Soc Int, 2008; Elected Fel, Wis Acad Sci Arts and Letts, 2010. *Bibliog:* Laura Murphy (auth), Art in Wisconsin, 4/87; Printworld Directory/87-88, 91-92; article, Am Crafts Mag, 4-5/96; Hannah Heidi Levy (auth), Famous Wisconsin Artists and Architects, 2004; Ray Chi (auth), Drawn from Life-The Art of Joanna Poehlmann (DVD film), 2009. *Mem:* Printforum Milwaukee Art Mus; Ctr Bk Arts, NY; Columbia Col, Chicago Ctr Book Paper Arts. *Media:* Hand Color Stone Lithography; Artists Books. *Publ:* Illusr, The chimp who went fishing, Int Wildlife Mag, 78; auth & illusr, The Day Before Christmas, Western Publ Co, 79; illusr, A Nutrition Monograph for Taking Off Pounds Sensibly, Tops Club, 80; auth & illusr, So have a Canary, self publ, 87; Love Letters, Food for Thought & Cancelling Out, Abbeville Press, Inc, 91. *Dealer:* Priscilla Javelis Rare Books Kennebunk Port Me; Grace Chosy Gallery Madison Wi; Katie Gingrass Gallery Milwaukee Wi. *Mailing Add:* 1231 N Prospect Ave Milwaukee WI 53211-3013

POGANY, MIKLOS
PAINTER, PRINTMAKER
b Budapest, Hungary, Feb 4, 1945. *Study:* St Procopins Col, BA, 65; Univ Chicago, MA, 65, PhD, 72. *Work:* Metrop Mus Art, NY; Philadelphia Mus Art, Pa; Phillips Collection, Washington, DC; Victoria & Albert Mus, London, Eng; Nat Mus Am Art, Washington. *Exhib:* The Am Artist as Printmaker, Brooklyn Mus, NY, 83; Contemp Am monotypes, Chrysler Mus, Norfolk, Va, 85; 1987 Invitational, New Britain Mus Am Art, Conn, 87; Contemp Art Exhib, Spencer Mus, Lawrence, Kans, 87. *Awards:* SECA Award Painting, San Francisco Mus Mod Art, 77; Grant for Printmaking, Conn Comn Arts, 80; Louis Comfort Tiffany Found Award, 81. *Dealer:* Victoria Munroe Gallery 415 W Broadway New York NY 10012

POHLMAN, LYNETTE
MUSEUM DIRECTOR, CURATOR
Study: IA State Univ, BA, 1972, MA in applied art, 1976. *Exhib:* Cur Emperors, Shoguns and Kings, 1981, Fiber to Glass, 1987, Land of Fragile Giants: Landscapes, Environs and Peoples of the Loess Hills, 1994-96, The Golden Age of Glass: 1875-1939, 1999. *Pos:* Dir, chief cur, Univ. Mus at IA State Univ. *Teaching:* Adj prof art & design IA State Univ; organizer Art in State Bldgs Progressive. *Awards:* Recipient Christian Petersen Design Award, 2004. *Mem:* Asn Coll and Univ Mus and Galleries (found mem). *Mailing Add:* Iowa State Univ Brunnier Art Mus Iowa State Ctr Schman Continuing Edn Bldg Ames IA 50011

POLAN, ANNETTE
PAINTER, DRAFTSMAN
b Huntington, WVa, Dec 8, 1944. *Study:* Hollins Col, Va, BA (art hist), 63-67; Ecole du Louvre, Paris, 64-65; Tyler Sch Art, Philadelphia; Corcoran Sch Art, Washington. *Work:* Huntington Mus, Huntington, WVa; WVa Coun Arts & Humanities, Charleston, WVa; Nat Drug Abuse Coun, Washington; Columbia Hosp Women, Washington; Hill & Knowlton, Washington; and many others pub & pvt. *Comn:* Portraits: Am Pharmaceutical Asn, Washington, 90; Hon Sandra Day OConnor, US Supreme Ct; Bergen Brunswig Corp, Orange, Calif, 90; Coun For Relations, NY, 95; Gov Gaston Caperton, Charleston, WVa, 96. *Exhib:* Am Genius, Corcoran Gallery, Washington, 76 & Hemicycle, 92; one-person exhibs, Foundry Gallery, 76 & 83, Wallace Wentworth Gallery, Washington, 85, Marywood Mus Art, Marywood Col, Scranton, Pa, 89, Montrose Gallery, Fredricksburg, Va, 90, Agardhs Gallery, Bastad, Sweden, 92, Gustaf Nord, Stockholm, Sweden, 92; Ann Art Auction, Washington Proj for the Arts, Wash, 91-98; Figure, Ctr Street Gallery, Manassas, Va, 92; The Woman's Show, Cur for Hon Eleanor Holmes Norton, Washington, 92; Stockholm Art Fair, Sweden, 93; Portraits, Georgetown Univ, Washington, DC, 93; Susan Conway Gallery, Washington, DC, 95; Cult Ctr, Charleston, WVa, 96; Gallery Samtah, Seoul, Korea, 96; Sunrise Mus, Charleston, WVa, 98; Md Art Place, Baltimore, 98; Huntington Mus of Art, Huntington, WVa, 2000; and many others. *Pos:* Artist-in-residence, Art Therapy Italia, Vignale, Italy, 86; vis artist, Landscape Painting Prog, La Napoule, France, 87; dir Corcoran Summer Prog, La Napoule, 88; pres, Fac Asn, Corcoran Sch Art, Washington, DC, 88-89, chmn painting dept, 91-92; guest lectr Contemp Am Portraiture, China, & Japan, 89, Nat Trust Sydney, 96 & Seoul, Korea, 97; artist-in-residence, La Napoule, France, 90; juror, many orgns & galleries, 90-93; presenter, Mod Artists' Mat & Their Conservation Implications, Smithsonian Inst, Washington, DC, 91. *Teaching:* Asst prof fine art, Corcoran Sch Art, Washington, DC, 74-. *Awards:* DC Comn Arts & Humanities Grants in Aid, 85 & 93; Distinguished Alumnae Award, Baldwin Sch, Bryn Mawr, Pa, 98; Award Batuz Found, Soc Imaginaire Pgm, Altzella, Ger, 99. *Mem:* Corcoran Fac Asn (pres, 88-89); Washington Proj for the Arts, Washington (bd dir, 94-). *Media:* Painting, Drawing. *Publ:* Illusr, Say What I Am Called, Selected Riddles from the Exeter Book, Sibyl-Child Press, 88; illusr, Relearning the Dark, Washington Writers Publ House, Washington; cover designer, Doers of the Word, Oxford Univ Press, 95. *Dealer:* Susan Conway Gallery Washington DC 20007. *Mailing Add:* 4719 30th St NW Washington DC 20008

POLCARI, STEPHEN
HISTORIAN, ADMINISTRATOR
b Boston, Mass, Jan 22, 1945. *Study:* Columbia Col, BA, 67; Columbia Univ, MA, 71; Univ Calif, Santa Barbara, PhD, 80. *Pos:* Cur, DeCordova Mus, Lincoln, Mass, 76; dir, Archives Am Art, NY. *Teaching:* Asst prof mod art, Univ Ill, Urbana, 79-83; State Univ NY, Stony Brook, 83-90. *Awards:* Rubinstein Mus Fel, Whitney Mus Art, 77; Nat Endowment Humanities, 82; Inst Advan Study, Princeton, 82; Nat Mus Am Art, 91. *Mem:* Coll Art Asn; Alumni of Inst Advanced Studies. *Res:* Intellectual, cultural & political history and the development of modern art, especially abstract expressionism, modern and American Art, the Depression and War, 1930-1950s. *Publ:* Martha Graham & Abstract Expressionism, Smithsonian Studies in Am Art, 90; Orozco & Pollock: Epic Transfigurations, Am Art, 92; Barnett Newman, The Broker Obelisk, Art J, 94

POLEDNA, MATHIAS
VIDEO ARTIST
b Vienna, Austria, 1965. *Study:* Student Univ Applied Arts; Student, Univ Vienna, Austria. *Exhib:* Principal works include: Produktion Pop (with Martin Beck & Jon Savage), 1996; Fondazione, Generali Found,Vienna, Austria, 1998; Actualite, 2001; Sufferers' Version, 2004; Zones of Disturbance, Graz, Austria, 1997; Grazer Kunstverein, 2001; Richard Telles Fine Art, Los Angeles, 2002 & 2005; Mus Mod Art Found, Austria, 2003; MUMOK, Vienna, Austria, 2003; Galerie Meyer Kainer, 2004; Witte de With Center Contemp Art, Neth, 2006; Open Space Art Cologne, Ger, 2006; How Soon is Now, La Corvina, Spain, 2007; LA Desire (Part 2), Galerie Dennis Kimmerich, Dusseldorf, Ger, 2007; UCLA Hammer Mus, 2007; Galerie Daniel Buchholz, Cologne, 2007; Galerie Meyer Kainer, Vienna, 2007; group shows: 3 Berlin Biennale, Martin-Gropius-Bau, Berlin, 2004; 20/20 Vision, Stedelijk Mus Post CS, Amsterdam, Neth, 2004; Liverpool Biennial, Tate Liverpool, Eng, 2004; Occupying Space/Wasting Time, Haus, London, 2005; Whitney Biennial: Day for Night, Whitney Mus Am Art, 2006. *Mailing Add:* c/o Richard Telles Fine Art 7380 Beverly Blvd Los Angeles CA 90036

POLESKIE, STEPHEN FRANCIS
ARTIST, PRINTMAKER
b Pringle, Pa, June 3, 1938. *Study:* Wilkes Coll, BS, 59; New Sch Social Res, 61; studied with Raphael Soyer. *Work:* Whitney Mus Art, Metrop Mus Art, Mus Mod Art, NY; Victoria & Albert Mus; Tate Gallery, London. *Comn:* Aerial Theatre, Toledo, Ohio, 84 & Richmond, Va, 85; Int Video Festival, Locarno, Switz, 85; Zone Art Ctr, Springfield, Mass, 88; Aerial Theatre, Southampton Performance Festival, Eng, 89. *Exhib:* Word & Image-Posters and Typography (1945-1975), Mus Mod Art, New York, 68; Recent Acquisitions: Prints and Drawings, Metrop Mus Art, 69; Oversize Prints, Whitney Mus Am Art, 71; solo exhibs, Palace of Cult & Sci, Warsaw, Poland & Gallery of Mod Art, Gdansk, 79; Stadt Mus, Kassel, Fed Ger Repub, 86; John Hansard Gallery, Univ S Hampton, United Kingdom, 89; Lee Art Gallery, Clemson Univ, SC, 90; Nine Columns Gallery, Brescia, Italy, 91; Glenn Curtis Mus, Hammodsport, NY, 93; Caproni Mus, Trento, Italy, 95; Friedman Art Gallery, Misericordia Univ, Pa, 2011; Brucken in Himmel, Okoffenes Kulturhus, Linz, Austria, 2011; and others. *Pos:* Founder & dir, Chiron Press, New York, 63-68. *Teaching:* Instr, Sch Visual Arts, New York, 66-68; assoc prof silk-screen & contemp art issues, Cornell Univ, 68-81, prof, 81-200, prof emer, 2000-; vis prof, Univ Calif, Berkeley, 76; vis artist, Alfred Univ, 2010. *Awards:* Carnegie Found, 67; New York State Coun Arts, 73; Best Found, 85. *Bibliog:* Peter Frank (auth), Flights of Fancy, catalog essay, Richmond, Va, 85; Enrico Crispolti (auth), catalog essay, Rome, 87; Alison Lurie (auth), catalog essay, Eng, 89. *Mem:* Authors Guild. *Media:* Aerial Theatre Performance, Screen Printing, Digital Photography. *Publ:* Auth, Dell'arte e del Volo, Dars Milano, 84; Art and Flight: Historical Origins to Contemporary Works, Leonardo, 85; Reasons for Aerial Theatre, Art Criticism, 86. *Dealer:* Terrain Gallery 141 Greene St NY 10012. *Mailing Add:* OnagerEditions PO Box 849 Ithaca NY 14851-0849

POLLARD, HERSCHEL NEWTON
PAINTER, INSTRUCTOR
b Chadbourn, NC, Apr 6, 1938. *Study:* Vanderbilt Univ, BA, 60, PhD, 72. *Work:* Nat Gallery, London; Ave Maria Univ Mus, Naples, Fla. *Comn:* Portrait of Sir Denis Mahon, Nat Portrait Gallery, London. *Exhib:* Solo exhibs, The Parthenon, Nashville, Tenn, 72 & Nat Trust Larson Gallery, Naples, Fla, 2000 & Goff Gallery at Visual Arts Ctr, Punta Gorda, Fla, 2003; Glimpses of the Sea, Mus of Everglades, Naples, Fla, 98; The Easter Exhib, Cape Coral Arts Studio, Fla, 99; People, Places, Things, Impac Univ, Punta Gorda, Fla, 2004; The Entombment, Ave Maria Univ, Naples, Fla, 2004-05; Solo retrospective, Arts & Humanities Gallery, Port Charlotte, Fla, 2005. *Pos:* Proj coord, Television, Radio & Film Comn, 62-64; bd chmn, Von Leibig Ctr Arts, Naples, Fla, 2003-04; bd chmn, Visual Arts Ctr, Punta Gorda, Fla, 2005-; pres, Art Inst Fla Inc, Punta Gorda, 2006-. *Teaching:* Instr, Pollard Studio, Chattanooga, Tenn, 86-; instr drawing & painting, Art League Bonita Springs, Fla, 96-99; instr painting, Cape Coral Arts Studio, Fla, 99-2004; instr painting & sculpture, Von Leibig Ctr Arts, Naples, Fla, 99-2003 & Visual Arts Ctr, Punta Gorda, Fla, 2001-; lectr, Fla Gulf Coast Univ Renaissance Acad, 2007-2009, Ringling Coll Art & Design, Continuing Educ, 2007-2008. *Awards:* First Judges Award, Visual Arts Ctr Fifth Nat Art Exhib, 2004; Bowles Award for Portraiture, Faces & Figures, Bill & Susanne Bowles, 2005; First Place, Nat Aviation Art Exhib, 2006. *Bibliog:* M Gomez (auth), The 2005 H Pollard Retrospective, CESA Press, 2005. *Mem:* Von Leibig Ctr Arts (pres, 2002-03); Art Coun SW Fla (rep, 2002-03); Visual Arts Ctr (pres, 2005-06); Peace River Nat Arts Festival (plan bd chmn, 2006); Nat Aviation Art Exhib (chmn, 2006). *Media:* Acrylic, Oil. *Res:* Italian baroque art; Ancient Greek, Chinese &

Roman coin-making techniques; Portraiure, religious themes, landscapes. *Interests:* Psychology of art, psychopathology of Vincent Van Gough, Tolous Lantree. *Collection:* Baroque religious art, mod masters. *Publ:* Auth, The Art of Frances Morton Pollard, 2000, The Madman of Arles, 2003, Pollard's Brief Handbook for Painters, 2004 & Pollard's Infinite Palette, 2006, CESA Press; ed, A Life Remembered, CESA Press, 2004. *Dealer:* L M Gomez 1001 Montlake Rd Soddy-Daisy TN 37379

POLLARD, JANN LAWRENCE
FINE ARTIST, INSTRUCTOR

b Mt Pleasant, Iowa, Apr 11, 1942. *Study:* Univ Colo, BFA, 63; Coll San Mateo, studied tech arts, San Mateo, Calif. *Work:* Duke Cancer Ctr, Durham, NC; Providence Gallery, Charlotte, NC; Numerous works. *Comn:* Princess Cruise, 2005. *Exhib:* Solo exhibs, The Gallery, Burlingame, Calif, 91, 93, 95-96, 98-99, 2001-2002, 2004-2005 & 2007, The Cottage Gallery, Carmel, Calif, 91, 93, 95 & 98; Images of Filoli, Filoli Gardens, 98; juried shows, Calif Watercolor Asn, 98, Nat Watercolor Soc, 99; California Watercolorist Invitational, 99; Watercolor USA, 2001; Providence Gallery, Charlotte, NC, 2012; Inspiring Destinations, Fibli, Woodside, 2013; Southern Watercolor Annual Juries, Clarksville, Tenn, 2015. *Pos:* fine art. *Teaching:* Instr, watercolor workshops, France, Italy, Eng, Mex, Calif, 95- & Filoi Nat Trust Garden, 96-2014; instr, Calif Watercolor Asn, 2001. *Awards:* 3rd Prize, 30 & 1 Artists Ann, San Mateo, Calif, 96; Patron Purchase award, Watercolor USA, 2001; Outstanding Achievement award, Calif Watercolor Asn, 2002; Southern Watercolor Soc Annual Juried Exhib Merchandise award Dr. PH Martin, 2015; and others. *Bibliog:* Jan Wright Bressler (auth), Almost Famous Recipes, Gentry Mag, 2002; Theodora Philcox (auth), Landscapes in Watercolor, AVA Publ, SA, Switzerland, 2002; Margot Schulzke (auth), A Painter's Guide to Design & Composition, N Light Bks, 2005; Best of Worldwide Landscape Artists, Vol 1, Kennedy Publishing; An Artists Portfolio-Jann Lawrence Pollard. *Mem:* Calif Watercolor Asn (signature mem, ann show dir, 97-98, fundraising dir, 97-98, newsletter editor, 99 & 2000 & newsletter dir, 2000 & 2001); Nat Watercolor Soc (signature mem); Soc Western Artists (signature mem); ASID (profl mem). *Media:* All Media. *Specialty:* Original art work, all media. *Interests:* Computer for artists. *Publ:* Cover artist, Karen Brown Travel Books, 91-; auth, The Artist & Computer can be Friends, Int Artist mag, Issue 5, 99; coauth, Creative Computer Tools for Artists, 2001, Watson Guptill Publs; Feature arteicle, Watercolor Mag Am Artist, Spring, 2012, Inspired Impressions; illustrator for Karen Brown Travel Books, 1990-2009; Paintings for Covers, numerous. *Dealer:* The Gallery Burlingame CA; New Masters Gallery Carmel CA; Providence Gallery, Charlotte, NC. *Mailing Add:* 10307 Wabeek Ct Charlotte NC 28278

POLLARO, PAUL
PAINTER

b Brooklyn, NY. *Study:* Flatiron Sch Art, NY; Art Students League, Pratt Graphic Ctr. *Work:* Mus NMex, Santa Fe; Jan Perry Mayer Collection; Chrysler Mus; Orlando Mus Art, Fla; Notre Dame Univ Mus Art, South Bend, Ind. *Exhib:* Ann, Pa Acad Fine Arts, Philadelphia, 64; Nat Inst Arts & Lett, 69 & 72; Artists of the 20th Century, Mus Mod Art, NY, 70; Artists at Work, Finch Coll Mus, 71; Babcock Gallery, NY, 73; Louis Newman Gallery, Beverly Hills, Calif; L K Meisel Gallery, NY; Solo exhib, Chrysler Mus, 91; Janus Gallery, Santa Fe, NMex, 92. *Pos:* Assoc dir, The MacDowell Colony, 73-77. *Teaching:* Instr painting, New Sch Social Res, 64-69; asst prof painting, Wagner Col, 69-72; vis artist, Notre Dame Univ, summers 65 & 67. *Awards:* Second Prize, Jersey City Mus, 62; MacDowell Colony Fels, 66, 68 & 71; Tiffany Found Grant, 67. *Media:* Acrylic, Oil. *Publ:* Articles in: Art in America, Art News, Arts, NY Times, Art Space, Art New Eng, Art Int. *Mailing Add:* Norway Hill Hancock NH 03449

POLLEI, DANE F
MUSEUM DIRECTOR, CURATOR

b Fond du Lac, Wis. *Study:* Beloit Coll, BA. *Collection Arranged:* Wayang Puppets: Art of Indonesia, Logan Mus Anthropology, 84; German Expressionism, Wright Mus Art, 85; Beloit and Vicinity, Wright Mus Art, 86; Franklin Boggs and V O Schaffer: Art and Architecture, Freeport Art Mus, Ill, 88; Scenes of Madagascar: Ethnographic Portraits 1890-1930, Freeport Art Mus, Ill, 88; The Art of Persuasion: Posters from the World Wars, Kenosha Hist Mus, 90; The Art of the Wheel: Nash Advertising; It Came from Hollywood: B-Movies of the 50's & 60's; The Photographs of Louis Thiers (auth catalog), 97. *Pos:* Asst cur, Logan Mus Anthropology, 83-85; asst to dir, Wright Mus Art, 85-86; dir, Freeport Art Mus, Ill, 87-89; exec dir, Kenosha Hist Mus, 89-97; dir admin, John Michael Kohler Arts Ctr, Sheboygan, 97-2004; dir, Brevard Mus Art & Sci, Melbourne, Fla, 2004-2006; dir, chief cur, Mabee-Gerrer Mus Art, Shawnee, Okla, 2006-; co-founder & pres, HMMGG Festival Arts & Cult, Wis. *Teaching:* Instr, mus studies, Univ Wis, Oshkosh, 87; instr, Am Indian art, Highland Community Coll, 88-89, instr anthropology, 88-89. *Awards:* D.A.N. award, HMMGG Festival of Arts & Culture, 2012. *Bibliog:* The Earth Chronicles Project: The Artist's Process (documentary), 2012. *Mem:* Am Asn Mus; Okla Mus Asn. *Res:* art education, art management. *Publ:* Ed, Westword Traveller, Wis Heritage Tourism Newspaper; auth, Focus on Louis Thiers: A Photographers View of Kenosha, 98; Board Member Mag, 2011. *Mailing Add:* Mabee-Gerrer Mus Art 1900 W MacArthur Dr Shawnee OK 74804

POLLI, ANDREA
ENVIRONMENTAL ARTIST, EDUCATOR

b Nov 13, 1968. *Study:* Johns Hopkins Univ, Balitmore, BA, 1989; Sch Art Inst Chicago, MFA, 1992. *Exhib:* Solo exhibs, Colfax Cult Ctr, Sount Bend, Ind, 1993, Alfred Univ, NY, 1997, Mus Contemp Art, Chicago, 1998, Chicago Cult Ctr, 2000, Whitney Mus Am Art, 2004, Beall Ctr for Art & Technol, Irvin, Calif, 2007, Atlas Ctr, Univ Colo, 2008; Perform.Media, Sch Fine Arts Gallery, Ind Univ, Bloomington, 2006; Global Eyes, San Diego Convention Ctr, Calif, 2007; Feeling the Heat - Artists, Scientists and Climate Change, Deutsche Bank Art, New York, 2008; Cloud Car and Hello, Weather!, Ctr for Contemp Art, Santa Fe, 2009; Sonic Antarctica, Hunt Gallery, Webster Univ, St Louis, 2010. *Pos:* Artist-in-residence, Columbia Coll, 1998-99; co-chmn, Am Soc Acoustic Ecology New York Chpt, 2004-08 & Leonardo Educ Forum, 2006-09; vpres, Am Soc Acoustic Ecology, 2009-. *Teaching:* Instr, Sch Art Inst Chicago, 1991-92, IHM High Sch, Westchester, Ill, 1992-93, St Joseph High Sch, Westchester, Ill, 1993-94, Robert Morris Coll, Chicago, 1994-96; assoc adj prof, Univ Ill, Chicago, 1996-97, Columbia Coll, Chicago, 1996-98; chmn art & design, Robert Morris Coll, 1996-98; adj fac, Sch Art Inst Chicago, 1998-2001; assoc prof film & media, Hunter Coll, 2001-08; assoc prof fine arts & eng, Univ NMex, 2009-, Mesa Del Sol endowed chmn, currently. *Awards:* Spl Assistance Grant, Ill Arts Coun, 1998; Project Grant, Community Arts Partnership, Columbia Coll, 2001; Visual Arts Res Grant, 2005-06 & Travel Grant, 2008, Hunter Coll; Individual Artist Grant, Queens Coun on the Arts, 2008; New York Found Arts Fel, 2009. *Bibliog:* Fred Camper (auth), Nineteen Ninety-Nine in Chicago, Chicago Reader, 9/17/1999; Leah Oates (auth), Dark Nature: Part 1, NY Arts Mag, 9-10/2005; Shana Ting Lipton (auth), An Eye and Ear on the Earth, Los Angeles Times, 1/18/2007; Rachel Corbett (auth), Global Warming: A Portfolio, ARTnews Mag, 6/2008; Kristen Peteson (auth), For Members of one Artist Residency, the Desert is their Muse, Las Vegas Sun, 6/7/2009. *Mem:* Int Soc Electronic Arts; Coll Art Asn; Leonardo Int Soc for the Arts, Sci, and Technol

POLLITT, JEROME JORDAN
HISTORIAN, EDUCATOR

b Fair Lawn, NJ, Nov 26, 1934. *Study:* Yale Univ, New Haven, Conn, BA, 57; Columbia Univ, New York, PhD, 63. *Pos:* Ed-in-chief, Am J Archeol, 74-78. *Teaching:* Prof classic art & archeol, Yale Univ, 62-. *Publ:* Auth, The Art of Greece: Sources and Documents, 64 & The Art of Rome: Sources and Documents, 65, Prentice-Hall & Cambridge Univ Press, 83 & 90; Art and Experience in Classical Greece, Cambridge Univ Press, 72; The Ancient View of Greek Art, Yale Univ Press, 75; Art in the Hellenistic Age, Cambridge Univ Press, 86 & Personal Styles in Greek Sculpture, 96; The Cambridge History of Painting in the Classical World, 2014. *Mailing Add:* Dept History of Art PO Box 208272 New Haven CT 06520

POLLOCK, LINDSAY
EDITOR-IN-CHIEF

Study: Barnard Univ, majored in Art History; Columbia Univ Graduate School of Journalism, Masters Degree. *Pos:* Reporter New York Sun and The Art Newspaper; cultural news reporter, Bloomberg, 2005-2011; editor-in-chief, Art In America, 2011-; blogger Art Market News, 2009. *Bibliog:* auth biography of art dealer Edith Halpert, The Girl with the Gallery, 2006. *Mailing Add:* Brant Publications 110 Greene St New York NY 10012

POLONSKY, ARTHUR
PAINTER, EDUCATOR

b Lynn, Mass, June 6, 1925. *Study:* Boston Mus Sch, with Karl Zerbe, dipl (with highest honors), 48; Europ Traveling Fel, 48-50. *Work:* Fogg Mus, Harvard Univ, Cambridge; Mus Fine Arts, Boston; Addison Gallery Am Art, Andover; Walker Art Ctr; Stedelijk Mus, Amsterdam, Holland; The High Mus, Atlanta, Ga; Zimmerli Art Mus, Rutgers Univ; Danforth Mus Art, Framingham, Mass; Decordova Mus, Lincoln, Mass; Univ NH, Durham, NH. *Comn:* Stone with the Angel (portfolio of ten original lithographs), Impressions Workshop Inc, Boston, 69; portraits, comn by Harvard Univ Med Sch, Brandeis Univ & Emerson Coll, 56-86. *Exhib:* Art Today-50, Metrop Mus Art, New York, 50, Pittsburgh Int Exhib of Contemporary Painting, Carnegie Inst, 52; Solo exhibs, Boston, NY & Washington, 51-2005; Starr Gallery, Boston, 87; Fitchburg Art Mus, Mass, 90; Boston Pub Libr, 90, 93, 96 & 99; Palais Universitaire, Strasbourg, France, 95; Boston Expressionism, Paul Creative Arts Ctr, Univ NH, 2000; Kantar Fine Arts, Newton, Mass, 2002; Decordova Mus, Lincoln, Mass, 2003, 2010; St Botolph Gallery, Boston, 2005; Retrospective, Danforth Mus Art, Framingham, Mass, 2008; Expressive Voice, St. Botolph Gallery, Boston, Danford Mus, Framingham, Mass, 2011. *Pos:* Founding mem & dir, Artists Equity Asn (New England Chap), 48-67. *Teaching:* Instr painting, Boston Mus Sch, 50-60; asst prof painting, drawing & design, Brandeis Univ, 54-65; assoc prof painting, drawing & design, Boston Univ, Coll of Fine Arts, 65-90, prof emer, 90. *Awards:* Tiffany Found Grant for Painting, 51-52; First Prize, Boston Arts Festival, 54; Purchase Award, Drawings '74, Wheaton Nat Exhib, Wheaton Coll, Norton, Mass, 74; Named Copley Master, Copley Soc Boston, 86. *Bibliog:* Revs of exhibs In: Art News, Arts Mag, NY Times, Time Mag, Life Mag Int Ed, New Yorker Mag & others, 2008; Archives Am Art, Smithsonian Inst, 72; Nathan Goldstein (auth), The Art of Responsive Drawing, Prentice Hall, 73, 77 & 84; Nathan Goldstein (auth), Figure Drawing, Prentice-Hall, 76; Judith Bookbinder (auth), Boston Expressionism, Univ Press New Eng, 2005; and others. *Media:* All. *Interests:* French literature; Philosophy. *Publ:* Léo Bronstein (auth), Kabbalah And Art, Brandeis Univ Press, 78; illusr, Sexual Decisions, Little, Brown & Co, 80; Richard Jones (auth), The Dream Poet, Schenkmann Bks, 81; Poetry in Motion, 87 & Sadie, Remember, 92, Sundance Publ; and others. *Dealer:* Kantar Fine Arts Newton MA 02458; Francesca Anderson Fine Art Lexington MA. *Mailing Add:* 364 Cabot St Newtonville MA 02460

POLSHEK, JAMES
ARCHITECT

b Akron, Ohio, Feb 11, 1930. *Study:* Case Western Reserve Univ, BS, 51; Yale Univ, MArch, 55. *Hon Degrees:* Pratt Inst, Hon DFA, 95; New Sch Univ, Hon DFA, 99; NJ Inst Technol, LHD, 2002. *Comn:* designer, Brooklyn Mus, entry pavilion & plaza, Brooklyn, NY; co-designer, Am Mus Nat Hist, Rose Center for Earth & Space, NY; designer, The Santa Fe Opera, NMex; designer, Scandinavia House: The Nordic Center in Am, NY; designer, William J Clinton Presidential Ctr, Little Rock, Ark, 2004. *Pos:* I M, Pei & Assocs, New York City, 55-56; Ulrich Frazen & Assoc, New York City, 57-60; Westermann & Miller & Assocs, 60-61; pvt Practice Archit, 62-80; special adv for planning & design to the Pres, Columbia Univ, 72-87; founder, Polshek Partnership Architects, 80-. *Teaching:* Columbia Univ, Grad Sch Archit, Planning & Preservation, dean, 72-87, prof archit, 72-2002, prof emeritus archit, 98-.

Awards: Fulbright Fel, 56-57. *Mem:* Am Acad Arts & Sciences (fel); Archit, Designers & Planners for Social Responsibility (founder, mem bd adv); Nat Acad (fel); Cathedral of St. John the Divine (regent); NY Sch Design (adv bd); Temple Hoyne Buell Center, Study of Am Archit, Columbia Univ (founder, former mem bd dir); Regional Plan Asn (bd mem); Lycée Français de NY (adv comt); Am Inst Archit (Coll of fel). *Mailing Add:* Polshek Partnership Architects LLP 320 W 13th St New York NY 10014

POLSKY, CYNTHIA HAZEN
ADMINISTRATOR, COLLECTOR
b New York, NY, Feb 16, 1939. *Study:* Art Students League; New Sch Social Res; Marymount Manhattan Col, BA; Fordham Univ, MBA. *Work:* Corcoran Gallery Am Art, Washington, DC; Israel Mus, Jerusalem; Ulrich Mus of Art, Wichita, Kans; Fogg Art Mus, Cambridge, Mass; USIA Collection, London, Eng; and others; Johnson Mus at Cornell Univ, Ithaca, NY; NY Acad Scis and Rockefeller Univ, NY. *Exhib:* One-person shows, Benson Gallery, Bridgehampton, Long Island, NY, 68, Comara Gallery, Los Angeles, 69, Artisan Gallery, Houston, Tex, 70, Palm Springs Desert Mus, 72-73 & Crispo Gallery, NY, 73 & 74; Ulrich Mus of Art, Wichita, Kans, 77. *Pos:* Trustee, Metrop Mus Art, chmn comt membership & visiting comt for 20th cent art, mem exec comn, acquisitions comt, adv comt Asian Art, educ comn, currently; hon trustee, Storm King Art Ctr, Mountainville, NY, chmn, acquisitions comt, mem exec comt, nominating comn; hon life trustee, Friends Asian Arts, Asia Soc, NY; chmn, Patrons Pierpont Morgan Libr, NY; trustee, Am Acad in Rome, co-chair, comn for Sch of Fine Arts, mem executive comn, nominating comn; adv comn, Cult Affairs NY. *Bibliog:* Judith Denham (auth), article, in: Art Week, 73; Alfred Frankenstein (auth), article, in: San Francisco Chronicle, 73. *Mem:* Comm on Indo-US Ed, Asia Soc; Collectors' Comt, Nat Gallery Art, Washington, DC; Collections Comt, Harvard Univ Art Mus; New York City Comn to the UN. *Publ:* Auth, Indian Paintings from the Polsky Collection, The Art Mus, Princeton Univ, 82; Cynthia Polsky, Paintings 1973-1974, 90. *Mailing Add:* 667 Madison Ave 15th Fl New York NY 10021

POLTA, VOLEEN JANE
SCULPTOR, STAINED GLASS ARTIST
b Summit, NJ, Dec, 21, 50. *Study:* Jersey City State Coll, BA, 71; Teachers Coll, Columbia Univ, MA & EdD, 74 & 75. *Work:* Milwaukee Art Mus. *Exhib:* Ponce Mus Art; Studio Mus of Harlem; High Mus Art; DC Moore Gallery; Peabody Essex Mus; The Drawing Ctr; Nepa Art Mus; Fine Art Manheim; Arnot Art Mus; Crazy Mountain Mus; Missoula Art Mus. *Pos:* sculpting consult, Jamenson Space, Slocumnelli Fine Art; space consult, Meriks Sculpting Space. *Teaching:* adj prof, scuplting, Univ NC; vol instr, Ronda High Sch. *Bibliog:* Abraham Linonel (auth), The Sculpture of a Possessed Artist, 2000; Francois Fontanel (auth), See Her Emotion in Every Sculpture: The Art of Voleen Jane Polta, 2013; John Carolina (auth), Jane Polta: Sculpting Queen, 2016. *Mem:* Nat Found Advancement Arts; Int Sculpture Ctr. *Media:* Stone. *Specialty:* Contemporary Sculpture. *Collection:* Edgar Degas, J. Paul Getty. *Publ:* auth, True & False: Decoding Pottery in Ghost, 2015; auth, Sculpting the Truth, 2012

POLZER, JOSEPH
HISTORIAN
b Vienna, Austria, May 7, 1929; US citizen. *Study:* Univ Iowa, BA (art), 50, MA (art hist), 52; Inst Fine Arts, NY Univ, PhD (art hist), 63. *Teaching:* Instr, Univ Kans, 57-58; lectr, Univ Buffalo, 58-62; from asst prof to prof, Univ Louisville, 62-73; prof art, Queen's Univ, Kingston, formerly, Univ Calgary, Alberta, Can, formerly, prof emeritus, currently. *Res:* Late Rome, Middle Ages, Renaissance. *Publ:* Auth, articles in Late Antique Medieval & Renaissance Art

PONCE DE LEON, MICHAEL
PRINTMAKER, PAINTER
b Miami, Fla, July 4, 1922. *Study:* Univ Mex, BA; Art Students League; Nat Acad Design; Brooklyn Mus Art Sch; also in Europe. *Work:* Mus Mod Art & Metrop Mus Art, NY; Nat Gallery Art & Smithsonian Inst, Washington, DC; Brooklyn Mus; collection of prints added to NY Pub Libr Collection, 02; and others. *Comn:* Many print editions, 60-; ten prints, US State Dept, 66; glass sculpture, Steuben Glass, 71; 100 prints, Pioneer Moss, Inc, annually, 68-83. *Exhib:* Mus Arte Mod, Paris; Victoria & Albert Mus, London; Venice Biennale, 70; Mus Mod Art & Metrop Mus, NY; Smithsonian Inst, Washington, DC; and others. *Pos:* Int Cult Exchange, US State Dept, teaching, lect & travel, Yugoslavia, 65, India & Pakistan, 67-68, Spain, 71 & SAm. *Teaching:* Instr printmaking, Hunter Col, 59-66; prof, New York Univ, 77 & Pratt Inst, 78; instr printmaking, Art Students League, 78, Berkeley Univ, Calif, Univ Calif, Los Angeles, and others. *Awards:* More than 65 medals & awards, incl Tiffany Found Grants, 54 & 55; Fulbright Grants, 56 & 57; Guggenheim Found Grant, 67. *Bibliog:* G Peterdi (auth), Printmaking, Macmillan, 72; F Eichenberg (auth), The Art of the Print, Abrams, 77; D Saff (auth), Printmaking History and Process, Holt, Rinehart & Winston, 78. *Mem:* Soc Am Graphic Artists (treas, 68); Asn Am Univ Prof. *Media:* All Graphic Media. *Publ:* Contribr, Experiments in three dimensions, Art Am, 68; auth, The collage intaglio, 72; The collage-intaglios of Michael Ponce de Leon, Am Artist, 8/74; History of an Art, Skira (in 4 languages), 81; History of International Art, Academia Italia (in 4 languages), 81. *Dealer:* AAA Gallery 663 Fifth Ave New York NY

PONDICK, RONA
SCULPTOR, ENVIRONMENTAL ARTIST
b Apr 18, 1952. *Study:* Queens Col, BA, 74; Sch Art, Yale Univ, MFA, 77. *Work:* Whitney Mus Am Art; Los Angeles Co Mus; Mus Contemp Art, Los Angeles; Brooklyn Mus; Israel Mus, Jerusalem. *Exhib:* Solo shows, Inst Contemp Art, Boston, 89; Israel Mus, 92, Cincinnati Art Mus, 95, Brooklyn Mus, 96-98; Whitney Biennial, Whitney Mus Art, 91; Corporal Politics, MIT List Visual Arts Ctr, Cambridge, Mass, 92; Vber-Leben, Bonner Kunstuerein, Bonn, Ger, 93; Configura 2, Erfurt, Ger, 95. *Awards:* Mid-Atlantic Arts Grant, 91; Guggenheim fel, 92; Rockefeller Found Fel, 96. *Bibliog:* Terry R Myers (auth), Presenting pleasures: Urgent sculpture of Rona Pondick, Arts Mag, 90; Jerry Saltz (auth), The Living Dead Life of the Body, Balcon, 91; Mark Wilson (auth), Het liminale lichaam: De Deelden van Rona Pondick, Metropolis, 94. *Mailing Add:* 32 Cooper Sq New York NY 10003

PONSOT, CLAUDE F
EDUCATOR, PAINTER
b Rabat, Morocco, May 29, 1927; US citizen. *Study:* Atelier Perrier/Jaudon, 47-50; Atelier Andre L'hote, 48-50; Atelier Fernand Leger, 49-50. *Work:* Associated Metals & Minerals Corp, NY; pvt collections, Monique Ponsot, Barbara Baranowska, NY; pvt collection Mr & Mrs M Kesdekian, Tex; Boltax Gallery, Shelter Island, NY. *Comn:* Graphics, LaGuardia Community Col, NY, 79-80 & St John's Univ, 81; South Oaks Hospital, Amityville, 81; and others. *Exhib:* Solo exhib, Galerie Maitre Albert, Paris, 76; Cabinet des Estampes, Bibliotheque Nat, Paris, 78; Brand X, Glendale, Calif, 80; In the Best Tradition, Heckscher Mus, Huntington, 81; Firehouse Gallery, Nassau Community Col, NY, 82 & 83; and others. *Collection Arranged:* Philippe Tailleur, Nimes, France. *Teaching:* Prof art, St John's Univ, New York, formerly. *Awards:* Pat Lambert Award, Shreveport Art Guild; Purchase Award, Images-Shapes 76, Plattsburgh; Patron Purchase Award, Watercolor USA, Springfield Mus, 77. *Bibliog:* Jean Parris (auth), articles, Newsday, 79-81; biog, WCUSAHS newsletter, 97. *Mem:* Watercolor USA Hon Soc. *Media:* Oil, Watercolor. *Res:* Lascaux, The Painters of Yesterday. *Specialty:* Boltax Gallery, One man show 1002. *Interests:* Romanesque art France; caves arts. *Dealer:* Kimberly Greer Gallery Northport Village NY 11768. *Mailing Add:* 8047 235th St Queens Village NY 11427

PONTYNEN, ARTHUR
EDUCATOR, ADMINISTRATOR
b Brooklyn, NY, Mar 23, 1950. *Study:* Univ Iowa, Iowa City, PhD, 83. *Teaching:* Asst prof art hist, Stephen F Austin State Univ, 85-89, Univ Wis, Oshkosh, 89-95, assoc prof, 95-, dept chair, 97-2003, full prof, 2006. *Awards:* Fel, Smithsonian Inst, Washington, DC, 79-80; Salvatori Fel, Heritage Found, Washington, DC, 91-93. *Mem:* Coll Art Asn. *Res:* Art theory and philosophy. *Publ:* Auth, A Winter landscape: Reflections on the theory & practice of art history, Art Bull, 86; A cosmopolitan critique of multiculturalism & Oedipus wrecks: PC & liberalism, Measure, 92-93; Beauty vs aesthetics, chapter in Moral Education: An Interdisciplinary Approach, 94; Taoism & Confucianism, Dictionary of Art, 96; Ready Reference: Censorship, Nat Endowment Arts; Art, Science and Postmodern Society, Am Outlook, 11-12/2000; Beauty and the Enlightened Beast, Am Outlook, 2001; The Aesthetics of Race vs The Beauty of Humanity, Am Outlook, 2002; For the Love of Beauty: Art, History, and the Moral Foundation of Aesthetic Judgment (Transaction Pub, 2006); co-auth, Western Culture at the American Crossroad: Conflicts Over the Nature of Science and Reason (ISI/The James Madison Program in American Ideals and Institutions, Princeton Univ, 2011. *Mailing Add:* Univ Wis Oshkosh WI 54901

POOLE, LESLIE DONALD
PAINTER, PRINTMAKER
b Halifax, NS, May 3, 1942. *Study:* Prince of Wales Col, Charlottetown, PEI, 60; Univ Alta, Edmonton, BFA, 67; Yale Univ, MFA, 70. *Work:* Can Coun Art Bank, Ottawa; Beaverbrook Art Gallery, Fredericton, NB; Confederation Ctr Art Gallery, Charlottetown, PEI; Hyatt Hotel, Chicago, Ill; Vancouver Art Gallery, BC. *Comn:* Portrait lieutenant gov, Prov Alta, 73; mural, Minto Suite Hotel, Ottawa, Ont, 89; Trimark Mutual Funds, Toronto, Ont, 94. *Exhib:* Solo exhibs, Confederation Ctr Art Gallery, Charlottetown, PEI, 73, Edmonton Art Gallery, 74, Encounters with the Goddess, Surrey AG, BC, 91, Kamloops Art Gallery, BC, 92-94, SFU Art Gallery, Vancouver, 95, Shadow/Light: new paintings, Heffel Gallery, 98, Aspen paintings, Scott Gallery, 99 & Leslie Poole's Diary, Gallery at Coperley House, Burnaby, BC, 2000; Memento Mori, Teck Gallery, Simon Fraser Univ at Harbor Ctr, Vancouver, 96; Shadow Paintings, Canadian Art Galleries, Calgary, Alta, 97; Landscapes with Cows paintings, Bauxi Gallery, Toronto, 99; After Bonnard, Winchester Galleries, 2000; Simon Fraser Univ, Vancouver, 2004; Scott Gallery Edmonton, 2005; Las Meninas, Scott Gallery, Edmonton, 2007; Off Road Landscapes, Marilyn Mvlrea Art Gallery, Vancouver, 2008. *Teaching:* Lectr design, Univ Alta, Edmonton, 71-72; instr painting, Banff Sch Fine Arts, 73; lectr drawing, Vancouver Community Col, 75-87. *Awards:* Can Coun Arts Grants, 72, 74, 75 & 80. *Bibliog:* Glenn Howarth (auth), An ecumenical intent, Vanguard Mag, Vancouver, 78; David Watmough (auth), Not exactly limpid Pooles, Interface, Alta, 81; Capilano Rev, No 34, 85. *Media:* Acrylic; Lithography. *Dealer:* Gary Maier New Westminster BC Can; Winchester Galleries Victoria BC; Wallace Galleries Calgary AB; Scott Gallery Edmonton AB. *Mailing Add:* 526 Fourth St New Westminster BC V3L 2V6 Canada

POOLE, NANCY GEDDES
GALLERY DIRECTOR
b London, Ont, May 10, 1930. *Study:* MacDonald Col, McGill Univ, dipl, 49; Univ Western Ont, BA, 55; Univ Western Ont, LLD, 90. *Hon Degrees:* Univ Western Ont, LLD, 90; ORDGR of Canada, 2004. *Collection Arranged:* SW18-London, Rothman Gallery, Stratford, Can, 69; Canadian Printmakers, 70 & Jack Chambers, 79, Canada House Gallery; British Printmakers, Ont galleries tour, 71; Victorian Artists, London Regional Art Gallery, 86. *Pos:* Dir & owner, Nancy Poole's Studio, 69-78; chmn governing coun, Ont Col Art, 73-74; gov, Univ Western Ont, 74-95; interim dir, London Regional Art Gallery, 81, exec dir, London Regional Art & Hist Mus, 85-95. *Awards:* Mayor's New Year's Honours List, 84; Women of Distinction Award, 84; Award of Merit, Univ Western Ont, 85. *Mem:* Hardy Geddes House (bd dir); London Health Asn (bd dir); London Social Planning Coun (vchmn). *Specialty:* Living Canadian artists with emphasis on London painters. *Publ:* Auth, Jack Chambers, pvt publ, 78; The Art of London: 1830-1980, Blackpool Press, 84. *Mailing Add:* 420 Fashawe Park Rd London ON N5X 2S9 Canada

POON, HUNG WAH MICHAEL
PAINTER
b Canton, China, Oct 30, 1942. *Study:* Sir Robert Black Col, Hong Kong; Hwa Kui Col; Hong Kong Acad Fine Arts. *Work:* Int Young Men's Club, Osaka, Japan; Hong Kong Acad Fine Arts. *Exhib:* Hong Kong Acad Alumnus Club Fine Arts; Hong Kong Art's Festival; Hist Mus Southern Fla, 98-99; traveling exhib, Tallahassee, Orlando & Tampa, Fla, 98-99. *Teaching:* Vpres, Int Studio Chinese Art, 76--88; teacher, Hong Kong Govt Middle Sch. *Mem:* Chinese Art Asn, Hong Kong; Kwong Ngar Calligraphy Soc, Hong Kong. *Media:* All media. *Mailing Add:* 15221 SW 89th Ave Miami FL 33157

POON, YI-CHONG SARINA CHOW
PAINTER, CALLIGRAPHER
b Canton, China; Jan 26, 1944. *Study:* Sir Robert Black Coll of Educ, Hong Kong; Hwa Kui Col; Studio of Chinese Art. *Work:* Univ Toronto, Canada; Mus Miami, Fla; Int Y's Men's Club, Osaka, Japan; Sir Robert Black Coll Educ. *Exhib:* Asia Mod Art Exhib, Art Gallery Tokyo, Japan; Mus Hist, Taiwan; Art Mus of Korea; Hong Kong Art's Festival; The Burger King World Hq, Miami, Fla. *Teaching:* Pres, Int Studio Chinese Art, 67-88; prof, dept extramural studies, Chinese Univ, Hong Kong, 79-80; principal, Kei Yam Sch, 70-85; Kei Ho Sch, 85-88. *Mem:* Chinese Art Asn, Hong Kong; Kwong Ngar Calligraphy Soc; Asia Artist Asn. *Mailing Add:* 15221 SW 89th Ave Miami FL 33157

POONS, LARRY
PAINTER
b Tokyo, Japan, Oct 1, 1937. *Study:* New England Conservatory, 57; Boston Mus Fine Arts Sch, 59. *Work:* Mus Mod Art, Metrop Mus Art, Solomon R Guggenheim Mus, Whitney Mus Am Art, NY; Albright-Knox Art Gallery; Stedelijk Mus, Holland; Woodward Found, Washington, DC; Mus Fine Arts, Boston, MA; Philadelphia Mus Art, PA; Tate Gallery, London, Eng. *Exhib:* Solo exhibs, Helander Gallery, Palm Beach, Fla, 90, Salander-O'Reilly Galleries, NY, 90, 92, 94-96, Beverly Hills, 91, Berlin, Ger, 92, Gallery Afinsa, Madrid, Spain, 91, Meredith Long & Co, Houston, 91, Univ Miami, 93, Frederick Spratt Gallery, San Jose, Calif, 94 & 96 & Ruth Bachofner Gallery, Santa Monica, 95, Danese Gallery, NY, 2007, Bernard Jacobson, London, 2004-2007, Camino Real, Boca Raton Fla, 2008, Jacobson Howard, NY, 2008, Loretta Howard Gallery, 2010, SAGG, New Berlin, NY, 2011, Lori Bookstein Fine Art, NY, 2011; Group exhibs, Art Inst Chicago, 66; Corcoran Gallery Art, 67; Whitney Mus Am Art Ann, 68 & 72 & Whitney Biennial, 73; Albright-Knox Art Gallery, Buffalo, NY, 68 & 70; retrospective, Boston Mus Fine Arts, 80; Mus Fine Arts, Boston, Mass, 82; Fort Worth Art Mus, Tex, 85; Galleria Chisel, Milan, Italy, 86; Hokin Gallery, Bay Harbor, Fla, 87; Meadow Brook Art Gallery, Rochester, MI, 88; Daniel Newburg Gallery, NY, 89-90; The Brushstrokes and its Guises, NY Studio Sch, 94; Seven Painters, Nicholas Alexander Gallery, NY, 95; Addison Gallery of Am Art: 65 Yrs, Addison Gallery, 96; Color Field, the Classic Years: 1960-75, Andre Emmerich, 96. *Teaching:* Vis fac, NY Studio Sch, 67, Bennington Col & Art Students League, 97-. *Awards:* Francis J Greenburger Found Award, 88. *Bibliog:* Roberta Smith (auth), Art Review, NY Times, 8/9/96; Karen Wilkin (auth), Partisan Review, Vol LXIII, No 3, 96; Karen Wilkin (auth), Partisan Review, No 4, 96; David Ebony (auth), Art in Am, 1/97; Karen Wilkin (auth), Art in America, 5/2006. *Media:* Painting acrylic on canvas. *Publ:* Auth, The Structure of Color, 71. *Dealer:* Loretta Howard Gallery 525 W 26th St New York NY; Danese 525 W 24th St New York NY. *Mailing Add:* 831 Broadway New York NY 10003

POOR, ROBERT JOHN
HISTORIAN
b Rockport, Ill, July 10, 1931. *Study:* Boston Univ, BA, 53 & MA, 57; Univ Chicago, with Ludwig Bachhofer, PhD (art hist), 61. *Collection Arranged:* Art of India (exhib catalog), 69 & Far Eastern Art in Minnesota Collections (exhib catalog), 70, Univ Minn Gallery; Hanga, The Modern Japanese Print (exhib catalog), Minn Mus Art, St Paul, 72. *Pos:* Consult Asian art, Minneapolis Inst Art, formerly; cur Asian art, Minn Mus Art, St Paul, formerly. *Teaching:* Asst prof Asian art, Dartmouth Col, 61-65; from assoc prof Asian art to prof art hist, Univ Minn, Minneapolis, 65-. *Res:* Chinese bronzes. *Publ:* Auth, Notes on the Sung archaeological catalogs, 65 & auth, Some remarkable examples of I-Hsing ware, 66-67, Arch of Chinese Art Soc Am; auth, Ancient Chinese Bronzes, Inter-Cult Arts Press, 68; auth, Evolution of a secular vesseltype, 68 & On the Mo-tzu-Yu, 70, Oriental Art. *Mailing Add:* Dept Art Hist Univ Minn 338 Management & Economics 271 19th Ave S Minneapolis MN 55455

POPE, MARY ANN IRWIN
PAINTER
b Louisville, Ky, Mar 8, 1932. *Study:* Art Ctr, Louisville; Univ Louisville; Cooper Union. *Work:* Mint Mus, Charlotte, NC; Huntsville Mus Art; Fine Arts Mus S, Mobile, Ala; Zerox; McGraw Hill; Springfield Mus Art, Mo; Tenn Valley Authority; Southern Progress Corp. *Comn:* Boy Scouts Am; Kaiser, Atlanta, Ga; and numerous pvt commissions. *Exhib:* Watercolor USA, 82-83, 87-89, 2003-04, 2007-9, 2012; Birmingham Biennial, 83 & 85; Art Quest, 85; Nat Biennial Invitational, Watercolor USA, 89; Voices Rising, Nat Mus Women Arts, 2000; Adirondacks Nat Exhib Am Watercolors, 2002, 2011; Butler Inst Am Art, 2005; Nat Watercolor Soc, 2006, 2008-9; Nat Art Mus, Tokyo, Japan, 2010; Watercolor Now, 2003, 2008, 2011, 2012; Watercolor Soc Ala, 2012. *Awards:* Gallery Award, Grand Nat Exhib, Miss Mus Art, 98; Merit Award, Exhib S, 95 & 98; Watercolor USA, 89, Greg C. Thielen Award, 2004; Philadelphia Award, Nat Watercolor Soc, 2006; SW Mo Mus Award, 2008; M Graham Award, Southern Watercolor Soc Exhib, 2008; Energen Landscape Award, 2009; Signature Award, Watercolor Society of Alabama Nat Exhib, 2011; Signature award, Ala Watercolor Soc, 2001, 2012; Purchase award, Watercolor USA, 2012. *Bibliog:* Patricia Seligman (auth), Painting Skies; Ruth Appelhof (auth) Voices Rising (catalog), 2000; Splash 7, 2002 & Splash 8, 2004, Northlight Publ; Master Painters of the World, US Showcase, Int Artist; Int Artist Mag, 6-7/2004, Apr/May 2008; Watercolor Mag, winter/2007; Water Works, Watercolor Artist, 2012. *Mem:* Kentucky Watercolor Soc; Ala Watercolor Soc; Nat Honor Soc-Watercolor USA; Nat Watercolor Soc; S Watercolor Soc; Ga Watercolor Soc. *Media:* Oil, Watercolor. *Specialty:* Contemp Art. *Interests:* Conservation. *Dealer:* Corporate Art Source Montgomery AL; Artistic Images Huntsville Ala; Dragonfly Gallery Fayetteville TN; Artistic Images Huntsville Al. *Mailing Add:* 1705 Greenwyche Rd SE Huntsville AL 35801

POPE, WILLIAM L
CONCEPTUAL ARTIST
b Newark, NJ, 1955. *Study:* Pratt Inst, Brooklyn, NY, 1973-75; Montclair State Coll, BA, NJ, 1978; Whitney Mus Independent Studio Prog, New York, 1977-78; Rutgers Univ, Mason Gross Sch Visual Arts, NJ, MFA, 1981; Skowhegan Sch Painting & Sculpture, Skowhegan, Maine, 1996. *Exhib:* Solo exhibs include Hallwalls Contemp Arts Ctr, Buffalo, NY, 1993, Horodner Romely Gallery, New York, 1994, Franklin Furnace, New York, 1995, Touchstone Theater, Bethlehem, Pa, 1996, The Project, New York, 1998, 2001, 2002, Univ Art Mus, Univ Albany, NY, 2004, Artists Space, 2004, North Adams, Mass, 2004, Cleveland Inst Art, Ohio, 2005, Art Inst Chicago, 2007; Group exhibs include Exquisite Corpse, Drawing Ctr, New York, 1993; Ed Art, Artist Space, New York, 2005; Available Culture, Here Art Gallery, New York, 1997; Freedom, Liberation & Change, Bronx Council, New York, 1998; Pix, Lance Fung Gallery, New York, 2000; Art & Outrage, Robert Miller Gallery, New York, 2002; The Big Nothing, Inst Contemp Arts, Philadelphia, 2004; Watch What We Say, Schroeder Romero, Brooklyn, NY, 2004; Plug, Sister, Los Angeles, 2007; Retail Value, Dorsky Gallery, Long Island City, New York, 2008. *Awards:* Art Matters Grant, 1990 & 1993; Franklin Furnace/Jerome Found Art Grant, 1992; Solo Performance Fel, NEA, 1993, Individual Collaborative Fel, 1994, Visual Art Fel, 1995; Maine Arts Comn Fel, 1994 & 1999; Tanne Found Fel, 2000; Creative Capital Found Grant, 2001; Andy Warhol Found Grant, 2001; Japan-US Friendship Commission Fel, 2001; Found Contemp Performance Art Grant, 2002; Rockefeller Found Grant, 2003; Guggenheim Fel, 2004; USA Rockefeller Fel, 2006; Louis Comfort Tiffany Found Grant, 2008

POPLAWSKA, ANNA
EDUCATOR, CRITIC
Teaching: teacher, in field. *Mem:* Chicago Art Critics Asn. *Publ:* Contribr to monthly art columns in the following publs: Footlights Playbill, Yoga Chicago, Wednesday Jour of Oak Park; freelancer Chicago Artist's News

POPOVAC, GWYNN
PAINTER, SCULPTOR
b Wilmington, Del, Dec 1, 1948. *Study:* Univ Calif, Los Angeles, Eng lit, honors, 66-71. *Work:* Detroit Med Hosp. *Comn:* Mask for Kabuki play, The Dream of Kitamura, Sierra Repertory Theatre, 92. *Exhib:* Behind the Disguise, Olive Hyde, Fremont City Gallery, Calif, 89; The Art of the Mask, Hearst Gallery, Moraga, Calif, 91; Habitat masks & hexapods, Wellspring Gallery, Santa Monica, 94; Chicago Sch Fine Arts. *Bibliog:* Liz Winter (auth), Behind the disguise, Monitor, Fremont, Calif, 10/25/89; Gary Linehan (auth), Working in the bugs, Union Democrat, Sonora, Calif, 4/3/92; Ann Batchelder (ed & auth), Swatches, Fiberarts, 94. *Media:* Mixed Media, Oil, Fibers. *Publ:* Auth, Ripe plums, Ms Mag, 7/84; Wet Paint, Houghton Mifflin & Ballantine, 86; illusr, Wet Paint (dust jacket for hardback ed), Houghton Mifflin & Ballantine, 86; auth & artist, Conversations with Bugs (Writing J & calendar), Pomegranate, 93; Limited Editions-Insect Series, Apple Jack, 96. *Dealer:* Vault Gallery 42 S Washington Sonora CA 95370; Anderson Gallery 7 N Saginaw Pontiac MI 48342. *Mailing Add:* 17270 Robin Ridge Sonora CA 95370

PORGES, MARIA FRANZISKA
SCULPTOR, PRINTMAKER
b Oakland, Calif, 1954. *Study:* Yale Univ, BA, 75; Univ Chicago, Ill, MFA; studied with Bob Peters. *Work:* Mus of Modern Art, San Francisco, Calif; Scottsdale Mus of Art, Ariz; di Rosa Found; Phillip Morris Collection; Oakland Mus of Calif; Berkeley Art Mus. *Comn:* 6 pieces, CalPERS HQ, 2006. *Exhib:* Albuquerque Mus Art, NMex, 2000; Palo Alto Art Ctr, Calif; Pratt Inst, Brooklyn, NY; Midway Gallery, Chicago, Ill; John Berggruen Gallery, San Francisco; Solo exhib, James Harris Gallery, Seattle, Wash, 2001, David Beitzel Gallery, New York City, Mus of Modern Art, San Francisco, Calif, Sheppard Art Gallery, Univ Nev, Reno. *Teaching:* instr, Stanford Univ, currently; instr, Univ Calif, Berkeley; adj prof, Calif Col Arts, San Francisco, currently. *Awards:* SECA Award, Mus Modern Art, San Francisco, Calif; Individual Artists Grant, Calif Arts Coun, 90; John McCarron Criticism Grant, San Francisco Artspace, Calif. *Mem:* AICA; Coll Art Asn. *Media:* Wax, Bronze & Paper. *Dealer:* John Berggruen Gallery San Francisco. *Mailing Add:* 5174 Trask St Oakland CA 94601

PORTA, SIENA GILLANN
SCULPTOR, PAINTER
b New York, NY, Nov 5, 1951. *Study:* Art Students League, 69-70; Brooklyn Coll, NY, BS (studio arts), 77; Pa State Univ, MFA (sculpture) 79; Studied with Lee Bonticu, Philip Pearlstein. *Work:* Fulbright Comn, Reykjavik, Iceland; Hafnarborg Mus, Iceland; Robert L Yaeger Health Ctr, Pomona, NY; Jacob Riis Nat Park, Ft Tilden, NY; Brisons Veor Trust, Cornwall, Eng; Hveragerdi Municipality, Iceland; Univ Iceland; Agric Coll, 2012. *Comn:* Co Rockland, NY; St Philip Church, Norwalk, Conn. *Exhib:* Solo exhibs, Dominican Coll, Blauvelt, NY, 80 & Mari Galleries, Ltd, Mamaroneck, NY, 85, 14 Sculptors Gallery, 85, 87 & 90, Mid Hudson Arts & Sci Ctr, Poughkeepsie, NY, 92-93, Noho Gallery, NY, 2003, 2005 & 2008; group exhibs, A B Condon Gallery, NY, 82-83; 14 Sculptors Gallery, 82-83; Notre Dame Univ, 90; Lehigh Univ, 92; Blue Hill Cult Ctr, Pearl River, NY, 95; NJ City Univ, 98; Nassau Community Col, NY, 98; Adelphi Univ, 2000; St Thomas Aquinas Coll, 2000; Ramapo Coll, Kresge & Pascal Gallery, NJ, 2001, 2009; Hafnarborg Mus, Iceland, 2002-2003; Snaeflsnes Reg Mus, 2002-2003; McLevy Green, Bridgeport, Conn, 2005; Sculpture at Lockwood Mathews Mansion Mus, Norwalk Conn, 2006; NJ City Univ, Jersey City, 2007-2012; Planet in Crisis, Azanian- McCullough, St Thomas Aquinas Coll, Sparkill, NY, 2008; Salem Art Park, Albany, NY, 2009-; Gov Island, 2011;

Edward Williams Gallery, Fairleigh Dickenson Univ, Teaneck, NJ, 2012; Art Ctr of Northeastern NJ, Milford, NJ, 2012; Arthur Berger Gallery, Manhattanville Coll, Purchase, NY, 2013; City of NY Parks & Recreation, Highbridge Park, Manhattan, NY, 2014. *Pos:* Scenic artist, Metrop Opera, New York, 87-92 & numerous broadway shows, 92-; vpres, 14 Sculptors Gallery, 87-89, pres, 89-91; cult comt co-chair, Partners Americas, Rockland Co, NY, 92-97. *Teaching:* Adj prof, Bergen Community Coll, Paramus, NJ, 84-85, St Thomas Aquinas Coll, Sparkill, NY, 2000-2009, Ramapo Coll, Mahwah, NJ, 2001-2013. *Awards:* NY State Coun Arts Grant, 86; NYFA, decentralization grantee, 86 & 2002; USIA Grantee, Partners of the Americas, 92; Artist-in-Residence, Brisons Veor, Cape Cornwall, England, 2003; Visiting Artist, Fritz Eager Found, New Canaan, Conn; Artist in residence, Varmahlid Haus, Hveragerdi, Iceland, 2010. *Bibliog:* Aspects of the Arts, Siena Porta, Sculptor (video), TKR Channel 30, 91; Broadcast, TKR Channel 30, 91; Vivien Raynor (auth), NY Times, 7/16/95; Oscar Corall (auth), Newsday, 4/2000; Ed McCormack (auth), Gallery & Studio, 10/2005. *Mem:* Coll Art Asn; Art/Science Collab, Staten Island, NY; Mem, Zen Ctr San Diego, 87-2006 & Prescott Zen Ctr, Ariz, 2006-2010. *Media:* Mixed Media, Acrylics. *Specialty:* contemporary sculpture, outdoor installations. *Interests:* shukokai karate. *Publ:* Illusr, Southern Ocean Atlas, Columbia Univ Press, 82; auth, Spray metal (article), Marquette Mag, Int Sculpture Soc, Washington, 94; Gallery & Studio (rev), 9/03. *Dealer:* 14 Sculptors Inc 168 Mercer St New York NY 10012. *Mailing Add:* PO Box 46 Palisades NY 10964

PORTER, JEANNE CHENAULT
EDUCATOR, HISTORIAN
b New York, NY, Mar 18, 1944. *Study:* Barnard Col, Columbia Univ, BA, 65; Univ Mich, Ann Arbor, MA, 66 & PhD(Ford Found Graduate Fel & Fulbright Grant), 71; Univ Florence, Rome & Ghent (Belgian Govt Grant). *Collection Arranged:* Bradley Tomlin: A Retrospective View, traveling exhib (auth, catalog), Hofstra Univ, 75-76; Bradley W Tomlin, City Univ NY. *Teaching:* Assoc prof, Finch Col, New York, 72-74 & Pa State Univ, 74-. *Awards:* Fulbright Grant to Rome, 68-69; Belgian Govt Grant, 68. *Mem:* Coll Art Asn Am. *Res:* Abstract Expressionism (American), and Spanish, French and Italian Baroque Painting. *Publ:* Auth, Bradley Walker Tomlin: Early paintings & intimations, Archives Am Art J, 74; Bradley Walker Tomlin: A painter's painter, Arts Mag, 75; Painting and Sculpture in the Samuel Gallu Collection (catalog), 80 & Works on Paper: Henry Varnum Poor (catalog), 83, Pa State Press; Tomlin (catalog), Munson-Williams-Proctor Inst, Utica, NY, 89; contribr, Munson-Williams-Proctor Inst (catalog), Baroque Publ

PORTER, KATHERINE PAVLIS
PAINTER, EDUCATOR
b Cedar Rapids, Iowa, 1941. *Study:* Boston Univ, 62; Colo Col, BA, 63; Colby Col, LHD, 82; Bowdoin Col, LHD, 92. *Work:* Metrop Mus Art, Mus Mod Art, Whitney Mus Am Art, Guggenheim Mus, New Mus Contemp Art, NY. *Exhib:* Collaboration, Inst Contemp Art, Boston, 69; Annual, Whitney Mus Am Art, NY, 69; Katherine Porter: Works on Paper, Fine Arts Mus San Francisco, 80; Recent Acquisitions, Mus Mod Art, NY, 83; I am an Am Drawings, Cape Split Pace Gallery, Addison, Maine, 84; Contemp Drawings from the Last Three Decades, Mus Mod Art, NY, 85; 1988 Invitational, New Britain Mus Am Art, 88; On the Edge, Portland Mus, Maine, 93; and many others. *Collection Arranged:* Painting Self-Evident, Picolo Spoleto Festival, 92. *Teaching:* Instr, Stanford Univ, Columbia Univ & Sch Visual Arts, Tyler. *Bibliog:* Peter Frank (auth), Rev, Art News, 2/76; Stacey Moss (auth), Rev, Art in Am, 6/76; William Zimmer (auth), Airing out the grid, SoHo News, 8/78; and others. *Dealer:* Les Yeux de Monde 841 Wolf Trap Rd Charlottesville VA 22911; Salander O'Reilly 79th St New York NY

PORTER, LILIANA
VISUAL ARTIST
b Buenos Aires, Arg, Oct 6, 1941; US citizen. *Study:* Nat Sch Fine Arts, Buenos Aires; printmaking, Iberoamericana Univ & La Ciudadela, Mexico City. *Work:* Mus Mod Art & Metrop Mus Art, NY; Mus Fine Arts, Philadelphia; Mus de Bellas Artes, Buenos Aires, Arg, Caracas, Venezuela & Santiago, Chile; La Bibliot Nat, Paris; Hunter Mus Art, Chattanooga, Tenn; Bronx Mus, NY; Tate Modern, London, Eng; NY Public Libr, NY; Museo de Arte Moderno, Buenos Aires, Argentina; plus many others. *Comn:* Alice; The Way Out, 4 Mosaic Murals, MTA Subway Line 1-9, 50th station, New York City; Untitled with Rabbit, Mural, three dimensional installations; The Traveler, glass mosaic mural, Domenech Train Station, San Juan, Puerto Rico, 2003; Situations with Them, (permanent installation mural), PS/IS 210, NY, 2007; Alice Goes Back, (8'x 28' mosaic mural), One Miami River Walk, 2005; Further Away, (permanent installation, porcelain figurine, mirror, metal and glass box on elevator shaft), Belmar Complex, Denver, Colo, 2003; El Viajero/The Travelor, (1700 sq. ft, glass mosaic mural), Domenech Station, Tren Urbano, San Juan, Puerto Rico, 2004; 6 faceted glass, windows, & 3 scultprues, MTA, Scarborough Train Station, 2010. *Exhib:* Solo Exhibs: Mus Mod Art, NY, 73; Weatherspoon Art Gallery, Univ NC, Greensboro, 91; Inst de Cult, San Juan, PR, 91; Bronx Mus Arts, NY, 92; Archer M Huntington Art Gallery, Univ Tex, Austin, 93; Steinbaum Krauss Gallery, NY, 93; Gallery Contemp Art, Sacred Heart Univ, Fairfield, Conn, 94; Galleria Valentina Bonomo, Rome, Italy, 2007; Hosfelt Gallery, NY, 2007; Barbara Krakow Gallery, Boston, Mass, 2008; Leo Fortuna Gallery, Hudson, NY, 2008; Brito Cimino, Sao Paulo, Brazil, 2008, Hosfelt Gallery, NYC, 2011, Luciana Brito Galeria, S. Paulo, Brazil, Lucia de la Puente, Lima, Peru, 2011, Espacio Minimo, Madrid, Spain, 2011, Fragment of the Cast, Sicanti Gallery, Houston, Tex, 2012, Barbara Krakow Gallery, Boston, Mass, 2012, The Task, Carrie Secrist Gallery, Chicago, Ill, 2012, Recent Works, Baginski Gallery, Lisbon, Portugal, 2012, Centro Cultural di Espana in Santiago de Chile, 2012; A Retrospective of Graphic Art 1968-1993, Reading Pub Mus, Pa, 93; Reclaiming Hist, El Mus del Barrio, NY, 93; El desdoblamiento, el simulacro y el reflejo, Inst de Cooperacion Iberoamericana, Buenos Aires, Argentina, 94; Toys/Art/Us, Castle Gallery, Coll New Rochelle, NY, 94; Art & the New Novel, Arnot Art Mus, Elmira, NY, 94; Latin Am Women Artists 1915-1995 (traveling), Milwaukee Art Mus, 95; Poetry in Paradox, Univ Art Gallery, NMex State Univ; Monique Knowlton, 96; Group Exhibs: Perspectivas de género y políticas de representación, Centro Cultural de España en Montevideo, Uruguay, 2006; Outside the Box, Hosfelt Gallery, San Francisco, Calif, 2006; Contemp Cool and Collected, Mint Mus Art, Charlotte, NC, 2007; Beginning with a Bang! From Confrontation to Intimacy: An Exhibit of Argentine Contemp Artists 1960/1970, Am Society, NY, 2007; Bienal Do Mercosul, Porto Alegre, Brazil (Conversas), 2007, Casas Riegner Gallery, Bogota, Columbia, Alice in Wonderland, Tate, Liverpool, 2011. *Pos:* Co-dir, Studio Porter-Wiener, 79-. *Teaching:* Instr etching, NY Graphic Workshop, 65-68; adj lectr graphics, State Univ NY, Purchase, 87; instr, printmaking workshop, NY, 88; prof, Art Dept, Queens Col, NY, 91-2007 (retired). *Awards:* Travel Grant, Nat Endowment Arts Int, 94; Regional Fel, Nat Endowment Arts Mid Atlantic, 94; NY Found Arts Grant, 96; Film Fel, NY Found Arts, 99; Civitella Ranieri Found Fel, (Artist in residence), Umbertide, Italy, 99; PSC-CUNY Research Award (Visual arts-digital prints award), 2006; Premio Aldo Pellegrini, Artista del año, Asociatión Argentina de Críticos de Arte, Buenos Aires, 2004; Premio Konex, Buenos Aires, Argentina, 2002; Academica Coorespondent for Argentina, 2003. *Bibliog:* James Collins (auth), articles in Artforum, 73 & Arts Mag, 5/77. *Media:* Video, photography. *Specialty:* Visual arts. *Interests:* Visual art, theater. *Publ:* Contribr, Wrinkle, 68, Nail, 73 & String, 73, New York Graphic Workshop; For You (16 mm film), 99; Drum Solo (19 minute video), 2000; Fox in the Mirror (20 minute digital video), NY, 2007; 20 min video, Matinee, 2009. *Dealer:* Hosfelt Gallery San Francisco CA; Sicardi Gallery Houston TX; Ruth Benzacar Gallery Buenos Aires Argentina; Barbara Krakow Gallery Boston Mass; Galeria Luciana Brito Sao Paolo Brazil; Galeria Espacio Minimo Madrid Spain. *Mailing Add:* 720 Greenwich St 10G New York NY 10014

PORTER, RICHARD JAMES
HISTORIAN, COLLECTOR
b Bellefonte, Pa, Jan 2, 1950. *Study:* Pa State Univ, BA, 71, MA, 73, PhD, 83. *Collection Arranged:* Sidney Goodman: Paintings, Drawings & Graphics 1959-1979 (coauth, catalog), Mus Art, Pa State Univ, Queens Mus, Columbus Mus Art & Del Art Mus, 80-81; Henry Varnum Poor (coauth, catalog), Mus Art, Pa State Univ, Burchfield Ctr, Everson Mus & Nat Acad Design, 83-84. *Pos:* Registrar & cur Am art, Mus Art, Pa State Univ, Pa 78-85; dir, Joe & Emily Lowe Art Gallery, 85-86; chmn, Grad prog in Mus Studies, Syracuse Univ, 85-86; sales assoc, Villager Realty, 86-87 & Assoc Realty, 87-90; assoc broker, Assoc Realty, 90-92; broker/partner ReMax Ctr Realty, 92; dir, Wally Findlay Galleries, 2005-2007, retired. *Teaching:* Instr art hist, Middle Tenn State Univ, 73-76; adj assoc prof art hist, Juniata Coll, 84; chair, Grad Program in Mus Studies, Syracuse Univ, 85-86. *Mem:* National Arts Club, NYC; English Speaking Union of NY; Saint Andrew's Soc of the State of New York (bd dirs, 2013-). *Res:* American and European art, 17th century to present, particularly American & French 18th-20th centuries. *Collection:* American art: 19th century to contemporary. *Publ:* Auth, A newly discovered painting by Ammi Phillips, Conn Hist Soc Bull, 79; Introduction, selected works from the collection of Samuel Gallu, Pa State Univ, 80; Jerome Witkin, A Decade of Work (exhib catalog), 82; Henry Varnum Poor, 1887-1970 (exhib catalog), 83; The oil paintings of Henry Varnum Poor, Arts Mag, 85; Henry Varnum Poor (exhib catalog), James Grahan Jans, 2004. *Mailing Add:* 308 E 79th St Apt 9J New York NY 10021

PORTMAN, JOHN C, JR
ARCHITECT, COLLECTOR
b Walhalla, SC, Dec 4, 1924. *Study:* Us Naval Acad, Midshipman, 44; Ga Inst Tech, BS in Archit, 50; Ga Inst Tech, DFA, 93; Emory Univ, DFA, 93; Atlanta Coll Art, DFA, 93. *Hon Degrees:* Hon Dr Philosophy, Ga Inst Tech, 2012; Hon Dr Economic Develop & Urban Policy, Ga State Univ, 2008. *Work:* Prin works incl: Beijing Yintai Ctr, China, Bund Ctr, Shanghai, Shanghai Ctr, Tomorrow Square JW Marriot, Shanghai, Indian Sch Bus, Hyderabad, India, Taj Wellington Mews, Mumbai, India, Capital Square, Kuala Lumpur, Malaysia, Westin Warsaw, Poland, The Regent Hotel, Marina Sq, both Singapore, Embarcadero Ctr, San Francisco, The Pan Pacific-San Francisco, San Francisco Fashion Ctr, Hyatt Regency O'Hare Hotel, Chicago, Peachtree Ctr, Atlanta, SunTrust Plaza, Atlanta; George W Woodruff Physical Educ Ctr, R Howard Dobbs Student Ctr, both Emory Univ, Atlanta, Atlanta Merchandise Mart, Atlanta Apparel Mart, Atlanta Decorative Arts Ctr, Atlanta Gift Mart, Inforum, One Peachtree Ctr, Kennedy Community Ctr and Middle Sch, Hyatt Regency Hotel, Westin Peachtree Plaza Hotel, Atlanta Marriott Marquis, Northpark Town Ctr, Riverwood, Greenbriar Shopping Ctr, Olympic Village Housing, all Atlanta, Blue Cross-Blue Shield Bldg, Chattanooga, Ft Worth Nat Bank Bldg and Garage, Brussels Int Trade Mart, Dana Fine Arts Bldg at Agnes Scott Col, Decatur, Ga, Renaissance Ctr, Detroit, Bonaventure Hotel, Los Angeles, NY Marriott Marquis, Rockefeller Ctr renovation, New York, Dream Lake Villas, Hangzhou Qiantang River City, Shandong Bldg, Guomai Bldg, BAODA Bldg, Senfuli Building, S Renzhill Complex, Peoples Republic of China. *Exhib:* A Retrospective Exhib, SunTrust Plaza, Atlanta, 99; Recent Accessions 1997-1998, Nat Acad Design, New York, 99; 178th Ann Exhib, Nat Acad Design, New York, 2003; Up, Down, Across: Elevators, Escalators & Moving Sidewalks, Nat Bldg Mus, Washington, DC, 2003-2004; John Portman: Art & Architecture, Atlanta High Mus of Art, 2009-2010; Shanghai Urban Planning Exhib Ctr, 2010; Beijing Capital Mus, 2011. *Pos:* Individual practice, 53-56; partner, Edwards and Portman (Archit), 56-68; princ, John Portman and Assocs, 68-; chmn, Chief Exec Officer, The Portman Cos., Atlanta, 71-; bd dir, Nations Bank; pres Cent Atlanta Progress, 70-72; bd dir, Aaron Rents, Inc, 2006-. *Awards:* Named Outstanding Young Man of Yr, Ga Junior CofC, 59; Silver medal for innovative design Ga chap Am Inst of Archit, 81; Atlanta Downtown Partnership's Resurgens award, Design of Peachtree Plaza; Award of Excellence, The Atlanta Urban Design Comn, 2006; Bldg of the Decade, 1956-1965, Peachtree Ctr, 1966-1975, Atlanta Hyatt Regency, AIA Atlanta 100 Years Atlanta Archit, 2006; and many others. *Bibliog:* The Master Architect Series VI, John Portman & Associates, Selected & Current Works, Images Publ, Australia, 2002 ; and many others. *Mem:* Fel Am Inst of Archits; Nat Coun Archit Registration Bd; Am Inst Interior Designers; Soc Int Bus Fel; World Trade Club (founding); Nat Acad. *Media:* Acrylic, Oil, Clay, Fabricated Elements. *Interests:* Archit, art, painting, sculpture, furniture, lighting design; travel & reading. *Publ:*

Co-auth, The Archit as Developer, 90; co-auth, John Portman, L'Arcaedizioni, Milan, 90; co-auth, John Portman: An Island on an Island, L'Arcaedizioni, Milan, 98; John Portman Art & Architecture, Univ Ga Press, 2009; John Portman: Form, Philip Jann Press, 2009. *Mailing Add:* 303 Peachtree Ctr Ave, NE Ste 575 Atlanta GA 30303

PORTNOW, MARJORIE ANNE
PAINTER
b New York, NY, Sept 30, 1942. *Study:* Western Reserve Univ, with Dr Sherman E Lee, BA (art hist), 64; Skowhegan Sch Painting, with Lenart Anderson, A Leslie & A Katz, 65; Brooklyn Col, with P Pearlstein & G Laderman, MFA (painting), 72. *Hon Degrees:* Nat Acad (National Acadamicicum From Member national Acad of Design). *Work:* Metrop Mus Art, Chase Manhattan Bank, New York, NY; Albany Inst Art, NY; Gibbs Mus, SC; Middlebury Coll Mus; Sheldon Art Mus, Lincoln, Nebr; and others. *Exhib:* Am Acad & Inst Arts & Lett, NY, 80, 90, 92, 94 & 96; Recent Developments in Am Landscape, Whitney Mus, Stamford, Conn; Graham Gund Collection, Mus Fine Arts Boston, 82; The Ital Tradition on Contemp Landscape Painting, Gibbs Mus, Charleston, SC; The Landscape in 20th Century Am Art: Selections from the Metrop Mus Art, 91; Rediscovering the Landscape of the Americas, Gerald Peters Gallery, Santa Fe; A Century, Painters and Sculptors at MacDowell Colony, Currier Gallery; Green Woods and Crystal Waters: The Am Landscape Tradition Since 1950, Philbrook Mus Art, 99; Peter Rose Gallery, New York City, 2003; Hollins Univ 2000; Oxbow Gallery, 2005. *Pos:* Fac, NY Studio Sch, 94-95 & Pa Acad Fine Arts, 95-2003; Western Conn State Univ, Fac, 2003-2006; Fine Arts Work Ctr, Provincetown, MA,. *Teaching:* Fac, Vt Studio Sch, 87-2000, Univ Pa (Grad Sch), 88-91, Pa Acad Art, 88-91 & 94-2000, Skowhegan Sch, 89, Univ Calif, Santa Cruz, 92-93, & NY Studio Sch, 95. *Awards:* Bunting Fel, Radcliff, 70-72; Louis Comfort Tiffany Found Grant, 72 & 78; Nat Endowment Arts Grant, 80 & 94; NY Found Arts Award, 86; Hassam Purchase Prize, Am Acad & Inst Arts & Lett, 90 & 94-95. *Bibliog:* R Milazzo (auth), Realism After 7PM-Realist Painting After E Hopper, 90; A Gussow (auth), The Artist as Native, Babcock, 93 & Rediscovering the Landscape of the Americas, 96; R S Torr & T Wolf (auths), Community of Creativity: A Century of MacDowell Artists, 96; The American Landscape Tradition Since, 1950; Greenwoods and Crystal Waters, John Author. *Mem:* NY Artists Equity Asn; Nat Acad. *Media:* Oil. *Specialty:* Contemporary oil Paintings. *Dealer:* Contemp Realist Gallery San Francisco CA; Fischbach Gallery 29 W 57th St New York NY 10019; Grigr Clark Gallery, Burlington, UT; Julie Heller Gallery, Provincetown, MA. *Mailing Add:* 67 Vestry St New York NY 10013

PORTNOY, THEODORA PREISS
DEALER
b New York, NY. *Study:* Manhattanville Col; Sarah Lawrence Col, BA. *Pos:* dir, Theo Portnoy Gallery, formerly, bd mem, currently; bd dir, Cornell Art Mus; chmn acquisitions, Rollin's Col. *Specialty:* Sculpture with emphasis on work that has evolved from craft media, clay, glass, wood and forged steel

POSKAS, PETER EDWARD
PAINTER
b Waterbury, Conn, Oct 29, 1939. *Study:* Univ Conn, 57-60; Paier Sch Art, 60-62; Univ Hartford, BS, 62-65. *Work:* Mint Mus, Charlotte, NC; Gen Foods Corp, White Plains, NY; FMC Corp, Chicago; Raht-West Mus, Wis; Frye Mus, Wash. *Comn:* Landscape, Metropolitan Life, NY, 89. *Exhib:* Solo exhibs, Mazur Mus, Monroe, La, 72, Mattatuck Mus, Waterbury, Conn, 74 & Hunter Mus Art, Chattanooga, Tenn, 84; Hassam Speicher, Am Acad & Inst Arts & Lett, NY, 77; Butler Inst, Youngstown, Ohio, 77; Artists of Am, Colo Heritage Ctr, Denver, 82-83; The Conn View, P P William Benton Mus Art, Storrs, Conn, 84; The Recognizable Image, Bruce Mus, Greenwich, Conn, 85; Acts of Season, Southern Alleghenies Mus Art, Loretto, Pa, 86; Brigham-Young Mus, Provo, Utah, 97. *Bibliog:* John Arthur (auth), Peter Poskas, Arts Mag, 83; Theodore Wolf (auth), Mondrian would have liked it, Christian Sci Monitor, 84; Michael Brenson (auth), Peter Poskas, NY Times, 84. *Media:* Oil. *Publ:* Coauth, Peter Poskas, Watson-Guptill, 87 & 92. *Dealer:* Spanierman Gallery 45 E 58th St New York NY. *Mailing Add:* Nettleton Hollow Rd Washington CT 06793

POSLITUR, INGA
PAINTER, ILLUSTRATOR
b Sochi, Russia; US citizen. *Study:* Sch Acad Fine Arts, Russia, 1978-1985; Acad Applied & Fine Arts, BA, 1986-1989; Fashion Inst Technol, AAS (gen illus), 1992-1996, BFA (gen illus), 2009; Univ Hartford, MFA (illus), 2012. *Exhib:* Catherine Lorillard Wolfe Group Show, Water Mill Mus, Water Mill, NY, 2006; TWSA, Nat Watercolor Competition, San Pedro, Calif, 2006; A Family Is, North West Cult Coun, Kent, NY, 2006; 30th Int Exhib, North East Watercolor Soc, 2006; Free Play, Islip Art Mus, East Islip, NY, 2007; Small Matters of Great Importance, Hopper House Art Center, Nyack, NY, 2007; The Best in Watermedia, Brother Kenneth Chapman Gallery, Iona College, NY, 2007; Audubon Artists 65th Ann Exhib, Salmagundi Club, NY, 2007; Contemporary Illustration, Grace Inst, NY, 2011. *Teaching:* instr, Animation & Illus Dept, SJSU, Calif. *Awards:* Best in Show, Being & Self, Afif Gallery, Pa, 2005; Fourth Place, A Family Is, North West Cult Coun, 2006; Aileen & Manuel de Torres Award, Allied Artists of Am 96th ann exhib, 2009; Allied Artsits of Am Merit Award, Audubon Artists 67th Group Show, New York, 2009; SUNY Chancellor's Award for Student Excellence, Albany, NY, 2009. *Bibliog:* Don Evans (auth), Atlantic Avenue Art Work, Brooklyn Daily Eagle, 6/4/2006. *Mem:* Audubon Artists Soc; Catherine Lorillard Wolfe Art Club; Soc of Illustrators NY. *Media:* Watercolor, Oil. *Publ:* Neighbor News, Mountain Lakes, NJ, 2006; Brooklyn Eagle, 2007; Creative Quarterly, 2009

POSNER, HELAINE J
GALLERY DIRECTOR, CURATOR
b New York, NY, Nov 17, 1953. *Study:* Georgetown Univ, BA (art hist), 1975; George Washington Univ, MA, 1978. *Collection Arranged:* Jasper Johns Prints: Three Themes (coauth, catalog), Whitney Mus Am Art, 1978; Selection from the Chase Manhattan Bank Art Collection (auth, catalog), 1981, Martin Puryear Sculpture (coauth, catalog), 1983 & Anish Kapoor, 1986, University Gallery, Univ Mass, Amherst. *Pos:* Cur asst to dir, Chase Manhattan Bank Art Prog, New York, 1978-81; cur, Univ Gallery, Univ Mass, Amherst, 1981-84 & dir, 1984-88; chief cur, Nat Mus of Women in the Arts, Washington, 1988-90; cur, List Visual Arts Ctr, MIT, 1991-98; dir exhibs, Int Ctr of Photography, formerly; co-commissioner, US Pavilion, Venice Biennale, 1999; adj cur, Am Fedn Arts, New York, 2003-08; chief cur & dep dir curatorial affairs, Neuberger Mus Art, State Univ NY, Purchase, 2008-. *Teaching:* Asst prof, dept art, Univ Mass, Amherst, 81-88, cur collections & educ, University Gallery, 81-84, dir, 84-88. *Mem:* Am Asn Mus; New Eng Mus Asn. *Res:* Modern and contemporary art. *Specialty:* Development of permanent collection of 20th century works on paper. *Publ:* Co-auth, Kiki Smith: Telling Tales, 2001; After the Revolution: Women Who Transformed Contemp Art, 2007. *Mailing Add:* Neuberger Mus Art Purchase Coll SUNY 735 Anderson Hill Rd Purchase NY 10577

POSNER, JUDITH L
DEALER, PUBLISHER
b Milwaukee, Wis, Sept 22, 1941. *Study:* Univ Wis, BFA. *Work:* Broward Co Libr - AGAM; Milw Exhbn/Conv Ctr-Arena Mecca. *Comn:* Bead Wall, Cantor Fitzgerald, New York. *Collection Arranged:* Tradewinds, Los Angeles, Calif; NWQ Corp, Los Angeles, Calif; Nuveen Financial; Boston Consulting; Christenson Miller. *Pos:* Dir & pres, Posner Fine Art, currently. *Teaching:* Instr, Comprehensive Employment & Training Act, Milwaukee, formerly. *Awards:* Hands That Svc, Mt Sinai Hosp, Milwaukee. *Bibliog:* Curtis Casewitt (auth), Making a Living in the Fine Arts, Macmillan. *Mem:* Indust Found Am Soc Interior Designers; Prof Tempo, Milwaukee Art Dealers Asn (past pres); Int Soc Appraisers; Picture Framers Asn; Woman in Hospitality NEWH Orgn; Siam Soc; Soroptimist Int of Dusit. *Specialty:* Nineteenth and Twentieth century American and European painting, sculpture and graphics and tribal art, Asian Accessories. *Interests:* Golf, Travel. *Publ:* Publisher of posters & prints. *Mailing Add:* 1212 S Point View St Los Angeles CA 90035

POST, ANNE B
SCULPTOR, GRAPHIC ARTIST
b St Louis, Mo. *Study:* Bennington Col, BA (fine arts); study with Simon Moselsio, Stephen Hirsch & Edwin Park; study in Europe. *Work:* Israel Mus, Jerusalem; Maison Francaise; Cooper Union Mus Gallery; Norfolk Mus; Va Bennington Visual Arts Mus; S Vermont Art Asn; Toledo Mus Art; St Louis Mus Art; Soc Independent Artists; JB Neuman Gallery. *Exhib:* St Louis Mus Art; Univ NJ Mus; benefit exhib, Acad Medicine, NY; Bennington Mus Art; Bennington Coll Visual Arts Mus; AIR Gallery, NY; and others. *Teaching:* Drawing & sculpture, Army Hosps, WVa, Tex, Mo & Settlement House, St Louis, 42-46. *Awards:* Represented Mo, Contemp Art Exhib, World's Fair, 39. *Bibliog:* Gunter Klotz (auth), Zcichnunsen und skulpturen der Anne Post, Klotz-Makowckie, 65. *Mem:* Artists Equity; Metrop Mus; Native Am Found. *Media:* Wood, Stone; Watercolor, Gouache. *Publ:* Am Art Today, 39. *Mailing Add:* 29 Washington Sq W New York NY 10011

POSTIGLIONE, COREY M
PAINTER, EDUCATOR, CRITIC
b Chicago, Ill, July 25, 1942. *Study:* Univ Ill, Circle Campus, BA; also with Martin Hurtig & Roland Ginzel; Sch Art Inst Chicago, MA (20th century Art Hist). *Exhib:* Solo exhibs, Evanston Art Ctr, Ill, 72, Mayer Kaplan JCC, Skokie, Ill, 73, Jan Cicero Gallery, Chicago, 76, 78, 83, 85, 95 & 97, Columbia Coll Gallery, Chicago, 81 & 97-98 & Passages, Oakton Community Col, 98; New Works on Paper, Jan Cicero Gallery, Chicago, 91; Labyrinth Series, Jan Cicero Gallery, Chicago, 93; Exquisite Corpse, Transmission Gallery, Glasgow, Scotland, 94; Lakeside Views, Evanston Art Ctr, 94; Blink (installation work) Northern Ill Univ Gallery, Chicago, 2000; Brad Cooper Gallery, Tampa, Fla, 2003; Hot Mix: John Phillips, 1979-2004, 2004; Travel Documents, 2006; Retrospective of Works on Paper 1972-2007, Evanston Art Ctr, Evanston, Ill, 2008. *Collection Arranged:* Art in Chicago, 96, 98, 2000 & 2002. *Pos:* Contribr ed, New Art Examiner, New Art Asn, 75-76; asst dir, Jan Cicero Gallery, Chicago, 77-84; contrib ed Dialogue, 89-2002, ArtForum, 2003. *Teaching:* Instr painting, Evanston Art Ctr, Ill, 71-79, Ill Inst Technol, 75-83, Columbia Col, Chicago, 79-89, Art Inst Chicago, 81-83 & Univ Ill, Chicago, summer 83; Art Inst Chicago, 81-; Instr art history and criticism, Columbia Col, Chicago, 90-, tenured prof, 96-, 2D design studio, 99-. *Awards:* 3rd Prize, Italian American Exhib; Merit Award Evanston and Vicinity Exhib, Ill. *Bibliog:* James Yood (auth), Chicago draws, New Art Examiner, 12/86; Michael Rooks (auth), article, New Art Examiner, 3/98; Esther Hammer (auth), article, Tampa Tribune, 11/2/2002; Michael Paglia (auth), Three Abstract Shows, Westwood Arts, 2012; Lauren Weinberg (auth), Re: Chicago, ARTnews, 2012. *Mem:* Chicago Art Critics Asn; Am Abstract Artists, NY. *Media:* Multimedia. *Publ:* Contribr, Dictionary of American Biography, Macmillan, 94. *Dealer:* Kathie Shaw Chicago IL; Brad Cooper Tampa FL; Thomas Masters Gallery Chicago IL; Space Gallery Denver Co. *Mailing Add:* 4508 N Monticello Chicago IL 60625

POTOTSCHNIK, JOHN MICHAEL
PAINTER, INSTRUCTOR
b St Ives, Cornwall, Eng, Nov 14, 1945; US citizen. *Study:* Wichita State Univ, BFA, 68; Art Ctr Coll Design, 69-71; Lyme Acad Fine Arts, 93. *Work:* Blue Cross Blue Shield, SC; City of McKinney, Tex; City of Carrollton, Tex; Kansas City Southern Railroad, Mo; Schlumberger, Tex; US Air Force, Washington, DC; Leggett & Platt, Mo; City of Murphy, Tex; Gold Bank, Kans; Cathedral Church of St Matthew, Dallas, Tex; Wichita Sedgwick Co Historical Mus; City of Wylie, Tex; De Bruce Gain Co, K.C., Mo; Emprise Financial Corp, Wichita, Kans; Wichita Ctr Arts, Wichita, Kans. *Exhib:* Am Art in Miniature, Thomas Gilcrease Mus, Tulsa, Okla, 93-94, 99-2001, 2004-2008; Miniatures, Albuquerque Mus, NMex, 93-2002; Oil Painters of Am Nat Show, 94, 96-97, 99 & 2001-2003 & 2007; Great Am Artists Exhib, Cincinnati, Ohio, 99-2005; Stewart Haley Mem Libr, 99-2006, 2008, 2010; Arts for the Parks, 2001-2003; Salon Int, San Antonio, Tex, 2004-2009; Nat Western Art Found, 2005-2007; Outdoor Painters Soc, 2006-2013; Oil Painters of America, 2009-2013;

Stewart Haley Libr, 2010-2013; C. M. Russell Mus, Great Falls, Mont, 2010-2013. *Pos:* Newsletter ed, Artists & Craftsman Assoc, 83-85, first vpres, 85-86, pres, 86-88. *Teaching:* Assoc prof art, Collin Co Community Coll, 94-; pvt lessons, 89-98. *Awards:* George Washington Honor Medal, Freedom's Found Valley Forge, 84, 86, 92 & 95; John Steven Jones Fel, Bosque Co Conservatory of Fine Arts, Roland & Joyce Jones, 92; Oil Painters of Am, 2001 & 2007; 1st Place, Landscape, Art Renewal Center, 1st Int Salon, 2004; Finalist, Midwest Gathering Artists Award, 94-95, 97-98, 2002; 3rd place, Int Artist Mag, 2009, Hon mention, 2001, 2003, finalist, 94, 95, 97, 98, 99, 2001, 2003. *Bibliog:* Peter Anderson (auth), Introductions, Southwest Art Mag, 87; Paul Soderberg (auth), Masters and Mentors, Plein Air Magazine, 2005; 100 Ways to Paint Landscapes, 100 Ways to Paint Flowers and Gardens & 100 Ways to Paint Seascapes, Rivers and Lakes, Int Artist Publ, 2004; Devon Jackson (auth), Everyday Realism, Southwest Art Mag, 2008; Diana Comer (auth), In a Perfect World, Country Life Mag, 2008; Michael Chesley Johnson (auth), The Artists Mag, 2009. *Mem:* Outdoor Painters Soc (sig mem); Oil Painters Am (sig mem); Art Renewal Ctr (assoc living master, 2013). *Media:* Oil. *Publ:* Contribr, Am Artist, BFI Communs, 90; The Artist's Mag, 8/94, 5 & 12/95, 4 & 6/96; 200 Great Painting Ideas for Artists, North Light Bks, 98; Int Artist, Oct/Nov 2000; Expressing the Visual Language of the Landscape, Int Artist Publ, 2002. *Dealer:* American Legacy Gallery 5911 Main St Kansas City MO; G Stanton Gallery 3412 Rosedale Dallas TX; Greenhouse Gallery of Fine Art 6496 N New Braunfels San Antonio TX; Rutledge Street Gallery 508 Rutledge St Camden SC; Southwest Gallery 4500 Sigma Dallas TX; Cherry's Art Gallery Carthage MO; Abend Gallery Fine Art Denver, Colo. *Mailing Add:* 6944 Taylor Ln Wylie TX 75098

POTRC, MARJETICA
ARCHITECT, PRINTMAKER
Exhib: Sao Paulo Biennial, Brazil, 1996, 2006; solo exhibs, Guggenheim Mus, New York, 2001, Galerie Nordenhake, Berlin, 2003, 2007, 2010, MIT List Visual Arts Ctr, Cambridge, 2004; Venice Biennial, Venice, Italy, 2003, 2009; Van Abbemus, Eindhoven, Neth, 2008; Smart Mus Art, Univ Chicago, 2009. *Awards:* Pollock-Krasner Found Grant, 1993, 1999; Hugo Boss Prize, Guggenheim Mus, 2000; Vera List Ctr for Arts & Politics Fel, New Sch, New York, 2007; Named one of 10 Most Imporant Artists of Today, Newsweek mag, 2001. *Bibliog:* Eleanor Heartney (auth), A House of Parts, Art in Am, 5/2004; Jennifer Higgie (auth), Form Follows Function, Frieze, 5/2006

POTTER, (GEORGE) KENNETH
PAINTER, PRINTMAKER
b Bakersfield, Calif, Feb 26, 1926. *Study:* Acad Art, San Francisco, 47 & 48; Acad Frochot, Paris, with Metzinger, 50-52; Inst Statale Belli Arte, Florence, Italy, summer 51; study in Sicily, 53; San Francisco State Univ, BA, 74, teaching credential San Francisco State Univ, 1976. *Work:* Admiral's Conference Room, USS Enterprise; Univ San Francisco Collection; City of San Francisco Art Comn; San Diego Mus Fine Art. *Comn:* Dome (stained glass & resin), Soc Calif Pioneers, Hale Mem Gallery, Civic Ctr, San Francisco, 74; triptych (stained glass & resin windows), Univ Calif, San Francisco, Moffitt Hosp, San Francisco, 76; hist mural (ink & acrylic on canvas), Corte Madera Recreation Ctr, Calif, 99; watercolors & prints, Embassy Suites Hotel, Sacramento; 100 Watercolors of Switz, for Robert Suter, Basel, Switz, 1991-2005. *Exhib:* Solo Exhibs: Brazilian-Am Inst, Rio de Janeiro, 1955; Univ Santa Clara, Calif, 1958; Univ Calif-Berkeley, 1959; Rosacrucian Mus, San Jose, Calif, 1959; Palo Alto Cultural Ctr, Calif, 77; Marin Civic Ctr Galleries, San Rafael, Calif, 85; Oakland Watercolor Ann, Oak Mus Art, Calif, 48, 52; Kingsley Ann, EB Crocker Art Mus, 48, Sacramento, Calif, 58, 61, 62, 64, 65; Phelan Awards Competition, San Francisco Mus Art, 49; Phelan Awards, Calif Palace of the Legion of Hon, San Francisco, Calif, 58, 60; Am Watercolor Soc, New York, 61, 74, 76, 79, 2003; AWS Nat Traveling Exhibs, 61, 76; Calif Watercolor Asn Open Ann, 2004-2009; Watercolor USA, Springfield, Mo, 73/74; Regional Watercolors 1930-1960, Calif Heritage Mus, Santa Monica, Calif, 2004; Cities of Promise, Orange Co Mus Art, Irvine, Calif, 2004; Modernist Watercolors of 1950's, Pasadena Mus Calif Art, 2006; Mother Lode Ann, Sonora, Calif, 57, 58, 65, 69; Soc of Western Artists, MD De Young Memorial Mus, San Francisco, Calif, 56-64; Marin Soc of Artists Ann, Ross, Calif, 48, 49, 58, 61, 65-73, 75, 95-98, 64-08; Marin Co Ann, San Rafael, Calif, 62, 65-67, 70, 71, 76; Invitationals exhibs, Springville, Utah Watercolor Invitational, 63; Fukuoka, Japan (with sister city, Oakland, Calif), 64; A City Buys Art, Calif Palace of the Legion of Hon, San Francisco, Calif, 67; Royal Watercolor Soc Exchange Traveling Show of West Coast, Watercolor Soc Shows, RWS Galleries, London & Leeds Mus of Art, England, etc, 75. *Pos:* Art dir, McCann-Erickson Inc Advert, Rio de Janeiro, 54-55, Johnson & Lewis Advert, San Francisco, 57 & Michelson Advert, Palo Alto, 59-60; artist demonstr, Grumbacher Inc, New York, 78-79. *Teaching:* Instr watercolor, Civic Art Ctr, Walnut Creek, Calif, 68-70, Acad Art, San Francisco, 70, San Francisco State Univ, 74 & 75 & Richmond Art Ctr, Calif, 78-79. *Awards:* Best of Show, Vacaville Art Festival, 2005, 2009 (printmaking), 1st prize (watercolor), 2009; Award of Excellence, Calif State Fair, 2006, Award of Merit, 2007, 2008, 2009; Best of Show, Magnum Opus Fine Arts Ctr, 2008, Award of Excellence, 2009; Best of Show, Watercolor Artists of Sacramento Horizons, Member's Show, 2008 ; Best of Show, Northern Calif Arts-members, 2008, First place, 2009; Kay Boron Mem Award, Calif State Fair, 2008; Non-Purchase (printmaking/watercolor), Calif State Fair, 58, 72; First Award, Marin Soc of Artists, Ross, Calif, 2006; First Popular Award, Sacramento Business Show, Sacramento Fine Arts Ctr, 2009; First Place (painting) & Best of Show, Environ Show, Sacramento Art Ctr, 2008; 2nd Best in Show, Univ Art Show, Sacramento, Calif, 2008. *Bibliog:* Christian Sci Monitor cover spread, 2/26/1949; California Style Watercolor Artists 1925-1955, Gordon McClelland Hillcrest Press, 1985; Charlotte Berney (auth), Antiques & Fine Art, 3-4/91; Gordon McClelland (auth), California Watercolors 1850-1970, Hillcrest Press, 2003. *Mem:* Signature mem, Am Watercolor Soc (AWS); signature mem, Calif Watercolor Asn (CWA); life mem, Marin Soc of Artists; signature mem, Soc of Western Artists (SWA). *Media:* Watercolor, Printmaking, Sculpture. *Publ:* Toward Diversity California Post War Watercolors, Gordon McClelland (auth), Antiques & Fine Art 1-2/91. *Dealer:* California Watercolor PO Box 1000 Fallbrook CA 92088. *Mailing Add:* 4824 Skyway Dr Fair Oaks CA 95628

POTTS, TIMOTHY
MUSEUM DIRECTOR
Pos: Dir media and telecommunications group, corporate finance department Lehman Brothers, NYC and London; head Nat Gallery of Victoria, Australia; dir, Kimbell Art Mus, Ft Worth, Tex, 1998-2007; dir Fitzwilliam Mus, Univ Cambridge, 2007-2012; dir J. Paul Getty Museum 2012-. *Teaching:* prof Univ Melbourne; adjunct prof, La Trobe Univ, Melbourne. *Publ:* Author: (monograph) Mesopotamia and the East: An Archaeological & Historical Study of Foreign Relations 3400-2000 BC, 1995; editor: Kimbell Art Museum: Handbook of the Collection, 2003; co-editor: Culture Through Objects: Ancient Near Eastern Studies in Honour of P. R. S. Moorey, 2003. *Mailing Add:* c/o J Paul Getty Mus 1200 Getty Ctr Dr Los Angeles CA 90049

POULET, ANNE LITLE
MUSEUM DIRECTOR
b Washington, Pa, Mar 20, 1942. *Study:* Sweet Briar Col, BA (cum laude), 1964; NY Univ Inst Fine Arts, NYU, MA, 1970. *Exhib:* Corot to Braque, Mus of Fine Arts, Boston, 1979; Clodion Terracottas in North Am Collections, The Frick Collection, 1984; Clodion, Musee du Louvre, 1992; Jean-Antoine Houdon: Sculptor of the Enlightenment, Nat Gallery of Art, Wash, DC, 2003. *Pos:* Cur, Dept European Decorative Arts and Sculpture Mus Fine Arts, Boston, cur emer, 1999-; dir, The Frick Collection, New York, 2003-. *Awards:* Recipient Ford Found Grant, 1970; Iris Found Award, 2000; Kress Fel, Nat Gallery Art; Chevalier de l'Ordre des artes et des lettres. *Mem:* French Heritage Soc (co-founder, vchmn bd, 1982-2003); Am Acad Arts & Sciences. *Publ:* Co-auth: (catalogue) Clodion (1738-1814), Jean-Antoine Houdon (1741-1828): Sculptor of the Enlightenment; (co auth) Nudity and Chastity: Houdons Statue of Diana in the Light of Newly Discovered Documents, Sculptures Journax X, Sept 03; Auth: (exh catalogue) Jean-Antoine Houdon: Sculptor of the Enlightenment, National gallery of Art. *Mailing Add:* The Frick Collection 1 E 70th St New York NY 10021-4967

POULIN, ROLAND
SCULPTOR
b Apr 17, 1940. *Study:* Ecole des Beaux-Arts de Montreal, 64-69, Atelier Mario Merola, 69-70, Univ Laral, PhD, 80. *Work:* Mus d'Art Contemporain, Montreal, PQ; Mus du Quebec; Nat Gallery, Ottawa, Ont; Mus des Beaux-Arts de Montreal; Art Gallery Ont, Toronto. *Exhib:* Solo exhibs, Mus D'Art Contemporain, Montreal, Can, 71 & 83, Agnes Etherington Art Ctr, Kingston, Can, 84, Olga Korper Gallery, Toronto, Can, 88, 90, 91, 93 & 96, Mus Folkwang Essen, 92, Galerie Rochefort, Montreal, Que, 92, Nat Gallery Can, Ottawa, Ont, 94 & Art Gallery North York, Ont, 95; Quebec '88--A Selection, Art Gallery Toronto Art Rental, 88; Historical Rouse: Art in Montreal, Power Plant, Toronto, 88; 49th Parallel, NY, 89; Cologne Art Fair, Ger. *Pos:* Instr sculpture, Univ du Que a Montreal, 71-72; instr composition, Col du Vieux-Montreal, 72-74, Col Brebeuf, 75-76; instr sculpture, Univ Laval, Quebec, 73-81, Concordia Univ, Montreal, 82-83, Univ Ottawa, 87-. *Awards:* Ozias Leduc Prize (Visual Arts), Emile Nelligan Found, 92. *Bibliog:* Gilles Daignault (auth), La nouvelle sculpture de Roland Poulin, Le Devoir, Montreal, 5/17/86; Norman Theriault (auth), L'oeuvre d'art prend le pas sur l'histoire, Forces, No 84, Montreal, winter 89; Chantal Pontbriand (auth), Roland Poulin, No 53, Parachute, Montreal, 89

POULOS, BASILIOS NICHOLAS
PAINTER, EDUCATOR
b Columbia, SC, Dec 15, 1941. *Study:* Atlanta Sch Art, BFA, 65; Tulane Univ, MFA, 68; Univ SC. *Work:* Mus Fine Arts, Houston; Chase Manhattan Bank, NY; Voores Mus, Athens; Tulane Univ, New Orleans, La; New Orleans Mus Art; and others. *Exhib:* Solo exhibs, High Mus Art, Atlanta, 65, LaGrange Coll, Ga, 84, McIntosh/Drysdale Gallery, Houston, 85, Harris Gallery, Houston, 86, Caroline Lee Gallery, Houston, 87, Meredith Long Gallery, Houston, 92 & Galveston Arts Ctr, Tex, 94; Contemp Reflections, Aldrich Mus Contemp Art, 74; 35th Biennial, Corcoran Gallery Art, Washington, 77; Fresh Paint: The Houston Sch, Mus Fine Arts, Houston, 85; Petit Format, Kouros Gallery, NY, 87; Large Scale/Small Scale, Sewall Art Gallery, Houston, 89; A Sense of Place, Transco Gallery, Houston, 93; Foreign Influences, Mus ETex, Lufkin, 93; New Gallery, Houston, Tex, 96, 98, 2001; Selini Gallery, Athens, Greece, 98; Theophilos Gallery, Athens, 2001. *Teaching:* Prof studio art, Rice Univ, Houston, 85-. *Awards:* Fine Arts Found Grant, Atlanta, Ga, 65; French Govt Grant, 65-66; Guggenheim Found Fel, 73-74. *Bibliog:* Mimi Crossley (auth), Poulos at Watson De Nagy, Art in Am, 77. *Media:* Acrylic on Canvas, Wood. *Res:* Figuration/Structure

POVSE, MATTHEW R
EDUCATOR
Study: Ohio Univ, BFA; Cranbrook Acad of Art, MFA; Univ of Guanajuato, Mexico, MFA. *Teaching:* Asst prof, Marywood Univ, currently, chair dept of art, 2010-. *Mailing Add:* Marywood University Studio Art Center Room 217 2300 Adams Ave Scranton PA 18509

POWELL, DAN T
PHOTOGRAPHER
b Richland, Wash, July 12, 1950. *Study:* Cent Wash Univ, with Jim Sahlstrand, BA, 73, MA (art), 77; Univ Ill, with Art Sinsabaugh & Luther Smith, MFA (art), 80. *Work:* Hallmark Collection, Kansas City, Mo; Calif Inst Arts; Art Inst Chicago, Ill; Midwest Mus Am Art, Elkhart, Ind; Ill State Univ, Normal; Polaroid Corp; Mus Fine Art, Houston; Portland Art Mus. *Exhib:* Summer Light, Light Gallery, NY, 82; Group

exhib, Fifth Vienna Int Biennial, Austria, 82, Chicago Art Inst, 88, San Francisco Mus Mod Art, 88; four-person exhib, San Francisco Camerawork, 83; Susan Spiritus Gallery, Los Angeles, 83; Evolving Abstraction in Photog, Anita Shapolsky Gallery, New York City, 89; Royal Coll Art, London, 93; Am Made, The New Still Life, Isetan Mus Art, Tokyo, Japan; Comdeso/Cawler Gallery, New York City, 94; Elizabeth Leach Gallery, Portland, 95. *Teaching:* Asst prof, Univ Northern Iowa, 80-; assoc prof, Univ Ore, Eugene, 87-. *Awards:* Second Award, Contemp Photoworks, Univ NMex, 80; Best of Show, Midwest Photo 80, Midwest Mus Am Art, 80; Best of Prints & Drawings, Iowa Artists, Des Moines Art Ctr, 82. *Bibliog:* Joan Murray (auth), rev of New Photographics, 79 & Diane Neumaier (auth), Visual & Verbal Language, 80, Artweek; Barbara Westerfield (auth), Constructed Realities, Art News, 86. *Media:* Photography. *Dealer:* Olson/Larsen Gallery Des Moines IA

POWELL, EARL ALEXANDER, III
MUSEUM DIRECTOR, HISTORIAN
b Spartanburg, SC, Oct 24, 1943. *Study:* Williams Coll, BA, 66; Harvard Univ, MA, 70, PhD, 74. *Hon Degrees:* Otis Parsons Inst, DFA, 87; Williams Coll, DFA, 93. *Pos:* Cur, Michener Collection, Univ Tex, Austin, 74-76; mus cur & asst to asst dir, Nat Gallery Art, Washington, DC, 76-78, exec cur, 79-80, dir, 92-; dir, Los Angeles Co Mus Art, 80-92. *Teaching:* Teaching fel fine arts, Harvard Univ, 70-74; asst prof Am art, Univ Tex, Austin, 74-76. *Awards:* King Olav Medal, Norway, 78; Officier dans l'Ordre des Arts & Lett Award, France, 2004; Grand Off Order Infante D Henrique Med, Govt Portugal, 95; Williams Coll Bicentennial Medal, 95; Mexican Cult Inst Award, 96; Commendatore dell 'Ordine al Merito della Republica Italiana, Govt Italy, 98; Chevalier of Legion Honor Award, French Govt, 2000; Officier dans l'Ordre des Arts & Lett Award, France, 2004; Centennial Medal, Harvard Grad Sch Arts & Sci, 2008; Officer's Cross of the Order of Merit of the Rep Hungary, 2009. *Mem:* Am Fedn Arts (trustee); Nat Trust Hist Preservation (trustee); White House Hist Asn (trustee); Asn Art Mus Dirs; Comt Preservation White House; Fed Coun Arts & Humanities; Pres Comt Arts & Humanities; Morris & Gwendolyn Cafritz Found (trustee); John F Kennedy Ctr Performing Arts (trustee); Am Acad Arts & Sci; Am Philosophical Soc; US Comn of Fine Arts (chmn 2005-); Norton Simon Mus (trustee); Mariner's Mus. *Res:* English influences in the art of Thomas Cole. *Publ:* Coauth, American Art at Harvard (catalog), 73; auth, Catalogue Raisonne of the Michener Collection, 78; Thomas Cole, (monogr), Abrams, New York, 90; plus articles & catalogue essays on Am art; and others. *Mailing Add:* Nat Gallery Art 2000B S Club Dr Hyattsville MD 20785

POWELL, GORDON
SCULPTOR
b Decatur, Ill, May 4, 1947. *Study:* Sch Art Inst, Chicago, BFA, 75; Univ Ill, MFA, 80. *Work:* Cresap, McCormick and Paget, Chicago; Levy Organization, Chicago; Prudential Insurance; Saks Fifth Ave, Portland, Ore; State Ill Collection, Springfield; Millikin Univ. *Comn:* Wine Label Imagery Series, Benziger Family Wines. *Exhib:* New Horizons in Art, Cult Ctr, Chicago, 84; 81st Exhib Artists of Chicago & Vicinity, Art Inst Chicago, 85; Fetish Show-Obsessive Expressions, Rockford Art Mus, 86; Extended Boundaries, Cult Ctr, Chicago, 86; Columnar, Hudson River Mus, Yonkers, 88; Body Fragments, Shea and Beker Gallery, NY, 89; The Chicago Show, Chicago Cult Ctr, Ill, 90; Summer 1990, Rosa Esman Gallery, NY, 90; one-person exhibs, Roy Boyd Galleries, Chicago, 82, 83, 85, 86 & 89, Santa Monica, Calif, 87 & Vaughan & Vaughan, Minneapolis, Minn, 90, Univ N Iowa, Cedar Falls, Roy Boyd Gallery, Chicago, 91, Chicago Cult Ctr, 96, William Rainey Harper Coll, Palatine, Ill, 2000, Perimeter Gallery, Chicago, 2001; Rockford (Ill) Art Mus, 92, Ukrainian Inst Modern Art, Chicago, 97; Perimeter Gallery, Chicago, 98, Elgin (Ill) Coll, 2001. *Teaching:* Instr, Rockford Col, 90; adj asst prof Sch of Art, Art Inst Chicago, 96. *Awards:* Artist-in-Residence, ArtPark, Lewiston, NY, 85, Yaddo, Saratoga Springs, NY, 93; Fel Nat Endowment Arts, 86; Prix de Rome, Am Acad Rome, 87-88; Vis artist Am Acad, Rome, 94; Visual Artists fel, Ill, Arts Coun, 97, Enrichment grant, Sch of Art Inst Chicago, 98, 2000. *Bibliog:* Emerging Sculptor Show, The New York Times, 12/11/87; reviews, Chicago Tribune, 7/16/82, 89, 91, 93, Los Angeles Times, 11/17/87, Evanston Rev., 95. *Media:* Wood. *Dealer:* Gordon Powell Studio 1117 W Lake St Chicago IL 60607. *Mailing Add:* 319 N Thatcher River Forest IL 60305

POWELSON, ROSEMARY A
PAINTER, PRINTMAKER
b La Junta, Colo. *Study:* Univ Nebr, Lincoln, BFA, 71; Mich State Univ, East Lansing, MFA, 74. *Work:* Art Inst Chicago; Cranbrook Acad Art, Bloomfield Hills, Mich; Hackley Art Mus, Muskegon, Mich; Kalamazoo Inst Art, Mich; Sioux City Art Ctr, Iowa; Lower Columbia Col, Longview, Wash. *Comn:* Mich bicentennial portfolio prints in collotype, Nat Endowment Arts, Alma, Mich, 76; Prints 83 (portfolio), Lower Columbia Coll Found, Longview, Wash, 83. *Exhib:* Solo exhib, Alma Coll, Mich, 78; Kans 5th Nat Small Paintings & Drawings, Art Gallery, Ft Hayes State Univ, 81; Wash Women Art, Art Gallery, Eastern Wash Univ, Cheney, 81; Print Exhib, Fort Steilacoom Community Col, Tacoma, Wash, 83; Print Exhib, Ore State Univ, Corvallis, Ore, 84; Invitational Group Show, Clatsop Community Coll, Astoria, Ore, 85. *Pos:* Humanities consult, Wash Humanities Project, Olympia, 81-. *Teaching:* Instr painting & drawing, Alma Col, Mich, 75-78; instr design & drawing, Ft Steilacoom Community Col, Tacoma, Wash, 78-79; instr art hist & design, Lower Columbia Col, Longview, Wash, 79-. *Awards:* Purchase Award, 33rd Ann Fall Show, 71; Merit Award, Saginaw Ann Area Art Exhib, 77. *Media:* All Media. *Publ:* Producer, Women in Art (film), Wash State Humanities Project, Olympia, 81

POWERS, DONALD T
PAINTER
b Madison, Tenn, May 20, 1950. *Study:* Tenn Technol Univ, 69-70; David Lipscomb Col, 70-72. *Work:* Smithsonian Inst Nat Portrait Gallery, Washington, DC; Emory Univ, Atlanta; Ga Mus Art, Univ Ga, Athens; Am Acad & Inst Arts & Lett, New York, NY; Mus Mod Art, Haifa, Israel. *Comn:* Portrait of Jimmy Carter, Friends of the President, Washington, DC, 85; portrait of His Holiness the Dalai Lama, 90. *Exhib:* Jimmy Carter in Plains, Hunter Mus Art, Chattanooga, Tenn, 86; Art and the Law, Minn Mus Art, St Paul, Minn & Moscarelle Mus, Coll William & Mary, Williamsburg, Va, 87; The Eternal Landscape, Southeastern Ctr for Contemp Art, Winston-Salem, NC, 91; 17th Art & the Law Exhib, Kennedy Galleries, NY & Loyola Law Sch, Los Angeles; The Artist as Native, Babcock Galleries, NY, Middlebury Coll Mus Art, Albany Inst Hist & Art, Owensboro Mus Art, Westmoreland Mus Art & Md Inst & Coll Art; Coast to Coast: The Contemp Landscape in Fla (with catalog), Daytona Mus Arts & Sci, Gulf Coast Art Mus, Bel Aire, Lowe Mus, Miami & Pensacola Mus Art, 98-; Am Embassy, Rome, 2001-04. *Pos:* Art Dir, TN State Mus, Nashville, 73-76. *Teaching:* Priv teaching to Pres Jimmy Carter. *Awards:* Lyndhurst Prize, Lyndhurst Found, 84-86; Purchase Award, West Publ Co, 87. *Media:* Egg Tempera, Oil. *Specialty:* Realism. *Publ:* Auth, The Artist As Native, Pomegranate Books, 93; Illustrator The Silver Donkey, Candlewick Press, Cambridge, 2005. *Dealer:* Stonehenge Gallery, Montgomery, AL. *Mailing Add:* 217 Edgewood Dr PO Box 3295 Thomasville GA 31799

POWERS, JOHN & KIMIKO
COLLECTOR
b Mt Vernon, NY, Aug 5 (Mr Powers); b Tokyo, Japan, Aug 26, 36 (Mrs Powers). *Study:* Mr Powers, Princeton Univ, BA, 38; Harvard Law Sch, LLB, 41; studied with John McRosenfield, 68-98; Colo State Univ, LLD, 90; Mrs Powers, Int Christian Univ, Tokyo, grad, 58. *Collection Arranged:* Traditions of Japanese Art, Harvard, Seattle, Princeton, 70; Extraordinary Persons: Japanese Artists (1560-1860), 88; Edo Period Art, Harvard Univ, 98. *Teaching:* Adj prof, Aspen Inst Humanistic Studies, Colo State Univ. *Bibliog:* John M Rosenfield & Shujiro Shimada (auths), Traditions of Japanese Art: selections from the Kimiko & John Powers Collection, Fogg Art Mus, Harvard Univ, 70. *Collection:* Antique Japanese painting, sculpture, ceramics, bronze from pre-history to 1868; contemporary art 1958-1998. *Mailing Add:* 13114 Hwy 82 Carbondale CO 81623

POWERS, W ALEX
PAINTER
b St Charles, Va, Apr 25, 1940. *Study:* Emory & Henry Col, Emory, Va, BA, 62; Eliot McMurrough Sch Art, Indialantic, Fla, 67-69; Art Students League, Woodstock, NY, 69. *Work:* SC State Art Collection, Columbia; Trammel Crowe Co, Charlotte, NC; Waccamaw Art & Crafts Guild, Myrtle Beach, SC; Coca Cola, Charlotte, NC. *Exhib:* Am Watercolor Soc, NY, 76, 88, 90 & 92; Nat Watercolor Soc, Los Angeles, 84-86 & 94; San Diego Watercolor Soc Int Exhib, 85-86 & 91-92 & 94; Rocky Mountain Nat, Golden, Colo, 90; Watercolor USA, Springfield, Mo, 91. *Teaching:* Self-employed teacher, watercolor workshops throughout US, Canada & Abroad, 72-. *Awards:* Best-of-Show, Okla Patrons Gala Watercolor Exhib, 86; Best-of-Show, Ky Watercolor Soc, 93 & 94; 2nd Award, Watercolor Soc Ala Nat Exhib, 93 & 94. *Bibliog:* Everything You Always Wanted to Know About Watercolor, Watson-Guptill, 92; Splash 2, Northlight Publ, 93; Exploring Transparent Watercolor, Davis Publ, 93. *Mem:* Nat Watercolor Soc; Southern Watercolor Soc; Waccamaw Arts & Crafts Guild, SC (pres, 76, vpres, 86); SC Watercolor Soc. *Media:* Watercolor, Drawing. *Publ:* Am Artist Mag, 2/85; Artist's Mag, 2/85; auth, Painting People in Watercolor, Watson-Guptill Publ, 89. *Mailing Add:* 401-72nd Ave N Apt 1 Myrtle Beach SC 29572-3814

POZZATTI, RUDY O
PRINTMAKER, PAINTER
b Telluride, Colo, Jan 14, 1925. *Study:* Univ Colo, BFA & MFA; Hon LHD, Univ Colo, 73; also with Wendell H Black, Max Beckman & Ben Shahn. *Work:* Mus Mod Art, NY; Libr Cong, Washington, DC; Art Inst Chicago, Ill; Sheldon Mem Art Mus, Lincoln, Nebr; Cleveland Mus Art, Ohio; Univ Art Mus, Bloomington, 2002, Evansville Mus Art, 2002; rep in permanent collections, Mus Modern Art, New York, Libr Cong, Washington, DC, Art Inst Chicago, Cleveland Mus Art. *Comn:* Spec Print Eds, Cleveland Print Club, Cleveland Mus Art, 54; Int Graphic Arts Soc, NY, 58-61 & 63; Conrad Hilton Hotel, NY, 61; Clairol, Inc, comn for NY World's Fair, 63; Ferdinand Roten Galleries, Baltimore, Md, 67 & 68; Rochester Print Soc, NY, 98; Int Print Symposium, Cortona, Italy; Corcoran Mus, Washington DC, 2001; Wall Comn, Ruth N Halls Theatre, Ind Univ, 2006; and others. *Exhib:* Young Americans, Whitney Mus Am Arts, NY, 61; Stampe di Due Mondi: Prints of Two Worlds, Tyler Sch Art, Rome, Italy, 67; 20 Yr Retrospective, Sheldon Mem Art Gallery, Univ Nebr, 69; Artists Abroad, Inst Int Educ, Am Fedn Arts, NY, 69; Int Cult Conf, Budapest, Hungary, 85; Rudy Pozzatti, Four Decades of Printmaking (82 works with catalog), Mitchell Mus, Mt Vernon, Ill, Traveling Show, 92-93; solo retrospective, Ind Univ Art Mus, 2001-2002; Mini Retrospective, McCutchen Art Ctr, Evansville, In, 2013; Mini Retrospective, Mcutchen Art Ctr, 58 works, Evansville, IN, 2013; Mini Retrospective, 53 works, McCutchon Art Ctr, Evansville, Ind, 2013. *Pos:* US State Dept Cult Exchange Proj, USSR, 61, Yugoslavia, 65 & Brazil, 74; artist-in-residence, Roswell Mus & Art Ctr, 79. *Teaching:* Asst prof printmaking & painting, Univ Nebr, 50-56; prof printmaking, Ind Univ, 56-72, distinguished prof, 72-91. *Awards:* Guggenheim Fel, 63-64; George Norlin Silver Medal, Asn Alumni of Univ Colo, 72; Rockefeller Grant, Belaggio, Italy, 95; Robert Foster Cherry Award Distinguished Teaching (top 3 finalists), Baylor Univ, Waco, Tex, 10/2007. *Bibliog:* Norman Geske (auth), Rudy Pozzatti; American Printmaker, Univ Kans, 71; Richard Taylor (auth), Pozzatti (film), Artists in America, NETV, 71; Rudy Pozzatti: A Printmaker's Odyssey, Ind Univ Art Mus & Ind Univ Press, 2002. *Mem:* Soc Am Graphic Artists; Am Color Print Soc; Coll Art Asn, NY; Nat Acad (assoc, 81, acad, 91). *Media:* All Media. *Dealer:* The Gallery 109 E Sixth St Bloomington IN 47401. *Mailing Add:* 1025 East Sassafras Circle Bloomington IN 47408

POZZI, LUCIO
PAINTER, PRINTMAKER
b Milano, Italy, Nov 29, 1935; US citizen. *Study:* Sculpture with Michael Noble. *Work:* Mus Modern Art, NY; Mus Contemp Art, Chicago; Detroit Art Inst; Fogg Mus, Cambridge, Mass; Museo Pecci, Prato, Italy. *Exhib:* John Weber Gallery, NY, 93, 96, 2000; Carlo Grossetti, Milan, 96; ESSO Gallery, NY, 99; Hindsight/Foresight, Bayly

Mus, Charlottesville, Va, 2000; Ben Shahn Gallery, Paterson Univ, NJ, 2002; Kalamazoo Inst Arts, Mich, 2002; Anderson Gallery, Drake Univ, Des Moines, 2002; Grossetti Arte, Milan, 2003; retrospectives, Kunsthalle, Bielefeld, Ger, 82, Badischer Kunstverein, Karlsruhe, Ger, 83, Mus New Art, 2001, Kalamazoo Inst Art, Mich, 2002. *Pos:* Art writer & critic various art publications. *Teaching:* Asst prof art & art hist, Cooper Union, 69-75; vis prof art, Princeton Univ, 75; instr art, Sch Visual Arts, 78-; sr critic, Yale Univ grad sculpture prog, 90. *Awards:* Nat Endowment Arts Fel, 83. *Bibliog:* David Shapiro (auth), An interview with Lucio Pozzi, NY Art J, 11/79; J Van Der Marck (auth), Reconnecting (exib catalog), Detroit Art Inst, 87; Tiffany Bell (auth), Lucio Pozzi Peccolo, Haley, 91. *Mem:* Am Abstract Artists. *Media:* Acrylic, Oil; All Media. *Publ:* Auth, Five Stories, 75 & 78; 475 years, 80-; A User's Manual to Approach the Art of Lucio Pozzi, 2000

PRACZUKOWSKI, EDWARD LEON
PAINTER, EDUCATOR
b Norwich, Conn, May 25, 1930. *Study:* Norwich Art Sch, fine arts dipl, 50; Sch Mus Boston, cert with hons in painting, 56, Clarrisa Bartlett travel fel & grad cert, 59; Tufts Univ, BS (art educ), 58; Cranbrook Acad, MFA, 65. *Work:* Slater Mem Mus, Norwich, Conn, 81; City of Seattle, Wash. *Exhib:* Drawing USA, St Paul Art Ctr, Minn, 66 & 69; Nat Polymer Exhib, EMich Univ, 67 & 68; 11th Ann Nat Drawing Exhib, Oklahoma Art Ctr, 69; Solo exhibs, Greenwood Gallery, Seattle, Wash, 81 & 83, Foster White Gallery, 86 & Pima Community Coll, Tucson, Ariz, 89; Living With the Volcano, The Artists of Mt St Helens, Mus Art, Wash State Univ, 83; Int Artist Exchange Exhib, Seattle Chap Artists Equity, 90, 92 & 93. *Teaching:* Assoc prof drawing & painting, Univ Wash, 65-. *Awards:* First Prize Painting, Int Arts Festival, Detroit, 65; MacDowell Colony Grants, 66 & 69; Wash Water Power Award, Spokane Ann, 81. *Mem:* Edward MacDowell Colony, NY; Allied Artists, Seattle, Wash; Artists Equity, Seattle Chap (pres, 91-92). *Media:* Oil, Acrylic. *Res:* Cosmic Space Painting

PRADA, MIUCCIA BIANCA
COLLECTOR
b Italy, 1949. *Study:* Teatro Piccolo, Milan, 1973-78. *Pos:* Inherited family-owned luxury goods manufacturer Prada SpA, Milan, 1978-, expanded from luxury goods to high end clothing introducing various product lines, including handbags, 1985, women's ready-to-wear, 1989, Miu Miu line, 1992, debut in NYC, opened London boutique, 1994, launched Prada Linea Rossa, 1997, launched Prada Sport, 1998, men's wear, Collezione Uomo, 1993, acquired Fendi, Helmut Lang, Jil Sander and Azzedine Alaia to its portfolio of brands. Founder PradaMilanoarte (now Prada Found.), Milan, 1993-. *Awards:* Accessories award, Coun. Fashion Designers of America, 1993, Internat. award, 2004, McKim Medal Laureate, American Acad., 2010; named one of The 30 Most Powerful Women in Europe, Wall St. Jour., 50 Women to Watch, 2005, The World's Most Influential People, TIME mag., 2005, Top 200 Collectors, ARTnews mag., 2005-12, The 100 Most Powerful Women, Forbes mag., 2011. *Collection:* Contemporary art. *Mailing Add:* Fondazione Prada Via Andrea Maffei 2 Milan 20135 Italy

PRADO-ARAI, NAMIKO
VISUAL ARTIST
b Mexico City, Mex. *Study:* Universidad Iberoamericana, Mex, 87; Escuela Nacional de Artes Plasticas, UNAM, Mex, Maestría, 92; Univ Paris VIII, Maîtrise, 96; Ecole des Hautes Etudes en Sciences Sociales, Paris, DEA, 98; Escuela Diseno INBA, Mex, Diplomado Compugafia, 2000. *Work:* Bibliotheque Nationale de France-Estampes, Paris; Fondation Culturelle du Mexique, Paris; Aeroports de Paris; Colegio de España, Paris; Maison du Mexique-Cite Int Universitaire, Paris; Ambassade de France, Mex; Museo de Ciencias Universum, UNAM, Mexico City; Museo de la Mujer, Mexico City. *Comn:* mural Museo de Ciencias-Universum, UNAM, Mex City, 00-01. *Exhib:* Encuentro Nacional Arte Joven, Mus Carrillo Gil, Mexico City, 92; Arte Joven en San Carlos, Mus de la Ciudad de Mex, Mexico City, 92; Cinco en la Grafica, Mus Universitario del Chopo, Mexico City, 93; Salon D'Art Contemporain, Mairie de Montrouge, France, 96; Biennale de Jeune Peinture, Mus D'Art Contemporain, Nice, France, 96; Novembre a Vitry, Galerie Guy Moquet, France, 97; Prize Johnny Walker, Museo de Arte Moderno, Mexico City, 98; Casa de Francia, Mex City, 2000 & 2001; Catalogo de Ilustradores, Centro Nacional de las Artes Mex City, 2000; Cuerpo en Movimiento, Mus Universum, 2003; Niche Gallery, Tokyo, Japan, 2003, 2006; Trajectoires, Espace Beaurepaire, Paris, 2002; Nippon Int Contemp Art Festival, Tokyo, 2003; Casa Lamm, Mexico, 2004; La Source, Villarceaux Chateau, 2005 & 2007; La Source, La Guéroulde, 2006; l'Avant Seine, Colombes, 2011; Maison du Mexique Pans, 2011. *Awards:* Intern, Peggy Guggenheim Found, 92; Spadem Prize, Paris, 93; Residence Association La Source, France, 2006. *Bibliog:* Aline Brandauer (auth), Travail Recent, Paris-Mexico, France, 93; Christine Frerot (auth), La Realite de L Abscence, Mex Embassy, France, 94; Elia Espinosa (auth), Lo Infinito Cotidiano, Revista UNAM, Mex, 96; Santiago Espinosa del los Monteros (auth), Energia Entranable, 2001. *Mem:* Soc des Auteurs Arts Graphiques & Plastiques; Asn Artistas Plasticos Mex; Asn Int d'Arts Plastiques, UNESCO, Fed Mexicana de Univ; Fed Mexicana de Universitanas. *Media:* Mixed media, works on paper, oil pastel, experimental supports. *Specialty:* Painting, drawing, etching, illustration, jewelry creations. *Dealer:* Niche Gallery 3-12 Ginza 3 Chome Tokyo Japan; Sum-Arte Cerro del Jabali 9 Pedregal de San Francisco CP 04320 Mexico. *Mailing Add:* 18 Rue du Plan de l aitre Bailly France 78870

PRAKAPAS, DOROTHY
DIRECTOR
b New York, NY, May 13, 1928. *Study:* Hunter Col, New York, BA (art), 49; Fashion Inst Technol, BS (drafting & design), 51; Parson's Sch Design, with Hananiah Harari, 52; Sch Visual Arts, Advert Design, 54. *Pos:* Animator, Lee Blair Film Graphics, 52-54; stylist, Playtex, 55-62; fashion design, Mercantile, 62-76; dir, Prakapas Gallery, 76-93; retired. *Mem:* Art Dealer's Asn Am; Asn Int Photog Art Dealers. *Specialty:* Twentieth century modernism with special emphasis on photography. *Mailing Add:* One Northgate 6B Bronxville NY 10708

PRALL, BARBARA JONES
PAINTER, INSTRUCTOR
b Cedar Rapids, Iowa, July 4, 1932. *Study:* Kirkwood Community Col, AA, 1973; Upper Iowa Univ, BA in Art Educ (magna cum laude), 1975; Iowa Univ, 1978-85; studies with Burt Silverman, John Howard Sanden, Daniel Green & Bob Gerbracht among others. *Comn:* Lake Louise (mural), comn by Erwin Besler, Dyersville, Iowa; Last Supper (mural), Open Bible Ch, Des Moines; Dyersville, USA (mural), Dyersville Nat Bank; mural, Harvs Auto Body, Iowa City. *Exhib:* Kalispell Mt Boyd Tower West Lobby, Univ Iowa Hosp; Marion Hist Soc, Racine, Wis, Cannon Falls, Minn, Owatonna, Minn & Edina, Minn, others; Operation Wildlife Art Show, Kansas City, Kans. *Pos:* owner, artist, Barb's Art Barn, Delhi, Iowa, Pinicon Acres Fine Art's Farm,Central City, Iowa & Barb's Fine Art Gallery & Studio, Marion, Iowa. *Teaching:* art teacher, grades 1-8, Central City Community Schs, Iowa; art instr, Barb's Art Barn, Delhi, Iowa, Pinicon Acres Fine Arts Farm, Central City, Iowa & Barb's Fine Art Gallery & Studio, Marion, Iowa. *Awards:* Best of Show landscape, Operation Wildlife; Artist of Yr, Upper Iowa Univ; winner calendar choice, Farmer's State Bank. *Mem:* Am Soc Portrait Artists; NY Portrait Soc. *Media:* Oil, Acrylic, Watercolor, Pastel. *Mailing Add:* c/o Barb's Fine Art 788 6th St Marion IA 52302

PRAMUK, EDWARD RICHARD
PAINTER
b Akron, Ohio, Feb 14, 1936. *Study:* Kent State Univ, BFA, MA; Queens Col, grad study; Akron Art Inst; also with John Ferren, James Brooks & Louis Finkelstein. *Work:* New Orleans Mus Art; Cornell Univ; Pan Am Life Corp; Banc Texas, Houston. *Comn:* Paintings, James Talcott Inc, NY, 74. *Exhib:* Pelham-Von Stoffler Gallery, Houston, Tex, 78; Edinboro State Univ, Edinboro, NY, 78; Solo exhibs, Contemp Art Ctr, New Orleans, 80, First St Gallery, NY, 83 & 85 & Entergy Ctr, New Orleans, 97; Landscape, Cityscape, Seascape, Contemp Art Ctr, New Orleans, 86; La Landscape, Downtown Gallery, New Orleans, 90; Sylvia Schmidt Gallery, New Orleans, 91, 93-94, 96 & 98; and others. *Teaching:* Prof art, La State Univ, 64-. *Awards:* Award, La Prof Artists, Baton Rouge, 71; Purchase Award, 7th Nat Drawing & Sculpture Show, 73; Purchase Award, New Orleans Mus Art, 74. *Media:* Acrylic. *Publ:* Contribr, two colorplates, How to Make an Oil Painting, Watson-Guptill, 90; Nine colorplates, Georgia Rev, Winter 98

PRANGE, SALLY BOWEN
CERAMIST, SCULPTOR
b Valparaiso, Ind, Aug 11, 1927. *Study:* Univ Mich, Ann Arbor, BA. *Work:* Victoria & Albert Mus, London, Eng; William Hayes Ackland Mem Art Ctr, Univ NC, Chapel Hill; NC Mus Art, Raleigh; Smithsonian Inst, Washington; Mus Art, Pa State Univ, University Park; Mus Int Ceramics, Faenza, Italy; J Patrick Lannan Found Cont Art, Palm Beach, Fla; Everson Mus Art, Syracuse, NY; Hickory Mus Art, Hickory, NC; NC State Univ, Raleigh; Southern Prog Corp, Birmingham, Ala, 90. *Comn:* Booke & Co, Winston-Salem, NC; Wachovia Bank, Winston-Salem, NC; Glaxo-Welcome, Res Triangle Park, NC; SAS Inst Res, Triangle Park, NC. *Exhib:* Am Ceramic & Sculpture Show, Butler Inst Am Art, Youngstown, Ohio, 67-68 & 71; Kyoto Crafts Ctr, Japan, 86; Tyndall Galleries, Durham, NC, 92 & 95; Durham Art Guild, NC, 93; Lee Hansley Gallery, Raleigh, NC, 92, 95 & 96; Greenville Art Mus, NC, 95; Green Hill Ctr NC Art, Greensboro, 97; Fayetteville Mus Art, NC, 97; Am Embassy, Tokyo, Japan; A Different Turn, NC Pottery Mus, Pinehurst, NC; Ceramics Viewpoint 98, Grossmont Col, El Cajon, Calif; Monarch Nat Competition, Kennedy, Douglas Ctr; Durham Art Coun, NC, 2000; Gallery C Raleigh, NC, 2000. *Pos:* Juror & vis lectr. *Teaching:* Instr ceramic pottery, Univ NC, Chapel Hill, 65-66; instr, Arrowmont, Gatlinburg, Tenn, 79 & 80, Penland Sch Crafts, NC, 81, NC State Univ Crafts Ctr, Raleigh, 82, Univ Calif, San Diego Craft Ctr, 82 & Greenwich House Pottery, New York, 83; guest lectr, Brit Craftsmen Potters Asn, London, 80, Int Mus Ceramics, Faenza, Italy, 80, Octagon Ctr, Ames, Iowa, 84, Kansas City Inst, Mo, 85 & Greenhill Ctr NC Arts, 85. *Bibliog:* Lloyd Herman (auth), American Porcelain: New Expressions in an Ancient Art, 80; Peter Lane (auth), Studio Potter, 81, Studio Ceramics, 85 & Studio Porcelain, 86; Katherine Pearson (auth), Am Crafts, 83. *Mem:* Tri-State Sculptors Guild; Am Crafts Coun; World Crafts Coun; Piedmont Crafts Guild, Winston-Salem; Nat Coun Educ Ceramic Art. *Media:* Clay. *Publ:* Ceramic Form: Shape & Decoration, 88; Hist of Am Ceramics, Elaine Levin, 89; The Best of Pottery, Rockport Publ, 89; The Craft & Art of Clay, Susan Peterson, 89. *Dealer:* ART Gallery New Bern NC; Gallery C Raleigh NC; Tyndall Galleries Durham NC; Penland Gallery NC; WDO Gallery Charlotte NC

PRANGER, BEN
SCULPTOR
Study: Oberlin Coll, BA, 1985; Sch Art Inst Chicago, MFA, 1989. *Exhib:* Solo exhibs, MWMWM Gallery, Chicago, 1992, Kohler Arts Ctr, Wis, 1993, Hudson D Walker Gallery, Provincetown, Mass, 1997, Hollins Univ Art Gallery, Va, 1999, Alleghany Art & Craft Ctr, Va, 2007, Arlington Arts Ctr, Va, 2008; In Praise of Folly, Kohler Arts Ctr, Wis, 1992; The Nature of the Machine, Chicago Cult Ctr, 1993; 55th Anniversary Show, Hyde Park Art Ctr, Chicago, 1994; FAWC: Small WOrk, Cape Cod Art Mus, 2002; Endless Forms, Univ Mich Sch Art & Design, 2006; Re-Surfacing, Ohio State Univ Art Gallery, 2007. *Teaching:* Instr, Sch Art Inst Chicago, 1995-96; adj asst prof, Southampton Coll, Long Island Univ, NY, 1998; lectr, Randolph-Macon Women's Coll, Va, 1999; lectr art, Hollins Univ, 1999-2003, vis artist, 2000-02, asst prof performance & new media, 2003-07. *Awards:* Visual Fel, Fine Arts Work Ctr, Provincetown, 1996; Marie Walsh Sharpe Space Program Fel, 1997; Sculpture Grant, Va Comn for the Arts, 2001; Individual Artist Grant, Va Mus Fine Arts, 2002; Pollock-Krasner Found Grant, 2008. *Bibliog:* Garrett Holg (auth), Perimeter Gallery Review, ARTnews, 1993; Alan Artner (auth), Points of View, Chicago Tribune, 9/8/1995; John Brunetti (auth), MWMWM Gallery Review, New Art Examiner, 1996. *Mailing Add:* 42 E Loantaka Way Madison NJ 07940

PRAT, LOUIS-ANTOINE & VERONIQUE
COLLECTOR, WRITER
Pos: Proj leader, Graphic Arts Dept, Louvre Mus, Paris; vpres, Friends of the Louvre. *Teaching:* instr French history of drawing, Ecole du Louvre, 2007-. *Awards:* Named one of Top 200 collectors, ARTnews mag, 2004-13. *Collection:* 17th- to 19th-century French drawings. *Publ:* Auth, La Cigue Avec Toi, 1984, Un Requiem Allemand, 1985, Trois Reflets D'Argetine, 1986, Le Tombeau Du Nouvelliste, 1988, Dessins Romantiques Francais, 2001, Ingres, 2004; co-auth (with Pierre Rosenberg), Nicolas Poussin 1594-1665, 1997, Antoine Watteau 1684-1721, 1997, Jacques-Louis David 1748-1825, 2003. *Mailing Add:* Graphic Arts Dept Musée du Louvre Paris 75058 France

PRATT, ELIZABETH HAYES
PAINTER, INSTRUCTOR
b Dayton, Ohio, 1927. *Study:* Dayton Art Inst, 45; Coll William & Mary, BA (art), 49; Workshops with Eliot O'Hara Na, Charles Demotropolis & James Twitty, 56-60; Studied with Murray Wentworth & Joan Rothermel, 78-85. *Work:* Cape Mus Fine Arts, Dennis, Mass; Int Monetary Fund, Washington DC; US Cath Conf, Washington DC; Superior Ct DC; Citibank, NY; Cahoon Mus, Cotuit, Mass. *Comn:* King of Morocco (portrait), comn by king's cousin, 59; watercolor landscape, Nat Asn Manufacturers, Washington DC, 74; paintings, Inst Irish Studies Stonehill Col, North Easton, Mass, 82; painting, Harvard Law Sch Libr, 83; illus, June Fletcher, What Should I Do?, Snow Libr, Orleans, Mass, 96; painting, Orleans CofC, Mass, 97. *Exhib:* Solo exhibs, Art Complex Mus, Duxbury, Mass, 79 & Cape Mus of Fine Arts, 2008; Face of Am (nat portrait show), Art Ctr Galleries, Old Forge, NY, 94; Audubon Artists Ann Nat, 94-2000; Ga Watercolor Soc Nat, Chattahoochee Valley Art Mus, La Grange, Ga, 95; Rocky Mountain Nat, Foothills Art Ctr, Golden, Colo, 96; Masters of Watercolor, New Bedford Art Mus, 2006. *Pos:* Bd dir, Washington Watercolor Soc, 71-77; dir, Spectrum Gallery, Georgetown, Va, 72-73. *Teaching:* instr watercolor, Creative Arts Ctr, 79-86, 98-2002, Castle Hill Ctr for Arts, 82-2001, Cape Mus Fine Arts, 90-92; lectr art, Cape Mus Fine Arts, 96. *Awards:* Rocky Mountain Nat Golden Artist Award, New Berlin, NY, 86; Dean L Rubin Award, Audubon Artists, 99. *Bibliog:* James Hanson (auth), Artists in Residence, Boston Mag, 86; Cindy Nickerson (auth), Watercolorist Loves Spontaneity, Cape Cod Times, 89; Carol K Dumas (auth), Going for the Gold, Cape Codder Arts Sect, 93. *Mem:* Audubon Artists (juried mem); Copley Soc (juried mem); New Eng Watercolor Soc (juried mem); Provincetown Art Asn; Creative Arts Ctr Chatham. *Media:* Watercolor. *Specialty:* Oils, watercolors, pastels, original works of fine art. *Publ:* Auth, Experiments with Watercolor, Artists Mag, 89; contribr, C LeClair, The Art of Watercolor, Watson Guptall, 94, The Best of Watercolor, Vol I & 3, 95, 99, Best of Watercolors-Painting Composition, 97 & Watercolor Expressions, Rockport Publ, 2000; Cape Arts Rev, 7/2008; Am Art Collection, 7/2007 & 8/2008. *Dealer:* Addison/Holmes Box 2756 43 Rt 28 Orleans MA 02642; The Capley Soc of Boston 158 Newbury St Boston 02116

PRAVDA, MURIEL
INSTRUCTOR, RESTORER
b Brooklyn, NY, 1925. *Study:* Brooklyn Coll Journalism, AA, 47; Traphagan Sch Fashion (cert), 47; S Fla Art Inst, (cert), 75-92, Bruno Luchese Seminars, 80-91, (cert); Atterbury Sch Sculpture, (cert). *Work:* N Miami Mus, Fla; Int Boat Show, Miami Beach; Hollywood Art Guild, Fla; Community Art Alliance, Hollywood, Fla. *Exhib:* One-woman show, S Fla Art Inst, Miami, 87; Sculpture Show, Gallery Turnberry, NMiami Beach, 89; Faculty Show, Discovery Ctr, Ft Lauderdale, 89; Miniature Show, Del Bello Gallery, Toronto, Can, 90; Leonard Art Gallery, Ft Lauderdale, 90; and others. *Pos:* Restorer paintings, Lang Gallery, Jamaica Estates, NY, 70-80, asst sales, 70-80. *Teaching:* Instr clay sculpture, S Fla Art Inst, 80-, lectr sculpture workshop, 82-84; taught sculpture for 15 yrs. *Awards:* Second Place Sculpture, Fresh Meadows, Merchants, 78; First Place Sculpture, 81 & Merit Award Sculpture, 82, Miami Art League; Silver Poet, Writer's Lullaby, 90 & Gold Poet, Song of the World, 91, World of Poetry. *Bibliog:* M L Pesora (auth), Art show sizzles, Hollywood Sun, 91; Cindy Stauger (auth), News item, Sun Sentinel, 89; Florence Gould (auth), Inside Art (Hallandale) Sculpture, Hallandale Press, 87. *Mem:* Community Art Alliance; charter mem Nat Mus Women Arts; assoc mem Nat Sculpture Soc; Int Sculpture Soc. *Media:* Clay, Painting, Sculpture. *Interests:* swimming, dance, painting, sculpture, writing, articles, poetry. *Publ:* Sculptures, Friends and Neighbors Column, 88, Hallandale Press; Poem, The Survivors, Miami Herald, 9/92. *Mailing Add:* 8308 NW 80th St Tamarac FL 33321-1628

PRECIADO, PAMELA
PAINTER, ILLUSTRATOR
b Evanston, Ill. *Study:* Univ Kans, Fine Art & Com Art, 1967; San Francisco Accad Fine Arts, Figurative Art, 1968; Am Accad Art, Figurative & Com Art, 1971-1979; Palatte & Chisel Acad Fine Art, 2004-. *Work:* US 104th Cong Black Caucus Portrait Montage, Washington, DC; Nat Women's Hist Mus, Year of the Women, Washington, DC; Chicago Artists Coalition (online gallery), Chicago, Ill. *Comn:* Wild West Portraits (campaign ad), Wells Fargo Bank Hqs, Hist Rm, San Francisco, Calif, 1969; Winston Churchill (portrait sepia oil), Park Ridge, Ill, 1973; Collection 25 Paintings (acrylic), Booth Fisheries Consolidate Foods Corp, Chicago, Ill, 1974; Scenes of Farm Landscapes (5), DeKalb-Ag Res Corp, DeKalb, Ill, 1975; and numerous other portrait comns for private parties, Chicago, Ill, 1968-2008. *Exhib:* Calif Macy's Dept Stores, 1968-1969; Joseph Alioto Gallery, San Francisco, Calif, 1969; Wells Fargo Bank Hist Rm, San Francisco, Calif, 1969; Amsterdam Whitney Mus, Gallery Show, New York, 2011. *Pos:* Portrait artist for, Babies R Us stores (Schaumburg, Lombard & Naperville, Ill) & Deck the Walls (Aurora, Ill). *Teaching:* instr portrait art, Union St Gallery Art Ctr, 2013. *Awards:* Grant, Ill Arts Coun, 2008. *Bibliog:* Glenview Times (article), 1974; La Petite Art Gallery, Park Ridge, Ill. *Mem:* Chicago Women's Bus Develop Ctr, Chicago Ill (1994-); Portrait Soc Am (2002-); Palette & Chisel Acad Fine Arts (2003-); Chicago Pastel Soc (2005-); Chicago Plein Air Painters, Chicago, Ill (2006-); Nat Asn Porf Women; Business Advantage Gold. *Media:* Oil, pastel acrylic, charcoal, watercolor. *Res:* began in 2003, Portraits of Great Am Women Achievers, Inc, A non-profit collection of outstanding women & their contributions a to humanity in a traveling exhib to 16 venues around the US in 2 more years. *Interests:* art hist, travel, teaching. *Collection:* portraits of great American women. *Mailing Add:* Fine Art & Portraiture 2706 W 85th Place Chicago IL 60652

PREEDE, NYDIA
PAINTER, ILLUSTRATOR
b Manhattan, NY, Nov 7, 1926. *Study:* Art Students League, Fine & Applied Arts Diploma, 45; Pratt Inst, 45-46; Columbia Univ, 49; Sch Visual Arts, 57; Monmouth Col, BA, 62, MA, 73. *Work:* Yergeau Mus Int D'Art, Que; Coast Guard Art Prog 4 Works, Washington DC; Plucking Strings, Monmouth Co Libr System; Collage, Award sale, Fells Point Gallery; Oceanport, car repair inspection station, 3 works tech; Plane Firsta, pvt, seascapes; Grace Christian Church, Tinton Falls, NJ; Lutheran Church of the Reformation, Long Branch, NJ; Seascape, Salmagundi Club, New York. *Exhib:* Nat Asn Women Artists Traveling Exhib, 91-92; Small Works, Concordia Coll, 92; Contemp Artists, Gelabert Studios, 93; Points of View, Agora Gallery, 93; Europa Bombal Palace, Lisbon, Port, 94; You, Me & Them, Women in the Arts, Cork Gallery, Lincoln Ctr Performing Arts, NY, 96; Earth-Water, Agora Gallery, 97; solo exhibs New Yorker Show, Barcelona, 90, Gallery 402, NY, 99, Monmouth County Libr System; WIA Peekskill Flat Iron Gallery, 99; Ceres Hallelujah Invitational, 99; Coast Guard Art Program, Washington, DC, 2000; Search & Rescue, Salmagundi, 2005; 3rd World Fedn Min Art, 2004 & 4th World Fedn Min Art, 2008, Tasmania, Australia; Aububon-online, 2013; NSPCA, Salmagundi Club, 2013; NAWA, Sylvia Wald Po Kim Gallery, 2013, 2015; AAPL, 2013; In-Visable, Point Park Univ, 2016; group shows in Portugal, Argentina, Paris, Jerusalem, Sweden, Venice, Canada, Japan. *Pos:* prof adv bd, Am Biographical Inst, 2003; art dir, Am Artists Prof League, 2004-2012, recording secy, 2012-, adv emeritus, presently. *Teaching:* Educational specialist, DOD, 1928-51; Prof, Art worshop, MAECOM; art instr, Long Branch High School, 73. *Awards:* Charles Horman Mem Prize, Nat Asn Women Artists, 88; 1st Place, Alternate, Nat Forest Stamp Prog (tour USA), 91-92; Nat Arts Club Award, 96; Audubon Artists; Pratt Alumni Asn; Marquis Who's Who in American Art Reference award in Aquamedia, Audubon Artists, 2014; Elsie Ject-Key Award, Nat Asn Women Artists; Dorothy Seligson Memorial award, Nat Asn Women Artists, 2001; Award, Nat Asn Am Pen Women Biennial, Atlanta, Ga, 2014. *Bibliog:* Alexandra Shaw (auth), The Enigmatic Images of Nydia Preede, Manhattan Arts Int, 09-10/1994, Gordon Dane (auth), Nydia Preede: Probes Beneath the Surface, Manhattan Arts Int, 11-12/1994. *Mem:* Nat Asn Women Artists (juror, 90-92); Women in Art; Nat Endowment Arts; NJ Educ Asn (formerly); Coll Art Asn; Nat Arts Club Asn; Coast Guard Art Program; Am Artists Prof League (fel); Am Asn Univ Women (formerly); Nat Soc Painters; Nat Asn Am Penwomen; Miniature Painters Sculptures & Gravers; Nat Collage Soc; AAPL (bd dir, 2002-); Artist Equity; Catherine Lorillard Art Club. *Media:* Acrylic, All Media. *Publ:* Time & Memory, Prentice Hall, 96; Creative Inspirations Composite Book, Rockport Publ, 97; 2 works in The Best of Acrylic Painting, Rockport Publ, 97. *Dealer:* Pen & Brush 116 E 10th St New York NY; Ward-Nasse New York. *Mailing Add:* 249 B Eatoncrest Dr Eatontown NJ 07724

PREISS, ALEXANDRU PETRE
DESIGNER, ILLUSTRATOR
b Bucharest, Romania, Oct 4, 1952. *Study:* N Grigorescu Fine Arts Inst, Bucharest, BA & dipl, 76 cert, 77; Purdue Univ, MA, 81. *Work:* Greater Lafayette Mus Art, Ind. *Comn:* Homage: The Soldier (environmental sculpture), Greater Lafayette Mus Art, Ind, 82. *Exhib:* Smithsonian Inst Traveling Exhib, 82; Summer Invitational Show, Pleiades Gallery, NY, 83; Solo exhib, Second Street Gallery, Charlottesville, Va, 84; 11th Biennial Graphic Design, Brno, Czech, 84; Great Ann Int Exhib, Ctr Int D'Art Contemporain, Paris, France, 86; and others. *Pos:* Owner, Kennedy & Preiss Design, Honolulu, HI, 86-. *Teaching:* Asst prof graphic design, Purdue Univ, W Lafayette, Ind, 81-86 & Univ Hawaii at Manoa, Honolulu, 86-88. *Awards:* Silver Medal, 11th Biennial Graphic Design, Brno, Czech, 84; Pele Award of Excellence in Illus, AAF Hawaii, 89; Award of Excellence, IABC, Hawaii, 89. *Bibliog:* Marion Garmel (auth), Purdue designer creates superb homage, Indianapolis News, 82. *Media:* Mixed, Photo-collage. *Interests:* Dog Agility. *Publ:* Contribr, American Illustration 2, Am Illus Inc, New York, 83; illusr, Heart to Heart: A Discussion of Sexual Assault, Honolulu, 91; No Way Out, Honolulu Mag, 9/93; The Stress of Paradise, Honolulu Mag, 4/94. *Mailing Add:* 2118 Kuhio Ave No 701 Honolulu HI 96815

PREKOP, MARTIN DENNIS
PAINTER, SCULPTOR
b Toledo, Ohio, July 2, 1940. *Study:* Cleveland Inst Art; Cranbrook Acad Art, MFA; RI Sch Design, MFA; Slade Sch Art, London, Eng. *Work:* Univ Ill, Edwardsville. *Exhib:* Roof Works, Mus Contemp Art, 72; Art Inst Chicago, 74 & 75; Solo exhibs, Photographs, Yale Univ, 75, Name Gallery, Chicago, 75; Jan Cicero Gallery, Chicago, 79 & 84; LYC Gallery, Cumbria, Eng, 81. *Pos:* Dean, Art Inst Chicago, 88. *Teaching:* Prof & grad prog chmn painting, sculpture & photog, Art Inst Chicago, 66-, chmn Freshman Found, 70-73, chmn grad div, 73-77, chmn painting dept, 78- & chmn undergrad div, 82-93; dean, Col Fine Arts, Carnegie-Mellon Univ, Pittsburgh, 93-. *Awards:* Fulbright Fel, US State Dept, 65; Artists grant, Ill Arts Coun, 85; Fel, Nat Endowment Arts, 87. *Bibliog:* Jan Vendermark (auth), Roof Works Rev, Artforum, 72. *Media:* All. *Mailing Add:* Col Fine Arts Carnegie-Mellon Univ 5000 Forbes Ave Pittsburgh PA 15213

PRENT, MARK
ENVIRONMENTAL ARTIST, SCULPTOR
b Montreal, Que, Dec 23, 1947. *Study:* Sir George Williams Univ, Montreal, 66-70, BFA, 70, study with John Ivor Smith. *Work:* Art Gallery of Ont, Toronto; Art Bank of Can; Mus Du Quebec; Mus D'Art Contemporain; Nat Gallery Can; Mus D'Art Joiette, Quebec; Reflex Modern Art Mus, Amsterdam, Holland; Mus Des Beaux Arts De Sherbrooke, Quebec. *Comn:* Le Festin Chez la Comtesse Fritouille, staged by Suzanne Lantagne, Espace Libre, Montreal, 87. *Exhib:* Eighth Biennale de Paris, Nat Mus Mod Art, France, 73; Solo exhibs, Akademie der Kunste (auth, catalog), Berlin,

Ger, 75-76, Kunsthalle Nuremberg, Ger, 76, Stedelijk Mus (auth, catalog), Amsterdam, The Neth, 78, Mus d'Art Contemporain (auth, catalog), Montreal, 79 & Galerie Esperanza, Montreal, 86, Power Plant (catalog), Toronto, Ont, 87, Chaffee Gallery, Rutland, Vt, Galerie Esperanza, Montreal, Que, 88, Isaacs Gallery, Toronto, 90, Galerie De La Tour, Basel, Switz, 93 & Centre Exhib Circa, Montreal, Que, 93, Espace D Rene Harrison, Montreal, 2000, Galerie Bernard, Montreal, 2001; Maison Cult Rennes, France, 80-81; Performances, Le Festin Chez La Comtesse Fritouille, Espace Libre, Montreal, Can, 87; Tetsuro Fukuhara and Bodhi Sattva with Mark Prent and Sue Real, traveling show, 91; Winds from the future, Tokyo, Japan, 92; Pupae, Montreal, Can, 96. *Awards:* Guggenheim Mem Found Fel, 77; Can Coun Sr Arts Award, 78-81, 85-88, 91 & 96; Art Matters Inc, 87, 88 & 94; Can Coun Proj Cost Grant, Japan-Can Fund, 90, 92 & 93. *Bibliog:* Hartmut Kraft (auth), Antiasthetica 1978, Helmut Braun Kg, Koln, WGer, 78; Brian McNeil (dir film documentary), Mark Prent: Overmood, 80; Martial Ethier (dir film documentary), Prent's Universe, 97. *Mem:* Can Artists Representatives; Royal Can Acad; Int Sculpture Asn. *Media:* Polyester Resin, Fiberglass. *Mailing Add:* 35 Bank St Saint Albans VT 05478

PRENTICE, DAVID RAMAGE
PAINTER, PRINTMAKER
b Hartford, Conn, Dec 22, 1943. *Study:* Hartford Art Sch. *Work:* Wadsworth Atheneum, Hartford; Yale Univ, New Haven, Conn; Mus Mod Art, NY; Corcoran Gallery Art, Nat Gallery, Washington, DC; Aldrich Mus, Ridgefield, Conn. *Exhib:* Solo exhibs, Livingstone-Learmonth Gallery, 75, NY & Genesis Gallery, NY, 78; Other Ideas, Detroit Inst Fine Arts, Mich, 69; Prospect, Dusseldorf, Ger, 69; Whitney Mus Am Art Ann, NY, 70; From Los Angeles & other places, Silverman Gallery, Los Angeles, 78. *Teaching:* Guest instr painting, Hartford Art Sch, Univ Hartford, fall 70. *Media:* Acrylic. *Mailing Add:* 654 Broadway New York NY 10012-2327

PRESCOTT, KENNETH WADE
MUSEUM DIRECTOR, ADMINISTRATOR
b Jackson, Mich, Aug 9, 1920. *Study:* Western Mich Univ, BS; Univ Del, EdM; Univ Mich, MA & PhD. *Collection Arranged:* Ben Shahn Retrospective Exhib, Nat Mus Mod Art, Tokyo & other Japanese mus (with catalog), 70 & 91; Jack Levine Retrospective Exhib, Jewish Mus, NY, 79-80; Burgoyne Diller Exhibs, Meredith Long & Andre Emmerich & Harcourts Gallery, 79-92; Complete Graphic Work of Ben Shahn, KWP. *Pos:* Dir, Kansas City Mus, Mo, 54-58 & NJ State Mus, 63-71; managing dir, Acad Nat Sci, Philadelphia, 58-63; prog officer, Div Arts & Humanities, Ford Found, New York, 71-74. *Teaching:* Adj prof changing perspectives in the humanities, Grad Sch, Temple Univ, 60-70; prof art & chmn art dept, Univ Tex, Austin, 74-84, emer prof, currently. *Mem:* Tex Asn Schs Art; Am Color Print Soc (hon vpres, 68-71); Coll Art Asn Am; Nat Coun Art Adminr (chmn, 79-80); Am Fedn Arts; Nat Mus of the Pacific War, Fredericksburg, Tex (bd mem). *Res:* Preparation for exhibitions and Catalogue Raisonne on contemp American artists (Shahn, Levine, Diller, Browne, Hunt, de Creeft, Lorrie Goulet, James Chapen, Hunt Slonem & others). *Collection:* Works of contemporary American artists. *Publ:* Auth, Ben Shahn: A Retrospective (catalog), 76-77; Jack Levine: A Retrospective (catalog), 78; Burgoyne Diller 1938-1962, Paintings, Drawings and Collages (catalog), 79; The Prints and Poster of Ben Shahn, 82; The Prints and Posters of Jack Levine, 83. *Mailing Add:* 1 Towers Park Lane Suite 2302 San Antonio TX 78209

PRESLAN, KRIS
PAINTER
b Dresden, Germany Feb 15, 1945. *Study:* Madison, Wisc, BA, 71, MA, 73. *Work:* Portland Art Mus, Ore. *Exhib:* Watercolor W, Transparent Watercolor Soc 42nd Ann Exhib, 2010; Nat Watercolor Soc, 2010, 2012; Transparent Watercolor Soc Am, 35th Ann Nat Exhib, Kenosha, WI, 2011; Western Fed Watercolor Soc, 36th Ann Exhib, Albuquerque, NMex, 2011; Am Watercolor Soc, 144th Ann Exhib, New York, 2011; La Watercolor Soc, 2013; Am Watercolor Soc, 2013; La Watercolor Soc Exhib, 2013; Internat Watercolor Biennial, Estampus, Belgium, 2014; Royal Inst of Painters in Watercolor Exhib, London, 2015; Signature American Watercolor Exhib, Fallbrook, Calif, 2015. *Awards:* Merit Award, Watercolor Art Soc Houston, 2011; Best of Show, Watercolor Soc Ore, 2011, 2012; First Place, Nat Waterworks Exhib, Northwest Watercolor Soc, 2011; Best Watercolor Artists of the Year, Splash 12, Splash 14 Annual North Light Publication of Best Watercolor Artists of the Year, 2010, 2012, 2013; John Diozegl Mem award, Transparent Watercolor Soc Am Exhib, 2012; Transparent Watercolor Soc Am award, Kenosha, Wisc, 2012; Grand Prize winner, Internat Artist Contest; Presidents award, Northwest Watercolor Soc, 2013; Memorial award, Transparent Watercolor Soc Am, 2014; Grand Prize award, Internat Artist Mag, 2014. *Mem:* Nat Watercolor Soc (signature mem); Transparent Watercolor Soc Am (signature mem); Watercolor Soc Ore; Northwest Watercolor Soc; Fed Canadian Artists; Watercolor Art Soc Houston (signature mem); Am Watercolor Soc; Watercolor West Int Transparent Watercolor Soc (signature mem). *Media:* Watercolor, Transparent. *Publ:* contribr, SPLASH 12, North Light, 2011, Splash 14, 2013, Splash 15, 2014; contribr, American Art Collection Mag, 2014; contribr, SPLASH 16, SPLASH Retrospective, 20 Yrs Watercolor Excellence, North Light Publishers; feature article, Art Collector Mag, 2014. *Dealer:* Valley Art Gallery 2022 Main St Forest Grove OR 97116; Portland Art Mus. *Mailing Add:* PO Box 1511 Lake Oswego OR 97035

PRESSER, ELENA
ASSEMBLAGE ARTIST
b Buenos Aires, Nov 3, 1940; US citizen. *Study:* Dade Community, AA, 75. *Work:* Fla Capitol, Dept Nat Resources & Art Pub Places, Fla; Ala Power Co, Birmingham, Ala; IBM, Gaithersburg, Md. *Comn:* Anna Magdalena Bach Notebook, Ruth & Marvin Sackner Arch, Miami Beach, Fla, 85; Italian Concerto-J S Bach, comn by Dr & Mrs Roley Kohen, Miami Beach, Fla, 87. *Exhib:* Solo exhibs, Elena Presser: Bach's Goldberg Variations, Frances Wolfson Art Gallery, Miami, Fla, 85, Meadows Mus & Gallery, Dallas, Tex, 87, Mus Contemp Hispanic Art, NY, 87 & Elena Presser: Transpositions, Moore Coll Art, Philadelphia, Pa, 88; group shows, Calligraffitti, Leila Taghinia Micani Gallery, NY, 84, Collage: The State of the Art, Bergen Mus, Paramus, NJ, 85, Southern Abstraction, City Gallery Contemp Art, Raleigh, NC, 87 & Expresiones Hispanas, Ctr Fine Arts, Miami, Fla, 89. *Awards:* Purchase Award, House of Repr, 79; Purchase Award, Fla Dept State, 81; Artist-in-Residence Fel, D Jerassi Gounf, 85. *Bibliog:* John & Joan Digby (auth), The Collage Handbook, Thames & Hudson Inc, 85; Marvin Sackner (auth), Ruth & Marvin Sackner Arch Concrete & Visual Poetry, Ruth & Marvin Sackner, 86. *Mem:* Women's Caucus For Art, Miami Chap, (bd dir 83-85); Lowe Art Mus, 78-88; Ctr Fine Arts, 88; Bass Mus, 84-88; Soc Layerists Multi-Media, 87-88. *Media:* Wall Relief Assemblage. *Mailing Add:* 7020 SW 100th St Miami FL 33156

PRESSLY, NANCY LEE
CURATOR, ADMINISTRATOR
b Suffern, NY, Feb 11, 1941. *Study:* Goucher Col, BA, 62; Columbia Univ, with T Reff, L Hawes & O Brendel, MA, 69; Inst Fine Arts, with W Rubin, R Rosenblum & G Schiff, 69-71. *Collection Arranged:* The Pursuit of Happiness: A View of Life in Georgian England (auth, catalog), 77 & The Fuseli: Circle in Rome: Early Romantic Art of 1770s (auth, catalog), 79, Yale Ctr Brit Art; A Birthday Celebration: Recent Gifts and Acquisitions, 1981 (auth, catalog), 82, Salome: La belle dame sans merci (auth, catalog), 83 & Revealed Religion: Benjamin West's Commissions for Windsor Castle and Fonthill Abbey (auth, catalog), 83, San Antonio Mus Art. *Pos:* Cataloger Am art, Metrop Mus Art, New York, 69-71; assoc res & asst cur, Yale Ctr Brit Art, 71-79; chief cur, San Antonio Mus Art, 81-84; asst dir, Mus Prog, Nat Endowment Arts, Washington, DC, 84-92; pres, Nancy L Pressly & Assocs, 92-. *Awards:* Paul Mellon Vis Sr Fel, CASVA, Nat Gallery Art, fall 92. *Bibliog:* Hilton Kramer (auth), Henry Fuseli: A leader in Romanticism, Sunday New York Times, 9/16/79; John Ashbery (auth), Dark satanic mills, New York Mag, 10/6/79; Gert Schiff (auth), article, Arts Mag, 12/79. *Mem:* Coll Art Asn; Am Asn Mus; Soc 18th Century Studies. *Publ:* Auth, Whistler in America: An album of early drawings, Metrop Mus J, 72; James Jefferys and the master of the giants, Burlington Mag, 4/77; Guy Head and his echo flying from Narcissus: A British artist in Rome in the 1790s, Bull Detroit Inst Arts, 82; Museum Design: Planning & Building for Art (intro & proj dir), Oxford Univ Press, 93. *Mailing Add:* 1090 Seaboard Ave NW Atlanta GA 30318

PRESSLY, WILLIAM LAURENS
HISTORIAN, EDUCATOR
b Chattanooga, Tenn, Apr 1, 1944. *Study:* Princeton Univ, BA, 66; Inst Fine Arts, New York Univ, PhD, 73. *Teaching:* Asst & assoc prof 18th-19th century European art, Yale Univ, 73-82; sr lectr, Univ Tex, Austin, 82-83; assoc prof, Duke Univ, 85-87; assoc prof, Univ Md, 87-93, prof, 93-. *Awards:* Morse Fel, Yale Univ, 75-76; Guggenheim Mem Fel, 83-84; Inst Advan Study, Princeton, 94-95. *Mem:* Fel Royal Soc Arts, London; The Am Soc for Eighteenth Century Studies; Coll Art Asn; Phi Beta Kappa Soc. *Publ:* The Life and Art of James Barry, Yale Univ Press, 81; James Barry: The Artist as Hero, Tate Gallery, London, 83; A Catalogue of Paintings in the Folger Shakespeare Libr, Yale Univ Press, 93; The French Revolution as Blasphemy: Johan Zoffany's Paintings of the Massacre at Paris, August 10, 1792, Univ Calif Press, 99; auth, The Artist as Original Genius: Shakespeare's Fine Frenzy, in Late Eighteenth Century British Art, Univ Del Press, 2007; Envisioning a New Public Art, Cork Univ Press, 2014. *Mailing Add:* 1090 Seaboard Ave NW Atlanta GA 30318

PRESTON, ANN L
SCULPTOR
b Seattle, Wash, 1942. *Study:* Swarthmore Col, Pa, 59-61; Sch Mus Fine Arts, Boston, 62-66; Tufts Univ, Boston, BFA, 68; Calif Inst Arts, Valencia, MFA, 80. *Work:* Chase Manhattan Bank, NA, NY; Carnation Corp, Los Angeles; Phoenix Art Mus, Ariz; Anaheim Marina, San Francisco, Calif. *Comn:* Los Angeles Cent Publ Libr; Los Angeles Transportation Comn, Willow Sta; San Francisco Courthouse, Family Court; San Francisco Int Airport. *Exhib:* Solo exhibs, Atlantic Richfield Co, Ctr Visual Arts, Los Angeles, Calif, 81, Pence Gallery, Santa Monica, Calif, 86-91, Barbara Toll Fine Arts, NY, 87, 88, 91 & 94, Los Angeles Contemp Exhibs, 88, Guggenheim Gallery, Chapman Univ, Orange, Calif, 92 & Rosamund Felsen Gallery, Los Angeles & Santa Monica, Calif, 93, 95; Selections from the Carnation Co Collection, Armory Ctr Arts, Pasadena, Calif, 90; In Her Image, Barbara Toll Fine Arts, NY, 90; The Lick of the Eye, Shoshana Wayne Gallery, Santa Monica, Calif, 91; From Studio to Station: Pub Art on the Metro Blueline, FHP Hippodrome Gallery, Long Beach, Calif, 92; Recent Work, Rosamund Felsen Gallery, Los Angeles, Calif, 93; The Figure as Fiction: The Figure in Visual Art and Lit, Contemp Arts Ctr, Cincinnati, 93; Gallery Artists, Barbara Toll Fine Arts, NY, 93; DAMNED, Life, Death & Surface, John Thomas Gallery, Santa Monica, 94; Hooked on a Feeling, Kohn Turner Gallery, Los Angeles, 94; Wax, Nohra Haime Gallery, NY, 95; The Anamorph, Anaheim, Calif, 95; From LA With Love, Galerie Praz-Delavallade, Paris, 95; Chimera, Angels Gate Cult Ctr, San Pedro, Calif, 97; Plastered, Shoshana Wayne Gallery, Santa Monica, Calif, 97. *Awards:* Nat Endowment Arts Fel, 88. *Bibliog:* Benjamin Weissman (auth), rev, Artforum, 10/93; Michael Duncan (auth), LA rising, Art Am, 12/94; Peter Frank (auth), Art pick of the week, LA Weekly, 6/15/95; numerous newspapers, mags, art publs. *Dealer:* Rosamund Felsen Gallery Bergamot Sta B-4 2525 Michigan Ave Santa Monica CA 90404. *Mailing Add:* 24618 Golf View Dr Valencia CA 91355

PRESTON, GEORGE NELSON
HISTORIAN, EDUCATOR
b Dec 14, 1938; US citizen. *Study:* City Coll New York, BA, 62; Columbia Univ, MA, 68, PhD, 73. *Collection Arranged:* African Art: Rare and Familiar Forms (auth, catalog), State Univ NY Art Gallery, Potsdam, 76; The Innovative African Artist (auth, catalog), Ithaca Coll Mus Art; Permanent Installation, African Hall, Brooklyn Mus, 68-78; Ancient Terracottas of Ghana and Mali (with catalog), 81-82. *Pos:* Spec consult, Brooklyn Mus, 68. *Teaching:* Asst prof art, Rutgers Univ, Livingston Col, 70-72; asst prof art, City Col, City Univ New York, 72-80, assoc prof, 81-, prof art hist, 95-. *Awards:* Fels, Ford Found, 68-70 & 72 & Kress Found, 69; Res Award, Res Found City Univ New York, 81-82. *Mem:* Columbia Univ Seminar Primitive &

Pre-Columbian Art; Washington Hq Asn, NY (bd dir, 79-); Int Asn Art Critics. *Res:* Conceptual and culture historical aspects of African art; contemporary American artists whose styles are outside the definition of the most popular isms. *Publ:* Auth, Dynamic/Static, African Art as Philosophy, Interbook, New York, 74; Jay Milder: Painter of discovery, resolution and rediscovery, 11/76 & Against the grain: The paintings of Ann Tabachnik, 2/79, Arts Mag; Reading the Art of Benin, Images of Power: Royal Court Art of Benin, New York Univ, 81. *Mailing Add:* c/o Art Dept City Col City Univ NY Convent Ave & 138th New York NY 10031

PRESTON, MALCOLM H
CRITIC, PAINTER
b West New York, NJ, May 25, 1920. *Study:* Univ Wis, BA; Columbia Univ, MA & PhD. *Work:* Hofstra Univ Collection; Portland Mus; Queens Mus, NY; Islip Art Mus; Cape Cod Mus Fine Arts; and others. *Exhib:* Mourlot Galerie; ACA Gallery; Eggleston Gallery; SAC Gallery; AAA Gallery; and others. *Pos:* Dir, Inst Arts, Hofstra Univ, 60-64; art critic, Newsday, 68-85 & Boston Herald Traveler, 70-72; writer, Christian Science, 85-90. *Teaching:* Asst instr fine arts, New Sch Social Res, 40-41; instr, Adelphi Univ, 47-48; prof, Hofstra Univ, 49-74. *Awards:* Joe & Emily Lowe Found Educ Res Grant, 50; Ford Found Grant, 56 & 57; Shell Oil Res Grant, 64. *Mem:* Nat Soc Lit & Arts; CAA. *Media:* Oil, Serigraphs. *Res:* Florality of Am Art; use of computer data to identify artists style. *Publ:* Contribr, Christian Sci Monitor, Arts Mag, Boston Globe & other mag & newspapers; writer, producer & principal performer, Arts Around Us & American Art Today (Ford Found-sponsored nat educ television series), 55-56. *Dealer:* Heller Gallery Provincetown, MA

PREWITT, MERLE R(AINEY)
PAINTER
b Fayetteville, NC, Mar 15, 1928. *Study:* Duke Univ, 50; Fayetteville Tech Community Coll with Tom Moore, Lyn Padrick, Petra Gerber & Kerstin Weldon. *Work:* Fayetteville Diagnostic Ctr, Cape Fear Studios & Jr League Fayetteville, NC; Cooperative Savings & Loan, Wilmington, NC; MacPherson Presbyterian Church, Fayetteville, NC; First Presby Church, Fayetteville, NC; New S Bank; pvt collections. *Comn:* 3 dogs - Singleton, Crab-Arts & Crab Dog. *Exhib:* Pembroke Art Mus, Pembroke Univ, NC, 93; solo exhibs, Cape Fear Studios, Fayetteville, NC, 93, 95 & 2011; Miniature Painters, Sculptures & Graphics Soc Washington DC, Art Club Washington, 94; Colored Pencil Soc Am, Oswego, Wash, 94; Moore Co Competition, Campbell House, Southern Pines, NC, 94; 1998 Winter Olympics, Nagano Japan, 98; Marilyn Wilson Gallery; Seaside, Nags Head, NC, 93; El Dorado Gallery, Colorado Springs; Moore Co Competition, 97, 2002; Olympics Show, Nagano Japan, 97-2005; and others; Up & Coming, Fayetteville Mus Art Show, 2008; Fayetteville, Cumberland Co Art Coun, 2009. *Pos:* Bd dir, Fayetteville Art Guild, 88-93; Cape Fear Studios, 91-2011. *Awards:* Cooperative Savings & Loan Purchase Award, Artquest of Wilmington, 91; Emerging Artist Grant, NC/Cumberland Co/Fayetteville Art Coun, 93 & 2006; Best local artist, Fayetteville, NC, 2004; Campbell House, New York, 2004; Artist of Year, Fayetteville Cumberland Co Art Coun, 2006; Mary Lynn McCree Bryan Leadership Award, Cumberland Community Found, 2011. *Mem:* Fayetteville Art Guild; Miniature Painters, Sculptors & Grafters of Washington, DC; Moore Co Art Coun; Fayetteville/Cumberland Co Art Coun; Fayetteville Art League; Colored Pencil Soc Am; NC Watercolor; Miniature Art Soc Fla; Fayetteville Mus Art Colored Pencil Soc Am; Am Watercolor Soc. *Media:* Watercolor, Colored Pencil, Pen, Scratch Board. *Interests:* Knitting, gardening, flower arranging & needlepoint. *Publ:* Best of Colored Pencil, 93. *Dealer:* Cape Fear Studios 148-1 Maxwell St Fayetteville NC 28305-5205; Not Quite Antiques Raeford Ave Fayetteville NC 28303; Fayetteville Art Guild Gillespie St Fayetteville NC 28301. *Mailing Add:* 416 Devane St Fayetteville NC 28305-5205

PREY, BARBARA ERNST
PAINTER
b Manhasset, NY, Apr 17, 1957. *Study:* Williams Col, Williamstown, Mass, BA(honors in art), 79; Univ Wurzberg, Ger, (Fulbright scholar, 80; Harvard Univ, MDiv, 86. *Work:* Williams Coll Mus Art, Williamstown, Mass; GE Capital Gallery, Stamford, Conn; Henry Luce Found, NY; Farnsworth Art Mus, Rockland, Maine; pvt collection of Pres & Mrs George Bush; and others; Pres and Mrs George Bush, The White House; Office of the First Lady of NY; Brooklyn Mus; Smithsonian Am Art Mus; Hood Mus, Dartmouth Coll; NY Historical Soc; Kennedy Space Ctr. *Comn:* Paintings, Prince Castell, Ger, 80; President's House, Williams Col, Williamstown, Mass, 86; Site of New Art Complex, Shadyside Acad, Pittsburgh, Pa, 93; US Embassy, Paris, France; Bloomberg Bus News Holiday Card, 95 & 97; NASA Art Collection; The White House Christmas Card, 03; NASA: The Internat Space Station; Commission X-43, Shuttle relaunch, 2005; US Arts in Embassies Program, Oslo, 03. *Exhib:* Brooklyn Mus, NY, 75; Farnsworth Mus Art Benefit Auction Exhib, Rockland, Maine, 94; Westmoreland Mus Art; Recent Acquisitions, Farnsworth Art Mus, 97; Guild Hall Mus, East Hampton, NY, 97; Express Yourself, Portland Mus Art, Maine, 97; Young Collectors Choice, Hecksher Mus, Huntington, NY, 99; Art in Miniature, Gilcrease Mus, 2000; Lightscapes, Jensen Fine Arts Mus, 2001; Retrospective, Blue Water Fine Arts, Maine, 2007, The Mona Bismarck Found, Paris, France, 2007; Smithsonian Nat Air & Space Mus, 2011; Heckscher Mus, 2011; US Embassy France, Spain, Norway, Czech Republic. *Collection Arranged:* Pres and Mrs. George Bush; The White House; The Farnsworth Art Mus; Williams Coll; The Brooklyn Mus; Smithsonian Am Art Mus; New York Hist Soc. *Pos:* Mod Painting Dept, Sotheby's Auction House, NY, 81-82; illusr, The New Yorker, 81-; Gourmet Mag, 82-; travel sect, New York Times, 87-88; poetry columnist, Good Housekeeping, 87-92; Nat Coun Arts, Adv Bd to Nat Endowment for the Arts, 2008-. *Teaching:* Vis lectr Western Christian Art, Taiwan Col & Sem, 86-87; Artist in Residence, Westminister Sch, Simsbury, Conn, 97. *Awards:* Henry Luce Found Grant, 86; Jean Thoburn Award, Pittsburgh Watercolor Soc, 94; Best Show, Westmoreland Mus Art, 96; NY Senate Women of Distinction Award, 2004; Raynham Hall Mus award, 2010; Celebrate Achievement award, Heckscher Mus, 2011. *Bibliog:* Art Market, Int Art Newspaper, 1/99; Critic's Choice, NY Daily News, 1/99; Inspirations, Maine PBS, 2001; CBS Evening News, 2011; CBS Sunday Morning, NY Times, 2011; Wall St Jour; and many others. *Mem:* Nat Mus Women in Arts. *Media:* Watercolor. *Publ:* Profiles, The Observer-Reporter, 1/93; illusr, Williams Coll Bicentennial Calendar, 92-93; Watercolor Wins Award, Pittsburgh Watercolor Soc, 94; cover, Am Artist Mag Watercolor, 94 & Dan's Papers, The Hamptons, 99, 2000; Barbara Ernst Prey: The Trace in the Mind-An artists Response to 9/11, 02; Works on Water, 2005. *Dealer:* Blue Water Fine Arts. *Mailing Add:* 22 Pearl St Oyster Bay NY 11771

PREZIOSI, DONALD A
HISTORIAN, CRITIC
b New York, NY, Jan 12, 1941. *Study:* Fairfield Col, BA, 62; Harvard Univ, MA, 63, PhD, 68. *Teaching:* Asst prof art hist, Yale Univ, 67-73 & Mass Inst Technol, 73-77; assoc prof, State Univ NY, Binghamton, 78-86; prof, Univ Calif Los Angeles, 86-. *Awards:* Fels, Nat Endowment Humanities, 73-74, Ctr Advan Study Visual Arts, Nat Gallery, 81-82 & Ctr Advan Study, Stanford Univ, 83-84; Am Coun Learned Soc, 89-90. *Mem:* Coll Art Asn Am; Archaeol Inst Am; Semiotic Soc Am (vpres, 83-84, pres, 84-85). *Res:* Ancient art and architecture; contemporary theory and criticism. *Publ:* Auth, The Semiotics of the Built Environment, Ind Univ Press, 79; Architecture, Language and Meaning, 79 & Minoan Architectural Design, 83, Mouton; Constructing the origins of art, Art J, 83; Rethinking Art Hist, Yale Univ Press, 89

PRICE, ANNE KIRKENDALL
CRITIC
b Birch Tree, Mo, June 14, 1922. *Study:* Univ Mo, Columbia, BJ; Univ Ga, Athens, art seminars; Southern Regional Educ Bd workshop for art critics. *Pos:* Art critic, Morning Advocate, Baton Rouge, La, 60-. *Awards:* Humanities Coun Award for Serv to the Arts, Greater Baton Rouge Arts, 86; Award, Women Achievement, Arts & Humanities, 94; Governor's Award for Lifetime Achievement in the Arts, 98. *Mem:* Capitol Corresp (pres, 68); Baton Rouge Arts Coun; Baton Rouge Little Theater (bd mem). *Mailing Add:* c/o Morning Advocate 525 Lafayette Baton Rouge LA 70802

PRICE, BARBARA GILLETTE
ADMINISTRATOR, PAINTER
b Philadelphia, Pa, June 26, 1938. *Study:* Univ Ala, BFA, 66, MA, 68. *Work:* Univ Ala, Tuscaloosa; Dept Health, Educ & Welfare N Portal Bldg, Washington, DC; Ferris State Col, Mich. *Exhib:* Solo exhibs, Foundry Gallery, Washington, DC, 76, Spiritscapes, Cranbrook Acad Art Mus, Bloomfield Hills, Mich, 80, Landscapes of the Mind, Ferris State, Big Rapids, Mich, 81, Md Inst, Coll of Art, Baltimore, 82, Schweyer Galdo Galleries, Birmingham, Mich, 82, Notre Dame Col, Baltimore, 85, Columbia Asn Ctr for Arts, Md, 89; Faculty Show, Md Inst Coll of Art, 83 & 85-92; Artscape, Baltimore, 86; Art in the Bell Tower, Baltimore, 88; Intimate Works, Morris Mechanic Theatre Gallery, 89; Solo exhib, Le Ninfee, Loyola Coll, Baltimore, Md, 91; Group exhibs, Members Only Premiere, Artshowcase, Baltimore, Md, 90, Reverberations: 4 Voices, Barbara Price, Nancy K Roeder, Jann Rosen-Queralt and Jo Smail, Roper Gallery, Frostburg State Univ, 91, Media-Mix, Artshowcase, Baltimore, Md, 91; Finding Beauty in the Ordinary, John Dorsey, Baltimore Sun, 91. *Pos:* Dean, Cranbrook Acad Art, 78-82; vpres, Acad Affairs, Maryland Inst, Col Art, 82-93; pres, Moore Col Art & Design, 94-. *Teaching:* Asst prof art, Corcoran Sch Art, DC, 70-78, dir summer prog, 75-78. *Bibliog:* Marsha Miro (auth), Celebration of legacy, Detroit Free Press, 2/21/82; Jeanne Heifeitz (auth), Price landscapes explore territory of Psyche, Jewish Times, 83; Mike Guliano (auth), Barbara Price at the Columbia Art Center, Columbia Flyer, 89. *Mem:* Nat Coun Art Adminr; Coll Art Asn; NASAD; Am Asn of Higher Educ. *Media:* Oil, Acrylics. *Publ:* Ed, Sculpture at Cranbrook (catalog), Cranbrook Acad Art Mus, 79; Spiritscapes (catalog), Ferris State Col, 81

PRICE, DIANE MILLER
ASSEMBLAGE ARTIST, COLLAGE ARTIST
b Paterson, NJ, Sept 13, 1943. *Study:* RI Sch Design, 61-63; Parsons Sch Design, New York, 63-64; Montclair State Univ, NJ, papermaking as art form with Anne Chapman, BA, 84. *Work:* Reader's Digest, Pleasantville, NY; Educ Testing Serv, Princeton, NJ; Blue Cross/Blue Shield, Wilmington, Del; Crane Mus Papermaking, Dalton, Mass. *Exhib:* NJ State Mus, Trenton, 86; Noyes Mus, Oceanville, NJ, 2009; In the Spotlight, Nat Asn Women Artists Gallery, New York, 2004; Solo Exhibs, Paper: By Hand, Lib Gallery, Printmaking Coun NJ, North Branch, 94; Paper Works & Habitats, Pierro Gallery, South Orange, NJ, 95; Interchurch Ctr Galleries, New York City, 2000; Reconnecting, Lippman Gallery, Short Hills, NJ, 2006; Great South Bay Gallery, Stageworks, Hudson, NY, 2009; Nat Acad Gechtoff Galleries, NY, 2014. *Awards:* Fel Grant, NJ State Coun, 86-87; Medal of Honor & Elizabeth S Blake Meml Award, Nat Asn Women Artists, 2004; Dorothy Tabak Mem Award for Collage, Nat Asn Women Artists, 2009. *Bibliog:* Jane Freeman (auth), The Art of the Miniature, Watson-Guptill Pubs, 02. *Mem:* Nat Asn Women Artists (asst awards chair, 86-98); Friends of Dard Hunter; Textile Study Group NY. *Media:* Handmade Paper, Found Objects, Found Papers. *Dealer:* Rabbet Gallery 360 Georges Rd North Brunswick NJ 08902. *Mailing Add:* 246 W End Ave Apt 4B New York NY 10023-3619

PRICE, HELEN BURDON
PAINTER, PRINTMAKER
b St Louis, Mo, Sept 23, 1926. *Study:* La State Univ, Baton Rouge, BS, 46; Johns Hopkins Univ, Baltimore, Md, BS & RN, 49; studied with Gerry Samuels, Budd Hopkins, DeLaMonica, John Heliker, Ken Nishi. *Work:* Dames & Moore, Blue Hill Ctr, NJ; Women's Ctr, Hackensack, NJ; Morgan Lewis & Bockius, New York City; Berlex Lab Inc, Montville, NJ; and others. *Exhib:* Thirty-five solo exhibs in NY & NJ; many 2 to 4 person & group exhibs; several traveling painting & printmaking exhibs in US, India & Italy. *Pos:* Dir & cur, Vineyard Theatre Gallery & Gallery 108, NY, 77-87; critique, Teen Festival, NJ, 95-2001. *Teaching:* individual guidance, workshops, panels, and lectures. *Awards:* Found Award, Nat Asn Women Artists Ann Exhib, Zuita & Joseph Akston, 87; Exhib Award, Ringwood Manor Exhib, W Wing Gallery, 88; Blake Mem Award, Nat Asn Women Artists Ann Exhib, Elizabeth Stanton Blake, 91; NAWA Medal of Honor, 95, Doris Kreindler Meml Award, 98, Gladys B

Blum Meml Award, 99; Showcase Award, 2004; Award of Excellence, 2004. *Mem:* Nat Asn Women Artists Inc (vpres, 89-92, pres, 93-)95; Salute to Women in Arts; Painting Affil Art Ctr Northern NJ; Artists Equity NY. *Media:* Acrylic, Collage. *Publ:* Contribr (auth P Knapp), Strictly business, Artist's Mag, 1/93. *Dealer:* Broadfoot & Broadfoot Boonton, NJ; Broadfoot & Broadfoot 484 Broome St New York NY. *Mailing Add:* 2110 Kendal Way Tarrytown NY 10591

PRICE, JOE (ALLEN)
SERIGRAPHER, WATERCOLORIST
b Ferriday, La, 1935. *Study:* Northwestern Univ, Evanston, Ill, BS, 57; Art Ctr Coll Design, Los Angeles, with Glenn Vilppu, 67-68; Stanford Univ, Calif, MA, 70. *Work:* Philadelphia Mus Art, Pa; Nat Mus Am Art, Washington; Libr Cong, Washington; Achenbach Found Graphic Art, Legion Honor, San Francisco; San Francisco Mus Mod Art; Mus Int Contemp Graphic Art, Fredrikstad, Norway. *Comn:* Print, Int Graphic Arts Found, Darien, Conn. *Exhib:* Solo exhibs, Tahir Gallery, New Orleans, 82, New Talent in Printmaking, Asn Am Artists, NY & Philadelphia, 84, Triton Mus Art, Santa Clara, 86, Ankrum Gallery, Los Angeles, Calif, 86, Huntsville Mus Art, Ala, 87, Gallery 30, San Mateo, Calif, 88, 91 & 97, Arches Paper Printed on Paper, Talens Hq, South Hadley, Mass, 98, Robert Wright Community Gallery, Coll of Lake Co, Grayslake, Ill, 2003, Carnegie Visual Arts Ctr, Decatur, Ala, 2005 & The Reality Show (2-5 solo exhibs), Peninsula Fine Arts Ctr, Newport News, Va, 2007; Sixth Int Exhib Botanical Art, Hunt Inst, Carnegie-Mellon Univ, Pa, 88; Fourth Int Biennial Print Exhib '89, Taipei Fine Arts Mus, Taiwan; Directions in Bay Area Printmaking: Three Decades, Palo Alto Cult Ctr, 92-93; Alabama Impact: Contemp Artists with Alabama Ties, Fine Arts Mus of the South & Huntsville Mus Art, 95; Agart World Print Festival, Ljubljana, Slovenia, 98; Am Botanical Prints of Two Centuries (with catalog), Hunt Inst, Carnegie-Mellon Univ, Pa, 2003; Robert T Wright Gallery. *Pos:* Chmn art dept, Coll San Mateo, Calif, 76-94. *Teaching:* Prof studio drawing & chair art dept, Coll San Mateo, Calif, 70-94. *Awards:* Louis Lozowick Mem Award, Audubon Artists 36th Ann, 78; Lessing J Rosenwald Prize, Philadelphia Print Club Int, 79; Ture Bengtz Mem Purchase Award, 39th NAm Print Exhib, New York, 86; Creative Achievement Award, Calif State Legislature, 89; Audubon Artists Silver Medal Honor in Graphics, 91. *Bibliog:* Duane Wakeham (auth), Joe Price: Serigraphs in light and tone, Am Artist, 10/77; Tom Cervenak (auth), Bay area printmakers, Visual Dialog, spring 78; Prints Charming, Pol, Sydney, Australia, 1/80; Mary Ann & Mace Wenniger (coauths), Secrets of Buying Art, 10/90. *Mem:* Calif Soc Printmakers; Boston Printmakers; Am Color Print Soc; Audubon Artists; Print Club, Philadelphia. *Media:* Serigraphy, Watercolor. *Interests:* Still lifes. *Dealer:* M Lee Stone Fine Prints Inc 2101 Forest Ave Ste 130 San Jose CA 95128. *Mailing Add:* 20501 Ventura Blvd Woodland Hills CA 91364

PRICE, JOE D & ETSUKO
COLLECTORS
Pos: Founder, Shin'enkan Found for Japanese Art, Corona del Mar, Calif; bd dir, Friends of Kebyar, 83. *Awards:* Names one of Top 200 Collectors, ARTnews Mag, 2004. *Collection:* Edo-period Japanese art. *Mailing Add:* PO Box 1111 Bartlesville OK 74005

PRICE, LESLIE KENNETH
PAINTER, EDUCATOR
b New York, NY. *Study:* Sch Visual Arts, NY, 63-64; Pratt Inst, with James Gahagan, Ernest Briggs, G Laderman, BFA, 69; Mills Col, Oakland, Calif, MFA, 71. *Work:* Oakland Mus, Calif; Johnson Publ Co, Chicago. *Exhib:* Blacks USA, NY Cult Ctr, 73; New Directions in Afro-Am Art, Cornell Univ, Ithaca, NY, 74; Berkeley Art Ctr, Calif, 76; San Jose Mus, Calif, 76; Studio Mus in Harlem, NY, 77. *Teaching:* From assoc prof painting to prof art, Humboldt State Univ, Arcata, Calif, 72-. *Awards:* Painting Award, Pratt Inst, 68; Award of Merit, Calif Palace Legion Honor, 73; Honorarium, Cornell Univ, 74. *Bibliog:* Alfred Frankenstein (auth), article, San Francisco Chronicle, 11/77. *Mem:* Nat Conf of Artists. *Media:* Acrylic, Graphite. *Publ:* Contribr, Black Artists on Art, Vol II, Contemporary Crafts, 72; Existence Black, Southern Ill Univ, 72; contribr, Directions in Afro-American Art, Cornell Univ, 74. *Mailing Add:* Humboldt State Univ Dept Art Arcata CA 95521

PRICE, MARLA
MUSEUM DIRECTOR, CURATOR
Study: PhD in Art Hist. *Pos:* Assoc cur, of 20th-century art Nat Gallery Art, Washington, DC; chief cur, Modern Art Mus Ft Worth, Tex, 1986-91, dir, 1991-. *Mailing Add:* Modern Art Mus Ft Worth 3200 Darnell St Fort Worth TX 76107-2872

PRICE , MARY SUE SWEENEY
MUSEUM DIRECTOR
Study: Allegheny Col, BA in Eng, 73. *Hon Degrees:* Caldwell Coll, 94; Rutgers Univ, 2004; Drew Univ, 2008; NJIT, 2012. *Pos:* supvr pub relations, Newark Mus, 75-80, dir prog, 80-86, asst dir, 86-90, deputy dir, 90-93, dir & CEO, 93-2013. *Mem:* Asn Art Mus Dir; Am Asn Mus; NJ Asn Mus; Art Table; Art Pride NJ; Newark Art Coun

PRICE, MORGAN SAMUEL
PAINTER, INSTRUCTOR
b Cleveland, Ohio, Feb 9, 1947. *Study:* Ringling Sch Art, Cert, 68, with Loran Wilford, 66-68 & Carl Cogar, 76. *Work:* Goddard Art Ctr, Ardmore, Okla; Libr Cong, Washington, DC; Kirchman Corp Gallery, Orlando, Fla. *Comn:* Oil painting, St Mary's Catholic Church, Annapolis, Md, 68, Walker Oil, 73, painting, comn by Mr & Mrs Norman Yodi, 78, 79, 80 & 81, Gant Oil Co, 78, Woodruff Oil Co, 80, Ardmore, Okla, Law Offices of Tanya Plant 78, Law Offices of Mort Rosenblum 75-80, Orlando, Fla. *Exhib:* Salmagundi Club, NY, 88, 90-91; 78th Ann Exhib, Allied Artists Am, NY, 89 & 91 & 92; Brevard Cult Alliance, Savannahs, Merritt Island, Fla, 90; Quintuple Galerie, Argenteuil, France, 91; one-woman show, State of Fla, Capitol Bldg, Tallahassee, 91, McDonald Douglas Corp, Kennedy Space Ctr, 91 & Brevard Mus Art, Melbourne, Fla, 92, Marie Ferrer Gallery, 92; The Cloisters, Sea Island, Ga, 91; Arts of the Park (Top 100), Nat Park Acad, Jackson Hole, Wyo, 92; Pastel Soc Am, NY, 92; Annual Combined Exhib, Salmagundi Club, NY, 2008. *Pos:* artist, Hallmark Cards, Kansas City, Mo; vpres, Knickerbocker Artists, New York, 91-92. *Teaching:* Instr oil painting, Goddard Art Ctr & Mus (oil, watercolor & pastel), Ardmore, Okla, 72-; workshops, oil, painting, watercolor & pastel, Throughout US & Europe, 72-. *Awards:* Joseph Hartley Award, Ann Open Show, Salmagundi Club, 90; Leon Stacks Mem, 78th Ann Exhib, Allied Artists, 91; Salmagundi Club, New York, New York, Antonio Cirino Award for a Pastel 1991; New Mems Show Oil Award Copley Soc Boston, Mass, 91; Best of Show, A Morning Walk, Central Fla Plein Air Artists, 2008; and many others. *Bibliog:* Dorothy Michaels (auth), Knowing How to Determine Value and Intensity, Am Artists, 6/91; Stephen Doherty (ed), Painting with a Positive Attitude, Am Artist (Spring Ed), 2008; Christine McHugh (auth), Studio Tour, Published Artist Mag, F&W Publ, Inc, Altamonte Springs, 2008. *Mem:* Fel, Am Artists Prof League; Salmagundi Club; Copley Soc Boston; Pastel Soc Am; Knickerbocker Artists, NY (vpres, 91-92); Allied Artists Assoc, NY; Audubon Artists Assoc, NY; Oil Painters of Am; Asn Pour La Promotion Du Patrimoine Artistique Francais. *Media:* Oil, Watercolor. *Publ:* Oil Painting with a Basic Palette; auth, Turn on the Light, MSP, L.L.C., 2008

PRICE, RITA F
PAINTER, PRINTMAKER
b Bronx, NY. *Study:* Art Inst Chicago, BFA, 82; Univ Ill, Chicago, 83-MFA Studies. *Work:* Carter Presidential Libr & Policy Ctr Mus, Atlanta, Ga; Int Mineral & Chemical Corp, Northbrook, Ill; Schiff, Hardin & Waite, Chicago, Ill; Ctr Prof Advan, E Brunswick, NJ; Renaissance No Shore Hotel, Northbrook, IL. *Comn:* A Place Where a Dreamer Goes, comn by Mr & Mrs Marshall Field, Chicago, 88; Cheries Garden, comn by Cherie Melchiorre, Chicago. *Exhib:* Curs Choice Collectibles, Prints & Drawings, Art Inst Chicago, 86; Ill Regional Print Show, Dittmar Gallery, Northwestern Univ, Evanston, Ill, 87 & 98; Ann Exhib, Am Jewish Arts Club, Spertus Mus, Chicago, 87, 88, & 89; 100 Yrs/100 Artists Traveling Exhib, 89; Nat V Print Exhib, Haggin Mus, Stockton, Calif, 90; Traveling Print Exhib, India, 90-91 & Nat Asn Women Artists, NY, 98-99; Women in the Visual Arts, Boca Raton, Fla, 1st place, 2011; Boca Mus Artists Guild, Boca Raton, Fla; NAWA Fla, Judges Recognition, 2004-2005, 1st place, 2009, 2011-2012. *Pos:* Asst dir admis, Art Inst Chicago, 83-85, asst dir, non-degree progs, 85-88 & dir alumni affairs, 88-93. *Teaching:* Instr experimental printmaking N Shore Art League, Winnetka, Ill, 84-; instr printmaking, Sch Art Inst, Chicago, 88-94; instr printmaking, Ox-Bow, Saugatuck, Mich, 88 & Evanston Art Ctr, Ill, 95. *Awards:* Award of Excellence, N Shore Art League, Ann Exhib, 82, Am Jewish Arts Club, 86, 87, 88, 90, 91, 92, 93, 97 & 98, Munic Art League, Chicago, 89 & Old Orchard Art Festival, 91; Women in the Visual Arts, Boca Raton, Fla; Nat Asn Women Artists Fla, Judges recognition, 2004-2005; Best in Show Exhib Nat Asn Women Artists, Palm Beach, Fla, 2007; 1st Prize, Women in Visual Arts, Fla, 2009; 1st Prize, Nat Asn Women Artists, 2009; 2nd Prize, Nat Asn Women Artists, 2009; 1st Prize, American Jewish Artists, 2011; honorable mention, Nat Asn Women Artists Fla; Judges recognition, Women in the Visual Arts Fla; Works on Paper award, 2012; Nat Assn Women Artists, 2012. *Bibliog:* Les Krantz (auth), The Chicago Art Rev, Am Reference Inc, 89; Louise Dunn Yochim (auth), Harvest of Freedom, Am Reference Inc, 89; Ivy Sundell (auth), The Chicago Art Scene, Woods Publ, 98. *Mem:* Nat Asn Women Artists; N Shore Art League (bd dir, vpres & pres, 73-); Chicago Soc Artists; Chicago Arts Coalition; Evanston Art Ctr (bd trustees, 92-); Nat Alumni Asn of Sch of Art Inst/Chicago (pres); Am Jewish Artists Club Chgo (pres, 2013). *Media:* Acrylic, Oil; All Media. *Mailing Add:* 1665 Dartmouth Ln Deerfield IL 60015

PRICE, SARA J
PAINTER, PHOTOGRAPHER
b 1952. *Study:* Pratt Inst, BFA, 76; New Sch Soc Res, 77-80; study with Burt Silverman, William Katavolos & Don Stacy. *Exhib:* Nat Exhib, Heckscher Mus, Huntington, NY, 85 & 86; Talent, Allan Stone Gallery, NY, 86 & 88-91; Giannetta Gallery, Philadelphia, Pa, 89; Nat Asn Women Artists, traveling exhib, Washington Cty Mus Fine Arts, Hagerstown, Md, 88, Greenville Mus Art, NC, 89, Butler Inst Am Art, Youngstown, Ohio, 89, Jesse Besser Mus, Alpena, Mich, 90 & Sansker Kendra Mus, Amedabad, India, 89-90; Mus Southwest, Midland, Tex, 91; Richmond Art Mus, Ind, 92. *Pos:* Freelance photogr, Tomlin Art Co, 77-92. *Awards:* Silver Medal/Printmaking, Int Art Competition, 84; Award of Excellence, Huntington Township Art League, 85; Purchase Award, Hoyt Inst Fine Arts, 86. *Mem:* Nat Asn Women Artists (exec bd 90-); NY Artists Equity Asn; Asn Flatbush Artists. *Media:* Oil on Paper, Watercolor. *Mailing Add:* 59 Sullivan St New York NY 10012-4306

PRICE, SETH
SCULPTOR, PAINTER
b Palestine, 1973. *Exhib:* Solo exhibs include Artists Space, New York, 2002, Art Gallery of Ontario, Ontario, 2003, Reena Spauldings, New York, 2004, 2006, Friedrich Petzel, New York, 2006, Galerie d'arte Moderna, Bologna, Galerie Isabella Bortollozi, Berlin, 2006; Group exhibs include Charley, PS 1, New York, 2002, Greater New York, 2005; Radical Entertainment, Inst Contemp Arts, London, 2003; Blinky, Tate Britain, London, 2003; So Few the Opportunities, So Many the Mistakes, Champion Fine Arts, New York, 2004; Last One On Is A Soft Jimmy, Paula Cooper Gallery, New York, 2004; Archives Generations Upon, Year, New York, 2004, Group Exhib, 2004; Make It Now, Sculpture Center, New York, 2005, Grey Flags, 2006; Whitney Biennial, Whitney Mus Am Art, 2002, 2008; 54th Int Art Exhib Biennale, Venice, 2011. *Teaching:* Fac, Bard Coll Milton Avery Grad Sch Arts, 2003. *Mailing Add:* Reena Spauldings Fine Art 165 E Broadway New York NY 10002

PRIEST, ELLEN
PAINTER
Study: Lawrence Univ, Appleton, Wis, BA, 1972; Yale Divinity Sch, 1977. *Work:* Astra Zeneca Corp, Wilmington, Del; Pfizer Corp, New London, Conn. *Exhib:* Solo exhibs include Mellon Arts Ctr, Wallingford, Conn, 1979, 2000, Yale Divinity Sch, 1982, Alva Gallery, New London, Conn, 2004, Philip & Muriel Berman Mus Art,

Collegeville, Pa, 2007; group exhibs include Artists Choice, 3rd Street Gallery, Philadelphia, 2001; Form & Color, Alva Gallery, New London, Conn, 2001; Jazz Series, Cosmopolitan Club Philadelphia, 2006. *Teaching:* Adjunct Fac, Pa Acad Fine Arts, Philadelphia, 2002; Prof, Univ Arts, Philadelphia, 2002-Present. *Awards:* Pollock-Krasner Found Grant, 2001, 2007

PRIEST, TERRI KHOURY
PAINTER
b Worcester, Mass, Jan 20, 1928. *Study:* Worcester Art Mus Sch, Mass, 47-48; Quinsigamond Community Coll, Worcester, 72 & 73; Univ Mass, Amherst, BFA (painting), 75, MFA (painting), 77. *Work:* Worcester Art Mus, Mass; Aldrich Mus Contemp Art, Ridgefield, Conn; DeCordova Mus, Lincoln, Mass; Bundy Art Ctr, Waitsfield, Vt; Springfield Art Mus, Springfield, Mass. *Comn:* Three color serigraph, Worcester Art Mus, 77; ltd ed print, Holy Cross Coll, Worcester, 81; Bishop Ireton Hish Sch, Alexandria, Va, 2004; 9 panel painting, Five Major Religions of the World, Coll Holy Cross, Worcester, Mass, 2007-; Holy Cross Coll, Worcester, Mass, 2008; and others. *Exhib:* New Eng Women, DeCordova Mus, Lincoln, Mass, 75; Painting Invitational, Brockton Art Ctr, Mass, 75; solo exhibs, Drawings, Worcester Art Mus, Mass, 76 & Wash World Gallery, Washington, DC, 81; Paperworks, Hudson River Mus, NY, 80; Classical Visions, Freddie Fong Gallery, San Francisco, 2004; Survey Show, Cantor Art Gallery, Holy Cross Coll, Worcester, Mass, 2005. *Pos:* Instr, Hampshire Coll, Amherst, Mass, 75; vis cur, Coll Art Gallery Prog, Worcester Art Mus, 79; artist-in-residence, Dorland Mt Artist Colony, (one month) 87. *Teaching:* assoc prof intermediate painting, visual design & color, Coll Holy Cross, Worcester, formerly; retired. *Awards:* Res & Publ Award, Holy Cross Coll, 82, 84 & 86. *Bibliog:* Nina Kaiden & Bartlett Hayes (auth), Artist and Advocate, Renaissance, 67; Roger T Dunn (auth), Terri Priest Interactions: Paintings & Works on Paper (monogr & catalog), Coll Holy Cross, Iris & B Gerald Cantor Gallery, Worcester, Mass; auth, The Visual Experience, 3rd Ed, Davis, Inc, Worcester, Mass, 2005. *Mem:* Worcester Art Mus; Boston Mus Fine Art. *Media:* Oil; Pastel. *Mailing Add:* 5 Pratt St Worcester MA 01609

PRIETO, MONIQUE N
PAINTER
b Los Angeles, Calif, 1962. *Study:* UCLA, BFA, 87; Calif Inst Arts, BFA, 92, MFA, 94. *Exhib:* Solo exhibs, ACME, Santa Monica, Calif, 94, 95, 96, 97, 99, 00, 01, Bravin Post Lee, NY, 96, Anderson Gallery, Va Commonwealth Univ, Richmond, 97, Pat Hearn Gallery, NY, 97, 98, 99, Robert Prime, London, Eng, 98, Corvi-Mora, London, 2000, 2002, Cheim & Read, NY, 2002, 2005 Il Capricorno, Venice, Italy, 2003, Out of the Blue, ACME, Los Angeles, 2004, A Great Stink of Burning But No Smoke, ACME, Los Angeles, 2005, Scottsdale Mus Contemp Art, Ariz, 2005; group exhibs, Wight Gallery, Univ Calif, Los Angeles, 87; Corazon Mexicana, Bacilla Hernandez Gallery, Long Beach, Calif, 89; Happy Show, Lockheed Gallery, Valencia, Calif, 94; Temporary, Thesis Show, Mus Contemp Art, Los Angeles, Calif, 94; The Speed of Painting, Pat Hearn Gallery, NY, 96; Chalk, Factory Place Gallery, Los Angeles, 96; LA Current: New View, Univ Calif Los Angeles/Armand Hammer Sales & Rental Gallery, Los Angeles, 97; Pat Hearn Gallery, NY, 2001, Tate Liverpool, 2001, Palm Beach Inst Contemp Art, Lake Worth, Fla, 2001, Kerling Gallery, Dublin, 2001, Mus Contemp Art, Denver, 2001, Cirrus Gallery, Los Angeles, 2002, Portland Art Mus, Ore, 2002, ACME, Los Angeles, 2002, 2003, Royal Acad, London, 2002, Kresge Art Mus, East Lansing, Mich, 2002, Kunstmus Wolfsburg, Ger, 2003, Marella Arte Contemporanea, Milan, Italy, 2003; Tete a Tete, Greenberg Van Doren, NY, 2005; Shape of Colour: Excursions in Colour Field Art, 1950-2005, Art Gallery of Ontario, 2005; Drunk vs Stoned, Gavin Brown's Enterprise, NY, 2005. *Collection Arranged:* Mus Contemp Art, San Diego; Mus Contemp Art, Los Angeles; Los Angeles Co Mus Art; Whitney Mus Am Art, NY City; Orange Co Mus Art, Newport Beach, Calif; Kresge Art Mus, Mich State Univ, East Lansing. *Awards:* Louis Comfort Tiffany Found Biennial Competition, 97, Grant, 98. *Bibliog:* David Pagel (auth), Adding a splash of fun to abstraction, Los Angeles Times, 12/5/97; Peter Frank (auth), article, LA Weekly, 12/12/97; Dave Hickey (auth), Top ten X 12, Artforum, 12/97; Martin Coomer (auth), Monique Prieto, Time Out, London, 10-11/2000; David Pagel (auth), A Breakthrough in Dark, Abstract Dramas, LA Times, F36, 12/21/2001; Blake Gopnik (auth), LA Consequential, Washington Post, 1, G6-7, 2002. *Dealer:* Acme, 6150 Wilshire Blvd, 1&2, LA 90048. *Mailing Add:* 1942 N Alvarado St Los Angeles CA 90039

PRINCE, ARNOLD
SCULPTOR, EDUCATOR
b Basseterre, St Kitts, West Indies, Apr 17, 1925. *Study:* Brit Coun with John Harrison, Jose DeCreeft, William Zorach & John Hovvannes; Art Students League. *Work:* First Vest Pocket Park, NY; Art Students League. *Comn:* Concrete sculpture, City North Adams, Mass, 68; gate post sculpture, Spruces Residential Park, 72; concrete sculpture, comn by Robert Potrin, Stamford, Vt, 73. *Exhib:* St Marks on the Bowery, 64; Sculptors Guild Exhib, Mus RI Sch Design, 69-75; Slide Show Collection of Afro-Am Artists, Univ Ala, 71; Boston Pub Libr, 73; Group exhib, RI Sch Design, 75. *Teaching:* Dir sculpture educ, Fed Govt Poverty Proj Harlem, HARYOU, 64-67; adj prof sculpture, North Adams State Col, 70-72; asst prof fine arts & sculpture, RI Sch Design, 72-82. *Bibliog:* Article in Village Voice, 12/65; article in NAdams Transcript, 66-71. *Mem:* Sculptors Guild NY. *Media:* Wood, Stone. *Publ:* Auth, Carving Wood and Stone, Prentice Hall, 80. *Dealer:* Sculptors Guild Inc 75 Rockefeller Plaza New York NY 10020. *Mailing Add:* c/o Sculptor's Guild Inc 110 Greene St New York NY 10012

PRINCE, EMILY
ARTIST
b Gold Run, Calif, 1981. *Study:* Stanford Univ, grad; Univ Calif, Berkeley. *Exhib:* Projects include Familar, 2004, Bury My Heart at Wounded Knee, 2006, American Servicemen and Women Who Have Died in Iraq and Afghanistan (but Not Including the Wounded, nor the Iraqis nor the Afghans), in progress; solo exhibs include Backroom Gallery, San Francisco, 2004, Jack Hanley Gallery, San Francisco, 2006, Eleanor Harwood Gallery, San Francisco, 2006; group exhibs include The Bay Area Show, Art Inst Detroit, 2004; The San Francisco show, New Image Art Gallery, Los Angeles, 2004; Bay Area Now 4, Yerba Buena Ctr Arts, San Francisco, 2005; Kapital, Kent Gallery, New York, 2007; Think with the Senses-Feel with the Mind, Venice Biennale, 2007

PRINCE, RICHARD
PHOTOGRAPHER
b Panama Canal Zone, Aug 6, 1949. *Work:* Whitney Mus Am Art & Mus Mod Art, NY; Haus due Kunst, Munich, Ger; San Francisco Mus Art, Calif; IVAM Centre del Carne, Valencia, Spain. *Exhib:* Inst Contemp Art, London, Eng, 83; Centre Nationalidad Art Contemporian, Grenoble, France, 88; Spirinal Am, IVAM Centre del Carne, Valencia, Spain, 89; Whitney Mus Am Art, NY, 92; Whitney Biennial, Whitney Mus Am Art, NY, 97; solo exhibs, White Cube, London, Eng, 97, Mus Haus Lange, Krefeld, Ger, 97, Barbara Gladstone Gallery, NY, 98, 2000, Sabine Knust, Munich, Ger, 99, Sadie Coles HQ, London, Eng, 99, 2001, Jabklonka Galerie, Köln, Ger, 2000, Partobject Gallery, Weaver Carboro, NC, 2000, MAK Ctr for Art and Archit, Los Angeles, 2000, Micheline Szwajcer, Antwerp, 2001, Skarstedt Fine Art, NY, 2001, Mus für Gegenwartskunst, Basel, Switz, 2001, Neue Galerie im Höhmann-haus, Augsburg, 2001, Kunsthalle Zurich, Switz, 2001, Barbara Gladstone Gallery, NY, 2002, Patrick Painter, Inc, Santa Monica, Calif, 2002; Marianne Boesky Gallery, NY, 98; Cleveland Mus of Art, Ohio, 98; Mus of Am Art, Pa Acad Fine Arts, 98; Whitney Mus Am Art, NY, 99; Mus Contemp Art, Chicago, 99; Whitechapel Art Gallery, London, 99; Barbara Gladstone Gallery, NY, 99; Galleria Franco Noero, Turin, Italy, 2001; Royal Acad of Arts, London, Eng, 2001; Mus of Contemp Art, Miami, Fla, 2001; Jablonka Gallery, Cologne, Ger, 2001; Mus of Mod Art, NY, 2001; Aldrich Mus Contemp Art, Ridgefield, Conn, 2001; Cheim & Reid Gallery, NY, 2001; Short Stories, Henry Art Gallery, Seattle, Wash, 2002; Pub Affairs, Kunsthaus, Zurich, 2002; Chic Clicks: Creativity and Commerce in Contemp Fashion Photog, the Inst of Contemp Art, Boston, Mass, 2002. *Pos:* Odd jobs Time Life, New York City, 1973-1985; ed cover photog Mademoiselle Mag, 1985; full-time artist, 1985-; Mem "Picture" Generation of artists 1970s, New York City. *Awards:* Recipient Nat Endowment award, 1985. *Bibliog:* David Humphrey (auth), New York Fax, Art Issues, No 54, 3-4/98; Richard Price Party, Dazed and Confused, London, 3/98; Richard Prince & Glen O'Brien (auths), Are we having fun yet, Blind Spot, 11/98. *Mem:* Mem The Off, NY (pres 1979-80). *Media:* Mixed Media. *Mailing Add:* c/o Barbara Gladstone Gallery 515 W 24th St New York NY 10011

PRINCE, RICHARD EDMUND
SCULPTOR, EDUCATOR
b Comox, BC, Apr 6, 1949. *Study:* Univ BC, BA (art hist), 71 & study, 72-73; Emma Lake Artists Workshop, Sask, with Ron Kitaj, 70. *Work:* Nat Gallery Can, Ottawa; Vancouver Art Gallery, BC; Govt of BC, Victoria Art Collection; Can Coun Art Bank, Ottawa, Can; Glenbow Mus, Calgary, Can; and others. *Comn:* Can Pavilion, Expo 86, Vancouver, Can; Concord Pac Developments Ltd, City of Vancouver, 96; CK Choi Inst Asian Research, 97. *Exhib:* Solo exhibs, Issacs Gallery, Toronto, 78 & 82 & Figure Structures, Burnaby Art Gallery, BC, 79, Hamilton Art Gallery, Ont, 84; Canadian Cult Ctr, Rome, Italy, 87; 49th Parallel Gallery, NY, 89; A New Decade: Vancouver, Alta Coll Art Gallery, Calgary, 79; Vancouver Heritage, Vancouver Art Gallery, 83; Reflecting Paradise, World Expo 93, Seoul, South Korea, 93; Strangers in the Arctic, Rundertaarn Mus, Copenhagen, Denmark & Mus Contemp Art, Helsinki, Finland, 96; MacLaren Art Ctr, Barrie, Can, 2000; and others. *Teaching:* Instr sculpture, Vancouver Community Col, BC, 74-75; instr fine arts & sculpture, Univ BC, 75-; vis lectr sculpture, Univ of BC, 77-78, asst prof sculpture, 78-83, assoc prof, 83-2003, prof 2003-. *Awards:* Art Vancouver for 74 Award, City of Vancouver, 74; Can Coun Arts Grant, Govt Can, 75; Can Coun Arts Grant, 77-78. *Bibliog:* Joan Lowndes (auth), Richard Prince: bringing the outdoors in, Artscanada, Toronto, 10-11/78; Arthur Perry (auth), Richard Prince: figure structures, Vanguard Vancouver, BC, 11/79; Joel Kaplan (auth), Richard Prince, Parachute, Montreal, Que, summer 85; Stephen Godfrey (auth), Focus on Richard Prince, Can Art, fall 88; JP Borum (auth), Richard E Prince, Artforum, New York, 1/90; Ian Thom (auth), Art BC, Douglas & MacIntyre, Vancouver, BC, 2000; Anne Newlands (auth) Canadian Art Fire Fly Books, Buffalo, NY, 2000; Arthur Williams (auth), Beginning Sculpture, Davis Publ Inc, Worcester, MA, 2004; Arthur Williams (auth), The Sculptor Reference, Davis Publ Inc, Worcester MA, 2004. *Mem:* Life mem Royal Can Acad; Univ Art Asn Can. *Media:* Multimedia. *Dealer:* Equinox Gallery 2321 Granville St Vancouver BC Can V6H 3G3. *Mailing Add:* Univ BC Dept Art Hist & Vis Art 6333 Memorial Rd Vancouver BC V6T I2Z Canada

PRINTZ, BONNIE ALLEN
PAINTER, PHOTOGRAPHER
b Luray, Va. *Study:* Va Commonwealth Univ, Richmond, BFA, 68; Hunter Coll, New York, MA, 70. *Work:* Baltimore Mus Art, Baltimore Life & Ballard Spahr Andrews & Ingersoll, Baltimore, Md; Corcoran Gallery Art & Bechtel Corp, Washington, DC; Towson Univ, Baltimore, Md. *Exhib:* Solo exhib, Baltimore Mus Art, 79; Corcoran Gallery Art, Washington, DC, 79, 82 & 88; William Penn Mem Mus, Harrisburg, Pa, 79-80 & 82; Va Mus Fine Arts, Richmond, 80 & 83; Baltimore Mus Art, 80, 83 & 86; McIntosh/Drysdale Gallery, Washington, DC, 87; Galerie Des Saints Peres, Paris, France, 92; Exposition D'Art Contemporain, Paris, France, 93; Fraser Gallery, Georgetown, Washington, DC, 97, 98 & 99; Bendann Art Gallery, Baltimore, Md, 99; Md Art Place, Baltimore, 99; Fish out of Water, Baltimore Pub Art Exhib, 2001; Art Works, Pub Television, MPT, MD; Party Animals, Arts Commn, Washington, DC, 2002; Group exhib, Baltimore Mus Art, 2011. *Pos:* Tech asst spec collections, Mus Mod Art, New York, 68-70. *Teaching:* Instr fine arts, Md Inst, Coll Art, Baltimore, 72-73, 76 & 79-89. *Awards:* Alliance Independent Coll Art Grant, 85; Yaddo Fel, 88 & 89; Fel Painting, Md State Arts Coun, Baltimore, 98. *Bibliog:* Allan Ripp (auth), Polaroid photos allow artists to develop their talents, News Am, Baltimore, 12/31/78.

Media: Oil. *Publ:* Illusr, Frank Young's Visual Studies: A Foundation Course for the Visual Arts, Minneapolis Coll Art & Design, 85; New American Paintings, Whitney Mus Am Art, New York, Open Studios Press, Mass, 94. *Dealer:* Barbara Feeser Art Assocs Baltimore MD; Susan Perrin Art Consult Baltimore MD. *Mailing Add:* 1104 Regester Ave Baltimore MD 21239

PRIP, JANET
CRAFTSMAN, SCULPTOR
b Hornell, NY, June 17, 1950. *Study:* Moore Coll Art, 68-70; RI Sch Design, BFA, 74. *Work:* RI Sch of Design Mus, Providence; Boston Mus Fine Arts; Am Craft Mus, NY. *Exhib:* Feature Show, Joanne Rapp Gallery, Scottsdale, Ariz, 93; Am Craft Mus, NY, 93; New Acquisitions Show, Craft Today USA, 93; Peter Joseph Gallery, NY, 94; Contemp Art RI, RI Sch Design Mus Art, Providence, 94; and others. *Awards:* Fel, Nat Endowment Arts, 86; Merit Award, Guild Am Craft Awards, 87. *Bibliog:* Jamie Bennet (auth), American Holloware: Changing Criteria, Metalsmith, summer 84; Sarah Bodine (auth), Janet Prip, Metalsmith, fall 88. *Media:* Bronze, Pewter. *Mailing Add:* 38 Rosemary Ln Jamestown RI 02835

PRITIKIN, RENNY
GALLERY DIRECTOR, EDUCATOR
Study: New Sch for Social Rsch, BA; San Francisco State Univ, MA. *Pos:* Chief curator, Yerba Buena Ctr for the Arts, formerly; dir, New Langton Arts, formerly; dir, Richard L Nelson Gallery and the Fine Arts Collection, Univ Calif, Davis, formerly; chier curator, Contemporary Jewish Mus, San Francisco, 2014-. *Teaching:* Tchr art admin, Calif State Univ, San Francisco State Univ, Golden Gate Univ, formerly; vis lectr, Pacific Northwest Col of Art, 2010; sr adj prof curatorial practice, Calif Col of Arts, currently. *Publ:* Auth, How We Talk, 2007. *Mailing Add:* Richard L Nelson Gallery & The Fine Arts Collection University of California, Davis One Shields Ave Davis CA 95616

PRITZKER, LISA & JOHN A
COLLECTORS
Study: Menlo Coll, grad; Univ Denver Coll Hotel and Restaurant Management, grad. *Pos:* Var positions to divisional vpres Calif, Hyatt Corp; pres, Hyatt Ventures Inc; founder & pres, Red Sail Sports Inc, 1988-; exec vpres bus develop, Key3Media Events Inc, 2000; bd dirs, Zoomedia Inc & Univ Calif San Francisco Found; trustee, San Francisco Mus Mod Art; dir, Pritzker Found, Pritzker Cousins Found, Children Now. *Awards:* Named one of Forbes 400 Richest Americans; named one of Top 200 Collectors, ARTnews mag, 2005-13. *Collection:* Photography. *Mailing Add:* 5 Pier the Embarcadero Ste 102 San Francisco CA 94111

PRITZKER, PENNY S
COLLECTOR
Study: Harvard Univ, BS, 1981; Stanford Univ, JD, MBA. *Pos:* Bd chmn, TransUnion, Classic Residence by Hyatt, The Parking Spot & Pritzker Realty Group; mem, President's Econ Recovery Adv Bd; nat finance chmn, Obama Presidential Campaign; co-chmn, Presidential Inaugural Comt, 2009; bd mem, Global Hyatt Corp; chmn, Chicago Pub Educ Fund; life trustee, Mus Contemp Art. *Awards:* Named one of Top 200 Collectors, ARTnews mag, 2009-11. *Collection:* Contemporary art. *Mailing Add:* Pritzker Realty Group 71 South Wacker Dr Ste 4700 Chicago IL 60606

PRITZLAFF, (MR & MRS) JOHN, JR
COLLECTORS
b Milwaukee, Wis, May 10, 25 (Mr Pritzlaff); b St Louis, Mo (Mrs Pritzlaff). *Study:* Mr Pritzlaff, Princeton Univ, BA, 49; Mrs Pritzlaff, Briarcliff Col. *Pos:* Mr Pritzlaff, US Ambassador to Malta, 69-72; Ariz State Sen, formerly; mem bd dir, Heard Mus, Phoenix, Ariz, 76-77; Mrs Pritzlaff, pres, bd dir, Phoenix Art Mus. *Mailing Add:* 7352 E McLellan Blvd Scottsdale AZ 85250-4523

PROBST, ROBERT
ADMINISTRATOR, EDUCATOR, GRAPHIC ARTIST
Study: Univ Essen, Germany, BS (design), 1972; Col of Design Basel, Switzerland, MS (design), 1974. *Work:* Ohio Arts Coun, Cooper-Hewitt Nat Mus for Design, NY, Nat Mus Modern Art, Tokyo. *Teaching:* Prof graphic design, Col Design, Architecture, Art, and Planning, Univ Cincinnati, 1978-, dean, 2008-, dir, Sch Design, 2001. *Awards:* SEGD fellow. *Mem:* Alliance Graphique Internationale. *Mailing Add:* University of Cincinnati College of DAPP 5470 Aronoff Center PO Box 210016 Cincinnati OH 45221-0016

PRODGER, PHILLIP
CURATOR, HISTORIAN
Study: Williams Coll, BA; Stanford Univ, MA; Darwin Coll, Cambridge Univ, PhD (art hist). *Pos:* Curatorial asst, Stanford Univ Mus Art, formerly; intern, dept prints, drawings, paintings & photog, Victoria & Albert Mus, London, formerly; asst archivist, photog & manuscript collections, Dept Experimental Psychology, Cambridge Univ, formerly; asst cur prints, drawings & photog, St Louis Art Mus, 2001; fel, Smithsonian Inst, Nat Mus Am Hist, Washington, 2001; Lisette Model & Joseph G Blum fel in hist of photog, Nat Gallery Can, 2007-08; cur photog, Peabody Essex Mus, Salem, Mass, 2008-. *Teaching:* Lectr art, Hong Kong Arts Ctr, formerly. *Publ:* Auth, Annotated Catalogue of Illustrations of Human & Animal Expression from the Collection of Charles Darwin, Edwin Mellen Press, 1998; Time Stands Still: Muybridge & the Instantaneous Photog Movement, Oxford Univ Press, 2003; coed, Impressionist Camera: Pictorial Photography in Europe, 1888-1918, Merrell Publishers, 2006; auth, E O Hoppé's Amerika: Modernist Photographs from the 1920s, W W Norton & Co, 2007. *Mailing Add:* Peabody Essex Mus East India Sq 161 Essex St Salem MA 01970

PROMUTICO, JEAN
PAINTER
b Baltimore, Md, Nov 23, 1936. *Study:* Md Inst Coll Art, Baltimore, with Lila Katzen & Jon Schueler, BFA (painting & drawing), 66; Univ NMex, Albuquerque, with John Kacere, MA (painting, art hist), 68, Art History, Univ NMex Grad Sch. *Work:* Fine Arts Mus NMex, Santa Fe; Univ Art Mus, Univ NMex, Albuquerque; Roswell Mus & Art Ctr, NMex; Lynn Mahew Gallery, Ohio Wesleyan Univ, Del; Roanoke Mus Fine Arts, Va; Anderson Mus Contemp Art, Roswell, NMex. *Exhib:* Mus Fine Arts NMex, Santa Fe, 73, 75, 89; Roswell Mus Art Ctr, NY, 74, 79, 90, 2007; NJ Ctr Visual Arts, Summit, NJ, Arco Ctr Visual Art, Ga, 76; First Western States Biennial traveling exhib, Nat Gallery Art, Wash DC, 79; San Francisco Mus Modern Art, 81; Bruce Mus, Greenwich, Conn, 85; The Painter's Light, PMWG, Stamford, Conn, 89 & Port Washington Pub Libr, Port Washington, NY, 93, Kornblee Gallery, New York, 80, 81, 82, 84; La Mama La Galleria, NY, 95; Fay & Friends, Md Inst, Baltimore, 97; China G, New York, 2007; "705" G, Stroudsburg, Pa, 2008; Westbeth Gallery, New York, 2005-; Gallery 307, New York, 2012. *Awards:* Nat Endowment Arts Grant, 74; Artist-in-Residence Grant, Roswell Mus & Art Ctr, 78-79 & 90-91; Nat Studio Prog Grant, PSI Mus, New York, 81. *Bibliog:* Leroy Perkins (review), Fields & Patterns, Albuquerque Jour, 1975; William Peterson/Jean Promutico (article), Artspace, spring 79; Gerrit Henry/Jean Promutico (review), Art News, 1981-. *Mem:* Retrograde, NY. *Media:* Acrylic, Miscellaneous Media, Oil, Paper, Canvas, Linen, Wood. *Specialty:* Fine Art, Contemporary. *Dealer:* Carter Burden G # 534; 547 W 27th St NY. *Mailing Add:* 55 Bethune St A507 New York NY 10014-2032

PRONIN, ANATOLY
PHOTOGRAPHER
b Leningrad, USSR, Oct 28, 1939; US citizen. *Study:* State Univ Leningrad, Russia, (journalism), 62-65. *Work:* Brooklyn (NY) Mus; Metrop Mus Art, NY; Libr Congress, DC; Bibliot Nat, Paris; Staatliche Mus Berlin, Ger; Mus Hist St Petersburg, Russia; State Mus Theatre and Music Arts, St. Petersburg, Russia; NY Public Libr; George Balanchine Found, NY; Salvador Daly Mus, St Petersburg, Fla; Portland Art Mus, Portland, Ore; Mass Inst Technol, Cambridge, Mass, Harvard Univ; Royal Coll; Royal Geographical Soc. *Exhib:* 33 Photo Salon, Photographic Asn Calcutta, India, 89; 128 Int Exhib Pictorial Photog, Edinburgh (Scotland) Photo Soc, 90; 43 South African Int Salon, Johannesburg, 90; Ghetto - Traces of Memory, NY Pub Libr, 90; Old Voices, New Faces, Nat Jewish Mus, Washington DC, 92; USE, Contacts/Proofs, Jersey City (NJ) Mus, 90, 93; Natural History, Katlin Ewing Gallery, Washington DC, 93; Children of Leningrad, MBM Gallery, NY, 96; Fellow Exhib 99, Hunterdon Mus Art, Clinton, NJ, 99, CHUBB Atrium Gallery, NJ, 2000; Propagandist and Romantic: Contemp Russian Photog, Priebe Art Gallery, Univ Wis, Oshkosh, 2002; New York City Photog in Black and White, Michael Ingbar Gallery, NY, 2003; 150 yrs Anniversary Tretyakov Gallery (Moscow, Russia), Lincoln Ctr, NY, 2006. *Awards:* Silver Medal, Int Photo Exhib, Berlin, Ger, 71; First place, USSR Photog Exhib, Moscow, 78-79; Best Photog (Time Life, Years), Mus Hist Leningrad, USSR, 1978; Cert of Excellence, Art Dir Club NJ, 88; NJ State Coun Arts Fel, 90, 99. *Publ:* contribr, Encyl Britannica, 86, 92; contribr, Graphis Photo 89, Graphis mag, Switzerland, 89; contribr, Power of Art, Harcourt Brace, 95; contribr, Facing the Music, Simon & Schuster, 96, 97; contribr, Encarta, Microsoft, 97, 2006; Power of Art, Harcourt Brace, 97; Stonehenge, Lusent Books, 98; Art in Focus, McGraw-Hill, 2000-05; Perspective from the Past, WW Norton, 2002-05; Medieval Jewish Civilization, Routlege, UK, USA, 2003; Islam-Artand Architecture, Tandem Verlaq, Germany, 2005; Italien-Die Schönsten Bilder, GEO, Germany, 2005; Civilization, Random House, United Kingdom, 2006; Timeline Art Hist, Barnes & Noble, 2006; Islamic Invention of Europe, WW Norton, 2007; God's Cruciblem WW Norton, 2007; A History of Philanthropy (film), Cynthia Hall Production, 2007; McDougal Littell, Write Smart, 2007. *Mailing Add:* 315 Eastern St Apt D-1613 New Haven CT 06513

PROPERSI, AUGUST J
ART DEALER, PAINTER
b Bronx, NY, Apr 3, 1926. *Study:* Sch Art Studies, with Isaac Soyer & Sol Wilson, 46-47; Sch Visual Arts, with Jack Sheridan, Ben Dale & Francis Criss, grad, 50; Conference Conservation of Paintings, Brooklyn, Mus, 62. *Work:* Veterans Administration Hospital, Montrose, NY. *Exhib:* Artists USA, Bohman Gallery, Stockholm, Sweden, 68; 50 State Competition, Duncan Galleries, Paris, France, 68; Am Artists, Propersi Gallery D'Arte, Scarsdale, NY, 68 & 80; Propersi Galleries, Greenwich, Conn, 77-84; Conn Inst of Art Galleries, 95-01. *Collection Arranged:* Am Artist (auth catalog), 68; American's 1930 (auth catalog) Depression Artists, 75. *Pos:* founder and dir, Propersi Galleria D'Art, Scarsdale, NY, 68-70; founder & pres, Propersi Galleries & Sch Art Inc, 70-84; founding pres & chmn, Conn Inst Art, 94-; chmn Conn Inst Art, 95-01; art consult, Art res, Art broker. *Teaching:* Dir & instr life drawing, The Little Studio, Pelham, NY, 59-68; dir & instr fine arts, Propersi Gallerie D'Arte, 68-70; chmn fine and commercial art, Propersi Sch Art, Inc, 70-84. *Awards:* Prix d'Paris, 50 States Competition, Raymond Duncan Galleries, 68; Skills 2000 Recognition Award, Coll Career Asn; Cert Achievement, Team Leader Workshop, Nat Asn Trade & Tech Schs, 86. *Bibliog:* Dorothy Friedman (auth) Personal Key to Success, Greenwich Time Newspaper, 10/13/75; Kathy Beals (auth), Dealer Bullish on Am Art Gannet, Westchester Newspaper, 6/13/75; Les Krantz (ed & publ), American Artist-an illustrated survey of contemporary Americans, 85; Les Krantz (auth), American References Inc, NY Art Rev, 88; John Branea and Steve Aconto (profiles), Artists in Sports WVOX-WFAS Radio Westchester, 76-77. *Mem:* Artist Guild (bd dirs, 53); Am Veterans Soc Artists (bd dir, 68); Alpha Beta Kappa Hon Soc, 85. *Media:* Pastels, Oils. *Res:* Art restoration; Art in its historical context. *Specialty:* Listed American painters and European painters--19th & 20th centuries. *Interests:* Collecting art. *Collection:* Old masters-16th and 17th Century Italian Paintings; 19th Century English and American Oils, Watercolors, and Etchings; Ralph Albert Blarelock. *Mailing Add:* 225 Magnolia Ave Mount Vernon NY 10552-3732

PROSIA, DEANN
PRINTMAKER, PAINTER
b Chgo, Ill, March 22, 1963. *Study:* N Ill Univ, BSA in Comm, 85; studied with Nina Weiss, Art Inst Chgo, 1994-1995. *Work:* NY Historical Soc Mus Coll, NY; NY Public Libr Print Coll, NY; Univ Conn Health Ctr, Farmington, Conn; Rutgers Univ Archives, New Brunswick, NJ; Syracuse Univ Art Coll, NY; NY Historical Soc Mus and Libr, NY; Jundt Art Mus, Gonzaga Univ, Spokane, Wash. *Comn:* Soc of Am Graphic Artists, 2014. *Exhib:* Solo exhibs, Mein Mainz, Eisenturm Gallerie, Mainz, Ger, 2009, Black and White, Blue Door Gallery, Yonkers, NY, 2013, Ridgefield Art Guild, Ridgefield, Conn, 2015; Group exhibs, Lessendra World Art Print, Lessendra Gallery, Sofia, Bulgaria, 2012, 3 Contemporary Printmakers, The Old Print Shop, NY, 2012, 100th Ann Exhib, Allied Artists of Am, Nat Arts Club, NY, 2013, Mem Exhib, New Britain Mus Am Art, New Britain, Conn, 2013, Pendle Print Fest, Lancashire, Eng, 2014, Pacific States Biennial Nat Printmaking Exposition, Hilo, Hawaii, 2014, Footprint, Ctr for Contemp Printmaking, Norwalk, Conn, 2014, Silvermine Guild Galleries, New Canaan, Conn, 2015, Kehler Liddell Gallery, New Haven, Conn, 2015, 10th Internat Miniature Print Biennial, Ctr for Contemp Printmaking, 2015, The Art Complex Mus, Duxbury, Mass, 2015, Watercolor USA, Springfield Art Mus, Springfield Mo, 2015, Notre Dame of Md Univ, Balt, Md, 2015. *Awards:* Shirley Kraus Memorial Printmaking award, Art of Northeast Exhib, 2003; Turnbull, Hoover, Kahl Purchase award, Will's Creek Survey, 2006; Marvin Bolotsky Purchase award, Internat Miniature Print Biennial, 2011; Rosenhouse award, Soc Am Graphic Artist Mem Exhib, 2013; Pauline Law Meml award, Allied Artists Am, 100th Ann Exhib, Pauline Law Meml, 2013; Marquis Who's Who in Am Art References award in Graphics, Audubon Artists, NY, 2013. *Mem:* Boston Printmakers; SAGA; Silvermine Art Guild; SGCI; Ctr Contemporary Printmaking; Allied Artists of Am. *Media:* Etching. *Publ:* editor, Etching Artist Turns to a New Medium to Color Her World, Newtown Bee, 2010; auth, Watercolor Artist: Etch-A Sketch, E&W Media Inc, 2012; editor, Splash 13:Alternative Approaches, North Light Books, 2012. *Dealer:* The Old Print Shop 150 Lexington Ave New York NY 10016; The Old Print Gallery 1220 31st St NW Wash DC 20007; EBO Gallery Millwood NY

PROSS, LESTER FRED
EDUCATOR, PAINTER
b Bristol, Conn, Aug 14, 1924. *Study:* Oberlin Coll, BA, 45, MA, 46; Ohio Univ, with Ben Shahn, summer 52; Skowhegan Sch Painting & Sculpture, summer 53; with Simon, Zorach, Levine, Hebald & Bocour; Univ Colo Kyoto Sem, Japan, 75-76; study painting with Kono Shuson. *Exhib:* More than Land or Sky: Art from Appalachia, Nat Mus Am Art, Smithsonian Inst, Washington, 81-82, Traveling Exhib, 82-84; Headley-Whitney Mus, Lexington, Ky, 83, 89, Kentucky to Ecuador, 89-90; one-person exhibs, Ky Guild Gallery, 88 & Prestonsburg Coll, 90; retrospective, Doris Ulmann Galleries, Berea Coll, 90; group exhib, Yeiser Art Ctr, Paducah, 92; Morgan Gallery, Transylvania Univ Lexington, 93; Paramount Gallery, Ashland, KY, 93; Kentucky Guild, Lexington, 94; Ky Mus Art & Craft, Louisville: 50 Years of KGAC, 2011; Ky Artisan Ctr at Berea, 2011; and others. *Pos:* Bd dir, Doris Ulmann Found, 60-84; chmn adv bd, Appalachian Mus, Berea Coll, 69-84. *Teaching:* Prof art, Berea Coll, 46-91, chmn dept, 50-84; Fulbright lectr painting & art hist, Univ Panjab, Pakistan, 57-58; vis assoc prof art educ & hist, Union Coll, summer 61; vis prof art, Am Univ Cairo, 67-68; Bryant Drake guest prof art, Kobe Coll, Japan, 84-85. *Awards:* Haskell Traveling Fel, Oberlin Coll, 57-58; Fulbright Lectureship, Pakistan, 57-58; Merit Award, UK Appalachian Ctr, 87; Fel, Ky Guild of Artists and Craftsmen. *Mem:* PKP, Berea Arts Council; fel Ky Guild Artists & Craftsmen (pres, 61-63). *Media:* Oil, Watercolor. *Publ:* Auth, Five Expressionists, Allen Mem Art Mus, Oberlin, Ohio, 46; illusr, The Passion, Mountain Life & Work, Berea, 51; Celebration, Berea Coll, Ky, 78. *Mailing Add:* 104 Peachbloom Cir Berea KY 40403

PROVAN, DAVID
SCULPTOR
b Los Angeles, Calif, Oct 3, 1948. *Study:* Yale Univ, BA, 79; Royal Coll Art, MA, 81. *Work:* Univ Calif, San Diego; Ise Art Found, Tokyo; Brooklyn Union Gas Co, NY; Metrop Transportation Authority, NY; Yale Univ Art Gallery. *Comn:* Mural, Santa Barbara City Col, 77. *Exhib:* Freedom of Speech, Univ Calif, Berkeley, 90; Invitational 1990, Grace Borgenicht Gallery, NY, 90; Lyric Thought, Lyric Form, Parkland Coll Art Gallery, Champaign, Ill, 92; Influenced by Architecture, Fitchburg Art Mus, Mass, 94; Cultured Pearl, Seoul Metrop Mus Art, Korea, 96. *Bibliog:* Edith Newhall (auth), Installation, New York Mag, 12/4/95; Walter Robinson (auth), Subway spinners, Art in Am, 1/96; Natasha Duré, Underground movement, Metropolis Mag, 5/96. *Mem:* Int Sculpture Ctr; Am Crafts Asn. *Media:* Welded Steel, Aluminum

PROVDER, CARL
PAINTER, INSTRUCTOR
b Brooklyn, NY, Feb 7, 1933. *Study:* Pratt Inst, BFA; Columbia Univ, MA, prof dipl; Inst Allende, MFA; Educ Alliance Art Sch; Art Students League; NY Univ; Acad Belli Arti, Perugia; with Samuel Adler. *Exhib:* Contemp Artists of Brooklyn, Brooklyn Mus, 72; Painters & Sculptors Soc, Jersey City Mus, NJ, 72; La Jolla Mus, 74 & 75; San Diego Mus, 75 & 79; Laguna Beach Mus, Calif, 77; and others. *Pos:* Mem, San Diego Mus Art & La Jolla Mus Contemp Art. *Teaching:* Instr fine arts, Bd Educ, New York, 64-73 & San Diego Community Coll, 74-83; pvt instr, 75-; instr, Mira Costa Coll, 76-77 & Mendocino Art Ctr, 80-81. *Awards:* First Prize-Mixed Media, Southern Calif Expo, Del Mar, 77 & Third Prize Mixed Media, 79; Purchase Award, Small Image Art Show, San Diego, 78-80; First Prize Painting, San Diego Art Inst Ann, 80 & Hon Mention, 81; Second Prize Painting, 82; Third Prize Painting, 83. *Bibliog:* Denise Draper (auth), An exhibit that passes the test, Coast Dispatch, 1/21/78; Richard Reilly (auth), Artist's work is from within, 1/22/78 & Joan Levine (auth), Art on a cul-de-sac, 10/19/78, San Diego Union. *Mem:* Artists Equity Asn (vpres, 76-79); San Diego Artists Guild; Soc Layerists in Multi-Media. *Media:* Oil, Mixed Media. *Publ:* Auth, A colorists approach to abstract painting, Today's Art, Vol 26, No 11, 78. *Mailing Add:* 1416 Elva Terr Encinitas CA 92024

PROVISOR, JANIS
ARCHITECT
b Brooklyn, NY, 1946. *Study:* Univ Mich, Sch archit & Design, 66; Univ Cincinnati, Coll Design, Art & Archit, 68; San Francisco Art Inst, BFA, 69, MFA, 71. *Work:* Albright-Knox Art Mus, Buffalo, NY; The Annex, Tucson, Ariz; Ludwig Mus, Aachen, Ger; Univ Art Mus, Berkeley, Calif; Oakland Art Mus, Calif; and others. *Comn:* Times Square Project, Proskauer Rose Goetz & Mendelsohn, NY, 91. *Exhib:* One-person exhibs, Gloria Luria Gallery, Miami, Fla, 90, Lisa Sette Gallery, Scottsdale, Ariz, 90, Dorothy Goldeen Gallery, Santa Monica, Calif, 90, Eugene Binder Gallery, Cologne, Ger, 91, San Francisco Art Inst, Calif, 91, Barbara Toll, NY, 92, Timothy Brown Fine Art, Aspen, Colo, 92, Plum Blossoms Gallery, Art Asia Hong Kong, 93 & Dorothy Goldeen Gallery, Santa Monica, Calif, 93; Contemp Prints, Gallery 44, 90, 20th Anniversary Visiting Artist Prog, Univ Art Gallery, Colo Univ, Boulder, 92; Post Earthquake Prints, Crown Point Press, San Francisco, Calif, 90; The Common Wealth Exhibition, Roanoke Mus Fine Art, Va, 90; Woodcuts, Crown Point Press, 90, The Tree, Elysium Art Gallery, 91, Sheh Zand Proj, NY, 92; Works on Paper, Timothy Brown Fine Arts, Aspen, Colo, 91; Presswork: The Art of Women Printmakers, Nat Mus Women in the Arts, Washington, DC, 91; Vital Forces, Hecksher Mus, Huntington, NY, 91; Miniatures, Lisa Sette Gallery, Scottsdale, Ariz, 92; Big Ideas, Tucson Mus Art, Ariz, 92; Abstract Paintings, Dorothy Goldeen Gallery, Santa Monica, Calif, 92. *Teaching:* Vis artist, Anderson Ranch Arts Ctr, Snowmass, Colo, 90 & 92, State Univ NY, Purchase, 92. *Awards:* Ford Found Grant, Univ Tex, 78; Nat Endowment Arts, Individual Artist's Fel, 80, 85 & 91; Colo Coun Arts & Humanities Fel, 88. *Bibliog:* B A M (auth), Anish Kapoor, Janis Provisor, Crown Point Press, Art News, 4/92; Allan Schwartzman (auth), Landscapes of the Mind, Aspen Mag, midsummer 92; Jane Wilson (auth), Artist Comes 'Home' with New Work, Aspen Times, 8/8/92. *Mailing Add:* c/o Crown Point Press Gallery 20 Hawthorne St San Francisco CA 94105

PROWN, JULES DAVID
ART HISTORIAN
b Freehold, NJ, Mar 14, 1930. *Study:* Lafayette Col, AB, 51; Harvard Univ, AM (fine arts), 53; Univ Del, AM (early Am cult), 56; Harvard Univ, PhD (fine arts), 61. *Hon Degrees:* Yale Univ, Hon AM, 71; Lafayette Col, Hon DFA, 79. *Collection Arranged:* John Singleton Copley Exhib (auth, catalog), 65-66 & Am Art from Alumni Collections, 68, Yale Univ Art Gallery; traveling exhib, 65-66 & Am Art from Alumni Collections, 68, Yale Univ Art Gallery. *Pos:* Asst to dir, William Hayes Fogg Art Mus, Harvard Univ, 59-61; cur, Garvan & Related Collections of Am Art, Yale Univ, New Haven, 63-68; dir, Yale Ctr Brit Art, New Haven, 68-76; assoc dir, Nat Humanities Inst, New Haven, 77. *Teaching:* Fel art hist, Harvard Univ, Cambridge, Mass, 56-57; from instr to prof, Yale Univ, 61-86, Paul Mellon prof hist of art, 86-99, Paul Mellon prof emeritus, 99-. *Awards:* Guggenheim Fel, 64-65; Blanche Elizabeth MacLeish Billings Award, Yale Univ, 66; Robert C Smith Award, Soc Arch Historians, 83; George Washington Kidd Award, Lafayette Col, 86; Iris Found Award for Outstanding Contrib to the Decorative Arts, Bard Grad Ctr for Studies in the Decorative Arts, 01; Lawrence A Fleischman Award for Scholarly Excellence in Field of Am Art Hist, 01; William Clyde DeVale Award for scholarship and teaching, Phi Beta Kappa, Yale Univ, 2005; Distinguished Scholar Session, Coll Art Assn Conf, 2010. *Mem:* Am Soc 18th Century Studies (exec bd mem, 73-76); Coll Art Asn (bd dir, 75-79); Benjamin Franklin Fel Royal Soc Arts; Am Antiquarian Soc (mem coun, 77-94). *Res:* American and English art; John Singleton Copley; Benjamin West; Winslow Homer; material culture; Louis Kahn. *Publ:* Thomas Eakins' Baby at Play, Studies in the History of Art, Nat Gallery Art, Washington, Vol 18, 121-7, 85; Benjamin West's Family Picture: A Nativity in Hammersmith, in John Wilmerding, ed, Essays in Honor of Paul Mellon, Washington, 269-81, 86; Charles Willson Peale in London, Charles Willson Peale: New Perspectives, A 250th Anniversary Celebration, Univ Pittsburgh Press, 91; Expedition against the Ohio Indians under Colonel Bouquet: Two Early Drawings by Benjamin West, in Guilland Sutherland, ed, British Art 1740-1820: Essays in Honor of Robert R Wark, Huntington Library, 92; The Truth of Material Culture: History or Fiction, in Steven Lubor and W David Kingery, eds, History from Things: Essays on Material Culture, Smithsonian Inst Press, 93; John Singleton Copley, 2 vols, 66; American Painting from Its Beginnings to the Armory Show, 69; The Architecture of the Yale Center for British Art, 77; ed with Kenneth Haltman, American Artifacts: Essays in Material Culture, Mich State Univ Press, 2000; Art as Evidence: Writings on Art and Material Culture, Yale Univ Press, 02. *Mailing Add:* Dept Art Hist Box 208272 Yale Univ New Haven CT 06520

PRUITT, LYNN
SCULPTOR, ASSEMBLAGE ARTIST
b Washington, DC, May 24, 1937. *Work:* Marlboro Hall, Prince George Com Col, Largo, Md. *Comn:* Sculptured canvas wall relief, Naval Acad, Annapolis, Md, 76. *Exhib:* Corcoran Gallery Art, Washington, DC, 65 & 72; one-person shows, Md Artists Today, East Coast Univ Tour, Baltimore Mus, 75 & 76, Nat Audubon Soc, Chevy Chase, Md, 77 & Nourse Gallery, Washington, DC, 80; Am Chairs, Form, Function & Fantasy, John Michael Kohler Arts Ctr, Sheboygan, Wis, 78; Washington Proj for the Arts, DC, 80; and others. *Pos:* Juror, Prince George's Community Col, 72-75, Nat Inst Health, 73-75, Md Col Art, 76 & Scholastic Art Awards, Washington, DC, Md & Va, 77-78; dir & consult, Holden Gallery, Inc, Kensington, Md, 76-. *Teaching:* Instr basic art, Jewish Community Ctr, Rockville, Md, 74-. *Awards:* First in Painting, 68, 69 & 70, Best in Show, 68, 69 & 70 & First in Sculpture, 70, 71, 73 & 74, Nat Inst Health, Bethesda, Md. *Mem:* Washington Women's Arts Ctr; Am Crafts Coun. *Media:* Plaster. *Dealer:* Nourse Gallery Washington DC 20013. *Mailing Add:* 12806 Poplar St Silver Spring MD 20904

PRUITT, ROBERT A
ASSEMBLAGE ARTIST
b Houston, Tex, 1975. *Study:* Tougaloo Art Colony, Jackson, Miss, 1999; Tex Southern Univ, BFA, 2000; Skowhegan Sch Painting & Sculpture, 20002; Univ Tex at Austin, MFA, 2003. *Work:* The Studio Mus Harlem, NY; Dallas Mus Art; Mus Fine Arts, Houston; Cleveland Mus Art. *Exhib:* Solo exhibs, Project Row Houses, Houston,

2004, Galveston Art Ctr, Tex, 2004, Clementine Gallery, New York, 2004, 2006, Contemp Art Mus, Houston, 2006, Mary Goldman Gallery, LA, 2007, Hooks-Epstein Gallery, Houston, 2010; Fresh Beginnings, African Am Mus, Dallas, 1998; Our New Day Begun, LBJ Libr & Mus, Austin, 2000; Come Forward: Emerging Art in Tex, Dallas Mus Art, 2003; Splat Boom Pow! The Influence of Cartoons in Contemp Art, Contemp Arts Mus Houston, 2003, Perspectives 144, 2005, Double Consciousness, 2005; The Big Show, Lawndale Art Ctr, Houston, 2003; Farm to Market, ArtPace, San Antonio, 2004, New Works: 07.1, 2007; Art on Paper, Weatherspoon Art Mus, Greensboro, NC, 2006; Whitney Biennial, Whitney Mus Am Art, New York, 2006; Sweet Sweetback's Badasssss Song, Von Lintel Gallery, New York, 2007; S & M Shrines and Masquerades in Cosmopolitan Times, NYU, Steinhardt Galleries, New York, 2008; Drawing for Projection, SITE Santa FE, PS!/Mod Mus Art, New York, 2010. *Pos:* Mem Otabenga Jones & Assoc, Houston, 2002; arts coord, Project Row Houses. *Awards:* Emerging Artist Grant, Cult Arts Coun Houston, 1999; Kimbrough Fund Award, Dallas Mus Art, 1999; First Prize, The Big Show, Lawndale Art Ctr, Houston, 2003; Artadia Award, 2004; Louis Comfort Tiffany Found Grant, 2008; Art Matters Found Grant, 2009. *Bibliog:* Martha Schwendener (auth), Robert Pruitt at Clementine, Time Out New York, 8/2004; Holland Cotter (auth), The Collective Conscious, The New York Times, 3/2006; Sarah Hill-Gajkowski (auth), Perspectives 154: Robert Pruitt, Arts Houston Magazine, 2/2007. *Mailing Add:* 1236 E Madison Park Chicago IL 60615

PRUNEDA, MAX
SCULPTOR

b Laredo, Tex, 1948. *Study:* Univ Tex, Austin, BFA, 73. *Exhib:* One-person shows, Brigitte Schluger Gallery, Denver, Colo, 89 & 91, Gallery Elena, Taos, NMex, 89, 90 & 91, Quintana Gallery, Portland, Ore, 89, 90, 91 & 92, Ralph Greene Gallery, Albuquerque, NMex, 92-, Bentley Gallery, Scottsdale, Ariz, 94-, Okun Gallery, Santa Fe, NMex, 94- & Art of the People, Portland, Ore, 98; Gallery Elena, Taos, NMex, 92; Guadalajara Int Book Fair, Mex, 94; Klein Horowitz Gallery, Santa Fe, 95 & 96; Gallery 10, Carefree, Ariz, 97; Crossing Cultures, Lewallen Contemp Gallery, Santa Fe, 98; Pedestals and Stretchers, Lewallen Contemp Gallery, Santa Fe, 98; and others. *Awards:* Nat Endowment Arts Fel, 88; Cult Arts Coun Houston Grant, 89. *Bibliog:* Mag of Arts, 1/94; Wesley Pulkka (auth), Renacimiento, NU-CITY, 11/93; Raquel Tibol & Maria Elena Alvarez (auth), Critic digs deep into New Mexican art, Albuquerque J, 12/11/94. *Dealer:* Art of the People Portland OR. *Mailing Add:* 2226 C Los Padillas Rd SW Albuquerque NM 87105-7168

PUCKER, BERNARD H
ART DEALER

b Kansas City, Mo, Oct 19, 1937. *Study:* Columbia Univ, BA, 59; Hebrew Univ, Jerusalem, 60; Brandeis Univ, MA, 66. *Pos:* Dir, Pucker Gallery, Boston, currently. *Mem:* St Botolph Club. *Specialty:* Contemporary artists; Chagall graphics; Israeli artist Bak, Sharir; New England artists such as Ali and Jim Schantz; fantastic realist artists like Shigeru Matsuzaki; Southern African works; bronzes by David Aronson, Igor Galanin, porcelains by Brother Thomas, Tetsuzo Shinzaka Hamzar, W Tsuchiya, K Masuzaki; photogs Baking, Marin Mutter. *Mailing Add:* Pucker Gallery 171 Newbury St Boston MA 02116-2839

PUCKETT, RICHARD EDWARD
PAINTER, ADMINISTRATOR

b Klamath Falls, Ore, Sept 9, 1932. *Study:* Southern Ore of Educ; Lakeforest Coll; Univ of San Fran, BA. *Exhib:* Seaside, Calif City Hall Avery Gallery, 1987-2001 & 2003-07; Ft Ord, Calif Art Gallery, 67, 73, 79, 81, 84, 86; Presidio of Monterey, Calif Art Gallery, 71-72, 79; Salinas Valley Art Gallery, Salinas, Calif, 1990-98; Int Art & Commun Congress, Fairmont Hotel, San Francisco, Calif, 1998; Del Mesa Art Gallery, Carmel, Calif, 1990-2007; Southern Ore Art Gallery, Medford, Ore, 2000; Sasoontsi Gallery, Salinas, Calif, 2004; juried show: Sasoontsi Gallery, Salinas, Calif, 2006; miniature shows: Monterey Art Mus, Monterey, Calif, 2004-2008; Special 7-month exhib, Fort Ord Arts & Crafts, Richard Puckett Collection, donated to Univ Calif, Monterey Bay, Monterey Airport, 2008. *Teaching:* Instr, Ft Sheriden Arts & Crafts, 57-68; instr, Camp Irwin, Calif, 58-60; instr, Ft Ord Arts & crafts Cntr, Calif, 60-86. *Awards:* First place Army, Dept of Army Shown at Smithsonian Mus, 78-85; First place sculpture, Monterey Fair, 79; Champion of the Arts-Friend sculpture from the Arts Coun Monterey Co, Calif, 2007; Cert Spec Cong Recognition, Us Cong, 2007; First place Juried Show, Mum Show, Steinbeck Mus, Salinas, Calif, 2009; and other awards. *Bibliog:* David Nordstrand (auth), A Passion for Painting, Californian, May 25, 2002; Brenda Moore (auth), Honoring Champions of the Arts, Monterey Herald, Jan 15, 2007; Kevin Howe (auth), The Artful Scrounger, Monterey Herald, Jun 9, 2008. *Mem:* Salinas Valley Art Assoc, (pres, 2000-2008); Monteren Mus of Art; Int Soc of Acrylic Painters. *Media:* Acrylic, Oil. *Interests:* Art, hist, antiques & gardening. *Collection:* Over 1200 paintings, graphics, art objects, sculptures & antiques. *Publ:* David Nordstrand (auth), Honoring Artistry, Salinas, Calif, Jan 17, 2007. *Mailing Add:* 210 San Miguel Ave Salinas CA 93901-3021

PUELZ, SUSAN P
PAINTER

b 1942. *Study:* Univ Nebr, Lincoln, BFA (art), MFA (painting). *Exhib:* Represented in permanent collections Mus Nebr Art, Springfield Art Mus, Great Plains Art Collection, Univ Nebr. *Teaching:* Adj prof, art & art hist, Univ Nebr, Lincoln. *Bibliog:* Joni Kinsey (auth), Plain Pictures: Images of the American Prairie, 96. *Media:* Watercolor. *Dealer:* Anderson O'Brien Fine Art 8724 Pacific St Countryside Village Omaha NE 68114. *Mailing Add:* Anderson O'Briend Fine Art 1108 Jackson St Omaha NE 68102

PUGH, GRACE HUNTLEY
PAINTER, ART HISTORIAN

b Schenectady, NY, Sept 25, 1912. *Study:* Wellesley Col, 30-32; Barnard Col, BA (fine arts), 34; Nat Acad Design, with Leon Kroll, Charles Hinton & Ivan Olinsky, 34-36; with Samantha Littlefield Huntley, 34-38; Parsons Sch Design, summer 37; Art Students League, with Reginald Marsh, summer 38. *Work:* Barnard Col; 100 Friends of Pittsburgh Art & Montefiore Hosp, Pittsburgh; Mamaroneck Free Libr, NY; Westchester Co Art in Pub Places, White Plains, NY. *Comn:* Harbor mural, St Thomas Episcopal Church, Mamaroneck, 63-66; paintings, Mamaroneck Harbor, Dime Savings Bank, Mamaroneck, 75, Mill Stream, Harrison, NY, 76 & Scarsdale Summer, Scarsdale, NY, 77. *Exhib:* Artist Equity Exhib, Whitney Mus Am Art, NY, 51 & Riverside Mus, NY, 53; NY State Painters, NY State Bldg-World's Fair, Flushing, 65 & Butler Art Inst, Pa; Solo exhibs, Sails, Wildcliff Mus, New Rochelle, NY, 75 & Rockport Art Asn, Mass, 76 & 80; Franklin & Marshall Col, 74, Pa; Gloucester Sawyer Libr, 78, Mass; 13 Artist Exhib, Rockport Art Asn, Mass, 93; 36th Nat Open Juried Exhib, Mamaroneck Artists Guild, 94; and others. *Pos:* Chmn art, Mamaroneck Free Libr, 50-87; artist-in-residence & adv fine arts, Village of Mamaroneck, 77-; first chmn, Mamaroneck Hist Preserv Adv Comt, archit art, 82. *Teaching:* Artist-in-residence & head dept art, Briarcliff Jr Col, Briarcliff Manor, NY, 36-40; art instr, Westchester Co Workshop, White Plains, 61-63. *Awards:* Grace Huntley Pugh Day, Village Mamaroneck, with commendation from Pres Bush, 10/17/82 & 6/14/91; Cert, Federated Conservationists Westchester Co, NY, 91; 50 Year Cert Appreciation, Rockport Art Asn, 94. *Bibliog:* Jim Kinter (auth), Show mirrors artist's strong moods, Intel J Newspaper, 74; Herb Rosoff (auth), The pro's nest meet with Grace Huntley Pugh, Palette Talk Mag, 77. *Mem:* Am Watercolor Soc; Rockport Art Asn; Mamaroneck Artists Guild (pres, 53-55, 61-63, dir, 53-80); Artists Equity. *Media:* Oil, Watercolor. *Publ:* auth, Buoy 16, Mamaroneck Harbor, Village of Mamaroneck; illusr, Sound Seasonings (cookbook), Jr League Westchester, NY, 90; 10 Year Recognition as Creator/producer/host of Down Memory Lane (film), Mamaroneck Hist Soc, 94; illusr, Rebuilding the Pigeon Cove Breakwater, Town Rockport Ann Report, Mass, 94; auth, The Last 100 Years, Village of Mamaroneck Centennial Book-Celebration, 95; and others. *Mailing Add:* 823 Stuart Ave Mamaroneck NY 10543

PUJOL, ELLIOTT
EDUCATOR, MEDALIST

b Memphis, Tenn, June 4, 1943. *Study:* Southern Ill Univ, BS (theatre), 68, with Brent Kington, MFA (art), 71; Penland Sch, with Arline Fisch, 70. *Work:* Minn Mus Art, St Paul; Sheldon Mem Art Gallery, Lincoln, Nebr; Topeka Public Libr; Wichita Art Mus; La Sch Visually Impaired; Samuel Dorsky Mus Art, New Paltz, NY; Nat Ornamental Metal Mus, Memphis, Tenn. *Comn:* Pendulum (sculpture), Kansas State Univ Coll Eng, 83. *Exhib:* First Blacksmith Conference, Carbondale, Ill, 70; Third Nat Student Metal International (auth, catalog), Tyler Sch Art, 72; Summer Vail Metal Symposium, Colo, 74; Am Metal Work (auth, catalog), Sheldon Mem Art Gallery, 76; First Nat Ring Show, Athens, Ga & Manhattan, Kans, 77; Brookfield Craft Ctr, Conn, 80; Basketry: Tradition in New Form (traveling), Inst Contemp Art, Boston, Mass, Cooper-Hewitt Mus, New York & Greenville Co Mus Art, NC, 83; Super Bowls - Gallery Eight, La Jolla, Calif, 88; Am Craft at the Armory, New York, 88; Traveling Metals Exhib, Univ Ore Mus Art, 88-89; Fiber/Metal Invitational USA, Craft Alliance Gallery, St Louis, 92; Kansas Chooses Kansas II, Mulvane Art Mus, Topeka; Steel City: Contemp Am in Metal, Sangre de Crist Arts Ctr, Pueblo Co; Kansas Artist Craftsmen Assoc Exhib & Conference, Manhattan Arts Ctr, KS, 2005; and others; Emprise Bank, Wichita, Kans. *Pos:* Guest artist, Penland Sch, NC, 71, 73, 76, 79, 89, 92, 96 & 2003, Arrowmont Sch, Gatlinburg, Tenn, 73, 79, 86 & 92, Brookfield Craft Sch, Conn, 73, 76 & 79, Summer Vail, Colo, 74-84 & 47th Ann Conf Mid Am Coll Art Asn, St Louis. *Teaching:* Instr jewelry & silversmithing, Tyler Sch Art, Philadelphia, 71-73; prof metalsmithing, Kans State Univ, Manhattan, 73-; studies abroad, Univ Ga, Cortona, Italy, 93. *Awards:* First Place, Mus Contemp Crafts, Copper Develop Asn, 71; 50 Outstanding Craftsmen, Penland Sch, Nat Endowment for Arts, 71; Purchase Award, Renwick Gallery, DC, 74; Master Metalsmith, Nat Ornamental Metal Mus, Memphis, Tenn, 2005; Kansas Gov Artist Award, 2010. *Bibliog:* Philip Morton (auth), Contemporary Jewelry, Holt, Rinehart, Winston, 70; Oppi Untracht (auth), Jewelry Concepts and Techniques, Doubleday, 71; plus var newspaper articles. *Mem:* Am Crafts Coun; Artist Blacksmith Asn N Am; Kans Artist Craftsmen Asn (pres, 96-98); Soc N Am Goldsmiths. *Media:* All. *Res:* Argentium Sterling Silver. *Publ:* Metalsmith, Vol 27, No 1, spring, 2007. *Dealer:* J Cotter Gallery Vail CO 81657. *Mailing Add:* 2002 Rockhill Cir Manhattan KS 66502

PUJOL, ERNESTO
PAINTER

b Havana, Cuba, 1957. *Study:* Universidad de Puerto Rico, Rio Piedras, BA (visual arts), 79. *Work:* Bronx Coun Arts, Longwood, NY; Int Univ, Miami; Mus Art, Ft Lauderdale, Fla; Asociacion de Artistas Plasticos de Cuba, Havana; El Museo del Barrio, NY. *Exhib:* Solo exhibs, Experimento en Tematica Religiosa, Taller D'Jevarez, San Juan, PR, 84, New Work, Cavin-Morris, NY, 93, Installations, Int Arts Relations, NY, 94, Taxonomies, Galeria Ramis Barquet, Monterrey, Mex, 95, The Children of Peter Pan, Casa de las Americas, Havana, Cuba, 95, Collapses, Frederic Snitzer Gallery, Miami, Fla, 95 & Winter, Iturralde Gallery, Los Angeles, 96; One Hundred Hearts, Nat Arts Club, NY, 90; 11th Ann Exhib, Bronx Mus Arts, NY, 91; Material Revisions, Brattleboro Art Mus, Vt, 92; Paper Visions V, Housatonic Mus Art, Bridgeport, Conn, 94; Inquisitive Art, Reed Coll Art Gallery, Portland, Ore, 94; Iconography of Exile, Seton Hill Col, Pa, 95; Other Choices Other Voices, Islip Art Mus, Long Island, NY, 95, & Recent Acquisitions, 96; Reaffirming Spirituality, El Museo del Barrio, NY, 95; Boat Images from South Fla Collections, Miami-Dade Pub Libr, 95; The House Project, Mus Contemp Art, Los Angeles, 95; Cuba Siglo XX - Modernidad y Sincretismo, Centro Atlantico de Arte Moderno, Las Palmas, 96; and others. *Awards:* Cintas Found Fel, Arts Int, Inst Int Educ, NY, 91; Visual Arts Fel, Pollock-Krasner Found, NY, 93; Reg Painting Fel, Mid Atlantic Arts Found/Nat Endowment Arts, Baltimore, Md, 94; Art Matters Found Grant, 2008. *Bibliog:* Yolanda Woods (auth), Ernesto Pujol - Signos de la Memoria, Revista Casa, Havana, Cuba, 95; Ruth Behar (auth), Bridges to Cuba, Puentes a Cuba, Univ Mich Press, 95; Victoria Looseleaf (auth), Home is where the heart is, Los Angeles Downtown News, 11/27/95. *Mailing Add:* 210 Dean St Brooklyn NY 11217-2298

PULITZER , EMILY RAUH
COLLECTOR, CONSULTANT
b Cincinnati, Ohio, July 23, 1933. *Study:* Bryn Mawr Coll, AB, 1955; Harvard Univ, MA, 1963. *Hon Degrees:* Univ Mo, LHD, 1989; Aquinas Inst, St Louis, DFA, 2002; St Louis Univ, DFA, 2003, HHD, 2005; Washington Univ, St Louis, HHD, 2005. *Pos:* Mem staff, Cincinnati Art Mus, 1956-57; asst cur drawings, Fogg Art Mus, Harvard, 1957-64, asst to dir, 1962-63; cur, City Art Mus, St Louis, 1964-73; mem painting and sculpture comt, Mus Mod Art, New York, 1975-, trustee, 1994-, vice chmn paintings & sculpture comt, 1985-, vchmn 1996-, mem drawings comt, 2003-, chair, Libr & Archives Trustee comt, 2010-; chmn visual arts comt, Mo Arts Coun, 1976-81; bd dirs, Mark Rothko Found, 1976-88, Grand Ctr, 93-95, 99-, Grand Ctr Arts Strategy chair, 2003-; mem bd, Inst Mus Serv's, 1979-84; bd dirs, Forum, St Louis, 1980-2003, pres, 1990-95; comnr, St Louis Art Mus, 1981-88, vpres 87-88, honorary trustee 90-, colls comt, 2006-, chmn 2006-08, nominating comt, 2010-; overseers comt to vis art mus, Harvard Univ, 1990-, colls comt, 92-, chmn, 2004-; Fogg Fels 1978-, co-chmn 78-94; bd dirs, Pulitzer Inc, 1993-2005; founder & bd chmn, Pulitzer Found for the Arts, 2001-; bd mem, Contemp Art Mus, St Louis, 2005-, strategic planning ctr, 2004; bd overseers, Harvard Univ, 2006-2012, exec comt 2009-2012; comt to visit the grad sch art design 2009-, humanities & arts, 2006-2012, vchair, 2009-2011, chair, 2011-2012, sch coll continuing edu, 2006-2012, comt to visit the dept hist art & archit, 2009-, comt to visit the dept of visual & environmental studies, 2011-; St. Louis Symphony, Exec Bd, 2009-; ARTstor, Advisory Council, 2009-. *Awards:* Woman of Yr, St Louis Variety Club, 2002; St Louis award for contrib to arts community, 2003; named one of Top 200 Collectors, ARTnews mag, 2003-2012; Gertrude Vanderbilt Whitney Award (outstanding patronage of the arts), Skowhegan, 2006; Civic Leadership Award, St Louis Found, 2009; Duncan Phillips Award, Phillips Collection, Washington, DC, 2009; Outstanding Contribr Arts, Contemp Art Mus, St. Louis, 2010; Nat Medal of Arts, Nat Endowment for the Arts, 2011; Am Acad Arts & Sci, 2013; Cin Art award, Cin Art Mus, 2013. *Mem:* Am Fedn Arts (dir, 1976-89); St Louis Mercantile Libr Asn (bd dir, 1987-93); Mo Women's Forum; Sterling & Francine Clark Art Inst, Williamstown, Mass (dirs coun, 2006-). *Collection:* Abstract Expressionism; Cubism; Post-Impressionism

PUNIA, CONSTANCE EDITH
PAINTER
b Brooklyn, NY. *Study:* Brooklyn Mus Art Sch; oil with Edwin Dickinson & Yonia Fain; oil and sumi-e with Murray Hantman. *Exhib:* Les Surindependants, Paris, 75; Grand Prix Humanitaire de France, Paris, 75; Des Artistes Francais, Grand Palais, Paris, France, 76 & 77; Sun Yat Sen Ctr of Asian Studies at St John's Univ, Jamaica, NY, 76; Nat A Arts Club, New York, NY, 77; Meridian House Int, Washington, DC, 86. *Awards:* Silver Medal & Laureate of Honor, Grand Prix Humanitaire de France, 75; Bronze Medal, Akad Raymond Duncan, 75; Order of Merit Medal, Acad of Sci & Human Rels, Dominican Repub; Palme D'Or. *Mem:* Nat League Am Pen Women; Sumi-E Soc Am. *Media:* Oil, Sumi-e. *Mailing Add:* 519 Magnolia Ave Brielle NJ 08730

PUNIELLO, FRANÇOISE SARA
LIBRARIAN
b Boston, Mass, June 3, 1947. *Study:* RI Coll, BA, 69; Rutgers State Univ NJ, MLS, 70, MA (art hist), 77. *Pos:* Assoc dir pub service, Douglass Lib, 85-88; dir, Mabel Smith Douglass Libr, 88-97; assoc dir, New Brunswick Campus Librs, Rutgers Univ, 97-2003; acting dir, New Brunswick Campus Libr, 2003-2006; assoc univ librarian, Facilities Planning and Management, Rutgers Univ, 2006-. *Mem:* Am Libr Asn (art section). *Res:* Women artists and how to research their lives and works. *Interests:* Women artists. *Publ:* Auth, Elsie Driggs in Past and Promise: Lives of New Jersey Women, Scarecrow, 90; Women Painters born after 1900 in Women Artists in the United States, GK Hall, 90; coauth, Abstract Expressionist Women Painters: An Annotated Bibliography, Scarecrow Press, Lantham, Md, 96. *Mailing Add:* 302 Harrison Ave Highland Park NJ 08904

PURA, WILLIAM PAUL
PRINTMAKER, PAINTER
b Winnipeg, Man, Dec 19, 1948. *Study:* Sch Art, Univ Man, BFA, 70; Ind Univ, Bloomington, MFA, 73. *Work:* Art Bank, Can Coun, Ottawa, Ont; Miller Brewing Co, Milwaukee, Wis; Prudential Life Insurance Co, Minneapolis; Gallery III, Univ Man, Winnipeg; Wilfred Laurier Univ, Kitchener, Ont. *Exhib:* Solo exhibs, Gallery III, Univ Man, Winnipeg, 80, Ukrainian Inst Mod Art, Chicago, 84 & Winnipeg Art Gallery, 85; Virginia Beach Art Ctr, Va, 79; Charlotte Printmakers, NC, 79; Contemp Can Printmaking, Australia, 85-86. *Teaching:* Prof, Sch Art, Univ Man, 73-. *Awards:* Print & Drawing Coun Can, Opus Frames Ltd, Vancouver, 80; Art Ventures Grant, Man Arts Coun, 85; Explorations Grant, Can Coun, 86. *Mem:* Man Printmakers Asn; Can Artists Representation. *Media:* Lithography; Acrylic, Oil. *Publ:* Auth, A quiet in the land, Arts Manitoba, spring 85; George Flynn interview, Border Crossings, winter, 88. *Dealer:* Can Art Galleries 110 8th Ave SW Calgary AB T2P 1B3; The New Van Straaten Gallery 742 N Wells St Chicago IL 60610

PURCELL, ANN
PAINTER
b Arlington, Va, Nov 18, 1941. *Study:* Corcoran Sch Art, DC; George Washington Univ, BA (fine arts), 73; NY Univ, MA (lib studies), 95. *Work:* Corcoran Gallery Art, Washington; Phillips Collection, Washington; Albright-Knox Mus, Buffalo, NY; Nat Gallery Art, Washington; Milwaukee Art Mus; Baltimore Mus Art; New Orleans Mus. *Exhib:* 19th Area Exhib, Corcoran Gallery Art, Washington, 74; Solo exhibs, 5 Washington Artists, 76 & Corcoran Fac Exhib, 76, Osuna Art, DC, 2008; Group exhib, Selected, Southern Alleghenies Mus Art, Loretto, Pa, 78; 5 Artists, Mus Fine Arts, St Petersburg, Fla, 78; Selected Works from Tibor de Nagy, Mint Mus, Charlotte, NC, 79; plus many others; Osuna Art, 2008, 2009. *Collection Arranged:* Nat Gallery Art; Phillips Collection; Nat Mus Women in the Arts; and others; Baltimore Mus; New Orleans Mus. *Teaching:* Instr painting & drawing, Smithsonian Inst, Washington, 74-78, Corcoran Sch Art, 74-79, Parsons Sch Art & Design, 83-. *Awards:* Pollock-Krasner Grant (painting), 89; Lester Hereward Grant (mid-career painting), Nat Gallery Art, 88. *Bibliog:* Jane Livingston (auth), Five Washington Artists, Garamond Press, 76; article, Arts, 11/83. *Mem:* New York Artists Equity Asn; Coll Art Asn. *Media:* Acrylic, All Media. *Dealer:* Tibor de Nagy Gallery 29 W 57th St New York NY 10019; Osuna Art & Antiques 7200 Wisconsin Ave Bethesda MD 20814. *Mailing Add:* 155 Henry St 8F Brooklyn NY 11201-2527

PURDUM, REBECCA
PAINTER
b Idaho Falls, Idaho, June 16, 1959. *Study:* St Martins Sch Art, London, Eng 80; Skowhegan Sch Painting & Sculpture, Maine, 81; Syracuse Univ, NY, BFA, 81. *Work:* List Visual Arts Ctr, Mass Inst Technol, Cambridge, Mass; Mus Mod Art, Ft Worth, Tex; Herbert F Johnson Mus Art, Cornell Univ, Ithaca, NY; Hood Mus Art, Hanover, NH. *Exhib:* 10 plus 10: Contemp Soviet & Am Painters, Mod Art Mus Ft Worth, traveling exhib, San Francisco Mus Art, Albright-Knox Gallery, Corcoran Gallery, Moscow, Tbilisi & Leningrad, 89-90; Jack Tilton Gallery, NY, 89, 91, 93, 95, 98 & 2000; List Visual Arts Ctr, Mass Inst Technol, 90; Whitney Biennial, NY, 91; Repicturing Abstraction, Va Mus Fine Arts, Anderson Gallery, Marsh Gallery & 1708 Gallery, Richmond; The Poetic Object: Paintings of Rebecca Purdum, Marywood Univ, Scranton, Pa, 97; After the Fall, Snug Harbor Ctr, Staten Island, NY, 97; After Nature, Herter Arts Gallery, Univ Mass, Amherst; solo exhib, Lebanon Valley Coll Mus Art, Annville, Pa, Jaffe-Friede Gallery, Dartmouth Col, Hanover, NH, 2009; No Greater Love: Abstraction, Tilton/Kustera Gallery, NY, 2002; Regional Selections 30, Hood Mus, Dartmouth Mus, Hanover, NH, 2003; Tilton Gallery, 2006; Art Now: Rebecca Purdum, Middlebury Coll Mus Art, Middlebury, Vt, 2007; Tilton Gallery, 2011; Arcadia Now, Castleton Coll, 2011, NJCU, 2012; Atea Ring Gallery, 2011, 2012, 2013. *Pos:* Artist-in-Residence, Dartmouth Col, Hanover, NH, 2009. *Awards:* Eugene M McDermitt Award, Mass Inst Technol; Louis Comfort Tiffany Found Award; Joan Mitchell Found Grant, 2005. *Bibliog:* Mary Haus (auth), Rebecca Purdum, Artnews; Wendy Beckett (auth), The Mystical Now Art and The Sacred, Universe Press; Rebecca Purdum, New Yorker, 4/2000, 10/2001; Art in America, Rev of Exhibs, 3/2007. *Media:* Oil. *Dealer:* Jack Tilton Gallery 8 East 76th St, NY

PURDY, DONALD R
PAINTER
b Conn, Apr 10, 1924. *Study:* Univ Conn, BA; Boston Univ, MA. *Work:* New Britain Mus; Colby Col; Chase Manhattan Bank Collection; Univ Kans; Chrysler Mus; Butler Inst, Ohio. *Exhib:* USA Int Show; Silvermine Guild Artists; Audubon Artists; Allied Artists Am; Hudson Valley Exhib, 85. *Awards:* Gold Medal, Allied Artists Am; First Prize, Silvermine Guild Artists; Jane Peterson Award, Audubon Artists; Hudson Valley Award. *Bibliog:* F Whitaker (auth), article, Am Artist. *Mem:* Am Fedn Arts; Allied Artists Am; Silvermine Guild Artists. *Media:* Oil. *Collection:* American and Barbizon; Impressionist. *Dealer:* Hammer Gallery E 57th St New York NY 10022; Flemington Art Gallery Main St Flemington NJ 08822; Greenwich Gallery 6 West Putnam Ave Greenwich CT 06830. *Mailing Add:* 8 Equestrian Ridge Rd Newtown CT 06470-1872

PURI, ANTONIO
PAINTER
b Chandigarh, India. *Study:* Academy of Art, San Francisco, Calif, 1986; Coe Co, IA, BA, 1989; Univ of IA, Coll of Law, JD, 1995. *Exhib:* Foot in the Door, Minneapolis Inst of Art, Minneapolis, Minn, 2000; Four Visions, Bergen Mus of Art, Paramus, NJ, 2004; Outside the Mandala, Philadelphia Art Alliance, Philadelphia, Pa, 2005; Path of Technology & Cosmology, Noyes Mus of Art, Oceanville, NJ, 2006; Micro to Macro, W Chester Univ, W Chester, Pa, 2006. *Collection Arranged:* Noyes Mus, NJ; Bergen Mus of Art & Sci, NJ; Planet Art Mus, S Africa; Post & Schell, Philadelphia, Pa; Ritz Theatre, NJ. *Media:* Acrylic, Oil, All Media. *Dealer:* Heineman Myers Comtemp Art Bethesda MD; Robert Roman Gallery, Scottsdale, AZ. *Mailing Add:* PO Box 1981 West Chester PA 19380-0075

PURNELL, ROBIN BARKER
PAINTER
b Norwood, Mass, Jul 5, 1951. *Study:* Mass Coll Art, BFA, 71; Samos Sch Art, studied with Aristotle Solunias, 73-74; Mukina Inst Art, Ste Petersburg, Russia, studied with Alexander Kondractieu, 99-2000. *Hon Degrees:* Mass Coll Art, Honors, 75. *Work:* Rappahannock Pub Libr, Wash, Va. *Comn:* Mary Mochary, Nat Mus of Women in Arts; Linda Dietel, Wife of former headmaster of Emma Ward Sch; Jon Purnell, Am Ambassador to Uzbekistan; Ambassador & Mrs Julius Walker, Ambassador to West Africa; many more. *Exhib:* Portrait Exhib, Soviet Cult Found, St Petersburg, Russia, 91; Painters St Petersburg, Hermitage Mus, Russia, 91; One Woman Show, Dostoyevsky Mus, St Petersburg, Russia, 92, Catherine's Palace, Catherine's Palace, Pushkin, Russia, 92, Walker Arts Ctr, Woodberry Forrest, Orange, Va, 97; Russian Artists, Anna Gallery, Brussels Belgium, 92; Journey's, Kasteey Mus, Almaty, Kazakhstan, 99; Summer Exhib, Royal Acad Art, London, 2002; group exhib, Mass Coll Art, 72-74, Middle St Gallery, Wash, Va, 86-98, 90 & 93, Ariadna Gallery, St Petersburg, Russia, 92, Kasteev Mus, Almaty, Kazakhstan, 99, Royal Acad Arts, London, Eng, 2002,. *Pos:* Display dir, Lodge at Harvard Sq, Boston, Mass, 75-78. *Teaching:* instr, life drawing, anatomy, Middle St Gallery Wash, Va, 86-87, instr, origami workshop, 86; instr, pastel portraiture, Artists Studio Wash Va, 87-88. *Bibliog:* B Martinenko (auth), Robin B Purnell, Evening Leningrad News, 5/91; Dr Vacheslau Mukin (auth), Robin B Purnell, Universal Commodity Exchange, 9/92; Janet Wilson (auth), From Russia with Love, Wash Post, 6/19/93. *Mem:* Middle St Gallery Wash, Va (bd dir, 86-87); Ki Theatre, Wash, Va (bd dir, 86-87); RAAC, Rappahannocr Asn for Arts in Community (bd dir, 87-88); Artists Group, Wash, Va (founder, 2001-05). *Media:* All Media, Lecturer. *Dealer:* Robin B Purnell PO Box 416 Washington VA 22747

PURTLE, CAROL JEAN
HISTORIAN, EDUCATOR
b St Louis, Mo, Feb 20, 1939. *Study:* Maryville Univ, St Louis, BA (magna cum laude), 60; Manhattanville Col, MA, 66; Washington Univ, St Louis, PhD, 76. *Teaching:* Instr art hist, Washington Univ, St Louis, 70-76; assoc prof art & coordr art hist, Univ Memphis, 77-93, prof art, 94-; prof art hist, Benjamin Rawlins, 2005-. *Awards:* Advan Res Fel, Belgian-Am Educ Found, 74-75; Nat Endowment Humanities Summer Fel, 82 & 88; Coolidge Fel, 85; NEH Travel Grant, 89; Kress Found Grant, 97; Royal Flemish Acad Science & Arts, Belgium, 2003; Visiting Foreign Res Scholar, Ghent Univ, 2005. *Mem:* Historians Netherlandish Art (nat pres, 83-85); Coll Art Asn Am; Southeastern Coll Art Conf; Midwest Art Hist Soc; Centre Europ d' Etudes Bourguignonnes. *Res:* Painting of Jan van Eyck; 15th century devotional images; relationship between word and image in church-related art. *Publ:* Auth, Marian Paintings of Jan Van Eyck, Princeton, 1982; auth, The iconography of Campin's Madonnas in interiors: a search for common ground, Robert Campin, New Directions in Scholarship, London, 96; Le Sacerdoce de la vierge et l'enigme d'un parti iconographique exceptionnel, Revue du Louvre, 12/96; ed, Rogier van der Weyden: St Luke Drawing the Virgin, Selected Essays in Context, Brepols, 97; auth, Rogier's St Luke and the Crossroads of Scholarship, 97; Narrative time and metaphoric tradition in the development of Jan Van Eyck's Washington Annunciation, Art Bulletin, 3/99; Assessing the Evolution of Van Eyck's iconography through technical study of the Washington Annunciation II, Investigating Jan Van Eyck, London, 2000; H. Verougstraeto Leuven (ed), Jan Van Eyck's Madonna in a Church: Re-viewing Stylistic Assumptions in Jeronic Bosch et son Entourage, 2003; The Context & Jan Van Eyck's Approach to the Thyssen Diptych in Prayers and Portraits: Unfolding the Netherlandish Diptych: Essays in Context, New Haven, 2006. *Mailing Add:* 8519 Hunters Horn Germantown TN 38138-6290

PURYEAR, MARTIN
SCULPTOR
b Chicago, Ill, May 23, 1941. *Study:* Cath Univ Am, Washington, BA (art), 63; studied wood craftsmanship with African carpenters, Sierra Leone, 64-66; Swed Royal Acad Art, Stockholm, guest student, 66-88; Yale Univ Sch Art & Archit, MFA (sculpture), 71. *Hon Degrees:* Yale Univ, hon degree, 94. *Work:* Mus Mod Art & Whitney Mus Am Art, NY; Art Inst Chicago; Walker Art Ctr, Minneapolis, Minn; Los Angeles Co Mus; Addison Gallery Am Art, Andover, Mass; Getty Center, Los Angeles; and others. *Comn:* Ampersand, Minneapolis Sculpture Garden, Walker Art Ctr, 88; GRIOT New York (set design), collab with Garth Fagan Dance Co, Garth Fagan & Wynton Marsalis, Brooklyn Acad Music, 91; Steven Oliver Art Ctr, San Francisco, 94; Battery Part Authority, NY, 95; Univ Wash Pub Art Comn, Seattle, 96; set design, Garth Fagan Dance Co. *Exhib:* Retrospectives include Art Inst Chicago, 1991, Hirshhorn Mus & Sculpture Garden, Washington, 1992, Mus Contemp Art, LA, 1992, Phila Mus Art, 1992, Cleveland Ctr Contemp Art, 1993, San Fran Mus Art, 2008; solo exhibs include Corcoran Gallery Art, Washington, 1977, Donald Young Gallery, Chicago, 1983, 1985, 1987, Seattle, 1997, Mus Fine Arts, Boston, 1990, McKee Gallery, New York, 1995, 2003, Am Acad, Rome, 1997, Contemp Arts Ctr, Cincinnati, 1999, Studio Mus Harlem, New York, 2001, Mus Mod Art, New York, 2007, Nat Gallery Art, Washington, 2008; group exhibs include Whitney Biennial, Whitney Mus Am Art, New York, 1979, 1981; McKee Gallery, NY, 2000, 2002-2003, 2005, 2007; Berkeley Art Mus and Pacific Film Arch, Calif, 2001; Addison Gallery Am Art, Andover, Mass, 2002; Donald Young Gallery, Chicago, 2002-2003, 2005; Corcoran Gallery Art, Wash, DC, 2003; Mus Fine Arts, Boston, 2003; Irish Mus Mod Art, Dublin, 2004; St Louis Art Mus, 2005; Mus Contemp Art, Cleveland, 2006; Rhona Hoffman Gallery, Chicago, 2007; Paintings, Drawings and Sculpture Part II, John Berggruen Gallery, San Francisco, 2008. *Pos:* Vis artist, Skowhegan Sch Painting & Sculpture, Maine, 80 & Am Acad Rome, 86. *Teaching:* Secondary sch instr Eng, French, biology & art, Sierra Leone, W Africa, 64-66; asst instr, Yale Univ, New Haven, Conn, 69-71; asst prof art, Fisk Univ, Nashville, 71-73 & Univ Md, College Park, 74-78; prof art, Univ Ill, Chicago, 78-88. *Awards:* Grand Prize for best artist, Sao Paulo Bienal, Brazil, 90; Skowhegan Medal for Sculpture, Skowhegan Sch Painting & Sculpture, New York, 90; Coll Art Asn Award, 93; Nat Medal of Arts, Nat Endowment for the Arts, 2011. *Media:* All Media. *Dealer:* representing Barbara Krakow Gallery, Boston, Donald Young Gallery, Chicago, McKee Gallery, NY, Greg Kucera Gallery, Seattle. *Mailing Add:* Donald Young Gallery 224 S Michigan Ave Suite 266 Chicago IL 60604

PUTMAN, MARY T
PAINTER
Study: Carnegie Mellon Univ, BFA, 1968. *Work:* Southern Alleghenies Mus Art; Gen Elec Corp; Blue Cross, Pa; Dupont Corp; First Union Bank. *Exhib:* Against the Grain 1960-1990: Images in American Art, Southern Alleghenies Mus Art, 1991; Butler Inst Am Art, Ohio, 1995; Nine Women Painters - Nine Distinct Voices, Lichtenstein Ctr Arts, Pittsfield, Mass, 1995; Conviviality & Confetti, Noyes Mus, Oceanville, NJ, 1998; Am Acad Arts & Letts Invitational, New York, 2010. *Bibliog:* Ellen Kaye (auth), Full of Surprises, Philadelphia Inquirer, 11/25/1984; Penelope Bass Cope (auth), Kent County is Her Canvas, Metrop HOme, 5/1985; Denise Pajerowski (auth), Stilling Life, Wilmington News J, 10/9/1988. *Mailing Add:* c/o Gross McCleaf Gallery 127 S Sixteenth St Philadelphia PA 19102

PUTNAM, ADAM
INSTALLATION SCULPTOR
b New York, NY, 1973. *Study:* Parsons Sch Design, BFA, 1995; Yale Univ Sch Art, MFA, 2000. *Exhib:* Solo exhibs include Artists Space, New York, 2004, Sandroni Rey, Los Angeles, 2005, Andrew Kreps, New York, 2005, Taxter & Spengemann, New York, 2007; Group exhibs include Benefit Auction, Los Angeles Contemp Exhibs, 2001; Staged/Un-Staged, Riva Gallery, New York, 2002; Drawings, Derek Eller Gallery, New York, 2003, Benefit Raffle for Into the Abyss, 2003; NeoQueer, Ctr Contemp Art, Seattle, 2004; The Uncertain States of Am, Astrup Fearnley Mus, Oslo, 2005; Annotations, Champion Fine Art, Los Angeles, 2005; Plain of Heaven, Creative Time and Friends of the Highline, New York, 2005; 2nd Moscow Biennial, Moscow, 2007; Whitney Biennial, Whitney Mus Am Art, 2008. *Awards:* Artists Space Independent Proj Grant, 2003; Rema Hort Mann Artist Grant, 2004. *Dealer:* Taxter & Spengemann 504 W 22nd St New York NY 10011

PUTRIH, TOBIAS
INSTALLATION SCULPTOR
b Kranj, Slovenia, 1972. *Study:* Acad Fine Arts, Ljubljana, Slovenia, 1997; Kunstakademie Dusseldorf, Germany, 1998. *Work:* Mus Mod Art, New York; Mus Boijmans Van Beuningen, the Netherlands; Mod Galerija Ljubljana; Mudam, Musee d' Art Mod Grand-Duc Jean, Luxembourg; Queensland Art Gallery, Australia. *Comn:* Maxine and Stuart Frankel Found for Art; Logan Collection; Margulies Collection at Warehouse, Miami. *Exhib:* Solo exhibs include Max Protetch Gallery, New York, 2003, 2005, 2007, Laumeier Sculpture Park, St Louis, MO, 2006, Neuberger Mus Art, Purchase, New York, 2007; Group exhibs include Max Protetch Gallery, New York, 2002; Downtime: Constructing Leisure, New Langton Arts, San Francisco, 2005; Monuments for Am, Wattis Inst Contemp Art, San Francisco, White Columns, New York, 2005; 52nd Venice Biennale, Venice, 2007. *Awards:* Vordemberge-Gildewart Found Award, 2002. *Mailing Add:* c/o Max Protetch Gallery 245 8th Ave New York NY 10011

PUTTERMAN, FLORENCE GRACE
PAINTER, EDUCATOR
b Brooklyn, NY, Apr 14, 1927. *Study:* New York Univ, BS; Bucknell Univ; Pa State Univ, MFA, 73. *Work:* Metrop Mus Art, Everson Mus, Brooklyn Mus, NY; Art Inst Chicago; Nat Mus Women Arts, Washington, DC; Philadelphia Mus, Pa; NJ State Mus, Trenton; and others; State Mus Pa, Harrisburg Pa; Palmer Mus, Penn State Univ; Polk Mus, Lakeland, Fla; Telfair Mus, Savannah, Ga; Ringling Mus, Sarasota, Fla. *Comn:* Harris Saving Bank, Harrisburg, Pa, 80; Geisinger Med Ctr, Women's Hosp, Sunbury Community Hosp, Sunbury, Pa. *Exhib:* Solo Exhibs: Lancaster Mus, Lancaster, Pa, 2001; Albany Art Mus, Albany, Ga, 2002; Ten Yr Retrospective, Lore Degenstein Gallery, Susquehanna Univ, Selinsgrove, Pa, 2003; Walton Art Ctr, Fayetteville, Ark, 2004; Projects Gallery, Philadelphia, 2006; Susquehanna Art Mus, Harrisburg, Pa, 2006; Gallery 10, Washington, DC, 2006; Ormond Beach Mus, Ormond Beach, Fla, 2006; The Gallery at Penn Coll, Williamsport, Pa, 2007; Projects Gallery, Philadelphia, Pa, 2008; Franklin and Marshal Col, Lancaster Pa, 2008, Allyn Gallup Contemp Art, Sarasota, Fla, 2009, Walter Wickiser Gallery, New York, 2010, Baisden Gallery, Tempa, Fla, 2010, Noir et Blanc, Susquehanna Art Mus, Harrisburg, Pa, 2010, Villanova Univ, 2011, Payne Galleries Fryeburg Academy, Fryeburg, Maine, 2011, A Survey of Works 1950-2010, Ringling Coll Art, 2011, Walter Wickiser Gallery, NY, 2012; Group Exhibs: Abstraction: Monotype, Univ Mus, Indiana, Pa; Valdosta National, Ga, 2008; Philadelphia Watercolor Soc Ann, Woodmere Mus, 92; Fla Artists Statewide Exhib, Ringling Mus, Sarasota, Fla, 94; Erie Art Mus Ann, 95; Haggin Mus Ann, Stockton, Calif, 95; Saginaw Art Mus, Saginaw, Mich, 2000; Chattahoochee Valley Mus, La Grange, Ga, 2002, 2004; Butler Inst Am Art, Youngstown, Ohio, 2002; Boca Raton Mus, Fla, 2003; Toronto Art Fair, 2005; Chicago Art Fair, 2007; Miami Art Fair, 2007; Basel Art Fair, Miami, 2007; Franklin & Marshall Coll, Lancaster, Pa, 2008; Philadelphia Int Airport, 2009; Art on Paper, Md Fed Art, 2009; Philadelphia Watercolor Club, Ursinus Coll, Pa, 2009; Paper in Particular, Columbia Coll, Mo, 2009; Keystone Nat Print, Mechanicsburg, Pa, 2009; Think, Boston Printmakers, Emmanuel Coll, Boston, 2010; Art as Emotion, Whitaker Ctr, Harrisburg, Pa, 2010; Fla Mus Women Artists, Deland, Fla, 2010; Nathan D Rosen Mus Gallery, Boca Raton, Fla, 2010; Brand Lib, Glendale, Calif, 2010; Art on Paper, Maryland Fed of Art, Annapolis, Md, 2011; Latent Images, State Mus, Harrisburg, Pa, 2011; Fla Mus Women in the Arts, Deland, Fla, 2011; SAGA Hands On, Projects Gallery, Phila, Pa, 2012; Black & White, Gallery 705, Stroudsburg, Pa, 2012; Artists that Made Sarasota Famous, Art Ctr Sarasota, 2012; Doshi 40, State Mus, Harrisburg, Pa. 2012; Across the Waters, Galerie Recolte, Fukuoka, Japan, 2013; SAGA-Delind Gallery, Milwaukee, Wisc, 2013. *Pos:* Founder & pres, Arts Unlimited, Selinsgrove, Pa, 65-78; cur, Milton Shoe Co Print Collection, Pa, 70-; bd dir, Art Gallery, Bucknell Univ, Lewisburg, Pa. *Teaching:* Artist in residence, Fed Title III Prog, 67-70; instr, Lycoming Coll, Williamsport, Pa, 73-75; instr, Susquehanna Univ, 84-; instr, Monotype Workshop, Bennington Coll, Vt, 89. *Awards:* Nat Endowment Arts, 79-80; Distinguished Alumni Award, Sch Arts & Archit, Pa State Univ, 88; Nat Medal Hon, Nat Asn Women Artists, 94; Award of Excellence, Philadelphia Watercolor Club, 95; Daniel Serra V Nevas Mem Award, Audubon Artists, 96; Purchase Award, Del Mar Coll Ann, 97; Stockton Print & Drawing Purchase Award, 98; Purchase Award, La Grange Nat XXII Biennial, 2002; Renaissance Graphic Arts Material Award, Saga 71st Ann Exhib, 2004; Graphic Chemical Award, Colorprint Soc, 2005; Patron Award, Brand Libr, 2007; Graphic Award, Soc Am Graphic Artists, 2010; Lifetime Achievement Award, Soc Am Graphic Artists, 2010; Donor Award, Brand Lib, Glendale, Calif, 2010. *Bibliog:* New American Monotypes, 79-80; articles, Am Artist, 7/79 & 2/81; The Nation, Art News, 1/83; New Art Examiner, 90; Art News, Nov, 2002; Art News, summer 2006; Patriot News, 4/06; Sarasota Herald Tribune, 3/08; Philadelphia Inquirer, 4/08; Carlsen (auth), Pelican Press, Sarasota, Fla, Jan 2009; Kiepiela (auth), Critics Choice, Longboat Observer, Feb 2009; Kiepiela, Go-Flo, Longboat Observer, Mar 2010; Susan Rife (auth), Entwined Metaphors, Sarasota Herald Tribune, April 2010; Mark Ormond (auth), A Survey of Works, Ringling Coll, 2010; Sarasota Herald Tribune Style Arts, 2013. *Mem:* Boston Printmakers; Nat Asn Women Artists; Soc Am Graphic Artists (vpres); Nat Colorprint Soc; Florida Printmakers; Graphic Chemical Colorprint Soc; Los Angeles Printmaking Soc; Philadelphia Watercolor Club. *Media:* Oil, Acrylic, Monotypes. *Publ:* Southwest Art, 6/88; Twenty Year Survey, Palmer Mus, Pa State Univ Publ, 90; Encountering the Narrative In Florence Putterman's Work, Susquehanna Univ Publ, 93; Cryptic Tidings, 97, Metaphoric Fables, 99, Art at the 4 Corners, 2000; Allusive Metaphors, 2002; Interwoven Dialogues, 2007; Surface and Substance, 2008; Legendary Fables catalogue, Walter Wickiser Gallery; Entwined Metaphors, Autobiography by Florence Putterman. *Dealer:* Walter Wickiser 210 11th Ave #303 New York NY 10001; Proj Gallery 629 N 2st Philadelphia PA 19123; Baisden Gallery 442 Grand Central Pk

Tampa Fla 33606; Lynden Gallery 117 S Market St Elizabethtown PA 19020; Grand Central West Palm Beach FL; Hudson Gallery Sylvania OH; Lebanon Art Gallery Lebanon PA; Faustina Lewisburg PA; Dancing Crane Gallery 1014 10th Ave Bradenton Fl 34205; Post & Lintel Gallery 34 S Market St Selinsgrove Pa 17870. *Mailing Add:* 3 Fairway Dr Selinsgrove PA 17870

PUTTERMAN, SUSAN LYNN
CURATOR, ADMINISTRATOR
b Zurich, Switzerland; US citizen. *Study:* Bennington Col; Barnard Col, BA, 75; Hunter Col, MA (art hist). *Collection Arranged:* Inside/Outside/On the Wall: Sculpture Invitational, 2003; Portraits, Myths & Stories: Three Photographers, 2004; Barbara Schwartz: Shaped Paintings (1998-2004), 2004; Are you Ready for Social Security?, 2005. *Pos:* Dir, Gallery Ilene Kartz, New York, 90-92; cur, Hebrew Home for the Aged, Riverdale, 94-. *Bibliog:* William Zimmer (auth), An artist with a sharp eye for the seams, NY Times, 5/21/95; Francine Silverman (auth), Two exhibits focus on parent/child relationship, Riverdale Rev, 11/23/97; Vivien Raynor (auth), From the famous to the nameless, NY Times, 6/14/98; Jonathon Goodman (auth), Inside/Outside/On the Wall, Hebrew Home for the Aged, Sculpture Magazine, 6/04; Pre-Teen Turf, The Riverdale Review, 3/11/04; Alex Friedman (auth), Getting Better with Age, the Riverdale Press, 2/3/05. *Mem:* Nat Asn Corp Art Mgrs; Am Asn Mus; Arts & Bus Coun; Mayo Smith Soc; IAPAA, ArtTable, Am Asn Mus; Arts & Business Council. *Specialty:* Contemporary Art. *Collection:* 20th C Art, including works by Christian Boltanski, Frederic Brenner, Christo, Amy Cutler, Joan Mitchell, Joel Perlman, Pablo Picasso, Andy Warhol, William Wegman. *Publ:* Auth, Art in the nursing home, Nursing Homes Mag, 6/97

PYLE, MELISSA BRONWEN
PAINTER, SCULPTOR
b Neptune, NJ, May 7, 1963. *Study:* Moore Coll Art and Design, BFA, 85. *Comn:* mural, Mrs Wilhamena Hardee, Alicante, Spain, 95; botanical oil painting, Dr Jason Connor, Villanova, Pa, 95; botanical oil painting, Ms Jeanette Petti, Oceanport, NJ, 2000; landscape oil painting, Mr & Mrs Joel Lizotte, Red Bank, NJ, 2000; landscape oil painting, Mr & Mrs Keith Olson, Naples, Fla, 2000. *Exhib:* Color Now, Main Line Ctr for the Arts, Bryn Mawr, Pa, 96; From Paper to Cloth, Moore Coll Art and Design, Philadelphia, Pa, 96; solo exhib, Thistledown Gallery, Spring Lake, NJ, 98 & Elzeard Gallery, Baltimore, Md, 2000; Monmouth Co Arts Coun juried exhib, Monmouth Mus, Lincroft, NJ, 99; 13th Ann juried exhib, Art Alliance, Red Bank, NJ, 99; An Affair of the Art, Walt Disney Imagineering, Los Angeles, Calif, 2000-2001; mem exhib, Woodmere Art Mus, Chestnut Hill, Pa, 2001; group exhib, Jersey Shore Ctr for the Arts, Ocean Grove, NJ, 2004 & Frederick Art Gallery, Allenhurst, NJ, 2006; Audubon Artists Juried Nat exhib, Salmagundi, New York City, 2006. *Pos:* Master Designer & Mgr, Smudges Inc, Chestnut Hill, Pa, 87-92; Sole Proprietor, M Bronwen Pyle Hand Painted, Philadelphia, Pa, 91-95. *Teaching:* Facilitator, The Artist's Way, Abington Art Ctr, Jenkintown, Pa, 97; Adj Prof, Color Theory, Moore col Art and Design, Philadelphia, Pa, 97-2003. *Awards:* MCAC Award, Monmouth Co Arts Coun, Monmouth Mus, Lincroft, NJ, 99; Wall Found for Educ Excellence, Wall High Sch, Wall, NJ, 2000. *Mem:* The Guild Creative Art, Shrewsbury, NJ (assoc mem); The Artists Group, Philadelphia, Pa (co-creator/facilitator, 95); Artsbridge, Lambertville, NJ (assoc mem); Audubon Artists Nat Art Soc, NY. *Media:* Acrylic, Oil; Mixed Media. *Publ:* auth, Wall township artist gives new life to conventional form, The Herald of Wall Township, 98; auth, Melissa Bronwen Pyle, The Times at the Jersey Shore, 98; auth, On display, Asbury Park Press, 99; auth, Living the material world, MCAC 21st ann show, Asbury Park Press, 2000. *Dealer:* Frederick Art Gallery 401 Spier Ave Allenhurst NJ 07711; Web of the Quill Gallery 5 Bay Rd Brooklin ME 04616

PYZOW, SUSAN VICTORIA
PAINTER, PRINTMAKER
b Bronx, NY, Oct 27, 1955. *Study:* Cooper Union, BFA, 76; Buffalo Univ, 78. *Exhib:* Art & Law Exhib, Minn Mus Art, St Paul, 80; Committed to Print, Mus Mod Art, NY, 88; Committed to Print, Spencer Art Mus, Kansas City, Kans, 90; Art at the Armory: Occupied Territory, Mus Contemp Art, Chicago, Ill, 92; Am Artists Prof League Nat Competition, Salmagundi Club, NY, 92; 57th Midyear Exhib, Butler Inst Am Art, Youngstown, Ohio, 93; 58th Midyear Exhib, Butler Inst Am Art, Youngstown, Ohio, 94; Pastel Soc of Am Nat Competition, Nat Arts Club, NY, 94; Contemp Printmakers, Seton Hall, NJ, 2004; Paul Marcus & Susan Pyzow, Two Contemp Printmakers, The Old Print Shop, NY, 2006; Graphic Studio Gallery, Dublin, Ireland, 2006; The Old Printshop, Go Contemp Printmakers, 2007; Never Routine, Grace Inst, NY, 2008; New Yorkers by New Yorkers, NY Etchers Soc, 2008; Soc Am Graphic Artists 76th Exhib, Lore Degenstein Gallery, Susquehannah Univ, Pa, 2009; Different at Evert Turn: Contemporary Painters of the Hudson River, Hutchins Gallery, CW Post, Long Island, Kingsborough Community Col, Brooklyn, Lake Champlain Mariteim Mus, Vergennes, Vt, Albany Inst Hist and Art, Gibson Gallery, SUNY Potsdam & US Milit Acad, West Point, 2009; SAGA 76th Exhib, Lore Degenstein Gallery, Susquehana Univ, Selingrove, Pa; Contemporary Printmakers, Old Print Shop, NY. *Teaching:* Instr intaglio & drawing, Buffalo Univ, NY, 77-78; drawing & watercolor, Parsons Sch Design, New York, 84-. *Awards:* Purchase prize, Fed Res Bank of NY, 2000; First place acrylic, Joyce Dutka Arts Found, 2002; Nat League of Am, Pa Women Grant in Art, 2004. *Mem:* Soc Am Graphic Artists. *Media:* Oil, Acrylic, Printmaking. *Specialty:* The Old Print Show (Printmaking)

Q

QUACKENBUSH, ROBERT
PRINTMAKER, PAINTER
b Hollywood, Calif, July 23, 1929. *Study:* Art Ctr Coll Design, Pasadena, Calif, BA, 56; Pratt Graphic Art Ctr, with John Ross & Clare Romano, 61. *Hon Degrees:* Int Univ for Grad Studies, PhD in Educ, 1999. *Work:* Whitney Mus, NY; Smithsonian Inst, Washington, DC; Mazza Collection Gallery, Findlay Col, Ohio; Lena Y de Grummond Collection, Univ Southern Miss; Kerlen Collection, St Paul, Minn. *Comn:* Paintings, US Dept Interior, 68 & US Air Force Mus, 69, Washington, DC. *Exhib:* Audubon Artists Ann, Nat Acad Art Galleries, 60; Continental American Print Show, Whitney Mus, 62; Nat Acad Arts Ann, 66; Soc Illustrators Ann, Soc Illustrators Gallery, 68, 70 & 84; New Acquisitions, Mus Am Illus, 84, NY. *Collection Arranged:* Soc of Illustrators' Retrospective of paintings, prints and illustrations by the artist, 2007. *Pos:* Artist, writer, art therapist, lectr. *Teaching:* Instr painting & bk illus, Sch Visual Arts, 68-73; instr painting & illus, Robert Quackenbush Studio-Gallery, 68-; guest lectr, worldwide tours to universities, schs & libraries, 68-. *Awards:* Citation, 50 Best Books Exhib, Am Inst Graphic Arts, 62; Edgar Allen Poe Spec Award for Best Juvenile Mystery, Mystery Writers Am, 82; Citations (2), Best Children's Books of 1992, Soc Illustrs, 92; Gradiva Award for best children's book of 1998; Holland Soc Gold Medal for distinction in art and literature, 2000. *Bibliog:* The art of Robert Quackenbush, Am Artist Mag, 65; Morton Schindel (dir), Signature Collection, Weston Woods Studio, 76; Something about the author, Gale Research Inc, Vol 7, 89; Something about the author, Gale Research Inc, Vol 133, 02. *Mem:* Auth Guild; Holland Soc, NY; Mystery Writers of Am; Soc Illustrators; NAAP. *Media:* All Media. *Res:* Understanding the Symbolic Communications of Children through their Art, Intl Univ for Grad Studies. *Specialty:* Woodcuts, oils, watercolor, and original art from children's books. *Interests:* Psychoanalytic Research. *Collection:* Mrs George Roy Hill; Mrs Norton Simon; Beulah Campbell, NC; Mrs Mayra Makepeace; Mrs Kathryn Tyree. *Publ:* Illusr, The Pilot (by James Fenimore Cooper), 68 & The Life of Washington (by Rev Mason L Weems), 74, Ltd Ed Club; The Scarlet Letter (by Nathaniel Hawthorne), Reader's Digest Bks, 84; auth & illusr, Robert Quackenbush's Treasury of Humor, Doubleday, 90; Batababy, Random House, 97; Daughter of Liberty, Disney Hyperion, 99; Miss Mallard Mysteries, animated film series, Cinar in co-prodn with Shanghai Animation Film Studio, 2000. *Dealer:* Robert Quackenbush Studios 223 E 78th St New York NY 10075. *Mailing Add:* 460 E 79th St New York NY 10075

QUAM, CAROLE C
PAINTER
b Grass Valley, Calif, Mar 22, 1944. *Study:* Univ Idaho, 62-65; Univ Alaska, Anchorage, BFA, 91. *Work:* Univ Alaska Mus, Fairbanks. *Exhib:* Solo shows, Univ Alaska, Anchorage Campus Ctr Gallery, 91, Rogue Community Col, Grants Pass, Ore, 93, Civic Ctr Gallery, Fairbanks, Alaska, 94, Alaska Pac Univ, 95, 99, Clatsop Community Col, Astoria, 96, La State Univ, Shreveport, 96; Northern Nat, Nicolet Coll Gallery, Rhinelander, Wis, 93; XXV All Alaska Juried, Anchorage Mus, Alaska, 94 & 96; group show, Sinclair Community Col, Dayton, Ohio, 94, Artists Gold Rush, Collector Art Gallery, Washington, 95, Fairbanks Arts Asn, 96, Alaska State Mus, 96; Mary, Woman Made Gallery, Chicago, 96; Solo shows, Erb Mem Union Gallery, Univ Ore, Eugene, 97, The Barn Gallery, Middle Tenn State Univ, Mur Freesboro, 97, Nordic Heritage Mus, Seattle, Wash, 97 & Univ Gallery, Univ Mass, Lowell, Mass, 98; group shows, Narratives, Woman Made Gallery, Chicago, 97 & Figuresque, The Art Ctr, Mt Clemens, Mich, 98. *Awards:* Anchorage Mus Best Fibre, Earth, Fire & Fibre, 87; Career Opportunity Grant, Alaska Arts Coun, 94; Residency Ragdale Found, 99. *Bibliog:* Dimetra Makris (auth), First Prize Quilts, Simon & Schuster, 84; Heather Robertson (auth), In the gallery, Fairbanks Arts, 94; Tom Nicholas (auth), The Best of Oil Painting, 96. *Mem:* Mensa. *Media:* Oil. *Publ:* Contribr, Hayden's Ferry Review, Ariz State Univ, 94

QUAYTMAN, HARVEY
PAINTER
b Far Rockaway, NY, Apr 20, 1937. *Study:* Syracuse Univ; Tufts Univ; Boston Mus Fine Arts Sch, BFA & grad degree. *Work:* Tate Gallery, London; Whitney Mus Am Art & Mus Mod Art, NY; Israel Mus, Jerusalem; Carnegie Inst of Technol, Pittsburgh, Pa; and others. *Exhib:* Solo exhibs, David McKee Gallery, NY, 75, 77, 78, 80, 82, 84, 86, 87, 88, 90, 93, 96, 98 & 2000, Galerie Nordenhake, Malmo, Sweden, 82, 86, 87, 90, 93 & 96, Nielsen Gallery, Boston, Mass, 76, 78, 80, 83, 86, 89, 93, 95 & 2000, Gilbert Brownstone Gallery, Paris, 90; Henie-Onstaad Art Center, Oslo, Norway, 96; Corcoran Biennale, Corcoran Gallery Art, Washington, DC, 87; Generations of Geometry, Whitney Mus Am Art, Equitable Ctr, NY, 87; Mus Mod Art, NY, 87-88; Germans Van Eck Gallery, NY, 89; 1989 Ljubljana Bienale 18, Int Centre Craphic Art, Yugoslavia, 89; 50 Yrs Collecting: Art at IBM, IBM Gallery Sci & Art, NY, 89; Abstraction in the Eighties, Rose Art Mus, Brandeis Univ, Waltham, Mass, 90; Tel Aviv Mus Art, Israel, 92; 48th Ann Am Acad Purchase Exhib, Am Acad Arts & Lett, NY, 97; Queens Artists: Highlights of the 20th Century, Queens Mus Art, NY, 97; The Edward R Broide Collection, Orlando Mus Art, Fla, 98; Then and Now: Nielson Gallery 35th Ann Exhib, Nielsen Gallery, Boston, Mass, 99; and others. *Teaching:* instr, Boston Mus Fine Arts Sch, Middlebury Col, Essex Col Art, Colchester, Eng & Sch Visual Arts, NY, formerly; instr, Cooper Union, Parsons Sch Design, NY; vis lectr, Harvard Univ, 82 & 83; adj asst prof, Hunter Col, 83. *Awards:* Guggenheim Fel, 79 & 85; Artist Fel, Nat Endowment Arts, 83; Am Acad Arts & Letters Award, 97. *Bibliog:* Peter Clothier (auth), Harvey Quaytman, Artnews, 5/88; Charles Hagan (auth), Harvey Quaytman, Artforum, 12/88; Ellen Handy (auth), Harvey Quaytman, Arts, 1/89. *Media:* Miscellaneous Media. *Mailing Add:* McKee Gallery 745 5th Ave New York NY 10151

QUAYTMAN, R.H.
PAINTER
b Boston, Mass, 1961. *Study:* Skowhegan Sch Painting & Sculpure, Maine, 1982; BA, Bard Coll, New York, 1983; Grad prog in painting, NatColl Art & Design, Dublin, Ireland, 1984; Inst des Hautes Etudes en Arts Plastiques, Paris, 1989. *Work:* Whitney Mus Am Art, New York; Mus Mod Art, New York; San Francisco Mus Mod Art; ICA, Boston. *Exhib:* Solo exhibs, Spencer Brownstone Gallery, New York, 1998, 2001, China Art Objects Galleries, Los Angeles, 1999, Revolution, Ferndale, Mich, 2002, Momenta Art, Brooklyn, 2004, Miguel Abreu Gallery, New York, 2008, Inst Contemp Art, Boston, 2009, San Francisco Mus Mod Art, 2010; group exhibs, A Gallery Project, Ferndale, Mich, 1995; Women and Geometric Abstraction, Pratt Manhattan

Gallery, New York, 1999; Dirty Realism, Robert Pearre Gallery, Tucson, Ariz, 2000; Pictures, Green-Naftali Inc, New York, 2002; The Big Nothing, Arcadia Univ Art Gallery, Pa, 2004; Out of Place, UBS Art Gallery, New York, 2005; Regroup Show, Miguel Abreu Gallery, New York, 2007; Electioneering, Fort Worth Contemp Arts, Tex Christian Univ, 2008; The Man Whose Shoes Sqeaked, Richard Telles Gallery, Los Angeles, 2008; Cave Painting, Greshams Ghost, New York, 2009; Blue, James Graham & Sons Gallery, New York, 2009; Guilty Feet, 179 Canal, New York, 2010; 54th Int Art Exhib Biennale, Venice, 2011. *Teaching:* lectr, Barnard Coll, New York, 2006, Brooklyn Coll, 2007, Columbia Univ Sch Arts, 2007, Yale Sch Art, 2008, Cooper Union, 2008, Princeton Univ, 2009. *Awards:* Rome Prize Fel, Am Acad Rome, Italy, 2001. *Bibliog:* TJ Carlin (auth), From One O to the Other, Time Out New York, 2008; RH Quaytman, The New Yorke, 2009; Roberta Smith (atuh), Chapter 12Liamb, The New York Times, 2009; Lauren O'Niell-Butler (auth), Ladies First, Artforum, 2010; Linda Yablonsky (auth), Women's Work, New York Times Mag, 2010; Steel Stillman (auth), In the Studio, Art in America, 2010; Steven Stern (auth), Past Present, Frieze, 2010. *Mailing Add:* Miguel Abreu Gallery 36 Orchard St New York NY 10002

QUENTEL, HOLT
PAINTER
b Milwaukee, Wis, 1961. *Study:* Lawrence Univ, 79-83; Sch Art Inst Chicago, 84-85; Princeton Univ, 86-87. *Work:* Milwaukee Art Mus. *Exhib:* Solo exhibs, Stux Gallery, Boston, 87, Stux Gallery, NY, 87, 88 & 90, Wriston Mus, Lawrence Univ, 89, State of Ill Gallery, Chicago, 89; All Quiet on the Western Front, Espace Dieu, Paris, 90; Bayly Mus, Va, 90; Mayor Rowan Gallery, London, 90; Stuttering, Stux Gallery, NY, 90; Outside Am: Going into the 90's, Fay Gold Gallery, Atlanta, 91; The Fetish of Knowledge, Real Art Ways, Hartford, 91; Invitational, Tony Shafrazi Gallery, NY, 91; Theoretically Yours, 92; and many others. *Awards:* Elizabeth Richardson Award, 83; Smith Merit Scholar, Sch Art Inst Chicago, 84-86; Nat Endowment Arts, 89. *Bibliog:* Michael Archer (auth), I Don't Like Eggs: Janet Green, British Collector, On Art & The Art World, Artscribe, summer, 90; Phyllis Freeman (auth), New York: Harry N Abrams Inc, New Art, 90; Gretchen Faust (auth), Holt Quentel, Arts, 1/91; and others. *Mailing Add:* 114 Bridgemann Rd London United Kingdom N11 BH

QUICK, EDWARD RAYMOND
MUSEUM DIRECTOR
b Los Angeles, Calif, Mar 22, 1943. *Study:* Univ Calif, Santa Barbara, with Dr Herbert Cole, BA, 72, MA, 77. *Collection Arranged:* Art Inc, 79; George Sugarman, 81; Views of a Vanishing Frontier, 84; Johann Berthelsen, 88; Swope Art Mus Collections, 87. *Pos:* Asst cur, Santa Barbara Mus Art, Calif, 77-78; registrar, Montgomery Mus Fine Arts, Ala, 78-80; dept head, Joslyn Art Mus, Omaha, Nebr, 80-85; dir, Sheldon Swope Art Mus, Terre Haute, Ind, 86-95, Berman Mus, Anniston, Ala, 95-. *Teaching:* Mus Mgt, Ind State Univ, Terre Haute, 89-. *Mem:* Am Asn Mus (map surveyor, 85-); Inst Coun Mus; Arts Illiana (bd pres, 86, secy, 88); Asn Ind Mus (bd, 88-); Midwest Mus Conf. *Publ:* Contribr, Regional styles of drawing in Italy: 1600-1700, Univ Calif, Santa Barbara, 77; Registrars on Record: essays on museum collections management, Am Asn Mus, 88; ed, Johann Berthelsen: An American master painter, Swope Art Mus, 88. *Mailing Add:* 5363 Brenda Ave San Jose CA 95124

QUIDLEY, PETER TAYLOR
PAINTER, PHOTOGRAPHER
b Boston, Mass, Dec 20, 1945. *Comn:* Paintings, Westinghouse, Ft Lauderdale, Fla, 68; portraits of 4 kings, Kingdom of Saudi Arabia, Raytheon Corp, Saudi Arabia, 79; Death of Socrates (copy), Anheuser-Busch, St Louis, 93. *Exhib:* Solo exhibs, Gallery Juarez, Palm Beach, Fla, 73 & Luminous Interiors, Copley Soc, Boston, Mass, 96; Int Art Expos, Jeddah Dome, Saudi Arabia, 78-79; Evolution of an Artist, Cahoon Mus Am Art, Cotuit, Mass, 94; Federal Reserve Group Show, 94; Portrait Group Show, Copley Soc Boston, 94; Places for the Muse, Cape Mus Fine Art, 98; Group exhib tour, Cornell Mus Art in Am Culture, Mobile Mus Art, Delray, Fla, Art Mus Southeast Tex, Beumont, Tex, Art Mus South Texas, Corpus Christi, Tex, Mus Southwest, Midland, Tex, Hagin Mus, Stockton, Calif, Coas Art Mus, Coos Bay, Ore, Minnesota Mus Marine Art, Winona, MN, American Soc Artists. *Awards:* Robb Saggandorf Mem Award, Copley Member Show, Yankee Mag, 92; First Prize Painting, Winter Member Show, Copley Soc Boston, 93; Evelyn Strand Dibner Award, Cape Cod Art Asn Show, 93. *Bibliog:* Tim Wood (auth), Introducing Peter Quidley, A Plus, 12/93; Anna Crebo (auth), Artist Peter Quidley, Cape Cod Life Mag, 4/94; Debbie Forman (auth), Master of romance paints with purpose, Cape Cod Times, 7/22/94; Charles Robinson (auth), Peter Taylor Quidley: Colorfulife Luminous Art, Fine Arts Connoisseur, 2010. *Mem:* Copley Soc Boston; Am Soc Marine Artists; Am Soc Portrait Artists; US Coast Guard Artists. *Media:* Oil. *Specialty:* Traditional Art. *Interests:* Sailing. *Publ:* Fine Art Connoisseur. *Dealer:* Quidley & Company 26 Main St Nantucket MA 02554. *Mailing Add:* PO Box 129 South Chatham MA 02659

QUIGLEY, ROBERT WELLINGTON
ARCHITECT
b Calif, 1945. *Study:* Univ Utah, Bachelor, 69. *Comn:* Prin works include San Diego New Main Libr (Honor award, Am Inst of Archit San Diego, 98), Sherman Heights Community Ctr (Citation, Am Inst of Archit San Diego, 90, Orchid, San Diego Chap Am Inst of Archit, 92, Merit award, Am Inst of Archit San Diego, 96), Baltic Inn, San Diego (Honor award, Am Inst of Archit San Diego, 87, Panda award, City of San Diego, 88), 202 Island Inn (One of "Ten Best Designs of 1992," Time Mag., 93, Nat Am Inst of Archit Honor award, 93, Merit award, Am Inst of Archit San Diego, 93, Honor award with Distinction, Am Inst of Archit Calif Coun, 94), Solana Beach Transit Station (Orchid, San Diego Chap, Am Inst of Archit, 96, Honor award, Am Inst of Archit Calif Coun, 98), Escondido Transit Station (Citation, Am Inst of Archit San Diego, 90, Orchid, Am Inst of Archit San Diego, 91, Beautification award, City of Escondido, 90); San Diego Children's Mus, Calif, Student Academic Services Facility, Univ Calif San Diego, San Diego Historic Harbor Front, West Valley Branch Libr (Divine Detail, Am Inst of Archit San Diego, 2003, Merit award, Am Inst of Archit Santa Clara, 2004), Leslie Shao-ming Sun Field Station, Stanford Univ (Merit award, Am Inst of Archit San Diego, 2003, Honor award, Am Inst of Archit Santa Clara, 2004, COTE Top Ten Green Buildings, Nat Am Inst of Archit, 2005), Opportunity Ctr for the Midpeninsula (Advocacy Planning award, Northern Sect Am Planning Asn, 2003), Shaw Lopez Park, Casa Feliz, and several others. *Exhib:* solo exhibitions, Retrospective, Southern Calif Inst of Archit, Santa Monica, 82, Exhibit of Recent Work, UCLA, 84, Recent Work, Portland State Univ, 91, exhibitions include Visual Communication Towards Architecture, Installation Gallery, San Diego, 82, Don Clos Pegase Competition, San Francisco Mus Contemp Art, 85, The Emerging Generation in the USA, Global Architecture Gallery, Tokyo, Japan, 87, Five Choose Five, Nat Am Inst of Archit Conf, St Louis, 89, Fabrications, San Francisco Mus Modern Art, 98, Books, Bytes and Mortar, Mus Contemp Art, San Diego, 2001, Modern Trains and Splendid Stations, Art Inst Chicago, 2002, and several others. *Pos:* Archit Peace Corps, Chile; prin, Quigley Archits, San Diego, Palo Alto, 74-. *Teaching:* Adj prof, archit Univ Calif, San Diego; vis design prof, Harvard Univ Grad School Design, 91, Univ Tex, Austin, 94, Univ Calif, Berkeley, 97 & 98; spkr. in field; invited juror and advisor. *Awards:* Named Headliner of Yr in Archit, San Diego Press Club, 95; named one of 100 Foremost Architects of the World, AD 100, Archit Digest, 91, 88 San Diegans to Watch in '88', San Diego Mag, 88, The San Diego 50 People to Watch in 1997; recipient Presidential Commendation for Exemplary Community. Serv, 88, Firm award, Am Inst of Archit Calif Coun, 95, The Irving Gill award, Am Inst of Archit San Diego, 97, Maybeck award, Am Inst of Archit Calif Coun, 2005, several mag. and community program awards, several awards for design excellence from the Nat Am Inst of Archit, Am Inst of Archit Santa Clara, Am Inst of Archit San Diego, and Am Inst of Archit Calif Coun; fellow Inst for Urban Design, 96. *Mem:* Fel, Am Inst of Archit; Nat Acad of Design. *Publ:* co-auth: Bldgs & Projects, 1996. *Mailing Add:* 416 13th St San Diego CA 92101

QUILLER, STEPHEN FREDERICK
PAINTER, PRINTMAKER
b Osmond, Nebr, Aug 15, 1946. *Study:* Colo State Univ, BA, 68. *Work:* City Medford Art Collection, Ore; Colo Coun Arts; Colo Springs Fine Arts Ctr; Luther Bean Mus & Adams State Coll, Alamosa, Colo; Berman Mus Art, Collegeville, Pa; Charles & Nancy Wallisk Collection. *Comn:* Gov's Export Award (painting), Colo Coun Arts, Denver, 79; City of Creede (mural), Colo Coun Arts. *Exhib:* Solo exhibs, Foothills Art Ctr, Golden, Colo, 73; Am Watercolor Soc, 73, 76, 94-99, 2001-05 & Nat Soc Painters Casein & Acrylic, 74 & 76-78, Nat Acad Design, New York; Rocky Mountain Nat, Foothills Art Ctr, Golden, Colo, 74-75, 77-79 & 81; Watercolor USA, Springfield Art Mus, Mo, 77; Am & Ital Printmakers, Sangre de Cristo Art Ctr, Pueblo, Colo, 80; and others. *Teaching:* Instr art, SW Watercolor Soc, Dallas, spring 76; instr art, NMex Watercolor Soc, Albuquerque, spring 79; guest artist-in-residence intaglio, Adams State Coll, Alamosa, Colo, fall 81 & instr painting & printmaking, 81-89. *Awards:* Gov's Award, Colo Coun Arts, 79; Greathouse Award & Medal, Am Watercolor Soc, 97; Louis Kaep Award, Am Watercolor Soc, 99; Philadelphia Watercolor Soc Award, Nat Watercolor Soc, 2004; Winsor & Newton Award, Am Watercolor Soc, 2005; Hal P. Moore Award, Am Watercolor Soc, 2006; Dolphin Fel Am Watercolor Soc. *Bibliog:* Web Allison (auth), Steve Quiller: Creede's artist-in-residence, Colo Country Life, San Luis Valley, 11/72; GA Minshew (auth), Spotlight on the artist, Scene, SW Watercolor Soc, 4/75; Susan Meyer (auth), 40 Watercolorists And How They Work, Watson-Guptill, 78. *Mem:* Nat Soc Painters Casein & Acrylic; Watercolor West; Artists Equity Asn; Watercolor Asn Ala; Am Watercolor Soc; Nat Watercolor Soc. *Media:* Watercolor, Acrylic; Casein, Intaglio. *Publ:* Auth, Water Media: Watercolor & Gouache (video), Water Media: Acrylic & Casein (video), Color Concepts (video) & Color for the Painter (video), Crystal Productions; Water Media Techniques, Watson-Guptill, 83, Water Media: Processes and Possibilities, 86, Color Choices, 89, Acrylic Painting Techniques, 94, Painter's Guide to Color, 2000; Mastering Color and The Plein Air Experience (video), 04; Watercolor Workshop (video), 2004. *Dealer:* Mission Gallery, Taos, NMex; Quiller Gallery, Creede, Colo. *Mailing Add:* PO Box 160 Creede CO 81130

QUINLAN, EILEEN
PRINTMAKER
b Boston, 1972. *Study:* Sch Mus Fine Arts, BFA, 1996; Columbia Univ, MFA, 2005. *Exhib:* Solo exhibs include Sutton Lane, London, 2006, Miguel Abreu, New York, 2007, Art Basel, Switzerland, 2008, Galerie Daniel Buchholz, Cologne, Germany, 2008; two-person exhibs (with Cheyney Thompson) Life is Elsewhere, Can Gallery, New York, 2001, S&M, Sutton Lane, Paris, 2005, (with Elena Pankova) Dialog #1: Puzzled, White Columns, New York, 2006; group exhibs include Bebe le Strange, D'Amelio Terras, New York, 2005; How to Build a Universe That Doesn't Fall Apart Two Days Later, Wattis Inst, San Francisco, 2006; Silicone Valley, PS1 Contemp Art Ctr, Long Island City, NY, 2007; Art Politiquement Engage, Sculpture Ctr, New York, 2007; Undone, Whitney Mus at Altria, New York, 2007; Update, White Columns, New York, 2008. *Dealer:* Sutton Lane 1 Sutton Lane London EC1M 5PU England UK; Galerie Edward Mitterand 52 rue des Bains 1205 Geneva Switzerland. *Mailing Add:* c/o Miguel Abreu Gallery 36 Orchard St New York NY 10002

QUINN, BRIAN GRANT
SCULPTOR, PAINTER
b Wahoo, Nebr, Oct 21, 1950. *Study:* Nebr Wesleyan Univ, BAE; Ariz State Univ, MFA; Univ Puget Sound. *Work:* Nebraska Wesleyan Univ; Weber State Col, Ogden, Utah; Ariz State Univ, Tempe; Plains Art Mus, Moorhead, Minn; Tucson Art Mus, Ariz; Yuma Art Ctr, Ariz; Shemer Art Ctr, Phoenix, Ariz; Phoenix Children's Hosp; Catholic Diocese Wichita; Scottsdale Public Schools, Scottsdale, Ariz; Newman Univ, Wichita; Quinn Mem Collection, Scottsdale Community Coll, Ariz; Bone Creek Mus Agrarian Art; Northern Ariz Univ, Flagstaff; and others. *Comn:* sculpture, Median Inst, Pittsburgh, Pa, 83; sculpture, Northern Ariz Univ, 83; sculpture, Nebr Wesleyan Univ, 87; sculpture, Lincoln Nebr Pub Sch, 87; sculpture, Glendale Community Col, 90; relief sculpture/painting, Phoenix Children's Hosp, Ariz. *Exhib:* Ariz Biennial, Tucson Art Mus, 80-84; 1st & 2nd Northern Ariz Univ Sculpture Invitational, 80 & 81; 13th-18th Midwestern Invitationals, O'Rourke Gallery, Moorhead, Minn, 81-86;

17th Ann Nat Drawing & Small Sculpture Show, Del Mar Col, Tex, 83; Redefining the Lathe-Turned Object, Ariz State Univ, 93; solo exhib, Shemer Art Ctr, Phoenix, Ariz, 2001; and others. *Pos:* Preparator, Phoenix Art Mus, 75; artist-in-residence, Nat Endowment Art, 75-76; dir bd, Japanese Sword Soc US, 94-2004; Pres, Japanese Sword Soc US, 2004-. *Teaching:* Vis instr sculpture, Glendale Community Col, 76-90; lectr sculpture, Ariz State Univ, Tempe, 80 & 81; prof sculpture & jewelry, Glendale Community Col, 90-94, cur art collection, 90-94. *Awards:* Fred Wells Purchase Award, Small Sculpture and Drawing Exhib, Nebr Wesleyan Univ, 76; Jurors Award, First & Third Ariz Wood-in-Art Exhib, 77-79, Ariz State Univ; Jurors Award, Galeria Mesa, 85; Fulbright Mem Fund Scholar, Japan, 2001; The Sch the Art Inst Chicago's Teacher Inst in Contemp Art Scholar, 2005. *Bibliog:* Barbara Cortright (auth), Brian Quinn at Northern Arizona Univ and the University of New Mexico, Artspace, spring 84; Jessica Benton Evans (auth), Brian Quinn an interview, The Ashes, 4/94; Jennifer Franklin (auth), The shape of things/gardens of stone, life, Scottsdale Progress, 4/7/94. *Mem:* Southern Asn of Sculptors; Japanese Sword Soc of the US; Cent Ariz Mus Asn; Orders & Medals Soc Am; Am Soc Military Insignia Collectors; and others. *Media:* Mixed Media, Stone, Steel, Bronze, Wood. *Interests:* Art; Militaria & Antique Arms Collector. *Dealer:* Faust Gallery 7103 E Main St Scottsdale AZ 85251; Ann Jacob Gallery Phipps Plaza 3500 Peachtree Rd NE Atlanta GA 30326

QUINN, THOMAS PATRICK, JR
PAINTER
b Honolulu, Hawaii, June 5, 1938. *Study:* Coll of Marin, Kentfield, Calif, 56-58, Art Ctr Coll Design, Pasadena, Calif, BA, 58-63. *Work:* Leigh Yawkey Woodson Art Mus, Wasau, Wis; Nat Wildlife Art Mus (permanent collection), Jackson, Wyo. *Comn:* Painting, Monterey Bay Aquarium, Calif, 84. *Exhib:* Nat Exhib Alaskan Wildlife, Alaskan Mus Art, Anchorage, 82; The Nature of the Best, Southern Alleghenies Mus Art, Loretto, Pa, 86; solo exhib, Frederic Remington Art Mus, Ogdensburg, NY, 88; NY Mus Natural Hist; Alexander Koenig Mus, Bonn, Ger; Nat Acad Western Art, Nat Cowboy Hall Fame, Oklahoma City, 93; Nat Wildlife Art Mus, Jackson, Wyo; Gilcrease Mus, Tulsa, Okla, 92; 25 Artists Nature Exhib, Zeist, The Neth, 92. *Awards:* Gold Medal, Nat Acad Western Art, Okla City, 93; Master Wildlife Artist Award, Leigh Yawkey Woodson Art Mus, Wausau, Wis, 98. *Bibliog:* Thomas Fox (auth), The elusive quality of a wild thing, Southwest Art, 83; Tom Davis (auth), Influencing the eye, Wildlife Art News, 87; M Stephen Doherty (auth), Thomas Quinn, Am Artist, 88. *Mem:* Trumpeter Swan Soc. *Media:* Mixed Media. *Publ:* Auth, First Person, Sports Illus, 83; The Working Retrievers, E P Dutton, 83; contribr, Wildlife Painting Techniques of Modern Masters, Watson Guptill, 85; Wildfowl Art, Ward Found, 86; Auth, R Riviere, Thomas Quinn on Art: Illustration and Inspiration, Art Today, 87; Wind, Wad & Waterverf (Dutch), 91. *Dealer:* Gerald Peters Gallery 1011 Paseo de Peralta Santa Fe NM 87501. *Mailing Add:* PO Box 225 Point Reyes Station CA 94956-0225

QUINN, WILLIAM
PAINTER, SCULPTOR
b St Louis, Mo, Sept 5, 1929. *Study:* Washington Univ, BFA, study with Paul Burlin & Carl Holty; Univ Ill, MFA, 57. *Work:* Brooks Mem Art Gallery, Memphis, Tenn; Nelson-Atkins Gallery, Kansas City, Mo; St Louis Art Mus; Weatherspoon Art Gallery, Univ NC; High Mus, Atlanta, Ga; Tampa Mus, Fla; Mus of the Arts, Ft Lauderdale, Fla; Mulvane Art Ctr, Washburn Univ, Topeka, Kans; Drury Col, Springfield, Mo; Univ Mo, Columbia; Webster Univ, St Louis,. *Comn:* Oil painting, Sea Watch (48x60), Four Seasons Hotel, Fayence, France, 2006. *Exhib:* Thirty-six solo exhibs, US, Europe & Mex. *Pos:* Formerly Prof painting & drawing, Washington Univ,. *Awards:* Miliken Travel Scholar, Washington Univ, 58; Fulbright Alternative, 1962; Cité Des Arts Fel, Paris, France, 82; Painting Fel, Nat Endowment Art, 86; and over 36 other awards in regional museums & galleries. *Bibliog:* Numerous newspaper & magazine articles & photos. *Media:* Oil, Gouache, Acrylic. *Dealer:* Duane Reed Gallery 4729 McPherson St Louis MO 63108. *Mailing Add:* 5 Schooner Ln Apt 11 Milford CT 06460

QUIÑONES KEBER, ELOISE
ART HISTORIAN, EDUCATOR
b Los Angeles, Calif. *Study:* Columbia Univ, PhD, 84. *Teaching:* Prof art hist, Baruch Col, City Univ New York, 86-; prof art hist, Graduate Ctr, City Univ, New York, 1991. *Awards:* Getty Publ Award, 92-93; Fel, Am Coun Learned Soc, 87-88 & 93-94, Nat Endowment Humanities, 93-94; John Simon Guggenheim Found Fel, 98-99. *Mem:* Coll Art Asn; Asn Latin Am Art; Am Soc Ethnohistory; Seminar Arts Africa, Oceania & Americas, Columbia Univ. *Res:* Aztec art and culture; early colonial Mexican art; manuscripts and early ethnohistorical texts. *Publ:* Coauth, Art of Aztec Mexico: Treasures of Tenochtitlan, Nat Gallery Art, 83; co-ed, The Work of Bernardino de Sahagun, Univ Tex Press, 88; Mixteca-Puebla: Discoveries and research in Mesoamerican art and archaeology, 94 & ed, Chipping Away on Earth: Studies in Prehispanic and colonial Mexico, 94, Labyrinthos Press; auth, Codex Telleriano-Remensis: Ritual Divination and History in a Pictorial Aztec Manuscript, Univ Tex Press, 95; ed, Precious Greenstone, Precious Quetzal Feather: Mesoamerican Essays in Honor of Doris Heyden, Laybrinthos Press, 2000; ed, Representing Aztec Ritual: Performance, Image & Text in the Work of Sahagún, Univ Colo Press, 2002. *Mailing Add:* Dept Fine & Performing Arts Baruch College 1 Bernard Baruch Way New York NY 10010

QUIRARTE, JACINTO
HISTORIAN, ADMINISTRATOR
b Jerome, Ariz, Aug 17, 1931. *Study:* San Francisco State Col, BA, 54, MA, 58; Nat Univ Mex, PhD, 64. *Pos:* Dir cult affairs, Ctr Venezolano Am, Caracas, 64-66; bd mem & vpres, San Antonio Arts Coun, 73-77; mem visual arts & humanities panel, Tex Comn on the Arts & Humanities, 76-80. *Teaching:* Art instr, Colegio Americano, Mexico City, 59-61; asst to Alberto Ruz Lhuillier, Seminario de Cultura Maya, Nat Univ Mex, 61-62; dir cult affairs, Centro Venezuelan Americano, Caracas, 64-66; vis prof hist contemp art Latin Am & pre-Columbian art, Yale Univ, New Haven, Conn, 67; prof hist pre-Columbian, Colonial & contemp art of Mex & Guatemala, Univ Tex, Austin, 67-72; vis prof hist pre-Colombia art of Mesoamerica & Colonial art of Latin Am, Univ NMex, 71; dean, Col Fine & Applied Arts, Univ Tex, San Antonio, 72-78; dir & prof art hist, Res Ctr Visual Arts, 77-98. *Mem:* Mid-Am Coll Art Asn; Soc for Am Archaeol; Int Cong of Americans; Int Cong of the Hist of Art; Int Cong of Ethnology & Anthrop. *Publ:* Auth, El estilo artistico de Izapa, Cuadernos de Historia del Arte, No 3, Instituto de Investigaciones Esteticas, Univ Nac Autonoma de Mexico, 73; auth, Izapan style art--a study of its form and meaning, Studies in Pre-Columbian Art & Archaeology, No 10, Dumbarton Oaks, Washington, DC, 73; auth, Mexican American Artists, 73 & Maya Vase, (in prep), Univ Tex Press, Austin, Art and Architecture of the Texas Missions, Univ Tex Press, Austin, 2002

QUIRK, JAMES
DIRECTOR
Study: Carroll Coll, BA, 1972. *Pos:* Pres & CEO, Milwaukee Envelope, Oconomowoc, Wis; owner, Quirk Reality, Watertown; exec dir, Charles Allis & Villa Terrace Art Mus, Milwaukee, 2007-. *Mem:* bd mem, Int Folk Art Mus, formerly; treas, Friends of Folk Art, Santa Fe, formerly; bd dirs, Earlier European Art Acquisitions, Milwaukee Art Mus, 2003-, Santa Fe Film Festival, 2006-. *Mailing Add:* Charles Allis Art Museum 1801 N Prospect Ave Milwaukee WI 53202

QUIRK, THOMAS CHARLES, JR
PAINTER, SCULPTOR
b Pittsburgh, Pa, Dec 31, 1922. *Study:* Edinboro Univ PA, BS, 48; Univ Pittsburgh, Med, 64; studied ceramics at Alfred Univ. *Work:* Butler Inst Am Art, Youngstown, Ohio; Chatham College, Pittsburgh, Pa; Pittsburgh Public Schools, Pittsburgh, Pa; Millersville Univ, PA; Rutgers Univ, NJ. *Comn:* Assumption of the Blessed Mother (sculpture), St Mary's Church, Kutztown, Pa; Holy Spirit Lutheran Church, Emmaus, Pa; Stations of the Cross, St Mary's Church, Kutztown, Pa. *Exhib:* Pa Acad Fine Arts Ann, Philadelphia, 69; Drawing & Small Sculpture Ann, Ball State Univ, 71; Nat Acad Design Ann, New York, 74; Philadelphia Watercolor Club Ann, 74, 76 & 79; Ann Nat Soc Painters Casein & Acrylic, New York, 76 & 79; Mary in Art, Milwaukee, Wis, Dayton, Ohio & Washington, DC, 98-99; and others. *Pos:* Artist-in-residence, Everhart Mus, Scranton, Pa, 72-. *Teaching:* Emer prof art, Kutztown Univ, Pa, 66-89. *Awards:* Dawson Mem Prize, Philadelphia Watercolor Club, 74; Crest Award, Philadelphia Watercolor Club, 97; Religious Art Award in Visual Arts-Sculpture, AIA, St Mary's Church, Kutztown, Pa, 99; Stations of the Cross. *Bibliog:* James J Kelly (auth), Sculpture as History, Ch. 2, The Sculptural Idea, Waveland Press, Inc, Long Grove, Ill, 2004. *Mem:* Nat Sculpture Soc; Philadelphia Watercolor Club. *Media:* Multimedia, Stone, Wood, Clay. *Publ:* Auth, Reptiles and Amphibians & Fishes of the Western Atlantic, Dover Publs; illusr, Ghost Garden, Hela Feil (auth), Atheneum Press. *Mailing Add:* 310 E Main St Kutztown PA 19530

QUIROZ, ALFRED JAMES
PAINTER, EDUCATOR
b Tucson, Ariz, May 9, 1944. *Study:* San Francisco Art Inst, BFA, 71; RI Sch Design, MAT, 74; Univ Ariz, MFA, 84. *Work:* Mus Fine Arts NMex, Santa Fe; Tucson Mus Arts; Scottsdale Mus Contemp Art; NY Pub Libr Print Collection, Manhattan. *Comn:* Housing projs, City of Tucson, Ariz, 86; Novus Ordo (mural), San Francisco Ctr Arts, 93. *Exhib:* Evidence, San Antonio Mus Art, 86; Counter Colonialism, Heard Mus, Phoenix, 92; Year of the White Bear, Mex Fine Arts Mus, Chicago, 92 & Walker Art Ctr, Minneapolis, 92; Chicago Codices, Mex Mus, San Francisco, 92; La Frontera, Mus Contemp Art, San Diego, 93; In Out of the Cold, Ctr Arts, Yerba Buena Gardens, San Francisco, 93; Works: On Paper, Galeria Mesta Bratislavy, Slovkia, 94. *Pos:* Resident artist (mural), Ariz Comn Arts, Phoenix, 85-89. *Teaching:* Prof painting & drawing, Univ Ariz, Tucson, 89-. *Awards:* Best of Show, Ariz Biennial, Tucson Mus Art, 86; Ariz Arts Award Fel, Tucson Comn Found, 88; Visual Arts Fel, Ariz Comn Arts, 89-95. *Mem:* Coll Art Asn; Nat Artists Arts Orgn; Asn Latin Am Art. *Media:* Oil, Wood panel. *Dealer:* Davis-Dominquez Gallery Tucson AZ. *Mailing Add:* 2726 E Winchester Vista Tucson AZ 85713

QUISGARD, LIZ WHITNEY
PAINTER, SCULPTOR
b Philadelphia, Pa, Oct 23, 1929. *Study:* Md Inst Coll Art, dipl, 49, BFA(summa cum laude), 66; studied with Morris Louis, 57-60; Rinehart Sch Sculpture, MFA, 66. *Work:* Univ Baltimore; Johns Hopkins Univ; Libyan Mission UN, Englewood, NJ, Can Imperial Bank Com, NY, Great Northern Nekoosa Corp, Norwalk, Conn, Quality Inns, Newark, NJ, Datalogy Corp, Valhalla, NY, Rosenberg Diamond Corp, NY, Ctr Club, Baltimore, Md; Fordham Univ, NY; Miss Mus, Jackson; Am Airlines, Dallas, Tex; Coca Colo Co of Brazil, Sao Paulo, Brazil; plus others. *Comn:* Mural painting, Urban Wall, Atlanta, Ga, 90; floor painting, Vets Stadium, Philadelphia, 92; mural painting, Royal Caribbean Cruise Line, Oslo, Norway, 96; mural painting, Sinai Hosp, Baltimore, 96; mural painting, Meridian Co, Indianapolis, 96. *Exhib:* Corcoran Biennial Am Painting, 63; Univ Colo Show, 63; Am Painting & Sculpture Ann, Pa Acad Fine Arts, 64; Art Inst Chicago Ann, 65; solo exhibs, Henri Gallery, Washington, DC, 87, Savannah Coll Art & Design, Savannah, Ga, 87, Three Financial Plaza, Chicago, 88, Franz Bader Gallery, Washington, DC, 89, Fairleigh Dickinson Univ, Hackensack, NJ, 90, Herr-Chambliss Gallery, Hot Springs, Ark, 90 Retrospective Gallery, La Jolla, Calif, 90; Broadway Windows, NY, 92; Asheville Mus, NC, 95; Richmond Mus, Ind, 96; Austin Mus, Tex, 97. *Pos:* Theatre designer, Goucher Col, Theatre Hopkins & Ctr Stage, Baltimore, 66-; art critic, Baltimore Sun, 69 & 70; area reviewer, Craft Horizons Mag, 69-75. *Teaching:* Instr painting & design, Baltimore Hebrew Congregation, 62-; instr painting & color theory, Md Inst, Baltimore, 65-80; lectr design, Goucher Col, 66-69; lectr art hist, Univ Md, Catonsville, 69-70; instr painting, Baltimore Jewish Community Ctr, 62-80. *Awards:* Rinehart Fel, Md Inst, 64-66; Best in Show, Loyola Col, 66; Florsheim Art Fund Grant, 91; and others. *Bibliog:* B Rose (auth), article, Art Int, 11/62; articles, Arts Mag, 11/62 & Art News, 11/62, Baltimore Sun, 4/78 & 10/88, Artspeak, 11/84 & 9/85, Manhattan Arts, 3/84,

New Art Examiner, 3/89, NY Times, 2/90 & 7/92. *Media:* Oil, Acrylic, Fiber; All media. *Publ:* Auth, Baltimore's top twelve, Baltimore Mag, 5/69; auth & illusr, An artist's travel log, Baltimore News Am, 71; illusr, Shore Writers' Sampler, Friendly Harbor Press, 87. *Mailing Add:* 113 Elizabeth St New York NY 10013

QUON, MICHAEL GEORGE
DESIGNER, PAINTER
b Los Angeles, Calif. *Study:* Univ Calif Los Angeles, BFA, 70; Art Ctr Coll Design, 71; studied with, Ed Ruscha, Richard Diebenkorn, Jan Stussy, Brice Marden, 65-70. *Work:* Libr Congress, Wash DC; NY Historical Soc; US Air Force Art Coll, Wash DC; Wakita Design Mus, Tokyo, Japan; NY Times Permanent Coll. *Comn:* int road rally race, Jacob Javits Convention Ctr, NY, 84; travel murals for Am Express, Am Express, NY, 86; city wide outdoor spring banners, Tokyo Dept Stores, Tokyo, Japan, 90; Sydney Olympic M Ali Poster, NBC Olympics, Sydney, Australia, 2000. *Exhib:* Greater NY, MoMA PS1/Group Show, NY, 83; Artworks of Mike Quon, Artlink Gallery, Fort Wayne, 88; From, Philbrook Mus Art, Tulsa, Okla, 2002; 9/11 Exhib, NY Historical Soc Mus, NY, 2003; Drawings, Paintings, and Collages, Soc Illustrators, NY, 2005; From NY to Red Bank, Monmouth Beach Cultural Ctr, Monmouth Beach, NJ, 2009; Art & Democracy Show, Gallery H, NY, 2009; Chairish Exhib, Monmouth Mus, Lincroft, NJ, 2011; Rema Hort Mann Found, 2011, 2012; Quon Artist Exhib, Starbucks, Red Bank, NJ, 2011; Art Alliance, Red Bank, NJ, 2011; Oceanic Public Libr, Mike Quon Drawings and Paintings, Lincroft, NJ, 2011; Middle Cultural Ctr, Middletown, NJ, 2012; Shine a Light Show, McLoone's Pier House Art Gallery, Long Branch, NJ, 2012; Red Bank & More, No Joes Cafe and Gallery, Red Bank, NJ, 2012; Guild of Creative Arts, Shrewsbury, NJ, 2013; Audubon Artists Exhib, 2013. *Teaching:* adj prof, art & illusr, Parsons Sch Design, 77-78, Sch Visual Arts, 91-92, Brookdale Comm Coll, 2004-2012. *Awards:* Temple Coun award, Dickson Art Gallery Presentation, UCLA, 70; Certificate of Merit, Print Ann Show, Print Mag, 82; Hon Mention, Advertising and Graphics, Art Dirs Club of NY, 84; Silver Medal award, Ann Show, Art Dirs Club of Phila, 85; Desi awards, Ann Awards Show, Graphic Design: USA, 95-2000; Jean Townsend award Winner, Art Alliance, Red Bank, NJ, 2011; Best in Show award, Middle Cultural Ctr, Middletown, NJ, 2012; Mixed Media/Collage First Prize award, Audubon Artist Exhib, 2013; Red Bank Comes Alive, Oyster Point Hotel, Red Bank, NJ, 2014; Belmar Arts Council, Belmar, NJ, 2014; AJ Dillon Art Gallery, Atlantic Highlands, NJ, 2014. *Bibliog:* Herb Lubalin (auth), Chinese Zodiac/U & l c, Int Typeface Corp, 81; Ilise Benum (auth), Self Promotion Online, North Light Books, 2001; Michael Fleishman (auth), Exploring Illustration, Delmar, 2003; Robin Landa (auth), Graphic Design Solutions, Wadsworth Cengage Learning, 2005; Norio Mochizuki (auth), NoAH Package Design, Int Creators Org, 2009. *Mem:* Art Alliance of Monmouth Co; Guild of Creative Arts; Monmouth Co Arts Coun. *Media:* Acrylic, Pen & Ink, Collage Assembly. *Res:* bold, spontaneous, and colorful Quon style, Chinese heritage, Chinese brush strokes. *Specialty:* personal artwork from travels, pop art, and everyday objects. *Interests:* photography, illustration, pop art, collage, abstract expressionism, acrylic paintings. *Collection:* focus on archit subject matter, landmarks, cities, everyday objects. *Publ:* auth, Non-Traditional Design, PBC Int, 92; contbr, The Creative Stroke, Rockport Pub, 92; editor, Corporate Graphics, PBC Int, 95; contbr, 1,000 Artist Jour Pages, Quarry Pub, 2008; contbr, Drawing Inspiration, Delmar, Cengage, 2010. *Mailing Add:* 543 River Rd Fair Haven NJ 07704

R

RAAB, GAIL B
COLLAGE ARTIST, PAINTER
b New York, NY, Jan 15, 1934. *Study:* Univ Colo with Louis Shanker, 53; Univ Mex, 54; Tyler Sch Fine Arts, BFA with honors, 55; Queens Col. *Work:* Philadelphia Mus; Seventeen Mag, NY; Scherling-Plough Corp, NJ; CBS Recordings, NY. *Comn:* Paintings, Columbia Broadcasting, NY, 86; wall assemblage, Schering-Plough Corp, NJ, 88; wall collages, Haines, Lundberg Waehler, NY, 89; Miniature Mus, Amsterdam, 96. *Exhib:* Solo-exhibs, Viridian Gallery, NY, 80, 82, Whitney-Clark Gallery, Lenox, Mass, 88 & Bachelier, Cardonsky, Kent, Conn, 90 & 96, Pepper Gallery, Boston, Mass, 99, OK Harris Gallery, New York City, 2000; Paper Works, Berkshire, Pittsfield, Mass, 88 & 89 & Nassau Co, NY, 88 & 89; Nat Asn Women Artists Juried Show, Nat Acad Design, NY, 88 & 89; Marabella Gallery, Bks & Co, NY, 90; OK Harris, NY, 1995, 1997, I Love NY Benefit, 2001, Collage & Assemblage, 2002; OK Harris Gallery, NY, 97, 2004; UTE Stebich Gallery, Lennox, Mass, 98; Ensembles, Pepper Gallery, Boston, 2003; Hidell Brooks Gallery, Charlotte, NC, 2004; SKH Gallery, Great Barrington, Mass, 2005. *Pos:* Art Reach dir, Whitney Mus, NY, 89-90. *Awards:* Medal of Honor, 80 & C Winston Mem Prize, 88, Nat Asn Women Artists; Martha Reed Mem Award. *Bibliog:* Jeanne Paris (auth), The artists inspiration, Newsday, 6/2/78; Jerry Tallmer (rev), New York Post, 6/3/78; Margaret Pomfret (rev), Arts Mag, 1/80. *Mem:* Nat Asn Women Artists (exec bd); Long Island Craftsman Guild. *Media:* Mixed Media, Acrylic, Collage, Paper. *Interests:* Collecting found objects to incorporate in collages of hist meaning. *Dealer:* OK Harris Gallery, 383 W Broadway, New York, 10012; Pepper Gallery,38 Newbury St, Boston, 02116. *Mailing Add:* 300 E 74th St No 25G New York NY 10021

RAAD, WALID
MEDIA ARTIST
b Chbanieh, Lebanon, 1967. *Study:* Boston Univ; Rochester Inst Technol, BFA; Univ Rochester, MA; PhD (visual and cult studies). *Work:* Walker Art Ctr, Minn; Solomon R Guggenheim Mus, New York; Hirschhorn Mus Sculpture Garden, DC; Mus Mod Art, New York; Hamberger Bahnhof, Berlin; Tate Mod, London; MUMOK, Vienna, Austria; Ctr Georges Pompidou, Paris. *Exhib:* Solo exhibs include The Truth Will Be Known, World Wide Video Festival, Amsterdam, 2003, La Galerie, Noisy-le-Sec, France, 2003, Krannert Art Mus, Champaign, Ill, 2004, Prefix Inst, Toronto, Can, 2004, Anthony Reynolds Gallery, London, 2003, I was Overcome with a Momentary Panic, York Univ, Toronto, 2004, Agnes Etherington Art Ctr, Queen's Univ, Kingston, Can, 2005, Art Basel 36, 2005, Sfeir-Semler, Hamburg, Ger, 2004, FACT, Liverpool, 2005, The Kitchen, NY City, 2006, Henry Art Gallery, Seattle, 2006, Paula Cooper Gallery, NY City, 2007, Sfeir-Semler, Beirut, Lebanon, 2008, Redcat, Los Angeles, Calif, 2009, Reina Sofia Mus, Madrid, Spain, 2009, Sweet Talk, Commissions, Camera Austria, Graz, Austria, 2010; group exhibs include Whitney Biennale, 2000; Kunst-Werke, Berlin, 2000; Kunsten Festival des Arts, Brussels, 2001; Atlanta Ctr for Arts, 2002; Documenta 11, Kassel, Ger, 2002; Barbican Art Galleries, London, 2003; Venice Biennale, 2003; Mus Contemp Art, Sydney, 2004; Taipei Biennial, 2004; LIFT, London, 2004; Int Photo Triennale, Esslingen, Ger, 2004; Anthony Reynolds Gallery, London, 2005; Sfeir-Semier Gallery, Hamburg, Ger, 2005, Beirut, 2005; Mus Mod Art, Ny City, 2005, 2006; Apex Art, NY City, 2006; Taipei Fine Arts Mus, Taiwan, 2006; Miami Art Central, 2006; in Situ, Paris, 2006; Photographers Gallery, London, 2007; Int Ctr of Photography, New York, 2008; Color Chart: Reinventing Color, Mus Mod Art, New York, 2008; Quiet Politics, Zwirner & Wirth, New York, 2008; Reality Check, Statens Mus Kunst, Copenhagen, Denmark, 2008; Pratt Manhattan Gallery, New York, 2008; Commentary, Paula Cooper Gallery, New York, 2009; Contemplating the Void, Interventions in the Guggenheim Mus, Solomon R Guggenheim Mus, New York, 2010; Vernacular of Violence, Invisible Experts, New York. *Pos:* Founder, Atlas Group, 1999-. *Teaching:* instr, dept art and hist, Univ Rochester, 1991-95, dept film studies, 1994-95; asst prof, sch humanities, Hampshire Coll, Amherst, Mass, 1995-98, dept media studies, Queens Coll, Univ NY, 1998-2002, sch art, Cooper Union, NY City, 2002-07. *Awards:* Best Conceptual Innovation Award, New Eng Film and Video Festival, Boston, 1997; Award of Accomplishment, Missouri Film Festival, 1998; Best Short Film and Best Scenario For a Short Film, Beirut Film Festival, 1999; Dirs Citation, Black Maria Film Festival, Jersey City, NJ, 1999; Grand Prize, Biennial of the Moving Image, Switzerland, 1999; Spec Jury Prize, Biennial for Arabs Cinemas, Inst de Monde Arabe, Paris, 2000; First Prize, Video Ex, Zurich, 2000, 2001; Rhineland Award, Oberhausen Film and Video Festival, Jersey City, 2001; Media Arts Award, ZKM, Karlsruhe, Ger, 2002; First Prize, Onion City Experimental Film and Video Festival, 2002; Rockefeller Fel, 2003; Hamburger Bahnhot, Berlin, Germany, 2006; Alpert Award Visual Arts, 2007. *Bibliog:* Okwui Enwezor, Archive Fever: Uses of the Document in Contemporary Art (exhib catalogue), Int Ctr of Photography, New York, Germany, 2008; Kassandra Nakas & Britta Schmitz, The Atlas Group (1984-2004): A Project by Walid Raad, 2007; Walid Raad, My Neck is Thinner Than a Hair: Engines, Cologn:Verlag der Buchhandlung Walther König, 2006; David Frankel (auth), Walid Raad, Art FOrum, Feb 2010. *Mem:* Arab Image Found. *Dealer:* Paula Cooper Gallery 543 W 21st St New York NY 10011. *Mailing Add:* c/o Paula Cooper Gallery 534 W 21st St New York NY 10011

RABB, MADELINE M
CONSULTANT
b Jan 27, 1945. *Study:* Univ Md, College Park, 61-63; Md Inst Coll Art, Baltimore, BFA (painting), 66; Ill Inst Technol, Inst Design, MS (visual design), 75. *Exhib:* In Our Own Image: Works by Woman, Capital East Graphics, Washington, DC, 80; The Chicago Exchange Group, Chicago State Univ Gallery, 81; The Young Collector's Sale, Renaissance Soc Invitational, Univ Chicago, 82; Jazzonia Gallery, Detroit, Mich, 83; Members Show, Arts Club Chicago, 84-85; Exhibs of Artists Mems, Arts Club, Chicago, 84-2001. *Collection Arranged:* Corp Collections, Ariel Capital Mgt, Brown Capital Mgt, John H Stroger Jr Hosp, Cook Co, Northwestern Mem Hosp, Chicago, Northern Trust S Financial Ctr; Museum Collections, The Minneapolis Inst Arts, Wadsworth Atheneum Mus Art, The Studio Mus in Harlem, Baltimore Mus Art, Univ Galleries at Fla Atlantic Univ, Camden Art Ctr, London & The Network Mus Art; Art Antiques & Archit Collections & Content, Chicago Int Antiques & Fine Art Fair, Merchandise Mart, 4/99; Chicago Art in Corp Collections, Art Inst Chicago, 10/2004; The Union League Club, Chicago, 10/20/2005; Valuation of African Am Art, The Art Market & Collecting African Am Art Conf, David Driskell Ctr, Univ Md, College Park, 10/28/2006; Women in the Arts: Building an Arts Community & Building an Art Collection, River East Art Ctr, Chicago, Schiff Hardin's Women's Networking Group, 11/1/2006. *Pos:* Asst dir art & production, Tuesday Publs, Chicago, 66-68; vpres-bus manager, Myra Everett Designs Inc, Chicago, 77-78; account exec, Corporate Concierge, Chicago, 78-79; owner, Madeline Murphy Rabb Studio, Chicago, 79-83; exec dir, Chicago Office Fine Arts, 83-90; pres, Murphy Rabb Inc, Chicago, 91-. *Awards:* Numerous Awards for work and service to publ. *Bibliog:* Big City Cultural Bosses (article), Ebony Mag, 88. *Mem:* Arts Club Chicago; Nat Conf Artists; Chicago Artists Coalition; Art Table Inc; Ill Arts Alliance; Md Inst Coll of Art (women's bd & alumni adv bd); Columbia Coll, Chicago (mem bd); Art Inst Chicago (women's bd & leadership adv comt). *Media:* Fine Arts. *Publ:* Auth, Removing Cultural Viaducts: Initiatives for Traditionally Underserved Audiences, Connections Quarterly, 86; Chicago: An Artistic Renaissance Under Way, Am Visions Mag, 87; An Artful Collection, Woman News, Baltimore Magazine, 12/15/99; The Art of the Deal, The Chicago Tribune, 2/15/2000; What the Pros Know, Chicago Tribune Magazine, 4/3/2005; Artful Investing, Satisfaction Magazine, 7-8/2006; and others. *Mailing Add:* c/o Murphy Rabb Inc 161 E Chicago Ave Apt 34A Chicago IL 60611

RABBIT, RUNNING See Red Star, Kevin (Running Rabbit)

RABINOVICH, RAQUEL
PAINTER, SCULPTOR
b Buenos Aires, Arg, Mar 30, 1929; Am citizen. *Study:* Univ Cordoba, Arg; Univ Edinburgh; Atelier Andre Lhote, Paris. *Work:* Ark Art Ctr, Little Rock; Miami Art Mus; Reading (Pa) Pub Mus; World Bank Fine Art Collection, Washington, DC; NJ State Mus, Trenton; Memory of Water Portable Works Collection, Phoenix, Ariz, 2007. *Comn:* Emergences (site specific sculpture installations on Hudson River shores), ongoing; sculpture mem, Threshold, Marbletown, NY. *Exhib:* Eric Stark Gallery, NY, 91-92; Presence/Absence, Trans Hudson Gallery, NJ, 95; Lehigh Univ Art Galleries, Pa, 96; Trans Hudson Gallery, NY, 2000; Collaborative Concepts, NY, 2003; Hudson River Mus, NY, 2003; Weatherspoon Art Mus, NC, 2004; Yellow Bird

Gallery, NY, 2005; Lesley Heller Gallery, NY, 2006; Kingston Biennial, NY, 2007; Alon found, Buenos Aires, Argentina, 2008; River Library (site specific installation), USA rep to the Xth Int Cuenca Biennial, Cuenca, Ecuador, 2009; Marc Strans, Y Gallery, NY, 2014; Creon, NY, 2014. *Teaching:* Lectr, Whitney Mus, 83-86 & Marymount Manhattan Col, 84-90, NY. *Awards:* Fel, Nat Endowment Arts, 91 & US/France Paris residency award, 92; NY State Coun Arts Grant, 95; Pollock-Krasner Found Grant, 2001 & 2006; Lee Krasner Lifetime Achievement Award, 2011. *Bibliog:* Michael Kimmelman (auth), Art Rev, NY Times, 90; Fatima Bercht (auth), catalog essay, 90; Patrick Smith (auth), article, catalog essay, 92; Nicole Krauss (auth), Art in Am, 1999; William Zimmer (auth), Art Review, NY, 2004; Linda Weintraub (auth), Environ Mentalities, 2007; Julia P Herzberg (auth) & Patricia C Phillips (auth), Anthology of the Riverbeds, 2008; Luisa Valenzuela (auth), Una Sucinta biblioteca de los ríos del mundo, Perfil, Buenos Aires, Argentina, 2009; David Levi Strauss (auth), From Head to Hand, 2010; Robert C Morgan (auth), Raquel Rabinovich: Fluid Equilibrium, Sculpture, Wash DC, 2010; Julia P. Herzberg (auth), Raquel Rabinovich: Stone Sculptures, ARTE Brasileiros, Brazil, 2011; Linda Weintraub (auth), Chronicles of Time, 2013. *Mem:* Am Abstract Artists. *Media:* Oil; Stone, Rivers & Mud. *Publ:* Auth, The Dark is the Source of Light, Contemporary Artists Collection, Sta Hill Arts; Antología del lecho de los ríos/Anthology of the Riverbeds, Fundacion Alon, Bueos Aires, Argentina. *Mailing Add:* 141 Lamoree Rhinebeck NY 12572

RABINOVICH, RHEA SANDERS See Sanders, Rhea

RABINOVITCH, WILLIAM AVRUM
PAINTER, FILMMAKER
b New London, Conn, Sept 16, 1936. *Study:* Worcester Polytech Inst, BSME, 58; Boston Mus Sch Fine Arts; San Francisco Art Inst, MFA, 73; Whitney Mus, independent study prog, 73. *Work:* Mus Mod Art, Wendy's, NY; Fairmont Hotel, San Francisco; Mercedes Benz Show Room, San Rafael, Calif. *Comn:* Mural, Fairmont Hotel, 77-2005; US Post Off, Canal St, NY, 87-2005; Pablo Picasso (video doc), comn by Marc Ham, Metrop Mus Art, 94. *Exhib:* Solo exhibs, Pac Grove Art Ctr, 91, Wendy's, NY, 95-2005, Soho Arts Festival, Artist's Studio Tour, 96-, Ross Power Gallery, Miami, Fla, 98-2001; Cineprobe Series, Mus Mod Art, NY, 2001; plus many others. *Pos:* Dir, Whitney Counterweight, 77, 79 & 81; dir & producer, Art Seen (cable show), NY, 93-99; bd dir, Artist Talk on Art Symp Series, NY, 93-2005; proj dir, DVD Arts Proj, 2001; producer cable TV, Manhattan Neighborhood Network, NY, 93-2003; dir, producer, creator, Pollock Squared, feature film, 99-2005. *Awards:* Nat Endowment Arts Grant, 77; Video Prod Grant, Time/Warner-Manhattan Neighborhood Network, 94 & 2000; Leonhardt Found, 99. *Bibliog:* New York Arts Mag, 2003; Fine Arts Guide to Marketing and Self-Promotion, 2003; Don Wigal (auth), Jackson Pollock: Veiling the Image, 2005. *Media:* Multi. *Res:* DVD 15 Year Video Archive of Visual Arts in NY. *Publ:* Cover artist, Jacob Boehme & Gregory of Nyssa: The Life of Moses, Paulist Press, 78; dir, Full Length Feature Movie on Jackson Pollack, 2001. *Dealer:* Ross Power Gallery 3701 NE 2nd Ave & 37th St Miami FL 33137. *Mailing Add:* PO Box 403 Canal St Station New York NY 10013

RABINOWITCH, ROYDEN LESLIE
SCULPTOR
b Toronto, Ont, Mar 6, 1943. *Study:* Self taught. *Work:* Guggenheim Mus, New York; Kunsthaus Zurich, Switz; Stedelijk Mus, Amsterdam, Neth; Watari Mus Contemp Art, Tokyo, Japan; Kunstmuseum, Düsseldorf, Ger. *Comn:* Rotation and Translation of the Top, comn by Sarabhai family, The Retreat Ahmedabad, India, 83; Eloges de Fontenelle, Toronto Conv Ctr, Can, 84; Tomb Dr Josef Hoet, Ghent, Belg, 87; Judgement on the Keplerian Revolution, Furkapasshohe, Swiss Alps, 87; Bell for Kepler, Waterloo, Can, 2008. *Exhib:* SMAK, Ghent, 99; Stedelijk Mus, Amsterdam, 2000; Galerie Foksal, Warsaw, 2001; Irish Mus Mod Art, Dublin, 2003; Musée des Beaux-Arts, La Chaux-de-Fonds, Switz, 2004; Marta Herford, Ger, 2009. *Pos:* Life mem, Clare Hall, Cambridge Univ, Eng, 86-. *Teaching:* Adj prof hist art, Leiden Univ, Neth, 94; Maxwell Cummings Distinguished lectr, McGill Univ, Montreal, 2002. *Awards:* Lynch Staunton Award of Distinction, Can Coun, 85; Officer of the Order of Can, 2002; Queen Elizabeth Golden Jubilee Medal, 2003. *Bibliog:* Adolf Krischanitz (auth), Royden Rabinowitch, Wiener Secession, Vienna, 91; R H Fuchs (auth), Royden Rabinowitch, Sculpture 1962/1992, Haags Gemeentemuseum, The Hague, 92; Robert Kwak (auth), Royden Rabinowitch's Judgment on the Copernican Revolution: The Virtual Documentary, DXNet, Toronto, 2002; Roland Nachtigaller (auth), Royden Rabinowitch, Marat Herford, 2009. *Media:* Mixed. *Publ:* Auth, Development of the Early Sculpture Leading to the Most Recent Sculpture, Orchard Press, 83; Mankind Breaking Through the Clouds of Heaven Recognizing New Spheres, Determining the Ethics of Stan Laurel & Oliver Hardy, Technical Univ, Berlin, Ger, 2006; Mod ontology, The Corollary of Mod Physic & the Content of my Work, Dir, Inst Quantum Computing, Univ Waterloo. *Dealer:* Timothy Northum-Jones. *Mailing Add:* Jan Verspeyenstraat 15 B-9000 Ghent Belgium

RABKIN, LEO
SCULPTOR, PAINTER
b Cincinnati, Ohio, July 21, 1919. *Study:* Univ Cincinnati; NY Univ. *Work:* Mus Mod Art, Whitney Mus Am Art, Guggenheim Mus, NY; Smithsonian Inst; Bass Mus, Fla; Brooklyn Mus, NY; NC Mus, Raleigh; Newburger Mus, Purchase, NY; Cincinnati Ar Mus, Ohio; Baruch Gallery, SUNY, NY; Tel-Aviv; Rutgers Univ; Newark Mus. *Exhib:* Seven Painting & Sculpture Biennials, Whitney Mus Am Art, 59-69 & Drawings & Watercolor, 74 & 75; A Plastic Presence, San Francisco Mus Art, Milwaukee Art Ctr & Jewish Mus, 70; Storm King Art Ctr, Mountainville, NY, 70; solo exhibs, La Jolla Mus Contemp Art, 81 & Marilyn Pearl Gallery, NY, 81, 83, 84, 86, 89 & 90, Drew Univ, NJ & Herbert Lust Gallery, NY, 96; Art Concrete, Nuremberg, WGer, 83; Persistence of Abstraction, Wichita, Kans, 92; Va Lust Gallery, NY, 96; Lust Gallery, NY, 99; Boxes Exhib, Roslyn Libr, NY, 2000; and others. *Awards:* Ford Found Award for Watercolor, 61; First Prize for Watercolor, Silvermine Guild Artists, 61; Richard Florsheim Art Fund, 98. *Bibliog:* Clarence Bunch (auth), Acrylic for Sculpture & Design, Van Nostrand Reinhold, NY, 72; Robert Bishop (auth), American Folk Sculpture, EP Dutton & Co Inc, NY, 79; Robert Bishop (auth), Treasure of American Folk Art, Harry N Abrams Inc, NY, 79. *Mem:* Am Abstr Artists (pres, 64-78); US Comn Int Asn Art (secy, 68-70); Fine Arts Fedn (bd dir), NY. *Media:* Shadow Box Constructions, Works on Paper, Digital Print, Shadows. *Specialty:* American Turn of the Century thru 1950. *Collection:* Dorothea & Leo Rabkin: outsiders art; 20th Century American Art (outsider), Shaker Artifacts & Furniture; Glyptic (Sumerian); Primitive American Folk Art, AAA Journals, 2000, 2003. *Publ:* Ed, American Abstract Artists 1936-1966; AAA Js, 2002-2005. *Dealer:* Conner-Rosenkranz 19 E 74th St New York NY 10021. *Mailing Add:* 218 W 20th St New York NY 10011

RABY , JULIAN
GALLERY DIRECTOR
b London, Eng, 1950. *Study:* Magdalen Coll Univ Oxford, BA, 71, PhD (Oriental studies), 81. *Collection Arranged:* Return of the Buddha: The Qingzhou Discoveries, 2004; Style and Status: Imperial Costumes from Ottoman Turkey, 2005; Hokusai, 2006; Encompassing the Globe: Portugal and the World in the 16th and 17th Centuries, 2007; Garden and Cosmos: The Royal Paintings of Jodhpur, 2008; Tsars and the East: Gifts from Turkey and Iran in the Moscow Krelin, 2009. *Pos:* Chmn curs Oriental Inst, Oxford Univ, 91-93 & 95-2000, chmn bd fac Oriental studies, 93-95; monogr ed, British Inst Archeol & Hist, Amman, Jordan, 91-93; founder, former co-owner Azimuth Eds publ; dir, Freer Gallery Art & Arthur M Sackler Gallery, Smithsonian Inst, Washington, 2002-. *Teaching:* Lectr Islamic Art & Archit, Oxford Univ, Eng, 79-2002. *Mem:* Fel, Soc of Antiquaries; Coun of Britis Inst of Archeol and Hist, Amman, Jordan. *Publ:* Series founder & ed, Oxford Studies in Islamic Art, Oxford Univ; auth, Venice, Durer, and the Oriental Mode, 82, IZNIK: The Pottery of Ottoman Turkey, 89, Turkish Bookbinding in the 15th Century, The found of a Court Style, 93, Qajar Portraits, 99. *Mailing Add:* Freer Gallery of Art Smithsonian Institution PO Box 37012 MRC 707 Washington DC 20013-7012

RACHOFSKY, CINDY & HOWARD
COLLECTOR, PATRON
Pos: bd dirs, Dallas Symphony Asn, Dallas Mus Art, New York Dia Ctr Arts, E Dallas Community Sch, Tate Lecture Series & Southern Methodist Univ; adv dir, Booker T Washington Magnet High Sch for Performing and Visual Arts, Dallas Theater Ctr, Dallas Archit Found, Univ Tex Sch Archit; founder & bd dirs, Dallas Ctr for Performing Arts Found; mem adv bd, Wharton Club, Dallas/Ft Worth, Dallas Bus Comt for the Arts; founder, Howard Earl Rachofsky Found; mem investment comt, St Phillips Acad. *Awards:* Named one of Top 200 Collectors, ARTnews mag, 2003-13. *Collection:* Contemporary art. *Mailing Add:* Rachofsky House 8605 Preston Rd Dallas TX 75225

RACITI, CHERIE
PAINTER
b Chicago, Ill, June 17, 1942. *Study:* Univ Ill, Urbana, 60-61; Memphis Coll Arts, Tenn, 63-65; San Francisco State Univ, BA, 68; Mills Col, Oakland, MFA, 79. *Work:* San Francisco Mus of Mod Art, Calif; Mills Col, Oakland; San Francisco Redevelopment Agency. *Exhib:* Whitney Mus Am Art Biennial, NY, 75; Los Angeles Inst Contemp Art, Calif, 76 & 78; solo exhibs, Adaline Kent Award Exhib, San Francisco Art Inst, 77, Fuller-Goldeen Gallery, San Francisco, 79, Marianne Deson, Chicago, 80, Long Beach Mus, Calif, 82 & Mills Coll Art Mus, 98; Angles Gallery & Fresno Mus, 87; Reese Bullen Gallery, Humboldt State Univ, Arcadia, Calif, 90; Terrain, San Francisco, Calif, 92; In/Out of the Cold, Inaugural Exhib, Ctr Arts, San Francisco, 93; two person show, Santa Monica Col, 98; 25/25 Southern Exposure 25th Ann Exhib, 99; Art Coun Awards, Jernigan Wicker Fine Arts, 2000; Conceptual Color, Santa Cruz Mus, 2003; New Geometries, Thatcher Gallery, Univ San Francisco, 2004. *Teaching:* prof art, San Francisco State Univ, 89-; prof, Calif State Univ, Hayward, 74; prof, San Francisco Art Inst, 78; prof, San Francisco State Univ, Col Creative Arts, 77-; prof emer, 2007. *Awards:* Trefethen Fel, Mills Col, 79; Eureka Fel, Fleishhacker Found, 88; Djerassi Resident Artist Prog, 94; Brit Travel Grant, 95; Tyrone Guthrie Ctr, Ireland, 95; Millay Colony Arts, Austerlitz, NY, 99; Juror's Award, The Art Coun, Inc, San Francisco, 2000; Va Ctr Creative Arts, 2005. *Bibliog:* Thomas Albright (auth), Art in the San Francisco Bay Area, 1945-1980, Univ Calif Press, 85; Marlena Donohue (auth), Los Angeles Times, 87; Moira Roth (ed), Connecting Conversations: Interviews with 28 Bay Area Woman Artists, Eucalyptus Press, 88; Judy Moran (ed), New Langton Arts, The First Fifteen Years, New Langton Arts, San Francisco, 90; Keith Lachowicz & Mark Johnson (auths, catalog) Mills College Museum 15 Year Survey, 98; Alicia Miller (auth), Art Week, 99; Jeff Kelley (auth), Art Week, 99; DeWitt Cheng (auth), Art Week, 10/2004; Colin Berry (auth), Art Week, 11/2004. *Mem:* San Francisco Art Inst Artist Comt (mem, 74-85); New Langton Arts (bd mem, 88-92). *Media:* Acrylic, Mixed Media. *Mailing Add:* 365 San Jose Ave San Francisco CA 94110

RACKUS, GEORGE (KEISTUS)
PAINTER, PRINTMAKER
b Lithuania, 1927; Can citizen. *Study:* Wayne Univ, 48-50; Ont Coll Art, 50-52; with Andre L'Hote, 52-55; Ecole des Beaux Arts, Paris, 52-55. *Work:* Victoria & Albert Mus, London; New York Cent Libr; Nat Gallery Can; NB Mus, St John; Contemp Mus, Sao Paulo, Brazil; Lithuanian Art Mus, Vilnius; R McLaughlin Gallery, Can; Art Gallery Ont, Can; and others. *Comn:* Murals (anodized aluminum), Howoco, Brussels, 69, Alcan Aluminum Ltd, Toronto, 70, Shell Can, Oakville, Ont, 70, Univ Western Ont, London, 71 & Dental Arts Bldg, Dunnville, Ont, 75. *Exhib:* Solo exhib, Galerie Foyer des Artists, Paris, 54-59, Anodized Aluminum Works, Commonwealth Inst, London, 70 & Anodized Aluminum Works & Prints, NB Mus, St John, 73; Agnes LeFort Galerie, Montreal, 60; Picture Loan Soc - Gallery, Toronto, 60, 63, 65, 66, 69 & 71; Gallery Moos, Toronto, 62; Fifth Ann Exhib Can Art, Montreal Mus, 62; Can Nat Art Gallery Tour for Australia, Nat Art Gallery, Victoria, 67, Nat Gallery, S Australia, Adelaide, 67 & Art Gallery New SWales, Sydney, 68; Vilnius Contemp Mus, Lithuania, 79, 87 & 88; Brand Libr Art Gallery, Glendale, Calif, 81; Grimsby Art Gallery, Can, 86; Peel Region Art Gallery, Brampton, Can, 87; Goethe Inst, Toronto,

87; traveling exhibs, Lithuania Mus Tour, 88 & art exhib, Dum Polonii, Warsaw & Paltusky, Poland, 89-90. *Pos:* Admin & Cur, Glenhyrst Arts Coun, Brantford, Can, 62-63; admin, Colour & Form Soc, Can, 85-89, admin, 89-. *Teaching:* Instr art, Dundas Valley Art Sch, Ont, 65-66, McMaster Univ, Hamilton, Ont, 68-69 & Brock Univ, St Catharine's, Ont, 77-78. *Awards:* Print of Yr, Soc Can Painter-Etchers & Engravers, 71; Graphic Award, Baltic Roots, Baltic Studies Asn, 78; First Prize Anodized Aluminum Work, Colour & Form Exhib, 81. *Bibliog:* Robert Ayre (auth), article, Montreal Star, 62; Robert Percival (cur), doc, New Brunswick Mus; Paul Duval (auth), doc, 88. *Mem:* Ont Soc Artists Can (pres, 86-88); Colour & Form Soc Can (pres, 74-76 & 79-84); Print Consortium, USA. *Media:* Anodized Aluminum, Lithography. *Publ:* Auth, British sculpture at Montreal Museum, Wkly, 61; A painter speaks up, Globe & Mail, 62; Anodized aluminum as an art media, 71 & Exploring new media, Vol II, 71, Arts Mag, Can

RADAN, GEORGE TIVADAR
ADMINISTRATOR, HISTORIAN
b Budapest, Hungary, Dec 31, 1923; US citizen. *Study:* Univ Budapest, MA, 46 PhD, 48, with Peter Pazmany; Ecole de Louvre, Paris AEM, 67. *Work:* Nat Maritime Mus, Haifa, Israel. *Collection Arranged:* Ships through the Ages (with catalog), Nat Maritime Mus, 55. *Pos:* Dir archeol, Ky State Univ & Wayne State Univ, 70-76; dir archeol excavations, Siena, 84. *Teaching:* Prof art hist, Villanova Univ, Pa, 60-, chmn dept art, 63-; prof art hist, Am Coll Paris, 66-67. *Awards:* Am Coun Learned Soc Scholarship to Hungary Acad Sci, 73 & 75; Outstanding Fac Publ Award, 85. *Mem:* Coll Art Asn; Asn Ancient Historians; Italian Art Soc. *Media:* Archaeologist. *Res:* Art historian dealing with ancient art and archeology. *Interests:* Naval Decoration. *Publ:* Auth, An Introduction to Ancient Art and Architecture, 67, Del Villanova Press; coauth, The Archeology of Roman Pannonia, Univ Ky Press, 80; The Sons of Zebulon, Jewish Maritime Hist, 80; The Villanova University Art Collection: A Guide, Villanova Press, 86; Lecceto, Silvania Editoriale, 91; Augustine in Iconography, Lang, 98; and 38 more articles. *Mailing Add:* Dept History Villanova Univ Villanova PA 19085

RADECKI, MARTIN JOHN
ADMINISTRATOR, CONSERVATOR
b South Bend, Ind, Jan 4, 1948. *Study:* Ind Univ, AB, 70; Intermuseum Conserv Lab (internship), 74-75. *Exhib:* Forgery: The Steele/Forsyth Controversy, 89. *Collection Arranged:* Conservation of Indiana Governors Portraits, Indianapolis Mus Art, 78. *Pos:* Apprentice conservator, Indianapolis Mus Art, 71-73, asst conservator, 73-74, actg chief conservator, 75-; conserv intern, Intermuseums Conserv Lab, 74-75, chief conservator, 75-. *Mem:* fel Am Inst Conserv Historic & Artistic Works; Int Inst Conserv Historic & Artistic Works. *Res:* Treatment of blanched paintings; methods of forgery detection, specifically on late 14th-early 20th century American paintings

RADES, WILLIAM L
PAINTER, SCULPTOR
b Milwaukee, Wis, Aug 13, 1943. *Study:* Univ Wis, Milwaukee, BFA, 65, MFA, 68; San Francisco Art Inst, with Ron Nagle & Jack Jefferson, 66. *Work:* Santa Barbara Mus Art, Calif; Am Telephone & Telegraph, NY; Minneapolis Inst Art, Minn; Georgia Pacific Corp, Portland, Ore; Eastern Wash Univ, Cheney. *Comn:* Drawing on paper, Wash State Arts Comn & Evergreen State Col, Olympia, 79; painting on paper, Wash State Arts Comn, Olympia, 80; painted wood relief, Wash State Arts Comn, Spokane, 82. *Exhib:* Oregon Artists Under 35, Portland Art Mus, 74 & 77; Drawing USA, Minn Mus Art, 77; Washington Painting, Tacoma Art Mus, 77, 79 & 81; 21st Nat Chautauqua Exhib Am Art, NY, 78; Illusionism: Handmade, Henry Art Gallery, Univ Wash, Seattle, 81; Northwest Perspectives, traveling exhib in US, 82-84. *Teaching:* Instr drawing, Univ Wis, Milwaukee, 65-68; asst instr ceramics, San Francisco Art Inst, 66; vis asst prof drawing, Ore State Univ, 72-74. *Awards:* Purchase Awards, Pensacola Nat Drawing Competition, Visual Arts Gallery, 76, Drawing USA, Minn Mus Art, 77 & Fourth LaGrange Nat Competition, CVAA Gallery, 78. *Bibliog:* Bill Rades paintings, Artweek, 74; Mus interview, KTRS Pub TV, 82; Harvey West (auth), The Washington Year, Univ Wash Press, 82. *Mem:* Coll Art Asn. *Mailing Add:* 12709 Lake City Blvd SW Tacoma WA 98498-4211

RADICE, ANNE-IMELDA MARINO
ADMINISTRATOR
b Buffalo, NY, Feb 29, 1948. *Study:* Wheaton Col, Norton, Mass, AB, 1969; Villa Schifanoia, Florence, Italy, MA, 1971; Univ NC, Chapel Hill, PhD, 1976; Am Univ, MBA, 1984. *Collection Arranged:* Two on Two at the Octagon (auth, catalog), Drawings from the Collection of the Architect of the Capitol, US Capitol, 1980. *Pos:* Asst cur & staff lectr, Nat Gallery Art, Washington, 1972-76; archit historian for the architect, US Capitol, 1976-80, cur, 1980-85; dir, Nat Mus Women Arts, 1985-89; Chief, Div Creative Arts, USIA, 1985-89; deputy chmn, Nat Endowment Arts, 1990-91, actg chmn, 1992-93; exec vpres, Gray & Co II, Miami, 1993; producer, World Affairs TV Production, 1993; assoc producer, New River Media, 1994; chief adv & chief of staff, Courtney Sale Ross, 1994-96; vpres, chief operating officer, ICL Int, 1996; exec dir, Friends of Dresden Inc, 1998-2001; exec dir appeal, Conscience Found, New York, 2001-03; chief of staff to sec, US Dept Educ, Washington, 2003-05; acting asst chmn programs, Nat Endowment Humanities, Washington, 2005-06; dir, Inst Mus & Libr Services, Washington, 2006-2012; dir, Am Folk Art Mus, NY, 2012-; bd trustees, African Art Mus, Smithsonian Inst, Historic Gettysburg Found, Coll Art Asn, Tom Lea Inst, Police Mus, NY, currently. *Awards:* Forbes Medal for Distinguished Contrib to Conservation, Am Inst Conservation of Hist & Artistic Works, 2008; Presidential Citizens Medal, 2008. *Res:* Italian renaissance architecture, architecture of Thomas Jefferson and US Capitol. *Publ:* Auth, Il Cronaca: Fifteenth Century Florentyne Architect, Univ Microfilms, 76; ed, ann reports of architect of Capitol, 76- & contribr, The Capitol, Govt Printing Off, 80; auth, US Capitol, Art J, fall 80, The Original Libr Congress, 81. *Mailing Add:* American Folk Art Museum 2 Lincoln Sq Columbus Ave at 66th St New York NY 10023

RADY, ELSA
CERAMIST, SCULPTOR
b New York, NY, July 29, 1943. *Study:* Chouinard Art Sch, 62-66. *Work:* Smithsonian Inst, Renwick Gallery, Washington, DC; Boston Mus Fine Arts; Victoria & Albert Mus Art, London, England; Brooklyn Mus, NY; Los Angeles Co Mus Art; Metrop Mus Art; NYNEX Corp, White Plains, NY; Chase Manhattan Bank, NY; General Motors, NY; Am Med Int Inc, Beverly Hills, Calif; Denver Art Mus; Detroit Inst Art; Long Beach Mus Art, Calif; and many more. *Comn:* Sculptures, Jules Stein Eye Inst, Univ Calif, Los Angeles, 66 & Disneyland, 67. *Exhib:* solo exhibs: Garth Clark Gallery, NY, 85, Jan Turner Gallery, Los Angeles, 87 & 88, Holly Solomon Gallery, NY, 87 & Lily (catalogue), 90, Ochi Gallery, Suny Valley, Idaho, 90 & Still Life (catalogue), Isetan Fine Arts Inc, Tokyo, Japan, 91, Santa Barbara Mus Art, Calif 93, Holly Solomon Gallery, New York, 95, Long Beach Mus Art, Long Beach, Calif, 2005, Craig Krull Gallery, Santa Monica, 2006; Am Porcelain, Renwick Gallery, Smithsonian Inst, Washington, DC, 80; Pacific Connections, Los Angeles Co Mus Art, 85; Craftsmen USA '66, Los Angeles Co Mus Art, 66; Am Potters Today, Victoria & Albert Mus, London, Eng, 86; World War II Holdings, Metrop Mus Art, NY, 89; Selections from the Joyce & Jay Cooper Collection of Contemp Ceramics, Nelson Fine Arts Ctr, Ariz State Univ Art Mus, 89-90; Building a Permanent Collection: A Perspective on the 1980s, Am Craft Mus, NY, 90; 28th Ann Ceramic Exhib (catalogue), Everson Mus Art, Syracuse, NY, 90; Southeast Bank Collects, A Corporation Views Contemp Art, Harn Mus Art, Univ Fla, West Palm Beach; Newark Mus, NJ, 2003; Palto Alto Art Ctr, Calif, 2005; Yale Univ Art Gallery, 2007; Palos Verdes Art Ctr, Calif, 2009. *Awards:* Nat Endowment Fel, 81; Calif State Arts Comn Grant, 83; Krasner-Pollack Found Grant, 2002; Adolph & Esther Gottlieb Found Grant, 2002; Artists' Fel, Inc, New York, 2008. *Bibliog:* William Wilson (auth), California ceramics: shape of things to come, Los Angeles Times, 8/9/84; Mac McCloud (auth), Elsa Rady: porcelain vessels, Am Ceramics, Vol III, No 4, 85; Gerrit Henry (auth), Elsa Rady, Art News, Vol 85, No 2, 86; and others; David Pagel (auth), Color & Fire, Defining Moments in Studio Ceramics 1950-2000, Los Angeles Times, 2000; Reed Johnson (auth), Function Follows Form, Contemp Craft Mus, 2000; Michael Web (auth), Back to Basics, Archit Digest, 2002; Telhen Keramelki (auth), Standing Room Only, Sixth Scripps Ceramic Ann, 2004; George Melrod (auth), Elsa Rady at Craig Krull, Lifescapes, 2006; Stephanie Cash & David Ebony (auth), Art in America, 2008. *Media:* Ceramics; Porcelain. *Publ:* Ornaments and Surfaces on Ceramics, Kunst & Handwerk, 77; Studio Porcelain, Chilton Book Co, 80; Porcelain: Traditions and New Visions, Watson-Guptill, 81; Ceramics of the 20th Century, Rizzoli, 82; American Crafts: A Source Book for the Home, Stewart, Tabori, Chang, 83. *Dealer:* Craig Krull Gallery Santa Monica CA

RAEBURN, CARRIE R.
PAINTER
b Tulsa, Okla, 1953. *Study:* Univ Tulsa, BS, 78; attended, Tulane Univ, Oral Roberts Univ; studied with Marilyn Simpson, PSA. *Work:* Dale Med Ctr, Ozark, Ala. *Exhib:* Solo exhibs, Pastel Soc N Fla, Fort Walton Beach, Fla, 2001, Carillon Inst, Carillon, Beach, Fla, 2002; Pastel Soc Am, Nat Arts Club, NY, 99, 2001, 2002, 2009, 2012, & 2014. *Pos:* mem bd govs, Pastel Soc Am. *Awards:* PSA awards in 99 & 2002, ALA Pastel Soc, 1st Place, 2001, Best of Show, 2010; Best of Show, Pastel Soc N Fla, 2012. *Bibliog:* Master Pastel Artist of the World USA Showcase, Pastel Artist Int, Elladrent Pty Ltd, Australia, 2001; Pastel 100 Competition, Pastel Jour, EW Pub, 2002, 2010, 2011. *Mem:* Pastel Soc N Fla (1st vice pres, 2008-2010, pres 2010-2014); Pastel Soc Am (signature mem); Degas Pastel Soc; Ala Pastel Soc; Salmagundi Club NY. *Media:* Pastel, Mixed Media. *Interests:* Landscapes, City Scapes, Nudes. *Mailing Add:* 262 County Rd 664 Coffee Springs AL 36318

RAFFAEL, JOSEPH
PAINTER, PRINTMAKER
b Brooklyn, NY, Feb 22, 1933. *Study:* Cooper Union, 53-54, Yale Sch Fine Arts, BFA, 56, studied with Josef Albers. *Work:* Metrop Mus Art, Whitney Mus Am Art, NY; San Francisco Mus Mod Art; Libr Cong, Hirshhorn Mus & Smithsonian Inst, Washington; Oakland Mus, Calif; Mint Mus, Charlotte, NC; and many others. *Exhib:* The Modern Era: Bay Area Update, San Francisco Mus Mod Art, 77; Eight Contemp Am Realists, Pa Acad Fine Arts, Philadelphia, 77; Drawings of the 70's, Soc Contemp Art, Art Inst Chicago, 77; one-man exhibs, San Francisco Mus Mod Art, 78-79, Butler Inst Am Art, 91, Hunter Mus Art, Chattanooga, Tenn, 92, Naples Philharmonic Ctr, Fla, 92, Louis Newman Galleries, Los Angeles, 92, Nancy Hoffman Gallery, NY, 92, 94, 96, 97 & 98 & Images Gallery, Toledo, Ohio, 95, The Canton Mus Art, Ohio, 98-99, Nancy Hoffman Gallery, NYC, 99, 01, 02; Art at Work: Recent Art from Corporate Collections, Whitney Mus Am Art, 78; New Am Monotypes, Smithsonian Inst, 79; The Decade in Review-Selections from the 1970's, Whitney Mus Am Art, 79; New Dimensions in Drawing, Aldrich Mus Contemp Art, 81; Contemp Am Realism since 1960 (traveling), Pa Acad Fine Arts, 81-83; A Private Vision: Contemp Art from the Graham Gund Collection, Mus Fine Arts, Boston, 82; Purchases of the Hirshhorn Mus, 1974-1983, Hirshhorn Mus & Sculpture Garden, 83; The Am Artist as Printmaker: Twenty-Third Nat Print Mus Exhib, Brooklyn Mus, NY, 83; Albright-Knox Art Gallery, 83; Reflections of Nature: Flowers in Am Art, Whitney Mus Am Art, 84; 50th Ann Midyear Show, Butler Inst Am Art, 86; Modern Am Realism, Sara Roby Found Collection, Nat Mus Am Art, Smithsonian Inst, 87; Close Focus: Prints, Drawings and Photographs, Smithsonian Inst, 87; California A to Z and Return, Butler Inst Am Art, 90; The Flower in Am Art, Butler Inst Am Art, 91; Nat Midyear Exhib, Butler Inst Am Art, 92; First Sightings, Denver Art Mus, 93; 57th Ann Midyear Exhib, Butler Inst Am Art, 93; Collector's Show, Ark Arts Ctr, Little Rock, 95-96; Small Scale, Nancy Hoffman Gallery, NY, 96; Painting '96, Kutztown Univ, Pa, 96; In Bloom, NJ Ctr Visual Arts, Summit, 96; Health & Happiness in Twentieth-Century Avant-Garde Art, Binghamton Univ Art Mus, NY, 96; Canton Mus Art, Ohio, 98-99; group exhibs, Nancy Hoffman Gallery, 01, 02, Taipei Gallery, New York City, 01, Ark Art Ctr, Little Rock, 01, 02, Yale Univ Sch Art, New Haven, Conn, 01, Art Foundry Gallery, Sacramento, 02, Selby Gallery, Ringling Sch of Art and Design, Sarasota, Fla, 02, TIAA/CREF, New York City, 02. *Collection Arranged:* Art

Inst Chicago; Butler Inst Am Art, Youngstown, Ohio; Denver Art Mus; Fort Worth Art Mus, Tex; Smithsonian Inst; Joslyn Art Mus, Omaha, Nebr; Libr Congress, Washington, DC; Los Angeles Co Mus Art; Metrop Mus Art; Mint Mus, Charlotte, NC; Oakland Mus, Calif; Philadelphia Mus Art; San Francisco Mus Modern Art; Va Mus of Fine Arts, Richmond; Walker Art Ctr, Minneapolis; Whitney Mus Am Art, NY. *Teaching:* Instr art, Univ Calif, Davis, 66, Sch Visual Arts, New York, 67-69; assoc prof art, Univ Calif, Berkeley, 69; prof art, Calif State Univ, Sacramento, 69-74. *Awards:* Fulbright Fel to Florence & Rome, 58-59; LC Tiffany Found Fel, 60; First Prize & Purchase Award, Oakland Mus, Calif, 75. *Bibliog:* Gloria Smith (auth), The Eyes Have It: Joseph Raffael (film), NBC-TV, 72; Wm S Wilson (auth), The paintings of Jos Raffael, Studio Int, 5/74; Jerome Tarshis (auth), Nature upclose, Horizon, 9/78. *Media:* Oil, Watercolor; Lithography. *Mailing Add:* c/o Nancy Hoffman Gallery 520 W 27th St Ste 301 New York NY 10001-5548

RAFFAEL, JUDITH K See North, Judy K Rafael

RAFFERTY, ANDREW
PAINTER, PRINTMAKER
Study: Boston Univ, BFA, 84; Yale Univ, MFA, 88. *Work:* Rhode Island Sch Design, Providence. *Exhib:* Mary Washington Col, Fredericksburg, Md, 87; Srathmore Hall Art Ctr, Rockville, Md, 88; Gallery Ohio, Nagoya, Japan, 92; Trenton State Col, NJ, 93; solo exhib, Hackett-Freedman Gallery, San Francisco, 94. *Teaching:* Lectr lithography, Yale Univ Sch Art, New Haven, Conn, 89-91; asst dir/instr etching, Yale Summer Sch Art, Norfolk, 88-93; fac printmaker, RI Sch Design, Providence, 91-93. *Bibliog:* Portraying the world as he finds it: The narrative paintings of Andrew Rafferty, American Artist, 95; Realism, Artnews, 96. *Mailing Add:* 2319 12th Ave San Francisco CA 94116-1907

RAFFERTY, EMILY
RETIRED MUSEUM ADMINISTRATOR
b New York, Mar 13, 1949. *Study:* Boston Univ, BA, 1971. *Pos:* Arts and philanthropy asst to David Rockefeller Jr, Boston, 1971; dep dir edn Inst Contemp Art, 1973-75; admin corp found and individual fundraising Metrop Mus Art, New York, 1976-81, manager development, 1981-84, vpres development and membership, 1984-96, sr vpres development and membership, 1996-99, sr vpres external affairs, 1999-2005, pres, 2005-2015, pres. emertia, 2015-. *Mem:* Independent Sector; Am Asn Museums (development com 1984-94); Asn Fundraising Professionals; ArtTable (bd dirs, 1991-94; Award for Distinguished Serv to Visual Arts, 2007). *Mailing Add:* Metrop Mus Art 1000 5th Ave New York NY 10028

RAFFERTY, JOANNE MILLER
PAINTER, COLLAGE ARTIST
b Morristown, NJ, May 31, 1948. *Study:* Daemen Coll, NY, with James Kuo & Jay Jodway, BS (art educ), 70; State Univ NY, Buffalo, 75, Art Educ, permanent cert. *Work:* Albright Knox Art Gallery, Buffalo, NY; Master Charge Int, New York; Bankers Trust, New York; Equitable Life Insurance, Atlanta, Ga; Dun & Bradstreet, New York; USBS Corp Hq, Hartford, Conn; General Motors; Exxon Corp; IBM; Am Express; AT&T; Marriott Hotels; Nabisco Corp; Merril Lynch; CompuServe, New York. *Comn:* Lobby, Int Bus Machines, comn by Armand Avakian, archit, Harrison, NY, 89; main lobby, Clark State Performing Arts Ctr, Springfield, Ohio, comn by Art Exchange, Columbus, Ohio, 93; main lobby, Crestar Bank, Richmond, Va, 92; main lobby, CompuServe, 5th Ave, New York, 95; main lobby, Warner Lambert Corp Hq, comn by Cloninger Fine Art, NJ, 97; int hq, Pub Svc Electric and Gas, Newark, NJ, 2002; main lobby, Chubb Insurance, Philadelphia, Pa, 2003. *Exhib:* Nat juried Exhib Painting & Sculpture, Mus Great Plains, 84; People's Choice Exhib, Long Beach Island Fdn Arts & Sci, Loveladies, NJ, 90; solo exhibs, Broden Gallery, Madison, Wis, 91-99 & 2006, Chasen Galleries, Sarasota, Fla, 93-99 & 2006 & Rima Fine Art, Scottsdale, Ariz, 2001 & 2007; AmeriFlora, 92; Huntington Nat Bank, Columbus, Ohio, 92; Starfish Found Invitational Exhib, 93; Nat Asn Women Artists, W Broadway, New York, 94; NJ Favorite Artists Exhib, Nabisco Corp Hq, Hanover, NJ, 98; Nat Asn Women Artists Millennium Collection Exhib, Comn Status Women, UN lobby, New York, 2002; A Decade of Papermaking, Visual Arts Ctr, NJ, 2003; Gallerie des Artes, Sarasota, Fla, 2003; Artists Who Happen to be Women, J Wayne Starke Galleries Nat Exhib, Tex A&M Univ, 2004; Blank Canvas Benefit: For Art's Sake, Visual Arts Ctr, NJ, 2006; Mona Lisa Gallery, NJ, 2007; Chasen Galleries, Richmond, Va, 2007; Chairs: Form Follows Function, Visual Arts Ctr, NJ, 2007; Images in Art from Tulsa Collection, The Sherwin Miller Mus Jewish Art, 2007; The Sketchbook Project, Brooklyn Art Libr, 2011. *Teaching:* Instr art, Middleport Cent Schs, NY, 70-71; Amherst Central Schs, NY, 71-76; Educ Dept, Montclair Mus, 94. *Awards:* NJ Watercolor Soc Award, 89; Winsor & Newton Award of Achievement, NJ Watercolor Soc Found 45th Anniversary Show, 92; Phillips Award, 50th Ann Open Exhib, Monmouth Mus, 92. *Bibliog:* J Taylor Basker (auth), Art at the Reece Galleries, Art Speak, 4/87; Susan Fields (auth), Publishers refine lines and grow, Art Bus News, 4/89; Robert Merritt (auth), Rafferty paintings, Richmond Times Dispatch, 5/92; F B Glucksman (auth), Turn your passion into your profession, Income Opportunities, 1/94; Kevin Lynch (auth), Abstract art is in again, The Capital Times, 5/2000; Cindy Potters (auth), Home is where the art is, Newark Star Ledger, 9/2005; Helena Miehle (auth), Joanne Rafferty: Beyond the Horizon, Fine Art Mag, 3/2006. *Mem:* Nat Asn Women Artists; NJ Watercolor Soc; New York Artists Equity. *Media:* Acrylic, Watercolor. *Dealer:* Rime Fine Art 7077 E Main St Scottsdale AZ; Uphouse Fine Art Publ Scottsdale AZ; Landmark Gallery 119 W 57th St New York NY 10019-2150; Chasen Galleries Richmond Va. *Mailing Add:* 14 Mackenzie Ln N Denville NJ 07834

RAFTERY, ANDREW STEIN
PRINTMAKER
b Goldsboro, NC, 1962. *Study:* Boston Univ Sch Arts, BFA, 1984; Yale Univ Sch Art, MFA, 1988. *Work:* Yale Univ Art Gallery, CT; Jane Voorhess Zimmerli Art Mus, New Bunswick, NJ; Metrop Mus Art, NY; Princeton Univ Art Mus, NJ; Whitney Mus Am Art, NY. *Exhib:* Solo exhibs include Narrative Paintings & Prints, Contemp Realist Gallery, San Francisco, 1994, Narrative Impulse, Frye Art Mus, Seattle, 1998, Drawings & Prints, Lenore Gray Gallery, Providence, RI, 1998, Real Estate Chiaroscuros, 2002, A Shopper's Paradise, Hackett-Freedman Gallery, San Francisco, 1998; group exhibs include Objects & Everyday Life, Montserrat Coll Art, Beverly, MA, 1993; RISD Collects RISD, RISD Mus, Providence, 1996, Chiaroscuro, 2004; South Coast New England Printmaking, Univ Mass, North Dartmouth, 2003; Newer Genres, Jane Voorhees Zimmerli Art Mus, New Brunswick, NJ, 2003; Drawn to Representation, Corcoran Gallery Art, Washington, 2005; Invitational Exhib, AAAL, 2006; Portfolios & Series, New York Pub Libr, New York, 2007; 60 Yrs North Am Prints, Boston Univ Art Gallery, 2007; Ann Invitational Exhib Contemp Am Art, Nat Acad Mus, New York, 2008. *Awards:* Fritz Eichenberg Fel Printmaking, Narrative Engraving Proj, Rhode Island State Coun Arts, 2001; Louis Comfort Tiffany Award, 2003; Purchase Award, AAAL, 2006; John Simon Guggenheim Mem Found Fel, 2008. *Dealer:* Mary Ryan Gallery 527 West 26th Street New York NY 10001. *Mailing Add:* 76 8th St Providence RI 02906

RAGINSKY, NINA
PAINTER
b Montreal, Que. *Study:* Rutgers Univ, BA, 62; Studied with George Segal, Allan Kaprow, Roy Lichtenstein. *Work:* Nat Film Bd Can; Edmonton Art Gallery; George Eastman House; Nat Gallery Can; Sol Lewitt Collection; Univ of Victoria: Canadian Mus Contemp Art & Photog, Ottawa; Maltwood Mus, Univ Victoria, British Columbia; Old Crow Mus, Yukon Territory, Can. *Exhib:* Int Photo Show, Nat Gallery Can, 68; Vision and Expression, George Eastman House, Rochester, NY, 69; solo exhibs, San Francisco Mus Art, 75 & Art Gallery Ont, 79; Between Friends, Field Mus, Chicago, 76; Nancy Hoffman Gallery, New York City. *Teaching:* Instr photog, Emily Carr Col Art, Vancouver, 72-81; workshops, Univ Ottawa, Univ Victoria & Banff Sch Fine Arts. *Awards:* Can Coun Grant, 76; Officer, Order of Can, 85. *Bibliog:* Geoffrey James (auth), An inquiry into the aesthetics of photography, Arts Can, 12/74. *Mem:* Royal Can Acad Art (founding mem coordr Waterbird Watch collection, 1994); Soc Advancement of Slow, Salt Spring Island Chap, 2002; Soc Advancement of Inconvenience, Salt Spring Island Chap, 2007. *Media:* Oils, Watercolors. *Interests:* The conservation of native fauna & flora and their habitat preservation. *Publ:* Vision & Expression, Horizon Press, 69; An Inquiry into the Aesthetics of Photography, Arts Can, 75; Banff Purchase, Wiley, 79; Aperture 88, Aperture, 82; Between Friends; Nat Film Board Image Series, 1, 2, 3, 5, 6. *Dealer:* Volume II Books Salt Spring Island BC. *Mailing Add:* 272 Beddis Rd Salt Spring Island BC V8K 2J1 Canada

RAGLAND, BOB
PAINTER, INSTRUCTOR
b Cleveland, Ohio, Dec 11, 1938. *Study:* Rocky Mountain Sch Art, Denver, Colo; study with Phil Steele. *Work:* Denver Pub Libr; Karamu House, Cleveland; Irving St Ctr, Cult Arts Prog, Denver; Created Mayor's Awards, Denver, Colo, 92; Kaiser Permanente, Colo; Colo State Univ; Channel 4 TV-Denver, Colo; Denver Pub Schs, Colo; Kirkland Mus Fine and Decorative Art, Denver, Colo. *Comn:* Logo, Metro State Coll Black Student Union, 74; art print, Big Sisters Colo, 75, art poster, 2007; Mayor's Arts Awards, Denver, Colo, 93; Governor's Recycling Awards, Denver, Colo, 94. *Exhib:* 16th Ann Drawing Exhib, Dallas Mus Fine Art Traveling Exhib, 67; Solo exhibs, Cleveland State Univ, 68, Denver Nat Bank, Colo, 80-81, Century Bank Cherry Creek, Denver, Colo, 80-81; Survival Techniques, PBS Series, 78, 79; Group Exhib, Boston, Mass Tubman Gallery, 81; Anniversary Art Exhib, Channel Six PBS, 91-93; Colo Pub Educ & Business Coalition Art Exhib, 93-96; Savageau Gallery, 96; North Am Sculpture Exhib, Foothills Art Ctr, Golden, Colo, 2006. *Pos:* Chmn, Arts & Humanities Comt, 68-69; lectr, Afro-American art of the 60's & 70's; founding fac mem, Auraria Campus, Community Col, Denver, 70-72; visual arts coordr, City Spirit Proj, 78; Free Counseling, Art Career Coach, Denver Colo; art career coach dir, Art Information Ctr, Denver, Colo; coaching art life, After Art Sch Business Focus. *Teaching:* Instr painting & drawing, Denver Pub Libr, 69-71 & Eastside Action Ctr, Denver, 69-71; artist-in-residence, Model Cities Cult Arts Ctr Workshop, 71-73; artist/teacher, KRMA-TV; instr, Gove Community Sch, 79-; instr, Metrop State Col, Denver, Colo; instr, Arapahoe Community Col, Littleton, Colo; vis artist, Cole Sch Arts, 93-95 & Urban Peak Ctr Homeless Youth, 96-97; artist-in-residence, Denver Pub Sch, 96-97 Denver Post, 1/81; artist-in-residence, A.I.R. Career Educ Ctr, 96-2009, Art Career Coach, 80-; Bob Ragland Talks About Art and Artists, Mary Motian-Meadows, Denver, Urban Spectrum, 11/2002; career educ ctr, Middle Coll Denver, 96-2009. *Awards:* Recognition Award, KCNC-TV & Denver Ctr Performing Arts, 86, Foot Hills Art Ctr, Golden, Colo, 2001; Invents Non-Starving Artists Project, 1997. *Bibliog:* Diane Wengler (auth), Bob Ragland- He's learned to survive by using his wits and considerable talent, Gazette-Telegraph, Colo Springs, 4/81; Alexandra King (auth), article, Street Talk Mag, Denver, 10/81; Bonnie McCune (auth), What to do until rich & famous, This Week in Denver, 11/22/82; Carson Reed (auth), Denver artist is more method than madness, Up the Creek Newspaper, 1/25/85; James J Lewis (auth), Making the Art is only Half of the Job, Sol Day News Arts & Entertainment, 98; Outlaw Artist's Work Reflects Neighborhood, Denver Post, 3/28/2005. *Mem:* Colo Black Umbrella. *Media:* All Media; Metal, Welded, Oil, Charcoal. *Res:* Oral history project with Colorado artists over the age of fifty. *Interests:* Collecting art books, artists lives, research. *Collection:* Traditional renderings of the figure and landscape in all mediums. *Publ:* Publ, Colorado Gallery Guide, 78-; contribr, Black Umbrella/Black Artists Denver; Dick Kreck, Artist will throw in a sculpture at this half off sale, Denver Post, 9/28/98 & 3/28/2005; GoGo Mag, Bob Ragland, Non Starving Artist, 10/2002; Art Talk Mag, Ariz, 12/98; Colorado Artscape Gallery Guide; How to Become an Art Collector (art); Life on Capital Hill, Mar 2008; Irene Rawinglin (auth), The Clothes Line Book, Denver, Colo. *Dealer:* Bob Ragland Studio 1723 E 25 Ave Denver Co 80205. *Mailing Add:* 1723 E 25th Ave Denver CO 80205

RAGLAND, JACK WHITNEY
PAINTER, PRINTMAKER

b El Monte, Calif, Feb 25, 1938. *Study:* Ariz State Univ, BA & MA, with Dr Harry Wood, Arthur Jacobson & Ben Goo; Univ Calif, Los Angeles, with Dr Lester Longman, Sam Amato & William Brice; Akad Angewandte Kunst; Akad Bildenden Kunste; Graphische Bundes-Lehrund Versuchsanstalt, Vienna; with Bill Bowne, San Diego, Calif, Ted Goerschner, Fallbrook, Calif, Tim Clark, David Leffel, Sherry McGraw, John Cosby, Ken Auster, Pasadena, Calif. *Work:* (in permanent collections) Albertina Mus, Vienna, Austria; Phoenix Art Mus, Ariz; Bibliotheque Nat, Paris; Kunstmuseum, Basel, Switz; Los Angeles Co Mus, Calif; Vintage Car Poster Designs, Fallbrook, 2003-05; Equity Life Assurance, Des Moines, Iowa; J D Enterprises, Stockton, Calif; Malabar Estates, Fallbrook, Calif. *Comn:* Portrait, Henry Nollen, Equitable Life Insurance, 73; stained glass windows, Methodist Church, Perry, Iowa, 74; mural sized commissioned paintings, Alan & Jean Silberman, 2006; signature painting, Beucler Signature Homes & Malabar Rancho (hqs), Fallbrook, Calif, 2006; Thundering Hooves (mural sized painting), Stockton Adventures, JD Properties, Stockton, Calif, 2007. *Exhib:* Exhib Nat Recognized Artists, Seattle, 63 & Ft Lauderdale, Fla, 64, 65; Iowa Ann Exhib, Des Moines, 70 & 72; Artists Fedn Traveling Exhib, Eight Midwest States, 75; Southern Calif Exhib, Del Mar, Calif, 81-2015; Designer Show Case, Pasadena, 95 & San Diego, 95-98; Desert Plein Air Master Show, 2000, 2001, 2002. *Pos:* Owner, Jack Ragland Atelier, 76-. *Teaching:* Grad asst drawing & painting, Univ Calif, Los Angeles, 61-64; instr drawing & painting, Ariz State Univ, summer 63; art dept head & assoc prof art hist, drawing, printmaking & painting, Simpson Coll, Indianola, IA, 64-76; pvt workshops, 84-2015. *Awards:* Grand Purchase Prize, Ariz Ann, Phoenix Art Mus, 61; Painting Selected for Prize Winning Paintings, Book II, Allied Publ, 62; First Prize, Prints & Graphics, Iowa State Fair, 74; First award, Acrylic Painting, Southern Calif Exhib, Del Mar, 1984, 2007 (4 awards); San Diego Co Fair Awards: 2nd award, 2003; Best of Show, 1st award, 3rd award (2 hon mentions), 2005; 1st award, 3rd Prize (hon mentions), 2006; 2nd award, 2 3rd Prizes, 2007; 1st Prize, 2 3rd Prizes (4 hon mentions), 2008, 2nd award & Hon Mention, 2009, 1st award, 2014, 1st award for City Scape, 2014, 1st award in Still Life & Hon Mention, 2015; Next Great Am Artist Contest (one of top three paintings), Kirklands, 2007; Grand Nat Art Show (Invitational), Best of show, Cow Palace, San Francisco, Calif, 2008; Top Mini 50, Nat Paint the Parks Competition, 2009; 2nd place, Paint Am, 2009; 3rd, 100 of the Top 100, 2009; Best of Show, Ralph Love, Plein Air, Temecula, Calif, 2011, 2012; 2nd award, Temecula City Hall, Plein Air award, 2014; 1st award and People Choice, Temecula Valley Art League, 2014. *Bibliog:* Am Artist Mag, 10/94; Decor and Style, 95-2006; San Diego Life Styles, 95-98; Present Art Scene, 2000-2008. *Mem:* Calif Art Club (past mem); Fallbrook Art Assoc; Oil Painters of Am (past mem). *Media:* Acrylic, Oils; Serigraphy. *Specialty:* European & Calif landscapes, portraits, figures, still life, animals. *Interests:* Singing, dancing, traveling the world. *Dealer:* Desert Art-Source Palm Desert CA. *Mailing Add:* 5555 8th St Fallbrook CA 92028-9602

RAGUIN, VIRGINIA C
HISTORIAN, CONSULTANT

b New York, NY, Feb 24, 1941. *Study:* Marymount Col, Tarrytown, NY, BA (magna cum laude), 63; Univ Toulouse, France, cert, 64; Yale Univ, with Summer McK Crosby, PhD, 74. *Collection Arranged:* Coll Gallery Prog, Worcester Art Mus, 75-84; Northern Renaissance Stained Glass (with catalog), Cantor Gallery, Holy Cross, 87; Glory in Glass (with catalog) Am Bible Soc, NY, 98. *Pos:* Dir, Census Stained Glass Windows Am, 82-2000; hist res consult, Stained Glass Mag, 83-; consult, Mem Hall Restoration, Harvard Univ, 85-; stained glass res, Boston, Charleston & Birmingham dioceses (currently). *Teaching:* Prof art hist, Col Holy Cross, 74-2010, distinguished prof humanities, 2010-. *Awards:* Fulbright Scholar, 64; Woodrow Wilson Fel, 64; Nat Endowment Humanities Educ Proj Grant, 77-80; Nat Endowment Humanities Tech, 96-99; Graham Found, 2001; Nat Endowment Arts, 2009. *Mem:* Int Ctr Medieval Art; Coll Art Asn; Soc Archit Historians. *Res:* Medieval Renaissance and Modern stained glass; Medieval iconography. *Publ:* Auth, Isaiah master of the Sainte-Chapelle in Burgundy, Art Bull, 77; Stained Glass in Thirteenth-Century Burgundy, Princeton, 82; Worcester's Tradition of Stained glass, Worcester Art Mus J, 83; coauth, Stained Glass Before 1700 in American Collections, Nat Gallery, 85-88; auth, Revivals Revivalists and Architectural Stained Glass, Soc Archit Historians J, 90; co-ed, Artistic Integration in Gothic Buildings, Toronto, 95; auth, Stained Glass from its Origins to the Present, Abrams, 2003; auth, Kikismith: Lodestar, Pace, 2010; coauth, Pilgrimage and Faith: Buddhism, Christianity, and Islam, 2010. *Mailing Add:* 280 Boston Ave Medford MA 02155

RAGUSA, ISA
HISTORIAN

b Rome, Italy, Dec 30, 1926; US citizen. *Study:* New York Univ, BA (magna cum laude), 47, Inst Fine Arts, MA, 51, PhD, 66. *Pos:* Reader & acting dir, Index Christian Art, formerly; res art hist, Princeton Univ, formerly. *Teaching:* Vis scholar, Inst Fine Arts, NY Univ, 83-84; vis prof, Univ Cattolica del Sacro Cuore, Milan, 92-93. *Mem:* Medieval Acad Am; Coll Art Asn; Renaissance Soc; Int Ctr Medieval Art. *Publ:* Coauth (with RB Green), Meditations on the Life of Christ, Princeton Univ Press, 61 & 77; auth, Porta patet vitae Sponsus vocat Intro venite and the Inscriptions of the lost Portal of the Cathedral of Esztergom, Zeitschrift fur Kunstgeschichte, 43, 77; Il manoscritto ambrosiano L 58 Sup: L'infanzia de Cristo e le fonti apocrife, Arte Lombarda, 83, 87; The iconography of the Abgar Cycle in Paris, Ms lat 2688 and its Relationship to Byzantine Cycles, Miniature, 2, 89; Mandylion-Sudarium: the 'Translation' of a Byzantine Relic to Rome, Arte Medievale, V, 91

RAHJA, VIRGINIA HELGA
PAINTER, ADMINISTRATOR

b Aurora, Minn, Apr 21, 1921. *Study:* Hamline Univ, BA, 44. *Exhib:* Walker Art Ctr; Minn State Fair, Minn Art Inst; Hamline Galleries; Coll of Visual Arts, Univ Minn; plus many other exhibs & ann. *Pos:* Asst supt fine arts, Minn State Fair, 44-48. *Teaching:* Assoc prof painting, Hamline Univ, 43-48 & dir, Hamline Galleries, 45-48; prof painting, Co of Visual Arts, St Paul, 48-65, dean, 48-73, dir and pres, 75-86. *Mem:* Coll Art Asn Am; Am Asn Univ Women. *Media:* Oil. *Interests:* Travel, reading, archeology. *Mailing Add:* 2940 E 94th Pl Apt 1019 Tulsa OK 74137-8724

RAIMONDI, JOHN
SCULPTOR

b Boston, Mass, May 29, 1948. *Study:* Mass Coll Art, BFA, 73. *Work:* Nat Mus Am Art, Smithsonian Inst, Washington, DC; Milwaukee Art Mus, Wis; Mus Fine Arts, Boston; Newark Mus, NJ; Okla Mus Art, Oklahoma City. *Comn:* Lupus, Cabot, Cabot & Forbes, Lotus Corp, Cambridge, Mass, 85; Aquila, Lincoln Prop Co, Miami, Fla, 86; Dance of the Cranes, Omaha Airport Auth, Nebr, 88; Artorius, Stanhope PLC Stockley Park Ltd, London, Eng, 89; Athleta, Univ Nebr, Kearney, 90. *Exhib:* C Grimaldis Gallery, Baltimore, 90; Helander Gallery, Palm Beach, Fla, 91; Stars in Fla, Mus Art, Ft Lauderdale, 92; Romantic Abstraction: A 20-Year Survey of Works by John Raimondi, traveling exhib (catalog), Stuart & Vero Beach, Fla, 92; The Hyde Collection, Glens Falls, NY, 92; and others. *Teaching:* Artist-in-residence, Portland Regional Vocational Tech Ctr, Maine, 75, San Angelo Independent Sch Dist, Tex, 79 & Univ Nebr, Kearney, 89. *Awards:* MacDowell Colony Fel, 82. *Bibliog:* John Raimondi: Artist-in Residence, Nat Endowment Arts, Guggenheim Productions, Washington, DC, 75; Harry Rand (auth), cover story, Arts Mag, 4/83; Dance of the Cranes, Pub Broadcasting System Documentary (film), 89. *Mem:* Mass Coun Arts & Humanities. *Media:* Bronze, Steel. *Mailing Add:* 4637 E Lake Harriet Blvd Minneapolis MN 55419-5265

RAINER, YVONNE
FILMMAKER, EDUCATOR

b San Francisco, Calif, Nov 24, 1934. *Hon Degrees:* Mass Coll of Art, Hon Dr Fine Arts, 88; RI School of School of Design, Hon Dr Fine Arts, 88; Art Inst Chicago, Hon Dr Fine Arts, 93; CA Inst of Arts, Hon Dr Fine Arts, 93. *Work:* Mus Mod Art, NY; Pac Film Arch, Berkeley, Calif; British Film Inst, London, Eng; Munich Film Mus, Ger; Australian Film Inst, Canberra, Australia. *Exhib:* retrospective, Whitney Mus, NY, 86; Carnegie Mus Art, Pittsburgh, 91; Vienna Film Casino, Vienna, 94; Am Ctr, Paris, 95; San Francisco MOMA, 97; Walter Reade Theater, 97; Ctr for Media Cult/NYU, NY, 99. *Teaching:* instr, Art Inst Chicago, 98, Columbia Univ, 99 & Whitney Mus, NY, 74-. *Awards:* Guggenheim, 69 & 98; NEA, 72, 74, 85, 88, 90 & 95; MacArthur, 90-95. *Bibliog:* Teresa deLauretis, Technologies of Gender, Indian Univ Press, 87; Peggy Phelan (auth), Unmarked: The Politics of a Performance, Routledge, 93; Shelly Green (auth), The Films of YR, Scarecrow Press, 94

RAINTREE, SHAWN
DIRECTOR

Study: USAF Acad, Grad, 1970; Univ Colo, MS (Health Admin). *Pos:* sr vpres, VHA, Inc, formerly; found, exec dir, Kaiser Permanente Colo Springs Health Plan, 1997-2007; interim pres, CEO, Colo Springs Fine Arts Ctr, 2007-. *Mem:* bd member, Colo Springs CofC, Colo Springs Symphony, formerly; chmn bd dir, mem, found, bd, Goodwill Industries, 2004. *Mailing Add:* Colorado Springs Fine Arts Center 30 W Dale St Colorado Springs CO 80903

RAISELIS, RICHARD
PAINTER, EDUCATOR

b Bridgeport, Conn, July 15, 1951. *Study:* Skowhegan Sch painting & sculpture, 72; Yale Univ, BA, 73; Tyler Sch Art of Temple Univ, MFA, 76. *Work:* Chemical Bank, NY; Exxon Corp; Fidelity Investments; Mich Bell, Detroit; Univ Iowa Mus Art; Boston Univ Photonics Ctr; Wellington Mgmt Co, Boston; Boise Mus Art, Idaho; Butler Inst of Am Art; Wright State Univ, Dayton, Ohio, 2003. *Comn:* Boston Univ, Photonics Ctr, 98; paintings, Boston Golf Club, Hingham, Mass, 2007. *Exhib:* Am Realism: 20th drawings & watercolors, San Francisco Mus Mod Art, 85; Am Acad of Arts and Letters, NY, 90, 2001; Robert Schoelkopf Gallery, NY, 91; Gerold Wunderlich & Co: The Urban Landscape, NY, 95; Nat Acad of Design, 171st Ann, NY, 96, 175th Ann, 2000; solo exhibs, Elevated Outlook: Urban Landscapes, Cedar Rapids Mus Art, Iowa, 95, Gallery NAGA, Boston, Mass, 96, 99, 2002, 2006, 2012, Roanoke Coll, 2007; Landscapes, Wright State Univ, 2003; Realism Now, Vose Contemp, Boston, 2003; Ocean View, Monserrat Coll Art, Beverly, Mass, 2004; Different Views, Washington Art Asn, Washington Depot, Conn, 2006; 181st Ann, Nat Acad Mus, NY, 2006, 185th Ann, 2010; The First Ten Years, Simmons Col, Boston, 2006; Galvanized Truth, Art Complex Mus, Duxbury, Mass, 2012; Small Matters of Great Importance, Hopper House, Nyack, NY, 2010; I-95 Triennial, Univ Maine Mus Art, 2010; Phoenix Gallery, NY, Nat Exhib, 2010; Regeneration, Painting Ctr, NY, 2012; Galvanized Truth, Art Complex Mus, Duxbury, Mass, 2012; Prince St Gallery, NY, 2011; Twist, SW Minn State Univ, Art Mus Marshall, MN, 2012. *Collection Arranged:* Pittura Figurativa Americana, Temple Univ, Rome, Italy, 88. *Teaching:* Asst prof art, Univ Mich Sch Art, 83-89 & Temple Univ, Rome, Italy, 86-88; asst prof art, Boston Univ Sch Visual Arts, 89-96, assoc prof, 96-, head painting, 2007-. *Awards:* Louis Comfort Tiffany Found Grant, 99; Purchase Prize, Am Acad of Arts and Letters, NY, 2001; Phil Desind Painting Prize, Butler Inst Am Art, Youngstown, Ohio, 2004; Artists Resource Trust Grant, Berkshire Taconic Community Found, 2005; Giovanni Martino Prize for Landscape Painting, Nat Acad Invitational Exhib Contemp Art Awards, 2010; Mass Cultural Council Fel, 2012. *Bibliog:* Judith Reynolds (auth), Out in the Open, Rochester City Newspaper, 6/89; Miles Unger (auth), Art New Eng, 4-5/96; Holland Cotter (auth), article, NY Times, 7/26/96; Andrew Forge, Ten Figurative Painters in New England: An Artist's Choice, 2000. *Mem:* AAM. *Media:* Oil. *Publ:* Auth, Don Shields, Detroit Focus Quarterly, Vol 3, No 3, 9/84. *Dealer:* Gallery NAGA 67 Newbury St Boston MA 02116. *Mailing Add:* 21 Arapahoe Rd Newton MA 02465-2202

RAISSNIA, RAHA
PAINTER
b Tehran, Iran, 1968. *Study:* Sch Art Inst Chicago, BFA, 1992; Pratt Inst, Brooklyn, MFA (Delacroix Award), 2002. *Exhib:* Works on Paper, The Drawing Room, Point Reyes Station, 2001; Art in General, Williamsburg Art & Hist Ctr, Brooklyn, 2002; solo exhibs, Court House Gallery, Anthology Film Archives, New York, 2002-03, Isfahan's Mus Contemp Art, Iran, 2004, Thomas Erben Gallery, New York, 2004-05, Miguel Abreu Gallery, New York, 2006 & 2008; Art on Paper, Weatherspoon Art Gallery, Greensboro, 2004; Report from NYC, Susquehanna Arts Mus, 2005; Holy Land: Diaspora and the Desert, Heard Mus Native Cultures & Art, Phoenix, 2006; Strip/Stripe, Emily Harvey Found, 2009; Engaging the False Mirror, Mus Contemp Art, St Louis, 2010. *Awards:* Vt Studio Ctr Fel, 1999; Pollock-Krasner Found Grant, 2008. *Bibliog:* Aaron Yassin (auth), Painting Epitaphios and Performing Systems, New York Arts Mag, 5-6/2004; Stephanie Buhmann (auth), Fall frontier on the Lower East Side: New dimensions of digital art and installations, Vol 78, No 17, The Villager, 9/24-30/2008. *Media:* Oil

RAKOCY, WILLIAM (JOSEPH)
PAINTER, HISTORIAN
b Youngstown, Ohio, Apr 14, 1924. *Study:* Butler Inst Am Art, with Clyde Singer, 39-41; Am Acad Art, 44; Kansas City Art Inst, with Ross Braught, Ed Lanning & Bruce Mitchell, MFA, 51. *Hon Degrees:* Kansas City Art Inst, MFA, 1952. *Work:* US Naval Training Sta, Great Lakes, Ill; YMCA, Youngstown; Butler Inst Am Art; El Paso Mus Art, Tex; Kid Forbes Collection, NY, Tex, NMex, Ariz, and Calif. *Comn:* Mural, Woodrow Wilson High Sch, Youngstown, 46; four murals (with Robert Sonoga & Chet Kwiecinski), McSorleys Colonial Rest, Pittsburgh, Pa, 55; three murals, YMCA, Youngstown; three murals, Mesa Inn, El Paso, Tex, 75; fourteen dioramas, Cavalry Mus & Wilderness Park Mus, El Paso, Tex, 78; 6 murals, El Paso Cancer Ctr, 2007; murals, El Paso Mus Art. *Exhib:* Butler Inst Am Art Ann, 55; Solo exhibs, Juarez, Mex, 79 & 81, El Paso Mus Art, 86, Quintas Gameros Mus, Chic City, Mex, Tapia de Oro Gallery, Ranchos de Taos, NMex, 90, Cherie Hanson show, Ruidoso, NMex. *Pos:* Founder, Bill Rakocy-Fine Arts, El Paso, Tex; cur educ, El Paso Mus Art, 71-73; cur var mus, El Paso, Tex, 73-85; installation cur, Wilderness Park Mus, 77. *Teaching:* Instr painting & drawing; prof painting & drawing, Col Artesia, 67-71; vis prof, Sull Ross State Univ, 89-; art inst, classes and lectures. *Awards:* Art Travel Grant to Study in Italy, Ital Businessmen, Kansas City, Mo, 53; Area Award in Watercolor, Butler Inst Am Art, 56-60. *Bibliog:* The Art and Times of Bill Rakocy, Bravo Press, El Paso, Tex. *Mem:* Kansas City Area Artists Asn; El Paso Art Asn; founder Rio Bravo Watercolorists; Western Asn Art Schs & Univ Mus; El Paso Hist Soc; Am Soc Appaisers. *Media:* Oil, Watercolor. *Res:* Pancho Villa Raid of Colonial New Mexico 1916. *Specialty:* Murals, Watercolors, Publications. *Interests:* Promote art auctions to assist artists via sales and scholarships; publisher of art and history books; founder and manager of Raks Art and History Museum, Ruidoso, New Mexico. *Publ:* Auth, A Western Portfolio, 65; Art Reporter, 72; Sketches & Observations, 72; Images, Paso del Norte, 79 & Villa Raids 80, Coll NMex; Mogollon Diary No 2; Auth, Taos Artists Founders, Bravo Press, El Paso, Tex, 2002; Auth, Mogollon Diary III, Bravo Press, El Paso, Tex; Taos Artists Founders, Sketch Book Documentary. *Dealer:* Prince Charming Gallery El Paso Tex; Mesila Book Store. *Mailing Add:* 4210 Emory Way El Paso TX 79922

RAKOVAN, LAWRENCE FRANCIS
PRINTMAKER, PAINTER
b Eleria, Ohio, Oct 26, 1939. *Study:* Detroit Soc Arts & Crafts; Wayne State Univ, BS; RI Sch Design, MA. *Work:* Brooklyn Mus, NY; Colby Col; Calif Coll Arts & Crafts, Oakland; Bowdoin Coll Mus Art; Univ Maine, Orono; Bates Col, Lewiston, ME. *Comn:* 14 Stations of the Cross & exterior monumental cross with stoneware reliefs of The Four Evangelists, St Charles Borromeo Church, Brunswick, Maine, 75. *Exhib:* Two-person exhib, St Peter's Ctr, NY, 73; Maine 75, Bowdoin Coll, 75; Sculpture in Wood, Maine Festival of Arts, Bowdoin Col, 77; Solo exhibs, Treat Gallery, Bates Coll, 76, Univ Southern Maine, 84 & Merrill Art Gallery, Nichols Coll, Dudley, Mass, 85; Juried competitions, Mamaroneck Artist Guild, Nat Exhib, 85, Chautauqua Nat Exhib Am Art, Chautauqua Inst, NY, 85, Fine Arts Inst, San Bernardino Co Mus, Redlands, Calif, 85, 13th Int Dogwood Arts Fest, Atlanta, Ga, 86, Springfield Art League 67th Nat, Mus Art, Mass, 86, & Arts Asn Harrisburg, Pa, 86; Sketch Book of Tibet, Univ Southern Maine Environ Studies Ctr, 98-99; Ctr Maine Contemp Art, Rockport, 2006. *Collection Arranged:* Maine to Tibet, Me Art Gallery, 99. *Pos:* Dir, Chocolate Church Art Gallery Ctr Arts, Bath, Maine, 84- 91. *Teaching:* Assoc prof painting & printmaking, Univ Southern Maine, 67-2006; vis prof art, Univ Maine, Augusta, 79-80. *Awards:* State of Maine Res Grant, 73. *Mem:* Copley Soc, Boston, Mass; Skowhegan Sch Painting & Sculpture. *Media:* Oil, Stone Lithography. *Interests:* Paintings and Textiles of Ctrl Asia; History of the ancient silk road. *Mailing Add:* 327 Maine St Brunswick ME 04011

RALAPATI, MEGHA
CURATOR, DIRECTOR
Study: Columbia Univ, BA (art hist & anthrop). *Collection Arranged:* Young Curators, New Ideas II, PPOW Gallery, 2009; Perfect Human, Dorsch Gallery, 2009. *Pos:* Dir, Bose Pacia. *Mailing Add:* 163 Plymouth St Brooklyn NY 11201

RALEIGH, HENRY PATRICK
PAINTER, WRITER
b New York, NY, Feb 5, 1931. *Study:* Pratt Inst, BS, 56 & MS, 59; New York Univ, PhD, 63. *Exhib:* The New Response, 86; Mus Hudson Highlands, 87; Rice Gallery, Albany, NY, 87; Woodstock Sch Art, 88; Park W Gallery, Kingston, NY, 94; and others. *Teaching:* Chmn art dept, Pratt Inst Art Sch, 61-68; prof painting, art criticism & aesthet, State Univ NY, New Paltz, 68-, chmn studio art & art hist, 68-74 & co-dean fac fine & performing art, 71-73. *Awards:* Travel Grant, 7th Int Am Coun Learned Soc, Cong, Rumania, 72; Prize Winner, 4th Nat Painting Exhib, Woodstock, NY. *Media:* Oils. *Res:* Application of value study to examinations of contemporary art and art criticism. *Publ:* Auth, Art and the public, 79 & The Ambiguous Art (film), 82, J Aesthetic Educ; Post Modernism in the Visual Arts, Hofstra Univ, 86; auth, Art Times (film); The Liberal Education of the Artist & Ortegay Gasset, Sch Visual Arts, NY, 87; Myth of the Artist, Sch Visual Arts, NY, 90. *Mailing Add:* 16 Deerpath Dr New Paltz NY 12561-2811

RALES, EMILY AND MITCHELL P
COLLECTOR
b 1956. *Study:* DePauw Univ, BA; Miami Univ, Ohio, grad, 1978. *Pos:* Partner, Equity Group Holdings, Washington, 1979-; pres, Danaher Corp, 1984-, bd dirs, chmn exec comt, 1990-; founder &, dir, Colfax Corp, 1995-; chmn, Capital Campaign for Hosp Sick Children; treas, trustee, and chmn, Capital Campaign of Norwood Sch; mem adv coun, Miami Univ, Ohio; bd trustees, Hirshhorn Mus and Sculpture Garden; mem trustees coun, Nat Gallery Art. *Awards:* Named one of Top 200 Collectors, ARTnews mag, 2003-13. *Collection:* Modern and contemporary art. *Mailing Add:* Danaher Corp 2099 Pennsylvania Ave Northwest 12th Fl Washington DC 20006-6800

RALES, STEVEN M
COLLECTOR
b Pittsburgh, Pa, Mar 31, 1951. *Study:* DePauw Univ, BA, 1973; America Univ, JD, 1978. *Pos:* Partner, Equity Group Holdings, 1979-; chmn bd & chief exec officer, Danaher Corp, Washington, DC, 1984-2001, chmn, 2001-. *Awards:* Named one of Top 200 collectors, ARTnews mag, 2003-13; named one of Forbes' Richest Americans, 2006. *Collection:* Modern and contemporary art; Impressionism. *Mailing Add:* Danaher Corp 2099 Pennsylvania Ave NW 12th Fl Washington DC 20006

RAMANAUSKAS, DALIA IRENA
PAINTER, DRAFTSMAN
b Kaunas, Lithuania, Jan 10, 1936; US citizen. *Study:* Southern Conn Coll, BS (art educ). *Work:* Prudential Insurance Co; Smithsonian Inst, Washington, DC; Va Mus, Richmond; Chase Manhattan Bank; Calif Palace, Legion Hon; New Britain Mus Am Art; Minneapolis Inst Art; Univ Mass Art Gallery; Dade Community Coll, Miami, Fla; Yale Art Gallery, New Haven, Ct. *Comn:* Spec drawing, Fidelity Investments, Boston, Mass, 95; Harvard Bus Sch; Parthenon Investments, Boston. *Exhib:* Am Drawing 1927-1977, Minn Mus Art, St Paul; solo exhibs, O K Harris Gallery, NY, 77-79, Capricorn Gallery, Washington, DC, 77, 82, 85, 90, 93 & 96, Stockholm Int Art Expo, 81 & Payson Weisberg, NY, 84, Playing Reality, Amarillo Mus Art, 2010; Chicago Expo, 82; Mainstream America, Butler Inst, Ohio, 87; 41st Ann Art Northeast USA, Silvermine, Conn, 90; Earth Art, Tokyo, Japan, 90; Irving Galleries, Palm Beach, Fla, 91-92; and others. *Awards:* Am Drawing 20th Ann Purchase Award, Norfolk Mus Arts & Sci, 63; Purchase Award American Drawing, Minn Mus Art, St Paul. *Bibliog:* Rev, Artforum, 4/74; M L D'Otrange Mastai (auth), Illusionism in Art, Abaris, 76; Watercolor, fall 92; Paris Rev, 76; Watercolors, Am Artist Publ, 92. *Media:* Acrylic, Oil, Watercolor. *Dealer:* Capricorn Gallery Washington DC; ALVA New London CT; Stephen Foster Fine Arts. *Mailing Add:* PO Box 264 Main St Ivoryton CT 06442

RAMIREZ, JOEL TITO
PAINTER, CALLIGRAPHER
b Albuquerque, NMex, June 3, 1923. *Study:* Univ NMex, with Randall Davey, Kenneth M Adams & Ralph Douglass; also with Enrique Montenegro & Raymond Jonson. *Work:* Mus NMex, Santa Fe; Univ Albuquerque; NMex State Univ; Univ NMex; Arthritis Found; Special Collections, Public Library 100 years Celebration, Albuquerque, NMex, Presentation and Investiture Sculpture of Immaculate Conception, 95. *Comn:* Arrival (mural), Volunteer Calvary From Pa (mural) & Modern Age (mural), Rio Rancho Hawk Missile Armory; Santa Fe Trail (mural), Fort Union, Springer, NMex; portrait, La Casa Senior Ctr, Clovis, NMex; Moon Glow (painting), Clayton Patrol Yard; San Ysibro (painting) & Toward Windmill (painting), Eunice Community Ctr, NMex; 100 Years (poster), Friends of the Libr; St. Vincent Coloring Book, Knights of Columbus Council, Village of Corrales; and many others. *Exhib:* War with Japan, 47; Fiesta Show, Mus NMex, 62; Art Intimates, Galerie de Paris, NY, 65; Museo Ibariano Arte De Norte America, Madrid, Spain, 85-86; 300 Centennial Poster Celebration, Albuquerque, NMex; Frazer Gallery, Washington, DC; Spec Collections, Ala Pub Libr; Art Exhib, Kimo Theater, 2007; State Senate, Hispanic Coll, Santa Fe, NMex, 2007. *Pos:* First vpres, NMex Art League, 58-59; assoc ed & art dir, El Clarin; art dir, Quijotes De Am. *Teaching:* Teacher oil painting, Ramirez Art Studio, 65-73. *Awards:* Anitiqua, Fine Arts Mus, Santa Fe, James T Forrest, 62; Los Trampas, Fiesta Show, Bernique Longley, 63; Nat Contest Columbus & the New World First Prize, Art Studio League, Denver, 91 & 92; and others. *Bibliog:* Jacinto Quirate (auth), Southwest Artists, Exxon Oil Co, 73 & Mexican-American Artists, Univ Tex, Austin, 74; Frank Duane (auth), Pilgrims to the West, KLRN-TV, San Antonio, Tex, 73. *Mem:* Int Soc Artists. *Media:* All Media, Oil. *Interests:* reading, history & contemporary events. *Publ:* Contribr, After Cortez, 73; illusr, Juan Diego and the Virgin of Guadalupe, 75; St Bernadette of Lourdes, 75; Across America, McDougal, Littell & Co, 86; text books for 8th grade literature 87-88 & art work studies, 88-89; Insignia, for 98th Bombardment Gr, Freedom Force, 90; Hispanic Notables of US of North America, Saquaro Publ; Ariz Highway Mag; Mexican American Artists, Quiarte Tex Libs. *Dealer:* Langell's Art Supplies 2900 Carlisle Blvd NE Albuquerque, NM 87110

RAMIREZ, LUIS SANCHEZ
FILM AND VIDEO ARTIST
Study: Art Inst Chicago, BFA; Univ Ill Chicago, MFA. *Exhib:* Seamless/Themeless: Works by Chicago Film and Video Makers, 2004; New York Int Ind Film and Video Festival, 2004; Chicago Underground Film Festival, 2004, 2007 & 2008; Hyde Park Cult Ctr, 2007; Gallery 2, 2007; Project Space, 2007; Blue Line Studio, 2008; The

Nightingale, 2008; 2008 CNEX Taiwan, Documentary Film Festival; Estacion Tijuana, Mexico. *Teaching:* Multimedia specialist, editor, Univ Ill Chicago, 2004-07, visual arts instructor, 2007-08; lectr, Depaul Univ. *Awards:* Provost Award, Univ Ill Chicago, 2006; Abraham Lincoln Fel Award, 2006-07 & Diversifying Faculty in Ill Fellowship Award, 2007, Univ Ill Chicago; Made In Chicago Award, Chicago Underground Film Festival, 2007; Art Matters Found Grant, 2008

RAMIREZ, MARI CARMEN
CURATOR
Study: Univ Puerto Rico, Rio Piedras, BA (magna cum laude), 75; Univ Chicago, MA (art hist), 76, PhD (art hist), 89; Mus Management Inst, W Asn Art Mus, Univ Calif, Berkeley, 79. *Work:* co-cur, (with Hector Olea) (exhib) Inverted Utopias: Avant-Garde Art in Latin Am, 2004, co-cur, (with Beverly Adams) Encounters/Displacements: Alfredo Jaar, Luis Camnitzer, Cildo Meireles, cur, David Alfaro Siqueiros, Cantos Paralelos: Visual Parody in Contemp Argentinean Art, Global Conceptualism: Points of Origin (Latin Am section). *Collection Arranged:* Puerto Rican Painting: Between Past and Present, Squibb Gallery, Princeton, NJ, 87; De Oller a los Cuarenta: La Pintura en Puerto Rico de 1900 a 1948, Univ Puerto Rico Mus, Rio Piedras, 87-88; Abstraccion-Figuracion/Figurative-Abstract (reinstallation), Permanent Collection Latin Am Art, Archer M Huntington Gallery, Univ Tex, Austin, 89; Liliana Porter: Retrospectiva de Obra Grafica, 1964-1990, Exposicion Homenaje, IX Bienal de San Juan del Grabado Latinoamericano y del Caribe, 91; Domingo Garcia: Icons of our History, Univ Puerto Rico Mus, Rio Piedras, 91; The School of the South: El Taller Torres-Garcia and Its Legacy, Archer M Huntington Art Gallery, Univ Tex, Austin, Centro de Arte Reina Sofia, Madrid, Spain, Mus de Arte de Monterrey, Mex, Mus Tamayo, Mex City & Bronx Mus Arts, NY, 91; Liliana Porter: Fragments of the Journey, 1968-1991 (with catalog), Bronx Mus Arts, NY, 91; Encounters/Displacements: Alfredo Jaar, Luis Camnitzer, Cildo Meireles, Archer M Huntington Art Gallery, Univ Tex, Austin, 92; Universalis (with catalog), XXIII Sao Paulo Bienal, 96; Re-Aligning Vision: Alternative Currents in South Am Drawing (with catalog), El Mus del Barrio, NY, 97, Ark Art Ctr, Little Rock, 97, Archer M Huntington Art Gallery, 98, Mus de Bellas Artes, Caracas, 98, MARCO, Monterrey, 98-99 & Miami Art Mus, 99; David Alfaro Siqueiros (with catalog), XXIV Bienal de Sao Paulo, Nucleo Historico, 98; Cantos Paralelos: Visual Parody in Contemporary Argentinean Art (with catalog), Jack S Blanton Mus Art, Austin, 99 & Phoenix Art Mus, Ariz, 99; Global Conceptualism: Points of Origin (with catalog), Queens Mus Art, NY, 99. *Pos:* Asst dir, Ponce Mus Art, 77-79; cur, Epstein Photog Arch, Dept Art, Univ Chicago, 81-82; dir, Mus Anthropology, Hist & Art, Univ Puerto Rico, Rio Piedras, 85-88; cur Latin Am Art, Jack S Blanton Mus Art & adj lectr Art Dept, Univ Tex, Austin, 89-2000; Worthman Cur, Latin Am Art Mus Fine Arts, Houston, 2001-; dir, Inter Ctr for the Arts of the Am, 2001-. *Teaching:* Instr Hist W Painting Survey, Docent Prog, Ponce Mus Art, 78-79; Mod Art Europe & Latin Am, Dept Fine Arts, Univ Puerto Rico, Rio Piedras, 88; Mex Avant-Garde, Art Hist & Inst Latin Am Studies, Dept Art, Univ Tex, Austin, 90 & 95; Multiculturalism & Visual Arts, Art Hist & Inst Latin Am Studies, Dept Art, Univ Tex, Austin, Spring 93; Globalization & Art Am, Ctr Curatorial Studies, Bard Col, Fall 98. *Awards:* Mellon Summer Res Grant, Inst Latin Am studies, Univ Tex, Austin, 91; Peter Norton Family Found Award Curatorial Excellence, 97; Getty Curatorial Residence Fel, Ctr Curatorial Studies, Bard Col, 98-99. *Mem:* Am Soc (visual arts bd, 97-); Coll Art Asn (bd dir, 90-94); Latin Am Studies Asn. *Publ:* Auth, Blue-Print Circuits: Conceptual Art and Politics in Latin America, Latin Am Art Twentieth Century, Mus Mod Art, New York, 93; Con-Sensualismo Caribeno: Las Casas de Antonio Martorell, Art Nexus, 1-3/94; co-ed, Beyond Identity: Globalization and Latin American Art, Univ Minn Press, in press; Ed & contribr, Latin American Art in the Collection of the Archer M Huntington Art Gallery, Univ Tex Press, in press; plus many others; Editor: (books) El Taller Torres-Garcia: The Sch of the South and Its Legacy, 1992; Collecting Latin America Art for the 21st Century, 2002; Questioning the Line: Gego in Context, 2003; co-auth (with Hector Olea): Inverted Utopias: Avant-Garde Art in Latin Am, 2004. *Mailing Add:* Mus Fine Arts PO Box 6826 Houston TX 77265-6826

RAMIREZ, MICHELE
PAINTER
b Calif. *Study:* Calif State Univ Stanislaus, BFA, 1992, Certificate Printmaking, 1993; Univ N Carolina Greensboro, MFA, 1995. *Work:* Envirotrans Solutions, Corp Headquarters, Oakland, Calif ; Alameda County Transportation Authority, Oakland, Calif; Kaiser Permanente, Corp Headquarters, Oakland, Calif. *Exhib:* Exhibs include Yo Soy Americana, Greensboro Cultural Arts Ctr, NC, 1996; MMMM, Abstrakt Zone, Emeryville, Calif, 1999; Obra Grafica, Carnegie Ctr Arts, Turlock, Calif, 2001; Re:Figuration, Ardency Gallery, Oakland, Calif, 2002; Ojos Indigenas, Corazon Del Pueblo Gallery, Oakland, Calif, 2004; Bay Area Celebration Arts, ArtSFest, San Francisco, 2006; Salud, Womens Cancer Resource Ctr, Oakland, Calif, 2006; Chicano Encounters: Local Places & Global Communities, de Young Mus, San Francisco, 2006; Un Lugar Solitario, Gallery Urban Art, Oakland, Calif, 2007; Nueve Mujeres, Mission Cultural Ctr Latino Arts, San Francisco, 2007. *Awards:* George Sugarman Found Grant, 2007

RAMIREZ, PAUL HENRY
PAINTER, SCULPTOR
b El Paso, Tex. *Study:* attended, Univ Tex, El Paso. *Work:* Whitney Mus Am Art, New York; Newark Mus, NJ; Hirshhorn Mus, DC; Austin Mus, Tex; NASA, DC; Smithsonian Am Art Mus, DC; Hammer Mus, LA, Calif. *Comn:* Mural, canvas, furniture, sound, Whitney Mus Am Art at Altria, New York, 2002; Mural & canvas painting, Aldrich Mus, Conn, 2004; Aluminum sculptural relief, Percent for Art, Queens, NY, 2005; Mural, canvas paintings, relief, furniture, lighting, Newark Mus, NJ, 2010. *Exhib:* Pop Surrealism, Aldrich Mus Contemp Art, Conn, 98; Space Addiction, Whitney Mus at Altria, New York, 2002; Elevatious Transcendsualistic, Tang Mus, Saratoga Springs, NY, 2002-2003; Elevatious Transcendsualistic, Contemp Arts Ctr, Cincinnati, Ohio, 2001; Extreme Abstraction, Albright-Knox Art Gallery, Buffalo, NY, 2005; NASA/Art: 50 Years of Exploration, Smithsonian's Nat Air & Space Mus, DC, 2008-2012; Blackout, Newark Mus, NJ, 2010; Smithsonian Am Art Mus, DC, 2013. *Awards:* Emerging award, Aldrich Mus, Conn. *Bibliog:* Ian Berry, Paul Henry Ramirez: Elevatious Transcendsualistic, Tang Mus, 2003; Kate Bonasinga, Lilly Wei, Natasha Goldman (auths), Seriously Playful: Paul Henry Ramirez 1995-2004, Stanlee & Gerald Rubin, Ctr Visual Arts, 2004; Adam D Weinberg, Shamin M Momin (auths), Whitney Mus Am Art at Altria 25 Years, Whitney & Yale Univ Press, 2008; Michele Cohen, Pub Art for Pub Sch, Monacelli Press, 2009; David S Rubin, Psychedelic: Optical & Visionary since the 1960s, MIT Press, 2010; Desert Modern and Beyond: El Paso Art 1960-2012. *Mem:* Whitney Mus Art, 2002-2012. *Media:* Painting, Drawing, Print, Sculpture, Ceramic, Site-Specific Installation. *Dealer:* Diane Villani Editions 285 Lafayette New York NY 10012

RAMÍREZ-MONTAGUT, MÓNICA
CURATOR
Study: MA (art & archit); PhD (theory & hist archit). *Collection Arranged:* Dennis Oppenheim: Indoors/Outdoors, Price Tower Arts Ctr, 2005, Bruce Goff: The Drunken Boat, 2005,; Prairie Skyscraper: Frank Lloyd Wright's Price Tower, traveling, 2006; Zaha Hadid, Solomon R Guggenheim Mus, NYC, 2006, Cai Guo Qiang: I Want to Believe, 2008. *Pos:* Dir, Carlos Taché Gallery, Barcelona, formerly; cur, Price Tower Art Ctr, Bartlesville, Ohio, formerly; asst cur archit & design, Solomon R Guggenheim Mus, New York, 2006-08; cur, Aldrich Contemp Art Mus, Ridgefield, Conn, 2008-. *Awards:* 2nd Place Award for Best Archit or Design Show, AICA, 2006. *Mailing Add:* Aldrich Contemp Art Mus 258 Main St Ridgefield CT 06877

RAMIREZ (ERRE), MARCOS
INSTALLATION SCULPTOR
b Tijuana, Baja California, Mexico, 1961. *Study:* Univ Autónoma de Baja Calif, Tijuana, Mex, 1978-82 . *Work:* Mus Contemp Art, San Diego, La Jolla, Calif. *Exhib:* Solo exhibs include Galería del Mar, Rosarito, Baja Calif, Mex, 1993, Cent Cultural Tijuana, Tijuana, Mex, 1996, Iturralde Gallery, Los Angeles, 1996, 1999, 2000, 2003, VI Bienal de la Habana, Havana, Cuba, 1997, Mus Contemp Art, San Diego, 1999, Intersection Arts, San Francisco, 2002, Quint Contemp Art, La Jolla, Calif, 2002; Group exhibs include UBA Unidos por el Arte, Robert Freeman Gallery, Escondido, Calif, 1993; Heroes and Sheroes, Intersection Gallery, San Diego, 1994; Artistas de Tijuana, Intersection Gallery, San Diego, 1994 ; All Am, Porter Troupe Gallery, San Diego, 1995; inSITE '97, San Diego-Tijuana, Installation, San Ysidro Border Crossing, 1997; Group Show, Iturralde Gallery, Los Angeles, 1999; Made in Calif, Los Angeles County Mus Art, Los Angeles, 2000; Whitney Biennial, Whitney Mus Am Art, New York, 2000; Interstate Five: Five Decades of Contemp Art in Calif, San Diego Mus Art, San Diego, 2001; Lateral Thinking: Art of the 1990's, Mus Contemp Art, San Diego, 2001; Here/There, Flux Gallery, San Diego, 2002; Away from Home, Wexner Ctr Arts, Columbus, Ohio, 2003 . *Awards:* US Artists Fel, 2007

RAMOS, JULIANNE
ADMINISTRATOR, CONSULTANT
b New York, NY. *Study:* Dominican Col, BA, 75; Columbia Univ, MFA, 91. *Pos:* Exec dir, Rockland Ctr Arts, 84-. *Teaching:* Adj prof, Marketing the Arts, New York Univ, spring 93; adj lectr, Goucher Coll. *Awards:* JP Getty Trust Fel, Getty Leadership Inst. *Mem:* Am Fedn Art (dirs forum); Am Asn Mus. *Dealer:* Rockland Ctr Arts New York NY. *Mailing Add:* 5 Old Farm Ct West Nyack NY 10994

RAMOS, (MEL) MELVIN JOHN
PAINTER, EDUCATOR
b Sacramento, Calif, July 24, 1935. *Study:* Sacramento Jr Col, with Wayne Thiebaud, 54; San Jose State Col, 55; Sacramento State Col, BA, 57 & MA, 58. *Work:* Mus Mod Art, NY; Neue Galerie, Aachen, Ger; Oakland Art Mus & San Francisco Art Mus, Calif; Guggenheim Mus; Indianapolis Mus; Nat Gallery, Washington, DC; DeYoung, San Francisco. *Comn:* Paintings, Time Inc, NY, 68 & Syracuse Univ, NY, 70. *Exhib:* Pop Art USA, Oakland Mus & Six More, Los Angeles Co Mus, Calif, 63; Human Concern, Personal Torment, Whitney Mus Am Art, NY, 69; Pop Art Revisited, Hayward Gallery, London, 69; Looking West, Joslyn Art Mus, Omaha, Nebr, 70; Am Pop Art, Whitney Mus Am Art, 74; Krannert Mus, Univ Ill, Champaign, 74; Cornell Univ, Ithaca, NY, 74; Retrospective, Mus Havs Lange, Krefeld, WGer, 75; solo exhib, Schaufenstergalerie, Frankfurt, Ger, 91, Louis K Meisel Gallery, NY, 91, ARTAX, Düsseldorf, Ger, 92 & Galerie B Haasner, Wiesbaden, Ger, 92; Hand-Painted Pop: Am Art in Transition, 1955-62 (catalog), Mus Contemp Art, Los Angeles, 92; Crocker Art Mus, Vienna, Austria, 2012; Modernism, San Francisco, Calif, 2013. *Teaching:* Assoc prof painting, Calif State Univ, Hayward, 66-92, prof art, 80-, prof emer. *Awards:* Nat Endowment Artist Fel, 86; US-France Exchange Fel, 86. *Bibliog:* Liz Claridge (auth), Mel Ramos, Mathews Miller Dunbar, London, 75; Mel Ramos--Watercolors, Lancaster-Miller, 79; Claudia Betti & Teel Sale (auths), Drawing: A Contemporary Approach, Chicago, 245,246, 92; Donald Kusdit (auth), Mel Ramos: Pop Art Fantasies. *Mem:* Visual Artists & Galleries Asn Inc. *Media:* Oil, Watercolor. *Interests:* Summers in Spain. *Collection:* Thiebaud, Wesselman, Warhol, Benton, Olivera. *Publ:* Contribr, History of Modern Art, 69, Erotic Art 2, 70, Art Now/New Age, 71. *Dealer:* Louis K Meisel Gallery 141 Prince St New York NY 10012; Galerie Levy Hamburg; Ernst Hilger Vienna Austria. *Mailing Add:* 5941 Ocean View Dr Oakland CA 94618

RAMOS, THEODORE
PAINTER, MURALIST
b Oporto, Portugal, Oct 30, 1928; British citizen. *Study:* Royal Acad Schs, London, Eng, RAS Dipl, 54. *Work:* Nat Portrait Gallery, London; Guildhall Chamber, Windsor, Berks, Eng; Royal Acad Arts, London; Government House, Perth, W Australia; Guards Mus. *Comn:* H M Queen Elizabeth the Queen Mother, Irish Guards, 78 & 94; mural, The Transfiguration, Distillers Company, London, 79; H R H the Duke of Edinburgh Grenadier Guards, 89; H M Queen Elizabeth II, Grenadier Guards, 91; J

Ortiz-Patiño, pres of Valderama Golf Club, the Duke of Devonshire, the Grand Duke of Luxembourg, 96. *Exhib:* Bicentenary Exhib, Royal Acad Arts, London, 68; 20th Century Portraits, Nat Portrait Gallery, London, 80 & 89. *Pos:* professional portrait painter. *Teaching:* Vis lectr fine art, Brighton Col Art, Eng, 59-65; Harrow Sch Art, Eng, 64-67; Royal Acad Arts, London, 60-84. *Awards:* Silver Medal, Royal Acad Schs, 54. *Mem:* Painter Stainers; Founders Co; E India Club; hon freeman of the Barber-Surgeons Co; Devonshire Soc of St James; Devonshire Soc St James (founder, 66). *Media:* Oil. *Interests:* classical music, illuminate manuscripts. *Publ:* Illusr, Chinese Art, Pelican & Thames & Hudson, 55; Monumental Brasses, Penguin Books, 57. *Dealer:* Portraits Inc 985 Park Ave New York NY 10028; Harley Art Brokers 13 Overstrand Mansions Prince of Wales Dr London SW11 4HA. *Mailing Add:* Studio 3 Chelsea Farm House Milmans St London United Kingdom SW10 OBY England

RAMSEY, DOROTHY J
PAINTER, WRITER
b Northampton, Mass, May 1, 1935. *Study:* Northampton Commercial Col, 54; Smith Col, 75-76; pvt study with Helen Van Wyk, Roger Curtis & Michael Stoffa. *Work:* New England Telephone. *Exhib:* Burr Artists Ann Exhibs, NY, 82-85; Salmagundi Club Ann Exhibs, NY, 82-87 & 90-; North Shore Arts Asn, Gloucester, Mass, 82-; Rockport Art Asn, Mass, 84-. *Pos:* Dir & instr oil painting, Ramsey Art Studio, 77-80; owner & operator, Michael Stoffa Gallery, Rockport, Mass, 80-. *Teaching:* Ramsey Art Studio, Northampton, MA,77-80. *Mem:* Rockport Art Asn; North Shore Arts Asn, Gloucester, Mass (secy, 80-84, mem bd, 80-90); Salmagundi Club, NY; Artist Fel, NY. *Media:* Oil. *Specialty:* Paintings & Prints, Traditional. *Publ:* Best Poems of 2000, "Wintry Day", In: Poetry's Elite. *Dealer:* Michael Stoffa Gallery. *Mailing Add:* c/o Michael Stoffa Gallery 5 Wildon Heights Rockport MA 01966

RANALLI, DANIEL
ARTIST, EDUCATOR
b New Haven, Conn, Oct 17, 1946. *Study:* Clark Univ, Worcester, Mass, BA, 68; Boston Univ, MA, 71. *Work:* Boston Mus Fine Arts; San Francisco Mus Mod Art; Mus Mod Art, NY; Baltimore Mus Fine Arts; Rose Art Mus, Brandeis Univ, Waltham, Mass; and others. *Comn:* New Works, Mass Council Arts, Photographic Resource Ctr, 81. *Exhib:* Solo exhibs, Mass Inst of Technol Photog Gallery, 77, Foto Gallery, NY, 78, Carl Siembab Gallery, Boston, 78-79 & 82, Brent Sikemma Gallery, Boston, 83, Vision Gallery, Boston, Alfred Univ, NY, 94 & DNA Gallery, Provincetown, 95-97, 99, 2001-2002; Group exhibs, Worcester Art Mus, 78, Addison Gallery Am Art, 80, RH Fleming Mus, Univ Vt, 80, Southern Alleghenies Mus Art, 81, Inst Contemp Art, Boston, 81, Boston Mus Fine Arts, 81, 2001, San Francisco Mus Mod Art, Baltimore Mus Fine Arts, 81, 89, Provincetown Art Mus, 82, Fuller Art Mus, 83, Franklin Institute Mus, 83, DeCordova Mus, Mass, 87, 2000, St Petersburg Mus Fine Arts, 87, Harvard Fogg Art Mus, 89, Fitchburg Art Mus, 91, Rose Art Mus, Mass, 92, Provincetown Art Mus, 99, Duxbury Art Mus, 99; and many more. *Collection Arranged:* Elements of Landscape, Boston Univ Art Gallery, 83 & Earthworks, 89. *Pos:* Prog dir, The Artists Found, 75-79; exec dir, Truro Ctr Arts, 79-81; actg dir, Boston Univ Art Gallery, 82-83; dir, Arts Admin Prog, Lesley Coll Grad Sch, Cambridge, Mass, 84-92, Boston Univ, 92-, founding dir & assoc prof, grad prog arts admin. *Teaching:* Prof, Lesley Coll Grad Sch, Cambridge, 84-92; assoc prof art hist dept, Boston Univ, currently. *Awards:* Individual Artist Fel, Nat Endowment Arts, 81; Mass Arts Lottery Grant, 83; Earthwatch Artists Fel, 93. *Bibliog:* article, Camera Arts, 5/83; C Temin (auth), Mingling scientific detachment & personal passion, Boston Globe, 12/7/89; numerous others. *Mem:* Mass Alliance Art Educ (bd trustees, 76-79); Photog Resource Ctr, Boston; Boston Visual Artists Union (vpres, 77); Am Asn Mus; Coll Art Asn. *Publ:* Auth, Forum (monthly column), Art New Eng, 82; coauth, Darkroom Dynamics, Curtin & London, 78; contrib ed, Provincetown Arts, Mass; Daniel Ranalli: Projects & Photographs, 94; auth, Daniel Ranalli-Asian Work (exhib catalog), 2004. *Dealer:* Artstrand Gallery Provincetown MA; Gallery Kayafas Boston MA. *Mailing Add:* 75 Richdale Ave Cambridge MA 02140

RAND, ARCHIE
PAINTER, MURALIST
b New York, NY, Aug 13, 1949. *Study:* City Coll New York, 65-66; Art Students League NY, 67-68; Pratt Inst, Brooklyn, BFA, 70. *Work:* Montclair Art Mus; Bibliotheque Nationale, Paris; San Francisco Mus Mod Art; Jewish Mus, NY; Casa Italiana, Columbia Univ. *Comn:* 12 stained glass windows, Anshe Emet Synagogue, Chicago, 80; three stained glass windows, Temple Sholom, Chicago, 83; exterior murals, Michlalah Col, Jerusalem, 83; murals, Fresco, Hebrew Home Greator Wash, 87, Chapters, Freyer Found, NY, 88; Castellani Art Mus (with Robert Creeley), Buffalo, 98. *Exhib:* Solo exhibs, Columbia Univ, 95, Univ Wis, 97, Aljira Ctr Contemp Art, NJ, 98, Jewish Mus Md, 98 & Interchurch Ctr, NY, 98; Columbia Univ, 92; Centre l'Echange de Perrache, France, 93; Worcester Mus, Mass, 94; Feigensen-Preston Gallery, Detroit, Mich, 91 & 92; Schmidt-Dean Gallery, Philadelphia, 91, 92 & 95; Baum Gartner Gallery, Washington, 91 & 95; John Post Lee Gallery, NY, 92; Philadelphia Mus Art, 92; and others. *Pos:* Designer, Rambusch Stained Glass Studios, 83, Edward Fields Tapestries Inc 83-84 & Xicon Animation Inc, 87; US rep, UNICEF Art Coun, 85-; acting dir, Hoffberger Grad Sch Painting, Md Inst, 89-90; co-chair, Studio Arts Prog, Col Art Asn, 92-94, chair, 94-; acq comt, George Mus, NY, 92-. *Teaching:* Vis prof, State Univ Ill, Normal, 84, Va Commonwealth Univ, 85, Columbia Univ, RI Sch Design, State Univ NY, Albany, Brooklyn Col, 90 & Univ Syracuse, 91; grad fac, Bard Col, 86-91 & Sch Visual Arts, 88-91 & 93-; assoc dir grad prog, Md Inst Col Art, 89-; prof art, Columbia Univ, 92-; artist-in-residence, Hoffberger Grad Sch Painting & Mt Royal Grad Sch Art, Md Inst, Col Art, 92-93; dir painting & drawing, Columbia Univ, NY, 97-. *Awards:* Engelhard Award, 85; awards, Visual Arts, 87; NY Found Arts Fel, 90; The Sienna Award, Ital Acad Advanced Studies in Am, 95; Lifetime Achievement Award for contrib to Visual Arts. *Bibliog:* Barry Schwabsky (auth), Archie Rand connections, Art Mag, 6/84; John Yau (auth), Archie Rand, Art Forum, 86; Barry Schwabsky (auth), What is painting about--a conversation with Archie Rand, ARTS Mag, 4/87. *Mem:* Nat Soc Mural Painters (bd mem); Int Soc Film Animators; IFRAA Am Inst Architects. *Media:* Acrylic on Canvas; Stained Glass, Fresco. *Publ:* Auth, The victory of the futile, ARTS Mag, 11/88; Trevor Winkfield's good show, Arts, 9/89; illusr, Two or Three Things, Collective Generation, 90; coauth (with Malcolm Morley), Sensation without memory, Tema Celeste, No 32-3, autumn 91. *Mailing Add:* 326 55th St Brooklyn NY 11220

RAND, HARRY
HISTORIAN, EDUCATOR
b New York, NY, Jan 10, 1947. *Study:* City Coll New York, BA, 69; Harvard Univ, AM, 71, PhD, 74. *Pos:* Contrib ed, Arts Mag, New York, 75-92; cur 20th century painting & sculpture, Nat Mus Am Art, Washington, 79-93, Sr cur, 93-; hon ed, Leonardo, Berkeley, 83-; consult, Nat Acad Sci, 84, Consanti Found, 89-, World Bank, 94-95; sr cur cult history, Smithsonian Inst, Wash. *Teaching:* Asst prof mod art & methodology, State Univ NY, Buffalo, 74-76. *Awards:* Rockefeller Found Develop Grant, 83; Smithsonian Inst Res Opportunities Grant, 85, 87, 90 & 91; Scholarly Studies Grant, Smithsonian Inst, 87-95; Getty Found Curatorial Fel, 2003. *Bibliog:* Hilton Kramer (auth), The pictures in the paintings, 6/21/81 & A true museum of record, 2/14/82, NY Times; Washington Times, Black Angel: The Life of Arshille Gorky, by Eric Gibson, April 30, 2000, pg B 7-8; Christian Science Monitor, A Building With Wavy Floors and Rooftop Tress, May 10, 2000, Shira J. Boss, p 14; New York Times, July 12 2000, Life Story of an Artist Who Embraced Mystery, by Roberta Smith, p B 8; German Life, June/July 2000, Jochen Seidel by Ferdinand Protzman, pg 16-19; New Times (Phoenix, AZ) October 21, 2002, Exile Adrift by Deborah Sussman Susser; Washington Post, December 5, 2002, Preserving A Tradition and Views of a Capital, by Judith Havemann; New York Observer December 8, 2003, Gorky's Oeuvre: Despite Hommages, Works Were Diary by Hilton Kramer, p1; 20; David M. Knight Playing God with the World, Endeavor (UK) vol 28, #3, September 2004, p 90-91; Beth Py-Lieberman, George Washington Sat Here, From the Attic, Smithsonian Mag, February, 2005, p 48. *Mem:* Explorers Club, NY. *Res:* History of modern art; problems of methodology and implications. *Publ:* Auth, Manet's Contemplation at the Gare St Lazare, UCal Press, 87; Paul Manship, Smithsonian Press, 89; Hundertwasser, Taschen, 91; Gorky, UCBC Press, 91; Julian Stanczak, State Univ NY, 92; auth, Color: Suite in Four Parts, DOV Press, 93; auth, The Clouds, DOV Press, 96; contbr, The Dictionary of Art, MacMillan Ltd; coauth, From Idea to Matter, Anderson Gallery Publ, 2005; auth numerous exhibition catalogs including Vincent Pepi, Art Gallery, NY State Univ at Stony Brook, 96, Merrill Mahaffey: Cue from Manet, Palm Springs Desert Mus, 00, From Idea to Matter: 9 Sculptors, Anderson Gallery, Va Commonwealth Univ, 00, William Scharf: History Painter, essay in Phillips Collection, Washington, 00. *Mailing Add:* 5511 Greystone St Chevy Chase MD 20815-5556

RANDALL, COLLEEN
PAINTER
b Sauk Ctr, Minn, 1952. *Study:* Macalester Coll, St Paul, Minnesota, BA (Art History), 1975; Univ Iowa, BFA (Painting), 1980; Queens Coll, MFA (Painting), 1983. *Exhib:* Solo exhibs include Paul Klapper Libr, Queens Coll, New York, 1986, Hood Mus, Dartmouth Coll, NH, 1989, Room 308, New York, 1997, Elliot Smith Contemp Art, St Louis, 2001, Painting Ctr, New York, 2001, 2005, Spheris Gallery, New York, 2002, New England Coll Art Gallery, NH, 2003; Group exhibs include Invitational Show, 55 Mercer St Gallery, New York, 1987; National Juried Show, Bowery Gallery, New York, 1993; Gallery Group Show, Elliot Smith Gallery, St Louis, 1993, 1994; Annual Exhib, National Acad Design, New York, 1994, 2002, 2008; Artists & Poets, Grayson Gallery, Woodstock, Vt, 1997; Works on Paper, Armory Show, New York, 1998, 1999; Works on Paper Invitational, Oxbow Gallery, Northampton, MA, 2005; Inaugural Exhib, Spheris gallery, Hanover, NH, 2006, Selected Works, 2006. *Mailing Add:* Ober Gallery 14 Old Barn Road Kent CT 06757

RANDALL, LILIAN M C
CURATOR
b Berlin, Ger, Feb 1, 1931. *Study:* Mt Holyoke Col, BA, 50; Radcliffe Col, MA, 51, PhD, 55; Hon degree, Towson State Univ, 93. *Work:* Walters Art Gallery, Baltimore, Md. *Collection Arranged:* Armenian Manuscripts, Walters Art Gallery, Baltimore, Md, 74; Printed Books before 1500, Walters Art Gallery, 77; Splendor in Books, Grolier Club, NY, 77-78; An Am Art Agent in Paris, George A Lucas (1857-1909), Walters Art Gallery, 78-79; Illuminated Manuscripts: Masterpieces in Miniature, Highlights from the Collection of the Walters Art Gallery, 84-85. *Pos:* Asst dir, Md Arts Coun, 72-73; cur manuscripts & rare books, Walters Art Gallery, 74-95. *Teaching:* Vis lectr medieval illumination, Johns Hopkins Univ, 64-68. *Awards:* Phi Betta Kappa, Sesquicentennial Award, Mount Holyoke Col, 87. *Mem:* Grolier Club; Int Ctr Medieval Art (bd dir, 78-82, 95-98); Baltimore Bibliophiles (pres, 81-83). *Res:* Medieval and Renaissance European illumination. *Publ:* auth, The Diary of George A Lucas: An American Art Agent in Paris, (2 vols), Princeton Univ Press, 79; auth, A Nineteenth-Century Medieval Prayerbook Woven in Lyon, In: Art the Ape of Nature: Studies in Honor of HW Janson, Harry N Abrams, 81; auth & ed, Medieval and Renaissance Manuscripts in the Walters Art Gallery: France, 875-1420, 89 & 1420-1540, 92, & Belgium 1250-1530, 97, Johns Hopkins Univ Press

RANDLETT, MARY WILLIS
PHOTOGRAPHER
b Seattle, Wash, May 5, 24. *Study:* Whitman Col, BA, 47; photog with Hans Jorgensen, Seattle, 48. *Work:* Dept Photog & Prints, Metrop Mus Art, NY; Arch Am Art, Nat Collection Fine Arts, Nat Portrait Gallery, Washington, DC; Manuscripts Div & Spec Collections, Univ Wash Collections, Seattle; Wash State Capitol Mus, Olympia, Wash; Western Wash State Univ, Bellingham; Bruce Mus, Greenwich, Conn; Cheney Cowles Mem Mus, Spokane, Wash; Henry Gallery, Seattle, Wash; The Burke Mus, Seattle, Wash; over 40 permanent collections. *Comn:* Wash State Artists (photog), Wash State Libr, Olympia, 68; doc ser (photogs), Noguchi Skyviewing sculpture, Western Wash Univ, Bellingham, 70, Tony Angell's "Owls", Pacific NW Bell, Seattle, 78, Artists, Everett, 80, 4 artists for Kingdome, King Co Arts Comn, Seattle, 78-80, Wash. *Exhib:* Solo Exhibs: Northwest Portfolio: The Photog of Mary

Randlett, Off of the Gov, Olympia, Wash, 91; Stonington Gallery, Seattle, Wash, 92; Grad Sch Design, Dept Landscape Archit, Harvard Univ, 96; Inside Back Cover: Lit Portraits of Mary Randlett,Tacoma Pub Libr, Tacoma, Wash, 97; The Light and The Landscape, Hendersons House, Tumwater, 98; Portraits of Writers, Northwest Bookfest, Pier 48, Seattle, 98; In Love With Light, Mus Northwest Art, 99 Liquid Light, Port Angeles Fine Arts Ctr, 2000; Mary Randlett and The Creative Neighborhood Safeco Plaza, Seattle, 2002; Mary Randlett Portraits on the Arts Community, Wright Exhib Square, Seattle, 2002-2003; Northwest Masters Selection, City of Seattle's One Percent For Art City Space, 2004; Walla Walla Community Col, Wash, 2004; Wash State Libr, Olympia, 2005; Ecology Building, Lacey, Wash, 2005; Skinner Bldg, Univ Wash, Seattle, 2005-2006; Veiled Northwest: Mary Randlett Landscapes, Tacoma Art Mus, 2007; Portraits of Writers, Univ Wash Press, Seattle, 2007-; Mary Randlett Photographs Special Collections, Univ Wash, 2007; Group Exhibs: Blue Prints: 100 Yrs of Seattle Architecture, Mus Hist & Indust, Seattle, Wash, 94; Sequoia Miller Transplants: Pottery, Place & the Pacific Northwest, Univ Portland, 2006; Building Tradition: Northwest Art from the Collection, Tacoma Art Mus, 2007; Seattle Public Market Special Collections, Univ Wash, 2007; Rain: A Group Exhib, Stonington Gallery, Seattle, 2007; Retrospective, Port Angeles Fine Art Center, 2007; Stumps & Clear Cuts, Grays Harbor Coll, Aberdeen, Wash, 2007; Artist's Portraits, Tacoma Art Mus, 2007; Celebrating Puget Soundscape, Stonington Gallery, 2007; River History, Skagit Valley Hist Mus, Wash, 95; Seattle Comes to Christ Church, Christ Church, NZ, 96; Guy Anderson: In Celebration, Mus NW Art, Wash, 96; Northwest Landscape: Clayton James, Mary Randlett, Paul Havas, Lucia Douglas Gallery, Wash, 96; Present & Future: Architecture in Cities, XIX Congress of the Int Union of Architects Barcelona, Spain, 96; Guy Anderson Northwest Master, Seattle Art Mus, 96; Philip McCracken Bronzes, Valley Mus Northwest Art, La Conner, Wash, 93 & Jacob Lawrence, 97; Jacob Lawrence, Instrument of Change: James Schoppert 1947-1992, Anchorage Mus Hist & Art, Anchorage, Alaska, 97 & Burke Mus Nat Hist & Cult, Seattle, Wash, 98; A Century of Photographs of the Western Landscape: The Paving of Paradise, Seattle Art Mus, Seattle, Wash, 98; 18th Ann Northwest Inter Art Comp, Whatcom Arco Exhib Gallery, Bellingham, Wash, 98; George Tsutakawa, Seattle Art Mus, 98; A Tribute to Del McBride, Henderson House Mus, Tumwater, Wash, 98 & Wash State Capital Mus, Olympia, 99; From Tractors to Tornadoes: Photographers of the Rural Landscape, Whatcom Mus, Bellingham, Wash, 99; 14th Ann Works from the Heart, Cheney Cowles Mus, Spokane, Wash, 99; Rock, Paper, Scissors, Henderson House Mus, Tumwater, 99; The View from Here: 100 Artists Mark the Centennial of Mount Rainier Nat Park, Mus Northwest Art, Laconner, Wash, 2000; Instrument of Change: James Schoppert Retrospective, Mus Am Indian, New York City, 99; Olympia Through Artists Eyes, Wash State Capitol Mus, 2000; Morris Graves: Journey Mus of Northwest Art La Conner, Wash, 2000; Leo Kenny: Celebrating the Mysteries, A Retrospective, Mus of Northwest Art, 2000; The Governors Heritage Award 1989-2000, Olympic, Wash, 2001; Over the Line: The Art and Life of Jacob Lawrence, The Phillips Collection, Washington, DC, 2002; Roderick Haig-Brown Exhib, Campbell River Mus, BC, 2002; Iridescent Light Artists and Portraits, Rainier Club, Seattle, 2002; Jacob Lawerence Seattle Art Mus, Seattle WA, 2003; New Acquisition for the Collection Tacoma Art Mus, Tacoma, 2003; John Cole Whatcom Mus, Bellingham, WA, 2003; Philip McCracken: 600 Moons, MONA, La Conner, Wash, 2004; Mary Randlett: Nature Photographs, Lucia Douglas Gallery, Bellingham, Wash, 2005; Sequoia Miller-Transplants: Pottery, Place & the Pacific Northwest, Univ Portland, Ore, 2006; Mary Randlett: Artist's Portraits, Hallie Ford Mus Art, Salem, Ore, 2009; Harry Widman: Image, Myth and Modernism, Hallie Ford Mus Art, Salem Ore, 2009; Tacoma Art Mus, 2010; Grays Harbor Coll, Wash, 2010; Wessel Leiberman, Seattle, Wash, 2010; Stonington Gallery, Seattle, 2009; Fishtown & the Skagit River, Wash, 2010; Show of Hands, North West Women Artists, Whatcom Mus, Wash, 1880-2010. *Awards:* Gov Award, Wash, 83; Individual Artists Award, King Co Arts Comn, Seattle, 89; GAP Award, Artists Trust, 89 & 92; Allied Arts Grants, 98; Matrix Table, Woman of Achievement, Seattle, Wash, 99; Allied Arts Found Grant, 2000; Nancy Blankenship Pryor Award Recipient, 2001; Artists Trust Lifetime Achievement Award, 2001; Honorary Mem of Seattle Chap of Am Inst of Architects, 2002; Hist Makers Award-Mus of Hist and Industry, Seattle, 2003; Alumnus of Merit Award Whitman Col, 2003. *Bibliog:* Robert Atwan & Valeri Vinokurov (auths), Openings: Original Essays by Contemporary Soviet and American Writers, Univ Wash Press, Seattle, Wash, 90; Arthur Kruckeberg (auth), The Natural History of Puget Sound Country, Univ Wash Press, Seattle, Wash, 91; Jim Rupp (auth), Mary Randlett (photogr), Art in Seattle's Public Places, Univ Wash Press, Seattle, 92; Marilyn Symmes (ed), Fountains: Splash and Spectacle, Water and Design from the Renaissance to Present, Rizzoli Int, 98; Mark Tobey (artist), Museo Nat Centro de Arte Reina, Sofia, Spain, 98; Clark Humphry (auth), Vanishing Seattle, Arcadia Press, 2006; Richard Rapport (auth), Physician: The Life of Paul Beeson, 2007; Ruth Kirk & Richard Daugherty (coauths), Archaeology in Washington, Univ Wash Press, 2007; Rebecca Alexander (auth), Mary Randlett's Landscape Photography: An Eye to See, Wash Park Aboretum Bulletin, winter 2009. *Mem:* Am Soc Mag Photogr; AIA Seattle (hon mem), 2002. *Publ:* Chinese Influence on the American West Coast Contemporary Art, Taiwan Mus Art, Taiwan, 88; Auth, To Know a River, Roderick Haig-Brown, Lyons Burford, New York, 96; The Confederate Raider in the North Pacific: The Saga of the SCC Shenandoah, 1864-65, Wash State Univ Press, 96; Sine Die: A guide to the Washington State Legislative Process, 1977 edition, Edward D See Berger, Univ Wash Press, 96; Seeing with Music: The Lives of Three Blind African Musicians, Simon Ottenberg, Univ Wash Press, 96; The Eighth Lively Art, Wesley Wehr, Univ Wash Press, Seattle, 2000; Seattle Waterways, J Scott Rohrer, Pudget Sound Maritime Hist Soc, Seattle, 2001; Geology & Plant Life, Arthur Kruckeberg, Univ Wash Press, Seattle, 2001; John Hoover, Art & Life, Julie Decker, Univ Wash Press, Seattle, 2002; John Cole, Deloris Tarzan Ament, Whatcom Mus, Bellingham, 2003; 600 Moons: 50 Years of Philip McCracken's Art, Deloris Tarzan Ament, Univ Wash Press, Seattle, 2004; The Quick, Katrina Roberts, Univ Wash Press, Seattle, 2005; Sketchbook: The 30s & the Northwest School, William Cumming, Univ Wash Press, Seattle, 2006; auth, Mary Randlett Landscapes, Univ Wash Press, 2007; Archaeology in Washington, Ruth Kirk, Richard Daugherty, Univ Wash Press, Seattle, 2007; Mark Di Suvero: Dreambook, Mark Di Suvero, Univ Calif Press, 2008; Joe Feddersen: Vital Signs, Rebecca J Dobkins, Univ Wash Press, Seattle, 2009; Harry Widman: Image, Myth and Modernism, Roger Hull, Univ Wash Press, Seattle, 2009; Henry Klein, Architect: Pilgrim On a Journey, Richard Lee Francis; Puget Sound Through an Artist's Eye: Tony Angell, Univ Wash Press, Seattle, 2009; Robert B Heilman: His Life in Letters, Univ Wash Press, 2009; The car that brought you here still runs, Frances McCue, Mary Randlett, Univ Wash Press, 2010; The Visionary Art of Morris Graves, Meridian Gallery, San Francisco, 2010; Henk Pander by Roger Hull, Memory and Modern Light, Hallie Ford Mus. *Dealer:* Martin/Zambito 1117 Minor Ave Seattle WA 98101. *Mailing Add:* PO Box 11238 Olympia WA 98508-1238

RANDOLPH, LYNN MOORE
PAINTER
b New York, NY, Dec 19, 1938. *Study:* Univ Tex, Austin, BFA, 1961. *Work:* The Mary Ingraham Bunting Inst, Radcliffe/Harvard; The Menil Collection, Houston; Ariz State Univ Mus; Nat Mus Women in Arts; San Antonio Mus Fine Arts; The Houston Mus Fine Arts; Harvard Univ, Mass; and others. *Exhib:* solo shows incl Contemp Arts Mus, Houston, 1978, Graham Gallery, 1984, 1986 & 1991, The Texas Landscape 1900-1986, Mus Fine Arts, Houston, 1986, Bunting Inst, Radcliffe Coll, 1990, Everyday Miracles: Retablos, Ex Votos and Contemp Texas Artists, Contemp Art Mus, Houston, Tex, 1990 & Virgins in Vertigo and Juicy Women, Lynn Goode Gallery, 1995, Joan Wich Gallery, 2003 & 2006; group shows incl The Vulnerable Body, Artscan Gallery, 2000; Waco Art Center, Tex, 2001; D Berman Gallery, Austin, Tex, 2002; Spirits on the Coast, Joan Wich Gallery, 2003; Democracy in Am, Ariz State Univ Mus, Tempe, Ariz, 2004; Cover Art, The Nation, Sept 13, 2004 & May 21, 2007; Joan Wich Gallery, Houston, 2006; Thrive, Diverse Works, Houston, Tex, 2008; Lines of Attach, Nasher Mus, Duke Univ, 2010; Substantiis Corpus Mixti the Synergies Exhib of the Bask, Rotterdam & Stockholm Conventions, United Nations, New York, 2010; Human Rights Exhib, South Tex Coll, 2014; Mural, Total Plaza, Houston, 2014; The Station Mus, Houston, 2013. *Awards:* Residency at Yaddo, June 1987; Fel, The Bunting Inst, Radcliffe Coll, 1989-90. *Bibliog:* Articles in Houston Press, 1993-97; Donna Harawa (auth), Modest Witness, Second Millennium, 1996; Deborah J Haynes (auth), The Vocation of the Artist, Cambridge Univ Press, 1997; Jeffrey Kripal Wiley (auth), Comparing Religions, Blackwell, 15 images, 2014. *Mem:* Nat Women's Caucus Art (regional vpres, 1982-86); Houston Women's Caucus Art (pres, 1979-80); Lawndale Art Ctr (artist bd, 1992-95). *Media:* Oil. *Publ:* Auth, Beyond political and economic equality, Women Artists' News, 1983; A Return to Alien Roots: Painting Outside Mainstream Western Culture, Radcliff Papers, 1990. *Dealer:* Joan Wich Gallery, Houston, TX. *Mailing Add:* 1803 Banks Houston TX 77098

RANKAITIS, SUSAN
MIXED MEDIA ARTIST, PHOTOGRAPHER
b Cambridge, Mass, Sept 10, 1949. *Study:* Univ Ill, Champaign, BFA (painting), 71; Univ Southern Calif, Los Angeles, MFA (painting & photog), 77. *Work:* Ctr Creative Photog, Tucson, Ariz; San Francisco Mus Mod Art, Calif; Los Angeles Co Mus Art, Calif; Nat Mus Am Art; Art Inst, Chicago; Mus Contemp Art, San Diego; MOCA, Los Angeles. *Exhib:* Solo exhibs, Los Angeles Co Mus Art, 83, Meyers/Bloom, Santa Monica, Calif, 89 & 90, Schneider Mus, 90, Ctr Creative Photog, 91, Ruth Bloom Gallery, Santa Monica, 92, Robert Mann Gallery, NY, 94 & 97, 2007, Mus Contemp Photog, Chicago, 94, Mus of Photog Arts, 2000 & Europos Parkas, Vilnius, Lithuania, 2005; group exhib, San Francisco Mus Mod Art, 87 & 89, Santa Fe Art Mus, 87, Axiom Ctr Arts, Eng, 87-88, Los Angeles Co Mus Art, 88 & 2000, Nat Mus Am Art, 89, Tokyo Metrop Mus Photog, 96; NC Mus Art, 2004; Kunstmuseums Ahen, Wortzberg, 2007; Pulse Miami, 2008; Mus Photographic Art, 2010; Am Art Mus, Smithsonian, 2013. *Pos:* Selector, Bingham Educ Trust, 97-2002. *Teaching:* Fletcher Jones chair in art (prof), Scripps Col. *Awards:* Avery Fel to China, 2001; Artist Scholar in Residence, Borchard Found, 2004; Award in Visual Arts, Flintridge Found, 2004. *Bibliog:* Andy Grundberg & Kathleen Gauss (auths), Photography and Arts Interactions Since 1946, Abeville Press; Susan Kandel (auth), Susan Rankaitis, Meyers/Bloom Gallery, 90; Denise Miller Clark (auth), Susan Rankaitis, Abstracting Technology, Science & Nature, 94, Mus Contemp Photog, Chicago; Diana Gaston (auth), Susan Rankaitis: Drawn From Science, 2000; Lyle Rexer (auth), The Antiquarian Avant-Garde, 2002; Paschal & Dougherty (auths), Defying Gravity: Contemporary Art & Flight; Michael Ned Holte (auth), Limbicwork, 2007; Lyle Rexer (auth), The Edge of Vision, 2009; Lynn Keinholz (auth), LA Rising, 2010; Gary Badger (auth) The Pleasure of Good Photographs, 2010. *Mem:* Coll Art Asn. *Media:* Miscellaneous Media. *Interests:* Neuroscience, politics, Los Angeles hist. *Dealer:* Robert Mann Gallery 525 W 26th St New York NY 10001. *Mailing Add:* 3117 Lansbury Claremont CA 91711

RANKIN, DON
PAINTER, INSTRUCTOR
b Dec 9, 1942. *Study:* Famous Artists' Sch; also with Bill Yeager; Samford Univ, BA (fine art & psychol); Union Inst, Cincinnati, PhD Visual Art. *Comn:* Birmingham Centennial Commemorative Coins, Arlington Shrine, 70, Univ Ala Med Complex, 71 & Birmingham-Jefferson Civic Ctr, 71; prints, First Nat Bank, Tuscaloosa, 74-76; painting, Country Club Birmingham, 79; Watercolor & print, comn by Air War Coll, class 90, Maxwell AFB, Montgomery, Ala; and others. *Exhib:* The Am Barn & Its Translation in Watercolor, Chautauqua Art Asn Exhib Am Art, New York, 79; 3rd Ann Exhib Southern Watercolor Soc, N Tex State Univ Galleries, Denton, 79; Southern Connections - a Nat Invitational, Blount Collection, Montgomery, Ala, 86; Invitational Exhib, Southern Watercolor Painters, Takarazuka, Japan, 90; 16th Ann Juried Exhib, Southern Watercolor Soc, Strathmone Hall, Baltimore, 93; Ala Artists Traveling Exhib, Wiregrass Mus Art, Dothan, Ala; 17th Ann Juried Exhib, Southern Watercolor Soc, The Parthenon, Nashville, Tenn, 94; PhD exhib, Samford Univ, 98; Energen Corp, 2013. *Teaching:* Instr, nat & int watercolor workshops, var art asns; asst prof, Samford Univ. *Bibliog:* Featured artist, watercolor page, Am Artist, 3/80; Elizabeth Leonard (auth), Painting the Landscape, Watson-Guptill; Watercolor 89, Am Artist; revs, New York Art Rev, 89, Am Artist (video), 6/90 & Artist's Mag (video), 7/90.

Mem: Ala Watercolor Soc; charter mem La Watercolor Soc; Southern Watercolor Soc; Indian Arts & Crafts Asn; patron Portrait Soc Am; assoc mem Oil Painters of Am; Coll Art Assn. *Media:* Watercolor, Egg Tempera, Oil. *Res:* Papermaking among N Am Indians. *Interests:* Shawnee Hist. *Publ:* Auth, Mastering Glazing Techniques in Watercolor, 86, Painting from Sketches, Photographs and Imagination, 87, Fifty Most Asked Questions About Watercolor Glazing Techniques, 91 & All You Ever Wanted to Know about Watercolor, 7/93, Watson-Guptill; Mastering Glazing Techniques in Watercolor, Vol I, 2011. *Mailing Add:* 3412 Wellford Cir Birmingham AL 35226

RAPOPORT, SONYA
CONCEPTUAL ARTIST
b Boston, Mass. *Study:* Mass Coll Art; New York Univ, BA; Univ Calif, Berkeley, MA. *Work:* Stedelijk Mus, Amsterdam, Holland; Grey Art Gallery, New York Univ; Indianapolis Mus Art, Ind; Oakland Art Mus, Calif; Crocker Art Mus, Sacramento, Calif; NY Mus Mod Art. *Comn:* Abstract painting (acrylic/canvas), Hall of Justice, Hayward, Calif, 76. *Exhib:* One-person shows, Calif Palace Legion Honor & Crocker Art Mus, 64 & 74, Peabody Mus, Harvard Univ, Cambridge, Mass, 76 & Kuopio Mus, Finland, 92; Art Scene, San Francisco Mus Mod Art & Baltimore Mus Art, 65 & 73; Book Arts III, Nat Mus Women, Washington, 90; Books as Metaphor for Art: Beyond Words, vol 1 & 2, Crafts & Folk Art Mus & Calif Craft Mus, San Francisco, 90; 4th Int Symp Electronic Art, FISEA, Minneapolis, Minn, 93; NY Digital Salon, 95-96; Coll Art Asn, Montreal, Can, 2001; Biennial, Buenos Aires, 2002; SETI Workshop, Paris, 2003. *Pos:* Reviewer, Leonardo Mag. *Teaching:* San Francisco Art Inst, 74; New Sch Social Res, New York, 81; Sarah Lawrence Col, Bronxville, NY, 84; Univ Calif, Berkeley, 88; Ohio State Univ, 92. *Awards:* Vera Adams Davis Mem Award, 63 & Rhea Keller Mem Prizes, 65, San Francisco Mus Art; Individual Juror's Award, Richmond Art Ctr Ann, Calif, 66; Eyes & Ears Found Grant, 82; Calif Art Coun Grant for Telecommun, 88. *Bibliog:* Stephen Moore (auth), Sonya Rapoport--An Aesthetic Response, Union Gallery, San Jose State Univ, 78 Rapoport, Ctr Visual Arts, 79; Edgar Buonagurio (auth), Interaction art & science, Truman Gallery review, Arts Mag, 4/79; Patricia Zimmerman (auth), Metaphysical or Virtual Reality, Soma Mag, Vol 18, spring 92; and others in LAICA J, 82 High Performance, 83, 88 & Heresies, 86; Judy Malloy (ed) Artswire, 99, 2000; Terri Cohn (auth), The Life and Art of Sonya Rapaport, 2012, Keyday Press, Berkeley Calif, 2012. *Mem:* Womens Caucus Art; Pacific Ctr Book Arts; Ylem; Kala Inst. *Media:* Scanning, Copy Images; Computer interactive. *Specialty:* Gender, Genetic Engring, Religion. *Interests:* Digital Art Theory, Gender Theory, Installation Art. *Publ:* Auth, About Me, 79, Surface, 80, Chelate, 80 & The Remainder, 80, The Animated Soul-Gateway To Your Ka, pvt publ; Transgenic Bagel, 1998; Redeeming the Gene, 2001

RAPP, M YVONNE
ART DEALER, LECTURER
b Lancaster, Pa, July 27, 1935. *Study:* Thomas More Col, BA (arts admin), 78. *Pos:* Gallery guide, Cincinnati Art Mus, Eden Park, Ohio, 70-78; docent, J B Speed Art Mus, Louisville, Ky, 79-81; own-dir, Yvonne Rapp Gallery, 82-2010. *Teaching:* Instr contemp art, Bellarmine Col, 92-. *Specialty:* Contemporary painting, drawings and sculpture. *Mailing Add:* c/o Yvonne Rapp Gallery 2117 Frankfort Ave Louisville KY 40206

RASCHKA, CHRIS
ILLUSTRATOR
b Huntingdon, Pa, Mar 6, 1959. *Study:* St Olaf Coll, Minn, grad. *Exhib:* Solo exhib, Art Inst Chicago, 2008. *Awards:* Caldecott Honor for Yo! Yes?, 2004; Caldecott Medal for The Hello, Goodbye Window, 2006. *Publ:* Auth & illus, Charlie Parker Played Be Bop, 1992, Yo! Yes?, 1993, Can't Sleep, 1995, Mysterious Thelonius, 1997, Arlene Sardine, 1998, Ring! Yo?, 2000, Waffle, 2001, John Coltrane's Giant Steps, 2002, Talk to Me About the Alphabet, 2003, Boy Meets Girl, Girl Meets Boy, 2004, New York is English, Chattanooga is Creek, 2005, Five for a Little One, 2006, The Purple Balloon, 2007, Peter & the Wolf, 2008; illus, The Genie in the Jar, by Nikki Giovanni, 1996; Simple Gifts: A Shaker Hymn, 1998; Another Important Book, by Margaret Wise Brown, 1999; Happy to be Nappy, by bell hooks, 1999, Be Boy Buzz, 2002 & Skin Again, 2004; Fishing in the Air, by Sharon Creech, 2000; A Poke in the I, ed Paul B Janeczko, 2001 & A Kick in the Head, 2005; Movin', ed Dave Johnson, 2000; The Four Corners of the Sky, by Steve Zeitlin, 2000; Little Tree, 2001; Table Manners, by Vladimir Radunsky, 2001; I Pledge Allegiance, by Bill Martin Jr & Michael Sampson, 2002; A Child's Christmas in Wales, 2004; The Hello, Goodbye Window, by Norton Juster, 2005; Good Sports, by Jack Prelutsky, 2007; contrib, The Art of Reading, 2005. *Mailing Add:* 599 W End Ave Apt 6A New York NY 10024-1737

RASKIND, PHILIS
SCULPTOR, INSTRUCTOR
b New York, NY. *Study:* Art Students League; Nat Acad Sch Fine Arts, cert, 73. *Work:* Elizabeth T Greenshields Mem Found, Montreal, Can. *Comn:* Peace Medal US & N Vietnam, pvt comn, NY, 73; theatre masks for New York City Opera, Conn Opera Co, 73-75; bust: Pompidou, Waxworks, Can, 74; miniature series, Quantum Arts, NY, 78-79; life-size figure for WAM Satta, 82; portrait bust, Sculpture Group, New Am Libr, 84. *Exhib:* Catharine Lorillard Wolfe Art Club, Nat Arts Club, NY, 72-79; Nat Sculpture Soc, NY, 72-80; Pen & Brush Club, NY, 75, 76, 78 & 79; Nat Acad Fine Arts Exhib, Nat Acad Fine Arts, 76-78; Salmagundi Club, NY, 79. *Pos:* Ed newsletter, Catharine Lorillard Wolfe Art Club, 75-78. *Teaching:* Instr sculpture, Manhattan Community for Psychotherapy, 73-75; instr sculpture, Am Telegraph & Telephone Adult Educ Prog, New York, 73-74; instr, Fashion Inst Technol, New York, 85-87. *Awards:* Gold Medal, Pen & Brush Club, 78; Bronze Medal, Catharine Lorillard Wolfe Art Club, 77; Kalos Kagathos Found Award, Nat Sculpture Soc, 82; and others. *Mem:* Catharine Lorillard Wolfe Art Club (sculpture chmn, 75-78); Nat Art League; Vis Artists & Galeri Galleries Asn; Int Soc Artists; Artists Equity Asn. *Media:* Clay; Wood. *Dealer:* Belanthi Gallery 142 Court St Brooklyn NY. *Mailing Add:* 330 Third Ave No 15G New York NY 10010-3705

RASMUSSEN, ANTON JESSE
PAINTER, ADMINISTRATOR
b Salt Lake City, Utah, Nov 12, 1942. *Study:* Univ Utah, BFA, 67, MFA, 74. *Work:* Utah Mus Fine Arts, Eccles Health Sci Libr, Univ Utah, Salt Lake City; Davis Co Libr, Farmington, Utah. *Comn:* Oil painting, Bountiful, 76 & three panels, Clearfield, 77, Davis Co Libr, Utah; oil painting, four panels (4 ft x 5 ft), Salt Lake Int Airport, Utah. *Exhib:* Utah Painting 75, Utah Mus Fine Arts, Salt Lake City, 75; Solo exhibs, Davis Co Libr, S Davis Br, Bountiful, Utah, 76, N Davis Br, Clearfield, Utah, 76 & Eccles Health Sci Libr, Univ Utah, Salt Lake City, 76; Two Utah Artists, Boise State Univ, Idaho, 77. *Pos:* Dir, Bountiful Art Ctr, Univ Utah Exten, Bountiful, 74-84; asst dir, Prog for Higher Educ, Davis Co/Univ Utah, Bountiful, 75-84. *Teaching:* Adj asst prof art, Univ Utah, Salt Lake City, 74-84. *Bibliog:* Claudia Sisemore (producer, color film), Anton J Rasmussen--painter of abstractions from nature, pvt publ, 77. *Media:* Oil. *Mailing Add:* 1321 Penn St Salt Lake City UT 84105

RASMUSSEN, ROBERT (REDD EKKS) NORMAN
SCULPTOR, CERAMIST
b Oslo, Norway, Feb 11, 1937. *Study:* San Francisco Art Inst, BFA, 59; Calif Coll Arts & Crafts, MFA, 70. *Work:* San Francisco Mus Mod Art, San Francisco; Los Angeles Co Mus Art, Los Angeles; Mills Coll Art Gallery, Oakland. *Exhib:* Mix, San Francisco Mus Art, 73; Ceramic Sculpture, San Francisco Art Inst, 74; Newport Harbor Art Mus, Newport Beach, Calif, 81; New Mus, NY, 81; Artists Space, NY, 82; Joseph Chowning Gallery, San Francisco, 83 & 86; Ten Yrs Later, Calif State Univ Fullerton, Calif, 87; New Langton Arts, San Francisco, 87; and others. *Teaching:* Instr ceramics, San Francisco Art Inst, 71-; instr ceramics, Univ Wis-Madison, summer, 75. *Awards:* Nat Endowment Arts, 81. *Mailing Add:* PO Box 210462 San Francisco CA 94121-0462

RASTO See Hlavina, Rastislav

RATH, ALAN T
SCULPTOR
b Cincinnati, Ohio, 1959. *Study:* Mass Inst Technol, BSEE, 82. *Work:* Denver Art Mus, Colo; Oakland Mus, Calif; San Diego Mus Contemp Art, La Jolla, Calif; Walker Art Center, Minn; Orange Co Mus Art, Newport Beach, Calif; Albert-Knox Art Gallery, Buffalo, NY; de Young Mus, San Francisco, Calif; Whitney Mus Am Art, New York; Hara Mus, Tokyo; San Jose Mus Art, Calif. *Exhib:* Solo exhibs, ctr Advanced Visual Art, MIT, 84 & 94, Walker Art Ctr (traveling), 91, Haines Gallery, San Francisco, 95, 96 & 98, Contemp Arts Mus, Houston (with catalog), 95, Nelson Gallery, Univ Calif, Davis (with catalog), 96 & Aspen Art Mus, Colo, 96; Site Santa Fe, NMex, 98; Dorfman Projects, NY, 98; Yerba Buena Ctr for Arts, San Francisco, 98; Mus Contemp Art, Scottsdale, Ariz, 99; Mus Art, Austin, Tex, 99; Track 16 Gallery, Santa Monica, Calif, 2002; Haines Gallery, San Francisco, 2003; Carl Solway Gallery, Cincinnati, 2004; Bryce Wolkowitz Gallery, New York, 2005; Rosa Preserve, Napa, Calif, 2006; Wolkowitz Gallery, NY, 2012; Hosfelt Gallery, San Francisco, 2013. *Awards:* Nat Endowment Arts Fel, 88; John Simon Guggenheim Mem Found Fel, New York, 94. *Bibliog:* Peter Boswell (auth), Alan Rath (brochure), Walker Art Ctr, Minneapolis, Minn, 91; Alan Rath (catalog), Gallery 210, Univ Mo, St Louis, 92; Ken Baker (auth), Alan Rath: digital world, Artnews, 5/92; Alison Bing (auth), Alan Rath: Meta Mechanics, Sculpure, vol 25, No 7, 2006. *Dealer:* Carl Solway Gallery 424 Findlay St Cincinnati OH 45214; Bryce Wolkowitz Gallery 505 W 24th St New York NY 10001; Hosfelt Gallery 260 Utah St San Francisco Ca 94103. *Mailing Add:* 830 E 15th St Oakland CA 94606

RATHBONE, ELIZA EURETTA
CURATOR, ART CONSULTANT
b St Louis, Mo, Sept 3, 1948. *Study:* Smith Coll, 67-68; New York, with Horst W Janson, William Rubin, Gert Schiff & Robert Rosenblum, BA, 72; Courtauld Inst, Univ London, with John Golding, MA, 74. *Collection Arranged:* Modigliani: An Anniversary Exhibition, 83; Mark Tobey: City Paintings (auth, catalog), 84; Susan Rothenberg (auth, catalog), 85; Duncan Phillips: A Centennial Exhib, 86; Bill Jensen (auth, catalog), 87; Nicolas de Stael in Am (coauth, catalog), 90; Brancus: Photographs and Sculpture, 94; Impressionists on the Seine: A Celebration of Renoir's Luncheon of the Boating Party, (coauth, catalog), 96; Jake Berthot: Drawing into Painting, 96; Impressionists in Winter: Effects de Neige (coauth, catalog), 98; Honore Daumier, 2000; The Eye of Duncan Phillips, 2000 (co-auth); Impressionist Still Life (co-auth catalog), 2001; Discovering Milton Avery, 2004; Modigliani: Beyond the Myth, 2005; Degas, Sichert & Toulouse-Lautrec, 2006; Impressionists by the Sea, 2007; Degas to Diebenkorn: The Phillips Collects (auth, catalog), 2008; Dieberkorn, NMex, 2008; Morandi: Master of Modern Still Life, 2009; Pousette-Dart: Predominantly White Paintings, 2010; Degas Dancers at the Barre: Point and Counterpoint (auth, catalog), 2011; Snapshot: Painter-Photographers, Bonnard to Vuillard (co-auth catalog), 2012; Van Gash Repetitions, 2013. *Pos:* Asst cur 20th century art, Nat Gallery Art, Washington, DC, 77-85; from assoc cur to chief cur, Phillips Collection, Washington, DC, 85-2014. *Awards:* Chevalier in the Order of Arts and Letters, French Govt, 02. *Publ:* Coauth, Art at Mid-century: The Subjects of the Artist, Nat Gallery of Art, 78 & The Morton Neumann Family Collection, 80; Mark Tobe: City Paintings, 84; Susan Rothenberg, 85; Bill Jensen, 88; Nicholas de Stael in Am, 90; Impressionists on the Seine, 96; Impressionists in Winter, 98; Impressionist Still Life, 2001; auth, Art Beyond Isms: Masterworks from El Greco to Picasso in the Phillips Collection, 2002; Discovering Milton Avery, 2004; Degas' Dancers at the Barre: Point and Counterpoint, 2011; Master Paintings from the Phillips Collection, 2011; Snapshot: Painter-Photographers (Henri Evenepoel: An Abundance of Gifts) 2012; Van Gogh...Repetitions, 2013; Made in the USA (The Rothko Room), 2014. *Mailing Add:* c/o The Phillips Collection 1600 21st St NW Washington DC 20009

RATHLE, HENRI (AMIN)
PAINTER
b Cairo, Egypt, Nov 4, 1911; US citizen. *Study:* Self-taught; Royal Palace, with El Hawawini, 29-30; also studied with Henry Gasser, 70; Fac de Medecine de Paris, MD, 38. *Work:* Phoenix Fire Mus & Mus of City, Mobile, Ala. *Comn:* President Nixon, Washington, DC, 69; Oakley and Southern Belle, Emperor Clocks, WGer, 73; President Charles deGaulle, comn by J F Bezou, New Orleans, La. *Exhib:* Solo exhibs, Percy Whiting Art Ctr, Fairhope, Ala, 68, Biloxi Municipal Art Gallery, Miss, 68, Jackson Co Col, Gautier, Miss, 68 & Fine Arts Mus South, Mobile, Ala, 72. *Awards:* Purchase Award, Bellingrath Gardens, Mobile, Ala, 70; Purchase Award, Fine Arts Mus South, Mobile, Ala. *Bibliog:* John Fay (auth), Masculinity found in art, Mobile Register, 3/67; J F Bezou (auth), Exposition a Biloxi, France-Amerique, 2/68; German & Swedish Monographs, 78. *Mem:* Mobile Art Asn; Easte. *Media:* Acrylic, Watercolor, Oil. *Mailing Add:* 3836 Hillcrest Ln Mobile AL 36693-2827

RAUF, BARBARA CLAIRE
INSTRUCTOR, PAINTER
b Covington, Ky, Mar 13, 1944. *Study:* Thomas More Col, AB, 68; Univ Cincinnati, BFA, 74; Univ Pa, MFA, 77. *Work:* Atkins & Pearce Manufacturing, Co, Cincinnati, Ohio; Saint Clair Med Ctr, Morehead, Ky; Admin Bldg, Sci Wing & Chancellors Room, Thomas More Col, Crestview Hills, Ky. *Comn:* Amy (portrait), comn by Mr & Mrs George Deitmaring, Ft Mitchell, Ky, 80; Asa (portrait), Atkins & Pearce Co, Cincinnati, 81; pres series & chancellor series (portraits), Thomas More Col, 84-86 & 96; Pat (portrait), comn by Dr & Mrs Forrest Calico, Ft Mitchell, Ky, 85. *Exhib:* Inst Contemp Art, Philadelphia, 75-77; solo exhibs, Carnegie Art Ctr, Covington, Ky, 92, Clermont Art Gallery, Eatavia, Ohio, 93, The Gallery, Covington, Ky, 93 & Dayton Visual Art Ctr, 95; Southern Ohio Mus, 96; Univ Cincinnati Gallery, 97; Cathedral Gallery, 98, 2002-04; Annex Gallery, 2005; Thomas More Gallery, 2007. *Pos:* Dir, Thomas More Gallery, Thomas More Col, 78-. *Teaching:* Asst prof art & dept chair, Thomas More Col, 77-83, assoc prof, 83-97, prof, 98. *Awards:* Advan Inst Development Grants, US Govt; Ky Found Women, 90; Outstanding Teacher of the Year, 2001. *Bibliog:* B Wheatley (auth), Carnegie Center today, Kenton Co Recorder, 84; Mary McCarty (auth), Portrait painter, Cincinnati Mag, 85. *Mem:* Contemp Art Ctr, Cincinnati; Coll Art Asn; Carnegie Art Ctr. *Media:* Oil, Pencil. *Mailing Add:* 840 Tater Knob Rd Peebles OH 45660

RAVENAL, JOHN B
CURATOR
b Providence, RI. *Study:* Wesleyan Univ, BA (art hist), 82; Columbia Univ, MA (art hist), 87, MPil (art hist), 90. *Work:* Cur (exhibs) Robert Lazzarini, Va Mus Fine Arts, 2003-04 (Award for Best Exhib of Digital Art, Asn Independent Art Critics/USA, 2005). *Collection Arranged:* Co-cur, From the Collection of Sol LeWitt (traveling), Wadsworth Atheneum, 84; co-cur, Ian Hamilton Finlay: The Garden and the Revolution, Wadsworth Atheneum, 91, Philadelphia Mus Art, 91-92; co-cur, Sherrie Levine, 93, Richard Long, 95, Lawrence Weiner, 94-95 & Rirkrit Tiravanija, 98, Philadelphia Mus Art; cur, Sidney Goodman, Philadelphia Mus Art, 96; cur, Twenty Philadelphia Artists, Philadelphia Mus Art, 98; cur, Vanitas: Meditations on Life and Death in Contemporary Art, Va Mus Fine Arts, 2000; cur, Outer and Inner Space: A Video Exhibition in Three Parts, Va Mus Fine Arts, 2002; cur, Robert Lazzarini, Va Mus Fine Arts, 2003; cur, Artificial Light, Anderson Gallery, Va Commonwealth Univ, Richmond, 2006, Mus Contemp Art, N Miami, 2006. *Pos:* Res, contemp art, Wadsworth Atheneum, Hartford, Conn, 82-85; asst cur 20th-century art, Philadelphia Mus Art, 91-97 & assoc cur 20th-century art, 97-98; cur mod & contemp art, Va Mus Fine Arts, Richmond, 98-. *Mem:* Asn Art Mus Curs (pres). *Publ:* Co-auth, From the Collection of Sol LeWitt (exhib catalog), 84; Sidney Goodman (exhib catalog), Philadelphia Mus Art, 96; Twenty Philadelphia Artists (exhib catalog), Philadelphia Mus Art, 98; Vanitas: Meditations on Life & Death in Contemporary Art (exhib catalog), Va Mus Fine Arts, 2000; Outer & Inner Space: A Video Exhibition in Three Parts (exhib catalog), Va Mus Fine Arts, 2002; auth, Shirin Neshat: Double Vision, in: Reclaiming Female Agency: Feminist Art History After Postmodernism, Univ Calif Press, 2005; Modern & Contemporary Art at the Va Mus Fine Arts (collection survey), 2007; Ivan Navarro: Bright Lights, Bad Dreams (exhib catalog), Galerie Daniel Templon, Paris, 2007; and others. *Mailing Add:* Va Mus Fine Arts 200 N Blvd Richmond VA 23220-4007

RAVETT, ABRAHAM
FILMMAKER, PHOTOGRAPHER
b Poland, Aug 2, 1947; US citizen. *Study:* Brooklyn Col, BA, 68; Mass Coll Art, BFA (film-photog), 75; Syracuse Univ, MFA (filmmaking), 78. *Exhib:* Cineprobe, Mus Mod Art, NY, 86; New Eng Film Festival, Boston, Mass, 86 & 90; Image Forum, Tokyo, 87; Anthology Film Archives, NY, 89; Collective for Living Cinema, NY, 90; Mus Mod Art, NY, 91; Edison Black Maria, 91. *Pos:* Artist-in-residence, The Artist Found, Boston, 79. *Teaching:* Assoc prof film-photog, Hampshire Col, Amherst, Mass, 79-. *Awards:* Andrew Mellon Found Grant, 81, 87, & 90; Artist Found Fel, Boston, 83; Nat Endowment Arts Grant, 85, 87 & 92; Japan-US Friendship Comn Grants, 83, 85, 87 & 90; Mass Productions, 88-89. *Mailing Add:* 193 Nonotuck St Florence MA 01062-1907

RAVIV, ILANA
PAINTER, PRINTMAKER
b Tel Aviv, Israel, Nov 29, 1945; US & Israeli citizen. *Study:* League NY, with Robert Delamonica, Knox Martin & Bruce Dorfman, 80-84. *Work:* Holocaust Mem Mus, Washington, DC. *Comn:* mural, City of NY, 87. *Exhib:* Solo exhibs, Nat Arts Club, New York City, 2000, Castra Gallery, Haifa, Israel, 01, Wilfrid Israel Art Mus, 01-02, Painters and Sculptors Asn, Tel-Aviv, 02, BoxHeart Gallery, Pittsburgh, 04. *Mem:* NY Artist Equity Asn; Painters & Sculptors Asn, Israel; Nat Asn Acrylic Painters. *Media:* Acrylic, All media; Serigraphy, Silkscreen

RAWLINS, SHARON ELIZABETH ROANE
PAINTER
b Athens, Ga, July 2, 1948. *Study:* Mary Washington Univ Va, 66-68; Univ Md, 72-74; Coastline Community Coll, AA, Fountain Valley, Calif, 92; Studied with Harry Carmean & Vern Wilson, Art Ctr Coll Design, Pasadena, Calif, 92; Studied with Timothy J Clark, Art Students League advanced study, Italy, New York, 2002; Marchutz Sch Fine Art, 2013; BLS Studio Art, Univ Mary Wash, 2013. *Comn:* Installation for lobby, Melles Griot Corp headquarters, Irvine, Calif, 99. *Exhib:* The Human Form, Anaheim Mus, Calif, 2002; 38th Ann Nat Juried Exhib, Palm Springs Art Mus, Calif, 2007; Belles of Capistrano, Four Women & Their Art, Mission San Juan Capistrano, Calif, 2008; Catharine Lorillard Wolfe Art Club, Nat Arts Club, New York, 2008, 2009, 2011, 2013, 2014; Nat Midyear Show, Butler Inst Am Art, Youngstown, Ohio, 2009, 2013; Laumeister Fine Art Competition, Bennington Ctr Arts, Vt, 2010; Brushes with Friendship, Nottingham Fine Art, Calif, 2010, Nat Watercolor Soc, Ann Exhib, 2010, Blossoms II, Art of Flowers, Naples, Fla, 2011, Ann Statewide Landscape Exhibs, Santa Cruz, Calif, 2011, 2012, 2015, San Diego Watercolor Soc 31st Ann Int Exhib, Calif, 2011, 2014; 8th Biennial Nat Art Exhib, Punta Gorda, Fla, 2012; Landscape Light & Color, Santa Cruz, Calif, 2012; Less is More, Small Works in a Great Space, St Johns Coll, Mitchell Gallery, Annapolis, Md, 2013, 2014; Ann Made in California Exhib, 2014, 2015; Drawin-In II, Q Art Salon, Santa Ana, Calif, 2015; Into the Light Plein Air Invitational, City of Brea Gallery, Brea Calif, 2015; NWS Int Small Image China Exchange Exhib, 2015-16. *Awards:* Best in show, Plein Air Painting, Tustin, Calif, 2002; award, Keyes Gallery, Springfield, Mo, 2006; Merit award, 8th Biennial Nat Art Exhib, Punta Gorda, Fla, 2012; 2nd Pl Water Media, Catharine Lorillard Wolfe Mems Exhib, 2013. *Bibliog:* Ann Kalayil (auth), A Soulful Workshop, Watercolor, Am Artist, 2002. *Mem:* Nat Watercolor Soc (sig mem); Catharine Lorillard Wolfe Art Club. *Media:* Watercolor, Printmaking. *Dealer:* Nottingham Fine Art 4229 Birch St Newport Beach CA 92660; Q Art Salon 205 N Sycamore St Santa Ana CA 92701. *Mailing Add:* PO Box 26382 Santa Ana CA 92799

RAY, ANDREA
INSTALLATION ARTIST
Study: RI Sch Design, BFA (printmaking), 1989; Cranbrook Acad Art, MFA (printmaking), 1994. *Exhib:* Apex Art, New York; DAC; White Columns; IPO lecture series, Whitney Mus Am Art, New York. *Teaching:* Vis faculty, Vt Col Fine Art, 2007-; teacher, Kans City Art Inst, Hunter Col, Cooper Union, Col NJ, Parsons The New Sch & Malmo Art Acad, Sweden. *Awards:* Art Matters Found Grant, 2008. *Mailing Add:* c/o Lower Manhattan Cult Coun 125 Maiden Ln 2nd Fl New York NY 10038

RAY, CHARLES
SCULPTOR
b Chicago, Ill, 1953. *Study:* Univ Iowa, Iowa City, BFA (cum laude), 1975; Mason Gross Sch Art, Rutgers, MFA, 1979. *Work:* Whitney Mus Am Art, NY; Newport Harbor Art Mus. *Exhib:* Solo retrospective, Whitney Mus Am Art, NY, 1998, Mus Contemp Art, LA, 1998 & Mus Contemp Art, Chicago, 1999; Solo exhibs, 64 Market St, Venice, Calif, 1983, Mercer Union, Toronto, 1985, Feature, Chicago, 1987, NY, 1989, 1990, 1991 & 1992, Burnett Miller, Los Angeles, 1988, The Mattress Factory, Pittsburgh, 1989, Galerie Claire Burrus, Paris, 1990, Donald Young Gallery, Seattle, Wash, 1992, Galerie Metropol, Vienna, Austria, 1993, Rooseum-Ctr for Contemp Art, Malmo, Sweden, 1994, Kunsthalle Bern, Switz, 1994, Kunsthalle Zurich, Switz, 1994, Studio Guenzani, Milan, 1996, Regen Proj, Los Angeles, 1997, Whitney Mus of Am Art, 1998, Mus of Contemp Art, Los Angeles, 1998, Mus of Contemp Art, Chicago, 1998, Matthew Marks Gallery, NY, 2006, 2007, 2009, 2011, 2012, Regen Proj II, Los Angeles, 2007; Group exhibs, Recent Drawings, Whitney Mus Am Art, NY, 1990, Whitney Biennial, 1997, The Am Century: Art and Cult 1900-2000, 1999, Pollock to Today: Highlights from the Permanent Collection, 2002; Helter Skelter: LA Art in the 1990's (with catalog), Mus Contemp Art, Calif, 1992; Regarding Beauty: A View of the Late Twentieth Century, Hirshhorn Mus & Sculpture Garden, Smithsonian Inst, 1999; Let's Entertain, Walker Art Ctr, 2000, Walk Around Time, 2002-04, Mythologies, 2005-08; Barbara Gladstone Gallery, NY, 2000; Made in Calif: Art, Image and Identity 1900-2000, Los Angeles County Mus Art, 2000; Au-dela du Spectacle, Centre Pompidou, Paris, 2001; Open Ends: Art Since 1960, Mus Mod Art, NY, 2001, Take Two-Worlds & Views, 2005-06; A Room of Their Own, Mus Contemp Art, Los Angeles, 2001, After Cezanne, 2005-06, Collecting Collections, 2008; Venice Biennale, 2003; Singular Forms (Sometimes Repeated), Guggenheim Mus, NY, 2004; Yes Bruce Nauman, Zwirner & Wirth, NY, 2006; The Lath Picture Show, Friedrich Petzel Gallery, NY, 2007; Whitney Biennial, Whitney Mus Am Art, New York, 2010; The World Belongs to You, Palazzo Grassi, Venice, 2011; Sculpture Show, Scottish Nat Gallery of Modern Art, Edinburgh, 2011; Lifelike, Walker Art Ctr, Minneapolis, 2012; NYC 1993: Experimental Jet Set, Trash and No Star, New Mus, NY, 2013; 55th Int Art Exhib Biennale, Venice, 2013. *Pos:* head sculpture dept, Univ Calif, Los Angeles, 81-present. *Awards:* NJ Coun on the Arts Grant, 1980; Nat Endowment Arts, 1985 & 88; Larry Aldrich Found Award, 1997. *Bibliog:* Christopher Knight (auth), An Art of Darkness at MOCA, Los Angeles Times, F1, F4-F5 (reproduction), 1/28/92, Charles Ray's Hinoki: A Wooden Record of Life, Los Angeles Times, 2007; Susan Kandel (auth), LA in Review, Arts, 98-99, 4/92; Hunter Drohojowska (auth), LA Raw, Artnews, 78-81, 4/92; Lane Relyea (auth), Charles Ray: In the No, Artforum, 92; Virginia Rutledge (auth), Ray's Reality Hybrids, Art in America, 11/98; Anne Wagner (auth), Review of Charles Ray at the Mus Contemporary Art, Los Angeles, Artforum, 5/99; and others. *Mem:* Fel Am Acad Arts & Sciences. *Publ:* auth, Thinking of Sculpture as Shaped by Space, NY Times, 10/7/2001; A Four Dimensional Being Writes Poetry on a Field with Sculptures, Matthew Marks Gallery, NY, 2006; 1000 Words: Charles Ray Talks about Hinoki, Artforum, 4/2007. *Mailing Add:* c/o Matthew Marks Gallery 523 W 24th St New York NY 10011

RAY, DEBORAH See Kogan, Deborah

RAY, DONALD ARVIN
PAINTER
b July 29, 1945. *Study:* Texas A&M Univ, BA, 71; Baylor Univ, JD, 74; Studied with Knox Martin, Art Students League, 98-99. *Exhib:* Visual Prayer, Klara Kohl Gallery, NY, 98; Donray: American Painter, The Rivington Gallery, London, 99, Wild Things, 2006; Donray: A Cross Section, Arlington Mus Art, Arlington, Tex, 2009. *Bibliog:* Ruth Bass (auth), Visual Prayer (catalogue), Klara Kohl Gallery, 98; Edward Lucie Smith (auth), Donray: American Painter (catalogue), The Rivington Gallery, 99; Donald G Kuspit (auth), Donray's Expressionism (catalogue), So Hyun Gallery, 2000; Dominic Lutyens (auth), Wild Things, The Rivington Gallery, 2006. *Media:* Acrylic, Pastel, Charcoal. *Mailing Add:* 1705 Stagecoach Dr Pantego TX 76013

RAY, KATERINA RUEDI
ART SCHOOL ADMINISTRATOR
Study: Duncan of Jordanstone Col of Art/Univ of Dundee, UK, Architecture, 1978; Diploma with honors, Architectural Asn, london, AA, 1986, Univ London, MS with Distinction, History of Modern Architecture, 1991, Univ of London, PhD in Architecture, 1998. *Exhib:* Chicago: Ten Visions, Art Inst of Chicago, 2004. *Pos:* staff mem. Bowling Green State Univ, 2002-, dir sch of art, currently. *Res:* Bauhaus pedagogy, capitalism, patriarchy, modernization and globalization, history of design education and practice, Chicago architecture, Bertrand Goldberg and Marina City, public art, art & economic development. *Publ:* co-auth, The Dissertation: An Architecture Student's Handbook, 2000, The Portfolio: An Architecture Student's Handbook, 2003, Practical Experience: An Architecture Student's Guide to Internship/Year Out, 2004, Chicago Architecture: Histories, Revisions. Alternatives, 2005, marina City: Bertrand Goldberg's Urban Vision, 2010; auth, Bauhaus Dream-house: Modernity and Globalization, 2010. *Mailing Add:* 1000 Fine Arts Center Bowling Green State University Bowling Green OH 43403-2786

RAYBURN, BOYD (DALE)
PAINTER, PRINTMAKER
b Carriere, Miss, May 12, 1942. *Study:* Univ Southern Miss, BS, 64; Univ Miss, MFA, 70. *Work:* DeCordova Mus, Lincoln, Mass; High Mus, Atlanta; Mint Mus, Charlotte, NC; Southeastern Ctr Contemp Art, Winston-Salem, NC; Yale Univ Art Gallery; Ga Mus Art, Athens, Ga. *Exhib:* 20th Southeastern Exhib, High Mus, Atlanta, 65; Piedmont Painting & Sculpture, Mint Mus, Charlotte, NC, 71; Audubon Artist Ann, Nat Acad Gallery, NY, 73; two-person show, Mint Mus, Charlotte, NC, 74 & Miss Mus Art, Jackson, 77; Hunterdon Print Exhib, Hunterdon Art Ctr, Clinton, NJ, 78; The Mississippi Story, Miss Mus Art, 2007. *Pos:* Bd dir, Nat Asn Independent Artist. *Teaching:* Instr art, Univ Miss, 69-70; instr printmaking, Ga Southwestern Col, 72-73; asst prof, La State Univ, Shreveport, 80-82. *Awards:* Purchase Award, DeCordova Mus, 77 & Southeastern Ctr Contemp Art, 78; Rembrandt Graphic Award, Boston Printmakers Exhib, 90; 1st Place Printmaking, Coconut Grove Arts Festival, 2002. *Mem:* Boston Printmakers; Southeastern Printmakers Asn; Nat Asn Independent Artists. *Media:* Monotype. *Dealer:* Lagerquist Gallery 3235 Paces Ferry Place NW Atlanta GA 30305. *Mailing Add:* 1538 Jones Rd Roswell GA 30075-2726

RAYEN, JAMES WILSON
PAINTER, EDUCATOR
b Youngstown, Ohio, Apr 9, 1935. *Study:* Yale Univ, BA, BFA & MFA; with Josef Albers, Sewell Sillman & Rico Lebrun. *Work:* Addison Gallery Am Art, Andover, Mass; Yale Univ, New Haven, Conn; Wellesley Col, Mass; First Nat Bank, Boston; Mint Mus, NC; Harvard Univ, Cambridge, Mass. *Comn:* Marriott Hotel Corp; Hyatt Hotel Corp. *Exhib:* Solo exhibs, Durlacher Brothers Gallery, NY, 66 & Eleanor Rigelhaupt Gallery, Boston, 68; 10 Yr Retrospective, Brockton Art Ctr, Mass, 73; Recent & Revised, Wellesley Coll Mus, 78; Chapel Gallery, Boston, 84; Rice Pollack Gallery, Provincetown, Mass, 95. *Pos:* Bd dir, N Bennet St Sch, Boston; bd dir & vpres, Boston Acad Music. *Teaching:* Prof, Wellesley Col, 61-, Elizabeth Christy Kopf chair in studio art, 83. *Awards:* Ital Govt Grant in Painting, 59-60; Ford Found Grant in the Humanities, 69-70; Wellesley Coll Fac Grant, summer 75, spring 84, 85, 91, 92 & 93; Mass Coun Arts Grant Printmaking, 88. *Bibliog:* Robert Taylor (auth), Boston Globe, 73; Christine Temon (auth), Boston Globe, 83, 90. *Media:* Acrylic, Watercolor; Monotype, Oil. *Dealer:* Gallery 79 Boston Mass. *Mailing Add:* Wellesley Col Art Dept Jewett Arts Ctr Wellesley MA 02481

RAYMOND, LILO
PHOTOGRAPHER
b Frankfurt, Ger, June 23, 1922; US citizen. *Study:* Photog Sem, with David Vestal, 61-63. *Work:* Sheldon Mus Art Gallery, Mus Mod Art & Metrop Mus, NY; High Mus, Atlanta; New Orleans Mus Art. *Exhib:* Still Life in Photog, Helios Gallery, NY, 76; Contrasts Gallery, London, Eng, 80; Woodman Gallery, Morristown, NJ, 81; Photo West, Carmel, 82; Baker Gallery, Kans, 82; and many solo exhibs. *Teaching:* Mem sem photog, Sch Visual Arts, New York, 78-, Maine Photog Workshop, Rockport, summer 79 & Int Ctr Photog, New York, winter 79. *Awards:* Creative Artists Pub Serv Prog Grant, 78. *Bibliog:* Sir Cecil Beaton (auth), The Magic Image, Little Brown & Co, 75; Alicia Wille (auth), Lilo Raymond, gravure portfolio, Popular Photog, 77; Richard Blodgett (auth), A Collectors Guide, Ballatine Bks, 79. *Publ:* Photogr, Classic County Inns of America, Knapp Press & Holt, Rinehart & Winston, 78. *Dealer:* Marcuse Pfeifer 825 Madison Ave New York NY 10021. *Mailing Add:* 16 Adams St Fl 2 Kingston NY 12401

RAYMOND, YASMIL
CURATOR
b Puerto Rico. *Study:* Art Inst Chicago, BFA (fine arts), 1999; Bard Coll, MA (curatorial studies), 2004. *Collection Arranged:* Andy Warhol/Supernova: Stars, Deaths, and Disasters 1962-64 (with Douglas Fogle), 2005; Kara Walker: My Complement, My Enemy, My Oppressor, My Love (with Philippe Vergne), 2007; Tino Sehgal, 2007; Brave New Worlds (with Doryun Chong), 2008; Statements: Joseph Beuys, Dan Flavin, Donald Judd, 2008. *Pos:* Coord pub programs, Mus Contemp Art, Chicago; curatorial fel to asst cur, Walker Art Ctr, assoc cur, 2004-2009; cur, Dia Art Found, 2009-. *Awards:* Guggenheim Fel; Monique Beudert Curatorial award, Bard Coll, 2004. *Mailing Add:* Dia Art Foundation 535 W 22nd St New York NY 10011

RÉ, PAUL BARTLETT
GRAPHIC ARTIST, SCULPTOR
b Albuquerque, NMex, Apr 18, 1950. *Study:* Calif Inst Technol, BS, 72, with honors. *Work:* Univ Calif Art Mus, Berkeley; Oakland Mus, Calif; Fine Arts Mus NMex, Santa Fe; J B Speed Mus Art, Louisville, Ky; Wichita Art Mus, Kans; Paul Ré Gallery & Sculpture Garden, Univ NMex Art Mus, Albuquerque. *Comn:* Series of 6 large drawings, comn by Jim Freeman, Kyoto, Japan, 76; series of 7 large drawings, comn by Fredrick Shair, Altadena, Calif, 81; Touchable Art for the Blind and Sighted (hand made bk), Perkins Sch Blind, Watertown, Mass, 83, Can Nat Inst Blind, Edmonton, Can, 83 & Deutsche Blindenstudienanstalt, Marburg, Ger, 86. *Exhib:* Solo exhibs, Triangle Gallery, San Francisco, 74, 75, Baxter Art Gallery, Calif Inst Tech, 81, Paul Ré: Drawings and Paintings, Jonson Gallery, Univ NMex Art Mus, Albuquerque, 78, Touchable Art: An Exhibit for the Blind and Sighted by Paul Ré, J B Speed Mus Art, Louisville, Ky, 85, Sumter Gallery Art, SC, 90; Wichita Art Mus, Kans, 86; Albuquerque Mus Art, NMex, 86; Aitken Bicentennial Exhib Centre, St John, NB, Can, 89; Colo Springs Pioneers' Mus, Colo, 90; Santa Barbara Mus Art, Calif, 91; New Works by Paul Ré, Jonson Gallery, Univ NMex Art Mus, 2001, Paul Ré: Shaping Serenity, Karpeles Mus, Newburgh, NY, 2002; group exhib, Graphic Design, XIII Biennale, Monrovia Gallery, Brno, Czech, 88; NMex Biennial, Fine Arts mus NMex, Santa Fe, 73; Southwest Biennial, Fine Arts Mus NMex, Santa Fe, 78; Gump's Art Gallery, San Francisco, Calif, 77, 78. *Pos:* Adv bd, Mus Am Folk Art, 86-94; dir, Paul Ré Collection and Archives, 96-. *Teaching:* Leonardo da Vinci Art & Sci, Osher Inst, Univ NMex, 2009. *Awards:* Helene Wurlitzer Found Residency Grant, Taos, NMex, 82 & 84; Publ Award for Touchable Art (book chpt) Spirit of Enterprise: The 1990 Rolex Awards, Geneva, Switzerland, 90; Legion of Hon (one of five worldwide for promoting peace through art), United Cult Convention, 2005; Paul Bartlett Ré Peace Prize; named to The Global 100 for Elevating, Unifying Art, 2011. *Bibliog:* Dennis Wepman (auth), Ré, Paul B, Contemp Graphic Artists, 88; Beryl Dakers & Mark Shaffer (auths), Touchable Art by Paul Ré (TV doc), SCETV, 90; Interview by Dennis Wepman, The Dance of the Pencil, J Print World, 94. *Mem:* Int Soc Art Sci & Technol; Int Soc Interdisciplinary Study of Symmetry; Order of Am Ambassadors. *Media:* Drawings, Thermoformed Reliefs, Réograms (hybrid hand-digital prints). *Publ:* Auth, My Drawings and Paintings, Leonardo XIII-2, 80, My Drawings and Paintings: An Extension, Leonardo XIV-2, 81 & On the Progression of My Figurative Drawings, 82, Leonardo XV-2; Touchable Art: A Book for the Blind and Sighted, 83 & The Dance of the Pencil: Serene Art by Paul Ré, 93, Paul Ré Archives; Art, Peace, and Transcendance: Réograms That Elevate and Unite, UNM Press, 2015. *Dealer:* The Paul Ré Archives. *Mailing Add:* 10533 Sierra Bonita Ave NE Albuquerque NM 87111

READ, DAVE (DAVID) DOLLOFF
PHOTOGRAPHER, EDUCATOR
b Belfast, Maine, July 14, 1938. *Study:* Ohio Univ, BFA, 63, MFA, 65. *Work:* Mus Mod Art, NY; Libr Cong, Washington, DC; Mus Fine Arts, St Petersburg, Fla; Univ Mich, East Lansing; Univ Louisville, Ky. *Exhib:* Photog Fine Arts, Metrop Mus Art, NY, 67; Photog Art Form, Ringling Mus, Sarasota, 77; Dave Read Photog, Mich State Univ, 77 & Light Factory, Charlotte, NC, 78; Dave Read: 1st Mid-west Photogs, Sheldon Art Gallery, Lincoln, Nebr, 80; Photographs by Dave Read, Friends Photog, Carmel, Calif, 83. *Collection Arranged:* Flash (photog by Mertin, Hume, Cohen & Bishop, auth, catalog), Miami Dade Community Col, 76. *Teaching:* Instr photog, Univ NMex, Albuquerque, 65-66; assoc prof photog, Miami-Dade Community Col, Fla, 69-77; prof photog, Univ Nebr, Lincoln, 78-. *Awards:* Artist's Fel, Mid-Am Arts Alliance & Nat Endowment Arts, 83. *Mem:* Soc Photog Educ; Friends of Photog. *Media:* Silver Prints. *Publ:* Contribr, Afterimage, Visual Studies Workshop, 81; Electronic Flash Photography, Van Nostrand Reinhold, 80; contribr, Exposure, 79. *Mailing Add:* Univ of Nebraska-Lincoln 120 RH Lincoln NE 68588-0114

READMAN, SYLVIE
PHOTOGRAPHER
b Quebec City, Que, Aug 10, 1958. *Study:* St-Foy Col, DEC, 80; Laval Univ, Que, BA, 81; Concordia Univ, Montreal, MA (photog), 89. *Work:* Can Contemp Mus Photog, Ont; Contemp Art Mus Montreal, Que; Mus Que; Winnipeg Art Gallery, Man; Bibliotheque Nat De Paris, France. *Exhib:* Group exhibs, Can Mus Contemp Photog, 91 & 92, Nickle Art Gallery, 93 & Frac De L'ile De France, Paris, 96; Les Decennies De La Métamorphose, Musee Du Que, 92; solo exhibs, Contemp Art Montreal, 93 & Edmonton Art Gallery, 96. *Bibliog:* Daniel Leger C Simon (auth), Sylvie Readman, Gallery S Lallouz, 92; Paulette Gagnon (auth), Sylvie Readman, Contemp Art Mus Montreal, 93; Lucy R Lippard (auth), The Lure of the Local, spring 97. *Dealer:* Samuel Lallouz 4295 St Laurent Montreal PQ H2W 1Z4 Canada. *Mailing Add:* 1747 boul Boucherville Rd Saint Bruno PQ J3V 4H2 Canada

REAGAN, ROURK C
PAINTER, PHOTOGRAPHER
b Baltimore, Md, Jan 5, 1970., 1970. *Study:* Scuola Lorenzo de Medici, Florence, Italy, BFA prog, 1990; Art Inst Chicago, BFA, 1991; Claremont Grad Univ, MFA, 2000. *Exhib:* Love, Power & Magic, Atelier 751, Taos, NMex, 1994; Lachsa Retrospective, Downey Mus Art, Calif, 1996; Am Signature, Fine Art Living, Melbourne, Australia, 1997; Agora Gallery, NY, 1997; La Casa de la Cultura Mex, San Jose, Calif, 1997; D C Gallery, Claremont, Calif, 1998; 1st Int Biennial Contemp Art, Trevi Flash Art Mus, Italy, 1998. *Teaching:* instr, Los Angeles Co High Sch for Arts; instr, San Antonio Coll; instr, The Buckley Sch. *Media:* Oil, Mixed Media. *Dealer:* Gunther Nachtrab Atelien 751 Box 22 Taos NM 87109

REBAUDENGO, PATRIZIA SANDRETTO RE
COLLECTOR
b Turin, Italy. *Pos:* Founder & chmn, Fondazione Sandretto Re Rebaudengo, Turin, Italy, 1995-, Centro per l'Arte Contemporanea, Turin, Italy, 2002-. *Awards:* Named one of Top 200 Collectors, ARTnews mag, 2003-10; Montblanc Arts Patronage award, 2003. *Mem:* Tate Gallery, London (int coun); Mus Mod Art, New York (int coun & Friends of Contemp Drawing). *Collection:* Contemporary art. *Mailing Add:* Fondazione Sandretto Re Rebaudengo Via Modane 16 Turin i 10141 Italy

REBBECK, LESTER JAMES, JR
GALLERY DIRECTOR, PAINTER
b Chicago, Ill, June 25, 1929. *Study:* Art Inst Chicago & Univ Chicago, hist with K Blackshear, BAEd, MAEd, 59; also painting with Wieghardt, drawing with Isoble McKinnon. *Comn:* Paintings & prints, comn by William Fischer, 69. *Exhib:* Mus Sci & Industry, Chicago, 83; Ill State Mus, Springfield, 83; Peace Mus, Chicago, 83; Fort Wayne Mus Art, Indiana Ex, 89-90; Ninth Biennial Nat Small Print Exhib, Sixty Sq Inches, Purdue Univ Galleries, 94; and others. *Pos:* Gallery dir, Countryside Art Gallery, Arlington Heights, Ill, 63-68; gallery dir, Chicago Soc Artists Gallery, 67-68. *Teaching:* Asst prof art appreciation & painting, Harper Col, 67-71. *Awards:* GI Show Medal Award, Art Inst Chicago, 53; First Place Oils, McHenry Art Fair, 60, Best of Show, 62. *Bibliog:* Nicolo Pan Epinto & Calogero Panepinto (coauths), Tendenze E Testimonianze Del Arte Contemporanea, Acad Italia, 83; Lis Krantz (auth), American Artists, Facts on File Publs, New York/Oxford, Eng, 85; Les Krantz (ed), The New York Art Review, Am References Inc, 88. *Mem:* Coll Art Asn Am. *Media:* Oil on Canvas; Wood Sculpture. *Dealer:* Nahan Galleries 381 W Broadway New York NY 10012. *Mailing Add:* 2041 Vermont St Rolling Meadows IL 60008

REBHUN, PEARL G
PAINTER, PRINTMAKER
b New York, NY, Feb 20, 24. *Study:* Studied with Isaac Soyer, Leo Manso, Shirley Gorelik, Jerry Okomoto & Jerry Samuels. *Work:* Nassau Mus Fine Art, Roslyn, NY; Trinity Col, Hartford; Public Serv Gas & Elec Utility, NJ; Martha Lincoln Gallery, Vero Beach, Fla; Isis Gallery, Port Washington, NY; Ft Lauderdale Mus, Juried Exhib: Hortt. *Comn:* Oppenheim, Appel Dixon & Co, NY, 78; Brookhaven Bursing Corp, Nassau Co, 79; Fleischmanns Distilling Corp, New Hyde Park, 80; Forest Elec Corp, NY, 87. *Exhib:* Palazzo Vecchio, Florence, Italy, 83; Mencul Ctr Arts, Cairo, Egypt, 83; Parrish Mus Art, Southampton, NY, 83; Heckshер Mus Art Ann, Huntington, NY, 85; Ft Lauderdale Mus Art, 90-91; Karen Lynn Gallery, Boca Ratan, 2008; and others. *Awards:* Grumbacher Award for Outstanding Contrib to the Arts, 76; Elizabeth Erlanger Award of Merit, Nat Asn Women Artists, 79; Chase Manhattan Bank Purchase Award, Nassau Mus Fine Art, 85; First prize, Boca Raton Mus Art, Artists Guild, 2001; 1st Prize, Boca Ratan Mus Art, Artists Guild. *Mem:* Nat Asn Women, New York (bd mem 80-91); Old Sch Square Cult Arts Ctr, Delray, Fla, 91-92; Boca Raton Mus Art, 92. *Publ:* NY Times, Newsday

RECANATI, DINA
SCULPTOR
b Cairo, Egypt. *Study:* Art Students League, with Jose de Creft, 59-62. *Work:* Israel Mus, Jerusalem; Tel Aviv Mus; Ben Gurion Airport, Tel Aviv; Tel Aviv Univ, Israel; Jewish Mus, NY; Herrzliah Mus, Continental Grain Collection, NY. *Comn:* Gate (bronze), Ministry of Transportation, Israel, 74; Gates (spec bronze ed), Am-Israel Cult Found, NY, 76; Israel Chancellery, Washington, DC, 80; President's Garden Collection, Jerusalem; Weizmann Inst Sci, Rehovot, Israel. *Exhib:* July M Gallery, Tel-Aviv, 81-84; Jewish Mus Sculpture Garden, NY, 81-84; Mus Contemp Art (with catalog), Ramat Gan, Israel, 89; Barbican Art Gallery, London, Eng, 90; Installation Ben Gurion Airport, 92; and others. *Bibliog:* Amnon Barzel (auth), Pillars and Parchments, 86; Prof M Omer (auth), Transformation from Within, Cimaise, 87 & Signs of Survival in the Culture of Decay, 89; Gil Goldfine (auth), Through the Trees, Jerusalem Post, 89; and others. *Media:* Bronze, Wood. *Publ:* Contribr, The Artist's Notebook, Gordon Galleries, Israel, 75. *Dealer:* Julie M Gallery Tel Aviv Israel. *Mailing Add:* 136 Grand St Apt 6E New York NY 10013

RECTOR, MARGE (LEE)
PAINTER, GRAPHIC ARTIST
b Norman, Okla, Aug 4, 1929. *Study:* Tex Tech Univ, BA(com art), 50; studied at Dallas Mus Fine Arts (painting & life drawing), 65-66, Chapman Kelley (critique & life drawing), 65-66 Coll Marin (ceramic & sculpture), 75-78. *Work:* Public; McDermott-Smyzer Collection, Dallas Tex; Private: Donald W Seldin-Dallas Tex, Ellen Hansen, Columbus, NC; Christine & Bill Berry-Tiburon, CA. *Exhib:* Tex Painting & Sculpture Exhib, Dallas Mus Fine Arts, 66 & 71; Butler Inst Am Art, Youngstown, Ohio, 66 & 70; 8th Ann Eight State Exhib Painting & Sculpture, Okla Art Ctr, 66; Color Talk & Personal Motives, Agora Gallery, NY, 93 & 94; Coastal Arts League Ninth Ann Juried Exhib, Coastal Arts League Mus, Half Moon Bay, Calif, 1993; Expanding Consciousness, Abney Galleries, NY, 94; Critics Choice, Montserrat Gallery, NY, 94; San Bernadino Art Asn Inland Exhib XXXI, San Bernadino Co Mus, Redlands, Calif, 1995. *Pos:* Artist, Bozell & Jacobs, 50-52; free lance com artist, Dallas, Tex, 52-65; fine arts gallery affil, Atelier Chapman Kelly, 66-73. *Awards:* Humble Oil & Refining Co Award, 66; Best in Show Circuit Award, Tex Fine Arts Asn, 67; Minnie Belle Heep Award, Tex Fine Arts Asn, 68. *Bibliog:* Timothy Rose & Marge Rector, Ways to Shape Space, Artweek, 76; Marge Rector's Abstracts Start 6 week Show at Library, Marin Scope, 2/77. *Mem:* Marin Arts Coun. *Media:* Acrylic, Abstract Painting, Ink Drawing. *Interests:* Free flow & hard edge abstractions. *Publ:* Contribr, California Art Review, Am References, 89; Encyclopedia of Living Artists 8, Art Network, 94; Color Talk Agora, Manhattan Arts Int, 1-2/94. *Mailing Add:* 25 San Carlos Sausalito CA 94965

REDD, RICHARD JAMES
PRINTMAKER, MISCELLANEOUS MEDIA
b Toledo, Ohio, Oct 22, 1931. *Study:* Toledo Mus Sch; Univ Toledo, BEd, 53; Univ Iowa, MFA, 58, study with Eugene Ludins & Mauricio Lasansky. *Work:* Allentown Art Mus, Pa; Lehigh Univ, Bethlehem, Pa; Philip & Muriel Berman Collection, Allentown; Kutztown Univ, Pa; East Stroudsburg Univ, Pa; Joan Miller Moran Collection; Allentown Symphony Orchestra Collection; Community Music School, Allentown. *Exhib:* Solo exhibs, Allentown Art Mus, 61, Kemerer Mus, Bethlehem, Pa, 80 & Zhejiang Art Acad, Hangzhou, China, 89 & 92, Home and Planet, Bethleham, Pa, 2007, Encaustic paintings, Zoellner Art Ctr, 2008 & 50 yrs at Lehigh Univ, Bethlehem, Pa; Mushroom Magic, Reading Mus, 82; Breaking with Tradition, Int Quilt Exhib, 83; 30 yr Print Retrospective, Lehigh Univ, 88; Jiangsu Art Gallery, Nanjing, China 92; Banana Factory, Bethlehem, Pa, 99; Hill Sch, Pottstown, Pa, 2000; Raab Gallery, Phila, Pa, 2002; 21 Years of Collagraph Prints Retrospective, Banana Factory, Bethlehem, PA, Aug-Sept 2005; 80 yr Retrospective, Banana Factory, Bethlehem, 2012; Home & Plane, Bethlehem, Pa, 2012. *Pos:* Cur, Masks: Other Faces, Kemerer Mus, 88; cur, Lets Face it, Bethlehem Town Hall, 2010. *Teaching:* Prof, Lehigh Univ, 58-95, prof emer, 96-; chmn dept fine art, 70-76; lectr in China, 89 & 92. *Awards:* Tribute to the Arts Award, Bethlehem Fine Arts Commission, 94; Prize, 9th Nat Print Show, Moravian Coll, 94 & Woodmere Art Mus, Philadelphia, 96; Print Prize, Phillips Mill, New Hope, Pa, 2001; Am Color Print Soc Print Prize, Philadelphia, 2006; 1st Prize, Lehigh Art Alliance, 2008; founder, Printmakers Soc Lehigh Valley, 2013. *Mem:* Lehigh Art Alliance (bd dir, 72-75 & 86-96, pres, 76-77); Kemerer Mus, Bethlehem (bd dir, 78-88); Am Color Print Soc (Phila chap); Printmakers Society of Lehigh Valley (founder 2013). *Media:* Intaglio, Collagraph, Encaustic. *Specialty:* prints. *Dealer:* Chestnut Hill Gallery Philadelphia PA; Zoellner Art Center Bethlehem PA; Art of Framing Jenkintown PA; Annex Galleries Santa Rosa Ca. *Mailing Add:* 1749 Stonesthrow Rd Bethlehem PA 18015-8935

REDDINGTON, CHARLES LEONARD
PAINTER, EDUCATOR
b Chicago, Ill, Mar 22, 1929. *Study:* Art Inst Chicago, with Paul Wieghardt, dipl, 54, BFA, 58; Southern Ill Univ, MFA, 70. *Work:* Commonwealth Govt Collection, Canberra, Australia; Art Gallery NSW, Sydney; Nat Gallery Victoria, Melbourne; Western Australian Art Gallery, Perth; Southern Ill Univ, Carbondale. *Comn:* Harold Mertz Pub Collection, NY, 63; Four Color Lithographs, Nat Gallery Victoria, Melbourne, 64. *Exhib:* Australian Painting Today, 64; Young Contemporaries of Australia, Japan, 65; Travel Exhib of Art, Ind, 71; Solo exhib, Swope Art Gallery, Terre Haute, Ind, 73; G Bablo, Acad D'Arts, Rivera dei Fiori, Bordighera, Italy; and many others. *Pos:* Dir educ abroad, Ind State Univ, Terre Haute, 75-93. *Teaching:* Lectr drawing & painting, NSW Univ, Sydney, 63-66; prof painting, Ind State Univ, Terre Haute, 70-93. *Awards:* Willis Painting Award, H O Willis Corp, Inc, Sydney, 65; Louis Comfort Tiffany Grant, 70; Works on Paper Prize, Indianapolis Mus, 72; and many others. *Bibliog:* Robert Hughes (auth), Art in Australia, Pelican Books, 70; James Gleeson (auth), Modern Painters, Landsdowne Press, 71; Alan McCulloch (auth), Encyclopedia of Australian Art, Hutchinson & Co. *Mem:* Coll Art Conf; Art Inst Chicago Alumnae; Int Inst Conserv Historic & Artistic Works; Ind Arts Comn. *Media:* Acrylic, Oil. *Mailing Add:* 735 W Division Chicago IL 60610-1005

REDDIX, ROSCOE CHESTER
PAINTER, EDUCATOR
b New Orleans, La, Nov 15, 1933. *Study:* Southern Univ, BA; Univ New Orleans; Ind Univ, Bloomington, MS (art educ); Univ Southern Miss; also with Dr Eddie Jordan; Vanderbuilt Univ, Nashville, Tenn, PhD. *Comn:* Pastic painting, Southern Univ New Orleans; painting, Superdome, New Orleans, La. *Exhib:* Expo 72, La Artist Exhib, Ill State Univ; NJ State Mus; Black Artist, Ind Univ; Solo exhibs, Ala State Univ, Southern Univ New Orleans & DeWitt Hist Soc, Ithaca, NY. *Pos:* Bd dir, New Orleans Mus Art. *Teaching:* Instr art, Shreveport, La & New Orleans, La; from asst prof to assoc prof art, Southern Univ New Orleans, 74-, asst to chancellor, 92-. *Bibliog:* Samella S Lewis & Ruth Waddy (auth), Black artist on art, Contemp Crafts. *Mem:* Nat Conf Artist (state dir, 73); Coll Art Asn; Creative Artists Alliance New Orleans. *Media:* Oil. *Publ:* Contribr, Black Artist on Art, Vol 2, 71. *Mailing Add:* 1330 Cambronne St New Orleans LA 70118-2002

REDDY, KRISHNA N
PRINTMAKER, SCULPTOR
b Chittoor, Andhra State, India, July 15, 1925. *Study:* Int Univ Santiniketan, India, dipl (fine arts), 47; Univ London Slade Sch Fine Arts, cert (fine arts), 52; Acad Grande Chaumiere, Paris, with Zadkine, cert (fine arts), 55; Atelier 17, Int Ctr Gravure, Paris, 55; Academie DiBelle Arti DiBrera, Milan, with Marino Marini, cert (fine arts), 57. *Work:* Marble sculpture, Carrara, Ital, 76; bronze sculpture, Demonstrators, Collectors Guild, NY, 77; Mus Mod Art, NY & Paris; Libr Cong, Nat Galleries, Smithsonian Inst, Washington, DC; Metrop Mus Art, NY; British Mus, London; Albertina Mus, Vienna; Chicago Art Inst. *Comn:* Monumental sculpture in marble, Int Sculpture Symposium, St Margarethan, Austria, 62 & Montreal, 64. *Exhib:* Solo exhibs, Madison Art Ctr, 73, Assoc Am Artists, NY, 74, Univ Calif Gallery, Santa Cruz, 75 & Galerie Vivant, Tokyo, 78; Retrospectives, Bronx Mus Arts, NY, 81; Lalitkala Akademi, New Delhi, 84; Museo del Palacio de Bellas Artes, 88. *Pos:* Dir art dept, Col Fine Arts, Kalakshetra, Madras, 47-49. *Teaching:* Prof & co-dir printmaking, Atelier 17, Int Ctr Graphics, Paris, 57-76; prof & dir graphics, printmaking prog, Dept Art & Art Educ, NY Univ, 77-, prof emeritus art & art educ, 2001-. *Awards:* Padma Shree, Pres India, 72; Printmaker Emer Award, Southern Graphics Council, 2000; Lifetime Achievement Award, Soc Am Graphic Art, 2005; Kala Ratna Award, Nat Acad Fine Arts, Govt of India, 2007. *Bibliog:* S W Hayter (auth), About Prints, 64 & New Ways of Gravure, 66, Oxford Univ Press, London; Gabor Peterdi (auth), Printmaking, Macmillan Co, New York, 71; Una Johnson (auth), American Prints and Printmakers, NY, 80; The Great Clown, Gallerie Borjeson, Malmo, Sweden, 85; Peggy Roalf (auth), Looking at Paintings: Circus, 93. *Mem:* Soc Am Graphic Artists. *Media:* Engraving, Etching; Stone, Bronze. *Interests:* Art education. *Publ:* Auth, Intaglio Simultaneous Color

Printmaking, State Univ New York Press, Albany, 88; New Ways of Color Printmaking: Significance of Materials and Processes, Aianta Press & Vadehra Art Gallery, New Delhi, 97. *Dealer:* Sylvan Cole Gallery 101 W 57th St New York NY 10019. *Mailing Add:* 80 Wooster St New York NY 10012

REDGRAVE, FELICITY
PAINTER, PRINTMAKER
b UK, 1920; Can citizen. *Study:* Sheridan Col, Oakville, Ont, dipl (hon; graphic design), 70; Univ Guelph, Ont, BA (hon; fine arts), 73; Univ Toronto, BEd (art), 75. *Work:* Can Art Bank, Ottawa; Esso Resources Ltd, Calgary, Alta; Lavalin Inc, Montreal; Teleglobe, Montreal; Telesat, Ottawa. *Exhib:* Solo exhib, Images of Nova Scotia & Newfoundland, Harbour Front, Toronto, 77, Art Gallery of Nova Scotia, 78, Confederation Ctr, Charlottetown, PEI, 80, Night-Spaces, St Mary's Univ, Halifax, NS, 84 & Moncton Univ, 86; Night Radio, Galerie Sans Nom, Moncton, 87; McPherson Libr, Univ Victoria, 92; Videographe, Montréal, Que, 94. *Pos:* Contrib ed, Art mag, 78-82; art critic, Discussion Concordia Univ, Montreal, 80; contrib writer, Arts Atlantic, 81. *Teaching:* Vis artist, Univ Toronto, York Univ, 77 & Univ Waterloo, 79 & 81; lectr, Owens Art Gallery, Mt Allison Univ, NS, 85. *Awards:* Can Coun B Grant, 83-84; Intermedia Group & video Grants, 87-88; Exploration Grant, 89. *Bibliog:* Susan Gibson (auth), article, Vangard Mag Review, 85; Univ Guelph Alumni Mag, 94. *Mem:* Visual Arts NS; Can Artists Representation; NS Printmakers Asn; Community Arts Coun, Victoria, BC. *Media:* Acrylic, Graphite. *Publ:* Auth, Tom Forrestal, Arts Atlantic, 79; Marlene Creates and Pat Martin Bates at Mt St Vincent's Art Gallery, 85; Brian Porter at Dalhousie Art Gallery, 85; John Neville, Art Gallery NS, 88. *Dealer:* Winchester Galleries 1545 Fort St Victoria BC V8S 1Z7. *Mailing Add:* 1545 Fort St Victoria BC V8S 1Z7 Canada

REDING, BARBARA ENDICOTT
ARTIST
b New York, NY, Jan 31, 1939. *Study:* b Brigham Young Univ, BA, 60; grad work, Univ Calif. *Work:* Art Mus of Santa Cruz; Tate Mus, London; Bank of Am; Plantronics Corp; Landmark Properties. *Comn:* Double Tree Hotel, Monterey, Calif. *Exhib:* NAPA Exhibit, Santa Fe, NM, 2002. *Collection Arranged:* Westminster exhib, London, Tate Mus, London, Colton Hall Cult Arts exhib, Monterey, Calif, Napa Signature exhibs, Monterey, Calif, New Orleans, La. *Pos:* Plein Air Instr, Santa Cruz Art League, 94-96; Plein Air Instr, Ireland, 96-2002. *Teaching:* studio private and group instructions. *Awards:* Best of Show, Capitala Plein Air Competition, 02; Best of Show, Santa Cruz, 99. *Bibliog:* Monterey Co Herald, 00; Santa Cruz Sentinel, 70-89. *Mem:* Nat Acrylic Painters Asn (signature mem); Cent Coast Painters; Carmel Colorist; Carmel Art Found; Santa Cruz Art League. *Media:* Oils. *Specialty:* Calif Plein Air Works, Calif Impressionists. *Mailing Add:* PO Box 755 Capitola CA 95010

REDINGER, WALTER FRED
SCULPTOR, MURALIST
b Wallacetown, Ont, Jan 6, 40. *Study:* Beal-Spec Art, London, Ont; Meinsinger Sch Art, Detroit; Ont Coll Art, Toronto. *Work:* Nat Art Gallery, Ottawa; Stratford Art Gallery; St Thomas Art Gallery; Univ Western Ont; Univ Sask; Art Bank of Ottawa; Het National Ballet. *Comn:* Nat Parks Comn, Ottawa, 78; Por & Assocs, 79; Oakville Art Gallery, Ont; Garlick Gardens, 83; Dr R Redinger, Louisville, Ky. *Exhib:* Montreal Mus Fine Arts, Que, 64; Survey 68, Montreal Mus Fine Arts, 68; Group exhib, Montreal Mus Fine Arts, 68; Ont Centennial Exhib, Toronto, Art Gallery Ont, 68; The Hart of London, Nat Gallery Can, 68; Can Artists, Art Gallery Ont, 68; Plastic Presence, Milwaukee Art Ctr, 69; Plastics, San Francisco Mus Art, 69; Sensory Perceptions, Art Gallery Ont, 70; 3 D's into the 70's, Art Gallery Ont, 70; St Thomas Art Gallery, Ont, 73; London Regional Art Gallery, 77; Opening Celebrations, London Regional Art Gallery, 80; Group exhib, Ctr Contemp Art St Thomas, 92; Three Elgin Co Artists, St Thomas Art Gallery, 92; Hart of London, London Regional Art Gallery, 93; Solo exhibs, Beyond Survival, London Regional Art Gallery & Christopher Cutts Gallery, Toronto, 94; Group exhib, Mitchel Algus Gallery, NY, 95; Michael Gibson Gallery, London, Ontario, Small & Mighty, small works by maj artists, 2003; St Thomas Pub Art Ctr, Organic Works on Paper, 2004; Mitchell Algus Art Gallery, NY, God Seekers, 2005; Project for Revolution, Mathew Marks Gallery, NY, 2007; Apparition, Canada Southern Railway Station and St Thomas Elgin Public Arts Centre, 2007; Return to the Void, The Ghost Ship and Other Tales from the Ether, Mus Contemp Art Toronto (MOCCA), 2007; The Garden Party, Woodstock, 2008. *Pos:* Resident artist, Univ Western Ont. *Awards:* Sculpture Prize, Montreal Mus Fine Art, 68; Can Coun Jr Awards, 68-71, Sr Awards, 73, 74, 78-80 & 87; Victor Lynch-Staunton Award, 77; Pollack-Krasner Award, 2004-2005. *Bibliog:* Peter Crass, 75 & 76; Phil Ross & Walter Redinger, Landscape Vision & Dreams, 82; Beyond Survival, Int Film Festival, Halifax, NS, 96; Redinger at work-Documentary, 2005; CBS Radio Here and Now, Interview by Lupe Rodriguez, Feb 2007; articles in Time Mag, Art in Am, Sculpture Now, Toronto Life, The Globe, Mail Toronto, La PRess, Canadian Art, New York Times. *Mem:* Royal Can Acad Arts. *Media:* Fiberglass, Steel, Mixed Media, Canvas. *Interests:* Walter Redinger Blues Band (Leader). *Dealer:* Mitch Algus, 511 West 25th St New York, NY, 212-242-6242. *Mailing Add:* 25761 Silver Clay Hene R #3 West Lorne ON NOL2PO Canada

REDMOND, CATHERINE
PAINTER, EDUCATOR
b Jamestown, NY, June 3, 1943. *Study:* Cornell Univ, Ithaca, NY, 61-62; Harpur Col, State Univ NY, Binghamton, AB, 66; Art Students League, New York, 69-74. *Work:* Butler Inst Am Art; Art Students League NY; Luther Col, Decorah, Iowa; Progressive Insurance Corp & Cleveland Clinic Found Collections, Cleveland, Ohio; Reading Mus, Reading, Pa; Swetbriar Coll, Va. *Comn:* View from Euclid, Cleveland Clinic Found, Ohio, 85; Winter Westside, Cardinal Fed Savings Bank, Cleveland, Ohio, 86; View from Downtown, Transohio Bank, Cleveland, 87; 17 Views of NY, Dreyfus Corp, 92. *Exhib:* Biennial One, Contemp Art Ctr, Cincinnati, 86; The City as Subject, Butler Inst Am Art, 88; Urbanology, Mary Grove Coll Gallery, Detroit, 89; The Artist as Native, Babcock Galleries, NY, 93-94; Rediscovering the Landscape of the Americas, Gerald Peters Gallery, Santa Fe, NMex, 96-97; NY Collection, Albright-Knox Art Gallery, NY, 98; NY Night and Day, David Findlay Jr Contemp Art, NY, 01; Kindred Spirits, David Findlay, Jr Contemp Art, 02; Points of View, David Findlay Jr Contemp Art, NY, 02; Value and Presence, List Gallery, Swarthmore Col, Pa, 03; Twelve: Catherine Redmond, David Findlay Jr Contemp Art 2003, Thru the Ether, Dean's Gallery, Pratt Inst; Small Photos, Deans Gallery, Pratt Inst, 2008. *Teaching:* Asst prof painting, Cleveland Inst Art, 85-90; instr, Art Students League, NY, 90-2000; vis asst prof, Sch of Art and Design, Pratt Inst, NY, 1999; Aju Associate Prof Sch of Art and Design, Pratt Inst 2005-. *Bibliog:* Erica-Lynn Gamino (auth), Creations at Goodheart, Southampton Press, 4/29/98; John Driscoll (auth), The Artist & American Landscape, First Glance Bks Inc, 98; Phyllis Braff (auth), 3 artists & a solid view of individual directions, NY Times, 4/19/98; Christopher Willard, "Creating Contrasts with Conte Crayons," American Artist, 2/99; Cynthia Dantzic (auth), 100 New York Painters, Schiffer Publ Co, fall 2006; Suzanne Slesin, To Each Her Own, NY Times, 1/22/2009; Steve Litt (auth), Cleveland Urban, Cleveland Plain Dealer, Mar 2009; Everything to See, An Artist's Life in the City, David Findlay Fine Art, New York, 2009. *Mem:* Art Students League NY (bd control, 72-74); Artists Fel; Coll Art Asn. *Media:* Oil. *Publ:* Mary Abbott (cat essay), Arlene Bujese Gallery, E Hampton, NY, July 2005; CJ Fields, Catalog essay, DSFA Gallery, New York, 2008. *Mailing Add:* 361 W 36th St New York NY 10018

REDMOND, ROSEMARY
PAINTER
b Anchorage, Alaska, Mar 16, 1952. *Study:* Univ Alaska, BFA, 82; Pratt Inst, grant & fel, MFA, 85. *Work:* Anchorage Mus Hist & Art, Alaska; Alaska State Coun Arts; Mat-Su Coll; Palmer, Alaska; Mus North, Fairbanks Mus; Juneau State Mus, Anchorage. *Comn:* Dr & Karen Compton, Anchorage, Alas. *Exhib:* solo exhibs, Visual Arts Ctr Alaska, Anchorage, 91, Kendall Gallery, New York, NY, 91, Stonington Gallery, Anchorage, Alaska, 94, Anchorage Mus Hist & Art, Alaska, 95, Alaska Pac Univ, 98, Bunnell Gallery, Homer, Alaska, 2000, Decker Morris Gallery, Anchorage, Alaska, 2000, Alaska Pacific Univ, 2004, Bitoz, Anchorage, Alaska, 2004 & Bunnell Gallery, Homer, Alaska, 2006, Alaska Pacific Univ, 2009, Through a Glass Lightly, Fireweed Gallery, Homer, Alaska, 2012, Jens Anchorage, Alaska, 2012, High Boat, Conoco Phillips Gallery, Anchorage, 2014, Int Gallery Contemp Art, Anchorage, Alasaka, 2015, Vienna Woods Gallery, Los Angeles, Calif, 2016; Group exhibs, Nat, New Am Talent, traveling, Tex Fine Arts Assoc, Austin, 89; Nat, Current Visions, Germanow Gallery, Rochester, NY, 86; Garr Gottstien Gallery, 98; Alaska Pacific Univ, 2004; Conoco Phillips Gallery, Anchorage, Alaska, 2009; Carr Gottstein Gallery, 2007; MTS Gallery, Anchorage, Alaska, 2008; Bunnell Gallery, Homer, Alaska, 2009. *Teaching:* adj prof art, Univ Alaska, Anchorage, beginner painting, 97-, beginner & intermediate painting, 2010; taught art appreciation, Mat Su Coll, 95, 96. *Awards:* Fel, Yaddo Corp, 89; Grants, Artists Space, New York, 90 & 91; Alaska State Coun Arts, 2000, 2012; Website Award, Northwestern States Art coun, 99; Grant, Alaksa State Coun Arts, 2004; Grant, Ak State Arts Council, 2012. *Bibliog:* Julie Decker (auth), Icebreakers-Alaska's Most Innovative Artists, textbook, Alaska State Coun on Arts and Alaska Humanities Forum, 99; John Branson (auth), Bristol Bay, From Hinterlands to Tidewater, textbook, Nat Park Svc; Painting the Railroad, Anchorage Daily News, 08/11/2006; Wild & Free Bristol Bay Artist, Anchorage Daily News, 12/15/95; Abstract Artist Returns to Alaska with a Purpose, Anchorage Times, 90; Masterful Exhib Revels in Hi Tech, Anchorage Daily News, Jan 2005; Inter Gallery of Contemporary Art, Anchorage; Road & Track Mag, March & April, p 68, 2014. *Mem:* Anchorage Mus. *Media:* Acrylic, Oil. *Res:* Art History. *Publ:* Auth, An Eskimo in Touch with Two Cultures, Alaska Mag, 11/79. *Dealer:* Blue-Holomon Gallery Anchorage AK. *Mailing Add:* 440 E 15th Terr Anchorage AK 99501

RED STAR, KEVIN (RUNNING RABBIT)
PAINTER, PRINTMAKER
b Lodge Grass, Mont, Oct 9, 1943. *Study:* Inst Am Indian Art, Santa Fe, NMex, 62-65; San Francisco Art Inst, 65-67; Mont State Univ, 68-69; Eastern Mont Col, Billings, BA, 72. *Work:* Northern Plains Mus, Browning, Mont; Inst Am Indian Art Mus, Santa Fe, NMex; Denver Art Mus, Colo; Shenyang Nat Art Mus, Liaoning, China; Rocky Mountain Coll, Billing, Mont; and others. *Comn:* Mural, Crow Tribal Office, Crow Agency, Mont. *Exhib:* Wheelwright Contemp Indian Artist Show, Wheelwright Ceremonial Art Mus, Santa Fe, 78; 100 yrs of Native Am Painting, Okla Mus Art, 78; Indian Images '80, Natural Hist Mus, Denver; Peking Exhibit of Am Western Art, China, 81; Lublin Collection, NY, 86 & Greenwich, Conn, 87; Segal Gallery, New York City, 87; El Taller Gallery, 88; Mus of the Rockies, Bozeman, Mont, 95; Kevin Red Star Gallery, Red Lodge, Mont, 97, 2000, 2001, 2002; Ramscale Gallery, New York City, 97; Autry Mus of Western Heritage, Los Angeles, 97, 98-2003; Red Lodge North Gallery, Billings, 98, 99; Ventana Fine Art Gallery, Santa Fe, 98, 99, 2000, 2001 & 2003; Denver Art Mus, 98; Wilde Meyer Gallery, Scottsdale, Ariz, 2000; Sutton West Gallery, Missoula, Mont, 2000, 2002 & 2003; Frame Hut & Gallery, Billings, 2000; Martin-Harris Gallery, Jackson Hole, Wyom, 2000; Big Horn Gallery, Cody, Wyom, 2000n; Mus Nebr Art, Kearney, 2000, 2002; Buffalo Bill Hist Ctr, Cody, 2000; Coeur d'Alene Tribal Art Show & Auction, 2001, 2002; Sorrel Sky Gallery, Durango, Colo, 2002; Lloyd Kiva New Gallery, Santa Fe, 2002; Eiteljorg Mus, Indianapolis, 2002 & 2003; Buffalo Bill Hist Ctr, Cody, 2002; Indian Artist's of Am Show, Scottsdale, 2003; Yellowstone Art Mus, Billings, 2003; one-person shows, Northcutt Steele Gallery, Billings, 89, El Taller Gallery, Santa Fe, 90, Ventana Fine Art Gallery, Santa Fe, 98, 2001, 2002, Healing Environ Gallery, Billings Deaconess Hosp, 98, Kevin Red Star Gallery, 98, 99, CM Russell Mus, 99, Carbon Co Arts Guild & Depot Gallery, Red Lodge, Mont, 2000, Holter Mus, Helena, 2000, Martin-Harris Gallery, 2001, Rich Haines Gallery, Jackson Hole, 2002 & Mt San Antonio Coll Gallery, 2002; two-person show, Sutton West Gallery, 2001. *Collection Arranged:* 77 West Coast Experience (auth, catalog), Tokyo, Japan; Am Indian Art Exhibition, Espace Pierre Cardin, Paris, 79; The Real People, Havana, Cuba, 79; Santa Fe Festival of the Arts, 78-81; Am Indian Art in the 80's, Native Am Ctr Living Arts Mus (auth, catalog), Niagara Falls, NY, 81. *Teaching:* Instr art, Lodge Grass, Mont, 73-74, Inst Am Indian Art, Santa Fe, 75-76. *Awards:* Governor's Trophy, Scottsdale Nat Indian Art Exhib,

65; First Place, Cent Wash State Coll Art Exhib, Ellensburg, Wash, 74. *Bibliog:* Scott E Dial (auth), Visual portrayals of Kevin Red Star, Southwest Art, 2/76; Penny Cox (auth), Red Star: Modern mystic and on the move, Santa Fe Profile Mag, 12/79; Jamake Highwater, The Sweet Grass Lives On, Harper & Row, 79-80. *Mem:* Harvard Project. *Media:* Acrylic, Oil; Lithography, Etchings. *Mailing Add:* PO Box 269 Roberts MT 59070

REECE, MAYNARD
PAINTER, ILLUSTRATOR
b Arnolds Park, Iowa, Apr 26, 1920. *Work:* Cent Nat Bank, Des Moines, Iowa; Norwest Bank, Des Moines; Leigh Yawkey Woodson Art Mus, Wausau, Wis; Iowa State Univ Mus, Ames, Iowa. *Comn:* Designs for postage stamps, Govt of Bermuda, 65; First Iowa Duck Stamp, State Conserv Comn, 72; Marshlander Mallards, Ducks Unlimited Inc, 73; Canada Geese & Mallards, Winnebago Indust; Canada Geese, Remington Arms, Bridgeport, Conn, 76; Am Artist Collection, 85. *Exhib:* Various mus throughout the US & Can. *Awards:* Five Time Winner, Fed Duck Stamp Competition; Ark Duck Stamp Award, 82; Tex Duck Stamp Award, 83; Master Artist, Leigh Yaukey Woodson Art Mus, Wausau, Wis. *Bibliog:* John Diffely (auth), Maynard Reece: Wildlife artist, Am Artist, 78; Chuck Wechsler (auth), I've been there with Maynard Reece, Wildlife Art News, 84; M Stephen Doherty (auth), Am Artist, 85; Mark E Stegmaier (auth), Maynard Reece: Celebrator of the marsh, Midwest Art, 85. *Mem:* Grand Cent Art Galleries New York; hon trustee Ducks Unlimited Inc; Soc Animal Artists; Nat Audubon Soc; Outdoor Writers Asn Am (past bd mem). *Media:* Oil, Watercolor; Stone Lithography. *Specialty:* Wildlife, scenic views. *Publ:* Illusr, Life, Outdoor Life, Sports Afield & others; auth & illusr, Fish & Fishing, Meredith, 63; illusr, Waterfowl in Iowa & Iowa Fish & Fishing, Iowa Conserv Comn; auth & illusr, Waterfowl Art of Maynard Reece, Abrams, 85; Upland Bird Art of Maynard Reece, Abrams, 97. *Dealer:* Mill Pond Press Inc 310 Center Court Venice FL 34292. *Mailing Add:* 5315 Robertson Dr Des Moines IA 50312

REED, CLEOTA
HISTORIAN, LECTURER
b Chicago, Ill. *Study:* Syracuse Univ, BFA, 75, MA, 76. *Awards:* Am Philos Soc Grant, 76 & 98; Nat Endowment Humanities Fel, 80 & 91; Merit Award, NY Regional Coun Hist Agencies, 85; Onondaga Hist Asn Medal, 2009. *Mem:* Am Ceramic Circle; Tile Heritage Found; Am Antiquarian Soc. *Res:* American & English ceramic tiles; Spanish arts and crafts móvement; John Gough Nichols and the Gothic revival. *Publ:* Auth, Irene Sargent: A Comprehensive Bibliography, Syracuse Univ: Courier, 81; William Ittner & H Mercer: Art & Architecture, Erie Co Hist Soc, 82; ed, Henry Keck Stained Glass Studio 1913-1974, Syracuse Univ Press, 85; auth, Henry Chapman Mercer and the Moravian Tile Works, Univ Pa Press, 87; Syracuse China, Syracuse Univ Press, 97; The Tiles of Erie, Erie Mus Art, 99; Madrid's Pictorial Tiles, A Walking Tour, 2007; The Golden Fountain & The Grill Room, TACS, 2009; Felicity Ashbee: A List of her Literary Works, 2009; Felicity as We Knew her, 2011; Irene Sargent at the Keystone, 2012; Irene Sargent and the American Arts and Crafts Movement, 2012. *Mailing Add:* 329 Westcott St Syracuse NY 13210

REED, DAVID
PAINTER
b San Diego, Calif, Jan 20, 1946. *Study:* Reed Coll, BA; New York Studio Sch; Skowhegan Sch Painting & Sculpture. *Work:* Metrop Mus Art, New York; Mus Contemp Art, San Diego; Mus Nat d'Art Mod, Centre George Pompidou, Paris; Wexner Ctr Arts, Columbus, Ohio; Mus Moderner Kunst, Frankfurt & Main, Ger; Mus Moderner Kunst, Stiftung, Ludwig, Vienna, Austria; Albright Knox Art Gallery, Buffalo, NY; Hirshhorn Mus, Washington, D.C.; Kunstmuseum St. Gallen, St. Gallen, Switz; Kaiser Wilheim Mus, Krefeld, Ger. *Exhib:* Solo Exhibs: Max Protetch Gallery, 89, 91-92, 95, 98-99, 2002, 2004, 2007; Galerie Rolf Ricke, Cologne, Ger, 91, 93, 97, 2000, 2003, & 2007; David Reed, Lives of Paintings, Douglas F Cooley Mem Art Gallery, Reed Coll, Ore, 2008; Galerie Schmidt Maczollek, Cologne, Germany, 2006, 2010, Hausler Contemp, Munich, Germany, 2009, Works on Paper, Peter Blum Gallery, New York, 2010 ; Asher/Faure Gallery, Los Angeles, 88, 97 & 2002; Leave Yourself Behind, Paintings & Special Projects 1967-2005, Ulrich Mus Art, Witchita, Kans, Roswell Mus & Art Ctr, NMex & Luckman Gallery, Los Angeles; William Eggleston & David Reed, Peder Lund, Oslo, Norway, 2011. *Teaching:* Vis artist, Calif Inst Arts, Valencia, 94; prof, Visiting Arts Council, Univ Calif, Los Angeles, 2001. *Awards:* Rockefeller Found Grant, 66; Fel, Guggenheim Found, 88; Nat Endowment Arts, 91; Skowhegan Medal for Painting, 2001; Ursula Blickle Stiftung Kunstforderpreis fur Malerei. *Bibliog:* Arthur Danto & Hanne Loreck (auths), David Reed (exhib catalog), Kolnischer Kunstverein, 95; Elizabeth Armstrong, Dave Hickey & Mieke Bal (auths), David Reed Paintings: Motion Pictures (exhib catalog); David Reed: You Look Good in Blue (exhib catalog), Kunstmuseum St. Gallen, Switz, 2001; High Times, Hard Times: New York Painting 1967-1975 (exhib catalog), 2006; Richard Shiff and John Yau (auths), David Reed: Leave Yourself Behind Paintings and Special Projects 1967-2005 (exhib catalog), Ulrich Mus Art, Wichita, Kansas, 2005. *Media:* Oil & Alkyd on Canvas. *Publ:* Auth, Memories of Rome, New Observations, #68, 6/89; Reflected light; In siena with Beccafumi, Arts Mag, 52-53, 3/91; Two Bedrooms in San Francisco (essay, exhib catalog), San Francisco Art Inst, 92; Step into Liquid, In: Richard Allen Morris Retrospective, 1958-2004 (exhib catalog), 2004; Rock, Paper, Scissors, Kienbaum Artists Book, Snoeck Pub: Ghent, Belgium, 2009. *Dealer:* Galerie Schmidt Maczollek Schonhauser Strasse 8 D-50968 Loln; Peter Blum Gallery 99 Wooster St New York NY 10012; Hausler Contemp Maximilian Strasse 35 D-80538 Munich. *Mailing Add:* 506 Greenwich St New York NY 10013

REED, DENNIS JAMES
CURATOR, DESIGNER
b Culver City, Calif, Oct 30, 1946. *Study:* Calif State Univ, Fullerton, BA, 69, MA, 71; MMI, Univ Calif, Berkeley, 83. *Collection Arranged:* Japanese Photography in Los Angeles, 1920-1945 (auth, catalog), 82 & The Furniture of Gustav Stickley, 83, Art Gallery, Los Angeles Valley Col; Japanese Photography in Am 1920-1940 (auth, catalog), Japanese-Am Cult Ctr, 86; Travel Exhib 88-89: Oakland Mus, Rahr-West Art Mus; Whitney Mus Am Art, Corcoran Gallery Art; Southern Calif Pictorialism: Its Mad Aspects, The Huntington; and other exhibs. *Pos:* Dir, Conejo Valley Art Mus, 78-80 & Art Gallery, Los Angeles Valley Col, 80-91. *Teaching:* Prof art, Los Angeles Valley Col, 80-91, dean fine, performing and media arts, 91-. *Awards:* Award of Excellence, Am Fed of the Arts; Award, Parallels and Contrasts, Am Inst Graphic Arts, 89. *Res:* Pictorial photography. *Publ:* Auth, Japanese Photograph in Am 1920-1940, 86; Richard Pettibone, Forty Years of California Assemblage, Wight Art Gallery, Univ Calif-Los Angeles, 89; Pictorialism in California: Photographs, 1900-1940, J Paul Getty Mus & Huntington Libr, 94. *Mailing Add:* c/o Los Angeles Valley Col Dean of Arts 5800 Fulton Ave Valley Glen CA 91404

REED, JAMES M
PRINTMAKER
b Wash DC, Dec 11, 1945. *Study:* Univ Missouri, Kans City, BA, 70; San Francisco State Univ, MA, 77; Tamarind Inst, 73-75. *Work:* NY Public Lib; Ohio Wesleyn Univ Mus; Metropolitan Mus Art; Smithsonian Inst; Achenbach Print Found, San Francisco, Calif. *Comn:* lithograph, Tamarind Inst, ALBQ, 74; lithograph, Little Egypt Ent, Houston, Tex, 75; lithograph, Blue Sky Press, San Francisco, Calif, 2000, 2006; Water Street Studio, Norwalk, Conn, 2005. *Exhib:* Solo Exhibs, Work on Paper, Inst Techinoglico, Monterney, Mass, 70, NW Mich Coll, Traverse City, Mich, MoMA, San Francisco, 78, Mus Art Sci, Bridgeport, Conn, 83, San Diego Mus, Calif, 2000, Portland Mus Art, Portland, 2004. *Pos:* owner, Milestone Graphics, Fine Printmaking, 76-; gallery dir, Univ Conn, Stamford, Conn, 2000-2003; mgr, curator, Gabor Pererdi Int Print Coll, 2010-. *Teaching:* Ford found, Ford, 73-75; Rocketfeller scholarship, 79; urban mentor, Connect Comn on Arts, 99-2000; park fellow, invited residence, 2012. *Bibliog:* Richard Byrnes (auth), Lithograph with Master Double Diamond, 97; Double Diamond Prodn, Etching with Master Double Diamond, 98; Venu Mag, 2012; Li Eisenstein (auth), Milestone, Journal of the Print World, 2013; A Chernow (auth), A Printmaker, Journal of Print World, 2014. *Mem:* SAGA; Silvermine Guild of Artists (bd trustees, 1983); Bridgeport Arts Council (gallery coord, 2010). *Media:* Printmaking. *Dealer:* Conn Fine Arts; Allinson Gallery Inc 23 Dunham Pond Rd East Storrs Conn 06268; Silvermine Art Ctr New Caanan Conn. *Mailing Add:* PO 5286 Bridgeport CT 06610

REED, JEFFREY
PAINTER
Study: Md Inst Coll Art, BFA, 1976; Skowhegan Sch Painting & Sculpture, 1979; Univ Pa, MFA, 1983. *Exhib:* Solo exhibs, Watermark Gallery, Annapolis, Md, 1980, Blair Acad, 1983, Gross McCleaf Gallery, Philadelphia, 19984, 1986, 1988, 1993, 1995, 1997, 1999, 2001, 2003, 2005 & 2007, List Gallery, Swarthmore Col, 1995 & George Billis Gallery, New York, 2004; Gross McCleaf Gallery, 1983, 1984, 1994, 1997 & 2003; The Spirit of hte Coast: American Artists (1850-1984), Monmouth Mus, Lincroft, NJ, 1984; Leo Castelli Gallery, New York, 1986; Cudahy's Gallery, New York, 1989; Hicks Art Ctr, Bucks County Community Col, 1990; Harn Mus, Univ Fla, 1991; Concepts in Drawing, Wayne Art Ctr, 1995; 55 Mercer, New York, 1996; Fleisher Art Mem, Philadelphia, 1998, MCS Gallery, Easton, Pa, 2000; Ballinglen Arts Found, Co Mayo, Ireland, 2001; Pa Acad Fine Arts, 2002; Ballinglen: The Artist in Rural Ireland, Castlebar, Co Mayo, Ireland, 2003; Embassies Program of USA, US Embassy, Dublin, 2004; Am Acad Arts and Letts Invitational, New York, 2009. *Awards:* Visual Arts Fel, Pa Coun Arts, 1994. *Media:* Oil. *Mailing Add:* c/o Gross McCleaf Gallery 127 S Sixteenth St Philadelphia PA 19102

REED, PAUL ALLEN
PAINTER
b Washington, DC, Mar 28, 1919. *Study:* San Diego State Coll, Calif; Corcoran Sch Art, Washington, DC. *Work:* Hirshhorn Mus, Washington, DC; Corcoran Gallery Art, Smithsonian American Art Mus, Wash DC; Detroit Inst Art; Walker Art Ctr, Minneapolis; Phillips Collection, Washington, DC; Georgetown Univ, DC; Nat Gallery Art, Wash DC; and in over 50 pub collections, including: San Francisco Mus Art; Nat Gallery of Art, Wash DC. *Exhib:* 25th Ann Soc Am Art, Art Inst Chicago, 65; Washington Color Painters, Washington, DC, Tex, Calif, Mass & Minn, 65-66; 250 Yrs Am Art, Corcoran Gallery Art, 66; Jackson Pollock to the Present, Steinberg Gallery, Washington Univ, St Louis, 69; Inaugural Exhib, Wadsworth Atheneum, Hartford, Conn, 69; Washington 20 Yrs, Baltimore Mus Art, 70; solo exhibs, Phoenix Art Mus, 77, Watkins Gallery, Am Univ, The Arts Club, Washington, DC, 97, Montgomery Coll, Takoma Park Md, 2001, Marymount Univ, Arlington, Va, 2002; Local Color, Am Art Mus, Washington, DC, 2008; Georgetown Univ, Wash DC, 2011; Nat Gallery of Art, Wash DC, 2012; A Career Exploring Color and Visual Perception, David Richard Gallery, Santa Fe, NMex, 2013; Reed & The Shaped Canvas, D Wigmore Fine Art Inc, NY, 2013. *Pos:* US Peace Corps, Graphics dir, 62-71. *Teaching:* Instr painting, Art League Northern Va, 71-74; asst prof & coordr first yr core prog, Corcoran Sch Art, 71-80. *Bibliog:* Barbara Rose (auth), The primacy of color, 5/64 & Legrace Benson (auth), Washington Scene, 69, Art Int; Walter Hopps (auth), The Vincent Melzac Collection, Corcoran Gallery Art, 71; Claudine Humblet (auth), The New American Abstraction, 1950-1970; Archives of American Art, Oral History; David Gariff (auth), The Art of Paul Reed: Color, Creativity, Curiosity, Nat Gallery Art, 2010. *Media:* Acrylic, Gouache. *Dealer:* D Wigmore Fine Art Inc 730 Fifth Ave New York NY; David Richard Gallery 544 S Guadalupe St Santa Fe NM. *Mailing Add:* 3541 N Utah St Arlington VA 22207

REEDER, SCOTT
PAINTER
b 1970. *Study:* Univ Iowa, BFA, 1994; Skowhegan Sch Painting & Sculpture, 1995; Visva Barhati Univ, Santiniketan, India, 1996; Univ Ill, Chicago, MFA, 1998. *Work:* Lambert Art Collection, Geneva, Switz ; Hirshhorn Mus & Sculpture Garden, Smithsonian Inst; and var pvt collections. *Exhib:* Yeah, Loyola Arts Res Ctr, Chicago, 1996; solo exhibs, Hermetic Gallery, Milwaukee, 1998, Pat Hearn Gallery, New York,

1999, Bronwyn Keenan, New York, 2001, Daniel Reich Gallery, New York, 2002, Gallery 400, Chicago, 2003, Midway Contemp Art, Minneapolis, 2005, Jack Hanley, San Francisco, 2006, Liste Art Fair, Basel, Switz, 2007 & Gavlak Projects, Fla, 2008; The Speed of Painting, Pat Hearn Gallery, NY, 2000; Mortal, Betty Rymer Gallery, Art Inst Chicago, 2001; Painting: for and aft, ACME, Los Angeles, 2002; Utopia Station, Venice Bienale, Italy, 2003; Spacemakers, The Suburban / Lothringer Dreizen, Munich, Ger, 2004; Kids of the Black Hole, Stalke Gallery, Copenhagen, 2005; The Armory Show, Jack Hanley Gallery, New York, 2006; Space is the Place, Portland Inst Contemp Art, 2007; Tales of the Grotesque, Karma Int, Zurich, 2008; There There, INOVA, Peck Sch Arts, Milwaukee, 2009. *Bibliog:* Michael Bulka (auth), A-OK, The New Art Examiner, 35, 12/1996; Christopher Knight (auth), The Next Wave, Los Angeles Times, 6/12/2000; Mary Louise Schumacher (auth), Calm, cool, collective, Milwaukee J Sentinel, 2/8/2003; Ken Johnson (auth), Karaoke Death Machine, NY Times, 5/25/2003; Ellen Fox (auth), The Cutting Edge Crashes the Dance Yet Again, Chicago Tribune, 5/7/2004; Rachel Comer-Green (auth), Drunk vs Stoned 2, TimeOut, 8/18-24/2005; Roberta Smith (auth), Last Chance: Listings, NY Times, 2/7/2007; Carol Lee (auth), Art of Darkness, Papermag, 4/2009. *Media:* Oil

REEDY, MITSUNO ISHII
PAINTER

b Osaka, Japan, Jan 18, 1941; US citizen. *Study:* Laguna Gloria Art Mus Sch, 76; Elizabeth Ney Mus Sch, 77-79; Scottsdale Art Sch, 92; Studied with Daniel Greene & Albert Handell; Studio Incamminati, 2011, 2012, 2013. *Work:* Okla Heritage Mus, Okla City; Greenwood Cult Ctr, Tulsa, Okla; Univ Oklahoma, Norman; US District Court House, Okla City; Purdue Univ, West Lafayette, Ind; Okla Capitol Rotunda, Okla City; US Bankruptcy Ct, Western Dist of Okla, Okla City; Gaylord-Pickens Okla Heritage Mus, Okla. *Exhib:* Pastel Soc Am Ann; Catherine Lorillard Wolfe Art Club Ann; Contemp Pastel Soc of Japan Ann; solo exhibs, Firehouse Art Ctr, Norman, Okla & Kirkpatrick Ctr, Okla City; Governors Gallery, Okla City. *Bibliog:* Article in Focus, Santa Fe, 6-7/95; article, Nichols Hills News, Okla City, 2/2002; Art Treasures of Okla Capitol, 2003. *Mem:* Pastel Soc Am; Portrait Soc Am. *Media:* Pastel; Oil. *Publ:* The Best of Oil Painting, Rockport Publ, Mass, 96; The Best of Pastel, 96, Portrait Inspirations, 97, Floral Inspirations, 97 & The Best of Pastel II, 99, Rockport Publ

REEDY, SUSAN
PAINTER, COLLAGE ARTIST

b Buffalo, NY. *Study:* State Univ NY, Buffalo, MFA (painting), 81. *Work:* Mem Art Gallery, Univ Rochester, NY; Roswell Park Cancer Ins, Buffalo, NY; 48 LEX; Castellani Art Mus, Niagara Falls; Mobil Oil Corp, New York; Rich Products Corp, Buffalo, NY; Standard Fed Bank, Troy, Mich; Automobile Asn Am, Amherst, NY; Hospice Found, Buffalo, NY. *Exhib:* Works on Canvas, OK Harris Gallery, New York, 88; Ann Midyear Exhib, Butler Inst Am Art, Youngtown, Ohio, 90 & 92; Recent Works on Canvas & Paper, Castellani Art Mus, Niagara Falls, 93; Ann Rochester Finger Lakes, Mem Art Gallery, NY, 95-96; Nat Varied Exhib, Gallery 84, New York, 96-97; Silent Soliloquy, Amherst Mus, NY, 97; Selected Works II, Albright-Knox Gallery, Buffalo, NY, 97; Marymount Manhattan Coll Art Gallery, New York, 2002; From NY to Western NY Collectors Gallery, Albright-Knox Art Gallery, Buffalo, NY; The Last Book, Mus Nat Libr, Buenos Aires, Argentina; Paper Explorations, Anderson Gallery, Bridgewater, Mass, 2009; Abstraction Now, Finehouse Plaza Art Gallery, 2009; Text 440 Gallery Brooklyn, NY, 2011; Visual Phrasing, Maloney Art Gallery, Coll of St Elizabeth, Morristown, NJ, 2011; An Exchange with Sol Lewitt, Cabinet Mass MoCA, 2011; Strange Glue: Collage at 100, Thompson Gallery, Cambridge, Mass, 2012; Post No Bills, Huntington Arts Center, Long Island, NY, 2013; Unhinged Pierogi Gallery, Brooklyn, NY, 2013; Mash Up: Collages in Mixed Media Islip Art Mus, 2014; 75 x 12 BT&C Gallery, Buffalo, NY, 2014. *Pos:* Artist-in-residence, Arts in Healthcare Initiative, State Univ NY, Buffalo, 2008-2015. *Awards:* Directors Choice Award, 54th Rochester-Finger Lakes Exhib, Mem Art Gallery, Rochester, NY, 95; Dorothy Cripps Salo Mem Award for Outstanding Non-Representational Painting, 55th Rochester Finger Lakes Exhib, Mem Art Gallery, Rochester, NY, 96. *Bibliog:* Richard Huntington (auth), Show full of surprises reflects penney's sensibilities, 7/15/97 & Measured skill, 9/95, The Buffalo News; Lynn Nicholas (auth), Reedy's mixed media, The Niagara Gazette, 2/93. *Media:* Vintage paper, Acrylic, Canvas, Paper, Mixed Media. *Interests:* Figure skating. *Dealer:* Pierogi Flatfiles; Mus Editions NYC; BT&C Gallery, Buffalo, NY. *Mailing Add:* 51 Glen Oaks Dr East Amherst NY 14051

REEL, DAVID MARK
MUSEUM DIRECTOR, CURATOR

b Pa, Nov 21, 1969. *Study:* Dickinson Coll, Carlisle, PA, BA, 92; NY Univ, NY, MA, 94. *Collection Arranged:* Ordered Chaos: Surrealist Art from the Coll, Dickinson College, Carlisle, PA, 91-92; Papers opf Joseph Huston, Pennsylvania State Capitol Preservation Committee, Harrisburg, PA, 91; Leon Golub: Worldwide, Dickinson College, Carlisle, PA, Chicago Cultural Ctr, Chicago, IL, 93; The Words of War: Documents of WWII, from Forbes Magazine Coll, Forbes Gallery, NY, 94-95; Faberge in Am, Metropolitan Mus Art, New York, HM DeYoung Memorial Mus, San Francisco, Mus Fine Art, Richmond, VA, New Orleans Mus Fine Art, LA, Cleveland Mus Art, Ohio, 96-97; The Great Am Place: Saratoga Springs, Forbes Gallery, NY City, 97; Carl Faberge: Goldsmith to the Tsar, Natl Mus, Stockholm, Sweden, 97; Highlights from the Forbes Magazine Collection, Forbes Gallery, NY, 97; Art of the Panama Canal, West Point Mus, US Military Acad, NY, 99; The Panama Canal and the Art of Construction, Williams Coll, Mass, 99-2000; Come Join us Brothers: African-Am in the US Army, West Point Mus, US Military Acad, NY, 2001-2003; Timeless Treasures: 200 yrs of West Point Memories, West Point Mus, US Military Acad, NY, 2001-2002; Tabletops and Tradition: The Officers Mess and Cadet Mess at West Point, West Point Mus, US Military Acad, NY, 2002-2003; Gallantry...Above and Beyond the Call of Duty...Civil War Medals of Honor, West Point Mus, US Military Acad, NY, 2003-2004; The West Point Mus: A mus for the Army, West Point Mus, US Military Acad, NY; Touched with Fire, Sesquicentennial of American Civil War, 2011-2012; Remember Fort Sumter; Operations Against Charleston 1861-1865, 2012-2013; Dark Blue is the National Color, 2013; Robert W Weir, Poetry in Art, Boscobel, 2013. *Pos:* Cur, Forbes Mag Collection, New York, NY, 93-98; Chief cur art, West Point Mus, US Military Acad West Point, New York, 98-2005, dir & chief cur, 2005-. *Teaching:* Instr arts, US Military Acad, West Point, NY, 98-. *Mem:* Am Asn Mus; Army Mus Asn, USA; Nat Trust for Historic Preservation; NY Univ Arts Alumni Adv Council, VPres 2002-03; Highlands CofC; Mus Asn NY; Greater Hudson Heritage Network. *Res:* Artwork depicting Am Army actions, Military portraiture and battle scenes. *Publ:* Auth, Western Passages, West Point, Points West, Denver Art Mus, 2002. *Mailing Add:* West Point Mus US Mil Acad West Point NY 10996

REEP, EDWARD ARNOLD
PAINTER, WRITER

b Brooklyn, NY, 1918. *Study:* Art Ctr Coll Design, cert, 41; also with E J Bisttram, Stanley Reckless, Willard Nash & Barse Miller. *Hon Degrees:* East Carolina Univ, MA, 56. *Work:* Los Angeles Co Mus, Calif; 66 works, US War Dept, Pentagon; Grunwald Graphic Arts Collection, Univ Calif, Los Angeles; Lytton Collection, Los Angeles; State of Calif Collection, Sacramento; Nat Mus Am Art, Smithsonian Inst, Washington, DC. *Comn:* Three panels of early conquests in Calif, SAm & US (with Gordon Mellor), USA Private's Club, Ft Ord, Calif, 41; Painter's Impression of International Airports (10 pages in full color), Life Mag, 6/56; Impressions of the Berlin Wall, Ger, US Govt, 71. *Exhib:* Whitney Mus Am Art Ann, NY, 46-48; Los Angeles Co Mus Ann, 46-60; Corcoran Gallery Art Biennial, Washington, DC, 49; Nat Acad Design, NY; Nat Gallery Art, Washington, DC. *Pos:* Coord art chmn, Los Angeles City Art Festival Exhibs, 51; official war artist & corresp, World War II. *Teaching:* Instr painting & drawing, Art Ctr Coll Design, Los Angeles, 46-50; instr painting & drawing & chmn, Dept Painting, Chouinard Art Inst, Los Angeles, 50-69; prof painting, artist-in-residence, E Carolina Univ, 70-85, prof emer, currently. *Awards:* First Prize in Oil Painting, Los Angeles All City Ann, 63; Nat Endowment Arts Grant, 75; Lifetime Achievement Gold Medal, Watercolor USA, 99, Nat Watercolor Soc, 2002; and others. *Bibliog:* Schaad (auth), Realm of Contemporary Still-life, 62 & Mugnaini (auth), Drawing, a Search for Form, 65, Van Nostrand Reinhold; James Jones (auth), World War II, Grosset & Dunlap, 75; Robert Henkes (auth), Themes in American Painting, 95. *Mem:* Life mem Nat Watercolor Soc (pres, 57-58); Watercolor USA Soc. *Media:* Oil, Watercolor. *Interests:* Gardening. *Publ:* Auth, The Content of Watercolor, Van Nostrand Reinhold, 83; A Combat Artist in World War II, Univ Press, Ky, 87; They Drew Fire, TV, Book, 2000. *Dealer:* Gordon McClelland. *Mailing Add:* 5508 Via Ravenna Bakersfield CA 93312

REESE, MARCIA MITCHELL
SCULPTOR

b Cleveland, Ohio. *Study:* Case Western Reserve Univ, BA, 51. *Work:* Hofstra Mus, Hofstra Univ, Godwin-Ternbach Mus, Queens Col, NY, Filderman Gallery, Hempstead, NY; MONY Financial Services World Headquarters, NY; Village of North Hills, North Hills, NY; many nat & int collections. *Exhib:* Solo shows, CAPA Rotational Art Exhib, 80, Bloomingdale's, Model Room #3, NY, 81, Chemical Bank, North Shore Towers, 82, Port Washington Libr Gallery, 82, Bryant Libr Gallery, 86, Gallery Lincoln Ctr, 86, Plandome Gallery, 91, Shelter Rock Gallery, 95; Elaine Benson Gallery, Bridgehampton, NY, 83; Nat Asn Women Artists, NY, 84-2004; Guild Hall Mus, East Hampton, NY, 87-90; Shelter Rock Gallery, 95; Heckscher Mus Art, 96; A Jain Marunouchi Gallery, New York City, 99-02. *Awards:* Cleo Hartwig Mem Award, Nat Asn Woman Artists, 89; Dr Max Ellenberg Award, Nat Asn Women Artists, 91; Nassau Co Mus Art, 92; Artists Network of Great Neck, 90, 93, 95, 96; Nat Asn Women Artists, 2003; and others. *Bibliog:* interview, On Long Island, WLIW-TV, 91; Stone Stories (video), 97; Artscene on Long Island (video), Cablevision Channel 44 & 25, 9/97; Cablevision Channel 20, 1/08. *Mem:* Nat Asn Women Artists (exec bd, 94- & chmn sculpture jury 94-96, chmn jury awards, 96-98); Sculptors Inc (pres); Stone Sculpture Soc NY; Artists Network Great Neck (archivist, 88-90 scholarships, 90-); Archeol Inst Am, LI Soc (vpres, grants chair). *Media:* Granite, Marble, Onyx, Alabaster. *Publ:* Hofstra Univ, Catalog of Art in Their Museum Collection, 89; Capturing the Essence of Their Vision & Form (catalog), Hofstra Univ, 94; Art Calendar Monograph, ps 92-93, 98

REESE, THOMAS FORD
HISTORIAN, ADMINISTRATOR

b New Orleans, La, Oct 9, 1943. *Study:* Fac Filosofia y Letras, Univ de Madrid, 63-64; Tulane Univ, BA, 65; Yale Univ, MA, 69, PhD, 73. *Collection Arranged:* Buenos Aires 1910: Memorias del Porvenir, Mercado del Abasto, Buenos Aires, May-June 99. *Pos:* exec dir, Stone Ctr Latin Am Studies, Tulane Univ, New Orleans, La. *Awards:* John Simon Guggenheim Mem Found Fel, 76-77; Academico correspondiente, Real Acad de Bellas Artes de San Fernando, Madrid, 77; Samuel H Kress Sr Fel, Ctr Advan Study in Visual Arts, Nat Gallery Art, Washington, 83. *Mem:* Coll Art Asn Am; Soc Archit Historians; Am Soc Hispanic Art Hist Studies; Asn Latin Am Art; Asn Res Insts in Art Hist. *Res:* History of the arts of Spain and Portugal; Latin American Colonial Art; European architecture since 1400. *Publ:* Auth, The Architecture of Ventura Rodriguez, Garland Publ Inc, 76; intro to Libro de diferentes pensamientos unos imbentados y otros delineados por Diego de Villanueva, Real Academia de Bellas Artes de San Fernando, 80; ed, Studies in Ancient American and European Art--The Collected Essays of George Kubler, Yale Univ Press, 85, Buenos Aires: Centro de estudios avenzados de la Universidad de Buenos Aires, 99; introd to La configuracion del tiempo--Observaciones sobre la historia de las cosas, Editorial Nerea, Madrid, Spain, 88; coauth, Boehm, Gehry, Hollein and Stirling in Los Angeles--The Competition Entries for the Walt Disney Concert Hall, Zodiac 2, Milan, Italy, 9/89. *Mailing Add:* 5825 Pitt St New Orleans LA 70115

REESER, ROBERT D
EDUCATOR, ADMINISTRATOR
b Orangeville, Ill, Mar 4, 1931. *Study:* Northern Ill Univ, BS, 53; Univ Denver, MA (art), 59; Ohio State Univ, PhD (art educ), 74. *Work:* Burpee Art Gallery, Rockford, Ill. *Pos:* Assoc dean, Sch Arts & Letters, Calif State Univ, Los Angeles, 87-94; retired. *Teaching:* Prof art, Calif State Univ, Los Angeles, 71-94. *Awards:* Douc Langur award. *Mem:* Calif Art Educ Asn (pres, 76-78); Nat Art Educ Asn; Artists Equity Asn; Int Soc Educ Art. *Res:* Teaching of secondary school art; aesthetics, art criticism and art history. *Mailing Add:* 1308 Emerald Dr Santa Maria CA 93454-3242

REEVE, DEBORAH B
ADMINISTRATOR, PAINTER
Pos: With US Dept Educ, formerly; assoc exec dir develop & spec projects, Nat Asn Elem Sch Principals, formerly, dep exec dir, formerly, advocacy & prof develop, 2001-07; exec dir, Nat Art Educ Asn, Reston, Va, 2007-. *Teaching:* Adj prof, Lesley Coll, Cambridge, Mass, formerly. *Dealer:* Gallery West 1213 King St Alexandria VA 22314. *Mailing Add:* National Art Education Association 1916 Association Dr Herndon VA 20191-1590

REEVES, DANIEL MCDONOUGH
VIDEO ARTIST, INSTALLATION ARTIST
b Washington, DC, Aug 1, 1948. *Study:* Ithaca Col, BS, 76. *Work:* Mus Mod Art; Pac Film Archives. *Exhib:* High Mus Contemp Art, Atlanta, Ga; Mus Mod Art & Whitney Mus Am Art, NY; Tate Gallery, UK; Pearce Inst, Glasgow, Scotland; Long Beach Mus Art, Calif; Nat Video Festival/Am Film Inst, Los Angeles, Calif; and others. *Pos:* Exec dir, Shakti Productions, Greenwich Village, NY & Tarbert, Scotland, UK. *Awards:* Fel & Grant Nat Endowment Arts, 80-94; NY State Coun on the Arts Prodn Grants, 80-94; Fel, John S Guggenheim Found, 83-84; NY Found Arts Fel, 87; Scottish Arts Council Grants, 90-92. *Mem:* Media Alliance; Asn Independent Video & Filmmakers. *Media:* Video, Film. *Publ:* Single channel video tapes, Smothering Dreams, Nat Video Festival Blue Ribbon Winner, 82; Mosaic for the Kali Yuga, 85; Sabda, Nat Video Festival Blue Ribbon Winner, 85; Ganapati/A Spirit in the Bush, 86; Sombra a Sombra, 88; video installations, The Well of Patience, 89, Eingang/The Way In, 90 & 93, Jizo Garden, 92, Obsessive Becoming, 95 & Forty Nine Bodhisattvas, 97. *Mailing Add:* 12 Glasgow St Scotland United Kingdom G129PR

REEVES, ESTHER MAY
PAINTER
b Riverside, Calif, Oct 12, 1937. *Study:* Calif State Univ-Fullerton, MA, 86, MFA, 88; studied with H Ralph Love. *Work:* United First Methodist Church, Riverside, Calif; Truth Consciousness-Poona Ashram, India; Riverside City Col. *Comn:* Angel of Light (mural), Truth Consciousness, Boulder, Colo, 81; Fallopian Tissue & Dermal Pore, Riverside City Col-Life Sci Dept, Calif, 83 & 84; Landscape with Ducks, comn by Jones, Riverside, Calif, 83; portrait, comn by Headman, Orange, Calif, 88; portrait, comn by Bavaresco, Sacramento, Calif, 92; Mondavi Wines, comn by Mr and Mrs Robert Mondavi, 2003; 2 paintings, portraits, comn by Mrs. Brenda Yeager, 2003. *Exhib:* Solo shows, Progressive Creativity, Inland Empire Gallery, 83 & Arising from Scripture, Riverside Art Mus, Calif, 92; Images 87, Bowers Mus, Santa Ana, Calif, 87; Grace Street Artists, Corona Gallery Ltd, Calif, 87; In Praise of Maleness, Piret's Gallery, Costa Mesa, 87; Celebration, Grand Hotel, Anaheim, 87; The Art of Love, Riverside Art Mus, 90; Wildlife Art, San Bernardino Art Mus, Calif, 90; Invitational, Capitol Bldg, Sacramento, Calif, 2000; Ontario Art Mus Invitational, 2000, 08. *Pos:* Illusr & secy, Riverside Unified Sch Dist, 60-61; instr, Calif State Univ-Fullerton, 88-89. *Teaching:* Instr beginning drawing, Calif State Univ, 88-89. *Awards:* Best of Show, Grumacher Award, M Grumbacher Inc, 89; Best of Show, Ann Exhib, Clarks, 90; Best of Show, Riverside Art Mus, 99; Award, Palm Springs Mus Open. *Bibliog:* Melody Rogers (host), Two on the Town (CBS-TV), Joel Tator, 87; Joey Bavaresco (host), The World of Joey Bavaresco, Daniel Foster, 08; Marie Hempy (video), Arising From Scripture, Riverside. *Mem:* Riverside Art Mus; Ontario Art Mus; Riverside Plein-Air Painters; RCAA. *Media:* Oil on Canvas. *Specialty:* Decorative Art; Western Art Landscapes; Surreal Landscapes. *Interests:* Gardening, Traveling. *Collection:* Dr. Robert Rogers, Rand Brooks Estate, Brenda Yeager, Ron Gallup, Jack Miller. *Publ:* Book by Authors: N Long Beach Anthology. *Dealer:* Reeves Studios Riverside Calif 92506. *Mailing Add:* 5415 Via San Jacinto Riverside CA 92506-3650

REEVES, JAMES FRANKLIN
HISTORIAN, COLLECTOR
b Huntsville, Ala, July 4, 1946. *Study:* Univ Ala, Huntsville, BA (art hist), 72; Vanderbilt Univ, Nashville, Tenn, MA (art hist), 75. *Collection Arranged:* Gilbert Gaul, (with catalog), Tenn Fine Arts Ctr, Nashville & Huntsville Mus Art, 75. *Pos:* Asst, P L Hay House Mus, Macon, Ga, 66-67; asst to dir, 73-75, cur Huntsville Mus Art, 75-77. *Mem:* Coll Art Asn Am; Southeastern Coll Art Conf; Kappa Pi (pres local chap, 71-72). *Res:* Gilbert Gaul, 1855-1919; Huntsville architecture, 1820-1975. *Collection:* 19th and 20th century American paintings; 18th and 19th century American decorative arts; 19th century European paintings; Oriental porcelains and sculpture. *Mailing Add:* 4800 Whitesburg Dr S #331 Huntsville AL 35802-1698

REEVES, JOHN ALEXANDER
PHOTOGRAPHER
b Burlington, Ont, Can, Apr 24, 1938. *Study:* Sir George Williams Art Sch, Montreal, 56-57; Ont Coll Art, Toronto, 57-61, AOCA. *Work:* Nat Film Bd Can, Ottawa; Archives Canada; Dept Indian & Northern Affairs, Ottawa; Can Mus Contemp Photog, Ottawa; Nat Libr Can, Ottawa; Art Gallery Northumberland, Coburg, Ont; The Varley Gallery, Markham, Ont; Art Gallery Ont, Toronto. *Exhib:* Solo exhibs, 30 Portraits of Women, Deja Vu Gallery, Toronto, 77, The Magic Word, Nat Archives Can, 81, Inuit Art World, Can Ctr Photog, Toronto, 82, Corkin Gallery, Toronto, 83, Can Cult Ctr, Rome, 91, About Face (traveling exhib), Cambridge, Simcoe & Brantford Art Galleries, Ont, 92 & Exile's Exiles, Bystriansky Gallery, Toronto, 92; Academic Images, Can Ctr Photog, 82; Creative Canadians (traveling exhib), Dept External Affairs, Ottawa, 82; Authors, Harbourfront Gallery, Toronto, 83; The Johnny Wayne Portrait (with Mary Pratt), Mem Univ Art Gallery, St John's, Nfld, 90; Portraits, Can Cult Ctr, Rome, 91; Burlington Art Centre, Ont, 95; Jazz Lives, Mendel Gallery, Saskatoon, Sask, 97; Appleton Mus Art, Ocala, Fla, 99; The Moore Gallery, Toronto, 2003; Facing Art, Art Gallery of Northumberland, Coburg, Ont, 2005; Surfacing for Atwood, The Varley Gallery, Markham, Ont, 2008; and others. *Pos:* Critic, host, Toronto Rev, Can Broadcasting Corp, Radio, 68- 71. *Teaching:* Instr photog, Ontario Coll Art. *Awards:* Am Inst Graphic Arts Award, 63 & 68; Award of Merit, Art Dir Club, Toronto, 71, 72, 76 & 77; Int Asn Printing House Craftsmen, 77. *Bibliog:* Charles Oberdorf (auth), articles, 11/72 & 6/77 & Gunter Ott (auth), Sand on the beach, 87, Camera Can Mag; Gary Michael Dault (auth), article, Toronto Star, 6/77; Gary Michael Dault (auth), Inuit Art World Catalogue, 82. *Mem:* Royal Can Acad Art; Can Asn Photogs & Illusrs Communs. *Interests:* Visual arts, music. *Publ:* Auth, John Fillion--Thoughts About My Sculpture, Martlet Press, 68; God's Big Acre--Life in 401 Country, Methuen, Can, 86; About Face, 90 & Exile's Exile, 92, Exile Eds, Toronto; Jazz Lives, McClelland & Stewart, Toronto, 92; Incontro, Where Italy & Canada Meet Exile Eds, Toronto, 96. *Dealer:* Feheley Fine Arts 14 Hazelton Ave Toronto ON M5R 2E2 Canada. *Mailing Add:* 33 St Paul St Toronto ON M5A 3H2 Canada

REFF, THEODORE
HISTORIAN
b New York, NY, Aug 18, 1930. *Study:* Columbia Col, BA, 52; Harvard Univ, MA, 53, PhD, 58. *Collection Arranged:* Cezanne Watercolors (ed, catalog), M Knoedler & Co, NY, 63; Degas in the Metropolitan, Metrop Mus, NY, 77; Cezanne: the Late Work, Mus Mod Art, NY, 77; Manet and Modern Paris, Nat Gallery, Washington, DC, 82-83. *Teaching:* Prof art hist & mod art, Columbia Univ, 57-, prof emer European painting & sculpture, currently; vis prof, Univ Mich, Princeton Univ, John Hopkins Univ & NY Univ; Slade prof, Cambridge Univ; plus others. *Awards:* Chevalier, Ordre des Palmes Academiques, 87. *Mem:* Coll Art Asn Am (dir, 77-81); Int Found Art Res (dir, 80-); Swann Found Caricature (dir, 82-89); Psychoanalytic Perspectives Art (dir, 84-90); Soc Paul Cezanne (pres, 98-). *Res:* 19th and 20th century art; relations between art and literature. *Publ:* Auth, Manet: Olympia, Penguin, 76; ed, Modern Art in Paris, 1850-1900, Garland, 81; auth, Manet and Modern Paris, Univ Chicago Press, 83; co-auth, Two Cezanne Sketchbooks, Philadelphia Mus Art, 90; Jean-Louis Forain: The Impressionist Years, Memphis, 95

REGAN, BETSEY
PAINTER
b Long Branch, NJ, Feb 22, 1954. *Study:* Monmouth Univ, BA, 82; Temple Univ, MS, 89. *Work:* Pfizer Collection, NY; Common Health Collection, Parsippany, NJ; Quantum Group, Parsippany, NJ. *Comn:* portrait, comn by Julie Corbisiero, Toms River, NJ 98 & 2000; portrait, comn by Annie Santulli, Rumson, NJ, 99; paperworks, comn by Maryann Sciarappa, Ocean NJ, 2000. *Exhib:* MCAC Show, Monmouth Mus, Middletown, NJ, 94-2001; New Jersey Arts Ann, NJ State Mus, Trenton, 94 & 99; Juried National, Aljira, Newark, NJ, 95 & 96; Watchung Arts Ctr Invitational, Watchung, NJ, 96; Noyes State Mus, Oceanville, NJ, 99. *Awards:* Best of Show, City W/O Walls Gallery, 94, 95 & 97; Best of Show, Art Alliance, 99. *Bibliog:* Barry Schwabsky (auth), Familiar Made Different, NY Times, 9/21/97 & New Jersey Arts Annual, 8/1/99; Pat Summers (auth), New Jersey Arts Ann, The Trentonian, 8/11/99. *Mem:* Art Alliance, Red Bank, NJ (cur, 90-2000). *Media:* Oil; Plaster

REGAT, JEAN-JACQUES ALBERT
SCULPTOR, MURALIST
b Paris, France, Sept 12, 1945. *Study:* Univ Alaska, BA; Soc Beaux Arts, France. *Work:* Sheik Zayed Ben Sultan Al-Nahyan, Pres of United Arab Emirates, Abu Dabi; Fairbanks North Star Borough Pub Libr, Alaska; Soroptimist Int of Anchorage; RCA Alascom, Anchorage; Kobuk Valley Jade Co, Alyeska. *Comn:* The Man Who Became Caribou (bas relief wood), Noatak Artic Sch Dist, 81; Miners of the Yukon (tryptic bas relief wood), Yukon Off Supplies Co, 82; Delta Pastoral (bas relief wood), Delta Greely Sch Dist, 82; The Resolution (bronze & bas relief wood), Carr-Gottstein Ltd; St Joseph & St Francis, St Anthony Cath Church Anchorage, 83. *Exhib:* Solo exhibs, Artique Ltd, Anchorage, 72-77; Heritage Northwest Gallery, Juneau, 73-74; House of Wood, Fairbanks, 74-80; Erdon Gallery, Houston, Tex; Rendezvous Gallery, Anchorage. *Bibliog:* Judy Shuler (auth), Jacques & Mary Regat, Alaska J autumn 77; Nancy Cain Schmitt (auth), Ancient legend of Sedna is captured in bronze, Anchorage Times, 5/20/79; Mary Sawyer-Albert (auth), Stories carved in wood and stone, Jacques and Mary Regat, Southwest Art, 8/79; plus others. *Media:* Stone, Wood. *Dealer:* House of Wood 529 Fourth Fairbanks AK 99701. *Mailing Add:* 518 Pearl Dr Anchorage AK 99518-1833

REGAT, MARY E
SCULPTOR, MURALIST
b Duluth, Minn, Nov 12, 1943. *Study:* Univ Alaska. *Work:* Anchorage Fine Arts Mus, Alaska; Soroptimist Int of Anchorage; Kobuk Valley Jade Co, Alyeska, Alaska; Fairbanks North Star Borough Pub Libr; RCA-Alascom, Anchorage. *Comn:* Trail of 98 (bas relief wood), Pioneers Asn Alaska, 79; Creek Woman (bas relief wood & bronze), Kokanok, Peninsula Sch Dist, 80; Huskies (bronze), Kotzebue Artic Sch Dist, 82; Dance of the Oomialik (sculpture), Gottstein Inc, 82; High, Wild and Free (sculpture), Greyling, Iditarod Sch Dist, 83. *Exhib:* Solo exhibs, Artique Ltd, Anchorage, 72-77; House of Wood, Fairbanks, 74-80; Erdon Gallery, Houston, Tex; Boreal Traditions Gallery, Anchorage; plus others. *Awards:* Sculpture Award, Design I, 71; Purchase Award, Anchorage Fine Arts Mus, 71. *Bibliog:* Judy Schuler (auth), Jacques and Mary Regat, Alaska J, autumn, 77; Nancy Cain Schmitt (auth), Ancient legend of Sedna is captured in bronze, Anchorage Times, 5/20/79; Mary Sawyer-Albert (auth), Stories carved in wood and stone, Jacques and Mary Regat, Southwest Art, 8/79; plus others. *Mem:* Artist Guild; Anchorage Fine Arts Mus Asn. *Media:* Wood, Bronze. *Dealer:* Boreal Traditions 939 W 5th Ave Suite J Anchorage AK 99501; New Horizons 519 1st Ave Fairbanks AK 99701. *Mailing Add:* 518 Pearl Dr Anchorage AK 99518-1833

REGIER, RANDY J
CONCEPTUAL ARTIST, HISTORIAN
b. Omaha, Nebr, June 16, 1964. *Study:* Kansas State Univ, BFA, 2003; Maine Coll Art, MFA, 2007. *Work:* Spencer Mus Art, Lawrence, Kans; Beach Mus Art, Manhattan, Kans; Mulvane Art Mus, Topeka, Kans. *Exhib:* Everything Must Go: Toys of Randy Regier, The Beach Mus Art, Manhattan, Kans, 2003; Baseball, Apple Pie & Earl Browder, Mulvane Art Mus, Topeka, Kans, 2007; Fallen Spacecraft installtion, Bonnaroo Mus Festival, Manchester, Tenn, 2009; Comic-al, Ctr Maine Contemp Art, Rockport, Maine, 2009; DeCordova Mus Biennial, DeCordova Mus, Lincoln, Mass, 2010; NuPenny Toy Store, traveling through Maine and US, 2010. *Bibliog:* Sebastian Smee (auth), All Over the Map, Boston Globe, 2010; Greg Cook (auth), Reboot, Boston Phoenix, 2010; Bob Keyes (auth), Imaginarium of Randy Regier, Portland Press Herald, 2010; Erik Almstead (auth), Randy Regier ADTI documentary, 2010. *Media:* Mixed Media, Digital Print

REGINATO, ANGELA
VIDEO ARTIST
Study: Univ Calif Berkley, Architecture. *Exhib:* Works has been featured in SFInternational, the Rotterdam Int Film Festival, Berlin Film Festival; Broadcasted in various PBS stations. *Pos:* Film editor, The Rise and Fall of Jim Crow, 2002, The Weather Underground, 2002, Ending Aids: The Search for a Vaccine, 2002, Runners High, 2006, Independent Lens, 2007. *Awards:* Creative Capital Found Grant, 2008

REHBERGER, TOBIAS
SCULPTOR
b Esslingen, Germany, 1966. *Study:* Hochschule fur Bildende Kunst, Frankfurt, Germany, MFA. *Exhib:* Solo exhibs, 9 Skulpturen, Wohnung K. Koenig, Frankfurt, 1992, Galerie Luis Campana, Cologne, 1994, Anastasia, Friedrich Petzel Gallery, NY, 1997, Standard Rad, Ltd., Transmission Gallery, Glasgow, 1999, Matrix 180. Sunny Side Up, Univ Calif Berkeley Art Mus and Pacific Film Archive, Berkeley, 1999, Dusk, Gio Marconi, Milan, 2000, Night Shift, Palais de Tokyo, Paris, 2002, Galerie Ghislaine Hussenot, Paris, 2003, Half the Truth, neugerriemschneider, Berlin, 2004, Reina Sofia, Madrid, 2005, American Traitor Bitch, Friedrich Petzel Gallery, NY, 2006, On Otto, Fondazione Prada, Milan (catalog), 2007, The Chicken-and-Egg-No-Problem Wall Painting, Stedelijk Mus, Amsterdam, Mus ludwig, Cologne (catalog), 2008, Pilar Corrias, London, 2009 and others; Give Me a Hand Before I Call You Back, Galerie Bleich-Rossi, Graz (catalog), 1991, SS.SS.R, Galerie Baerbei Grasslin, Frankfurt, 1992, Kunstverein Ludwigsburg, Villa Franck, Germany, 1993, Regal, Regal, Forum, Frankfurt, 1995, Biennale di Venezia, Venice, 1997, 2003, 2009, Heaven, P.S. 1, NY, 1997, Ain't Ordinarily So, curated by Daniel Birnbaum, Casey Kaplan, NY, 1998, Who, if not we?, Elizabeth Cherry Contemporary Art, Tucson, 1999, Kemper Mus of Contemporary Art, Kansas City, 2000, Project #0004, Friedrich Petzel Gallery, 2000, The Sky is the Limit, Taipei-Biennale, 2000, Painting at the Edge of the World, Walker Art Ctr, Minn, 2001, EU2, Stephen Friedman Gallery, London, 2002, Outlook, International Art Exhib, Athens, 2003, Suburban House Kit, Deitch Projects, NY, 2004, Extreme Abstraction, Albright-Knox Art Gallery, Buffalo, 2005, Present Perfect, Friedrich Petzel Gallery, NY, 2005, Cohabitats, Galerie Ghislaine Husenot, Paris, 2005, Post Notes, Midway Contemporary Art, Minn, 2005, HyperDesign, Shanghai Biennale, Shanghai Art Mus, 2006, Sculptor's & Drawing, Aspen Art Mus, 2007, Pilar Corrias Gallery, London, 2008, The Quick and the Dead, Walker Art Ctr, Minn, 2009, Green Acres, Abbington Art Ctr, 2009 and others. *Awards:* Golden Lion Award, Venice Biennial, Italy 2009. *Mailing Add:* c/o Friedrich Petzel Gallery 535 W 22nd St New York NY 10011

REIBACK, EARL M
SCULPTOR, KINETIC ARTIST
b Brooklyn, NY, May 30, 1948. *Study:* Lehigh Univ, Pa, BA (lit) & BS (eng physics); Mass Inst Technol, MS (nuclear eng). *Work:* Whitney Mus Am Art & Mus Mod Art, NY; Philadelphia Mus Art; Milwaukee Art Ctr; New Orleans Mus Art; and 34 other mus; David Bemant Light Collection; Dennos Mus Center, Mich; Brevard Coll, NC; and many other private collections. *Comn:* 70' Lumia light sculpture, Las Vegas Hilton, Nev, 68; Coty Awards (mural of light), Metrop Mus Art, 70; Lumia light sculpture, comn by Hugh Heffner, 71. *Exhib:* Solo exhibs, Metrop Mus Art, NY, 67, Moos Gallery, Montreal, Can, 70, Waddell Gallery, NY, 72 & 73, Colibri Gallery, San Juan, PR, 74, Estes Robles Gallery, Los Angeles, Calif, 75 & 82, Electric Gallery, Toronto, Can, 71, 76 & 84 & OK Harris Gallery, NY, 95; Brooklyn Mus, NY, 68 & 69; Milwaukee Art Ctr, Wis, 69; Metrop Mus Art, NY, 69; Philadelphia Mus Art; Albright-Knox Art Gallery, Buffalo, NY; Long Beach Mus Contemp Art, Calif; Aldrich Mus Contemp Art, Ridgefield, Conn; Mus d'Art Contemporain, Montreal, Que; US Cult Ctr, Tel Aviv, Israel; Fine Arts Gallery, Ankara, Turkey; Mus Mod Art, NY; Baltimore Mus Art, Md; Walker Art Ctr, Minneapolis, Minn; Hayden Gallery, Cambridge, Mass; Whitney Mus Art, 94; Cite des arts et des nouvelles technologies, Montreal, Can, 96; Long Beach Mus Art, Calif, 97; Age of Technology, San Jose Mus Art, 98; Summer of Love, Whitney Mus Am Art, New York, 2007; Through the Looking Glass, Dennos Mus Ctr, Traverse City, Mich, 2008; Modernist Gallery, Zimmerli Art Mus, New Brunswick, NJ, 2000-2011. *Collection Arranged:* New Am Films & Videos at Whitney Mus Am Art, 94. *Teaching:* Instr, NY Univ Sch Continuing Educ, currently; lectr, Met Mus Art, NY Univ, Columbia Univ, City Coll NY, Univ Denver, Mass Inst Tech, many others. *Mem:* Art & Sci Collaborations Inc; Whitney Mus Art (permanent artist mem). *Media:* Electronics, Light. *Interests:* Human develop. *Publ:* Auth, articles, Fortune Mag, 68, House & Garden, 1/69 & Electronics Age, spring 70, Encyclopedia Britanica Yearbook of Science & the Future, 71; The Art of Light & Color, 1972; The American Century Art & Cult 1950-2000; The 20th Century Art Book, 96; Wichita Art Mus 75 Years of Am Art, 2010. *Mailing Add:* Cooper Station PO Box 148 New York NY 10276

REICH, OLIVE B
PAINTER
b Brooklyn, NY, Mar 1, 1935. *Study:* Mt Holyoke Coll, South Hadley, Mass, BA, 56; Art Students League, 66-67; Craft Students League; Parsons Sch Design. *Work:* Brooklyn Botanic Garden/Nature Conser, NY; Health & Hospital Corp, NY; Mount Holyoke Coll Mus of Art; Brooklyn Botanic Garden Health & Hosp Corp, NY; Cantor Fitzgerald, NY. *Comn:* Series of drawings, comn by Union Chapel Grove, Shelter Island, NY, 76-86; Centennial Celebration (painting), comn by Fox River Paper Co, Appleton, Wis, 84; Series of homes on Shelter Island, NY, 2000-04. *Exhib:* Solo exhibs, Present Day Club, Princeton, NJ, 78 & Brooklyn Botanic Garden, NY, 86, Mayer, Brown & Platt Law Firm, NY, 96, Nat Arts Club, NY, 2001, 2005, 2007, Cook Pony Farm Gallery, Sag Harbor, NY, 2002, Clayton Libertore Gallery, Bridgewhampton, NY, 2002, UBS, Southampton, NY, 2008 & East End Arts Coun, Riverhead, NY, 2009; Monmouth Mus, Lincroft, NJ, 90; Adelphi Univ, NY, 90; CW Post Univ, Brookville, NY, 92; Brooklyn Borough Hall, 96; Art Ctr, Sarasota, Fla, 2000; Walter Greer Gallery, Hilton Head, SC, 2000; Gallery at Quoque Libr, Quoque, NY, 2010; Springsteel Gallery, Greenport, NY; Town Hall, Shelter Island, NY, 2011. *Pos:* Instr watercolor, YWCA, 74-77, own studio, 78-, Brooklyn, NY & Aquarelle Studio, Shelter Island, NY, 83-88. *Awards:* Catharine Lorillard Wolfe Art Club Award, 99; Halpern Mem Award, Nat Asn Women Artists, 99; Four Awards, Nat Asn Women Artists, 99-2004; 1st Place, East End Arts Coun, 2005; Visual Arts Award, Nat Arts Club, NY, 2007. *Bibliog:* Barbara Dunne (auth), Reich exhibits watercolor, Shelter Island Reporter, 84; Dawn Goris (auth), From Art of the Bay Ridge/Profile Olive Reich, Here's Brooklyn Mag, 89; Kim Covell (auth), Olive Reich, An artist in search of happy homes for her work, Shelter Island Reporter, 2000; An Island Sheltered - Olive Reich, Sally Flynn, Dans Papers, 2001; Featured Artist, N Fork Section, Dan's Papers. 2005; Marion Wohlbergweiss (auth) Dan's Papers (featured artist), 2006. *Mem:* Artists Alliance East Hampton; Audubon Artists; Artists Equity; Contemp Artist Guild (corresp secy, 80-); Catharine Lorillard Wolfe Art Club (exec bd, 85-88); Nat Arts Club (exhibiting mem); Nat Asn Women Artists; Brooklyn Watercolor Soc; Shelter Island Community Artists. *Media:* Watercolor. *Interests:* Theatre, ballet, decorating, traveling and gardens; Environ preserv; Animal protection/rights. *Publ:* Illusr, God's Summer Cottage, Shelter Island Hist Soc, 80; Chronicle of Shelter Island churches, MIT Graphics, 83; Shelter Island Yacht Club-A History, Mad Printers, 86; Cover, Art Calendar, 92; contribr, Manhattan Arts Int Mag, 96; auth, Watercolors, 2008. *Dealer:* Wishrock Gallery Shelter Island NY. *Mailing Add:* 7518 Third Ave Brooklyn NY 11209

REICHEK, ELAINE
CONCEPTUAL ARTIST
b New York, NY, Apr 30, 1943. *Study:* Brooklyn Col, BA, 63; Yale Univ Sch Art & Archit, BFA, 64. *Work:* Norton Gallery Art, West Palm Beach, Fla; Portland Art Mus, Ore; Arthur Anderson & Assoc; AT&T; New Sch Social Res. *Exhib:* Out of the House, Whitney Mus Am Art, 78; NY Collection, Albright-Knox Art Gallery, 78; Site Seeing Travel & Tourism in Contemp Art, Whitney Mus Am Art, 91; Whitney Biennial, Whitney Mus Am Art, 2012; solo exhibs, Jewish Mus, NY, 94, Stichting de Appel, Amsterdam, 94, Ctr Res Contemp Art, Univ Tex, Arlington, 94, Michael Klein Gallery, NY, 95, Univ Arts, Philadelphia, Van Every Smith Gallery, Davidson Col, NC, 96 & Mus Mod Art, NY, 99; Labor of Love, New Mus, NY, 96; A Bare Wall, Michael Kelin Gallery, NY, 96; Model Home, PS1, The Clocktower, NY, 96; Embeded Metaphor (traveling), 96; Making Pictures: Women and Photog, 1975-Now, Nicole Klagsbrun, NY, 96; Art on the Edge of Fashion, Ariz State Univ Art Mus, Tempe, 97; Ethno Antics, Nordiska Museet, Stockholm, 98; Loose Threads, Serpentine Gallery, London, 98; Dimensions of Native Am: the Contact Zone, Mus Fine Arts, Fla State Univ, Tallahassee & Appleton Mus Art, Ocala, Fla, 98; Palais Des Beaux Arts, Brussels, 2000; "When This You See," MoMA Project Room and Nicole Klagsbrun Gallery, 1999; "MADAM I'M ADAM," Shoshana Wayne Gallery, Los Angeles, 2003; "Online Project," Gardner Museum, Boston, 2003. *Teaching:* Guest lectr, Bryn Mawr, Pa, 89, Kent State Univ, Ohio, 89, Hobart-William Smith Col, Geneva, NY, 89, Everson Mus, Syracuse, NY, 90, Syracuse Univ, NY, 90, Art of the Middle Ages: Recent Work by Mid-Career Feminists, Women's Caucus Art, NY, 90, Ethnicity/Ethnography: The Uses and Misuses of Traditional Aesthetics by Contemp Artists, Col Art Asn, NY, 90. *Awards:* Creative Artists Pub Serv Grant, NY State Coun Arts, 83; New York Found Grant, 88; Louis Comfort Tiffany Found Award, 94. *Bibliog:* Arnd Schneider (auth), Uneasy Relationships, Contemporary Artists & Anthropology, J Mat Cult, 7/96; Robin Rice (auth), Now Who's Laughing, Philadelphia City Paper, 10/96; Jeanne Nugent (auth), Museum Focus, Philadelphia Weekly, 9/18/96; Fall Preview, Seven Arts, Philadelphia, 9/96. *Mem:* Women's Caucus Art. *Publ:* Auth, Liberals at War (article, book review), Artforum, 1/90, 23-24. *Dealer:* Nicole Klagsbrun 526 W 26th St New York NY 10001; AIR Gallery 63 Crosby St New York NY 10013. *Mailing Add:* c/o Nicole Klagsbrun 526 W 26th St No213 New York NY 10001

REICHEL, MYRA
TAPESTRY ARTIST, WEAVER
b Philadelphia, Pa, June 19, 1951. *Study:* Philadelphia Coll Art, 69-71, apprenticed with Nora Johnson, 81-82, study workshops with Mary Lane, 88-89; Bryn Mawr Col, BA, 95. *Work:* Hercules Corp, Wilmington, Del; Fox Co, Chesterbrook, Pa; Educ Testing Serv, Princeton, NJ; Wolf Block Schorr Solis, Cohen, Philadelphia, Pa; Dupont Corp, Wilmington, Del. *Comn:* Colo Mountains (tapestry), comn by Dr Richard Small, Reading, Pa, 80; Spring Dreams (tapestry), comn by George & Toni Wiswessler, Reading, Pa, 81; Miroian Dream (tapestry), comn by Helene & Walter Sencer, NY, 85; Night tales (tapestry), comn by Arthur Gershkoff, Merion, Pa, 88; Star Flower (tapestry), comn by Jean Bradley, Philadelphia, Pa, 88; Daybreak, Lee MacIlhenney, 89. *Exhib:* Solo Exhibs: Hudson River Mus, Yonkers, NY, 85, Del Ctr Contemp Arts, Wilmington, 85, Bryn Mawr Coll, 1993; Am Express Fin Svcs, Plymouth Meeting, PA, 2000; National Healing Solo Arts, 2005-2006, Community Art Center, Pa, 2006; Reiki Healing Center, Media, Pa, 2007, Wallingford Community Arts Center; Group Exhibs: Henry Chauncy Conf Ctr, Educ Testing Serv, Princeton,

NJ, 87; Biennial Art/Craft Exhib, Del Art Mus, Wilmington, 89; Philadelphia Guild of Handweavers, Swedish Mus, Pa, 92; Abington Art Ctr, 94; Liberty Place, Philadelphia, Pa, 98; Art of the State, Susquehanna Art Mus, Harrisburg, Pa, 2002; Sedwick Art Center, Alma Gallery, Philadelphia, 2003; Windsor Art Gallery, Pa, 2005, This Space for Rent, Media Arts Council. *Pos:* dir, Reiki Healing Center, Media, Pa. *Teaching:* Philadelphia Guild of Handweavers, 84-92; Community Arts Ctr, Wallingford, Pa, 91; artist-in-residence, Pa Coun Arts, 93-95; Powell Elem Sch; Gillespie Middle Sch. *Mem:* Philadelphia Guild of Hand Weavers. *Media:* Fibers. *Publ:* Contribr, Handmade Charter Issue, FiberArts, 81. *Dealer:* Reiki Healing Center 20 S Olive St Media PA 19063. *Mailing Add:* 121 E Sixth St Media PA 19063

REICHERT, DONALD KARL
PAINTER, PHOTOGRAPHER
b Libau, Man, Jan 11, 1932. *Study:* Univ Man Sch Art, with Robert A Nelson & George Swinton, BFA, 56; Inst Allende, Mex, with James Pinto; Emma Lake Artist's Workshops, with Jules Olitzki, Stepan Wolpe, Lawrence Alloway, John Cage & Frank Stella. *Work:* Nat Gallery Can; Art Gallery Ont; Winnipeg Art Gallery; Can Coun Art Bank; Montreal Mus Fine Arts. *Exhib:* Winnipeg Show Nat Biennial; Montreal Spring Show Nat; Nat Gallery Biennial; solo-exhibs, Winnipeg Art Gallery, 60, 69, 75, 83 & 92; Visua '67, Nat Exhib. *Pos:* Founding pres, Winnipeg Artists Co-op Inc, Site Gallery, 95. *Teaching:* Artist-in-residence, Univ NB, 61-62; prof painting, Univ Man Sch Art, 64-88, emer prof, 90. *Awards:* Can Coun Sr Nat Awards, 67 & 74; Visual Arts Grant, Manitoba Arts Coun, 89. *Bibliog:* Don Reichert, Artist in the Landscape, CBC Film, 82; Robert Enright (auth), Balancing the instrument of art, Arts Manitoba Mag, 83; Don Reichert, A Life in Work (monogr), Winnipeg Art Gallery, 95. *Mem:* Royal Can Acad Arts. *Media:* Acrylic, Watercolor. *Mailing Add:* 228 Glenwood Crescent Winnipeg MB R2L 1J9 Canada

REICHERT, MARILYN F
MUSEUM DIRECTOR
b Cincinnati, Ohio. *Study:* Bryn Mawr Col, BA, 58; Xavier Univ, MEd, 78. *Exhib:* William Zorach Paintings & Sculpture, 94; Jerusalem Album: Vintage Photographs 1860-1905, 96; Henry Mosler Rediscovered: Drawings & Paintings, 96; Artisans in Silver: Judaica Today, 97; Kenneth Treister: A Sculpture of Love and Anguish, 98; June Wayne: The Dorothy Series, 99. *Mem:* Am Asn Mus; Asn Coll & Univ Mus; Ohio Mus Asn. *Mailing Add:* Hebrew Union Col-Jewish Inst Religion Skirball Mus 3101 Clifton Ave Cincinnati OH 45220

REICHMAN, LEAH CAROL
PAINTER
b Kansas City, Mo, Aug 9, 1951. *Study:* Oxbow Summer Sch Painting Saugatuck, Mich, 70; Univ Wis, Madison, BS, 73; Whitney Mus Independent Study Prog, New York, NY, 73, 74; Hunter Col, New York, MA, 80. *Work:* Mus Mod Art, New York; Mus Bilbao, Spain; Archives Am Art, New York; Univ Wis, Madison; De Warande, Belgium; Best Products Co Inc, Richmond, Va. *Exhib:* A Piece of Cake, 75 & The Object and the Viewer, 78, 3 Mercer St Store, New York; Art Now 2-3, Woman Art Gallery, New York, 77; Pie in the Sky, Soho Art Fair, New York, 78; $100 Gallery, New York, 78; The Emerging Collector, New York, 91; and others. *Mem:* Nat Asn Female Execs. *Media:* Oil, Watercolor. *Publ:* Auth, Robert Indiana and the Psychological Aspects of his Art, Hunter, 80. *Mailing Add:* 249 6th Ave Brooklyn NY 11215

REID, CHARLES CLARK
WRITER, PAINTER
b Cambridge, NY, Aug 12, 1937. *Study:* S Kent Sch; Univ of Vt, 57; Art Students League, study with Frank Reiley, 59. *Work:* Yellowstone Art Ctr, Billings, Mont; Brigham Young Univ, Salt Lake City, Utah; Smith Coll Mus, South Hampton, Mass. *Comn:* US Postage Stamp to Commemorate Family Planning, US Postal Dept. *Exhib:* Nat Acad of Design, Am Watercolor Soc & Am Inst of Arts & Letters, NY; Far Gallery, NY; Munson Gallery, Mass & NMex; exhibs incl Govt House, Madeira, Portugal, 1961; Roko Gallery, New York City, 1973-74; Gallery Fair, Mendocino, Calif, 1991-92; Stremmel Gallery, 2005. *Pos:* Assoc, Nat Acad, New York City, 1980-83, academician, 1983-. *Awards:* Salmagundi Award, Allied Artists, 75; Silver Medal, Soc Illustrs, 83; Adolph & Clara O'Brig Prize, Nat Acad, 87 & 92. *Mem:* Mem Nat Acad of Design (assoc, 75, acad, 83, 1st Altman prize, 2nd Altman prize, Julius Hulgarten award, Clark prize, Salmagundi award 1975, Ranger fund, Emil Dines award, Obrig prize), Nat Watercolor Soc, Century Assoc. *Media:* Watercolor; Oil. *Publ:* Auth & illusr, Figure Painting in Watercolor, 72, Portrait Painting in Watercolor, 73, Flower Painting in Oil, 76 & Flower Painting in Watercolor, 79, Watson-Guptil; Painting What You Want To See, 83; Pulling Your Paintings Together, 85; Painting by Design, 88; Painting Flowers in Watercolor with Charles Reid, 2001. *Dealer:* Munson Gallery Chatham MA. *Mailing Add:* Munson Gallery 800 Main St Chatham MA 02633-2735

REID, FREDERICK W
PATRON
Study: Univ Calif, Berkeley, BA, 73. *Pos:* Va positions, Pan Am World Airways, Am Airlines, 76-87; commercial managing dir, Am Airlines, London, 87-91; sr vpres, Lufthansa, 91-97; exec vpres, chief marketing off, Delta Airlines Inc, Atlanta, 98-2004; Chief Exec Officer, Virgin Am, Inc, New York City, 2004-; bd trustees, Solomon R Guggenheim Found, currently; bd dir, High Mus Art, Atlanta; adv bd, Taub Inst for Res on Alzheimer's Disease & the Aging Brain

REID, KATHARINE LEE
MUSEUM DIRECTOR, CURATOR
Study: Harvard Univ, MFA, 1966; Instiut d'Art et Archaeologie, Sorbonne, Paris; BA magna cum laude, Vassar Coll. *Pos:* Cur Toledo Mus Art, Ohio, David and Alfred Smart Mus, Univ Chicago, Ackland Art Mus, Univ NC, Chapel Hill; asst dir Art Inst Chicago, 1982-86, deputy dir, 1986-91; dir Va Mus Fine Arts, 1991-2000, Cleveland Mus Art, 2000-2009; Chair vis comt Frances Lehman Loeb Art Ctr, Vassar Coll. *Mem:* Am Fedn of Arts, Am Asn Mus, Am Asn Mus Dir (pres 2000-01, mem bd trustees, formerly)

REID, LESLIE
PAINTER, PHOTOGRAPHER, VIDEO ARTIST
b Ottawa, Ont, Feb 8, 1947. *Study:* Queen's Univ, Kingston, Ont; Byam Shaw Sch Art, London, Eng; Chelsea Sch Art, London, Eng; Slade Sch Art, London, Eng. *Work:* Nat Gallery Can, Ottawa; Can Coun Art Bank, Ottawa; Agnes Etherington Art Ctr; Montreal Mus Fine Arts; Mus d'Art Contemp, Montreal; Winnipeg Art Gallery; Glenbow Mus; Art Gallery of Nova Scotia; Canada Council Art Bank; and others. *Exhib:* Nat Gallery Can, Ottawa, 75, 78, 84, & 2012; Biennalede de Paris, 77; Mira Godard Gallery, Toronto, 78, 81 & 84; Can Cult Ctr, Paris, 80; Can House Gallery, London, 80; Galerie Jolliet, Montreal, 82; Ottawa Art Gallery, 90; Mary Porter Sesnon Gallery, Santa Cruz, 91; Galerie St Laurent & Hill, Ottawa, 93, 96, 98, 2003, 2006, 2011, 2013; Robert Mclaughlin Gallery, Oshawa, 94; Agnes Etherington Art Ctr, Kingston, 96; Carleton Univ Art Gallery, Ottawa, 96; Galerie Rene Blouin, Montreal, 2000; Retrospective exhib, Carleton Univ Art Gallery, 2011; Builders: The Canadian Biennial Nat Gallery Can, 2012; and others. *Teaching:* Prof painting & drawing, Univ Ottawa, Ont, 72-2007, chmn art dept, 80-81 & 85-88, co-chair, 96-98 & dir grad studies, 2007-, prof emerita 2008. *Awards:* Ed Award, First Can Biennial Prints & Drawings, Can Coun, 74-77, 79, 83, 89, 94 & 97; Ont Arts Coun Grant, 78, 83-84, 90 & 95-96 & 2011; Arts 2000 Jury Prize for Excellence in Visual Arts, RCA, 2000; Queen Elizabeth Diamond Jubilee medal, 2012. *Bibliog:* Rolando Castellon (auth), Leslie Reid, Meridian Gallery, San Francisco, 91; Sandra Dyck (auth), Surfacing - Leslie Reid, Carleton Univ Art Gallery, 96; Jan Allen (auth), Fertile Ground, Agnes Etherington Art Ctr, 96; Diana Nemiroff (auth) Leslie Reid A Darkening Vision, Carleton Univ Art Gallery, 2012; and others. *Mem:* Royal Can Acad; Can Artist Representation. *Media:* Oil. *Dealer:* Galerie St Laurent & Hill 293 Dalhousie St Ottawa Canada K1N 7E5. *Mailing Add:* 50 Glen Ave Ottawa ON K1S2Z9 Canada

REID, SHEILA
ASSEMBLAGE ARTIST, WRITER
b Minneapolis, Minn. *Study:* Monteith Experimental Coll, Wayne State Univ; Ctr Creative Studies Art Coll; Ecole Nationale Superieure des Beaux-Arts, Paris, France. *Work:* Solomon Guggenheim Mus, NY; Musee d'Art Moderne, Saint-Etienne, France; Davis Mus, Wellesley, Boston; Mus Arts & Sci, Daytona Beach, Fla; RB Ginsburg Chambers, Supreme Court of the US; Utah Mus Fine Arts, Salt Lake City; Fyns Kunst Mus, Denmark; Harrison Mus Art, Logan, Utah; Univ Jacksonville Mus, Fla; McAllen Int Mus, Tex; Midwest Mus Am Art, Ind; Mus Biblistec, Alexandria, Egypt; Kyoto Inst Mus, Japan; Mus Artists Books, Baku; Downey Mus, Calif; Light Installation (13 structures with solar lights), Vence, France. *Exhib:* Musee de Luxembourg, Grand Palais, Paris, 84; Maier Mus, Lynchburg, Va, 86; Mus Univ Miss, 86; Nexus Found Today's Art, Philadelphia, 87; New Am Art, Inst Contemp Art, London, 88; Thoughts Without Words, Art Gallery Greater Victoria, Can, 90 & Gulbenkian Mus, Lisbon, Port, 91; FYNS Kunst Mus Odense, Denmark, 91; Musee d'Art Contemporain, Chamaliéres, France, 91; Uncensored, Davis Mus, Boston, Harrison Mus Art, Logan, Utah, 94; Imperceptible Icons, Midwest Mus Am Art, Elkart, Ind, 96; Biannale Mus, Alexandria, 2003; Paper Mus, Tokyo, 2006; Artists Books, Baku, Azerbayan, 2009; Palazzo Arengario, Milan, Italy, 77. *Awards:* Premio di Grafica di Pitture, Italy, 74. *Bibliog:* Nat Endowment for the Art without Rejection, 2011; Entre Les Pensees, 2013; A Place Between Thoughts, 2013; Three Contemporary Artists, Negri Found; Uncensored, Davis Mus, Boston, Harrison Mus, Utah; Donation Vicky Remy, Musee d'Art Moderne, St. Etienne, France; Art Without Rejection, Columbia Univ; Art Without Rejection, Maine Arts Commission. *Media:* Installation, Assemblage Art, Structures. *Publ:* Auth, Art Without Rejection, Rush Ed, 94; ed, Irony & Rude Questions, A Journal, Rush Ed, 96; A Place in the Future, 1/2 hour Film; auth, The Major Works of Sheila Reid, Rush Eds, 2007; Uncensored, 92; Three Contemp Artists, 83; A Place Between Thoughts, the Art of Sheila Reid, 2011; auth, Art Without Rejection, 93; auth, Art & Memories, Artist Book, 2011. *Dealer:* Jenny Vigneau, Vicent Delhomel. *Mailing Add:* c/o Rush Editions BP 13 Vence 06141 Cedex France

REID JENKINS, DEBRA L
PAINTER, ILLUSTRATOR
b Grand Rapids, MI, Mar 24, 1955. *Study:* Kendall Sch of Design Grand Rapids, 73-75; Aquinas Coll, 78-90. *Work:* Muskegon Mus Art, Mich; Butterworth Hosp Helen Devos Women & Children's Centre, Grand Rapids, Mich; Spectrum Fred & Lena Meijer Heart Centre, Grand Rapids, Mich; Am South Bank, Birmingham, Ala; Grand Valley State Univ, Grand Rapids, Mich; RDV Corp; pvt collection of Dick & Betsy DeVos. *Exhib:* Regional, Muskegon Mus Art, Mich, 93; solo exhib, Frederick Meijer Botanical Gardens, Grand Rapid, Mich, 97, Button Gallery, Douglas, MI, Art Prize, Grand Rapids, Mich, 2010, Between the Shining Seas, Wisconisn Maritime Mus, Minnesota Marine Art Mus, 2010-11; 15 Nat Exhib, Am Soc Marine Artists, 2011-2013; 33rd Int Marine Art Exhib, Mystic Seaport, 2012; Art of the Sleeping Bear Dunes, Dennos Mus, Traverse City, Mich, 2013; 34th Int Marine Art Exhib, Mystic Seaport, 2013; Butler Inst Am Art, 78th Mid Yr Exhib, 2014; 35th Int Marine Art Exhib, Mystic Seaport, 2014; 36th Int Marine Art Exhib, Mystic, Conn, 2015. *Awards:* Emerging Artist, Am Artist Mag, 95; 3rd place, Int Artist Mag, 2010, Hon Mention, 2014. *Bibliog:* Emerging Artist, Am Artist Mag, 95. *Mem:* Sig mem, Pastel Soc Am; Soc Gilders; Am Soc Marine Artists (signature mem); Portrait Soc Am. *Media:* Oil. *Interests:* Tai chi, feldenkrais, philos, kayaking. *Publ:* Illus, I Wanted to Know all About God, 93 & I See the Moon, 97 & Glory, 2001, Eerdmans; My Freedom Trip,

Boyds Mills Press, 98; Here is Christmas, Waterbrook Press, 2000; Grand Rapids Vision, Pagoda Group, 2007; The Saugatuck Dunes, 2008; Int Artist Mag, June/July 2010, Feb/March, 2014; Mich Artists Gallery, Sultons Bay, MI; Today's Masters, Fine Art Connoisseur Mag, Dec, 2014; International Artist Mag Seascapes Competition, June/July, 2015. *Dealer:* Arthur Frederick Button Gallery 161 Blue Star Hwy Douglas MI 49406-0400; Sychronicity Gallery Glen Arbor MI 49636. *Mailing Add:* 1323 Alden Nash Ave NE Lowell MI 49331

REILLY, BERNARD FRANCIS
HISTORIAN, CURATOR
b Philadelphia, Pa, June 7, 1950. *Study:* Villanova Univ, BA, 72; Bryn Mawr Col, with Arthur Marks, MA (hist art), 74. *Exhib:* Caricature Since 1870, Libr Cong, Washington, DC, 79. *Collection Arranged:* Am Political Prints (cataloged), Libr Cong, 78; Applied Graphic Art, Libr Cong; Photographs from 1845 to 1876 (cataloged), Libr Co Philadelphia. *Pos:* Cur prints & drawing, Libr Co Philadelphia, 74-77; cur popular & applied graphic art, Prints & Photographs Div, Libr Cong, 78-87; head cur, Prints & Photog Div, Libr Congress, formerly; dir res & access, Chicago Hist Soc, 97-. *Teaching:* Am political art, Humanities Prog, Georgetown Univ, 81-92. *Mem:* Am Asn Mus. *Res:* History of 19th century painting, graphic art and photography, particularly landscape; history of political art from Renaissance to current times with emphasis on theory of expression. *Publ:* Auth, Drawings of Nature and Circumstance, Caricature since 1870, contribr, Posada's Mexico, Libr Cong, 79; auth, American Political Prints in the Library of Congress, GK Hall, 89. *Mailing Add:* Chicago Hist Soc Clark St at North Ave Chicago IL 60614-6099

REILLY, JACK
PAINTER, VIDEO ARTIST
b Pittsburgh, Pa, Nov 4, 1950. *Study:* Fla State Univ, BFA, 76, MFA, 77. *Work:* Oakland Mus Art, Calif; Matthews Ctr Mus, Ariz State Univ, Tempe; Arco Ctr Visual Arts, Am Airlines, Los Angeles; Fresno Metrop Mus, Calif; Co of San Diego Pub Art Fredric Weisman Found, Los Angeles; Retrospective, Channel Islands Art Ctr, Camarillo, Calif, 2002; Magnum Opus, Ventura Co Govt Ctr, Ventura, Calif, 2003; Electronics Alive, Univ Tampa, Fla, 2003. *Comn:* Pub Art Comn, San Diego Co, Calif; Painting, Am Airlines. *Exhib:* Solo exhibs, Palm Gallery, CI Exhibs, Old Town Camarillo, Calif, 2009, Artamo Gallery, Santa Barbara, Calif, 2010, McNish Art Gallery, Oxnard Coll, Calif, 2011, Robert Graves Gallery, Wenatchee Coll, Wash, 2011, Corporale Bleicher Gallery, Los Angeles, Calif, 2012, Calif State Univ Channel Islands, Camarillo, Calif, 2013, and many others; Group exhibs, Inside/Insight L.A., Jose Drudis-Biada Gallery, Mt St Mary Coll, Los Angeles, Calif, 2009, Gallery Artists: Breaking Away 24/7, Artamo Gallery, Santa Barbara, Calif, 2010, Eclectic Visions, John Spoor Broome Gallery, CSU Channel Islands, Calif, 2011, Los Angeles Modernism, Santa Monica Air Ctr, Santa Monica, Calif, 2012, Art and Humor, Bleicher/Golightly Gallery, Santa Monica, Calif, 2013, Atrium Gallery, Ventura Gov Ctr, Ventura, Calif, 2013. *Pos:* Chair, art dept, Calif State Univ, Channel Islands, prof, 2001-; bd dir, Ventura Co Arts Coun, Calif. *Teaching:* Adj instr painting, Fla State Univ, 78; vis prof painting, Ariz Western Coll, Yuma, 80-81; instr, Otis-Parsons Art Inst, Los Angeles, 85-86; prof, Calif State Univ, Northridge, 87-2001. *Awards:* Best Show, Alexandria Mus Art, 94; Best Experimental Film, Univ Cincinnati Film Festival, 94; Best Captioned Video Poem, Nat Poetry Asn, 96; Best 3D Art, Carnegie Mus, Oxnard, Calif, 2001; Jury Award for Best Screenplay, Silver Spocket Film Competition, Fla, 2002; Rsch and Instructional Development Grant, CSU Channel Islands, 2005; Painting Commission, City of Ventura Music Festival, Ventura, Calif, 2006; Award of Distinguished Contributions to the Regional Arts, Ventura Arts Council, Calif, 2011. *Bibliog:* Linda Jacobson (auth), article, Arts Mag, 12/81; Edward Lucie-Smith (auth), article, Am Art Now, 85; Morrow Marva (auth), Inside the Los Angeles, Artist, 88; Shauna Snow (author), Article, The Fugue A Public Art Commission, Los Angeles Times, 10/90; Josef Woodard (auth), A Wild Ride Through Art History, Los Angeles Times, 9/2002; Jessica White (auth), Island Passages, VC Life and Style, pp 39, 40, 45, 2006; Matthew Singer (auth) California Thinkin, VC Reporter, p 15, 12/20, 2007; Aly Comingore (auth), Three Reasons Why Jack Reilly's Art in Shape Makes Math Fun, Santa Barbara Independent, 1/24 (color reproduction), 2008; Josef Woodard (auth), Where Leafage Meets Geometries-Jack Reilly's Show Poses Riddles and Mixes References, Santa Barbara News Press, 2/1 (two color reproductions), 2008; Heather Wills (auth), Jack Reilly's 3.5, CI View, 12/17 (color reproductions), 2009; More Cowden (auth), CI Opens New Studio, Ventura Co Star, 10/26, 2010; Zeke Barlow (auth) Eyesore to Artwork, Ventury Co Star, 9/15, 2011; Tracey Harnish (auth), Jack Reilly at Bleicher Gallery, Artweek L.A., Vol 6, 1/30, 2012. *Mem:* Coll Art Asn Am; Los Angeles Contemp Exhibs. *Media:* Acrylic, Oil; Digital Media. *Res:* Investigation into the relationships between digital media & traditional painting techniques. *Publ:* Auth, Shelia Ruth, A Discourse on Flowers Rev, 1/85 & Ed Paschike, Exhib Rev, Artweek, 12/90. *Dealer:* Image Mod Gallery 2674 Main St Ventura CA 93003. *Mailing Add:* PO Box 6151 Malibu CA 90264

REILLY, JOHN JOSEPH
PAINTER, INSTRUCTOR
b Brooklyn, NY, June 9, 1942. *Study:* Sch Art & Design, New York, 56-60; Pratt Inst, Brooklyn, NY, 60-62; Sch Visual Arts, New York, 63-64; Mechanics Inst, New York, 63-64; duCret Sch Arts, Plainfield, NJ, 87-89; NJ Ctr Visual Arts, Summit, NJ, 89-90; Art Students League, New York, 90-91; Newark Sch Fine Arts, NJ, 91-93; Nat Acad Fine Arts, New York, 92-94; studied with Jim McGinley (landscape/figure), Plainfield, NJ, 91-94, Burton Silverman (figure), New York, 95-97 & Everitt Raymond Kinstler (portrait), New York, 97-. *Work:* Joy Malin Fine Art, NYC; Richland Fine Art, Nashville, Tenn; Rinee Bank, Stacton; Lambersville, NJ, Riverside; Cancel, France; Glillers Wash Crossing Pa; Children's Specialized Hosp; Nabisco Corp Collection. *Comn:* Portrait, comn by Judge Macstein, Long Island, 99; mural (30'x40'), Dal Archit, Bayonne, NJ, 2000; Kearny Bank, Kearny, NJ, 2003; Ste John on the Mountain, comn by Mary E Bittrich, 2006; Vanderneer House, comn by Mary E Bittrich, 2006; portrait, Ernest Hemingway, Players Club, New York. *Exhib:* Salmagundi Club, NY, 90-2000; Nabisco Gallery, Hanover, NJ, 97; solo exhibs, Watchung Art Ctr, NJ, 98, NJ Ctr Visual Arts, Summit, 99, Barron Art Ctr, 2000, Bouras Properties, Summit, 2001, Johnson & Johnson, Stillwell, NJ, 2002, Ryland Inn, Whitehouse, NJ, 2003; Robert Wood Johnson, Mountainside, NJ, 2001. *Collection Arranged:* Salmagundi Club, NY, 90-2002; Nabisco Gallery, Hanover, NJ, 97; Children's Specialized Hosp, Mountainside, NJ, 2001; Johnson & Johnson, 2002; Clarence Dillon Libr, Bedminster, NJ, 2006. *Pos:* Dir, Elliot J Axelrod, NYC, 65-90; owner & oper, sales promotion agency, 84-89; Somerset Art Asn, Somerset, NJ, 2001-2004; Ridgewood Art Asn, 2003-2005. *Teaching:* Sch Visual Arts, New York, 80. *Awards:* Gold Medal, Dr Ralph Weiler Award, 2/95 & Gold Medal, William Auerbach Levy Award, 6/95, Nat Acad; 1st Prize, Timothy Shacknow Hannon Mem Award & Audubon Award, Salmagundi Club, New York, 9/98; Best of Tewksbury & 1st Prize, Tewksbury Hist Soc, 10/2002; 1st Place, Riverside Festival Arts, 2002; 2nd Place, 5th Ann Juried Show, Louisa Melrose, 2003. *Mem:* Artist Fel; Somerset Art Asn; Summit Art Asn. *Media:* Oil. *Publ:* TV (short segment on Channel 9), John Rouland, 2002; ed, NJ section NY Times, 2004; ed (article), Bernardsville News, 2005; ed (article), Weekender Local News, 2006. *Mailing Add:* 211 Pickle Rd Califon NJ 07830

REILLY, MAURA
CURATOR
Study: Inst Fine Arts, NYU, MA & PhD. *Collection Arranged:* The Dinner Party; Global Feminisism (with Linda Nochlin); Ghada Amer: Love Has No End; La Mirada Iracunda, 2008; Nayland Blake: Behavior, 2008; Carolee Schneemann: Painting, What It Became, 2009; Richard Bell: I Am Not Sorry, 2009. *Pos:* Critic & contribr, Art in Am, 1998-; founding cur, Brooklyn Mus Elizabeth A Sackler Ctr for Feminist Art, 2003-2008; sr cur, Location One, 2008-2009 & Am Fedn of Arts, 2009-2014; interim dir, Academy Art Mus, 2014-. *Teaching:* Prof contemp art hist & women's studies, Tufts Univ; instr art hist, Pratt Inst, Vassar Coll & NYU. *Awards:* Future Women Leadership Award, ArtTable, 2005; Lifetime Achievement Visual Arts Award, Women's Caucus for Art, 2006. *Mem:* Nat Org for Women; Int Asn Art Critics; ArtTable; Nat Comt Feminist Art Project. *Mailing Add:* 1083 Fifth Avenue at 89th St New York NY 10128

REILLY, NANCY
PAINTER
b Bryn Mawr, Pa, Mar 29, 1927. *Study:* Portraiture with Samuel E Brown, Westport, Conn & Mimi Jennewein, NY. *Work:* The Black Cape, Smithsonian Inst, DC; Study of a Child, Univ Conn, Farmington, Conn. *Comn:* Numerous portraits & landscapes, pvt collections. *Exhib:* Nat Arts Club, NY, 1971-2008; Am Artists Prof League, Salmagundi Club, NY, 1985-2008; Salmagundi Club, NY, 89; Acad Artists, 90-96; Butler Inst of Am Art, Youngstown, Ohio, 2001; New Britain Mus Am Art, Conn, 2001; incl in invitational traveling exhib with Allied Artists of Am to 8 mus throughout US, 2003-2005, Bennington Center Arts (with Allied Artists Am), Bennington, Vt, 2007. *Pos:* volunteer artist Norwalk Hosp Rehabilitation Unit, 84-95. *Teaching:* demonstr lectr portrait painting Bridgeport Art League, Conn, Milford Art League, Conn, New Haven Brush and Palette Club, Conn Classic Arts Asn, Allied Artists Am, Kent Art Asn, Conn, SCAN, Newtown, Conn. *Awards:* Bruce Stevenson Award, Nat Arts Club, 78, 88 & 91; Claude Parsons Mem Award, Nat Arts Club, NY, 2003; First prize, 106th Annual Exhib Artist Mem Exhib, 2005; Thora M Jensen Award, Hudson Valley Art Asn, 2005; Leila Gardin Sawyer Mem Award, Am Artists Professional League, 2005; James H Aiken Award Best Pastel, Kent Art Asn, 2006; Anna Liffey Award, New Haven Brush & Palette Club, 2008. *Bibliog:* Contrib, Westport, Conn artistic legacy (film), 2008. *Mem:* Allied Artists Am Inc (hon, bd dir, 91-98); Nat Arts Club; Pastel Soc Am; fel Am Artists Prof League; Hudson Valley Art Asn; Artists Fel NY. *Media:* Oil, Pastel. *Collection:* Slide collection; Smithsonian Institute, Washington, D.C.; University of Connecticut, Farmington. *Mailing Add:* Nine Marilane Rd Westport CT 06880

REILLY, RICHARD
DIRECTOR, HISTORIAN
b New York, NY, Mar 13, 1926. *Pos:* Consult, James S Copley Libr & Art Collection, La Jolla; fine arts adv, James S Copley Found. *Publ:* Auth, A Promise Kept, 83. *Mailing Add:* PO Box 1530 La Jolla CA 92037

REIMANN, ARLINE LYNN
PRINTMAKER, PAINTER
b St Louis, Mo, Nov 25, 1937. *Study:* Rutgers Univ, BA, 74; Montclair State Univ, NJ, MA, 80. *Work:* Newark Pub Libr Fine Print Collection, NJ; Montclair State Univ, Upper Montclair, NJ; Jane Voorhees Zimmerli Art Mus, New Brunswick, NJ; Bailey Matthew Mus, Sanibel, Fla; Black Hills Inst, SD. *Exhib:* Jane Voorhees Zimmerli Art Mus, 98 & 99; Prince St Gallery, Soc Am Graphic Artists, NY, 99; Worldwide Feminist Expo, Baltimore, Md, 2000; Nat Asn of Women Artists United Nations, 2002; Soc Am Graphic Artists, Old Print Shop, New York, 2004 & 2007; Ringling Mus Sch Art, Sarasota, Fla, 2006; Venezuelan Consulate, New York, 2006; Goggleworks, Reading, Pa, 2006-2013; Long View Mus of Fine Arts, Longview, Tex, 2007; Audubon artists, Salmagundi Club, New York City, 2007, 2008, 2009, 2010, 2011; NY Hall Sci, Nat Asn Women Artists, 2008; Nat Asn Women Artists Gallery, New York, 2008; Ormond Mem Art Mus, Soc Am Graphic Artists, Ormond Beach, Fla, 2008; Civic Arts, Shadelands, Walnut Creek, Calif, 2009; Howland Cult Ctr, Int Exhib, Beacon, NY, 2010; Nat Assoc Women Artists, Nat Arts Club, New York, 2010; Soc Am Graphic Artists, Ebo Gallery, NY, 2010; Nat Asn Women Artists, Nawa Gallery, 2011; Nat Asn Women Artists, Sylvia Wald, Po Kim Gallery, NY, 2011, 2012, 2013; Soc Am Graphic Artists, Prince St Gallery, NY, 2011; Nat Asn Women Artists, Armory Art Ctr, West Palm Beach, Fla, 2011-2012; Nat Asn Women Artists, Riverside Public Lib, NY, 2012, Point Park Univ, Pittsburgh, Pa, 2012, Midday Gallery, Englewood, NJ, 2012; Society Am Graphic Artists, The Old Print Shop, NY, 2012; Audubon Artists (online), 2012, 2013; Valley Art Gallery, Walnut Creek, Calif, 2012, 2013; Delind Gallery of the Arts, Milwaukee, Wisc, 2013. *Awards:* Best Show,

Lincoln Ctr, 81; Hon Mention, Nat Juried Exhib Small Works, Montclair State Univ, NJ, 95; Aida Whedon Mem Award, Nat Asn Women Artists, NY, 96; Miriam Russo Enders Award, Nat Asn Women Artists, NY, 2011. *Bibliog:* cover art, Am Conchologist Vol 37 No1, March 2009, Vol 37, No 2, June 2009; Art of Arline Reimann (include cover art), Am Conchologist Vol 36 No1, March, 2008. *Mem:* Nat Asn Women Artists (chmn travel printmaking exhib, 84-86 & 87-89 & printmaking jury 87-89 & 95-97); Audubon Artists (recording secy, 91-97); Soc Am Graphic Artists; Phi Beta Kappa; Calif Soc Printmakers. *Media:* Intaglio-Etching, Monotype, Linocuts. *Interests:* Paleontology & conchology. *Mailing Add:* 546 Hillrise Pl Walnut Creek CA 94598

REIMANN, WILLIAM P
SCULPTOR, EDUCATOR
b Minneapolis, Minn, Nov 29, 1935. *Study:* Yale Univ, BA, 57, BFA, 59, MFA, 61; with Josef Albers, Rico Lebrun, Robert M Engman, James Rosati, Gilbert Franklin, Seymour Lipton, Gabor Peterdi, Neil Welliver & Bernard Chaet. *Work:* Mus Mod Art, Whitney Mus Am Art & Rockefeller Univ, NY; Boston Mus Fine Arts; Nat Gallery Art, Washington; City of Holyoke, Mass. *Comn:* Relief-mural, First Church of Christ, Boston, Mass, 81; suspended sculpture, Shell Oil Corp, Houston, Tex, 81 & Southwestern Bell Telephone Co, 86; Designated Artist, Radnor Twp, Pa, Blue Route Enhancement Proj, 89-96; Sandblasted Relief, Boston Red Sox Baseball Club, Fenway Park, Mass, 90; water feature, Mass Turnpike Authority, 96; relief sculpture, Mass Port Authority, 96. *Exhib:* Structured Sculpture, Galerie Chalette, NY, 61-68; Sculpture Ann, 64-65 & Young Americans, 65, Whitney Mus Am Art; Int Exhib Contemp Painting & Sculpture, Carnegie Inst, Pittsburgh, 67-68. *Teaching:* Asst prof art, Old Dom Col, 61-64; lectr visual & environ studies, Harvard Univ, 64-, Carpenter Ctr Visual Arts, spring 71, sr preceptor visual & environ studies, 75-, head tutor dept visual studies, 86-. *Media:* Plexiglas, Stone. *Mailing Add:* One Gerry's Landing Cambridge MA 02138-5511

REIMERS, GLADYS ESTHER
SCULPTOR, INSTRUCTOR
b Yonkers, NY. *Study:* Art Students League, New York, 60; Sculpture Ctr, New York, 65-69; Studied metal sculpture with Herb Kallems, 66. *Work:* Newark Mus, NJ; AAUW Traveling Collection; Rockwell Int, Pittsburgh, Pa; British Petroleum, London. *Comn:* Caring (marble sculpture), Union Co / Westlake Special Sch, NJ, 86. *Exhib:* one-women shows, Morris Pine Gallery, Fair Lawn, NJ, 79, Caldwell Coll Gallery, NJ, 80 & Palmer Mus, Springfield, NJ, 2001; Cork Gallery, Lincoln Ctr, NY, 87; Audubon Artists Ann Exhib, Salmagundi Club, NY, 98; Biennial Exhib, Trenton State Mus, NJ & Newark Mus, NJ. *Teaching:* instr sculpture workshop, Town of Westfield, NJ, 82-94 & Somerset Art Asn, Bedminster, NJ, 90-. *Awards:* Hirsch Award, Audubon Artists Nat Show, 96, Cleo Harting Award, 98; Women of Achievement Award for Union Co, NJ State Legislature, 99. *Mem:* Audubon Artists; New York Soc Women Artists; NJ Ctr for Visual Arts; Somerset Art Asn. *Media:* Stone, Wood. *Dealer:* Braunsdorf Gallery Westfield NJ. *Mailing Add:* 837 Fairacres Ave Westfield NJ 07090

REINERTSON, LISA
SCULPTOR
b Washington, DC, May 15, 1955. *Study:* Univ Calif, Davis, BA, 82, MFA, 84; Skowhegan Sch Painting & Sculpture, Scholar, 83. *Work:* Martin Luther King (bronze bust), Calif State Univ, Chico; ceramic, Davis Art Ctr, Calif. *Comn:* Martin Luther King Jr (terra cotta portrait), King Law Sch, Univ Calif, Davis, 87; portrait, George Washington HS, San Francisco, Calif, 89; Martin Luther King Jr (full size bronze), City of Kalamazoo, Mich, 89. *Exhib:* Fifty-ninth Ann Crocker-Kingsley Exhib, Crocker Art Mus, Sacramento, Calif, 84; City of Savona, Italy; Introductions, Dorothy Weiss Gallery, San Francisco, 89; Reynolds Gallery, Univ Pac, Stockton, Calif, 90; Figures in Ceramics, La State Univ, Baton Rouge, 90. *Teaching:* Vis artist & instr ceramics, La State Univ, Baton Rouge, 84; lectr ceramics & drawing, Calif State Univ-Stanislaus, 86-87; asst prof ceramics, Calif State Univ, Chico, 87-. *Awards:* Grand Central Gallery Educational Asn Award, New York, 85; Research Award, Calif State Univ, Chico, 89. *Bibliog:* Saunthy Singh (auth), Lively ceramic sculpture, Artweek, 10/86; Craig Thomas (auth), Kalamazoo Gazette, 89; Elaine Levin (auth), Contemporary Ceramics: The Artists of TB9 (exhib catalog), 89. *Mem:* Coll Art Asn. *Media:* Clay

REININGHAUS , RUTH
PAINTER
b New York, NY, Oct 4, 1922. *Study:* Studied with Bob Maione & Rudy Colao, 57-62, Nat Acad Design, with Morton Roberts, 62; Frank Reilly Sch Art, with Frank Reilly, 63; Art Student's League, with Robert Philip & Robert Beverly Hale, 68; New York Univ. *Work:* Murtugh D Guinness; Salmagundi Club; US Navy Art Prog; US Coast Guard Art Prog; Horace Singer Collection. *Comn:* numerous pvt collections. *Exhib:* Allied Artists Am Ann, Nat Acad Design, New York, 72 & 87; Hammer Gallery, New York, 74; Salmagundi Club Ann, New York, 74-; Far Gallery, New York, 75; Catharine Lorillard Wolfe Art Club Ann, New York, 78-; Hong Kong, 1976; Knickerbocker Artists, 85-; A Fertile Fellowship, Thomas A Walsh Gallery, Fairfield Univ, Conn, 87; solo exhib, Petrucci Gallery, 88; Pastel Soc Am Ann, 88-; Heidi Neuhoff Gallery Inc, New York, 90; Heckscher Mus Art, Huntington, NY, 97; John Lane Gallery, Rheinbeck, NY; Regianni Gallery, New York. *Pos:* Draftsmen, Engineering Aide, Allied Control Co, 41-45 & 52-68; Freelance tech illusr, 60's; Management Info, Bell Helicopter, Iran, 77-79; Sr artist, Economics, Bankers Trust, 80-85; 1st woman pres, Salmagundi Club, NY, 83-87; Electrical Testing Lab liaison between management and production, 68-76. *Teaching:* Instr oil painting, Bankers Trust, New York, 71-99 & Kittredge Club for Women, 72-77. *Awards:* Anna Hyatt Huntington Horse's Head Trophy (Best in Show), Catharine Lorillard Wolfe Exhib, 78; J Giffuni Purchase Award, Pastel Soc Am Ann, 1988; Medal Hon, Salmagundi Club, 89; Dianne B. Bernhard Silver Medal Award for Excellence in Pastel, Art Spirit Found, 2006; over 150 awards in juried ann shows. *Bibliog:* Lucien Mandose (auth), 58th Ann Allied Artists Am Exhib, La Rev Mod, Paris, 72; Raymond Steiner (auth), Profile, Art Times, 8/89; Jennifer McGhee Siler (alumnae ed), New York artist pursues international following, Adelphean, summer 91; 200 Great Painting Ideas for Artists, in Carole Katchen; The Best of Pastel 2, by Pastel Soc Am; Pastel Artist Intl, Jan/Feb, 2001. *Mem:* Salmagundi Club (dir at large, 74-77, chmn admiss, 81-83, pres, 83-87 & cur, 89-2004); Fel Am Artist's Professional League; Knickerbocker Artists, 1983-89; Catharine Lorillard Wolfe Club (bd dir, 87-); Hudson Valley Art Asn; Pastel Asn Am (bd dir, 87-89); Pen & Brush Club, 80-90; NACAL (Navy Art Cooperation & Liaison) 70-80; COGAP (Coast Guard Art Program) 80-90; Am Artist Professional League, 71-; Music Box Soc, 1959; and others. *Media:* Oils, Pastels. *Specialty:* Representational: oil, watercolor, pastels, graphics, sculpture, and photog. *Interests:* 18th & 19th century music boxes & watches. *Collection:* Johann Schrettiger, Augsberg, 1700 Horologe, 1865 Music Box (8 songs), 1885 Nicole Frerers Large Cylinder Music Box with Bells and Zither, and 2 changeable cylinders, 1811 Gold Musical watch by PM in a diamond, 1820 Musical Watch, silver. *Dealer:* Salmagundi Club New York NY. *Mailing Add:* 222 E 93rd St Apt 26A New York NY 10128-3758

REINKER, NANCY CLAYTON COOKE
PAINTER, SCULPTOR
b Owensboro, Ky, July 6, 1936. *Study:* Kent State Univ; Cleveland Inst Art; Silvermine Sch Art; Critique with Robert Reed, Sculpture with Stanley Bleifeld; ConnGraphicarts Ctr with Robert Reedat, etching with Vijay Kumar. *Work:* New Haven Paint & Clay Club, New Haven, Conn; Housatonic Community Col, Bridgeport, Conn. *Exhib:* solo exhib, Silvermine Hayes Gallery, New Canaan, Conn, 92 & Farrell I Gallery, Art Place, Southport, Conn, 93, 95 & 98, Westport Art Ctr, 2009; Conn Art, Stamford Mus, Conn, 92; Faber Birren Color Show, Stamford Mus, Conn, 93; Art Place, Southport, Conn, 93, 95, 98 & 2000; Farrell I Gallery, 98; United Nations Regeneration Exhib, New York City, 99; Norwalk Community Col, 99 & 2000; Artspace, Hartford, Conn, 99; Gallery Irohani, Sakii City, Japan, 2000; 100th Ann Exhib, New Haven Paint and Clay Club, 2000; Katonah Mus Art, 2001; Art of Northeast, 2001, 2002; Erector Square Gallery, New Haven, Conn; Silvermine Now, 2008; Years in the Making, Westport Hist Soc, 2009; Double/Vision, Ariz State Univ Commons Libr, 2009; Wilton Libr, Conn, 2009. *Pos:* vpres, Art Place Gallery, 91-92; pres, Inst for Visual Artists, 92, 93; Chmn, Western Comn Arts, 93-94; bd mem, Silvermine Guild of Artists, 94-99. *Awards:* Painting Award, Conn Women Artists, 91; Merit Award, New Haven Paint & Clay, 93; R Chitwood Prize, Greenwich Art Soc, Randolph Chitwood, 94; Painting Awardm Westport Art Ctr, 2007. *Bibliog:* Ann R Langdon (auth), Art New Eng, June-July, 94; Wm Zimmer (auth), NY Times, 12/17/95 & 1/20/91; Kate Jennings (auth), Westport News, 11/17/96. *Mem:* Nat Asn Women Artists; Inst Visual Arts (pres, 92-93); Conn Women Artists; Art Place (vpres, 91-92, pres, 94); Women's Caucus Art; Silvermine Guild Artists; Phoenix Mus (contemp forum scholar comt); and others. *Media:* Mixed Media on Wood, Canvas, Vellum & Ink. *Dealer:* Silvermine Guild of Artists 1037 Silvermine Rd New Canaan CT 06840. *Mailing Add:* 682 Fairfield Beach Rd Fairfield CT 06824

REINKRAUT, ELLEN SUSAN
PAINTER
b East Orange, NJ Jul 3, 1949. *Study:* Univ of Cincinnati, BFA, 71; Arts Students League, studied with Bruce Dorfman/Norman Lewis, New York, 75-79. *Work:* Muhlenberg Coll, Pa; McCarter and English, Law Off, NJ; McBride Corp, NJ; Maxwell Us Headquarters, NJ; JMS Advisory, Mass; Aronsohn & Weiner, NJ; Bev Max Properties, NY; Biotracx Medical Corp, NJ; Hanover Insurance, NJ; and numerous other corp collections. *Exhib:* Paterson Mus, Paterson, NJ, 92; Morris Mus, Morristown, NJ, 2002-04; Phillips Mus of Art, Lancaster, Pa, 2003; Bergen Mus, Paramus, NJ, 2004; Monmouth Mus, Monmouth, NJ, 2004. *Teaching:* Instr art & dir, Dunellen Pub Sch, 75-91; instr art, Art Ctr of Northern NJ, 2003-04 & var workshops, currently. *Awards:* Art Asn Award, Maurice Pine Gallery, 93; 2nd Prize, Int Exhib, 93 S Art Gallery, NY, 98; First Prize, PCFL Art Festival, NJ, 98; Mary K Karasick Mem Award, NAWA, New York, 2004; Best in Show, Avila Ann Art Exhib, NJ, 2006-2007. *Bibliog:* NY Gallery Guide, 96; Art News, 2001; Art in Am, 2002. *Mem:* Nat Asn of Women Artists; The Soc of Layerist in Multi Media; Studio Montclair; Salute to Women in the Arts. *Media:* Oil. *Publ:* Cover art, Inner Realm Mag, 7/2001. *Mailing Add:* 706 Clove Ln Franklin Lakes NJ 07417

REIS, MARIO
PAINTER
b Weingarten, Ger, 1953. *Study:* Dusseldorf Art Acad, 73-78; study with Prof Gunther Vecker, 78-79. *Work:* Ministerium fur Wissenschaft und Kunst des Landes; Baden-Wurttemberg; Stadische Galerie Ludenscheid; Mus der Stadt Gelsenkirchen; Ulmer Mus. *Exhib:* One-man shows, Unge Kunstneres Samfund, Oslo, Norway, 86, Galerie Vayhinger, Radolfzell, 86, Fenderesky Art Gallery, Belfast, Ireland, 86, Galerie Dorothea van der Koelen (with catalog), Mainz, 86, Galerie Monochrom, Aachen, 87, Gallery Carla Fuehr, Munchen, 88, Salon des Modernes Mus, Belgrad, Yugoslavia, 88; Stadisches Bodenses-Mus (with catalog), Freidrichshafen, 86; Nur Rost---? (with catalog), Skulpturenmuseum Glaskastn, Marl, 86; Kunstmuseum Karlsruhe, 88; Kunstmuseum Dusseldorf, 88. *Media:* Watercolor

REISMAN, CELIA
PAINTER
Study: Carnegie-Mellon Univ, Pittsburgh, Pa, BFA, 1971; Yale Sch Art, New Haven, Conn, MFA, 1978. *Exhib:* Solo exhibs, Hood Mus Art, Hanover, NH, 1988, List Gallery, Swarthmore, Pa, 1990, Cleaver Callahan Gallery, New York, 1992, Gross McCleaf Gallery, Philadelphia, 1995, 1997, 1999, 2001, 2004 & 2007, Fifteen Year Survey, James A Michener Art Mus, Doylestown, Pa, 2000, Kathryn Markel Fine Arts, New York, 2001 & Les Yeux du Monde, Charlottesville, Va, 2006; The Artist as Native: Reinventing Regionalism, Babcock Gallery, 1994; Spirit of Nature, MB Modern, New York, 1996; Rediscovering the Landscape of the Americas, Gerald Peters Gallery, 1996; In Her Own Voice: Self Portraits, Berman Art Mus, Collegeville, Pa, 1998; Small Things, Kathryn Markel Fine Arts, New Yorks, 2002; FIVE Princelet

Street Gallery, London, 2002; Landscape: The Painting Center, New York, 2007; Marking the Landscape, SUNY Genesco Sch Art, 2008; Lenore Gray Gallery, Providence, RI, 2009; Am Acad Arts and Letts Invitational, New York, 2009. *Teaching:* Vis asst prof, Art Dept, Dartmouth Coll, 1985-2002; asst prof, Swarthmore Coll, 1990-2008; vis artist, Trinity Coll, 2001. *Awards:* Window of Opportunity Award, Leeway Found, 2001; SOS Grant, Pa Coun Arts, 2001; Faculty Res Award, 2003 & Faculty Res Grant, 2007, Swarthmore Coll; Purchase Award, Am Acad Arts and Letts, 2009. *Media:* Oil. *Dealer:* Lex Yeux du Monde Gallery 841 Wolf Trap Rd Charlottesville Va 22911; Ruth Morpeth Gallery 43 West Broad Hopewell NJ 08525

REISS, ROLAND
SCULPTOR, PAINTER
b Chicago Ill, May 15, 1929. *Study:* Univ Calif, Los Angeles, BA, 55, MA, 57; also at Am Acad Art, Chicago. *Work:* Los Angeles Co Mus Art; Laguna Art Mus, Laguna Beach, Calif; Oakland Mus, Calif; Hallmark Inc; Newport Harbor Art Mus, Newport Beach, Calif. *Exhib:* Biennial, Whitney Mus Am Art, NY, 75; one-person exhib, Los Angeles Co Mus Art, 77; Documenta 7, Kassel, Ger, 82; 20 Am Artists, Mus Mod Art, San Francisco, 82; Currents, Inst Contemp Art, Boston, 83; Boxes, Mus Tamayo, Mexico, 85; Avant Garde in the 80s, Los Angeles Co Mus Art, 87; Contemp Calif, Taipei Fine Arts Mus, Taiwan, 87; Ace Contemp Exhibs, 87, 88 & 89; solo exhib, Ace Contemp Exhibs, Los Angeles, 88; Montgomery Art Gallery, Claremont, Calif, 90; Barnsdall Munic Art Gallery, Los Angeles, 91; Univ Ariz Mus Art, Tucson, 92; Neuberger Mus Art, State Univ NY, Purchase, 92; Palm Springs Desert Mus, 92. *Teaching:* Asst prof art, Univ Calif, Los Angeles, 57; from asst to assoc prof, Univ Colo, Boulder, 57-61; chmn & prof, Claremont Grad Univ, 71-. *Awards:* Visual Arts Fel, Nat Endowment Arts, 71, 77, 80 & 87. *Publ:* Auth, Roland Reiss, A Seventeen Year Survey, Fels Contemp Art. *Mailing Add:* Dept Art Claremont Grad Univ 251 E Tenth St Claremont CA 91711

REITZENSTEIN, REINHARD
SCULPTOR, ENVIRONMENTAL ARTIST
b Uelzen, Ger, May 27, 1949; Can citizen. *Study:* Ont Coll Art. *Work:* Art Gallery of Ont; Can Coun Art Bank; Nat Gallery Can; Mem Univ Art Gallery; Government of Ont; Gov Canada Art Gallery of Hamilton. *Comn:* Wall relief, Govt of Ont, Can, 85; outdoor sculpture, Mem Univ Art Gallery, St John's Newfoundland, 85; Pergola (sculpture), Western Univ, 93; Arch (sculpture), McDonald Stewart Art Gallery, Ont, 94. *Exhib:* Nat Gallery Can, 74 & 77; Landscape Canada Traveling Exhib, Art Gallery Ont & Edmonton, 76; solo exhibs, Carmen Lamanna Gallery, Toronto, 75-90, Olga Korpa Gallery, Toronto, Ont, 93-, Can; Royal Botanical Gardens, Sculpture Symposium, 83; Lutz Teutluzf Gallery, Brock Univ, 99; Royal Botanical Gardens, Burlington, Ont, 2000; Rideau Hall, Ottawa, Can, 2002; Tridel Corp, Toronto, 2003; Greatland Corp, Toronto, 2010; Larkin Group, Buffalo, NY, 2010; Daniels Corp, Toronto, 2011. *Pos:* dir sculpture & assoc prof, State Univ NY, Buffalo, 2000-. *Teaching:* Instr, Univ Guelph, 80-98, Brock Univ, 90-94, Univ Waterloo, 83, Toronto Sch Art, 98-2000, Sheridan Col, 2000. *Awards:* Can Coun Proj Cost Grants, 74 & 76-84 & Art Grants, 78-2011; Warhol Found Grant, 2006. *Bibliog:* Carol Corbel (auth), article, Globe & Mail, Toronto, 3/86; Kate Tayler (auth), Can Art, 90; John K Grand (auth), Sculpture Mag, 94, 99, 2000, & 2011, Vies Des Arts, 2000, Le Sabord, 2000, Espace, 2000, Circa Mag, Dublin Ire, 2001; Gil Meavoy (auth), Sculpture Mag, 2003; Jacqueline Bouchard (auth), Espace Mag, 2008; Andre Seleanu (auth), Vie des Arts, 2008. *Media:* Mixed Media, All Media. *Publ:* Auth, Natural Areas Divisions Charter, 75; According (record album), 80; Reinhard Reitzenstein, C Dewdney Art Gallery of Hamilton, 89; World Tree, Ted Fraser Confed Centre Arts, PEI, 93; For the Joy of It, Newfoundland Sound Symposium, 96; Let the Work Begin, UB Art Gallery, 2003; Plutos Cave, New Jersey City Univ Art Gallery, 2006; Shift Happens, Barlington Cultural Centre, 2009. *Dealer:* Olga Korper Gallery 17 Morrow Ave Toronto Can. *Mailing Add:* 146 Ridge Rd W Grimsby ON L3M 4E7 Canada

REKER, LES
PAINTER, EDUCATOR
b Indianapolis, Ind, Aug 7, 1951. *Study:* Ind Univ, Bloomington, BFA, 73; Queens Col, MFA, 75; study with Robert Birmelin & Gabriel Laderman. *Work:* Reading Mus, Reading, Pa. *Comn:* Landscape paintings, Hawk Mountain Sanctuary, Kempton, Pa, 82 & Republic Bank, Dallas, 84. *Exhib:* In Praise of Space, Westminster Col, New Wilmington, Pa, Gross-McCleaf Gallery, Philadelphia, Pa & Parsons Sch Design, NY, 77-78; Christmas Invitational, Allentown Art Mus, Allentown, Pa, 77 & 78; Co-op Invitational, Philadelphia Art Mus, 81; Queens Alumnus, Godwin-Ternbach Mus, Flushing, NY, 82; Sherry French Gallery, NY, 83-86; Art of Our Time, Temple Emanuel, Woodcliff-Lake, NY, 84; Emerging Realists: Sherry French Gallery, NY, 84; Emerging Realists: East Meets South, Coll Mainland, Texas City, Tex, 86. *Collection Arranged:* Contemporary Narrative Figure Painting (auth, catalog), 85 & Landscapes of the Hudson River Sch (auth, catalog), 86, Payne Gallery, Moravian Col; Artificial Light: Paintings by William Haney (auth, catalog), 85; Robert Arneson (auth catalog), 87; Clarence Carter. *Pos:* Dir & cur, Payne Gallery, Moravian Col, Bethlehem, Pa, 84-; asst prof art, Moravian Col, Bethlehem, Pa, 84. *Teaching:* Instr art hist, Leigh Co Community Col, Schnecksville, Pa, 78-83; asst prof drawing, Kutztown Univ, Kutztown, Pa, 83-84; asst prof studio & art hist, Moravian Col, 84-. *Bibliog:* Hedy O'Beil (auth), reviews, Arts Mag, 6/78 & 1/84; Freddie Kaplin (auth), Landscape painting in America, Am Artist, 2/84. *Mem:* Asn Coll & Univ Gallery & Mus; Am Asn Mus. *Media:* Oil on canvas. *Dealer:* Sherry French Gallery 41 W 57th St New York NY 10019

RELKIN, MICHELE WESTON
PAINTER, INSTRUCTOR
b Calif, Jan 17, 1946. *Study:* Santa Monica Coll, Lucille Brown Green Studio, AA, 66. *Work:* Clinton Libr, Ark; Whitehouse, Presidential Coll, Washington, DC; Galleria Ortiz, San Antonio, Tex; Johnson Corp Gallery Coll, Los Angeles, Calif; Ronald Raegan Pres Libr and Mus, Simi Valley, Calif; Gabriells Gallery, Santa Fe, NMex; pvt collection of Governor Richardson, Santa Fe; "Capitol" of NMex, Santa Fe; Sweeney Convention Center; Capitol Rotunda, Book Arts, Santa Fe, 2011. *Comn:* CD Cover Art, George Gamez, Los Angeles, Calif, 2004; Socks in Blue Room, Los Angeles Mus Art, Los Angeles, Calif; Children Art & Music Festival, Dorothy Chandler Pavillion, Los Angeles, Calif. *Exhib:* Black Tie & Blue Jeans, Conejo Valley Art Mus, Thousand Oaks, Calif, 92; Internet Mail Art, Pasadena Armory Ctr, Pasadena, Calif, 92; From Washington to Clinton, Ronald Reagan Mus, Semi Valley, Calif, 93; Parade of Animals, Lancaster Mus Art, Lancaster, Calif, 94; Los Angeles Co Mus, Los Angeles, Calif, 97; Atkinson Gallery, Santa Barbabra Coll, Santa Barbara, Calif, 97; Permanent Collection, Clinton Pres Libr, Ark, 2004; Mining the Unconcious, Coll Art and Design, Sweeney Convention Center Gallery, Santa Fe, NMex, 2011; Mining the Unconcious, Sweeney Convention Ctr Gallery. *Collection Arranged:* Cur, Gallery 9, 98; The Red Book, Sweeney Convention Ctr Gallery, 2011. *Pos:* Supvr, Elem Arts; UCLA. *Teaching:* Artist-in-residence, Walnut Canyon Elem, 97-2004; vis artist, pub & pvt sectors, Santa Fe, NMex; supvr & dir, Cult Arts Prog, Santa Fe, NMex; supervisor enrichment prog, Eldorado Elementary, Santa Fe, NMex; lecture on creativity (Carl Jung), Symposium on Schizophrenic Art. *Awards:* Woman of the Yr, Santa Monica Coll, Calif, 65; Printmaking Award, Moorpark Coll, Santa Monica, CA, 91; Honorable Mention, Thousand Oaks Juried Exhib, Katherine Leiu, 99. *Bibliog:* Dialogue with Georgia O'Keefe, Studio Zine Magazine, 2001; Patty Jean Levine (auth), Presidential Pets, Thousand Oaks Star, 2004; Claudia Jacobs (auth), Focus Magazine, 2007; One Heart. *Mem:* NAWA, 95-; Book Artists Group, 2005-; N Gallery, Santa Fe. *Media:* Mixed Media, Acrylic, Found Objects. *Res:* Numinous studies & mythological, Carl Jung. *Interests:* Archeology, nature, music, symbology of the universal. *Collection:* Beany Babies. *Publ:* Santa Fean Mag; Focus NMex; Southwest Mag; New Mexican Newspaper, One Heart Mag. *Dealer:* Gabriells Gallery Santa Fe NM; Zipp Gallery Santa Fe NM; Galleria Ortiz San Antonio TX. *Mailing Add:* 125 Overlook Rd Santa Fe NM 87505

RELYEA, LANE
ADMINISTRATOR, EDUCATOR
Pos: Delivered lectures at NY Mus of Modern Art, Harvard Univ, Art Inst of Chicago, and others; editor-designate Art Journal, 2012-. *Teaching:* Faculty mem, Calif Inst of the Arts, Valencia, 1991-2001; dir Core Program and Art History, Glassell Sch of Art, Houston, Tex, formerly; assoc prof, chair, art theory & practice department, Northwestern Univ, currently. *Publ:* Essays and Reviews have appeared in Artforum, Parkett, Frieze, Modern Painters, Art in America and Flash Art; auth (monographs on) Polly Apfelbaum, Richard Artschwager, Jeremy Blake, Vija Celmins, Toba Khedoori, Monique Prieto, Wolfgang Tillmans and others; contribr (exhibition catalogs) Helter Skelter and Public Offerings (both Mus of Contemporary Art, Los Angeles, 1992. 2001); auth, D.I.Y. Culture Industry: Signifying Practices, Social Networks and Other Instrumentalizations of Everyday Art, 2012. *Mailing Add:* Northwestern University Art Theory & Practice 1880 Campus Dr Office Kresge 3-404 Evanston IL 60208

REMSEN, JOHN
PAINTER, CONSULTANT
b Glen Cove, NY, Apr 21, 1939. *Study:* Pratt Inst, BFA; NY Univ, MA (art educ); painting studies with Richard Lindner, Stephen Greene, Fred Mitchell. *Work:* Larsa USA, Melville, NY. *Exhib:* Postcards From Our Friends, AIR Gallery, NYC, 2003; Alpan Gallery, Huntington, NY, 2003, 2005-08, 2010; Abstraction at 40, Gallery North, Setauket, NY, 2005; Of Nature and the Hand (curator & exhib), Port Jefferson Village Ctr, NY, 2006; Re/Opening, Alpan Gallery, Huntington, NY, 2002; Solo exhibs, Canios Bookshop, Sag Harbor, NY, 1992, New Works on Paper, Nesé Alpan Gal, Roslyn, NY, 1992, horse show paintings, Prism Gallery, Port Jefferson, NY, 1999, Abstract Landscapes, West Beth Gal, NYC, 2001 & paintings from 1980-2001, Gallery Rood, Eastport, NY, 2001. *Collection Arranged:* John T Mather, sculpture, Mem Hosp, Port Jefferson, NY. *Pos:* Mgr & dir contemp art gal, NYC, Calif & Long Island, NY; independent cur & reviewer of fine arts for various publ. *Teaching:* Instr, high schools, Long Island, NY. *Media:* Acrylic on canvas. *Specialty:* Contemporary painting, assemblage, sculpture & environments. *Collection:* Larsa USA, Melville NY. *Dealer:* Alpan Fine Arts. *Mailing Add:* PO Box 2803 East Setauket NY 11733-0860

REMSING, JOSEPH GARY
PAINTER, SCULPTOR
b Spokane, Wash, Sept 18, 1946. *Study:* San Jose State Univ, BA & MA. *Work:* De Saisset Mus, Univ Santa Clara; Oakland Mus. *Comn:* Maj sculptural comn, State of Calif, 78. *Exhib:* Solo exhibs, Willima Sawyer Gallery, San Francisco, 71 & 73-74; Int Sculpture Competition, State of NJ, traveling, 79-80; Djurovich Gallery, Sacramento, Calif, 85; Palo Alto Cult Ctr, 85; Chuck Levitan Gallery, NY, 86; Lighting Collaborative, NY, 87; Modesto Coll Calif, 89 & 94; and others. *Teaching:* Instr, Modesto Jr Col, 71-. *Awards:* Award, Maryville Col, Tenn, 70; Award, Calif Arts Comn, 70. *Bibliog:* Articles in San Francisco Chronicle, 9/8/69 & 5/7/71, Artforum, 11/69 & Art Wk, 5/71, 4/72 & 6/74; and others

RENDL, M(ILDRED) MARCUS
PAINTER, WRITER
b New York, NY, May 30, 1928. *Study:* NY Univ, BS, 48, MBA, 50; Radcliffe-Harvard, PhD, 54. *Hon Degrees:* Dean Brown Cronkite Fel, Radcliffe Coll, 50-51; Anne Radcliffe Fel, SubSahara Africa, 58-59. *Comn:* Cover for ann meeting, Allied Social Sci Asn, 94. *Exhib:* Art of the Northeast, Silvermine Guild Ctr Arts, New Canaan, 86; Phoenix Gallery, New York, 89; Lever House Gallery, New York, 90; Cork Gallery, New York, 90; Greater Hartford Archit Conserv, Conn, 91; Barnum Festival Art Exhib, Discovery Mus, Bridgeport, Conn, 95-96; Ward Nasse, 99-; Fine Art Liliana Gallery, Lenox, Mass, 2001-2003; Nat Asn Women Artists, 115 yr Anniversary Show, World Trade Ctr, New York, 2004; Pen & Brush Non-Member Show, New York, 2004; Nat Asn Women Artists, New York, 2005-2007; Catherine Lorilland Wolfe Art Asn, 2005-2007; Real Art Ways, Hartford, Conn, 2005-2007; Nat Mus of Women in the Arts, Fall Benefit, 2007. *Pos:* Art econ consult; organizer, Rendl Fund Conserv Slavic Artifacts, Mus Mod Art, New York; Harvard Univ Art Mus,

Busch Reisinger Mus, 99-; Peabody Mus Archeology and Ethnology, Cambridge, Mass & Harvard Mus Nat Hist, 2000; organizer, Rendl Fund for Czech Art, Metrop Mus of Art, NY, 2006-; cur, Peabody Mus, Harvard Univ; cur, Rendl Fund for Exhibs of Native Am Art, 2011. *Awards:* Faber Birren Color Award; Metrop New York Award. *Mem:* Women's Caucus Arts, Miami, San Antonio; Artists Equity Asn; Southwest Soc Economists; Western Economics Asn; Women Arts Found, New York; Nat Asn Women Artists, New York; Allied Artists Am Inc, Asn Artist; Catherine Lorilland Wolfe Art Asn, New York. *Media:* Oil, Acrylic; Ink. *Res:* Economics of art; complex art appraisals and pricing art; art as investment or money substitute; art as consumer durable good and valuation. *Interests:* Piano. *Collection:* black & white series, political-economic. *Publ:* Auth, Economics of the fine arts: Fad, fashion and value, Eastern Community Coll Asn, 84; Pricing contemporary art & Economic issues in the arts, Women Arts Found, 86-90; When Is a Price of Fine Art, The Price ?, Am Soc Bus & Behav Sci, 96 & Price Distortion (Fine Art) Caused by Source of Purchase, 96. *Dealer:* Art Commun Int On-Line Gallery 210 W Rittenhouse Sq Philadelphia PA; Liliana Fine Arts Gallery Lenox MA; Ward-Nasse Gallery, New York, NY; Chelsea Ward-Nasse Gallery, New York, NY

RENEE, LISABETH
SCULPTOR, ASSEMBLAGE ARTIST

b Brooklyn, NY, July 28, 1952. *Study:* Univ Puget Sound, Tacoma, Wash, 72-73; State Univ NY, Buffalo, BA, 77; Art Students League, New York, studied drawing with Marshall Glasier & Anthony Palumbo, sculpture with Jose Decreeft & Sidney Simon, painting with Knox Martin & Theodoros Stamos, 78-80; New Sch Social Res, New York, with Dorothy Gillespie & Alice Baber, 79; Long Island Univ, MFA, 82; Rollins Col, Winter Park, Fla, teaching cert, 84; Univ Cent Fla, Orlando, EdD, 96. *Comn:* Mural (8ft X 11ft), State Univ NY, Buffalo, 76; Peaches on the Roof (mural), comn by Dr Michael Reeves, Montgomery, Ala, 84; Jet (floor installation), McCoy Elementary Sch, Orlando, Fla, 85. *Exhib:* Solo exhibs, The Painted Box, Ctr Arts, Vero Beach, Fla, 86 & Harris, Atlantic Ctr Arts, New Smyrna Beach, Fla, 92; Creatures of Creativity Invitational Exhib, Seminole Community Col, Sanford, Fla, 93; Underwraps Invitational Exhib, Harris House, Atlanta Ctr Arts, New Smyrna Beach, Fla, 93, 94 & 95; Nat Art Educ Asn Exhib, Baltimore, Md, 94; Traditions, Translations & Transformations Invitational, Orlando, Fla, 96; and others. *Pos:* Dir, Southern Artists' Registry, Winter Park, Fla, 84-87; juror, Riverfront Fine Arts Festival, Seminole Community Col, 90 & Ponce Inlet Art Festival, 92; dir, W Campus Art Gallery, Valencia Community Col, Orlando, 96-. *Teaching:* Instr studio art, Long Island Univ, Greenvale, NY, 80-82, Orange Co Pub Schs, Fla, 83-86 & Seminole Co Pub Schs, Fla, 86-94; adj fac drawing, Rollins Col, Winter Park, Fla, 83; adj fac art educ, Univ Cent Fla, 94-95, vis instr & coordr art educ, 95-96; adj fac humanities, Valencia Community Col, 95-96, prof humanities & fine arts, 96-. *Awards:* Ace Scholar, 92 & 96; Kimball Grant, Fla Dept Educ, 95; Invision Grant, Fla Div Blind Servs, 95. *Bibliog:* Art Rev, Tampa Art Today, Channel 8, Tampa, Fla, 10/85; Teacher excels in art fields, Wings, spring 88; Jim Murphy (auth), Contemporary art lost and found, Orlando Sentinel, 11/6/92. *Mem:* Women's Caucus Art; Coll Art Asn; Int Sculpture Ctr; Nat Art Educ Asn; Fla Art Educ Asn, (central Fla regional rep). *Media:* Mixed. *Publ:* Ed, Children and the Arts: A Sourcebook of Arts Experiences for School Age Childcare Programs, 90 & Children of the Arts: A Sourcebook of Arts Experiences for Pre-Kindergarten Programs, 90, Fla Dept Educ, Tallahassee; Cooperative Art, The ARTISTeacher, 91; auth, the Phenomenological significance of aesthetic communion, Univ Cent Fla, Orlando, 96. *Mailing Add:* 20 Cobblestone Court Casselberry FL 32707-5410

RENEE, PAULA
PAINTER, TAPESTRY ARTIST

b Hackensack, NJ. *Study:* Rockland Community Col, Suffern, NY, 70-71; Ramapo State Col, Mahwah, NJ, 73; Fairleigh Dickenson Univ, Teaneck, NJ, 73-77; Art Ctr Northern NJ, Tenafly, 77-80; Thomas A Edison Col, Princeton, NJ, 78; OCCC Sch Art, Demarest, NJ, 78-80; State Univ NY, Empire Col, AS, 90; studied with John McQueen, Albertje Koopman & Hugh Mesibov. *Work:* handmade book "100 Words", Nat Inst Design, Ahmedabad, India; The Wood Sch, NY; tapestry, Sealy Mattress; woven painting, AT&T; tapestry, pvt collection of Mary Tyler Moore; AT&T Internat Marketing, NY; mixed media, Bramwell Capital Management, NY; Travelers Insurance, Hartford, Conn; tapestry, Warner Lambert, Morris Plains, NJ; The Wood School, NY; woven painting, Worthington Hotel, Ft Worth, Tex; IBM, Lincoln Financial Group, New Haven, Conn; dimensional paper construction, Montessori School, New Preston, Conn; many others. *Comn:* Tapestry, Sheraton Hotel, Chicago, Ill, 88; handwoven Moroccan bldgs, Stouffers' Resort, Indian Wells, Calif, 89; Our Lady of Peace Mausoleum at St Nicholas Cemetery, Lodi, NJ, 91; tapestry (with Sidney Simon), West Point Jewish Chapel "Tree of Life", US Army Military Acad; tapestries, GE Capital, Stamford, Conn; woven paintings, Tobu Hotel, Kinshicho, Japan, Presidential Suite and 17 lobbies; woven painting, Ramada Inn, Albuquerque, NMex; tapestries, dimensional fiber construction, woven painting, Biomatrix, Ridgefield, NJ; dimensional paper construction, A T Clayton, Greenwich, Conn; woven paintings, gouache on paper, Tetko Corp, Briarcliff Manor, NY; University Club, Durham, NC; Town Club, Corpus Christi, Tex; Olin Corp, Stamford, Conn; and others. *Exhib:* Hudson River Mus Westchester, Yonkers, NY; New London Art Soc Gallery, Conn; L'Atelier Gallery, Piermont, NY; Images Gallery, Briarcliff Manor, NY; Bergen Mus Arts & Sci, Paramus, NJ; Silo Gallery, New Milford, Conn; Reece Galleries, NY; Rawls Mus Art, Courtland, VA, 2000-01; Longwood Ctr Visual Arts, Portsmith, Va, 2000-01; Picture This Gallery, Westport, Conn, 2000-01; ENMU-R, Roswell, NM, 2002; Am Crafts Gallery, Cleveland, Ohio, 2002; Wooster Art Ctr, Danbury, Conn, 98; New Canaan Soc for Arts, New Canaan, Conn, Ann Photog Show 2006-2007 & Spectrum, ann juried art show, 2006, 2008 (first prize), Rockwell Gallery, Wilton Conn, Solo Exhib 2006, Merging Elements & Rockwell Gallery, Ridgefield, Conn, 2010-11; Norwalk Symphony, Conn, 2004; Vertrue, Norwalk, Conn, 2008; Bergen Mus Art, Paramus NJ, 81; Trenton City Mus, NJ, 91; Hopper House Fed, NY, 88; Long Beach Island Fed Arts, Loveladies, NJ, 87; Am Cult Ctrs, traveling to New Delhi, Bombay, Calcutta, Bhopal, Madras, Goa, Ahmedabad, India, Galleria d'arte, 2010; Stamford Ctr Arts, 2007; Pittsburgh Ctr Arts, 2003; Blue Hill Art & Cult Ctr, Pearl River, NY, 98, 2002; Am Crafts Gallery, Cleveland, Ohio, 98; St Johns univ, Jamaica, NY, 98; Michael Ingbar Gallery, Soho, NY, 89; Seeing Trees, A Fine Art Exhib, Blue Hill Art & Cultural Ctr, Pearl River, NY, 2011; Peace & Joy: Magical Images, The Art Gallery at the Rockefeller State Park Preserve, 2011-2012; Easton Arts Coun, Conn, 2012; Odyssey Guild, Ridgefield Guild of Artists, 2012; Flowers, Art and Frame, 2012; Earth's Treasures, Barn Gallery, 2012; Richter Asn for the Arts, Danbury, Conn, 2012; Soc Creative Arts, Newtown, Conn, 2012; Solo exhib, Art & Frame, Danbury, Conn, 2012; Trees, PS Gallery, Litchfield, Ct, 2013. *Pos:* Artist-in-residence, Bergen Community Col, Paramus, NJ, Studio/Gallery-Hackensack, NJ, 78-79. *Teaching:* OCC Sch Art, Demarest, NJ, 85. *Awards:* 9th Place, Int Art Competition, Harrison, NY, 85; David Blick Award, SCAN, 2000; 1st Place, Richter Art Ctr, Danbury, Conn, 2001, 02, 04, 2nd Place 03, 1st Place, 11; Best in show, Society of Creative Arts, Newtown, Conn, 2008; New Canaan Soc for Arts, 1st place, mixed media, 2008; numerous others. *Bibliog:* June Avignon (auth), Colorful masks can't disguise her whimsical art, North Jersey Suburbanite, 2/1/84; Edith Sobel (auth), Artist fabricates symbolic tapestry, Fed News, 8/85; Betty Freutenheim (auth), NY Times, 1/20/91; Tracey O'Shaughnessy (auth), Republican American, 10/4/06; Travis R Moore (auth), The Mercurial (article). *Mem:* Soc Creative Arts Newtown Conn; Ridgefield Guild Artists; Richter Art Ctr. *Media:* Acrylic; Gouache, Oil; Loom-woven Fiber, tapestry, multimedia dimensional paper, photography, constructions, woven paintings. *Interests:* nature, abstracts, color, people, new ways of expressing. *Publ:* Illusr, Photo Covers, Shuttle Spindle & Dyepot Mag (Handweavers Guild of Am), 81 & 86; auth, Shuttle, Spindle & Dyepot (mag, cover), Handweavers Guild Am, Bloomfield, Conn, 86; photograph and article, Fiberarts, Asheville, NC, 9-10/84, 11-12/86, 9-10/98; Creative thought, Religious Sci Int, Spokane, Wash, 5/90; mag cover, Sci of Mind Mag, Church Relig Sci, Los Angeles, Calif, 7/90, 4/91, 10/92 & 6/95, Connecticut Mag, 6/2000; Savvy Living mag, 11-12, 2000; Westport Mag, 10/02; auth, Pages of Revelations, Artbuilders Inc Collection Metropolitan Mus Art and Newark Libr. *Dealer:* Rockwell Gallery Main St Ridgefield CT; PS Gallery on the Green Litchfield CT; Barn Gallery 82 Rte 27 Creative Crns New Fairfield CT. *Mailing Add:* Birchwood 27 Crow's Nest Ln - 16D Danbury CT 06810

RENK, MERRY
GOLDSMITH, PAINTER

b Trenton, NJ, July 8, 1921. *Study:* Sch Indust Arts, Trenton, NJ; Inst Design, Chicago. *Work:* Boston Mus Art; San Francisco Art Comn & Calif Craft Mus, San Francisco; Am Craft Mus, NY; Oakland Mus Art, Calif; Smithsonian Inst; Renwick Gallery; Private Collections. *Comn:* Wedding crown, comn by Johnson Wax, Objects, USA; copper sculpture, Contra Costa Jr Coll Dist, Martinez, Calif; iron sculpture, Walnut Creek Pub Libr, Calif. *Exhib:* Messengers of Modernism, traveling through Quebec, US, Europe; Solo exhibs, De Young Mem Mus, San Francisco, 71 & Mus Hist & Technol, Smithsonian Inst, 71-72; Retrospective, Calif Craft Mus, San Francisco, 81; Le Trou Gallery, San Francisco, Watercolors, 86 & 88-90; Depot Gallery, Mill Valley, Calif, 94; Smithsonian Am Art Mus, 2007-; Jewelry by Artists, Daphine Farago Collection Mus Fine Arts, Boston, 2007-; and others. *Pos:* Founder, 750 Studio, Chicago, 46-47; self employed Goldsmith, until 83; watercolor printer, 83-2005. *Teaching:* Instr enamel for jewelry, Haystack Mt Sch Crafts, Deer Isle, Maine; instr design, Univ Calif, Berkeley. *Awards:* Craftsman Grant, Nat Endowment Arts, 74; San Francisco Comn Awards Hon, 86-; Fel, Am Craft Coun, 94. *Bibliog:* Toni Greenbaum (auth), Messengers of Modernism; A Fried (auth), article, San Francisco Examiner, 3/71; Joan Watkins (auth), article, AM Crafts Mag, 4/81; Opulent and Organic The Jewelry of Merry Renk, JP Watkins, April / May 81, American Craft Mag; Women Designers in the USA-1900-2000-Toni Greenbaum; Modernist Jewelry, 1930-1960, Marbeth Schon-2004. *Mem:* Metal Arts Guild Life (pres, 53); distinguished mem Soc NAm Goldsmiths. *Media:* Metal. *Interests:* Painting life memories for my grandchildren. *Publ:* Auth, Design Autobiography, Goldsmith J, Summer, 80. *Dealer:* Mobilia 358 Huron Ave Cambridge MA 02138. *Mailing Add:* 17 Saturn St San Francisco CA 94114-1420

RENNER, ERIC
PAINTER, PHOTOGRAPHER

b Philadelphia, Pa, Nov 6, 1941. *Study:* Univ Cincinnati, BS, 64; Cranbrook Acad Art, MFA, 68. *Work:* Mus Mod Art, New York; Nat Gallery Can, Ottawa; Mus Mod Art, Mexico City; Mus Art Sao Paulo, Brazil; Inst Contemp Art, Chicago; Graham Nash Collection; Bibliothèque Nationale, Paris. *Comn:* Photographs, State Ohio, State Off Tower, 74. *Exhib:* Nat Gallery Can, 71, 73 & 75; solo exhibs, Mus Mod Art, Mexico City, 71 & Mus Sao Paulo, Brazil, 78, Solo Photo, New York, San Francisco Art Inst, RI Sch Design, Mus Modern Art, Mexico City, Museu de Arte de Sao Paulo, Brazil, Nat Sch Photog, Buenos Aires, Univ NMex, Hollins Coll, State Univ NY at Alfred; The Great West, Univ Colo, Denver, 79; The Extended Frame, Visual Studies Workshop, Rochester, NY, 80; Handmade Cameras, Tyler Sch Art, Temple Univ, 82; The Panoramic Image, Univ Southampton, Eng, 82; The Pinhole Image, Va Mus, Richmond, 83; Through a Pinhole Darkly, Fine Arts Mus Long Island, Ctr Contemp Arts Santa Fe & Museo de Arte Contemporaneo Sevilla, Spain, 88; Centre Photographique d'Ile de France, Paris, Photog Mus Charleroi, Belgium, & Saidye Bronfman Center, Montreal, 89; Optical Alchemy, Rencontyres Int de la Photog d'Arles, France, 96; The World Through a Pinhole, Michael Fowler Center, Wellington, New Zealand, 97; Magiae Naturalis, Lonsdale Gallery, Toronto, Images from the Collection Nat Gallery Can, Ottawa, 99; Sténopé Photog 1985-2000, Mediatheque Jean Levy, Lille, France, 2000; Pin: Whole, Univ Essex, Eng, 2001; Why Pinhole?, Visual Studies Workshop, Rochester, NY, 2001; Dis/Content, Coll Santa Fe, 2001. *Pos:* Founder & dir, Pinhole Resource, 84-. *Teaching:* Asst prof design, State Univ NY, Alfred, 68-71; adj prof photog, Visual Studies Workshop, 75; tchr various workshops and lectrs, various cities, 75-; teacher, Espanola (NMex) Pub Schs, 76; adult ed painting tchr, Coll Santa Fe, 76-78; adj prof art appreciation, Western NMex Univ, 79; instr photog, Tyler Sch Art, Philadelphia, summer session, 85-88; vis prof photog, Hollins Coll, Roanoke, Va, 91; vis artist-in-residence with

Nancy Spancer, Hollins Univ, Va, Spring semester, 2002. *Awards:* Nat Endowment Arts Fel, 76 & 79; Aaron Siskind Found grant, 90; Am-Scandinavian Found Grant, 87; J Paul Getty Trust grant, 86. *Mem:* Soc Photog Educ. *Publ:* Auth, The Horsefetter, 77, Visual Studies Workshop; Pinhole Photography - Rediscovery of a Historic Technique, Focal Press, 95, 2d ed, 99, 3d ed, 2004; Pinhole J, 85-2006; American Disguise, 2007; coauth (with Nancy Spencer), on deaf ears. *Dealer:* Blue Dome Gallery Silver City NM. *Mailing Add:* Star Rte 15 Box 1355 Hanover NM 88041

RENNINGER, LEE
CERAMIST
Study: Univ Fla, Gainesville, BA, MA. *Exhib:* Solo exhibs include Ohr-O'Keefe Mus Art, Biloxi, Miss, 2001, Univ Southern Miss, 2002; group exhibs include San Angelo Nat Ceramic Competition, Tex, 2002; Mastery in Clay Invitational, Clay Studio, Philadelphia, 2002, 2005; Miss Invitational, Miss Mus Art, Jackson, 2003, 2005, 2007; Fiberart Int: Biennial Exhib Contemp Fiberart, 2004, 2005; Forested Landscape, Kent State Univ, Ohio, 2006; Crowning Achievement, Mint Mus Craft & Design, Charlotte, NC. *Awards:* Visual Arts Fel, Miss Arts Comn, 2003; Dir's Award for Innovative Use of Materials, Fiberarts Int, 2004; Andy Warhol Found Grant, 2006; Emergency Grant, Joan Mitchell Found, 2006; Pollock-Krasner Found Grant, 2006-07. *Media:* Clay

RENOUF, EDDA
PAINTER, PRINTMAKER
b Mexico City, Mex, June 17, 1943; US citizen. *Study:* Academie Julian, Paris, 63-64; Sch Art, Columbia Univ, MFA, New York, 71; Academie der Bildende Kunste, Munich, 69-70; Columbia Univ, Paris, France, painting fel, 71-72. *Work:* Art Inst Chicago, Ill; Nat Gallery Art, Washington, DC; Metrop Mus Art, Mus Mod Art & Whitney Mus Am Art, New York; Australian Nat Gallery, Canberra, Australia; Centre Georges Pompidou & Bibliotheque Nationale, Paris; British Mus, London; Collection Lambert, Avignon, France; Corcoran Gallery, Washington, DC; Kunstmuseum, Winterthur, Switz; Mus Contemp Art, Los Angeles; Philadelphia Mus Art, Philadelphia, Pa; Tel Aviv Mus, Israel; Walker Art Ctr, Minneapolis, Minn; Blanton Mus Art, Univ Texas, Austin; Brooklyn Mus Am Art, Brooklyn, NY; Cincinnati Mus Art, Cincinnati, Ohio; Delaware Art Mus, Wilmington, De; Detroit Mus Art, Detroit, Mich; High Mus Art, Atlanta, Ga; Yale Univ Art Gallery, New Haven, Conn; Speed Art Mus, Louisville, KY; Harvard Univ Art Mus, Cambridge, Mass; Phoenix Art Mus, Ariz; Miami Art Mus, Fla; Pa Acad Fine Arts, Philadelphia; Memphis Brooks Mus Art, Tenn; Univ Mich Mus Art, Ann Arbor; Dallas Mus Fine Art, Tex; Frac Pays de la Loire, Carquefou, France; Group Lhoist, Limelette, Belgium; Kemper Mus Contemp Art, Helsinki, Finland; Louisiana Mus, Denmark; Milwaukee HHK Found for Contemp Art, Wisc; MIT Visual Art Center, Mass; Montclair Art Mus, Montclair, NJ; Seattle Art Mus, Wash; Honolulu Acad Arts, Honolulu; Saint Louis Art Mus; Albright-Knox Art Gallery, Buffalo, NY; Akron Art Mus, Ohio; Portland Mus Art, ME; LAM Lille Metropole, Lille, France; Hood Mus Art, Hanover, NH; Portland Art Mus, Portland, Ore; Power Art Inst Australia, Sydney; Mus Art, Rhode Island; Sch Design, Providence, RI. *Comn:* etching proj, CNAP, France, 96. *Exhib:* Solo exhibs, Galerie Yvon Lambert, Paris, 72, 74-75, 78, 80, 84 & 93, Françoise Lambert Gallery, Milan, 73, 75, 76, 79 & 83, Daniel Weinberg Gallery, San Francisco, 77 & 79, Blum Helman Gallery, New York, 78, 79, 82, 85, 87 & 89, Elisabeth Kaufmann, Basel, Switz, 94 & 96, Galerie Sollertis, Toulouse, France, 94, 96, 98 & 2007, Univ Mich Mus Art, Ann Arbor, 95, Staatliche Kunsthalle Karlsruhe, Ger, 97, Hubert Winter, Vienna, 98, Joseph Helman Gallery, New York, 2002, Nat Mus Women Arts, Washington, DC, 2004, Galerie Arnaud Lefebvre, Paris, 2006 & Galeria Charpa, Valencia, Spain, 2007, Galerie 1900-2000, Paris, 2010, Annely Juda Fine Art, London, 2013, Senior and Shopmaker Gallery, NY, 2013; Group exhibs, Mus Mod Art, New York, 73, 77, 90 & 98; Stedelijk Museum, Amsterdam, Fundamental Painting, 75, Musée d Art Moderne, Paris, 75, MoMA, New York, Extraordinary Women, 77; Whitney Mus Am Art, New York, 78, 79 & 85; Contemp Drawing-NY, Univ Calif, Santa Barbara, 78; Biennial Exhib, Whitney Mus of Am Art, 79; Drawing Acquisitions 1981-1985, Whitney Mus Am Art, 85; 20th Century Art, Metrop Mus of Art, NY 87; Lines of Vision: Drawings by Contemp Women (traveling exhib), Hillwood Art Gallery, Long Island Univ Brookville, NY, 89; From Bonnard to Baselitz-Ten Yrs of the Collection 78-88, Bibliot Nat de Paris, 92; Musee d'Art Moderne, Lille, Villeneuve d'Aseq, France, 92; From Minimal to Conceptual Art: Works From the Dorothy & Herbert Vogel Collection, Nat Gallery Art, Washington, DC, 94 & 98; Prints, Galerie Gisele Linder, Basel, Switz, 96 & 2004; Paper Assets, Collecting Prints & Drawings, British Mus, 96-2001; Heureux le Visionnare, Centre National de l 'Estampe et de l'Art Imprime, Chatou, France, 97; From Minimal to Conceptual Art: Works from the Dorothy & Herbert Vogel Collection, Tel Aviv Mus Art, 98; La Collection Yvon Lambert, Yokoham Mus Art, Japan, 98; Prints & Drawings, Recent Acquisitions, Corcoran Gallery, Washington, DC, 2000; La Cult Pour Vivre, De Georges Braque Aurelie Nemours, Centre Georges Pompidou, Paris, 2002; Matisse to Freud: A Critic's Choice-The Bequest of Alexander Walker, The British Mus, London, 2004; Matisse to Freud, Hayward Gallery, British Mus, London, 2006-07; Les 40 Ans de La Galerie Yvon Lambert-Message Personnel, Galerie Yvon Lambert, 2006; Summertime, Galerie Gisele Linder, Basel, Switz, 2006; Galerie Arnaud Lefebvre, Paris, France, 2007; Gifted: Recent Additions to the Permanent Collection, Delaware Art Mus, Wilmington, Del, 2008; 30 Años de Arte y Artistas, Galeria Charpa, Universidad Politécnica, Valencia, Spain, 2008; Collected Thoughts: Works from the Dorothy and Herbert Vogel Collections, Indianapolis Mus Art, Ind, 2008; Jeffmute, Mamco, Geneva, Switzerland, 2009; New York/New Drawings 1946 - 2007, Museo de Arte Contemporaneo Esteban Vicente, Segovia, Spain, 2009; Elles, Ctr Pompidou, Paris, 2010-2011; Dorothy & Herbert Vogel Collection, Penn Acad Fine Arts, 2010; Primary of Paper, Mus Art, RI Sch Design, 2010; Mus des Beaux Arts, Lyon, France, 2010; Miss Mus Art, Jackson, Miss, 2010; Dela Art Mus, Dela, 2010; Albright-Knox Gallery, Buffalo, NY, 2010; LAM Lille Metropole Musee d'art Moderne art contemporain, 2011; Brit Mus, London, 2011; Katonah Mus Art, Westchester, NY, 2011; High Mus Art, Ga, 2011; Portland Mus Art, 2011; Honolulu Acad of Arts, 2011; Art Inst Chicago, 2011; Blanton Mus Art, Austin, Tex, 2012; Hood Mus Art, Hanover, NH, 2012; Seattle Art Mus, Seattle, Wash, 2012; Yellowstone Art Mus, Billings, Montana, 2012; Maison de la Culture, Namur, Belgium, 2013; Virginia Mus Fine Arts, Richmond, Va, 2013; Fine Arts Ctr, Colo Springs, Colo, 2013; Senior & Shopmaker Gallery, NY, 2013; Belvedere Mus, 2013; Univ Colo Art Mus, Boulder, 2013; Many Things Placed Here and There: The Dorothy and Herbert Vogel Collection, Yale Univ Art Gallery, 2013-2014; 50 Works for 50 States, NMex Mus Art, Santa Fe, 2013-2014; Bowdoin Coll Mus Art, Brunswick, Me, 2014. *Teaching:* Vis prof, Ecole Nat Superieure de Beaux Arts, Paris, 95-96. *Awards:* Printmaking Grant, Nat Endowment Arts, 76; Pollock-Krasner Found Inc Grant, 90. *Bibliog:* C Beret, Interview with Edda Renouf, Art Press 1/73; Susan Larsen (auth), rev, Art in Am, 2/77; Steven Henry Madoff (auth), Edda Renouf at Blum-Helman, Art in Am, 143, 5/82; Thomas Clark (auth), From Dawn to Dusk to Midnight, Contemporary Art, London, 93; Maiten Bouisset (auth), Edda Renouf, Art Press 216, 9/96; Rolf-Gunter Dienst (auth), Sprache, Sichtbar-Die Malerin Edda Renouf in Karlsruhe, Frankfurter Allegmeine Zeitung, 5/97; Alvaro de los Angeles (auth), El Soporte Como Discurso-Edda Renouf, Levante, El Mercantil Valenciano, 5/2007. *Media:* Acrylic, Oil; Pastel Chalk, Oil Pastels. *Publ:* Lines, Edizione Flash Art, Milan, 74; Lines and Non-Lines, Lapp Princess Press & Printed Matter Inc, New York, 77; Echoes, Graeme Murray Gallery, Edinburgh, Scotland, 79; Lines of Vision-Drawings by Contemporary Women, Hudson Hills Press, New York, 89; auth, 24 Signes, Editions Galerie Arnaud Lefebvre, Paris, 2006. *Dealer:* Galerie 1900-2000 8 rue Bonaparte 75006 Paris France; Annely Juda Fine Art 23 Dering St London W15 1AW London; Senior & Shopmaker Gallery 210 Eleventh Ave at 25th St New York NY 10001. *Mailing Add:* 37 Rue Volta Paris 75003 France

RENSCH, ROSLYN
HISTORIAN, COLLECTOR
b Detroit, Mich. *Study:* Northwestern Univ, BM & MM; Univ Ill, MA (art hist); Univ Wis-Madison, PhD (art hist), 64. *Pos:* Bd dir, Sheldon Swope Art Gallery, Terre Haute, Ind, 77-82, World Harp Congress, 83-89; harpist spec events, The Cloister, Sea Island, Ga, currently. *Teaching:* Lectr art hist & humanities & chmn div humanities, Nat Col Educ, 62-65; prof art hist & humanities, Ind State Univ, 65-88; lectr art hist & humanities, Elder hostel progs, Ga Southwestern Col & Mercer Univ, Golden Isles, Ga; adj fac Univ N Fla, Jacksonville, 2002-. *Mem:* Coll Art Asn Am; Midwest Art Hist Soc; Int Ctr Medieval Art; life mem Art Inst Chicago. *Res:* Pre-Romanesque stone carving in the British Isles; representations of the harp in art monuments; American landscape painting; 18th-20th century harps. *Collection:* Harps (antiques & modern); art representations featuring the harp. *Publ:* Auth, Harp, its History, Technique & Repertoire, Praeger, 69 & Duckworth, 69; Development of the medieval harp: A re-examination of the evidence of the Utrecht Psalter and its progeny, Gesta, Vol 11, No 2; Harp carvings on the Irish crosses, Am Harp J, winter 74; Landscape painting in America to c 1900, Ind State Univ, 75; Harps & Harpists, Duckworth, 89 & Ind Univ Press, 89; Three centuries of harpmaking, Victor Saln Found, 2002. *Mailing Add:* 315 Forest Oaks Saint Simons Island GA 31522-2490

RENTSCH, ANDREAS
PHOTOGRAPHER
Study: Col St Michel, Freiburg, Switzerland, BS (Economics), 1978-82; Ecole des Arts Appliqués, Vevey, Switzerland, BFA (Photography), 1983-87; Int Ctr Photography, New York, 1989-90. *Work:* Mus Fine Arts, Houston; Polaroid Collection, Waltham, Mass; Swiss Found Photography, Zurich, Switzerland; Mus Checkpoint Charlie, Berlin. *Exhib:* Solo exhibs include Midtown Y Gallery, New York, 1993, Old Pink Sch House, Tres Piedras, NMex, 1994, Houston Ctr Photography, Houston, 1996, Ctr de la Photographie, Geneva, 1998, Sag Harbor Picture Gallery, Sag Harbor, NY, 2001; Group exhibs include Fondation Gianada, Martigny, Switzerland, 1985; Spiritual Travels, Robin Rice Gallery, New York, 1992; A Grand Tour, Swiss Inst, New York, 1993; Disposable Generation, CB's 313 Gallery, New York, 1993; San Miguel De Allende, Inst Nacional De Bellas Artes, Mex, 1996; Spirit in the Flesh, Stuart Levy Gallery, New York, 1996 ; Shots, Afterimage Gallery, Dallas, 1996; Outer Boroughs, White Columns, New York, 1999; Preview 2000, Cheryl McGinnis Gallery, New York, 2000; Summer Show, Rosenberg & Kaufman Fine Art, New York, 2005, Gallery Artist's, 2006; Free Play, Islip Art Mus, E Islip, New York, 2007; Picturing Long Island, Heckscher Mus, Huntington, NY, 2007 . *Dealer:* Stephen Rosenberg Fine Art 115 Wooster St #4R New York NY 10012. *Mailing Add:* 19 Lake Pl Huntington NY 11743

REPLINGER, DOT (DOROTHY THIELE)
WEAVER, DESIGNER
b Chicago, Ill, Jan 30, 1924. *Study:* Sch Art Inst Chicago, BA (educ), study with Carolyn Howlett & Else Regensteiner. *Work:* Amerinvesco, Chicago; Caterpillar Int, Peoria, Ill; Haskins & Sells, Stand Oil Bldg, Chicago; State of Ill Bldg, Chicago; Waterfront Place, Seattle, Wash. *Comn:* Ark curtain, Sinai Temple, Champaign, Ill, 76; wall piece, Friends of Champaign Pub Libr, Ill, 78; Citizens Bank, Ind. *Exhib:* Craft Multiples, Renwick Gallery, Smithsonian Inst, Washington, DC, 75; Marietta Crafts Nat, Ohio, 75 & 77; Clay & Fiber--15 Viewpoints, Wustum Mus Fine Arts, Racine, Wis, 78. *Awards:* Craftsmen's Fel, Nat Endowment Arts, 76-77; Creativity Award, Miss River Craft Show, Brooks Mem Art Gallery, Memphis, Tenn, 76; Purchase Award, Mid-States Craft Exhib, Evansville, Ind, 77. *Mem:* Am Crafts Coun (state rep, 70-76); Handweavers Guild Am; Midwest Weavers Cong. *Media:* Fiber. *Mailing Add:* 403 Yankee Ridge Ln Urbana IL 61802

RESEK, KATE FRANCES
PAINTER
b Cleveland, Ohio. *Study:* Univ Wis, Madison, BS (fine arts); Columbia Univ, MFA, 69. *Work:* Aldrich Mus of Contemp Art, Ridgefield, Conn; Neuberger Mus, Purchase, NY; Housatonic Mus, Bridgeport, Conn; Columbia Univ. *Exhib:* Solo exhibs, Soho 20, NY, 74 & 76, Noyes, Van Cline & Davenport, NY, 77 & Bertha Urdang Gallery, NY, 77; Contemp Reflections 1974-1975, Aldrich Mus of Contemp Art, 75; 40th Ann

Show, Butler Inst of am Art, Youngstown, Ohio, Ohio; New Acquisitions, Neuberger Mus, 76; New Acquisitions, Aldrich Mus of Contemp Art, 78; Penthouse Show, Mus Mod Art, 80-81; Adam Gimbel Gallery, NY, 81; and others. *Teaching:* Instr drawing/painting, State Univ NY, Purchase, 75-76, Fairleigh Dickinson Univ, Teaneck, NJ, 78-82, Brooklyn Mus, 83. *Awards:* Silver Hill Award/Painting, & Inez Leon Greenberg Award/Drawing, Silvermine 22nd New Eng Exhib; Yaddo Fel, 78 & 82; NJ State Coun Arts Grant, 83. *Bibliog:* Ellen Lubell (auth), Kate Resek, Arts Mag, 12/76; Holland Cotter (auth), article in NY Arts J, 9/77; Carrie Rickey (auth), Village Voice, 10/82. *Mem:* Women's Caucus of Art; Women in the Arts; Coll Art Asn. *Media:* Pastel on Canvas. *Dealer:* Adam Gimbel Gallery 17 E 49th St New York NY

RESIKA, PAUL
PAINTER
b New York, NY, Aug 15, 1928. *Study:* With S Wilson, 1940-44 & Hans Hofmann, 1945-47, New York; also in Venice & Rome, 1950-54. *Work:* Sheldon Mem Gallery, Univ Nebr-Lincoln; Univ Wyo, Laramie, Wyo; Whitney Mus, NYC; Hood Mus Dartmouth Hanover, NH; Mills Col, Oakland, Calif; Metropolitan Mus Art, NY; Memorial Art Mus, Rochester, NY; Addison Gallery, Andover, Mass. *Exhib:* Solo exhibs include Artist's Choice Mus, NY, 1985, Crane Kalman Gallery, London with Robert De Niro, 1986, Kornbluth Gallery, Fairlawn, NJ, 1986, 1995, 1997, Meredith Long Gallery, Houston, 1986, 1997, 2005, Long Point Gallery, Provincetown, 1988, 1992, 1995, Mead Art Mus, Amherst Col, Mass, 1991, Salander, O'Reilly Galleries, NY, 1993, 1994, 1996, 1999, 2001, 2002, 2005, Gerald Peters Gallery, Santa Fe, 1996, Lizan Tops Gallery, East Hampton, NY, 1997, 1998, Berta Walker Gallery, Provincetown, Mass, 1998-2012, Alpha Gallery, Boston, 1998, 2002, 2012; Peridot Gallery, NY, 1964-71; Washburn Gallery, NY, 1973; Graham Gallery, NY, 1977-84; Century Asn, NY, 1982; Hackett-Freedman Gallery, San Francisco, Calif, 1997, 1998, 2000, 2002, 2006; Air-Light-Color, Provincetown Art Asn & Mus, Mass, 8/97 & Berta Walker Gallery, 1998; Lori Bookstein Gallery, NY, 1998, 2001, 2006, 2010, 2011; Lizan-Tups Gallery, East Hampton, NY, 1998; Group Exhibs: Ctr Figurative Paintings, New York City, 2000, 2001; NY Studio Sch, 2002; Contemp Am Art in Embassies Program, Embassy of US of Am, Vienna, 2002; Benucci Gallery, Rome, 2005; and others. *Collection Arranged:* Am Acad Arts and Letters; Ark Art Ctr; Chase Manhattan Bank; Dartmouth Col; Indianapolis Mus Art; Metrop Mus Art; Nat Acad Design, NYC; Nat Mus Am Art; Weatherspoon Art Gallery, NC; Mus Mod Art, NY. *Pos:* Artist in residence, Dartmouth Col, 1972; chmn masters prog, Parsons Sch Design, NY, 1978-90. *Teaching:* Adj prof painting & drawing, Cooper Union, 1966-78; instr painting, Art Students' League, 1968-69; instr, Skowhegan Sch Painting, 1973 & 76; instr, Grad Sch, Univ Pa, 1974 & 1979. *Awards:* Fel, Guggenheim Mem Found, 84; Purchase Awards, Hassam Fund & Speicher Fund, Am Acad & Inst Arts & Letts, 1986, 1988 & 1991; Benjamin Altman Landscape Prize, Nat Acad Design, 91, Adolph and Clara Obrig Prize, 96, Benjamin Altman Landscape Prize, 97; and others. *Bibliog:* Arturo Vivante (auth), Figures on the Beach, High Head Press, 1992; W S DiPiero & Karen Wilkin (auths), Paul Resika Paintings, Salander-O'Reilly Galleries, New York, 1993; David Bonetti (auth), Gallery Watch, San Francisco Examiner, 3/24/2000; and many others; Hilton Kramer (auth) NY Observer, NY Times; Vivian Raynor (auth), NY Times. *Mem:* Nat Acad Design (assoc, 1976, acad, 1978); Century Asn, NY; Am Acad Arts & Lett. *Publ:* Figures on the Beach, 1992; Provincetown Pier Paintings, 1995; John Russell (auth), NY Times. *Dealer:* Meredith Long Gallery Houston TX; Lori Bookstein Fine Art 138 Tenth Ave New York NY 10011; Berta Walker Gallery Provincetown Ma; Alpha Gallery Boston Ma. *Mailing Add:* 175 Riverside Dr New York NY 10024

RESNICK, DON
PAINTER
b New York, NY, May 19, 1928. *Study:* Hobart Coll, BA, 49; Int Acad of Fine Art, Salzburg, Austria, Cert, 57; studied with Oskar Kokoschka, 56-57, Raphael Soyer, Seymour Lipton, 58-59. *Work:* Hood Mus Art, Dartmouth Coll, Hanover, NH; JB Speed Mus, Louisville, Ky; Portland Mus Art, Maine; Sheldon Mem Art Gallery, Univ Nebr, Lincoln; Nat Mus Am Art, Washington, DC; Bowdoin Coll Mus Art; Colby Coll Mus Art; Williams Coll Mus Art; Univ Mich Mus Art; Rose Art Mus, Brandeis Univ; Bates Coll Mus Art; Farnsworth Art Mus, Rockland, Maine; others. *Exhib:* Long Island Artists, Nassau Co Mus Fine Art, Roslyn, NY, 89; Figurative Abstraction, Andrea Marquis Fine Arts, Boston, 89; Five over Five, Hobart Coll, 94; Long Island Landscape, Firehouse Art Gallery, Nassau Community Coll, 96; The Poetry of His Painting (with catalog), Odon Wagner Gallery, Toronto, 96; In Good Company, Heckscher Mus Art, Huntington, New York, 97; Poets and Artists: Collaborations, CW Post Hutchins Gallery, 98; Landscapes, Wright Gallery, New York, 98; Overview, Hobart Coll, Geneva, New York, 99; Odon Wagner Gallery, Toronto, 2000 & 2005; Earth, Sea and Sky (with catalog), Odon Wagner Gallery, 2002; Century Asn Ann, FAN Gallery, Philadelphia; Flanders Gallery, The River Gallery, Damariscotta, Maine; Mint Mus Art, Charlotte, NC, 2003; Kresge Mus Art, Lansing, Mich, 2003; US Embassy, NATO, Brussels, Belg, 2003; The Round Top Ctr for the Arts, Damariscotta, ME, 2005; Hammer Galleries, Contemp Artists, 2005; The Long Island Mus of Art, The Little Continent of Long Island-Paintings from the Permanent Collection, 2005; Union Coll, Mandeville Gallery, 2005; The Century Asn, New York, 2006; Hammer Galleries, New York, 2006; River Gallery, Damariscotta, ME, 2006; Illuminated Landscapes, Odon Wagner Gallery, Toronto, 2007. *Awards:* First Prize, Long Island Artists, 58; Nominated, Am Acad Arts & Lett, 82 & 86; Millay Colony Found Arts, 89; Medal of Excellence, Hobart Coll, 99. *Bibliog:* Joanna Silver (auth), Artist illuminates Africa, Boston Herald, 2/6/94; Terry Sullivan (auth), From eye to heart to hand, Am Artist, 8/96; Louis Simpson (auth), Donald Resnick Drawings, Grenfell Press, New York, 2000. *Mem:* Artist's Equity; Artists Fel; Century Asn. *Media:* Oil, Watercolor, Etching. *Publ:* Illusr, The King My Father's Wreck & There You Are, Louis Simpson (auth), Story Line Press; contribr, The Best of Drawing and Sketching, Rockport Publ; transl, cover design & drawing, Francois Villons-The Legacy and The Testament; Susan Keggan (auth), The Eye of God, a Life of Oscar Kokoschka. *Dealer:* Hammer Galleries 33 W 57th St New York NY 10019; Andrea Marquit Fine Arts 71 Pinckney St Boston MA 02114; Odon Wagner Gallery 196 Davenport Rd Toronto Ont M5R1J2; The River Gallery Damariscotta ME; Gakkery North Setauket NY. *Mailing Add:* 15 Revere St Rockville Centre NY 11570

RESNICK, MARCIA
PHOTOGRAPHER, CONCEPTUAL ARTIST
b New York, NY, Nov 21, 1950. *Study:* NY Univ, 67-69; Cooper Union, BFA, 72; Calif Inst Arts, MFA, 73; Hunter Col, Tchng Cert, 92. *Work:* Metrop Mus Art & Mus Mod Art, NY; Tampa Mus Art, Fla; George Eastman House, Rochester, NY; Mus Fine Arts, Houston; San Francisco Mus; Santa Barbara Mus, Calif; Univ S Calif, Los Angeles; NY Pub Lib; Hallmark Collection, Nelson-Atkins Mus Art, Kansas; Rijksmuseum, Amsterdam; Jewish Mus, New York City; Getty Mus, Calif. *Exhib:* Photog Unlimited, Fogg Mus, Harvard Univ, 74; Women of Photog, San Francisco Mus & Traveling Show, 75; Punk Art, Washington Proj Arts, 78; Book Art, Art Inst Chicago, 78; Kunst als Photographie 1879-1979, Tiroler Landesmuseum Ferdinandeum, Innsbruck, Austria, 79; Galerie Ricke, Cologne, 81; John Belushi, Univ Dallas, Tex, 87; Gallery Mod Objects, Los Angeles, Calif, 87; Suzan Cooper Gallery, NY, 87-88 & 93; New Photographs, Old Friends, Oregon Sch Arts & Crafts, Portland, Ore, 89; Photog Collection of Robert Olden, Arles, France, 90; Open Mind: The Sol Lewitt Collection, Wadsworth Atheneum, Hartford Ct, 91; Beat Art, Washington Sq, NY Univ, 94; The Cool & the Crazy, Earl McGrath Gallery, NY, 96; Half a Dozen Roses, Venice, Calif, 96-97; Luhring-Augustine Gallery, NY, 99; Revelations-Familiar Faces, Greely Square Gallery, New York City, 2000; New Wave Levis Internet Show, 2001; Bande á Part, Galerie du jour Agnes B (traveling), Paris, London, Tokyo, 2006 & Los Angeles, Hong Kong, 2007; Deborah Bell Photographs, NYC, 2009, Revisions, 2011, Bad Boys, and others. *Teaching:* Instr photog, Queens Col, Cooper Union, Int Ctr of Photog, Staten Island Col, City Univ NY & La Guardia Community Col, NY, 73-88; Instr photog, Pratt Manhattan, Manhattanville Col. *Awards:* Creative Artists Pub Serv Prog Grant, 77; Nat Endowment for Arts grant, 76, 78. *Bibliog:* Pop up people, Time-Life Yearbk, 74; Layered eye, Camera 35 Mag, 7/74; Peter Frank (auth), Picture books, Soho Weekly News, 7/17/75; Twelve hot photographers, Rolling Stone Mag, 5/77; Ben Lifson (auth), Growing pains..., Village Voice, 5/1/78; Alex Sweetman (auth), Exposure Mag, 78; Alan Sondheim (auth), Art Papers, 5/6/87; Ken Winokur (auth), Contemporary Photographers, St James Press, 88; Vinee Aletti (auth), The New Yorker, apr 2009. *Publ:* Auth, Landscape; See; & Tahitian Eve, 75; Re-visions; & Landscape-Loftscape, 78. *Dealer:* Paul M Hertzmann Inc PO Box 40447 San Francisco Calif 94140. *Mailing Add:* 2 Grove St 1F New York NY 10014

RESNICK, STEWART ALLEN
COLLECTOR
b Jersey City, NJ, Dec 24, 1936. *Study:* Univ Calif, Los Angeles, BS, 1959, LLB, 1962. *Pos:* Co-chmn, chief exec officer & pres, Roll Int Corp, Los Angeles; chmn & chief exec officer, Franklin Mint, Aston, Pa, 1985-; bd trustees, J Paul Getty Trust, Los Angeles, 2005-. *Awards:* Named one of Top 200 Collectors, ARTnews, 2008. *Collection:* Old Masters. *Mailing Add:* Roll Int Corp 10th Fl 11444 W Olympic Blvd Los Angeles CA 90064

REUTER, LAUREL J
MUSEUM DIRECTOR, CURATOR
b Devils Lake, NDak. *Study:* Univ NDak, MA, 74, Hon Doctorate of Letters, 2008; interned at Minneapolis Inst Arts. *Collection Arranged:* cur, Light & Shadow: Japanese Artists in Space, 94; Snow Country Prison: Interned in NDak, regional tour, 2003-; Mouths of Ash: Juan Manuel Echavarria, nat tour, 2005-; The Disappeared, int tour, 2005-; Artists & War, NDak Mus Art, 2008, 2009. *Pos:* Founder & dir, NDak Mus Art, 70-; vis specialist, Nat Mus Jakarta, 90; vis critic, Univ Hawaii, 92 & Univ Ore, 95; served on numerous panels & as juror for founds & art groups; site vis, mus progs, 92-. *Teaching:* Lectured and conducted workshops at 13 nat mus in Pac Rim countries & China; lectr, Ann Humanities Lecture, Univ Tex, El Paso & Scripps Coll, Claremont, Calife, 2009. *Awards:* NDak Gov's Award for Individual Contrib to the Arts, 2007. *Bibliog:* Articles in New York Times, 11/23/97, Art News, 11/98 & Notable N Dakotans, 98. *Res:* Contemp art. *Publ:* Autobiography (catalog), 96; auth & co-ed Under the Whelming Tide: The 1997 Flood of the Red River of the North, 97; coauth (with Mildred Constantine), Whole Cloth, Monacelli Press, NY, 97; Will Maclean: From Scotland (catalog), 98; The Disappeared, Milan: Charta Publ, 2006; Marking the Land: Jim Dow in NDak, NDak Mus Art & Ctr for Am Places, 2007; auth, Brian Paulsen, NDak Mus Art, 2009; auth, Zoran Mojsilov, NDak Mus Art, 2009

REVINGTON BURDICK, ELIZABETH
COLLECTOR
Collection: Modern American painting and sculpture exhibited at major museums throughout the United States. *Mailing Add:* 3000 Woodkirk Dr Columbia MO 65203

REVITZKY, DENNIS L
PRINTMAKER, PAINTER
b Titusville, Pa, Apr 28, 1947. *Study:* Gannon & Mercyhurst Cols, BA (Art Educ), 69; Suny Brockport, NY, Grad studies (Fine Arts), 71-76. *Work:* Patron Print, Mem Art Gallery, Rochester, NY; Western Ill Univ, Macomb, Ill; Print Archives, Corcoran Gallery of Art, Washington, DC; State Univ NY, Brockport, NY; Nelson-Atkins Mus Art, Kansas City, Mo. *Comn:* Edition of Serigraphs (Patron Print), Mem Art Gallery, 84; Edition of 40 Linocuts, Print Soc of Nelson Atkins Mus of Art, Kans City, Mo, 90. *Exhib:* solo exhibs, Recent Prints & Drawings, Gallery 34, Finger Lakes Community Coll, Canandaigua, NY, 91, 96, Reflections on the Nature of Things (solo), Ohringer Gallery, RIT, Henrietta, NY, 2005, Linoleum Printmaking, Arts & Cult Coun of Rochester, NY, 2008, Black and White: Linocuts by Dennis Revitzky, Canton Mus Art, Canton, Ohio, 2015; Finger Lakes Exhib, Mem Art Gallery, Rochester, NY, 80-81, 2013; Everson Biennial, Everson Mus of Art, Syracuse, NY, 94; 171st Ann Exhib, Nat Academy of Design, NY, 96; Nat Print & Drawing Exhib, Bradley Univ,

Peoria, Ill, 98; 2000 Pacific States Biennial Nat Exhib, Univ of HI, Hilo, HI, 2000; 18th Los Angeles Printmaking Soc, Nat Print Exhib, Armory Ctr for the Arts, Pasadena, Calif, 2005; 71st & 76th Nat Midyear Exhib, Butler Inst Am Art, Youngstown, Ohio, 2007, 2012; New York State Landscapes, Edward Hopper House Arts Ctr, Nyack, NY, 2010; SAGA 77th Members Exhib, Fyre Gallery, Braidwood, Austrailia. *Teaching:* Instr Visual Arts, Livonia Cent Sch Dist, Livonia, NY, 1970-2002. *Awards:* Roy M. Mason Mem Award (Nat Exhib), Batavia Soc of Artists, 88; Jurors Award (Juried Spring Show), Erie Art Mus, 93; Merit Award (Images 2002 Robeson Gallery, Penn State Univ), Cent Pa Festival of Arts, 2002; 1st Place Award, Prints & Graphics, 80th Int Exhib, Art Asn of Harrisburg, Pa, 2008. *Bibliog:* Sherry Chayat (auth), Landscape Show Graces Gallery's New Home, Syracuse Herald Am, 1994; Elizabeth Forbes (auth), Etch A Sketch, Rochester Democrat & Chronicle, 1995; Los Angeles Printmaking Soc 18th Nat Exhib Catalog, Kitty Maryatt, Two Hands Press, CA, 2005; Tracy H Kroft (auth), Not Your Father's Linoleium: Dennis Revitzky's Printmaking, Metropolitan Mag, Arts Coun of Rochester, NY, 2008. *Mem:* Soc of Am Graphic Artists (91-); Los Angeles Printmaking Soc (96-2005); Rochester Contemp (2002-); Boston Printmakers (2005-); Spectrum Gallery, Rochester, NY, 2013. *Media:* Serigraphy, Woodcut, Linocut, Oil & Mixed media on canvas. *Mailing Add:* 131 Monroe St Honeoye Falls NY 14472

REVRI, ANIL
PAINTER, GRAPHIC ARTIST
b New Delhi, India, Jan 8, 1956. *Study:* Sir J J Sch Art, BFA (interior design), 76; Corcoran Sch Art, BFA (graphic design), 95. *Work:* Tempra Mus, Malta; DC Commn Arts & Humanities. *Exhib:* Senior Show, Corcoran Mus Art, Washington, DC, 95; Veiled Doorways '96 (coauth, catalog), Am Inst Architects, Washington, DC, 97; Baltimore Print Fair, Baltimore Mus Art, 98; Art Mus Am, Washington, DC, 98; Pyramid Atlantic: A Study in Collaboration, Fed Reserve Bd, Washington, DC, 98; 21st Ann Art on Paper, Md Fedn Art Gallery Circle, Annapolis, 98; Ctr Visual Arts, Int Show, Summit, NJ, 98; Malta Biennale, 99; solo exhib, Cult Crossings, The Millennium World Peace Summit, NY, 2000; F Donald Kenny Mus, St Bonaventure Univ, NY, 2001; Lichtenstein and Beyond; Recent Acquisitions of Modern Prints, Corcoran Gallery of Art, 2001; India; Contemp Art from Northeastern Pvt Collections, Jane Voorhees Zimmerli Mus, Rutgers Univ, NJ, 2002; In Search of Self (Solo) Corcoran Gallery of Art 2004. *Collection Arranged:* Ministry Energy, Oberoi Hotels, New Delhi; Air India, Great Eastern Shipping Co & Tata Sons, Ltd, Bombay; The Corcoran Gallery of Art; Library of Congress. *Awards:* Fel, Washington DC Comn Arts & Humanities, Nat Endowment Arts, 98. *Bibliog:* Suneet Chopra (auth), Art equity: opt for Indian images, Financial Express, India 12/22/96; Cornelia Ravenal (auth), Coming in from the cold, Interiors & Lifestyles, India Biannual, 97; Mahoney, J.W. Anil Revri's Inner Order, Washington Review, 2001-2002; Prakash, Uma, Keeping Faith, Asian Art News, March/April, 2001; Shaw-Eagle, Joanna, Print Masters at Corcoran, The Washington Times, 12/08/2001; O'Sullivan, Michael, Anil Revri's Doors of Perception at Corcoran, Washington Post, Weekend, 6/25/2004; McLaughlin, Caitlin, Painter of All Times, Asian Art News, Nov/Dec 2004; Amy, Michael, Anil Revri at the Corcoran, Art in America, Jan, 2005. *Mem:* Am Inst Graphic Arts; Art Dirs Club Metrop Washington DC; Allied Artists Am. *Media:* Oil on Canvas, Mixed media on Handmade paper. *Publ:* Illusr, Femina, 76-77 & Youth Times, 77, Times India; Highlights, Washington Art Assocs, fall 96. *Dealer:* Sundaram Tagore Gallery, NY. *Mailing Add:* 3201 Wisconsin Ave NW No 802 Washington DC 20016

REXROTH, NANCY LOUISE
PHOTOGRAPHER
b Washington, DC, June 27, 1946. *Study:* Marietta Col, Ohio, 64-65; Am Univ, BFA, 65-69; Ohio Univ, MFA (photog), 69-71. *Work:* Mus Mod Art, NY; Smithsonian Inst & Libr Cong, Washington, DC; Biblioteque Nat, Paris, France; Ctr Creative Photog, Tucson, Ariz; Mus Fine Arts, Houston, Tex; Columbus Mus Art, Columbus, OH; Minneapolis Art Mus; Corcoran Gallery Art, Wash DC; Univ Mass, Amherst; Santa Barbara Mus Art, Calif; Univ Ariz. *Exhib:* One-person shows, Corcoran Gallery Art, Washington, DC, 73, Light Gallery, 75, 77 & 80, Grapestake Gallery, San Francisco, 78, Ctr Creative Photog, Tucson, 82, Silver Image Gallery, Columbus, Ohio, 78, Jefferson Place Gallery, Washington DC, 74, Antioch Col, Noyes Gallery, Yellow Springs, 75, Weinstein Gallery, Minneapolis, 2000 & Steven Wirtz Gallery, San Francisco, 2000; Group shows, Baltimore Mus Art, Md, 73, 81; Smithsonian Inst, Washington, DC, 73; Halstead 381 Gallery, Birmingham, Mich, 77; Int Ctr Photog, NY, 78; Rochester Inst Tech, NY, 80; Nat Mus Am Art, Washington, DC, 84; Kennedy Ctr, Wash DC; Light Gallery, NY; Santa Barbara Mus Art, Calif; Robert Mann Gallery, NY. *Teaching:* Instr beginning-advan photog, Antioch Col, Yellow Springs, Ohio, 77-79 & Wright State Univ, 79-82. *Awards:* 2 Grants, Nat Endowment Arts, Ohio Arts Council. *Bibliog:* Janis Crystal Lipzin (dir), Trepanations (film); Artweek Mag, 76, 78; Holiday T Day (auth), Art in America Mag, 79; Ken Johnson (auth), Art in Review, NY Times, 12/31/2004. *Media:* Photography. *Publ:* Auth, IOWA, 76 & The Platintotype 1977, 76, Violet Press; contribr, The Diana and the Nikon, Godine, 79; contribr, The Platinum Print, Graphic Arts Res Ctr-RIT, 80; and others. *Dealer:* Exclusive Weinstein Gallery 908 W 46th St Minneapolis MN 55409

REYNARD, CAROLYN COLE
PAINTER, INSTRUCTOR
b Wichita, Kans, Aug 6, 1934. *Study:* Wichita State Univ, BFA; Ohio Univ, MFA. *Work:* Wichita State Univ; State Univ NY Coll Oswego. *Exhib:* Santa Barbara Art Mus, Calif, 60; Artists Santa Barbara, Faulkner Gallery, Santa Barbara, 60-62; Artists Cent NY, Munson-Williams-Proctor Inst Mus Art, Utica, NY, 64-65 & 67; Barrett House Gallery, 70-; Mid-Hudson Armory Show, 90-91; Vassar Coll, 2006. *Pos:* speaker, Rochester Mineralogical Symposium, 2012, 2013, 2014. *Teaching:* Instr art, Ohio Univ, 58-59; asst prof art, State Univ NY, Coll Oswego, 63-69; instr art, Wappingers Cent Sch Dist, NY, 69-97, adminr & coordr fine arts dept, 78-79. *Awards:* Artist-in-residence, WCSD, 2003-2006. *Mem:* Eastern Fedn Mineralogical & Lapidary Soc. *Media:* Acrylic. *Interests:* Graphic design, mineralogy; illustrating topes for rocks & minerals magazine. *Publ:* Auth, I can't draw, 71 & Getting it all together, 74, Sch Arts. *Mailing Add:* 110 College Ave Poughkeepsie NY 12603

REYNOLDS, HUNTER
PHOTOGRAPHER
Study: Otis-Parsons Art Inst, Los Angeles, BFA, 1984. *Exhib:* Experimental Bookworks, Women's Caucus for Art Invitational, Brand Libr, Glendale, Calif, 1985; solo exhibs, Home for Contemp Theatre & Art, New York, 1986, White Columns, New York, 1988, Hallwalls Contemp Art Ctr, Buffalo, 1990, Usdan Gallery, Bennington Coll, 1995, Yerba Buena Ctr for the Arts, Calif, 1997, Schwulen Mus, Berlin, 1998, Parsons Sch Design, New York, 2001; Selections from the Artists, Artists' Space, New York, 1987; Up-Date Show, White Columns, New York, 1989; AIDS Timeline, Wadsworth Antheneum, Hartford, Conn, 1990; The Spatial Drive, New Mus Contemp Art, New York, 1992; Dress Codes, Inst Contemp Art, Boston, 1993; Altered Egos, Santa Monica Mus Art, Calif, 1994; In a Different Light, Univ Calif Art Mus, Berkeley, 1995; Acts of Art, Aldrich Mus Art, Conn, 2000; Drawing Now, Armory Art Ctr, Fla, 2005; Out of the Blue, Abington Art Ctr, Pa, 2006. *Pos:* Artist-in-residence, Kunstlerhaus Bethanien, Berlin Ger, 1992, Yaddo Studio, 1995, Yerba Buena Ctr for the Arts, Calif, 1997, St Norberts Arts & Cult Ctr, Can, 1998, Banff Ctr for the Arts, Can, 2000, Braizers Studio, UK, 2001, Armory Art Ctr, Fla, 2004. *Awards:* Art Matters Fel, 1988 & 1993; Individual Grant, Artists Space, 1989; Pollock-Krasner Found Grant, 1998 & 2008. *Bibliog:* Lyndy Kay Zoeckler (auth), The Books that Artists Make, Artweek, 2/4/1984; Glen Helfand (auth), Situation, Art Issues, 9-10/1991; Robert Atkins (auth), Queer for You, Village Voice, 6/28/1994; Nancy Stapen (auth), The Poignancy and Pitfalls of Tragic Art, Boston Globe, 2/27/1996; Michael Ducnan (auth), Critics Diary, Art in AM, 11/2006

REYNOLDS, JAMES ELWOOD
PAINTER
b Taft, Calif, Nov 9, 1926. *Study:* Kann Inst Art, Beverly Hills, Calif; Sch Allied Arts, Glendale, Calif. *Work:* Phoenix Art Mus, Ariz; Cowboy Hall Fame, Oklahoma City; Mus Southwest, Midland, Tex. *Comn:* Design gold & silver medals Cowboy Artists Am 8th Ann Exhib & future competitions, Cowboy Artists Am & Franklin Mint, 73; painting used by Marlboro for spec Christmas advert, Philip Morris Co, 85; plus many others paintings. *Exhib:* Cowboy Hall Fame, Oklahoma City, 69-73; Ann Cowboy Artists Am Show, Phoenix Art Mus, 73-75; Texas Art Gallery; Settlers West Gallery; O'Briens Gallery; Main Trail Gallery. *Teaching:* Instr, Scottsdale Artist's Sch, 83 & 84. *Awards:* Gold Medal First Prize, Cowboy Hall Fame, 71 & 78; Most Outstanding Western Painter, 74-75; Artist of the Yr, Tucson Festival of Arts, Ariz, 77; plus others. *Mem:* Cowboy Artists Am (secy, 72-73, vpres, 74-75, pres, 75-76); Western Art Asn, Phoenix; Ariz Artists in Action. *Media:* Oil. *Publ:* Contribr, Cowboy in Art, 68; West & Walter Bisom, Univ Ariz, 71; American cowboy in life & legend, Nat Geographic, 72; Renaissance of Western Art, Franklin Mint, 74; Western Painting Today, Watson-Guptill, 75

REYNOLDS, JOCK
CURATOR, EDUCATOR, GALLERY DIRECTOR
Study: Univ Calif, Santa Cruz, BA, 1969; Univ Calif, Davis, MFA, 1972. *Work:* Smithsonian Nat Mus Am Art; Corcoran Gallery Art; Walker Art Ctr; Minneapolis Inst Arts; Univ Wash Henry Art Gallery. *Pos:* Co-founder, 80 Langton St (now New Langton Arts), 1975; dir, Wash Project of the Arts, Wash, 1983-89, Addison Gallery Am Art, Andover, Mass, 1989-98; Henry J Heinz II dir, Yale Univ Art Gallery, New Haven, 1998-. *Teaching:* Assoc prof, dir, grad prog, Ctr for Experimental and Interdisciplinary Art San Francisco State Univ, 1973-83; adj prof, Yale Univ, 1998. *Awards:* Recipient Fulbright Fel

REYNOLDS, JOHN (JOCK) M
DIRECTOR, WRITER
Study: Harvard Univ, AB, 66, MAT, 67. *Work:* Center Gallery, Bucknell Univ, Lewisburg, Pa; Freedman Gallery, Albright Col, Reading, Pa; Anderson Gallery, Va Commonwealth Univ, Richmond; Washington Project for Arts, Washington, DC. *Collection Arranged:* The First Texas Triennial, 88, Works From a Decade (with catalog), 88, The Border/La Frontera, 89, Everyday Miracles, 90 & Happy Families (with catalog), 90, Contemp Arts Mus, Houston, Tex. *Pos:* Dir, Yale Univ Art Gallery, 98-. *Teaching:* Asst prof art hist, Bucknell Univ, Lewisburg, Pa, 74-77, Albright Col, Reading, Pa, 77-81 & Va Commonwealth Univ, 81-86. *Res:* Contemporary art with sepecial interest in social and political content. *Publ:* Auth & ed, Sue Coe: Police State, 87 & Hunt Slonem: Baroque Beatitudes, 87, Va Commonwealth Univ; Belchite/South Bronx, Univ Mass, 88; Bill Viola: Works From a Decade, 88 & Ida Applebrong: Happy Families, 90, Contemp Art Mus, Houston. *Mailing Add:* c/o Yale Univ Art Gallery PO Box 208271 New Haven CT 06520-8271

REYNOLDS, ROBERT
PAINTER, EDUCATOR
b San Luis Obispo, Calif, Mar 7, 1936. *Study:* Art Ctr Coll Design, Los Angeles, Calif, BPA; Calif Polytech State Univ, San Luis Obispo, MA; also with Lorser Fettelson, Harry Carmean, Robert Clark, Arne Nybak & Joe Henninger. *Work:* San Luis Obispo Co, Calif; Mus Nat Hist, Morro Bay, Calif; Mus Nat Hist, Santa Barbara, Calif; Calif Polytechnic Univ, San Luis Obispo; Cuesta Community Coll, San Luis Obispo, Calif; over 1200 pvt collections. *Comn:* ltd ed print, Natural Hist Asn Central Coast, Calif, 82; painting & prints, Mozart Festival, San Luis Obispo, Calif, 88; paintings & serigraphs, San Luis Obispo Co Symphony, 88; post card stamp design, US Postal Serv, 88; Ser of Paintings, Bear Valley Lodge, Bear Valley, 96; S L O Mus Art, 2012. *Exhib:* Solo Exhibs: retrospective, Art Ctr, San Luis Obispo, 75; Allan Hancock Col, Santa Maria, 80; Clark Galleries, Bakersfield, 88; Hutchins Gallery,

Cambria, 88 & 90; Calif Polytechnic Univ Union Galeria: 89 & 93; Vision Art Gallery, Morro Bay, Calif, 91 & 94; Johnson Art Gallery, San Luis Obispo, Calif, 98, 99, 2000; San Luis Obispo Arts Center, 6-7/2007 and 8-9/2008, Talley Vineyards Gallery, Stillpoints 2, San Luis Obispo Mus Art, 2011; traveling exhib, Ford Motor Co, Dearborn, Mich, 77-78; Cunningham Art Mus Watercolor Exhib, Bakersfield, Calif, 78; solo exhibs, Harbinger Gallery, Arnold, Calif, 98, 2000 & 2002, Johnson Art Gallery, San Luis Obispo, Calif, 98, 99, 2000-2002 & 2005, Elverhoj Mus Hist & Art, 2004; Featured Artist/Poster, Bear Valley Music Festival, Bear Valley, Calif; Biennale Internazionale Dell'Arte Contemporanea, Florence, Ital, 2003; San Luis Obispo Mus Art, 2011; Hearst Castle, San Simeon, Calif, 2012; Salisbury Art Gallery, Avila, Calif, 2013. *Pos:* Pres, Art Asn, San Luis Obispo, Calif, 68-69; mem design & review bd, City of San Luis Obispo, 68-73; mem bd of trustees, San Luis Obispo Art Ctr, 69-78; founding mem, Cent Coast Watercolor Soc, Calif, 77-, pres, 80-81. *Teaching:* Prof art, drawing & painting, Dept Art, Calif Polytech State Univ, 64-, actg dept head, 82-83, chmn, dept art & design, 84-86; art instr drawing & painting, Evening Div, Cuesta Community Col, 72-76, Robert Reynolds Watercolor Workshop, 74-; 2 painting workshops, San Luis Obispo Mus Art, 2012; conducted, over 50 Outdoor Watercolor Workshops in the High Sierra, Calif Central Coast, 1972-2010. *Awards:* Bronze Award Winner, Nat Painting Competition, Artist's Mag (Landscape Div), 96; Calif Poly President's Art Award, Calif Poly Univ, San Luis Obispo, Calif, 93; Gold Award Winner, Calif Discovery Awards Art Competition, 94; Purchase Prize, Ironstone Vineyard's Nat Art Competition, 2000; Selected The Central Coast Wine Classic Commemorative Artist, 99, 2000; Central Coast Wine Classic Commemorative Artist, 99, 2000 & 2002. *Bibliog:* Stephen L Smith (auth), The Art of Robert Reynolds, Cent Coast Art Guide, 93; Splash 3, North Light Bks, 94; April Karys (auth), Learning from nature's art, Focus/Telegram-Tribune Newspaper, 3/94; James Hayes (auth), feature article, Robert Reynolds, Central Coast Magazine, CA, 2004; The Art of Robert Reynolds: Quiet Journey, Calif Poly Tech Univ, San Luis Obispo, 2006; The Art of Robert Reynolds: Quiet Journey (178 pages), Cal Poly Univ, San Luis, Obispo, Calif; Work is highlighted in over 20 art books, including seven in Biannual book series, Splash; the Best in Watercolor. *Mem:* San Luis Obispo Mus Art, Slo Arts Coucil. *Media:* Multimedia. *Interests:* traveling. *Publ:* Watercolor Page, Am Artist, 3/88; Artist's Mag, 90; coauth, Design Secrets, Watercolor Magic Mag, 93; illusr, Painting Nature's Peaceful Places, North Light Bks, 93; How to be a rock star, Artist's Mag, 94; Painting the Figure, Watercolor Mag (Am Artist), 96; Rediscovering Reynolds, New Times, 6/1/2000, 98; Painting the Wild Fields, Telegram Tribune Focus, 6/98, San Luis Obispo, 98; A Discovery of 25 Artists Around the World, Pratique Des Arts Mag, 2010, 2012; To Capture the Light, San Luis Obispo Tribune, 2011. *Dealer:* Robert Reynolds Studio

REYNOLDS, VALRAE
CURATOR
b San Francisco, Calif, Dec 18, 1944. *Study:* Univ Calif, Davis, BA, 66; New York Univ, MA, 68, cert mus training, 69. *Collection Arranged:* Chinese Art from the Newark Mus, China Inst, 80; Tibet, A Lost World (auth, catalog), 81-82 & Japan, The Enduring Heritage, 83, Newark Mus; 16 permanent galleries of Asian Art, Newark Mus, 89; Cooking for the Gods: The Art of Home Ritual in Bengal, 95-96; From the Sacred Realm, Treasures of Tibetan Art (auth, catalog), Newark Mus, 99; Tibet: Mountains and Valleys, Castles and Tents, Paine Webber Art Gallery, NY, 2001; Williams Coll Mus of Art, 2003. *Pos:* Ford Fel arms & armor dept, Metrop Mus Art, New York, fall 68; Ford Fel Islamic ceramics, Asian Art Mus, San Francisco, spring 69; asst cur Oriental collection, Newark Mus, 69-70, cur Oriental collection, 70-. *Teaching:* Instr Tibetan art & civilization, Columbia Univ, 96. *Awards:* Nat Endowment Humanities Grant Film Production, 72-74; Nat Endowment Arts Grant Publ, 82-83, 85-86 & 99; J Paul Getty Grant Publ, 86, 88-91; Nat Endowment Arts Spec Artistic Initiative Grant galleries & progs, 88; Asian Cult Coun grants, travel, 89; Nat Endowment Humanities galleries & progs, 90-91; nat Endowment Arts Grant Exhib, 98-99; Freeman Found Grant progs, 02-03. *Mem:* Comt SAsian Art; Asia Soc; Japan Soc; Tibet Soc. *Res:* Arts of Tibet, India and Himalayas. *Publ:* Auth, Tibet, A Lost World, Ind Univ Press, 79; Chinese Art from the Newark Museum, China Inst, 80; The Newark Museum Tibetan Collection, Vol I, 83 & Vol III, 86; Japan, the enduring heritage, Newark Mus Quart, 83; A Tibetan Buddhist Altar, Newark Mus, 91. *Mailing Add:* Newark Mus 49 Washington St Newark NJ 07101

REYNOLDS, WADE
PAINTER
b Jasper, NY, 1929. *Study:* Self-taught. *Work:* Santa Barbara Mus Art, Calif; Cleveland Mus Art, Ohio; Miami Inst Fine Art, Fla; Times-Mirror Corp, Los Angeles; Palm Springs Desert Mus, CA; Arnot Mus. *Comn:* Official Portrait Gov Deukmejian, State of Calif, 89. *Exhib:* Solo Exhib, Realism, Calif Palace Legion Honor, 67-68 & California Visions, Santa Barbara Mus, Calif, 77; Prints, Miami Inst Art, 79; Retrospective, Pioneer Mus, Stockton, Calif, 82; Selections from Ellen & Jerome Westheimer Collection, Okla Art Ctr, 88; Johnson & Johnson Gallery, San Francisco, Calif, 2003; Arnot Mus, 2004; About Face: Portraiture Now, Long Beach Mus Art, 2007-8; Re-Presenting the Nude Evoke Contemp, Santa Fe, 2010. *Teaching:* Acad Art Col, San Francisco, 96-98; Art Inst Southern Calif, Laguna, 97-2003. *Awards:* Best Show, Madonna Festival, San Luis Obispo, Calif, 77 & Miami Print Biennial, 79. *Bibliog:* Frankenstein (auth), New realists, San Francisco Chronicle, 67; Stowens (auth), Intense realism, Am Artist, 1/81; Pincus (auth), Los Angeles Times, 6/25/82. *Media:* Oil, Acrylic. *Specialty:* Contemp Realism. *Interests:* Intense but not photo realism. *Publ:* Auth, Painting Faces and Figures, Carole Katchen/Watson-Guptil, 86. *Dealer:* Scape-Corona Delmar; Jenkins Johnson Gallery San Francisco and New York. *Mailing Add:* 5022 Medalist Ct Oceanside CA 92057

RHODE, ROBIN
PHOTOGRAPHER
b Cape Town, South Africa, 1976. *Study:* Witwatersrand Technikon, Nat Diploma Fine Art, 1998; South African Sch Film, Television & Dramatic Arts, Johannesburg, 2000. *Work:* Mus Mod Art, New York; Solomon R Guggenheim Mus, New York; Walker Art Ctr, Minneapolis; Studio Mus, New York; Johannesburg Art Gallery, South Africa. *Exhib:* Solo exhibs include Market Theatre Gallery, Johannesburg, 2000, South African Nat Gallery, Cape Town, 2000, Rose Art Mus, Brandeis Univ, Mass, 2004, Artists Space, New York, 2004, Perry Rubenstein Gallery, New York, 2004, 2007, Rubell Family Collection, Miami, 2006, Haus der Kunst, Munich, 2007, Galleria Tucci Russo, Turin, 2008, White Cube, London, 2008, Hayward Gallery, London, 2008; group exhibs include How Latitudes Become Forms, Walker Art Mus, Minneapolis, 2004; Adaptive Behavior, New Mus Contemp Art, New York, 2004; I Still Believe in Miracles/Drawing Space 1, Mus d'Art Moderne, Paris, 2005; The Experience of Art, Venice Biennale, 2005; New Photography, Mus Mod Art, New York, 2005, Out of Time: A Contemp View, 2006; Collection in Context: Gesture, Studio Mus Harlem, New York, 2006; Animated Painting, San Diego Mus Art, 2007; For the Love of the Game, Wadsworth Atheneum, Hartford, Conn, 2008; Street Level, Inst Contemp Art, Boston, Nasher Mus Art, NC & Contemp Arts Ctr, New Orleans, 2008; Currents: Recent Acquisitions, Hirshhorn Mus & Sculpture Garden, Washington, 2008. *Mailing Add:* Perry Rubenstein Gallery 1215 N Highland Ave Los Angeles CA 90038

RHODES, CURTIS A
PAINTER, PRINTMAKER
b Butler, Mo, Nov 5, 1939. *Study:* Univ Kans, BFA, 62; Ohio Univ, MFA, 66. *Work:* Univ Kans Spencer Mus Art, Lawrence; Flint Inst Arts, Mich; Grand Rapids Art Mus, Mich; Kalamazoo Art Ctr, Mich; Trisolini Gallery, Ohio Univ; Bathurst Regional Art Gallery, NSW, Australia. *Comn:* Multi-color lithograph, Oxbox Sch Art, Sagituck, Mich, 73; multi-color photo-etching, Detroit Print Workshop, Mich, 76; five multicolor lithographs, comn by Terry Allen, 81; four multicolor lithographs, comn by new art examiner of artist Ed Paschke, 85; three color lithograph, comn by Dan Leary, 93-94. *Exhib:* Butler Ann, Butler Inst Art, Youngstown, Ohio, 60; And Another, Western Mich Univ, Kalamazoo, 66; Nat Painting & Sculpture Invitational, Flint Inst Art, Mich, 66-67 & 70; 3rd Nat Drawing-Prints (auth, catalog), Juried Drawing-Prints, 68; Multiples USA (auth, catalog), Nat Juried Invitational Exhib Prints, 70; Markings, Major Int Exhib of Prints, 75; Paper as Medium, Smithsonian Invitational & Traveling Exhib, Washington, DC, 79-81; Strike/Restrike-The Revitalized Print (with catalog), traveling exhib, 83-86; Another View, Nat Invitational Contemp Prints, Fosdick-Nelson Gallery, Alfred Univ, NY, 90; Progressive Proofs, Celebrating 40yrs of Collecting at Western Mich Univ, Kalamazoo Inst Arts, Mich, 2003; solo exhibs, Kalamazo Inst Arts, 98 & Bathurst Regional Art Gallery, NSW, Australia, 2005. *Pos:* Visual arts adv, Mich Coun Arts, 75-78. *Teaching:* Prof, Western Mich Univ, Kalamazoo, 66-2003, prof emer. *Awards:* Nat Endowment Arts Fel, 74-75; Ford Found Awards, 77-82; Mich Coun Arts Fel, 84-85 & 90-91. *Bibliog:* Kathy Clark (auth), Twinrocker: Collaboration in Custom Papermaking, Fine Print, 77 & Pigments and Dyes in Hand Papermaking, Tamarind Tech Papers, 78. *Media:* Color Lithography, Paint. *Publ:* Mayan Legends/Replies, Limited Ed, Twinrocker Paper Mill, 81. *Dealer:* Thomas Holowitz Gallery Detroit MI. *Mailing Add:* Western Mich Univ Dept Art Kalamazoo MI 49008

RHODES, DAVID
ADMINISTRATOR, EDUCATOR
Study: Wesleyan Col, BA (philos); Columbia Univ (attended). *Pos:* Pres Sch Visual Arts, New York City, 78-. *Awards:* Spirit of NY award, 2014. *Mem:* Comn Higher Educ Middle States Asn Coll & Sch, (appointment 2003-04), Regents Adv Council Inst Accreditation, Comn Higher Educ, Asn Proprietary Coll (bd trustees 89-, chmn fed affairs comt 89-). *Mailing Add:* Sch Visual Arts Office of the Dean 209 E 23d St New York NY 10010

RIBAS, JOAO
CURATOR, EDUCATOR
b Braga, Portugal, 1979. *Collection Arranged:* Ryan Gander: Loose Associations, Performa, 2007; New Economy, Artists Space, 2007; Frederick Kiesler: Corealities, Drawing Ctr, 2008; Rirkrit Tiravanija: Demonstration Drawings, Drawing Ctr, 2008. *Pos:* Cur, The Drawing Ctr, New York, formerly & MIT List Visual Arts Ctr, 2010-. *Teaching:* Adj fac, Sch Visual Arts, New York; prof dept painting, RI Sch Design; vis lectr, Secession, Vienna, Stedelijk Mus, Amsterdam, Kunstnernes Hus, Oslo, COlumbia Univ, NYU, RI Sch Design, Cranbrook Acad Art, Boston Univ, Cooper Union. *Awards:* Emily Hall Tremaine Found Award, 2010. *Mailing Add:* 20 Ames St Bldg E15 Cambridge MA 02139

RICCIO, LOUIS NICHOLAS
PAINTER, CURATOR
b Jersey City, NJ, Oct 19, 1931. *Study:* Art Instructions Inc, 1947-1950; Instr with John Grabach, 1955-1957; Newark Sch of Fine & Industrial Art, Carmella DeFronzo Art Sch, 1965-1968. *Work:* Noyes Mus (signature mem), Oceanville, NJ; Ocean Co Coll Gallery, Toms River, NJ; Bordentown Gallery-Laurelton Art Gallery, Bordentown, NJ; Audubon Artist-Salmagundi Club, NY; NJ State Show Gallery, Flemington, NJ. *Comn:* Billboard, O'Mealia Outdoor Adv Co, Jersey City, NJ, 1950-1970; House murals, Jersey City, NJ, 1950-2006; portrait, EXPO 67, Montreal, Can, 67; Outside wall murals, Jersey City, NJ, 1970-1987; 2 oil portraits, Lakewood, NJ, 2007. *Exhib:* 15 Ann statewide Exhib, Jersey City Mus, NJ, 1967; NJ State 1st Place Pen-Ink, Manalapan Munic Libr, Manalapan, NJ, 1993; Audubon Artists Art Soc, Salmagundi Art Club, NY, 2005-2015; NJ State Juried Exhib, Ocean Co Guild, Island Heights, NJ, 2006; Allied Artists Centennial Exhib, Canton Ohio Mus Group Exhib, 2015. *Collection Arranged:* Ocean Co Coll NJ Anns, Seniors Exhib, 1998-2006; NJ Open State Juried, Am Artists Pro League, 2006. *Pos:* Billboard pictorial artist, O'Mealia Outdoor Adv Co, Jersey City, NJ, 1950-1973; sign painter, Lou Riccio Sign Co, 1973-2000. *Teaching:* Instr sign painting, Newark Sch of Fine & Indust Art, NJ, 1984-1986; instr art (oil pen-ink drawing), Manasquan High Sch, Leisure Knoll, NJ 1987-2006; instr, Ocean Co Col, NJ, 2000-2006; instr, Leisure West Village, Manchester, NJ, 2007-; instr, pvt lessons, currently. *Awards:* John Grabach Award, Am Artist Prof League, 1997-2004, 2010; Beatrice Jackson Award, Salmagundi Club, Audubon Artists Inc, NY, 2005; Best in Show, Am Artist Prof

League, 2006; Pen & Ink Award, Sr Citizens Show, Flemington, NJ; Watercolor Award, Ocean Co Artist Guild, Island Heights, NJ, 2006; First Place, Oil, Laurelton Art Soc, NJ, 2007; Distinguished Merit Award, Oil Portrait, NJ Chap, Am Artists Prof League, 2007; Hon Mention Still Life, Am Artist Prof League, 2010, Special Judges Award, 2011; Best in Show, Lacey Show, 2010; Gamblin Artist Material Award, Audubon Artists, 2011; 2nd Place, WC Portrait, Lacey United Methodist Church, Warrtown, NJ, 2012, 1st Place, Still Life, 1st Place, Pen-Ink-Figurative Portrait, 3rd Place Oil; Best in Show, Laurelton Art Soc, Lakewood, NJ, 2012; 1st Place, Oil Portrait, Senior Citizen Show, Ocean Co Coll, 2012; Best in Show, Watercolor Portrait, Lacey, NJ, 2014; Best in Show-Open, Oil Portrait, Middletown Art Ctr, NJ, AAPL Orgn, 2014; 1st Place, Watercolor, American Dreamer, Portrait, Lacey-Forked River, NJ, 2014; Lifetime Achievement Award for Art and as a Teacher of Art, Cult and Heritage Comt of Ocean County, NJ, 2014; Best in Show, Pen & Ink Portrait, Lacey, NJ, 2015; Best in Show, Oil Portrait, Laurelton Art Asn, Lacey, NJ, 2015; Best in Show-Open, Watercolor Portrait, Lacey, Forked River, NJ. *Bibliog:* Susan Weiner (auth), Show Recognizes Talent of Artist, Senior Scoop, 2000; Carolyn Van Houten (auth), seniority/Art, Ocean Co Observer, 2006; Lynne Salisbury (auth), Festival of Art 2006, Community News, 2006. *Mem:* Am Artist Prof League, NJ; Ocean Co Artist Guild, NJ; Manasquan River Group, NJ; Laurelton Art Soc, NJ; Audubon Artists Inc, NYC; Noyes Mus, NJ (sig mem); Allied Artists of Am, NYC, 2014. *Media:* Oil, Watercolor, Pen & Ink. *Publ:* Auth, Portraits and Still Life in Oils, Manasquan River Group Artists, 2002; contrib, illusr, Coffee House, Carpenter Gothic Press, 2005. *Mailing Add:* 12 Dartmoor Rd Brick NJ 08724

RICE, ANTHONY HOPKINS
HISTORIAN, ARTIST

b Angeles Pampanga, Philippine Islands, July 21, 1948. *Study:* Va Commonwealth Univ, Richmond, BFA, 70; Univ NC, Chapel Hill, MFA, 72. *Work:* NY Pub Libr; Nat Mus Am Art, Smithsonian Inst, Washington; Victoria & Albert Mus, London, Eng; Nat Mus Am Art, Washington, DC. *Comn:* Indoor environmental sculpture, Sarasota Sq Mall, Sarasota, Fla, 89. *Exhib:* New Sculpture, Washington, Baltimore, Richmond, Corcoran Gallery, Washington, DC, 70; Translucent and Transparent Art, St Petersburg Mus Art, Fla, 71; Renwick Gallery, Smithsonian Inst, Washington, 81; Brooklyn Mus Art, NY, 88; Nat Sculpture '89, Libr Congress, Washington, 89; Gallery Camina Real, Boca Raton, Fla, 90; solo exhibs, Mary Ryan Gallery, NY, 89, Kathy Albers Gallery, Memphis, Tenn, 90, 92, 93 & 96, McIntosh Gallery, Atlanta, Ga, 92, 94 & 95 & Miramar Gallery, Sarasota, Fla, 92, 93, 94, 95 & 96. *Teaching:* Coordr art hist prog, Ringling Sch Art & Design, Sarasota, Fla, 85-, fac mem, 85-; actg dean liberal art, 95-96. *Awards:* Visual Arts Fel Award in Painting, Nat Endowment Arts. *Bibliog:* Greg Thielew (auth), article, Art Voices, 3/81. *Mem:* Coll Art Asn; Am Asn Univ Prof. *Media:* Modern Art. *Dealer:* Mary Ryan Gallery New York NY. *Mailing Add:* 2319 Roselawn Cir Sarasota FL 34231

RICE, DANIELLE
MUSEUM DIRECTOR

Study: Wellesley Coll, BA, 1973; Yale Univ, PhD, 1979. *Pos:* Educ dept, Wadsworth Athenium, Hartford, Conn, formerly; educ dept, Nat Gallery, Washington, formerly; Cur of Educ, Philadelphia Mus Art, 1986-97, senior cur of educ, 1997-2001, assoc dir of prog, 2001-2005; exec dir, Dela Art Mus, Wilmington, Dela, 2005-. *Awards:* Mus Educ Award, Am Asn Mus, 1988; Mus Educ of the Year, Pa Art Educ Asn, 1996. *Mailing Add:* Delaware Museum of Arts 2301 Kentmere Parkway Wilmington DE 19806

RICE, EDWARD
PAINTER

b Augusta, Ga, Feb 24, 1953. *Study:* Freeman Schoolcraft, 72-80. *Work:* Gibbes Mus Art, Charleston, SC; Morris Mus Art, Augusta, GA; NationsBank, Charlotte, NC; State SC, Columbia; Springs Industries, NY. *Exhib:* Mint Mus Biennial, Charlotte, NC, 88; SC Arts Commission Fel Retrospective, SC State Mus, Columbia, 90; solo exhib, Tree Paintings, Heath Gallery, Atlanta, 90; SC Expressions, Columbia Mus Art, 92; The Artist as Native, Babcock Galleries, NY, 93; Lure of the Lowcountry, Gibbes Mus Art, Charleston, SC, 94; Vividly Told, Morris Mus Art, Augusta, Ga, 94; and others. *Awards:* Merit Award, Mint Mus Biennial, Charlotte, NC, 88; SC Arts Commission Visual Arts Fel, 88; Nat Endowment for Arts Regional Fel, Southern Arts Fedn, 88. *Bibliog:* Jeffrey Day (auth), Resurrecting the mundane, The State, 3/1/92; Estill Pennington (auth), A Southern Collection, Augusta, 92; Allan Gussow (auth), The Artist as Native: Reinventing Regionalism, San Francisco, 93. *Dealer:* Hodges Taylor Gallery 227 N Tryon St Charlotte NC 28202. *Mailing Add:* 502 Lucerne Ave North Augusta SC 29841

RICE, NANCY NEWMAN See Newman-Rice, Nancy

RICE, SHELLEY ENID
CRITIC, HISTORIAN

b Bronx, NY, Aug 20, 1950. *Study:* Smith Col, 68-69; State Univ NY, Stony Brook, BA (summa cum laude), 72; Inst Fine Arts, New York Univ, MA, 75; Princeton Univ. *Work:* Parisian Views, 1997; Inverted Odysseys, 1999. *Exhib:* Deconstruction/Reconstruction, New Mus, NY,1980; The Eye of the Beholder, ICP, 1997; Inverted Odysseys, Grey Art Gallery, 1999-2000; consult & coauth, Role Modles: Feminine Identity in Contemp Am Photography, Nat Mus Women Arts, DC, 2008-2009; The View from Left Field, Taminent Libr, NY Univ, 2012-2013. *Collection Arranged:* Avon Collection of Contemporary Women's Photography, 97. *Pos:* Photog critic, Village Voice, 76-77; columnist, SoHo Weekly News, 78-79; freelance cur & critic, 78-; staff writer, Artforum Mag, 80-82; invited blogger, Jeu de Paume Mus, Paris, 2012. *Teaching:* Arts Prof, NYU. *Awards:* PEN/Jerard Award for Non-Fiction Essay, 89; Fulbright Seniors Fellowships, 89, 99; Hasselblad Rsch Grant, 92; Guggenheim Found Fel, 92-93; AICA award for Best Photography exhib, 2000; Chevalier dans l'ordre des Arts et des lettres, France, 2010. *Mem:* Coll Art Asn; Am Sect Int Asn Art Critics; PEN/Am. *Res:* Historical and contemporary photography; contemporary multi-media art. *Publ:* Fields of Vision (exhib catalog), Landmarks, Bard Col, 84; Lartigue: Le Choix du Borheur, Paris, Minister of Culture, France, 92; Parisian Views, MIT Press, 97; Inverted Odysseys, MIT Press, 99; The Book of 101 Books, A Roth (D.A.P.), 2001; American ed, The New History of Photography, Bordas Paris, 94; Candida Hofer: In Portugal, 2007; Role Models, NMWA, 2008; Am Photography, 2012; JH Lartigue, 2013. *Mailing Add:* New York Univ Dept Art History 303 Silver Ctr 100 Washington Sq East New York NY 10003

RICH, DAVID
PAINTER, EDUCATOR

b Chicago, Ill, Sept 21, 1952. *Study:* Philadelphia Coll Art, 70-72; Kansas City Art Inst, BFA, 74; Univ Ore, MFA, 76. *Work:* Walker Art Ctr, Minneapolis, Minn; Minneapolis Inst Arts, Minn; Piper Jaffray Collection, Abbott-Northwestern Collection, Minneapolis, Minn; Weisman Mus, Minneapolis. *Comn:* Three murals, City of St Paul, 84; two paintings, Marquette Bank, Minneapolis, 85; four paintings, McCormick Place, Chicago, Ill, 98. *Exhib:* Solo exhibs, Dolly Fiterman Fine Art, Minneapolis, 85, 92 & 98, Franz Bader Gallery, Washington, DC, 86, Minn Inst Arts, 87, Satori Fine Art, Chicago, 97, First St Gallery, NY, 91, 93, 95, 98 & 2000 & Gallery Co, Minneapolis, 2005; group exhibs, Minneapolis Inst Arts, 89, Minn Mus Am Art, St Paul, 92, ann exhib, Nat Acad Mus, NY, 96, Frye Mus, Seattle, 2002, Grimaldis Gallery, Baltimore, MD, 2004 & Robert Steele Gallery, New York, 2007. *Teaching:* Instr painting & drawing, Minn Mus Art, 77-87; fac, Minn Coll Art & Design, 85-. *Awards:* Fac grants, Minneapolis Coll Art & Design, 2001, 03, 05, 07; Minn State Arts Bd, 84. 90, 2005; Puffin Found, 96, 99, 2004. *Bibliog:* Nancy Roth (auth), Meetings & Archetypes, Minneapolis Inst Arts, 87; David Nye Brown (auth), David Rich (exhib essay), Dolly Fiterman Fine Arts, 98; Norman Lundin (auth), A Decade of Contemporary American Figure Drawing, 2002; Patricia Briggs (auth), www.mnartists.org, 2005. *Mem:* Coll Art Asn. *Media:* Oil. *Publ:* Contribr, Exploring Painting, Davis Publs, 88; Tikkun, Inst Labor & Mental Health, 89; Journal of the American Planning Association, Hunter Coll, NY, 90. *Mailing Add:* 436 Smith Ave N Saint Paul MN 55102

RICH, GARRY LORENCE
PAINTER

b Newton Co, Mo, Nov 11, 1943. *Study:* Kansas City Art Inst, BFA; New York Univ, MA. *Work:* Whitney Mus Am Art, NY; Aldrich Mus Contemp Art, Ridgefield, Conn; Phoenix Art Mus, Ariz; Nelson Gallery Art, Kansas City, Mo; Miami Art Ctr, Fla. *Exhib:* Whitney Mus Am Art Ann, 71; Highlights of the Season, Aldrich Mus Contemp Art, Ridgefield, 71; solo exhibs, Max Hutchinson Gallery, NY, 71-72, 74, 77, 79, 81, 83 & 85, Henri Gallery, Washington, DC, 72 & Gallery A, Sydney, Australia, 72. *Teaching:* Asst prof painting, New York Univ, 65-71, Hofstra Univ, 71-72 & Bard Col, 72. *Awards:* Max Beckman fel, Brooklyn Mus, 66; Nat Coun Arts Award, 67; Nat Endowment Art, 74. *Bibliog:* Domingo (auth), Color abstractionism, 12/70 & Bowling (auth), Color & recent painting, 72, Arts Mag; Ratcliff (auth), Young New York painters, Art News, 70. *Mailing Add:* 167 Crosby St New York NY 10012-2709

RICHARD, JACK
PAINTER, RESTORER

b Akron, Ohio, Mar 7, 1922. *Study:* Chicago Prof Sch Art, scholar; Univ Ohio, Athens; Kent Univ; Akron Univ; also with R Brackman, A Bohrod, Y Kunioshi, B Shahn, J Carroll & many others. *Work:* Canton Art Inst, Ohio; Umbaugh Pole Bldg Collection, Ravenna, Ohio; Woodrum Ins Collection, Stow, Ohio; Good Year Tire Co; Firestone Country Club; and many others; over 2,000 pvt and instnl collections. *Comn:* President & Mrs Eisenhower, Tupperware Int, Orlando, Fla; murals, Central Christian Church Kettering, Dayton; Valley Savings & Loan, Cuyahoga Falls; mural, First United Church of Christ, Akron; portraits, comn by Bing & Catherine Crosby, Byron Nelson, Juan Rodrigues, President Gerald Ford, Bob Hope, Dinah Shore, Arnold Palmer, Nancy Lopez, President George Bush & Raymond Firestone; portrait, Abigail Adams, Nat First Ladies Libr; portrait, Hugh Glosser, Hugh Glosser School of Music Building, Kent State Univ; portrait, Dan Sullivan CEO Fed Ex Ground; portrait, William Considine, CEO Children's Hospital; portrait, Peggy Elliot (pres Univ Akron), Akron Univ Building; over 2,400 comn works; over 600 portraits. *Exhib:* Retrospective, Ambassador Col, Pasadena, 70; City Ctr Gallery, NY; Fifty Am Artists, Gallerie Int & Salmagundi Club, NY; Butler Inst Am Art Nat, Youngstown, Ohio. *Pos:* Illusr, Stevens-Gross Studios, Chicago; Cinecraft Productions, Cleveland, Ohio. *Teaching:* Instr painting & design & dir, Cuyahoga Valley Art Ctr, Cuyahoga Falls, 53-63; instr, Woman's City Club, Akron, Ohio, 60-; instr painting & design & dir, Almond Tea Galleries, Cuyahoga Falls, 63-; instr, Madison Sch Art, Conn, 81; pvt students in US, Japan, Eng and China. *Awards:* Purchase Award & Second Award Painting, Canton Art Inst; Best in Show Award, Akron Art Inst, 48; Huntington Hartford Fel, 58; Best in Show Award, ASA, 2001 & 02; Contemp Personalities; Am Artists of Renown; Dir Am Portrait Painters; over 200 awards. *Bibliog:* Six Rotos, Beacon J, Knight Newspapers; M M (auth), Jack Richard Al Lavoro, Il Pungold Verde, Italy, 74, Asahi Press, Japan. *Mem:* Artists, Ohio; Ohio Arts & Crafts Guild; Tri-Co Art Soc, Ohio; Akron Soc Artists; Cuyahoga Valley Art Ctr. *Media:* Acrylic, Oil, Watercolor, Pastel. *Specialty:* portraits; murals; national and local exhibits. *Interests:* Assisting in training of young artists and rehabilitation use of arts. *Publ:* Illusr, Staley J, Ind, 43-45; The Helm Mag; Ohio Edison Ann Report, 60; Ohio Story, TV prog, Ohio Bell Tel; Asahi Press, Japan. *Dealer:* Almond Tea Galleries. *Mailing Add:* c/o Almond Tea Galleries 2250 Front St Cuyahoga Falls OH 44221

RICHARD, PAUL
CRITIC

b Chicago, Ill, Nov, 22, 1939. *Study:* Harvard Col, BA, 61; Univ Pa Grad Sch Fine Arts. *Pos:* Art critic, Washington Post, DC, 67-. *Mailing Add:* 1707 Columbia Rd NW Apt 519 Washington DC 20009

RICHARDS, BILL
PAINTER
b Grantsville, WVa, July 15, 1936. *Study:* Ohio Univ, with Dwight Mutchler, BFA; Ind Univ, with Leon Golub & James McGarrell, MFA; Skowhegan Sch Painting & Sculpture. *Work:* Philadelphia Mus Art; Brooklyn Mus & Guggenheim Mus, NY; NJ State Mus Art, Trenton; Westinghouse Corp, Pittsburgh; and others. *Comn:* Diptych painting & performance, The Travelers Corp, TV Commercial, 86. *Exhib:* Friends Collect 20th Century, Philadelphia Mus Art, 67; Pa Acad Fine Arts Ann, 68; Whitney Mus Am Art Biennial, 75; solo exhibs, Marian Locks Gallery, Philadelphia, 75, Olympia Galleries Ltd, Philadelphia, 76, La Bertesca Gallery, Dusseldorf, 77, Ohio Univ, Athens, 79 & Ricco/Maresca Gallery, NY, 96; 19 Artists--Emergent Americans, Exxon Nat Exhib, Guggenheim Mus, 81; Westinghouse Collection, Loch Haven Art Ctr, Orlando, Fla, 83; NY Painting Today, Three Rivers Arts Festival, Pittsburgh, 83; Pa Acad Fine Arts, 85; Traveling Exhib, US & Canada, Independent Curators, Inc, 85-87; Painting, Beyond the Death of Painting, Kuznetsky Most Exhib Hall, Moscow, USSR, 89. *Pos:* Originator & dir Harlem Horizon Art Studio, Harlem Hosp Ctr, New York, 88-. *Teaching:* Assoc prof, Moore Col Art, 67-81, prof, 81-82. *Bibliog:* Victoria Donohoe (auth), rev in Philadelphia Inquirer, 5/75; Ann Jarmusch (auth), article, Art News 1/77; Peter Frank (auth), article, Art Am, 3/77. *Media:* Acrylic

RICHARDS, BILL (WILLIAM) A
DRAFTSMAN
b Brooklyn, NY, Sept 19, 1944. *Study:* Pratt Inst, BFA, 66; Univ Iowa, MA, 68; Univ NMex, MFA, 70. *Work:* Chase Manhattan Bank, NY; Ill Bell Tel, Chicago; Asheville Art Mus, NC; Nat Mus Art, Washington, DC. *Exhib:* On Paper, Va Mus Fine Arts, 80; The Am Landscape: Recent Developments, Whitney Mus Am Art Fairfield Co Br, Stamford, Conn, 81; Contemp Am Realism Since 1960, Pa Acad Fine Arts, Va Mus Fine Arts, Oakland Mus Art & mus in Europe, 81-83; Nature Transformed, Anderson Gallery, Va Commonwealth Univ, 82; solo exhibs, Hite Art Inst, Univ Louisville, 83 & Moravian Col, Bethlehem, Pa, 85; Am Realism, Twentieth Century Drawings and Watercolors, San Francisco Mus Mod Art, 85; Tomasulo Gallery, Union Col, Cranford, NJ, 86; Divergent Styles: Contemp Am Drawing, Univ Gal, Univ Fla, Gainesville, 90. *Teaching:* Asst adj prof drawing, State Univ NY, Purchase, 77-78; instr, Sch Visual Arts, 77-79 & Parsons Sch Design, 85-90. *Awards:* Creative Artists Pub Serv Grant, 75-76; Nat Endowment Arts Fel, 77-78. *Bibliog:* Vivian Raynor (auth), Art: A tranquil show of American landscape, New York Times, 5/15/82; Ronny Cohen (auth), Drawing the meticulous realist way, Drawing, 3-4/82; Antony Nicoli: (auth), Bill Richards, Arts, summer 85. *Mailing Add:* c/o Nancy Hoffman Gallery 520 W 27th St Ste 301 New York NY 10001-5548

RICHARDS, BRUCE MICHAEL
PAINTER, PRINTMAKER
b Dayton, Ohio, Jan 28, 1948. *Study:* Univ Calif, Irvine, BA, 70, MFA, 73. *Work:* Los Angeles Co Mus Art; San Francisco Mus Mod Art; Grunwald Ctr Graphic Arts, Los Angeles; La Jolla Mus Contemp Art, Calif; New Port Harbor Art Mus, Calif. *Comn:* Print, Graphic Arts Coun, Los Angeles Co Mus Art, 92. *Exhib:* Southern California Styles of the 60's & 70's, La Jolla Mus Art, 78; solo exhibs, Laguna Beach Mus, Calif, 81 & 86, Los Angeles Munic Art Gallery, 84; 20th Century Watercolors Yesterday & Today, Long Beach Mus Art, Calif, 88; Individual Realities in the California Art Scene, Se Zon Mus Art, Tokyo, Japan, 91; End of the Century, Los Angeles Co Mus, 97. *Awards:* Painting Fel, Nat Endowment Arts, 76; 8th Nat Exhib 1st Award, Los Angeles Print Soc, 84; City of Los Angeles Individual Artist Grant, Los Angeles Munic Art Gallery, 97-98. *Bibliog:* Michael Smith (auth), Bruce Richards - A Selection of Paintings and Watercolors, Baxter Art Gallery, 79; Donald Carrol (auth), Bruce Richards: Recent Images (exhib catalog), Los Angeles Munic Art Gallery, 84; Joan Hugo (auth), Bruce Richards (exhib catalog), Laguna Beach Mus, 86. *Media:* Oil, Watercolor. *Mailing Add:* c/o Hamilton Press Gallery 1317 Abbott Kinney Blvd Venice CA 90291

RICHARDS, DAVID PATRICK
PAINTER, WRITER
b Abington, Pa, Sept 14, 1950. *Study:* Kutztown Univ, BS, 73; Lehigh Univ, 78-80; Studied with Michael Kessler, 93. *Work:* Muhlenberg Col, Allentown, Pa; Salisbury Univ, Md. *Exhib;* Allentown Arts Mus Biennial, Pa, 84; Nat Watercolor Soc, Muckenthaler Cult Ctr, Los Angeles, 84; Am Watercolor Soc, Salmagundi Club, NY, 84, 87, 91; Pa Watercolor Soc, Port Hist Mus, Philadelphia, 87; Allied Artists Am, Nat Arts Club, NY, 99; Rotunda, Bethlehem, Pa, 2014. *Pos:* Freelance auth, 84-. *Teaching:* Spec educ art instr, Vitalistic Therapeutic Ctr, Allentown, Pa, 74-80; gen art workshop facilitator, 80-95; vis artist, Northern Lehigh Sch Dist, Pa, 90-92. *Awards:* Shalin Award, AWS, 84; Muckenthaler Award, Nat Watercolor Soc, 88; Law Award, Allied Artists Am, 99; Gold brush, Audubon artists, 2005. *Bibliog:* Greg Albert (auth), Splash: America's Best Watercolors, North Light Books, 91; Daniel J Lombardo (auth), Arts and Humanities, Libr Jour, 9/1/95; Rachel Wolf (auth), A Variety of Personal Textures, Painting Textures in Watercolor, F & W Publ, 98; Betsy Dillard Stroud (auth), The Artist's Muse, North Light Book, 2006. *Mem:* American Watercolor Soc; Nat Watercolor Soc (Regional rep); Nat Soc Painters Casien & Acrylic (bd dir & publicity chmn 98-2006); Allied Artists Am; Audubon Artists. *Media:* Acrylic, Oil, Watercolor, Photography. *Publ:* Auth, David P Richards, Am Artist Mag, 84; The Peacefulness of Pointillism, Watercolor Magic, 93; How to Discover Your Personal Painting Style, N Light Books, 95; Becoming a Message Maker, Artists Mag, 96; contribr, Basic Nature Painting, N Light Bks, 98; Moving on to move ahead, Watercolor magic, 2006. *Mailing Add:* 1006 Caravan Way Salisbury MD 21804

RICHARDS, EUGENE
PHOTOGRAPHER, LECTURER
b Dorchester, Mass, Apr 25, 1944. *Study:* Northeastern Univ, Boston, BA (Eng), 67; Mass Inst Technol, grad level study with Minor White. *Work:* Mus Mod Art, NY; Mus Fine Arts, Boston; Addison Gallery Am Art, Andover, Mass; J B Speed Art Mus, Louisville, Ky; Everson Mus, Syracuse, NY. *Comn:* Art in Public Places, Mass Artists Found, Boston, 78. *Exhib:* We the People, Smithsonian Inst, DC, 75; Photogs, J B Speed Art Mus, Louisville, Ky, 76; Recent Acquisitions, Mus Fine Arts, Boston, 76 & Fourteen New Eng Photogrs, 78; Recent Acquisition Show, Addison Gallery Am Art, Andover, Mass, 77; Solo exhib, Photogs, Folkwang Mus, Essen, WGer, 79; Mass Art Found Winners, Worcester Art Mus, Mass, 80. *Pos:* Artist-in-residence, Maine Photo Workshop, Rockport, 77-78 & Int Ctr Photog, New York, 78-79; nominee mem, Magnum Photos, New York, 78-. *Teaching:* Instr photog, Art Inst Boston, 74-76 & Union Col, Schenectady, NY, 77. *Awards:* Nat Endowment for Arts grant, photog, 74 & 83; Mass Artists Found, 78 & fel, 79; Guggenheim fel, photog, 80. *Bibliog:* Lou Stettner (auth), A look at forgotten books, Camera 35, 3/78; Vickie Goldberg (auth), Half dirty realities, Am Photogr, 78; Julia Scully (auth), Dorchester days, Mod Photog, 6/79. *Mem:* Photog Resource Ctr. *Publ:* Auth, Few Comforts or Surprises: The Arkansas Delta, Mass Inst Technol, 73; Contribr- Photographer's Choice, Addison House, 76; contribr, Family of Children, 77 & contribr, Family of Women, 78, Ridge Press; auth, Dorchester Days, Many Voices Press, Wollaston, Mass, 78. *Mailing Add:* c/o Many Voices 472 13th St Brooklyn NY 11215-5207

RICHARDS, ROSALYN A
DIRECTOR
b Palo Alto, Calif, Sept 21, 1947. *Study:* RI Sch Design, BFA, 69; Yale Univ Sch Art, MFA, 75. *Work:* Chicago Art Inst; Yale Univ Art Gallery; Minneapolis Inst Art; Hood Mus, Dartmouth Col; Grunwald Ctr for Graphic Arts, UCLA. *Exhib:* 6th Ann Mid Yr Exhib, Butler Inst Am Art, Youngstown, Ohio, 00; two-person exhib, Munson Williams Proctor Inst, Sch Art, Utica, NY, 01; Global Matrix Int Print Exhib, Purdue Univ Galleries, W Lafayette, Ind, 02, Wright State Univ, Dayton, Ohio, 02; Three Artists, Dowd Fine Arts Gallery, SUNY, Cortland, NY, 03; Solo Show, Howard Co Ctr for the Arts, Ellicott City, Md, 02. *Teaching:* Asst prof art, Dartmouth Col, Hanover, NH, 76-82; prof art, Bucknell Univ, Lewisburg, Pa, 82-. *Awards:* Purchase Award, Delta Small Prints Exhib, Ark State Univ, 00; Purchase Award, Mid Atlantic New Painting, Mary Washington Col, 97; Ragdale Found Fel, Lake Forest, Ill, 03. *Mem:* Womens Studio Workshop; CAA; SAGA; Print Ctr. *Media:* Prints, Drawings. *Publ:* Diane Lesko, Rosalyn Richards Catalogue, Center Gallery, Bucknell Univ, 90. *Dealer:* Sande Webster, 2081 Locust St, Philadelphia, PA, 19103. *Mailing Add:* 1195 Smoketown Rd Lewisburg PA 17837

RICHARDS, SABRA
PRINTMAKER, PAINTER
b Utica, NY. *Study:* Syracuse Univ BFA (cum laude), 58; Bennington Coll & Parsons Sch Design, 83-86. *Work:* Mus Arts & Sci, Daytona Beach, Fla; Mem Art Gallery, Univ Rochester, NY; Syracuse Univ Fine Arts Collection, NY; NY State Fine Arts Collection, Albany; City of Ann Arbor Fine Arts Collection, Mich. *Comn:* Six Works, IBM, Atlanta, Ga, 84; 4 ft x 5 1/2 ft piece, Humana Hosp, Louisville, Ky, 85; 12 pieces, Temple Univ, Philadelphia, 86; 2 pieces, IBM lobby installation, San Francisco, 87; 4 ft X 9 ft piece, Ann Arbor Pub Libr. *Exhib:* Hunterdon Nat Print Show, traveling exhib, 79-83; Nat Asn Painters Acrylic, traveling exhib, 80-82; solo exhibs, Visions of the Sea, Krasl Mus Art, St Joseph, Mich, 85 & State Univ NY, Rockefeller Ctr Art, Fredonia, NY, 86; Six Artists, Rochester Inst Technol, NY, 87; Collages, Neville Sargent Gallery, Chicago, 88; Hand Made Paper, Rubiner Gallery, Detroit, 88. *Teaching:* Instr, painting, St John Fisher Col, Rochester, NY, 78-82; Artist-in-residence, Artpark, Lewiston, NY, 81. *Awards:* Miller Mem Award, Nat Asn Women Artists; 1st Prize painting, Syracuse Univ, 73; 1st Prize graphics, World Orchid Show, Am Orchid Soc, 84. *Bibliog:* Karen Wenger (auth), Not just hand painted, Screen Printing, 85; Sebby Jacobson (auth), Sabra Richards, Rochester Times-Union, 86; Jan Serasky (auth), Sabra Richards, Artist Mag, spring 89. *Mem:* Nat Asn Women Artists; Arena Group (treas, 88, vpres, 90), Rochester, NY; Ohio Designer Craftsmen. *Media:* Collage; Handmade Paper

RICHARDSON, FRANK, JR
MURALIST
b Baltimore, Md, Jan 14, 1950. *Study:* Community Coll Baltimore, AA; Md Inst Coll Art, BFA; Towson State Col; Riverside Art Ctr with Jacob Laurence, Romare Bearden. *Work:* ILE-IFE Mus Afro-American Cult, Philadelphia; ThirdWorld Mus, 111 & Assoc, Baltimore; Merabash Mus, Inc, Willingboro, NJ; Old Slave Mart Mus, Charleston, SC; Nat Ctr Afro-American Artists, Inc, Dorchester, Mass. *Comn:* Mural for film Amazing Grace, 74; mural, Enoch Pratt Free Libr, Baltimore, 74; Black Art (murals), FAN: Baltimore Arts Tower, 74; Amen America, (murals with Berkeley S Thompson), Asn Black Arts/East, Nat Endowment Arts, 75. *Exhib:* First and Second Wide-Regional, Black Art Show, Baltimore; Black Mural Painter, Inst Art Ctr, Lima, Peru, 75; Mural Painter, Univ Pretoria, Repub South Africa, 75. *Collection Arranged:* An Evening With the Links, 74; Awards Extravaganza 74. *Teaching:* Dir graphics, Sinai Druid Camp, Baltimore, 71-72; dir, Mus Prep Sch, 72-; instr printing, Career Opportunities Inc, Baltimore, 71-. *Awards:* Best Black Art Work in Show, Black Cult Endowment, 69; Children's Hour Prog, Md Art Coun, 74; Third World Prep Sch, Nat Endowment Arts, 75. *Bibliog:* Averil Jordan-Kadis (auth), Colorful mural, Baltimore Sun, 67; Priscilla Coger (auth), Mr Richardson's beautiful wall, Baltimore Afro-American, 72; James Kelmartin (auth), Museum unit to expand, News American, 75. *Mem:* Asn Black Arts/East. *Media:* Paint. *Mailing Add:* 3016 Baker St Baltimore MD 21216

RICHARDSON, JEAN
PAINTER, SCULPTOR
b Hollis, Okla, Feb 10, 1940. *Study:* Wesleyan Col, Macon, Ga, BFA, 62; Arts Student League, New York, 78. *Work:* Arthur Anderson Cos, St Charles, Ill; State Collection of Okla, Oklahoma City; Fed Reserve Bank of Kansas City; US State Dept, Copenhagen, Denmark; Coll Law, Univ Okla. *Comn:* Murals, State Capitol Okla, Okla House of Reps, Oklahoma City, 76; mural, Co Courthouse, Okla Co, Oklahoma City, 92; murals, Sarkey Law Ctr, Oklahoma City Univ, Okla, 94. *Exhib:* West 80 Exhib, Minn Mus Art, Minneapolis, 80; Okla Artist Showcase, Goddard Mus Arts, Ardmore, 81; Arts Place Exhib, Okla Art Mus, Oklahoma City, 91; Am Art in

Miniature Ann, Thomas Gilcrease Mus, Tulsa, Okla, 93 & 94; Oklahoma Illustrations, Mabee Gerrer Mus, Shawnee, Okla, 94. *Pos:* Judge design & illus, Okla Book Awards, 95-. *Bibliog:* Joan Carpenter (auth), Plains Myths & Other Tales, John Szoke Graphics, 88 & Turning Toward Home: The Art of Jean Richardson, 98; Sandy Clarke (auth), Jean Richardson, A certain mystique, Equine Images, summer 90. *Mem:* Nat Women Arts; Okla Visual Artists Coalition. *Media:* Acrylic; Miscellaneous Media. *Publ:* Santa Fean Mag, 84 & 87; Southwest Profile Mag, 85; Art Gallery Mag, 85; Western Art Digest, 86. *Dealer:* John Szoke Edits 591 Broadway 3rd Flr New York NY 10012. *Mailing Add:* 12700 N Council Rd Oklahoma City OK 73142

RICHARDSON, SAM
SCULPTOR, EDUCATOR

b Oakland, Calif, July 19, 1934. *Study:* Calif Coll Arts & Crafts, BA, 56 & MFA, 60. *Work:* Dallas Mus Fine Art, Tex; Denver Art Mus; M H De Young Mem Mus, San Francisco; Milwaukee Art Ctr; Nat Mus Am Art, Smithsonian Inst, Washington, DC. *Exhib:* Plastic as Plastic, 63 & Creative Casting, 73, Mus Contemp Crafts, NY; New Media, New Methods, Mus Mod Art, NY, 69; Whitney Mus Am Art, 68-69; Stanford Univ, Calif, 72; Vassar Col, 72; Rutgers Univ, 75; Vpres US Home, Artists Pac Coast States, 80; and others. *Teaching:* Instr art, Oakland City Col, 60-61; art dir, Mus Contemp Crafts, New York, 61-63; asst prof art, San Jose State Univ, 63-66, assoc prof art, 67-72, prof art, 72-. *Dealer:* Martha Jackson Gallery 521 W 57th St New York NY 10019; Hansen Fuller Goldeen Gallery 228 Grant Ave San Francisco CA

RICHARDSON, TREVOR J
GALLERY DIRECTOR, CURATOR

b Nov 7, 1950; United Kingdom citizen. *Study:* Univ Mass, Amherst, MFA, 82. *Collection Arranged:* Fantasies, Fables & Fabrications: Photoworks from the 1980's, Herter Gallery, Univ Mass, Amherst, 89; Meg Webster: Sculpture Projects (auth, catalog), Weatherspoon Art Gallery, Univ NC, Greensboro, 89, Ida Applebroog: Selected Paintings: 1982-90 (auth, catalog), 93 & Pink Lady (auth, catalog), 94. *Pos:* Cur exhib, Weatherspoon Art Gallery, Univ NC, Greensboro, 90-95; cur galleries, Manchester Col, St Paul, Minn, 95-97; dir, Herter Gallery, Univ Mass, Amherst, 97-. *Teaching:* Asst prof, Univ Mass, Amherst, 97-. *Awards:* Spec Proj Award, Southeast Mus Asn, 92. *Mem:* Am Asn Mus; Coll Art Asn; Mass Soc Prof. *Res:* Contemporary American and European art. *Publ:* Auth, Contemporary American College: 1960-85, Univ Mass, Amherst, 86; Fractions of the Self: The Portrait in Contemporary Photography, Univ NC, Greensboro, 93. *Mailing Add:* Univ Mass 125A Herter Hall Amherst MA 01003

RICHARDSON, W C
PAINTER, EDUCATOR

b San Diego, Calif, May 15, 1953. *Study:* Univ NC, Chapel Hill, BFA (studio art, with hons), 75; Wash Univ, St Louis, MFA, 77. *Work:* Hirshhorn Mus & Sculpture Garden, Washington; Ackland Art Ctr, Chapel Hill, NC; Corcoran Gallery of Art, Washington; US Embassy in Algiers, Town Hall, Washington, DC; Ctr for Physics, College Park, Md; US Dept of State, Algiers; DC Town Hall; Prudential Life, NY; IBM Corp, DC; Northrop-Grumman, Va; Reston Town Ctr. *Comn:* Reston Town Ctr, Va, 90; Ronald Reagan Nat Airport Terminal, 94-95. *Exhib:* Md Biennial, Baltimore Mus Art, 80, 83; one-person shows, Osuna Gallery, Washington, 82, 85 & 87, Baumgartner Galleries Inc, Washington, 89, 91, 93, 95 & 98, Univ NC, Chapel Hill, 94 & Baumgartner Gallery, NY, 2000, Fusebox, Washington 02, 03 & 05, Kiang Gallery, Atlanta, 04, Webster Univ, St Louis, Mo, 07; Wash Show, Corcoran Gallery Art, Washington, DC, 85; two-person show, Va Mus Fine Arts, Richmond, 86; Washington/Moscow Art Exchange, Tretyakoff State Mus, Russia, 90; Abstract Icons, Roanoke Mus Fine Arts, Va, 92; WPA at the Hemicycle, Corcoran Gallery Art, Washington, DC, 92; The Far Light, Fine Arts Gallery, Millersville Univ, Pa, 94; Art Sites 96, WPA/Corcoran Cent Armature Annex, 96; Fine Arts Ctr, Provincetown, Mass, 96; Remote Sensing, Cheryl Numark Gallery, Washington, DC, 97; Chance and Necessity, Md Art Place, Baltimore, 97; Kiang Gallery, Atlanta, 2000; Broadway Gallery, NY, 2005; Gallery Siano, Philadelphia, Pa, 2006; Amman Gallery, Jordon, 2006; James Backas Gallery, Md State Arts Coun, Baltimore, Md, 2007, 08; Townson Univ, Baltimore, Md, 2008; Lump Gallery, Raleigh, NC, 2009. *Pos:* Active vis artist, lecturer, and juror at academic institutions and museums throughout the region and across the country. *Teaching:* With Dept Art, Univ Md, College Park, 78-, prof painting and drawing, chair, currently. *Awards:* First Prize, Md Biennial, Baltimore Mus Art, 83; Artist's Fel, Md State Arts Coun, 81, 87, 98 & 02; First Prize, McLean Proj Arts, Va. *Bibliog:* Ferdinand Protzman (auth), City Focus, Art News, 11/97; JoAnna Shaw-Eagle (auth), WC Richardson, Wash Times, 3/22/98; Ferdinand Protzman (auth), WC Richardson, Wash Post, 4/2/98; Ingrid Perez (auth), WC Richardson, ArtNews, 11/2000; Jonathan Gilmore (auth) WC Richardson, Art in America 5/01; Glen Dixon (auth), Swing Shift, Wash City Paper, 6/03. *Mem:* Wash Proj Arts; Md Art Place; Sch 33 Art Ctr, Baltimore; CAA. *Media:* Oil, Alkyd. *Res:* Contemporary Art. *Specialty:* Contemporary Art. *Interests:* Contemporary Art Theory, mathematics, physics, music, non-western art. *Publ:* Substance and Doubt (catalog essay), Recent Paintings, Proj Space, WPA/Corcoran, Washington, DC, 98; Enter Decatur Blue (catalog essay), DB Sides, The Wardhouse, Wash, 02. *Dealer:* Fusebox 1412 14th St NW Washington DC, formerly; Kiang Gallery 1545 Peachtree St NE Atlanta GA, formerly; G Fine Arts 1515 14th St NW Washington DC; Baumgartner Gallery, DC and NY, formerly. *Mailing Add:* University of Maryland Department of Art m2319 Art/Sociology Building College Park MD 20742

RICHMOND, REBEKAH
PRINTMAKER, PAINTER

b Ashland, Ky. *Study:* Ringling Sch Art; Univ Ky, Lexington; Art Inst Pittsburgh. *Work:* Coos Art Mus, Coos Bay, Ore; Mus Prints & Printmaking, New York; Nat Arts Club, New York; Libr Cong, Washington, DC. *Comn:* Presentation Print, Print Club Albany, 76-77. *Exhib:* Ann Artists Salon, Okla Mus Fine Art, 75 & 77; solo exhib, Albany Inst Hist & Art, 77; April Salon, Springville Mus Art, Utah, 77-78, 80 & 82; Colorprint USA, Tex Tech Univ, 80; Audubon Artists Ann, Nat Arts Club, New York, 81; 3rd Brit Int Miniature Exhib, 97; Irish Int Print Exhib, 98. *Awards:* Gold Medal Hon, Acad Artists Asn, Mass, 78-79; Anna Hyatt Huntington Bronze Medal, Catharine Lorillard Wolfe Art Club, 79; Hugh P Botts Award, Salmagundi Club, 92. *Mem:* Salmagundi Club; Hudson Valley Art Asn; Soc Am Graphic Artists; Am Artists Prof League; Acad Artists Asn. *Media:* Etching, Oils. *Dealer:* Kerwin Galleries 1107 California Dr Burlingame CA 94010. *Mailing Add:* PO Box 468 Ashland KY 41105-0468

RICHTER, HANK
PAINTER, SCULPTOR

b Cleveland, Ohio, Oct 10, 1928. *Study:* Philadelphia Mus Sch of Art. *Work:* DeGrazia-Gonzales Cult Ctr & Mus, Casa Grande, Ariz; Valley Nat Bank Collection, Phoenix; First Nat Bank Collection, Tucson, Ariz; Read Mullan's Gallery Western Art, Ariz State Univ; Principia Coll, Elsah, Ill; Wells Fargo Bank, Tucson, Ariz; City Art Collections, Glendale, Ariz & Peoria, Ariz; and others. *Comn:* Ted DeGrazia portrait (ltd edition pewter bas-relief plate). *Exhib:* San Dimas Am Indian & Cowboy Artists Soc Show, Calif, 77-93; First Fed Savings & Loan Traveling Exhib; Western Gallery, 1st Interstate Bank, Tucson, Ariz; Gene Autry Mus Western Heritage, 95-96; Mountain Oyster Club Ann; and others. *Pos:* Owner, Hank Richter Studio. *Teaching:* Student instr anat, Philadelphia Mus Sch Art, 49-50; instr creative design, Kachina Sch Art, Phoenix, 54-56; sculpture instr & drawing instr, Principia Coll, Elsah, Ill; instr pvt classes, currently. *Awards:* Gold Medal, Atlanta Film Festival, 69; Golden Eagle, CINE/USA, 69; Silver Medal, W/C Sandimas Art Festival, Calif, 2001, Gold Medal, 09. *Bibliog:* The West & Walter Bimson, Univ Ariz Press, 72; Pat Broder (auth), Bronzes of the American West, Abrams, 75; Lil Rhodes (auth), A man and his art, Southwest Art, 78. *Mem:* Am Indian & Cowboy Artists Soc (past pres); Art Group 12, Payson, Ariz; Artists of Renown; Peoria Fine Art Assoc, Ariz; Oil Painters Am. *Media:* Oil, Watercolor, Acrylic; Graphite, Pastel. *Res:* Artist Morgue from 1960. *Specialty:* Oils, watercolors of ranch life giclees ltd ed prints. *Interests:* Reading-illustrations (book). *Publ:* auth, illustrator, Look Look Im Writing a Book, Little Ray of Light, Little Red Truck; Cartooning Made Easy (how-to book). *Dealer:* Espritdecor 5533 N 7th St Phoenix AZ 85014; Metamorphosis Gallery Patagonia AZ. *Mailing Add:* 1221 W Carol Ann Way Phoenix AZ 85023-4497

RICO-GUTIERREZ, LUIS
ARCHITECT, EDUCATOR, ADMINISTRATOR

Study: Instituto Tecnologico y de Estudios Supenores de Monterrey, Queretaro, Mexico, Bachelor's in Architecture, 1986; Fundacion Rafael Leoz, Madrid, Spain, Graduate Degree, 1988; Carnegie Mellon Univ, Pittsburgh, Pa, Master's in building performance, 1997. *Teaching:* Dean, design administration, prof architecture, Iowa State Univ, Col of Design, currently. *Mailing Add:* Dean's Office Iowa State Univ 134 College of Design Ames IA 50011

RIDDLE, JOHN THOMAS, JR
SCULPTOR, PAINTER

b Los Angeles, Calif, Mar 18, 1933. *Study:* Los Angeles City Col, AA, 60; Los Angeles State Col, BA, 66; Calif State Univ, MA, 73. *Work:* High Mus Art, Atlanta, Ga; Golden State Mutual Life Inst Co, Calif State Univ, Los Angeles; Oakland Mus, Calif; Albany Mus Art, Ga. *Comn:* Murals, Bank of Am (2 br), Los Angeles, 70; The Operation (welded steel), Los Angeles Co Mental Health Clinic, 72; relig murals, Shrine of Black Madonna, Atlanta, 74; Expelled Because of Their Color (bronze), State of Ga, Atlanta, 77; Spirit Bench 1, City of Atlanta, 78; Painted, Welded, Sculpture Walls, Mid-Town Marta Sta, Atlanta, Ga. *Exhib:* Black Artists, Oakland Mus, Calif, 73; Calif Artists, Calif State Univ, Sacramento, 74; Artists in Ga, High Mus Art, Atlanta, 75-80; Calif Artists, the Black Experience, State Capitol, Sacramento, Calif, 76; Black Artists S, Huntsville Mus Art, Ala, 78; 8th Ann Art Festival, Martinique, WI, Port de France, 79; Calif African-Am Mus, Los Angeles, 89; William Grant Still Gallery, Los Angeles, Calif, 92. *Pos:* Dir, Neighborhood Arts Ctr, Inc, Atlanta, 75-81. *Teaching:* Instr ceramics & sculpture, Pub Schs, Los Angeles & Beverly Hills, Calif, 66-73; asst prof painting, Spelman Col, Atlanta, 79-80; asst dir, Atlanta Civic Ctr, 84-92. *Awards:* Emmy Award, TV Acad Arts & Sci, 71; Ga Gov Award Visual Art, 81. *Bibliog:* Lewis Productions, Three artists, Lewis, Riddle, Pajaud, 68; Larry Stuart (auth), Renaissance in black, KNBC, 10/71; Lewis & Waddy (coauth), Black Artists on Art, 2 vols, Contemp Crafts, 72. *Mem:* Black Artists Atlanta; Ga Coun for Arts; Gov Artist-in-Schs; Atlanta Urban Design Comn, 90-91. *Publ:* Contribr, Prints by American Negro Artists, Cult Exchange Ctr, 67; Black Artists on Art, 2 vols, Contemp Crafts, 71; Art: African American, Harcourt-Brace, 78. *Dealer:* Camille Love 3230 Kingsdale Dr SW Atlanta GA 30311. *Mailing Add:* 3034 Rebecca Dr SW Atlanta GA 30311-1920

RIDER BERRY, TARAH J
PHOTOGRAPHER, INSTRUCTOR

b New York, NY, 1963. *Study:* Ariz State Univ, BA (art hist). *Work:* Scottsdale Mus Contemp Art & Scottsdale Cult Coun; Phoenix Arts Comn & PMH Found, Phoenix. *Comn:* Picture This (photographic portfolio), Phoenix Arts Comn, 95 & 98; Documentary, Scottsdale Cult Coun, 96; Animal Rites, Ariz Comn Arts, 97. *Exhib:* I Can Fly: Photographs by Tarah Rider Berry (with catalog), Scottsdale Ctr Arts, 96; Annual Collectors Exhibition, Houston Ctr Photog, 96; Souls, AP Tell Gallery, Phoenix, 97; Tucson Biennial, Tucson Mus Art, 97; My Life: Photographs of Children Living in Phoenix, Ariz Comm Arts Traveling Exhib, 97-98; Another Arizona, Nelson Art Mus, Ariz State Univ, Tempe, 98; Building for the Millennium, Scottsdale Mus Contemp Art, 98. *Teaching:* Instr photog, Pub Art Projs City of Phoenix, 95 & 98. *Awards:* Visual Arts Grant, Ariz Comm Arts, 96 & Artist Proj Grant, 97; Flow Fund Grant, Rockefeller Found, 98. *Bibliog:* Gia Cobb (auth), By the people, for the people, Ariz Repub, 9/14/97; Richard Nilsen (auth), The jury is in, Arizona State University exhibit, Ariz Repub, 3/29/98. *Mailing Add:* 6212 S 8th Pl Phoenix AZ 85040

RIDLON, JAMES A
SCULPTOR, ASSEMBLAGE ARTIST
b Nyack, NY, July 11, 1934. *Study:* Syracuse Univ, BA, 57, MFA, 65; San Francisco State Col, 58-59. *Work:* Munson-Williams-Proctor Inst, Utica, NY; Julliard Sch, NY; Rochester Mem Gallery, NY; Everson Mus, Syracuse, NY; Smithsonian Inst, Washington; and others. *Comn:* Assemblage, ABC, NY, 58; Outland Trophy, Football Writers Asn Am, 88; Disneyland, 89; HSE, 90. *Exhib:* New Paintings, Everson Mus Art, 74; Solo retrospective, Logan Alexander Ctr Creative Arts, Concord Coll, 75; Lubin House Gallery, NY, 77; Herbert F Johnson Mus, Cornell Univ, Ithaca, NY, 77; Canton Art Inst, Canton, Ohio, 89; and others. *Pos:* Chmn, CORE Dept, Syracuse Univ, 82-. *Teaching:* Prof sculpture & studio arts, Syracuse Univ, 68-74, prof sculpture & synaesthetic educ, 74-81, prof, Sch Art Design, 82-. *Awards:* Purchase Prize, 32nd Ann Exhib, Munson-Williams-Proctor Inst, 68; First Prize in Sculpture, 10th Ann Westchester Art Soc Exhib, 70; First Prize Sculpture, NY State Fair, 92; and others. *Publ:* Contribr, Synaesthetic Education, Syracuse Univ, 71; auth, Synaesthetic education as a basis for symbolic expression, Humanities J, 5/73; co-producer & dir, Icons and Eclecticism (film), Syracuse Univ, 81; producer & dir, Artist-Athlete (film), Syracuse Univ, 82; co-producer & dir, The Wonder of Friction (film), Syracuse Univ, 83. *Dealer:* Oxford Gallery 267 Oxford Rochester NY 14607. *Mailing Add:* 4468 E Lake Rd Cazenovia NY 13035

RIEBER, RUTH B
PRINTMAKER, PAINTER
b New York, NY, Mar 9, 1924. *Study:* New York Univ, BS, 45; Art Students League, 47; Columbia Univ, MFA, 48. *Work:* Westinghouse Electric, Pittsburgh, Pa; Pub Serv Electric & Gas Co, Newark, NJ; State NJ Dept Treasury, Trenton; Newark Teachers Union, NJ; Jane Voorhees Zimmerli Art Mus, Rutgers, NJ; and others. *Exhib:* NJ Invitational Graphics, Morris Mus Art & Sci, 80; Nat Asn Women Artists Centennial Celebration (juried, travel), India, 89; solo exhibs, Insights, Saint Peters Church Gallery, NY, 87, Relief Print, Johnson and Johnson World Hq, New Brunswick, NJ, 90 & Works on Paper, Int Church Ctr, NY, 91; Hudson River Open 91, Hudson River Mus, Yonkers, NY, 91; SUNNY Westchester Community Col, NY, 96. *Teaching:* Teacher art, Bd Educ, NY, 46-49; art therapist, Teaneck Sch System Spec Educ, NJ, 68-74; printmaker specialist, Project Impact Arts in Educ Found, NJ, 85-92. *Awards:* Medal of Honor, Catharine Lorillard Wolfe Art Club, 83, 84, 86, 94, 95 & 97; Graphics Award, Nat Asn Women Artists, Janet Turner, 84; Purchase Award, Nat Print 86 Exhib, Trenton State Col, 86 & 96; and others. *Bibliog:* Dori Halasz (auth), A Show in Trenton Survey's States Art, NY Sunday; Eileen Watkins (auth), Shedding Artistic Light on Women's Issues, The Star Ledger, 3/5/88; Vivian Raynor(auth), Well Known Artists Join the Crowd at NY Art Gallery Auction, NY Times, 6/21/92. *Mem:* Nat Asn Women Artists; Print Coun NJ; Painting Affiliates, NJ; Audubon Artists; Catharine Lorillard Wolfe Art Club; NY Soc Women Artists. *Media:* Woodcut. *Publ:* Collaborative Artist Book Project, Int Printed ed, ed VIII, 96, ed IV, 97 & 98. *Mailing Add:* 140 Cedar St Lexington MA 02421-5518

RIEGLE, ROBERT MACK
ART DEALER, COLLECTOR
b Sedan, Kans, Nov 11, 1924. *Study:* Tex A&M Univ, College Station, 43; Univ Kans, Lawrence, BS (archit), 50. *Pos:* Dir, Wichita Gallery Fine Art, currently. *Specialty:* Original fine paintings and sculpture; realism, impressionism and expressionism. *Collection:* Contemporary realists and impressionists of the southwest; oils, watercolors and pastels; bronze sculpture. *Mailing Add:* Wichita Gallery of Fine Art 437 Lexington Rd Wichita KS 67218

RIES, MARTIN
PAINTER, PRINTMAKER
b Washington, DC, Dec 26, 1926. *Study:* Corcoran Gallery Art, 40-44; Am Univ, with William Calfee, Jack Tworkov & Leo Steppat, BA, 50; Hunter Col, MA, 68, with Leo Steinberg, William Rubin, Ad Reinhardt & E C Goossen; Post Grad Mus Admin with Everett Ellin, Wilder Green, and James Elliot, 1968. *Work:* Pace Univ Mus; Riverside Mus Collection, Rose Art Mus, Brandeis Univ; Corcoran Mus, Washington,; NY Pub Libr Print Collection; Netherlands Consulate; Housatonic Mus, Bridgeport, Conn; Rose Art Mus, Brandeis Univ; Manhattan Psychiat Ctr, Ward's Island, NY; William Calfee Found, Md; Rabobank of the Netherlands, Chicago; Watkins Gallery, Am Univ. *Exhib:* Corcoran Gallery Art, 52; Mus Mod Art, 56; Paul Gallery, Tokyo, Japan, 68; Verfeil, France, 73; Stamford Mus, Conn, 87; Inst Contemp Art, London, 88; Raja Idris Gallery, Melbourne, Australia, 89; Homages, Images, Juxtapositions, 2/20 Gallery, NY, 96; Watkins Gallery, American Univ Washington, DC, 2000; Retrospective: Karpeles Mus, Newburgh, NY, 2002; Visual Diversities, Katoneh Museum Artists Asn, Mt Kisco, NY; Solo Exhibs: Mystic Landscapes: Intuitions of an Order, Hammond Mus, North Salem, NY; others. *Pos:* Asst dir pub rels, Nat Cong Comt, 51; asst dir, Hudson River Mus, Yonkers, NY, 57-67; adv, Westchester Cult Ctr, 65-67; contrib ed, Arts Mag; art ed, Greenwich Village News; bd dir, Artists Representing Environ Art; juror Inst Int Educ, J William Fulbright Art Scholarships, UN. *Teaching:* Instr medieval art hist, Marymount Col, 59; instr mod art hist, Hunter Col, 63-67; prof hist art, color theory, printmaking, drawing & painting, Long Island Univ, 68-94. *Awards:* Honorable Mention, 52nd Nat Soc Arts & Lett Award, Corcoran Gallery Art; Critics Choice, Whyte Gallery, 57; Yaddo Fel; Research-Time Award, Long Island Univ. *Bibliog:* Masters & Houston, Psychedelic Art, Grove Press, NY, 68; C Dantzic (auth), Design Dimensions, Prentice-Hall, NJ; G. Battcock (ed), The New Art, Dutton Co, NY, 1965; Robert C Morgan (auth), The Interior Landscape and the Value of Mysticism: Paintings by Martin Ries, 2007; Into the Light: Paintings by Vivian Tsao, Nat Mus History. *Mem:* Asn Int des Critques d'Art, Am Sect; Artists Equity Asn; Am Soc Contemp Artists; Katonah Mus Art Asn. *Media:* Acrylic, Silk Screen Printing. *Res:* Braque's Atelier and the Symbolic Bird; Abstract-Perspectivism of John Hultberg; Andre Masson: Surrealism and its Discontents; Willem de Kooning's Asheville; Gorky's Centauromachia: Betrothal and Betrayal. *Interests:* classical music, Greco-Roman culture. *Publ:* Endowments for Great Society, Art Voices Mag, 65 & New Art: Anthology, Dutton, 66; Picasso and the Myth of the Minotaur, Art J, winter 72-73, portion reprinted in: Picasso in Perspective, Prentice Hall, 75; Environmental Art: Working with Elements, video produced by AREA; Braque's ateliers and the symbolic bird, J Aesthetic Educ, summer 95; US ed, Irony & Rude Questions, Nat Writers Union; Art research & visuals for TV documentary, The Feuding Tombs of Christopher Columbus, Newman Assocs, Washington, 92; The Ecstasy of Discontent, Art e Dossier, Florence, Italy, 4/2002; Andre Masson: Surrealism and His Discontents, Art Jour, 2002; numerous reviews, introductions to catalogs, gallery/artists news releases; De Kooning's Asheville & Zelda's Immolation, Art Crticism Journ, State Univ New York Stony Brook, 2005; John Hultberg's Abstract Perspectivism, Art Criticism Journ, State Univ New York Stony Brook, 2006; Gorky's Centauomachia: Betrothal & Betrayal, Art Criticism Journ, State Univ New York Stony Brook, 2007; Andre Masson: Surrealist, Survivor, Sage, Artandeducation.net, 2009; Gorky's Roofs, Goats, Letters & Documents, Art Criticism Jour, vol. 25, no 1&2, 2010. *Dealer:* Francesca Fine Arts 116 Duane St New York NY 10007; Blue Door Gallery 13 Riverdale Ave Yonkers NY 10701. *Mailing Add:* 36 Livingston Rd Scarsdale NY 10583

RIESS, LORE
PAINTER, PRINTMAKER
b Berlin, Ger; US citizen. *Study:* Art Acad, Contempora (Bauhaus Sch), Berlin; Sumi Drawing & Calligraphy, Tokyo; Art Students League. *Work:* Corcoran Gallery Art, Washington, DC; Tel Aviv Mus & Israel Mus, Jerusalem; US Embassy, Japan & Korea; pvt collections in US, Japan, Belg, Eng & Israel; AT&T; and others. *Comn:* Ed of etchings, Mickelson Gallery, Washington, DC, 71. *Exhib:* Solo exhibs, Old Jaffa Gallery, Israel, 70, 73, 75 & 79, Nora Art Gallery, Jerusalem, 71, 74 & 82, Jeanne Frank Gallery, NY, 78 & Park Village West, London, 79-80; Linden Galleries, NY, 81, Artist Studio, NY, 82, 85 & 90, Park West Gallery, London, Eng, 83, Lillian Heidenberg Gallery, NY, 84, Zack Schuster Gallery, Boca Raton, Fla, 85, 86 & 89. *Awards:* William McNulty Merit Award, Art Students League, 64; M J Kaplan Prize, Nat Asn Women Artists, 69; Gallery of Graphic Art Award, Int Miniature Print Exhib, 71. *Bibliog:* T Ichinose (auth), Colorful abstract oils by Lore Riess, Mainichi Daily News, 65; articles in Jerusalem Post, 7/70 & 3/71. *Media:* Acrylic, Pastel. *Dealer:* Margaret Lipworth, FL; Adler Arts Int Washington DC. *Mailing Add:* One Lincoln Plaza Apt 23B New York NY 10023

RIETH, SHERI FLECK
EDUCATOR, ADMINISTRATOR
Study: Univ of Kansas, BFA (drawing & painting); Memphis Col of Art, MFA (studio arts). *Collection Arranged:* Collections include Meridian Mus of Art, Mississippi, Mobile Mus of Art, Ala, Opryland Hotel Third Tennessee and Watkins Col of Art and Design, Nashville. *Pos:* Puppeteer, artist, Puck Players Puppet Theatre, Bloomington, Ind; mem State Bd of the Tennessee Asn of Crafts Artists; reader, Educational Testing Servicces Advance Placement Studio Arts; bd mem Number Inc. *Teaching:* Taught Watkins Inst of Art and Design, Nashville, Memphis Col of Art, & Univ Memphis; assoc Prof, chair, printmaking, Univ of Mississippi, currently. *Awards:* Artist's Fellowship, Mississippi Arts Commission. *Mem:* Southern Graphic Council; Southeastern Col Art Conference; Col Art Asn; Nat Mus of Women in the Arts. *Mailing Add:* University of Mississippi The Department of Art-116 Meek Hall PO Box 1848 University MS 38677

RIFKA, JUDY
PAINTER
b New York, NY, Sept 25, 1945. *Study:* NY Studio Sch, Cert, 67; Suny Empire Westbury, BA, 94; Adelphi Univ, MA, 95. *Work:* Boston Mus Fine Arts; NY Pub Libr; Eli Broad Family Found, Los Angeles; The Mint Mus, Charlotte, NC; Kemper Mus Contemp Art, Kans City, Mo. *Comn:* Bistro 110, Levy Corp & Doug Roth, Chicago; Bistro 100, Nations Bank Bldg, Levy Corp & Nations Bank, Charlotte, NC; Union Square Cafe, Daniel Meyer, NY, 86 & 04; Madison Square Garden, MSG Corp, NY, 89; Ericcson Stadium, Charlotte, NC, 96. *Exhib:* Biennial, Whitney Mus, NY, 75, 83; Documenta 7, Kassel, Ger, 82; Back to USA, Kunst Mus, Luzerne, 84; Borrowed Embellishments, Kansas City Art Inst, Kansas City, 87; Making Their Mark, Cincinnati, Denver, New Orleans Mus & Pa Acad, 89; The Future Now, Bass Mus, Miami, 89; Beyond the Pale, Irish Mus Modern Art, Dublin, 94; Grey Art Gallery, NY Univ, 2006; Berkeley Art Mus, 2006; Andy Warhol Mus, 2006. *Teaching:* asst prof, Hofstra Univ, 95-96. *Bibliog:* Joseph Masheck (auth), Modernities, Pa Univ Press, 93; Ann-Sargent Wooster (auth), Judy Rifka, Arts Mag, 91; Vincent Carducci (auth), Judy Rifka at Alley Culture, Art in Am, 98; Brooklyn Rail, Political Cartoons, 2004. *Mem:* Whitney Mus; Friend New Mus. *Media:* Oil. *Collection:* Metrop Mus Art, NY; NY Pub Libr. *Publ:* Auth/illusr, Judy Rifka's Polaroid Album of Premiere, Kunst Forum, 85; illusr, Opera of the Worms, Solo Press, 85; Making Their Mark, Cincinnati Art Mus, 89; illusr, A Still Small Voice, Delacorte, 2000. *Dealer:* C Hendricks Alley Culture PO Box 441261 Detroit Michigan 48244. *Mailing Add:* 53 Market St Apt 4B New York NY 10002

RIGBY, IDA KATHERINE
CRITIC, HISTORIAN
b Los Angeles, Calif, May 10, 1944. *Study:* Stanford Univ, BA, MA; Ecole des Beaux Arts, Tours, France; Univ Calif, Berkeley, MA, PhD (art hist), 74. *Teaching:* Asst prof mod art hist, Univ Montana, Missoula, spring 72; instr, Newcomb Col, Tulane Univ, New Orleans, 72-74; asst prof, Univ Victoria, BC, 74-76; prof mod & contemp art, San Diego State Univ, 76-. *Awards:* Kress Found Grant; Grant, Deutscher Akademischer Austauschdienst, Bonn. *Mem:* Coll Art Asn; Art Historians of Southern Calif. *Res:* German Expressionism; German Expressionist artists and politics; politics of opposition and official collaboration in Germany during the 1930's; art criticism. *Publ:* Auth, Karl Hofer, Garland Publ, 76; The Expressionist Artist and Revolution, 1918-1922 & Entartte Kunst, 1933-1938, In: German Expressionist Art: The Robert Gore Rifkind Collection, Univ Calif, Los Angeles Press, 77; Franz Marc's wartime

letters from the front, 1880-1916, Univ Calif Berkeley, 79; Wichner Collection, Long Beach Mus Art, 81; An Alle Kunstler War Revolution Weimar: German Expressionist Prints, Drawings, Posters and Periodicals for the Robert Gore Rifkind Foundation, San Diego State Univ Press, 83. *Mailing Add:* Sch Art Design & Art Hist San Diego State Univ San Diego CA 92182

RIGG, MARGARET R
ASSEMBLAGE ARTIST, CALLIGRAPHER
b Pittsburgh, Pa, Dec 14, 1929. *Study:* Carnegie-Mellon Univ, 45-50; Fla State Univ, BA, 51; Scarrett Col; Presby Sch, MA, 55; George Peabody Col; Chicago Art Inst, 63; painting with Edmund Lewandowski & Florence Kawa; design & theory with Mathias Goeritz; Chinese calligraphy with Tsutomu Yoshida, Kim Kee-Sung, Kim Hahn & Tennyson Chang; Am calligraphy with Corita Kent & Jan Steward; Brit calligraphy with George L Thompson. *Work:* Tenn Collection, Smithsonian Inst; Yamada Gallery, Kyoto, Japan; Turku Univ Mus, Finland; NH Mus, Manchester; Korea Fulbright House, Seoul. *Comn:* Stained glass windows, Mexico City Nat Cathedral, 61; stained glass window, communion table, lectern & celtic cross, Univ NC, Chapel Hill, 62; calligraphy mural, Experiment House, Vere, Jamaica; calligraphy, CBS-TV News, 69 & 71; calligraphy letterhead & gates to campus, Eckerd Col, 72. *Exhib:* Solo shows, calligraphy, Hannover, Ger, 84, calligraphy & paintings, Montreal, NC, 85, calligraphy, Buenos Aires, Argentina & Salvador, Bahia, Brazil, 86 & calligraphy, Cult Olympics, Seoul, Korea, 87; calligraphy, Tokyo, Japan, 88, Galeria Pequena, St Petersburg, Fla, 90; Gararia Pequena, St Petersburg, Fla, 91; Aura group, Philadelphia, Pa, 92; St Petersburg visual artists, Univ SFla, 92; and others. *Pos:* Art dir, Bd Publ, Fla State Univ, 51-53; owner & publ, Possum Press; art ed, Motive Mag, Nashville, Tenn, 54-65. *Teaching:* Artist-in-residence, Fla Presby Col, 65-67; prof visual art, Eckerd Col, 67-; dir, Elliot Teaching Gallery, Eckerd Col, 81-88. *Awards:* Stone Lectr, Princeton Seminary, Princeton, NJ, 71; Fulbright-Hays Sr Res Grant in Chinese Calligraphy, Korea, 72. *Bibliog:* Contribr, Amenu Alphabet Workbook, 89; The Cherry Tree Alphabet, 94; A SHAHN Alphabet Workbook, 95; The Cherry Tree Alphabet, 98. *Mem:* Int Soc Women Calligraphers; Soc Italic Handwriting; Nashville Artist Guild (pres, 63-64); Fla Artist Group, Inc; St Petersburg Soc Scribes (founder & 1st pres, 78-); Soc Arts, Religion & Contemp Cult (ARC), NY. *Media:* Acrylic, Mixed Media; Pen & Ink, Markers, Calligraphy. *Interests:* Go (Chinese board game), Chess, Go Moku. *Publ:* Pro-Nica, logo & art, Religious Soc Friends (Quakers) (relief to Nicaragua), 89; front cover logo design, Human Quest Mag, 90. *Dealer:* Carol Ridge St Petersburg Fla

RIGGIO, LOUISE & LEONARD
BOOK DEALER, COLLECTOR
b 1941. *Hon Degrees:* Baruch Coll CUNY, PhD; Bentley Coll, PhD. *Pos:* Merchandise mgr, NY Univ Bookstore, New York, 1962-65; pres, chief exec officer & bd dirs, Barnes & Noble Bookstores, Inc, 1965-86; founder, chief exec officer, pres, and treas, Barnes & Noble Inc, New York, 1986-2002, chmn bd, 1986-; chmn bd & principle beneficial owner, Software Etc Stores Inc, Minneapolis, MBS Textbook Exchange Inc, Columbia, Mo; chmn bd, Dia Art Found, 1998-2006, bd mem, 2006-; bd dirs, Childrens Defense Fund, Black Childrens Community Crusade, Brooklyn Tech Found, Italian Am Found. *Awards:* Recipient Ellis Island Medal of Honor, Frederick Douglas Medallion, Americanism award, Anti-Defamation League, 2002; Named one of Top 200 Collectors, ARTnews mag, 2003-13; Named to Acad of Distinguished Entrepreneurs, Babson Coll, Retailing Hall of Fame, Tex Agr & Mechanical Univ, 2005. *Collection:* Modern and contemporary art. *Mailing Add:* Barnes & Noble Inc 122 5th Ave 4th Fl New York NY 10011-5605

RILEY, BARBRA BAYNE
PHOTOGRAPHER, EDUCATOR
b Brooklyn, NY, Dec 20, 1949. *Study:* Sch Visual Arts, New York, cert (fine arts), 70; Calif State Univ, Sacramento, BA, 72, MA, 74. *Work:* Dallas Mus Art; Mus Fine Art, Houston; Laguna Beach Mus Art; Chase Manhattan Bank, NY; Atlantic Richfield Co. *Comn:* Photographers Portray the Family, Women & Their Work, Nat Endowment Arts, Austin, Tex, 81; 24 photographs, Corpus Christi Nat Bank, 81; Texas Commerce Bank, Corpus Christi. *Exhib:* Solo exhib, Art Mus STex, Corpus Christi, 79; Contemp Photog as Phantasy, Santa Barbara Mus Art, Calif, 82; Texas Landscape 1900-1986, Mus Fine Arts, Houston, 86; Houston Ctr for Photog, 86; Texas Women, Nat Mus Women in Arts, Washington, DC, 88; 150 Yrs of Photog, Laguna Gloria Art Mus, Austin, Tex, 89. *Collection Arranged:* Return to Beyond the Valley of Photography, Weil Gallery, Corpus Christi State Univ, 81; Touched by Man--Landscape Photographs from Around the World, Weil Gallery, Corpus Christi State Univ, 90. *Teaching:* From asst prof to prof photog & design, Corpus Christi State Univ, Tex, 82-. *Bibliog:* Ellen Wallenstein (auth), Ties that bind, Artweek, 12/81; Suzanne Winkler (auth), Where's the family, Tex Monthly, 1/82. *Mem:* Tex Photog Soc; Houston Ctr for Photog; Art Mus S Tex (bd trustees). *Media:* Silver Prints, Non-Silver Processes. *Dealer:* Carrington/Gallagher 7979 Broadway San Antonio, TX 78209. *Mailing Add:* 327 Katherine Corpus Christi TX 78404

RILEY, BRIDGET LOUISE
PAINTER
b London, Apr 24, 1931. *Study:* Goldsmith's Sch Art, London, 49-52; Royal Coll Art, 52-55; Ulster Univ, 86. *Hon Degrees:* Manchester Univ, Dlit (hon), 76. *Pos:* With, J Walter Thomspon, London, 58-59; trustee, Nat Gallery London, 81-88. *Teaching:* Part time teacher, Hornsey Col Art, London, 60-61. *Awards:* AOCA critics prize John Moores Exhib, Liverpool, 63; travel bursary, 64; Int Prize, Painting XXXIV Venice Biennale, 68; Ohara Mus Prize, Tokyo Print Biennale, 72; Decorated comdr; Order Brit Empire; Recipient Peter Stuyvesant Found; City of Siegen's Rubens prize, 2012. *Publ:* auth, Paintings from the 60's & 70's, London, Serpentine Gallery, 99; auth, Selected Paintings 1961-1999 (Dusseldorf: Kunstverein fur die Rheinlande und Westfalen; Ostfildern: Cantz Publishers, 99); auth, Works 1961-1998 (Kendal, Cumbria: Abbot Hall Art Gallery & Mus, 98); auth, Dialogues on Art (London: Zwemmer, 95). *Mailing Add:* Pace Wildenstein Galleries 32 E 57th St 2nd fl New York NY 10022

RILEY, DUKE
INSTALLATION ARTIST, SCULPTOR
Study: RI Sch Design, BFA (painting), Providence, 1995; Pratt Inst, MFA (sculptor), Brooklyn, 2006. *Exhib:* Bernard Toale Gallery, Boston, 1996; C Francis Gallery, Providence, RI, 1999; Of Earth and Sky, Am Mus Natural Hist, New York, 2000; Night Swimming, State of Art Gallery, Brooklyn, 2001; National Arts Club, New York, 2002; Book, Weir Space, Belfast, 2004; T&AIV, GV/AS Gallery, Brooklyn, 2004; Benefit Show, Robert Miller Gallery, NY, 2004; Magnan Projects, New York, 2005; We Could Have Invited Everyone, Andrew Krepps Gallery, NY, 2005; A Knock At The Door, Lower Manhattan Cult Coun, 2005; Pulse Miami Contemp Art Fair, 2006-07; Pulse New York Contemp Art Fair, 2007-08; Volta 4, Magnan Projects, Basel, Switzerland, 2008; Rent Control: NYC Documented and Imagined, The Maysles Inst, Harlem, NY, 2009; Chelsea Visits Havana, Havana Biennial, Museo de Bellas Artes, 2009; Seaworthy, Corridor Gallery, Brooklyn, 2009; solo exhibs, Climate 8, New York, 2001, Sarah Lawrence Coll, NY, 2005, Magnan Projects, NY, 2006, Pulse Armory, New York, 2006, White Box, New York, 2006, Contemp Art Fair, New York, 2007, Havana Biennial, 2009. *Pos:* Tattoo artist, East River Tattoo, Brooklyn. *Awards:* Belfast Arts and Bus Partners Found Grant, 2003; Lagenside Develop Corp Grant, 2004; Ind Proj Grant, Artist Space, 2005; Art Matters Found Grant, 2009. *Dealer:* Magnan Projects 521 West 26th St New York NY 10001

RILEY, ENRICO
PAINTER
b Waterbury, Connecticut, 1973. *Study:* Dartmouth Coll, BA (Visual Studies), 1995; Yale Univ, MFA, 1998; Vt Studio Ctr, Resident, 2000 & 2001. *Exhib:* Solo exhibs include Karl Drerup Art Gallery, Plymouth, NH, 2004, Pageant Gallery, Philadelphia, 2005; group exhibs include Invitational Exhib Visual Arts, AAAL, New York, 2004; Rhythmic Brushwork, Mus Nat Ctr Afro-Am Artists, Roxbury, Mass, 2005; The Grid, Reeves Contemp, New York, 2006; Color as Structure: Structure as Color, Lori Bookstein Fine Art, New York, 2007. *Teaching:* Sr Lectr Studio Art, Dartmouth Univ, Hanover, NH. *Awards:* Purchase Prize, AAAL, 2004; John Simon Guggenheim Mem Found Fel, 2008. *Media:* Acrylic, Oil

RILEY, PHILIP DUKE
PAINTER
b Mass. *Study:* RI Sch Design, BFA, 95; Pratt Inst, MFA, 2006. *Work:* Brooklyn Mus Art, New York; Queens Mus Art, New York; Cleveland Mus Contemp Art, Ohio; Toledo Mus Art, Ohio; Jane Voorhees Zimmerli Art Mus Rutgers Univ, New Brunswick, NJ. *Comn:* MTA Arts Comm Subway Site-Specific Work, MTA, New York, 2008. *Exhib:* Emergency Room, PS 1 Ctr Contemp Art, New York, 2007; Grow Your Own, Palais de Tokyo, Paris, 2007; Chelsea Visits Havana: Havana Biennial Mus de Bellas Artes, Havana, Cuba, 2009; Those Who Are About to Die Salute You, Queens Mus Art, New York, 2009; An Invitation to Lubber Land, Clveland Mus Contemp Art, Ohio, 2010; Bienal do Mercosul, Porto Alegre, Brazil, 2011. *Awards:* Grad Acad Achievement Award, Pratt Inst, 2005; Launch Pad, Those Who Are About to Die Salute You, Queens Mus Art, 2009; Art Matters, 2009; AICA Award, 2nd Pl Best Project in a Public Space, Duke: Riley: Those About to Die Salute You, 2011. *Bibliog:* Eleanor Heartney (auth), Duke Riley: After the Battle of Brooklyn, Magnan Proj, 2007; Randy Kennedy (auth), An Artist & His Sub Surrender in Brooklyn, NY Times, 8/4/2007; Brian Boucher (auth), Duke of Hazards, Art in Am, 11/2009; Jerry Saltz, The Best Art in New York, NY Mag, 12/23/2009; Ann Landi, Artists to Watch: Maritime Mischief, ArtNews, 2/2010. *Dealer:* Magnan Metz Gallery 521 West 26th St New York NY 10001

RILEY, SARAH A
PAINTER, PRINTMAKER
b Richmond, Va, July 1, 1947. *Study:* Tyler Sch Art, Rome; Va Commonwealth Univ, BFA; Univ Mo, Columbia, 77, MFA, 82. *Work:* Chesapeake & Pacific Telephone Co; Springfield Art Mus, Mo; Vivian & Gordon Gilkey Ctr Graphic Arts, Portland, Ore; Air Touch Communications, DC, 82. *Comn:* Painting, Univ Mo Hosp & Clinics, 83. *Exhib:* Va Mus Fine Arts Next Juried Show, 83; Watercolor USA, Springfield Art Mus, Mo, 83 & 88; 2nd Nat Small Print & Drawing Exhib, Cobleskill, NY, 84; Solo exhibs, Wichita State Univ, 85 & Leedy-Voulkes Gallery, Kansas City, Mo, 90; Mid-Four Ann Juried Exhib, Nelson Atkins Mus, Kansas City, 87; Greater Midwest Int, Warrensburg, Md, 96; Ceres Gallery, New York, 2009; Schoolhouse Gallery, Provincetown, Mass, 2009; New Media Exhib, Provincetown Art Asn & Mus, 2010; New Viridian Artists & Affiliates Exhib, 2011; Viridian Affiliate Artists, Meridian Gallery, NY, 2012. *Collection Arranged:* Viridian Gallery exhib, Fountain St Gallery, Mo, 2006. *Pos:* Dir, Davis Art Gallery, Stephen's Col, Columbia, Mo, 83-94; dir, Fountain St Gallery, Cape Girardeau, Mo, 2005-2007. *Teaching:* Prof drawing & painting, Stephens Col, 82-94, actg head art dept, 85-86, prog dir art area, 86-94; prof & chairperson, SE Mo State, 94-2000; head printmaker, Southeast Mo State Univ, 2001-. *Awards:* Purchase Award, Springfield Mus Art, 88; 1st Place Award, 47th Spiva Ann Competition, Spiva Art Ctr, Joplin, Mo, 97; and others. *Bibliog:* Donald Hoffman (auth), article, Kansas City Star, 6/20/82; article, New York Art Rev, 88. *Mem:* Watercolor USA Hon Soc; assoc mem, Kans Watercolor Soc; Southern Graphics Coun; MAPC. *Media:* Drawing, Paint, Printmaking. *Publ:* Charlottesville First Folio, 71; Practical Mixed Media Printmaking Techniques, A & C Black, 2012. *Dealer:* Sherry Leedy Contemp Art 1919 Wyandotte Kansas City MO 64111; Viridian Artists NYC. *Mailing Add:* 1105 Bella Vista Dr Jackson MO 63755

RILEY, TERENCE
MUSEUM DIRECTOR, ARCHITECT
Study: Univ Notre Dame, BA (archit), 78; Columba Univ, MA (archit and urban planning). *Collection Arranged:* Cur, Paul Nelson: Filter of Reason, Arthur Ross Archit Galleries, Columbia Univ, 89; Light Construction; The Un-Private House; Mies in Am, 2001; On-Site: New Architecture in Spain, 2006. *Pos:* Partner, Keenen/Riley Architects, currently; dir, Arthur Ross Archit Galleries, Columbia Univ, until 91; cur

dept archit and design, Mus Modern Art, NY, 91, chief cur, 92-2002, staff liaison to architect selection comt, Philip Johnson chief cur archit and design, 2002-2006; dir, Miami Art Mus, Fla, 2006-2009; trustee, Fundació Mies van der Rohe, Barcelona, Spain, currently; mem adv bd, Parsons Grad Sch Design, currently. *Teaching:* Prof, Harvard Univ & Columbia Univ. *Mem:* Am Inst Architects. *Publ:* Contribr articles to prof jour. *Mailing Add:* 508 W 26th St #9A New York NY 10001

RINDFLEISCH, JAN
DIRECTOR, CURATOR
Study: Purdue Univ, BS, 62, San Jose State Univ, MFA, 79; Mus Mgt Inst, J Paul Getty Trust, 89. *Collection Arranged:* Art Collectors in and Around Silicon Valley, 4/85; Art of the Refugee Experience, 3/88; Drawing from Experience: Artists over Fifty, 2/90. *Pos:* Dir, Euphrat Gallery, De Anza Col, Cupertino, Calif, 79-. *Teaching:* Instr studio art/art hist, De Anza Col, Cuperinto, Calif, 79-85. *Awards:* Asian Heritage Coun Arts Award, 88; Woman Achievement, Santa Clara Co, 89. *Bibliog:* Cordell Koland (auth), Euphrat Gallery fights cultural deprivation in the valley, Bus J, 3/25/85; Theresa Hong Bailar (auth), Focus on Jan Rindfleisch, Silhouette Mag, 4/89; Eric Reyes (auth), A Room of One's Art, Metro, 4/90. *Mem:* Am Asn Mus; Calif Confederation Arts; Western Mus Conf; Comt Arts Policy, Santa Clara Co (comt mem, 85-); Arts Coun Santa Clara Co (bd mem, 88-). *Publ:* Auth, Art, Religion, Spirituality, Euphrat Gallery, 82; Art Collectors in and Around Silicon Valley, Euphrat Gallery, 85; Content: Contemporary Issues, Euphrat Gallery, 86; Art of the Refugee Experience, Euphrat Gallery, 88. *Mailing Add:* Euphrat Mus Art De Anza Col 21250 Stevens Creek Blvd Cupertino CA 95014

RINEHART, MICHAEL
EDITOR
b Miami, Fla, Dec 27, 1934. *Study:* Harvard Univ, BA, 56; Courtauld Inst, Univ London, 57-59. *Pos:* Ed-in-chief, BHA Bibliography of the History of Art. *Mem:* Coll Art Asn; ARLIS/NA. *Publ:* Ed, B Berenson, Italian Pictures of the Renaissance, Florentine School, London, 63; auth, A Drawing by Vasari for the Studiolo of Francesco I, Burlington Mag, 64; auth, Practical Support on an International Basis for the Bibliography of Art History, CNRS, Paris, 69; auth, A Document for the Studiolo of Francesco I in Art the Ape of Nature, Abrams, 81; auth, Art databases and art bibliographies: A survey, Art Librs J, 82; and others. *Mailing Add:* 415 Central Park W New York NY 10025-4856

RINGGOLD, FAITH
PAINTER, SCULPTOR
b New York, NY, Oct 8, 1930. *Study:* City Coll New York, BS, 55, MA, 59, DFA, 89; DFA, 91; Moore Coll Art, DFA, 86; Wooster Coll Art, DFA, 87; Brockport State Univ, DFA, 92; Calif Coll Arts & Crafts, DFA, 93; DFA MA Coll Art, 91; DFA RI Sch Design, 94; DFA Parsons Sch of Design, 96; DFA Russell Sage Coll, 96; DEd Wheelock Coll, 97; DHL Molloy Coll, 97; DHL Bank St Coll Edu, 99; DFA Marymount Manhattan Coll, 99; DHL Mary Grove Coll, 2000; DHL St Joseph Coll, 2004; DFA Bloomfield Coll, 2005; DFA, Lafayette Coll, 2007. *Hon Degrees:* Hon Dr, William Paterson Univ & Sch of Chicago Art Inst, 2001. *Work:* Chase Manhattan Bank, NY; Studio Mus, Harlem, NY; High Mus Art, Atlanta, Ga; Philip Morris Collection, NY; Newark Mus, NJ; Metrop Mus Art, Solomon R Guggenheim Mus, NY; Boston Mus Fine Art. *Comn:* Williams Coll, Williamstown, Mass, 88; High Mus Art, Atlanta, 88; Committed to Print, Mus Mod Art, NY, 88; Tradition & Conflict: Images of a Turbulent Decade, 1963-1973, Studio Ms Harlem, NY; Oprah Winfrey, Harpo Prod, 90-91. *Exhib:* Solo exhibs, Wooster Coll, Columbus, Ohio, 85, Bernice Steinbaum Gallery, NY, 86, Baltimore Mus, Md, 87, Deland Mus Art, Fla, 87 & Bernice Steinbaum Gallery, NY, 88, Faith Ringgold: Coming to Jones Rpad and Other Stories, ACA Galleries, 2001; group exhibs, Mem for Martin Luther King, Mus Mod Art, NY, 68; Women Choose Women, NY Cult Ctr, 73; Retrospectives, Rutgers Univ Art Gallery, 73, Studio Mus Harlem, NY, 84 & Fine Arts Mus of Long Island (traveling), 90-93; Jubilee, Boston Mus, 75; Second World Black & African Festival Arts & Cult, Lagos, Nigeria, 77; Whitney Biennial, 85; The Decade Show, Studio Mus Harlem, 90; Hudson River Mus Westchester, Yonkers, NY, 96; San Diego Children's Mus, 97; Adams Art Gallery, Dunkirk, NY, 98; Jane Voorhees Zimmerli Art Mus, Rutgers Univ, NJ, 99. *Pos:* Founder, Coast to Coast: A Women of Color Nat Artists' book proj, 88; independent cur, Detroit Focus Gallery, 89, African Am Mus Fine Art, 90 & SoHo 20 Gallery, New York, 90. *Teaching:* Prof art, Univ Calif, San Diego, 84-; prof emer, Univ Calif, 84-2002. *Awards:* Nat Endowment Arts, 78 (sculpture), 89 (painting); Fel (painting), Solomon Guggenheim, 87; La Napoule Found Award, 90; Coretta Scott King Award, 92; Caldecott Hon, 92; Visionary Woman Award, Moore Coll Art & Design, 2005; Distinguished Feminist Award, Coll Art Asn, 2011. *Bibliog:* Leslie Sills (auth), Inspirations: Stories about Women Artists, Albert Whitman & Co, Ill, 88; Arlene Raven, Cassandra L Langer & Joanna Frueh (co-eds), Feminist Art Criticism: An Anthology, 88; Faith Ringgold, A 25 Yr Survey, Fine Arts Mus Long Island, 90. *Mem:* Women's Caucus Art; Coll Art Asn; Nat Acad Design. *Media:* Mixed Media. *Interests:* Art, children & philanthropy. *Publ:* Contribr, Confirmation: An Anthology of African American Women Writers, William Morrow, 83; auth, Tar Beach, Crown Publ, 91; Dinner at Aunt Connie's House, Hyperion, 93; Bonjour Lonnie, Hyperion, 96; My Dream of Martin Luther King, Crown Publ, 95; Talking to Faith Ringgold, Crown Publ, 95; Invisible Princess, Crown Publ, 99; Aunt Harriet's Underground Railroad in the Sky, Crown Publ, 93; auth, If a Bus Could Talk: The Story of Rosa Parks, Simon Schuster, 99; Counting to Tar Beach, Crown Publ, 99; Cassie's Colorful Day, Crown Publ, 99; Cassie's Word Quilt, Crown Publ, 2000; O Holy Night, Harper Collins Publ, 2004; Three Witches, Harper Collins Publ, 2005; Bronzeville Boys & Girls, Harper Collins Publ, 2006. *Dealer:* ACA Gallery 529 West 20th St New York NY 10022; Mary Ryan Gallery 527 W 26th St New York NY 10001. *Mailing Add:* PO Box 429 Englewood NJ 07631

RINGIER, ELLEN & MICHAEL
COLLECTOR
b Switz. *Pos:* With Grüner & Jahr, H Bauer; mgt team, Ringier Group, Zurich, Switz, 1984-85, chmn dir, 1985-90, pres bd dirs, 1990-97, chief exec officer, 1991-2003; pres bd dirs, Ringier Holding AG, 2003. *Awards:* Named one of Top 200 Collectors, ARTnews mag, 2004-13; named one of Power 100, The ArtReview. *Mem:* Bilderberg Group. *Collection:* Contemporary art; Russian avant-garde art. *Mailing Add:* Ringier AG Pressehaus 1 Dufourstrasse 23 Zurich CH-8008 Swaziland

RINGNESS, CHARLES OBERT
EDUCATOR, PRINTMAKER
b 1946. *Study:* St Cloud State Univ, BS, 68; Univ NMex, 70; Tamarind Lithography Workshop, Los Angeles, Master Printer (Ford Fel Grant), 70; Univ Cincinnati, MFA, 83. *Work:* Mus Mod Art, NY; Los Angeles Co Mus Art, Calif; Amon Carter Mus Western Art, Ft Worth, Tex; Canada Coun Art Bank, Ottawa; Pasadena Art Mus, Calif; Art Gallery, Ont, Toronto. *Exhib:* Solo exhibs, Univ Cincinnati, Art Gallery, 73, Gallery Moos, Toronto, 79, 81, 83 & 85, Phillis Needlman Gallery, Chicago, 83, Condesso Lawler Gallery, NY, 83 & 84, Art Gallery, Ont, Toronto, 84, Helandenr Rubinstein Gallery, Palm Beach 85 & Malton Art Gallery, Cincinnati, 86 & 90, Lydon Fine Art, Chicago, 90, Peter M David Gallery, Minneapolis, 90; Canadian Biennial, Winnipeg Art Gallery, Man, 81; Condesso/Lawler Gallery, NY, 83 & 84; Van Straaten Gallery, Chicago, 85. *Teaching:* Asst prof, Univ SFla, 70-76, graphic's studio mgr, 71-76; assoc prof, Univ Sask, 76-85, prof, 85-. *Awards:* Ford Fel Grant, 68-70; Prizes for prints & drawing, Art Gallery Brant Inc, Brantford, Ont, 80 & 81; Kathleen Fenwick Award, Edmonton Art Gallery, 80; Sask Sr Arts Bd Grant, 82-83. *Bibliog:* Marshall Webb (auth), article, Arts West, 12/79; Carol Phillips (auth), article, Artscanada, 4/80; Charlie Crane (auth), Anti-multiple printmaker, Artmagazine, 6/80; articles in Palm Beach Daily News, Cincinnati Post & NY Times. *Mem:* Coll Arts Asn, NY; Print & Drawing Coun Can; Canada Artists Representation. *Media:* Mixed. *Dealer:* Gallery Moos 136 Yorkville Ave Toronto ON Canada M5R 1C2; Lydon Fine Arts Chicago Ill. *Mailing Add:* Univ Sask Dept Art & Art History 3 Campus Dr Saskatoon SK S7N 5A4 Canada

RIPPE, DAN (CHRISTIAN)
PAINTER
b Giradote, Columbia, May 26, 1934. *Study:* North Texas Univ, 53-57; Famous Artist Sch, 60-63; Studied with Paul Strisik. *Work:* US Army Med Training Ctr, San Antonio; Stockholm Univ Sch Med, Sweden,; Univ Tex Law Sch, Austin; E/Sys Ross Perot, Dallas. *Comn:* murals, US Army Med Training Ctr, San Antonio, 59; mountain & Aspen scenes, comn by Dr Christian D Rippe IV, Denver, 2000. *Exhib:* Coppini Acad Show, Panhandle Plains Hist Mus, Canyon, Tex, 68-74; Nat Acad Design, NY, 76; D'Art Mus & Gallery, Dallas, 79; Am Watercolor Ann, Nat Acad Design, NY, 76; Salmagundi Club, NY, 80, 97; Law Sch Mus, Univ Tex, Austin, 81; Land & Light Show, Mary Bryan Mem Gallery, Jeffersonville, Vt, 98 & 2001; Audubon Artists, Inc, Nat Acad Design, NY, 76; and others. *Pos:* artist, engineer, Heath & Co, Dallas, 62-78; art dir, engineer, Tandy Electronics, Arlington, Tex, 85-96. *Teaching:* instr oil painting, Artisan Shop, Ruidoso, NMex, 74-75; instr oil techniques, Carrizo Lodge, NMex, 76-78; instr oil & aquamedia, Williamson Gallery, Dallas, 78-80. *Awards:* Outstanding Mural Award, Med Training Ctr, US Army, 59; Best of Show, Tex Fine Arts Asn, 75; Tara Fredrix Canvas Award, Audubon Artists 55th Ann, 97; and others. *Bibliog:* Living - New Approach, Dallas Times Herald, 77; From Field to Studio (film), Metrop Libr System, Okla City, 83; Profile, Dan Rippe, Hensley Gallery Southwest, 98; feature reviews, various galleries. *Mem:* Whiskey Painters Am; Audubon Artists, Inc; Salmagundi Club; and others. *Media:* Oil, Watercolor, Pencil. *Publ:* illusr, Drawing for the Student, N Tex Univ Press, 56-. *Dealer:* Hensley Gallery Southwest 311 N Pueblo Rd Taos NM 87571. *Mailing Add:* 717 W Cheryl Ave Hurst TX 76053-4905

RIPPEY, CLAYTON
PAINTER, MURALIST
b La Grande, Ore, Apr 24, 1923. *Study:* Northwestern Univ; Stanford Univ, with Daniel Mendelowitz, Ray Faulkner & Anton Refrigier, BA & MA; San Jose State Col, with George Post; Inst Allende, Mex, with James Pinto & Fred Samuelson. *Work:* Pepsi Cola, Bakersfield, Calif; Dance Mag Hq, NY; Wakayama Castle, Japan; Missions of Calif, Mexicali, Bakersfield, Calif; World of Legends, Los Altos, Calif. *Comn:* 2 murals (12' x 48'), Valley Plaza, Calif; Calif mural (12' x 46'), Tenneco Corp; mural (4' x 10') & mural (9' x 25'), Bakersfield, Calif; set of doors, Leo Lambile, Orras, Wash. *Exhib:* Lucian Labaudt Gallery, San Francisco, 55; Bakersfield Mus Art, Calif, 58, 61 & 66; Circulo de Belles Artes, Palma, Spain, 60; Haggen Mus, Stockton, Calif, 64; Galerie Yves Jaubert, Paris, France, 73; Cezanne Gallery, 67-; and over 100 solo shows. *Pos:* Chmn art dept, Bakersfield Col, 69-72. *Teaching:* Prof art, Bakersfield Col, 49-67 & 69-80; prof art, Maui Comm Col, 68-69. *Awards:* Top 100 Arts for Parks, 90; Artist of the Year, 97, Sponsor Artist, 98, Wash. *Bibliog:* Contemporary Personalities, Parma, Italy, 81; murals by Mueller; Elan Mag, 90. *Media:* Acrylics, Watercolor, Mosaics. *Dealer:* Cezanne Gallery 420 H St Bakersfield CA

RIPPON, RUTH MARGARET
SCULPTOR, CERAMIST
b Sacramento, Calif, Jan 12, 1927. *Study:* Calif Coll Arts & Crafts, with Antonio Prieto, BA, 47, MFA, 51; San Francisco Sch Fine Arts, with Joan J Pearson, scholar. *Work:* Crocker Art Mus, Sacramento; Vice President's House, Washington; Bemidji State Univ; Calif Expos & Fair, Sacramento; Mem Gallery Rochester; and many pvt collections. *Comn:* Life-size sculpture group, Mother w/children, Pavilions, A Robert Powell Development, Sacramento, 89; Freeport Sq, Sacto Sculpture Lifesize, 91; The Children's Hour, life-size sculpture group, Sierra Health Found, Garden Hwy, Calif; 3 discs (large wall), comn by Mr & Mrs Michael Heller, Gold River, Calif, 97; Leaping Koi (pond Sculpture), comn by Mr & Mrs Paul Fong, Sacramento, Calif, 98; Walting, UC Med Ctr, Sacto, CA; Life Size Bronze Woman Reading Circa, 2004. *Exhib:* solo

exhibs, Univ Pac, Stockton, Calif, 76, Univ Rochester, NY, 76, Artists Contemp Gallery, Sacramento, 79, 82 & 86, Michael Himovitz Gallery, Sacramento, 90 & John Natsoulas Gallery, Davis, Calif, 95 ; Oakland Mus, 74; Crocker Kingsley Retrospective, Sacramento, 75; 20-Yr Retrospective, Crocker Art Mus, Sacramento, 71; Drawing Show, Sacramento City Coll, 78; Coll Holy Names, 82; Retrospective Calif State Univ, 87; Exhib Ceramic Conf, John Natsoulas Gallery, Davis, Calif, 91-94; Bronze UCD Med Ctr, Sacramento, Calif, 2000; 50 Year Retrospective, Fresno Art Mus, 2002-2003; and others. *Teaching:* Crafts dir, Presidio of San Francisco, 54-56; prof ceramics, Calif State Univ, Sacramento, 56-87, prof emer, 87-. *Awards:* Many Purchase Awards, Calif State Fair & Expos, Sacramento, 48-66; Presidents Wives Series, San Francisco Potters Asn, DeYoung Mus, 69-70, Excellence in craftsmanship, AIA for Lollies, Powell Pavilion, 87; designated Woman Artist of the Year, Coun of 100, Fresno; designated as a Calif Living Treasure, Creative Arts League of Sacramento, 2002; Golden Bear Award, Artist of the Yr, Calif State Fair, 2008. *Bibliog:* Oppi Untracht (auth), Ruth Rippon, Sgraffito Through Glaze, 57 & Fred Ball (auth), Ruth Rippon Retrospective, 71, Ceramics Monthly Mag; Ruth Holland (auth), Rippon Retrospective, Creative Arts League 71 Catalog, 71; Calif State Univ Retrospective catalog, 87; brochure, Fresno Art Mus, 2003; John Natsoolas (press) and Nancy Servis (essay), Ruth Rippon (catalog), 2011. *Mem:* Creative Arts League Sacramento; Asn Calif Clay Artists; Crocker Art Mus Asn. *Media:* Stoneware Clay, Watercolor, Pencil. *Collection:* Anne & Malcolm McHenry; Jeanette Powell; Thomas Minder. *Dealer:* John Natsoulis Gallery Davis CA. *Mailing Add:* 98 Sandburg Dr Sacramento CA 95819

RIPPS, RODNEY
PAINTER
b New York, NY. *Study:* York Col, BA, 72; Hunter Col, MA, 72-73. *Work:* Israel Mus, Jerusalem; Rothchild Bank, Zurich, Switz; Brooklyn Mus; New Orleans Mus; LaJolla Mus; and others. *Exhib:* Critics Choice, Munson-Williams-Proctor Inst, Utica, NY, 77; Solo exhibs, Nancy Lurie Gallery, Chicago, 77, Brooke Alexander Gallery, NY, 77 & 78 & Galerie Daniel Templon, Paris, 78, Univ Art Mus, Calif State Univ, Long Beach, 84, Carl Solway, Cincinnati, Ohio, 86, Berkshire Mus, Pittsfied, Mass, 88 & Kim Foster Gallery, NY, 97-98; Holly Solomon Gallery, NY, 80-81; Univ Kentucky Art Mus, Lexington, 82; Joslyn Art Mus, Omaha, Nebr, 82; Univ Tex, Austin, 83; Jacksonville Art Mus, Fla, 83; Ronald Felman Gallery, NY, 84; Jewish Mus, NY, 86; Berkshire Mus, Pittsfield, Mass, 90; Marisa Del Re Gallery, NY, 91. *Pos:* Vis artist, Art Inst Chicago, 77, Ill State Univ, Bloomington, 78, Marisa Del Re, New York, 85 & Princeton Univ. *Teaching:* Instr painting, Brooklyn Mus Art Sch, 74-76. *Awards:* Nat Endowment Arts, 79 & 90. *Bibliog:* John Russell (auth), Painting 1985, The New York Times, 2/1/85; Anthony Bannon (auth), Anything goes, Buffalo News, 1/18/85; Stephen Westfall (auth), Ripps romantic theatre, Art in Am, 1/86. *Mem:* Abstract Artist Asn

RIPSTEIN, JACQUELINE
PAINTER, WRITER
b Mex City, Mex. *Study:* Self taught. *Work:* Posada Hermandad, Toledo, Spain; Mus/Biblioteca Galeria Dos Puertas, Mex City, Mex; Biblioteca Cuernauaca, Mex. *Exhib:* St Carmen Mus, Mex City, Mex, 90; Jewish Community Ctr, Mus Community Ctr, Houston, 92; Centro Arte Cult, Posada Hermandad, Toledo, Spain, 94; Plastique Found Napoleon, Art Plastique Found, Paris, 95; Grand Prix Acquitaire & Grand Prix Paris Art, Mus Art Mod, Unet, France, 95; Kolel Art Show, Synagogue Caracas, Venezuela, 96. *Pos:* Staff artist, City Aventura, 96. *Teaching:* Instr children's art, South Beach Alternative Sch, 95 & Aspira of Fla United Way Educ Prog, 95; Dancing hands art, Moca Mus, 96. *Awards:* Dipl Honneur Encourgemont Pub, Oevre Francaise d'entraide Sociale, 95. *Bibliog:* Alberto Peldez (auth), Art Inquisitions Events Spanish TV; Joaquin Bravo, Hola Mag, 94; Cover Art Expressions, Henk Abbink, 96. *Media:* Oil, Poetry. *Publ:* Auth, Voices Esteticas II, Govt Mex, Ignacio Flores Autura, 79. *Dealer:* William Levine 761 Palmer Ave Holmdel NJ 07733; Wilm Fine Arts 168 Mercer St 2nd Floor Soho NY. *Mailing Add:* 2800 Williams Island Blvd No 804 Miami FL 33160-4935

RISBECK, PHILIP EDWARD
GRAPHIC ARTIST, EDUCATOR
b Kansas City, Mo, July 25, 1939. *Study:* Univ Kans, BFA, 62, MFA, 65. *Work:* Sheldon Gallery Art, Lincoln, Nebr; Union Soviet Artists Collections, Moscow; Libr Cong; Wilanov Poster Mus, Warsaw; Moravian Mus, Brno, Czechoslovakia. *Exhib:* Int Poster Biennale, Zacheta Mus, Warsaw, 66, 68, 70, 72, 74, 76, 78, 84, 86, 88, 90, 92, 94, 2000 & 2002; Graphic Design Biennale, Moravian Mus, Brno, Czechoslovakia, 66, 70, 74, 78, 82, 84, 86, 88, 90, 92, 94, 98, 2000 & 2002; Posters USA, Mead Libr Ideas, NY, 75; Am Poster, 45-75, Smithsonian Inst, 76; Jurors Exhib, Cordegarda Gallery, Warsaw, 80; solo exhibs, Gallery Union Soviet Artists, Moscow, 83, traveling exhib, 83-84 & Porto Museo de Los Soares, Portugal, 84, M'ARS Gallery, Moscow, Russia, 2004, Rother Gallery, Nat Univ, Bogota, Columbia, Salon of Cult & Design, Rosario, Argentina, Gallery Cent Univ of City of Rio de Janeiro, Brazil, Cent Cult Mus Fed Supreme Ct Bldg, Rio de Janeiro, Gallery Do Sala Verde, Arapei, Brazil, 2006; COGRADA, Respect Cult Exhib, World Cong, Havana, Cuba, 2007; Alphabet of Europe, Sophia, Bulgaria, 2008; and many others. *Pos:* Co-dir, Colo Int Poster Exhib, 79-. *Teaching:* Prof art, Colo State Univ, 65-, dept chmn, 93-03. *Awards:* Durrell Award Res, Colo State Univ, 82; Outstanding Prof, Coll Arts, Humanities & Soc Sci, Colo State Univ, 83; Honorable Diploma, Un Coun for Publ Awards for Outstanding Contrib to Graphic Design, 2004; First Distinguished Alumni Award, Sch Fine Arts, Univ Kans. *Bibliog:* Richard Coyne (auth), Colorado State University Poster Exhibition, Commun Arts Mag, 79; Silas Rhodes (auth), Colorado State University Art Program in Graphics, Graphis, Zurich, 82; Oleg Savostiuk (auth), Philip Risbeck-An artist of the USA, Art Mag, Moscow, 84; Lanny Sommese (auth), Showroom: Phil Risbeck Novum, Gebrachs Graphik, 2000; Lanny Sommese (auth), Colo State Univ Graphic Design, Novum Gebrachsgraphik, 2004. *Mem:* Art Dirs Club Denver (pres, 81-82, mem bd, 81-); Univ & Coll Designers Asn; Int Typography Alliance; Int Cong Graphic Design. *Publ:* Auth, Eighth International Poster Biennale in Warsaw, Graphis Press, Zurich, 80; Third, Fourth & Fifth Colorado International Poster Exhibition, Graphis, 84, 86 & 88; Poster Exhibition International, CA Mag, Colo, 91, 93, 95, 97, 99, 2001, 2003, 2005 & 2007. *Mailing Add:* 1113 Parkwood Dr Fort Collins CO 80525-1928

RISELING, ROBERT LOWELL
EDUCATOR, PAINTER
b Sioux City, Iowa, June 5, 1941. *Study:* Univ Northern Iowa, BA, 63, MA, 66; State Univ Iowa, 64; Univ Wis-Madison, MFA, 72. *Work:* Memphis Brooks Mus Art, Memphis Coll Art, Tenn; Tenn State Mus, Nashville; Hamline Univ, St Paul, Rochester Art Ctr, St Cloud Univ, Anoka-Ramsey St Jr Col, Wilmar & City of St Cloud, Minn; Univ Northern Iowa, Cedar Falls; and many others. *Exhib:* Solo exhibs, Maka Gallery, Rock Island, Ill, 65 & 71, Univ Northern Iowa, Cedar Falls, 66, Rochester Art Ctr, Minn, 67, Hamline Univ, Minn, 67, 71 & 73, St Cloud State Univ, Minn, 68, 70 & 72, Edythe Bush Theatre, St Paul, Minn, 71 & Univ Wis, Madison, 72; Memphis Coll Art, Tenn, 75 & 82, Commerce Sq Gallery, Tenn, 77, Theatre Memphis, Tenn, 78, Galveston Arts Ctr, Tex, 80, Clark Turner Gallery, Tenn, 82, Alice Bingham Gallery, Tenn, 83 & Albers Gallery, Tenn, 86; Jewish Community Ctr, Memphis, Tenn, 87 & Crown Plaza Hotel Gallery, Memphis, Tenn, 88; Group exhibs, Luther Coll Fine Arts Festival Exhib, 65 & 67, Luther Coll Watercolor, Prints and Drawing, 65-66, 3rd Ann, Waterloo, Iowa, 66, Charles E MacNider Mus Painting and Drawing Exhib, Mason City, Iowa, 66, Minn State Fair, 66, Luther Coll Drawing, Water, Print Show, 69 & Minn Printmakers, 70; Midwest Drawing Invitational, N Hennepin State Jr Col, 71, 8th Ann, Waterloo, Iowa, 71, 40th Ann Arrowhead, Tweed Gallery, Duluth, Minn, 73, 17th Ann Delta, Ark Arts Ctr, Little Rock, 74, Tenn Bicentennial, Nashville, 76, 11th Ann Prints and Drawings, Ark Art Ctr, Little Rock, 78 & Memphis in May Exhib, 81; Art in the Eighties, Tenn State Mus, Nashville, 81, Tenn State Mus, Nashville, 84, Memphis Ctr Contemp Art, Tenn, 89 & Flora, Goldsmiths Botanic Gardens, Memphis, Tenn, 90. *Teaching:* Instr art, Monticello, Iowa, 63-65; grad asst, Dept Art, Univ Northern Iowa, 65-66; asst dir & resident artist, 66-67, dir art, Rochester Art Ctr, 67; instr dept art, St Cloud State Univ, 67-71; teaching asst, Dept Art, Univ Wis, 71-72; asst prof, Dept Art, St Cloud State Univ, 72-74; asst prof, Memphis Col Arts, Tenn, 74-78, assoc prof, 78-, prof, 90-; vis artist, Lake Placid Sch Arts, NY, 81, Univ Northern Iowa, Cedar Falls, 83, Alfred Univ, NY, 83, Pac Northwest Col Art, Portland, Ore, 86 & fac, Gov Sch Arts Murfreesboro, Tenn, 89 & 90. *Awards:* First Award Painting, 8th Ann, Waterloo, 71; Second Award Painting, 40th Ann Arrowhead, Tweed Gallery, Duluth, Minn, 73; Purchase Award, Tenn Bicentennial, 76. *Media:* Acrylic, Collage. *Mailing Add:* 1273 N Pkwy Memphis TN 38104

RISHEL, JOSEPH JOHN, JR
CURATOR
b Clifton Springs, NY, May 15, 1940. *Study:* Hobart Col, BA, 62; Univ Chicago, MA, 65. *Exhib:* Art in France Under the Second Empire, Philadelphia, 78-79, Detroit, 78-79, Paris, 78-79; Masters of 17th-Century Dutch Landscape Painting, Rijksmus Amsterdam & Mus Fine Arts, Boston, 87-88. *Collection Arranged:* Painting in Italy in the 18th Century: Rococo to Romanticism (co-ed, catalog), Chicago, Minneapolis & Toledo, 70-71; Art in France Under the Second Empire (auth, catalog), Philadelphia, Detroit, Paris, 78-79; Sir Edwin Landseer (auth, exhib catalog); Cezanne in Philadelphia Collections (auth, exhib catalog); British Painting in the Philadelphia Mus of Art from the Seventeenth through the Nineteenth Century; Claude Monet: Philadelphia, 87; Henry P McIlhenny Collection, 87-88; Masters of 17th-Century Dutch Landscape Painting, 87-88; Masterpieces of Impressionism and Post-Impressionism: The Annenberg Collection, 89. *Pos:* Sr cur, European painting before 1900 & John G Johnson Collection, Philadelphia Mus Art, 71-; cur, Rodin Mus, Philadelphia, formerly. *Teaching:* Instr art hist, Wooster Coll, Ohio; lectr spec exhibs, Art Inst Chicago. *Mem:* Mus Loan Network; William Penn Found; Am Fedn Arts; Fel Am Acad Arts & Scis; Chevalier dans l'Ordre des Arts et des Lettres. *Publ:* The Hague School: some forgotten pictures in the collection, Philadelphia Mus of Art Bull, 15-27, 7-9/71; auth, Landseer: Queen Victoria's favorite painter copied in America, 19th Century Mag, Vol 7, autumn 81; A Lyonnais flower piece by Antoine Berjon (1754-1843), Philadelphia Mus Art Bull, Vol 78, No 336, 16-24, fall 82; contribr, Great French Paintings from the Barnes Found, (catalog), New York, Knopf, 93; co-editor Mus Studies, jour of Art Inst of Chicago; Degas and the Dance, exhib catalogue, Detroit Inst Arts, 02, Philadelphia Mus Art, 03. *Mailing Add:* 2322 Delancey St Philadelphia PA 19103

RISLEY, JACK
ADMINISTRATOR, SCULPTOR
Study: Oberlin Coll, BA, Ohio; Cooper Union, BA, NY; Yale Sch Art, MFA, New Haven, Conn, 86. *Exhib:* Solo exhibs, Postmasters Gallery, NY, 89, 91, 92, 93, 97, 2004, Galerie Burgis Geisman, Cologne, Ger, 91, Baklar Gallery, Mass Coll Art, 96, Real Art Ways, Hartford, Conn, 98, Pacific Northwest Coll Art, Ore, 2001; Group exhibs, Cristinerose Gallery, NY, 2000, Flipside Gallery, Brooklyn, NY, 2001, Palm Beach Inst Contemporary Art, Fla, 2001, The Workspace, NY, 2002, Dietch Projects, NY, 2002, Ace Gallery, 2002, Postmasters Gallery, NY, 2003, The Brooklyn Mus, NY, 2004, and many others. *Teaching:* academic postions at Yale Sch Art, NYU, & Cooper Union, formerly; grad & undergrad art courses, Cleveland Inst Art, Harvard Univ, Rhode Island Sch Design, formerly; Ruth Head centennial prof, chair dept art & art history, Univ Tex, Austin, currently. *Awards:* Art Matters Inc grant, NY, 86, 87; MacDowell fellow, Petersboro, NH, 87; Louis Comfort Tiffany Found award, 91; Studio fellow, Marie Walsh Sharpe Found, NY, 93; Mid Atlantic Arts, Regional fellow, Nat Endowment for the Arts, 95; Rome Prize, Am Acad Rome, 98-99; Pollack Krasner Found grant, 99. *Mem:* Coll Art Assn; Int Council of Art Administrators; Foundations in Art Theory and Edn (think tank adv bd). *Dealer:* Postmasters Gallery 459 W 19 St New York NY. *Mailing Add:* University of Texas at Austin Art Building 23rd & San Jacinto Campus Box D1300 Austin TX 78712

RISS, MURRAY
PHOTOGRAPHER, EDUCATOR
b Poland, Feb 6, 1940; US citizen. *Study:* City Univ New York, BA; Cooper Union Sch Art; RI Sch Design, with Harry Callahan, MFA. *Work:* Mus Mod Art, NY; Bibliot Nat, Paris; Art Inst Chicago; Nat Gallery Art, Can; New Orleans Mus Fine Arts; Richmond Mus Art, Va; Libr Cong; Minneapolis Mus Fine Art; David Logan Found; Mus Rhode Island Sch Design; Nat Gallery of Canada, Ottawa; Ryerson Inst, Ontario Canada. *Comn:* Photograph Reelfoot Lake, State of Tenn, 72. *Exhib:* Mus Mod Art, NY, 70-71; solo exhibs, Minneapolis Mus Fine Art, 71, Visual Studies Workshop (traveling show), NY, 76-78, Projects Inc, Cambridge, 79 & Southern Artist (worldwide traveling exhib), US Info Agency, 76; Fantastic Photog USA, six maj mus in Europe, 78; Photographer's Gallery, London, Eng, 79; Rhodes Coll, Memphis, 80; Big Shot, Univ Ala, 83; Askew Nixon Gallery, 94-; Christian Brothers Univ Gallery, 2007; One More with Feeling, Memphis Coll Art, 2013. *Pos:* Vis sr lectr, Univ Haifa, Israel, 75-76; cur, Emerging Southern Photographers, Memphis Coll Art, 92. *Teaching:* Prof photog, Memphis Coll Art, 68-86, head dept photog, 68-86. *Awards:* Nat Endowment Arts Grant, 79. *Bibliog:* William Parker (auth), Introduction to my portfolio, Ctr Photog Studies, 75. *Media:* photography. *Publ:* Illusr, Sleep Book, Harper & Row, 74; Good Abode: Architectural History of Shelby County, Towery Press, 83; The Guide to Mud Island, MM Publ, 87; Elmwood 2002, Elmwood Publ, 2003; First Shooting Light, Art Memphis Publ, 2008; A Bridge to Peter, 2014. *Dealer:* Visual Studies Gallery Rochester NY; Joseph Bellows Gallery La Jolla CA. *Mailing Add:* 1306 Harbert Ave Memphis TN 38104

RISTAU, JACOB ROBERT
DESIGNER, EDUCATOR
b Lawrence, Kans, Jan 3, 1978. *Study:* Abilene Christian Univ, BFA, 2000; Sch Art Inst Chicago, MFA, 2005; studied with Stephen Farrell and Ann Tyler, Sch Art Inst Chicago, 2005. *Work:* Joan Flasch Artists Book Collection, Chicago. *Exhib:* Print: Regional Design Ann, Print Mag, New York, 2003; Communication Arts: Design Ann, Menlo Park, Calif, 2003; Graphis: Design Ann, Graphis, New York, 2004; Logo Lounge Vol II, Beverly, Mass, 2005; Graphis: Logo Design 6, Graphis, New York, 2005; 26 Temptations: Typographic Engagements, Peppers Art Gallery, Redlands, Calif, 2007. *Collection Arranged:* The Edge of Conscience: The Long Shadow of Lynching, Prints, Artist Books & Installations by Ann Tyler & Constance White, 2008; Andrew Scott Ross, Sculptures, Installations & Drawings by Andrew Ross & Installations by Vanessa Mayoraz, 2008. *Teaching:* Vis assist prof, Art & Design, Univ Redlands, Calif, 2005-2006, assist prof, 2006-2008; Prog Leader: Visual Communication Design & Lecturer, Auckland Sch Design, Massey Univ, 2008-2010. *Awards:* Four Awards of Excellence, Houston Art Directors Club, 2002. *Mem:* Am Inst Graphic Arts; Coll Art Assoc. *Publ:* auth, Book Review: Signs of Inka Khipu: Binary Coding in the Andean Knotted-String Records, Design Issues, Vol 22 No 2, MIT Press, 2006

RITCHEY, RIK
PAINTER, SCULPTOR
b Mountainhome AFB, Idaho, Mar 3, 1953. *Study:* Wash State Univ, BA (fine art), 78; Mills Col, MFA (painting), 83. *Work:* Art Beam, Seoul, Korea; San Jose Mus Art, Calif; City of Pusan, Korea; Calif State Univ, Bakersfield. *Comn:* The Four Seasons after SFB Morse (bronze), Symp 94 Open Air, Pusan, Korea, 94. *Exhib:* Solo exhibs, Pascal de Sarthe Gallery, San Francisco, 89, IPOMAL Gallery, Landgraaf, The Neth, 90, New Sculpture, William Sawyer Gallery, San Francisco, 91, Tissue, In Khan Gallery, NY, 94, Fong Gallery, San Jose, Calif, 97 & New Paintings and Works on Paper, Klein Art Works, Chicago, Ill, 98; Oakland Artists '90, Oakland Mus, Calif, 90; Monoprints, Riverside Mus Art, Calif, 91; Material Abstraction (with catalogue), Seomi Gallery, Seoul, Korea, 92; Codified Desires (with catalog), traveling, 96 & 97; Blue, In Khan Gallery, NY, 97; Contemp Abstraction, Klein Art Works, Chicago, Ill, 98. *Pos:* Chairperson, Educ Subcomt ISC 1994 Biennial, Int Sculpture Ctr, Washington, DC, 93-94. *Teaching:* Instr studio art/theory, Univ Calif, Berkeley, 92- & Acad Art Col, San Francisco, 92-95; instr sculpture, Sierra Nev Col, Incline Village, Nev, 98. *Awards:* Inventor '89: La Cite du Bicentenaire Concours, La Villette Grand Halle, Paris, 87; Ann Flanagan Fel, Fel Exhib, KALA, 89-91; Artist Fel in Visual Arts, Calif Arts Coun, 90. *Bibliog:* Peter Selz (auth), Rik Ritchey, Art News, 5/89; Kenneth Baker (auth), Vigor and diversity in Oklahoma, San Francisco Chronicle, 14, 5/18/90; Roger Anderson (auth), Oaklandish art, Eastbay Express, 30-31, 6/22/90. *Mem:* Int Sculpture Ctr, Washington, DC. *Media:* All Media. *Publ:* Contribr, Small Arena for Heroics, Eye Mag, San Francisco, 85. *Dealer:* Dong Jo Chang In Khan Gallery 415 W Broadway New York NY 10012. *Mailing Add:* 667 11th St Oakland CA 94607

RITCHIE, CHARLES MORTON, JR
PAINTER, PRINTMAKER
b Pineville, Ky, Nov 21, 1954. *Study:* Univ Ga, Athens, BFA, 77; Carnegie Mellon Univ, MFA (grad fel), 80. *Work:* Nat Gallery Art, Washington, DC; NY Pub Libr; Boston Pub Libr, Mass; Butler Inst Am Art, Youngstown, Ohio; Va Mus Fine Arts, Richmond; Fogg Art Mus, Harvard Univ Art Mus, Cambridge, Mass; Balt Mus Art, Md; Boise Art Mus, Idaho; Chrysler Mus, Norfolk, Va; Corcoran Gallery Art, Washington; Phila Mus Art, Pa. *Exhib:* Solo exhibs, The Interior Landscape, Marsh Art Gallery, Univ Richmond & Va Mus Fine Arts, 93-95, Works on Paper 1983-96, Butler Inst Am Art, Youngstown, Ohio, 96, recent work, Numark Gallery, Washington, DC, 98, drawings & prints, Mary Baldwin Col, Staunton, Va, 98 &Spheris Gallery, NY, 2000; 171st Ann Exhib, Nat Acad Design, NY, 96; Prints Washington 1997, Corcoran Gallery Art, Washington, DC, 97; 61st Ann Mid-Year Exhib, Butler Inst Am Art, Youngstown, Ohio, 97; 40th Chautauqua Nat Exhib Am Art, NY, 97; group exhibs, Butler Inst Am Art, 99 & 2000, Washington Art Club, DC, 2001, Pepper Gallery, Boston, 2002, Swarthmore Col, Pa, 2003 & others. *Pos:* Staff artist, Univ Ga, 76-77; art dir, TFC Inc, Atlanta, Ga, 77-78; staff asst, Nat Gallery Art, Washington, DC, 81-85, res asst, 85-88 & asst cur dept mod prints & drawings, 88-. *Teaching:* Instr drawing, Carnegie Mellon Univ, Pittsburgh, Pa, 78. *Awards:* Individual Artist Fel, Arts Coun Montgomery Co, Md, 96; Individual Artist Award, Md State Arts Coun, 98; The MacDowell Colony Fel, 99; Individual Artist Award, Md State Arts Coun, 2000. *Bibliog:* Richard Waller (auth), Charles Ritchie: The Interior Landscape, Marsh Art Gallery, Univ Richmond, 94; Gabriella Fanning (auth), Working Proof: Charles Ritchie, On Paper, Vol 1, No 1, 29, 9-10/96; Jacqueline Brody (auth), Prints and Photographs Published: Charles Ritchie, Print Collector's Newsletter, Vol XXVII, No 1, 29, 3-4/96; Steven Zevitas (auth), New American Painting 33, Open Studios Press, Wellesley, Mass, 2000; Joanna Shaw-Eagle (auth), Print Masters at Corcoran, The Washington Times, 8/2001. *Mem:* Washington Print Club, DC; Print Coun Am. *Media:* Watercolor, Conte Crayon; Intaglio Printmaking, Lithography. *Publ:* Coauth, The 1980's: Prints from the Collection of Joshua P Smith, 89, Art for the Nation: Gifts in Honor of the 50th Anniversary of the National Gallery of Art, 91 & The Robert and Jane Meyerhoff Collection 1945-95, 95, Nat Gallery Art; auth, Gemini GEL: Recent Prints and Sculptures, Nat Gallery Art, 94; auth, Max Webers Modern Vision, 2000; and many others. *Dealer:* Center Street Studio 369 Congress St Boston MA 02210. *Mailing Add:* 3107 Lee St Silver Spring MD 20910-1052

RITCHIE, WILLIAM (BILL) H, JR
PRINTMAKER, VIDEO ARTIST
b Yakima, Wash, Dec 24, 1941. *Study:* Cent Wash State Col, BA, 64; San Jose State Col, MA, 66; studied with Rolf Nesch, Norway, 69; intern Nat Ctr for Experiments in Television, 74; Studied Worldwide, 83. *Work:* Philadelphia Mus Art, Pa; US Info Agency, Japan; Seattle Art Mus, Wash; Tacoma Art Mus, Wash; Segovia Biennial, Spain. *Comn:* Print, Henry Gallery Asn, Seattle, Wash, 70; sculpture, City of Seattle, Wash, 77; prints, CDROM Publisher's Club, Seattle, Wash; Videotape, King Co Arts Comn, 80. *Exhib:* Nat Print Exhib, Libr of Cong, Washington, 71; Brit Int Print Biennale, Bradford Galleries, Eng, 72; NWest Film & Video Exhib, Portland Art Mus, Ore, 73 & 74; Am Printmaking, Brooklyn Mus Art, NY, 76; Boston Printmakers 29th Nat, DeCordova Mus, Lincoln, Mass, 77; Portopia, Kobe, Japan, 81; Perspectives: 100 Yr Washington Art, Tacoma Art Mus, 89; Northwest Vision, Seattle Art Mus, Wash, 90. *Collection Arranged:* Ritchie's Video Archives Northwest Regional Multimedia Arts. *Pos:* Art prof, Univ Wash, Seattle, 66-85; corp exec artist, Ritchie's, Inc, 90-96. *Teaching:* Prof art, Univ Wash, Seattle, 66-85; vis prof media arts, Evergreen State, Wash, 87, Univ Ore, 89 & Highline Community Col, 94; instr, Myartpatron.com, 2000-. *Awards:* Research Grants, Printmaking, Video & Computer Art, 70-76; First Prize, First NWest Film & Video Festival, Portland Art Mus, Ore, 73; Nat Endowment Arts Fel, 74. *Bibliog:* Korot & Schneider (coauths), Video Art, Harcourt, Brace, Jovanovitch, 76; F Eichenberg (auth), The Art of the Print, Harry N Abrams, 76; V Ancona (auth), Bill Ritchie: Video in the Northwest, Videography Mag, Vol 12, No 6; Lois Allan (auth), Contemporary Printmaking in NW, 97. *Mem:* Washington Software Asn (found mem digital media alliance 96-97). *Media:* All print media; Video and Computer Graphics. *Specialty:* diplays tech assisted arts, research & dev. *Publ:* Auth, Behind Time in the Electronic Age, Ritchie's Video, 82; Print 'N Video News, Ritchie's Video, 85-87; Art of Selling Art, Ritchie's Perfect Press, 89; Reinventing Art Studios: Between Tradition and Technology, 93. *Dealer:* Emeralda Works Artist's Gallery 5th & Aloha PO Box 9627 Seattle WA 98109. *Mailing Add:* 500 Aloha-105 Seattle WA 98109-3901

RITTER, RENEE GAYLINN
PAINTER
b Bronx, NY. *Study:* Queens Col, NY, BA; Long Island Univ, Greenvale, NY, MFA. *Work:* Islip Art Mus, NY; Muscarelle Mus Art, Col William and Mary, Williamsburg, Va; Family Mus, Hempstead, NY; Danville Mus Art, VA; Jane Voorhees Zimmerli Art Mus, Rutgers, NJ. *Exhib:* Sivermine Guild for Arts, New Canaan, Conn, 81, 83, 86, 92 & 94; Heckscher Mus Art, Huntington, NY, 90, 92, 94 & 96; Del Mus Art, Wilmington, 92; Art on Paper, Md Fedn Art, Md, 94, 95 & 96; Eleftherias Park Art Ctr, Athens, Greece, 96; Rathbone Gallery, Sage Col, Albany, NY, 96; Islip Art Mus, Islip, NY, 2009. *Pos:* Lectr, Nassau Co Mus Art, 79-91; exec bd, Nat Drawing Asn, 91-98. *Teaching:* Adj prof, art, CW Post Ctr, Long Island Univ, NY, 82-2008; adj prof, art, Nassau Community Col, 2000-. *Awards:* Award of Excellence, Long Beach Mus, 87 & 88; Donn Steward Graphic Award, Heckscher Mus, 90; Purchase Prize, Muscarelle Mus Art, Williamsburg, Va, 96. *Bibliog:* Numerous articles including, NY Times, Newsday, Artspeak & Artists Mag, Christian Sci Monitor. *Mem:* Nat Asn Women Arts. *Media:* Paint, Collage. *Dealer:* Reece Gallery 24 W 57 St New York NY; Nese Alpan Gallery Huntington NY. *Mailing Add:* 62 Birchwood Park Dr Jericho NY 11753

RITTS, EDWIN EARL, JR
ADMINISTRATOR, MUSEUM DIRECTOR
b Pittsburgh, Pa, Nov 11, 1948. *Study:* Wilmington Col, AB, 70; Univ Cincinnati, grad prog, 71; Univ NC, cert arts mgt, 85. *Collection Arranged:* Andrew Wyeth in Southern Collections, 76; Richard Hunt, Mountain Flight, 77; Pvt collection of Arthur & Holly Magill, 81; New Modern Painting, Harsh Images on Canvas, 84; America's Impressionists, 86. *Pos:* Pres, SC Artist's Guild, 74-75; treas, SC Mus Asn, 74-76; chmn art sect, NC Mus Conf, 89-91. *Teaching:* Lectr art markets, SC Gov Sch, 82; adj prof mus studies, Univ NC, 84-86. *Mem:* Am Asn Mus; NC Mus Conf. *Mailing Add:* c/o Historic Greenville Foundation 540 Buncombe St Greenville SC 29601-1906

RITZ, LORNA J
PAINTER, SCULPTOR
Study: Worcester Art Mus, 63-65; Boston Mus Fine Arts, 65; Art Students League, 66; Skowhegan Sch Painting & Sculpture, Scholar, 68; Pratt Inst, BFA, 69; Cranbrook Acad Art, Bloomfield Hills, Mich, MFA (painting & sculpture), 71. *Work:* Bank of Boston, Int Bank New Eng & High Voltage Eng, Shrafts Ctr, Boston; Mt Holyoke Coll Art Mus; Hale & Dorr Lawfirm, Boston & NY; Veridex; Johnson & Johnson. *Exhib:* Solo exhibs, Nat Arts Mus, Teguciagalpa, Honduras, 83, Boston Visual Artists Union, 85, Augusta Savage Gallery, New Africa House, Univ Mass, Amherst, 87, Nicole C Gallery, Boston, 90, NACUL Archit Ctr, Amherst, Mass, 90 & Harriet Tubman House, Boston, 91; Art in Embassies Program, Washington, DC, paintings located in Guatemala City, Brazzaville, the Congo, Banjul, The Gambia, Valetta,

Malta and Praia & Cape Verde; Lopoukhine Gallery, Boston, 88; Nat Asn Women Artists, Jacob Javits Ctr, NY, 89; Grossman Gallery, Sch Mus Fine Arts, Boston, 89; Lacoste Exhib, Mona Bismarck Found, Paris, 91; Portland Mus Art, Maine, 99; The Painting Center, 2003; Oxbow Gallery, Northampton, MA, 2004. *Teaching:* Asst prof painting, Univ Minn, 76-77; vis asst prof, Brown Univ, RI, 78 & Dartmouth Col, NH, 78-79; lectr, univs & insts throughout US and world; New York Studio School, New York, NY. *Awards:* US Info Agency Grant Awards, Vt, Partners of Americas, to paint, exhibit, lectr & teach at Univ Honduras, 83, Mass Partners of Americas, to teach, lectr & exhib at Inst de Belles Arted, Medelin, Columbia, 90; Esther & Adolph Gottlieb Found Emergency Grant Award, 88; Pollock-Krasner Found Grant Award, 90, 99, 2004; George Sugarman Found Grant, 2007. *Media:* oil on linen. *Dealer:* Watkins Gallery 142 Main St Northampton MA 01060. *Mailing Add:* c/o Oxbow Gallery 275 Pleasant St Northampton MA 01060

RITZER, GAIL L
COLLAGE ARTIST, CERAMIST
b Indianapolis, Ind, Jan 9, 1954. *Study:* Univ Mo-Columbia, BS (art educ), 74; E Carolina Univ, MFA (ceramics/painting), 82. *Work:* Greenville Mus Art, NC; NC Mus Crafts; Psychology Clinic, Va Commonwealth Univ; Mendenhall Galleries, E Carolina Univ; Community Coun Arts, Kinston, NC. *Comn:* Ceramic sculpture, Bloomingdale's, NY, 85; ceramic mural, Southern Women's Show, Raleigh, NC, 86; ceramic sculpture, NC Solar Asn, Raleigh, 86; ceramic sculpture, Sch Textiles, NC State Univ, 90; tile mural, NC Arts Coun/Elmhurst Sch, Greenville, 96. *Exhib:* NC Artists Exhib (with catalog), NC Mus Art, 80; NC Sculpture Exhib (with catalog), Northern Telecom Corp, Research Triangle, 84; Fantastic Fibers (with catalog), Yeiser Art Ctr, Paducah, Ky, 96; Form & Freedom (with catalog), Int Quilt Festival, Houston, 96; one-women show, E Carolina Univ, Greenville, NC, 96; Expressions of Freedom (with catalog), Int Quilt Study Ctr, Lincoln, Nebr, 98; NC 20th Century Masters, Lee Hansley Gallery, Raleigh, NC, 2000; Reformations (with catalog), The Courthouse Galleries, Norfolk, Va, 2000; Remembrance: Women, Bloomsburg Univ, Pa, 2000; Women Artists: Works from the Greenville Mus Art Collection (with catalog), NC, 2001; NC Art Quilts (with catalog), Green Hill Ctr for NC Art, 2001; Story Quilts (with catalog), Univ Mo, St Louis, 2001; Story Quilts, Greenville Mus of Art, Greenville, NC, 2002; Art Quilts, East Carolina Univ, 2004; Women of the GMA, E Carolina Univ, 2005; Imago Dei (with catalog), E Carolina Univ, 2006; Juried Nat Art Exhib, Chadron State Col, Nebr, 2006; Small Works Invitational Salon Exhib (with catalog), New Arts Program, Kutztown, Pa, 2006; Space, Place, Life: National Juried Exhib, Eastern Kentucky Univ, 2008; Fifteen, Lee Hausley Gallery, 2008; Spiritual Provocations, East Carolina Univ, 2008; No Frigate Like a Book: Handmade Books by Gail Ritzer, Joyner Libr, East Carolina Univ, 2007; Short Stories, Nelle Hayes Gallery, Greenville, NC, 2008; Sweetening the Sour Apple: Celebrating Woman's Heritage Month, Joyner Libr, E Carolina Univ, 2009; Freedom, Nat Juried Exhib, E Ky Univ (with catalog), 2008; Space Place, Life (with catalog); Darwin Day Juried Art Exhib, E Carolina Univ, Biology Dept, Second Place, 2009; Down East Sculpture Exhib, Nat Juried Exhib, E Carolina Univ, 3rd Place,2008; What's New? Fresh Works by Stable Artists, Lee Hansley Gallery, 2009; nquiries Nat Juried Exhib, Eastern Kentucky Univ, 2010; Greenville Artists Asn, Greenville Mus Art, 2010; Paul Hartley Legacy, Lee Hansley Gallery, Raleigh, NC, 2010; In Full Bloom, Nelle Hayes Gallery, Greenville, NC, 2010; Natures Human, Eastern KY Univ, 2011; Greenville Mus Art, 2011; Down East Sculpture Exhib, E Carolina Univ, 2012; Preyed Upon, Art Alley, Greenville, NC, 2012; The Love Show, Nelle Hayes Gallery, Greenville, NC, 2013; Greenville Mus Art, 2013. *Teaching:* instr classes in mixed media, Greenville Mus of Art, 90-, Emerge Arts Ctr, 2008-; Outreach Coordr, Greenville Mus Art, 2009-. *Awards:* Visual Artists Proj Grant, NC Arts Coun, 96, Emerging Artist Grant, 96, Regional Artist Proj Grant, 97 & 2001; Regional Artist Proj Grant, 2005; Regional Artist Proj Grant, 2007; Regional Artist Proj Grant, NC Arts Coun, 2010. *Bibliog:* Lynn Lewis Young (auth), The Quintessential Quilt, Quilts Inc, 96; Gail L Ritzer (auth), Mommy, sew me a Story, Art/Quilt Mag, Lynn Lewis Young Publ, 97. *Mem:* Greenville Artists Asn. *Media:* Mixed Media. *Publ:* auth, Expressions of Freedom: Quilts Celebrating Human Rights, Quilters Newsletter Mag, 3/99; auth, Fiberarts Design Book 7, Susan Mowery (ed), Kieffer Lark Books, 2004; auth, Quilting Arts Magazine, John P. Bolton Publ, summer 2005, No 18; juror, Rebel 53, East Carolina Univ Art and Literature Pub, 2011. *Dealer:* Lee Hansley Gallery, 225 Glenwood Ave, Raleigh, NC, 27603. *Mailing Add:* 1318 Red Banks Rd Greenville NC 27858

RIVERA, ELIAS J
PAINTER
b Bronx, NY, April 18, 1937. *Study:* Art Students League, 55-61, with Frank Mason; pvt study with Steve Raffo, 61-64. *Work:* Ga Mus Fine Arts, Athens; Adelphi Univ, Long Island, NY; Vassar Mus, Poughkeepsie, NY. *Comn:* Mural, Banco de Ponce, Rockefeller Plaza, NY, 73; four paintings and one bronze plaque, pvt comn by Fortunoff family, NY, 80. *Exhib:* Community Gallery, Brooklyn Mus, NY, 69; Nat Acad Design, NY, 71, 73-74 & 77-78; Crimes of Passion, Chrysler Mus, Norfolk, Va, 81; Santa Fe Festival Arts, NMex, 83 & 84; Ctr Contemp Arts, Santa Fe, 85; Miniature Show (91, 92), Albuquerque Art Mus, NMex, 93; Cacciola Gallery, NY, 93; The Americas: A Latin Connection, Nev Inst Contemp Art, 93; Solo exhib, Visions of Solola, Riva Yares Gallery, Santa Fe, NMex & Scottsdale, Ariz, 95; Riva Yares Gallery, Santa Fe, NMex, 95 & 97. *Awards:* Best Painter, De Puerte Rico Inst, 72; Purchase Prize, Ann Show, Am Acad & Inst Arts & Lett, 78; Creative Artists Pub Serv Award, 81. *Media:* Oil. *Mailing Add:* c/o Riva Yares Gallery 123 Grant Ave Santa Fe NM 87501

RIVERA, FRANK
PAINTER
b Cleveland, Ohio, Aug 28, 1939. *Study:* Yale Univ Grad Sch Fine Arts, with Alex Katz & Jack Tworkov, BFA, 62; Univ Pa, with Pi Dorazio, Savelli, Helen Frankenthaler & Ludwig Sander, MFA, 67. *Exhib:* Ann Am Painting & Sculpture, Pa Acad Fine Arts, 68; NJ State Mus Painting & Sculpture Ann, 72; Univ Rochester Gallery Art, 72; Susan Caldwell Gallery, New York, 74; 1975 Biennial Exhib Am Art, Whitney Mus Am Art, 75; Ellarslie Mus, Trenton, NJ, 84; Abington Art Ctr, Pa, 87; Considine Gallery, Princeton, NJ, 89; Mariboe Gallery, Swig Art Ctr, Hightstown, NJ, 95 & 97; City Without Walls, Urban Gallery; New Art & Artists, Newark, NJ, 99; Luise Ross Gallery, New York, 2007-2010, one man show, Mariboe Gallery, Hightstown, NJ, 2008; NJ State Mus Fine Arts Ann, 99; Salon d'Automme de Paris, 2000; Festival Int d'Art Contemporain, Paris, France, 2000. *Teaching:* Guest artist/critic, Md Inst Coll Art, Baltimore, Md, 2008-2010. *Awards:* Nat Endowment Humanities Grant for Study & Travel in France, 72-73. *Bibliog:* Wendy Heisler (auth), Windsor-Heights-Herald, Princeton, NJ, 95; Richard Shea (auth), Time Off Mag, Princeton, NJ, 97; Dan Bischoff (auth), Newark Star Ledger, 99; Chris Rywalt (auth), Gallery Slog, 2008; Janice Purcell (auth), Trenton Times, 2010. *Media:* Oil on Canvas. *Publ:* Critic/art reviewer US1, Princeton, NJ. *Mailing Add:* 110 Broad St Hightstown NJ 08520

RIVERA, GEORGE
MUSEUM DIRECTOR, PAINTER
b Japan, Nov 5, 1955; US citizen. *Study:* San Jose State Univ, BA, 79, MA, 82. *Exhib:* San Jose Mus Art, 88; de Saisset Mus, 93; Los Gatos Mus Art Hist, 99; Washington Sq Gallery, 2001; D P Fong Galleries, 2001, 02, 03; Euphrat Mus Art, Cupertino, Calif, 2003-2004; Los Gatos Mus Art, Los Gatos, Calif, 2005. *Pos:* cur, Triton Mus Art, Santa Clara, Calif, 86-94, asst dir & chief cur, 94-97, exec dir, 97-. *Teaching:* Assoc fac art, Mission Col, Santa Clara, Calif, 86-; instr, Exten Prog, Univ Calif, Berkeley, 96- & Pac Art League, Palo Alto, 98-; instr, DeAnza College, Cupertino, CA. *Awards:* Asian Heritage Award, 92; Critics Choice Award, 96; Jean Bock Spirit of Art Award, 2000. *Media:* Oil, Charcoal, Acrylic, Watercolor, Mixed Media. *Dealer:* dp Fong Gallery San Jose CA; Michael Himovitz Gallery Sacramento CA; Washington Square Gallery San Francisco CA; Togonon Gallery San Francisco Gallery San Francisco CA. *Mailing Add:* Triton Museum of Art 1505 Warburton Ave Santa Clara CA 95050

RIVO, SHIRLEY WINTHROPE
PAINTER
b Toronto, Ont; US citizen. *Study:* Kean Univ, BA, & teaching certification, 77, MA, 80; studied with Carl Burger, Vito Giacalone, James Howe, Wanda Gromodska, Joseph Loeber, Nicholas Reale, Michael Metzger. *Work:* pen & pencil sketch, Nat Baseball Hall of Fame Mus, Cooperstown, NY, 98, painting, 2012; Winter in the Park, Schering-Plough, Corp Hq, Madison, NJ; painting, Johnson & Johnson, World Hq, New Brunswick, NJ, 94; Statue of Liberty Nat Monument, Liberty Island, NY, 99; Yankee Stadium, Bronx, NY, 98 & 2009; Cooperstown, NY, 98; Brooklyn Botanic Garden, NY; Morris Mus, Morristown, NJ; Nabisco Corp Hqs, Hanover, NJ; The New York Botanical Garden, Bronx, NY 2005; Summit Free Pub Libr, Summit, NJ, 2006; Statue of Liberty (2 Photographs), Ellis Island; Nat Baseball Hall Fame & Mus, Cooperstown, NY, June 2007; Law Off, Alan L Zegas, Chatham, NJ, 2008; Yankee Stadium; Nat Baseball Hall of Fame & Mus, Cooperstown, NY, 2012. *Comn:* Revelation For Centennial of Brooklyn Bridge, Morris Mus, Morristown, NJ, 83. *Exhib:* Solo exhibs, Chemical Bank, NY, 77, St Barnabas Med Ctr, Livingston, NJ, 78, NJ Ctr Visual Arts, Summit, NJ, 79 & 85, Ciba-Geigy Corp, Summit, NJ, 79, Exxon Corp, Linden, NJ, 84, Chubb Corp World Hq, Warren, NJ, 85, Johnson & Johnson, World Hq, New Brunswick, NJ, 94, Schering Plough, Kenilworth, NJ, 94, Johnson & Johnson Health Care, Piscataway, NJ, 2004 & Photographs, Visual Arts Center NJ at Summit Free Pub Libr, 2006, New Prov Mem Libr, 2008-09, Morris Mus, 2010-11; Images, Members Gallery, NJ Ctr Visual Arts, AT&T, Prudential, Chubb, 88 & 90-91; Arts Counc of Morris Area at Schering Plough, Madison, NJ, 92; Award of Merit, Paper Mill Playhouse, Millburn Short Hills Arts, 95; Salmagundi Club, NY, Nat Soc Painters, 96-98 & 2000; Union Co Arts Exhib, NJ Ctr Visual Arts, 96, 2010; paintings, NJ Sen Robert C Torricelli Senate Off, Washington, DC, 97-98; Seton Hall Univ, 98; Paper Mill Play House, Renee Foosaner Gallery, 98; two-person exhibs, Schering-Plough, Madison, NJ, 2000 & Overlook Hospital, Summit, NJ, 2003; Morris Mus, 2010-2011. *Pos:* Window display designer, Display Craft & Belg Stores, 44-53; theatrical design & decor, Actors Co, Toronto, Ont, 51-53; needlepoint design, Creative Yarn Kits Inc, New York, 65-72. *Teaching:* Substitute teacher art, various high schs NJ, 77-90. *Awards:* Award of Excellence, Renee Foosaner Gallery, Paper Mill Playhouse, NJ, 90, 91 & 95; Award of Merit, Atrium Gallery, Morristown, NJ, 97; Award of Excellence in Photograph, Atrium Gallery, 99; The Outstanding Achievement in Amateur Photography Award for 2004 from The Int Soc of Photographers, Owing Mills, MD; Merit Award for photography, Renee Foosaner Gallery, Papermill Playhouse, NJ, 2003 & Millburn Short Hills Arts Ctr, Madison Libr, 2008. *Bibliog:* Andrea Kannape (auth), New York Times, 11/1/98; Kristie Hanley (auth), The Star-Ledger, 10/22/98; Mitchel Seidel (auth), The Star-Ledger, 10/23/99, 3/8/2006; Liz Keill (auth), Summit Herald, 2/18/2006; Independent Press, July 2007 & Dec 2008; Dan Bischoff (auth), The Sunday Star Ledger, 11/28/2010; Independent Press, 2012; Linda Haase (auth), Palm Beach Post, 9/23/2012. *Mem:* NJ Ctr Visual Arts (prog chmn, 1979-1984); Millburn-Short Hills Art Ctr (bd trustees, 1986-2006); NJ Ctr Visual Arts (chmn of classes, 1990-1998); Nat Mus Women in Arts; Nat Soc Painters in Acrylic & Casien. *Media:* Oil, Acrylic, Photography. *Interests:* Writing, film, science. *Mailing Add:* 6061 Palmetto Cir N AptA305 Boca Raton FL 33433

RIZZI, JAMES
PAINTER, PRINTMAKER
b Brooklyn, NY, Oct 5, 1950. *Study:* Miami Dade Jr Col, AA, 72; Univ Fla, BFA, 74. *Work:* Brooklyn Mus, NY; Isetan Sagamihara, Kanagawa, Japan; Seibu Parco, Chiba, Tokyo, Japan; Int Olympic Mus, Lausanne, Switz, 96. *Comn:* 45-meter outdoor mural, Eric's Bar & Grill, NY, 75; painting, Werzalit AG, Ger; ltd ed collector's China vase, candlestick holders, canister, plate, espresso cup, decorative box & pitcher, Rosenthal China, 94-95; exterior of Boeing 757 in celebration of their 40th anniversary, 96; paintings, Int Olympic Mus, Lausanne, Switz; Painted Smart Car, Spiral Garden, Tokyo; Original Art, Siemens Corp, 01; Exterior of train, City of Heilbronn, Ger, 02. *Exhib:* 30 Yrs of Am Printmaking, Brooklyn Mus, NY, 76; solo exhibs, Fine Art Mus, Hempstead, Long Island, Tsukuba City Mus, Japan, 92, Kunst Mus Limburg, Ger, 96,

Univ Fla, Gainesville, 96, Int Olympic Mus, Lausanne, Switz, 96 & Ctr Arts, Vero Beach, Fla, 97. *Awards:* Guest of Hon, United Hospital Fund, 92; Guest of Hon, Am Anorexia/Bulimia Asn, 93; Citation, Atlanta Olympic Comt, 96; Sport Artist of Yr, US Sports Acad, Ala; Invited Artist World Economic Forum, Davos, 98. *Bibliog:* Gerrit Henry (intro auth), James Rizzi 3-D, Constructions, 88 & Glenn O'Brien (auth), Rizzi, 92, John Szoke Graphics; Juan Antonio Samaranch (intro auth) & George Plimpton (auth), James Rizzi-Dreams of Sport, Olympic Mus & Study Ctr, 96. *Media:* Acrylic, Oil; Miscellaneous Media. *Publ:* Auth, 3-D Constructions, John Szoke Graphics Inc, New York, 88; Rizzi, John Szoke Graphics Inc, New York, 92; feature article with cover, Dan's Papers, 8/96; The New York Paintings, Prestel-Verlag, Ger, 96; Christmas Cooking in NY, Mary Hahn verlag, Muenchen, Germany, 97; American Cookies & More, Sudwest Verlag, Germany, 00

RIZZIE, DAN
COLLAGE ARTIST, PAINTER
b Poughkeepsie, NY, May 23, 1951. *Study:* Hendrix Col, Conway, Ark, BA, 73; Southern Methodist Univ, Dallas, Tex, MFA, 75. *Work:* Dallas Mus Fine Arts & Univ Gallery, Southern Methodist Univ, Tex; Witte Mus, San Antonio, Tex; Brooklyn Mus, NY; Mus Mod Art, NY Pub Libr, Metrop Mus Art, NY; Univ Tex, Austin. *Comn:* Akard Mall banners, City of Dallas, Tex, 79; Signa Life Insurance, Dallas, 94. *Exhib:* solo exhibs, Lizan Tops Gallery, East Hampton, NY, 97, 99, Allene Lapides Gallery, Santa Fe, 97, 98, 99, Dan Rizzie: Works on Paper, Dueringer Gallery, Jackson, Miss, 98, Liz Mayer Fine Art, New York City, 97, West End Fine Arts Gallery, West Palm Beach, Fla, 97; Black and, Flatbed Gallery, Austin, Tex, 99; Flatbed Press Impressions, Amarillo Mus Art, Tex, 99; Multiple Impressions, ACA Gallery, Austin, 99; Flatbed at Ten, Flatbed Press, Austin, 99; 3 Americans, Wilson Stephens Fine Art, London, 99; Flatbed Selections, Flatbed Gallery, Autstin, 2000. *Teaching:* Instr lithography & drawing, Southern Methodist Univ, Dallas, 74-75; instr drawing, Richland Col, Dallas, 75-76; instr painting & drawing, Eastfield Col, Dallas, 76-80. *Awards:* Best of Shows, Tex Painting & Sculpture, 76, Shreveport Ann, 77 & Tarrant Co Ann, 78. *Bibliog:* Festival, The East Hampton Star, 20, 10/28/99; Marion Walberg Weiss (auth), Honoring the Artist: Dan Rizzie, Dan's Papers, 10/15/99. *Media:* Drawing, Collage. *Publ:* Betsy Craz (auth), A Cinema Toast, In Style, 304, 6/99,. *Dealer:* Allene La Pedes Gallery 217 Johnson St Santa Fe NM. *Mailing Add:* PO Box 1672 Sag Harbor NY 11963

RIZZOLO, LOUIS (LOU) B M
ENVIRONMENTAL ARTIST, PAINTER
b Ferndale, Mich, Oct 8, 1933. *Study:* Western Mich Univ, with Harry Hefner, BS (art), 56; Univ Iowa, with Frank Wachowiak & Maurico Lasansky, Ky, MA (art), 60, post grad studies, Univ Ga, with Lamar Dodd, 69-70. *Work:* Mich Artist Permanent Collection, Battle Creek Mus Art; Western Mich Univ Collection, Kalamazoo; Kalamazoo Inst Art, Mich; Chicago Inst Arts, Oxbow Prog; Univ Iowa. *Comn:* Mind Energy (multi-media performance), Mich Found Art, Detroit, 85; Mind Events (multi-media performance), Upjohn Co, Kalamazoo, Mich, 86; Skye Gondola (interactive light art work), Dow Corning/Midland Ctr Art, 86-87. *Exhib:* Construction to Performance, Minn Mus Am Art, St Paul, Minn, 86; North Skye, Mich Technol Univ, Hancock, Mich, 88; Oxbow Light, Chicago Inst Arts, Oxbow Prog, Saugatuck, Mich, 88 & 89; Calgary Skye, Mt Royal Conserv Int Workshop, 90; Swiss Skye, Nat Conserv, Lake Geneva, Lausanne, Switz, 91; Lyon Skye, Lyon Conserv Nat de Region, Lyon, France, 94; Scottish Royal Acad Int Workshop, 95; Konserthus Norway Int Workshop, 97; Palais des Festivals, Int Workshop, Biarritz, France, 98; Bjergsted Install, Stavanger Norway, 2002; Fear/Fun, Multimedia Performance WMU, 2002; Starr Earthwork, Albion, 2002. *Pos:* Dir & artist, Rizzolo & Assoc, ILWC (Art/Tech Collaborative), Glenn, Mich, 1979-2003. *Teaching:* Prof art painting, drawing & multi-media, Western Mich Univ, 1964-2003, Int Workshops, Md, 1989-2003; watercolor painting instr, Kalamazoo Inst Arts, 1968-81. *Awards:* W K Kellogg Found Expert-in-Residence, Kellogg Skye Environ Art, 92; Mich Millennium Proj State Grant, Mich Coun Arts & Cult Affairs, 96-97 & Nat Endowment Arts Regrant, 98; Fetzer Inst, 1999, 2000; Richard Florsheim Art Fund, 2002; Starr Commonwealth, 2000-2002; artist residency, W R Kellogg Found World Peace Art Initiatives. *Bibliog:* Review, New Art Examiner, Chicago, Ill, 11/84; Fetes d'etc, Int Workshops, Lyon, France, 7/94; Rizzolo Ganther (dir), Michigan Millennium (film), Ganther Films, Chicago, 11/96; Art for Peace, Reclaiming Children & Youth, Sculpture Nat Jour Beijing, 2003. *Mem:* Mich Watercolor Soc; Int Soc Arts & Technol; World Forum on a Coustic Ecology. *Media:* Environmental Light Art; Watercolor. *Publ:* Contribr, Int Skye Art Catalog, 1st & 2nd ed, MIT Press, 83 & 91; Emphasis Art, Int Textbook, 89; The Fourth Coast, Penguin Books, 95; Best of Watercolor, 95, Creative Inspirations, 96, Rockport Publ. *Mailing Add:* PO Box 62 Glenn MI 49416

ROACH, STEPHANIE
GALLERY DIRECTOR
Study: Univ Pa, BA (art hist & Spanish, magna cum laude). *Pos:* Bd mem, Inst Contemp Art, Univ Pa; cur, Galeria Senda, Barcelona, Spain; dir, FLAG Art Found. *Mailing Add:* 545 W 25th St 9th Fl New York NY 10001

ROATZ See Myers, Dorothy Roatz

ROBB, CHARLES
PAINTER
b Toronto, Ont, June 28, 1938. *Study:* Ont Coll Art, AOCA, 59, with Jock MacDonald, John Alfson & Carl Schaefer. *Work:* Can Coun Art Bank, Ottawa; Citicorp Ltd, Toronto; Kitchener/Waterloo Art Gallery, Ont; Esso, Calgary, Alta; Art Gallery London, Ont, Can; and others. *Exhib:* Solo exhibs, Pollock Gallery, Toronto, 77-82 & Gallery One, Toronto, 82-90; Group exhib, Agnes Etherington Art Centre, Queens Univ, Kingston, Ont, 77; Art for Bus Sake, Art Gallery Ont, Toronto, 75; Lefebvre Galleries, Edmonton, Alta, 81; Kitchener/Waterloo Art Gallery, Ont, 81; and others. *Bibliog:* D Adlow (auth), Stripes by Robb, Christian Sci Monitor, 64; Kay Woods (auth), Charles Robb, Arts Canada, 77 & 81; Seeing it Our Way, Portrait of Charles Robb (film), Canadian Broadcasting Corp. *Media:* Acrylic. *Mailing Add:* 121 Nymark Ave No 104 Willowdale ON M2J 2H3 Canada

ROBB, DAVID METHENY, JR
HISTORIAN, CONSULTANT
b Minneapolis, Minn, Apr 12, 1937. *Study:* Princeton Univ, BA, 59; Yale Univ, MA, 67; Attingham Summer Sch, 78; Mus Mgt Inst, Univ Calif, Berkeley, 83. *Collection Arranged:* The Book of Hours of Charlotte of Savoy, 73; Star Spangled History, 75-77; Louis I Kahn: Sketches for the Kimbell Art Mus (auth, catalog), 78; Elisabeth Louise Vigee Le Brun, 82; Vivid Colors: Three Pastel Artists, 93; co-cur, Early Alabama: Our Land and Lifeways, 98. *Pos:* Res asst, Nat Gallery Art, DC, 63; cur, Collection of Mr & Mrs Paul Mellon, 63-65; curatorial fel, Walker Art Ctr, Minneapolis, 67-69; cur, Kimbell Art Mus, Ft Worth, Tex, 69-74, chief cur, 74-83 & acting dir, 79-80; dir, Telfair Acad Arts & Sci, Savannah, 84-85 & Huntsville Mus Art, Ala, 85-95; dir emer, Huntsville Mus Art, 95-. *Awards:* Ford Found Cur Training Fel, 68-69. *Mem:* Coll Art Asn; Am Asn of Mus; Soc Archit Historians; Ala Historical Assn; Friends of Ala Archives. *Res:* American and European portrait painting; architectural and landscape photography; southern landscape painting; 18th century cartography; 19th century southern photography. *Publ:* Ed, Kimbell Art Mus Catalogue, 72; Louis Kahn: Sketches for the Kimbell Art Mus, 78; Kimbell Art Mus Handbook, 81; Frances Benjamin Johnston-1939 Tennessee Valley Architectural Photography, Hist Huntsville Quart, Vol XXVI, 1&2 (entire issue), 2000; Articles, Encyclopedia Ala, 2009; Alabama's Invisible Man of 1818 revealed. *Mailing Add:* 506 Lanier Rd Huntsville AL 35801

ROBB, LAURA ANN
PAINTER, INSTRUCTOR
b Winfield, Kans, Apr 5, 1955. *Study:* Art Students Acad, 70-71; studied with Michael Aviano, 72-73, with Richard Schmid, 74. *Exhib:* Miniatures 2000, Albuquerque Mus Art, NMex, 2000; Am Art in Miniature, Gilcrease Mus, Tulsa, Okla; Salon D'Arts, Denver, Colo, 2002-2006; Western Rendezvous of Art Ann Exhib, Helena, Mont, 2007-2010, 2011; Nat Mus Wildlife Art Western Visions, Wy, 2007-2010, 2011; Am Masters at SCNY, Salmagundi Club, NY, 2011; Three Graces, Clagett Rey Gallery, Vail Colo, 2012; Taos Living Legends, Taos Art Mus & Fechin House, 2012; Western Rendezvous of Art, 2012; American Art in Miniature Gilcrease Mus, Tulsa, Okla, 2012; Rims to Ruins, Mesa Verde, Denver, Colo, 2013; Rims to Ruins, Denver, Colo, 2014. *Pos:* Guest artist, Western Rendezvous Art, Helena, Mont, 2006-2007. *Teaching:* Instr oil painting, Scottsdale Artists Sch, Ariz, 93-99, Valdes Art Sch, Santa Fe, 94-2001, 2009, 2010, 2011, 2012 & Fechin Art Inst, Taos, NMex, 2000-2001, First Brush of Spring, New Harmony, Ind, 2012, Valdes Art Sch, Santa Fe, 2013, Mainstreet Art Ctr, Lake Zurich, Ill, 2013, Peninsula Sch Fine Art, Fish Creek, Wisc, 2013. *Awards:* Grumbacher Gold Medal, Catharine Lorillard Art Club, 86; John F and Anna Lee Stacey Scholar award, 91; Liquitex Award, Oil Painters of Am juried exhib, 96; John Scott People's Choice Award for Painting, Western Rendezvous of Art. *Mem:* Western Rendezvous of Art. *Media:* Oil, Watercolor. *Publ:* Contribr, The Subject is Merely A Vehicle, Art of the West, 90; Laura Robb, Southwest Art, 92; Emerging Realist Painters, Art-Talk, 96; Contemporary American Oil Painting, Jilin Publ House, 99; A Personal Sense of Beauty, Southwest Art, 4/2001; In the Studio, Southwest Art, 1/2002; An All-Consuming Passion, Arts of the West, 5/2003-6/2003; A Sharp Eye, The Artist's Mag, 9/2003; The Cultural Times, 9/2006; The Studio Art of the West, July/Aug 2007; A Visual Conversation, Southwest Art, Feb 2010; Im Not Trying to Stay Safe, Art of the West, 2013; Entre Realisme et Abstraction, Pratique des Arts, 2013. *Dealer:* Claggett / Rey Gallery 100 East Meadow Dr Vail CO 81657; Nedra Matteucci's Fenn Galleries 1075 Paseo de Peralta Santa Fe NM 87501

ROBB, PEGGY HIGHT
PAINTER, INSTRUCTOR
b Gallup, NMex, Sept 14, 1924. *Study:* Univ NMex, BFA & MA, with Raymond Jonson & Kenneth Adams; Art Students League, New York, 64. *Work:* Univ NMex, Albuquerque; Guangzhuo Art Inst, China, 84. *Comn:* Stained glass window & portraits, Christian Ctr, Albuquerque, 75; McDonnell-Douglass Aircraft, St Louis, Mo, 79. *Exhib:* Southwestern Fiesta, NMex Art Mus, Santa Fe, 66; Sun Carnival Art Exhib, El Paso, Tex, 71; Centre Int D'Art Contemporian, Paris, 83; Inst Art, Guangzhuo, China, 84; NMex State Fair, 86; Biennial exhib, Ariz, Colo, NMex, Tex & Utah, 87; Expressions of Faith, Scottsdale, Ariz, 87; Christians in the Visual Arts, Washington, 87; Graham Ctr Mus, Wheaton, Ill, 87 & 89; Sacred Arts 200, Civic Ctr Mus, Philadelphia, 89; Nat Exhib, Farmington Gateway Mus, NMex, 2007. *Pos:* Juror, Statewide Exhib, 81, 87, 89, 91; bd dir, Col Fine Arts, Univ NMex, 89-. *Teaching:* Univ NMex, Continuing Educ. *Awards:* First Prize, NMex State Fair, 59 & 63; Exhib Awards, St John's Episcopal Cathedral, Albuquerque, 78 & 79; Jurors Award, Nat Christian Fine Arts Exhib, Farmington, NMex, 96. *Bibliog:* Conceptions Southwest, Southwest Art Mag, Univ NMex, 85. *Mem:* Albuquerque Asn United Artists; Christians in the Visual Arts; Albuquerque Arts Alliance. *Media:* Acrylic, Oil. *Mailing Add:* 7200 Rio Grande Blvd NW Albuquerque NM 87107

ROBBIN, TONY
PAINTER, SCULPTOR
b Washington, DC, Nov 24, 1943. *Study:* Columbia Univ, BA, 65; Yale Univ, MFA, 68. *Work:* Whitney Mus Am Art, New York; Neuberger Mus, Purchase, NY; Loch Haven Art Ctr, Orlando; Chrysler Mus, Norfolk, Va; Del State Mus, Wilmington. *Comn:* Prudential Insurance, Newark, NJ, 82; Southeast Bank, Miami, Fla, 83; United Bank, Houston, 83. *Exhib:* Le Wouvean Mus, Lyon, France, 80; McNay Art Inst, San Antonio, 83; Loch Haven Art Ctr, Orlando, 83; Concepts in Construct, Neuberger Mus, Purchase, NY, 84; Computers & Art, IBM Gallery, New York, 88; Kaos, Chicago Acad Sci, 89; solo exhibs, Am Asn Advan Sci, Washington, DC, 92 & Boston Meeting, 93, Fordham Univ, New York, 92 & Williams Gallery, Princeton, 92; Structure of Symmetry, Hungarian Nat Gallery, Budapest, 89; Bronx Mus Arts, 91; The William Collection, Princeton, 92; Contemp Develop Design Sci, 95; Building for the Future, Istanbul Mus, 96; Am Asn Advan Sci, Fordham Univ, Univ Sci, Philadelphia & Univ Fla, Greenville, 2006. *Awards:* Artist Fel, Nat Endowment Arts, 75; Nat Science Found Grant, 89. *Bibliog:* Linda Henderson (auth), Princeton Univ Press, 83; David Curtis (auth), To the Nth Dimension, Innovations/PBS, 87; Cynthia

Goodman (auth), Distal Visions, Henry Abrams, 87; Tony Robbin, A Retrospective, Hudson Hills Press, Manchester, 2011; Mood Swings: A Painters Life, Kindle, 2011. *Media:* Acrylic, Sculpture. *Publ:* Chuangtze, Main Currents, 75; Painting & Physics--4 Dimensions, Leonardo, 84; Quasi crystals for Architecture, Leonardo, 89; auth, Fourfield: Computers, Art & the 4th Dimension, 92; Engineering a New Architecture, Yale University Press, New Haven, 96; auth chpt, Beyond the Cube, by J Francis Gabriel, 97; Shadows of Reality: The Fourth Dimension in Cubism, Relativity, and Modern Though, Yale Univ Press, New Haven, 2006; auth numerous articles. *Mailing Add:* 423 Broome St New York NY 10013

ROBBINS, EUGENIA S
WRITER, EDITOR
b New York, NY, Apr 22, 1935. *Study:* Smith Col, BA. *Pos:* ed, Art & Auction, 80; news ed, Art Express, 81-; secy, Iroquois Co, formerly & Ctr Can Archit Adv Bd, formerly; dir, Friends of the Vt State House; chmn, Langeview House Restoration, 82-84. *Teaching:* Instr, Union Col, Schenectady, NY. *Media:* Print. *Res:* Persian art and architecture; modern art and architecture; Art books; history of photography; historical preservation on prints and drawings; early photography, American art. *Collection:* 19th and 20th century paintings, drawings, and prints. *Publ:* Auth & coauth, articles in Studio Int, Art in Am, Art and Auction & NY Post; auth, Art, Collier's Yr Bk; auth, regular column in Art J & rev in Art in Am & Art J; Toulouse Lautrec; and others

ROBBINS, HULDA D
PAINTER, PRINTMAKER
b Atlanta, Ga, Oct 19, 1910. *Study:* Pa Mus Sch Indust Art, Philadelphia; Prussian Acad, Berlin, with Ludwig Bartning; Barnes Found, Merion, Pa. *Work:* Metrop Mus Art, NY; Victoria & Albert Mus, London, Eng; Bibliot Nat, Paris; Art Mus Ont; Smithsonian Inst, Washington; 16 Prints in Philadelphia Mus Art Col, 2006-2007. *Exhib:* Portrait of Am, NY & Tour, 45-46; Current Am Prints, Carnegie Inst, Pittsburgh, 48; Nat Print Ann, Brooklyn Mus & Tour, 48-49; Nat Exhib Prints, Libr Cong, Washington, 56; US Info Agency Print Exhib Europ Tour, 72-. *Teaching:* Instr basic & advan serigraphy, Nat Serigraph Soc Sch, 54-60; instr creative painting, Atlantic Co Jewish Community Ctr, Margate, NJ, 60-67. *Awards:* Purchase Award, Prints For Children, Mus Mod Art, 41; Paintings by Printmakers Award, 47 & Babette S Kornblith Purchase Prize, 49, Nat Serigraph Soc. *Mem:* Print Club; Am Color Print Soc. *Media:* Oil. *Dealer:* The Picture Store Boston MA; William P Carl Fine Prints Boston. *Mailing Add:* 11 Lenwood Ct Egg Harbor Township NJ 08234-5342

ROBBINS, JACK C
PAINTER, SCULPTOR
b Dallas, Tex. *Study:* Univ NTex, study with Robert Wade, BFA, 77; Univ Tex, San Antonio, MFA, 94. *Work:* Mus Mod Art, Ft Worth, Tex; ARTPACE Found Contemp Art, San Antonio, Tex; City Pub Art Coll, Dallas; Barrett Coll Tex Art, Dallas. *Comn:* City billboard, Patrick Media Co, Arlington, Tex, 87; pedestrian tunnelway, City of Dallas, 96. *Exhib:* Social Distortions, Los Angeles Contemp Exhibs, 86; Tornadoes Twister of Fate, Vanderbilt Univ, 90; Prints from Permanent Collection, Ft Worth Mus Mod Art, 90; 40 Texas Printmakers, Laguna Gloria Mus, Austin, Tex, 92; Return of Cadavre Exquis, The Drawing Ctr, NY, 93. *Bibliog:* Janet Kutner (auth), Dallas Morning News, 9/90; Joel W Barna (auth), Tex Architect, 2/94; Dan Goddard (auth), San Antonio Expos News, 6/95. *Media:* Installation. *Dealer:* Parchman-Stremmel Presa St San Antonio TX

ROBBINS, JOAN NASH
PAINTER, COLLAGE ARTIST
b Kalamazoo, Mich, Nov 24, 1941. *Study:* Western Mich Univ, BA, 63; Oakland Univ, MA, 69. *Comn:* Jungle Story (series of 4 collages), St Louis Fed Savings & Loan, 84; Growth (series of 4 collages), Gen Am Life, St Louis, 85; Rivers Run (diptych collage), AT&T, St Louis, 85; Dance (diptych collage), AT&T, St Louis, 86. *Exhib:* An Art Affair, Westport, St Louis, 82 & 84-86; San Diego Int, 85; Watercolor Missouri, William Woods Col, Fulton, Mo, 85; 10th Okla Ann, Norman Gallery, Lawton, Okla, 85; 10th Nat Ann, Southern Watercolor Soc, Okla Art Ctr, Oklahoma City, Okla, 86. *Teaching:* Pvt instr, collage & watermedia, in studio & in workshops. *Awards:* Moerschel Award, St Charles 17th Ann Show, 82; Merit Award, An Art Affair, Show, St Louis, 83; Norman Gallom Award, Watercolor, Okla 10th Ann, 85. *Mem:* Southern Watercolor Soc; Midwest Watercolor Soc; St Louis Art Guild; North Coast Collage Soc. *Media:* Watercolor, Collage. *Mailing Add:* 204 N Gilmore St Charleston MO 63834

ROBBINS, MICHAEL JED
PAINTER, PRINTMAKER
b New York, NY, June 15, 1949. *Study:* High Sch Music & Art, New York, dipl, 66; Cooper Union, New York, BFA, 70; Syracuse Univ, MFA (teaching fel), 71. *Work:* Mus City New York; Brooklyn Mus; Mus Liege, Belg; Smithsonian Inst Nat Gallery Art, Washington, DC; Rutgers Univ, NJ; Univ NC, Greensboro; Mus Boverie Park, Brussels, Belg; Richard Brown Baker pvt collection, New York; Metrop Mus Art, New York. *Comn:* Posters, Molissa Fenley Dance co, New York, 80; on site oil on panel mural, ESPA Dept Store, 84; banners & posters, 84-85, Ito Yokado Corp, Tokyo; outdoor banners, St Marks Church, New York, 87. *Exhib:* Drawings, Czech Mus Mod Art, 76; Recent Drawings by Younger Artists, Whitney Mus, 78; Art in the 70's-Richard Brown Baker Collection, Rochester Univ Mus, 79; The Block Print, Whitney Mus, 82; NY in Print, Mus City New York, 82; Paintings, Prints, Trustees Collection, Albright-Knox Mus, 86; Am Expressionists, Montclair Mus, NJ, 87; Prints, Rutgers Univ, 88; traveling exhib, Robi Collection, Smithsonian Inst Nat Gallery Art, 98; Narrative Prints from the Rutgers Archives, Zimmerli Art Mus, Rutgers Univ, NJ, 2005. *Pos:* Fine Artist, currently; Minister, currently. *Teaching:* Asst instr art & drawing, Syracuse Univ, 70-71; sub-instr painting, Cooper Union, 76 & 80-85. *Awards:* CAPS Grant, NY, 78; NEA Grant, 85. *Media:* Oil Painting; Linocuts. *Specialty:* Sragow Art of the 20th century & art of the 1930's and 40's. *Interests:* Art, ministry, lecturing. *Dealer:* Ellen Sragow 67-73 Spring St New York NY. *Mailing Add:* 136 E 208 Norwood NY 10467

ROBBINS, PATRICIA
PAINTER
b Brooklyn, NY, Oct 27, 1951. *Study:* Am Univ, Washington, DC, BA, 73; Johns Hopkins Univ, Baltimore, MD, MLA, 77. *Work:* Morgan Stanley Regional Hq, San Luis Obispo, Calif. *Comn:* Painting, Botanical Garden, Calif, 2005-2007; painted Violin Mozart Int Music Festival, 2006. *Exhib:* Solo exhibs, City of Paso Robles, Paso Robles, Calif, Postcards, Excellent Experiences Gallery, San Luis Obispo, Calif, Postcards 2, Excellent Experiences Gallery, Santa Cruz, Calif, 2006, Picking Daisies, San Luis Obispo, Calif, 2009, Equilibrium, 2009; New Art, Fogg Mus Contemp Art, Boston, Mass, Asian Style 2005; Excellent Experiences Gallery, San Luis Obispo, Calif; Miniatures & Biennial Exhib, Monterey Mus Art, Monterey, Calif; Small Works Exhib, Bakersfield Mus Art, Bakersfield, Calif, 2005 & 2007; Configurations, San Luis Obispo Art Ctr, Calif; Sacred Women, Art Harvest, Sacramento, Calif; Nat Asn Women Artists Small Works Exhib, Karpeles Libr Mus; 54th Haggin Juried Exhib, Haggin Mus, Stockton, Calif; Nat Asn Women Artists 117th Ann Exhib, Reading, Pa, 2006; Asian Style, McConnell Gallery, In the Tin Gallery & Roofs, Doors, Windows, San Luis Obispo Art Ctr, Calif, 2004; Women Working, Studio Channel Arts Ctr, Calif State Univ, Camarillo; Personal Totems, Adelphi Univ Gallery, Garden City, NY; Moving Forward, Belskie Mus Art, Closter, NJ; Harper Coll, Pallatine, Ill; September Competition, Alexandria Mus Art, La; Int Asn Acrylic Painters Exhib, San Luis Obispo, Calif; 11th Exhib, Int Asn Acrylic Painters, Santa Cruz, Calif, 2008; Nat Asn Women Artists (NAWA), 118 Ann Exhib & 120 Ann Exhib, Penn & New York, 2008, 2009; 79th Ann Statewide Exhib, Irreplaceable Places, Santa Cruz, Calif, 2009; Art the First Language, Jeannet Haire Gallery, Northwood Univ, Fla, 2009; Haub Gallery, Avila, Calif, 2009; Gallery Los Olivos, Calif, 2009; NAWA 121st Ann Exhib Natil Arts Club, New York 2010; Seaside GalleryPismo Beach, CAIIF, 2010; Inspirations, Coral Springs Mus Art, 2010; Red, Viva Gallery, SHerman Oaks, Calif, 2010. *Awards:* Elizabeth Horman Mem Award, 2005; Hon Mention, 2nd City Coun Gallery Exhib. *Mem:* Nat Asn Women Artists (juried mem); Nat Asn Independent Artists; San Luis Obispo Oil, Pastel & Acrylic Group; Women Painters West (juried); Women Caucus Art; Int Asn Acrylic Painters (sig mem); Nat Asn Women Artists (juried mem); Women Painters West (juried); Nat Asn Acrylic Painters (signature mem). *Media:* Acrylic, oil. *Mailing Add:* 7170 Cerro Robles San Luis Obispo CA 93401

ROBBINS, TRINA
CARTOONIST, ILLUSTRATOR
b Brooklyn, NY, Aug 17, 1938. *Exhib:* Corcoran Gallery, Washington, DC, 69; Global Space Invasions, San Francisco Mus Mod Art, 78; Pork Roasts, Univ BC Fine Arts Gallery, Vancouver, 81. *Awards:* Inkpot Award, San Diego Comic Art, 77. *Bibliog:* Ronald Levitt Lanyi (auth), Trina, Queen of underground comics, Univ Calif, Davis, 78; Sharon R Gunton (ed), Contemporary Literary Criticism, Vol 21, Gale Res, 82. *Publ:* Ed & contribr, It ain't me, Babe, 70 & contribr, Wimmen's Comix No 1-6, 72-76, Last Gasp; Wet Satin No 1 & 2, Krupp/Last Gasp, 76 & 78; auth & illusr, Flashback Fashions, Price, Stern, Sloan, 83; coauth, Women and the Comics, Eclipse Enterprises, 85; and others. *Mailing Add:* 1982 15th St San Francisco CA 94102

ROBERSON, SAMUEL ARNDT
ARCHITECTURAL HISTORIAN, EDUCATOR
b Honolulu, Hawaii, May 5, 1939. *Study:* Williams Col, BA, 61, MA, 63; Salzburg-Klessheim Sch, cert, 65; Yale Univ, PhD, 74. *Collection Arranged:* Am Paintings from a Private Long Meadow Collection, Amherst Col, 71; Five College Modern Architecture, Amherst Col, 72; Early Chicago Architecture, Herron Sch Art, 80. *Pos:* Consult, Eye of Thomas Jefferson Bicentennial Exhib, Nat Gallery Art, Washington, DC, 74-76; acad coordr, Nat Endowment Humanities Learning Mus Prog, Indianapolis Mus Art, 76-80; dir, Historic Indianapolis Inc, 80-; comnr, Ind Film Comn, 83-; adj assoc prof Am studies, Sch Liberal Arts, Ind Univ, 84-. *Teaching:* Instr art hist, Williams Col, 61-63, Yale Univ, 64-66, Princeton Univ, 66-68 & Amherst Col, 69-72; asst prof, Herron Sch Art, 72-76, chmn art hist, 72-80, assoc prof, 76-; vis assoc prof, Ind Univ, Bloomington, 76. *Mem:* Soc Archit Historians; Coll Art Asn; and others. *Res:* Eighteenth and nineteenth century American architecture and landscape gardening. *Publ:* Auth, The Technical Creation of the Greek Slave, 65 & coauth, The Greek Slave, 65, Newark Mus; contribr, Praeger Encyclopedia of Art, Praeger Publ, 71; auth, Indiana Historic Sites and Structures Reports, 80-; Historic American Buildings Survey in Indiana Catalog, 83

ROBERSON, SANG
CRAFTSMAN
b Greenville, Miss, Feb 7, 1938. *Study:* Sophie Newcomb Col, Tulane Univ; Daytona State Coll; Arrowmont, Gatlinburg, Tenn; Penland Sch, NC; Univ Miss, BA. *Work:* Mus Arts & Sci, Daytona Beach, Fla; Off Chief Exec Officer, Walt Disney World, Fla; Orlando City Collection, Fla; DeLand Mus Art, Fla; also pvt collections of Dan Rather, CBS News, Steffi Graf, Ger, Jane Fonda & others. *Exhib:* Solo exhibs, Decorative Touch, Greenville, Miss, 89, Gallery 500, Elkins Park, Pa, 93, Albers Gallery, Memphis, Tenn, 93, Hibbard-McGrath Gallery, Breckenridge, Colo, 94 & 96, Sampson Galleries, Stetson Univ, DeLand, Fla, 95 & Ormond Mem Art Mus, Ormond Beach, Fla, 96; Pa Acad Art, Philadelphia, 92; Philadelphia Mus Art, 92 & 94; Florida's NEA & SAF Recipients Exhib, Fla Craftsmen Gallery, St Petersburg, Fla, 97; SOFA-MIAMI, Gingrass Gallery, Milwaukee, Wis, 97; Smithsonian Craft Show, Washington DC, 97 & 2007; Beyond Function, Columbus Mus Art, Ga, 97; Sophia Wanamaker Gallery, San Jose, Costa Rica, 2001; Fla Craftsmen Gallery, St Petersburg, Fla, 2001; Wyndy Moorhead Fine Arts, New Orleans, La, 2001; Gayle Wilson Gallery, Southampton, NY, 2001; Brevard Mus, Melbourne, Fla, 2009. *Awards:* Nat Endowment Arts Visual Artist Fel, 94; Award Excellence Southeastern Crafts Regional Exhib, Tampa Mus Art, Fla, 95; First Place Ceramics, Am Craft Expo, Evanston, Ill, 96; Award Excellence, Am Craft Coun Atlanta, 2000. *Bibliog:* Southern Homes Mag, 7/90; Ceramics Monthly, 5/92; The Year of American Craft Desk Diary, Harry N Abrams Publ, New York, 93. *Mem:* Am Craft Asn (bd dir, 93); Piedmond Craftsmen; Arts Coun Volusia Co; Am Craft Coun; Fla Craftsmen (secy exec bd,

88-89); Fla Dept Cult Affairs (visual arts fel panel). *Media:* Terra Cotta, Terra Sigillata. *Dealer:* Blue Spiral Ashville NC; Albers Fine Art Gallery Memphis TN; Hibberd McGrath Breckinridge Coll CO; Telluride Gallery of Fine Art CO. *Mailing Add:* 19 Orchard Lane Ormond Beach FL 32176

ROBERSON, WILLIAM
TAPESTRY ARTIST, COLLAGE ARTIST
b Ripley, Miss, Feb 15, 1939. *Study:* Memphis State Univ; Memphis Coll Art, BFA; Ind Univ. *Work:* Ark Art Ctr, Little Rock; Tenn Craft Collection, Craft Mus, Nashville; 1st Nat Bank, Orlando, Fla; Falls Creek State Park, Tenn; and others. *Comn:* Tapestries, comn by Lausanne Sch, Memphis, 70, Jewish Community Ctr, Memphis, 71, Holiday Inns of Am, Aberdeen, Tex, 73, Opryland Hotel, Nashville & First Tenn Bank, Memphis. *Exhib:* Young Americans, Mus Contemp Crafts, NY, 69; Piedmont Craft Exhib, Sneed Mus, Charlotte, NC; Miss Arts Festival, Jackson; Southeastern Craftmen Show, San Antonio, Tex. *Pos:* Assoc dean. *Teaching:* Assoc prof fiber design, Memphis Col Art, 69-. *Mailing Add:* 694 N Trezevant St Memphis TN 38112

ROBERTS, DARRELL KEITH
PAINTER
b Ottumwa, Iowa, 1972. *Study:* Univ Northern Iowa, BA (Art History); Sch Art Inst Chicago, BFA, MFA. *Exhib:* Solo exhibs include Hyde Park Art Center, Chicago, 2007; Group exhibs include L2 Kontemporary, Los Angeles, 2007; MN Gallery, Chicago . *Awards:* Robert Rauschenberg Found Grant, 2007; George Sugarman Found Grant, 2007; Dedalus Found Grant, 2007; Ludwig Vogelstein Found Grant, 2007. *Dealer:* Thomas McCormick Gallery 835 W Washington Blvd Chicago IL 60607. *Mailing Add:* 1800 W Cornelia 205 Chicago IL 60657

ROBERTS, DONALD
EDUCATOR, PRINTMAKER
b Wolfeboro, NH, Nov 24, 1923. *Study:* Vesper George Sch of Art, Boston, cert; RI Sch of Design, Providence, BFA; Ohio Univ, Athens, MFA. *Work:* Cleveland Mus of Art; Tate Gallery, London; Rosenwald Collection, Los Angeles; Seattle Mus, Wash; Libr of Cong, Washington, DC. *Exhib:* Dayton Art Inst, Ohio, 60, 65 & 74; 1st-3rd Lithography Ann, Tallahassee, Fla, 64-67; The Print Club, Philadelphia, 68; Contemp Am Prints, Krannert Mus, Champaign-Urbana, Ill, 70; Huntington Galleries, WVa, 71; and others. *Teaching:* Prof printmaking, drawing & painting, Ohio Univ, Athens, 53-. *Awards:* Tamarind Lithography Grant, 62; Purchase Award, 9th Ann Paint of the Yr, Mead Corp, 63; Pennypacker Award, 4th Ann Soc Am Graphic Artists, 65. *Bibliog:* William Sargent (auth), American Printmakers, Ashland Oil Corp, 76. *Mailing Add:* 6555 Frum Rd Athens OH 45701

ROBERTS, MARK
PAINTER, DESIGNER
b Detroit, Mich, April 10, 1928. *Study:* Wayne Univ, Detroit, Mich; Traphagen Sch Fashion, New York, NY; Central Park Sch Art, New York, NY; studied with Howard Hayward, WM Duncalf, Victor Perard, and Arthur Black. *Work:* Eleanor Mann, New York; Mr William Hernstadt, Las Vegas, Nev; Clyta Montllor, Chicago, Ill; Georgia Medical Coll, Augusta, Ga. *Exhib:* several small exhibs in NYC, Mountain Lakes, and Morristown, NJ. *Pos:* textile designer, Golding Decorative Fabrics, NYC, 1949-55, Seneca Textiles, NYC, 1955-64, M Lowenstein & Sons, NYC, 1964-65. *Media:* Oil, Pastel, Charcoal, Watercolors. *Mailing Add:* 64 Highland Avenue Bloomingdale NJ 07403

ROBERTS, MARK DENNIS
PHOTOGRAPHER, CURATOR
b Los Angeles, Calif, Mar 10, 1943. *Study:* Stanford Univ, Palo Alto, Calif, MA, 62; studied photog with Ansel Adams, 56-57, Imogen Cunningham, 63-64 and Pierre Cordier, 82. *Work:* Minn Mus Art, St Paul; Minn Inst Arts, Minneapolis; Mus Mod Art, NY; Huntington Hartford, Los Angeles; Ecole Nationale de la Photographia, Arles, France; Vatican Mus, Italy; Mus D'Arte Moderna, Milan; Paul Getty Mus, Malibu, Calif. *Exhib:* Lincoln Ctr Gallery, NY, 77; Provincetown Art Mus, Mass, 85; Am Acad, Paris, France, 90; Ecole Nat De La Photographis, Arles, France, 95; one-person, Am Acad Rome, Italy; Miami Nat Expo, 2000; Miami Mayors Exhib, 02; Art Basel, Miami, 02. *Collection Arranged:* Vera Stravinsky Gouaches and Watercolor, 85; Photographs by Igor and Vera Stravinsky, 87-88; Kirlian Imagery, 92; Alternative Image, 96; Contemp Nudes, 96. *Pos:* Dir, J Hunt Gallery, 72-80 & Imprimator, Ltd, 80, Minneapolis; Dir, Roberts & Assocs, Palm Beach, Fla. *Bibliog:* Tom Adair, Wyld Rice, KTCA-PBS, 77; John Barnier, Images, KUOM Radio, 81; Tom Adair (auth), Belle Russe, Renaissance House, Ltd, 86. *Publ:* Illusr, Hennepin Government Center, Archit Forum, 80; Mark Roberts, Photogrs Forum, 80; Adam without Eve, Christopher Street, 84 & Artnews, 85; Ideas and images, Photo Design, 86; 200 Photographic Innovators; Salon Album of Vera Stravinsky, Princeton Univ Press. *Dealer:* Roberts and Assocs Palm Beach FL

ROBERTS, RANDY
MUSEUM DIRECTOR
Pos: Mgr, Visitor Studies Assn; dep dir, Crocker Art Mus, 2009-. *Mailing Add:* 216 O St Sacramento CA 95814

ROBERTS, RUSSELL L
PAINTER
b Sept 9, 1953. *Study:* Vassar Col, BA (eng lit); Sch Mus Fine Arts, dipl; Boston Univ, MFA (painting). *Exhib:* Tsai Performance Art Ctr, Boston Univ, 95; MFA Thesis Exhib, Boston Univ Art Gallery, 95; Traveling Scholars Exhib, Mus Fine Arts, Boston; Outside the Box, Horn Gallery, Babson Col, Mass; Spirit of Landscape, V, Nielsen Gallery, Boston, 2000; Boston Drawing Project, Bernard Toale Gallery, Boston, 2001; solo exhibs, Danforth Mus, Framingham, Mass, 2001, Sherman Gallery, Boston Univ, 2001, Farrell-Pollock Gallery, Brooklyn, NY, 2001 & Hanes Art Ctr, Univ NC, Chapel Hill, 2003; Intersection: Couples in Mixed Media, DNA Gallery, Provincetown, Mass, 2002; Merry II, Sideshow Gallery, Brooklyn, NY, 2002. *Pos:* Artist-in-residence, Univ NC, 2003. *Teaching:* Asst prof painting, Mass Col Art, 2000-01; vis asst prof, Pratt Inst, 2001-2002 & 2002. *Awards:* Charles Cumming Mem Travel Grant, Sch Mus Fine Arts, Boston, 96; Guggenheim Fel Painting, 97-98; Artist Books Finalist Grant, Mass Cult Coun, 2002. *Mailing Add:* 15 Gramercy Park S #11A New York NY 10003-1705

ROBERTS, STEVEN K
SCULPTOR, PRINTMAKER
b San Diego, Calif, Dec 2, 1954. *Study:* Washington & Lee Univ, Va, BA, 76; also with Ju Ming, Taiwan, 76. *Work:* Nat Mus Am Art & Fed Deposit Insurance Corp, Washington, DC; Nat Mus Hist, Taipei, Taiwan; Gen Motors, Detroit; Am Tel & Tel, Rosalyn, Va. *Comn:* Poster, comn by City Councilman John Wilson, Washington, DC, 80; stained glass window, Rivertown Gen, Occuquan, Va, 80; painting, Am Systs Corp, Annandale, Va, 82; sculptural portrait, pvt comn by Melvin Watson & family, Lynchburg, Va, 84; wall murals, pvt comn by Anita & Burton Reiner, Bethesda, Md, 86. *Exhib:* 36 Hours, Mus Temporary Art, Washington, DC, 78; Sculpture Conference, Lansburg Bldg, Washington, DC, 80; 57th Ann Int, Print Club, Philadelphia, 81; Am Printmakers in Moscow, US Embassy, Moscow, USSR, 84; North Miami Mus & Art Center, N Miami, Fla, 84; Kathleen Ewing Gallery, Washington, DC, 85. *Bibliog:* Paul Waley (auth), US sculptor deeply influenced, The China News, 9/19/76; Ellen Edwards (auth), Art-Show & Tell, 4/26/80 & Jo Ann Lewis (auth), Art in boxes: surprises inside, 3/12/83, Washington Post. *Mem:* Washington Proj Arts, DC; Print Club, Philadelphia. *Media:* Wood, Steel; Serigraphy. *Dealer:* Kraskin Gallery 9812 Falls Rd Potomac MD 20854. *Mailing Add:* 1731 Harvard St NW Washington DC 20009

ROBERTS, WILLIAM EDWARD
PAINTER, EDUCATOR
b Cleveland, Ohio, July 1, 1941. *Study:* Kent State Univ, BFA, 68, MA, 71; Cornell Univ, lithography with Arnold Singer, 73. *Work:* Everson Mus Art, Syracuse, NY; Kent State Univ, Ohio; IBM Corp, Albany, NY; NY Racing Asn, Elmont; Seagrams Inc, NY. *Exhib:* Solo exhib, Everson Mus Art, 74; 55 Mercer, NY, 81; Saratoga Performing Art Ctr, NY, 82; Hartell Gallery, Cornell Univ, 82; Dayspring Gallery, Saratoga Springs, NY, 82-86; Handwerker Gallery, Ithaca Col, 83; Schweinforth Art Ctr, Auburn, NY, 85; Shearson Lehman Am Express, Ithaca, NY, 86; Herbert Johnson Mus, Cornell Univ, 91; Tyler Art Gallery, SUNY Oswego, NY, 91. *Pos:* Instr, Cayuga Correctional Facility, 90-. *Teaching:* Assoc prof painting, Wells Col, Aurora, NY, 71-86, prof, 86-; instr painting, Auburn Prison, NY, 75-77. *Awards:* Purchase Awards, State Univ NY, Potsdam, 73 & Erie Pa Ann, Marine Midland Bank, 73; Purchase Award, Erie, Pa Ann, Marine Midland Bank, 73; First Place in Painting, Skaneateles Art Assoc, NY, 90. *Bibliog:* Millie Wolff (auth), Artist's racing series has King's excitement, Palm Beach Daily News, 3/14/79; Charlene Johnson (auth), Saratoga on a grand scale, Horsemen's J, 8/83; Lee Scott (auth), Aurora artist paints life on the fast track, Ithaca J, 2/20/84; Message to the Future, Binghamton, NY, 91; and others. *Mem:* Coll Art Asn; Am Asn Univ Prof. *Media:* Oil,. *Mailing Add:* Wells Rd Aurora NY 13026

ROBERTSON, CHARLES J
ADMINISTRATOR
b Houston, Tex, Sept 12, 1934. *Study:* Univ Va, BA, 56; Harvard Univ, MA, 58; Courtauld Inst, Univ London, 60; George Wash Univ, JD, 64. *Pos:* Assoc dir, NC Mus Art, 75-77; asst dir mus resources, 77-86; dep dir, Smithsonian Am Art Mus, 86-2001; asst to dir, 2002-. *Mem:* Octagon House Mus (adv comt, 89-97, chmn, 93-96); Victorian Soc Am (bd dir, 90-, vpres, 94-2000, 2006-); Am Asn Mus (treas, 81-83); Am Archit Found (regent, 93-96); Hist Preservation Review Bd Washington DC (1992-2004); Cosmos Club Hist Pres Found (trustee, 93-, tres 99-2003); Comt of 100 on the Fed City (trustee, 2006-). *Publ:* Auth, Temple of Invention: History of a National Landmark, Scala Pub Ltd, 2006. *Mailing Add:* Nat Mus Am Art Smithsonian Inst Washington DC 20560

ROBERTSON, DAVID ALAN
MUSEUM DIRECTOR
b Jefferson City, Mo, Oct 10, 1950. *Study:* Univ Mo, BA, 73, MA, 76; Kress fel, London, 76, Vienna, 80; Penfield Scholar, Studies in Vienna, Austria, 81-82; Univ Pa, PhD, 83; Fulbright, Munich, 89. *Collection Arranged:* Context & Collab in Contemp Art, Dickinson, 86; On Loan from the Metrop Mus, Dickinson, 87; Leon Golub: World Wide (auth, catalog), Dickinson/Chicago Cult Ctr, 93; Sacrificial Images of Christ (1350-1750) (auth, catalog), Loyola D'Arcy Gallery, 94. *Pos:* Curatorial asst, Yale Ctr Brit Art, New Haven, Conn, 77-78; staff supervisor Rosenbach Mus and Libr, 80-82; dir, Dickinson Col, Carlisle, 82-2002; founding dir, Trout Art Gallery, Dickinson Col, 82-91; mem selection comt, Fulbright Comn, Bonn, Ger, 89; Fulbright professorship, Univ Munich, 89-90; grant reviewer, Inst Mus Serv's, Wash, 89-91; dir, Martin D'Arcy Gallery, Loyola Univ, Chicago, 92-95 & Univ Ore Mus Art, 96-2000; assoc dir, Smart Mus, Univ Chicago, 2000-2002; dir, Block Mus, Northwestern Univ, 2002-; exec dir, Assoc Acad Mus and Galleries, 2012-2013. *Teaching:* Teaching asst art hist, Univ Pa, Philadelphia, 78-81; assoc prof, Dickinson Col, Carlisle, Pa, 82-91; lectr, Dept of Art History, Northwestern, 2003-. *Awards:* Kress fel Kress Found, London, 1976, Vienna, 1980; Penfield fel Univ Pa, Vienna, Austria, 1981-82; Fulbright Univ, Munich, 89-90; emeritus dir bd, Asn Academic Mus and Galleries, 2011. *Mem:* Ill Medieval Asn (pres, 94); Am Asn Mus; Historians Netherlandish Art; Asn Acad Mus and Galleries (bd mem, 2006-2008, pres 2008-); Univ Mus Comt, Icom (2007-); Task Force Coll Univ Mus (co chair, 2009-); Assoc Art Mus Dir. *Res:* Late-medieval German art; contemporary American art. *Specialty:* Prints & drawings. *Publ:* Coauth, Toshiko Takaezu: ceramics, textiles, bronzes, Dickinson Col, 83; auth, Michelangelo's St Proculus reconstructed, Art Bull, 83; coauth, The art & science of Eadweard Muybridge, Dickinson Col, 85; co-ed, Essays in Medieval Studies, 94-96; auth, Bridging the Pacific through Art, UNESCO Mus Intl, 2000; forward to Marion Mahony Griffin: Drawing the Form of Nature, 2006; film, Casting a Shadow: Creating the Alfred Hitchcock, 2007. *Mailing Add:* Telford House 511 Park Ave Galena IL 61036

ROBERTSON, E BRUCE
HISTORIAN, CURATOR
b Dunedin, New Zealand, May 14, 1955. *Study:* Swarthmore Col, BA (hons), 76; Yale Univ, MA, 78, MPhil, 80, PhD, 87. *Collection Arranged:* The Art of Paul Sandby (auth, catalog), Yale Brit Art Ctr, 85; Dutch Landscape Prints, Allen Art Mus, 86. *Pos:* Assoc cur Am paintings, Cleveland Mus Art, 87-91; chief cur, Ctr for Am Art. *Teaching:* Instr, Univ Del, Newark, 82 & Oberlin Col, Ohio, 83-87; asst prof, Case Western Reserve Univ, Ohio, 87-90; assoc prof, Univ Calif, Santa Barbara, 94-98, prof, 98-. *Mem:* Coll Art Asn; Am Studies Asn. *Res:* British and American painting to 1945. *Publ:* Coauth, Views and visions, Corcoran Gallery Art, 86; auth, Reckoning with Winslow Homer: His Late Paintings and Their Influence, 90; Marsden Hartley, 95; Am Realist Prints, 95; auth & coauth, Perils of the Sea & Yankee Modernism (essays), Picturing Old New England: Image and Memory, Nat Mus Am Art, 99; Ruth Harriet Louise and Hollywood Glamour Photography, 2002; Sargent and Haly, 2003. *Mailing Add:* c/o Art Hist Dept Univ Calif Santa Barbara CA 93106

ROBERTSON, JOAN ELIZABETH MITCHELL
GRAPHIC ARTIST
b Washington, DC, June 11, 1942. *Study:* Bucknell Univ, Lewisburg, Pa, BA (art), 64; Univ Iowa, MA (printmaking), 67, studied with Mauricio Lasansky. *Work:* Kemper Group, Long Grove, Ill; Chemical Bank, NY; First Nat Bank, Chicago; Southland Corp, Dallas, Tex; Ill State Mus, Springfield; Blount Inc, Montgomery, Ala. *Exhib:* Works on Paper by Artists of Chicago and Vicinity, Art Inst Chicago, 78; one-person shows, Donnelly Libr Gallery, Lake Forest Col, Ill, 79 & Loyola Univ, Chicago, 81 & Saginaw Art Mus, 98; Nat Prints & Drawing Competition, DeKalb, Ill, 81; Ill State Fair, Prof Art Exhib, 89; Flora 88 & 90, Chicago Botanic Garden, 88, 90 & 96; Karga Art Ctr, St Joseph, Mich, 97; Jan-Cicero, Chicago, 98. *Collection Arranged:* Kemper Nat Insurance Companies art collection, purchase, brochure preparation & monthly exhibs, 73-; Couples I and Couples II, Suburban Fine Arts Ctr, Highland Park, Ill, 83 & 84; A Celebration of Women (catalog), David Adler Cult Ctr, Libertyville, Ill, 92. *Pos:* Art cur, Kemper Nat Insurance Companies, Long Grove, Ill, 73-; gallery coordr, Lake Forest Col, Ill, 81-84. *Awards:* Award Merit, Flora, 88; Chicago Botanic Garden, 88; President's Purchase Award, Elgin Community Col, Ill, Works on Paper, 90; and others. *Bibliog:* Lydia Murman (auth), Joan E Robertson, New Art Examiner, 6/81; Sandy Riemer (auth), Color puts life into her pencil drawings, Sunday Herald, 4/81; Garrett Holg (auth), An exhibition for art and nature lovers at Botanic Garden, Waukegan News-Sun, 2/11/88; and others. *Mem:* Asn Corp Art Curators, Chicago; Nat Asn Corp Art Mgt, NY; David Adler Cult Ctr, Libertyville, Ill (bd dir, 90-93). *Media:* Colored Pencil. *Mailing Add:* c/o James S Kemper Found Long Grove IL 60049

ROBERTSON, LORNA DOOLING
PAINTER
b New York, NY, Aug 29, 1929. *Study:* Purdue Univ, BS, 51; Cornell Med Ctr, MS, 52. *Hon Degrees:* Hans Hofman Sch, New York, 60-64; Art Students League, New York. *Work:* Curwen & Chilford Mus, Cambridge, Eng; Tate Mus Print Collection, London, Eng. *Exhib:* Solo exhib, Willow Gallery, New York, 92 & Gallery Herouet, Place de Voges, Paris, France, 94; Exhib Hall & Mus, Palais des Congres, Marseille, France, 94; Osaka Int Art Festival, Osaka, Japan, 94; 12th Int Biennial Humor & Satire in Art, Gabrovo, Bulgaria, 95; Ann Juried Exhib, Hui-No eau, Maui, Hawaii, 2000; Benefit show, Aspen, Colo, 2005. *Awards:* Gold Medal, Palais DeCongres, Mme Grimaldi, 94; First Prize, First Int Female Artist Exhib, 94; Bronze Medal, L'Bradem Francouse Soc, 95. *Mem:* founding mem Vt Studio Ctr. *Media:* Oil, All Media. *Publ:* Illusr, Social Problems, Allyn & Bacon, 2000

ROBERTSON, NANCY ELIZABETH See Dillow, Nancy Elizabeth Robertson

ROBERTSON, RUTH
ART DEALER, PAINTER
b Philadelphia, Pa, Dec 22, 1949. *Study:* Va Commonwealth Univ, BFA, 73. *Work:* James F Lewis Mus, Baltimore; CID Collection, Sao Paolo, Brazil; Santos Cult Inst, Sao Paolo; Mus of Contemp Art, Washington, DC. *Exhib:* Between the Light & Dark, Nat Theater, Havana, Cuba, 2002; Recent Works, Mus of Contemp Art, Wash, DC, 97; Stations of the Cross, DC AA Ctr, Wash, DC, 99. *Pos:* Photography Cur, Mus of Contemp, DC, 98-2000; Gallery Dir, Dist West Fine Art, Leesburg, VA, 2000; dir, E-Moca.com, 95-, mem bd 2003-; owner, dir, Ruth Robertson Fine Art, 2004-. *Teaching:* Art Instr, Bishop O'Connell HS, 91-98; instr, VA Commonwealth Univ, Graduate Sch Fine Art, 2004-. *Awards:* Presidential Citation, Univ Richmond, 94; Nominated for Whitney Biennial, Whitney Mus of Am Art, 98, 2000. *Mem:* NVCC adv comt fine arts, 2001-; Am Soc Landscape Painters. *Media:* Painting, Photography, Mixed Media. *Specialty:* Contemporary Fine Art. *Publ:* DC Arts, At MOCA DC, 99; Arts/Corcoran Dir, 2002; Washington Review, The Cabinet of Good & Evil, 98. *Dealer:* District West Fine Art 3 1/2 S King St Leesburg VA 20175. *Mailing Add:* 602 Third St Herndon VA 20170

ROBINS, JOYCE
SCULPTOR, LANDSCAPE ARCHITECT
b Greenville, SC, Aug 23, 1944. *Study:* Cooper Union, BFA, 66; Yale Summer Sch, 66; City Coll NY, BSLA, 95. *Exhib:* Solo shows, Nobe Gallery, NY, 79, 55 Mercer St Gallery, NY, 80-81, 83-84, 86-88, 90-91, 93-94 & 96, Vassar Coll Art Gallery, Poughkeepsie, NY, 92; Function, Gallery 128, NY, 95; Domestic Policies, Art Gallery State Univ NY, 95; Insites II: Lower East Side Artists Re-think Neighborhood Streets, Abrons Art Ctr, Henry St Settlement, NY, 96; Vis Fac, Coll Ctr Gallery, Vassar Col, Poughkeepsie, NY, 96. *Pos:* Bd mem, 55 Mercer St Gallery, New York, 90-96, Springside Landscape Restoration, Poughkeepsie, NY, 95-2001. *Teaching:* Instr sculpture, Vassar Col, Poughkeepsie, NY, 96-2001. *Awards:* NY State Creative Artists Pub Serv Grant for Sculpture, 82. *Bibliog:* David Carrier (auth), Joyce Robins, Art in Am, 3/87; Yanick Rice Lamb (auth), Flag deconstruction, NY Times, 1/94; Holland Cotter (auth), NY Times, 9/97 & 10/97. *Media:* Bronze, Ceramic. *Dealer:* Pierogi 2000 177 N 9th St Brooklyn NY 11211

ROBINSON, AMINAH BRENDA LYNN
SCULPTOR, PAINTER
b Columbus, Ohio, 1940. *Study:* Columbus Art Sch (now Columbus Coll Art and Design), BA, cum laude, 1960. *Hon Degrees:* DFA, Ohio Dominican Coll, Columbus, Oh, 2002. *Work:* Poindexter Village Quilt, 1966-84; (sculpture) Gift of Love, 1974; Journal, 1980; To Be a Drum (Jazz), 1996-98. *Comn:* Murals, Columbus Metrop Library. *Exhib:* Columbus Mus Art; Akron Art Mus; Oakland Mus; Baltimore Mus Art; Studio Mus, Harlem; San Francisco Craft and Folk Mus; Retrospective, Brooklyn Mus Art, 2006; Summer Favorites, Hammond Harkins Gallery, 2006; Brooklyn Mus, NY; Columbus Mus Art, Oh; Nat Underground Railroad, Freedom Ctr, Cincinnati, Oh; Toledo Mus Art, Toledo, Oh. *Teaching:* Tchr art, Columbus Dept Recreation and Parks, since 1972. *Awards:* Int Studios Fellow; Bob Blackburn Print Shop Fellow, NY; Governor's Award for Visual Arts, 1984; Individual Artist Fellowship, Ohio Arts Council, 1980 and 1987, 1991-92; John D and Catherine T MacArthur Found Fellow, 2004. *Bibliog:* Carol Miller Genshaft, Leslie King-Hammond, Ramona Austin and Annegreth Nil (authors) Symphonic Poem: The Art of Aminah Brenda Lynn Robinson, 2003. *Mailing Add:* c/o Hammon Harkins Galleries Ltd 2264 E Main St Columbus OH 43209

ROBINSON, AVIVA
PAINTER
b May 24, 1933. *Study:* Univ Mich, 1951; Wayne State Univ, BS, 1951-55. *Work:* Detroit Inst Arts, Mich; Univ Mich, Dearborn; Ford Motor Co; Kmart Int Headquarters; Merrill Lynch Pierce Fenner & Smith Inc. *Exhib:* Rubiner Gallery, 84; Cantor & Lemberg Gallery, 86; Kidd Gallery, 88, 90; Edge Gallery, 94; Nat Paper Invitational, Univ of Mich Sch of Art, 96; Uzelac Gallery, 98. *Teaching:* teacher, art, Oak Park High Sch, 1954-55. *Awards:* Johns Manville award, Rocky Mountain Nat Watercolor, 76; Mich Watercolor soc, award, 79, 80 & 82; Mich Women's Found Painting award, 88; Brotherhood awardm AME Bethel Church, 90; Mich Artrain Painting award, 92; Outstanding Philanthropist award, Nat Soc Fund Raising Execs, 99; Mich Gov Arts award, 2003. *Mem:* Detroit Inst Arts (bd of dir, 1995-); Mus of Arts & Design (bd, 1996-); Arts Found Mich (former bd mem); Concerned Citizens of the Arts of Mich (former bd mem). *Media:* Watercolor. *Publ:* Corinne Abatt (auth), Variations on the Theme, The Birmington Eccentric (11/1984); Aviva Robinson at Cantor & Lemberg Gallery, The Detroit News (9/1986); Corinne Abatt (auth), Crating Dimensional Relationships, The Birmington Eccentric (9/1986); Bonita Fike (auth), A Passion for Glass - The Aviva and Jack A Robinson Studio Glass Collection, The Detriot Inst Arts, 07/2006; Uzbek Embroidery in the Nomadic Tradition, The Jack A and Aviva Robinson Collection, Minneapolis Inst of Arts, 1/2007. *Mailing Add:* 1589 Kirkway Bloomfield Hills MI 48302

ROBINSON, CHARLOTTE
PAINTER, PRINTMAKER
b San Antonio, Tex, Nov, 1924. *Study:* Art Students League, 48; New York Univ, 49; Corcoran Art Sch, 51-53. *Work:* Mus Espanol de Arts Contemporaneo, Madrid; Philip Morris Inc, New York; McNay Art Mus, San Antonio, Tex; Nat Mus Women Arts, Washington, DC; The White House, Washington, DC; Musea al De Arte Contemporanes, Lisbon, Portugal New Sch for Social Res, NY; Mus Reina Sofia, Madrid; Imperial Colcasiew Mus, Lake Charles, La; The White House, Wash, DC. *Exhib:* Solo exhibs, McNay Art Mus, San Antonio, Tex, 86, Lowenstein Libr Gallery, Fordham Univ, NY, 90, San Antonio Art Inst, Tex, 91 & Masur Mus Art, Monroe, La, 93, Savannah Coll Art & Design, 97 & Duke Univ Law Sch, Durham, NC, 98, Lee Hansley Gallery, Raleigh, NC, 2002, Emerson Gallery, McLain Art Ctr, VA, 2003; retrospectives at Lee Hansley Gallery, NC, 2007; Group exhibs, Mint Mus, Charlotte, NC, 77; Twentieth Yr Invitational Show, Rutgers Univ, New Brunswick, NJ, 92; Emerson Art Ctr, McLean, Va, 93 & 96; Northern Va Community Coll, Fairfax, 99; Tiknor Hall, Harvard Yard, Cambridge, Mass, 96; Southwest Ctr for Art & Crafts-San Antonio, Tex, 2004; The Am Ctr for Physics, 2005, College Park, MD. *Pos:* Trustee, Bronx Mus, NY, 76-77; vis artist, Southwest Craft Ctr, San Antonio, Tex, 85 & 86. *Teaching:* Instr painting, Torpedo Factory, Alexandria, Va, 67-75; instr drawing, Smithsonian Assoc Prog, Washington, DC, 76-; instr art world sem, Washington Women's Art Ctr, Washington, DC, 76-80. *Awards:* Scholar, Student Exhib, Corcoran Art Sch, Washington, 51; Grants, Nat Endowment Arts, 77, 78 & 81; Fel, Va Ctr Creative Arts, 90. *Bibliog:* A New Kind of Art, NY Times Mag, 82; The Artist & The Quilt, Time Mag, 83; Joan Arbeiter (auth), Talks with Women Artists, Scarecrow Press, 96; Dan Goddard (auth), Nature in painting, San Antonio Express, 97; Mary Shuter (auth), Underwater art, Savannah Morning News, 97; Energy Leaps in Feminist Art Pioneer's Work, News and Observer, Raleigh, NC, 6/10/2007. *Mem:* Nat Women's Caucus Art (bd dir, 82-84); Coll Art Asn. *Media:* Oil; Lithography. *Res:* Agricultural water withdrawal that protects Va waterways & downstream residents. Part of ongoing (since 96) project for "Waterworks" series of paintings. *Interests:* Environment (clean water), Swimming. *Publ:* Ed, The Artist & The Quilt, Knopf, 10/83. *Dealer:* Lee Hansley Gallery 225 Glenwood Ave Raleigh NC 27603

ROBINSON, CHRIS (CHRISTOPHER) THOMAS
CONCEPTUAL ARTIST, EDUCATOR
b Huntington, NY, Mar 18, 1951. *Study:* Fla State Univ, BFA, 73; Univ Mass, MFA, 75. *Work:* Arch Am Art, Washington, DC; Univ South; SC State Art Collection, Columbia; Southern Graphics Coun; Univ Miss. *Comn:* Installations, Ninth Nat-Int Sculpture Conf, New Orleans, 76, Nat Sculpture Conf, Jonesboro, Ark, 77, Arcosanti Festival Art in the Environment, Cordes Junction, Ariz, 78, Coll Art Asn, New Orleans, 80 & Eastern Ill Univ, 81; The Laser (installation), SC State Mus, Columbia, 89; Viscom, Southern Bell Regional Hq, Charlotte, NC, 91; 25th Annual Governors Carolighting, State Capitol, Columbia, SC, 92; First Night, Releigh Bicentennial, NC, 92. *Exhib:* Artists Biennial, New Orleans Mus Art, 77; solo exhibs, Atlanta Art Workers Coalition Gallery, 80, Univ NC, Coll at Charleston, 87, Art in Transit, Arts Festival Atlanta, 89; Fact, Fiction and Fantasy: Recent Narrative Art in the Southeast, Traveling Exhib, Ewing Art Gallery, Univ Tenn, Knoxville, 87; Traces, Proposals, Plans & Documentations, Trahern Gallery, Austin Peay State Univ, Clarksville, Tenn,

93; Centennial Exhib, SC State Mus, Columbia, 94; Art in Transit, Arts Festival Atlanta, Ga, 94; Emblems, Yale Univ Art Gallery, 95; Clemson Nat Print & Drawing Exhib, Clemson Univ, 98; Ormond Meml Art Mus, 99; Views From the Edge of the Century, Florence Mus of Art, 2000; SC State Mus, SC Arts Comn, Triennial Exhib, 2001; With/Without Distance, Volksbank, Kaiserslautern, Ger, 2002; Dream or Nightmare, Images of Air and Space in Contemp Art, Asheville Mus ARt, NC, 2003; Space Artists: The Cultural Frontiers of Space Travel, SETI Inst, Mountain View, Calif, 2005; Do not Fold, Bend, Spindle, or Mutilate: Computer Punch Card Art, Washington Pavilion Arts & Sci, Sioux Falls, SDak, 2006; DegradArte Expo, Mattatoio di Testaccio, Macello IV, Rome, Italy, 2008. *Collection Arranged:* Nat Sculpture Exhib, 76, 78 & 79. *Pos:* Dir, Northern Projects, Operation Raleigh, Chile; bd trustees, Lexington Co Sch Dist Five; leader, US Expeditions (sci, serv, adventure), Operation Raleigh, Alaska, Colo & NC, 88; dir grad studies, Univ SC, 90; pres, SC Sch Bd Asn, Columbia, 98; prin, Preston Coll, Univ SC LPM, 2002-2006; assoc chair, dept art, Univ SC, 2004-2006. *Teaching:* Assoc visual arts, Univ Mass, Amherst, 73-75; from instr to assoc prof, Univ SC, Columbia, 75-; guest artist, Univ Ala, Huntsville, 77, Univ South, Greensboro Coll, Brevard Coll & Univ Cent Ark. *Awards:* Merit Award, 18th Ann Juried Show, Anderson Co Arts Ctr, 93; Distinguished Serv Award, Nat Sch Bds Asn, 98; Merit Award, What is Drawing Now, Weber State Univ, 2000; Hewlett Initiative Grant, 2002; John Gardner Motivational Fac Award, Univ SC, 2005; Leonardo da Vinci Space Art Award, Planetary Soc/ISDC, 2006. *Bibliog:* Elizabeth George (auth), Laser artist beams brush towards space shuttle, Greenville Piedmont, 3/10/78; Ron Jones (auth), Techno-aesthetics in South Carolina, Art Papers, 3-4/81; Linda Shrives (auth), Outline of a dream, Columbia Record, 4/13/84; Michael Farley (auth), USC art instructor lives life full of adventure, The Charlotte Observer, 7/7/85; Beverly E Simmons (auth), University professor leads five month research mission, The State, 1/16/86. *Mem:* Coll Art Asn; Southern Asn Sculptors (bd mem, 75-80); Southeastern Coll Art Conf. *Media:* Computers, Light. *Res:* Experiential investigation of exploratory processes in science and technology as an impetus to the expansion of the visual arts process. *Publ:* Auth, Astronautics as an impetus to visual art, In: Proceedings of the 33rd International Astronautical Federation Congress, 82; Cultural dichotomy: An artist's role in scientific and space exploration, Art Papers, 5-6/85; Sky Art and Power chap Sky Art Book Ctr for Adv Visual Studies, Mass Inst Technol, in press; Art & Technol, Koger Ctr Prog, 89; The Visual Artist's Role in Scientific & Space Exploration, 41st Int Art Found Congress, Dresden, Ger; What Happens When the Lights Go Out, SECAC, Norfolk, VA; Idea vs Object Revisiting Conceptual Art Through the Digital Looking Glass, SECAC?MACCA; Laser Light Scanning, Mixed Messages Conf, Univ North Carolina, Charlotte; and many more lects & papers. *Mailing Add:* 212 S Edisto Ave Columbia SC 29208

ROBINSON, DONALD WARREN
PAINTER, INSTRUCTOR

b New Bedford, Mass Sept 18 1932. *Study:* Art Student's League NY (scholar), 50; Univ Ga (scholar), 53; Columbia Univ, MFA, 54; Rutgers Univ, EdD (curric theory & develop), 83; Workshops with Skip Whitcomb, Timothy Thies, 2007. *Exhib:* 54th Ann Open Juried Show, Monmouth, Mus, Lincroft, NJ, 96; 5th Juried Art Exhib, Hunterdon Art Center, Clinton, NJ, 96; 17th Ann Regional Juried, Ridgewood Art Inst, Ridgewood, NJ, 97; 8th Ann Open Juried, Guild Creative Art, Shrewsbury, NJ, 2000; Open Juried Show, Ocean Co Artists, Island Heights, NJ, 2001; 75th Ann Nat Juried, Nat Arts Club, New York, 2006; Open Juried Show, Guild Creative Artists, Shrewsbury, NJ, 2007; MCAC 29th Ann Juried Art Show, 2008; Plein Air Paintings of Jersey Coast, Ann Exhib, 2008; 9th Nat Juried Exhib, Am Impressionists Soc, 2008; Audubon Artists Nat Open Juried Show, Salmagundi Club, New York, 2009; Am Artists Prof League, Ann Exhib, NJ, 2009; 31st Ann Open Juried Show, Monmouth Mus, NJ, 2010; Guild Creative Art, 2012; Art of Illusion, Monmouth Mus, NJ, 2012; NJ/AAPL, 2012; NJ/AAPL, 2013. *Pos:* Instr dept head, Elem & Sec Schs, Edison Twp Schs, Edison, NJ, 57-67. *Teaching:* Instr fine arts, Wagner Coll, Staten Island, NY, summer 53; Instr, Gettysburg Coll, Gettysburg, Pa, 54-55; instr art educ, Staten Island Mus, NY, 61-63. *Awards:* Artists Mag Award, 8th Ann Open Juried, Guild Creative Art, 2000; Recognition Award, 13th Open Juried Show, Guild Creative Art, 2005; Merit Award, Open Juried Show, Am Artists Professional League, NJ, 2007; John Grabach Award painting in oils, Am Artists Prof League, 2009; Monmouth Mus Award, 31st Ann Juried Art Show; Friedlander Award for Abstraction, Guild Creative Arts, 2011; Best in Show, NJ/AAPL, 2012. *Mem:* Am Artists Professional League (NJ chap); Plein Air Painters Jersey Coast; Printmaking Coun of NJ; Art Alliance. *Media:* Oils. *Dealer:* Guild of Creative Art 620 Broad St Rt 35 Shrewsbury NJ 07702. *Mailing Add:* 55 Frost Ave W Edison NJ 08820-3157

ROBINSON, DUNCAN (DAVID)
DIRECTOR, HISTORIAN

b Kidsgrove Staffs, Eng, June 27, 1943. *Study:* Clare Coll, Cambridge, Eng, BA, 65, MA, 69; Yale Univ, Mellon Fel, 65-67, MA, 67. *Collection Arranged:* Stanley Spencer (auth, catalog), 75 & William Nicholson, 80, Arts Coun Gt Brit; British Watercolors, Brisbane, Australia, 82; and several exhibs of British Contemp Art. *Pos:* Asst keeper paintings & drawings, Fitzwilliam Mus, Cambridge, Eng, 70-76, keeper, 76-81; dir, Yale Ctr Brit Art, 81-95 & Fitzwilliam Mus, Cambridge, Eng, 95-2007; master, Magdalene Coll, Cambridge, Eng, 2002-12, hon fel, 2013-; chmn, The Henry Moore Found, 2007-14, The Prince's Drawing Sch, 2007-13, Cambridge City Coun Pub Art Panel, 2009-13. *Teaching:* Lectr art hist, Univ Cambridge, Eng, 70-81, 95-2012; adj prof hist Art, Yale Univ, 81-95; fel, Clare Coll, Cambridge. *Res:* History of British Art concentrating on later 18th and 19th century contemporary art. *Specialty:* World-wide fine & decorative arts. *Interests:* travel, wine, gardening. *Publ:* Auth, Companion Volume to the Kelmscott Chaucer, Basilisk Press, 75; Stanley Spencer, Phaidon, 79 & rev, 90; coauth, Morris & Company in Cambridge, Cambridge Univ Press, 80; auth, Town Country, Shore and Sea: British Drawings and Watercolors from Van Dyck to Nash, Cambridge, 82; Yale Ctr for British Art: A Tribute to Louis I Kahn, 97; The Fitzwilliam Mus, Cambridge: 150 Years of Collecting, 98; Paul Mellon: A Cambridge Tribute, 2007. *Mailing Add:* 3240 Windham Hill Rd Townshend VT 05359

ROBINSON, FRANKLIN W
MUSEUM DIRECTOR, HISTORIAN

b Providence, RI, May 21, 1939. *Study:* Harvard Univ, BA, 1961, MA, 1963, PhD, 1970. *Pos:* Dir, Williams Coll Mus Art, 1976-79, Mus Art, RI Sch Design, 1979-92 & Herbert F Johnson Mus Art, Cornell Univ, 1992-2011. *Teaching:* Asst prof art hist, Dartmouth Coll, 1969-75; assoc prof & dir grad prog art hist, Williams Coll, 1975-79. *Res:* Baroque art; prints and drawings. *Publ:* Auth, 100 Master Drawings from New England Private Collections, 72; Gabriel Metsu, 75; Dutch Life in the Golden Century, 75; Seventeenth Century Dutch Drawings from American Collections, 77; Dutch and Flemish Paintings from the Ringling Museum, 80; Fresh Woods and Pastures New, 99. *Mailing Add:* Herbert F Johnson Mus Art Cornell Univ Ithaca NY 14853

ROBINSON, JAY
PAINTER

b Detroit, Mich, Aug 1, 1915. *Study:* Yale Coll, BA; Cranbrook Acad Art, MFA. *Work:* Cranbrook Mus, Bloomfield Hills, Mich; Detroit Inst Art; Houston Mus Fine Arts; J B Speed Mus, Louisville, Ky; Philbrook Art Ctr, Tulsa; Georgia Mus Art, Athens. *Exhib:* Carnegie Inst Int, Pittsburgh; Corcoran Gallery Art Biennial, Washington, DC; Nat Acad Design, NY; Pa Acad Fine Arts, Philadelphia; Ga Mus Art, Athens. *Teaching:* Private lessons. *Awards:* Louis Comfort Tiffany Found Fel, 49; seven Childe Hassam Fund Purchase Awards, Am Acad Arts & Lett. *Media:* Miscellaneous, Acrylic & Mixed. *Collection:* Jason Schoen. *Mailing Add:* 305 E Landing Williamsburg VA 23185-8254

ROBINSON, LILIEN FILIPOVITCH
HISTORIAN, EDUCATOR

b Ljubljana, Yugoslavia, Feb 7, 1940; US citizen. *Study:* George Washington Univ, BA, 62, MA, 65; Johns Hopkins Univ, PhD, 78. *Pos:* Chmn dept art, George Washington Univ, 76-2000. *Teaching:* Lectr art introd & surveys of Western art, George Washington Univ, 64-65, asst prof 19th century art & surveys of Western art, 65-76, assoc prof 19th century Europ art, 76-79 & prof 19th century Europ art, 80-. *Awards:* Outstanding Teacher Award, Columbian Col, George Washington Univ, 88; Trachtenberg Serv Award; The George Washington Award; Jane Lingo Outstanding Achievement award, 2013. *Bibliog:* Boris Weintraub (auth), The professor's enthusiasm is contagious, Washington Star, 10/27/79. *Mem:* Coll Art Asn; Asn for Slavic, East European, & Eurasian Studies; N Am Soc Serbian Studies. *Res:* 19th-century French painting and academic painting; Serbian 19th-century secular art. *Publ:* Auth, Clarice Smith, Wildenstein Galleries, 86; Barye & the Nineteenth Century Sculptural Tradition, Barye and Patronage in Antoine-Louis Barye, Corcoran Gallery Art, Washington, DC, 88; Anna Klumpke in Context, Anna Elizabeth Klumpke: Duty and the Dedicated Spirit, Ariz State Univ, 93; Arthur Hall Smith: Works on Paper, LRC Gallery, Charles County Community Col, 93; Nineteenth-Century Serbian Painting: A Confluence of Nationalism & Secularism, Serbian Studies, Vol 16, 2/2003; introduction, Clarice Smith: Patterns in People, Places and Things, Richard Green Galleries, London, 2002; Clay Variance, The Lyons Agy, Alexandria, Va, 1995; Inspiration and Affirmation of Revolution in Nineteenth-Century Serbian Painting, Serbian Studies, Vol 19.2, 2005; Interpreting Western Academic Traditions in 19th-Century Serbian Painting, Serbian Studies, Vol 20, 2, 2006; La Vie Moderne, Cocoran Gallery Art, 83; Exploring Modernity in the Art of Krstic Jovanovic, and Predic, Serbian Studies, Vol 21 No1, 2007; Paja Jovanovíc and the Imaging of War & Peace, Serbian Studies, Vol 22.1, 2008; Belgrade: Transformations and Confluences, Serbian Studies, Vol 24 (1-2), 2010; Orientalism through the Balkan Lense & PajaJovanovic, Serbian Studies, Vol 25, 2014; On the Very Edge Modernism and Modernity in the Arts and Architecture of Interwar Serbia (1918-1941), Jelena Bogdanovic, Lilien Filipovitch Robinson, Igor Marjanovic (editors), Leuven Univ Press, 2014; From Tradition to Modernism: Uros Predic and PajaJovanovic. *Mailing Add:* Dept Art George Washington Univ 801 22nd St NW Washington DC 20052

ROBINSON, MARC ANDRÉ
SCULPTOR

b Los Angeles, 1972. *Study:* Pa Acad Fine Art, BFA, 1998; Md Inst Coll Art, MFA, 2002; Whitney Mus Am Art, Independent Study Prog, 2002-03; Studio Mus Harlem, Artist in Residence, 2004-05. *Exhib:* Group exhibs include Divergence, Rush Arts Gallery, New York, 2002; Off the Record, Skylight Gallery, Brooklyn, 2003; 24/7: Wilno-Nueva York (Visa Para), Contemp Art Ctr, Vilnius, Lithuania, 2003; Float, Socrates Sculpture Park, Long Island City, NY, 2003; In the Poem About Love You Don't Write the Word Love, Ctr Contemp Arts, Glasgow, 2005 & Artists Space, New York, 2006; Frequency, Studio Mus Harlem, New York, 2005, Scratch, 2006; Propeller, Steve Turner Gallery, Los Angeles, 2005; When Artists Say We, Artists Space, New York, 2006; Unmonumental: The Object in the 21st Century, New Mus Contemp Art, New York, 2007. *Awards:* Art Matters Found Grant, 2009. *Mailing Add:* Steve Turner Contemporary 6026 Wilshire Blvd Los Angeles CA 90036

ROBINSON, MARGOT STEIGMAN
PAINTER, SCULPTOR

b New York, NY. *Study:* Art Students League, with Harry Sternberg, 47; Robert Blackburn's Creative Workshop, 49-55; painting with John Von Wicht, 53-55; Gerard Koch Studio, Paris, 68; Donald Mavros Studio, New York, 71-72. *Work:* Am Express Co, New York; Data Processing Co, Boston & Chicago; Continental Grain Co, Columbus, Ohio; Bronze mem, Jervis Pub Libr, Rome, NY. *Comn:* Bronze memorial, Jervis Pub Libr, Rome, NY. *Exhib:* Whitney Mus Am Art, NY; Womens Caucus Art Painters Puzzle Project, Port Authority, NY, 90; solo exhibs, Tom Kendall Gallery, NY, 90 & Noho Gallery, NY, 92; Cincinnati Art Mus, Ohio; Brooklyn Mus, NY; Cie Mod et Contemporaine, Paris, France, 91; Contemp Artists for Global Peace, Casa Argentina en Israel Tierra Santa, 93; Forgiveness/or Not, Ceres Gallery, New York, 96; Hallelujah, Ceres Gallery, New York, 2002. *Pos:* Dir, Creative Graphic Workshop, New York, 52-54; registr, Nat Acad Sch of Fine Arts, New York, 55-57; vpres, Noho Gallery, New York, 76-77, secy, 77-78. *Bibliog:* Edgar Buonagurio (auth), Arts Mag,

4/78; James T McCartin (auth), essay, 82; Ellen Lee Klein (auth), 85; Sean Simon (auth), Artspeak, 11/89; Claude Le Suer (auth), Artspeak, 1/90; Bruno Palmer Poroner (auth), article, Artspeak, 6/92. *Mem:* New York Artists Equity; Women in the Arts; Womens Caucus Art, New York & Nat. *Media:* Acrylic, Oil; Miscellaneous Media, Bronze & Stone. *Publ:* Contribr, Modern Sculpture, calendar, Cedco Publ Co, San Rafael, Calif, 90. *Dealer:* Aldona M Gobuzas 215 E 79 St New York NY 10075. *Mailing Add:* 141 Joralemon St Brooklyn NY 11201

ROBINSON, MARY ANN
PAINTER, EDUCATOR
b McPherson, Kans, Sept 24, 1923. *Study:* Kans State Univ, BS, 45; McCormick Theological Sem, MA, 55; Wichita State Univ, MA, 72; studied under Maude Ellsworth, Jan Lundgren, Robert Kisskaden, Robert Wood & James Pike. *Work:* Galaxy Series. *Exhib:* Am Contemp Arts & Crafts, Fla, 73; Birger Sandzen Mem Gallery, 80-92; Kans Watercolor Soc Mem Exhib, Lawrence, Kans, 88; Wichita Art Mus Watercolor Exhib, 89; Ellsworth Art Gallery, Kans, 91; Pratt Art Gallery, Pratt, Kans, 92; Friendship Gallery, McPherson Col, 96; The Gallery, McPherson Col, 95-2000. *Collection Arranged:* Nat Art Exhibition, 1989-1998. *Pos:* Supvr art pub sch, McPherson, Kans, 47-49; dir, Friendship Hall Gallery, McPherson Col, Kans, 63-86; co-sponsor & dir, Aesthetics Nat Art Exhib, 89-98. *Teaching:* Assoc prof art educ & art hist & chmn dept art, McPherson Col, Kans, 63-86, emer prof, 86-. *Mem:* Kans Watercolor Soc (bd mem, 77-79); McPherson Mus & Art Found (bd mem, 86-90); Opera House Preserv Co (bd mem, 86-90); McPherson Arts Coun; charter mem Nat Mus Women in the Arts; Aesthetics Ltd (bd mem, 89-98); Rayner Soc. *Media:* Watercolor, Acrylic. *Publ:* Illustrated Survey of Leading Contemporaries, 90. *Mailing Add:* 601 S Walnut McPherson KS 67460

ROBINSON, NADINE CAROLINE
INSTALLATION SCULPTOR
b London, Oct 16, 68; arrived in US, 75. *Study:* State Univ NY, Stony Brook, BFA, 95; New York Univ, MFA, 97. *Work:* Altoids Curiously Strong Collection, New Mus Contemp Art, New York; Studio Mus in Harlem, New York; Norton Family Collection. *Exhib:* Solo exhibs include Black Listing, Longwood Arts Project, Bronx, NY, 98, White We, Caren Golden Fine Art, New York, 2003, Ramp Projects - Das Hochzeitshaus, Inst Contemp Arts, Philadelphia, 2003, Flip Flop, Susanne Vielmetter Los Angeles Projects, Culver City, Calif, 2005, Conclusion of the System of Things, Grand Arts, Kansas City, 2005, Alles Grau, Studio Mus Harlem, New York 2006, The Colored Congregation, Vienna Artweek, 2007; group exhibs include Artsfeast, Union Coll, Schenectady, NY, 96; Women's Hist, Union Gallery, Stony Brook, Long Island, 96; Re-Bates, LC Bates Mus, Hinckley, Maine, 97; Artists in the Marketplace, Bronx Mus Arts, NY, 98; Ruido/Noise, Mus del Barrio, New York, 98; Genealogies, Miscegenations, Missed Generations, Williams Benton Mus, Conn, 2000; Greater New York, PS1 Contemp Art Ctr, New York, 2000; The Project, New York, 2000; For the Record, Studio Mus in Harlem, New York, 2001, Freestyle, 2001, African Queen, 2005, Harlem Postcards, 2006; Rappers Delight, Yerba Buena Ctr Arts, San Francisco, Calif, 2001; One Planet Under a Groove: Hip Hop & Contemp Art, Bronx Mus Arts, Walker Art Ctr, Minneapolis, & Mus Villa Stuck, Munich, 2001-04; One Hand Clapping, Smack Mellon Gallery, Brooklyn, NY, 2002 & Sunrise Sunset, 2004; Mass Appeal, Gallery 101, Ottawa, Can, 2002; Hair Stories, Adam Baumgold Gallery, New York, 2002; Inside Out, Festival New Art, Bunker Reinhardtstrasse, Berlin, 2002; Tempo, Mus Mod Art, Queens, NY, 2002; 4 und 4, Muller DeChiaria Gallery, Berlin, 2004; Arco, Die Neue Aktionsgalerie, Madrid, 2004; Great White, Ctr Curatorial Studies, Bard Coll, Annandale-on-Hudson, NY, 2004; Open House, Brooklyn Mus Art, NY, 2004; Hot Town Summer in the City, Caren Golden Fine Art, New York, 2005; Crossing the Line, Cornell Fine Arts Mus, Rollins Coll, Ithaca, NY, 2007; She's So Articulate, Arlington Arts Ctr, Va, 2008. *Collection Arranged:* Ziggy & the Black Dinosaurs, Longwood Arts Gallery, Bronx, NY, 99. *Teaching:* Artist-in-Residence, Skowhegan Sch Painting & Sculpture, Skowhegan, Maine, 97, Millay Colony Arts, Austerlitz, NY, 98, Studio Mus in Harlem, 2000, Smack-Mellon, Brooklyn, NY, 2002, Chashama Found, New York, 2007; Harvestworks artist-in-residence, Media Technol Ctr, New York, 99; World Views artist-in-residence at World Trade Ctr, Lower Manhattan Cult Coun, New York, 99. *Awards:* Emerging Artist Fel, NY Community Trust, 2002; William H Johnson Prize, 2003. *Mailing Add:* c/o Caren Golden Fine Art 170 East 87th St New York NY 10128

ROBINSON, NATHANIEL
INSTALLATION ARTIST
b Providence, Rhode Island, 1980. *Study:* Amherst Coll, BA, summa cum laude, 2002; Sch Art Inst Chgo, MFA, 2005. *Exhib:* Solo exhibs, 12x12 series, Mus Contemporary Art, Chgo, Ill, 2005, Pseudorandom, Denler Gallery, Northwestern Coll, St Paul, MN, 2008, Civil Twilight, Feature Inc, NY, 2010, Twig Gallery, Brussels, 2010, de facto, Devening Projects, Chgo, Ill, 2010, Congealed Daydreams, 2012, Parts of a World, Feature Inc, NY, 2012, Outer Air, 2013; Group exhibs, Form and Color, Lenore Gray Gallery, Providence, RI, 2002, Body of Work, Gallery Agniel, Providence, RI, 2003, Inrathin, Gahlberg Gallery, Coll DuPage, Glen Ellyn, Ill, Peridolia, Orange Co Ctr Contemporary Art, Santa Ana, Calif, 2004, Drawn to Drawing, Betty Rymer Gallery, Sch Art Inst Chgo, Gallery 2, 2005, Lookers, Heaven Gallery, Chgo, Ill, 2005, A Sense of Place: Emerging Chgo Sculpture, The Lobby Gallery, Chgo, Ill, 2005, Four Ways to Tell a Story, Eli Marsh Gallery, Amherst Coll, Mass, 2006, Hope, Linda Warren Gallery, Chgo, 2006, Action Stop Action, Vox Populi, Phila, Pa, 2008, Paper Love, Devening Projects, Chgo, Ill, Little Triggers 2009, All My Friends are Dead, Maerzgalerie, Leipzig, Ger, 2009, Skulture, Feature, Inc, NY, 2009, I am not Monogomous, I Heart Poetry, 2011, Looking Back: The Fifth White Columns Annual, White Columns, NY, 2010, We Regret to Inform You There is Currently No Space or Place for Abstract Painting, Martos Gallery, NY, 2011, Creature from the Blue Lagoon, 2012, Color: Fully Engaged, A + D Gallery, Columbia Coll, Chgo, Ill, 2011, If Loss Could Weigh, TCB Art Inc, Melbourne, 2011, Upstream, NADA, Hudson, NY, 2012, July/Core Club, NY, 2012. *Awards:* Jacob Javits fellow, 2003-2005. *Bibliog:* Deborah Wilk (auth), Studio City, Chicago Mag, 2005; Jeffrey Kastner (auth), review, Artforum, 11/2010; Ken Johnson (auth), Nathaniel Robinson, New York Times, 9/2010; Kathleen Massara (auth), Trash Talks Back, The L Mag, 9/2010; Ben Sutton (auth), Martos Gallery Makes for the Hamptons, Filling a Collector's Beach House with High-Priced Hipster Art, Artinfo.com, 8/2012. *Mailing Add:* Feature Inc 131 Allen St New York NY 10002

ROBINSON, SALLY W
PRINTMAKER, PAINTER
b Detroit, Mich, Nov 2, 1924. *Study:* Bennington Coll, BA; Wayne State Univ, MA & MFA; Cranbrook Acad Art; also with Hans Hofmann, Paul Feeley, Karl Knaths & Leon Kroll. *Work:* Chase Manhattan Bank, New York; Detroit Inst Arts; K-Mart Hq; and pvt collections; Williams Coll. *Exhib:* Toledo Mus, Winston Traveling Show; Zella 9 Gallery, London, Eng; Troy Art Gallery, 78; Detroit Inst Arts, 78; Cliche-Verre, nat exhib, Detroit Inst Arts & Houston; and others. *Pos:* Mem, Gov Comn for Art in State Bldgs, Mich, 78-79; bd mem, Mus Art, Univ Mich, currently; vis fel, Williams Col Mus Art, currently. *Teaching:* Instr silk screen, Wayne State Univ, 73-74. *Awards:* Second Prize, Bloomfield Art Asn, 72; Second Prize, Soc Women Painters, 74 & First Prize, 75. *Mem:* Friends Mod Art; Founders Soc; Detroit Artists Market; Soc Women Painters; Bloomfield Art Asn; Fel Williams Coll Mus Art; Guggenheim Mus; Cooper Hewitt Mus; Whitney Mus Mod Art; and others; Selby Gardens Sarasota Rescaugh Com. *Media:* Painting, Printmaking, Collage. *Interests:* Botany, art. *Publ:* Contribr, Mich Art J, 76; auth, Cliche-Verre: Hand Drawn, Light Printed, 80. *Dealer:* Klein-Vogel Gallery 4520 N Woodward Royal Oak MI 48053; Rina Gallery E 74th St & Madison New York NY 10021. *Mailing Add:* 209 Hills Pl Charlotte VT 05445

ROBINSON, THOMAS V
DEALER, COLLECTOR
b Ft Worth, Tex, Feb 9, 1938. *Study:* Tex Christian Univ, 56-57; Carlsbad-Oceanside Col, 57-58; Tex Wesleyan Col, 59-60; Univ Houston, 88-89. *Exhib:* Inst Allerde, San Miguel de Allerde, Mex, 81; Edinburgh Int Festival, 83-86; Am Festival, Glasgow, Scotland, 85; Casa de la Cultura, Quito, Ecuador, 87; Mus Mod, Cuenca, Ecuador, 87; Mus Munic de Guayaquil, Ecuador, 94. *Collection Arranged:* Ben Shahn 1930-1969, 70; Auther G Dove 1920-1940, 71; Am Landscape, 73; Western Am Art 1860-1940 (auth, catalog), 74; Networking, Int Exchange Prog, 82-86 & 87-95. *Pos:* Dir, Robinson Galleries, 69-, pres, 77-90; dir, Ben Shahn Foundation, New York, 71-75; bd mem, Houston Art Dealers Asn, 81-83 & 94-97, pres 95-96; chmn, art travel studies & bd mem, Instituo de Arte Grace, Ecuador, 88; publ, Pasaporte Á USA; chmn, Kuumba House Found, 93-94; rep, Paul Suttman Sculpture Estate, currently. *Awards:* Consulor Corps Comt, 89; Inst Hispanic Cult, 90; Leadership Award, Ecuadorian-Am Chamber Commerce, 90. *Bibliog:* Thomas V Robinson, SW Art Mag, 71; Donna Tennant (auth), Gallery-Inst Exchange, Houston Chronicle, 81; Internation exchange, Artscene, Houston, 83; International networking, Houston Chronicle, 84; El Commercial, Quito, Ecuador, 87 & 94. *Mem:* Cultural Arts Comt Houston Chamber Com; Tex Arts Alliance; Cultural Arts Coun Houston; Houston Art Dealers Asn (treas, 80-81, dir, 83-97, pres 95-96). *Specialty:* Twentieth century figurative expressionists and outsider artists of the Americas; Contemporary painting, sculpture, performance, video and all media objects. *Publ:* Coauth, Kachinas-Paone, Encino Press, 76; International Fine Art Collector, 90; auth, PasaporteÁ Houston, 94-95; A Traves de los Ojos de Texas, 95. *Mailing Add:* Robinson Galleries Inc 2022 Banks St Houston TX 77098

ROBISON, ANDREW
MUSEUM CURATOR, WRITER
b Memphis, Tenn, May 23, 1940. *Study:* Princeton Univ, AB & PhD; Oxford Univ, MA; Fulbright Res Scholar, India. *Exhib:* Giovanni Battista Piranesi & Picasso Prints, 70, Princeton Univ; diverse print & drawing exhib, Nat Gallery of Art, 74-; 18th century Venetian Illus Bks, Grolier Club, 81; Uncommon Piranesis, Grolier Club, 88; The Glory of Venice, Royal Acad, London, 94-95; Ernst Ludwig Kuichner, Nat gallery of Art and Royal Acad, London, 03; German Master Drawings, Nat Gallery Art, 2010; Albrecht Durer, 2013. *Pos:* Cur & head dept prints & drawings, Nat Gallery Art, 74-, sr cur, 83-91, Mellon sr cur 91-; pres, Print Coun Am, 75-81; mem ed adv bd, Master Drawings, 81-; pres, Int Adv Comn Keepers Pub Collections Graphic Art, 84-88; bd dir, Drawing Soc, 84-. *Teaching:* Instr & asst prof, Univ Ill, 70-74. *Awards:* Ateneo Veneto, 90. *Bibliog:* Der Zusammendenker, Weltkunst, 10/04. *Mem:* Grolier Club, NY; Master Drawings Asn (int ed adv bd, 81-); Drawing Soc (bd dir, 84-); Print Coun Am (pres, 75-81). *Res:* Eighteenth century Italian graphic art; early German prints and drawings; German expressionism. *Collection:* Prints and 18th century Italian drawings and illustrated books. *Publ:* Paper in Paris, 77; German Expressionist Prints from the Collection of Ruth & Jacob Kainen, 85; Piranesi: Early Architectural Fantasies: A Catalogue Raisonne of the Etchings, 86; Durer to Diebenkorn, 92; The Glory of Venice: Art in the Eighteenth Century; Building a Collection, 97; A Century of Drawings, 01; and others. *Mailing Add:* 2000 B South Club Dr Landover MD 20785

ROBLES-GALIANO, ESTELA
PAINTER, WRITER
b Mayaguez, PR, Mar 28, 1943. *Study:* Univ PR, Mayagüez, BA, 1963; Art Ctr Francisco Oller, Aguadilla, PR, 1973-78. *Work:* Clínica San Francisco, Guadalajara, Mexico; U PR, Aguadilla; Autoridad Comunicaciones, San Juan, PR; Aguadilla Art Mus. *Comn:* cover and interior for telephone directory (12 paintings), Autoridad Comunicaciones, Caguas, PR, 92-93; cover telephone directory (25 paintings), PR Telephone Co, San Juan, 92-93; cover, The Tourist's Telephone Directory Quickguide, ITT Intermedia, Inc, Hato Rey, PR, 92-93; cover for Maldita Sea la Justicia (auth Jorge Chear Cacho), 97; Literature in Painting (10 paintings), Hewlett-Packard Caribe, Aguadilla, PR, 2000. *Exhib:* 10th Ann NDak Nat Exhibit, Minot, NDak Art Gallery, 87; Int Art Competition, Pfeiffer Gallery, NY, 88 & Agora Gallery, NY, 93; 48th Ann Anniversary Nat Art Competition, Lake Worth, Fla Art League, 89; Watercolor Asn PR Ann Exhib, Graphic Art Mus, San Juan, 90; Int Showcase Traditional Marine Art, Gloucester Fine Arts, Mass, 91; Las Americas en Encuentro Musical, Las Americas Mus, San Juan, 93; 22nd Ann Pa Watercolor Soc, So

Alleghenies Mus, Ligonier Valley, Pa, 2001; Master Painters of the World, Int Artist Mag, Australia, 2003; Int Art Contest, Art Dept, Australia, 2002, 2003, 2004; San Juan Mus, PR, 2003; LatinAm Art Mus, Miami, Fla, 2003; My Watercolors Gallery, Argentina, 2003-2009; Caracas Venezuela, Raul Leoni Libr, HispanoAm Watercolorists Group, 2004; Interamerican Univ PR, Bayamon Campus, Caribbean Artists Asn, 2004; Art Mus La Princesa, San Juan, Tourist Co, Water Asn PR, 2005; The Capitol, San Juan, Nat Day of PR Painter Artist, Watercolor Asn PR, 2005; Art Mus El Plata, Dorado, PR, 2005; Moxie Fire Cracker Films, NY, 2006; Caracas Venezuela, Univ Tec, HispanoAmerican Watercolorists Group, 2007; Art & Hist Mus Arecibo, PR, 2007; Mus Ramirez de Arellano, San German, 2007; Hist Mus, Guanica, Puertorican, 2007; Mus Castillo Serralles, Ponce, PR, 2009; 3rd Int Triennale of Watercolor, Bolivariano Art Mus, Santa Marta, Colombia, 2009, 4th Triennale, 2012; Mus Reyes Magos, Juana Diaz, PR, 2009; Ibero Am Biennial of Watercolor, Mus Casa de la Moneda, Madrid, Spain, 2009; Mus Castillo Serralles, Ponce, PR, 2009, 2011; Mus City Hall, Aguadilla, PR, 2009-2012. *Collection Arranged:* 10 watercolors, Hewlett Packard Caribe Ltd, Aguadilla, PR, Painting Literature in Honor of Puerto Rican Writers Enrique Laguerre y Abelardo Diaz Alfaro, 2000; 8 paintings, Lic Eugenio Cabanillas, Mayaguez, PR, 2000; Dr Salvador Recio, King Wood Med Ctr, Houston, Tex, 2005. *Pos:* juror, lectr watercolor, Ramey Sch, CABA, Aguadilla & Univ PR, Mayagüez, 99-2000; pres, AAPR, 2005; pres exhibs, PWFAA, 2008; pres exhibs, APPRA, 2009-2011, pres, 2011-2013. *Teaching:* prof humanities I & II, Cath Univ PR, Aguadilla, 64-71; art instr drawing & painting, Colegio San Carlos, Aguadilla, 78-80 & Univ PR, Aguadilla, 82-84; workshop instr, Centro Arte Borinké, Aguadilla, 94-96; lectr, Univ PR, Centro Mujer y Salud, San Juan, 96. *Awards:* Cert of Excellence, Internat Art Competition, I a C, NY, 88; Langnickel award, 48th Annual Nat Art Competition, Lake Worth Art League, 89; Second Place award, 10th Anniv Watercolor Asn PR, Citibank, Ctr, Cupey, PR, 93; Disting Woman, Senate of PR, 95 & 98; homage, Exch Club, 92, Union Am Women, 92 & Women Civic Club, 98; UNESCO of PR Medal, 2004; Trophy, VI Int Biennale Watercolor, Nat Mus Watercolor, Mexico, 2004; Int Art Contest, Agora Gallery, Soho, NY, 94. *Bibliog:* Reinaldo Silvestri (auth), Estela Robles y su mundo pictórico, Visión de Puerto Rico, 5/89; subject of video Down to Sea, North Am Marine Art Soc, 91; Randi Hoffman (auth), Mysticism at Agora Gallery, ARTSPEAK, 94; and many more. *Mem:* Watercolor Asn PR (publicity chmn 1997, 98 & 99); Nat Exhib Day PR Painter (founder, pres. assessor, 1998-99, 2000-03); Aguadilla Art Mus (assessor 1980-2003); Am Soc Portrait Artists; Nat Mus Women in the Arts; PR Watercolorists Asn; Puertorican Women Fine Arts Asn, (pres, 2007-2009); Hispano Am Watercolor Asn, (2005-2009); Caribbean Artists Asn, (2004-2009); APPRA (2009-2012); PAUA (2009-2012); AAC (96-2012); COAPR (2006-2012). *Res:* 20 Hispano-American painters to be included in her book "Tu Puedes ser Artista Pintor". *Specialty:* Transparent watercolor, acrylic, oil, landscape, flowers, architecture, portraits, still life with bold, tropical colors. *Interests:* reading, photography, travel, computers. *Collection:* more than 200 paintings, more than 1500 art & history books, international pins, international Catholic rosaries, international coin purses, music boxes, pallete pendants and miniatures. *Publ:* auth, Tu Puedes ser Artista Pintor. *Dealer:* Marco de Oro Gallery Asdrubal Ruiz Galle Rotario #1 Apt 1 Aguada PR 00602. *Mailing Add:* PO Box 462 Aguadilla PR 00605-0462

ROBLETO, DARIO
ASSEMBLAGE ARTIST, SCULPTOR

b San Antonio, 1972. *Study:* Univ Tex, San Antonio, 1991-93, BFA, 1997; Univ Tex, El Paso, 1993-96; Yale Summer Sch Music & Art, 1996. *Work:* Altoids Curiously Strong Collection, New Mus Contemp Art & Whitney Mus Am Art, New York; Austin Mus Art & Blanton Mus Art, Univ Tex, Austin; Mus Fine Arts, Houston; Mus Contemp Art, San Diego; Los Angeles Co Mus Art. *Exhib:* Solo exhibs, ArtPace, San Antonio, 2000; ACME, Los Angeles, 2000, 2002, 2004; Contemp Arts Mus, Houston, 2001; Mus Contemp Art, San Diego, 2003; Inman Gallery, Houston, 2003, 2008; Whitney Mus Am Art at Altria, 2003; Weatherspoon Art Mus, Univ NC, Greensboro, 2006; D'Amelio Terras, New York, 2006; Frye Art Mus, Seattle, 2008; Altoids Curiously Strong Collection, Bowery Ballroom, New York, 1999; Paradise 8, Exit Art, New York, 1999; Fresh: The Altoids Curiously Strong Collection 1998-2000, New Mus Contemp Art, New York, 2001, A Work in Progress: Selections from the New Mus Collection, 2001; Rapper's Delight, Yerba Buena Ctr Arts, San Francisco, 2001; Gene(sis): Contemp Art Explores Human Genomics, Henry Art Gallery, Seattle, 2002; Int Abstraction, Seattle Art Mus, 2003; Dust Memories, Swiss Inst, New York, 2003; Perspectives @ 25, Contemp Arts Mus, Houston, 2004; Treble, Sculpture Ctr, New York, 2004; Whitney Biennial, Whitney Mus Am Art, New York, 2004; Estranged Objects, Bard Ctr Curatorial Studies, NY, 2005; A Historic Occasion, Mass Mus Contemp Art, North Adams, Mass, 2006; America/Americas, Blanton Mus Art, Austin, 2007; Martian Museum of Terrestrial Art, Barbican Art Gallery, London, 2008. *Teaching:* Vis lectr, Corcoran Coll Art & Design, Wash, 2001; instr, Univ New Orleans, 2001, Calif Inst Arts, Valencia, 2002, Calif Coll Arts & Crafts, San Francisco, 2002 & Loyola Marymount, Los Angeles, 2002. *Awards:* Ellen Battel Stoeckel Fel, 1996; Altoids Tin Canvas Proj Award, 2000; AICA Award, 2004; Joan Mitchell Fel, 2007; Tobin Grand Prize for Artistic Excellence, Artistic Found San Antonio, 2007; US Artists Rasmuson Fel, 2009. *Media:* Miscellaneous Media. *Mailing Add:* c/o Acme 6150 Wilshire Blvd #1 Los Angeles CA 90048

ROBSON, AURORA
SCULPTOR

b Toronto, Can, 1972. *Study:* Columbia Univ, BA (visual art & art hist, magna cum laude), 2000. *Work:* Aliante Hotel, Las Vegas; Four Seasons Hotel, St Louis; Merrill Lynch; Poipu Beach Hotel, Kauai; numerous pvt collections. *Exhib:* Re-Surface Showroom, Brooklyn, 2004; Introduction, Pentimenti Gallery, Philadelphia, 2005; solo exhibs, Richard Levy Gallery, Albuquerque, 2005, Project Space, New York, 2006, Islip Art Mus Carriage House, New York, 2007, Rice gallery, Houston, 2008; Eleven Ten Gallery, Brooklyn, 2006; Wallworks 3, Traywick Contemp Art, Berkeley, Calif, 2007; Discarded to Distinctive, Ross Art Mus, Del, 2008; New Now, Schoolhouse Gallery, Provincetown, Mass, 2009. *Pos:* Artist-in-residence, Maho Bay, St John, US Virgin Islands, 2002 & Islip Mus Carriage House, NY, 2007. *Teaching:* Instr photog, 144 Music & Arts, New York, 2001; instr electric & gas welding, Educ Alliance Art Sch, New York, 2004-2006. *Awards:* Pollock Krasner Found Grant, 2008; NY Found Arts Fel, 2009. *Bibliog:* Wesley Pulkka (auth), Artist Executes Work with Skill, Sunday Jour, 2005; Ruth La Ferla (auth), Fashion & Art, NY Times, 2006; David Cohen (auth), Pollinium, Artworld Digest Mag, 2007; Julia Ramey (auth), The Great Indoors, Houston Press, 2008; Cate McQuaid (auth), Exhibit is a fun way to take in the trash, The Boston Globe, 2009

ROCAMORA, JAUME
PAINTER

b Tortosa, Spain, July 6, 1946. *Study:* Taller Sch Art, Tortosa, Spain, 56; studied with Joan Llimona, Cercle Artistic Sant Lluc, Barcelona, 69. *Hon Degrees:* Socio de honor del Centro Picasso de Horta de Sant Joan. *Work:* Mus Popular Contemp Art, Villafamés, Spain; Zabaleta Mus, Quesada; Munic Mus Fine Arts, Cholet, France; Mus Leopod-Huesch, Dûren, Alemania; Mus Dibujos, Larres, Spain; Museo Vostell de Malpartida, Cáceres, Spain; Museo d'Art Contemporani, Eivissa, Spain; Universidad de Alcalá de Henares, Madrid, Spain; Biblioteca Nacional, Madrid, Spain; Museo Saturo Sato de Tome, Japan. *Comn:* Mural collage, Casa Diocesana d'Espiritualitat, Tortosa, Spain, 86; mural collage, Hotel Berenguer IV, Tortosa, Spain, 86; Serigrafia, Ministry of Trabajo, Madrid, 89 & 90; Asesor de la Fundació Privada Duran Marti, Tortosa, Spain, 92; Espacios Picassianos de Horta de Sant Joan, 93; Co-dir, Coloquio Int, L'abstracció geomètrica, Fundación Noesis, 94. *Exhib:* Elements Primaris, Mus Popular Contemp Art, Villafamés, 84; Oeuvres 1983-1988, Mus Munic Fine Arts, Cholet, 89; Sala Caixa de Tarragona y Biblioteca Comarcal Sebastià Juan Arbó, Amposta, 06; Museu d'Art Modern, Tarragona, 07; Museu de l'Ebre, Tortosa, Spain, 07; Museu de la Norguera, Balaguer, 07; Rietveld: a language, Rocamora: a form of dialogue, Instituto Cervantes, Utrecht, 08. *Teaching:* instr, Workshop on Transformation of Space, Horta de San Joan, Spain, 98. *Bibliog:* J Corredor Matheos (auth), El Arte Mental de Jaume Rocamora, catalog, 85; Josep Miquel Garcia (auth), La percepció implica pensament, catalog, 86; Arnau Puig (auth), Intención ensimismada, catalog, 91; W. Ramba (auth), Jaume Rocamora, una geometrica de nuestro tiempo, Mediterraneo, Castellon, 2000; W. Ramba (auth), Principales itinerarios artisticos del XX, Publicaciones de la Universidad Jaume I, Castellon, 2000; W. Rambla and S. Tena (auths), Forma y Construccion en la plastica de Jaume Rocamora, Contratalla, 2006. *Mem:* Noesis Found, Calaceite, Spain (vpres, currently); Amics, gues de l'Ebre, Spain; Comite de Defense des artistes du Grand-Palais, Paris, France. *Media:* Collage. *Res:* Septima island; artists that have been inspired in the final section of the Rio Ebro; Museu del Montsia. *Specialty:* contemporary Art. *Interests:* constructivism. *Publ:* Illusr, Textos Bàsic de Edicions de Filosofia, Santa Coloma de Gramenet, 91; Xle, Festival de Música Felip Pedrell, Tortosa, 91; Ediciones del Ministerio de Trabajo, Madrid, 91; L'Organització Territorial en Vegueries, Tortosa, 91. *Dealer:* Printworld Int Inc West Chester PA. *Mailing Add:* Argentina 13 Tortosa Spain 43500

ROCHAT, RANA
PAINTER

b Memphis, Tenn, 1960. *Study:* RI Sch Design, BFA, 83. *Exhib:* Sandler Hudson Gallery, Atlanta, Ga, 200, 2001; Fay Gold Gallery, Atlanta, Ga, 2001, 2002, 2005, 2006; Palm Beach Internat Art Fair, Fla, 2001, 2003; David Lusk Gallery, Memphis, Tenn, 2001, 2002, 2004, 2006; 15th Anniversary Works on Paper, The Park Avenue Armory, NY, 2003; The Armory Show, NY, 2003; Convergence of Contemp Painting, Jacksonville Mus Modern Art, Fla, 2005. *Mailing Add:* c/o David Lusk Gallery 4540 Poplar Ave Memphis TN 38117

ROCHE, (EAMONN) KEVIN
ARCHITECT

b Dublin, Ireland, Jun 14, 1922. *Study:* Nat Univ Ireland, BArch, 45; Ill Inst Tech, Postgrad, 48. *Hon Degrees:* Wesleyan Univ, DFA (hon), 81; Nat Univ Ireland, DSc (hon), 77; Yale Univ, DFA (hon), 95, Albertus Magnus, DFA (hon), Iona Coll, DFA (hon). *Comn:* Prin works incl Ford Found Hdqs, 67, Oakland (Calif) Mus, 68, Metrop Mus Art, NY, Creative Arts Ctr, Wesleyan Univ, Middletown, Conn, 71, Fine Arts Ctr, Univ Mass, 71, Union Carbide Corp World Hdqs, Conn, General Foods Corp Hdqs, Rye, NY, 77, 78, Conoco Inc Hdqs, Houston, 79, Central Park Zoo, NY, 80, DeWitt Wallace Mus Fine Arts, Williamsburg, Va, 80, Bouygues World Hdqs, Paris, 83 JP Morgan and Co Hdqs, NY, 83, UNICEF Hdqs, NY, 84, Leo Burnett Co Hdqs, Chicago, 85, Corning (NY) Inc Hdqs, 86, Merck & Co Hdqs, NJ, 87, Dai Ichi Hdqs./Norinchukin Bank Hdqrs, Tokyo, 89, Nations Bank Hdqs, Atlanta, 89, Pontiac Marina Pvt Ltd; Singapore, 90, Metrop, Madrid, 90, Borland Inter Headquarters, Scotts Valley, Calif, 90, Tanjong & Binariang/Ampang Tower, Kuala Lumpur, Malaysia, 93, Mus Jewish Heritage Holocaust Mem, NY, 93, Tata Cummins Private Ltd, Jamshedpur, India, 94, Vis Ctr, Columbus, Ind, 94, Cummins Engine Co APEX Manufacturing Facility, 94, Lucent Techs. Hdqs, Murray Hill, NJ, 96, Wuxi Newage Cummins Wuxi, China, 96, Total Systems Serv Corp. Headquarters, Columbus, Ga, 97, student housing and student union NY Univ, NY 2003, central athletic facility Mass Inst of Tech, Cambridge, 2000, Lucent Tech. Research and Development Facilities, various locations incl The Neth and Ger, 2001, Shiodome Block B Devel, Tokyo, 2003, Santander Central Hispano, Madrid, 2001-, Securities & Exchange Comn Hdqrs, Wash, 2001-, Bouygues SA Holding Co Hdqrs, Paris, 2002-, Conf Ctr, Dublin, 2011. *Exhib:* Yale Univ, New Haven, Conn, 2011; Mus City of NY, 2011; Nat Bldg Mus, Wash DC, 2012; Eric Arthur Gallery, Univ Toronto, 2013. *Pos:* With Eero Saarinen & Assocs Bloomfield Hills, Mich, 50-61; partner, Kevin Roche John Dinkeloo & Assoc, Hamden, 66-. *Awards:* Recipient Creative Arts award Brandeis Univ, 67; AS Bard award City Club NY, 68, 77, 79; Pritzker Archit Prize, 82; Gold Medal Award for Archit, Am Acad Arts and Letts, 90; Albert S Bard award, 90; Gold Medal award, Am Inst Architects, 93; Ulysses award, Univ Coll Dublin, 2012. *Bibliog:* Kevin Roche, John Dinkeloo and Associates 1962-1975, 75; Francesco Dal Co (auth), Kevin Roche, Electa Editrice, Milan, Italy, 85; Kevin Roche, Architecture and Urbanism Extra Edition, Yoshio Yoshida, 87; Nobuo Hozumi (auth), Latest Works of Kevin Roche, John Dinkeloo and Associates, Architecture & Urbanism, Yoshio Yoshida, 88; EEva-Liisa Pelkonen (co-auth, with Kathleen John-Alder, Olga Pantelidou, and David Sadighia), Kevin Roche: Architecture as Environment, Yale Univ Press, 2011; numerous articles in The Architectural Forum. *Mem:* Fel Am Inst of Archits; Am Asn for Advancement of Sci; Nat Acad (assoc, 67, acad, 73); Am Acad of Arts and Letters (pres, 94-97); Munic Art Soc, NY; Woodrow Wilson Inst Scholars (founding bd mem); Royal Inst British Architects; Royal Inst Architects of Ireland; Japanese Inst Architects. *Mailing Add:* Kevin Roche John Dinkeloo & Assoc 20 Davis St PO Box 6127 New Haven CT 06517-3501

ROCHE-RABELL, ARNALDO
PAINTER
b Santurce, PR, 1955. *Study:* Sch Archit PR, 74-78; Art Inst Chicago, BFA (James Nelson Raymond Fel), 82, MFA, 84. *Work:* Art Inst Chicago; Hirshhorn Mus & Sculpture Garden, Washington, DC; Metrop Mus Art & Mus del Barrio, NY. *Exhib:* Recent Acquisitions, Hirshhorn Mus & Sculpture Garden, Washington, DC & Museo del Barrio, NY, 91; Myth and Magic: Am Art of the 1980's, Museo de Arte Contemporaneo, Monterrey, Mex, 91; Cruciformed: Images of the Cross Since 1980, Cleveland Ctr Contemp Art, Ohio, 91-92; Awards in the Visual Arts 10, Southeastern Ctr Contemp Art, Hirshhorn Mus & Sculpture Garden, Washington, DC, Albuquerque Mus Art, Hist & Sci, NMex & Toledo Mus Art, Ohio, 91-92; 40th Anniversary Exhib: Selections from the Richard Brown Baker Collection, Frumkin/Adams Gallery, NY, 92; Latin Am Artists of the Twentieth Century, Mus Mod Art, NY, Estacion Plaza de Armas, Seville, Centre Georges Pompidou, Paris, Mus Ludwig, Cologne, 92-93; Selections from the Collection, Hirshhorn Mus & Sculpture Garden, Washington, DC, 94; Caribbean Visions: Contemp Painting and Sculpture, Art Serv Int, 95; The Reconstructed Figure: The Human Image in Contemp Art, Katonah Mus Art, NY, 95; Azaceta, Bedia, Roche, George Adams Gallery, NY, 95 & Going Places, 96; Art in Chicago: 1945-1995, Mus Contemp Art, Ill, 96-97; Caballos: Political Animals, Azaceta, Bedia, Benedit, Elso, Roche, George Adams Gallery, NY, 97; FIA 1997, Caracas, 97; Annual Collectors Show, Ark Arts Ctr, Little Rock, 98; Latin-Am Group Show (Azaceta, Bedia, Roche, Palazyan), George Adams Gallery, NY, 98; and many others. *Awards:* Medallion of Lincoln Award, presented by Mr James Thompson, Gov Ill, 81; 2nd Ann Biennial Painting Prize, Cuenas, Ecuador, 89. *Bibliog:* Enrique Garcia Gutierrez (auth), Arnaldo Roche-Rabell: Los Premeros Diez Anos (exhib catalog), Museo de Arte Contemp, 92; and many others. *Mailing Add:* c/o George Adams Gallery 525 W 26th St New York NY 10001

ROCKBURNE, DOROTHEA
PAINTER, SCULPTOR
b Montreal, Que; US citizen. *Study:* Black Mountain Col, Ecole Des Beaux Arts, Montreal; Montreal Mus Sch, Can. *Hon Degrees:* Coll for Creative Studies, DFA, 2002. *Work:* Mus Mod Art, Whitney Mus Am Art & Metrop Mus Art, NY; Philadelphia Mus Art; Corcoran Gallery, Washington; Guggenheim Mus, NY; J Paul Getty Trust, Calif; Nat Mus of Women in Art; Philadelphia Mus of Art; Auckland City Art Mus; Brooklyn Mus of Art; Nat Galleries, Washington, DC; Houston Mus of Fine Arts; Carnegie Mus, Pittsburgh; Nat Acad Design Mus, NY; Parrish Art Mus, Southampton, NY; Cranbrook Art Mus, Mich; Mus Fine Arts, Boston; MoCA, La; LACMA. *Comn:* Northern Sky, Southern Sky (mural), Sony Corp, NY, 93; Time Sequence (mural), Ganek Residence, NY, 93; Sensor, (mural), Hilton Hotel, San Jose, Calif, 93; The Virtues of Good Government, (mural), Portland Maine Courthouse, 94; Euclid's Comet (mural), Univ Mich, Ann Arbor, 97; The Virtues of Good Government, Conn, 2000; Am Embassy Wall Mural, Kingston, Jamaica, 2008; Tribute to Colin Powell (mural), FAPE, US Embassy, Kingston, Jamaica, 2009. *Exhib:* Solo exhibs, Bykert Gallery, 70-73, Sonnabend Gallery, Paris, 71, Galleria Schema, Florence, 73, 75, 92, Tex Gallery, 73, 75, 79, 81, 92, John Weber Gallery, 74, 76, 78, Dorothea Rockburne: Locus, Mus Modern Art, NY 81, Margo Leavin Gallery, Los Angeles, Calif, 82, Xavier Fourcade, NY, 81, 82, 83, 85, 86, Arts Club, Chicago, Ill, 87, Ten Yr Painting Retrospective, Rose Art Mus, Brandeis, 89, Andre Emmerich Gallery, 88, 90, 91, 92, 94, 95, Guild Hall Mus, 95, Portland Mus Art, 96, Art in General, 99, Lawrence Rubin, Greenberg, Van Doren Fine Art, NY, 2000, 2011, 2012, Beard Gallery, Wheaton Col, Norton, Mass, 2009, Black Mountain Col Mus & Arts Ctr, Asheville, NC, 2009, NY Studio Sch, New York, 2010, Parris Art Mus, Southampton, NY, 2011, Dorothea Rockburne: In My Minds Eye, Mus Fine Arts, 2011-12, Works 1967-1972, Craig Starr, 2012; Group exhibs, Eight Contemp Artists, MoMA, 74, Drawing Now, MoMA, Whitney Biennial, 73, 77, 79, Constructivism & the Geometric Tradition, Albright Knox, 79-84, The NY Sch: 4 Decades, Guggenheim, 82, A Century of Modern Drawing, MoMA, 82-83, Contemporary Works from the Collections, MoMA, 85-86, Strong Statements in Black & White, James Goodman, 87, Am Masters, Corcoran Gallery, 87, Viewpoints: Postwar Painting & Sculpture, Guggenheim Mus, NY, 89; Making Their Mark, Cincinnati Art Mus, 89, Lines of Vision, 89-91, From Minimal to Conceptual Art, Nat Gallery, 94; More than Minimal: Feminism & Abstraction in the 70's, Rose Art Mus, Brandeis Univ, Mass, 96; Serial Attitude, Addison Gallery Am Art, Phillips Acad, Mass, 97, Tracing the Sublime, 2004; Thirty-five Years at Crown Point Press (traveling), Nat Gallery of Art, Washington, 97; Gemini GEL at Joni Moisant Weyl, NY, 1998, New Editions, 99; Afterimage: Drawing Through Process, Mus Contemp Art, Los Angeles, 99; Drawing in the Present, Parsons Sch Design, NY, 99; Limerick City Art Gallery, Ireland, 2000; Ceremonial Exhib, Am Acad Arts & Letts, 2001; I Love NY, Artemis Greenberg Van Doren Gallery, NY, 2001, All American, Part II, 2002; Three Decades of Contemp Art: The Dr John & Rose M Shuey Collection, Cranbrook Art Mus, Mich, 2001 & 2002; Best Impressions: 35 Yrs of Prints and Sculpture from Gemini GEL, 2001-2002; Nat Gallery Art, 2001-2002; Painting & Drawing, Lawrence Rubin Greenberg Van Doren Fine Art, NY, 2001; Across the Universe; 177th Ann, Nat Acad Design, NY, 2002, Recent Acquisitions, 2006; Armory Show, Art in General, NY, 2002; Drawing Modern, Cleveland Mus Art, Ohio, 2003; Black Mountain Coll: Experimenting with Power, Reina Sophia Mus, Madrid, 2003; Drawings of Choice from a NY Collection, Krannert Art Mus, 2002-2003; Recent Acquisitions to Permanent Collection, Mus Fine Arts, Boston, 2003; A Minimal Future?, Geffen Contemp, Los Angeles, 2003 & 2004; Singular Forms (Sometimes Repeated), Guggenheim Mus, NY, 2004; Tracing the Sublime, Addison Gallery Am Art, Andover, Mass, 2004; High Times, Hard Times: NY Painting 1965-75, Ind Curators Int, 2006-2008; Sets, Series, and Suites, Mus Fine Arts, Boston, 2005; Tete a Tete, Greenberg Van Doren Gallery, NY, Women's Work, 2006; Transforming Chronologies, Mus Modern Art, NY, 2006; What is Painting, MoMA, 2007; Drawing Connections, Morgan Libr, NY, 2007; 182nd Ann Exhib Contemp Am Art, Nat Acad Mus, NY, 2007; Multiplex: New Directions in Art, 1970 to Now, Mus Mod Art, NY, 2007-2008; Equinox, MoCA, LA, 2007-2008; The Abstract Impulse, Nat Acad Mus, 2007; Geo/Metric, Mus Mod Art, NY, 2008; Lines, Grids, Stains, Words, Mus Mod Art, traveled, 2008-; Geometry as Image, Russell Bowman Art Adv, Chicago, 2009; Paper: Pressed, Stained, Slashed, Folded, Mus Mod Art, New York, 2009; 184th Ann, Nat Acad Mus, NY, 2009; Richard Brown Baker Collection, Hood Mus Art, Dartmouth Col, Hanover, NH, 2009-10; A Perfect Measure, Trust for Mus Exhibs, Washington, DC, 2010-11; I am the Cosmos, State Mus, Trenton, NJ, 2011; On Line: Drawing Through the 20th Century, Mus Modern Art, NY; Esteban Vicente: Portrait of the Artist, Parrish Art Mus, Southampton, NY, 2011; Black Mountain Coll and its Legacy, Loretta Howard Gallery, NY, 2011; Selections from the Private Collection of Robert Rauschenberg, Gagosian Gallery, NY, 2011; Time Out of Mind, Spruth Magers, Berlin, 2011-12; Contemp Drawings from Irving Stenn Jr Coll, Art Inst Chicago, 2011-12; Art Basel Miami Beach, 2011; Nat Acad Mus; From Protest to Process, Recent Gifts by Women Academicians, White: The Anatomy of a Color, The Annual, 2012; Art Basel Miami, Greenberg Van Doren, 2012; Weights & Measures, Eleven Rivington, 2012; Geometric Abstraction, James Goodman Gallery, EXPO Chgo, 2012. *Collection Arranged:* cur, Emerging Artists Selected by Dorothea Rockburne, Art in General, NY 87. *Pos:* Art in General, NY; bd mem, The Brooklyn Rail. *Teaching:* Instr, Columbia Univ, NY, Sch of Visual Arts, NY, Harvard Univ, New York Studio Sch, UC Davis, San Francisco Art Inst, Yale Univ, Am Univ Washington, Princeton Univ. *Awards:* Guggenheim Fel, 72-73; Painting Award, Art Inst Chicago, 72; Nat Endowment Arts Fel, 74-75; Brandeis Univ Creative Arts Award, 85; Am Acad in Rome Fel, 92; Bellagio award, 97; Am Acad Arts & Letts Jimmy Ernst Lifetime Achievement Award, 99; Nat Acad Design Adolph & Clara Abrig Prize, 2002, Pike Award, 2002; Francis J Greenburger Award, Art Omi Int, 2003; Lee Krasner Award, Pollock-Krasner Found, 2003, 2007; Lifetime Achievement Award, Nat Acad Mus, 2009. *Bibliog:* Mel Bochner, Robert Pincus-Witten, Jennifer Licht, (auths), Robert Pincus-Witten (auth), Reviews, Artforum, 70-72, Bruce Boice (auth), Review, Artforum, 73, Thomas Hess (auth), Rules of the Game, Part II: Marden & Rockburne, NY mag, 74, Naomi Spector (auth), New Color Works by Dorothea Rockburne (catalog, essay), 76, Bernice Rose (auth), Drawing Now, MoMA catalog, 76, Deborah Phillips (auth) ArtNews, 81, Brice Marden (auth), Dorothea Rockburne, ArtNews, 83; Robert Storr (auth), Painterly Operations, Art Am, 2/86 & Rockburne's Wager (exhib catalog), Andre Emmerich Gallery, 1988; Michael Brenson (auth), A new-world painter views the masterpieces of old-world innovators, 4/29/88 & Egyptian art is alive & well in the West, 12/31/89, NY Times; Lilly Wei (auth), Dorothea Rockburne, Stargazer, Art in Am, 10/94; John Yau (auth), Light and Dark (exhib catalog), Andre Emmerich Gallery, 1989; Chuck Close (auth), The Portrait's Speak, ART Press, NY, 97; Carter Ratcliff, Out of the Box: The Reinvention of Art, 1965-75, NY, 2000; Jerry Saltz (auth), The Village Voice, 2001 & 2003; David Reed (auth), Art Forum, 2001 & 2003; Dorothea Rockburne and Klaus Kertess in Conversation with Bill Bartman, The Brooklyn Rail, 2005; Greg Allen (auth), NY Times, 2003; Denise Green (auth), Metronymy in Contemporary Art: A Paradigm, 2005; Katy Siegel (editor), High Times, Hard Times, New York Painting 1967-1975, DAP, 2006; Barbara A MacAdam (auth), The New Abstraction, ArtNews, 2007; Raphael Rubenstein (auth), It's Not Made by Great Men, Art in Am, 2007; Christine Ratlemyer (auth), Lines, Grids, Stains, Words (exhib catalog), 2008; Karen Rosenberg (auth), Of the Academy, by and for Academicians, NY Times, 2009; Robin Shulman (auth), Colin Powell Art Reaches for the Sky, The Washington Post, 2009; Joan Waltemath (auth), Dorothea Rockburne's Astronomy Drawing, the Brooklyn Rail, 2010; Robert C Morgan (auth), Astronomy Drawings at the New York Studio Sch, Artcritical.com, 2010; Alfred MacAdams (auth), Dorothea Rockburne, New York Studio Sch, ARTnews, 2010; Cornelia Butler & Catherine de Zegher (auths), Online Drawing Through the 20th Century, MOMA, 2010; Esteban Vicente, Concrete Improvisations: Collages and Sculpture, Grey Art Gallery, NYU, 2010; David Levi Strauss & Christopher Bamford (auth), In Conversation: Dorothea Rockburne, Brooklyn Rail, 2011; Alicia Long Well & David Anfam (auths), Dorothea Rockburne: In My Mind's Eye, Woman's Art Jour, 2011; Anna Lovatt (auth), Dorothea Rockburne: In My Minds Eye, Artforum Int, 2011; Barbara A MacAdam (auth), American Abstract Artists: Ok Harris Works of Art, ARTnews, 2011; David Ebony (auth), The ADAA Art Show Top 10, Art in Am, 2012. *Mem:* Nat Arts Club; Art in Gen Century Club; Nat Acad; Am Acad Arts & Letts; Nat Found Advancement Arts (adv bd); Nat Asn Women Artists (hon vice pres); Am Abstract Artists. *Media:* Various Media. *Res:* Astronomy, Physics, Mathematics, Philosophy. *Specialty:* Estab and Emerging Contemp Artists. *Interests:* Art, Astronomy, Mathematics, Science, Philosophy, Ancient Egypt. *Dealer:* Artemis Greenberg Van Doren Fine Art 730 5th Ave 7th Fl New York NY 10019. *Mailing Add:* 140 Grand St # 2WF New York NY 10013

ROCKEFELLER, JOHN (JAY) D, IV
COLLECTOR
b New York, NY, June 18, 1937. *Study:* Int Christian Univ, Tokyo, 1957-60; Harvard Univ, BA, 1961. *Hon Degrees:* Eleven from US Coll & Univ. *Awards:* Named one of 200 Leaders in Am, Time Mag, 1975; named one of Top 200 Collectors, ARTnews mag, 2004-09. *Mem:* Charleston Rotary; Nat Gov Asn (chmn, formerly). *Collection:* 19th- and early 20th-century American art, especially American Impressionism; modern and contemporary art. *Publ:* Auth, The Japanese Student, New York Times Mag, & Life 6/60. *Mailing Add:* 531 Hart Senate Off Bldg Washington DC 20510

ROCKEFELLER, SHARON PERCY
COLLECTOR
b Oakland, Calif, Dec 10, 1944. *Study:* Stanford Univ, BA (cum laude), 1966. *Hon Degrees:* DPS, Alderson-Broaddus Coll, WVa, 1977; LLD, Univ Charleston, WVa, 1977 & Beloit Coll, Wis, 1978; LHD, W Liberty State Coll, WVa, 1980, Hamilton Coll, NY, 1982 & Wheeling Coll, WVa, 1984. *Awards:* Named Washingtonian of Year, Washingtonian Mag, 1994; Nat Endowment for the Humanities, 1994; Distinguished Broadcaster Award, 1994; named one of Top 200 Collectors, ARTnews mag, 2004-09; Charles Frankel Prize; Woman of Vision Award; Women in Film & Video Award; CINE Lifetime Achievement Award. *Mem:* Stanford-in-Washington Coun (chmn, formerly); Fel, Am Acad Arts & Sciences; Smithsonian Am Art Comn (bd mem, currently). *Collection:* 19th- and early 20th-century American art, especially American Impressionism; modern and contemporary American art

ROCKLEN, RY
SCULPTOR
b Los Angeles, Calif, 1978. *Study:* Calif Inst Arts, Valencia, 1998; Univ Calif, Los Angeles, BFA, 2001; Univ Southern Calif, MFA, 2006. *Work:* Thomas J Watson Libr, Metrop Mus Art, New York; Mus Contemp Art, Los Angeles. *Exhib:* Solo exhibs include Black Dragon Soc, Los Angeles, 2003, Dangerous Curve, Los Angeles, 2004, Zack Feuer Gallery, New York, 2006, Half Craft, Black Dragon Soc, Los Angeles, 2007, Bernier/Eliades, Athens, Baronian Francey, Brussels, 2008, Marc Jancou Contemp, New York, 2009, BFAS Blondeau Fine Arts Serv, Geneva, 2010; Group exhibs include Face Off, The Smell, Los Angeles, 2001; I'm From Orange County and I Drink Johnny Walker Red, Galerie Julius Hummel, Vienna, Austria, 2002; Low Overhead, Todd Hughes Fine Art, Pasadena, CA, 2002; The Daily Circus, The Latch, Los Angeles, 2002, Something Else, 2003; 3D 7DEEP, Black Dragon Society, Los Angeles, 2003; Black Dragon Society, Apex Art, New York, 2004; Los Angeles Juried Exhibition, Hollywood, 2005; 11:59, Compact/Space Gallery, Los Angeles, 2006; Whitney Biennial, Whitney Mus Am Art, 2008; Second Nature, The Valentine-Adelson Collection, Hammer Mus, 2008; Country Music, Blum & Poe, Los Angeles, 2010. *Collection Arranged:* cur, Spoils, Sarah Coleman Gallery, Los Angeles; cur, Trance Plants, Latch Gallery, Los Angels, 2003. *Dealer:* Marc Jancou Contemp 524 W 24th St New York NY 10011. *Mailing Add:* Marc Jancou Contemporary 524 W 24th St New York NY 10011

ROCKMAN, ALEXIS
PAINTER
b New York, 1962. *Study:* Rhode Island Sch Design, Providence, RI, 1982; Sch Visual Arts, New York, 1985. *Work:* Baltimore Art Mus; Brooklyn Mus; Carnegie Mus; Cincinnati Art Mus; Solomon R Guggenheim Mus; Israel Mus; Los Angeles Co Mus Art; Mus Fine Arts, Boston; Mus Sex, New York; Mus Mod Art, New York; Newark Mus, NJ; NY Pub Libr; Rose Art Mus, Brandeis Univ, Mass; Whitney Mus Am Art, New York; Wurth Mus, Germany; Zimmerli Mus, Rutgers Univ, NJ. *Exhib:* Solo exhibs, Carnegie Mus Art, Pa, 1992, Jay Gorney Mod Art, New York, 1993, 1995, Contemp Art Mus, Houston, Tex, 1997, London Projects, Eng, 1998, Works on Paper, Los Angeles, Calif, 1999, Baldwin Gallery, 2002, 2004, 2008, Gorney Bravin & Lee, New York, 2004, Leo Koenig Inc, New York, 2006, 2008, Franklin Parrasch Gallery, New York, 2009, Smithsonian Am Art Mus, DC, 2010; group exhibs, Screen, Friedrich Petzel Gallery, New York, 1996; The Empire Strikes Back, The ATM Gallery, New York, 2002; Future Noir, Gorney Bravin & Lee, New York, 2005; Crypotozoology: Out of Time, Place, Scale, Bates Coll Mus Art, Portland, Maine, 2006; Surrealism, Dada and Their Legacies in Contemp Art, Israel Mus, Jerusalem, 2007; Landscape: Form & Thought, Ingrao Gallery, New York, 2008; Feeling the Heat, Art, Sci & Climate Change, Deutche Bank Gallery, New York, 2007; Hunt & Chase, Salomon Contemp, East Hampton, NY, 2010. *Teaching:* lecture at Cooper Union, Inst Contemp Art, Boston, Carnegie Mus, Portland Mus, Ill State Univ, Detroit Zoo, Montana State Univ, Contemp Art Ctr, Houston, Sch Visual Arts, Univ Wash, Univ Tex, Henry Art Gallery, Guggenheim Mus, Orlando Mus, Royal Coll Surgeons, Am Mus Natural Hist, United Nations Paris, Wexner Ctr Arts, Sch Visual Art, Brooklyn Mus, Harvard Club, Getty Mus, Addison Muc, RI Sch Design Mus, Sch Mus Fine Arts, Boston, Nat Acad Mus & Sch Fine Arts, Bates Mus, Contemp Art Ctr, Cincinnati, NYU Fine Art Dept, Mass Moca, Rose Mus, Utah State, Smithsonian Am Art Mus, Sch Art Inst Chicago, Explorers Club. *Mailing Add:* Leo Koenig Inc 459 W 19th St New York NY 10011

RODA, RHODA LILLIAN SABLOW
PAINTER, TAPESTRY ARTIST
b Port Chester, NY, 1926. *Study:* Univ Wis; Rochester Inst Technol; Art Students League; also with Frank Vincent DuMont & Frank Reilly. *Comn:* Cranbrook 50th Anniversary (needlepoint rug), Cranbrook Acad, Bloomfield Hills, Mich, 73; needlepoint designs of main altar area & furniture, Christ Episcopal Church, Detroit, Mich, 75 & main altar rug, 82; needlepoint designs altar seats & kneelers, St James Church, Birmingham, Mich, 83; needlepoint design, Church of the Holy Sepulcher, Jerusalem, 94. *Exhib:* Allied Artists Am, Nat Acad, NY, 69; Ahda Artzt Gallery, NY, 70; Needle Arts Gallery, Birmingham, Mich, 71, 74 & 76; Lever House, NY, 77. *Pos:* chmn, organizer juried craft show, Purchase Coll Performing Arts Center, Purchase, NY, 98-2000, (co-chmn) 2008. *Bibliog:* Lesley Umans (auth), Encaustic painting, Reporter Dispatch, AP, 7/70 & Creative stitchery, Women's Wear Daily, 8/71; Lillian Braun (auth), 3-D needlepoint, Detroit Free Press, 10/74. *Media:* Oil, Acrylic; Silk, Wool. *Interests:* Working on wall hangings, wool, calling hangings, knottings, all sizes & shapes & lengths. Abstract designs. *Mailing Add:* 23 Rural Dr Scarsdale NY 10583

RODE, MEREDITH EAGON
PRINTMAKER, EDUCATOR
b Delaware, Ohio, Mar 27, 1938. *Study:* Corcoran Sch Art, 55-58; George Washington Univ, BA, 58; Art Students League, New York, (scholar), study with George Grosz & Harry Sternberg, 59; Univ Md, MFA, 74; Union Inst, PhD, 94. *Work:* Southern Graphics Print Collection, Univ Miss, Oxford; Univ Md Coll Permanent Collection; Dundalk Col; Univ Dist Columbia Permanent Collection; Nat Mus Women in Arts. *Exhib:* Baltimore Mus Art, Md, 77; Utah Mus Fine Arts, Salt Lake City, 77; Contemp Printmaking in Maryland, (juried) Baltimore, MD, 83; Dundalk Coll Gallery Invitational, self-portraits, 91; US Dept State Art in the Embassies Prog, Nassau, Bahamas, Kinshasa, Zaire, Vienna, Austria, Port-Au-Prince, Haiti, Brazzaville, the Congo & Geneva, Switz; Mus Modern, in New Delhi, India, Beijing, China, 2002. *Pos:* Actg chmn, Federal City Col, Washington, DC, 71-72, chair, Mass Media, Visual & Performing Arts, Univ DC, 2007; Art Prog Dir, Univ, DC, 2003. *Teaching:* Instr studio art, Corcoran Sch Art, 62-68; assoc prof studio art, Univ DC, 68-78, prof, 78-. *Awards:* Fac Res Grant, Univ DC, 85-86, 86-87; Fel, Ctr Applied Res, 88-89; Sussman Award, Union Inst, 94; Nat Educ Asn Award, 2000; Participant & Speaker, Oxford Round Table, Oxford Univ, Oxford, UK, 2006; Distinguished Educator's Award, UDC, 2009. *Bibliog:* UDC Special Art Collection catalog, 84. *Mem:* Women's Caucus Art (nat vpres, 75-76); Founds Art Theory & Educ; Arts Coun African Studies Asn; Coll Art Asn; and others. *Media:* Multimedia. *Res:* Visual Culture (global). *Interests:* cultural diversity in world art; race and ethnicity; perception and cognition. *Publ:* Auth, articles, Art J, Coll Art Asn, 75; illusr, Earth Day, 90, Quicksilver Comm, Inc; auth, Thought on Action, The NEA Higher Educ J, 2000; auth, Fate in Review, Foundations in Art, Theory and Education, 2000. *Mailing Add:* Univ DC 4200 Connecticut Ave NW Washington DC 20008

RODEIRO, JOSE MANUEL
PAINTER, MURALIST
b Tampa, Fla, Feb 5, 1949. *Study:* Univ Tampa, Fla, BA, 71; Pratt Inst, Brooklyn, MFA, 73; Ohio Univ, Athens, Ohio, PhD, 76. *Work:* Washington Co Mus, Hagerstown, Md; Oscar Cintas Found, NY; City of Tampa, Fla; Oscar Cintas Found Collection, Fla Int Univ Mus, Miami, Fla; MDC Mus of Art & Design, Miami, Fla; NJ City Univ. *Comn:* Arrival of De Soto in Florida (mural), Convention Center, Tampa, Fla, 2004; Tampa the Cradle of Cuban Independence (mural), Fla, 90; The Ransoming of Frederick (mural), Walkersville, Md, 92. *Exhib:* Four Allegheny Artists, Md Art Place, Baltimore, 83; one-person shows, Nicholas Roerch Mus, NY, 85 & Washington Co Mus, Md, 88; Inaugural Exhib, Casal de Sarria, Barcelona, Spain, 86; Grace Harkin Gallery, NY, 88; Rosenberg Gallery, Baltimore, Md, 90; Lucia Gallery, NY, 90; Washington Co Mus, Md, 97; Face-to-Face, Washington Co Mus, Hagerstown, Md, 2001; Visual Imagery of Latinas/os Exhib, Mason Gross Sch Art Gallery, Rutgers, State Univ NJ, 2001; Corazones Unidos, Newark Mus, 2002; Kenkelaba Gallery, New York City, 2002; Transcultural NJ, Perth Amboy Gallery, Perth Amboy, NJ; Kraft-Nabisco Gallery Exhib, NJ, 2005; East-Here/Neo-Latino, Gallery Korea, New York, 2003; Int Immigrants Found, United Nations Economic & Social Coun, New York, 2009; New Classicism, Theresa Maloney Gallery, Coll St Elizabeth, Morristown, NJ, 2010, Responding to Cuba, 2009, Contemp Portraits Show, 2010; 17th & 18th Ann Jersey City Artist Studio Tour, Rotunda Gallery, Jersey City, NJ, 2008; Melting Pot show, Passaic Libr Gallery, NJ, 2010. *Pos:* Assoc Prof of Art, New Jersey City Univ, Jersey City, NJ, 1993 and Prof of Art, 2003-2015. *Teaching:* Vis prof, Pratt Inst, Brooklyn, 75-77; adj prof art, Univ SFla, Tampa, 77-79; asst prof, Frostburg State Univ, Md, 79-84, assoc prof, 84-92; artist-in-residence, Md State Arts Coun, 92; visiting prof, Univ Central Am, Managua, Nicaragua, 95. *Awards:* Oscar B Cintas Fel in painting, 82; Best of Show, Washington Co Mus, 85; Vis Artist Fel in painting, Nat Endowment for the Arts, 86-87; Best of Show, Lucia Gallery, 88; Lectr Res Fulbright Grant, Nicaragua, 94-95; grant, Inter-Am Develop Bank, DC, 91. *Bibliog:* Nico Suarez (auth), Amnesis Art, Lascaux Pub, 88; Murals article, St Petersburg Sun Times, 11/11/90; Presencia Revista, La Paz, Bolivia, 9/12/93; The Hispanic Outlook in Higher Education, Paramus, NJ, 1/2002; Transcultural New Jersey Vol II, 2005; Neo-Latino, Perth Amboy Galleries Publ, Perth Amboy, NJ, 2004-2005; Visual Imagery of Latinoas/os in New Jersey, Rutgers Univ, 2002; Martin Espada (ed), El Coro, Univ Pass Press, 97; Charles Hayes & Peter Seeger (ed), From the Hudson to the World, New York, Clearwater Sloop Press, 78; The Immanentist Anthology, Smith Press, New York, 72; Walter Lowenfels (auth), For Neruda, for Chile, Beacon Press, Boston, 75. *Mem:* Art South Inc; Md Fedn Art; Md State Arts Coun Visual Arts Panel; Friends of Art NJ; Ctr for Latino Arts & Culture; Council on Hispanic Affairs; Neo-Latin Group, Newark, NJ; La Ruche Art Consortium, Union City, NJ; We Are You Proj, Jersey City, NJ. *Media:* Oil, Acrylic. *Res:* Aesthetics section, Cuban-Am & Dominican-Am Art sections, Encyclopedia Latina, Groliers Inc, Danbury, Conn, 2007; Intro, Carta a la Amnesia #2.046, De Los Escribanos de Loen, Altamira Press, Northampton, Mass, 94; Ben Jones: Washed in the Blood, monogram for the SAMA Mus, SAMA, Altoona, Pa, 2010. *Interests:* Poetry. *Publ:* Art of the 60's & 70's, Wash Co Mus Fine Arts, Hagerstown, 90; Contemporary Nicaraguan Art, Frostburg State Univ Press, 91; Ron Felber's Searchers (cover), Omni Mag, St Martins Press, NY, 11/94; and others; cover design, illusr, Amnesia Tango, Cedar Hill Pub, 98; cover design, Infinite Days, BOP Press, 2003; Harriet Febland, New York, 2008; Sheenkai Stanislai, Int Gallerie, Mumbai, India, Feb 2009; Bori4arte, Four Puerto Rican Artists monogram, Lemmerman Gallery, Jersey City, Coun Hispanic Affairs Publ, 2007; Ultra Violet, Coun Hispanic Affairs Publ, 2004, Wash Co Mus Fine Arts, Hagerstown, Md, 2004; Neo-Latino Visual Artistic Creativity, The Academic Forum, Acad Affairs Publ, NJ City Univ, 2004; Mascaras (Latin-Am Masks), Wash Co Mus Fine Arts Publ, 2003. *Dealer:* Clayton Galleries Tampa FL; Lucia Gallery New York NY; Alan Britt, Baltimore, MD; La Ruche Art Union City NJ. *Mailing Add:* 208 Park Ave Madison NJ 07940

RODENSTOCK, INGE
COLLECTOR
Awards: Named one of Top 200 Collectors, ARTnews mag, 2009-13. *Collection:* Contemporary German, American and British art

RODRIGUEZ, BERT
INSTALLATION SCULPTOR
b Miami, Fla, May 5, 1975. *Study:* Univ Fla, New World Arts, BFA, 1998; Skowhegan Sch Painting & Sculpture, Portland, ME, 1999. *Work:* Rubell Family Collection, Miami; Mus Contemp Art, North Miami, Fla; Kemper Mus Art, Kansas City. *Exhib:* Solo exhibs include Centre Gallery, Miami, 2000; Group exhibs include 52, the Art

Nucleus, Portland, OR, 2004; Becoming Father, Becoming Infant, Bronx Mus, NY, 2004; Faith, Champion Fine Art, Los Angeles, 2004; Brought Together Again, New World Gallery, Miami, 2005; Mus Contemp Art & Miami, Mus Contemp Art, North Miami, 2005; Something, Locust Projs, Miami, 2006; Native Seeds, ArtCenter, South Fla, Miami, 2006; Advertising Works!, Fredric Snitzer Gallery, Miami, 2007; Whitney Biennial, Whitney Mus Am Art, New York, 2008; Disappearances, Shadows & Illusions, Miami Art Mus, Miami, 2008. *Mailing Add:* Fredric Snitzer Gallery 2247 NW 1st Place Miami FL 33127

RODRIGUEZ, GENO (EUGENE)
PHOTOGRAPHER, MUSEUM DIRECTOR, CURATOR
b New York, NY, June 2, 1940. *Study:* Hammersmith Coll Art, London, NDD, 66; Int Peoples Col, Elsinore, Denmark. *Work:* Metrop Mus Art; Everson Mus Art; Int Ctr for Photog, NY; Am Mus Natural Hist, NY; Mus Contemp Art, Caracas, Venezuela; Mus City NY. *Exhib:* One & two-person exhibs, Wadsworth Atheneum, Hartford, Conn, 76, Alternative Ctr for Int Arts, NY, Studio Arte 2001, Castressata, Italy & Centro Arte Galeter, Brescia, Italy, 77, Mus Contemp Art, Caracus, Venezuela & II Diaframma Gallery, Milan, Italy, 79, Cayman Gallery, NY & Real Art Ways Gallery, Hartford, Conn, 80, Jayne H Baum Gallery, NY, 86, CEPA Gallery, Buffalo, NY, 87 & Sheldon Memorial Art Gallery, Univ Nebr, Lincoln, 89; Graham Mod, NY, 87; San Diego Mus Art, Calif, 87; Photog on the Edge (catalog), The Patrick & Beatrice Haggerty Mus Art, Marquette Univ, Milwaukee, Wis, 88; The Photog of Invention: Am Photogrs of the Eighties (catalog), Nat Mus Am Art, Smithsonian Inst, Washington, DC, 89; Fantasies, Fables and Fabrications: Photoworks from the 80's traveling exhib, Univ Mass, Amherst, Herter Art Gallery, also traveling: Delaware Art Mus, Wilmington; Lamont Gallery, Phillips Exeter Acad, Andover, Mass; Univ Mo, Gallery Art, Kansas City; Mus Contemp Art, Ostende, Belgium; Mus Contemp Photog, Antwerp, Belg & Mus Contemp Art, Florence, Italy, 89; and others. *Collection Arranged:* Dia Dos Los Muertos III: Homelessness, 90; Peter Dean: A Retrospective, 90; Keith Morrison: Recent Paintings, 90; Syncretism: Art of the 21st Century, 91; Artists of Conscience: 16 Years of Social & Political Commentary, 92; Disinformation: Manufacture of Consent, 85; Made in Am: Art of the Great Lakes States, 86; Thy Brother's Keeper, Flint Inst Arts, Flint, Mich; We the People, Occupy Wall St, Brik Gallery, Catskill, NY. *Pos:* Founder, Cur, Inst Contemp Hispanic Art, 72-74, Enfoco: Latin Am Photog Collaborative, 73-74, Alternative Mus, 75-2001; served, Clinton-Gore Presidential Transition Team, Arts & Humanities, 92. *Teaching:* Instr photog, Rutgers Univ, 77-78; instr photo critique, Sch Visual Arts, New York, 77-. *Awards:* Distinguished Am Vis to Africa, Phelps Stokes Fund, 77; Artist Nat Endowment Arts fel, 79; Ludwig Vogelstein Found Fel, 81. *Mem:* Am Asn Mus (cur comt, exec mem, 85-86). *Media:* Photography. *Specialty:* socio-political contemporary art. *Interests:* books, film, scuba diving, archery. *Publ:* The Islands: Worlds of the Puerto Ricans, Harper & Row, 74; auth, Mira Mira Mira Puerto Rican New Yorkers, Forum Press, 75. *Mailing Add:* 32 W 82nd St Apt 9A New York NY 10024

RODRIQUEZ, ERNESTO ANGELO
PAINTER, DESIGNER
b New York, NY, 1947. *Study:* Parsons Sch Design, 65-68; New Sch Social Res/Parsons, BFA, 79. *Work:* Hudson River Mus, Yonkers, NY; pvt collection, Dr Livette Johnson, New York; pvt collection, Louisa A Turner; pvt collection, Paul Farfard; pvt collection, Hazel V Rodriguez; Sheila Willard, Marvin Raps, Shirley Brathwaite. *Comn:* Linen fabric design, comn by Miss Iris Roberts, New York, 89; linen designs, comn by D Calahan, New York, 89; floral fabric designs, comn by H Rodriquez, New York, 90 & 2002; football fabric, comn by S Brathwait, New York, 90; marine fabric design, comn by S Willard, New York, 90-91; grand piano, comn by P Candide, New York, 2002; Portrait and Egyptian Temples, comn by James Patton, New York, 2004. *Exhib:* Hudson River Mus, Yonkers, NY, 81; Hispanic Experience, Long Beach Mus Art, NY, 82; St Francis Assisi, New York, 84; Int Art Gallery, Bogota, Colombia, 86; Art Communication Int, Philadelphia, 96; Pa Hotel, NY, 89; Madison Square Garden, New York, 89; Durban Art Gallery, S Africa, 99; Hilltop Inc, New York, 2002-03; Jano R co, New York, 2002-03; Mercer Gallery, Rochester, NY, 2012. *Pos:* art instr. *Teaching:* Instr art & actor, Studio Sch Asn, New York, 79-81; coordr, Camp Oakhurst, NJ, 82-86; instr art, St Francis Assisi, New York, 84-89, 91-93 & 2010-2011; instr crafts, Jewish Guild for Blind, 86-87; pvt art tutor, 2003-09; instr, St Francis Assisi, NY, 2012; art instr, St Francis Assisi, NY, 2010-2013. *Awards:* Max Beckman Fellowship, 68; Change Incorporated grant, 78. *Bibliog:* Mantle Fielding's Dictionary of American Painters, Sculptors and Engravers, 2001; Biographical Encyclopedia of American Painters, Sculptors and Engravers of the US, Colonial to 2002; New Art Int, 2007. *Mem:* Metrop Mus Art; St Francis Advisory Bd (advisory bd, 2011-2013). *Media:* Oil, Acrylic, color pencils, conte crayon, mixed media, ink. *Res:* Portraiture, studying landscape photography; abstract's & semi-abstracts; Hieronymus Bosch, Paul Klee study artist's usage of light, color & composition; making discoveries in balance, form and color applications in Leonardo da Vinci; Vincent Van Gogh. *Specialty:* representational & abstract. *Interests:* Developing and acquiring a unique artistic expression in painting; obtaining ideas from hotels, conventions, and cruise lines; developing simple art message to reach more people. *Collection:* Hazel V Rodriguez, James Patton; Ms Livette Johnson, MD; Ms Sheila Willard; Mrs Shirley Brathwaite; Mr Marvin Raps; Mr Paul Fafard. *Publ:* Arts Mag, 72, NY Times, 80, Oxidized Look, 81, Long Beach Mus, Hispanic Experience, 82, Prydent Pub Calandar, 84; Intergalactic Poetry Messenger, 94; New Art Int, 2006-2007. *Dealer:* Ernesto Rodriguez. *Mailing Add:* 55 Overlook Terr 4H New York NY 10033

ROESCH, ROBERT ARTHUR
SCULPTOR, DESIGNER
b Buffalo, NY, June 25, 1946. *Study:* State Univ NY; Pratt Inst, study with David Lee Brown. *Work:* Fidelity Bank, Philadelphia; Marine Midland Bank, NY; State Univ NY, Farmingdale. *Comn:* Sculpture, Cynmark Group, Suffern, NY, 84; sculpture, Boca Raton Redevelopment, Fla, 85. *Exhib:* New Directions in Sculpture, Heckscher Mus, NY, 77; Wistariahurst Mus, Holyoke, Mass, 77; Art Alliance, Philadelphia, 80; Bennison Bldg, Long Island, NY, 81; Beaver Col, Pa, 83. *Teaching:* Adj prof, 3-D design, Southampton Col, NY, 75-84, Parsons Sch Design, New York, 84-85 & Acad Fine Arts, Philadelphia, 86-. *Bibliog:* Jessica Darraby (auth), article, in: Designer's West, 86. *Media:* Steel and Similar Metals. *Dealer:* David Segal Gallery 568 Broadway New York NY 10012; Nerlino Gallery 96 Green St New York NY

ROFMAN, JULIE
PAINTER
Study: Tulane Univ, BFA (Ruth G Hanaw Prize, Mary LS Neill Prize & Class of 1914 Prize), 1999; Calif State Univ, Long Beach, MFA (Creative Achievement Award), 2006. *Exhib:* Solo exhibs include Gallery Ocho, Santa Barbara, Calif, 2007; group exhibs include Debut, Carl Berg Gallery, Los Angeles, 2006, When Worlds Collide, 2007; Civil Twilight, Electric Works Gallery, San Francisco, 2007; TerraUnFirma, Caren Golden Fine Art, New York, 2008; Future Tense: Reshaping the Landscape, Neuberger Art Mus, Purchase, NY, 2008. *Awards:* Pollock-Krasner Found Grant, 2007

ROGERS, ART
PHOTOGRAPHER
b Wilson, NC, Sept 13, 1948. *Work:* Joseph Seagrams & Sons Calif Photog Collections, NY; Arch Univ Ariz, Tucson; San Francisco Mus Mod Art, Calif; Ctr Creative Photog/Archive, Tucson, Ariz; Int Ctr for Photography, NY; The Archive, Tucson, Ariz. *Exhib:* SECA, San Francisco Mus Mod Art, Calif, 82; Photographs, CEPA Gallery, Buffalo, NY, 83; 10,000 Eyes, ASMP, Int Ctr Photog, NY, 91; Time and Motion, Int Ctr Photog, NY, 93; Family Values, PHOTOS Gallery, San Francisco, 93; Portraits for Families, Old Bank Bldg Gallery, Point Reyes, Calif, 95; Yesterday and Today, Bolinas Mus, Calif, 99. *Teaching:* San Francisco Art Inst, 68-73, Indian Valley Col (Col Marin), Ignacio, Calif, 76-79 & Point Reyes Nat Seashore Field Sem, 78-80. *Awards:* Guggenheim Fel; Fel, Nat Endowment for the Arts; Fel, Marin Arts Coun; SECA/San Francisco Mus of Modern Art Award. *Mem:* Am Soc Mag Photogs; Marin Arts Coun. *Dealer:* Photos 403 Francisco St San Francisco CA 94133. *Mailing Add:* 6 Cypress Rd PO Box 777 Point Reyes Station CA 94956-0777

ROGERS, BARBARA
PAINTER, EDUCATOR
b Newcomerstown, Ohio, Apr 28, 1937. *Study:* Ohio State Univ, BSc; Univ Calif, Berkeley, MA. *Work:* San Francisco Mus Mod Art; Oakland Art Mus, Calif; Univ Calif, Berkeley; San Jose Mus Art; Ariz State Univ Mus Art, Tempe; Scottsdale Mus Contemp Art; Frick Art Mus, Univ Pittsburgh; corp collections incl Prudential Ins Co, AT&T, Bank of Am, Kaiser Permanente Hosp, Duke Power & Energy & Estee Lauder Found. *Exhib:* Solo exhibs, San Francisco Mus Mod Art, 73, Michael Berger Gallery, Pittsburgh, Pa, 78 & 81, Fuller Goldeen Gallery, San Francisco, Univ Pac Gallery, Stockholm, Calif, 87, Frauen Mus, Erfurt, Ger, 92, Ga State Univ, 93, Selby Mus Bot & Arts, Sarasota, Fla, 94 & Univ Ariz Mus Art, 94, Frederick Spratt Gallery, San Jose, Calif, 95, One West Art Ctr, Ft Collins, Colo, 96, Sandy Carson Gallery, Dever, 97, Etherton Gallery, Temple of Music & Art, Tucson, 98, Eleanor Jeck Galleries, Tucson, 99, Vanier Galleries, Scottsdale, 2000, Tucson Mus Art, 2001, Chiaroscuro Gallery, Santa Fe, NMex, 2003, Dosi Gallery, Pusan, S Korea, 2004, Gardens of Paradise, Coll Fine Arts, Univ Sharjah, United Arab Emirates, 2005, & Gebert Contemp, Santa Fe, 2007-2008; 71st Am Exhib, Art Inst Chicago, 74; two-person exhib, Embracing Change, San Jose State Univ, Calif, 89; Bridges: Artists Responses to Disaster, Berkeley Art Ctr, Calif, 90; Human Nature, Allrich Gallery, San Francisco, Calif, 92; Recent Paintings, Sandy Carson Gallery, Denver, Colo, 97; Earthly Pleasures: the Garden as Source, Jewish Community Ctr, Tucson, Ariz, 97; The Permanent Collection 1997: Recent Acquisitions, San Jose Mus Art, Calif, 97; Recent Paintings: Her Garden, Objects and Sites Remembered, Temple Gallery, Tucson, 98; Retrospective: Works on Papers, Ohio State Univ, Columbus, 98; Pleasures of the Palettess Auction, The Phoenician, Scottsdale, Ariz; Another Arizona: A State Wide Juried Exhib, Nelson Fine Arts Ctr, Ariz State Univ, Tempe, 98; 43rd Ann Painting Invitational, Longview Mus Fine Arts, Tex, 2003; Fac Exhib, Univ Ariz Mus Art, Tucson, 2004; Summer Show, Chiaroscuro Gallery, Santa Fe, NMex, 2005; Small Works, Davis Dominguez Gallery, Tucson, 2006; Looking Closer: Inspired by the Beauty of the Sonoran Desert, Ariz-Sonora Desert Mus, Tucson, 2007; Bodacious Botanicals, Phoenix Airport Mus, 2008. *Pos:* Mem, exhib comt, San Francisco Art Inst, 75, bd trustees, 80; artist consult, Adv Coun, Grumbacher Inc, Cranbury, NJ, 94. *Teaching:* Vis fac, Univ Calif, Berkeley, 72-73, San Francisco Art Inst, 75-76 & Univ Wash, Seattle, 75; instr painting & drawing, Contra Costa Coll, El Sobrante, Calif, 77-78 & San Jose State Univ, 78-83; vis artist to var sch & univ, 76-2008; prof & chmn, dept painting, San Francisco Art Inst 83-87, chmn grad prog, painting, sculpture & ceramics, 87-90; prof painting & drawing, Univ Ariz, Tucson, 90-2007, grad coordr, Dept Art, 91-92. *Awards:* Int Travel Grant, Univ Ariz, 91; Prof Develop Grant, Com on Arts, Ariz, 91; Fine Arts Summer Res Incentive Grant, Univ Ariz, Tucson, 92-93; Richard Florsheim Art Fund Grant, 99. *Bibliog:* Thomas Albright (auth), Art in the San Francisco Bay Area, 1945-1980, Univ Calif Press, 85; Angelika Storm-Rushe (auth), Reverence for the Water, General-Anzeiger, 1/92; New American Paintings, Open Studios Press, Wellesley, Mass, 97; Bonnie Gangelhoff (auth), A Contemporary Eye, Southwest Art, 1/2004; plus many revs in mags & newspapers. *Mem:* Coll Art Asn; Women's Caucus for Art. *Media:* Oil, Mixed Media. *Mailing Add:* 6161 N Camino Padre Isidoro Tucson AZ 85718

ROGERS, BRYAN LEIGH
SCULPTOR, EDUCATOR
b Amarillo, Tex, Jan 7, 1941. *Study:* Yale Univ, New Haven, Conn, BE, 63; Univ Calif, Berkeley, MS, 66, MA, with Jim Melchert, Peter Voalkos, Mark DiSuvero, Arnaldo Pomodoro, Eduardo Paolozzi & Robert Morris, 69, PhD, 71; Akademie der bildenden Künste, Munich, Ger, 74-75. *Work:* San Francisco Mus Mod Art, Calif. *Comn:* Mannesmann Demag Corp, Pittsburgh, Pa, 93. *Exhib:* Umbrella Show, San Francisco Mus Mod Art, Calif, 74 & Laguna Beach Mus Art, Calif, 74; San Francisco/Science Fiction, Clocktower Gallery, NY, 85; Mechanical Contraptions, Objects Gallery, Chicago, 92; ARTEC 93, Nagoya, Japan, 93; On the Nature of the

Machine, Chicago Cult Ctr, 93; Pittsburgh Biennial, Pittsburgh Ctr Arts, 94; Allegheny Coll Gallery, Meadville, Pa, 97; Aichi Art Gallery, Nagoya, Japan, 97; and others. *Pos:* Ed, Leonardo Journal, San Francisco, Calif, 82-85; dir, Studio for Creative Inquiry, Carnegie Mellon Univ, 89-2000. *Teaching:* Lectr art, Univ Calif, Berkeley, 72-73; prof art, San Francisco State Univ, 75-88; prof art & dept head, Carnegie Mellon Univ, 88-2000; prof art & dean, School Art & Design, Univ Michigan, An Arbor, 99-2012, dean emeritus, prof art 2012-. *Awards:* Artist's Fel, Nat Endowment Arts, 81 & 82; Res Fel, Mass Inst Technol, 81; fel, Deutscher Akademischer Austauschdienst, Ger, 74-75. *Bibliog:* Gerhard Lischka (auth), Das Poetische ABC, Benteli Verlag, Bern, 85; Jim Jenkins/Dave Quick (coauth), Motion Motion Kinetic Arts, Gibbs-Smith, 89. *Media:* Electromechanical Installations. *Publ:* The Umbrella Series, Leonardo, Pergamon, 76, Timepieces, 81 & Odyssetron, 84; Apples and Bouillabaisse, Art/Cognition, 92

ROGERS, EARL LESLIE
PAINTER, EDUCATOR
b Oakland, Calif, July 8, 1918. *Study:* Los Angeles Valley Col, 49-52, AA, Pierce Col, 58, Northridge State Univ, 58-59, Univ Calif in Los Angeles, 67, Sergei Bongart Sch Art, 67-68, MA equivalency, Merced Col, 96, Earl Rogers, SAG, Mariposa, Calif. *Work:* Bear Valley Mus, Calif; Mariposa Co Historical Mus, Calif; Seattle Pub Libr Capitol Hill Branch, Seattle, WA; John C Fremont Hosp Mariposa, Calif; Merced Coll Merced, Calif; Merced Court House Mus, Calif; N Mariposa Co Hist Ctr, Coulterville, Calif. *Comn:* John C Fremont portrait, Soroptimists Int, Mariposa, Calif, 69; memorial painting, John C Freemont Hosp staff, 72; Early Mariposa (mural), Mariposa Mus & Hist Ctr, Inc, 79; portrait of Yosemite Indian leader, Mariposa Arts Coun, 84; memorial portrait painting, Friends of Mariposa Co Libr, 86. *Exhib:* Yosemite Art Pl, Yosemite Nat Park, Calif, 71; Society of Western Artists, Fashion Fair, Fresno, Calif, 77; 31st Ann Soc Western Artists, Hall of Flowers, Golden Gate Park, San Francisco, Calif, 78; Cong Washington Art Show, Cannon Bldg Rotunda, Washington, 82; solo exhib, US Post Off, Mariposa, Calif, 86, Bear Valley Hist Bon-Ton, Calif, 99, Sierra Artist Gallery 2006. *Pos:* Pres, West Valley Artist Asn, San Fernando Valley, 67-68; art dir, Yosemite Nat Park, Calif, 73; mem, 15th Cong Dist Arts Comt, 80-82. *Teaching:* Teacher art, Mariposa Co High Sch, 69-70; instr oil & watercolor painting, Earl Rogers Studio Workshops, 69-96, 70-2003; instr art, Merced Col, 69-2007. *Bibliog:* Janis McCrae (auth), Mariposa's gold rush mural, Merced Sun Star, 80; Doris Jamgotchian (auth), Earl Rogers exhibit, Mariposa Gazette, 86; Leslie Bonner (auth), portrait workshop, The Catalyst-Merced Col, 94. *Mem:* Mariposa Arts Coun, Inc; Sierra Artists (signature mem, 2010); Allied Arts of Whatcom County. *Media:* Oil, Acrylic. *Specialty:* Contemp Traditional Paintings, all media & subject matter. *Interests:* Piano, Books. *Publ:* Illusr, Model Cities Program-City of Los Angeles, Off of the Mayor, 67; City of Los Angeles-Engineering Procedure, Los Angeles City Coun, 67; From the Kitchen of Ruth Robeson, Robeson Realty, 71; Mariposa History Center Tour Guide, Mariposa Mus & Hist Ctr Inc, 72; The Catalyst, Merced Col, 90; illusr, Yosemite (1958-1961): Exploits of a Former Employee, 2005; auth, 60 Years of Timeless Tips and Observations. *Dealer:* Arbor Gallery 645 W Main St Merced CA 95340. *Mailing Add:* 700 N Shore Dr #4 Bellingham WA 98226

ROGERS, JOHN H
SCULPTOR, CONSULTANT
b Walton, Ky, Dec 20, 1921. *Study:* Eastern Ky Univ; Tyler Sch Art, Temple Univ, BFA & MFA. *Work:* Ala Archives, Montgomery; Marine Corps Art Collection, Marine Corps Mus, Washington, DC; Auburn Univ, Ala; Dept Defense, Pentagon, Washington, DC; NDak Mill & NDak Mus Art, Grand Forks, 81 & 92. *Comn:* Bust of Gen H M Smith USMC, Ala Archives, Montgomery, 69; mem plaque of Lt Gen J A Chaisson, USMC, 75; baptistry, St Paul's Episcopal Church, Grand Forks, NDak, 83; Peace Garden Award Medallion, Univ NDak, 85; bust of Gen C B Cates USMC, Tenn State Mem Mus, Nashville & Marine Corps Univ, Quarntico, Va. *Exhib:* Artists in Vietnam, Smithsonian Traveling Exhib Serv, 68-70; Atlanta Coll Art Fac Exhib, High Mus Art, Ga, 72; Inaugural Exhib, USMC Hist Ctr, Wash, DC, 77; solo show, Art Gallery, Univ NDak, 81; John Rogers, Elder & Younger, Art Gallery, Univ NDak, 92; Sculptures in the Garden, NC Botanical Garden, Chapel Hill, 93-2001; Bronze Sculpture, Keep Morisi, dedicated to NCO's, 2003. *Pos:* Acad dean, Minneapolis Col Art & Design, 64-68; asst head, Marine Corps Combat Art Prog, Washington, DC, 68-69, head, 69-70; dean, Atlanta Col Art, Ga, 70-73; dean col fine arts, Univ NDak, 73-80; sculptor in residence, Syracuse Univ, 80-81; pres, Docents NC Mus Art, 97-98. *Teaching:* Sr sem humanities, Atlanta Col Art, 70-71; prof fine arts & sr symp, Univ NDak, 73-80, prof visual arts, 81-85; adj prof basic design, Syracuse Univ, 80-81, emer prof visual arts, 85-; vis lect sculpture, Earlham Coll, 89; docent, NC Mus Art, Raleigh, 91-2002. *Mem:* Fel & life mem Nat Asn Schs Art & Design; Am Crafts Coun; Int Sculpture Ctr; Tri-State Sculptors Guild. *Media:* Wood; Miscellaneous. *Res:* Arts & Aging. *Publ:* Coauth, Aging & creativity, In: Lifelong Learning and the Visual Arts, Nat Art Educ Asn, 80

ROGERS, JOSEPH SHEPPERD See Nevia, Joseph Shepperd Rogers

ROGERS, MALCOLM AUSTIN
MUSEUM DIRECTOR
b Scarborough, Yorkshire, England, Oct 3, 1948. *Study:* Oxford Univ, BA, MA, 1976, DPhil, 1976. *Hon Degrees:* Emmanuel Coll, Hon DFA, 2011; Boston Architectural Coll, LHD, 2014. *Pos:* Asst keeper, Nat Portrait Gallery, London, 74-83, deputy dir, 83-85, dep keeper, 85-94; Ann & Graham Gund dir, Mus Fine Art, Boston, Mass, 94-; trustee, Found for the Arts, Nagoya, Japan. *Teaching:* humanitas visiting prof museums, Galleries and Libraries, Univ Oxford, 2012. *Awards:* Comdr, Order Brit Empire, 2004; Chevalier de l'Ordre des Arts et des Lettres, 2007; Encomienda de la Orden de Isabel la Catolica, Spain, 2010; Excellency Award, Found for Italian Art and Culture, 2010; Award of Merit, British Soc, 2012. *Mem:* Fel Soc Antiquities; Am Alliance of Museums; Beefsteak Club; Liveryman Girdlers Co; Algonquin Club (hon); Wednesday Evening Club; Thursday Evening Club; Asn Art Mus Dir; Comt to visit the Harvard Art Mus, Harvard Univ; Am Acad Arts and Sciences; trustee, British Soc; overseer, Boston Lyric Opera. *Publ:* Blue Guide Museums and Galleries of London, 83; contribr, The Companion Guide To London, Blue Guide, 92; William Dobson 1611-46: The Royalists at War, 83-84; Camera Portraits, 89-90; auth, Dictionary of British Portraiture, 4 Vols, 79-81. *Mailing Add:* Mus Fine Arts 465 Huntington Ave Boston MA 02115-5597

ROGERS, MICHAEL
EDUCATOR, SCULPTOR
Work: Carnegie Mus; Corning Mus Glass, New York; L'Viv Nat Mus, Ukraine; Grand Crystal Mus, Taiwan; Museo del Vidrio, Mex. *Teaching:* Assoc prof, Aichi Univ Educ, Kariya, Japan, 1991-2002; chmn, Sch for Am Crafts, Rochester Inst Technol, 2002-05, prof, 2002-08. *Awards:* New York Found Arts Fel, 2009. *Mem:* Glass Art Soc (pres, 2002-04). *Media:* Glass. *Mailing Add:* Rochester Institute for Technology School for American Crafts-Glass 73 Lomb Memorial Dr Rochester NY 14623

ROGERS, MURIEL I
PAINTER, INSTRUCTOR
b Dec 5, 1937. *Study:* Georgian Court Col, graduate. *Work:* Georgian Court Coll; Monmouth Co Park System; Am Reinsurance Corp; Kirkland & Ellis; KFR Consult & Adminr Inc; Nationwide Insurance; numerous pvt collections in US corps & businesses. *Exhib:* NJ Watercolor Soc Ann Open Juried Show, 97, 99, 2001 & 2005-2006; Garden State Watercolor Soc Open Juried Show, 98-2004 & 2006; Guild of Creative Art Juried State Show, 2000-07; Am Artist Prof League, NJ, 2000-2002; New Am Gallery Juried Nat Watercolor Show, 2003-2007. *Teaching:* Instr, watercolor painting, pvt sessions, currently. *Awards:* NJ Watercolor Soc Peoples' Choice Award, 97; Am Artists Prof League, NJ, 99; Guild of Creative Art State Show Award, 2000 & 2003; First Place Watercolor Award, Anchor & Patelle Gallery, NJ, 2006; Award of Excellence, NJ Watercolor Soc Member Show, 2006; Special Judges Award, Am Artists Prof League NJ Open Juried Exhib, 2007; Distinguished Merit Award, NJ Am Artists Professional League, 2011. *Mem:* NJ Watercolor Soc; Garden State Watercolor Soc; Am Artist Prof League; Guild of Creative Art; Manasquan River Group Artists. *Media:* Oil & Watercolor. *Publ:* Articles in Am Artist; articles, Winter Watercolor, 97; cover artist, Jersey Shore Home & Garden, 2000 & 2004; articles, To the Shore Once More, Vol I & II; articles, Jersey Shore Mag, 98-2006. *Dealer:* Anchor Palette Gallery Bay Head; Matawan Art Gallery Aberdeen; New America Internet Gallery. *Mailing Add:* 33 Beaver Dam Rd Colts Neck NJ 07722

ROGERS, P J
PRINTMAKER, COLLAGE
b Rochester, NY. *Study:* Wells Coll, BA; Univ Buffalo; Acad Fine Arts, Vienna; Art Students League; also with Victor Hammer, Lazlo Szabo & Robert Brackman. *Work:* Akron Children's Hosp; Ohio Arts Coun, 98; Cleveland Art Mus; Art Complex Mus, Duxbury, Mass; Hahn, Loeser and Parks, Law Off, Cleveland, Ohio. *Comn:* Portrait of founder, Novatny Electric co, Akron, 67; poster for opening of new theater, Akron Weathervane Theater, 70; portrait of Dr DJ Guzzetta, pres, Univ Akron, 75; Ohio Arts Coun, 94; Children's Hosp, 94. *Exhib:* Maison des Arts et de la Cult, Quebec, 98; Olin Art Col, Kenyon Coll, 2000; PJ Rogers Retrospective, Harris-Stanton Gallery, Akron, Ohio, 2001; SAGA 69th Nat Juried Exhib, The Art Students League, New York, 2002; All Ohio Landscape Juried Rosewood Gallery, Kettering, Ohio, 2002; Wooster Mus Art, New York, 2003; Susan Teller Gallery, New York, 2004; solo exhibs, Harris Stanton Gallery, Akron, Ohio, 2005 & 808 Gallery Boston Univ, Boston, Mass, 2005; Hollar Soc Gallery, Prague, 2006; Harris Stanton Gallery, Akron, Ohio, 2007, 2010-2012; Zullo Gallery, Boston, 2010; Guren Art Gallery, Cleveland, Ohio, 2010. *Pos:* Art preparator, Buffalo Mus Sci, 52-55. *Teaching:* Instr painting, Buffalo Mus Sci, 55; instr arts & crafts, Univ Akron Spec Progs, 58. *Awards:* Purchase Award, Print Club, Philadelphia, 90-91; Prof Develop Assistance Award, Ohio Arts Coun, 93; Purchase Award, Coll NJ, 97; Lifetime Achievement award, Akron Arts Alliance, 2011. *Bibliog:* Stevens (auth), Aux Etats-Unis, expositions diverses, PJ Rogers, La Rev Mod; David Acton (auth), 60 Years of North American Prints 1947-2007, Worcester Art Mus, Mass, 2009. *Mem:* Boston Printmakers; Soc Am Graphic Artists, New York. *Media:* Aquatint-etching, Mixed Media & Digital Inkjets Prints. *Publ:* Contribr, The Gamut, (six aquatints), Cleveland State Univ, Ohio, 80 & 90; American Artists, Krantz Co Publ, 85 & 92; David Acton (auth), 60 Years of North American Prints 1917-2007 (in prep), Boston Printmakers. *Dealer:* Harris Stanton Gallery 2301 W Market St Akron OH 44313. *Mailing Add:* 954 Hereford Dr Akron OH 44303

ROGERS, PETER WILFRID
PAINTER, WRITER
b London, Eng, Aug 24, 1933. *Study:* St Martins Sch Art, London, Eng. *Work:* Bristol Art Gallery, Eng; Roswell Mus, NMex; Macnider Mus, Mason City, Iowa; Mus Southwest, Midland, Tex; Fine Arts Mus, Santa Fe, NMex; ARCO Collection, Los Angeles. *Comn:* Mural, Tex State Arch & Libr, Austin, 64; 48 paintings & drawings of Alaska, Atlantic Richfield co, Los Angeles, 70-71; mural, Tex Tech Mus, 74; mural, Anaconda Co, Denver; mural, Arcomex, Mexico City. *Exhib:* Solo exhibs, Fairmount Gallery, Dallas, 69, Artium Orbis, Santa Fe, 71-72, Grace Cathedral, San Francisco, 73 & Janus Gallery, Santa Fe, 75; Heard Mus, Phoenix, Ariz, 75; plus others; Retrospective exhib, A Painters Progress 1949-2012, Roswell Mus, 2011, 2012. *Bibliog:* Mary Carroll Nelson (auth), Peter Rogers: Journeyman Artist, Am Artist, 76 & Profiles: Peter Rogers, Art Voice S, 3/80; Isabelle Howe (auth), The Murals at Texas Tech; Mary Carroll Nelson (auth), Artists of the Spirit, New Prophets in Art and Mysticism, 94. *Media:* Oil, Acrylic. *Res:* Edward de Vere and the sonnets of William Shakespeare. *Interests:* Ancient history and the Shakespeare authorship controversy. *Publ:* Auth & illusr, A Painter's Quest, Bear & co. *Dealer:* Wyeth Hurd Gallery 206 E Palace Ave Santa Fe NM 87501. *Mailing Add:* PO Box 214 San Patricio NM 88348

ROGERS, RICHARD L
EDUCATOR, ADMINISTRATOR
b New York, NY, Sept 17, 1949. *Study:* Yale Coll, BA, 71; Yale Divinity Sch, MAR, 73; Univ Chicago, 77-80; Bankstreet Coll Educ, MSed, 89. *Pos:* Vpres & secy, New Sch Soc Res, 82-94; pres, Coll Creative Studies, 94-. *Teaching:* Foote Sch, New Haven, Conn, 74-77; instr liberal arts, Parsons Sch Design, New York, 87-94. *Mailing Add:* 201 E Kirby Detroit MI 48202

ROGERS, SARAH
CURATOR
b Buffalo, NY, Aug 8, 1956. *Study:* Wells Col, Aurora, NY, BA, 78; Northwestern Univ, Evanston, Ill, MA, 80. *Collection Arranged:* Doug & Mike Starn, Contemp Arts, Cincinnati, 85-90; Trilogy Inaugural Exhibs, Wexner Ctr, 89-90; Lorna Simpson: Interior/Exterior-Full/Empty, Wexner Ctr, 97; The Body and the Object: Ann Hamilton, Wexner Ctr & tour, 96-98; Evidence: Photography & Site, Wexner Ctr & tour, 97-98; Body Mecanique: Artistic Explorations of Digital Realms, Wexner Ctr, 98. *Pos:* Intern, Nat Endowment Arts, Walker Art Ctr, Minneapolis, 80-81; asst dir, New Gallery Contemp Art, Cleveland, 81-82; cur, Contemp Arts Ctr, Cincinnati, 82-; dir exhibs, Wexner Ctr Arts, Columbus, currently. *Teaching:* adj prof, Dept Art, Ohio State Univ, currently. *Awards:* Abby Grey Fel, Nat Endowment Arts, 80. *Mem:* Coll Art Asn. *Publ:* Segments I-III (catalogs), Contemp Arts Ctr, 84-85; Nam Jine Paik, Video Flag X (catalog), Contemp Arts Ctr, 85; interview, Doug & Mike Starn, Abrams, 90. *Mailing Add:* c/o Wexner Ctr Arts Ohio State Univ N High St at 15th Ave Columbus OH 43210-1393

ROGOVIN, MARK
MURALIST, MUSEUM DIRECTOR
b Buffalo, NY, July 31, 1946. *Study:* Mexico, with Elizabeth Catlett Mora & David Alfaro Siqueiros, 64-68; RI Sch Design, Providence, BFA, 68; Art Inst Chicago, MFA, 70. *Comn:* Outdoor mural (18ft x 89ft), side of Am Nat Bank, comn by Rockford Evening Cosmopolitan Club, Ill, 75; indoor mural, Coll of Dupage, Glen Ellyn, Ill, 75; outdoor mural, comn by several neighborhood orgn on Chicago's West Side, 76. *Exhib:* Murals for the People, Mus of Contemp Art, Chicago, 71; Street Art-Pub Murals in the USA (Bicentennial traveling exhib), Amerika-Haus, W Berlin, 76; Mural Art USA (traveling exhib); porcelain enamel mural, Percent for Art Comn, Chicago. *Pos:* Dir & co-founder, Pub Art Wkshp, 72-81 & Peace Mus, 81-86. *Teaching:* Sch prog artist, Urban Gateways, Chicago, 73-81; artist-in-residence murals, Coll DuPage, Glen Ellyn, Ill, spring 75, Univ Nebr, Omaha, 77, Univ Ill, Champaign, 78. *Mem:* Chicago Artists Coalition. *Publ:* Auth, Mural Manual, Beacon Press; The Day Will Come, Illinois Labor History Soc, 1994, 2011, 2014. *Mailing Add:* 930 Dunlop Ave Forest Park IL 60130

ROHM, ROBERT
SCULPTOR
b Cincinnati, Ohio, Feb 6, 1934. *Study:* Pratt Inst, BID, 56; Cranbrook Acad Art, Bloomfield Hills, Mich, MFA, 60. *Work:* Mus Mod Art, Metrop Mus Art & Whitney Mus Am Art, New York; Kunsthalle, Zurich, Switz; Mus Fine Art, Boston; The Rose Art Mus, Brandeis Univ, Waltham, Mass; Newport Art Mus, Newport, RI; Tucson Mus Art, Ariz; Munson-Williams Proctor Mus Art, Utica, NY; Flint Inst of Arts, Mich; Butler Inst Am Art, Youngstown, Ohio; Harn Mus, Univ Fla, Gainsville; Amarillo Mus Art, Tex; Erie Art Mus, Pa; Wadsworth Atheneum Mus Art, Hartford, Conn. *Exhib:* Solo exhibs, OK Harris Works of Art, New York, 70-2002, 2005, 2009, Worcester Art Mus, Mass, 78, Nielsen Gallery, Boston, Mass, 85-86, 92-93 & 2002, Cumberland Gallery, Nashville, Tenn, 86 & 93, New Work: Sculpture & Drawing, Fine Arts Ctr, Univ RI, Kingston, 88 & 94, Lenore Gray Gallery, Providence, RI, 90, 93 & 95, Salve Regina Univ, Newport, RI, 93 & 2003, Bannister Gallery, RI Coll, Providence, 98 & Wheaton Coll, Norton, Mass, 2002, Robert Rohm Sculpture, Fine Arts Ctr, Univ Rhode Island, Selections, Charlestown Gallery, Rhode Island; Totem: Sculpture by Ellen Driscoll, Christopher Hewat, Robert Rohm, Ursula von Rydingsvard, Addison Gallery Am Art, Phillips Acad, Andover, Mass, 89; 10 Yrs of Boston Art, Nielsen Gallery, Boston, Mass, 91; Drawing, Lenore Gray Gallery, Providence, RI, 91; Whats Next, Soma Gallery, San Diego, 93; Concept in Form: Artistd Sketchbooks & Maquettes, Palo Alto Cult Ctr, Calif, 95; The Minimalist Aesthetic, Wadsworth Atheneum Mus Art, Conn, 2011; and others. *Teaching:* Instr sculpture, Columbus Coll Art & Design, 56-59 & Pratt Inst, 60-65; prof sculpture, Univ RI, 65-95, prof emer, 95-. *Awards:* Guggenheim Found Fel, 64; Fel, RI Coun Arts, 73, 82 & 93; Nat Endowment Arts Award, 74 & 86. *Bibliog:* Kenneth Baker (auth), review, Art Am, 5/84; Ronald J Onorato (auth), Robert Rohm, Arts Mag, 1/85; Robert C Morgan (auth), Review, Arts Mag, Summer, 89; J Bowyer Bell (auth), Review Robert Rohm, Review Mag, 11/99. *Media:* Welded Metal with other materials. *Publ:* Robert Rohm: Selected Works 1975-1985, Nielsen Gallery, Boston, Mass, 85; Robert Rohm, Nielsen Gallery, Boston, Mass, 2001. *Dealer:* OK Harris Works of Art 383 W Broadway New York NY 10012; Clark Gallery 145 Lincoln Rd Lincoln MA 01775; Charlestown Gallery 5000 South County Trail Charlestown RI 02813. *Mailing Add:* PO Box 1679 Charlestown RI 02813

ROHOVIT, MARAH BROWN
PAINTER
b Arkansas City, Kans, Apr 28, 1942. *Study:* studied sculpture with Ron Hicks, Kansas City, 1970; Johnson Co Community Coll, 1970-1971; studied with Jean Howard, Kansas City, 1971; Univ Utah, 1972; Salt Lake City Art Center, 1972-1973; Vt Studio Center, studied with Bill Jensen, Lois Dodd, Phoebe Adams & Robert Lobe, 2007. *Work:* Salt Lake Co permanent Collection, Salt Lake City, Utah; State of Utah permanent Collection, Salt Lake City, Utah. *Exhib:* Women Artists of Utah, Utah Mus Fine Art, Salt Lake City, Utah, 1983; Utah 84, Utah Mus Fine Art, 1984; Int Exhib Worlds Fair, Exhib Hall, New Orleans, La, 1984; Art Extra Ordinare, Springville Mus Fine Art, Springville, Utah, 1988; Regional Juried Exhib, Kimball Art Center, Park City, Utah, 1988; Int Exhib, Stage Gallery, Long Island, NY, 2003; 13th Utah Biennial Women Artist, Rose Wagner Performing Art Center, Salt Lake City, Utah, 2006; Florence Biennal, Exhib Center, Florence, Italy, 2007; Art for Life, Woodbury Mus Fine Art, Orem, Utah, 2007; 83rd Spring Salon, Springville Mus Fine Art, 2007; MMAS Exhib, Fla Int Univ, Miami, Fla, 2007; Infusion Gallery, 2008; Spring Salon, Springville Mus Art, Springville, UT, 2008; solo exhib: Infusion Gallery, Los Angeles, Calif, 2008; RED, Berkeley Art Ctr, Calif, 2009; The Truth of Abstraction, Patrick Moore Gallery, Utah, 2009; Art for Animals, Patrick Moore Gallery, Utah, 2009; AAUW Biennial, Celebarting the Diversity of Women, Utah, 2009; Black & White, State wide juried eccles Art Ctr, Utah, 2010; Spring Salon Springville Mus Art, Utah, 2010; Artprize, Grand Rapids, Mich,2010; United States Florence Biennale Artiste, Broadway Gallery, New York, 2010; Nine Torres Fine Art, Miami, 2010. *Awards:* Purchase Award, Utah Women Artists, Utah Mus Fine Art, 1983; Jurors Award, Regional Exhib, Kimball Art Center, 1988; Second Place Award, Int Exhib, Nat Cong Art & Design, 1988; Travel Award, Utah 88, Salt Lake Art Center, 1988; Solo Exhib, Celebrating the Soul & the Spirit, Salt Lake Co, 2006; Merit Award, 83rd Spring Salon, Springville Mus Fine Art, 2007; Vt Studio Ctr Month Artist Residence, 2007; Florence Biennale Florence, Italy, 2007; Awarded a venue in ArtPrize, Grand Rapids, Mich, 2010; Guest Artists 66th Spring Salon, Springville Mus Art, Utah, 2010. *Bibliog:* Richard P Christensen (auth), Utah '84, Deseret News, 1984; Richard P Christensen (auth), Freedom of Expression, Deseret News, 1987; George Dibble (auth), Revisiting Veteran Artists, Salt Lake Tribune, 1987; Vern Swanson (auth), Utah Art Extra-Ordinaire, Springville Mus Fine Art, 1988; Dr Robert Olpin (auth), Art Life in Utah, Kued TV for Univ Utah, 2004-2005. *Mem:* Bountiful Davis Art Center; Berkeley Art Ctr, Women Made Gallery. *Media:* Acrylic, Mixed Media. *Publ:* auth, Women Artists of Utah, Springfield Mus Fine Art, 1984; auth, Artists of Utah, Springville Mus Fine Art, 1999; auth, Salt Lake Co Art Collection, Salt Lake Co, 2003; auth, Florence Biennal Catalog, Art Studio, 2007; auth, 83rd Salon Catalogue, Springville Mus Fine Art, 2007. *Dealer:* Infusion Gallery 719 S Spring Los Angeles CA. *Mailing Add:* 1017 S 1500 E Salt Lake City UT 84105

ROHRBACHER, PATRICIA
PAINTER, INSTRUCTOR
b Marblehead, Mass, Dec 4, 1940. *Study:* Studied with Harvey Dimmerstein, 87-98, David Leffel, BS (92-94), DL (85-93) & Burton Silvermain, privately, 91-99. *Comn:* Still life paintings, Silonex Inc, Montreal, 95; Floral landscape, Frances Kalil, Montreal, 96; Floral landscape, Pamela Foss, Bronxville, NY, 98; Floral painting, Paintings Direct.com, NY, 99; numerous portraits. *Exhib:* Soc Illusr, Mus of Am Illus, NY; Art Club Mem Exhib, Broome St, NY, spring 99; Exhib Akron Soc Artists, Emily Davis Gallery, Akron Univ, fall 2000; Oil Painters of Am, Dunton Gallery, Arlington Hgts, Ill, 2000; Hilligoss Galleries, Chicago; Nicholas Taos Fine Art Gallery, Taos, NMex; Mather Gallery; Woman Art Exhib, Case Western Reserve Univ, Cleveland, Ohio; Cincinnati Art Club, 2002; Pastel Soc Am Sig Mem Exhib, Bennington Ctr for the Arts, 2008; Greenhouse Gallery of Art Ann Exhib, San Antonio, Tex, 2008; Oil Painters of Am Exhib, Fla, 2009; Am Women Artists, Nat South St Art Gallery, Md, 2009; Oil Faints of Am Nat Exhib, 2010; Legacy Tally, Scottsdale, Ariz, 2010. *Teaching:* Pvt lessons at art studio since 96; instr, Peninsula Art Acad, 2008; instr, Cliffside Artists Collaborative. *Awards:* scholar, Pastel Soc Am, 89; merit scholar, Art Student League, 90; award, Catharine Lorillard Wolfe, 95; Margaret Dole Portrait Award, 99; Award of Excellence, Oil Painters of Am, 2000; Silver Medal, Bosque Conservatory Art Classic, 2007; Am Women Artists Award of Recognition, 2007; Honorable Mention for Still Life Painting, OPA Natural 22nd Exhib; Am Women Artists award for Excellence, 2014. *Bibliog:* Review Pastel Soc 89 Exhib, Park E Publ, 10/89; J Sanders Eaton (auth), Review of CLWAC 99 Members, Gallery Studios, 5-6/99. *Mem:* Art Students League NY, 85-99; Akron Society Artists; PSA; Am Artists Prof League; Audubon Artists; Knickerbocker Artists; Oil Painters of Am; Catharine Lorillard Wolfe Art club; Bosque Art Classic, Tex, 2008, 2009; Am Women Artists (signature mem); Oil Painters Am; Master Signature Mem, Am Women Artists. *Media:* Oil, Pastel. *Publ:* Illus, Annual of American Illustration, Madison Square Press, 88, 90-91 & 93-94; How did you paint that?, still life & portrait, Int Artist Publ, 2004; still life and florals, Richeson 75 Publ, 2/2008; Richeson 75 Still Life & Floral, 2009, 2010. *Dealer:* Lawrence Churski Gallery Ghent Rd Ghent OH 44333; Art and Frame Gallery 85 Pondfield Rd Bronxville NY 10708; Hudson Fine Art Hudson OH; Fredericksburg Art Gallery, Tx. *Mailing Add:* 971 Gavington Pl Akron OH 44313-8002

ROKEACH, BARRIE
PHOTOGRAPHER, WRITER
b Huntington Beach, Calif, Mar 11, 1950. *Study:* Univ Calif, Berkeley, BA, 70, MA, 74. *Work:* Oakland Mus Nat Hist; Bank Am, San Francisco; Hewlett Packard, Consolidated Freightway, Palo Alto; Citicorp, New York. *Exhib:* Images From Above, Ryder Gallery, Chicago, 83; An Intimate Look, Neikrug Gallery, New York, 84; Aerial Photog, Art Ctr, Waco, Tex, 86; Aerial Photog, Tweed Mus, Duluth, Minn, 87; Oakland Mus, Calif, 90; Calif Mus Sci & Indust, Los Angeles, 91; and others. *Teaching:* Instr, Univ Calif Berkeley, 77-78 & 84. *Awards:* Calif Design Award, Art Dirs, 92. *Bibliog:* Paul Raedeke (auth), article, Photo Metro, 83; Lucas Blok (auth), Portfolio, Vantage Point, 84; Brenda Kahn (auth), Aerial photography, Zoom, 86. *Mem:* Am Soc Media Photogrs (exec bd & ed, 68-). *Publ:* Contribr, 24 Hours in the Life of Los Angeles, Van der Marck, 84; Ireland: A Week in the Life of a Nation, Century Hutchinson, 86; Thailand: Seven Days in the Kingdom, Times Ed, 87; auth-illusr, Timescapes: California Aerial Images, Westcliffe, 89; Kodak Guide to Aerial Photography, Silver Pixel, 96. *Mailing Add:* 499 Vermont Ave Berkeley CA 94709

ROLLA, MAUREEN J
MUSEUM DIRECTOR
Study: Carnegie Mellon Univ, BA (Eng); Columbia Univ, MA (Eng & comparative lit). *Pos:* Admin dir, Getty Leadership Inst Mus Mgt, Los Angeles, formerly; asst dir, Carnegie Mus Art, Pittsburgh, 1999-2006, dep dir, 2006-08, co-dir, 2008. *Mailing Add:* Carnegie Mus Art 4400 Forbes Ave Pittsburgh PA 15213-4080

ROLLAND, PETER GEORGE
ARCHITECT
b Frankfurt, Ger, Jul 2, 1930. *Study:* Del Valley Coll, BSc, 52; Harvard Univ, MLA, 55. *Work:* Principal landscape archit, New Parliament House, Canberra, Australia, 1980, State Univ of NY, Coll at Purchase, 1964-75. *Pos:* Chief site planner, Perkins & Will Archits, White Plains, NY, 55-60; project landscape archit, Lawrence Halprin & Assoc, San Francisco, 60-63; prin, Peter G Rolland & Assoc, Rye, NY, 63-89; partner, Rolland/Towers UC, New Haven, 81-. *Teaching:* Andrew Mellon vis prof Yale Univ Sch Forestry, 1979; fac Sch Archit, Yale Univ, 1973-; vis prof Harvard Grad. Sch Design, 1990. *Awards:* Design award Am Inst of Archits, 75, 78, 85, 90, 92, 94; Recipient Arthur Brown award Del Valley Coll, 78; Rome Prize fel Am Accad in Rome, Pierson Coll fel Yale Univ, 82-92. *Mem:* Fel Am Soc Landscape Archits; Nat Acad (assoc, 91, acad, 94, coun); Australian Inst Landscape Archits. *Mailing Add:* Rolland/Towers Site Planners & Landscape 85 Willow St New Haven CT 06511-2668

ROLLMAN, CHARLOTTE
PAINTER
b Harrisburg, Ill, Oct 15, 1947. *Study:* Murray State Univ, Ky, BFA, 69; Univ Ill, Champaign, MFA, 71. *Work:* Capitol State Bank, Continental Banking Co, St Louis, Mo; McDonald's Corp, Heart Hanks Radio, Phoenix, Ariz; State of Ill Bldg, Harris Bank, Chicago; Nev State Univ, Reno; Evansville Mus Art & Sciences, Ind; and others. *Comn:* John Gardener Tennis Resort, Sedona, Ariz; Jan Cicero Gallery, Chicago; Locus Gallery, St Louis, Mo; Suzanne Brown, Scottsdale, Ariz. *Exhib:* One person exhibs, Roy Boyd Gallery, Chicago, 84, Suzanne Brown Gallery, 85, Locus Gallery, 88, Univ Wis Ctr/Rock Co, Janesville, 91, Cornucopia, Dorothea Thiel Gallery, S Suburban Col, S Holland, Ill, 91, River of Life, Perry Rotunda Theatre Gallery, Aurora Univ, 93, Riverscapes, Campbell House, Kane Co Forest Preserve Cult Ctr, 93, Midstates Contemp Gallery, Evansville, Ind, 93, River of Life, Kishwaukee Col, 93, Source, Strategy, Reflection, Northern Ill Univ, Art Mus, 94, Flood Plain, AES Gallery, Chicago, Ill, 94 & Eastern Influence, New Harmony Contemp Gallery Art, Ind, 94; Utopia: Envisioning a Dream, The Forum Gallery at Jamestown Community Col, NY, 92; 16th Harper Nat Print & Drawing Exhib, Harper Col, Palatine, Ill, 92; Owensboro Nat Bank & the Arts: Part IV, Owensboro Mus Fine Arts, Ky, 92; Art on Paper 92, Md Fedn Art, MFA Gallery on the Circle, Annapolis. *Pos:* Colorist & textile designer, Gallery Studio, NY, 76-77; supvr silk painting & textile designer, Nicole Ltd, Chicago & Rio Rancho, NMex, 80-84; textile design & stylist, Thybony Wallcovering, Chicago, Ill, 84-88. *Teaching:* Instr drawing & design, Ball State Univ, 71-75; asst prof art, Northern Ill Univ, 86-92, assoc prof art, 93-. *Bibliog:* Judd Tulley (auth), Icons in Art (review), Am Artist Pub, spring 94. *Media:* Watercolor, Drawing. *Publ:* Illusr, New American Dictionary of Music, Penguin Bks, NY, 91; New International Dictionary of Music, Penguin Bks, NY, 92 & 93. *Mailing Add:* 184 McLaren Dr S #4-C Sycamore IL 60178

ROLLY, RONALD JOSEPH
ART DEALER, GALLERY DIRECTOR
b Waterbury, Conn, Dec 31, 1937. *Collection Arranged:* On Their Own, Robert Castagna, Art Complexx Mus, Duxbury, Mass. *Pos:* Dir, Rolly-Michaux Galleries, Boston, 1969-. *Specialty:* 20th century Europ masters and contemporaries; paintings, sculpture, rare etchings and graphics; French Impressionists and Post-Impressionists. *Mailing Add:* c/o Rolly-Michaux Galleries LTD 290 Dartmouth St Boston MA 02116

ROLOFF, JOHN (SCOTT)
SCULPTOR, ENVIRONMENTAL ARTIST
b Portland, Ore, Sept 20, 1947. *Study:* Univ Calif, Davis, BA; Calif State Univ, Humboldt, MA. *Work:* Nat Mus Am Art, Wash; San Francisco Mus Mod Art, Calif; Oakland Mus, Calif; Newport Harbor Mus, Newport Beach, Calif; Art Mus, Univ Calif, Berkeley; and others. *Comn:* Deep Gradient/Suspect Terrain (Seasons of the Sea Adrift), Yerba Buena Gardens, San Francisco, Calif, environmental sculpture, San Francisco Redevelopment Agency, 93; Fragment: The Hidden Sea (Island of Refuge), environmental sculpture, Stanford Univ, Stanford, Calif, 93; The Middle of the World, mult-media sculpture, Staten Island Ferries, NY (with W Klotz), 2000-05; Site Index, environmental sculpture, Sch of Archit and Landscape Archit, UM, Minneapolis, Minn (with R Krinke), 2000-2006; Untitled environmental sculpture I-5 Open Space Project, Pro Parks Levy, Seattle, Wash, 2003-05. *Exhib:* Whitney Biennial, Whitney Mus of Am Art, NY, 75; OK Art Contemp Art Ctr, Ohio, 75; Second Newport Biennial; The Bay Area, Newport Harbor Mus, Newport, Beach, Calif, 86; Vanishing Ship (Greenhouse for Lake Lahontan), Matrix Exhib, Univ Art Mus, UC Berkeley, Berkeley Calif, 87; The Boat Show, Smithsonian Inst, Washington, DC, 89; Facing Eden; 100 Yrs of Landscape Art in the Bay Area, MH De Young Memorial Mus, San Francisco, Calif, 95, 98; The Rising Sea, Mus of Contemp Art, Lake Worth, Fla, 98; Morphology of Change, Lance Fung Gallery, NY, 99; John Roloff; Displacement, John Michael Kohler Art Ctr, Sheboygan, WI, 2000; Original Depositional Environment, Gallery Paule Anglim, San Francisco, Calif 2001; Holocene Passage, Archivio Emily Harvey, NEXT, Venice Architectural Biennale, Venice Italy, 2002; The Snow Show, Kemi Finland, 2004; Technological Sublime, Univ of Colo, Boulder, Colo, 2005. *Teaching:* Prof, Sculpture Dept, Univ Ky, 74-78 & Univ Southern Calif, 87-88; Prof, Chmn of Sculpture Dept, Co-Coord, Ctr for Art and Sci, San Francisco Art Inst, 88-present. *Awards:* Visual Arts Award, Nat Endowment Arts, 77, 80 & 86; Guggenheim Fel, 83; Visual Arts Award, Calif Arts Coun, 90. *Bibliog:* John Roloff, Univ Art Mus, Artforum, Nov 87, pg 144; Becker, Lisa Tamaris, John Roloff; Displacements, solo exhib catalog, J.M Kohler Arts Center, Sheboygan, WI 2000; Morgan, Robert, John Roloff's Rising Sea, catalog essay, Mus of Contemp Art, Lake Worth, FL, 98. *Publ:* Auth, Kiln projects, Artery Mag, 2-3/83; Untitled Essay, Ten Years Later, Exhib, catalog, CSU, Fullerton, CA, 87; 51 Million BTU's, documentation catalog, 90; Organic Logic, New Observations Mag, #127, NY, co-editor, with Mark Barlett, Fall/Winter, 2000; Devonian Shale; Aquifer I, limited first edition of 4 books, Fractal Terror Press, Oakland, CA, 2001. *Dealer:* Gallery Paule Anglim 14 Geary St San Francisco CA 94108; Lance Fung Gallery 537 Broadway New York NY 10012. *Mailing Add:* 2020 Livingston St Oakland CA 94606

ROMAN, SHIRLEY
PRINTMAKER, PAINTER
b New York, NY. *Study:* Am Artists Sch; Brooklyn Mus Sch; Queens Col; also with Gregorio Prestopino, Raphael Soyer, Ruth Leaf & Agnes Mills. *Work:* De Cordova Mus, Lincoln, Mass; Readers Digest, Pleasantville, NY; Slater Mus, Norwalk, Conn; Butler Mus Am Art; Libr Cong, Washington, DC; Fed Reserve Bank, Richmond, Va. *Exhib:* Philadelphia Print Club, 69-74; Soc Am Graphic Artists; Pratt Graphics Miniature Show; Boston Printmakers Asn, 73; Audubon Artists, Taipei, Taiwan, 80; Nat Asn Women Artists, 80-99; Madison Art Guild, 1997-2003. *Awards:* Purchase Prize, Boston Printmakers 25th Ann, 73; Medals of Hon, Nat Asn Women Artists, 76, 79, 82 & 86; and others. *Bibliog:* Ruth Leaf (auth), Intaglio Printmaking Techniques. *Mem:* Madison Art Guild; Nat Asn Women Artists; Soc Am Graphic Artists; Nat Art League. *Media:* Etching; Watercolor

ROMANO, ANTONIO
MURALIST, PAINTER
b Bojano, Italy, April 5, 1953. *Study:* attended, Alfred Pells Sch Art, NY, 78; Sch Visual Arts, NY, BFA, 81; studied with, Luigi Fallai, NY, Antenucci, Bojano, Italy. *Work:* City Bank of NY; Dalva Antiques, Colo; Vigano Architectural Co, NY; Estee Lauder Co, Chicago, Ill; Bloomingdales Co, NY. *Comn:* Florentine fresco scenes, Michael Fuchs, NY, 84; oil on canvas to walls, St. Joseph Church, Raritan, NJ, 85; fresco murals, St Mary's Cathedral, Albany, NY, 87; fresco puro murals, Church of Pompeii, NY, 89; fresco murals, St Agnes Cathedral, Brooklyn, NY, 90; fresco puro murals, Immaculate Conception Church, Astoria, Queens, NY, 90. *Exhib:* From Realism to Abstraction, Spring Lake Art Gallery, Spring Lake, NJ, 2012; E-Scribble Modern, Nat Inst Art, Bojano, Italy, 2012. *Teaching:* fresco puro teacher, La Bottega del Buon Fresco, NY, 85-90; fresco teacher, Metropolitan Mus Art, NY, 89; fresco artist/teacher, Sch of Sacred Arts, NY, 90-93. *Awards:* 1st Prize Still Life, Nat Drawing Contest, Antennucci of Italy, 65. *Bibliog:* Adam Gopnik (auth), Born to Paint, New Yorker mag, 89. *Mem:* The Vagerrian Soc Am, Rochester, NY. *Media:* Mixed Media, Fresco. *Publ:* auth, Al Fresco, 90-92. *Dealer:* Spring Lake Art Gallery 217 Jersey Ave Spring Lake NJ 07762

ROMANO, CLARE
PAINTER, PRINTMAKER
b Palisade, NJ, 1922. *Study:* Cooper Union Sch Art, 1939-43, BFA; Ecole Beaux-Arts, Fontainebleau, France. *Work:* Mus Mod Art, Whitney Mus Am Art & Metrop Mus Art, NY; Libr of Cong & Nat Collection Fine Arts, Washington, DC; British Mus, London; Ftizwilliam Mus, Cambridge, England; Brooklyn Mus; Smithsonian Inst; Philadelphia Mus; Mus Modern Art, Cairo, Egypt; White House. *Comn:* Tapestry, Mfrs Hanover Bank, NY, 69; mural, Northern Valley Savings & Loan, Englewood, NJ, 79; Texas Tech, Portfolio, 1998; Casanatense, Rome, Italy, Portfolio, 1997; Nat Acad Design, Portfolio, 1997. *Exhib:* 2nd Triennial Int Exhib Woodcuts, Ugo Carpi Mus, Italy, 72; Am Prints, US Info Agency, Australian Nat Mus, Canberra, 72; Hane Haslem Gallery, Washington, DC, 81, 88 & 93; Queensland Coll Art, Brisbane, Australia, 82; AAA Gallery, NY, 82; NJ State Mus, Trenton, 85; Benton Gallery, Southampton, NY, 91; Steinbaum-Krauss Gallery, New York City, 97; Mus Modern Art, Cairo, Egypt, 98; Denise Bibno Gallery, New York City, 99; Rutgers Univ, 2002; Nat Acad Design, 2000, 2002; Houghton Col, 2000. *Pos:* Asst to Herbert Bayer, 43-46. *Teaching:* instr printmaking, New Sch Social Res, 60-73; adj assoc prof printmaking, Pratt Graphic Arts Ctr, 63-87; prof printmaking, Pratt Inst, 64-94, emeritus; vis artist, Brisbane Col Art, Australia, 82; vis artist Baltimore Col Art, Pa; Pratt in Venice, Italy, drawing & printmaking, 88-. *Awards:* MacDowell Fel, 74, 76, 78, 82 & 87; Distinguished Teacher Award, Pratt Inst, 79; NJ State Counc Arts Grant, 80; Lifetime Achievement Award, Soc Am Graphic Artists, 2002; Fulbright Grant, Inst Statale Arte, Florence, Italy, 58-59; Clinedinst Art Achievement Award, Artist Fel, New York, 1991. *Bibliog:* Jules Heller (auth), Printmaking Today, Holt, Rinehart & Winston, 72; Fritz Eichenberg (auth), The Art of the Print, Abrams, 77; Eldon Cunninham (auth), Printmaking, A Primary Form of Expression, Univ Press Colo, 92. *Mem:* Soc Am Graphic Artists (pres, 70-72); Nat Acad Design (assoc, 70, acad, 79, vpres, 87-). *Media:* Painting, Acrylic & Oil, Printmaking, Collagraph, Woodcut & Etching, Art of the Book. *Publ:* Co-illusr, Leaves of Grass, 64; auth, Artist's Proof, 64 & 66; American Encyclopedia, 71; coauth, The Complete Printmaker, 72 & 89 & The Complete Collagraph, 80, Free Press. *Dealer:* Susan Teller Gallery 568 Broadway New York NY 10012; Jane Haslem Gallery 406 Seventh St NW Washington DC 20004. *Mailing Add:* PO Box 1122 New York NY 10159-1122

ROMANO, SALVATORE MICHAEL
SCULPTOR, INSTALLATION SCULPTOR
b Cliffside Park, NJ, Sept 12, 1925. *Study:* Art Students League, with Jon Corbino; Acad Grande Chaumiere, Paris, with Edouard Georges & Earl Kerkam. *Work:* Brooklyn Bridge Cent (by Creative Time NY), 83; The Children's Mus of Manhattan, NY, 97; Chase Manhattan Bank, NY; Nassau Co Mus Fine Art, NY; Mass Mus Fine Art, Amherst; Mus Mod Art; Rutgers University, 2003; Herbert H Lehman Coll, City Univ NY. *Exhib:* Bali Miller Gallery, NY, 88; Water Installation, Sculpture Ctr (with catalog), NY, 90; solo exhib, Andrea Zarre, NY, 94; Robert Parde Gallery, 2000; Pratt Inst Campus, 2001; sculpture, 2005-; Galleria Bate Leur, Rome, Italy; Rutgers State Univ NJ Art Libr, New Brunswick, 2003; Samuel Dorsky Mus Art, New Paltz, NY, 2004; Delaware Valley Arts Alliance, Narrowsburg, NY, 2005; BLT Gallery, New York, 2009; Wooster Art Space, 2007; 307 Gallery, NY, Unison Ctr, New Paltz, NY, 2012. *Teaching:* Adj instr sculpture, Cooper Union Sch Arts & Archit, 68-70; lectr painting & sculpture, Lehman Coll, 69-71, prof, 72-; lectr kinetic sculpture, US Info Serv, Brazil, 72 & Rutgers Univ, 79; prof emer, Herbert H Lehman Coll, CUNY, Bronx, NY. *Awards:* Nat Endowment Arts, 79-80; Fac Res Award, City Univ NY, Lehman Coll, 80-81; McDowell Coloy Fel, 80 & 81; NY Found Arts Award, 85-86, 89-90; Delaware Valley Art Alliance Award, 2002. *Bibliog:* Michael Brenson (auth), Time, 9/7/90; Elena Hartney (auth), Art in Am, 11/90; Bruce Altshuler (auth), The Avant Garde in Exhibit, 94; Robert Morgan (auth), Int Sculpture Mag, 5/2001 &

6/2007. *Mem:* Artist Equity; Int Sculpture Ctr. *Media:* Plastics, Wood; Metal, Water, Copper Brass. *Specialty:* Painting, sculpture, performances. *Publ:* Auth, article, Lehman Coll Art News Lett, 71. *Dealer:* Gallery 307 7 Ave New York NY 10011. *Mailing Add:* 83 Wooster St New York NY 10012

ROMANS, VAN ANTHONY
SCULPTOR, DESIGNER
b Baltimore, Md, Jan 13, 1944. *Study:* Univ Calif, Fullerton, BA (art design), studied with Dextra Frankel; Univ Southern Calif, studied 3-D arts & mus design with Lee Chesney, MFA. *Work:* Claremont Grad Sch Gallery, Calif; Univ Southern Calif, Los Angeles; Calif State Univ, Fullerton; Orange Coast Col, Costa Mesa, Calif. *Comn:* Westcliff Shopping Ctr (designed), comn by Richard Marowitz, 76; Courtyard Shopping Ctr (designed), comn by Jerry Stout, 77. *Exhib:* Solo exhibs, Oakland Mus Art, Calif, 71 & Univ Southern Calif, Los Angeles, 72; Six Promising Young Sculptors, Claremont Cols, Calif, 73; Environments/Spaces, Orange Coast Col, 75; Spaces, Pac Design Ctr, Calif, 76; and others. *Collection Arranged:* Thonet & Thereafter, show of chair hist incl Bauhaus (auth, catalog), Japanese Sword Show, collection from collectors & from Los Angeles Co Art Mus, Western Indian Show--Dan Namingha & Persian Rug Show (designed exhib), 57 rugs from cols & collections, Orange Coast Coll Art Gallery. *Pos:* Dir display prog, Orange Coast Col, Costa Mesa, Calif, 73-, dir galleries interior design, 75-; mem, Orange Co Art Alliance, Calif, 77; lectr, Newport Harbor Art Mus, Newport Beach, Calif. *Teaching:* Prof design & exhib design/visual promotion, Orange Coast Col, Costa Mesa, Calif, 73-, prof design & visual promotion, currently; asst prof design, Univ Southern Calif, Los Angeles, 73-82. *Awards:* Most Outstanding Educator, Orange Coast Col, 75. *Bibliog:* Wilson (auth), Sculpture, 74. *Mem:* Am Soc Interior Designers. *Media:* Metal. *Mailing Add:* Dept Art PO Box 5005 Orange Coast Col 2701 Fairview Rd Costa Mesa CA 92628-5005

ROMERO, MEGAN H
PAINTER, DEALER
b Chicago, Ill, Sept 22, 1942. *Study:* Ind Univ, BA, 65; Univ Chicago, with Max Kuhn; Univ NMex, with Charles Mattox, MA, 69. *Work:* Univ NMex Fine Arts Mus, Albuquerque; Mus NMex, Santa Fe. *Exhib:* Intrinsic Art, Friends Contemp Art, 71, Denver; Fall Invitational, Roswell Mus & Art Ctr, NMex, 72; Solo exhib, Lerner Heller Gallery, NY, 72; Fine Arts Mus NMex, Biennial, 73; Seven Artists, Francis McCray Gallery, Western NMex Univ; and others. *Pos:* Owner, Hill's Gallery, Santa Fe, currently. *Awards:* Southwest Biennial, Mus NMex, 72. *Bibliog:* Donna Meilach (auth), Leather Book, 71; article, Art in Am, 8/72; article, Southwest Art Gallery Mag, 12/72. *Mem:* Mus NMex Found. *Specialty:* Contemporary New Mexico fine arts and crafts. *Publ:* Auth, Aiming at the creative environment, SW Art Gallery Mag, 11/71 & 1/73; contribr, Craft Horizons, 12/71. *Mailing Add:* 1469 Canyon Rd Santa Fe NM 87501

ROMEU, JOOST A
CONCEPTUAL ARTIST, DESIGNER
b Bremerhaven, Ger, Jan 16, 1948; US citizen. *Study:* Drexel Univ, BS. *Work:* Kansas City Art Inst; MTL Gallery, Belg. *Exhib:* Deurle, Belg, 73; Projekt '74, Koln, Ger; Diskussies Omtrent Joost A Romeu, Univ Antwerp, Belg, 75; Idea Warehouse, NY, 75. *Bibliog:* Foote (auth), The apotheosis of the crummy space, Artforum; J L Mackie (auth), The Direction of Causation; Merleau Ponty (auth), Primacy of Perception. *Publ:* Art after philosophy, 73; auth & illusr, ONCE1, ONCE2. *Mailing Add:* PO BOX 1322 Gualala CA 95445-1322

ROMNEY, HERVIN A R
ARCHITECT
b Havana, Cuba, 1941; US citizen. *Study:* Cooper Union, 62-65; L'Ecole Speciale d'Architecture, Paris, 70; Catholic Univ, Washington, DC, BArchit, 73; Yale Univ Sch Archit, Master's, 75. *Comn:* Il Gattopardo, Ambassador J A Correa, Quito, Ecuador, 76; Babylon (condominium), Pac Developers, Miami, 77; Atlantis (condominium), Stonecrest Development, Miami, 79; Palace (condominium), Helmsley-Spear, Miami, 79, Helmsley Ctr, 81. *Exhib:* Inst Archit & Urban Studies, Rome, 79; Cooper Hewitt, NY, 79; Yale Art Gallery, New Haven, Conn, 80; Inst Fine Arts, Chicago, 80; Mus Contemp Arts, La Jolla, 81; Contemp Arts Mus, Houston, 82. *Pos:* Designer, Harrison & Abramovitz, New York, 61-65; proj designer, Andrault-Parat, architects, Paris, 69-70; architect & environmental designer, South Am, 75-76; principal & founder, Arquitectonica Int Corp, Miami, 76-; founder & pres, Hervin Romney Architect Inc, Miami, 85-. *Awards:* Cintas Fel, UN Inst Int Educ, 74-75; Design Citations, Progressive Archit, 78 & 80; Fla Am Inst Archit, 82; First Prize, Dade Co Prototype Sch Competition, Miami, 85; Miami Design Preservation League, 90; Fla AIA Design Award, 89. *Bibliog:* Color-architecture, Life Mag, 4/81; articles, Newsweek 11/8/82 & House & Garden, 6/83. *Publ:* Ed, Perspecta 15, Yale Archit Papers, 75. *Mailing Add:* 2940 S Le Jeune Rd Miami FL 33134-6604

ROOD, KAY
PAINTER, PRINTMAKER
b Omaha, Nebr, May 19, 1945. *Study:* Univ Iowa, BA, 68, with Maurico Lasansky, Stuart Edie & James Lechay; Ecole des Beaux Arts, 68. *Work:* Seattle Art Mus; City of Seattle, One Percent For Art, Portable Works Collection; Washington State, One Percent For Art, Art in Public Places; King Co Arts Commission Portable Purchase Collection; Portland, Art Mus. *Exhib:* Washington Women Artists, Eastern Wash State Univ, Cheney, 81; Ten Monotype Artists, 82 & Contemp Seattle Art, 83, Bellevue Art Mus, Wash; Northwest Print Council in China, Cent Fine Arts Acad, Beijing, China, 86; Northwest Now, 86 & Kay Rood: Recent Monotypes, 87, Tacoma Art Mus, Wash; Sixth Ann Northwest Int Art Competition, 86 & Kay Rood, 92, Whatcom Mus, Bellingham, Wash; First Impressions: Northwest Monotypes, Seattle Art Mus, 89. *Pos:* Artist-in-residence, Centrum Found, 84 & 88, Marrowstone Press, Pt Townsend, 86. *Awards:* Juror's Award Painting & Drawing, Sixth Ann Northwest Int Art Competition, 86. *Bibliog:* Matthew Kangas (auth), Kay Rood: The gesture and the void, West Art, 10/22/82; Lynn Smallwood (auth), Studies in monotype, The Seattle Weekly, 10/17/84; Ron Glowen (auth), The fascination of process, Artweek, 5/24/86. *Mem:* Northwest Print Coun, Portland, Ore (bd dir, 84-92). *Media:* Miscellaneous Media; Monotype. *Publ:* Contribr, Perspectives in New Music, Six Images, vol 28, no 2, 90; Five Pears or Peaches (cover art), short stories by Reginald Gibbons, Broken Moon Press, Seattle, 91; Modernism & Beyond: Women Artists of the Pacific Northwest, ed, Laura Brunsman, Midmarch Arts Press, New York, 93. *Mailing Add:* 5954 31st St Seattle WA 98126-2910

ROOKE, FAY LORRAINE (EDWARDS)
ENAMELIST, INSTRUCTOR
b Chatham, Ont, Dec 22, 1934. *Study:* Ont Coll Art, Toronto, AOCA, 56; internat specialized enamel techniques; Royal Canadian Acad Arts; RCA. *Work:* Royal Can Acad Arts, 86; Claridge Investments, Montreal, Quebec, 89; Can Craft Collection, Mus Civilization. *Comn:* Enamel celebratory object, Claridge Invest, Que; enamel object, Glenn Gould Prize, Toronto, Ont, 90; enamel triptych, Capex 78; enamel Cross & objects/containers, Loretto Abbey Chapel, Toronto; champleve chandelier panels, St Elaias Byzantine Rite Catholic Church, Homestead, Pa. *Exhib:* Solo exhibs, Koffler Gallery, North York, Ont, 86, Can Clay & Glass Gallery, Waterloo, Ont, 93 & Harbinger Gallery, Waterloo, Ont, 95; Peninsula Fine Arts Gallery, Hampton, Va, 95; Mus Contemp Art, Caracas, Venezuela, 96; Burlington Art Ctr, Ont, 97; int invitational exhibs, South Korea, Tokyo, France, US, 2000, 2003, 2012, 2013; Canadian Mus Civilization, 2007. *Pos:* Vpres & exec bd mem, South Hills Arts League, Mt Lebanon, Pa, 70-72; found bd dir, Renaissance Ctr Arts, Pittsburgh, Pa, 71-72; dir, Enamelist Soc, Newport, KY, 89-95; adj panel, Pereny Flat Bed Enamel Furnace, Cleveland, Ohio, 93-, Can Clay & Glass Gallery, Waterloo, Ont, 94-; juror, Designer Crafts 94, Hamilton Regional Arts Coun Ont Enamelist Soc IV Biennial, Cleveland, Ohio, 93-, The Color of Fire: Mississauga, ON, 2002; conf. chair & exhibs coord, Crossing Boundaries, Enam Soc, Waterloo, 99. *Teaching:* Prog coordr enamel, Ont Col Art & Design,Toronto, 79-95; guest enamel instr, NS Col Art & Design, Halifax, 94; instr enamel, Brock Univ, St Catherines, Ont, 87, 88 & 92, St Lawrence Col, 84-2006; Int Workshops, Caracas, Venezuela 96, Sydney & Brisbane, Australia, 98, 2010, San Diego, Calif, 2000, 01, Newark, NJ, 2005. *Awards:* Thompson Enamels Award & Alice Wilick Robyns Mem Award, 85; Grand Prize Winner, 9th Cloisonne Jewelry Contest, Tokyo, Japan. *Bibliog:* Current Exploration in Glass & Enamel, Koffler Gallery, North York, Ont, 86; film, Faces in small places: Fay Rooke, CKUR Barrie, Ont-TV Series, 84 & CBC Nat Television, Sunday Arts, 90, 91 & 92. *Mem:* Royal Can Acad Arts (coun mem, 86-88 & exec bd mem, 86-); Metal Arts Guild; Ont Coll Art Alumni Asn (mem-at-large, 84-85); Enamelist Soc (trustee, 89-95, conf chair, 99); Ont Crafts Coun; Enamel Guild South Fla. *Media:* Enamelled Forms, Fine Art Objects. *Res:* Larger fine art objects in multiple enamel techniques, specializing in plique-à-jour. *Interests:* Enamel art hist, fine needle work. *Collection:* Claridge, Stonefields, Raymond, Loretto Abbey. *Publ:* Ornament and Object, Barros, 97; The Art of Enameling, 2004; The Art of Enameling, 2004; The Art of Fine Enameling, 2002; Craft Arts: International # 50, 2000, #81, 2012; The Color of Fire, 2002; Mag! 2010; Glass on Metal, 2012. *Mailing Add:* 842 Forest Glen Ave Burlington ON L7T 2L2 Canada

ROOKS, MICHAEL
CURATOR
Study: Sch Art Inst Chicago, BFA, 1988 & MA (in mod art history, theory & criticism), 1995. *Collection Arranged:* AA Bronson: Negative Thoughts, 2001; The Body Present: Effigies, Decoys and Other Equivalents, 2002. *Pos:* Asst cur, Mus Contemp Art, Chicago, 1998-2009; Wieland Family Cur Mod & Contemp Art, High Mus Art, Atlanta, 2009-. *Mem:* Weiss Mem Hosp (bd mem, 1999-2000) & Friends Against AIDS (bd mem, 2000-), Univ Chicago. *Publ:* Auth, Landlocked and Ceremonial: Prairie Sculpture, New Art Examiner, 34-37, 5/1998; Mark Booth on Wool Mammoths, the Language of Porn, and More, Dialogue, 42-43, 5-6/1999. *Mailing Add:* 1280 Peachtree St NE Atlanta GA 30309

ROOSEVELT, MICHAEL ARMENTROUT
PRINTMAKER, ART APPRAISER
b Philadelphia, PA, 1948. *Study:* Carnegie-Mellon Univ, BFA, 70; Tyler Sch Art, MFA, 86; Atelier 17, Paris - SW Hayter (pvt study), 67-85; NY Acad Fine Arts, Grad Sch of Figure Study, 95; NAA Educ Inst, GPPA & USPAP, 2010, 2012. *Work:* Woodmere Mus Art, Philadelphia, PA; Sherman Hines Mus, Liverpool, NS, Can; Lessing Rosenwald Coll, Abington, PA. *Exhib:* Solo exhibs, The Print Club, Philadelphia, PA, 70, NS Coll Art & Design, Halifax, NS, 71, Galerie Harriet Woolley, Paris, France, 86, The Print Club, Philadelphia, PA, 86, Sherman Hines Mus, Liverpool, NS, Can, 97 & Woodmere Art Mus, Philadelphia, PA, 98, Lyndon State Coll, Lydonville, Vt, 2009, Inverness Co Ctr for Arts, Inverness, NS, Can, 2009; group exhib, RI Coll, Providence, RI, 89; 62nd Int of the Print Club, Philadelphia, PA, 86; PA Painters & Printmakers, PA State Univ, Univ Park, PA, 88; Parigi 1927-2007 Dall'Atelier 17, Museo Civico, Cremona, Italy; Oyster Bay Hist Soc, Oyster Bay, NY. *Pos:* partner, Roosevelt Fine Art LLC. *Teaching:* instr printmaking, NS Coll Art & Design, Halifax, NS, Can, 70-71; Adj prof visual design, drawing, Lyndon State Coll, Lyndonville, Vt, 2008-. *Mem:* The Print Ctr (formerly Print Club), Philadelphia, PA, (bd mem, 84-86); Vis Arts NS; NS Printmakers Asn; Vt Crafts Coun; The Authors Guild; Soc Can Artists; Nat Auctioneers Asn. *Media:* Printmaking. *Res:* Harold Liebmann. *Publ:* Auth, Universal Multiplication of Intelligence, Institutes Press, 80; illusr, Enough, Inigo, Enough, Institute Press, 84; auth, Joseph Hecht, Dolan/Maxwell, 85; Stanley William Hayter (1901-1988), www.contrepoint.com, 2004. *Mailing Add:* PO Box 162 West Danville VT 05873-0162

ROOTS, GARRISON
SCULPTOR, EDUCATOR
b Abilene, Tex, June 25, 1952. *Study:* Mass Coll Art, with George Greenmayer, Harris Barron & Jana Longacre, BFA (with hon), 79; Wash Univ, with Howard Jones & James Sterritt, MFA, 81. *Work:* Denver Art Mus, Colo; City of Dallas; Laumeier Sculpture Park, St Louis; City of Miami, City of Memphis. *Comn:* Aspen Art Mus,

Colo, 89; City of Denver, New Denver Airport Proj, 90; City of Dallas, 1993 Dallas Conv Ctr Expansion Proj, 91-93; Miami Int Airport 96-; Memphis/Shelby Co Airport, 99. *Exhib:* solo exhibs, Contemp Arts Ctr, New Orleans, 84, Alternative Mus, NY, 86, Cincinnati Artist Group, 89, Inst Design & Experimental Art, Sacramento, Calif, 92, SW China Normal Univ, Chongqing, Beibei, 93, Art Galleries, Univ Colo, Boulder, 93 & Laumeier Sculpture Mus, St Louis, 96; ARTPARK, Lewiston, NY, 86; Aspen Art Mus, Colo, 89; Contemp Art Ctr Santa Fe, N Mex, 90; SPACES S, Cleveland, Ohio, 91; FUSE, Boulder, Colo, 95; Lawndale Art Ctr, Houston, Tex, 95; Buffalo Bayou Artpark, Houston, Tex, 95; Larumeier Sculpture Mus, St Louis, 96; Bemis Ctr Contemp Art, Omaha, Nebr, 99. *Pos:* Med artist/photogr, Mass Eye & Ear Infirmary, Boston, 76-79; asst to dir, Laumeier Sculpture Mus, St Louis, 79-81; artist/consult, Denver Art Ctr, Denver Comn on Cult Affairs, Colo, 86-87. *Teaching:* Teaching/tech asst, Wash Univ, St Louis, 79-80; instr, Swain Sch Design, New Bedford, Mass, 81-82; asst prof, Univ Colo, 82-88, assoc prof & dir sculpture, 88-97, assoc chmn grad studies, 96-98, prof, 98-. *Awards:* Fel Award for Sculpture, Nat Endowment Arts, 81 & 84; Travel Grants Mex, China, Ecuador & Chile, Univ Colo, 92-98; Fel Award, Westaf/ Nat Endownment Arts, 95. *Bibliog:* Beth Chic (auth), Dialouge, 91; Steven Litt (auth), The Plain Dealer, 91; Randall Davis (auth), Artweek, 92; and many others. *Mem:* Nat Endowment Arts; Colo Coun Arts & Humanities; Coll Art Asn; FUSE, Boulder, Colo. *Dealer:* Robischon Gallery 1122 E 17 Ave Denver CO; William Campbell Gallery Ft Worth TX. *Mailing Add:* 1923 Marti Cr Longmont CO 80501-8665

ROPHAR
PAINTER
b Los Angeles, Calif, Dec 19, 1935. *Study:* Self taught. *Work:* Bolshoi Theatre, Moscow, Russia; Am Cancer Prevention Ctr, Los Angeles, Calif; Bank Yokohama, Japan. *Comn:* Dancer/Portraits, comn by Ruth St Denis, Los Angeles, Calif, 59; Study of Anna Pavlova, comn by James A Doolittle, Los Angeles, Calif, 72; Total Design Concepts, comn by Liberace, Los Angeles, Calif, 73; 17th Century Fantasy (portrait), comn by Dr Richard Ellenbogen, Los Angeles, 83; White Tigers, comn by Jim Simon, Scottsdale, Ariz, 92. *Exhib:* One-man shows, 21 Turtle Creek Club, Dallas, 71, residence of Baroness von Boehm, Berlin, Ger, 73, Marina City Club, Marina Del Rey, Calif, 76 Regional Conf ASID, Los Angeles, Calif, 81, Pomeroy Gallery Fine Arts, Carmel, Calif, 89 & Ctr Arts Galleries, Hawaii, Honolulu, 90-91. *Awards:* Rotary Club Award, Art Contest, Rotary Club Int, 51-57; Hon Mem, Regional Conf ASID, Los Angeles Chap, 81. *Media:* Acrylic, All Media. *Mailing Add:* 369 S Doheny Dr Beverly Hills CA 90211

ROPP, ANN L
PAINTER, GALLERY DIRECTOR
b LaCrosse, Wis, Nov 14, 1946. *Study:* Univ Ill, BFA, 71; Columbia Univ, MFA, 89. *Work:* Evansville Mus Art, Ind; NY Pub Libr, NY. *Pos:* Gallery dir, East Tenn State Univ, Johnson City, Tenn, 89-. *Teaching:* Instr printmaking, East Tenn State Univ, 92-. *Awards:* Fel, Nat Endowment Arts, 94. *Media:* Oil, Watercolor. *Mailing Add:* Slocumb Galleries Dept Art East Tenn State Univ Johnson City TN 37614-0708

ROREX, ROBERT ALBRIGHT
EDUCATOR, HISTORIAN
b Alexandria, La, Sept 9, 1935. *Study:* Hendrix Col, BA, 57; Univ Ark, MFA, 60; Princeton Univ, MA, 69, PhD, 75. *Teaching:* Asst prof, Hendrix Col, 60-61; actg asst prof, Univ Kans, Lawrence, 68-70; instr, Univ Iowa, Iowa City, 70-75, asst prof art hist, 75-79, assoc prof, 79-. *Mem:* Coll Art Asn; Mid-Am Coll Art Asn; Midwest Art Hist Soc. *Res:* Chinese art & archeology; Japanese art & archeology; Sung, Ming & Liao painting. *Publ:* Coauth, Eighteen Songs of a Nomad Flute: The Story of Lady Wen-Chi, Metrop Mus Art, 74; auth, Setting out at dawn on an autumn river: A painting by Wang Hui, Artibus Asiae, 79; auth, Eighteen songs of a nomad flute, 8/81 & Chunghi Choo: Works in metal and silk, 10/82, Orientations; auth, Some observations on Harold Osborne's The Aesthetics of Chinese Pictorial Art, J Theory & Criticism Visual Arts, 82. *Mailing Add:* 610 Beldon Ave Iowa City IA 52246

RORICK, WILLIAM CALVIN
PAINTER, INSTRUCTOR
b Elyria, Ohio, June 23, 1941. *Study:* Studied drawing, painting & sculpture at NY Acad Art, Art Students League, Nat Acad Design, Sch Visual Arts & Lyme Acad Art. *Comn:* Many comn portraits in corp, institutional, public & pvt collections. *Exhib:* Portraits Only Int Juried Competition, Washington, DC Soc Portrait Artists, 98; Juried Exhib, NY Soc Portrait Artists, Salmagundi Club, NY, 2002; Faces of Newtown, Booth Libr, Newtown, Conn, 2005; Drawings Only Exhib, Portrait Soc of Atlanta, 2005; 55th Ann Nat Exhib Contemp Realism in Art, Acad Artists Asn, First Church Gallery, Springfield, Mass, 2005; Am Artists Prof League, 2010, Hudson Valley Art Asn, 2011. *Teaching:* Instr (cert leader), Portrait Club of Greater Southbury, Conn. *Awards:* Randolph Chitwood Award, Greenwich Art Soc, 96; 1st Place Award in Pastel, Graphics, Mixed Media, Conn Classic Arts, 2001; Meritorious Serv, NY Soc Portrait Artists, 2002; Vernon W Hill Mem Award, Conn Pastel Soc, 2003; Hon Mention, Conn Soc Portrait Artists, 2004; Acad Artists Award, Pastels Acad Artists Asn, 2005; Jerry's Artarama Award, Conn Pastel Soc, 2007; Ridgewood Art Inst Award, Kent Art Asn, 2007; The Pauline Law Memorial award for Graphics, Allied Artists of Am Inc, 2012; Conn Sr Juried Art Show, The Art of Experience, 2011-2012 awards; and others. *Bibliog:* Who's Who in the East, 1995-1996; Who's Who in Am, 1997-; Who's Who in the World, 2004-; Who's Who in Educ, 2005-. *Mem:* Conn Classic Arts (publicity chair, 96-99); Soc Creative Artists Newtown (bd dir, corresp secy & mem, 99-2002); NY Soc Portrait Artists (leadership team, 2002); Acad Artists Asn (elected artist, 2004); Audubon Artists; Arts & Crafts Asn Meriden; Kent Art Asn (elected mem, bd dir, 2003-2007); Conn Soc Portrait Artists (Founding mem, 2002-, secy, 2008-2010). *Media:* Oil, Pastel. *Res:* Locator Index to the Portraits of Thomas Sully, 1783-1872. *Interests:* Portraiture, Historical Portrait Series of Famous Composers, and others. *Dealer:* Gallery at Kent Conn. *Mailing Add:* 63 Beacon Hill Dr Southbury CT 06488-1914

RORSCHACH, KIMERLY
MUSEUM DIRECTOR
Study: Brandeis Univ, BA; Yale Univ, PMA, PhD in art hist. *Pos:* Cur, Philadelphia Mus Art, Rosenbach Mus & Libr, Philadelphia, formerly; Dana Feitler dir, Smart Mus Art, Univ Chicago, 1994-2004; dir, Nasher Mus Art, Duke Univ, Durham, NC, 2004-12; dir, Seattle Art Mus, 2012-. *Teaching:* adjunct prof, Dept Art, Art Hist & Visual Studies, Duke Univ, formerly. *Mem:* Asn Art Mus Dir. *Mailing Add:* Nasher Mus Art PO Box 90732 Durham NC 27708

ROSAS, MEL
PAINTER, EDUCATOR
b Des Moines, Iowa, June 1, 1950. *Study:* Drake Univ, with Jules Kirschembalm, BFA, 71; Tyler Sch Art, with John Moore & Steven & Dave Greene, MFA, 74. *Exhib:* Corcoran Gallery Art, 74; Eastern Mich Univ, Ypsilanti, 78, Cantor/Lemberg Gallery, Birmingham, Mich, 81 & 84 & Community Arts Gallery, Wayne State Univ, Detroit, 88; Cranbrook Art Mus, 79 & 80; Brooklyn Mus, 81; Butler Inst Am Art, 87; Portals, Maxwell Davidson Gallery, NY, 95; Maxwell Davidson Gallery, 2000, 2001; Art Palm Beach, Fla, 2001; Water and Other Stories, Maxwell Davidson Gallery, NY, 2003; Everyday Mysteries: Paintings by Mel Rosas, The Muskegon Mus, Muskegon, Mich, 2005; The Enigma of Return, Davidson Contemporary Gallery, NY, 2007; After the Rain, Maxwell Davidson Gallery, NY, 2005, La Calle Desconocida (The Unknown Street), 2009, Davidson Contemporary Gallery, NY; Perdido en el tiempo/Lost in Time, NY, Davidson Contemporary Gallery, NY, 2011; Un Verso Sincillo/A Simple Verse, Davidson Contemporary Gallery, 2013. *Teaching:* Instr, Univ Calgary, Alberta, 75-76; prof, Wayne State Univ, Detroit, 76-. *Awards:* Fac Res Grants, Wayne State Univ, Detroit, 87 & 90; Creative Artists Grant, Mich Coun Arts, Detroit, 87; Nat Endowment Arts Grant, 93; Creative Artist Grant, Artserve of Mich, 99-2000; The Elizabeth Found for the Arts Grant, NY; Pollock-Krasner Found Grant, 2008-09; Elaine L Jacob Chair in Fine Arts, James Pearson Duffy Dept Art and Art History, Wayne State Univ, Detroit, Mich, 2013-. *Bibliog:* Harry N Abrams (publ), Tools as Art, Thr Hechinger Collection; Nathan Goldstein (auth), The Art Responsive Drawing, Prentice Hall. *Media:* Oil, Drawing. *Dealer:* Maxwell Davidson Gallery

ROSE, DEEDIE POTTER
COLLECTOR, PATRON, ADMINISTRATOR
Study: Tex Christian Univ, BA (French). *Pos:* Bd trustees, Dallas Mus Art, pres, 1994-98; bd trustees & bd dirs, Dallas Ctr Performing Arts; life trustee & bd dirs, Dallas Theater Ctr, chmn bd, formerly; bd dirs, Dallas Inst Humanities & Cult, Dallas Archit Forum, Pub Radio Int, Channel 13/KERA, Tex Int Theatrical Arts Soc, Dallas Found, Tex Christian Univ; adv bd, Univ Tex Sch Archit; mem Nat Coun Arts, Nat Endowment Arts, 2002. *Awards:* Legend Award, Dallas Visual Arts Ctr, 1995; Neiman Marcus Silver Cup Award, TACA Dallas, 1997; named one of Top 200 Art Collectors, ARTnews mag, 2007-13. *Collection:* Contemporary German, American, and South American art. *Mailing Add:* c/o Bd of Trustees Dallas Mus Art 1717 N Harwood Dallas TX 75201

ROSE, EDWARD W, III
COLLECTOR
b Dallas, Tex. *Study:* Harvard Bus Sch, MBA. *Pos:* Founder & principal, Cardinal Investment co, Inc, Dallas, 1974-; co-gen partner (with George W Bush), Tex Rangers, 1989-98. *Awards:* Named one of Top 200 Collectors, ARTnews mag, 2007-12. *Collection:* Contemporary German, American and South American art. *Mailing Add:* Cardinal Investments 500 Crescent Ct Ste 250 Dallas TX 75201

ROSE, LEATRICE
PAINTER, INSTRUCTOR
b New York, NY, Jun 22, 1924. *Study:* Cooper Union, 45; Art Students League, 46; Hans Hofmann Sch, 47. *Exhib:* Artists Ann, Whitney Mus Am Art, 50; Solo exhibs: Zabriske Gallery, 65; Landmark Gallery, 74; Tibor de Nagy Gallery, 75, 78,81; Armstrong Gallery, 85, Cyrus Gallery, 89; Women Choose Women, NY Cult Ctr, 73; Nat Acad Design Ann, 74-76; Whitney Mus Am Art, Downtown, 78; Hans Hofmann as Teacher: Drawings by his Students, Metrop Mus Art, 79; Contemp Naturalism, Nassau Co Mus Fine Arts, 80; Contemp Still Life, One Penn Plaza, NY, 85; Am Academy of Arts & Letters, 91,92; Nat Acad of Design Ann 92-2003; Cherry Stone Gallery, Wellfleet, MA, 2004. *Teaching:* Instr painting, State Univ NY, Stony Brook, 74-75, Sch Visual Art, New York 77, Art Students League, currently. *Awards:* Nat Endowment Arts Grant, 77; Gottlieb Found Award, 80; Esther and Adolph Gottlieb Found Grant, 88; Am Acad Arts and Letts Painting Award, 92; Nat Acad Design Painting Award, 92; Carlson Award Best Still Life, Nat Acad Design, 99. *Bibliog:* John Ashbery (auth), Dash, Dodd & Rose, 3/74 & Lawrence Campbell (auth), article, 10/85, Art in Am; April Kingsley (auth), The Lugano review, Art Int, 3/20/74; Lawrence Alloway (auth), Art, The Nation, 10/25/75; Barbara Guest (auth), article, Arts, summer 85; Woman's Art Journal 94-95. *Mem:* Nat Acad of Design (assoc, 92, acad, 94). *Media:* Oil on canvas. *Collection:* Lisa Felgy-Chemical Bank, Metropolitan Mus

ROSE, PEGGY JANE
PAINTER, INSTRUCTOR
b Plainfield, NJ Oct 4, 1947. *Study:* Univ Tex, BA with high hon, Austin, Tex, 1971; Acad of Art Col, BFA with distinction, 1980; Private studios: Peter Blos, 1982-1984; Daniel Greene, 1983; Burton Silverman, Hudson River Valley Studio, NYC, spring & summer 1998; Teachers as Scholars, Princeton U, 2006 & 2008; Marygrove Coll, MAT, 2010. *Work:* Mercer Co Cult & Heritage Comn Collection, Trenton, NJ. *Comn:* Private portrait commissions. *Exhib:* Pastels USA, Pastel Soc W Coast, Roseville Art Center, Sacramento, Calif, 1996-1999; Pastel Soc Am Ann Exhib, Nat Arts Club, NY, 1998-2010; Catharine Lorillard Wolfe Art Club, Nat Art Club, NY, 2000, 2002, 2004; Allied Artists Am Ann, Nat Arts Club, NY, 2002-2015; Princeton Arts Council, 2002-2012; Audubon Artists Inc Ann Exhib, Salmagundi Club, NY, 2002-2015; 21st

& 22nd Ellerslie Open Exhibits, City of Trenton Mus, Trenton, NJ, 2003-2004; Present Day Club, 2005; Butler Inst Am Art-PSA Exhib, 2009-2010, 2012-2013, 2014-2015; Canton Mus Art, Allied Artists of Am 100 Years, 2015. *Pos:* bd govs, Pastel Soc Am, NY. *Teaching:* Fac, Figure, Portrait, color drawing & Painting, Acad Art Col (Univ), San Francisco, Calif, 1983-1997; Fac, Illus drawing & painting, Calif Col Arts & Crafts, Oakland, Calif, 1985-1986; Fac, gen art, Montgomery Twp, Sch Dist, Skillman, NJ, 2005-2013. *Awards:* Best of Show, Pastels in Light, Pastel Soc W Coast, 1996; Gold Medal of Honor, Catharine Lorillard Wolfe Art Club 106th Exhib, 2002; Gold Medal of Honor, Allied Artists of Am 89th Exhib, 2002; Bernhard Gold Medal in Pastel, 2013. *Bibliog:* Nancy Cushing (auth), Rose Paintings are Pure Pleasure, Mill Valley Record, 1987; Ian Seldon (auth), Three Cheers, Diablo Arts Mag, 1992; Int Showcase Prize Winners, Int Artist Mag, 2003. *Mem:* Pastel Soc W Coast (signature mem), 1999-; Allied Artist Am (signature mem), 2002-; Pastel Soc Am (master pastellist), 2004-; Catharine Lorillard Wolfe Art Club (full mem), 2005-; Audubon Artists Am (signature mem), 2006-. *Media:* Pastel, Oil. *Publ:* Auth, Whistler's Pastels in Venice, Their Innovations & Their Impact on Pastel in Am, Pastel Soc Am, 2003; Auth, A Celebration of Pastel, Ann Exhib, Pastelagram Mag, winter 2004. *Mailing Add:* 12 Perry Dr Princeton Junction NJ 08550-2803

ROSE, PETER HENRY
DEALER
b New York, NY, Feb 25, 1935. *Study:* Hamilton Col, BA; Univ Pa, MA; Columbia Univ; Ecole Superieure, Univ Paris. *Exhib:* Curated exhibs of several sculptures: Clement Meadmore, Nations Rapopart, James Rosati, Itzik Benshalom, Bozidar Kemperle, Butler Inst Am Art. *Pos:* Co-owner, Peter Rose Gallery, currently. *Mem:* Arts & Bus Coun New York. *Specialty:* Nineteenth and twentieth century contemporary American art; major French impressionist paintings. *Collection:* Currently emphasizes sculpture including, Clement Meadmore, Bradford Graves, James Rosari, Nathan Rapoport and others; works on paper by Russian artist, Anatoli Zverev

ROSE, ROBIN CARLISE
PAINTER, SCULPTOR
b Ocala, Fla, Sept 3, 1946. *Study:* Fla State Univ, BFA, 68, MFA, 70. *Work:* Corcoran Gallery, Phillips Collection & Nat Mus Am Art, Washington, DC; Jacksonville Mus Fine Art, Fla; Hirshhorn Mus & Sculpture Garden, Washington, DC. *Comn:* IBM, Gaithersburg, Md; Signet Bank, Washington, DC; Shea Beker Gallery, NY; Grand Hyatt, Washington, DC. *Exhib:* M-13 Gallery, NY; WPA, Washington, DC; Corcoran Gallery Art, Washington, DC; White Columns, NY. *Bibliog:* Stephen Westfall (auth), rev, Art in Am, 5/86. *Media:* Encaustic, Silverpoint. *Dealer:* Fendrick Gallery 3059 M St NW Washington DC 20007. *Mailing Add:* 2900 Fessenden St NW Washington DC 20008

ROSE, ROSLYN
DIGITAL PHOTOGRAPHER, COLLAGE ARTIST
b Irvington, NJ, May 28, 1929. *Study:* Rutgers Univ; Pratt Graphic Ctr; Skidmore Coll, BS. *Work:* NJ State Mus, Trenton; Newark Mus, NJ; Citibank of NY, Moscow, Russia; Newark Pub Libr, NJ; Zimmerli Mus, Rutgers Univ, New Brunswick, NJ; McAllen Int Mus, Tex; Noyes Mus, Oceanville, NJ; Readers Digest Collection, Pleasantville, NY; Voorhees-Zimmerli Mus, New Brunswick, NJ; Stevens Inst, Hoboken, NJ; and others; Hoboken Historical Mus, Hoboken, NJ. *Comn:* Etchings, NY Graphic Soc, Ltd, Greenwich, Conn, 70-80 & John Szoke Gallery, New York, 81-85; UNICEF Card, 79-80; etched metal wall-relief, Pub Serv Elec & Gas Co, Newark, NJ, 80. *Exhib:* Liberated Printmakers (traveling), NJ Coun Arts, 72; Solo exhibs, Robins Hutchins Gallery, 78, George Frederick Gallery, Rochester, 81, Arnot Art Mus, Elmira, 82, Nathans Gallery, West Paterson, 84, 86, 89, 97, 99, Gallery 3, Hoboken, NJ, Pen & Brush Club, New York, 98, New Century Artist Inc, New York, 2003, Symposia, Hoboken, NJ, 2005, Hoboken Hist Mus, Hoboken, NJ, 2006,2012, Ceres Gallery, New York, 2008, 2010, hob'art Gallery, Hoboken, NJ, 2012, 2013; Group exhibs, Western Colo Art Ctr, Grand Junction, Colo, Catherine Lorillard Wolfe Art Club, New York & Penn & Brush Club, 2000; Faces, Period Gallery, Omaha, Nebr, Bristol Art Mus, Bristol, RI, 2001; Mt Art Show, Bernardsville, NJ & Cambridge Art Asn, Cambridge, Mass, 2002; Case Western Reserve Univ, Cleveland, Ohio, Nat Asn Women Artists, New York, Seton Hall Univ, South Orange, NJ, 2003; Lee Co Alliance of the Arts, Fort Myers, Fla, Studio Seto, Boston, Mass, 2004; Somerville Art Mus, Somerville, Mass, AIR Gallery, New York, Stevens Inst Technol, 2005; DeVos Mus, Northern Mich Univ, Marquette, Mich, Ceres Gallery, New York & Goggle Works Ctr for the Arts, Reading, Pa, 2006; Lexington Art League, Ky, 2006; Longview Mus Fine Arts, Longview, Tex, 2007; Ceres Gallery, New York, 2008; New York Hall of Sci, Queens, NY, 2008; Washington Gallery of Photog, Bethesda, MD, 2008; Viridian Gallery, New York, 2008; exhibit & cur, Hoboken Hist Mus, NJ, 2009; Calif Inst Integral Studies, San Francisco, 2009; 1978 Arts Ctr, Maplewood, NJ, 2009; Banana Factory Mus, Bethlehem, Pa, 2009; Morris Mus, NJ Ann, 2009; Robeson Gallery, Penn State Univ, 2009; NJ Ann, NJ State Mus, Trenton, NJ, 2010; Watchung Arts Ctr, NJ, 2010; George Segal Gallery, Montclair Univ, NJ, 2010; Frances Young Tang Mus, Skidmore Coll, Saratoga Springs, NY, 2011; GDP Studios, Shelton, Wash; Justice Brennan Ct House Gallery, In Her Strength, Jersey City, NJ. *Collection Arranged:* Black-White & Color, Printmaking Coun, NJ, 82. *Pos:* Bd dir, Printmaking Coun NJ, 80-85; jury ch printmaking, Nat Asn Women Artists, 86-88, jury chair works on canvas, 93-96, vpres, 97-2000; co-founder, hob'art cooperative gallery, Hoboken, NJ, corresponding secy, 2002-2006 & pub relations secy, currently. *Teaching:* Instr printmaking, Newark Mus, 72-82. *Awards:* Ga Memorial Graphic Prize, 77, Innovative Painting Prize, 90, Nat Asn Women Artists; Mixed Media Award, Salmagundi Club, 95; Mixed Media Award, Pen & Brush Club, 96-98; Innovative Award, Western Colo Art Ctr, Grand Junction, 2000; Nat Asn Women Artists Computer Art Award, 2003; Lee Co Alliance, 2004; Best in Show Award, Mt Art Show, 2004; Computer Art Award, Intl Soc of Experimental Artists, 2007; Best in Show, Int Soc Experimental Artist, 2008; Nat Asn Women Artists Annual Photog award, 2012. *Bibliog:* J H Newman & L S Newman (auths), Plastics for the Craftsman, Crown, 72; Thelma R Newman (auth), Innovative Printmaking, Crown, 77; Manhattan Arts Mag, 1/98. *Mem:* Nat Asn Women Artists (printmaking jury ch, 86-88 & 2000-03, vpres, 97-99); Printmaking Coun NJ (bd dir, 80-85); Assoc Artists NJ (exec bd, 86); hob'art cooperative gallery (bd dir, 2002-); Int Soc Experimental Artists (sig mem); ProArts, Jersey City, NJ. *Media:* Digital Media Montage. *Publ:* Auth, Outline of Printmaking, NJ Coun Arts, 72. *Dealer:* Ceres Gallery 547 W 27th St New York NY 10001; Hob'art Gallery 120 Monroe Ave, Hoboken, NJ. *Mailing Add:* PO Box 6129 Hoboken NJ 07030-7203

ROSE, SAMUEL
PAINTER, MURALIST
b Cleveland, Ohio, Sept 17, 1941. *Study:* Cape Cod Sch Art, Provincetown, with Henry Henche; Cooper Sch & Kent State Univ; Boston Atelier, with R H Ives Gammell; also with Basil Kalashnifoff, Cleveland. *Work:* Maryhill Mus Art & St Ignatius Church, Washington, DC; Nat Fire Protection Asn; Brockton Mus; Pierce Galleries Inc, Hingham, Mass. *Comn:* Many, incl Maharaj Ji, Mrs F Lee Bailey, Patricia Barlow & Patricia Pierce. *Exhib:* Nat Arts Club, NY, 69; Copley Art Soc & Concord Art Asn, 71; Jordan Marsh, Boston, 72-73; Solo exhibs, Concord Art Asn, 75, Pierce Galleries, Inc, 79-80, 88 & 90, Hammer Galleries, NY, 85; and others. *Teaching:* Pvt art classes. *Awards:* First Prize, Concord Art Asn, 63, 67 & 69; Greenshields Grant, Montreal, 63-70; Nat Fire Protection Asn; Julias Hallgarten Prize, NAD, 68. *Mem:* Copley Soc; Salmagundi Club; Guild Boston Artists; Concord Art Asn; Am Artists Prof League. *Media:* Oil. *Publ:* Edmund C Tarbell and the Boston School, 80; Samuel Rose, Surrealist, 76. *Dealer:* Pierce Galleries Inc Hingham MA 02043. *Mailing Add:* c/o Pierce Galleries Inc 721 Main St Hingham MA 02043-3326

ROSE, THOMAS ALBERT
SCULPTOR, PHOTOGRAPHER
b Washington, DC, Oct 15, 1942. *Study:* Univ Wis, Madison, 60-62; Univ Ill, Urbana, BFA, 65; Univ Calif, Berkeley, MA, 67, study grant to Univ Lund, 67-68. *Work:* Univ NMex Mus, Albuquerque; Libr Cong, Washington; Minneapolis Inst Art; Walker Art Ctr, Minneapolis; Brooklyn Mus, NY; Whitney Mus Am Art; Getty Inst, Los Angeles, Calif; Yale Univ Archit Libr. *Comn:* Park St Loft One, Springfield, Mass; chapel, St Lukes Episcopal Church, Minneapolis; set design, Fool for Love, Cricket Theater, Minneapolis; set design, Circus, Theater de Jeune Lune, Minneapolis; Minn Zoological Gardens; Dunwoody Inst Technol, Minneapolis; Mary Vaughan Garden, Minneapolis. *Exhib:* Walker Art Ctr, Minneapolis, 74; Small Objects, Whitney Mus Am Art, NY; Scale & Environment, Walker Art Ctr; outdoor sculpture exhib, Wave Hill, NY, 81; Sheldon Mus Art, Univ Nebr, Lincoln; Thomson Gallery, Minneapolis, 91; Minneapolis Inst Art, 92; Frederick R Weismann Mus, Minneapolis, 94; Nat Mus Art, Tirana, Albania, 94; Tweed Mus Art, Univ Minn, 95; Steinbaum/Krauss Gallery, NY, 96 & 97; Socrates Sculpture Park, NY, 96; Bernice Steinbaum Gallery, Miami, Fla, 2001, 2003; Luxun Acad Art, Shenyang, China, 2006; Gallery Lipanjeuntin, Trieste, Italy, 2006; Beijing Film Acad, China, 2007; Mus Contemp Art, Terhan, Iran, 2007; Weisman Art Mus, Minneapolis, 2008; 798 Photo Gallery, Beijing, China; Ping Yao Int Festival of Photog, Ping Yao, China; Midnight Party, Walker Art Ctr, 2012; Timeless Gallery, Beijing, China; Artist Multiples 3-D, Minneapolis Inst Art, 2012; Minn Ctr for Book Arts, 2012. *Collection Arranged:* Cur, Exercises, The Drawings of Merce Cunningham, Nash Gallery, Univ Minn, 2005; cur, Encounters: The Past Re-Configured, Liu Xuguang & Li Shuan, Nash Gallery, Univ Minn; American Imaging, Beijing, China; GuoGui Artist from Beijing Art, Soap Factory; Wang Youshen, Artist From Beijing at MPLS Photo Ctr & Regis Ctr MPLS. *Teaching:* Instr sculpture, Univ Calif, Berkeley, 68-69; instr sculpture & graphics, NMex State Univ, 69-72; instr sculpture, Univ Minn, Minneapolis, 72-81, assoc prof, 81-83, prof art, 83-. *Awards:* Bush Found, 79; Nat Endowment Arts, 79 & 81; Jerome Found Fel, 93-94; Rockefeller Found, Bellagio, Italy, 93; Dayton Hudson Travel Grant, Italy, 94; McKnight found fel, 95; McKnight Fel/photog, 2002; Fesler/Lampert Chair in Humanities, J of Minn, 2004. *Bibliog:* John Ligon (prod), Encounters with Minnesota Artists (film); Eleanor Heartney (auth), Tom Rose: Access to Hidden Worlds (article); Ann Klefstad (auth), Five McKnight Artists; Mark Cohen (auth), Provisional Locations, Review Mag, 3/99. *Media:* Mixed Media; Photography. *Publ:* Auth, Winter Book, Minn Ctr Book Arts, 95; Where do we Start, 2000; 1018 W Scott, 2005; Time Frames, 2008; Arthur & Barbara: A Portrait; auth, The Artists Philosopher: And the Open Work (essay), Library of Living Philosophies; Secrets, 2012. *Dealer:* Bernice Steinbaum Gallery 3550 N Miami Ave, Miami FL. *Mailing Add:* 91 Nicolet St Minneapolis MN 55401

ROSELIONE-VALADEZ, JUAN
MUSEUM DIRECTOR
Study: Cooper Union Advan Sci & Art, BFA. *Pos:* Collections mgr & acting dir, Rubell Family Collection-Contemp Arts Found, 2001-2010, dir, 2010-. *Mailing Add:* 95 NW 29th St Miami FL 33127

ROSEMAN, SUSAN CAROL
PRINTMAKER, PAINTER
b Philadelphia, Pa, June 20, 1950. *Study:* Art Inst Pittsburgh, 67; Pa Acad Fine Arts, cert, 68-73. *Work:* Allentown Art Mus, Pa; Springfield Free Pub Libr. *Exhib:* Japan Int Artists Soc, Prefectural Mus, Nara, China, 81-82; Nat Print Exhib, Trenton State Col, NJ, 86; James A Michener Art Mus Bucks Binnial I, Doylestown, Pa, 92; 10th Biennial Nat Printshow, Payne Gallery, Moravian Col, Bethlehem, Pa, 96; Donald B Palmer Mus, Springfield, NJ, 96; The Learning Studio, Longhorn, Pa, 99; PC NJ Newark Mus, NJ, 99. *Pos:* exhib committee, fel, Pa Acad Fine Arts, 91-; Pres, Riverbank Arts Inc, Stockton, NJ, 94-. *Awards:* Fel, Pa Acad Fine Arts, Ft History Mus, 88; 2nd Place, Graphics Art Show at the Dog Show, 95; Purchase Prize Award, 98th Ann Juried Exhib Fel, PASA, Westchester Univ, 95 & 10th Biennial Nat Print Show, Payne Gallery, Bethlaham, Pa, 97. *Mem:* Printmaking Coun NJ; Pa Acad Fine Arts; Woodmere Art Mus. *Media:* All. *Publ:* Auth, rev, Art Matters, 12/84, 10/89. *Mailing Add:* 6588 Groveland Rd Pipersville PA 18947

ROSEN, ABY J
COLLECTOR
Pos: Co-founder, RFR Holding LLC, New York. *Awards:* Named one of Top 200 Collectors, ARTnews mag, 2006-13; recipient Man of Yr Award, Spring Ahead Gala, Jeffrey Modell Found, 2000. *Collection:* Modern and contemporary art; contemporary photography

ROSEN, ANDREA
GALLERY DIRECTOR
Pos: pres, Andrea Rosen Gallery, NY, currently. *Specialty:* contemporary socio-political art. *Mailing Add:* Andrea Rosen Gallery 525 W 24th St New York NY 10011

ROSEN, DIANE
PAINTER, WRITER
b New York, NY. *Study:* Goucher Coll, BA (cum laude), 70; Art Students League, with Robert Beverly Hale & Daniel Greene, 78-80; Nat Acad Design, with Harvey Dinnerstein, 79; French Govt Fel Painting, Independent Study, 81; Teacher's Coll, Columbia Univ, MA (Eng educ), New York, 2008. *Work:* Pastel Soc Am, Nat Arts Club, NY. *Comn:* Mural (oil, 7 x 10 ft), comn by Victoria Hunter-Gohl, NY, 92; mural (acrylic 6 x 16 ft), Robert Vissichio, NY, 93; mural (acrylic 8 x 17 ft), Bruce Selfon, Washington, DC, 94; mural (oil, 60 x 54 ft) comn by Constance Slaughter, London, Eng, 95; mural (acrylic 5 x 13 ft), comn by Pamela Swedelson, Woodbury, NY, 96; mural (acrylic 8 x 6 ft), comn by M E Bernal, San Antonio, Tex, 97; and others. *Exhib:* Bard Coll, Annandale-on-Hudson, NY, 79; 19th Ann Pastel Soc Am, Nat Arts Club, NY, 91; True Love & Other Stories, Gallery Stendhal, NY, 91; Ann Combined Media Exhib, Salmagundi Club, NY, 92; Pastels USA, 6th Ann Pastel Soc West Coast Int Open Exhib, Sacramento Fine Arts Mus, Carmichael, Calif, 92; solo exhibs, Two Visions Gallery, Washingtonville, NY, 94, Walter Wickiser Gallery, NY, 95, 2004, S E Feinman Gallery, NY, 96, Wyckoff Gallery, NJ, 95-2000, Mark Gruber Gallery, New Paltz, NY, 95-2002; Hammond Mus Invitational, N Salem, NY, 95; Gayle Clark Fedigan Gallery, Cornwall Univ, 2002-; Catharine Lorillard Wolfe Art Club Ann Nat Arts Club, NY, 2002, 2006-2012; Butler Inst Am Art Nat Show, Youngstown, Ohio, 2002, 2004-2005; Pastel Soc Am Curator Series Show, 2002-2003; Pastel Soc Am Ann, NY, 2003, 2006-2012; Allied Artists Am Ann, NY, 2003; Women's History Month Invitational Show, Howland Cult Ctr, Beacon, NY, 2005; Hopper House Art Ctr, Nyack, NY, 2006, 2013; Broome St Gallery, NY, 2007-2010; Game Show NYC: The Art of Learning Through Games, NY, 2011; Enduring Brilliance: Pastel Soc Am at 40, Noyes Mus Art, NJ, 2012. *Pos:* Creative dir, vpres, Wilcox & Assoc, NY, 84-88; creative dir/owner, Diane Rosen Communs, NY, 89-90; Sole proprietor, Diane Rosen Studio, 91-2005, Curiosity Matrix Studio, 2005-. *Teaching:* Teacher art, Drawing the Face and Hands, Parsons Sch Design, NY, Birch Wathen Sch, NY & Pastel Soc Am Sch, NY; RCC State Univ NY, NY. *Awards:* President's Award, 6th Ann Pastel Soc West Coast Int Open, 92; A & A Giffuni Purchase Award, Pastel Soc Am, 95; Salmagundi Club Award, Catharine Lorillard Wolfe Art Club 106th Ann Exhib, 2002; elected Master Panelist, Pastel Soc Am, 2003; Joseph V Giffuni Mem Award, Pastel Soc Am, 2003; Dianne Bernhard Gold Medal award for Pastel, Allied Artists Am, 2003; HK Holbein Award, Pastel Soc Am, 2006; William Alfred White Mem Award, Salmagundi club, 2007; Anna Hyatt Huntington Award, First for Painting, 2007, First for Mixed Media, 2008, Catharine Lorillard Wolf Club; Harry A Ballinger Award, 2008; CLWAC Award, Pastel Soc Ann, 2009. *Bibliog:* Elizabeth Exler (auth), The classical in the contemporary art of Diane Rosen, Manhattan Arts, 92; Kathy Swanwick (auth), Giving form to humanity, The Times Herald-Record, 94; EC Lipton (auth), New Voices, Artspeak, 94; Barbara Fischman (auth), Seeing the World Afresh, Pastel Soc Am Mag, 96; Kristina Feliciano (ed), Best of Pastel 2, Rockport Pub, 98; Keith Crandell (auth), Remembering Adam In Noho, The Villager, 2000; J. Sanders Eaton (auth), Pastels Only Celebrates a Major Medium, Gallery Studio Mag, 2004; Loraine Crouch (auth), Diane Rosen, Pastel Journal, 2005; Maureen Bloomfield & James Markle (ed), Pure Color - The Best of Pastel, North Light Bks Publ, 2006; David Neilson (auth), Life Laid Bare: Diane Rosen Explores the Human Form, The Hook, 2012. *Mem:* Pastel Soc Am; Salmagundi Club, NY; Allied Artists Am; Am Artists Prof League; Hudson Valley Pastel Soc; Arts Coun Orange Co; Coll Art Asn; Catharine Lorillard Wolfe Art Club. *Media:* Pastel, Acrylic. *Res:* Creative process across disciplines; role of curiosity. *Interests:* Hiking, cycling, photography. *Publ:* Auth & ed, Pastelagram, Newsletter Pastel Soc Am, 91, 92; auth, Interpreting Classical Form with Abstract Underpainting, Am Artist Mag, 2003; Create Evocative Figures, Pastelagram, Newsletter, Pastel Soc Am, 2004; auth, Bringing Inquiry In: A Curriculum Guide, 2010; auth, The Curiosity Habit' in Perspectives on Creativity, vol. II., 2011; auth, Spielraum: Play, Chance, and Creativity Across Disciplines, 2011; auth, A Jester's Guide to Creative See(K)ing Across Disciplines, Am Jour Play, 2012; auth, Creativity in the Classroom: Beware! The Irascible Professor, 2012; auth, How to Encourage Your Child's Curiosity and Creativity, NY Metro Parents Mags, 2012. *Dealer:* Walter Wickiser Gallery NY

ROSEN, JANE
SCULPTOR
b New York, NY 1950. *Study:* New York Univ, BA, 1972. *Work:* Albright-Knox Art Gallery, Buffalo; Brooklyn Mus; Mus Contemp Art, San Diego; Scottsdale Mus Art, Ariz; Yellowstone Mus, Mont. *Exhib:* Shifting into Balance, Buckhorn Sculpture Park, Petaluma, Calif, 2006; The Fine Art of Banking, Heritage Bank, San Jose, Calif, 2008; Ashes to Ashes, Life and Death in Contemporary Glass, Va Commonwealth Ctr, 2009; Natural Blunders, de Saisset Mus, Santa Clara, Calif, 2009; Am Acad Arts & Letts Invitational, New York, 2010; Sears Peyton Gallery, 2010. *Pos:* Spl lectr, Univ Calif, Berkeley, 1994-95 & 1996-2005; res fel, LaCoste Sch Arts, France, 1998. *Teaching:* Sr fac, Sch Visual Arts, New York, 1978-89; vis prof, Md Inst Coll Fine Arts, 1985, Univ Calif, Davis, 1990-92, Stanford Univ, Calif, 1993, Bard Coll, NY, 1995-96. *Awards:* Madein / Luso-Am Found Grant, 1988; Pilchuck Glass Sch Fel, Seattle, 1999, 2008; Purchase Award, Acad Arts & Letts, 2010. *Bibliog:* Matthew Kangas (auth), The Seattle Times, 10/2006; Alan Artner (auth), rev, Chicago Tribune, 5/18/2007; Jan Garden Castro (auth), rev, Sculpture Mag, 10/2008

ROSENBAUM, ALLEN
MUSEUM DIRECTOR
b New York, NY, 1937. *Study:* Queens Coll, New York, BA, 58; Inst Fine Arts, New York Univ, MA, 62. *Pos:* Lectr, Educ Dept, Metrop Mus Art, 64-69, sr lectr, 71-72; asst dir, Shickman Gallery; asst dir, Art Mus, Princeton Univ, 74-, dir, 80-98; vis comt, Meadows Mus, SMU, Dallas; vis comt dept art, Africa, Oceania and the Americas, Metrop Mus Art; Board Godwin Ternbach Mus, Queens Coll, New York; consult, Henry & Rose Pearlman Found, New York. *Teaching:* Instr, Sch Gen Studies, Queens Coll, City Univ New York, 61 & Sch Fine Arts, Univ Calif, Irvine, 72. *Awards:* Fulbright Fel Hist Art, Rome, 62-63. *Mem:* Asn Art Mus Dirs. *Publ:* Auth, Titian and Giotto in Padua, Marsyas, Studies Hist Art, Vol 8, 66-67; Old Master Paintings from the Collection of Baron Thyssen Bornemisza, Int Exhibs Found, Washington, DC, 79; The museum program vis-a-vis the art department & other disciplines, In: Museum in Academe II, Vassar Coll Art Gallery, 4/8/88; Peter Jay Sharp, In: The Peter Jay Sharp Collection (exhib catalog), Sotheby's, New York, 94; lects, Nat Gallery London, 2000 & Metrop Mus Art, New York, 2001. *Mailing Add:* 205 E 78th St Apt 10C New York NY 10075

ROSENBAUM, EVELYN ELLER See Eller, Evelyn Eller Rosenbaum

ROSENBAUM, JOAN H
MUSEUM DIRECTOR
b Hartford, Conn. *Study:* Hartford Coll Women, AA; Boston Univ, BA; Hunter Col (art hist). *Hon Degrees:* Jewish Theological Sem Am, D Hebrew Letters, 1993. *Pos:* Cur asst, Mus Modern Art, NY, 1966-72; dept head, Mus Prog, NY State Coun Arts, 1973-79; trustee, Artist Space, NY, 1982-92, Creative Time, 97-2001, Artis, 2011-; consult, Michael Washburn & Assocs, 1979-80, Am Asn Mus, Mus Assessment Prog, 1979-; dir, Jewish Mus, NY, 1981-2011, dir emerita, 2011-. *Awards:* European travel grantee, Int Coun Mus, 1972; Knighthood from Denmark, 1983; Navassah Woman of Distinction, 1994; Distinguished Alumni Award, Boston, Mass, 1994; Diploma, Chevalier Order Arts & Letters, 1999; Jewish Women's Found NY Edn award, 2004; Art Table 30 Yrs Anniversary Honoree, 2011. *Mem:* Asn Art Mus Dirs; Am Alliance Mus; ICOM. *Res:* History of Jewish museums in America and Europe. *Publ:* Introd, Treasures of the Jewish Museum (catalog), Universal, 26; Inside the Minds: The Business Behind Museums, Aspatore Books, 2004; Masterworks of the Jewish Mus, Yale, 2004

ROSENBERG, ALEX JACOB
ART DEALER, CONSULTANT, APPRAISER
b New York, NY, May 25, 1919. *Study:* Philadelphia Mus Art; Albright Coll, Philadelphia Univ, BS, 48; Instituto Superior de Arte, ScD (art), 2003. *Hon Degrees:* HLD, Hofstra Univ, 89. *Work:* Art gifts in over 30 coll collections; Major Collections, Hofstra Univ; Savannah Coll Art & Design; Albright Coll. *Collection Arranged:* An Am Portrait 1776-1976 Traveling Exhib (original print & multiple sculpture portfolio; ed, catalog), 76-77; Marc Tobey Retrospective, 77 & 81; James Coignard Traveling Exhib, 82-83; Henry Moore (Mother & Child, co-cur & assoc ed, catalog), Mus Traveling Exhib, 87-88; co-cur, The Prints of Romare Bearden, co-ed catalog, Mus Traveling Exhib, 92-96; Henry Moore Traveling retrospective, Havana, Cuba & 4 other Latin Am Venues, 97-99; Alex & Carole Rosenberg Coll, Freedman Gallery, Albright Coll, Reading, PA; Sculpture of Degas Nat Mu Fine Arts, Havana Cuba, 2010; Tel Aviv Mus Art, 2010. *Pos:* Publ & ed-in-chief, Transworld Art Corp, NY, 69-88; dir & bd mem, Artist's Rights Today Inc, 76-86; dir, Alex Rosenberg Gallery, NY, 77-88; assoc dir, Snug Harbor Cult Ctr, 83-88; dir, Ardmore Affiliates Ltd, 85-; trustee, Mus Borough Brooklyn, 86-88; Abbott Group, 87-89; Neikrug-Rosenberg Assoc Inc, 89-90; adv comt mem, Hofstra Mus, 89-93; trustee, Philadelphia Coll Textiles & Sci, 91-95; dir, Tel Aviv Mus Art, 2001; chair, Salvador Dali Research Center, New York, 2006. *Teaching:* Lectr, New Sch Social Res, Parsons Div, 79-88; Appraising Modern Art, NY Univ, 92-95, Adjunct Asst Prof & Business of Appraising, 93-; vis prof, Instituto Superior de Arte, Havana, Cuba, 93-; Cencrem, Havana, Cuba, 2011. *Awards:* Alex Rosenberg Gallery-Hofstra Univ, 95; Repub Cuba-Order of Cult, 95; Graham J Littlewood Award, Philadelphia Coll Textiles & Sci, 96; Honorary fel Tel Aviv Mus Art, 2002; Silver Circle mem, Alex & Carole Rosenberg Studio, Albright Coll; Service Diploma, Nat Mus Fine Art, Havana, Cuba; Lifetime Achievement Award, Nat Arts Club, 2004; President's Award, Appraisers Assoc Amer, 2005. *Mem:* Asn Artist Run Galleries (bd dir, 79-83); Fine Arts Publ Asn (vpres & dir, formerly); Fine Arts Publ Asn (pres, 84-86); sr mem Am Soc Appraisers (bd examiners, 87-); Cert Mem, Appraisers Asn Am (vpres, 92-94, pres, 94-96); Nat Arts Club, 90-; Bd Gov, 2011; Hon Vice Pres, 2012. *Specialty:* Modern art. *Interests:* Appraising, authenticating. *Publ:* Ed, The 12 Tribes of Israel-Dali, 73, The Prophets-R Rubin, 73, Homage to Tobey, 74, Our Unfinished Revolution-Calder, 76 & An American Portrait 1776-1976, 76, Transworld Art; The Art, Science and Business of Appraising, 2000; An Approach to Advanced Problems in Appraising, 2011; Friendly Rememberances, 2012; Embracing Posthumous Bronze Sculpture, 2012. *Mailing Add:* Alex Rosenberg Fine Art and Appraisers 3 E 69th St New York NY 10021

ROSENBERG, BERNARD
PUBLISHER, BOOK DEALER
b New York, NY, Aug 2, 1938. *Study:* City Coll of New York, cert advert. *Pos:* Owner, Olana Gallery. *Res:* American art; decorative art; libr bldg consult. *Interests:* gardening, wine, photography, jewelry design. *Publ:* Auth, Olana's Guide to American Artists, A Contribution Toward a Bibliography, Olana Gallery, 2/78, supplement, vol 2, 80; Edward Shiesis Collection, Nat Gallery DC, 2010. *Mailing Add:* 2 Carillon Rd Brewster NY 10509

ROSENBERG, CAROLE HALSBAND
ART DEALER, PHILANTHROPIST
b New York, NY, Nov 16, 1936. *Study:* Hunter Col, Brooklyn Col, BA; Yeshiva Univ; New York Univ. *Exhib:* Women Beyond Borders, Havana, Cuba. *Collection Arranged:* An Am Portrait 1776-1976; Mark Tobey Retrospective (ed, catalogue), 77 & Yaacov Agam (ed, catalogue), 77; Belkis Ayon, Mass Coll Art. *Pos:* vp, Alex

Rosenberg Fine Art; pres, Am Friends of the Ludwig Found of Cuba. *Awards:* Lotos Medal of Merit, 1995; Cuba's Nat Medal for cult, 2004. *Bibliog:* Metaphor/Commentaries: Artists from Cuba, forward. *Mem:* Nat Arts Club; Women's City Club; Lotos Club; Art Table; Am Friends Ludwig Found Cuba (pres). *Specialty:* contemporary, modern, Cuban art, *Interests:* Gardening. *Collection:* Int contemporary & modern art, Cuban art. *Dealer:* Ardmore Affiliates Ltd; Rosenberg Fine Art. *Mailing Add:* 3 E 69th St New York NY 10021

ROSENBERG, CHARLES MICHAEL
HISTORIAN, EDUCATOR
b Chicago, Ill, Aug 3, 1945. *Study:* Swarthmore Col, Pa, BA, 67; Univ Mich, Ann Arbor, MA, 69, PhD, 74. *Teaching:* Asst prof renaissance art, State Univ NY, Brockport, 74-80; Prof renaissance art, Univ Notre Dame, 80-. *Awards:* Fel, Harvard Ctr, 85-86; Rome Prize, NEH, 2000-01. *Mem:* Renaissance Soc Am; Centro di Studi Europa delle Corti; Italian Art Soc; Coll Art Asn. *Res:* Renaissance patronage; portraiture; Renaissance coinage. *Publ:* Auth, Courtly decorations and the decorum of interior space, 82, Raphael and the Florentine Istoria, 86 & Borsian imagery in the heavenly zone in the Sala dei Mesi, 89; Fifteenth Century North Italian Painting & Drawing: Bibliography, GK Hall, 86; Four Este Monuments and Urban Development in Renaissance Ferrara, Cambridge Univ Press, 97; ed, The Court Cities of Northern Italy, Cambridge Univ Press, 2010. *Mailing Add:* 410 Manitou Pl South Bend IN 46616

ROSENBERG, HERB
SCULPTOR, EDUCATOR, ADMINISTRATOR
Study: Harpur Col, State Univ NY, BA; Pratt Inst, MFA; Ecole des Beaux Arts in Paris, certificate. *Exhib:* Exhibited throughout the US, England, France, Italy, Australia, Cuba, New Zealand, Hong Kong, and China; exhibitions include American Macho, Dialogue with and Ancient Forest, Working Hands, and Black Cloud Over America. *Pos:* Juror, Hong Kong Biennial. *Teaching:* Prof art, NJ City Univ, 1971-, chair, currently. *Mailing Add:* New Jersey City University Visual Arts Building Room 120 2039 Kennedy Blvd Jersey City NJ 07305-1597

ROSENBERG, JANE
ILLUSTRATOR, PAINTER
b New York, NY, Dec 7, 1949. *Study:* Beaver Col, with Jack Davis, BFA, 71; New York Univ, with Sol Lewitt, MFA, 73. *Work:* Amerada Hess, NY. *Comn:* Scenes of the Operas (notecard ser), Metrop Opera Guild, NY, 86. *Exhib:* Review, Preview, Judith Christian Gallery, NY, 81; Invitational Show, 55 Mercer Gallery, NY, 82; The Original Art: Celebrating the Fine Art of Children's Book Illustration, Master Eagle Gallery, NY, 85-86; The Art of the Fairy Tale, Every Picture Tells A Story Gallery, Los Angeles, 91; Jane Rosenberg-Theatreworks, Summerlin Libr & Performing Arts Ctr, Las Vegas, 95. *Bibliog:* Tessa Rose Chester (auth), Children's Literature, London Times, 4/11/86; San Francisco Chronicle, Bk Rev, 12/3/89; Deirdre Donahue (auth), Tune in to classical music, USA Today, 12/5/94. *Mem:* Soc of Children's Books Writers and Illustrators. *Media:* Children's Books; Watercolor, Gouache. *Specialty:* Children's book illustration. *Publ:* Auth & illusr, Dance Me a Story: Twelve Tales from the Classic Ballets, Thames & Hudson, 85; Sing Me a Story: The Metropolitan Opera's Book of Opera Stories for Children, 89; Play Me a Story: A Child's Introduction to Classical Music Through Stories and Poems, Alfred A Knopf, Inc, 94. *Dealer:* Every Picture Tells A Story: A Gallery of Original Art from Children's Books 1318 Montana Ave Santa Monica CA 90403. *Mailing Add:* 2925 Nichols Canyon Rd Los Angeles CA 90046

ROSENBERG, MARILYN R
VISUAL POET, GRAPHIC ARTIST
b Philadelphia, Pa, Oct 11, 1934. *Study:* Pratt Graphic Ctr, studied with Andrew Stasi; Empire State Coll, State Univ NY, BPS (studio art), 78; New York Univ, MA, 93. *Work:* Ohio State Univ Libr, Columbus, Ohio; King St Stephen Mus, Hungary; Tate Gallery Libr, Eng; Chelsea Sch of Art Libr, Eng; Canberra Sch Art Libr, Australia; Harvard Univ, Yale Univ Libr, Ind Univ Libr, Brown Univ Libr, Georgetown Univ Libr, Getty Rsch Inst Hist Art & Humanities, Calif; London Coll Printing; NY Pub Libr; Oberlin Coll Libr, Ohio; Mus Fine Arts, Boston; Mus Mod Art Libr, New York, NY; Rutgers Univ Libr, New Brunswick, NJ; Amherst Col Libr, Mass; Bibliotheque Nationale, Paris, France; Brooklyn Mus Libr, Brooklyn, NY; Victoria & Albert Mus National Art Libr, London Eng; Va Commonwealth Univ Cabell Libr, Richmond, Va; Everson Mus, Syracuse, NY; and many others. *Exhib:* Solo exhibs: Westchester Community Coll Gallery, Valhalla, NY, 2002; Visual Poetry/Artists' Bks, Chappaqua Libr Gallery, 2007, and others; Group exhibs: MN Ctr for Book Acts; An Am Avant Garde, Ohio State Univ Libr, Columbus, 2002; Printed and Bound, Peck Arts Ctr Gallery, Central Wyoming Coll, Reneiton, Wyo, 2003; The Book Unbound Redux, Durango Arts Ctr, Colo, 2004; New Editions, O'Hanlon Ctr Arts (with cat), Mill Valley, Calif, 2005; The Artist and the Book, Pelham Art Ctr, New York, 2006; Book Structures, Kyoto Inst Technol, 2006; Fuller Craft Mus, Brockton, Mass, 2007; Para Stamps, Budapest Mus Fine Arts, 2007; Singular Objects, Brooklyn Coll Libr, 2007; Women of the Book, 97-2003, Visual Poetry in Artists' Bks (18 titles), Brooklyn Pub Libr, Brooklyn, NY, 2008; Journeys, Treasures of Ohio State Univ Libr Special Collection, Thompson Mem Libr, Columbus, Ohio, 2009-2010; Last Vispo Prints, Lbulleria, Moscow, Russia, Windsor, Ontario, 2010; Israel-Light of the Land, Temple Israel Gallery, New Rochelle, NY, 2012; The Internat Plain Notebook Project, Beit Hair Urban Culture, Mus Tel Aviv, Israel, 2013; Prints: Nourim 3d, MN Center for the Book, 2010; The Illustrator Accordian, KBAC Gallery, Kalamazoo, Mich, 2010; Avant Writing Symposium, Columbus Exhib, Ohio State Univ, 2010; Handmade/Homemade, Pace Univ, Pleasantville, NY, 2011; Fla Atlantic Univ Lib, Boca Raton, Fla, 2011; Of Line and Form, WCC, Peekskill, NY, 2011; Language to Cover, SUNY, 2011; Apocryphal, State Univ Milledgeville, Ga, 2011-2012; Object Poems, 23 Sandy Gallery, Portland, Ore, 2011; Write Now, Chgo Cultural Ctr, Ill, 2011-2012; Triennal Visual and Experimental Poetry, Serbia, 2011; Women of the Book, Park Sch Baltimore, Md, 2011; Rejoice, Ceres Artist Friends Exhib, NY, 2012; Point of View, WC College Gallery, Peekskill, NY, 2012; Feminism and the Artists Book, Brooklyn, NY, 2012; Visual Poetry Exhib, Mount Baker, South Australia, 2012. *Teaching:* Fac, Pratt Inst, Manhattan, (Graphic Ctr), New York, 85-86; visiting artist, lectr various art insts and orgns, 85-2000; pvt teaching, 80-2013. *Bibliog:* Jason Thompson (auth), Making Journal by Hand, Rockprot Pub, 2000; Bob Grumman and Craig Hill (coauth), Writing to Be Seen, Runaway Spoon Press & Score Pub, 2001; Ori L Saltes (auth), Fixing the World, Univ Press of New England/Brondius Univ Press, 2003; Steve Miller (juror), 500 Handmade Books: Inspiring Interpretations, Lark Bks, NY, 2008; Visual Poetry in the Avant Writing Collection, Ohio State Univ, 2008; MPR (auth), Red, Otoliths, 2008; Mark Young (ed), Otoliths, Part Two, 2008; Mekal ed Anthology Spidertangle, West Leira, X exoxial ed, 2009; MRR (auth), Etceteras, Luna Bisonte Prod, 2010; MRR (auth), This is Visual Poetry, Nassance, 2010; Mark Young (ed), Otoliths Part II, 2010; Hand Made Books, Lark Studio Series, 2010; MRR with C. Mehrl (coauth), The Book of Soles, Luna Bisonte Prods, 2011; MRR (auth), NOISE, Redfoxpress, 2012; Sandra Salamony & Peter and Donna Thomas (auths), 1000 Artists' Books, Duary Books, 2012. *Media:* Artists Books, Visual Poetry. *Publ:* 7 Poets, 7 Poems: A Portfolio of Visual Poems, Hermetic Press, 94; auth & illusr, Xerolage No 25, Rumble-Strips, Xexoxial Eds, 94; contribr, Visuelle Poesie aus den USA Experimentelle Texte, Siegen Univ, Gesamthochschule, 95, Bibliophilos, Vol IV, No 3, winter 2000, Movable Stationery "Interfolds", Vol 7, No 2, May 99; contribr, (with David Cole), A Point of View, Visual Poetry: The 90's, Kaliningrad-Koenigsberg, Russia, 98; Martha Hellion (ed), Artists' Books... Vol 1 pf 2, 184 & 201, 2003; contribr, Book Arts Classified, Cover Feature, 2, Interfolds, spring 2003; contribr, Visual Poetry in the Avante Writing Collection, Ohio Univ Libr, 2008; Last Vispo Anthology: Visual Poetry, 1998-2008; Speechless 3, Alberta, Canada, pgs 8-9, 2009; Anthology Supertangle, Miekal and Xexoxial ed, pgs 56, 57, & 104, 2009; Handmade Books, Lark Studio Series (image) p. 24, NY, London, 2010; Otoleiths, Australia, pgs 76-88, 2010; Art Stamp Line, Andy Landio, Chicago, Il, 2011. *Dealer:* Printed Matter 77 Wooster St Chelsea NY 10012; Vamp and Tromp Booksellers LLC South Hall Bldg 1951 Hooper Ct Suite 105 Birmingham AL 35226-3606; Central Booking Gallery New York, NY. *Mailing Add:* 67 Lakeview Ave West Cortlandt Manor NY 10567

ROSENBERG, TERRY
PAINTER, SCULPTOR
b Hartford, Conn, 1954. *Study:* Miami-Dade Community Col, AA, 74; Univ Miami, Coral Gables, BFA, 76; NY State Coll Ceramics, Alfred Univ, MFA, 78. *Work:* Albright-Knox Art Gallery, Buffalo; Walker Art Ctr, Minneapolis; Smart Gallery, Univ Chicago; Brooklyn Mus, NY; Nelson Atkins Mus, Kansas City; Smithsonian Am Art Mus; Fine Arts Mus, San Francisco, Calif; Berkeley Art Mus, Calif; Albertina, Vienna; and others. *Exhib:* The UFO Show, Queens Mus, Flushing, NY, 82; Raw Edge: Ceramics of the 1980's, Everson Mus, Syracuse, NY, 83; Modern Masks, Whitney Mus Am Art, NY, 84; A Passionate Vision: Contemp Ceramics, DeCordova Mus, Lincoln, Mass, 84; Between Sci & Fiction, Sao Paulo Bienal, Brazil, 85; The Eloquent Object, Traveling Exhib, Philbrook Art Ctr, Tulsa, Mus Fine Arts, Boston & Oakland Mus, Calif, 86-; Solo Exhibs: Drawings Inside the Dance (auth, catalog), Sheldon Mem Art Gallery, Lincoln, Nebr, 94; Coral Springs Mus of Art, Coral Springs, Fla, 2002; Univ of Wyoming Art Mus, 2004; Laramie, WY; Berman Art Mus, Collegeville, Pa, 2005; Tenri Cult Inst NY, NYC, 2007; Museo de Arte, Contemporaneo de Yucatan, Merida, Mex, 2008, Tufts Univ Art Gallery, 2011, Centro Nacional de las Artes, Mexico City, 2012. *Awards:* Kohler Company Arts/Industry, 1979 & 1982; Award, Bemis Found, Omaha, 87; Award, NY Found Arts, 89; Nebr Arts Coun, 96. *Bibliog:* Nicholas Moufarrege (auth), Terry Rosenberg, Arts Mag, 9/82; Alan Artner (auth), Chicago Tribune, 11/26/82; Grace Glueck (auth), Terry Rosenberg, NY Times, 11/9/84; Kendall, Richard, NY Arts; Anderson, Jack, NY Times, 2001; Carpenter, Kim, NY Arts, 2006. *Media:* Oil. *Publ:* Terry Rosenberg: Drawings/Sculpture, 1984; Terry Rosenberg: Berlin/New York, 1986; Inside the Dance, Sheldon Mem Art Gallery, Lincoln, Nebr, 94; Projections, Leonardo Mag, 96; Generatrix, Uno Editions, Univ Nebr, Omaha, 96; Hypersurface Architecture II, Ad, 99; Figuring Motion: Terry Rosenberg, Smart Art Press, 2002. *Dealer:* Bette Stoler Gallery; Galerie Silvia Menzel; Nowhere Gallery Milan Italy. *Mailing Add:* 96 Grand St Apt 3F New York NY 10013-2660

ROSENBLATT, ADOLPH
PAINTER, SCULPTOR
b New Haven, Conn, 1933. *Study:* Sch Design, Yale Univ, BFA, 56, with Albers, Brooks & Marca-Relli, Peterdi, Chait. *Work:* NY Times; Libr Cong, Washington; Ft Wayne Mus Art, Ind; Carlisle Mus Art, Pa; Milwaukee Art Mus, Wis. *Exhib:* Solo exhibs, Toledo Mus Art, Ohio, 78, Minneapolis Inst Art, 82 & Tibor de Nagy Gallery, NY, 82; Cooperstown Hall of Fame, NY, 83; Haggerty Mus Art, Marquette Univ, 96; Charles Allis Art Mus, Milwaukee, 1999 & 04; Piano Gallery, Milwaukee, 2000-01; Betty Brinn Mus, Milwaukee, 2000-; Chapman Hall, Univ Wis-Milwaukee, 2000-; Artist Marketplace, Milwaukee Art Mus, 2005-2009; Rosenblatt Gallery, Milwaukee, 2007; Univ Wis, Oshkosh, 2007; Univ Wisc, Milwaukee, 2010. *Teaching:* From assoc prof to prof, Univ Wis-Milwaukee, 66-99; prof emeritus, Univ Wis-Milwaukee, 1999-. *Awards:* Wis Arts Bd, 85-86; Res Award, Univ Wis-Milwaukee, 86; Midwest Arts Grant, 95-96; Wisc Visual Art Lifetime Achievement award, 2013. *Bibliog:* Robert Berlind (auth), Adolph Rosenblatt, Art in Am, 9-10/78; Milwaukee Journal; Milwaukee Sentinel. *Mem:* Milwaukee Artists Resource Network; Allis Art Mus; Milwaukee Art Mus; Walkers Point Ctr for Art. *Media:* Polychrome, Clay. *Publ:* Auth, Book of Lithographs, Peter Deitsch Gallery, New York, 71; producer, dir & ed, Underpass (film), 74 & Daydream Diner (film), 75. *Dealer:* www.rosenblattgallery.com. *Mailing Add:* 4211 N Maryland Ave Milwaukee WI 53211

ROSENBLATT, SUZANNE MARIS
PAINTER, WRITER
b Hackensack, NJ, 1937. *Study:* Cent Sch Arts & Crafts, London, 57-58; Oberlin Col, Ohio, BA, 59; Cooper Union, 60; Art Students League, 61-63. *Work:* City Ctr, Libr Performing Art, Guggenheim Mus & Mus Mod Art, Artists Books Collections, NY. *Comn:* Courtroom drawings, WISN-TV, Milwaukee, 73-77 & Milwaukee's Pub TV, 74. *Exhib:* Solo exhibs, Oshkosh Pub Mus, Wis, 72, New York City Ctr Gallery, 76 & others; Ft Wayne Mus Art, Ind, 76; Performing Arts Ctr, Milwaukee, 76-87; Long Island Univ, Brooklyn, NY, 80; Gallery Wis Art, 92; Piano Gallery, Milwaukee, 2000-01; Charles Allis Art Mus, Milwaukee, Wis, 2004; Artist Marketplace, Milwaukee Art Mus, 2005-2009; Univ Wis, Oshkosh, 2007; Univ Wis, Whitewater, 2007; Rosenblatt Gallery, Milwaukee, 2007-. *Teaching:* Artreach, 1989-98. *Awards:* Hon Mention, Media Am, Seattle, Wash, 75; Artreach Teaching Grants, Junior League, 89 & 94, Milwaukee Found, 90, Bader Found, 93 & Poets & Writers, 94; Taparts Grant, 94. *Bibliog:* Donald Key (auth), Show of painted people shadowed by circus, Milwaukee J, 71; Edith Brin (auth), Milwaukee J, 91; Harvey Taylor (auth), Shepherd Express, 91. *Mem:* Milwaukee Artists Resource Network; Wis Painters & Sculptors; Milwaukee Earth Poets; Grass Roots. *Media:* Acrylic, Ink. *Interests:* Tai chi; environmental causes; dance; gardening. *Publ:* Producer, dir & ed, Animated film paintings & drawings of dancers, 76; auth, Memorandance, Marcel Dekker, 78; Changes in the Lake, 82; Some Poems, 87; Shorelines, Gallery of Wis Art, 91; illus in On the Waterbed They Sank To Their Own Levels, Carnegie Mellon, 2000; illus, One Season Behind Carnegie Mellon, 2007; Three Ladies in Their Eighties, 2011. *Dealer:* www.rosenblattgallery.com. *Mailing Add:* 4211 N Maryland Ave Milwaukee WI 53211

ROSENFELD, RICHARD JOEL
DEALER
b Philadelphia, Pa, May 31, 1940. *Study:* Pratt Inst, New York, MFA, 64; Univ Pa, Philadelphia & Pa Acad Fine Art (coordinated prog), BFA, 62. *Pos:* Mgr, Artists Galleries, Cheltenham, Pa, 67-72; co-dir, Longman Gallery, Pa, 72-75; dir-owner, Rosenfeld Gallery, Philadelphia, Pa, 76-. *Teaching:* Instr painting & art hist, Perkiomen Sch, Pennsburg, Pa, 63-65. *Bibliog:* Susan Perloff (auth), article, Pa Gazette, 6/77. *Mem:* Fel Pa Acad Fine Arts. *Specialty:* Contemporary art, all media including crafts. *Mailing Add:* Rosenfeld Gallery 113 Arch St Philadelphia PA 19106

ROSENFELD, SAMUEL L
ART DEALER, APPRAISER
b New York, NY, July 27, 1931. *Study:* Univ Pa, BS, 51; Harvard Univ, MBA, 53. *Pos:* Owner, Rosenfeld Fine Art, New York, currently. *Awards:* Pres Award, Appraisers Asn Am, 2008. *Mem:* Appraisers Asn Am (cert life mem). *Specialty:* American art in the realist & modernist tradition in all media, mainly from 1910 to World War II emphasizing the WPA period, the Eight & Ash Can school. *Collection:* Modern American realists, especially WPA period; Trench art; Rogers groups; Doulton Lambeth stoneware pottery; cast iron boot jacks. *Mailing Add:* Rosenfeld Fine Art 300 E 56th St #33C New York NY 10022

ROSENFELD, SARENA
PAINTER
b Elmira, NY, Oct 17, 1940. *Study:* Otis Art Inst, currently; Idylwild Sch Music & Art, currently. *Work:* Tishman Corp, Los Angeles; Ruhr Univ Bochum, Ger; South Africa Asn Arts South Transual, Johannesburg; Univeritatlinikum Benjamin Franklin, Berlin, Ger; Gallery 444, San Francisco; Home Art Corp. *Exhib:* Gallery 444, San Francisco; Coda Gallery, Palm Desert, Calif; Carmel by the Sea, Gallery Diamonte. *Awards:* Tapestry in Talent, San Jose Arts Coun, 89; Best of Show, Glendale Reg Arts Coun, 95; Sweepstakes Award, Santa Monica Arts Coun, 98. *Bibliog:* Michael Colbruno (auth), Fauvism Live at Robert Dana Gallery, San Francisco Sentinel, 91; Chris Culwell (auth), Wild about Sarena, San Francisco Sentinel, 92; Patrick Lagreca (auth), On the Wall & Off the Wall, Marina Union, 98. *Mem:* Nat Mus Women Arts, Washington, DC. *Media:* Oils on canvas. *Specialty:* figurative expressionism. *Interests:* Volunteer animal keeper, Los Angeles Zoo. *Collection:* Robert Gore Rifkind. *Dealer:* Gallery 444 Post St San Francisco CA 94102; CODA Gallery Palm Desert CA; Gallery Diamonte Carmel By the Sea CA. *Mailing Add:* 6570 Kelvin Ave Canoga Park CA 91306

ROSENFELD, SHARON
PAINTER
b New York, NY, Apr 8, 1954. *Study:* Pratt Inst, BFA, 77; NY Univ, MA, 83. *Work:* Mus Nat Arts Found, NY. *Exhib:* Solo exhibs, 80 Washington Sq E Gallery, NY, 83, Mead Data Cent, Pan Am, NY, 90, Mighael Ingbar, NY, 91, Righetti Knie Fine Arts Trading, Muri-Bern, Switz, 92, Century Galleries, Henley on Thames, Eng, 92 & Gallery Galimberti, Vaduz, Liechtenstien, 92; State of the Art, Boston, 93; Art Addiction (with catalog), Stockholm, Sweden, 93; Le Livre d'or des Collectionneurs et Amateurs d'Art, Paris, 93; Jadite Gallery, NY, 96; Martha's Vineyard, Old Sculpting Gallery, 96; Mayer, Brown & Platt, NY, 97; Sylvia White Gallery, NY, 98; and others. *Awards:* Ford Found Studio Art Award, 77; Artist in Residence Grant, Millay Colony Arts, 85. *Media:* Acrylic on Linen, Watercolor. *Publ:* Reviews, Arts Mag, 4/84; Contribr, Profile, Manhattan Arts, 6/89; Le Livre d'or des Collectionneuers et Amateurs d'Art, Paris, 93. *Dealer:* Sylvia White Gallery 560 Broadway New York NY 10012. *Mailing Add:* 16 E 96th St Apt 4B New York NY 10128

ROSENFIELD, JOHN M
EDUCATOR, CURATOR
b Dallas, Tex, Oct 9, 1924. *Study:* Univ Calif, Berkeley, BA, 45; Univ Iowa, Iowa City, MFA, 49; Harvard Univ, PhD, 59. *Collection Arranged:* Japanese Art of Heian Period (auth, catalog), Asia House, NY, 67; Traditions of Japanese Art (auth, catalog), Fogg Mus, Harvard, 70; Courtly Tradition in Japanese Art & Literature (coauth, catalog), Fogg Mus, Harvard, 73; Journey of the Three Jewels (coauth, catalog), Asia House, NY, 79; Masters of Japanese Calligraphy (coauth, catalog), Japan Soc, NY, 84. *Pos:* Cur Asian art, Fogg Art Mus, Cambridge, Mass, 76-91; actg dir, Harvard Univ Art Mus, 82-85. *Teaching:* Asst prof oriental art, Univ Calif, Los Angeles, 57-60; prof E Asian art, Harvard Univ, Cambridge, Mass, 65-91, emer prof, 91-. *Awards:* Order of the Rising Son, Japan, 88; Distinguished Teaching Award, Coll Art Asn, 94. *Publ:* Auth, Dynastic Arts of the Kushans, Univ Calif, 67; ed, Song of the Brush: Japanese Paintings from the Sanso Collecion, Seattle Art Mus, 79; coauth, The Japanese Courtier: Painting, Calligraphy and Poetry from the Fogg Art Mus, The Philip Hofer Collection, Santa Barbara Mus Art, 80; Masters of Japanese Calligraphy 8th-19th Century, Japan Soc, NY, 84; Extraordinary Persons: Works by Eccentric, non-conformist Japanese Artists. *Mailing Add:* Harvard Univ Dept History of Art and Architecture Cambridge MA 02138

ROSENSAFT, JEAN BLOCH
CURATOR, MUSEUM DIRECTOR
b New York, NY, Jan 6, 1954. *Study:* Barnard Col, BA, 73; New York Univ Inst Fine Arts, 73-77. *Collection Arranged:* The Eichmann Trial, Chagall and the Bible, Justice in Jerusalem Revisited, Jewish Mus, 86, 87; David Newman, Ran Oron, Rage/Resolution, Rebirth After the Holocaust: The Bergen-Belsen Displaced Persons Camp, 45-50, Hebrew Union Col, Jewish Inst Relig, 95, 96, 97, 2000. *Pos:* Spec asst publs, Mus Mod Art, New York, 83-84; dir pub progs, Jewish Mus, New York, 84-86, asst dir educ, 86-89; exhib dir, Hebrew Union Col-Jewish Inst Relig, 94; mus dir, Hebrew Union Col, Jewish Inst Relig Mus, 2000. *Teaching:* Gallery lectr modern art, Mus Mod Art, New York, 77-80, Nat Endowment Arts lectr (collections), 79-80, spec asst independent sch prog, 80-83. *Bibliog:* Chagall & the Bible, 87; Maty Grunberg: Selected Works, 1966-2006; Vision of Sigmund R Balka, 2006. *Mem:* Chmn, UJA Womens Task Force Arts Comt, 95; Coun Jewish Am Mus (officer, 96-2001). *Specialty:* Contemporary art. *Publ:* Auth, Giorgio De Chirico, Mus Mod Art, 82; Chagall and the Bible, Universe Books, 87; ed, The Collectors Room: Selections from the Steinhardt Collection, 93, David Newman - Breaking the Tablets, 95 & Ran Oron - Planes, 96, Hebrew Union Col-Jewish Inst Relig; 30 Pieces/30 Years, Sculpture by Ann Sperry, 2003; auth, Archie Rand: The 19 Paintings, 2004; Aliza Olmert: Tikkun, 2005; Carol Hamoy: Psalm Song, Journey Through Jerusalem, 2005; Vision/Action: Designers of the Next Generation, 2006; Tamar Hirschl: Cultural Alarm, 2006; Judy Chicago: Jewish Identity, 2007; The Eye of the Collector: The Jewish Vision of Sigmund R. Balka, 2006; The L.A. Story, 2007; Paul Weissman (auth), Elements of Alchemy: Prints, 2007. *Mailing Add:* Hebrew Union College Jewish Inst Religion 1 W 4th St New York NY 10012

ROSENTHAL, DEBORAH MALY
PAINTER, EDUCATOR
b New York, NY, Jan 16, 1950. *Study:* Smith Col, with Leonard Baskin, 66-68; Barnard Col, BA, 71; Pratt Inst, with George MacNeil, MFA, 74; Queens Col, with Ilya Bolotowsky, 74. *Comn:* Stained Glass Windows, Ansche Chesed Congregation, NY. *Exhib:* Solo exhibs incl Bowery Gallery, NY, 86, 87, 91, 93, 96, 99, Eve's Vocabulary, Hebrew Union Col, NY, 99, others. *Pos:* Critic, Arts, Artforum & New York Arts J, 75-; artist & cur, Cult Coun Fedn, 78-80. *Teaching:* Guest lectr, Queens Col, Univ NH & Parsons Col, 77-; lectr, Sch Visual Arts, New York, 80-82; fac mem, New Sch Social Res, 81-; prof of art, Rider U, Lawrenceville, NJ; guest lectr Sch of the Art Inst of Chicago, Am Univ. *Awards:* Critic's Award, Nat Endowment Arts, 79-80. *Mem:* Coll Art Asn; Int Asn Art Critics. *Media:* Oil. *Publ:* Auth, Metaphor in Painting, 78, auth, The lesson of the master: Paul Klee, 78, auth, Interview with Andre Masson, 80 & coauth, Zone painting, 81, Arts Mag; auth, Ilya Bolotowsky, Harry N Abrams, 82. *Dealer:* Bowery Gallery New York NY. *Mailing Add:* 250 W 85th St No 5D New York NY 10024

ROSENTHAL, DONALD A
HISTORIAN, CRITIC
b Jersey City, NJ, Oct 7, 1942. *Study:* Yale Univ, BA; Princeton Univ; Hunter Coll, MA; Columbia Univ, MPhil, PhD. *Collection Arranged:* Charlotte Dorrance Wright Collection, Philadelphia Mus Art, 78; George Eastman Collection, Mem Art Gallery, Rochester, 79; Monet in London, High Mus Art, Atlanta, 88; Thomas Cornell: Paintings, Bowdoin Coll Mus Art, 90; Latin Am Colonial Art from the Mabee-Gerrer Mus, Chapel Art Ctr, 94; Carl Barnas 1879-1953; Crossing Continents, Chapel Art Ctr, 2000. *Pos:* Res asst, Metrop Mus Art, New York, 74-77; asst cur Europ painting, Philadelphia Mus Art, 77-79; cur collections, Mem Art Gallery, Rochester, NY, 79-85; chief cur & cur europ art, High Mus Art, Atlanta, 86-89; assoc dir, Bowdoin Coll Mus Art, 89-91; dir, Chapel Art Ctr, St Anselm Coll, Manchester, NH, 91-2001; critic, Art New Eng, Boston, 2001-. *Bibliog:* An Arcadian Photographer in Manhattan: Edward Mark Slocum, Callum James Books, 2012. *Mem:* Coll Art Asn; Int Coun Mus; Phi Beta Kappa. *Res:* European art of the 18th & 19th centuries; history of photography. *Publ:* Géricault's Expenses for The Raft of the Medusa, Art Bull, 80; Orientalism: The Near East in French Painting, 1800-1880, 82 & La Grande Manière: Historical and Religious Painting in France, 1700-1800, 87, Rochester; The Photographs of Frederick Rolfe, Baron Corvo, 1860-1913, Asphodel Ed, 2008. *Mailing Add:* 2050 Massachusetts Ave #306 Cambridge MA 02140

ROSENTHAL, JUDITH-ANN SAKS See Saks, Judith-Ann (Judith-Ann Saks Rosenthal)

ROSENTHAL, MARK L
CURATOR, HISTORIAN
b Philadelphia, Pa, Aug 9, 1945. *Study:* Temple Univ, AB, 63; Univ Iowa, MA, 71, PhD, 79. *Collection Arranged:* Andre, Buren, Irwin, Nordman: Space as Support (auth, catalog), 79; Franz Marc (auth, catalog), 79; Neil Jenney (auth, catalog), 81; Juan Gris (auth, catalog), 83-84; Jonathan Borofsky (auth, catalog), 84-85; Anselm Kiefer (auth, catalog), 87-88; Joseph Johns (auth, catalog), 88-89. *Pos:* Assoc cur, Wadsworth Atheneum, Hartford, Conn, 74-76; cur collections, Univ Art Mus, Berkeley, Calif, 76-83; cur 20th century art, Philadelphia Mus Art, Pa, 83-, Nat Gallery Art, Washington, DC & Solomon R Guggenheim Mus, NY, 97-; cur, 20th

century art, Nat Gallery Art, Washington, DC; cur, 20th century art, Solomon R Guggenheim Mus, NY, currently. *Mem:* Coll Art Asn. *Res:* Various topics in twentieth century art. *Publ:* Auth, Paul Klee, Phillips Collection, 81; The prototypical triangle of Paul Klee, 82 & Picasso's night fishing at Antibes, 83, Art Bulletin; auth, Picasso's night fishing at Antibes, Art Bulletin, 83. *Mailing Add:* c/o Solomon R Guggenheim Mus 1071 5th Ave New York NY 10128

ROSENZWEIG, DAPHNE LANGE
HISTORIAN, MUSEUM CONSULTANT
b Evanston, Ill, July 7, 1941. *Study:* Mt Holyoke Col, AB; Columbia Univ, MA & PhD; Univ Wis; Corcoran Sch Art; Fulbright Fel, Nat Palace Mus, Taiwan. *Collection Arranged:* Art of the Orient: Eighth Century to the Present; Fine Arts Group Collection of Later Chinese Painting (with catalog), 94; Yangtze River Collection of Later Chinese Jade (with catalog), 95; Power and Pride in Later Korean Painting, 96. *Pos:* Owner, Rosenzweig Assoc Inc (personal property appraisals); Bd mem, vis collections committee, Morikami Mus Japanese Art; bd dirs, Int Soc Appraisers, 2007. *Teaching:* Lectr Oriental art, Univ NMex, Albuquerque, 69-73; asst prof Oriental art, Oberlin Col, 73-77; asst prof, Univ SFla, 78-94; from inst to prof Art hist, Ringling Coll Art & Design, 92-. *Mem:* Fla Token Kai; Coll Art Asn; Royal Asiatic Soc, Seoul; Int Soc Appraisers. *Res:* Painting the Qing Dynasty of China, with emphasis on court painting and modern Chinese jades; Japanese prints, Korean painting. *Collection:* Chinese paintings, Oriental ceramics; modern Japanese prints. *Publ:* Reassessment of Painters and Paintings at the Early Ch'ing Court, Artists and Patrons: Some Social and Economic Aspects of Chinese Painting, Univ Wash Press, 89; auth, A Chinese Chronology & Appraisal of Chinese Jade, Jade, Anness Publ & Nostrand-Reinhold, 92; coauth, Collection of the Museum of Fine Arts, St Petersburg, Fla, 93; auth, The Paintings of Cheng Haw-chien, Taipei, 94; Appraisal of Japanese Prints (3rd edition). *Mailing Add:* Ringling Coll of Art & Design 2700 N Tamiami Tr Sarasota FL 34234

ROSENZWEIG, PHYLLIS D
CURATOR
b Brooklyn, NY, Dec 27, 1943. *Study:* Hunter Col, City Univ New York, BA, 64; Inst Fine Arts, New York, MA, 95. *Collection Arranged:* The Thomas Eakins Collection (auth, catalog), Hirshhorn Mus & Sculpture Garden, Smithsonian Inst, Washington, 77, Arshile Gorky: The Hirshhorn Mus & Sculpture Garden Collection, 79; The Fifties: Aspects of Painting in New York, 80; Larry Rivers, The Hirshhorn Mus and Sculpture Garden Collection, 81; Directions 83 & 86; Content: A Contemporary Focus, 84; Sol Lewitt Works, 87; Directions: Sherrie Levine, 88; Krzysztof Wodiczko Works, 88; Daniel Buren Works, 89; Directions, Susana Solano, 89; Lawrence Weiner Works, 90; Thomas Struth: Mus Photographs, 92; Joseph Kosuth Works, 92; Glenn Ligon: To Disembark, 93; Cindy Sherman: Film Stills, 95; Byron Kim: Grey-Green, 96; Kiki Smith:Night, 97; Directions: Dana Hoey, 2001; Directions Marina Abramovic-The Hero, 2002; Directions: Gabriel Oruzco-Photographs, 2004. *Pos:* Curatorial asst, Hirshhorn Mus & Sculpture Garden, 71-76, assoc cur, 76-00; curator, works on paper, 2000-. *Mem:* Coll Art Asn. *Res:* contemp and modern prints, drawings, and photos. *Mailing Add:* Hirshhorn Mus & Sculpture Garden Smithsonian Inst MRC 350 PO Box 37012 Washington DC 20013-7012

ROSER, CE (CECILIA)
PAINTER, VIDEO ARTIST
b Philadelphia, Pa. *Study:* Hochschule Fur Bildende Kunste, Berlin, Ger, 52-53. *Work:* Guggenheim Mus, NY; Mus Mod Art, NY; Brooklyn Mus, NY; Nat Mus Art, Washington, DC; The Brit Mus, London, Great Britain; Newark Mus Art, NJ; Bibilotheque Nat, Paris, France; Herbert F Johnson Mus; Ithaca NY Heckscher Mus, Huntington, NY; NJ State Mus; Bronx Mus, New York; Jacksonville Mus Mod Art, Fla; and others. *Comn:* Stained Glass Windows, Irwin Residence, East Hampton, NY. *Exhib:* Int Watercolor Biennial, Brooklyn Mus, 63; Women Choose Women, NY Cult Ctr, 73; Works on Paper/Women Artists, Brooklyn Mus, 75; Art & Poetry, Tweed Mus Art, Duluth, Minn, 77; New Acquisitions, Guggenheim Mus, 82; Am Abstr Artists, Bronx Mus, 86; New Spaces/New Faces, East Hampton Guild Hall Mus, 87; Int traveling exhib Tikanoja, Rovaniemi & Josensuu Art Mus, Finland, 88-92; Ulrich Mus, Witchita, Kans, 92; Baruch Coll, NYC, 96; Hillwood Art Mus, Brookville, NY, 2000; Hamptons Art Hist Gallery, Hampton, NY, 2001; Hunterdon Mus, Clifton, NJ, 2004; Missoula Art Mus, Mont, 2005; Feminist Film Festival, Ceres Gallery, NYC, 2006; St Peter's Coll Art Gallery, NJ, 2007; plus many others. *Pos:* Producer & pres, Artists Video Arch, New York, 77-; juror, Women Choose Women Show, NY Cult Center, 1973; found Women in the Arts (first exec & coordr), 1974-1976; lectr, Douglas Coll, NJ, 1975; moderator, Conferences Panel, Southampton Coll, 1994. *Awards:* Honoree Medal Veteran Feminist of Am, 2003. *Bibliog:* Rosemary Daniell (auth), Elegant explosions East and West mingle in Roser act, Atlanta Constitution, Ga, 7/5/67; Lane Dunlop (auth), article, 9/77 & Joan Marter (auth), article, 2/80, Arts Mag; Talks with Women Artists Vol II, Scarecrow Press, 96; Women Artists Series-25 yrs, Rutger Univ, NJ, 96; plus others. *Mem:* Founder Women in the Arts (first exec-coordr, 74-76, bd mem at large, 76-78); Women's Caucus for Art; Am Abstr Artists. *Media:* Oil, Watercolor; Collage. *Publ:* Works on Paper, Women Artists, Brooklyn Mus, NY, 75; producer, narration: The Circle of Charmion von Wiegand (video Documentary), 78; On Edge, Am Abstract Artists, 2006. *Mailing Add:* 355 Riverside Dr New York NY 10025

ROSS, CHARLES
ENVIRONMENTAL ARTIST, SCULPTOR
b Philadelphia, Pa, Dec 17, 1937. *Study:* Univ Calif, AB, 60, MA, 62. *Work:* Centre Pompidou; Whitney Mus Am Art; French Ministry of Culture; Indianapolis Mus Art; Walker Art Ctr, Minneapolis; Los Angeles Co Mus Art, Calif; Lannan Found, Mus NMex; Frederick A Weisman Mus, Minneapolis, Minn; French Min of Culture; Nat Mus Am Indian, Smithsonian Inst. *Comn:* Dwan Light Sanctuary, United World Col, Montezuma, NMex; Cook Inst, Grand Rapids, Mich; Plaza of the Americas, Dallas; Solar Spectrum, Harvard Bus Sch Chapel; Year of Solar Burns, Chateau D'Oiron, France; Saitama Univ, Japan; US Fed Courthouse, Tampa, Fla; Meiji Univ, Tokyo; Nat Mus Am Indians; Highlands Univ, Las Vegas, NMex. *Exhib:* Renwick Gallery, Smithsonian, Washington, DC; Stadtizches Mus, W Ger; Centre Georges Pompidou, Paris, 77; Albright Knox, Buffalo; Hirshhorn Mus, Washington, DC; Mus Contemp Art, Chicago; Yale Univ Art Gallery; Stadtisches Mus, WGer; Mus Fine Arts, Boston; solo exhibs, Richard Humphrey Gallery, NY, 95 & Mus d'Arte y Diseno Contemporaneo, San Jose, Costa Rica, 96; NTT Intercomm Ctr, Tokyo, 97; Lyon Biennal, Lyon, France, 2000; Chiaroscuro Gallery, Santa Fe, NMex, 2004; Harwood Mus Art, Taos, NMex, 2004-2005; Artempo Palazzo Fortuny, Venice, Italy, 2007; Braunstein/Quay Gallery, San Francisco, Calif, 2007. *Teaching:* Assoc prof, Cornell Univ, 64; instr, Univ Calif, 65, Sch Visual Arts, New York, 67, 70 & 71 & Herbert Lehman Coll, 68; adj prof, Coll Santa Fe, NMex, 94-2007. *Awards:* Am Inst Graphic Arts Award, 76; Boston Soc Architects, 92; Interfaith Forum Relig Art & Archit, 92; NCAA Award Distinction, 97; Washington Bldg Cong Award, Spectrum 8, Nat Mus Am Indian (NMAI), 2005. *Bibliog:* Patrick Werkner (auth), Star Axis, Diadelos, 6/15/93; Giles Tiberghein (auth), Land Art, C Eds, Carre, Paris, 93, Princeton Archit Press, 95; Baile Oaks (auth), Sculpting with the Environment, Int Thomson Publ Inc, London, pages 46-55, 95; Jan Adlmann, Contemporary New Mexico Artists: Sketches & Schemas, Craftsman House, Australia, 96; Harold Linton (auth), Color in Architecture, McGraw-Hill, 99; Anne-Marie Charbonneaux and Norbert Hillaire (eds), Architectures de Luriere, Marvel, 2000; Jean-Herbert Martin (auth), Le Chateau d'Oiron, Editions du Patrimoine, 2000; Amy Dempsy (auth), Destination Art, Univ Calif Press, Thames & Hudson, 2006; Michael Lailach (auth), Land Art, Taschen, 2007. *Publ:* Auth, Sunlight Convergence-Solar Burn, Univ Utah Press, 76; Charles Ross: The Cosmos, Architecture, 5/84; Sculpting the Environment-A Natural Dialogue, Van Nostrand & Rienhold, 94; Ben Tufnell (auth), Land Art, Tate Publ, 2007. *Dealer:* Loic Malle 167 Blvd Haussmann Paris France 75008

ROSS, CONRAD H
PAINTER, PRINTMAKER
b Chicago, Ill, Apr 26, 1931. *Study:* Univ Ill, BFA, 53; Univ Chicago, 54; Univ Iowa, MFA, 59; Masereel Ctr Graphic Arts, Kasterlee, Belg, 87, 92 & 95, Fulbright Summer Seminar in China, 93. *Work:* Libr Cong, Washington; Springfield Art Mus, Mo; Norfolk Mus Arts & Sci, Va; Dallas Mus Fine Arts, Tex; Macon Mus Arts & Sci, Ga; Mus Tex Tech Univ, Lubbock, Texas. *Exhib:* Solo exhibs, Augusta Coll, Ga, 79, Univ Ctr Gallery, Huntsville, Ala, 96, Malone Univ, Troy, Ala, 98 & Jacksonville State Univ, Ala, 99, China On My Mind, Wiregrass Mus of Fine Arts, Dothan, Ala, 2009, Temessee Valley Art Asn, 2010; Southeastern Graphics Invitational, 81; Art Dept Gallery, Jacksonville State Univ, Ala, 85; Exhib US-UK Print Connection, An Int Exchange, Los Angeles Printmakers Soc & Printmakers Coun Great Brit, 88-89; Artsplosure, Raleigh, NC, 89; Artist Selects, Comer Art Mus, Sylacauga, Ala, 89; Through the Yrs, Drawing, Painting, Prints, Chattahoochee Valley Art Mus, LaGrange, Ga, 2003. *Pos:* Bd dir, Southeastern Coll Art Conf, 79-82; publ, Wycross Press, 89-. *Teaching:* Instr drawing, design, lettering & art appreciation, La Polytech Inst, 61-63; asst prof drawing & printmaking, Auburn Univ, 63-81, assoc prof, 81-83, prof, 83-97, prof emer art, 97-; vis lectr drawing & printmaking, Kans Univ, 68; instr, Arrowmont Sch Arts & Crafts, Gatlinburg, Tenn, 83; artist-in-residence, Univ Ga Summer Abroad Prog, Cortona, Italy, 84. *Awards:* Louis Comfort Tiffany Found Grant printmaking, 60; Auburn Univ Res Grant-in-Aid, 65-68, 70 & 73; Purchase Award, LaGrange Nat II, Prints and Drawings, Ga, 75; Tech Asst Grant, Ala State Arts Coun, 97; 35th Ann Montgomery Art Guild Mus Exhib Award, Montgomery Mus Fine Arts, 2003; Best of Show, Tenn Valley Art Asn Exhib S, 2005; and others. *Bibliog:* Stevens Seaberg (auth), The Daemons Face: An Artists Discovery of the Metaphors of Child Abuse, Vol 28, Leonardo; Noble Press, Vol XXII No 4, The Print Collectors Newsletter, 9-10/91; The China Collés, Vol 22 issue No 1, Auburn Circle, winter 96; Jason Nix (auth), Fine Print, Opelika, Auburn News, 9/04; Wycross Press, The Jour of the Mid Am Print Coun, Vol 11, 1, Spring/Summer, 2005; Wellbeing..., Jour of the Print World, page 15, Spring, 2005. *Mem:* Ala Art League (pres, 78-80); Southern Graphics Coun (vpres, 78-80); Coll Art Asn Am. *Media:* Oil, Intaglio. *Publ:* Contribr, Artists' Proof the annual of prints and printmaking, 70; The monoprint and the monotype: a case of semantics, Art Voices/South, 78/79; Approaches to Drawing: Activity in the Southeast, SECAC Rev, 81; auth, Perceptual Drawing, A Handbook for the Practitioner, Edwin Mellon Press, NY, 2011; auth, Reconsidering Regionalism, Prints Inspired by the South, 1951-2011 (exhib catalog), Jule Collins Smith Mus Fine Art, Auburn Univ, 2011. *Mailing Add:* 447 Wrights Mill Rd Auburn AL 36830-5914

ROSS, DAVID ANTHONY
MUSEUM DIRECTOR
b New York, NY, Apr 26, 1949. *Study:* Syracuse Univ, BS, 71. *Collection Arranged:* Traveling exhib, Circuit: A Video Invitational (survey of video art, 68-72), 72-74; Southland Video Anthology (survey of video art in Southern Calif, 68-75, with catalog), Long Beach Mus Art, 75 & 77; Richard Avedon: Retrospective, Univ Art Mus, Berkeley, 80; Inst Contemp Art, Boston, 82-84 & 86; The BiNational: Am and German Art of the Late 80's, Inst Contemp Art, Boston & Kunsthale, Dusseldorf, 89-98; Between Spring and Summer: Soviet Conceptual Art in the Era of Late Communism (traveling exhib), Inst Contemp Art, Boston, Tacoma Art Mus, Wash & Des Moines Arts Ctr, Iowa, 90; William Wegman, Kunstmuseum Lucerne & Whitney Mus Am Art, 91-92; Multiple Identity (traveling exhib), Whitney Mus Am Art, NY, Nat Gallery, Athens, Greece, Contemp Art Mus, Barcelona, Spain, Kunst Mus, Bonn, Ger & Costello de Rivoli, Turin, 96-97; Bill Viola: a 25 Year Survey (traveling), Whitney Mus Am Art, NY, 98-99; Diebenkorn, San Francisco Mus Modern Art, Calif, 98-99. *Pos:* Asst dir, Everson Mus Art, Syracuse, 71-72, cur video arts, 71-74; deputy dir TV & film, Long Beach Mus Art, 74-77; chief cur, Univ Art Mus, Univ Calif, Berkeley, 77-81; dir, Sam Rayburn House, Bonham, Tex, formerly, Boston Inst Contep Art, 82-91, Whitney Mus Am Art, NY, 91-98 & San Francisco Mus Mod Art, 98-. *Teaching:* Lectr video performance, San Francisco Art Inst, 70-82; lectr video art, Grad Sch, Univ Calif, San Diego, 74-82; lectr, Calif Col Arts and Crafts, 82, Harvard Univ, 83-91 & Sch Art, Columbia Univ, NY, 97-98. *Awards:* John D Rockefeller III Found Res Study Grant, 74. *Mem:* Am Asn Mus; Advocates for Arts; Am Asn Mus Dirs; Trustee, Tiffany Found, NY. *Res:* Relationship between development of new art

and context that supports art in American society and development of new support structures. *Publ:* Coauth, Douglas Davis: Videotapes, Manifestos, Drawings and Objects, 72; Frank Gillette: Video Process & Metaprocess, 73; Nam June Paik: Video & Videology, 74; Peter Campus: Video Works, 74; auth, Southland Video Anthology, 75 & 76-77. *Mailing Add:* San Francisco Mus Modern Art 151 Third St San Francisco CA 94103-3159

ROSS, DOUGLAS ALLAN
PAINTER, PRINTMAKER
b Los Angeles, Calif, Jan 23, 1937. *Study:* Carleton Col, BA, 59; Minneapolis Coll Art & Design, 59-61; Univ Minn, MFA, 65. *Work:* The Weisman Art Mus; Ill State Univ, Normal; Sheldon Art Gallery, Lincoln, Nebr; Prudential-Bache Securities, NY; McDonalds Corp, Chicago, Ill; Price, Waterhouse, Cooper, Minneapolis, Minn; DeLoitte & Touche, Lincoln, Nebraska; The Brunswick Corp, Lake Forest, Ill. *Exhib:* Okla State Univ, Stillwater, 88; 20th Ann Joslyn Biennial, Joslyn Art Mus, Omaha, Nebr, 88; Cent Time Zone Sculpture Exhib, Nebr Wesleyan Univ, Lincoln, 89; 6th Ann Exhib, Kansas City Artists Coalition, Mo, 89; 60th Ann Exhib, Art Asn Harrisburg, Pa, 89; 12th Ann Art Exhib, Milford Fine Arts Coun, Conn, 89; Chicago Int New Art Forms, Navy Pier, Chicago, 89; Sculpture Now, Spokane Ctr Gallery, Wash, 89; solo exhibs, Drury Col, Springfield, Mo, 90, Eastern Mont Col, Billings, 90, MC Gallery, Minneapolis, Minn, 90 & Ralston Fine Arts, Johnson City, Tenn, 91; MAA Juried Art Exhib, Midland, Tex, 2003; 12th Nat Northern Colo Art Asn, Ft Collins Co, 2003; Frank Stone Gallery, Minn, 2005; 19th Northern Nat, Rhinelander, Wis, 2006; Univ Mich Health Serv, Ann Arbor, Mich, 2010; Abbot Northwestern Hosp, Minneapolis, 2014. *Collection Arranged:* First Great Plains sculpture Exhib, Sheldon Mem Art Gallery, Lincoln, Nebr, 75; Drawings by Sculptors, SW Mo State Univ, 75 & Syracuse Univ, NY, 76; Second Ann Great Plains Sculpture Exhib, Sheldon Mem Art Gallery, 76; Nebr Alumni, Nebr Mus Fine Arts, 76. *Teaching:* From asst prof to prof emeritus sculpture/drawing, Univ Nebr, Lincoln, 66-79; lectr grade II sculpture, Manchester Polytech, Eng, 69-70. *Awards:* Purchase Award, solo exhib, Muhlenberg Coll, 76; Juror's Award, NJ Ctr Arts, 90; First Prize, Greater Midwest Int III, Warrensburg, Mo, 90; Award Merit, Anderson Winter Show, Ind, 93; Benefactor's Award, 19th Northern Nat Rhinelander, Wis, 2006. *Mem:* Mid-Am Coll Art Asn (prog dir & exhib dir, 75-76). *Media:* Mixed

ROSS, JAIME
GRAPHIC ARTIST, PAINTER
b New Haven, Conn, Aug 14, 1946. *Study:* Princeton Univ; Univ Colo, BA, 69, MFA, 71, studied with Roland Reiss and George Woodman. *Work:* Oslo Fine Arts Mus, Norway; Alvord Mus Fine Art, Portugal; Univ Colo, Boulder; Los Angeles Inst Contemp Art. *Comn:* Billboard, ABC Records, Los Angeles, 76; mural, Fiat, Milan, 78; distributional sculpture, Alvord Inst, Oporto, Portugal, 84; mural, Santa Fe Pub Schs, 85 & NMex Arts Comn, Ojo Caliente, NMex, 86. *Exhib:* Wit and Whimsey, Cambridge Mus Fine Arts, Eng, 77; Small Wonders, Univ BC, Vancouver, 81; Contemp Cartoons, Lisbon Fine Arts Mus, Portugal, 84; Western States Biennial, Fine Arts Mus NMex, Santa Fe, 82; Color, Oslo Fine Arts Mus, Norway, 83. *Pos:* Artist-in-residence, NMex Arts Comn, 85-86; painter, designer & illusr for various ad agencies, animation studios & mags, Los Angeles, 76-78. *Teaching:* Instr painting & drawing, Univ Ill, 71-72; instr painting, Univ Colo, 75. *Media:* All. *Dealer:* Ed Thomas Fine Art Taos NM; El Zocalo Santa Fe NM. *Mailing Add:* Catchwater Farm PO Box 44 Carson NM 87517

ROSS, JAMES MATTHEW AKIBA
ASSEMBLAGE ARTIST, PHOTOGRAPHER
b Ann Arbor, Mich, Sept 8, 1931. *Study:* Univ Mich, AB, 51; Cranbrook Acad Art, MFA (painting), 60; Rockham Sch Grad Studies, Ann Arbor; Acad Belle Arti, Rome. *Work:* Butler Inst Am Art; Cranbrook Mus Art; Wustum Mus, Racine, Wis; Madison Art Ctr, Wis; Detroit Inst Art. *Exhib:* Detroit Inst Art & Pa Acad Fine Arts, 59-60; Walker Art Ctr, 59-60; Wis Painters & Sculptors Ann, Milwaukee Art Ctr, 63-65; 100 Yrs of Navajo Weaving, Univ Wis-Platteville, 91; Uncommon Thread, West Bend Mus Art, Wis, 94; In a Modern Vernacular Navajo Textile, Chicago Cult Ctr, 95; and others. *Teaching:* Asst prof art, Univ Wis-Platteville, 62-80, assoc prof fine arts, 80-90. *Awards:* Fulbright Grant Painting to Italy, 60 & 61; Prizes, Wis Painters & Sculptors, 63 & Mich Fine Arts Exhib, 64; Individual Artist Fel, Wis Arts Bd, 92-93. *Bibliog:* Surface Appearances: The Painted Photograph, Kohler Art Ctr (pending). *Mem:* Coll Art Asn Am; Wis Painters & Sculptors Soc; Am Asn Univ Prof. *Mailing Add:* 310 High St Mineral Point WI 53565-1219

ROSS, JANICE KOENIG
PAINTER
b Harrisburg, Pa, 1926. *Study:* Pa State Univ, BA, 47; Univ Ill, MFA, 54; Fulbright-Hays seminar, Pakistan, summer 86. *Work:* Mr & Mrs Harper; Beauregard Family; Family Portrait; Conversation, Sarah & Emily, Birthday, & many others. *Comn:* portraits Auburn Univ Coll Vet Med. *Exhib:* Solo exhibs, Ga Inst Technol Student Ctr Gallery, 80 & Chattahoochee Valley Art Asn Gallery, 83; The Human Figure, Arts Festival of Atlanta, 89; Hearthstones I, Space One Eleven, Birmingham, Ala, 91; Patchwork of Many Lives, Huntsville Mus Art, 92; Montgomery Mus Fine Arts, 93; Red Clay Survey, Huntsville Mus Art, 98; Albany Arts Gallery, Calif, 2000; (with Conrad Ross), Through the Yrs, Chattahoochee Valley Art Mus, LaGrange, Ga, 03. *Pos:* Artist-in-residence, Art Studios Abroad Prog, Univ Ga, 84; founder, Studio 218, Auburn, Al, 1980. *Teaching:* Prof art, Tuskegee Univ, Ala, 68-91. *Awards:* Nat Endowment Humanities Fel, 81-82; Fulbright-Hays Fel, Pakistan, 86; Residency, Hambidge Ctr, Rabun Gap, Ga, 97, 2000. *Bibliog:* Susan Hood (auth), Through the years, Auburn Univ, Montgomery, 2003; John M. Williams (auth), Art papers, 1/89 & 2/89. *Mem:* Coll Art Asn; Women's Caucus Art (nat adv bd, 88-91); Southeastern Women's Caucus Art (mem secy-treas, 78-80); and others. *Media:* Oil, Pastel. *Specialty:* Alabama Artists. *Collection:* Alabama Power Co, Auburn Univ, Montgomery Al; Craig & Goulden Architects, Greenville, SC; Intertape Systems, Inc., Winston-Salem, NC; & many private collections. *Publ:* Co-Auth, MFA Survey, Coll Art Asn, fall 78; Eight from Auburn, Art Voices South, 1-2/80; Agnes Bradley Taugner profile, Artcraft, 2-3/80. *Mailing Add:* 447 Wrights's Mill Rd Auburn AL 36830

ROSS, JOAN M
PAINTER, INSTRUCTOR
b Brooklyn, NY, Apr 23, 1931. *Study:* St Joseph's Coll, Brooklyn, New York, BA, 53; St Elizabeth's Coll, Convent Station, NJ (continuing educ), 80-84; studied with Betty Lou Schlemm, Robert Laessig & Robert Wade, art workshops 84-85. *Work:* Lakeland State Bank, Sparta, NJ, 91; Sussex Co Libr, Vernon, NJ, 93; Permanent Collection, US Coast Guard; Operation Smile HQ, Va, 96; Intrawest-Mt Creek, Vernon, NJ, 2000. *Comn:* Watercolor-landscapes, J Kane, Hygrade Corp, Philadelphia, Pa, 80; watercolor-landscapes, comn by Senator & Mrs Robert E Littell, Franklin, NJ, 91 & 95; Dr & Mrs Joseph D'Onofrio, Sparta, NJ, 93, 95 & 97; watercolor-landscapes, comn by Dr & Mrs William R Magee, Norfolk, Va, 94-96; Mr & Mrs Samuel Lewin Highland Lakes NJ, 2002-2004; Senator & Mrs Steve Oroho, 2006; Mr & Mrs Robert Firmenich, Sussex, NJ, 2009; Mr & Mrs Joseph Sweeney, Highland Lakes, NJ, 2010. *Exhib:* NE Watercolor Soc, Hall Fame Mus, Goshen, NY, 76-98; Salmagundi Club Ann, New York, 85-2010; Am Artists Prof League, Grand Nat, Salmagundi, New York, 86-2010; NJ Watercolor Soc, Monmouth Mus, 95-2007; Hudson Valley Art Asn, Hastings on Hudson, 91-2010; NJ Watercolor Soc, Monmouth Mus, 91-2010; Morris Mus, 2001-2002; Nat Arts Club, New York, 2006-2007. *Pos:* Treas, vpres & chmn adv bd, Sussex Co Arts Coun, 77-98; pres, Vernon Township Cult Soc, 80-82 & Northeast Watercolor Soc, 86-94; vpres, NJ Watercolor Soc, 99-2000, pres, 2004-2006. *Teaching:* Chmn & vprincipal dept art & sci, Immaculate Conception Regional Sch, 68-90; instr art & watercolor workshops, demonstr art groups, NY, NJ & Pa, 90-2010; Official US Coast Guard Artist, 90-2010. *Awards:* John Pike Mem Award, Northeast Watercolor Soc, 91-92; Ogden Pleissner Mem Award, Salmagundi Club Ann, 96-2004; Helen G Ohler Mem Award, 97 & Claude Parson Mem Award, 99, Am Artists Prof League; Award of Excellence, RI Watercolor Soc, 2000; Award of Excellence, Northeast Watercolor Soc, 2002-2008, 2009; Award of Excellence, NJ Water Color Soc, 2004; Presidents Award, Am Artist Prof League, 2005; David H. Wright Award & Best of Show, Skylands Juried Exhib, 2005; Essex Watercolor Club Award of Merit, 2006-2007; John Loughlin AWS Award, Hudson Valley Art Asn, 2007-2010; Second Place, Warwick Art League, 2009. *Bibliog:* Mark Fitzgibbon (auth), Immortalizing Vernon, Vernon News, 3/86; Jim Cordes Beacon (auth), Recording a vanishing scene, NJ Herald, 8/86; Maura Rossi (auth), Beauty around her, The Beacon, Paterson, NJ, 86; Beth Ambrose Vernon Artist, NJ Herald, 2002, 2004 & 2006-2009; and others. *Mem:* Am Artist Prof League; Salmagundi Club; Essex Watercolor Club; Hudson Valley Art Asn; Northeast Watercolor Soc (vpres, 83-86 & 93-94, pres, 86-88); NJ Watercolor Soc (vpres, 2003-2004, pres 2005-2006); NJ Am Artists Prof League; Ecology Comt, Highland Lakes, NJ (chmn). *Media:* Watercolor, Oil. *Mailing Add:* 1181 Lakeside Dr E Highland Lakes NJ 07422

ROSS, JOAN STUART
PAINTER, PRINTMAKER
b Boston, Mass, Sept 21, 1942. *Study:* Conn Col, with R Lukosius & W McCloy BA, 64; Yale Univ, with J Albers, G Peterdi & Sillman, 65; Univ Iowa, with M Lasansky & E Ludins, MA, 67, MFA, 68. *Work:* Seattle City Light Collection; Oregon Arts Found, Salem; Seattle Art Mus; Sea First Bank; King Co Harborview Hosp. *Comn:* Environ sculpture, Seattle Arts Comn & Nat Endowment Arts, Seattle, 76; five woodcut prints, King Co Arts Comn, 78-79; 7 mixed-media panels, King Co Archit Div, 80; painting, Seafirst Bank, Seattle, 86; King Co Justice Ctr, 97. *Exhib:* Original Ed, traveling exhib, Oregon Arts Found, 78; 31st Spokane Ann Exhib, Cheney-Cowles Mem Mus, 79; Rutgers Nat Drawing, Rutgers Univ Mus, 79; New Ideas IV, Seattle Art Mus, 81; Northwest Now, Tacoma Art Mus, 86; Focus: Seattle, San Jose Art Mus, 86; NW Monotypes, Seattle Art Mus, 89; Betty Bowen Mem Exhib, Seattle Art Mus; Familie-Portrait Exhib, Norway, Nordic Heritage Mus, Vesterheim Mus, 1999-2000; Univ Puget Sound, Tacoma Wash, 2005; WA County Mus, Portland, Ore, 2010; Summer Pages: Past & Present, Patricia Cameron Gallery, Seattle, 2012; Ink This! Tacoma Art Mus, 2014. *Pos:* Mem, Seattle Arts Comn, 81-85; chair, Art in Pub Places Comn, 83-85; Bumbershoot Festival Comn, 85-91. *Teaching:* Instr printmaking & drawing, Seattle Pac Univ 68-88; instr printmaking, Factory Visual Art, 74-76; instr drawing, Green River Community Col, 78; instr drawing, Univ Wash, 88-91; instr drawing, Edmonds Community Col, 92-96; instr art, monotype & painting, N Seattle Community Col, 96-2009. *Awards:* Gaiser Award, Cheney-Cowles Mem Mus, 79; Betty Bowen Award, Seattle Art Mus, 81; Rome Fel, Northwest Inst Archit & Urban Studies in Italy, 93; Fulbright Hays Study Grant, Vietnam, 2005. *Bibliog:* L. Allan, Contemp Printmaking in NW, 97; M. Kangas, Family Portrait Seattle Times, 2000; Doc, Artists Express, SCC-TV; M Kangas, Relocations, 2008; Return to the Viewer, 2011. *Mem:* Northwest Print Coun (charter mem); Seattle Bk Arts Guild; founding mem Seattle Print Arts. *Media:* Acrylic, Mixed Media, Encaustic, Oil. *Res:* Encaustic Research, Louvre Mus, Sabbatical Leave, 2001. *Interests:* Published poet, member, Village Idioms, Seattle. *Publ:* Backbone: Seven Northwest Poets, 77 & Talk and Contact, 78, Seal Press; Fifty Northwest Artists, Chronicle Books, 83; two covers, Copper Canyon Press, 86-89; Bumbershoot Arts Festival, poster, 92; NW Originals, Matrimedia Press, 1992; Contemporary Printmaking in the Northwest, 96; Nature, Paris, France, 2009. *Dealer:* Seattle Art Mus Gallery Sales & Rental; Patricia Cameron Gallery Seattle; Waterworks Gallery Friday Harbor WA; RiverSea Gallery Astoria Or. *Mailing Add:* 8034 26th Ave NW Seattle WA 98117

ROSS, JOHN T
PRINTMAKER, EDUCATOR
b New York, NY, Sept 25, 1921. *Study:* Cooper Union Art Sch, with Morris Kantor & Will Barnet, BFA; New Sch Social Res, with Antonio Frasconi & Louis Schanker; Columbia Univ, 53. *Work:* Libr Cong, Hirshhorn Mus & Nat Collection Fine Arts, Washington; Metrop Mus Art, & Whitney Mus, NY; Brit Libr, Victoria & Albert Mus, London; NY Pub Libr; Smithsonian Inst; collected in 80 museums and libraries. *Comn:* Ed prints, Hilton Hotel, 63, Asn Am Artists, 64, 66 & 72, Philadelphia Print Club, 67, NY State Coun Arts, 67 & Int Poetry Forum, 68. *Exhib:* Second Int Color Print Exhib, Grenchen, Switz, 61; Int Biennale Gravure, Cracow, Poland, 68; Prize-winning Am Prints, Pratt Graphic Art Ctr, NY, 68; Nat Acad Fine Arts, Amsterdam, The Neth, 68; Biennial Print Exhib, Calif State Coll, Long Beach, 69;

Century Assoc, Masters Exhib, 2008; Jersey City Mus, 2010; Old Print Shop Exhib, 2010. *Pos:* Chmn, dept art Manhattanville Coll, Purchase, NY, 64-86; pres, US Comt-Int Asn Art, 67-69. *Teaching:* Instr printmaking, New Sch Social Res, 57- & Pratt Graphics Ctr, 63-; prof art, emer, Manhattanville Coll, 64-, prof emer, currently; demonstr & lectr, US Info Agency Exhib, Romania & Yugoslavia, 64-66. *Awards:* Louis Comfort Tiffany Found Grant Printmaking, 54; citation for prof achievement, Cooper Union Art Sch, 66; McDowell Colony Fel, 78, 82, 87; B W Clinedinst Award Artists Fel, 91. *Bibliog:* Articles, Am Artist, 52-81, Artists Proof, 64 & Art in Am, 65; auth, F Geierhaas, The Creative Act, Int Print Soc, 84. *Mem:* Soc Am Graphic Artists (pres, 61-65, exec coun, 65-); Nat Acad Design (assoc, 70, acad, 83); Ctr Book Arts, NY; Grolier Club, NY; Century Assoc, NY. *Media:* Prints, Artists Books. *Res:* The collagraph print. *Specialty:* Prints, Drawings. *Publ:* coauth, The Complete Printmaker, 72 & 90 & The Complete Collagraph, 80, Free Press, NY; dir, High Tide Press, New York, NY, 91-; illusr, many bks; Artists Books, High Tide Press. *Dealer:* Old Print Shop 150 Lexington Ave New York NY; Joshua Heller Rare Books Washington DC Box 39114 20016

ROSS, RHODA HONORE
PAINTER, INSTRUCTOR

b Boston, Mass, Dec 24, 1941. *Study:* Carnegie-Mellon Univ; RI Sch Design, BFA; Yale Univ, with Jack Tworkov, Al Held, Lester Johnson & Bernard Chaet, MFA; Skowhegan Sch Painting & Sculpture, Fashion Inst Technol, AAS. *Work:* Mus City NY; The White House, Washington; Julliard Sch, Chemical Bank, & Can Imperial Bank of Commerce, NY. *Comn:* Paintings, Russian Tea Room, NY; paintings, Smith Barney, Harris, Upham & Co, NY; Waldorf Astoria Hotel, NY; paintings, First Deposit Corp, San Francisco, Calif; portrait, retiring pres, Lehman Col, NY; and others. *Exhib:* Watercolor USA, Springfield Art Mus, Mo; The Subway Show, Lehman Coll Art Gallery, NY; Art in the Garden, Cape Mus Fine Arts, Dennis, Mass; Nat Asn Women, Pace Univ Art Gallery, NY; Artists traveling exhib, Nicolasen Art Mus, Wyo, Lewiston Art Ctr, Mont, Jesse Besser Mus, Mich & S Roper Gallery, Md; Am Univ, Washington; NY Studio Sch, NY. *Pos:* Treas, RI Sch Design Alumni Exec Comt, formerly; juror, Nat Asn Women Artists, formerly. *Teaching:* Instr New York Univ, presently. *Awards:* First Prize, Mademoiselle Mag; Susan B Whedon Prize, Yale Univ; Grumbacher Gold Medal. *Mem:* Nat Asn Women Artists; Womens Caucus Art; Graphic Artists Guild; Nat Asn Women Artists. *Media:* Oil, Watercolor. *Publ:* Am Artist; UNICEF; Am Psychologist Mag. *Dealer:* The North End Gallery Boston MA; Wally Findlay Galleries NY, Palm Beach FL & Chicago IL. *Mailing Add:* 473 W End Ave New York NY 10024

ROSS, SUEELLEN
PAINTER, PRINTMAKER

b Oakland, Calif, July 12, 1941. *Study:* Univ Calif, Berkeley, BA, 65, MA, 69, Sch Visual Arts, New York, 78-79. *Work:* Leigh Yawkey Woodson Art Mus; Sajco Insurance; Shell Oil. *Comn:* Bittern in reeds, Safeco Insurance co, Seattle, Wash, 86. *Exhib:* Survival to Sport, Whatcom Mus Hist & Art, Bellingham, Wash, 86; Birds in Art, Leigh Yawkey Woodson Art Mus, Wausau, Wis, 87, 89, 91-95, 97, 99, 2000-2005 & 2007, 2009-2012; Arts for Parks, 91-92; Naturally Drawn, Leigh Yawkey Woodson Art Mus, Wausau, Wis, 92; Wildlife: The Artists View, 93 & 96; Wildlife Art Sale, Christie's, South Kensington Ltd, London, Eng, 96; and others; Featured Artist, Western Wash State Fair, 2008. *Teaching:* Instr fine arts, Frye Art Mus & Daniel Smith Inc, 97, 99; instr fine arts, Dillman's, 2000-01 & 2005-06. *Awards:* Region I Winner, poster, Arts for Parks, 91; Poster, Birds in Art, 2007. *Bibliog:* Bart Rulon (auth), Painting Birds Step by Step, N Light Bks, 96; Rachel Wolf (ed), The Best of Wildlife Painting, N Light Bks, 97; Bart Rulon (auth), Artist's Photo Reference: Songbirds, N Light Bks, Cincinnati, 2004; Rachel Wolf (ed), Strokes & Genius 3, The Best of Drawing, N Light Bks, 2011; Rachel Wolf (ed), Splash 13, The Best of Watercolor, N Light Bks, 2012; plus others. *Mem:* Signature mem NW Watercolor Soc; Colored Pencil Soc Am. *Media:* Hand Colored Etchings; Mixed Media. *Interests:* Animals, Art, Photography. *Publ:* Auth, Paint Radiant Realism with Mixed Media, N Light Bks, 99; auth, Living Color, The Artist's Magazine, Jan, 2001; Jamie Gildow, Colored Pencil Explorations, N Light Bks, 2002. *Dealer:* Howard/Mandville Gallery 120 Park Ln Kirkland, WA 98033; Trailside Galleries 130 E Broadway Jackson NY 83001. *Mailing Add:* 1909 SW Myrtle Seattle WA 98106

ROSS, WILBUR LOUIS, JR
COLLECTOR

b Weehawken, NJ, Nov 28, 1937. *Study:* Yale Univ, AB, 59; MBA with distinction, Harvard Univ, 61. *Pos:* Assoc, Wood, Struthers and Winthrop, New York City, 63-64; pres, Faulkner, Dawkins & Sullivan Securities Corp, 64-76; sr managing dir, Rothschild, Inc, 76-2000; Chief Exec Officer, News Comms, Inc, 96-98; chmn, chief investment off, Rothschild Recovery Fund, 97-2000; chmn, Chief Exec Officer W L Ross & Co LLC, 2000-; bd dir, Biocraft Labs Inc, Rutherford, NJ, FurVault Inc, New York City, Investors Insurance Co, Lawrence Harbor, NJ, Revere Copper and Brass Co, Stamford, Syms Corp, Secaucus, NJ, Am Bankruptcy Inst, Wash, Allis Chalmers Corp, Milwaukee, KTI Inc, RH Cement Co, Seoul, Korea, Tong Yang Life Insurance Co, Seoul, Kansai Sawayaka Bank, Osaka, Fresca Credit Card Co, Osaka; fin adv equity holders comt Texaco Co, AH Robins Co, Pub Serv NH; hon economic ambassador from Korea to APEC Investment, Montana, 99; chmn Asia Recovery Fund LP, WL Recovery Fund LP, Asia Co, Investment Partners L.P; chmn, Clarent Hosp Corp, Int Steel Group, Inc, Cleveland, 2002-, Ohizumi Manufacturing Co, Japan, 2003- Burlington Industries, 2003-, Marquis Who's Who LLC, 2003-; dir, Nikko Electrical Co, Japan; treas, NY State Dem Comt, 80-83, Am Fedn Arts, 93-, The New Mus, 93-; vchmn, Brooklyn Mus, 81-; chmn, univ coun comt, on art Yale Univ, 83-88; chmn, Nat Acad Design, New York City, 85-, Am Art Forum, Smithsonian Inst, 87-; trustee, vchmn, Nat Mus Am Art, Wash, 86-91, chmn, 91-; trustee, Mus Am Fin Hist; trustee, Sarah Lawrence Col, 86-, chmn art gallery, 84-; pres, Parrish Art Mus, 91-95; chmn, NY Hist Soc, 93-94; bd dir, Smithsonian Inst Nat Bd, 94-, chmn bd, 95; nat chmn, Smithsonian Bicentennial Celebration, 96; trustee Gustave Hyde Ctr Nat Mus Am Indian, 2001-, Nat Mus Am Fin Hist; bd dir, Turnaround Mgt Asn, 2001-; chmn, Absolute Recovery Hedge Fund, Ltd, Hamilton, Bermuda, Taiyo Fund, 2003-, Japan Real Estate Recovery Fund, 2003-, With US Army, 61-63. *Mem:* Fel, Jonathan Edward Coll Yale Univ, Metrop Mus Art; mem Fin Analysts Fedn (chartered), Century Asn, The Bus Round Table, Southampton Bath & Tennis Club (chmn bd dir), Harvard Bus Sch Club NY (bd dir), Beach Club, Club Colette, Palm Beach Fla. *Mailing Add:* WL Ross and Co LLC 1166 Avenue of the Americas New York NY 10036-2708

ROSSEN, SUSAN F
HISTORIAN, EDITOR

Milwaukee, Wis. *Study:* Smith Col, AB (art hist), 63; Univ of Mich, Wayne State Univ, MA (art hist), 71. *Pos:* Asst cur educ, Detroit Inst Arts, 64-68, assoc cur Europ art, 71-72, sr ed & coordr of publ, Detroit Inst Arts, 72-81; exec dir publs, Art Inst Chicago, 81-2009, consult, ed, 2009-. *Teaching:* Lectr 19th century art, Univ Detroit, 71. *Awards:* Am Art Mus Asn; Art Mus Asn, Chicago Book Clinic; ARLIS, Coll Art Asn. *Mem:* Int Asn Mus Pubs; Coll Art Asn. *Res:* Nineteenth and twentieth century art and women artists, women as patrons of the arts. *Interests:* 20th century illustrated books. *Publ:* The Photography of Gustave Le Gray; Ed, Henri Matisse Paper Cut-Outs, 77; The Golden Age of Naples: Art and Civilization Under the Bourbons 1734-1805, 81; auth, Primer for seeing: The Gallery of Art interpretation of Katharine Kuhs crusade for modernism in Chicago, Art Inst Chicago Mus Studios, Vol 16, No 1, 90; ed, Ivan Albright, 96

ROSSER, DONNA KING
PHOTOGRAPHER, CONSULTANT

b Fredericksburg, Va, Jul 29, 1961. *Exhib:* Solo exhib, A Novel Experience, Zebulon, Ga, 2009; Glynn Art Asn, St Simons Island, Ga, 2005; Ga Nat Fair Photog Exhib & Competition, Perry, Ga, 2005, 2006, 2007; Fayette Art Ctr Photog Show, Fayetteville, Ga, 2006; Fayette Art Ctr, exhibit artist, Fayetteville, Ga, 2007, 2008; Southeastern Flower Show, Juried Photog Show, Atlanta, Ga, 2008, 2009; Viewpoint: Variations on Landscape, Dogwood Gallery, Tyrone, Ga, 2008; Slow Exposures, Juried Photog Exhib, Concord, Ga, 2008, 2009; Arts Clayton, Juried Photog Competition, Jonesboro, Ga, 2008; Dogwood Gallery, exhib artist, Tyrone, Ga, 2008, 2009 ; The Art Chamber event at Beyond the Door, Senoia, Ga, 2009 . *Collection Arranged:* dir, Nature Undisturbed juried photography exhib, Tyrone, Ga, 2009-. *Pos:* owner, Barefoot Photographer, Fayetteville, Ga, 2000-2009; co-owner, The Art Chamber, Peachtree City, Ga, 2009-. *Awards:* Hon Mention, Welcome to My World exhibit, Glynn Art, 2005; 1st Place, Macro, Fayette Art Ctr Photog Show, 2006; 1st, B&W, Animals, Ga Nat Fair, 2006 ; Purchase Award, 2008; 1st Place, Arts Clayton, 2009; Patrons Award, Arts Clayton, 2009 . *Bibliog:* Clayton News Daily, Ga; The Citizen, Ga; Fayette Daily News, Ga; Work featured in four issues of Arts & Expressions Mag, Ga; Peachtree City, a 50 Year Perspective, Ga, 2009; Barefoot Living (podcast), 2009; Slow Exposures, 2008, 2009 . *Mem:* Co-found, Art Chamber artists network, 2009; found, Fayette Photo Club, 2006; Glynn Art Asn; N Am Nature Photog Asn. *Mailing Add:* The Barefoot Photographer 105 Whitehall Place Fayetteville GA 30215

ROSSER, PHYLLIS F
SCULPTOR, PAINTER

b Rochester, NY, Dec 30, 1934. *Study:* Smith Coll (studied art hist with Henry Russell Hitchcock, Clarence Kennedy, Phyllis Lehman), BA, 1956; NY Sch Interior Design (completed one yr), 1957. *Work:* Smith Coll Mus Art, Northampton, Mass; Microsoft Art Collection, Redmond, Wash. *Exhib:* Solo Exhib: Ties That Bind, Johnson & Johnson World Hq, New Brunswick, NJ, 1997; Ceres Gallery, 2005-2007; Smith Coll Alumnae Art Gallery, Northampton, Mass, 2006 & 2008; Group Exhib: Aljira Nat 4, Aljira Gallery, Newark, NJ, 1998; Ceres Gallery Artists, Krasdale Gallery (satellite Bronx Mus), NY, 2006; As if Alive: Animate Sculpture, NJ Center Visual Arts, Summit, NJ, 2000; Breaking New Ground: The Power and Variety of Landscapes, Iona Coll, New Rochelle, NY, 2007; Southern Vt Arts Ctr, Manchester, Vt, 2009; Gallery at the Rhodes Art Ctr, Northfield Mt Hermon, Mass, 2010; Groundbreaking: Women of the Sylvia Sleigh Collection, Rowan Univ, Art Gallery, Glassboro, NJ. *Pos:* bd meme, NY Feminist Art Inst, 1985-1990; Art critic, Women Artist News, New Directions for Women, NY & High Performance, Los Angeles, Calif, 1986-1994; Public art review, St Paul, Minn, 1994; arts adminr, Ceres Gallery, bd trustees, 2000-, pres, 2000-2004, exhib organizer. *Awards:* 107th Ann Exhib, Catharine Lorillard Wolfe Art Club, Coun Am Artist Socs. 2003; 110th Ann Exhib, Catharine Lorillard Wolfe Art Club, Coun Am Artist Socs, 2006; Harriet W Frishmuth award, 2010. *Bibliog:* William Zimmer (auth), In white Plains, Krasdale Provides Views of City Life, NY Times, 8/14/1991; Barry Schwabsky (auth), Signposts in Driftwood, NY Times, 7/17/1997; Sara Lynn Henry (auth), As If Alive: Animate Sculpture Catalog, NJ Center Visual Arts,; Dan Bischoff (auth), The Mojo of Masks, The Star Ledger, Newark, NJ, 7/28/2000; Anne Swartz (auth), A Place for Beauty, New York Arts Mag, 1/7/2007. *Mem:* Nat Asn Women Artists; Int Asn Art Critics; Feminist Art Project, Rutgers Univ; NY Artists Circle; Art Table. *Media:* wood, Acrylic. *Interests:* Depiction of the forms and colors of the natural world, the gestures of nature, garden designs. *Collection:* Sylvia Sleigh. *Publ:* auth, Feminism & Art: A Lecture by Arlene Raven, Women Artist News, 1985; auth, Education Through Collaboration Saves Lives, Art in the Pub Interest, UMI, 1989; auth, Art & the Invisible Reality, High Performance #49, 1990; auth, There's No Place Like Home, New Feminist Art Criticism, 1994; auth, Mel Chins Invisible Architecture, Pub Art Review, fall/winter 1994. *Dealer:* Chris Quidley Quidley & Co 38 Newbury St Boston Ma 02116. *Mailing Add:* 14 E Fourth St New York NY 10012

ROSSI, ROGER
PAINTER

b Penn, Aug 17, 1936. *Study:* Mercersburg Acad, 56; Lafayette Coll (business admin), 60; Sch Visual Arts, 96; Studied with Nancy Chunn, John A Parks, Sch Visual Arts. *Work:* Chrysalis Gallery, Southampton, NY; Marshall Le Kae Gallery, Scottsdale, Ariz. *Comn:* Sailing the Hudson, Thomas Clynes, Australia, 99; Temple to Love, Chrysalis Gallery, Southampton, NY. *Exhib:* Solo exhib, Painted Gardens, Rodale

Publ, New York, 2010; Grand Nat Exhib, Salmagundi Club, New York, 2009, Mem Show, 2009, 2011, Fall Auctions, 2009, 2011, Spring Auctions, 2010, 2012, Black and White Exhib, 2011, Thumbox Exhib, 2011, Eternal Landscape, 2011, Audubon Artists, 2011, Am Artists Professional League, 2011; Chrysalis Gallery Reception, 2011; Allied Artists Am, Nat Arts Club, 2011. *Awards:* Jefferson Market Garden, Salmagundi Club, F Ballard Williams 2009; New York Botanical Gardens, Salmagundi Club, Herbert L & R Harmer Smith, 2010; Fontaine de Vaucluse, Eternal Landscape Exhib, Salmagundi Club, 2010. *Mem:* Salmagundi Club (bd dir, 2009, 2010, juried art committee, 2010-, vchmn, 2009-, art committee, 2009-); Am Artists Prof League (bd dirs); Audubon Artists (bd dirs); Allied Artists (bd dirs); Washington Sq Outdoor Art Exhibs (bd dirs); Oil Painters of Am. *Media:* Oil. *Specialty:* contemporary realism in floral landscapes, gardens. *Interests:* travelling. *Dealer:* Chrysalis Gallery 2 Main St Southampton NY 11968; Marshall LeKae Gallery 7106 E Main St Scottsdale Az

ROSSMAN, RUTH SCHARFF
PAINTER, INSTRUCTOR
b Brooklyn, NY. *Study:* Cleveland Inst Art; Case-Western Reserve Univ, BS; Kahn Inst Art; Univ Calif, Los Angeles; also with Sueo Serisawa & Rico Lebrun. *Work:* Pa Acad Fine Arts; Univ Redlands; Nat Watercolor Soc; Brandeis Inst; Ahmanson Collection, Calif; plus others. *Exhib:* Recent Paintings USA: Figure, Mus Mod Art, NY, 61; Crescent Gallery, New Orleans, 77, 78; Rocky Mountain Nat, Colo, 77 & 81; Denver Art Mus; Venice Art Walk, Venice, Calif, 92-98, 99; Platt Art Gallery, Univ Judaism, Los Angeles, 94; A Retrospective, 98; and others. *Teaching:* Teacher art, Pub Sch Syst, Canton, Ohio; teacher art, Canton Art Inst; instr, Arts & Crafts Ctr, Los Angeles. *Awards:* Purchase Award, Pa Acad Fine Arts, 65; All-City Ann Purchase Awards, Los Angeles, 65 & 69; Rocky Mountain Nat, 77; plus others. *Bibliog:* William Wilson & Henry Seldis (auths), articles, Los Angeles Times, 63 & 6/66; States Item, Times-Picayune World Art, New Orleans, 12/77; Robert Perine (auth), The California Romantics - Harbingers of Watercolorism, Artra Publ Inc, 86. *Mem:* Nat Watercolor Soc (secy, 73-74, 1st vpres, 74-75, pres, 75-76). *Media:* Acrylic, Oil. *Mailing Add:* 1843 El Camino De La Luz Santa Barbara CA 93109-1924

ROSTER, FRED HOWARD
SCULPTOR, EDUCATOR
b Palo Alto, Calif, June 27, 1944. *Study:* Gavilan Col, AA; San Jose State Col, BA & MA; Univ Hawaii, MFA & with Herbert H Sanders. *Work:* Honolulu Acad Art, Hawaii; State Found Cult & Arts, Honolulu; Contemp Arts Ctr Hawaii; Hawaii Loa Col, Kailua; St Francis Hosp, Honolulu. *Comn:* Sand cast mural, Ft Derussy, 75; bronze bust of former Gov John Burns, State Found Cult & The Arts; Kekuanaoa bronze portrait, 79; bronze & stainless steel mural, Physical Educ Facility, Univ Hawaii, Manoa, 82; bronze, stone & stainless steel sculpture, Honolulu Int Airport, 83. *Exhib:* Artists of Hawaii Ann, Honolulu Acad Art, 75-76, 79 & 81; Hawaii Craftsmen's Ann, Honolulu, 69-72 & 75-80; one-man shows, Contemp Arts Ctr Hawaii, 72, Gima's Art Gallery, Honolulu, 75 & 78 & Corpus Christi Univ, Tex, 80. *Teaching:* Instr ceramics, San Jose State Col, 68-69; asst prof sculpture, Univ Hawaii, 69-78, assoc prof, 78-. *Awards:* Elizabeth Moses Award, San Francisco Potter's Asn, 68; Sculptural Grant Award, Windward Artists Guild, 71; Hawaii Craftsman Award, 74. *Mem:* Honolulu Acad Art. *Media:* Mixed. *Mailing Add:* 1841 Halekoa Rd Honolulu HI 96821

ROTENBERG, JUDI
PAINTER, ART DEALER
b Boston, Mass. *Study:* Boston Univ, BFA; studied privately in Paris, Mex & Israel. *Exhib:* Le Salon 80, Soc des Artistes Francais, Paris, 80; DeCordova Museum; Holyoke Mus Show; Societarian de Societe des Beaux Art. *Pos:* Dir, Judi Rotenberg Gallery, Boston & Square Circle Gallery, Rockport, Mass. *Teaching:* Spain Univ, Madrid, 98; Young President's Orgn, 98. *Mem:* Rockport Art Asn. *Media:* Acrylic, Watercolor. *Specialty:* 20th century American art

ROTH, FRANK
PAINTER
b Boston, Mass, Feb 22, 1936. *Study:* Cooper Union, 54; Hofmann Sch, 55. *Work:* Albright-Knox Art Gallery, Buffalo, NY; Whitney Mus Am Art, Metrop Mus Art, Mus Mod Art, NY; Santa Barbara Mus Art, Calif; Baltimore Mus Art; Walker Art Ctr, Minneapolis; Tate Gallery, London, Eng; David Rockefeller Collection, NY; and others. *Exhib:* one person exhibs, Martha Jackson Gallery, NY, 67, 68, 70 & 71, Gimpel & Weitzenhoffer, NY, 74, O K Harris Works Art, NY, 75, Louis K Meisel Gallery, NY, 81, 82, 84 & 85, Martha White Gallery, Louisville, Ky, 81, Sindin Gallery, NY, 91 & 93; Va Mus Fine Arts, Richmond, 70; Indianapolis Mus Art, Ind, 70; Louise Himmelfarb Gallery, Bridgehampton, NY 77 & 78; David Anderson Gallery, Buffalo, NY, 91, 93 & 99; Bologna Lawdi Gallery, East Hampton, NY, 92, 93; Sindin Gallery, NY, 94, 97, 99; Hermitage Arts, Amsterdam, The Neth, 96; Radford Univ Mus, Va, 99; many others. *Pos:* panelist, Col Art Asn, New York, 78. *Teaching:* Instr painting, State Univ Iowa, summer 64; instr painting & drawing, Sch Visual Arts, NY, 63--; Ford Found artist-in-residence, Univ RI, 66; artist-in-residence, Univ Wis, Madison, 70; instr, Univ Calif, Berkeley, 68 & Univ Calif, Irvine, 71; vis lectr, Bellville Area Col, Ill, 76, Maryland Inst Art, Baltimore, Md, 77; vis critic, Md Inst Art, Baltimore, 78-88; prof emer, Sch Visual Arts. *Awards:* Prix de Rome, Chaloner Prize Found Award, 61; Guggenheim Fel, 64; Minister Foreign Affairs Award, Int Exhib Young Artists, Tokyo, Japan, 67; Nat Endowment for Arts, 77. *Bibliog:* Phyllis Braff (auth), The Emotional Intensity of Devotion, NY Times, 1/3/93; Jacquely Campbell (auth), Precise in Speech and Painting, spec to J Bull, 96; James Michner (auth), Art Voices Who's Who in American Art, NY Times Mag, 4/7/96. *Media:* Acrylic. *Mailing Add:* 120 Accabonac Rd East Hampton NY 11937

ROTH, LELAND M(ARTIN)
HISTORIAN, WRITER
b Harbor Beach, Mich, Mar 22, 1943. *Study:* Univ Ill, Urbana, BA (archit), 66; Yale, MA, 71, PhD, 73. *Teaching:* Instr, Univ Ill, Urbana, 66-67 & Ohio State Univ, Columbus, 71-73; asst prof, Northwestern Univ, 73-78; assoc prof, Univ Ore, Eugene, 78-90, prof, 90-, Marion Dean Ross prof archit hist, 92-2010, prof emeritus, 2010-. *Awards:* Founders Award, Soc Archit Historians, 79; Nat Endowment Humanities Fel, 82-83; Kamphoefner Fel, 85. *Mem:* Coll Art Asn; Soc Archit Historians (dir, 77-80); Nat Trust Hist Preserv; Vernacular Archit Forum. *Res:* American archit, 1700-1950; history of urban America; history of American art, 1850-1930; Native American archit; Oregon hist & archit. *Publ:* Ed, Monograph of the Work of McKim, Mead & White, B Blom, 73; auth, The Architecture of McKim, Mead & White, 1870-1920: A Building List, Garland Publ, 78; A Concise History of American Architecture, 79, ed, America Builds: Source Documents in American Architecture, 83, auth, McKim, Mead & White, Architects, 83 & Understanding Architecture, 93, Harper Collins; American Architecture; A History 2001, Westview Press; Understanding Architecture, Westview Press, 2nd ed, 2006; Understanding Architecture, Westview Press, 3rd ed, 2014. *Mailing Add:* Dept Art & Architectural History Univ Ore Eugene OR 97403-5229

ROTH, MICHAEL S
ADMINISTRATOR, EDUCATOR
Study: Wesleyan Univ, BA; Princeton Univ, MA; Princeton Univ, PhD (hist). *Comn:* Archit, Film, Photog & Urban Landscape, 2001, Disturbing Remains: Memory, Hist, & Crisis in Twentieth Century, 2001. *Exhib:* cur, (exhib) Sigmund Freud: Conflict & Cult, Libr Congress, 1998. *Pos:* Assoc dir, Getty Res Inst, chmn, Res & Educ Dept; pres, Calif Col Arts, San Francisco, 2000-07, Wesleyan Univ, 2007-. *Teaching:* HB Alexander Prof, Humanities & Cult Studies Claremont Grad Sch. *Publ:* Auth: Freud: Conflict & Culture, 1998; auth: Looking for L.A. *Mailing Add:* Wesleyan Univ Off of Pres Wesleyan Sta Middletown CT 06459

ROTH, MOIRA
EDUCATOR, HISTORIAN, CURATOR, POET, PLAYWRIGHT
b London, Eng, July 24, 1933. *Study:* New York Univ, BA, 59; Univ Calif, Berkeley, MA, 66, PhD, 74. *Hon Degrees:* San Francisco Art Inst, Hon Dr, 94. *Exhib:* Blogger for the 18th Biennale of Sydney, Australia, 2012; Through the Eyes of Rachel Marker, A Literary Installation, The Magnes Collection of Jewish Art and Life, Berkeley, 2013. *Pos:* Dir Univ Calif San Diego Manderville Art Gallery, 74-76; curated Barbara Smith Retrospective, 74, Miriam Schapiro Retrospective, 75, Theresa Hak Kyung Cha: Echoes, Mills Col, 89, Carlos Villa: ForceField, Mills Col, 90, and Bernice Bing (co-curator), SOMAR, San Francisco, 99; co-founder, Visibility Press, 91; co-published a series of catologs: Bernice Bing, 91, Betty Kano, 92, Flo Oy Wong, 92, Brian D Tripp, 92, Carlos Villa, 94, Library of Maps Rachel Marker, 2006; Theater productions (with Mary Sano): Dancing/Dreaming: Izanami and Amaterasu, Cascade Theater, Tokyo, Japan, 2004; Amaterasu, The Blind Woman and Hiroshima (with koto, biwa and flute players, and Noh actor, dancer and other performers), Kyoto Concert Hall, Japan; (with Pauline Oliveros) The Map and The Magnifying Glass, American Haus, Berlin, Germany, 2001; dir, scriptwriter, The Library of Maps, An Opera in Many Parts, Oakland, Calif, 2001; artist advisor and script writer, Library of Maps: Experience of Art & Technology, An Exchange Between Students of Mills College Children's School and Ark Community Charter School, Troy, NY, Oakland, Calif, 2002; script writer, The Library of Maps, Rensselaer Polytechnic Institute, Troy, NY, 2002; City of Maps Production, Rare Book Room, Mills Col, Oakland, Calif, 2002; Library of Maps performance by Oliveros and Roth ath the Firehouse North, Berkeley, Calif, 2009. *Teaching:* Lectr, Ind Univ, Bloomington, 68-69; acting asst prof art hist, Univ Calif, Irvine, 70-72; lectr art hist, Univ Calif, Santa Cruz, 73-74; from asst to assoc prof, Univ Calif, San Diego, 74-86, chmn, Visual Arts Dept, 82-83; prof art hist & Trefethen endowed chair, Mills Col, 86-. *Awards:* Lifetime Achievement Award, Women's Caucus Art, 98; Frank Jewett Mather Lifetime Achievement Award in art criticism, 2000. *Bibliog:* Annika, Maria, ed, All Over the Map: A Festschrift, Celebration and Exhibition Honoring Moira Roth,, Poor Farm Press, Manawa, Wis, 2012 (contains texts by and about Roth); Fragments of an Autobiography or Remembering in the House of Time: From London to Wisconsin, 1933-2010 (together with poem, The House of Time, issue 55, Women's Voices from the House of Time, online American Studies Journal: http://asjournal.zusas.zusas.uni-halle.de/, published as a book, 2012. *Mem:* Coll Art Asn (bd dir, 92-96); Asian Am Women Artists Asn. *Res:* Performance art, Marcel Duchamp, American Multicultural & women's contemporary art, contemporary global art. *Publ:* Interviews: Robert Smithson on Duchamp, an interview, Artforum, October, 73; John Cage on Marcel Duchamp: An Interview, Art in America, Nov/Dec, 73; Allan Kaprow, An Interview by Moira Roth, Sun and Moon, Fall, 78; An Interview with Linda Montano, High Performance, Dec, 78; Of Self and History: Exchanges with Linda Nochlin, Art Journal, Fall, 2000, reprinted in Aruna d'Souza, ed, Of Self and History, In Honor of Linda Nochlin, NY: Thames and Hudson, 2001; Marcel Duchamp in America: A Self Readymade, Arts Magazine, May, 77; The Aesthetic of Indifference, Artforum, 11/77, reprinted, 90, 98, 2012; Toward a History of California Performance: Part II, Arts Magazine, June, 78; Visions and Re-Visions, Artforum, Nov, 80; ed & contbr, The Amazing Decade: Women and Performance Art in America 1970-1980, A Source Book, Los Angeles, Astro Artz, 83; ed & contbr, Connecting Conversations: Interviews with 28 Bay Area Women Artists, Eucalyptus Press, Mills Col, 88; auth, The Dual Citizenship: Art of Carlos Villa, Visions, fall 89; auth, A Trojan Horse (essay), Faith Ringgold: A Twenty Year Retrospective (catalog), 90; contribr, Shigeko Kubota: Video Sculpture (catalog), 91; Social Protest: Racism and Activism (co-auth Yolanda Lopez), The Power of Feminist Art: The American Movement of the 1970s, History and Impact, 94; ed, We Flew Over the Bridge: The Memoirs of Faith Ringgold, 95; ed & contbr (introduction), Rachel Rosenthal, John Hopkins University Press, Baltimore, 97; Difference/Indifference: Musings on Postmodernism, Marcel Duchamp and John Cage, Critical Voices in Art, Theory and Culture Series, Gordon and Breach, Amsterdam, Holland, (commentary by Jonathan D Katz), 98; Remnants &

Reverberations: Drawing(s) from the American-Vietnam War, in Persistent Vestiges: Drawing from the American-Vietnam War, ed by Catherine de Zegher, The Drawing Center, NY, 2006; Obdurate History: Dinh Q Le, the Vietnam War, Photography, and Memory, Art Jour, 2001, Reprinted, Humor US cat, p7, Los Angeles Municipal Art Gallery, Barnsdall Park, 9/2007-12/2007; Introduction, Suzanne Lacy: Three Decades of Performing and Writing/Writing and Performing, Leaving Art: Suzanne Lacy's Writings on Performance, Politics and Publics, Duke Univ Press, Durham, NC & London, 2010; Introduction, Martha Wilson: A Woman With a Mind of Her Own, Martha Wilson Sourcebook: 40 Years of Reconsidering Performance, Feminism, Alternative Spaces, Independent Curators Int, NY, 2011; contbr, Of Vietnam & America: the Life, Art & Memories of Dinh Q Le, Dinh Q Le: Memory for Tomorrow, Mori Art Museum, Tokyo, 2015. *Mailing Add:* Dept Art Mills College Art Center 107 5000 MacArthur Blvd Oakland CA 94613

ROTH, RICHARD
PAINTER
b Brooklyn, NY, June 22, 1946. *Study:* Cooper Union, BFA, 69; Tyler Sch Art, Temple Univ, MFA, 77. *Work:* Akron Art Inst, Ohio; Chase Manhattan Bank Collection, NY; NY Univ Art Collection; Wexner Ctr for the Arts, Columbus; Va Mus Arts. *Exhib:* 1969 Ann Exhib of Contemp Am Painting, Whitney Mus Am Art, NY, 69-70; Group shows, Calif Mus Photog, Univ Calif Riverside, 98, McKenzie Fine Art, NY, 2012; Solo shows, Tomlinson Kong Contemporary, NY, 2011, Reynolds Gallery, Richmond, Va, 2013. *Teaching:* Asst prof & dir, Prog Fundamentals & Spec Classes, Art Inst Chicago, 77-81; prof, Dept Art, Ohio State Univ, 81-99; prof, painting & printmaking dept, Va Commonwealth Univ. *Awards:* Nat Endowment Arts, Visual Artists Fel, Painting, 91; Ohio Arts Coun Individual Artists Fel, 91; Fellowship in Painting, Va Mus Fine Arts, 2008. *Publ:* Beauty Is Nowhere: Ethical Issues in Art and Design, G & B Arts Int, with Susan King Roth; also Color Basics, with Stephen Pentak, Thompson-Wadsworth; Design Basics 3D, with Stephen Pentak, Wadsworth Cenfage Learning

ROTHAFEL, SYDELL
PAINTER
b Brooklyn, NY, June 11, 1931. *Study:* Goucher Coll, Towson, Md, 53; Brooklyn Coll, NY, studied with Anderson, D'Arcangelo, BA (fine arts), 80; post grad studies, 81-82; New Sch, studied with Anthony Toney & Henry Pearson. *Work:* Queensboro Pub Libr, NY; World Women Online, Ariz State Univ; pvt collections, C Mackenzi & A Goebel. *Exhib:* Brooklyn Mus, 77; Sun Yat Sen Gallery, St Johns Univ, 77; Seaman's Church Inst, 77; Creativity, Bentley Gallery, Lawrence, NY, 90; New Yorkers In Barcelona, Banco-Hispano-Americano Cartoon Gallery, Barcelona, Spain; Visions & Diversity, Staten Island Mus, NY, 92; Perceptions of Beauty, Ariel Gallery, 92; Int Bienniale, Tonniens, France, 93; Beams of Light, Salon du vieux Columbiers, Paris, 93; A Woman's Place, Prince Street Gallery, 95. *Pos:* Exhib chmn, Sumi-e Soc Am, 77-78; pres, Japan-Am Sumi-e Club, 83-86; artist-in-residence, Hilai Int, Ma'alot, Israel, 93. *Teaching:* Instr art, Freeport Arts Coun, 81-82, adult ed, Brookside Jr HS, 82-83, Alley Pond Environ Ctr, 87-88, Ryan Ctr Gateway Nat Park. *Awards:* Presidents Award, Japan House Gallery, Sumi-e Soc Am, 76; Hon First Prize, Cork Gallery, Japan Am Sumi-e Soc, 83; Soho NY Int Prize Winner, Agora Gallery, 92; Finalist, Broome St Gallery, 2008. *Bibliog:* Ariel Gallery (auth), Perceptions of Beauty, Manhattan Arts, 91; Jeanne Russel (auth), The beauty that winter was, Newsday, 3/96. *Mem:* NY Artists Equity Asn; Women's Caucus Art; Burr Artists. *Media:* Acrylic. *Dealer:* Lenox Artisans Gallery Lenox MA; Bradford Collection. *Mailing Add:* 326 Beach 142nd St Neponsit NY 11694

ROTHENBERG, BARBARA
PAINTER, EDUCATOR
b New York, NY, June 21, 1933. *Study:* Univ Mich, 52-54; Bennington Col, with Paul Feeley, BA (cum laude), 56; Columbia Univ Teachers Col, MA, 56; NY Univ, with Esteben Vicente & Samuel Adler, 56-58. *Work:* Housatonic Mus Art, Bridgeport, Conn; Readers Digest Corp, Pleasantville, NY; CDC Financial, Farmington, Conn; Smithsonian Inst; United Nations, NY; Pitney-Bowes, General Elec; Sacred Heart Univ. *Comn:* Tapestry, Sofia Assocs, NY, 85; Jacob's Ladder (20' mural), Temple Israel, Westport, Conn, 94. *Exhib:* Northeast Ann, Silvermine Guild Arts Ctr, 76, 79-80, 82-83, 93-94, 97-98, 2007, 2011; Collage, Silvermine Guild Arts Ctr, 79; New Dimensions in Drawing, Aldrich Mus, 81; Solo Exhibs: Ingber Gallery, NY, 88, Conn Gallery, Marlborough, 88, Newspace Gallery, Manchester Community Col, Conn, 91, Conn Comn Arts, Hartford, 94, Mort Rosenfeld Gallery, Westport Art Ctr, Conn, 96, Discovery Mus, Bridgeport, Conn, 97 & Silvermine Guild Arts Ctr, 98, UN Invitation, 99, Gallery of Contemp Art, Sacred Heart Univ, 2000; Out of Longing and Out of Song, Silvermine Guild Arts Ctr, 2005; Timelines, 2012 Flinn Gallery, Greenwich, Conn, 2007, 2012, Arc Gallery, Conn, 2012; The Big Hike, Silvermine Guild Arts Ctr, 90; Modern Times, Katonah Mus, NY, 92; Investing in Dreams, William Benton Mus Art, Storrs, Conn, 95; Silvermine Invitational, Kohn, Pederson, Fox, NY, 95; India: Reflections of a Country, Krasdale Gallery, NY, 95; Archeology of the Spirit, Gallery Brocken, Koganei, Japan, 96; Paessagio Gallery, Hartford, Conn, 98; West Wind Gallery, Up from Earth, 2004; Hebrew Union Inst Mus, The Art of Aging, 2003-2004; Song of the Earth, Van Brunt Gallery, 2006; Earth, Sight and Sound Silermine Guild, 2008, Gallery Contemp Art, Sacred Heart Univ, 2009. *Collection Arranged:* cur, Word/Image, Westport Art Ctr, 2003. *Pos:* Moderator-organizer, Inst Visual Artists, Silvermine Guild Arts Ctr, 85, 2000; lectr, Friends Music, 85, Fairfield Univ, 87 & 89 Westport Arts Ctr, 87, 89 & 2009, Westport Continuing Educ, 87; moderator & panelist, Inst Visual Artists, Silvermine Guild Arts Ctr & Conn Gallery, Marlborough, 89; lectr & vis artist, Silvermine Guild Arts Ctr, 89, Westport Arts Ctr, 91-92, 93 & 95, New Brit Mus Art, 91-93, Fairfield Univ, 91-93, Harvard Club India, 91-93, Univ Hyderabad, India, 91-93, Discovery Mus, Bridgeport, Conn, 92, Great Neck Libr, 92, Delhi Col Art, 92, India Int Ctr, 92, Friends Music, 93, Port Wash Libr, 93, Hewlett-Woodmere Libr, 95, Inst Asian Studies, NY, 95, Long Beach Island Found Arts & Sci, Loveladies, NJ, 96 & Weir Farm Historic Site, 98. *Teaching:* Instr art, City Col NY, 58-60 & Silvermine Sch Arts, 80-83 & 96-2009; adj assoc prof art, Housatonic Community Col, 70-82, Sch Visual Arts, NY, 80-82, Sacred Heart Univ, 80-88 & Fairfield Univ, Conn, 86-98; adj prof fine arts, Fairfield Univ, 88-98; guest lectr & critic, RI Sch Design, 92; instr, Silvermine Guild Sch Arts, 94-2012 & Victor D'Amico Inst Art, Amagansett, Long Island, 96, 97, 98, 2000 & 2001. *Awards:* Indo-Am Fulbright Grant, 92-93; Best Show for Painting on paper, Discovery Mus, Conn, 96; Artist-in-Res, Weir Farm, 98; Artist-in-Res, Virginia Ctr for the Creative Arts, 2000; Outstanding Women of Conn, 2002; 1st Prize Sculpture, Northeast Ann, 2007. *Bibliog:* Vivian Raynor (auth), review, NY Times, 1/96; Sachidananda Mohanty (auth), In search of Ragamala, SPAN Mag, 1/96; Art New Eng, 97; LP Streitfeld Review, The Advocate, 2003; Nancy Hull-Duncan (auth), Out of Longing & Out of Song (catalog), 2005; Laura Einstein (auth), Fragments, Stamford Advocate, Bridgeport Post, 2012. *Mem:* Coll Art Asn; Women's Caucus Arts; Westport-Weston Arts Coun; Silvermine Guild Ctr Arts (mem bd, 78-80); Fulbright Asn. *Media:* Oil, Pastel; Collage. *Res:* All lectrs in art hist. *Specialty:* Contemp Art. *Interests:* Music, Poetry, Travel, Dance. *Publ:* Auth, On painterly painting, Women Artists News, 81; Connecticut women artists, Conn Mag, 81. *Dealer:* Silvermine Guild New Canaan CT; Westport Art Ctr; Arc Gallery Fairfield CT. *Mailing Add:* 303 Bayberry Ln Westport CT 06880

ROTHENBERG, STEPHANIE
VIDEO ARTIST, EDUCATOR
Study: Md Inst Coll Art, BFA; Dept Film, Video & New Media, Sch Art Inst Chicago, MFA, 2003. *Exhib:* Sundance Film Festival; ISEA; Zer09/01SJ Global Festival of Art on the Edge; Banff New Media Inst; Amsterdam Int Film Festival; Hallwalls Media Art Ctr; ConFlux Festival; Interaccess Media Arts Ctr; Bent Festival; Chicago Underground Film Festival; Radiator Festival New Technol Art; Knitting Factory; Studio XX & Ctrl Acad Fine Art, Beijing. *Pos:* Dir & founder, Pan-O-Matic, 2001-. *Teaching:* Asst prof visual studies, SUNY, Buffalo. *Awards:* Individual Artist Award, NY State Coun on the Arts, 2008; Grant for Emerging Fields, Creative Capital Found, 2009. *Mailing Add:* Univ Buffalo North Campus 229 Center for the Arts Buffalo NY 14260-6010

ROTHENBERG, SUSAN
PAINTER, PRINTMAKER
b Buffalo, NY, Jan 20, 1945. *Study:* Cornell Univ, BFA, 1966; George Wash Univ, 1967; Corcoran Mus Sch. *Work:* Mus Mod Art, Whitney Mus Am Art, NY; Albright-Knox Art Gallery, Buffalo, NY; Walker Art Ctr, Minneapolis, Minn; Mus Fine Arts, Houston; Fogg Art Mus, Harvard Univ, Cambridge, Mass. *Exhib:* Solo exhibs, Recent Work (with catalog), Walker Art Ctr, Minneapolis, Minn, 1978, Los Angeles Co Mus Art, Calif, traveling, 1983-85, Paintings & Drawings 1974-1192 (with catalog), Albright-Knox Art Gallery, Buffalo, NY, traveling, 1992-94, Focus Series, Va Mus Fine Arts, Richmond, 1995, Mus Art Contemp Monterrey, Mex, 1996, Drawings & Prints (catalog) Herbert F Johnson Mus Art, Cornell Univ, Ithaca, NY, 1998-99 & Paintings from the 90's (catalog) Mus Fine Arts, Boston, 2000, Sperone Westwater, NY City, 2006, Craig F Starr Associates, 2007; Group exhibs, New Acquisitions, Extraordinary Women & Am Drawn & Matched (with catalog), 1977, Prints from Blocks, Gauguin to Now (with catalog), 1983, An Int Survey of Recent Painting & Sculpture (with catalog), 1984 & Allegories of Modernism: Contemp Drawing (with catalog), 1992, Thinking Print: Books to Billboards, 1980-95 (with catalog), 1995, Mus Mod Art, NY; New Image Painting (with catalog), 1978-79, 1979 Biennial Exhib (with catalog), 1979, A Decade in Review: Selections from the 1970's, 1979, Focus on the Figure: Twenty Years (with catalog), 1982, Block Prints, 1982, 1983 Biennial Exhib (with catalog), 1983, Minimalism to Expressionism: Painting & Sculpture Since 1965 from the Permanent Collection, 1983, Visions of Childhood: A Contemp Iconography, 1984, 1985 Biennial Exhib (with catalog), 1985, Four Printmakers, 1985, Three Printmakers, 1986 & Evolutions in Expression, 1994, Whitney Mus Am Art; Am Paintings of the 1970's, Albright-Knox Gallery, NY, traveling, 1978-80; A New Bestiary: Animal Imagery in Contemp Art, Va Mus Fine Arts, 1981; 74th & 75th Am Exhib (with catalog), Art Inst Chicago, Ill, 1982 & 1986; New Figuration in Am (with catalog), 1983, 1988-The World of Art Today (with catalog), 1988, & 25 Americans: Paintings in the 90s, 1995, Milwaukee Art Mus, Wis; 47th Ann Mid-Yr Exhib (with catalog), 1983 & 50th Nat Mid-Yr Exhib, 1986, Butler Inst Am Art, Youngstown, Ohio; Images & Impressions: Painters Who Print (with catalog), Walker Art Ctr, Minneapolis, Minn, 1984; States of War: New European & Am Paintings (catalog) & Virginia & Bagley Wright Collection, 1999, Seattle Art Mus, 1985; Boston Collects: Contemp Painting & Sculpture, Boston Mus Fine Arts, Mass, 1986-87; The Int Art Show for the End of World Hunger, Minn Mus Art, St Paul, traveling, 1987-91; Timely & Timeless (with catalog), Aldrich Mus Contemp Art, Conn, 1993-94; A NY Time: Selected Drawings of the Eighties, Bruce Mus, Greenwich, Conn, 1995; 7 Artists, Cleveland Mus Art, 1995; XXV Years, John Berggruen Gallery, San Francisco, 1995; Diary of the Human Hand, Galerie Centre Arts Saidye Bronfman, 1995; Powerful Expressions: Recent Am Drawings (with catalog), Nat Acad Design, 1996; Thinking Print: Books to Billboards 1980-95 (catalog), Mus Mod Art, NY, 1996; Hirshhorn Collects: Recent Acquisitions 1992-96 (catalog), Hirshhorn Mus & Sculpture Garden, Washington, 1997; Eye of Modernism, Georgia O'Keeffe Mus, Santa Fe, NMex, 2001; Sperone Westwater, NY, 2001, 2002. *Collection Arranged:* A Guide to the Collection of the Mus Fine Arts, Houston, Tex; The Image in Am Photography & Sculpture 1950-1980 (auth, catalog), Akron Art Mus. *Awards:* Creative Artists Pub Serv Prog Grant, NY State Coun Arts, 1976-77; Guggenheim Fel Painting, 1980; Award Painting, Am Acad Arts & Letts, 1983. *Bibliog:* Anne Midgette (auth), Words Worth a Thousand Pictures, Wall St J, 9/22/1999; Jason Edward Kaufman (auth), The Gallery: Chaos and Crowds, Wall St J, 1/5/2000; Elisa Turner (auth), Mythic Proportions, Artnews, 5/2001. *Mem:* Nat Acad. *Media:* Acrylic and Flashe or Oil on Canvas or Paper, Aquatint; Lithography. *Publ:* Contribr, New Image Painting, Whitney Mus, 1978; American Paintings: The Eighties, Barbara Rose/Vista Press, 1979. *Dealer:* Evelyn Aimis Fine Art 3780 NE 199th Terr Miami FL 33180; Baldwin Gallery 209 S Galena St Aspen CO 81611; Adam Baumgold Gallery 74 E 79th St New York NY 10021; Alan Brown Gallery Naples FL 34102; Gemini GEL 8365 Melrose Ave Los Angeles CA 90069; Gemini

GEL at Joni Moisant Weyl 980 Madison Ave New York NY 10075; Larissa Goldston Gallery 530 West 25th St New York NY 10001; Dean Jensen Gallery 759 N Water St Milwaukee WI 53202; Greg Kucera Gallery 212 Third Ave S Seattle WA 98104; Anthony Meier Fine Arts 1969 California St San Francisco CA 94109; Craig F Starr Assocs 5 E 73rd St New York NY 10021; John Szoke Editions 591 Broadway New York NY 10012-3232; Diane Villani Editions 285 Lafayette St New York NY 10012; Waddington Galleries 11 & 12 Cork St London W1S 3LT United Kingdom; Sperone Westwater New York NY. *Mailing Add:* c/o Sperone Westwater 257 Bowery New York NY 10002

ROTHKOPF, SCOTT
CURATOR, CRITIC
Study: Harvard Univ, BA & MA (in art history & archit). *Collection Arranged:* Mel Bochner Photographs 1966-1969, 2002 & Pierre Huyghe This is Not A Time for Dreaming, 2004, Fogg Art Mus. *Pos:* Vis critic, Yale Univ Sch Art & Mus Fine Arts Sch Boston; sr ed, Artforum, 2004-2009; cur, Whitney Mus Am Art, 2009-. *Mailing Add:* 945 Madison Ave New York NY 10021

ROTHOLZ, RINA
PRINTMAKER
b Israel; US citizen. *Study:* Pratt Graphic Arts Ctr, New York; Brooklyn Mus Art Sch, NY. *Work:* Boston Mus Fine Arts; Rose Art Mus, Brandeis Univ; Mus Mod Art, NY; Israel Mus, Jerusalem; Albright-Knox Art Gallery, Buffalo, NY; and others. *Comn:* Ed of 50 prints, 69 & ed of 200 prints, Commentary Libr Collection of Art Treasure; Blue Disc (greeting card design), UNICEF, 72; 36 ingots (reprod by Franklin Mint), Judaic Heritage Soc, 73-78. *Exhib:* Solo exhibs, Pucker/Safrai Gallery, Boston, 72, 74, 77 & 81 & Port Washington Libr, NY, 75; Boston Printmakers Ann & Traveling Shows, 67-79; Queens Mus, NY, 74; Potsdam Print Exhib, State Univ NY Col, Purchase, 76; and others. *Teaching:* Lectr & demonstr, Bd Coop Educ Serv, Scholars in Residence Prog, Nassau Co, NY. *Awards:* First Prize for Graphics, Port Washington Ann, 70; Purchase Prize, Nassau Community Graphic Exhib, 72 & 73; Prize in Graphics, Nat Asn Women Artists, 72 & 74. *Mem:* Boston Printmakers; Graphic Arts Coun NY; Nat Asn Women Artists; Prof Artists Guild. *Res:* Discovered process of Tullegraphy, which is the carving of vinyl asbestos tiles while they are still warm, then printing the tiles as intaglio plates to achieve a variety of textures, shapes, and high reliefs. *Publ:* Auth, Tuilegraphy, Artist's Proof, Vol 7. *Mailing Add:* 42 Shepherd Ln Roslyn Heights NY 11577

ROTHSCHILD, BARBARA R SIMON
PAINTER
b Chicago, Ill. *Study:* Art Inst Chicago; Am Acad Art, Chicago; Coll New Rochelle, BA (art ed), 74, MA (art ed), 78. *Work:* Greenburgh Pub Libr, Elmsford, NY; Larchmont Libr, NY; Free reading room, Rye, NY. *Exhib:* Artists Guild, Norton Gallery, W Palm Beach, Fla, 91-93; Palm Beach Watercolor Soc, Cornell Mus, Delray Beach, Fla, 93; Bay Ann Tri-State, Visual Arts Ctr, Panama City, Fla, 95; Tallahassee Watercolor, Le Moyne Art Found, 95 & 96; Best of the Gallery, Mus New Arts, Ft Lauderdale, 96; Boca Raton Mus Art, Fla, 98, 2000; Mus Fine Arts, St Petersburg, Fla; Hudson River Mus, Yonkers, NY; Coral Springs Fla Mus, 98. *Pos:* Instr contemp painting, Boca Mus Art, Fla, 88-96. *Teaching:* Prof drawing, Mercy Col, Dobbs Ferry, NY, 85-87. *Awards:* Second Prize, Gold Coast Watercolor Soc, 92 & 95; Merit Award, Arizona Aqueous, 93; Second Prize and Special Award, Palm Beach Watercolor Soc,; Several awards, Prof Artists Guild, Fla, 98-. *Bibliog:* J Pat & Cindy Breedlove (dirs), Artists of Florida III, Mountain Productions, 94; Linda Selichia (auth), Barbara Rothschild, XS Mag/Sun Sentinel, 2/6/96. *Mem:* Exhibiting mem, Florida Watercolor Soc; signature mem, Gold Coast Watercolor Soc; Women in the Visual Arts; Palm Beach Watercolor Soc; Boca Mus Artists Guild. *Media:* Water Media, Acrylic. *Dealer:* Conservant Boca Raton FL; Lupine Gallery Monhegan ME

ROTHSCHILD, ERIC DE
COLLECTOR
Pos: Head, Chateau Lafite-Rothschild, 1974-. *Awards:* Named one of Top 200 Collectors, ARTnews mag, 2009-12. *Collection:* Old masters; modern and contemporary art. *Mailing Add:* Chateau Lafite-Rothschild Pauillac 33250 France

ROTHSCHILD, JOHN D
DEALER
b Chicago, Ill, June 22, 1940. *Study:* Mass Inst Technol, BS, 62; Columbia Univ, MBA, 64. *Pos:* Owner, Rothschild Fine Arts Inc, currently. *Specialty:* European and American paintings, drawings and sculptures by the masters, from French impressionists up through the present. *Publ:* Contribr, I Love New York Guide, Macmillan, Danger: Poets at Play; A Story for the Eleventh Hour, E M Donahue. *Mailing Add:* 5346 E Sapphire Ln Paradise Valley AZ 85253-2531

ROTHWELL, JUNKO ONO
PAINTER
b Yamaguchi, Japan, Apr 16,1952. *Study:* Okayama Univ, Japan. *Work:* George Wash Univ Hosp; Southern Co; Continental Telephone; Northwest Mem Hosp Chicago; Prime Bank, Nations Bank; MC Anderson Cancer Ctr, Univ Tex. *Comn:* Kaiser Permanente Atlanta, Oil, 1995; Southern Company, Oil, 1996; Emory Clinic, Emory Univ Hosp, Oil, 1997; Northwest Mem Hosp Chicago, Pastel, 1999; George Washington Univ Hosp, Oil, 2002. *Exhib:* Nat Exhib: Am Artists Prof League Nat Exhib, Pastel Soc Am, NY, Patel Soc Japan, Tokyo; solo exhib, Morehouse Coll, Ga; group exhibs: Marietta/Cobb Mus, Ga; Butler Inst Am Art; Huntsville Mus Art, Al; Oglethorpe Univ Mus, Ga. *Bibliog:* Best of Pastel, Rockport Publishers, 96; Best of Flower Painting 2, North Light Books, 99; articles: Unforgettable Landscapes, Different Approaches to Light and Texture, Pastel J, 5/200-6/200; Caroling Purtell (auth), Junko Ono Rothwell, The Pastel J, 8/2004; Pure Color, North Light Bks, 2006. *Mem:* Pastel Soc Am (Master Pastelist); Am Artist Prof League, NY (fel mem); Pastel Soc Japan (signature mem); Atlanta Artists Club (mem of Excellence); Southeastern Pastel Soc (mem of Excellence); Plein Air Painters of the Southeast. *Media:* Oil, Pastel. *Publ:* A Lesson from the East, Artist Mag, 6/2004. *Dealer:* Anderson fine Art Gallery; St Simons Island; Portfolio Art Gallery SC; Wells Gallery Kiawah SC; Frameworks Gallery GA. *Mailing Add:* 3625 Woodstream Circle Atlanta GA 30319

ROTTER, ALEX
ART APPRAISER
Pos: With Sothebys, New York, 2000-, sr vp head dept contemp art, currently. *Mailing Add:* Sotheby's 1334 York Ave New York NY 10021

ROTTERDAM, PAUL ZWIETNIG
PAINTER
b Austria, Feb 12, 1939; US citizen. *Study:* Acad & Univ Vienna. *Work:* Graphische Sammlung Albertina, Vienna, Austria; Metrop Mus, Mus Mod Art & Guggenheim Mus, New York; Mus Nat d'Art Moderne, Paris; and others. *Exhib:* 8th Biennial, Tokyo, 65; Whitney Biennial Am Art, 75; Acquisitions, Guggenheim Mus, 75; Susan Caldwell Gallery, New York, 75; Mus de l'Abbaye St Croix, Les Sables d'Olonne, France, 76; Mus de Nice, France, 77; Birmingham Mus Art, Ala, 77; Ark Arts Ctr, 95; Leopold Museum, Vienna, 2007. *Teaching:* Lectr painting, Harvard Univ, 68-88 & Cooper Union Sch Art, 74-75. *Awards:* Cross of Honor, Sci & Art, Austrian Govt, 2007. *Bibliog:* Alvin Martin (auth), Paul Rotterdam: The 14 Stations of the Cross, Univ Tex, 80; Carter Ratcliff (auth), Paul Rotterdam: Selected Paintings, Storrer, 82; Townsend Wolfe (auth), Paul Z Rotterdam, A Drawing Retrospective, The Ark Arts Ctr, Littlerock, 95; Carl Aigner, Paul Rotterdam Work list 53-2004; Prestel Publ., London, NY. *Dealer:* Denise Cade 1024 Madison Ave New York NY 10021; Jayne Baum Grove St New York NY 10014; Galerie Erich Storrer Scheuchzerstr 25 8006 Zurich Switzerland. *Mailing Add:* PO Box 952 North Blenheim NY 12131-0952

ROUILLARD, MICHAEL
PAINTER
Study: Hunter Coll, BA. *Work:* Albright-Knox Art Gallery, Buffalo; San Jose Mus Art, Calif; Ege Kunst-und Kulturstiftung, Ger; Crawford Art Gallery, Ireland. *Exhib:* Hudson River Mus, Yonkers, NY, 1988; Otis Coll Art & Design, Los Angeles, 1999; Dumbo Art Ctr, Brooklyn, 2003; Albirght-Knox Gallery, Buffalo, 2008; Olschewski & Behm, Frankfurt, Ger, 2009. *Awards:* NY Found Arts Fel, 1988, 1995, 2009; Artist Space Grant, 1990-91. *Bibliog:* Grace Glueck (auth), Drawing a Bead on Public Monuments, NY Times, 10/3/1982; Lilly Wei (auth), Michael Rouillard at Stark, Art in Am, 6/1995; Peter Frank (auth), A Slice of Apple, Los Angeles Weekly, 10/1998

ROUSSEAU, IRENE VICTORIA
SCULPTOR, PAINTER
Study: Hunter Coll, with Tony Smith, AB; Claremont Grad Univ, MFA; NY Univ, PhD. *Work:* Metrop Mus Art, Mus Mod Art & Guggenheim Mus Art, NY; Smithsonian Inst, Washington; Philadelphia Mus Art; Brit Mus, London; Whit Mus Am Art, NY; Mus Contemp Art, Geneva, Swtiz; Valett Mus Fine Art, Malta. *Comn:* Mosaic mural, Holocaust Mem, The Brotherhood Synagogue, NY; series of metal wall relief sculptures, Capital Sports Inc, Stamford, Conn; mural wall relief, Beacon Hill Club, Summit, NJ; mosaic mural, Overlook Hosp Found, Summit, NJ, 93; mosaic murals, Concert Hall, La Roche, Switzerland, 95 & 96. *Exhib:* Solo exhib, Gallery Saint Agnes, Denmark & Bridges '97, Univ Calif, Berkeley, 97, Weston Gallery, Sch Artchit, NJ Inst Tech, Newark, 2003; Drawing Exhib, Philadelphia Mus Art, Pa; Weatherspoon Art Gallery, Univ NC, Greensboro; Moody Art Gallery, Univ Ala; 50th Anniversary 1936-1986 Am Abstract Artists, Bronx Mus Arts, 86; Int Art Competition, Gallery 54, NY; Noyes Mus, NJ, 94; Columbia Mus, SC, 95; 1st Int Art Bienniale, Malta, 95; Mosaic: Ancient Medium/Modern Expressionism, Int AIEMA Conf, Lausanne, Switz, 97; Ecole Francaise de Rome, Italy, 2001; Polytech Inst, Freiburg, Ger, 2002; NJ Inst Tech Sch Architecture, 2003; Univ Granada, Spain, 2003; NJ Inst Tech, Weston Art Gallery, 2004; Yellow Bird Gallery, Newburg, NY, 2005; Science & Art, Int Interdisciplinary Conf, Athens, Greece, 2005; Renaissance Banff, Banff Art Ctr, Alberta, Can, 2005; trav exhib, Soc Math, France & The Min Culture, 2005; Coll St Elizabeth, Madison, NJ, 2008; Centre Cult, Paris, France, 2008; Galatasaray Univ, Turkey, 2008; Ramanujan Inst, Turkey, 2008; Am Abstract Artists, Painting Ctr, New York, 2008; Painting Ctr, New York, 2008; Mathematics & Art, traveling exhib throughout Europe, Henry Poincare Inst & Ministry of Cult Affairs, 2010, 2011, Towson Univ, Md, 2012; Join Mathematics Meeting exhib, Mathmatical Art, 2010; Am Abstract Artists 75th Anniversary Exhib, OK Harris Gallery, NY, 2011, Crane Art Ctr, Phila, Pa, 2011, Otrano, Italy, 2011, Kunstverein, Berlin, Germany, 2011, Concrete Art Gallery, Paris, 2011. *Collection Arranged:* Language of Abstraction & Works on Paper, Am Abstract Artists, Betty Parsons Gallery; Am Abstract Artists: The Early Years, mus traveling show; Abstraction in Action, City Gallery, NY; Am Abstract Artist, Visual Arts Ctr, NJ; Ilya Bolotowsky Exhib, Visual Arts Ctr, NJ. *Pos:* Invited speaker, Noyes Mus, NJ, 94 & Mus African Art, NY, 94, Univ Sydney, Australia, 96, Int Soc Arts, Mathematics & Architecture, Freiburg, Germany, 2002, Mathematical Connections in Art, Music & Sci/Int Soc Arts, Mathematics & Architecture, Granada, Spain, 2003, NJ Inst Tech, 2004; invited artist, Harold Berg Endowment, Art Dept, Colo Coll, Colo Springs, 2002; invited Lehman lectr & exhib artist, Morristown Beard Sch, NJ, 2007; Speaker, Int-Interdisciplinary Conf, Albany, NY, 2009; invited speaker, Princeton Univ, 2011. *Teaching:* prof, William Paterson Coll, Wayne, NJ, formerly. *Awards:* ER Squibb and Sons Sculpture Award; Presentation Design Award, Am Inst Architects, 95; Installations Winner, Biennale for US, Malta, 97; Lehman lectr, Morristown Beard Sch, Morristown, NJ, 2007. *Bibliog:* Roskilde Avis (auth), Drom, fantasi realiteter og Illusioner; Synagogue to Unveil Mosaic Mural, Town and Village, NY; Jennifer Lawson (auth), Holocaust mural, The Jewish Week, Inc, New York; Arthur Williams (auth), Sculpture: Technique-Form-Content, Davis Publ, Inc, Worcester, Mass, 88; Ed McCormack (auth), World Class Winners at Art Gallery 54, Artspeak, NY; Mosaic of 16,000 parts

the piece de resistance, 5/13/93; Dan Bishoff (auth), Malta Biennale Awards, Star Ledger, NJ, 7/24/98; Art Mathematique, Societe Mathematique de France ed de la Culture, 2006. *Mem:* Coll Art Asn; ISC; Fine Arts Fedn; Am Inst Architects (chair archit dialogue comt, 94-95); AIEMA; Am Abstract Artist (past pres). *Media:* Stone, Glass; Acrylic Paint. *Res:* Mosaics: ancient medium/modern expression, a series of lectures based on research of ancient mosaics, how these were used to structure space in architecture, and how these methods have evolved in the contemporary use of mosaics as a medium; Mathematical & scientific concepts found in patterns of nature, how these patterns have been used in the visual arts. *Interests:* interdisciplinary creative art using concepts of science and mathematics. *Publ:* Contrib, Perle Fine Arts, 6/82; Hiroshi Murata, Arts; Nassos Daphnis: An Artist in the Art World, Arts; Offset Technology as a fine arts medium, Arts; auth, Spectral Light as Sculptured Space, BRIDGES, 2001; auth, Geometric Mosaic Tiling on Hyperblic Sculptures, Univ Granada, Spain, 2003; auth, Mosaics as a Concept for Mathematics & Science, AIEMA Publ, Int Conf Antique & Medieval Mosaics, Rome, Ital, 2004; auth, Language of Abstraction, Pan Hellenic Soc, Athens, Greece, 2005; auth, Mosaic Art from Pebbles to Pixels, Renaissance Banff, BRIDGES, 2005; Art as a Metaphor for the Fourth Dimension, Int Soc of Arts, Mathematics & Architecture, ISAMA Publ, 2009; Hyperbolic Mosaic Sculptures: A Metaphor for the Intellectual Understanding of the Unseen, L'Association Internationale Pour L'Etude de la Mosaique Antique N Am Branch, Princeton Univ, 2011. *Mailing Add:* 41 Sunset Dr Summit NJ 07901

ROUSSEL, CLAUDE PATRICE
SCULPTOR, EDUCATOR

b Edmundston, NB, July 6, 1930. *Study:* Ecole Beaux-Arts, Montreal, PQ, 50-56; Can Coun Sr Traveling Fel, Europe, 61. *Work:* Smithsonian Inst, Washington, DC; NB Mus, St John; Can Coun Art Bank; Portland Mus, Maine; NB Art Bank; Seoul Olympic Sculpture Garden; Confederation Art Gallery; Beaverbook Art Gallery; and numerous others. *Comn:* Exterior sculpture & interior mural, Univ Moncton Nursing Pavilion, 71; Sailing Olympics, Kingston, Ont, 76; Int Sculpture Garden, Seoul Olympics, 88; Moncton 100 Monument, 90; Clement Cormier Monument, Univ Moncton, 90; Exterior mural, Caisse Populaire Moncton, 99; mosaic murals, comn by The Assomption Cathedral, Moncton, NB, 2005; and numerous others. *Exhib:* Survey 69, Montreal Mus Fine Arts, 69; Owens Art Gallery, 75 & 79; Ctr d'Art du Montreal, Royal, 82; Beaverbrook Art Gallery, 84-88; Univ Moncton Art Gallery, 84; retrospective, Univ Moncton Art Gallery, 93; Claude Roussel Virtual Gallery; Topomania, NB Mus, 2000; Festival Int Des Artvisuels, Caraquet, NB, 2003; Crea-Passion Univ Monicton Art Gallery, 2004; Random Impulses, Centre Culturel, Deippe, NB, 2013; Off the Grid, Beaver Brook Art Gallery, 2014. *Pos:* Asst cur, Beaverbrook Art Gallery, Fredericton, 59-61. *Teaching:* Instr art, Edmundston Pub Schs, 56-59 & Univ Moncton, 63-91, retired; prof emer, Univ Moncton, 98 & Royal Canadian Acad, 2000. *Awards:* Order of Can, 84; McCain Exhib, Beaverbrook Art Gallery, Fredericton, NB, 89; Current Award, Can Soc Educ Art, Ont, 96, RCA, 2012; Order of NB, 2002; Diplome De Medaille Dargent, Art-Sci-Lett, France, 2004; Lifetime Award (Lt Gov), 2005; Hall of Fame for the Arts, Endmundston, NB, 2007; Queen's Jubilee medal, 2012. *Bibliog:* Articles, Arts Atlantic, fall 77 & spring 83; Claude Roussel, Sculpteur, Sculptor, Edition D'Acadie, 87; Calude Roussel, Retrospective (video), 95; Bravo TV, Shaping Art, 2005. *Mem:* Asn Des Artistes Acadiens. *Media:* Wood, Enamel, Mixed Media. *Res:* works on paper. *Interests:* Documenting Biog Documents. *Publ:* Coauth, The Visual Arts, In: The Acadians of the Maritimes, 82. *Mailing Add:* 50 allee des Arts Cap-Pele NB E4N 1R2 Canada

ROUTON, DAVID F
PAINTER, DRAFTSMAN

b Jackson, Tenn, Dec 6, 1931. *Study:* Mexico City Coll, BFA, 59; Univ Iowa, MFA, 63. *Work:* Sheldon Mem Art Gallery, Lincoln, Nebr; Univ Nebr, Lincoln; Univ Minn Art Mus, Minneapolis; Sioux City Art Ctr, Iowa; Coll Notre Dame Md, Baltimore; Doane Coll, Crete Nebr; Mus Nebr Art, Kearney, Nebr; and others. *Comn:* Portrait Carl T. Curtis, US Nat Park Serv, NPS Regional Bldg, Omaha, Nebr. *Exhib:* 24th Bradley Nat, Bradley Univ, Peoria, Ill, 93; 10th Art in the Woods Exhib, City Overland Park, Kans, 93; Galerie Tempo, Roeselane, Belgium, 93-94; Galerie Magenring, Hagen, Ger, 94; 28th Ann Nat Drawing & Small Sculpture Show, Del Mar Coll, Corpus Christi, Tex, 94. *Teaching:* Instr, Mich State Univ, E Lansing, 63-64; Asst prof drawing & painting, State Univ NY, Plattsburg, 64-66 & Univ Minn, Minneapolis, 66-72; prof drawing & painting, Univ Nebr, Lincoln, 76-97, emer, 97-. *Awards:* Canson/Mi-Teintes Award Pastel, 29th Ann Chautauqua Nat, Chautauqua Inst, NY, 86; Jurors Merit Award, La Grange Nat XV, 90; Merit Award, Anderson Winter Show, Anderson Fine Arts Ctr, 93. *Mem:* Coll Art Asn. *Media:* Oil; Drawing. *Publ:* illusr, Sod House Days, Univ Press, Kans, 83; illusr, Ten Years in Nevada, 85, All is But a Beginning, 86, Martha Maxwell, Rocky Mountain Naturalist, 86, Emily: The Diary of a Hard Worked Woman, 87 & Life in Alaska, 88, Univ Nebr Press. *Mailing Add:* 430 Haverford Dr Lincoln NE 68510-2316

ROUX, BARBARA AGNES
ENVIRONMENTAL ARTIST, SCULPTOR

b Huntington, NY, Feb 28, 1946. *Study:* State Univ NY, Coll Old Westbury, BA, 79; Hunter Col, City Univ NY, MFA, 85. *Work:* Islip Art Mus, East Islip, NY; Heckscher Mus, Huntington, NY; Brooklyn Mus, Brooklyn, NY; Metropolitan Mus Art, NY; Cincinnati Mus, Cincinnati, Ohio; Libr, Whitney Mus, NY; Nat Mus of Women in eth Arts, Libr Collection. *Exhib:* Outdoor Sculpture Now, Islip Art Mus, East Islip, NY, 89; Collaborations: Word and Image, Pages Turned, Miami Univ Art Mus, Oxford, Ohio, 91; Featured Artists of the Permanent Collection, Islip Art Mus, 93; Eighteen Suffolk Artists, Univ Art Gallery, State Univ NY at Stony Brook, 95; What on Earth?, Wave Hill, Bronx, NY, 97; Country Pleasures, Heckscher Mus, Huntington, NY, 98; Elements 2000, Saug Harbor Cult Ctr, Newhouse Ctr Contemp Art, Staten Island, NY, 2000; Utopia/Dystopia, Byrdcliffe Arts Colony, Woodstock, NY, 2000; Invisible Forest, Walter Wickiser Gallery, NY, 2003; Within the Land, Islip Art Mus, NY, 2003; Artists, Neighbors, Friends, Heckscher Mus, NY, 2003; Hidden Forrest Exhibit, AIR Gallery, NY, 2005. *Awards:* Alumni Award of Excellence, Communications & Creative Arts, Coll Old Westbury, State Univ NY, 4/98; Artist Residency, Andy Warhol Preserve, The Nature Conservancy, 2005. *Bibliog:* Judy Collischan Van Wagner (auth), Barbara Roux, Arts Mag, 5/90; Helen A Harrison (auth), Pitting Man Against Nature Roux review, New York Times, 8/90; Interview with Barbara Roux, Artscene on Long Island, CableTV, 2/2000; Vivien Raynor (auth), A Show That Tweaks Ecological Concers, NY Times, 9/97; Phyllis Braff (auth), The Intellectual Translated into the Visual, NY Times, 1/99; Amy Storts (auth), Barbara Roux, NY Arts Mag, 2/02; Islip Art Mus, Within the Land, 2003; David Everitt (auth), The Woods and Wetlands Are Her Inspiration, NY Times, 11/03. *Mem:* Artists in Residence, New York. *Media:* Installation Art, Sculptural Environments. *Publ:* Coauth, The Opaque Glass, Water Mark Press, 84; Soc of Plants, Barbara Roux, 2001; Barbara Roux, Huntington, NY. *Mailing Add:* 20 Lloyd Pt Dr Huntington NY 11743

ROW, DAVID
PAINTER

b Portland, Maine, Aug 31, 1949. *Study:* Yale Univ, BA (cum laude), 72, Yale Sch Art, with Al Held, MFA, 74. *Work:* Carnegie Mus Art, Pittsburgh, Pa; Brooklyn Mus Art, NY; Cleveland Mus Art; Hood Mus Art, Dartmouth Col; Wash Nat Airport; and others. *Comn:* Triptych, Richard Lewis Assocs, NY, 87; mural, Washington Nat Airport, 94. *Exhib:* Solo exhibs, John Good Gallery, NY, 87, 89, 91 & 93, Richard Feigen Gallery, Chicago, Ill, 91, Fujii Gallery, Tokyo, Japan, 91, Pamela Auchincloss Gallery, NY, 94, Locks Gallery, Philadelphia, Pa, 95 & Andre Emmerich, NY, 95 & 96, Von Lintel Gallery, 2007; Group exhibs, Armand Hammer Mus Art, Univ Calif Los Angeles, 95; Galerie Thomas von Lintel, Munich, 95 & 97; Turner, Byrne & Runyon, Dallas, 96 & 98; Contemp Arts Forum, Santa Barbara, 96; Mus Beaux Arts, La Chaux de Fonds, 96; Brandstelter & Wyss, Zurich, 98. *Teaching:* Instr drawing & photo, Rutgers Univ, NJ, 77-78; instr drawing & color, Sch Visual Arts, NY, 77-91; vis critic, Tyler Sch Art, 81, Bates Col, 87, Pratt, 88, NY Studio Sch, 90, Syracuse Univ, 93 & Kent State, 94; asst prof, Pratt Inst, Brooklyn, NY, 86-87; vis prof advan painting, Cooper Union Arts & Sci, NY, 94-95, Sch Visual Arts, graduate program, NY, 96-99; vis lectr & painting critic, Mt Royal Sch Art, Md Inst, 96 & Princeton Univ, NJ, 98. *Awards:* Scholar of the House in Painting, Yale Univ, 71-72; Yale-Norfolk Scholar, Norfolk Summer Sch Art & Music, 71; Grant in Painting, Nat Endowment Arts, 87. *Bibliog:* Roberta Smith (auth), Palettes full of ideas about what painting should be, NY Times, 11/1/96; John Zinsser (auth), Continuous Model: The Paintings of David Row, Edition Lintel, Munich, Ger; Alfred MacAdam (auth), Studio: David Row, Art News, 6/97; and others. *Mem:* Am Abstract Artists. *Media:* Oil, Fresco. *Dealer:* Andre Emmerich Gallery 41 E 57th St New York NY 10022; Galerie Thomas Von Lintel 10 Residenzstrasse Munich Germany. *Mailing Add:* 476 Broadway New York NY 10013

ROWAN, DENNIS MICHAEL
PRINTMAKER, EDUCATOR

b Milwaukee, Wis, Jan 6, 1938. *Study:* Univ Wis, BS, 62; Univ Ill, MFA, 64. *Work:* Art Inst Chicago; Boston Mus Fine Arts; Seattle Art Mus, Wash; Okla Art Ctr, Oklahoma City; Honolulu Acad Arts, Hawaii. *Exhib:* Boston Mus Fine Arts, 61, 64-65, 68-69 & 70; Walker Art Ctr, Minneapolis, 62; Chicago Art Inst, 62 & 66; Pa Acad Fine Arts, 63; Seattle Art Mus, Wash, 63-65, 67, 70 & 71; Okla Art Ctr, 68, 70 & 72; Miami Art Ctr, 73; Brooklyn Mus, NY, 73; Calif Palace Legion Honor, San Francisco, 73; Vienna Graphics Biennale, Austria, 73; US Nat Mus, Washington, DC, 74; Kansas City Art Inst, 75; 3rd Biennale Int de l'Image, Epinal, France, 75; and many others. *Teaching:* Prof art, Univ Ill, Urbana-Champaign, 64-, assoc ctr advan study, 71-, prof sch art & design, currently. *Awards:* Purchase Award, 2nd Biennale Int Gravure, Cracow, Poland, 68; Yorkshire Arts Asn Purchase Prize, Brit Int Print Biennale, 70; Juror's Prize, Graphikbiennale Wien, Europahaus, Vienna, Austria, 72. *Media:* Intaglio. *Publ:* Contribr, Prize-winning graphics, Vol 3, 65 & Vol 4, 66; contribr, John Ross & Clare Romano's Complete Printmaker, Free Press, New York & Collier-Macmillan Ltd, Toronto, 72; contribr, Walter Chamberlin's Etching & Engraving, Thames & Hudson, London, 72 & Viking Press, New York, 73. *Mailing Add:* 101 S Scarborough Sidney IL 61877

ROWAN, FRANCES PHYSIOC
PAINTER, WOODCUTTER

b Ossining, NY, Dec 17, 1908. *Study:* Randolph-Macon Woman's Col, 29-30; Cooper Union, BFA, 36; also graphics with Harry Sternberg & woodcuts with Carol Summers, 65-73. *Work:* Randolph-Macon Woman's Col, Lynchburg, Va; Freeport High Sch, NY; Cotton Inc. *Exhib:* Brooklyn Mus 11th Nat Print Show, 58; Audubon Artists, 58 & 59; Am Fedn Arts Traveling Show, 58-59; Knickerbocker Artists, 61; Silvermine Guild Artists 6th & 14th Nat Print Show, 66 & 80; Solo exhib, Sarasota Art Asn, 81. *Teaching:* Instr drawing & painting, Country Art Gallery, Westbury, NY, 55-66; instr drawing & painting, Five Towns Music & Art Found, 70-72; instr drawing, still life & figure, Longboat Key Art Ctr, 77-. *Awards:* First Prizes, Hofstra Univ, 57 & Sarasota Art Asn, 79 & 82; Flax Award, Knickerbocker Artists, 61; and others. *Mem:* Prof Artists Guild; Silvermine Guild Artists; Longboat Key Ctr for the Arts. *Media:* Graphics; Oils. *Mailing Add:* 601 Broadway Longboat Key FL 34228

ROWAN, HERMAN
PAINTER, EDUCATOR

b New York, NY, July 20, 1923. *Study:* Cooper Union; San Francisco State Col; Kans State Col, BS; State Univ Iowa, MA & MFA. *Work:* Walker Art Ctr, Minneapolis; Brooklyn Mus, NY; Univ Notre Dame, South Bend, Ind; Columbus Mus, Ohio; San Diego Gallery Fine Arts, Calif; Tweed Mus, Duluth, Minn. *Exhib:* Grand Central Moderns, NY, 60, 63 & 65; San Francisco Mus Nat Ann, 63; Southwest Ann, Houston Mus, 63; Walker Art Ctr Exhib, 65; Box-Top Art, Tour NZ Galleries, 71-72; Mitzi Landau Gallery, Los Angeles, 82; Tweed Mus Art, Duluth, Minn, 86; retrospective, Katherine Nash Gallery, Univ Minn, 93. *Teaching:* Prof painting, Univ Minn, Minneapolis, 63-93, emer prof, 93-. *Awards:* Lyman Award, Albright Gallery, 59; Purchase Prize, San Diego Gallery Fine Arts, 63. *Media:* Oil. *Collection:* Brooklyn Mus, Tweed Mus, Duluth. *Mailing Add:* University of Minnesota Regis Center for Art 405 21st Ave S Minneapolis MN 55455

ROWAND, JOSEPH DONN
GALLERY DIRECTOR, ART DEALER
b Champaign-Urbana, Ill, July 11, 1942. *Study:* Southern Ill Univ, BFA, 64; Ont Sch Art; Parsons Sch Design, New York. *Collection Arranged:* Vic Huggins, 78, 81, 85, 89 & 93, Dorothy Gillespie, 81, 84, 88 & 92 Maud Gatewood, 83, 87, 89, 91 & 93, Mary Lou Higgins, 84, 87 & 91, Edith London, 82, 84, 86, 89 & 91; Raymond Chorneau, 85, 88 & 91, Andrew Braitman, 92, Will Dexter, 90, Claytopia, 90 & Thomas Sayre, 92; Group Fiber Show 87, Somerhill Gallery, Chapel Hill, NC. *Pos:* Panel mem, How to Buy & Enjoy Contemp Art, City Gallery Contemp Art, Raleigh, NC, 88; adv bd, City Mag, 91 & NC Home Mag, 92; Town Chapel Hill Pub Art Endowment Coun, 91 & 92; owner & dir, Somerhill Gallery, currently; plus numerous juror & adminr positions for arts orgns. *Teaching:* Guest lectr, Sandhills Community Col, Carthage, NC, 85, Arts on the River Festival, Savannah Arts Asn, Ga, 88, Duke Univ Continuing Educ Fac, 89 & 90 & Wake Visual Arts Asn, Raleigh, NC, 92; NC Cent Univ Fine Art of Collecting Symp, 87. *Bibliog:* Kay McClain (auth), Chapel Hill Newspaper, 89; Jo Schwarts (auth), Art Bus News, 90; Kathleen Christiansen & Fred Park (auths), article, Bus Properties, 91; and others. *Mem:* NC Mus Art Found; Duke Univ, Mus Art (bd dir, 92-95); Art Advocates NC; Akland Mus Assocs; Southeastern Ctr Contemp Art; and others. *Specialty:* Contemp American Artists of Southeastern US

ROWE, CHARLES ALFRED
PAINTER, EDUCATOR
b Great Falls, Mont, Feb 7, 1934. *Study:* Mont State Univ, 52-53; Southern Methodist Univ, 56-57; Univ Chicago, 59-60; Art Inst Chicago, BFA, 60; Tyler Sch Art, Temple Univ, Philadelphia, MFA, 68; also with John Rogers Cox, Boris Margo, Max David Brill, Leroy Neiman & James Paulus. *Work:* Victoria & Albert Mus, London; Noel Goldblatt Collection, Chicago; Michael Landon Productions, Hollywood; Banco De Granda, Spain; Star Shower Found, Graveson-en-Provence, France; NASA Space Mus, Cape Canaveral, Fla; CM Russell Mus, Great Falls, Mont. *Comn:* Designed a coord arts coun symbol & related printed materials for Mont Arts Coun, Missoula, 73; designed numerous fabrics for major accounts for Galleon Fabrics, Inc, NY, 74-; USAF Pentagon, Washington, DC, 89, 91 & 92; NASA Mus, Cape Kennedy, Fla, 89. *Exhib:* Dallas Mus Fine Art, 57; Art Inst Chicago, 59; Los Angeles Co Mus, Calif, 65; Solo exhibs, Newark Gallery, Del, 67-69, Mickelson Gallery, Washington, DC, 70 & 74, C M Russell Mus, Great Falls, 72-74, 76, 78, 80, 82-87, 89, Pleiades Gallery, NY, 77 & 81, Sala de Exposiciones, Almunecar, Spain, 88, West Chester Univ, Pa, 92 & Soc Illusrs, NY, 93 & 2004; Mid-Year Show, Butler Inst Am Art, Youngstown, Ohio, 69; 37th Mid-Year Show, Butler Inst Am Art, Youngstown, Ohio, 73; Ball State Nat Drawing & Small Sculpture Show, Ball State Univ, Muncie, Ind, 74; C M Russell Mus Invitational, Great Falls, Mont, 86-91; Nat Drawing Exhib: Exhibits USA, Kansas City, Mo, 89-91; USAF Exhib, Soc Illusrs, NY, 89 & 91; Our Own Show, Soc Illusrs, NY, 90-2008; Atrium Gallery, NY, 95; Hauptman & Greenwood Collections, NY, 94; Kevin Costner, Hollywood, Calif, 95; Howard Pine Studio, Wilmington, DE, 2005; plus over 200 other exhibs. *Collection Arranged:* Univ Del, Mont. State Collection, Mont. State Univ Del State Collection, Great Falls Pub Schs, Michael Landon Prodns, Calif, Jerry Pinkney, Croton-on-Hudon, NY, Kay Collection, Charlotte, NC, Meredith Corp, Des Moines, Collection Knissel, Austria, Duncan Collection, Spokane, Wash, Archives Victoria and Albert Mus, London, artists USAF Nat. Collection, Washington, Jacqueline Pierson, Nice, France, Banco De Granada, Granada, Spain, artists USAF Nat Collection, Washington; NASA Space Mus, Hauptman and Greenwood Collections, NYC, Bush Collection, Swampscott, MA, Kernaghan Collection, Great Falls, Mont, Star Shower Foundation, Graveson, Provence, France, Vera Haas, Dallas, Baker, Honolulu; fabric designer Galleon Fabrics, Inc, NYC, Jones of NY, Saks Fifth Ave, Kevin Kilner, Jordan Baker, Hollywood, Calif, 1987, Steele Big Fork, Mt, Kevin Costner Collection, 1997, designer graphics Mont. State Arts Coun, Del. state duck stamp, 1981. *Pos:* Graphic designer & consult, Chicago, Ill, 57-60; graphic package designer, Am Can Co, Bellwood, Ill, 60-62; graphic designer, Abrams-Bannister Engraving, Inc, Greenville, SC, 62-64; life drawing prog, Greenville Mus Art, 62-64; artist-in-residence, Nat Endowment Arts & Humanities, 72-73; design consult, Galleon Fabrics, Inc, First Run Fabrics, Inc & TAGS, 74-83. *Teaching:* Prof drawing, painting, illustration & graphic design, Univ Del, 64-; exchange prof, Univ Ariz, 83-84; Prof Emeritus, 97. *Awards:* Nat Endowment Arts & Humanities Grant, 72-73; Del Duck Stamp Print, 1981; Unidel Grant, 89; President's Grant, 1/90; and many others. *Bibliog:* Three present rewarding results of sabbatical leaves, Univ Del, News Update, 88; Sara Albert (auth), Potpourri, Cecil Co Arts Coun, 89; Article in Grand Rapids Press, 12/4/89. *Mem:* Soc Illusrs, NY. *Media:* All Media. *Res:* Italy, Spain, France, Mex, Belgium, Germany, Eygpt, Japan, Irealand and Can. *Publ:* Illusr, State duck stamps, New York Art Review, Harshman & Houk; Artists in the Schools-Communities, 72-88, Mont Arts Coun, 88; Duck Stamps and Prints, the Complete Federal and State Ed, Hugh Lauter Levin Assoc Inc, 88, rev ed 91; The New York Art Review, Am References, Inc, 88; artist, Huang Trial, WNSTV Channel 2 & WPVI Channel 6, 89. *Dealer:* Hardcastle Gallery Newark DE. *Mailing Add:* Chapel Hill 133 Aronimink Dr Newark DE 19711

ROWE, HEATHER
INSTALLATION SCULPTOR
b New Haven, Conn, 1970. *Study:* Boston Univ, Sch Fine Arts, 1988-90; Mass Coll Art, BFA, 1993; Columbia Univ, Sch Arts, MFA, 2001. *Exhib:* Solo exhibs include D'Amelio Terras, New York, 2007, Dicksmith Gallery, London, 2008; Group exhibits include The Artist and the Artifact, Fed Reserve Gallery, Boston, 1997; Part 01, Wallach Art Gallery, Columbia University, 2000; Cannibal Delicacies, Neiman Ctr Gallery, New York, 2001; Things Fall Apart All Over Again, Artists Space, New York, 2005; Bunch Alliance and Dissolve, Pub-Holiday Projs, Contemp Arts Ctr, Cincinnati, 2006; Open Wall #2, White Columns, New York, 2006; Practical F/X, Mary Boone Gallery, New York, 2007; Whitney Biennial, Whitney Mus Am Art, New York, 2008; Undone, Whitney Mus at Altria, New York, 2008. *Teaching:* Vis Critic, Basic Drawing, Univ Penn Sch Design, Landscape Architecture, Summer Session, 2003; Basic Drawing, Columbia Univ Scho Arts, New York, 2003-04. *Awards:* Art Sch Assocs Trust Fund Award, Mass Coll Art, 1992; Patrick Gavin Award for Drawing & Painting, Mass Coll Art, 1993; Merit Fels, Visual Arts Div, Columbia Univ, 1999-2001; Hayward Prize Salzburg Stiftung, Am Austrian Found, 2001. *Dealer:* D'Amelio Terras 525 W 22nd St New York NY 10011. *Mailing Add:* c/o D'Amelio Terras 525 W 22nd St New York NY 10011

ROWE, MICHAEL DUANE
PAINTER
b Lykens, Pa, Nov 5, 1947. *Study:* Art Inst Pittsburgh, 71-72. *Work:* Southern Allegheny Mus Art, Loretto, Pa. *Exhib:* Pa Coun Arts, Pa State Mus, Harrisburg, 86-87 & 2007; Dia de los Muertos, Alternative Mus, New York, 90 & 94-95; 56th Nat Mid Yr, Butler Inst Am Art, Youngstown, Ohio, 90 & 92; Images, Pa State Univ, 92-93; Works on Paper, Del Cent Conte Art, Wilmington, 93; Magic Realism, Southern Allegheny Mus, Loretto, Pa, 96-97, 99, 2008; Whitaker Arts & Scis, Harrisburg, Pa, 2000. *Awards:* Grant, Art Matters, 88; First Prize, Delaplaine Gallery, 89; Fel, Pa Coun Arts, 93. *Bibliog:* Michael Tomor (auth), Magic Realism, Art Rev, 99. *Mem:* Southern Allegheny Mus Art, Loretto, Pa. *Media:* Oil. *Interests:* Running, travel, reading. *Dealer:* Mangel Gallery 1714 Rittenhouse Sq Philadelphia PA 19103. *Mailing Add:* 814 Meadow Ln Camp Hill PA 17011-1545

ROWLAND, ADELE
PHOTOGRAPHER
b Ft Rodman, Mass, Dec 4, 1915. *Study:* Carnegie Mellon Univ, 34-35; Univ Southern Calif, BS, 38, MS, 42; Univ Calif, Berkeley, PhD, 49. *Work:* Bibliotheque Nationale, Paris, France; Grunwald Ctr Graphic Arts, Univ Calif, Los Angeles; San Francisco Mus Mod Art, Calif; Libr Cong, Washington, DC; Nanjing Mus Art, China. *Comn:* Greek photomontage, Occidental Life, Los Angeles, Calif, 77; wall mural (7 ft), Kapalua Bay Hotel, Maui, Hawaii, 78; seven wall murals, Torrey Pines Bank, La Jolla, Calif, 85; two wine-country murals, comn by pvt home, Napa, Calif, 89; three Wis photomontages, Hitachi Data Systems, Palo Alto, Calif, 93. *Exhib:* Light Images, Chrysler Mus Art, Norfolk, Va, 78; Haiku Photog Prints, San Jose Mus Art, Calif, 79; Adele's Recent Counterpoint Images, Hearst Gallery, St Mary's Col, Moraga, Calif, 89; Counterpoint Images of Am Dr Adele, Nanjing Mus Art, China, 92; Les Artistes Francais, Le Salon 93, Grand Palais, Paris, France, 93; 138th Ann Int Print Exhib, Royal Photog Soc Gt Brit, Octagon House, Bath, Eng, 94; Panorama de l'Art Vivant '97, Salon d'Automne, Espace Eiffel Branly, Paris, France, 97; Int Dominican Artists, Piazza della Minerva, 42, Rome, 00; Imaginary Imagery, Oakland Munic Water Gallery, Calif, 01; Salon d'Automne, Espace Auteuil, Paris, 01; Int Artists, La Galerie Int, Palo Alto, Calif, 01; Am Artists, France-Ameriques, Paris, 02; Int Artists, Alliance Francaise, San Francisco, 03. *Teaching:* Assoc prof Eng, Calif State Univ, Fresno, 40-50; assoc prof humanities, hist art & photog, Dominican Col, San Rafael, Calif, 51-75 & resident artist, 75-. *Awards:* Award of Distinction, Royal Photog Soc Gt Brit, 94; Most Talented Artist Silver Medal, 7th Int Exhib, Peder Russu, Stockholm, Sweden, 97; Fra Angelico Award for Excellence in Art, Lifetime Achievement Award, Dominican Inst Arts, 98; US Dominican Artist Rep, Convocation of Leading Internat Dominican Artists, Rome, 00. *Bibliog:* Gary Peterson (auth), Marvelous transformation, San Rafael News Pointer, 3/2/94; Unsigned, Spirit and Tradition in American Art, Art Pictorial, Tokyo, Vol 10, 96; B Winegarner (auth), Dominican artist honored with art award, News Pointer, 9/22/98. *Mem:* Alliance Women Artists; Royal Photog Soc Gt Brit. *Interests:* the photomontage aspect of photography. *Mailing Add:* Artist-in-Residence Dominican Univ Calif 50 Acacia Ave San Rafael CA 94901

ROWLAND, ANNE
PHOTOGRAPHER
b Washington, DC. *Study:* Am Univ, 79; Sch Mus Fine Arts, Boston, BFA, 82; Calif Inst Arts, 87-89. *Work:* Bank of Boston; Spencer Mus, Kans; Houston Mus Fine Art, Tex. *Exhib:* Solo exhibs, Hera Coop Gallery, Wakefield, RI, 83, Sch Art, Univ Denver, Colo, 84, Burlington Co Col, Pembrerton, NJ, 84, Zoe Gallery, Boston, 86, 87 & 91, Tartt Gallery, Washington, DC, 90, Greg Kucera Gallery, Seattle, 90-91 & Jayne Baum Gallery, NY, 93; Twelve on 20 x 24, Mus Fine Arts Sch, Boston, 84; Boston Now: Photog, Inst Contemp Art, Boston, 85; 50th Anniversary Celebration, Inst Contemp Art, Boston, 86; The Photog of Invention: Am Pictures of the 1980's, Nat Mus Am Art, Smithsonian, Washington, DC, 89, travelled to Walker Art Ctr, Minneapolis, 89; This is My Body, Greg Kucera Gallery, Seattle, 94; Sum of the Parts, Univ Hawaii Art Gallery, Honolulu, 94; Contemp Collections of the Los Angeles Ctr for Photog Studies, Gallery at 777, Los Angeles, 94; About Face, Real Art Ways, Hartford, Conn, 94; and others. *Awards:* Fel, Nat Endowment Arts, 86; Photog Fel, Mass Coun Arts & Humanities, Artists' Found, 85. *Bibliog:* Miyoshi Barosh (auth), Photo essay, Now Times, Los Angeles, 92; Michael Duncan (auth), Hollywood, Hollywood, Art Issues, Los Angeles, No 26, 1-2/93; Vince Aletti (auth), Voice Choice, Village Voice, NY, 3/9/93. *Dealer:* Tartt Gallery 2017 Q St NW Washington DC 20009. *Mailing Add:* c/o Jayne H Baum Gallery 26 Grove St 4C New York NY 10014

ROY, RAJENDRA
CURATOR
Study: Univ Calif San Diego, BA (polit sci & French lit); Sorbonne Nouvelle, Paris. *Collection Arranged:* Name June Paik and the Worlds of Film and Video, 2000; Between Shadows and Light: Italian Cinematography, 2001; Drama Queens: Women Behind the Camera, 2001. *Pos:* Exec dir, MIX Festival, 1996-2000; prog assoc, Guggenheim Mus, 1995-2000, prog mgr, 2000-2002; dir programming, Hamptons Int Film Festival, 2002-2006, artistic dir, 2006-2007; juror Student Acad Awards, Acad Motion Picture Arts & Sci, 2003-2007; Celeste Bartos chief film cur, Mus Mod Art, 2007-. *Mem:* Berlin Int Film Festival (mem Int Competition Selection Comt). *Mailing Add:* 11 W 53 St New York NY 10019

ROYBAL, JAMES RICHARD
SCULPTOR, PAINTER
b Santa Fe, NM, Aug 23, 1952. *Study:* Highlands Univ, Las Vegas, NMex, 71-72; NMex State Univ, 73-75; Albert Handel-Pastel Hall of Fame, 94-95. *Comn:* Life size Geronimo, Mr. James Garrow, Santa Fe, NMex, 2003; life size nude, Susan Hart Henegar; bronze, Eyes of Vision, Brown Co Mus, Minn; Ella Corothers Dunegan

Coll, Bolivar, Mo; bronze, Keeping a Close Eye. *Exhib:* NMex State Fair Prof Fine Arts, Albuquerque State Fair Grounds, Albuquerque, NMex, 71; NMex State Fair Prof Fine Arts, NMex State Fair, Albuquerque, NMex, 78-81, 86 & 88; Santa Fe Festival of the Arts, Convention Ctr, Santa Fe, NMex, 79-80; Taos Arts Asn, Vistas, Stables Art Ctr, Taos, NMex, 86; NMex State Fair, Permanent Collection, Gov's Gallery, Santa Fe, NMex, 87; Miniatures, Albuquerque Mus of Art, Albuquerque, NMex, 91-94; Invitational Show, Mitchell Mus, 2010. *Teaching:* Instr, Pastel Painting, Valdes Art Workshops, Santa Fe, NMex, 2005-2013, Art Expo, Santa Fe Conv Ctr, 2008. *Awards:* First Place & Purchase Award, NMex Fair Prof Fine Arts Show, 78; Best of Show, NMex State Fair Prof Fine Arts Show, Fair, 86 & 88; Southwest Art Magazine Award, 2003; Hon Mention, Pastel J 100, 2007; 1st place, Oil & Acrylic Contemp Spanish Market, Santa Fe, NMex, 2010; Best of Show, Colores award, 2012. *Bibliog:* Daniel Gibson (auth), Artist of the Year, Santa Fean Mag, 78; Peggy & Harold Samuels (auths), Contemporary Western Artist, Southwest Art Mag, 82; Joy Waldren Murphy (auth), Best Part is Art, Santa Fean Mag, 87; Sara Ford (auth), Focus Sante Fe, 2007. *Mem:* NMex Pastel Soc; Nat Sculpture Soc. *Media:* Painter, All Media, Sculptor, Bronze, Metal cast w/stone. *Specialty:* Representational Art - Western. *Interests:* Oil painting proficiency. *Publ:* Auth, Sculptor James Roybal (cover), 79; Exploring all Possibilities, Santa Fean Mag, 94. *Dealer:* The Edmund Craig Gallery 3550 W 7th Fort Worth TX 76107; Jordan & Roybal Fine Art 924 Ste 5 Paseo de Peralta Santa Fe NM 87501; Santa Fe Fine Art Collector 217 Galesteo Santa Fe NM 87501; Long Coat Fine Art 2825 Sudderth Dr St Ridoso NM 88345. *Mailing Add:* 25 Lone Pine Spur Santa Fe NM 87505

ROYCE-SILK, SUZANNE
CONSULTANT, CURATOR
b Oakland, Calif, Dec 26, 1935. *Study:* Univ Calif, Berkeley, BA (hist art), 83. *Collection Arranged:* Parker Edwards, George Scott Miller, Louis Siegriest, Bolinas Mus, Calif, 92; Gordon Onslow Ford (auth, catalog), Bolinas Mus, Calif, 93; Richard & Martha Shaw, Robert Hudson, Cornelia Schulz-The Stinson Years (auth, catalog), Bolinas Mus, Calif, 93; Calif Contemporary: Three Coastal Collections, Bolinas Mus, Calif, 98; Gordon Onslow Ford Mirando en lo profundo, Seeing in Depth, Fundacion Eugenio Granell, Santiago de Compostela, Spain, 98; Fletcher Benton, Solid Geometry, Sheldon Mem Art Gallery, Univ Nebr, Lincoln, 99; JB Blunk California Spirit; Bolinas Mus, 2000. *Pos:* Spec projs coordr, Phillips Collection, Washington, DC, 83-84, corp progs mgr, 84-86; art communs consult, Suzanne Royce & Assocs, San Francisco, 87-. *Mem:* Am Asn Mus; Nat Asn Corp Art Mgt; Coun Univ Art Mus, Berkeley; Coll Art Asn. *Publ:* Auth, The Years at White Gate Ranch (exhib catalog), Bolinas Mus, Calif, 95. *Mailing Add:* 1408 Kearny St San Francisco CA 94133

ROYER, MONA LEE
PAINTER
b Washington, DC, June 5, 1944. *Study:* Dayton Art Inst, 53; Famous Artists Sch, 66; Wright State Univ, BFA (hons), 78; Georgetown Univ, 85; Alliance Francaise, Paris, 85; Casa Italiana, Washington, 95; Riverbend Art School, Ohio, Roberson Studio, Hawaii, Tepping Studio, Ohio. *Work:* Joan Rivers, NY; The Embassy of Europ Economic Community, Washington; Xerox Corp & Ohio Vision Serv, Columbus, Ohio; Nat Portrait Gallery, Washington; Pat Summerall, Dallas, Tx; Neiman Marcus, Washington, DC; KY Fried Chicken, Louisville, KY; I Magnin, MD; Burke & Herbert Bank, VA; Kettering Foundation, Ohio; Nolan Miller, Hollywood. *Comn:* Andy Williams, Branson, Mo; Visitors Service Staff, Nat Gallery Art, Washington; DM Graves Jr, Asn Old Crows; Hist Soc Bermuda; Joan Rivers, NY; Judith Lieberer Handbags; Painted Violin for Arlington, Symphony, VA; National Gallery Orchestra, Washington, DC; Gold Cup Title & Escrow, VA; Rolls Royce, USA, 2006; Nat Symphony Orchestra, 2006. *Exhib:* Galerie Julian, 92-; solo exhibs, Nat Gallery Art, Washington, You'll Love It Gallery, Palm Beach, 94 & 95, Fashion Accessories Expo, NY, 94, Gramercy Park Gallery, NY, 94 & 95, Saks Fifth Ave, Washington, 94, 95 & 96, Christina's, Martha's Vineyard, 94 & 95 & Russell Senate Rotunda, Washington, 97; Broadway Gallery, Fairfax, Va, 98; Toledo Mus Art, Ohio; Columbus Mus Fine Art, Ohio; Iranian Embassy; Brit Embassy; Capitol Hill; Phillips (mus) Mansion; Marin Price Gallery, Chevy Chase, Md, 2000; Foliograph Gallery, DC, 2001-2005; Art & Frame by Valentino, 2002-2003; Mt Vernon Plantation, Va, 2003; Sisco Systems Beastie Bizaar, 2004-2006; Washington Int Horse Show, 2004; Riverbend Designs, WVa, 2005; Watercolors of Columbus Gallery, 9 Yrs; Nat Symphony Show House, 2006; Daughters Am Revolution, Washington, DC, 2007-2008; Washington Club, Nat Pen Women, 2007; Elizabeth Stone Gallery, Alexandria, Va, 2007. *Pos:* Prof painter (artist), Sales Art/Dayton, selling through galleries and out of her own studio, 67-68; dealer & consult, 69-; exhib aide & art info specialist, Nat Gallery Art, Washington, DC; licensed tour guide, (Art Specialists Tours); sketch artist, Nat Gallery of Art Concert Series, Washington, DC, 94-2008. *Teaching:* Independent Art Marketing, 94-. *Awards:* Second in Painting, Nat Arboretum, Washington, 89; One Artist Hon, Toledo Mus Art, 95; and over 70 total awards. *Bibliog:* Jacqueline Hall (auth), Enjoying paintings, Columbus Dispatch, 78 & 79; Kay Blue (auth), article, Wright State Alumni News, 91; Kristen Hartke (auth), Hill Rag, Art Critic, Washington, 91; Alexandria Gazette, 2000, plus others. *Mem:* Guild Prof (Art) Tour Guides; Nat Trust Hist Preserv; Nat Capitol Hist Soc; Blair House. *Media:* Oil, Watercolor. *Publ:* Delta Queen Cover, CFA program, Cincinnati, 68; Eight art covers, Hill Rag, Washington, 85-91; art covers, Foxhall Gazette, Fagon Publ, Washington, 90-91; auth, Journal of Electronic Warfare, 92; cover art, Wright State News, 92; self-pub Pastel Cats, 92, 2000; My Mother's Friends, The Siamese Cats & Romantic Watercolors, self publ. *Mailing Add:* PO Box 34 Mount Vernon VA 22121

ROYSDON, EMILY
INSTALLATION SCULPTOR, CONCEPTUAL ARTIST
Study: Hampshire Coll, BA, 1999; Univ Calif, Los Angeles, MFA, 2006. *Exhib:* When Artists Say We, Artists Space, New York, 2006; Read Me, Armory Ctr for Arts, Pasadena, Calif, 2007; The Way That We Rhyme, Yerba Buena Ctr for Arts, 2008; The Generational: Younger Than Jesus, New Mus, New York, 2009; Whitney Biennial, Whitney Mus Am Art, New York, 2010. *Awards:* Hoyt Award, UCLA, 2006; Art Matters Grant, 2008; Franklin Furnace Grant, 2009. *Bibliog:* Cate McQuaid (auth), Something Borrowed, Boston Globe, 5/30/2003; Suzanne Muchnic (auth), Feminism Looks to the Horizons, Los Angeles Times, 3/12/2007; Holland Cotter (auth), Ecstatic Resistance, NY Times, 12/18/2009

ROZIER, ROBERT L
PAINTER
Study: St Mary's Seminary Col, Perryville, Mo, BA, 72; Mich State Univ, East Lansing, MFA, 81. *Exhib:* Columbia Art League Ann Exhib, Columbia, Mo, 77; Knollwood Gallery, Western Mich Univ, Kalamazoo, 80; All Area 1985 Exhib, Saginaw Art Mus, Mich, 86; Nat Juried Exhib, Arlington Art Asn, Arlington Mus Art, Tex, 87; Four Views of the Figure, Pontiac Art Ctr, 88; solo exhibs, Flora Kirsch Beck Gallery, Alma Col, 83, Colby-Sawyer Col, New London, NH, 84, Creative Arts Gallery, Mt Pleasant, Mich, 87, Saginaw Valley State Univ, 88. *Teaching:* Instr painting, drawing, watercolor, Art Reach Mid-Mich, Mt Pleasant, 81-82; instr illus, Lansing Community Col, 82; asst prof, Alma Col, Mich, 83-. *Media:* Watercolor. *Dealer:* Cade Gallery, Royal Oak, MI. *Mailing Add:* 416 Yale Ave Alma MI 48801

ROZMAN, JOSEPH JOHN
PAINTER, EDUCATOR
b Milwaukee, Wis, Dec 26, 1944. *Study:* Univ Wis, Milwaukee, BFA (with honors), 67, MFA, 69. *Work:* Southwest Tex State Coll; Carroll Coll, Waukesha, Wis; Racine Art Mus, Wis; Georgetown Univ, Washington, DC; Milwaukee Art Mus; and others. *Comn:* Complete ed of etchings for membership drive, Milwaukee Art Ctr, 69; Award Emblem Design, Lakefront Festival of Arts, Milwaukee Art Ctr, 73 & 77; PBS Great TV Auction (poster), WMVS TV, 78. *Exhib:* 19th, 20th & 21st Boston Printmakers Nat, Boston Mus Fine Arts, 67-69; Nat Print & Drawing Exhib, Okla Art Ctr, Oklahoma City, 67-68 & 72; Int NW Printmakers Exhib, Seattle Art Mus & Portland Art Ctr, 68 & 69; Printmaking: Wisconsin Editions, Milwaukee Art Mus, 72; solo exhib, Milwaukee Art Mus, 73 & Joy Horwich Gallery, Chicago, 80 & 83; Artists/Toys Exhib, Milwaukee Art Mus, 77 & 79; Works on Paper, Art Inst Chicago, 78; Wisconsin Directions Two: Here & Now, Milwaukee Art Mus, 78; Watercolor USA, Springfield Art Mus, 81; Prints & Multiples, Art Inst Chicago, 81; Wis Masters Exhib, Wis Acad Arts & Scis, 86; The Aesthetic Excursion: Artists Look at Travel & Transportation, Wustum Mus Fine Arts, Racine, 89; Fourth Int Biennial Print Exhib, Taipei Fine Arts US, Taiwan, Rep of China, 90; Watercolor Wisconsin: Celebrating 25 Years, Charles A Wustum Mus Art, Racine, 91; Hometown Heritage: Racine & Kenosha Artists in Ram's Collection, Racine Art Mus, Racine, Wis; and others. *Pos:* Prof & chair art dept, Mount Mary Coll, Milwaukee, Wis, 1975-2008. *Teaching:* Instr design & printmaking, Univ Wis-Milwaukee, 67-69 & 72-73; instr printmaking, Milwaukee Art Mus, 68-76; instr printmaking & painting, Carthage Coll, 69-72; vis lectr art, Univ Wis-Parkside, 70-71; instr printmaking & design, Layton Sch Art & Design, 73-74; prof printmaking, painting & photography, Mt Mary Coll, Wis, 75-2008; artist-in-residence, Univ Wis-Platteville, 83. *Awards:* Logan Award, Art Inst Chicago, 66, Curtis Award, Art Inst Chicago, 81; Edgewood Coll Award, Madison Nat Watercolor Exhib, 88; Janey & Carl Moebius Award for Excellence, Alumni Art Show 15, Univ Wis-Milwaukee Art Mus, 89; William Bushel Purchase Award, Watercolor Wis, 92; many others. *Bibliog:* Dean Jensen (auth), Art in a cold climate, Wisc Acad Rev, 3/83; James Auer (auth), Rozman combines patience craft & vision, Milwaukee J, 91; Elizabeth McGowan (auth), Wet & wild, J Times, 6/13/96. *Mem:* Milwaukee Art Mus; Racine Art Mus. *Media:* Watercolor; Mixed Media. *Mailing Add:* 5125 Darby Pl Racine WI 53402

RUB, TIMOTHY F
MUSEUM DIRECTOR
b New York, NY, Mar 9, 1952. *Study:* Middlebury Coll, BA (art hist), 74; NYU, MA (art hist), 79; Yale Univ, MBA, 87; Harvard Univ, Postgrad, 98. *Pos:* Curatorial intern, Met Mus Art, 83; guest cur, Bronx Mus Arts, NY, 85-86; cur, Cooper-Hewitt Mus, New York, 83-87; assoc dir, Hood Mus, Dartmouth Coll, Hanover, NH, 87-91, dir & COO, 91-2000; dir, Cincinnati Art Mus, 2000-06; dir & chief exec officer, Cleveland Mus Art, 2006-2009; George D Widener dir, CEO, Philadelphia Mus Art, 2009-. *Teaching:* Lectr art & archit history, Cooper-Hewitt Mus/Parsons Sch Design, Stevens Inst Technol, 79-84. *Mailing Add:* Philadelphia Mus Art PO Box 7646 Philadelphia PA 19101-7646

RUBELL, DONALD
COLLECTOR
Pos: Gynecologist and hotel executive; retired. *Awards:* Named one of Top 200 Collectors, ARTnews mag, 2004-12; Smithsonian Archives of Am Art Medal, 2010. *Collection:* Contemporary art. *Mailing Add:* The Rubell Art Collection 95 Northwest 29th St Miami FL 33127

RUBELL, MERA
COLLECTOR
Awards: Named one of Top 200 Collectors, ARTnews mag, 2004-13; Smithsonian Archives of Am Art Medal, 2010. *Collection:* Contemporary art. *Mailing Add:* 46 E 73d St New York NY 10021

RUBELLO, DAVID JEROME
PAINTER, PHOTOGRAPHER
b Detroit, Mich, Sept 3, 1935. *Study:* La Acad Di Belli Arti, Rome, with Franco Gentilini, BFA, 61; Det Kongelige Akademi, Copenhagen, with Richard Mortensen, 63-66; Univ Mich, Ann Arbor, with Guy Palazzola, MFA, 72. *Work:* Philip Morris Collection, Washington, DC; Tate Gallery, London; Victoria & Albert Mus, London; Brit Libr; Mus Mod Art, New York; Stanford Univ; Rijksmuseum, The Hague; Book Mus, The Hague; and others; Kresge Foundation Collection. *Comn:* Mural-painting, New Detroit, Inc, Mich, 72; mural-painting, Residential Coll, Ann Arbor, Mich, 73.

Exhib: Solo exhibs, Slusser Art Gallery, Univ Mich, 78, Shippensburg State Univ, 84, GM Design Ctr, Warren, Mich, 2007, Ellen Kayrod Gallery, Detroit, Mich, 2012; Konkrete Miniatures Invitational, Amsterdam, 81; Null Dimension, Fulda, Ger, 88; Systemica Constructive Art, Madrid, 89; Reform Function, Detroit Arts Mkt, 93; Ann Celebrate Mich Artists, P Cart Ctr, Rochester, 94, 95 & 96; Photo Nat 2, Ella Sharp Mus, Mich, 95; Patrimonio Invitational, Wayne State Univ Gallery, Detroit, 96; Planet Art Gallery, Capetown, S Africa, 99; New Life Forms, Maniscalco Gallery, Grosse Point, Mich, 2000; Detroit Focus, 2000; Archive 90s, Amsterdam, London; Invitational Drawing Exhib, Paint Creek Art Ctr, Rochester, Mich, 2007; Dennos Mus, Traverse City, Mich, 2007; Oakland Community Coll, Auburn Campus, Auburn, Mich, 2008; Invitational, Geometry, Robinson Gallery, BBal, Bloomfield Hills, Mich, 2009. *Pos:* Artist coordr, Italian-Am Archives, Warren, Mich, 87, dir, 88. *Teaching:* Lectr, Univ Mich, Ann Arbor, 73-74; asst prof art, Pa State Univ, University Park, 74-80; assoc prof art, Towson State Univ, Md, 80-81 & Univ Mich, Ann Arbor, 87-90; lectr, Ctr Creative Studies, Detroit, Mich, 97-99; adj prof art, Daytona State Coll, Fla, 2007-. *Awards:* Fel, Va Ctr Creative Arts, 81; Mich Coun Arts Grant, 87; Mich Coun Arts Grant, 87-88. *Bibliog:* Blank page, B-4 Publ, London 90; Structurist, No 37-38, 97-98, No 41-42, 2001-02 & No 45-46, 2005-2006; New Life Forms, Black & White Fine Art Photog, 6/2001. *Mem:* Mich Photog Hist Soc. *Media:* Acrylic, Wood. *Publ:* Auth, Reflection and Form; contribr, articles to prof journals including: The Structurist, 99-2002; featured prof artist profile B&W Fine Art Photog Mag, June, 2001; My Sicilian Garden, Poetry & Photographs, 2004; auth, Moment to Moment, Away at Home, story poems & photographs, 2007; auth, Drawing on Words, 2009-10. *Dealer:* Arnold Klein Gallery Royal Oak MI. *Mailing Add:* 22062 27 Mile Rd Ray MI 48096

RUBEN, ALBERT
PAINTER
b New Orleans, La, Dec 4, 1918. *Study:* Univ Calif, Los Angeles, BA (hon; art), 41; Art Students League, with Robert Brackman & F V Dumond, 44-46. *Work:* Elizabeth Greenshields Found, Montreal. *Exhib:* Solo exhib, Regina Gallery, NY, 55, Studio Gallery Workshop, NY, 59 & Doll & Richards, Boston, 61; Butler Mus Am Art, 60; Nat Acad Ann Exhib, NY, 72; Allied Artists Am Ann Exhib, NY, 75-78. *Teaching:* Instr painting, Pels Sch Art, NY, 65-66 & Montserrat Sch Art, Mass, 73-74. *Awards:* Gold Medals, Am Veterans Art Soc, 57 & Rockport Art Asn, 68 & 80. *Mem:* Allied Artists Am; Rockport Art Asn; North Shore Art Asn; life mem Art Students League NY

RUBENSTEIN, EPHRAIM
PAINTER
b Brooklyn, NY, 1956. *Study:* Columbia Univ, AB (Art History), 1978, MFA, 1987; Brooklyn Mus Art Sch, 1970-74, 1978-79; Nat Acad Design, Sch Fine Arts (Merit Scholar), 1979. *Work:* Metrop Mus Art, New York; Longwood Ctr Visual Arts, Longwood College, Farmville, VA. *Exhib:* Solo exhibs include Tibor de Nagy Gallery, New York, 1986, 1988, 1990, 1992, 1994, 1995, 1997, Nicholas Roerich Mus, New York, 1985, Marsh Gallery, Richmond, VA, 1991, 1994, Peninsula Fine Arts Ctr, Newport News, VA, 1991, Olin & Smoyer Gallery, Salem, VA, 1995, Tatistcheff & Co, New York, 1997, Flippo Galery, Ashland, VA, 2001, Laurel Tracey Gallery, NJ, 2002; Ann Invitational Exhib Contemp Am Art, Nat Acad Mus, New York, 1984, 1994, 1998, 2000, 2004 & 2008; Group exhibs include The Sentient Object, Emerson Gallery, McLean, VA, 2001; Painting, Laurel Tracey Gallery, Red Bank, NJ, 2002, Recent Landscape Paintings, 2003, Bread & Fruit, 2004. *Teaching:* Assoc Prof Arts, Univ Richmond, VA, 1987-98. *Awards:* Distinguished Educ Award, Univ Richmond, 1993; Emil & Dines Carlsen Award, Nat Acad Design, 2004 & Beatrice & Sidney Laufman Award, 2008. *Dealer:* Laurel Tracey Gallery, 10 White St, Red Bank, NJ 07701. *Mailing Add:* 215 W 57th St New York NY 10019

RUBIN, DAVID S
CURATOR, WRITER
b Los Angeles, Calif, June 18, 1949. *Study:* Univ Calif, Los Angeles, AB, 72; Harvard Univ, MA (art hist), 74; Mus Mgt Inst, 89. *Work:* Ogden Mus of Southern Art. *Exhib:* Drawing Conclusions I & II, NY Arts Gallery, 2003; Cursive, Tenri Cultural Inst, 2005; Draw, Scissors, Paper, Domestic Setting, 2006; Bihl Haus, San Antonio, 2007-2012; Cursive 2, Artist-Commune, Hong Kong, 2007; Loyola Univ, New Orleans, 2008; Talento bilingue de Houston, 2011; Solo Exhibs: Blue Star Contemp Art Center, San Antonio, 2008; Barristers Gallery, New Orleans, 2010, Highwire Arts, San Antonio, 2012. *Collection Arranged:* Black and White are Colors (auth, catalog), Galleries Claremont Cols, 79, & Contemporary Triptychs (auth, catalog), 82; Jay DeFeo (auth, catalog), San Francisco Art Inst, 84, Wally Hedrick (auth, catalog), 85 & Concerning the Spiritual (auth, catalog), 85; William Baziotes (auth, catalog), Freedman Gallery, 87, Computer Assisted (auth, catalog) 87 & Edward Albee Collection, 88; Painting from the San Francisco Bay Area (auth, catalog), Paine Art Ctr, 88; Cynthia Carlson (auth, catalog), 89; Contemp Hispanic Shrines (auth, catalog), Freedman Gallery, 90; Art About AIDS, 89, Donald Lipski (auth, catalog) 90, Freedman Gallery; Cruciformed (auth, catalog), Cleveland Ctr Contemp Art, 91; Petah Coyne (auth, catalog), Cleveland Ctr Contemp Art, 92; Ellen Brooks (auth, catalog), Cleveland Ctr Contemp Art, 93; Old Glory: The Am Flag in Contemporary Art (auth, catalog), Cleveland Ctr Contemp Art, 94; It's Only Rock & Roll: Rock & Roll Currents in Contemporary Art (auth, catalog), Exhib Mgt Inc, 95; Elusive Nature (auth, catalog), Cuenca Biennial, 96; Phoenix Triennial (auth, catalog), 98; Photography Now (auth, catalog), 2000; Chelsea Rising (auth, catalog), 2001; Al Held (auth, catalog), 2002; Douglas Bourgeois (auth, catalog), 2003; Birdspace: A Post Audubon Artists Aviary, (auth, catalog) 2004; Tomer Ganihar: Raving in the Desert (auth, catalog), 2005; The Culture of Queer: A Tribute to JB Harter (auth, catalog), 2005; Celebrating Freedom: The Art of Willie Birch (auth, catalog), 2006; Stuart Allen: Mapping Daylight (auth, catalog), 2007; Playing with Time, Blue Star Conempt Art Ctr, San Antonio, 2008; Chocolate: A Photog Exhib, San Antonio Mus Art, 2008; Marcia Gygli King (auth, catalog), San Antonio Mus Art, 2009; Waterflow (auth, catalog), San Antonio Mus Art, 2009; David Halliday, San Antonio Mus Art, 2009; Ry Cooder/Vincent Valdez (auth, catalog), San Antonio Mus Art, 2009; John Hernandez (auth, catalog), San Antonio Mus Art, 2009; Psychedelic: Optical & Visionary Art since the 1960's (auth, catalog), San Antonio Mus Art, 2010; Photos of the Brothers Montiel Klint, San Antonio Mus Art, 2010; Daniel Lee, San Antonio Mus Art, 2011; Adad Hannah, San Antonio Mus Art, 2012. *Pos:* Asst dir, Galleries Claremont Cols, 77-82; asst prof, Art History, Scripps Coll, 77-82; contrib ed, Arts Mag, NY, 79-81; cur, Los Angeles Visual Arts, 82; dir, Santa Monica Coll Art Gallery, 82-83; dir exhibs, San Francisco Art Inst, 83-85; adj cur, San Francisco Mus Mod Art, 83-85; guest cur, Paine Art Ctr, Oshkosh, Wis, 86-88; dir, Freedman Gallery, Albright Col, Reading, Pa, 86-90; assoc dir & chief cur, Cleveland Ctr Contemp Art, 90-94; cur 20th century art, Phoenix Art Mus, 94-99; US Comnr, 1996 Cuenca Biennial of Painting, 96; cur visual arts, Contemp Arts Ctr, New Orleans, 2000-06; cur contemp art, San Antonio Mus Art, 2006-. *Teaching:* Lectr art hist, Sch Visual Arts, NY, 76-77; asst prof art hist, Scripps Coll, Claremont, Calif, 77-82. *Awards:* Nat Endowment Arts Mus Fel, Fogg Art Mus, 75-76; summer fel, Guggenheim Mus, 76; Visual Arts Achievement Award, N Ohio LIVE Mag, 92 & 94. *Mem:* Coll Art Asn; Int Asn Art Critics; Am Asn Mus; Assoc Art Mus Cur. *Media:* drawing. *Res:* Contemporary art, twentieth century art, automatism, abstract expressionism, Californian art. *Publ:* Jean St Pierre, Re-Dact, 84; Fritz Scholder: Flirting with Possessions, 97; American Dreamer: The Art of Philip C Curtis, 99; auth, The Art of Beth Ames Swartz, 2002; auth, Baby-Boom Daydreams: The Art of Douglas Bourgeois, 2003; Willie Birch, 2005; Psychedelic: Optical & Visionary Art since the 1960's, 2010. *Dealer:* Barristers Gallery New Orleans. *Mailing Add:* 427 Quentin Dr San Antonio TX 78201

RUBIN, DONALD VINCENT
SCULPTOR
b New York, NY, July 10, 1937. *Study:* studies with CE Monroe Jr & Ernest Berke. *Work:* Hunstville Mus of Art. *Comn:* US Army War Col, Carlisle Barracks, Pa; Am Polled Hereford Asn; Del River & Bay Auth. *Exhib:* Soc Animal Artists Exhib Conv, NY, 79; solo exhibs, Brass Door Galleries, Houston, 77, Hunter Gallery, San Francisco, 77, Indian Paint Brush, Vail, Colo, 77-94 & Huntsville Mus Art, Ala, 78; Nat Sculpture Soc 47th Ann Exhib, NY, 80; and many others. *Pos:* Bd Dirs, Huntsville Mus Art, 81-89. *Bibliog:* Ralph Perril (auth), Donald Rubin (Huntsville Alabama), Art Voices South Mag, 7-10/78; Cover Photo Polled Hereford World, 10/88; Francis Robb (auth), Don Rubin American Realistic Sculptor (monogr), Art Press, 11/88. *Mem:* Signature Artists; Soc Animal Artists; Am Artists Prof League (fel); Salmagundi Club. *Media:* Bronze. *Specialty:* Western Art. *Interests:* Portrait Relief Sculpture. *Publ:* Auth, The Cattail Ranch & An American Realist Sculptor - Four Decades of Sculpture. *Dealer:* J N Bartfield Art Galleries 30 W 57th St New York NY 10019. *Mailing Add:* PO Box 49656 Colorado Springs CO 80919

RUBIN, LAWRENCE
ART DEALER, COLLECTOR
b New York, NY, Feb 22, 1933. *Study:* Brown Univ, BA, 55; Univ Paris. *Pos:* Pres, M Knoedler, New York, formerly; art adv panel, IRS; principal, Galleria Lawrence Rubin, Milan Italy, formerly; principal partner, Lawrence Rubin Greenberg Van Doren Fine Art, New York, 99-. *Mem:* Art Dealers Asn (vpres). *Specialty:* Twentieth century contemporary paintings sculpture and drawings; artists Adolph and Esther Gottlieb Found, Inc, Michael David, Richard Diebenkorn, Estate of Herbert Ferber, Glenn Goldberg, Nancy Graves, Howard Hodgkin, Robert Motherwell, Robert Rauschenberg, Estate of David Smith, Frank Stella, Donald Sultan, John Walker. *Collection:* Contemporary painting and sculpture. *Mailing Add:* Van Doren Waxter Gallery 23 E 73rd St New York NY 10021

RUBIN, PATRICIA
HISTORIAN, ADMINISTRATOR
Study: Yale Univ, BA (summa cum laude), 1975; Courtauld Inst Art, London Univ, MA, 1978; Harvard Univ, PhD, 1986. *Pos:* Judy and Michael Steinhardt dir, New York Univ Inst Fine Arts, 2009-. *Teaching:* Instr Italian Renaissance art, Courtauld Inst, London Univ, 1979-2009. *Awards:* Eric Mitchell Prize, 96. *Res:* 15th and 16th century central Italian painting; Rafael, Italian Renaissance drawings, Vasari's Lives, collecting of renaissance art. *Publ:* Auth, Giorgio Vasari: Art and History, Yale Univ Press, 1995; co-ed (with G Ciappelli), Art, Memory, and Family in Renaissance Florence, Cambridge Univ Press, 2000; auth, Images and Identity in Fifteenth-century Florence, Yale Univ Press, 2007; and others. *Mailing Add:* NYU Inst Fine Arts James B Duke House 1 E 78th St New York NY 10075

RUBIN, SANDRA MENDELSOHN
PAINTER
b Santa Monica, Calif, Nov 7, 1947. *Study:* Univ Calif, Los Angeles, BA, 76, MFA, 79. *Work:* Los Angeles Co Mus Art; Santa Barbara Mus Art; Univ Calif, Los Angeles; Boise Art Mus, Idaho. *Exhib:* Exhib of Contemp Los Angeles Artists, Nagoya City Mus, Nagoya, Japan, 82; A Heritage Renewed, Univ Art Mus, Santa Barbara, 83; solo exhib, Los Angeles Co Mus Art, Calif, 85, Claude Bernard Gallery, NY, Pieces from Life, LA Louver, Venice, Calif, 1992, 2003, 2007, 2011; Am Realism: Twentieth-Century Drawings & Watercolors, San Francisco Art Mus, 86; The Janss Collection, Boise Art Mus, Idaho, 88; Calif Cityscapes, San Diego Mus Art, 91; Cityscapes, Community Arts Inc & Los Angeles Stories, Jack Rutberg Fine Arts, Los Angeles, Calif, 93; Place in Time: Contemporary Landscape, Scripps Coll, 2008. *Awards:* Young Talent Purchase Award, Los Angeles Co Mus Art, 80; Nat Endowment Arts Artist's Fel Grant, 81 & 91. *Bibliog:* David Hale (auth), Capturing the Californias, Fresno Bee, 10/4/92; Andy Brummer (auth), The face of the place-the city of Los Angeles gets itself painted, Visions, winter 92; Pat Leddy (auth), Dreamtown, Los Angeles stories at Jack Rutberg Fine Arts, Artweek, 3/93. *Media:* Oil on Canvas. *Dealer:* LA Louver Gallery 55 N Venice Blvd Venice CA 90291. *Mailing Add:* PO Box 627 Boonville CA 95415

RUBINFIEN, LEO H
PHOTOGRAPHER, WRITER
b Chicago, Ill, Aug 16, 1953. *Study:* Reed Col; Calif Inst Arts, BFA, 74; Yale Univ Sch Art, MFA, 76. *Work:* Cleveland Mus Art; San Francisco Mus Mod Art, Calif; Metrop Mus Art, New York; Mus Mod Art, New York; Corcoran Gallery Art; Seattle Art Mus; Yale Univ Art Gallery; Cincinnati Art Mus; Mus Fine Arts, Houston; Tokyo Metropolitan Mus Photog. *Comn:* Grandola Alentejo Province, Portugal, 2000-01; Citigroup, 2005-06. *Exhib:* Solo Exhibs: Metrop Mus Art, NY, Philadelphia Coll Art, Robert Mann Gallery, NY, Seattle Art Mus, Seibu Art Forum, Tokyo & Cleveland Mus Art, Fraenkel Gallery & Castelli Graphics, Corcoran Gallery Art, 2008, San Francisco Mus Mod Art, 2008, Nat Mus Modern Art, Tokyo, Yale Univ Art Center, Cantor Art Center, Stanford Univ, Taka Ishi Gallery, Tokyo; Group Exhibs: The New Color, Int Ctr Photog, NY, 81; New Am Color Photog, Inst Contemp Arts, London, 81; Color & Colored, San Francisco Mus Mod Art, Calif, 81; Color as Form, George Eastman House, Rochester, NY & Corcoran Gallery, Washington, DC, 81; Recent Acquisitions, Mus Mod Art, NY, 84; New Directors, New Films, Mus Mod Art, NY, 89; Met Mus Art, NY, Robert Mann Gallery. *Collection Arranged:* Home, Tomatsu, Skin of the Nation, San Francisco Mus Modern Art, 2002-2005; Garry Winogrand, San Francisco Mus Modern Art and Nat Gallery of Art, 2010-. *Teaching:* Instr photog, Swarthmore Col, 77 & Sch Visual Arts, NY, 78-87; assoc prof art, Fordham Univ, 81-87; vis lectr, Cooper Union, 82; instr, Reed Col, 2001; instr, NY Univ, 2001-; Sch Visual Arts, 2000-04; artist in res, Corcoran Sch Art, Wash, 2008; Lightbourne Guest Artist, Art Academy of Cincinnati, 2011. *Awards:* Guggenheim Found Fel, 82-83; Asian Cult Coun Fel, 84; fel, Int Ctr Advanced Studies, NY Univ, 98; Japan Found, 2002. *Bibliog:* Pepe Karmel (auth), The anxious moment, Soho News, 11/4/81; Prudence Carlson (auth), article, Art in Am, 3/82; Ian Buruma (auth), New York Review of Books, 10/92; Max Kozloff (auth), Face Value; Liz Jobey (auth), The Guardian; and others. *Media:* Photography. *Publ:* Auth, Love-Hate Relations, Artforum, 78 & The Man in the Crowd, In: Photography in Print, 81, Touchstone Press; 10 Photographs in Camera Mainichi, 5/84; dir & co-writer, The Money Juggler (56 min film), 88; dir & coauth, My Bed in the Leaves (film), 90; auth (bks), A Map of the East, Godine, Thames, and Hudson Inc, Boston, 92; auth, The Poetry of Plain Seeing, 12/2000, Perfect Uncertainty, 3/02, The Mask Behind the Face, 6-7/04, Where Diane Arbus Went, 10/05, Art in America; auth (bk), Shomei Tomatsu: Skin of the Nation, Yale Univ Press & San Francisco MOMA, 2004; (auth) Wounded Cities, Steidl, 2008; auth, A map of the East, Godine, 92; and many others; auth, The Ardbeg, 2010. *Dealer:* Robert Mann Gallery 210 11th Ave New York NY 10001; Taka Ishii Gallery, Tokyo

RUBINSTEIN, CHARLOTTE STREIFER
WRITER, CURATOR
b New York, NY, Dec 14, 1921. *Study:* Brooklyn Col, BA, 41; Teachers Col, Columbia Univ, MA, 46; Otis Art Inst, Los Angeles, MFA, 69. *Collection Arranged:* Women USA Nat Exhib (with catalog), Nat Endowment Arts, 73; Women Sculptors of the Nineties, 96. *Teaching:* Instr art hist, appreciation & design, Fullerton Col, 71-74. *Awards:* Best Humanities Bk of 1982, Asn Am Publ, 82; Individual Res Grant, Am Asn Univ Women, 84-85; Nat Award, Women's Caucus Art, 94. *Mem:* Coll Art Asn; Women's Caucus Art; Art Lib Soc NAm. *Res:* All aspects of history of American women artists. *Publ:* Auth, The early career of Frances Flora Bond Palmer (1812-1876), Am Art J, fall 85; The first American women artists, Women's Art J, spring-summer 82; American Women Artists: From Early Indian Times to the Present, G K Hall/Avon Bks, 82; American Women Sculptors: A History of Women Working in Three Dimensions, G K Hall, 90; Fanny Palmer: The Work Horse of Currier & Ives, 97

RUBINSTEIN, RAPHAEL
CRITIC
b Lawrence, Kans, July 22, 1955. *Study:* Bennington Col, BA, 79. *Pos:* Managing ed, Flash Art, 89-90; Assoc ed, Art in Am, 94-96, sr ed, 97-. *Awards:* John McCarron Award. *Publ:* Auth, Europa resurgent: nouveau realisme, 88, Outstations of the post modern, 89 & A hemisphere decentered: Mexican art comes north, 91, Arts Mag; Sight unseen: Derrida at the Louvre, 91 & The painting undone: supports/surfaces, 91, Art Am. *Mailing Add:* Art in America 575 Broadway New York NY 10012

RUBINSTEIN, SUSAN R See SuZen, Susan R Rubinstein

RUBIO, ALEX
PAINTER, PRINTMAKER
b San Antonio, 1968. *Study:* San Antonio Art Inst; Univ Tex, San Antonio; studied printmaking with Sam Coronado. *Exhib:* Solo exhibs include Blue Star Ctr Contemp Art, San Antonio, 2003, ArtPace, San Antonio, 2007; group exhibs include Chicano Visions: Painters on the Verge, San Antonio Mus Art, 2001; Arte Caliente, South Tex Inst Arts, Corpus Christi, 2004; Contemp Wall Painting, Univ Tex San Antonio Art Gallery, 2005; Four Horsemen, McNay Art Mus, San Antonio, 2006. *Pos:* Mural coord, San Anto Cult Arts Org. *Teaching:* Artist in Residence, Inmate Creative Arts Prog, Bexar County Jail, Tex; instr, Guadalupe Cult Arts Ctr; Int Artist in Residence, ArtPace, San Antonio, 2007-08. *Awards:* Joan Mitchell Found Grant, 2007

RUBY, LAURA
SCULPTOR, PRINTMAKER
b Los Angeles, Calif, Dec 7, 1945. *Study:* Univ Southern Calif, BA (English), 67; San Francisco State Coll, MA (English), 69; Univ Hawaii, MFA (art), 78. *Work:* Honolulu Acad Arts, Hawaii State Fedn Cult & Arts, Honolulu; Erie Mus, Pa; Soc Am Graphic Artists, NY; McNeese State Univ, La, Univ of Dallas, Tex. *Comn:* Richard Street YWCA (screenprint), Hawaii YWCA, 86; Film Crew at Diamond Head (screenprint), Honolulu Printmakers, 88; Stage Set--Mise en Scene (site specific mixed media sculpture), Hawaii St Fedn Cult & Arts, Honolulu, 91; Site of Passage-Chinatown (site-specific mixed media sculpture), City & Co of Honolulu, 94; Elvis & Marilyn (site-specific installation), Honolulu Acad Arts, Hawaii. *Exhib:* Honolulu Acad Arts, 87, 95, 2005, 2010; 12th Nat Los Angeles Printmaking Soc, Marymount Univ Gallery, Los Angeles, 93; Univ Iowa Mem Union, 95; Georgia Southern Univ Art Gallery, 96; Mus Nebr Art, 97; Tex Wesleyan Univ East Rm Gallery, 2001; Morningside Coll Eppley Art Gallery, Iowa, 2002; Denison Univ Art Gallery, Ohio, 2003; Walking on Water, SUNY Brockport Tower Fine Arts Gallery, NY, 2005; Printmaking Currents, Ore, 2006; Peoria Art Guild, Ill, 2007; East Hawaii Cultural Ctr, Hawaii, 2008; Hawaii Pacific Univ Art Gallery, 2011; Koa Gallery, Hawaii, 2012; and others. *Pos:* Ed, Fate in Review, 93-2001. *Teaching:* Instr, Univ Hawaii, Honolulu, 77- & Chaminade Univ, Honolulu, 80-81. *Awards:* Award in Sculpture, Artquest 86, Los Angeles; Lace Artist Proj Grant New Forms Regional Initiative, Los Angeles, 91-92; Purchase Awards & Catalogue Cover Art Award, 65th Soc Am Graphic Artists Nat Print Exhib, New York, 93; Hawaii Individual Artist Fel, 2008. *Bibliog:* Marcia Morse (auth), A Tribute to Diamond Head, Honolulu Star Bull, Hawaii, 3/16/86; Joan Rose (auth), Installation Sculptures Invite Viewer Participation, Honolulu Star Bull, 4/5/92; Reuel Denney (auth), Laura Ruby's Nancy Drew Series, Honolulu Acad Arts Catalogue, 4/95; Joanne Yamada (auth), Chaucer on the Brain, Honolulu Weekly, 5/18/2011. *Mem:* Coll Art Asn; Found Art Theory & Edn; Asn Art Editors; Jean Charlot Found; Honolulu Printmakers; Am Print Alliance,; Moiliili Community Center Bd. *Media:* All; Screenprinting. *Res:* Land & Power in Hawaii, Moiliili, (a Hawaii Community), Honolulu Downtown & Chinatown. *Publ:* Drawing on a Sleuth: The Case of the Nancy Drew Series, Rediscovering Nancy Drew (ed by Carolyn Stewart & Nancy Tillman Romalov), Univ Iowa Press, 95; Diamond Head Contemporary Impressions, Am Print Alliance, Vol 6, No 2, fall 98; Cultural Determination of Visual Perception: The Unavoidable Condition that could Liberate, FATE in Rev, vol 23, 2001; editor, Moili'ili-The Life of a Community, 2005; of orthigraphy, etymology and cartography, Kennedy Theatre, 2009; Talking Hawaii's Story, Journal of Hawaii History, 2011; Honolulu Town, 2012. *Dealer:* Ramsay Mus 1128 Smith St Honolulu HI 96817. *Mailing Add:* 509 University Ave 902 Honolulu HI 96826

RUBY, STERLING
SCULPTOR
b Bitburg, Germany, 1972. *Study:* Pa Sch Art & Design, BA (fine arts, magna cum laude, Merit Scholar), 1996; Sch Art Inst Chicago, BFA (Merit Scholar), 2002; Art Ctr Coll Design, Pasadena, Calif, MFA (Art Ctr Scholar), 2005. *Work:* Guggenheim Mus, New York; Hammer Mus, Los Angeles; Seattle Art Mus. *Exhib:* Solo exhibs include 1R/Van Harrison Gallery, Chicago, 2003, 2004, Foxy Prodn, New York, 2004, 2005, 2007, Sister, Los Angeles, 2005, Guild & Greyshkul, New York, 2005, Marc Foxx, Los Angeles, 2005, 2006, Emi Fontana, Milan, 2006, Metro Pictures, New York, 2007, 2008, Drawing Ctr, New York, 2008, Mus Contemp Art, Los Angeles, 2008; group exhibs include Blinky 2, Tate Britain, London, 2003; Depression: What is it Good For?, Gene Siskel Film Ctr, Chicago, 2004; Voiceovers, LACE, 2005; All the Pretty Corpses, Renaissance Soc, Univ Chicago, 2005; Having New Eyes, Aspen Art Mus, Colo, 2005; Only the Paranoid Survive, Hudson Valley Ctr Contemp Art, 2006; Calif Biennial, Orange County Mus Art, Newport, Calif, 2006; Circumventing the City, D'Amelio Terras, New York, 2007; Fit to Print, Gagosian Galley, New York, 2007; Substraction, Deitch Projects, New York, 2008. *Dealer:* Metro Pictures 519 W 24th St New York NY 10011. *Mailing Add:* c/o Foxy Productions 623 W 27th St New York NY 10001

RUDA, EDWIN
PAINTER
b New York, NY, May 15, 1922. *Study:* Columbia Univ, MA, 49; Sch Painting & Sculpture, Mexico City, 49-51; Univ Ill, MFA, 56. *Work:* State of NY Collection, Albany Mall; Indianapolis Mus Art, Ind; Dallas Mus Art, Tex; Nat Gallery of Australia, Canberra; Mass Inst Technol, Cambridge; Corcoran Gallery, Washington; Port Authority of NY. *Exhib:* Smithsonian Traveling Exhib, Latin Am, 66; Systemic Painting, Guggenheim Mus, 66 & Whitney Mus Am Art Painting Ann, 69, NY; Paintings on Paper, Aldrich Mus Contemp Art, Ridgefield, Conn; 73 Biennial, Whitney Mus Am Art, NY; Contemp Am Painting & Sculpture, Krannert Art Mus, Univ Ill, Urbana, 74; 10th Anniversary Exhib 1964-1974, Aldrich Mus Contemp Art, 74; Baltimore Mus, 75, Drawing Show, 76; Benefit Exhib for Udine, Italy, NY Univ, 76; June Kelly Gallery, New York, NY, 87-95; Condeso Lawler Gallery, New York, NY, 87-88; one-person exhib, Paula Cooper Gallery, NY, 69, 71, 73 & 75, Gallery A, Sydney, Australia, 73, June Kelly Gallery, NY, 88, 92 & 95 & Condeso/Lawler Gallery, NY, 88; and others. *Pos:* Co-founder, Park Pl Gallery Art Res. *Teaching:* Instr painting, Univ Tex, Austin, 56-59 & 78, Sch Visual Arts, NY, 67-71, Pratt Inst, Syracuse Univ & Ohio State Univ, 78 & Tyler Sch Art, Philadelphia, 79. *Awards:* Creative Artists Pub Serv Fel, 78-79. *Bibliog:* Carter Ratcliff (auth), Striped for action, Artnews, 2/72; Dore Ashton (auth), New York commentary, Studio Int, 2/70; Peter Schjeldahl (auth), In and out of step in Soho, New York Times, 10/73; and many others. *Publ:* Auth, Park Place 1963-67: some informal notes in retrospect, Art Mag, 67. *Dealer:* June Kelly Gallery 591 Broadway New York NY 10012. *Mailing Add:* 8921 24th Ave East Elmhurst NY 11369

RUDELIUS, JULIKA
VIDEO ARTIST
b Cologne, Ger, 1968. *Study:* Rietveld Akademie, BFA, 1998. *Exhib:* Solo exhibs, Kunsthaus Glarus, Switz, 2003, Centre Culturel Suisse, Paris, 2004, Frans Hals Mus, Neth, 2005, Grazer Kunstverein, Austria, 2006, Dumbo Arts Ctr, Brooklyn, 2009; ICP Triennial, Int Ctr for Photog, New York, 2003; Tennage Kicks, Royal Hibernian Acad, Dublin, 2004; Populism, Stedelijk Mus Bureau, Amsterdam, 2005; Temporarily Disconnected, Ctr for Curatorial Studies, Bard Coll, New York, 2007; The Possibility of an Island, Mus Contemp Art, Miami, Fla, 2008; Actors and Extras, Argos Centre for Art & Media, Brussels, 2009. *Awards:* Louis Comfort Tiffany Found Grant, 2009

RUDENSTINE, ANGELICA ZANDER
HISTORIAN, CURATOR
b Ger. *Study:* Oxford Univ, Eng, BA, 59, MA, 60; Smith Col, MA, 61. *Hon Degrees:* Univ Del, Hon Dr Humanities, 2012. *Collection Arranged:* Art of the Russian Avant-Garde: The George Costakis Collection Traveling Exhib (auth, catalog), 82-84; Kazimir Malevich, 90-91; Piet Mondrian, 94-96. *Pos:* Cur, Mus Fine Arts, Boston,

60-68 & Guggenheim Mus, NY, 69-82; freelance cur, 82-; prog off, mus & conserv, Andrew W Mellon Found, 93-2010. *Teaching:* Adj prof 19th & 20th century art hist, Inst Fine Arts, NY Univ, 85-86. *Awards:* Guggenheim Fel, 83; Alfred H Barr Award, 87; Mitchell Prize, 88. *Mem:* Coll Art Asn Am; Am Acad, Rome (trustee & chmn, fine arts comt, 80-92); Int Coun Mus; Pulitzer Found for the Arts (trustee); Phila Art Mus (trustee); Marlboro Music (trustee). *Res:* 20th century European and American art. *Publ:* Auth, Guggenheim Mus Collection: Paintings 1880-1945, 76; Russian Avant Garde Art: The George Costakis Collection, 81; Peggy Guggenheim Collection, Venice, Abrams, 85; Modern Painting-Drawing-Seulpture Collected by Emily & Joseph Pulitzer, Jr, Harvard Univ Press, 88; Piet Mondrian 1872-1944, Mondadori, 94

RUDINSKY, ALEXANDER (JOHN)
PAINTER
b Corvallis, Ore, Feb 4, 1957. *Study:* Ore State Univ, 75-76; Univ Mass, 76-77; Syracuse Univ, BFA (studio arts), 79; Univ Calif, Irvine, MFA (studio arts, Regents fel), 89. *Work:* Portland Art Mus, Ore; Univ Calif, Irvine; Hewlett Packard, Corvallis, Ore; Hufstedler, Miller, Kaus & Beardsley, Newport Beach, Calif; Williamette Valley Co, Eugene, Ore. *Comn:* Mural, Crescent Valley High Sch, Corvallis, Ore, 75; mural, Benton Co Courthouse, Corvallis, Ore, 76; stage set for Journey, Univ Mass, Amherst, 77; neighborhood photomural, Mt Scott/Arleta Community Ctr, Portland, Ore, 82; mural, Show Biz Expo, Los Angeles, Calif, 92. *Exhib:* Fine Arts Inst 28th Ann, San Bernardino Co Art Mus, Redlands, Calif, 93; 58th Nat Exhib, Cooperstown Art Asn, NY, 93; Nat Small Oil Painting Exhib, Wichita Ctr Arts, Kans, 94; Neighborhoods of the '90's, 53rd Ann Nat, Braithwaite Fine Arts Gallery, Southern Utah Univ, Cedar City, 94; City Art Invitational, Millard Sheets Gallery, Los Angeles Co Fair, Pomona, Calif, 94. *Pos:* Installation consult, Alexander Rudinsky Studios, Portland, Ore, 85-87; gallery preparator, Elizabeth Leach Gallery, Portland, Ore, 86; self-employed fine artist, 85-94. *Teaching:* Instr drawing & bus art, Pac Northwest Coll Art, Portland, Ore, 86-87; instr film & video, Marylhurst Coll, Ore, 86-87; teaching asst contemp art, Univ Calif, Irvine, 87-89. *Awards:* Multi-Arts Grant, Metrop Comn, Portland, Ore, 82; Fine Arts Res Grant, Univ Calif, Irvine, 89. *Bibliog:* Cathy Curtis (auth), The preoccupation behind creation, LA Times, Orange Co Ed, 5/8/88; Randy Gragg (auth), Gallery's mixed bag of new works, Oregonian, 2/17/90; Nancy Kapitanoff (auth), Sharing life's crosses, LA Times, San Fernando Ed, 7/2/93. *Mem:* Seeing It Through Exhibs. *Media:* Oil on Canvas, Ceramics. *Publ:* Illusr, Seven Slovak Stories, Gregorian Univ Press, Rome, 80; Jozef Mak, Slavica Pub, Columbus, 85

RUDMAN, BETTY & ISAAC
COLLECTOR
Awards: Named one of Top 200 Collectors, ARTnews mag, 2009-13; Top Latin American Art Collectors, Latin American Art Jour. *Collection:* Latin American art; numismatics; pre-Columbian art; rare coins. *Mailing Add:* 6000 Island Blvd Miami FL 33160

RUDMAN, JOAN (COMBS)
PAINTER, INSTRUCTOR
b Owensburg, Ind, Oct 7, 1927. *Study:* Mich State Univ, BA (art educ), MA (art); Art Student's League, Woodstock, NY, with Arnold Blanch, Walter Plate & Richard Segalman also with Edgar A Whitney, Walter DuBois Richards, Diana Kan & Charles Reid. *Work:* Combe Inc, Kresgie Mus; Connolly-McMullen Watercolor Collection, Baylor Univ, Tex. *Exhib:* Wadsworth Atheneum; Acad Fine Arts & Watercolor Soc, New Brit Mus Am Art; Nat Arts Club Open Watercolor Show, 69 & 78; Am Watercolor Soc, 74, 77 & 84; Mus Fine Arts, Springfield, Mass, 77; Salmagundi Club, 78; Nat Acad Design, NY, 86; solo show, Vt Arts Ctr, 2005; and others. *Pos:* Asst Ed, Newsletter (Am Watercolor Soc); pres, Hudson Valley Art Asn, 2000-2009. *Teaching:* Instr, King Sch, Stamford, Conn, Round Hill Community House, Greenwich, Conn & Continuing Educ Classes, Stamford, currently; artist-in-residence, Southern Vermont Art Ctr, Manchester, currently. *Awards:* Best in Show & Russell Purchase Award, Old Greenwich Art Soc, 91; Winsor-Newton Plaque & Award, Hudson Art Asn, 91; Hon Mention in Graphics, Catharine Lorillard Wolfe Art Club, 91; first in watercolor, Founder's Show Art Soc, Old Greenwich, 99; Mrs John Newinton 1st Award (pencil), HVAA 69th Ann, 2000; and others. *Mem:* Am Watercolor Soc, 84- (bd dir, 87-); Am Artists Prof League; Hudson Valley Art Asn (bd dir, 71-, vpres, 99, pres, 2000); hon mem, Columbia Univ Alumni Club; Nat Press Club, Washington; Mich State Univ Alumni Club; and others. *Media:* Watercolor. *Publ:* Artist in Special Tribute, HVAA Catalog Ann, Newspaper Press Releases, Gannett Chain, 72-; and others. *Mailing Add:* 274 Quarry Rd Stamford CT 06903

RUDOLPH, JEFFREY N
MUSEUM DIRECTOR
Study: Univ Calif, Berkeley, BA; Yale Univ, New Haven, MBA. *Pos:* deputy dir, Calif Sci Ctr, LA, exec dir, pres, CEO, currently; pres, Calif Sci Ctr Found, currently; mem, Calif Coun on Sci and Tech, bd dirs, Nat Health Sci Consortium, Sci Museums Exhib Collaborative, Mus Trustees Asn Adv Coun of Dirs, EXPO Ctr. *Mem:* Asn Sci-Tech Centers (past pres); Am Asn Museums (chmn, 2004-2006). *Mailing Add:* California Science Ctr 700 Exposition Park Dr Los Angeles CA 90037

RUDY, HELEN
PAINTER, INSTRUCTOR
b New York, NY Aug 2, 1925. *Study:* Hunter Col, BA; Ridgewood Art Inst; Art Sch Northern NJ. *Comn:* Pvt Collections. *Exhib:* Ann Exhibs, Hudson Valley Art Asn; Grand Nat, Am Artists Prof League; Ann Juried Exhib, Allied Artists Am; Ann Juried Exhib, Audubon Artists; Butler Mus, Youngstown, OH; Valley Hospital, Ridgewood, NJ; Cork Gallery, Lincoln Ctr, NY. *Pos:* Coast Guard Artist; juror, West Essex Art Asn & Kent Art Asn, Conn. *Teaching:* Instr, painting; teaching asst, Ridgewood Art Inst; Art Sch Northern, NJ. *Awards:* Awards for Juried Shows; Am Artists Prof League, Kent Art Asn, Hudson Valley Art Asn, Suburban Art League, Allied Artists Am; Silver Medal Honor, Ann Exhib, Audubon Artists. *Mem:* Allied Artists Am (bd dir, currently); Am Artists Prof League (bd dir, currently); Catharine Lorillard Wolfe Art Club; Hudson Valley Art Asn (bd dir); Kent Art Asn; Audubon Artist (bd dir). *Media:* Acrylic, Oil & Pastels. *Mailing Add:* 856 Hillcrest Rd Ridgewood NJ 07450

RUEHLICKE, CORNELIA IRIS
PAINTER, PRINTMAKER
b Berlin, Ger. *Study:* Acad Fine Arts, Stuttgart, Hamburg, Ger, MFA, 83; studied painting with Kurt Sonderborg; studied sculpture with Alfred Hrdlicka. *Work:* Hampton Arts Comn, Va; Somerset Co Col, NJ; Haag & Haag Gmbh, Leonberg, Ger; Duszinsky Gmbh, Hoefingen, Ger; Art Space, Nishinomiya, Japan; Binghamton Univ Art Mus, NY; The Community Theatre, Morristown, NJ; Kalani Honua Cultural Center, Hawaii. *Comn:* Artists of Worldwide Attention, ARS Nova. *Exhib:* Palm Springs Desert Mus, Calif; San Diego Art Inst; Nat Exhib of Women's Work on Paper, Women's Found Genesee Valley, Rochester, NY; Time Capsule, Paula Cooper Gallery, NY; HUB Galleries, Pa State Univ; O'Keefe Ctr for Arts, Toronto, Can; Monmouth Coll Art Gallery, NY; Consulate Gen of Ger Cult Ctr, NY; Goethe Inst, Toronto, Can; Gasteig Cult Ctr, Munich; San Francisco Mus Mod Art; Allentown Art Mus, Pa; Guggenheim Mus; San Bernardino Co Mus, Calif; Berkshire Mus, Mass; Mus Mod Art, Bordeaux, France; Newport Art Mus, RI; Atlantic Ctr for the Arts, Fla; NJ Ctr Vis Arts, Morristown, NJ; Mus Nat d'Histoire Naturelle, Paris, Fr; Abu Dhabi Cultural Foundation, Abu Dhabi, UAE; Rajasthan Lalit Kala Akademy, Daiput, India; Indira Gandhi Nat Centre for the Arts, New Dehli, India. *Pos:* lectr, Consulate Gen Fed Repub Ger; Home for Contemp Theatre and Art, ATOA Foundation for the Community of Artists, NY; Linhards Foundation, Prague, Czechoslovakia; Atlantic Center for the Arts, Fla; Goethe Inst, Toronto, Calif; Somerset County Col, NJ & Kalani Honua Cult Center, HI. *Awards:* Hub Galleries Cent Pa Fest Arts Merit Award, Pa State Univ, 93; Hampton Arts Comn Mayor's Purchase Award Charles H Taylor Arts Ctr, 93; Marc Printmaking Award, Peninsula Fine Arts Ctr, 94; Elizabeth Found for the Arts Studio Ctr, 00, 02; Cons Gen of Ger Grant, 99. *Bibliog:* Lynn Gamwell (auth), Drawings of Complexions Contemp Ballet on Exhib, Univ Art Mus, Binghamton, NY, 2007; Lynn Gamwell (auth), Cornelia Ruelicke Captures Complexions Dancers in Motion, On STAGE, Anderson Center for the Arts, Binghamton, NY, 2007. *Mem:* Brooklyn Waterfront Artists Coalition; Elizabeth Found for the Arts; Robert Blackburn Printmaking; Manhatten Graphics Center; NJ Center Visual Arts. *Media:* Oil, Acrylic, Watercolor. *Publ:* Auth, Promotional Copy, M Somerby, New York, 93; Diversions, Hampton Arts Comn, 94; Time Capsule, Creative Times & SOS Int, 95; Crossings, Vol III, Brooklyn Waterfront Artists Coalition, 96; disc covers, Louisville First Editions, for music by Morton Gould, Walter Piston, and Roy Harris; The Swan Culture and Jewelry, Tokyo, Japan, 2004; Campus Stage: INSIDE B.U, Binghamton Univ, NY, 2007. *Mailing Add:* 35 W 16th St No 4 New York NY 10011

RUFFING, ANNE ELIZABETH
PAINTER
b Brooklyn, NY. *Study:* Cornell Univ, BS; Drexel Inst Technol; also studied with John Pike. *Work:* Metrop Mus Art, NY; Brooklyn Mus, NY; Nat Gallery Art, Washington, DC; Whitney Mus Am Art, NY; Libr of Nat Collection of Fine Arts, Smithsonian Inst, Washington, DC; and many others. *Comn:* Four Wildlife Drawings, Johnston Hist Mus, North Brunswick, NJ, 76; four hist landmark lithographs, NY State Senate, comn by City of Kingston, NY, 76; porcelain series, Danbury Mint, Norwalk, Conn, 81-82; porcelain series, Oxmoor House, Birmingham, Ala, 83-85; ltd ed print, Nat Wildlife Fedn, Washington, DC, 88. *Exhib:* Rocky Mountain Nat Watermedia Exhib, Golden, Colo, 76; 25th Ann Exhib Painting & Sculpture, Berkshire Mus, 76; Solo exhibs, Art in Industry, IBM Corp, NY, 66 & A E Ruffing Exhib, Hall of Fame, Goshen, NY, 71; 4th Ann Exhib, Midwest Watercolor Soc, Manitowoc, Wis, 80; and others. *Awards:* Int Women's Year Award, Int Women's Festival, D Gillespie, 76; Spec Merit Award, Midwest Watercolor Soc, 80. *Bibliog:* Bruce Henry Davis (auth), Introducing the art of A E R, 1/77, Memories of Childhood, 2/77 & Glimpses of yesterday, 7/77, Collector's News, Am Masters Found. *Media:* Watercolor, Ink. *Publ:* Illusr, Ideals Old Fashioned Issue (title page plus two others), Ideals, 75

RUFFNER, GINNY MARTIN
SCULPTOR, GLASSBLOWER
b Atlanta, Ga, June 21, 1952. *Study:* Univ Ga, BFA (drawing, painting, cum laude), 74, MFA, 75. *Work:* High Mus, Atlanta, Ga; Corning Mus Glass, NY, Cooper-Hewitt Mus, NY; Toledo Mus Art, Ohio; Mus des Arts Decoratif, Lausanne, Switz; Metrop Mus Art, NY. *Comn:* Sculpture & mural, S Park Community Ctr, Seattle, 89; sculpture, Security Pacific Bldg, Seattle, 90; sculpture, Absolut Vodka, 90; playground, William T Machan Sch, Phoenix, Ariz, 93. *Exhib:* Mus Louvre, Paris, 89; Am Craft Mus, NY, 90; Detroit Inst Arts, Mich, 91; Espace Duchamp-Villon, Rouen, France, 91; Renwick Gallery, Smithsonian Inst, Washington, 92; Museo Correr, Venice, Italy, 96; Metrop Mus Art, NY, 96; and others. *Pos:* Dir, Glass Art Soc, 88-91, pres, 90-91; ed adv, Glass Mag, New York, 89-94; trustee, Pilchuck Glass Sch, Stanwood, Wash, 91-, vpres, 94-; comnr, Seattle Arts Comn, 91; dir, New York Experimental Glass Workshop, 92-94; contemp art coun prog comt, Seattle Art Mus, currently. *Teaching:* Adj instr watercolor & art appreciation, DeKalb Col, Clarkston, Ga, 77; vis scholar glassblowing, Penland Sch Crafts, NC, 79; lectr, Nat Sculpture Conf, Cincinnati, 87; lectr, Bellevue Mus, Wash, 88; instr, Pilchuck Glass Sch, 84-89 & Univ d'été, Sars-Poteries, France, 90; conf coordr, Glass Art Soc, Seattle, 90; exhib cur, Tacoma Art Mus, Wash, 91. *Awards:* Visual Artist Fel, Nat Endowment Arts, 86; Outstanding Contrib Award, UrbanGlass, New York, 95; Woman of the Year, Palm Springs Desert Mus, Calif, 96. *Bibliog:* Matthew Kangas (auth), Unraveling Ruffner, Glass Mag, spring 91; Bonnie Miller (auth), Why Not?: The Art of Ginny Ruffner, Tacoma Art Mus, in asn with Univ Wash Press, Seattle & London, 95; Ellen Pall (auth), Starting from scratch, NY Times Mag, 9/25/95. *Mem:* Glass Art Soc; Am Craft Coun; Am Sci Glassblowers Soc. *Media:* Glass, Metal. *Publ:* Auth, Speaking of glass/women sculptors, Am Craft Mag, 10/88; co-ed, Glass: Material in the Service of Meaning, Tacoma Art Mus, in asn with Univ Wash Press, Seattle & London, 91; and others. *Mailing Add:* 5000 20th Ave NW Seattle WA 98107

RUFFO, JOSEPH MARTIN
PRINTMAKER, ADMINISTRATOR
b Norwich, Conn, Dec 6, 1941. *Study:* Pratt Inst; Cranbrook Acad Art. *Work:* Ark Art Ctr, Little Rock; Mus Mod Art, Salvador, Brazil; Memphis Coll Art, Tenn; Miss Art Asn, Jackson; Sheldon Mem Art Gallery, Lincoln, Nebr; and others. *Comn:* American Tool Co; Cliffs Notes Inc. *Exhib:* Third Biennial Rutgers Nat Drawing Exhib, State Univ NJ, Camden Coll Arts & Sci, 79; Potsdam Prints, 16th Nat, 82; 11th Nat Prints & Drawing Exhib, Minot State Col, 82; La Grange Nat, 82; 23rd Nat Print Exhib, Hunterdon Art Ctr, Clinton, NJ, 79; Images Aluminum, Tamarind Prints Traveling Exhib, Macalester Col, 79-80; solo exhib, Sheldon Mem Art Gallery, Lincoln, Nebr, 87. *Pos:* Head dept art, Univ Northern Iowa, Cedar Falls. *Teaching:* Instr art, Memphis Acad Arts, 64-68; instr art, Fla Mem Col, 69-77; asst prof art & chmn dept, Barry Col, 69-74, chmn div fine arts, 74-77; prof art, Univ Northern Iowa, 77-84; chmn dept art and art hist, Univ Nebr, 84. *Awards:* Fulbright Grant, Brazil, 63; Best in Show, 12th Ann Mid South Exhib, 67; Purchase Prize, 10th Dixie Ann Prints & Drawings, 68. *Mem:* Nat Coun Art Adminrs; Nat Asn Schs Art & Design; Coll Art Asn; Am Arbitration Asn. *Media:* All Media. *Mailing Add:* Dept Art & Art Hist Univ Nebr Lincoln 14th & R St Lincoln NE 68588

RUFO, CAESAR ROCCO
MEDALIST, SCULPTOR
b Philadelphia, PA, Aug 15, 1929. *Study:* Temple Univ, with Raphael Sabatini, Philadelphia; Studied at Pa Academy Fine Arts; Studied at Philadelphia Coll Art. *Work:* La Scala Mus, Milan, Italy; Metrop Opera House Mus, New York; Franklin Mint Mus, Franklin Center, PA; Smithsonian Inst, Washington, DC; Belskie Mus Art & Science, Closter, NJ. *Comn:* bronze bust, comn by Dr. John Esposito, PA, 1971; plaque, Nat Liberty Corp, Springfield, PA; monument, Virginia Military Inst, Lexington, VA, 1983; life size statue, Villanova Univ, PA, 1985; bronze relief wall plaques, comn by Dr PM Lincoln Jr, Boston, MA, 1986. *Exhib:* Metrop Centennial Medal, 21st World Expos, New York, 1987. *Pos:* Sr medallic sculptor, Franklin Mint, PA, 1965-1978; chief sculptor, Roger Williams Mint, Attleboro, MA, 1978-1983; vpres art dept, Highland Mint, Melbourne, FL, 1991-. *Teaching:* Instr sculpting tech, Delaware County, PA, 1960-1965. *Mailing Add:* 504 Eaton Way West Chester PA 19380

RUGGERI, GINA
PAINTER
b Milwaukee, Wisconsin, 1970. *Study:* Yale Summer Sch Music & Art, Norfolk, Conn, 1991; Md Inst, Coll Art, Baltimore, BFA, 1992; Yale Sch Art, New Haven, Conn, MFA, 1996. *Exhib:* Solo exhibs include Vassar Coll, Poughkeepsie, NY, 2002, Tenri Biennale, Japan, 2003, Red Dot, New York, 2003, Kevin Bruk Gallery, Miami, 2004, 2006, 2008; group exhibs include Jan Weiner Gallery, Kansas City, Mo, 1996; Resurfaced, Boston Univ Art Gallery, 2005; 181st Ann Exhib, Nat Acad Design, New York, 2006; Refined, Lyons Wier Ortt Contemp, New York, 2006; Queens Int, Queens Mus Art, Flushing, NY, 2006; Eclectic Eye, Contemp Art Ctr, New Orleans, 2007; Paper now, I-Space, Chicago, 2007; Running Around the Pool, Mus Fine Arts, Tallahassee, Fla, 2007; Outer Space, Pluto Gallery, Brooklyn, NY, 2008. *Awards:* New York Found Arts Fel, 2008. *Dealer:* Kevin Bruk Gallery 2249 NW 1st Pl Miami FL 33127; Lyons Weir 175 7th Ave New York NY 10011

RUGGIERO, LAURENCE J
MUSEUM DIRECTOR
b Paterson, NJ, Mar 25, 1948. *Study:* Univ Pa, BA, 69, MA, 73, PhD, 75; Boston Univ, MBA, 79. *Pos:* Consult projs, J Paul Getty Mus Found, Los Angeles & Boston Mus Fine Arts; asst to pres, Metrop Mus Art, New York, 78-81; exec dir, Oakland Mus Asn, Calif, 81-85; dir, John & Mable Ringling Mus Art, Sarasota, 85-92; assoc dir, Charles Hosmer Morse Mus Am Art, Winter Park, Fla, 92-, dir, 95. *Teaching:* Asst prof hist art, Univ Ill, Chicago Circle, 73-77. *Awards:* Kress Found Fel, 72. *Mem:* Coll Art Asn; Am Asn Mus. *Mailing Add:* c/o Charles Hosmer Morse Mus Am Art 445 Park Ave N Winter Park FL 32789

RUGGLES, JOANNE BEAULE
PAINTER, EDUCATOR
b New York, NY, May 19, 1946. *Study:* Akron State Univ; Ohio State Univ, with Sidney Chafetz, BFA (painting) & MFA (painting, printmaking & photography). *Work:* Ohio State Univ, Columbus; Calif Polytech State Univ, San Luis Obispo; Calif State Library, Sacramento; Wesleyan Coll, Macon, Ga; The City of San Luis Obispo; Mindt State Univ; Cabo Frio Int Print Collectiom. *Exhib:* 6th, 7th, 8th & 9th Int Exhib Original Drawings, Mus Mod Art, Rijeka, Yugoslavia, 78, 80, 82 & 84; Eigth Premio Biella Per L' Incisione, Italy, 80; Second Int Exhib of Prints and Drawings, Mus Arts & Sci, Wesleyan Coll, 83-84; Cabo Fio I & II Int Print Biennal, Brazil, 83 & 85; Intergraphic '84, Exhibit Ctr, Berlin, 84; Int Print Exhib: 1983 Repub China, Taipei City Mus Fine Arts, Taiwan, 83-84; Prints USA, Nat Mus, Singapore & Nat Gallery, Bangkok; Art Ctr, 84, Silpakorn Univ, Bangkok, 97; Royal Soc Artists Gallery, Birmingham, Eng, 97; Prints USA Museo Carvillo Gil, Mex, DF, 87; Westminster Gallery, London, 99; Black Sheep Gallery, Hawarden, Wales, 99; US Embassy, Luanda, Angola, 99-2003; Durham Art Gallery, 2000; AIM for Arts Int Open, 2000, Performance Works Gallery, Vancouver, BC, Can, 2000; US Embassy, Freetown, Sierra Leone, 2005-; Best of Am Nat Oil and Acrylic Painters Soc, Caruthers Dunnegan Gallery, 2005; All Calif Invitational, Laguna Art Mus, 2005; Palm Springs Art Mus, 2006; Corpora in Extremis, San Luis Obispo Mus Art, 2009; Philippine Consulate, NY, 2010; Soma Arts, Man As Object, Reversing the Gaze, 2011; Kinsey Inst, 2011; Solo exhibs, A Stone of Hope, Arc Gallery, Chgo, Ill, 2006, Eye, Hand, Heart, Western Colo Ctr Arts Grand Junction, 2010, Hanging by a Threat, Mother Earth in Peril, Foxworthy Gallery, Santa Maria, Calif, 2011. *Pos:* Cur, Exhibs Univ Art Gallery, Cal Poly, 89-98; reviewer, Applications for Dorland Mountain Arts Colony, 89-2004; panelist to rev art in pub places applicants, San Luis Obispo Co, 92; mem, San Luis Obispo Co Arts Coun Adv Bd, 2000-02; bd mem, San Luis Obispo Art Ctr, 2008-; vis artist, Esalen Inst, Big Sur, Calif. *Teaching:* Lectr drawing & painting, Ohio State Univ, 70-71, Allan Hancock Coll, 71-76 & Cuesta Coll, 77-79; lectr drawing & printmaking, Calif Polytech State Univ, 73-80, assoc prof, 83-88, prof, Dept Art & Design, 88-2004; prof emer, 2004. *Awards:* Jurors Award, Cabo Frio Int, Brazil, 83; Purchase Award, Minot State Univ, 96; Selected Artist of 1997, US State Dept Art Embassies Prog, 97; Cal Poly award, Outstanding Res, Creative Activity & Prof Develop, 2004; Individual Artists Grant, James Irvine Found Art Inspires Grant Prog in Conjunction with SLO Community Found, 2005; Miriam Russo Enders Award, Nat Asn Women Artists 116th Ann, 2005; Artist Grant, Capelli di Angeli Found, 2006; Puffin Found Grant, 2008; Evylynn Nann Miller Award, Women Painters West, 2008; ASCA award, 2011; Featured Artist, Womens Caucus for Arts, 2011. *Bibliog:* Glen Starkey (auth), The arts: Earth Angels, New Times, 7/18-25/96; Monica Fiscalini (auth), Searching for celestial & other heavenly bodies, San Luis Obispo Co Telegram Tribune, 8/16-27/96; Teresa Mariani (auth), What is it with you artists, always drawing nudes, San Luis Obispo Co Telegram Tribune, 8/16-27/96; Shannon Marsh McClure (auth), Joanne Beaule Ruggles Receives Cal Ply's Distinguished Research Award, Art Rag, 2004; Ashley Schwellen Bach (auth), Figures, Spirits, & Survivors, New Times, 1/2007; Ann Weltner (auth), Whispers of Humanities, New Times, 9/2011, The Artists Happenings of 2011, New Times, 1/2012; Who's Who in Am, the World's Whos Who of Women, Who'S Who of Am Women, Who's Who in Am Art, Who's Who in the West, 2000, Notable Am Women, Who's Who in Am Educ. *Mem:* Nat Asn Women Artists; Calif Soc Printmakers; Am Soc Contemp Artists; US Art in Embassies Prog Artist; Los Angeles Print Makers Soc; Boston Print Makers Soc; Women Painters West; Womens Caucus for Art. *Media:* Acrylic, charcoal, ink, and mixed media. *Res:* A Stone of Hope, 30 piece painting series. *Publ:* Coauth, Darkroom Graphics: Creative Photographic Techniques for Photographers and Artists, Amphoto, 75; contribr, Encyclopedia of Photography, Amphoto/Eastman Kodak, 78. *Mailing Add:* Box 46 San Luis Obispo CA 93406

RUGOLO, LAWRENCE
PRINTMAKER, EDUCATOR
b Milwaukee, Wis, Oct 2, 1931. *Study:* Univ Wis, Milwaukee, BA (art & art educ), 54; Univ Iowa, MFA, 59. *Work:* IBM, St Louis, Mo; Hunterdon Art Ctr, Clinton, NJ; State Univ NY Col, Potsdam; Ark Arts Ctr, Little Rock; Arts Coun Collection, Tulsa, Okla; plus others. *Comn:* Mural, First Nat Bank, Columbia, Mo, 79. *Exhib:* Solo exhibs, Albrecht Art Mus, 75, NE Mo State Univ, 81 & Lindenwood Col, St Louis, Mo, 88; La Grange Nat XVII, Nat Exhib Painting, Drawing & Prints, CVAA, Ga, 92; Valdosta Works on Paper IV, Valdosta State Col, 92; 24th Bradley Nat Print & Draw Exhib, Bradley Univ, Peoria, Ill, 93; 38th Nat Print Exhib, Hunterdon Art Ctr, Clinton, NJ, 94; NPVAG Nat Exhib, Scottsbluff, Nebr, 94. *Teaching:* Prof screenprinting & design, Univ Mo, Columbia, 74-95, chmn art dept, 73-96. *Media:* Screenprinting. *Mailing Add:* 2509 Cimarron Dr Columbia MO 65203

RUHE, BARNABY SIEGER
PAINTER, CRITIC
b New York, NY, Aug 10, 1946. *Study:* US Naval Acad, BS, 68; Md Inst, Coll Art, with Ed Dugmore, Sal Scarpitta & Babe Shapiro, MFA (painting), 75; NY Univ, PhD, 89. *Work:* Lincoln & Great Neck Schs; Muhlenberg Col, Lincoln & Great Neck; Sidney Lewis Mus; Patterson Mus; Conejo Valley Art Mus. *Comn:* Marathons, City Allentown, 80; Conejo Valley Art Mus, 90. *Exhib:* Pleiades, NY, 76, 77 & 79; 5 solo-shows, Barbara Braathen Gallery, NY, 85-88; Conejo Valley Art Mus, 90. *Collection Arranged:* WC4 Box 83 10,000, NY Mail Concept Exhib. *Pos:* Dir, cur & producer, Whitney Counterweight, NY, 77, 79, 81 & 83; Sr art ed, Art World, 80-90; artist & lectr, Mus Mod Art, NY, 90-91. *Teaching:* Instr, Art hist, US Naval Acad, 72-75; instr Shamanistic painting workshops, Muhlenberg Col & Great Neck Ctr, 81-. *Awards:* Nat Endowment Arts Dirs Grant, 77; Prize, Allentown Art Mus, 79; Comn Visual Arts Grant, NY, 83, 86. *Bibliog:* Vic Miles (interviewer), Ruhe marathon painting, CBS TV, New York, 1/79 & NBC TV, 2/80; Myra Goldfarb (auth), Zen in Ruhe Painting, Call Chronicle, 5/79; Brad Swift, Bill Paige & Nina Barbier (dirs), Movies on Ruhe. *Mem:* Valley Arts Coun (founding mem, 76-); Artists Talk on Art, NY (bd dir, 89-91). *Media:* Oil, House Paint. *Publ:* Auth, Art of Making Boomerangs, American Woodworking, Rodale Press, 91. *Dealer:* Helen Turner 185 E 85th New York NY 10028. *Mailing Add:* 4926 Mountain Dr Emmaus PA 18049

RUILOVA, AIDA
VIDEO ARTIST
b Wheeling, West Virginia, 1974. *Study:* Univ S Fla, BFA, 1999; Sch Visual Arts, MFA, 2001. *Work:* Altoids Curiously Strong Collection, New York; Bard College, NY; Solomon R Guggenheim Mus, New York. *Exhib:* Solo exhibs include White Columns, New York, 2000, Salon 94, New York, 2002, 2007, The Moore Space, Miami, 2004, Franklin Art Works, Minneapolis, 2005, The Kitchen, New York, 2007, Contemp Art Mus, St Louis, MO, 2008; Group exhibs include Collectors Choice, Exit Art, New York, 2000; Special Projects, PS 1 Contemp Art Ctr, Long Island City, NY, 2001; Altered States, Stefan Stus Gallery, New York, 2002; Monitor II, Gagosian Gallery, New York, 2002; Videodrome II, New Mus Contemp Art, New York, 2002; I, Assassin, Wallspace, New York, 2004; Whitney Biennial, Whitney Mus Am Art, New York, 2004; Disturbing the Peace, Danese Gallery, New York, 2004; Eflux Video Rental, Eflux, New York, 2004; Black & White, Greenberg Van Doren Gallery, New York, 2004; Phillip: Divided by Lightning, Deitch Projs with John Connelly Presents, Brooklyn, 2004; Irreducible: Contemp Short Form Videio, 1995-2005, Bronx Mus, New York, 2005; Reverse Engineers, Carnegie Art Ctr, North Tonawanda, NY, 2005; Greater New York, PS1 Contemp Art Ctr, New York, 2005, Into Me/ Out of Me, 2006; The Beat, Haswellediger Gallery, New York, 2006; Sympathy for the Devil, Mus Contemp Art, Miami, 2008; Slightly Unbalanced, Chicago Cultural Ctr, 2008. *Awards:* Rema Hort Mann Found Grant, 2001; Hugo Boss Guggenheim Prize Finalist, 2006; Louis Comfort Tiffany Found Grant, 2007. *Mailing Add:* Van Doren Waxter Gallery 23 E 73rd St New York NY 10021

RUIZ, JOSE
INSTALLATION ARTIST, CURATOR
b Lima, Peru, 1975. *Study:* Univ Md, BA (studio art), 1999; San Francisco Art Inst, MFA, 2004. *Work:* Starwood Urban Investments, Miami, Fla; Barrick Gaming Corp, Las Vegas; Core Group, Washington, DC; SAP Software, Washington, DC; Dorsey & Whitney LLP, Washington, DC. *Exhib:* Escalate, Antennae Gallery, Washington, DC, 1999; Penta Luna, Decatur Blue, Washington, DC, 2000; Lucky 7, Millenium Arts Ctr, Washington, DC, 2001; Take Me to the River, The Opera Gallery, Cairo, Egypt, 2002; solo exhibs, DC Arts Ctr, Washington, DC, 2002, Steven Wolf Fine Arts, San Francisco, 2005, Barbara Walters Gallery, Sarah Lawrence Coll, Bronxville, NY, 2006, Jamaica Ctr for Arts & Learning, Queens, 2007 & Cuchifritos, New York, 2008; Space Invaders, Penrose Gallery, Tyler Sch Art, Temple Univ, 2003; DC Now, Second Street Gallery, Charlottesville, Va, 2004; Wall Mountables, DC Arts Center, Washington, DC, 2005; Black Now, Longwood Arts Project, Bronx, NY, 2006; Drift, Rush Arts Gallery, New York, 2007; Bandwagon, Vox Populi Gallery, Philadelphia, PA, 2008; Preemptive Resistances, Westport Arts Ctr, Conn, 2009. *Collection Arranged:* Dauxbs, Decatur Blue, Washington, DC, 2000; San Francisco Video Artist's Festival, San Francisco Art Inst, 2004; Concrete Domain, Bronx River Art Ctr, Bronx, NY, 2006; Laura Napier: Spontaneous Formations, PS122 Gallery, New York, 2008; The Individual & The Family, PPOW Gallery, New York, 2009. *Awards:* 1st Place Prize, 3rd Nat Juried exhib, Galeria Galou, Brooklyn, 2005; Artist-in-Residence, Jamaica Ctr for Arts & Learning, Queens, 2006-2007; Artist fel, Emerge 10, Aljira Ctr for Contemp Art, Newark, NJ, 2008

RUMFORD, RONALD FRANK
PRINTMAKER, PAINTER
b Ft Meade, Md, May 28, 1962. *Study:* Univ Arts, Philadelphia, BFA, 84. *Work:* NY Pub Libr, New York; Camden Co Cult & Heritage Soc, Haddonfield Twp, NJ; Ballinglen Arts Found, Bally Castle, Rep Ireland; Philadelphia Mus Art; Print and Picture Collection, Free Libr, Philadelphia, Pa; Palmer Mus Art, Penn State Univ; Fine Art Collection, Western Carolina Univ, NC; Watson Gallery, Wheaton Coll, Norton, Mass; Cleveland Mus Art. *Comn:* Lunamoth, Univ Print Club, Cleveland, Ohio, 96. *Exhib:* Images of N Mayo Fel Exhib, Philadelphia Art Alliance, Pa, 94; solo exhibs, The Print Ctr, 95 & Univ Arts, 95; One Over One, Rubicon, Dublin, Ireland, 97; New Prints: Bridgewater Lustberg, Blumenfeld Gallery; Challenge Exhib: Fleisher Art Mem, Philadelphia, Pa; New Prints, Locus Gallery, St Louis, Mo, 2000; The Print Ctr, 2002; Sch House Ctr, Provincetown, Mass, 2002; Abington Art Ctr, Jenkintown, Pa, 2003; Whats New: Recent Acquistions, Palmer Mus Art, State College, Pa, 2004; From Tamarind to 1026: New Acquistions, Free Libr Philadelphia, Pa, 2005; Community Arts Ctr, Wallingford, Pa, 2008. *Pos:* Assoc dir, Dolan/Maxwell Inc, Philadelphia, 88-91, dir, 91-. *Awards:* Alexander Award, Cheltenham Art Ctr, 89; Purchase Prize, Camden Co, NJ, 89; Miriam McCall Award, 90; Cohen Award, Philadelphia Cult Fund. *Bibliog:* Edward Sozanski (auth), Museums and Galleries, Philadelphia Inquirer, 6/16/95, 10/22/2000 & 6/16/2002; Victoria A Donohoe (auth), Philadelphia Inquirer, 5/11/2003; Victoria A Donohoe (auth), Philadelphia Inquirer, 5/10/2008. *Mem:* Printcenter, Philadelphia (bd dir 2004-09); Int Fine Print Dealers Asn; Greene St Artists Cooperative (found pres, 90-92); Philadelphia Print Ctr (bd dirs, 2004-); Print & Picture Collection Friends, Free Libr, Philadelphia; Philagrafika, New Philadelphia Print Collab. *Media:* Print Making. *Publ:* Working Proof: Art on Paper, 2000. *Dealer:* Sears Peyton 210 11th Ave #802 New York NY; School House Gallery 494 Commercial St Provincetown MA 02657; McGowan Fine Art 10 Hills Ave Concord MA 03301. *Mailing Add:* 5225 Greene St Philadelphia PA 19144

RUPP, SHERON
PHOTOGRAPHER
b Mansfield, Ohio, Jan 14, 1943. *Study:* Denison Univ, BA, 65; Univ Mass, MFA, 82. *Work:* Mus Mod Art, NY; Fogg Art Mus, Harvard Univ; Columbus Mus Art, Ohio; Smithsonian Mus, Washington, DC; J Paul Getty Mus, Los Angeles, Calif; Mus Fine Arts, Boston; Rose Art Mus, Brandeis Univ, Waltham, Mass; Mus Fine Arts, Boston; Gallery of Art, Wash DC; Corcoron; Sir Elton John Photog Collection, England; Nelson-Atkins Mus Art, Kans City, Mo. *Exhib:* Recent Acquisitions, Mus Mod Art, NY, 87; Rose Art Mus, Waltham, Mass, 88; Portland Sch Art, Maine, 89; Pleasures & Terrors of Domestic Comfort, Mus Mod Art, NY, 91; The Magic of Play, Dir Guild of Am, Los Angeles, Calif, 94; Columbus Mus Art, Ohio, 98; Cleveland Mus of Art, Ohio, 00; Smithsonian Inst, Game Face, DC, 01; Getty Mus, Los Angeles, 2006-2007; Garden Eden (group int exhib), Emden, Ger, 2008; Sheron Rupp: Dialogue with a Collection, Univ Fine Arts Center, Univ Mass, Amherst, 2009; Pictures by Women: A History of Modern Photography, Mus Mod Art, NY, 2010; Everyday America, Steven Kasher Gallery, Berman Coll, NY, 2013; Character Study, de Cordova Sculpture Park & Mus, Lincoln, Ma, 2013. *Teaching:* Instr photog, Northfield Mt Hermon Sch, 82-83 & Holyoke Community Col, 86-88; vis asst prof, Hampshire Col, 85-87; vis lectr, Amherst Col, Mass, 94. *Awards:* Mass Artists Fellowship, 84 & 87; Visual Arts Fel, Nat Endowment Arts, 86 & 94; John Simon Guggenheim Mem Award, 90. *Bibliog:* For Kids' Sake - Photographs of Today's Youth, PRC-Boston, 85; Cross Currents, Cross Country, PRC Boston & San Francisco camera work, 88; Northampton Postcards, Smith Coll Art Mus, Northampton, Mass, 90; Peter Galassi (auth), Pleasures & Terrors of Domestic Comfort, Mus Mod Art, New York, 91. *Media:* Photography. *Interests:* writing, kayaking, nature. *Publ:* Auth, Sheron Rupp Color Photographs, Helicon Nine, J Women's Arts & Lett, 86; Doubletake Mag (front cover), Winter Issue #11, 98; An American Century of Photography: From Dry-Plate to Digital, Hallmark Photographic Coll, Harry Abrams, NY, 99; Modern Starts: People, Places, Things, Mus Mod Art, NY, 1999; Photography in Boston (1955-1985), MIT Press, Cambridge, Mass, 2000; Jane Gottesman (auth), Game Face: What Does a Female Athlete Look Like?, Random House, NY, 2001; Color Photographs: Fifty Postcards, Mus Mod Art, NY, 2005; Where We Live: Photographs of Am from The Berman Collection, Getty Trust Publ, Calif, 2006; Kunsthalle, Emden, Germany, 2008; Garten Eden: Der Garten Inder Kunst Seit 1900. *Mailing Add:* 3 The Lope Haydenville MA 01039-9726

RUPPERSBERG, ALLEN
CONCEPTUAL ARTIST
b Cleveland, Ohio, Jan 5, 1944. *Study:* Chouinard Art Inst, BFA, 67. *Work:* Guggenheim Mus Art, Mus Mod Art, Whitney Mus Am Art, NY; Los Angeles Co Mus, Calif; Addison Gallery Am Art, Andover, Mass; Milwaukee Art Mus, Wis; Los Angeles Co Mus Art, Mus Contemp Art, Los Angeles, Calif. *Exhib:* 557,087, Seattle Art Mus, Wash, 69; Ann exhib, Contemp Am Sculpture, Whitney Mus Am Art, NY, 70; 24 Young Los Angeles Artists, Los Angeles Co Mus Art, Calif, 71; Pier 18, Mus Mod Art, NY, 71; Biennial Exhib, Whitney Mus Am Art, NY, 75; Calif Painting & Sculpture, The Modern Era, Smithsonian Inst, Washington, DC, 76; Theodoran Awards: Nine Artists, Solomon R Guggenheim Mus, NY, 77; Am Narrative Story Art, Contemp Arts Mus, Houston, 77; Book Works, Mus Mod Art, NY, 77; Ft Worth Art Mus, Tex, 77; Am Exhib, Art Inst Chicago, Ill, 80; LA Hot & Cool, Mass Inst Technol, Cambridge, 87; Boys and Girls, Men and Women, Addison Gallery Am Art, Andover, Mass, 90; Word as Image (with catalog), Milwaukee Art Mus, Wis, 90; Biennial 1991 (with catalog), Whitney Mus Am Art, NY, 91; Solo exhibs, frac Limousin, France, 92, Jay Gorney Mod Art, NY, 93 & 94, Linda Cathcart Gallery, Los Angeles, 93, Raum fur Aktueller Kunst, Vienna, Austria, 94, Galerie de Expeditie, Amsterdam, The Neth, 94, Galerie Gabrielle Maubrie, Paris, France, 94, Studio Guenzani, Milan, Italy, 94 & Pontikus, Frankfurt, Ger, 98; The Elusive Object, Recent Sculpture from the Permanent Collection of the Whitney Mus Am Art (with catalog), Whitney Mus Am Art, 93; For 35 Yrs: Brooke Alexander Editions, Mus Mod Art, NY, 94; L'Hiver de lAmour (with catalog), Mus Mod Art, Paris, 94; Ideas and Objects: Selected Drawings and Sculptures from the Permanent Collection, Whitney Mus Mod Art, NY, 94; Drawn in the 70's, Brooke Alexander Gallery, NY, 94; In the Field: Landscape in Recent Photog, Margo Leavin Gallery, Los Angeles, 94; Five Longish Wood Sculptures, Feature, NY, 94; Cocido y Crudo (with catalog), Mus Nac, Ctr de Arte Reina Sophia, Madrid, Spain, 94; Musee d'art Modenne et contemporian, Geneve, Switz, 98; Fonds Regional d'Art Contemporain, Marseille, France, 98; and others. *Awards:* Grant, Nat Endowment Arts, 76 & 82; Theodoran Award, Guggenheim Mus, 77; Guggenheim Fel, 97. *Bibliog:* Judd Tully (auth), Galeries de New York, Beaux Arts, Paris, 6/94; Raphael Rubenstein (auth), Gorney review, art in Am, 11/94; Alain-Henri Francois (auth), Maubrie review, Voir, Switz, 11/94. *Publ:* Auth, The Secret of Life and Death, Black Sparrow Press, 85; Art Paper, 4-9/88, Art Paper, 9/88, Artist's Page; Our House is very Beautiful at Night, Alti Novri (Utrecht), Vol 2, No 1, 92; Western/Allen Ruppersberg: A Different Kind of Never-Never Land (exhib publ), De Appel, Amsterdam, 92

RUPPRECHT, ELIZABETH
INSTRUCTOR, PROFESSOR, PAINTER
b Paris, France, Mar 28, 1932; US citizen. *Study:* Sch of Art Inst Chicago, BFA, 54, MFA, 65. *Work:* Lubenick Mus, Mich City, IN. *Comn:* portraits, Wyler Children's Hosp, Chicago, Ill, 80. *Exhib:* Grand Rapids Mus, Mich, 2010; Luminous Ground, Ill State Mus, 2011-12. *Pos:* dir, Oxbow Sch Art, Saugatuck, Mich, 58-63, bd dir, 57-, pres, 66, secy, 67-89. *Teaching:* prof drawing, painting & color, Sch of Art Inst Chicago, Ill, 60-. *Awards:* John Quincy Adams Foreign Traveling Fel, 55; Key to the city of Iron River, Mich, 80; Ox-Bow School of Art & Artist Residency, Saugatuck, Mich, 2004. *Media:* Acrylic, Oil. *Mailing Add:* 5421 N Laporte Chicago IL 60630

RUSAK, HALINA R
LIBRARIAN, PAINTER
b Navahradak, Belarus; US citizen. *Study:* Douglass Col, New Brunswick, NJ, BA, 54; Rutgers Univ, New Brunswick, MLS, 56, MA, 76. *Work:* Nat Art Mus, Belarus; Douglass Col, NJ; Zimmerli Art Mus, New Brunswick, NJ; Jane Voorhees Zimmerli Art Mus, New Brunswick, NJ. *Comn:* outside sculpture, Batiment de loisirs, Lac-Beauport, Quebec, 2013. *Exhib:* Solo exhibs, NJ State Mus, Trenton, 77, Georgian Court Col, Lakewood, NJ, 77, SOHO 20, NY, 79, 84 & 87, 89 & 94, Byelorussion Inst Arts & Sci, NY, 82, Franklin Libr, Somerset, NJ, 82, Ortho Pharmaceutical Corp Art Gallery, Raritan, NJ, 86, Johnson & Johnson Int Hq Gallery, New Brunswick, NJ, 87, Symbols of Resiliency, SoHo 20, NY, 94 & Miracles & Disasters, 97, Mille eclats, Gallery of the Neufchatel Libr, Quebec, 2013, Mille Eclats, suite, Gallery of the Gabrielle Roy LIbr, Quebec, 2013; Women Artists, Paul Robeson Gallery, Newark, NJ, 79-80 & Nabisco World Hq, East Hanover, NJ, 80; Women Artists Series, Walters Hall Gallery, New Brunswick, 81 & Douglass Coll Libr, 84; Women's Spheres, Middlesex Co Mus, Piscataway, NJ, 83-84; Slavic Art Exhib, NY, 88; Double Blind, SoHo 20, NY, 96; Belarus: 10 Yrs After Chemoby, Capital Children's Mus, Washington, DC, 96 & Johnson & Johnson World Hq, New Brunswick, NJ, 97; Graphic Work, Hunterdon Art Mus, 96; Transmission, NY-Amsterdam, De Zaaijer, The Neth, 98; Mem Exhib 1999, Hunterdon Mus of Art, Clinton, NY, 99; La noblesse du bois, Bibliotheque Etienne-Parent, Beauport, Quebec, 2012; Art Sans Frontiere, Espace Frere Jerome, Quebec, 2013; A Toutes Mailles! Maison Marie Uguay, Montreal, 2013. *Pos:* Art bibliographer & slide librn, Douglass Col, New Brunswick, 56-83; art librn & head, Rutgers Univ, New Brunswick, 83-; consult ed, Art Reference Services Quarterly, 91-. *Teaching:* Bibliog instr, art, Rutgers Univ, New Brunswick, NJ, 83. *Awards:* Preservation Grant for Elephant Folio, State of NJ; Res Coun Grant for Publ, Am Abstract Women Painters; Res Coun Grant for Publ, Art & Archit Polacak Principality. *Bibliog:* Women Artists Series Representative Works, 1971-84, Douglass Col, 84; Women Artists Series: 25 Years 1971-1996; My Land Minsk, Rutgers Univ, 96. *Mem:* Art Libr Soc NAm (vchmn, 84-85 & pres, 85-86, NJ chap); Women's Caucus Art; Coll Art Asn. *Media:* Acrylic. *Res:* Women's art history; Belarusan arts history; architectural history and preservation; abstract expressionist woman artists. *Publ:* Auth, New and adequate space for the art library, ARLIS/NJ Newsletter, spring, 90; Ann Ryan, In: Past and Promise: lives of New Jersey Women, Scarecrow Press, 90; co-auth, American Women Painters Born After 1900, In: Women Artists in US, GK Hall, 90; The Art Library: A New Landmark, J Rutgers Univ Libr, 92; Coauth, Abstract Expressionist Women Painters, Scarecrow Press, 96. *Dealer:* SOHO 20 Gallery 469 Broome St New York NY 10013. *Mailing Add:* Art Libr Voorhees Hall-Rutgers Univ CAC-71 Hamilton St New Brunswick NJ 08903

RUSCHA, EDWARD JOSEPH
PAINTER, PHOTOGRAPHER
b Omaha, Nebr, Dec 16, 1937. *Study:* Chouinard Art Inst, Los Angeles, Calif, 1960. *Work:* Mus Mod Art & Whitney Mus Am Art, NY; Los Angeles Co Mus Art; Joseph Hirshhorn Collection, Washington, DC; San Francisco Mus Mod Art; retrospective of works on paper J Paul Getty Mus Los Angeles, 1998; retrospective of career Hirshhorn Mus, 2000; Sculpture Garden, Washington, DC, 2000; Mus Contemp Art, Chicago, Miami Art Mus, Modern Art Mus, Ft Worth, Tex; Harry Ransom Ctr, Univ Tex, Austin. *Comn:* Mural, Metro Dade Co Art in Pub Places, 85; mural, Denver Pub Libr, 94-95; painting, JP Getty Ctr Auditorium, Los Angeles, 97. *Exhib:* Mus Contemp Art, Los Angeles, 81; Solo exhib tour, San Francisco Mus Mod Art, 82-83; Whitney Mus Am Art; Los Angeles Co Mus Art; Contemp Arts Mus, Houston; Vancouver Art Gallery; ICA, Nagoya, Japan, 88; Whitney Biennial, Whitney Mus Am Art, NY, 97; Gagosian Gallery, Beverly Hills, 99, Metro Plots, NY, 99; Kunst, Munich, Moderne Museet, Stockholm, 2009-2010; Hamilton Press, Calif, 2010; Retrospectives, Denver Art Mus, 2011, Mus Contemporary Art, Fla, 2012. *Pos:* US Rep, Venice Biennale, 2005. *Teaching:* Lectr painting, Univ Calif, Los Angeles, 69-70. *Awards:* Nat Coun Arts Grant, 67; Nat Endowment Arts Grant, 69 & 78; Tamarind Lithography Workshop Fel, 69; Guggenheim Found Fel, 71; Skowhegan Sch Painting & Sculpture Award in Graphics, 74; Nat Arts Award, Americans for the Arts, 2009; Named One of the Most Influential People in the World, TIME mag, 2013. *Bibliog:* Geoffrey Haydon (dir), Edward Ruscha (film), British Broadcasting Corp, 79; Dave Hickey (auth), Available Light, Hudson Hills Press, 82; Peter Plagens (auth), Ed Ruscha, Seriously, Hudson Hills Press, 82; plus many others. *Mem:* Fel: Am Acad Arts & Sci; Am Acad Arts and Letters (mem dept art). *Publ:* Auth, Twenty Six Gasoline Stations, 63, Various Small Fires, 64, Every Building on the Sunset Strip, 66, Real Estate Opportunities, 70, A Few Palm Trees, 71, Colored People, 1972, Hard LIght, 1978, Country Cityscapes, 2001, ME and THE, 2002, Ed Ruscha and Photography, 2004, OH/NO, 2008, Dirty Baby, 2010. *Dealer:* Gagosian Gallery 456 North Camden Beverly Hills CA 90210; Anthony d'Offay Gallery 9 Dering St London W1R 9AA England. *Mailing Add:* Gagosian Gallery 980 Madison Ave New York NY 10021-1848

RUSH, ANDREW
PRINTMAKER, SCULPTOR
b Mich, Sept 24, 1931. *Study:* Univ Ill, BFA (hons), 53; Univ Iowa, MFA, 58; Fulbright fel, Florence, Italy, 58-59. *Work:* Uffizi Mus, Florence, Italy; Libr Cong, Washington; Dallas Mus Art; Seattle Art Mus. *Comn:* Law Prints (portfolio of three offset lithographs), Lawyers Publ Co, 68 & 74; ed etchings, Tucson Art Ctr, 71; large scale tile mural, Univ Ariz Health Sci Libr, 95; public art, Sentinal Plaza, Ariz, 2003. *Exhib:* US Info Serv Traveling Exhib to Europe & Latin Am, 60-65; Graphic Art USA, Am prints to Soviet Union, 63; Brooklyn Mus Biennial, 64; 50 Am Printmakers, Am Pavilion, NY World's Fair, 64-65; Intag 71, 30 Printmakers, San Fernando State Univ, 71; Tucson Gateway Project, 02; Univ Ariz retrospective, 2003-2004. *Pos:* Founding mem, Rancho Linda Vista Community Arts, 69; guest cur, Tucson Mus Art, 88. *Teaching:* Assoc prof art, Univ Ariz, 59-69; vis artist-in-residence, Ohio State Univ, 70. *Awards:* Seattle Mus Int Printmakers Award, 63; Purchase Award, Brooklyn Mus Biennial, 64; Lifetime Achievement Award, City Tucson, 2006. *Bibliog:* Article, Southwest Art Gallery Mag, 3/72. *Media:* All. *Publ:* Prog cover artist, Tucson Symphony & Ariz Theatre & Opera Co, 78-83; illusr, The Rule of Two, Oracle Press, 84; A Voice Crying in the Wilderness, St Martins Press, 90; Ask Marilyn, St Martins Press, 92; illusr, Intaglio Prints of Andrew Rush, Univ Ariz Mus Art, 2003; illusr, Voice of the Borderlands, Rio Nuevo Press, 2006; auth, The Nature of Drawing, Draw Studio, 2010. *Mailing Add:* Rancho Linda Vista PO Box 160 Oracle AZ 85623

RUSH, JEAN C
EDUCATOR, PAINTER
b Bloomington, Ill, Nov 21, 1933. *Study:* Ill Wesleyan Univ, BFA, 55; Univ Iowa, MFA, 58; Univ Ariz, PhD, 74. *Work:* Libr Congress, Washington, DC; Dallas Mus Fine Arts, Tex. *Exhib:* 13th Nat Exhib Prints, Libr Congress, Washington, DC, 55; 11th Exhib Southwest Prints & Drawings, Dallas Mus Fine Arts, Tex, 61; Ariz Women's Caucus for Art Statewide Show, 79. *Pos:* Coordr art educ prog, Univ Ariz, 78-80 & 81-88; co-ed, Studies in art education, Nat Art Educ Asn, 81-83, sr ed, 83-85; dir, Ariz Inst Elementary Art Educ, 86-87. *Teaching:* Lectr art educ, Univ Ariz, 71-75, asst prof art educ, 75-80, assoc prof, 80-89, prof, 89, emer prof, 89-; prof & admin chmn art dept, Ill State Univ, 89-91, prof, 91-96, emer prof, 96-. *Awards:* First Prize, Ariz State Fair, 60; Purchase Prize, Dallas Mus Fine Arts, 61; June King McFee Award, Nat Artists Equity Asn, 85. *Mem:* Coll Art Asn; Int Soc Educ through Art; Nat Art Educ Asn. *Media:* Oil, Pencil. *Res:* Visual perception, art learning discipline-based art lesson, Studies in Art Educ, 87. *Publ:* Coauth, Teaching Children Art, Prentise Hall, 97

RUSH, JOHN
PAINTER, ILLUSTRATOR, PRINTMAKER
b Indianapolis, Ind, June 27, 1948. *Study:* Univ Cincinnati, BA (industrial design), 1971; Art Ctr Col, (illustration), 1975. *Comn:* painting, French Government, Bicentennial Celebration, 1989; painting, Musical Theatre, Branson, Mo, 1994; Battle of Lexington and Concord (mural), US Nat Parks Serv, 1997; mural, Hoover Dam, US Dept Interior, 2005; Hippocrates Teaching (painting), 2006. *Exhib:* Exhib include Eleanor Ettinger Gallery, NY, 1991-, Frederick Baker Gallery, Chicago, 2003-; also exhib at Chicago Cultural Ctr, Hong Kong Art Expo, French Bicentennial Expo, Soc Illustrators; represented in permanent collections of US Dept Interior, French Nat Government, US Steel, British Petroleum, Zurich-American Insurance. *Pos:* Industrial designer, Philips Corp, Holland, 1970-71; machine tool designer, Structural Dynamics Rsch Corp, Cincinnati, 1971-72; city planner, City of Cincinnati, 1972; staff member, Jack O'Grady Inc and Handelan-Pedersen Inc, 1975-78; freelance illustrator, NY, 1978, Chicago, 1980. *Awards:* Gold Medal Award, Soc of Illustrators, 1980, David Usher Memorial Award, 1998, Silver Medal, 2000. *Publ:* Illusr, Ivanhoe, 2004. *Dealer:* Frederick Baker Gallery 1230 West Jackson Chicago IL; Eleanor Ettinger Gallery 119 Spring St Ground Floor NY NY 10012. *Mailing Add:* 123 Kedzie St Evanston IL 60202

RUSH, JON N
SCULPTOR, EDUCATOR
b Atlanta, Ga, Sept 24, 1935. *Study:* Art Inst Chicago, 53-55; Cranbrook Acad Art, with Tex Schiwetz, 55-59, BFA & MFA. *Work:* Columbus Mus Art, Ohio; Univ Mich, Ann Arbor. *Comn:* Sculpture, Southwestern Mich Col, Dowagiac, 84; sculpture, Domino World Hq, Ann Arbor, 89; sculpture, ISR, Univ Mich, 89; sculpture, Wallenberg Mem, Univ Mich, Ann Arbor, 95. *Exhib:* Hong Kong Int Competition, China, 62; Bundy Art Gallery, Waitsfield, Vt, 63; Fifteen Mich Sculptors, City of Lansing, 76; Meadowbrook Outdoor Sculpture, Rochester, Mich, 81; Mich Outdoor Sculpture II, S Field, 89; Mich Sculpture, Midland Ctr Arts, 02. *Teaching:* Prof sculpture, Univ Mich, 62-2007. *Awards:* Sculpture Award, All Mich Artists, Flint Inst Art, 72; Sculpture Prize, Mich Outdoor Sculpture II, S Field, 89; 1st Place, Art in Pub Places, Mich Coun Arts, 90. *Media:* Metal, Stone. *Mailing Add:* 7930 Fifth St Dexter MI 48130

RUSH, KENT THOMAS
PHOTOGRAPHER, PRINTMAKER
b Hayward, Calif, Jan 16, 1948. *Study:* Calif Coll Arts & Crafts, BFA, 70; Univ NMex, Albuquerque, MA, 75; Univ Tex, Austin, MFA, 79. *Work:* Oakland Mus, Calif; McNay Mus, San Antonio; Albuquerque Mus, NMex; Inst De Obra Grafica De Oaxaca, Oaxaca, Mex; Humanities Res Ctr, Univ Tex, Austin; Ctr Fine Print Res, Coll W Eng, Bristol, Eng; Auchenbach Found Graphic Arts, San Francisco, Calif; St Bride Printing Libr, London, Eng. *Exhib:* Solo exhibs, Univ Art Mus, Univ NMex, Albuquerque, 90, Inst Cult Peruano Norte Americano, Lima, Peru, 90, Dowd Fine Arts Ctr, State Univ NY, Cortland, 92, Martin Mus Art, Baylor Univ, Waco, Tex, 94, Art Pace, San Antonio, Tex & Legion Arts/CSPS, Cedar Rapids, Iowa, 2002; group exhibs, Retrospective, McNay Art Mus, 98, Blue Star Art Space, San Antonio, Tex, 93, Amarillo Mus Art, Tex, 2003, Art Gallery, Ctr Fine & Performing Arts & Texas A&M Int Univ, Laredo, Tex, 2006; Ctr for Photog, Woodstock, NY, 93; Santa Fe Mus Fine Arts NMex, 93; San Antonio Mus Art, Tex, 94; Diverse Works, Houston, Tex, 94; SE Mus Photog, Daytona Beach, Fla. *Pos:* Printer's asst, Tamarind Inst, Univ NMex, 73-74. *Teaching:* Instr, San Antonio Art Inst, 76-79; lectr, Calif Coll Arts & Crafts, Oakland, 80-81, San Francisco Art Inst, 82; prof, Univ Tex, San Antonio, 82-06; instr, Santa Reparata Grafic Arts Ctr, Florence, Italy, 84 & 97, Taller Delas Artes Plasticas Rufino Tamayo, Oaxala, Mex, 88 & Universidad Catolica, Lima, Peru, 90. *Awards:* Sr Fulbright Fel, Taller Rufino Tamayo, Oaxaca, Mex, 88; MidAm Arts Alliance & Nat Endowment Arts Fel in Photog, 90-91; Partners of the Americas Grant, Univ Catolica, Lima, Peru, 90. *Bibliog:* Diane Armitage (auth), Kent Rush, Recent Photographs, THE Mag, Santa Fe, NMex, 12/93; Lyle Williams (auth), Kent Rush: A retrospective, San Antonio: Marian Koogler McNay Art Mus, 98; Anjali Gupta (auth), Foundabstraction, San Antonion Current Mag, 6/14/2000. *Mem:* Southern Graphics Coun; Soc Photog Educ. *Publ:* Auth, Collotype: An Extension of Lithography, Tamarind Papers, 87. *Dealer:* Parchman-Stremmel Galleries San Antonio TX; Hare & Hound Press San Antonio TX. *Mailing Add:* Dept Art & Art History Univ Tex San Antonio One UTSA Circle San Antonio TX 78249-0642

RUSH, MICHAEL JAMES
MUSEUM DIRECTOR, WRITER
b Orange, NJ, Apr 30, 1949. *Study:* St Louis Univ, BA, 1971, MA, 72; Harvard Univ, PhD, 80. *Work:* Centre Georges Pompidou, Paris; Kunsthalle, Zurich; Whitney Mus, NY. *Exhib:* Brooklyn, 2001; Video Jam, 2001; Sue Williams, 2002; Sculpture Now, 2002. *Pos:* founding dir, New Haven Artists' Theater, 85-2000; dir, Palm Beach Inst of Contemp Art, 2000-. *Teaching:* Harvard Univ, 79-80, Boston Col, 80, Yale Univ, 87-90, Duke Univ, 90. *Awards:* Found for Contemp Performing Arts, 92; Nat Endowment for the Arts, 93; New Eng Found for the Arts, 94. *Bibliog:* A Klein (auth), NY Times, 86-95. *Mem:* Am Asn Mus; Int Asn of Art Critics; Dramatists' Guild; Asn Independent Video and Filmmakers. *Media:* Video. *Publ:* auth, New Media in Late 20th Century Art, Thames and Hudson, 99; auth, Video Art, Thames Hudson, 2003; featured writer in NY Times, Art in Am, Newsweek.com

RUSHWORTH, MICHELE D
PAINTER, INSTRUCTOR
b Toronto, Ont, Can, Oct 16, 1958, US citizen. *Study:* Queen's Univ, BFA, 76-78; Ont Coll Art and Design, with William Whitaker, Tony Ryder, Juliette Aristides & Calvin Goodman, 78-80. *Work:* State of Wash, State of Nev, State of Wyo, US Coast Guard. *Comn:* Official Portrait of Washington Governor Gary Locke, State Wash, Olympia, Wash, 2005; Portrait of Pacific NW Ballet Directors, Pacific NW Ballet, Seattle, Wash, 2005; Official Portrait of Nevada Gov Kenny Guinn, State Nev, Carson City, Nev, 2006; Portrait of 3 Law Deans, Campbell Univ, Buies Creek, NC, 2006; mural with 30 portraits, Peel Co Bd Educ, Toronto, Can; Official Portrait, Norman Zoller, 11th Circuit Ct, State Wash; Portraits of four doctors, Univ Ala Med Center; Official Portraits of US Senator Clifford Hansen, Ambassador Michael Sullivan, Wyo Gov James Geringer, US Coast Guard Commandant Thad Allen; Wyoming Gov Hunt, Wyoming Gov Brooks, Fed Judge Alan B Johnson, Fac Portrait Soc Am. *Exhib:* Salmagundi Club Allied Artists Am Nat Arts Club Am Watercolor Soc juried exhib, New York, NY; Rutgers Univ Regional Int show, NJ; Pa Watercolor invitational show, Pa. *Teaching:* Fall City Fine Arts Studio, Gage Academy; Guest lectr, Kirkland Art Studios. *Bibliog:* CBS News (television), Portrait of a Hero, CBS News The Early Show, 9/3/2002; Sherry Grindeland (auth), Portrait colorful tribute to former state leader, Seattle Times, 1/4/2006; Cy Ryan (auth), Seattle artist picked to paint Guinn, Las Vegas Sun, 8/23/2006. *Mem:* Portrait Soc Am. *Media:* Oil on Canvas. *Dealer:* Portraits Incorporated New York NY. *Mailing Add:* 22930 SE 27th Ct Sammamish WA 98075

RUSSELL, CHRISTOPHER RYAN
PAINTER
b Boulder, Colo, 1983. *Study:* Mikie Hara Scholar (creative achievement award), 2002-2005; Calif Coll Arts, BFA (Painting & Drawing), 2006. *Exhib:* Tautologicolloquialligature, 2005; A Bahl Beemsh, Boontling Gallery, Oakland, Calif, 2005; Awesome: Contemp Sublime, PlaySpace Gallery, San Francisco, 2006; Velotree, Space Gallery, San Francisco, 2006; You, Me, Now, Hangar 1018, Los Angeles, 2006; Magic Stones in the Secret Cave, Floral Gallery, Fruitvail, Calif, 2006; Joy Ride, Don O'Melveny Gallery, Los Angeles, 2006; Boontling Gallery, Oakland, Calif, 2006; solo exhibs, Bruce Gallery, San Francisco, 2006, Art D'Core, Danville, Calif, 2007, Rowan Morrison, Oakland, Calif, 2008, Park Life, San Francisco, 2009; RoMoLoCo, Rowan Morrison, Oakland, Calif, 2007; Rowan Morrison, Oakland Calif, 2007; Fourthrite, Oakland Calif, 2007; Forthrite Gallery, Oakland, 2008; Freak of Nature, Ill Minna Gallery, San Francisco, 2008; High Points, Galley Glance, Italy, 2010; Fort Big Mountain, San Fran, Calif, 2010. *Bibliog:* New American Painting, Issue 79, 12/2008; New American Painting, Issue 91, 12/2010. *Media:* Acrylic, Oil. *Publ:* Isabelle Ringer (auth), Piedmont Post (review), 2008. *Mailing Add:* 927 Grace Ave Oakland CA 94608

RUSSELL, JEFF
PAINTER, PHOTOGRAPHER
b Oakland, Calif, 1942. *Study:* Univ NMex, BFA, 1971; Univ Wis-Madison, MFA & MA, 1973. *Work:* Mus Mod Art, NY; Metrop Mus Art, NY; Moderna Museet, Stockholm, Sweden; Art Inst Chicago, Ill; Seattle Art Mus, Wash; Libr Congress, Washington, DC; Art Inst Chicago, Chicago, Ill; Fogg Art Mus, Harvard Univ, Cambridge, Mass; High Mus Art, Atlanta, Ga; Israel Mus, Jerusalem, Israel; Montclair Art Mus, Montclair, NJ; Mus Mod Art, New York, NY; and numerous others; Whitney Mus Am Art. *Exhib:* Recent Acquisitions, Metrop Mus Art, NY, 1979; one-person exhibs, OK Harris Works Art, 1979, The Destroyed Print (with catalog), Pratt Manhattan Ctr, 1982, Univ Colo, 1984, Bronx Mus Arts, 1984, City Univ Grad Ctr Mall, 1984, Orange Co Ctr Contemp Art, 1989 & Univ Nev, Reno, 1995; Recent Acquisitions, Art Inst Chicago, 1984; Aldrich Mus Contemp Art, 1988; 100th Birthday Celebration, Denver Art Mus, 1993; 20th Century Art: Recent Accessions, Snite Mus Art, Univ Notre Dame, 1993; Across Borders/Sin Fronteras (with catalog), Art Mus Americas, Washington, 1994; What is a Print, Montclair Art Mus, NJ, 1995; Temporarily Possessed: The Semi Permanent Collection (with catalog), New Mus Contemp Art, NY, 1995. *Teaching:* Asst prof, Fashion Inst Technol, 1975-2008. *Awards:* Res Found Grant, State Univ NY, 1983-85; Fel, Nat Endowment Arts, 1986-87. *Bibliog:* Grace Glueck (auth), Art: Beauties & Beasts at the Pratt Gallery, NY Times vol CXXXIII, 4/6/1984; Michael Arkush (auth), Valley Calendar: Fall Brings a Diversity of Arts, Its New Its Local, Los Angeles Times, 9/21/1990; Cathy Curtis (auth), Art Review: The focus of Death Has Clearly Departed, Los Angeles Times, 9/13/1991. *Media:* Acrylic, Oil. *Mailing Add:* 114 Fulton St New York NY 10038

RUSSELL, ROBERT S
SCULPTOR
b Fitchburg, Mass, Nov 10, 1919. *Study:* Univ of NH, Keene, BA, 66; Columbia Univ, MA, 69; Columbia Univ, EdD, 76. *Work:* Perm Collections: Fitchburg Art Mus, Fitchburg, MA, Mills Col, Oakland, Calif; City Univ NJ, Three Bronze Sculptors, Jersey City, NJ; Wavehill Ctr, Eagle Garden Sculptor, Riverdale, NY City. *Exhib:* Solo exhib, Dow Gallery, TC Columbia, New York City, 67; World Craft Conf, Lima, Peru, 68; Hudson Co Paints & Sculpture Show, Jersey City, NJ, 70; Group exhib, Juried New York City Loeb Ctr, Univ Coun for the Arts, New York, 84. *Pos:* Cur, Mus Am Indian Art, formerly. *Teaching:* Student asst, Columbia Univ, 65-66; instr, CUNJ, Jersey City, NJ, 66-89; prof emer, NJCU; retired, currently. *Mem:* Univ Coun for the Arts (treas, formerly). *Mailing Add:* 44 College Dr Jersey City NJ 07305

RUSSO, ALEXANDER PETER
PAINTER, EDUCATOR
b Atlantic City, NJ, June 11, 1922. *Study:* Pratt Inst, 40-42; Swarthmore Col, 47; Bard Col, summer 47; Columbia Univ, BFA, 52; Acad Fine Arts, Rome, Fulbright Grant, 52-54; Univ Buffalo, 55. *Work:* Albright-Knox Gallery, Buffalo, NY; Nat Collection Fine Arts, Washington, DC; Fed Ins Deposit Corp, Washington, DC; Acad Arts & Lett, NY; Delgado Mus of Art, New Orleans, La. *Comn:* Encaustic mural, Telesio Interlandi, Capo San Andrea, Sicily, 53; var design comns, Doubleday Publ Co, Dutton Publ, Birge Co & Cohn Hall Marx, 56-60; acrylic painting series, US Navy Dept, 64; acrylic mural, Dr Martin Cherkasky, NY, 70; Vet Mem sculpture, Frederick, Md, 75. *Exhib:* Carnegie Nat, Pittsburgh, 46; Int Exhib, Bordighera, Italy, 53 & 54; Four Am Artists Exhib, Biblioteca, Rome, 54; Albright-Knox Gallery Regional, Buffalo, NY, 56; Corcoran Biennials, Washington, DC; and many solo exhibs. *Pos:* Combat artist, US Navy Dept, Washington, DC, 42-46; actg art dir, Sewell, Thompson, Caire Advert, New Orleans, 48-49; freelance artist & designer, var agencies & orgns, New York, 58-60; guest lectr art, Roanoke & Hollins Cols, Univ Southern Ill, Miss Art Asn, and others; art consult, Univ Publications of Am, Frederick, Md, 80-; guest art critic, Southampton Press, summer 88 & 91. *Teaching:* Assoc prof painting & drawing, Corcoran Sch Art, 61-70, chmn fac & painting dept, 66-69; prof art & chmn dept, Hood Col, 71-85, prof art, 86-90, prof emer, 90; vis prof art, Inst Allende; San Miguele de Allende, Mex, 92 & 93. *Awards:* Guggenheim Fel, Painting, 47-48, 49-50; Fulbright Grant (painting), Rome, 52-54; Grantee, India, US-Indo Subsomm, on Ed & Culture, 84; Breevort-Eickenmeyer Fel, 52. *Bibliog:* Carl Fortes (auth), Tape on aesthetics and teaching methods of Alexander Russo, Boston Univ, 68; Anne M Jonas (auth), Focus on: Alexander Russo, The Art Scene, 70/71. *Mem:* Coll Art Asn; Arts Club Washington (chmn exhibs, 70-71); Artists Equity; Soc Washington Artists; Edward McDowell Colony; Md State Arts Coun. *Media:* Acrylic, Oil. *Publ:* Illusr, To All Hands, an Amphibious Adventure, 44 & Many a Watchful Night, 45, McGraw; auth, Profiles on Women Artists, Univ Publ Am, 83; The Challenge of Drawing, Prentice-Hall, 86; Vigmettes, poems by Alexander Russo, Morris Publ, 96; Poems & Images, xlibris, 2008; Combat Artist, A Journal of Love and War, Authorhouse, 2014. *Dealer:* Arthur T Kalaher Gallery Southampton NY; Julian Beck Fine Paintings Bridgehampton NY. *Mailing Add:* PO Box 1377 Wainscott NY 11975

RUSSOTTO, PAUL
PAINTER, EDUCATOR
b New York, NY, May 28, 1944. *Study:* Art Students League, 62-63. *Work:* Metrop Mus Art, NY; Heckscher Mus Fine Art, Huntington, NY; Tokai Bank Ltd, Chicago; Gen Electric Corp; Novartis Corp, East Hanover, NJ; Brooklyn Mus; NY Pub Libr; Rochfort-en-Terre FDN, Brittany, France; Asheville Art Mus; Acad D'Arte Dino Scalabrino, Montelatiniterme, Italy; Circolo La Scaletta, Matera, Italy; Dallas Mus Art; Nat Acad Mus, New York; Mus Art Bates Coll, Lewiston, Maine; Mus Della Ceramica Contemp, Deruta, Italy; Mus Palazzo Lepri, Bevagna, Italy; Ctr per L'Arte Moderna & Contemp Luigi Grosso, Altomonte, Italy; Museo Internatzionale Della Grafica (MIG), Castronuovo, Italy; Museo della Scultura Contemporane a Matera, Italy. *Comn:* Work for Permanent Installation for Mus of Peace, Comune Di Murlo (si) Italy, 2004. *Exhib:* NY/Beijing, Beijing Art Inst, Shanghai Mus, 87; Invitational, Am Acad Arts & Letters, NY, 93 & 97; Recent Acquisitions, Heckscher Mus Fine Art, Huntington, NY, 2000; Omaggio A Marino Marini, Acad Scalabrino, Montecatini Terme, Italy, 2000-2001; Angeli, Rome, Florence, Montecatini Terme, Venice, Romania, 2001-02; Libro d' Artista, XIX Premio Letterario, Lido Di Camaiore, Italy, 2006; Group shows: 40 Peintres Americains a Rochefort-en-Terre, One Hundred Years of American Artistic Tradition, Brittany, France, 2003; Nat Acad Mus, New York, 2007, 2009; In Chartis Mevaniae, Bevagna, Italy, 2008; L'Arte e Magia, Deruta, Italy, 2008; Sfilata di Pittura, Milano, Italy, 2010; Inaugural Exhib, Museo Internazionale della Grafica (Mig), Castronuovo, Italy, 2011; Alberto Zanmatti e I Compagni di Strada, Museo Della Scultura Contemporanea (Musma), Matera, Italy, 2012. *Teaching:* instr painting & drawing, Parsons Sch Design, NY, 78-80, NY Studio Sch of Drawing, Painting & Sculpture, NY, 80-82 & Vt Studio Ctr, Johnson, Vt, 85-2001, Int Sch Art, Montecastello Di Viblo, Italy, 93, 94. *Awards:* Rouchefort-en-Terre Found Award, 95; Purchase Award, Am Acad Arts & Letters, 97; Edwin Palmer Mem Prize, Nat Acad Design, 2000; Henry Ward Ranger Purchase award, 2001. *Bibliog:* Eleanor Heartney (auth), Paul Russotto at Ingber, Art In America, 12/86; Gerard Haggerty (auth), Crux of Change, Cover Mag, 1/94; Vincent Katz, Paul Russotto, Art in America, 5/94; Valentine Tatransky (auth), Men & their Bodies, Cover Mag, 80-81; Peter Bellamy (auth), The Artist Project: Portraits of the Real Art World / New York 1981-1990, In Pub, NY, 91; Alan Jones (auth) Drawing the Line, Paul Russotto Drawing Disegni, 2002; Alan Jones, 8 Artisti Da New York, Acad Darte Dino Scalabrino, Montecatini terme, Italy; Mark Stevens & Annalyn Swan (auth), de Kooning: An American Master, Knopf, 2004. *Mem:* Nat Acad Design (assoc, 93, acad, 94); cert. of merit 1996; Palmer Mem prize 2000; Henry Ward Ranger award 2001. *Media:* Oil. *Publ:* Boundary 2: A Journal of Postmodern Literature & Culture, SUNY Binghamton, 85-86. *Mailing Add:* PO Box 385 Canal St Sta New York NY 10013-0385

RUST, DAVID E
CURATOR, COLLECTOR
b Bloomington, Ill. *Study:* Harvard Col, BA; NY Univ Inst Fine Arts, MA, 63. *Collection Arranged:* English Drawings & Watercolors, 62; Old Master Drawings from Chatsworth, 69; Nathan Cummings Collection, 70; Francois Boucher: 100 Drawings (asst auth, catalog), 73; French Paintings from the Alisa Mellon Bruce Collection (auth, catalog), 78; Manet and Modern Paris, 82-83. *Pos:* Cur Fr, Brit & Spanish Paintings, Nat Gallery Art, Washington, DC, 61-83; adv panel, Art Pub Places, Dade Co, Fla; dir, Tissot Exhib, 84-85. *Collection:* Paintings and drawings, mostly European sixteenth-nineteenth century; American nineteenth century and some contemporary. *Publ:* Auth, Twentieth Century Paintings & Sculpture of the French School in the Chester Dale Collection, 65; Eighteenth & Nineteenth Century Paintings & Sculpture of the French School in the Chester Dale Collection, 65; The drawings of Vincenzo Tamagni da San Gimignano, Report & Studies Hist Art, 68; Small French Paintings from the Bequest of Alisa Mellon Bruce, 78

RUST, EDWIN C
SCULPTOR, ADMINISTRATOR
b Hammonton, Calif, Dec 5, 1910. *Study:* Cornell Univ; Yale Univ, BFA; also with Archipenko & Milles; Southwestern at Memphis, Hon DFA, Memphis Coll Art, Hon DFA. *Work:* US Ct House, Washington; Univ Tenn Ctr Health Serv; Univ Miss, Oxford; Univ Tenn, Knoxville; Memphis Acad Arts, Tenn; Ouchita Baptist Univ, Arkadelphia, Ark; Memphis Brooks Mus Art. *Exhib:* Whitney Mus Am Art, NY, 40; Carnegie Inst Int, Pittsburgh, 40; Philadelphia Mus Art, 40 & 49; Mus Mod Art, NY, 42; Brooks Mem Mus, 50 & 52. *Pos:* Dir, Memphis Acad Arts, 49-75, emer dir, 75-. *Teaching:* Assoc prof sculpture, Col William & Mary, 36-43, head, Dept Fine Arts, 39-43. *Mem:* Nat Sculpture Soc

RUTHLING, FORD
PAINTER, SCULPTOR
b Santa Fe, NMex, Apr 23, 1933. *Study:* With Randall Davey; largely self taught. *Work:* Mus NMex; Wichita Falls Fine Art Mus; Univ Utah Collection; and others. *Comn:* US Pueblo Pottery Postage Stamp (4 thirteen cent stamps), 77; and others. *Exhib:* Nelson Atkins Mus; Mus NMex; Oklahoma City Mus Fine Art; Dallas Mus Fine Art; Wichita Falls Mus Fine Art; Roswell Art Mus, 79; and others. *Pos:* Cur Exhibs, Mus Int Folk Art, 65-68. *Teaching:* NMex State Penitentiary, 73-. *Awards:* 2006 Governor's Art Award; 4 Top Awards at competition for Int Incarcerated Prisoners. *Media:* Oil, Graphics; Metal, Wood, Mono Prints. *Collection:* Folk Art, Latin Religious Santos, Retablos, Reliquaries & Paintings; African Antique Art; Indian Jewelery; Pottery; Textiles. *Publ:* Various. *Mailing Add:* 313 E Berger St Santa Fe NM 87501

RUTHVEN, JOHN ALDRICH
PAINTER, LECTURER
b Cincinnati, Ohio, Nov 12, 1924. *Study:* Univ Cincinnati Art Acad; Ctr Acad Com Art; Miami Univ, Ohio, DHL; St Francis Col, Loretto, Pa, DHL. *Work:* Hermitage Mus, Leningrad, Russia; Neil Armstrong Space Mus, Wapakoneta, Ohio; Ruthven Conf Ctr, Middletown, Ohio; White House, Washington; Cincinnati Natural Hist Mus. *Comn:* Cardinals for Gov Conf, State Ohio, Columbus, 68 & Eagle to the Moon, 69; Colonial Williamsburg Ser, Va, 70-75; Cardinal, USSR, 70; Miami Indian, Miami Univ, 74; Bankers' Life & Casualty. *Exhib:* Ducks Unlimited, Hilton Head, SC, 72; Ohio State Fair, Columbus, 74; White House Reception, 76; Leigh-Yawkey-Woodson Mus, Wausau, Wisc, 76 & 77; Wildlife Festival, Easton, Md, 77; Artists Am, Denver; Soc Animal Artists; Bennington Ctr Arts, NJ, 96; Cannon House, Washington, 96. *Pos:* Mem bd dir, Cincinnati Nature Ctr, 69; trustee, Cincinnati Natural Hist Mus, 75; trustee, Ducks Unlimited, Ohio Nature Cons Bd, currently. *Awards:* Sachs Fine Art Award, Cincinnati Art Acad, 69; Ducks Unlimited, 1st Art of Yr, 82; 1st Ohio Animal Stamp, 88; Pacific Flyaway Artist, Ducks Unlimited, 1989; recipient Irma Lazarus Award for sustained arts excellence, Ohio Govs Awards for the Arts, 2001; Nat Medal of Arts, 2004. *Bibliog:* Jerry Bowles (auth), John Ruthven, Acquire Mag, 73; Cincinnati Art, Town & Country, 75; Art of Life, film-doc, WCET-TV, 96. *Mem:* Soc Animal Artists NY; Audubon Soc; Nature Conservancy; Grouse Soc; Wild Turkey Fedn. *Media:* Opaque Watercolor. *Publ:* Coauth, Topflight, 69; auth, Carolina Paraquet, Audubon Mag, 72; auth, In the Audubon Tradition, Hennegan, 94; Wings of Encouragement, Helen Steiner Rice Found, 95; Ohio Wildlife Guidebook, Ohio Div Wild, 96

RUTLAND, LILLI IDA
PAINTER, ILLUSTRATOR
b Dothan, Ala, Jan 3, 1918. *Study:* Univ Ala, 50-52; study with Claude Peacock, 50-52. *Work:* Governors Mansion, Montgomery, Ala; Houston Mem Libr & Rose Hill Elem Sch, Dothan, Ala. *Comn:* Yearbook cover, Young Jr High Sch, Dothan, Ala, 33. *Exhib:* King Alfred Daffodils, Panama City Art Mus, Fla, 60; First Snow and Wild Flowers, Montgomery Mus Fine Arts, Ala, Daytona Mus Arts & Sci, Daytona Beach, Fla, Mobile Art Gallery, Ala & Birmingham Mus Art, Ala, 76; Daybreak, 84 & Southern Magnolias, 84, City Nat Bank Gallery, Dothan, Ala; solo exhib, Southeast Ala Med Ctr Gallery, Dothan, Ala, 85. *Pos:* Illusr, Training Aids, Ft Rucker, Ala, 67-75. *Awards:* First in Watercolor, Houston Co Fair, City of Dothan, 60; First in Watercolor, Dothan Wiregrass Art League, 73; Best of Show in Watercolor, Dothan Bank & Trust Co, 73. *Mem:* Dothan Wiregrass Art League (secy, 62); Portrait Club, Washington, Conn. *Media:* Watercolor

RUTTINGER, JACQUELYN
PAINTER, PRINTMAKER
Study: Univ Wash, Seattle, 58-60; Art Inst Chicago, BFA (hon), 63; Northern Ill Univ, MA, 76, MFA, 77; Gov's State Univ, 81-83, Post-grad work in Printmaking. *Work:* Ill State Mus, Springfield; State Ill Percent Art, Northern Ill Univ, DeKalb & Eastern Ill Univ, Charleston; Millikin Univ, Decatur, Ill; Sheldon Swope Art Mus, Terre Haute, Ind; Western Mich Univ, Kalamazoo, & Downtown Grad Ctr, Grand Rapids, Mich; Am Council on Education, Washington, DC; Western Mich Univ (40 works); Northern Ill Univ Art Mus; El Paso Mus Art. *Comn:* 2 paintings, Appl Technol Bldg, Grand Rapids Community Col, Mich, 92; Woodcut print, comn by Bestiario & Nahnales II (portfolio 20 artist prints), Arceo Press, Chicago, Ill, 2007. *Exhib:* Solo exhibs, Kalamazoo Inst Arts, Mich, Saginaw Art Mus, Mich & Jesse Besser Mus Alpena, Mich; Four from Kalamazoo Krasl Art Ctr, St Joseph, Mich, 99; Farnham Galleries, Simpson Col, Indianola, Iowa; 75th Muskegon Mus Art Regional, MI, 2004; Recent juried: Jackson Area Show, Ella Sharp Mus, Jackson, MI, 2005, Best of Show Award; Nat Art Premiere, Elmhurst Art Mus, Elmhurst, Ill, 2007; Bestiario & Nahnales I & II: Casa Michoacan, Chicago, Ill, 2007; Centro Cultural Taxco, Guerrero, Mex, 2007-2008; Univ Tex-Pan American, Edinburg, Tex, 2008; Drawing & Print Nat, Long Beach Arts, Calif, 2008; Midwest Nat Abstract Art IV, Garfield Park Arts Ctr, Indianapolis, Ind, 2008; PaperWorks Nat, Marin MOCA, Novato, Calif, 2008. *Pos:* Dir exhib & vis artist progs, Sch of Art, Western Mich Univ, Kalamazoo, 86-2006. *Awards:* Ill Art Coun, Grant, 81-82; Best of Show, Jackson Area Show, Ella Sharp Mus, Mich, 96, 2005. *Mem:* Friends of Sch Art, Western Mich Univ; Kalamazoo Inst Arts. *Media:* Acrylic Airbrush Paintings, Prismacolor Drawings, Prints. *Interests:* hiking & gardening. *Mailing Add:* 1110 Dwillard Dr Kalamazoo MI 49048-2259

RUYLE, LYDIA MILLER
PRINTMAKER, EDUCATOR
b Denver, Colo, Aug 4, 1935. *Study:* Univ Colo, Boulder, BA (magna cum laude), 57; Univ Northern Colo, MFA, 72; Syracuse Univ, int study, Renaissance Art, Italy; Romanesque Art, France, Spain, 85; Santa Reparata Graphic Arts Ctr Workshops, Florence, Italy, 1988-2000; Sch Art Inst Chicago, study in Indonesia, 93; Phi Beta Kappa. *Work:* Nat Mus Women Arts, Washington; Citicorp, Denver; McDougal-Littell Publs, Evanston, Ill; Lincoln Ctr, Ft Collins, Colo; Union Colony Civic Ctr, Sr Ctr, Greeley, Colo. *Comn:* print ed of lithographs, Am Hist Soc Gers from Russia, Lincoln, Nebr, 80; print eds for United Way, Weld Co, Colo, 80-91; environ sculpture, Artspicnic Festival, Greeley, Colo, 85; graduation banners, Univ Northern Colo, 96; cast paper sculptures, Children's Hosp, Denver, 92. *Exhib:* Nat Asn Women Artists Ann Exhibs, NY, 82-92; Exchange Exhib, Traveling Printmaking, Bombay, India, 89-90, throughout US, 92-93; solo exhibs, The Goddess in the Desert, Palm Springs, Calif, 98, Language of the Goddess & Crop Circle, Loveland, Colo, 98, Re-Imaging Revival: The Divine Feminine, Minneapolis, Minn, 98, Nat United Methodist Churches Conf, Orlando, Fla, 98, The Language of the Goddess Conf, Calif Inst Integral Studies, San Francisco, 98, circles of Light/Techno Cosmic Mass with Mathew Fox, Glen Miller Ballroom, Univ Colo, 98 & The Greenest Branch: Conf for 900th Birthday of Hildegard of Bingen, Burlington, Vt, 98; Univ Tex Health Scis Ctr, San Antonio, Tex, 92; Quattro Amici, Santa Reparata Graphic Arts Ctr, Florence, Italy, 92; Goddesses in the Himalayas, Fatan Mus, Nepal, 2000; Goddess in Eastern Europe, Hady Gallery, Brno, Czech Repub, 2001; Daily Ctr Visual Arts, Boulder, Colo, 2003; Boise State Univ, ID, 2003; Univ Missouri, Columbia, MO,2003; New Col, San Francisco, Calif, 2003; Serbian Academy of Arts & Sci, Novi Siad, Serbia, 2004; UCLA's Fowler Mus, Los Angeles, Calif, 2004; Women's AIDS conf Kenya, 2004; UC Boulder, Colo 2005; Marin Servs Women Gala, 2006; Sekmet Festival, Indian Springs, Nev, 2006; Healing Retreat, Machu Picchu, Peru, 2006; Mysteries of Ancient Greece, 2006; Goddess Conversations, Paris, France, 2006; and many others. *Pos:* Gov appointed bd mem, Colo Coun Arts Humanities, 77-82; comnr, Colo Comn Higher Educ, 83-85; Presenter/owner, Goddess Tours, Ya-Ya Journeys, 93-. *Teaching:* Creative Arts Ctr, Greeley, Colo, 68-78; adj fac, Printmaking, art hist & art appreciation, Univ Northern Colo, 80-; workshop presenter, univs serv clubs, prof asns throughout US & abroad, 85-; Vis artist, Col of the Desert, Palm Springs, Cal, 94-95; Univ of CO, Boulder, 2005. *Awards:* Juror's Award, Manhattan Nat Print, 84; Printmaking, 86, Works on Paper, 91, Nat Asn Women Artists Ann; Honored Alumni Award, Univ N Colo, 96; Arts Alive! Award, City of Greeley, Colo, 2005. *Bibliog:* Judy Chicago (auth), The Birth Project, Doubleday & Co, 85; Linda Anderson (auth), Greeley's Goddesses, Spectrum UNC, 90; Mary Carroll Nelson (auth), Affirming Wholeness, Southwest Art/CBH Publ, 6/92. *Mem:* Nat Asn Women Artists, NY; Los Angeles Printmaking Soc; Women's Caucus Art, Philadelphia; Soc Multi-Media Layerists, Albuquerque, NMex; Colo Art Educs Asn. *Res:* Research and use inherited images of divine feminine in collagraph print & icon banners; Black Madonnas as icon images of healing. *Specialty:* Artist Cooperative. *Interests:* travel. *Publ:* Contribr, Layering, Soc Layerist in Multimedia, Albuquerque, 91 & 98; illusr, The Great Goddess, An Introduction to Her Many Names, Shef, Boulder, 92; auth & illusr, The Goddess Has A Thousand Faces, Inner Eye Press, Tucson, Ariz, 92; auth, Goddess Icons, Spirit Banners of the Divine Feminine, Woven Word Press, 2002; illusr, Dark Mother, African Origins and Godmothers, Lucia Chiavola Birnbaum, iUniverse, 2002; (auth) Turkey Goddess Icons Spirit Banners of the Divine Feminine, Hitit Publ, Istanbul, 2005; (cover & illusr) Prayers and Seven Contemplations of the Sacred Mother, Mary E Kingsley, 2004; auth & illustr, Lydia Ruyle: Fifty Years of Herstory in Art, 1955-2005 (exhib catalog), 2005; cover, Making Place, Making Self, Ashgate Press, Eng, 2005. *Dealer:* Madison & Main Gallery. *Mailing Add:* 2101 24th St Greeley CO 80631

RUZ, THELMA
SCULPTOR
b Mexico, June 4, 1949. *Study:* Haddox Acad, 66; study with Enrique Jolly, Moyado, Palma Cajiga. *Work:* Grupo Arte Contemporaneo, Mexico. *Comn:* Bronze sculpture, Patrimono de la Nacion. *Exhib:* Galena Ultra, Galena Alexandra, Galena Nona, Mex; 8 solo exhibs in Mex & Los Angeles. *Media:* Bronze. *Mailing Add:* Privada de Ahuehuetes Sur No #18 Bosques de las Lomas Mexico 17000 Mexico

RYBCZYNSKI, WITOLD MARIAN
ARCHITECT, EDUCATOR
b Edinburgh, Scotland, Mar 1, 1943. *Study:* Loyola Col, Montreal, 60; McGill Univ, BArch, 66, March, 72, Stet, 2002 (hon). *Hon Degrees:* McGill Univ, DSc, 2002; Univ Western Ontario, LLD, 2006. *Pos:* res assoc, McGill Univ, 72-75, asst prof, archit, 75-80, assoc prof, 80-86, prof, 86-93; Consult UN, Manila, 76, Int Devel. Res Ctr, Ottawa, 77, Banco de Mex, 79-80; sr fel, Design Futures Inst, 2003. *Teaching:* Pvt practice, archit, Montreal, 70-82; Meyerson prof, of Urbanism Univ Pa, 94-2012, emeritus prof, Univ Pa, 2012-. *Awards:* Progressive Architect Design award, 91; Jurzykowski Found award, 93; Athanaeum Lit prize, 97 & 2001; J. Anthony Lucas Prize, 2000; Vincent Scully Prize, 2007; Seaside Prize, 2007; AIA (Inst Honors for Collab Achievement), 2007; Nat Design award, 2014. *Mem:* Hon Fel Am Inst Archit; US Commission Fine Art; Hon Mem Am Society Landscape Archit. *Publ:* Auth: Paper Heroes: A Review of Appropriate Technol, 1980, Taming the Tiger: The Struggle to Control Technology, 1983, Home: A Short History of an Idea, 1986, The Most Beautiful House in the World, 1989, Waiting in the Weekend, 1991, Looking Around: A Journey Through Archit, 1992, A Place for Art, 1993, City Life: Urban Expectation in a New World, 1995, A Clearing in the Distance, 1999 (Christopher award), One Good Turn, 2000, The Look of Archit, 2001, The Perfect House, 2002; Vizcaya (with L Olin), 2007; Last Harvest, 2008, My Two Polish Grandfathers, 2009; Makeshift Metropolis, 2010; The Biography of Building, 2011, How Architecture Works, 2013; contrib ed: Saturday Night, 1990-2001; contributing auth Booknotes: Stories from Am Hist, mem adv. board Encyclopedia Americana; founding editor: Wharton Real Estate Rev, 1996-2012

RYCHLAK, BONNIE L
SCULPTOR, CURATOR
b Culver City, Calif, July 7, 1951. *Study:* Univ Calif, Los Angeles, BA, 73; Univ Mass, Amherst, MFA, 76. *Work:* Harvard Univ. *Comn:* Wall sculpture, NY, 94. *Exhib:* Rastovsky Gallery, NY, 88; Solo shows, Rastovsky Gallery, NY, 89, Shoshana Wayne Gallery, Santa Monica, Calif, 91, Sculpture Ctr 2d Gallery, NY, 93, Gallery Three Zero, NY, 94; Shoshana Wayne Gallery, Santa Monica, 89; Stux Gallery, NY, 90; Penine Hart Gallery, 90; Emily Sorkin Gallery, NY, 90; Sue Spain Fine Art, Los Angeles, Calif, 90; Hallwalls Pleasure, Buffalo, NY, 91; Int House, NY, 92; 55 Ferris St, NY, 92; T'zart - Test Wall, NY, 93; Adam Baumgold Gallery, NY, 94; Otis Fine Arts, NY, 96; Silverstein Gallery, NY, 98; R&F Gallery, Kingston, NY, 99; Momenta Benefit Exhib, NY, 2000. *Collection Arranged:* Isamu Noguchi-Rosanjin Kitaoji (auth, catalog), Sezon Mus Art, Tokyo, Japan, 96; Noguchi and The Figure (auth, catalog), Mus Arte Contemporaneo Monterrey and Mus Rufino Tamayo, 99. *Pos:* Asst, Isamu Noguchi, 80-88; dir collections & cur, Isamu Noguchi Found, 80-. *Awards:* NEA, 76-77; Bellagio Residency, Rockefeller Found, 85; Prix de Rome Am Acad Rome, 90. *Bibliog:* Arlene Raven (auth), Well healed, The Village Voice, 2/94. *Mem:* Coll Art Asn; Asn Am Mus; Int Cong Art Historians; Orgn Independent Artists. *Media:* Found objects. *Mailing Add:* 248 Lafayette St New York NY 10012

RYDEN, KENNETH GLENN
SCULPTOR
b Chicago, Ill, May 16, 1945. *Study:* Univ Wis, Superior, BFA; Univ Kans, Lawrence, MFA; study with Bernard Frazer, Eldon Tefft & Victor Timmerman. *Work:* Grover Hermann Fine Arts Ctr, Marietta, Ohio; Swope Art Gallery, Terre Haute, Ind; Southern Ill Univ Art Collection, Edwardsville; Wabash Coll Art Collection, Crawfordsville, Ind; Kans State Univ; and others. *Comn:* Delyte Morris Mem, Southern Ill Univ at Edwardsville, 76 & John Rendleman Mem, 76; Greenville City Sq, 80; 10 Yr Mem, Southern Ill Univ, Sch Med, Springfield. *Exhib:* Mainstreams 73, Grover M Hermann Fine Arts Ctr, Marietta, Ohio, 73; Solo exhibs, Univ Wis-Superior, Ark State Univ, Jonesboro, Univ Notre Dame, Kans State Univ, Manhattan & Roberts Wesleyan Col, Rochester; Houghton Coll, NY, 80; and many others. *Teaching:* Instr sculpture, Univ Mo, Columbia, 70-73; asst prof sculpture, Southern Ill Univ, Edwardsville, 73-78; assoc prof & chmn art dept, Greenville Col, Ill, 78-; assoc prof, Anderson Col, Ind, 83-. *Awards:* Purchase Award, Mainstreams 73, Grover M Hermann Fine Arts Ctr, 73; Top Purchase Award, 33rd Ann Wabash Valley Sheldon Swope Art Gallery, 77; First in Sculpture, Int Platform Asn Artists Exhib, 82. *Mem:* Nat Coll Art Asn; Southern Sculptors Asn; Nat Sculpture Ctr; Int Platform Asn; Washington Arts Club, Washington, DC. *Media:* Multimedia, Metals. *Dealer:* Prairie House Gallery 3013 Lindburgh Blvd Springfield IL. *Mailing Add:* Dept Art Anderson Univ 1100 E 5th St Anderson IN 46012

RYMAN, WILL
SCULPTOR
b New York, NY, 1969. *Study:* The McBurney Sch, 1988; The New Sch, New York, 1989. *Exhib:* Christies Auction House, Los Angeles, 2003; solo exhibs, Studio Space, New York, 2003, Klemens Gasser & Tanja, New York, 2004, Grunert Inc, New York, 2005, Galerie Bernd Kluser, Munich, Ger, 2006, Howard House, Seattle, Wash, 2006, Scope Basel, Switz, 2007, Marlborough Chelsea, New York, 2007, Saatchi Gallery, London, 2009 & Marlborough Gallery, New York, 2009; New Work, Studio Space, New York, 2004; Flower Power, Klemens Gasser & Tanja Grunert Inc, New York, 2005; PS1 Contemp Art Ctr, Long Island City, 2005; Ben Shahn Gallery, William Patteson Coll, Wayne, NJ, 2006; Sanctuary and the Scrum, Black and White Art Gallery, New York, 2006; Summer exhib, Marlborough Gallery, New York, 2007; Invitational exhib, Acad Arts & Letts, New York, 2007-2008; Sobre el Humor, Galeria Marlborough, Madrid, Spain, 2008; The Shape of Things to Come, Saatchi Gallery, London, 2009. *Bibliog:* Noelle Hancock (auth), The Eight Day Week, New York Observer, 22, 8/4/2003; Ken Johnson (auth), Art in Review, NY Times, 7/2/2004; Roberta Smith (auth), rev, NY Times, 7/2005; Nate Lippens (auth), Ryman Turns the Intimage into the Outrageous, Seattle Post-Intelligencer, 9/29/2006; Brook S Mason (auth), The World Comes to Basel, Art and Antiques, 40-42, 9/2007; Robert C Morgan (auth), rev, Sculpture Mag, 3/2008; Imogen Carter (auth), Pillow talk with a bunch of artists, The Observer, London, 1/4/2009. *Mailing Add:* c/o Marlborough Gallery 40 W 57th St New York NY 10019

S

SAAR, ALISON M
SCULPTOR
b Los Angeles, Calif, Feb 5, 1956. *Study:* Scipps Coll, BA, 78; Otis Art Inst, MFA, 81. *Work:* Metrop Mus Art & Studio Mus Harlem, New York; Trenton Mus Art, NJ; Newark Mus, NJ. *Comn:* Bronze gates, Metro Transit Authority, New York, 90-91; Monument, Great Northern Migration, Bronzeville Renovation, Chicago, Ill, 96. *Exhib:* Solo shows incl High Mus, Atlanta, Ga, 93, Va Mus Fine Arts, 94, Newhouse Ctr Contemp Art, Staten Island, NY, 95, Phyllis Kind Gallery, New York, 95, Brooklyn Mus, 95-96, Jan Baum Gallery, Los Angeles, Calif, 97, 2001, Swarthmore Col, Pa, 97, Santa Monica Mus Art, 99, Herron Gallery, Indianapolis, 99, Springfield Art Mus, Mo, 2003; group shows incl Recent Acquisitions, Metrop Mus Art, New York, 87; Urban Figures, Whitney Mus Am Art, New York, 88; The 1980's: A New Generation, Metrop Mus Art, New York, 88; Advocacy Art, Aldrich Mus, 91; Biennial Exhib, Whitney Mus Am Art, 93; Landscape as Metaphor, Denver Art Mus, Colo & Columbus Mus Art, Ohio, 94; A Labor of Love, New Mus Contemp Art, New York, 96; Subjective Vision, Kipp Gallery, Ind Univ Pa, 96; Bearing Witness: Contemporary Works by African American Women Artists (traveling), 96-99; Remembrance of Exhibitions Past, Jan Baum Gallery, Los Angeles, Calif, 97; On the House, Santa Monica Mus Art, 97; Fassbender Gallery, Chicago, 99; The Getty Ctr, Los Angeles, 2000; New Mus Contemp Art, New York, 2000; Phyllis Kind Gallery, New York, 2001. *Awards:* Nat Endowment Arts, 85 & 88; John Solomon Guggenheim Award, 89; COLA Fel, City of LA Cultural Affairs Dept, 2005. *Bibliog:* William Zimmer (auth), The ties that bind mother & daughter, NY Times Sunday, 1/1/95; Edward Lucie-Smith (auth), Art Today, Phaidon, London, 95; Christopher Knight (auth), Saar's spare forms resonate with richness, Los Angeles Times, 1/15/99. *Dealer:* Blumenfeld/Lustberg Fine Art 23 Fiske Pl Brooklyn NY 11215; The Frostig Collection 971 N Altadena Dr Pasadena CA 91107; Gallery Karl Oskar 3008 W 71 Prairie Village KS 66208; LA Louver Gallery 45 N Venice Blvd Venice CA 90291; Peltz Gallery 1119 E Knapp St Milwaukee WI 53202; Sightlines PO Box 750430 Forest Hills NY 11375-0430; Diane Villani Editions 285 Lafayette St #3-d New York NY 10012. *Mailing Add:* 2456 Green Valley Rd Los Angeles CA 90046

SAAR, BETYE
ASSEMBLAGE ARTIST, COLLAGE ARTIST
b Los Angeles, Calif, July 30, 1926. *Study:* Univ Calif, Los Angeles, BA; Univ Southern Calif; Long Beach State Col; San Fernando Valley State Col. *Work:* Univ Mass, Amherst; Wellington Evest Collection, Boston; Golden State Mutual Life Ins Collection, Los Angeles; Los Angeles Co Mus Art; Univ Calif Mus, Berkeley. *Comn:* Mural, Los Angeles, 1983; mural, Newark Sta, NJ, 1984; Metrorail Sta, Miami, Fla, 1986. *Exhib:* Solo exhibs incl Whitney Mus Am Art, 1975, Jan Baum/Iris Silverman Gallery, Los Angeles, 1977, 1979 & 1981, Univ Art Gallery, Univ NDak, 1979 & Mandeville Art Gallery, Univ Calif, San Diego, 1979, Personal Icons, Univ Art Mus, Univ NMex, 1999, Betye Saar: As Time Goes By 1591-1591, IconsSavannah Coll of Art & Design, Ga, 2000; group exhibs incl Sculpture Ann, 1970 & Contemp Black Artists in Am, 1971, Whitney Mus Am Art, NY; Black Artist Exhib, Los Angeles Co Mus Art, 1972; Painting/Sculpture in Calif: Mod Era, San Francisco Mus Mod Art, 76 & Smithsonian Inst, Washington, DC, 1977; Monique Knowlton Gallery, NY, 1976 & 1981; San Francisco Mus Mod Art, 1977; Studio Mus Harlem, NY, 1980; Connections, Mass Inst Tech, Cambridge, 1987; African Am Art: 20th Century Masterworks, VII, Michael Rosenfeld Gallery, NY, 2000; Migrations/Transformations, Michael Rosenfeld Gallery, NY City, 2006; Family Legacies: The Art of Betye, Lezley, and Alison Saar, Ackland Art Mus, Univ NC, 2006. *Teaching:* Vis artist, Calif State Univ, Hayward, fall 1971; prof art, Calif State Univ, Northridge, 1973-75 & Otis Art Inst, 1976-84; instr, Univ Alaska, summer 1979 & Univ Calif, Los Angeles, 1984-. *Awards:* Purchase Award, Calif State Col, Los Angeles, 1972; Nat Endowment Arts Award, 1974 & 1984; The Visual Arts Award, The Flintridge Found, Pasadena, Calif, 1997-98; Nat Artist Award, Anderson Ranch Art Ctr, Colo, 1999; Artist Award for Distinguished Body of Work, Coll Art Asn, 2007. *Bibliog:* Spirit Catcher: The Art of Betye Saar, The Originals: Women in Art series, WNET-PBS, NY; Houston Conwill (auth), Interview with Betye Saar, Black Art, 1979; Eleanor Munro (auth), Originals: American Women Artists, Simon & Schuster, 1979; Lynn Miller & Sally Swenson (auths), Lives & Works: Talks with Women Artists, Scarecrow Press, NJ, 81; Clothier (auth), Betye Saar (catalog), Mus Contemp Art, Los Angeles, 1984. *Media:* Multi. *Publ:* Auth, Handbook, 1967. *Dealer:* Monique Knowlton New York NY. *Mailing Add:* c/o Michael Rosenfeld Gallery 100 11th Ave New York NY 10011

SAAR, LEZLEY
PAINTER
b Los Angeles, Calif, 1953. *Study:* L'Institute Fracais de Photographic, Paris, 72; San Francisco State Univ, 76; Calif State Univ Northridge, BA, 78. *Exhib:* Solo shows incl Art Works, Los Angeles, 90, Koplin Gallery, Santa Monica, Calif, 91, 93, Jan Baum Gallery, Los Angeles, 94, 96, David Beitzel Gallery, New York, 97, 2000, 2001, Kemper Mus Contemp Art, Kans City, 2000, Contemp Arts Ctr, Cincinnati, 2000, Forum Contemp Art, St Louis, Mo, 2001; group shows incl Conejo Valley Art Mus, 84; Franklin Furnace, New York, 85; Scottsdale Cult Ctr, Ariz, 92; Art Gallery-Visual Arts Ctr, Calif State Univ, Fullerton, Calif, 93; Nat Mus Women in Arts, Wash, DC; 5th Biennial, Havana, Cuba; Jan Baum Gallery, Los Angeles, 94, 95; Mus Contemp Art, Sydney, 94; David Beitzel Gallery, New York, 97, 99, 2001; Katonah Mus Art, NY, 99; Todd Madigan Gallery, CSU Bakersfield, Calif, 99; UFA Gallery, New York, 2000; Ruth Chandler Williamson Gallery, Scripps Coll, Calif, 2000; Calif Ctr for Arts, Escondido, 2000. *Awards:* J Paul Getty, Mid Career Grant; Seagram's Gin Perspective in African Am Art Fel. *Media:* Acrylic on Paper. *Dealer:* Jan Baum Gallery 170 S LaBrea Ave Los Angeles CA 90036. *Mailing Add:* 667 Calle Miramar Redondo Beach CA 90277

SAARI, PETER H
PAINTER, SCULPTOR
b New York, NY, Feb 15, 1951. *Study:* Sch Visual Arts, 69-70; C W Post Col, BFA, 74; Tyler Sch Art, Rome, Italy, study with Stephen Greene, 72-73; Yale Sch Art, study with William Bailey & Al Held, MFA (fel), 76. *Work:* Hirshhorn Mus, Washington, DC. *Comn:* John O Shoosan (Co), Baliston, Va; Bruce Kouner (residence), Millbrook, NY. *Exhib:* Solo exhibs, Helander Gallery, Palm Beach, Fla, 87, OK Haris Works of Art, NY, 87 & 93, Robert Schoelkopf Gallery, NY, 88, Tortue Gallery, Santa Monica, Calif, 89, Fendrick Gallery, Washington, DC, 90 & OK Harris Works Art, NY, 93, 98, 2001, Disjecta Membra, Broadway Windows, NY, 2001; New York-NY, Helander Gallery, Palm Beach, Fla, 86-87; Mainstream Am: The Collection of Phil Desind & 51st Ann Nat Mid-Year Exhib, Butler Inst Am Art, Youngstown, Ohio; Classical Myth and Imagery in Contemp Art, The Queens Mus, Flushing, NY, 88; Art After Art (with catalog), Nat Co Mus Art, Roslyn Harbor, NY, 94 & 95. *Collection Arranged:* Hirshhorn Mus & Sculpture Garden, Smithsonian Inst, Washington, DC; Israel Mus, Jerusalem. *Teaching:* Asst instr advan painting, Yale Sch Art, New Haven, Conn, 75-76; guest lectr, St Lawrence Univ, 78. *Bibliog:* Ninon Gaulthier (auth), Impressions de New York, Finance, France, 4/87; A Question of Space: Architectural Inquiries (catalog), The Rye Arts Ctr, NY, 87; Richard Martin and Harold Koda (coauthor), The Historical Mode: Fashion and Art in the 1980's, Rizzoli, New York, 80. *Dealer:* OK Harris 383 W Broadway New York NY 10012

SAATCHI, CHARLES
COLLECTOR
b Jun 9, 1943. *Pos:* Assoc dir, Collett Dickenson Pearce, 1966-68; dir, Cramer Saatchi, 1968-70; co-founder & dir, Saatchi & Saatchi, plc, London, 1970-93, pres, 1993-95; partner, M & C Saatchi Agency, 1995-; founder, Saatchi Gallery, London, 2003. *Awards:* Named one of Top 200 Collectors, ARTnews mag, 2004-13. *Collection:* Contemporary art, especially British. *Mailing Add:* 36 Golden Sq London United Kingdom W1R 4EC

SABLOW, RHODA LILLIAN See Roda, Rhoda Lillian Sablow

SABO, BETTY JEAN
PAINTER, SCULPTOR
b Kansas City, Mo, Sept 15, 1928. *Study:* Univ NMex; with Randall Davey, Carl von Hassler, Charles Reynolds & Al Merrill. *Work:* Albuquerque Mus; Mus Sasebo, Japan; Pub Serv Co, NMex; United NMex Bank; Wells Fargo Bank. *Comn:* Christmas Greeting, Phelps-Dodge Collection, 81; 36 Collographs, St Joseph Rehabilitation Hosp, 90; 5 bronze figures (sculpture), Sun Health Care, 94; 2 bronze figures (sculpture) & group 24 bronze figures (sculpture), City of Albuquerque, NMex; 7 bronze figures (sculpture), Univ NMex; Bronze Figure, Mt Union Coll Alliance, Ohio; Bronze Figure, Juan Diego High School, Draper, UT. *Exhib:* Albuquerque I,

Albuquerque Mus, 68; Catharine Lorillard Wolfe Exhib, Nat Acad, NY, 71 & Nat Arts Club, NY, 72-73; Allied Artists, 78-80; Am Acad Art, NY, 80; Margaret Jamison Presents, NMex, 84-86; NMex Tapestries, 84-85; Magnifico, Gov Exhib, Albuquerque; Arte Grande Outdoor Sculpture, Albuquerque, 91; Magnifico 90-94, Albuquerque; Sedona Sculpture Walk, Ariz, 91-94; NM Community Found, 91-92. *Collection Arranged:* Miniatures, Albuquerque Mus, 91-2002. *Pos:* Chmn, Albuquerque Arts Bd, 88-90; guest cur, Miniatures, 91-94, Albuquerque Mus; chmn, Bernalillo Co Arts Bd, 93-94. *Bibliog:* Flo Wilks (auth), The colorful way of the land, SW Art, 12/77; Women on the Arts, Southwest Art, 4/81; M C Nelson (auth), New Mexico is warm when its Cold, Art Lines, Winter 86-87; S H McGarry (auth), Schooled in the Art of Collecting, Southwest Art, 1/87; J A Baldinger (auth), Colorful Artists Run the Spectrum, NMex Mag, 6/91; Fabulous Fountains, Southwest Art, 8/92. *Mem:* Catharine Lorillard Wolfe Art Club; NMex Art League; Am Artists Prof League. *Media:* Oil; Metal Cast

SABOL, FRANK ROBERT
ADMINISTRATOR, EDUCATOR
Study: Indiana Univ, BS, 1971, MS, 1977, PhD (Curriculum and Instruction), 1994. *Pos:* Presenter in the field; Nat Assessment of Educational Progress (NAEP) Visual Arts Development Team, 1994-97, NAEP Visual Arts Exercise Review Bd, 1995-97; many roles for the Indiana, Fla, & Minnesota Department of Educ Service; mem arts educ adv com, Indiana Arts Commission, 2008-12. *Teaching:* Elementary art teacher, Crawfordsville Community Sch Corp, 1972-95; assoc instructor, art educ department, Indiana Univ, Bloomington, 1989-90; asst prof art and design, Rueff Sch of Visual and Performing Arts, Purdue Univ, West Lafayette, 1995, assoc prof, 2001, interim chair, 2002, chair Art Educ, Department of Art and Design, 2002-11, 2012-, prof Visual and Performing Arts, 2008-, chair department of Art and Design, 2009-12. *Awards:* Getty Educ Institute for the Arts Doctoral Research Fellowship, 1992; Nat Art Educ Asn Manual Barkan Memorial award, 2003, Distinguished Service within the Profession award, 2009; Art Educ Asn of Indiana Indiana Art Teacher of the Yr, 1992, Art Higher Educ Educator of the Yr, 1998. *Mem:* Nat Art Educ Asn (Western region vpres-elect, 2004-06, vpres, 2006-08, mem exec com bd dirs, 2006-2008, 2009-, pres-elect, 2009-11, distinguished fellow, 2009 and several other roles); Art Educ of Indiana (pres-elect, 1992-94, pres 1994-1996, past pres, 1996-98, parliamentarian, 1992-94, 2005-09, distinguished fellow chair, 2005-11 and several other roles). *Publ:* Numerous articles in professional journals; co-auth Assessing Expressive Learning and Through the Prism: Looking into the Spectrum of Writings by Enid Zimmerman. *Mailing Add:* 1221 W Watson Dr Crawfordsville IN 47933

SABORSKY, TERESA
SCULPTOR, DIRECTOR
Work: Port Warwick Art & Sculpture Festival, 2007. *Pos:* Geologist and geochemist, Conoco Oil Co, formerly; bd dirs, Nat Asn Independent Artists, 2007-, chmn, 2010-. *Media:* Metal, Cast, Wood. *Mailing Add:* 1412 Old Taylor Trail Goshen KY 40026

SACCOCCIO, JACQUELINE
ARTIST
b Providence, RI, 1963. *Study:* RI Sch Design, BFA in painting, 1985; Sch of the Art Inst of Chicago, MFA in painting, 1988; L'Universita per Stranieri, Perugia, Italy, 1990. *Exhib:* Solo exhibs incl, Lauren Wittels Gallery, New York City, 1997; White Columns, New York City, 2001; Galerie Michael Neff, Frankfurt, Ger, 2003; Black and White Gallery, NY, 2006; Eleven Rivington Gallery, 2008. *Teaching:* Adj fac, RI Sch Design. *Awards:* Edward L Ryerson Traveling Fel, 1988; Fulbright-Hays Found Grant/Miguel Vinciguerra Award, 1990-91; John Simon Guggenheim Mem Found Fel, 2000; Harold M English/Jacob H Lazarus-Met. Mus Art Rome Prize Fel; Am Acad in Rome, 2004-05. *Bibliog:* Jerry Saltz (auth), Maximum Voracity: Jackie Saccoccio's Retinal Thought Storm (pg 43), 1/2007; Steven Maine (auth), Call and Response (pg 15), The New York Sun, 1/2008. *Mem:* Coll Art Asn. *Dealer:* Eleven Rivington Gallery NY. *Mailing Add:* c/o Augusto Arbizo Eleven Rivington 11 Rivington St New York NY 10002

SACHS, SAMUEL, II
MUSEUM DIRECTOR, HISTORIAN
b New York, NY, Nov 30, 1935. *Study:* Harvard Univ, AB (cum laude); NY Univ Inst Fine Arts, AM. *Collection Arranged:* The Past Rediscovered, XIX Century French Painting 1800-1900, 69; Fakes and Forgeries (with catalog), 73; Grant Wood, 83. *Pos:* Asst prints & drawings, Minneapolis Inst Arts, 58-60, chief cur, 64-73, dir, 73-85; asst dir, Univ Mich Mus Art, 62-64; dir, Detroit Inst Arts, 85-97; dir, Frick Collection & Frick Art Ref Libr, 97-03; pres, Pollock-Krasner Foundation, 2003-. *Teaching:* Lectr art hist, Univ Mich, Ann Arbor, 62-63. *Mem:* Am Fedn Arts; Coll Art Asn Am. *Res:* Fakes and forgeries; American 19th and 20th century painting. *Publ:* Auth, Reconstructing the whirlwind of 26th St, Art News, 2/63; Drawings and watercolors of Thomas Moran, In: Thomas Moran (catalog), Univ Calif, Riverside, 63; American Paintings at the Minneapolis Institute of Arts, 71; Art forges ahead, Auction Mag, 1/72; Favorite Paintings from the Minneapolis Institute of Arts, Abbeyville Press, 81

SACHS, TOM
PAINTER, SCULPTOR
b NY, 1966. *Study:* Bennington Coll, Vt, BA, 1989. *Work:* Met Mus Art; Costime Inst, New York; Solomon R Guggenheim Mus, New York; Whitney Mus Am Art, New York; Centre Georges Pompidou, Paris. *Exhib:* Solo exhibs, Jacob Javitz Ctr, New York, 1993, Whitney Mus Am Art, New York, 1994, Morris-Healy Gallery, New York, 1995, Mario Diacono Gallery, Boston, 1996, John Berggruen Gallery, San Francisco, 1997, Thomas Healy Gallery, New York, 1998, Galerie Thaddeus Ropac, Paris, 1999, Mary Boone Gallery, 1999, Tomiyo Koyama Gallery, Tokyo, 2000, A/D Gallery, New York, 2001, Bohen Found, New York, 2002-03, Deutsche Guggenheim Berlin, 2003, Baldwin Gallery, Aspen, 2005, Fondazione Prada, Milan, 2006, Gagosian Gallery, Beverly Hills, 2007, Sperone Westwater, New York, 2008; Group exhibs, Allied Cult Prosthetics, New York, 1992; Alleged Gallery, New York, 1994; Paul Morris Gallery, New York, 1995; Gramercy Int Art Fair, New York, 1995, 1996, 1997, 1998; Linda Kirkland Gallery, New York, 1996; Sperone Westwater Gallery, New York, 1997, 2000, 2001; Thomas Healy Gallery, New York, 1998; Holly Solomon Gallery, New York, 1999; Exit Art, New York, 1999; Art/31/Basel, 2000; Apex Art, New York, 2001; Marianne Boesky Gallery, New York, 2001; Albright-KnoxArt Gallery, Buffalo, NY, 2003; Bienal de Sao Paulo, 2004; Cooper Hewitt Nat Design Mus, 2004-05; Herron Sch Art Design, 2005; Krannert Art Mus, Univ Ill at Urbana-Champaign, 2007. *Awards:* Archit Asn Furniture Prize, London, 1987. *Media:* Mixed Media. *Dealer:* Baldwin Gallery 209 S Galena St Aspen CO 81611; Galleria Cardi Corso di Porta Nuova 38 20121 Milan Italy; Dranoff Fine Art 591 Broadway 3D New York NY 10012; Galerie Michael Haas Niebuhrstraße 5 D-10629 Berlin Ger; Galerie Thaddaeus Ropac 7 Rue Debelleyme 75003 Paris France; Sebastian + Barquet Showroom 601 W 26th St New York NY 10001; Sperone Westwater New York NY. *Mailing Add:* c/o Sperone Westwater Gallery 257 Bowery New York NY 10002

SACKS, BEVERLY
ART DEALER, CONSULTANT
Study: Brooklyn Coll, BA. *Exhib:* African-Am Artists; Woman at Her Easel; The Fine Line; Wondrous Imagery; All the Isms; City Views. *Pos:* Beverly: Consult, Phillips & Son & Neale, Am Illusr; owners, Sacks Fine Art; permanent collection, Comt Soc Illusr Mus Am Illus. *Bibliog:* Antique & Arts Weekly, 10/17/80; Maine Antique Digest, 11/80; Buying American painting, Boston Sunday Globe, 11/23/80; Antiques & Art Weekley, 9/2010. *Mem:* Appraisers Asn Am; Soc Illusr (trustee); Nat Arts Club; Nat Acad Design; Asher B Durand Soc. *Specialty:* American paintings; 19th and early 20th century American illustrations and paintings; American works on paper; African American, modernist, WPA, regional, abstract; women artists; modernist jewelry. *Interests:* Women artists 19th & early 20th century. *Collection:* African American, abstract and surrealists. *Publ:* Rube Goldberg Early Works; African-American artists of the Harlem Renaissance period and later, 91. *Mailing Add:* 40 W 25th St #131 New York NY 10010

SACKS, STEVE G See Sax, (Steve G Sacks)

SADAN, MARK
ARTIST, PHOTOGRAPHER
b Syracuse, NY, Dec 15, 1939. *Study:* Am Acad Dramatic Arts, NY, 63; NYU, (film & TV), CFA, 69; Univ Mass, Amherst, MEd, 74. *Exhib:* Solo exhibs, Latvia Nat Photo Gallery, 89-90; Golden Lands, Golden Dreams, 2004; Nat Mus of Dance & Hall of Fame, 2004; Mus of New Art, 2005; Am Mus Dance, 2000, 2002; Photo-Art Mus, Norway, 2003; The Young Dancer, Nat Mus Dance & Hall of Fame, Saratoga, Springs, Fla, 5/2006-4/2007; Julia Margaret Cameron, Mus on the Isle of Wight, UK. *Pos:* Photo film unit Anti Poverty Prog, NYC, 66-67; 1st director film video workshop, 69-74; producer & dir short films, Sesame Street, 69, 72; directed numerous award winning documentaries; Artist in residence; Instr, film & photog; dir, Nat Road Safety Found. *Awards:* Medal Excellence for Photog Art, Latvian Nat Photog Soc, 90; Cine Film Awards, 2003. *Bibliog:* Circle of Life, Harper Press, San Francisco; Meditations, Tablet of Carmel & the Most Holy Tablet, Nightingale Bks, UK. *Mem:* Film Video Workshop (found, dir, 69, 74); Sunday Photo Group (dir, lectr, 82, 2004). *Interests:* Dance, Cinema, Swimming, poetry, reading, travel. *Publ:* Frente Desnudo, Udyat Publ, Barcelona. *Mailing Add:* PO Box 207 Ossining NY 10562

SADAO, AMY
MUSEUM DIRECTOR
Study: The Cooper Union Sch of Art, BFA, 1995; Univ of California, Berkeley, MA in cooparative ethnic studies, MA, 2000. *Pos:* Exec dir, Visual AIDS, NYC, 2002-2012; The Daniel W Dietrich, II dir, Institute of Contemporary Art, Univ Pennsylvania, 2012-. *Mailing Add:* Institute of Contemporary Art University of Pennsylvania 118 S 36th St Philadelphia PA 19104-3269

SADEO, AMY
MUSEUM DIRECTOR
Study: Cooper Union Sch Art, BA, 95; Univ Calif, Berkeley, MA, 2000. *Pos:* exec dir, Visual AIDS, NY, 2002-2012; Daniel Dietrich II Dir, Inst Contemp Art, Univ Pa, Phila, 2012-. *Mailing Add:* University of Pa Inst Contemp Art 118 S 36th St Philadelphia PA 19104

SADIK, MARVIN SHERWOOD
DEALER
b Springfield, Mass, June 27, 1932. *Study:* Harvard Univ, AB, 54, AM, 61. *Hon Degrees:* Bowdoin Col, DFA, 78. *Pos:* Curatorial asst, Worcester Art Mus, Mass, 55-57; cur & dir, Bowdoin Col Mus Art, 61-67; dir, Univ Conn Mus Art, 67-69; dir, Nat Portrait Gallery, Smithsonian Inst, 69-81. *Teaching:* Instr fine arts, Harvard Col, 58-60. *Awards:* Knight of Dannebrog, Denmark; Smithsonian Gold Medal For Exceptional Service, 81. *Mem:* Colonial Soc Mass; Am Antiquarian Soc; fel Morgan Libr; Century Asn; Grolier Club. *Publ:* Auth, Leonard Baskin, 71; auth, Christian Gullager, Portrait Painter to Federal America, 76; auth, Wedgewood Portraits and the American Revolution, 76; co-auth, American Portrait Drawings, 80; auth, Portraits of George Bellows, 81; auth, Colonial and Fed Portraits at Bowdoin Col, 66; auth, The Drawings of Hyman Bloom, 68; auth, The Paintings of Charles Hawthorne, 68; auth, Edith Halpert and the Downtown Gallery, 68; auth, The Life Portraits of John Quincy Adams, 70

SADLE, AMY ANN BRANDON
PRINTMAKER, PUBLISHER
b Council Bluffs, Iowa, Aug 3, 1940. *Study:* State Univ Iowa, 58-61; Ed Whitney Watercolor, 73; Univ RI, 65-. *Work:* Statute of Liberty Mus, NY; Des Moines Art Ctr, Des Moines, Iowa; Univ Nebr Ed TV & Agr Dept; Mc Cook Col, Nebr. *Comn:* St Theresa Church, Sta of the Cross, Mitchell, Nebr, 80; stained glass window, Cath

Church, Torrington, Wyo, 80; portrait, Indian Comn, Lincoln, Nebr, 83. *Exhib:* East Meets West, Jacob Javitz Ctr, NY, 89; Nat Tour of Impact; Mus Art, Kearney, Neb, 2001; Blosson Art of Flowers, Houston, Tex, 2008; Endangered Species, Calif, 2008. *Collection Arranged:* Impact the Art of Nebraska Women, 88-90; Unitarian Gallery, Kansas City, Mo, 94; McCook Col, McCook, Nebr, 94; Needles & Thread, 95-98. *Pos:* Art gallery dir, W Nebr Art Ctr, 74-76; corp dir, Impact, Nebr, 87-94. *Teaching:* Instr, Painting, W Nebr Community Col, Scottsbluff, Nebr, 72-81; workshop instr, Midwest 72-00; residence artist, Nebr Arts Coun, 2000-, assoc instr, 2008-. *Awards:* Nebr Arts Award, ANAC, 88; Top Award, Ottawa Nat, Sylvania, Ohio, 95; Amsterdam Art Competition Award, 98; First Place, San Diego Nat Print. *Bibliog:* Krantz, Calif Art Review. *Mem:* Fla Print Club; Asn Nebr Art Clubs, (pres comts 75-96). *Media:* Woodcut, Watercolor. *Res:* Encaustic Book; monoprint book. *Specialty:* Woodcut. *Interests:* Travel; research. *Publ:* Auth, ed & illusr, Home of Wooden Men and Iron Ships, private publ, 79; ed, Her Barnyard Brush, Country People, 81; auth, Doing My Thing in Tune, Pallet Talk Mag, 88; ed, Impact, art of Nebr women, private publ, 89, Hunter Hall, 2001 & 2004; Creating a Winner in Any media, Praire Sage Publ, 2008. *Dealer:* Praire Sage Publishing; White Crane Omaha. *Mailing Add:* Box H Syracuse NE 68446

SADOW, HARVEY S, JR
CERAMIST, SCULPTOR
b New York, NY, June 29, 1946. *Study:* Knox Coll, Ill, BA, 68; Sch Art & Art Hist, Univ Iowa, MA (ceramics), 70, MFA (ceramics, sculpture), 71. *Work:* Yingge Mus Art, Taipei, Taiwan; Mus Fine Arts, Boston; High Mus Art, Atlanta; Mus Ceramic Art, Alfred, NY; Everson Mus Fine Art, Syracuse, NY; Biseul Art Ctr, Gyungbuk, S Korea; Boca Raton Mus Art, Boca Raton, Fla; Canberra Art Inst, Canberra, Australia; Decorative Arts Mus, Little Rock, Ark; Columbia Mus Art, Columbia, Sc; Hawaii State Art Mus, Honolulu. *Comn:* Mixed media wall installation, Decatur Mem Hosp, Ill, 73; mixed media sculpture, World Bank, Washington, DC, 85; mixed media sculpture, MNC Financial Ctr, Columbia, Md, 87; ceramic wall installation, Williams & Connolly, Washington, DC, 93; ceramic vessel, White House, 93. *Exhib:* 20 Year Retrospective Exhib (traveling), William Benton Mus Art, Tampa Art Mus, Racine Art Mus & Decorative Arts Mus, Little Rock, Ark, 88; Int Raku Invitational Biseul Art Ctr, Gyungbuk, S Korea, 2001; Int Contemp Ceramic Art, Shijingyi Art Mus, Foshan, China, 2002; Generations: Impending Lineage, Art & Industry Gallery, San Diego, Calif, 2003; 21st Century Ceramics, Columbus Coll Art & Design, Columbus, Ohio, 2003; Taiwan Biennial, Yingge Mus of Art, Taipei, Taiwan, 2004; American Masterpieces, Tradition/Innovation, traveling exhib, Southern Arts Fedn, Ogden Mus Am Art, New Orleans, 2007-2009; Mastering Raku, Memorial Gallery, Needham, Mass, 2010; Atmospheres, Blue Spiral Gallery, Asheville, NC, 2012. *Pos:* Dir, Paducah Sch Art, Paducah, Ky, 2007-2012; studio artist, Jupiter, Fla. *Teaching:* Millikin Univ, Decatur, Ill, 71-73; Univ Wis, Whitewater, 73-77; Canberra Art Inst, Australia, 88 & 91; numerous lect & workshops, Smithsonian Inst, Washington, DC, Sydney Coll Art, Sydney, NSW, Australia, Am Ceramics Soc, Los Angeles, Corcoran Sch Art, Washington, DC, Coll William & Mary, Williamsburg, Va & Purdue Univ, West Lafayette, Ind; hd ceramics & sculpture dept, Armory Art Ctr, West Palm Beach, Fla, 98-2004; chmn ceramics dept, Armory Art Ctr, West Palm Beach, Fla. *Awards:* Juror's Award, Md Biennial, Baltimore Mus Art, 80; Lennox Award for Excellence in Ceramics, Lennox China Co, 84; Fla Artists Fel, State of Fla, 91; Presidential Citation, 94. *Bibliog:* Hildegard Cummings (auth), Harvey Sadow: Toward a vessel aesthetic, Univ Conn, 88; Robert Ellison (auth), Harvey Sadow, Am Ceramics, 7/89; Linda Marx (auth), Sadow lands, Ocean Drive Mag, 10/94; Gerry Williams (auth), Harvey Sadow, Studio Potter Mag, 12/98. *Mem:* Nat Coun Educ Ceramic Arts; Am Crafts Coun; Fla Craftsmen; Int Sculpture Ctr; Coll Art Asn. *Media:* Ceramics, Mixed Media, Digital Imaging. *Publ:* Auth, Contemp Ceramics in Am Pub Art & Architecture, Design & Use of World Bldg Ceramics, pub Artrend Studios, Guangzhou, china, 2002; My Secret Life as a Shino Addict & Carbon Trapper, Studio Potter Mag, 2002; The Relevance of Handmade Pottery in the Twenty First Century, Ceramics Monthly, 2004. *Dealer:* Blue Spiral Gallery Asheville NC. *Mailing Add:* c/o Sadow Art Studios 9540 Quail Trail Jupiter FL 33478

SADOWSKI, CAROL (LOUISE) JOHNSON
PAINTER
b Chicago, Ill, 1929. *Study:* Art Inst Chicago Scholar, 42-43; Wright Jr Coll, AAS, 49. *Work:* Mus Fla Hist, Tallahassee; Elliot Mus, Stuart, Fla; Hollywood Art & Cult Ctr, Fla; Ernest Hemingway Home & Mus, Key West, Fla; Hemingway Mus, San Francisco; Presidential Palace, Havana, Cuba; The Vatican; pvt collections, Burt Reynolds, Jamses Caan, Nadji Jameel (Emir of Bahrain), David Usher Pres & Harcourt Sylvester & Carolyn and Clem Pearce. *Comn:* Paintings, San Augustin Antiqua Found, St Augustine, Fla, 85; Atlantic Bank, Fort Lauderdale; Bonnet House Fla Trust, Ft Lauderdale. *Exhib:* Solo exhibs, Scenes of Fla, Mus Fla Hist, Tallahassee, 84, Hemingway's Haunts, Elliot Mus, Stuart, Hemingway's Home & Mus, Key West, Hist Mus S Fla, Miami, 86, Marjorie Kinnan Rawlings-Cross Creek, Thomas Ctr Arts, Gainesville, Fla, 85 & Mus Fla Hist, Tallahassee 85 & 87; Marjorie Kinnan Rawlins-Cross Creek, Mus Fla Hist, Tallahassee, 85; Debruyn Fine Art Gallery, 89, 90, 2008, 2007. *Teaching:* Art teacher, adult educ, Malverne High Sch, 68-69. *Awards:* Appreciation Award, City Hollywood, Fla; Hemingway Medal, Ernest Hemingway Mus, San Francisco de Paula, Cuba. *Bibliog:* Paul Heidelberg (auth), Canvassing Hemingway's life, Ft Lauderdale Sun Sentinal, 5/15/88; Stuart McIver (auth), Hooked On Hemingway's Haunts, Gold Coast Mag; Stuart McIver (auth), Hemingway's Key West, Pineapple Press Inc. *Mem:* Mus Art Fort Lauderdale, Fla; Fla Hist Assocs; charter mem Women Arts Nat Mus, Washington, DC; Chopin Found US. *Media:* Oil, Watercolor. *Interests:* Swimming, bike riding. *Dealer:* Gingerbread Sq Gallery Key West FL; De Bruyne Fine Art Gallery Naples FL; Patricia Cloutier Gallery Tequesta FL. *Mailing Add:* Sheridan By The Beach 1480 Sheridan St Apt B-17 Hollywood FL 33020

SAFER, JOHN
SCULPTOR
b Washington, DC, Sept 6, 1922. *Study:* George Washington Univ, AB, 47; Law Sch, Harvard Univ, LLB, 49. *Hon Degrees:* Lees-McRae Coll, LLD, 94; Daniel Webster Coll, Dlitt, 2003; George Wash Univ, DFA, 2009. *Work:* Anabasis, Baltimore Mus Art; Flare, Corcoran Gallery Art; Dancer & the Dance, Frederik Meijer Sculpture Gardens, Grand Rapids, Mich; Limits of Infinity & Golden Quill, George Washington Univ; Quest, Milwaukee Mus Art; Cube on Cube, Philadelphia Mus Art & San Francisco Mus Art; Chandelle, Smithsonian Am Art Mus; Bird of Peace, United Nations; Quest, US Embassy, Beijing; Bird of Peace, US Embassy, London; Wave, US Embassy, Nassau, Bahamas; Pisces, Lawrenceville Acad. *Comn:* Pathway II, Am Hosp of Paris; Leading Edge, Bank of Am; Pathway, Dayton Art Inst; Multicube V & Promise, Duke Univ Med Ctr; Symbol of Courage & Symbol of Caring, Georgetown Univ Med Ctr; Search, Harvard Bus Sch; Judgment, Harvard Law Sch; Interplay, Bird of Peace III & Phoenix, Hofstra Univ; Cube on Cube, Johns Hopkins Univ; Ascent, Challenge & Web of Space, National Air & Space Mus; Limits of Infinity, Royal Collection of Spain; Cosmos & Flame of Knowledge, Scripps Research Inst; Line of Flight, Vanderbilt Univ; For Charlie, Williams Coll; Swing, World Golf Hall of Fame, Wilmer Eye Inst, Quest; and many others. *Exhib:* Solo exhibs, US Embassies, Belgrade, Bern, Brussels, Bucharest, Dublin, Lisbon, London, Nassau & Paris, 74-92; David Findlay Galleries, New York, 74 & 82; High Mus Art, Atlanta, 78; Nat Acad Sci, Washington, DC, 80; Nat Air & Space Mus, Washington, DC, 85; Norton Gallery Art, Palm Beach, Fla, 86; Cheekwood Fine Art Ctr, Nashville, Tenn, 86; Mint Mus Art, Charlotte, NC, 86; Cosmos Club, Washington, DC, 87, & 2011; Espace Pierre Cardin, Paris, 90; Harvard Law Sch, 92; Duke Univ Mus Art, NC, 2000; International Monetary Fund, Washington, DC, 2001; Frederik Meijer Sculpture Gardens, Grand Rapids, Mich, 2002; Dayton Art Inst, 2003; Daniel Webster Coll, Nashua, NH, 2005, Nassau, Bahamas, 2008, George Washington Univ, 2011. *Collection Arranged:* Pathway II, Am Hosp Paris; Pathway, Dayton Art Inst, Nashua, NH; The Dancer & the Dance, Friends of Art in Embassies. *Pos:* Guest lectr, Duke Mus Art, Durham, NC, Harvard Law Sch, Cambridge, Mass, Mint Mus Art, Charlotte, NC, Philips Collection, DC, Smithsonian Inst, DC. *Teaching:* Am Univ, 58; George Wash Univ, 61; Harvard Law, 96. *Awards:* Hodges Leadership Award, Georgetown Univ, Lombardi Cancer Ctr, 2007; Distinguised Alumni Award, George Wash Univ, 2008. *Bibliog:* Frank Getlein (auth), John Safer, 82; A Shaping Hand, Harvard Business Review, 84; Articles including, An Artistic Bent, Pursuits, 88; The Art of John Safer, Dossier, 90; Walter Boyne (auth), Art in Flight, 91; David Finn (auth), Art of Leadership, 98; Ascent, Cosmos, 2001; David Finn (photo); Yoichi Okamoto (photo). *Mem:* Cosmos Club, Washington, DC; founder & dir, Wash Gallery Modern Art. *Media:* Metal, Lucite. *Mailing Add:* 183 Chain Bridge Rd Mc Lean VA 22101

SAFF, DONALD JAY
PAINTER, EDUCATOR
b New York, NY, Dec 12, 1937. *Study:* Queens Col, City Univ NY, BA, 59; Columbia Univ, MA, 60; Pratt Inst, MFA, 62; Teachers Col, Columbia Univ, EdD, 64; Univ So Fla, DFA 1999; Fulbright Grant (Italy), 64-65; Inst Statale Di Belle Artis Urbino, Italy, 65. *Work:* Metrop Mus Art, Mus Mod Art, Brooklyn Mus, & Nelson Rockefeller Collection, NY; William Hayes Fogg Art Mus, Harvard Univ & Mus Fine Arts, Boston, Mass; Philadelphia Mus Art; Nat Gallery Art, Libr Cong, Washington; Butler Inst Am Art, Ohio; and many others. *Comn:* Int Graphic Arts Soc, 67, 68 & 71. *Exhib:* Smithsonian Inst, 61; Fanesi Gallery, Ancona, Italy, 64; solo exhibs, Galleria Academia, Rome, 65, La Colomba Gallery, Bologna, Italy, 66, Byron Gallery NY, 68, Toronto Art Gallery, 70, Galleria D'Arte Moderna, Udine, Italy, 81 & Gemini, GEL, Los Angeles, 85; Canadian Int Print Exhib, Vancouver, 67; Loch Haven Art Ctr, Orlando, 70; Edison Community Col, Ft Myers, Fla, 80; Huntsville Mus Art, Ala, 81; Libr Congress, 84; retrospective, Tampa Mus Art, 89 & Va Beach Ctr Arts, 91; and many others. *Pos:* Co-dir, Pyramid Arts Ltd, Tampa, Fla, formerly; dir graphic studio, Univ SFla, 68-76 & 85-90 & dean, Col Fine Arts, 71-82; dir & cur, Rauschenberg Overseas Cult Interchange, 84-91; consult, Art J, formerly; dir, Saff Tech Arts, Inc, 90- & Knoedler & Co, New York, 94-95. *Teaching:* Instr printmaking & design, Teachers Col, Columbia Univ, summers 65 & 66; assoc prof printmaking & design, Univ SFla, Tampa, 65-67, chmn visual arts dept, 67-71, distinguished prof, 82, distinguished prof emer, 96 & emer dean, 89. *Awards:* Individual Artist Grant, Fla Endowment Arts, 80; Pennell Comt, Libr Cong, 79-86; Univ Serv Medallion, Univ S Fla, 93. *Bibliog:* article, Print Collector's Newslett, 7-8/72, 5/79, 1/81; Graphic studio: Contemporary Art from the Collaborative Workshop at the University of South Florida, Nat Gallery Art, Washington, 91; Interview: Donald Saff, Sculpture Mag, 11/94. *Mem:* Nat Coun of Art Adminrs (mem bd dir, 73-75); Int Coun Fine Arts Deans; Coll Art Asn; mem & founder, Nat Coun of Art Adminrs, (bd dir, 73-75). *Publ:* Coauth, Fables, 79 & Constellations, 80, Getler/Pall Gallery, NY; Jim Dine: Youth and the Maiden, Waddington Graphics, 89; Rauschenberg Overseas Culture Interchange (catalog), Nat Gallery Art, 91; Conservation of matter: Robert Rauschenberg's art of acceptance, Aperture Mag, 91. *Mailing Add:* PO Box 408 Royal Oak MD 21662

SAFTEL, ANDREW P
PAINTER, SCULPTOR
b New Bedford, Mass, June 13, 1959. *Study:* San Francisco Art Inst, BFA, 81. *Work:* Knoxville Mus Art, Tenn; Tenn State Mus, Nashville; Nashville Int Airport; Metro Atlanta Chamber of Commerce; Asheville Art Mus. *Comn:* Paintings, Southcentral Bell, Nashville, 94; Painting & Sculpture, Hartsfield Int Airport, Atlanta, 96; sculpture, St Andrews Sewanee Sch, Tenn, 2000; sculpture, Episcopal Sch, Portland, Oreg, 2002; sculpture, Knoxville Conv Ctr, Tenn, 2002. *Exhib:* Solo exhib, Confluence, Knoxville Mus Art, 95; Serenade the Procession, Tenn State Mus, Nashville, 96; Spirit Sq Ctr Arts, Charlotte, NC, 96; Cheekwood Mus Art, 99. *Teaching:* printmaking, Penland Sch Crafts, 2001, Haystack Mt Sch Crafts, 2002, Arrowmort Sch Arts & Crafts, 2002. *Awards:* Fel, Tenn Arts Comn. *Bibliog:* Catherine Fox (auth), The Southern Artist, Southern Accents, 5/91; Suzanne Stryk (auth),

Confluence: Objects by Andrew Saftel, Art Papers, 7/95; Bilen Mesfin (auth), Emerging Artist: Andrew Saftel, Art & Antiques, 12/2002. *Dealer:* Lowe Gallery 75 Bennett St Atlanta GA 30309; Cumberland Gallery Hillsboro Cir Nashville TN 37215. *Mailing Add:* Cumberland Gallery 4107 Hillsboro Cir Nashville TN 37215

SAGER, ANNE
PHOTOGRAPHER
Study: Studied with Phillippe Halsmann, Lisette Model, George Tice; worked with Alfred Eisenstaedt. *Work:* Int Ctr Photography, New York; Mus Photographic Arts, San Diego; Wyoming Mus Art; Nat Acad Mus; Sch Fine Arts, New York. *Exhib:* Solo exhibs, Beacon Gallery, Bellport, NY, 2000; Group exhibs, Women Over Fifty, Konica Plaza, Tokyo, Japan, 90; United Nations, New York, Copenhagen, Beijin, 94; Women Byond Borders, Contemp Arts Forum, Cailf, 95; Guild Hall Mus, E Hampton, NY, 98; Cornel Med Libr, 2002; Compassion, St Vincents, New York, 2006; Small Works juried show, New York Univ, 2005, 07, 08, 09; Arlene Bujese Gallery, E Hampton, 94-2006; Antikenmuseum Basil, Switzerland, 97; Southampton Cult Ctr, 2010; Delany Cooke Gallery, Sag Harbor, New York, 2010. *Awards:* Best in Show, Guild Hall Mem Show, 98; Theo Hios Award, Best Landscape, 2006. *Mailing Add:* 35 E 75th St New York NY 10021

SAHAGIAN, ARTHUR H
PAINTER, INSTRUCTOR
b Cleveland, Ohio, Oct 16, 1924. *Study:* Western Reserve Univ, & Cleveland Inst Art, 47; Northeastern Ill Univ, MA, 72. *Work:* John Fitzgerald Kennedy Libr, Boston, Mass; Eisenhower Nat Site Mus, Gettysburg, Pa; Miss Mus Art, Jackson, Miss; Nat Civil Rights Mus, Memphis, Tenn; DuSable Mus, Chicago, Ill. *Comn:* Oil portrait, Nancy Reagan, Say No Found, Ventura, Calif, 87; oil portrait, Chicago Transit Authority, Chicago, Ill, 88; oil portrait, Gerald Ford, Pres, Calif, 89. *Exhib:* Watts in Calie, DuSable Mus, Chicago, Ill, 80; Presidential Showing, Herbert Hoover Mus, Iowa, 88; permanent collection, Lyndon Baines Johnson Mus, Houston, Tex, 89; permanent collection, Miss Mus Art, Jackson, Miss, 95; 6 Squares, Clown Hall Fame Mus, Delavan, Wis, 98; Lillies Won't Do, Mus Human Rights, Memphis, Tenn, 2006; and many others. *Pos:* Art Supv, Garfield Heights bd educ, Cleveland, Ohio, 47-50; dir, Nat Arts Found, Chicago, Ill, 94-98; owner, Arthurian Gallery, Skokie, Ill, 98-2002. *Teaching:* Art teacher, Chicago bd educ, Chicago, Ill, 67-90, Smith Ctr, Skokie, Ill, 85-98 & Highland Park, Ill, 2000-2001. *Awards:* 1st Place, Renata Gallery, 87; Special Recognition, Skokie Art Show, 90-93; 1st Place, Prism Art Gallery, Evanston Ill, 93. *Bibliog:* Nation Medal of Arts, Arts Nomination, Armenian Mirror, 98; Myrna Petlicki, Artists Surveys, Pioneer Press, 2001; Unveiled in Skokie, Lerner Papers, Alen Kaleta 2004. *Mem:* Nat Art Found (bd mem, 85); progs, Skokie Artists Guild, 88 & Armenian Artist Asn, 98; Skokie Fine Arts Comt (bd mem, 92-96). *Media:* Acrylic, Oil; All Media. *Publ:* Auth, Arthurian Approach, Arthurian Gallery, 82; Sahagians Armenia, St Vartans, 2000; Reflections on the Century, Nat Arts Found, 2001; Reflections on America, Nat Arts Found, 2004. *Dealer:* Harry Hagen NAF Gallery 4448 Oakton Ave Skokie IL 60076

SAHLSTRAND, JAMES MICHAEL
PHOTOGRAPHER
b Minneapolis, Minn, May 4, 1936. *Study:* Univ Minn, BA, MFA. *Work:* New Photographics Exhib, Central Wash Univ, 1972-88. *Comn:* Photographs SE Wash, Walla Walla Community Col, 76-77 & photographs E Wash, Eastern Wash Univ & Turnbull Game Reserve Res Sta, 77, Wash State Arts Comn. *Exhib:* Young Photographers Traveling Exhib, 68-70; Be-ing without Clothes, Mass Inst Technol, 70; Photo-Media, Mus Contemp Crafts, NY, 71; San Francisco Mus Art, 72; Synthetic Color, Univ Southern Ill, 74. *Pos:* Pres, Roslyn Arts, 72-. *Teaching:* Assoc prof photog, Cent Wash Univ, Ellensburg, 65-. *Mem:* Soc Photog Educ. *Media:* Color, Multiple Image. *Mailing Add:* 12060 Hwy 10 Ellensburg WA 98926

SAHLSTRAND, MARGARET AHRENS
PRINTMAKER, CRAFTSMAN
b St Louis, Mo, Oct 1, 1939. *Study:* Lindenwood, Col, St Charles, Mo, 61; Univ of Iowa, Iowa City, printmaking, MFA, 64; also in Japan, 81-83. *Work:* Kobe Mus Fine Arts, Hygo Prefecture Mus Collection, Japan; Okla Art Ctr, Oklahoma City; Wash State Printmakers Collection, Evergreen State Col, Olympia; Nat Collection Art, Washington, DC. *Comn:* Cast paper murals, W Valley Sr High Sch, Yakima, Wash, 80 & Western Paper Co, Kent, Wash, 81. *Exhib:* Solo exhibs, Cast Paperworks, Slocumb Gallery, E Tenn State Univ, Johnson City, 77; 1st Editions Graphics Competition, Ore Arts Comn, Salem, 76; World Print Competition, San Francisco Mus Art, 77; Paper as Medium, SITES, Smithsonian Inst, Washington, DC, 78-; Cast Paper, Pratt Graphics Ctr, NY, 78; Works in Handmade Paper, Jerusalem Theater, Israel, 83; Paper Innovations, Mingei Int Mus, La Jolla, Calif, 85; Arts of the Book, The Akuin Soc, Vancouver, BC, 86. *Pos:* Proprietor, Icosa Studio & Papermill, Ellensburg, currently. *Teaching:* Retired. *Awards:* Cannon Prize, Printmaking, Nat Acad Design, New York, 66; Purchase Award, Statewide Services, Univ Ore, Eugene, 75; Fac Res Grant, Cent Wash Univ, 78; First prize, Paper Fair III Exhib, Vancouver, BC, 85. *Mem:* Northwest Book Arts Guild; Northwest Designer Craftsmen. *Publ:* Auth, Paper clothing, Fiberarts, Vol II, No 2, 84 & Hyakomantoh, No 61, Tokyo, 85; Japanese paper textiles, Paper Innovations, Mingei Int Mus, 85. *Mailing Add:* 12060 Hwy 10 Ellensburg WA 98926

SAID, WAFIC RIDA
COLLECTOR
b Damascus, Syria, 1939. *Pos:* Banker UBS, Geneva, 62; founder TAG System Construction, Saudi Arabia, 69, SIFCORP Holdings, 81, Sagitta Asset Mgt, London & Dublin, 95; Founder, Karim Rida Said Found, Eng, 82, chmn, Said Holdings Ltd. *Awards:* Named to Ordre Cherifien, Morocco; recipient Sheldon medal, Oxford Univ, 2003; named one of Top 200 Collectors, ARTNews Mag, 2004. *Mem:* Court Benefactors Oxford Univ; trustee Said Bus Sch Found; gov Royal Shakespeare Co, London. *Specialty:* Old Masters, British Sporting Art & Impressionism. *Mailing Add:* c/o Karim Rida Said Foundation 4 Bloomsbury Place London United Kingdom WC1A 2QA

SAINSBURY, DAVID
COLLECTOR
Study: Univ Cambridge, BA; Columbia Univ, MBA. *Pos:* Mgr, Sainsbury's supermarkets; Minister Sci & Innovation. *Awards:* Named one of Top 200 Collectors, ARTnews mag, 2009-13. *Collection:* Impressionism; modern and contemporary art. *Mailing Add:* Sainsburys 33 Holborn London United Kingdom EC1N 2HT

ST CLAIR MILLER, FRANCES
PRINTMAKER, PAINTER
b Croydon, Eng, Feb 15, 1947. *Study:* Slade Sch Art; Univ Col, London. *Work:* Adelphi Univ, Long Island, NY; Citibank, AT&T, IBM, NY. *Comn:* Portfolio of Prints, Shell Oil, UK, 80; Edition of Prints, P&O; Eng, 94. *Exhib:* Solo exhibs, Graffiti Gallery, London, 78 & 79 & Hereford City Art Gallery, 92; Tolly Cobbold Eastern Arts, Fitzwilliam Cambridge, 83; Slade Ladies, Mall Galleries, London, 90. *Pos:* Master printer, Studio Prints, formerly & Octopus Press, currently. *Teaching:* Art of printmaking, Sir John Cass Col, Eng, currently. *Mem:* Printmakers Coun; Chelsea Arts Club. *Media:* Etching

ST DENIS, PAUL ANDRE
PAINTER, INSTRUCTOR
b Chicago, Ill, Nov 16, 1938. *Study:* Cleveland Inst Art, BFA; Kent State Univ, MA; additional study with Julian Stanczak. *Work:* Tweed Mus, Duluth, Minn; Massillon Mus, Ohio; Utah State Univ, Logan; Columbia Mus Art, SC. *Comn:* Cleveland Pub Libr. *Exhib:* Butler Inst Am Art, Youngstown, Ohio, 68 & 70; Canton Art Inst, Ohio, 73; Aqueous Open, Pittsburgh Watercolor Soc, 74 & 75; Watercolor West, Utah State Univ, 76-79; Nat Watercolor Soc, Laguna Beach Mus Art, Calif, 76-88 & 92; Adirondacks Nat Exhib Am Watercolors, 91; and others. *Pos:* Chmn art dept, Interlochen Ctr Arts, Mich, summers, 69-81; chmn found, Cleveland Inst Art, 94-. *Teaching:* Prof painting, Kent State Univ, Ohio, 68-70, Cooper Sch of Art, Cleveland, 70-80 & Cleveland Inst of Art, 73-. *Awards:* First Prize Gold Medal, Ohio Watercolor Soc, 89, 90 & 94; William Kowalsky Award, Adirondacks Nat Exhib Watercolors, 91; First Prize, Nat Watercolor Soc, 92. *Bibliog:* The Artist Mag, 9/90, 9/93 & 7/94; Splash, 90 & Splash II, 91, North Light/FW Publ. *Mem:* Am Watercolor Soc; Nat Watercolor Soc; Ohio Watercolor Soc. *Media:* Acrylic, Watercolor. *Dealer:* Belstone Gallery Traverse City MI; Vigland Gallery Benzonia MI. *Mailing Add:* 28007 Sites Rd Bay Village OH 44140

ST FLORIAN, FRIEDRICH GARTLER
EDUCATOR, ARCHITECT
b Graz, Austria, Dec 21, 1932; US citizen. *Study:* Tech Univ Graz, dipl (archit), 58; Ecole Nat Superiure d'Archit, Brussels, Belg, 55-56; Atelier, with Victor Bourgeois; Columbia Univ, March, 62. *Work:* Mus Mod Art, NY; Mass Inst Technol, Cambridge; Mus Art, Providence; Pompidou Centre, Paris. *Exhib:* Solo exhibs, Mod Museet, Stockholm, 69, Hayden Gallery, Mass Inst Technol, 73, Mus Art, Univ Tex, 76, Drawing Ctr, NY, 79 & Walker Art Ctr, Minneapolis, 80; Archit Studies & Proj, Mus Mod Art, NY, 75; RI Sch Design Mus Art, 77; Centre Georges Pompidon, 94; Visionary Architecture in Austria, Biennale Di Venezia, 96; From Bauhaus to Pop, Mus Mod Art, NY, 96. *Teaching:* From asst to prof archit design, RI Sch Design, 63-, chmn archit div, 77-78, dean archit, 78-88. *Awards:* Fulbright Fel, 61-62; Fel, Ctr for Advan Visual Studies Fel, Mass Inst Technol, 71-77; Nat Endowment Arts Awards, 73-74 & 76-77; Fel, Am Acad in Rome, 85-; Finalist, Nat World War II Mem, Am Battle Monuments Comn, 96. *Mem:* Am Inst Architects. *Publ:* Auth, On my imaginary architecture, Leonardo, 77. *Mailing Add:* 146 Westminster St Fl 2 Providence RI 02903-2229

ST GEORGE, WILLIAM (M)
PAINTER, INSTRUCTOR
b Canton, Mass, Jan 13, 1939. *Study:* Sch Mus Fine Arts, Boston, Mass, 69-. *Work:* Scudder, Stevens & Clark Mutual Funds, Int Place, Wertheim Schroder & Co Inc, Colonial Mgt, Exec Off Gillette, Boston, Mass, The Alexander Law Firm, San Jose, Calif, Can Imperial Bank of Commerce, Ackerley Communications, Seattle, Wash, Kuhns Brothers Investment Banking, Greenwich, Conn, Societ'mmobilier Trans, Qu'c; also pvt collections of John Davidson, Undersecy Finance, Nuevo Leon, Mex, Gulston & Storrs, Attys Law, Law Off Hale & Dorr, Law Off Atwood & Cherney; Boston Globe Newspaper. *Comn:* corp bldg, New World Power Corp, Lime Rock, Conn, 95; Boston paintings, Boston Globe, Mass, 95; Boston Coll & Middlebury Col, Alexander Law Firm, San Jose, Calif, 96; Baupost Financial Group, Cambridge, Mass, 98; Citizen's Bank, Boston, Mass, 98, Bank of Canton, Canton, Mass, 99. *Exhib:* Solo exhibs, J Todd Galleries, Wellesley & Lexington, Mass, 91, Lime Rock Galleries, Lakeville, Conn, 91, E L Wilde Gallery, Avon, Conn, 92, Michael Thompson Galleries, San Francisco, Calif, 93, Open Studios, Boston, Mass, 94 & 96, S Rotunda Art Gallery, Hynes Auditorium, Boston, Mass, 96; Boston Painters, Judi Rotenberg Gallery, Boston, Mass, 95; Fall Exhib, Copley Soc, Boston, Mass, 95; Corp Prog, De Cordova Mus, Waltham, Mass, 96; Kennedy Galleries, Provincetown, Mass & Key West, Fla, 96; St George Gallery, Boston, 2001-; Boulevard Gallery, Newport, RI, 2003; Linden Galleries, Rowley, Mass, 2005; Willoughby Galleries, Martha's Vineyard, Mass,; Boston Art, Boston, Mass, 2005. *Pos:* Guest demonstr oil painting, various New Eng art groups, 91-; producer & host, Impressions (weekly art show), Cablevision Television Group; artist instructor, gallery owner, St George Gallery, Boston, Mass. *Teaching:* Instr oil painting, Blackburn Hall, Walpole, Mass, 98, Steinert Hall, Boston, 98, 2001, St. George Gallery, Boston, Mass, on going. *Awards:* Am Artist Ser Feature Artist, PAK 2000, 92; Two Collection Best Show, Channel Two Auction, WGBH Boston, 94; Artist of the year, Santa Monica charity horse show, Santa Monica, Calif, 2005. *Bibliog:* Showcase: A celebration of the arts, Newbury Street Guide salutes William St George, Newbury St Guide, Boston, Mass, 3/3/94; Art of all styles, Boston Herald, 11/17/95; Alexander Berman (dir), The Painter (film), 95; Equine Vision Mag, The Horse in Landscape, Fall 2004. *Mem:* Copley Soc Boston; Mus Fine Arts Advan Painting Group, Boston, Mass; Cambridge Art Asn. *Media:* Oil. *Specialty:* Boston Cityscapes, Equestrian, Swimmers, Still life, Landscapes, Portraits.

Interests: Location for DNC Reception July 2004; Woman's Caucus Group/Maryland and Delaware Delegates Reception; NABB Reception and wine tasting, charity event. *Publ:* Auth, Expressions (newsletter), St George Gallery, Boston, Mass; contribr, The Two Collection Catalog (cover), WGBH, Boston, Mass, 94; auth, Final touches: Painting en plein air, Pleiades, 3-4/95; contribr, Boston Bar J (cover), 11-12/95, 96, 97. *Mailing Add:* c/o St George Gallery 162 Boylston St Ste 49 Boston MA 02116-4613

ST JOHN, ADAM
CRAFTSMAN
b Tampa, Fla, Feb 24, 1952. *Study:* Self-taught. *Work:* Mus Fine Arts, Houston, Tex; San Antonio Mus Asn Collection, Texas. *Comn:* Future Perfect One table, Houston, Tex, 86; Paradise: The Chair, West Palm Beach, Fla, 86; Remember the Alamo, Amarillo, Tex, 87; Pueblo Santa Fe chair, Santa Fe, NMex, 89; Texas Virgin Bed, Houston, 90. *Exhib:* The Chair Fair, Int Design Ctr, NY, 86; Materials: Hard & Soft, Denton Arts Coun, Tex, 87; Furniture of the 80's, Hokin-Kaufman Gallery, Chicago, IL, 88; solo exhib, Parkerson Gallery, Houston, Tex, 86; two-person show, O'Kane Gallery, Houston, Tex, 90. *Pos:* Int exec dir, Am Soc Furniture Artists, 91-. *Teaching:* Painted illusions, Trompe l'Oeil, Art League Houston, 88-; continuing educ Faux finishes, Univ Houston, 90-; art for detained youth, Harris Co Juvenile Detention Ctr, 90-. *Awards:* Honor Award, 1986 Furniture Design, Texas Homes Mag, 86; Meadows Found Award, 87; Outstanding Artist Award, IAC New York '88, 88. *Bibliog:* 397 Chairs, Archit League NY, Abrams, NY, 88. *Mem:* Art League Houston (bd dir, 88-90); Am Craft Coun; Am Soc Interior Designers; Am Soc Furniture Artists (found & Pres, 89-). *Media:* Mixed. *Publ:* Article, Los Angeles Mag, 86, ID, 87, Ambienture, 87, Ultra, 88

ST JOHN, TERRY N
PAINTER, CURATOR
b Sacramento, Calif, Dec 24, 1934. *Study:* Univ Calif, Berkeley, AB; San Francisco Art Inst, spec study with James Weeks; Calif Coll Arts & Crafts, Oakland, MFA. *Work:* Mills Coll, San Francisco; Oakland Mus; Fine Arts Mus, San Francisco. *Exhib:* James D Phelan Award Show, Calif Palace Legion Honor, 65; solo exhibs, Crown Coll, Univ Calif, Santa Cruz, 75 & Contemp Realist Hackett-Freedman Gallery, San Francisco, 94, 2006; Contemp Realist Hackett-Freedman Gallery, San Francisco, 90 & 2001-03, Art Los Angeles Expos, 92, Chicago Int Art Expos, 93 & New Bay Area Painting, 94; Gallery North, Setauket, NY, 90; Dolby Chadwick Gallery, San Francisco, Calif, 2011, 2014. *Collection Arranged:* Dilexi Years Revisited, (co-cur, auth & catalog), 83. *Pos:* Assoc cur, Oakland Mus, 69-90; head art dept, Coll Notre Dame, Belmont, Calif, 90-97. *Teaching:* Outdoor Painters Proj, Univ Calif, Santa Cruz, 79-88; Coll Notre Dame, Belmont, 90-2000. *Bibliog:* Thomas Albright (auth), Art in the San Francisco Bay Area, Univ Calif Press, 85; San Francisco Chronicle, 2006; Art Critical, 2014. *Media:* Oil. *Publ:* Auth, Society of Six (catalog), Oakland Mus, 72; Louis Siegriest: A painter's topography, Currant Mag, 75; Impressionism: The California View, Oakland Mus, 81. *Dealer:* Dolby Chapwick Gallery San Francisco. *Mailing Add:* 5340 Locksley Ave Oakland CA 94618

ST LIFER, JANE
ART APPRAISER
b New York, NY, April, 19, 1956. *Study:* Syracuse Univ, BFA, 79; NJ City Univ, MA, 96. *Collection Arranged:* Milton Glaser: Retrospective, Hammer Graphics Gallery, New York, 85; Emotions: Diego Rivera & Frida Kohle, Gallery Int 57, New York, 89; 20th Century Artists Posters, NJ City Univ, Jersey City, 96; Common Ground: 6 Artists view the landscape together, Gallery@NYITC, 2000, Miros posters, 2000 & Wolves on Wall Street, 2001; Will Barnet Pastors, 2003-2006. *Pos:* dir print dept, Hammer Galleries, New York, 81-86; sales dir, Gallery Urban, Naguya, Japan, 86-88; pres, Jane St. Lifer Fine Art Inc, New York, 88-; asst dir, Grand Central Art Galleries, New York, 93-94. *Teaching:* inst print art, Pace Univ, 95-97. *Bibliog:* Melisa Chapman (auth), The Fine Art of Modern Posters, Downtown Express, New York, 3/30/99; Alison Simke (auth), New Galleries Relaunch Financial District's Art Scene, Battery Park City Broadsheet, 2/19/2000. *Mem:* Auctioneers Asn Inc, New York (vpres, 98-); Int Found Art Research; Am Soc Appraisers; Nat Art Club, New York; Metrop Day Club (treas); Foreign Press Assoc, New York. *Publ:* coauth, Art Publishers & Dealers Need Contact, Art Business News, 84; Will Barnet Print Catalogue Raisonne, John Szeke Pub, 2009

ST MAUR, KIRK
SCULPTOR, PAINTER
b July 7, 1949. *Study:* Quincy Col; Univ Minn; Carleton Col, BA, 72; Academia di Belle Arti, Florence, Italy, 72-75, studied anat with Harkevitch; asst to R Puccinelli, Univ Int de Belle Arte, 73 & 74; Villa Schifanoia, Florence, MA, studied with E Manfrini; Simi Studio, Florence, 74-78. *Work:* State of Ill Mus; Lindbergh Mus, St Louis; H M Seymour Libr, City of Le Bourget, France; Pere Marquette State Park (monument); St Louis Univ. *Comn:* Heroic bronze of St Michael, Church of Buriano, Italy, 79; Quest (bronze monument), Ore State Univ, 83; The Sentinel (monument), City of Richmond, Calif, 84; Indian monument, City of Duluth, 92; Marathon, St Louis Univ, 94. *Exhib:* Quincy Art Ctr, 74 & 85; Am Artists Prof League, 82, 86, 87,92, 93 & 96; Knickerbocker Artists, 1983-1989; John Pence Gallery, 84; Acad Artists Asn, 1986-1989, 1991; Int Art Expo, Los Angeles, 88; and others. *Teaching:* Prof sculpture, Gonzaga Univ, 78-79. *Awards:* Knickerbocker Artists Award, 84; Acad Artist Asn Award, 86; Medal of Honor, City of LeBourget, France, 88; Best of Show, Billy Graham Mus, 95. *Bibliog:* Mario Bucci (auth), Kirk McReynolds, Sansoni Editrice, Florence, Italy, 77; articles in Rome Daily Am, San Francisco Examiner, 79 & 83, Oakland Tribune, 84 & St Louis Post Dispatch, 93 & 96. *Mem:* Fel Am Artists Prof League; Hudson Valley Art Asn. *Media:* Bronze, Oils. *Publ:* Am Arts Quart, spring 92; Christianity and the Arts, spring 96. *Mailing Add:* PO Box 158 Payson IL 62360-0158

ST TAMARA
PAINTER, PRINTMAKER
b Navahradak, Repub Belarus; US Citizen. *Study:* Western Coll, Oxford, Ohio, BA; Columbia Univ, MFA, with John Heliker; Art Students League, with Seong Moy. *Work:* Nat Mastacki Mus, Minsk, Repub Belarus; Hrodzienski Historyka-Archealahichny Mus, Hrodno, Repub Belarus; Mus Belaruskaha Knihadrukavannia, Polatsak, Repub Belarus; Ablasny Krayaznauchy Mus, Vitsiebsk, Repub Belarus; Navahradski Hist-Krayaznauchy Mus, Navahradak, Repub Belarus; Soros Found, Minsk, Belarus; Columbia Univ, NY; NY Pub Libr, NY; Zimmerli Art Mus, Rutgers Univ, New Brunswick, NJ; Belarusan Embassy to the UN, New York; Belarusan Consulate, New York; Mus F Skaryna, Homiel, Belarus. *Comn:* Four Icons, Belarusan Church, Cleveland, Ohio; woodcut portrait of Dr Francisak Skaryna, comn by Dr V Kipel, NY Pub Libr, 68. *Exhib:* Vitsiebski Ablasny Krayaznauchy Mus, Vitsiebsk, Repub Belarus, 97; solo exhibs, Nat Art Mus, Repub Belarus, 94, Hrodzienski Dziarzauny, Hist-Archeol Mus, Repub Belarus, 96, Vitsiebski Ablasny Krayaznauchy Mus, Vitsiebsk, Belarus, 97, Lidzea Nat Gallery, Lida, Belarus, 96, Mus Belaruskaha Knihadrukavannia, Polatsak, 97; Clwac, New York, 94, 98, 99, 2001 & 2003; Western Coll, Oxford, Ohio, 96; The Capital Children's Mus Washington, DC, 96; Hunterdon Art Ctr Clinton, NJ, 96; Zimmerli Art Mus, New Brunswick, NJ, 96-97; Johnson & Johnson World Hq, New Brunswick, NJ, 97; Everhart Gallery, Basking Ridge, NJ, 97; Guild of Creative Art, Shrewsbury, NJ, 2000; Art Alliance, Red Bank, NJ, 2001; Salmagundi Club, New York City, 2001-2003; Custer Co Art Ctr Miles City, MT, 2001; Halshany Mus, Belarus, 2001; National Drawing, Ewing, NJ, 2002; Wiford & Vogt Fine Art, Snata Fe, NMex, 2004; CLWAC, Nat Art Club, New York, 2005-2008; Salmagundi Club, 2006-2007; Benefit Exhib, Nat Mus Women in Arts, 2007. *Awards:* Gold Medal, CLWAC, Nat Acad Design, NY, 71; 1st Place, FACET, Taos, NMex, 85; Samuel Ballin Mem Award, Salmagundi Club, 2001; Honorable Mention, Custer Co Art Ctr, Miles City, MT, 2001. *Bibliog:* Tatsiana Antonava (auth), St Tamara: Her Cosmos Began in Navahrudak, Zviazda, 10/6/94; S Y Kryshtapovich (auth), Stahanovich Tamara, Belarus-Belarusan Encyclopedia, 95; Valyantsina Tryhubovich (auth), St Tamara: My-America, My-Belarus, Mastatstva, 4/98. *Mem:* Guild Creative Art, NJ; Catharine Lorillard Wolfe Art Club, NY; Belarusan Inst Arts & Sci, NJ; Art Alliance, NJ; Salmagundi Club, New York City; The Nat Mus of Women in the Arts, Washington, DC; Nat Mus Am Indian; Nat Mus Afro-Am History & Culture. *Media:* Oil, Graphics. *Interests:* Nature, Photography; ethnic folk art; AM Indian Art;. *Collection:* Hudson River Painter; Icons. *Publ:* Auth & illusr, Save that Racoon & Chickaree, a Red Squirrel, Harcourt, Brace, Jovanovich; Asian Craft, Lion Press, 70; illusr, Biography of a Polar Bear, G P Putnam's Sons, 72; Animal Games, Holiday House, 76. *Mailing Add:* Skyline Tower 60 Paterson St New Brunswick NJ 08901

SAITO, SEIJI
SCULPTOR
b Utsunomiya, Japan, 1933. *Study:* Tokyo Univ Art, BFA (sculpture), clay modeling with Tsuruzo Ishii & MFA (stone carving), with Kametaro Akashi; Brooklyn Mus Art Sch, Scholar, 8 yrs; granite carving with Odillo Begg; Ottavino Granite Corp, NY. *Work:* Methodist Hosp, Brooklyn, NY; Isaac Delgado Mus Art, New Orleans; Non-Ferros Int Corp & Kowa Realty, NY; The Toyo Trust & Banking co, Ltd, NY; Wichita Mus; Tochigi Mus, Japan; Taiyo Kobe Bank, NY; Utsukushigahara Open Air Mus, Japan; Salisbury State Univ, Md; Daiwa Security & Trust co, NJ; Utsunomiya Mus Art, Tochigi, Japan; PepsiCo Inc, New York; Sagamihara Cent Hosp, Kanagawa, Japan; and many others. *Comn:* Buddha (stone sculpture), Gyokusendo, Okinawa, Japan, 81. *Exhib:* Solo exhibs, Samanthe' Gallery, NY, 68 & 70, New Sch, NY, 78, Warner Commun Bldg, 79, Tokyo Gallery, Tokyo, Japan, 79, Yokyo Hall Gallery Ctr, Tokyo, 79 & Gallery Seiho, Tokyo, 90; Azuma Gallery, NY, 75; Mid-Hudson Art & Sci Ctr, Poughkeepsie, NY 80; FIDEM Int Exhib, Florence, Italy, 83; Nat Sculpture Soc Ann Show, 70, 89 & 93, 100th Ann Show, Seravessa, Italy, 94; 3 Person Show, Utsunomiya Mus Art, Japan, 2013. *Teaching:* Instr sculpture, Brooklyn Mus Art, summer 74, 76, 84, 85; Art Student League New York, 98-. *Awards:* Cert Merit, Ann Exhib of Nat Acad Design, New York, 73; Many Awards, Nat Sculpture Soc Ann Exhibs, New York, 76-96, 2004 & 2006; Merit Prize, Hakone Open-Air Mus, Japan, 80. *Mem:* Nat Sculpture Soc (fel). *Media:* Stone, Bronze, Wood. *Specialty:* Gallery Seiho (specializing in sculpture), Tokyo, Japan. *Publ:* Art Text book, article, Expressions, McMillan, New York & Sculpture Rev. *Mailing Add:* 925 Union St Apt 1G Brooklyn NY 11215

SAITO, YOSHITOMO
SCULPTOR
b Tokyo. *Study:* Jiyugakuen Col, Tokyo, BS-E, 80; Calif Coll Arts & Crafts, Oakland, MFA, 87. *Work:* Hawaii State Found Cult & Arts, Honolulu, Hawaii; MH de Young Mus, San Francisco, Calif; Oakland Mus Calif. *Exhib:* Solo exhibs, Fuller Gross Gallery San Francisco, 88; Shidoni Contemp Gallery, Tesque, NMex & Mincher/Wilcox Gallery, San Francisco, 90, Haines Gallery, San Francisco, 91, 93, 95, 2008, Zwillingswerke AG, Solingen, Ger, 92, Univ Art Gallery, Sonoma State Univ (with catalog), Rohnert Park, Calif, 95 Haines Gallery, San Francisco, Calif, 97, 99, 01, Marshall Univ Art Gallery, Huntington, WV, 03. *Teaching:* Lect, Sonoma State Univ, 89, Univ Calif, Berkeley, Southern Ill Univ, Carbondale, 90, Calif State Univ, Hayward, 90-96; Artist-in-Residence, Southern Ill Univ, Carbondale, 90. *Awards:* Gold Award, Art Calif Mag Discovery Award, 92; Reg Fel, Western States Art Fedn/Nat Endowment Arts, 93; Fel Grant, Nat Endowment Arts, 94; Hawaii State Found Cult Arts Award, 2003. *Bibliog:* Jamie Brunson (auth), San Francisco/Pleasanton Fax, Art Issues, 11-12/97; Topics - Sculptor Yoshitomo Saito, Mon Mag, 12/97; John Rapko (auth), article in Art Week, 11/95. *Media:* Bronze. *Dealer:* Haines Gallery. *Mailing Add:* c/o Haines Gallery 49 Geary St 5th fl San Francisco CA 94108

SAJET, KIM
MUSEUM DIRECTOR
b Nigeria, 1951. *Study:* BA, in Art History, Melbourne Univ, MBA; M, in Art History, Bryn Mawr Coll. *Pos:* dir corporate relations, Phila Mus Art, 1998-2001; vp deputy dir, Pa Acad Fine Arts, 2000-2007; pres, chief exec, Historical Society of Pa, 2007-2013; launched, Digital Ctr for Americana, 2009; dir, Nat Portrait Gallery, 2013-. *Mailing Add:* National Portrait Gallery 8th & F St NW Washington DC 20001

SAKAI, KIYOKO
PAINTER, COLLAGE ARTIST
b Osaka, Japan. *Study:* Doshisa Univ, Kyoto, Japan, BA. *Hon Degrees:* Art Students League, 77. *Work:* Move 21, Osaka, Japan; Zen Society, NY; NY Stock Exchange; Deloitte, Haskins, and Sells, NJ; Amsak Corp, Ramsey, NJ. *Exhib:* Solo exhibs: Osaka Contemp Art Ctr, Japan, 93; Myunsuk Lee Gallery, Soho, NY, 99; Kunner Kurzon Mus, New Rochelle, NY, 99; Johnson and Johnson, World Hq, New Brunswick, NJ, 2006; Gallery G2, Tokyo, Japan, 2009; Group exhibs: In-a-Sense, Bergen Mus Art and Sci, Paramus, NJ, 84; Mt. Fuji Exhib, Cultural Ctr Japanese Embassy, Brussels, Belgium, 2010. *Awards:* 2nd Prize Painting, Bergen Mus, Bergen Mus Arts and Sci, 86; 1st Prize Mixed Media, Ramapo Coll, 89; Artists Showcase Award, Manhatten Arts Int, 90. *Bibliog:* John Zeaman (auth), Better than Whole Pies, The Record, NJ, 86; Eileen Watkins (auth), Layering Colors with a Sense of Order, The Star Ledger, NJ, 88; Angela Moore (auth), Kiyoko Sakai, Cover Mag, NY, 99. *Mem:* Art Students League. *Media:* Acrylic, Oil, Mixed Media. *Dealer:* Art Front Gallery Tokyo Japan

SAKAOKA, YASUE
SCULPTOR, EDUCATOR
b Himaji-City, Hyogo-Prefecture, Japan, Nov 12, 1933; Nat US. *Study:* Reed Coll, BA, 59; Portland Mus Art Sch, cert; Univ Ore, MFA, 63; Rinehart Inst Sculpture, 63-65; CUNY, Brooklyn, 72-73; Ohio Univ, PhD (comparative arts), 77-79. *Work:* Portland Mus Art, Ore; Arnot Mus, Elmira, NY; Zanesville Art Ctr, Ohio; Schumacher Gallery, Capital Univ, Columbus; Upper Arlington Municipal Bldg, Ohio; Columbus Public Libr, Ohio. *Comn:* Concrete Panels, Jasper Park, Ore, 63; a play sculpture, Columbus Acad, Ohio, 80-81 & Godman Guild, 83; a tapestry, Epiphany Lutheran Church, Pickerington, Ohio, 84-85; Four Seasons, Worthington Arts Coun, 93; Goodwill Rehabilitation Ctr, Columbus, Ohio, 93-94; St Helen's Church, Dayton, Ohio, 99-2000; Worthington Comm Ctr, 2004; Columbus Public Libr. *Exhib:* Paper Exhibs, 81 & Best of 1986, 86, Columbus Cult Arts Ctr, Ohio; Pub Sculpture in Columbus, Ohio State Univ Art Gallery, 84; Ohio Selection Dayton Art Inst, 89; Pebbles Cast on the Water (with catalog), Worthington Arts Coun, Ohio, 93; Reflections of Japan in Ohio Visual Arts (with catalog), Ohio State Univ, 94; Dayton Univ, Artstreet, 2011; ArtSpace, Lima, Ohio, 2011; Triangle Gallery, Sinclair Community Coll, 2013; Decorative Art Ctr, Lancaster, Oh, 2013; Ohio Designer Craftsman Inc, 2013. *Collection Arranged:* Many exhibs at St Paul's Coll in Va including Robert Dilworth's work, 66-77; View of Columbus (with catalog), Artreach Gallery, Columbus, Ohio, 82; A Photographic Exhib: Sculpture on the Grass (with catalog), 83; Franklin Co Sculptors (a catalogue), Columbus, Ohio, 83; Stivers Sculpture Invitational, Ohio, 96 & 99; Installation, Nat City Bank Center, IMPEL Design with Miami Valley Arts Cooperative, Dayton, Ohio, 2001; Upper Arlington Cult Arts Comn, Five Women Scultpors & others, 2008, 2009. *Pos:* Vis artist, Stivers Sch for the Arts, Dayton, Ohio, 89-2006; artists' cur, Miami Valley Coop Gallery, Dayton, Ohio, 89-2006; cur, Asian Artists in Central Ohio, 2001, Miami Valley Corp Gallery, Bank Ctr, Oh. *Teaching:* Asst prof art, St Paul's Coll, Va, 67-77; asst prof sculpture & art hist, Mansfield State Univ, Pa, 77-78; lectr, Ohio State Univ Continuing Educ, 80-2008; resource fac, Capital Univ Without Walls, Colo, Ohio, 81-86; vis prof studio art & humanities, Ohio Dominican Coll, 95; vis artist, Stivers Sch of the Arts, Ohio, 89-2006. *Awards:* Pollock-Krasner Found Award, 87-88; Apprenticeship Award, Ohio Arts Coun, 89-92, 97 & 2001-2002; Best, Outdoor Sculpture Competition, Olde Towne East, Columbus, Ohio, 94; Ohioana Libr Asn, 2006; Heritage Fel Award, Ohio Arts, 2007; Pollock-Krasney Found Award, 2010-2011. *Bibliog:* Fred Kalister (auth), Yasue Sakaoka in Dialogue, Ohio Found Arts, 82; Charles Dietz (auth), Yasue Sakaoka (exhib catalog), Zanesville, Art Ctr, Ohio, 85; John Seto (auth), Sakura in Buckeye, Lima Art Asn, 90-91; and others. *Mem:* Coll Art Asn; Int Sculpture Ctr; Dayton Visual Arts Ctr; Ohio Alliance for Arts in Educ. *Media:* All. *Res:* Japanese Folk Art; Italian Sculptors. *Interests:* visual arts & cultural practices. *Collection:* Jeanne Phillip, Dayton, Ohio. *Publ:* Auth, article, Sculpture Quart, Vol II, No 1, 74; Fragments: A review of a Whitney exhibition in sculpture, Southern Asn Sculptors, summer 76; auth (Arthur Williams), The Sculpture Reference, Sculpture Bks, 2005; many catalogs & videos; and many more. *Dealer:* Mary Baskett Cincinnati OH; Terra Gallery Columbus OH. *Mailing Add:* PO Box 09428 Columbus OH 43209-0428

SAKOGUCHI, BEN
PAINTER
b San Bernardino, Calif, 1938. *Study:* San Bernardino Valley Col, 56-58; Univ Calif, Los Angeles, BA, 60, MFA, 64; Calif State Univ, Los Angeles, 82-83. *Work:* Brooklyn Mus, NY; Chicago Art Inst; Mus Mod Art, NY; Nat Mus Am Art, Smithsonian Inst, Washington; Philadelphia Mus Art, Pa; Hirshhorn Mus, Smithsonian Inst, Washington. *Comn:* Etching, Container Corp Am, 65. *Exhib:* Solo exhibs: Los Angeles City Col, 03; Shifting Perceptions: Contemp Los Angeles Visions, Pacific Asia Mus, Pasadena, Calif, 2000; Made in Calif: Art, Image and Identity, 1900-2000, Los Angeles Co Mus of Art, 2000; 46th Biennial Exhib: Media/Metaphor, Corcoran Gallery of Art, Washington, 2000; Represent, Kellogg Gallery, Calif State Polytechnic Univ, Pomona, 2001; 3rd Int Biennial Exhib of Contemp Art, Florence, Italy, 2001; Smile, Oceanside Mus of Art, Calif, 2002; The Story is in the Telling, Armory Ctr for the Arts, Pasadena, Calif, 2002; In Their Own League, Saddleback Coll Art Gallery, Mission Vielo, Calif, 2003; Issho/Together, Meridian Gallery, San Francisco, 2004; and many others pre-2000. *Teaching:* Prof art, Pasadena City Col, Calif, 64-97. *Awards:* Nat Endowment Arts Fel, 80 & 95; Pasadena Arts Comn Fel, 91; J Paul Getty Trust Fund Visual Arts Fel, Calif Community Found, 97; Lila Wallace-Reader's Digest Fund Artists at Giverny Fel, 97; Calif Arts Council Fel, 03; and others. *Bibliog:* Lucy Lippard (auth), A Different War (exhib catalog), Whatcom Mus Hist Art, 90; Walter Gabrielson (auth), Ben Sakoguchi, Addictions (exhib catalog), Santa Barbara Contemp Arts Forum, 91; Andrew Perchuck (auth), Ben Sakoguchi's America, Artists of Conscience II (exhib catalog), Alternative Mus, 92; Michael Duncan (auth), Ben Sakoguchi at Luckman Fine Arts Gallery, California State University, Art in America, Nov 99, p 150. *Publ:* Special issue on nuclear disarmament, Village Voice, 6/15/82; 10: Artist as Catalyst (portfolio), ed/100, Alternative Mus, 92. *Mailing Add:* 1183 Avoca Ave Pasadena CA 91105

SAKS, JUDITH-ANN (JUDITH-ANN SAKS ROSENTHAL)
PAINTER
b Anniston, Ala, Dec 20, 1943. *Study:* Tex Acad Art, Houston, 57-58; Houston Mus Fine Arts, 62; Rice Univ, 62; Sophie Newcomb Col, Tulane Univ, BFA (Arthur Q Davis Prize, Scholars & fel, art ed the Tiresian), 66; Univ Houston, 67. *Work:* Marine Transportation Collection, Smithsonian Inst; Royal Libr, Windsor Castle, England; Univ Houston; Harris Co Heritage Soc Mus, Houston; Johnson Manned Space Mus, Clear Lake, Tex; St Lukes Hosp, Houston, 2011. *Comn:* Christmas card design (oil painting), Houston CofC, 70; Drawing of the Straithard, Roberts Steamship Agency, New Orleans, 75; Am Revolution Bicentennial Proj (six oil paintings), Port of Houston Authority, 75-76; four hist paintings, Pin Oak Charity Horse Show Asn, 77; painting, Cruiser Houston Mem Room, Univ Houston. *Exhib:* 59th Ann Exhib, Birmingham Mus Art, Ala, 67; 1st Nat Space Art Show, Brown Palace Hotel, Denver, 69; Images on Paper, Miss Arts Festival & Munic Art Gallery, Jackson, 70; 7th Ann Art Exhib, Mobile Art Gallery, Ala, 72; and others. *Pos:* Cur student art collection, Univ Houston, 68-72. *Awards:* Selected Print, Miss Art Asn, 70-71; Nat First Places, Prints, Am Heritage Comt, NSDAR, 87; 1st place watercolor, Art League Houston, 1st place sculpture, 1st place graphics; 1st place acrylics, Fourth of July, Tex, 2004; 1st place drawing, Tex State, NSDAR award, 2002; 1st place, Tex Notecards of Artist Paintings, 2010; 1st place, South Central Div(6 states), 2010; Nat Hon Mention, 1st Nat Drawing & Small Sculpture show, Del Mar Coll; Nat Hon Mention, Hear the Bells, Let Freedom Ring, 2006; Nat 3rd place acrylics, Memories, 2003; Nat 3rd place, Acrylics-Proclaim Liberty, 2005; Nat 1st place acrylics, Women's Spirit Unity & Purpose, 2000; Nat 1st place acrylics, Jamestown 1607, A New Day, 2007; Nat 1st place collage, Am Heritage Contest, Am Heritage Remembered, 2009; Nat 1st place, Cult Events & Traditions, NSDAR Am's Heritage Remembered, Houston, 2010; Nat 3rd place, Am Heritage Acrylics, 2012; Tex Women in the Arts award, 2013; Nat 2nd place Am Heritage Acrylics, 2013; CDA 85th Ann Celebration award, 2013. *Bibliog:* Ann Absher (auth), Painter on the roof, The Milepost, Columbia Gulf Transmission Co, 6/69; Susanna Friedman (auth), Southern artist, Bull Asn Jewish Libr, 9/79; Judith-Ann Saks, Arch Am Art, Smithsonian Inst, 79; Jewish Herald Voices: Saks Wins 1st Place in Am Heritage Contast, 2009, Local Artist Wins Nat 1st Place, 2007; Southwestern Art, Vol II no 1, Nov 1967; Absolutely! The Artist Among Us, 2007; The Arkas, The Container Revolution, 50 Years of Containerization, 2006; Memorial Examiner, Saks Wins 1st place in Am Heritage Contest, 7/9/2009; Bicentennial Times, Commemorative Reprints; History of the Women's Club, painting of Houston; JoAn Martin (auth), Retrieving Morning, 2009; Ann Becker (auth), Images of Am: Houston 1860-1900, 2010. *Mem:* NSDAR; Art League, Houston; Daughter Repub Tex; Mus Fine Arts, Houston; Colonial Dames Am (2nd vice pres chapter VIII); Daughters of Am Colonists; Daughters of the Am Revolution; Lady Washington (recording secy, 2013-); Jamestown Soc; Colonial Dames of the 17th Century. *Media:* Oil on Linen; Pen and Ink Etchings; Acrylic. *Res:* Bicentennial proj, Port o Houston; Am Heritage Paintings & Cult events & traditions. *Interests:* hist, writing. *Publ:* Illusr, Southwestern Art Inc, 11/67; illusr, seven covers, Port Houston Mag, 71, 75 & 76; The Catline, Desk & Derrick Club, 72; Maersk Post, A P Moller, Denmark, 8/77; Texas Sesquicentennial drawing for Texas Daughters of the American Revolution, Nat Soc Daughters Am Revolution Nat Mag, 86; The Arkas, 2006; Absolutely, 2007; Jewish Herald Voice, 2009; Memorial Examiner, 2009

SAKSON, ROBERT (G)
PAINTER
b Trenton, NJ, Feb 13, 1938. *Study:* Trenton Jr Col, AA, 58. *Work:* Hunterdon Co Libr, Felmington, NJ; AT&T Longlines, Bedminster, NJ; US Coast Guard, Mich; Ellarslie, Trenton City Mus, NJ; Princeton Univ Art Mus, NJ. *Comn:* Paintings for Calendar, Best Foods Corp, Ridgewood, NJ, 86; paintings of Phillipsburg, NJ, Carteret Savings Bank, 86, 87 & 88; location paintings, Avon Corp, NY, 89 & 90; series paintings, Waterloo Village, Horizon Bank, Morristown, NJ, 88, 89 & 90; painting of Palmer Square, Collins Develop Corp, Princeton, NJ, 90; Best Portfolio- 9 paintings of Philadelphia for The Chubb Insurance Group Corp offices, Philadelphia, PA. *Exhib:* Am Watercolor Soc Ann Exhibs, NY, 68-95; Allied Artists Am, Nat Arts Club, NY, 83, 86 & 87; Audubon Artists Ann, Nat Arts Club, NY, 88; Knickerbocker Artists Ann, Salmagundi Club, NY, 89; In Our Circle, James Michener Art Mus, Doylestown, Pa, 91; Historic NJ: A Contemp View, Bristol Myers-Squibb Gallery, Princeton, 91; Phillips Mill Art Exhib, New Hope, Pa, 2010; Traveling exhib: 144th Annual Exhib, Am Watercolor Soc, NY, 2011. *Pos:* Watercolorist. *Teaching:* Instr master classes watercolor, Somerset Art Asn, FarHills, NJ, 70-; Perkins Ctr Arts, Moorestown, NJ. *Awards:* Silver Medal of Honor, NJ Watercolor Soc, 76, 83 & 92; Gold Medal, Allied Artists Am, 83; Elizabeth Callan Mem Medal & Dolphin Fel, Am Watercolor Soc, 93; Conti Award, Phillips Mill Ann, 2005; Riverside Gallery Award, Artist Paints Hunterdon Co, 2006; Dagmar Tribble Award, 2007; Invited Artist, Phillips Mill Ann, 2007; Mayors Award Excellence, 25th Ellarslie Open, 2007; Garden State Watercolor Society, 2007; Bob & Byers Award, Coryell Gallery, 2007; Bud Chavoosian Award, NJ Watercolor Soc, 2007; Fred Beans Family of Automotive Dealerships Award, 2010. *Bibliog:* Featured Artist, Am Artist (watercolor issue), 9/2007; Stephen Doherty (auth), Tried and True (featured article), Am Artist (watercolor issue), 2007. *Mem:* Am Watercolor Soc; Allied Artists Am (juror, currently); Audubon Artists Am (juror, currently); Knickerbocker Artists (juror, currently); Pastel Soc Am (juror, currently); NJ Watercolor Soc & Garden State Watercolor Soc; Phila Watercolor Soc. *Media:* Watercolor, Pastel. *Publ:* Contribr,

Painting Light & Shadow, Painting Texture, Best of Watercolor 1 and 2, Rockport Publ; Painting with the White of Your Paper, Splash 2 and 4, North Light Bks; Painters of the River towns, River Arts Press, 2002; Long Beach Island Rhapsody-35 paintings; Splash 10, Passionate Brush Strokes; contribr, American Artist (feature article), 2007. *Dealer:* Things Adrift Shipbottom NJ. *Mailing Add:* 10 Stacey Ave Trenton NJ 08618-3421

SAKUYAMA, SHUNJI
PRINTMAKER, PAINTER
b Harbin, Manchuria, July 29, 1940; Japan citizen. *Study:* Tokyo Gakugei Univ, BA, 65; Brooklyn Col, MFA, 72; Pratt Graphics Ctr. *Work:* Brooklyn Mus; Berkshire Mus, Pittsfield, Mass; City Mus, NY; New Sch Art Ctr, NY; NY Hist Soc; 21 Century Pear Mus, Tottori, Japan. *Exhib:* Solo exhibs, Paintings, 72 & Prints, 94, Berkshire Mus, Takano Gallery, Tokyo & Chinoh Gallery, NY; 21st Nat Print Exhib, 78; NY Album, Brooklyn Mus, 79; NY Collects, City Mus, NY, 81; Gene Baro Collects, Brooklyn Mus, 83; Gallery Blanche, Osaka, Japan, 2003, 2005, 2007, 2010. *Teaching:* Instr Japanese brush work, Long Island Univ, Brooklyn Ctr, 77-78. *Awards:* Painting Awards, New Eng Art Exhib, New Canaan, Conn, 72 & Berkshire Art Asn Exhib, 75. *Media:* Lithography; Acrylic, Oil. *Publ:* Auth, Cynthia Dantzic, Design Dimensions, Prentice Hall; auth, Cynthia Dantzic, NY 100 Painters. *Dealer:* Chino Art Gallery 575 5th Ave New York NY 10017. *Mailing Add:* 915 President St Brooklyn NY 11215

SAL, JACK
PHOTOGRAPHER, PAINTER
b Waterbury, Conn, Mar 28, 1954. *Study:* Philadelphia Coll Art, BFA, 76; Art Inst Chicago, MFA, 78. *Work:* Detroit Inst Arts, Mich; Ctr for Creative Photog, Tucson, Ariz; Mus Mod Art, NY; Int Mus Photog, Rochester, NY; Yale Univ Art Gallery, New Haven, Conn; Mus Ludwig, Köln, Ger; and others. *Comn:* Earth Work, Off Cult Affairs, New Haven, Conn, 79; Grant, Conn Comn for Arts, 80; Fresco mural, Univ Bridgeport, 84; Fresco mural, Padua, Italy, 86; Am Cult Heritage Abroad and City of Kielce, Poland, 2005. *Exhib:* Prints in the Cliche-Verre, Houston Mus Fine Art, 80; solo exhibs, Northlight Gallery, Tempe, Ariz, 80 & Recent Camera Works, Photog Workshop, New Canaan, Conn, 80, Mus Ludwig, Köln, Ger, 95; Light Gallery, NY, 81; Int Ctr Photog, NY, 81; Ferns Gallery, Hull, Eng, 82; Mus Mod Art, NY, 83; Hudson Ctr, 85; Gallery Multigraphic, Venice, 01; Salt Ctr, Denmark, 02; and others. *Pos:* Cur, Light Gallery, 85-. *Teaching:* Assoc prof, Int Ctr Photog-NY Univ, Rutgers Univ, 85; chmn photog dept, Moore Col Art & Design. *Awards:* Mellon Fel, 82; Vis Artist Am Acad in Rome, 86-87. *Bibliog:* S D Peters (auth), Interview/Jack Sal, Int Mus Photog, 79; Roger Baldwin (auth), Jack Sal/camera images, Views, 80; Glassman/Symmes, Prints in the Cliche-Verre, Detroit Inst Arts, 80; Wire/works (auth) Salon Verlag, 2000; M & M (editors), Primary drawings, 2001. *Media:* Pigment, Light-Sensitive Paper. *Publ:* Auth, Cliche-Verre: cameraless images, Portfolio Mag, 79; contribr, Prints in the Cliche-Verre, Detroit Inst Arts, 80; contribr, Connecticut Photographers, Art Resources of Conn, 80; contribr, Photographers Hand, Int Mus Photog/George Eastman House, 80; auth, Mark/Making, Combinations Press, 81. *Dealer:* Brigitte Schenk Gallery Köln Ger. *Mailing Add:* 431 E Sixth St New York NY 10009

SALADINO, TONY
PAINTER, PRINTMAKER
b New Orleans, La, June 5, 1943. *Study:* La State Univ, BS, 64, New Orleans, La; self-taught as artist. *Work:* Nat Mus Fine Arts, Hanoi, N Vietnam; Mus Int Art, Bahia, Brazil; Tex State Univ; Wichita Falls Mus & Art Ctr, Tex; Mus Art & Archaeol, Univ Mo; Bank of Laredo, Tex; Michale & Susan Dell Found, Austin, Tex; Fort Worth Pub Libr Found, Tex; Winstead Seachrest & Minick, PC, Austin, Tex. *Comn:* Mem Hosp, San Antonio, Tex; Circle Theatre, Fort Worth, Tex; GSX Corp, Tex, 2010. *Exhib:* Central Texas Biennial, The Art Center, Waco, Tex, 89 & 92; Nat Works on Paper, Univ Miss, 90; Small Impressions 1990, The Printmaking Coun of NJ, Somerville; Pac States Nat Print Exhib, Univ Hawaii, Hilo, 90; Am Realism Competition, Parkersburg Art Center, WVa, 90; The Print Club of Albany, NY, 92; 5th Ann Nat Art Exhib, Cooperstown Art Asn, NY, 92; New Traditions: Contemp Mezzotints, Bradley Univ, Peoria, Ill, 94; and others. *Teaching:* monotype workshop, Oxbow Summer Sch Art, Saugatuck; instr painting, Mod Art Mus, Ft Worth, Tex, 92-; instr, workshop, Painting Abstractly in Acrylics, Creative Arts Ctr, Bossier City, La; instr abstract painting workshops, La & Tex; Workshop, Going from the Real to the Absract, 2009. *Awards:* Purchase Award, Am Realism Competition, Parkersburg Art Ctr, Va, 90; Purchase Award, Univ Wis, Parkside, 90; Delta Nat Small Prints Exhib Purchase Award, Ark State Univ, 97; Bank Am Award, Presentation is the Art of City, Ft Worth, Tex, 2004. *Bibliog:* Article, NY Times, 12/17/89; article, the Art Calendar, 2/92; David Band (auth), Enrich Your Paintings with Texture, North Light Bks, 94; others; Head Games (article), Southwest Art, 7/2007. *Mem:* Int Mezzotint Soc. *Media:* All Media. *Interests:* Argentine Tango, Span Study. *Publ:* The Artist's Mag, 89; The Art Calendar, 92; La Semana, Fort Worth, 6/2000; Austin American Statesman, Austin, Tex, 12/2004; Crosswinds Weekly, Albuquerque, 7/2004; Southwest Art Mag, July 2007; Kentucky Homes & Gardens, 2010. *Dealer:* B Deemer Gallery Louisville KY; Gallery at Snoal Creek 1500 W 34th St Austin Tex; Edmund Craig Gallery Ft Worth TX. *Mailing Add:* 756 Norwood Hurst TX 76053

SALDANA, ZOE SHEEHAN
WEAVER, SCULPTOR
Study: Oberlin Coll, BA, 1994; Rochester Inst Technol, MFA, 1998; Skowhegan Sch Painting & Sculpture, Maine. *Exhib:* Solo exhibs, Castellani Art Mus, Niagra Univ, 1997, Choate Gallery, Pace Univ, NY, 2006, Southwest Sch Art & Craft, Tex, 2008; Simulacrum, Soc Contemp Photog, Kans City, 2005; Altered, Stitched & Gathered, PS1/Mus Mod Art, 2006; Transactions, Blanton Mus Art, Tex, 2007; Resistance, NJ Book Arts Symposium, Rutgers Univ, NJ, 2008; Dress Codes, Katonah Mus Art, NY, 2009. *Pos:* Vis artist, Univ Calif, Riverside, 2003, Texas A&M Univ, 2004, Parsons Sch Design, NY, 2008; resident artist, Ucross FOund, Wyo, 2008, Ctr for Bk Arts, NY, 2008. *Teaching:* Assoc prof, CUNY Baruch Coll, NY, 2009-. *Awards:* NY Found Arts Fel, 2009. *Bibliog:* Korky Vann (auth), Swap and Shop, Hartford Courant, 9/26/2005; Sarah Schmerler, Point of Purchase, Time Out New York, 64, No 56, 8/10-16/2006; Daniel Morgan (auth), Exploring Exhibits Before It's Too Late, New York Sun, 1/4/2007; Dan Goddard, Works mix media, tackle issues, San Antonio Express-News, 10/12/2008; Michael Shaw (auth), Saldana in Mid-Wilshire, ARTslant Los Angeles, 10/5/2009

SALGIAN, MITZURA
ARTIST
b Bucharest, Romania; US citizen. *Study:* Nicolae Grigorescu Art Inst, Bucharest, MA, 1976. *Work:* New Britain Mus Am Art. *Exhib:* solo exhibs, Escada Quatro Gallery, 1995, Arte Varia Gallery, 1996, Portals Gallery, 1999-2004; group exhibs, Saginaw Art Mus, 98, Midwest Mus Am Art, 98-99; 92nd Exhib, Conn Acad Fine Arts, 2003; Danville Mus of Fine Arts & Hist, Danville, Va, 2004; The Butler Inst Am Art, 2004; Bergstrom-Mahler Mus, 2004; Huntsville Mus Art, 2004; Mus Texas Tech Univ, 2005; Catharine Lorillard Wolfe Art Club 109th Ann Open Juried Exhib, Nat Arts Club, NY, 2005; Conn Accad Fine Art, 2005; New Britain Mus Am Art, 2006; Bennington Center for the Arts, 2007; Attleboro Arts Mus, 2007-2008; Butler Ins Am Art, 2008. *Collection Arranged:* Marquis Luc de Clapiers; Angelo Loggia, Rome; Onik Sahakian, Lisbon & NY, many others; Mimi Adler, NY; Gilbert Kahn, Newport, RI. *Awards:* John Young Hunter Award, Allied artists of Am, 1990; Honorable Mention Midyear Show Award, Butler Inst of Am Art, 2004; Tamsin L Holzer Memorial Award, Catharine Lorillard Wolfe Art Club, 2005; Mervin Honig Memorial Award, Allied Artists Am; 4th Place, Conn Accad Fine Art, 2005; Award for Oil, New Britain Mus Am Art, 2006; Dorothy Barberis Mem: Catharine Lorillard Wolfe Art Club, 2006; MidAmerica Pastel Soc Award, Pastel Soc Am, 2007; Award for Oil/Acrylic, New Britarie Mus Am Art, 2006. *Mem:* Allied Artists of Am; Flushing Coun Culture & Arts. *Media:* Oil, Egg Tempera, Pastel, Watercolor. *Mailing Add:* 60-11 Broadway Apt 1F Woodside NY 11377

SALINAS, BARUJ
PAINTER, PRINTMAKER
b Havana, Cuba, July 6, 1935; US citizen. *Study:* Kent State Univ, BArch. *Work:* San Antonio Mus Art; Museo Arte Moderno Mex; Art Inst Chicago; Museo Maria Zambrano, Velez-Malaga, Spain; Museo Nacional D'Art de Catalunya, Barcelona, Spain; Mus Jose L Cuevas, Mexico; MOLAA, Los Angeles. *Comn:* Murals, Sephardi Sch, Mex DF; paintings, Edificio la Victoria, Mex DF, 79; paintings, Europ Am Bank, Miami, 82; Stained Glass Windows (3) and a Mural, Inst Cult Mexico-Israel, Mexico City, 93. *Exhib:* Solo exhibs, Harmon Gallery, Fla, 75 & 83, EditArt, Geneva, Switz, 75, 77, 79, 83, 85, 88 & 91, 94, 96, 2000, 2002, 2004 & 2006, Mus Carrillo Gil, Mex, 81; Galeria Joan Prats, NY, 82; Mus de Arte Mod, Mexico City, Mex, 88; Shuyu Art Gallery, Tokyo, Japan, 94; Musee Des Tapisseries, Aix-en-Provence, 98; retrospective, Espace Vallon, Editart, Geneva, 2000; New Works, Central Conn State Univ, S Chen Art Ctr, Hartford, Conn, 2002; Pintar de Palabras, Centro Cult Espanol, C Gables, Fla, 2003; Claros Del Bosque, Frances Wolfson Gallery, Miami, Fla, 2004; Layers, Univ Buffalo Art Center, Buffalo, NY, 2006; La Mirada del Que Mira, Diputacion de Malaga, Malaga, Spain, 2007; Casa Bacardi (retrospective), Univ Miami, Coral Gables, Fla, 2007; Flares, Americas's Collection, Coral Gables, Fla, 2007; Caminos, Mus Jose Luis Cuevas, Mexico, 2011; Baruj Salinas, Ayuntamiento de Soria, Spain, 2011. *Teaching:* Instr seminars graphic work, Winchester Sch Art & Sch Visual Arts, Barcelona, Spain, 92-94; instr seminar paintings, Sch Visual Arts NY, summer 93; instr, Miami Dade Coll, 99-2007; prof painting, MDC Interamerican Campus, Miami, 2005-2013. *Awards:* Cintas Fel, Inst Int Educ, 69 & 70; First Prize, VI Biennale, Degrabado Latino-Americano de San Juan, PR, 83. *Bibliog:* Wifredo Fernandez (auth), Baruj Salinas su mundo pictorico, Ed Punto Cardinal, 71; Gloria Moure, Carlos Franqui, Wifredo Fernandez & Jose A Valente (auths), Baruj Salinas, Ediciones Poligrafa, Espana, 79; Octavio Armand, Carlos Monsivais, Michel Butor, Jose A Valente, (auths), Baruj Salinas, Mus Arte Mod, Mexico City, 88; Carlos M Luis (auth), Pintar De Palabras, Centro Cult Espanol, Miami, 2003; Maria Zambrano, Rogelio Blanco, Jesus Moreno, Jose C Matheos, Jose Kozer, Lorenzo G. Vega, Et Al (coauths), Catalog (200 pages), La Mirada del Que Mira, Malaga, Spain, 2007. *Media:* Acrylic, Miscellaneous Media. *Interests:* Reading, classical music, travel. *Publ:* Resumen AIP, 71; Narradores Cubanos de Hoy, 75; Revista Escandalar, NY, 81; co-illusr, Tres Lecciones de Tinieblas, with J A Valente, Ediciones la Gaya Ciencia, Barcelona, 82; Antes De La Ocultacion: Los Mares, Maria Zambrano, 83; Trois Enfants Dans La Fournaise, Michel Butor, 88. *Dealer:* Galerie Editart Route de Pre-Bois 20 1215 Geneva Switzerland; Masters Latin Am Art 2020 N Main St #239 Los Angeles Ca 90031; The Americas Collection 4213 Ponce de Leon Coral Gables Fl 33134. *Mailing Add:* 2740 SW 92nd Ave Miami FL 33165

SALINGER, ADRIENNE
PHOTOGRAPHER, EDUCATOR
b Los Angeles, Calif. *Study:* Sch Art Inst Chicago, with Joyce Neimons, MFA (photog), 86. *Work:* Los Angeles Co Mus Art; Mus Fine Arts, Houston; Nat Gallery Can, Ottawa; Bibliotheque Nationale, Paris; Int Polaroid Coll, Cambridge, Mass. *Exhib:* The Photog of Invention, Nat Mus Am Art, Washington, 89; Pleasures & Terrors of Domestic Comfort, Mus Mod Art, NY, 91; Recent Acquisitions, Mus Fine Arts, Houston, 91; Observing Traditions: Contemp Photog, Nat Gallery Can, 93; solo exhib, San Jose Mus Art, Calif, 95; Sala El Tunel, Inst Chileno Norteamericano, Santiago, Chile, 96; In My Room, Scottsdale Ctr Arts, Ariz, 96; Alt Youth Media, New Mus, NY, 96. *Teaching:* Assoc prof photog, Syracuse Univ, 88-. *Awards:* James D Phelan Award in Photog, 87; MacDowell Colony, fel, 96. *Bibliog:* Dennis Cooper (auth), Teenage fan club, SPIN, 6/95; Dulcie Leimbach, A room of their own, NY Times, 10/15/95; Bobbie Ann Mason (auth), Overdue books, Doubletake, winter 96. *Mem:* Coll Art Asn; Soc Photog Educ. *Media:* Photography. *Publ:* Auth, In My Room: Teenagers in Their Bedrooms, Chronicle Books, 95. *Dealer:* Stephen Wirtz Gally 49 Geary St San Francisco CA 94109

SALLICK, LUCY ELLEN
PAINTER, INSTRUCTOR
b Boston, Mass, Sep 21, 1937. *Study:* Univ Mich, 55-58; New York Univ, BA, 59, painting, 60-62; Art Students League, 64-65; Corcoran Sch Art, 66-68. *Work:* Bruce Mus, Greenwich, Conn; Rahr West Mus, Manitowoc, Wis; Housatonic Mus Art, Bridgeport, Conn; Univ Mich Art Mus, Ann Arbor; Town of Westport, Conn. *Comn:* Painting, Brunswick Savings Inst, Maine, 75. *Exhib:* Contemp Reflections, Aldrich Mus, Ridgefield, Conn, 75; solo exhibs, Rutgers Univ, New Brunswick, NJ, 77, Canton Art Inst, Ohio, 80 & Bowdoin Coll Mus Art, Brunswick, Maine, 87; Childe Hassam Purchase Exhib, Am Acad & Inst Arts & Lett, 76-83; Contemp Naturalism, Nassau Co Mus Fine Arts, NY, 80; Conn Painters, Wadsworth Atheneum, 83; Contemp Landscape Painting, Wesleyan Univ, Conn, 83; Contemp Am Still Life, One Penn Plaza, NY, 85. *Teaching:* Instr painting, Silvermine Guild Sch Arts, 77- & Lyme Acad Fine Arts, 85-. *Awards:* Eloise Egan Mem Award, New Eng Ann Silvermine Guild, 75 & Guild Award, 79. *Bibliog:* Lawrence Alloway (auth), Lucy Sallick, Fairleigh Dickinson Univ, 75; John Russell (auth), article, New York Times, 9/23/77; Gerrit Henry (auth), article, Art in Am, 2/83. *Mem:* Women's Caucus Art; Silvermine Guild; Soho 20. *Media:* Oil, Watercolor. *Dealer:* G W Einstein Co Inc 591 Broadway New York NY 10012. *Mailing Add:* 77 Long Lots Rd Westport CT 06880

SALMINEN, JOHN THEODORE
PAINTER, INSTRUCTOR
b Minneapolis, Minn, Jan 18, 1945. *Study:* Univ Minn, Duluth, BS (art educ) 1968, MEd (art educ) 1974; Univ Minn with Cheng Khee Chee -1982-84. *Hon Degrees:* TWSA, Master Status. *Work:* Nat Watercolor Soc, San Pedro, Calif; Univ Minn, Tweed Mus, Duluth; Springfield Art Mus, Mo; 1st Bank Fine Arts Collection, National. *Comn:* Paintings, Duluth Visitors & Conv, Minn, 1983; paintings, Seaway Port Auth, Duluth, Minn, 1996; mag covers, Seaway Port Auth, Duluth, Minn, 1998-; purchased paintings, St Mary's Duluth Clinic, Minn, 2005; Shanghai Biennial Collection, China. *Exhib:* Tweed Mus of Art, Duluth, Minn, 1988; Allied Artists, New York City, 1995, 96, 98, 99; Am Watercolor Soc, Salmagundi Club, New York City, 1995-2001, 2003, 05, 06; Audubon Artists, New York City, 1997, 2002-03; Neville Mus, Green Bay, Wis, 1998; Nat Acad 173rd Annual Exhib, New York City, 1998; Nat Arts Club Open Exhib, New York City, 1998. *Collection Arranged:* San Marino Galley, Pasadena, Calif, 4/2008. *Pos:* Nominations chmn, TWSA, 2000-05; dir, Am Watercolor Soc, 2002-04. *Teaching:* Instr art, I.S.D., Duluth, Minn, 1969-2001; instr, Col St Scholastica, Duluth, Minn, 1984; instr, Fulbright Exchange, Edinburgh, Scot, 1984-85; instr, watercolor, 2001-. *Awards:* Grant recipient, Marie Walsh Sharpe Found, Colorado Springs, Colo, 1995; 1st Place Experimental, Artists Mag Art Comp, 2000, 2nd Place in landscape art,; Silver Star, Nat Watercolor Soc, 2005; Gold Medal, Am Watercolor Soc, 2006, 2010; Dolphin Fellow, AWS. *Bibliog:* Michael J. Burlinham (auth), An Urban Realist Takes on the Big Apple, Am Artist Watercolor, 1999; Loraine Crouch (auth), Staying in the Flow, Watercolor Magic Yearbook, 2004. *Mem:* Dolphin fellow Am Watercolor Soc (dir, 2002-2004); signature mem Nat Watercolor Soc; master status Transparent Watercolor Soc of Am (nom chair, 2000-2005); Sylvian Groose Pennsylvania Watercolor Soc; signature mem Watercolor West. *Media:* Watercolor. *Publ:* Auth Bright Lights, Dark City, Watercolor Magic/FandW, 1999; East Meets West (interview of Cheng Khee Chee), Watercolor Magic/Fiw pub, 2000; Auth Expressing the Language of the Landscape, Int Artist Pub Inc, 2002; On the Street, Artists Mag, F&W Pub, 2004; Crough, Mesch & Moorman (auth), View from the Top, Watercolor Magic Fiw Pub, 2005; Every Picture Tells a Story, Int Artist Pub Inc, 2006. *Dealer:* American Legacy Gallery Jack Olsen 5911 Main St Kansas City MO 64113; San Marino Gallery 70 N Raymond Ave Pasadena Ca. *Mailing Add:* 6021 Arnold Rd Duluth MN 55803

SALMON, DONNA ELAINE
ILLUSTRATOR
b Los Angeles, Feb 23, 1935. *Study:* Univ Denver Sch Art. *Exhib:* Univ Denver, 55; Univ Northern Colo, 64. *Pos:* Freelance illusr, Salmon Studios, Calif, 60-. *Teaching:* Pvt instr painting, 70-74. *Awards:* Book Design Illusr Award for Symmetry, Freeman Pub. *Media:* Pen and Ink, Gouache, Oil, Printmaking. *Interests:* Volunteering community art and art instruction. *Publ:* Illusr, The Psychology of Consciousness, Freeman Publ. Co, 72 & Harcourt Brace 76; Illusr, Biochemistry/Stryer, 75; Illusr & Contribr, Chemistry/Linus Pauling, 75; Illusr, An Introduction to Genetic Analysis, 76; Illusr, The Handbook of Scientific Photography, Freeman Publ Co, 77. *Dealer:* Studio 2901 Gallery Fulford-Ganges Rd Salt Spring Island BC V8K 1X6. *Mailing Add:* 717 Alabama St Vallejo CA 94590

SALMON, MARGARET
PHOTOGRAPHER, VIDEO ARTIST
b Suffern, NY, 1975. *Study:* Sch Visual Arts, New York, BFA (Photog), 1998; Royal Coll Art, London, MA (Fine Art, Photog), 2003. *Exhib:* Solo exhibs include Collective Gallery, Edinburgh, Scotland, 2006, Whitechapel Art Gallery, London, 2007, Witte de With Ctr Contemp Art, Rotterdam, 2007; group exhibs include John Kobal Photographic Awards Exhib, Nat Portrait Gallery, London, 2000; Montebello Read, Wallspace, New York, 2002, Holiday Shopping, 2002, Photography for People, Like Us, 2003; Beck's Futures Student Film & Video Award Exhib, Inst Contemp Art, London, 2002; New Contemporaries, Liverpool Biennial, 2004; New Contemporaries, Barbican Art Gallery, London, 2004; Think with the Senses-Feel with the Mind, Venice Biennale, 2007. *Awards:* John Kobal Photog Award, 2000; 2nd Prize, Beck's Futures Student Film & Video Award, 2002; Am Acad in Rome Residency, 2006; MaxMara Women's Art Prize, 2006; Le Prix Giles Dusein, 2006; Hospital Club Film Award, 2007. *Mailing Add:* c/o STORE 27 Hoxton St London N1 6NH United Kingdom

SALMON, RAYMOND MERLE
ILLUSTRATOR, CARTOONIST, EDUCATOR
b Akron, Colo, Sept 6, 1931. *Study:* Mesa Coll; Univ Denver; Chicago Acad Fine Arts; Univ Colo; Calif Coll Arts & Crafts; San Francisco State Univ; Colorado Springs Fine Arts Ctr; Univ Northern Colo, BA & MA (fine arts). *Work:* Libr Community & Graphic Arts, Ohio State Univ. *Exhib:* Univ Denver Art Mus, 55; Colorado Springs Fine Arts Ctr, 61; Tacoma Art Mus, Wash, 64; State Univ Mo, 65; Master Cartoonists Exhib, Parke-Bernet, New York, 71. *Pos:* Free lance graphic artist, Salmon Studios, Calif, 60-; cartoonist; creator cartoon panel, The Little Man. *Teaching:* Art educ, John F Kennedy Univ, 66-74; art educ, commercial dept, Solano Community Coll, 71-; Chapman Coll, 88; Emeritus Prof Art, 2013. *Mem:* Nat Cartoonists Soc, New York. *Media:* Pen and Ink, Watercolor, Printmaking. *Publ:* Cartoons in Saturday Review, FM and the Fine Arts Mag, Writer's Digest, Life Mag & Newspapers. *Dealer:* Studio 2901 Gallery Fulford-Ganges Rd Salt Spring Island BC V8K 1X6. *Mailing Add:* 717 Alabama St Vallejo CA 94590

SALOMON, JOHANNA
PAINTER, INSTRUCTOR
b Passaic, NJ, Jan 29, 1944. *Study:* Art Ctr NJ, with Denise Collins, Florence Hurewitz, Leonard Agronsky, Gerald Samuels, Philip Pearlstein and Charles Reid, 86-96; Art Students League, with Knox Martin & Christine Jordan, 90-91. *Comn:* mural, Holley House for Children, Hackensack, NJ, 87. *Exhib:* Catherine Lorrilard Exhibit, Nat Arts Club, NY, 90, 92; Gallery 108, Vineyard Theater, NY, 90; Three Worlds of Realism, Williams Ctr Arts, Rutherford, NJ, 91; Festival Exhibit, Bergen Mus Arts & Sci, Paramus, NJ, 91; Figuratively Speaking, Art Ctr NJ, New Milford, 91; Paterson Mus, NJ, 92; Cork Gallery, Avery Fisher Hall, NY, 94; Belskie Mus Art and Sci, 2002. *Teaching:* instr watercolor, acrylic, oil, Emerson Bd Educ, NJ, 92-2001, Art Ctr Northern NJ, 99-, Bergen Community Coll, Paramus, NJ, 2000-; instr watercolor, Ridgewood Bd Educ, NJ, 93-. *Awards:* Winsor & Newton Painting Award, Hackensack Art Club, 85; Grumbacher Award, Hackensack Art Club, 89; Best in Show, Westwood Chamber Com, NJ, 89. *Bibliog:* Will Grant (auth), About NY in the Galleries, Artspeak, 5/1/90; Alexandra Shaw (auth), Salute to Women in the Arts, Manhattan Arts Int, 9-10/94. *Mem:* Art Ctr NJ Watercolor Affiliates (pres, 90-95, educ com, 90-94); Salute to Women in the Arts; Art Ctr NJ Painting Affiliates; Community Arts Asn; Ridgewood Arts Coun. *Media:* Watercolor, Acrylic. *Dealer:* Michael Fitzsimmons Westwood Gallery 10 Westwood Ave Westwood NJ 07675. *Mailing Add:* 29 Powell Rd Emerson NJ 07630-1446

SALOMON, LAWRENCE
SCULPTOR, EDUCATOR
b Chicago, Ill, July 18, 1940. *Study:* Art Inst Chicago; Univ Ill, BFA; Univ Chicago. *Exhib:* Chicago Biennial, 68 & Critic Choice, 69, Art Inst Chicago; Lyman Wright Art Ctr, Beloit, Wis, 70; The Five: Pub Works, Univ Chicago, 71; Art for Pub Places, Dept Housing & Urban Develop Nat Competition, 73; Cool Abstraction, Richard Gray Gallery, Chicago, 76; Romantic Structures: Abstract Art in Chicago Traveling Exhib, Univs Mo & Kans, 78; and others. *Teaching:* Assoc prof fine art, Univ Ill, Chicago Circle, 65-. *Awards:* Art in Pub Places Award, Nat Competition, Dept Housing & Urban Develop, 73. *Bibliog:* Amy Goldin (auth), Greasy kid stuff, Art Gallery Mag, 73; articles, Art in Am, 77; C L Morrison (auth), Chicago dialectics, Art News, 2/78. *Mem:* The Five; Participating Artists Chicago (secy, 68-70); Art Pub Places (bd dir, 78-). *Media:* Metal. *Dealer:* Jan Cicero Gallery 433 N Clark Chicago IL. *Mailing Add:* 2116 N Bissell Chicago IL 60614

SALT, JOHN
PAINTER
b Birmingham, Eng, 1937. *Study:* Slade Sch Fine Arts, London, 60; Birmingham Coll Art, Eng, 68; Md Inst Coll Art, Baltimore, MFA, 69. *Exhib:* Die Metamorphose des Dinges, Palais des Beaux-Arts, Brussels, 71; Relativerend Realisme, Stedelijk van Abbemuseum, Eindhoven, The Neth, 72; Sharp-Focus Realism, Sidney Janis Gallery, NY, 72; Verkehrskultur, Westfalische Kunstverein, Munster, WGer, 72; solo exhibs, Louis Meisel Gallery, NY, 94, White Chevy Red Trailer: John Salt Paintings, Prints and other Works from 1953-1997, Wolfhampton Mus & Art Galleries, Silk Top Hat Gallery, Ludlow, Eng, 97; Paperwork, Louis W Meisel Gallery, NY, 96; Our Century: Selections (with catalog), Housatonic Mus Art, Bridgeport, Conn, 97; Photorealists (with catalog), Savannah Coll Art & Design, Ga, 97. *Teaching:* Instr, various cols of art, Eng, 60-67 & Md Col Art, Baltimore, 67-68. *Bibliog:* Helen Harris (auth), Town and Country, Art and Antiques: The New Realists, 242, 244, 246-247, 10/78; The New Republic (cover), 3/15/80; Gerrit Henry (auth), John Salt, O K Harris, 121, 7/91. *Media:* Oil. *Mailing Add:* c/o O K Harris Works of Art 383 W Broadway New York NY 10012

SALTER, RICHARD MACKINTIRE
PAINTER
b Iowa City, Iowa, May 7, 1940. *Study:* Northern Ariz Univ, BA, 64; Univ Guanajuato, Inst Allende, Mex, MFA, 68. *Work:* Arthur Adams Western Collection, Beloit, Wis; US Dept Interior, Washington, DC; Miller Brewing Co, Milwaukee, Wis; Univ Wis, Green Bay; Northern Ariz Univ. *Comn:* Com Design, US Borax Co, Boron, Calif, 65-66; Photography, Orput & Orput, Architects, Rockford, Ill, 71. *Exhib:* Mitchell Mus, Mt Vernon, Ill, 81; Smithsonian Inst, 82; Kennedy Ctr, 82; Solo exhib, Alverno Coll, Milwaukee, 82; Appleton Gallery Fine Arts, Wis, 83; and many other solo & group exhibs. *Teaching:* Instr painting, Stanislaus State Col, 68; instr creative photog, Univ Wis-Green Bay, 73. *Awards:* First Prizes, Red Cloud Indian Art Show, Pine Ridge, SDak & Heard Indian Art Show, Phoenix. *Bibliog:* Platt Cline (auth), NAU Show, Ariz Daily Sun, 73; Barbara Manger (auth), Salter Exhib, Mid-West Art Mag, 74 & 77. *Mem:* Rockford Art Asn; Wis Painters & Sculptors Asn; Coll Art Asn Am. *Media:* Acrylic, Mixed. *Dealer:* Segal Gallery New York NY; Cudahy Gallery Milwaukee Art Ctr Milwaukee WI. *Mailing Add:* 414 Forest Rd Mount Dora FL 32757

SALTZ, JERRY
CRITIC, CURATOR
b Chicago, Ill, Feb 19, 1951. *Study:* Art Inst Chicago, BFA, 73; Fashion Inst Tech, Grad Studies, 89 & 90. *Collection Arranged:* Recent Tendencies in Black & White, Sydney Janis Gallery, 73; A Drawing Show, Cabel Gallery, NY, 87; and over 75 shows at NAME Gallery, Chicago, 73-78. *Pos:* Founder & dir, NAME Gallery, 73-78;

contrib, ed Arts Mag, 87-; contrib ed, Balcon Mag, 89; contribr, Flash Art; sr art critic, Village Voice, 98-, NY Magazine, 2007-. *Awards:* Nat Endowment Arts Grant, 80; Frank Jewett Mather Award, Coll Art Asn, 2007. *Publ:* Coauth, Sketchbook with Voices, Alfred Van der Marck, 86; auth, Beyond Boundaries: New York's New Art, Alfred Van der Marck, 87; numerous exhibition catalog essays

SALTZMAN, MARVIN
PAINTER, DRAFTSMAN
b Chicago, Ill, 1931. *Study:* Art Inst Chicago, 54-56; Univ Southern Calif, BFA, 58, MFA, 59. *Work:* Nat Mus Am Art, Washington; Univ Calif, Berkeley Art Mus; Ackland Art Mus, Chapel Hill, NC; NC Mus Art; Nat Acad Sci, Washington, DC. *Exhib:* Los Angeles Artists & Vicinity Ann, Los Angeles Co Mus, 57-59; solo, Nat Acad Sci, Washington, 87; Durham Arts Coun, NC, 91; Peninsula Fine Arts Ctr, Newport News, Va, 92; Greenville Mus Art, NC, 93; Waterworks Ctr, Salisbury, NC, 93; Ackland Art Mus, NC, 97; French Embassy, Washington, DC, 99-2007; and many others. *Teaching:* prof painting, Univ NC, Chapel Hill, 67-97, studio chmn, 67-74 & 86-88, chmn fine arts div, 76-79, emer prof, 97-. *Awards:* Pogue Fel, 78-79; Sam Ragan Award, St Andrews Col; NC award, Fine Arts, 98. *Media:* Oil, Graphite. *Publ:* Places: Graphite Drawings, 98; Serigraphs & Poems, Chapel Hill Gravel, 72. *Dealer:* info@themahlerfineart.com (The Mahler Fine Art); Minta@mintabell.com (Minta Bell Design). *Mailing Add:* 717 Emory Dr Chapel Hill NC 27517-3011

SALVESEN, BRITT
CURATOR, EDUCATOR
Study: Trinity Univ, San Antonio, BA (art hist, magna cum laude), 1989; Courtauld Inst, London, MA, 1991; Univ Chicago, PhD (art hist), 1997. *Collection Arranged:* Danny Lyon: The Bikeriders, Pictures and Audio from the 1960s, 2003 & Super Hits of the 70s: Photographs from the Collection, 2004-2005, Milwaukee Art Mus; Harry Callahan: The Photographer at Work, Ctr for Creative Photog, 2006; Garry Winogrand: Four Edges and the Facts, Phoenix Art Mus, 2007; Making a Photograph: Iconic Images and Their Origins, Ctr for Creative Photography, 2007-2008. *Pos:* Assoc ed scholarly publ, Art Inst Chicago, 1994-2003; assoc cur prints, drawings & photographs, Milwaukee Art Mus, 2003-2004; cur, Univ Ariz Ctr for Creative Photog, 2004-2008, interim dir, 2007-2008, dir & chief cur, 2008-2009; dept head & cur prints & drawings, Wallis Annenberg Dept Photog, Los Angeles County Mus Art, 2009-. *Teaching:* Adj prof hist photog, Columbia Coll, 1999; adj prof art hist, Univ Ariz, 2008-. *Awards:* Getty Curatorial Rsch fel, 2007; artist-in-residence, Rockefeller Found, Bellagio Ctr, 2008. *Mem:* Print Coun Am; Asn Art Mus Curators; Coll Art Assn; Oracle. *Publ:* Auth, Eric Payson and the Idea of America, In: You Can't Spell America without Eric, PowerHouse Bks, 2006; Geoffrey James and the Art of Description, In: Utopia/Dystopia: The Photographs of Geoffrey James, Nat Gallery Can, 2008

SALVEST, JOHN
SCULPTOR, EDUCATOR
b Kearny, NJ, Feb 13, 1955. *Study:* Duke Univ, BA, 77; Univ Iowa, MA (English), 79, MFA, 83. *Work:* NJ State Mus, Trenton; Bristol-Myers Squibb Collection, Princeton, NJ; DePauw Univ Permanent Art Collection, Greencastle, Ind; Zimmerli Mus Rutgers Univ, New Brunswick, NJ; Univ Iowa Mus Art, Iowa City. *Comn:* Sculpture, Salina Art Ctr, Kans, 98; sculpture, Ark State Univ, Jonesboro, 99; sculpture, Memphis Pub Libr, Tenn, 2001; sculpture, Cannon Ctr Performing Arts, Memphis, 2003; sculpture, Hartsfield Int Airport, Atlanta, 2004. *Exhib:* Brooks Biennial, Memphis Brooks Mus Art, Tenn, 92; Tijd Tekens (Marking Time), Gallery Quartair, The Hague, The Neth, 95; New Am Talent, Austin Mus Art, Tex, 96-97; Triennial, New Orleans Mus Art, 98; Birdspace, Contemp Arts Ctr, New Orleans, 2004; What Business Are You In?, Atlanta Contemp Ctr, 2005; solo exhib, Inventory: Selections & Evaluations, City Gallery Chastain, Atlanta, Ga, 96; Meditation 7.21, Forum for Contemp Art, St Louis, Mo, 97; Nothing Endures, New Mus Contemp Art, New York, 98; Time on His Hands, Phoenix Art Mus, Ariz, 99-2000; Texture, Ark Arts Ctr, Little Rock, 2002; New Glory, Cheekwood Mus Art, Nashville, Tenn, 2002; Fly, etc, Bernice Steinbaum Gallery, Miami, Fla, 2005; No Time for Sorrow, Morgan Lehman Gallery, New York, 2006. *Teaching:* Vis artist, sculpture, Univ Memphis, Tenn, 85-86; prof art, sculpture, Ark State Univ, Jonesboro, 89-. *Awards:* Ark Arts Coun Fel, 92; Nat Endowment for the Arts Fel, 93; Pollock-Krasner Found Grant, 98. *Bibliog:* Felicia Feaster (auth) Inventory: Selections & Evaluations, City Gallery at Chastain, 96; Debra Wilbur (auth) Studio View: John Salvest, New Art Examiner, 3/98; Kim Levin (auth) Time on His Hands, Phoenix Art Mus, 99. *Mem:* Coll Art Asn; Southeastern Coll Art Conf. *Media:* Mixed Media, Objects and Installations. *Publ:* Coauth, Composition Book, Salina Art Ctr, 95. *Dealer:* Rudolph Projects 1836 Richmond Ave Houston TX 77098; Morgan Lehman Gallery 317 10th Ave New York NY 10001; Bernice Steinbaum Gallery 3550 N Miami Ave Miami FL 33127

SAMBURG, GRACE (BLANCHE)
PAINTER, LITHOGRAPHER
b New York, NY. *Study:* Art Students League, painting with Morris Kantor & Raphael Soyer; New Sch Social Res, stage design & lighting; Contemp Art Gallery Graphic Workshop, with Michael Ponce de Leon; also with Philip Guston. *Work:* Slide Collection, Mus Fine Arts, Boston. *Exhib:* Silvermine Guild Artists Ann, New Canaan, Conn, 59; Works on Paper, Brooklyn Mus, New York, 75; Chatham Coll, Pittsburgh, Pa, 76; Randolph-Macon Women's Coll, Lynchburg, Va, 77; solo exhibs, Kornbluth Gallery, Fairlawn, NJ, 83 & Péne DuBois Gallery, New York, 86; Green Mt Gallery, New York, 73; John McEnroe Gallery, New York, 96; Prince St Gallery Invitational, New York, 2001; Long Beach Island Found 3rd Ann Juried Competition, 2002; Juried exhib, Studio Montclair, NJ, 2005; Art Ctr Northern NJ, Natdo Juried Show, 2006; and others. *Bibliog:* Lawrence Campbell (auth), article, Art News, 9/73; Gordon Brown (auth), article, Arts Mag, 11/73; Lucy Lippard (auth), From the Center, Feminist Essays on Women's Art, Dutton, 76; Lucy Lippard (auth), Household images in art, Ms Mag, 9/73. *Mem:* Women in the Arts. *Media:* Oil on Canvas. *Publ:* Contribr, Arts Mag, & Art News, 67. *Dealer:* Kornbluth Gallery Fair Lawn NJ; Péne DuBois Gallery New York NY. *Mailing Add:* 63 Highwood Terrace Weehawken NJ 07087-6814

SAMIMI, MEHRDAD
ILLUSTRATOR, PAINTER
b Mashad, Aug 14, 1939; US citizen. *Study:* Sch Archit, Univ Ariz, 64. *Work:* Calif State Capitol, Sacramento; Cosmopolitan Fine Arts, La Jolla, Calif; Lynn House, City Comn Art, Antioch, Calif. *Comn:* Governor's portrait, Sacramento, Calif, 92; portrait of Clarence Woodard of Orinda, Calif, comn by Woodard's children, 92; mayoral portrait, New Orleans Gallier Hall, 93; recreation of fire destroyed portrait, comn by Judith Woods, Oakland, Calif, 93; portrait, comn by Dr & Mrs Safavi, Dallas, Tex, 94. *Exhib:* Solo exhibs, Art Circle, Vancouver, BC, 86, Los Angeles, Calif, 87; group exhib, Kertesz Fine Art, San Francisco, Calif, 90; Oakland Art Asn, Kaiser Ctr, Oakland, Calif, 91, Pan Pacific, Oakland, Calif, 92; Inside/Outside, Lynn House, Antioch, Calif, 94. *Teaching:* Pvt lessons landscape, still lifes & portrait, 90-94. *Awards:* Art Calif Mag Discovery Award, Juried Traditional Realist, 93. *Bibliog:* Doc, Univ Ariz, 63; Portrait lost in Oakland fire reborn, San Francisco Chronicle, 93; Portrait lost in fire reborn, Assoc Press, 93. *Mem:* Calif Art Club; Smithsonian Nat Portrait Gallery. *Media:* Oil. *Dealer:* Cosmopolitan Fine Art 7932 Girard Ave La Jolla CA 92037

SAMPLE, HILARY
ARCHITECT
Study: Syracuse Univ, BA (archit); Princeton Univ, MA (archit). *Exhib:* Young Architects Program PSI/Mod Mus Art, New York, 2004 & 2007; SoftCell, Henry Urbach Archit, New York, 2005; Living Spaces, ICFF, New York, 2007; Design Triennale - iVY, Design Life Now, ICA, Boston, 2007; Venice Biennale Experimental Archit Padiglione Italia Pavillion, 2008; Overhang, Tobias, Putrih & MOS, Baltic Centre Contemp Art, New Castle, England, 2009. *Pos:* Proj architect, Office for Met Archit, Rotterdam & Skidmore, Owings and Merrill, New York; founding principal, MOS. *Teaching:* Instr, Univ Toronto, Northeastern Univ & SUNY Buffalo; asst prof, Yale Sch Archit. *Awards:* Reyner Banham Teaching Fel, SUNY Buffalo; Young Architects award, PS1/Mod Mus Art, 2009; Archit award, Am Acad Arts & Letts, 2010

SAMPSON, FRANK
PAINTER, PRINTMAKER
b Edmore, NDak, Mar 24, 1928. *Study:* Concordia Coll, BA, 50; Univ Iowa, MFA, 52; studied printmaking with Mauricio Lasansky, 56-59. *Work:* Libr Cong, Washington, DC; Walker Art Ctr, Minneapolis; Nelson-Atkins Mus, Kansas City; Sheldon Mem Art Ctr, Lincoln, Nebr; Joslyn Art Mus, Omaha, Nebr. *Exhib:* Solo exhibs, Walker Art Ctr, Minneapolis, 54, Sheldon Mem Art Ctr, Lincoln, Nebr, 64 & Denver Art Mus, 75; Mid-Am, Nelson-Atkins Mus, Kansas City, 65; 13th Am Drawing Biennial, Norfolk Mus Arts, Va, 69; 21st Nat Exhib Prints, Libr Cong, Washington, DC, 69; Drawings from Nine States, Mus Fine Arts, Houston, Tex, 70; Regionalism: Seven Views, Joslyn Art Mus, Omaha, Nebr, 79; Hanga Ann, Tokyo Metrop Art Gallery, Japan; retrospective, Boulder Mus Contemp Art, Boulder, Colo, 97; Arvada Art Ctr, Colo, 2003. *Teaching:* Prof painting, drawing & printmaking, Univ Colo, Boulder, 61-90, prof fine arts emer, 90-. *Awards:* Fulbright Grant (painting & printmaking), Brussels, Belg, 59-60; Ford Purchase, Walker Biennial, 64; Purchase Prize, Minn Mus Art, St Paul, 71. *Bibliog:* Michele de Ghelderode (auth), D'ou Viens Tu, Beau Nuage?, Le Cahier des Arts, Bruxelles, Belg, 4/61; Walter Simon (auth), The collector, Colo Quart, Univ Colo, summer 77; Merrill Mahaffey (auth), Contemporary western painting, the new western art, Southwestern Art, fall 77. *Media:* Oil, Acrylic. *Dealer:* Sandra Phillips Gallery 420 W 12th Ave Denver CO 80204. *Mailing Add:* 1912 Columbine Ave Boulder CO 80302

SAMSON, CARL JOSEPH
PAINTER, INSTRUCTOR
b Sandusky, Ohio, Jan 7, 1961. *Study:* Study under Allan R Banks, 1975-79 & 1981-83, R H Ives Gammell, 1979-80 & Richard (Atelier) Lack, 1983-85. *Work:* Music Hall Grand Gallery, Cincinnati, Ohio; Ohio State Senate Chambers, Capitol Bldg, Columbus; Northminster Presby Church, Tucson, Ariz. *Comn:* Sen Stanley Aronoff (portrait), 93, Sen Theodore Gray (portrait), 94, State of Ohio, Columbus; Hershel Farmer (portrait), Cintas Corp, Cincinnati, Ohio, 93; James DeBlasis (portrait), Cincinnati Opera Inc, Ohio, 93; Patricia Corbett, Corbett Found, Cincinnati, Ohio, 95. *Exhib:* Solo show, Cincinnati Art Galleries, 95; PAPA Ann Catalina Show, Avalon, Calif, 95; ASCR Traveling Exhib, Boston, Minneapolis, Milwaukee, 96; The Legacy Lives, Lever House Gallery, NY, 96; Am-Rus Plein-Air Exhib, Kolomna, Russ, 96. *Teaching:* Instr drawing, Atelier Fine Arts, Sandusky, Ohio, 1981-83; pvt instr, Cincinnati, Ohio, 1986-; asst dir drawing & painting, Atelier Plein Air Studies, Safety Harbor, Fla, 1994-. *Awards:* John Howard Sanden Award for Excellence in Portrait Painting, Nat Portrait Sem, Atlanta, 1993; Artist's Mag Award, Cincinnati Art Club Viewpoint Exhib, 1995; Portrait Inst Award for Distinguished Achievement in Portrait Painting, Nat Portrait Competition, New York, 1996. *Bibliog:* Mary McCarty (auth), It's the real thing, Cincinnati Mag, 10/92; Owen Findsen (auth), Prized portraits-Cincinnatian Carl Samson paints his way to top prize in prestigious competition, Cincinnati Enquirer, 5/24/93; M Stephen Doherty (auth), Prize-winning portrait-painting techniques, Am Artist, 12/96. *Mem:* Am Soc Classical Realism; Am Artists Prof League; Cincinnati Art Club (vpres); Am Soc Portrait Artists (chmn 2002-). *Media:* Oil on Linen Canvas. *Publ:* Auth, A journey through Monet country, 6/91 & Cincinnati past & present, spring 1992, Classical Realism Quart, Am Soc Classical Realism; Three steps to polished portraits, Artists Mag, 6/94; contribr, Realism in Revolution-The Art of the Boston School, Taylor Publ Co, 1985. *Dealer:* Cincinnati Art Galleries 605 Main St Cincinnati OH 45202. *Mailing Add:* 2152 Alpine Pl Cincinnati OH 45206

SAMUELS, JOHN STOCKWELL, III
COLLECTOR, PATRON
b Galveston, Tex, Sept 15, 1933. *Study:* Tex A&M Univ, BA, 54 & MS, 54; Harvard Univ, BL, 60. *Collection:* American, French, Italian & Pre-Columbian paintings and decorative arts. *Mailing Add:* 1702 Broadway Galveston TX 77550

SAMUELS (JOESAM), JOE
SCULPTOR
b Harlem, NY, 1939. *Study:* Univ Mass, Amherst; self taught. *Work:* Cleveland Rapid Transit System, Ohio; Anchorage Mus Hist & Art; Univ of Central Fla, Orlando; 53 sculptures, Hide n Seek; Sadie, Wilmington/Imperial Metro Rail Station, Los Angeles, Calif. *Exhib:* Oakland Mus, Collectors Gallery, Calif; No Am Sculpture Exhib, Golden, Colo; Nat Black Arts Festival, Atlanta, Ga; Museo Nat de Belles Artes, Santiago, Chile; Solo exhib, Albertson-Peterson Gallery, Winter Park, Fla, Morgan/Monceaux Gallery, Seattle, Wash, Mus of African Art, Los Angeles, Calif, 2000, Richmond Art Ctr, Calif, 2001. *Awards:* Compton Found Fel; Nat Endowment for Arts, 85-86; Artist-in-Residence, Djerassi Found, 99. *Media:* Mixed. *Mailing Add:* 221 Trumbull St Apt 2403 Hartford CT 06103

SAMUELSON, FRED BINDER
PAINTER, EDUCATOR
b Harvey, Ill, Nov 29, 1925. *Study:* Univ Chicago, 46-53; Sch Art Inst Chicago, BFA, 51 & MFA, 53. *Work:* Denver Art Mus, Colo; Witte Mus, San Antonio, Tex; Ohio Univ, Athens; Tex Fine Arts Asn, Laguna Gloria Mus, Austin. *Comn:* Acrylic mural, Hemisfair 68, San Antonio. *Exhib:* 60th Ann Exhib Western Art, Denver Art Mus, 54; 20th Ann Tex Painting & Sculpture Exhib, Dallas Mus Fine Art, 58; Southwest Am Art Ann, Okla Art Ctr, 60; Segundo Festival Pictorico Acapulco, 64; 53rd Tex Fine Arts Asn Ann, 64; 35th Westmreland Art Nat, Westmoreland Co Community Coll, 2009. *Teaching:* Prof painting & drawing, Inst Allende, San Miguel de Allende, Mex, 55-63, head grad studies & painting, 65-80; chmn fac, San Antonio Art Inst, 63-64. *Awards:* Purchase Award, Denver Art Mus, 54; Purchase Award, Tex Fine Arts Asn, Laguna Gloria Mus, Austin, 64; Purchase Award, Ohio Univ, Athens, 64; Art Students League Award, Nat Soc Painters in Casein & Acrylic Inc, 2010; NS PCA award, Nat Soc Painters & Casein & Acrylic Inc, 2010; Artist In Res, Daytona Art League, 2010-. *Bibliog:* Leonard Brooks (auth), Oil Painting Traditional and New, 59 & Wash Drawings, 61, Van Nostrand Reinhold; interview, Time-Life, 65. *Media:* Acrylic. *Publ:* The Daytona Beach News Jour, 2014; Artifacts Revival News, Smyrna Beach, Fla

SANABRIA, ROBERT
SCULPTOR, WRITER
b El Paso, Tex, Aug 20, 1931. *Study:* Univ Md, BA, 65, MFA, 79. *Work:* Wichita Art Mus, Kans; Tweed Mus Art, Duluth, Minn; Miss Mus Art, Jackson; Univ Md, College Park; Four Seasons Hotel, Chgo, Ill; DC Arts & Humanities Coun; Equity Residential, NY, 2013. *Comn:* bronze/copper abstract tree sculpture, comn by Dr Wm Rutherford, Wash, 91; bronze/copper abstract tree sculpture, comn by Beth Sholom Synagogue, Fredrick, Md, 94; bronze/copper fountain sculpture, Dr & Ms Ronald Hodges, Eugene, Ore, 96; abstract bronze/copper flame sculpture, comn by Kemp Mill Synagogue, Silver Spring, Md, 2000; Menorahs, Beth Sholom Synagogue, 2004; bronze/copper abstract tree sculpture, Ralph Terkowitz, McLean, Va, 2005; bronze/copper abstract tree sculpture, Shady Grove Adventist Hosp, Rockville, Md, 2006; Bronze/copper fountain, Butterball Farms, Grand Rapids, Mich, 2008; Bronze/copper abstract sculpture, Village of Palestine, Ill, 2008; triple step, Paul Lawrence, Princeton, NJ, 2010; Volante II, Paul Lawrence, Princeton, NJ, 2010; copper/bronze sculpture, Viento, Weinberg Galleries, Pacific Palisades, Calif, 2012. *Exhib:* Md Coll Art & Design, Silver Spring, 90; Fridholm Fine Arts Gallery, Asheville, NC, 91; Invitational Outdoor Sculpture Exhib, Montgomery Col, Rockville, Md, 92; Invitational, Washington Abstract Sculpture, The Am Univ, Washington, DC, 93; Art in Pub Places, Glenview Mansion, Rockville, Md, 96; Sculpture on the Grounds, Rockville Civic Ctr Park, Rockville, Md, 98; Flora: Sculptures of Natural World, Botanic Garden, Washington, DC; Dulles Int Airport, Washington, DC, 2007; and others. *Pos:* Artist-in-residence, Fairfax Co Sch, Mobil Oil Co, 92. *Teaching:* Instr sculpture, Art League Workshops, Alexandria, Va, 75-78. *Bibliog:* CB Tomlins, (auth) Water Sculpture: USA, 86; Galleries, Washington Post, 90; Gale Woldron (auth), On a Grand Scale, Loudoun Mag, summer 2006. *Mem:* Loudoun Arts Coun, Leesburg, Va (vpres, 87-92); Washington Sculptor's Group, Washington, DC; ISC Sculpture.org. *Media:* All Media, Metal-Welded. *Publ:* Auth, Fees for commissions, Sculptors' Int, Vol 1, No 6, 83; A World Apart, A World of Art, Vol 5, No 6, 11-12, 2000; Stewing in the Melting Pot, Capital Books, 2001; The Memoir of a Real American; Make Love to Me, Tertulia Mag, 2007; The Last Californio, Paraguas Books, 2011. *Mailing Add:* 18163 Canby Rd Leesburg VA 20175

SANCHEZ, JOHN
PAINTER, PHOTOGRAPHER
b 1973. *Exhib:* Solo exhib, Emblems of a Prior Order, UCLA, Los Angeles, Calif, 2004; Resident Artists' Exhib, Cooper Union, New York City, 2004; Portraits, Cooper Brook Gallery, 2004; An American Album, J Paul Getty Mus, Los Angeles, Calif, 2004; Amory Ctr for the Arts, Los Angeles, Calif; Berkeley Art Ctr, Berkeley, Calif; Contemp Arts Forum Gallery, Santa Barbara, Calif; group exhib: Robert Miller Gallery, New York, 2005, Sikkema Jenkins Gallery, New York, 2006, Gallery 402, New York, 2007, Santa Monica Mus Art, Calif, 2007, James Cohan Gallery, New York, 2007, Anderson Ranch Arts Ctr, Snowmass Village, Colo, 2008. *Awards:* Artist's Residency, Cooper Union for the Advan of Sci & Art, New York City, 2004. *Bibliog:* Articles: Artnews, 6/2000, Los Angeles Times, 6/13/2004, Los Angeles Times West Mag, 4/22/2007, 50,000 Beds exhibit catalog: Aldrich Contemp Art Mus, Artspace, Real Art Ways, 7/2007, New York Times, 7/8/2007 & 8/5/2007, Impermanence: Editions of Contemporary Music, Munich, Germany, spring 2008, Aperture, spring 2008. *Media:* Painting, Photography, Filmmaking

SANCHEZ, THORVALD
PAINTER
b Havana, Cuba, June 11, 1933; US citizen. *Work:* Milwaukee Art Ctr, Wis. *Exhib:* Pintura Cubana, Caracas, Venezuela, 72; 15th Ann Hortt Competition, Ft Lauderdale, Fla, 73; 35th Ann Exhib, Soc Four Arts, Palm Beach, Fla, 73; East Coast Painters, Longboat Key Art Ct0, Sarasota, Fla, 74; Fla Artists, Norton Mus, West Palm Beach, 75. *Awards:* Best of Show Award, Fla Gulf Coast 9th Show, High Mus Art, Atlanta, Ga, 74. *Bibliog:* Georgia Dupuis (auth), Transition theme of Sanchez work, Palm Beach Post, 74. *Mem:* Fla Artist Group. *Media:* Acrylic, Collage. *Dealer:* Center Gallery 327 Acadia Rd West Palm Beach FL 33401. *Mailing Add:* 1029 N Palmway Lake Worth FL 33460-2313

SAN CHIRICO, JOANIE
ARTIST
Comn: Public Art Library Project, Atrium, Ocean County Library Headquarters, Toms River NJ; Wallhanging,World Trade Center Memorial, NY. *Exhib:* Uncommon Threads/Uncommon Women, Cleopatra Steps Out Gallery, Asbury Park, NJ, 2000; Fiber Revolution, Brodsky Gallery, Chauncey Conference Ctr, Princeton, NJ, 2003; Beyond the Stitch, Ocean Co Artists' Guild, Island Heights, NJ, 2004; Common Thread, Phoenix Gallery, NY, 2005; Beyond the Stitch II, Ocean Co Artists' Guild, Island Height, NJ, 2006. *Collection Arranged:* E-Conversation Keeps a Group Connected, Surface Design Asn Newsletter, summer 2004; Creating Opportunities in Art Galleries, The Professional Quilter, winter 2005; Spotlight on Education: The Quilt/Surface Design Symposium, Surface Design Asn J, spring 2005. *Bibliog:* Footnotes, Jersey Footlights, NY Times, 2003; Feature Story, Weekend, Ocean Co Observer, 2004; New Zealand Quilter, 2005. *Media:* Independent Curator. *Publ:* Surface Design Asn Newsletter, Summer, 2004; The Prof Quilter, Winter, 2005; Surface Design Asn Journal, Spring, 2005. *Mailing Add:* 1064 Lake Placid Dr Toms River NJ 08753

SANDELMAN, JONATHAN (JON) E
PATRON
Study: Adelphia Univ, BA; Cardozo Sch Law, JD. *Pos:* Deputy head global equities, managing dir, equity derivatives Salomon Brothers, formerly; head equity fin, prod NationsBank (now Bank Am Securities), New York City, 98-2002; head equities, Bank Am Securities LLC, 2002-04, pres, 2004-, head debt & equities, 2004-. *Mem:* Whitney Mus Am Art (trustee, currently)

SANDEN, JOHN HOWARD
PAINTER, INSTRUCTOR
b Austin, Tex, Aug 6, 1935. *Study:* Minneapolis Sch Art, BFA, 56; Art Students League, New York; Houghton Col, DFA, 94. *Work:* US Capitol & NASA Hq, Washington, DC; Fifth Ave Presby Church & New York Univ, NY; Royal Palace, Oyo, Nigeria; NY Presbyterian Hospital, NY; Weill-Cornell Medical College, NY; Carnegie Hall, NY; US Dept Defence, NY. *Pos:* Pres & found, Portrait Inst, New York, 74-; chmn & found, Nat Portrait Sem, 79-. *Teaching:* Instr, Art Students League, 71-. *Awards:* John Singer Sargent Medal, Am Soc Portrait Artists, 94; Portrait Brokers Lifetime Achievement Award, 2006. *Bibliog:* Doreen Mangan (auth), Portrait of a portraitist, Am Artist Mag, 3/75; Joe Singer (auth), Painting Men's Portraits, Watson-Guptill, 76 & 77; Eunice Agar (auth), John Howard Sanden, Am Artist Mag, 11/83. *Mem:* Leading Am Portrait Painters (coun mem). *Media:* Oil. *Publ:* Auth, Painting The Head in Oil, 76 & Successful Portrait Painting, 81, Watson-Guptill; Portraits from Life, North Light Publications, 1999; Portraits of John Howard Sanden, Madison Square Press, 2001; Face to Face with Greatness, The Adventure of Portrait Painting, The Portrait Inst Press, 2009. *Dealer:* Portraits Inc 7 W 51st St NY 10019; Portraits South 4008 Barrett Dr Raleigh NC 27609; Portrait Brokers of America Birmingham Alabama 35213. *Mailing Add:* 100 Cains Hill Rd Ridgefield CT 06877

SANDER, SHERRY SALARI
SCULPTOR
b McCloud, CA, July 16, 1941. *Work:* Denver Zoo, Denver, Colo; Nat Mus Wildlife Art, Jackson, Wyo; City of Bend, Bend, Ore; Okla City Zoo, Oklahoma City, Okla; Benson Park Sculpture Garden, Loveland, Colo; Leanin' Tree Mus Western Art, Boulder, Colo; Buffalo Bill Mus, Cody, Wyo; Genesee Country Mus, Mumford, NY; Gerald Ford Amphitheater, Vail, Colo; High Desert Mus, Bend, Ore; Leigh Yawkey Woodson Art Mus, Wausau, Wis; Big Sky Resort, Huntley Lodge, Big Sky, Mont; Kentucky Dept Fish & Wildlife Resources, Frankfort, Ky; Int Mus Contemp Masters Fine Art, San Antonio, Tex; City of Kalispell, Kalispell, Mont. *Comn:* Grizzly Monumental, Big Sky of Montana, Big Sky, Mont, 90; Whitetail Deer Monumental, Private Party, Aspen, Colo, 95. *Exhib:* Soc Animal Artists 79-98, 2002, 2008-2015; Nat Acad Western Art, 82-95; Nat Sculpture Soc, 85, 90-96, 99, 2001, 2006, 2009; Birds in Art, Leigh Yawkey Woodson Art Mus, Wausaw, Wis, 90, 92, 94-96, 98-99, 2007, 2011, 2012; Rendezvous '95, Thomas Gilcrease Mus, Tulsa, Okla, 95; Prixde West, Nat Cowboy and Western Heritage Mus, 96-2012; 100 Years of NSS of USA in Italy, Palazzo Mediceo, Seravezza, Italy, 98; Masterworks of Am Sculpture, Fleischer Mus, Scottsdale, Ariz, 99; Wildlife Art for a New Century II, 2005, Western Visions, 1992-2015, Nat Mus of Wildlife Art, Jackson, Wyo, 2104 Exhib and Tour, America's Parks II. *Pos:* Juror, CM Russell Auction, 80, Soc Animal Artists, NY, 93 & AmWomen Artists, 2015. *Teaching:* Instr, Scottsdale Artists Sch, Scottsdale, Ariz, 89. *Awards:* Gold Medal, Nat Acad of Western Art (NAWA), 83, Silver Medal, 86; Best of Show, CM Russell Auction, CM Russell Mus, 88; CM Russell Featured Artist, 2007; Purchase Award, Patron's Choice, Int Masters, Int Mus of Contemp Masters, 2002; Best of Show, Soc Animal Artists, 83, Awards of Excellence, 79, 84, 86, 88, 2009, 2010; Ethology Award for Best Depiction on Natural Behavior 3-D, 2014; WmE Weiss Purchase Award, 87, Buffalo Bill Hist Ctr, Cody, Wyo, Peoples Choice Award, 87, Artists Choice Award, 95; Best of Show for Extraordinary Artistic Achievement in any Media, 2006, 1st Place 3D Art, Desert Cabellaros Western Mus, Wickenburg, Ariz, 2010, 2011, 2012; Purchase Award, 2015; 1st Place Sculpture, Western and Wild

Horse Art Show, 2011; Allied Artists of Am Helen Gapen Oehler Mem Award, 89; Silver Medal 91 & 93; Raymond H. Brumer Mem Award, 2000; Elliot Liskin Mem Award, 2004; Ranieri Sculpture Casting Award, 2008; Leonard J. Meiselman Award, 2009; Pietro & Alfrieda Montana Mem Award, 2011; Gold Medal, 2012; Nat Sculpture Soc Pietro & Alfrieda Montana Mem Award, 1992; Bedi-Makky Foundry Award, 1996; The Briscoe Mus Artists Choice Award, 2012; Am Women Artists Best in Show, 2013. *Bibliog:* Greenhouse Gallery (auth), Leading Ladies Part I, Am Art Collector, 2006; Joan Brown (auth) Sculptor Creates a Wildlife Haven, Wildlife Art, 2006; Vickie Stavig (auth), Magical Medium, Art of the West, 2006; Western Art Collector, Intense Expressions: Sherry Salati Sander, 2007; Emily Van Cleve, The Studio, May/June 2007; ForbesLife Mountain Time, Bronze Sculpture, 2009; Vicki Stavig (auth), Art of the West, Great Challanges, Great Rewards, 2010; Michele Corriel (auth), Western Art & Architecture, Illuminations, 2013; John Orrelle (auth) The Red Fox in Art (book), 2013. *Mem:* Allied Artists of Am; Nat Acad of Western Art (NAWA); Nat Sculpture Soc Fel; Soc of Animal Artists (master signature artist); Am Women Artists. *Media:* Metal, Cast (Bronze). *Mailing Add:* PO Box 5448 Kalispell MT 59903-5448

SANDERS, IDA
COLLECTOR
Awards: Named one of Top 200 Collectors, ARTnews mag, 2009-11. *Collection:* Modern and contemporary art, especially sculpture; African art

SANDERS, JEANNETTE & MARTIJN
COLLECTOR
b Scheidam, Netherlands. *Study:* Univ Mich (bus admin). *Hon Degrees:* Univ Nyenrode, PhD, 2002. *Pos:* Mng dir, Jogchem's Theaters, formerly, Het Concergebouw, Amsterdam, 1982-2006; chmn, AVRO, Amsterdam, formerly; cons, 2006-; chmn, Found Bernard Haitink Scholarship, Worldwide Video Festival, Sahel Opera Found; bd dirs, Jogthem's Theater, Found Het Willem Mengelberg Archief, Rembrandt Soc, Amsterdam Arena, Intermusica. *Awards:* Gold Medal of the City of Amsterdam; Knight, Order of Oranje Nassau, 1996; Named one of Top 200 Collectors, ARTnews mag, 2003-13; Hon Commander, Order Brit Empire, 2005; Int Citation of Merit, Int Soc Performing Arts', 2010. *Collection:* Post-1980s American and European art. *Mailing Add:* Sahel Opera Found Hoge Nieuwstraat 30 The Hague 2514 EL Netherlands

SANDERS, JOOP A
PAINTER
b Amsterdam, Holland, Oct 6, 21; US citizen. *Study:* Art Students League, with George Grosz; also with De Kooning. *Work:* Stedelijke Mus, Amsterdam; Munic Mus, The Hague; Belzalel Mus, Jerusalem; Dillard Univ. *Exhib:* Ninth St Show, 51; Stable Shows, 52-55; Solo retrospective, Stedelijke Mus, 60; Carnegie Inst, 60; Options, Mus Contemp Art, Chicago, 68; Solo exhib, Alfred Kren Gallery, NY, 86; Gallery Biderman, Munich, Ger, 92. *Teaching:* Vis lectr, Carnegie Inst Technol, spring 65; prof painting, State Univ NY Col, New Paltz, 66-; vis lectr, Univ Calif, Berkeley, spring 68. *Awards:* Longview Found Fel, 60-61; Carnegie Inst Technol Res Found Awards, 71-72. *Media:* Oil, Acrylic. *Mailing Add:* 157 Lake Dr Lake Peekskill NY 10537

SANDERS, MARIEKE
COLLECTOR
Study: Vrije Univ Amsterdam, 1982-85. *Pos:* Statenlid, Provinciale Staten van Noord Holland, 1987-99; mem European Parliament, 1999-2004; pres commissaris, Probiblio, 2005-06; rector of pres, Stichting Reprorecht, 2004-2010; mem com of experts on charter for minority languages, Coun of Europe, 2004-; hon consul of Botswana in the Netherlands, 2004-; advisor to coun of ministers on framework convention protection of minorities, Coun of Europe, 2006-. *Awards:* Named one of Top 200 Collectors, ARTNews mag, 2011, 2012. *Collection:* Dutch art; sculpture; contemporary American and European Art

SANDERS, PIET
COLLECTOR
b Schiedam, Neth, 1912. *Pos:* Former sec, Queen Wilhelmina of The Neth; co-founder & hon pres, Neth Arbitration Inst & Int Coun for Commercial Arbitration; principal drafter, UN Convention on Recognition and Enforcement of Foreign Arbitral Award, 1958 & UNCITRAL Arbitration Rules, 1976. *Teaching:* Emer prof & founder, Fac Law, Erasmus Univ, Rotterdam. *Awards:* Named one of Top 200 Collectors, ARTnews mag, 2009-11. *Collection:* Modern and contemporary art, especially sculpture; African art

SANDERS, PIETER, JR
COLLECTOR
Study: Univ Leiden, 1990-96. *Pos:* Advocaat, Loeff Claeys Verbeke, 1996-2003; lawyer, Allen & Overy (formerly Loeff Claeys Verbeke), 1996-2003; art consultant, PS Art Consultancy, 2007-; project dir, Nieuw Dakota International Space for Contemporary Art, 2010-. *Awards:* Named one of Top 200 Collectors, ARTNews Mag, 2011, 2012, 2013. *Collection:* Dutch art; sculpture; contemporary American and European Art

SANDERS, RHEA
PAINTER, WRITER
b Charleston, SC, Nov 6, 1923. *Study:* With Maurice Sterne, 40-44; Pratt Graphics, NY, 83; Cooper Union Sch Continuing Educ, New York, 92. *Work:* High Mus, Atlanta, Ga; Univ SC, Columbia; British Mus Libr, London; Rare Bks Collection, New York Pub Libr; Gibbes Art Mus, Charleston, SC; and others. *Exhib:* NY Tech Col, Brooklyn, 93; First Street Gallery, NY, 94; Ctr for Book Arts, NY, 94; Members Gallery, Albright-Knox Mus, Buffalo, NY, 94; Made by Hand, NGO Forum on Women, Beijing, 95; Juried Arts Competition, Jacques Marchais Mus Tibetan Art, Staten Island, NY, 95; New Work, First St Gallery, NY, 96; NY Pub Libr, 1997; Saho 20 Gallery, New York City, 2000; Prince St Gallery, New York City, 2000; Biennial 2001, Flushing Town Hall, 2001; Queens Community Col, New York City, 2002; Snug Harbor Cult Ctr, NY, 2002; LaGuardia Community Col, Queens, NY, 2002; Berliner Kunsthalle, Berlin, Ger, 2002; NY Pub Libr, NY, 2002; Prince Street Gallery, NY, 2004; Coll of Charleston Libr, Charleston, SC, 2005; numerous local group shows, Broome St Gallery, Prince St Gallery, Frist St Gallery, Blue Mountain Gallery, 2005-2010; Gibbbes mus Art, Charleston, SC, 2006, 2008, 2009. *Awards:* Artist Space Grant, 80, 83; Orgn Independent Artists Grant, 80; Visual Artists Fel Grant, Nat Endowment Arts, 85; Resident Fel, Karolyi Found, Vence, France, 89; Resident Fel, Mishkenot Sha'ananim, Jerusalem, Israel, 93. *Media:* Miscellaneous Media. *Publ:* Auth & illusr, The Fire Gardens of Maylandia, Tradd St Press, 80; Lecture on Egg Tempera (film), Paragon Cable, New York, 90; Rhea Sanders Talks About Her Solo Show (film), Paragon Cable, New York, 94; auth & illusr, At Ravemel 1927, 83. *Mailing Add:* 617 W End Ave New York NY 10024-1607

SANDERSON, WARREN
ART HISTORIAN, LECTURER, ARCHITECT
b Boston, Mass, Feb 9, 1931. *Study:* Boston Univ, MA, 56; NY Univ Inst Fine Arts, PhD, 65. *Pos:* Pres Emer, Can Nat Comt of Int Comt of Hist of Art (Paris); pres asn Villard de Honnecourt for the Interdisciplinary Study of (Medieval) Sci, Tech & Art (Avista, 1992-2000; pres asn for Art Hist, 2001-2002. *Teaching:* Prof hist art & archit, Univ Ill, Chicago, 66-70; prof art hist & criticism, Concordia Univ, Montreal, 76-2006, prof emeritus, 2006-; vis prof art hist, Univ Trier, Ger, 77, 78 & 83; vis prof archit hist, Univ Cologne, Ger, 89; vis scholar, Harvard Fine Arts, 90. *Awards:* Fulbright Fel, 66, 82, 83; Deutsche Forschungsgemeinschaft, 77, 78 & 83; Can Coun Award, 80, 86-89, 96-99; Thyssen Found Award. *Bibliog:* Jeffrey Horrell (auth), article, Art Doc, 10/82; Diane Kay (auth), article, Art Int, 1/3/83; Elaine Cohen (auth), Sharing the joy & discovery of fine works of art, Suburban, 9/28/83; Nigel Hiscock (auth) The Wise Master Builder: Platonic Geometry in Cathedrals, Ashgate Publ (in Speculum), 2002-2004. *Mem:* Soc Archit Historians; Int Comt Hist Art (pres emer, Can Sect); Univ Arts Asn Can; Asn Art Hist (pres 99-01); Coll Art Asn Am; Asn Villard d'Honnecourt for Interdisciplinary Study of Medieval Sci, Technology & Art (pres 92-2000). *Res:* Western art and architecture; Carolingian & Ottonian; art and architecture since 1950. *Interests:* Archit, politics, educ, scis, art & music. *Publ:* Coauth, Hommage--Joseph Beuys 1986, Vie Des Arts, 87; auth, Considerations on the Ottonian Monastic Church of Saint Maximin at Trier, Baukunst Des Mittelalters in Europa Hans Erich Kubach Zum Ft Geburtstag, 89; Art Et Hyperactivite Un perspective Tres Visuelle, Prisme (Psychiatrie, Recherche et Intervention en Sante Mentale de L'enfant), Montreal 93; Early Christian Buildings, 300-600, Astrion Publ, 94; auth, Carolingian, Ottonian & Romanesque Buildings, 760-1130, Astrion Publ; auth, The Plan of St Gall Reconsidered, in Speculum, A Journal of Medieval Studies (Cambr.MA) 60/3, p615-632, 85; auth, Medieval Architecture and Liturgy 750-1400, in Macmillan Dictionary of Art, London, 96; auth, Carolingian Aachen., in Avista Forum Journal, 13/1, p1-14 / 8 illus, 01; auth Geometry on a Carolingian Wall, chapter 1 in Ad Quadratum: Practical Application of Geometry in Medieval Architecture, Ashgate Publ, London, 02; auth, The Practical Application of Geometry in Medieval Architecture, Nancy Wu (ed), Ashgate Publ, London, 2002; auth, Monastic Architecture and the Gorze Reforms Reconsidered, chapter 4 in The White Mantle of Churches...Around the Millennium, Ashgate Publ, UK, 03; auth, review of CB McClendon, Origins of Medieval Archit, CAA Reviews, 2007; and others

SANDGROUND, MARK BERNARD, SR
COLLECTOR, PAINTER
b Boston, Mass, June 6, 1932. *Study:* Univ Mich, BA, 52; Univ Va, LLB, 55, JD, 71 & PhD, Johnson & Wales Univ, 2000. *Work:* The First Chartered Collection, Cracked Eggshells from Pacifica, Delmura Art Inst, 2004. *Exhib:* Hard on the Cutting Room floor, demonstration of film gastronomics, 92. *Pos:* Chmn, The Orient House, Istanbul, Turkey, 2000; chief judge, KC-BBQ-The Jack, (Lynchburg term), 2005-2006. *Teaching:* Prof humanities & cooking, Free Coll, Belgravia, Lower Sch, 65-66; lectr, Johnson & Wales Univ, RI. *Awards:* Star of Mex, 92; Order of the Grand Papal Soc for Peace & Friendship, Columbia, 92; Order of the Grand Enchalata, Mex, 93. *Bibliog:* D Kane (auth), Killer Kane and the White Princess, McGraw, 72; The Gypsie princess (film), Anon, 72. *Mem:* Friends of Corcoran Gallery Art (bd dir, 67-, pres, 68-70); Osuna Gallery Inc, Washington, DC, Miami, Fla & Santa Fe, NMex. *Res:* Graphic works of Jose Louis Cuevas. *Specialty:* Masterpieces from Eastern Shore, Oil on Crab Shells; Unique Collection of paintings and recipes. *Collection:* Cuevas, Rico Lebrun & Anne Truitt. *Publ:* Auth, Collected letters from unknown artists, 1846-1871, pvt publ, 52; Erotica from the Falls Church Collection, 72; Specialties at The Sign of The Whale, 92; HARD on the Cutting Room Floor, pvt publ, 99. *Dealer:* Osuna Gallery Bethesda MD

SANDITZ, LISA
PAINTER
b St Louis, Mo, 1973. *Study:* Studio Art Ctr Int, Florence, Italy, 1994; MacAlester Coll, Minn, BA, 1995; Pratt Inst, Brooklyn, MFA, 2001. *Exhib:* Solo exhibs include The Rite Spot, San Francisco, Calif, 1998, Pratt Inst, Brooklyn, 2001, Onefront Gallery, NY, 2001, PS 122, NY, 2003, CRG Gallery, NY, 2003, 2005, Rodolphe Jansen Gallery, Brussels, 2004, Kemper Mus Contemp Art, Kansas City, Mo, 2006, ACME, Los Angeles, 2006; groups exhibs include Filler, Three Blue Lights, San Francisco, 1998; Pier Show, Brooklyn Working Artist Coalition, NY, 2000; No Comment, Blake-Sherlock Gallery, NY, 2000; Six Artists Drawings, im n il Gallery, Brooklyn, 2000, Hello Franklin, 2003; Need to Know Basis, Geoff Young Gallery, Great Barrington, Mass, 2002; Sugarfree, The Puffin Room, NY, 2002; Singing My Song, ACME, Los Angeles, 2004, Tugboat, 2007; Galerie Tanit, Munich, 2004; No Man's Land, Shoshana Wayne Gallery, Los Angeles, 2005; Landscape Confection, Wexner Ctr for Arts, Ohio, 2005, Orange County Mus Art, Newport Beach, Calif, 2006; New Prints 2005/Autumn, Int Print Ctr, NY, 2005; Ridykeulous, Participant Inc,

NY, 2006; Grounds for Progress, Ctr Curatorial Studies, Bard Coll, NY, 2008; Beware of the Wolf II, Am Acad Rome, 2008; Am Acad Arts & Letts Invitational, New York, 2010. *Awards:* Guggenheim Fel, 2008. *Bibliog:* Sarah Schmerler (auth), Lisa Sanditz, TimeOut New York, 10/2005; Holly Myers (auth), Casinos and myth of the frontier, LA Times, 11/2006; Hilarie Sheets (auth), Strip Malls in Paradise, ARTnews, 4/2007; Roberta Smith (auth), Chelsea: Art Chockablock with Encyclopedic Range, NY Times, 11/2008 & Summer Pictures, 10/2009. *Mailing Add:* c/o ACME 6150 Wilshire Blvd Spaces 1&2 Los Angeles CA 90048

SANDLER, BARBARA
PAINTER
b New York, NY, Sept 14, 1943. *Study:* Art Students League, George Bridgeman scholar, 63, also with Edwin Dickenson & Robert Beverly Hale. *Work:* Mus Mod Art, NY; Chicago Art Inst; Joseph Hirshhorn Mus, Washington, DC; Chase Manhattan Bank; Manufacturers Hanover Trust; Hearst Corp; Royal Saudi Arabian Naval Base; Dance Collection Lincoln Ctr. *Comn:* Poster & lithograph for Bicentennial, Spec Proj Group, Chicago, 75; posters, Circle in the Square Theatre, NY, 77-78; covers for Harpers & Sat Rev Mag; var record covers for Columbia & Verve Records; poster PBS Mobil Oil Mystery Series. *Exhib:* one-person shows, Segal Gallery, NY, 81 & 83-85, Mary Martin Gallery, Aspen, Colo, 83, Trabia-Macafee Gallery, 89, The Ctr Show, 89, Art in Embassies-US State Dept, 89 & Dance Collection Lincoln Ctr, 91; Micro '83 Int Exhib, Stockholm, Sweden, 83; Zeus Trabia Gallery, 86; group exhib, Art in General, 93; group exhib, Lennon Weinbers, 94; Pavel Zoubok Gallery, New York, 2003 & 2006. *Awards:* Elizabeth T Greenshields Mem Found Grant, 74. *Bibliog:* Articles, Archit Digest, 2/76, Print Mag, 79, Graphis Mag, 80, Arts Mag, 5/83, 5/84, 4/86 & 5/89, Downtown Mag, 12/86, Village Voice, 89, NY Native, 89, Dance Mag, 1/89, NY Sun, 2006 and others. *Media:* Oil, Graphite. *Publ:* Illusr, The Long View, Knopf, 74; Indian Oratorio, Ballantine Bks, 75; contribr, Super Realism, Dutton, 75. *Dealer:* Pavel Zoubok Gallery New York NY. *Mailing Add:* 221 W 20th St New York NY 10011

SANDLER, IRVING HARRY
CRITIC, HISTORIAN
b New York, NY, July 22, 1925. *Study:* Temple Univ, BA, 48; Univ Pa, MA, 50; NY Univ, PhD, 76. *Pos:* Art critic, Art News, 56-62 & NY Post, 60-65; contrib ed, Art Am, 72. *Teaching:* Instr art hist, NY Univ, 60-71; prof, State Univ NY Col Purchase, 71-. *Awards:* Tona Shepherd Fund Grant Travel in Ger & Austria; Guggenheim Found Fel, 65; Nat Endowment Humanities Fel, 80; AICA Lifetime Achievement Award, 2008. *Bibliog:* Jay Jacobs (auth), Of myths and men, Art Am, 3-4/70; Rosalind Constable (auth), The myth of the myth-makers, Washington Post Bk World, 11/29/70; Gesture-makers and colourfieldsmen, Times Lit Suppl, 6/8/71. *Mem:* Int Asn Art Critics (pres, Am Section, 70-75); Coll Art Asn Am (bd dir, 86); Artists Space (co-founder, 73). *Res:* American art since 1930. *Publ:* Auth, The New York School: Painters and Sculptors of the Fifties, Harper & Row, 78; Alex Katz, Abrams, 79; Al Held, Hudson Hills, 84; American Art of the 1960s, 88; Mark di Suvero, 96. *Mailing Add:* SUNY Purchase Col Humanities Div 735 Anderson Hill Rd Purchase NY 10577-1400

SANDLIN, DAVID THOMAS
PAINTER, PRINTMAKER
b Belfast, N Ireland, Nov 9, 1956. *Study:* Univ Ala, Birmingham, BA, 79. *Work:* Gallery X, Kansas City; Chase Manhattan Bank, NY. *Exhib:* Birmingham Art Asn Show, Birmingham Mus, 79 & 80; Excerpts from East Village, Va Beach Arts Ctr, 84; Innocence and Experience, Greenville Co Mus, 85; New Work from NY, Barbara Farber Gallery, Amsterdam, The Neth, 85; Painting and Sculpture 1986, Indianapolis Mus, 86; Prints, Pub and Pvt 1986, Brooklyn Mus, 86; Focus NY, Moos Art Gallery, Miami, 86; Investigations, McIntosh-Drysdale Gallery, Washington, DC, 86; solo exhibs, Kwok Gallery, NY, 83, Gracie Mansion Gallery, NY, 84-86 & Brunswick Gallery, Missoula, Mont, 85. *Pos:* Founding mem, Print Co-op, NY, 80-81. *Teaching:* Mgr, printmaking shop, Sch Visual Arts, 82-, teacher lithography, 85-. *Awards:* Jurors Award, Birmingham Art Asn, Birmingham Mus, 79; NY Found Arts Fel, 2009. *Bibliog:* M Brenson (auth), rev, New York Times, 85; M Cone (auth), Prints about prints, Print Collectors Newsletter, 85; D Rubey (auth), Sarcastic quotations, Arts Monthly, 85. *Media:* All

SANDMAN, JO
PHOTOGRAPHER, CONCEPTUAL ARTIST
b Boston, Mass, Mar 22, 1931. *Study:* Brandeis Univ, AB, 52; with Hans Hofmann, Provincetown and NY, 52-53; Hunter Col, with Robert Motherwell, 53; Univ Calif, Berkeley, MAn (art), 54; Radcliffe Col, MAT, 56. *Work:* Addison Gallery Am Art; Dallas Mus Fine Arts; NY Univ; Mass Inst Technol; Portland Mus of Fine Art, OR; Rose Mus, Brandeis Univ, Mass; Rhode Island Sch Design, RI. *Comn:* Video piece for TV, Nat Endowment Arts, Rockefeller Found & Mass Coun Arts, Boston, 75; Removal Drawing, Bicentennial Painting Comn, Boston 200, 75. *Exhib:* Flush with the Walls, Mus Fine Arts, Boston, 71; Drawings from Two NY Galleries, Va Mus Fine Arts, (traveling), 73-75; solo exhibs, Addison Gallery Am Art, Phillips Acad, Andover, Mass, 74, Stux Gallery, Boston, 81 & 83, O K Harris Works of Art, NY, 73, 75, 82 & 94, 2001, Grey Art Gallery, NY Univ, NY, 78, Group Gallery, Provincetown, Mass, 83, 84 & 85, DeCordova Mus, (installation) Lincoln, Mass, 86 & Mobius, Boston, Mass, 88 & Thomas Segal Gallery, 89; On the Wall (installation), Inst Contemp Art, Boston, 76; Boston Now: Abstract Painting, 81 & Boston Now: Works on Paper, Inst Contemp Art, Boston, 88; Andrea Marquit Gallery, Boston, 94 & 95; Gallery Kayafas, Boston 2003, 2007; Mercer Gallery, NY, 2001; New Eng Sch of Art & Design, Boston 2002; and others. *Teaching:* Vis artist, lectr & critic painting, various art sch & col, 56-. *Awards:* Sculpture Fel, Mass Coun on Arts & Humanities, 84; Citation for Excellence, Boston Soc Architects, 90; 2nd place, Best Mid-career Show, IAAC, Boston, MA. *Bibliog:* Cate McQuaid, Two Artists Explore Their X-Ray Vision, Boston Globe, July 2003; Robert C Morgan (auth), Jo Sandman: The Elusive Image, Provincetown Arts, 2001; D Lynne Plummer (auth), Unreasonably Beautiful, Arts Editor, 2011. *Media:* Antique photographic processes. *Specialty:* photography. *Dealer:* Gallery Kayafas 450 Harrison Ave Boston MA 02118. *Mailing Add:* 1 Fitchburg St Studio C-507 Somerville MA 02143

SANDOL, MAYNARD
PAINTER
b Newark, NJ, 1930. *Study:* Newark State Coll, 52; also with Robert Motherwell. *Work:* Newark Mus Art; Wadsworth Atheneum, Hartford, Conn; Princeton Univ, NJ; Finch Coll Mus, NY; Joseph Hirshhorn Collection, Washington, DC; also pvt collections. *Comn:* Dr John Murray, Clinton, NJ; Salvatore & Sandra Tobia, Toms River, NJ. *Exhib:* Corcoran Gallery of Art, Washington, DC; Mus Mod Art, NY; NJ Pavilion, NY World's Fair; NJ State Mus, Trenton; NJ Masters, 80; Art Center of the Ozarks; Vineyard Gallery, Bentonville, Ariz; and others. *Teaching:* Instr, US Army, 53-55; tchr, art, Newark Pub Schs, NJ, 55-56, East Paterson, NJ, 65-67; tchr art & humanities, Hackettstown High Sch, NJ, 64-98; instr art hist, Farleigh Dickinson Univ, Madison, 65-67, Co Coll Morris, NJ, 81, 82. *Bibliog:* William H Gerdts, Jr (auth), Paintings and Sculpture in New Jersey, Van Nostrand, 64. *Mem:* Plein Air Painters Ozarks (PAPO); Artists Northwest Ark (ANA); Ozark Pastel Soc (OPS). *Media:* Oil, Acrylic. *Mailing Add:* 2073 N Barrington Dr Fayetteville AR 72701-3061

SANDOVAL, ARTURO ALONZO
EDUCATOR, WEAVER
b Española, NMex, Feb 1, 1942. *Study:* Univ Portland, Ore, 59; Calif State Univ, Los Angeles, with Virginia Hoffman & Michael Schrier, BA, 64, MA, 69; Cranbrook Acad Art, with Richard Devore, Robert Kidd & Gerhardt Knodel, MFA, 71. *Work:* Mus Mod Art, Design & Archit, NY; Smithsonian Inst Art, Renwick Gallery, DC; Rocky Mt Quilt Mus, Golden, Colo; Mus of Art and Design, NY; Nat Hispanic Cult Ctr, Albuquerque, NMex; Cityscape No 6, JB Speed Art Mus, Louisville, Ky, 2000; Columbus Mus Art, 2010; Evansville Mus Art, History, and Science; and others. *Comn:* Fiber art quilt, Citizens Fidelity Bank & Trust, Louisville, Ky, 90; fiber art quilt, Fed Reserve Bank, Cincinnati, Ohio, 91; fiber art, UFCW of the AFL/CIO, Washington, 92; The Atlanta Clock (with Aaron Alvic Schroeder), Atlanta Hartsfield Airport, 99; Sparkle, Horsemania, Lexington Arts and Cult Coun, Lexington, Ky, 2000; GSA, AIA, 6th District Courthouse, London, Ky. *Exhib:* Pacesetters and Prototypes, Detroit Inst Art, 73; Textiles: Past & Prologue, Greenville Co Mus Art, SC, 76; 8th Int Biennial Tapestry, Mus Cantonal des Beaux Arts, Lausanne, Suisse, 77; New Acquisitions: Design Collection, Mus Modern Art, NY, 79; Art Fabric: Mainstream, Mus Mod Art, San Francisco, Calif, 81; solo exhibs, J B Speed Art Mus, Louisville, Ky, 81, Indianapolis Art Ctr, Ind, 2000, Commonwealth Int Conv Ctr, Louisville, Ky, 2000, Wingspan Gallery, Lexington, Ky, 2000, Cult Arts Gallery, Indianapolis, Ind, 2002, Cult Arts Gallery, Indianapolis, Ind, 2002, Southwest Art and Craft Ctr, San Antonio, Tex, 2003 & Cerlan Gallery, Lexington, Ky, 2003; 8 State Crafts, J B Speed Art Mus, Louisville, Ky, 84, New Works/New Artists IV, 89; retrospectives, Network Gallery, Cranbrook Acad Art Alumni Art Space, Pontiac, Mich, 98, Art Mus, Univ Ky, Lexington, 98, Columbus State Univ, Ga, 99, Campbell Hall Gallery, Western Ore Univ, Monmouth, 99, Reed Gallery, Univ Cincinnati, Ohio, 2000, St Louis Community Col, Mo, 2001 & La Col, Pineville, 2003; 3rd Ann Renaissance Regional, Visual Arts Gallery, Renaissance Ctr, Dickson, Tenn, 2001; Ahora, Visual Arts Galleries, Albuquerque, NMex, 2002; Homage to 911, Cerlan Gallery, Lexington, Ky, 2002; Breaking from Tradition: Quilt Explorations, Mus Am Quilter's Soc, Paducah, Ky, 2003; Arturo Alonzo Sandoval: 35 Year Survey of Fiber Art Forms, Foundry Art Centre, St. Charles, Mo, 2008; Pattern Fusion, Logsdon Gallery, Chicago, Ill, 2008; JE Smith Gallery, Evansville, In, 2009; 35 Year Survey of Fiber Art Forms, Lieu Gallery, Belmont Univ, Nashville, Tenn, 2011. *Pos:* Freelance designer & illusr, Western Lighting Corp, Los Angeles, 64; supervisor, Carding Mill, Edison Inst, Dearborn, Mich, 71; cur, Barnhart Gallery, Univ Ky, Lexington, 79, Student Ctr, Lexington, 84, State Capitol, Frankfort, Ky, 84; co-cur, Chandler Medical Ctr, Lexington, Ky, 91; bd dir, Lexington Arts and Cultural Ctr, Ky, 2002. *Teaching:* Asst, Calif State Univ, Los Angeles, 68 & 69, instr, 70; instr, Sch Art and Design, Southern Ill Univ, Carbondale, 71; asst prof, head weaving/textiles prog, Coll Commun and Fine Arts, Edwardsville, Ill, 71-74; from asst prof to assoc prof, Coll Arts and Scis, Univ Ky, Lexington, 74-86, head fiber prog, 76-, prof, 86-, acting dir undergrad studies, 88; UK Alumni Endowed Prof, 2007-. *Awards:* Craftsman's Fel, Nat Endowment Arts, 73, Visual Arts Fel, 92; Al Smith Fel, Ky Arts Coun, 87; NEA Artist Residency, Pyramid Atlantic, 96; Al Smith Profl Svc Award, Ky Arts Coun, Frankfort, Ky, 97; Rude Osolnik Award, Ky Craft Mktg Program, and the Ky Art and Craft Found, Frankfort, 97; First place, Reverse Raffle, Lexington Art League, Ky, 99; Ky Gov Artist Award, 2003; KAC Al Smith VAF, 2006; Univ Ky Kirwan Prize for Creativity, 2007; elected Fel Am Craft Coun, New York, 2008. *Bibliog:* Art Jester (auth), Faith and values: crown jewel, Lexington Herald-Leader, 02/14/2001; Christine Zoller (auth) Local talk, southeast, Surface Design Newsletter, Vol 14, No 2, 2001, Vol 15, No 2, 2002; Charles Talley (auth), Sandoval's Double Terrorist - deja vu all over again?, Friends Fiber Art Int, 4/2002; Pattern Fusion, Shuttle, Spindle, & Dyepot, 2009; Pattern Fusion No. 9 (illustration), News & Notes: Artists Awards Announced, FiberArts, 2010; Makers and Shakers: Columbus Gets a Sandoval, Am Craft, 2011. *Mem:* Am Craft Coun; Surface Design Asn; Ky Guild Artists and Craftsmen; Fiber Guild Lexington; Ky Mus Art & Craft (cur, 85); Louisville Visual Arts Asn. *Media:* Non-Woven Man-Made Materials, Mylar. *Res:* Active investigation in using recycled industrial linear tapes, films and cables in the creation of mixed media art works. *Specialty:* Fine arts and craft work. *Interests:* Cinema, Cards, Gardening, Opera, Theatre. *Collection:* Textiles from around the world. *Publ:* Coauth, The creative process, Fiberarts, 48-50, 11-12/83; auth, The Artist as Revelator, Fiberarts/Lark Press, 1/2 90; coauth, Quilt National: The Best Contemporary Quilts, Lark Bks, 2001. *Dealer:* Carl Solway 424 Findley Ave Cincinnati OH 45214. *Mailing Add:* PO Box 25153 Lexington KY 40524

SANDROW, HOPE
PHOTOGRAPHER
b Philadelphia, Pa, Dec 31, 1951. *Study:* Philadelphia Coll Art, 72-75. *Work:* Metrop Mus Art; Baltimore Mus Art; Houston Mus Fine Arts; Minn Mus Art; Henry Art Gallery, Mus Mod Art. *Comn:* Dakis Joannou, Athens, Greece, 87; Artforum Mag, 90; Vera List, 92; Artist in the Community, Southeastern Ctr Contemp Art, 94; Material Matters, Creative Time, NY, 95. *Exhib:* Solo exhibs, Philadelphia Coll Art, 84, Haggery Mus, Milwaukee, Wis, 86, Gracie Mansion Gallery (with catalog), NY, 86, 88, 89 & Southeastern Ctr Contemp Art (with catalog), 95, Whitney Mus (with catalog), Philip Morris, 98; Painting & Sculpture Today-Biennial, Indianapolis Mus, 86; Directions-Biennial (with catalog), Hirshhorn Mus, Washington, 86; The New Shape of Content, Whitney Mus Art (with catalog), 87; Photo on the Edge, Haggerty Mus, Milwaukee, 88; Am Photos of the 80s (with catalog), Nat Mus Am Art, Washington, 89; Sequence (con) Sequence, Blum Art Inst, Bard Col, 89; Fantasies, Fables & Fabrications, Herter Art Gallery, Univ Mass, 89-91; Grey Art Gallery, NY Univ, 91; Dia De Los Muertos, Alternative Mus, 91; Tradition & the Unpredictable, Houston Mus Art, 94. *Pos:* Founder & pres, Artist & Homeless Collaborative. *Awards:* Art Matters Award, 91; Manhattan Borough Pres Citation for Excellence in Arts, 91; Mayor Dinkins Superstar Award, 92; Govs Award Skowhegan Sch of Painting & Sculpture, 94; Nat Endowment Arts, Artists Fel, 90 & 94. *Bibliog:* Nina Felshin (ed), The Spirt of Art as Activism, Bay Press; Reading in Comtemporary Poetry, Dia Found, 88; Julia Ballerini (auth), Sequence con Sequence, Aperture, 89. *Mem:* Women's Action Coalition. *Media:* Photography, Mixed Media. *Publ:* Art Forum, 80 90 & 91; Art in Am, 84, 90, 93 & 94; Village Voice, 87, 89, 90, 93, 95, 97 & 98; Boston Review, 89; Flash Art, 10/91; Vogue, 91; and others

SANDSTRÖM, SIGRID
PAINTER
b Stockholm, Sweden, 1970. *Study:* Cooper Union Sch Art, New York, 1995; Acad Minerva, Groningen, Netherlands, BFA, 1997; Skowhegan Sch Painting & Sculpture, ME, 2000; Yale Univ Sch Arts, MFA, 2001. *Work:* Mod Museet, Stockholm, Sweden; Mus Fine Arts Houston; Ulrich Mus Art, Wichita, KS; Yale Univ Art Gallery. *Exhib:* Solo exhibs include I Know Where I'm Going, Inman Gallery, Houston, 2002, Ginnungagap, 2004, Action, 2006, 2008, Tillflykter, Galleri Gunnar Olsson, Stockholm, 2003, Hrönir, 2004, Märkt, 2007, Sighting, Brant Gallery, Mass Coll of Art, Boston, 2004, Her Black Flags, Mills Coll Art Mus, Oakland, CA, 2005, Ginnungagap, Frye Mus, Seattle, 2006, Recent Paintings, Edward Thorp Gallery, New York, 2007; group exhibs include Core Artists Residence, Mus Fine Arts, Houston, 2002, 2003; Pertaining to Painting, Contemp Art Mus, Houston, 2003; Edge of Darkness, LeRoy Neiman Gallery, Columbia Univ, NewYork, 2005; Aqua, Inman Gallery, Miami, 2006, Probably, Houston, 2008; Gallery Artists, Edward Thorp Gallery, New York, 2007; Sylvia Rivera Law Proj Art Benefit, Sara Meltzer Gallery, New York, 2007; Learning by Doing, Mus Fine Arts Houston, 2008. *Teaching:* Asst Prof of Studio Arts, Bard Coll, Annandale-on-Hudson, NY, 2005-. *Awards:* De Groote Brugmans fond, Groningen, 1995; Cult Award, Am Soc, New York, 1997; Alice Kimball Eng Traveling Fel, Yale Univ, 2001; Core Fel, Glassell Sch Art, Mus Fine Arts, Houston, 2001-03; Eliza Randall Prize, 2002, 2003; Artadia Award, Fund Art & Dialogue, New York, 2003; Barbro Osher Found, San Francisco, 2004; John Simon Guggenheim Mem Found Fel, 2008. *Dealer:* Edward Thorp Gallery 210 11th Ave 6th Fl New York NY 10001; Inman Gallery 3901 Main St Houston TX 77002; Galleri Olsson Fredsgatan 12 SE-11152 Stockholm Sweden. *Mailing Add:* c/o Inman Gallery 3901 Main St Houston TX 77002

SANDUSKY, BILLY RAY
PAINTER, PRINTMAKER
b Bowling Green, Ky, Oct 23, 1945. *Study:* John Herron Sch Art, Ind Univ, BFA, 68, Tulane Univ, New Orleans, La, MFA, 70; Academia di Belle Arte, Florence, Italy, 75. *Work:* Midwest Mus Am Art, Elkhart, Ind; Evansville Mus Arts & Sci, Ind; South Bend Regional Mus Art, Ind; Santa Raparta Graphic Art Ctr, Florence; Tulane Univ, New Orleans; Wilfrid Laurier Univ, Waterloo, Ont, Can. *Exhib:* One-person shows, Palazzo Strozzi, Florence, 76, S Bend Art Ctr, 82 & 90 & Purdue Univ, Lafayette, Ind, 86; Ind Artists Show, Indianapolis Mus Art, 83; Realism Today, Mus Arts & Sci, Evansville, 85-86; La Grange National XI, Lamar Dodd Art Ctr, Ga, 86; Art USA, Grand Junction, Colo, 89; South Bend Regional Mus Art, 96; Colfax Cult Ctr, South Bend, 96. *Teaching:* Assoc prof painting, chmn dept art, St Mary's Col, Notre Dame, Ind, 80-. *Awards:* Saint Mary's Coll Fac Teaching Grants, 90 & 94; Lilly Open Fel, Lilly Found, 92; 1st place Fine Arts, 4th Airbrush Excellence Nat Competition, Airbrush Action Mag; and others. *Mem:* Coll Art Asn; Mid-Am Coll Arts Asn (exec bd); Mid-Am Print Coun (exec bd). *Media:* Acrylic, Oil; Lithography, Etching. *Mailing Add:* St Mary's Col Art Dept Notre Dame IN 46556

SANDWEISS, MARTHA ANN
MUSEUM DIRECTOR
b St Louis, Mo, Mar 29, 1954. *Study:* Harvard Univ, BA, 75; Nat Endowment for Humanities Fel, Nat Portrait Gallery, Washington, 75-76; Yale Univ, MA, 77, Fel, Ctr Am Art & Mat Cult, 77-79, PhD, 85. *Collection Arranged:* A Knot of Dreamers: The Brook Farm Community, Nat Portrait Gallery, 76; Pictures from an Expedition: Early Views of the Am West (auth, catalog), Yale Univ Art Gallery, 78; Carlotta Corpron: Designer with Light (auth, catalog), 80; Masterworks of Am Photography (auth, bk), 82; Carleton E Watkins: Photographer of the Am West (introd, bk), Amon Carter Mus; 83; Carl Mydans, Amon Carter Mus, 85; Richard Avedon: In the Am West, 85; Laura Gilpin: An Enduring Grace (auth, bk), Amon Carter Mus, 86; Eliot Porter (introd, bk), Amon Carter Mus. *Pos:* Cur photographs, Amon Carter Mus, Ft Worth, Tex, 79-86, adj cur photographs, 87-89; dir, Mead Art Mus, Amherst Col, 89. *Teaching:* Assoc prof Am studies, Amherst Col, currently. *Awards:* George Wittenborn Award, 87; Nat Endowment Humanities Fel for Independent Scholars, 88; Am Coun Learned Soc Fel, 96. *Publ:* Ed, Historic Texas: A Photograhic Portrait, Tex Monthly, 86; Contemporary Texas: A Photographic Portrait 86; coauth, Eyewitness to War: Prints and Daguerreotypes of the Mexican War, 1846-1848, Smithsonian Press, 89; ed & coauth, Photography in Nineteenth-Century America, Abrams, 91; co-ed, Oxford History of the American West, 94. *Mailing Add:* Amherst Col Mead Art Mus Amherst MA 01002

SANGIAMO, ALBERT
EDUCATOR, PAINTER
b Brooklyn, NY. *Study:* Brooklyn Col, AB; Yale Univ, BFA & MFA. *Work:* Baltimore Mus, Md. *Exhib:* Smithsonian Am Drawing Exhib (traveling), 65; Solo exhibs, Baltimore Mus, 69, Towson State Coll, 71, Decker Art Gallery, Md, 75 & Md Arts Coun (traveling), 75. *Teaching:* Instr painting & drawing, Md Inst Col Art, 61-, chmn found dept, 61-73, chmn dept fine arts, 73-. *Awards:* Grand Prize, Baltimore Mus, 59; Purchase Prizes, St Paul Arts Ctr, 64. *Media:* Synthetic Charcoal, Acrylic. *Mailing Add:* 1715 Bolton St Baltimore MD 21217

SANGRAM, MAJUMDAR
PAINTER, PRINTMAKER
b Kolkata, India, 1976. *Study:* RI Sch Design, BFA, 1999; Indiana Univ, MFA, 2001. *Exhib:* Solo exhibs, Wright State Univ, Dayton, 2004, Rose Lehrman Art Gallery, Harrisburg Area Community Coll, 2008, Kresge Art Mus, Mich State Univ, 2008, Univ Baltimore, 2008, Laguna Coll Art & Design, 2009, Jerusalem Studio Sch, 2010; Drawing Invitational, Aichi Prefectural Mus Art, Nagoya, Japan, 2005; Here and Now, Md Inst Coll Art, 2006; US Embassy, Freetown, Sierra Leone, 2007; 35/25: Twenty-Five Painters Under Thirty-Five, Painting Ctr, New York, 2009; Am Acad Arts & Letts, New York, 2010. *Teaching:* Asst prof, Univ Wis, Eau Claire, 2001-03; prof painting, Md Inst Coll Art, Baltimore, 2003-. *Awards:* Marie Walsh Sharpe Studio Space Program Grant, 2009; Elizabeth Greenshields Found Grant, 2010; Individual Artist Grant, Md State Arts Coun, 2010. *Bibliog:* Tom Rhea (auth), Blueprints for a Ruin, Bloomington Ind, 4/5/2001; Mike Giuliano (auth), Baltimore Weekly Highlights, CityPaper, 10/20/2004; Cate McQuaid (auth), Exhibit charms with its twists on being Handsome, Boston Gloe, 6/24/2009

SANIN, FANNY
PAINTER
b Bogota, Colombia, US Citizen, Nov 30, 1938. *Study:* Chelsea & Cent Schs of Art, London, 69; Univ Los Andes, Bogota, MFA, 60; Univ Ill, 63. *Work:* Univ Essex Coll Latin Am Art, Colchester, Gt Brit; Nat Mus Women Arts, Washington, DC; New Orleans Mus Art; Mus of Art of the Americas, Washington, DC; Interamerican Develop Bank, Washington, DC; Greater Lafayette Mus Art, W Lafayette, Ind. *Comn:* Set for Walt Whitman's A Clear Midnight, Am Soc, NY. *Exhib:* Mus Fine Arts, Caracas, 67; 1st Edinburgh Open 100, 67; Internat Sao Paulo Art Biennial, 79; Mus Modern Art, Mexico City, 79; Jersey City Mus 86; Mus Modern Art, Retrospective, Bogota, 87; Latin-Am Women Artists 1915-1995, Milwaukee Art Mus, 95; Colors: Contrasts & Cultures, Discovery Mus, Bridgeport, Conn, 97; Color and Symmetry-Retrospective, Luis Angel Arango Cult Ctr, Bogota, 2000; Mus of Abstract Art Manuel Felquerez, Zacatecas, Mex, 2001; Italo Latin Am Inst, Rome, 2007; Latin Collector, NY, 2008; Durbin Segnini Gallery, Miami, 2010; Frederico Seve Gallery, NY, 2012. *Awards:* Medellin Award, Coltejer Internat Biennial, 70; Canadian Club Award, US Art Tour, NY, Canadian Club, 85; Colombia External Excellence Award, Miami, 2006. *Bibliog:* Michel Ragon & Michel Seuphor, L'Art Abstrait 1945/70, v IV, 74; Marta Traba, Latin Am Art 1900-80, IDB, 94; Jules & Nancy Heller (coauths), North American Women Artists of the Twentieth Century, Garland Press, 95; Edward Sullivan (auth), Latin American Art in the Twentieth Century, Phaidon Press, London, Eng, 96; Margaret Barlow, Women Artists, Hugh Lauter Levin Asn, 99; Nancy G Heller, Why a Painting is like a Pizza, Princeton Univ Press, 2002; Holland Cotter (auth), Bulletins from a Bustling Undiscovered Land, NY Times, 11/19/2007; Agnes Berecz (auth), Fanny Sanin Latin Collector, Art in Am, 2/2009; Jason Dubs (auth), Fanny Sanin - Latin Collector, Art Nexus, No 71, 2009; Peter Plagens (auth), Fanny Sanin: Drawings and Studies 1960 to Now, Wall St Jour, 2012; John Angeline (auth), Fanny Sanin Frederico Seve, Art Nexus, No 85, 2012. *Mem:* Nat Arts Club, NY. *Media:* Acrylic, Watercolor. *Dealer:* Andrea Marquit 71 Pinckney St Boston MA 02114; Frederico Seve Gallery 37 W 57th St New York NY 10019; Alonso Garces Galeria Cra 5 No 26-92 Bogota Colombia; New Arts Gallery 513 Maple St Litchfield CT 06759. *Mailing Add:* 345 E 86th St Apt 17C New York NY 10028

SANSONE, JOSEPH F
CRAFTSMAN
b Mt Vernon, NY, Oct 20, 1922. *Exhib:* Milton Glazer, Univ Minn, Minneapolis, 88; Frank Stella, Los Angeles; Richard Haas, San Francisco. *Pos:* Pres, Archit Wallcovering Inc, 60-; Painting & Decorating Contractors Am, 70-71. *Teaching:* Instr mural installation, various trade unions (CETA sponsored), 60-. *Awards:* First Prize, Painting & Decorating Contractors Am, 87, 88 & 89, Second Prize, 88. *Mem:* Painting & Decorating Contractors Am. *Publ:* Coauth, PWC Mag, Finan Publ, 70-90; coauth, American painter-decorator, Voss Publ, 70-90; coauth, Journal of Property Mgt, NAR, Chicago, 90

SAN SOUCIE, PATRICIA MOLM
PAINTER, INSTRUCTOR
b Minneapolis, Minn, Nov 4, 1931. *Study:* Univ Wis, graphics with Warrington Colescott, John Wilde & Alfred Sessler, painting with Dean Meeker & Santos Zingale, BS (applied art), 53; NJ Ctr Vis Arts, NJ, painting. *Work:* Springfield Art Mus, Mo; Chattahoochee Art Mus, Ga; Butler, 85; and others. *Comn:* Casio Int Off, NJ & NY. *Exhib:* Am Watercolor Soc, 72-76; solo exhib, Acad Arts, Easton, Md, 83; Butler Inst Am Art, 86; Watercolor USA Hon Soc, 89-2008. *Collection Arranged:* Invitational exhib at Parkland Coll Art Gallery, Champaign, IL, State of the Art Exhib, Feb-Mar, 99, curated by Glenn Bradshaw,; Butler Inst of Am Art Midyear, 85; Touring exhibs in Chateau de Tours, France and Taiwan Art Mus, China; Cultural Exchange, Zheljiang Art Mus, Hangzhow, China, 94; Jane Voorhees Zimmerli Art Mus, New Brunswick, NJ, permanent collection, two watercolors, 94; Artists Collab Books Editions IV, V, VI

in collections, Newark Mus and Mus of Modern Art Librs, Artists Libr of the Victoria and Albert Mus, London, Nat Gallery of Art Libr, Washington; Chattahoochee Valley Art Mus, LaGrange, GA, 96; Southwestern WC Milan, Ital Invitational Exchange, 2001; 40 Watercolorists Selected to show in Irvine, Tex & Milan, Ital; Myrtle Beach, SC; Bill Naito, Portland, Ore, 2004. *Pos:* Jury selection chmn, St Louis Artists Guild, 68-71; gallery exhib comt, Summit Art Ctr, NJ, 73-79; pres, NJ Watercolor Soc, 88-90; bd, Watercolor USA Honor Soc, 94-2003; mem chmn, Watercolor Hon Soc, 2007-2008. *Teaching:* Instr, Princeton Art Asn, NJ, 75-76; fac mem, Summit Art Ctr, NJ, 83- & ARTWORKS, Trenton, NJ, 92-; instr numerous workshops, Kanuga, NC, Acapulco, Mex, Canada; Oregon College of Arts & Craft, Sitka Ctr of the Arts, Otis, OR; Frameworld Beaverton, Ore, pvt lessons in studio. *Awards:* Walser Greathouse Award & Gold Medal, Am Watercolor Soc, 91; Arches Special Papers, Third Award, Ajomari Inc, 91; Ariz Aqueous Award for Excellence, Tubac Ctr Arts, 91, 98; Watercolor Society Oregon, 98, 99, 01, 07, & 08; Tenn Art League, Nashville, Tenn, 2009; Western Co Watercolor Award, 2007; Pike's Peak, Pueblo, Colo, 2009. *Bibliog:* Color section, Master Class in Watercolor, Edward Betts, 75; Watermedia Techniques for Releasing the Creative Spirit, Marilyn Hughey Phillis, 92; color inclusion, Splash I and II, Rachel Wolf, 93; How to Discover Your Personal Painting Style, David P Richards, 95; Abstracts, 96; Exploring Color II, Nita Leland, 98; How to Use and Control Color; Rachel Wolf (auth), Splash 10, 2007; Splash XI; Rachel Wolf (auth), Fifteen Artists, 2009. *Mem:* Nat Watercolor Soc; Signature mem Am Watercolor Soc; Watercolor USA Honor Soc; AWS; Dolphin Fel; Northwest Watercolor Soc; NJW Watercolor Soc; Rocky Mountain Watercolor Soc; Watercolor Soc Oregon; Ala Watercolor Soc; Ga Watercolor Soc; Miss Watercolor Soc. *Media:* Watercolor, Gouache, Dyes, Natural colors. *Interests:* Landscapes; Whimsies; abstracts. *Publ:* Auth, article, Artists Mag, 1/91; auth, article, Watercolor, Fall, 97; auth, article, Watercolor Magic, Fall, 99; Beth Patterson (auth), Artists Mag, 2003. *Dealer:* Lawrence Gallery Rt 18 Sheridan Ore; Howden Arts Gallery Oregon City Ore; The Attic Gallery Portland Ore; Frame World Beaverton Ore. *Mailing Add:* 11777 SE Timber Valley Dr Clackamas OR 97086-8388

SANT, VICTORIA P
MUSEUM DIRECTOR
Study: Stanford Univ, BA. *Pos:* Docent, Nat Gallery Art, Wash, DC, 83-85, chmn trustees coun, 2001—2002; pres, The Phillips Collection, 2003—; Co-founder, pres, Summit Found, Summit Fund of Wash, currently. *Mailing Add:* Summit Found Ste 525 2100 Pennsylvania Ave NW Washington DC 20037

SANTIAGO, RICHARD E
SCULPTOR, EDUCATOR
b Mar 29, 1948. *Study:* Univ S Fla, Tampa, BA (art educ), 74, MA (art educ) 77; Univ Utah, Salt Lake City, MFA (sculpture), 84; studied with Stephen Antonakos, Sculptor, NY. *Work:* Tampa Mus Art & Berkeley Prep Sch, Tampa, Fla; First Fla Bank, Clearwater, Fla; Univ Utah, Mus Fine Arts, Univ Utah, Art Dept & Salt Lake City Art Ctr, Salt Lake City; Nora Eckles Harrison Mus Fine Art, Logan, Utah; also pvt collections of Stephen Antonakos, Peter Frank & James Whitecotton. *Exhib:* ASA Gallery, Albuquerque, NMex, 83; solo exhibs, Gittins Gallery, Salt Lake City, Utah, 83 & 84, Univ Utah, Mus Fine Arts, Salt Lake City, 83 & 84, Univ S Garage Gallery, Sarasota, Fla, 86, Fla Ctr Contemp Art, Tampa, 88, Michael Murphy Gallery, Tampa, Fla, 89, Fla Towers Bldg, Tampa, 90, Tampa Mus Art, Fla, 90 & C Company, Chicago, Ill, 91; Utah Arts Coun, Salt Lake City, 84; Bellair Art Ctr, Bellair, Fla, 87; Ridge Art Asn, Winter Haven, Fla, 87; The Arts Ctr, St Petersburg, Fla, 87, 88 & 92; Fla Ctr Contemp Art, Tampa, 87 & 88; PSA Architects Inc, St Petersburg, Fla, 89; N Miami Ctr Contemp Art, Fla, 91; PJC Gallery, Pensacola, Fla, 92. *Teaching:* Instr art, Hillsborough Co Pub Schs, Fla, 75-; instr design & sculpture, Univ Utah, Salt Lake City, 80-82 & 91. *Awards:* Emerging Artists Grant, Arts Coun Tampa/Hillsborough, Tampa, Fla, 89; Master Assoc, Atlantic Ctr Arts, New Smyrna Beach, Fla, 89; Individual Artist Fel, Fla Arts Coun, Div Cult Affairs, Tallahassee, Fla, 90. *Media:* Neon, Site Specific Installation. *Mailing Add:* 7107 N 18th St Tampa FL 33610-1257

SANTIAGO-IBARRA, BEATRICE MAYTE
EDITOR, CRITIC
b Santurce, PR, Feb 17, 1949. *Study:* Univ PR, Rio Piedras, BA (comparative lit), 75; Centro de Estudios Avanzados, MA (lit & arts), 98. *Work:* Museo Casa del Rey, Dorado, PR; Arsenal de la Marina, Instituto de Puerto Rican Cultura & Museo las Americas, San Juan, PR; Museo Casa Alonso, Vega Baja, PR; Feria de Arte Contemporanio, Madrid, Spain. *Comn:* Cultural Doradina, Municipo de Dorado, PR, 85-86; Organizadora Brenal de San Juan, Instituto de Puerto Rican Cultura, PR, 86-98; Monumentos Turismo, Compania de Turismo, San Juan, PR, 88. *Pos:* Pub relations art, Univ Sacred Heart, 80-84; dir cult affairs, Casa del Rey, Dorado City Hall, 85-86; gen coordr, San Juan Print Biennial Latin Am & Caribbean Countries, Instituto Puerto Rican Cultura, 86-98; critic, 80-. *Teaching:* Prof, Acad Santa Teresito, 77-80; prof art & pub relations, Univ Sacred Heart, PR, 80-84. *Awards:* First Prize of Literature, Book of Poems, La Habana, Cuba, 74. *Bibliog:* Several articles in El Mundo Newspaper, 77-82. *Mem:* Am Asn Mus; Asn Art Critics. *Res:* Financial aspects supporting biennials. *Publ:* Auth, Siembra Para No Decir Adios (poetry), Taller Quinque, 71; En el Silencio de las Desgarradurcas (poetry) & El Asesinato de Casandra Ramirez (fiction), 86, Coqui-Zahori-Editorial. *Mailing Add:* Institute of Puerto Rican Culture Apartado 9024184 Toa Baja PR 00949

SANTOLERI, PAUL D
PAINTER, MURALIST
b Philadelphia, Pa, 1965. *Study:* Tyler Sch Art, Temple Univ, BFA (painting), 1987; Visual Artist Residency, Banff Centre for the Arts, 1990; Univ Ariz, MFA (painting), 1991; Showhegan Sch Art, 1991; MacDowell Fel, MacDowell Colony, NH, 1992, 1998; Visual Arts Fel, Pa Coun Arts, 1992, 2005; Residency Fel, Altos de Chavon, Dominican Republic, 1994, 1998; Residency Fell, Fundacion Valparaiso, Spain, 1998; Visual Arts Fel, Independence Found, 2004. *Work:* State Mus Pa, Harrisburg, Pa ; Philadelphia Mus Art,; Philadelphia Free Libr; Rohm & Haas Art Collection, Philadelphia, Pa; Reading Anthracite Mus. *Comn:* Five Story Oil Tank, Sunoco, City of Philadelphia, Philadelphia, Pa, 1999; murals, mosaics at entry Philadelphia Zoological Gardens, Philadelphia, Pa, 2003, 2006; fresco mural in soffitt, Philadelphia Free Libr, Walnut W Branch, Philadelphia, 2004; three story interior murals, Univ Pa, WXPN/World Cafe Live, Philadelphia, Pa, 2005; Thomas Eakins' house mural, Mural Arts Project, Philadelphia, 2007. *Exhib:* New and Black and White, Pa State Mus, Harrisburg, Pa, 2002; Illusions of Greeneur, Del Center for Contemp Art, Wilmington, Del, 2005; Effemera Meravigliosa, Primo Piano Gallery, Lecce, Italy, 2006; Linear Interference, Painted Bride Art Center, Philadelphia, Pa, 2006; Kentler Drawing Space, Brooklyn, NY, 2007; Spinning Worlds, Noyes Mus Art, Oceanville, NJ, 2007; Surface Tension, Arts Center of Troy, Troy, NY, 2007; Installation Exhib, Cesta, Tabor, Czech Republic, Arts Festival, 2007. *Teaching:* Instr, murals, Mural Arts Project, Philadelphia, Pa, 1997-2007. *Awards:* Visual Artist Residency, Banff Centre for the Arts, 1990; Pollock-Krasner Found Grant, 2008. *Bibliog:* Chris Emmanuelidis (auth), To Your Island (film), 1999; Ed Sozanski, Paint, Philadelphia Inquirer, 2005; Sarah Schmerler (auth), Confluence (article), Kentler Drawing Space, 2007. *Mem:* Painted Bride Arts (mem, 1998-); Del Center Contemp Arts (mem, 2000-2007). *Media:* Drawing, painting (ink, fresco, oil, acrylic). *Publ:* Contribr, Philadelphia Murals & the Stories They Tell, Temple Univ Press, 2005. *Mailing Add:* 1123 N Orianna Philadelphia PA 19123

SANTORE, JOSEPH W
PAINTER
b Philadelphia, Pa, Dec 15, 1945. *Study:* Philadelphia Coll Art, BFA, 69; Univ Ariz, 70-71; Yale Univ, MFA, 73. *Exhib:* Solo exhibs, Yale Univ, 73, Edward Thorp Gallery, 82, 84, 87, 90 & 93, NY Studio Sch, 95, Philadelphia Art Alliance, Pa, 97 & Phoenix Art Mus, 2000; Whitney Biennial, Whitney Mus Am Art, 91; Leo Castelli Gallery, NY, 93; Skowhegan 93, Colby Coll Mus Art, 93; Waterworks, Edward Thorp Gallery, NY, 94; Summer Group, Edward Thorp Gallery, NY, 94; 70th Ann Exhib of the Nat Acad Design, NY, 95; A Gift of Vision: The William and Susan Small Collection, Tucson Mus Art, Ariz, 95; Painting Faculty Exhib, NY Studio Sch, 96; Am Still Life, Aspen Art Mus, Colo, 96; The Figure Revisited, Gallery at Hasting-on-Hudson, NY, 97; Gallery Group Exhib, Edward Thorp Gallery, NY, 97 & 98; Contemp Selections from the Nat Acad at Silvermine, Silvermine Guild Galleries, New Canaan, Conn, 98; Drawing Plus One, NY Studio Sch, NY, 98; 174th Ann Exhib, Nat Acad Design, NY, 99; Kinds of Drawing: NY, NC, Western Carolina Univ, Cullowhee, NC, 99; The Figure: Another Side of Modernism, Newhouse Ctr Contemp Art, Snug Harbor, NY, 2000; 178th Annual Exhibition, Nat Acad Mus, New York, 2003; 49th Anniversary exhib, New York Studio Sch. New York, 2005; 184th AnnExhib Contem Am Art, Nat Acad Design, New York, 2009; Am Acad Arts & Letts Invitational, New York, 2010. *Teaching:* Fac, NY Studio Sch, New York City. *Awards:* John Simon Guggenheim Mem Fund Fel Grant, 88-89; Am Acad & Inst Arts & Letters Award, 89; Nat Endowment Arts Fel, 93-94. *Bibliog:* Haines Sprunt Tate (auth), At home with the paradoxical, the ambiguous and the random, Maine Times, 9/10/93; Eileen Watkins (auth), Review, Star-Ledger, 7/4/93; Alisa Tager (auth), Patrick Dunfey, Joseph Santore, Artnews, 9/93; Edward J Sozanksi (auth), Traditional fare rendered unconventionally, The Philadelphia Inquirer, 6/27/97; Karen Sandstrom (auth), Exhibit captures a place in memory, The Plain dealer, 4/30/98; Dorothy Shinn, Show disproves adage "Those who can't...", The Beacon Jour, 4/12/98. *Mem:* Am Acad & Inst Arts & Lett; Nat Acad (assoc, 93, acad, 94-)

SANTOS, ADELE NAUDE
ARCHITECT, DESIGNER
Study: Archit Asn, London, dipl, 61; Univ Pa, MArch & MP; Harvard, MArch in UD. *Pos:* Professorships grad prog at Harvard, Rice Univ & Univ Pa, chmn dept archit, 81-87; founding dean, Sch Archit, Univ Calif, San Diego, formerly; Univ Calif, Berkeley, 94-. *Awards:* Int design competitions. *Publ:* Published work in journals world-wide. *Mailing Add:* c/o Adele Santos & Assoc 33 Zoe St San Francisco CA 94107

SAPHIRE, LAWRENCE M
WRITER, ART DEALER
b Brooklyn, NY, Jan 12, 1931. *Study:* Yale Univ, BA, 52, writing with Robert Penn Warren; Yale Sch Fine Arts, 51-53; Univ Paris I at Sorbonne, two dipl. *Pos:* Dir, Blue Moon Gallery, NY; ed, Blue Moon Press, Yorktown Heights, NY. *Res:* Modern prints, particularly Leger, Andre Masson. *Specialty:* Modern European painting, sculpture, graphics, original print publications in books and albums. *Publ:* Auth & ed, Sea Bird Saga (including Wallace Putnam lithographs), Blue Moon Gallery, 66; Poems (including Andre Masson etchings), Ed de la Lune Bleue, 74; Andre Masson/Second Surrealist Period, 75, The Genius of Andre Masson (catalogs), 76, Fernand Leger/Complete Graphic Work, 78, Blue Moon Press; Andre Masson/The Illustrated Books, 94, Patrick Crater Publ; Andre Masson, Complete Graphic Work, Blue Moon Press, 90. *Mailing Add:* 808 Broadway New York NY 10003

SAPIEN, DARRYL RUDOLPH
PAINTER
b Los Angeles, Calif, Mar 12, 1950. *Study:* Fullerton Col, AA, 71; San Francisco Art Inst, BFA, 72, MFA 76. *Work:* Art Mus, Univ Calif, Berkeley; Oakland Mus, Calif; San Francisco Mus Mod Art; Solomon R Guggenheim Mus, NY. *Comn:* This is Not A Test, Soc Encouragement Contemp Art, San Francisco, 76; "Pixellagem," Commissioned Set Design for San Francisco Ballet, 83; Lobby Installation, Nat Automobile & Casualty Co, Pasadena, Calif, 93. *Exhib:* Within the Nucleus (performance), San Francisco Mus Mod Art, 76; Painting & Sculpture in Calif: The Mod Era, Nat Collection Fine Art, Washington, DC, 76; Space, Time, Sound, a Decade in the Bay Area, San Francisco Mus Mod Art, 79; Hero (performance), Newport Harbor Art Mus, Calif, 80; 19 Artists--Emergent Americans, Solomon R Guggenheim Mus, NY, 81; Am Roulette, Solomon R Guggenheim Mus, NY, 81; Artspace Painting Grant Award, San Francisco Artspace, 88; Digital Visions: Computers and Art, Everson Mus Art, Syracuse Univ, NY, 88; The Written Word,

Richmond Art Ctr, Richmond, Calif, 90; San Francisco Art Comn Gallery, 91; Recent Work, San Francisco City Col, 96; Facing Eden 100 Yrs of Landscape Art in the Bay Area, MH de Young Mus, San Francisco, 95; Recent Work, Opts Art Gallery, San Francisco, 94; Eyecharts, Wienstien Gallery, San Francisco, 98. *Pos:* Sr computer graphics artists, Amdahl Coop, 84-86. *Teaching:* Lectr, San Francisco State Univ, San Francisco Inst. *Awards:* Nat Endowment Arts Awards, 73, 79 & 92; Louise Riskin Award, Video Pavillion, San Francisco Art Festival, 75; Artspace Painting Grant, 88. *Bibliog:* Charles Csuki (auth), Music & Dance J a Paint Machine, Computer Graphics & Applications, 8/85; Christine Tamblyn (auth), Darryl Sapien at Art Space, Artnews, 11/88; Ken Baker (auth), Darryl Sapien at Opts Art, San Francisco Chronicle, 11/30/94. *Media:* Paintings; Multi-Media Installations. *Publ:* Auth, Splitting the axis & Video art and the ultimate cliche, La Mamelle, 76; contribr, Other Sources (catalog), San Francisco Art Inst, 76; Oggi in California, Data, 77; auth, Crime in the streets, High Performance, summer 79; What is performance art?, Intersection Newslett, 81. *Dealer:* Mendoza Gallery Latin American Art. *Mailing Add:* 4333 Balboa St San Francisco CA 94121

SAPP, WILLIAM ROTHWELL
SCULPTOR, EDUCATOR
b Cape Girardeau, Mo, July 4, 1943. *Study:* Univ Mo, Columbia, MA, 67; Wash Univ, MFA, 78; Southeast Mo State Univ. *Work:* Univ Ark & State Capitol, Little Rock; Comptroller of the US Currency, Oklahoma City; N Ark Med Ctr, Harrison, AK; Harlin Mus, West Plains, MO. *Comn:* J P Harlin Portrait Sculpture, comn by Harlin family, 73; Ark Gov Bailey, 88; St Redhead, Casa de la Cultura, Santa Cruz, Bolivia, 88; Ark Gov Faubus, 89; Claude Parrish Onc Hosp, 90. *Exhib:* Ark Arts Coun Fel, Winners, pub Serv Gallery, Little Rock, Ark, 85; Mid Am Arts Asn/NEA Winners Exhib, Salina Arts Ctr, Kans, 86; Casa dela Cultura/Taller de Artes Visuales, Santa Cruz, Bolivia, 88; Dogs, Memphis Ctr Contemp Arts, 89; SAF/NEA Winners, New Orleans Cont Arts Ctr, 94; Mus Univ, Medellin, Colombia, 95; Casa de la Cultura, Santa Cruz, Bolivia, 96; Biblioteca Luis Angel Arango, Bogota, Colombia, 96; Instituto Iberoamericano, Santa Cruz, Bolivia, 98; Centro Colombia Americano, Medellin, Colombia, 98. *Teaching:* Asst Prof, Adams State Col, Alamosa, Co, 67-73; assoc prof, Univ Ark, Little Rock, 78-89; assoc prof, sculpture, Univ Ga, Athens, 89-95. *Awards:* MAAA/NEA Fel, 85; AAC Vis Arts Fel, 86; SAF/NEA Fel, 93; Sculpture Award, Fla Nat, Tallahassee, Fla, 94. *Mem:* Int Sculpture Ctr; Mid-Am Coll Art Asn. *Media:* All Media, Handformed Paper. *Mailing Add:* Lamar Dodd Sch Art Dept Art Univ Georgia Athens GA 30602

SARABIA, EDUARDO
INSTALLATION SCULPTOR
b Los Angeles, Calif, 1976. *Study:* Otis Coll Art & Design, BFA, Los Angeles, 99. *Exhib:* I Candy, Rosamund Felsen Gallery, Santa Monica, Calif, 99; solo exhibs, I-20 Gallery, New York, 2001, 2003 & 2006, Santa Monica Mus Art, Calif, 2002, Sutton Lane, London, 2003, 404 Arte Contemporanea, Naples, Italy, 2004, 4-F Gallery, Los Angeles, 2005, Art Basel Miami Beach, Miami, 2005-2006, LA Louver, Los Angeles, 2008, Tokyo Wonder Site, Japan, 2009, Galerie Anne de Villepoix, Paris, France, 2009; Liste, Art 32 Basel, Switzerland, 2001; The Armory Show, New York, 2002; Works for Giovanni, China Art Objects, Los Angeles, 2003; Art Basel Miami Beach (I-20), Miami, 2003; Democracy Was Fun, White Box, New York, 2005; Rogue Wave '07, Los Angeles, 2007; Whitney Biennial, Whitney Mus Am Art, New York, 2008. *Bibliog:* Peter Frank (auth), Art Pick of the Week, LA Weekly, 8/21-27/98; Clayton Campbell (auth), i-CANDY: LA in Flux, Flash Art, 1-2/99; Liz Goldwyn (auth), LA Story: Eduardo Sarabia, Hanatsubaki, 8/2001; Lisa Boone (auth), My Favorite Weekend: Eduardo Sarabia, Calendar Weekend, LA Times, 12/12/2002; Christine Kim (auth), Color Blind: For A Generation of Artists, Race is a Metaphor, But Not An Ism, V Mag, 3-4/2003; Tatiana Flores (auth), The Armory Show, ArtNexus, No 53, Vol 3, 2004; Robin Symes (auth), The Art House, Marie Claire, 244-247, 5/2005; Eleanor Heartney (auth), Eduardo Sarabia at I-20, Art in Am, 191, 10/2006; Benjamin Genocchio (auth), Fresh Eyes on a Colorful Movement, NY Times, 12/9/2007; Richard Lacayo (auth), The Simple Life, Time Mag, 71-74, 5/24/2008. *Mailing Add:* I-20 Gallery 314 E 51st St #2 New York NY 10022

SARACENO, TOMAS
INSTALLATION SCULPTOR
b Tucuman, Argentina, 1973. *Study:* Escuela Superior de Bellas Artes Ernesto de la Carova, Buenos Aires, Postgraduate in Art & Archit, 1999-2000; Universidad Nacional de Buenos Aires, Licencuado en Archit, 1992-99; Staatliche Hochschule fur Bildende Kunst, Postgraduate in Art & Archit, Frankfurt, 2001-03. *Exhib:* Solo exhibs, Walker Arts Ctr., 1990, 2009, Lucas de estrella, Escuela Nacional de Bellas Artes Ernesto de la Carcova, Buenos Aires, 1998, 612 Planetas, Parque Planetario, Buenos Aires, 2000, in-migration, Universitat Kaiserslautern, Germany, 2003, on-air, Pinksummer, Genoa, Italy, 2004, Air-Port-City, Tanya Bonakdar Gallery, NY, 2006, 2008, Matrix 224, Univ Calif, Berkeley, 2007 and others; Objetos de Jovenes Artistas, Centro Cultural Recoleta, Buenos Aires, 1998, Real Presence, Tito Mus, Berlin, 2001, Peace and Love, Palazzo Buonauguro, Bassano, Italy, 2002, Biennale de Venezia, Venice, 2002, 2003, 2009, Un-build Cities, Kunstverein, Bonn, 2003, Universal Outstretch, Flaca Gallery, London, 2004, Dialectic of Hope, Moscow Biennale of Contemporary Art, 2005, The Opening, Anderson S Contemporary Art, Copenhagen, 2005, Longing Ballons Are Floating Around the World, Green Light Pavillion, Berlin, 2005, Buenos dias Santiago, Mus Contemporary Art, Santiago de Chile, 2006, The History of a Decade that Has Not Yet Been Named, Lyon Biennial, France, 2007, Brave New Worlds, Walker Art Ctr, Minn, 2007, 48 Degrees Celcius Public Art Ecology, Delhi, India, 2008, The Liverpool Biennial, 2008, Seeing the Light, Tanya Bonakdar Gallery, NY, 2008-09. *Mailing Add:* c/o Tanya Bonakdar Gallery 521 W 21st St New York NY 10011

SARAI, MAYUMI
SCULPTOR
b Aichi, Japan. *Study:* Nihon Univ Coll Art, Tokyo, BFA (Sculpture), 1988; New York Studio Sch, 1995. *Exhib:* Solo exhibs include Senyu Gallery, Tokyo, 1986, Cooper Gallery, Jersey City, 1998, Washington Art Asn, Washington Depot, Conn, 1998, Coll Ozarks, Point Lookout, Mo, 2003, Cidnee Patrick Gallery, Dallas, 2003, Lohin Geduld Gallery, New York, 2005, Cecille R Hunt Gallery, Webster Univ, St Louis, 2006; Group exhibs include Tokyo Metrop Mus, 1988; Select Paintings & Sculpture, Pleiades Gallery, New York, 1995; Bright Light, Masquerade Am Vision, Cooper Gallery, Jersey City, 1997, United Water, 1998; Wayne Art Ctr, Wayne, Pa, 2000; Native Voices: New Jersey & Westward, Mason Gross Sch Arts, Rutgers Univ, New Brunswick, NJ, 2002; Elizabeth Harris Gallery, New York, 2002; New Jersey State Mus, Trenton, NJ 2002; Studio Selections, Dallas Mus Art, 2003; Seismic Disturbance, Lohin Geduld Gallery, New York, 2004; 183rd Ann: Invitational Exhib Contemp Am Art, Nat Acad Mus, New York, 2008. *Awards:* George Spaventa Memorial Sch, NY Studio Sch, 1993-95; NJ Printmaking Fel, 2001; J Sanford Saltus Award & Medal, Nat Acad, 2008

SARANTOS, BETTIE J
PAINTER, INSTRUCTOR
b Aug 15, 1934. *Study:* Workshops with Dong Kingman, Betty Lou Schlem, Charles Movali, Frank Webb, Charles Reid, Gerald Brommer & others, 79-; Zhejiang Acad Arts, Hangzhou, China, cert, 86. *Work:* Nat Croquet Gallery, Newport, RI; RI Hosp Corp Collection, Providence; Arts & Crafts Inst, Weifang, China; Smithsonian Inst-White House Easter Egg Collection, Washington, DC. *Exhib:* Providence Art Club, 81-95; Taipei Exhib, Am Brush Painters, Taipei, 84; solo exhib, Univ Conn, Storrs, 85; Zhejiang Acad Arts, Hangzhou, China, 86, 2009; Newport Art Mus, RI, 95 & 97-2003; Art Complex Mus, Duxbury, Mass, 2003; Jessica Hagen Fine Art, 2006; Rhode Island Sch Design, 2010; Japan Craze, Newport Art Mus, 2010; Spring Bull Gallery, Newport RI, 2010. *Pos:* Dir, Roger King Gallery Art, Newport, RI, 85-95. *Teaching:* Oriental brush painting, Newport Art Mus, RI, 74-94 & RI Sch Design Continuing Educ; Classes in her own studio; Instr workshops, Newport Art Mus; Instr Workshops, RI Sch Design Continuing Educ. *Awards:* First, Channel 36, Providence, RI, 84; First & Best of Show, War Coll Mus, 95; Florence Brevoort Kane, Providence Art Club, 98. *Bibliog:* Spencer Berger (auth), Bettie J Sarantos-Not just the lady artist of the croquet world, RI First Online Mag, 98; studio tour & interview, Cox Cable Television, 98. *Mem:* Copley Soc, Boston; SUMI-E Soc Am Inc; Am Artists Chinese Brush Painting; Nat Mus Woman Artists, Washington, DC; Providence Art Club; Art League of RI. *Media:* All Media. *Publ:* Featured artist, Best of 2007, Newport Life Mag; Elaine Colton (auth), Art Work on cover, The Newport Girls, 2010. *Dealer:* Roger King Fine Art 21 Bowens Wharf Newport RI 02840; Spring Bull Gallery Bellevue Ave Newport RI 02840. *Mailing Add:* Studio One 1 Hope St Newport RI 02840

SARET, ALAN DANIEL
SCULPTOR, PAINTER
b New York, NY, Dec 25, 1944. *Study:* Cornell Univ, BArch, with Peter Kahn & Alan Atwell; Hunter Col, with Robert Morris. *Work:* Mus Mod Art, Whitney Mus Am Art, NY; Detroit Inst Art; Art Gallery Ont; Ft Worth Art Mus, Tex; Dallas Art Mus & Art Mus STex; Allen Art Mus, Oberlin Col. *Comn:* Ghosthouse, Artpark, Niagara, NY, 75; Home and Away (environ mosaic), Greater Pittsburgh Int Airport, 92. *Exhib:* Whitney Ann, 69 & Whitney Biennial, 77, Whitney Mus Am Art, NY; Recent Acquisitions, Mus Mod Art, NY, 75-76; solo exhibs, Charles Cowles Gallery, NY 80 & 82, Rudolph Zwirner Gallery, Cologne, Ger, 81, Nigel Greenwood Gallery, London, 82, Daniel Weinberg Gallery, Los Angeles, 83 & 89, Albright-Knox Gallery, Buffalo, NY, 83 Alan Saret: Recent Sculpture & Drawings, Margo Leavin Gallery, Los Angeles, 86 & Lorence Monk Gallery, NY, 89; Recent Developments in Sculpture, Whitney Mus Am Art, 81; Images of the Unknown, PS 1, Long Island City, NY, 86; Natural Form and Forces, MIP Bank Boston, Mass, 86; Eccentric Abstraction, Blum Helman Gallery, NY, 86; Retrospective exhib, Inst Art Urban Resources, PS 1, Long Island City, NY, 90; Web of Pythagoras, 99. *Pos:* Founder & dir, ALAEL, 74-77. *Teaching:* Vis artist sculpture, Univ Calif, Irvine, 78. *Awards:* Guggenheim Fel, 69; Nat Endowment Arts Fel, 75; CAPS Grant, 76. *Bibliog:* Suzanne Muchnic (auth), A show that is wired for brightness, Los Angeles Times, 6/9/86; Cynthia Goodman (auth), Digital Visions, Everson Mus Art, 87; Michael Brenson, rev, NY Times, 5/29/87; Robert Morgan (auth), Eccentric abstraction and post-minimalism, Flash Art, 1/2/89; Michael Kimmelman (auth), Exploring the connections in a multi-faceted Career, NY Times, 1/26/90. *Media:* Multimedia. *Publ:* Auth, The Ghosthouse, ALAEL, 76; coauth (with Klaus Kertess), Matter Into Aether, Newport Harbor Art Mus, Newport Beach, Calif, 82

SARETZKY, GARY DANIEL
PHOTOGRAPHER, HISTORIAN
b Newton, Mass, 1946. *Study:* Univ Wis, BA, 68, MA, 69; Thomas Edison Coll, BA; studied with Peter Bunnell, William Barksdale, Duane Michals, Frederick Sommer, Eva Rubinstein & Charles Harbutt. *Work:* Hist Soc of Princeton, NJ; Hopewell Mus, NJ; George Eastman House, Rochester, NY; Mercer Co Cult & Heritage Comn, Trenton, NJ. *Exhib:* 2nd Biennial NJ Artists Exhib, NJ State Mus, 79; Images: The Art of Photog, Monmouth Mus, 81; Living in Am, Noyes Mus, 88; Stated as Fact, NJ State Mus, 90; TAWA in the USSR, Soviet Artists Gallery, Moscow, 90; Rutgers Univ, Newark, 2007; Rider Univ, Lawrenceville, NJ, 2007; Bucks Co Blues, Levittown, Pa, 2008; Blue Musicians, JB Kline Gallery, Lambertville, NJ, 2011. *Collection Arranged:* Educ Testing Serv Arch, Princeton, NJ; Herman Witkin Papers; Louis H Draper Papers; exhibs curated, Margaret Bourke-White: In Print, Rutgers Univ, 2006. *Pos:* Archivist, Monmouth Co, 94; self-employed photogr, photo conservator & consult, presently. *Teaching:* Assoc prof photog, Mercer Co Community Coll, 77- & Trenton State Coll, 85-93; vis prof, Rutgers Univ, 93-, Thomas Edison Coll, 2011-. *Awards:* Purchase Award, Mercer Co Photography, 78, 80, 82 & 83; First Prize, Princeton Art Asn, 79; Best in Show, Mercer Co Photography, 80; Maureen Ogden

award, 2012. *Bibliog:* Gary Saretzky Retrospective, 1972-2007 (exhib catalog). *Mem:* Am Inst Conserv Photo Materials Group; History Photog Group; Trenton Artists Workshop Asn (pub relations dir, 85-87); Soc Photog Educ; Princeton Preservation Group (pres, 2004-). *Media:* Silver Gelatin, Digital Prints. *Res:* History of photography. *Interests:* 19th century New Jersey photographers. *Publ:* Auth, The effects of electrostatic copying on modern photographs, 86 & Recent photographic conservation and preservation literature, 87, Picturescope; Photographic conservation, Conservation Admin News, 88; North American business archives, Business History Bull, 90-91; Elias Goldensky: Wizard of Photography, Pa History, 97; Margaret Bourke-White: Eyes on Russia, Photo Review, 99, She Worked Her Head Off: Edwin and Louise Rosskam & the Golden Age of Documentary Photography Books, 2000; Nineteenth Century NJ Photographers, NJ Hist, 2004; Margaret Bourke-White: In Print (auth, catalog), Rutgers Univ, 2006. *Mailing Add:* 700 Trumbull Ave Lawrenceville NJ 08648

SARGENT, MARGARET HOLLAND
PAINTER
b Hollywood, Calif, 1927. *Study:* Univ Calif, Los Angeles, 45-47; Tokyo, Japan, 56; with Herbert Abrams, NY, 59-61 & Marcos Blahove, Fairfax, Va, 69; Art Students League, with John Sanden, 74. *Work:* British Piano Mus, Middlesex, Eng; US Military Acad Mus; US Air Force Acad; USA Pentagon; US Naval Acad; US Naval War Col; Hawaii State Found; Navy Combat Artists; Nat Portrait Gallery, US. *Comn:* Portrait, President Gerald Ford, Time, Inc; Judge Wm Matthew Byrne, Jr, US District Ct; Secretary of State and Mrs Alexander M Haig; playwright Tennessee Williams; Jules S Stein; Prince Turki Saud; Governor George Ariyoshi, Hawaii; Army Chief of Staff, General John A Wickham; Lew R Wasserman; Dorothy Stimson, Bullitt; Kent Kresa, CEO, Northrop Grumman, 2003; portrait, Mary Maxwell Gates & William Gates Sr; Jonathan Varat, Dean, UCLA School of Law, 2004; Los Angeles Mayor, James K. Hahn; Hearst Cord Coll; Frank A Bennack, CEO Hearst Corp; Michael Foster, Pres Bus Sch, Univ Wash; Michael AJ Farrell CEO Annaly Capitol Mgmt. *Exhib:* Solo exhibs, Turkish Am Asn, Ankara, 63, Frye Art Mus, 71 & 84, Woodside Gallery, Seattle, 72 & Excelsior Club, NY, 74-75; Group exhibs, Salmagundi, NY; plus many others. *Pos:* Owner-dir, Sargent Portraits, Los Angeles, currently. *Teaching:* Lectr,Metrop Mus Art, 2001; instr video, Camelot Productions, currently. *Awards:* H M Salmagundi Award; Naval Award Outstanding Achievement in Oil Painting, 77; First Prize Prof Oils, AFL-CIO's 10th Ann, Los Angeles, 79; and others. *Bibliog:* numerous articles in Town & Country, Forbes, Time, Inc, Am Artist, Southwest Art, Money, Palm Springs Life, Baltimore Sun & many others, 76-2000. *Mem:* Salmagundi Club; Am Portrait Soc; Coun Leading Am Portrait Painters (founder); Am Soc Portrait Artists; West Coast Soc Portrait Artists (judge); Portrait Soc of Am. *Media:* Oil. *Specialty:* Oil Portraits. *Dealer:* Portraits Inc NY. *Mailing Add:* 2750 Glendower Ave Los Angeles CA 90027

SARICH, MICHAEL
PAINTER, CERAMIST
b Chicago. *Study:* Northern Ill Univ; Univ Okla. *Work:* Art Inst Chicago; Univ Nev, Las Vegas & Reno; Bemis Ctr Contemp Arts, Omaha. *Exhib:* Solo retrospective: Like, Love, Lust, Nev Mus Art, 2008. *Teaching:* Assoc prof painting/ceramics, Univ Nev, Reno, 1989-. *Awards:* NEA Nev State Award Visual Arts; Bemis Found Fel, 1992; Joan Mitchell Found Grant, 2007. *Dealer:* Stremmel Gallery 1400 S Virginia St Reno NV 89502. *Mailing Add:* Dept Art 224 Univ Nevada Reno 1664 N Virginia St Reno NV 89557

SARKISIAN, AMY
SCULPTOR
b Cleveland, 1969. *Study:* Kent State Univ, BFA, 1994; Univ Calif Los Angeles, MFA, 1997. *Exhib:* Solo exhibs include 1234 gallery, Los Angeles, 1999, Marella Arte Contemporanea, Milan, 2002, Suzanne Vielmetter Los Angeles Projs, 2003, Atelier Cardenas Bellanger, Paris, 2005, 2006, Sister, Los Angeles, 2005, 2007,; Group exhibs include Malibu Sex Party, Purple, Los Angeles, 1997; Ideas, Beyond Baroque, Los Angeles, 1998; Young & Dumb, Acme, Los Angeles, 2000; People are Animals, Three Day Weekend, Los Angeles Projs, 2000; Mysterious Prey, Roberts & Tilton Gallery, Los Angeles, 2000; Funeral Home, Marc Foxx, Los Angeles, 2002; We Are Electric, Deitch Projs, New York, 2003; Losing My Head, Sister, Los Angeles, 2004 ; Fast Forward, House of Campari, Los Angeles, 2005; All I Want Is Everything, Small A Projects, Portland, Ore, 2005; Altoids Curiously Strong Collection 7, New Mus Contemp Art, New York, 2005; Symmetry, Mak Ctr, Los Angeles, 2006; Pub Park, Los Angeles, 2007 ; Globetrotters, Cottage Home, Los Angeles, 2008; Against the Grain, Los Angeles Contemp Exhibs, Los Angeles, 2008 .

SAROFIM, FAYEZ S
COLLECTOR
b Nov, 19, 1928. *Study:* Univ Calif, Berkeley, BS (food technology), 1949; Harvard, MBA, 1951. *Pos:* Founder, chmn, and pres, Fayez Sarofim & co, 1958-; bd mgr, Mem Sloan-Kettering Cancer Ctr, currently; council mem, Rockefeller Univ; bd dirs, Alley Theatre, Houston Ballet Found, Mus Fine Arts, Houston, Tex Heart Inst. *Awards:* Named one of Top 200 Collectors, ARTnews mag, 2004-13. *Mem:* Houston Symphony Soc (vice chair bd dirs, formerly). *Collection:* Coptic art; 19th-century American art; Old Masters; American Impressionism; modern and contemporary art. *Mailing Add:* Fayez Sarofim & Co Ste 2907 Two Houston Ctr Houston TX 77010

SAROFIM, LOUISA STUDE
COLLECTOR
Pos: Chmn, Houston Grand Opera Studio; pres bd trustees The Menil Collection, currently; trustee adv, Rice Univ; hon chmn, The Drawing Ctr, New York. *Awards:* Named one of top 200 collectors, ARTnews mag, 2006-13. *Bibliog:* Coauth (with Matthew Drutt and Anna Gaskell), Anna Gaskell: Half Life, 2003. *Collection:* Modern and contemporary art and works on paper. *Mailing Add:* The Menil Collection 1511 Branard Houston TX 77006

SARSONY, ROBERT
PAINTER, PRINTMAKER
b Easton, Pa, Jan 1, 1938. *Work:* Butler Inst Am Art, Youngstown, Ohio; NJ State Mus, Trenton; Joslyn Art Mus, Omaha, Nebr; Nat Mus Am Art, Smithsonian Inst, Washington; Univ Kans Mus Art, Lawrence; and others. *Exhib:* Allied Artist Show, NY, 63-65; Solo exhibs, Capricorn Galleries, Bethesda, Md, 67-78; Christopher Gallery, NY, 78-80; Meinhard Galleries, Houston, Tex, 82-83; Harris Gallery, Dallas, Tex, 85-87; Huckleberry Galleries, Bethesda, Md; The Little Gallery, Moneta, Va; Zantman Galleries, Carmel, Calif. *Bibliog:* John S Le Maire (auth), Robert Sarsony, NJ Bus Mag, 69; Philip Desind (auth), article, Southwest Art, 4/80; Dennis Wepman (auth), article, Sunstorm Arts Mag, fall 91. *Media:* Oil, Watercolor, Serigraph, Lithography, Acrylic. *Publ:* Contribr, Sunstorm Arts Mag, 10/91; US Art, 8/97; Robert Sarsony An Artists Album, 2013. *Dealer:* Robert Sarsony Portfolio Cary NC; The Little Gallery Moneta VA; Huckleberry Fine Art Rockville Md; Zantman Galleries Carmel CA

SASAMOTO, AKI
INSTALLATION SCULPTOR, KINETIC ARTIST
Study: Wesleyan Univ, Conn, BA, 2004; Columbia Univ Sch Arts, MFA, 2007. *Exhib:* Salvage/Salvation, Queens Botanical Garden, Long Island City, 2004; Construct, Exit Art, New York, 2007; Freeway Balconies, Deutsche Guggenheim, Berlin, 2008; Whitney Biennial, Whitney Mus Am Art, New York, 2010; Greater New York: 5 Year Review, PS1 Contemp Art Ctr/Mus Mod Art, New York, 2010. *Teaching:* Instr sculpture programs, Columbia Univ, 2009, Wesleyan Univ, 2009, Whitney Mus Am Art, 2010. *Awards:* Jessup Prize, Wesleyan Univ, 2004; Toby Fund Award, Toby Fund, 2007; Visual Art Grant, Rema Hort Mann Found, 2007. *Bibliog:* Susan Yung (auth), Dancing Asia/New York, Dance Mag, 8/2004; Deborah Jowitt (auth), Yvonne Meier: Monkey Do: Could this dance be a poster for recycling?, Village Voice, 12/25/2007; Linda Yablonsky (auth), Women's Work, NY Times, 2/12/2010

SASNAL, WILHELM
PAINTER
b Tarnow, Poland, 1972. *Study:* Krakow Polytech (Architecture), 1994; Krakow Acad Fine Art, Poland, 1999. *Work:* Carnegie Mus Art, Pittsburg; Mus on Seam, Jerusalem; Saatchi Gallery, London; Tate Britain, London; MuHKA Mus, Antwerp, Belgium. *Exhib:* Solo exhibs include Ctr Contemp Art, Warsaw, 1999, Anton Kern Gallery, New York, 2002, 2007, MuHKA Mus voor Hedendaagse Kunst Antwerpen, Belgium, 2003, Zawa Srod, Johnen & Schöttle, Cologne, Germany, 2004, Berkeley Art Mus & Pac Film Arch, CA, 1995, Sadie Coles HQ, London, 2006, Swiss Inst, New York, 2007, Johnen Galerie, Berlin, 2007, CaixaForum Barcelona, 2007; group exhibs include Johann Korec, Galerie Susanne Zander, Cologne, Germany, 1999; Scene 2000: All-Polish Art Exhib, Ctr Contemp Art, Warsaw, Poland, 2000, Foksal Gallerys Deposit, The Young Are Realists Really, 2002, A Need for Realism, 2002, 1 2 3 AVANT-GARDE, 2006, At the very centre of attention Part 10, 2006, MANUAL CC, 2008; Tirana Biennale, 2001; In Between, Chicago Cult Ctr, 2001; Semiotic Landscape, Charim Galerie, Vienna, 2002; Funny Cuts, Staatsgalerie Stuttgart, Germany, 2004; T-ow, Anton Kern Gallery, New York, 2004; Triumph of Painting Part 2, Saatchi Gallery, London, 2005; Grey Flags, Sculpture Ctr, Long Island, NY, 2006; Lights Camera Action, Whitney Mus Am Art, New York, 2007; Painting of Mod Life, Mus d'arte contemp Castello di Rivoli, Turin, Italy, 2008; Selections, Hara Mus Contemp Art, Tokyo, 2008. *Dealer:* Zwirner & Wirth 32 E 69th St New York NY 10021; Sadie Coles HQ 35 Heddon St London England W1B 4BP UK; GALERIA RASTER Hoza 42 apt 800-516 Warsaw Poland; Johnen & Schöttle Maria-Hilf-Str 17 Cologne Germany 50677; Johnen Galerie Schillingstr 31 Berlin Germany 10179. *Mailing Add:* Anton Kern Gallery 532 West 20th Street New York NY 10011

SASSONE, MARCO
PAINTER, PRINTMAKER
b Florence, Italy, July 27, 1942. *Study:* Ist Galileo Galilei, Florence; Acad Fine Arts, with Silvio Loffredo, Florence. *Work:* Los Angeles Co Mus Art; Nat Art Gallery, Wellington, NZ; Galleria d'Arte Int, Florence; Hunt-Wesson; Laguna Art Mus, Calif. *Comn:* Mural, Palio D'asti, San Francisco; mural, Bellagio on bloor, Toronto, Can. *Exhib:* Solo exhibs, Wally Findlay Galleries, Beverly Hills & NY, 77-79, Wally Findlay Galleries, Beverly Hills, Calif, 82, Bernheim-Jeune, Paris, France, 88, Diane Nelson Gallery, Laguna Beach, Calif, 87, Buschlen-Mowatt Gallery, Vancouver, Can, 90, Ital Cul Inst, San Francisco, Calif, 89 & 91 & Pasquale Iannetti Galleries, San Francisco, 93, Cloisters of S Croce, Florence, Italy, 97, Palazzo Ducale, Massa-Carrara, Italy, 2002, Scape, Corona del Mar, Calif, 2007, Nat Shrine S Francis, San Francisco, 2010, Price Tower Arts Ctr, Bartlesville, Okla, 2012, Berenson Fine Art, Toronto, Canada, 2012, San Angelo Mus Fine Art, Tex, 2013, Berenson Fine Art, Toronto, Can, 2013; group exhibs, Nat Acad Design, NY, 77, Basel Art Fair, Ger, 90, Chicago Int Art Expo, 90; Laguna Art Mus, Laguna Beach, Calif, 79; Munic Art Gallery, Los Angeles, 88; Los Angeles Contemp Exhib, 92; Mus Italo Americano, San Francisco, 94; Springfield Art Mus, Mo, 98; Toronto Int Art Fair, 2001; Art Miami, 2004; San Francisco Int Art Exposition, 2005; David Findlay Jr Fine Art, New York, 2008; Palm Beach 3, Fla, 2009, David Findlay Jr, NY, 2010, Berenson Fine Art, Toronto, 2012. *Pos:* Lectr-guest artist, Bowers Mus, Santa Ana, Calif, 70, San Bernardino Mus Art, Calif, 78, Laguna Beach Mus Art, 78, Orange Coast Coll, Costa Mesa, Calif, 78, Laguna Beach Arts Comn, Calif, 78-81 & Kern Co Art Educ Asn, Bakersfield, Calif, 79. *Awards:* Gold Medal, Ital Acad Arts, Lit & Sci, 78; Off Knight, Ital Repub, 82; Day named in honor, Mayor Frank Jordan, San Francisco, 3/30/94. *Bibliog:* Donelson F Hoopes (auth), monogr, 79, Arti Grafiche Il Torchio, Florence, Italy; John Wilson (producer), Sassone (film), Fine Arts Films Inc, 76; Peter Clothier (auth), Home on the Street (catalog), 94. *Media:* Oil; Watercolors. *Publ:* Critic, William Wilson, Los Angeles Times, 11/14/75; Sassone Serigraphs, Arti Grafiche, Florence, Italy, 9/84; Janet Dominik (auth), Sassone (catalog), Bernheim-Jeune, Paris, France, 88; Peter Clothier (auth), Sassone (catalog), Ital Cult Inst, San Francisco, Calif, 91; Kenneth Baker (critic), San Francisco Chronicle, Apr 17, 94; and others.

Dealer: Pasquale Iannetti Art Gallery 565 Sutter St San Francisco CA 94102; Scape 2859 East Coast Highway Corona Del Mar California 92625; Berenson Fine Art 212 Avenue Rd Toronto ON M5R 2J4 Canada. *Mailing Add:* Marco Sassone Studio 300 Bloor St East Ste 1910 Toronto ON Canada M4W 3Y2

SATO, MASAAKI
PAINTER
b Kofu, Japan, Feb 28, 1941. *Study:* Kofu Saito Fine Arts Inst, Japan; Heatherley Sch Fine Arts, London, Eng; Brooklyn Mus Art Sch, NY; Pratt Inst. *Work:* Aldrich Mus Contemp Art, Ridgefield, Conn; Mus Honolulu Acad Art; Minn Mus Art, Minneapolis; ETenn State Univ; Mus Mod Art, La Tertulia, Cali, Columbia; and others. *Comn:* Big Apple (sculpture), Eye Messe Yamanashi, Yamanashi Prefectural, Japan, 95. *Exhib:* Solo exhibs, Brooklyn Mus Little Gallery, 73, Soho Ctr Visual Artists, NY, 76 & Edward Williams Col, NJ, 77; Yamanashi Prefectural Mus (auth, catalog), Japan, 90; OK Harris Works of Art, NY, 92, 95 & 96; and many others. *Awards:* 9th Nat Print & Drawing Exhib, Minot, NDak; Rockford Int Print Exhib, Ill, 79; 40th N Am Print Exhib, Brockton Art Mus, Mass, 88. *Bibliog:* Richard Walker (auth), Gallery reviews, Art Rev, 8/31/68; Arthur Bloomfield (auth), An artist of many styles, San Francisco Examiner, 9/24/73; Malcolm Preston (auth), Westbeth connection, Newsday, 7/31/75; John Canaday (auth), It's spring in Connecticut and new talent blooms, 5/9/76; Michael Brenson (auth), Off the beaten paths at city treasure houses, 1/13/84 & Michael Brenson (auth), Weekend reviews, 6/21/85, New York Times. *Mem:* Contemp Artists Orgn; Am Soc Contemp Artists. *Media:* Acrylic, Oil. *Publ:* Auth, The Frederick R Weisman Foundation Collection of Art, Tsurumoto Room Co Ltd, Japan, 86; Japanese Anti-Art: Now and Then, Nat Mus Art Osaka, Japan, 91; ARTODAY, Phaidon Press Ltd, London, 95. *Dealer:* OK Harris 383 W Broadway New York NY 10012. *Mailing Add:* 55 Bethune St New York NY 10014

SATO, NORIE
ENVIRONMENTAL ARTIST, SCULPTOR
b Sendai, Japan, July 19, 1949. *Study:* Univ Mich, BFA, 1971; Univ Wash, MFA, 1974. *Work:* Brooklyn Mus; Philadelphia Mus Art; Seattle Art Mus; Guggenheim Mus; Tacoma Art Mus. *Comn:* Westside Light Rail, Portland, Ore, 1992-98; Miami Int Airport, 1996-2007; Univ Wash/Cascadia Community Col, Bothell, 2000; Seattle Justice Ctr, 2000-02; Mountain Ranch Aquatic Ctr, Scottsdale AZ, 2007; Arabian Libr, Scottsdale, AZ, 2008; Intermodal Transit Ctr, Salt Lake City, UT, 2009; Sound Transit, Seattle, 2008-; Hygienic Lab, Univ Iowa, 2010; Port of Portland Headquarters, 2010; Hach Hall, Iowa State Univ, 2011; Cary Arts Ctr, NC, 2011; San Francisco Int Airport, 2011; Biochemistry addition, Univ Wisc, Madison, 2012; Reflection Room, San Diego Int Airport, 2014. *Exhib:* Thirty Yrs Am Printmaking, 1976 & Eight West Coast Printmakers, Brooklyn Mus, 1978; 5th Int Brit Print Biennale, Bradford, Eng, 1976; Northwest '77, Seattle Art Mus, 1977; Proj Video XXIV, Mus Mod Art, NY, 1979; Lande, Ritchie & Sato, Vancouver Art Gallery, BC, 1979; Videoviewpoints, Mus Mod Art, NY, 1980; 19 Artists-Emergent Americans, Guggenheim Mus, 1981; solo shows, Linda Farris Gallery, 1981, 1982, 1983, 1986, 1987, 1990, 1993 & 1995 & Elizabeth Leach Gallery, 1989, 1991, 1994 & 1997; Seattle Art Mus, 1984; Reed Col, 1987; 15th Ave Studio II, Henry Art Gallery, Seattle, 1987; Home Show, Santa Barbara Contemp Arts Forum, 1988; Contemp Voices: Washington Sculptors, Bellevue Art Mus, 1993; Alcott Gallery, Univ NC, Chapel Hill, 2000. *Teaching:* Cornish Col, Seattle, 1984-87; Western Wash Univ, Bellingham, fall 1989; Univ Mich, Ann Arbor, 1998. *Awards:* Wash State Arts Com, 1990; Artist Trust Fel, 1994; George Tsutakawa Award for Advancement of Pub Art, 1997; Crescordia Award Environmental Art, Phoenix, AZ, 2007; Year in Review, Pub Art Recognition, Am Arts, 2007, 2008, 2010, 2012; Twining Humber award, Artist Trust, Seattle, 2013; Public Art Network/Americans for the Arts Leardership award, 2014. *Mem:* COCA, Seattle, (bd mem); Reflex, Seattle, (bd mem); WESTAF, Santa Fe, (bd mem); Coll Art Asn (bd mem); Pub Art Network Coun; On The Boards (bd mem, secy); Seattle Design Comn; Am Inst Architects (hon mem, 2010). *Media:* Electronic, Mixed. *Mailing Add:* 1045 NE 88th Seattle WA 98115

SATTLER, JILL
PHOTOGRAPHER, PAINTER
b New York, NY, Jan 3, 1947. *Study:* Chouinard Art Inst, Los Angeles, 68 (with scholarship & honors), Univ Calif, Santa Barbara; pvt study as well as manuscript painting with student of Royal Scribe to Queen of Eng. *Work:* Pvt collections of Cher (worn during acceptance of Acad Award for Moonstruck), Diane English (writer, exec producer of Murphy Brown & featured in ELLE Mag); photog portraits of Beatrice Wood (100th birthday), Chantal of Good Morning Am & Sandy Duncan. *Comn:* Many public & pvt comns. *Exhib:* CL Clark Galleries, Bakersfield, Calif, 91; Painting & Photog Exhib, Karpeles Manuscript Mus, 93-94; Photog Exhib, Carnegie Art Mus, Ventura, Calif, 94; Art Mus Santa Cruz Co; Ron Breeden Gallery, Orange Co, 95; Contemp Arts Forum Santa Barbara; De La Guerra Gallery & Frameworks, Santa Barbara, Calif, 97; Photog portrait, Beatrice Wood's 105th Birthday (with catalog), Milagros Nest Gallery, Ojai, Calif, 98; Photog portrait with Beatrice Wood's Vessels and Figures, Ojai Valley Mus, Calif, 98. *Pos:* Own, Jill Sattler Embellishments & Jill Sattler Photog. *Teaching:* Instr photog hand tinting, Carnegie Art Mus, Santa Barbara City Col, Santa Barbara Photog & Learning Tree Univ, Thousand Oaks. *Bibliog:* Chouinard: An Art Vision Betrayed, Astra Publ Inc, 86; A Survey of the States Museums, Galleries and Artists, Calif Art Rev, 90 & A Survey of Leading American Contemporaries, 90, Am References Publ Co. *Publ:* Jewelry photos only in Elle Mag, Ladies Home J Memories Mag (front cover), Artspace Mag Scene, Los Angeles Times, Vanity Fair Mag

SATUREN, BEN
PAINTER, EDUCATOR
b Somerset, Pa, Dec 10, 1948. *Study:* Iowa State Univ, BS, 70; Calif Coll Art & Crafts, 84; Santa Rosa Jr Col, 2000-05, Calif NAUI, 99-2000; Adobe Photoshop cert, 2004. *Work:* Chinese Med Acad Sci, Beijing, China & Shanghai Second Med Univ; Leigh Yawkey Woodson Art Mus, Wausau, Wis; Bell Mus Natural Hist, Minneapolis, Minn. *Comn:* Silkscreen seriagraph, comn by Dr William Bigler, San Francisco State Univ, Calif, 85; World Wildlife Fund/Sao Tome Cachets & Stamps, Comn by Intercontinental Philatelics, Inc, Southampton, NJ, 92; Marine Wildlife Poster, Nature Discovery Press, 90; A Tribute to Tidepools (mural), Petaluma Wildlife & Natural Sci Mus, Calif, 93; Sea Turtles of the World, Nature Discovery Press, 95; Fit n Furry Murals, Petaluma, Calif, 2006. *Exhib:* Wildlife in Crisis, Cent Park Wildlife Conserv Ctr, NY, 93 & 94; Art and the Animal, Bennington Ctr Arts, Vermont, 94 & 96; Houston Mus Natural Sci, 95; Scripps Inst Steven Birch Aquarium & Mus, La Jolla, Calif, 95; Detroit Zoological Gardens, 96; Romberg Tiburon Ctr (SFSU), 2000-2001; Red Star Blue Ring mural, Encloe Med Hosp, Chico, Calif, 2008; Snow Goose Festival, Gallery 9, Chico, Calif, 2009; Gold Nugget Craft Fair, Paradise, Calif, 2011. *Teaching:* Instr 3D modeling & animation, Col of Marin, 2000, Santa Rosa Jr Col, 2001, 02; instr, Acad Art Univ, San Francisco, Calif, 2004; instr animal illus, Sonoma State Univ, 2005-2011; instr botanical & wildlife illustration, Paradise Recreation & Parks District, Paradise, Calif, 2011. *Awards:* Cash Award Winner, Artist's Liaison, 88; Third Place, Seascape, and Merit Awards, Wildlife Art Show, Los Angeles Audubon, 87; Artist of the Year, Proj Reefkeeper, Miami, Fla, 94. *Bibliog:* Colleen Francis (auth), Diving for Art, Calif Diving News, 88; Colleen Francis (auth), Below the Surface, Artist's Mag, 4/89; Colleen Francis (auth), Artist Vignette: Ben Saturen, Wildlife Art News, 3-4/90. *Mem:* Soc Animal Artists; Artists Guild San Francisco; San Francisco Soc Fine Arts; Chico Art Ctr. *Media:* Oil; Silkscreen Serigraphy, Acrylic, Color Pencil. *Publ:* Bay Area Naturalist, Marjorie Ruegg, 82; 1987 Artists' Profile, Wildlife Art News, 87, 89, 90; Profile of Wildlife Artists, Southwest Art, 88; Tropical sea creatures for all to see, The Press Democrat, 94; Undersea Artistry, Petaluma Argus-Courier, 95. *Dealer:* Saturen Studio Paradise CA

SATZ, JANET
PAINTER, EDUCATOR
b Chicago, Ill, Apr 20, 1933. *Study:* Pratt Inst, BFA, 74; New York Univ, MA, 77, DA Fel, 77-79. *Work:* Smithsonian Inst; Southern New Eng Tel, Fairfield, Conn; Housatonic Coll Mus Art, Bridgeport, Conn; Town Westport Collection Art, Conn; Spencer Mus Art, Univ Kans, Lawrence, Kans; Fairfield Univ, Conn; Marlboro Coll, Marlboro, Vt; Sprint Collection Art, Kansas City, Mo; Albert A Arenberg Collection, Chicago; Sch Engineering, Univ Kans, Lawrence; Gen Elec HQ, Fairfield, Conn; AM Century, Kansas City, Mo; and others. *Exhib:* Chicago & Vicinity Ann, Art Inst Chicago, 69; New Reflections, Aldrich Mus Contemp Art, Ridgefield, Conn, 77; Women's Art, Grad Ctr, City Univ New York, 78; Solo exhibs, Carlson Gallery, Bridgeport Univ, Conn, 79, Henry Chauncey Conf Ctr, ETS, Princeton, NJ, 81, Stamford Mus, ART/EX Gallery, Conn, 87, Joy Horwich Gallery, Chicago, 94, Norman R Eppink Art Gallery, Emporia State Univ, Kans, 94 & Morgan Gallery, Kansas City, 2001, Theater Lawrence Gallery of Art, Environments, Lawrence, Kans, 2015; Int Delle Arti Palasso Grassi, Venice, Italy, 79; White House Easter Egg Collection, Mus Art, Sci & Indust, Bridgeport, Conn, 85; 40th Art of Northeast USA, Silvermine Guild Ctr Arts, New Canaan, Conn, 89; Central Mo State Univ, Warrensburg, 91; Kans Ten, Mulvane Art Mus, Washburn Univ, Topeka, 91; 12th Benefit Art Auction, Mus Contemp Art, Chicago, 96; White Gallery, Butler Community Coll, El Dorado, Kans, 97; Shaffer Gallery, Barton Community Coll, Great Bend, Kans, 97; Manhattan Ctr Arts, Kans, 98; Suburban Fine Arts Ctr, Highland Park, Ill, 97; Wichita Art Mus, Wichita Kans, 98; Stockdale Gallery, William Jewel Collape, 2002; Strecher-Nelson Gallery, Manhattan, Kans, 2004; Fields Gallery, Lawrence, Kans, 2006; Foundry Art Ctr, Ft Charles, Mo, 2007; Wall Work, Flatfile Galleries, Chicago, Ill, 2008; Selected Works on Paper and Canvas, Signs of Life Gallery, Lawrence, Kans, 2010; Artists Choose Artists, Burkholder Project, Lincoln, Nebr, 2010; Urban Suburban, Kansas City Jewish Mus Contemporary Art, Epstein Gallery, Kansas City, Mo, 2011, 2012; Lawrence Art Ctr, Kans, 2012; Exhibit A Revisited, Cultural Ctr Chgo Ill, 2013. *Pos:* Dir educ, Whitney Mus Am Art Branch, Fairfield Co, Stamford, Conn, 81-89, educ consult, 89-90; major grants panelist & prof develop panelist, Kans Arts Comn, 90-93; appointment, Lawrence Arts Comn Bd, 2001-2004. *Teaching:* Lectr & dir mus docent training, Whitney Mus Am Art, Stamford, Conn, 81-90. *Awards:* Collborate Lithography Project grant, Kans Arts Comn, 91; Prof Develop/Kans Artist Fel, Nat Endowment Arts & Kans Arts Comn, 94; Exhib Award, Muchnic Gallery, Atchinson, Kans, 97; Barbara Rensner Cash Award, Wichta Mus, Kans, 98; Cover of the Year Award, Kansas City Voices #9 Pub, Kansas City, Mo, 2011; Residency: Escape to Create, Seaside, Florida, 2015. *Bibliog:* William Caxton Jr (auth), The Art of Janet Satz, American Artist, (issue 275), 5/64; J Burnham (auth), monogr, Arts Mag, 2/73; Jacqueline Moss (auth), Stamford Museum celebrates, The Advocate, 4/13/82; Vivien Raynor (auth), Contemporary Solo Shows in Hartford and Marlborough, NY Times, 1/24/88; Mindy Paget (ed), City Seen: Art hails urban landscapes, Lawrence J World; Mindy Paget (auth), City Seen: Art Hails Urban Landscapes, Journal World, Lawrence, Kans, 2007; Michael Weinstein (auth), Janet Satz, Photog, NewCity Pub, Chicago, Ill, 2008; Michael Auchard (auth), Exploring the Urban Landscape, Journal-World, Lawrence, Kans, 2010; A Profile of the Artist Janet Satz, EReview Arts Pub, Kansas City, Mo, 2011. *Media:* Acrylic, Mixed Media, Collage. *Interests:* Contemp art. *Publ:* A Community of Artists: A Chronicle of Painters, Sculptors and Cartoonists of Westport-Weston, 1900-1985. *Mailing Add:* 3713 Quail Creek Ct Lawrence KS 66047

SAUER, JANE GOTTLIEB
SCULPTOR, CURATOR
b St Louis, Mo, Sept 16, 1937. *Study:* Washington Univ, St Louis, Mo, BFA, 59; studied with Leslie Laskey, 76-78. *Work:* Wash Univ Steinberg Mus, St Louis Art Mus, Mo; Erie Art Mus, Pa; Nordenfjeldske Kunstinndustrimuseum, Tronndheim, Norway; Wadsworth Atheneum, Hartford, Conn; Mus Suwa, Japan; and others. *Exhib:* Denver Art Mus, traveling to JB Speed Art Mus, 86; Mus Cantonal Beaux-Arts, Lausanne, Switz, 92; St Louis Art Mus, 93 (two exhibs), 94 & 95 (two exhibs); Newport Harbor Art Mus, 93; Fiber: Five Decades from the Collection, Am Craft Mus, NY, 95; Breaking the Barriers: Recent Am Craft (traveling), Portland Art Mus, Madison Art Ctr, Wis, Albany Art Mus, Ga & Am Craft Mus, NY, 95; Thread, Baribican Ctr, London, Eng, 98; Mint Mus Craft & Design, Inaugural Gift, 2000; Ark

Art Mu Fiber Forms, 2000; Univ Nebr, 2001; R Duane Reed Gallery, St Louis, 2001; Mus Fine Arts, Santa Fe, 2003. *Collection Arranged:* Baskets & Beyond, St Louis, 98; Under The Japanese Influence, St Louis, 99; Inventions & Construction, St Petersburg, Fla, 2000; The Art of Basketry, Santa Fe, 2003. *Pos:* Studio artist, lectr & workshop leader, 76-; lectr, various univs & orgns, US, 77-; vis artist/lectr numerous schs & mus, 77-94; consult, Harris Stowe Col, St Louis, Mo, 80-84. *Teaching:* Art teacher, Jefferson Barrocks Sch Dist, St Louis, Mo, 59-63; artist-in-residence, New City Sch, St Louis, Mo, 76-78. *Awards:* Visual Artists Grant, Nat Endowment Arts, 84 & 90; 15th Biennale Int de la Tapisserie Lausanne, Mus Cantonal Des Beaux-Arts, Switz, 92; Distinguished Alumni Award, Wash Univ, St Louis, Mo. *Bibliog:* Rita Reif (auth), Weavers aren't the whole story in fiber art, NY Times, 4/23/95; Jane Sauer (auth), Janet Kaplos, Catalogue for Making A Difference: Fiber Sculpture, 2000; Bruce Pepich (auth), Impassioned Form (catalogue), Univ Nebr, 2001. *Mem:* Am Craft Coun (bd trustees, 92- & chmn, 97-2000); St Louis Artist Coalition (bd trustees, 84-86); Forum Contemp Art, St Louis, Mo (bd dir, 90-); Nat Coun Sch Art, Wash Univ, 95-; Int Women's Forum; Mus Found NMex (bd dir, 2002-03). *Media:* Structured Fiber. *Dealer:* R Duane Reed Gallery 7513 Forsyth, St Louis, MO 63105; Thirteen Moon Gallery Santa Fe NM 87501. *Mailing Add:* 1379 Cerro Gordo Santa Fe NM 87501

SAUL, ANDREW M
COLLECTOR
b New York, 1946. *Study:* Wharton Sch Fin, Univ Pa, BS, 1968. *Pos:* Exec vpres, Brooks Fashion Stores, 1968-80, pres, 1980-85, BR Investors, 1985-86; gen partner, Saul Partners, 1986-; dir, Caché Inc, 1986-, chmn, 1993-2000; chmn, Fed Retirement Thrift Investment Bd; comnr, Metrop Transportation Authority, New York, 1996-; mem exec comt & chmn audit comt, Mt Sinai Med Ctr; trustee, Fedn Jewish Philanthropies, United Jewish Appeal, Sarah Neuman Nursing Home; trustee & chmn coun, Metrop Mus Art. *Awards:* Named one of Top 200 Collectors, ARTnews mag, 2004-12. *Collection:* Chinese bronzes; modern & contemporary art, especially postwar American. *Mailing Add:* Caché Inc 1440 Broadway New York NY 10018

SAUL, DENISE
COLLECTOR
Awards: Named one of Top 200 Collectors, ARTnews mag, 2009-12. *Collection:* Modern and contemporary art, especially postwar American; Chinese bronzes. *Mailing Add:* 9 W 57th St Ste 3405 New York NY 10019

SAUL, PETER
PAINTER
b San Francisco, Calif, Aug 16, 1934. *Study:* Stanford Univ; Calif Sch Fine Arts, San Francisco, 1950-52; Wash Univ, with Fred Conway, BFA, 1956. *Work:* Art Inst Chicago; Whitney Mus Am Art, Metrop Mus Art, Mus Mod Art, NY; San Francisco Mus Mod Art; Carnegie Inst, Pittsburgh; Los Angeles Co Mus Art; Carnegie Inst, Pittsburg; Madison Art Mus, Wis; Yale Univ Art Gallery; Mus Ludwig; Moderna Museet, Stockholm; and many others. *Exhib:* Solo exhibs, Frumkin/Adams Gallery, NY, 1989-90, 1992, 1993, 1995, Galerie Bonnier, Geneva, Switz, 1990, 1995, Krannert Art Mus, Univ Ill, Champaign, 1990-91, Art Mus, Washington Univ, St Louis, 1990-91, Galerie Du Ctr, Paris, (with catalog) 1991, 1997 & 2000, Herbert Palmer Gallery, Los Angeles, 1994, George Adams Gallery, NY, 1996, 1998-99 & 2004, Nolan Eckman Gallery, 1998, (with catalog) 2000, 2002 & 2004, Galerie Charlotte Moser, Switz, 2002, David Nolan Gallery, NY, 2006, Leo Koenig Gallery, NY, 2006, Galerie Charlotte Moser, Geneva, 2007, Orange Co Mus Art, Newport Beach, Calif, 2008, Pa Acad Fine Arts, Philadelphia, 2008, New Orldans Mus Art, 2009; group exhibs, Soc Contemp Am Art, Art Inst Chicago, 1962-65, 67th Ann Am Exhib (with catalog), 1964, 70th Am Exhib (with catalog), 1972, 72nd Am Exhib, Art Inst Chicago, 1976; Social Comment in Am, Mus Mod Art, NY, 1968, Committed to Print, 1988, Grotesque, 1995, Multiplex: Directions in Art 1970 to Now, 2008; Paris Biennale Int (with catalog), Mus Mod Art, Paris, 1968; Human Concern/Personal Torment (with catalog), Whitney Mus Am Art, NY, 1969-70, Art About Art (with catalog), 1978, The Figurative Tradition and the Whitney Mus (with catalog), 1980, Hand-Painted Pop: Am Art in Transition, 1955-1962 (with catalog), 1992-93, Summer of Love, 2007; Made in the USA: Art from the '50s and '60s (with catalog), Va Mus Fine Arts, Richmond, 1987; Calif A to Z and Return (with catalog), Butler Inst, Youngstown, Ohio, 1990; Quotations (with catalog), Aldrich Mus Contemp Art, Ridgefield, Conn, 1992, Pop Surrealism (with catalog), 1998; Masters of Satire (with catalog), William King Regional Arts Ctr, Abingdon, Va, 1994; Old Glory: The Am Flag in Contemp Art (with catalog), Cleveland Ctr Contemp Art, Ohio, 1994; Auction 98, Denver Art Mus, 1997; Made in Calif: Art, Image and Identity 1900-2000 (with catalog), Los Angeles Co Mus Art, 2000-01; Snug Harbor Cult Ctr, Staten Island, NY, 2000-2001; George Adams Gallery, 2002, 2003; Eye Infection, Stedelijk Mus (with catalog), Amsterdam, 2002; Contemp Arts Mus, Houston, Tex, traveling to Inst of Contemp Art, Boston, Mass, 2003; Disparities & Deformations: Our Grotesque (with catalog), Site Santa Fe, NMex, 2004-2005; Action/Abstraction (with catalog), Jewish Mus, NY, 2008; Bad Painting, Good Art (with catalog), MUMOK, Vienna, 2008. *Awards:* New Talent Award, Art in Am Mag, 1962; William & Norma Copley Found Grant, 1962; Nat Endowment Arts Grant, 1980 & 1985; Guggenheim Fel, 1993; Am Acad Arts & Letts Award, 2001; Artist's Legacy Found Award, 2008. *Mem:* Am Acad Arts & Letts; Nat Acad. *Dealer:* George Adams Gallery 41 W 57th St New York NY 10019; David Nolan Gallery 560 Broadway New York NY 10012. *Mailing Add:* PO Box 571 Germantown NY 12526-0571

SAUNDERS, EDITH DARIEL CHASE
PAINTER, INSTRUCTOR
b Waterville, Maine, Mar 19, 1922. *Study:* Univ NC, Greensboro, with Robert Partin, Boris Margo, Gilbert Carpenter & Madam Sun To-Ze Hsu; John Brady Sch Art, Blowing Rock, NC; studied with Maria D'Annuzio in Florence, Italy & Leroy Neiman, Philip Moose, Blowing Rock, NC. *Work:* Wachovia Bank; Reynolds Tobacco; Southport Libr, NC; Hunt Mfg Co Collection; Westminster Presbyterian Church, Knoxville, Tenn. *Exhib:* Island Gallery, Manteo, NC; Contemp Graphic Artists (traveling exhib); Weatherspoon Art Gallery, Greensboro; Regional Gallery, Boone, NC; Assoc Artists of NC; Mint Mus Art, Charlotte, NC; Art Gallery Originals, Winston-Salem, NC, 94; and others. *Collection Arranged:* Arts Coun Gallery, Winston-Salem, 57, 62, 64, 65, 77 & 81; Southeastern Art Festival, Winston-Salem; Arts & Sci Mus, Statesville, NC; Herman Art Gallery, Statesville, NC; Contemp Graphic Artists (nat traveling exhib); Regional Gallery, Boone, NC; Hickory Mus of Art, NC; Greenville Art Gallery, NC; Caldwell Arts Coun, Lenoir, NC. *Pos:* Art chmn-coordr, Winston-Salem Women's Club, 60-61; columnist, Edy and Art (weekly), The Suburbanite, 74-76 & 77-78. *Teaching:* Inst privately in home, painting. *Awards:* Purchase Prizes, Northwest Art Exhib, Lowe's Collection, Lowe's Co, 62 & Southport Art Festival, City of Southport, NC, 63; Hunt Mfg Purchase Award, Watercolor Soc of NC, 75. *Mem:* Assoc Artists Winston-Salem; Watercolor Soc NC. *Media:* Acrylic, Watercolor. *Publ:* Artists of Florida vol II, Mountain Productions Tex, Inc; Artists of North Carolina vol I, Mountain Productions Tex, Inc. *Dealer:* Lewis Interiors 2809 Gates Head Dr Winston-Salem NC 27106

SAUNDERS, J BOYD
PRINTMAKER, EDUCATOR
b Memphis, Tenn, June 12, 1937. *Study:* Memphis State Univ, BS; Univ Miss, MFA; Bottega Arte Grafica, Florence, Italy. *Work:* Denison Univ; SC State Collection, Mus Art, Columbia; Bottega Arte Grafica; Cent Art Acad, Beijing, China. *Comn:* Mixed media altar panel, Guess Chapel, Univ Church, Oxford, Miss, 62; mem portrait comn, Tipoff Club, Columbia, SC, 69; oil mural, Univ House, Univ SC, 72. *Exhib:* Soc Washington Printmakers 24th Nat, Smithsonian Inst, 62; First Int Printmaker's Exhib, Gallerie Bottega & Arte Grafica, Florence, 67; 34th Graphic Arts & Drawing Nat, Wichita, Kans, 69; Fifth Dulin Print & Drawing Competition Nat, Knoxville, Tenn, 70; 15th NDak Print & Drawing Ann, Grand Forks, 72. *Pos:* Staff artist, Dan Kilgo & Assocs, Tuscaloosa, Ala, 59-60; designer & illusr, Chaparral Press, Kyle, Tex, 63-65. *Teaching:* Instr art, Univ Miss, 61-62; instr art, Southwest Tex State Col, 62-65; prof art, Univ SC, 65-. *Awards:* Third Prize, Sixth Ann Mid-South Exhib Paintings, Prints & Drawings, Memphis, Tenn, 61; Grand Prize, Guild Columbia Artists, 71; Purchase Prize, 15th NDak Ann Print & Drawing Competition, 72. *Bibliog:* Jack Morris (auth), Boyd Saunders, printmaker, Contemp Artists SC, 69; Beryl Dakers (producer), Boyd Saunders (video tape), WSCE-TV, 79; Gita Maritzer Smith (auth), The Storyteller's Art of Boyd Saunders, WLC Press, 84. *Mem:* Print Coun Am; Guild SC Artists; Columbia Art Asn; Southeastern Graphics Coun; Am Asn Univ Prof. *Publ:* Illusr, Bosque Territory: A History of an Agrarian Community, 64; illusr, Lyndon Baines Johnson: The Formative Years, 65; auth, A summer's printmaking in Florence, Art Educ J, 68. *Dealer:* Trans Designs Inc 1000 Transart Pkwy Woodstock GA 30188. *Mailing Add:* 533 Mallard Dr Chapin SC 29036

SAUNDERS, MARR
PAINTER
b Tacoma, Wash, 1975. *Study:* Harvard Col, Cambridge, Mass, AB (visual & environ studies), 1997; Yale Sch Art, MFA (painting/printmaking), 2002. *Exhib:* Solo exhibs include Sert Gallery, Cambridge, Mass, 2003, Lombard-Freid Fine Arts, NY, 2003, Grimm/Rosenfeld, Munich, 2004, Geneva, 2004, Galerie Almine Rech, Paris, 2006, HarrisLieberman, NY, 2006; group exhibs include Am Coun for Arts, NY City, 1993; Carpenter Ctr for Visual Arts, Cambridge, Mass, 1997; Adams House Art Space, Cambridge, Mass, 1997; Galerie-Atelier A48, Grenoble, France, 1999; Art Unlimited, Basel, Switzerland, 1999; In Vitro Alternative Space, Geneva, 1999; Matthew Marks Gallery, 2000; Yale Norfolk Summer Exhib, 2001; Wight Biennial 2001, New Wight Gallery, Los Angeles; Lombard-Freid Fine Arts, NY City, 2002; Galerie Andreas Grimm, Munich, 2002; Momenta Art, Brooklyn, NY, 2002; Sara Meltzer Gallery, NY, 2003; Grimm/Rosenfeld, Munich, 2003, 2004, 2005; Prague Biennial 1, 2003; Southfirst, Brooklyn, 2004; Artemis Greenberg VanDoren Gallery, NY, 2004; Galerie Almine Rech, Paris, 2005; Artists Space, NY, 2005; represented in permanent collections Mus Mod Art, NY City, Whitney Mus Am Art, Harvard Univ Mus Art, Yale Univ Art Gallery. *Awards:* Louis Sudler Prize, 1997; Thomas T Hoopes Prize, 1997; Robert Schoelkopf Fel, 2001. *Media:* Oil, ink. *Dealer:* Analix Forever 25 rue de l'Arquebuse Geneva Switzerland 1204. *Mailing Add:* c/o Galerie Almine Rech 19 rue de Saintonge Paris 75003 France

SAUNDERS, MATT
PAINTER
b Tacoma, Wash, 1975. *Study:* Harvard Univ, BA, 1997; Yale Univ Sch Art, MFA, 2002. *Work:* Yale Univ Art Gallery; Harvard Univ Art Mus; Guggenheim Mus; Whitney Mus Am Art; Mus Mod Art, New York. *Exhib:* B-Hotel, PS1 Contemp Art Ctr, 2001; Lazarus Effect, Prague Biennial, Veletrzni Palac, Prague, 2003; Log Cabin, Artists Space, New York, 2005; All the Best: The Deutsche Bank Collection and Zaha Hadid, Singapore Art Mus, 2006; Passageworks: Contemporary Art from the Collection, San Francisco Mus Mod Art, 2008; Untitled (History Painting), Univ Mich Mus Art, 2009. *Awards:* Louis Comfort Tiffany Found Grant, 2009. *Bibliog:* Roberta Smith (auth), Founders Day at Grimm/Rosenfeld, NY Times, 8/19/2005; Charlie Blightman (auth), The Ultimate Fan Club, ArtReview, 2/2006; Nick Stillman, Harris Liberman Gallery rev, Artforum, 2009

SAUNDERS, RAYMOND JENNINGS
PAINTER, EDUCATOR
b Pittsburgh, Pa, Oct 28, 1934. *Study:* Pa Acad Fine Arts, nat scholastic scholar, 53-57; Univ Pa, nat scholastic scholar, 54-57; Carnegie Inst Technol, BFA, 60; Calif Coll Arts & Crafts, MFA, 61. *Work:* Pa Acad Fine Arts, ARA Serv, Philadelphia; Mus Mod Art, & Whitney Mus Am Art, NY; San Francisco Mus Mod Art; Crocker Art Mus, Sacramento, Calif; Oakland Mus, Calif; Hunsaker/Schlesinger Fine Art, 2001; Centre Jerome Cuzin, France, 2002; Schneider Mus Art, Southern Ore Univ, 2004; rep in permanent collections, Mus Modern Art, New York City, Whitney Mus Am Art, New York City, Philadelphia Mus Art, Chrysler Mus, Va; Corcoran Gallery Art; Carnegie Inst Mus Art; Mus Contemporary Art, Los Angeles; MH de Young Memorial Mus, San Francisco; and others. *Comn:* US Bicentennial Ltd Ed Print Portfolio, 76; US

Olympic poster, 84; exhib poster, Hunsaker/Schlesinger Gallery, Los Angeles, 87. *Exhib:* Mus Mod Art, NY, 68, 70, 72-73 & 74; Philadelphia Art Mus, Pa, 68, 72-73, 74 & 78; Thirty Contemp Black Artists, San Francisco Mus Art, Calif, 69; Metrop Mus, NY, 70; Card Design, Mus Mod Art, NY, 70; Whitney Mus Am Art, NY, 70 & 74; Recent Acquisitions, Mus Mod Art, NY, 71; Contemp Black Artists in Am, Whitney Mus Am Art, NY, 71; Pa Acad Fine Arts, Philadelphia, 72-73, 74 & 79; San Francisco Mus Mod Art, Calif, 72-73 & 74; Biennale, Whitney Mus Am Art, NY, 72-73; Corcoran Gallery Art, Washington, 74; Tweed Mus Art, Duluth, Minn, 74; Va Mus Fine Arts, Richmond, 74; Graffiti, San Francisco Mus Mod Art, Calif, 78; Paper on Paper, San Francisco Mus Mod Art, Calif, 79; Masterpieces from the Permanent Collection, San Francisco Mus Mod Art, Calif, 80; Resource/Reservoir: Collage and Assemblage, San Francisco Mus Mod Art, 82; Second Western State Exhib/The 38th Corcoran Biennial Exhib of Am Painting, Corcoran Gallery Art, Washington, 83, Brooklyn Mus, NY, 84, Long Beach Mus, Calif, 84 & San Francisco Mus Mod Art, Calif, 84; Resource/Reservoir: CCAC 75 Years, San Francisco Mus Mod Art, Calif, 83; The Human Condition: SFMMA Biennial III, San Francisco Mus Mod Art, Calif, 84; Made in USA Traveling Exhib, Univ Art Mus, Berkeley, Calif, Nelson-Atkins Mus Art, Kans, Mo & Va Mus Fine Art, Richmond, 87; Raymond Saunders: New Work, Oakland Mus, Calif, 94; Recent Acquisitions, Metrop Mus Art, NY, 95; Seven African-Am Artists, Encino Art Gallery, Sacramento, 96; It's Only Rock and Roll Traveling Exhib, Contemp Arts Ctr, Cincinnati & Addison Gallery Am, Phillips Acad, Andover, Mass, 96; Seeing Jazz, Smithsonian Inst, Washington, DC, 97-99; solo exhibs, Raymond Saunders: Distinguished Fac Exhib, Calif Coll Arts & Crafts, Oakland, Calif, 97; Strength & Diversity: A Celebration of African-Am Artists, Carpenter Ctr for the Visual Arts, Harvard Univ, Mass, 2000; Hunsaker Schlesinger Fine Art, Santa Monica, Calif, 97 & Hunter Col, City NY Fine Arts Bldg Gallery, NY, 98; New Works, Stephen Wirtz Gallery, San Francisco, 99, 2001; Cooley Gallery, Reed Col, Portland, Ore, 2000, Art with Elders, MH DeYoung Mus, San Francisco, 2000; Zoetrope, 2004. *Pos:* Nat consult urban affairs, Vol Teaching Serv, NY, 68; art consult, Dept Black Studies, Univ Calif, Berkeley, 69; prof emer, Calif State Univ, East Bay, Hayward. *Teaching:* Prof painting, Calif State Univ, Hayward, 68-88; Ais critic, RI Sch Design, 68, vis artist, 72; vis artist, Yale Univ, 72; prof, Calif Col Arts & Crafts, Oakland; prof, painting, drawing Calif Col Arts and Crafts, Oakland, 1988-. *Awards:* Nat Inst Arts & Letts Award, 63; Guggenheim Award, 76; Nat Endowment Arts Award, 77 & 84; Visual Arts, Southeastern Ctr Contemp Art, 90; Rome Prize Fel, 64-66. *Bibliog:* David Memet (auth), Glengary, Glen Ross (book cover & poster), 84; Kenneth Baker (auth), Raymond Saunders' signs of the times, San Francisco Chronicle, 7/10/94; Victoria Dalkey (auth), Exhibits give two views, Sacramento Bee, 2/18/96; Donald Miller (auth), Colorful, Cool and Colorblind: The Life and Art of Raymond Saunders, Pittsburgh Post Gazette, 4/11/96; Richard Powell (auth), Black Art and Culture in the 20th Century; H.W. Jansen (auth), History of Art; and multiple articles in Art Forum, Art in America, San Francisco Chronicle, Los Angeles Times, and New York Times. *Mem:* Fel Am Acad Rome; Nat Acad (assoc, 92, acad, 94-). *Media:* All. *Publ:* Auth, Black is a color, pvt publ, 68; Raymond Saunders, Stephen Wirtz Gallery, San Francisco, Intro by Toni Morrison, fall 93; Raymond Saunders: Recent Work, Oakland Mus, 94. *Dealer:* Stephen Wirtz Gallery San Francisco CA. *Mailing Add:* Painting & Drawing Dept Calif Col Arts & Crafts 5212 Broadway Oakland CA 94618-1426

SAUNDERS, RICHARD HENRY
MUSEUM DIRECTOR, HISTORIAN

b Rochester, NY, Aug 13, 1949. *Study:* Bowdoin Col, BA, 70; Univ Del (Winterthur Prog), MA, 73; Yale Univ, MA, 76, PhD, 79. *Collection Arranged:* Daniel Wadsworth: Patron of Arts, Wadsworth Atheneum, 81; Celebrating Vermont: Myths and Realities, Middlebury Col; The Brook Collection, 2005. *Pos:* Cur, Am paintings, Wadsworth Atheneum, Hartford, Conn, 78-81; dir, Christian A Johnson Mem Gallery, Middlebury Col, Vt, 85-91; Middlebury Col Mus Art, 92-. *Teaching:* Lectr, art hist, Yale Univ, 77-88; asst prof art hist, Univ Tex, Austin, 81-85; asst prof art, Middlebury Coll, Vt, 85-95, assoc prof, 95-. *Awards:* Samuel H Kress Found Fel, Courtalld Inst, London, 76-77; Andrew Wyeth Fel, Yale Univ, 75-76; Walter Cerf Distinguished Coll Prof, 2003. *Mem:* Coll Art Asn; Nat Trust Hist Preserv; Yale Club, NY. *Publ:* Coauth, American Colonial Portraits: 1700-1776, Smithsonian Inst, Ore, 87; auth, Collecting the West: The CR Smith Collection of Western American Art, Univ Tex Press, 88; auth, John Smibert: Colonial Americas First Portrait Painter, Yale Univ Press, 95. *Mailing Add:* Middlebury College Museum of Art Middlebury VT 05753

SAUTER, GAIL E
PAINTER

b San Antonio, Tex, July 16, 1949. *Study:* Univ Okla, BFA, 70; Va Ctr Creative Arts, fel, 91-92; Vermont Studio Colony, fel, 91; Atlin Center, fel, 98; I Park Center, fel, 05. *Work:* Painting, Solomon Brothers, NY; painting, Chubb Life Am, Concord, NH; painting, Browning Ferris Industs, Boston; painting, Northern Telecommunications, Manchester, NH; painting, Arthur Anderson & Co, Concord, NH. *Exhib:* Nat Ann Exhib, Pastel Soc Am, New York, 83-90; Statewide Asn Exhib, Currier Mus, Manchester, NH, 83-92; Invitational Nat, Salmagundi Club, New York, 86-87; The Subject is Water, Newport Art Mus, RI, 87; Nat Color Show, Faber Birren Exhib, Stamford, Conn, 88 & 92; Europastel, Russian Fedn, St Petersburg, Russia; UNESCO "Pastellisti Contemporanei", Cuneo, Italy; Art du Pastel, Normandy, France; and others. *Awards:* Isenberg, Giffuni, Armstrong, Pastel Soc Am Nat, 83, 86 & 88; Grumbacher Gold Medal, Pastel Soc Can, 85; McCarthy, Salmagundi Club, 86. *Mem:* Pastel Soc Am (elected master status); Copley Soc (elected artist status); NH Art Asn; League NH Craftsmen; Womens Caucus, Boston Chap. *Media:* Oil, Pastel. *Publ:* Illusr, Sudden Harbor, Orchises Press, 91; auth, The Best of Pastels, Rockport Press; Auth, Pastellagram, Pastel Society of America, 03; Illusr, Chautauqu Literary Journal, 05-06; Auth, L'Art du Pastel/The Art of Pastel, APF, 06. *Mailing Add:* 9 Government St Kittery ME 03904

SAVAGE, ROGER
PAINTER, PRINTMAKER

b Windsor, Ont, Sept 25, 1941. *Study:* Mt Allison Univ, Sackville, NB, Can, BFA, 63; study with Alex Colville, Lawren Harris, Jr & E B Pulford. *Work:* Confederation Ctr Art Gallery & Mus, PE; Art Gallery NS, Halifax, NS; Can Coun Art Bank, Ottawa, On; Glenbow Mus, Calgary, AB; Can Found, Ottawa, Ont. *Comn:* Can $100 Gold Commemorative Coins, Royal Can Mint, Ottawa, 78 & 81; watercolors, Bowater Mersey Paper Co, 81; Serigraphs, Halifax Sheraton Hotel, 85; drawings, Liverpool Int Theatre Festival, 92, 94, 96, 98, 2000 & 2002; portrait, Queens Gen Hosp Found, Liverpool, 97. *Exhib:* Arctic in Palmengarten, Palmengarten, Frankfurt, 91; Gotlands Konst Mus, Visby, 92; Malschule Gallery, Weimar, DE, 99; Sable Island Watercolors, Savage Gallery, Liverpool, 2005; Owens Gallery, Sackville, New Brunswick, Can, 2007; Watercolors Cuba & Nova Scotia, Savage Gallery, Liverpool, 2010; Landscapes, Savage Gallery, Liverpool, 2012, 2013. *Pos:* Vis artist, Univ Moncton, 79, Arctic Awareness Prog, 91 & Camp Otto Fiord, 92; Printworkshop BBK, Berlin, 88-92; juror, Far & Wide exhib, Art Gallery NS, Halifax, 96; vis artist, Weimar, Ger, 99, Masterworks Found, Bermuda, 2002 & Sable Island, Nova Scotia, 2005. *Teaching:* Bermuda, 98, Tatamagouche Ctr, 99, Weimar, DE, 99-2001 & 2007-2008, Cuba, 2011, 2012. *Awards:* Can Coun Grants, 70 & 80; Award, Province NS, 80; Int Cult Relations, Foreign Affairs Dept, Ottawa, 99. *Bibliog:* Pat Laurette (auth), Roger Savage: A Survey, Art Gallery NS, 79; Elizabeth Jones (auth), Roger Savage: An intractable essence, Arts Atlantic, 3/81; John Murchie (auth), New Acquisitions, Roger Savage, Art Gallery, 99; Janice Carbert (auth), Canadian Encyl, 2000; Mora O'Neill (auth), The Artist's Halifax, 2003; Dee Appleby (auth), From Land and Sea: Nova Scotia's Contemporary Landscape Artists, 2009. *Mem:* CARFAC; Royal Can Acad Arts; CARFAC Copyright Collective. *Media:* Watercolor; All Media. *Specialty:* Original savage watercolors, serigraphs and giclees. *Interests:* sea kayak, swimming, xc ski. *Dealer:* Roger Savage 611 Shore Rd Mersey Point Liverpool NS B0T 1K0. *Mailing Add:* 611 Shore Rd Mersey Point Liverpool NS B0T 1K0 Canada

SAVENOR, BETTY CARMELL
PAINTER, PRINTMAKER

b Boston, Mass, Sept 2, 1927. *Study:* Jackson von Ladau Sch Fashion; Mass Coll Art; Brandeis Coll, with Mitchel Siporin; Mass Coll Art, BFA. *Hon Degrees:* Mass Coll Art. *Work:* Liberty Mutual Insurance Co; Bank Boston; First Capital Bank, Concord, NH; New Eng Life Insurance Co; TECO Energy Corp, Fla; Sheraton Corp; Fairfield Med Asn, Calif; Meadows Country Club, Fla; Creator & Collectors Tour, Fine Arts Soc of Sarasota, 2008-2009; Fla Art Soc. *Comn:* Needlepoint design, Temple Sinai, Springfield, Mass, 88. *Exhib:* RI Watercolor Soc Nat Exch, Tokyo, Japan, 87-88; Nat Asn Women Artists USA Centennial (traveling), New York, 88-89; Nat Asn Women Artist 100 Works (traveling), India, 89-90; Ga Watercolor Soc (traveling), 96; solo exhibs, Cataumet Arts Ctr, Mass, 96, Market Barn Gallery, Mass, 98, Mazur Art Gallery, Mass, 98; Nat Asn Women Artists, US traveling painting exhib, 98-99; Fla W Coast Symphony, Harmony Gallery, 2007. *Pos:* Instr demonstrations; juror. *Teaching:* Instr in home studio & cruises. *Awards:* First Prize Graphics, All New Eng Exhib, Cape Cod Art Asn, 93-95 & 98-2000, First Place Mixed Media, 2002; Best In State, Nat League Am Pen Women, 95 & 38th Nat Biennial Award Excellence, 98; Juror's Choice, Falmouth Artists' Guild, Open Exhib, 96; Bronze Medal, Catherine L Wolfe Art Club, New York, 2000; Belle Kramer Mem Award, Nat Asn Women Artists, 2002. *Bibliog:* Mary Ann Wenninger (auth), Collograph Printing, Watson Guptil, 80; Best of Watercolor Painting Textures & Best of Watercolor II, Rockport Publ, 98-99. *Mem:* Nat Asn Am Penwomen; New Eng Watercolor Soc (past dir); Monotype Guild New Eng; Womens Contemp Artists; Northwest Watercolor Soc, Wash; Nat Asn Women Artists, New York; FLAG Fla; ISEA (Int Soc Exp); Northeast Watercolor Soc; Southern Watercolor Soc; Fine Arts Society of Sarasota. *Media:* Watercolor; Graphics; Mixed Media. *Interests:* Sculpting; tennis, swimming, decorating, jewelry designs. *Publ:* Painting Textures, Collected Best of Watercolors, 2002, The Best of Watercolor 2 & The Best of Watercolor, Rockport Publ; Collograph Printing, Watson Guptil. *Dealer:* Art Three Manchester NH; Gallery 333 MA Diane Levine Fine Arts MA. *Mailing Add:* 4305 Highland Oaks Cir Sarasota FL 34235-5173

SAVILLE, KEN
SCULPTOR, CRAFTSMAN

b Hanging Rock, WVa, Jan 9, 1949. *Study:* Austin Peay State Univ, BS, 71. *Work:* Albuquerque Mus; Mus NMex, Santa Fe; Libr Cong; New Mus, NY; Univ Idaho. *Comn:* Sculpture, City Albuquerque, one percent for the Arts Prog, 86. *Exhib:* Drawings USA, Minn Mus Art, 77; Artwords and Bookworks, Los Angeles Inst Contemp Art, 78; New Epiphanies, Gallery Contemp Art, Univ Colo, 82; Arteder, Muestra Int Arte Grafico, Bilboa, Spain, 82; Arts New Mexico, Gallery Contemp Art Latin Am, Washington, DC, 84; Mus NMex, 91-93; Roswell Mus, 91-93; Gusty Winds May Exist, 20 Yr Retrospective, Artspace 116, Albuquerque, NMex, 2006. *Pos:* NMex Arts Div Grants Awards Juror, 84. *Teaching:* Artist-in-residence, NMex Arts Div, 78-83 & 88-97, Tex Comm Arts, 90 & Mus Int Folk Art, Santa Fe, 96-97; Vis artist-in-residence, Austin Peay State Univ, 99; artist-in-residence, Buddy Holly Ctr, Lubbock, Tex, 2001; Albuquerque Public Sch, 2000-2012. *Awards:* Jurors Award, Southwest Fine Arts Biennial, 76; Award Merit, Craftworks V, 83. *Bibliog:* Michael Reed (auth), article, Artspace, summer 83; Sandy Ballatore (auth), New Mexico Sculptors, El Palacio, spring/summer 90; Mary Carroll Nelson (auth), Ken Saville salvages joy from sorrow, NMex Mag, 5/93. *Media:* Polychromed Wood; Colored Pencil. *Dealer:* Mariposa Gallery 3500 Central SE Suitek Albuquerque NM 87106. *Mailing Add:* Box 4662 Albuquerque NM 87196

SAVOY, CHYRL LENORE
SCULPTOR, EDUCATOR

b New Orleans, La, May 23, 1944. *Study:* La State Univ, BA(art); Acad Fine Arts, Florence, with Gallo & Berti; diploma di Profitto, Universita degli Studi di Firenze, Florence; Wayne State Univ, MFA(sculpture); TH Harris Vocation Tech Sch, diploma (welding), 72. *Work:* Alexandria Mus Art, La; Couvent St Dominique de la Gloire de Dieu, Maison Mere des Dominicaines, Flavigny, France; Our Lady Star of the Sea,

Cameron, La; Sixtus Vezie, Cath Mission, Willowvale, Transkie, SAfrica; Savoy Med Ctr, Mamou, La; Frank R Savoy Cancer Ctr. *Comn:* New Orleans Mus of Art, St John the Baptist (sculpture design), Our Lady Star of the Sea, Cameron, La, 73; portrait, comn by FC Barksdale Assocs, Savoy Med Ctr, Mamou, La; Digittactus (sculpture), comn by Alexandria Mus Art, 91. *Exhib:* Detroit Inst Arts, 71; Ark Art Ctr, 71; New Orleans Mus Art, 72; Mint Mus Art, 73; Am Painters in Paris, Palais de Congres, Paris, 75; Galeria de Artes Plasticas, Monterrey, Mex, 87; Wang Cult Art Ctr, Columbia, Mex, 87; New Orleans Contemp Art Ctr, 89; Alexandria Mus Art, 90 & 93; Escuela de Humanidades, Univ de las Americas, Pueblo, Mex, 96; Circumscriber-Drawing the Line, Northeastern State Univ, Tahleguah, Okla, 2001; one-person exhib, Univ de las Americas, Puebla, Mex, 2003. *Pos:* Art comm chmn & bd mem, RS Barnwell Garden & Art Ctr, Shreveport, La, 76-77; juror, numerous local, regional and state art exhibs. *Teaching:* Asst prof fine arts, La State Univ, Shreveport, 73-77; Assoc prof sculpture & drawing, Univ La, Lafayette, 78-. *Awards:* Artist Exhib Award, New Orleans Mus Art, 71; Samuel Wiener Sculpture Award, 73; Instrnl Improvement Grants, Dept Fine Arts, Univ Southwestern, 86 & 87; Octava Premio Naz Danza Mex 1987 Finalist, Palacio Bella Artes, Mexico City, 87; Beacon Club Teacher of the Year Award, Univ, of LA, Lafayette, 2000; Borst Grant; Interdisciplinary Foundry and Mold Making Studio Development Spring, 2004. *Bibliog:* Virginia Watson-Jones (auth), Contemporary American Women Sculptors, Oryx Press, 86; Arthur Williams (auth), Sculpture: Technique-Form-Content, Davis Publ Inc, 89; Making Their Mark-Women Artists Move Into the Mainstream, Abbeville Press, 89; Beginning Sculpture by Arthur Williams, Davis Studio Series, Davis Pub, 2004; The Sculptural Reference, by Arthur Williams, Sculpture Books, Sculpture Books Pub, 2004; Who's Who Among America's Teachers, 2003-2004. *Mem:* Artist's Alliance. *Media:* Wood, Mixed Media. *Interests:* Music, Intramedia Collaborations. *Collection:* New Orleans Mus of Art, Alexandria Mus of Art, Alexandria LA. *Mailing Add:* PO Box 573 Youngsville LA 70592

SAWADA, IKUNE
PAINTER
b Japan, Aug 30, 1936. *Study:* Kyoto Art Univ, BFA. *Work:* Seattle Art Mus; Art Gallery Gtr Victoria, BC; Brooklyn Coll; Art Univ Kyoto; Whatcom County Mus; Tacoma Art Mus. *Comn:* Mural, Puget Sound Mutual Savings Bank, Seattle, 75; King Co Bldg, Seattle, Wash, 76; Safeco Insurance co, Seattle, 80. *Exhib:* Ann Exhib Northwest Artists, Seattle Art Mus, 71-75; Wash State Artmobile Exhib, 72; Ann Puget Sound Area Exhib, Charles & Emma Frye Art Mus, Seattle, 72 & 75; Nat Art Competition, Springfield Art Mus, Utah, 75; Asian Artist Exhib, Western Wash State Coll Mus, 75. *Teaching:* Teacher art & art hist, Pub High Sch, Japan, 60-65. *Awards:* Lulu Fairbanks Award, Found Int Understanding Through Students, 70; Second Place Award, Fed Way Arts Festival, Washington, DC, 72; Hon Mention Award, Ann Exhib Northwest Artists, Seattle Art Mus, 74. *Bibliog:* Natsuhiko Tsutsumi (auth), People in Seattle, Katei-Zenka, 75. *Media:* Oil, Watercolor. *Mailing Add:* 637 Pleasant Walla Walla WA 99362

SAWAI, NOBORU
PRINTMAKER
b Takamatsu, Japan, Feb 18, 1931; US citizen. *Study:* Augsburg Col, Minneapolis, BA, 66; Univ Minn, MFA, 69; Yoshida Hanga Acad, Tokyo, woodcut printmaking with Toshi Yoshida, 70. *Work:* Nat Gallery Can, Ottawa; Glenbow Mus, Calgary, Alta; Edmonton Art Gallery, Alta; Winnipeg Art Gallery, Man. *Comn:* Sculpture, Trinity Lutheran Congregation, Minneapolis, 67. *Exhib:* 38th Ann Exhib, Japan Printmakers Asn, Tokyo, 70; Can Nat Exhib, Toronto, 73; 1st Ann Nat Print Exhib, Los Angeles, 73; 2nd NH Int Graphics Ann, 74; 11th Int Biennial Graphic Art, Ljubljana, Yugoslavia, 75. *Teaching:* Instr printmaking, drawing & art hist, Berea Col, Ky, 70-71; asst prof printmaking, Univ Calgary, 71-94. *Awards:* Manisphere Award, Manisphere 10th Ann Show, 73; Purchase Award, London Mus, Ont, 74; Edition Award, Art Gallery Brant, Brantford, Ont, 75. *Bibliog:* Dennis Elliot (auth), 12th Annual Calgary Graphic Show, Arts Can Mag, 72; Ruth Weisberg (auth), Prints of wit and humor, W Coast Art Works, 5/4/74; Rino Boccaccini (auth), Noboru Sawai, Voce di Ferrara, 9/21/74. *Media:* Woodcuts, Etching. *Mailing Add:* 662 Alexander No 4 Vancouver BC V6A 1C9 Canada

SAWYER, ERROL FRANCIS
PHOTOGRAPHER
b Miami, Fla, Aug 8, 1943. *Study:* New York Univ, Hist & Political Sci, 62-66. *Work:* Bibliothèque Nationale, Paris; Schomberg Lbr of Black Cult, New York; Mus Fine Art Houston, Tex; Le Musée de la Photographie, Bièvre, France; Victoria & Albert Mus, London, Eng. *Exhib:* Solo exhibs, 4th Street Gallery, New York, 89, Royal Photographic Soc, Bath, Eng, 92, Le Musée de la Photographie, Bièvre, France, 92, Foto Huset Gallery, Gothenburg, Sweden, 92, No Name Gallery, Basel, Switzerland, 93, La Chambre Claire Gallery, Paris, France, 2000; Two person exhibs, Dominikaner Kloster, Frankfurt, Germany, 2003, RCA, Amsterdam, Holland 2005. *Teaching:* Guest lectr photography, Technical Univ, Delft, Netherlands, 2003-. *Bibliog:* Herman Hoeneveld (auth), Errol Sawyer, Duotone (article), PF Mag, Holland, 2001; Jos Bloemkolk (auth), Amsterdammers en New Yorkers look alive (article), Her Parool, 2010

SAWYER, MARGO
SCULPTOR, ENVIRONMENTAL ARTIST, INSTALLATION ARTIST
b Washington, DC, May 6, 1958. *Study:* Brighton Polytechnic Fac Art, Gt Britain, 76-77; Chelsea Sch Art, London, Hon BA, 77-80; Skowhegan Sch Painting & Sculpture, 80; Yale Univ, MFA, 80-82. *Work:* Leon Hess; Chemical Bank; Samuel P Harn Mus Art, Univ Fla; Progressive Corp; El Paso Mus Art, Tex; Prudential Insurance; Austin Mus Art, Tex; McNay Art Mus, San Antonio, Tex; City of Houston; City of Austin; City of Dallas. *Comn:* Birdhouse Proj, Hong Ning Apts, NY, 86; Austin Convention Center, Tex, 2002; San Antonio Int Airport, 2006; Discovery Green, Houston, Tex, 2008; One Arts Plaza, Dallas, Tex, 2008. *Exhib:* Solo exhibs, Spec Proj, PS1, Long Island, NY, 89, Barbara Toll Fine Arts, NY, 89 & 91, Women & Their Work, Austin, Tex, 92 & 98, Projects, Diverworkds, Houston, Tex, 94, Sagacho Exhib Space, Tokyo, 96, Austin Mus Art, 98 & Galveston Art Ctr, 99, Holly Johnson Gallery, 2008; Skowhegan ten yr retrospective, Leo Castelli Gallery, NY, 86; Meyers-Bloom Gallery, Santa Monica, Calif, 89; Archer M Huntington Art Gallery, Austin, Tex, 90; Contemp Sculpture, Harn Mus Art, Univ Fla, 92; Drawing-Crossing the Line Diverse works, Houston, Tex, 94; plus many others; Art Pace, San Antonio, Tex, 2000; Mattress Factory, Pittsburgh, Pa, 2003-2004; Blaffer Gallery, Houston, Tex, 2004. *Collection Arranged:* Austin Mus Art. *Teaching:* prof, Univ Tex, Austin, 88. *Awards:* Nat Endowment Visual Arts, 86; Fel, Acad in Rome, 86-87 & Japan Found Visual Arts, 96; Grant, NY State Coun Arts, 87, Fulbright Sr Res to India, 82 & 83 & to Japan, 95-96; Louis Comfort Tiffany Found, 2001. *Bibliog:* Patricia Phillips (auth), Margo Sawyer & Mark Walczak the bird house project, Artforum, 12/86; Michael Kimmelman (auth), Margo Sawyer,NY Times, Living Arts, 2/24/89; John Clarke (auth), Margo Saywer at diverseworks, Art in Am, 9/94. *Mem:* ISC. *Media:* metals, glass, light, mist. *Res:* Site specific work that unites sculpture, archit, painting, & landscapes. *Publ:* Pub Art Network, Year in Rev, 2009. *Dealer:* Holly Johnson Gallery Dallas TX. *Mailing Add:* Univ Tex Dept Art & Art Hist Art 3-338 Austin TX 78712

SAWYER, MARIA ARTEMIS PAPAGEORGE See Artemis, Maria

SAX, (STEVE G SACKS)
PAINTER, CARTOONIST
b Brooklyn, NY, Jan 2, 1960. *Study:* Sch Visual Arts, 82-84; Art Students League, 84-89. *Work:* Nat Baseball Hall Fame, Cooperstown, NY; Basketball Hall Fame, Springfield, Mass; Hockey Hall Fame, Toronto, Ont; Pelham Art Ctr, NY; Del Art Mus, Wilmington; and others. *Comn:* Ball Park, Queens, NY; Sargent Garcias, Queens, NY; 3 Sticks on a Fat Lady, NY; Popilini, NY; Alamo, Brooklyn, NY. *Exhib:* Teamwork, Krasdale Foods, Lehman Coll Art Gallery, White Plains, NY; "Batter Up" the Art of Baseball, Pelham Art Ctr, NY; Nat Baseball Hall Fame, Cooperstown, NY, 89-94; The Artist and the Baseball Card, Syracuse Univ Lowe Gallery, NY, 92, Tex Christian Univ, Ft Worth, 94 & Brigham Young Univ, Provo, Utah, 94; Great Moment from the 50s, Basketball Hall Fame, Springfield, Mass, 93; Rock & Roll, Ambassador Gallery, NY, 97-98; solo exhib, Paintings & Sculpture, Butler Inst Am Art, Youngstown, Ohio, 98. *Bibliog:* Joe Gerson (auth), Cooperstown, Newsday, 8/93; Georgett Gouveia (auth), Baseball Art, Gannett, 94. *Media:* Acrylic, Oil

SAXE, HENRY, OC
SCULPTOR
b Montreal, Que, Sept 24, 1937. *Study:* Ecole Des Beaux Arts, Montreal, 56-62. *Work:* Nat Gallery Can; Montreal Mus Fine Arts; Mus Art Contemp, Montreal; Mus de Que; Queens Univ, Ont; Musee Que; Nickle Art Gallery, Calgary; Art Gallery Ont; Hamilton Art Gallery. *Comn:* Govt Ocean Bldg, Calgary Alta. *Exhib:* Bienale de Paris, 68; Salon Int Pilot Galleries, Lausanne, Switz, 70; Int Sculpture, Middleheim, Antwerp, 71; Bienale, Venice, 78; Retrospective, Mus d'Art, Contemp Montreal, Que, 94; Freedman Gallery, Albright Coll, Reading, Pa; and many others. *Awards:* Grants, 67-69 & Sr Awards, 73, 77, 81, 84, 87 & 91, Can Coun Arts; Order Can, 88; Paul Emile Borduas Prize, 94. *Bibliog:* Jennifer Lynton (auth), Abstract Beauty in Sculpture, Queen's J, Kingston, 10/83; Elio Grazioll (auth), Aurora Borealis, Flash Art, No 124, Milan, 10/11/85. *Dealer:* Galerie Kozen 552 Duluth E Montreal H2L1A9 Quebec

SAXTON, CAROLYN VIRGINIA
DIRECTOR
b Charleston, W Va, June 24, 1948. *Study:* Wesleyan Coll, BA, 1971; Loma Linda Univ, Postgrad, 1991. *Hon Degrees:* Cert Fund Raising Exec. *Pos:* Coun Open Door, Annapolis, Md, 1971-1973; social worker, Salvation Army, Charleston, 1977-1979; patient educ, Womens Health Ctr, 1979-1983; community educ specialist, Shawnee Hills Mental Health, 1983; exec dir, W Va Nat Abortion Rights Action League, 1983-1986; exec dir, Community Hospice, Ashland, Ky, 1986-1989; dir, home hospice, Home Hospice NVA North, Evanston, Ill, 1989-1990; exec dir, Community Chest Oak Park/River Forest, 1990-2004; exec dir, Oak Park/River Forest Comt Found, 1993-2005; exec dir, Lubeznik Ctr for the Arts, Mich City, Ind, 2005-. *Mem:* mem, Asn Fundraising Prof, 1991-1995; Nat Hospice Orgn; Ky Asn Hospice; Coun for Non-Profits; Women in Mgt, 1993-1995; Rotary, 1993-2004; Comt Founds, Advan Network. *Mailing Add:* Lubeznik Center for the Arts 101 Avenue of the Arts Michigan City IN 46360

SAYLES, EVA
PAINTER
b June 10, 1928. *Study:* Brooklyn Col, BA, 49; Art Students League (scholar), with Will Barnet, Burban & Palumbo, 60-62 & 84-86; Sch Visual Arts; Pratt Inst. *Exhib:* Marcolio Ltd, NY, 69; Pen & Brush Club, NY, 70; solo exhibs, St Bartholemew's Church, NY, 70, Pen & Brush Club, 71 & Amos Eno Art Gallery, Port Chester Coun Arts, 92; Knickerbocker Artists; Queens Mus, 83; Port Chester Coun for the Arts, NY, 92; Nat Asn Women Artists; Greenwich Art Soc. *Awards:* Oil Painting Award, Pen & Brush Club, New York; Scholarships, Art Students League, 84 & 85. *Bibliog:* Numerous reviews. *Mem:* Nat Asn Women Artists (chairperson pub relations comt, 86-88); Pen & Brush Club. *Media:* Oil, Pencil. *Interests:* Art, music, science, philosophy, literature, poetry, dance & singing. *Publ:* Article in Greenwich Time Newspaper, 4/92; plus poems and articles published in The Am Bard, Greenwich Times and others

SAYLORS, JO AN
SCULPTOR, INSTRUCTOR
b Lewisberg, Tenn, Apr 23, 1932. *Study:* Scottsdale Artists Sch, studied with Edward Fraughton, 86. *Work:* Will Rogers Mus, Claremore, Okla; Collection of Pres Suharto, Jakarta, Indonesia; Territorial Mus, Guthrie, Okla; Am Petroleum Mus, Ponca City, Okla; Childrens Hosp, Dallas. *Comn:* Stations of the Cross, Episcopal Church, Ponca City, 80; seal fountain, comn by Margo Kay Shorney, Oklahoma City, 82; life-sized

bronze, Ponca City Libr, 88; Lady of Justice, Okla Found, 91; One & 1/4 life size Centennial Bronze, Centennial Found, 93; and others. *Exhib:* Am Royal Art Show, Am Royal Bldg, Kansas City, Mo, 81; Art Ann III & IV, Oklahoma City & Tulsa, 82-83; Nat Audubon Soc Invitational, Tulsa, 83; N Am Sculpture Show, Golden, Colo, 84; Artists of Am Rotary Show, Denver, Colo; Am Rotary Show, Denver, Colo, 98; and others. *Teaching:* Instr, Scottsdale Artists Sch, Ariz & Loveland Acad Art, Colo. *Awards:* Gallery Owners Award, Art Ann III, Oklahoma City, 82; First Prize for Sculpture, Nat Audubon Soc, 83; Merit Award, Int Western Wildlife Show, Okla Gallery Owners Asn, 85. *Bibliog:* Article, Southwest Art, 4/89, Vail Mag, winter 90; cover, Santa Faen, 12/89. *Media:* Bronze. *Dealer:* Knox Galleries Denver Vail Beaver Creek CO & Naples FL; Alterman-Morris Galleries Dallas Houston TX Santa Fe NM & Hilton Head Island SC. *Mailing Add:* Knox Galleries 1512 Larimerst R 15 Denver CO 80202

SAYRE, ROGER L
SCULPTOR, PAINTER
b Sandusky, Ohio, Sept 19, 1941. *Study:* Sch of Dayton Inst, BFA, 73; Univ Cin, MFA, 76, MA, 77. *Work:* Ind Univ Mus, Ohio; Dayton Art Inst, Ohio; Brooklyn Mus, NY; Wooster Coll Mus, Ohio; Opposing Sculptural Forms, Contemp Art Ctr, Cinncinati, Ohio. *Comn:* sculpture, Ohio State Univ Hosp, Columbus, 73; prints, Sears Bldg, Chicago, Ill, 74; sculpture, UCF Cincinnati, Ohio, 76; sculpture, Citizen Fed Ctr, Dayton, Ohio, 91; sculpture, City of Dayton, Ohio, 92. *Exhib:* City of Chicago, Pub Sch, Ill; All Ohio Painting Sculpture, 69; Honor Exhib Ohio Arts Coun, 73; City of Toronto, Can, 75; Nat Gallery, Washington, DC, 94; Dayton Art Inst, Ohio, 2000; Steve Martin's Gallery, New Orleans. *Teaching:* asst prof 3-D design, Univ Dayton; asst prof drawing, Univ Cin; head program sculpture, Ind Univ East. *Awards:* Scholar, Ford Found, 67; Purchase awards, All Ohio Painting & Sculpture Exhib, 94 & All-Ohio Graphics Biennial; Atelier scholar Dayton Art Inst; Individual Artist fel Montgomery Co Arts & Cult Dist. *Mem:* Ohio Arts Coun; Dayton Art Inst; Cin Contemp Arts Ctr; Dayton Visual Arts Ctr; Montgomery Co Cooperative Arts Coun. *Media:* All Media. *Publ:* major works published in Le Revue Moderne, Exponent, Art in Am, Art Forum, Dialogue Mag, Dayton Mag, Am Contemp Artists, Viva Mag & The New Art Examiner. *Dealer:* TRA Art Gallery Troy Mich

SAZEGAR, MORTEZA
PAINTER
b Teheran, Iran, Nov 11, 1933; US citizen. *Study:* Univ Tex, El Paso, BA, 55, BS, 56; Baylor Univ Coll Med, 56-57; Cornell Univ, 58-59. *Work:* Whitney Mus Am Art, NY; San Francisco Mus Art; Corcoran Gallery Art, Washington, DC; Prudential Ins Co, Newark, NJ; Tehran Mus Contemp Art. *Exhib:* Solo exhib, Poindexter Gallery, NY, 64-77; Group exhibs, Art Inst Chicago, 65; Whitney Mus Am Art Ann, 69-70; Cleveland Mus Art, 72; Corcoran Gallery Art, 73. *Bibliog:* Donald B Goodall (auth), Color Forum, Univ Tex Art Mus, 72; Gene Baro (auth), The Way of Color, Corcoran Gallery Art, 73; Lucy R Lippard (auth), Intricate Structural Repeated Image, Tyler Sch Art, Temple Univ, Philadelphia, 79. *Media:* Acrylic, Watercolor. *Mailing Add:* 1223 Homeville Rd Cochranville PA 19330

SBARGE, SUZANNE
DIRECTOR, PAINTER
b Hartford, Conn, 1965. *Study:* Barnard Coll, New York, BA (art hist & studio art), 1987; Univ NMex, MA (art educ), 1991; Penland Sch Crafts, NC, 1998 & 2000. *Exhib:* Salon, Site 21/21, Albuquerque, 1996; No Edition, Lucy Gallery, Albuquerque, 1997; The Manipulated Photographic Image, Facet, Taos, 1998; Cleavage: An Exhib on the Breast, Jonson Gallery, Albuquerque, 1999; Guadalupe Fine Art, Santa Fe, 2000; Grace Lost & Found, Indications Gallery, 2001; 3 Corners, Eye Lounge, Phoenix, 2002; Faces & Figures, Gallery Urbane, Silver City, NMex, 2003; Opening Show, Volakis Gallery, Yountville, Calif, 2004. *Pos:* Former dir, Magnifico Arts & Harwood Art Ctr; exec dir, 516 Arts, Albuquerque. *Awards:* Bravos Award for Excellence in Visual Arts, Albuquerque, 1998. *Dealer:* Nuart Gallery 670 Canyon Rd Santa Fe NM 87501. *Mailing Add:* 516 Central Ave SW Albuquerque NM 87101

SCALA, JOSEPH A
SCULPTOR, PAINTER
b Queens, NY, Feb 20, 1940. *Study:* C W Post Col, BS, 62; Cornell Univ, MFA (sculpture), 71. *Work:* Metrop Mus Art, NY; Herbert Johnson Mus, Ithaca, NY; Battelle Mem Inst, Acad Contemp Problems, Columbus, Ohio; Lehigh Univ, Penn. *Comn:* Laser sculpture, Andrew Dickson White Mus, Ithaca, NY, 70; Sound/Light Sculpture, Rochester Jr League, 70; Cybernetic Fountain, Cornell Univ Physics Dept, 72. *Exhib:* Some More Beginnings, Brooklyn Mus, 68; Mirrors, Motors, Motion, Albright-Knox Gallery, Buffalo, NY, 70; one-person shows, Everson Mus, Syracuse, NY, 72 & W Broadway Gallery, NY, 76; Can Comput Show Art Exhib, Toronto, Ont, 75; Computers & Art, IBM Gallery, New York, NY & traveling, 87-88. *Collection Arranged:* Current-New York (auth, catalog), Syracuse Univ Lowe Art Gallery, 80; Tibor de Nagy Collection, Syracuse Univ Lubin House Gallery, 80; A Contemporary Art Collection: Clement Greenberg, Syracuse Univ. *Pos:* Pres & founder, Collaborations in Art, Sci & Technol Inc, 69-79; dir, Lowe Art Gallery, Syracuse Univ, 78-85, dir, Lubin House Gallery, 79-82. *Teaching:* Instr multi-media, Cornell Univ, 70 & 71; assoc prof art & technol, Syracuse Univ, 71-85, chairperson museology prog, 78-85, prof computer graphics & museology, 85-86, prof computer graphics art, 85-92, emer prof, 92-; exec dir, Stone Quarry Hill Art Park, Cazenovia, NY, 2009-. *Awards:* Winner Young Sculptors Competition, Sculptors Guild, New York, 69; New York State Coun Arts Grants, 70-85; Inst Mus Serv, Nat Endowment Arts, 85-86. *Bibliog:* Milford Kime (auth), Laser art, Laser Focus, 73; Arts Magazine, A Brief History of Siggraph Art Exhibition, 4/1982, page 13; Patric D. Prince, Brave New World; ACM Siggraph 89-Leonardo, 7/1989, page 3. *Media:* Ceramic, wood, acrylic, Mixed media, computer. *Publ:* Auth, Teaching Art Through Computer Graphics, Nat Computer Conf Proceedings, ed Stanley Winkler, AFIPS Press, 1976, Vol 45, No 1, 185-189; auth, Current/New York: Recent Works in Relief, 1980. *Mailing Add:* 2381 Fairbanks Rd New Woodstock NY 13122

SCALERA, MICHELLE ANN
CONSERVATOR, EDUCATOR
b Montclair, NJ, May 7, 1952. *Study:* Kean Univ, BA (art hist & fine arts), 74; Universita Internazionale dell' Arte, Florence, Italy, MA, 74-76; Conservation Studio apprentice to Prof Paolo Gori, Florence, Italy, 76-80. *Hon Degrees:* Kean Univ, Phi Kappa Phi. *Pos:* Conservator, Ringling Mus Art, Sarasota, Fla, hired Sept 1981, appointed Chief Conservator, 1985-. *Teaching:* Ringling Mus Art, 2001-06; adj fac, Fla State Univ, interior design & mus studies practicum, summer 2007, 2008. *Awards:* Gold ADDY Award, Arts & Sci, Techno-Vouet CD, 2004; Davis Productivity Award, Fla Asn Mus, 2005 & 2007; Caterina Cornaro Award, 2006; Silver ADDY Award, Encore, 2007; Distinguished Alumni Award, Kean Univ, 2009. *Mem:* AAM-ICOM Am Asn Mus; Am Inst Conserv; FAM (Fla Asn Mus); Materials Res Soc; Int Inst Conserv; IIC (Int Inst Conservation); Aic-Am Inst Conservation; MRS (Materials Res Soc). *Res:* Scientific investigations, UV, infra-red, X-Ray, microscopy, Raman Spectroscopy of mus collection artworks. *Interests:* European old master paintings; Cypriot antiquities; Italian, French, Dutch & Spanish decorative arts & drawings, guilded period frames. *Publ:* Auth, JRS Micro Raman Spectroscopic Studies, of Lapatsa Cypriote clay vessels, 2005; auth, JRS Micro-Raman Study Della Robbia, 2005; contrib auth, Encore! The Historic Asolo Theater, chap, The Restoration and Conservation of the Historic Asolo Theater, 8/2006; auth, Ca d'Zan The Restoration of Ringling Mansion, 9/2006; multiple auths, Encore! The Historic Asolo theater: Chap The Restoration & Conservation of the Historic Asolo Theater, 8/2006. *Mailing Add:* 8019 Indigo Ridge Terr University Park FL 34201

SCALZO, JOYCE ANN
CERAMIST, CURATOR
b Utica, NY, Sept 29, 1946. *Study:* Munson-Williams-Proctor Art Inst, with Vincent Clemente & John Von Bergen, 79-81. *Comn:* Wall sculptures, Breckenridge Resort Hotel, St Petersburg Beach, Fla; vessels & wall sculptures, Girard Jewelers Corp Off, St Petersburg, Fla & pres Weight Watchers, Palm Beach, Fla, 93. *Exhib:* Contemp Relig Works, Schumacher Gallery, Capitol Univ, Columbus, Ohio; In Perspective/Out of Bounds, Fla Ctr Contemp Art, Ybor City, Fla, 87; Festival of States, Theodore Wolf, Juror Arts Ctr Asn, St Petersburg, Fla, 89; Arts in Embassies, Am Embassy, Madrid, Spain, 89-92; Crafts at the White House, White House, Washington, DC, 93; Water Lillies (exterior wall), comn by Ambassador & Mrs Mel Sembler, Treasure Island, Fla. *Collection Arranged:* Arts in Embassies (with catalog), Am Embassy, Madrid, Spain, 89; Rubadoux, Washington Irving Ctr, Madrid, 92; Return Engagement, Anderson-Marsh Galleries, 92. *Pos:* Dir, Gallery Mido, Clearwater, Fla, 94-; owner & dir, Scalzo Gallery, Bellair Bluffs, Fla. *Teaching:* Clay, Lee Co Pub Schs-Adult Educ, Fla, 81-83, St Petersburg Arts Ctr, Fla, formerly & Dunedin Arts Ctr, Fla, 93-. *Awards:* 2nd Place-Ceramics, Art at the Bluffs, 83-84; 2nd Place-Sculpture, Bay Pine Show, 84; First Place-Sculpture, Suntan Arts Ctr, 85. *Bibliog:* Angela Savko (auth), Arts critic, Ft Myers News Press; Charles Benbow (auth), Arts critic, St Petersburg Times, 84, 85 & 86; Mary Ann Marger (auth), Arts critic, St Petersburg Times, 88 & 89. *Mem:* Fla Craftsmen Inc (juried exhibitor, 93-); Womens Caucus Art; Clay Workers Guild Fla (pres, formerly); Arts Ctr Asn; Pinellas Arts Coun. *Media:* Porcelain. *Mailing Add:* c/o A Scalzo Gallery 8208 Forest Cir Seminole FL 34646

SCANGA, CARRIE
INSTALLATION SCULPTOR, EDUCATOR
b 1977. *Study:* Bryn Mawr Coll, Pa, BA, 1999; Univ Wash, Seattle, MFA, 2001. *Exhib:* Solo exhibs, Women's Studio Workshop, Rosendale, NY, 2002, El Conteiner, Quito, Ecuador, 2005, Artspace, Raleigh, NC, 2005, Hudson D Walker Gallery, Provincetown, Mass, 2005-06, Salina Art Ctr, Kans, 2009, Univ Arts, Philadelphia, 2009; Delta Nat Small Prints Exhib, Bradbury Gallery, Ark State Univ, 2002; Projects '03, Islip Art Mus, NY, 2003; New Prints 2003/Spring, Int Print Ctr, New York, 2003; Works in Progress, Sculpture Space, Utica, NY, 2005; Domestic Policy, Dist Fine Arts Gallery, Washington, DC, 2005; 4 Aces Wide Format Print Exhib, Washington Univ, St Louis, 2007; The Medium is the Message, Samuel Dorsky Mus Art, New Paltz, NY, 2008. *Pos:* Asst prof art, Bowdoin Coll, currently. *Awards:* MacDowell Colony Fel, 2003; New York Found for the Arts Fel, 2004; Fine Arts Work Ctr Fel, 2004-05; Ludwig Vogelstein Found Grant, 2007; Pollock-Krasner Found Grant, 2008. *Bibliog:* Helen A Harrison (auth), When Native Heritage Meets Colonialism, NY Times, 2003; Cate McQuaid (auth), Energetic Fellows, Boston Globe, 2005; Paul Smart (auth), Medium Cool, New Paltz Times, 6/5/2008. *Mailing Add:* Bowdoin Coll 308 Visual Arts Ctr Brunswick ME 04011

SCANLAN, JOE
INSTALLATION ARTIST, PHOTOGRAPHER
b Circleville, Ohio, 1961. *Study:* Columbus Coll Art & Design, BFA, 1984. *Exhib:* Aperto, Le Nouveau Musee, Institut d'Art Contemporain, France, 1995; Solo exhibs, Mus Haus Lange, Krefeld, Ger, 1996, Mus Contemp Art, Chicago, 1998, Jewish Mus, New York, 2000, Kunstmuseum Herford, Ger, 2001, Institut d'Art Contemporain, Villeurbanne, France, 2002; 12th Biennale of Sydney, Sydney, Australia, 1998; Waste Management, Art Gallery of Ontario, Toronto, 1999; Against Design, Inst Contemp Art, Philadelphia, 2000; Curious Crystals of Unusual Purity, PS1 Contemp Art Ctr, NY, 2004; Still Life, 8th Sharjah Biennial, Sharjah, United Arab Emirates, 2007; Double Agent, Inst Contemp Arts, London, 2008. *Awards:* Louis Comfort Tiffany Found Grant, 2009

SCARBROUGH, CLEVE KNOX, JR
MUSEUM DIRECTOR, HISTORIAN
b Florence, Ala, July 17, 1939. *Study:* Univ NAla, BS, 62; Univ Iowa, MA, 67. *Collection Arranged:* Pre-Columbian Art of the Americas, 70, Graphics by Four Modern Swiss Sculptors, circulated by Smithsonian Traveling Serv, 72- & Completed Charlotte Mus Hist, 76, Mint Mus Art, Charlotte, NC. *Pos:* Dir, Mint Mus Art, 69-76, Hunter Mus Art, Chattanooga, Tenn, 76-; mem visual arts adv panel, Tenn Arts Comn, 76, chmn comt, 77-81, rev comt, Art in Pub Places, 78. *Teaching:* Grad asst, Univ

Iowa, 64-67; asst prof art hist, Univ Tenn, Knoxville, 67-69. *Mem:* NC Mus Coun (bd mem, 70-75); Southeastern Mus Assoc (bd mem & adv comt, 78-81 & 86-89); Chattanooga Cent City Coun (adv, 81-); Coun Am Asn Mus, 86-89; and others. *Publ:* Ed, North Carolinians Collect, 71; Graphics by Four Modern Swiss Sculptors, 72; British Painting from NC Mus Art, 73; Mountain Landscapes by Swiss Artists, 75. *Mailing Add:* Hunter Mus Art 10 Bluff View Chattanooga TN 37403

SCHAAD, DEE
EDUCATOR, CERAMIST
b Sutton, Nebr, Sept 6, 1943. *Study:* Univ Nebr, Kearney, BA (art educ), 66, MS (art educ), 71; Univ Nebr, Lincoln Coll Fine Arts, MFA, 73. *Work:* Univ Evansville, Ind; Mus Nebr Art, Kearney; Sheldon Swope Art Mus, Terre Haute, Ind; Citizens Gas co, Indianapolis, Ind; Am Clay co Collection, Indianapolis, Ind; Skutt Ceramic Products Inc, Portland, Ore. *Comn:* Risen Christ sculpture, St Vincent's Hosp, Indianapolis, Ind, 82; commemorative plaques, Pan Am Games, Indianapolis, Ind, 84. *Exhib:* Materials Hard & Soft, Ctr Visual Arts, Denton, Tex, 90; Int Ceramic Competition, San Angelo Mus Fine Art, Tex, 90; Clayfest VIII, Ctr Contemp Art, Indianapolis, Ind, 92; Natural Wonders, Culver Stockton Col, Canton, Mo, 94; Bald Headed Potters of Am, Grossmont Col, El Cajon, Calif, 95; Artists Who Teach, Concordia Coll, St Paul, Minn, 95, Muskingum Coll, New Corcord, Ohio, McMurray Univ, Abeline, Tex, 96; Plates & Platters, Studio Potters Network, Rochester, NY, 96, Ind Univ SE, New Albany, Ind, 96; Wall to Wall Ceramics, Univ Evansville, Ind, 97; Glazed Expressions, The Gallery at Studio B, Lancaster, Ohio, 98; Dinner Works, Louisville Visual Arts Assoc, Louisville, Ky, 99; Arthur Butcher Gallery, Concord Col, Athens, WVa, 2000; Hair Today Gone Tomorrow, Artists on Santa Fe, Denver, Colo, 2000; Clayfest 2001, Herron Gallery, Indianapolis, 2001; Contemp Hoosier Artists Sculpture Walk, Crown Hill Cemetery, Indianapolis, 2003; Sheldon Swope Mus, Terre Haute, Ind, 2004; Nat Coun on Educ for Ceramic Arts Invitational, Indianapolis, 2004; Ind Univ, Purdue Univ, Ft Wayne, 2004; Richmond Mus Art, Ind, 2004; Am Ceramic Soc Invitational, Ind Convention Ctr, Indianapolis, 2004; Pleasure of the Table Exhib, NCECA Nat Invitational Exhib, Indianapolis, Ind, 2004; Earth in Balance Regional Juried Competition, Rosewood Gallery, Kettering, OH, 2004; Ceramic Invitational Exhib, Armory Art Ctr, Palm Beach, Fla, 2005; Works on Walls Exhib, Texas Tech Univ, Lubbock, Tex, 2005; XXX Exhib, Santa Fe Clay, NMex, 2005; Ceramic Invitational Exhib, Thaddeus Gallery, LaPorte, Ind, 2005; Skin Deep Exhib, Francis Marion Univ, Florence, SC, 2006; Functionality, Dean Johnson Gallery, Indianapolis, Ind, 2006; Bourbon in the Bluegrass, Louisville, Ky, 2007; Ceramic Work by Contemp Artists, Florence Ala, 2007; Recent Works Artists Santa Fe, Denver, Colo, 2007; Clay Fest, Ctr Contemp Art, Herron Sch Art, Ind, 2008; Ctr Contemp Ceramics (solo exhib), Ind, 2009; Hist Myth & Current Event, Carrend Gallery, Ind, 2010; Works on Walls, Tex Tech Univ, 2010. *Teaching:* Prof, Univ Indianapolis, Ind, 75-, chair, Art Dept, 94-. *Awards:* Jurors Merit Award, Mat Hard & Soft Nat Craft Competition, 90; Dorothea Schlechte Merit Award, Mid-States Craft Exhib, 90; John Gormley Award, Clayfest VIII, Am Art Clay Co, 92; first place winner, Clayfest 2001, Herron Gallery, Indianapolis, Ind, 2001; Artists Fel, Indianapolis Arts Coun, 2007-2008; 1st place, Clayfest, Herron Gallery, Ind, 2008. *Mem:* Ind Artist-Craftsmen (bd dir, 96-); Cent Ind Scholastic Awards (bd dir, 96-); Potters Guild Ind (pres, 90-91); Nat Coun Educ Ceramic Arts (bd dir, 2002-04, onsite liaison, 2002-04); Midwest Coll Art Asn; ARTITUDE (bd mem, 2004-); Munce Fine Art Exec Comt. *Media:* Ceramics. *Publ:* Auth, A conversation with Carl Martz Potter, Arts Ind, 80; Light catcher - the work of Curt & Susan Benzelle, Dialogue Mag, 85; Hand Built Figures, 2/2004; Packing Pots, 3/2007; Pottery Making Illustrated. *Mailing Add:* Art Dept Univ Indianapolis 1400 E Hanna Ave Indianapolis IN 46227

SCHAB, MARGO POLLINS
ART DEALER
b Cincinnati, Ohio, Aug 4, 1945. *Pos:* Pres, Margo Pollins Schab, NY. *Mem:* Pvt Art Dealers Asn. *Specialty:* Important prints, drawings, paintings and sculpture of the 19th and 20th century; Paintings, drawings & prints of the 19th and 20th Centuries. *Mailing Add:* 1000 Park Ave New York NY 10028

SCHABACKER, BETTY BARCHET
PAINTER
b Baltimore, Md, Aug 14, 1925. *Study:* Conn Coll Women; Marian Carey Art Asn, Newport, RI; Coronado Sch Art, Calif, with Monty Lewis; also with Gerd & Irene Koch, Ojai, Calif. *Work:* St John's Col, Santa Fe, NMex; Erie Art Mus, Pa; Western Union, NY; McGraw Edison, Columbia, Mo; Erie Zoo, Pa; and others. *Exhib:* 20 solo shows, Muses de Arte Moderne, Paris, France, Nat Acad Design; Butler Inst Am Art Ann, 64-77; St John's Col, Santa Fe, NMex, 90, 99; Soc Animal Artists (traveling), 91-92; Lightside Gallery, Santa Fe, NMex, 93; Sangre Cristo Arts Ctr, Pueblo, Colo; and others. *Pos:* Artist-in-residence, Lake Erie Col, 71. *Awards:* Nancy Hubbard Lance Award, Lake Erie Col, 71; First Toastmaster, Ann Fine Art Series, 73; Second Award, Nature Interpreted, Cincinnati Mus Natural Hist, 80; and others. *Bibliog:* Gerald Brommer (auth), Art of Collage, 77 & Collage Techniques, 94, Watson Guptil Publ. *Mem:* Nat Watercolor Soc; Collage Artists Am; Audubon Artists; Soc Animal Artists. *Media:* Watercolor, Mixed Media. *Mailing Add:* 33 Speyside Circle Pittsboro NC 27312

SCHACHTER, JUSTINE RANSON
GRAPHIC ARTIST, ILLUSTRATOR
b Brooklyn, NY, Dec 18, 1927. *Study:* Tyler Sch Fine Arts, Temple Univ, scholar; Brooklyn Mus Art Sch, with John Bindrum, Milton Hebald & John Ferren; Art Students League, with Will Barnett. *Work:* Bellmore Pub Libr, NY; Island Trees Pub Libr, Levittown, NY; Wantagh High Sch, NY. *Comn:* Poster, NY State Parent-Teacher Asn, 70-73. *Exhib:* Solo exhib, Ruth White Gallery, 61; Nat Asn Women Artists Traveling Graphics Show, US & Europe, 69-70; Am Soc Contemp Artists, NY, 49-95 & 2000-06, 2008, 2009; and others. *Pos:* Dir graphic arts, Audio-Visual Educ TV, Mineola Pub Sch, 64-65; exec dir, Art Forms Creative Ctr, 71-73; owner, The Artist's Studio Gallery, 74-; designer & partner, Justine & Ruth Cards, 85-91; art dir, Long Island Pride Parade, 94-96, 97-02; ed/designer, Long Island Tidings Publ, 92-; mem, bd trustees & 5 times pres, Island Trees Pub Libr, 68-98. *Teaching:* Artist-in-residence, Community Arts Prog, Wantagh High Sch, 72 & Syosset High Sch, 74. *Awards:* Awards for Mixed Media, Nassau Co Off Cult Develop, 70 & Am Soc Contemp Artists, 71 & 75; Lifetime Achievement Award Arts in Publ, Long Island Pride Parade, 2002; Dedication to PFLAG Award, 15 yrs of Artistic Serv, 2002. *Bibliog:* Elyse Sommer (auth), Rock and Stone Craft, Crown, 72. *Mem:* Am Soc Contemp Artists (chmn admis, 68-71); Nat Asn Women Artists; Artists Equity Asn; Int Asn Arts. *Media:* Pen, Ink; Paper, Stone. *Publ:* Illusr, Long Island Free Press, 70-71; Make a Glad Sound, Consort Music, Inc, 74; You Can Play a Recorder, Music Minus One, illusr, Treasury of Stories, Waldman, 78; Long Island Pride Press, 94-; LI Pride Guide, 94-96, 2000. *Mailing Add:* 14 Trumpet Ln Levittown NY 11756

SCHAECHTER, JUDITH
STAINED GLASS ARTIST, PAINTER
b Gainesville, Fla. *Study:* RI Sch Design, BFA (sculpture), 1983. *Work:* Julie & Neil Courtney, Robert Ingersoll & John Wineman, Philadelphia, Pa; Corning Mus Glass, NY; Renwick Gallery, Nat Mus Am Art, Washington. *Exhib:* One-woman shows, La Luz De Jesus Gallery, Los Angeles, 1992, Helander Gallery, 1992, 1993, Snyderman Gallery, Philadelphia, 1994, 1997, 2000, 2002, Inst Contemp Art, 1995, John Michael Kohler Art Ctr, 1995, Cincinnati Art Ctr, 1996, Pa Acad Fine Arts, Morris Gallery, 1998, Agni Fine Arts, The Hague, The Neth, 1999, Smalands Mus, Vaxjo, Sweden, 2000, Huntington Mus Art, WVa, 2001, Claire Oliver Fine Art, New York, 2003, 2005, 2007, 2008, Kemper Mus Contemp Art, Kans City, Mo, 2005, Mus Glass, Tacoma, Wash, 2005; Art Around the Edges, Port Hist Mus, 1989; Contemp Philadelphia Artists, Philadelphia Mus Art, Pa, 1990; Renwick Gallery, Smithsonian Inst, 1990; Newport Art Mus, 1993; Del Art Mus, 1998; Tampa Mus Art, 1999; Cornell Fine Arts Mus, Winter Park, Fla, 2000; DC Moore Gallery, New York City, 2000; Whitney Biennial, 2002; Mus fur Angewandte Kunst, Frankfurt, Ger, 2003; Cheongju Int Craft Biennale 2005, Korea; Los Angeles County Mus, 2006; Newark Mus, 2007; Laguna Art Mus, 2007. *Teaching:* artist-in-residence, glass prog, RI Sch Design, 1985 & guest lectr, glass prog, 1988; guest lectr glass prog, Tyler Sch Art, Temple Univ, 1988, RI Sch Design, 1988-90 & Glass Art Soc Conf, Kent State, Ohio, 1988; guest lectr painting dept, Univ Arts, 1989, adj prof, Crafts Dept, 1994-; panelist, New Art Forms Expos, Chicago, Ill, 1991; vis instr, NY Accad Art, 2008-. *Awards:* Fels in Visual Arts, Nat Endowment Arts, 1986, 1988; Louis Comfort Tiffany Found Award, 1989; Pa Coun Arts Fel Grant, 1991; Joan Mitchell Award, NYC, 1995; Leeway Found Award in Crafts, 1999; Innovation and Techniques, Urban Glass, 2000; Fel, Crafts and Traditional Arts, US Artists, 2008. *Bibliog:* Shawn Waggoner (auth), The seduction of pain Judith Schaechter's stained glass world, Glass Art, 3-4/1994; Jeanne Nugent (auth), Schaechter: wretched beauty, Glass, spring 1994; Deni Kaurel (auth), Judith Schaechter: she cast pains in visions of beauty, Art Matters, 1/1995; and others. *Mem:* Found Today's Art, Nexus, 1983-. *Media:* Stained Glass. *Dealer:* Snyderman Gallery 303 Cherry St Philadelphia PA 19106

SCHAEFER, GAIL
SCULPTOR
b NJ, June 11, 1938. *Study:* Art Students League, with Kaz-Simon, 77-80, Scholar, 85-86; Ramapo Col, NJ, BA, 79; Nat Acad Design, Lucchesi scholar, 80-83. *Comn:* North Jersey Automobile MEM Plaque; BEC Manufacturing Corp; Trautwein Farms Inc. *Exhib:* Catherine Lorrilard Wolfe Nat Arts Club, NY, 78, 82 & 83; Allied Artists Am, Nat Acad Galleries, NY, 78, Am Acad & Inst Arts & Lett, 80 & Nat Arts Club, 81, 83, 87, 89, 90 & 91; Salmagundi Club, NY, 80; Nat Acad Design 157th Ann, NY, 82. *Teaching:* Instr studio classes, 77-; instr sculpture, Old Church Cult Ctr, Demarest, NJ. *Awards:* William Averbach-Levy Award, Nat Acad Design, 81; Medal Hon, Printers & Sculptors Soc NJ, 82; Anna Hyatt Huntington Award, Catherine Lorrilard Wolfe Art Club, 83. *Bibliog:* David Spengler (auth), Women of the arts, Record, 10/28/76; Diana Drew (auth), Sculptress has a way with children, Town News, 6/21/78; Terry Meyer (auth), Gail Schaefer's talent, Sunday Post, 7/16/78. *Mem:* Allied Artists Am; Painters & Sculptors Soc NJ; Catherine Lorrilard Wolfe Art Club; Nat Sculpture Soc. *Media:* Clay, Bronze. *Mailing Add:* 103 Commander Black Oradell NJ 07649

SCHAEFER, ROBERT ARNOLD, JR
PHOTOGRAPHER, DIRECTOR
b Cullman, Ala, Dec 1, 1951. *Study:* Auburn Univ, BA, 75; Tech Univ Manchester, Eng, cert merit, 76; Techn Univ, Munich, dipl ingenieur, 78. *Work:* Biblio Nat, Paris; Stadt Mus, Munich, Ger; Philip Morris, Inc, NY; Huntsville Mus Art, Ala; Birmingham Mus Art, Ala; Mus Modern Art, NY; Mus Fine Arts, Houston; Montgomery Mus Fine Art; City Mus, Münich, Ger; Amerika Haus, Münich, Ger. *Comn:* Wall mural, Interstate 280, City Birmingham, Ala, 71. *Exhib:* New Acquisitions, Birmingham Mus Art, Ala, 93; Am Zoo, 2 1/2 x 4 1/2 Galerie, Amsterdam, The Neth, 94; New Visions, Md Fedn Art, 94; Alabama Impact, Fine Arts Mus, Mobile, Ala, 95; Berlinier Ansichten, Aroma, Berlin, 95-96; New Works, Huntsville Mus Art, Ala, 96; Raab Gallery, Berlin, Ger, 97; Berlin Blau, Aroma Gallery, Berlin, 97-98; Robert A Schaefer Jr-25 Yrs of Photog, Huntsville Mus Art, Ala, 99-; Art on the Line Comes Inside, Philadelphia, Pa, 2000; The Silver Eye Ctr for Photog, Pittsburgh, PA, 2005; Goethe Institut/Max Mueller Bhavar, Delhi India; Gov MW and Art Gallery, Chandigarh, India; Windows on Columbus, Jersey City, NJ; Mus Fine Arts, Montgomery, Ala; Gallery DeFragi History, Tex; plus others. *Pos:* Dir pub relations, Soho Photo, 84-90; writer, www.doublexposure.com, currently. *Teaching:* Instr darkroom tech, Int Ctr Photog, NY, 82-84; instr, Palladium Printing, Soho Photo, NY, 87-91; instr digital printing, Apple Computers, NY, 2001; NY Univ, currently; New Sch, NY; instr, New School, 2003-2005; Center for Alternative Photog, NY. *Awards:* SOS Award for New Works of Robert Schaefer in Orient, NY State Coun Arts, Long Island, 94. *Bibliog:* The Star Ledger, Newark, NJ, 2002; Photo Insider, Florham Park, NJ, 2000. *Mem:* NY Photogr; Am Soc Picture Professionals. *Media:* Photography. *Res:* Alternative Photographic Developing Processes Platinum, Paladium and Cyanotype. *Specialty:* Fine Art & Photography. *Interests:* Fine Art

Films. *Collection:* William Hunt Dancing Bear Coll, Kofi Annan, Peter Hay, Michael Mazzeo, James Maloney. *Publ:* Coauth, American pie, Foto Mag, 88; Bilder Leben (Art Life), Viktor Publ Co, Cologne, 94; Orient photographers 1885-1995, 95, Voyager, 96, Suffolk Times; Brennpunkt, Berlin, Ger, 97; Fotophile Photog Mag, NY, 97; Photography's Antiquarian Avant-garde, by Lyle Rexer, Abrams, 2002; Architectural Blue, Delhi, 2010. *Dealer:* Domeishel Gallery NY; Frog Gallery Houston Tex; William Floyd NY. *Mailing Add:* 44 E 21st St Apt 2R New York NY 10010-7220

SCHAEFER, RONALD H
PRINTMAKER, EDUCATOR
b Milwaukee, Wis, June 2, 1939. *Study:* Univ Wis-Milwaukee, BS (art), 62; Univ Wis-Madison, MS (art), 63, MFA, 64. *Work:* Joslyn Mus, Omaha, Nebr; Tampa Pub Libr; First Nat Bank Minneapolis; and others. *Exhib:* Five Okla Printmakers Ann, 64-72; three Boston Printmakers Ann, 65-67; 12th & 19th Ball State Univ Drawing & Small Sculpture Ann, 66 & 73; Miami Biennial Print, 73; NH Int Ann, 73; and others. *Teaching:* Prof printmaking & chmn dept, Univ NDak, 65-. *Awards:* Twenty-five Printmakers Nat Invitational Purchase Award, Minot State Col, 71; Graphic Chem & Ink Co Award, First NH Print Int, 73; Purchase Award, Los Angeles, Print Exhib, 73. *Mem:* Print Club. *Media:* Etching, Intaglio

SCHAEFER, SCOTT JAY
CURATOR, HISTORIAN
b Chicago, Ill, Mar 30, 1948. *Study:* Univ Ariz, BA, 70; Bryn Mawr Col, MA, PhD, 75. *Pos:* Asst cur paintings, Philadelphia Mus Art, 74; asst cur prints, Fogg Art Mus, Cambridge, Mass, 76-78; asst cur paintings, Mus Fine Arts, Boston, 78-80; cur Europ paintings and sculpture, Los Angeles Co Mus Art, 80-87; dir mus serv, Sotheby's, NY, 88-91, sr vpres, Old Master Paintings, 91-99; cur paintings, J Paul Getty Mus, 99-2014. *Teaching:* Lectr, Philadelphia Coll Art, 71-72 & Harvard Univ, Cambridge, Mass, 76-79. *Mem:* Southern Calif Art Hist; AAM. *Res:* Late 16th & 17th century Italian painting, 19th century French paintings. *Publ:* Auth, Drawings of the Studiolo of Francesco; a catalogue, Master Drawings, XX, 83; Drawings by Martin Freminet, Gazette Des Beaux-Arts, 1371, 83; Europe and beyond: Some paintings for the studiolo, Coun Europe, 3/84; A day in the country, Impression and the French Landscape, 84; Guido Reni, 88

SCHAEFFER, S(TANLEY) ALLYN
PAINTER, INSTRUCTOR, AUTHOR
b Franklin, NJ, Nov 3, 1935. *Study:* W Lester Stevens Studio, 50-60; Nat Acad Design, with Ivan Olinsky, 54-55; Art Students League (Schanackenberg Merit Scholarship), with Robert Brackman, 54-56, NY. *Work:* Schering Plough, Madison, NJ; Pastel Soc Am, NY; NJ Sports & Exposition Authority, East Rutherford, NJ; Monmouth Park, Oceanport, NJ; NJ Bell Telephone Co, Newark. *Comn:* Racing Paintings, Monmouth Park, Oceanport, NJ, 80-92; Revolutionary War Mural, (6x12), State Bank NJ, Springfield, 79; Mural School Life, (8x12), Long Branch Pub Sch, NJ, 83; Historic Drawing, Muhlenberg Hosp, Plainfield, NJ, 84; History of the Hambletonian, NJ Sports Authority, East Rutherford, 92. *Exhib:* Hudson Valley Art Asn Ann, White Plains Co Ctr, NY, 75-92; Pastel Soc Am Ann, Nat Arts Club, NY, 80-92; Hudson Valley group show, Hammond Mus, NY, 80; Pastel Soc Am Traveling Show, Eastern States, Fla & New Eng, 86; Salmagundi Ann; Thoroughbred Hall of Fame, Aiken, SC. *Pos:* Art ed, NJ Life Mag, Maplewood, 70-76 & NJ Music & Arts Mag, Chatham, 81. *Teaching:* Instr anatomy figure drawing, Du Sch Arts, Plainfield, NJ, 70-76; instr anatomy figure drawing, Spectrum Inst, Hillsboro, NJ, 75-80; instr painting, NJ Ctr Visual Arts, Summit, 82-. *Awards:* Mrs John Newington Award, Hudson Valley Art Asn, 95; Uschi Grueterica Award 23 Ann, Paste Soc of Am, 96; William O Zann Mem Award & Antonio Cirini Mem Award, Salmagundi Club, 2000. *Bibliog:* Wendon Blake (auth), Painting in Alkyd, Am Artists Mag, Billboard Publ, 80; George Maganan (auth), Interview S Allyn Schaeffer, Todays Art & Graphics, Sindicate Mag Inc, 81. *Mem:* Pastel Soc Am (bd mem, 91-); Hudson Valley Art; master pastelist, Pastel Soc Am; Salmagundi Club (New York City Art Comn), 41st Vice Pres; Served on the Board of all these Groups; Audubon Artists. *Media:* Oil, Pastel. *Publ:* Auth, The Oil Painter's Guide to Painting Trees, The Oil Painter's Guide to Painting Skies, 85, The Oil Painter's Guide to Painting Water, 86, Color Composition & Light in the Landscape, 87 & Big Book of Painting Nature in Pastel, 93, Watson/Guptill; auth, Best of Pastel 2, Rockport Publ, 98. *Dealer:* The Sporting Gallery Inc 11 W Washington St Middleburg VA 22117; Windsor Gallery 41 Highway 34 S Colts Neck NJ 07722; Swain Gallery Plainfield NJ, Contemporary Am Painting. *Mailing Add:* 104 Jefferson Dr Brick NJ 08724-3210

SCHAFF, BARBARA WALLEY
ARTIST
b Plainfield, NJ, May 6, 1941. *Study:* Syracuse Univ, BA, 1963; Pa Acad Fine Arts, cert degree, 1994; China Nat Acad Fine Art, cert degree, Hangzhou, 1994. *Work:* Fuller Craft Mus, Brockton, Mass; Independence Found, Philadelphia, Pa; McGraw Hill Publishers, NY; NJ State Mus, Trenton, NJ; Pfizer Int, NY; Newark Mus, Newark, NJ; Sloan Kettering Hosp, Basking Ridge, NJ; Temple Univ Sch Law, Philadelphia, Pa; Philip & Muriel Berman Mus Art, Ursinus Coll, Collegeville, Pa; Atlantic Richfield Chemical Corp, Philadelphia, Pa; Prince Theater, Philadelphia, Pa; Chubb Corp, Warren, NJ; Golkow Technologies, Philadelphia; Schering Plough, Kenilworth, NJ; Pfizer Int, New York; Pa Acad Fine Arts Mus; Lehigh Magnetic Imaging Ctr, Allentown, Pa; Cephaloa Inc, Pa; Marriott Corp, Princeton, NJ; Public Service Electric & Gas, Newark, NJ; Va Ctr for the Creative Arts; Pa Acad Fine Art. *Comn:* NJ Natural Gas, Wall, NJ, 1983; Bell Communications Res, Red Bank, NJ, 1985; Barbara & Leon Goldstein, Mountain Lakes, NJ, 1985; Meldisco Corp, Mahwah, NJ, 1987; Temple Univ Sch Law, Phila, 2004; Newark Mus, NJ, 2005. *Exhib:* NJ Designer Craftsmen, Newark Mus, NJ, 1973; NJ Artists Series, Reflections/Abstractions, NJ State Mus, Trenton, 1985; In Recognition of Excellence, Montclair Mus of Art, NJ, 1986; The Expressionist, Gesture Berman Mus Art, Collegeville, Pa, 1994; The Mus Restaurant, Philadelphia Mus of Art, Pa, 1999; Grounds for Sculpture, Toad Hall Gallery, Hamilton, NJ, 2003; 6th Biennial, AIR Gallery, NY, 2005; 66th Ann Juried Exhib, Woodmere Art Mus, Philadelphia, Pa, 2006; Perkins Center for the Arts, Moorestown, NJ, 2007; Gallery St Martin, Philadelphia, Pa, 2007; Big Work Invitational, Perkins Ctr for the Arts, Collingswood, NJ, 2008; A Cause for Art, Sande Webster Gallery, Philadelphia, 2009; Solo show, Sande Webster Gallery, Philadelphia, 2010; Art Trust Gallery at Meridian Bank, West Chester, Pa, 2011; Abstractions of Nature, Oxford Art Ctr, Oxford, Pa, 2011; Artists We Admire, William Penn Found, Phila, Pa, 2011-2012; Drawn to the Dance, Water Gallery, Lansdale, Pa, 2011; Cosmopolitan Club, Phila, Pa, 2011; Woodmere Art Mus, 2012; The Linda Lee Alter Collection of Art by Women, Pa Acad Fine Arts, Phila, Pa, 2012; The Female Gaze, Pa Acad Fine Arts, Phila, Pa, 2012; Contain Yourself, Kline Inst Gallery, York, Pa, 2013; Artists We Admire, William Penn Found, Phila, 2013; Summer Show, Bridgette Meyer Gallery, Pa, 2013. *Pos:* Fel Coun mem, Va Ctr for Creative Arts, Amherst, Va, 2005-08; adv to the fac, BFA prog, Kean Col, Union, NJ, 1988-94; adv artists coun mem, Hunterdon Art Ctr, Clinton, NJ, 1988-89; adv bd mem, Coalition, Inginue, Philadelphia, Pa, 2006-; adv, Louise Nevelson Found, Artist Advisory, Philadelphia, Pa, 2006. *Teaching:* Long Beach Island for the Arts & Sci, summer 2005. *Awards:* Fel, NJ State Coun on the Arts, 1985; Blue Ribbon award, outstanding achievement, Long Branch Island Found for the Arts and Sciences, 1998-99; Fel, Pa Coun on Arts, 2004; Prize and Jurors award, Newark Mus, Perkins Ctr Art, 2005. *Bibliog:* Victoria Donohoe (auth), The Expressionist Gesture, Philadelphia Inquirer, 9/26/2004; Janet Purcell (auth), Allure of Orchids transforms potter to painter, The Times, Trenton, NJ, 8/1/2003; Eileen Watkins (auth), Former Potter turns her talent to porcelain tile paintings, The Sunday Star Ledger, 2/19/1989; Vitoria Donohoe (auth), Natural Light, Philadelphia Inquirer, 5/23/2010. *Mem:* Nat Arts Club, NYC. *Media:* All media. *Mailing Add:* 1111 Locust St #4B Philadelphia PA 19107

SCHAFFER, DEBRA S
COLLAGE ARTIST, SCULPTOR
b New York, NY, Nov 22, 1936. *Study:* Montclair State Coll, BA, 58; Univ Md, with Kenneth Campbell, 79; Westchester County Ctr, with Anthony Padovano, 82; Art Life Studio with Sebastiano Mineo; Pietra Santa Italy; Jane B Armstrong, VT. *Work:* Blue Heron Gallery, Wellfleet, Mass; Images Gallery, Briarcliff, NY; Tully Healthcare Ctr, Stamford Hosp, Conn; Temple B'nai Yisrael, Armonk, NY; North Castle Libr, Armonk, NY; Morse Life Insurance, West Palm Beach, Fla. *Comn:* Owls & seals, comn by Dr & Mrs Bruce Brofman, Armonk, NY; harp seal, comn by Dr & Mrs David Schaffer, Philadelphia, Pa; Dr & Mrs George Ubogy, Greenwich, Conn; Mr & Mrs Paul Frankel, Armonk, NY; Dr & Mrs Steven Winter, Briarcliff, NY; Mr and Mrs Joe Altman. *Exhib:* Allied Artists Am, NY, 89; two-person exhib, Westchester Community Coll, NY, 90; Bergen Co Mus Arts & Sci, NY, 91; Art of NE USA Exhib, Silvermine, Conn, 94, 95, 96, 97, 99, 2000, 2002 & 2005, 2007; Katonah Mus, NY, 98, 2005, 2009; Hammond Mus, N Salem, 98 & 2004; Solo shows, Director's Choice, Silvermine Art Guild, 2003, H Pelham Curtis Gallery, New Canaan Libr, Conn, 2009, Pound Ridge Lib Gallery, 2012; Katonah Mus (Benny Andrews, juror), 2005; Westchester Biennial, Coll New Rochelle, Castle Gallery, 2006; Housatonic Mus Art, Helen During (juror), Conn, 2008; Montclair State Univ, George Segal Gallery, 2013. *Pos:* Pres, bd mem, juror, Mamaroneck Artists Guild, 77-88; juror, Nat Asn Women Artists; judge Am Fedn of Women's Clubs. *Teaching:* Instr sculpture, Heritage Hills, Somers, NY, 82-; Home Studio, 77-2000. *Awards:* Mixed media award, Art of the Northeast Silvermine Cora Rosevear, MOMA, 97; First prize mixed media, Art of the Northeast Silvermine Alan Stone, 99; First prize Katonah Mus Artists Asn, 2000, Ellen Keiter, Hudson River Mus; First Prize mixed media, New Canaan Art Soc, 2002; Best in Show, William Zimmer, Art of the northeast at Silvermine, 1999; Jens Risom Award, Valerie Smith, Queens Mus Art, 2007; Second Prize, Ridgefield Guild Ann Competition, 2011. *Mem:* Silvermine Guild Arts Ctr; Katonah Mus Artists Asn. *Media:* Mixed Media Photo Collage, Wood, Stone. *Interests:* Bicycling, Knitting and travel. *Dealer:* Images Gallery Briarcliff Manor NY 10510; Silvermine Guild of Art New Canaan CT. *Mailing Add:* 638-22 Danbury Rd Ridgefield CT 06877

SCHAFROTH, COLLEEN
DIRECTOR
Study: Ore State Univ, BA (English & Arts), MA (Art Hist & Mus Studies). *Pos:* Intern, Smithsonian, formerly; design & implement educ progs & exhibs, Horner Mus, Williamette Science & Technol Ctr, formerly; cur of educ, Maryhil Mus, 1985-, co dir, 1992, acting dir, 2000-2001, dir, 2001-. *Mem:* secy & pres, Columbia Gorge Arts Coun; mem, Ore Art Educ Asn. *Mailing Add:* Maryhill Mus Art 35 Maryhill Museum Dr Goldendale WA 98620

SCHAPP, REBECCA MARIA
DIRECTOR
b Stuttgart, Ger, Dec 12, 1956. *Study:* DeAnza Coll, AA, 1977; San Jose State Univ, BA (Art), 1979, MA (Art Admin), 1985. *Pos:* Admin dir, Union Gallery, San Jose, Calif, 1979-1982; Mus Coordr, deputy dir, de Saisset Mus Santa Clara Univ, 1982-1992, dir, 1993-. *Mem:* mem, San Francisco Mus Mod Art; bd dirs, Works of San Jose, vpres, 1983-1985; mem, bd dirs, Non-Profit Gallery Assn. *Mailing Add:* Santa Clara Univ de Saisset Mus 500 El Camino Real Santa Clara CA 95053-0550

SCHAR, STUART
ADMINISTRATOR, EDUCATOR
b Chicago, Ill, Aug 27, 1941. *Study:* Univ Chicago, BFA, 63, MFA, 64, PhD (arts admin), 67. *Comn:* Painting for Frank Lloyd Wright house, Brookfield, Ill, 73; lithograph for Lyons Twp High Sch, City of LaGrange, Ill, 74; painting for Aurora Pub Libr, City of Aurora, Ill, 75. *Exhib:* Art Inst Chicago, 60-64, 70 & 74; Lexington Studios, Chicago, 64-65, 75-76; Printmaking 1969, Northern Ariz Univ, Flagstaff, 69; John Hancock Ctr, Chicago, 73; Columbus Gallery Fine Arts, Ohio, 76; Oberlin Col, Ohio, 77; Western Art League Asn, 77; and others. *Pos:* Res assoc higher educ, NCent Asn Cols & Sec Schs, 65, asst to exec secy, 66; admin asst to chmn art dept, Univ Ill, Chicago Circle, 66-69, actg chmn art dept, 69; artist-in-residence, Joliet Art League, Ill, 70-72; dir, Sch of Art, Kent State Univ, 75-83; co-dir, Blossom Kent Art, Music &

Theatre summer progs, 75-83; dir, James A Michener Mus, Univ Galleries, Eells Outdoor Gallery & Jack Lord Purchase Collections, 75-83; coordr, Div Res & Serv, La State Univ, 84-86; dean, Hartford Art Sch, 86-; assoc vpres, Arts, 89-; actg dean, Hartt Sch Music, 89-90. *Teaching:* Asst prof rendering & drafting, Chicago Tech Col, 64, asst prof design & graphics, 65; asst prof art, Univ Ill, Chicago Circle, 66-70, assoc prof urban sci, 70-75; prof art, Kent State Univ, 75-83; Distinguished Prof, La State Univ, 83; prof art, Hartford Art Sch, 86-. *Awards:* Best of Show, Midway Studios, 72; Gen Motors Purchase Award, Art Inst, Chicago, 74; Best of Show, Western Art League Asn, 77; Lady Bing Fel Award, 86. *Mem:* Coll Art Asn; Am Asn Univ Prof; Am Inst Planners. *Publ:* Coauth, Guide for the Evaluation of Institutions of Higher Education, NCent Asn Cols & Sec Schs, 66; auth, The education of an art student, Tallyrand, Vol 3, 70; coauth, A Self Study Report: The University of Illinois at Chicago Circle, Univ Ill, 71; Central Themes of Louisiana Architecture, Art & Humanities Coun, Baton Rouge, 84; Pathways to Art through Numbers, Apple Educ Found, 86; A Video Pilot: Significant Interiors Survey, Am Soc Interior Designers

SCHARF, WILLIAM
PAINTER
b Media, Pa, Feb 22, 1927. *Study:* Samuel Fleisher Mem Art Sch, Philadelphia, Pa; Pa Acad Fine Arts, Philadelphia; The Barnes Found, Merion, Pa. *Work:* Neurosciences Inst, San Diego, Calif; Telfair Mus, Savannah, Ga; Frederick Weissman Mus, Malibu, Calif; Nat Acad Design Mus, NY City, 2003; Rose Art Mus, Brandeis Univ; Guggenheim Mus, New York; The Phillips Collection, Washington, DC; Ark Art Ctr; Boston Int Contemp Art; Carnegie Corp, New York; Carnegie Mus Art, Pittsburgh, Pa; Mercer Coll, Pa; Nat Acad Mus, New York; Philadelphia Mus Art; Ireland Mus Modern Art; Mus Modern Art, NY; Nat Acad Mus, NY; Yale Univ Art Gallery, New Haven; Smith Coll, Mus Art, North Hampton, Mass; Rutgers Univ, New Brunswick, NJ; Nat Mus Am Art, Smithsonian, Wash DC; Miss MUs, Jackson, Miss; High Mus, Atlanta, Ga; The Brooklyn Mus, Brooklyn, NJ; Nat Mus Am Art, Wash DC; Miss Mus, Jackson, MS; Colo Springs Fine Art Mus, Colo Springs, Colo. *Exhib:* Am Acad & Inst Arts & Lett, New York, 91; Univ Mich Mus, 92; Phillips Collection, Washington, DC, 2000; Weissman Mus, Malibu, Calif, 2001; PSI/Moma, New York, 2002; Richard York Gallery, New York, 2002 & 2004-2005; Meredith Ward Gallery, New York, 2005 & 2009. *Teaching:* Instr painting, San Francisco Art Inst, 63, 66, 69, 74 & 89, Sch Visual Arts, NY, 65-69; lectr, Art Students League, 86-. *Awards:* Emmlen Cresson fel Pa Acad Fine Arts, 48. *Bibliog:* Cynthia Dantzic (auth), 100 New York Painters, book of biography & reproductions, 2006; Melinda Dodd (auth), Tangerine Dreams, NY Mag, 2004; Hilton Kramer (auth), The Paintings of William Scharf, Phillips Collection Catalogue, 2000-2001; Ann Landi (auth), Great Planes, Art News, Feb 2003; Cate McQuaid (auth), William Scharf, The Boston Globe, 12/27/2007; Mario Naves (auth), Belligerent Elements Battle with Blissful, Biomorphic Blips, New York Observer, 2/16/2004. *Mem:* Artists Equity Asn; Soc Illusrs; Nat Acad (acad, 2002-). *Media:* All. *Publ:* Art in Am, 7/2009. *Dealer:* Meredith Ward New York NY. *Mailing Add:* 75 Central Park W New York NY 10023

SCHARFF, MARGI
PAINTER
b Memphis, Tennessee. *Exhib:* Solo exhibs include Thinking Eye Gallery, Los Angeles, 1988, Michael Folonis Archit Studio, Santa Monica, Calif, 1994, Galeria de Ciudad, Tijuana, Mexico, 1996, Sanskriti Kendra Art Gallery, Delhi, India, 2002, L2kontemporary Gallery, Los Angeles, 2006, Rio Hondo Art Gallery, Whittier Calif, 2006; two-person exhibs include Overtones Gallery, Los Angeles, (With S E Barnet), 2006; group exhibs include Calif Women Artists, Corp Ctr, Sacramento, 1984; Mod Mountain Concert, Chi Chi-Bu, Saitama, Japan, 1991; Cross Current & Intersection, LA Artcore, Los Angeles, 2003; Present Art XI, Couturier Gallery, Los Angeles, 2004; Close Calls, Headlands Ctr Arts, San Francisco, 2005; After the F Word, I-5 Gallery, Los Angeles, 2006. *Awards:* Flintridge Found Grant, 1993; Pollock-Krasner Found Grant, 2006

SCHATZ, HEATHER
PAINTER
b 1968. *Study:* Univ Calif, Berkeley, Grad, 90; Columbia Univ, MFA, 98. *Exhib:* Exhibs with Eric Chan (as ChanSchatz) include Columbia Univ, New York, 98, Deep Thought, Basilico Fine Arts, New York, 98, XXIV Bienal de Sao Paulo, Brazil, 98, Open House, Shiffler Found, Greenville, Ohio, 98, The Production of Production, Apex Art, New York, 99, Too Wide Enough, Swiss Inst, New York, 99, Basilico Fine Arts, New York, 99, Real Art Ways, Hartford, Conn, 2000, Representing, Parrish Art Mus, Southampton, NY, 2000, Grand Arts, Kansas City, Mo, 2001, Lemon Sky, Los Angeles, 2002, Before & After Science, Marella Contemp Art, Milan, 2003, Life By Design, Beall Ctr, Univ Calif, Irvine, 2003, Lukas & Sternberg, Inc, New York, 2003, Portrait Masterworks, New York, 2003, Augmentation, Massimo Audiello, New York, 2003, Here & There, 2006 & Remix, 2006, Starring, Armory Art Fair, New York, 2004, One in a Million, Austrian Cult Forum, New York, 2004, Ctr Curatorial Studies, Bard Coll, NY, 2004, INterVENTIONS, Bowling Green State Univ Art Gallery, Ohio, 2004, FloorPlay, Brooklyn Coll Art Gallery, NY, 2004, Multiple Studies, Contemp Art Ctr, Cincinnati, Ohio, 2004, Crib Sheets, Univ Calif, Los Angeles & Monacelli Press, 2005, Extreme Abstraction, Albright-Knox Art Gallery, Buffalo, NY, 2005 & Ideas First, 2006, Mutiny, The Happy Lion, Los Angeles, 2006, Meeting in the Drawing Project, Univ NC, Greensboro, 2007, In Situ, Galerie Michael Janssen, Berlin, 2007, Cress Gallery, Univ Tenn, Chattanooga, 2007, Hunter Mus Am Art, Chattanooga, Tenn, 2007. *Teaching:* Adj asst prof visual arts, Columbia Univ, New York. *Media:* Serigraphy, Silkscreen. *Mailing Add:* ChanSchatz 423 W 14th St 2R New York NY 10014

SCHEER, SHERIE (HOOD)
PHOTOGRAPHER, PAINTER
b Estherville, Iowa, Feb 15, 1940. *Study:* Univ Iowa, 58-60; Univ Calif, Los Angeles, BA, 69, MA, 71. *Work:* Metrop Mus Art, NY; Fogg Art Mus, Harvard Univ; Israel Mus, Jerusalem; Minneapolis Inst Art, Minn; San Francisco Mus Mod Art. *Exhib:* Contemp Hand-Colored Photog, DeSaisset Mus, Santa Clara, Calif, 81; Summer Show V, Los Angeles Co Mus Art, 81; Five Photographers, Los Angeles Inst Contemp Art, 82; Artists' Tribute to Bertha Urdang, Israel Mus, Jerusalem, 82; Invitational: Bertha Urdang, London Regional Gallery, Ont, 83. *Teaching:* Instr photog, Univ Calif, Los Angeles Exten, 82-84. *Bibliog:* Barbara Noah (auth), J Golden & S Scheer at the Womens Building, Art in Am, 3-4/78; Colin Westerbeck (auth), Reviews: New York, Artforum, 3/81; Anne Wagner (auth), Selections from An Interview with Sherie Scheer together with some suggestions for their use, J Womens Studies, winter 92. *Media:* Painted Photographs, Mixed Media. *Dealer:* Sherie Scheer Studio 31 Park Ave Venice CA 90291. *Mailing Add:* 31 Park Ave Venice CA 90291

SCHEIN, EUGENIE
EDUCATOR, GRAPHIC ARTIST
Study: Hunter Col, BA; Columbia Univ, MA; Art Students League, with De Muth & Bridgeman; studies in art & aesthetics at New York Univ & Univ NMex; Martha Graham Sch Dance. *Work:* Carvell Mus, La; Ga Mus Art, Athens; Lowe Art Mus, Coral Gables, Fla; Miami Mus Mod Art, Fla. *Exhib:* Int Watercolors, Brooklyn Mus; Soc Four Arts, Palm Beach; Lowe Mus, Univ Miami, Coral Gables, Fla; Hollywood Art & Cult Ctr, Fla; Butler Inst, Youngstown, Ohio; one-person shows, Midtown Gallery, Uptown Gallery & Salpeter Gallery, NY, Mexico City, Havana, PR, Barzasky Gallery, NY; Metamorphosis, Galleo, Miami Beach, 95; and others. *Teaching:* Instr, Hunter Col, 26-55 & Univ Miami, 56-60. *Mem:* Artists Equity Asn (vpres, 72-); Fla Artists Group; Nat Asn Women Artists. *Mailing Add:* 1070 Stillwater Dr Miami FL 33141

SCHENCK, WILLIAM CLINTON
PAINTER, PRINTMAKER
b Aug 19, 1947; US citizen. *Study:* Columbus Coll Art & Design, 65-67; Kansas City Art Inst, BFA, 69. *Work:* Whitney Gallery of Western Art, Cody, Wyo; Brandeis Univ Mus, Boston, Mass; Smithsonian Inst, Washington, DC; Clymer Mus, Ellensburg, Wash; Brigham Young U, Provo, Utah; Tucson Mus Art, Tucson, Ariz; plus others. *Comn:* Paintings, Sky Harbor Int Airport, Phoenix, 79; paintings, IBM Corp, Tucson, Ariz, 81; Wells Fargo, Los Angeles, Calif, 83. *Exhib:* Wadsworth Atheneum, Hartford, Conn, 74; Rose Art Mus, Boston, 75; Grand Hornu Gallery, Belg, 76; Edwin Ulrich Mus, Wichita, Kans, 76; Navy Pier, Chicago, 81; 15-Year Retrospective, Scottsdale Ctr for the Arts, Ariz, 83; and others. *Bibliog:* Gregory Battcock (auth), Super-Realism: A Critical Anthology, E F Dutton, New York, 75; John Perrault (auth), Impressions of Arizona, Art Am, 81; Barbara Perlman (auth), Schenck's brand, Ariz Arts & Lifestyle, 81; Julie Sasse (auth) The Irony and the Ecstasy, The Paintings of Bill Schenck (catalog for Vanier Gallery Show), Nov, 99; Elizabeth Claire Flood (auth) Cowboys and Indians, 7/2000. *Media:* Oil; Serigraph. *Publ:* plus others. *Dealer:* Martin-Harris Gallery 268 Los Pinos Rd Santa Fe NM 87505. *Mailing Add:* 268 Los Pinos Rd Santa Fe NM 87505

SCHENNING, MATTHEW
PHOTOGRAPHER
b Baltimore, Md, 1977. *Study:* Univ Md Coll Park, BA (fine arts), 1999. *Comn:* Indoor installation, West Gallery, Univ Md College Park, 1999. *Exhib:* Solo exhibs, Recent Works, Geometrics, Baltimore, 2000, Questions, Planet on the Corner, Baltimore, 2001, Blackbirds Feeding, Atlantico, Brooklyn, NY, 2005, Night Stories, Sch Visual Arts, NY, 2005, Suburban Renewal, AG Gallery, Brooklyn, NY, 2006; Group exhibs, Fresh Outlook, Rosenberg Gallery, NY Univ, 1999; Ann Open Studio Tour & Auction, Sch 33 Art Ctr, Baltimore, 2000 & 2001; Emerging Artist Exhib, Sheppard Art Gallery, Ellicott City, Md, 2000; Baltimore Juried All Arts Festival, Creative Alliance, Baltimore, 2001; Employee Art Exhib, Met Mus Art, NY, 2003; Ides of March, Abc No Rio, NY, 2004, Clothesline Show Benefit Auction, 2004; The Photo Show, Gallery 402, NY, 2004; Looking South, 70NY Internat Photog Gallery, Milford, Pa, 2004; 15th Ann Juried Exhib, Viridian Artists, NY, 2004; Real Party Benefit, Real Art Ways, Hartford, Conn, 2005 & 2006; Pairs Groups & Grips, Leslie Tonkonow Artworks + Projects, NY, 2005; Re-Make/Re-Model, D'Amelio Terras, NY, 2006; New '06 Nurturing the Edge, Nurture Art, NY, 2006; New Work, Design Within Reach, Tribeca, NY, 2006; EV+A 2007, Limerick, Ireland, 2007. *Pos:* Registrar & preparator, Leslie Tonkonow Artworks + Projects, NY. *Mailing Add:* Leslie Tonkonow Artworks + Projects 535 W 22nd St New York NY 10011

SCHEPIS, ANTHONY JOSEPH
INSTRUCTOR, PAINTER
b Cleveland, Ohio, Mar 6, 1927. *Study:* Cooper Sch Art, dipl; Cleveland Inst Art, cert; Kent State Univ, MA. *Work:* Canton Mus Art, Ohio; Massillon Mus Art, Ohio; Butler Inst Am Art, Youngstown, Ohio; Richmond Art Mus, Ind; Hoyt Art Inst Fine Arts, Pa. *Exhib:* Nat Mid-Yr Show, Butler Inst Am Art, 55-74; Avanti Gallery, New York, 71; May Show, Cleveland Mus Art, 55-56, 66 & 73-89; Univ Mus, Ind Univ, Pa, 83; Cleveland/Toronto Exhib, Harbourfront Gallery, Toronto, 78; Univ Columbia Fine Arts Gallery, Mo, 80; Ft Wayne Mus Art, Ind, 80; Albion Coll, Mich, 85; Hoyt Art Inst, Pa, 96; Arnot Art Mus, New York, 96; Richmond Art Mus, Ind, 2005; Cavalier Gallery, New York, 2005; Canton Mus Art, 2007; Ormond Mem Art Mus, Fla, 2010. *Teaching:* Prof drawing & painting, Cleveland Inst Art, Ohio, 79-96 & prof emer, 99-. *Awards:* Purchase Award, Butler Inst Am Art, 74; Painting Awards, Cleveland Mus Art, 78 & 88-89; Corning Award, Arnot Art Mus, New York, 96; and others. *Bibliog:* Article, Cleveland Mag, 6/78; article, Ft Wayne J Gazette, 80; Cleveland Mus Art Bull, 5/88. *Mem:* Cleveland Artists Found. *Media:* Oil, Silkscreen. *Dealer:* Tregoning Fine Art Cleveland OH; Lyons Fine Art Consulting Charlotte NC; Bonfoey Gallery Cleveland OH. *Mailing Add:* 125 Osprey Heights Dr Winter Haven FL 33880

SCHER, JULIA
CONCEPTUAL ARTIST, VIDEO ARTIST
b Mar 9, 1954. *Study:* Univ Calif Los Angeles, BA, 75; Univ Minn, MFA, 84. *Work:* Musee d'Art Moderne, Centre Georges Pompidou, Paris; Musee Art Moderne, Geneve, Switz; Musee d'Art Contemporani de Barcelona, Spain; Neue Galerie am Landesmuseum Joanneu, Graz, Austria; Kôlnischer Kunstverein, Cologne, Ger. *Exhib:*

1989 Whitney Biennial, Whitney Mus Am Art, NY, 89; solo exhibs, Occupational Placement, Wexner Ctr Arts, Columbus, Ohio, 89-90, Don't Worry, Koln Kustverein, Cologne, Ger, 94, Forecast, Maurine & Robert Rothschild, Gallery, Bunting Inst, Radcliff Col, Cambridge, Mass, 97, The Komputer Kings, Schipper & Krome, Berlin, Ger, 98, Wonderland, Andrea Rosen Gallery, NY, 98, Predictive Engineering II, San Francisco Mus Mod Art, 99; The Raw & the cooked (cociday crudo), Reina Sofia, Madrid, Spain, 94; The End of the Avantgarde, Kunsthalle der Hypo-Kultur, Munich, Ger, 95; Push-ups, Factory-Athens Sch Fine Art, Greece, 96; The Art of Detection: Surveillance in Society, Mass Inst Tech Visual Art Ctr, Cambridge, 97; Performance Anxiety, Site Santa Fe, NMex, 98; Roommates, Mus Van Loon, Amsterdam, The Neth, 98. *Teaching:* Asst prof media & performing arts, Mass Col Art, 95-96; vis artist video, Mass Inst Technol, 95-96; Rensselaer Polytechnic Inst, Troy, NY, 97; Lectr Archit, Visual Arts, Mass Inst Tech, 97-2002; lectr, Mass Inst Tech, 2005-2006. *Awards:* Bunting Fel, Harvard Univ, 96-97. *Mem:* Coll Art Asn. *Media:* Mixed Media Installation; Audio, Web. *Mailing Add:* MIT Visual Arts Program N51-328 265 Massachusetts Ave Cambridge MA 02139

SCHERER, HERBERT GROVER
EDUCATOR
b Brooklyn, NY, May 16, 1930. *Study:* Western Reserve Univ, BA (art), 53, MA (art hist), 60, MLS, 63. *Collection Arranged:* Marquee on Main Street: Jack Liebenberg's Movie Theaters, 1928-1941 (auth, catalog), Univ Minn Art Gallery, 82. *Pos:* Art librn, Syracuse Univ, 63-66 & Univ Minn, Minneapolis, 66-98; mem, Gorman Art Libr Endowment Adv Bd, 89-99; mem, Pub Art Rev Adv Comt, 94-98. *Teaching:* Instr art hist & methodology, Univ Minn, Minneapolis, 66-; lectr, 84-98. *Mem:* Art Libr NAm (charter mem & founder, 72) (Wittenborn Art Book Comt, 95). *Interests:* Art deco archit. *Publ:* Auth, Program of the thirty-nine ceiling paintings of the Jesuit Church of St Ignatius in Antwerp, painted by P P Rubens in 1620, Am Philos Soc Yearbk, 68; auth, Minneapolis art deco extravaganza, Arts Mag, summer 71; dir, Streamlined Dreams (TV doc), KTCA, 80; auth, Marquee on Main Street: Jack Liebenberg's Movie & Theatres, J Decorative Arts, spring 86; Tickets to Fantasy, Hennepin Co Hist, fall 87; A tarnished Art Deco Gem, Minneapolis-St Paul, 3/88; Merging Subject Collections or Love's Labor Lost, The Architecture Library of the Future: Complexity and Contradiction, Ann Arbor Univ, Mich Press, 89, 105-111; Modernism at Norwest: An Interview with David Ryan, Journal of Decorative and Propaganda Arts, 14, Fall 89, 112-127. *Mailing Add:* 170 Wilson Library 309 19th Ave S Minneapolis MN 55455

SCHERPEREEL, RICHARD CHARLES
EDUCATOR, PAINTER
b Mishawaka, Ind, Dec 1, 1931. *Study:* Univ Notre Dame, BFA & MFA; McMurry Col, MEd; George Peabody Coll for Teachers, EdD. *Comn:* STex totems, Tex A&I Univ, Kingsville, 75. *Exhib:* Mid States Artist Exhib, 66-68; Found Exhib, Art Mus S Tex, 70-78; Del Mar Nat Drawing & Small Sculpture Exhib, 71; Tex Fine Arts Asn, 72-74. *Teaching:* Instr art, Irving Pub Schs, Tex, 59-60 & Elkhart, Ind, 60-63; prof & chmn dept art, Bloomsburg State Col, Pa, 64-68 & Tex A&M Univ, Kingsville, 68-. *Mem:* Nat Coun Art Adminr (bd dir, 72-78, secy-treas, 72-78); Art Mus STex (bd mem, 74-96, exhib policy bd, 96-); Tex Fine Arts Asn (bd dir, 71-74); S Tex Art League (pres, 72-73); Coastal Bend Art Educ Asn (pres, 73-74). *Mailing Add:* 1631 Santa Cecilia Dr Kingsville TX 78363

SCHEUER, RUTH
PAINTER, TAPESTRY ARTIST
b Wilson, NC, Aug 20, 1952. *Study:* Univ NC, BFA (cum laude), 70; Les Manufactures Nationales Des Gobelins, Paris, France, invitational studies, 79-80; Univ Calif, San Francisco, MA (fine art), 81. *Work:* Am Embassy, Warsaw, Poland; Univ NC, Weatherspoon Gallery, Greensboro. *Comn:* Tapestry, IBM, White Plains, NY, 87; tapestry, Nabisco-RJR, Atlanta, Ga, 87; tapestry, Touche-Ross, Houston, Tex, 88; tapestry, Wilmington Trust Bank, Del, 89; tapestry, Bell Atlantic Hq, Philadelphia, Pa, 91. *Exhib:* Solo exhib, NJ State Mus, Trenton, 85, Weatherspoon Gallery, Univ NC, Greensboro, 91 & Va Ctr Arts, Richmond, 92; Int Textile Exhib, Kyoto Cult Mus, Japan, 87 & 92; The Narrative Voice (touring), Musée D'Aubusson, France, 89; Int Tapestry, Anchorage Mus, Alaska, 90 & Textile Mus; World Tapestry Today (touring), West Pac Gallery, Melbourne, Australia, 88. *Pos:* Founder & dir, Scheuer Tapestry Studio, 82-89; founder & pres, Ctr Tapestry Arts, NY, 89-92, InterArt Ctr, NY, 92-. *Awards:* Visual Arts Fel, Midatlantic/Nat Endowment Arts, 89; Fel Grant, NY Found Arts, 90. *Bibliog:* Manson Kennedy (dir), Narrative Voice (film), 89; Pamela Scheinman (auth), cover article, Urban Tapestry, Am Craft, 89; Beatrijs Sterk (auth), Stromungen Der Zeit Tap, Deutsches Textilforum, 90. *Mem:* Distant Lives/Shared Voices, Lodz, Poland (int steering comt, 92); Am Tapestry Alliance (vpres & bd dir, 82-89); San Francisco Tapestry Workshop (co-founder, 76-79). *Media:* Miscellaneous

SCHIAVINA, LAURA M
PAINTER, COLLAGE ARTIST
b Springfield, Mass, Nov 27, 1917. *Study:* Traphagen Sch Fashion, NY, cert, 44-46; Art Students League, with Will Barnet, 73; studied with Paul Puzinas, Carl Molno & Don Stacy. *Work:* Metrop Club, NY; Queensborough Community Coll Art Gallery, Bayside, NY; and other pvt collections. *Exhib:* Solo Exhibs, 93 S Art Gallery, Nyack, NY, 98; Z Gallery, NY, 93, 94; NYC Coll Technol, Grace Gallery 2005; and others; Salmagundi Club, NY 74-2009; Priva B Gross Int, Queensborough Community Coll, Bayside, NY, 94, 96; Art Ctr of Munic of Athens, Eleftherias Park, Greece, 96; Flushing Coun Cult & Arts Membs Exhib, 97, 99, 2000, 2002, 2004, 2005, 2006, 2008, 2009; Queens Mus Art, 2001-02; Nat Asn of Women Artists, 89-2009; and many other group exhibs. *Awards:* Kenneth W Fitch Award, Salmagundi Club, 96; Samuel T Shaw Mem Award, Salmagundi Club, 1998; Cash Award, Postcard Exhibit, Nat Collage Soc, 2000; Audrey Hope Shirk Mem Award, 2005; Dorothy L Irish Award, 2006; Nat Asn Women Artists; First Prize, Small Works Nat Art League, 2006; R&C Stephens Award, Jackson Heights Art Club, 2006; 2nd Prize, SCNY Contemp Expressions Exhib, Salmagundi Club, 2009; and others. *Bibliog:* Rev, France-Amerique, Le Courrier des Estats Unis, 69; Dorothy Hall (auth), rev, Park East, New York, 69; article, Mixing pensions and painting, Marsh & McLennan News, 90; Artist in the 1990's, Manhattan Arts Mag, 9-10/92; Prof Cynthia Maris Dantzic (auth) 100 New York Painters, 2006. *Mem:* Salmagundi Club; Nat Collage Soc; Burr Artists; Nat League Am Pen Women; Nat Art League; NY Artist's Equity; Nat Asn Women Artists; Audubon Artists; Jackson Heights Art Club; and others. *Media:* Acrylic on Canvas & Paper, Watercolor & Collage Artist. *Mailing Add:* 35-25 78th St Jackson Heights NY 11372

SCHIEBOLD, HANS
PAINTER
b Freiberg, Ger, Feb 12, 1938; US citizen. *Study:* Brigham Young Univ, Utah, BA, 68; Hartford Art Sch of Univ Hartford, Conn, MFA, 70. *Work:* Aldrich Mus Contemp Art, Conn; New Britain Mus Am Art, Conn; Brownsville Art Mus, Tex; Southern Conn State Col, New Haven; Lake Oswego Town Hall & Libr, Ore; Farmington Town Hall, Farmington, Conn; Mus Art, Norman, Ok; Wichita Art Mus, Wichita, Kansas; Edwin A Ulrich Mus Art, Wichita State Univ, Kans; Am Energy Corporation, Wichita, Kans; Sedgwick County Court House, Wichita, Kans. *Comn:* Mural, Sedgewick Co Courthouse-Co Comnr, Kans, 81; 12 public murals, Kans Arts Commission & Wichita Arts Board, Kans, 80; 3 outdoor murals, Wesleyan Univ, Conn, 76. *Exhib:* Solo Exhibs: Ctr Arts, Wesleyan Univ, Conn, 74, Razor Gallery, NY, 77, Mus Art, Okla, 80 & Wichita Art Mus, Kans, 81; Lawrence Gallery, Pearl District and Sheridan, Ore, 2002; Bronze Coast Gallery, Cannon Beach, Ore, 2004; Lawrence Gallery, Salisan, Ore, 2005; Stormy Weather Festival, Bronze Coast Gallery, Cannon Beach, 2006; Lawrence Gallery, Pearl District, Portland, Ore, 2007; Group exhibs, Contemp Reflections, Aldrich Mus, Conn, 74; Invitation Acad Exhib, Wadsworth Atheneum, Conn, 71-73; Holloman Gallery, Colorado Springs, Colo, 1997-2001; Lanning Gallery, Sedona, Ariz, 1997; Freed Gallery, Lincoln City, Ore, 1998-2004; Contemp Fine Arts of Vail, Vail, Colo, 1999; Rich Haines Gallery, Park City, Utah, 1999. *Teaching:* Asst prof painting & drawing, Wesleyan Univ, Conn, 70-78 & Wichita State Univ, Kans, 78-82. *Awards:* Best in Show, Greater Hartford Arts Festival, 72; First Prize, Conn Acad, 74 & Springfield Art League, Mass, 75. *Media:* Acrylic, Graphite. *Dealer:* Lawrence Gallery Portland OR; Lanning Gallery Sedona AZ; Bronze Coast Gallery Cannon Beach OR; Gallery 903 Portland OR. *Mailing Add:* 13705 SW 118th Ct Portland OR 97223

SCHIEFERDECKER, IVAN E
PRINTMAKER, PAINTER
b Keokuk, Iowa, Apr 14, 1935. *Study:* Univ Ill, BFA; Univ Iowa, MFA. *Work:* Colorado Springs Art Ctr; Ohio Univ; Dulin Art Gallery, Knoxville, Tenn; Springfield Art Mus, Mo; Montgomery Art Mus, Ala; and others. *Exhib:* Pa Acad Fine Arts Ann Prints & Drawings, 65; J B Speed Art Mus, Louisville, Ky, 77; Southeastern Juried Exhib, Fine Arts Mus South, Mobile, Ala, 87; Border To Border Nat Drawing Competition, Austin Peay Univ, Clarksville, Tenn, 87 & 89; Dwight Merrimon Davidson Print Exhib, Elon Col, NC, 91; Ky On Paper, Quito, Ecuador, 91; Swanson Cralle Gallery, Louisville, Ky, 90 & 93; and others. *Teaching:* Prof printmaking, Western Ky Univ, 64-81. *Mem:* Coll Art Asn. *Mailing Add:* 1701 Dunlaney Way Bowling Green KY 42103

SCHIETINGER, JAMES FREDERICK
SCULPTOR, EDUCATOR
b Baltimore, Md, Sept 27, 1946. *Study:* Fla Presby Col, 64-66; Fla Atlantic Univ, 67; Univ SFla, BA, 68, MFA, 71. *Work:* Univ SFla; Norton Gallery Art, West Palm Beach. *Exhib:* Twenty-fifth Ceramic Nat, Everson Mus, Syracuse, 69; New Photog, Cent Wash State Col, 71; Photo-Media Show, Mus Contemp Crafts, NY, 71; Light and Lens: Methods of Photog, Hudson River Mus, NY, 73; Images-Dimensional, Moveable, Transferable, Akron Art Inst, 73. *Teaching:* Instr art hist, Fla Atlantic Univ, 71; instr ceramics, Univ SFla, 71-72; instr art, Miami-Dade Community Col, Miami, 72-73; asst prof art, Univ Vt, Burlington, 77-78 & Millikin Univ, 78-. *Awards:* First Prize in Sculpture, Winter Park Art Show, 70; Technol & Artist-Craftsman Symposium Award, Octagon Art Ctr, 73; Best in Show, Los Olas Art Festival, Ft Lauderdale, 75. *Mem:* Am Crafts Coun. *Media:* Clay. *Mailing Add:* RR 1 Mount Auburn IL 62547-9732

SCHIFF, JEFFREY ALLEN
SCULPTOR, INSTALLATION ARTIST
b Rolla, NDak, Aug 23, 1952. *Study:* Brown Univ, with R Fleischner, BA, 1974; Univ Mass, Amherst, MFA, 1976. *Comn:* Second Mesa (performance), Inst Contemp Art, Boston, 1983; Separate Ground (permanent outdoor sculpture), Univ Mass, Amherst, 1984; Mooring (bench), Conn State Comn Arts, Univ Conn, Storrs, 1987; Destinations (permanent sculpture), Fed Railroad Adminstrn & Mass Bay Transportation Authority, South Station Railroad Terminal, Boston, 1995; Rail of Justice(permanent sculpture), Superior Court, New Britain, Conn 2008; From L'Encyclopedia"(permanent sculpture), Office of Chief Medical Examiner Forensic Biology Lab, New York City, digital print. *Exhib:* Solo exhibs, Univ RI, Kingston, 1980, Univ Mass Gallery, Amherst, 1981, Stux Gallery, Boston, 1982 & Danforth Mus, Framingham, Mass, 1983; exhibs: Inst Contemp Art, Boston, 1979; group exhibs, Boston Mus Fine Arts, 1982; Brown Univ, 1983; Hayden Gallery, Mass Inst Technol, 1983; Rose Art Mus, Brandeis Univ, Mass, 1986; San Diego Mus Contemp Art, 1987; Williams Coll Mus, 1988; Sculpture Ctr, New York, 1993; Katonah Art Mus, NY, 1996; Real Art Ways, Hartford, Conn, 1998; San Jose Mus Art, 2000; Cathedral of St John the Divine, NY, 2001; Olin Mem Libr, Wesleyan Univ, 2003; Exit Art, New York, 2005, 2006; Proteus Gowanus, Brooklyn, 2006. *Teaching:* Instr, Boston Col, 1980-81; lectr, Clark Univ, Worcester, Mass, 1981; assoc prof art, Wesleyan Univ, Conn, 1987-. *Awards:* Mass Artists Found Fel, 1975, 1980, 1985; Rome Prize for Sculpture, Am Acad Rome, 1976; NEA Fel, 1976, 1979, 1984; Boston/Kyoto Sister City Traveling Grant, 1984; Boston Soc Archits Award for Design Collaboration, 1991; Fulbright Sr Scholar Research Fel, 1998; Rockefeller Found Residency, 2002; Ctr Humanities, 2003; NY Found Arts Fel in Sculpture, 2003; Bogliasco Found, 2005; Guggenheim Fel, 2008. *Dealer:* Stux Gallery 36 Newbury St Boston MA 02116. *Mailing Add:* Dept Art & Art Hist Wesleyan Univ Middletown CT 06459

SCHIFF, MELANIE
PHOTOGRAPHER
b Chicago, Ill, 1977. *Study:* Univ London, Goldsmiths Coll, 1995; Colorado Coll, 1996; New York Univ, Tisch Sch Arts, BFA, 1999; Univ Ill-Chicago, MFA, 2002. *Work:* Kempter Mus Contemp Art, Kansas City; Mus Contemp Art, Chicago. *Exhib:* Solo exhibs include Kavi Gupta Gallery, Chicago, 2004, 2006, Mus Contemp Art, Chicago, 2007, Uschi Kolb, Karlsruhe, Germany, 2007; Group exhibs include Tainted Love, Unit B Gallery, Chicago, 2003; Push Pin Proj, Deluxe Projs, Chicago, 2003; Sitting, Standing, Reclining, Modern Culture, New York, 2004, 2005; Into the Woods, Thomas McCormick Gallery, Chicago, 2005; Sympathy for the Devil: Art & Rock and Roll Since 1967, Mus Contemp Art, Chicago, 2007; Whitney Biennial, Whitney Mus Am Art, New York, 2008. *Awards:* UIC Neisser Award, 2000-01; Artadia Jury Award, 2006. *Dealer:* Kavi Gupta Gallery 835 West Washington Chicago IL 60607

SCHIFF, MOLLY JEANETTE
PAINTER, PRINTMAKER
b Chicago, Ill, Oct 19, 1927. *Study:* Sch of the Art Inst of Chicago, BFA, 62, MFA, 63, MAE, 69; Studied with Richard Keane (MFA) & John Fabian (BFA), Robert Lifvandhal (BFA & MFA), 58-63. *Work:* Ill State Mus, Springfield, Ill; Loyola Univ Mus Fine Art, Chicago,; Art Heritage Gallery, New Delhi, India; Standard Oil Corp, Chicago; Borg Warner Corp, Chicago; Art Inst Chicago. *Exhib:* Solo exhibs, Windows- In & Out, City of Chicago Treasure's Office, 2008, Water Images, City of Chicago Cult Ctr, 1999; Ann Exhib, Ill State Mus, Springfield, Ill, 78; Primarily Primary, Art Inst Mus, Chicago, 86; Illinois Inst Art, Chicago, 2000; Engaging with the Present, Spertus Mus, Chicago, 2004-2005; Biennale Int, Fortezza da Basso, Florence, Italy, 2003; I Remember Purim, Loyola Mus Of Fine Art, Chicago, 2007; Art in the Embassies, USA State Dept Int, Marshall Island, 96-2000; Biennial Exhib, The Arts Club Chicago, 99-2009; The Arts Club Chigaco, 99-2012; Water Images & Still Life, Art Heritage Gallery, New Delhi, India, 84; Chicago Cultural Center, 2008; Two person exhib, A Colorful Journey, Cong Beth Shalom, Naperville, Ill, 2009; As The Spirit Moves You, Highland Pk Art Ctr, 2009; Reality & Beyond, Chicago Soc of Artists, 2009; The Arts Club of Chicago, 2009-2010; The Gift, Am Jewish Artists Cub, 2009-2010; I Remember Purim, Temple Israel Mus, West Bloomfield, Mus, 2009; Celebrating Chicago, Chicago Soc Art, 2010; Bloomingdale Park Art Mus, 2010; Anderson Art Ctr, Chicago Soc Art, 2010; A Gathering of Waters, Beverly Art Ctr, 2010; Arts Club of Chicago, 2011; Swedish Am Mus, 2011; Anderson Art Ctr, Chicago Society Art, 2010, 2012; I Remember Purim, N.S., Synagogue Beth El, Highland Park, 2012. *Pos:* Prog chmn, Am Jewish Artists Club, Chicago, 80-90, exhib chmn, 90-95, pres, 2004-2006, website chmn, 2005-2009. *Teaching:* Instr drawing, Art Inst Jr Sch, Chicago, 69-70; instr drawing, Gov State Univ, Park Forest, Ill, summer 72, instr etching, summer 73. *Awards:* Purchase Award, Ill State Ann, Ill State Mus, 78; Exhib Award, Group at Beacon St Gallery, Nat Endowment Arts, 73; General Award, Coal Miners Resources, Ill Dept Energy, 88; First Place, Latest Impressions, Chicago Sr Art League, 90; Best Club Award, Am Jewish Artist Club, 2000. *Bibliog:* PN Margo & Iqbal Singh (auths), MS Paintings Expression of Life, Patriot, New Delhi, India, 9/8/84; Joan M Plaisted (auth), From the Chicago Reef, USA Embassy-Marshall Islands, 7/30/98; Dorothy Ives (auth), Contrast of Artists' Works, Post-Tribune, Ind, 12/19/71; G Jurer Polanski (auth), Women Do Figure: Body Works, Art Scope, Chicago, 4/25/2000; Harold Hayden (auth), Galleries, Chicago Artists, Chicago Sun Times, 4/27/81. *Mem:* Alumni Asn of Art Inst Chicago (Bd mem, 65-70); Chicago Soc Artists; Chicago Artist Coalition; Arts Club of Chicago; Am Jewish Artists Club (pres 2004-2006); Int Soc Artists; Saatch Gallery. *Media:* Acrylic, Oil, Misc Media, Etching, Lithography, Silkscreen. *Res:* Markal oil, Markal Corp, 78-95. *Interests:* Photography. *Publ:* Role & Impact, Grant Ill Art Coun, 79; Harvest of Freedom, Libr Cone Catalog, 89; Int Libr Photography, Libr Cone Catalog, 93; Biennale Internazionale Dell Arte Contemp, Art Studio Riproduzione, 2003. *Dealer:* Anatomically Correct. *Mailing Add:* 744 Sheridan Rd Evanston IL 60202

SCHILDKNECHT, DOROTHY E
PAINTER
b Chicago, Ill, Sept 30, 1943. *Study:* Am Acad Art. *Work:* St Patrick High Sch, Chicago; Lillian Berkley Collection, Calif, 2000. *Exhib:* Women Artists on the West, Calif, 90-91; Nat Asn Women Artists, NY, 91; Mountain Oyster Exhib, Tucson, Ariz, 93-94; Old West Mus Exhib, Cheyenne, Wyo, 94; Am Art Miniatures, Gilcrease Mus, Tulsa, Okla, 94; and others. *Teaching:* Oil painting, Mt Prospect Park Dist & Glenview Park Dist, 88-; adult educ, Oakton Community Col. *Awards:* Third Place, Nat Exhib NMex Small Picture, 91. *Mem:* Nat Asn Women Artists, NY; Palette & Chisel Acad Fine Art, Chicago; Women Artists of West. *Media:* Oil. *Publ:* Chicago Tribune, 8/92 & 7/96; Daily Herald, 1/94. *Dealer:* White Oak Gallery Edina MN; Cain Gallery Oak Park IL. *Mailing Add:* 1356 Whitcomb Des Plaines IL 60018

SCHILDKROUT, ENID
CURATOR, EDUCATOR
Study: Sarah Lawrence Coll, BA; Newnham Coll, Cambridge Univ, MA & PhD (social anthrop). *Collection Arranged:* African Reflections: Art from Northeastern Zaire, 1990; Spirits in Steel: The Art of the Kalabari Masquerade, 1998; Body Art: Marks of Identity, 1999. *Pos:* Cur, Am Mus Natural Hist, New York, 1972-, chmn divsn anthrop, 1997-2002; chief cur & dir exhibs & publ, Mus for African Art, New York, 2005-; ed adv bd, Rutgers Univ Press Childhood Studies; adv bd, Margaret Mead Film Festival; adv ed, Yale Univ Encyclopedia of National Cultures; ed bd, Curator: The Mus Jour & Jour Childhood Studies. *Teaching:* Adj prof dept anthrop & art, Columbia Univ; adj prof, CUNY Grad Ctr. *Mem:* African Studies Asn (bd dirs Arts Coun); Am Anthrop Asn; Coun for Mus Anthrop; Royal Anthrop Inst (fel). *Publ:* Auth, People of the Zongo: The Transformation of Ethnic Identities in Ghana, 1978; co-auth (with Curtis A Keim), African Reflections: Art from Northeastern Zaire, Univ Washington Press, 1990; co-ed (with Curtis A Keim), The Scramble for Art in Central Africa, Cambridge Univ Press, 1998. *Mailing Add:* c/o Museum for African Art 3601 43rd Ave #3 Long Island City NY 11101-1736

SCHIRA, CYNTHIA
TAPESTRY ARTIST
b Pittsfield, Mass, June 1, 1934. *Study:* RI Sch Design, BFA, 56; L'Ecole D'Art Decoratif, Aubusson, France, 56-57; Univ Kans, MFA, 67. *Hon Degrees:* RI Sch Design, hon DFA, 89. *Work:* Am Craft Mus, NY; Chicago Art Inst, Ill; Renwick Gallery, Nat Mus Am Art, Smithsonian, Washington; Metrop Mus Art, NY; Philadelphia Mus Art, Pa; Boston Muc of Fine Arts; De Young Mus, San Francisco; Mus Bellerive Zurich; Mus Art, RI Sch Design; Indianapolis Mus Art; Cooper-Hewitt Mus; Smithsonian, NY. *Comn:* Wall Hanging, Arrow Corp, 94; Horsley Bridge Partners, San Francisco, 2005. *Exhib:* Solo exhibs, Mus Bellerive, Zurich, 79, Spencer Mus Art, Univ Kans, Lawrence, 87, Renwick Gallery, Nat Mus Am Art & Smithsonian, Washington, 87; group exhib, The Art Fabric: Mainstream, San Francisco Mus Mod Art, 81; Craft Today, Am Crafts Mus, 87; Int Textile Competition '89, Kyoto, Japan; Jacquard Proj, Mus Indust Kultur, Nuremberg, Ger, 91; First Textile Miniature Triennale, Gdynia, Poland, 93; 2010-Textiles & New Technology, Brit Craft Ctr, London, 94; Technology as Catalyst, Textile Mus, Wash, DC, 2002; Miniature Textiles 2000, Mus of Art and Design, Helsinki, 2000. *Pos:* Chairperson bd trustees, Haystack Mountain Sch Crafts, Maine, 89-92; Honorary Trustee, Haystack School of Crafts, Deer Isle, ME, 2004-. *Teaching:* Prof textile design, Univ Kans, 76-99, prof emer, 99-. *Awards:* Fel Am Crafts Coun, 91; Gold Medal, Am Crafts Coun Coll of Fel, 2000; Distinguished Educator Award; James Renwick Alliance, Smithsonian. *Bibliog:* Susan Axy (auth), A World of Costume & Design (exhib catalog), Mus Art, RI Sch Design, Providence, 89; Beatrijs Sterk (auth), High tech textilkunsk, Deutsches Textileforum Heft, 12/4/92; Joan Simon (auth), Cynthia Schira, portfolio collection, Telos Art Publ, 2003. *Mem:* Am Crafts Coun; Textile Soc Am. *Media:* Textiles. *Dealer:* Snyderman Works Gallery 303 Cherry St Philadelphia PA 19106. *Mailing Add:* Box 303 Westport NY 12993

SCHIRM, DAVID
PAINTER, EDUCATOR
b Pittsburgh, Pa, Mar 31, 1945. *Study:* Carnegie Mus, BFA, 67; Ind Univ, MFA, 72. *Work:* Albright-Knox Art Gallery; Carnegie Mus Art; Nat Mus Art, Hanoi, Vietnam; Kaufman & Broad, Los Angeles; Burchfield Penny Art Ctr. *Exhib:* Directions, Hirshhorn Mus, Washington, 79; Painting & Sculpture Today, Indianapolis Mus Art, 80; Carnegie Int, Carnegie Mus, 82. *Teaching:* Lectr painting, Univ Calif Los Angeles, 77-81; asst prof, Univ Southern Calif, 82-83; prof, Dept Visual Studies, Univ Buffalo, 85-. *Awards:* NY Found for Arts, 91; Fulbright Fel, Fragile Petals, Fulbright Comn, 94-95; Fullbright Regional Res, India & Sri Lanka. *Bibliog:* Howard Fox (auth), Directions, Hirshhorn Mus, 79; Lucy Lippard (auth), A Different War, Vietnam in Art, 90; Susan Larsen (auth), David Schirm, Ind Univ, 94. *Mem:* Coun Int Exchange Schs. *Mailing Add:* 3602 Rose Rd Batavia NY 14020

SCHJELDAHL, PETER
CRITIC, EDITOR
b Fargo, NDak, 1942. *Study:* Carlton Col; New Sch, 1960-65. *Pos:* Art critic, New York Sunday Times, 1970-75, Village Voice, 1981-82, Vanity Fair, 1983-84, 7 Days, currently; contrib ed, Art Am, currently. *Awards:* Frank Jewett Mather Award, Coll Art Asn, 1980; Clark Prize for Excellence in Arts Writing, 2008. *Publ:* Auth: (poetry collections) White Country, 1968, An Adventure of the Thought Police, 1971, Dreams, 1973, Since 1964; New and Selected Poems, 1978, Sun, (books) Hydrogen Jukebox: Selected Writings of Peter Schjeldahl, 1978-1990, 1991, The Seven Days Art Columns, 1991, Columns and Catalogues, 1994; Auth, Cindy Sherman, Pantheon Books, 1984; Eric Fischl, Art Am/Stewart, Tabori & Chang, 1988; and articles in Artforum, Art News, Art Int, Art & Antiques, Camera Arts, Am Craft; co-founder poetry mag Mother; contributing editor Art in Am; contribr articles to art jours. incl Artforum, Art News, Art Inter, Art & Antiques, Camera Arts, Am Craft and others. *Mailing Add:* The New Yorker 4 Times Sq New York NY 10036-6592

SCHLANGER, GREGG
ADMINISTRATOR
Study: attended Univ Oregon, Eugene, 1978-1980; Boise State Univ, Idaho, BFA, 1987; Northern Ill Univ, MFA (Sculpture), 1989. *Exhib:* One person exhibitions include: Prairie State Waterway, Prairie State Col, Ill (part 1), ARC Gallery, Raw Space, Chgo, Ill (part 2), 1990, Bridged Waterway, Galerie Neue Raume, Berlin, Germany, 1992, Cutthroat Trout, New Rivers, New Dreams, Fassbender Gallery, Chgo, Ill, 1995, Sockeye Waters, Sockeye Dreams, Refish Lake, Idaho, 1998, 10 Ways to Make a River, Univ Memphis, 2002, Mr Peabody's Coal Train, Tennessee Arts Commision Gallery, 2006, BWR Basic Water Requirements 50 Liters, Twist Art Gallery, Nashvillee, 2009, Renaissance Ctr, Dickson, Tennessee, 2010, Storefronts Seattle, 2012, Mapping the Spokane River, Spokane Falls Community Col Art Gallery, 2013 and others; Group exhibitions include: Rocky Mountain Nat Juried Watermedia Exhibition, Foorhills Art Ctr, Golden, Colorado, 1988, Chgo International New Art Forms, Navy Pier, Chgo, 1990, Spurlos, Altes Rathaus, Potsdam, Germany, 1993, 3-D From P-C, Gallery II, Univ Arkansas, Little Rock, 1999, Welt Wesser, KunstHaus Potsdam, Germany, 2007, The Value of Water, The Cathedral Church of Saint John the Divine, NY, 2011-2012, Works on Water, Marin Community Foundation, Novato, Calif, 2012-2103 and others. *Teaching:* Chair, prof art, Central Washington Univ, Ellenburg, Washington, 2011-. *Mailing Add:* Central Washington University Art Department 400 E University Ellensburg WA 98926

SCHLANGER, JEFF
SCULPTOR, PAINTER
b New York, NY, 1937. *Study:* Swarthmore Col, BA; Cranbrook Acad Art, with Maija Grotell. *Work:* Sheldon Mem Art Gallery, Univ Nebr, Lincoln; Am Craft Mus, NY; Cranbrook Art Mus, Bloomfield Hills, Mich; Acad Art Mus, St Petersburg, Russ; Mus Art & Design, New York, NY; St. Petersburg Art Acad, Russia. *Comn:* Tile mural, Performing Arts Ctr, Eugene, Ore, 82. *Exhib:* Total Cup, Kanazawa City, Tokyo, Kyoto, Japan, 73; Contemp Crafts of the Americas: 75, Ft Collins, Colo, 75; The

Object as Poet, Renwick Gallery, Smithsonian Inst, Washington & Mus of Contemp Crafts, NY, 77; Solo exhibs, State Coll Ceramics, Alfred, NY, 78 & City Univ NY Grad Ctr Mall Gallery, 80; CUE Art Found, New York, 2005; and others; Abrons Art Ctr, New York, 2010; Clay Art Ctr, Port Chester, NY, 2008-2010; Roulette, Brooklyn, NY, 2014. *Teaching:* Instr ceramics, Hunter Col, 75 & Pratt Inst Grad Sch, 77; instr sculpture, State Univ NY, Purchase, 82; ceramics, Cranbrook Acad Art, 84. *Awards:* LC Tiffany Found award, 68; NEA Fel, 73; Fel NY State Creative Artists Pub Serv, 81. *Media:* Clay, Wood, Paint. *Publ:* Auth, Maija Grotell, Studio Potter Books, 96; Spiritworld (dvd), Witnissimo, 2007 . *Mailing Add:* c/o Studio Spirale 556 Stratton Rd New Rochelle NY 10804-1108

SCHLEEH, HANS MARTIN
SCULPTOR
b Konigsfeld Schwarzwald, Ger, Oct9, 1928; Can citizen. *Work:* Montreal Mus Fine Arts; Tel Aviv Mus, Israel; Art Gallery Winnipeg; Vancouver Art Gallery; Univ Sherbrooke, Can; Musée Contemporain. *Comn:* Limestone sculpture, Ciba Ltd, Montreal, 56; Swan (carrara marble), Pl Arts, Montreal, 65; copper sculptures, Arthur Maron Enterprises, Montreal, 67; limestone sculpture, Freiman Stores, Ottawa, 73. *Exhib:* Solo exhibs, Dominion Gallery, Montreal, 60-70, Que Sculptors Asn, Montreal, 65-70, Salon Jeune Sculpture, Paris, 66-67 & Expo 67, Montreal, 67; Exposition Int, Rodin Mus, Paris, 71; and others. *Bibliog:* Guy Robert (auth), L'Art au Quebec Depuis 1940, 40 & Ecole de Montreal, 64, La Presse. *Mem:* Royal Can Acad Arts. *Media:* Stone, Metal. *Mailing Add:* 2209 av Oxford Montreal PQ H4A 2X7 Canada

SCHLEINER, ANN-MARIE
GRAPHIC ARTIST
b Providence, 1970. *Study:* Univ Michoacan, Mex; Univ Kiel; Univ Calif, Santa Cruz; San Jose State Univ, MFA. *Work:* Madame Polly Game Patch, 1998; Epilepsy Virus Patch, 1999; Cracking the Maze, 1999; mutation.fem, 2000; Luckykiss xxx, 2000; Skool, 2001; Snow Blossom House, 2001; Anime Noir, 2002; Velvet Strike, 2002; Parangari Cutiri, 1999-; PS2 Diaries, 2004-; OUT: Operation Urban Terrain, 2004-. *Teaching:* Asst prof, interactive arts Technol, Univ British Columbia, Can, 99-2000; adj fac, of digital art Univ Calif, Irvine, 2001; asst prof, Univ Colo, Boulder, 2003-. *Mem:* fel, Akademie Schloss Solitude, 2003

SCHLEMM, BETTY LOU
PAINTER, INSTRUCTOR
b Jersey City, NJ, Jan 13, 1934. *Study:* Phoenix Sch Design, New York, scholar; Nat Acad Design, New York, scholar. *Work:* US Navy; 1st Nat Bank Boston; Andrew Mellon Collection; American Telephone & Telegraph; also in many other pvt & public collections. *Exhib:* Am Watercolor Soc; Butler Inst Am Art; Nat Acad Design; Allied Artists Am; Audubon Artists. *Pos:* Vpres, Boston Watercolor Soc; regional vpres, Am Watercolor Soc, 89-90 & dir, 90-92. *Awards:* Gold Medal, Rockport Art Asn, 81; Frederick B Robinson Award, Academic Artists, 81; Dolfin Fel, Am Watercolor Soc, 81 & Silver Medal, 64; and others. *Bibliog:* 100 Watercolor Techniques, Watson-Guptill, 69; Stephen Doherty (auth), Being An Artist, 92; Lewis Lehrman (auth), North Light, 92; and others. *Mem:* Am Watercolor Soc; Rockport Art Asn (pres, 95-97); Boston Watercolor Soc (vpres, 76-); and others. *Media:* Watercolor, oil. *Publ:* Auth, Watercolor page, Am Artist, 64 & 76; Painting with Light, Watson-Guptill, 78, 2nd ed, 79 & 3rd ed, 92; Learning from today's art masters, Am Artist Mag, 95; Watercolor Secrets for Painting, Light-North Light, 96. *Dealer:* Guild of Boston Artists 162 Newbury St Boston MA 02116; Rockport Art Asn 10 Main St Rockport MA 01966; State of the Art Gallery 1&2 Wanson St Gloucester MA 01930 & Pleasant St Gloucester MA 01930. *Mailing Add:* Caleb's Ln Rockport MA 01966

SCHLESINGER, CHRISTINA
PAINTER, MURALIST
b Washington, DC, Dec 19, 1946. *Study:* Radcliffe Col, Harvard Univ, BA, 68; Zhejiang Acad Fine Arts, Hangzhou, China, 88; Mason Gross Sch Arts, Rutgers Univ, MFA, 95. *Comn:* The Peaceable: Kingdom, Kennedy Child Study Ctr, Bronx, NY, 91; The Big Splash, Greyhound Inc & City of Los Angeles, Percent for Art, Calif, 91; Fire Mural, DP Bean & Co, Jaffrey, NH, 92; East NY, Past, Present & Future, Sites Proj, Percent for Art, NY, 94; Chaqall Returns to Venice Beach, Cult Affairs Dept, City of Los Angeles, Venice, Calif, 96. *Exhib:* Mixed Use District, Clock Tower, NY, 90; Artists & Homeless Collaborative World Wall, Henry Street Settlement House, NY, 93; Other Choices, Other Voices, Islip Mus Art, NY, 95; Trees, Provincetown Art Asn, Mass, 95; Celebrity Hood, Bronx Ctr Arts, NY, 96; Altered Egos, Hallwalls Contemp Art Ctr, Buffalo, NY, 97. *Pos:* Co-found, Social & Pub Art Resource Ctr, Venice, Calif, 76-. *Awards:* Grant, Pollock-Krasner Found Inc, 88; Grant, Adolph & Esther Gothlieb Found Inc, 89. *Bibliog:* Alan Barnett (auth), Community Murals: The People's Art, Art Alliance Press & Cornwall Bks, 94. *Media:* Oil; Acrylic. *Mailing Add:* 16 Deep Six Dr East Hampton NY 11937-1603

SCHLITTER, HELGA
PAINTER, SCULPTOR
b Mexico City, Mex; Can citizen. *Study:* Studied with Marcel Jean, 68-75. *Work:* Musee du Quebec; Ministry Multicultural Communities, Quebec Govt; Loto Quebec. *Comn:* Laure Gaudreault, Clermont, Québec, Andiwish:Lestortues, Interior floor mosaic, École L' Apprentisage, Québec, 99; Cirque, exterior wall installation, Ecole De Cirque De Québec, 2003; Un Drôle Ó Animal, exterior sculpture, École Primaire, 2003; Azi Mut Le Gardiev De L' École, exterior sculpture, École La Rose-Des-Vents, St Jean Chrysostome, Québec; Centre de recherches sur les nutraceutiques et les aliments fonctionnel, Laval; Installation of Four outside sculptures, Univ Quebec, 2003; outside sculpture, Bibliotheque Charles H Blais, Quebec, 2004; outside sculpture, Maison Vezina, Boischatel, Quebec, 2005; inside installation of five panels of sculpted wood covered with colored glass, Ecole l'accueil, St Emile, Quebec, 2006; outside sculpture, Ecole primaire de Portneuf, 2009; La Guadeloupe, Centre sportif Armand-Racine, Quebec, 2009. *Exhib:* Pret d'oeuvres d'art, Musee du Que, 83, 85 & 86; Femmes-Forces Musee du Que, 87; Noel Reinvente, Musee du Civilisation, Que, 88; Quetzalpapalotl, le temple de l'oiseau-papillon, 84 & Recent Work, 86, La Chambre Blanche; Recent Work, Powerhouse, Montreal, 86; Des jaguar-des serpents-et des temples, Axe-Neo 7, Hull, Que, 86; BBK-Werkstattev, Freiburg, Ger, 92; De Quebec A Chicomoztoc Museo Carrillo Gil, Mex, D F, 94; Universidad La Salle, Mex, DF, 95; Galerie De L'Universite Laval, Que, 95; Centre D'Expositions De St-Jerome, Que, 97; Galerie Du Parc, Trois-Rivieres, Que, 98; Sculptures Et Mosaïques Galerie Trompe L'oeil, Cegep Ste-Foy, Qué, 2000; Jeux En Mosaique, Maison De La Cult, Notre-Dame-De-Grace, Montreal, Qué, 2001; Jardins De Cristal, Centre D'art De Baie-St-Paul, Qué, 2003; Bibliotheque de neufchatel. *Pos:* Mem exec coun, La Chambre Blanche, Quebec, 80-83, pres, 82-83; pres, Atelier le 88, Quebec, 80-88; mem exec coun, L'Oeil du Poisson, Quebec, 88. *Awards:* Quebec Cult Ministry Scholar, 88 & 94; Scholar of artistic exchange between Que & Mex, Ministry of External Affairs, 94; Scholar for Prof Studies in Barcelona, Ministry Art, Quebec, 98; Ministry of External Affairs of Can and Fonca (Fondo Nacinal Para La Cultura Mexico) Scholarship-Mexico/Can Exchange. *Bibliog:* Marie Delagrave (auth), Architec & paysages imaginaires, 1/28/84 & Helga Schlitter et le temple des papillons, 4/14/84, Le Soleil; Chantal Boulanger (auth), Atelier de l'artiste, Vanguard, 84; Dany Qunie (auth) Joies Exotiques, Le Soleil, Québec, 2/5/2000; Nathalie Côté (auth), La Menagerie De Verre, Voir, Québec, 2/10/2000. *Media:* Multimedia. *Mailing Add:* 169 St-Olivier Quebec PQ G1R 1G2 Canada

SCHLODER, JOHN E
DIRECTOR
Study: Duquesne Univ, BS, 1969; L'Ecole du Louvre, Paris, Diplôme d' Ancien Elève; L'Institut d' Archéologie Univ Paris-Sorbonne, 1973; Lurcy Fel, Columbia Univ, 1975; Traveling Fel, Univ Cambridge Eng, 1975-1976; Leverhulme Fel, 1977; Kellogg Project Fel, Smithsonian Inst, 1987; Columbia Univ, MPhil, 1980; L'Institut d' Art et d'Archéologie, Univ Paris-Sorbonne, PhD, 1988; J Paul Getty Trust, scholar, 1989; Japan Found vis schol, 1995. *Pos:* Chargé de Mission Musée du Louvre, Paris, 1979-1982; Asst cur, Cleveland Mus Art Edn Dept, 1982-1985, assoc cur, 1985-1986, adminr pub progs, 1986-1988, asst dir, edn & pub progs, 1988-1992; Dir Birmingham (Ala) Mus Arts, 1992-1996; Dir, Joslyn Mus Art, Omaha, 1997-2000; Dir, Mus Fine Arts, St. Petersburg, Fla, 2001-. *Teaching:* Vis prof, Colégio Andrews, Rio de Janeiro, Brazil, 1980-1981; Vaculdade Candido Mendes, Rio de Janeiro, 1981-1982; Adj prof art hist, Case Western Reserve Univ, Cleveland, 1984-1992. *Awards:* French Govt Award of Achievement, 1975; Northern Ohio Live Mag, 1991. *Mem:* Am Asn Mus; Asn Art Mus (dirs); Int Lab Visitor Studies; Visitor Studies Asn; Ala Mus Asn; Birmingham Area Mus Asn; Soc de l'Historie de l'Art Francais; Rotary Club Birmingham. *Mailing Add:* Mus Fine Arts 255 Beach Dr NE Saint Petersburg FL 33701

SCHLOSS, ARLEEN P
PAINTER
b Brooklyn, NY, Dec 12, 1943. *Study:* Parsons Sch Design, cert; New York Univ, BA; Art Students League. *Work:* Aldrich Mus Contemp Art, Ridgefield, Conn; Am Tel & Tel Longlines, NJ; Mus Mod Art Libr, NY; Lenbachhaus Mus, Munich, Ger. *Exhib:* Tenth Anniv Exhib, Aldrich Mus, Conn, 74; Contemp Reflections, 1971-74 Traveling Show, Am Fedn Arts, 75-77; Artists Books USA, Allen Mem Art Mus, Oberlin Col, 79; Solo exhib, Diagrams, Rush Rhees Gallery, Rochester Univ, 75; Stadtische Galerie im Buntentor, Bremen, Ger, 94. *Teaching:* Artist-in-residence art & music, NY Pub Schs, 67-75; guest lectr art, Rochester Univ, 75; guest prof, Hochschule fur Kunste, Bremen, Ger, 93. *Awards:* Video Fel, NY Found Arts, 92. *Bibliog:* Jill Dunbar (auth), Avant-Garde--The other end, The Villager, 12/8/77; Enrico Baj (auth), Panorama Mag, 6/86; Frances DeVuono (auth), New York Art Examiner, 89; Tobey Crockett (auth), High Performance Mag, 92. *Media:* Audio & Visual Materials. *Publ:* Contribr, Weaving: A Handbook of The Fibre Arts, Holt, Rinehart & Winston, 78

SCHMALTZ, ROY EDGAR
PAINTER, EDUCATOR
b Belfield, NDak, 1937. *Study:* Otis Art Inst, Los Angeles, 59-60; Univ Wash, Seattle, 57-59, 60-61; Akademie Der Bildenden Kunste, Munich, Ger, 65-66; San Francisco Art Inst, BFA, 63, MFA, 65. *Work:* Frye Art Mus, Seattle; San Francisco Art Inst & M H De Young Mem Art Mus, San Francisco; Mills Col, Oakland; Amerika-Haus, Munich, Ger; Univ Hawaii, Hilo; and others. *Exhib:* M H De Young Mem Art Mus, San Francisco, 69; San Francisco Mus Mod Art, 71; Oakland Art Mus, 79; Springfield Art Mus, Mo, 81; Butler Inst Am Art, Youngstown, Ohio, 81; Crocker Art Mus, Sacramento, 82; Appalachian State Univ, NC, 82; Univ Hawaii, Manoa, 83; and others. *Pos:* Artists bd, San Francisco Art Inst, 89-92. *Teaching:* Lectr, Col Notre Dame, Belmont, Calif, 68-70; lectr, M H De Young Art Mus, San Francisco, 69-70; prof, St Mary's Col, Moraga, Calif, 69-, chair, Dept Art. *Awards:* Fel, Fulbright, Munich, Ger, 65; Walnut Creek Civic Art Ctr Award, 82; San Francisco Art Comn Award, 85. *Bibliog:* Thomas Albright (auth), Art of the San Francisco Bay Area 1945-1980, Univ Calif Press, Berkeley; Bay Area Artists Calendar-1984, KQED TV; Les Krantz (auth), The Calif Art Review, Second ed, Am References, Chicago. *Media:* Oil, Watercolor. *Dealer:* Hackett-Freedman Gallery 250 Sutter St 4th Floor San Francisco CA 94108; Hearst Art Gallery Saint Mary's Coll Moraga CA. *Mailing Add:* 1020 Whistler Dr Suisun City CA 94585

SCHMANDT-BESSERAT, DENISE
HISTORIAN, ARCHAEOLOGIST
b Ay-Champagne, France, 1933. *Study:* Ecole du Louvre, Paris, 65. *Hon Degrees:* Kenyon Col, PhD (hc), 2008. *Collection Arranged:* Permanent exhib, Near Eastern Collections (with catalog), Peabody Mus, Harvard Univ, 68; The Legacy of Sumer, the First Civilization (with catalog & children's catalog), 75 & Ancient Persia--The Art of an Empire, 78, Univ Tex Art Mus. *Pos:* Adv ed, Technology & Cult, 78-92; adv bd, Visible Language, 85-; ed bd, Written Commun, 93-95, Media Ecology, 2002- & Archaeol Odyssey, 2003-; curator, Legacy of the Middle East, exhib, Jeddah, Saudi

Arabia. *Teaching:* Prof ancient Near East, Univ Tex, Austin, 72-; vis assoc prof, Dept Near Eastern Studies, Univ Calif, Berkeley, 87; guest scholar, Ger Archaeological Inst, Berlin, WGer, 87; guest scholar, Tsukuba Univ, Hiroshima Univ, Japan, 90; 2004 Retired from teaching. *Awards:* Nat Endowment Humanities, 79-80, 91 & 96; Ger Acad Exchange Serv Grant, 86; USIA Fel, Am Ctr Oriental Res, 95, 97, 2001, 2009; Named One of the 100 Authors of the 20th Century, Am Scientist, 99; Kayden Nat Univ Press Book Award, 92; Robert W Hamilton Author Award, 98, 2008; Walter J Ong Award Media Ecology Asn, 2004; and others. *Mem:* Archaeol Inst Am (pres, Cent Tex Chap, 74-76, gov bd, 85-); Am Oriental Studies; fel Am Anthropological Asn; Am Sch Oriental Res; Ctr Int Ricerche Archeologiche Antropologiche e Storiche. *Res:* Symbolism in the Ancient Middle East. *Interests:* The Middle East. *Publ:* auth, The origins of writing, Written Commun, Vol 13, No 1, 86; Before Writing, 92, When Writing Came About, 96, Univ Tex Press; History of Counting, 2000; From Behind the Mask, Origini, Vol XXIV, 2002; Stone Age Death Masks, Archaeol Odyssey, Vol 6, No 2, 2003-; others; Auth, When Writing Met Art, 2007

SCHMELTZ, L AILI
SCULPTOR, PAINTER
Study: Kans City Art Inst, BFA (printmaking & painting), 1997; Univ Ariz, Tucson, MFA (sculpture), 2003; Sculpture Space Fel, Utica, 2005; Prof Develop Grant, Ariz Comn Arts, Phoenix, 2006; Bemis Ctr for Contemp Art Fel, 2008; Pollock-Krasner Found Grant, 2008. *Exhib:* This American Lawn, Mus Contemp Art, Tucson, 2003; solo exhibs, Fuller Projects, Ind Univ, 2004, Tilt Gallery & Project Space, Portland, Ore, 2006, Gardiner Art Gallery, Okla State Univ, 2008, Greenleaf Gallery, Whittier Coll, Los Angeles, 2010; Fac Exhib, Ind Univ Mus Art, Bloomington, 2005; Console, Portland Art Ctr, Ore, 2007; Los Angeles Biennial Exhib, Los Angeles Munic Art Gallery, 2008; The Sketchbook Project Volume 3 (traveling exhib), Mus Contemp Art, Washington, DC, 2009. *Bibliog:* Chas Bowie (auth), Nowadays, Portland Mercury, Vol 4, No 39, 2/26/2004; Candace Jarrett (auth), A Haven for Artists, Observer-Dispatch, Utica, 6/23/2005; Deborah McLead (auth), Road to Nowhere, Blatimore City Paper, 4/16/2008

SCHMID, RICHARD ALAN
PAINTER
b Chicago, Ill, Oct 5, 1934. *Study:* Am Acad Art, Chicago, 52-55, with William Mosby. *Exhib:* Invitational Drawing Exhib, Otis Art Inst, Los Angeles, 66; 33rd Ann, Butler Inst Am Art, Youngstown, Ohio, 68; 23rd Ann Drawing Biennial, Norfolk Mus Arts & Sci, 69; 164th Ann, Pa Acad Fine Arts, Philadelphia, 69; Am Watercolor Soc Ann, Nat Acad Design Galleries, NY, 70-71; and many solo exhibs throughout US, 58-72. *Awards:* Jane Peterson Prize, Allied Artists Am, 67; Gold Medal of Honor, Am Watercolor Soc, 71, Gold Medal of Honor for Marianne, Am Artist, 72; and others. *Media:* Oil, Watercolor. *Publ:* Auth, Richard Schmid Paints the Figure, 73 & auth, Richard Schmid Paints Landscapes, 75, Watson-Guptill. *Dealer:* Talisman Gallery 115 SE 12th Bartlesville OK 74003

SCHMIDT, CHARLES
PAINTER, CURATOR
b Pittsburgh, Pa, Mar 4, 1939. *Study:* Carnegie-Mellon Univ, Pittsburgh, BFA (painting), 60; Cranbrook Acad Art, Bloomfield Hills, Mich, MFA (painting), 67. *Work:* Nat Air & Space Mus, Nat Gallery Art Rosenwald Collection, Washington, DC; San Francisco Mus Art; Philadelphia Mus Art; Butler Mus, Youngstown, Ohio; Europ Space Agency, Paris, France; Museo Aeronautico, Rome, Italy; VA Air and Space Mus, Hampton, VA; US Capitol Bldg, Washington, DC; Syracuse Univ, Lowe Art Mus, Syracuse, NY; NASA, Washington, DC; Ark Art Ctr, Little Rock, Ark; McGraw Hill cos, New York; Glaxo Smith Line Corp, Philadelphia, Pa; West Publ co, St Paul, Minn; Cigna Corp, New York; Donaldson, Lufkin & Jenrette, New York. *Comn:* Painting, Nat Aeronautics & Space Admin, 80, 82-83 & 86-87; Mem mural of Challenger astronauts, US Senate for US Capitol, dedicated 87. *Exhib:* 164th Ann Exhib, Pa Acad Fine Arts, Philadelphia, 69; Nat Drawing Exhib, San Francisco Mus Art, 70; solo exhibs, Lowe Art Mus, Syracuse Univ, NY, 73 & Rosenfeld Gallery, Philadelphia, 76, 80 & 83; Small Works, Newcastle upon Tyne Polytech Mus Art, Eng, 79; Artist and the Space Shuttle int tour, 82-87; The Art of Silverpoint, nat tour, 89; Myth & Psych, The More Gallery, Philadelphia, Pa, 98; Figure and Object, The More Gallery, Philadelphia, Pa, 2000. *Collection Arranged:* Silverpoint Etcetera: Contemp Am Metalpoint Drawings, traveling exhib, 10/92-10/93. *Pos:* Calligrapher, White House Social Staff, Washington, DC, 61-62. *Teaching:* Instr, Atlanta Coll Art, Ga, 63-65; prof, Tyler Sch Art, Temple Univ, Philadelphia, 67-72, assoc prof, 72-81, prof, 81-; asst prof, Temple Abroad Tyler Sch Art Rome, Italy, 70-72 & 2006. *Awards:* Dana Watercolor Medal, Pa Acad Fine Arts, 69; Purchase Award, Southern Ill Univ, Carbondale, 75; Purchase Award, West Collection, West Publ Co, St Paul, 84. *Bibliog:* Life on the new frontier, Look Mag, 1/2/62; The watercolor page, Am Artist Mag, 10/77; Roger Winter (auth), On Drawing, Coll Press, 97; Mary Settegast (auth), Mona Lisa's Moustache, Phanes Press, 2001. *Media:* Oil. *Publ:* Illusr, Bioscience, by Platt & Reid, Reinhold Publ, 67. *Dealer:* Grey McGear Modern Inc Santa Monica CA. *Mailing Add:* 209 Ft Washington Ave Fort Washington PA 19034

SCHMIDT, EDWARD WILLIAM
PAINTER
b Ann Arbor, Mich, Apr 19, 1946. *Study:* Art Students League, 66-69; Skowhegan Sch Painting & Sculpture, 67; Ecole Beaux Arts, Paris, with R Chaplain-midi, 67-68; Pratt Inst, BFA, 71, Brooklyn Col, MFA, 74; Atelier 17, Paris with Stanley Hayter, 78. *Work:* Bayly Mus Art, Univ Va, Charlottesville; Am Acad Rome; Nat Acad of Design, NY; Ark Art Ctr, Little Rock; Elizabeth Greenshields Found, Montreal, Can. *Comn:* Mural, Alwyn Court, NY, 77; eight statues, Cincinnati Orchestra Pavilion, comn by M Graves, 85; four murals, Hotel Giorgio, Denver, 87; Quantum Corp, NY. *Exhib:* Salon Nat Beaux Arts, Grand Palais, Paris, 68; solo exhibs, Robert Schoelkopf Gallery, NY, 82, Stiebel Mod, NY, 92 & 94, NY Acad Art, NY, 92, Contemp Realist Gallery, San Francisco, 93, Hackett Freedman Gallery, San Francisco, 95 & More Gallery, Philadelphia, 97; Art & Archit & Landscape, San Francisco Mus Mod Art, 85; Centre Georges Pompidou, Paris, 88. *Teaching:* Assoc prof, New York Acad Art, 82-98; instr, Art Students League, 96-98. *Awards:* Nat Endowment Arts Grant, 85-86; Adolph & Ester Gottlieb Found Grant, 94-95; Arthur Ross Award in Painting, 98. *Bibliog:* Mark Helprin (auth), Arcadian lyricism of Edward Schmidt, Am Arts Quart, Spring 93; Edward Lucie-Smith (auth), Art Today, 95; Michael Graves (auth), Reading Edward Schmidt, Contemp Realist Gallery, 96. *Mem:* Soc Fel Am Acad in Rome; Nat Soc Mural Painters. *Media:* Oil. *Publ:* Ed cartoonist, Wall St J, 3/25/94, 7/25/94, 11/25/94 & 1/3/95. *Dealer:* Salander-O'Reilly Galleries 20 E 79th St New York NY; Hackett Freedman Gallery 250 Sutter St San Francisco CA 94108

SCHMIDT, FREDERICK LEE
PAINTER
b Hays, Kans, Dec 11, 1937. *Study:* Univ Northern Colo, BA; Univ Iowa, with Eugene Ludins & Stuart Edie, MFA; also with Joe Patrick & Howard Rogovin. *Work:* Joint Educ Consortium, Arkadelphia, Ark; Worthen Bank, Ark Arts Ctr, Hist Capitol Hotel, Ark State Capitol, Little Rock; Kimberly-Clark, Conway, Ark; Systematics-Little Rock, Ark; La Gas Co, Little Rock; St Vincents Hosp, Little Rock; KPMG Peat, Marwick, Cleveland, Ohio; Univ Ark Medical Ctr Aging, 2000; Penrose Cancer Ctr, Colo Springs, Colo. *Comn:* Stuck, Frier, Lane, Scott Archit, 82; Allison, Moses & Redden Archit, 86; J B Hunt Trucking Co & Cromwell Archit, 90. *Exhib:* Little Rock Arts & Design Fair, 77; 12th Ann Ark Artists Exhib, 78 & 79; 23rd & 24th Ann Delta Exhibs, Little Rock, Ark, 80-81; Arkansas Art Exhibit, Arkadelphia, 82; solo exhibs, Heights Gallery, 86 & Territorial Restoration, Little Rock, Ark, 87; Territorial Restoration, 89; Ark Art Ctr, Vineyard, Little Rock, 92; Pueblo State Bank, Salida, Colo, 2002. *Pos:* Artist/painter, 96-2005, retired prof art. *Teaching:* Asst prof art, Northwestern Coll, 68-70, Western Carolina Univ, 70-72 & Va Polytech Inst & State Univ, 72-76; instr, Ark State Univ & Ark Arts Ctr, 76-77, Univ Ark, Pine Bluff, 77-78 & Ark Arts Ctr, 78-96. *Awards:* Purchase Awards, 12th Ann Ark Artists Exhib, 79 & 24th Ann Delta Exhib, 81; Governor's Award, Little Rock Arts & Design Fair, 80; Painting Invitational, Hendrix Coll, Ark. *Media:* Acrylic, Oil. *Mailing Add:* PO Box 344 Nathrop CO 81236

SCHMIDT, JULIUS
SCULPTOR
b Stamford, Conn, June 2, 1923. *Study:* Okla Agr & Mech Coll; Cranbrook Acad Art, BFA & MFA; with Ossip Zadkine, Paris, France, 53; Acad Belle Arti, Florence, Italy, 54. *Work:* Mus Mod Art, New York; Art Inst Chicago; Albright-Knox Art Gallery, Buffalo; Hirshhorn Mus; Whitney Mus Am Art, New York; and 38 pub collections. *Exhib:* Sixteen Americans, Mus Mod Art, New York, 59; Hirshhorn Collection, Guggenheim Mus, New York, 62; Seventh Biennial, Sao Paulo, Brazil, 63; Sculpture in the Open Air, Battersea Park, London, Eng, 63; Biennial, Middleheim, Belg, 71; and 38 solo exhibs. *Teaching:* Chmn dept sculpture, Kansas City Art Inst, 54-59; vis artist sculpture, RI Sch Design, 59-60 & Univ Calif, Berkeley, 61-62; chmn dept sculpture, Cranbrook Acad Art, 62-70; head dept sculpture, Univ Iowa, 70-93; retired. *Awards:* Guggenheim Fel, 64; Lifetime Achievement Award in Sculpture Education, Int Sculpture Ctr, 98. *Bibliog:* H Read (auth), Concise History of Modern Sculpture, Praeger, 64; Redstone (auth), Art in Architecture, McGraw, 68; Feldman (auth), Varieties of Visual Experience, Prentice-Hall; Empire State Plaza Art Collection & Plaza Memories, Rizzoli Int Publ. *Media:* Cast Bronze & Cast Iron. *Dealer:* Robert Kidd Gallery Birmingham MI; Karolyn Sherwood Gallery Des Moines IA. *Mailing Add:* 5 Highview Knoll NE Iowa City IA 52240

SCHMIDT, MARY MORRIS
LIBRARIAN, HISTORIAN
b Minneapolis, Minn, June 28, 1926. *Study:* Univ Minn, BA, 47, MS (libr sci), 54 & MA (art hist), 55; Univ Paris, Fulbright fel, 56-57; New York Univ, 62-65. *Pos:* Art librn, Univ Minn, Minneapolis, 53-55; cataloger-reference librn, Metrop Mus Art, New York, 57-58; indexer, Art Index, H W Wilson Co, Bronx, 58-65, ed, 65-69; fine arts librn, Columbia Univ, New York, 69-77; librn, Marquand Libr, Princeton Univ, NJ, 77-89; spec projs librn, Princeton Univ, NJ, 89-91. *Awards:* ALA award, 99. *Mem:* Art Libr Soc NAm; Coll Art Asn Am. *Res:* Rare 19th century art periodicals. *Interests:* Romantic book illustration; 19th century American art journals. *Publ:* Index to Nineteenth Century American Art Periodicals, Sound View Press, Madison, Conn, 99. *Mailing Add:* 29 Sergeant St Princeton NJ 08540

SCHMIDT, RANDALL BERNARD
SCULPTOR, EDUCATOR
b Ft Dodge, Iowa, Oct 2, 1942. *Study:* Hamline Univ, BA; Univ NMex, MA. *Work:* Univ NMex Art Mus, Albuquerque; Univ Art Collections, Ariz State Univ, Tempe; Coll Art Collection, Ariz Western Col, Yuma; Univ Art Collections, Pac Lutheran Univ, Tacoma, Wash; Yuma Fine Arts Asn. *Exhib:* Nat Crafts Exhib, Univ NMex Art Mus, 68; 25th Ceramics Nat, Everson Mus Art, Syracuse, NY, 68-70; Media 68 & Media 72, Civic Arts Gallery, Walnut Creek, Calif, 68-72; Southwest Crafts '70, Am Crafts Coun, Los Angeles, 70; Crafts 72, Richmond Art Ctr, Calif, 72. *Teaching:* Asst prof ceramics, Ariz State Univ, 68-75, assoc prof, 75-; guest artist, Pac Lutheran Univ, summer 71. *Awards:* Best of Show, 1st Ann Art Exhib, Phoenix Jewish Community Ctr, 68; Award, Media 68, Civic Arts Gallery, 68; Award, Four Corner Painting & Sculpture Biennial, Phoenix Art Mus, Ariz, 71; and others. *Mem:* Ariz Designer-Craftsmen; Nat Coun Educ Ceramic Arts. *Media:* Ceramics, Vinyl. *Res:* Exploration of expanded vinyl as a sculptural material. *Publ:* Contribr, Teaching Secondary School Art, W Brown Co, 71

SCHMIDT, TERESA TEMPERO
PRINTMAKER, DRAFTSMAN
b Moscow, Idaho, July 16, 1947. *Study:* Cent Wash Univ, BA, 69, MA 70; Wash State Univ, MFA, 72. *Work:* Fogg Art Mus, Harvard Univ, Cambridge, Mass; Springfield Art Mus, Springfield, Mo; Minot State Univ Art Dept, NDak; Norwich Sch Art & Design, Eng; Helen Spencer Mus Art, Lawrence, Kans. *Exhib:* Solo exhib, Manhatten

Arts Ctr, Kans, 96, Norwich Sch Art & Design, Eng, 97, Leslie Powell Found Gallery, Lawton, Okla, 98, Union Gallery, Kans State Univ, 98, Emporia State Univ, Kans, 98 & Columbia Col, Mo, 98; 32nd Ann Nat Open, San Bernardino Co Mus Fine Arts Inst, Calif, 97; Small Works, Norwich Arts Coun Gallery, Conn, 98; Georgetown Int Fine Arts Competition, Fraser Gallery, Washington, DC, 99; St Johns Univ, Jamaica, NY, 2000; 24th Juried Art Exhib, Dodge City Arts Coun, Kans, 2000; Drawing Connections, Beach Art Mus, 2000. *Teaching:* Teaching asst, Wash State Univ, Pullman, Wash, 70-72; instr, Kans State Univ Art Dept, 72-76, asst prof, 76-96; assoc prof, Kansas State Univ, 98-. *Awards:* Kans Arts Comn Matching Grant, Lawrence Lithography Workshop, 90; Fac Res Award, Kans State Univ, 85 & Fac Develop Award, 95; Artist's Residency Grant, Vt Studio Ctr, 97. *Publ:* Contribr, The Best of Printmaking, Rockport Publ, 97; The Sage National (catalog), Sage Col, Albany, NY, 97; 40th Chautauqua National Exhibition of American Art (exhibit catalog), Chautauqua Ctr Visual Arts, NY, 97. *Mailing Add:* 500 Oakdale Dr Manhattan KS 66502-3738

SCHMIT, RANDALL
PAINTER, COLLAGE ARTIST
b Newark, NJ. *Study:* Tex A&M Univ, Coll Station, 73-75; Tex A&M Univ, Commerce Tex, BFA, 77 & MFA, apprentice to Ray Parker, 78-79. *Work:* Metrop Mus Art, New York, NY; New Orleans Mus Art & Ogden Mus Southern Art, New Orleans, La; Castellani Art Mus, Niagara, NY; Birmingham Mus Art, Birmingham, Ala; Mus Contemp Art, Jacksonville, Fla; Art Mus Western Va, Roanoke, Va; Nasher Mus Art, Duke Univ, Durham, NC; Frederick Weisman Mus Art, Malibu, Calif. *Exhib:* Small Paintings, Betty Cuningham Gallery, New York, NY, 81; Romantic Science, One Penn Plaza Gallery, New York, NY, 87; New Acquisitions, New Orleans Mus Art, New Orleans, La, 87 & Apel Galeri, Istanbul, Turkey, 2000; Collage: New Applications, Lehman Coll Art Gallery, New York, NY,91; The New York Collection, Albright-Knox Art Gallery, Buffalo, NY, 95; Seeing Jazz (catalog), Int Gallery, Smithsonian Inst, Washington DC; Hunter Mus Am Art, Chattanooga, Tenn; Huntington Mus Art, Huntington, WV; Mus of the SW, Midland, Tex; Bass Mus Art, Miami Fla; Muson-Williams-Proctor Inst Mus Art, Utica, NY, 99; Winter Exhib, N Pointe Cult Ctr, Kinderhook, NY, 2005; Corpus, David Bruner Gallery, Hudson, 2008; Private View: Res Nova, NY, 2007; Solo exhib, David Bruner Gallery, Hudson, NY, 2010. *Teaching:* guest critic & adj fac, Studio Prog, SUNY at Empire State Col, New York, NY, 83; guest lectr, painting, Delgado Col & Univ New Orleans, New Orleans, La, 84, Parsons Sch Design, New York, NY, 95-96, SUNY at Purchase Schs Fine Art, 97 & US Consulate Gen, Instanbul, Turkey, 2000; guest lectr, Collaborative Master's Degree Prog, Bank St Col Educ/Parsons Sch Design, New York, NY, 94; guest critic & lectr, Md Inst Grad Sch Fine Arts, Baltimore, Md, 91, Skidmore Col, Saratoga Springs, NY & Bennington Col, Bennington, Vt, 92; guest critic & lectr, Studio Prog, SUNY at Empire State Col, New York, NY, 95; visiting artist, Sch Visual Arts, NY, 2012. *Awards:* Ludwig Vogelstein Found Grant, Ludwig Vogelstein Found, 83; Invitational Travel Grant, Apel Galeri, US Consulate Gen, Instanbul, Turkey, 2007; Adolph & Ester Gottlieb Individual Artist Support Grant, 2011. *Bibliog:* Lowery Stokes Simms (auth), Randall Schmit (catalog), EM Donahue Gallery, NY, 90; Linda Yablonsky (auth), Randall Schmit, Artforum Vol XXXIII, No 3, 11/94; Tom Breidenbach (auth), Randall Schmit, The Country and Abroad, 12/2000. *Mem:* Mental Health Asn Columbia Greene Counties, Hudson, NY (bus adv coun, 2000-2006); Columbia Co CofC, Hudson, NY (mem comt, 2003-2006); Valatie Free Libr, NY (bd of dir, 2007-, vice pres bd trustees, 2010-). *Media:* Painting, Collage. *Res:* Renaissance Hermetic Philosophy; Greek Hermetic Philosophy; Painting & the Psychedelic Experience. *Interests:* Waterfalls, cats, football. *Dealer:* David Dew Bruner Hudson NY. *Mailing Add:* PO Box 445 Hudson NY 12534-0445

SCHMUKI, JEFF
CERAMIST
Study: N Ariz Univ, Flagstaff, BFA, 1993; NY State Coll Ceramics at Alfred Univ, MFA, 1998. *Work:* Smithsonian Inst, Washington, DC. *Exhib:* Solo exhibs include Osterle Gallery, N Cent Coll, Naperville, Ill, 1999, George Ohr Mus, Biloxi, Miss, 2001, CW Woods Art Gallery, Univ S Miss, Hattiesburg, 2002, Malone Gallery, Troy Univ, Troy, Ala, 2006, Richard E Peeler Art Ctr, DePauw Univ, Greencastle, Ind, 2008; group exhibs include ANA-24, Holter Mus Art, Helena, Mont, 1995; Fletcher Challenge, Auckland Mus & Inst, Auckland, New Zealand, 1996, 1997; Sydney Myer Fund Int Ceramic Exhib, Shepparton Art Gallery, Victoria, Australia, 2000, 2003, 2006; Invitational, Miss Mus Art, Jackson, 2003, 2005, 2007; Southeastern Juried Exhib, Mobile Mus Art, Mobile, Ala, 2004; Topographies, Ortlip Art Gallery, Houghton Coll, Houghton, NY, 2006. *Teaching:* Assoc Prof Ceramics, William Carey Coll, Gulfport, Miss, 1999-2005; Vis Assoc Prof Ceramics, DePauw Univ, Greencastle, Ind, 2007-Present. *Awards:* Governor's Art Award, Miss Arts Comn, Jackson, 2004; Artist & Writers Grant, AAAL, 2005; Pollock-Krasner Emergency Grant, 2006, Found Grant, 2007

SCHMUTZHART, BERTHOLD JOSEF
SCULPTOR, EDUCATOR
b Salzburg, Austria, Aug 17, 1928; US citizen. *Study:* Acad Appl Art, Vienna, Austria; masterclass for ceramics & sculpture. *Work:* Mr & Mrs Hirshhorn Collection; Fredericksburg Gallery Mod Art, Va. *Comn:* Christ (wood), St James Church, Washington, DC, 62 & Christ (bronze), 64; bacchus fountain, Fredericksburg Gallery, 67; Christ (steel), St Clements Church, Inkster, Mich, 68 & processional cross (bronze), 71; cross (guilded wood), Church of Reformation, Washington, DC, 74. *Exhib:* Washington Artists, Massilon Mus, Ohio, 69; Twenty Washington Artists, Nat Collection Fine Arts, Washington, DC, 70; Art Barn, US Dept Interior, Washington, DC, 71; Franz Bader Gallery, Washington, DC, 78-81; Nat Gallery Mod Art, New Delhi, India, 90; and others. *Pos:* Chmn, Franz & Virginia Bader Fund. *Teaching:* Assoc prof sculpture & chmn sculpture dept, Corcoran Sch Art, Washington, DC, 63-81, prof, 81-94, prof emer, 94-. *Awards:* First Prizes, Wash Relig Arts Soc, 60 & Southern Sculpture, 66; First Prize Silver Medal, Audubon Soc, 71. *Bibliog:* Off Econ Opportunity (auth), A Face for the Future (film), Booker Assocs, Reston, Va, 65; Tools for Learning (film), Kingsbury Ctr, Washington, DC, 71. *Mem:* Am Asn Univ Prof; Guild Religious Archit; Artist's Equity Asn (pres, Washington, DC Chap, 73). *Media:* Multimedia. *Publ:* Auth, The Handmade Furniture Book, Prentice-Hall, 81. *Mailing Add:* 32 Layline Ln Fredericksburg VA 22406-4061

SCHNACKENBERG, ROY
PAINTER, SCULPTOR
b Chicago, Ill, Jan 14, 1934. *Study:* Miami Univ, Oxford, Ohio, BFA. *Work:* Whitney Mus Am Art, NY; Art Inst Chicago. *Exhib:* Whitney Recent Acquisitions Show, 67 & Whitney Ann, 67-69; New Am Realists, Goteberg, Sweden, 70; Beyond Illustration, The Art of Playboy World Tour, 71-; Recent Acquisitions Show, Art Inst Chicago, 71; Dept Interior Bicentennial Exhib, Corcoran Gallery, Washington, DC; and numerous solo & int group exhibs. *Media:* Oil, Canvas; Mixed Media. *Mailing Add:* 731 W 18th St Chicago IL 60616

SCHNEEMANN, CAROLEE
PAINTER, FILMMAKER
b Fox Chase, Pa, Oct 12, 1939. *Study:* Bard Coll, NY, BA; Univ Ill, Urbana, MFA; Columbia Univ Sch Painting & Sculpture, New York; New Sch Social Res, New York; Univ de Puebla, Mexico. *Hon Degrees:* Calif Inst Arts, Valencia, DA, 2003. *Work:* Mus Contemp Art, Chicago; Mus Mod Art, NY; Philadelphia Mus Art; Inst Contemp Art, London; San Francisco Mus Mod Art. *Exhib:* Palazzo Reale, Milan, 81; Max Hutchinson Gallery, NY, 82-83; Contemp Arts Ctr, Cincinnati, 90; Biennale Venezia, Italy, 90; San Francisco Mus Mod Art, 91; solo exhib, Kunstraum, Vienna, 95; Ctr Nat Art & Cult Georges Pompidou, Paris, 94-96; solo retrospective, New Mus Contemp Art, NY, 96; Frauen Mus, Bonn, Ger, 97; New Mus Contemp Art, NY, 97; Mus Contemp Art, Los Angeles, 98; Emily Harvey Gallery, NY, 2000; Dorsky Mus, SUNY, New Paltz, 2010. *Pos:* Founder-dir, Kinetic Theatre, NY; vis artist, San Francisco Art Inst, Calif, 92. *Teaching:* Instr art, Art Inst Chicago, Ill, Univ Colo, Univ Ohio & Univ Calif, Los Angeles, Pratt Inst, NY. *Awards:* Individual Artist Grant, Gottlieb Found, 87; Guggenheim Fel, 93; Pollock-Krasner Grant, 96; Lifetime Achievement Award, Chicago Caucus for Women in the Arts, 2000; Distinguished Artist Award for Lifetime Achievement, Coll Art Asn, 2001; Rockefeller Found Fel, 2001; Jimmy Ernst Award, Am Acad Arts & Letts, 2003; Lifetime Achievement Award, Women's Caucus for Art, 2010. *Bibliog:* Linda M Montano (auth), Performance Artists Talking in the Eighties, Univ Calif Press, 83; Jitka Hanzlova (auth), Female, Deichtorhallen publ,; David Burrows (auth), Making a Scene, Univ of Central England; Art Monthly, Apr 2000. *Mem:* Women's Caucus Art; Coll Art Assoc. *Publ:* Auth, Kenneth Anger's Scorpio Rising, Film Culture No 32, New York, 64; Love Paint Ritual Technicians of the Sacred, New York, 69; Banana Hands, Plays for Children to Direct, London, 70; More Than Meat Joy (complete performance works & selected writings), 78 & Carolee Schneemann: Early & Recent Work (monography of painting--constructions 1963-1983), 83, Documentext; Imaging Erotics: Carolee Schneemann's Body Politics, 97. *Dealer:* Elga Wimmer Gallery 560 Broadway New York NY 10012; Galerie Samuel Lallouz Montreal

SCHNEIDER, GARY
PHOTOGRAPHER, EDUCATOR
b East London, South Africa, Nov 25, 1954; American Citizen. *Study:* Univ Cape Town, South Africa, BFA, 77; Pratt Inst, Brooklyn, NY, MFA, 79. *Work:* Whitney Mus Am Art, NY; Nat Gallery Canada, Ottawa; Mus Fine Art, Boston; Metrop Mus Art, NY; Art Inst Chicago. *Exhib:* Solo exhibs, Naming, Artists Space, NY, 77, Recent Photographs, Haggerty Mus, Milwaukee, 97, Genetic Self-Portrait, Int Ctr Photography, NY, 2000, Le Siecle du Corps (Genetic self portrait), Musee de L'Elysee Lausanne, Switzerland, 2000, Portraits, Sackler Mus, Cambridge, Mass, 2004, Nudes, Aperture, NY, 2005; The Naked Portrait, Scottish Nat Portrait Gallery, Edinburgh, Scotland, 2007; FLESH, Mus of Photographic Art, San Diego, Calif, 2008. *Teaching:* Adj prof photography, The Cooper Union, 1989-2005; distinguished vis artist grad photog and film, Va Commonwealth Univ, Richmond, Va, 2005; artist-in-residence photography, Stony Brook Univ, NY, 2006-2010; lectr, Princeton Univ, 2007 & 2010. *Awards:* Alfred Eisenstaedt Award, Life Mag & Columbia Univ, 2000; NEA, Gary Schneider: Portraits & Harvard Univ Art Mus, Boston, 2004; Lou Stoumen Prize, Mus Photographic Arts, San Diego, 2005. *Bibliog:* Lauren Sedofsky (auth), Through a Glass Darkly, Artforum, March, 95; John Noble Wilford (auth); Inside Out: Genetic Self-Portrait by Gary Schneider, NY Times Mag, Oct, 99; Trevor Fairbrother (auth), Gary Schneider: Facing Time, Art in America, Feb, 2005. *Publ:* John in Sixteen Parts, PPOW Gallery, NY, Howard Yezerski Gallery, Boston, Mass, Stephen Daiter Gallery, Chicago, 97; Genetic Self-Portrait, Light Work, Syracuse, NY, 89; Yezerski Family Portrait, Howard Yezerski Gallery, Boston, Mass, 2001; Gary Schneider Portraits, Yale Univ Press, HUAM, New Haven, Conn, 2004; Gary Schneider: Nudes, Aperture Found, NY, 2005. *Dealer:* Stephen Daiter Gallery 311 W Superior St Chicago IL 60610; Howard Yezerski Gallery 460 Harrison Ave Boston MA 02118. *Mailing Add:* 320 Beaver Dam Rd Brookhaven NY 11719

SCHNEIDER, JANET M
MUSEUM DIRECTOR, PAINTER
b New York, NY, June 6, 1950. *Study:* Queens Col, City Univ New York, BA (fine arts, summa cum laude), 72; Boston Univ Tanglewood Inst, special study, fine arts, 71. *Exhib:* Solo Exhibs, Prince Street Gallery, 74, 76 & 81; Long Island Invitational, C W Post Art Gallery, 81; The First Eight Yrs, The Artists Choice Mus, 84. *Collection Arranged:* Sons and others: Women Artists See Men (auth, catalog), 75; Urban Aesthetics (auth, catalog), 76; Masters of the Brush: Chinese Painting and Calligraphy from the Sixteenth to the Nineteenth Century (auth, catalog), 77; Symcho Moszkowicz: Portrait of the Artist in Postwar Europe (auth, catalog), 78; Shipwrecked 1622: The Lost Treasure of Philip IV (auth, catalog), 81; Michelangelo: A Sculptor's World (auth, catalog), 83; Joseph Cornell, Revisited, (auth, catalog), 92; Blueprint for Change (coauth, catalog), Queensborough Pub Libr, 96. *Pos:* Cur, Queens Mus, 73-75, prog dir, 75-77 & exec dir, 77-89; exec dir, Cult Inst Group, 95-2006; consult

dir, Flushing Town Hall, NY, 2007-2008. *Teaching:* Instr mus cert prog, Hofstra Univ, 85-86. *Mem:* Gallery Asn NY State (bd dir, 79-81); Artists Choice Inc (bd trustees, 79-82); Cult Inst Group (chmn, 86-87); Mayor's Adv Comn Cult & Arts, NY. *Media:* Oil. *Dealer:* Prince St Gallery 121 Wooster New York NY 10012. *Mailing Add:* 35-39 159th St Flushing NY 11419

SCHNEIDER, JO ANNE
PAINTER
b Lima, Ohio, Dec 4, 1919. *Study:* Sch Fine Arts, Syracuse Univ. *Work:* Butler Inst Am Art, Youngstown, Ohio; Syracuse Univ; Allentown Mus, Pa; St Lawrence Univ; Metrop Mus Art, New York; and others. *Exhib:* Corcoran Gallery Art, Washington, DC; Whitney Mus Am Art Ann, NY; 50 Yrs of Am Art, Am Fedn Art, 64; Childe Hassam Fund Exhib, Am Acad Arts & Lett, 71; plus solo exhibs, 54-85. *Awards:* First Prize, Guild Hall, 67; Marion K Haldenstein Mem Prize, Nat Asn Women Artists, 70; Stanley Grumbacher Mem Award, Audubon Artists, 72. *Media:* Oil. *Mailing Add:* 35 E 75th St New York NY 10021

SCHNEIDER, JULIE SAECKER
PAINTER, DRAFTSMAN
b Seattle, Wash, Mar 7, 1944. *Study:* Univ Wis, Madison, BS (art); Univ Wis, MFA (painting & drawing), 76. *Work:* Minn Mus Art, St Paul; Algur Meadows Mus, Shreveport, La; Rutgers Univ, Camden, NJ; State Univ NY Col, Potsdam; Indianapolis Mus Art. *Exhib:* Drawings USA Nat Exhibs (traveling show), Minn Mus Art, Saint Paul, 75 & 77; Am Drawings, Tidewater Art Coun & Portsmouth Community Art Ctr, Va, 76 & 78; Davidson Nat Print & Drawing Competition, Appalachian Nat Drawing Competition, Boone, 76, NC; Smithsonian Travel Exhibs, 76 & 78; Bradley Print & Drawing Competition, Bradley Univ, Peoria, Ill, 77, 79 & 85; Drawing Invitational, Goucher Col, Towson, Md, 85; Washington Community Artists, Jane Haslem Gallery, Washington, DC, 85; solo exhibs, Am Int Col, 80, Arlington Arts Ctr, Va, 85, Drawings, Fairweather-Hardin Gallery, 86, Jane Haslem Gallery, Washington, DC, 89 & 93, Tretyakov Gallery, Moscow USSR, 90-91, recent work, Arlington Arts Ctr, Va, 93, Legends Revisited, Peninsula Fine Arts Ctr, Newport News, Va, 96; Am realists (with catalog), San Francisco Mus Mod Art, Calif, 85-86; Realism/Idealism (with catalog), Jane Haslem Gallery, Washington, DC; Am Drawing, Boca Raton Mus Art; 12th Ann Int Drawing Invitational, Emporia, Kans; and others. *Pos:* Chair visual arts, Interlochen Ctr Arts. *Teaching:* Adj prof, Williams Col, 82-84; assoc prof, Northern Va Community Col, Alexandria; vis lectr, Va Mus Artists-in-residence series, Md Inst Col Art, Interlochen Ctr Arts, Towson State Univ; assoc prof & undergrad chair, Univ Pa, Philadelphia, 95-. *Awards:* Purchase Awards, Rutgers Nat Drawing 77, Drawings USA-77, Minn Mus of Art, St Paul, 77 & Bradley Print & Drawing, 79; Finalist, Mass Artist Found Grants, 80; Fel, Mid Atlantic Found, 88; Va Comn for the Arts Grant, 92; Arlington Comn for the Arts Grant, 94. *Bibliog:* American Realism, San Francisco Mus Mod Art & Abrams Press, 85; Pamela Kessler (auth), Galleries, Washington Post, 5/20/87; Brown & McLean (auth), Drawing from Life, Holt, Rinehart & Winston, 92 & 97; Nathan Goldstein (auth), Figure Drawing 4th ed, text bk, 93. *Mem:* Coll Art Asn; FATE. *Media:* Graphite, mixed media. *Mailing Add:* c/o Jane Haslem Gallery 2025 Hillyer Pl NW Washington DC 20009

SCHNEIDER, KENNY
SCULPTOR, PAINTER, FILMMAKER
b Ellenville, NY, Jan 3, 1939. *Study:* Univ Miami, BA in Art, 60; Summer Acad Bildende Kunst, Salzburg, Austria, 63; Adams State Univ, MA in Art. *Work:* Palm Beach Int Airport; Musee de Cinema, Paris; Donnell Library, Brooklyn Coll Film Libr. *Comn:* Sculpture Art in Public Places, Seattle Arts Comn, 83; sculpture, Community Redevelopment Agency, Los Angeles, 91-95; sculpture, David W Bermant Found, Santa Barbara, Calif, 95; sculpture, City of Miami Beach, Fla, 97; sculpture, Buell Childrens Mus, Pueblo, Colo, 99; Homestead Park Proj, City of Collins, Colo. *Exhib:* Solo exhibs, Galerie 99, Bay Harbor, Fla, 1st Ann Prize Competition, Provincetown Art Asn, 83, Ground Zero Gallery, Miami Beach, Fla, 88, Fiona Whitney Gallery, Los Angeles, 91; 4th Ann Small Works, Wash Sq E Galleries, NY Univ, 79; Mus Contemp Art, N Miami, Fla, 86; 29th Ann Hortz Mem Exhib, Mus of Art, Ft Lauderdale, Fla, 87; Humor in Art, Tempe (Ariz) Arts Ctr, 88; Nemiroff-Deutch Fine Art, Santa Monica, Calif, 91; Two-person exhib The Artists Gallery, Ojai, Calif, 95; Colorado Call, The Art Ctr Douglas Co, Castle Rock, Colo, 96; Awareness Alert Breast Cancer, WomenMade Gallery, Chicago, 98; Co-Excellence 98 Traveling Exhib Alternative Arts Alliance, Denver, 98; 20th Ann Show Barbara Gillman Gallery, Miami Beach, Fla, 99; Rocky Mt Biennial, Moca, Ft Collins, Colo; Film Colorado, Sangre de Cristo Art Ctr, Pueblo, Colo, 2008; Electronic 4Culture, Media Gallery, Seattle, WA, 2010. *Collection Arranged:* Pvt collections of Mel Brooks & Ann Bancroff, Gerald Robins, Michelle Isenberg, Barbara Marcus, Sen Howard Metzenbaum, Ohio, Walter Annenburg Collection; Amos Vogel Film Collection. *Pos:* Presenter, Pueblo (Colo) Regional Arts Dialogue, Pueblo Community Coll, 97; Panelist, Media Fel Awards, Colo Coun on the Arts; trustee & bd chmn, Spanish Peaks Regional Health Ctr; pres, Huerfano Co Art Coun, 98-; vpres LaVeta Re-2 sch bd Art Advisory Comt, Harp Project, Pueblo, Colo; fine arts gallery dir, Colo St Univ, Pueblo. *Teaching:* Instr Art Hist, Art Appreciation, Drawing, Film Making, Trinidad State Jr Coll, Walsenburg, Colo, 96, Multimedia Arts, Trinidad, 99-; adj prof drawing, digital media, sculpture, exhib design, art history, visual dynamics, introduction to Cinema, Colo State Univ, Pueblo. *Awards:* Kokoschka Prize Sommerakad for Bildende Kunst; Art in Cauly Sq Award; 8th Ann Small Works Nat Jurors Award, 24th Ann Small Painting Exhbn Jurors Award; NY Film Festival Silver Medal; Tampere Film Festival Award of Merit; Directors Award Colo Coun on Arts, 97; Visual Arts (3-D) Artist Fel, Colo Coun for the Arts & NEA, 99; NY State Caps Grant. *Bibliog:* S Derickson Moore (auth) World Class Art, Palm Beach Coun of Arts, Fla, 88; Helen Kohen (auth) Summer Dreams, Miami Herald, 88; Peter Frank (auth), Art Picks of the Week, LA Weekly, 91; James Rupp (auth) Art in Seattles Public Places: An Illustrated Guide, Univ Wash Press, 92; Pancho Doll (auth), Ojai Artist Kenny Schneider, LA Time, 95; Maja Beckstrom (auth) Pluggen In, Ventura Co Star, 95; Joseph Woodward (auth) This Artists Sense of Humor, LA Times, 95; Ronald Lee Fleming (auth) The Art of Placemaking (page 271), 2007. *Mem:* Screen Actors Guild. *Media:* All Media. *Res:* Directed feature length dramatic film "Adonde Fue Juan Jose?", 2002. *Dealer:* Barbara Gillman 3814 NE Miami Ct Miami FL Tel 305-573-1920 800-688-7079. *Mailing Add:* PO Box 542 La Veta CO 81055

SCHNEIDER, LAURIE See Adams, Laurie Schneider

SCHNEIDER, LISA DAWN
DEALER, CRITIC
b Brookline, Mass, Nov 16, 1954. *Study:* Boston Mus Fine Arts Sch, Mass; DeCordova Mus; Syracuse Univ, Visual & Performing Arts Sch; Finch Coll; Arts Sch League; Marymount Coll, BA (fine arts). *Pos:* Asst dir, Galerie Denise/Rene, 76-77; art critic & art ed, Women's Week, 77-79; dir, Robert Freidus Gallery, NY, 78; assoc dir, Bertha Urdang Gallery, NY, 79-; exec dir, Cur Consul & Galleries, New York & Boston, 80-; cur, Fisher Brothers Collection, 82-; art correspondent, CNN, 99-. *Awards:* Third Ann Interiors Award, Ramco Co Art Collection. *Specialty:* Nineteenth & twentieth century Europe & American paintings, drawings, photography & sculpture. *Mailing Add:* 135 E 54th St New York NY 10022

SCHNEIDER, RICHARD DURBIN
CERAMIST, INSTRUCTOR
b Toledo, Ohio, April 5, 1937. *Study:* Univ Toledo, BA, 63; Bowling Green State Univ, MA, 68. *Work:* Utah Mus Fine Arts, Salt Lake City; Cleveland Mus Art; Ohio Wesleyan Univ; Libbey-Owens, Ford Collection, Toledo; Kaiser Permanente Hosp. *Exhib:* Eighteenth Nat Las Vegas Art Exhib, Las Vegas Art Mus, 75; Materials & Techniques of 20th Century Artists, Cleveland Mus Art, 76; Lake Superior 4th Biennial Int Exhib, Tweed Mus Art, Duluth, Minn, 77; Beaux Art Designer, Columbus Mus Art, Ohio, 79; Eighth State Ann Craft Exhibition, JB Speed Art Mus, Louisville, Ky, 80; 28th Ann National Drawing & Sculpture, Ball State Univ, Muncie, Ind, 82; First Ann Am Ceramic Nat, Downey Mus Art, Calif, 83. *Collection Arranged:* Cleveland Clinic Found, Cleveland Mus Art. *Teaching:* Asst prof ceramics, Monroe Co Community Coll, Mich, 69-71; assoc prof, Cleveland State Univ, Ohio, 71-. *Awards:* Special Award Sculpture, Cleveland Mus Art, 72; Purchase Award Ceramics, Butler Mus Am Art; Juror's Award for Drawing, Kansas 6th Nat Exhib, Ft Hays State Univ, 81. *Bibliog:* Lynette Rhodes (auth), Nine artisans, Craft Horizons, 74; Elizabeth McClelland (auth), Ceramic sculpture, Nat Orgn Visual Artists News, 80; Roger Welchans (auth), Dialogue, Ohio Arts J, 83. *Media:* Clay. *Specialty:* Painting & ceramics. *Publ:* Auth, Large thrown forms, 76 & Surface decoration on ceramic functional ware, 82, Ceramics Monthly. *Dealer:* River Gallery Old Detroit Rd Rocky River OH 44145. *Mailing Add:* 2610 Exeter Rd Cleveland Heights OH 44118

SCHNEIDER, ROSALIND L
VIDEO ARTIST, PAINTER
b New York, NY. *Study:* Sch Fine Arts, Syracuse Univ; State Univ NY, BA, 74. *Work:* US Info Agency, Washington, DC; Nynex Collection, New York; Dance Archives, Lincoln Ctr, New York; Donnell Film Libr, New York; Video Art Collection, Locarno, Switzerland; Metro Media Fibre Network; Libr Cong; Mus Mod Art Film Archive, NY; Exit Art, NY; Hudson Valley Hospital Ctr, NY; Syracuse Univ Art Gallery; Mt Sinai Hospital; Westmed Medical Group. *Exhib:* Yosemite Loop Extension, Mus of the Hudson Highlands, Cornwall, NY, 84; Ancient History, Bronx Mus, New York, 88; 10 Artists From NY, Kulturforum, Monchengladbach, Fed Repub Ger, 90; The Nature of the Beast, Hudson River Mus, Yonkers, NY, 90; Contemp Bestiary, Islip Art Mus, NY, 90; Women Avant Garde Filmmakers 1930-2000, Whitney Mus, New York, 2000; Chelsea Art Mus, New York, 2003; Monique Goldstrom Gallery, NY, 2003; Imaging the River, River Meditations, Hudson River Mus, NY, 2004; Landscape Show, Van Brunt Gallery, Beacon, NY, 2005-2007; Wave Transformations, 911 Media Arts Ctr, Seattle, 2005; River Fragmentations, Diva Art Fair, New York, 2005; Donnell Libr Media Ctr, 2005; Miami Beach Cinematheque, 2006, 08; Art Miami (auth, catalog), 2006; Women's Int Video Festival, Tucson, Ariz; Sparks Int Exhib, Tel Aviv, Israel; Maxwell Fine Arts, video projection, Peekskill, NY, 2008; Lyndhurst Historic Site, NY, 2008; Exit Art Underground, NY, 2008; Art Now Exhib, NY, 2008; The Affordable Art Fair, NY, 2008, 2012; Bridge Art Fair, 2009; Quadricentennial Celebration of the Hudson Lyndhurst Hist Site, 2009; Brecht Forum, New York, 2010; Art Hamptons, New York, 2010; Becket Arts Ctr, Mass, 2010; Saatchi & Saatchi, New York, Benefit for Free Arts, 2010; Art and Technology, Elisa Contemp Art, NY; Tidal Transformation at the Bay of Fundy, 2011; Vimeo, Ikono: TV Broadcast Arabsat; Jacobs Burns Film Ctr, 2013; Artifact Solo show, 2013; Artery NY, 2013, Online mag. *Pos:* Exec dir, Film & Video Workshop Inc. *Awards:* Directors Award, Biennial 2000, Westchester, 2000; Finalist, MTA Transit Comn for Dobbs Ferry Station, New York, 2003; Film Preservation Grant, NY Women Film & TV, 2006 & 2008. *Bibliog:* Jayanta Chatterjee & Hector Currie (eds), Women/Artists/Filmmakers, Univ Cincinnati Press, 76; Cynthia Nadelman (auth), Light & Lascaux, 92; Matt Freedman (auth), Wave Transformations, NY Hall Sci, 2000; William Zimmer (auth), Lights, Videos & Photos in a Biennial, 2000; Carlos Suarez de Jesus (auth), Riding the Earth's Curl, The New Times, 2006; Sara Blazej (auth) The Alaska Series, Artifact, 2013. *Mem:* Art Students League of NY. *Media:* Video Installation, Digital/Fusion Paintings. *Res:* Internet site art in context. *Specialty:* Contemporary art. *Publ:* 10 Artists from New York, Kulturforum, Monchengiadbach, Fed Repub Ger, 90; Jules & Nancy Heller (eds) Encyclopedia of 20th Century Women Artists, Garland Publ, 92; Auth, Feminists Who Changed America 1963-1975, Univ Ill Press, 2006; Sage Mag, Vol III, Yale Sch Environ Studies & Forestry, 2009. *Dealer:* Artifact NY. *Mailing Add:* 40 Cottontail Lane Irvington NY 10533

SCHNEIDER, SHELLIE
PAINTER, COLLAGE ARTIST
b Brooklyn, NY, Oct 12, 1932. *Study:* Cooper Union Art Sch, with Nick Marsicano & Leo Manso, 54; Hunter Col, with Tony Panzera, BA (cum laude, printmaking), 74; Queens Col, with Walter Kendra, MS (art educ), 77. *Work:* Voluntary Hosps Asn, Tampa, Fla; Chalgrin Co Ltd, Osaka, Japan; Am Stock Exchange, NY; Computer

Assoc International, Islandia, NY; mural, On the Bay, Mill Pond Acres Condo, Port Wash, New York, 2008; and others. *Comn:* Triptych (collage), comn by Mr & Mrs Kurtz, Long Island, NY, 90; acrylic collage, comn by Dr & Mrs R Edwards, Long Island, NY, 92; acrylic collage, comn by Mr & Mrs I Levy, Long Island, NY, 93; mural 6'x8', On the Bay, Mill Pond Acres, Port Wash, NY, 2008; and others. *Exhib:* Nat Works on Paper '88, Firehouse Gallery, Nassau Community Col, Garden City, NY, 88; Traveling Nat Print Show, Nat Asn Women Artists, 89, 91, 96 & 99; Multi-Media Art Forum & Exhib, Hempstead House, Sands Point, NY, 91; one-person shows, From There to Here--In a Decade, Graphic Eye Gallery, Port Washington, NY, 91 & Manhasset Libr, Manhasset, NY, 94, Gallery North, Setauket, NY, 2000, Haddad Lascono Gallery, Great Barringten, Mass, 2004, Shelter Rock Gallery, Manhasset, NY, 2010; Berkshire Artisans, Pittsfield, Mass, 2003; Dorian Grey Gallery, NY, 2011. *Pos:* Co-pres, Graphic Eye Coop Gallery, Port Washington, New York, 86, 87, 98 & 99; secy, Art Adv Coun, Port Washington Libr, NY, 93-2012. *Teaching:* Art instr K-12 & adult educ, Port Washington, New York, 74-92; adj instr printmaking, C W Post Univ, New York, 80; adj asst prof art educ, Hofstra Univ, NY, 2001-2002. *Awards:* First Place, Sheffield Art League, 86; Award Excellence, Nassau Co Mus Fine Art, 86; Medal Honor, Nat Asn Women Artists, Leila Sawyer Mem, 88; Cecile Holzinger Award, Nat Asn Women Artist, 2000. *Bibliog:* Articles in Newsday, 10/84 & New York Times, 9/93 & 12/2002, 1/2005; Berkshire Eagle, 7/2003; Hows it Made, Berkshire Record, 8/2003. *Mem:* Nat Asn Women Artists (jury selection, printmaking, 88); Sheffield Art League; Art Adv Coun, Port Washington Libr, 90-2014; Art League of Long Island. *Media:* Acrylic Paint, Mixed Media Collage. *Interests:* Reading, sketching, theatre. *Dealer:* Graphic Eye Coop Gallery New York; Lenox Gallery of Fine Art, MA. *Mailing Add:* 4 Miro Pl Port Washington NY 11050

SCHNEIDERMAN, RICHARD S
MUSEUM DIRECTOR
b NJ, June 27, 1948. *Study:* Hartwick Col, BA, 70; Univ Cincinnati, MA, 73; State Univ NY Binghamton, PhD, 76. *Collection Arranged:* West Meets East, Impressionism in Nineteenth Century Prints, 78-80; J M W Turner Watercolors from the British Mus (auth introd, catalog), 82; Guardians of the Spire: The Gargoyle Image in Prints, 84; Drawings as Drawings: Works from the Ackland and the Weatherspoon, 87-88; Robes of Elegance: Japanese Kimono from the Sixteenth-Twentieth Centuries, 88; Nature into Art: English Landscape Watercolors from the British Mus, 91. *Pos:* Cur prints & drawings, Ga Mus Art, Univ Ga, Athens, 76-86, dir, 81-86; dir, NC Mus Art, Raleigh, 86-94. *Teaching:* Adj prof hist art, Tompkins-Cortland Community Col, Cortland, NY, winter 76; lectr mod art, State Univ NY Binghamton, summer 76; adj assoc prof, dept art, Univ Ga, 83-86. *Mem:* Am Asn Mus; Am Soc Aesthet; Coll Art Asn; Asn Art Mus Dirs; Print Coun Am. *Res:* History of prints, primarily English and northern European. *Publ:* Contribr, A Catalogue Raisonne of the Prints of Sir Francis Seymour Haden, Robin Garton Fine Art Publ, 83; Masterpieces of European Printmaking: 15th-19th Centuries, Ga Mus Art, 84; A Catalogue Raisonne of the Prints of Charles Meryon (with Frank W Raysor II), Garton & Co, Scolar Press, 90. *Mailing Add:* 13232 N Valley Pike Timberville VA 22853-3119

SCHNEIER, DONNA FRANCES
DEALER
b St Louis, Mo, Mar 30, 1938. *Study:* Brandeis Univ, BA; NY Univ, MFA; Inst Fine Art, NY Univ, PhD (art history). *Pos:* Pres, Gallery 6M, NY, 66-73 & Donna Schneier Fine Arts; consult contemp works art, Sothebys, 1990-1994. *Awards:* Visionary, Mus Art & Design, 2005. *Mem:* Am Craft Coun (bd trustees); Am Craft Mus (chairman & collections comt); First NY Bank For Business (bd advisors); Sch For Serv, Georgetown Univ (bd govs). *Specialty:* Post World War II Ceramics, Glass, Fiber, Metal & Wood. *Interests:* Contemp jewelry by artists. *Collection:* Zero Karat: contemp jewelry by artists. *Mailing Add:* PO Box 443 Claverack NY 12513-0443

SCHNITGER, LARA
SCULPTOR
b Haarlem, Netherlands, 1969. *Study:* Koninklijke Academie voor beeldende Kunsten, Den Haag, 1987-91; Academie Vyvarni Umeni, Prague, 1991-92; Ateliers '63, Amsterdam, 1992-94; CCA, Kitakyushu, Japan, 1999-2000. *Exhib:* Solo exhibs include Anton Kern Gallery, New York, 1996, 1999, 2002, 2005, Univ Buffalo Art Gallery, 1997, Galerie Daniel Blau, Munich, 1998, Up & Co, New York, 1999, Bur Amsterdam, 2000, Kunstwerke, Berlin, 2000, Santa Monica Mus Art, 2001, Basel Art Fair, 2001, Chinese European Art Ctr, Xiamen, China, 2002, Air 2 Paris, 2004, Magasin 3, Stockholm, Sweden, 2005, Stuart Shave Mod Art, London, 2007, Galerie Gebr Lehmann, Berlin, 2008; group exhibs include Sublieme Vormen, Stedelijk Mus, Amsterdam, 1996; The Centre Holds, Gmurzynska Gallery, Cologne, 1997; Raumkorper, Netze und andere Gebilde, Kunsthalle Basel, 2000; Shanghai Biennial, 2002; Building Structures, PS1 Contemp Art Ctr, New York, 2002; Thing: New Sculpture from LA, Hammer Mus, LA, 2005; USA Today: New Am Art from the Saatchi Gallery, Royal Acad Arts, London, 2006; Fantastic Politics, Nat Mus Contemp Art, Oslo, 2007; Unmonumental: The Object in the 21st Century, New Mus Contemp Art, New York, 2007. *Awards:* Pollock-Krasner Found Grant, 1998. *Dealer:* Galerie Gebr Lehmann Lindenstrasse 35 10969 Berlin Germany. *Mailing Add:* Anton Kern Gallery 532 W 20th St New York NY 10011

SCHNITZER, ARLENE
PATRON
b Salem, Ore, Jan 10, 1929. *Study:* Univ Wash, Seattle, 47-48; Portland Art Mus Sch, 59-61; studied with Michele Russo. *Pos:* Dir, Fountain Gallery of Art, Portland, Ore, 61-87; Exec vpres, Harsh Investment Corp, 50-; pres, Fountain Assoc, 86-; bd trustees, McCallum Theatre, Palm Desert, 2002-. *Awards:* Pioneer Award, Univ Ore, 85 & Distinguished Service Award, 91; Portland First Citizen Award, 95; Outstanding Philanthropist Award, 96. *Mem:* Nat Comt Performing Arts, Kennedy Ctr, 95-; Nat Coun Fine Arts Mus San Francisco, 95-. *Collection:* Primarily most noted artists of the Northwest; largest collection outside a museum of works by C S Price, including carvings. *Mailing Add:* 1121 SW Salmon St Portland OR 97205

SCHNITZER, KLAUS A
PHOTOGRAPHER
Study: State Univ NY, Albany, BA, 67; Ohio Univ, Athens, MFA, 71. *Work:* Mus Mod Art, NY; Witkin Gallery, NY; Brookdale Community Col, Lincroft, NJ. *Exhib:* Invitational, Bertha Urdang Gallery, NY, 77; Solo exhibs, Newark Mus, NJ, 77, Mem Fine Arts Ctr, Univ Colo, Boulder, 81 & Art Inst Chicago, Ill, 81; Hunterdon Art Ctr, Linton, NJ, 78; NY Univ East Galleries, 78; and many others. *Awards:* Nat Endowment Arts Photog Fel, 80; Montclair State Coll Alumni Asn Grants, 78 & 80; Montclair State Coll Research Grant & Release Time, 81-82. *Publ:* Ed & contribr, Sans Silver, Camera 25 Mag, 10-12/74; illusr, Ancient Glass at the Newark Mus, Newark Mus, 77; auth, New Jersey: Unexpected pleasures, United Jersey Banks & NJ Monthly, 80; auth, Capitol Story, New York State Publ, 82. *Mailing Add:* 551 Upper Mountain Ave Upper Montclair NJ 07043-1608

SCHNURR, ELINORE
PAINTER
b Sandusky, Ohio, 1932. *Study:* Cleveland Inst Art, BFA. *Work:* Cleveland Mus Art; Mus City New York; Mus of Fine Art, St Petersburg, Fla; National Mus Am Art, Washington, DC; Pfizer Inc, New York; Brooklyn Historical Soc., NY; Cahoon Mus of American Art, Cotuit, Cape Cod, Mass. *Exhib:* Recent Paintings USA/The Figure, Mus Mod Art, New York, 62; Butler Inst Am Art, Youngstown, Ohio, 62, 75, 81, 83-84, 87, 98, 2001-2002 & 2004; Cleveland Inst Art, Ohio, 83; Capricorn Galleries, Bethesda, Md, 84, 87 & 93; Nat Acad Design, New York, 86, 88, 90 & 93; Mus City New York, 94-95 & 2000; DFN Gallery, New York, 97-98; Walter Wickiser Gallery, New York, 2003; Atlanta Art Gallery, Atlanta, Ga, 2008; Nordart, 2011; Kunstwerk Carlshutte, Budelsdorf, Ger, 2011; Port Washington Pub Libr, NY, 2011; La Guardia Community Col, Long Island City, NY, 2012; South Huntington Libr, NY, 2012; New Canaan Libr, Conn, 2014; Edward Hopper House Art Center, Nyack, NY, 2015. *Awards:* CAPS Fel, NYSCA, 79; Thomas B Clarke Award, Nat Acad Design, New York, 86; Mid-Atlantic Nat Endowment Arts, Fel, 94; Juror's Award, Armory Art Ctr, West Palm Beach, Fla, 2001; Golden Found, 2001; Nat Midyear 2nd Place Award, Butler Inst Am Art, Youngstown, Ohio, 2002. *Bibliog:* New York, New York, Cleveland Inst Art Bull, fall 79; A Barnhill Portrait (film), 94; Painting the Town: Cityscapes of NY, 2000. *Media:* Oil, Watercolor. *Dealer:* Hudson Gallery Sylvania OH. *Mailing Add:* 21-25 44th Ave Ste 105 Long Island City NY 11101

SCHOEN, (MR & MRS) ARTHUR BOYER
COLLECTORS
b Pittsburgh, Pa, Apr 17, 23 (Mr Schoen); b New York, NY, Sept 27, 15 (Mrs Schoen). *Study:* Mr Schoen, Princeton Univ, BA; Mrs Schoen, Columbia Univ; Grand Cent Sch Art, NY. *Pos:* Mr Schoen, bd adv, Ocean Learning Inst, West Palm Beach, Fla; dir & secy, Aqua Sol Inc; dir, Solar Micro Inc. *Mem:* Parrish Art Mus (Mrs Schoen, pres, 70-76, trustee); Meadow Club, Southampton. *Collection:* Paintings: 18th century English and American furniture; archaeological artifacts; Chinese porcelains; 10th & 12th century Persian pottery

SCHOENER, ALLON
DESIGNER, CONSULTANT
b Cleveland, Ohio, Jan 1, 1926. *Study:* Yale Univ, BA, 46, MA, 49; Courtauld Inst Art, Univ London, 47-48. *Collection Arranged:* Lower East Side: Portal to Am Life, Jewish Mus; Erie Canal: 1817-1967, NY State Coun Arts, 67; Harlem on My Mind, Metrop Mus Art, 69; Word From Jerusalem, Jewish Mus, 72; Life Aboard the Tall Ships for South Street, Seaport Mus, 76; The Family of Nations for the United Nations, Vienna, Austria, 79; Jewish Life in Am, NY Pub Libr, 83; The Italian Americans--per terre assai lontane, Archivi Alinri, Florence, Italy, 89; Ellis Island, NY, 92. *Pos:* Asst dir, Jewish Mus, 66-67; visual arts prog dir, NY State Coun Arts, 67-72; consult traveling exhib, Smithsonian Inst, Washington, DC & Jewish Mus, NY; consult multiple exhib prog, Libr of Cong, Washington, DC. *Awards:* Nat Endowment Arts Proj Fel, 82. *Publ:* Ed, Portal to America, Holt, Rinehart & Winston, 67; Harlem on My Mind, Random House, 69, Dell, 79 & The New Press, 95; The American Jewish Album, Rizzoli Int Publ, 83; The Italian American, Macmillan, 87; illusr, History of the People, Norton, NY, 98

SCHOFIELD, ROBERTA
PAINTER, PHOTOGRAPHER
b Ronceverte, WVa, July 9, 1945. *Study:* Univ S Fla, BA, 73, MFA, 79. *Work:* Federal Reserve Bank, Richmond, Va & Miami, Fla; Polk Mus Art, Lakeland, Fla; Jamestown Community Coll, Olean, NY; Strathmore Hall Found, Rockville, Md; Gulf Coast Mus Art, Largo, Fla; and others. *Comn:* Painting, Jamestown Community Coll, 88; 4 pvt commissions. *Exhib:* Port Royal Plantation, Hilton Head Island, SC, 95; ISE Art Found, New York, 96; Waterworks Visual Arts Ctr, Salisbury, NC, 96; Cudahy's Gallery, Richmond, Va, 97; Valencia Community Coll, Orlando, Fla, 98; Cudahy's Gallery, Richmond, Va, 93, 97, 99 & 2002; Clayton Galleries, Tampa, Fla, 93, 99 & 2005; 22nd Floor Capitol Gallery, Tallahassee, Fla, 2000; Greely Square Gallery, NY, 2001; Polk Mus, Lakeland, Fla, 2002; Seton Hall Univ, Orange, NJ, 2002; Gulf Coast Mus Art, Key Largo, 2005; Boca Raton Mus Art, Fla, 2005, 2010; Pakhuis 6 Gallery, Rotterdam, Neth, 2006; Turner Ctr Arts, Valdosta, Ga, 2006; Mus Arts & Scis, Daytona Beach, Fla, 2007; Tampa Mus Art, 2008; Leepa Rattner Mus Art, St Petersburg Coll, 2009, 2012; TECO Public Art Gallery, Tampa, Fla, 88, 2005, 2011; Cornell Mus Art & Culture, Delray Beach, Fla, 2011; Old Courthouse Art Ctr, Woodstock, Ill; Selby Gallery, Ringling Coll Art, 2012; Eastern Ky Univ, 2013; and others. *Pos:* Artistic dir, Fla Ctr Contemp Art, 87-88; exhib coordr, Tampa City Coun, 87-89 & 92-94; independent cur, 92-; Photographer, Tampa Tribune, 2005-. *Teaching:* Independent lectr, 1979-, instr, S Fla Jr Coll, Avon Park Fla, 79-82, Univ Wis, Eau Claire, Wis, 83-84 & St Petersburg Jr Coll, Clearwater, Fla, 89. *Awards:* Fla Arts Coun Fel, 87-88; Arts Grants, Hillsborough Co, Fla, 90, 2001; Best in Show, Arts Ctr, St Petersburg, Fla, 2002; Best In Show, St Augustine Arts Ctr, Fla, 2004; Merit Award, Boca Raton Mus Art, Fla, 2010; 2nd prize, Scanfone/Hartley Gallery, Univ Tampa,

Fla, 2010; Hon Mention, 3rd Annual Media Art Biennial, Art Addiction, London, England, 2011; and others. *Bibliog:* Adrienne Golub (auth), Art Papers, Atlanta, Ga, 10-11/93 & 9-10/98; Martha Mabey (auth), Schofield Unsettles, Pleases, Richmond Times-Dispatch, Va, 5/4/97; Roy Proctor (auth), Roberta Schofield's Vision of Interior Life on Display, Richmond-Times Dispatch, 10/31/99; and others; Aaron Todunau (auth), Slope, Color & Texture, Tampa Bay Magaginer, 2006. *Mem:* Women Caucus Art (chap secy, 87, treas, 88, publicity, 90); Nat Asn Women Artists, 92-94; Fla Artists Group; Las Damas de Arte. *Media:* Manipulated Photography, Oil, Color Pencil, Graphite, Photography. *Publ:* Auth & illusr, Gallerie Women's Art, Gallerie Pubs, 88; Cultural Affairs, Cult Affairs Publ, 2002-2003 & 2005; auth, South Tampa People, Tampa Tribune, 2008; Studio Visit Mag, 2011. *Dealer:* Clayton Galleries 4105 S MacDill Ave Tampa FL 33611. *Mailing Add:* PO Box 10561 Tampa FL 33679

SCHOLDER, LAURENCE
PRINTMAKER, EDUCATOR
b Brooklyn, NY, Nov 23, 1942. *Study:* Carnegie Inst Technol, BFA; Univ Iowa, MA. *Work:* Ft Worth Art Ctr, Tex; Houston Mus Fine Arts; Brooklyn Mus, NY; Dallas Mus Fine Arts, Tex. *Exhib:* Am Graphic Workshops '68, Cincinnati Art Mus, 68; Multiples USA, Western Mich Univ, Kalamazoo, 70; Midwest Biennial, Joslyn Art Mus, Omaha, Nebr, 70 & 72; Seattle Print Int, Seattle Art Mus, 71; Libr of Cong 22nd Print Nat, Washington, DC, 71. *Teaching:* Asst prof printmaking, Southern Methodist Univ, 68-73, assoc prof, 73-81, prof, 81-. *Awards:* Purchase Awards, Young Printmakers, Herron Art Inst, 67 & Print & Drawing Nat, Okla Art Ctr, 68; Merit Award, Southwest Graphics, San Antonio, 72; Nat Endowment Arts Printmaker's Fel, 75. *Media:* Intaglio. *Dealer:* Gerald Peters Gallery 2913 Fairmount Dallas TX 75201. *Mailing Add:* 5239 Goodwin Ave Dallas TX 75206

SCHON, NANCY QUINT
SCULPTOR
b Boston, Mass, Sept 24, 1928. *Work:* Children's Patio Newton Free Libr, Mass; Plotkin Mus, Phoenix, Ariz; M Maloney Properties, Boston, Mass; Beth Shalom, Needham, Mass; Sarah Pryor Living Mem, Wayland, Mass, 96. *Comn:* Nat Acad Sci, Washington, DC; Sweet Briar Col, Va; Jewish Home for the Elderly, Fairfield, Conn; Make Way for Ducklings, Boston Pub Garden, Mass & Novodevichy Park, Moscow, Russ, 91; Raccoons, Belle Meade, Nashville, Tenn, 94; and others. *Exhib:* One-person shows, Bristol Art Mus, RI, 78, Jerusalem Theatre Gallery, Israel, 79, Mass Inst Technol, Cambridge, Pierce Galleries, Hingham, Mass & Schönhaus Preview, Newton, Mass, 85; Concourse Art Gallery, Boston, 78; Richards Galleries, Hyannis, Mass, 80-81; Riji Gallery, NY, 81; Small Works, Rochester, NY, 84; Aetha Inst, Hartford, Conn, 84-85; Catherine Lorrilard Wolfe Ann, NY, 84-85; New Eng Sculptors' Asn Invitational, Boston, Mass, 85; Worcester Craft Mus, 86; Boston Mus, Mass, 86; Galleria de Tour, San Francisco; Rae Landers Gallery, East Brunswick, NJ; Raphael Galleries, La Jolla, Calif, Las Vegas, Nev; Wellesley Coll Mus, Mass; Univ of New Hampshire, Durham; Two Squares Gallery, Boulder, Colo; Springfield Mus of Fine Arts, Mass; George Walter Vincent Smith Art Mus, Springfield, Mass; and others. *Pos:* Gov's task force, Accessibility of the Arts (gov's comm), Boston, Mass, 72-74; Gov's Coun on Arts & Humanities, Boston, Mass, 72-75; founder, mem, Pub Media Found; adv bd Newton free Libr, Senior Citizens of Newton; bd dir, Newton Senior Ctr, Friends of Copley Sq. *Awards:* Good Samaritan Award, Easter Seal/Sculpture Competition, 73; Fel, Va Ctr Creative Arts, 85; Boston Preserv Award, Pub Art, 88; Joseph Henry Keenan Award, Mass Inst Technol, Cambridge; Browne Found Grant, 96; Wayland Cult Coun Grant, 96; Coll Club Ann Career Award, 96; Woman of Distinction, Spar & Spindle Nat Girl Scouts Bachrach VIP Portrait Show, Newton Free Libr, 94; Historic Neighborhood Found Award; Cert of Recognition, Boston Mayor Raymond Flynn: for Art Award, Stamford Conn. *Media:* Bronze. *Mailing Add:* 291 Otis St Newton MA 02465-2531

SCHORR, COLLIER
ARTIST
b NY City, 1963. *Study:* Sch Visual Arts, NY City, BFA. *Exhib:* Solo exhibs include Cable Gallery, NY, 1988, Standard Graphik, Koln, Germany, 1990, 303 Gallery, NY, 1990, 1991, 1993, 1994, 1997, 1999, 2001, 2004, Galerie Drantmann, Brussels, Belgium, 1995, 1997, Stockholm Kultur 98, Sweden, 1998, Georg Kargl, Vienna, 1999, Partobject Gallery, NC, 1999, Emily Tsingou Gallery, London, 2000, Consorcio Salamanca, Spain, 2002, Modern Art, London, 2004, 2006, Fotogalleriet, Oslo, Norway, 2004, Mus Contemp Art, Denver, 2007; group exhibs include Foul Play, Thread Waxing Space, NY, 1999; Lightness, Visual Arts Gallery, NY, 2000; Prepared, Georg Kargl Gallery, Vienna, 2000; Innuendo, Dee Glasgoe, NY, 2000; Uniform: Order and Disorder, PS 1, NY, 2001; Chick Clicks, Inst Contemp Art, Boston, 2001; American Tableaux, Walker Art Ctr, Minneapolis, 2001; Biennial, Whitney Mus Am Art, 2002; Some Options in Realism, Carpenter Ctr, Harvard Univ, Mass, 2002; Screen Memories, Contemp Art Ctr, Art Tower, Mito, Japan, 2002; Attack! Art and War in Times of the Media, Kunsthalle Wien, Vienna, 2003; Strangers, Triennial of Int Ctr Photography, NY, 2003; Terror Chic, Spruth Magers, Munich, Germany, 2003; Beyond Compare: Women Photographers on Beauty, Toronto, Canada, 2004; Open House - Working in Brooklyn, Brooklyn Mus Art, NY, 2004; The Muse, Leslie Tonkonow Artworks + Projects, NY, 2004; The Lost Paradise, Stiftung Opelvillen, Frankfurt, Germany, 2005; Seeing Double: Encounters with Warhol, The Andy Warhol Mus, 2005; Sport, Socrates Sculpture Park, Queens, NY, 2005; Modern Photographs: The Machine, The Body and The City, Miami Art Mus, 2006; Youth of Today, Schirn Kunsthalle, Frankfurt, Germany, 2006; Human Game, Stazione Leopolda, Florence, Italy, 2006; Reality Bites: Making Avant-Garde Art in Post-Wall Germany, Sam Fox Art Ctr, Washington Univ, St Louis, 2007. *Mailing Add:* c/o 303 Gallery 525 W 22nd St New York NY 10011

SCHOTTLAND, M
ILLUSTRATOR, PAINTER
b Brooklyn, NY, Nov 18, 1935. *Study:* Pratt Inst, BFA, 57; New Sch, printmaking with Antonio Frasconi, painting with Gregorio Prestodino, 58-60. *Work:* Soc of Illustrators Permanent Collection, NY; US Army Military Hist, US Air Force Art Prog, Pentagon & Nat Parks Serv, DC. *Comn:* Postage stamp, US Postal Serv, DC, 76; painting, US Air Force, DC, 77; paintings for nat advert, Ingersoll Rand Corp, NJ, 78; painting for bk illus, Franklin Libr, NY/Philadelphia, 79; NASA, 83; and others. *Exhib:* Indust Arts Methods Ann Show, NY, 76; 200 Yrs Am Illus, NY Hist Soc, 77; Soc Publ Designers Ann Show, NY, 78-79; Soc Illustrators Ann Show, NY, 78 & 79 & 50 Yrs of Award Winners, 79; Art in Sci, Cincinnati Mus Art, 79; Smithsonian Inst, 83. *Pos:* Chmn Air Force Art Prog, US Air Force/Soc Illustrators, 76-79. *Teaching:* Guest lectr illus, Soc Illustrators, New York, 77, Sch Visual Arts, New York, 78, Fashion Inst Technol, New York, 79 & Philadelphia Col Art, 79. *Awards:* Hamilton King Award, Soc Illustrators Ann Show, 71; Best of Show, Indust Arts Methods Ann Show, 76; Awards of Distinctive Merit, Soc Publ Designers Ann Show, 77 & 79. *Mem:* Soc Illusrs; Comt to Save NY Libr Picture Collection (vpres, 78-80); Graphic Artists Guild, NY. *Media:* Tempera. *Mailing Add:* 2201 Massachusetts Ave NW Washington DC 20008

SCHREFFLER, MICHAEL
EDUCATOR, HISTORIAN
Study: Univ Chicago, PhD, 2000. *Teaching:* Assoc prof art hist, Va Commonwealth Univ, 2000- & co-dir study abroad prog, 2002-. *Awards:* Arthur Kingsley Porter Prize, Coll Art Asn, 2010. *Publ:* Auth, No Lord Without Vassals, Nor Vassals Without a Lord: The Royal Palace and the Shape of Kingly Power in Viceregal Mexico City, Oxford Art J, 27, No 2, 155-171, 2004; Emblems of Virtue in Eighteenth-Century New Spain, In: Woman and Art in Early Modern Latin America (eds, Kellen McIntyre and Richard Phillips), Brill, 265-87, 2006; The Art of Allegiance: Visual Culture and Imperial Power in Baroque New Spain, Penn State Univ Pres, 2007; Their Cortes and Our Cortes: Spanish Colonialism and Aztec Representation, The Art Bull, 12/2009. *Mailing Add:* Va Commonwealth Univ Dept Art History 922 W Franklin PO Box 843046 Richmond VA 23284-3046

SCHREIBER, EILEEN SHER
PAINTER, PRINTMAKER
b Denver, Colo, 1925. *Study:* Univ Utah, 42-45; NY Univ Exten, 66-68; Montclair State Coll, 75-79. *Work:* Citibank; AT&T co; Johnson & Johnson; Georgia Pac; Champion Int Paper; Nabisco; Independence Bank, New York; Barclay Bank Eng; IBM; Mitsubishi; PSE&G; plus others; Sovereign Bank. *Comn:* NJ Beach Area, Broad Nat Bank, Newark, 70; Mitsubishi, Barclay Bank Eng. *Exhib:* NJ Mus, Trenton, 69 & 73; Am Watercolor Soc Nat, Nat Acad Galleries, New York; Audubon Artists, New York; Pallazzo Vecchio, Florence, Italy; Va State Mus, 75; Art Expo, New York, 86-87; Traveling show, Art Cult Ctr in Athena, Livingston Art Asn, 96. *Teaching:* Instr art, Jewish C Ctr, W Orange, NJ, formerly. *Awards:* Best Show Cash Award, Short Hills State Show, 76; Purchase Award, Tri-State Exhib, Somerset Co Coll, 77; Best Show, Tri State Exhib, Somerset Coll, 80; First Prize, Nat Asn Women Artist, 95; Accepted as one of 30 artists for permanent exhibiting artist, Noyes Mus, NJ, 2009; Lifetime Achievement Membership Award, Nat Asn Women Artists, 2009. *Bibliog:* M Lenson (auth), article, Newark Eve News, 4/70; article, Newark Star Ledger, 6/74; Addison Parks (auth), article, Arts Mag, 12/79; Eileen Watkin (auth), article, Star Ledger; Dianne Bainbridge (auth), article, NJ Music & Arts. *Mem:* Nat Asn Women Artists (chmn, 73-2012); Artists Equity Asn, New York; Printmakers Coun; NJ Visual Arts; Noyes Mus, NJ, 2006, 2012. *Media:* Acrylic, Watercolor; Collage, Monoprints. *Interests:* gardening, photography, travel, reading, art. *Dealer:* South West Gallery Barnegat Light NJ; Many galleries in New York and Florida

SCHRERO, RUTH LIEBERMAN
SCULPTOR, PRINTMAKER
b New York, NY. *Study:* Columbia Univ, with Oronzio Maldarelli; Art Students League, with George Grosz; Tyler Sch Art, Temple Univ; Pratt Graphics Workshop & Manhattan Graphics Workshop; studies with Tony Kirk & Vijay Kumar. *Work:* Maywood Pub Libr, NJ; Harsen & Johns, Architects, Rochelle Park, NJ; Nabisco Brands Corp, Parsippany, NJ; NY Univ Sch Law; Bergen Mus Art & Sci. *Comn:* Bronze portrait Hon Edward Weinfeld, comn by New York Univ Sch Law, 77. *Teaching:* Community Schools, Fairlawn & Glen Rock, NJ. *Awards:* Estelle Goodman Prize, Nat Painters & Sculptors Soc, 75; Exhib Am Drawings, Morris Mus, 84; Anna Hyatt Huntington Bronze Medal for Sculpture, 84, 89 & 98 & Gold Medal of Honor for Sculpture, Catharine Lorillard Wolfe Art Club, 97; Leila Gardin Sawyer Award for Etching, 99; plus others. *Bibliog:* NY Times, 79 & 84; Star Ledger, 80, 95 & 96. *Mem:* Artists Equity Asn NY; NY Soc Women Artists; Nat Asn Women Artists; Catharine Lorillard Wolfe Art Club; life mem Art Students League. *Media:* Clay, Miscellaneous Media; Etching, Mixed Media. *Interests:* pen & ink, drawing, sketching. *Dealer:* Wyckoff Gallery Wyckoff NJ. *Mailing Add:* 377 Rutland Ave Teaneck NJ 07666-2844

SCHREYER, CHARA
COLLECTOR
Pos: Chmn, Kadima Found, Mill Valley, Calif; trustee, Mus Mod Art, San Francisco & Contemp Jewish Mus. *Awards:* Named one of Top 200 Collectors, ARTnews mag, 2004-13. *Mem:* Mus Mod Art, San Francisco, Calif; Contemp Jewish Mus. *Collection:* Modern and contemporary art and photography. *Mailing Add:* Kadima Found PMB 200 38 Miller Ave Mill Valley CA 94941

SCHROECK, R D
PAINTER, CONCEPTUAL ARTIST
b Buffalo, NY, June 28, 1949. *Study:* Rosary Hill Col, BFA, 76. *Work:* Dartmoth Coll Mus & galleries, Hanover, NH; Georgia State Univ, Atlanta; Cleveland Coll Art & Design, Middlesbrough, Eng; Burchfield-Penney Art Ctr, Buffalo, NY; Cleveland Co Coun, Middlesbrough, Eng. *Exhib:* Western NY Exhib, Albright Knox Art Gallery, Buffalo, NY, 76, 80, 86, 94 & 96; 16th Biennale De Sao Paulo, 81; New Art of 1980-1990, Atelier Galeria, Dijon, France, 81; The Charles Rand Penney Collection of 20th Century Art, Rochester Art Gallery, NY, 83-84; Recent Acquisitions, Burchfield Penney Art Ctr, Buffalo, NY, 96. *Media:* Acrylic, Oil. *Mailing Add:* 14 Danforth St Buffalo NY 14227-1609

SCHROHENLOHER, SALLY A
PAINTER
b Cincinnati, Ohio, Feb 12, 1957. *Study:* Univ Cincinnati, BFA, 79. *Work:* Borden Inc, Columbus, Ohio; Fidelity Investments, Atlanta, Ga; Cincinnati Bell Tel, Ohio; Southern Ohio Mus, Portsmouth; EW Scripps Inc, La Jolla, Calif. *Exhib:* Faber Birren Color Show, Stamford Art Mus, Conn, 90; The Allen Collection, Miami Univ Art Mus, Oxford, Ohio, 94; Southern Ohio Mus, Portsmouth, 2000; South Bend Regional Mus Art, Ind, 2000; The Object Considered, Columbus Coll Art & Design, Ohio, 2000. *Awards:* Special Exhib Grant, Inst Mus Svcs, Nat Endowment for Arts, Washington, DC, 82; Individual Artist Grant, Summerfair Inc, Cincinnati, Ohio, 91; Ohio Arts Coun Award Fel, State of Ohio, Columbus, 2001. *Mem:* Oil Painters Am. *Media:* Oil. *Dealer:* Hueys Fine Art 217 W San Francisco St Sante Fe NM; Eisele Gallery 5729 Dragon Way Cincinnati Oh 45227. *Mailing Add:* 4010 Hanley Rd Cincinnati OH 45247

SCHROTH, PETER
PAINTER
Study: Syracuse Univ, BFA, 1977; Univ Colo, MFA, 1981. *Work:* Jersey City Mus; Johnson & Johnson; MET Life; Chase Manhattan; GE Corp. *Comn:* Breast Ctr, Chilton Meml Hosp, Pompton Plains, NJ. *Exhib:* 8th Int Print Biennale, Krakow, Poland, 1980; 59th SAGA Nat Print Exhib, Soc Am Graphic Artists, New York, 1982; Clemson Nat Print & Drawing Exhib, Clemson Univ, NC, 1983; Fla Ctr for Contemp Art, Ybor City, 1985; Ann Small Works Exhib, New York Univ, 1988; NJ Arts Ann, Jersey City Mus, 1990; Surroundings, NJ Ctr for Visual Arts, Summit, 1991; solo exhibs, Victoria Munroe Fine Art, New York, 1994, Watchung Art Ctr, NJ, 1996, Morris Mus, Morristown, NJ, 1998, Adam Baumgold Fine Art, New York, 2000, Hammond Harkins Galleries, Columbus, Ohio, 2002; One View/Two Visions, Leepa Ratner Mus, Tarpon Springs, Fla, 2005; Artists In Rural Ireland: American Artists at the Ballinglen Arts Found, Concord Arts Asn, Concord, Mass, 2006. *Teaching:* Assoc prof, Univ South Fla, Tampa, 1981-86; instr, Penland Sch Crafts, NC, 1983, Sch Visual Arts, New York, 1993, Marymount Manhattan Coll, New York, 1993-97, Raritan Valley Community Coll, NJ, 1995-97, Cooper Union, New York, 1994-2005 & Western Conn State Univ, Danbury, 2005; prof foundations, Savannah Coll Art & Design, Ga, 2005-07. *Awards:* Individual Artist Fel, Fla State Arts Coun, 1983; Pollock-Krasner Found Grant, 1991, 2008; Dodge Found Fel, Vt Studio Ctr, 1997; Individual Artist Fel, NJ State Coun Arts, 1998; Pres Fel, Savannah Coll Art & Design, 2007

SCHRUT, SHERRY
PAINTER, PRINTMAKER
b Detroit, Mich, Apr 27, 1928. *Study:* Wayne State Univ, Detroit, BA (art), 50; Long Beach State Col, Calif & Univ Calif, Los Angeles. *Work:* Security Pac Nat Bank, Palm Desert, Calif; Cedars-Sinai Med Ctr, Thalians Bldg, Los Angeles; Int Cult Ctr for Youth, Jerusalem, Israel; Hebrew Union Coll Skirball Mus, Los Angeles; Atlantic Richfield Co, Los Angeles; Wayne State Univ, Mich; IBM, Atlanta, Ga; Xerox Corp; Univ Calif Med Center, Los Angeles. *Comn:* Southern Calif Psychoanalytic Inst, Beverly Hills, 71 & 74; Sheraton Grande Hotel, Tokyo, Japan; MGM Grand Air, Lax Terminal Airport, Los Angeles; Princess Cruise Lines, London, Eng; Univ Minn Hosp, Minneapolis, Minn. *Exhib:* Wayne State Univ, Detroit, Mich, 50; Los Angeles Inst Contemp Art, Century City, 75; Laguna Beach Mus Art, 76; Works on Paper, Newport Harbor Art Mus, Calif, 77; Am Embassy, London, Eng, 77; Solo exhibs, Brand Libr & Art Ctr, Glendale, 72 & 79 & Galeria Del Sol, Santa Barbara, 76; Calif Mus Sci & Indust, 81; Hank Baum Gallery, San Francisco, 82; Eva Cohon Gallery, Chicago, Ill, 86. *Teaching:* Instr, Craft & Folk Art Mus, Los Angeles, 73-74; Los Alamitos Sch Distr, Calif; Cent High Sch, Detroit, Mich. *Awards:* Nat Scholastic Art award, New York 42; Second Prizes, Wayne State Univ, Detroit, 51 & Long Beach Mus Art, 53; First Prize, Westwood Ctr Arts, 68 & Riverside Mus Art, 80, Calif; Lucille Simon Purchase Award, Skirball Mus, Los Angeles. *Bibliog:* Barbara Probstein (auth), The fiery art, Home Mag, Los Angeles Times, 73 & Cloisonne enameling, Sch Arts Mag, Davis Publ, 1/75; W F Alexander (auth), Cloisonne Extraordinaire, California Contemporary Artists, In: Cloisonne & Related Arts, Wallace-Homestead Bk Co, 77; Designers West, Calif, 86. *Mem:* Southern Calif Designer-Crafts, Inc (treas, 75-78); Enamel Guild-West (mem bd, 77); Am Crafts Coun; World Crafts Coun. *Media:* Collage, Calligraphy. *Publ:* Contribr, Creative Stitchery, Crown Publ, 70; Porcelain Enamel, Historical, Contemporary, Industrial and Artistic, San Diego Univ Press, 76; Enameling for Secondary Schools, Lawrence Univ Press, RI, 76; Crafts 1976, Southern Calif Designer-Crafts, Inc, 76; The Center Mag, Ctr Democratic Insts, Santa Barbara, Calif, 78 & 79. *Dealer:* Ruth Bachofner Gallery Beverly Hills CA

SCHULE, DONALD KENNETH
SCULPTOR, INSTRUCTOR
b Madison, Minn, June 17, 1938. *Study:* Univ Minn, sculpture with Richard Randall, Robert Mallory & James Wines, BFA, 64, MFA, 67. *Work:* Walker Art Ctr, Minneapolis; Sheldon Art Mus, Lincoln, Nebr; Univ Notre Dame, South Bend, Ind; Wichita Art Mus, Kans; Minn Mus Art, St Paul. *Exhib:* Walker Art Ctr, Minneapolis, 62 & 64; solo shows, Minneapolis Inst Arts, 70, Contemp Arts Mus, Houston, 75, Sheldon Art Mus, Lincoln, Nebr, 78 & Phyllis Kind Gallery, Chicago, 78; Allan Stone Gallery, NY, 73 & 77; Whitney Mus Am Art, NY, 77; Indianapolis Mus Art, 78; Nelson Mus, Kansas City, 83; Karen Lennox Gallery, Chicago, 83; Janet Fleisher Gallery, Philadelphia, 83; and others. *Teaching:* Assoc prof, Wichita State Univ, 67-78; lectr, Southwest Tex State Univ, San Marcos, 81-88 & Pa State Univ, 89-94. *Awards:* Purchase Prizes, Ford Found, 64 & Nat Endowment Arts, 70; 1st Prize, Wichita Art Asn, 72. *Bibliog:* Dona Z Meilach (auth), Woodworking: The New Wave, Crown Publ Inc, 81. *Media:* Wood, Stone. *Mailing Add:* 1721 Linden Hall Rd Boalsburg PA 16827

SCHULEIT, ANNA
ARTIST
b Mainz, Ger, 1974. *Study:* RI Sch Design, BFA, 98; Dartmouth Col, MFA, 2005. *Exhib:* Solo exhibs include Nada Mason Gallery, Northfield, Mass, 2000, Northampton Ctr Arts, 2000; group exhibs include A Transatlantic Project, Muhle der schoenen Kunste, Ger, 95; Off the Wall, 16 S Main St Gallery, Providence, 98; Nat Prize Show, Cambridge Art Asn, Mus Fine Art, Boston, 98; Summer Show, Harvard Univ, 99; Kaelin Gallery, Boston, 2002; Pioneers of Public, Revolving Mus, Lowell, Mass, 2002; Inch x Inch, Arlington Ctr Arts, 2002; Chi of Ancestry, Gallery Luna, Salem, Mass, 2004; Medfield State Hospital Closing: Projections, Dept Mental Health, Westborough, Mass, 2004; The Matzo Files, NYC, 2004-2005; 1939 The Missing Year, New Art Ctr, Newton, Mass, 2005; Goliath, Brooklyn, 2006. *Pos:* Consultant Metrop Transit Authority, NY City, 2005. *Teaching:* Art instr Nightingale-Bamford Sch, 2005; guest lectr dept sociology Brown Univ, 99, 2002, 2005, Smith Col, 2000, River Valley Hospital, Middletown, Conn, 2000, Springfield Col, 2001, Brattleboro Mus and Art Ctr, 2001, The Delaney House, Holyoke, Mass, 2001, RI Sch Design, 2005; presenter Forum on Historical Records, Univ Mass Amherst, 2001, Nat Convention State Art Agencies, 2001, Sch Architecture McGill Univ, Montreal, 2003; vis artist Westborough State Hospital, Mass, 2001-2004; distinguished visitor Sch Art and Design, Univ Mich, 2006. *Awards:* Grad Alumni Award, Dartmouth Col, 2005, Thesis Res Award, 2005; MacDowell Colony Fellow, 2002, 2005, Chubb Life Am Fellow, 2000-2001; Artist Grant, Elizabeth Greenshields Found, 96; Artist Grant, Northampton Arts Council, 2000; Artist Grant, Mass Found Humanities, 2000; MacArthur Fellow, John D and Catherine T MacArthur Found, 2006

SCHULMAN, ARLENE
PHOTOGRAPHER, WRITER
b Bronx, NY, Aug 13, 1961. *Study:* Suffolk Community Coll, AAS; Hunter Coll, BA. *Work:* Mus City New York; NY Pub Libr; Nat Baseball Hall Fame, Cooperstown, NY; Int Boxing Hall Fame, Canastota, NY; Westinghouse Corp, Pittsburgh, Pa; plus pvt collections. *Exhib:* Solo exhib, Martin Luther King Jr Mem Lib, Washington, 86, Aurora, NY, NY 93 & Henry Street Settlement, NY, 95; Vassar Col, 96; and others. *Pos:* Freelance writer, 86-. *Teaching:* Instr, Ohio State Univ, Columbus, 96; instr, NY pub schs, 97-2001; instr, NY Pub Libr, 97-2001; instr, Hunter Coll Sch Continuing Edu, 2003-2006. *Mem:* PEN, 1995; Women in Communications, 2005; Soc Silvarians; Newswomen's Club of NY. *Media:* Photography. *Interests:* writing, art. *Publ:* Auth & illusr, The Prizefighters, Lyon & Burford, 94; auth, Muhammad Ali, Lerner, 96; auth & illusr, Carmine: The Story of a Boy Living with AIDS, 97; Robert F Kennedy: Promise for the Future, 98; TJ's Story: A Boy Who is Blind (bk), 98; 23rd Precinct: The Job, 01; Cop on the Beat, 2001; auth, Arlene's Scratch Paper (blog), 2012; filmmaker: Provincetown Sky, The Tides of Norman Mailer, My Hands Talk for me - A Boxing Journey, The Perfect Coverup, 2012

SCHULNIK, ALLISON
PAINTER, VIDEO ARTIST
b San Diego, Calif, 1978. *Study:* Calif Inst Art, BA (experimental animation), 2000. *Work:* Nerman Mus, Kans City, Mo; Mus Contemp Art, San Diego, Calif. *Exhib:* Solo exhibs, No Luck, Rokeby Gallery, London, Eng, 2007, Fools, Rejects, & Sanctuaries, Mark Moore Gallery, Santa Monica, Calif, 2007, No Luck Too, Mike Weiss Gallery, New York, 2008, Allison Schulnik, Mark Moore Gallery, Pulse Fair, New York, 2009, Go West, 1/9 Unosunoma, Rome, Italy, 2009; Group exhibs, San Diego Art Asn 45th Ann Int Exhib, San Diego, 2001; The Armory Show, Black Dragon Soc, New York, 2005; Epic, Bellwether Gallery, New York, 2005; Sex & Horses, Mark Moore Gallery, Santa Monica, Calif, 2005; Bluemen, Galerie Huebner, Frankfurt, Germany, 2008; Warm, Red, Salt & Wet, 31 Grand, New York, 2008; Phenomenon, Al-Sabah Art, Dubai, 2009; New Now: Building the Mus Collection, Nerman Mus, Overland Pk, Mo, 2009. *Bibliog:* Christopher Bollen (auth), Modern Art's Three Hot Trends, Domino Mag, 2006; Debut: Allison Schulnik at Rokeby, London, Saatchi Daily Mag, 2007; Rachel Potts (auth), Forward Motion Previews, Garangeland, Spring 2007; Christopher Knight (auth), Gobs Create Romantic Themes, LA Times, Mar 2007; Christopher Knights (auth), 45 Painters Under 45, LA Times, 12/2/2007; Future Greats-- Ones to Watch, Art Rev Mag, Mar, 2008; Stephen Maine (auth), Allison Schulnik, Mike Weiss Gallery, Art in Am, 2009. *Dealer:* Mike Weiss Gallery 520 W 24th St New York NY 10011; Mark Moore Gallery 2525 Michigan Ave Space A1 Santa Monica CA 90404

SCHULSON, SUSAN
PAINTER, SILVERSMITH
b Racine, Wis, Nov 21, 1941. *Study:* Lawrence Univ, BA, 63; Univ Ill, MFA (teaching asst), 78. *Work:* Mus Contemp Art, Chicago. *Exhib:* With Paper, About Paper, Albright-Knox Art Gallery, Buffalo, NY, 80; Navy Pier, Chicago, 81; Heresies, Grey Art Gallery, NY, 81; Swen Parson Gallery, 83; Ornaments as Sculpture, Sculpture Ctr, NY, 83; Critical Mixage, Galerie Lara Vincey, Paris, 85; and others. *Pos:* Ed, Le Corbusier Sketchbooks vols II-IV, Archit History Found, New York, 81-82; film producer & educator commercials & features in development, 83-94. *Teaching:* Instr printmaking, Evanston Art Ctr, Ill, 75-76, Univ Ill, 76-78, Searing Sch, New York, 80-81; guest lectr, Univ Chicago, 75-76, Sch Visual Arts, New York, 87 & 88. *Bibliog:* Joanna Frueh (auth), Susan Schulson at Zolla/Lieberman, Art Am, 79. *Mem:* Coll Art Asn; Artist Equity; NY Acad Arts & Scis. *Media:* Miscellaneous Media. *Mailing Add:* 121 Wooster St New York NY 10012

SCHULTE, ARTHUR D
COLLECTOR
b New York, NY, 1906. *Study:* Mr Schulte, Yale Univ; Mrs Schulte, Hunter Col, Columbia Univ, NY Univ. *Collection:* French, American, Italian and Greek paintings and sculpture. *Mailing Add:* 825 5th Ave New York NY 10021

SCHULTZ, DOUGLAS GEORGE
DIRECTOR
b Oakland, Calif, Oct 3, 1947. *Study:* Univ Calif, Berkeley, BA (art hist), 69, MA (art hist), 72; Inst Arts Admin, Harvard Univ, 71. *Collection Arranged:* Antoni Tapies: Thirty-Three Years of His Work, 77, In Western New York (coauth, catalog), 77, Piero Dorazio: A Retrospective, 79, Kenneth Nelson, 81, Chryssa: Urban Icons, 82, Robert Motherwell, 83, Beverly Pepper, 86, Albright-Knox Art Gallery. *Pos:* Curatorial intern, Albright-Knox Art Gallery, 72-73, asst cur, 73-75, assoc cur, 75-76, cur, 77-79, chief cur, 80-83, acting dir, 83, dir, 83-; mem professional adv comt, Arts Develop Servs, Buffalo, NY. *Teaching:* Adj prof art hist, State Univ NY, Buffalo, 75-79. *Mem:* NY State Coun Arts; Arts Develop Serv. *Mailing Add:* 1285 Elmwood Ave Buffalo NY 14222

SCHULTZ, JOHN BERNARD
EDUCATOR, HISTORIAN
b Pittsburgh, Pa, Nov 26, 1948. *Study:* John Carroll Univ, BA, 70; Univ Pittsburgh, MA, 73, PhD, 82. *Pos:* Bd dir, Monogalia Arts Ctr, Morgantown, WVa, 82-84 & 94-; chmn, div art, WVa Univ, Morgantown, 89-94, assoc dean, Coll Creative Arts, 94-2000, dean, Coll Creative Arts, 2000-. *Teaching:* Instr art hist, John Carroll Univ, Cleveland, Ohio, 74-75; from instr art hist to prof, WVa Univ, Morgantown, 77-90. *Awards:* Outstanding Teacher, 81, Innovation-Excellence Award, 85, Art Div, WVa Univ; Distinguished Prof Art, WVa Art Alumni Asn, 88; Frick Fine Arts Distinguished Alumnus, Univ Pittsburgh, 93; Governor's Arts Award, Arts Leadership & Service, 2006. *Mem:* Coll Art Asn Am; Am Asn Hist Med. *Res:* Historical interrelationships between medicine and art, Art history pedagogy, Art history survey. *Publ:* Auth, Art and Anatomy in Renaissance Italy, UMI Res Press, 85; A Fifteenth Century Papal Brief on Human Dissection, Medical Heritage, 86; coauth, Art Past/Art Present, Abrams, Prentice-Hall, 90, 2nd ed, 94, 3rd ed, 97, 4th ed, 2000 & 5th ed, 2005; Study Guide for Janson's History of Art, 4th ed, Prentice-Hall, 91, 5th ed & rev, 95-97 & 6th ed, 2001; With Gratitude to Eva Hubbard: A Celebration of Women Artists at WVa Univ (exhib catalog), 91; coauth, Art Studies in America at the beginning of the twentieth century, Blanche Lazzell: The Life and work of an American Modernist, WVa Univ Press, 2004. *Mailing Add:* WVa Univ Coll Creative Arts PO Box 6111 Morgantown WV 26506-6111

SCHULTZ, MARILOU
WEAVER, INSTRUCTOR
b Safford, Ariz, Nov 6, 1954. *Study:* Ariz State Univ, BA, 78, MA, 79. *Work:* Am Indian Sci & Eng Soc, Albuquerque, NM. *Comn:* Weaving, Intel Corp, Chandler, Ariz, 94; Germantown blanket, comn by a friend of Kevin Johnson, Phoenix, Ariz, 97; Ten Rugs in One Rug, comn by Mr & Mrs Craig Cummings, Paradise Valley, Ariz, 98; Ganado Red (on a loom), United Properties Inc, Sedona, Ariz, 98. *Exhib:* Ann Santa Fe Indian Market, SW Asn Indian Arts, NMex, 81-; Ann Navajo Show, Mus N Ariz, Flagstaff, 86-90; Ann Indian Fair & Market, Heard Mus, Phoenix, Ariz, 90-. *Pos:* Demonstr weaving, SW Mus, Mesa, Ariz, 97, Redhouse Inc, Scottsdale, Ariz, 98- & Heard Mus, Phoenix, Ariz, 98; Native Am adv bd, SW Mus, Mesa, Ariz. *Teaching:* Instr Navajo weavings, Omega Inst, Rhinebeck, NY, 98-2001 & Split Rock Arts Prog, Univ Minn, Minneapolis, Minn, 99-2005; Spinning Lofr, 2003-2005. *Awards:* Ariz Comn Arts Fel, 97; Best of Division Weavings, Heard Mus, Phoenix, Ariz, 97; Challenge Award, 96, 97, 2000. *Bibliog:* Fabric of Time (TV doc), KNXV-Channel 15, 12/97; CD Screen Saver, Santa Fe Indian Market, NMex, 98. *Mem:* SW Asn Indian Arts; Am Tapestry Alliance; ATALT; Heard Mus (Guild Member); and others. *Mailing Add:* 844 E Eighth Pl Mesa AZ 85203

SCHULTZ, MICHAEL
PHOTOGRAPHER
Work: NC Mus Art St; Petersburg Mus Fine Art; Fed Reserve Bank, Charlotte. *Awards:* Guggenheim Found Fel, 2010. *Publ:* Auth, Foundry Work, Am Foundry Soc, 2008. *Dealer:* Sherry Leedy Gallery 2004 Baltimore Ave Kansas City MO 64108; Joie Lassiter Gallery 1430 S Mint St Sute 105A Charlotte NC 28203

SCHULTZ, SAUNDERS
SCULPTOR
b July 16, 1927. *Study:* Wash Univ, St Louis, Mo, BFA, 50; Univ Ill, Urbana, MFA, 52; special study with Max Beckman, Paul Burlin & Fred Conway. *Work:* Morris Arboretum/Sculptural Park, Philadelphia; Broward Co--Art in Public Places Collection, Pompano Beach, Fla; Univ Ark Art Collection, Little Rock; Sculpture Fountain, Kansas City; St Louis Univ Hosp, Mo. *Comn:* Cosmos, is Prize-International Competition, Juffall Hq, Jedda, Saudi Arabia, 83; Light Rays, Maridian Hotel, Singapore, 83; Battle Bows-resulted from international Competition; Nurturing, Cath Cemeteries, St Louis, Mo, 89; Battle Bows, Tri-State Vet Mem, Dubuque, Iowa, 89; Flamma, One Pacific Place, Omaha, Nebr, 90-91. *Exhib:* Sculpture in Architectural Context, Fordham Univ, NY, 79; Centennial Alumni Exhib, Bixby Hall Gallery, Wash Univ, St Louis, Mo, 79; Sculpture Outdoors, Temple Univ, Philadelphia, Pa, 80; Int Sculpture Competition, Mercer Col, Trenton, NJ, 80; Interfaith Forum Exhibition on Religion, Art & Architecture, Washington, DC, 84; Sch Environ Design, Calif State Polytechnic, 88; Miss State Univ, 89; The Good Shepherd & The Good Shepherd Cross Archdiocese of City of Chicago & Catholic Cemeteries Chicago, Ill, 2005. *Teaching:* Guest lectr, numerous cols & univs incl Harvard Univ Sch Grad Sch Design, Columbia Univ Archit, Planning & Preserv, 77-. *Awards:* First Prize, Univ Wis, Green Bay, 75, Broward Co Housing Authority, 80, Washington, DC Hebrew Cong, 83, Nat Competition to create sculpture for Washington Hebrew Congregation, DC, 84, Tri-State Vets Mem, 87; Preservation by Design Award, Swain Sch Design, 89. *Bibliog:* George McCue (auth), Sculpture City: St Louis, Hudson Mills Press, 88; Lineatus, Hotel & Motel Mgt, Harcourt Brace & Jovanovich, cover photo, 88; plus others; Has delivered 11 Keynote addresses. *Media:* stainless, bronze, wood, marble, All. *Collection:* Umo Art Gallery, College of Fine Art, Univ of Neb, Omaha; US Embassy Fountain, Moscow, 83, Triyud, Temple Shaave Emerth, Crev Coeur, Mo. *Publ:* contribr, Nat Community Arts Program, US Dept Housing Urban Development, 73; auth, Washington Univ Mag, Washington Univ, St Louis, Mo, 79; auth, Religion and Theatre, Bethel Col, St Paul, Minn, 8/80; contribr, A Christian Response to the Holocaust, Stonehenge Books, 81; coauth, Art Guidelines, Salt River Project, Phoenix, 89. *Mailing Add:* 27 Covington Rd Saint Louis MO 63132

SCHULTZ, STEPHEN WARREN
PAINTER, EDUCATOR
b Chicago, Ill, Aug 28, 1946. *Study:* RI Sch Design, 65-67; San Francisco Art Inst, BFA, 71; Stanford Univ, MFA, 74. *Work:* Equitable Life Assurance Corp, New York; Univ Iowa Mus, Iowa City; Stanford Univ; Boise Mus, Idaho; Brunier Mus, Iowa State Univ; McNay Art Mus, San Antonio, Tex; Hallmark, St Louis, Mo; Touchstone Pictures, Los Angeles; Story/Crossroads Films; Syntex Corp, Saratoga, Calif; Regis Corp, Minneapolis, Minn; Verona Foundation, Hydra, Greece. *Exhib:* Braunstien/Quay Gallery, San Francisco, 75; Walker Art Ctr, 77; Awards in Visual Arts, Nat Mus Am Art, Washington, DC, 82, Denver Art Mus, 83 & Des Moines Art Ctr, 83; Iowa Artists, Des Moines Art Ctr, 82; Sid Deutsch Gallery, New York, 84 & 86; Minneapolis Mus Art, 86; Artists Who Teach, Fed Res Gallery, Washington, DC, 87-; Ovsey Gallery, Los Angeles, 91; Lowe Gallery, Santa Monica, 93; Lowe Gallery, Atlanta, 93 & 95; Sinoway Gallery, Chicago, 96; Chac Mool Gallery, Los Angeles, Calif, 98; Paris Gibsons Mus, Great Fall, Mont, 99; Victoria Boyce Gallery, Tucson & Scottsdale, Ariz, 2000; Frye Mus, Seattle, 2002; Salt Lake Art Ctr, 2003; Mus Art, Spokane, Wash, 2006; Daniel Besseiche Gallery, Paris, France, 2006; N Idaho Coll, 2007; Verena Found, Hydra, Greece, 2007; Galerie Fatiha Selam, Paris, Fr, 2012, 2013, 2015; Prographica Gallery, Seattle, Wash, 2012. *Pos:* Artist-in-residence, Yaddo/George Rickey Workshop, East Chatham, NY, 82, Rockefeller Found, Bellagio Ctr, Lake Como, Italy, 84 & Camargo Found, Cassis, France, 85; juror, Ill Art Coun Fels, 90; vis artist, Univ Tex, Arlington, 80, Belgrade Acad Fine Arts, Yugoslavia, 86-87 & Am Acad Rome, 97. *Teaching:* Prof, Univ Iowa, 75-94, Stanford Univ, 75 & Univ Wash, Seattle, 2003. *Awards:* Tiffany Found Fel, 79; Awards in Visual Arts, Southeastern Ctr Contemp Arts, 81; Fel, Idaho Comn for the Arts, 84; Faculty Scholars Award, Univ Iowa, 84-86; Fulbright Fel, Int Exchange Scholars, 86; Fels painting, Nat Endowment Arts/Westaf, 90. *Bibliog:* RS Coburn (auth), Raising veil of emerging artist, Smithsonian Mag, 5/82; All art considered (interview), Nat Pub Radio, 5/19/82; Southeastern Ctr Contemp Art, Awards in Visual Arts (film), PBS TV, 83; Stephen Schultz, Selected Works (catalog), 88-94; Johanna Hays, essay, 95; Stephen Schultz, A Classic Vision, Paris Gibson Mus, 97. *Media:* painting and drawing. *Dealer:* Galerie Fatiha Selam Paris Fr; Prographica Seattle Wa; SWSpaint.com. *Mailing Add:* 915 Poplar St Sandpoint ID 83864

SCHULZ, ANNE MARKHAM
HISTORIAN, EDUCATOR
b New York, NY, 1938. *Study:* Radcliffe Col, BA, 59; New York Univ, Inst Fine Arts, MA, 62, PhD, 68. *Pos:* Visiting scholar, Brown Univ. *Teaching:* Asst prof Renaissance art, Univ Ill, Chicago Circle, 1967-68; vis lectr to vis prof & res assoc, Brown Univ, 1968-. *Awards:* Basic Res Grant & Sr Fel, Nat Endowment Humanities, 1982-1986, 1998; Am Coun Learned Soc Sr Fel, 1987-88; Fulbright Fel, Italy, 1961-1962, 1996-1997; Delmas Fel, 1978, 2003, 2005; Associate, Villa I Tatti, Florence, Italy, 1983-84; Kress Fel, 1974-75, 1993-95, 2005-06. *Mem:* Coll Art Asn; Renaissance Soc. *Res:* Venetian Renaissance sculpture; early Renaissance art. *Publ:* The sculpture of Giovanni & Bartolomeo Bon, Transactions Am Philos Soc, 78; Niccolo di Giovanni Fiorentino and Venetian Sculpture of the Early Renaissance, CAA Monographs Series 33, New York Univ Press, 78; Giambattista and Lorenzo Bregno: Venetian Sculpture in the High Renaissance, Cambridge Univ Press, 91; Luciano Bellosi, Brunella Teodori & Giorgio Semmoloni (contrbs), Nanni di Bartolo e il portale della Basilica di San Nicola a Tolentino, Centro Di, Florence, Italy, 97; Giammaria Mosca called Padovano: a Renaissance Sculptor in Italy and Poland, (2 vols), Penn State Press, 98; The Sculpture of Bernardo Rossellino and his Workshop, Princeton Univ Press, 77; Antonio Rizzo, Sculptor and Architect, Princeton Univ Press, NJ, 1983; Manuela Moresi & Toto Bergamo Rossi (contrbs), The Badoer - Giustiniani Chapel in San Francesco della Vigna, Venice, Centro Di, Florence, Italy, 2003; Woodcarving and Woodcarvers in Venice 1350-1550, Centro Di Florence, Italy, 2011. *Mailing Add:* Brown Univ Dept Art History & Archit Box 1855 64 College St Providence RI 02912

SCHULZ, CHARLOTTE
DRAFTSMAN, EDUCATOR
b Massillon, Ohio. *Study:* Univ S Fla, BA, 1983, MFA, 1993. *Work:* Mills Coll Art Mus, Oakland; Ringling Mus Art, Fla; Univ S Fla Phyllis P Marshall Ctr; NCNB Bank, Tampa; William R Hough Co, St Petersburg. *Exhib:* Selection of Recent Acquisitions, Ringling Mus Art, Sarasota, 1994; Small Works!, Valencia Community Coll, Orlando, 1995; 57th Ann Nat Exhib Contemp Am Paintings, Soc Four Arts, Palm Beach, 1995; Insights and Outlooks: Figuring Ourselves In A Postmodern World, Dunedin Fine Art Ctr, Fla, 1996; solo exhibs, Lee Scarfone Gallery, Univ Tampa, 1996, Azarian McCullough Gallery, St Thomas Aquinas Coll, 2005, Aldrich Contemp Art Mus, 2007, Mills Coll Art Mus, 2008; underCURRENT/overVIEW, Tampa Mus Art, 1997; Drawings, St John's Univ, Jamaica, NY, 1999; The Art of Oil, Lowe Gallery at Hudson Guild, New York, 2002; Radius, Aldrich Contemp Art Mus, Ridgefield, 2003; Timeless/Timeliness, Aljira Ctr Contemp Art, 2004; Paperworks, Pace Univ, New York, 2005; Stilled Life, Islip Art Mus, NY, 2006; Home Girls, NJ City Univ, 2007; Dark Poets, Md Inst Coll Art, Baltimore, 2008; Lucid Dreaming, Michener Art Mus, Pa, 2009. *Teaching:* Instr, Ringling Sch Art & Design, Sarasota, Fla, 1993-98, Northeastern Univ, Boston, 1998-99, St Johns Univ, NY, 1999-2000, Manhattan Community Coll, 2000-04, Parsons New Sch for Design, New York, 2000- & Pace Univ, NY, 2005-. *Awards:* Skowhegan Sch Painting & Sculpture Fel, 1992; Govs Award Excellence, Univ Mobile, 1994; Artist Fel, State Fla, 1996; NY Found Arts Fel, 2001 & 2009; Pollock-Krasner Found Grant, 2005; Guggenheim Found Fel, 2010. *Bibliog:* Ben Genocchio (auth), Opening a Window on the Creative Mind, NY Times, 1/27/2008. *Media:* Charcoal. *Mailing Add:* 1503 Saratoga Ln Fishkill NY 12524

SCHULZE, FRANZ
HISTORIAN, CRITIC
b Uniontown, Pa, 1927. *Study:* Northwestern Univ; Univ Chicago, PhB, 45; Sch Art Inst Chicago, BFA, 49, MFA, 50; Acad Fine Arts, Munich, 56-57. *Hon Degrees:* Sch Art Inst Chgo, DFA, 2014. *Work:* Art Inst Chicago, Ill; Mus Contemp Art, Chicago, Ill. *Exhib:* Solo exhib Jan Cicero Gallery, Chicago, 98; Printworks, Chicago, 2011. *Collection Arranged:* Art Collection, North Trust Bank, Chicago, 98. *Pos:* Art critic, Chicago Daily News, 62-78; corresp ed, Art in Am, 65-; contrib ed, Art News, 75-2005, Inland Architect, 75- & Chicago Sun-Times, 78-85. *Teaching:* Instr, Purdue Univ, 50-52; prof, Lake Forest Coll, 52-74 & Hollender prof art, 75-91. *Awards:* Ford Found Critics Fel, 64; Harbison Award, Danford Found, 71; Graham Found Advan Fine Arts Fel, 71 & 80; and others. *Mem:* Coll Art Asn Am (bd dir, 81-82); Arch Am Art; Am Asn Univ Prof; Ragdale Found. *Media:* Painting; Drawing. *Res:* Art and architecture in the Midwest, especially Chicago. *Specialty:* Painting and drawing. *Publ:* Auth, Mies van der Rohe: A Critical Biography, 85; co-auth with Edward Windherst, Mies van der Rohe: A Critical Biography, revised and expanded edition; ed, Chicago's Famous Buildings, 93; Philip Johnson: Life & Work, 94; The Farnsworth House, 97; Rosemary Cowler & Arthur H Miller (auths), 30 Miles North, a History of Lake Forest College, Its Town and Its City of Chicago, 2000; coauth (with Kevin Harrington), Chicago's Famous Buildings, 5th ed, 2004; Helmut Jahn, 2012. *Dealer:* Paintworks Chicago IL. *Mailing Add:* Lake Forest Coll Dept Art Lake Forest IL 60045

SCHULZE, PAUL
DESIGNER
b New York, NY, Feb 7, 1934. *Study:* Parsons Sch Design, cert; NY Univ, BS (indust design), 60. *Work:* Corning Mus Glass; Nat Air & Space Mus, Washington, DC; NC State Univ; also numerous pvt collections. *Comn:* Crystal cross, Steuben Glass, St Clement's Episcopal Church, NY. *Exhib:* Studies in Crystal 1966, Steuben Glass, NY, 65; Islands in Crystal, Steuben Glass, NY, 66; New Glass, Corning Mus Glass, 79. *Pos:* Off interior design, Bus Equip Sales Co, New York, 60-61; designer, Steuben Glass, 61-69, asst dir design, 69-70, dir design, 70-87; prin, Paul Schulze Design, 87-. *Teaching:* Instr eng drawing & three dimensional design, Parsons Sch Design, 62-70. *Awards:* Student Competition Award, Am Soc Indust Designers, 59. *Bibliog:* Harry Abrams (auth), Contemporary Glass, Glass Animals, others. *Mem:* Guild for Organic Environment; Nat Alumni Coun Parsons Sch Design; NY State Craftsmen. *Media:* Glass, Mixed. *Publ:* Illusr, Organics, Steendrukkerij & Co, Holland, 61. *Mailing Add:* PO Box 134 New Suffolk NY 11956-0134

SCHULZKE, MARGOT SEYMOUR
PAINTER, WRITER
b San Francisco, Calif. *Study:* Brigham Young Univ, BA, 59, additional study with Albert Handell, Constance Flavell Pratt, William Schultz, Richard Yip & Frank Zuccarelli. *Work:* Sutter Auburn Faith Hosp, Calif; Blanning & Baker Inc, Sacramento; Auburn Diagnostic Soc & Surgery Ctr, Auburn, Calif; US State Dept, Moldova US Embassy. *Comn:* Shirley Canyon (pastel painting), Squaw Valley Auburn Diagnostic Ctr, Calif; 7 paintings, Sutter Auburn Faith Hosp, Auburn, Calif; Phipps Family At Home (group), comn by Wendy Brown, Auburn, Calif; Megan (portrait), comn by Mr & Mrs Steven Martini, Bellingham, Wash; Lee Remmel (portrait), comn by Richard Remmel; Jason & Dallin, comm by Wendy Brown, Auburn, Calif. *Exhib:* Pastel Soc Am Nat Open Exhibs, Nat Arts Club, NY, 86-94; Pastel Soc West Coast Nat Open Exhibs, Ctr Galleries, Sacramento Fine Arts Ctr, Calif, 86-2007; 3rd Ann Orig Art Showcase, Prestige Gallery Ltd, Toronto, Can, 91; 69th Ann Spring Salon, Springville Mus, Utah, 93; Monmouth Mus, Lincroft, NJ, 94; NW Pastel Soc, Washington, 97; Ore Pastel Soc, Coos Bay Mus, 97; Audubon Artists of Am, Salmagundi Club, New York City, 2002; Triton Mus, Santa Clara, Calif, 2004, 2009; Degas Pastel Soc, 10th Biennial, New Orleans, 2004-05; Lauren Rogers Mus, Laurel, Miss, 2004-05; Haggin Mus, Stockton, Calif, 2006, 2008; Southwest Society Open Exhib, Tacoma, Wash, 2008 ; Pastel Joun, Cinn, Ohio, 2004; Chisinaw Moldova Exhib, 2011. *Collection Arranged:* judge, Pastels USA, Haggin Mus, Calif, 2007, Northwest Pastel Soc, Tacoma, Wash, 2008, Emerald Art Ctr Nat Open Exhib, Sprinfield, Ore, 2009. *Pos:* Pres (founding), Pastel Soc West Coast, 85-88, & adv bd mem, 88-, pres, 95-97 & bd dir 85-; juror selection, Pastels USA, 2003, Sierra Pastel Soc Nat Open Exhib, 2002; juror nat art exhibs, 2002-2008; judge, Northwest Pastel Soc Nat Open, 2008; judge, Bold Expressions Nat Open, Calif, 2011. *Teaching:* Lectr, creativity, oil painting, Educ Week Tours, Brigham Young Univ, Educ, 66-67; instr pastel & oil, Roseville Arts Ctr, 85-2005; instr pastel, Ultima Nat Art Symp, Yellowstone, 91; workshops, Mex, 98, 2001, 2002; High Sierra Workshop, 2003, 2006; instr pastel & oils painting workshops in US, Mex, 90-2010; instr arts, pastel & oil classes, 1985-. *Awards:* Awards in nat competitions since 1986; Distinguished Pastelist, Pastel Soc West Coast, 89; awards in 14 Pastels USA Internat Exhibs; Pastel Laureate Award, PSWC Hall Fame, 2006. *Bibliog:* Calif Season Mag (cover & feature article), May/June 1999; Perspectives (feature article), Arts Coun Mag, May/June 2005; Sierra Heritage Mag (feature article), May/Apr 2006; feature article, The Pastel Joun, Nov/Dec 2008. *Mem:* Am Artists Prof League, NY; Pastel Soc Am, NY; Pastel Soc West Coast, Sacramento (dist pastelist); Calif Art Club; Degas Pastel Soc. *Media:* Pastel, Oil. *Interests:* Hispanic women & children; mountains, rivers & shore Sierras, Pacific Coast & SW; archit wealth of Europe, Near East & Mex. *Publ:* Artists Mag & Am Artists, 1986-1992; featured artist, Pastel Interpretations by Madlyn Ann C Woolwich, Northlight, fall 93; featured artist, Best of Pastel, 96 & Landscape Inspirations, 97, Rockport Publ, 99; Artspeak & The Westsider, New York City; contribr, Pure Color: The Best of Pastel, Northlight, Cincinnati, 2006; auth, Guide to the Arts Mag, Grass Valley, Calif, 2001; contribr, Best of Pastel, Rockport Pubs, Mass, 1992; auth, A Painter's Guide to Design & Composition, North Light, Cincinnati, Ohio, 2006; Guide to the Arts (cover & feature article) summer 2002, featured the Pastel Joun, Dec 2008; auth, The Artist's Viewpoint (column), Pastel J, 1999-2010; Pastel 100, Pastel Journ, Cincinnati, 2004; Emerald Art Ctr Nat Open, Springfield, Ore, 2009; Stockton Art League, Haggin Mus 56th Ann Open Exhib, Calif, 2010. *Dealer:* Margot Schulzke Studio Auburn, Calif. *Mailing Add:* 1840 Little Creek Rd Auburn CA 95602

SCHUMACHER, JUDITH KLEIN
SCULPTOR
b Pittsburgh, Pa, 1947. *Study:* Drew Univ, BA, 95; Mason Gross Sch Arts, Rutgers Univ, MFA; studied with John Goodyear, Robert Cooke & Lynne Allen. *Exhib:* Hunterdon Mus Art, NJ, 99; Greenwich St Studio Ctr, New York City; Gallery at Bristol-Myers Squibb, Princeton, NJ; Jane Voorhees Zimmerli Art Mus, Rutgers Univ, NJ, 2001. *Teaching:* instr, Visual arts, Middlesex Co Col, Edison, NJ, 97-2000; instr, ceramic sculpture, Rutgers Univ, 97-2000. *Media:* Ceramic. *Specialty:* Site Specific Installations

SCHUPP, RONALD IRVING
SOCIAL JUSTICE ARTIST, WRITER
b Syracuse, NY, Dec 10, 1951. *Work:* Smithsonian Inst, Wash DC; Chicago Historical Society, Chicago History Mus, Ill; World Center for Peace, Freedom, and Humain Rights, Verdun, France; Sch Art Inst Chicago. *Pos:* mem, Uptown Multi-Cultural Art Ctr, organizer, Free Speech Artist's Movement, lead organizer, T-Shirt Art Harvest Festival, Chicago, Ill, 2010-2012. *Awards:* Best Poem award, People's Tribune, 1992. *Bibliog:* Poetry published in People's Tribune, 1990s. *Publ:* auth, Grassroots Poetry (book), 1982, People's Poetry in Motion (book), 2015. *Mailing Add:* 4541 N Sheridan Rd Apt 409 Chicago IL 60640

SCHURR, JERRY M
PAINTER, PRINTMAKER
b Philadelphia, Pa, May 4, 1940. *Study:* Univ Pa, 58-59; Pa Acad Fine Arts, 58-60 & 65-69; Univ Hawaii, 59-60; Temple Univ, 61-63. *Work:* Philadelphia Mus Art, Pa; Del Art Mus, Wilmington; Portland Mus Art, Ore; Minneapolis Mus Art, Minn; US Dept State (Vienna Embassy), Vienna. *Exhib:* Ann Fel Show, Pa Acad Fine Arts, Philadelphia, 68, 69, 70, 74 & 86; Philadelphia Print Club, 74, 77, 78 & 86; The Philadelphia Civic Ctr Mus Exchange Exhib, Tel Aviv, Israel, 80; 65th Ann Multiple Impressions Traveling Show, Philadelphia Print Club, 80; Fel Show PAFA, Noyes Mus, NJ, 86; Nat Acad Art for the Parks, Smithsonian Inst, Washington, 87. *Teaching:* Instr serigraphy, Tyler Sch Art, Elkins Park, Pa, 77-78. *Awards:* Thouron Prize, Pa Acad Fine Arts, 66; Eugene Feldman Mem Prize, Philadelphia Print Club, Philadelphia Mus Art, 77; Nat Arts Club Purchase Prize, 79. *Bibliog:* Talking Posters, Art Bus News, 11/85; Victoria Donahoe (auth), The panorama of the west, Philadelphia Inquirer, 4/11/86; Roni Henning (auth), Silkscreen Painting, 10/94. *Mem:* Artist Equity; Philadelphia Print Club; Pa Acad Fine Arts (alumni). *Media:* Acrylic; Serigraphy, Silkscreen. *Dealer:* Summa Gallery 85th & Amsterdam New York NY; Ira Genstein 1121 Fox Chase Rd Jenkintown PA 19046

SCHUSELKA, ELFI
PAINTER, SCULPTOR
b Vienna, Austria, Feb 13, 1940. *Study:* Art hist & theatre, Univ Vienna; Acad Arts, Vienna; photog, Graphic & Experimental Inst, Vienna; studied with Oskar Kokoschka, Sch of Vision, Salzburg, Austria; Art Students League, NY; Pratt Graphics Ctr, NY. *Work:* Albertina, Vienna, Austria; Amon Carter Mus Western Art, Ft Worth, Tex; Bibliot Nat, Paris, France; Nat Mus Hist, Taipei, Taiwan; Mus Mod Art, NY; Mus Contemp Art, Ibiza, Spain; Mus Int Contemp Graphic Art, Fredrikstad, Norway; Mus d'Art Contemporian, Skopje, Yugoslavia; Nat Mus Hist, Taipei, Taiwan; NY Pub Libr; Univ Dallas, Tex; Xantus Janos Mus, Gyor, Hungary; and many others. *Exhib:* Brooklyn Mus Print Exhib, NY, 70 & 76; Exhib Graphic Art, Frechen, Ger, 76, 78, 83 & 90; solo exhibs, 55 Mercer Gallery, NY, 77, 79, 82 & 84, Condeso/Lawler, 80, 83, 85 & 87, Joan Hodgell Gallery, Sarasota, Fla, 85, Broadway Windows, NY Univ, 88 & Neue Galerie, Vienna, 88, Henry Chauncey Conf Ctr, Princeton, NJ, 90, Al Galerie, Stuttgart, 93, Glaskasten, Leonberg, Stuttgart, 96, Austrian Trade Comn, 2000; Monumental Drawing, Brooklyn Mus, 86; Int Biennial Graphic Art Ljubljana, Tokyo, Japan, 88-89; Int Biennale Varna, Bulgaria, 89; Plaster in Contemp Art, Queens Mus, NY, 90; Int Triennial Graphic Art, Bitola, Macedonia, 94, 97, 2000; Group shows: Musee du Petit Format, Couvin, Nismes-Viroinval, Belgium, 87, 89, 91, 93, 98, 2000, 2002, 2004, 2006, 2008, 2010, 2012, Int Biennale Bharat Bhavan, Roopankar, India, 89, 91, 95, 2002, Int Biennale Varna, Bulgaria, 89, 2003, 2005, 2007, 2009, 2011, 2013, Prahova Co Mus, Ploiesti, Romenia, 2009, 2011, 2013, World Gallery of Drawings, Skopje, Macedonia, 2009, 2010, 2012, Tribuna Graphic, Art Mus of Cluj, Romania, 2010, Prahova County Mus, Ploiesti, Romenia, 2009, 2011. *Teaching:* Instr printmaking, Sch Visual Arts, New York, 70-73; instr art, Pratt/Phoenix Sch of Design, New York, 74 & Pratt Graphics Ctr, 78-80 & Baruch Col, City Univ New York, 89, 90, 91; vis artist Rutgers Univ, NJ, 76. *Awards:* Int Exhib Graphic Art Medal, Frechen, Ger, 78; Award, Ibizagraphic 82, Spain; NY Found Arts Grant, 86; Artist space, NYC, 88; Raciborz 2000, Poland, 00; Invitational Exhib Contemp Art, Nat Acad Mus, New York, 2006; Honorable Mention, Screen Print Biennial, Japan, 2011. *Bibliog:* Tiffany Bell (auth), article, Arts Mag, 1/78; Vivien Raynor (auth), NY Times, 8/6/78 & 12/26/82; Nancy Unger (auth), Gannett Newspaper, 1/21/83; Grace Glueck (auth), article, NY Times, 3/29/85; C Braunsteiner, Studio Interview for Seitenblicke, 99; Nora Novak, Cetatea Culturala, 01. *Mem:* NY Artist Equity. *Dealer:* Al Galerie Löportar U 14B H-1134 Budapest, Hungary; Studio 13 133 Eldridge St New York NY 10002. *Mailing Add:* c/o Studio 13 133 Eldridge St New York NY 10002

SCHUSTER, CITA FLETCHER (SARAH E)
APPRAISER, CONSULTANT
b El Paso, Tex, Sept 12, 1929. *Study:* Vassar Coll, AB, 50; Univ Tex, El Paso, with David Deming & Sally Bishop; Univ Calif, Los Angeles, Am Soc Appraisers sem fine arts; conserv & restoration with Nikoli Poloskov, 81; Cornucopia V, Am Soc Appraisers sem fine arts, London, 85. *Exhib:* Solo exhibs, Univ Tex, El Paso, 75 & 78; Int Woman's Art Slide Festival, 76; 19th Ann Sun Carnival Nat, El Paso Mus Art, Tex, 76-77; El Paso Designer Craftsmen Invitational, Univ Tex, El Paso, 78; Toys Designed by Artists, Ark Art Ctr, 79-80. *Pos:* Owner-dir, Two-Twenty-Two Gallery, El Paso, 63-72; fine art appraiser, 63-82; chair art adv bd, El Paso Mus Art, 92-95; class I, curric adv & session leader, Leadership Art, El Paso; bd mem, Art Resources Dept, El Paso, Tex, 95-; bd, SW Art History Conference, Taos, NMex, 98-2011; mem

development, AD BRA Edma, 2012-. *Teaching:* Session presenter, Leadership Art El Paso, 94; Ctr Lifelong Learning, Univ Tex El Paso, 96-98. *Bibliog:* Betty Chamberlain (auth), Professional page, Am Artist, 11/74; guest appearance, Spectrum - appraising fine arts, KCOS-TV, 86. *Mem:* Charter mem Visual Artists & Galleries Asn Inc; Appraisers Asn Am; founder Valuors Consortium, Houston; La Watercolor Soc; co-founder, Univ Tex El Paso, Friends Art, 87; sr mem Am Soc Appraisers (recertified, 98-2003); El Paso Mus Art (adv bd develop, 2012-). *Media:* Watercolor, Acrylic, Collage. *Res:* Southwestern modernist. *Specialty:* Nineteenth and twentieth century painting, print and sculpture. *Publ:* Coauth, The Status Game, Avalon Hill, 82; Harri Kidd Modernist in the Desert, with Bcky-Duval-Reese; EP Historical Society Publication, 2011. *Mailing Add:* 5854 Mira Serena Dr El Paso TX 79912

SCHUSTERMAN, GERRIE MARVA
ART DEALER, GALLERY DIRECTOR
b Chicago, Ill, July 6, 1928. *Study:* Univ Mich; Soc Arts & Crafts, Detroit; Univ Southern Calif, Irvine. *Pos:* Gallery dir, Art Angles Gallery, Orange, Calif, 71-. *Teaching:* Teacher & coordr, Rancho Santiago Community Col, 80-; Walker Elementary Sch, Santa Ana, Calif, 95. *Mem:* Prof Picture Framers Asn; Art Dealers Asn (bd mem). *Specialty:* Established regionalist artists

SCHUTTE, THOMAS FREDERICK
ADMINISTRATOR
b Rochester, NY, Dec 19, 1935. *Study:* Valparaiso Univ, Ind, AB, 57; Ind Univ, Bloomington, MBA, 58; Univ Colo, Boulder, DBA, 63. *Pos:* Asst dean, Wharton Sch, Univ Pa, Philadelphia, 73-75; pres, Philadelphia Col Art, 75-83; dir, Union Independent Cols Art, 75; pres, RI Sch Design, 83-93; pres, Pratt Inst, Brooklyn, NY, 93-. *Interests:* American 18th and 19th century decorative arts. *Publ:* Auth, Is the antiques dealer aware of his economic position in the market place?, 1-5/63 & A salesmanship model for the antiques dealer, 4/64, Antiques Dealer; ed, An Uneasy Coalition: Design & Corporate America, Univ Pa, 75. *Mailing Add:* Pratt Institute 200 Willougby Ave Brooklyn NY 11205

SCHUTZ, DANA
PAINTER
b Livonia, Mich, 1976. *Study:* Skowhegan Sch Painting & Sculpture, Maine, 1999; Norwich Sch Art & Design, England, 1999; Cleveland Inst Art, BFA, 2000; Columbia Univ, New York, MFA, 2002. *Work:* Colby Mus Art; Corcoran Gallery Art; Guggenheim Mus, New York; Hammer Mus, Los Angeles; Los Angeles County Mus Art; Mus Contemp Art, Los Angeles; Mus Fine Art, Boston; Mus Mod Art, New York; Whitney Mus Am Art. *Exhib:* Atavism, Inside Gallery, Tremont, Ohio, 2000; Portraits, PS1 Mus Mod Art, New York, 2001; Young, Free and Single, Zinc Gallery, Stockholm, 2002; solo exhibs, LFL Gallery, New York, 2002, Mario Diacono Gallery, Boston, 2004, Nerman Mus Contemp Art, Overland Park, Kans, 2004, Contemp Fine Arts, Berlin, Ger, 2005 & 2010, Site Santa Fe, NMex, 2005, Zach Feuer Gallery, 2007 & 2009, Douglas Hyde Gallery, Dublin, Ireland, 2010, Atlanta Contemp Art Center, Georgia, 2011, Neuberger Mus of Art, Purchase, NY, 2011; Clandestine, Venice Biennale, Venice, 2003; Unforseen: Four Painted Predictions, Portland Inst Contemp Art, Ore, 2004; Corcoran Biennial, Corcoran Mus Art, Washington, DC, 2005; Once Upon a Time in the West, Contemp Fine Arts, Berlin, Ger, 2006; From Here to Infinity, Cleveland Inst Art, 2007; Encounters, Pace Beijing, China, 2008; Saints and Sinners, Rose Art Mus, Brandeis Univ, 2009; Open, Zach Feuer Gallery, NY, 2010; Shifting the Gaze: Painting and Feminism, The Jewish Mus, NY, 2010; Creating the New Century: Contemp Art from the Dicke Collection, Dayton Art Inst, Ohio, 2011; Inside the Painter's Studio, Massachusetts Coll of Art and Design, Boston, 2011; Cryptic: The Use of Allegory in Contemporary Art with a Master Class from Goya, Contemp Art Mus, St Louis, Missouri, 2011. *Awards:* Grant, Rema Hort Mann Found, New York, 2002; Louis Comfort Tiffany Found award, New York, 2003; Am Acad Arts & Letts award, New York, 2007; John Koch Award for Painting, Nat Acad Invitational Exhib Contemp Art Awards, 2010; Columbia Univ Medal for Excellence, NY, 2010. *Bibliog:* Jerry Saltz (auth), A Stumblebum's Progress, The Village Voice, 62, 5/21/2003; Benjamin Carlson (auth), The Dreamland Artist Club, Time Out New York, 51, 8/5-12/2004; Carly Berwick (auth), Where the Scenes are, New York Mag, 38-39, 3/7/2005; Dottie Indyke (auth), rev, ARTnews mag, 3/2006; Holland Cotter (auth), Leaving Her Mark, Sometimes with Tape, NY Times, 5/17/2007; Adda Birnir (auth), Death! Fire! Mayhem! Art!, The Village Voice, 8/13-19/2008; Dodie Kazanjian (auth), Secrets of the Flesh, Vogue, 222-227, 4/2009. *Mem:* Nat Acad. *Media:* Oil. *Mailing Add:* c/o Zach Feuer Gallery 548 W 22nd St New York NY 10011

SCHWAB, CHARLES R
COLLECTOR
b Sacramento, Calif, 1937. *Study:* Stanford Univ, 1959, MBA, 1961. *Pos:* Mutual fund mgr, Marin co, Calif, formerly; founder & chmn, Charles Schwab Corp, San Francisco, 1971-, chief exec officer & chmn, 1971-2003, 2004-, chmn, 2003-2004, exec chmn 2008-; bd dirs, The Gap, Inc, 1986-2004, Seibel Systems, Inc; co-founder (with Helen Schwab) & chmn, Charles & Helen Schwab Found, 2001-; chmn, All Kinds of Minds Inst; bd trustees, Stanford Univ; chmn, Pres's Coun on Financial Literacy, 2008-. *Awards:* Achievements inc pioneer in discount brokerage bus since 1974; named one of Forbes' Richest Americans, 1999-, Forbes' Exec Pay, 1999-, World's Richest People, 1999-; named one of Top 200 Collectors, ARTnews mag, 2004-09, & 2011, 2012, 2013; named one of 50 Most Generous Philanthropists, BusinessWeek, 2005. *Collection:* Modern and contemporary art. *Publ:* Auth, How to be Your Own Stockbroker, Dell, 1986; Guide to Financial Independence, Three Rivers Press, 1998; You're Fifty - Now What?, Three Rivers Press, 2002. *Mailing Add:* Charles Schwab & Co Inc 101 Montgomery St San Francisco CA 94104

SCHWAB, HELEN O'NEILL
COLLECTOR
Pos: Bd pres, Charles and Helen Schwab Found; mem bd governors, San Francisco Symphony; vice chmn, San Francisco Mus Mod Art; bd assoc, Golden Gate National Parks Conservancy. *Awards:* Named one of Top 200 Collectors, ARTnews mag, 2009-13. *Collection:* Modern and contemporary art

SCHWAB, JUDITH A
SCULPTOR, CURATOR
b Philadelphia, Pa, Feb 22, 1935. *Study:* Kean Coll, BA (fine art & art educ), NJ, 75; Univ Dela, MFA (sculpture), Newark, Dela, 86; pvt study with Jacob Landau, Roosevelt, NJ, 81. *Hon Degrees:* Xi'an Art Sch, China, 98. *Work:* One on One Fitness Training Ctr, Wilmington, Dela; Skadden Arps Slate Meagher & Flom, Wilmington, Dela; Youth & Creative Art Ctr, Triosk, Russia; Georgian Int Friendship Ctr, Tbilisi, Repub Georgia; Dela Hist Mus, Wilmington, Dela; Skadden Arps Meahger & Flam. *Comn:* Archmere Acad, Xi'an Art Sch, People to People Int, Int Dela Chapter, 98; S African-Shortlidge Acad, Pacem-in-Terris, Neumours Found, 2003. *Exhib:* Solo exhibs, Peregrination, N Ariz Uni Art Gallery, Flagstaff, Ariz, 85, From Nature to Neon & Back, Univ Tenn at Chatanooga, 87, Stretching My Skin, Susan Isaacs Gallery, Wilmington, Dela, 87, Rhythms of the Future, Convention Gallery, Univ Dela, Newark, Dela, 90, Revisiting Nature, Artemis Gallery, Richmond, Va, 2001, Nature-Revisited II, Cecil Community Coll, North East, Md, 2005, Making Waves, with poetry by Charles Fishman, Bakehouse Art Complex, 2013; Group exhib, Sacred Spaces, Jewish Mus, Miami, Fla, 2007; cur, assembled, & arr, Women Collared for Work, Coral Springs Mus Art, 2009, Delaplaine Arts Educ Ctr, 2009, Delaware Art Mus, 2010, Villanova Univ Art Gallery, 2011, & W Chester Univ Art Gallery, 2012; Red Eye, Art Serve, 2012; Ledbetter Gallery, 2012; Plus Factor, Glass Gallery, Penbroke Pines, Fla, 2012; Making Waves (with poetry by Charles Fishman), F.A.T. Village Sculpture Ctr, 2013, BAC Bakehouse Art Complex, Miami, Fla, 2013, Posnack J.C.C., Davie, Fla, 2013 . *Collection Arranged:* cur, assembled, & arr, Women Collared for Work, Coral Springs Mus Art, 2009, Delaplaine Arts Educ Ctr, 2009, Delaware Art Mus, 2010, Villanova Univ Art Gallery, 2011, & W Chester Univ Art Gallery, 2012. *Pos:* vis artist, Girls & Boys Clubs, 97-99, Xi'an Art Sch, China, 98; art facilitator, InkonjanieSch Soweto Art Found 97-98, Human Services Inc, Wilmington, Dela, summer 2003; resident artist, Bellevue State Pk Art Ctr, Bellevue Dela, summer 2001. *Teaching:* prof art educ, exhibit & lect, Xi'an Art Sch, China, 98; facilitator, art educ, Shortlidge Acad, Wilmington, Dela, 97-99. *Awards:* Honorarium, Responses: Art for Young Children, Please Touch Mus, 82; Art for Peace Prog, People to People Int, Troisk, Russia, 96; Emerging Artist Fel, NEA Fund Div Arts, 87-88, Established Artists Fel, 94-95; Opportunity Grant Arts, Dela Div Art, 2005; Individual Artist Grant, Women Collared for Work, Broward Co Comn, 2009; Hon prof art, Xi'an Art Sch, Xi'an, China, 98. *Bibliog:* Penelope Bass Cope (auth), A Media Mix, Schwab exhibits her performance art, the News Journ, 12/4/83; Belena S Chapp (auth), Delaware Judith Schwab, Dela State Arts Coun, May-June 89; Gary Mullinax (critic), Art & myth come together, the News Journ, 11/16/90, Georgia on her mind, the News Journ, 4/2/91; Scott Fishman (auth), Exhibit celebrates women's strength, Sun Sentinel, Fla, 6/14/2009; Diane C Lade (auth), Artistic Merger, Sun Sentinel, 2/16/2013, Today Art, Making Waves, 4/4/2013. *Mem:* The Prof Artist's Org (mem at large), 2007-2009; Coral Springs Mus Art, Fla, 2005-2009; The Prof Art Org; Puppetry Guild, Ft Lauderdale; World and Eye Art Ctr; Art Serve Ft Lauderdale; 2+3 The Artists Org; Flagler Art Tech Village Art District Org; Puppet Network; Art Serve, Ft Lauderdale. *Media:* acrylic, fiberglass, wood. *Res:* Hist of women's issues, hist of costume. *Specialty:* painted sculpture. *Interests:* Voice, exercise, healthy life style, puppetry. *Publ:* auth, Puppetry Language on the Special Child, a Multi-Media Approach to Language, Nancy Renfo Studios, 82. *Dealer:* Elizabeth Torregrossa 91 Green Meadow Dr Elkton MD 21921; Coral Springs Museum of Art 2855 Coral Springs Dr Coral Springs FL 33065; Creative A Frame 1743 N Univ Dr Plantation Fl

SCHWAGER, MICHAEL R
EDUCATOR, CURATOR
b New York, NY, June 25, 1953. *Study:* Calif Coll Arts & Crafts, BFA, 75; John F Kennedy Univ, MA (mus studies), 82. *Collection Arranged:* One By Two: Artists in Collaboration, 92; Dangerous Pleasures: The Art of Judith Linhares (ed, catalog), 94; Private Visions: Artists' Sketchbooks, 95; The Urban Landscape: Recent Photographs, 95; Re-Presenting the Figure: The Body as Image & Object, 96. *Pos:* Exhib coordr, San Francisco Mus Mod Art, 84-88; cur, Richmond Art Ctr, Richmond, Calif, 88-90; dir, Univ Art Gallery, Sonoma State Univ, 91-. *Teaching:* Asst prof art hist, Sonoma State Univ, 94-; instr mus studies, Univ Calif, Berkeley, 96. *Mem:* Am Asn Mus. *Res:* Modern and contemporary art with an emphasis on Northern California art. *Publ:* Auth, Alvin Light: A Memorial Exhibition (brochure), San Francisco Mus Mod Art, 82; Viewpoints: 8 Installations (exhib catalog), Richmond Art Ctr, 91; Views from Afar: Contemporary German Art (exhib catalog), 93, Yoshitomo Saito: Bronze Sculpture 1986-1995 (exhib catalog), 95, Sonoma State Univ. *Mailing Add:* c/o Sonoma State Univ Art Gallery 1801 E Cotati Ave Cotati CA 94928

SCHWALB, SUSAN
DRAFTSMAN, PAINTER
b New York, NY, Feb 26, 1944. *Study:* Carnegie-Mellon Univ, BFA, 65; Fel, Va Ctr Creative Arts, 73, 92, 2007 & 2009; MacDowell Colony, 74, 75 & 89; Yaddo, Saratoga Springs, NY, 81, UCCA, 2010. *Work:* Brit Mus, London; Brooklyn Mus & Chase Manhattan Bank, NY; Ark Arts Ctr, Little Rock; Achenbach Found Graphic Arts, Fine Arts Mus San Francisco; Rose Art Mus, Waltham, Mass; Libr of Congress, Washington, DC; Israel Mus, Jerusalem; Nat Gallery of Art, Washington, DC; Mus of Fine Arts, Houston, Tex; Mus of Modern Art, NY; Fogg Art Mus, Cambridge, Mass; Mus of Fine Arts, Boston; Kupferstich Kabinett Staatliche Mus, Berlin, Ger; Victoria & Albert Mus, London; Ashmolean Mus, Oxford; and others. *Exhib:* Sacred Artifacts, Objects of Devotion, Alternative Mus, 82-83; solo exhibs, SOHO 20 Gallery, NY, 85 & 89, Brad Cooper Gallery, Tampa, Fla, 89, Yeshiva Univ Mus, 90, B'nai B'rith Klutznick Nat Jewish Mus, Wash, DC, 92-94, Andrea Marquit Fine Arts, Boston, 94, 96 & 99 & Am Cult Ctr, Jerusalem, Israel, 94, MY Art Prospects, 2001, Robert Steele Gallery, NY, 2003, 2005, 2006, Simon Gallery, Morristown, NJ, 2003, 2006 & 2009, Galeriae Mourlot, 2008, 2011, K Imperial Gallery, San Francisco, Calif, 2011, Gallery Simen, NY, 2013, Gerald Peters Gallery, Santa Fe, 2013; Pino Molica Gallery (with catalog), 92-93; Cevini Haas, Scottsdale, Ariz, 2002 & 2004; Solo Solomon Fine Arts, Seattle, 2005; Silverpoint Etcetra: Contemp Am Metalpoint Drawings, Art Arts Ctr, Little Rock, 92-93; Sanctuaries: Recovering the Holy in Contemp Art, Mus Contemp

Relig Art, St Louis Univ, Mo, 93; Power, Pleasure, Pain: Contemp Women Artists and the Female Body, Fogg Art Mus, Harvard Univ, 94; Mus of Fine Arts, Houston, Tex, 2002; Danforth Mus, 2004; and many more; RI Sch Design, Mus Art, 2010; Acad Art Mus, 2010. *Pos:* Art dir, Aphra, Literary Mag, 74-75 & Women Artist News, 75-77. *Teaching:* Instr, Kean Coll of NJ, 78-79, City Univ New York, 79-82 & Parsons Sch Art, 82; spec instr, Simmons Coll, 88; vis assoc prof, Mass Coll Art, Boston, 82-91; artist-in-residence, Tel Aviv Artists Studios, Mishkenot Sha'ananium, Jerusalem, Israel, 94. *Awards:* Comt for the Visual Arts Grant, New York, 77, 85 & 89; Int Commun Agency Travel Grant, 80. *Bibliog:* Cassandra Langer (auth), The Creation Series: 15 years of silverpoint, Women Artists News, fall 90; Helen A Harrison (auth), Contemporary metalpoint drawings, NY Times, 4/3/94; Alicia Faxon (auth), Doing nature in the 20th Century, Art New Eng, 6/94; Orisoltes Fixing the World Jewish American Painters in the 20th Cent, NE; Margaret Mathews Bernron, Light Touch, American Artist, Drawing, 2005; Amy Eshoo, 560 Broadway A New York Drawing Collection at Work, 1991-2006, Yale Univ Press, 2007; Elizabeth Mandel, Intricate Enigma, Artseditor.com, 2009; Doug McClement (auth), Susan Schwalb at Galerie Mourlot, ArtNews, 4/2011. *Mem:* Coalition of Women's Art Orgn (exec comt, 77-78, vpres, 85-86); Coll Art Asn; Women's Caucus Art (bd mem, 78-79, coord, Boston chap, 82-83); AICA. *Media:* Silverpoint Drawing, Acrylic. *Publ:* Illusr, Issue of Aphra, 73; contribr, Crafting with Plastics, Chilton Bk Co, 75; Women Artist News, Mid-March Assoc, 75-77; auth, Notes From Houston, Womanart, 78; contribr, Art New England, 95-2004; contrbr & writer, Artscope, Mass, 2007-. *Dealer:* Andrea Marquit Fine Arts Boston; Galerie Mourlot New York NY; Gerald Peters Gallery Santa Fe NM; Garvey Simon Art NYC. *Mailing Add:* 10 Winsor Ave Watertown MA 02172

SCHWARM, HAROLD CHAMBERS
PAINTER, INSTRUCTOR
b Fairmont, WVa, May 5, 1925. *Study:* Univ Iowa, Iowa City, 45-48; Bradley Univ, Peoria, Ill, BFA, 51, MA, 52. *Work:* Kaiser Hosp, Milpitas, Calif; Univ Calif Cancer Ctr, Sacramento; Subway, Nuremburg, Ger; Galeria Aguntamiento, Naquera, Spain. *Comn:* Pier 66 (painting), Ft Lauderdale, Fla, 81; painting, Raley's Corp, Sacramento, Calif, 82; Kronick, Moskowitz, Tredmann & Girand (painting), Sacramento, Calif, 88; painting, McCuen & Steele, Rancho Condovg, Calif, 89; triptych, Hyatt Regency, Sacramento, 90. *Exhib:* Iowa Print Group, Philadelphia Mus Art, 47; Nat Print Ann, Brooklyn Mus, 48; Student show, Univ Iowa, Iowa City, 48; Painting, Butler Inst Am Art, 50; Bradley Prints, Art Inst Chicago, 54; Painting, Denver Art Mus, 63; Miniature show, Frye Art Mus, Seattle, 65; Claudia Chapline Gallery, Stinson Beach, Calif, 87-2005; Anagma Arte Contemp, Valencia, Spain; Galerie IM Gassla, Erlangen Ger, 95; Bay Model, Sausalito, Calif, 97; Bolinas Mus, Calif, 97; Civic Arts Plaza, Thousand Oaks, Calif, 99; Sf Art, Stasbourg, France, 2003; Strasbourg, France, 2003-04. *Pos:* Supervisor art serv, Southern Ill Univ, Carbondale, 55-59; designer, JB Talmadge Inc, Reseda, Calif, 72-74. *Teaching:* Instr sculpture & design, Bradley Univ, Peoria, Ill, 52-55; assoc prof graphic design, Calif State Univ, Northridge, 59-72; supervisor art serv, S Ill Univ, 55-59. *Bibliog:* The Fine Art Index, 93, International Fine Art Reference, Chicago; Art Fair Seattle, 93, Catalog; US Art Catalog, 95, Caskey, Lees. *Media:* Acrylic, Pastel, Watercolor. *Publ:* Contribr, California & the Western States, Roberts Publ co, 63; illustr, many books for pvt & univ presses. *Dealer:* Claudia Chapline Gallery Stinson Beach CA. *Mailing Add:* c/o Claudia Chapline Gallery 3445 Shoreline Hwy PO Box 1117 Stinson Beach CA 94970

SCHWARTZ, ADRIENNE CLAIRE See Mim, Adrienne Claire Schwartz

SCHWARTZ, AUBREY E
PRINTMAKER, SCULPTOR
b Brooklyn, NY, Jan 13, 1928. *Study:* Art Students League; Brooklyn Mus Art Sch. *Work:* Nat Gallery Art, Washington, DC; Brooklyn Mus Art; Philadelphia Mus Art; Libr Cong, Washington, DC; Art Inst Chicago; NY Pub Libr; Jewish Mus, NY. *Comn:* Ed lithographs, Predatory Birds, Gehenna Press, 58, Midget & Dwarf, Tamarind Workshop, 60 & Bestiary, Kanthos Press, 61. *Exhib:* Young Am, Whitney Mus Am Art, 57; Print Coun Am Show, 57; solo exhib, Grippi Gallery, New York, 58 & Odon Wagner Gallery, Toronto, Can, 2003; Art USA, New York Coliseum, 59; Contemp Graphic Art, US State Dept, 59; retrospective, SUNY, Binghamton, NY, 97 & McClaren Center, Barrie, Ont, Can, 2003. *Teaching:* Prof art, State Univ NY, Binghamton, formerly, prof emer, currently; retired. *Awards:* Guggenheim Found Fel Creative Printmaking, 58-60; Tamarind Fel Creative Lithography, 60; First Prize Graphic Art, Boston Arts Festival, 60. *Mailing Add:* PO Box 6 Afton NY 13730-0006

SCHWARTZ, DANIEL BENNETT
PAINTER, SCULPTOR
b NY City, Feb 16, 1929. *Study:* Art Students League, 46; studied with Y Kuniyoshi; RI Sch Design, BFA, 49. *Comn:* Walter Peyton Man of the Year Award, Nat'l Football League, 71. *Exhib:* Solo exhibs, Davis Galleries, NY, 55-56, 58, 60, Hirschl & Adler Galleries, NY, 63, Maxwell Galleries, San Francisco, 64, Badcock Galleries, NY, 67, FAR Galleries, NY, 70, Armstrong Galleries, NY, 85, 87, Hammer Galleries, NY, 94, Hudson River Gallery, Dobbs Ferry, NY, 2001; Group exhibs, Albany Inst Hist & Art, Am Fedn Arts, Bulter Inst Am Art, Libr Cong, Nat Acad, Pa Acad Fine Art, Whitney Mus Am Art, Collection Nat Portrait Gallery, Munson-Williams-Proctor Inst, Bates Coll, Brit Mus, Century Asn, and many others. *Teaching:* Instr private painting classes, 65-03, Parsons Sch Design, 83. *Awards:* Louis C Tiffany Found Grant, 56, 60; 11 Gold Medals, Soc Illustrators, NY, 60-85; Purchase Prize, Am Acad Arts and Letters, 65, 84; Obrig Prize Painting, Nat Acas, 90; Benjamin Altman Figure Prize, 92; Soc Illustrators Hall Fame, 2002. *Bibliog:* David Finn (auth), Portrait of the Artist, Running, 2005; Communication Arts, Profile 75; Am Artist, Profile 71. *Mem:* Nat Acad (acad, 97); Century Asn

SCHWARTZ, DAVID
CURATOR
b Queens, New York. *Study:* SUNY Purchase, BFA. *Collection Arranged:* Changing the Picture: The Emergence of African-Americans in Television; The Living-Room Candidate: Television and Presidential Campaigns 1952-1992; Independent America: New Film 1978-188; Films That Tell Time: A Ken Jacobs Retrospective. *Pos:* Programmer, Cinema Arts Centre, Huntington, NY; chief film cur, Mus Moving Image, 1985-; dir programming, Hamptons Int Film Festival, 1988; panelist, Nat Endowment for the Arts, NY State Coun on Arts, Jerome Found, MacDowell Colony for the Arts, Ind Tv Svc

SCHWARTZ, LILLIAN (FELDMAN)
FILMMAKER
b Cincinnati, Ohio, July 13, 1927. *Study:* Univ Cincinnati. *Hon Degrees:* Kean Col, NJ, LHD, 88. *Work:* Mus Mod Art, NY; Moderna Museet, Stockholm, Sweden; Stedlijk Mus Art, Amsterdam, Holland; Los Angeles Co Mus Art; Newark Mus Art, NJ. *Comn:* Painting/collage, Columbia Univ, NY, 67; murals, Int Bus Machines, Zurich, Switz, 72, sculpture, Miami, Fla, 77; New York Philharmonic, 76; mural, Am Telephone & Telegraph, Basking Ridge, NJ, 76; Hitachi, 88. *Exhib:* Mus Mod Art, NY, 68-69; Metrop Mus, NY, 72 & 73; Whitney Mus Am Art, NY, 73; 25th Int Film Festival, Cannes, France, 74; Hirshhorn Mus, Washington, DC, 75; Albright-Knox Art Gallery, Buffalo, NY, 76; Huntsville Mus, Ala, 78; Venice Biennial, 80; Grand Palais, Paris, 80; ELECTRA, La Musee d'Art Moderne de la Ville de Paris, France, 83; Lavillette, 88; IBM Gallery Sci & Art, 88; trav solo show, Retrospectives of Film, 2006. *Collection Arranged:* Archive Coll, Ohio State Univ. *Pos:* Consult, Lucent Technologies Bell Labs Innovations, 2001. *Teaching:* Prof, Univ Md, 77-; adj prof, Kean Univ, Union, NJ, 81- & Rutgers Univ; grad fac, Sch Visual Arts, New York City, 90-92. *Awards:* Video Expos, Victor Co, Japan, 80; Artist of the Month, Hitachi, Japan, 88; Fel, World Acad Art & Sci; and others. *Bibliog:* Keating Productions, The Artist and the Computer (film), Am Telephone & Telegraph, 76; Jankel (auth), Creative Computer Graphics, Cambridge Press, 84; BBC special, Battle of the Wills, 94. *Mem:* Artists Equity Asn (NY & NJ); Artists League Cent NJ; Nat Acad Television Arts & Sci; Soc Motion Pictures & Television Engineers; Independent Cinema Artists & Producers; and others. *Media:* Computer, Video Books, DVD, DV. *Res:* artists & art analysis. *Publ:* Auth, The Computer Artist's Handbook (with Laurens R Schwartz), Norton Publ, 92; The Mask of Shakespeare, Pixel, 92; Electronic Restoration, Piero delle Francesca, Visual Computer, 92; Scientific American, 94; Leonardo: Appropriation Art, 96; co-auth, Leonardo da Vinci-The Hidden Mona Lisa, 2006. *Mailing Add:* 215 E 96th St Apt 8D New York NY 10128

SCHWARTZ, MARIANNE & ALAN E
COLLECTOR
b Detroit, Mich, Dec 21, 1925. *Study:* Univ Mich, BA, 1947; Harvard Law Sch, LLB, 1950. *Hon Degrees:* Wayne State Univ, LLD, 1983; Univ Detroit, LLD, 1985. *Pos:* Special asst, counsel NY State Crime Comn, 1951; assoc, Kelley, Drye & Warren, New York, 1951-52; dir, Detroit Symphony Orchestra; mem, Honigman, Miller, Schwartz & Cohn, Detroit, 1952-; bd dir, Pulte Corp, Detroit Renaissance, New Detroit, Jewish Welfare Fedn Detroit, Wayne State Univ Found & United Found; trustee, Community Found for Southeastern Mich; adv mem, Arts Comn, City of Detroit; past mem, investment comt, Skillman Found. *Awards:* Mich Heritage Hall of Fame award, 1984; George W Romney Award for Lifetime Achievement in Volunteerism, 1994; Max M Fisher Community Serv Award, 1997; named one of Top 200 Collectors, ARTnews mag, 2004-13. *Mem:* Mich Bar Asn Clubs; Franklin Hills Co; Detroit, Econ. *Collection:* Old masters; modern prints. *Publ:* Ed, Harvard Law Rev, 1950. *Mailing Add:* 4120 Echo Rd Bloomfield Hills MI 48302-1941

SCHWARTZ, MARVIN D
HISTORIAN
b New York, NY, 1926. *Study:* City Coll New York, BS, 46; Inst Fine Arts, NY Univ, 47-51; Univ Del, MA, 54. *Collection Arranged:* 19th Century Am Tupperware Collection, Mus Modern Art. *Pos:* Jr cur, Detroit Inst Arts, 51-52; cur decorative arts & indust design lab, Brooklyn Mus, 54-68, ed publ, 59-60; adv dept design, Sears, Roebuck & Co, 64-72; auth, weekly antiques column, New York Times, 66-72; lectr & consult, Metrop Mus Art, 68-; NY ed, Antique Monthly, 74-93. *Teaching:* Lectr, City Col NY, 48-51 & 56-64, State Univ NY, Purchase, 69-82 & NY Sch Interior Design, 94-. *Awards:* Stipend, Belg-Am Educ Found. *Mem:* Soc Archit Historians; Coll Art Asn Am; fel HF DuPont Winterthur Mus; Nat Trust. *Res:* History of furniture. *Interests:* 19th century silver. *Publ:* Auth, Collectors Guide to American Clocks, 75; auth, Collectors Guide to American Silver, 75; plus many others; auth articles Grove Dict Art. *Mailing Add:* Educ Dept Metrop Mus of Art 5th Ave & 82nd St New York NY 10028

SCHWARTZ, RUTH
PAINTER, INSTRUCTOR
b Sept 24, 1927. *Study:* studied with Leo Manso, Great Neck, Long Island, NY Art Studio Sch, Art In America; Empire State Col, 84, Harry Sternberg, Art Students League, Jerry Okimoto, Great Neck, Long Island, NY, Sch Art in America, Great Neck, Rd, Long Island, NY. *Work:* John T Mather Mem Hosp, Port Jefferson, NY; Atlantic Co Pub Libr, Atlantic City, NJ; Albright-Knox Art Gallery; and many other private & public collections here & abroad. *Exhib:* Long Island Artists, Nassau Co Mus Fine Arts, Roslyn Harbor, NY, 85; 43rd Western NY Exhib, Albright-Knox Gallery, Buffalo, NY, 90; Chautauqua Inst, NY; Burchfield Ctr, State Univ NY, Buffalo; State Col, Buffalo; Silvermine Guild of Artists, Inc, New Canaan, Conn; The Breakers, Palm Beach, Fla; Am Acad & Inst Arts & Letters, NYC; Nat Arts Club, Gramercy Park, NYC; Veridian Gallery, NYC; Central Hall Gallery, NYC; Century Village Art Exhibs, Fla. *Teaching:* Instr, USDAN Ctr Performing & Creative Arts, Wheatley Heights, Long Island, NY, 81-88, Jewish Ctr, NY Forest Rd, Amherst, NY, Birchfield Art Ctr, Buffalo, NY, Elmwood Ave; Albright-Knox Art Gallery, Buffalo, NY, 89-; Art with Artists, Century Village, W Palm Beach, Fla; art instr, Century

Village, West Palm Beach, Fla, Tradition Retirement Res, West Palm Beach, Fla. *Awards:* NAWA Award, 78, 80, 83, 85 & 88; Audubon Artists Citation of Merit, Am Acad & Inst Arts & Letters, 80; C Whinston Memorial Works on Canvas Award, Nat Asn Women Artists, 88. *Bibliog:* Park East (auth), article, Artspeak, 82; Malcolm Preston (auth), An invitational show, Newsday, 84. *Mem:* Nat Asn Women Artists (oil jury chmn, 80-81); Audubon Artists; Artist's Equity of NY; Buffalo Soc Artists (steering comt, 90). *Media:* Collage, Painting, Drawing. *Specialty:* 2 dimensional works on paper and canvas. *Interests:* Int Folk Dancing, Theater, Opera, Ballet, Piano, Reading, Crocheting, Pvt Collectors, Film, Concerts, Creative Writing, Poetry. *Collection:* Here (USA) and Abroad, Israel, Panama Canal, Rev Pederson, United Methodist Church. *Publ:* Park East (periodical), Merrick Life. *Dealer:* Art Dialogue Gallery One Linwood Ave Buffalo NY 14209-2203; Albright-Knox Art Gallery, Buffalo, NY. *Mailing Add:* 1 Cambridge A West Palm Beach FL 33417-1301

SCHWARTZ, SING-SI
PHOTOGRAPHER
b New York, NY, Oct 20, 1954. *Study:* New Sch for Social Res, advan photo printing with George Tice; psychol portraiture with Phillippe Halsman, 73; Rochester Inst Technol, AAS, 75, BS, 77; Artist in Res, Vermont Studio Ctr. *Comn:* Photograph, Burma Airline & posters, Burma Govt, 71; photograph, Vt Bi-Centennial Comn, 75; photographic mural, Wool Bur, Chicago Hq, 81; Eastern Spirit Western World, Transparencies in the film on artist, Diana Kan, 88. *Exhib:* Solo exhibs, Pen & Brush Club, NY, 77 & 85, Rochester Inst Tecnol, NY, 77, Dawson Gristmill Gallery, Vt, 77, Portchester Libr, NY, 78, Photographers Place, 86, Backer and Spielvogel, 86 & Nat Arts Club, NY, 88, Salmagundi Club, 2005. *Pos:* Mem staff, Villager Newspaper, New York, 68-74; photogr/correspondent, Cosmorama Pictorial, Hong Kong, 70-; photogr ed, New York Air, 83-85, & The New York Scene, 83-87. *Teaching:* Instr, Int Ctr Photog, New York, 81-88; adj prof, New York Univ, 83-84; Instr, New Brunswick Craft Sch, British Columbia, Can, 85. *Awards:* Elected as one of 100 outstanding Chinese abroad for accomplishments in photography, Chinese Govt, Taiwan, 71-77. *Bibliog:* Beautiful girls of Hong Kong seen through the eyes of photographer Sing-Si Schwartz, Ming-Pao Weekly, Hong Kong, 8/15/71; article, Interior Design, 10/81. *Mem:* Nat Arts Club; Am Soc Mag Photogr; assoc Allied Artists Am; Overseas Press Club. *Publ:* Photogr, Creating with Card Weaving, Crown Publ Inc, 73; photogr, The How and Why of Chinese Painting, Van Nostrand, 74; contribr, 40 American Watercolorists & How They Work, Watson-Guptill, 77; photogr, Joan Whitney Payson Gallery of Art, Westbrook Col, Maine, 77; photogr, A guide to flowers and flower painting, North Light, 80; Scientific Experiments for Kids, Harper & Row, 88; From the Desk of, Harcourt Brace Jovanovich, 89

SCHWARZ, JUDITH
SCULPTOR, DRAFTSMAN
b Can, Nov 26, 1944. *Study:* Univ BC, BA, 66; York Univ, MFA, 78. *Work:* Art Gallery Ont; Art Gallery Windsor; Hamilton Art Gallery; Nat Gallery Can; Oakville Galleries. *Comn:* Bronze sculpture, Skydome Corp, 90; Bronze & Steel sculpture, Waterpark Pl, 92. *Exhib:* Judith Schwarz, AGYU, York Univ, Toronto, 90; 9 x Toronto, Polytechnic Gallery, Newcastle-Upon-Tyne, Great Brit, 90; Legal Perspective, McMichael Can Art Collection, Kleinburg, Ont, 92; 64-94 Contemp Decades, ECIAD, Vancouver, Brit Columbia, 94; Fictive Space, Illingworth Kerr Gallery, Calgary, Alta, 94; Looking Back 111: 1986-1990, SAAG, Lethbridge, Alta, 95; Review 11, Mercer Union Gallery, Toronto, 96; Threshold, Power Plant, Toronto, Ont, 98. *Pos:* Mem bd, Mercer Union Gallery, 80-, Toronto Sculpture Garden, 84-88; pres, Mercer Union Gallery, 83-88; bd mem, Art Gallery York Univ, Toronto, 89-; bd mem, Art Gallery Ont, Toronto, 91-97. *Teaching:* Asst prof sculpture & drawing, York Univ, Toronto, Can, 78-, Assoc dir MFA Prog, 87-89, dir, MFA Prog, 94-97. *Awards:* Sr Grant Award, Ont Arts Coun, 93; Sr A Grant Award, Can Coun, 91, 92 & 96; Release Time Teaching Fel, York Univ, 96. *Bibliog:* Grant Arnold (auth), Disjunctions of Experience (exhib catalog), Art Gallery Windsor, 89; Annette Mangaard (dir), A Dialogue with Vision: The Art of Spring Hurlbut and Judith Schwarz (film), 90; Thomas McEvilley (auth), Fictive Space: The Collaboration of Judith Schwarz and Arlene Stamp (exhib catalog), Illingworth Kerr Gallery, 94. *Mem:* Adv mem Ont Arts Coun. *Dealer:* S L Simpson Gallery 515 Queen St W Toronto Ont M5V 2B4. *Mailing Add:* 26 Noble St Unit 7 Toronto ON M6K 2C9 Canada

SCHWEBEL, RENATA MANASSE
SCULPTOR
b Zwickau, Ger, Mar 6, 1930; US citizen. *Study:* Antioch Coll, BA, 53; Columbia Univ, MFA, 61; Art Students League, 68. *Work:* Am Airlines, Irvine, Calif; Jule Collins Smith Mus, Auburn, Ala; Comcraft Indust, Nairobi, Kenya; Southwest Bell, Houston; Heinrich Gruber House, Berlin, Ger; Colt Industs, NY; Columbia Univ, NY; Mus For Art, Sofia, Bulgaria; Housatonic Mus, Conn. *Comn:* Var pvt collections. *Exhib:* Art of Northeast, Silvermine Guild, US Ann, 72, 76, 80, 95 & 98; Hudson River Mus Competitions, NY; Wadsworth Atheneum; New Britain Mus, Am Cult Ctrs, Egypt, Israel, Stamford Mus & Chesterwood Mus; Grounds for Sculpture, Kyoto, Japan & Stockholm, Sweden; Governors Island, New York; solo exhib, Sculpture Ctr, NY; Katonah Gallery, Pelham Art Ctr, Berman/Daferner Gallery, NY; Carriage Barn Art Ctr, New Canaan Ct, 2013. *Pos:* Pres, Sculpture Guild, 80-83; trustee, Sculpture Ctr, NY, 80-86, cmn exhib comt, 84-86; bd dir, Fine Arts Fedn NY, 84, 85, 86 & Ams for Peace Now, 91-2001. *Awards:* Chaim Gross Found Award, 80; Medal of Honor, Nat Asn Women Artists, 81; Medal of Honor, Audubon Artists, 82; and many others. *Bibliog:* Padavano (auth), The Process of Sculpture, Doubleday, 81; Watson-Jones (auth), Contemporary American Women Sculptors, Oryx Press; Benton (auth), The Art of Welded Sculpture, Van Nostrand Reinhold; Les Krantz (auth), American Artists, Facts on File Publications. *Mem:* Sculptors Guild (pres, 80-83); Audubon Artists; Nat Asn Women Artists; NY Soc Women Artists; Silvermine Guild; Conn Acad Fine Arts. *Media:* Welded Metal, Cast Metal and Wood. *Mailing Add:* 10 Dogwood Hills Pound Ridge NY 10570

SCHWEDER, ALEX
ARCHITECT
Study: Sch Archit, Pratt Inst, BArch, 1993; Sch Archit, Princeton Univ, NJ, MArch, 1998. *Exhib:* Latent Space, Henry Urbach and Neth Archit Inst, Rotterdam, 2002; solo exhibs, Parsons Sch Design, New York, 2004, Henry Urbach Archit, New York, 2005, Tacoma Art Mus, 2007, Chinati Found, Marfa, Tex, 2009 & San Francisco Mus Mod Art, 2009; Three Rooms, Am Acad in Rome, 2006; Sparkle then Fade, Tacoma Art Mus, 2007; Dark Matters, Yerba Buena Ctr for Arts, Calif, 2007; 246 and Counting, San Francisco Mus Mod Art, 2008; Murmurs, Cranbrook Mus, Detroit, 2009. *Pos:* Intern, Edward Larabee Barnes & Assocs, New York, 1990; draftsman, Beckhard Richland Architects, New York, 1991-93, Leo Blackman Archit, New York, 1993-97; project architect, Reserve Consultants Ltd, Seattle, 2001-08. *Teaching:* Lectr, Univ Greenwich, London, 2005, Pratt Inst, Brooklyn, 2006, Portland Art Mus, 2008, Colgate Univ, NY, 2008, Harvard Univ, 2008, San Francisco Mus Mod Art, 2009; adj prof, Southern Calif Inst Archit, Los Angeles, 2007. *Awards:* Rome Prize, Am Acad in Rome, 2005; Artist Pension Trust, Los Angeles, 2006; Pollock-Krasner Found Grant, 2008. *Bibliog:* Anna Fahey (auth), Pee and Sympathy, Seattle Weekly, 10/4/2001; Ann Landi (auth), Interior Motives, ARTNews, 1/2002; Regina Hackett, Lively 'Ergonomicon' plumbs environments awash in fantasy, Seattle-Post Intelligencer, 2/25/2005; Martha Schwendener (auth), Proof That Objects Are People too (Well, Almost), NY Times, 5/18/2007; Michael H Hodges (auth), Artology, Science and Art Collide, The Detroit News, 11/18/2009. *Dealer:* Jack Hanley Gallery 163 Watts New York NY 10013; Lawrimore Project 831 Airport Way S Seattle WA 98134

SCHWEITZER, JOHN ANDREW
COLLAGE ARTIST, CURATOR
b Simcoe, Ont, Can, Oct 6, 1952. *Study:* Univ Western Ont, London, with Paterson Ewen & Michael Ondaatje, scholar, 73, Gold Medal Visual Arts, 73, BFA (hons, visual arts), 74; York Univ, Toronto, with Vera Frenkel & Sir Anthony Caro, MFA(painting), 78, Clement Greenberg, 79; Robert Motherwell, 89 & 91; Northrop Frye, 90. *Work:* York Univ, Toronto, Ont; Lynnwood Arts Ctr, Simcoe, Ont; Nat Capital Comn; La Citadelle, Quebec City; McIntosh Gallery, Univ Western Ont, London; Univ de Montreal, Que; Art Gallery Windsor, Ont; Mc Gill Univ, McCord Mus, Montreal, Que, Batcrest Ctr, Toronto, Ont; Bibliotheque Nat, Montreal; Musee de Joliette, Que; Univ Cape Brenton, Nova Scotia. *Comn:* Mus emblem, Ont Heritage Ctr, Delhi, Ont, 90; Mnemosyne (libr mural), Grand Erie Dist Bd Educ, Brantford, Ont, 91; The Equine Trilogy book design, comn by Dr JL Southin, McGill Univ, Montréal, Que, 94; Hosp Gén Montréal, Que, 96; Restaurant Toqué, Montréal, Que, 97; Astral Media, Montreal, Que, 99; comn by Charlie Trotter, Chicago, 2000; emblem, Montreal Print Collectors Soc, 2001. *Exhib:* Homage to Duchamp, London Regional Art Gallery, Ont, 78; Accrochage Gallerie Suzanne Bollag, Zurich, 74; No Solution-A Suspense Thriller, Vancouver Art Gallery, BC, 78; Re:union, Art Gallery York Univ, Toronto, Ont, 80; Parallels; Girardoni: Schweitzer, Stephen Haller Fine Art, NY, 91; Sunt Lacrimae Rerum, Champigny, Montréal, Que, 92; Power Plant, Toronto, Ont, 97; The Pilgrimage, McGill Univ, Montreal, 97; Of Porphyry, Univ Western Ont, London, 99; The Erehwon Cycle, Centaur Theatre, Montreal, 99; The Arcadian Suite, Goethe-Institut, Toronto, Ont, 99; Galerie Christine Chassay, Montreal, Que, 2000; The Shapes of Time: 1991-2001, Visual Art Ctr, Montreal, Que, 2001. *Collection Arranged:* Mapplethorpe: 1978-1984, Galerie John A Schweitzer, 84; Bauhaus: Zweite Generation, Galerie John A Schweitzer, 85; Art Against AIDS (auth, catalog), Galerie John A Schweitzer, 86; Domus via Domus, Galerie John A Schweitzer, 88; Five Architectures (coauth, catalog), Galerie John A Schweitzer, 89; Duane Michals: Upside Down, Galerie John A Schweitzer, 89; Bolley Calzetta: Une Perspective de XV Ans (coauth, catalog), Galerie John A Schweitzer, 89. *Pos:* Vpres, Can Cult Progs, Montréal, Que, 80-84; trustee, La La La Human Steps Dance Co, Montréal, Que, 85-90; pres, Found John A Schweitzer, Montréal, Que, 94-; art comt, UNICEF, 95-; acquisition comt, Univ de Montreal, Que, 2000-. *Teaching:* Asst prof painting, York Univ, Toronto, Ont, 76-78; Bishop's Univ, Lennoxville, Que, 83, McGill Univ, Montréal, Que, 85 & 95 & Banff Ctr, Alta, 87; Goethe Inst, Toronto, 2000. *Awards:* John G Rowe Fine Arts Scholar, Univ Western Ont, London, 73; Grant Hall Soc, Queen's Univ, Kingston, Ont, 96; Rector's Circle, Universite de Montreal, Que, 98; N C James Soc, Univ Western Ont, 99; President's Circle, Mus des Beaux-Arts de Montreal, 2000; Prix des Amisdm Mus d'Art Contemp, Montreal, Que, 2000. *Bibliog:* Howard Reitman (dir), Art Appreciation: City Beat (film), Can Broadcasting Corp, 94; Margaret Atwood (auth), Underbrush Man, 97; Ricardo L Castro (auth), The Pilgrimage, 98; James Miller (auth), Of Porphyry, 99; The Arcadian Suite, 99; John K Grande (auth) Border Crossings, 2000; Melanie Reinblatt (auth), ETC: MTL, 2000; Monique Brunet Weinmann (auth), Vie des Art, 2001; Ricardo L Castro (auth), The Shapes of Time: 1991-2001, 2001. *Mem:* Docomomo Int, Montréal, Que; Art & Design Coun Embassy Row, Montréal, Que (chmn, 92-); Montréal Print Collectors Soc. *Media:* Collage, Painting. *Collection:* 20th Century American & European painting, sculpture, photography, architectural and decorative arts; outsider and tribal art. *Publ:* Auth, Louis Comtois and the hagiographical icon, ELAAC, 90; Parallels; Girardoni: Schweitzer, Stephen Haller Fine Art, 91; Marcel Saint-Pierre, a theatrical prescience, ELAAC, 91; Anish Kapoor drawings at the Tate Gallery, London, ETC Montréal, 91; Peter Dickinson, ETC, Montréal, 96; XXV Reunion, Univ Western Ont Press, London, 99. *Dealer:* Galerie Christiane Chassay 358 rue Sherbrooke Est Montréal Québec Canada H2X 1E6. *Mailing Add:* 1545 Ave Docteur-Penfield Ste 503 Montreal PQ H3G 1C7 Canada

SCHWEIZER, PAUL DOUGLAS
MUSEUM DIRECTOR EMERITUS, ART HISTORIAN
b Brooklyn, NY, 1946. *Study:* Marietta Coll, Ohio, BA, 1968; Univ Del, MA, 1974, PhD, 1979. *Collection Arranged:* Avant-Garde Painting & Sculpture in Am: 1910-25 (collab effort, co-auth, catalog), Del Art Mus, spring 1975; Edward Moran, Del Art Mus, 1979; North Country Folk Art, 1982, Cole's Course of Empire, 1983 & The Voyage of Life: Paintings, Drawings, & Prints, 1985, Munson-Williams-Proctor Inst, Utica, NY; 200 Yrs of Am Art, 1986-87, The Art of Trenton Falls, 1989, Munson-Williams-Proctor Inst, Utica, NY, 1986-87; Alex Katz: A Drawing

Retrospective, 1991; Life Lines - Am Master Drawings, 1788-1962, Munson-Williams-Proctor Inst, Utica, NY, 1994; Ferdinand Richardt's Drawings & Am: 1855-1859, 2007. *Pos:* Res consult, Choptank Collection, Middletown, Del, 1976-77; cur collections, St Lawrence Univ, Canton, NY, 1977-78, dir, Richard F Brush Art Gallery, 1978-80; dir & chief cur, Mus Art, Munson-Williams-Proctor Inst, Utica, NY, 1980-2012, dir emer, 2012-; pres, bd of trustees, Williamstown Regional Art Conservation Lab, 1987-91 & Gallery Asn NY State, 1998-2000. *Teaching:* Instr art hist, Univ Del, Wilmington, 1976; instr art hist, St Lawrence Univ, 1977-78, asst prof fine arts, 1978-80; adj fac Pratt at Munson-Williams-Proctor Arts Inst, 2000-. *Awards:* Unidel Fel, Univ Del, 1972-76. *Mem:* Coll Art Asn; Asn Art Mus Dirs. *Res:* American Painting drawings & Sculpture of the 19th & 20th centuries; Historial American Drawings. *Publ:* Edward Wales Root and American Modernism, co-auth, Auspicious Vision: Edward Wales Root and American Modernism, Utica, NY: Munson-Williams- Proctor Arts Institute, 2-55, 2008; Fernnand Richardt: Draftsman, Ferdinand Richardt: Drawings of America, 1855-1859, Utica, NY: Munson-Williams-Proctor Arts Institute, 17-23, 2008; Catalog essay on Edward Moran's Marsh Landscape in The Sewell C Biggs Collection of American Art, Dover, DE: Biggs Museum of American Art, 2002; William J Weaver and His 'Chymical and Mechanical' Portraits of Alexander Hamilton, American Art Journal, 82-101, 1999; Fruits of Perseverance: The Art of Rubens Peale, 1855-1865, The Peale Family: Creation of a Legacy, New York: Abbeville Press, 169-85, 1996; William J Weaver's Secret Art of Multiplying Pictures, Portrait and Portrait Making in the American Northeast, The Dublin Seminar for New England Folklife: Annual Proceedings, Boston University, 151-66, June 24-26, 1994; Thomas Cole's The Voyage of Life, Manson-Williams-Protctor Arts Inst, Utica, NY, 2014. *Mailing Add:* Munson-Williams-Proctor Arts Inst 310 Genesee St Utica NY 13502

SCHWENINGER, ANN ROZZELLE
ILLUSTRATOR
b Boulder, Colo, Aug 1, 1951. *Study:* Univ Colo, 69-72; Calif Inst Arts, BFA, 73-75; also with Uri Shulevitz and Peter Hopkins, 75-. *Awards:* Notable Bk Award, Am Libr Asn, 82. *Media:* Watercolor, Pencil. *Publ:* Illusr, ABC Cat, Harper & Row, 83; illusr, Tales of Amanda Pig, Dial Press, 83; illusr, The Musicians of Bremen, 83 & illusr, Silent Night, 83, Western Publ; auth & illusr, Christmas Secrets, Viking Press, 84; and many others. *Mailing Add:* 2261 Rte 82 Ancram NY 12502

SCHWIEGER, C ROBERT
EDUCATOR, PRINTMAKER
b Scottsbluff, Nebr, Dec 5, 1936. *Study:* Nebr Western Col, AA; Chadron State Col, BFA (educ); Univ Northern Colo, MA; Univ Denver, MFA. *Work:* Ohio State Univ; Miss Art Asn; Ga Inst Technol; Olivet Col, Mich; Oklahoma Art Ctr, Oklahoma City; and others. *Comn:* Gilded gold & mixed media on glass mural, Univ Northern Colo, 66. *Exhib:* Am Printmakers Invitational, Univ SDak; St Cloud State Univ; Univ Dallas; Prints of the 80's, Pratt Manhattan Gallery & Schafler Gallery, NY, 90; Nat Invitation Screenprint Traveling Exhib, Sch Mus Fine Arts, Boston, Mass; and others. *Teaching:* Assoc prof, Minot State Univ, 67-81, coordr art & prof, 81- 90, prof & chmn, dept art; prof & chmn, art dept, Mo Southern State Col, 90-91, prof art, 91-2000; adj prof art, Neb Wesleyan Univ, 2002-. *Awards:* Purchase Award, Univ Tex, Austin; Northwest Printmakers Int Jury Commendation, Seattle Art Mus, 71; 16th Nat Print & Drawing Exhib Jury Commendation, Okla Art Ctr, 74. *Bibliog:* The Complete Printmaker, Ross-Romano-Ross, rev ed, 89; Printmaking Techniques, Ayers Watson-Guptil Publ, 93; Waterbased Printing Inks Watercolor, Am Artist Publ, 93. *Mailing Add:* 7121 Shamrock Rd Lincoln NE 68506

SCOATES, CHRISTOPHER
ART SCHOOL ADMINISTRATOR, CURATOR
Study: attended Salisbury Coll Art; Univ Fla, BFA, 1984; Cranbrook Acad Art, MFA, 1986. *Collection Arranged:* Pieces of 9: Reframing the Collection, Univ Art Mus, CSULB, 2010, Perpetual Motion: Michael Goldberg, 2010, Goldmine: Contemporary Works from the Collection of Sirje and Michael Gold, 2011, Peace Press Graphics: Art in the Pursuit of Social Change, 2011, Lou Reed, Metal Machine Trio: The Creation of the Universe, 2012, Static Noise: The Photographs of Rhona Bitner, 2012, Gabe Bartalos: Abhorance and Obsession, 2013; and many others. *Pos:* dir, curator, Churchman Fehsenfeld Gallery, Indianapolis, Ind, 86-89; curatorial assoc contemporary art, Indianapolis Mus Art, 89-90; co-founder, Cowboys and Indians, 1989-2007; curator contemporary art, Wash Univ Gallery Art, St. Louis, Mo, 90-93; dir, Atlanta Coll Art Gallery, Ga, 1993-2000; prodr, Razorfish, Los Angeles, Calif, 2000-2001; acting dir, chief curator, Univ Art Mus, Univ Calif, Santa Barbara, 2002-2003, chief curator, 2002-2005; dir, Univ Art Mus, Calif State Univ, Long Beach, Calif, 2005-2014; founder, co-dir, 5D Institute: The Future of Immersive Design Conference, 2006-; dir, Cranbrook Acad Art, Bloomfield Hills, Mich, 2014-. *Publ:* A Conversation with Allan Wexler, Custom Built: A Twenty-Year Survey of Work by Allan Wexler (exhib catalog), Atlanta Coll Art Gallery, City Gallery at Chastain, 99; Ada Tolla and Giuseppe Lignano Speak with Christopher Scoates, LOT-EK: MDU (exhib catalog), Univ Art Mus, Univ Calif Santa Barbara, NY, D.A.P., 2003; Going Underground: The Nuclear Weapons Series by Paul Shambroom, Paul Shambroom: Picturing Power (exhib catalog), Weisman Art Mus, Univ Minn, NY, D.A.P., 2007; Bullet Proof...I Wish I Was: The Lighting and Stage Design of Andi Watson, Essays by Dick Hebdige, J Fiona Ragheb, and Christopher Scoates, San Francisco, Chronicle Books, 2011; Brian Eno: Visual Music, essays by Steve Dietz, Brian Dillon, and Christopher Scoates, San Francisco, Chronicle Books 2013; and many others. *Mailing Add:* 39221 Woodward Ave Bloomfield Hills MI 48303

SCOGIN, MACK
ARCHITECT, EDUCATOR
Study: Ga Inst Tech, Atlanta, BArch, 66. *Pos:* Sr design, archit Heery & Heery Archits & Engs, Inc, 67-81, vpres, coordr, 78-81, pres, COO, dir design, 81-84; principal, Scogin Elam & Bray Archits, Inc, Atlanta, 84-2000, Mack Scogin Merrill Elam Archits, Inc, Atlanta, 2000-. *Awards:* Arnold W Brunner Meml Prize in Archit, Am Acad Arts and Letts, 2011. *Mem:* Nat Acad (assoc, 92, acad, 94-), Archit Soc, Atlanta (founding mem, mem bd sponsors 83—88); Am Inst of Archit's (nat comt on design, chmn steering comt 1987). *Mailing Add:* Mack Scogin Merrill Elam Archit Inc 111 JW Dobbs Ave Atlanta GA 30303

SCOTT, ARDEN
SCULPTOR
b Port Chester, NY, Oct 21, 1938. *Comn:* Nassau Co Mus Fine Arts, NY, 77; pub sculpture, Riverhead, NY, 81; Atlanta Arts Festival, 83; Greenport Maritime Monument, 86. *Exhib:* one-person shows, 112 Greene Gallery, NY, 74, AIR Gallery, NY, 97, Erie Art Mus, Pa, 99, AA Sites, NY, 2000, Oysterponds Mus, Orient, NY, 2004, Sculpture in the Garden, Greenport, NY, 2002, Van Deb Editions, 2006, Kathryn Markel Gallery, NY, 2007; Whitney Mus Biennial, 73; Aberdeen Arts Mus, Scotland, 83; Ways of Wood, Queens Col, NY, 84; Sculpture Ctr, NY, 84; Guild Hall Mus, EHampton, NY, 85; Live Steam Voices (performance), NY Harbor, 87 & Erie Canal, 88; Nat Print Exhib, Brooklyn Mus Art, 89; Cleveland Inst Art, Ohio,92; Printmaking Workshop Gallery, NY, 93; Sculpture Fest, Vt Arts Coun, Woodstock, 95; Outdoor Sculpture, SVt Art Ctr, Manchester, 96; Outdoor Sculpture Expo, Bristol, RI, 96; Parrish Art Mus, Southampton, NY, 98; Spirit of Place, Vt Arts Coun, Huntington, 98; Ahab's Wife, Newhouse Ctr Contemp Art, Staten Island, NY, 98; Van Deb Editions, Albright Knox, Buffalo, NY, 2002 & 2006; Long Island Maritime Mus, Sayville, NY, 2003; Northfork/Southfork, Parish AA Mus, Southampton, NY; Anthony A Giordano Gallery, Dowling col, Oakdale, NY, 2006; Current 2008, Garrison Art Ctr, Garrison, NY, 2008; Pollack-Krasner Fel Gallery North, NY, 2008; Kathryn Markel Fine Arts, 2009; River Journey, Cornwall on Hudson, NY, 2009; Women Printmakers, van Deb Ed, 2010; Benton-Nyce Gallery, NY, 2010; Hillwood Art Mus, CW Post, Long Island, NY, 2011; Art Encounters Preservation, Wentworth-Coolidge, Portsmouth, NH, 2011; Tension/Balance, Full Moon Art Ctr, 2012; Pratt Sculpture Garden, Brooklyn, NY; Peconic Landing Sculpture Garden, Greenport, NY. *Teaching:* Prof sculpture, Bard Col, 75-, Parsons Sch Design, 78-85 & Long Island Univ (semester prog), 91-95. *Awards:* NY State Coun Arts Award, 77; Guggenheim Fel, 81; Fel, NY State Found Arts, 88; Grant, Pollock-Krasner Found, 2001. *Bibliog:* Marcia Tucker (auth), Making it big, Ms Mag, 4/74; Brentano & Savitt, 112 Workshop/112 Greene, NY Univ Press, 81; Jack Somer (auth), A modern monument, Yachting Mag, 1/86; New York Times, 5/12/02, 8/4/02, 9/1/02, 5/15/04. *Media:* Miscellaneous. *Publ:* auth, (with Poppy Johnson), Sculpture and fiction, Bomb Mag, No 6, 83. *Dealer:* Richard Eagan Fine Art 72-74 Third St Hudson NY 12584; Kathryn Markel Fine Art 529 W 20th St 6W NY NY 10011; Van Deb Editions NY NY

SCOTT, B NIBBELINK (BARBARA GAE SCOTT)
PAINTER, SCULPTOR
b Columbia, Mo, July 23, 1944. *Study:* With Daniel Greene, 82-83, Albert Handell, 84 & Herman Margulies, 85. *Work:* Wichita Art Asn & Fourth Financial Ctr, Wichita, Kans; Am Ambassador's Collection, London; Mr & Mrs Gerald Michaud pvt collection, Wichita, Kans. *Exhib:* Kans Pastel Soc First Nat, Wichita Art Asn Gallery, 86-87; Pastel Soc Am, Nat Arts Club, NY, 86-90; Third Salon des Pastellistes France, Centre Culturel de la Ville, Lille, France, 87; Am Aid Soc, Mall Gallerie's, London, 88; Fourth Salon des Pastellistes France, Centre Culturel de la Ville de Compiegne, France, 88; Cassatt Pastel Soc, Berkley Gallery, Scottsdale, Ariz, 89. *Pos:* Prog chmn, Community Art Guild, Wichita, Kans, 83-84, pres, 84-85. *Teaching:* Pvt lessons. *Awards:* Honorary Award, Kans Small Oil Painting Exhib, 82; Prix de International Honneur, Third Salon des Pastellistes de France, 87; First Place US, Fifth Salon des Pastellistes de France, 89. *Mem:* Kans Pastel Soc (founder, pres, 84-90); Pastel Soc Am; Salmagundi Club; Societe des Pastellistes de France (hon pres US, 87-90); Kans Acad Oil Painters. *Media:* Pastel, Oil; Clay. *Publ:* Auth, Discovering my potential with pastel, Am Artists, 7/87. *Mailing Add:* 8801 E Bradford Cir Wichita KS 67206-4044

SCOTT, BILL EARL
PAINTER
b Cumberland, Md, May 6, 1935. *Study:* Self taught. *Work:* Barnett Bank, Tampa, Fla; Busch Gardens, Tampa, FL; Havatampa Inc,Tampa, FL; Leigh Yawkey Woodson Art Mus, Wausau, WI; Tampa Parks Dept, Tampa, FL. *Comn:* 300 hand colored prints, Arthur Andersen, Tampa, 93; painting, Art in State Bldg, Starke, Fla, 96; 6 pieces, Art in Public Places, City of Tampa, FL; 11 Brush and ink paintings, Tampa Parks Dept, Tampa, FL; 6 paintings, USAA, Tampa, FL. *Exhib:* Watercolor USA, Springfield Art Mus, Mo, 91; Southeastern W/C VI, Deland Mus Art, Fla, 91; Bird in Art Exhib, Leigh Yawkey Woodson Mus Art, Wis, 93; Fla Artists Group, Mus Art Sci, Daytona Beach, 94; Watercolor Soc of Ala, Gladsden Ctr, 95; 25th Ann Fla Watercolor Soc, St Petersburg, Mus Art, 96; Albemarle Gallery, London, 2006; Looking Through, Hollis Taggart Galleries, NY, 2007. *Mem:* Nat Watercolor Asn; Fla Watercolor Soc; Fla Artists Group; Prof Asn Visual Artists. *Media:* Watercolor, Acrylic. *Mailing Add:* 5504 Bandera Rd Ste 510 San Antonio TX 78238-1946

SCOTT, CAMPBELL
PRINTMAKER, SCULPTOR
b Milngavie, Scotland, Oct 5, 1930; Can citizen. *Study:* Studied with S W Hayter, Paris; Glasgow Sch Art, Scotland. *Work:* British Mus, London; Bibliot Nat, Paris; Scottish Nat Gallery Mod Art; Montreal Mus Art Can; Victoria & Albert Mus; Art Gallery Ont Can; and others. *Comn:* Bronze sculpture, Pub Libr, Niagara Falls, Can; wood sculpture, Pub Libr, St Catharines, Can; Niagara on the Lake (mural), The Pumphouse Art Ctr; designer, St Mark's Church, Niagara-on-the-Lake, Can, 2005,

Addison Libr, Ont, Can, 2006. *Exhib:* FAAP Gravura, Sao Paulo, Brazil, 68; 1st British Int Print Biennale, Gt Brit, 69; Traveling Exhib, Nat Gallery Can, Ottawa, 69; 4th Am Biennial Engraving, Santiago, Chile, 70; Exhib Can Graphics, Can Embassy, Washington, DC, 71 & Pratt Inst, NY, 71; Niagara Pumphouse Visual Art Ctr, Can, 94, 99. *Media:* Sculpture (bronze, aluminum), Graphics (woodcuts, etchings, engravings, computer laser prints), Jewelry (gold and silver), Architecture. *Publ:* Auth, article, City and Country Home, Maclean Hunter Publ, 9/85; article, House and Garden (Brit ed), Conde Publ, 11/87. *Mailing Add:* 89 Byron Niagara on the Lake ON L0S 1J0 Canada

SCOTT, CONCETTA CIOTTI
PAINTER, INSTRUCTOR

b Philadelphia, PA, Jan 17, 1927. *Study:* Moore Coll of Arts and Design, Assoc, 46-51. *Work:* Les Amis de la Grande Vigne Coll, Dinan, Brittany, France. *Exhib:* To Everything a Season, Charles Summer Sch Mus, Washington, DC, 90; Selections from Series, Barry Gallery, Marymount Univ, Arlington, VA, 94; Ann Juried Art Show, The Decoy Mus, Havre de Grace, MD, 95; 96th Int Jury Show, PWCS-Berman Gallery-Ursinus, Bryn Mawr, PA, 96; Int Miniature Show, MBGGS, Strathmore Hall, Bethesda, MD, 97-2004; Regional Juried Exhib, N Va Coll Cult Ctr, Annandale, VA, 99; 101st Int Philadelphia Watercolor Soc, Gregg Ctr, Am Col, Bryn Mawr, PA, 2001; Multiples Exhib, Juried Wilson Hall, Moore Coll Art, Philadelphia, PA, 2005; Vienna Mini Show, Va, 2005; Wash Watercolor Exhib, Strathmore Hall, Md, 2005; Juried Show, McLean Soc, 2005; 27th Juried Show, Va Watercolor Soc, 2006; 15th Juried Show, Central Va, 2006; Juried Show, Cumberland Art, Hagerstown, Md, 2006; Juried Int Miniature, Strathmore Hall, Bethesda, Md, 2007; The Baltimore Watercolor Soc, Strathmore Hall, Bethesda, Md, 2007; Miniature Show, Cobblestone Gallery, Alexandria, Va, 2007; Small Works, Carlisle Arts Learning Ctr, Carlisle, Pa, 2007; and others. *Pos:* Dir Art, Woodward & Lothrop Stores, Washington, DC, 59-63; chmn, convention, Nat Women's League Am Pen Women, Washington, DC, 83-84; chmn, programs & workshops, McLean Arts Club, McLean, VA, 2003-2005; prog chair, Mclean Art Soc, 2005-2007; vpres, McLean Art Soc, 2006-; art rep, Coun Arts Fairfax City, 2006-2007. *Teaching:* teacher, Melrose Acad, Melrose Park, PA, 51-53; teacher, Montesorri Sch of McLean, McLean, VA, 75-95; instr, Design/Miniature Pkg, Art Asn Fairfax Cty, 95-2004; demonstr & lectr, Md & Va, 2007-. *Awards:* Winsor Newton & Plaque, Fourteenth Virginia Watercolor Show, Winsor Newton, 93; The Archers-D Smith Award, 101st Intl, PWCS, Philadelphia Watercolor Soc, Oct-Dec, 2001; Grant to paint, 1 month, at La Grande Vigne Dinan, France; and others. *Bibliog:* Art News Editor, Fax News, C Scott, VA Tech, Fairfax Council of Arts Publ, 90; Rachel Woet (ed), Splash 6-Textures, North Light Books, Spring 2000; Tabitha Yeatts (auth), Framing the Still Life, Elan Magazine, D Reynolds Publ, Aug 2000 & 2005. *Mem:* Baltimore Watercolor Soc, Baltimore, MD; Philadelphia Watercolor Soc, Philadelphia, PA; Virginia Watercolor Soc, Roanoke, VA; Miniature Painters Sculptors, Gravers Soc, Washington, DC; Nat league Am Pen Women, Washington, DC; Potomac Valley Watercolor; Wash Watercolor Soc, Washington DC; Mclean Art Soc Art League, Alexandria, Va, Cider Paint Am Miniature Soc. *Media:* Pastels, Alkyds, Watercolor. *Res:* Miniature Art Hist: Middle E, India, W Europe. USA, 4th-20th century. *Interests:* painting; reading World News; music. *Collection:* MPR Asn, Alexandria, Va; Rosenberg Realtors MD; City of Dinan, France; Plv College Sweden, US. *Publ:* illusr, Move Over Mother Goose, Gryphon House, 87; Splash 6, North Light Books, 2000; Elan Magazine, 10/2000. *Mailing Add:* 1111 Dead Run Dr Mc Lean VA 22101-2126

SCOTT, DEBORAH EMONT
CURATOR

b Passaic, NJ. *Study:* Livingston Col, Rutgers Univ, BA; Oberlin Col, MA. *Collection Arranged:* Veda Reed, 79; Alan Shields (auth, catalog), Memphis Brooks Mus Art, Memphis, Tenn, 83-84; David Saunders, 84; 50 Years of Collecting: The Friends of Art at the Nelson, 84; Highlights from Kansas City Art Institute Alumni, 85; Jonathan Borofsky (auth, catalog), 88; Judith Shea, 89; Gerhard Richter, 89; John Ahearn, 90; Kathy Muehlemann, 91; Nate Fors, 91; Julian Schnabel, 91; Shuttlecocks: the Making of a Sculpture (auth, brochure), 94; Joel Shapiro, 95; Lewis deSoto, 96. *Pos:* Asst cur, Allen Mem Art Mus, Oberlin, Ohio, 77-79; cur, Memphis Brooks Mus Art, Memphis, Tenn, 79-83; cur, 20th century art, Nelson-Atkins Mus Art, Kansas City, 83-, chief cur, 98-2009; dir, CEO, Taft Mus Art, 2009-. *Bibliog:* Interview with Ursula Von Rydingsvard, Nelson Gallery Found & Yorkshire Sculpture Park, 97. *Mem:* Coll Art Asn. *Res:* 20th century art. *Publ:* Auth, Winners, Nat Endowment for the Arts/Mid-America Arts Alliance, 3/87; The Nelson-Atkins Museum of Art Henry Moore Sculpture Garden, Nelson-Atkins Mus Art, 6/89; Joan Backes, Hafnarborg Inst Cult & Fine Art, Hafnarfjordur, Iceland, 8/91; Joel Shapiro: the Figure in Nature, In: Joel Shapiro: Outdoors, Walker Art Inst & Nelson-Atkins Mus Art, 6/95; A modern sculpture initiative recent acquisitions at the Nelson-Atkins Museum, Apollo Mag, 11/96; contrib Celebrating Moore: Works from the Henry Moore Foundation, 98, Modern Sculpture at the Nelson-Atkins Mus Art: An Anniversary Celebration, 99, (CD Rom) Masterworks for Learning: A College Collection Catalogue, Allen Memorial Art Mus, Oberlin Col, 98. *Mailing Add:* 316 Pike St Cincinnati OH 45202

SCOTT, JOHN BELDON
HISTORIAN, EDUCATOR, WRITER

b Scottsburg, Ind, Aug 3, 1946. *Study:* Ind Univ, BA (history), 68; Rutgers Univ, MA (art history), 75, PhD (art history), 82. *Pos:* Ed, Rutgers Art Rev, 78-79; US Nat Comt, for the Hist of Art Int Congress of the Hist of Art, 2001-02; assoc editor, Cambridge World History of Religious Architecture. *Teaching:* Instr, Rutgers Univ, 77-79; lectr, Univ Pa, 81-82; asst, assoc prof to prof, Univ Iowa, 82-, Elizabeth M Stanley prof of arts, 2004-, dir, Sch Art and Art History, currently; vis mem Inst Advanced Study, Princeton, NJ, 1991-92, 2007, Robert Janson-La Palme Vis Prof in Art and Archaeology, 2007. *Awards:* Am Acad Rome Fel, 79-81; Delmas Found Fel, 82; Am Coun Learned Soc Fel, 84, 89; Am Philos Soc Grant, 84; Andrew W Mellon Fel, Univ Pa, 85; Nat Endowment of the Humanities Travel to Collections Grant, 1986; Gladys Krieble Delmas Found for Venetian Studies Grant, 1986; Nat Humanities Ctr Fel, 1993-94; Trinity Coll Barbieri Grant in Italian Hist, Barbieri Endowment for Italian Culture, 1994; Marta Sutton Weeks Fel, Stanford Humanities Ctr, Stanford Univ, 1999-2000; Graham Found for Advanced Studies in the Visual Arts Research Grant, 1999; Am Philos Soc Sabbatical Fel, 2000. *Mem:* Coll Art Asn (bd dir, 98); Soc Archit Historians (bd dir, 97-2000); Renaissance Soc Am; Midwest Art Hist Soc (bd dir, 1986-89); Coll Art Asn (bd dir nominating comt, 1998); Soc Archit Historians (bd dir, 1997-2000). *Res:* Italian Renaissance and Baroque; northern Baroque. *Publ:* S Ivo Alla Sapienza and Borromini's symbolic language, J Soc Archit Historians, 82; Urban VIII, Bernini and the Contess Matilda, L'Age D'or Du Mecenat (1598-1661), Paris, 85; The Meaning of Perseus and Andromeda in the Farnese Gallery and on the Rubens House, J of the Warburg and Courtauld Inst, 88; Pietro da Cortona's Painted Ceilings of Palazzo Barberini, Princeton Univ Press, 90; and others; Auth: Images of Nepotism: The Painted Ceilings of Palazzo Barberini, 1991, Archit for the Shroud: Relic and Ritual in Turin, 2003 (Charles Rufus Morey Book Award, Coll Art Asn, 2004), (articles have appeared in) Art Bulletin, Burlington Mag, Memoirs of Am Acad Rome, Storia dell'Arte, J of the Warburg and Courtauld Inst, J of Soc Archit Historians. *Mailing Add:* University Iowa School Art & Art History 150ABW 141 N Riverside Dr Iowa City IA 52242

SCOTT, JULIE
DIRECTOR

b St Louis, Mo, Aug 24, 1958. *Study:* Calif Inst of Integral Studies, MA (Cultural Anthropology); Regis Univ, MBA. *Pos:* Grand Master, pres, CEO, English Grand Lodge for the Ams of the Ancient Mystical Order Rosae Crucis, 2000- ; Dir on the Bd, Supreme Grand Lodge of AMORC; Dir, Rosicrucian Egyptian Mus, San Jose, California, 1995-. *Mailing Add:* Rosicrucian Egyptian Museum and Art Gallery 1342 Naglee Ave San Jose CA 95191

SCOTT, MICHAEL
PAINTER, PRINTMAKER

b Lawrence, Kans, 1952. *Study:* Kansas City Art Inst, BFA (Skowhegan Fel), 76; Univ Cincinnati, MFA, 78. *Work:* AT&T, Piscataway, NJ; Cincinnati Art Mus, Ohio; City of Covington, Ky; Ky Utilities, Carrollton, Ky; Manhattan Life Co, NY; and many others. *Comn:* Mural, Cincinnati Pub Libr, Ohio, 76; mural, comn by Bruce Shock, Cincinnati, 87. *Exhib:* Works on Paper, DeGraff Gallery, Holland, Mich, 88; solo exhib, DeGraff Gallery, Chicago, Ill, 88 & Sherry French Gallery, NY, 90, Joseph Chowning Gallery, San Francisco, Calif, 95, Cincinnati Art Gallery, 96, Cladbeck Gallery, Rockland Maine, 97, Linda Swartz Gallery, Lexington, Ky, 98 & Gerald Peters Gallery, Santa Fe, NMex, 99; Phoenix Installation, The Phoenix, Cincinnati, 89; Harmony & Discord, Va Mus Fine Arts, Richmond, 90; Waiting for Cadmium, Sherry French Gallery, NY, 90; The New Whitney Dissenters (traveling exhib), Sherry French Gallery, NY, Anchorage Mus Hist & Art, Alaska, Rockford Coll Art Gallery, Ill & Fitchburg Art Mus, Mass, 92-93; Expedition: Everglades--River of Grass (traveling exhib), Sherry French Gallery, NY, Henry Morrison Flagler Mus, Palm Beach, Fla, Deland Mus Art, Fla, Ctr Arts, Vero Beach, Fla, Alexander Brest Gallery & Mus, Jacksonville, Fla, 94-96; 61st Ann Nat Competition, Butler Mus Art, 97; Expedition: Great Lakes-The Power of Water (traveling exhib), Sherry French Gallery, NY, Krasl Art Ctr, St Joseph, Mich, Flint Inst Art, Mich & Dennos Mus, Traverse City, Mich, 99. *Teaching:* Instr drawing, Art Acad Cincinnati, 80-. *Awards:* Bououn Award, 77. *Bibliog:* Jackie Barrett (auth), This event would make Cinderella proud, Cincinnati Enquirer, D-5, 3/29/89; Ivan Amoto (auth), Singing the Cadmium Blues (color reproduction), Sci News, 168-169, 9/15/90; James F Cooper (auth), American realists get back to nature (reproduction), NY City Tribune, 16, 10/11/90. *Media:* All Media

SCOTT, SAM
PAINTER

b Chicago, Ill, Apr 7, 1940. *Study:* Univ Mich, BFA, 65; Md Inst Coll Art, MFA, 69; also with Grace Hartigan, David Hare, Joseph Goto, Zubel Kachadoorian. *Work:* Mus NMex, Santa Fe; Roswell Mus Fine Art, NMex; AT&T Corp Bldg, NY; Univ Iowa Fine Arts Mus, Iowa City; Phoenix Fine Arts Mus, Ariz; Midlands Bank, Denver; Albuquerque Mus Contemp Art, NMex; and others. *Comn:* Mural painting, Westinghouse Elec Corp Bldg, Norman, Okla, 72; mural, Jelco Corp Bldg, Minneapolis, Minn, 72. *Exhib:* Keats Gallery, Santa Fe, 85; Conlon Grenfelly Gallery, San Diego, 86; Robischon Gallery, Denver, 87; Sena West Gallery, Santa Fe, 87; Tucson Fine Art Mus, Tucson, 87; 10 Take 10 (retrospective), Colorado Springs Fine Arts Mus, 77; Phoenix Art Mus, 79-80; Sacred Dimension, Robischon Gallery, Denver, 93; A Sacred Embrace, Mindy Oh Gallery, Chicago, Ill, 94; Recent Paintings, Univ Club Chicago/Mindy Oh Gallery, Chicago, 94, Select Art Gallery, Sedona, 95 & Robischon Gallery, Denver, 96; Sandra D'Emilio: A Curator's Vision, NMex Mus Fine Arts, Santa Fe, 95. *Pos:* Artist-in-residence, Sun Valley Ctr Arts & Humanities, Idaho, 75 & 76, Tucson Fine Art Mus Sch, Ariz, 87 & E Carolina Univ, Greenville, 88; panel coord mem, Tucson Vis Artists Consortium, 78-80. *Teaching:* Instr painting, Md Inst Col Art, 67-69; instr painting, St Johns Col, Santa Fe, 71; asst prof art, Univ Ariz, 78-83; vis assoc prof painting & drawing, Univ Tex, San Antonio, 90, Adams State Col, Alamosa, Colo, 92 & NMex Highlands Univ, Las Vegas, 92; vis prof painting, Tex A & M Univ, Corpus Christi, 96. *Awards:* Res & Mat Grant, Univ Ariz, Tucson, 80; Panel mem, Art in NMex, Int Contemp Art Fair, Los Angeles, 86; NMex Arts Comn Prize, 73. *Bibliog:* Linda Durham (auth), Artists of New Mexico, 88; Ernesto Mayans (auth), Men of the River, 88. *Media:* Oil on Canvas. *Publ:* Auth, Sam Scott, Southwest Profiles Mag, 87; 12 books and others. *Dealer:* Watson de Nagy Gallery 1106 Berthea Houston TX 77006; Sebastian Moore Gallery Denver CO; Artifold Gallery Santa Fe NMex. *Mailing Add:* 149 Mesa Verde St Santa Fe NM 87501

SCOTT, SANDY (SANDRA) LYNN
SCULPTOR

b Dubuque, Iowa, July 24, 1943. *Study:* Kansas City Art Inst. *Work:* Wildlife World Mus, Monument, Colo; El Paso Zoo, Tex; Gilcrease Mus, Tulsa, Okla. *Comn:* Rodeo Events (etchings), Nat Cowboy Hall Fame, Oklahoma City, 78; Grand Slam, 79 & Bears of North America, 80, Nat Sporting Fraternity Ltd, NY; Kodiak Bears, WesTex

Oil Co, El Paso, 80; Wood Ducks, Albuquerque, NMex, 81. *Exhib:* Am Artists Prof League, NY, 82 & 83; Catharine Lorillard Wolfe Art Club, NY, 82 & 83; Salmagundi Open Sculpture Exhib, NY, 83; NY Pen & Brush, 83; Ann Soc Am Impressionists Show, 84; more than fifty solo exhibs at galleries throughout the country. *Pos:* Background artist, Calvin Motion Pictures, Kansas City, Mo, 62-65. *Awards:* New York Pen & Brush Award, Ann Sculpture Exhib, 83; Medal Hon Sculpture, Catharine Lorillard Wolfe Art Club, 83; Barett-Colea Award & Salmagundi Club Cert Merit, Salmagundi Club Open Sculpture Exhib, 83; Sculpture Award, Pen & Brush, 83; Graphics Award, Am Artists Prof League, 84, Medal of Honor, sculpture, 85; Harriett W Frishmuth Mem Award, Catharine Lorillard Wolfe Art Club, 85. *Bibliog:* Sandy Scott: Etchings, Prints Mag, 7-8/81; Carrol Nelson (auth), Sandy Scott, In: Masters of Western Art, Watson-Guptill, 82; article, Artists of the Rockies, spring 83. *Mem:* Soc Animal Artists; Am Artists Prof League; New York Pen & Brush; Soc Am Impressionists. *Media:* Cast Bronze, Bronze. *Publ:* Illusr, The Ultimate Fishing Book, Houghton-Mifflin, 81. *Mailing Add:* c/o Knox Gallery 1512 Larimerst St R 15 Denver CO 80202-1514

SCRIBNER, CHARLES, III
HISTORIAN, LECTURER
b Washington, DC, May 24, 1951. *Study:* Princeton Univ, AB, 73, MFA, 75, PhD, 77. *Pos:* Vpres, MacMillan Publ co, 84-94; ed, Scribner, 94-2004; mem adv coun, dept art & archeol, Princeton, Univ, 83-91 & 99-, adv comt, Libr, 80-90. *Teaching:* Instr Baroque art, Princeton Univ, 76-77, mem adv coun, Dept Art & Archaeol, 83-91. *Awards:* Thesis Prize, Princeton Univ, 73. *Mem:* Asn Princeton Univ Press. *Res:* Baroque art, especially religious art of Rubens, Bernini and Caravaggio--cultural world of the Counter-Reformation. *Publ:* Auth, Sacred architecture: Rubens' Eucharist tapestries, Art Bulletin, 75; Daniel Hopfer's Venus and Amor, Princeton Univ Art Mus Rec, 76; In Alia Effigie: Caravaggio's London Supper at Emmaus, Art Bulletin, 77; The Triumph of the Eucharist: Tapestries by Rubens, UMI Res Press, 82; Rubens and Bernini, Ringling Mus J, 83; Rubens: Baroque Artist, Renaissance Man, Abrams, 89; Gianlorenzo Bernini, Abrams, 91; The Shadow of God, Doubleday, 2006. *Mailing Add:* 155 E 72nd St # 5C New York NY 10021-4371

SCUCCHI, ROBIE (PETER), JR
EDUCATOR, PAINTER
b Lake Village, Ark, Apr 10, 1944. *Study:* Ark State Univ, with Dan F Howard, BS (painting), 67; Southern Ill Univ, Edwardsville, painting with John Richardson, 70-71; Inst Allende, Univ Guanajuato, Mex, with James Pinto & Fred Samuelson, MFA (painting), 71. *Work:* Claypool-Young Art Gallery, Morehead State Univ, Ky; Matrix Art Gallery, Ind Univ, Bloomington; Grinstead Art Gallery, Cent Mo State Univ, Warrensburg; Jackson Hall Art Gallery, Ky State Univ, Frankfort; Gallery Fine Arts, Univ Ark, Little Rock. *Exhib:* Washington & Jefferson Coll Gallery, Washington, Pa, 73 & 79; Birmingham Mus Art, Ala, 74; Solo exhibs, Jackson Hall Art Gallery, Ky State Univ, Frankfort, 81, Claypool-Young Art Gallery, Morehead State Univ, Ky, 81 & Matrix Art Gallery, Ind Univ, Bloomington, 82; Nat Arts Club, NY, 82-85, 87 & 88; Int Trade Mart Ctr, New Orleans, La, 82, 84 & 90; Ark Arts Ctr, Little Rock, 83, 84 & 88; Parthenon Art Mus, Nashville, Tenn, 83 & 86; W Nebr Art Ctr, Scottsbluff, 88, 90 & 92; Cottonlandia Mus, Greenwood, Miss, 92 & 95; Tenn Valley Art Mus, Tuscumbia, Ala, 96; and others. *Teaching:* Instr & head painting, drawing & design, NW High Sch, House Springs, Mo, 67-71; assoc prof art, Miss State Univ, Starkville, 71-96. *Awards:* Best Show Awards, St Charles Art Guild 4th Ann, Mo, 69 & Ark Bicentennial, 76; 2nd Place Purchase, Am Inst Architects, 72; Ann Art Exhib, Miss Artists, 92 & 95. *Mem:* Nat Soc Painters Casein & Acrylic; Coll Art Asn Am; SE Coll Arts Conf; Nat & Miss Art Educ Asn (state assemblyman, 78-79, state vpres, 78-80). *Media:* Charcoal, Acrylic. *Mailing Add:* 2402 Maple Dr Starkville MS 39759

SCULLY, SEAN
PAINTER
b Dublin, Ireland, Jan 3, 1945; arrived in US, 1975; Am citizen, 1983. *Study:* Croydon Coll Art, London, 65-68; Newcastle Univ, 68-72; Harvard Univ, 72-73. *Hon Degrees:* Mass Coll Art, 2003; Nat Univ Ireland, 2003. *Exhib:* Metrop Mus Art, NY, 2000; David Winton Bell Gallery, Brown Univ, 2001; Kouros Gallery, NY, 2002; LA Louver Gallery, Los Angeles, Calif, 2002, 2006; Galeria Calres Tache, Barcelona, 2003; Galerie Lelong, NY, 2003, 2005, Paris, 2004; Irish Mus Modern Art, Dublin, Ireland, 2005; Phillips Collection, Washington, DC, 2005; Timothey Taylor Gallery, London, 2006. *Teaching:* Teacher, Chelsea Sch Art and Goldsmith's Sch Art, London, Eng, 73-75, Princeton Univ, 77-83; prof painting, Akademie der Bildenden Kunste, Munich, Germany, 2002. *Awards:* Guggenheim Fellowship, 83; Artists Fellowship, Nat Endowment Arts, 83. *Mem:* London Inst (hon mem)

SCULLY, VINCENT JOSEPH, JR
ARCHITECT, EDUCATOR, WRITER
b New Haven, Conn, 1920. *Study:* Entered Yale Univ at age 16; Yale Univ, BA in English, 40; MA in art history, Yale Univ, MA in art hist, 47; Yale Univ, PhD in art hist, 49. *Teaching:* Mem fac, art hist Yale Univ, New Haven, 49-91, prof, art hist, 61-91; master Morse Col, 69-75; Sterling Prof, Emer of the Hist of Art, 91-; distinguished vis prof, Sch Archit Univ Miami, 92-. *Awards:* Named Jefferson Lectr, Nat Endowment of the Humanities, 95; inaugural Vincent Scully Prize, Nat Bldg Mus, Wash, DC, 99; Nat Medal of Arts, 2004. *Publ:* Auth: (books) The Shingle Style: Architectural Theory and Design from Richardson to the Origins of Wright, 55, Frank Lloyd Wright, 60, Modern Architecture: The Architecture of Democracy, 61, Louis I Kahn, 62, The Architectural Heritage of Newport, RI, 1640-1915, 67, American Architecture and Urbanism, 69, Pueblo Architecture of the Southwest, 71, The Shingle Style and The Stick Style: Architectural Theory and Design from Richardson to the Origins of Wright, 71, The Shingle Style Today: Or the Historian's Revenge, 74, Pueblo: Mountain, Village, Dance, 75, The Earth, the Temple, and the Gods: Greek Sacred Architecture, 79, Robert Stern, 81, Studies and Executed Buildings by Frank Lloyd Wright, 86, The Villas of Palladio, 86; auth: New World Visions of Household Gods and Sacred Places: American Art and the Metropolitan Museum, 1650-1914, 88, The Architecture of the American Summer: The Flowering of the Shingle Style, 89, The Architecture of Robert Venturi, 89, The Great Dinosaur Mural at Yale: The Age of Reptiles, 90, Architecture: The Natural and the Man-Made, 91, French Royal Gardens: The Design of Andre Le Notre, 92; book of essays: Modern Architecture and Other Essays, 2003; co-auth: (with C. Lynn, E. Vogt, P. Goldberger) Yale in New Haven: Architecture & Urbanism, 2004. *Mailing Add:* Yale Univ Dept Hist of Art 56 High St PO Box 208272 New Haven CT 06520

SEABERG, LIBBY W
ARTIST, HISTORIAN
b New York, NY. *Study:* Queens Coll, BA (cum laude), 57; Columbia Univ with Meyer Schapiro, MA, 64; Bryn Mawr Grad Sch; City Coll grad painting prog; New Sch with Jacob Lawrence. *Exhib:* Group exhib, Works on Paper/Women Artists, Brooklyn Mus, 75; Dimenseraction, Ammo's New Waterfront Mus, Brooklyn, 89; Physicality: An Exhib on Color Dimensionality in Painting, Hunter Coll Art Galleries, New York, 91; Bubbles, Blisters and Pearls, Stern Sch, New York Univ, 92; Private Papers: A Decade of Drawings, Queens Coll Art Ctr, Flushing, NY, 95; Brushes with Sculpture, 55 Mercer Gallery, New York, 95; Clairvoyance, Dietz Gallery, New York, 2000; AIR Gallery, New York, 2003, 2005, 2007; New York Arts Gallery, 2003; Brooklyn Borough Hall, 2003; Holland Tunnel, 2004-2007; Locus Media Gallery, 2004; NURTUREart Gallery, 2004; Diesel Gallery, Brooklyn, 2004; Asian American Arts Ctr, 2005; Spike Gallery, New York, 2005; CUE Art Found, 2006; Chelsea Art Mus, 2006; Guild Hall, 2008, 2009, 2010. *Pos:* Libr researcher, Whitney Mus Am Art, 68-76; asst cur contemp art & exhib coordr, Yeshiva Univ Mus, New York, 89-90; cur & co-cur, several exhibs. *Teaching:* Lectr art hist & appreciation, Philadelphia Coll Art, 64-65; lectr, Queens Coll, Flushing, NY, 66; instr, Borough Manhattan Community Coll, New York, 66-67. *Awards:* Vt Studio Colony (fel & artist in res), 89. *Bibliog:* Hilton Kramer (auth), A monumental muddle of American sculpture, NY Times, 3/28/76; Greg Gattuso (auth), Entertainment best bets, New York Newsday, 3/12/95; Joy Walker (auth), New York gallery walking, Next, No 36, spring, 96. *Mem:* Coll Art Asn; Am Asn Mus; Artists Talk On Art (advisory bd mem); Int Sculpture Center; NY Artists Circle. *Media:* Two- & three-dimensional, glue, mixed media. *Res:* Contemp art; merging painting & sculpture; Am & 19th-21th-century art. *Publ:* Contribr, Contemporary Black Artists in America (exhib catalog), 71 & Two Hundred Years of American Sculpture, Whitney Mus Am Art, 76; ed, Japanese Literati Painters: The Third Generation (exhib catalog), Brooklyn Mus, 77; ed, American Ceramics: 1876 to the Present, rev ed, Abbeville Press, 87; Judy Hoffman, rev, Sculpture, Vol 22, New York, 7-8/2003; Will The Real Janet Sobel Please Stand Up?, www.janetsobel.com, 2009

SEABERG, STEVE (STEVENS)
ASSEMBLAGE ARTIST, PERFORMANCE ARTIST
b Evanston, Ill, Sept 30, 1930. *Study:* Northwestern Univ, BS, 52, MA, 61; Academie Grande Chaumiere, Paris, 56. *Work:* Art Bus Collection, State Ga, Atlanta; Albany Mus Art, Albany, Ga. *Comn:* Mural, comn by Ted Berrigan, NY, 66; mural, comn by Melvin Wildberger, Brooklyn, NY, 67; Lex et Domus (mural), The Law Office, Atlanta, 76; The Black Arts (mural), Nat Endowment Arts, Atlanta, 78; Hulsey Yard (murals), Seaboard Railway, Atlanta, Ga, 86. *Exhib:* Chicago and Vicinity, Art Inst Chicago, 60, Biennial Print & Drawing Exhib, 62; solo exhibs, Here Come de Judge-ment, Clocktower Gallery, NY, 79 & Ancestors, Malmo Konsthall, Sweden, 81; Artists in Georgia, High Mus Art, Atlanta, 80; Collage & Assemblage, Miss Mus Art, Jackson, 82; Leisure Am, Tampa Mus Art, Fla, 83; Birmingham Biennial, Birmingham Mus Art, Ala, 83; Centro Cult, Buenos Aires, 89; Children of Alcoholism, Little Beirut Art Space, Atlanta, 90; Children of Abuse, 800 East Art Space, Atlanta, 92. *Pos:* Artist & artist preparator, Field Mus Natural Hist, Chicago, 67-65; painter in residence, Neighborhood Art Ctr, Atlanta, 76-79; program dir, Arts Interface, Atlanta, 80-83, Atlanta Urban Design Comn, 85-; mgr, Nexus Theater, Atlanta, 88-90. *Teaching:* Vis lectr art hist, Northwestern Univ, 61-64; lectr & asst prof studio & art hist, Rutgers Univ, 67-70; instr humanities, Clark Col, Ga, 70-73. *Awards:* Nat Endowment Arts Visual Artist Fel, 78; Site Work Grants, Arts Festival Atlanta, 79-81; Third Prize, Birmingham Biennial, Birmingham Art Asn, 83. *Bibliog:* Oyvind Fahlstrom (dir, film), Sweden's TV, 68; Ann Livet (auth), Steve Seaberg's skeletons, Art Papers, 6/79; Tom Patterson (auth), Who is Steve Seaberg?, Brown's Guide to Ga, 8/82. *Publ:* Auth, Sunlight in Jungleland, private publ, 65; illusr, Om Baddrakter, Forfatterforlaget, 77; Song of Atlanta, Ali Baba, 81; The Iconography of Abuse, Seaberg, Atlanta, 94; The Demon's Face: An artist's discovery of the metaphors of child abuse, Leonardo, Mass Inst Technol, 95; and others. *Mailing Add:* 683 Queen St SW Atlanta GA 30310-2611

SEABOURN, BERT DAIL
PAINTER, PRINTMAKER
b Iraan, Tex, 1931. *Study:* Famous Artists Schs, Westport, Conn, cert (art); Univ Cent Okla; Okla Univ. *Hon Degrees:* Okla City Univ, LHD, 97. *Work:* Am Embassy, London; Smithsonian Mus Nat Hist, Washington, DC; Pres Geral Ford Libr Collection, Mich; Vatican Mus Mod Religious Art, Italy; Nat Palace Mus, Taipei, Taiwan. *Comn:* Bronze sculpture, Southwestern Bell Tel, Okla City, 86; mural, Fox Television Channel 25, Okla City, 96; acrylic on linen, Episcopal Diocese, Okla, 2000; 15 ft acrylic mural, Supreme Ct Bldg, Okla City, 2011. *Exhib:* New Britain Mus Am Art, Conn, 79; Denver Mus Natural Hist, Colo, 80; Native Am Ctr Living Arts, Niagara Falls, NY, 81; Mus Natural Hist, Smithsonian Inst, Washington, DC, 83; Ming Chaun Coll, Taipei, Taiwan, 89; Mandarin Galleries, Singapore, 89; Moskow Univ, Ulyanovsk, Russia, 96. *Pos:* Artist & journalist, USN, 51-55; art dir & artist, Okla Gas & Elec Co, Okla City, 55-77. *Teaching:* Instr, watercolor, acrylic & printmaking, City Arts Ctr, Okla City, 97-2011; adj instr session classes, mixed media & surface texture, Univ Central Okla, 2002-2004. *Awards:* First Prize (Watercolor), Okla Watercolor Asn, 74-75, 86, 96-97 & 2004; Gov Art Award, Okla, 81; Grand Award, Master Artists, Five Civilized Tribes Mus, 88, 97 & 2005-2006; Distinguished Alumnus Award, Okla City Univ, 88; First Prize (Oil), Inter-Tribal Indian Ceremonial Art Show, Gallup, NMex, 89; Okla Living Legend Award, 2004; Okla Artist of the Year, 2009; Lifetime Achievment Award, 2009. *Bibliog:* Dick Frontain (auth), Cherokee artist Bert

D Seabourn, Prairie Hawk, 79; Tricia Hurst (auth), Bert Seabourn common ties, Southwest Art, 81; Cecil Lee (auth), Bert Seabourn Paintings, Univ Sci & Arts, 2000; Mary Ellen Meredith (auth), Bert Seabourn: A retrospective, Okla Ctr Sci & Arts & Kirkpatrick Ctr; John Brand (auth), Bert Seabourn: An American Expressionist, 2008. *Mem:* Okla Art Guild (pres, 70); Okla Watercolor Asn; Master Artists Five Civilized Tribes; Okla Visual Arts Coalition; Individual Artists of Okla. *Media:* Watercolor, Acrylic; Etching, Monotype. *Publ:* Auth & illusr, Indian Gallery, 72; Master Artists of the Five Civilized Tribes, 76; Vanishing Americans, 84; Seabourn Prints & Posters, 90; illusr, The Father & Son Indian, Y Guide Manual. *Dealer:* 50 Penn Place Art Gallery 5000 N Pennsylvania Oklahoma City 73118. *Mailing Add:* 6105 Covington Ln Oklahoma City OK 73132

SEABOURN, CONNIE
PAINTER, PRINTMAKER
b Purcell, Okla, Sept 20, 1951. *Study:* Univ Okla, BFA, 81. *Work:* Gilcrease Mus, Tulsa; Talley Indust, Phoenix; Southwestern Bell Tel Co, Washington, DC; Heritage Ctr, Red Cloud Indian Sch, Pine Ridge, SDak; Tyson Foods Corp, Fayetteville, Ark. *Exhib:* Nat Printmaking & Drawing Show, Okla Art Ctr, 81; Night of the First Americans, John F Kennedy Ctr, Washington, DC, 82; Selected Works from Night of the First Americans, Smithsonian Mus, 82; Traditions & Transformations, Somerstown Gallery, Somers, NY, 83; Native Am Art--Three Artists, Twenty Six Horses, NY, 83; two-person exhib, New Trends Gallery, Santa Fe, 83; Eye of My Mind, San Diego Mus Man, 85; Southern Plains Indian Mus, Anadarko, Okla, 86; Kimball Art Ctr, Park City, Utah, 89. *Awards:* Powers Award, Red Cloud Art Show, 83. *Bibliog:* Jimmie Marshall (auth), The emerging of an artist, Art Gallery Mag, winter 80; Jimmie Marshall (auth), The best of both worlds: Connie Seabourn Ragan, Okla 81, 11/81; Dick Frontain (auth), The rising star of Connie Seabourn Ragan, Indian Trader, 10/82. *Mem:* Soc Layerists Multi Media. *Media:* Watercolor, Serigraphy. *Publ:* Auth, The Artist as Printmaker, 8/86

SEAMANS, BEVERLY BENSON
SCULPTOR
b Boston, Mass, Oct 31, 1928. *Study:* Mus Sch Fine Arts, Boston, 48-50; with George Demetrios & Peter Abate, 46-48. *Work:* Essex Inst & Peabody Mus, House of Seven Gables, Salem, Mass; Salem Hosp, Mass; Am Cathedral, Paris, France. *Comn:* Bronze, First Nat Bank Boston, Mass, 69; bronze, Salem Hospital, Mass, 76; bronze, Mass Inst Technol, 80; bronze, Camp Kieve, Nobleboro, Maine, 81; and other pvt collections. *Exhib:* Nat Sculpture Soc, NY, 73, 76-80; one-person shows, Essex Inst, Salem, 74, Mus Sci, Boston, 76, Pingree Sch, Hamilton, 75 & 77, Peabody Mus, Salem, 79-80, House of Seven Gables, Salem, Mass, 86, North Haven Gallery, Maine, 87 & Mem Art Gallery, Rochester, NY, 88, plus others; Abbot Pub Libr, Marblehead, Mass, 85; Trustees of Reservations, Beverly, MA, 2000; Marblehead HS, Marblehead, MA, 2001; Memorial Children's Sculpture, Prouts Necks, ME, 2003. *Awards:* First Prize, Marblehead Arts Asn, 76, 78 & 87; Silver Medal, Nat Sculpture Soc, 78. *Bibliog:* Sharron King (auth), Woman 75, Channel 4, Boston, 75. *Mem:* Fel Nat Sculpture Soc; New Eng Sculptors Asn; Copley Soc; Cambridge Arts; Marblehead Arts; Rockport Art Asn, Mass; Rebohoth Art League. *Media:* Bronze, Marble. *Mailing Add:* Ten Harbor View Marblehead MA 01945

SEARLE, WILLIAM ROSS
PAINTER
b Oak Bluffs, Mass, Sept 25, 1936. *Study:* Mass Coll Art, BFA, 57-61; RI Sch of Design, MFA, 61-63. *Work:* West Point Mus, NY; Rev Martin Luther King Jr Mus, Atlanta, Ga; New England Mus of Sports, Boston, Mass; Cape Cod Mus of Art, Dennis, Mass; Cahoon Mus of Am Art, Cotuit, Mass; Heritage Mus & Gardens, Sandwich, Mass; Martha's Vineyard Mus, Edgartown, Mass; Braintree Hist Soc Mus, Braintree, Mass. *Comn:* 1797 and 1849 Salem Mass, Eastern Bank, Mass, 85; 350th Anniversary Mural of Braintree Mass, 90. *Exhib:* 1969 Invitational Exhib, Fitchburg Art Mus, Fitchburg, Mass, 69; Art Galleries Invitational, Thayer Gallery, Braintree, Ma, 79-2014, China Trade Mus, Milton, Mass, 79; Edge of the Sea, Cape Cod Mus of Art, Dennis, Mass, 2002; 2004 Invitational Exhib, Cape Cod Mus of Art, Dennis, Mass, 2004-2014; Animal King Dom, Cahoon Mus of Am Art, Cotuit, Mass, 2005; World of Words, 2006; Children and Childhood, 2007; RISD Art Mus, Providence, RI, 63; Attleboro Mus, Mass, 84; Solo exhib, Memories, 2010. *Pos:* Chmn art dept, Lawrence Acad, Groton, Mass, 63-70, gallery dir, 68-70; chmn, gallery dir, art dept, St. Margarets-McTernan Sch, Waterbury, Conn, 74-77 & Thayer Acad, Braintree, Mass, 77-2013, art gallery dir, 77-2000. *Teaching:* Architectural Design, Thayer Acad, 2000-2013. *Media:* Watercolor, Acrylic. *Publ:* Leigh Harrington (auth), Art Imitates Life on Cape Cod, Where Mag, (spring/summer 2002); Judith Montminy (auth), Vogues Catch up Artists Vision, Boston Globe, (1/9/1994); Gerald R. Kelley (auth), The Arts of Summer, Grapevine, (7/12/1978); Saundra Tobins (auth), Inside Cape Cod Magazine, 8/2006; Rob Duca (auth) A Seashore Laureate in Paint, Cape Cod Life Mag, 2010. *Dealer:* J Miller Gallery Rte 28 Mashpee MA 02649; Island Gallery Main St Vineyard Haven MA 02568; Kendall Gallery Wellfleet Mass; Angles & Art Gallery, Haverhill, Mass. *Mailing Add:* 59 Shields Rd Mashpee MA 02649

SEARLES, CHARLES
PAINTER, SCULPTOR
b Philadelphia, Pa. *Study:* Pa Acad Fine Arts, four-year cert, 73. *Work:* First Pa Bank, Philadelphia; Harlem State Bldg, NY; Smithsonian Inst; Howard Univ; Philip Morris Corp; Arco Chemical Co; First Dist Self-Help Inc, Philadelphia, Pa, 90. *Comn:* Celebration (mural), Gen Serv Admin, Philadelphia, 76; Playtime (mural), City Philadelphia, 78. *Exhib:* Black Artist in Am, Whitney Mus Am Art, 71; Invisible Artist, Philadelphia Mus Art, 73; Jubilee, Boston Mus Fine Arts, 75; Afro-Am Abstract, PS1 Gallery, NY, 81; one-person shows, Landmark Gallery, NY, 81, Peale Gallery, Pa Acad Fine Arts, 82 & Sande Webster, Philadelphia, 83, 85, 87, 90 & 92; Black Art: Ancestral Legacy, Dallas Mus Art, Tex, High Mus, Atlanta, Ga. *Teaching:* Lectr drawing, Philadelphia Col Art, 73-. *Awards:* Cresson Award, Sr Show, Pa Acad Fine Arts, 71; Nat Endowment Fel Arts, 78; Creative Artists Pub Serv Fel, 80 & 81. *Media:* Acrylic; Painted Wood Sculpture

SEARS, ELIZABETH L
EDUCATOR, HISTORIAN
b Glen Ridge, NJ, July 21, 1952. *Study:* Duke Univ, BA (art hist), 1974; Yale Univ, MA, 1977, PhD, 1982. *Pos:* Ed, Gesta, Int Ctr Medieval Art, 2000-03; Ctr Adv Study Visual Art Fel, 2010; Inst Hum Univ Mich Fel, 2014. *Teaching:* Lectr, Yale Univ, 1981; asst prof dept art & archeol, Princeton Univ, 1982-89, acting dir, Index Christian Art, 1987-88; vis prof, Universitat Hamburg, 1991-92; asst prof dept art hist, Univ Mich, 1992-95, assoc prof, 1995-2001, dir grad studes, 1998-2001, prof, 2001-09; prof, George F Forsyth Jr, 2009-. *Awards:* Getty Found Fel, 1989; John Nicholas Brown Prize, Medieval Acad Am, 1990; Getty Res Inst Scholar, 2000; Brit Sch Rome Fel, 2004; Am Acad in Berlin Res Fel, 2008; Guggenheim Found Fel, 2010. *Mem:* Int Ctr Medieval Art (bd adv, 1993-96, nominating comt, 1993-95, bd dirs, 1996-99, publ comm chair, 2011-); Medieval Acad Am (councilor, 2007-2010). *Res:* European representational art from the 8th-14th century; current project: study of international movement in art history and cultural study emanating from the Warburn Library in Hamburg, Warburg Circles, 1929-1964. *Publ:* Auth, The Ages of Man: Medieval Interpretations of the Life Cycle, Princeton Univ Press, 1986; The Iconography of Auditory Perception in the Early Middle Ages: On Psalm Illustration and Psalm Exegesis, In: The Second Sense, Warburg Inst, 1991; ed, The Religious Symbolism of Michelangelo: The Sistine Ceiling, Oxford Univ Press, 2000; co-ed, Reading Medieval Images: The Art Historian and the Object, Univ Mich Press, 2002; The Afterlife of Scribes, In: Pen in Hand, Red Gull Press, 2006; Craft Ethics & the Critical Eye, In: Gesta, 2006; co-auth, Verzettein als Methode: Der Humanistischen Ikonologe William S Heckscher, Akademie Verlag, 2008; The Warburg Institute, 1933-1944, Art Libraries Journal, 2013; co-auth, An Emigre Art Historian and America: HW Janson, Art Bull, 2013. *Mailing Add:* Univ Michigan 110 Tappan Hall Ann Arbor MI 48109-1357

SEARS, KELLY
VIDEO ARTIST
Study: Hampshire Coll, Amherst Mass, BA (Media Practice & Theory), 2000; Univ Calif San Diego, MFA (Video, Film, & Animation), 2005. *Exhib:* Exhibs include Domesticity, Herbert Marcuse Gallery, Univ Calif San Diego, 2003; Becomings, Mus Contemp Art, La Jolla, Calif, 2003, Fresh, 2005; Video Scoring, Machine Proj, Los Angeles, 2003, Underground Film Festival, 2007; Remade, Re-remade and Re-re-remade, Aurora Picture Show, Houston, 2004; Film/Stills, New Langton Arts, San Francisco, 2005; Supersonic, LA Design Ctr, Los Angeles, 2005; Fine Line, Cirrus Gallery, Los Angeles, 2005, The Latest Fiction, 2006; Silverlake Film Festival, Los Angeles, 2005; How the West Might Save Us Yet, NY Underground Film Festival, New York, 2006; Broken Screen Happening, Schindler House, Los Angeles, 2006; Brooklyn Int Film Festival, Brooklyn, 2006; Off-Screen, Hammer Museum, Los Angeles, 2007; Against the Grain, Los Angeles Contemp Exhibs, Los Angeles, 2008. *Awards:* Waggerman Grant, 2003; Russell Grant, 2003; Honorable Mention, Ann Arbor Film Festival, 2006. *Dealer:* Cirrus Gallery 542 S Alameda St Los Angeles CA 90013

SEARS, STANTON GRAY
PAINTER, SCULPTOR
b Bethlehem, Pa, Oct 22, 1950. *Study:* RI Sch Design, BFA, 73; Pa State Univ, MFA, 76. *Comn:* Sculptures, NH Art Asn, Manchester, 79 & 80; sculptures, Phillips Exeter Acad, NH, 81. *Exhib:* Stedman Art Gallery, Rutgers Univ, Camden, NJ, 79; Lee Hall Gallery, Northern Mich Univ, Marquette, 79; Allentown Art Mus, Pa, 79; De Cordova Mus, Lincoln, Mass, 79; Currier Gallery Art, Manchester, NH, 81; solo show, Plymouth State Coll Art Gallery, Plymouth, NH, 81; Silvermine Guild Artists, New Canaan, Conn, 81; and others. *Teaching:* Instr, Pa State Univ, State Col, 75-78; instr, Univ NH, Durham, 80-81; instr, Manchester Inst Arts & Sci, NH, 81-83. *Awards:* Drawing Award, Educ Ctr Arts, New Haven, Conn, 78; Currier Award, NH Art Asn 34th Ann, Currier Gallery, 80; Award for Advanc Am Art, Arts Coun Holyoke, Mass, 81. *Bibliog:* David Elliot (auth), What are those stripes in the ravine, Univ NH Newspaper, 81; Laura Holland (auth), Sears' high overhead, Valley Advocate, 81; John Wharton (auth), David Fullam, Stanton Sears, Art New Eng, 81. *Mem:* Coll Art Asn Am; NH Art Asn. *Media:* Graphite, Pastel; Welded Aluminum. *Dealer:* Boston Art Work 2345 Washington St Newton Lower Falls MA 02162. *Mailing Add:* McCalister-Art Dept-Dewitt Wallace Library 1600 Grand Ave Saint Paul MN 55105-1801

SEAWELL, THOMAS ROBERT
PRINTMAKER, PHOTOGRAPHER
b Baltimore, Md, Mar 17, 1936. *Study:* Wash Univ, BFA, 58; Tex Christian Univ, MFA, 60. *Work:* Portland Mus Art; Libr Cong, Washington, DC; Mem Art Gallery of the Univ of Rochester, NY; Brooklyn Mus, NY; DeCordova Mus, Lincoln, Mass; Purdue Univ, West Lafayette, Ind, 83; JS Blanton Mus, Univ Tex, Austin; Dulin Gallery Art, Knoxville, Tenn; Pushkin Mus Art, Moscow; Del Mar Col, Corpus Christi, Tex; Brockton Art Ctr, Mass; US Info Agy; Univ ND; Alexandria Mus of Art; Ark Art Ctr; McNeese Univ Mus Art; many others; Portland Mus Art. *Comn:* Rochester Print Club; Geldermann Print Comn, 85-92; Merchants Nat Bank & Trust, 90; Print Club of Albany, 04. *Exhib:* 30 Yrs of Am Printmaking Including 20th Nat Print Exhib, Brooklyn Mus, 76; retrospective exhib, The Oswego Years, Tyler Art Gallery, State Univ NY, 91; Midwestern Univ, Wichita Falls, Tex, 93; Texas A&M Univ Commerce, 95; Columbia Col, SC, 96; Ceramic Vessel Making by Tex Artist, Richland Col, Dallas, 97, Irving Arts Ctr, Tex, 98, 13th San Angelo Nat Ceramic Competition, San Angelo Mus of Fine Art, Tex, 2000; Texas Prints, Univ Tex, Austin, 2001; Texas Mud, Ceramics by Texas Artists, Dallas Ctr Contemp Arts, 2002; The Pritnmakers Ceramics, Tarrant Co Coll, Northwest, 2010; and others. *Collection Arranged:* Art Ctr Plano, Tex, 2007; Art Doors Project, Brookhaven Col, Dallas, Tex, 2008. *Teaching:* Prof drawing & printmaking, State Univ NY, Oswego, 63-91; retired; Vis artist, numerous sch art, 77-89, Print Symposium, Ox Bos, summer 85, Univ Dallas, 89, Henderson State Univ, 97 & ETenn State Univ, 97, Lousiana Col, 04.

Awards: State Univ NY Res Found Printmaking Fels, 67, 70 & 74; over 65 prizes and awards, nat and regionals competitions. *Bibliog:* The Complete Collagraph, Romano & Ross, The Free Press, Macmillan, NY, 80; Eldon Cunningham (auth), Printmaking: A Primary Source of Expression; Richard Zakin (auth), Hand Formed Ceramics (Creating Form & Surface), Chilton Bk Co, 95. *Mem:* Boston Printmakers; Soc Am Graphic Artists; Tex Sculpture Soc. *Media:* Printmaking, Ceramics, Photography. *Dealer:* Old Print Shop New York NY. *Mailing Add:* 1513 Park Commerce TX 75428

SEAWRIGHT, JAMES L, JR
SCULPTOR, EDUCATOR
b Jackson, Miss, May 22, 1936. *Study:* Univ Miss, BA, 57; Art Students League, NY, 61-62. *Work:* Mus Mod Art, Whitney Mus Am Art & Solomon R Guggenheim Mus, NY; Larry Aldrich Mus, Ridgefield, Conn; Wadsworth Atheneum, Hartford, Conn. *Comn:* Electronic Environ, Seattle-Tacoma Int Airport, 73; outdoor sculpture, NJ State Mus, Trenton, 76; outdoor sculpture, Mobile Tech Ctr, Pennington, NJ; Sculpture Terminal C, Logan Int Airport, Boston. *Exhib:* Whitney Ann, Whitney Mus Am Art, 67; The Sixties, Mus Mod Art, 67; Focus on Light, NJ State Mus, Trenton, 68; Magic Theater, Nelson Gallery Performing Arts Found, Kansas City, Mo, 68; Cybernetic Serendipity, Inst Contemp Art, London, 69; Theodoron Awards Show, Solomon R Guggenheim Mus, NY, 69; Works for New Spaces, Walker Art Ctr, Minneapolis, 71; Art of the Space Age, Huntsville Mus Art, Ala, 78; Am Renaissance Mus of Art, Fort Lauderdale, Fla; solo exhib, David Bermant Found, NY. *Pos:* Dir visual arts prog, Princeton Univ, 74-2003. *Teaching:* Instr sculpture, Sch Visual Arts, New York, 67-69; lectr sculpture, Princeton Univ, NJ, 69-, prof visual arts, 92-; prof visual arts, Lewis Ctr for the Arts, Princeton Univ, 2007-, emeritus, 2009-. *Awards:* Nat Endowment Arts Comn, NJ State Mus, 76; Award of Merit, Miss Inst of Arts & Letters, 83; Acad Award in Art, Am Acad Arts & Letters, 97. *Bibliog:* Article, Life Mag, 4/67; Douglas Davis (auth), interview, Art Am, 1-2/68; Ralph T Coe (auth), The Magic Theater, Circle Press, 70. *Mem:* Am Abstract Artists. *Media:* Miscellaneous. *Publ:* Contribr, On the Future of Art, Viking, NY, 70. *Dealer:* OK Harris Works of Art 393 W Broadway NY NY 10012. *Mailing Add:* 421 Grahamtown Rd Middletown NY 10940

SEBASTIAN, JILL C
ENVIRONMENTAL ARTIST, SCULPTOR
b Libertyville, Ill, Mar 24, 1950. *Study:* Univ Wis-Milwaukee, MFA, 79. *Work:* Burpee Art Mus, Rockford, Ill; Haggerty Art Mus, Milwaukee Art Mus, Milwaukee, Wis. *Comn:* Toucan Du, New Orleans, La, 92; sculpture, Lake Terrace, Milwaukee, Wis, 98; Integrated Art, Midwest Express Conv Ctr, Milwaukee, Wis, 98. *Exhib:* Solo exhibs, Purdue Univ, W Lafayette, Ind, 83, Kit Basquin Gallery, Milwaukee, 83, Charles Wustum Mus, Racine, Wis, 84, Bertha Urdang Gallery, NY, 85, Loho Gallery, Louisville, Ky, 86 & Wis Conv Ctr, Milwaukee, 96; Kohler Art Ctr, Sheboygan, Wis, 86; Walkers Point Ctr for Arts, 87; Dean Jensen Gallery, Milwaukee, 88 & 90; Michael Lord Gallery, Milwaukee, 91-92. *Pos:* Mem, Milwaukee Arts Bd, 91-93, pub art com, 97-2000; chair, Art Futures, 96-98. *Teaching:* Lectr film, design & drawing, Univ Wis-Milwaukee, 79-84; asst prof sculpture, Univ Denver, Color, 84-85; assoc prof, Milwaukee Inst Art & Design, 88-98. *Awards:* Grants, Wis Arts Bd, 81, 82 & 87, Milwaukee Artists Found, 82; Nat Endowment Arts Fel, 85; Sacajawea Award, 89; Milwaukee Artist of Yr, 97; named Artist of Yr, City of Milwaukee, 99. *Bibliog:* Christine Buth-Furness (auth), Jill Sebastian, New Art Examiner, 4/83; John Mominee (auth), Jill Sebastian, Wis Acad Rev, 3/85; Whitney Gould (auth), Midwest Express Ctr, Milwaukee J/Sentinel, 7/98. *Mem:* Coll Art Asn; Riverwest Artist Asn. *Publ:* Auth & illusr, Cream City Rev, 81; Aviva Rahmani, rev, & Jim Brozak, rev, New Art Examiner, 84. *Dealer:* Michael H Lod Gallery 420 E Wisconsin Ave Milwaukee WI 53202

SEBEK, MIKLOS LASZLO
SCULPTOR, INSTRUCTOR
b Soskut, Hungary, Dec 6, 1941; US citizen. *Study:* Budapest State Atelier of Fine Arts, 66; Budapest Tech Inst of Archit, 68; Montclair State Univ, BA (sculpture), 78. *Work:* bronze reliefs, Am Hungarian Mus, Passaic, NJ; steel sculpture, Clifton Arts Ctr, NJ; bronze sculpture, Rutgers Univ, NJ, Univ Gottingen, Ger & Bergen Co, NJ; bronze relief, Vatican City. *Comn:* bronze portrait of Mayor Chenoweth, Nutley City Hall, Nutley, NJ, 97; One City, One Nation, stainless steel sculpture, Clifton City Hall Park, Clifton Beautification Comm, NJ, 94; bronze medallion, Am Inst Architects 9/11/2001; memorial award, 14 World Renown Architects, Wash DC, 2012. *Exhib:* The State of the Arts in NJ, Morris Mus, NJ, 84, 1st Open Juried Art Exhib, Bergan Mus, Paramus, NJ, 84; Art Expo, Jacob Javits Ctr, NY, 87; For Arts Sake, Hunterdon Arts Ctr, Clinton, NJ, 89; Audubon, Nat Arts Club, NY, 80-96; Audubon, Salmagundi Club, NY, 81-2010; Interiorscapes, Monmouth Mus, NJ, 91; Artists from Hungary, Hungarian Embassy, Wash, 94; Noyes Mus Art, 2008-2009; Allied Artist Invitational, Canton Mus of Art, Ohio, 2015, Allied Artists of America, Salmagundi Club, NY, 2015, Noyes Mus, NJ, 2015, Tycoon Galleries, Spring Lake, NJ, 2015. *Collection Arranged:* Saint Stephen Plaque, Bronze, American Hungarian Mus, NJ 1992; Sextet Marble, Morris Mus Arts & Sci, NJ, 2005; Reclining Figure, Bronze Noyes Mus Art, NJ, 2008; Trio Marble, The Butler Inst of American Art, Youngstown, Ohio, 2015. *Teaching:* instr, Bloomfield Art Ctr, NJ, 98; instr sculpture, Clifton Adult Sch, 94-2009; instr sculpture, Rutherford Adult Sch, 2011; instr sculpture, Montclair Adult Sch, 2012; instr sculpture, Bergen Community Coll, 2012. *Awards:* Best in Show Award, Art Ctr Caldwell, Coll ND, 2002; Best of Show, Millburn Art Show, 2004; Best Sculpture, West Essex Art Show, 2005; Gold Medal of Honor, Audubon Artists, 2007; Lindsey Morris Mem Award, Allied Artists of Am, 2008; Marquis Who's Who in Am Art References Award for sculpture, Audubon Artists, 2009; Cleo Hartwig Award, Audubon Artists, 2010; Josephine Beardsley Sandor Mem Award, Allied Artists Am, 2010; Elliot Liskin Mem award, Allied Artists Am, 2011; Marquis Who's Who in Am Art References award in Sculpture, Audubon Artists, NY, 2013; The Pietro and Alfrieda Montana award, Allied Artists Am, Salmagundi Club, NY, 2014; Marion and Gil Roller award, Audubon Artists, Salmagundi Club, NY, 2014; The Allied Artists of Am Gold Medal of Honor, Salmagundi Club, NY, 2015. *Bibliog:* NJ Coun on the Arts, Channel 50, 94; Tom Sullivan (auth) One City One Nation, Channel 19, 94; Steve Cooper (auth) Art in New Hampshire, WMUR-ABCTV, 2000; Spotlight of Miklos Sebek, Herald News, NJ, 2009. *Mem:* Audubon Artist (sr vpres, 99-2005, exhib chmn, 2003, 2011); Allied Artists Am (exhib chmn, 2006, 2011); S Vt Arts Center; Signature Artists, Noyes Mus Art. *Media:* Bronze, Marble, Steel, Wood. *Publ:* Public Art, The Guild Archit Sculpture, 98; Navarra, Tova (auth) New Jersey Artists Through Time, 2015. *Dealer:* Tycoon Art Gallery Spring Lake NJ. *Mailing Add:* 112 Lafayette Ave Passaic NJ 07055

SEBELIUS, HELEN
PAINTER
b Assiniboia, Sask, 1953. *Study:* Univ Regina, Sask, 71-72; Alberta Coll Art, Calgary, Dipl, 74-78; Banff Ctr, Alta, 80; Nova Scotia Coll Art & Design, Halifax, MFA, 87. *Work:* Alberta Art Found; Can Coun Art Bank & Dept External Affairs, Ottawa; Grant MacEwan Col, Edmonton; Nickle Arts Mus, Calgary; Red Deer Col. *Exhib:* Solo exhibs, Gallery O, Toronto, Ont, 81, Olga Korper Gallery, Toronto, Ont, 83, 85, 88 & 91, Anna Leonowens Gallery, Halifax, NS, 87, New Gallery, Calgary, Alta, 87; Visions of Alberta, Muttart Art Gallery, Calgary, 88; Drawings/Motivations, Glenbow Mus, Calgary, Alta, 88; Four: Toyo Kawamura, New Gallery, Calgary, Alta, 88; OR Gallery, Vancouver, BC, 94. *Pos:* Guest speaker, Calif Col Arts & Crafts, Oakland, 81; asst dir, Snyder Hedlin Fine Art Consult, Calgary, Alta, 81-83; bd dir, Off Centre, Calgary, Alta, 84-85; adv bd, New Gallery, Calgary, Alta, 88-. *Teaching:* Instr textile & foundations, Alta Col Art Calgary, 81-85; vis artist & instr textiles, 87-88, instr drawing, 88-; instr foundations, Univ Calgary, Alta, 84, instr drawing 88-; instr papermaking, David Thompson Univ, Nelson, BC, 84, Red Deer Col, Alta, 85; teaching asst, Nova Scotia Col Art & Design, Halifax, 85-87, instr drawing, 87. *Awards:* Alta Cult Assts Award, 79; Project Grant, 82-83, Short Term Grant, 84, Travel Grant, 85, Can Coun; Project Grant, Alta Cult Project, 82-83. *Bibliog:* Nancy Tousley (auth), 5 plus 5, 9/27/85 & Drawings/Motivations, 10/5/88, Calgary Herald; Christiane Laforge (auth), Papiers Transformes 11, Le Quotidien, 5/16/87. *Media:* All media

SECKEL, CORNELIA
PUBLISHER, WRITER
b Queens, NY, Jun 28, 1946. *Study:* Queens Col, NY, BA, 68; Mich State Univ, East Lansing, MA, 73. *Pos:* publ, Art Times. *Awards:* Governors Citation, Governor Cuomo, NY, 94; Friend of Pastel award, Pastel Soc Am, 2001. *Mem:* Artists Fel Inc; Catharine Lorillard Wolfe Art Club; Art Table Inc; Nat Asn Women Artists. *Res:* Cultural art. *Interests:* Travel; Gardening; Beach combing. *Publ:* columnist, Art Times. *Mailing Add:* c/o Art Times PO Box 730 Mount Marion NY 12456

SEED, SUZANNE LIDDELL
PHOTOGRAPHER, WRITER
b Gary, Ind, Mar 8, 1940. *Study:* Yale Univ Summer Sch Music Art, 1961; Ind Univ, with Henry Holmes Smith, BA, 1963; Art Inst Chicago, MFA, 1982. *Work:* Chrysler Mus; Chase Manhattan Bank, NY; Exchange Nat Bank, Chicago. *Exhib:* Los Angeles Inst Contemp Art's Photog, Downey Mus Art, 1980; Chicago Contemp Photog, Los Angeles Ctr Photog Studies, Calif, 1981; Women/Image/Nature, Tyler Sch Art, Philadelphia, Pa & Rochester Inst Technol, NY, 1981; and others. *Mem:* Soc Photogrs Communications; Soc Photogrs Educ; Writers' Guild; PEN Ctr USA; Poetry Ctr Chicago. *Publ:* Auth & illusr, Saturday's Child, J Philip O'Hara, 1973; contribr, Women See Men, McGraw Hill, 1977; contribr, Women Photograph Men, Morrow, 1977; auth & illusr, Fine Trades, Follett, 1979. *Dealer:* Marjorie Neikrug 224 East 68th St New York NY 10021. *Mailing Add:* 175 E Delaware Pl Apt 7511 Chicago IL 60611-7740

SEEGER, MATTHEW W
EDUCATOR, ADMINISTRATOR
Study: Indiana Univ, PhD, 1982. *Pos:* Worked closely with the US Centers for Disease Control and Prevention on communication and anthrax attack and on pandemic influenza preparednes; affiliate of the Nationla Center for Food Protection and Defense; co-private investigator on the National Science Foundation Grant Multi-Agency Jurisdictional Organized Response; works with the National Center for Border Security and Immigration. *Teaching:* Assoc Dean, Wayne State Univ Graduate Sch, formerly, prof communication, Dean, Col of Fine, Performing & Communication Arts, Wayne State Univ, currently. *Publ:* Contributor of several journal articles, book chapters and conference proceedings; (co-auth) Organizational Communication and Crisis, 2003, Effective Crisis Communication, 2006, Effective Risk Communication: A Message-Centered Approach, 2009; (auth) Organizational Communication Ethics: Decisions and Dilemmas, 1997. *Mailing Add:* 5104 Gullen Mall The Linsell House Wayne State University Detroit MI 48202

SEELBACH, ANNE ELIZABETH
PAINTER, SCULPTOR
b Detroit, Mich, 1944. *Study:* New York Univ, NY, BA, 67; Internationale Sommerakademie for Bildende Kunst, Salzburg, Austria, cert (painting), 68; Hunter College (City Univ of NY), MFA, 85. *Work:* The Newark Mus, Newark, NJ; Radcliffe Inst, Harvard Univ, Cambridge, Mass; Lyman Allyn Mus, New London, Conn; Frauen Mus, Bonn, Ger; Prudential Insurance Art Collection, Newark, NJ; Pfizer Inc, Groton, Conn; XTO Energy, Fort Worth, Tex. *Exhib:* Newark Mus, Newark, NJ, 84; Hudson River Mus, Yonkers, NY, 84; Frauen Mus, Bonn, Ger, 86, 88; Attleboro Mus, Attleboro, Mass, 96; Smolyan Art Ctr, Smolyan, Bulgaria, 2006; Palace of Culture, Sofia, Bulgaria, 2006; Univ Conn, Groton, 2009; Centre Coll, Danville, KY, 2010; PMW Gallery, Stamford, CT, 2012; Islip Art Mus, East Islip, NY, 2013; Univ Conn, Groton, 2013; Long Island Biennial Heckscher Mus Art, Huntington, NY, 2014. *Pos:* Curational asst, the Costume Inst, Metropolitan Mus of Art, NY, 74-78; curator, Monhegan Mus, Monhegan Island Maine, 92-95. *Teaching:* Instr, Univ RI, 90; instr fundamentals, 3-D design, Parsons Sch of Design, 94; instr watercolor, studio painting, Victor d'Amico Inst Art, Amaganset, NY, 94-. *Awards:* MacDowell Colony

Peterborough, NH, 87; Triangle Artists Workshop, Pine Plans, NY, 88; Honorary Prize, annual juried exhib, Monmouth Mus, NJ, 89; Painting Fellowship, The Bunting Inst, Radcliffe Coll, 90; Int Guest Artist, Orpheus Foundation, Bulgaria, 2006; NY Found Arts, Mark Program, 2011. *Bibliog:* Shirley L David (auth), Newark Whimsical Houses, NY Times (NJ sect, Pg 8), 12/84; Hank Hoffman (auth), The Big Picture, New Haven Advocate, New Haven, CT 4/2001; Ford (catalogue), Orpheus Publ House, Bulgaria, 2008; Nada Marjanovich (auth), 9 in Art, Long Island Pulse Mag, Patchoque, NY, July/August, 2013. *Mem:* Soc Bunting, Radcliffe Inst Advanced Studies, Cambridge, Mass (fel). *Media:* Watercolor, Oil, Welded Metal, Acrylic. *Dealer:* PMW Gallery 530 Roxbury Rd Stamford Conn 06902. *Mailing Add:* PO Box 606 Sag Harbor NY 11963-0014

SEGADE, ALEXANDRO
PERFORMANCE ARTIST
Study: Univ Calif Los Angeles, BA (english). *Exhib:* Whitney Mus; MOCA; LAXART; New Mus; PS1; Studio Mus, Harlem; Aspen Art Mus; Anton Kern Gallery; Contemporary Arts Forum; Mus Het Domein; Calif Biennials, 2006 & 2008; Performa Biennials, 2007; Montreal Biennial, 2007. *Pos:* Founder, performer, My Barbarian, 2000-. *Awards:* Art Matters Found Grant, 2008

SEGAL, BARBARA JEANNE
SCULPTOR, INSTRUCTOR
b Bronxville, NY, Jan 27, 1953. *Study:* Pratt Inst Technol, NY, 70-72, BFA, 96; L'Ecole Nationale Superieuve Des Beaux-Arts Paris, 72-74; Sch Visual Arts, 90-94. *Work:* Malcomb Forbes Collection, NY; Whitehouse Collection, City of Yonkers; Neuberger Mus of Art. *Comn:* sculpture park, Phillipse Manor Hall, The City of Yonkers, 2000-2001; Yonkers Sculpture Park on the Hudson, 2001-2003, comn by the City of Yonkers; Metropolitan Transportation Authority, 2005. *Exhib:* New Talent, Alan Stone Gallery, NY, 84-85; Art of Northeast Am, Silvermine Gallery, Conn, 86, 87 & 88; one-women shows, Gallery Henoch, 89, Westchester Gallery, 94, Over and Under, The Hudson River Mus, 98 & Women of Stone, Neuberger Mus Art, 2000; The Reality of Illusion, Contemp Grafts, Mus, Ore, 92; Musee Rodin, Hommagea Collamarini, Hokin Gallery, Fla, 93-94; Art as a Verb, Mus at Fashion Inst Tech, NY, 95; Virtual Bride, La Mama La Galleria, NY, 99. *Teaching:* Instr, private, formerly; instr stone carving, Sch Visual Arts, New York, 90-95; instr contemp sculpture, Westchester Art Workshop, 93-; instr, Nat Acad Design, 94; instr stone carving, Sch Visual Arts, 90-. *Awards:* Claudia & Maurice Stone Memorial Award, Silvermine Gallery, 88; Sculpture Award, Int Art Competition, 88; Hud Grant, 95; Mayoral Citation, 2000; Art Westchester Art, council, 2004; MTA/ Art for Transit. *Bibliog:* Patricia Malarcher (auth), 90's commentary in a classical medium (review), NY Times, 94; In Yonkers Hope is Chiseled in Stone, NY Times, 95, Roberta Hersenston (auth), NY Times, 98; Domenick Lombard, Art New England, 98; Beverly Russell (auth), Sculpture Mag, 98; Roberta Hershenson (auth), Works that Appear Soft but are Posed in Stone, NY Times, 2000; Carved in Stone, JournalNews, New York, 2000; Yonkers Waterfront Moves Ahead NY Times, Elsa Brenner, 3/2002; Sculpture Depicts City's River Links, Journal News, Caren Hatbfinger, 7/2003; Tograce Yonkers Station work that Mirrors the River, Roberta Hersherison, 2004. *Mem:* Art on Main Street, (chmn, 94); Yonkers Friends of the Arts, 2003-2005. *Media:* Stone, Metals. *Collection:* Small works & Public Art. *Publ:* Co-auth, Barbara Segal Sculptor, EGG, 90; New York Mode - Aus Marmor, Germany, 99. *Mailing Add:* 88 Alta Ave Yonkers NY 10705-1411

SEGAL, MARY
GRAPHIC ARTIST, PRINTMAKER
b Cincinnati, Ohio, Dec 25, 1933. *Study:* Brown Univ, BA, 55; RI Sch Design; Akademie der Bildenden Kunste, Munich, Ger, 55-56; Laguna Coll Art, with Paul Darrow, 65-69. *Work:* Sackner Arch of Concrete and Visual Poetry, Miami Beach; Ctr Arts, Vero Beach, Fla; Atlanta Women's Feminist Health Ctr; City Orlando; Larson Drawing Collection, Austin Peay State Univ, Clarksville, Tenn. *Exhib:* National Exhibit of Prints & Drawings, Bradley Univ, Peoria, 90-91; Autobiographical Subjects, Fla Ctr Contemp Art, Tampa, 91; one-person shows, Sarah Doyle Ctr, Brown Univ, Providence, 91, Wolfson Galleries, MDCC, Miami, 93, TULA Found, Atlanta, 94 & Atlantic Ctr Harris House, 94; Nat Mus Women, 96; South Fla Art Ctr, Miami; Dunedin Fine Arts Ctr, Fla, 97; Thomas Ctr Gallery, Gainesville, Fla, 97; Burns Rd Ctr Gallery, GardensArt, Palm Beach Gardens, 2001. *Pos:* Panelist nat conf, Women's Caucus Art, 95. *Teaching:* printmaking and mixed media, Ctr for The Arts, Vero Beach, Fla & Indian River Community Col, 90-2000. *Awards:* Hambidge Ctr Creative Arts Resident Fel, Rabun Gap, Ga, 91 & 94; Centrum Found Resident Fel Printmaking, Port Townsend, Wash, 92; SAF/Nat Endowment Arts Grant for Works on Paper, 92. *Bibliog:* Helen Kohen (auth), Text and images, Miami Herald, 93; Jo Ann Wein (auth), Mary Segal, SAF, 93; Philip E Bishop (auth), Some people call it eccentric, Orlando Sentinel, 94. *Mem:* Women's Caucus Art; Fla Printmakers Soc. *Media:* Collage, Mixed Media. *Dealer:* Mary Woerner PO Box 1647 Stuart FL 34995; Charles Kristen Gallery 3905 W 32nd Ave Denver CO 80212. *Mailing Add:* PO Box 861 Roseland FL 32957

SEGAL, TAMA & DAVID
DEALERS, CURATORS
b Tama, Brooklyn, NY, Feb 13, 49, b David, Bronx, NY, Aug 31, 40. *Study:* Tama, Brooklyn Mus; Pratt Inst; New Sch; David, City Col, New Sch Social Res, BFA, 64. *Exhib:* Peter Max in Charlotte, 93; Thomas Kinkade, 97-2005. *Pos:* Owners, Segal Fine Art, 77-. *Teaching:* Guest lectr contemp Native Am painting & sculpture, New Sch Soc Res. *Mem:* Munic Art Soc, New York; Santa Fe Festival Arts; Mus Am Indian; Mint Mus & Mint Mus Crafts. *Specialty:* Contemporary Native American art. *Publ:* Warhol Headlines, Nat Gallery Wash DC, 2012. *Mailing Add:* 8047 Tifton Rd Charlotte NC 28226

SEGAL, THOMAS H
ART DEALER
b New York, NY, Feb 18, 1940. *Study:* Univ Pa, BA, 61; Columbia Univ, MBA, 65. *Pos:* Pres, Thomas Segal Gallery, Boston, Mass, 76-96; trustee, Inst Contemp Art, 84-; vis comt, Dept Hist Art, Univ Pa, 91-97; trustee, Mass Col Art, 96-. *Mem:* Art Dealers Asn Am. *Specialty:* Impressionist, modern and contemporary art. *Publ:* Jasper Johns (catalog), Thomas Segal Gallery, 81; Helen Frankenthaler, Thomas Segal Gallery. *Mailing Add:* Thomas Segal Gallery 4 W University Pl Baltimore MD 21218

SEGALL-MARX, MADELEINE (MADDY MARX)
SCULPTOR, PAINTER
b New York, 1952. *Study:* Univ Mich, BA; Art Students League, anat with Robert Beverly Hale, sculpture with Nat Kaz & Jose de Creeft, 77-80; studies at Foundries & Stoneyards of Pietrasanta, Italy. *Work:* Art Students League Permanent Collection, NYC; public sculpture, Rothenberg Mem Mathematics Wall, Stuyvesant High Sch, NY, 99. *Comn:* NY Street Tree Consortium, 90; Save the Children Award Sculpture; The Childrens Ride, NYC Dept Parks, 95; Centennial Wall, Stuyvesant HS, NYC, 2004; Bihasaalih sculpure, Northern Dutchess Hosp, Rhinebeck, NY. *Exhib:* Sculptors League, Lever House, NY, 94; Audubon Nat Exhib; Woodstock Artists Asn; Soho Loft Pioneer Show, Puffin Found, NY, 96; Traveling Painting Exhib, Nat Asn Women Artists, 96-99; WaveCrest, Sculpture Park, Hyde Park, NY; Albert Shahinian Fine Art; Hyde Park Lib; Adelphi Univ; The Singing Bowl: Voices of the Enemy, Wavecrest, NY, 2013; Canton Mus of Art, Canton, Ohio, 2015. *Pos:* Bd control, Art Students League, NY, 79-80; pres, Nat Asn Women Artists, 99-2002. *Teaching:* Instr sculpture, PS 41, NY, 93-96, Childrens Aid Soc, NY, 93-96 & Barrett House Sch Art, Poughkeepsie, NY, 94-. *Awards:* Medal Honor, Catherine Lorillard Wolfe Art Club, 91, 2007; Medal Honor & Amelia Peabody Award, Nat Asn Women Artists, 93, 97 & 2005; Excalibur Foundry Award, Pen & Brush, 94; Audubon Artists Award, Sculpture; Dutchess Co Exec Arts Award, 2006; Puffin Found Grant, 2007; NY Coun Arts Grant, 2007. *Bibliog:* William Zimmer (auth), Sculpture on 4 lush acres, NY Times, 9/6/92; Eileen Watkin (auth), East Brunswick gallery sculpture competition, Sunday Star Ledger, 9/13/92; Toby Axelrod (auth), A sculpture that won't offend anybody, New York Observer, 1/16/94; Stuart Leung (auth), Stuyvesant Legend Remembered with Memorial Wall, The Spectator, 12/99; Artistic Expression of Madeline Segall, Daily Freeman; Hyde Park Townman on Library, Exhib of Singing Bowl; Artist Listens, Award Winning Artist, Poughkeepsie Jour; Catalog, Canton Mus of Art, 2015. *Mem:* Nat Asn Women Artists (1st vpres, 97-99, pres, 99-2002); Allied Artists Am; Audubon Artists; Catherine Lorillard Wolfe Art Club; Woodstock Artist Asn. *Media:* Miscellaneous Media. *Res:* Singing Bowl Project, War Stories Around the World. *Publ:* The Singing Bowl, Voice of the Enemy, 2013. *Dealer:* Albert Shahinian Fine Art Rhinebeck NY. *Mailing Add:* 148 Greene St New York NY 10012

SEGGER, MARTIN JOSEPH
HISTORIAN, MUSEUM DIRECTOR
b Felixtowe, Eng, Nov 22, 1946; Can citizen. *Study:* Univ Victoria, BA, 69, with Alan Gowans, dipl, 70; Warburg Inst, Univ London, with E H Gombrich, MPhil, 73. *Collection Arranged:* Arts of the Forgotten Pioneers (with catalog), Maltwood Mus, 71; Samuel Maclure-Architect, 74 & House Beautiful, An Exhibit of Decorative Arts 1860-1920 (with catalog), 75, BC Prov Mus; Colonial Painters of British Columbia, 79; The Victoria Portrait, 81; To Sir Yehudi Menuhin, 85; John Wright, Architect, 90. *Pos:* Dir, Maltwood Mus, Victoria, 71-2011, BC Heritage Trust, Provincial Heritage Adv Bd, Heritage Can & Int Coun Monuments & Sites Can; consult mus training, Egypt/UNESCO, 83; consult, Heritas Inc, 83; consult, Icom, Costa Rica, 89; chair, Int Comt Training of Mus Personnel, Int Coun Mus; vchair, BC Provincial Capital Comn; pres, Soc of Architectural Hist, Pacific Northwest Branch; pres, Commonwealth Assn of Mus; chmn bd, Queenswood Soc. *Teaching:* Lectr art hist & mus studies, Univ Victoria, BC, 71-. *Awards:* Lieut Gov Medal, BC Heritage, 89; Harley J McKee Award, Asn Preserv Technol; Award of Merit, Victoria Hallmark Soc; Queens Jubilee Medal. *Mem:* Soc Archit Historians; Can Mus Asn (nat exec mem, 75-77); Soc Study Archit Can; Royal Soc Arts Fel; Commonwealth Asn Mus (pres); and others. *Media:* Print. *Res:* Art of the Pacific Northwest, Museums & Civil Society. *Specialty:* fine & decorative arts. *Interests:* motor mechanics. *Publ:* Auth, Museum Operations Manual, 83; Samuel Maclure: An Architectural Biography, 86; The Development of the Gordon Head Campus, 88; Exploring Victoria's Architecture, 96; Victoria Modern: UVIC and the Regional Aesthetic in the Late 1950s and 60s, 2011. *Mailing Add:* Maltwood Art Mus & Gallery Univ of Victoria PO Box 3025 St C Victoria BC V8W 3P2 Canada

SEGUIN, JEAN-PIERRE
PAINTER, PHOTOGRAPHER
b Montreal, Que, Feb 12, 1951. *Study:* Cegep du Vieux-Montreal, DEC, 72; Univ de Que, Montreal, BA, 75, MA, 79. *Work:* Mus du Que; Conseil des Arts du Can, Ottawa; Univ du Que a Montreal; Steinberg; Mus d'Art Contemporain a Montreal. *Comn:* Stained-glass window, Govt du Que, Ville de la Baie, 86. *Exhib:* Gravure du Quebec, Mus d'Art Contemporain, Montreal, 74; Galerie Nat, Ottawa, Ont, 77; Jeune Contemporain 80, London Art Gallery, Ont, 80; ACTFART, Musée du Saguenay-Lac-St-Jean, Chicoutimi, Oue, 85; Nommage à A Wharol, Galerie 13, Montreal, 87; Histoire De Collections, Mus d'Art Contemporain, Montreal, 88; Passages, Mus Du Saguenay, Que, 89; Le Blanc of MFS Nuits, éoifice Belgo, Montreal, 91; Two Cities/Latitudes Exchange, Latitudes 53 Gallery, Edmonton, Alta, 95; Les Ateliers, S'Exposent, Montreal, 95; Autres Passages, CNE, Jonquiére, 95; Mobilier d'Artistes, Galerie Optica, 95. *Teaching:* Charge de cours activite de synthese, Univ Que, Montreal, 76-78 & prof painting & drawing, Univ Que, Chicoutimi, 79-717. *Awards:* Greenshield Fel, 75; ler Prix, Concours de Dessin & Biennale du Que, Govt du Que, 79; ler Prix Biennale Du, Que, 89. *Bibliog:* René Payant (auth), Dépeindre le photographique, Galerie Graff, 83; Giles Daigneault (auth), Jean-Pierre Seguin: Peindre ou feindre, Le Devoir, 83; Pierre Ouellet (auth), Le Savoir peint, Revue Protée, 85. *Media:* All. *Res:* Systems of representation &

production of both photographic & pictorial portraiture. *Publ:* Coauth, Du neuf a cinq, Articule, 80; Entre le corps et la matiére, Intervention, 81; Ou, Langage Plus, 83; illusr, Langage et savoir, Protée, 85; Un Printemps Costaud, Vie Des Arts, 91. *Mailing Add:* Univ Quebec a Chicoutimi Art Dept Chicoutimi PQ G7H2B1 Canada

SEIDE, PAUL A
GLASS BLOWER, SCULPTOR
b New York, NY, Feb 15, 1949. *Study:* Egani Neon Glassblowing Sch, cert, 71; Univ Wis, BS (art), 74. *Work:* Nat Mus Mod Art, Kyoto, Japan; Corning Mus Glass, Corning, NY; Chrysler Mus Art, Norfolk, WVa; Mus des Arts Decoratifs, Lausanne, Switz; Lannan Found Mus, Palm Beach, Fla; and others. *Comn:* Swarovski World of Crystal, Wattens, Austria, 95. *Exhib:* Solo exhibs, Heller Gallery, NY, 82, 84 & 88, Kurland Summers Gallery, Los Angeles, Calif, 84 & 86 & Habatat Galleries, Bay Harbour Islands, Fla, 85 & 87, Leo Kaplan Modern, NY, 98; Corning Mus Glass, NY, 78-79; Leigh Yawkey Woodson Art Mus, Wausau, Wis, 79, 81 & 88; Hokkaido Mus Mod Art, Sapporo, Japan, 82; Illumination: The Quality of Light, Pittsburgh Ctr for the Arts, Pa, 85; Luminosity, The Alternative Mus, NY, 86; The Saxe Collection, Mus Am Craft, NY, 87; Light and Transparency, Mus Bellerive, 88 & Illuminated Sculpture, Sanske Gallerie, 88, Zurich, Switz; Expressions en Verre II, Musee des Artes Decoratifs, Lausanne, Switz; Building a Permanent Collection, Mus Am Craft, NY, 90. *Teaching:* Instr, Milropa Studios, New York, 75-76 & New Sch Social Res, New York, 76-77. *Awards:* Res Grant, Union Molycorp, Los Angeles, 82. *Bibliog:* Judy Spurgin (auth), article, Art Craft Mag, 10-11/80; Sylvia Netzer (auth), Rays of Glass-Paul Seide, Neus Glas Mag, 3/88. *Mem:* Glass Art Soc. *Media:* Blown Glass, Neon. *Specialty:* Glass & wood sculpture. *Dealer:* Scott Jacobson Gallery 114 E 57th St New York NY 10022. *Mailing Add:* 49 Ward St Burlington VT 05401

SEIDEN, ARTHUR
PAINTER, ILLUSTRATOR
b Brooklyn, NY. *Study:* Queens Col, BA (cum laude), 74; Art Students League, 8 yrs study with Will Barnet, S Dickinson, Charles Alston & Mario Cooper; New Sch, with Stuart Davis. *Work:* Kerlan Collection, Univ Minn; Philip Morris Corp & Kennedy Gallery, NY; Rutgers Univ, New Brunswick, NJ; Mazza Collection, New Britain Youth Mus; Univ Southern Miss; New Britain Mus Am Art. *Comn:* Hoffmann-LaRoche, Eli Lilly, Gen Motors, Hearst Pubs, others. *Exhib:* Am Watercolor Soc, Nat Acad Design, NY, 64, 67 & 68; Solo exhibs, Lotos Club, NY, 74, 2002; Lotos Club, 75; Am Watercolor Soc 123rd Ann Exhib, 90; Nat Acad 169th Ann Exhib, 94. *Collection Arranged:* Lotos Club, NY. *Pos:* guest instr, NY Univ. *Teaching:* Guest instr, New York City Community Col. *Awards:* Bk Awards, Am Inst Graphic Arts, 54, 57 & 61. *Mem:* Am Watercolor Soc; life mem Lotos Club; life mem Art Students League; Artist's Equity NY Inc; Soc Illusr; Artists Fel, Inc. *Media:* Transparent Watercolor, Gouache. *Specialty:* original illustrations. *Interests:* collecting autographs. *Publ:* Illusr, Train to Timbuktu, Golden Bks, 51; Greek Gods and Heroes, 61, Big Treasure Book of Fairy Tales, 64 & Big Book of Kittens, 68, Grosset & Dunlap; Doc stops a war, Reader's Digest; Heroines of the American Revolution, 98. *Dealer:* Kendra Krienke Gallery. *Mailing Add:* 75 Lloyd Ln Lloyd Harbor NY 11743-9781

SEIDEN, KATIE
SCULPTOR, ASSEMBLAGE ARTIST
b New York, NY. *Study:* Sarah Lawrence Col, Bronxville, NY, BA, 58; New York Univ, New York, NY, MA, 60. *Work:* House of Humor & Satire, Gabrova, Bulgaria; Grand Manan Mus, New Brunswick, Can; Wash Co Mus Fine Arts, Hagerstown, Md; Helen S Keller Nat Ctr, Kingspoint, NY; Saint Mary Abbey, Mechanicsville, Md; Islip Art Mus, E Islip, Mid-Houston Arts & Sci Ctr, Poughkeepsie, NY. *Comn:* Sculpture (3 feet), comn by Mr & Mrs David Wood, Berkeley, Calig, 84; sculpture (7 feet), comn by Stephen Style, NY, 85. *Exhib:* Solo exhibs, Edward Williams Gallery, Hackensack, NJ, 84, Cent Hall Gallery, Soho, NY, 79, 82, 84, Five & Dime, East Village, NY, 87, Wash Co Mus Fine Arts, Hagerstown, Md, 88 & Sensory Evolution Gallery, NY, 87 & 88, San Francisco Int Airport, Calif, 88 & Myth & Reality, Gallery 10, Washington, DC, 90; Lines of Vision I: Drawings by Contemp Women Traveling Exhib, Islip Art Mus, E Islip, NY, 92, ARC Gallery, Chicago, 92; Lines of Vision II: Drawings by Contemp Women, US Info Agency Traveling Exhib, 89-90; Centennial Exhib Nat Asn Women Artists Traveling Exhib, 89- 90; The Expressionist Surface & Contemp Art in Plaster, Queens Mus, Flushing, NY, 90; Original Sin, Hillwood Art, Brookville, NY, 91. *Pos:* Arts ed & critic, Boulevard Mag, 87, 88 & 89; Exec ed & critic, Country Plaza Mag, 89, 90 & 91; arts ed & reviewer, The Gold Coast Gazette, Glen Cove, NY, 91-. *Awards:* Artists Grant, Artist Space, New York, 88-91; Puffin Found, 92; NY Found for the Arts & E End Arts Coun, 92. *Bibliog:* Michael Brenson (auth), Sculpture that springs from surrealism, The Sunday New York Times, 3/8/87; Karin Lipson (auth), Katie Seiden - The Outpost Artist, Newsday, 6/1/87; Diane Ketchum (auth), Katie Seiden - About Long Island, 12/4/88; Barbara Matilsky (auth), The Expressionist Surface: Contemporary Art in Plaster-Katie Seiden (exhib catalog), 90; Michael Brenson (auth), Plaster as a medium, not just an interim step, New York Times, 7/13/90. *Mem:* Nat Asn Women Artists; Hempstead Harbor Artists (bd mem, 84-85); Women's Caucus Arts. *Media:* Plaster, Miscellaneous Media. *Publ:* Auth, article, Central Hall Artists Newsletter, 76; Women Artists News, Midmarch Asn, 77; illusr, Sinister Wisdom, 84; feature art exhib (monthly), Boulevard Mag, 87, 88 & 89; illustr, Spiral Though, Front Cover, 89. *Dealer:* Country Art Gallery Locust Valley NY; Sensory Evolution Gallery 420 E 13th St East Village NY. *Mailing Add:* 52 Cromwell Pl Sea Cliff NY 11579

SEIDL, CLAIRE
PAINTER, PRINTMAKER
b Greenwich, Conn, May 17, 1951. *Study:* London Polytech, Sir John Cass Coll Art, 72; Syracuse Univ, Coll Visual & Performing Arts, BFA (cum laude), 73; City Univ New York, Hunter Col, MFA, 82; Int Ctr Photog, 96-99. *Work:* Albright Col, Pa; Aldrich Mus, Conn; Citibank & Mobil Oil Corp, NY; Portland Mus Art, Maine; Pfizer Electric, NY; and others. *Comn:* two paintings, Miller, Anderson, Sherrard, MOMA Tower, NY, 88; four paintings, Reliance Insurance, NY, 89; painting/mural, Oxford Hills Comprehensive High Sch, S Paris, Maine, 97. *Exhib:* Solo exhibs, Hunter Gallery, NY, 82, John Davis Gallery, Akron, Ohio, 83 & 85, Stephen Rosenberg Gallery, NY, 86, 88, 90, 94, 96 & 99 Rosenberg + Kaufman Gallery, NY, 96, 99 & 2001, Claudia Carr Gallery, NY, 99, Icon Gallery, Brunswick, Maine, 2000 & A Ramona Space, NY, 2000; Works on Paper, Frick Gallery, Belfast, Maine, 92; Contemp Abstraction, O'Farrell Gallery, Brunswick, Maine, 92; The Tenth Summer, Stephen Rosenberg Gallery, NY, 93,; Paint and Paper, Rosenberg + Kaufman Fine Art, NY, 95, Painting, 97, Spatial Relations - Photographs, 99, Sun Signs, 2000 & Land Photographs, 2000; The Language of Art: Res Ipsa Loquitor Art Initiatives, NY, 95; Icon Gallery, Brunswick, Maine, 96 & 97; and others. *Teaching:* Vis artist, Ill State Univ, 84 & Syracuse Univ, NY, 85 & 86; lectr, Hunter Col, City Univ, NY, 85-90, asst prof, 90-95. *Awards:* Nancy Ashton Mem Fund Prize, 82; William Graf Fel, 82; Fel, Cummington Community of the Arts, 83. *Bibliog:* Marina Vaizey in Berlin: New work--New York, London Sunday Times, 10/30/83; Benjamin Forgey (auth), article, Washington Post, 7/20/85; Vivien Raynor (auth), New Currents in Watercolor, NY Times, 8/4/91; Sue Scott (auth) Art News, 9/96; Mario Naves (auth), New Art Examiner, 9/96; Lilly Wei (auth), Art In America, 1/97; Dominque Nahas (auth), Review, 1/99; Grace Glueck (auth), NY Times, 2/5/99. *Mem:* 22 Wooster (treas, 79-80). *Media:* Oils, Watercolor; Black & White Photography. *Dealer:* Rosenberg + Kaufman Fine Art 115 Wooster St New York NY 10012; Icon Contemp Art 19 Mason St Brunswick ME 04011; Claudia Carr Gallery 478 W Broadway New York NY 10012. *Mailing Add:* c/o Stephen Rosenberg & Kaufman Fine Art 115 Wooster St New York NY 10012

SEIDLER, DORIS
PAINTER, PRINTMAKER
b London, Eng. *Study:* Atelier 17, New York, with Stanley William Hayter. *Work:* Smithsonian Inst, Washington, DC; Philadelphia Mus Art; Brooklyn Mus; Seattle Mus Art; Whitney Mus Am Art, New York; British Mus; V&A Lonson, Libr Cong, Washington, DC; Pallant House, Chichester, Eng. *Exhib:* First & Second Hawaii Nat Print Exhib, Honolulu Acad Arts; Pa Acad Fine Arts, Philadelphia; Soc Am Graphic Artists; Jewish Mus, New York; Atelier 17, Brooklyn Mus, 78; Whitney Mus Am Art; Libr Cong, Washington, DC; Nassau Co Mus Fine Art, NY; Pallant House, Chichester, Eng, 91 & 2006; British Mus, 96; Eds Alecto Exhib, Whitworth Gallery, Manchester, Eng, 2003; and others. *Awards:* MacDowell Artists Colony Fel, 66 & 75; Medal for Creative Graphics, Audubon Artists, 72; Awards, Soc Am Graphic Artists, 82-83 & 85. *Bibliog:* Joly Patterson (auth), Chicago Soc Etchers, Farleigh Dickinson Univ Press, 2002; Tessa Sidey (auth), Editions Alecto Graphics, 1960-1981, 2003. *Media:* Acrylic; All Media. *Interests:* Art, music, travel. *Collection:* Chas Dean, NY. *Publ:* Auth, articles in Artist Proof. *Dealer:* Anita Shapolsky Gallery 152 E 65th St New York NY 10012. *Mailing Add:* 205 Washington Ave Apt 504 Santa Monica CA 90403

SEIPEL, JOSEPH H
ADMINISTRATOR, EDUCATOR
Study: Univ Wis, Madison, BS (art), 1970; Rinehart Sch Sculpture, Md Inst Art, MFA, 1973. *Pos:* Sr assoc dean, dir grad studies, Va Commonwealth Univ Sch of the Arts, 2002-09, dean, 2011-; vpres academic services, Savannah Col Art and Design, Ga, 2009-11. *Teaching:* Instr, Va Commonwealth Univ, 1974-82, asst prof, Sculpture Dept, 1982-86, chair, 1985-2001, assoc prof, prof, 1999-. *Mailing Add:* Virginia Commonwealth University School of the Arts 325 N Harrison St Richmond VA 23284-2519

SEITZ-ELLIOTT, PATRICIA LYNNE
PAINTER
b San Diego, Calif, Dec, 2, 1962. *Study:* Univ Ariz, Scholarship, 93; Ventura Coll, AA, 95; Syracuse Univ, BA, 97; Studied with John Pototschnik, Daniel Edmondson & Johannes Vloothuis, 2011. *Work:* Everson Mus, Syracuse, NY. *Exhib:* Chasm Falls, Everson Mus, Syracuse, NY, 2011. *Awards:* Everson Mus 60/60, Chasm Falls, Everson Mus, 2011; Featured Art, Sacandaga River, Realist Paintings about Water, 2011; Permanent Feature Gallery, Spring Bouqet, Painters Universe, 2011; Featured Art, Sacandaga River, Impressionism Cafe, 2011; Featured Art, Winter Thaw, Landscape Painting, 2011; Featured Art, Higley Pond, Painting the Country Life, 2011. *Bibliog:* Bradford Gordon Wheler (auth), Horse Sayings, Book Collaborative, 2011; Snow Play, Upstate Medical Univ, The Healing Muse, 2011. *Mem:* Oil Painters of America; CNY Art Guild; Fingerlakes Artists and Crafters of NY; NY Plein Air Painters; Ask Art: Artists Bluebook. *Media:* Acrylic, Oil. *Publ:* illusr, Horse Sayings: Wit and Wisdom Straight from the Horses Mouth, 2011; illusr, The Healing Muse: A Journal of Literary and Visual Arts, Upstate Medical Univ, 2011; auth, Peaceful Glow, 2011. *Dealer:* Xandu Gallery 7039 E Main St 101 Scottsdale Az 85251; Patricia Elliot Seitz PO Box 303 Liverpool NY 13088-0303. *Mailing Add:* PO Box 303 Liverpool NY 13088

SELF, DANA RAE
CURATOR, WRITER
b Fort Lauderdale, Fla, June 5, 1959. *Study:* Stephens Col, BA, 81; Univ Kans, Lawrence, MA, 84. *Collection Arranged:* Subversive Domesticity, 95; Chihuly Over Venice: An Am Premier, 96; Christian Boeltamski - So Far, 98; Alex Katz: Small Paintings, 2000; Robert Therrien, 2000; Ken Aptekar, 2001. *Pos:* asst cur, John Michael Kohler Arts Ctr, 93-94; cur, Ulrich Mus, Wichita State Univ, Kans, 94-96; cur, Kemper Mus Contemp Art, 96-. *Teaching:* adj instr art hist, Johnson Co Community Col, 91-93. *Mem:* Coll Arts Asn; Am Asn Mus; PEO. *Res:* contemporary art. *Publ:* auth Subversive Domesticity, Wichita State Univ, 95; coauth Chihuly Over Venice, Portland Press, 96; auth Georgia O'Keefe: Intimate Landscapes, Univ Pub, 98; auth Shahzia Sikander, Kemper Mus, 98; coauth Alex Katz: Small Paintings, Kemper Mus, 2001

SELIGMAN, THOMAS KNOWLES
DIRECTOR
b Santa Barbara, Calif, Jan 1, 1944. *Study:* Stanford Univ, BA, 1965; Acad of Art Col, San Francisco, BFA, 1967; Sch of Visual Arts, New York, MFA, 1968. *Collection Arranged:* Eskimo Art from the Toronto-Dominion Bank, 1972, Man and Animals in Pre-Columbian Mesoamerica, 1973, Australian Aboriginal Art from the Louis Allen Collection, 1974, African & Ancient Mexican Art-The Loran Collection (coauth, catalog), 1974-75, Fire, Earth & Water-Sculpture from the Land Collection of Mesoamerican Art (ed, catalog), Honolulu Acad of Arts & Seattle Art Mus, 1975 & Masterpieces of Primitive Art from the Mus of Primitive Art in NY, 1977, San Francisco Mus Fine Arts; Form & Freedom, Rice Inst Arts; The Art of Being Huichol, Field Mus, Chicago & Am Mus Natural Hist, NY; Treasures of Ancient Nigeria, co-organized with Detroit Inst Arts & Metrop Mus Art, 1978-80; Bay Area Collects (coauth, catalog); Spirits, Gods and Kings; Forms and Forces: Dynamics of African Figurative Sculpture (coauth, catalogue), 1988; The Art of Being Tuareg: Sahara Nomads in a Modern World (coauth) 2006. *Pos:* Dir, Africana Mus, Liberia, Africa, 1969-71; deputy dir educ & exhibs, Fine Arts Mus, San Francisco, 1972-89; deputy dir operations and planning, Fine Arts Mus, San Francisco, 1989-1991; dir, Cantor Arts Ctr, Stanford Univ, 1991-. *Teaching:* Asst prof African art hist, Cuttington Col, Liberia, Africa, 1969-71; senior lectr, Dept Art, Stanford Univ. *Awards:* Aid to Mus Prof Award, Nat Endowment Arts, 1975 & 87; Award of Honor, Nat Inst Anthropology & History, Mex. *Mem:* Am Asn Mus; Friends of Ethnic Arts (dir, 1974-); Am Fedn Arts (trustee & vpres), 1982-1995; Cult Property Adv Comt to Pres of US, 1988-92; Asn Art Mus Dirs, 1992-. *Res:* African aesthetics; art in context in Liberia, Sierra Leone and Ivory Coast, Tuareg art of Niger Mali and Algeria. *Publ:* Auth, African art at the MH de Young Memorial Museum, African Arts, Univ Calif, Los Angeles, Vol 7 (4); Educational use of an anthropology collection in an art museum, Curator, fall 1974; An indigenous concept of fakes--authentic African art?, African Arts, Univ Calif, Los Angeles, Vol 9 (3); An Unexpected Bequest and an Ethical Dilemma featuring serpents and flowering trees, Fine Arts Mus of San Francisco, 1988. *Mailing Add:* Cantor Arts Ctr Stanford CA 94305-5060

SELLA, ALVIN CONRAD
PAINTER, EDUCATOR
b West Hoboken, NJ, Aug 30, 1919. *Study:* Yale Univ Sch Art; Art Students League, with Brackman & Bridgman; Columbia Univ, with Machau; Coll Fine Arts, Syracuse Univ; Univ NMex; also in Mex. *Work:* Bristol Iron & Steel Co; Collectors of Am Art; Sullins Col. *Exhib:* Am Fedn Arts Traveling Exhib, 61-62; solo exhibs, Centenary Col, Lauren Rogers Mus Art, Laurel, Miss, Munic Art Gallery, Jackson, Miss, Birmingham Mus Art, 69, Dick Jemison Gallery, Birmingham, 76, Moody Gallery Art, Univ Ala, Tuscaloosa, 95, Ala State Univ, Montgomery, 96, Stillman Col, Tuscaloosa, 98 & others; Birmingham Mus Art, 76; Watercolor Soc Ala, 76; Frank Fedele Fine Art, 84-86; Univ Ark, 85; and others. *Teaching:* Head, Dept Art, Sullins Col, 48-61; prof art, Univ Ala, 61-; vis prof, Spring Workshops, Miss Art Colony, 62-64 & Shreveport Art Colony, 64-68; artist-in-residence, Summer Sch Arts, Univ SC, 68. *Awards:* First Award, 54th Ann Miss Exhib; Third Prize, 7th Mobile Art Exhib, 72; 32nd Ann Watercolor Exhib First & Second Prize, Birmingham Mus Art, 72; others. *Mem:* Art Students League; Am Asn Univ Prof; Coll Art Asn Am; fel Int Inst Arts & Lett. *Media:* All Media. *Dealer:* Galleria Atenea San Miguel de Allende Mexico, 95. *Mailing Add:* Univ Ala Dept Art Tuscaloosa AL 35486

SELLDORF, ANNABELLE M
ARCHITECT
b Cologne, Germany, 1960. *Study:* Pratt Inst, BArch; Syracuse Univ, MArch. *Work:* Neue Galerie New York; Sterling and Francine Clark Art Inst; Inst for Study of the Ancient World; Sunset Park Materials Recycling Facility; Urban Glass House; Gladstone Gallery; Acquavella Galleries; Michael Werner Gallery; Hauser & Wirth; David Zwirner; Abercrombie & Fitch Flagship Stores in New York, London, Milan, Paris, Copenhagen, Tokyo; others. *Pos:* architect, Gluckman Mayner, New York; founder, principal, Selldorf Architects LLC, New York, 1993-; designer, Vica, New York; consultant, vis critic; bd dirs, Chinati Found, Marfa, Tex, Design Trust for Pub Space; pres bd, Archit League NY. *Awards:* finalist, Cooper-Hewitt Nat Design Award for Interior Design, 2006; named One of Top 100 Designers in World, Architectural Digest; Pub Design Comn Award, New York, 2010. *Mem:* Nat Acad; Fel Am Inst Architects. *Mailing Add:* Selldorf Architects 860 Broadway at Union Sq New York NY 10003

SELLER, LINDA
ARTIST
b Brooklyn, NY, Sept 29, 1954. *Study:* Hunter Col, 1972; Study with the Art Students League, 1973-82; Nat Acad of Design, 1985-88. *Work:* Trenton State Col, Trenton, NJ; Scott Mem Study Collection, Bryn Mawr, PA; Center for Book Arts, New York, NY. *Comn:* mural, comn by Lucinda C Collins, Brattleboro, Vt, 2005-06; mural, comn by HS Corwin, Boca Raton, FL, 2006. *Exhib:* HTAL Ann Juried Exhib, Heckscher Mus, Huntington, NY, 1990; Am Drawings Biennial, Muscarelle Mus Art, Williamsburg, VA, 1992; Selections from The Scott Mem Study Collection, Bryn Mawr Coll Ctr, Bryn Mawr, Pa, 1993. *Awards:* Juror Award, Art Assoc of Harrisburg, 1991; First Place Juror Award, Muscarelle Mus Art, 1992; Janet Royce Award, Pastel Soc Am, 1994. *Mem:* Center for Book Arts; Guild of the Bookworker, New York, NY; Guild of the N Am Goldsmiths; Pastel Soc of Am; Craft Coun Am. *Media:* On Paper, Graphite, Ink, Pastel Watercolor. *Interests:* bookarts, gold/silversmithing. *Collection:* Neil Lane, Lucinda Copeland Collins. *Mailing Add:* 1665 Glenwood Rd Brooklyn NY 11230

SELLERS, WILLIAM FREEMAN
SCULPTOR, PAINTER
b Bay City, Mich, June 1, 1929. *Study:* Univ Mich, BArch, 54, MFA, 62. *Work:* Suspension, Six Cubes & Converging Cubes, Mem Art Gallery, Rochester, NY. *Comn:* Four Squares (painted steel), Student Asn, State Univ NY, Cortland, 69; reprogression, Sentry Group, Rochester, NY. *Exhib:* Sculpture & Prints Ann, Whitney Mus Am Art, NY, 66, Contemp Am Sculpture Ann, 68; Plus by Minus: Today's Half-Century, Albright-Knox Art Gallery, Buffalo, 68; Am Sculpture of the Sixties, Grand Rapids Art Mus, Mich, 69; Painting and Sculpture Today, Indianapolis Mus Art, 70; Installation, Carleton Col, 81; Contemp Sculpture, State Univ NY, 83; sculpture installation, Pyramid Arts Ctr, Rochester, NY, 87; working drawing & studies, Monroe Community Col, Rochester, NY, 87. *Teaching:* Instr design, Rochester Inst Technol, 62-65; asst prof sculpture, Univ Rochester, 66-70; asst prof art, Lehman Col, 70-, chmn dept art, 75-77; vis artist-teacher, Carleton Col, 81-; instr sculpture, Nazareth Col, 87. *Awards:* Jurors' Show Award, Mem Art Gallery, 66; Faculty Res Grant, Lehman Col, City Univ New York, 72-73. *Media:* Metal, Wood; Acrylic, Oil. *Dealer:* Oxford Gallery Rochester NY. *Mailing Add:* 192 Aberdeen St Rochester NY 14619

SELSOR, MARCIA LORRAINE
CERAMIST, SCULPTOR
b Philadelphia, Pa, Feb 1, 1949. *Study:* Philadelphia Univ Arts, BFA, 70; Southern Ill Univ, MFA, 74. *Work:* Northern Ariz Univ Galleries, Flagstaff; Yellowstone Art Mus, Billings, Mont; Ill State Mus, Springfield; Mus Plastic Arts, Tumen, Russia; Mus Fine Art, Riga, Latvia; Archie Bray Found, Helena, Mont; Clay Studio, Philadelphia, Pa; Margaret Greenham Theater, Walter Phillips Permanent Collection Banff Centre, Alberta, Can; Int Ctr of Artists, Tashkent, Uzbekistan; Pushkin Mus, Moscow, Russia; and numerous pvt collections; Centro Leon, Santiago de los Caballeros, Dominican Republic; Jade Palace Restaurant, Helena, Mont; Instituto de Cultura Juan Gilbert Alicante, Spain; Int Ctr Artists, Tashkent, Uzbekistan; N Ariz Univ, Flagstaff, Ariz; Riga Mus Fine Arts, Riga, Latvia; Pushkin Mus, Moscow, Russia; Planned Parenthood of Billings, Mont; Security Bank, Laurel, Mont; Springfield Art Mus, Springfield, Ill; and many others. *Comn:* Raku plaques, Deaconess Med Ctr, Billings, Mont, 89; Horse plaques, Security Bank, Laurel, Mont. *Exhib:* N Ariz Univ Gallery, Flagstaff, 91; Dzintari Creative Arts, Ceramic Symp: Exhib Dzintari Creative Arts Ctr, Jurmala, Latvia, 91; solo exhibs, Marking the Millennium, Yellowstone Art Mus, Billings, Mont, 91 & Recent Raku, Minot Art Gallery, NDak, 92; Year Am Craft, WWC, Rock Springs, 93; Contemp Am Ceramics, Loveland Art Mus, 96; Fulbright Artists, Meridian Ctr, Washington, DC, 97; Wild Things, Peter's Valley, NJ, 98; Text and Texture, Broome St Gallery, New York, 98; 39th Ann Intl Exhib, Brownsville Mus Art, 2006; Tex 6-Pack Show, Austin, 2007; Archie Bray Int, 2006; Syracuse Ceramics Guild, 2009; Jackson Arts Asn, Jackson, Wyo, 2009; Hui Noeau Art Ctr, Maui, Hawaii, 2009; Fertile Ground, Yellowstone Art Mus, Billings, MT; 10th Anniv of 9/11, Every Life is a Book at the Int Tech, Educ and Commerce Center at the Univ Tex, Brownsville, 2011; AIR Vallauris, Fr, 2012. *Pos:* vis artist, Dzintari Creative Arts Ctr Soviet Artists Union, 91 & Uzbekistani Artists Union, 92; res artist, BANFF, 93; pres fac sen, Mont State Univ, Billings, 98-99; tech staff, Ceramics Monthly; bd dirs, Potters Coun. *Teaching:* Prof ceramics, Mont State Univ, Billings, 75-2000, prof emer; workshops, Centro Agost, Spain, Sierra Nev Coll, 98, Appalachian Ctr for Crafts, 2000, La Meridiana, Italy, 2001-2003 & 2007, Tex Ceramics Showdown UTPA/TSC, McAllen, Tex, 2008, LI Art League, 2008, self-employed artist, UT Brownsville, 2011-2012. *Awards:* Merit Award, Texas Six Pack Show; Merit Award, Vascfinder, 2007; Best of Show, First Place Mixed Media, Brownsville Mus Fine Art, 2010. *Bibliog:* James Watkins and Paul Wandless (auths), Alternative firing methods, 93, 84; Dr Louana Lackey (auth), Under a bigger sky, Montana's Marcia Selsor, Ceramics Monthly, 5/97; First Annual Clay Arters Exhibition, Ceramic Monthly, 98; Darryl Baird (auth), The Extruder Book, Am Ceramics Soc, 2000; Bill Jones (ed), Advanced Raku Techniques, 10-13; Michael Bailey (auth), Oriental Glazes, 35, 79, 89 & 100; Steven Branfman, Raku Mastering, Anderson Turner 9ed), Ceramics Sculpture, Inspiring Techniques, 2010; 500 Raku, Lark Books. *Mem:* Nat Coun Educ Ceramic Arts (dir-at-large, 90-91); Potters Coun (pres); Tex Clay Art Asn. *Media:* Terra Cotta, Raku, Porcelain. *Res:* Shellac carving multi-colored layers. *Specialty:* Ceramics, Vintage Art. *Interests:* Large scale hand building, thrown porcelain. *Publ:* Fulbright in Uzbekistan, Studio Potter, Vol 23, No 5, 95; Japanese Women Ceramists, Nat Coun Educ Ceramic Arts J, 43, 95-96; Once is Not Enough, An Historical Explanation of the Development of Multiple Firing Techniques, Nat Coun Educ Ceramic Arts J, 97-98; Political Ceramics in Voices of Art, 2010. *Dealer:* Charlie Blim/Charlie B Gallery 200 E Main St Ste 101 Fenley NV 89408. *Mailing Add:* 204 E Cowan Ter Brownsville TX 78521-0134

SELTZER, JOANNE LYNN
PAINTER, PRINTMAKER
b Philadelphia, Pa, June 21, 1946. *Study:* Northwestern Univ, cert, 63; Univ Mich, BFA (painting & ceramics), 69; New Sch Social Res, 73; Pratt Inst, 74; Pratt Graphics Ctr, 74; NY Univ, MA (photog & art history) 79; Parsons Sch Design, 86-88 (perspective drawing), AAS, 94. *Work:* Brooklyn Mus; Worcester Art Mus, Mass; Mus Contemp Art, Ghent, Belgium; Sunrise Mus, Charleston, WVa; Toledo Mus Art, Ohio; Indianapolis Mus Art, Ind; WVa Cult Ctr, Charleston; Ripley Mus, Ripley, WV. *Exhib:* Women Artists 1877-1977, Charlottenburg Palace, Berlin, 77; Travaux Sur Papier, Ctr Cult-Jacques Prevert, Paris, 81; Typich Frau, 81; Mapped Art, Charts, Roots, Regions traveling exhib, 81-83; Independent Cur Benefit, 85; 1978-79 Art-About the Strange Nature of Money, Stadtische Kunsthalle, Dusseldorf; and others. *Pos:* Inst, Nat Soc Col Dames State NY Art Archit & Decorative Arts Col Am, 86-88. *Teaching:* Guest lectr, Univ Iowa, 79, Univ Va, 79, Koninklijke Akad Bosch, Holland, 80 & 82, NY Univ, 81, Drew Univ, 81 & Conn Col, 82; lectr art history, Caring Comm Senior Ctr, NY, 2004-2005. *Bibliog:* Peter Frank (auth), article, Art News, 9/76; Lucy Lippard (auth), From the Center, EP Dutton, 77; Jos Knaepen (auth), article, Bulletin, Belg, 1/22/82; and others. *Media:* Oil, Silkscreen-Serigraphy, Ceramics, Watercolor. *Res:* Charles Willson Peale, Colonial Portraitist. *Interests:* Reading, Ballet, Museums. *Publ:* Contribr, Mus J, Amsterdam, 76, Kunstlerinnen Int, 77 & Flash Art, 77. *Mailing Add:* 210 Centre St New York NY 10013

SELTZER, PETER LAWRENCE
PAINTER
b 1947. *Study:* Studied with Daniel Greene. *Work:* Butler Inst Am Art; New Britain Mus Am Art; Harvard Univ; paint & clay, New Haven, Conn. *Comn:* portrait, Harvard Univ, 2006. *Exhib:* Nat Acad Design, NY; Nat Arts Club, NY; Butler Inst Am Art, Ohio; New Britain us Am Art, Conn; Various solo and group exhibs. *Collection Arranged:* Corporate and pvt collections. *Awards:* Dianne B Bernhard Gold Medal, Pastel Soc Am, 2001 & 2002; Allied Artists Am Gold Medal Hon, Allied Artists Am, 2004; Best in Show, Int Exhib Pastels, Taiwan Ctr, NY. *Bibliog:* Pastel Journal, 2001; American Artist, 2004; Maureen Bloomfield (ed), Pastel Journal, 2006. *Mem:* Allied Artists Am; Pastel Soc Am. *Media:* Oils and Pastels. *Mailing Add:* 87 Main St N Woodbury CT 06798

SELTZER, PHYLLIS
PAINTER, PRINTMAKER
b Detroit, Mich, May 17, 1928. *Study:* Univ Iowa, BFA & MFA; Lasansky's Workshop, sr study hist of technol, with M Kranzberg; Case Western Reserve Univ. *Work:* Brooklyn Art Mus; Cleveland Mus Art; Minn Mus Art, Minneapolis; Nat Gallery Art, Ottawa, Ont; Butler Mus, Youngstown, Ohio; Cleveland Clinic, Ohio; Citibank, NY; BP America, Cleveland, Ohio. *Comn:* Bicentennial print, Cleveland Area Arts Coun, 75; ed of 25, Exodus print, Cleveland Health Dept; elevators & etched mirrors, Stouffer's Inn on the Square, Cleveland, Ohio; Murals, Bistro des Artistes, Cleveland, Ohio. *Exhib:* May Show, Cleveland Mus Art, Ohio, 87 & 90 & Yr in Review, 90; Fla Printmakers Soc Ann, Tampa, 89; Art Expo, NY, 90; NY traveling, WGer, 90; NY Print Fair, 92; and others. *Pos:* Coordr fine arts, Cleveland Col, Case Western Reserve Univ, 66-70; interior designer, Dalton, Van Dijk, Johnson, Cleveland, 72-74; interior designer, 75-87. *Teaching:* Lectr art hist & printmaking, Lake Erie Col, Painesville, Ohio, 70-72; lectr art fund, Cleveland State Univ, 69-71. *Awards:* Purchase Award, Brooklyn Mus 19th Nat, 75; Tiffany Fel, Nat Congress Art & Design, 88; Artlink, 90. *Bibliog:* William Bierman (auth), Artist Improves on Technology, Akron Beacon J, 3/23/75; Helen Cullinan (auth), Venice is Source of Inspiration, Cleveland Plain Dealer, 8/7/88; Helen Cullinan (auth), A New Perspective on Spring Tradition, Cleveland Plain Dealer, 4/6/90. *Mem:* New Orgn Visual Arts (secy, 73, vpres, 74); Print Club Cleveland (pres, 83 & 84). *Media:* Oil; Heat Transfer Printing, Miscellaneous Media. *Publ:* Printworld, 83-87 & 90; Art Examiner, 90; An Illustrated Survey of Leading Contemporaries, Am Artists, 89 & 90; NY Gallery Guide, 90. *Dealer:* The Bonfoey Gallery Cleveland OH; John Szoke Gallery New York NY

SELVIN, NANCY
CERAMIST, SCULPTOR
b Los Angeles, Calif, 1943. *Study:* Univ Calif, Berkeley, BA, 69, with Voulkos & Ron Nagle, MA, 70. *Work:* Oakland Mus, Calif; Hokkoku Shimbun, Tokyo; Ariz State Univ Art Gallery, Tempe; Mint Mus, NC; Los Angeles Mus Mod Art; Nora Eccles Mus, Utah; Renwick Gallery, Smithsonian Inst, Washington, DC; Microsoft Art Collection, Redmond, Wash; Univ Iowa Mus Art; Celestial Seasonings, Boulder, Colo; Kohler Art Center, Sheboygan, Wisc; Racine Art Mus; Daum Mus. *Comn:* stone/text sidewalk inserts, In Berkeley 2000, City of Berkeley, Calif, 2000-01; Cafe Liliane, San Francisco, CA. *Exhib:* Mus Contemp Crafts, NY, 76; San Francisco Mus, 77; solo exhib, Calif Crafts Mus, Palo Alto, 82, Grossmont Col, Cajon, Calif, 90, Berkeley Civic Arts, Calif, 91, Richmond Art Ctr, Calif, 95, Works Gallery, Sonoma, Calif, 96, Charleston Heights Art Ctr, Las Vegas, Nev, 99 & Sybaris Gallery, Royal Oak, Mich, 99, Pence Gallery, Davis, Calif, 02, Tercera Gallery, Palo Alto, Calif, 03, Sybaris Gallery, Royal Oak, Mich, 04; Fac Exhib, San Francisco State Univ Art Gallery, 91; Artists Sketchbooks, Palo Alto Cult Ctr, Calif, 95; Kiddush Cup Invitational, Jewish Mus, San Francisco, 97; Teabowl Invitational, Lafayette Mus Art, Ind, 98; Celestial Seasonings, Boulder, Colo, 98; Ferrin Gallery, Northampton, Mass, 98; Survey of Int Ceramics, Laguna Beach Art Mus, Calif, 98; Artesans Gallery, Mill Valley, Calif, 98; traveling, Color & Fire: Defining Moments in Studio Ceramics 1950-2000, 2000; Glimpse of the Invisible, Arvada Ctr for Arts, Colo, 2000; Selections from the Chasanoff Collection, Mint Mus, Charlotte NC, 2001; Scripps Coll Collection, Claremont, Calif; Diverse Domain, Taipei, Taiwan, 2004; Calif Clay, Baltimore Clay Works, 2008; New Work Old Stories, San Francisco Contemp Jewish Mus, 2009; Diversity with Clay, Am Mus Ceramic Art, Pomona, Calif, 2009; Tu B'Shavat Jewish Mus, 2011; Do Not Destroy, Contemporary Jewish Mus, 2012; Bay Area Treasures, Berkeley Art Ctr, 2012; Nancy Selvin: Paintings & the Work on Paper, Lightroom, Berkely, Calif, 2013. *Collection Arranged:* Prater Collection, Univ Md. *Pos:* owner & founder, After School Arts, Cragmont Prospect Schs, 83-89; grants rev panelist, City of Oakland, 86-89 & 2000, pub art adv comt, 89-97, chair, 94-97; bd dir, ProArts, 87-94, pres, 89-91, chair nominations comt, 91-92, chair open studios comt, 90-91; dir, After Sch Art, 86- & San Francisco State Univ, 92; arts proj consult, Preserv Park, Oakland, 93 & Cult Arts Div, City of Oakland, 94; pub art adv comt, Alameda Co, 94-97; co-owner, Brushstrokes Studio, Berkeley, Calif, 95-98; art selection comt, Summit Hosp, Oakland, Calif, 96-; guest artist, Watershed Ctr Ceramic Arts, 98, bd trustees, 99-, pres bd trustees, 2000-04; CED coun bd, Univ Calif, 2005-2012; Alameda Co Public Art Comn, 2004-. *Teaching:* Instr ceramics, Laney Col, Oakland, 73-86, program dir workshop series, 78-86; vis fac, State Univ NY, Albany, 70-72, Fashion Inst Design, San Francisco, 73, Univ Calif, Berkeley, 88, San Francisco State Univ, 92 & Pitzer Col, Claremont, Calif, 99; lectr, Calif Col Arts & Crafts, 99, Merritt Col, Oakland, Calif, 2000, Univ Utah, Salt Lake City, 2000, Casper Col, Wyo, 2000, Brookhaven Col, Dallas, 2000 & many others; vis fac, Univ California, Berkeley, CA, 2004; Calif Col Arts, 2007-. *Awards:* Craftsman Fel, 80 & Artist Fel, 88, Nat Endowment Arts; Skaggs Found Prog Develop Grant, 86; Business Arts Award, Oakland, 90; others; NEA Artist Fel, 80; Fel, California Arts Council, 2003. *Bibliog:* Up Front, Ceramics Monthly, 9/96; David M Brin, Nancy Selvin's Abstracted Forms, Ceramic Art & Perception, 98; Scott Dickensheets, Great Bowls of Fire, Las Vegas Weekly, 10/12/99; Susan Peterson (auth), The Craft of Art and Clay, 99; Bai Ming (auth), Overseas Contemporary Ceramics, 2002; Ceramic Art Perception, 2010. *Mem:* CED Alumni Coun; NCECA; Alameda County Public Arts Commission, 2004-; Am Craft Council; Watershed Ctr Ceramic Arts. *Media:* Mixed, Ceramic. *Publ:* Auth, Tepcoware, 8-9/82 & Bulmer brick and tile, 85, Am Craft Mag; auth, How I Got Here, Ceramics Monthly, 11/89; Decorating tile, Fine Homebuilding, 1/93; Fundamentally Clay: Ceramic Abstraction, 2006; Ceramic Art Perception, 2010. *Dealer:* Tercera Gallery, Palo Alto, CA; Snyderman Works Gallery, Philadelphia, PA. *Mailing Add:* 745 Page St Berkeley CA 94710

SELZ, PETER H
ART HISTORIAN, CURATOR
b Munich, Ger, Mar 27, 1919. *Study:* Univ Chicago, fel, 46-54, MA & PhD; Univ Paris, Fulbright Award, 49-50. *Hon Degrees:* Calif Coll Arts & Crafts, hon DFA, 67. *Collection Arranged:* Directions In Kinetic Sculpture (catalog), 65; Funk (catalog), 67; Richard Lindner, 69; Pol Bury, 70; Excellence, 70; Harold Paris (catalog), 72; Ferdinand Hodler (catalog), 72; The Am Presidency in Political Cartoons (coauth, catalog), 76; German and Austrian Expressionism (catalog), 78; Two Decades of Am Painting: 1920-1940 (catalog), Dusseldorf, Zurich & Brussels, 79; Max Beckmann: Self Portraits, 92; Hans Burkhardt, 93; Tobi Kahn, 97; Spaces of Nature; Robert Colescott, 2001; Nathan Oliveira, 2002; Hassel Smith, 2003; Bob Freimark, 2007; Jerry Barrish, 2007; Morris Graves, 2010; The Painted Word, Patrick Graham, San Francisco, Calif; and many others. *Pos:* Head art hist prog, Inst Design, Ill Inst Technol, 53-55; chmn dept art & dir art gallery, Pomona Coll, 55-58; chief cur painting & sculpture exhibs, Mus Mod Art, 58-65; dir, Univ Art Mus, Univ Calif, Berkeley, 65-73; ed, Art Am; mem consult comt, Art Quart; proj dir, Christo's Running Fence Project, Calif, 74-76; Fine Arts Mus of San Francisco Aquisitions Comt, 96-. *Teaching:* Asst prof art hist, Inst Design, 53-54; chmn, Art Dept, Pomona Coll, 55-58; prof art hist, Univ Calif, Berkeley, 65-88, prof emer, currently; vis prof, Grad Sch Theology, Berkeley, 2007-. *Awards:* Belg-Am Educ Found Fel, 53; Order of Merit, Fed Ger Repub, 63; Sr Fel, Nat Endowment Humanities, 72; Rockefeller Found Study Ctr, Bellagio, 94; Charles Rufes Morey Award, Col Art Asn, 2007. *Mem:* Coll Art Asn Am (dir, 59-68); Neue Gallery, NY (trustee, 2000-); Kala Art Inst, Berkeley (trustee, 2002-); Meridian Gallery, San Francisco (trustee, 2003-, bd dirs); Neue Galerie, NY (bd dirs). *Res:* 20th/21st Century American and European Art. *Interests:* Art of the 20th Century-American & European. *Publ:* Art in Our Times, 81; Sam Francis, second ed, 82; Chillida, 86; Theories and Documents of Contemporary Art, 96; Max Beckmann, 96; Beyond the Mainstream, 97; Gottfried Helnwein, 97; Barbara Chase-Riboud, 99; Nathan Oliveira, 2002; Art of Engagement: Visual Politics in California and Beyond, 2006. *Mailing Add:* 861 Regal Rd Berkeley CA 94708

SELZNICK-DRUTZ, JUNE
PAINTER, EDUCATOR
b Toronto, Ont, Feb 14, 1920. *Study:* Cent Tech Sch; Ont Coll Art, grad (hons), 65. *Work:* McMaster Univ, Hamilton, Ont; Univ Waterloo, Ont; Royal Can Art Collection, Nat Gallery, Ottawa; Univ Guelph, Ont; London Trust Co, Ont; Citibank, Toronto; Hudson Bay Co, Toronto; and many others. *Comn:* Seeds of Spring Returning (serigraph ann print), Glenhyrst Art Asn, Brantford, Ont, 68-69. *Exhib:* Solo exhibs, Rebecca Sisler Gallery, Toronto, 78 & Prince Arthur Gallery, Toronto, 79; Ont Soc Artists, 80; Univ Ind, Elkhart, 80; Can Soc Painters Watercolor, 81; Second Int Watercolour Biennial, Mus Nac Aquarela, Coyoacan, Mex, 96; Cirle Art Gallery, Tohermoy, Ont, 2000; plus others. *Teaching:* Instr, Ont Col Art, Toronto, 67-86, Ont Dept Educ, summers 68-72, Ryerson Polytech Inst, Toronto, 72-73 & Toronto Art Sch, 66-75, retired. *Awards:* Honor award, Can Soc Painters Watercolor, 89; Honor Award & AJ Casson Medal, Soc Painters Watercolour, 93, Honour Award, 95, 97 & AJ Casson Award, 97. *Bibliog:* Robert Myers (auth), The youth cult maidens of June Drutz, Art Mag, Vol 6, No 22, 75. *Mem:* Royal Can Acad; Ont Soc Artists; Can Soc Painters Watercolor. *Media:* Tempera, Watercolor, Acrylic Tempera, Drawing. *Publ:* Article, Watercolor Magic, Cincinnati, Ohio, 99. *Dealer:* Circle Arts Gallery Tohermory Ont Canada. *Mailing Add:* 430 Annette St Toronto ON M6P 1R9 Canada

SEMAK, MICHAEL
PHOTOGRAPHER, EDUCATOR
b Welland, Ont, Jan 9, 1934. *Study:* Ryerson Polytech Inst, Toronto, cert archit technol, 59. *Work:* Nat Gallery Can, Pub Arch, Ottawa; George Eastman House, Rochester, NY; Mus Mod Art, NY. *Comn:* Photographing Canada, Nat Film Bd, Ottawa, 64, 66, 67, 72 & 74; Photographing Tunisia, Nat Geog Soc, Washington, DC, 67; Photographing WVa, Time-Life Bks, NY, 68; Photographing Italy, Can Coun, Ottawa, 71; Photographing USSR, York Univ, Toronto, 75. *Exhib:* Ghana Image 4, Nat Film Bd, Ottawa, 69; Ghetto, New Sch Social Res, NY, 70; Mixed Subjects, Image Gallery, NY, 71; Italy 1971, Il Diaframma Gallery, Milan, 73; Mixed Subjects, Deja Vue Gallery, Toronto, 75; Retrospective, Nat Gallery Can, Can Mus Contemp Photog, Ottawa, 2005. *Pos:* Toronto chmn interarts, Canada-USSR Asn, 73-. *Teaching:* Lectr photog, Visual Arts Dept, Fac Fine Arts, York Univ, Toronto, 71-73, asst prof, 73-76, assoc prof, 77-. *Awards:* Gold Medal for Photog Excellence for Ghana Show, Nat Film Bd, 69; Award of Excellence in Photo-Jour, Pravda Newspaper, Moscow, 70 & 72; Excellence Int Fedn Photog Arts Dipl, Switz, 72. *Bibliog:* Don Long (auth), Tell a story, Can Photo Ann, 75. *Mem:* Royal Can Acad Art; Canadian Artists Representation. *Media:* Photography. *Interests:* Art, Politics, Reading. *Publ:* Ed, Concerned photographer, Popular Photog, 70; Semak portfolio, Creative Camera, 70 & 73, Camera Can, 71 & Nuova Fotografia, 73; co-auth, Michael Semak monograph, Impressions Mag, 74; and others. *Mailing Add:* 1796 Spruce Hill Rd Pickering ON L1V 1S4 Canada

SEMEL, TERRY S
PATRON
b New York City, Feb 24, 1943. *Study:* LI Univ, BS, 1964. *Pos:* Domestic sales mgr, CBS Cinema Ctr Films, Studio City, Calif, 1970-72; vpres, gen mgr, Walt Disney's Buena Vista, Burbank, Cali, 1972-75; pres, WB Distribution Corp, Burbank, 1975-78; exec vpres, Chief Operating Officer, Warner Bros Inc, Burbank, 1979-80, pres, Chief Operating Officer 1980-94, chmn, co-Chief Exec Officer, 1994-99; chmn, Chief Exec Officer, Yahoo! Inc, 2001-; bd dir, Revlon, Polo Ralph Lauren Corp. *Mem:* Trustee, Solomon R Guggenheim Mus, Educ First, Cedars Sinai Med Ctr, Environ Media Asn

SEMMEL, JOAN
PAINTER
b New York, NY, 1932. *Study:* Cooper Union, New York, dipl, 52; Art Students League, with Morris Kantor, 58-59; Pratt Inst, New York, BFA, 63, MFA, 72. *Work:* Chrysler Mus, Norfolk, Va; Brooklyn Mus, NY City; Parrish Mus of Art, Southampton, NY; Jocelyn Art Mus, Omaha, Nebr; Guild Hall Mus, East Hampton, NY; Mus Fine Art, Houston, Tex; Jack Blanton Mus, Austin, Tex; Greenville County Mus Art, SC; The Jewish Mus, NY; Mus Modern Art, NY. *Comn:* Portraits of: Chris Connell, Evelyn Wexler, Robin Oz, Frank Oz, Taylor Reznick, Eric Nord, Virginia Smith (pres, Vassar Col), V O'Leary, (pres, State Univ NY, Albany), Mary Hartman (dean, Douglass Col) & Delores Sloviter (judge) Philadelphia. *Exhib:* Solo exhibs, Greenville Co Mus Art, SC, 91, Skidmore Col, Saratoga Springs, NY, 92, State Univ NY, Oswego, 92, State Univ NY, Albany, 92, Bypass, NY, 93, Pratt Manhattan Ctr, NY, 93 & Brenda Taylor, NY, 96, Guild Hall Mus, Easthampton, NY, 98, Mitchell Algus Gallery, NY, 99 & 2003, Jersey City Mus, NJ, 2000, Wexner Ctr Contemporary Art, Columbus, Oh, 2008, Alexander Grey Gallery, NY, 2011, 2013, Bronx Mus, NY, 2013; group exhibs: NJ Arts Ann, NJ State Mus, Trenton, 94, Sexual Politics, Armand Hammer, Mus, Berkeley, Calif, 96, The Figure, The Other side of Modernism, New House Ctr of Contemp Art, NY, 2000, Personal and Political, Guild Hall Mus, East Hampton, NY, 2003, Woman on Woman, The White Box, New York City, 2003, New York City DFN Gallery, 2004, Upstarts & Matriarchs Mizel Arts Ctr, Denver, Colo, 2005, Why the Nude? Contemporary Approaches, The Art Students League, NY, 2006, Splash, ACA Gallery, NY, 2006, Nat Acad Mus, NY, 2006, Rutgers Univ, New Brunswick, NJ, 2006, Blanton Mus Art, Austin, Tex, 2006, Jason McCoy Gallery, NY, 2007, All the More Real, The Parrish Mus Art, Southhampton, NY, 2007, Naked Portrait, Nat Mus Scotland, Edinburgh, 2007, Palazzo Delle Arti, Napoli, Italy, 2007, Dangerous Beauty, Chelsea Mus, NY, 2007, Vancouver Art Gallery, 2007, Women's Mus, Wash DC, 2007, Wack!, MOCA Los Angeles, Calif, 2007, New Adquisitions, Guild Hall Mus, Easthampton, NY, 2008, The Female Gaze, 2008, Cheim & Read, 2008, Shifting the Gaze, The Jewish Mus, NY, 2010, Ringling Coll Art & Design, Sarasota, Fla, 2010, Glee, Blum, and Poe, Los Angeles, Calif, Miami Basel, Miami, Fla, 2012, Pairings, Orange Co Mus, Calif, 2012, Remix, Chrysler Mus, Norfolk, Va, 2012. *Collection Arranged:* Contemporary Women: Content & Consciousness, Brooklyn Mus, NY, 1977; Private Worlds Art in General, NY, 2000. *Pos:* Prof Emer, Rutgers Univ, currently. *Teaching:* Md Inst Art, Baltimore, 73, Rutgers Univ, Livingston, NJ, 74-75, Brooklyn Mus Art Sch, 76-78 & Mason Gross Sch Arts, Rutgers Univ, New Brunswick, NJ, 78-2000, emer prof 2000-; Int Summer Acad of Fine Arts, Salzburg, Austria, 2000; Skowhegan Sch of Painting & Sculpture, 1991. *Awards:* Off Educ EPDA Fel, 70-72; Creative Artists Pub Serv Prog Award, NY State Coun on Arts, 75-76; Nat Endowment Arts Grant, 80 & 85; Richard Florsheim, Art Fund Grant, 96; Anonymous Was a Woman Award, 2008. *Bibliog:* Frances Borzello (auth) Seeing Ourselves, Women's Self-Portraits, Thams & Hudson, London, 98; Marie-Jo Bonnet (auth), Les Femmes Dans L'Art, Editions de la Martiniere Reproduction; Alan Tannenbaum (auth), New York in the 70's, Berlin, Ger; Erika Doss (auth), 20th Century Am Art, Oxford Hist of Arts Eries, Univ Press; Reckitt, (editor), Art and Feminism (Themes & Movements), Phaidon Press, London; David McCarthy (auth), The Nude in American Painting 1950-1980, Cambridge Univ Press, 98; Frances Borzello (auth), Seeing Ourselves, A History of Women's Self-Portraiture, Thames and Hudson Ltd., London, 99; Dan Bischoff (auth), Bodies in Motion and Joan Semmel: Recent Paintings, Star Ledger, NJ, 2000; Erika Doss (auth) 20th Century American Art, Oxford History of Art Series, Oxford Univ Press, 2002; Ken Johnson (auth), The New York Times, 2003, An Invitational Survey of Contemporary Art, 2006; Marie-Jo Bonnet (auth), Les Femmes Dans L'Art, Editions de la Martiniere, 2004; Alan Frame (auth), Pure Perception, Joan Semmel, Fahrenheit Arte Contemporaneo, 2007; Richard Meyers (auth), Its Not Me, Solitaire, Yale Univ Press, 2008; Roberta Smith (auth), The Female Gaze: Women Look at Women, New York Times, 2009; Karen Rosenberg (auth), A Raucous Reflection on Identity: Jewish and Feminine, New York Times, 2010; Alexander Adler (auth), Joan Semmel Paintings, The Huffington Post, 2011. *Mem:* Coll Art Asn. *Media:* Oil. *Dealer:* Alexander Gray Asn NY. *Mailing Add:* 508 W 26th St #215 New York NY 10001

SEMOWICH, CHARLES JOHN
HISTORIAN, PAINTER
b Binghamton, NY, 1949. *Study:* State Univ NY, Binghamton, BA, 71; Cath Univ Am, MFA, 72; Int Coll, PhD, 81; Woodstock Sch Art, NY, 89. *Work:* Roberson Ctr, State Univ NY, Binghamton, NY; Woodstock Sch Art, NY; Print Club Albany, NY; Newark Pub Libr, NJ; Albany Inst Hist & Art, NY. *Comn:* Murals, Rensselaer Riverfront Park, New York. *Exhib:* Schweinfurth Art Ctr, Auburn, NY, 92; spring exhib, Market Theatre Gallery, Albany, 94, RAMS, 95, State Univ NY, Binghamton, 96, Woodstock Sch Art, NY, 98 & Print Club Albany, 98; East of the Hudson, Fulton Street Gallery, Troy, NY, 99; Northeast Prints, William Patterson Univ, 2000; solo exhibs, Print Club of Albany, 2001 & LePetit Mus, Pittsfield, Mass, 2007; Interpreting Landscape, 2002; Mem, Fulton St Gallery, Troy, NY, 2005-06; Regional exhib, Woodstock Sch Art, NY, 2007; Upstate Artists Guild, Albany, 2007; Alumni Juried Exhibition, SUNY Binghamton, 2008; Fulton St Gallery, Troy, 2009-2012; Albany Ctr Gallery, 2012. *Collection Arranged:* Please Be Seated, Roberson Ctr, New York, 80; 16th Nat Print Show, Print Club Albany, NY, 89; D Lathrop Retrospective (with catalog), State Univ NY, Albany, 91; Nat Print Exhib, Print Club Albany & Schenectady Mus, 92 & 98; 10 Exhib of Albany, Ctr Galleries; Woodcuts, First Unitarian Universalist Soc, 2011, 2012. *Pos:* Pres, Print Club Albany, 88-99, cur currently; mem, Mayor's Task Force Arts, Albany, 90-; artist-in-residence, Fulton Street Gallery, Troy, NY, 2001; juror, Albany Tulip Festival, 2001-05; exec dir, Albany Ctr Galleries, Albany, NY, 2004-05; city historian, City Rensselaer, NY, 2006-; Juror, Seven Deadly Sins Exhib, Fulton St Gallery, Troy NY, 2008. *Teaching:* Adj fac, Empire State Coll, 78- & Chautauqua Inst, NY, summers, 88-90; lectr, NY State Coun Humanities, 96. *Awards:* NY State Fair Awards Art, 72; Cogswell Award, Print Club Albany (disting mem), 99; Hart-Cluett Awards, Rensselaer Co Hist Soc, Troy, NY, 2007. *Bibliog:* Article, Capital District Bus Rev, 1/18/92; Albany Times Union, 2007. *Mem:* Print Club, Albany; Soc Am Graphic Artists (adv coun). *Media:* All Media. *Res:* American art, both fine and decorative; Joseph Antonio Hekking; New York state furniture; American prints; African American furniture. *Publ:* Auth, Historical ceramics-Englebert, Bulletin NY State Archaeol Soc, 80; American Furniture Craftsmen Working Prior to 1920, Greenwood, 84; coauth, Dorothy Lathrop-A Centenary Celebration State Univ, NY, 92 & Flora, Fauna & Fantasy: The Art of Dorothy Lathrop (exhib catalog), Brandywine Mus, Chadds Ford, Pa, 2006; auth, William Buttre, Furniture Hist, 93; articles in Dictionary of Art, 96 & Grove's Encyclopedia of American Art, 99; The Dedication Concerts for the Albany City Carillon Dutch Settlers of Albany Yearbook, 2012. *Dealer:* LePetit Musee Housatonic MA. *Mailing Add:* 242 Broadway St Rensselaer NY 12144

SEMPLE, JOHN PAULUS
PAINTER
b Easton, Pa, 1930. *Study:* Hamilton Col, BA, 53; Mex City Col; Boston Univ, MFA; SKowhegan Sch Painting & Sculpture; studied with James Penney & Ivan Albright. *Work:* Univ Wis; Print Club Albany. *Exhib:* Pa Acad Fine Arts; San Diego Art Inst; Butler Inst Am Art, Youngstown, Ohio, 99; Boston Printmakers, 2001. *Awards:* Louis Comfort Tiffany Found Grant, 58; Grumbacher Gold Medal, Allied artists Am, 87; First prize, painting, Cape Cod Art Asn, 96. *Mem:* Boston Printmakers; Allied Artists Am; Audubon Artists; Print Club Albany. *Mailing Add:* PO Box 305 North Pomfret VT 05053

SENCIAL, GABRIEL JAIME
PRINTMAKER, PAINTER
b Medellin, Colombia, Jan 28, 1947; US & Colombian citizen. *Study:* Medellin Fine Arts Inst, cert, 61-63; Univ Miami, with Eugene Massin, BA(art, art in our cchs scholar), 66-70; Santa Rosa Col, with Max Hein, certs, 82-91. *Work:* Lowe Art Mus, Coral Gables, Fla; Nat Inst Cult Inc, Panama; Univ Antioquia Mus, Mus de Antioquia, Medellin, Colombia; Sonoma Co Mus, Santa Rosa, Calif; Bristol Myers Squibb, The Netherlands; plus numerous other pvt and public collections. *Comn:* A View of Our Valley (350 sq ft), Alexander Sch Dist, Healdsburg, Calif, 88. *Exhib:* IV Medellin Biennial, Palace of Exhibs, Medellin, Colombia, 81; Panamanian Art Inst Collection, Palace of Exhibs, Panama City, 83; 35th Ann Mill Valley Art Festival, Calif, 90; 18th Open Studios, Somar Gallery, San Francisco, 91; Festival Latino, Sonoma Co Mus, Santa Rosa, Calif, 93-94; solo exhibs, Soundscape Gallery, Santa Rosa, Calif, 94, Quicksilver Gallery, Sebastopol, Calif, 89 & 3D Dynamic Gallery, Healdsburg, Calif, 98-99; 35th-38th Sonoma Ann Art Show, Calif, 96-98. *Pos:* Art dir, Artist Guild San Francisco, 91-94; cons in field, 72-80. *Teaching:* Teaching asst painting, Univ Miami, 67-68; teaching asst silkscreen, Santa Rosa Col, 88-92; artist-in-residence art, Healdsburg Sch Dist, 88-93. *Awards:* First Prize, 10th Nat Art Competition, Mus de Antioquia, 79; Discovery Awards, Art of Calif, 93. *Bibliog:* Jean Millewics (auth), The Art of G Sencial, US Info Agency, 80; Roger Kerraker (dir), Video disc on Colombia, Santa Rosa Col, 90; Julie & David Allen (dirs), Studio Views, KRCB-TV 22 PBS, 91; Art antiques and collectibles, Santa Rosa, Calif Press Democrat, 7/90; plus others. *Mem:* Artist Guild San Francisco; Cult Arts Coun Sonoma Co; Int Asn Artists (UNESCO), Paris; Artist Guild Santa Rosa; Valley of the Moon Art Asn. *Media:* All Media. *Interests:* Archaeology, nature, ethnic and primitive art, photography. *Publ:* Award Winner, Miami Herald, 6/6/66; Folk art to pop, El Tiempo, 3/20/80; article in Vision Time Mag, 8/25/80; Video disc on Gabriel Sencial, Press Democrat, 7/16/90; Spiritual Inspiration in Contemporary Art, 92. *Dealer:* Gallery One 209 Western Ave Petaluma CA 94952. *Mailing Add:* Artists Guild San Francisco 601 Van Ness Ave #E3-140 San Francisco CA 94102

SENDER, LENORE & ADAM D
COLLECTOR
Pos: Gen partner, Exec Capital Mgt, New York, 1998-. *Awards:* Named one of Top 200 Collectors, ARTnews mag, 2004-13. *Collection:* Contemporary art

SENIE, HARRIET F
HISTORIAN, CRITIC
b New York, NY, Sept 23, 1943. *Study:* Brandeis Univ, BA, 64; Hunter Col, New York, MA, 71; Inst Fine Arts, New York, PhD (art hist), 81. *Collection Arranged:* Fabric into Art Traveling Exhib (auth, catalog), 80, William King Traveling Exhib (auth, catalog), 80, South Africa-South Bronx (auth, catalog), 81 & Landscape-Sculpture (auth, catalog), Amelie A Wallace Gallery, State Univ NY, Old Westbury; Sculpture for Public Spaces (auth, catalog), Marisa del Re Gallery, 86; George Rickey: Projects for Public Sculpture (auth, catalog), Neuberger Mus, 87; Memory as Metaphor, Pleiades Gallery, 96. *Pos:* Dir, Amelie A Wallace Gallery, State Univ NY, Old Westbury, 79-82; assoc dir, The Art Mus, Princeton Univ, 82-86; dir, Mus Studies Prog, City Col NY, 86-. *Teaching:* Adj prof art hist, Hunter Col, 74-78; asst prof, State Univ NY, Old Westbury, 79-82; prof, City Col NY, 86- & City Univ NY Grad Ctr, 97-; vis disting prof, Carnegie Mellon Univ, Pittsburgh, 2000. *Awards:* Eisner Scholars Award, City Col, 89; Nat Endowment Asn Mus studies grant, 87; PSC-City Univ UNY Res Grant, 88, 92, 95 & 96. *Mem:* Coll Art Asn; Am Asn Mus; Soc Am Art Historians; Am Studies Asn; ArtTable. *Res:* Public art and contemporary culture. *Publ:* Contemporary Public Sculpture: Tradition, Transformation and Controversy, Oxford Univ Press, 92; co-ed & contribr, Critical Issues in Public Art: Content, Context and Controversy, Harper Collins, 92 & Smithsonian Inst Press, reissued 98; auth, Public art and the legal system, Pub Art Rev, fall/winter 94; contribr, Encyclopedia of New York City, Yale Univ Press, 95; Public Art in Brazil, Sculpture, 2/98 & Re-approaching Tony Smith, 11/98; contribr Complex Identities: Jewish Consciousness and Modern Art, Rutgers, 2000; auth article Harvard Design Mag, Fall/99; plus others. *Mailing Add:* 215 Sackett St Brooklyn NY 11231-3604

SENSEMANN, SUSAN
PAINTER, EDUCATOR
b Glen Cove, NY, Oct 6, 1949. *Study:* Tyler Sch Art, Rome Italy, 70; Syracuse Univ, NY, BFA, 71; Tyler Sch Art, Philadelphia, MFA, 73. *Work:* Ill State Mus, Springfield; Southern Ill Univ Mus, Edwardsville; Lakeview Mus, Peoria, Ill; Univ Rochester, NY; Appalachian Col, Boone, NC. *Comn:* Five oil paintings, Ill Agricultural Asn,

Bloomington, Ill, 79; two acrylic paintings, Hyatt Regency Hotel, Flint, Mich, 81; two watercolors, Western Hotels, Houston, Tex, 84; five paper pieces, Paper Press, Chicago, Ill, 84; two oils, IBM Tower, Atlanta, Ga, 88. *Exhib:* Ill Painters, Western Ill Univ, Macomb, 92; Open Surface: Nardi, Sensemann, Tinsley, State Ill Gallery, Chicago, 92; Roy Boyd Gallery, Chicago, Ill, 92; Artemesia, Chicago, Ill, 92; solo exhibs, Artemisia, Chicago, 93 & 94, Locus Gallery, St Louis, Mo, 94, SACI, Florence, Italy, 94, Roy Boyd Gallery, Chicago, Ill, 94 & Gallery Woong, Seoul, Korea, 95; Kunstler Haus Gallery, Ger, 98; Faeroernes Kunst Mus, Faroe Island, 98; Mus Arco, Madrid, Spain, 99; and others. *Teaching:* Assoc prof, Univ Ill, Urbana, 73-81, Chicago, 81-. *Awards:* Rice Award, Vicinity Show, Art Inst Chicago, 79; Capital Develop Bd, State Ill, 91; Mucia Travel Grant, Chicago/Seoul, Korea, 94. *Bibliog:* Alan Artner (auth), Sensemann puts the unseen of canvas, Chicago Tribune, 8/85; Kristen Schleifer (auth), Susan Sensemann Review, New Art Examiner, 6/92; Maud Lavin (auth), Susan Sensemann, Book Review: Cut With the Kitchen Knife, Design Issues, Mass Inst Technol Press, summer 94. *Media:* Works on Paper. *Publ:* Patty Carroll, James Yood, Spirited Visions, Univ Ill Press, 91. *Mailing Add:* Univ Ill Chicago Sch Art & Design 929 W Harrison 106 Jefferson Hall Chicago IL 60607-7038

SEPLOWIN, CHARLES JOSEPH
SCULPTOR
b New York, NY, July 19, 1945. *Study:* Univ NH, BA (art); RI Sch Design, MFA (sculpture). *Work:* Municipal Fire House Ctr, NY; Titan Steel Corp, NY; Montclair State Col; Univ NH; Sherson-Hutton, NY. *Comn:* Gates, Caleia Fine Arts, Upper Montclair, NJ; One percent Prog for Art. *Exhib:* Aldrich Mus, 75; Solo exhib, Elizabeth Weiner Gallery, NY, 80; Sculpture Ctr, NY, 83; Cheltenham Art Ctr, Philadelphia, 83; Mus Mod Art Latin Am, Washington, DC, 83; Leslie Cecil Gallery, 86-; Recent Acquisitions, Art Mus Ams, Washington, DC, 92; and others. *Teaching:* Assoc prof, Montclair State Col, 74-. *Bibliog:* Articles in Craft Horizons, 8/74 & Arts Mag, 9/74. *Mailing Add:* 463 W St New York NY 10014

SERA, ASSUNTA
PAINTER, INSTRUCTOR
b Ceprano, Italy US Citizen. *Study:* Center Creative Studies, Detroit, Mich, BFA, 1980; Apprenticeship to Barbara Price (dean Cranbrook Mich Coun Arts), 1981-1982; Print Making Apprenticeship with Tom James, Pontiac, Mich, 1986; Brooklyn Coll, Brooklyn, NY, MFA, 1989. *Work:* Montclair Art Mus, Montclair, NJ; Rutgers Univ, New Brunswick, NJ; Vatican Collection, Rome, Italy; Tuttleman Collection, Wilmington, Del; Deerfield Management, NY. *Comn:* Grand Cent Renovation Painting, Metrop Transit Auth, NY, 1997; Organized, Directed & painted (9murals), Gen Motors, Pontiac, Mich, 1981-1982. *Exhib:* Collaboration: The Capital City Meets the Renaissance City, Trenton City Mus, Trenton, NJ, 1991; Europa/America, Molica Guidarte, NY, 1991; Solo Exhibs: New Paintings: In Transit, First St Gallery, NY, La State Univ, Shreveport La, 1996; Elizabeth Holden Gallery, Warren Wilson Coll, Ashville, NC, 1997; Measured Ground, Michael Ingbar Gallery, NY, 2005. *Pos:* Gallery Cur, Art in NY, Bloomfield Coll, Bloomfield, NJ, 1997; juror (MTA poster contest), Metrop Transit Auth, NY, 1998. *Teaching:* Adj prof drawing, NY Univ, 1989-1990; adj prof, Montclair State Coll, Montclair, NJ, 1993; adj prof drawing, painting intro to art in NY, Bloomfield Coll, Bloomfield, NJ, 1991-1997. *Awards:* Renaissance Center (hon), Ebb & Flow of an Artist's Work, Mich Water Bd, Detroit, Mich, 1983; Am Acad Arts & Letters (nominee), 1994, 1995; Arts for Transit Poster Prog, Bank St Coll Educ (MTA), 1999. *Bibliog:* Joy Colby (auth), Review, Detroit News, 1984; Herma Snider (auth), Assunta Sera Interview, Pontiac TV Sta, 1985; Suzanne, Bake, Mich Woman Mag, July, Aug 1986; Lisa Batitto (auth), Review, Essex J, Apr 1991; Stefania Severi (auth), Americans in Italy, Italians in Am Bk, 1997. *Mem:* Montclair Art Mus (fac 1990-1992); Artist Space; Women Artist Montclair, 1993-; Mus Mod Art. *Media:* Painting, Drawing. *Dealer:* Michael Ingbar Gallery 568 Broadway New York NY 10012; Frederick Galleries 111 Main St Allenhurst NJ 07711. *Mailing Add:* 580 Broadway #504 New York NY 10012

SERENYI, PETER
HISTORIAN, ADMINISTRATOR
b Budapest, Hungary, Jan 13, 1931. *Study:* Dartmouth Col, AB, 57; Yale Univ, MA, 58; Washington Univ, PhD, 68. *Collection Arranged:* Contemporary Architecture in India, 76 & Le Corbusier in India, 80, Northeastern Univ Art Gallery & traveling; Hungarian Art: 1920-1970, Northeastern Univ Art Gallery, 81; Additions to Buildings: 1972-1982, 83 & Boston Architectural Competitions: 1960-1983, 84, Northeastern Univ Art Gallery & Boston Archit Ctr; Northeastern Univ Centennial Exhib, 97-98. *Teaching:* Chmn dept art & archit, Northeastern Univ, 81-96, prof emer, 96-. *Awards:* Graham Found Advan Studies Fine Arts Grant, 74-75; Fulbright Sr Res Grant, 74-75; Northeastern Univ Fac Develop Grant, 91; and others. *Mem:* Soc Archit Historians (vpres, New Eng chap, 77-78, pres, 78-79, dir, 79-82); Mass Comt Preserv Archit Records (dir, 79-81); Citizen Ambassador Prog Art Educ Deleg to People's Repub China, 91; Fulbright Asn, Eastern Mass Chap (pres, 98-). *Res:* Le Corbusier; modern architecture in India. *Publ:* Auth, Le Corbusier, Fourier and the Monastery of Ema, Art Bull, 67; ed, Le Corbusier in Perspective, Prentice-Hall, 75; auth, Mies' New National Gallery, Harvard Archit Rev, 80; Le Corbusier's Architecture in India, Le Corbusier Archive, 83; Sixty years of housing in Delhi, Techniques et Architecture, 85. *Mailing Add:* Dept Art & Archit Northeastern Univ 239 Ryder Ave Boston MA 02115

SERRA, RICHARD
SCULPTOR, VIDEO ARTIST
b San Francisco, Calif, Nov 2, 1939. *Study:* Univ Calif, Berkeley; Univ Calif, Santa Barbara, BA (English lit), 61; Yale Univ, BFA & MFA, 64. *Hon Degrees:* Calif Coll Arts & Crafts, PhD in Art (hon), 94. *Work:* Whitney Mus Am Art & Guggenheim Mus, NY; Stedelijk Mus, Amsterdam; Tate Gallery, London; Yale Univ Art Gallery, New Haven, Conn; and numerous pvt collections. *Comn:* Tilted Arc (sculpture). US Fed Gov, Fed Plaza, New York, 81; London Stock Exchange, 87; sculpture, Rijksmuseum Kroller-Muller park, Otterlo, Neth, 88; Stacks, Yale Univ, New Haven, 90; Hall of Witness, US Holocaust Mem Mus, Wash; Mus Contemp Art, Barcelona,. *Exhib:* Solo exhibs incl Galleria La Salita, Rome, 66, Galerie Francoise Lambert, Milan, 69, Portland Ctr for Visible Arts, 75, Mus Boymans-van Beuningen, Rotterdam, 80, Akira Ikeda Gallery, Tokyo, 87, Galerie Nordenhaken, Stockholm, 88, Gagosian Gallery, 91, 96, 97, 99, 2001, 2002, 2003, 2006, 2008, 2009, 2010, 2011, 2013, Ctr of Art Reina Sofia, Madrid, 92, Solomon R Guggenheim Mus, 93, Ctr for the Fine Arts, Miami, 94, Ctr for Fine Arts, Miami, Fla, 95, Matthew Marks Gallery, 96, Geffen Contemporary Mus Contemporary Art, Los Angeles, Calif, 98, Solomon R Guggenheim Mus, Bilbao, Spain, 99, Van de Weghe Fine Art, NY, 2002, Saint Louis Mus Art, Mo, 2003, Freeman Gallery, NY, 2004, Godt-Cleary Projects, Las Vegas, NV, 2006, Mus Modern Art, NY, 2007, Kunsthaus Bregenz, Austria, 2008, The Metropolitan Mus Art, NY, 2011, Craig F Starr Gallery, NY, 2012; group exhibs incl Galerie M Bochum, Ger, 84; Stedilijik, The Neth, 88; Tony Shafrazi Gallery, 91-92; Pace Gallery, 92; IVAM Ctr, Valencia, Spain, 93; Jablonka Galerie, Cologne, Ger, 94; Mus Art Contemporaneo, Monterrey, Spain, 99; Whitney Mus Am Art, 2000; Whitney Biennial: Day for Night, Whitney Mus Am Art, 2006; Akira Ikeda Gallery, Berlin, Ger, 2007; 55th Int Art Exhib Biennale, Venice, 2013. *Awards:* Fulbright Grant, 66, Guggenheim fel, 70, Skowhegan Sch Painting & Sculpture award, 75, named Fel, Bezalei Acad, Jerusalem, 83, Chevalier de l'Ordre l' Arts et des Lettres, French Govt, 85, Officer, 91, Comdr, 2008, recipient Wilhelm-Lehmbruck award for sculpture, Sculpture Ctr award for Distinction in Sculpture, 92, Praemium Imperiale, Japan Art Asn, 94; Gold Medal for Sculpture, Am Acad of Arts and Letters, 2001; Int Art award Cristóbal Gabarrón Found, 2005; Prince of Asturias Award for the Arts, Prince of Asturias Found, Spain, 2010. *Bibliog:* Pincenthal, Nancy (auth.) The Print Collector's Newsletter, 91; Kimmelman, Michael (auth.), N.Y. Times, 99; and others. *Mem:* Fel Acad Arts and Sci; Acad Universelles des Cultures; Nat Acad Design. *Publ:* Richard Serra Writings & Interviews, Univ Chicago Press, 94; Richard Serra: Torqued Ellipses, Dia Center Arts, 97; Richard Serra Sculpture 1985-1998, Mus Contemp Art, Los Angeles, 98; and others. *Dealer:* Gagosian Gallery 980 Madison Ave New York NY 10021. *Mailing Add:* 173 Duane St Fl 5 New York NY 10013-3334

SERRA, RUDY
SCULPTOR
b San Francisco, Calif, Apr 9, 1948. *Study:* City Coll San Francisco, AA; San Francisco State Col, BA; Univ Calif, Berkeley, MA & MFA. *Exhib:* San Francisco Art Inst, 73 & 76; 1975 Whitney Biennial, NY, 75; San Francisco Mus Mod Art, 77; Faculty Exhib, Univ Conn, 80-82; one-person shows, Univ Houston, 80, Baruch Col, 82 & Marianne Deson Gallery, 83; Oakland Mus, 82; Nassau Mus, NY, 85; Tomoko Liguori Gallery, NY, 88. *Teaching:* Vis asst prof sculpture, Calif State Univ, Chico, 75; asst prof, Am River Col, Sacramento, 76-77; vis asst prof sculpture, Univ Calif, Davis, fall 78; asst prof sculpture & drawing, Univ Conn, Storrs, 79-; State Univ NY, Purchase, 84, Sarah Lawrence Col, NY, 86-87, Bennington Col, Vt, 88. *Awards:* Nat Endowment Arts Grant, 76, 78 & 85. *Bibliog:* Roberta Smith (auth), Biennial review, Artforum, 5/75; Amy Goldin (auth), The New Whitney Biennial, Art Am, 5-6/75; Judith Dunham (auth), Introduction 75, Artweek, 7/75; Michael Brenson (auth), article, New York Times, 88. *Media:* Concrete, Hydracol. *Mailing Add:* 16 Greene St New York NY 10013

SESLAR, PATRICK GEORGE
WRITER, PAINTER
b Fort Wayne, Ind, Sept 20, 1947. *Study:* Purdue Univ, BS (psychology), 69. *Exhib:* Coconut Grove Art Festival, Fla, 96; Cherry Creek Art Festival, Denver, 97; Masterworks in Miniature, Gallery One, Mentor, Ohio, 97-2000; Friends and Lovers, LeMoyne Art Found, Tallahassee, 2000. *Pos:* contribr editor, Artist's Mag, Cincinnati, 85-. *Awards:* Juror's Award, Cherry Creek Art Festival, Denver, Colo, 97; First place painting, Maitland Arts Festival, 98. *Mem:* Nat Asn Independent Artists. *Media:* Oil. *Res:* Contemporary art technique and art marketing,. *Publ:* coauth, Painting Seascapes in Sharp Focus, 87, Painting Nature's Peaceful Places, 93, (auth) Wildlife Painting Step by Step, 95, Painting From Photographs, 99, The One-Hour Watercolorist, 2001, North Light Books. *Dealer:* Art Sales and Rental Gallery Philadelphia Mus Art 26th St & Benjamin Franklin Pkwy Philadelphia PA 19130

SETFORD, DAVID F
GALLERY DIRECTOR
b Eng. *Study:* Leicester Univ, BA with honors, 1979; Univ Manchester, MA, 1980. *Pos:* chief cur, Norton Mus Art, West Palm Beach, Fla, 1990-99; founder, dir, ArtReach Int, 1999; dir, Palm Beach! America's 1nt Fine Art & Antique Fair, formerly; dir cur affairs, Naples Mus Art, Fla, 2005-08; exec dir, Hyde Collection, Glens Falls, NY, 2008-. *Mem:* Eng Mus Assn (assoc, 1992). *Mailing Add:* Hyde Collection 161 Warren St Glens Falls NY 12801

SETLOW, NEVA C (DELIHAS)
SCULPTOR, PAINTER
b New Haven, Conn, 1940. *Study:* Empire State Coll, BA. *Work:* Assoc Univs, Brookhaven Nat Lab, Upton, NY; Pittsfield City Bank, Mass; Islip Art Mus, NY. *Exhib:* Group exhibs, Aldrich Mus, Ridgefield, Conn, 76; Guild Hall, East Hampton, 86-2013; Ward Nasse Gallery, NY, 92-97; Faber Biren Color Award Show, Stamford, Conn, 97, 2001 & 2011; The Altered Image, Islip Art Mus, Long Island, NY, 97, Eden Revisited, 2000; Exploring the Art of Space, Planetary Art Soc, Pasadena, Calif, 97; Firehouse Gallery, Garden City, NY, 97 & 2004; Salon des Femes, Southampton Cult Ctr, NY, 97; Tribute, Smithtown Arts Coun, 98; Pleiades Gallery 16th Juried Exhib, NY, 98; Broome St Gallery, Soho, NY, 99-2010; Huchins Gallery, Brookville, NY, 2000; Shelter Park Art Gallery, 2000 & 2006; Edison Gallery, Piqua, Ohio, 2001; Huntington Arts Coun, Artrium, Melville, NY, 2001; Grounds for Sculpture, Hamilton, NJ, 2001; The Banana Factory, Bethlehem, PA, 2002; East End Arts Coun, Riverhead, NY, 2003; J Wayne Stark galleries, Texas A & M Univ, 2004; Rosetta stone Gallery, Juno, Fla, 2004; East End Arts Council, The Skys the Limit, 2005; Arts & Literature Laboratory, New Haven, Conn, 2006, Games, 2009; The Karpeles Libr

Mus, Newburgh, NY, 2006; Port of Call Gallery, Warwick, NY, 2006; Levitas Gallery, Southampton, NY, 2011; Women's Perspective, Marco Island, Fla, 2007; Kauffman Gallery, Shippensburg, Pa, 2008; NY Hall of Science, Queens, NY, 2008; Manhattan Borough President's Gallery, NY, 2008; Studio East, 2009; Hub-Robeson Galleries, Pa State, 2009; guest artist, The Crazy Monkey Gullery, NY, 2011; A Tribute to East Quogue Artists, Quogue, NY, 2011; Berkeley Coll, Brooklyn, NY, 2011; Armory Art Ctr, West Palm Beach, Fla, 2011; Midday Gallery, NJ, 2012; Art in the Alcove, Hauppage, NY, 2012; East End Arts Council, 2013; Watermill Mus, Watermill, NY, 2013. *Pos:* Biology assoc, Brookhaven Nat Lab, Upton, NY, 76-96, guest app, 2005-2009. *Awards:* Silvermine Guild Artists 50th Ann Award, 72; Sculpture House Award, West Chester Art Soc, 73; Award of Excellence, Huntington Art League, 74; North Shore Art Guild Painting Award, 98, Sculpture Award, 98; Am Icon-Outer Space Sculpture Award, 2001; Cleo Hartwig Award, Nat Asn Women Artists, 2002; Nat ASN Woman Artist; Gretchen Richardson Mem Award, 2004; Am Soc of Contemp Arts Award, 2004; East End Arts Coun, 2005; Third Place, Southampton Artists, 2008; Faber Biren 31st Color Award, 2011; 2nd Prize, East End Arts Council, 2012; 2nd prize, East End Arts Art & Sci, 2013. *Mem:* E End Arts Coun; Southampton Artists; Int Sculpture Ctr; Nat Asn Women Artists; Artist Equity of New York City; Am Soc Contemporary Artists, NY; ASCI, NY. *Media:* Plastic, Acrylic, Collage. *Interests:* Art & sci, light art, color. *Publ:* Contribr, Art & Science, Similarities Dissimilarities, Leonardo, Pergamon Press, Vol 27, No 3, 94; Am Soc Contemp Artists: The First 85 years, Best of Am, Sculpture Artist Artisans; Int Contemporary Artists Vol I. *Dealer:* Ward Nasse 178 Prince St New York NY 10012. *Mailing Add:* Four Beachland Ave East Quogue NY 11942

SETO, TAKAYO
PAINTER
b Kanagawa, Japan. *Study:* Sophia Junior Coll, English, 1984; Trinity Coll Washington, BA (Am Studies), 1986; Univ Ala, Painting, 1994; Pratt Inst, Masters (Painting), 1999. *Exhib:* Solo Exhibs include Anotheroom, New York, 2002, Meru Art Gallery, Brooklyn, NY, 2003, Domo Gallery, Summit, NJ, 2003, Plum Blossoms Gallery, New York, 2004; group exhibs include Asahi Seimei Gallery, Tokyo, 1994; Nat Prize Show, Univ Place Gallery, Cambridge, Mass, 2001; Oriental Philos from Ink, Amerasia Bank Exhib Gallery, Flushing, NY, 2002; 29th Ann Juried Arts Exhib, Mills Pond House Gallery, St James, NY, 2004; Blank Canvas Benefit, Vis Arts Ctr NJ, Summit, 2006; Medial 2 Art Biennial, Art Addiction Medial Mus, London, 2007; Woodstock Biennial, Woodstock Byrdcliffe Guild, Woodstock, NY, 2007; 15 Years, Thomas Masters Gallery, Chicago, 2008. *Awards:* Pollock-Krasner Found Grant, 2004, 2007; Award of Excellence, Manhattan Arts Gallery, NY, 2007; New York Found Arts Fel, 2008. *Dealer:* Thomas Masters Gallery 245 W North Ave Chicago IL 60610. *Mailing Add:* 379 Washington Ave #1C Brooklyn NY 11238

SEVIGNY, MAURICE JOSEPH, II
EDUCATOR, ADMINISTRATOR
b Amesbury, Mass, July 24, 1943. *Study:* Mass Coll Art, BSEd, 65; Ohio State Univ, MA, 69, PhD, 77. *Teaching:* Asst prof art educ, Western Ky Univ, 69-76; teaching assoc, Ohio State Univ, 76-78; assoc prof art, chair, Div Art Educ, Bowling Green State Univ, Ohio, 78-81, dir, Sch Art, 77-85, prof, 81-; chmn dept art & Marguerite Fairchild centennial prof, Univ Tex, Austin, 86; dean Col of Fine Arts, Univ Ariz, 91; pres, Int Coun Fine Arts Deans, 2005-07. *Awards:* Award Excellence Dissertation Res, Rev Res Visual Arts Educ, 79; Ann Hollis Moore Award Disting Serv, Bowling Green State Univ Student Union, 82; Disting Alumnus, Ohio State Univ, 87; Educator of Yr Pacific Region High Edn Divsn NAEA, 96; Father of Yr, Tucson, Ariz, 98; Ariz Gov Art Award, 2003; NAEA Distinguished Fel, 2005. *Mem:* Nat Coun Policy Studies Art Educ; Ohio Art Educ Asn (adv coun rep, 78, chmn Higher Educ, 79); Nat Art Educ Asn Higher Educ Div (chmn elect); Nat Coun Art Adminr; Nat Soc Schs Art & Design; Internat Coun of Fine Arts Deans (secy, 2003-2005, pres, 2005-2007). *Res:* Discipline based art education, studio learning and performance; assessment at the university level from the triangulated perspective of teacher, student, classroom ethnographer; language and gender differences in non-verbal communication. *Publ:* Auth, Triangulation and descriptive research, Rev Res Visual Arts, 5/78; auth, Utilizing recorded materials for the clinical component of teacher training, In: Human Relations and the Clinical Component, Ohio Dept Educ, 80; auth, Triangulate inquiry: A methodology for the analysis of classroom interaction, In: Analysis of Discourse: Ethnographic Approaches, Ablex Publ, 81; Discipline Based Art Education and Teacher Education, J P Getty Ctr Educ, 86; contribr, Jour of Aesthetic Edn, Studies, and NAEA News. *Mailing Add:* 6463 E Paseo Otono Tucson AZ 85750

SEWELL, DARREL L
CURATOR, HISTORIAN
b Cushing, Okla, Dec 21, 1939. *Study:* Univ Chicago, BA, 62, MA, 62. *Exhib:* Henry Ossawa Tanner, The Art Mus San Francisco, 91; Eastern State Penitentiary, Philadelphia, Pa, 94; The Cadwalader Family: Art and Style in Early Philadelphia, Philadelphia Mus Art, 96; The Peale Family: Creation of an Am Legacy, 1770-1870, Philadelphia Mus Art, 96. *Collection Arranged:* Modern Jewelry, 64-86; Philadelphia: Three Centuries of Am Art (auth, catalog), 76; Installation of Am Collections, 77; Am Presidential China, 77; The University of Pennsylvania: Collector and Patron of Art, 1779-1979, 79; Copley from Boston (auth, catalog), 80; Thomas Eakins: Artist of Philadelphia (auth, catalog), 81-82; One Hundred Years of Acquisitions, 83; Benjamin West in Pennsylvania Collections, 86; Diego Rivera, 86; The Helen Drutt Collection, 86-87; The Fairmount Waterworks, 88; Henry O Tanner (auth, catalog), 91. *Pos:* cur educ, Nat Collection Fine Arts, 70-73; cur, Am Art, Philadelphia Mus Art, 73-; chmn, Staff adv comt, Capitol Campaign, 86-89. *Teaching:* Instr art hist, Ohio State Univ, Columbus, 66-67 & Univ Ill, Chicago Circle, 68-70. *Publ:* Auth, What you see is what you get: An approach to the use of museums for education, Art Educ, 12/71; Auth, Henry O Tanner (with catalog), Philadelphia Mus Art, 91; Guide to the Thomas Eakins Research Collection with a Lifetime Exhibition Record and Bibliography, Philadelphia Mus Art, 96. *Mailing Add:* Philadelphia Mus Art PO Box 7646 Philadelphia PA 19101

SEWELL, JACK VINCENT
MUSEUM CURATOR
b Dearborn, Mo, June 11, 1923. *Study:* St Joseph Jr Col, Mo, 41-43; City Coll New York, 43-44; Univ Chicago, MFA, 50; Harvard Univ, 51-53. *Collection Arranged:* Complete reinstallation of Oriental Collections, Art Inst Chicago, 58; installation of Indian & SE Asian collections, Art Inst Chicago, 86. *Pos:* Mem staff, Oriental dept, Art Inst Chicago, 50-56, assoc cur Oriental art, 56-58, cur, 58-88, consult, 89-90, cur emer, 90-. *Mem:* Far Eastern Ceramic Group; Japan-Am Soc Chicago; The Cliff Dwellers; Arts Club Chicago. *Res:* Indian and Far Eastern art; arts of China; strength in delicacy--archaic Chinese bronzes and sculptures of Gandhara. *Publ:* Contribr, Archaeol & Chicago Art Inst Quart

SEWELL, LEO
ASSEMBLAGE ARTIST, SCULPTOR
b Annapolis, Md, Sept 7, 1945. *Study:* Univ Del, MA, 70. *Work:* Hartsfield Atlanta Airport, Ga; Express-Ways Children's Mus, Chicago; Ripley's Believe It or Not Mus, St Augustine, Fla; Philip & Muriel Berman Mus Art, Ursinus Col, Collegeville, Pa; Am Visionary Art Mus, Baltimore, MD. *Comn:* NBC Corp Hq, Comn by Brandon Tartikoff, NY, 80; The Family, comn by Philip & Muriel Berman, Allentown, Pa, 83; Rocky, comn by Sylvester Stallone, Los Angeles, Calif, 85; Nolan Ryan, comn by Nike Corp, Portland, Wash, 92. *Exhib:* solo exhib, Children's Mus RI, Pawtucket, 89, Danville Mus Fine Art & Hist, Va, 90 & Livlan Mus Art, Tokyo, Japan, 92; Trash Menagerie, Express-Ways Children's Mus, Chicago, Ill, 90; Penis Art, University City Arts League, Philadelphia, 94; Recycle Reuse Recreate, USIA Traveling Exhib, 95; Fuller Craft Mus, Brockton, Mass; Lost & Found, Princeton, NJ; Art Works Gallery, Newark, Ohio. *Bibliog:* Cultural Connections, Temple Univ Press, 91; Hand and Home: The Homes of American Craftsmen, Little Brown Co, 94; Art with a Sense of Humor, Davis Publ, 96. *Mem:* Dumpster Divers Asn. *Media:* Found Objects. *Interests:* Found objects. *Publ:* Featured on many TV productions including You Asked For It, 81, Ripley's Believe It or Not, 82, Captain Noah, 85 & Earth Week Celebration on Mr Roger's Neighborhood, 90; auth, Artful Jesters, 10 Speed Press, 2003; auth, Found Object Art Schiffer, Publ LTD, 2001; auth, Humor in Art, Davis Publ, 97. *Dealer:* Connell Gallery 333 Buckhead Ave Atlanta GA 30305; Twist Gallery Portland OR; Works Gallery Philadelphia PA. *Mailing Add:* 3614 Pearl St Philadelphia PA 19104

SEWELL, RICHARD GEORGE
PRINTMAKER, PAINTER
b St Louis, Mo, Aug 22, 1942; Can citizen. *Study:* Univ Nac Autonoma de Mexico, 65; Kansas City Art Inst, Mo, 66; Univ Mo, Kansas City, BA, 67. *Work:* Can Coun, Ottawa; The Gallery, Stratford, Ont; Nova Scotia Art Gallery, Halifax; Owens Art Gallery, Mt Allison, NB; Winnipeg Art Gallery, Man. *Exhib:* Beyond the Repeatable Image, Heywood, Tamasauskas, Sewell, Eng, Spain, Belg, Scotland, France, 84-85; New Work, May, Besant, Parker, Sewell, Alberta Coll Art, Calgary, 88; Agnes Etherington Art Ctr, Kingston, Ont, 85; Univ Toronto, Erindale Campus, 90; solo exhib, Mem Univ St John's Newfoundland, 90. *Pos:* Co-founder & dir, Open Studio, Print Workshop, Toronto, Ont, 70-82; chmn, Print and Drawing Coun Canada, Toronto, Ont, Can, 89-91. *Teaching:* Univ Saskatchewan, Saskatoon, 81; Alberta Col Art, Calgary, 84-86; prof visual arts, Sheridan Col, Oakville, Ont, 86-; Ontario Col Art, Toronto, 88-. *Bibliog:* Linda Beattie (auth), Beyond the Repeatable Image, Heywood, Tamasauskas, & Sewell, Visual Arts, Ont, Toronto, 84; Louise Dompierre (auth), Paratactic Images Agnes Etherington Art Ctr, Kingston, Ont, 85; Deidre Hanna (auth), Chaos/Relief, NOW Mag, Toronto, Ont, 1/90. *Media:* All; Acrylic, Oil. *Publ:* Contribr, Open Studio-Ten Years (catalog), Open Studio, Toronto, Ont, 80; auth, StoneGrain Cycle, The Prints of Mark Critoph, The Gallery/Stratford, Ont, 84. *Mailing Add:* 49 Appleton Ave Toronto ON M6E 3A4 Canada

SEXAUER, DONALD RICHARD
INSTRUCTOR, PRINTMAKER
b Erie, Pa. *Study:* Coll William & Mary; Edinboro State Col, BS; Kent State Univ, MA. *Work:* Butler Inst Am Art, Youngstown, Ohio; NY Pub Libr; Mint Mus Art, Charlotte, NC; Nat Mus Art, Smithsonian, Washington, DC; Libr of Cong, Washington, DC; and others. *Comn:* Print eds, Make Believe Print Club of Albany, Int Graphic Art Soc, 66, To Fly, To Fly, 66; Vietnam Fragments (folio), Off, Chief Mil Hist, Washington, DC, 71; Mecklenburg Bicentennial Comn (folio). *Exhib:* Soc Am Graphic Artists, 64-; New Talent In Printmaking, NY, 66; 140th Ann, Nat Acad Design, 66; San Diego Print Exhib, 71; 16th Hunterdon Nat, Clinton, NJ, 72. *Teaching:* Prof printmaking, Sch Art, E Carolina Univ, 60-. *Awards:* Print Prize, Nat Acad Design 140th Ann, 66; Purchase Awards, Piedmont Print Ann, Mint Mus, 69-74; Purchase Awards, Bradley Print Show, Peoria, Ill, Soc Am Graphic Artists, 79 & 80 & Hunterdon Art Ctr, Clinton, NJ, 83 & 86. *Mem:* Soc Am Graphic Artists; Boston Printmakers; Audubon Artists. *Media:* Intaglio. *Publ:* Illusr, Red clay reader number 5, Southern Lit Rev, 68. *Mailing Add:* 301 John Wesley Rd Greenville NC 27858

SEXTON, JANICE LOUISE
PAINTER, SCULPTOR
b Milwaukee, Wis, Oct 23, 1951. *Study:* Univ Mass, 73-74; Univ Nev, Reno, 84-85; Santa Rosa Community Coll, Santa Rosa, 86. *Work:* Univ Mass-Dartmouth; State House Rotunda, Boston; Westport Townhall, Westport, Mass; Quadrangle, Springfield, Mass; Peabody Essex Mus, Salem, Mass. *Comn:* Town of Westport pub libr (mural), Westport, Mass, 97; Chaney Instruments Nationwide Distribution (illus), Lake Geneva, Wis, 98; Ocean Graphics (mural), Westport Mass, 2002. *Exhib:* Waterfowl Stamp Competition (dept of fisheries and wildlife), Peabody Essex Mus, Salem, Mass, 99-2003; Waterfowl Stamp Competition (dept of fisheries and wildlife), Mus of Sci at the Quadrangle, Springfield, Mass, 2002; Am Soc Marine Artists, NE Regional Show, Wis, Minn Maritime Mus. *Pos:* Art Dept (art), The Imagination Station, Bridgewater, Mass, 84-87; Mgr (art), Ben Franklin Crafts, Reno, Nev, 88-90; Art, The Wisteria Vine, Westport, Mass, 91-94; Porcelain Painter, Sheryl Wagner, Int, art dept supv, 2012-. *Teaching:* Art instr, West Bridgewater High School; Adult Edu, Bridgewater, Mass, 84-85; The Wisteria Vine, Westport, Mass, 91-94; pvt art instr, oil painting,

95-99, China painting teacher, 2010-. *Awards:* Helen Ellis Trust Fund Grant, Town Hall-Westport, 94-2001; Mass Arts Lottery Grant, 95; Prof Category Univ Mass, Dartmouth, Women's Ctr at U-Mass, 97; Mass State Waterfowl (second pl), Peabody Mus, Mass Dept of Fisheries/Wildlife, 99-2003; Mass State Waterfowl Stamp Design, second pl, 2006, first pl, 2010; First place, Mass Waterfowl Deisng, 2010. *Bibliog:* Patricia O'Connor (auth), Times, 1993; Bill Hall (ed auth), Painting Wins Town Flag, The Chronicle, 1994. *Mem:* Am Soc of Marine Artists; Mass State Arts Lottery Coun, (treas, 88-90); Westport Art Group; Int Soc Marine Artists (prof mem). *Media:* Acrylic, Oil, Watercolor & Clay. *Dealer:* Roshambo Art Phoenix AZ. *Mailing Add:* PO Box 377 Westport Point MA 02791

SEXTON, JOHN (WILLIAM)
PHOTOGRAPHER
b Maywood, Calif, May 22, 1953. *Study:* Photog workshops with Ansel Adams, Wynn Bullock, Paul Caponigro & Brett Weston, 73-74; Cypress Coll, AA (photog), 74; Chapman Univ, BA, 76. *Hon Degrees:* Brooks Inst of Photog, Hon MS, 90. *Work:* Univ Ariz Ctr Creative Photog, Tucson; Polaroid Corp Collection, Clarence Kennedy Gallery, Cambridge, Mass; Newport Harbor Art Mus, Newport Beach, Calif; Monterey Peninsula Mus Art, Calif; China Photogrs Asn, Beijing, Chica. *Exhib:* Solo exhib, Chapman Coll, Orange, Calif, 76; Bell Gallery, Brown Univ, Providence, RI, 80; New Landscapes, Friends Photog Gallery, Carmel, Calif, 80; Message From The West Coast, Photo Gallery Int, Tokyo, 81; Focus Gallery, San Francisco, 81; and others. *Pos:* Co-dir & instr, Owens Valley Photog Workshops, Agoura, Calif, 76-; tech consult to Ansel Adams, Carmel, Calif, 79-82. *Teaching:* Instr, Cypress Coll, Calif, 77-79, Univ Calif, Santa Cruz, 80-81 & Ansel Adams Yosemite Workshops, 80-. *Bibliog:* Ron Eggers (auth), Working with the masters, Rangefinder, 80. *Mem:* Am Soc of Media Photogrs; North American Nature Photog Asn. *Publ:* Contribr, Photo-Image Mag, Lodestar Press, 76; Darkroom Photog Mag, Sheptow Publ, 79; The negative, New York Graphic Soc, 81; Zoom Mag, Joel Laroche-France, 81; coauth, Quiet Light, essays, 51 black & white reproductions, 4/90, 2nd printing, 5/90 & Listen to the Trees, 50 black & white reproductions, 4/94, 2nd printing, 1/95, Bulfinch Press/Little, Brown & Co; Places of Power, 86 black & white reproductions, 10/2000 & Recollections, 56 black & white reproductions, 10/2006, Ventana Eds. *Dealer:* Ansel Adams Gallery Yosemite National Park CA 95389. *Mailing Add:* PO Box 30 Carmel Valley CA 93924

SEYLER, MONIQUE G
PAINTER
b Jersey City, NJ, Dec 3, 1956. *Study:* Sorbonne, Paris, 76; Fu Jen Univ, Taiwan, ROC, 77-78; Seton Hall Univ, BA, 79; Art Students League, 76, 81-83; Sch Visual Arts, 83-85. *Work:* Zimmerli Mus, Rutgers Univ; Sanford C. Bernstein co. *Exhib:* Two-person exhib, Conscious Color, Lyrical Light, Westchester Community Coll, 93; Emerging Artists, Elaine Benson Gallery, 95; Transition, Reggio Gallery, New York, 96; An Organic Palette, Manhattanville Coll, 97; Recent Acquisitions, Zimmerli Mus, Rutgers Univ, 99; solo exhibs, Westchester Arts Coun, Valhalla, NY, 95, Nardin Galleries, Somers, NY, 97; and others. *Collection Arranged:* Gallery Saint Martin, Inc. *Pos:* Prog chair, Katonah Mus Artists Asn, 93-95; independent cur, Art & the Environ Exhib, Katonah Village Libr, 93, Waterworks, Paramount East Gallery, 94 & Multiples, Hastings Gallery, 95; founder/owner, Gallery Saint Martin, Inc, 2004-. *Awards:* Painting Scholar, NJ Ctr Visual Arts; Miriam E Halpern Award for Works on Paper, Nat Asn Women Artists, 93; Hon Mention, Putnam Arts Coun, 93. *Bibliog:* Vivian Raynor (auth), More fantasies natural and cultural in arts council survey, NY Times, 11/19/95; Rose Slivka (auth), From the studio, E Hampton Star, 5/12/96; William Zimmer, Women's Work, Not all of it Ladylike, New York Times, 1/24/99. *Mem:* Nat Asn Women Artists. *Media:* Acrylic, Oil; Pastel. *Dealer:* Gallery Saint Martin Inc 6732 Schooner Bay Circle Sarasota Fla 34231. *Mailing Add:* 6732 Schooner Bay Circle Sarasota FL 34231

SEYMOUR, CLAUDIA HULTGREN
PAINTER, ADMINISTRATOR
b St Paul, Minn, 1948. *Study:* Duke Univ, BA, 1970; NY Univ, MA, 1979; Silvermine Art Sch, Conn, 1997-2000; Cape Cod Sch Art, 1999; Art Students League, NY, 2001-2003. *Work:* Salmagundi Club. *Exhib:* Catharine Lorillard Wolfe Art Club; Hudson Valley Art Asn; Int Asn Pastel Soc; Nat Exhib Pastel Soc, NMex, N Fla & W Coast; over 150 juried reg & nat exhib; Pastel Soc Am; Audubon Artists; Allied Artists Am; Am Artists Prof League; Oil Painters Am; Salmagundi Club. *Pos:* Pres, Salmagundi Club, NYC, 2007-2013. *Teaching:* instr workshops, Pastel Soc Am, Int Asn Pastel Soc; instr master class, Int Asn Pastel Soc. *Awards:* Numerous First Prize Awards and Best in Show Awards; Gold & Silver medals, Art Spirit Found; Bernhard Gold Medal, Am Artists Prof League, 2006. *Bibliog:* Michael Chesley Johnson (auth), Claudia Seymour, Pastel Journal, July-Aug 2003; Linda Price (auth), Creating Movement in a Still Life, Am Artist, 9/2009; Anne Hevener (auth), One Still Life, Three Visions, Pastel Jour, 2009; Holly Davis (auth), Destined to Bloom, Artists Mag, 2013. *Mem:* master signature mem, Pastel Soc Am; Conn Pastel Soc; Painters Soc Cape Cod; Allied Artists Am; Am Artists Prof League; Hudson Valley Art Asn; Oil Painters Am (assoc); Acad Artists Asn; Salmagundi Club (vpres 2004-07, pres 2007-2013). *Media:* Oils and Pastel. *Publ:* auth, Controlling the Light, Int Artist, June-July 2006. *Dealer:* Handwright Gallery 93 Main St New Canaan CT 06840; JM Stringer Gallery 21-25 Claremont Rd Bernardsville NJ; Gladwell & Patterson 5 Beauchamp Pl London Eng; 3465 Ocean Dr Vero Beach Fl

SHACK, RICHARD
COLLECTOR, PATRON
b New York, NY, May 15, 1926. *Pos:* founder, chmn emer, Mus Contemp Art, Miami, Fla; chmn, Art Ctr S Fla, Miami Beach; print acquisitions comt, Whitney Mus; fine arts panel, Fed Reserve Bd. *Bibliog:* At Home With Art, Potter, 99; The World's Top 200 Collectors, Art News, summer 2000, 01 & 02. *Collection:* contemporary art. *Mailing Add:* 151 SE 15th Rd Miami FL 33129

SHACKELFORD, GEORGE T M
CURATOR
b 1955. *Study:* Dartmouth Coll, BA (summa cum laude), 1977; Yale U, MA (fine art), 1978, MA (philos), 1980, PhD, 1986. *Pos:* Asst cur European art, Mus Fine Arts, Houston, 1984-88, cur European painting & sculpture, 1988-95; cur European paintings, Mus Fine Arts, Boston, 1996-99, chmn Art Europe Dept, 1999-, Arthur K Solomon cur modern art. *Mem:* Asn Art Mus Curs (trustee 2003-2006, pres 2006-2009). *Mailing Add:* Museum Fine Arts 465 Huntingdon Ave Boston MA 02115-5597

SHADDLE BAUM, ALICE
SCULPTOR, COLLAGE ARTIST
b Hinsdale, Ill, Dec 21, 1928. *Study:* Oberlin Col; Univ Chicago; Sch Art Inst Chicago, BFA & MFA. *Work:* Smithsonian Inst, Washington, DC; Muskegon Mus, Mich; State Ill Ctr Mus; Mus Contemp Art, Chicago; pvt collections, Dr Alfred D Klinger, Ruth & Leonard Horowich, Dr & Mrs Charles Baum. *Exhib:* Soft Edges, 54-55, Made With Paper, 67, Chicago Needs Famous Artists, 69 & Alternative Spaces, 84, Mus Contemp Art, Chicago; Soc for Contemp Art, 69, Exhib by Artist in Chicago & Vicinity, 75 & 85 & Prizewinners, 79, Art Inst, Chicago; Indianapolis Mus Art, Ind, 76; 26th Ill Invitational, Ill State Mus, Springfield, 76; Nat Drawing Show, Kohler Arts Ctr, Sheboygan, Wis, 76; Ill Traveling Sculpture Exhib II, 78-79; Fragments in a Fractured Space, Hyde Park Art Ctr, 2007-2008. *Teaching:* Instr printmaking & drawing, Roosevelt Univ, Chicago, 65-67; children's painting & drawing teacher, Hyde Park Art Ctr, 55-2006 & Triangle Art Ctr, 78-88, Chicago; Hyde Park Art Center, 1955-2006. *Awards:* Logan Medal, 75th Exhib by Artist of Chicago & Vicinity, Art Inst Chicago, 75; Ill Arts Coun Grant, 78; Nat Endowment Arts Grant, 79. *Bibliog:* Meilach & Ten Hoor (auth), Collage & Assemblage, Crown, 73; C L Morrison (auth, rev), Artforum, 76 & 78; Holly Day (auth), revs, Art in Am, 78 & 79. *Mem:* Artemisia Gallery & Fund (treas, 77-79); Hyde Park Art Ctr, Chicago; Art Inst Chicago (life mem). *Media:* Paper, Oil on Canvas, All Media. *Publ:* Contribr, Art: Choosing & Expressing, Benefic Press, 77, Leonardo, Vol II, Pergamon Press, 78, London, Eng; contribr, Perpetually Strange, Hyde Park Art Center, 2005

SHADRACH, JEAN H
PAINTER, EDUCATOR
b La Junta, Colo. *Study:* Univ NMex; Constantine & Roman Chatov Studio, Atlanta, Ga; Alaska Methodist Univ, Sumie, with Diana Kan, Shozo Sato, Prof I-Hsing Ju, Ed Whitney, Gerald Brommer, Henry Wo, Katherine Liu, Skip Lawrence, Christopher Shink, & others. *Work:* Anchorage Fine Arts Mus & Aleyeska Pipeline co, Anchorage; Frye Mus, Seattle; Standard Oil co Calif; Price Waterhouse; pvt collections, Senator & Mrs Ted Stevens, B Donatello & F & V Prewitt; British Petroleum Corp Hqs, Anchorage; and others. *Comn:* Anchorage Beautification, 70; Executive suites, ARCO & Aleyska Pipeline, 75; SOHIO painting, 80. *Exhib:* All Alaska Art Exhib, Anchorage, 68-72; Northwestern Watercolor Soc Ann, Seattle, 70; Design I, Anchorage, 71; Artists of Alaska, traveling exhib, 71-75; Frye Mus, Seattle, 85; Sumie Soc Am, 87-88, 91-94 & 97-98; Providence Hops, 90; Charter N Hosp, 98; Cornerstone Clinic, 2003-; Virtue Gallery, 2010; Blue-Holoman Gallery, 2012, 2013. *Pos:* Founder, Artique Ltd, Fine Art Gallery, Anchorage, 71-87. *Teaching:* Workshops, Foothills Art Ctr, Golden, Colo, 89-90; artist-lectr aboard Cunard Lines cruise ships, 89-92, 94-95 & 97; lectr-teacher, Univ Alaska, Cordova, Homer & Anchorage, 93-94 & 97-2000; instr workshop, Sumie for cancer patients; workshop dir, Shadrach Arts, 98-; instr, Machetanz Art Festival, Wasilla, Ark, 2012-2013. *Awards:* Gov Award, Alaska, 70; Best Show, Alaska Watercolor, 88; Paul Schwartz Award, Sumie Soc Am, 93. *Bibliog:* Leo Krantz (auth), Contemporary Am Artists, 85 & 89; Article in Am Artist, 4/85 & Midwest Art, 9-10/87; Elizabeth Leonard (auth), Floral Painting, 86; Alaska People, 96; Symi-e Society of America, Fall, 2008. *Mem:* Alaska Artist Guild (pres, 70-71); Artists Equity Asn; Sumie Soc Am; Alaska Watercolor Soc. *Media:* Acrylic, Watercolor. *Interests:* Teaching, basics of Sumie and using magic & art in performance. *Publ:* Auth, Okinawa Sketchbook, 62; SHADRACH (collection of work). *Dealer:* Vickie Prewitt Anchorage AK; Birch Tree Gallery Soldotna Ark; Blue Holoman Gallery. *Mailing Add:* 3530 Fordham Dr Anchorage AK 99508

SHAFFER, FERN
PAINTER, LECTURER
b Chicago, Ill, Mar 29, 1944. *Study:* Univ Ill, BFA, 81, Columbia Univ, MA, 91; Studies in Univ Ill & Art Inst, Chicago, Ill. *Hon Degrees:* Honor Roll of Feminist Artist, Veteran Feminists of America. *Work:* Portland Art Mus; Midway Airport (painting for pedestrian walkway); John G. Shed Aquarium (painting for Amazon Rising Exhib); Chicago Flower and Garden Show; Chicago Flower and Garden Show; Fern Cow, Chicago Cows on Parade; Peggy Notebaert Nature Mus. *Exhib:* Solo exhibs, Artemisia Gallery, Chicago, 81, 83, 85, 86 & 91, Centro Colombo Americano, Colombia, 95, Johnson State Col, Vt, 96, Mus Mod Art, Colombia, 96, Int Art Festival of Medellin 1997, Colombia, 97 & Olin Gallery, Roanoke Col, Va, 98; Peregrinajes Hacia Lo Sagrado, Mus Mod Art, Pereira, Colombia, 96; Art in Chicago 1945-95, Mus Contemp Art, Chicago, 96; Myths & Legends, Anchorage Mus Hist & Art, Alaska, 98; Spiritual Passports, Ill Art Gallery, Chicago, 98, Southern Ill Art Gallery, 98, Lockport, Ill, 99 & Ill State Mus, Springfield, 99; Then & Now, Northern Ill Art Mus Gallery, Chicago, 98; Lithuanian Mus, Vicnius, Lithuania, 99; Centro Colombo Americano, Medellin, Colombia, SAm, 2000; Galeria De Arte Fotografico, San Miguel de Allende, Mex, 2000; Turchin Ctr for Vis Arts, Appalachian State Univ, 2004; Portland Art Mus, 2005; Mus Mod Art, Medellin, Columbia, SA, 2010, 2011; Peggy Notbaret Nature Mus, 2012; Int Photog Festival, Israel, 2012. *Pos:* Pres, Artemisia Gallery, 83-92. *Teaching:* Guest lectr, many incl Art Inst Chicago & Museo de Arte de Periera, Columbia, 84-98; instr, Humanities Inst, 89-90 & workshop, Art Inst Chicago, 97; lectr, Jewish Mus Lithuania, Vilnius, 99, Art Inst Chicago, 99 & 2000, Univ Antioquia, South America, 2003, Columbia College, 2004 & Nat Univ, Medillin, Columbia, 2005; Flash Point Accad, 2008. *Awards:* Nancy Grey Grant, 98; Copenhagen Grant, 98; Andrea Frank Found, 2000. *Bibliog:* Suzi Gablik (auth), Arts and the Earth, Orion, Autumn, 95; Boule Oakes (auth), Sculpture with the

Environment, Van Nostrand Reinhold, 95; Juan Alberto Gaviria (auth), Desde el silencio, El Mundo Mag, 8/97. *Mem:* Womens Caucus Art (chmn, 90-91); Chicago Artists Coalition. *Media:* Acrylic, Ink, Colored Pencil, Oil. *Interests:* Environment, Science. *Collection:* Chicago Cows on Parade, Morgan Freeman, Marshall Fields. *Publ:* Auth, (catalog) Artemisia, 1983-88 & 93, Sacred Wild, Apexart, 2005; Art in Chicago 1945-1995. *Mailing Add:* 2530 N Rockwell Chicago IL 60647

SHAFFER, MARY
SCULPTOR
b Oct 3, 1947. *Study:* Nat Endowment Arts Fel, 74; RI Sch Design, Nat Endowment Arts, 77; Wellesley Coll, Huber Grant (study art in Czech), 79. *Work:* Grounds for Sculpture, Hamilton, NJ; Metrop Mus Art, New York; Toledo Mus Art, Toledo, Ohio; Stadt Mus, Fraunau, WGer; Columbus Mus Art, Ohio; NBC, Canadian CBS, Networks of Ger, France, Switz & France. *Comn:* Blumenthal Performing Arts Ctr, Charlotte, NC; Sara Lee Corp; Am Craft Mus, NY; Huntington Mus, Huntington, WVa; Providence Park Dept, Providence, RI. *Exhib:* Honolulu Acad Arts, Hawaii; Oakland Mus, Calif; Mus Fine Arts, Boston; Kestner Mus, Hanover, Ger; Kunstindusfriemuseet, Copenhagen, Denmark; Gemeentemus Arnhem, The Neth; Manchester City Art Galleries, Eng; Mus Kunsthandwerk, Frankfurt, Ger; Stedlijk Mus, Amsterdam, The Neth; Nat Mus Fine Arts, Rio de Janeiro, Brazil, 91; Va Mus Art, 93; Ruffino Tamayo Mus, Mexico City; Halcone Open-Air Mus, Tokyo; Detroit Inst Art, Mich; Indianapolis Mus Art, Ind; Kunsthaus Am Mus, Koln, Ger; Corning Mus, NY; Am Craft Mus, NY; Tucson Mus Art, Ariz; Mus Mod Art, Koyto, Japan; Metrop Mus Art, NY, 96; Convergence IX; Int Sculpture Conf, RI Parks Dept, Providence, 96; New Look: Contemp Women Sculptors, Washington Sq, 96; 12 X 12, RI Sch Design, Providence, 96; People in Glass Houses, Robert Lehman Gallery, Brooklyn, NY, 96; solo exhibs, Sanske Gallery, 97, Habitat Galleries, Farmington Hills, Mich, 97, Marx Gallery, Chicago, 98, Heller Gallery, NY, 99, Mus Bellerive, Zurich, Switz, Mary Saunders Gallery, 2000, Chicago Art Fair, 2001; Hawk Gallery, Columbus, Ohio, 2003; Houston Ctr for Contemp Craft, Houston, Tex, 2004; group exhib, Breaking the Mold: Conceptual Glass, Arts Midland: Galleries and Sch of the Midland Ctr for the Arts, Midland, Tex, Cleveland, Ohio & Museo del Vidrio, Monterrey, Mex, 2001; group exhib, Sculpture in Glass, San Francisco Art Fair, Robert Berman Gallery, Los Angeles, Calif, Walton Arts Center, Fayetteville, Ark, 2002. *Teaching:* Instr, New York Univ, Wellesley Coll, & Univ RI. *Awards:* Fel Individual Artists, DC Comn Arts & Humanities, 87 & Nat Endowment Arts, Washington, 94; Visionary Award, Am Craft Mus, NY, 95; Innovated use of Glass and Sculpture Award, Urban Glass, NY, 98; US Artists Simon Fel, 2009. *Bibliog:* Bellerive Zurich GLAS, Band I 1945-1991, Zurich, 93; A Labor of Love: Distinction and Beyond, New Mus Contemp Art, New York, 96; Dan Klein & Attilia Dorigato (auths), International New Glass, Arenale Editrice, Italy, 96; Richard Wilfred Yelle (auth), Glass Art from Urban Glass, A Schiffer Art Book, 2000. *Media:* Glass, Metal. *Dealer:* Marx-Saunders Gallery Ltd 230 W Superior St Chicago IL 60610; The Gerald Peters Gallery Santa Fe NM

SHAFFER, RICHARD
PAINTER, PRINTMAKER
b Fresno, Calif, Mar 17, 1947. *Study:* Univ Calif, Santa Cruz, BA (philos), 69; New Sch Social Res, New York, grad study philos; San Francisco Art Inst, BFA (painting), 73; Stanford Univ, Palo Alto, Calif, MFA (painting), 75. *Work:* Santa Barbara Mus Art, Calif; Roswell Mus & Art Ctr, NMex; La Jolla Mus Contemp Art, San Diego; Dallas Mus of Art, Tex; Nova Corp, Canada. *Exhib:* Roswell Mus 20th Anniversary Exhib, Roswell, NMex, 87; Am Acad & Inst Arts & Lett, NY, 86; La Jolla Mus Contemp Art, La Jolla Calif, 88; Nat Mus Am Art, Washington, DC, 82; John Berggruen Gallery, San Francisco, Calif, 88; La Louver, Venice, Calif, 1990; and others. *Collection Arranged:* St Mary's Col, Moraga, Calif, 1999; Santa Cruz Inst Contemp Art, Santa Cruz, Calif, 2004; 418 Project, Santa Cruz, Calif, 2005; Tannery Arts, Santa Cruz, Calif, 2007. *Pos:* Artist-in-residence, Roswell Mus, 75-76, MacDowell Colony, Peterborough, NH, fall 77, Yaddo, Saratoga Springs, NY, spring 78, Ossabaw Found, Savannah, Ga, spring 79; vis artist, Univ Iowa, Iowa City, fall, 81; artist-in-residence, Bellagio Study & Conference Ctr, Lake Como, Italy, 83. *Teaching:* Instr printmaking, Univ Calif, Santa Cruz, summer 75; assoc prof painting & drawing, Univ Tex, Arlington, 78-83; instr, painting & drawing, Univ Calif, Santa Barbara, 1992-1994, Univ Calif, Santa Cruz, 1994-1996. *Awards:* Fulbright fel, Fulbright-Hays Exchange Act, 76-77; Nat Endowment Arts, painting, 81; Visual Arts Award for Painting, 82. *Bibliog:* Harry Rand (auth), Awards in the Visual Arts I, Southeastern Ctr Contemp Art, 82; Richard Shaffer (LA Lower, Susan Freudenheim) (coauth), article, Venice, Calif, 84; Annette Carlozzi (auth), 50 Texas Artists, Chronicle Books, San Francisco, Calif, 86. *Mem:* MacDowell Colony Fel. *Interests:* Installation Art. *Publ:* Auth, Andenken, L A Louver Publications Inc, 82; auth, Art Today, Phaidon Press, 1995; auth, Roswell Artist-in-Residence, Univ NMex Press, 2007. *Dealer:* Kenneth Paige 1531 Mission St San Francisco CA 94301. *Mailing Add:* 199 Sylvan Way Felton CA 95018-1507

SHAH, ELA
PAINTER, SCULPTOR
b Bombay, India, May 10, 1948; US citizen. *Study:* SNDT Univ, Bombay, India, BA, 65: CN Coll India, dipl (fine arts), 71; Montclair State Univ, MA, 80. *Work:* Permanent Mission of India to UN, NY; Univ Pa, Philadelphia; NJ State Mus, Trenton; Montclair Art Mus, NJ; and others. *Comn:* Indoor mural, Temple at Leicefer, comn by Temple Comt, Leicester, UK, 85; outdoor mural, Riker Hill Art Park, comn by Ben Schaffer, Livingston, NJ, 88. *Exhib:* Five from India, Brookhaven Cult Ctr, NY, 90; Monmouth Mus, NJ, 90; one-person show, Oakside Bloomfield Cult Ctr, NY, 91; Sometimes My Eyes Blur at Beauty, Asian Am Art Ctr, 92; Goddess Festival of India, Am Mus Natural Hist, NY, 94; and others. *Pos:* Foreign chairperson, Nat Asn Women Artist; bd mem, Sculptor's Asn NJ, 80-94 & Indian Am Artists, 90-94. *Mem:* Sculptor's Asn NJ; Riker Hill Art Park Artist; Indian Am Artists; Miniature Soc NJ. *Media:* All Media. *Mailing Add:* 550 Highland Ave Upper Montclair NJ 07043

SHAHEEN, GARY EDWARD
ADMINISTRATOR, COLLAGE ARTIST
b Binghamton, NY, Oct 21, 1952. *Study:* Royal Univ Malta, with Charles Eldred, 75; State Univ New York, Binghamton, with Angelo Ippolito & Aubrey Schwartz, BA (art), 75; Syracuse Univ Maxwell Sch, with Joseph Scala, 86. *Work:* Security Mutual Life Corp, Binghamton, NY. *Exhib:* State Univ NY-Binghamton Alumni Invitational, Univ Art Gallery, 83; Central Regional Exhib, Robinson Mem, Binghamton, NY, 86; Artists of Achievement, Lever House, NY, 88 & Stuhr Mus, Grand Island, Nebr, 90. *Pos:* Dir, Studio Sch & Art Gallery, Binghamton, NY, 80-87; bd mem, Broome Co Arts Coun, 85-87, Schenectady Co Arts Coun, 87-90; exhibs comt mem, Schenectady Mus, NY, 89-90. *Teaching:* Instr drawing, Robinson Mem, Binghamton, NY, 82-86; instr printmaking, Studio Sch/Art Gallery, Binghamton, NY, 84-86. *Awards:* Purchase Prize, Security Mutual Life, 82; Hon Mention, Visual Individualists, 89. *Mem:* Schenectady Co & Coun (bd dir, 87-90, visual arts comt, 90); Schenectady Mus & Planetarium (exhib comt, 89-90); A Place for Jazz Inc (bd mem, 90). *Mailing Add:* 1002 Bill Rd Schenectady NY 12303

SHAHLY, JEHAN
PAINTER
b Detroit, Mich, Dec 12, 1928. *Study:* Mich State Univ, BA; Art Students League; New Sch Social Res; Hunter Coll, MA. *Work:* San Francisco Mus Art; Univ Southern Ill; Univ Mass; Geigy Collection; Provincetown Art Asn Mus; Weatherspoon Gallery, Univ North Carolina; Benedictine Hospital, Kingston, NY. *Exhib:* Grand Cent Mod Gallery, NY, 62 & 63; Six Painters, Kansas City Mus, 63; solo exhibs, Green Mountain Gallery, NY, 73, Ulster Co Community Coll, 76 & Landmark Gallery, NY, 78; Caldbeck Gallery, Rockland, Maine, 86 & 88; Le Va-Tout, Waldoboro, Maine, 92; Coffey Gallery, Kingston, NY, 2001; Omega Inst, Rhinebeck, NY, 2002-05. *Pos:* Lectr, Guggenheim Mus, formerly; Gallery & mus tour guide, Great Neck Adult Prog, NY, formerly. *Awards:* Purchase Prizes, San Francisco Mus Art, 56 & Wichita Mus, Kans, 57; Creative Artists Pub Serv Grant, 76; Gottlieb Grant for Painting, 89. *Bibliog:* Lawrence Campbell (auth), article, Art News Mag, 11/73; April Kinsley (auth), article, Art Int, 1/74; Robbie Ehrlich (auth), article, Arts Mag, 12/78. *Media:* Oil. *Mailing Add:* 166 Moore Rd Germantown NY 12526

SHAHN, ABBY
PAINTER
b Long Branch, NJ, July 31, 1940. *Study:* Skowhegan Sch Painting & Sculpture, 59-61; Calif Sch Fine Arts, San Francisco, 60; Art Students League, 60-61. *Work:* Hirshhorn Mus & Sculpture Garden, Washington, DC; Portland Mus, Maine; Colby Col, Waterville, Maine; Union Carbide; Walker Mus, Bowdoin Col, Brunswick, Maine. *Comn:* Door panels, Railroad Square Cinema, Waterville, Maine, 81; three paintings, Solon Elem Sch, Maine, 83; four paintings, Dept Disability, Old Max Bldg, Augusta, Maine, 85; mural, Univ Southern Maine, 90. *Exhib:* All Maine Biennial, Bowdoin Col, 79 & Portland Mus, 85; Ghost Dance, Univ Maine, Farmington, 83; Abstraction, Maine Coast Artists, Rockport, 85; Here and Now in Maine, Westbrook, 85; solo exhibs, Midtown, NY, 87-89; Caldbeck Gallery, 99; Fitzpatrick Gallery, 2005; Stadler Gallery, Kingfield, Me, 2009, 2010. *Pos:* Mem, Maine Biennial Comt, Portland Mus Art, 81-83 & Visual Arts Panel, Maine State Comn, 79-83. *Teaching:* Instr mural proj, Skowhegan High Sch, 85 & Univ Southern Maine, 86; instr gifted class art, Madison High Sch, 86. *Bibliog:* Edgar Allen Beam (auth), 2 stars of the 3rd magnitude, Maine Times, 85; Susan Elizabeth Ryan (auth), Roy Slamm and Abby Shahn making art up country, Artists in Maine, summer 86; Ken Greenleaf (auth), One of the best artists, Maine Times. *Mem:* Union of Maine Visual Artists. *Media:* Egg Tempera. *Publ:* Illusr, Visions Mag, 70. *Dealer:* Davistown Mus Liberty Me. *Mailing Add:* Rowell Mountain Rd Solon ME 04979

SHAHN, JONATHAN
SCULPTOR
Work: exhib in group shows at Vatican Mus, Rome, Art Mus, Princeton, NJ. *Comn:* print works incl Martin Luther King Jr commission, NJ Transit, Jersey City, NJ, Franklin D Roosevelt Mem, Roosevelt, NJ. *Exhib:* Solo exhibs incl Mary Porter Sesnon Gallery, UC Santa Cruz, 1980, Hackett-Freedman Gallery, New York City, 2001; group exhibs incl Nat Acad of Design, 1998, Cantor Fitzgerald Gallery, Harvard Coll, 2001, O'Hara Gallery, New York; Rep in permanent collections Nat Portrait Gallery, Wash. *Mem:* Fel, Nat Sculpture Soc; Nat Acad (assoc, 90, acad, 94-, coun)

SHAINMAN, JACK S
ART DEALER, GALLERY DIRECTOR
b Pittsfield, Mass, July 21, 1957. *Study:* Am Univ, BA, 82. *Pos:* Owner, Jack Shainman Gallery, New York, NY. *Specialty:* Contemporary American, Canadian and European art of all media. *Publ:* Numerous reviews of the Jack Shainman Gallery in newspapers and mags. *Mailing Add:* Jack Shainman Gallery 513 W 20th St New York NY 10011

SHAKLEE, KIM
SCULPTOR
b Colo, 1956. *Study:* Colo State Univ, Forestry & Natural Resources. *Work:* Maytag Park, Newton, Iowa; Azalea Park, Summerville, SC; City of Northglenn, Northglenn, Colo at Croke Reservoir. *Exhib:* Am Art in Miniature, Thomas Gilcrease Mus, Tulsa, Okla, 2000-2002, 2004 & 2006; One artist Show, Marine Nat Bank, Naples, Fla, 2000; Plantation Wildlife Festival, Thomasville Cult Ctr, Ga, 2001; Southeastern Wildlife Expo, Charleston, SC, 1996-2010; Art of the Animal Kingdom VII, Bennington Ctr for Arts, VT, 2002, 2013; Mystic Int Maritime Exhib, Mystic Seaport Mus, Conn; Mystic Int, Mystic Seaport Gallery & Mus, 94-2013; Bennington Ctr for the Arts, Bennington, Vt. *Collection Arranged:* Smithsonian Nat Zoological Park; Okla City Zoo; Benson Park Sculpture Garden, Loveland, Colo; Steamboat Springs Art Coun, Colo; Smithsonian Nat Zoological Park, Wash, DC. *Pos:* bd dirs, Am Soc of Marine Artist, 2008-2010, secretary & managing fel, ASMA, 2010-2011; vice pres,

American Soc of Marine Artists, 2011-. *Awards:* Gold Medal of Hon, Allied Artists Am, NY, 2001; Best of Show, Am Acad Women Artists, Tucson, Ariz, 2005; Best in Show, Ruidoso, NM, 2009; Josephine Beardsley Sandor Mem Award, New York, 2005; Allied Artists of Am, Raymond H Brumer Mem Award, 2003; Award of Excellence, Int Marine Art Ehib, Mystic Point Gallery, Conn, 2011; Eliot Liskin Memorial award, Allied Artists of America, 2012. *Bibliog:* Cathy Abramson & Nancy Arbuthnot (auths), Wild Washington Animal Sculptures A to Z, Annapolis Publishing Co, 2005; Charles Raskob Robinson (auth), Notes from Brush Hill Studio, Am Soc of Marine Artists, 4/2002; Sculpture of the Rockies, 97 Contemp Sculptors, editors of Southwest Art, 2009. *Mem:* Allied Artists Am; Catharine Lorillard Wolfe Art Club; Pen & Brush Inc; Am Artists Prof League; Am Acad Women Artists; Women Artists of the West; Am Soc Marine Artists; elected fel, Am Soc Marine Artists, 2008; Women Artists of the West (master sculptor mem). *Media:* Metal, Bronze. *Specialty:* Maritime Art: Mystic Seaport Gallery, Mystic Conn; Kensington-Sotbart Gallery, Salem, Mass. *Interests:* birding & photography. *Publ:* auth, Zoogoer, Editorial feature, Smithsonian Nat Zoo, 7-8/99; auth, Art of the West, Editorial feature, 11-12/99; Heather Lampe (auth), Touchable Art, Wildlife Art Editorial, July 2007; Southwest Art, Ed, July 2008; Wildlife Art, Ed, July 2007. *Dealer:* Mystic Maritime Museum & Gallery Mystic CT; Lee Youngman Galleries Calistoga CA; Howell Gallery Oklahoma City OK; Gallery of the Rockies Colorado Springs CO; Kensington-Stobart Galleries Salem MA; Gallery on Merchant Square Williamsburg VA. *Mailing Add:* 14599 Piccadilly Rd Brighton CO 80603

SHALALA, EDWARD
GRAPHIC ARTIST
Work: Brooklyn Mus Art; Libr Cong, Washington. *Exhib:* Solo exhibs include St Peter's Church, New York 1994, Brokebridge Gallery, Cleveland, 2008; group exhibs include Optical Simulations, Am Abstract Artists, Yellow Bird Gallery, Newburgh, NY, 2005; Material Matter, Am Abstract Artists, AIR Gallery Sideshow, Brooklyn, NY, 2007; Ann Invitational Exhib Contemp Am Art, Nat Acad Mus, New York, 2008. *Pos:* Asst dir, Painting Ctr, New York, currently. *Awards:* Pollock-Krasner Found Grant; Leo Meissner Prize, Nat Acad Design, 2008. *Mem:* Am Abstract Artists; Painting Ctr (asst dir). *Mailing Add:* 50 Delancey St New York NY 10002

SHAMAN, SANFORD SIVITZ
MUSEUM DIRECTOR, CURATOR
b Pittsburgh, Pa, July 11, 1946. *Study:* Ohio Univ, Athens, BFA, 68; State Univ NY Binghamton, 70-71; Villa Schifanoia Grad Sch Fine Arts, Florence, Italy, MFA, 74. *Collection Arranged:* Contemporary Chicago Painters (auth, catalog), Ohio State Univ, Fla State Univ, Univ SFla & Univ Northern Iowa Gallery Art, 77-78; De Kooning 1969-1978 (auth, catalog), Univ Northern Iowa Gallery Art, St Louis Art Mus, Contemp Arts Ctr, Cincinnati & Akron Art Inst, 78-79; Standards by Allan Kaprow (auth, catalog), Univ Northern Iowa Gallery Art; The Contemporary Am Potter (ed & contribr, catalog), 80-82 & Noritake Art Deco Porcelains: Collection of Howard Kottler (auth, catalog), 82-84, Smithsonian Inst Traveling Exhibs; Philip Pearlstein: Painting to Watercolors (auth, catalog), Wash State Univ & Univ Northern Iowa, 83-84; Rodney Alan Greenblat's Reality & Imagination, Two Taste Treats in One (auth, catalog), Penn State Univ; Inst of Contemp Art, 86-87; Robert Yarber Paintings: 1980-88 (auth, catalog), Penn State Univ; Va Mus of Fine Arts; Mordecai Moreh, The Nocturnal Works (auth, catalog), Univ Haifa & Mishkan Le Omanut Mus Art Ein Harod, Israel; The Light of Yehoshua Grossbard, Univ Haifa, Omanut La'Am traveling exhib, Israel; Univ Haifa Oscar Ghez Collection: 18 Artists Who Perished in the Holocaust. *Pos:* Cur, Huntington Galleries, WVa, 74-75; asst cur, Mem Art Gallery, Rochester, NY, 75-77; dir, Gallery of Art, Univ Northern Iowa, Cedar Falls, 77-80; dir, Mus Art, Wash State Univ, Pullman, 80-84 & Palmer Mus Art, Pa State Univ, 80-89; evaluator, Am Asn Mus, Mus Assessment Prog, 85-88; dir fine arts exhib & collections, Univ Haifa, Israel, currently. *Teaching:* Vis lectr, WVa State Col, 75; adj fac, Univ Northern Iowa, 78 & mus studies, Univ Haifa, 89-. *Awards:* Villa Schifanoia Grad Sch Fine Arts Scholar, Florence, 72; Univ Northern Iowa Fac Res Award, 79-80; Nat Endowment Arts Fel, 83; B'nai B'rith Hillel Found Leadership Fel, Jewish Acad. *Bibliog:* Donald Miller (auth), A new art museum is his dream at Pennsylvania State, Pittsburgh Post Gazette, 2/24/87; Ethics and professionalism, Museum News, 12/88. *Mem:* Am Asn Mus; Pa Coun Arts, vchmn mus adv panel; Eastern Wash State Hist Soc (trustee, 82-84); Asn Coll & Univ Mus & Galleries (vpres, 81-82, pres, 82-83); Forum of Art Mus, Israel. *Publ:* Coauth, Museum Programs: Public Escapism or Education for Public Responsibility?, 7/88; Education, Sunflowers and the New Vulgarity, Mus Media, Message, Routledge, London, 95; contribr, Chronicle of Higher Education, The Journal of Museum Education, The International Journal of Museum Management and Curatorship, Museologist, Art Mag, Christian Sci Monitor & Studio Israel; Interview with Belu-Simon Fainaru, J Contemp Art, Vol 7, 2, 95; Public Spaces-Private Art, Visitor Studies: Theory, Research and Practice, Vol 8, 1, 96. *Mailing Add:* Dir Fine Arts Exhib Univ of Haifa Mt Carmel Haifa 31905 Israel

SHAMBROOM, PAUL D
PHOTOGRAPHER
b Teaneck, NJ, Jan 26, 1956. *Study:* Macalester Col, St Paul, Minn, 74-75; Minneapolis Coll Art & Design, BFA, 75-78. *Work:* Whitney Mus Am Art & Mus Mod Art, NY; San Francisco Mus Mod Art; Los Angeles Co Mus Art; Walker Art Ctr, Minneapolis. *Exhib:* Recent Acquisitions in Photog, Mus Mod Art, NY, 93; Truths and Trials: Color Photog Since 1975, Minneapolis Inst Arts, 96; Crossing the Frontier: 1849 to the Present, San Francisco Mus Mod Art, 96; Hidden Places of Power, Walker Art Ctr, Minneapolis, 95; Biennial, Whitney Mus Am Art, NY, 97; Extra Ordinary: Am Place in Recent Photog, Madison Art Ctr, Wis, 2001; solo show, Mus Contemp Photog, Chicago, 2003. *Teaching:* Vis artist photog, Minneapolis Col Art & Design, 97-2000. *Awards:* Bush Found Fel, St Paul, 92 & 2002; Grant, Creative Capital Found, 2001; Guggenheim Fel, 2003. *Dealer:* Julie Saul Gallery 535 W 22nd St New York NY 10011

SHANK, J WILLIAM
CONSERVATOR
Study: Villa Schifanoia, Florence, Italy, Studied art hist and art conservation; NY Univ Inst Fine Arts, Grad studies; Harvard Univ, Advanced training in art conservation. *Work:* Cur (conserv based exhib) A Hidden Picasso, Guggenheim Mus, Bilbao, Spain, 2004. *Pos:* With Ctr for the Conserv of Fine Arts; mem staff, San Francisco Mus Modern Art, 85-2000, chief conservator, 91-2000; now with Conserv Resources Mgt; Found, Rescue Pub Murals (in cooperation with Heritage Preserv). *Awards:* Booth Family Rome Prize Fel for Historic Preserv and Conserv, Am Acad in Rome, 2004-05

SHANKMAN, GARY CHARLES
PAINTER, EDUCATOR
b Washington, DC, Sept 30, 1950. *Study:* Sch Fine & Applied Arts, Boston Univ, BFA, 68-73; Sch Arts & Sci, Am Univ, MFA, 73-75; Koninklijke Academie voor Schone Kunsten, Belg, 75-76; Skowhegan Sch, 78. *Work:* Mabee-Gerrer Mus Shawnee, Okla; Superior Ct Art Trust, Washington, DC; Nat Home Furnishings Asn, Chicago, Ill; The Watkins Collection, Am Univ, Washington, DC. *Comn:* Cover design ITT Int Fel Yearbook. *Exhib:* Solo Exhibs: Still Life & Landscapes, Seta House, Antwerp, Belg, 76; H C Dickens, London, Eng, 82; Patterns of Light, Mickelson Gallery, Washington, 85; Reflections, 88; Confections, 92; Painters Light, Shelnutt Gallery Rensselaer Polytechnic Inst, Troy, NY, 89; Sunlight & White Lace, Mickelson Gallery, Washington, 96; Broadway Gallery, 94; Yates Gallery, Siena Coll, Loudonville, NY, 99; Canajohavic Libr & Art Gallery, Canajoharie, NY, 2001; Adirondack Lakes Center for the Arts, Blue Mountain Lake, NY, 2008; GCCA Catskill Gallery, Catskill, NY, 2008; Ten Brocck Mansion, Albany, NY, 2008, A Quarter Century of Painting, Clement Art Gallery, Troy, New York, 2010, Now & Then: A Retrospective, Sow's Ear Studio & Gallery, Schnetady, NY, 2011, Paintings, The Arkell Mus, Canajoharie, NY, 2012, Oil Painter, Sacandga Valley Arts Nework Gallery Program, Worthville, NY, 2011, An Artist's Albany, Albany Heritage Area Visitors Ctr, NY, 2015; Group exhibs, Color-Expression, Perception & Meaning, Dietel Gallery, Troy, NY, 93, The Martinez Gallery, NY, 2015, The Nat Bottle Mus, Ballston Spa, NY, 2015, The Shirt Factory Gallery, Glen Falls, NY, 2015; Landscape Show, Nisk Art Gallery, Wiskayuna, NY, 93; Quiet Elegance, Mickelson Gallery, Washington, 94; group exhibs, Broadway Gallery, Albany, NY, 94, Oak Room Artists Gallery, Schenectady, NY, 98, 2000 & 2003, Stillness, Parker Gallery, Washington, DC, 2002 & Train Station Gallery, West Stockbridge, Mass, 2003; Eastern State Regional, Local Color Gallery, Lutham NY, 2003; Arts and Eros, Parker Gallery, Washington DC, 2003; Winter Exhib, Firlefanz Gallery, Albany, NY, 2004; Welcome Home; GCCA Mountaintop Gallery, Windham NY, 2004; regional exhib, Woodstock Sch Art, NY; Vacancy, Washington Park Lake House, Albany, NY, 2005; small works show, Bennington Ctr Natural & Cult Arts, Vt, 2006; The Katzen at Am Univ Mus, Washington, DC, 2007; 24th Ann Small Works Show, Schoharie Art Coun, Cobleskill, NY, 2006-2008; Banks of the Hudson, Woodstock Sch of Art, Woodstock, NY 2009; Regional Exhib, Woodstock Sch Art, NY, 2010; Small Works Show, Bennington Ctr Arts, Vt, 2010, 2011, 2012; Summer Salon, Clement Gallery, Troy, NY, 2011, 2012; Illuminations, Broadway Art Ctr Inc, Albany, NY, 2013; Works by Oakroom Artists, Mimosa Gallery, Saratoga, NY, 2013; Fruit & Food, Brath & Hughes Fine Art, Mechanicsburg, Pa, 2013. *Pos:* Artist-in-residence, City Rockville, Md, 77 & State Okla, 81. *Teaching:* Instr drawing & painting, Smithsonian Inst, Washington, DC, 78- & Md Coll Art & Design, 81-86; prof drawing & design, Sage Coll Albany, NY, 86-. *Awards:* First Place, Nat Home Furnishing Asn, 85; First Place, Nat Landscape Competition, Tolley Galleries, Washington, DC, 83; First Place, Joys of Summer, Lansingburgh Art Studio, NY, 96; Friendship Award, Colonie Artograph Inc, 2000; Merchandise Award, Colonie Nat, 2000; Awarded summer residencies at Artists' Enclave, I-Park, East Haddam, Conn, 2002, The Constance Saltonstall Found for the Arts, Ithaca, NY, 2001 & The Byrdcliffe Artist Colony, Woodstock, NY, 97. *Bibliog:* John Greenya (auth), Painter's progress, Washington Post Mag, 80; Merrie Aiken (auth), An American artist paints English scene, 82 & Lucia Anderson (auth), Time to do something for themselves, 84, Potomac News. *Mem:* Oakroom Artists. *Media:* Oil. *Mailing Add:* 86 Lawnridge Ave Albany NY 12208

SHANNON, JOE
EDUCATOR, PAINTER
b Lares, Puerto Rico, 1933. *Work:* art shows, Art in Am; writer, (art related articles) Washington Times. *Exhib:* Studies Monuments & Variations, Haslem Gallery, 1983; Shoe Salesman, Corcoran Gallery, 1969. *Pos:* technician, Smithsonian Mus Nat Hist; cur, Hirshhorn Mus & Sculpture Garden. *Teaching:* prof, Corcoran Sch Art; instr, Md Inst Col Arts (MICA), Baltimore

SHANNON, R MICHAEL
PAINTER
b Lexington, Ky, Dec 29, 1950. *Study:* studied with Henry Lawrence Faulker, 67-70, Ralph Wolfe Cowan, 74-75. *Work:* Fifth Third Nat Bank, Cincinnati; First Security Nat Bank, Lexington, Ky; Am Savings & Loan, New York City; Stock Yard Bank, Louisville, Ky; Calumet Farm, Lexington, Ky. *Comn:* poster, Am Jazz festival, Lexington, Ky; paintings, Halleon Resort, Key West, Fla,; painting, comn by Mr & Mrs William DeVries, Louisville, Ky, Bank of Lexington, Ky, SCAPA, Lexington, Ky. *Exhib:* Henry Faulkner & Friends Spindletop, Lexington, Ky; World Equestrian, Ky Horse Park, Lexington; Nat Landscape Show, Martha White Gallery, Louisville, Ky; Our Fragile Environment, Martello Mus, Key West, Fla; Key West by Two, Living Arts & Sci Ctr, Lexington, Ky; solo exhibs, Heinsmith's, Lexington, Ky, Aristo's Gallery, Key West, Fla. *Media:* Acrylic, Oil. *Mailing Add:* 1935 Stanton Way Rm 233 Lexington KY 40511

SHANNONHOUSE, SANDRA
SCULPTOR
b Petaluma, Calif, May 19, 1947. *Study:* Univ Calif, Davis, BS, 69, MFA (dramatic art), 73. *Work:* Utah Mus Fine Arts, Salt Lake City. *Comn:* Bronze sculpture, Benicia Pub Libr, Calif, 93; bronze & stone sculpture, City of Davis, Central Park, Calif, 95; bronze baptismal font, Davis Community Church, Calif, 98. *Exhib:* Solo exhibs, The

Candy Store Gallery, 71, 74, 75 & 76, Quay Gallery, San Francisco, 75, 78 & 80, Memphis Acad Art, Tenn, 79, Pence Gallery, Davis, Calif, 80, Stephen Wirtz Gallery, Sacramento, Calif, 82, 84, 86, 90 & 91, City Gallery, Sacramento, 86, John Natsoulas Gallery, Davis, Calif, 92; Selections from the Joyce & Jay Cooper Collection of Contemp Artists, Ariz State Univ Art Mus, Nelson Fine Art Ctr, Tempe, 90; Hovikodden Int, Sonja Henie-Niels Onstad Mus, Oslo, Norway, 90; Elizabeth Leach Gallery, Portland, Ore, 91; Contra Costa Collects, Bedford Gallery, Walnut Creek Art Ctr, Calif, 91; Sculptural Perspective for the Nineties, Muckenthaler Cult Ctr, Fullerton, Calif, 91; Bronze, Frumkin/Adams Gallery, NY, 91; Art Studio Alumni Exhib, Walter A Buehler Alumni & Visitors Ctr, Univ Calif, Davis, 92; From the Fire: Incendiary Spirits, Palo Alto Cult Ctr, Calif, 93; Sculpture from the Walla Walla Foundry, Greg Kucera Gallery, Seattle, 93; Pacific Rim Ceramic Sculpture, Honolulu Acad Arts, Hawaii, 93 & 94; Robert Arneson: Changing the Face of Am Ceramics, A Tribute, Kingsborough Community Coll Art Gallery, Brooklyn, 94; Here and Now: Selections from the Rene and Veronica di Rosa Collection, Oakland Mus, Calif, 94; USA Within Limits, Documenta, Galleria de Arte & Ctr Book Arts, Sao Paulo, Brazil, 94; The Figure, John Natsoulas Gallery, Davis, Calif, 95; Concept in Form: Artists' Sketchbooks & Maquettes, Palo Alto Cult Ctr, Calif, 95-96; Cast Contemp Sculpture: Works from the Walla Walla Foundry, Sheehan Gallery, Whitman Col, Wash, 97; Ceramic Still Life: The Common Object, Oliver Art Ctr, Calif Coll Arts & Crafts, Oakland, 97; L'Chaim: A Kiddush Cup, Jewish Mus, San Francisco, Calif, 97; Sculptural Perspectives for the New Millennium, LEF Found, St Helena, Calif, 98; A Feast for the Eye, M H de Young Mem Mus, San Francisco, Calif, 98; Generations, B Sakala Garo Fine Art, Sacramento, 98; Kos Chaim--A Cup of Life, Margolis Gallery, Congregation Beth Israel, Houston, Tex, 99. *Teaching:* Lectr form in theatre, Univ Calif, Davis, 74; instr ceramics & drawings, Am River Col, Sacramento, Calif, 75-76; guest artist, Otis Art Inst, Los Angeles, Calif, 76-78; artist-in-residence ceramics, Oxbow Summer Sch Art, Saugatuck, Mich, 76-77. *Bibliog:* Suzanne Foley (auth), A Decade of Ceramic Art, San Francisco Mus Art, 72; Sandy Ballatore (auth), The California Clay Rush, Art in Am, 76; Mac McCloud (auth), Dealer's choice, Images & Issues, 9-10/83; Beth Coffelt (auth), Recent Bronzes, Stephen Wirtz Gallery. *Media:* Bronze, Clay. *Publ:* Illusr, Woman and Medicine (cover), Western J Med, 88; Modern Sculpture 1990 Calendar, Cedco Publ Co, San Rafael, Calif, 89; Cast Contemporary Sculpture, Walla Walla Foundry, Wash, 97. *Dealer:* Stephen Wirtz Gallery 345 Sutter St San Francisco CA 94108. *Mailing Add:* 430 1st St Benicia CA 94510

SHAP, SYLVIA
PAINTER, PHOTOGRAPHER
b Toledo, Ohio, March 29, 1948. *Study:* Otis Art Inst, 65; Univ Judaism, 68-71; pvt studies with mentor since childhood. *Work:* Art Mus S Tex, Corpus Christi; Atlantic Richfield Co, Anchorage, Alaska; Los Angeles Co Mus Art; Los Angeles Music Ctr, Calif; Smithsonian Nat Portrait Gallery, Washington, DC. *Comn:* Portraits, comn by Audrey & Billy Wilder, Los Angeles, Calif, Henry Mancini, Los Angeles, Eileen & Peter Norton, Los Angeles, Victoria Principal, Beverly Hills & Anna & Rupert Murdoch, New York. *Exhib:* Recent Acquisitions, Smithsonian Nat Portrait Gallery; Solo exhib, USC Fisher Mus De Art, 2011. *Teaching:* Gifted Children's Prog, Otis-Parsons, Los Angeles (formerly); lectr, mus & univs; TV appearances. *Bibliog:* The Portraits of Sylvia Shap: Explorations and Revelations, USC Fisher Mus Art, 2011. *Media:* Oil, Miscellaneous Media. *Interests:* Contemporary realism & portraiture. *Publ:* About Face (exhib catalog), by Jim Edwards, Art Mus S Tex, Corpus Christi, 84; American Art Today: The Portrait (exhib catalog), by Dr. William Betsch, Art Mus Fla, Miami, 5/8-6/3, 87; Contemporary Southern California Art (exhib catalog), by Marie de Alcuaz, Mus Fine Arts, Taipei, 87; Some Members of My Family: The work of Sylvia Shap (exhib catalog), by Jim Edwards, Los Angeles Municipal Art Gallery, 5/31-6/10, 88; Insatiable Desires (exhib catalog), by Lillian H Choy & others, USC Fisher Gallery, 3/2-4/16, 2005, 2011 ; The Portraits of Sylvia Shap Explorations and Revelations (exhib catalog), by Selma Holo, 2011

SHAPERO, ESTHER GELLER See Geller, Esther Geller Shapero

SHAPERO, MINDY
SCULPTOR
b Louisville, Ky. *Study:* Attended NY Studio Program, Independent Studio, 96; Md Inst Coll Art, Baltimore, BFA, 97; Univ Southern Calif, LA, MFA, 2003. *Exhib:* Solo and Two-person exhibs, Not really here, LA Contemp Exhib, 2001; Univ Southern Calif, LA, 2002, 2003; Anna Helwig Gallery, LA, 2004, 2006; Wexner Ctr for Arts, Columbus, Ohio, 2006; CRG Gallery, NY, 2006; The Breeder Project, Athens, Greece, 2007; Group exhibs, Bellwether, Brooklyn, NY, 2000, Flatfile, 2000; Stinky Stew, Richard Heller Gallery, Santa Monica, Calif, 2000; Snapshot, Contemp Mus Baltimore, 2000; Graphic, Curt Marcus Gallery, NY, 2002; Sometimes It's Dark, Practice Space, Los Angeles, 2002; To believe much more than that, Biennial, New Wight Gallery, 2002; T-shirt Show, Daniel Silverstein Gallery, NY, 2003; Stay Inside, Shoshana Wayne Gallery, Los Angeles, 2004; Calif Biennial, Orange Co Mus Contemp Art, 2004; There is no such thing as the real world, Galleri MGM, Oslo, Norway, 2005; Thing, New Sculpture from Los Angeles, The Hammer Mus, 2005; Rogue Wave, LA Louver, Venice, Calif, 2005; Nathalie Obadia Gallery, Paris, 2005; The Uncertainty of Objects and Ideas, Hirshhorn Mus, Washington, DC, 2006; LA Trash and Treasure, Milliken Gallery, Stockholm, Sweden, 2006; Like color in pictures, Aspen Art Mus, Colo, 2007; Exit Music, Grimm/Rosenfeld, NY, 2007. *Awards:* Will-Grohamm Award, Berlin, Germany, 2006

SHAPIRO, BABE
PAINTER
b Irvington, NJ, May 4, 1937. *Study:* NJ State Teachers Col, Newark, BS; Hunter Col, with Robert Motherwell, BS & MA, 58. *Hon Degrees:* Md Inst Coll Art, Hon DFA, 2000. *Work:* Albright-Knox Art Gallery, Buffalo; Corcoran Gallery Art, Washington, DC; Scottish Nat Gallery of Mod Art, Edinburgh; Baltimore Mus Art, Md; Bayley Art Mus Univ Va; and many others. *Exhib:* NY's Worlds Fair, NY, 65; Cincinnati Mus Art, Ohio, 66; Indianapolis Mus Art, IN, 70; Baltimore Mus Art, Md, 70; Krannert Art Mus, Champagne-Urbana, IL, 80. *Pos:* Founder, dir emeritus, Mount Royal Grad Sch Art, Md Inst Col Art, Baltimore, 75-2000. *Teaching:* artist in res, Quincy Club, Quincy, Ill, 66; dir emer, Mount Royal Graduate School Art, MICA, Baltimore, MD, 2000. *Awards:* First Prize in Painting, Monmouth Col, NJ, 63; Purchase Prize Award, Bamberger's, 66; Ford Found Grant, 66. *Bibliog:* Hilton Kramer (auth), Art Once Cold, Now Romantic, The NY Times, Oct 69; Lincoln Johnson (auth), Paintings of Babe Shapiro, New Lugano Review, vol 8-9, 76; John Dorsey (auth), Retrospective reveals major change in Babe Shapiro's work, Baltimore Sun, 1, 4/3/90. *Mem:* Am Abstr Artists, NY. *Media:* Acrylic. *Mailing Add:* 31 Walker St New York NY 10013

SHAPIRO, DAVID
PAINTER, PRINTMAKER
b Brooklyn, NY, June 26, 1944. *Study:* Skowhegan Sch Art, Maine, 65; Pratt Inst, BFA, 66; Ind Univ, Bloomington, MFA, 68. *Work:* Brooklyn Mus, Guggenheim Mus & Mus Mod Art, NY; San Francisco Mus Mod Art; Ft Lauderdale Mus Art, Fla. *Exhib:* Poindexter Gallery, NY, 71, 73, 74 & 77; Gloria Luria Gallery, Fla, 79, 81, 83, 85 & 88; Getler/Pall/Saper Gallery, NY, 81, 83 & 85; Jan Turner Gallery, Los Angeles, 87; Dolan/Maxwell Gallery, Philadelphia, 87 & 88; Fay Gold Gallery, Atlanta, 88. *Teaching:* Instr, Pratt Inst, 69-71; vis artist, Barnard Col, 72; guest artist, Kansas City Art Inst, 73; instr, Parsons Sch Design, 74-80. *Bibliog:* M L Thompson (auth), Cosmos and chaos, Arts Mag, 10/80; Jon R Friedman (auth), Elucidation in the art of David Shapiro, Arts Mag, 11/85. *Media:* Acrylic. *Dealer:* Dolan/Maxwell Gallery 154 Wooster St New York NY 10012. *Mailing Add:* 549 W 52nd St New York NY 10019-5012

SHAPIRO, DAVID JOEL
CRITIC, EDUCATOR
b Newark, NJ, Jan 2, 1947. *Study:* Columbia Col, BA, 68; Clare Coll Cambridge, Eng, BA, MA, 70- 74; Columbia Univ, PhD, 73. *Pos:* Ed Assoc, Art News, 69-70, Architectures Mag, 89-; ed bd, RES, Harvard. *Teaching:* Assoc prof, Wm Paterson, Wayne, NY, 80-; vis prof, architecture, Cooper Union, NY, 80-; asst prof, Columbia Univ, 73-79, Brooklyn Col, Princeton Univ. *Awards:* Zabel Prize, Nat Acad Inst Arts & Letters,77; Nat Endowment Humanities, for research in poetry & painting, 78; Nat Endowment Art, for poetry, 79. *Bibliog:* Stephen Paul Miller (auth), David Shapiro, Jasper Johns: An Analogy (Master's Thesis, City Col); Michael Simon, Padgett Shapiro Master's Thesis, Brown Univ. *Mem:* ed bd, RES Mag, Harvard/Peabody Mus; advisor, Poet's House. *Res:* Interdisciplinary modern Semiotics and aesthetics. *Publ:* Auth, John Ashbery's Poetry, Columbia Univ Press, 77; Jim Dine: Painting What One Is, Abrams, 80; Jasper Johns' Drawings, Abrams, 84; Mondrian Flowers, Abrams, 91; coauth, Artistic Collaboration in the 20th-Century Art, Smithsonian Inst Press, 84. *Mailing Add:* 3001 Henry Hudson Pkwy Bronx NY 10463-4717

SHAPIRO, JOEL ELIAS
SCULPTOR
b New York, NY, Sept 27, 1941. *Study:* NY Univ, BA, 64, MA, 69. *Work:* Fogg Art Mus, Cambridge, Mass; Metrop Mus Art, Mus Mod Art, Whitney Mus Am Art & Brooklyn Mus, NY; Philadelphia Mus Art, Pa; Corcoran Gallery Art, Nat Gallery Art, Hirshhorn Mus & Sculpture Garden, Washington, DC; Art Gallery Ontario, Toronto; and many others. *Comn:* Sony Music Entertainment, NY, 94-95; Friedrichstadt Passagen, Berlin, Ger, 94-95; Koln Sculpture Park, Cologne, Ger, 96-99; Embassy of the US, Ottawa, Can, 99; Koln Skulpture Park, Cologne, 2000; Communaute de Communes de L'Agglomeration Orleanaise, Orleans, Fr, 2001; Norton Mus Art, West Palm Beach, Fla, 2007; 23 Savile Row, London, 2009; Denver Art Mus, Colo, 2011; US Consulate, Guangzhou, China, 2013. *Exhib:* Retrospective of sculpture & drawing, Whitney Mus Am Art, NY & traveling, 82-84; Group show, Paula Cooper Gallery, NY, 96-97; Solo shows, Paula Cooper Gallery, 70-90, 2010, Susan Hilberry Gallery, Detroit, Mich, 77, 82, 88, 96, 2003-2004, Galerie Daniel Templon, Paris, 86, 88, 2001, 2004, & 2009, John Berggruen Gallery, San Francisco, Calif, 87, 91, 2000, 2005, & 2012, Pace Gallery, 93, 96, 98, 2001, 2003, 2005, 2007, & 2011, Galerie Jamileh Weber, Zurich, 97, 2006-07, Gerald B Cantor Rooftop Galleries, Metropolitan Mus Art, 2001, LA Louver Gallery, Los Angeles, Calif, 2004, 2006, 2009, & 2011, Musee d'Orsay, Paris, 2005, Davidson Coll, Davidson, NC, 2008, Gana Art Gallery, Seoul, 2008, Tex Gallery, Houston, Tex, 2008, 2012, Galerie Karsten Greve, St Moritz, 2009-10, Mus Ludwig, Cologne, 2011, Galerie Forsblom, Helsinki, Finland, 2011, Rice Univ Art Gallery, Houston, Tex, 2012; Craig F Starr Gallery, 2013. *Teaching:* instr, Princeton Univ, 74-76, Sch Visual Arts, NY, 77-82. *Awards:* Creative Arts Award, Brandeis Univ, 84; Skowhegan Medal for Sculpture, 86; Merit Medal for Sculpture, 90 & elected to Am Acad & Inst Arts & Letts, 98; Chevalier, Ordre des Arts et des Lettres, Fr, 2005; Smithsonian Archives of Am Art award, 2008; Alumni Achievement award, NYU, 2010. *Bibliog:* Sculpture and Drawings, Hendel Eicher and Michael Brenson, NY, 98; Sculpture in Clay, Plaster, Wood, Iron, and Bronze, interview by Jack Reynolds, text by Joel Shapiro, Addison Gallery American Art, 98; Wood/Painted Wood, text by Brad Thomas, interview by Richard Shiff, North Carolina: The Van Every/Smith Galleries, Davidson Coll, 2008. *Mem:* Swedish Royal Acad Art; Am Acad Arts & Letts; Nat Acad. *Dealer:* Pace Gallery 32 E 57th St New York NY 10022

SHAPIRO, LOIS M
COLLAGE ARTIST, INSTRUCTOR
b Elizabeth, NJ, Nov 18, 1932. *Study:* Fairleigh Dickinson Univ, BFA, 72; Kean Col, MA, 76; Montclair State Col, with Anne Chapman, 80-83. *Work:* Mus Mod Art, NY; Newark Mus, NJ; Noyes Mus, Oceanville, NJ; Montclair Mus, NJ; Library Congress, and others. *Exhib:* One-woman shows, Newark Mus, NJ, 84, Kent Place Gallery, Summit, NJ, 93, The Park Avenue Club, Florham Park, NJ, 96 & Icons/Iconography, Print Coun NJ, N Branch, 96; Contemp Papermakers, Print Coun NJ, North Branch, 93; Editions-The First Five Years, Newark Mus, NJ, 93; Papermade USA, Zimmerli Mus, New Brunswick, NJ, 93; Diversity in Paper, Univ of the Arts, Philadelphia, 94; Editions, Noyes Mus, Oceanville, NJ, 95; Spheres of Influence, NJ Ctr Visual Arts, Summit, 95, Celebrating Excellence, 96; Dimension Dementia, Print Coun, NJ, 95;

Paper Made NJ, Gloucester Col, Sewell, NJ, 97. *Pos:* Dir Artmakers Gallery, Coop Gallery, Garwood, NJ, 73-79; bd dir, Watchung Art Ctr, NJ, 80-85; membership dir, Print Coun NJ, 85-90; co-ed, Editions, 89-; founder, Artshare, 92; creator & cur, The Glove Project, 96. *Teaching:* Instr handmade paper, Newark Mus, NJ, 87-, NJ Ctr Visual Arts, Summit, 88- & Printcouncil, NJ, 94-95; res artist, 96-97. *Awards:* NJ State Fel, NJ State Coun Arts, 86-87; Merit Award, Int Juried Show, 98. *Bibliog:* Rachael Mullin (auth), Artshare/Bringing Artists Together, Recorder Publ, 93; Barbara Goldstein (dir), Video Interview with Lois Shapiro, Monmouth Festival of Art, 94. *Mem:* NJ Designer Craftsmen; Printmaking Coun NJ; Guild of Papermakers; Friends Dard Hunter Papermakers. *Media:* Mixed Media. *Publ:* Ed, A Letter to a Friend, 90, coauth, In My Wildest Dreams, 91, Earth Mother/Mother Earth, 92, Voices and Visions, 93 & contribr, Icons, Editions, 94. *Mailing Add:* 11 Hyde Cir Watchung NJ 07060

SHAPIRO, MICHAEL EDWARD
MUSEUM DIRECTOR, CURATOR
b New York, NY, Nov 15, 1949. *Study:* Hamilton Coll, BA, 72; Williams Coll, MA (Kress fel), 76; Harvard Univ, MA (teaching fel), 78, PhD, 80. *Collection Arranged:* Buffalo Bill Hist Ctr, Cody, Wyo, 88, Mus Fine Arts, Houston, Tex, 89 & Metrop Mus Art, NY, 89; Modern Art from the Pulitzer Collection: Fifty Years of Connoisseurship (auth, brochure), Fogg Art Mus, Harvard Coll, 88 & St Louis Art Mus, 88; New Sculpture/Six Artists, 88 & Currents 41: Judy Pfaff, 90, St Louis Art Mus; George Caleb Bingham, St Louis Art Mus & Nat Gallery of Art, Washington, DC, 90; Rings Five Passions in World Art, 96; Impressionism Paintings Collected by European Mus, 98-99. *Pos:* Guest cur, Nat Mus Am Art, 80-81; cur 19th & 20th Century art, St Louis Art Mus, 84-92, chief cur, 87-92, secr bd comnrs, 89-91; dir, Los Angeles Co Mus Art, 92-93; dir mus progs & chief cur, High Mus Art, Atlanta, Ga, 94-95, dep dir, chief cur, 96-99, Nancy & Holcombe T Green, Jr dir, 2000-; Harvard Univ Visiting Comt, Harvard Art Mus, formerly. *Teaching:* Asst prof dept art, Duke Univ, Durham, NC, 80-84. *Awards:* Chevalier Ordre Arts & Lettres, France, 2005. *Publ:* Auth, Bronze Casting and American Sculpture, 84; Twentieth-Century American sculpture, Bull St Louis Art Mus, winter 86; contrib auth Frederic Remington The Masterworks, 88; Gerhard Richter: Paintings, Photographs and Prints in the Collection of the St Louis Art Mus, Bull St Louis Art Mus, summer 92; and others. *Mailing Add:* Director High Mus Art 1280 Peachtree St NE Atlanta GA 30309

SHARBAUGH, KATHRYN K
CERAMIST, DESIGNER
b Norwich, Conn. *Study:* Norwich Art Sch, 67; Kansas City Art Inst, BFA, 72; Cranbrook Acad Art, MFA, 74. *Work:* RI Sch Design, Providence, RI; Cooper-Hewitt, Smithsonian; Slater Mus, Norwich, Conn; Cranbrook Mus Art, Bloomfield Hills, Mich; Ark Art Ctr, Little Rock, Ark; Mokpo (S Korea) Mus Ceramics; Mus Het Kruithuis, s' Hertogenbosh, The Netherlands; Renwick Gallery, Smithsonian Am Art Mus, Washington; Pfannebecker Collection, Lancaster, Pa; Crocker Art Mus, Sacramento, Calif; Garwin Art Collection, Carbondale, Ill; Flint Inst Arts, Mich. *Comn:* Columbarium, Chapel of the Resurrection, St Paul's Episcopal Church, Flint, Mich, 94; commemorative plate series, Flint Cult Ctr Corp; Besser Collection, Santa Fe, NMex. *Exhib:* Mich Invitational, Flint Inst Arts, 90; Black & White, Kavesh Gallery, Ketchum, Idaho, 91; Teapots: Contemp Views, Pro-Art, St Louis, Mo, 92; Artistic Generations, Works Gallery, Philadelphia, Pa, 92; Teatime, Miller Gallery, Cincinnati, Ohio, 97; Plates Pewabic Pottery, Detroit, Mich, 97; The Art of Dinning, Ball State Univ, Muncie, Ind; Concours Int Ceramique, Mus Caronge (Switz). *Collection Arranged:* Captured Glass, Flint Inst Arts, 2012. *Pos:* freelance pattern designer, Mikasa, Lauffer & Corning Glass Works; coord Capital Campaign, Endowment Campaign, Flint Inst Arts, Mich, dir develop, currently, adj decorative arts, currently. *Teaching:* instr Flint Inst Arts. *Awards:* Nat Endowment Arts, 80, 92; Fel, Mich Coun Arts, 85-94. *Bibliog:* Robert Bishop & Patricia Coblentz (auth), American Decorative Arts, Harry N Abrams, NY, 82; Duane Preble (auth), Artforms, Harper & Row, NY, 84 & The Best of Pottery, Quarry Books, 98; Ceramics: A Potter's Handbook, Nelson, Harcourt; Ceramics, Mastering the Craft, R Zakin, Krause; 500 Teapots, Lark Publ; Leslin Ferrin (auth), Teapots Transformed, Guild; Nelson (auth), Ceramics: A Potters Handbook; Bishop (auth), Am Decorative Arts. *Mem:* Univ Mich Citizens Adv bd; For-Mar Nature Preserve, Flint Mich (bd trustees); Former Cranbrook Acad Art, Bloomfield, Mich (bd trustees). *Media:* high fired porcelain. *Interests:* Birdwatching. *Collection:* historic and contemporary paperweights. *Mailing Add:* FIA 1120 E Kearsley Flint MI 48503

SHARLIN, JONATHAN
PHOTOGRAPHER, EDUCATOR
b Hackensack, NJ, Apr 20, 1950. *Study:* Goddard Col, BA, 72; Visual Studies Workshop, SUNY, MFA, 78. *Work:* Fogg Art Mus Harvard Univ; Rose Art Mus Brandeis Univ; Mus Fine Arts, Houston; RI Sch Design Mus; Fidelity Investments, Polaroid Collection; Mus Fine Arts, Houston, Tex; Mus Art, Providence, RI. *Exhib:* Representing Holocaust, Univ Southern Maine, Gorham, 96; Ancient Stones, Brown Univ List Art Center, Providence, RI, 97; Art Sentinels, RI Sch Design Mus, Providence, 99; Letters from the Middle East, St Mary's Coll, Notre Dame, Ind, 99, Artspace Gallery, Univ Va, Charlottesville, 99; Univ Mass, Lowell, Mass, 2001; Minn Ctr for Photog, 2002; Four Indias, Newport Art Mus, Newport, RI, 2006; The New England Survey, Photo Resource Ctr, Boston, Mass, 2008, Fruitlands Art Mus, Harvard, Mass, 2008; The Photograph Now, Grimshaw-Gudewiez Art Gallery, BCC, Fall River, Mass, 2008; Photo & Book, 23 Sandy Gallery, Portland, Ore, 2009; Here and There, Baminster Gallery, RI Coll, 2011; Rurel Revolution, Goddard Coll, Plainfield, Vt, 2013; RISCA Fellowships, Pawtucket, RI, 2014. *Teaching:* instr photog, RI Coll, 93-97, RI Sch Design, 1997-2003; instr photog, CC of RI, 84-05. *Awards:* Winner of self-publ photo books, Photo & Book, 23 Sandy Gallery, Portland, Ore, 2009; Merit award, Artist Fellowship Photography, RISCA, 2014. *Media:* Photography. *Interests:* Sea Kayaking. *Mailing Add:* 166 Lancaster St Providence RI 02906

SHARON, RUSSELL
PAINTER, SCULPTOR
b Minn, 1948. *Study:* Univ Ams, Sch of Liberal Arts, Mexico City, Mex, 68-72; MIT, Student Art Asn, Cambridge, Mass, MA, 74-75. *Comn:* Outdoor sculptures, comn by Mr & Mrs Orton, Calif, 88. *Exhib:* Solo exhibs, Ctr for Fine Arts, Miami, Fla, 87, The Gallery, NY, 89, Barbara Greene Gallery, Miami, Fla, 90, Minneapolis Inst Art, Minn, 90. *Bibliog:* John Herzfeld (auth), article, Art News, 4/87; Helen H Kohen (auth), article, Miami Herald, 2/16/88; Leslie Judd Ahlander (auth), On Site Sculpting at Art Center, Miami News, 3/11/88

SHARP, ANNE CATHERINE
PAINTER
b Red Bank, NJ, Nov 1, 1943. *Study:* Pratt Inst, Brooklyn, NY, BFA, 65, with Richard Lindner & Gabriel Laderman; Brooklyn Coll, MFA, 73, with Lee Bontecou & Jimmy Ernst, Laurence Campbell, Philip Pearlstein. *Work:* Albright-Knox Art Gallery, Buffalo, NY; St Vincent's Hosp, NY; NY Pub Libr; White House; Anchorage Mus Hist & Art, Alaska; Smithsonian, Nat Air & Space Mus, Washington, DC; US Geological Survey, Reston, Va; Univ Alaska, Anchorage; Int Mus Erotic Art, Kronhausen Collection, Sweden; Janco-bada Mus, Eil-Hod, Israel; Dalls Mus Art, Tex; Libr Congress, Wash DC; Art in Embassies prog, DC; New Rivers Press, New York; Sheraton Hotel, Waikiki, Hawaii; Budapest FMK Gallery, Hungary; Biskup, Lewin & Bravo, New Rochelle, NY; Contemp Gallery, Dallas, Tex; Ridgewood Public Libr, NJ. *Comn:* Libby Riddles - First Woman to Win the IDITAROD (poster), Libbys Blazing Stars, Alaska, 95; portraits, Vermica Scutaro, 2010-12. *Exhib:* Solo exhibs, Pace Edit, New York City, 74, Ten Down Town, New York, 74, Katonah Gallery, New York City, 74, Contemp Gallery, Dallas, Tex, 75, Eatontown Hist Mus, NJ, 80, NY Pub Libr, Epiphany Branch, 88, Books & Co, NY, 89, Kendall Gallery, NY, 90, Int Gallery Contemp Art, Anchorage, 93, US Geol Survey, Reston, Va, 94, Think Tank Gallery, NY, 94 & Stonington Gallery, Anchorage, 94, On Television Benefit, New York City, 98, 99, & 2000; group exhib, Coos Art Mus, Ore, 90; Univ Alaska, Anchorage, 90, 91, 94 & 95; Rochester Mus & Sci Ctr, NY, 90-94; Nat Mus Women Arts, Washington, 91; Kikbuartsctr Gallery, Lawrenceville Sch, NJ, 96; Blue Mountain Gallery, NY, 98; AIR Gallery, NY, 2002-2008; AIR Gallery, 2009, 2010, 2012; Mus Brasileivo da Escultura, Sao Paulo, Brazil, 2010. *Pos:* Family Hist Project bk, J Lindemann, Guild-Liddell, 2005-, Alverson-Steele 2011-. *Teaching:* Instr, NY Univ, 78, Sch Visual Arts, 78-89, Pratt Manhattan Ctr, 82-84, State Univ NY, Purchase, 83, Parsons Sch Design, NY, 84-90, Anchorage Mus Hist & Art, 90-95, Univ Alaska, Anchorage, 94-96 & Fashion Inst Technol, NY, 97-98. *Awards:* Teaching fel, Artist's Show, Brooklyn, NY, 72; Artist sponsor, Great Lakes Coll Asn Apprenticeship Prog, 73-76; Artist-in-residence, Va Ctr Creative Art, 75, Artpark, 80; Pippin Award, Our Town, 84. *Bibliog:* NY Post, 12/7/91; Jerry Tallmer (auth), A Sharp View of the World; Mike Dunham (auth), Artists expanding the landscape, capturing the wild land, Anchorage Daily News, 11/14/93; Refreshing Collages, Anchorage Daily News, 11/6/94, Faculty Show, 9/12/95; Matthew Campbell Roberts (auth), The Cortland Rev, Winter 2007. *Mem:* Nat Mus Women Arts; Pratt Alumni Asn; Coll Art Asn Am. *Media:* Oil, Acrylic; Collage. *Interests:* Travel, glaciology, astronomy, photography. *Publ:* Auth, Swimming in the mainstream with her, fall 86, Thoughtlines, fall 86, Univ Va Mag; Artists Vision of the Spirit, Anchorage Daily News, 7/31/94; The Art Scene - An Artists View, Anchorage Press, Alaska, 11/95-6/96; The Big Wow-Yup 'ik Art Excites New York, Anchorage Daily News, 4/6/97; New Rivers Press, NY. *Dealer:* Site 250 Contemporary Art 250 Cushman St Suite 2A Fairbanks AK 99701; ON Television, 388 Broadway, 2nd Fl, New York, NY 10013; Budapest Funk Gallery Hungary; Biskup and Bravo New Rochelle NY. *Mailing Add:* PO Box 1776 New York NY 10156-1776

SHARP, LEWIS INMAN
MUSEUM DIRECTOR
b New York, NY, Dec 22, 1941. *Study:* Lewis & Clark Coll, Portland, Ore, BA, 65; Univ Del, MA, 68 & PhD, 80. *Pos:* Asst cur Am paintings & sculpture, Metrop Mus Art, New York, 72-75, assoc cur Am paintings & sculpture, 75-82, adminr & cur, 82-89; Frederick & Jan Mayer dir, Denver Art Mus, 1989-2010. *Mem:* Asn Art Mus Dirs, 89-. *Publ:* Auth, John Quincy Adams Ward: History & contemporary influences, The Am Art J, Vol IV, 11/72; The Smith Memorial, Sculptures of a City: Philadelphia's Treasures in Bronze & Stone, Walker Publ Co, 74; New York Public Sculpture by 19th Century American Artists, Metrop Mus Art, 74; contribr, The Architecture of Richard Morris Hunt, Univ Chicago Press, 86

SHARP, SUSAN S
PAINTER
b North Bergen, NJ, Jan 4, 1942. *Study:* Syracuse Univ, 60-62; Univ Hartford, BS, 64. *Work:* Chase Manhattan Bank, Kidder/Peabody, NY; Town of Fairfield; General Elec, Conn; Huntington Bank, Columbus, Ohio; Trenwick Corp; Housatonnic Mus; Superior Courthouse State of Conn. *Exhib:* Conn Watercolor Soc, Wadsworth Atheneum, Hartford, 81; Winners Conn-Painters & Sculptors, Stamford Mus, 82; Art of Northeast, Silvermine Guild, 83, 85 & 89; Solo shows, Water & Memory, Soho 20, NY, 92, Walter Wilkiser Gallery, NY, 99, Housatonnic Mus, Bridgeport, Conn, 2001, & Heidi Cho Gallery, New York, 2010.; Abstract Connections, Silvermine Guild, 92; Kohn Pederson Fox Gallery, NY; Looking East, Butters Gallery, Portland, Ore, 95; Surround, Reece Gallery, NY, 97; Housatonnic Mus Art, Conn Comn Gallery. *Teaching:* Painting, independent projs, Silvermine Guild. *Awards:* Fel, Conn Comn in the Arts in Painting, 2002. *Bibliog:* Roger Baldwin (auth), Art on the Town, Art New Eng, 85; Jude Schwendenwien (auth), A survey of Connecticut art, Art New Eng, 9/90; James Fox (auth), Gallery reviews, Art & Antiques, summer 92; William Zimmer (auth), rev, 1/24/99 & Vincent Lombardi (auth), rev, 3/26/99, NY Times Conn sect; Pat Rosoff (auth), Art New England, 2002. *Mem:* Silvermine Guild (bd 85-86, trustee); Inst Visual Artists (pres 90-91). *Media:* Acrylic, Oil. *Mailing Add:* 53 Wyldewood Rd Easton CT 06612-1528

SHASHATY, YOLANDA VICTORIA
PAINTER
b Chicago, Ind, Aug 13, 1950. *Study:* Oberlin Col, BA, 72; Univ Wis-Madison, MA, 74. *Work:* Sunrise Mus, Charleston, WVa. *Exhib:* Directions 1986, Hirshhorn Mus, Washington, DC, 86; A View to Nature, Aldrich Mus Contemp Art, Ridgefield, Conn, 86. *Bibliog:* Michael Brenson (auth), New York Times, 86; Everett Potter (auth), Arts Mag, 88; Nancy Grimes (auth), Art News, 88. *Media:* Oil on Canvas. *Mailing Add:* 395 Riverside Dr Apt 8F New York NY 10025-7728

SHAVER, NANCY
SCULPTOR
b Appleton, NY, 1946. *Study:* Pratt Inst, BFA, 1969. *Exhib:* Solo exhibs, Pratt Manhattan Ctr, New York, 1972, Hundred Acres Gallery, New York, 1974, Curt Marcus Gallery, New York, 1987, 89, 91, 94, 97 & 99, Michael Kohn Gallery, Los Angeles, 1989, Feature Inc, New York, 2003-04 & 2007; Conn Coll Art Gallery, New London, 1976; Univ Art Gallery, SUNY Albany, NY, 1977; Vermont Photography, Robert Hall Fleming Mus, Univ Vt, 1985; Messages, Carlo Lamagna, Gallery, New York, 1987; Media Post Media, Scott Hanson Gallery, New York, 1988; The Mirror in Which Two are Seen as One, Jersey City Mus, 1989; Status of Sculpture, ELAC Art Contemporain, Lyon, France, 1990; Drawn in the Nineties, Katonah Mus Art, Katonah, 1992; Les Petits Rien de la Vie, La Galerie Volee a Une Muse, Lyon, France, 1993; Can You Always Believe Your Eyes: Recent American Drawings, Mus Contemp Art De Beyard, Breda, Neth, 1994; Coming off the Wall, Susquehanna Art Mus, Harrisburg, Pa, 1998; Living with Duchamp, Tang Teaching Mus Art Gallery Skidmore Coll, NY, 2003; Honey Bunches, Allston Skirt Gallery, Boston, 2005; Albany Int Airport, NY, 2008. *Teaching:* Instr, Milton Avery Grad Sch Arts, Bard Coll, Annandale-on-Hudson, NY, currently. *Awards:* MacDowell Fel, 1972-73; Yaddo Fel, 1974; Pollack-Krasner Found Grant, 1993; Anonymous Was a Woman Award, 2008; Guggenheim Found Fel, 2010. *Bibliog:* Gary Indiana (auth), Really Real, Village Voice, 10/13/1987; Tim Hilton (auth), Childish Things, Guardian, 9/26/1990; Deborah Gimmelson (auth), ARCO Takes Center Stage in Madrid, Art & Auction, 2/1992; Peter Schjeldahl (auth), Selective Affinities, New Yorker, 9/6/1999; Holland Cotter (auth), Another, Once Again, Many Times More, NY Times, 5/11/2001

SHAW, DONALD EDWARD
SCULPTOR, PAINTER
b Boston, Mass, Aug 24, 1934. *Study:* Boston Mus Sch Fine Arts. *Work:* Ark Arts Ctr, Little Rock; Atlantic Richfield Co, Los Angeles; Chase Manhattan Bank, NY; Mus Fine Arts, Houston, Tex; Smithsonian Inst, Washington, DC; Historic Ark Mus; Univ Ark, El Dorado, Ark. *Comn:* Ark Arts Ctr, Little Rock, 88; Ark Coll, Bateville, 92; Am Capitol, Houston; Bio-med Ctr, Univ Ark, Little Rock, 94; Univ Ark at Hope, Ark. *Exhib:* Tex 30, Nave Mus, Victoria, Tex, 77; Solo exhibs, Moody Gallery, Houston, Tex, 81 & 84; Mus Fine Arts, Houston, Tex, 89 & 94; Mid Am Mus, Hot Springs, Ark, 92; Historic Ark Mus, 2009, Santa Fe, NMex, 2010; Vellum drawings, Community Coll, Pine Bluff, Ark, 2001; Downtown Subscription, Santa Fe, NMex, 2011. *Awards:* Travel Grant to Arg, Casa De'Arg, 77. *Bibliog:* Ann Holmes (auth), Fantastic artists, Southwest Art Gallery Mag, 2/72; N Laliberte & A Mogelon (auths), Art in Boxes, Van Nostrand, Reinhold Co, 74; Susie Kalil (auth, essay cat), Don Shaw, Ark Arts Ctr, Little Rock, 89; Images from Space, David Braur, Mus Fine Art, Houston. *Media:* Mixed. *Publ:* Contribr, Agencia Noticias Mex, 69 & cover illus, Southwest Art Gallery Mag, 72; Poverty Point, Sky Drawings Video, 91. *Dealer:* Hooks Epstein Houston TX. *Mailing Add:* PO Box 417 Guadalupita NM 87722

SHAW, ERNEST CARL
SCULPTOR
b New York, NY, Apr 17, 1942. *Work:* Aldrich Mus Contemp Art, Ridgefield, Conn; Indianapolis Mus; Nelson Rockefeller; Wichita Art Mus, Kans; and others. *Comn:* Orlando Int Airport, Reading, Pa. *Exhib:* Storm King Art Ctr, Mountainville, NY, 77; Contemp Reflections, Aldrich Mus Contemp Art, 77; Solo exhibs, Storm King Art Ctr, 78, Hamilton Gallery Contemp Art, 78, Sculpture Now, NY, 78, Allentown Art Mus, 81, Wichita Art Mus, 81, Huntington Galleries, WVa, 81, Althea Viafora, NY, 86, Maxwell Davidson, NY, 88 & Williams Coll Art Mus, Williamstown, Mass, 88; Group exhib, Hamilton Gallery Contemp Art, 78; A M Sachs Gallery, 80; and other solo & group exhibs. *Media:* Steel, Wood

SHAW, ISABEL
SCULPTOR, GRAPHIC ARTIST
b New York, NY. *Study:* Bard Col, BFA, 52; Sch Visual Arts, Cooper Union. *Work:* numerous pvt collections in US, Eng, Hong Kong & Switz. *Exhib:* Solo exhibs, Anaya Gallery, Scarsdale, NY, 80, MAG Gallery, Larchmont, NY, 81 & 2000, Mari Gallery, Mamaroneck, NY, 81 & Gallery at Chappaqua Libr, NY, 95; Art Students League, NY, 90; Broome Street Gallery, NY, 91, 92 & 94; Pen & Brush Club, NY, 92; Westbeth Gallery, NY, 94; Kohn Pedersen Fox Gallery, NY, 96; and others. *Awards:* Merit Award, New Rochelle Artists, NY, 74; First Place Sculpture, Beaux Arts Finale, Westchester Co, NY, 74; Sculpture Award, Mamaroneck Artists Guild, Lyla J Weiss Mem, 84. *Bibliog:* Review, NY Times, 1/22/95; interview, Scarsdale Inquirer, 10/27/2000. *Mem:* NY Soc Woman Artists; NY Artists Equity; Contemp Artists Guild NY; Hudson River Contemp Artists; Sculptors League, NY; Art Studio Club, NY. *Media:* Bronze, Wood. *Publ:* Contemp Women Artists (calendar), 88. *Dealer:* Roslyn Sailor Fine Arts Ltd Margate NJ & Philadelphia PA

SHAW, JIM
PAINTER
b Midland, Mich, Aug 8, 1952. *Study:* Univ Mich, Ann Arbor, BFA, 74; Calif Inst Arts, MFA, 78. *Work:* Albright-Knox Art Gallery, Buffalo; CAPC musee d'art contemporain de Bordeux, Fr; Des Moines Art Ctr, Ia; Guggenheim Mus, NY; FNAC, Paris; FRAC Haute-Normandie, Fr; Fri-At Mus, Fribourg, Switz; Galleria d'Arte Moderna e Contemporanea, Palazzo Forti, Italy; Hammer Mus, Los Angeles; Patchett Coll, San Diego; Los Angeles Co Mus Art; Metropolitan Mus Art, NY; Mus Contemporary Art, Los Angeles; Mus Modern Art, NY; Walter Art Ctr, Minneapolis; Whitney Mus Am Art, NY. *Exhib:* Video and Dream, Mus Mod Art, NY, 90; Recent Drawings, Whitney Mus Am Art, NY, 90; Biennial Exhib, Whitney Mus Am Art, NY, 91; Solo exhibs, Tex Gallery, Houston, 92, Massimo de Carlo, Milan, Italy, 92 & 96, Metro Pictures, NY, 92 & 93, Linda Cathcart Gallery, Santa Monica, Calif, 92 & 93, Rena Bransten Gallery, San Francisco, 94, Donna Beam Fine Art Gallery, Univ Nev, 95 & Cabinet Gallery, London, 96, and others; Helter Skelter: LA Art in the 1990s, Mus Contemp Art, Los Angeles, 92; Songs of Innocence/Songs of Experience, Whitney Mus Am Art, Stamford, Conn, 92; Galleri Andreas Brändström, Stockholm, 95; Art on Paper, Weatherspoon Art Gallery, Univ NC Greensboro, 95; Pay-Fi, Real Art Ways, Hartford, Conn, 96; It's Only Rock & Roll: Rock & Roll Currents in Contemp Art (with catalog), Bedford Gallery/Dean Lesher Regional Ctr Arts, Walnut Creek, Calif, 96; Group exhibs, What Exactly is a Dream and What Exactly is a Joke, Donna Beam Fine Art Gallery, 95, Galerie Praz-Delavallade, Paris, 97, 99, 2002, Frankfort Kunstverein, 98, From Head to Toe: Concepts of the Body in 20th Century Art, Los Angeles Co Mus Art, 98, Jim Shaw: Thrift Store Paintings, Inst Contemp Art, London, 2000, La Bienniale de Montreal 2000, 2000, The Artist's World, Calif Coll Arts and Crafts, 2000, Biennale of Sydney, Mus Contemp Art, 2002, Metro Pictures, NY, 2005, 2006, 2007, Los Angeles County Mus Art, 2006, 2010, Hammer Mus, Los Angeles, 2007, BFAS Blondeau Fine Art Svcs, Geneva, 2008, Marres Ctr Contemporary Culture, The Netherlands, 2009, Los Angeles Municipal Art Gallery, Barnsdall Art Park, 2012, 55th Int Art Exhib Biennale, Venice, 2013. *Awards:* Nat Endowment Arts Grant, 87; Tiffany Found, 89; Fel Guggenheim Mem Found, 2004. *Bibliog:* David A Greene (auth), California Dreaming, The Village Voice, 96; Janet Preston (auth), New York Letter Bomb, Coagula Art J, No 24, 96; Ken Johnson (auth), California Dreamer, Art in Am, 12/96; Carroll Dunham (auth), Jim Shaw, ARTnews, 1/97; Amy Gerstler (auth), Jim Shaw: Rosamund Felsen, Artforum, 4/98; Ralph Rugoff (auth), Rules of the Game, Frieze, 99; Rachel Kushner (auth), A Thousand Words: Jim Shaw Talks about his Dream Project, Arforum, 11/2000; Tony Oursler (auth), Jim Shaw, ITS, Issue 3, 11/2001; Steven Stern (auth), Sweet Charity, Frieze, 2002; David Pagel (auth), Eye to Eye with Forgotten Codgers, Los Angeles Times, 2003; Jan Tumlir (auth), Destroy All Monsters-Jan Tummlir on Motor City Madness, ArtForum, 2004; Jordan Kantor (auth), Drawing from the Modern: After the Endgames: The Mus Modern Art, NY, 2005; Martha Schwendener (auth), Jim Shaw: The Donner Party, NY Times, 2007; Doug Harvey (auth), Jim Shaw's Real Mirage: A Partial Inventory, Afterall, Calif Inst Arts, Valencia, 2008; Doug Harvey (auth), Prop Department, Modern Painters, 2009; Catherine Lee (auth), Its a Stitch, Art & Music, 2010; Michael Wilson (auth), Jim Shaw at Metro Pictures, Time Out New York, 2012; Alfred Mac Adam (auth), Peter Saul/Jim Shaw Drawings at Mary Boone, ARTnews, 2013; and many others. *Publ:* Auth, Thrift Store Paintings, Heavy Industry Publ, 90; Dreams, Smart Art Press, Santa Monica, Calif, 95; and others. *Dealer:* Metro Pictures 150 Greene St New York NY 10012; Simon Lee Gallery 12 Berkeley St London Greater London W1J 8DT. *Mailing Add:* 6185 Buena Vista Terrace Los Angeles CA 90042

SHAW, JOHN PALMER
PAINTER, PRINTMAKER
b San Mateo Calif, Apr 23, 1948. *Study:* Art Students League; Pratt Inst; Md Inst Coll Art, BFA, 72. *Work:* Mus Mod Art, NY; Brooklyn Mus, NY; Bank Am, San Francisco; NY Pub Libr. *Exhib:* Five Baltimore Artists, Baltimore Mus Art, 73; Ritz Show, Ritz, Washington, 83; Terminal Show, Brooklyn Terminal, 83; The Great East River Bridge Show, 83 & New Acquisitions, 86, Brooklyn Mus; New Talent, Leo Castelli Uptown, NY, 84; Stornaway Gallery, Montreal, 92; Artifice 96, Place Victoria Show, Montreal, 96; Galerie DuGazon-Couture, Montreal, 98; Dugazon Couture, Montreal, Can, 99 & 2000; Yellowfish Gallery, Montreal, PQ, 08, 09, & 2013. *Bibliog:* Beverly Mitchell (auth), Home again, Montreal Gazette, 7/12/92; Lucinda Catchlove (auth), A painters painter John Shaw, Montreal Mirror, 11/10/92; Henry Lehmann (auth), Interiors, Exteriors, Montreal Gazette, 10/3/98. *Media:* Encaustic, Oil. *Publ:* Ed, New Observations No 8, Lucio Pozzi, 83. *Dealer:* Alessandro Mangiarotti Yellow Fish Art. *Mailing Add:* 624 Rue Sainte-Madeleine Montreal PQ H3K 2L3 Canada

SHAW, JOSEPH WINTERBOTHAM
HISTORIAN, EDUCATOR
b Chicago, Ill, July 6, 1935. *Study:* Brown Univ, BA, 57; Wesleyan Univ, MA, 59; Univ Pa, PhD, 70. *Hon Degrees:* Brown Univ, LHD, 87. *Teaching:* Asst prof, Univ Toronto, 70-73, assoc prof, 73-77, prof, 77-. *Awards:* Various res grants for Aegean Bronze Age archit and archaeology; Gold medal, Lifetime Achievement from the Archaeological Inst Am, 2006. *Mem:* Can Mediterranean Inst; Am Sch Classical Studies; Archaeological Inst Am (pres, Toronto chap, 79-88, vpres); Soc Antiquaries; Royal Soc Can. *Res:* Bronze Age Aegean archaeology and art. *Publ:* Excavation at Kommos, Crete, Hesperia, 76-93; Coauth, Kenchreai, Vol 1, Brill, 78; auth, Consideration of the Site of Akrotiri as a Minoan Settlement, Thera & Aegean World, 78; Evidence for the Tripartite Shrine, Am J Archaeol, 78; The Early Helladic II Corridor House, Am J Archaeol, 87; Phoenician Shrine at Kommos, Am J Archaeol, 89; coed & auth, Kommos An Excavation on the South Coast of Crete, I(1), I(2), II, III, IV, V, Princeton Univ Press, 90-2006; Kommos I, The Kommos Region and Houses of the Minoan Town, Part I, The Kommos Region, Ecology, and the Minoan Industries, Princeton, 95 & Part 2, 96; Kommos IV, The Greek Sanctuary, 2000; Kommos V, The Monumental Minoan Buildings, 2006; Kommos, A Minoan Harbor Town and Greek Sanctuary in Southern Crete, 2006; Elite Minoan Architecture, Its Development at Knossos, Phaistos, and Malia, 2014; Bathing at Tiryns, Am J Ardracol, 2012. *Mailing Add:* Univ Toronto Art/Grad Dept Art Toronto ON M5S3G3 Canada

SHAW, KAREN
PAINTER, CURATOR
b Bronx, NY, Oct 25, 1947. *Study:* Hunter Col, City Univ New York, BFA, 65; grad work Hunter Coll & C W Post, 70-71. *Work:* Herbert F Johnson Mus Art, Ithaca, NY; Israel Mus, Jerusalem; City Univ Grand Ctr, NY; Erasmus Haus, Basel, Switzerland; Mus Mod Art, NY. *Comn:* 11 large paintings, Mall, City Univ Grad Ctr, NY, 80;

Installation: Effects of Acid Rain on the Great Lakes, LI Univ, Southampton Campus, 88; Installation, Het Apollohus, Eindhoven, Netherlands, 90; Pandora's Box, The Effects of Burning Fossil Fuels on the Environment, 90; Plato's Box in Pandora's Cave, Dowling Col, 91. *Exhib:* Book Works, Albright Knox Art Gallery, Buffalo, NY, 77; solo exhibs, Bertha Urdang Gallery, NY, 76 & 83, Dany Keller Galerie, Munich, WGer, 78 & 81, City Univ Grad Ctr, NY, 80 & 86, Corinne Hummel Galerie, Basel, Switz, 83, C Kermit Ewing Gallery Art & Archit, Univ Tenn, Knoxville, 86 & 91, Southampton Col, Long Island Univ, NY, 88 & Het Apollohuis, Eindhoven, The Neth, 90; Artists Books, Walker Art Ctr, Minneapolis, Minn, 81; Albright Knox Art Gallery, Buffalo, NY, 82; Dowling Col, Oakdale, NY; Women's Art Caucus, The Environment Show, Bronx, NY, 90; Anchorage Mus Hist & Art, Alaska, 90; Vital Signs, Artists Address the Environ, Henry St Settlement, NY, 90; and others. *Pos:* Cur, Islip Art Mus, 81-. *Teaching:* Asst prof art, Univ Tenn, 89-90; instr, Silvermine Art Sch, New Canaan, Conn, 89-; lectr Princeton Univ, 95, 99. *Awards:* Nat Endowment Arts, US Govt, 78-79; Found Karolyi, Vence, France, 88 & 89; New York Found Arts Grant, 92-93. *Bibliog:* Lenore Malen (auth), Karen Shaw: The reckoner, Arts Mag, 4/79; Helen Harrison (auth), New York Times, 9/22/91. *Media:* Acrylic, Oil. *Publ:* Contribr, A Big Jewish Book, Anchor Press Doubleday, 78; auth, Market Research, Univ Akron, Ohio, 78. *Dealer:* Tony Zwicker 15 Gramercy Park NY 10003; Art Resources Transfer New York NY 10011

SHAW, KENDALL (GEORGE)
PAINTER
b New Orleans, La, Mar 30, 1924. *Study:* Ga Inst Technol, 44-46; Tulane Univ, BS, 49, MFA, 59; La State Univ, 50; New Sch Social Res, 50-52; Brooklyn Mus Art Sch, 53; also with Ralston Crawford, Stuart Davis, O Louis Guglielmi, George Rickey & Mark Rothko. *Work:* Mus Contemp Art, Nagaoka, Japan; NY Univ; Brooklyn Mus, New York; Everson Mus, Syracuse, NY; Neue Galerie Sammlung Ludwig, Aachen; Ogden Mus Southern Art, New Orleans, La; Miss Mus Art; Polk Mus Art, Lakeland, Fla; Orlando Mus Art, Fla; New Orleans Mus Art, La; Newcomb Art Gallery, Tulane Univ, New Orleans; Univ Richmond. *Comn:* Chase Manhattan Bank. *Exhib:* Solo exhibs, Orleans Gallery, New Orleans, 60-61 & 63, Tibor de Nagy Gallery, New York, 64-65 & 67-68, John Bernard Myers Gallery, New York, 72, Alessandra Gallery, New York, 77, Lerner-Heller Gallery, 79 & 81-82, Nature Morte Gallery, New York, 83, Bernice Steinbaum Gallery, New York, 91, Artists Space, New York, 92, Gallery S Orange, NJ, 98, Univ Richmond, Va, 99, Tulane Univ, New Orleans, 2001, Ogden Mus Southern Art, New Orleans, 2007 & Cambridge Univ, Eng, 2007, St Peter's Church, New York, 2011, Skoto Gallery, New York, 2011, Hudson Guild, NY, 2012; Contemp Painting, Mus Contemp Art, Nagaoka, Japan, 65; Galerie Simone Stern, New Orleans, 68; Modular Painting, Albright-Knox Art Gallery, 70; Sets for The First Reader by Gertrude Stein, Mus Mod Art & Metrop Mus Art, New York, 70-71; Pattern Painting, PS 1, New York, 77; Pattern & Decoration, Rice Univ, Houston, Tex, 77; Les Nouveaux Fauves, Die Neuen Wilden, Sammlung, Ludwig, 80; Pattern & Decoration, Ill Wesleyan Univ, Bloomington, 80; and others. *Teaching:* Columbia Univ, New York, 61-66; Hunter Coll, New York, 66-68; Parsons Sch Design, New York, 66-86; Lehman Coll, New York, 68-70; Brooklyn Mus Art Sch, Brooklyn, New York, 70-76; Brooklyn Coll. *Awards:* Disting Alumns, Tulane Coll, 2001. *Bibliog:* Art Forum, 11/77; articles, Arts Mag, 1/77 & Art News, 10/80; Art & Artists, 8-9/86. *Mem:* Coll Art Asn Am; NY Artists Equity Asn; Art Group, NY. *Media:* Acrylic, Collage. *Publ:* Modular Painting, 1970; The Painter and the Photographer, Van Deren Coke, Univ NMex, 72; Helicon Nine, 79; Richard Waller, Kendall Shaw, A Life's Journey in Art, Univ of Richmond, Va, 99; Tulane Univ, 2001; The Tulane Coll Rev, 2001-2002; CAC, New Orleans, 2003; Let there be light, Ogden Mus Southern Art, 2008; and others; Back Seat at the Drive In, Skoto Gallery, NY, 2010. *Dealer:* Skoto Gallery New York NY. *Mailing Add:* 916 President St Brooklyn NY 11215-1604

SHAW, LOUISE E
DIRECTOR
b Quincy, Mass, Mar 16, 1951. *Study:* Clark Univ, Worchester, Mass, BA, 73; Syracuse Univ, MFA, 81. *Exhib:* The World Unseen: When Science Meets Art; Shifting Planes: New Immigrants in the Deep South. *Collection Arranged:* Obsession: Who What and Why People Collect, Traveling Exhbn, 97; Between Space and Time: Contemporary Norwegian Sculpture and Installation, 2000-01; Georgia Triennial, 01-02. *Pos:* Exec dir, Nexus Contemp Art Ctr, 83-98; freelance cur & consult, 80-; cur, CDC Mus, 2002-. *Awards:* Nat Endowment Arts Mus Fel, 88; ORISE Fel, 2002-2006. *Mem:* Cult Olympiad; Bus Coun Arts; Ga Asn Mus & Galleries; Art & Cult Comt, Atlanta; Ga Citizen for Arts; Atlanta Pub Art legacy Comt; and others. *Publ:* Vital signs, Nexus Contemp Art Ctr, 91; auth, Harry Callahan and His Students: A Study in Influence, Ga State Univ, 81; Between Space and Time: Contemporary Norwegian Sculpture and Installation, Norwegian Sculpture Asn, 2000; Georgia Triennial, 01. *Mailing Add:* 225 Melrose Ave Decatur GA 30030

SHAW, NANCY (RIVARD)
ART HISTORIAN, INDEPENDENT SCHOLAR
b Saginaw, Mich. *Study:* Oakland Univ, Mich, BA (fine art & art hist), 69; Wayne State Univ, Mich, MA (art hist), 73; Attingham Summer Inst, Eng, 77. *Collection Arranged:* Thomas Hart Benton: An Am Original, 89; Am Paintings from the Manoogian Collection, 90; Gari Melchers: A Retrospective Exhibition, 90; Henry Ossawa Tanner, 91; Am Paintings from the Monoogian Collection: A Private View (catalog), 93; The Art of Thomas Wilmer Dewing: Beauty Reconfigured, 96; Heritage & Horizon, Am Painting 1776-1976, 76; Daniel Chester French, An Am Sculptor, 77; Arts & Crafts in Detroit, 1906-1976, 77; John Singer Sargent & the Edwardian Age, 79; Silver in Am Life, Selections from the Middle Brady Garvan & Related Coll, Yale Univ Art Gallery, 82; Am Masters, The Thyssen-Bornemisza Coll, 84; Sharing Traditions, Five Black Artists in 19th Century Am, 86; The Art that is Life, Arts & Crafts Movement in Am, 1875-1920, 88. *Pos:* Asst cur Am art, Detroit Inst Arts, 72-75, cur Am art, 75-98, cur emer, 98-. *Teaching:* Adj prof, Wayne State Univ, 86-98. *Bibliog:* Cotopaxi, Detroit Inst Arts Bull, 78; American Paintings Acquired During the Last Decade, Detroit Arts Bulletin, 77; American Paintings at the Detroit Inst Arts, Antiques Mag, 78; Rebellion, Defiance, and Beauty, Two Centuries of American Painting at the Detroit Inst Arts, Apollo Mag, 1986. *Mem:* Decorative Art Chap, Soc Archit Hist; Founders Soc; Detroit Inst of Arts; Wayne State Univ Alum Assoc; Am Asn Univ Women. *Res:* Late Nineteenth and early twentieth century American painting, sculpture, and dec arts. *Interests:* Painting. *Publ:* auth introd to, American Paintings in the Detroit Institute of Arts: Works by Artists Born Before 1816, (1st of 3 vol on the collections), 91; auth & contribr, From the Hudson River School to Impressionism: American Paintings from the Manoogian Collection (exhib, catalog), 96; auth, Introduction to American Paintings in the Detroit Institute of Arts, Works by Artists Born between 1817 & 1847, 97; Marriages, divorces and reconciliations: challenges in framing a museum collection, in The Gilded Age: The Art of the Frame, 2000; contribr, Calm in the Shadow of the Palmetto & Magnolia, 2003; American Paintings in the Detroit Institute of Arts, Works by Artists Born After 1847, 2005; Spot: Works on Paper from the Gallery's Collection, Charleston Renaissance Gallery, Charleston, SC, 2008; catalogue contribr, The Quest for Unity, Am Art Between World's Fairs 1876-1893 (exhib catalog), 83. *Mailing Add:* 9319 SE 137th St Rd Summerfield FL 34491

SHAW, PAUL JEFFERSON
CALLIGRAPHER, DESIGNER, HISTORIAN
b Ann Arbor, Mich, Sept 28, 1954. *Study:* Reed Coll, BA, 76; Columbia Univ, MA, 78, MPh, 80. *Comn:* Corp typeface, Origins, 91-92. *Exhib:* Brooklyn Art Mus, 83; Lettering Arts in the Zapftradition, Strathmore Hall, Bethesda, Md, 93; Alphabetics, Pratt Inst, Brooklyn, NY, 93; Calligrafia, Venice, Italy, 94; Paper, Art & the Book, Ctr Book Arts, NY, 96; solo exhibs, Asolo, Italy, 97 & St Paul, Minn, 98; group show, NY, 99; Blackletter: Type and National Identity, 98. *Collection Arranged:* Calligraphy in the Graphic Arts, 81-89; Werner Schneider: Schriftkunst, 99; Words & Images, 83-87; George Salter, Calligrapher 80-82. *Pos:* Corresp, Calligraphy Rev, formerly; contribr, PRINT, NY, Baseline, Lett Arts Rev, Eye Mag; editor in chief, Codex, 2012-. *Teaching:* Prof calligraphy, Sch Visual Arts, 79-85 & prof hist of graphic design, 2000-2014, Long Island Univ, 81-89 & Parsons Sch Design, 85-2014, NYC Col of Tech, 2001, calligraphy, Univ Arts, 2006; prof lettering design, NY Inst Technol, 81-97; Fordham Univ, 2009, 2011. *Awards:* Fel, Biblio Soc Am, 2002; Am Acad in Rome, Italy, 2002. *Bibliog:* WA Dwiggins: Jack of All Trades, Master of One, Linotype Matrix Vol 4, 2006; Bartolomeo Sanvito, Parts I & II, Letter Arts Rev, 2003 & 2004; Looking for Letters in NY: A Tale of Surprise and Dismay, Letters From NY 2, 2006; The Long & Complicated Saga of WA Dwiggins' Design of the Lakeside Press Edition of Tales by Edgar Allan Poe, Part I Bibliologia 2, 2007, Part II, Biliologia 4, 2009; The Philadelphia Story, Letterspace, 2006; Lord & Taylor: Times of the Sign, Print LXII:II, 2008; Poggio's Epitaph, Alphabet: Journal of the Friends of Calligraphy vol 33, 2008; The (Mostly) True Story of Helvetica & the NYC Subway, AIGA Voice, 2008; Andrea Bregno: Il Senso della Forma nella Cultura Artistica del Rinascimento, Rom: Artout - Maschietto Editor, 2008; Helvetica & the New York City Subway System, Blue Pencil, 2010; Philip Gushkin (auth), A Designers Archive, Glen Horowitz Books, 2013. *Mem:* Soc Scribes Ltd (bd gov, 78-85); Type Director's Club; Am Inst Graphic Artists; Asn Typografique Int; and others. *Media:* Ink, Gouache and Paper; Collage. *Res:* W A Dwiggins, Bartolomeo Sanvito, Andrea Bregno, George Salter; Philip Gushkin; Oswald Cooper. *Interests:* Cooking; baseball; hockey. *Publ:* WA Dwiggins, Design Issues, 84; Letterforms, pvt publ, 87; Font Piracy: another view, Print, 94; Touchstones, 96; Blackletter: Type & National Identity (monograph), 98; Blackletter Type & National Identity: The Catalogue, 2000; A Chronology of Letterforms 1850-2000, vols I & II, 2000 & 01; Helvetica and the New York City Subway System (2nd ed), 2011; Philip Gushkin: A Designer's Archive, 2013. *Mailing Add:* 785 W End Ave New York NY 10025

SHAW, REESEY
PAINTER, SCULPTOR
b Jacksonville, Fla, Jan 11, 1943. *Study:* Sch Fine & Appl Art, Boston Univ, 60-62; Md Inst Coll Art, BFA, 64, MFA, 66. *Work:* Kaufman & Broad Collections, Los Angeles, Calif; AT&T, Los Angeles, Calif; Arco Corp Collection, Los Angeles, Calif. *Exhib:* La Jolla Mus Contemp Art, Calif, 74, 78 & 86; solo exhibs, San Diego Mus Art, 75 & Los Angeles Inst Contemp Art, 80, Calif; Personal Myth, Queens Mus, NY, 78; Private Icons, Bronx Mus, NY, 79; Painted Sculpture, Munic Art Gallery, Los Angeles, Calif, 82; Sunshine & Shadow, Univ Southern Calif, Los Angeles, 85; Retrospective, Selected Works 1980-1990 (auth, catalog), Mesa Coll Art Gallery, San Diego. *Pos:* Cur, Felicita Found Arts, Calif, 87-89, artist dir, 89-91; dir galleries, Ctr for the Arts, Escondido, Calif, 91-93, vpres visual arts, 93-97; dir, Lux Art Inst, Rancho Santa Fe, Calif, 98-. *Teaching:* Asst prof art hist, Morgan State Univ, Baltimore, 66-69; lectr, Univ Calif, San Diego, 77-79; instr masters' classes, Claremont Col, Calif, 83. *Awards:* Art Guild Award, San Diego Mus Art, 75. *Bibliog:* John Russell (auth), When Art Imitates Anthropology, NY Times, 4/78; David Rubin (auth), Contemporary Tryptichs, Calif Technol-Pamona Col, 82; Ballatore (auth), The Psychological Tightrope, Images & Issues, 1/82. *Mem:* Am Asn Mus; Am Fed Arts; Calif Assembly Local Arts Agencies. *Media:* Encaustic Paint; Wood. *Publ:* Auth, Double Exposure, Images & Issues, 81; Inside: The Work of Saint Clair Cemin, Joel Otterson and Others, 96, coauth, Myths and Magical Fantasies, 96 & Tabletops Morandi's Still Lifes to Mapplethorpe's Flower Studies, 97, Calif Ctr Arts Mus, Escondido. *Mailing Add:* 7793 Senn Way La Jolla CA 92037

SHAW, RICHARD BLAKE
SCULPTOR
b Hollywood, Calif, Sept 12, 1941. *Study:* Orange Coast Col, 61-63; San Francisco Art Inst, BFA (Agnus Brandenstein Fel), 65; Alfred Univ, 65; Univ Calif, Davis, MA, 68. *Hon Degrees:* San Francisco Art Inst, Hon DFA. *Work:* Oakland Mus, Calif; Nat Mus Art, Tokyo; Stedelijk Mus, Amsterdam, Holland; De Young Mus, San Francisco; Di Rosa Preserve, Napa, Calif; Los Angeles Co Mus Art; San Francisco Mus Mod Art; Smithsonian Inst, Washington, DC; Whitney Mus Am Art, New York. *Exhib:* Solo Exhibs: Braunstein Quay Gallery, San Francisco, 69-2008; San Francisco Mus Art, 73; Franklin Adams Gallery, NY, 1990-1992; Perimeter Gallery, Chicago, Ill, 1995-99;

Robert Hudson and Richard Shaw, 1999-2000; A Survey, George Adams Gallery, NY, 98; Tempe Arts Ctr, Ariz, 98; Whitney Mus Am Art, NY, 70 & 81; Int Ceramics, 1972, Victoria & Albert Mus, London, 72; The Chosen Object: Europ & Am Still Life, Joslyn Art Mus, Omaha, Nebr, 77; Newport Harbor Art Mus, Calif, 81; San Jose Mus Art, Calif, 81; Boise Gallery Art, Idaho, 81; Palm Springs Desert Mus, 87. *Teaching:* Lectr, Col Marin, Kentfield, Calif, 77; lectr, Univ Calif Davis, 78; prof ceramics, Univ Calif, Berkeley, 87-. *Awards:* Nat Endowment Arts Grant, 70; Nat Endowment Arts Crafts Grant, 74; Fel, Am Crafts Coun, 98; Shigaraki Ceramic Park, Japan, 98; Marin Arts Coun Bd Award, San Rafael, Calif, 2002. *Bibliog:* Articles in Viking Press, 69 & Arts Can, summer 71; catalog, Ceramic Sculpture, 78 & 81-83; The Not-So-Still Life: A Century of California Painting and Sculpture, The San Jose Mus Art, 2003; 500 Figures in Clay: Ceramic Artists Celebrate the Human Form, A Lark Book Ceramic Book, 2004; Selections, The San Jose Mus Art Permanent Collection, San Jose Mus Art, 2004; Robin Hopper (auth), Making Marks: Discovering Ceramic Surfaces, Lark Books, 2005; Bai Ming (auth), World Famous Ceramic Artists Studios, Vol. 2, Hebei Fine Arts Publ House, Peoples Rep China, 2005; Kenneth Baker, (auth), Shaw in his Stride, San Francisco Chronicle, 2007. *Mem:* Order Golden Brush; Int Soc Ceramists. *Media:* Ceramics, Mixed Media. *Specialty:* Contemp. *Dealer:* Braunstein/Quay Gallery 430 Clementina St San Francisco CA 94121. *Mailing Add:* 231 Frustuck Fairfax CA 94930

SHAW-EAGLE, JOANNA
CRITIC
Pos: Art critic, Wash Times. *Publ:* Contribr articles to prof jour. *Mailing Add:* Wash Times 3600 New York Ave Washington DC 20002-1947

SHAY, ART
PHOTOGRAPHER
b 1922. *Work:* Mus Contemp Photography, Chicago. *Exhib:* Solo exhibs include Stephen Daiter Gallery 1999, 2007; Group exhibs include The Last Great Maxwell St Picture Show, Stephen Daiter Gallery, 2005 . *Dealer:* Stephen Daiter Gallery 311 W Superior St Chicago IL 60610

SHAY, ED
PAINTER
b Boston, Mass, Nov 12, 1947. *Study:* Murray State Univ, Ky, BFA, 69; Univ Ill, Champaign, MFA, 71. *Work:* Minn Mus Art, St Paul; Univ NDak, Grand Forks; Dulin Gallery Art, Knoxville, Tenn; Bradley Univ, Peoria, Ill; Calif Coll Arts & Crafts, San Francisco. *Comn:* Oil Planetarium, Ponderosa Collection, Dayton, Ohio, 74; wall graphic, Skate Away, Muncie, Ind, 77; billboard, Indianapolis Art League, Ind, 78. *Exhib:* 74th Chicago Artists & Vicinity Show, Chicago Art Inst, 73; World Print Competition, Calif Coll Arts & Crafts, San Francisco, 73; Works On Twinrocker Handmade Paper, Ind Mus Art, Indianapolis, 75; Crimes of Passion, Univ Ky, Lexington, 77; Rutgers Nat Drawing 77, Camden Coll Arts & Sci, NJ, 77; My Backyard: A Mid Career Retrospective of Paintings, Mt Vernon, Ill, 90 & State of Ill Art Gallery, Springfield, 91; Contemp Ill Watercolor Art Asn, 91; 8th Biennial Exhib, Tarble Arts Ctr, Charleston, Ill, 91; solo exhibs, Ctr Art Gallery, State of Ill, Chicago, 91, My Back Yard: A Mid-Career Retrospective of Painting, Ill Art Coun Traveling Exhib, 95; Cast in Carbondale, Evansville Mus Art, 93; Gallery Artists, Roy Boyd Gallery, Chicago, Ill, 94 & 95; Southern Ill Artists Open Competition, Mitchell Mus, Mt Vernon, Ill, 95; Twentieth Century Am Sculpture at the White House, Washington, DC, 96; Watercolor USA Honor Soc Biennial, Nat Invitational Exhib, Springfield Art Mus, Springfield, Mo, 97-98; Drawing/Watercolor: Illinois 12th Biennial Exhib, Tarble Art Ctr, E Ill Univ, Charleston, 98-99. *Collection Arranged:* Rollman-Shay, Not In NY Gallery, Cincinnati, Ohio, 74 & 76; Krannert Gallery, Univ Evansville, Ind, 74; Nancy Lurie Gallery, Chicago, Ill, 76; Roy Boyd Gallery, Chicago,. *Pos:* Vis artist, Studio Art Ctr Int, Florence Italy, 97, Burren Col Art, Ballyvaughn, Ireland, Ariz State Univ, Tempe, Ariz, 99. *Teaching:* Prof art & design, Southern Ill Univ, Carbondale, 86-. *Awards:* Purchase Awards, 55th Soc Am Graphic Artists Nat Print Exhib, New York, 77 & Drawings & Prints 77, Miami Univ, Oxford, Ohio, 77; Bronstein Purchase Award, Mid-States Exhib, Evansville Mus Art, Ind, 77; Special Asst Grant, Ill Art Coun, 88 & Exhib Grant, 91. *Bibliog:* Clinton Hillary Rodham & Tucker Marcia (auths), Twentieth Century American Sculpture at the White House, 96; Rob Erdle (auth), International Watercolor Biennial-East/West, Parkland Coll Art Gallery, Champaign, Ill, 97; Gisele Alterberry (auth), Watercolor exhibit at Parkland joins east and west, The News-Gazette, F-4, 3/23/97. *Media:* Oil, Watercolor. *Mailing Add:* 1601 E Walnut Carbondale IL 62901

SHEAD, S RAY
PAINTER, PRINTMAKER
b Cartersville, Ga, Nov 27, 1938. *Study:* Atlanta Art Inst, BFA, 60; Art Ctr Coll Design, BPA, 63; Ga State Univ, MVA; Inst Allende, Mex; also with John Rodgers & Loser Fiedelson, Los Angeles. *Work:* Columbus Mus, Ga; Montgomery Mus, Ala; Opelika Art League, Ala; Atlanta High Mus, Ga; Southwest Ga Art Mus, Albany. *Comn:* Painting, Chrysler Corp, Atlanta, 60; sculpture, Dibco-Wayne Corp, Atlanta, 68; painting, Callaway Gardens, Ga, 70; C & S Bank; First Nat Bank. *Exhib:* Dixie Ann, Montgomery, Ala, 60; 6th Ann Callaway Gardens Exhib, Ga, 69; 49th Shreveport Art Exhib, La, 70; Ga Artists Exhib I & II, Atlanta, 71-72; SC Artists, 74. *Pos:* Art dir, Compton Advert, New York, 63-67; art dir, Marschalk Co, Atlanta, 67; creative dir, Storer Studio, 67. *Teaching:* Assoc prof art & head dept, LaGrange Col, 68-74; head dept art, Presby Col, 74-76; chmn commercial art, Dekalb Col, 77-86; head com art, Dekalb Tech Inst, 86-. *Awards:* Second Dixie Ann Award, 60; Southern Contemp Award, 69; 6th Ann Columbus Exhib Award, 70. *Mem:* Coll Art Asn Am. *Media:* Acrylic, Epoxy; Etching. *Dealer:* Singlee Ltd, Atlanta, GA, 30507. *Mailing Add:* 5133 Strickland Rd Gainesville GA 30507

SHEARD, WENDY STEDMAN
HISTORIAN, EDUCATOR
b New Haven, Conn, July 24, 1935. *Study:* Vassar Col, BA, 57; Yale Univ, with Charles Seymour Jr, MA, 65, PhD, 71. *Exhib:* Antiquity in the Renaissance (auth, catalog), Smith Coll Mus Art, 78. *Teaching:* Asst prof art hist, Mt Holyoke Col, 78-79; vis asst prof, Univ Hartford, 79-80 & Boston Univ, 83-84; vis assoc prof, Boston Univ, spring 88; vis scholar in art, Wesleyan Univ, spring 90. *Mem:* Coll Art Asn; Asn Independent Art Historians. *Res:* Relationships between sculpture and painting in Renaissance Venice. *Publ:* Ed, Collaboration in Italian Renaissance Art, Yale Univ Press, 78; auth, Asa Adorna: The Prehistory of the Vendramin Tomb, Jahrbuch Berliner Mus, Vol 20, 78; auth, Giorgione and Tullio Lombardo in Giorgione, Convegno Int Studi, Castelfranco, Italy, 79

SHEARER, LINDA
MUSEUM DIRECTOR
b Long Island, NY, Feb 13, 1946. *Study:* Sarah Lawrence Col, Bronxville, NY, BA, 1968. *Pos:* Solomon R Guggenheim Mus, NY, 1969-80; exec dir, Artists Space, NY, 1980-85; cur, Dept Painting & Sculpture, Mus Mod Art, NY, 1985-89; dir, Williams Col Mus Art, 1989-2004; chmn bd, Am Fedn of Arts Exhib Comm, 1994-2000; comt mem, Mus Loan Network, 1998; dir, Contemp Arts Ctr, Cincinnati, 2004-06; interim dir, Contemp Arts Mus Houston, 2007-. *Teaching:* Instr, Sch Visual Arts, NY, 1973-79 & Williams Col Mass, 1991-. *Mem:* Asn Art Mus Dirs. *Mailing Add:* Contemp Arts Museum Houston 5216 Montrose Blvd Houston TX 77006

SHEARER, STEVEN
COLLAGE ARTIST, PAINTER
b New Westminster, Can, 1968. *Study:* Alliance Independent Colls Art, NY Summer Studio Prog, 1991; Emily Carr Coll Art & Design, BFA (studio art), 1992. *Exhib:* Solo exhibs include SL Simpson Gallery, Toronto, 1994, 1996, Am Fine Arts, Co, New York, 1999, 2002, Blum & Poe, Santa Monica, 2003, Galleria Franco Noero, Turin, 2003, 2006, Art 35, Basel, 2004, Contemp Art Gallery, Vancouver, 2004, Galerie Eva Presenhuber, Zurich, 2005, De Appel Ctr Contemp Art, Amsterdam, 2007; two-person exhib with Daniel Guzman, New Mus, New York, 2008; group exhibs include Three Artists, Contemp Art Gallery, Vancouver, 1994; Dark Memories, Marc Foxx Gallery, LA, 1995; New Vancouver Modern, Belkin Gallery, Univ Brit Columbia, Vancouver, 1998; Rock My World: Recent Art & the Momory of Rock'n Roll, Calif Coll Arts Wattis Inst, San Francisco, 2002; Baba to Vancouver, Seattle Art Mus, traveling, 2003; Go Johnny Go!, Kunsthalle Wien, Vienna, 2003; Pin up: Contemp Art & Collage, Tate Mod, London, 2004; Post no Bills, White Columns, New York, 2005; Mario Testino: At Home, Galerie Yvonne Lambert, New York, 2007. *Dealer:* Galeria Eva Presenhuber Limmatstrasse 270 PO Box 1517 CH-8031 Zurich Switzerland. *Mailing Add:* Stuart Shave Mod Art 10 Vyner St London United Kingdom E2 9DG

SHECHET, ARLENE J
ARTIST
Study: NYU, BA; BA, Skidmore Col; RI Sch Design, MFA. *Exhib:* Solo exhibs, Bernard Toale Gallery, Boston, 97, John Berggruen Gallery, San Francisco, 97, Mirror Mirror, Elizabeth Harris Gallery, 99, Galerie Rene Blouin, Montreal, 2000, Flowers Found, Elizabeth Harris Gallery, 2002, Harbor Cult Ctr, 2003, Out of the Blue, Shoshana Wayne Gallery, 2004, exhibited in group shows at Water, Water, Rotunda Gallery, 2003, Vessels, Greenwich House Poetry, 2003, Mystic, Mass Coll Art, 2003, Aldrich Contemp Art Mus, 2004, pub collections, Brooklyn Mus Art, Fidelity Investments, Boston, NY Pub Libr, Drawings & Prints Collection, Banff Sch Fine Arts, Can. *Pos:* Artist-in-residence Pilchuck Glass Sch. *Awards:* Fel Guggenheim Mem Found, 2004; grantee NY Found for Arts, Artist Fel, 99; Art award, Am Acad Arts and Letts, 2011. *Mailing Add:* 52 White St New York NY 10013

SHECHTER, BEN-ZION
PAINTER, ILLUSTRATOR
b Tel Aviv, Israel, Aug 7, 1940; US & Israel citizen. *Study:* Bezalel Sch Art, Jerusalem, BFA, 66; Sch Visual Arts, New York, 67-69. *Work:* Whitney Mus Am Art & New York Pub Libr, NY; Mus Fine Art, Boston; Brooklyn Mus; Houghton Libr, Harvard Univ, Cambridge, Mass; Univ Iowa Mus. *Exhib:* Interiors-Exteriors: Figurative Artist, Brooklyn Mus, 80; solo exhibs, Wustum Mus, Racine, Wis, 82, Capricorn Gallery Bethesda, Md, 89 & FDR Gallery, NY, 93; Ark Art Ctr, Little Rock, 86 & 92; Carnegie Inst, Pittsburgh, Pa, 88; Hunt Inst, Pittsburgh, Pa, 88; Buther Inst; Squibb Gallery, Princeton, NJ, 94; and others. *Awards:* Purchase Award, West Publ, 80. *Bibliog:* Lawrence Alloway (auth), Park Slope: The Urban Subject, Brooklyn Mus, 80; Susan Paul (auth), Interiors/Exteriors, Phoenix, Brooklyn, 80; N Scott Marraday (auth), Recent Press Book, Fine Print, 81. *Media:* Gouache; Pen & Ink, Watercolor, Silverpoint. *Publ:* Illusr, Common Ground, Bieler Press, 80. *Dealer:* Biddingtons 425 # 50th St New York 10022. *Mailing Add:* 429 4th St Brooklyn NY 11215

SHECHTER, LAURA J
PAINTER, DRAFTSMAN
b Brooklyn, NY, Aug 26, 1944. *Study:* Brooklyn Col, BA, 65. *Work:* Boston Mus Fine Arts, Mass; Brooklyn Mus, NY; Indianapolis Mus Art, Ind; Albright-Knox Art Gallery; Art Inst, Chicago, Ill. *Exhib:* Solo exhibs, Suffolk Mus, Stony Brook, NY, 71, Wuster Mus, Wis, 82, Greenville Co Mus Art, SC, 82, Univ Richmond, Va, 91, Rahur West Mus, Wis, 91 & Perlow Gallery, NY, 94, Pucker Gallery, Boston, 96 & 99; The New Am Still Life, Westmoreland Co Mus Art, Greenburg, Pa, 79; Am Drawing in Black & White, Brooklyn Mus, NY, 80 & 81; Still Life, Albright-Knox Art Gallery, Buffalo, NY, 81; West 81/Art & the Law, Minn Mus Art, St Paul, 81; Contemp Art-Gund Collection, Boston Mus, 82; Perspectives on Contemp Realism, Pa Acad Fine Art, 82 & Art Inst Chicago, 83; Am Realism, San Francisco Mus, 85; Metal Point etc, Ark Art Ctr, 92; Loring Gallery, Sheffield, Mass, 02. *Teaching:* Instr, Parson Col, 84 & Nat Acad Fine Art Sch, New York, 85-88, 94-98, 02. *Bibliog:* Ralph Poweroy

(auth), Laura Shechter, Arts Mag, 81; Eric Widing (auth), Laura Shechter, Am Artist, 83; Romen Cohen (auth), Laura Shechter (mus catalog, Wis & Va), 91. *Mem:* Nat Acad Art, NY; Nat Acad (acad, 95-). *Media:* Oil, Watercolor; Pencil, Silverpoint. *Dealer:* Michael Ingber Gallery 568 Broadway NY. *Mailing Add:* 429 4th St Brooklyn NY 11215

SHEDOSKY, SUZANNE
PAINTER, SCULPTOR
b Joliet, Ill, Sept 11, 1955. *Study:* Brookwood Gallery/Merfeld Atelier with Gerald Merfeld, 76-92. *Work:* Ore Ill Pub Libr; Loveland Comm House, Dixon, Ill. *Exhib:* Allied Artists Am, NY, 84, 87, 88, 91 & 92; Am Artists Prof League, NY, 86; Midwest Pastel Soc, Chicago, Ill, 86 & 87; Catharine Lorillard Wolfe Art Club, NY, 86; Nat Small Oil Painting Exhib, Wichita Art Asn, 88; Oil Painters Am Nat, Chicago, Ill, 93, Regional Exhib, 93 & 94; My Favorite Place, Pueblo, Colo, 93; Happy Canyon Western Art Invitational, Pendleton, Ore, 97; Ann Art Sangres Invitational Exhib & Sale, Westcliffe, Colo, 97 & 98. *Pos:* Studio asst, Brookwood Gallery/Merfeld Atelier, 83-92. *Teaching:* Brookwood Gallery, 89-91; Sauk Valley Cmty Col. *Awards:* Ann & Richard Sauter Award for Pastel, Allied Artists Am, 84; Ella Shaw Mem Best of Show Award, Lucille Warner Award, Anne Roe Mem Award, Caryl Crawford Award, Mary DeFrancisco Award, Phidian Art Club, Dixon, Ill, 88, 91, 07, 08, & 09; Best of Show, Oil Painters Am, 92; Silver Medal Honor, Allied Artists Am, New York, 92. *Bibliog:* Betty Harvey (auth), Suzanne Shedosky, Western Horseman Mag, 6/96. *Media:* All Media. *Publ:* The Best of Oil Painting & Flora Inspirations, Rockport Publ

SHEEHAN, EVELYN
PAINTER
b Hymera, Ind, Dec 27, 1919. *Study:* Scripps Col, with Jean Ames; also study with Phil Dike & Rex Brandt. *Work:* Lytton Collection, Los Angeles; Calif Bank, San Francisco; Mus Art, Univ Ore, Eugene; Tacoma Bank, Wash. *Exhib:* Spokane Ann Art Exhib, Cheney-Cowles Mus Art, Wash, 69; Watercolor USA, Springfield Art Mus, Mo, 70; 32nd Ann Northwest Exhib, Seattle Art Mus, Wash, 71; Dimensional Construction Exhib, Portland Contemp Craft Gallery, 77; Exhib of Paintings, Governor's Ceremonial Chambers, Salem, 77; Solo exhib, Mus Art, Univ Ore, Eugene, 71. *Awards:* Lytton Purchase Award, Watercolor USA, 1967; Mo Award, 32nd Ann Nat Watercolor Soc, 1971; Cash Award, 62nd Ann Nat Watercolor Soc, 1982. *Mem:* Nat Soc Painters in Casein; Nat Watercolor Soc; Portland Art Asn. *Media:* Water Media, Collage

SHEEHY, COLLEEN J
MUSEUM DIRECTOR
b Minneapolis, Aug 25, 1953. *Study:* Univ Minn, Minneapolis, PhD, 1991. *Pos:* Vpres, Minn Folklife Soc, Minneapolis, 1979-90; dir touring exhib prog, Univ Art Mus, Minneapolis, 1985-93; curator & dir educ, Weisman Art Mus, Univ Minn, 1993-2008; bd dirs, Forecase Pub Artwords, 1995-2000; dir & chief exec officer, Plains Art Mus, Fargo, ND, 2008-. *Teaching:* Affiliate faculty, Univ Minn, 1998-2007 & Univ St Thomas, St Paul, Minn, 1998-2007. *Awards:* Dayton Hudson Found Grant, 1995; Nat Endowment Humanities Fel, 1995; Outstanding Staff Achievement Award, Univ Minn, 2000; Target Corp Grant, 2006. *Mem:* Am Asn Museums; Coll Art Asn; Am Studies Asn. *Mailing Add:* Plains Art Mus 704 First Ave N Fargo ND 58102

SHEIKH, FAZAL
PHOTOGRAPHER
b New York, NY, 1965. *Study:* Princeton Univ, BA, 87. *Work:* San Francisco Mus Mod Art, Calif; Sprengel Mus, Hanover, Ger; Art Inst Chicago; Int Ctr of Photog, NY; Philadelphia Mus Art, Pa; Metrop Mus Art, NY; Los Angeles Co Mus of Art; Mus of Fine Arts, Houston; and several others. *Exhib:* Syracuse Univ (auth, catalog), 93; Other Africans: Photographs by Max Belcher, Fazal Sheikh, and Vera Vidits Ward, Photog Resource Ctr, Boston, 94; Rhode Island Sch Design, Providence, 96; A Sense of Common Ground, Int Ctr Photog, NY, 96 & Nederlands Foto Institut, Rotterdam, The Neth, 97; Diggs Gallery, Winston-Salem State Univ, NC, 97; Houston Ctr Photog, Tex, 97; Sprengel Mus (auth, catalog), Hanover, Ger, 98; Fotomuseum, Winterthur, Switz, 99; solo exhib Art Inst of Chicago, 2000; Smithsonian Inst, 2000; Am Univ of Beirut, Lebanon, 2000; Northwestern Univ, Chicago, 2000; The Corcoran Gallery of Art, Washington (traveling), 01-04; and others. *Awards:* Fulbright Fel Arts, Kenya, 92; Photog Fel, Nat Endowment Arts, 94; Infinity Award, Int Ctr Photog, 95; Mother Jones Int Documentary Award, 95; Leica Medal of Excellence, 95; Mondriaan Found & Netherlands Fofo Inst Award, 99; Humanitarian Award, Lucie Found, 2009. *Bibliog:* The Nature of Photography, Johns Hopkins Univ Press, Nat Pub Radio-Fresh Air, 3/96; Witness in our Time: Social and Documentary Photography, Smithsonian Inst Press, 98; Face Forward: Young African American Men in a Critical Age, Chronicle Books, 98; Vince Aletti (auth), Out of the past, The Village Voice, 12/29/98; Beyond Cliched Interpretations of Exile, Suffering & Death, The NY Times, 1/1/99. *Publ:* Auth, Herkunft, Winterthur Mus, Switz, 96; The Garden of Eden, Asn Aurora Borealis, Holland, 97; Linguna France, Encontras de Fotografia, Portugal, 97; The Victor Weeps, Afghanistan, Scalo, Zurich, Berlin, New York, 98; Innovation/Imagination: 50 Years of Polaroid Photography, Abrams/The Friends of Photography, 99; Documents: Artifacts of Modern Knowledge, Duke Univ Press, 01; In Response to Place, The Nature Conservancy's Last Great Places, Chronicle Books, 01; and others. *Mailing Add:* c/o Pace MacGill 32 E 57th St New York NY 10022

SHEIRR, OLGA (KROLIK)
PAINTER
b New York, NY, June 7, 1931. *Study:* Art Students League, with Reginald Marsh, 1948-50; Brooklyn Col, with Rothko, Reinhardt & Still, BA, 1953; Post grad, New York Inst Fine Arts, studied with Alfred Salmony, 1954; Pratt Graphics Ctr, with Michael Ponce de Leon, 1965-70; Art Students League, with Michael Ponce de Leon, 1970-72. *Work:* Springfield Art Mus, Mo; Southeast Mo State Univ, Cape Girardeau, Mo; Greenville Co Mus, SC; Libr collection, Nat Mus Women Arts, Wash; Bank of Tokyo, NY; NY Artists Equity, Art Bank, NY; Libr collection, Mus City New York; St Vincent's Hospital, NY; Brooklyn Coll Libr, New York. *Comn:* Serigraph eds, Art Resources and Treasures, NY, 1979 & Summit Fine Arts, NY, 1979. *Exhib:* Solo shows, Noho Gallery, 1975-92, New Sch Social Res, NY, 1984, Barbizon Gallery, Greenwich, Conn, 1984, Farleigh Dickinson Univ, 1985 & 1991, Kendall Gallery, NY 1986, Passaic Co Community Col, Paterson, NJ, 1990, San Giorio Island, Venice, Italy, 1994, Gallery Juno, NY, 1996, 1998 & 2002, The Jewish Ctr of the Hamptons, NY, 1996, Paul Edward Gingras Gallery, Southampton, NY, 2001, Woodward Gallery, NY, 2008; group shows, Sharjah Art Mus, United Arab Emerates, 2000 & 2005; Open Studio, Wills Art Deco Bldg, Long Island City, NY, 2003-05, 2007, 2010; Art Students League, NY, 2006; Springs Improvement Soc, East Hampton, NY, 2001-2010; Ashawagh Hall, Springs, NY, 98-2010; Broome St Gallery, NY, 91-2010; Guild Hall, E Hampton, 89-2010; Silvermine Guild Art Ctr, Conn, 66, 76, 93, 2005; Pace Univ, New York, 96, 2002; Butler Inst Am Art, Youngstown, Ohio, 95; Patterson Mus, NJ, 93; Nat Acad Design, 90; Nat Arts Club, New York, 88; Riyadh, Saudi Arabia, 82. *Collection Arranged:* Noho Gallery Invitational Exhib, 76, Madness on Mercer, 86, NY; Twenty Three Artists at Ten Studios (auth, catalog), NY, 77; Six at the Arsenal (auth, catalog), NY, 78. *Pos:* Instr, art workshop, Fla Gulf Coast Art Ctr, Belleair, 1987; Education Alliance, NY, 1989; watercolor workshop, Barkly Art Ctr, Custer, SDak, 1990; lectr, Rutgers Univ, New Brunswick, NJ, 1990, Art Student's League, 1993, NY Artists Equity, 1995, Synagogue for the Arts, 1996. *Awards:* Patrons Purchase Award, Springfield Mus Art, 1997; Best work on Paper, Guild Hall, 2004; New York Artists Equity Ann Award, 91. *Bibliog:* Stephen DeLauro (auth), Am Artist Mag, 1984; Arts & Antigue, 2009; Art News, 2008; In the Mindd of Me, Pollock Kormer House, News Papers, 4/29/2010. *Mem:* Women in Arts; NY Soc Women Artists; NY Artists Equity; Southampton Artists Asn; Nat Arts Club. *Media:* Watercolor, Oil. *Interests:* art hist, gardening, travel. *Dealer:* John Woodward 124 Eldadge St New York NY 10002. *Mailing Add:* 360 First Ave Apt 11G New York NY 10010

SHELLER, G A
PAINTER, PHOTOGRAPHER
b Altoona, Pa, June 20, 1936. *Study:* Coll New Rochelle, BFA, 58; Pa State Univ, 59; Visual Studies Workshop, Yale Univ, with Robert Reed, 81-83. *Work:* Xerox Corp, Stamford, Conn; IBM Corp, Armonk, NY; Chase Manhattan Bank; Eastman Kodak co; PriceWaterhouse, Rochester, NY; Mem Art Gallery, Univ Rochester, NY; Strong Mem Hosp, Rochester, NY. *Comn:* Diptych acrylic painting, Annandale, Va, 78; gum bichromate painting, Tokyo, Japan, 89; gum bichromate painting, Austin, Tex, 89; gum bichromate painting, Atlanta, Ga, 92; gum bichromate paintings, Rochester, NY, 94, 95, 96, 2002-2003; images, Eastman Sch Music, Rochester, NY, 2012. *Exhib:* Solo exhibs, Arnot Art Mus, Elmira, NY, 83, Gum Bichromate Paintings, Nazareth Coll, Rochester, NY, 94-96, 2000, Renaissance Art Gallery, 2009 & others; Nat Exhib, Virginia Beach, Va, 88, 99; Under the Oaks Exhib, Ctr for Arts, Vero Beach, Fla, 90; Skaneateles Art Expo, Skaneateles, NY, 91; Ann Exhib, Mem Art Gallery, Rochester, NY, 93-2000 & 2002-2008; Hilton Head Art League Ann, 94 & 95; Fac Exhib, mem Art Gallery, Univ Rochester, 97-2005 & 2009, 2010, 2011, 2012, 2013; Insights Exhib, Bausch & Lomb Gallery, 2006; Saint John Fisher Coll, 2011, 2012, 2013; Bausch & Lomb Gallery, World Headquarters, 2012; plus others. *Pos:* Libr liaison, Pittsford Art Group, NY, 82-2003; artist-in-residence, Irondequoit Schs, Rochester, NY, 2000; bd dir, Rochester Art Club, Rochester, NY, 2004-2009; panel mem, NY State Council on the Arts, 2004; juror, Grants Prog, NY State, 2004; commentator, NY Artists Guild, 2007, 2009-2012; juror, Irondequos Art Club, 2013. *Teaching:* Instr adult drawing/painting, Studio Sch, Mem Art Gallery, 83-2006, 2009-2012; instr painting, Inniemore Sch Art, Mull, Scotland, 92, Burren Painting Ctr, Co Clare, Ireland, 92-94 & 97, Provence Workshop, France, 97, 2000, 2007 & 2009, Greek Island Workshop, 97, Santa Fe Workshop, 98 & 2005, Dingle, Ireland Workshops, 2000, 2003 & 2006, 2010, Tuscany, Italy Workshop, 2009, Ireland Workshop, 2010; guest lectr, Univ Rochester, NY, 99, Univ Galway, Ireland, 97, Memorial Art Gallery, Rochester, NY, 2000, Savannah, Ga, 2003, Bluffton, SC, 2005 & Hilton Head Island, SC, 2007, 2008, 2009, 2010; prof, Saint John Fisher Coll, 2009, 2010; guest lectr, Memorial Art Gallery, 2011; guest lect, St John Fisher Coll, 2012. *Awards:* Finalist, NY State Artisans Award, Southern Tier Arts Asn, 82; Merit, Ann Exhib, Mem Art Gallery, 93; Named one of 2000 Outstanding Artists of 20th Century, Internat Biograph Ctr, Cambridge, Eng; Merit Award, Sonnenberg, NY Nat exhib, 2004; 2nd place painting, NY State, 2005; Jurors Award, Rochester Art Club, 2007 & 2008; Hon Men, Digital Art Rochester Inst Tech, 2010; Jurors Award, Rochester Art Club, 2011. *Bibliog:* Nancy Wellard (auth), Art League Show charms, Island Packet, 3/6/92; M Stephen Doherty (auth), Adding pattern and texture with light-sensitive materials, Watercolor, 2/97; Stuart Lowe (auth) Mixing Media - g.a. Sheller, Gannett Press, 4/13/97; Passports and Paintbrushes, Rochester Mag, 10/2007. *Mem:* Rochester Art Club, NY (prog chairperson, 78-85, 2004-2005); Pittsford Art Club, NY (vpres, 70 & libr liaison, 82-2012); Atlanta Artists Ctr, Ga (mem of excellence); Hilton Head Art League, SC; Print Club Rochester NY; Rochester Contemporary Gallery, NY. *Media:* Gum Bichromate, Watercolor, Acrylic. *Interests:* Commentary and research on the relevance of today's art and art criticism. *Publ:* Watercolor Mag; Rochester Mag. *Dealer:* Pat Rini Rohrer Gallery Canandaigua NY; Kelly's Fine Art Alexandria VA; Memorial Art Gallery Rochester NY

SHELLEY, WARD
SCULPTOR, PAINTER
b Auburn, New York. *Study:* Eckerd Coll, BFA (Art and Communications) ; New York Univ, MFA. *Exhib:* Solo exhibs include Ctr Contemp Art, N Miami, 1991, PS 122 Gallery, New York, 1992, Diversworks, Houston, Tex, 1993, Flipside Gallery, Brooklyn, 1998, Socrates Sculpture Park, New York, 1998, Smack Mellon Gallery, Brooklyn, 2001, Islip Art Mus, New York, 2002, Pierogi Gallery, Brooklyn, 2001, 2004, 2006; Group exhibs include Offbeat, Eyewash, Brooklyn, 1998, Valentines, 1999; Picture This, Flipside Gallery, Brooklyn, 2000, Outsourcing, 2001; Re-Construction Biennial, Exit Art, New York, 2003; Re-Do China, Ethan Cohen Gallery, New York, 2004; Open House: Working in Brooklyn, Brooklyn Mus Art, 2004; Archive Installation, Dumbo Art Ctr, New York, 2006; Twice Drawn, Tang Mus,

Saratoga, NY, 2006; The Accidentally Real, Sara Tecchia Gallery, New York, 2007; The Happiness of Objects, Sculpture Ctr, New York, 2007; Cosmologies, James Cohen Gallery, New York, 2007. *Awards:* NY Found Arts, Sculpture Fel, New Media Fel; Rema Hort Mann Found; Am Acad in Rome Fel, 2005-06; Joan Mitchell Found Grant, 2007. *Dealer:* Pierogi Gallery 177 N 9th St Brooklyn NY 11211

SHELNUTT, GREG W.
SCULPTOR, EDUCATOR
Study: East Carolina Univ, BFA, 1980-85; Univ of Georgia, MFA, 1988. *Comn:* Building the Arts, Community Council for the Arts, Kinston, NC, 1990, Chancellor's Ceremonial Mace, Univ of Miss, 1996, Chancellor's Ceremonial Medallion, NC Sch of the Arts, 2001. *Exhib:* work exhibited in over 350 solo, invitational and group exhibitions, 1985-. *Collection Arranged:* Amnesty International, Washington, DC, Community Council for the Arts, Kinston, NC, Univ of Mississippi, Walker & Associates, Reston, Virginia, Orange Frazier Press, Wilmington, Ohio, LaGrange Mus of Art, Georgia, Visual Arts Centre, Australia and William King Regional Art Center, Vir. *Pos:* Foundry technician, Maxcast Foundry, Iowa City, 1986; gallery dir, Craven Arts Council & Gallery, New Bern, NC, 1988; serves as juror, consultant, 1993-; bd dir, Theatre Art Galleries, High Point, NC, 2008-2011. *Teaching:* vis asst prof, dept of art, Univ of Mississippi, 1988-89, asst prof 1989-95, assoc prof 1995-2000; Sculpture instructor, Belvoir Terrance, Lennox, Mass., 1989; asst prof, sculpture, Univ of Georgia, Studies abroad in Cortona, Italy, 1991; lecturer Level II, Victorian Coll of Arts, Melbourne, Australia, 1992-93; artist-teacher, independent contractor in MFA-V program, Vermont Col of the Union Inst and Univ, Raleigh, NC, 2000; visual arts faculty, sculpture, school of design & production, Univ North Carolina School of Arts, Winston-Salem, 2000-2011; dir, visual arts program, 2005-11; department chair, prof sculpture, Department of Art, Coll of Architecture, Arts & Humanities, Clemson Univ, South Carolina, 2011-. *Mem:* Coll Art Asn, International Sculpture Ctr, Nat Art Edn Assn, Phi Kappa Phi, Southern Col Art Asn, Tri State Sculptors Edn Asn, Inc (pres 2005-08). *Mailing Add:* 1007 Berkeley Dr Clemson SC 29631-2301

SHELTON, ROBERT LEE
DESIGNER, EDUCATOR
b Memphis, Tenn, Apr 8, 1939. *Study:* Memphis State Univ, BFA; Univ Ala, MA. *Work:* South Central Bell, Regional Off, Birmingham, Ala; First Nat Bank, Montgomery, Ala; Ambassadors Off, Fed Repub Ger. *Exhib:* Nat Small Painting Biennial, Purdue Univ, 66; Nat Black & White Prints, Kans State Univ, 66; Mid-South Ann, Memphis, Tenn, 69; Hunter Gallery Ann, Chattanooga, Tenn, 69; Graphics USA, Dubuque, Iowa, 70. *Teaching:* Asst prof drawing & design, Auburn Univ, Ala, 64-68; prof printmaking & design, Birmingham-Southern Col, Ala, 68-. *Awards:* First Prize, Macon Mus, 68; First Purchase Award, Columbus Mus Art, 69 & 72; First Purchase Award, Montgomery Mus Art, 70. *Bibliog:* Martin Hames (auth), Robert Shelton, 1975 Birmingham Festival of Arts Bull, 3/75. *Mem:* Birmingham Art Asn (bd mem, 74-75, pres, 81-); Tenn Valley Art Asn. *Media:* Crayon, Oil. *Publ:* Auth, Contemporary printmaking in the US, Birmingham Festival Bulletin, 73. *Dealer:* Courtyard Gallery 2800 Sixth Ave S Birmingham AL 35208. *Mailing Add:* Ten Fifth St Birmingham AL 35217

SHEMDIN, AZHAR H
PAINTER, ASSEMBLAGE ARTIST
b Can citizen. *Study:* Al-Hikma Univ Baghdad, BSc, 68; Am Univ Beirut, MA, 74; Univ Toronto, BEd, 77, Ont Coll Art & Design, 1978-1987, Art Specialist, 1992, Sheridan Coll, 1997. *Work:* Oakville Munic Bldg, Ont; Westwood Sanitarium, Toronto; Oakville Community Living. *Exhib:* Ann Juried Art Exhib, Mississauga City Hall, Ont, 87; Peace at Home - TV Wars, Oakville Munic Bldg, 91; Every War Brings Its Peace, Oakville Art Soc, Ont, 92; 32nd Toronto Outdoor Art Exhib, Toronto City Hall, 93; A Celebration of the Shemdin Women, Oakville Munic Bldg, 97; Solo Exhibs: State of Mind, Oakville Munic Bldg, Oakville, Ont, 2000; Farewell 2000, Fireside Lounge, Burlington, Ont, 2000; Meadowvale theatre, Mississauga, Ont, Can, 2001; Gallery at Indust Art Space, Oakeville, Ont, Can, 2001;Interior-exterior, Oakville, Munic Bldg, 2003; Unknown Outcomes, Burlington Art Centre, Fireside Lounge Gallery, 2004; Exhib at the Artist's Union Centre, Zakho Iraqi, Kurdistan, Iraq, 2005; Spring Exhib, Cannington House Gallery, Oakville, Ont, Can, 2006. *Pos:* Juror, Art in the Park, Burlington, Ont, Can, 2003. *Teaching:* Instr painting, Humber Col, Toronto, formerly; instr visual arts, Halton Bd Educ, Ont, 89-96; instr art hist, color theory & painting, Sheridan Inst Art & Design, Oakville, Ont, 97-2006. *Awards:* Art of Halton TV 23 Prize Winner Contemp & Abstract Art, 1/1997; Alice Peck Award, 2002. *Bibliog:* Dennis Smith (auth), World Art Tour, The Burlington Past, 10/24/99; Carol Baldwin (auth), Millennium Art Show, The Oakville Beaver, 12/10/99; Patricia Frazier (auth), Local Bronte Artist to Display Work at the Millennium Art Show, The Bronte Villager, vol 2, no 1, spring 2000; Kumkum Ramchandani (auth), Expressions in Colour, The Arabian Woman, Duba, United Arab Emirates, 1/2003; Elaine Hujer (auth), Unknown Outcomes, Hamilton Spectator, 7/3/2004; Catherine O'Hara (auth), Homeland Journey to Kurdistan, Inspired Artist, Oakville Beaver, 4/19/2006. *Mem:* Oakville Art Coun; Burlington Fine Arts Asn; Art Gallery Hamilton; Oakville Camera Club. *Media:* Acrylic Oil, Mixed Media. *Mailing Add:* 2316 Millward Ave Oakville ON L6L 1W4 Canada

SHEMESH, LORRAINE R
PAINTER, SCULPTOR
b Jersey City, NJ, 1949. *Study:* Boston Univ, BFA (magna cum laude), 71; Tyler Sch Art, Rome, 71-72; Tyler Sch Art, MFA (painting fel), 73. *Work:* Butler Inst Am Art, Youngstown, OH; Nat Acad Mus, New York; DeCordova Mus, Lincoln, Mass; Mus RI Sch Design, Providence; Mus City of New York; Boise Art Mus, Idaho; Novartis Corp, Basel, Switzerland; Morgan Stanley, New York; Nat Acad Mus, New York. *Exhib:* Solo exhibs, RI Sch Design, 76, Alpha Gallery, Boston, 78, Allan Stone Gallery, NY, 83, 85, 88, 91, 95, 2000 & 2004, 2009, Butler Inst Am Art, 2006; group exhibs, Am Realism: 20th Century Drawings, San Francisco Mus Mod Art, 85-86; Duke Univ, Mus Art, Durham, NC, 87; Akron Art Mus, Ohio, 87; Sotheby's, NY, 93, 2012; Musee de Carouge (Switz), 99; Tryon Ctr Visual Art, Charlotte, NC, 99; Frye Art Mus, Seattle, 2002; Nat Acad Design Mus 2002, 2006, 2007, 2009, 2012; Allan Stone Gallery, NY, 2004; Mus of the City, NY, 94, 95; Mus RI Sch Design 77, 81. *Teaching:* Asst prof fine arts, RI Sch Design, 73-80 & Amherst Coll, 80-81; vis artist, Marie Walsh Sharpe Art Found, 2002; vis lectr, Bloomsberg Univ Pa, 2006, Univ NH, 2007 & Nat Acad Sch, 2008; vis critic, Md Inst Coll Art, 2009. *Awards:* RI State Coun Arts Grant, 79; Yaddo Fel, 81; Distinguished Alumni Award, Sch Visual Arts, Boston Univ, 92; Painting finalist, Nat Endowment Arts/Regional Fels, 96. *Bibliog:* Art in America, 9/88, 12/95, 12/2000, 2/2007, 2009; NY Times, 8/95, 5/2000, 4/2004, 1/2007, 2/2007, 2/2009; Dr Louis Zona (auth), Breaking the Surface, Butler Inst Am Art, 2006; Patrick Kennedy (auth), Seeing the Extraordinary in the Ordinary, Espirit, Boston Univ Press, 2006; Olympia Stone (auth) The Collector (film), 1/2007; The New Yorker, 5/95, 5/2000, 8/2011. *Mem:* Nat Acad Design (acad, 2004-, coun). *Media:* Oil. *Collection:* Marie Josee Kravis. *Publ:* American Realism-20th C Drawings and Watercolors, Harry N Abrams, 86; auth, A Guide to Drawing-m Fourth Ed, Holt, Rinehart & Winston, 88; A Decade of American Figure Drawing, Frye Art Mus, 2002; Drawing Space Form & Expression, Prentice Hall, 2003, 2011; Breaking the Surface-Lorraine Shemesh at the Butler Institute of American Art, 2006; Intersections, Donald Kuspit Catalogue Essay, Allan Stone Gallery, 2009. *Dealer:* Gerald Peters Gallery 24 East 78th St New York NY 10075. *Mailing Add:* 22 W 30th St # 4-5 New York NY 10001

SHEON, AARON
HISTORIAN, ADMINISTRATOR
b Toledo, Ohio, Oct 7, 1937. *Study:* Univ Mich, AB, MA, 60; Inst d'Art et d'Archeolgie, Paris, 62; Princeton Univ, MFA, PhD, 66. *Teaching:* Assoc prof, Univ Pittsburgh, Pa, 66-78, prof, 78-2003, prof emeritus, 2003-; vis mem, Inst Advan Study, Princeton, 84-85. *Awards:* Bowman Fac Award, Univ Pittsburgh, 76; Hon Award, Pa Soc Architects, 82; Gould Found Fel, 86. *Mem:* Coll Art Asn; Soc Fr Art Hist. *Res:* French 19th and 20th century art history; art and scientific thought; educational role of the museum. *Publ:* Auth, Monticelli, His Contemporaries, His Influence, 79; Organic Vision: The Architecture of Peter Berndston, 80; Octave Tassaert's Le Suicide, Arts, 81; Courbet, French realism and discovery of unconscious, Arts, 81; 1913: Forgotten cubist exhibitions in America, Arts, 83; Monticelli Centennial Exhib, Marseille, 86; Paul Guigou, 87. *Mailing Add:* 1212 Ventana Dr Coraopolis PA 15108

SHEPARD, LEWIS ALBERT
DEALER, HISTORIAN
b East Orange, NJ, May 24, 1945. *Study:* Rutgers Univ, New Brunswick, BA, 67; Ind Univ, Bloomington, MA, 70. *Collection Arranged:* Cowboys, Indians, Trappers & Traders (with catalog), Mead Art Gallery, Amherst Coll, 73 & Am Painters of the Arctic (with catalog), 75. *Pos:* Trainee catalog & dept head, Sotheby Parke Bernet, New York, 70-72; cur, Mead Art Gallery, Amherst Coll, 72-77; proprietor, dealer & appraiser, pvt pract, Boston, Mass, 77-; coord appraisers study program, RI Sch Design, 2001-2006. *Teaching:* Asst instr mod art, Ind Univ, Bloomington, 69-70; instr Am art, Amherst Coll, 73-76, Clark Univ, 80 & 84, Worcester State Col, 95- & Bentley Coll, 2002-2004; instr, RI Sch Design (RISD), 2006-2007. *Mem:* Worcester Heritage Preserv Soc (bd dir, 79-84); Appraisers Registry 80-92; Appraisers Asn of Am (mem, 2004-); B Fletcher & Assoc, 2005-. *Res:* American 19th and 20th century painting; Western Americana; Arctic exploration; arts and crafts movement. *Specialty:* American and European 19th and 20th century art. *Collection:* American drawings 1830-1930; Native American Art; Contemporary Art. *Publ:* Auth, Willard Metcalf Exhibition-a Review, Am Art Rev, 77; American Art at Amherst Collage-a Summary Catalogue, Amherst Coll, 78; The Diary of Anne Frank, Pennyroyal Press, 85. *Mailing Add:* 2400 Beacon St Chestnut Hill MA 02467

SHEPARD, MARK
ARCHITECT, EDUCATOR
Study: Cornell Univ, BArch; Hunter Coll, CUNY, MFA (combined media); Columbia Univ, MS (advanced archit design). *Exhib:* Baltimore Contemp Mus, Md; Conflux, Brooklyn, 2006; ISEA, San Jose, Calif, 2006; SIGGRAPH, San Diego, 2007; Futuresonic, Manchester, Eng; Sonar Festival, Barcelona, Spain; Electronic Language Int Festival, Sao Paolo, Brazil, 2007; Arte.Mov Festival for Mobile Media, Belo Horizonte, Brazil. *Pos:* Vis researcher, NetLab, Studio-X, Grad Sch Archit, Planning & Preservation, Columbia Univ; co-ed, Situated Technologies Pamphlet Series, Archit League New York. *Teaching:* Asst prof dept archit & media study, Univ Buffalo, SUNY, coordr, Media, Archit & Computing degree program. *Awards:* Peabody Award in New Media, Univ Ga Grady Coll Journalism & Mass Commun; Fel in Humanities, Jacob K. Javits Found; William Graf Travel Grant; Independent Project award, NY State Coun Arts; Finishing Funds Award, Experimental TV Ctr. *Bibliog:* Lytle Shaw (auth), Mark Shepard: Unformation Theory and Berlin Urbanism, Tripwire, fall 1998; Regine Debatty (auth), Re-defining a Sense of Space, Art Rev, No 7, 1/2007; Usman Haque (auth), Distinguishing Concepts: Lexicons of Interactive Art and Architecture, Archit Design, 8/2007. *Publ:* Auth, Situating the Device: Arverne, NY and an Urbanism of Stillborn Renewal, spring 1998 & Working Title: Industrian Pilz, spring 1999, Shark J Poetics & Art Criticism; Tactical Sound Garden Toolkit, 30 60 90: Regarding Public Space, Vol 9, Princeton Archit Press, 2005; coauth (with Adam Greenfield), Urban Computing and its Discontents, Situated Technologies, No 1, fall 2007; auth, Extreme Informatics: Toward the De-saturated City, chap in: Handbook of Research on Urban Informatics: The Practice & Promise of the Real-Time City (ed, Marcus Foth), Info Sci Ref, IGI Global, 2008. *Mailing Add:* Univ Buffalo SUNY 231 Center for the Arts Buffalo NY 14260-6020

SHEPARD, STEVEN L
PAINTER
b Port Arthur, Tex, Mar 23, 1955. *Study:* Univ S Ala, BFA, 77. *Work:* Miss Mus Art, Jackson; Mobile Mus Art, Ala. *Comn:* J L Scott Marine Educ Ctr, Biloxi, Miss; George Ohr Mus, Biloxi, Miss. *Exhib:* Urgent Messages, Chicago Pub Libr, 87; Contemp Drawing Invitational, Wake Forest Univ, Winston-Salem, NC, 88; Exchange

D'Experiences Culturelles Entre Le Burkina Faso et Les Estats-Unis, Poboye Konate et Steve Shepard, Am Cult Ctr, Ouagadougou, Burkina Faso, W Africa, 88; The Original Art, Mus Soc Bk Illustrs, NY, 91; 1996 Southern Arts Fedn/Nat Endowment Arts Regional Visual Arts Fels Painting, Drawing & Works on Paper, Southeastern Ctr Contemp Art, Winston-Salem, NC, 97; Miss Mus of Art Invitational, 99; La State Univ Works on Paper Exhib, 2001; one-person exhib, Univ S Ala, 02; one-person exhib, Montgomery Mus of Art, 03. *Awards:* Nat Endowment Arts/Southern Arts Fedn Visual Arts Fel, 96-97; Miss Arts Commission Grant, 97; W T Neal Residency Grant, Blountstown, Fla, 97. *Bibliog:* C E Licka (auth), Steve Shepard: works on paper (catalog), Southeastern Mass, Univ, 90; Joe Adams (auth), The Mississippi imagists: Steve Shepard and David Thomas Roberts, Raw Vision, winter 94-95; Tom Patterson (auth), Several works stand out, Winston-Salem J, 97. *Mem:* Nat Asn Independent Artists. *Media:* Mixed Media. *Publ:* Auth & illustr, Elvis Hornbill: International Business Bird, Henry Holt, 91. *Dealer:* America Oh Yes Gallery PO Box 3078 Hilton Head Island SC 29928. *Mailing Add:* PO Box 1295 Gautier MS 39553

SHEPHERD, HELEN PARSONS
PAINTER
b St John's, Nfld, Jan 16, 1923. *Study:* Mem Univ Nfld, LLD, 41-42; Ontario Coll Art, hons grad, 48. *Work:* Mem Univ Gallery, St John's Nfld, Can; Beaverbrook Gallery, Fredericton, New Brunswick, Can; Gov General Shreyer's Portrait, Readeau Hall, Ottawa, Ont, Can; Reader's Digest Coll, Can; Coll Northern Telecom, Can Ltd. *Comn:* Portraits, mayors, St John's, 73; portrait, Lord Taylor of Harlow, Mem Univ, 73; portrait, Prince Philip, Government House, St John's, Royal Canadian Legion, 76. *Exhib:* Maritime Art exhib, Beaverbrook Gallery, 64; Expo 67, Montreal; Montreal Mus Fine Arts Exhib, 68; Solo exhib, Mem Univ, Nfld, 75, Erindale Col, Toronto, 75, The Gallery-Mauskoph, St John's, Nfld, 85; Mem Univ Gallery 25th Ann Exhib, St John's, 86; Helen Parsons Shepherd & Reginald Shepherd - Four Decades, Mem Univ Gallery, 89. *Pos:* Co-founder & teacher, Nfld Acad Art, 49-61. *Teaching:* Instr drawing & painting, Nfld Acad Art, 49-61. *Awards:* Royal Can Acad Arts; Mem Univ, Nfld, LLD. *Bibliog:* Rex Murphy (dir), Here & Now (film), Can Broadcasting Corp TV, 76; Neil Murray (auth), Profile, Nfld Herald, 79; Helen Parsons Shepherd & Reginald Shepherd, Four Decades, Peter Gard (art critic). *Mem:* Royal Can Acad Arts; St Michael's Print Shop. *Media:* Oil, Graphic Drawing. *Mailing Add:* 26 Oxen Pond Rd Saint John's NL A1B 3J3 Canada

SHEPHERD, WILLIAM FRITZ
PAINTER
b Casper, Wyo, April 1, 1943. *Study:* Univ Wyo, BA, MFA, 72. *Work:* Amoco Oil Co, Houston; Univ Wyo Art Mus, Laramie; IT&T, Basking Ridge, NJ; NMex Fine Arts Mus, Santa Fe; pvt collection of Mrs Joseph Hirshhorn, Washington, DC. *Exhib:* New Works New Mexico, Blaffer Gallery, Univ Houston, 81; Rosalind Constable Selects, Sweeney Ctr, Santa Fe, 81; Best of Decade, Hills Gallery, Santa Fe, 81; Solo exhib, Amarillo Art Ctr, Tex, 86; Boundless Realism, Rockwell Mus, Corning, NY, 87; The Face of the Land, Southern Alleghenies Mus Art, Loretto, Pa, 88; The Art Collection of Ambassador and Mrs Keith Campham Brown, Am Embassy Residence, Copenhagen, Denmark, 90-92; Events About a Rectangle, Cedar Rapids Mus Art, Iowa, 91; Events About a Rectangle, Eiteljorg Mus, Indianapolis, Ind, 91. *Awards:* Spec Jurors Prize, Washington & Jefferson Col, 74. *Bibliog:* Harold Olejarz (auth), article, Arts Mag, 1/79; William Peterson (auth), Smoke Rings, Shinto Shrines, Doktor Thrill and the Snake Lady, Art News, 12/80; Carol Everingham (auth), Bi-lateral--bi-literal rocks, spring 83, Town & Country, 7/84 & Art & Antiques, 4/86, Artspace. *Media:* Oil on Canvas. *Mailing Add:* 1519 Canyon Rd Santa Fe NM 87501-6135

SHEPP, ALAN
GRAPHIC ARTIST, DIGITAL PHOTOGRAPHER
b Cleveland, Ohio, Nov 11, 1935. *Study:* Bowling Green State Univ, BA, 57; Cleveland Inst Art, BFA, 58; Univ Wash, Seattle, MFA, 63. *Work:* Seattle Art Mus, Wash; Walker Art Ctr, Minneapolis, Minn; Univ Wis, Menomie; Cleveland Mus Art; Univ Notre Dame, Idaho. *Comn:* Marble relief, Mill Valley City Hall, Calif, 82; slate relief, Bank Am, San Francisco, 83; Pan Pac Singapore Hotel, Singapore, 86; IBM, Alameda, Calif, 86; Hewlett Packard, Mountain View, Calif, 86. *Exhib:* Seattle Art Mus, 63; one-man shows, Calif State Univ, Hayward, 74, AND/OR Gallery, Seattle, 75, 80 Langton St Gallery, San Francisco, 75, Univ Waterloo, Ontario, 77, Neill Gallery, NY, 78-79, Steven Wirtz Gallery, San Francisco, 82, 85, 90, 92 & 96 & Monterey Peninsula Mus Art, 91; Aesthetics of Graffiti, San Francisco Mus Mod Art, 78; Wax & Lead, Steven Wirtz Gallery, San Francisco, 90; Uncommon Objects, Richmond Art Ctr, Calif, 90; traveling show, West Art and the Law (with catalog), San Francisco, Raleigh & Tacoma, 92; Images in Bronze, China Basin Build Gallery, San Francisco; California Eclectic, TransAm Pyramid Lobby, San Francisco, 93; Galerie Sho, Tokyo, Japan, 94. *Teaching:* Instr, Goldsmiths Col, Univ London, 64-66; Minneapolis Col Art, 66-70; Univ Victoria, 70; Calif State Univ, Hayward, 71-. *Awards:* Fulbright Fel to Italy, 63-64; Nat Endowment Arts Fel, 79; Fulbright Travel Grant to Egypt, 91. *Bibliog:* Jane Ayers (auth), Times Tribune, Palo Alto, Calif, 3/20/88; Rick Deragon (auth), Stone Cool, The Herald, 12/6/91; Anita Decarlo (auth), Shepp's Stone Works are at MPMA, The Weekly Sun, 12/5/91. *Media:* Slate. *Publ:* Auth, 1968 Biennial of Painting and Sculpture, Walker Art Ctr, 68; RE-DACT, Willis, Locker & Owens, 84. *Mailing Add:* c/o Stephen Wirtz Gallery 49 Geary San Francisco CA 94108

SHEPPARD, JOSEPH SHERLY
PAINTER, SCULPTOR
b Owings Mills, Md, Dec 20, 1930. *Study:* Md Inst Coll Art, cert (fine art); also with Jacques Maroger. *Work:* Butler Inst Am Art; Fine Arts Mus, Mobile, Ala; Baltimore Mus Art, Md; Carnegie Inst; Westmoreland Art Mus, Greenburg, Pa; Midwest Mus of Am Art, Elkhart, IN; Natl Portrait Gallery, Washington, DC; Consiglio Regionale Delle Toscana, Florence, Italy; Brooks Robenson Sculpture, Baltimore City, Md. *Comn:* Murals, Police Dept Hq Bldg, Baltimore; bronze, Holocaust Mem, Baltimore; mural, Palmer House Hotel, Chicago, Ill; President Bush (portrait), comn by Presidential Libr, Coll Station, Tex, 98; Archbishop J Foley (portrait), comn by Vatican City, 98; and others. *Exhib:* Solo exhibs, Butler Inst Am Art, 64 & 72, Westmoreland Co Mus, 66, 72 & 82 & Davenport Munic Art Gallery, Iowa, 67 & 83; consecutive shows, Florence, Italy, 77-; Walters Art Gallery, Balt, 2002-03; Forbes Gallery, NY, 2003; and others. *Collection Arranged:* Leroy Merrit Art Ctr for the Works of Joseph Sheppard, Univ Md. *Pos:* Owner studio, Pietrasanta, Italy. *Teaching:* Instr painting & artist-in-residence, Dickinson Col, 56-57; instr drawing, painting & anat, Md Inst Col Art, 60-75. *Awards:* Prize for Figure Painting, 63 & Paul Puzinas Award, 84, Allied Artists; John J McDonough Prize, Butler Inst Am Art, 67; Gov Prize, Md Artists Exhib, Baltimore Mus, 71; Tallix Foundry Prize, 83, Agop Agopoff Mem Prize, 86, & C Percival Dietch Prize, 94, Nat Sculpture Soc; Award of Merit, Soc Animal Artists, 83. *Bibliog:* The Work of Joseph Sheppard, Arti Grafiche Giorgi & Gambi, Italy, 82; Joseph Sheppard-Sculpture, Arti Grafiche Giorgi & Gambi, Italy, 93; Joseph Sheppard-Portraits, Arti Grafiche Giorgi & Gambi, Italy, 96; Joseph Sheppard-50 Years of Art, Arti Garfiche Giorgi & Gambi, Italy, 2000; Uomo Di Penna (Beast of Burden), Polistampe, Italy, 2005; Legacy (The Tradition Lives On), Grafichegelli, Italy, 2005; Sheppard on a Grand Scale, Art Ctr for the Work of Joseph Sheppard, 2014. *Mem:* Allied Artists Am; Nat Sculpture Soc; Soc Animal Artists; Knickerbocker Artists. *Media:* Oil; Bronze, Marble. *Publ:* Auth, Anatomy, 75, Drawing the Female Figure, 75, Drawing the Male Figure, 76, Learning From the Masters, 79 & Drawing the Living Figure, 84, Watson-Guptill; auth, Keeping Christmas, Stemmer House, 81. *Dealer:* Marin-Price Gallery 7022 Wisconsin Ave Chevy Chase MD. *Mailing Add:* 3908 N Charles St Baltimore MD 21218

SHER, ELIZABETH
VIDEO ARTIST, PRINTMAKER
b Washington, DC, Feb 13, 1943. *Study:* Smith Col, Mass, 60-62; Univ Calif, Berkeley, BA, 64, MA, 67; San Francisco Art Inst, 65-66. *Work:* US Info Agency, Washington, DC; Oakland Mus; Calif Palace Legion Hon; Sierra Mus Art; Carnegie Mellon Univ. *Exhib:* Fifty-seven Calif Printmakers, Calif Palace Legion Hon; Edinburgh Int Film Fest, 82; First Int Video Fest, Montbeliard, France, 82; San Francisco Int Film Fest, 82 & 83; Athens Int Film & Video Fest, Mich, 83; AFI Women in Film III, John F Kennedy Ctr, Washington, DC, 83; Ann Arbor Film Fest, Mich, 83; Milan Fest Am Independent Cinema, 83; Video on the Rock, La Rochelle, France, 84; Calif Collection, Fortuny Mus, Venice, Italy, 84; New Music USA, Musee d'Art Moderne de la Ville de Paris, 85. *Collection Arranged:* Guest cur, Mixed Media on Paper, Berkeley Art Ctr, 78. *Pos:* Dir, IV Studios, Berkeley, Calif, 82-. *Teaching:* Assoc prof, Calif Col Arts & Crafts, 77-. *Awards:* Purchase Award, Seventh Nevada Ann, 80; Union of Independent Art Coll Fac Grant, 82 & 83; Most Humorous Video, Hollywood Erotic Film & Video Fest, 84; Western Regional Media Arts Fel, 84. *Bibliog:* Articles, San Diego Mag, 81 & Artweek Mag, 82; Video, Ego Mag, 82; Showing a head for video, Chicago Tribune, 4/85; review, St Louis Post-Dispatch, 9/12/85; Totally tubular artists, Calif Living Mag, 9/15/85. *Mem:* Film Arts Found; Calif Soc Printmakers; Bay Area Video Coalition; Women's Caucus Art; Canyon Cinemateque Film Soc. *Media:* Mixed Media. *Publ:* Illusr, A Child's Library of Dreams, Celestial Arts, 78. *Mailing Add:* 985 Regal Rd Berkeley CA 94708

SHERBELL, RHODA
SCULPTOR, PAINTER
b Brooklyn, NY. *Study:* Art Students League, with William Zorach & Reginald Marsh, 50-53; Brooklyn Mus Art Sch, with Hugo Robies 59-61; study in Italy, France, Eng & Switz, with Meroiv Honig, 56. *Work:* William Benton Mus Art, Conn; Colby Coll Art Mus, Waterville, Maine; NY Pub Libr, Queens Mus & Brooklyn Mus, NY; Nat Arts Collection, Smithsonian Inst; Nat Portrait Gallery; Mus Mod Art, NY; Jewish Mus, NY; Nat Acad Mus; Hofstra Mus, NY; Heckscher Mus Art, Huntington, NY; Smithsonian Am Art Mus, Washington, D.C.; Nat Acad Design, NY; Jewish Mus Art, NY; Smithsonian Am Art Mus; William Benton Mus Art, Ohio; Butler Inst Am Art, Youngstown, Ohio; Brook Green Gardens, SC; Stanford Mus Art, Conn; Nat Acad of Design Mus, NY; Morris Mus, NJ; Baseball Hall of Fame, Cooperstown, NY; and others, 30 total. *Comn:* Marguerite & William Zorach Bronze, Nat Arts Collection, Smithsonian Inst, Washington, DC, 64; bronzes of Aaron Copland, Eleanore Roosevelt, & Yogi Berra, Montclair Art Mus; Casey Stengel, Country Art Gallery Long Island, Baseball Hall of Fame, Cooperstown, NY; Yogi Berra, comn by Percy Uris; Colonal Man (bronze), Hofstra Univ; The Am Baseball Family Group, Portland, ME, 2006; 5 foot portrait (head) of Professor Mohammad Yunus; outdoor monument, Sea Dogs Baseball Club, 8'5 figure, Portland, Me. *Exhib:* Pa Acad Fine Arts, 60; Brooklyn Mus Art Award Winners Exhib, 65; Nat Acad Design, 67, 72, 80, 82 & 98, 2002-2012; Jewish Mus, NY; Nat Arts Club, Allied Artists Am, William Benton Mus; Butler Mus Am Art, Youngstown, Ohio, 2013; Pastel Exhib, Chinese Art Asn, 2013; Solo exhibs, Brooklyn Mus, NY Cult Ctr & Bronx Mus Art, NY, Nat Asn Women Artists Inc, Women Artist of the Year, 2013. *Pos:* Pres bd, Friends Emily Lowe Gallery; dir sculpture, Allied Artists; dir pub rels, Audubon Artists, currently; bd mem, Portrait Soc Am; trustee, Nat Art Mus of Sport, Indiana; 1st vp, Bd Nassau County Mus Fine Art, NY. *Teaching:* Instr, Mus Mod Art, Art Students League, Nat Acad Design; prof art, Hofstra Univ, NY; private teaching. *Awards:* Am Acad Arts & Lett Awards; Louis Comfort, Tiffany Found Award; Ford Found Award; Gold Medals, Audubon Artists Am, Allied Artists & Nat Asn Woman; Allied Artists Am; guest at Dept of State Embassy Prog, Prague, Czech Rep, 2003-04; Nat Acad Design NY; PA Acad Fine Arts; Nat Sculpture Soc NY; 1st Prize Bronze Sculpture, Nat Arts Club NY, 2009, 1st Prize Bronze Portrait, 2012; Salmagundi Club, NY. *Bibliog:* Articles, Mus Mag, 4/82 & McCall's Mag, 8/82; Woman in Bronze (film), PBS TV; and many others. *Mem:* Allied Artists Am; Audubon Artists; life mem Art Students League; Am Inst Arts & Letters; assoc mem Am Watercolor Soc; Nat Acad (assoc, 79, acad, 82-); Nat Sculpture Soc (fellow); Portrait Soc Am. *Media:* Bronze, Pastel. *Collection:* Contemporary American realistic work, including M & R Soyer, W Zorach, Marguerite Zorach, Mervin Honig, Harry Sternberg, John Koch, Agostine, H Jackson, Margit Beck, Will Barnet, and others. *Mailing Add:* 64 Jane Ct Westbury NY 11590

SHERIDAN, SONIA LANDY
MEDIA ARTIST
b Newark, Ohio, Apr 10, 1925. *Study:* Hunter Col, AB, 45; Columbia Univ, 46-48; Taiwan She Da Univ, 58; Yoshida Studio, Tokyo, 60; Calif Coll Arts & Crafts, MFA, 60. *Work:* Art Inst Chicago; Fundacion Artey Technol, Madrid; San Francisco Mus Art; George Eastman House, Rochester, NY; Nat Gallery, Ottawa, Can; Tokyo Metrop Mus Photog; Hood Mus of Art, Dartmouth Daniel Langlois Foundation, Montreal, Canada; and others. *Comn:* pvt collections include Dr Douglas Dybvig, Minn, Dr Diane Kirkpatrick, Mich, and more. *Exhib:* Software, Jewish Mus, NYC, 1970; Two-person show, Projects, Mus Mod Art, NY, 74; Women of Photog, San Francisco Mus Art, 75; retrospective, Univ Iowa Mus Art, 76; Electra Exhib, Mus Mod Art, Paris, 83; Reine Sofia Mus, Madrid, 86; Photog & Art, Los Angeles Co Mus, 87; Am Women Artists: 20th Century, Knoxville Mus Art & Queensboro Community Art Col, NY, 89-90; Infinite Illusion, Smithsonian, 90; Tokyo Metrop Mus, 91; Vasarely Mus, Budapest, 92; Trivial Machines, Osthaus Mus, Hagen, Ger, 92; Circulo des Belles Artes, 92; Emblems, Yale Univ Art Gallery, 95; Moholy-Nagy Tribute, Magyar, Foto Grafia Mus, Hungary, 95; What Happened to the Pioneers?, Galerie Arts Technol, Montreal, 95; Kapieren, Scryption, Tilburg, The Neth, 98; Vidego Gallery, Hungary, 2000; Mus fur Communication, Frankfurt Ger, 2001; 2 NY Biennale Buenos Aries, Argentina, 2002; Lessaedra Bulgaria, 2005; Intermediale, Berlin, Ger, 2013; Solo show, Intermediale, Berlin, Ger, 2012, House of Danish Graphic Artists, 2014. *Pos:* Co-ed, Leonardo, Int J Art, Sci, Tech, currently; hon dir, Mus fur Fotocopie, Mulheim an der Ruhr; hon dir, Leonardo. *Teaching:* Instr art educ & design, Calif Col Arts & Crafts, 60-61; founder, prof & area head generative systems, Sch Art Inst Chicago, 61-80, prof emer, 80-; artist-in-residence, 3M Co, St Paul, 70 & 76, Xerox Corp, 81. *Awards:* NEA Workshop Grant, 74, Union Independent Cols Art Grant, 75; Pub Media Grant, 76 & Artist Grant, 81-82; Nat Asn Sch Art & Design Citation, 2006; Guggenheim Fel, 1974. *Bibliog:* Raymond Synard (ed), Color Theory and Imaging Systems, Soc Photog Scientists & Engrs, 73; Diane Kirkpatrick (auth), Chicago the City and Its Artists, Univ Mich, 78; Richard Wickstrom (auth), NMex State Univ, Art Science, 78; The Computer Revolution in Art, Univ Fla Press, 3/88; Gardner's Art Through the Ages (auth, 10th ed), De la Croix, Tansey, Kirkpatrick; Visual Resources, 2006; Generative Systems: Sonia Landy Sheridan (online publ, Kathryn Farley), 2007; Kathryn Farley (auth), Sonia Sheridan & Generative Systems, www.fondation-langlois.org, 1991; Michael R Peres, Focal Encyclopedia of Photography, 4th ed, 2007; The Art of Sonia Landy Sheridan, Dartmouth Hood Mus Art, 2009-2010. *Mem:* Founding mem Int Soc Interdisciplinary Study Symmetry, Budapest, Hungary; Coll Art Asn; ACLU; Dem for New Hampshire. *Media:* Electronic Imaging. *Publ:* Symmetry/Asymmetry: An Artist's View, Symmetry in a Kaleidoscope, Int Soc Interdisciplinary Study of Symmetry, Budapest, Hungary, 89; Guest ed & auth, New Foundations: Lessons in Art/Science/Technology, Leonardo: Int J Art, Sci, Tech, Vol 23, No 2/3 Pergammon Press, Berkeley, Calif, 90; Timescope: Patterns in Flow Symmetrically, Symmetry: Culture & Science, Budapest, Hungary, 92; auth, Generative Systems, Visual Resources, 2006; ed, Leonardo Vol 23, New Foundations, 90; auth, Artist in the Science Lab, 3M Publ, 76; book editor, writer, artist, Dawnings of the Electronic Era: Faces and Hands, 11/2013. *Mailing Add:* 80 Lyme Rd Apt 438 Hanover NH 03755-1225

SHERMAN, CINDY
PHOTOGRAPHER
b Glen Ridge, NJ, Jan 19, 1954. *Study:* State Univ NY, Buffalo, BA, 76. *Work:* Mus Mod Art, Metrop Mus Art, & Brooklyn Mus, NY; Tate Gallery, London; Walker Art Ctr, Minneapolis, Minn; San Francisco Mus Art, Calif; Corcoran Gallery Art, Washington; Stedelijk Mus, Amsterdam; Centre Pompidou, Paris; St Louis Art Mus; and many others. *Exhib:* Solo shows incl Contemp Arts Mus, Houston, 80, Stedlijk Mus, Amsterdam, 82, St Louis Art Mus, 83, Baltimore Mus Art, 84, Aldrich Mus Contemp Art, 86, Wadsworth Atheneum, 86, Whitney Mus Am Art, 87, Inst Contemp Art, Boston, 87, Dallas Mus Art, 87, Nat Art Gallery, NZ, 89, Whitechapel Gallery, London, 91, Milwaukee Art Mus, 91, Walker Art Ctr, 91, Linda Cathcart Gallery, Santa Monica, Calif., 92, Museo de Monterrey, Mex, 92, San Francisco Mus Mod Art, 95 & Kunstmus Lucerne, 95, Studio Guenzani, Milan, 2001, Centerfolds, 1981, Skarstedt Fine Art, NY, 2003, Mus Modern Art, NY, 2012; group shows incl Newport Harbor Art Mus & Israel Mus, Jerusalem, 91; Geementemus Arnhem, The Neth, Neth & Aarhus Kunstmus, Denmark, 93; Kunsthistorisches Mus, Vienna, Austria (with catalog), 93; Radical Images, 2nd Austrian Triennial on Photog 1996 (with catalog), Neue Galerie am Landesmus Joanneum, Graz, 96; Picasso: A Contemp Dialogue, Galerie Thaddeus Ropac, Salzburg/Paris, 96; Tableaux Vivants, Kunsthalle Wien, Vienna, 2002; Moving Pictures, Solomon R Guggenheim Mus, NY, 2002; 54th Int Art Exhib Biennale, Venice, 2011, 55th Int Art Exhib Biennale, 2013. *Awards:* MacArthur Found Fel, 95; NY State Gov's Arts Award, 2001; Nat Arts Award, 2002; Man Ray Award, Jewish Mus, 2009; Roswitha Haftmann Prize, Roswitha Haftmann Found, 2012. *Bibliog:* Cindy Sherman, BT Mag, 10/96; David D'Arcy (auth), Screen romance, Art & Auction, 10/96; Robert Hirsch (auth), Exploring Color Photography, third ed, State Univ NY, Buffalo, 97; Harry Abrams (auth), The Essential: Cindy Sherman, 99; Edsel Williams (auth), Early Work of Cindy Sherman, Glenn Horowitz Bookseller, 2001; Elisabeth Bronfen (auth), Cindy Sherman: Photographic Works 1975-1995, Schirmer/Mosel, 2002; and others. *Mem:* Nat Acad. *Publ:* Photog & auth, Fitcher's Bird, Rizzoli, New York, 92; coauth (with Andrea Dietrich), Cindy Sherman (exhib catalog), ACC Galerie Weimer, Ger, 94; coauth (with Peter Galassi), Cindy Sherman: The Complete Untitled Film Stills, Mus Mod Art, NY, 2003; and others. *Dealer:* Metro Pictures 519 W 24th St Manhatten NY 10011; Spruth Magers 7A Grafton St London Greater London W1S 4EJ; Gagosian Gallery 980 Madison Ave New York NY 10075. *Mailing Add:* c/o Metro Pictures 519 W 24th St New York NY 10011

SHERMAN, CLAIRE RICHTER
HISTORIAN, EDUCATOR
b Boston, Mass, Feb 11, 1930. *Study:* Radcliffe Coll, BA (Fulbright Scholar), 51; Univ Mich, with Marvin J Eisenberg, MA (Am Univ Women Fel), 58; Johns Hopkins Univ, with Adolf Katzenellenbogen, PhD, 64. *Collection Arranged:* Writing on Hands: Memory & Knowledge in Early Modern Europe (auth, catalog), The Trout Gallery, Dickinson Coll, 2000, The Folger Shakespeare Libr, 2000-01; Interpretation by Design: Contemp bookbindings by Stanley M Sherman, The Walters Art Mus, 2006. *Pos:* Sr fel, Ctr Advan Study Visual Arts, Nat Gallery Art, 81-82; consult, J Paul Getty Trust, 83; sr res assoc, Ctr Advan Study Visual Arts, Nat Gallery Art, 86-94. *Teaching:* Instr art hist, Univ Mich, 58-59; lectr art hist, Am Univ, 66-72; vis assoc prof of art, McIntire Dept of Art, Univ of Va, 76. *Awards:* Grant in Aid, Am Coun Learned Socs, 75 & 82; Grants, Am Philos Soc & Nat Endowment Humanities, 85. *Mem:* Coll Art Asn Am. *Res:* Illustrations of Aristotle's Ethics & Politics in fourteenth and fifteenth century manuscripts; women scholars in the arts; the inscribed hand in medieval & Renaissance culture. *Publ:* Auth, The Portraits of Charles V of France (1338-80), 69; The Queen in Charles V's Coronation Book, Viator, Medieval & Renaissance Studies, Vol 8, 77; Some visual definitions of the illustrations of Aristotle's Nifchomachean Ethics and Politics in the French translation of Nicole Oresme, Art Bull, Vol 59, 77; ed & contribr, Women as Interpreters of the Visual Arts, 1820-1979, 81; Imaging Aristotle: Verbal and Visual Representation in 14th Century France, 95; and many others. *Mailing Add:* 4516 Que Ln NW Washington DC 20007

SHERMAN, SARAI
PAINTER, SCULPTOR
b Philadelphia, Pa, 1922. *Study:* Tyler Sch Art, Temple Univ, BFA, BS (educ); Barnes Found; Univ Iowa, MFA. *Work:* Whitney Mus Am Art, Mus Mod Art, NY; Hirshhorn Collection, Smithsonian Inst, Washington, DC; Uffizi Gallery Print Collection, Florence, Italy; Collection Mod Art, Southwestern Methodist Univ, Dallas; Univ Nebr, Lincoln; Wichita Mus, Kans; Okla Art Ctr. *Comn:* 18th Century Chapel, 10 murals, ceramic altar wall, sculpture, Capella Guzzetti, Cortona, Italy, 88-93; Sculpture installation, State Off Complex, Waterbury, Vt, 96. *Exhib:* Recent Painting USA: The Figure, Traveling Show, Mus Mod Art, NY, 62-63; Venice Biennial, Int Graphics: USA, Italy, 72; Childe Hassam Acquisition Fund, 75; 30 Yrs--Painting, Sculpture, Drawing, Palazzo Acad, Tod, Italy, 83; Forum Gallery, NY, 86; Idiomi Della Scuttura Contemp, Verona, 89; Carnera Pieta, Il, Bisonte, Florence, Italy, 97; Premio Suzzara, Italy, 98; Premio Biella, 99. *Pos:* Juror for Artists' Awards, Fulbright Comn, 89-91. *Awards:* Award for Painting, Nat Inst Arts & Lett, 64; Europ Community Prize, Premio Marzotto, 67; Ann Painting Award, Repub San Marino, 75; Proctor Prize, Nat Acad Design, 76. *Bibliog:* Bryant (auth) & Venturoli (auth), Painting of Sarai Sherman (monogr), Galleria Penelope, Rome, 63; Sarai Sherman, Edizioni Enrico Vallecchi, Florence, 83; Geske (auth), American Painting Collection, Sheldon Mem Gallery, Univ Nebr, 83; Bellini, Busignani & Krulike (auths), Camera Picta, Univ Wash Press, Seattle, Valecchi, Florence, Italy, Capella Guzzetti, Cortona, 94. *Mem:* Nat Acad (acad, 99-). *Media:* All; Ceramic Sculpture. *Dealer:* Forum Gallery 745 Fifth Ave New York NY 10151; Appiani Arte via Appiano 1 Milan Italy

SHERMAN, Z CHARLOTTE
PAINTER, GALLERY DIRECTOR
b Los Angeles, Calif, 1924. *Study:* grad courses, Univ Calif, Los Angeles; Kann Art Inst; Otis Art Inst, scholar; Jepson Art Inst. *Work:* Munic Art Gallery, Los Angeles; Palm Springs Mus, Calif; Glass Container Corp Am; Winthrop Rockefeller Found, Ark; Laguna Art Mus; Vincent Price Gallery; Appraisers Asn Am. *Comn:* Glass Container Corp; F Fuller Collection; Mr & Mrs Winthrop Rockefeller. *Exhib:* Downey Mus, 67; Gallery Rene Barel, Paris, France, 72; Heritage Gallery, Los Angeles, 63-95, 97, 99-2001, 2003, 2005-2010; Habitant, Los Angeles, Calif, 2003; Metro Gallery, Bakersfield, Calif, 2006; plus others. *Collection Arranged:* Arthur Primas Collection; Robert Holmes Collection, Calif Pasadena Mus Art. *Pos:* Bd mem, Art Dealers Asn Calif, Mayor's Art Comn, Los Angeles; cur, Mus Special Exhibs. *Teaching:* Instr, cult arts dept, Munic Arts Dept, City of Los Angeles, Calif, 65-80. *Awards:* Phelan Found Award, 61; Pasadena Mus Ann Award, 61; All City Exhib Award, Barnsdale, Los Angeles, 63 & 65; and others. *Bibliog:* Joseph Mugnaini (auth), Oil Painting Techniques, Van Nostrand, 63; Bertrand Sorlot (auth), article, La Rev Mod, Paris, 74; Don Rothenberg (producer), Z Charlotte Sherman, Portrait of a Woman Artist (film), 77 & 79. *Mem:* Nat Watercolor Soc; signature mem Nat Watercolor Soc. *Media:* Oil, Watercolor, Acrylic, Prints, Sculpture. *Specialty:* American Art, Hispanic Art, African American Art. *Dealer:* Heritage Gallery 1300 Chautauqua Blvd. *Mailing Add:* 1300 Chautauqua Blvd Pacific Palisades CA 90272

SHERMAN-ZINN, ELLEN R
PAINTER, DESIGNER
b Newton, Mass, Mar 13, 1945. *Study:* Syracuse Univ, BFA, 66; Studies at Parsons Sch Design, 75; Montclair State Univ, MA (fine arts), 88; Studies at Int Ctr Photog, NY, Donald Stacy Studio, NY & Boston Univ, Mass. *Work:* Raritan Bay Med Ctr, Perth Amboy, NJ; Continental Airlines President's Club, Newark, NJ; Solomon A Berson Found, Long Island, NY; Raritan Bay Med Ctr, Perty Amboy, NJ; Syracuse Univ, NY; Lexus Corp, Bridgewater, NJ; Orloff, Lowenbach, Stifelman & Siegel, Roseland, NJ; Numerous pvt collections, NY, NJ & Pa. *Comn:* Mural, comn by Mr & Mrs J Weisglass, West Orange, NJ, 94; mural, comn by Dr Linda & Mr Michael Stone, Greenbrook, NJ, 96; mural (double wall), comn by Dr. Linda Stone offices, Livingston, NJ; mural, comn by Mr & Mrs Jay Weissglass, New York; mural comn by William E. Kinvig, British Columbia; mural comn by Mr & Mrs Bruce Goldstein, Warren, NJ; and many other pvt comns. *Exhib:* Solo exhibs, Post Logis, NY, Palmyra Gallery, Bound Brook, NJ, Everhart Gallery, Basking Ridge, NJ, Invitational, Libr Gallery, Maurice M Pine, Fairlawn, NJ, Straley Gallery, Livingston, NJ, Millburn Pub Libr, NJ, Montclair State Univ, Upper Montclair, NJ and many others; Group exhibs, Johnson & Johnson, Bridgewater, NJ, Continental Airlines Presidents Clube, Newark Liberty Int Airport, NJ, Focus on Art, NCJW, West Orange, NJ, Bridgewater Libr, Somerset Co, NJ, NJ Ctr Visual Arts, Summit, NJ, Frame of Mind Gallery, Miami, LA

Gallery & Frame, Greenbrook, NJ, Westbeth Gallery, Montclair State Univ, NJ, NJ State Mus, Trenton, Ridgewood Art Inst, NJ, Ben Shahn Gallery, William Patterson Coll, NJ, AJ Lederman Fine Art, Hoboken, NJ, David Gary Gallery, Millburn, NJ, Bloomfield Coll, NJ, Pargot Gallery, Edison, NJ, Lowe Art Ctr, Syracuse Univ, NY; CAA Midlantic Open Juried Show, Ridgewood Art Inst, NJ, 94; Nat Juried Show, Art Ctr Northern NJ, Passaic, 94; Corp Art Prog Invitational, Johnson & Johnson Hq, New Brunswick, NJ, 95; Invitational exhib, Nabisco Foods, E Hanover, NJ, 97; Union Co Coll Solo Invitational, Tamasulo Gallery, Cranford, NJ, 94; Warner Lambert Invitational, Morris Plains, NJ, 94; Andrews Art Mus, NC, 2009. *Pos:* Designers' group dir, New York City, 80-84; fashion dir, Nat Knitwear & Sportswear Asn, 80-84. *Awards:* Best Contemp Work, Kerygma Gallery, Ridgewood, NY, 94; outstanding graduate student, Montclair St Univ & Phi Kappa Phi, 1988; Liquitex Fine Art scholar, 1988; Most Accomplished Women, NJW Mag, 1993-94; grant, Vermont Studio Ctr, Johnson, Vt, 2008. *Bibliog:* Eileen Watkins (auth), Bergen exhibit confronts viewer with bold colors, Sunday Newark Star Ledger, 92; Sally Friedman (auth), Ellen Sherman-Zinn born to paint, NJ Women Mag, 93; Michelle Morris (auth), Woman leaves corporate world to fulfill dreams as an artist, Echoes Sentinel, 94. *Mem:* NJ Ctr Visual Arts; Watchung Art Ctr, NJ. *Media:* Acrylic, Oil. *Publ:* Auth, Viewpoint, Knitting Times Mag, 80-84; contribr, Spokesman for the knit industry, Am Fabric & Fashion Mag, 82. *Dealer:* Everhart Gallery 117 S Maple Ave Basking Ridge NJ 07920

SHERR, RONALD NORMAN
PAINTER
b Plainfield, NJ, July 17, 1952. *Study:* DuCret Sch Art, Plainfield, NJ; Nat Acad Design Sch Fine Art; also with Burton Silverman. *Work:* Phoenix Mus Art, Ariz; Nat Portrait Gallery, Washington, DC. *Exhib:* Ann Exhib, Nat Acad Design, NY, 78; Hassam Fund Exhib, Inst Arts & Letters, NY, 78; Painting & Sculpture Today, Indianapolis Art Mus, Ind, 78; Drawing Exhib, Univ NH, 79; A Heritage Renewed: Representational Drawing Today Traveling Exhib, 83. *Pos:* Instr painting seminar, Galeria San Juan, PR. *Teaching:* Instr painting, Nat Acad Sch Fine Art, & Art Students League, New York, currently. *Awards:* Benjamin Altman Figure Prize, Nat Acad Design, New York, 78; Award for Excellence, Int Ed Design Competition, 83; Allied Artists Am Gold Medal of Honor, New York, 86; Hubbard Art Award for Excellence, Ruidoso, NMex, 91. *Bibliog:* Smithsonian Mag, 7/88; Am Artist, 9/91; Southwest Art, 8/91. *Media:* Oil, Drawing. *Publ:* Illusr, Illusr 25, 29. *Mailing Add:* 400 Wireless Blvd Hauppauge NY 11788-3934

SHERRATT, HOLLY
ART APPRAISER
Study: Unic Calif, Los Angeles, BA; Univ Calif, Irvine, MA. *Pos:* Trainee, Laguna Art Mus, Laguna Beach, Calif; staff, Nat Mus Am Art, Smithsonian Inst, Washington, DC; cur staff, Huntington Beach Fine Arts Ctr, Calif; modern, contemp & Latin-American specialist, Bonhams & Butterfields, San Francisco, Calif, 2000-. *Mailing Add:* Bonhams & Butterfields 220 San Bruno Ave San Francisco CA 94103

SHERRILL, MILTON LOUIS
SCULPTOR, PAINTER
b New York, NY, May 30, 1949. *Study:* Cooper Union, NY, 72; State Univ NY, BA, 74; Pratt Inst, NY, MFA, 76. *Work:* Studio Mus in Harlem, New York; Schomburg Collection, New York; City New York; The Apollo Theater, New York; Hosp Joint Diseases Orthopedic Inst, New York; Columbia Law Sch, New York; Ford Motor co, Gary Found, Harris Bank, Chicago, Ill. *Comn:* Monument (steel sculpture), City of Mt Vernon, NY, 78; bronze abstraction, Selchow & Righter Co, NY, 83; lifesize bronze figures, City of NY, 83 & Apollo Theater, NY, 87; One Child Our Village Found, Los Angeles, Calif; Nat Bar Inst, Washington, DC; 12 ft bronze sculpture of Martin Luther King, Westchester Co, White Plains, NY. *Exhib:* Solo exhibs, SUNY Coll at Old Westbury, Pratt Inst, Brooklyn, NY, Studio Mus in Harlem, NY, Countee Cullen Libr, NY, Mt Vernon Coop Col, NY, Interfaith Ctr, NY, Mt Vernon Pub Libr, NY, White Plains Libr, NY; Emerging Artists, Neuberger Mus, Purchase, NY, 80; 35 Under 35, Lever House, NY, 80; Ideas in Bronze, Los Angeles Co Mus, Calif, 83; two-man exhib (with Robert P Dilworth), Isobel Neal Gallery, Chicago, Ill, 88; UFA Gallery, NY, NY, 99; Mount Vernon Fine Art Gallery, 2000; Federal Mem Hall, New York; National Sculpture Soc, New York. *Teaching:* Teacher sculpture, State Univ NY, Mt Vernon Co-Op Col, 70-72; dir, Artists in Schs Prog, Mt Vernon, 73-74; teacher, Studio Mus Co-Op Sch Prog, 74-75; teacher Westcher Art Coun, 2000. *Awards:* Westchester Arts Council CETA, Adolph & Ester Gittlieb Found; Arts Council Arts Alive Grants, 2000, 01 & 02. *Bibliog:* C Gerald Fraser (auth), Guide going out, New York Times, 83; Terrie S Rouse (auth), From painter to sculptor, Rev African Am Art, 84; Frank Oliveri Monument for Dr Martin Luther King Jr, J News. *Mem:* Artists' Equity Asn; Orgn Independent Artists; Nat Sculpture Soc. *Media:* Bronze, Steel; Oil, Acrylic. *Mailing Add:* PO Box 2421 Mount Vernon NY 10551

SHERROD, PHILIP LAWRENCE
ARTIST, POET, COMPOSER
b Pauls Valley, Okla, Oct 12, 1935. *Study:* Okla State Univ, BS, 57, BA (painting), 59; Art Students League, Am Fed Arts & Lett Scholar, NY, 63; Jacques Seligman Col, Postgrad, 68; Carrol Reese Mus, Postgrad, 68. *Work:* Herbert Johnson Gallery, Cornell Univ, Ithaca, NY; Smithsonian Inst, Hirshhorn Mus & Sculpture Garden, Washington, DC; Worcester Fine Arts Mus, Mass; Mus City NY; Newark Mus, NJ; and others. *Exhib:* Inside Out, Newport Harbor Art Mus, Newport Beach, Calif, 81; Solo exhib, Herbert Johnson Mus, Cornell Univ, Ithaca, NY, 85; Hirshhorn Mus & Sculpture Garden, Smithsonian Inst, Washington, DC, 89; Street Painters, Cork Gallery, Lincoln Ctr, NY, 97-98; Instructor's Exhib, Art Students League, NY, 98; Nat Acad Sch Fine Arts, NY, 98, 99; The Artist Interprets, NJ Ctr US Arts Summit, 98; Fed Mod Painters & Sculptors Exhib, Brooklyn Community Col, NY, 98; Art Students League, New York City, 99-2002; NJ Ctr Visual Arts, Summit, 2000-03; Fedn Modern Painters and Sculptors, Fordham Univ, New York City, 2000, 2002, 2003; Cork Gallery, New York City, 2000, 2002; Nat Acad Sch Design Mus, New York City, 2001; Limner Gallery, New York City, 2003. *Pos:* Pres & founder, Street Painters, NY. *Teaching:* Instr color & design, Okla State Univ, 59; asst painting, Art Students League, 60 & instr, 84-09; instr, Morristown Art Asn, NJ, 73-74 & NJ Ctr Visual Arts, 77-03; Nat Acad Sch Fine Arts, 94, 98-99; Baird Center (Master Class), S Orange, NJ, 2003-2009. *Awards:* Childe Hassam Purchase Award, Am Acad Arts & Letters 67, 69, 74; Adolph/Esther Gottlieb Found Grants, 81, 88, 96 & 2006; Nat Endowment Grant, 82; Prix de Rome Fel, Am Acad in Rome, 85-86; The Pollock-Krasner Found Grant, 89; Creative Public Serv Prog Grants, New York, NY. *Bibliog:* Barry Schwartz (auth), Arts in Society (Humanist Alternative), Univ Wis, 4/73; Barry Schwartz (auth) New Humanism: Art in a Time of Change, Praeger, 74. *Mem:* Nat Acad (assoc, 93, acad, 94-); Fel Am Acad in Rome, 1985-1986. *Media:* Oil, Etching. *Publ:* Auth, 30 Mentaltalia (poems & paintings), Merging Media Publ, 80; Black Truck (poems), Mirronic Pub, 81; Mr Wigley Cums (poems), Mirronic Pub, 83; Images Below the Belt (poems & paintings), Carrousel Pub, 84; Sex (I) Con (poem), Carrousel Pub, 85. *Dealer:* Allan Stone Gallery 113 E 90th St New York NY 10128. *Mailing Add:* 41 W 24th St New York NY 10010-3210

SHERWOOD, JAMES BLAIR
PATRON
b New Castle, Pa, Aug 8, 1933. *Study:* Yale Univ, BA, 1955. *Pos:* Mgr French ports, US Lines Inc, LeHavre, France, 1959-62, asst gen freight traffic mgr, New York, NY, 1962-63; gen mgr, CTI Inc, 1963-65; pres, Sea Containers Ltd, London, 1965-2006; chmn, Orient-Express Hotels Inc, 1987-2007; dir, Hotel Cipriani SPA, Venice, Italy; vpres, Transport Trust, London; bd dir, Peggy Guggenheim Mus, Venice, Italy, 1983-, Mus Modern Art, Oxford, Eng, 1987-; trustee, Solomon R Guggenheim Found, 1989-. *Mem:* Pilgrims, Hurlingham, Mark's, Annabel's, Harry's Bar (London). *Mailing Add:* Sea Containers Ltd 20 Upper Ground London United Kingdom

SHERWOOD, LEONA
PAINTER, INSTRUCTOR
b New York, NY. *Study:* Studied with John Chetcuti, New York, 46-48; workshop critiques with Philip Hicken, Mass, 58, Robert Gelinas, Fla, 65, Leon Berkowitz, New Col, 80, William Pachner, New Col, 81. *Work:* Hickory Mus Art, NC; Edison Col, Ft Myers, Fla; Collegiate Sch Boys, NY; Diamond Shamrock Co, Cleveland, Ohio; Barnett Bank, Sarasota, Fla; Town of Longboat Key, Fla. *Comn:* 42 paintings for Strathmore Co, Sarasota, Fla, 67-; painting, Lido Ambassador, Sarasota, 71; paintings, Thru Hang-up Gallery, Sarasota, Fla, 90; and others. *Exhib:* Metrop Art Mus, Miami, Fla, 77; one-person show, Hickory Mus Art, NC, 79 & Sarasota, Fla, 86; Boca Raton Art Mus, Fla, 83; Cornell Fine Arts, Rollins Col, 89; Polk Co Col, Winter Park, Fla, 90, Daytona, Fla, Racardi, Miami, Tampa; Sumner Mus, Washington, 92; Cork Gallery, NY, 94; and others. *Teaching:* Instr contemp painting & drawing, Longboat Ctr, for the Arts, Fla, 69- & Art League Manatee, Bradenton, Fla, 74-89; instr workshops, NC & Fla Art Ctrs, 79-, Chateau de La Napoule Art Found, France, 86, 87, 89, 91 & 93, Corfu, 89, O'Neill Art Ctr, Ireland, Madeira, Port, 90, Wilson Art Ctr, Wales, 91 & Malta, 92. *Awards:* First in Painting, Nat League Pen Women State Biennial, 71, 72, 76, 78, 79, 91, 93; Am Artist Award Watercolor, Fla Suncoast Ann, 90; Best of Show & Merit Award, Nat Biennial Nat League Am Penwomen, Washington, DC, 92; Best in Show, watercolor and acrylic, Longboat Key Art Ctr, 94, 95. *Bibliog:* Sheila Scotter (auth), An artist, cook & gardener, Australian Women's Weekly & Tatler, London, Eng, 79; Jane Roehr (auth) Art for the Artists Sake, Sarasota Times, 89; Penwoman, biennial issue, 92; Dora Walters (auth), Painting - A Colorful Life, The Longboat Observer, 01. *Mem:* Fla Artist Group; Nat League Am Pen Women; Fla Watercolor Soc; Artists Fel, NY; Women Contemp Artists; Nat Mus Women in the Arts. *Media:* Multimedia, Watercolor. *Publ:* Auth, Learn to really see, not just look, Islander, 81; The Best of Watercolor, 95; The Best of Watercolor - Painting Textures, 97, Creative Inspirations, 98, Rockport Publ Inc, The Best of Watercolor, 99, The Collected Best of Watercolor, 02. *Mailing Add:* 915 Oasis Ct Southlake TX 76092-6339

SHETTAR, RANJANI
SCULPTOR
b Bangalore, India, 1977. *Study:* Karnataka Chitrakala Parishath, Coll Fine Art, Bangalore, India, BFA (Sculpture), 1998, MFA (Sculpture), 2000. *Exhib:* Solo exhibs include Talwar Gallery, New York, 2004, 2006, Fine Arts Ctr, Univ Mass, 2005, Talwar Gallery, New Delhi, India, 2005, 2007, Inst Contemp Art, Boston, 2008; Group exhibs include How Latitudes Become Forms: Art in a Global Age, Walker Art Ctr, Minneapolis, 2003; Landscape Confection, Wexner Ctr Arts, Columbus, OH, 2005; (desi)re, Talwar Gallery, New York, 2005; Freeing the line, Marian Goodman Gallery, New York, 2006; Life on Mars: Carnegie Intl Exhib, Carnegie Mus Art, Pittsburgh, 2008. *Mailing Add:* Talwar Gallery 108 E 16th St New York NY 10003

SHIBATA, TOSHIO
PHOTOGRAPHER
b Tokyo, Japan, 1949. *Study:* Tokyo Nat Univ Fine Art & Music, Japan, BFA, 72, MFA, 74. *Work:* Mus Contemp Art, Art Inst Chicago; Metrop Mus Art, Mus Mod Art, NY; Los Angeles Co Mus Art; Mus Fine Arts, Houston; Nat Gallery Can, Ottawa. *Exhib:* New Acquisitions, New Work, New Directions, Los Angeles Co Mus, 92; New Photog 8, Mus Mod Art, NY, 92; Art Inst Chicago, 93; Inside Out: Japanese Contemp Photog, Light Factory, Charlotte, NC, 94; Santa Monica Col, Los Angeles, 94; Landmark Tower Gallery, Yokohama City, Japan, 94; Fabulous Photos, Worcester Art Mus, Mass, 95; Gallery RAM, Los Angeles, 95; Halsted Gallery, Detroit, 95; Yokohama Portside Gallery, Japan, 95; Cleveland Mus Art, 95; Photog and Beyond in Japan, Los Angeles Co Mus Art & Corcoran Gallery Art, Washington, DC, 96; Denver Mus Art, 96; Landscapes/People, Tepper Takayama Fine Arts, Boston, 97-98; People and Landscapes, Fitchburg Art Mus, Mass, 97-98; Beyond the Familiar, Mus Contemp Art, Chicago, 97-98. *Awards:* Ministry Nat Educ Dutch Cult Fel, Belg, 75 & 76; Ihei Kimura Prize, Asahi Newspaper Publ Co, 92. *Bibliog:* Jane Brettle (auth), Liquid crystal futures, transcript I, part I, 1/94; Catherine Grout (auth), Variations on process in Japanese photography, Art Press 209, 29-32, 1/96; Charles Hagen (auth), Review,

NY Times, 1/19/96. *Publ:* Auth, Photographs by Toshio Shibata, Asahi Shinbun Publ, Tokyo, 92; Terra: Photographs by Toshio Shibata (Essay by Yoshio Nakamura), Toshi Shuppan, 94; Landscape, Nazzaeli Press, Tucson, 96; View: Visions of Japan, Korinsha Press, Kyoto, 98. *Mailing Add:* c/o Tepper Takayama Fine Arts 20 Park Plaza Suite 600 Boston MA 02116

SHIE & ACORD, SUSAN & JAMES
CRAFTSMEN, PAINTERS
b Wooster, Ohio, Sept 28, 1950 (Shie); b Fairfield, Ill, Nov 26, 1953 (Acord). *Study:* Shie: Coll Wooster, Ohio, BA, 81; Sch Art, Kent State Univ, Ohio, MFA, 86 Acord: Self-taught. *Exhib:* Mus Arte Sao Paulo, Brazil, 89; solo exhibs, Wasmer Gallery, Ursuline Col, Cleveland, 94, MOBILIA Gallery, Cambridge, Mass, 95, River Oaks Sq Art Ctr, Alexandria, La, 95, Wayne Ctr Arts, Wooster, Ohio, 96, Art Gallery Univ Wis, La Crosse, Adams Art Gallery, Dunkirk, NY, 99, Fitton Ctr Creative Arts, Hamilton, Ohio, 2000 & Mt Vernon Nazarene Col, Mont, 2001; Renwick Gallery, Nat Gallery Art, Washington, DC, 95; Celebrations, Art Quilt Network, Mansfield Art Ctr, Ohio, 97; Stitchers & Beaders: America's Best, Ohio Craft Mus, Columbus, 97; Up in the Air: UFO Invitational, Roswell Mus & Art Ctr, NMex, 97; Quilt Nat '97, Southeastern Ohio Cult Arts Ctr, Athens (2 1/2 yr world tour), 99; The Kiss, Eastern Wash Univ Exhib Touring Svcs, 98; Tiger on the Hearth, Mansfield (Ohio) Arts Ctr, 98; Art Quilts: A Haystack Faculty Survey, Maine Arts Comn and Haystack Sch, Blaine House, Augusta, Maine, 98; Ohio Craft Invitational, Mansfield Art Ctr, 98; Colander Girls, Qult Art Internet Group, 99; Quilt and basket Invitational, Peninsula Art Sch, Fish Creek, Wis, 99; Fine Focus touring exhib, 99; The Good Earth, Aullwood Audubon Ctr, Dayton, Ohio, 2000; The Best of 2000, Ohio Designer Craftsmen, Columbus, 2000; CraftSummer Faculty Exhib, Hiestand Gallery, Miami, Univ, Oxford, Ohio, 2000; Linda Schwartz Gallery, Cincinnati; Mitakuye Oyasin, Wayne Ctr Arts, Wooster, Ohio, 2000; Remnants: The Thread of Memory, Spruill Ctr Arts, Atlanta, 2000; Tell Me a Story - Chapter 1: Narrative Themes in Contemp Fabric Arts, Cahoon, Mus Am Art, Cotuit, Cape Cod, Mass, 2001; Thirteen Moons Gallery, Santa Fe, NMex, 2001; Alegre Retreat Art Show, Sweeny Ctr, Santa Fe, NMex, 2001; Fantastic Fibers, Yeiser Art Ctr, Paducah, Ky, 2001; Quilt National '01, Dairy Barn Arts Ctr, Athens, Ohio, 2001; Craftsummer (faculy exhib), Miami U, Oxford, Ohio, 2001, Parallel Threads, New Eng Quilt Mus, Lowell, Mass, 2001; WAGE group exhib, Lowry Ctr, Coll Wooster, 2001; AQN Exhib, Fitton Ctr, Hamilton, Ohio, 2003; Dreaming the Garden, Touring Exhib, Laura Cater-Woods, Cur, 2003; group exhib, Claypool-Young Art Bldg, Morehead State Univ, Morehead, KY, 2004; and others. *Pos:* Founders, Turtle Moon Studios; Shie: founder, Green Quilts Proj, 89. *Teaching:* Mixed Media Healing quilts classes world wide; week long art camps, Turtle Moon Studios; workshops at craft schs, cols & mus; artist-in-residence, PS1, NY, 88 & Crafts Coun Ireland, 94; exchange artist to China, Ohio Arts Coun, 90; artist residency, Alfred Univ, NY, 97. *Awards:* Individual Artist Grants, Nat Endowment Arts, 90-91 & 94-95 & Ohio Arts Coun, 96 & 98; numerous other grants & awards. *Media:* Quilting, Mixed Media. *Mailing Add:* Turtle Moon Studios 2612 Armstrong Dr Wooster OH 44691-1806

SHIELDS, ANNE KESLER
PAINTER, ASSEMBLAGE ARTIST
b Winston-Salem, NC, Jan 27, 1932. *Study:* Hollins Col, Roanoke, Va, BA, 54; studied with Hans Hoffman, Provincetown, Mass, 57; Univ NC, Greensboro, MFA, 59. *Work:* NC Mus Fine Art, Raleigh; Mint Mus, Charlotte, NC; Weatherspoon Gallery, Univ NC, Greensboro; Mus Fine Arts, Montgomery, Ala; Cornell Univ, Ithaca, NY. *Comn:* Portrait of James English, Conn Bank & Trust, Hartford, 70; urban wall mural, Arts Coun, Winston-Salem, NC, 75; portraits (4), Wake Forest Univ, Winston-Salem, NC, 80, 82, 83 & 88; portraits (3), Trinity Col, Hartford, Conn, 88 & 89. *Exhib:* Xylon IV, Int Exhib Woodcuts, Musee d'art et d'historie, Geneva, Switz, 65; 20th Nat Exhib Prints, Libr Cong, Washington, DC, 66; Printmakers, US Pavilion, Japan Expo, 70; solo exhibs, Silvermine Guild, New Canaan, Conn, 70 & Southeastern Ctr Contemp Art, Winston-Salem, NC, 77; 200 Yrs of Art in NC, NC Mus Art, Raleigh, 76; Five Winston-Salem Printmakers, Southeastern Ctr Contemp Art, NC, 83; After Her Own Image, Woman's Work, Salem Fine Arts Ctr, NC, 85. *Awards:* Atwater Kent Award, Soc Four Arts, Palm Beach, Fla, 64; E J Arden Prize, Boston Printmakers, Mass, 70; Va Ctr Creative Arts fels, 87, 88 & 90. *Bibliog:* Joanna L Krotz (auth), New traditions, Money Mag, 6/90; Genie Carr (auth), Face to face, portrait-group, Winston-Salem J, 8/25/91; Jean S Rodgers (auth), Women of letters, a group portrait of North Carolina writers, Winston-Salem, 3/18/92. *Mem:* Artworks Gallery (Artists Cooperative, Winston-Salem). *Media:* Oil on Canvas. *Publ:* Illustr, Whedbee--Legends of the Outer Banks & Tarheel Tidewater, Blair Publ Co, 66. *Dealer:* Portraits Inc 985 Park Ave New York NY 10028. *Mailing Add:* c/o Portraits South 105 S Bloodworth Raleigh NC 27601

SHIFF, RICHARD
EDUCATOR
Study: Harvard Coll, BA (archit), 1965; Yale Grad Sch, MA, 1969, PhD (art hist), 1973. *Pos:* Dir, Univ Tex Ctr for Study of Modernism. *Teaching:* Prof art hist & Effie Marie Cain Regents art chmn, Univ Tex, Austin. *Awards:* Mellon Humanities Fel, Univ Pa, 1979-80; Nat Humanities Ctr Fel, 1986; Guggenheim Fel, 1985-86; Sr Res Grant, Getty Found, 1996-97; Disting Teaching of Art Hist award, Coll Art Asn, 2010. *Publ:* Auth, Cezanne and the End of Impressionism: A Study of the Theory, Technique, and Critical Evaluation of Modern Art, Univ Chicago Press, 1984; co-ed (with Robert S Nelson), Critical Terms for Art History, Univ Chicago Press, 1996; co-auth (with Carol Mancusi-Ungaro & Heidi Colsman-Freyberger), Barnett Newman: A Catalogue Raisonne, Yale Univ Press, 2004; auth, Doubt, Routledge, 2007; auth, Between Sense and De Kooning, Reaktion, 2011; Ellsworth Kelly: New York Drawings, 1954-1962, Prestel, 2014. *Mailing Add:* Univ Tex Dept Art & Art History Campus Mail Code D1300 Austin TX 78712

SHILSON, WAYNE STUART
PAINTER, ILLUSTRATOR
b Minneapolis, Minn, July 14, 1943. *Study:* Univ Minn, BS(art educ), 1971, MFA, 1972; study with Katherine Nash, 1968-70; Univ Minn, with GP Weisberg (prof), 1987-89. *Work:* Parks Fine Art Gallery, Sycamore, Ill; Arthur's Int Gallery, Las Vegas, Nev; Meadowcreek Gallery, Edina, Minn; Framestyles Gallery, Kenwood, Minneapolis, Minn; Southdale/Hennipen Publ Libr, Edina, Minn; and many other permanent collections; Libr Meeting Room, Park Rapids, Minn, 2004; St Peters Catholic Church, Park Rapids, Minn, 2005, 2010; Longville Centennial, Docksider Bldg, Longville, Minn, 2006; Liberty Park, Am Legion, Pine River, Minn, 2006; sculpture, Chamber of Commerce, Park Rapids, Minn, 2005. *Comn:* Paintings, Bernard Picture Co, Stamford, Conn, 1986; paintings, comn by William George, Minneapolis, 1988; paintings, Arthur's Int, Honolulu, 1988-90; paintings, Scafa-Tornabene, Nyack, NY, 1990; Lake Harriet Bandshell (painting), comn by Julie Andrews (actress); painting, Aunt Bell's Confectionary, Park Rapids, Minn, 99; Patriotic "ribbon" Am Legion, Pine River, Minn, 2003; painting to Crystal Gayle, country music hall of fame, Walker, Minn, 2008; painting, Bill Cosby, 2010; painting, Gov Jan Brewer, Ariz, 2011. *Exhib:* Solo exhibs include Sky Gallery, St Paul, Minn, 1976 & 1979, Minn Inst Arts, Minneapolis, 1979 & 1980, Horizon Gallery, Bloomingdale, Ill, 1986, Arthurs Int, Honolulu, Hawaii & Las Vegas, Nev, 1987-90, Minn State Fair, St Paul, 1990, The Stable Art Gallery, Maddens Resort, Gull Lake, Minn, 2001 & The Paul Bunyan Art Gallery, Bemidji, Minn, 2001; group exhibs include retrospectives, Normandale Cent Gallery, Bloomington, Minn, 1987-89 & Lutheran Brotherhood, Minneapolis, 1989; Eagan Auction, Eagan Rotary, Minn, 1990; Minn State Fair, 1990; N Country Mus Art, Park Rapids, Minn 1993-96 & 2006; C'mon Inn show, 35 works, Park Rapids, Minn, 2007; Grand Canyon CofC, Tusayan, Ariz, 2010. *Pos:* Artist & illusr, Honeywell, Minneapolis, Minn, 1974-; pres, Household Landscapes, 1987-; Judge, North Country Mus Art, 1994; art dir & artist, Top Dog Productions, Park Rapids, Minn, 1996; bd mem, N Country Mus Art, Park Rapids, Minn, 1997-98; design layout artist, Bemidji Pioneer Newspaper, Minn, 1998. *Teaching:* drawing, painting, art hist & caricatures, N Country Mus, Park Rapids, Minn, 1994-2000; painting & drawing, Park Rapids Comn Educ, Minn, 1997-98; art teacher Pine Point Sch, White Earth Indian Reservation, Minn, 1998-99, Remer-Longville Elem, Remer, Minn, 1999-2000, Pine River/Backus Elem and High Sch, Minn, 2000-09. *Awards:* Award, Sky Gallery, St Paul, 1976 & Art Ctr Minn, 1980; Second prize, Eagan Rotary Club, 1990; Artist grant McKnight Found, 1998; Region Two Arts Grant, 1999-2000, 2011. *Bibliog:* Liz Healy (auth), The Enterprise, Park Rapids, Minn, 1/1992; Chelsey Johnson (auth), The Enterprise, Park Rapids, Minn, 8/1994; Charmaine Barranco (auth), Bemidji Pioneer Newspaper, 7/26/1998, Our Northland Diocese, 8/2010. *Media:* Acrylic on Canvas. *Publ:* Park Rapids Enterprise, 11/1991; illusr, Keyboard Classic, Sept-Oct, 1992; Park Rapids Enterprise, 5/1994, 8/1994, 07/2010, 09/2010; The Maha-Leader, 9/1993, 3/1994; Summer Scene, 8/1993, 8/1994; The Forum of Fargo, 10/2010; Review Messenger, 10/2010, 08/2011; Northwoods Press, 2011. *Dealer:* Marvin C Arthur 2613 High Range Dr Las Vegas NV 89134. *Mailing Add:* 17767 Emerald Island Cir Park Rapids MN 56470

SHIMIZU, YOSHIAKI
HISTORIAN, CURATOR
b Tokyo, Japan, Feb 27, 1936. *Study:* Harvard Col, BA, 63; Univ Kans, MA, 68; Princeton Univ, MFA, 71, PhD, 74. *Pos:* Cur Japanese art, Freer Gallery Art, Smithsonian Inst, Washington, DC, 79-84; bd adv, Japan Soc NY, 81- & Arthur Sackler Gallery, Ctr Asian Art, Smithsonian Inst, Washington, DC, 84; ed bd, Arch Asian Art, 82-; consult cur, Nat Gallery Art, Washington, DC, 84-89; bd dir, Col Art Asn Am, 87-91; adv comt, Asia Soc Galleries, 92. *Teaching:* Asst prof art & archeol, Princeton Univ, 73-75, vis lectr, 81-84, prof, 84-, Marquand prof, 92-; asst prof Oriental art, Univ Calif, Berkeley, 75-78, assoc prof art hist, 78-79. *Awards:* Social Sci Res Coun Am Coun Learned Soc Grant, 78; Asian Cult Coun Grant, 95; Kajima Found Grant, 96. *Mem:* Japan Art Hist Soc; Coll Art Asn Am; Asn Asian Studies. *Res:* Primarily Japanese art of the medieval period with reference to Chinese art. *Publ:* Coauth, Masters of Japanese Calligraphy: 8th-19th Centuries, Asia Soc-Japan Soc, New York, 84; auth, A Chinese album leaf from the former Ashikaga Collection in the Freer Gallery of Art, Arch Asian Art, Vol 38; Zen Art? Zen in China, Japan and East Asian Art, Swiss Asian Studies, Vol III, Peter Lang, Berne-New York, 85; ed & coauth, Japan: The Shaping of Daimyo Culture 1185-1868, Nat Gallery Art, 88; The Vegetable Nehan of Ito Jakuchu, in Sanford, LaFleur and Nagatomi, Flowing Traces: Buddhism in the Literary and Visual Arts of Japan, Princeton Univ Press, 92; and others. *Mailing Add:* Dept Art & Archeol McCormack Hall Princeton Univ Princeton NJ 08544

SHIMOMURA, ROGER
PAINTER, PERFORMANCE ARTIST
b Seattle, Wash, June 26, 1939. *Study:* Univ Wash, BA (graphic design), 61; Syracuse Univ, MFA (painting), 69. *Work:* Seattle Art Mus; Nat Mus Am Art; Phoneix Mus Art; San Jose Art Mus; Denver Art Mus; Whitney Mus Am Art; Philadelphia Mus Art; Art Inst Chicago; and others. *Comn:* Mural (120" x 420"), Westlake Station, Metro, Seattle, 90. *Exhib:* Morgan Gallery, Kansas City, Kans, 77, 79; Dobrick Gallery, Chicago, 77, 80; Elaine Horwitch Gallery; Steinbaum Krauss Gallery, New York, 89-90, 92, 94 & 99; Folmenhaft Gallery, New York, 2006; and many others. *Teaching:* Distinguished prof art, Univ Kans, Lawrence, 69-. *Awards:* Nat Endowment for the Arts Grant, 77, 89 & 91; seventeen gen res grants, Univ Kans; McKnight Fel, 95; and numerous others. *Bibliog:* Harold Haydon (auth), An unexpected sensation, Chicago Sun-Times, 5/17/74; JoAnn Lewis (auth), The American ethic, Washington Post, 6/3/76; David L Shirley (auth), Twitting the Samurai style, NY Times, 11/23/76. *Media:* Acrylic, Serigraphs. *Dealer:* Greg Kucera Gallery Seattle WA; Flomenhaft Gallery NYC; Jan Weiner Gallery Kansas City Mo. *Mailing Add:* 1424 Wagon Wheel Rd Lawrence KS 66049

SHIN, JEAN
INSTALLATION SCULPTOR
b Seoul, South Korea, 1971. *Study:* Pratt Inst, Brooklyn, NY, BFA (Painting), 1994; Pratt Inst, Brooklyn, NY, MS (Art History & Criticism), 1996; Skowhegan Sch Painting & Sculpture, Maine, 1999. *Work:* Microsoft; Citicorp; Chase Bank; Smithsonian Mus Am Art. *Comn:* Dress Code, US Gen Servs Admin Art in Archit, Baltimore, Md, 2008; Celedon Remnants, MTA, Arts for Transit, LIRR Broadway Station, Queens, NY, 2008; New York Percent for Art, 2010. *Exhib:* Solo exhibs include Apex Art, New York, 1999, Socrates Sculpture Park, New York, 2003, Mus Mod Art, New York, 2004, Univ Art Mus, Albany, NY, 2005, Galerie Eric Dupont, Paris, 2005, Fabric Workshop & Mus, Philadelphia, 2006, Frederieke Taylor Gallery, New York, 2007, Location One, NY, 2008, Smithsonian Mus Am Art, Washington, DC, 2009; group exhibs include Pres Scholars in Vis Arts, Nat Mus Am Art, Washington, 1990; Exploring America's Cult, Macy Gallery, Columbia Univ, New York, 1999; Lost & Found, Rotunda Gallery, Brooklyn, NY, 2001; Counter Cult, New Mus Contemp Art, New York, 2004; Open House, Brooklyn Mus, 2004; Material Matters, Johnson Mus Art, Cornell Univ, Ithaca, NY, 2005; One Way or Another, Asia Soc & Mus, 2006; Red Hot, Mus Fine Art, Houston, 2007; We Interrupt Your Prog, Mills Coll Art Mus, Oakland, Calif, 2008; Second Lives, Mus Art & Design, New York, 2008; Contemp Outlook, Mus Fine Arts, Boston, 2009. *Teaching:* Prof, Pratt Inst, 1998-2010. *Awards:* Louis Comfort Tiffany Found Biennial Art Award, 2001; Fel Asian Cult Coun, 2001; Fel Award in Sculpture, NY Found Arts, 2003, Fel in Archit/Environmental Sculptures, 2008; Pollock-Krasner Found Grant, 2007; Fel Award in Archit/Environ Structures, NY Found Arts, 2008. *Bibliog:* Hilarie Sheets (auth), Because Everyone Deserves a Trophy, NY Times, 4/2009. *Dealer:* Art Projs Int 429 Greenwich St Suite 5B New York NY 10013; Frederieke Taylor Gallery 535 W 22nd St 6th Fl New York NY 10011; Solo Impression 601 W 26th St 2 Mez New York NY 10001

SHINER, ERIC C
MUSEUM DIRECTOR, CURATOR
Study: Honors Col, Univ Pittsburgh, BA (History of Art & Architecture and Japanese Language & Lit); Osaka Univ, MA (History of Art). *Collection Arranged:* Making a Home: Japanese Contemporary Artists in NY, Japan Soc, 2007. *Pos:* Prog dir, Japan-Am Soc of Pa; intern, Curatorial Dept, Nat Mus of Modern Art, Kyoto, Japan; asst curator, Yokohama Triennale, 2001; Milton Fine curator of art, Andy Warhol Mus, Carnegie Museums of Pittsburgh, 2008-11, acting dir, 2011, dir, 2011-. *Teaching:* Adj prof, Cooper Union for the Advancement of Sci and Art. *Mailing Add:* Andy Warhol Museum Office of Director 117 Sandusky St Pittsburgh PA 15212-5890

SHIPLEY, ROGER DOUGLAS
SCULPTOR, EDUCATOR
b Cleveland Heights, Ohio, Dec 27, 1941. *Study:* Am Sch Fontainebleau, France, with Monsieur Goetz, cert (painting), 62; Otterbein Coll, Ohio, BA, 64; Cleveland Inst Art, painting & sculpture, 64-65; Cranbrook Acad Art, Mich, MFA, 67. *Work:* Nat City Bank, Cleveland; Kalamazoo Inst Arts, Mich; Cranbrook Acad Art; Lock Haven Univ, Pa; M & T Bank; Sterling Drug Inc, Philadelphia; Pa Coll of Technol, Williamsport; Lycoming Coll & Otterbein Coll, Westerville, Ohio; Susquehanna Univ, Selinsgrove, Pa; Susquehanna Health, Williamsport, Pa. *Comn:* Achievement award, comn by Williamsport/Lycoming Found, 91; recognition award, comn by N Cent Pa Conservancy, 91. *Exhib:* 31st Ann Mid-Year Show, Butler Inst Am Art, 66; Cleveland Mus (May show exhib), 67-83; A Plastic Presence, Milwaukee Art Ctr, 69-70; Penn's Landing, Port Hist Mus, Philadelphia, 83; Henri Gallery, Washington, 86; AAV/108 Nat Competition Metal Sculpture, Millerville Univ, Pa, 84; B & S Galleries, Williamsport, Pa, 85-2004; Extension Gallery, Johnson Atelier, Mercerville, NJ, 88; Int Miniature Art Exhib, Seaside Art Gallery, 2006-2013; Sculpture Retrospective Docent, Arts Williamsport, Pa, 2007; Light and Form, Converge Gallery, Williamsport, PA, 2012, Sinners and Saints, 2012. *Pos:* Emer Prof of Art, Lycoming Coll; Logan Richmond Chair. *Teaching:* Prof painting, drawing, printmaking, two-dimensional design & color theory, Lycoming Coll, prof emer, currently. *Awards:* Second Place Sculpture Award & Charlie Gohn Sculpture Award, William Penn Mus, Harrisburg, Pa, 83; May show, Cleveland Mus Art, 83; Cultural Enhancement Award, Williamsport/Lycoming Found, 93; Best in Show, 5th Ann Juried Art Exhib, Williamsport, Pa, 2010. *Bibliog:* Bringing the art of plastics into focus, Chicago Tribune, 2/70; The brightness of lesser lights, Cincinnati Enquirer, 10/73; Penns landing sculpture show, in doors and out, Philadelphia Inquirer, 8/83; Artist La; Artists Laudeo For Work, Williamsport, Sun-Gazette, 99; and others. *Mem:* Lyco Co Hist Soc; Williamsport/Lycoming Arts Coun; Bald Eagle Art League; Clinton Co Arts Council. *Media:* Cast Bronze, Plexiglass, Oil, Watorcolor. *Publ:* Severin Roesen, Greater Williamsport Community Arts Coun, Bucknell Univ Press, 92; The Park Home Collection, 97 & The John Sloan Collection, Lycoming Co Hist Soc, Williamsport, Pa, 98; Beginning- Sculpture, Davis Publ, Inc, 2005; The Sculpture Reference, Sculpture Bks Publ, 2005. *Dealer:* Gold Leaf Gallery Williamsport PA 17701; Seaside Art Gallery Nags Head NC 27959; Faustina Gallery Lewsburg PA 17837; Eagles Mere Art Gallery Eagles Mere PA; Converge Gallery Williamsport PA; Gallery at Second; Station Gallery Lockhaven PA. *Mailing Add:* 264 Lehman Dr Cogan Station PA 17728-9228

SHIRE, PETER
SCULPTOR, DESIGNER
b Los Angeles, Calif, Dec 27, 1947. *Study:* Chouinard Art Inst, BFA, 70. *Work:* Mus Mod Art, Lodz, Poland; Art Inst Chicago; Los Angeles Co Mus Art; Brooklyn Mus, NY; Oakland Mus Art, Calif; Victoria & Albert Mus, London. *Comn:* Sculpture, McCarren Airport, Nev, 87; sculpture, Hokuden Electric, 94; sculpture, Sapporo Factory, Japan, 94; sculpture, Angels Point, Los Angeles, Calif, 94; sculpture, AIM Corp, Japan, 95; Colburn Sch Performing Arts, Los Angeles. *Exhib:* Seattle Art Mus, Was, 87; Los Angeles Munic Gallery, Calif, 88; Design Gallery, Milano, Italy, 89; Groninger Mus, The Neth, 90; Riva Yares Gallery, Ariz, 92; Ueda Gallery, Japan, 93; plus many others. *Teaching:* Calif State Univ, Los Angeles, 81-82; Hochschule Angewandte Kunst, Vienna, 83; Otis Parsons Sch Design, Los Angeles, 83; San Diego Univ, 85; Polytech Univ, Pomona, 86; Southern Calif Inst Arch, Santa Monica, 89-93. *Awards:* Design Team of XXIII Olympiad, Inst Architects, 84; Esquire Register, 85. *Bibliog:* Maria Porges (auth), Am Craft, 89; Peter Clothier (auth), Am Ceramics, 89; Hunter Drohojowska (auth), Ceramic Monthly, 89; Penny Smith (auth), Art & Perception, 2001. *Media:* Metal, Clay. *Publ:* Auth, Teatypes, Tea Garden Press, 80; Tempest in a Tea Pot, Rizzoli Int Publ, 91. *Dealer:* Modernism San Francisco; Frank Lloyd Gallery Santa Monica CA. *Mailing Add:* 1850 Echo Park Ave Los Angeles CA 90026

SHIRLEY, JON ANTHONY
COLLECTOR
b San Diego, Calif, Apr 12, 1938. *Study:* Mass Inst Technol, 1957. *Pos:* Several Radio Shack divisions Tandy Corp, Ft Worth, 1963-72, vpres, 1972-83; pres & chief operating officer, Microsoft Corp, Redmond, Wash, 1983-90, bd dirs, 2003; dir, Manzanita Capital, Seattle, currently, Mentor Graphics, formerly. *Awards:* Named one of Top 200 Collectors, ARTnews mag, 2004-12. *Mem:* Asn Data Processing Serv Orgn (bd dir, 1986-); Seattle Yacht Club. *Collection:* Modern and contemporary art

SHIRLEY, MARY
COLLECTOR
Awards: Named one of Top 200 Collectors, ARTnews mag, 2009-12. *Collection:* Modern and contemporary art

SHISHIM, FRANCIS See Bob & Bob

SHIVES, ARNOLD EDWARD
PAINTER, PRINTMAKER
b Vancouver, BC, Dec 27, 1943. *Study:* Univ BC, 62-64; San Francisco Art Inst, BFA, 66; Stanford Univ, MA, 69. *Work:* Tate Mod, London; Victoria & Albert Mus, London; British Mus, London; Art Gallery of Ontario, Toronto; Berkeley Art Mus, Berkeley, Calif; Mus Mod Art, New York. *Exhib:* Solo Exhibs: Pollock Gallery, Toronto, 75; Paul Kuhn Gallery, Calgary, Canada, 84, 86, 88, 89, 91, 92, 97; Heffel Gallery, Vancouver, 89, 90; Galerie Lindenthal, Cologne, Ger, 2000; Deleon White Gallery, Denver, Co, 2001; Gallery/Cafe Hanare, Kobe, Japan, 2006; DeLeon White Gallery, Toronto, 96; DeLeon White Gallery, Denver, 01; Bond Univ Art Gallery, Queensland, Australia, 2004. *Teaching:* instr, 2 & 3 dimensional design & printmaking, Trinity Western Univ, Langley, BC, Can, 2004. *Awards:* Distinguished Citizen Award, North Vancouver Centennial, 91. *Bibliog:* John K Grande (auth), Arnold Shives, Art Forum, New York, 3/96; Trevor Carolan (auth) The Wilderness Sacraments of Arnold Shives, Image Mag, Seattle, Wash, 2001. *Mem:* Canadian Artists Representation; Royal Canadian Academy of the Arts. *Media:* Mixed Media on paper, Canvas & board. *Publ:* Auth, The Valley of Melting Sand, Prospect Press, Vancouver, 99; auth, Mountain Journal, Prospect Press, 2004; Auth, Ron Dart: Mountaineering & the Humanities, 2007; auth, John Grande, Mystical Mosquito, Prospect Press, 2005; auth, John Grande, At Stonehenge & Avebury, Prospect Press, 2008 (received Alcuin Awards for Excellence in Book Design); auth, Pick Culbert, The Coast Mountains Trilogy, Tricouni Press, 2009. *Mailing Add:* 4217 Prospect Rd North Vancouver BC V7N 3L6 Canada

SHKURPELA, DASHA
PAINTER, SCULPTOR
b Bishkek, Kyrgyzstan. *Study:* Am Univ, Bishkek, Kyrgyzstan, BA (Liberal Arts/Journalism), 1999; Centr European Univ, Budapest, Hungary, MA (History), 2001; Mass Coll Art, Boston, MFA (Painting), 2002. *Exhib:* Solo exhibs include Kyrgyz State Mus Fine Arts, Bishkek, 1995, Prince Street Gallery, New York, 2008; Two person exhibs include Kyrgyz State Mus Fine Arts (with Konstantin Shkurpela), Bishkek, 1999 ; Group exhibs include Soundscape, Mass Coll Art, 2001; Boston High Tea, ARamona Studio Gallery, New York, 2004; The Cabin Fever, Gallery 125 Trenton Downtown Asn, Trenton, NJ, 2005; New Directions, Barrett Art Ctr, Poughkeepsie, NY, 2005, 2007 ; Portraits, Self-Portraits, Gallery 402 / OIA, New York, 2006. *Awards:* Soros Found, 1999; George Sugarman Found Grant, 2007; AAUW, Int Fel, 2000. *Bibliog:* A Yarkov (auth), Fish Therapy 1 in: Almanac Kurak 1, Bishkek: Soros Foundation, 1999; William & Mary Review, 2002, 2003; Chicago Art J (Univ Chicago), 2003; G Bokonbaev (ed), Fine Arts in Kyrgyzstan, Bishkek: AUB, 2007; Joe Bendik (auth), Shkurpela's view of the world, Chelsea Clinton News, Aug 14, 2008. *Collection:* Pvt collections in: Kyrgyzstan, Russia, Hungary, Czech Repub, Croacia, Ger, US

SHLIEN, HELEN S
CURATOR
b Kansas City, Mo. *Study:* Sarah Lawrence Coll, BA, 41; Univ Chicago, MA, 64. *Collection Arranged:* Four Installations, Mobius, Boston, 87; Social Concerns, The Space, Boston, 88; Layerings, Newton Art Ctr, Maine, 89; I Want a Child, Westfield State Col, Maine, 89; Boston-Montreal, Artists Found, Boston, 90; Other Views, Danforth Mus Art, 94; Over Seventy, Boston's Honored Artists, Danforth Mus Art, 95; Still Life and Portraits, Danforth Mus Art, 97. *Pos:* Owner, Contemp Prints & Drawings Gallery, Chicago, 65-67; cur, Inst Contemp Art, Boston, Mass, 69-72; gallery dir, Boston Visual Artists Union, 74-75; owner, Helen Shlien Gallery, Boston, 78-85; independent cur, 85-; appraiser, 20th Century and Contemp painting, sculpture and prints, 2001-. *Awards:* Nat Endowment Arts Grant, 77. *Mem:* Int Soc of Appraisers. *Specialty:* Contemporary painting and sculpture. *Publ:* Auth, Artists' Associations in the USA, A Descriptive Directory, pvt publ, 77; Ewa Kuryluk (auth), catalogue introduction, Fiberarts, Vol 15, #2, 88; Gabrielle Rossmer (auth), catalogue introduction, Aspeckte der Gegenwartskunst; Virginia Gunter (auth), catalogue introduction, Revelations, 97. *Mailing Add:* 11740 Wilshire Blvd A2006 Los Angeles CA 90025

SHOEMAKER, INNIS HOWE
CURATOR
b Reading, Pa, Feb 7, 1942. *Study:* Vassar Col, Poughkeepsie, NY, AB, 64; Columbia Univ, New York, MA, 68, PhD, 75. *Collection Arranged:* Paul Cezanne: Two Sketchbooks, Philadelphia Mus of Art, 89 (exhib & cat coauth); New Art on Paper 2 (coauth, catalog), Hunt Manufacturing Co Collection, 96; Encounters with Modern Art (coauth, catalog), Selections from Rothschild Family Collection, 97; Mad for Modernism: Earl Horter and His Collection (auth, catalog), 99; Jacques Villon and His Cubist Prints, 2001; Adventures in Mod Art: The Charles K Williams II Collection, 2009. *Pos:* Cur, Vassar Col Art Gallery, Poughkeepsie, NY, 73-76; asst dir, Ackland Art Mus, Univ NC, Chapel Hill, 76-78, acting dir, 78, dir, 83-86; sr cur prints, drawings & photogr, Philadelphia Mus Art, 86-. *Teaching:* adj prof, dept art, Univ NC, Chapel Hill; adj prof dept art history & archaeology, Univ Pa, 2002-. *Awards:* Rome Prize Fel, Hist Art, Am Acad Rome, 71-73. *Mem:* Am Asn Mus; Print Coun of Am; Coll Art Asn Am. *Publ:* Contrib, Some Observations on the Development of FIlippino Lippi's Figure Drawings, Florentine Drawing at the Time of Lorenzo the Magnificent, Bologna, 255-264, 94; Filippino Lippi and his Antique Sources, The Drawings of Filippino Lippi and his Circle, Metrop Mus Art, NY, 29-36, 97; Crossing Borders: the Weybe Gallery & the Vogue for Mexican Art, 1926-1940, Mex & Mod Printmaking: A Revolation in the Graphic Arts, Philadelphia Mus Art, 2006. *Mailing Add:* Philadelphia Museum of Art Philadelphia PA 19130

SHOOSTER, STEPHEN LEON (SHOOSTY)
CONCEPTUAL ARTIST, AUTHOR
b Chester, Pa, May 11, 1958. *Study:* Univ Fla, B (Fine Art, Painting), 1976-1982; Studied under: Hiram Williams (painting), Univ Fla; Nate Shiner (painting), Univ Fla; Marcia Isaacson (drawing), Univ Fla; David Kremgold (design), Univ Fla; Catriel Efroney (painting), Sfadt, Israel. *Work:* Historic 5th Avenue, 2014, Oil on Canvas with painted frame, 7ft x 5ft, Tribute to George Tandy, Athens, 2014, Oil on Canvas 4.5ft x 4ft, A Tribute to Django Rienhardt, 2013, Oil on Canvas, 6ft x 5ft; Dual Violins, 2013, Oil on Canvas with painted frame, 4.5ft x 4 ft, Tribute to Jascha Lieberman, El Arenal, 2012, Oil on Canvas with painted frame, 4.5ft x 4ft, The Party Favor, 2011, Oil on Canvas, Tribute to Galicia circa 1935, Frogs and Flowers, 2013, Oil on Canvas, 6.5ft x 5ft, Tribute to Yaakovt Thompson, Sax-o-Phony, 2011, Acrylic on Canvas, A Gift to Catholics, 2011, Oil on Canvas, 6ft x 5ft, Guitar on Fire, 2010, 6ft x 5ft, Acylic on Canvas; Public Places: Hello Friends, Univ N Fla Office of Admissions, Tallahassee, Fla, 2010, Shark Valley, 2004, Oil on Canvas, 4.5ft x 4ft, Univ Fla, Office of Special Donors, placed 2014; MET Bus Office, New York, NY; MoMA Security Office. *Exhib:* Summer, Iron River Mus, Iron River, Mich, 2006; Tours resulting in drawing sets: 2015, Dinosaur Tour, Salt Lake City, Utah - Vernal, Utah, 2014, Cassidy Shooster London-Greece Tour, Jamie Shooster Poland - Scotland Tour, 2012, Carly Shooster Poland - Liverpool Tour. 2011; Dr. Sketchy's, Burlesque Drawing, S Fla, 2011. *Pos:* Co-CEO, Global Response Corp, 1976-; Artist (owner), www.Shoosty.com, 1982-. *Mem:* AAM; MET; Iron River Mus; Behance Network. *Media:* Watercolor, Ink, Oil, Dye on Silk. *Interests:* Jewish History, Drawing musicians while they play, software development. *Publ:* Slow Mover, 2004; auth, The Horse Adjutant, A Jewish Boy's Life during the Nazi Holocaust, 2011. *Dealer:* Shoosty Gallery 777 St State Rd 7 Margate FL 33068

SHORE, STEPHEN
PHOTOGRAPHER
b New York, NY, Oct 8, 1947. *Work:* Metrop Mus Art, Mus Mod Art & Whitney Mus Am Art, NY; George Eastman House, Rochester, NY; Mus Fine Arts, Boston; Art Inst Chicago; San Francisco Mus Mod Art; Los Angeles Co Mus Art; and others. *Exhib:* Solo exhibs, Metropolitan Mus Art, NY, 71; Mus Mod Art, NY, 76; Art Inst, Chicago, 82Nederlands Foto Inst, Rotterdam, 97, Photog Resource Ctr, Boston, 97, CRAF, Villa Cini, Spilinbergo, Italy, 98, Gallery Contemp Art, Mestre, Italy, 99, Musei Comunali, Rimini, Italy, 99, Palazzo Civico, Rubiera, Italy, 99, SK Stiftung Kultur, Cologne, Ger, 99 & Victorian Arts Ctr, Melbourne, Australia, 2000, 303 Gallery, NY, 2000, 03, 06 & 09, Galerie Conrads, Ger, 2001, Galerie Rodolphe Janssen, Brussels, Belgium, 2002, 2003, Spruth Magers Lee, London, 2003, PS 1 Contemp Art Ctr, NY, 2005, Worcester Art Mus, Mass, 2006, Henry Art Gallery, Univ Washington, Seattle, 2006, Int Ctr Photography, 2007; group exhibs include Flora Photographica, S Bank Art Ctr, London, Eng, 92; Am Studies, Aktions Forum Praterinsel, Munich, 95; Breuer's Whitney, Whitney Mus Am Art, NY, 96; Metrop Mus Art, NY, 97 & 98; Photog Innovators, 1840s-1990s, Victoria & Albert Mus, London, 99; Places as Landscape, Uffizi Gallery, Florence, Italy, 2000; Galerie Sprüth Magers, Cologne, Ger, 2005; Jeu De Paume, Paris, France, 2005; Hammer Mus, Los Angeles, Calif, 2005; Henry Art Gallery, Seattle, Wash, 2006; 303 Gallery, NY, 2006; Galerie Sprüth Magers, Munich, Ger, 2006. *Teaching:* Chmn photog dept, Bard Col, 82-. *Awards:* Nat Endowment Arts Grants, 74 & 79; Guggenheim Fel, 75; Am Acad Rome, 80; MacDowell Colony Grant, 93; Aperture Award, 2005; Culture Prize, German Photographic Soc, 2010; Hon Fellow, Royal Photographic Soc, 2010. *Bibliog:* Tony Hiss (auth), The framing of Stephen Shore, Am Photog, 2/79. *Publ:* Auth, Uncommon places, 82 & The gardens at Giverny, 83, Aperture; Luzzara, Arcadia, Edizioni, 93; The Velvet Years, Pavilion Books, 95; Stephen Shore: Photographs, 1973-1993, Schirmer/Mosel, 95; The Nature of Photographs, Johns Hopkins, 98; American Surfaces, Schirmer/Mosel, 99; Uncommon Places, The Complete Works, Aperture, 2004; American Surfaces, Phaidon, 2005; Stephen Shore, Phaidon, 2007; A Road Trip Journal, Phaidon, 2008; The Hudson Valley, Blind Spot, 2011; Mose: A Preliminary Report, Konig, 2011. *Dealer:* 303 Gallery 547 W 21st St New York NY 10011-1100

SHORES, (JAMES) FRANKLIN
PAINTER
b Hampton, Va, Nov 9, 1942. *Study:* Pa Acad Fine Arts, Cresson Europe Traveling Scholar, Eakins Figure Painting Prize. *Work:* Pa Acad Fine Arts, Philadelphia; Camden Pub Libr, Maine. *Exhib:* Pa Acad Fine Arts Ann, 67 & 69; Philadelphia Watercolor Club Exhibs, 68-; Cabrini Col, 86. *Teaching:* Instr art, Pa Acad Fine Arts, 65-86. *Awards:* Harry Deitch Mem Prize, Philadelphia Watercolor Club, 78. *Mem:* Philadelphia Watercolor Club (hon pres, currently). *Media:* Watercolor, Oil. *Mailing Add:* 612 S Ninth St Philadelphia PA 19147

SHORR, HARRIET
PAINTER
b New York, NY. *Study:* Swarthmore Coll, BA, 1960; Yale Sch Art & Archit, BFA, 1962. *Work:* Bklyn Mus; Utah Mus Fine Arts, Salt Lake City; Citicorp, NY; Chemical Bank, NY; Estee Lauder Corp, NY. *Exhib:* Eight Women-Still Life, New Britain Mus, Conn, 1982; Painterly Realism, 1982 & Contemp Women Painters, 1983, Rahr West Mus, Manitowac, Wis; Am Realism, William Sawyer Gallery, San Francisco, 1985 & San Francisco Mus Fine Art, 1985-86; Artists Choosing Artists, Artists Choice Mus, NY, 1985; The Object Revitalized, Paine Arts Ctr, Oshkosh, Wis, 1985-86; Contemp Am Still Life, One Penn Plaza, NY, 1985-86; solo exhibs, Evelyn Segal Gallery, Fort Worth, Tex, 1993, 1998, Editions Ltd, Indianapolis, IN, 1993, Gallery of Contemp Art, Univ Colo, 1993, Gallery Camino Real, Boca Raton, Fla, 1994, Mus East Tex, Lufkin, 1995, Neuberger Mus, Purchase, NY, 1999, Purchase Col, SUNY, 1999, Cheryl Pelavin, New York City, 2001, 2002; Bristol Meyers Squibb Gallery, Princeton, NJ, 1997; Gischback Gallery, New York, 1997; Century Asn, New York, 1998; Univ NH, 1998; Nat Acad Design, New York, 1998; Am Acad Arts & Letts Invitational, New York, 1999; Qualita Gallery, Las Vegas, 1999; Qualita Fine Arts, Las Vegas, 1999; Erector Sq Gallery, New Haven, Conn, 2000; Del Ctr Contemp Arts, Wilmington, 2002; Am Acad Arts and Letts, 2009. *Teaching:* Prof painting, State Univ NY, Purchase, 1979-2006. *Awards:* Nat Endowment Arts Grant, 1980; Am Artist Achievement award, 1994; Purchase Award, Am Acad Arts & Letts, 1999; Pollock-Krasner Found Grant, 2000. *Bibliog:* Nathan Kernan (auth), Review, Art in Am, 6/2005-7/2005; Ken Johnson (auth), NY Times, 2001; Faye Hirsch (auth), Review, Art on Paper, 3/2001-4/2001. *Mem:* Nat Acad. *Media:* Oil. *Publ:* Auth, A painter's reflections on real painting, Arts, 1979; The Artist's Eye, Watson-Guptill, 1991. *Dealer:* Cheryl Pelavin 13 Jay St New York NY 10013. *Mailing Add:* 117 Mercer St New York NY 10012

SHORT, SCOTT
PAINTER
b 1964. *Study:* Ohio State Univ, BFA, 1988, MFA, 1990. *Exhib:* New American Talent 18, Jones Ctr for Contemp Art, Austin, Tex, 2003; Varied Marks: Contemporary Drawings and Works on Paper, Univ St Francis, 2004; Takeover, Hyde Park Art Ctr, Chicago, 2006; Not Fade Away, Evanston Art Ctr, Ill, 2007; Whitney Biennial, Whitney Mus Am Art, New York, 2010. *Mailing Add:* Christopher Grimes Gallery 916 Colorado Ave Santa Monica CA 90401

SHOTWELL, KENNETH E
PAINTER, PRINTMAKER
b McKeesport, Pa, Feb 11, 1950. *Study:* Carnegie-Mellon Art Inst, 68; Univ Pittsburgh, BSME, 72. *Work:* Slater Mem Mus, Norwich, Conn; Combustion Eng, Windsor, Conn; Nihon Gallery, Nagoya, Japan; Conn Pub Television, Farmington, Conn. *Comn:* Lobby, comn by Steve Macera, West Warwick, RI, 78; Fr cave reproduction mural, comn by pvt source, North Attleboro, Mass, 79; landscape mural, comn by Mr Wright, Sarasota, Fla, 93. *Exhib:* Ann Regional Exhib, Mystic Art Asn, Conn, 88; Machef Art Show, Milan, Italy, 88; Mus Art & Sci, New Britain, Conn, 89; Burmingham Art Exhib, London, Eng, 89; Spring Fair, Frankfort, Ger, 90; Nihon Garo/Art Stage Sakae/Villagio Italiano, Nagoya, Japan, 2007; Park West Gallery, Southfield, Mich; Red Dot Fair, Miami, Fla, 2011. *Pos:* pres, Contemp Multimedia Inc, 85-91 & Signature Gallery Ltd, Inc, 92-98; pres, Omni Studios Ltd Inc, 99-2007. *Teaching:* Instr drawing & perspective, Iindust design & packaging, RI Sch Design, East Providence, 82-83. *Awards:* Purchase Award of Distinction, United Technol Ann Emp, United Technol Corp, 74; Cert Design Excellence, 3rd Ann Nat, Print Mag, 88; 4th Asian Print Awards, Bronze Medal, Shanghai, China, 2006; US Patent Grant, Lighting System For Fluorescent Art, 2008; US Patent Grant, Depth Illusion Picture Frame, 2011. *Bibliog:* Ronald Roy (auth), Prolific Stonington artist, Norwich, Bull, 3/25/88; Clare Collins (auth), An artist for the masses, New York Times, 4/10/88; Eydie Cubarrubia (auth), Sarasota artist aims for surreal success, Bradenton Herald, 1/28/94. *Mem:* Life mem Mystic Art Asn. *Media:* Acrylic on Canvas; Giclee on Paper & Canvas. *Interests:* Fourth dimensional physics. *Publ:* Illusr, Audition Guide, McGraw-Hill, 88; auth, Fine art of frisk, Art Digest, 89; Artsmart, CM Inc, 90; COREL CD-ROM, 96; Mindscapes, Highland Press, 2006. *Dealer:* Art Force Co Ltd Tokyo Japan; Tom Binder Fine Art 825 Wilshire Blvd #708 Santa Monica Calif 90405; Artisan Direct Ltd Pittsford NY

SHOTZ, ALYSON
ASSEMBLAGE ARTIST, SCULPTOR
b Glendale, Ariz, 1964. *Study:* RI Sch Design, BFA, 1987; Univ Wash, Seattle, MFA, 1991. *Work:* Whitney Mus Am Art, Solomon R Guggenheim Mus, Brooklyn Mus Art, Mus Mod Art, New York; Hirshhorn Mus & Sculpture Garden, Washington; Harvard Univ Art Galleries; Yale Univ Art Gallery; LA County Mus Art. *Exhib:* Solo exhibs include Susan Inglett, New York, 1996, 1998, 1999, Lemon Sky Projects, LA, 1997, 2002, Susquehanna Art Mus, Harrisburg, Pa, 1999, Derek Eller Gallery, New York, 2003, 2005, 2006, 2007, 2008, Tang Teaching Mus, Saratoga, New York, 2003, Rice Univ Art Gallery, Houston, 2004, Locks Gallery, Philadelphia, 2004, 2008, Aldrich Mus Contemp Art, Conn, 2005, Madison Mus Contemp Art, Wis, 2006, Peeler Art Ctr,

DePauw Univ, Ind, 2006, Yale Univ Art Gallery, 2007, Derek Eder Gallery, 2009, Standing Waves, Wexner Art Ctr, 2010, Wavelength, Derek Eller Gallery, NY, 2011, Fundamental Forces, Carolina Nitsch, NY, 2011, Espace Louis Vuitton, Tokyo, Japan, 2011; Group exhibs include Pop-Surrealism, Aldrich Mus Contemp Art, Conn, 1998, Best of the Season, 1999; Greater New York, PS1 Contemp Art Ctr, New York, 2000; Pastoral Pop, Whitney Mus at Phillip Morris, New York, 2000; Digital Printmaking Now, Brooklyn Mus Art, 2001; Mirror Mirror, Mass Mus Contemp Art, 2002; Needful Things: Contemp Multiples, Cleveland Mus Art, 2004; Light x Eight, Jewish Mus, New York, 2006; The Shapes of Space, Guggenheim Mus, New York, 2007; Currents: Recent Acquisitions, Hirshhorn Mus & Sculpture Garden, Washington, 2008; San Francisco Mus Mod Art, 2008; Ways of Seeing: E.V. Day, Richard Dupont, Alyson Shotz, Carolina Nitsch Gallery, NY, 2010; The More Things Change, San Fran Mus Modern Art, Calif, 2011; Fracturing the Burning Glass: Between Mirror and Meaning, Inst Contemp Art, Maine Coll Art, Portland, ME, 2011. *Awards:* NY Found Arts Fel, 2004; Marie Walsh Sharpe Found Fel, 2004; Happy and Bob Doran Artist in Residence, Yale Univ Art Gallery, 2005-6; Saint-Gaudens Mem Fel, 2007. *Mailing Add:* c/o Derek Eller Gallery 615 W 27th St New York NY 10001

SHRIGLEY, DAVID
DRAFTSMAN
b Macclesfield, Cheshire, England, 1968. *Study:* Glasgow Sch Art, 1988-91. *Work:* Carnegie Mus Art, Pittsburgh. *Exhib:* Solo exhibs include Transmission Gallery, Glasgow, Scotland, 1995, Galleri Nicolai Wallner, Copenhagen, Denmark, 1995, 1997, 2000, 2003, 2005, Stephen Friedman Gallery, London, 1997, 1999, 2001, 2004, Francesca Pia, Bern, Switzerland, 1997, 1999, 2004, Bloom Gallery, Amsterdam, 1998, Galerie Yvon Lambert, Paris, 1998, 1999, 2001, 2004, 2006, Anton Kern Gallery, New York, 2002, 2005; group exhibs include In Here, Transmission, Glasgow, Scotland, 1992; Scottish Autumn, Bartok 32 Galeria, Budapest, Hungary, 2005; White Hysteria, Contemp Art Ctr of South Australia, Melbourne, 1996; Appetizer, Free Parking, Toronto, 1997; Habitat, Ctr Contemp Photog, Melbourne, 1998; Zac 99, Mus d'Art Mod Ville Paris, 1999; Under Bridges & Along The River, Casino Luxembourg, 2001; Jokes, MAMCO, Geneva, Switzerland, 2002; Contemp Arts Mus, Houston, 2003; Britannia Works, Xippas Gallery, Athens, 2004; Emotion Pictures, MUHKA, Antwerp, Belgium, 2005; Under God's Hammer, Art Gallery Western Australia, Perth, 2006; The Compulsive Line: Etching 1900 to Now, Mus Mod Art, New York, 2006. *Dealer:* Anton Kern Gallery 532 W 20th St New York NY 10011; Stephen Friedman Gallery 25-28 Old Burlington St London England W1S 3AN United Kingdom; Galerie Francesca Pia Limmatstrasse 275 Zurich Switzerland 8005; Yvon Lambert 108 rue Vieille du Temple Paris France 75003; Galerie de multiples 17 rue Saint Gilles Paris France 75003; Galleri Nicolai Wallner Njalsgade 21 Copenhagen Denmark 2300

SHUBIN, MORRIS JACK
PAINTER, LECTURER
b Mansfield, Wash, Feb 25, 1920. *Work:* Utah State Univ, Logan; Las Vegas Art Mus, Nev; Home Savings & Loan, Calif; City La Mirada, Calif; Philip H Greene Collection; Glendale Federal Savings & Loan, Calif; Springmaid Beach Le Roy Springs Co, SC; and others. *Comn:* Painting (brochure), Robert Mondavi Winery, Calif, 90. *Exhib:* Nat Watercolor Soc Ann, Palm Springs Art Mus, Calif, 81; Art and the Law, Atlanta, 83; Utah State Univ, Logan, 83; 161st Ann Exhib, Nat Acad Design, 86, 88 & 92; Am Watercolor Soc Invitational, Museo de la Acurela Mexicana, Mexico City. *Teaching:* Instr watercolor workshops, Fla, Tex, NMex, Ore, Colo, Mo & Mex, 74-84, Spain, 85 & Canada, 90. *Awards:* Addeso Franklin Page Award, Owensboro Mus, Ky, 83; Samuel J Bloomingdal Mem Award, Am Watercolor Soc, 118th Ann Exhib, Canton Art Inst, 85; Crandall Norton Award, Downey Art Mus, 90. *Bibliog:* Gerald Brommer (auth), Transparent Watercolor, Davis, 73; Susan Meyer (auth), 40 Watercolorists and How They Work, Watson-Guptill; McClelland & Last (coauths, publ), The California Style, 85. *Mem:* Am Watercolor Soc (vpres, 87-89); Nat Watercolor Soc (treas, 70-72, 89-90, vpres, 72-73); WCoast Watercolor Soc; Pasadena Soc Artists; Watercolor USA Hon Soc. *Media:* Multimedia. *Publ:* Auth, Watercolor page, Am Artists, 8/74; producer, Nat Watercolor Soc Ann Catalog, 89-90; cover art, Your Research: Data Analysis for Criminal Justice and Criminology, West Publ Co, 92. *Dealer:* Eileen Kremen's Gallery 619 N Harbor Blvd Fullerton CA. *Mailing Add:* 313 N 12th St Montebello CA 90640

SHUKMAN, SOLOMON
PAINTER, PRINTMAKER
b Bobr Prov, USSR, July 5, 1927; US citizen. *Study:* Coll Fine Arts & Theater Design, Moscow, BA, 49; Stroganoff Inst Art, Moscow, BA, 52. *Work:* Mankind and Work (monumental composition), Moscow; Energy/Metal (monumental composition), Paris; Summer, Spring, Autumn (monumental composition), Ehrfurt, EGer; Majakovski (collage), NY; Transport (3 decorative compositions), Prague. *Comn:* Mankind & Oil (mural), Art Found USSR, Moscow, 68; Morning, Union Soviet Artist, Moscow, 69; Cosmos, Union Soviet Artist, Moscow, 69; Country and Army (mural), Art Found USSR, Moscow, 71; Men and Cloth, Art Found USSR, Moscow, 72. *Exhib:* Solo exhibs, Loeb Rhode Market Gallery, 75, Panteon Gallery, 77 & Nathan Gallery, 78, San Francisco & Magnes Mus (with catalog), Berkeley, Calif, 78-79; Int Art Expo, NY Coliseum, NY & Los Angeles Convention Ctr, 85. *Awards:* First Praise, Int Expo, Moscow, 69 & 72, 2nd Praise, 73. *Bibliog:* Article, Best show of the year, Art in the USSR Mag, 72. *Mem:* Int Soc Artists; Graphic Arts Coun; Ctr Visual Arts; World Print Coun. *Media:* Murals, Graphics. *Mailing Add:* 554 Beresford Ave Redwood City CA 94061

SHULER, THOMAS H, JR
PHOTOGRAPHER, EDUCATOR
b Detroit, Mich, Apr 15, 1949. *Study:* Princeton Univ, BA, 71; Univ Del, MA, 78. *Work:* Corcoran Gallery Art; Mus Francais Photog, Bievres, France; Bibliot Nat, Paris; Libr Cong, Washington, DC. *Exhib:* Recent Acquisitions, 77 & Still Life, 78, Corcoran Gallery Art; Focus Gallery, San Francisco, 79; MFA Gallery-The Platinotype, Rochester Inst Technol, 79; Photographer's Gallery, London, Eng, 79; Nuages, Bibliot Nat, Paris, 80; Invisible Light, Harvard Univ, 81; and others. *Teaching:* Instr photog, Smithsonian Inst, 75-76; chmn, asst prof & prog head photog, Northern Va Community Col, 76-. *Awards:* Medaille Verrieres Buisson, Mus Francais Photog, 78. *Bibliog:* Ben Forgey (auth), A sense of the moment when everything's right, Washington Star, 5/5/78; Time-Life Photo Annual, 79; Hafey & Shillea (auth), The Platinum Print, Graphic Arts Res Ctr, Rochester Inst Technol, 80; and others. *Mem:* Soc Photog Educ. *Publ:* Ed, Places, Infrared Photographs 1976-1978, pvt publ, 78. *Mailing Add:* 3715 Cardiff Rd Chevy Chase MD 20815

SIAMIS, JANET NEAL
PAINTER
b Cleveland, Ohio, July 31, 1938. *Study:* Rollins Coll, Winter Park, Fla, 56-57; Antelope Valley Coll, Lancaster, Calif, 78-81; study with Ralph Love, Temecula, Calif. *Work:* Home Savings Am; Fluor Corp, Irvine, Calif; Kaiser Permanente; Security Pac Bank; Embassy Suites Hotel; Marriott Hotel, Presidential Suites, New Orleans, La; Marriott Lincolnshire, Exec Suites, Chicago, Ill; Marriott Hotel, Ballrooms & Hospitality Suites, Anaheim, Calif. *Exhib:* All Media Exhib, Lancaster Mus, Calif, 85; Tallahassee City Hall Art Show, 88 & 89; Fla Watercolor Ann, St Petersburg, 91 & 96; Monotypes, Philbrook Mus, Tulsa, Okla, 95; Fla State Univ, Mus Fine Arts, 2003. *Awards:* Judge's Choice Award, Fla Watercolor Soc, 91. *Bibliog:* JS Ayres (auth), Brushes, Am Artist Mag, 86, Making Watercolor Monotypes, 88, Monotypes, Mediums & Methods, Watson-Guptill, 91; Dorothy Hoyal (auth), Taking oneself seriously as an artist, Am Artist Mag, 6/86; JS Ayres (auth), Printmaking Techniques, 93. *Mem:* Fla Watercolor Soc. *Media:* Watercolor. *Publ:* Illusr, A Christmas to Remember, Antelope Valley Press, 80; cover painting, Forecast Mag, Fla State Univ, 95; Flowers in Watercolor, Rockport Publ, 96. *Dealer:* Siamis Studios PO Box 1383 Crawfordville FL 32326. *Mailing Add:* Hwy 98 PO Box 1383 Crawfordville FL 32327

SIBERELL, ANNE HICKS
PAINTER, SCULPTOR
b Los Angeles, Calif. *Study:* Univ Calif, Los Angeles; Chouinard Art Inst, BFA; studied with John Wheat, Richard Lytle & Antonio Frasconi. *Work:* Fine Arts Mus, San Francisco; Cleveland Art Inst; Victoria & Albert Mus, London; Nat Mus Women Arts; Library of Congress, Washington, DC; Oakland Mus, Calif; Victoria & Albert Mus, London; and others. *Comn:* Ed 100 woodcuts, Silvermine Guild Art, Silvermine Coll Art, 66. *Exhib:* Grad Theological Union, Berkeley, Calif, 2000; Unique Handmade Books, San Francisco Pub Libr, 2001; The Spirit of Handmade Prints, Triton Mus Art, Santa Clara, Calif, 2001; The Learning Curve, Ctr for the Book, San Francisco, 2001; 1st Ann Contemp Graphics Exhib, Galeria Nat, San Jose, 2002; Imagining the Book, Libr of Alexandria, Egypt, 2002; Imagining the Book 2, Libr of Alexandria, Egypt, 2005; Solo Exhibs: Meridian Gallery, San Francisco, 1991; Global Focus, Beijing, China, 1997; Pequenos Historias Mus Art & Design, San Jose, Costa Rica Sonoma State Univ, Sonoma, Calif, 1996; Graduate Theological Union, Berkeley, Calif, 2000; and others; Group Exhibs: The Learning Curve Center for the Book, San Francisco, 2000; Where or When Wustum Mus Art, Racine, Wis, 2000; The Spirit of Handmade Prints, Triton Mus Art, Santa Clara, Calif, 2001; Unique Handmade Books, San Francisco Pub Libr, 2002; Imagining the Book, Libr Alexandria, Egypt, 2002; Elements 1, San Francisco Presidio, 2004; Imagining the Book 2, Library of Alexandria, Egypt, 2005; Out of a Box, Sebastopol Ctr Arts, Sebastopol, Calif, 2009; Text'-o-&-Figura, Meridian Gallery, San Francisco, 2010. *Pos:* Asst art ed, Walt Disney Prods, Inc, 56-59; ed filmstrip prep from children's lit, Weston Woods Studios, Conn, 60; bd dir, Appletree Etchers, Inc, 72-74; artist-in-residence, Women's Graphics Ctr, Los Angeles & Nat Endowment Arts, 83 & Ragdale Found, Lake Forest, Ill, 90; panelists, Book Arts Conf & Exhib, San Francisco, 91; Invited lectr, Am Libr, Paris, 96; Invited auth & illus, Rabat Am Sch, Morocco. *Teaching:* Art for Children, Silvermine Col Art, 66-68 & Martin Luther King, Jr Ctr, San Mateo, 68-70; woodblock printmaking, San Mateo Adult Educ, 70, illus children's lit, 74-75 & teaching, 76-78; guest lectr, Bakersfield Col, Calif, 77, Univ Ky, 80 & Mills Col, Oakland, Calif, 86 & Sonoma State Univ, 92; Advisor, Grad Studies Book Arts, Acad Art Col, San Francisco, 96. *Awards:* San Francisco Art Festival Award, Palo Alto Cult Ctr, 77; Grant, Nat Endowment Arts & Women's Graphic Ctr Bk Prod, 82; Peninsula Community Found Grant, Burlingame, Calif, 87; Artist-in-Residence, Ragdale Found, Lake Forest, Ill, 90. *Bibliog:* Design without Clients, Fortune Mag, 75; TV interview, Festival of Arts, San Carlos, Calif, 75. *Mem:* Calif Soc Printmakers; Appletree Etchers, Inc; Ctr Bk Arts, NY; Pac Ctr Bk Arts. *Media:* Oil Based Paint, Ink; Collage, Metals. *Publ:* Illusr, Emanuel Thayer's, Climbing Sun - The Story of a Hopi Indian Boy, Dodd, Mead, 80; auth & illusr, Whale in the Sky, EP Dutton, 82; coauth & illusr, Who Found America, 83 & Feast of Thanksgiving, 84, Children's Press; auth & illusr, A Journey to Paradise, Henry Holt, 90, Arabic translation, 2005; Bravo! Brava! A Night at the Opera, Oxford Univ Press, 2001; The Valkyrie: A Warrir Maiden's Story, Kastle Press, 2009. *Mailing Add:* 1041 La Cuesta Rd Hillsborough CA 94010

SIBONY, GEDI
SCULPTOR
b NYC, 1973. *Study:* Brown Univ, BA, 1995; Student, Skowhegan Sch Painting & Sculpture, Maine, 1999; Columbia Univ, MFA, 2000. *Exhib:* Two Person Show, Gallery 16, San Francisco, 1998; Superimposition, Caren Golden Fine Art, New York, 2001; Silent Takeover, Staedtische Gallerie, Baden, Switz, 2002; One Fine Day, Block Gallery, Sydney, Australia, 2003; Breaking Ground, White Columns, NYC, 2003; Playpen: Selections Summer, The Drawing Center, NYC, 2004; Slouching Towards Bethlehem, The Project, NYC, 2004; Floorplay, Brooklyn War Mem, 2004; The Qualities Depend Upon Other Qualities, 2004; Art Rev 25, Philips De Pury, NYC, 2005; Greener Pastures Contemp Art, Toronto, Can, 2005; Make it Now, The Sculpture Center, NY, 2005; Walls'n Things, Nicole Klagsbrun Gallery, NYC, 2005; Some Places Exist, London, 2005; The Wrong Gallery, NYC, 2005; Poetry in the

Backyard, Galerie Art: Concept, Paris, 2006; Whitney Biennial: Day for Night, Witney Mus Am Art, 2006. *Awards:* Grantee, Rema Hort Mann Found, 2004; Willard L Metcalf Award in Art, Am Acad Arts and Letters, 2006; Louis Comfort Tiffany Found Grant, 2009. *Mailing Add:* Green Naftali Gallery 508 W 26th St 8th Fl New York NY 10001

SICKLER, MICHAEL ALLAN
PAINTER, COLLAGE ARTIST
b Milwaukee, Wis, Aug 11, 1945. *Study:* Layton Sch Art, Milwaukee, Wis, BFA, 70; Univ Wis-Milwaukee, MFA, 73. *Work:* Univ Potsdam, NY; Layton Sch Art, Milwaukee, Wis; Keith Corp, Salmon Brook, Conn; Oswego State Univ, NY; Syracuse Univ, NY, 2010; and over 100 pvt collections in US & Eng. *Comn:* Painting-mural, Keith Corp, Glastonbury, Conn, 84; 2 paintings, Birnbaum & Assoc, Syracuse, NY, 85; painting, comn by Sheraton Hotel, Liverpool, NY, 86; 2 covers, Comstock Review, winter/spring, 2006. *Exhib:* Regional, 76 & New Paintings, 77, Everson Mus, Syracuse, NY; 42nd Ann, Munson-Williams-Proctor, Utica, NY, 79; Recent Paintings, Univ London, Ctr Related Arts, Eng, 83; Six Syracuse Painters, Skidmore Col, Saratoga, NY, 85; Retrospective: John Mulroy Civic Ctr, Syracuse, NY, 6/2000; Edgewood Gallery, Syracuse, NY, 2007; Drawing on Purpose, Schweinfurth Mus, Auburn, NY, 2007; Collage & Assemblage, Schweinfurth Mus, NY, 2009; Palitz Gallery, Lubin House, Syracuse, Univ, NY, 2010; Limestone Gallery, 2011; Schwalbach Gallery, Univ Wisc, Baraboo, 2012; Edgewood Gallery, Syracuse, NY, 2013; Kirkland Art Ctr, 2014; James Schwalbach Gallery, 2013; Kirkland Art Ctr, 2014. *Collection Arranged:* Co-cur, Drawing Lives Exhibition, Lowe Gallery, Syracuse Univ, 2005; cur, Collage & Exhib, Joseph Scala Gallery, New Woodstock, NY, 2006, Collage-plus, 2007; Joseph Scala Gallery, 2005. *Pos:* editor, Comstock Review; Syracuse Poet Laureate Coun, Ted Kooser Project, 2006; panel moderator, Clement Greenberg: Memorial Exhib, Lowe Gallery, Syracuse Univ. *Teaching:* Assoc prof studio art & art hist, Syracuse Univ, NY, prof emer. *Awards:* First Prize, WCNY Invitational, PBS Sta, NY, 83; Golden Poet Award, World Poetry Press, 85-88; 3rd Place Defined Providence J Nat Poetry; Faculty Develop Grant, Syracuse Univ, 2005-2006; First Prize, League Amer Penwomen (Syr chapter) Poetry. *Bibliog:* He Draws Plein-air, Milwaukee Journ, 74; Bev Leesman (interview), 5 Yr New Times, 96; Carmen Livingston (auth), Artist Draws on Various Styles, Auburn Citizen, 4/96; Katherine Rushworth (auth), Snapshot of An Artist, Herald Am Stars, 4/2000. *Mem:* Am Acad Poets. *Media:* Acrylic on Canvas, Watercolor, Collage. *Specialty:* all media. *Interests:* Indian pottery, rugs, painting, drawing, ceramic & glass. *Collection:* Sleep Drawings. *Publ:* Poetry, Salt Hill J, Syracuse Univ, 94; contribr, Defined Providence J, Ia, 95-96; Int Asheville Poetry Rev, 96-2004; Red Brick Rev, 96; Controlled Burn, poetry mag, 97; Comstock Review, poetry mag, 2000-2014; Chapbook, Stereopticon, 2002; Threshold Press, Cathy Gibbons (ed); Eye of Language, Finishing Line Press, Georgetown, Ky, 2009; Pudding House, Greatest Hits, Chap Book, 2004-2005; Reviews: Nebo, Arqestes, Gihon River, Illya's Honey, Alehouse, Finishing Line Press, 2012, 2013, 2014. *Dealer:* Edgewood Gallery Syracuse NY

SIDEMAN, CAROL K
PAINTER
b Oakland, Calif, Feb 18, 1925. *Study:* UC Berkeley, Calif, BA, 47; UC Berkeley (Erle Loran) Calif, Secondary Cred, 48; Grad Sch, Coll Arts & Crafts (Harry Krell), 59. *Work:* Kaiser Permanente, Hospitals & Exec Offices, Oakland, Vallejo, CA; Glenborough Realtors, Corp Offices throughout US. *Exhib:* Collector's Gallery, Oakland Mus, Calif, 65-05; Annual Marin Soc Artists, Frances Young Gallery, Ross, Calif, 67; Featured Artist, OAA, Keith Gallery, St Mary's Col, Moraga, Calif, 71; California State Fair, Sacramento, Calif; Arts for the Parks, US Parks (Nat), Jackson Hole, WY. *Teaching:* Teacher art, Oakland PS, 49-52; teaching asst architectural rendering. *Awards:* First place, Marin Annual, Marin Soc Artists, 67; first place oils-figure, Alameda Co Fair, 75; first place, Kaiser Gallery Show, Oakland Art Asn, 2000. *Bibliog:* Kay Alexander (auth), Take 5 Art Prints-Teacher's Guide, Crystal Productions, 92-2005; Stacy Trevenson (auth), Art Reporter, Half Moon Bay Review, 2003. *Mem:* Oakland Art Asn, exhib coordr, 2003-2004; Marin Soc Artists, juror for numerous shows; Valley Art. *Media:* Oil, Watercolor. *Publ:* Prize Winning Art, Book IV, Allied Publ, 67; Art Education Resources, Take 5 Art Prints, Crystal Productions, 95-2005. *Dealer:* Sue Grim Langert, Langert Publishing, 300 Main St, Half Moon Bay, CA, 94019

SIDNER, ROBERT BROWN
DIRECTOR
Study: St Meinrad Coll, Ind, BA (English); Gregorian Univ, Rome, STB; Notre Dame Univ, Ind, MA (Liturgy). *Pos:* Assoc pastor, Ohio, 1969-1977; pastor, St John's Church, Delphos, Ohio, 1981-1985, St Charles Church, Lima, 1985-1991; owner & dir, Cable Gallery, San Diego, 1991-1992; membership coord, Mingei Int Mus, 1993-1994, dir pub relations, 1994-1996, asst dir, 1996-2005, acting dir, 2005-2006, dir, 2006-. *Teaching:* asst prof, dir formation, St Meinrad Coll, 1977-1981. *Mem:* San Diego/Tijuana Japan Soc; pres, Nat Fedn Spiritual Dirs, 1977-1981. *Mailing Add:* Mingei International Museum 1439 El Prado San Diego CA 92101

SIEG, ROBERT LAWRENCE
SCULPTOR, EDUCATOR
b Cement, Okla, 1938. *Study:* Cent State Univ, Okla, BA, 63; Inst Allende, Univ de Guanajuato, MFA, 68. *Work:* Ark Arts Ctr, Little Rock; Okla Art Ctr, Oklahoma City; Mus Art, Univ Okla, Norman; Okla Arts & Humanities Coun Collection, Oklahoma City. *Exhib:* Inter-D Exhib, McAllen Int Mus, Tex; Midwest Biennial Joslyn Art Mus, Omaha, Nebr; Monroe Ann, Masur Mus Art, La; Delta Art Exhib, Ark Art Ctr; Goddard Arts Ctr, Okla, 78; Since Statehood: Twelve Oklahoma Artists, Oklahoma City Art Mus, 96. *Teaching:* Asst prof art, E Cent Okla State Univ, 66-86, chmn art dept, 90-2000, retired. *Awards:* Sculpture Award, 15th Mid-Am, Nelson Gallery Art, Kansas City, 65; Inter-Am Craft Alliance Award, McAllen Int Mus, Tex, 70; Purchase Award, Toys Designed by Artists, Ark Art Ctr, 74. *Bibliog:* BJ Smith (auth), Features artist, Cimarron Rev, 4/73. *Mem:* Individual Artists of Okla. *Media:* Wood, Metal. *Mailing Add:* 20669 County Rd #3 Dr Stonewall OK 74871

SIEGEL, BARBARA
PAINTER, ARCHITECT
b Baltimore, Md, Oct 26, 1959. *Study:* Univ Wis, with Don Reitz, BA, 80; Univ Md, MArch, 85; Corcoran Gallery Sch Art, with Bert Schmutzhart and F L Wall, 85-92, 2008; studied with Joyce Jewell, Teach Artist Inst, Montgomery Coll, 2008; American Univ, 2012. *Comn:* Children's Nat Med Ctr, Washington, DC; Children's Inn, NIH. *Exhib:* Solo exhibs include Cafe Zino, Bethesda, Md, 95, Bethesda Regional Libr, 95, 97, 98, AIR Gallery 97, 2007, New Horizons Gallery, 98, 2000, Barnes and Noble, Bethesda, Md, 99; group exhibs include Then and Now: Twenty Yrs of A Salon, 98; Elements, Wilson Ctr Gallery, 99; Sweet and Sour, Wilson Ctr Gallery, 2000; Room with a View, Bethesda Artspace, 2000; Suburbanscape, Anne Arundel Community Col, 2000; Imaginary Landscapes, Irvine Nature Center, 2011. *Pos:* graphic recorder, Look 2 Listen. *Awards:* Bethesda Row Arts Festival, 98; Individual Artists Award, Md State Arts Coun, 2000-; Teaching Artist Inst Grant, 2008. *Mem:* Int Forum of Visual Practitioners. *Media:* Monoprint, Pastel. *Specialty:* Graphic Recording. *Interests:* Creativity Training. *Mailing Add:* 7107 Exfair Rd Bethesda MD 20814

SIEGEL, FRAN
PAINTER
b Mar 10, 1960. *Study:* Tyler Sch Art, Temple Univ, BFA (magna cum laude), 82; Yale Univ Sch Art, MFA, 87. *Work:* Paine Webber; Brown Found; ITT Sheraton; Caddell & Conwell Found Arts; Alta Light Productions; US Embassies. *Comn:* W Hollywood Pub Art. *Exhib:* Solo exhibs, Genovese Gallery, Boston, Mass, 92, 94, 97 & 2005, Margaret Thatcher Projs, NY, 2004 & 2006 & Bank Gallery, Los Angeles, Calif, 2005; Mus Szuki; Lodz, Poland; Cuenca Bienal, US Rep, Ecuador, 2007. *Teaching:* Painting & Drawing, Calif State Univ, Long Beach, assoc prof. *Awards:* Yaddo, 95, 2009; Albee Found, 97; ED Found, 97; City Los Angeles Individual Artist Fel, 2005-2006. *Bibliog:* Articles In: Artweek, 5/85, Boston Herald, 3/94, Art New Eng, 6-10/94 & rev, 5/97, Los Angeles Times, 10/99 & Art in Am, 2001 & 2007. *Mem:* CAA, Asn Colour Int. *Media:* Drawing, Installation. *Publ:* Light/Shadow, Art Mus Arad, Romania; Art in Am, 2001; Sculpture Mag, 2001; NY Times, 2001. *Dealer:* Genovese Gallery Boston MA; Margaret Thatcher Projects New York NY

SIEGESMUND, RICHARD
EDUCATOR
b Jan 10, 1951. *Study:* Trinity Col, Hartford, Conn, BA, 73; Univ Hawaii, Manoa, Honolulu, Hawaii, grad study, 73-75; Fel Arts Mgt, Visual Arts Prog, Nat Endowment Arts, Washington, DC, 81, Stanford Univ, MA 95, PhD, 2000. *Pos:* assoc dir, Wash Proj Arts, 86-89; dir, The Fabric Workshop, Philadelphia, Pa, 89-90, deputy dir, San Francisco Mus Mod Art, 91-92. *Teaching:* Asst, Stanford Univ, 95-98; asst prof, Art Ed, Univ Georgia, 2001-2007, assoc prof, 2007-2011; assoc prof, N Ill Univ, 2012-. *Awards:* Fulbright Fel, 2010. *Mem:* Nat Art Educ Asn; Am Educ Res Asn. *Res:* cognition and aesthetic theory, assessment. *Publ:* Roulledge 2008; book chapters & articles

SIEMS, ANNE
PAINTER
b Berlin, Ger, Feb 16, 1965. *Study:* Hochschule der Kunste, Berlin, Ger, MFA, 91. *Work:* Boise Art Mus, Idaho; Am Airlines, Seattle, Wash; Hallmark Collection, NY; Microsoft Collection, Redmond, Wash; Ark Art Ctr, Little Rock. *Comn:* Spiral Screen, Ore Coll Arts & Crafts, 95. *Exhib:* NW Juried Art Exhib, Cheney Cowles Mus, Spokane, Wash, 92; Figure 7, Bellevue Art Mus, Wash, 92; solo exhibs, Calif State Univ Art Gallery, San Bernardino, 95; Seventh Nat Juried Exhib, Viridian, NY, 96; Botanical Vision, Boise Art Mus, Idaho, 96; Out of Eden, Kemper Mus Contemp Art, Kansas City, Mo, 97; Botanically Inspired, Holter Mus Art, Helena, Mont, 97; Since 1907, Ore Coll Art & Craft, Portland, 97. *Teaching:* Ore Col Art & Craft, Portland, 97. *Awards:* First Prize Drawing, Artquake, Portland, Ore, 94; Alice Rooney NW Women Artist Stipend, Pilchuck Glan Sch, 95; Ore Coll Arts & Crafts 90th Anniversary Award, 97. *Bibliog:* Michael Lawrence (auth), Visions, 94; Tracy Smith (auth), Anne Siems at PDG, Art Am, 96. *Mem:* Artista Trust. *Media:* Beeswax, Acrylic on Paper. *Dealer:* Grover Thurston Gallery 309 Occidental Ave S Seattle WA 98104. *Mailing Add:* 6548 21st Ave NW Seattle WA 98117

SIENA, JAMES
PAINTER
b Oceanside, Calif, Oct 28, 1957. *Study:* Cornell Univ, BFA, 79. *Work:* San Francisco Mus Mod Art, Calif; Whitney Mus Am Art, NY, NY; Mus Modern Art, NYC; Metrop Mus Art, New York; Mus Fine Arts, Boston; Hammer Mus, Univ Calif Los Angeles, Calif. *Exhib:* San Francisco Art Institute, 2003; invited exhibitor Whitney Mus Art, 2004; Pace Wildenstein, New York, 2005-06, 2008; Daniel Weinberg, Los Angeles, Calif, 2007, 2010; Atlantic Ctr Arts, New Smyrna Beach, Fla, 2009; Johnson Mus Art, Cornell Univ, Ithaca, NY, 2010; Pace Prints, NY, 2011, Pace Gallery, 2011. *Teaching:* adj prof art, Va Commonwealth Univ, Richmond, 2000, 2002; adj prof art, San Francisco Art Inst, 2002; vis prof, New School, NYC, 2003; adj prof art, Sch Visual Arts, New York, 2008-09; adj prof art, Cooper Union Sch Art, New York, 2008-09. *Awards:* fel in painting NY Found for the Arts, 95; Tiffany Award, Louis Comfort Tiffany Found, 99; Acad Award in Painting, invitational, Am Acad Arts & Letters, 2000. *Bibliog:* Amy Michael (auth), James Siena at Cristinerose Gallery, Art in Am, 11/98; Goings on About Town/Galleries-Chelsea: James Siena at Gorney Bravin - Lee, The New Yorker, 10/29/2001; Ken Johnson (auth), Art in Review: James Siena at Gorney Bravin - Lee, NY Times, 10/26/2001; David Frankel (auth), Reviews: James Siena at Gorney Bravin - Lee, Artforum, 1/2001; Joe Fyfe (auth), Strange Loops, Art on Paper, Jan-Feb, 2003; Roberta Smith (auth), Art in Review, NY Times, 1/2006; Sarah Schmerler (auth), The Compulsive Line, Art on Paper, 7/2006; David Cohen (auth), Falling, Going, Following, and Breathing, His Own Rules, The NY Sun, 3/2008. *Mem:* Corp of Yaddo, Saratoga Springs, New York. *Dealer:* The Pace Gallery 32 East 57th ST New York NY 10022; Pace Wildenstein, New York

SIFF, MARLENE IDA
PAINTER, SCULPTOR

b New York City. *Study:* Hunter Coll, BA, 57. *Work:* B'nai B'rith Klutznick Nat Jewish Mus, Washington, DC; corp collections incl, Dial Corp, Ariz, Katzen Investments, Fla, Fairfield First Bank and Trust co, Conn, Cannon Mills, New York, J C Penney, NY, Stauffer Chemical, Conn, Easter Seal Found, NY, Lenox, Inc, NJ, Alcide Corp, Conn, and many more. *Exhib:* Cheesebrough Pond's Gallery, Westport Arts Ctr, Conn, 84-87, 91, 95; solo exhibs, David Segal Gallery, New York City, 87, Conn Pub Television Gallery, Hartford, 87, Paul Mellon Art Ctr, Choate Rosemary Hall, Wallingford, Conn, 89, Conn Nat Bank Hdqs, Norwalk, 90, Michael Stone Collection, Washington, DC, 92, Bergdorf Goodman Men, New York City, 93, Joel Kessler fine Art, Miami Beach, Fla, 94, Park Place, Stamford, Conn, 95, Westport Arts Ctr, 95, Mitchells, Westport, Conn, 98, NIH, Bethesda, Md, 99, Durst Lobby Gallery, New York, 99, Rosenthal Gallery at Rich Forum, Stamford, Conn, 2005, Walter Wickiser Gallery, New York City, 2007, Elements of Peace, Walsh Art Gallery, Fairfield Univ, Conn, 2012; Conn State Capital Bldg, 90; Aldrich Mus, Ridgefield, Conn, 91-92; Galleri Seven, Danbury, Conn, 91; Funding Ctr, Alexandria, Va, 92-93; Michael Stone Collection, Washington, DC, 92-93; Am Soc Interior Designers Nat Hdqs, Washington, DC, 92-93; Joel Kessler Fine Arts, Miami Beach, 93-94; Wave Gallery, New Canaan, Conn, 93-94; Galerie Début, Nagoya, Japan, 93-94; Int Cancer Alliance, Nat Inst Health, Bethesda, Md, 93; Boston Corp Art, 94; Art Miami Int Expos, 94; Share Gallery, Funibashi Japan, 95; Reece Gallery, New York City, 95; Whitney Gallery, Westport, Conn, 96; B'nai B'rith Klutznick Nat Jewish Mus, Washington, DC, 98; Studio Tour, Westport Arts Ctr, 2000; Kenneth Raymond Gallery, Boca Raton, Fla, 2001-06; River Road Gallery, Wilton, Conn, 2002-05; Hall-Brooke Behavioral Health Services Art Show, Westport, Conn, 2004; Bendheim Gallery, Greenwich, Conn, 2007; Toronto Int Art Fair, Can, 2007; Art Now Fair, Miami Beach, Fla, 2007; The Barnum Mus, Bridgeport, Conn, 2008; Walter Wickiser Gallery, New York, 2008; The Lichtenstein Ctr Arts, Pittsfield, Mass, 2008; Toronto Int Art Fair, Can, 2008; Calvin Charles Gallery, Scottsdale, Ariz, 2008, 2009; Nat Sept 11th Mem Mus, Artists Registry Visual Art Gallery, 2009; Walter Wickiser Gallery, New York, 2009, 2010; Fairfield Co Branch, Conn, 2010; Westport Arts Ctr, Conn, 2010; Upstream People Gallery, Omaha, Nebr, 2010, 2011, 2012; Kraft Ctr, Columbia Univ, NY, 2011; Fairfield Public Lib, Bruce S Kershner Gallery, Fairfield, Conn, 2011; Art About Town, Westport, Conn, 2011; ArtsWestchester, White Plains, NY, 2011; Housatonic Mus Art, Bridgeport, 2011; Katonah Mus Art, Katonah, NY, 2012; Bendheim Gallery, Greenwich, Conn, 2012; 14th Ann Contemporary Exhib, Upstream, Gallery, Greenwich, Conn, 2012; Local Color, Defying Boudareis, Flinn Gallery, Greenwich, Conn, 2012; Honoring Women's Rights: Visual Voices Together, Nat Steinbeck Ctr Mus, Salinas, Calif, 2012; Art Takes Times Square, The Times Square Billboard Premier Event, NY, 2012; Total Recall, Katonah Mus Art, Silvermine Arts Ctr, New Canaan, Conn, 2012. *Pos:* Freelance interior designer, Westport, Conn, 66-70; designer, Varo Inertial Products, Trumball, Conn, 70, signature collections, JP Stevens & Co, Inc, NY, 74-78, JC Penny Co, 78, CR Gibson Co, Norwalk, Conn, 80; art adv coun, Herbert F Johnson Mus Art Cornell Univ, Ithaca, NY. *Teaching:* Teacher, Stewart Manor Sch System, NY, 57-59, Teaneck Sch System, NJ, 59-60. *Awards:* Award for creating the most beautiful working environ in an indust facility in lower Conn, Lower Conn Manufacturers Asn, 70; Special Recognition, 13th Ann Painting, Drawing, Photography, and Print Exhib, 2011, 14th Ann Contemporary Exhib, Upstream People Gallery, 2012. *Bibliog:* Westport News, 10/18/89 & 10/19/90; NY Times, Conn Weekly, 12/16/90; American Society of Interior Designers Report, 9-10/93; Minuteman, 7/6/95; Why Art? Making a House a Home, The Homesteader, 1/96; The Advocate & Greenwich Time, 5/25/97; The Jewish Calendar, Nat Jewish Mus, 4/5/98-99; Mother's Day Art Show at Hall-Brooke, 4/30/2004 & Marlene Siff Work on View in Stamford, 10/12/2005, Westport News; Edward Lucie-Smith (auth), catalog essay. *Mem:* Anti Defamation League; Nat Coun Jewish Women; Kappa Pi. *Media:* Acrylic on linen, Watercolor; Oil, Pastel. *Mailing Add:* 15 Broadview Rd Westport CT 06880

SIGAL, LISA
PAINTER

b Philadelphia, Pa, 1962. *Study:* Temple Univ, Tyler Sch Art, BFA, 1985; Skowhegan Sch Art, ME, 1986; Yale Univ Sch Art, MFA (painting), 1989. *Comn:* Fed Reserve Bank, Atlanta, 2003. *Exhib:* Solo exhibs include White Columns Gallery, New York, 2000, Aldrich Mus, Conn, 2005, Frederieke Taylor Gallery, New York, 2001, 2004, 2005, 2007; Group exhibs include Outer Boroughs, White Columns, NY, 1999, Fast Forward, 2003; Summer Time, Tricia Collins Gallery, NY, 2000; Conversation Exhib, Art Resources Transfer, NY, 2000; Happy Medium, Clementine Gallery, NY, 2004; Orpheus Selection, PS 1/ Mus Modern Art, Long Island City, NY, 2007; Whitney Biennial, Whitney Mus Am Art, 2008; Museum as HUB: Six Degrees, New Mus, New York, 2008. *Awards:* Provincetown Fine Arts Work Ctr, 1988; Yaddo Fel, 1991; Elizabeth Found for Arts Grant, 1998; Joan Mitchell Found Grant, 1998; Ballinglen Arts Found Fel, Ireland, 1999; New York Found for the Arts Grant, 2002; Headlands Ctr for the Arts, San Francisco, 2004

SIGAL-IBSEN, ROSE
CALLIGRAPHER, PAINTER

b Bucharest, Romania, Aug 22; US citizen. *Study:* Fashion Inst Technol, 78; Parson Sch Design, 85-86; Koho Sch of Sumi-E, 79-90; Zhejiang Acad Fine Arts, China, 90. *Work:* NY Pub Libr; Manhattan Savings Bank, New York; Steinhardt Conservatory, Brooklyn Botanical Garden; Nat Mus Women in Arts, Washington DC; Chemical Bank, New York; Mobile Mus Art, Ala; Palm Beach State Coll; Denver Hosp; Freeman Ctr Asian Studies, Wesleyan Univ. *Exhib:* Solo exhibs, China-Gallery Weizhi Schubert, Hanover, Ger, 91, Manhattan Savings Bank, New York, 93-94, Roumanian Cult Found, Bucharest, 98, World Fine Art Gallery, New York, 98, NY Pub Libr & Berkeley Coll Gallery, 2006; China Nat Acad Fine Arts, Hangzhou, 94; group exhibs, Gallery Korea, New York City, 94, Golden West Coll, Huntington Beach, Calif, 95, Global Focus The Nat Mus of Women in the Arts, Washington, DC, 96, Seton Hall Univ, South Orange, NJ, 96, Conn 98 Int Contemp Calligraphy Exhibit, Weslyan Univ, Middletown, Conn, 98, JACCC, Los Angeles, 99, Art of Ink in Am (traveling exhib), Newark Mus, Nat Taiwan Art Educ Inst, Paris & Korea, 2000, 2004-2005 & 2007-; Fine Arts Gallery, Huntington Beach, Calif, 95; Seaton Hall Gallery, S Orange, NJ, 96; Cork Gallery/Lincoln Ctr, New York, 98; Broome St Gallery, 99; Doizaki Gallery, 99; Contemp Art guild, Corg Gallery, 2003; Romanian Cult Ctr, New York, 2003; NY Artists Equity, Holiday Invitational Exhib, 2005; Am Soc Contemp Artists, 87th Ann Exhib, Broome St Gallery, 2005; JAA NY, Hammond Mus, 2005; Municipal Mus Fine Art, Osaka, Japan, 2009; Tokyo Metropolitan Art Mus, Tokyo, Japan, 2010; Kyoto Municipal Mus Art, Kyoto, Japan, 2010; Japanese Paintings & Calligraphy on Cotton Scrolls, Berkeley Gallery, New York, 2011; Interchurch Ctr, Treasure Room Gallery Scrolls, Japanese Painting and Caligraphy, 2012; Gallery of the Office, Manhatten Borough Pres Municipal Bldg, 2012. *Pos:* Cur, Metrop NY Chap of Sumi-E Soc, 90-, vpres, 90-. *Teaching:* Lectr, Taiwan Art Edn Ctr, 2000, Bronx Sch Sci, 99; Demo in Calligraphy, Asian Festival, 2009-2012. *Awards:* Manhattan Arts Award Cover Art Competition, New York, 92, 94-95 & 97; Tenth Japanese Int Calligraphy Exhib Award, New York, 96; Award of Excellence, Calligraphy Competition, Kampo Cult Ctr, New York, 96; Emily N Hatch Mem Award, Pen and Brush Inc, 98; Shoe Ming Chao Award, Nat Sumi-e Soc, 99, 2010, Hallie Hazen Mem Award, 2001, Yasutomo award, 2002, Mingchao award, 2003, Soc Am Frame Award, 2004, Nancy Rupp Mem award, 2006. *Mem:* Nat Mus Women in Arts; Artist Equity of NY; Am Soc Contemp Artists; Oriental Brushwork Soc Am; Genesis 21 Am-Romania Artists; The Oriental Brushwork Soc Am; Am Soc Contemp Artists (ASCA); Contemp Artists Guild. *Media:* Watercolor. *Collection:* Andrew Rasiej, J Newman, Gay Fallow, Ira Hall, Keneth Eichler, RMD/JBS, and many more. *Publ:* New Art Int, 50-51, 2001; New Art, 54-55, 2003 & 144-145, 2005 & 2008. *Mailing Add:* 1 Irving Pl #P22B New York NY 10003-9741

SIGALA, STEPHANIE CHILDS
LIBRARIAN, EDUCATOR

b Berkeley, Calif, Nov 1, 1947. *Study:* Univ Calif, Los Angeles, BA, 68, MA, 70; Univ Ill, MLS, 84. *Pos:* Slide cur, Univ Wisc, Milwaukee, 73-74; archit librn, Auburn Univ, 84-85; head librn, St Louis Art Mus, 85-2000, actg dir educ, 2000. *Teaching:* Instr art hist, Univ Wis, Whitewater, 71-73; asst prof, Ill State Univ, 78-83; adj prof libr sci, Univ Mo, 88-96; sr educ, St Louis Art Mus, 2001-. *Awards:* Kress Found Grant, 69; Fel, Univ Ill, 74-75. *Mem:* Art Libr Soc of NAm (chap pres, 88-90, exec bd, 94-96); Spec Libr Asn (chap dir, 89-90); Am Libr Asn. *Res:* Greek and Roman art; mus librarianship; history of the St Louis Art Mus. *Publ:* Auth, A Decade of Professional Literature for Slide Curators, VRA Bulletin, 85; Exhibition Catalogs on Exchange, Art Documentation, 88; Art of the Ancient World, St Louis Art Mus, 89; auth, The Museum Building: Inside and Out, St Louis Art Mus, 90; contribr, History of American Mass Market Magazines, Greenwood Press, 90. *Mailing Add:* 815 Brookside Dr Saint Louis MO 63122-1804

SIGG, ULI
COLLECTOR

Study: PhD, Univ Zurich Law Faculty. *Comn:* over 40. *Exhib:* Mahjong: Chinese Contemporary Art from the Sig Collection, Mus Fine Arts, Bern, Switzerland, 2005, Kunsthalle, Hamburg, Germany, 2006-2007, Mus Modern Art, Salzburg, Austria, 2007, Berkeley Art Mus, Pacific Film Archive, Univ Calif, Berkeley, 2008, Peabody Essex Mus, Salem/Boston, Mass, 2009; China Window, Chinese Contemporary Art from Canton, Sigg Collection, Mus Fine Arts, Bern, Switzerland, 2006; The Year of the Golden Pig, Contemporary Chinese Art from the Sig Collection, Lewis Glucksman Gallery, Cork, Ireland, 2007; Art from China, Collection Uli Sigg, Centro Cultural Banco do Brasil, Rio de Janeiro, Brazil, 2007; Red Aside, Contemporary Chinese Art from the Sigg Collection, Fundacio Joan Miro, Barcelona, Spain, 2008; Big Draft, Shanghai, Chinese Contemporary Art from the Sigg Collection, Mus Fine Arts, Bern, Switzerland, 2010-2011; Shansui: Poetry without Sound? Landscape in Chinese Contemporary Art, Mus Art Lucerne, Switzerland, 2011; Nat Portray Gallery, Canberra, 2012. *Pos:* With, Shindler Elevator co; Swiss amb to China, Mongolia & North Korea; vchmn, Ringier AG; founder, Chinese Contemp Art Awards, 1997; founder, Art Critic Award, 2007. *Awards:* Southern Mississippi College of Arts and Letters, Wall of Fame, 2004; Named one of Top 200 Collectors, ARTnews mag, 2009-13. *Bibliog:* James Panero (auth), Gallery Chronicle, The New Criterion, Vol. 29, No. 6, p. 57, 2011. *Mem:* Advisory Bd China Develop; Int Council New York MOMA; Int Advisory Council, Tate Gallery, London. *Collection:* Contemporary art, especially Chinese; donated 1450 works of Chicago Contemporary art to M+ Museum for Visual Culture, 2012. *Mailing Add:* Schloss 6216 Mauensee Switzerland

SIGUROARDOTTIR, KATRIN
INSTALLATION SCULPTOR

Exhib: Solo exhibs include Reykjavik Mus Art, Iceland, 2000, 2004, Gallaeria Maze, Torino, Italy, 2003, PS1 Contemp Art Ctr, New York, 2006, Greenberg Van Doren Gallery, New York, 2009, The Suburban, Chicago, Ill, 2010, Metrop Mus Art, New York, 2010; group exhibs, Models of Resistance, Globe, Overgaden, Copenhagen, Denmark, 2000; Confronting Nature, Corcoran Gallery, DC, 2001; Carriage House proj, Islip Art Mus, New York, 2002; Indoor/Outdoor, LIMN Gallery, San Francisco, 2003; Not to Scale, Dorsky Gallery, New York, 2003; Microwave 4, Cristinerose/Josee Bienvenu Gallery, New York, 2003; Troy Story, Hosfelt Gallery, San Francisco, Calif, 2004; Models and Prototypes, Kemper Art Mus, Wash Univ St Louis, Mo, 2006; Acting in Utopia, Landesgalerie Linz, Austria, 2007; Garden of Acclimation, Villa Arson, Nice, France, 2008; It's Not Your Fault, Luhring Augustine Gallery, New York, 2008; Automatic Cities, Mus Contemp Art San Diego, Calif, 2009; Otherworldly, Mus Art & Design, New york, 2011. *Teaching:* Rutgers Univ, NJ, 1994; Univ Uceland, 1998-2002; Oslo Nat Acad Arts, 2001-2002; Nat Acad Art, Reykjavik, Iceland, 1999-. *Awards:* Nat Artist Fel, Icelandic Dept Cult, 1997, 2000; Residency, Nordic Com Art & Design, Norway, 1999, 2001; G Kristinsdottir Mem Award, Icelandic Dept Cult, 2000; Finalist, Carnegie Art Award, Icelandic Dept Cult, 2002; Rema Hort Found Grant, New York, 2005; Louis Comfort Tiffany Biennial Award,

2005; Nat Artist Fel, Icelandic Dept Cult, 2005, 2007. *Bibliog:* Russ Sabine & Gregory Volk (auths), The Force, NY Arts Internat, Vol 7, 2002; Eva Heisler (auth), Place Enfolded, Site Unfolded, NY Arts Mag, 2004; Ken Johnson (auth), Exceeding Paint/Expanding Paint, New York Times, July 5, 2005; Going on About Town, The New Yorker, 2006; Kristin Lentini (auth), It's Not Your Fault, Art Papers, 2008; Rachel Wolff, Turning OVer a New Leaf, Artnews, April 2009; Ken Johnson, Period Rooms Take on a Modern Gloss, New York Times, 2010

SIKANDER, SHAHZIA
PAINTER
b Lahore, Pakistan, 1969. *Study:* Nat Coll Arts, Lahore, Pakistan, BFA, 92; Rhode Island Sch Design, Providence, MFA, 95. *Exhib:* Solo exhibs, Pakistan Embassy, Washington, DC, 93, Veil: In Their Minds and on Our Heads, Rhode Island Sch Design, Providence, 94, Introduction 96, Barbara Davis Gallery, Houston, 96, Miniatures and Murals, Deitch Proj, NY, 97, Renaissance Soc, Univ Chicago, 98, Kemper Mus Contemp Art & Design, Kansas City, Mo, 98-99, Hishorn Mus, Washington, DC, 99, Acts of Balance, Whitney Mus, Phillip Morris Br, NY, 2000, The Renaissance Soc at the Univ of Chicago (catalog), 2001, Brent Sikeema, New York City, 2003, Aldrich Contemp Art Mus, Conn, 2004, Miami Art Mus, Florida, 2005-06, Sikkema Jenkins & Co, NY, 2006 & 2009, Mus of Contemp Art, Sydney, Australia, 2007-08, IKON Gallery, Birmingham, 2008, Cooper-Hewitt, Nat Design Mus, NY, 2009, San Francisco Art Inst, Walter and McBean Galleries, 2011; Biennial Exhib (auth, catalog), Whitney Mus Am Art, NY, 97; Out of India (auth, catalog), Queens Mus Art, Flushing Meadows, NY, 97; On the Wall, Forum Contemp Art, St Louis, Mo, 98; I love NY (auth, catalog), Ludwig Mus, Austria, 98; Pop Surrealism (auth, catalog), Aldrich Mus Contemp Art, Conn, 98; Cinco Continentes y una Ciudad, Museo de Ciudad de Mexico (catalog), Mexico City, 99; Negotiating Small Truths, The Blanton Mus of Art, Austin, Tex, 99; Art-Worlds in Dialogue, Ludwig Mus (catalog), Koln, Ger, 99; Third Asia-Pacific Triennial of Contemp Art (catalog), Brisbane, Australia, 99; The Am Century, Whitney Mus (catalog), NY, 99; Greater New York, PSI, in collaboration with MOMA, Queens, NY, 2000; 00, Barbara Gladstone Gallery (catalog), NY, 2000; New Works: 01.1 Rivane Neuenschwander, Shahzia Sikander, Tony Villejo, Art Pace, San Antonio, Tex, 2001; Elusive Paradise, Nat Gallery of Can, Ottawa, Ont, 2001; Expanding Tradition, Deutsche Bank Lobby Gallery, NY, 2001; ARS 01, Mus of Contemp Art, Kiasma, Helsinki, 2001; Conversations with Traditions, Asia Soc, NY, 2001; Threads of Vision: Toward a New Feminine Poetics, Cleveland Ctr for Contemp Art, Ohio, 2001; Mus Mod Art, 02, 05; Weatherspoon Art Mus, Greensboro, NC, 02-03; Fabric Workshop and Mus, Phila, Pa, 06; Scottsdale Mus of Contemp Art, 2007-08; The Big Bang, Museo Carlo Bilotti, Rome, Italy, 2008; Moving Perspectives: Shahzia Sikander and Sun Xun, Sackler Gallery, The Smithsonian, DC, 2009. *Pos:* co-cur The Stroke, an overview of contemp painting, Exit Art, 5/1-7/2, 99. *Awards:* Shakir Ali Award/Kipling Award, Nat Coll Arts, Lahore, 93; Louis Comfort Tiffany Found Award, 97; Joan Mitchell Award, 98-99; South Asian Women's Creative Collective Achievement Award, 99; MacArthur Fellow, John D and Catherine T MacArthur Found, 2006; Performing and Visual Arts Achiever of the Yr award, South Asian Excellence Awards, 2008; Inaugural Rockefeller Found Bellagio Center Creative Arts Fellowship, 2009. *Bibliog:* Thomas McEvilley (auth), Tracking the Indian Diaspora, Art Am, 74-79, 10/97; Edward Gomez (auth), Past is present, Art & Antiques, 60-66, 12/98; Phoebe Hoban (auth), The Mod Squad, NY Mag, 30-37, 1/11/99; Germaine Gomez-Haro (auth), Five Continents and a City-Museo de Ciudad de Mexico, Art Nexus, 8-10, 99; Francine Prose (auth), The Gallery: The Artist as Curator, The Wall St Jour, 5/20/99; Homi Bhabha (auth), Miniaturizing Modernity, Public Culture, Winter 99; Homi Bhabha (auth), Shahzia Sikander, a Happy dislocation, Elaine Kim and Margo Machida (eds), Fresh Talk: Daring Gazes, Univ of Calif Press, 99; Edith Newhall (auth), Installation, New York Mag, 4/24/2000; Holland Cotter (auth), Shahzia Sikander, Acts of Balance, The NY Times, 6/9/2000; Franklin Sirmans (auth), Shahzia Sikander, Acts of Balance, Time Out, 6/15/2000; Jonathan Goodman, Shahzia Sikander, Art Asia Pacific, 2001; Harriet Zinnes (auth), Projects 70, NY Arts, 1/2001; Jerry Saltz (auth), Good on Paper, The Village Voice, 57, 10-11/2002; The New Yorker, 1/27/2003; and many others. *Mem:* Nat Acad. *Mailing Add:* c/o Deitch Projs 76 Grand St New York NY 10013

SILBERSTEIN-STORFER, MURIEL ROSOFF
ART EDUCATOR, INSTRUCTOR
b Brooklyn, NY. *Study:* Carnegie-Mellon Sch Fine Arts, Drama Dept, BFA (scene design & acting), 44. *Comn:* Prog drawings, Philadelphia Symphony Orch Children's Concerts, 49; murals & other projs, Mt Sinai Hosp & West Philadelphia Psychiat Hosp. *Exhib:* Jewish Community Ctr Group Show, 71-72; solo exhibs, Panoras Gallery, NY, 72, Pacem in Terris Gallery, NY, 75 & Gallery 84, 78 & 83. *Pos:* co tech dir & co scene designer, Pittsburgh Playhouse, 44-46; interior display designer, var Pittsburgh Dept Stores, 46-47; art educ consult, Staten Island Ment Health Schs, Head Start, Staten Island Community Col Mus Mod Art, Metrop Mus Art & others; founder & creative dir, Doing Art Together, Inc, 82; art ed adv bd, Binney Smith Inc, 86-91. *Teaching:* Instr, Inst Mod Art, Mus Mod Art, New York, 63-70, Int Playgroups Art Workshops, New York, 70-71, Victor D'Amico Institute of Art, Amagansett, NY, Staten Island Community Col, 70-71, Metrop Mus Art, 72-; guest lectr art educ, var univs, cols & community education groups, New York, 67-. *Awards:* Art Commission Serv Award, Mayor of NY, 85; New York City Sch Art League Award, 95; Very Spec Arts Mayors Award, 96; and others; Art Educator Award New York City Art Teachers Asn & United Fedn Teachers, 2000. *Bibliog:* The Museologist, Vol 47, No 169, winter 85; NY Mag, 1/88; Art News, Vol 88, No 6, summer 89. *Mem:* New York Art Comn (comnr, 70-85); Metrop Mus Art (trustee, 71-77 & emer trustee, 77-); Assoc Art Comn City New York (pres, formerly); Snug Harbor Cult Ctr (trustee, 76-87); Nat Art Educ Asn; and others. *Media:* Assemblage, All Media. *Res:* Art education; community arts projects. *Interests:* Art mus & galleries, community art progs, Head Start sch prog. *Publ:* Auth, Parent-Child Workshops (pamphlet), Metrop Mus Art, NY; Doing Art Together, Simon & Schuster, 82, rev ed, Harry Abrams Inc, 97; Look What I See (CD-Rom), Mitsubishi Chemical Am, 96, new Look What I See! (CD-Rom), Metrop Mus Art; Design for Prog notes & drawings, Philadelphia Pa Synphony Orchestra Children's Concerts progs. *Mailing Add:* 2500 Johnson Ave #16N Riverdale NY 10463-4944

SILER, TODD (LAEL)
PAINTER, SCULPTOR
b Long Island, NY, Aug 21, 1953. *Study:* Smith Col, with Leonard Baskin, 73-74; Bowdoin Col, BA (cum laude), 75; Mass Inst Technol, MS (visual studies), 81, PhD (interdisciplinary studies in psychol & art), 86. *Work:* The Solomon R Guggenheim Mus; Whitney Mus Am Art; Metrop Mus Art; Mus Mod Art; Pushkin Mus Fine Arts, Moscow. *Comn:* Sculpture, Alvin I Schragis, New York City, 88. *Exhib:* Solo exhibs, Humanature-A Turbulent Integration, Mus Mod Art, Belo Horizonte, Brazil, 91, Metaphorms, Turman Gallery, Ind State Univ, 92, Radical Futures, Ronald Feldman Fine Arts, 93, Artscience, Crossman Gallery, Univ Wis-Whitewater, 94, Mind Icons, Allen Ctr, Houston, Tex, 95, Metaphorming Civilization, Ronald Feldman Fine Arts, 95 & Metaphorming Worlds, Taipei Fine Arts Mus, Taiwan, 95, Mind Icons, The Allen Ctr, Houston, Tex, 95, Changing Minds, Ronald Feldman Fine Arts, NY, 97, Ronald Feldman Gallery, 2007; Group exhibs, Schemes: A Decade of Installation Drawings, Mus D'Art Contemp, Montreal & traveling, 81; Revolutions Per Minute (The Art Record), Ronald Feldman Fine Arts, Tate Gallery, Documenta, Ger & Biennale De Paris, 82; Alea(s), Mus D'Art Mod, Paris, 82; Brainworks, Munic Art Gallery, Los Angeles, 85; Savoir-vivre, Savoir-faire, Savoir-etre, Centre Int D'Art Contemporain, De Montreal, Que, 90; Eighteen from NY, traveling Galerie Lohrl, Mochengladbach, Ger, 91; Blast 3, Remaking Civilization, X-Art Found, 93; The Unconscious at Work, Peyton Wright Gallery, Santa Fe, NMex, 93; traveling exhib, 25 Yrs: Light Space Time, 94-; Blast Art Benefit, The X-Art Found and Blast, NY, 94, 96; Withdrawing, Ronald Feldman Fine Arts, NY, 96; Baroque Bash: A Fan Fantasy, The John and Mable Ringling Mus Art, Sarasota, Fla, 98; Defining Structures, LaSalle Partners at NationsBank Plaza, Charlotte, NC, 98. *Pos:* Res fel, Ctr Adv Visual Studies, Mass Inst Technol, 81-; co-pres & consult, United Sciences & Arts, 83-; res affil, Computer-Aided Design Lab, Dept Mech Eng, Mass Inst Technol, 86-91; adv bd, Coun Art, Sci & Technol, Mass Inst Technol, Cambridge; founder, Psi-Phi Commun; founder, Art Sci Ctr, Mus Outdoor Arts, Greenwood, Colo. *Teaching:* Instr visual design, Mass Inst Technol, 82-83. *Awards:* Gold Medal Award, Int Book Fair, Jerusalem, 93; Grawemeyer Award Educ Nominee, Univ Louisville, 94; Artist of Yr Award, New York City Art Teachers Asn/United Fedn Teachers, 95; Colo Space Educ Distinguished Educator Award, Lt Gov Colo, 96. *Bibliog:* Gary Massaro (auth), This Genius Opens Minds, The Rocky Mountain News, 12/6/96; Robert Schwab (auth), Firm Sells Real Talent-Creativity, The Denver Post, 1/97; Helen Levin (auth), Try a little 'metaphorming', Staten Island Register, 5/5/98. *Media:* All. *Publ:* Healing and The Mind, Bill Moyer, Doubleday, NY, 93; METAPHORMERS: Connecting Our Work and Our World Through Metaphorms in R&D Innovator, 7/94; Metaphorming the Genetic Code, Art J, Coll Art Asn, 95; Freeing Your Mind: Thresholds of ArtScience, Artsci Publ, 95. *Dealer:* Ronald Feldman Fine Arts Inc 31 Mercer St New York NY 10013; Pas-Phi Communications 7070-B S Tucson Way Englewood NY 80112. *Mailing Add:* c/o Ronald Feldman Fine Arts 31 Mercer St New York NY 10013

SILL, GERTRUDE GRACE
CURATOR, WRITER
b New York, NY. *Study:* Smith Col, with Oliver Larkin, BA, 48; Wesleyan Univ, with Samuel Greene & Richard Field, MA, 78. *Collection Arranged:* George Cope: West Chester's Home Artist (consult, cur, catalogue, essay), Brandywine River Mus, Chadds Ford, Pa, 1978; Amon Carter Mus, Houston, Tex, 85; John Haberle, Master of Illusion (auth, catalog), Mus Fine Arts, Springfield, Mass, 85-86, NEw Britain Mus Am Art, 2009; Whitney Mus Am Art, 86; Realism and Romanticism in 19th Century New England Seascapes, Whitney Mus Am Art, Stamford, Conn, 89; George Cope (auth), An Artists Life, Chester Co Hist Soc, West Chester, Pa, 2004; John Haberle, Am Master of Illusion, New Britain us Am Art, Conn, 2009-2010; Brandywine River Mus, Chadd's Ford, Pa, 2010; Portland Mus Art, Maine, 2010. *Pos:* Writer & art critic, Connoisseur, Antiques, Art in Am, Portfolio, Art & Antiques & others, 68-; art critic, Brooks Community Papers, 86-90, Conn Post, 90-2009; cur, writer, New Britain Mus Am Art, Conn, 86-2010. *Teaching:* Lectr & consult, Metrop Mus Art, NY, 75-78; lectr, Southern Conn State Univ, New Haven, 80-81, Whitney Mus Am Art, 89, New Brit Mus Am Art, 89-95, 2009, Yale Univ, 89, 91, 93 & 98, Mus Fine Art, Houston, Tex, 90, Smith Col Sem, 91, Mus Fine Arts, Boston, Mass, 91 & 94, Portland Mus Art, Maine, 92 & Col Art Asn, 93; lectr, Fairfield Univ, Conn, 76-2003, Minneapolis Inst Art, 95 & Cummer Mus Art, 96, San Diego Art Mus, Yale Univ Art Mus & Cummer Mus Art, Jacksonville, Fla, 98, 99; adj prof, Fairfield Univ, Ct, 76-03; instr, Chester Co Hist Soc, 2004-; lectr, New Britain Mus Am Art, Conn, 2009, 2010; lectr, Portland Mus Art, Portland, ME, 2009, 2010; lectr, Brandywine Mus Art, Chadds Ford, Pa, 2009, 2010. *Awards:* Nat Endowment Humanities Grant, 78; Nat Endowment Arts Grant, 85 & 86; Furthermore Foundn, Longrock Found, Wyeth Fund, 2009; Luce Found Grant, 2009. *Mem:* Coll Art Asn; Archives Am Art; Asn Am Art Historians; New Britain Mus Am Art. *Res:* John Haberle, Am painter (1856-1933) monogr for publ; George Brainerd Burr (1875-1933) for exhib, Am Impressionists; John Haberle, Master of Illusion, 03-; George Cope, West Chester, Pa; John Haberle, Am Master of Illusion, New Britain Mus Am Art, 2009; D Origsby, CB Guelpa, T Hill; CJ Hamilton. *Interests:* John Haberle, 19th century Am trompe l'oeil painter; Am still life & landscape painters. *Collection:* 19th century Am still-life, landscape paintings & drawings. *Publ:* George Cope: West Chester's Home Artist, Brandywine River Mus & UMI, 78; John Haberle: Master of Illusion, Mus Fine Arts, Springfield, Mass, 95, New Britain Mus Am Art, New Britain, Conn, 2009; A Handbook of Symbols In Christian Art, Simon & Schuster/Touchstone, 96; Groves Dictionary of Art, Macmillan, London, 97; George Cope: An Artists Life, Chester Co Hist Soc, West Chester, Pa, 2004; article, Am Nat Biography, Oxford Univ Press, vol 10, Cary, NC; Reviews: Fakes & Forgeries: The Art of Deception; Gustav Klimt at the New Gallery;

Art for Love, Conn Post, 2006, John Haberte: Am Master of Illusion, Am Art Review, Vol. XXII, No. 3, Chadds Ford, Pa, 2010; John Haberle: Three Rediscovered Paintings, The Magazine Antiques, 135-41, 11/2007; Handbook of Symbols in Christian Art, Simon & Schuster, 2008, ebook, 2010. *Mailing Add:* 112 Southport Woods Dr Southport CT 06890

SILLMAN, AMY (DENISON)
PAINTER
b Detroit, Mich, Oct 6, 1955. *Study:* Sch Visual Art, New York, BFA, 79; Bard Col, MFA, 95. *Work:* Art Inst Chicago; Baltimore Mus Art; Brooklyn Mus; NY Pub Libr; Jewish Mus. *Comn:* print, Jewish Mus, 2000. *Exhib:* solo shows, Kanoria Ctr Art, Ahmedabad, India, 88, Ledis Flam, NY, 91, Lipton Owens Co, NY, 94, Casey Kaplan, NY, 96 & 98, Brent Sikkema, NY, 2000 & 03, Galleria Marabini, Bologna, Italy, 2001, Susanne Vielmetter Projects, Los Angeles, 2002, Jaffe-Friede Strauss Galleries, Hopkins Center, Dartmouth Col, Hanover, NH, 2002, Brent Sikkema, NY, 2003, Inst of Contemp Art, Univ of Pa, 2004, Susanne Vielmetter LA Projects, Calif, 2005, Sikkema Jenkins & Co, NY, 2006 & 2010, Blaffer Gallery, Art Mus of the Univ Houston, 2007, Crown Point Gallery, 2007, Hirshhorn Mus and Sculpture Garden, DC travels to Tang Tchg Mus at Skidmore Coll, NY, 2008 & 2010, Carlier Gebauer, Berlin, Germany, 2009; New Generations: NY, Carnegie Mellon Gallery, Pittsburgh, 91; Out West & Back East - New Work from NY & Los Angeles, Santa Monica Mus Contemp Art, Calif, 95; Imaginary Beings, Exit Art, NY, 96; Nu-Glu, Jospeh Helman Gallery, NY, 97; Team SHaG, Postmasters Gallery, NY, 97; Irredeemable Skeletons, Shillam & Smith, London, Eng, 97; Distraction, TBA Exhib Space, Chicago, 97; New York Drawers, Gasworks, London, Eng, 97; Current Undercurrent: Working in Brooklyn, Brooklyn Mus, NY, 97; Art on Paper, Weatherspoon Art Gallery, Univ NC, 97; Art and Provocation: Images From Rebels, Boulder Mus Contemp Art, 97; Drawings & Paintings, Wooster Gardens Gallery, NY, 97; The Secret Charts, Jonctions Festival, Brussels, 98; Drawings, Graham Mod Gallery, NY, 98; Codex USA, Entwistle Gallery, London, 98; Pop Surrealism, Aldrich Mus, Ridgefield, Conn, 98; From Here to Eternity: Painting in the 1990's, Max Protech Gallery, NY, 98; Commitment to Image, Univ NTex Art Gallery, Denton, 98; Personal Touch, Art in General, NY, 98; Cluster Bomb, Morrison-Judd, London, Eng, 98; The New Surrealism, Pamela Auchincloss Proj Space, NY, 98; Drawing in the Present Tense, Parsons Sch Design, NY, 99; James Van Damme Gallery, Brussels, 2000; Greater NY, PS1, 2000; The Approximative, Galerie Ghislaine Hussenot, Paris, 2001; A Long Drawing, Brent Sikkema, NY, 2002; Rendered, Sara Meltzer Gallery, NY, 2003; Wonderland, Judy Ann Goldman Fine Art, Boston, 2004; Post Modern, Greene Naftall, NY, 2005; Gifts Go in One Direction, Apexart, NY, 2006; Oranges and Sardines, Hammer Mus, UCLA, 2008; Abstract America: New Painting and Sculpture, Saatchi Gallery, UK, 2009; Blue, James Graham & Sons, NY, 2009; Team SHaG, Clough-Hanson Gallery, Rhodes Coll, Memphis, 2010. *Pos:* Vis artist, Sch Art Inst Chicago, 93 & 95; vis critic, MFA/Fine Art Prog, Parsons Sch Design, 96-. *Teaching:* Instr painting, Bennington Col, Vt, 90-95; asst prof art, Bard Col, 96- & fac mem painting, MFA Prog, 96-. *Awards:* Nat Endowment Arts Fel, 95; Pollock-Krasner Found Fel, 99; Civitella Ranieri Found Fel/Residency, Umbria, Italy, 99; Louis Comfort Tiffany Award, 99; John Simon Guggenheim Memorial Found Fellowship in Painting, NY, 2001; American Acad in Berlin: Berlin Prize in Arts and Letters, Guna S. Mundheim Fellow in the Visual Arts, Berlin, Germany, 2009. *Bibliog:* Thad Ziolkowski (auth), rev, Artforum, 98; Wayne Koestenbaum (auth), The best of-1998, Artforum, 98; Jonathon Goodman (auth), Medrie Macphee & Amy Sillman, Contemp Visual Art, 99; David Humphrey (auth), Bomb Mag, 2000; Gail Gregg (auth), Profile, Art News, 2001; Gregory Volk (auth), (catalog essays), Regarding Amy Stillman's Paintings, 1998; Gail Gregg, Art News, 2001; Helen Molesworth (catalog), 2002. *Mem:* Nat Acad. *Media:* Gouache, Oil. *Dealer:* Sikkema Jenkins & Company 530 W 22 St New York NY 10011. *Mailing Add:* 705 Driggs Ave Brooklyn NY 11211

SILOOK, SUSIE
SCULPTOR, CRAFTSMAN
Work: Anchorage Mus Hist & Art; Eiteljorg Mus Am Indians & Western Art, Indianapolis. *Exhib:* Solo exhibs include Grant Hall, Anchorage, 2001; group exhibs include Who Stole the Teepee?, Nat Mus Am Indian, Smithsonian Inst, Washington, DC, 2001. *Awards:* Gov's Arts Award, 2000; Eiteljorg Mus Am Indians & Western Art Fel, 2001; US Artists Rasmusen Fel, Crafts & Traditional Arts, 2007. *Media:* Ivory. *Dealer:* Alaska Gallery 1233 E 76th St Anchorage AK 99518

SILVA, JUDE HUTTON
ARTIST
b Springfield, Mass, Dec 15, 1939. *Study:* San Jose State Univ, BFA, 81; San Jose State Univ, MA, MFA, 91, 93. *Work:* Kaiser Hosp, Oakland, Calif, 82; Progressive Corp, Colo Springs, 98; Commerce Bank, Arvada, Colo, 02. *Exhib:* Installations, Univ Southern Colo, Pueblo, 02; Paradise Lost-Redefining, Univ Colo, Boulder, 98. *Teaching:* Artist in Residence, Sacred Heart Co Serv, 92, 94; Instr, Colo Mountain Col, 97-; Instr, Co Sch of Music & Art, 93-95. *Awards:* State of Colo Fel, Republic Plaza, 01. *Mem:* Bay Area Basketry Guild, pres, founding mem; Ark Valley Art Ctr. *Publ:* Donnaz Melack, Basketry Today, 79; Consuelo Underwood, Fiberarts, 90; Clint Driscoll, Fiber is Good for Your Art, Colo Central, 01. *Dealer:* Cultureclash 100 North F St Salida CO 81201. *Mailing Add:* 28875 County Rd 330 Buena Vista CO 81211

SILVER, LARRY ARNOLD
CURATOR, HISTORIAN
b Los Angeles, Calif, Oct 14, 1947. *Study:* Univ Chicago, BA, 1969; Harvard Univ, MA, 1971, PhD, 1974. *Collection Arranged:* Graven Images: The Rise of Professional Printmakers in Antwerp and Haarlem, 1540-1640, Mary & Leigh Block Gallery, Northwestern Univ & Ackland Art Mus, Univ NC, Chapel Hill, 1993; Theater of the World: The Golden Age of the Atlas in the Low Countries, 1570-1670, Newberry Libr, Chicago, 1997; A Transformation: Jews and Modernity, Arthur Ross Gallery, Univ Pa, 2001, The Painter-Etcher, 2006. *Pos:* Vis cur, St Louis Art Mus, 1981-82; vis res cur, Art Inst Chicago, 1981-84; vis cur, Block Gallery, Northwestern Univ, 1989-97. *Teaching:* Asst prof Medieval & Renaissance art, Univ Calif, Berkeley, 1974-79; prof Medieval, Renaissance & Baroque art & chmn dept, Northwestern Univ, 1979-97; Farquhar prof art hist, Univ Pa, 1997-. *Awards:* Porter Prize, Coll Art Asn, 1975; Coll Art Asn. *Mem:* Renaissance Soc Am; Soc Values in Higher Educ; Print Coun Am; Coll Art Asn (vpres 1990-92, pres 1992-94, editor in chief, 1999-2005); Historians of Netherlandish Art (vpres 1985-87, pres 1999-2001, bd mem 2001-05); Am Asn Netherlandic Studies; 16th Century Studies Conf; Am Asn Univ Profs. *Res:* Painting and graphics in northern Europe, 15th and 16th century. *Publ:* Coauth, Flemish Dutch Paintings (catalog), Ringling Mus, 1980; auth, Early Northern European Paintings (catalog), St Louis Art Mus, 1982; Forest primeval: Albrecht Altdorfer and --- landscape, Simiolus, 1983; auth, The Paintings of Quinten Massys, Allanheld & Schram, 1984; auth, Rembrandt, Rizzoli, 1992; auth, Art in History, Prentice-Hall, 1993; coauth, Graven Images: The Rise of Professional Printmakers in Antwerp & Haarlem, 1540-1640, Northwestern Univ, 1993; ed, Introduction, Blockpoints, 1995; ed & auth, Transformation: Jews & Modernity, Univ Pa Press, 2001; co-ed, Northern Renaissance Art, Prentice-Hall, 2004; auth, Peasant Scenes & Landscapes, Univ Pa Press, 2005

SILVER, RAWLEY A
WRITER, PAINTER
b New York, NY. *Study:* Cornell Univ, BA, 39; Art Students League, with George Grosz, 48, 50; Columbia Univ, MA (fine arts educ), 64, EdD (fine arts educ), 66. *Work:* Archives Nat Mus Women in Arts, 91-; Smithsonian Inst Archive; Metropolitan Mus Art; Cornell Univ Archives. *Exhib:* 19 solo invitationals, 55-92 & 2005, 2006, 2007 & 2008; Hudson River Mus Invitational, Yonkers, NY, 76. *Collection Arranged:* Shout in Silence (auth, catalog), 69-77 & Art as Language (auth, catalog), 79-82, Smithsonian Inst Traveling Exhib. *Teaching:* Instr art, 61-73; adj assoc res prof art therapy, Col New Rochelle Grad Sch, 74-81. *Awards:* Ann Award Res, Am Art Therapy Asn, 76, 80, 92 & 96; Res Grants, US Off Educ, Nat Inst Educ & NY State Dept Educ; Distinguished Alumni Award, Teachers Coll, Columbia Univ, 2009. *Bibliog:* Alexander Kopytin (auth), The silver drawing test standardization in Russia, Am J Art Therapy v 40 (4), May 2002; CD Allessandrini et al (auth), SDT: the Brazilian standardization of the silver drawing test of cognition and emotion, ARTherapy, J of the Am Art Therapy Asn, vol 15 (2) 1998; Linda Jo Pfeiffer (auth), The Arts in Psychotherapy, vol 29 (1), 2003; Amelia C Joynes (auth), Natl Arts Ed Assn News, vol 45 (2), April, 2003; Donna H Kaiser (auth), Art Therapy, J of Am Art Assn, vol 20 (4), 2003; Roberta Shoemaker-Beal (auth bk review), The Arts in Psychotherapy, Vol 33 (3), 2006. *Mem:* Hon life mem Am Art Therapy Asn; Hon life mem Art Therapy Asn Fla. *Media:* Watercolor, Oils. *Res:* Developing and assessing cognitive skills & depression. *Publ:* Art as Language, Brunner-Routledge, 2001; Aggression and Depression Assessed through Art, Brunner-Routledge (NY)/ Taylor & Francis (UK), Jan 2005; auth, The Silver Drawings Test and Draw A Story, Routledge, NY & Taylor & Francis, UK, 2007; Identifying Risks for Aggression & Depression through Metaphors, Purple Finch Press, 2010; 82 Journ Articles, research proj report, book chapters, book rev, & 6 books in print, digital access to 31 joun articles & other publ on the web; Developing Cognitive and Creative Skills Through Art, 1Universe.com Publ, 2012; translated and published in Russia and Korea. *Mailing Add:* 3114 Gracefield Rd Apt 305 Silver Spring MD 20904

SILVER, SHELLY ANDREA
VIDEO ARTIST, FILMMAKER
b Manhattan, NY, July 16, 1957. *Study:* Cornell Univ, Coll Arts & Sci, BA, 79, Coll Art & Archit, BFA, 79; Whitney Mus Am Art Independent Studio Prog, 80-81. *Work:* Mus d'Arte Moderne Centre Georges Pompidou, Paris, France; Long Beach Mus Art, Los Angeles, Calif; Stadtgalerie, Bern Switz; Werkleitz Biennal, Ger; Mus Art & Hist, Fribourg, Switz. *Comn:* Mus Art & Hist, Fribourg, Switz; Stadtgalene Bern, Switz; Werkleitz Bienial, Ger; Mus Chinese Am, NY; Mus Chinese in Am, 2009. *Exhib:* New York Film Festival, NY, 94; Nat Film Theaters, London, Eng, 94; Filmladen Dokumentarfilm & Videofestival, Kassel, Ger, 94; Cinevideo Festival, Karlsrube, Ger, 94; Yokohama Mus Art, Japan, 94; Yokohama Portside Gallery, 02; Singapore Int Film Festival, 02; Kunsthaus, Zurich, Switz, 02; Musee de L' Elysee, Switz, 01; Palm Beach Inst of Contemp Art, 01; Berlin Film Festival, 2005, 2010; and others. *Collection Arranged:* The Mus of Modern Art, NYC; Mus of Broadcasting, NYC; Centre Georges Pompidou, Paris; Yokohama Art Mus, Japan. *Teaching:* Assoc prof, visual arts dept, Columbia Univ. *Awards:* Nat Endowment Arts Fel, 89, 91; Checkerboard Found Grant, 90; US/Japan Artists Exchange Fel, 93; Anonymous Was a Women Award, 1998; Fel, John Simon Guggenheim Found, 2005. *Mem:* Media Alliance; Asn of Independent Video and Filmmakers. *Media:* Videos, Film, Photography, Installation. *Dealer:* EAI 536 Broadway New York NY; Video Data Bank 37 S Wabash 10th Floor Chicago IL 60603; Arsenal Experimental Berlin Ger; Argos Brussels Belg. *Mailing Add:* 22 Catherine St No 6 New York NY 10038

SILVERBERG, JUNE ROSELYN
PAINTER, GRAPHIC ARTIST
b Brooklyn, NY. *Study:* Brooklyn Col, BA, 56 cum laude, honors in design: Yale Univ, with Joseph Albers, 56-57 honors,; Art Students League, Concours honors, Pratt Inst, MS, 69. *Work:* Arthur Andersen Corp Collection, Minneapolis, Minn; Bryn Mawr Coll Libr Collection, Pa; Art Students League, NY. *Exhib:* NY Univ 9th, 25th, 26th Ann Small Works, 80 Wash Sq E Galleries, NY, 85, 02-03; Am Drawing Biennial II, Muscarelle Mus Art, Williamsburg, Va, 90; Int Exhib Miniature & Small Format Art, Metro Toronto Conv Ctr & Del Bello Gallery, Can, 90 & 91; Landscape Works by Women Artists, Bryn Mawr Coll, Pa, 94; 25th Anniversary Show, Bowery Gallery, NY, 94: Bowery Gallery Solo Shows 3/83, 3/93 & Group Shows 80-2005; Audubon Artists, Ann Exhib Nat Arts Club, NY, 91-95; Fed Hall, NY, 96; Salmagundi Club, NY, 97-03, 06; Butler Inst Am Art, 66th Nat Midyear Exhib, Youngstown, Ohio, 02; Life of the City, Moma, NY, 02; Allied Artists Am Ann, Nat Arts Club, NY, 2004, 2007; NY Artists Equity Int, Broome St Gallery, NY, 2008. *Pos:* Dir oils, Audubon Artists, 98. *Awards:* Premier Prix, Salon du Portrait de Montreal, 91; Hon Mention, Audubon Artists Ann Exhib, 95, SCAC Small Works Exhib, 94; The Conn Acad of

Fine Arts Graphic Award for Allied Artists of America Annual Exhib, 11/2004. *Bibliog:* Tallahassee Democrat 12/89- Betty Rubenstein; Archival Listing, Nat Mus Women Arts, Washington, DC, 93; The NY Sun, Pg 17, 1/6/2005- Work Cited with Photo. *Mem:* Audubon Artists; life mem Art Students League New York; Artists Equity; Bowery Gallery (assoc). *Media:* All media. *Mailing Add:* 32 Union Sq Rm 1205 New York NY 10003

SILVERMAN, BURTON PHILIP
PAINTER
b Brooklyn, NY, June 11, 1928. *Study:* Pratt Inst; Art Students League, 46-49; Columbia Univ, BA, 49. *Hon Degrees:* Sch of Humane Letters, Acad Art Univ, San Francisco, Calif, 2003. *Work:* Brooklyn Mus, NY; Philadelphia Mus Art; Butler Inst Am Art; Del Art Mus, Wilmington; New Britain Mus Am Art, Conn; Denver Art Mus, CO; Brigham Young Mus Art, Provo, UT; Nat Portrait Gallery, Smithsonian Inst Mus, Washington, DC; Columbus Mus Art, Columbus, Ohio; Mint Mus, Charlotte, NC. *Comn:* Portrait, Paul Moore, Jr, Episcopal Bishop of NY; portrait, Dr David Hamburg (chmn bd), Carnegie Corp; portrait, Robert McCormack Adams Retired Secy, Smithsonian Inst; portrait, Bruce Babbit (former secy Interior); Richard West (former dir), Mus Am Indian; Lewis Sharp (dir), Denver Art Mus; Jack & Suzy Welch (former CEO), Gen Electric Corp; Werner Polak, pres, Practicing Law Inst, New York; Eliz. Duffy, Headmaster, The Lawrenceville School, Lawrenceville, NJ; Elena Kagan, Assoc Justice, Supreme Court, Harvard Law School. *Exhib:* Nat Acad 59-2001, 2003-2007; Am Watercolor Soc Ann, 79-99; Face of Am, W/C Portraits 150 Contemp, Old Forge Mus, NY, 94; Int Waters, 3 Nation Traveling Show, Us, Can & United Kingdom, 92-94; South Bend Mus, 94; Retrospective, Butler Inst Am Art & Brigham Young Mus, 99; Artists of Am, 94, 2000; Re-Presenting Representation, Arnot Mus, 2001-02; Protest in Montgomery (50th anniversary Montgomery Boycott), Montgomery Mus Art, 2006, Del Art Mus, 2004; Intimate Eye (retrospective), Brigham Young Mus Art, 2006-07, Lyme Acad Art Coll, Lyme, Conn, 2007, Butler Inst Am Art, 2007; Realism Recovered, The Art of Burton Silverman, Miller Mus Jewish Art, Tulsa, Okla, 2010; Humanist Spirit, The Art of Burton Silverman, retrospective, Hofstra Univ Mus, NY, 2011; American Masters, Salmagundi Club, NY, 2012. *Pos:* asst treas, Coun Nat Acad Design; Membership subcomm Nat Acad Design; lectr, Sch Visual Arts, 2007; lectr (art & illus), Hartford Univ, 2008. *Teaching:* Instr drawing & painting, Sch Visual Arts, New York, 64-67; lectr & workshops, Nat Acad Design, New York, 90-94, 2004-05; distinguished vis prof, George Washington Univ, Washington, 92; Workshops, Scottsdale Artists Sch, 2004, 06; Lectr, The Creative Progressive, Scottsdale, 2005; lect, Syracuse Univ Grad Prog, 2007, 09; Art Students League, 2009, 2010, 2011, & 2013. *Awards:* Soc Illusrs Hall Fame, Pastel Soc Am, Hall of Fame, New York, 92; Silver Medal, Am Watercolor Soc, 94; Gold Medal, Nat Portrait Soc, 2004; Newington Gropsey Ann Award, Excellence in the Arts, 2005; Berkelson award, Nat Acad Mus, 2006. *Bibliog:* Fredrick Whitaker (auth), Four realists, 10/64, Elizabeth Case (auth), Burton Silverman captures the moment, 6/71 & Pat Van Gelder (auth), Drawing the human figure, an interview with Burt Silverman, 7/81, Am Artist Mag; Robert McGrath (auth) & others, Sight & Insight: The Art of Burton Silverman, Madison Square Press, 12/98; Herman Dutoit (auth), The Intimate Eye, The Drawings of Burton Silverman, Brigham Young Univ, 2006; Matthew Anderson (auth, Burton Silverman, Sight & Insight, Fine Art Connoisseur Mag, 2/12/2007; Gabriel Weisberg (auth), The Humanist Spirit, Lifelike Catalog, Hofstra Mus, 2011; John O'Hearn (auth), Everyday People, Americna Art Review, 12/2011; Wende Caporale (auth), A Day in the Life, International Artist, 2012. *Mem:* Am Watercolor Soc; Nat Acad (assoc, 69, acad, 72-); Century Asn, New York, 2005. *Media:* Oil, Watercolor. *Specialty:* realist. *Interests:* amateur guitar, essays, art critiques. *Publ:* Painting People, 77 & Breaking the Rules of Watercolor, 83, Watson-Guptill; Realism rediscovered, Artist's Mag, 90; What makes art great, Am Arts Quart; and others. *Dealer:* Gallery Henoch, 555 W 25th St, NYC, 10001; Total Arts Gallery, 122A Kit Carson Rd, Taos, NM, 87571; Gallery 1261 1261 Delaware Denver CO 80204; Haynes Galleries 1600 Division St #140 Nashville TN; 91 Main St Thomaston Me. *Mailing Add:* 324 W 71st St New York NY 10023

SILVERMAN, LANNY HARRIS
DIRECTOR, CURATOR
b Philadelphia, Pa, Oct 16, 1947. *Study:* Case Western Reserve Univ, BA, 69. *Collection Arranged:* Sowers of Myth (catalog), 91; Michiiko Itatani: Paintings Since 1984 (interview, catalog), 92; The Nature of the Machine (auth, catalog), 93; Con/textual: Art & Text in Chicago (catalog), 2001; Leon Golub: Works since 1947 (catalog), 2003; Kif Slemmons: Re: Pair & Imperfection (catalog), 2006; Nick Cave: Soundsuits (catalog), 2006; Karl Wirsum: Winsome Works (some), (catalog), 2007; William Coriger: Paintings 1958-2008 (catalog), 2009. *Pos:* Educ asst, Akron Art Mus, 80-81; cur educ & pub prog, Madison Art Ctr, Wis, 81-84; dir, NAME Gallery, Chicago, 85-87; asst dir, Evanston Art Ctr, 87-89; cur, Chicago Cult Ctr, 89-. *Teaching:* Instr art, poetry & performance, Cleveland Mus Art, 74-78. *Bibliog:* Barbara Newsom & Adele Silver (ed), The Museum as Educator, Univ Calif Press, 78. *Specialty:* Experimental art; mixed media; installations; performance art; new music. *Interests:* New Music and World Music. *Mailing Add:* Dept Cult Affairs Visual Arts Dept 78 E Washington 4th Fl Chicago IL 60602

SILVERMAN, LILA & GILBERT B
COLLECTOR
Study: Univ Calif Berkeley. *Pos:* Chmn and chief exec officer, Silverman Companies, Bingham Farms, Mich, currently; owner, Amurcon, currently; bd dirs, Univ Cancer Found, On My Own, Mich, and The Greening, Detroit. *Awards:* Named one of Top 200 Collectors, ARTnews mag, 2004-10. *Mem:* Bldg Indust Asn (pres, 1996). *Collection:* Fluxus and Conceptual art. *Mailing Add:* Silverman Companies Ste 220 32100 Telegraph Rd Bingham Farms MI 48025

SILVERMAN, RONALD H
EDUCATOR, WRITER
b Cleveland, Ohio, 1926. *Study:* Univ Calif, Los Angeles, BA, 52; Los Angeles State Col, MA, 55; Stanford Univ, EdD, 62. *Pos:* Consult, Nat Assessment Educ Progress Art; assoc dir, Getty Inst Educators Visual Arts. *Teaching:* Prof emer art, Calif State Univ, Los Angeles, 55-88. *Awards:* Bur Res grant, US Office Educ, 1967-69; Outstanding Prof Award, Calif State Univ, Los Angeles, 78; Award, Nat Art Educ Asn, 81; Distinguished Fel, Nat Art Educ Asn, 91; Best in Show, Artists Over 50, 2002. *Mem:* Life mem, Nat Art Educ Asn; Calif Art Educ Asn. *Media:* Acrylic, Oil. *Publ:* Auth, Spectrum of Music, Macmillan, 74; Goals and roles in art education of children, In: The Arts, Human Development and Education, McCutchan, 76; A comprehensive model for teaching art, In: Report of the NAEA Commission on Art Education, Nat Art Educ Asn, 77; ed, Art, Education and the World of Work, Nat Art Educ Asn, 80; The egalitarianism of discipline-based art education, Art Educ, 3/88. *Mailing Add:* 47 Hillgrass Irvine CA 92603

SILVERTOOTH, DENNIS CARL
SCULPTOR
b Killeen, Tex, Aug 20, 1957. *Study:* Corpus Christi Community Art Ctr, with Maurice Schmidt & Ann Armstrong, 74. *Exhib:* Am Cowboy: Fact & Fiction, Eastman Kodak, NY, 75; Tex Art Classic, Tarrant Co Convention Ctr, Ft Worth, 76-79; Shidoni Summer Sculpture Show, Shidoni Foundry & Gallery, Santa Fe, NMex, 77-81; Philbrook Presents Sculpture, Philbrook Mus, Tulsa, Okla, 78; Midland Coll Sculpture Show, Tex, 78-81; and others. *Awards:* Best Sculpture, Art About Town, Dallas Crippled Childrens Soc, 77; Best Sculpture, 34th Ann American Indian Artist Exhib, Philbrook Mus, Okla, 79; Artist of the Year, Santa Fean Mag, 80. *Bibliog:* Donn Puca (auth), A young artist working magic, Southwest Art Collector, 12/79; Marion Love (auth), article, Santa Fean Mag, 8/80; Joseph Cain (auth), article, Art Voices/South, 9-10/80. *Media:* Bronze, Plaster. *Mailing Add:* 3014 Pimlico St Corpus Christi TX 78418

SIMANSKI, CLAIRE DVORAK
EDUCATOR, VIDEO ARTIST
b Baltimore, Md, June 28, 1946. *Study:* Md Inst Col Art, BFA, 1968. *Pos:* Instr, Anne Arundle Co Pub Schs, 1969-1970; photogr, WMAR-TV, Baltimore, Md, 1968-1969; educ, Fairfax Co Pub Schs, 1992-2011; dept chair, Fine & Performing Arts, 2001-. *Teaching:* Instr, art, Fairfax Co Pub Sch, 1993-. *Awards:* Outstanding Volunteer, HC-TV for TV Shows, 1997, 1999, 2003-2005; Partnership in Educ Award, Optimists Herndon, 1998; Nat Found Arts, 2001, 2003. *Mem:* Art in Pub Places, 1995-2008; Herndon Comt Cult Arts Center, 2001-2002; Herndon Cable Access Television, bd dirs, secy, 2004-2008; Fairfax Educs Asn. *Media:* Acrylic, watercolor, pencil. *Interests:* antiques. *Publ:* Safe & Drug Free Schs (4 part TV show on character educ) 2001; Auth, Sch Arts, Davis, 2007; auth, Middle Matters, 2007. *Mailing Add:* 1136 Stevenson Center Herndon VA 20170

SIMKIN, PHILLIPS M
SCULPTOR
b Philadelphia, Pa, Jan 19, 1944. *Study:* Tyler Art Sch, Temple Univ, BFA; Cornell Univ, MFA; Univ Pa, post grad fel. *Comn:* Sculpture, Pub Ctr for Collection & Dissemination of Secrets, Inst Contemp Art, Univ Pa, 73; Displacement Proj I (with Doris Olafson), Inst Contemp Art, Boston, 74; Displacement Proj II (with Doris Olafson), Philadelphia Mus Art, 74; Artpark (with Thom Farmer), Lewiston State Arts Park, NY, 75. *Exhib:* Displacement Proj II-a Pub Event, Philadelphia, 74; Commodity Exchange, Human Puzzle, Lewiston, NY, 75; Choices Maze, Inst Art & Urban Resources, PS1, NY, 76; Project Looking Glass, Three Centuries of Am Art exhib, Philadelphia Mus of Art, 76; Proj--Is There Anything Else You Want to Tell Me?, Brooklyn Mus, 77; solo proj, Pa Acad of Fine Arts, Philadelphia, 78; Sculpture Performance Comn, Nat Fine Arts Comt, XIII Winter Olympics, Lake Placid, NY, 80; and others. *Pos:* Art dir, Earthweek Inc, Philadelphia, 71-73; co-dir (with John Formicola), The Luncheonette Inc Artist Ctr, Philadelphia, 75; adv bd mem, Dept Community Programs, Philadelphia Art Mus, 77-82. *Teaching:* Assoc prof studio fine arts, York Col, City Univ New York, 73-; adj asst prof studio fine arts, Moore Col Art, Philadelphia, 73-; artist-in-residence, Brooklyn Mus, 77. *Awards:* Nat Endowment Arts Artist Fel, 75-76; Creative Artists Pub Serv Sculpture Grant, New York, 76; Artist Fel Grant, Pa State Coun Arts, 80. *Mailing Add:* 1434 S Broad St Philadelphia PA 19146

SIMMONS, JOHN HERBERT
EDUCATOR, HISTORIAN
b Springfield, Mo, Mar 23, 1938. *Study:* Drury Col, BA, 60; Univ Ark, MA, 73; Univ Rome, DA, 78. *Collection Arranged:* All cataloged, Ernest Trova, Work by Contemp Sculptor, 71, Classical Greek Ceramics, Early Movement Through Gallo Rome, 75, Sung Dynasty Ceramics, Chinese Ceramics, 75, Egyptian Art, Works from the Duncan Collection, 78, Chinese Art, Neolithic Through Ching Dynasty, 79 & Alice Neel, 80. *Pos:* Chmn bd trustees, Springfield Art Mus, Mo, 79-80; art critic, Springfield News Leader, 87-. *Teaching:* Prof & chmn art dept, Drury Col, 69-83. *Mem:* Coll Art Asn; Am Inst Archaeol; assoc Am Inst Archit. *Res:* Chinese art with papers published and read on Ku kai chih; also early printing in Europe. *Interests:* Chinese art, especially ceramics, and early European printed books. *Publ:* Auth, Ku kai chih, an Early Chinese Painter, 73, Ching-te-Chan, 74 & The Loud Brothers of Philadelphia, 75, Gallery. *Mailing Add:* 2059 S Mayfair Ave Springfield MO 65804

SIMMONS, JULIE LUTZ
PAINTER, RESTORER
b San Diego, Calif. *Study:* Murray State Univ, BS, 64, with Miles Batt, Ed Betts, Virginia Cobb, Maxine Masterfield, Barbara Nechis, Charles Reid, Frank Webb & Daniel Green; Southeast Mo State Univ. *Work:* Southwestern Bell, St Louis, Mo; Coca Cola Inc, Atlanta, Ga; Marriot Hotels, Atlanta, Ga; First Bank Fla; First Bank Tenn. *Comn:* sculptured reredos wall and baptismal, Hillside Village, Chapel of the Running

Waters, Peoria, Ill; sculptured reredos wall, Trinity Lutheran Church, Bay City, Mich, 97; sculptured wire mesh tosos, comn by Dr Larry Shaw, Phoenix, 98; mural, Encian Meadows Chapel, Flagstaff, Ariz, 98; sculptured the wall Jesus speaks the Masses on the Sea of Galilee, Salen Lutheran Church, Peoria, Il, 2003; sculptured reredos wall, St Matthew Luthern Church, Sonora, Calif, 03. *Exhib:* Abstein Gallery, Atlanta, Ga, 86-90; Shawnee Col, Ill, 87; Barucci's Gallery, St Louis, Mo, 90; Sun Cities Mus, Sun City, Ariz, 92; Village Gallery, Scottsdale, Ariz, 96; Robb & Stuck, Phoenix, Ariz, 98; Postera 2004 Int Jazz Festival, Sedona, Ariz, 04. *Teaching:* Instr studio workshops watercolor, Charleston, Mo, 70-; instr, studio workshops, Medford, Ore, Monroe, La, 86 & 89, Sikeston, Mo, 86, Lighthouse Art Ctr, Crescent City, Calif, 88, 89 & 91, Geneseo Art League, Ill, 88 & 89, ECent Col, Union, Mo, 88, Ill Art League, Peoria, 89, Sun Cities, Ariz, 90-, Friends of Arts & Scis, Sarasota, Fla, 91 & Left Bank Art League, Moline, Ill, 91. *Awards:* First Prize, Midwest Watercolor Soc Seventh Ann Exhib, 83; Ky Watercolor Soc Exhib Award, 84; An Art Affair Award, St Louis, 85; Ga Watercolor Soc Award, 86; La Watercolor Int Award, 86; Ariz Watercolor Soc Award, 91 & 93. *Bibliog:* Article, The watercolor page, Am Artist, 1/86; articles in Phoenix Home & Garden, Am Artists & The Adelphean, 91-98; article, 101 North Magazine, 04. *Mem:* Soc Layerists Multi-Media; Ariz Watercolor Asn; Ariz Artists Guild; Sonoran Art League. *Media:* Watercolor; Mixed Media, Sculpture. *Publ:* Auth, article, The watercolor page, Am Artist, 1/86; Interior design, Southern Accents, 9/89; Architectural Design Collaborators 2, 91. *Mailing Add:* 11783 E Becker Ln Scottsdale AZ 85259

SIMMONS, LAURIE
PHOTOGRAPHER
b Long Island, NY, Oct 3, 1949. *Study:* Tyler Sch Art, Temple Univ, BFA, 1971. *Work:* Metrop Mus Art, Mus Mod Art, Whitney Mus Mod Art, NY; Mus Art Contemp, Montreal, Can; Stajdelik Mus, Holland; Fogg Mus Art, Boston; Albright-Knox Gallery, Buffalo, NY; and many others. *Exhib:* Solo exhibs, Galerie Rizzo, Paris, 1993, 1995, Metro Pictures, 1994, 1995, SL Simpson Gallery, Toronto, 1995, 1998 Sprengel Mus, 1995, Savannah Coll Art & Design, Ga, 1996, Baltimore Mus Art, 1997, Deitch Projects, New York, 2000, Baldwin Gallery, Aspin, Colo, 2001, Skarstedt Fine Art, New York, 2002, 2007, Sperone Westwater Gallery, New York, 2004, 2005, 2006, Nassau County Mus Art, Roslyn, NY, 2007, In and Around the House, Carolina Nitsch Project Room, NY, 2008, 2009, Tomio Koyama Gallery, Tokyo, 2009; Group exhibs, Biennial Exhib, Whitney Mus Am Art, NY, 1991; Mus Mod Art, NY, 1991, 1992, 2000, 2005; Whitney Mus Am Art, 1996, 1999, 2000; Galerie Philippe Rizzo, Paris, 1996; Metro Pictures, NY, 1996, 1998; Baltimore Mus Art, Md, 1997; Thomas Healy Gallery, New York, 1998; San Francisco Mus Mod Art, 2000; Int Ctr Photog, New York, 2000; Sean Kelly Gallery, 2001; Henie Onstad Kunstsenter, Norway, 2002; Walker Art Ctr, Minneapolis, 2003; SITE Santa Fe Fifth Int Biennial, 2004; Contemp Art Mus, St Louis, 2006; JGM Galerie, Paris, 2007; Galleria Rafaella Cortese, Milan, 2007; America Standard Gallery, NY, 2009; 55th Int Art Exhib Biennale, Venice, 2013. *Teaching:* Asst prof grad photog, Yale Univ; adj prof grad fine arts, Columbia Univ. *Awards:* Nat Endowment Arts, 1984; Guggenheim Fel, 1997. *Bibliog:* Robert Sabbag (auth), The invisible family, NY Times Mag, 2/11/1996; Modernism - Laurie Simmons (rev), San Francisco Examiner, 4/5/1996; Vicki Golberg (auth), Laurie Simmons, NY Times, 7/4/1997; and others. *Dealer:* Artware Editions 327 W 11th St New York NY 10014; Baldwin Gallery 209 South Galena St Aspen CO 81611; Cerealart 149 N 3rd St Philadelphia PA 19106; ClampArt 521-531 W 25th St New York NY 10001; Distrito Cu4tro Bárbara de Braganza 2 Madrid E-28004 Spain; Dorfman Projects 529 W 20th St New York NY 10011; G-C Arts 1217 S Main St Las Vegas NV 89104; Susan L Halper Fine Art Inc New York NY 10010; Joseph K Levene Fine Art Ltd 25 Cent Park W New York NY 10023; Meridian Gallery/Rita Krauss Fine Art 41 E 57th St New York NY 10022; Modernism Inc 685 Market St San Francisco CA 94105; Carolina Nitsch Contemp Art 537 Greenwich St New York NY 10012; Sperone Westwater Gallery 415 W 13 St New York 10014. *Mailing Add:* c/o Metro Pictures 519 W 24th St New York NY 10011

SIMMONS, XAVIERA VINCENTA
INSTALLATION SCULPTOR
b New York, New York, 1974. *Study:* Bard Coll, BFA (Photog), 2004. *Exhib:* Solo exhibs include Contemp Arts Mus, Houston, 2007, Santa Barbara Contemp Arts Forum, Calif, 2007; group exhibs include Re:source, Art in General, New York, 2004; Harlem Postcards, Studio Mus Harlem, New York, 2004, African QUeen, 2005, Frequerncy, 2005; When Artists Say We, Artists Space, New York, 2006; Emerge 7, Ctr Contemp Art, Newark, NJ, 2006; Passionate Attitudes, Ctr Photog Woodstock, Woodstock, NY, 2006; M*A*S*H New York, Cottelston Advs, New York, 2007; Red Badge of Courage, Newark Arts Coun, Newark, NJ, 2007. *Awards:* David C Driskell Prize, High Mus, 2008. *Mailing Add:* Jamaica Center for Arts & Learning 161-04 Jamaica Ave Jamaica NY 11432

SIMMS, JEANNIE
VISUAL ARTIST
Study: Univ Calif Irvine, MFA. *Exhib:* ICA, London, 2002; MIX festival, New York, 2002 & 2003; 4D project, Havana, Cuba, 2003; ARS Electronica Ctr, List, Austria, 2003; Kunstbuero, Vienna, 2003; Mus Fine Arts, Boston, 2004; solo exhib, OHT Gallery, Boston, 2004; Los Angeles County Exhibs, 2005; Courtisane Video and New Media Festival, Belgium, 2006; Int Film Festival Rotterdam, 2006. *Teaching:* Grad and photog faculty, Sch Mus Fine Arts, Boston. *Awards:* Art Matters Found Grant, 2008. *Mailing Add:* Sch Mus Fine Arts 230 The Fenway Boston MA 02115

SIMON, AMY
PHOTOGRAPHER
b New York, NY 1957. *Study:* Univ Fla, BFA, 1979; Fla Atlantic Univ, Miami, postgrad, 1979-1980; New York Univ, MA, 1982. *Exhib:* Fourteen Conversation Pieces, Kagelbanen, Djurgarden, Stockholm, 1996; Continuing the Conversation, F-Rummet, Malmo Konstmuseum, Malmo, Sweden, 1998; Galerie Christian Larsen, Stockholm, 2000; Swedish Cult Inst, Paris, 2003; Martenson & Persson, Paarp, Sweden, 2004; Kulturhuset, Stockholm, 2008; 53rd Int Venice Biennale, Venice, 2009. *Pos:* Co-owner & designer, Kinder's Kinder Inc, 1982-1985; ptnr, Simon/Neumann Gallery, New York, 1985-1994; bd mem, Magasin 3 Stockholm Konsthall, 1987-. *Awards:* Nat Swedish Grant for Visual Art, Konstnarsnamden, Sweden, 1997 & 2009

SIMON, BARBARA R See Rothschild, Barbara R Simon

SIMON, DAVID L
HISTORIAN, EDUCATOR
b Lawrence, Mass, June 14, 1946. *Study:* Boston Univ, BA, 69, MA, 71; Courtauld Inst Art, Univ London, PhD, 77. *Teaching:* Chmn & assoc prof, State Univ NY Coll, Cortland, 74-81; chmn & Ellerton M Jette prof art, Colby Coll, 81-. *Awards:* Am Coun Learned Soc Travel Grant, 78; US-Spanish Comt Educ & Cult Affairs Res Fel, 78-79 & 94; Mellon Found Fel, Metrop Mus Art, 80-81, 94 & 2009; Basset Teaching Award, Colby Coll, 2005. *Mem:* Coll Art Asn; Int Ctr Medieval Art. *Res:* Romanesque sculpture. *Interests:* medieval art. *Publ:* Romanesque Sculpture in North American Collections, The Metrop Museum of Art, Gesta, XXIII, XXV, XXVI, 84, 86 & 87; La Condesa Dona Sancha Y Los Orígenes De Aragón, Zaragoza, 95; Moses Capital at Jaca, Imagines y Promotores en el arte medieval: Homenaje Yaza Luaces, Bettatera, 2001; Eastman Johnson's Lunchtime, Colby Quarterly, XXXIX, 2003; Janson's History of Art, 8th ed, Upper Saddle River, 2011; A Basic History of Art, 9th ed, Upper Saddle River, 2013. *Mailing Add:* Colby Coll Art Dept 5640 Mayflower Hill Waterville ME 04901

SIMON, HERBERT BERNHEIMER
SCULPTOR, PRINTMAKER
b Nashville, Tenn, Sept 20, 1927. *Study:* Brooklyn Mus Art Sch; Hans Hofmann Studio, NY; Colorado Springs Fine Art Ctr; Hunter Col, study with Robert Motherwell; NY Univ, BA & MA, study with Philip Guston. *Work:* Everhart Mus, Scranton, Pa; Lehigh Univ, Bethlehem, Pa; Roberson Ctr Arts & Sci, Binghamton, NY; State Mus Pa, Harrisburg; Roberson Ctr for the Arts and Scis, Binghamton, NY; and others. *Comn:* Two Modules (sculpture), Coal St Park, Wilkes-Barre, Pa, 77; Facets (aluminum relief), Wilkes Col, Wilkes-Barre, Pa, 77; Aluminum Relief, Schaeffer Residence, Mountaintop, Pa, 78; Aloft (aluminum sculpture), Wilkes-Barre-Scranton Int Airport, Avoca, Pa, 2005. *Exhib:* Drawings USA, Mus Mod Art, NY, 55; Fed Hall, NY, 82; 84 Sculptors for 1984, Rodger LaPelle Gallery, 84-86 & 90; Five Sides & Some Tops, Southern Ohio Mus & Cult Ctr, Portsmouth, Ohio, 85; Sordoni Art Gallery, Wilkes Coll, Wilkes-Barre, Pa, 86; Susquehanna Regional Art Exhib, Roberson Mus, Binghamton, NY, 88 & 92; Mayfair Juried Art Exhib, Allentown Art Mus, Allentown, Pa, 89-91; Katharina Rich Perlow Gallery, New York, NY, 89; Penn State Univ, 90, State Mus Pa, 91-92; Contemp Gallery, Marywood Col, Scranton, Pa, 90-92; Bixler Gallery, Stroudsburg, Pa, 91; Riverwalk Juried Exhib, York, Pa, 92; Coll Misericordia Dallas, Pa, 92; Places & Things, Wilkes Univ, 93; Art Marries Industry, Alumni Tech, Atlanta, 94; Contemp Pa Sculpture Southern Alleghenies Mus Art, Loretto, 95; and others. *Teaching:* Instr painting & drawing, Sch Design, NC State Col, Raleigh, 56-58; prof sculpture & 3-D design, Wilkes Univ, Wilkes-Barre, Pa, 69-92. *Awards:* Award, William Penn Mus, Harrisburg, Pa, 71; Purchase Prize Regional Art Exhib, Everhart Mus, Scranton, Pa, 76; Artist-in-Residence, Johnson Atelier, Mercerville, NJ, 86. *Bibliog:* William Sterling (auth), Herbert Simon: Metal Sculpture 1976-1980, Wilkes Coll, Wilkes-Barre, Pa, 80; The Sculpture of Herbert Simon, Offset Paperback Press, Dallas, Pa, 2009. *Media:* Welded Steel, Aluminum; Cast Bronze, Etching. *Mailing Add:* 25 E Center St Shavertown PA 18708

SIMON, LEONARD RONALD
ADMINISTRATOR, WRITER
b Norristown, Pa, Dec 9, 1936. *Study:* Ohio State Univ. *Collection Arranged:* Two Centuries of Black Am Art (coauth, catalog), 75. *Pos:* Registr, Stanford Mus, 65-69; deputy dir, Calif Arts Coun, 77-80; vpres, Robert Brownlee Found, San Jose, Calif, 87-; pres, Celebration Theatre, Los Angeles, Calif, 92-. *Teaching:* Instr Black Am art, Univ Calif, Riverside, 76-77 & 80-. *Awards:* Oscar Micheaux Visual Arts Award, Int Black Writers & Artists, 94. *Mem:* Coll Art Asn. *Res:* Black American artists. *Publ:* Auth, The American presence of the Black artist, Am Art Rev, 76; The sound of people, Arts in Soc, Vol 12, No 1. *Mailing Add:* 360 S Mills Ave Claremont CA 91711

SIMON, MICHAEL A
PHOTOGRAPHER
b Budapest, Hungary, June 20, 1936; US citizen. *Study:* Budapest Tech Univ, 54-56; Pa State Univ, 57-58; Wis Arts Bd photog fel, 80, Rochester Inst Technol, MFA; Beloit Col, Wis, Hon BA. *Work:* Mus Mod Art, George Eastman House, Rochester, NY; Univ Kans, Lawrence; Minneapolis Inst Arts, Minn; Sheldon Mem Art Gallery, Lincoln, Nebr; Theodore Lyman Art Ctr, Beloit Col; Wis State Hist Soc, Madison. *Exhib:* Contemp Photog VII, George Eastman House, Rochester, NY, 72; Midwest Invitational, Walker Art Ctr, Minneapolis, 73; Solo exhibs, Wright Art Ctr, 77-78 & 80, Minneapolis Inst Arts, Minn, 79, Write Art Ctr, Beloit Coll, 80, TUBE Gallery, Write Art Ctr, Beloit Coll, 83, Write Art Mus, Beloit Coll, Univ Rochester, 85, Malone Gallery, Rochester, NY, 86 & The World is Beautiful, Wright Mus Art, 98; Recent Acquisitions, Minneapolis Inst Arts, Minn, 76; Madison Art Ctr, Wis, 83; Aspen Ctr Visual Arts, Colo, 83; Wright Art Mus, Beloit Col, 85; Univ Rochester, NY, 85; Malone Gallery, Rochester, NY, 86, The World is Beautiful, Wright Mus Art, 98; Wis Sesquicentennial Re-Photog Project, Wis State Hist Soc, 98. *Pos:* Cur photog, Wright Art Ctr, Beloit Col, currently; consult, Andre Kertes Retrospective exhib, Art Inst Chicago, 83-85; guest cur, exhib, Hungarian Photog from 1839 to Present, Fratelli Aliari, Florence, Italy, 87-89. *Teaching:* Assoc prof photog, Beloit Col, Wis, 69-; artist-in-residence photog, Univ Del, 74; vis artist photog, Art Inst Chicago, 78; artist-in-residence, Avila Col, Kansas City, Mo, 81; instr workshop, Chilmark Photog Workshop, Martha's Vineyard, Mass, 86; chmn dept art & art hist, Beloit Col, currently, emer prof art, 98-. *Awards:* Nat Endowment Arts Photog Survey Grant, 80; Nat Endowment Arts Exhib Grant, 81; grant, Wis Humanities Comt, 81; Purchase

Awards, Mus Mod Art, NY, George Eastman House, Rochester, NY, Univ Kans, Lawrence, Minneapolis Inst Arts, Minn & Sheldon Mem Art Gallery, Lincoln, Nebr. *Bibliog:* Diaframma Italiana, Milan, Italy, 1-2/75. *Mem:* Soc Photog Educ (nat bd mem, 76-84, chmn nat bd dir, 79-81, chmn reg affairs comt, 81-83, chmn educ comt & mem steering comt, 83-84); Szechenyi Soc Hungary. *Res:* Mellon Foundation grant for the research of the history of photography in Hungary (76-80). *Publ:* auth, three Hungarian Photographers (exhib catalogue), Wright Mus Art, Beloit Col, Beloit, Wis; auth, article, Newslett Photog teachers, Polaroid Corp, summer 85; auth, essay in exhib catalogue for Contemp Hungarian Photogr, Allen Mus, Oberlin Col, Ohio, 89; auth, three Hungarian Photographers (exhib catalogue), Wright Mus Art, Beloit Col, Beloit, Wis; Jewish Photographers of Hungary, Mus Jewish Diaspora, Tel Aviv, Israel, 98

SIMON, MICHAEL J
CERAMIST
b Springfield, Minn, Dec 27, 1947. *Study:* Univ Minn, BA, 70; Univ Ga, MFA, 80. *Exhib:* Solo exhibs, Baltimore Clayworks, Md, 89, Arvada Ctr Arts & Humanities, Denver, Colo, 89, Fla Gulf Coast Art Ctr, Belleair, Fla, 90; group shows, Pro Art Gallery, St Louis, Mo, 90; Expressive Teapot, Swidler Gallery, Royal Oak, Mich, 90; McKenzie Legacy, Manchester Craftsmen Guild, Pittsburgh, 91; Beyond the Body: Architectural Ceramics, LaCoste Gallery, Concord, Mass, 2000; Collaborating Couples, Ga Mus of Art, Athens, 2000; Color and Fire, Los Angeles Co Mus of Art, Calif, 2000; and many others. *Pos:* Many workshops & lectr including, Stetson Univ, Deland, Fla, 88, Fla Gulf Coast Art Ctr, Belleair, 90, Arrowmont Sch, Gatlinburg, Tenn, 91, Pa State Univ State Col, 91, Ga Mus of Art, 99, Baltimore Claywork, 2000. *Awards:* Fel, Ford Found, 81; Craft Fel, Nat Endowment Arts, 90. *Bibliog:* Michael Simon (auth), Old & New Pots: A Ceramics Monthly Portfolio, Ceramics Monthly, p 53-62, 6/83; Andy Nasisse (auth), A Coffee Bowl, Ceramics Monthly, p 63, 6/83; Am Craft, 92, 95, 97; Ceramics Monthly, 90, 95; Molded by Tradition, Atlanta Jour-Constitution, 96; Michelle Coaks (auth), Creative Pottery, Rockport Publ, 98; Don Davis (auth), Wheel Thrown Ceramics, 98; Karen Ann Wood (auth), Tableware in Clay: From Studio and Workshop, Croward Press UK, 99; Color and Fire: Defining Moments in Studio Ceramics, 1950-2000, Rizzoli Int Publ & Los Angeles Co Mus Art, 2000. *Media:* Salt Glazed Stoneware. *Dealer:* The Ferrin Gallery Lenox MA; The Signature Shop Roswell Rd Atlanta GA. *Mailing Add:* 357 Prince Ave Apt A Athens GA 30601

SIMON, PETER
COLLECTOR
b England, 1951. *Pos:* Founder & chmn, Monsoon, London, 1973-, Accessorize, London, 1984-, Monsoon Accessorize Trust, 1994-, Monsoon Art Collection, 2000-. *Awards:* Named one of Top 200 Collectors, ARTnews mag, 2005-13. *Collection:* Contemporary art. *Mailing Add:* Monsoon PLC Monsoon Bldg 179 Harrow Rd London United Kingdom W2 6NB

SIMON, ROBERT BARRY
ART DEALER, HISTORIAN
b New York, NY, Nov 27, 1952. *Study:* Columbia Col, BA, 73; Columbia Univ, MA, 75, MPhil, 76, PhD, 82. *Collection Arranged:* Sixteenth Century Portraits (auth, catalog), Soprintendenza, Florence, Italy, 80-82; US Info Agency Permanent Collection (auth, catalog), 82; Haggerty Mus, Marquette Univ (auth, catalog), 84; Discoveries in una nuova luce (auth catalog), 88 & Devotion and Delight (auth catalog), 89, Piero Corsini Gallery, NY; From Sacred to Sensual: Italian Paintings 1400-1750 (auth, catalog), Berry-Hill Galleries, NY, 98, Figure and Fantasy in French Painting 1650-1800 (auth, catalog), 99, Visions and Vistas: Old Master Paintings and Drawings (auth, catalog), 2000 & Old Master Paintings, 2001. *Pos:* Chester Dale Fel, Metrop Mus Art, New York, 76-78; dir, Fine Arts Group Crosson Dannis, 82-85 & Robert B Simon Fine Art Inc, 85-08; lectr, Fakes & Forgeries, Appraisal Inst Am, 97, Improving Old Masters & Mannerist Portraiture, Baylor Univ, 99, New Technology and Appraisal, Valuation, 2000 & Collecting Old Masters, Sotheby's Inst, 2000. *Teaching:* lectr appraisal old master paintings, Marymount Col, 91; lectr conservation & value, New York Univ, 94, El Greco in Venice, Univ Crete, 95 & Crivelli, Montreal Mus Fine Art, 95; Tracing Provenance in Old Master Paintings, 2002; Bronzino Working Methods, RSA, Toronto, 2003; Building a Significant Art Collection, Palm Beach, 2004; Art as an Investment, Palm Beach, 2005; Cleaning up Dirty Pictures, Montclair, NJ, 2007; Extreme Makeovers, Wadsworth Atheneum, Hartford, 2008. *Mem:* Coll Art Asn; Am Soc Appraisers; Am Asn Mus; Appraisers Asn Am (bd dir, 90, treas, 92, first vpres, 96, pres, 98-2000); Prv Art Dealers Asn & Antique Dealers League of N Am. *Res:* Bronzino, Salviati; American Impressionists; Mannerism; Richardsonian Romanesque architecture; Leonardo da Vinci. *Specialty:* old master paintings. *Publ:* Auth, Bronzino's portrait of Cosimo I De'Medici, Burlington Mag, 83, Giulio Clovio's Eleonora Di Toledo, 89; Sofonisba Anguisciola, 86 & Dore in the Highlands, 89, Walters Art Gallery J; Yo Pontormo, J Art, 89; The Renaissance of the 16th Century, Sotheby's, 2001; From Palace and Chapel: Important Old Master Paintings, 2005; Bronzino (review), Burlington Mag, 2011, 2012, Perino del Vaga (review); Maria Salviati, Florence, Italy, 2010; Reflections on a Once Lost Painting, Inst of Fine Arts NY, 2012; Finding Leonardo, Nelson-Atkins Mus, Kans City, 2013. *Mailing Add:* Satis House 53 Tower Hill Rd E Tuxedo Park NY 10987

SIMON, TARYN
PHOTOGRAPHER
b New York, 1975. *Study:* Brown Univ, BA. *Exhib:* Solo exhibs include PS 1 Contemp Art Ctr, Long Island City, NY, 2003, Gagosian Gallery, Beverly Hills, Calif, 2004, Mus Contemp Photography, Chicago, 2005, Cincinnati Contemp Art Ctr, 2006, Whitney Mus Am Art, New York, 2007; Group exhibs include Set Up, Recent Acquisition in Photography, Whitney Mus Am Art, New York, 2005; Greater New York, PS 1 Contemp Art Ctr, Long Island City, NY, 2005; New Photography, High Mus Art, Atlanta, 2006. *Dealer:* Gagosian Gallery 980 Madison Ave New York NY 10075

SIMONEAU, DANIEL ROBERT
PAINTER, PHOTOGRAPHER
b Lewiston, Maine, Aug 3, 1962. *Study:* Univ of Southern Maine, BFA, 1984. *Work:* Toledo Federation of Art Societies. *Comn:* Bowling Mural, Holiday Lanes, Lewiston, Maine, 1979; Beethoven Mural, Lewiston High Sch, Maine, 1980. *Exhib:* Toledo Area Artist's Exhib: Toledo Mus of Art, Ohio, 1992, 1994, 2009; Northwestern Ohio Watercolor Soc, Toledo, Ohio, 1994, 2006; Salon De Refuses Exhib, Spectrum Gallery, Toledo, Ohio 1994; Artlink Mem Exhib, Artlink Gallery, Ft Wayne, Ind, 1995; Along the Waterfront, Seebeck Gallery, Kenosha, Wis, 2001; Wis Watercolor Soc Group Exhib, 2005, 2006, 2010, 2013; Wis Portrait Artists Group Show, Milwaukee, Wis, 2007; Works (solo exhib), Artists Gallery, Racine, Wis, 2006; Winter Juried Exhib, Anderson Arts Ctr, Kenosha, Wis, 2003, 2006, 2009, 2011, 2012; Racine & Vicinity Exhib, Wustum Mus, Racine, Wis, 2008; Wis Visual Artists Southeast Chapter Exhib, Anderson Arts Ctr, Kenosha, Wis, 2008; Exhib, Reuss Fed Building, Milwaukee, Wis, 2008; People Exhib, Lemon Street Gallery, Kenosha, Wis, 2009; Go Figure exhib, Artworks, Kenosha, Wis, 2009; Watercolor Wis, Wustum Art Mus, Racine, Wis, 2009; myartcontest.com, Portrait exhib, 2009; AHA! Wis, Madison, Wis, 2009, 2010; 6x6 Gallery, New York, 2010; Photography exhib, Anderson Art Ctr, Kenosha, Wis, 2010, 2013; 13th Ann Int Exhib, Int Soc Acrylics Painters, Santa Cruz, 2010; Real People, Woodstock, Ill, 2010; 14th Ann Int Exhib, Int Soc Acrylic Painters, Santa Cruz, 2011; Sig Mem Exhib, Int Acrylic Painters, Paso Robles, 2011; Group exhib, Lemon St Gallery, Kenosha, 2011; Infinity Art Gallery, 2010; 4th Int Exhib, Int Soc Acrylic Painters; Nat Soc Painters in Casein and Acrylic 58th Ann Exhib, NY, 2012; Solo exhib, LGBT Ctr SE, Wisc, 2012; American Watercolor Soc, NY, 2013; Nat Oil and Acrylic Painters Online Exhib, 2013; 16th Ann Int Soc Acrylic Painters, Paso Robles, 2013; Salmagundi Club Summer Potpourri Exhib, NY, 2013. *Pos:* bd of dirs, Spectrum Friends of Fine Art, Toledo, Ohio, 1995, chmn (educ subcommittee, award winners show), dir of educ; mem chair, Transparent Watercolor Soc of Am, 2003-2005, vice pres, 2005, mus search chair, 2005, 2007, TWSA mktg chair, 2013; dir, Artists Gallery, Racine, Wis, 2008; Management Coun, Lemon Street Gallery, Kenosha, Wis, 2009. *Teaching:* Instr, Spectrum Gallery, Toledo, Ohio, 1993-94; instr, Auburn, Maine Adult Educ, 1989-90. *Awards:* People's Choice Award, Kenosha Racine Artist Network, 2010; Founders Award, Infinity Art Gallery, 2010; Honorable Mention, Int Soc Acrylic Painters 3rd Ann, 2010; Award of Excellence, Nat Oil and Acrylic Painters, 2013; Savoir Faire award, Int Soc Acrylic Painters, 16th Ann Int Exhib, 2013. *Mem:* Int Soc Acrylic Painters (signature mem); Nat Soc Painters in Casein & Acrylic; Wis Watercolor Soc (juried mem); Transparent Watercolor oc Am (life mem); Northwestern Ohio Watercolor Soc (juried mem); Portrait Soc Am; Am Watercolor Soc; Nat Oil and Acrylic Painters Soc; Salmagundi Club; Watercolor West. *Media:* Watercolor, Acrylic, Digital Photography. *Publ:* Expressions in Watercolor, LA Today Mag, 1991, Dan Simoneau. *Dealer:* Lemon St Gallery Kenosha Wi; Xanadu Gallery Scottsdale Az. *Mailing Add:* 9507 74th St Kenosha WI 53142-8194

SIMONIAN, JUDITH
PAINTER, COLLAGE ARTIST
b Los Angeles, Calif, 1945. *Study:* Calif State Univ, Northridge, BA, 67; MA, 74. *Work:* Chemical Bank, NY; Security Pac Bank, NY & Los Angeles; Prudential Savings Insurance Co, NJ, Kaufman & Broad, Los Angeles & Paris, France; Newport Harbor Mus, Calif; Mus Contemp Art, San Diego. *Comn:* Sculpture, Barbara Sinatra Children's Ctr, Palm Springs, Calif, 86; street installation, Washington Proj Arts, Washington, DC, 87; site sculpture, Art on the Beach, NY, 88; The Art Mall (dressing rooms), New Mus, NY, 92; 6 sculptures (installation), Long Island Univ, Brooklyn, NY, 94. *Exhib:* Fresh Paint, San Francisco Mus Mod Art, 82; one-person exhibs, Ovsey Gallery, Los Angeles, Calif, 82-84, 86, 88, 90, 91 & 94, Leila Taghinia-Milani, NY, 84, Newport Harbor Art Mus, Calif, 84, Peter Miller Gallery, Chicago, Ill, 84 & 91 & Jane H Baum Gallery, NY, 89; Hells Kitchen, Salon de Guerre, NY, 92; Am Embassy, Zurich, Switz, 94; FAO Gallery, NY, 96; NY Kunsthalle (installation), 96; Long Island Univ, Brooklyn, 97; Spensieri Contemp Art, San Francisco, 97-98; Chimeat, NY, 98; Jorgensen Gallery, NY, 99; The Passion/Passions of Art, Richard Anderson, NY, 99; Out of Y2k, Im n il, Greenpoint, NY, 99; NY/Arts Mag Collection, Artists Mus, Lodz, Poland, Emmanuel Heller, Tel Aviv, Isreal, Kulture Bahnhof, Ger, 2000; Facts and Figures, Margaret Bodell Gallery, 2000. *Teaching:* Instr drawing, Moorpark Community Col, 74-78; East Los Angeles Community Col, 78-82; instr color theory & graphic art, Calif State Univ, Long Beach, 80-81; instr drawings & painting, Otis Parson Sch of Design, Los Angeles, Calif, 81-85; vis artist, Clairmont Grad Sch, Calif, 83 & 88; instr, Cooper Union, 93-. *Awards:* Fel, Calif Confederation of Arts, 78; Fel, Nat Endowment Arts, 87; Site Installation Design Award, Dept Transportation, NY, 96. *Bibliog:* Kathy Norklon (auth), First Newport Biennial-Los Angeles, Newport Harbor Art Mus, 84; Robert L Pincus (auth), Art as Artifact, Flash Art, summer 85; Terry Bissell (auth), Art: Judith Simonian, Southern Calif Home & Garden, 11/88. *Media:* Acrylic, Mixed Media. *Mailing Add:* 231 E 5th St No 5 New York NY 10003

SIMONS, DONA
PAINTER, VIDEO ARTIST
b Bryn Athyn, Pa, Aug 10, 1953. *Study:* Univ of the Arts, 1974; Moore Coll Art, 1976; Pa Acad of Fine Arts, studied with Arthur DeCosta, Henry Pearson, Ben Kamihira, Morris Blackburn & Lou Sloan, 1977-79. *Work:* Pub Libr, New Orleans, LA; New Orleans East Regional Libr. *Comn:* Portrait of Nat Hero, Dept Cult, Gov Curacao, Neth, Antilles, 1990; oil paintings, Shell Offshore, Inc, New Orleans, LA, 1998. *Exhib:* Prix Internat d'Art Contemporain de Monte Carlo, Monaco, 1985; Curacao Mus, Curacao, The Neth Antilles, 1991; Sylvia Schmidt Gallery, 1992-2005; Allentown Mus Art, Allentown, Pa, 1998; Masur Mus Art, Monroe, La, 2001; Alexandria Mus Art, Alexandria, La, 2003; State Conference on the Cult Economy, New Orleans, La, 2005; Acadiana Ctr Arts Lafayette, La, 2006, 2007; Contemp Arts Ctr, New Orleans, La, 2006-2007; Chateau de La Napoule Mandelieu la Napoule, France, 2007; Art as Artifact, New Orleans, 2008; New Orleans Jazz & Heritage

Gallery, 2009; Acad Gallery, New Orleans, 2010. *Mem:* Pa Acad of the Fine Arts Fel. *Media:* Oil. *Publ:* Illus, Henry's Journey, Portals Press, 1992, The Green and the Burning Alike, 1992, Cafe Millennium, 2000 & Waterblind, 2002; Art as Artifact catalog, 2010. *Mailing Add:* 6151 Milne Blvd New Orleans LA 70124

SIMONSON, ANNE
ADMINISTRATOR, EDUCATOR
Study: Univ Calif Berkeley, BA; Univ Calif Los Angeles, PhD. *Pos:* came to San Jose State Univ, 1982, instr Medieval, Renaissance, Baroque art/architecture, coordr creative arts program, 1987-2001, prof, art dept chair, currently. *Interests:* Neolithic to Bronze Age art in Europe and Central Asia and the history of the book. *Mailing Add:* San Jose State University Dept Art and Art History One Washington Sq #116 San Jose CA 95192

SIMOR, SUZANNA B
LIBRARIAN, GALLERY DIRECTOR
b Prague, Czech; US citizen. *Study:* Inst Fine Arts, NY Univ, MA, 74; Grad Sch Libr & Info Sci, Pratt Inst, MLS, 76. *Collection Arranged:* Italian Art--15th to 18th Century (auth catalog), Godwin-Ternbach Mus, Queens Col, 86. *Pos:* Head Art Libr, dir Art Ctr, Queens Col, City Univ NY, 80-. *Teaching:* Asst prof art librarianship, Queens Col, City Univ NY, 77-. *Awards:* Nat Endowment Arts Grant, 85; PSC/City Univ NY Grant, 86-87. *Mem:* Art Librs Soc NAM (chmn, 77, NY chap chmn, 90-); Coll Art Asn; Special Librs Asn-Mus-Arts and Humanities Div; Am Libr Asn; Libr Asn City Univ NY (chmn, 77-). *Res:* Art librarianship; art bibliography and research methods; late medieval and Renaissance art; 20th century art. *Interests:* Medieval and Renaissance art; art of the 20th century contemporary art and artists. *Publ:* Auth, articles, Basic Materials for Reference & Research in Art History, Queens Col, 81-86; auth & ed, Art of E Africa Slide Collection, IFLA, Art Librs Sect, 84; ed, NY Membership Directory, ARLIS/NY, 85; coauth, Italian Art--15th to 18th Century, Queens Col, 86; auth, Necessary luxury: art exhibitions in academic libraries, 90; The Credo in Context: Endorsing Other Themes, Pensee - image et communication en Europe medievale, 91. *Mailing Add:* 13927 Coolidge Ave Jamaica NY 11435

SIMPSON, BENNETT
CURATOR, CRITIC
Study: Univ Va, BA, 94. *Exhib:* Apex Art, NY, 99; Elysian Fields, Centre Pompidou, Paris, 2000; Shoot the Singer: Music on Video, ICA, Philadelphia, 2002; Make Your Own Life: Artists in and out of Cologne, 2004. *Pos:* Former ed, ArtByte Mag, NY & Purple Mag, NY; Whitney Lauder cur fel, Inst Contemp Art, 2001-2002; assoc cur, Philadelphia, 2002-2003 & Boston, 2004-07, Mus Contemp Art, Los Angeles, 2007-. *Publ:* contribr, articles in many professional journals. *Mailing Add:* ICA Boston 100 Northern Ave Boston MA 02210-1802

SIMPSON, DAVID
PAINTER
b Pasadena, Calif, Jan 20, 1928. *Study:* Calif Sch Fine Arts, with Clyfford Still & others, BFA, 56; San Francisco State Col, MA, 58. *Work:* Panza Collection, Varese, Italy; Laguna Art Mus, Laguna Beach, Calif; Muses Di Arte Moderna E Contempornea Di Trento E Rovereto & Mart, Italy; Albright Knox Art Gallery, Buffalo, NMex; and others. *Comn:* The Camera ella Musica, Palazzo di Ducale, Sasupilo, Italy. *Exhib:* Americans 1963, Mus Mod Art, NY, 63; retrospective, Oakland Mus, Calif, 78; Angles Gallery, Santa Monica, Calif, 91-92 & 94; Bemis Found, Omaha, Nebr, 92; Haines Gallery, San Francisco, 96, 2002 & 2007, 2010; Studio La Citta, Verona, Italy, 97, 2001, 2008, & 2012; Renate Schroder Galerie, Cologne, 2002; Charlotte Jackson Fine Arts, Santa Fe, NMex, 2005 & 2008, 2010-2011; Galerie Sonta Roesch, Houston, Tex, 2005, 2007, & 2012; Giacomo Guidi Arte Contemporanea, Rome, Italy, 2011; Modernism Gallery, San Francisco, Calif, 2009, 2011, 2012; Univ Art Mus, Laramie, 2013. *Teaching:* Prof art emer, Univ Calif, Berkeley, 65-. *Awards:* Nat Endowment Arts Grant, 90. *Media:* Acrylic, Canvas. *Dealer:* Haines Gallery San Francisco CA; Studio La Citta Verona Ital; Charlotte Jackson Fine Art Santa Fe NMex; Galerie Sonja Roesch Houston Tex. *Mailing Add:* 565 Vistamont Berkeley CA 94708

SIMPSON, JOSH (JOSIAH) J L SIMPSON
GLASS BLOWER
b Aug 17, 1937. *Study:* Hamilton Col, Clinton, NY, BA, 72. *Work:* Renwick Gallery/Smithsonian Inst, Washington, DC; Mus Fine Arts, Boston, Mass; Corning Mus, NY; Chrysler Mus Art, Norfolk, Va; Sphere Mus, Tokyo, Japan. *Comn:* Mega Planet, Nortel Inc, Tex, 97 & Moritex Corp, Japan, 98; Mega, Mega Planets, Royal Caribbean Cruise, Norway, 98. *Exhib:* New Glass, Corning Mus, NY, 79 & Heidi Schneider, Switz, 88; solo exhibs, Arnot Mus, Elmira, NY, 91; Int Exhib Glass, Kanazawa, Japan, 92; New Work, New Worlds, Hamilton Col, Fred L Emerson Gallery, NY, 94; White House Collection, White House, Washington, DC, 95; Visionary Landscapes, Bruce Mus, Conn, 98. *Teaching:* Glass, Penland Sch Crafts, NC, 89; Aichi Univ, Hirosawa, 93; Corning Mus, NY, 97. *Awards:* Humanitarian Award, Niche, 93; Achievement in Limited Series Design, Urban Glass, 96. *Bibliog:* S Frantz (auth), Contemporary Glass, 89; Artists look at earth, Smithsonian, 11/96; K Conover (auth), From a fiery inferno, Christian Sci, 4/6/97. *Mem:* Am Craft Enterprises, 84-85; Craft Emergency Relief Fund (pres, 85-92); life mem Glass Art Soc (pres, 92-94). *Media:* Glass. *Mailing Add:* Frank Williams Rd Shelburne Falls MA 01370

SIMPSON, LORNA
PHOTOGRAPHER, FILMMAKER
b Brooklyn, NY, 1960. *Study:* Sch Visual Arts, NY, BFA (photog), 83; Univ Calif, San Diego, MFA (visual arts), 85. *Exhib:* Solo exhibs incl Consejo Nacional Para La Cultura y Las Artes, Mexico City, 2003, Corridor, Wohnmaschine, Berlin, 2004, Sean Kelly Gallery, NY, 2004, 31, Mary & Leigh Block Mus of Art, Northwestern Univ, 2004, Coll of Wooster Art Mus, Ohio, 2004, Videos and Photographs, Galerie Obadia, Paris, 2004, Walter E Terhune Gallery, Owens Community Coll, Ohio, 2004, Prefix Inst Contemp Art, Toronto, 2005, Am Federation of Arts, 2006, Whitney Mus Am Art, 2007; group exhibs incl Biennial, Whitney Mus Am Art, NY, 91, 93, 95, 2002; Prefix Inst Contemp Art, Toronto, 2004; Public/Private, Auckland Triennial, New Zealand, 2004; Beginning Here: 101 Ways, Sch Visual Arts, NY, 2004; Adams and 21 Eves: Women Photographers from the Vault, Univ Art Mus, Calif State Univ, 2005; Transcending Time, Hood Mus Art, Dartmouth Coll, 2005; Double Exposure: African Americans Before and Behind the Camera, Wadsworth Atheneum Mus Art, Conn, 2005; Double Consciousness: Black Conceptual Art Since 1970, Contemp Art Mus Houston, Tex, 2005; Contemporary Voices, MoMA, NY, 2005; Bodies of Evidence: Work by Women of Color, Mus Art, RI Sch Design, 2005; Artists Interrogate: Race and Identity, Milwaukee Mus Art, 2005. *Teaching:* Distinguished artist-in-residence, Christian A Johnson Endeavor Found, Colgate Univ, 2003. *Awards:* Louis Comfort Tiffany Award, Louis Comfort Tiffany Found, 90; Whitney Mus Am Art Award, Cartier Found Contemp Art, 2001; Joyce Alexander Wein Artist Prize, Studio Mus, Harlem, 2006; Infinity Award, Int Ctr Photog, 2010. *Dealer:* Galerie Nathalie Obadia 3 rue du Cloitre Saint-Merri 75004 Paris France; Barbara Krakow Gallery 10 Newbury St Boston MA 02116; Jean-Yves Noblet Contemporary Prints 429 S 5th St Brooklyn NY 11211; Rhona Hoffman Gallery 118 N Peoria St Chicago IL 60607; Graphicstudio/USF 3702 Spectrum Blvd Tampa FL 33612; Gallery Karl Oskar 3008 W 71 Prairie Village KS 66208

SIMPSON, MARILYN JEAN
PAINTER, INSTRUCTOR
b Birmingham, Ala, 1929. *Study:* Univ Ala; Art Students League, NY; Inst Allende, San Miguel Allende, Mex; Madison Art Sch, Conn; with Robert Brackman; Am Univ Avignon, France; Rome & Florence, Italy. *Exhib:* Smithsonian Inst, Wash, DC; Pastel Soc Am, NY; Pastel Soc NMex; Pastel Soc West Coast; Pastel Soc N Fla; Arts in the Park, Degas Pastel Soc; Pastel Soc Southwest. *Pos:* dir, Sch Pastel Painting, Ft Walton Beach, Fla. *Teaching:* Dir & instr, Acad Fine Arts, Ft Walton Beach, Fla. *Awards:* Arts Speak, PSA Award, Edith Barow, PSA Award; Pres Award, PSWC; Richardson Award, PSNF, First Place, PSNF, Best in Show, PSNF; American Artists Prof League Award; Dick Bleik Award; Kitty Wallies Award. *Mem:* Signature mem Pastel Soc Am, NY; Knickerbocher Artist, USA, NY; Pastel Soc N Fla (founder & pres), Ft Walton Beach, Fla; Int Asn Pastel Soc (vpres), NY; Degas Pastel Soc. *Media:* Pastel, Oil. *Specialty:* Fine Arts Gallery. *Interests:* Teaching and Reading. *Publ:* Auth, The Art of Pastel Portraiture; auth, 100 Arts for the Parks, Artists Int; Northlight Mag (cover contest); contribr, Artist USA; Pastel Artist, Int. *Dealer:* Gallery Fine Arts Hwy 98 East Destin FL. *Mailing Add:* 2991 W Highway 98 Mary Esther FL 32569-2336

SIMPSON, WILLIAM KELLY
HISTORIAN, EDUCATOR
b New York, NY, Jan 3, 1928. *Study:* Yale Univ, BA, 47, MA, 48, PhD, 54; Ecole Practique Hautes Etudes, Paris. *Hon Degrees:* DHL, Am Univ, Cairo, 2001. *Collection Arranged:* The Pennsylvania-Yale Expedition to Nubia, Peabody Mus, Yale Univ, New Haven, Conn, 63; Recent Accessions in Egyptian & Ancient Near Eastern Art & The Horace L Mayer Collection, 72, Mus Fine Arts, Boston; Metrop Mus, NY; Univ Pa Mus, Philadelphia; The Offering Chapel of Kayemnolnet, Mus Fine Arts, Boston, 92; The Inscribed Material from Pa-Yale Excavations, Abydos, 95. *Pos:* Cur, Egyptian art & ancient Near Eastern art, Mus Fine Arts, Boston, 70-86. *Teaching:* Prof Egyptol, Yale Univ, 65-2004, chmn dept Near Eastern langs, 66-69; vis prof Egyptol, Univ Pa. *Awards:* Guggenheim Found Fel, 65. *Mem:* Archaeol Inst Am; Am Oriental Soc; Am Res Ctr in Egypt; Int Coun Mus Mod Art, NY; and others. *Publ:* Auth, Papyrus Reisner I-Records of a Building Project, 63; auth, Papyrus Reisner II-Accounts of the Dockyard Workshop, 65; auth, Papyrus Reisner III-Records of a Building Project in the Early Twelfth Dynasty, 69; coauth, The Ancient Near East: A History, 71; coauth, The Literature of Ancient Egypt, 72; auth, The Mastaba of Queen Mersyankh III, 74. *Mailing Add:* Katonah's Wood Rd Katonah NY 10536

SIMS, LOWERY STOKES
ART HISTORIAN, CURATOR
b Washington, DC, Feb 13, 1949. *Study:* Queens Col, City Univ New York, BA, 1970, MPhil, 1990, PhD, 1995; Johns Hopkins Univ, MA, 1972. *Hon Degrees:* Md Inst Coll Art, DHL, 1988; Moore Coll Art & Design, DArt, 1991; Parsons Sch Design, DArt, 2000; Atlanta Coll Art, DArt, 2002; Brown Univ, DFA, 2003; Mass Coll Arts & Design, 2010. *Exhib:* Romare Bearden: An Artist's Odyssey, (catalog essay & organizer), 1986; Race and Representation, (catalog essay), Hunter Coll Gallery, NY, 1987; Art as a Verb, The Evolving Continuum, (co-cur & essay), Maryland Inst Coll of Art, Baltimore, Md, 1988-89; Next Generation, Southern Black Aesthetic, (catalog essay), Southern Ctr Contemp Art, Winston-Salem, NC, 1990; Challenge of the Mod African-Am Artists, 1925-1945, 2003; Curator's Choice: Install & Insight, Nat Gallery, Kingston, Jamaica, 2004; Legacies: Contemp Artists Reflect on Slavery, New Hist Soc, 2006; Second Lives: Remixing the Ordinary, Mus Arts & Design, 2008; Dead or Alive, 2010; The Global Africa Proj, 2010; Against the Grain, 2012. *Pos:* Asst mus educ, Metrop Mus Art, NY, 1972-1975, assoc cur 20th century art, 1975-1995, & cur, 1995-2000; dir, Studio Mus in Harlem, 2000-05; pres, 2005, 2006; cur, Mus Arts & Design; juror, guest cur, Queens Mus, Studio Mus in Harlem, Pratt Inst, Caribbean Cult Ctr, New York, Cooper Union, and others; panelist, mem bd numerous orgs; adj cur, Studio Mus, Harlem, 2006-2007. *Teaching:* Vis critic, Md Inst, 87, Pa Acad Arts, 88, Univ Pa & Univ Tex, Austin; vis prof, Hunter Col, 2005, 06; vis prof, Queens Col, 2006; AD White prof at large, Cornell Univ, 2006-; vis prof, Univ Minn, Minneapolis, Minn, 2007. *Awards:* Frank Jewett Award, Coll Art Asn, 1991; Distinguished Alumni, City Univ NY Grad Ctr, 2002; Fel, Clark AA Inst, 2007; Lifetime Achievement Award, Women's Caucas for Art, 2008. *Mem:* Col Art Asn; Art Table Inc. *Res:* 20th century painting, sculpture, studio craft and archit especially of the last 30 years, with special interest in Afro-American, Latin American, Asian and Native American artists. *Interests:* Needlepoint, black memorabilia. *Publ:* Race Riots - Cocktail Parties - Black Panthers - Moon Shoots and Feminists: Faith Ringgold's

Observations on the 1960's in America, (essay), Faith Ringgold: A 25 Year Survey, Fine Arts Mus Long Island, Hempstead, New York, 1990; Beulahland (for Marilyn Monroe), An Icon for America, (essay), IDA Applebroog: Happy Families, A Fifteen-Year Survey, Contemp Arts Mus, Houston, 1990; Cultural Diversity or the Americanist Canon: The Aesthetic Dialog of the 1990's, (catalog essay), The Decade Show, New Mus Contemp Art, Studio Mus Harlem & Mus Contemp Hispanic Art, New York, 1990; Wifredo Lam and his contemporaries, 1938-1952, Studio Mus Harlem, 1992; Stuart Davis, American Painter (exhib catalog), Metropolitan Mus Art, 1991; Wifredo Lam and the International Avant-Garde, 1923-1982, 2002; Challenge of the Modern African-American Artists, 1925-1945, 2003; Persistence of Geometry, 2006; African American Art: 200 Years, 2000, 2008; Fritz Scholder: Indian/Not Indian, 2008; Second Lives, 2008; Dead or Alive, 2008; The Global Africa Proj, 2010; Against the Grain, Wood in Contemporary Art & Craft Design, 2002. *Mailing Add:* 1125 Lexington Ave New York NY 10075

SINA, ALEJANDRO
KINETIC ARTIST
b Santiago, Chile, May 10, 1945. *Study:* Univ Chile, MBA, 73; Ctr Advan Visual Studies, Mass Inst Technol, with Gyorgy Kepes & Otto Piene, fel, 73-79. *Work:* Mus Sci & Indust, Chicago; Nat Mus Fine Arts & Museo Interactivo Mirador, Santiago; Nat Sci Mus, Veno Park, Tokyo; Saitama Childrens Mus, Higashi-Matsuyama, Japan; Bruce Mus, Greenwich, Conn; Children's Hosp, Boston; The Butler Inst Am Art; Museo de Bellas Artes, Santiago; MBTA, Alewife Sta, Cambridge; Morris Mus; Mus Art, Iowa Univ; El Mirador, A Children's Mus, Santiago; pvt collection, Dana Farber; Harvard Sch Dental Medicine, Cambridge, Mass. *Comn:* End of Redline/Alewife Sta, Mass Bay Transit Authority, Cambridge, 85; Sprouts, Fidelity Investments HQ, Boston, 89; Coca Cola Hq with Jonathon Spiers, London, Eng, 93; Six Helicoils, The Trocadero, Sega Floor, London, Eng, 96; MCI HQ, Arlington, Va; Hyatt Regency, Cambridge; MIT Student Ctr; RG Vanderweill HQ, Boston; Pvt villa, Milan; King Faisal Complex, Riyadh; Art Pub Space, David Bermant; Consul Chile, Dr Paul Garber. *Exhib:* Gaslight Phenomena, Inst Contemp Art, Boston, 77; Five Artists, Five Technologies, Grand Rapids Art Mus, Mich, 79; Art in Light and Illusion, Isetan Mus Art, Tokyo, 82; Color-Light-Motion, Wadsworth Atheneum, Hartford, Conn, 84; ARTEC 89, Inagural Bienal, Nagoya, Japan; Les Artistes et la Lumiere, Rheims, France, 91; Electrique, Mus de la Civilisation, Que, Can; Esculturas Luminicas, Sala de Arte, CTC, Santiago, Chile; Licht, Kunst, Werke, Technorama Sci Ctr, Winterthur, Switz, 2008-2009; Open House NY, Focus Lightin Gallery, New York. *Teaching:* Instr, Ctr Advan Visual Studies, Mass Inst Technol, 73-77. *Awards:* Art Landmark, Genjii Cluster, Boston Soc Archits, 73; Fulbright Fel, 73-75; Nat Endowment Arts Grant, 76-77; Gov's Citation, Outstanding Artists, Boston, 85; Lumina Award, Light Artists, Entel Tower, Santiago, Chile, 95. *Bibliog:* Milan Ivelic & Gaspar Galaz (auths), La Pintura en Chile desde la Colonia hasta, 81; Sixto Escobar (producer), The Art of Alejandro Sina, La Plaza Prog, TV Channel 7, Boston, 83; Michael Webb (auth), The Magic of Neon, 83 & Liquid Fire, 90, Peregrine Smith Bks; Rudi Stern (auth), Contemporary Neon, 91 & The New Let There Be Neon, Larry Fuersich Retail Reporting; Christian Schiess (auth), The Light Artist Anthology, ST Publ, 93; Frank Popper (auth), Art of the Electric Age; Sci & Art, The Asahi Shimbun, Tokyo; Feedback, Art Responsive to instructions input or its Environment, Laboral; Edward A Shanken (auth), Art and Electronic Media, Phaidon, 2009. *Media:* Neon, Electronics; Glass. *Publ:* Auth, Guide Internacional de Arts Electroniques, Guide Kanal, Paris, France; Art & Electronic Media, Edward A Shanken, Phaidon Press. *Mailing Add:* 21 Andem Pl Brookline MA 02445

SINCLAIR, ROBERT (W)
PAINTER, SCULPTOR
b Saltcoats, Sask, Can, Feb 9, 1939. *Study:* Univ Manitoba Sch Art, BFA, 61; Univ Iowa, MA, 65, MFA, 67. *Work:* Art Gallery, Windsor, Ont; Agnes Etherington Art Gallery, Queens Univ, Kingston, Ont; Confederation Art Gallery, Charlottetown, PEI; Glenbow Mus, Calgary, Alta; Edmonton Art Gallery, Alta; Royal Collection, Windsor Castle Libr, Eng; Whyte Mus of the Rockies, Banff, Ala. *Comn:* Foyer painting (acrylic stain), Oxford Develop Group, Royal Trust Tower, Edmonton, Alta, 79; Slumped Glass Landscape (sculpture), Brit Petroleum, Calgary, Alta, 89. *Exhib:* Changing Visions, Art Gallery Ont, Toronto, 76-77; Solo exhibs, Gallery-Stratford, Ont, 76 & Edmonton Art Gallery, Alta, 82-83; Pertaining to Space, Art Gallery Ont, Toronto, 76-77; Diamond Jubilee Collection, Royal Libr, Windsor Castle, Eng, 86; Spaces & Places, Alta Art Found, traveling China & Japan, 86-90; Heaven-and-Earth, Whyte Mus Can Rockies, Banff, Alta, 91; Artists in Wilderness: Images of a Vanishing Alberta, Provincial Mus, Edmonton, 92; A View of Nfld, Art Gallery Nfld & Labrador Univ, St Johns, 96; Scott Gallery, Edmonton, Ala, continuing; Willock & Sax Gallery, Banff, Ala, continuing. *Teaching:* Prof art painting & drawing, Dept Art & Design, Univ Alta, 65-97; vis artist, Univ Iowa, 73 & Banff Sch Fine Art, 76; prof emeritus. *Awards:* Acto Gas Award, Outstanding Lifetime Achievement by an Edmonton Artist, 2004; Alta Centennial Medal, 2005; Alberta Centennial medal, Outstanding Contrib Arts, 2006; City of Edmonton's Salute to Exellence, Hall of Fame, 2009. *Bibliog:* Four Praire Artists (film), Can Broadcasting Corp, 85; Mary-Beth Laviolette (auth), A Delicate Art: Artists, Wildflowers, and Native Plants of the West, 2012. *Mem:* Royal Canadian Acad Arts; Can Soc Painters Watercolour. *Media:* Watercolor, Acrylic Stain; Folded Paper, Oil Painting, Embossed Prints, Oriental Brush Paintings. *Res:* Alta Wildflower Series, Grasslands Series, Bow Valley Series, Jaspered Series, Waterton Series, Flower's Breath Series. *Specialty:* Paintings, drawings, prints & sculpture, photographs. *Interests:* Facilitating mindfullness & watercolor workshops, Canada & New Zealand. *Publ:* Contributing articles, Visual Arts Alberta Association newsletters, www.visualartsalberta.com. *Dealer:* Gallery at Jasper Park Lodge Box 1651 Jasper Alberta T0E 1E0; Willock & Sax 210 Bear St Banff AB T1L 1C2; Scott Gallery 10411-124st Edmonton AB T5N 3Z5; Gallery at Banff Springs Hotel 405 Spray Ave Banff AB; Gallery at Chateau Whistler 4559 Chateau Blvd Whistler BC Von 1B4; Leyton Galley Bairds Cove St Johns NL AIL 3V2. *Mailing Add:* 10819 52 Ave Edmonton AB T6H 0P2 Canada

SINDELIR, ROBERT JOHN
GALLERY DIRECTOR, ADMINISTRATOR
b Olivia, Minn, June 12, 1932. *Study:* Univ Miami, Coral Gables, Fla, with Virgil Barker, AB, 57. *Collection Arranged:* Christo, Wrapped Coastline, 72; Lee Krasner, Selected Paintings, 73; Duane Michals, Photographs, 77; Philip Pearlstein, Selected Paintings, 78; Komar and Melamid, Monotype Prints, 90. *Pos:* Dir, Art Pub Places Prog, Miami, Fla, 74-76, Mitchell Wolfson Gallery, 83-90, Kendall Campus Art Gallery, 90-. *Teaching:* Instr humanities, Miami-Dade Community Col, 70-74. *Publ:* Auth, African Tribal Art (exhib catalog), Miami-Dade Community Col, 83; contribr, Journal of Decorative and Propaganda Arts, Wolfsonian Found, 86; auth, Susana Sori (exhib catalog), Thomas Ctr, 88; Julio Antonio (exhib catalog), Elite Fine Art, 89; Lynn Davison (exhib catalog), Miami-Dade Community Col, 91

SINGER, ALAN DANIEL
PAINTER, PRINTMAKER
b Jun 19,1950. *Study:* The Cooper Union, BFA, 1972; Cornell Univ, MFA, 1975; Pratt, post grad. *Work:* Leigh Yawkey Woodson Art Mus, Wausau, WI; The US Postal Mus, Washington, DC. *Comn:* Birds and Flowers of 50 States, US Postal Service, Washington, DC, 1982; 5 Pathogens for Levaquin Johnson & Johnson, 2006; Everson Mus Art, Syracuse, NY, 2000, 06; Dr. Shirley Sherwood, the Alisa & Isaac M Sutton Collection. *Exhib:* State Birds & Flowers, Smithsonian, Washington, DC, 1988; Finger Lakes Invitational, Memorial Art Gallery, Rochester, NY, 1992; Biennial, Everson, Syracuse, NY, 2000; Pushing the Envelope, Norman Rockwell Mus, Stockbridge, MA, 2000; Everson Mus Art, Syracuse, NY, 2006; Schweinfurth Mus Art, Auburn, NY, 2007; Nat Watercolor Exhib, Art Ctr at Old Forge, NY, 2007; Juried Show, Bowery Gallery, New York, 2009; In Fullbloom, Mills Pond Gallery, St James, NY, 2009; Botanicals, Traveling Show, Hunt Inst for Botanical Documentation, Pittsburgh, Pa, 2009-2010; solo exhib, OCK Hee Gallery, Honeoye Falls,NY, 2010; Nat Adirondacks Watercolor Exhib, Old Forge, NY, 2011; Windsor Whip Works, Art Center, Windsor, NY, 2011; Bridges, Math and Art, Towson, Md, 2012; Guide to Nature, Roger Tory Peterson Inst, Jamestown, NY, 2012. *Pos:* pres, The Print Club of Rochester, Rochester, NY, 1995-2000. *Teaching:* vis artist, painting, Parson's School of Design (grad prog), 1986-87, Syracuse Univ, 2006; prof, fine art, Rochester Inst of Technology, 1987-. *Awards:* Purchase Prize, Watercolors, Nassau Community Col, 1983; S.O.S. Award, Slice of Life, Dyer Art Ctr, 2003. *Mem:* Print Club of Rochester, pres, 1995-2000; Coll Art Assoc; Am Soc of Botanical Artists. *Media:* Oil, Watercolor, Print making, Art writer. *Res:* Studio art practice, digital printmaking. *Interests:* Writing, gardening, hiking, art & antiques. *Publ:* Auth, Wildlife Art, Rockport Press, 1999; illusr, State Birds, Lodestar Books, 1986. *Dealer:* Mona Berman Fine Art 72 Lyon St New Haven CT 06511. *Mailing Add:* 3021 Elmwood Ave Rochester NY 14618

SINGER, ESTHER FORMAN
PAINTER, CRITIC
b New York, NY. *Study:* Art Students League, 39-41; Temple Univ, 41-44; NY Univ, 47-49; New Sch Social Res, 68-70; Fairleigh Dickinson Univ, pvt study with Hans Hoffman, Brackman, George Gross, Jackson Pollack, & Tosun Bayrak; Art Scholar in Elem and High School. *Hon Degrees:* Hon degree, Univ dell'Arte Contemp, Parma, Italy. *Work:* NJ State Mus, Trenton; Finch Mus Contemp Art, Whitney Mus Permanent Collection, New York; Yonkers Mus, NY; Morris Mus Arts & Scis, Morristown, NJ; Newark Mus, NJ; Libr Cong; pvt collections, Sen Nelson Stamler & Gov Richard J Hughes; State House, Morven, NJ; Seton Hall Univ Mus Collection, NJ; and others. *Comn:* Many works in pvt & pub collections worldwide. *Exhib:* Chubb Art Gallery, Warren, NJ, 86; Shering-Plough, Madison, NJ, 88; Johnson & Johnson Corp Hq, 90; Governors Club, Palm Beach, Fla, 90; Aids Project, Hyacinth Fund, 91; Biennale Int Dell Arte Florence, Italy, 11-12/2005, 2006, & 2007; and others. *Pos:* Guest panelist, Art Forms, WOR-TV, 67-68; ed, Newark News, 70-74; art critic, Am Artist Mag, 72-, Worrall Press, 74- & Suburban Life Mag, currently; art ed, Jersey J Newspaper, Suburban Mag & Newark Evening News; staff writer, Am Artist Mag; syndicated art column, Worrall Press; contribr, writer, Am Artist Mag, Suburban Life Mag. *Teaching:* Instr elementary art, Baird Community Ctr, South Orange, NJ, 69-; pvt instr at own studio, South Orange, NJ, 68-70; lectr, groups of women, NJ. *Awards:* Gov Purchase Award, Art from NJ 10; Painting Prize, Mus Mod Art, Paris, 73; and others. *Bibliog:* Articles in NJ Suburban Life Mag, 3/70; article, New York Art Rev Mag, 87; Art Views (film), Ch 36, 10/91; and others. *Mem:* Artists Equity Asn, NJ & NY; Old Bergen Art Guild; Painters & Sculptors Soc, NJ; Am Veterans Soc Artists. *Media:* Acrylic. *Res:* Painting, traveling to embassies of the world-rotating countries prog by US Gov. *Interests:* Traveling, Museums. *Collection:* Abstract art. *Publ:* American Artist Magazine; Art News Local Lectures (slide to groups on art). *Dealer:* Helander Gallery Palm Beach FL; Key Gallery Soho NY. *Mailing Add:* 36 Schweinberg Dr Roseland NJ 07068

SINGER, JONATHAN M
PHOTOGRAPHER
Study: Southampton Coll, grad (1st Prize Sculpture) 1966, study with Ilya Bolotowsky & Willem DeKooning; MD, 1974. *Work:* Smithsonian Libraries, Washington; Nat Mus Natural History, Washington. *Exhib:* Solo exhibs, Aurora Gallery, New York, 2005, Smithsonian Libraries, Nat Mus Natural History, Washington, 2008. *Awards:* Martin Luther King Award; Victor Hasselblad Del Award, 2008. *Publ:* Botanica Magnifica (5-vol folio set), Cone Editions Press, 2008. *Dealer:* Throckmorton Fine Art 3rd Fl 145 E 57th St New York NY 10022. *Mailing Add:* Westwood Gallery 10 Westwood Ave Westwood NJ 07675

SINGER, MICHAEL
SCULPTOR
b 1945. *Study:* Cornell Univ, BFA, 67; Rutgers Univ, New Brunswick, grad study, 68; Yale Univ, Norfolk Prog, 68. *Work:* Albright-Knox Art Gallery, Buffalo; Australian Nat Gallery, Canberra; Louisiana Mus Mod Art, Humrebaek, Denmark; Solomon R Guggenheim Mus, Mus Mod Art & Metrop Mus Art, NY; Yale Univ Art Gallery; and

others. *Comn:* Urban renewal waterfront park, Long Wharf, New Haven, Conn; recycling center, Dept Pub Works, Phoenix, Ariz; Those Who Survived (sculptural garden), Stuttgart, WGer; sculpture & walkway, Grand River East Bank, Grand Rapids, Mich, 94; interior sculpture garden, New Denver Airport. *Exhib:* Solo exhibs, Galerie Zabriskie, Paris, 81, J Walter Thompson Art Gallery, NY, 83, Solomon R Guggenheim, NY, 84, Sperone Westwater, NY, 86, Michael Singer Ritual Series, Retelling, Fine Arts Ctr, Art Gallery, State Univ NY-Stonybrook & Michael Singer-Ritual Series, Santa Barbara Contemp Arts Forum, 87, Artworks: Michael Singer, Williams Coll Mus Art, Williamstown, Mass, 90; Sculpture Inside Outside, Walker Art Ctr, Minneapolis, 88; Collage, Robinson Orange Gallery, Boston, 89; Arts on Paper, Weatherspoon Art Gallery, Univ NC, Greensboro, 90-91; The Transparent Thread: Asian Philosophy in Recent Am Art (travel), Hofstra Mus, Hofstra Univ, Hempstead, NY, 90 & many other mus, 90-92; Art for the Land, Five Points Gallery, E Chatham, NY, 91; Guggenheim's Ten Young Artists Theodorn Award Show, Documenta; The Kunsthaus Zurich's Mythos and Ritual; Sculpture in the Twentieth Century, Reihen, Switz. *Bibliog:* Patricia C Phillips (auth), Michael Singer: Williams College, Artforum, 131-132, 1/91; Michele Cone (auth), Baroque Nature, Arts Mag, 3/91; Ann Wilson Lloyd (auth), Michael Singer at Williams College Museum of Art, Art in Am, 4/91

SINGERMAN, HOWARD
EDUCATOR, ADMINISTRATOR
Study: Antioch Col, BA, 1975; Claremont Grad Sch, MFA, 1978; Univ Rochester, PhD, 1996. *Pos:* Mus editor, Mus of Contemporary Art, Los Angeles, 1985-88. *Teaching:* Assoc prof Contemporary Art and Theory, McIntire Dept of Art, Univ Virgina, formerly; Phyllis and Josef Caroff Prof Fine Arts, Dept Chair, Hunter Col Dept Art & Art History, NY, currently. *Publ:* Published regularly in Artweek and Artforum. *Mailing Add:* Hunter Art & Art History Department Main Campus 695 Park Avenue 11th Fl North Building New York NY 10065

SINGH, CAROLYN
PAINTER, CERAMIST
b St Paul, Minn, May 11, 1947. *Study:* Univ Minn, studied with Malcolm Myers, Raymond Hendler, Warren MacKenzie, BA (studio arts), 72, BFA (painting & drawing), studied with Raymond Hendler, Herman Somburg, George Morrison, Lynn A Gray, 72. *Work:* Museo de Arte del INBA, CD Juarez, Chih, Mex; Dept Art & Prinkmaking, Univ Minn, Minneapolis; Nat Bank Com San Antonio, Tex; El Paso Mus Art, Tex; The Bank of El Baso, El Paso, Tex. *Comn:* painting, comn by Hazel Johnson, Minneapolis, Minn, 80; watercolor painting, comn by Sean Jarem, Huntsville, Ala, 85; painting, comn by Elizabeth Jarem, Huntsville, Ala, 86; Lg Bowl, Comn by Rebecca Krasne, 97, 2000; paintings, comn by V. Ajay Singh & Morela Hernandez, Seattle, Wash, 2006; paintings, comn by Joseph & Irma Raseon, Phoenix, Ariz, 2006. *Exhib:* 16th Ann Exhib Western Fedn Watercolor Socs, Art Ctr Corpus Christi, Tex, 91; Ariz Aqueous VII, Tubac Arts Ctr, Ariz, 92; Artists on Art, El Paso Mus Art, Tex, 93; Seven Points of View, Americana Mus, El Paso, Tex, 93; Transpositions, Galerie M, Berlin, 96; Desert Echos: The DIVA Show (I),The Peoples Gallery, El Paso, Tex, 98, & The DIVA Show (II), El Museo de Arte del INBA, CD Juarez, Chih, Mex, 98; Desert Echo IV/Sacred Journey, Chamizal Nat Mem, Los Paisanos Galery, El Paso, Tex, 99; Adair Margo Gallery, El Paso, Tex, 2000; Desert Echo: Women Illuminate the Sacred, Women's Mus: An Inst for the Future, Dallas, 2001; Keith Batchelor (photograph) and Carolyn Singh (mixed media), Arts place Lexington, KY, 2002; The Other Nude Show, Miller Fine Art, 2003; Earth and Air Ceramics by Carolyn Singh, photographs by Leonor de Lohle, CTR Libr Gallery, Lexington, Ky, 2005; Kisses at the Gate: Painted Poems, Heritage Art Ctr, Lexington, Ky, 2010; Carolyn Singh The Butterfly Zone, Heritage Art Ctr, Lexington, Ky, 2011; Solo exhib, Family Affair, Heritage Art Ctr, Lexington, Ky, 2011. *Pos:* artist, Laudable Mud Studio. *Teaching:* Teacher drawing, painting & claywork, El Paso Mus Art Sch, 83-2000; instr figure drawing & sculpture, Dept Prof & Continuing Educ, Univ Tex, El Paso, 93-2000 & Sculpture Ctr Life Long Learning, 96-2000, Laudable Mud Studio, Lexington, KY, 2005-; instr, Carolyn Singh Studio, El Paso, 1985-2000. *Awards:* Second Place, Rio Bravo Watercolorists Ann Exhib, 94 & 95; Juror's Selection Award, Close to the Border: Biennial Exhib, 94; Second Place, NMex Watercolor Soc, 92; Best in Mixed Media, Visual Expressions of Love Exhibit, Gallery on Main, Eastern Ky Univ, 2003. *Bibliog:* Betty Ligon (auth), The Women's Voices Heard Through the Eyes, El Paso Inc, 10/11-17/98; NEUE Bildende Kunst (auth), Berlin, Ger, 10/11/96; Jaime Castaneda Reyes (auth), Acuarelas del Rio Bravo, Seccion Cultural, Periodico Norte, Juarez, Mex, 10/94; Scott Wampler (ed), Contemporary American Oil Painting, Jilin Fine Arts Publ, Chang Chun, China, 99; Jacquelyn Stroud Spier (auth), Desert Echo: Women Illuminate the Sacred, Women's Mus, Dallas, Tex, 2000; Tuland Review, Dept of Art, Tulane Univ, New Orleans, LA, Fall, 2000; David Milton (auth), In a High Traffic Area, Lexington Herald Leader, 8/11/02; Heather Lindquist (auth), Get Some Color at Gallery Hop, Heritage Center's Last Show, Nudes are Highlights, Lexington Herald Ledger, Weekender, p 26, 2/2004. *Mem:* Signature mem Rio Bravo Watercolorists (pres, 87-88 & 93-94, vpres, 91-92); signature mem NMex Watercolor Soc; signature mem Tex Watercolor Soc; Southwestern Watercolor Soc; Purple Sage Soc. *Media:* Mixed Media, Watercolor; Clay; Pearl & Gemstone Jewelry. *Publ:* Auth, Artists, donors deserve contributions break, El Paso Times, 83; Guest speaker, Rio Bravo Watercolorists Newsletter, 90; Earth and Air (video), LPL Gallery, Lexington, KY, Jan/Feb, 2005. *Dealer:* Laudable Mud Studio. *Mailing Add:* 4109 Kentucky River Parkway Lexington KY 40515

SINGLETARY, MICHAEL JAMES
PAINTER
b New York, NY, Jan 23, 1950. *Study:* Art Student League; Vt Acad, 68; Univ Ghana, W Africa, 69; Guadalajara Univ, Mex, 70; Ecole De Beaux Art, Fountainbleau, France, 71; Syracuse Univ, BFA, 72; RI Sch Design, 73; Lehman Col, New York, 74; State Univ New York, 88; Bob Blackburn Printmaking Workshop, 88. *Work:* Pvt collections of Kim Alexis, Don King, Dizzy Gillespie, Nancy Wilson, and others. *Comn:* Eight painting ser, Am Contract Designers, New York, NY; 12 painting ser for Grand Paradise Island Hotel, Creative Concepts, NY; 7 painting ser for hotel chain, Sheraton Inn, Roanoke, Va; Tribute to Woodie Shaw, New York Jazz Committee; Martin Luther King, painting, Ariel Mgt Corp, Chicago, Ill; 23 portraits, New York City Basketball Hall of Fame. *Exhib:* solo exhibs, US Fed Court House, NY, 82-84, 112 Greene St Gallery, Soho, NY, 90 Jazz Series, Dalcour Fine Art, 90, Mercy Col, Dobbs Ferry, NY, 90, Iona Col, New Rochelle, NY, 90, Heritage Show, NY Univ, 90; Printmakers Show, Kent State Univ, 90; Edwin A Ulrich Mus Art, Wichita, Kans, 90; The Humanist Icon, NY Acad Art, NY & Univ Va, 90; Bayly Art Mus, 90; and others. *Pos:* Assoc dir, CBS Inc, 75-86. *Teaching:* Artist-in-residence, Bronx Mus Art, 72-73; master teacher mosaic, Cloister Mus, Metrop Mus Art, New York, 73; teacher art, New York City Bd Educ, 74; artist-in-residence, Studio Mus, 74; Sarah Lawrence Col Gallery Sch, Bronxville, NY, 89-90. *Awards:* First Prize Portrait, Bridgeport Art League Exhib, Bridgeport Mus, 85. *Bibliog:* Television appearances, Best Talk in Town, WPIX, New York, 88, Phil Donahue Show, WNBC, New York, 89 & State of the Art Show, WDMC, 90; Fine arts and collectibles, Emerge Mag, 10/89; numerous other mag & newspaper articles. *Mem:* Dir Guild Am; Writers Guild Am; Harrison Art League; Found Community Artists; New York Artist Equity ASN. *Media:* Acrylic, Oil. *Publ:* The artist life - A Master of Improvisation, Artist Mag, 3/91; The art of Basketball, Daily News, New York, 9/24/91; Inside Track Michael Singletary: Guilding Light Gets Jazzy, Soap Opera Digest; Own Way, Art Sect, Kenichi Ishizuka, Tokyo, Japan, winter 91. *Mailing Add:* 308 Macs Farm Ct Silver Spring MD 20905-5034

SINNER, STEVE
SCULPTOR
b Omaha, 1942. *Study:* Iowa State Univ, BS (industrial educ), 65. *Work:* Mus Art & Design, New York. *Exhib:* Arrowmont Sch Arts and Crafts, Gatlinburg, Tenn, 2001; Minn Mus Art, St Paul, Minn, 2001; Univ Calif, Davis, 2001; Turned Wood-Small Treasures, del Mano Galleries, LA, 2003-2010; Beneath the Bark: 25 Years of Woodturning, BYU, 2004; SOFA Chicago, 2001-2010; SOFA, New York, 2003-2010; 500 Wood Bowls: A Western Perspective, 2007; Masters: Woodturning- Major Works by Leading Artists, Lark Books, 2009; Wood Art Today 2, Schiffer Publ, 2010; Selected Works, del Mano Gallery, 2004-2010; Our Turn Now: Artists Speak Out in Wood, Ohio Craft Mus, Columbus, Ohio, 2006

SIPHO, ELLA
PAINTER
b Kansas City, Mo, Aug 12, 1964. *Exhib:* Small Works, Limner Gallery, New York, 2002; Legler Barn Mus, Fem Canvas, Womens Art Hist, Kans, 2003; Paradigms of Conception, Amsterdam Whitney, New York, 2003; group exhibs, Galerie Gora, Montreal, Can, 2003 & 30+ KCAC Invitational, Kansas City, Mo, 2007; Regional River Market, Kansas City Artist Coalition, Kansas City, Mo, 2003; Lessedra World Print Ann, Lessedra Gallery Contemp Art Projects, Sofia, Bulgaria, 2004; Art Expo, New York, Sneak Preview Attraction Art, 2005; Int Experimental Film Festival, Florean Mus, Romania, 2005; Bohemian Gallery, 2005; The Mus Television & Radio, Beverly Hills, Calif, 2005; Int Videoart Festival, Sala Estense, Piazza Municipale, Ferrara, Italy, 2005; ARTV Award recipient collection, Marlene Tseng Yu Studio, New York, 2006; Snap to the grid, LACDA, Los Angeles, Calif, 2006-2007; 3rd Ed Int Experimental Film Festival Carbunari, Mus Florean, Romania, 2006; Gates Proj Exhib, ARC Gallery, Chicago, Ill, 2006. *Awards:* River Market Annual, Kansas City Artist Coalition, 2003; Frontice Piece Cover Award, New Art Int, 2003 & 2004; Manhattan Arts Award, 2003; ARTV Award, Venetian Resort Las Vegas, 2005; Prize of Excellence-Award of Distinction, Media 2 Art Biennial, Art Addiction Medial Mus, 2007. *Bibliog:* Peter Wiley (auth), Gallery & Studio, 2002-2003; Jeremy Sedley (auth), New Art Int, Book Art Press, 2003; Tom Palmer (auth), Am Art Collection, Alcove Bks, 11/2004; The View Grandview Parks, 2004; Art World News, 11/2002 & 1/2006; John M Ramirez (auth), Ella Sipho: An American Treasure, Artsource Newsletter, Vol I, No V, 11/2006. *Mem:* Chicago Artist Coalition. *Media:* Acrylic, Oil, Filmmaker. *Publ:* Art Exposed, 2002; Direct Art, 2003; Montreal Gallery Guide (catalog) 6/2003; American Art Collector, Vol 1, 2004. *Mailing Add:* 22952 W 220th St Spring Hill KS 66083

SIPIORA, LEONARD PAUL
MUSEUM DIRECTOR, MUSEOLOGIST
b Lawrence, Mass, Sept 1, 1934. *Study:* Vanderbilt Univ; Univ Mich, Ann Arbor, AB (cum laude), 55, MA, 56. *Collection Arranged:* Ann Nat Sun Carnival Exhib; Biennial, Int Designer Craftsmen; W S Horton Retrospective, 70; Tom Lea Retrospective, 71; Walter Griffin Retrospective, 71; Kress Collection, 19 & 20th Cent Am Art, Mexican Colonial Coll, Art on Paper Coll. *Pos:* Co-founder & pres, El Paso Arts Coun, 69-70, dir, 71-; dir, El Paso Mus Art, 67-91; ret. *Teaching:* Ctr for Lifelong Learning, Univ Tex, El Paso, Tex. *Awards:* Knight Grand Cross of Malta. *Mem:* Tex Asn Mus (pres, 77-79); Am Asn Mus; Am Fedn Arts; Am Platform Asn; Asn Art Mus Dir; Mt Plains Mus Asn (pres, 78-79); Appraisers Asn Am. *Res:* Nineteenth and twentieth century American painting. *Specialty:* American/European Fine Art. *Interests:* Am, European, Oriental Art. *Collection:* American paintings and graphics. *Publ:* Auth, The Universality of Tom Lea (catalog), 71; A Community Oriented Art Museum, Southwest Gallery Art Mag, 71; auth foreword, Biography of John Enneking, 72. *Mailing Add:* 1012 Blanchard El Paso TX 79902

SIRA, VICTOR
PHOTOGRAPHER
Study: Central Univ Venezuala, Caracas, 1987-99; Int Ctr Photog, New York, 1990-91; City Univ NY, 1994-97. *Exhib:* Latin Am Photog in New York, Puebla, Mex, 2001; 50 Crows Found, San Francisco, 2002; Rencountre D'Arles, France, 2003, 2005; Leica Gallery Solms, Germany, 2006; European Cult Capital, Luxembourt, 2007. *Awards:* 50 Crows Int Fund Documentary Photog Grant, 2002; W Eugene Smith Fel Grant, 2003; Mosaique Fel Grant, 2003; Guggenheim Found Fel, 2006; NY Found Arts Fel, 2008. *Mailing Add:* 38 Morton St Apt 5C New York NY 10014

SIRÉN, JANNE
MUSEUM DIRECTOR
Study: Coll Holy Cross, BA in Art History, Worcester, Mass; NYU, MA in Art History, PhD in Art History. *Collection Arranged:* Georg Baselitz: Remix; Surrealism and Beyond: Masterpieces from the Israel Museum; Defiance and Melancholy-German Painting from the Dresden Albertinum/Galerie Neue Meister and Helsinki School-Photography and Video Now. *Pos:* asst art history prof Hebrew U, Jerusalem, 2000-2004; dir Tampere Art Mus, Tampere, Finland, 2004-2007, Helsinki Art Mus, 2007-2013, Albright-Knox Art Gallery, Buffalo, 2013-. *Mailing Add:* Albright-Knox Art Gallery 1285 Elmwood Ave Buffalo NY 14222

SIRLIN, DEANNA LOUISE
PAINTER, ENVIRONMENTAL ARTIST
b Brooklyn, NY, Mar 7, 1958. *Study:* State Univ NY, Albany, BA, 78; Queens Col, City Univ NY, MFA, 80. *Work:* Macon Mus Arts & Sci, Ga; Ga Pac & Egleston Hosp, Atlanta; United Airlines Dalles Airport, Washington, DC; Penny McCall Found, NY; Woodruff Park, Atlanta, Ga; High Mus Art, Atlanta, Ga; Shenzhen Inst Art, China. *Comn:* Ceramic Tondos, Omni Hotel, Charlotte, NC, 91; Paintings, Omni Hotels, Miami, Fla, 94; Art on Digital Billboard, Arts Festival Atlanta, Ga, 96; Installation-Glass-Silkscreen & Etching, Fulton Co, Atlanta, Ga, 98; Atlanta Gas Light, Ga; Wells Corp, Minn; Hartsfield-Jackson Int Airport, Atlanta, 2005; Memorial, Sci Bldg, Agnes Scott Coll, Decatur, Ga, 2008; color transparency wall, Cousins Properties, Atlanta, Ga, 2009; color transparencies, Pope and Lard, Atlanta, Ga, 2009; Falling Water, exterior mosaic, Fire Sta 18, Atlanta, Ga, 2009; Round the Clock, color transparency, Fire Sta 13, Atlanta, Ga, 2009; C Flow of Atlanta, Day of Awe, Flux Projs, Atlanta. *Exhib:* Solo exhibs, Arnot Art Mus, Elmira, NY, 83, Catholic Univ, Washington, DC, 86, Forecasts, Cheekwood Fine Arts Ctr, Nashville, Tenn, 95, Quarnity, Nexus Contemp Art Ctr, Atlanta, Ga, 96, High Mus Art, Atlanta, Ga, 99, Vanishing Point Installation, Univ Ca'Foscari Venezia, Italy, 2001 & Installation, Saltworks Gallery, Atlanta, Ga, 2003, Plus Gallery, Denver, 2006, Ctr 4 Recent Drawing, London, 2006, Ferst Ctr for Arts, Atlanta, 2006, Whitespace Gallery, Atlanta, Ga, 2009; Multiple World: An Int Survey of Artists Books, Atlanta Coll Art, 94; Collaborating Couples, Ga Mus Art, Athens, 2000; New Orleans Triennial, New Orleans Mus Art, 2001; Kunsthaus Invitational, Heidenheim, Ger, 2002; Shenzhen Biennial, Guan Shanyue Art Mus, China, 2002; Shenzhen Biennial, 2002 & 2004; Antalya Cultural Ctr, Turkey, 2004; group shows, Color, Space 301, Mobile, Ala, 2006; Genius Loci, Venice, Ital, 2007; Whitespace, Atlanta, Ga, 2009; 5+15+5, Oyten, Ger, 2011; Bank of America Plz, 2012; Billboard Art, Atlanta, 2012; Kleine Art, Ger, 2012. *Awards:* Yaddo Found Fel, 83; Ga Women in the Visual Arts Honoree, Ga Dept Natural Resources, 97; Artist in Communities Grant, Fulton Co Arts Coun, Atlanta, Ga, 2002; Artist in residence, Padies Chateau, Lempaut, France. *Bibliog:* Jerry Cullum (auth), On Meteorological & Meditative Conditions: Reflections on the paintings of Deanna Sirlin, Fay Gold Gallery, 95; Blake Leland (auth), Into the Blue, Solomon Projects, 98; Carrie Przybilla (auth) Retracings, High Mus of Art, 99; W Eric Martin (auth) Art on High, Modern Reprographics, 2000; John Vilani (auth), Catching the World's Emerging Art Voices, Sirlin's Vanishing Point in Venice, Art World News, 44, 9/2001; Frances Colpitt (auth), Report from New Orleans, Art in Am, 58-63, 11/2001; Nancy Staab (auth), Art on a Grand Scale, Southern Living Mag, 10/2004; Larry Qualls, Arton Paper Mag, 2005; Rebecca Cochran, Sculpture Mag, 2005; Quadra Rodriguez (auth), Catalyst Magazine, 2006; Sandi Toksvig (auth), London Telegraph, 2006. *Mem:* CAA. *Media:* Painting and Site Works and Installation. *Publ:* Auth, Disappearance, Fulton Co Arts Coun, 93; Into the Blue, Solomon Projects, 98; auth, Shes Got What it Takes: American Women Artists in Dialogue, Chart Art Books, Milan, Italy, 2013. *Mailing Add:* 120 North Christopher's Run Alpharetta GA 30004-3100

SISSMAN, LIRON
PAINTER
b New York, NY, May 07, 1966. *Study:* Hebrew Univ Jerusalem, BSc, 1985-1987; Avni Fine Art Inst, 1987-1988; NY Univ, MBA, 1989-1991; NY Acad Art, 1996-1999; Landscape studies with David Dunlop, 2005-2006 & Skip Whitcomb 2008, Scott Tallman Powers, 2009, Donald Demers, 2011. *Work:* PeproTech Inc, Rocky Hill, NJ; Taro Pharmaceuticals, Hawthorne, NY; AtlantiCare Med Center, Atlantic City, NJ; Potomac Homes, Princeton, NJ; Lounge Zen, Teaneck, NJ; Square Business Products, Mahwah, NJ; Wex Trust Capital, NY; Glendale Adventist Med Center, Glendale, Ca; Ridgewood Oral and Maxillofacial Surgery, Ridgewood, NJ; Mount Sinai Medical Center, NY; Data Recovery, Scotch Plains, NJ; Jesta Group, NY; St Joseph Mercy Okland, Pontiac, Mich; Atlanticare Health Park, Hammonton, NJ; Valley Hosp Ctr, Cortlandt Manor, NY; Hackensack Univ Medical Ctr, Westwood, NJ; Atlanticare Cancer Care Inst, Cape May, NJ. *Comn:* Seascape, Dr Yitzhak Stabinsky, Tel Aviv, Israel, 2004; Adi & Donna, Dr Yitzhak Stabinsky, Lawrenceville, NJ, 2004; Leaving the Nest, Ms Miriam Coti, Bergenfield, NJ, 2004; Steve Finley, PeproTech co-found, PeproTech Inc, Rock Hill, NJ, 2005; Aviv, Dr Yitzhak Stabinsky, Tel Aviv, Israel, 2007; Princeton Golf, Dr. Yitzhak Stabinsky, Lawrenceville, NJ, 2007; Asaf, Dr Yitzhak Stabinski, Lawrenceville, NJ, 2008; Pelican on a Seashore, Dr Yitzhak Stabinsky, Lawrenceville, NJ, 2008; Asaf II, Dr Yitzhak Stabinsky, Lawrenceville, NJ, 2009; Yuval, Michal & Asaf, Shiloni, Oak Park, Calif, 2009; Sisters, Dr. Yitzhak Stabinsky, Tel Aviv, Israel, 2010; Inner Strength, Drs. Makiko & Albert Fliss, Cranberry, NJ, 2012. *Exhib:* Ridgewood Art Inst Juried Regional, Ridgewood Art Inst, Ridgewood, NJ, 2001-2003, 2005, 2007; Theme Exhib Flowers, Salmagundi Club, New York, NY, 2002, 2003; Women Artist Exhib, Salmagundi Club, New York, NY, 2003; Studio Montclair 8th Ann Int Exhib, Westminster Gallery, Bloomfield, NJ, 2003; Taboo, Gallery 214, Montclair, NJ, 2005; Am Artists Prof League 77th, 79th, 82nd, and 84th Grand Nat Exhibs, Salmagundi Club, New York, NY, 2005, 2007, 2010, 2012; Hudson Valley Art Asn, Newington-Cropsey Mus, Hastings-on-Hudson, NY, 2005; Nature as a Metaphor, Donald B Palmer Mus, Springfield, NJ, 2007; Visions of Landscapes, Johnson & Johnson World Headquarters Gallery, New Brunswick, NJ, 2006; Speaking about Flowers, Watchung Arts Center, Watchung, NJ, 2005; Spring Exhib, Peter McPhee Fine Arts, Stone Harbor, NJ, 2007; The Four Seasons, Hudson Guild Gallery, Chelsea, NY, 2008; Artists Invitational, Chelsea 32, NY, 2008-9; Summer Exhib, Sheldon Fine Art, Newport, RI, 2008; Artist Showcase, Burn Mills Gallery, Bernardsville, NJ, 2008; Appetizing Pictures: Unusual Still Lifes of Food & Kitchen Objects, Hudson Guild Gallery II, NY, 2009; Hudson Valley Art Asn, Nat Arts Club, New York, 2010; Featured Artist, Geary Gallery, Darien Conn, 2010, 2011; Eclectic Visions, Montclair Art Mus, Montclair, NJ, 2011; A Brush With Nature, The Gallery at Crooked Halo, Park Ridge, NJ, 2011; Examing Process, Montclair Art Mus, Montclair, NJ, 2013. *Pos:* Found, www.artistadvisory.com. *Teaching:* Art business & marketing workshops, Montclair Art Mus, NJ, 2010-2012, Newark Mus, NJ, 2010, Garrison Art Ctr, NY, 2009-2013, Edward Hopper House Art Ctr, NY, 2010, Rowayton Art Ctr, Norwalk, Conn, 2010, Guilford Art Ctr, Conn, 2010; Radius: Professional Practice Series for Artists Workshop, The Aldrich Contemporary Art Mus, Ridgefield, Conn, 2010; Visual Art Ctr NJ, Summit, NJ, 2010; Katonah Art Ctr, Katonah, NY, 2011-2013. *Awards:* Best in Show, Mid-Rockland Arts Festival, 2004; 1st Place Oil, Bergenfield Arts Festival, Bergenfield Arts Festival Coalition, 2005; Best of Art, Edgewater Arts Festival, 2006; 1st Prize-Oil/Acrylic, Trees, Salute to Women in the Arts, 2007; Hon Mention, Renewal Interpreted, Art Center Northern NJ, 2007. *Bibliog:* PKRG-TV Channel 77, Monday Night Live, Dr Ned Barber, 10/2006; Maggie Fazeli Fard (auth), A Painter's Life, Pascack Valley Mag, spring 2007; Erin Patricia (auth), Community Spotlight, Community Life, 1/2009. *Mem:* Salmagundi Club (2002-2004); Studio Montclair (2003-2007); Am Artists Prof League (2005-, elected fellow 2011-); Salute to Women in the Arts (treas, 2007); Landscape Artists Int (elected mem, 2006-2007); Oil Painters of Am, 2010. *Media:* Oil. *Publ:* Auth, Pascack Press, John J DeFina, 2004; auth, Decor, Kim R Feager, 2005; auth, Canvas, Norma Jean Wood, 2005; auth, Art Business News, Kim R Feager, 2005; auth, Pascack Valley Mag, Janice Friedman, 2007; auth, 201 Mag, Ryan Greene, 2011; auth, Pascack Press, Melissa Meisel, 2012; auth, Color and How to Use it, Marcie Cooperman, Pearson, Edn, 2013; auth, Community Life, Lianna Albrizio, 2013; auth, Jewish Standard, Beth Janoff Chananie, 2012; auth, Christine Cote, Stone Voices, 2011. *Dealer:* Geary Gallery 576 Boston Post Rd Darien CT; JSO Art Assoc 6 Nappa Dr Westport CT; Courtyard Gallery 12 Water Street Mystic Conn; William Ris Gallery 9400 Second Ave Stone Harbor NJ 08247; Beacon Fine Arts 61 Monmouth St Red Bank NJ 07701; Clinton Falls Art Gallery on the River 49-51 Main St Clinton NJ; Design Domain Gallery 67 Mine Brook Rd Bernardsville NJ; Evalyn Dunn Gallery 549 S Ave W Westfield NJ 07090; Soul Made Gallery 725 Arnold Ave Point Pleasant Beach NJ 08742; The Gallery at Crooked Halo 137 Kinderkamack Rd Park Ridge NJ 07656. *Mailing Add:* 82 Blackwood Ln Stamford CT 06903

SISSOM, EVELYN JANELLE See Lee-Sissom, E (Evelyn) Janelle Sissom

SKALAGARD, HANS
PAINTER, LECTURER
b Skuo, Faroe Islands, Europe, Feb 7, 1924; nat US. *Study:* Royal Acad Art, Copenhagen; with marine artist Anton Otto Fisher, New York. *Work:* Constitution, Dudley Knox Libr & War of 1812 Constitution & Guerriere, Hermann Hall, Naval Post Grad Sch, Monterey, Calif; Casco, Reid Hall, Robert Louis Stevenson Sch, Pebble Beach, Calif; Frigate Ship US, Salvation Army Hq & Savannah US Frigate, Allen Knight Maritime Mus, Monterey; Flying Cloud Clipper Ship, Carmel Community Hosp, 95; William P Frye, Petaluma Community Hosp, 2000; WWII North Atlantic Convoy Series, 11 Oils on Canvas; Pacific coast Lumber Schooner Series, 15 Oils on Canvas. *Comn:* Olivebank Deck View, comn by Dr Wm Rustad, Sea Cliff, San Francisco, 68; USN BB Maine, comn by Hal Whitten, Dean Witter & Assoc, San Mateo, Calif, 73; Anna Maerske, comn by Capt Olsen, Port Capt Maersk Line, San Francisco, 75; and other pvt collections; Oil paiting of Christopher Columbus, 2005; Torshaun's Fishing Schooner Mus, 16 watercolors, 2010. *Exhib:* Galerie De Tours, San Francisco, 72; Gallerie Vallombreuse, Biarritz, France, 75; New Los Angeles Maritime Mus, 80; Skaalegaard's Square-Rigger Art Gallery, Carmel, Calif, 66-97 & 2000-02; Stanton Hist Ctr, New Maritime Mus, Monterey, Calif, 92-95; 200 Yrs of USS Constitution, Maritime Mus, 97; Maritime Ventura Co Mus, 98; Monterey Stanton Ctr Maritime Mus, 99; Life Under Sail: 50 yr retrospective, Monterey Maritime & His Mus, 2006-2007; Santa Barbara Martime Mus, 2008, 2009; and over 75 others. *Pos:* Dir, Skaalegaard's Square-Rigger Art Gallery, Carmel, 66-97 & 2000-; Calif hist librn, Mayo Hayes O'Donnel Libr, Monterey Hist & Art Asn, 72-73; dir bd, Allen Knight Maritime Mus, 72-76; cult dir, Sons of Norway, Monterey, 74-76. *Awards:* Gold Medal & Title Master Painter, Tommaso Campanella Acad Arts, Lett & Sci, Rome, 72; Gold Medal, Academia Italia Delle Arti e Del Honoro, Parma, 80; Statua della Vittoria, Italian Premio Mondale dell Cultural, 85; and others. *Bibliog:* Judith A Eisner (auth), Carmel closeup, Pine Cone, Carmel, 9/14/72; Salinas Weekend Living, full page, 85. *Mem:* Life hon Academia Italia Delle Arti e Del Honoro; US Navy League, Monterey chap; Am Coun Master Mariners, San Francisco chap (speaker). *Media:* Multimedia. *Interests:* Maritime hist. *Collection:* Monterey's Historic Addbe Col. by 17 Artists Who donated their art to Monterey's Civic Club, Oldest Women Club House in America; Several latest 20 oils of Am Rev. War & US 200th Yr Constitution. *Publ:* Sea Classics 92-93. *Dealer:* Winters Fine Art Galleries Plaza San Carlos Carmel CA. *Mailing Add:* 602 Stony Point Rd Petaluma CA 94952-1048

SKELLEY, ROBERT CHARLES
EDUCATOR, PRINTMAKER
b Bellevue, Ohio, Jan 15, 1934. *Study:* Ind Univ, AB & MFA; Studied with Rudy Pozzatti, Arthur Deshaies, Alton Pickets, Jack Twarkov, James McGarrell, Richard Barnes, Leon Golub, David Smith, Robert Laurant, Carl Martz, George Rickey, plus others. *Work:* Libr of Cong, Washington, DC; Mint Mus, Charlotte, NC; Montgomery Mus Art, Ala; Springfield Col, Mass; Southern Ill Univ, Carbondale; Rockford Col, Rockford, Ill; Calif Soc Etchers, San Francisco, Calif; Jacksonville U, Jacksonville, Fla; plus many others. *Exhib:* Dixie Ann Graphic Exhib, Montgomery Mus Art; Boston Printmakers, Mass; Mint Mus Ann Graphics; Libr Cong Print Ann; Am Graphics, Coll of Pac, Stockton, Calif; Solo exhibs, Pensacola Jr Col, Pensacola, Fla, Brevard Jr Col, Cocoa Beach, Fla, Micanopy Mus Modern Art, Micanopy, Fla, Univ

Fla Tchg Gallery, Gainesville, Fla, plus numerous others; Pacific Print Exhib, Coll of the Pacific, Stockton, Calif; Mint Mus Ann, Charlotte, NC; Dixie Ann, Montgomery, Ala; Savannah Art Festival, Savannah, Ga; Mercyhurst Col, Erie, Pa; plus many others. *Teaching:* Prof graphic design, Univ Fla, Gainesville, 61-81. *Awards:* Dixie Ann Best in Show Purchase, Montgomery Mus Art; Boston Printmakers Hon Mention, Boston Mus Art; Libr of Cong Purchase Award; Humanities Coun Res Grant. *Bibliog:* Graphic rev in La Rev Mod, 1/65 & Art Rev Mag, 4/66; Norman Kent (auth), Robert Skelley wood cuts, Am Artist Mag, 1/71; Lanny Sommesse (auth), Robert Skelley Woodcuts, Novum Gebrauchs Graphik, 10/76. *Mem:* Soc Am Graphic Artists; Southern Graphic Artist Circle. *Media:* Woodcut, wood sculpture. *Publ:* Auth, articles in Am Artist Mag, Novum Gebrauchs Graphic Mag & 30 Years of Am Printmaking

SKLAR-WEINSTEIN, ARLENE (ARLE)
GRAPHICS ARTIST
b Detroit, Mich, Oct 25, 1931. *Study:* Parsons Sch Design; Mus Mod Art, New York, scholar & study with Bernard Pfreim; Albright Art Sch; New York Univ, with Hale Woodruff, BS, 52, MA(art educ), 55; Pratt Graphics Ctr, with Andrew Stasik; Ctr for Understanding Media, 74; Coll New Rochelle (cert prog, educ for gifted & talented), 75 & 81; Columbia Univ, 85-86. *Work:* Mus Mod Art, NY; NY Pub Libr Permanent Print Collection; Hudson River Mus Permanent Collection, Yonkers, NY; Metrop Mus Art, Slide Libr; Pepsico Art Collection. *Exhib:* Tirca Karlis Gallery, Provincetown, Mass, 67; The Visionaries, Easthampton Galleries, NY, 68-69; Manhattan Col, 75 & Neuberger Col, 75, Purchase, NY; Lending Art Gallery, Mus Mod Art, NY, 79; Boston Visual Artists Union Gallery, Mass, 80; Roundhouse, Copenhagen, Denmark, 80; Bridge Gallery, White Plains, NY, 82 & 84; Interchurch Ctr, NY, 95; Chappaua Libr Gallery, NY, 95 & 97; Contemp Textile, Rye Art Ctr, NY, 95 & 98; Left Bank Gallery, Bennington, Vt, 96; Northern Westchester Ctr Arts, Mt Kisco, Nt, 97; Peekskill Performing Arts Ctr, NY, 97; Columbia Univ Law Libr, NY, 97; Women Artists of the Hudson Valley, Howland Ctr, Beacon, NY, 98; Wave Hill/Glyndor Mansion Galleries, Riverdale, NY, 97-98; Solo exhib, Katonah Gallery, 75-96, South Church, Dobbs Ferry, NY, 94 & 98, Westchester Art Workshop Galleries, Peekskill, White Plains, NY, 95-96, Aisling Galleries, Durango, Colo, 95-96, Bloodroot Gallery, Bridgeport, Conn, 95 & NY Focus: Arle Sklar-Weinstein, The Gallery at Hastings on Hudson, 96 & Animazing Gallery, NY, 97; Columbus Mus of Art, Ohio, 2003; Katonah Mus Art, NY, 2003; Galerie du Bar Zinc, Paris, France, 2002; Cornell Mus, Del Ray Beach, Fla, 2001; Houston Int Quilt Festival, Tex, 01, 02, 03; San Diego Mus Hist, 99. *Collection Arranged:* Cur, Masks: The Alternative Self (40 artists), The Gallery of Hastings-on-Hudson, NY, 89-90. *Pos:* Visual arts coordr, Coun Arts Westchester, White Plains, NY, 69-70; co-found, Westbroadway Gallery, SoHo & NY, 72-79; bd mem, Hastings Creative Arts Coun, 73-93; artists adv bd, Katonah Mus Art, 92-; artist-in-residence, Washington ST Sch, Mt Vernon, NY, 94; lectr/workshop facilitator, Hudson River Mus, Westchester, Yonkers, NY, 94-95. *Teaching:* Art specialist, Hillside Sch, Hastings-on-Hudson, NY, 73-81; lower sch art specialist, Marymount Sch of NY, 81-87; Fieldston Lower Sch, NY Ethical Cult Soc, 87-94. *Awards:* Purchase Prize, Albright-Knox Galleries, Buffalo, NY, 51; First Prize, Hudson River Mus Regional, Yonkers Art Asn, 71; Print Competition Award, Gestetner Corp, 71; SOS Grant, NY Found for the Arts, 2002. *Bibliog:* Masters & Houston (auths), Psychedelic Art, Grove, 68; H H Arnason (auth), History of Modern Art, Abrams, 69; HH Arnason (auth), Contemporary Art, Abrams, 69. *Mem:* Manhattan Quilters Guild; Katonah Mus Artists Adv Bd; Textile Study Group. *Media:* Fabric Construction, Digital Photographs, Mixed Media. *Interests:* Computer Imaging, Photography, Travel. *Publ:* NY Sunday Times, 10/22/95, 11/97, 6/99, 11/01; Am Crafts Mag, 12/97; Oceanside Mus of Art Yardworks Catalog, Calif, 2001; Quilt 21 Catalog, 2002; Artnew, Westchester Arts Coun, 2000; Fiberarts Mag, 10/99; Fibrearts Design Book 6. *Dealer:* Katonah Museum Shop Katonah Mus of Art Rt 22 at Jay St Katonah NY 10536. *Mailing Add:* 18 Harvard Ln Hastings On Hudson NY 10706

SKOFF, GAIL LYNN
PHOTOGRAPHER
b Los Angeles, Calif. *Study:* Univ Calif, Berkeley, 67-69; San Francisco Art Inst, BFA, 72, MFA, 79. *Work:* Nat Mus Am Art, Smithsonian Inst; Bibliot Nat, Paris; Oakland Mus, Calif; Ctr Creative Photog, Tucson, Ariz; Smith Coll Art Gallery; Amon Carter Mus; Fort Worth, Tex. *Exhib:* Exchange, Ft Worth Mus Art & San Francisco Mus Mod Art, 75-76; Attitudes: Photog in the '70's, Santa Barbara Mus Art; Soc Encouragement Contemp Art Photog Invitational, San Francisco Mus Mod Art, 80; Contemp Hand-Colored Photographs, DeSaisset Mus, Univ Santa Clara, 81; Am Photogrs and the Nat Parks, traveling to NY Pub Libr, Los Angeles Co Mus, Amon Carter Mus, Corcoran Gallery; In Color: Ten California Photographers, Oakland Mus, 83; Exposed and Developed, Nat Mus Am Art, Smithsonian Inst, Washington, DC, 84; The Colored Image: Hand Applied Color in Photog, Friend of Photog, Carmel, Calif, 85; one-person exhibs, Badlands, Robert Koch Gallery, San Francisco, Calif, 87 & Cecile Moochnek Gallery, Berkely, Calif, 97, In Color-Triangle Gallery, San Fran, 2009; The Painted Photograph, Robert Koch Gallery, San Francisco, Calif, 86; Eye of the Beholder, ICP, NY, 97; New Realities, Hand Colored Photographs 1839-Present, Univ Wyo, 97; French Roots, SK Josefsberg Gallery, Portland, Ore, 99; The Art of the Book: 4th Annual Exhib of Handmade & Altered Artists Books, Donna Seager Gallery, San Rafael, 2009; In Color, Triangle Gallery, San Francisco, 2009; Donna Seager Gallery, 2010. *Teaching:* Instr photog and hand-colored photog, Univ Calif Extension, San Francisco, 76-; instr photog, Univ Calif, Berkeley, summer 80. *Awards:* Nat Endowment Arts Photogr Fel, 76. *Bibliog:* Contemporary hand-colored photography, Picture Mag, 81; Dana Asbury (auth), Gail Skoff/Judy Dater, Popular Photog, 83; Kermit Lynch (auth), Adventures on the Wine Route, Farran Straus, 88; Paul Bertolli (auth), Chez Panisse Cooking with Alice Waters, Random House, 88; Richard Olney (auth), Lulus Provencal Table, 2002; Kermit Lynch (auth), Inspiring Thirst, 2004. *Mem:* Friends of Photog, Carmel, Calif. *Publ:* Contribr, The young romantics, Newsweek, 79; New Landscapes & Untitled 24, Friends Photog, 81; Photography Year, Trends, Time-Life Books, 82; Cliches, Brussels, 84; Zyzzyva, San Fran, 2006. *Dealer:* Jones Troyer Gallery 1614 20th St NW Washington DC 20009; Terry Etherton Gallery 424 E 6th St Tucson AZ 85705; Triangle Gallery San Francisco. *Mailing Add:* 717 The Alameda Berkeley CA 94707

SKOGERSON, GRETCHEN
VIDEO ARTIST, INSTALLATION SCULPTOR
b Teaneck, NJ, 1970. *Study:* Columbia Coll, BA; New York Univ, Tisch Sch Arts, MA; Rensselar Polytechnic Inst, MFA; Columbia Coll, BA; Tisch Sch Arts, New York Univ, MA; Rensselar Polytechnic Inst, MFA. *Exhib:* Group exhibs include Anthology Film Archives, Boston Cyberarts Festival; G-niale, Independent Exposures; Kasseler Documentary Film & Video Festival; MadCat Women's Int Film Festival; New York Video Festival; Ann Exhib, DeCordova Mus & Sculpture Park, Boston, 2006; Whitney Biennial, Whitney Mus Am Art, New York, 2008. *Teaching:* Asst prof film/video, Mass Coll Art & Design, Boston, currently. *Awards:* Fulbright Grant; Charlotte Faculty Fel, 2006. *Mailing Add:* 70 W 93rd St Apt 16A New York NY 10025

SKOLER, CELIA REBECCA
CONSULTANT, GALLERY DIRECTOR
b Sioux City, Iowa, Apr 7, 1931. *Study:* Syracuse Univ, NY, BFA (music & art), 76. *Work:* Syracuse Univ, Marine Midland Bank Cent, Crouse Irving Mem, Syracuse, NY; Savannah Coll Art and Design, Ga. *Exhib:* Rochester-Finger Lakes, Univ Rochester Mem Art Gallery, NY, 70 & 73; Cooperstown Ann, Village Libr Bldg, NY, 72; Everson Mus Art Regional, Syracuse, NY, 73; Solo exhib, Assoc Artists, 73; Munson-Wms-Proctor Inst 38th Ann, Utica, NY, 75. *Pos:* Freelance artist, Syracuse, NY, 73-80; owner, dir & consult, New Acquisitions, Syracuse, NY, 81-2003; orgn supervisor gallery management, Syracuse Univ Community Internship Prog, 81-93; contrib writer of art critiques in Syracuse newspapers, NY, 89-91; partner, Gallery Metro, Syracuse, NY, 91-93; fine arts appraiser, Syracuse, NY, 89-. *Awards:* Purchase Prize, NY Art Open, 70 & 71; Fine Arts Exhib First Prize, NY State Fair, 74; Purchase Prize, Arena '75 Regional. *Bibliog:* In celebration of women, Oswego City Messenger, 3/21/84; Linda M Herbert (dir), State of the Arts (film), Cooke Cablevision, 89; Lynn Zerschling (auth), Central Grad Records Album, Sioux City J, 9/19/98. *Mem:* Everson Mus Art (corp mem). *Specialty:* Contemporary. *Publ:* Auth, Sharply compelling contrasts, 89, Luck of the draw, 90, Artist struggles against setting, 90 & Exhibit challenges views, 91, Syracuse Herald-Am; Going to extremes, Syracuse New Times, 10/24/90

SKUPINSKI, BOGDAN KAZIMIERZ
PRINTMAKER, PAINTER
b Pabianice, Poland, July 16, 1942. *Study:* Acad Fine Arts, Krakow, Poland, MFA (very good, with distinction), 1969; Ecole Nat Superieure Beaux Arts, Paris, cert, 1971; Pratt Graphics Ctr, cert, 1972. *Work:* Lib of Congress, Washington; Nat Gallery Art, Washington; State of NJ Dept Edn, Trenton; NY Pub Libr, NY; Nat Lib France, Paris; Smithsonian Am Art, Libr Collection; Smithsonian American Art Libr Coll. *Exhib:* Int Exhib of Graphic Art, Frechen Ger, 1978; Solo exhib, Atlantic Gallery, NY, 1980; X Int Exposition of Original Drawing, Mus Mod Art, Rijeka, Yugoslavia,1986; 9 Int Triennale of Graphic, Berlin, Ger, 1990; Boston Expo, Nat Exposition of Art, Boston, 1992. *Collection Arranged:* Libr Congress; Nat Gallery Art; NJ State Mus; NY Pub Libr; Nat Libr in Paris; Ministry of Cult, France; Salon D'Autome - Purchase, Paris. *Pos:* pres, Bogdan & Assoc, NY, 84-2002. *Awards:* Medal of Merit, Int Exhib of Graphic Art, Frechen Ger, 1976, Purchase award, 1978; Medal of Merit, Rep Presdl Task Force, 1990; Order of Merit, Rep Presdl Legion of Merit, 1994; Cannon prize for Graphic Art, Nat Acad Design, NY, 71; Acad prize for Print and Drawing, Conn Acad Fine Arts, 71. *Bibliog:* Boleslaw Wierzbianski, (auth), Bogdan Skupinski, New Horizon Polish American Review, 5/19/1976; Palmer Poroner (auth), Reality through ideas and symbols, Artspeak, Vol 3, No 7, 11/20/80; J.T. (auth), Exhibition reviews, Art/World, Vol 5, No 3, 11/20-12/20/80; Contemporary Prints of the World, 89; E Benezit, Dictionnaire, Critique and Documentaire, Fr, 99. *Mem:* Askart.com; Artprice.com. *Media:* Oil. *Res:* Life & work of John F Kennedy & Alber Michelson, 69-76. *Specialty:* Paintings, Graphics. *Interests:* Sports. *Collection:* Old Master Painting, 16c-19c. *Publ:* E Benezit, Dictionnaire, Critique and Documentaire, Paris, Fr, 99; Gwan Kim Chae (auth), Bk II Vol, Contemp Prints of the World, 89; Mark Ryden (auth), Bk, Blood, 2003; Lonnie Dunbier (auth), Bk, Artist Bluebook, 2005. *Dealer:* Art Commun Internat 210 W Rittenhouse Sq Ste 400 Philadelphia PA 19103. *Mailing Add:* PO Box 849 Cathedral Station New York NY 10025

SKURKIS, BARRY A
PAINTER, SCULPTOR
b Chicago, Ill, Nov 21, 1951. *Study:* Coll Du Page, with Karl Owen; AA, 71; Sch Art Inst Chicago, With T Karpalis, R Yoshida & C Wirsum, BFA, 75; Univ Notre Dame, with Don Vogl, MA, 78. *Comn:* watercolor, Robert Malorny, DDS, Westmont, Ill, 82; oil painting, Edward Mazurowski, Westmont, 82; watercolor, Dean Bunting, Downers Grove, Ill, 82; St Francis Residence, 95; John Dicken, 98; and others. *Exhib:* Solo exhibs, Aurora Univ, Ill, 88, N Cent Col, Naperville, 88 & Rainy River Col, Minn, 94 & 98; Historical Crosscuts: Private Response to World Events Flint, Mich, 92; 42nd Spiva Ann Competition, Joplin, Mo, 92; Salon Exhib, Windham, NY, 94; Yosemite Renaissance, Calif, 94; Mini Print Int 14 (traveling), Spain, Eng, Repub Korea, 95, 96, 97 & 98; Anderson Art Ctr, Kenosha, Wisc, 98; and many others. *Collection Arranged:* The Holocaust: 1933-1945, 89. *Pos:* Gallery cur, N Cent Col, Naperville, Ill, 83-90; mem bd dir & vpres, Sch Art Inst Chicago Alumni Asn, 88; bd dir, Riverwalk Sculpture Garden, 88-89 & chmn, 89-90; pres, Chicago Soc Artists, 89-98. *Teaching:* Instr, Col DuPage, Glen Ellyn, Ill, 75-83; vis lectr painting, drawing & design, N Cent Col, 80-83, chmn, dept art, 83-91, assoc prof, 91. *Awards:* Third Place, Linoleum Print Competition, Chicago Soc Artists, 90; Daniel Smith Award, Nat Small Works, Schohaire Co Arts Coun, Cobleskill, NY; 11th Ann Juried Exhib of Soc Watercolor Artists, Ft Worth, Tex, 92. *Bibliog:* Mementy's, Featured Artist, Linoleum

Prints, 88; Chicago Soc Artists Block Print Calendar, 86-. *Mem:* Chicago Soc Artists; Art Inst Chicago; Wedge Pub Cult Ctr Arts (bd mem, 78-84); Chicago Soc Artists (mem bd dir, 87-); Chicago Artists Coalition, 88. *Media:* Acrylics, Watercolor; Bronze, Wood. *Mailing Add:* N Cent Col 30 N Brainard St Naperville IL 60566

SKY, ALISON
ENVIRONMENTAL ARTIST
b New York, NY, Aug 1, 1946. *Study:* Columbia Univ, 62; Adelphi Univ, with Peter Lipman-Wulf, BA (fine arts), 67; Art Students League, with Jose de Creeft & John Hovannes, scholar, 67-69. *Work:* Smithsonian Inst, Washington, DC; Mus Mod Art & Avery Libr, Columbia Univ, NY; and others. *Comn:* Formica Corp, 83; McDonald Corp, 83; NJ Transit Arts, Hoboken, 98; New York City Dept Cult Affairs, Bronx, 98; sculpture, Conn Comn Arts, Univ Conn, Avery Pt, 98; and others. *Exhib:* Louvre, Paris, 75; Cooper-Hewitt Mus, NY 78; Am Now, traveling, Hudson River Mus, NY & Wadsworth Atheneum, Hartford, Conn, 79; Mus Mod Art, NY 79; Va Mus Fine Arts, Richmond, Va, 80; 1984-A Preview, Ronald Feldman Fine Arts, NY 83; Opening Exhib, Mus Mod Art, NY, 84; Boiler House Projects, Victoria & Albert Mus, London, Eng, 84; High Styles: Twentieth-Century Am Design, Whitney Mus Am Art, NY, 85-86; Museum of the Future, Documenta 8, Kassel, W Ger, 87. *Pos:* Vpres & co-founder principal, SITE Projects Inc, 78-91. *Teaching:* Instr, Parsons Sch Design, New York, 94 & Cooper Union, New York, 95; vis artist, Purchase Col, State Univ NY, 94-95. *Awards:* Award, Progressive Archit, 80; Ward for Showroom Design, Interiors Mag, 83 & 85; Nat Endowment Arts Design Fel, 84. *Bibliog:* Jutta Fedderson (auth), Soft Sculpture & Beyond, G&B Arts Int, Australia, 93; Ellis Seebohm & Sykes (auths), At Home with Books, Crown, New York, 95. *Mem:* Fel Am Acad Rome. *Media:* Multi-Media. *Publ:* Auth, Sky Book, Profile Press, 72; ed, On SITE On Energy, SITE/Scribners, 74; co-auth, Unbuilt America, McGraw-Hill, 76; SITE: Projects and Theories 1969-78, Dedalo Libri, 78; SITE: Architecture as Art, Acad Ed & St Martin's Press, 81. *Mailing Add:* 60 Greene St New York NY 10012

SKY, CAROL VETH
PAINTER, PHOTOGRAPHER
b Cleveland, Ohio, Aug 30, 1934. *Study:* Ohio State Univ, 52-53, Coll of the Mainland, Texas City, Tex, 71-74, Slade Sch of Art, Univ London, Eng, 79, Univ Houston, BFA cum laude, 79, Univ Iowa, MA, 82, MFA, 83, Corcoran Sch Art, 86. *Work:* Nat Mus Women Arts, Washington; Univ Iowa, Iowa City; Univ St Thomas, Houston; Coll Mainland, Texas City; Washington DC Arts Comn. *Exhib:* Nat Drawing & Sculpture, Del Mar Coll, Corpus Christi, Tex, 75; Nat on Paper Show, Terrance Gallery, Palenville, NY, 83; Focus Int: Am Women in Art, United Nations World Conf, Nairobi, Kenya, 85; Visions, Westbeth Gallery, NY, 90; Nat Oceanic and Atmospheric Admin 25th Ann, 95; Nat Mus of Women in the Arts, 91, 96; Corcoran Gallery of Art, Washington, 92, 97; Nat Acad Art, New Delhi, India, 99; Tsinghua Univ, Beijing, China, 2002; US Embassy, Vienna, Austria, 2002; Santa Fe Art Inst, 2004; St Johns Coll, Santa Fe, 2006; Ratner Mus, Md, 2007; US Embassy, El Salvador, 2007; Millicient Rogers Mus, Taos, NMex, 2007. *Collection Arranged:* Con Fao, San Antonio, Coll of the Mainland, 75, Orgn of Black Artists, 75, Primitive Art from Greenland, 76, The Art of Vodun, Sculpture and Dance from Haiti, 78; Washington Area Women in Surface Design, Md Coll Art and Design, Silver Spring, MD, 91. *Pos:* Admin art after sch, Contemp Arts Mus, Houston, Tex, 69-79; gallery dir, Coll of the Mainland, Texas City, Tex, 73-79; gallery prog admin, Univ Iowa Sch Art, Iowa City, 80-81, asst to dir, 82-83; asst registr, Univ Iowa Mus Art, 81-82; dean, Md Coll Art & Design, 88-92, acting pres & dean, 89, 92. *Teaching:* Instr drawing, arts appreciation Coll of Mainland, Texas City, 73-79; instr drawing, painting Capitol Hill Arts Workshop, Washington, DC, 87-89; instr drawing Md Col Art and Design, Silver Spring, MD, 87-88; instr drawing, painting, Smithsonian Resident Assocs Program, Washington, DC, 94-95; instr drawing, painting, Georgetown Univ, Washington, DC, 88, 92-95. *Awards:* 2nd prize Howard Fox, Arlington Art Ctr, 96; Best of Show, Laurie Hughes, Artists Equity, 96; Juror's Spl Award, Samuel Hoi, Touchstone Gallery, 97. *Bibliog:* Michael Welzenbach (auth), Landscapes of light & shadow, Wash Post, 7/11/92; John Dorsey (auth) School 33 shows work their way up, Baltimore Sun, Nov 11/94; Sara Wildberger (auth) Color it Brilliant, Washington Post, 12/22/99. *Mem:* Int Artists Support Group, Washington (bd dir, 99-); Corcoran Alumni Asn (steering com 94-); Nat Artists Equity (officers); Washington Chpt Artists Equity (pres 94-97); Women's Caucus for Art; Oil Painters Am. *Media:* Oil, Pastel. *Publ:* Auth, Brazilian Art & History; Focus on Modernism, Univ Iowa, 83; Ethical & political considerations of being an artist, Nat Artist Equity, 87; The Role of Art Colleges for the Artist, ACA/Inst Asn Art Critics, Pub Policy Forum, 88-92; Art, Funding, Choice, Accountability & Censorship: Orienting Students to Issues & Realities, Nat Asn Schs Art & Design, 90; Nat Artist Equity response to 1992 report of Lib Cong, J Copyright Soc USA, 92. *Dealer:* The Ralls Collection 1516 31st St NW Washington DC 20007; Rendezvous Gallery 5 Loudoun St SE Leesburg VA 20175; Coady Contemporary 205 Canyon Rd Santa Fe NM 87501. *Mailing Add:* 705 Pinon Dr Santa Fe NM 87501-1337

SLADE, GEORGE G
HISTORIAN, ADMINISTRATOR
b St Paul, Minn, Jan 2, 1961. *Study:* Yale Univ, with Alan Trachtenberg, Tod Papageorge & Ben Lifson, BA, 83. *Collection Arranged:* Automotive Minnesota, pARTs, Minneapolis, 93; Local Color, pARTs, 94; Democratic Processes, pARTs, 96; Roger Mertin: In Minnesota 91-2001, pARTs, 2001; Jerome Liebling: Selected Photographs, Minn Ctr Photography, Minneapolis, 2006, Hand in Hand, 2006, Choreographic, 2006 & Downriver, 2006; One on One, Icy & Three Gorges, 2007. *Pos:* Librn, Walker Art Ctr, 92-95; lectr, Walker Art Ctr, Minneapolis Inst Arts, 93-98; ed, pARTs J, pARTs Photogr Arts, Minneapolis, 95-98; dir, McKnight Photog Fels, 98-; project adv, Minn Hist Soc, St Paul, 95-2000; Artistic Dir Minnesota Ctr for Photog, Minneapolis, 2003-Present; adjunct asst cur, Dept Photog, Minneapolis Inst Art, 2008. *Teaching:* instr art history, Univ St Thomas Grad Sch, 2007. *Awards:* Arts Writers Grant Recipient, Creative Capitol/Andy Warhol Found, 2007. *Bibliog:* Bill Jay (auth), Endnotes, Lens Work, 8/2006; Stephanie Xenos (auth), Slade Show, MPLS St Paul Mag, 6/2008. *Mem:* Soc Photog Educ. *Publ:* Auth, Contact Sheet (article), Light Work, No 89, 96; ed & auth, Minnesota in Our Time: A Photographic Portrait, Minn Historical Soc Press, 2000; Public Art Rev, No 36, 2007

SLADE, ROY
PAINTER, MUSEUM DIRECTOR
b Cardiff, Wales, July 14, 1933. *Study:* Cardiff Coll Art, NDD, 54; Univ Wales, ATD, 54. *Hon Degrees:* Hon DFA, Art Inst Southern Calif. *Work:* Arts Coun Gt Brit; Contemp Art Soc; Nuffield Found; Westinghouse Corp; Brit Overseas Airways Corp; Corcoran Art Gallery; Cranbrook Art Mus; Wakefield City Art Gallery; VK Government Art Collection; Contemp Art Soc Wales. *Exhib:* Nat Print Club, Nat Coll Fine Art, Washington, DC, 72; Pyramid Gallery, Washington DC, 76 & 77; Robert Kidd Gallery, Birmingham, Mich, 81; The Cranbrook Vision, touring exhib, 86; Cranbrook Contemp, touring exhib in Latin Am, 86; & others. *Pos:* Chmn, Comt Art in Pub Places, State of Mich, 83-85; comnr, Comn on Inst Higher Educ, NCentral Asn Col & Sch, 83-; chmn, Design Mich Adv Coun, 78-; mem, Mus Prog Overview Panel, Nat Endowment Arts, 90-93; Misc lects, art show jurors, exhib judge, catalog essays, 95-. *Teaching:* Sr lectr post-grad studies, Leeds Col Art, Eng, 64-69; prof painting, Corcoran Sch Art, Washington, DC, 67-68, dean, 70-77, dir, Gallery, 72-; pres, Cranbrook Acad Art, Bloomfield Hills, Mich, 77-95. *Awards:* Fulbright-Hays Scholar, 67; Knight, First Class, Order of the White Rose, Finland, 85; Knight, Order of the Polar Star, Sweden. *Mem:* Nat Soc of Lit & Arts; Nat Coun Art Admin (chmn, 81-); hon mem Asn Art Mus Dir; Nat Asn Schs Art & Design; Soc Bolivariana de Arguitectors, hon mem; Am Inst Architects (hon mem, Detroit chap); Asn of Art Mus Directors (hon mem). *Publ:* Auth, Report from Washington, Studio Int, 1/72; Studio Int; A new cultural center, Yorkshire Post, 2/69; Artist in America, Contemp Rev, 5/69; The Temple Flourishes, Nat Council of Art Administrators Publ, 80; Toward understanding and collaboration, Nat Asn Sch Art & Design Publ & Asn Art Mus Dir Publ, 82. *Dealer:* Robert Kidd Gallery 107 Townsend Birmingham MI 48011

SLATE, JOSEPH FRANK
WRITER, PAINTER
b Holliday's Cove, WVa, Jan 19, 1928. *Study:* Univ Wash, BA, 51; printmaking, Tokyo, Japan, 57; Yale Univ Sch Art & Archit, Alumni fel & BFA, 60; study of sumi-e painting, Kyoto, Japan, 75. *Hon Degrees:* Kenyon Coll, hon DFA, 88. *Work:* Kenyon Coll; Yale Univ; Newberry Collection Rare Bks, Univ Chicago, Ill; Kerlan Coll, Children's Lit, Univ Minn; Proctor & Gamble corp collection. *Exhib:* 12th Nat Print Show, Brooklyn Mus, 60; Whitney Mus, NY, 74; Cent Ohio Watercolor Soc, Schumacher Gallery, Columbus, 75; Hopkins Hall Gallery, Columbus, Ohio, 76; Mus Art, Port Huron, Mich, 78; Retrospective, 1956-1988, Olin Gallery, 88. *Pos:* Consult, studies on aesthetic & perception, Yale Univ Dept Psychol, 60-65; mem exec comt, Kress Found Consortium Art Hist, 65-69; consult, Nat Endowment for the Arts, 77-78; Juror, Soc Children Book Writers & Illusrs, 86. *Teaching:* Prof Art, Kenyon Coll, 62-88, chmn dept, 64-72 & 81-82, chmn fine arts div, 67-69, emer prof, 88-. *Awards:* Ohioana Libr Asn Award for Distinguished Contribution to Children's Lit, 88; 100 Best Books, New York Pub Libr, 88 & 96; Outstanding Md Auth Award, Asn Childhood Educ Int, 2001; Alumni Hall of Fame, UW Communications Dept, 2010; NY State Master Reading List, 2012. *Bibliog:* Wash Alumnus, fall 82; numerous revs, In: Publishers Weekly, NY Times, Horn Bk, Wash Post and others, 82-2006; Something about the author, Vols 38 & 122, Contemp Auth, Vol 110, fall 88; Along Pub Row, Guild Bulletin, Fall 2011; iTunes, Apple, Audio-Video Interview, 2012. *Mem:* Auth Guild; Soc Children Book, Writers & Illusr. *Media:* Acrylic. *Res:* The preconceptual eye; study on Aesthetics with Irvin L Child, Yale University. *Interests:* Illustration, travel, children's books. *Publ:* short stories, New Yorker, 62-64; Miss Bindergarten Series, Dutton, 96, 98, 2000-2002 & 2005-2006; The Star Rocker, Harper & Row, 82; Who Is Coming To Our House?, Putnam, 88; The Secret Stars, Cavendish, 98; What Star Is This? Putnam, 2005; I Want To Free, Putnam, 2009; Miss Bindergarten and the Secret Bag, Penguin, 2013. *Dealer:* Anne Hawkins, John Hawkins & Associates Inc 71 W 23rd St Suite 1600 New York NY 10010. *Mailing Add:* 15107 Interlachen Dr Apt 701 Silver Spring MD 20906

SLATER, DAVID
PAINTER
b Nov 3, 1940. *Study:* State Univ New York Buffalo, BS(art educ); Rhode Island Sch Design, MFA(painting). *Work:* ISWP Art Mus, Rep Nat Bank. *Comn:* Ghost Train, NEA Grant Proj. *Exhib:* Solo exhib, Dreams & Nightmares, Opalka Gallery, Albany, NY, 1993; group exhibs include Dreams & Visions, Ross Sch, East Hampton, NY, 2007; Hampton Road Gallery, Southampton, NY, 2007-2008; Botanical Exhib, Christy Art Ctr, 2008. *Teaching:* Ross Sch, 2009. *Awards:* Nat Endowment Arts Grant, 1976; RI State Coun Arts Grant, 1976; Pollock-Krasner Found Grant, 2006-07. *Media:* Mixed Media. *Specialty:* Contemp art. *Interests:* Spirituality, history, photography. *Dealer:* Peter Marcelle Contemp. *Mailing Add:* 5 Elizabeth Sag Harbor NY 11963

SLATER, GARY LEE
SCULPTOR
b Montevideo, Minn, Oct 27, 1947. *Study:* Univ Minn, BFA, 70; Ariz State Univ, MFA, 73. *Work:* Sky Harbor Int Airport, Phoenix, Ariz; Mus Fine Arts, NMex; City Monterey Park, Calif; City Palo Alto, Calif; Tucson Mus Art, Ariz. *Comn:* Ambassador Row Ctr, Lafayette, La, 86; Gwinett Com Ctr, Atlanta, Ga, 87; Ctr Park II, Calverton, Md, 88; Univ Ariz, Cancer Ctr, Tucson, 89; Chase Manhattan Bank, Tempe, Ariz, 92; and others. *Exhib:* Corten Steel: Contemp Sculpture, Bowers Mus, Santa Ana, Calif, 74; SW Fine Arts Biennial, Santa Fe, NMex, 76; Summer Outdoor Sculpture Exhib, Palo Alto, Calif, 77; Ariz Biennial, Tucson Mus Art, 80; NAm Sculpture Exhib, Golden, Colo, 83; and others. *Awards:* Nat Endowment Arts Grant, 73-74; Purchase Awards, 9th Ann Drawing & Sculpture Show, Del Mar Col, Corpus Christi, Tex, 75 & Ariz Outlook 76, Tucson Mus of Art, 76; Master of Southwest,

Phoenix Home and Garden Mag; Architectural Excellence award, Art in Pub Places, Chandler, Ariz; Pred citation, Ariz AIA; Excellence award, Art in Pvt Develop, Tempe, Ariz. *Media:* Metal. *Dealer:* Victoria Boyce Gallery 7130 E Main Scottsdale AZ 85251. *Mailing Add:* 638 W Contessa Cir Mesa AZ 85201

SLATKIN, WENDY
HISTORIAN
b New York, NY, June 20, 1950. *Study:* Barnard Col, Columbia Univ, with Barbara Novak, BA, 70; Villa Schifanoia Grad Sch Fine Arts, Florence, Italy, MA, 71; Univ Pa, with John McCoubrey, PhD, 76. *Teaching:* Asst prof art hist, survey & post-renaissance, Camden Col Arts & Sci, Rutgers Univ, 76-83; vis lectr, Univ Calif, Riverside, 83-85, Univ Redlands, 85- 90; prof, Calif Polytech, Pomona, Calif, currently. *Publ:* Auth, The genesis of Maillol's la Mediterranee, Art J, spring, 79; The early sculpture of Maillol, Gazette des Beaux Arts, 10/80; Reminiscences of Maillol: A conversation with Dina Vierny, Arts Mag, 2/80; Maternity and sexuality in the 1890's, Woman's Art J, spring 80; Women Artists in History, Prentice-Hall, 84, 2nd rev ed, 90. *Mailing Add:* Art Dept Univ Redlands Redlands CA 92374

SLATTON, RALPH DAVID
PRINTMAKER, GRAPHIC ARTIST
b Trumann, Ark, March 19, 1952. *Study:* Ark State Univ, BFA, 81, MA, 86; Univ Iowa, MFA, 90. *Work:* Taiwan Mus Art, Taichung; Print Consortium, Kansas City, Mo; Proj Home, Baltimore, Md; Found Arts, Little Rock, Ark; Ark Artists Registry, Little Rock; Ino-Cho Paper Mus, Kochi-shi, Japan; Skagit Valley Coll, Whidbey Island, Wash. *Exhib:* 15th Harper Nat, William Harper Raney, Palatine, Ill, 91; 35th Anne Steele Marsh, Hunterdon Art Ctr, Clinton, NJ, 91; 2nd Sapporo Int Print Biennale, Osawa Bldg, Japan, 93; 2nd Kochi Int Triennial, Ico-cho, Japan, 93; Mini Print Slovenija 93, Maribor Art Gallery, 93; Art Link, Contemp Art Gallery, Ind, 97; Nineth Ann Nat, Coll Notre Dame, Md, 97; Pressed and Pulled, Ga Coll State Univ, 97; Southern Graphics Asn traveling Exhib, 98; Creatures, Lexington Art League, Ky, 2010; Naestved Int, Naestved, Denmark, 2008; Ormond Mem Art Mus, Fla, 2008; Studio Arts Ctr Int, Florence, Italy, 2008; The Old Print Shop, Soc Am Graphic Artists, 2012; ArtsAt1830 Gallery, Wash DC, 2012; East/West Portfolio, Univ LA at Lafayette, 2012. *Teaching:* Prof printmaking, E Tenn State Univ, Johnson City, formerly, prof, chmn dept art and design, currently. *Awards:* Purchase Award, 17th La Ann, Sulzer Escher Wyss Serv Ctr, 90; Purchase Award, Henley Southeastern Spectrum, 91; Purchase Award, 21st Prints & Drawings, Ark Arts Found, 91; Distinguished Res Award, Coll Art & Sci, 2010; Distinguished Alumni, Ark State Univ, 2011. *Bibliog:* The Tusculum Review, Tenn, 2010; Art View, Spectrum, Hunter Mus Am Art, 2000; Soc Am Graphic Artists, New York, 2010. *Mem:* Print Consortium; Philadelphia Print Club; Asociacion Difusora Obra Grafica Int; Soc Am Graphic Artists. *Media:* Etching. *Publ:* Best of Printmaking '97, Rockford Publ, 97

SLAUGHTER, KWABENA
PHOTOGRAPHER
Study: Oberlin Coll, BA (fine arts), 1998; Univ Ill, Chicago, MFA (studio arts), 2001; Smack Mellon Studios, Brooklyn, Resident, 2004, Bronx Mus Arts, 2005, Ctr Photog at Woodstock, 2006, Art Omi, 2007. *Exhib:* Solo exhibs include Spaces Gallery, Cleveland, 1998, Grand Projects, New Haven, 2004, Phoenix Gallery, New York, 2005, Smack Mellon Gallery, Brooklyn, 2008; group exhibs include Selzer Pants, Smart Project Space, Amsterdam, 2001; Unjustified, Apex Gallery, New York, 2002; Adaptive Behavior, New Mus Contemp Art, New York, 2004; 9X, Smack Mellon Gallery, Brooklyn, 2004; AIM 25, Bronx Mus Arts, 2005; Frequency, Studio Mus Harlem, New York, 2005; Structure & Stories, David Castillo Gallery, Miami, 2007; Essentiality, Lana Santorelli Gallery, New York, 2008; Holy Holes, Dumbo Arts Ctr, Brooklyn, 2008. *Awards:* NY State Coun Arts Grant, 2006; NY Found Arts Fel, 2008. *Mailing Add:* 161 Austin Ave NE Marietta GA 30060-1515

SLAVICK, SUSANNE MECHTILD
PAINTER, EDUCATOR
b South Bend, Ind, Apr 1, 1956. *Study:* Yale Univ, with B Chaet, Samia Halaby, R Reed, G Peterdi, BA, 78; Tyler Sch Art, with David Pease, Margo Margolis & John Moore, Philadelphia, MFA, 80. *Work:* Madison Art Ctr, Wis; Prairie State Col, Chicago Heights, Ill; Wabash Col, Crawfordsville, Ind; Mercyhurst Col, Erie, Pa; Heinz Foundation, Pittsburgh. *Exhib:* Anderson, Lane, Slavick, Minn Mus Art, St Paul, 83; 80th Chicago Vicinity Exhib, Art Inst Chicago, 84; Wisconsin Directions 4, Milwaukee Art Mus, 84; solo exhibs, Pittsburgh Ctr Arts, Pa, 88, CAGE Gallery, Cincinnati, 89, Foster Art Gallery, Univ Wis, Eau Claire, 89, Denison Univ, 94, Mercyhurst Col, 94 & Otterbein Col, Westerville, Ohio, 95 & Rose Lehrmann Art Ctr, Harrisburg, Pa, 98; Anxious Nature, Univ Nebr, Lincoln, 91; Parteciparte, Venice, Italy, 93; Violent Violence, Arti et Amicitiae, Amsterdam, 2003; Six Painters, Art Acad Cincinnati, 96; Made in Heaven, Utrecht, The Neth, 97; Flesh and Blood, Hewlett Gallery, Carnegie Mellon Univ, Pittsburgh, 97; Aichi Prefectural Art Mus, Nagoya, Japan, 97; George Billis Gallery, NY, 98; WVa Univ, Morgantown, 99; Cult of Class, MICA, Baltimore, 2000; Univ Galleries, Murray State Univ, Ky, 01; and others. *Pos:* head Sch of Art, Carnegie-Mellon Univ, Pittsburgh, 2000-. *Teaching:* Instr art, Kutztown State Col, Pa, 80-81; asst prof, Univ Wis, Madison, 81-84; prof, Carnegie-Mellon, Pittsburgh, Pa, 84-; Andrew W Mellon prof of art, Carnegie-Mellon, Pittsburgh, 2001-. *Awards:* Broadus James Clarke Mem Prize, 80th Chicago & Vicinity Exhib, 84; Pa Coun Arts Fel in Painting, 84, 95 & 98; Nat Endowment Arts Grant, 87; SOS grant, Pa Coun Arts, 2000. *Bibliog:* Michael Bonesteel (auth), rev, Art Am, 10/87; Mary Jean Kenton (auth), Perspectives from Pa, New Art Examiner, 89; Richard Schindler (auth), Susanne Slavick (rev), New Art Examiner, 95. *Media:* Oil, Acrylic. *Publ:* Dinah Ryan (auth), Perspectives from Pa, Flesh & Blood, Art Papers, 2000; Phyllis Leverich Evans (auth), Susanne Slavick, Art Papers, 2000. *Mailing Add:* 14 Swan Dr Pittsburgh PA 15237-2375

SLAVIN, ARLENE
SCULPTOR
b New York, NY, 1942. *Study:* Cooper Union, BFA, 64; Pratt Inst, MFA, 67. *Work:* Brooklyn Mus, Metrop Mus Art, Hudson River Mus, Yonkers, NY; Fogg Art Mus, Cambridge, Mass; Allen Mem Art Mus, Oberlin, Ohio; Berkeley Univ Art Gallery, Calif; Norton Mus Art, Palm Beach, Fla; Chase Manhattan Bank. *Comn:* Cut-steel stair rail main stairway, Desoto Sch, NY, 95; ornamental steel fencing & posts, Kissena Park, Steel Plate animal art panels & gates, Ft Tryon Park, New York City Parks & Recreation, NY, 97-98; Paving inserts, etched glass, tree grates & seating (artist designed), Liberty State Park, NJ Transit Sta, 97-98; Entry Sculptures (4 large scale steel), Junction Plaza, Zoological Park, Asheboro, NC, 98-99; Gateway Sculptures & Terrazzo Floor (artist designed), Richard Stockton Col, NJ, Percents for Art, 98-99, Court St Development, Handy Holzman Heiffer Assocs ornamental fence, 99-00; designed steel benches, Town of Chapel Hill, NC, 2002; 8 carved glass windscreen murals, Hoboken Transit Terminal, NJ, 2003; Assunpink Wildlife, NJ, 2004. *Exhib:* Whitney Biennial Contemp Art, 73 & Am Drawings 1967-1973, Whitney Mus; solo exhibs, Alexander F Milliken Gallery, NY, 79-83, Am Embassy, Belgrade, Yugoslavia, 84, Painterly Panels, Heckscher Mus, NY, 87 & Simultaneous Landscapes, Rich Perlow Gallery, 88, Chauncey Gallery, Princeton, NJ, 90, The Gallery: Benjamin N Cardozo Sch Law, Screen Retrospect, NY, 91; Large Drawings, Santa Barbara Mus Art, Calif, 86; group exhib, Noahs Art, NY Parks & Recreation, Central Park, 89; Screen Retrospect, Norton Ctr Arts, Danville, Ky, 92; Karesh Gallery, Ketchem, Idaho, 93; Hebrew Union Col, 96-97; paintings, Fischbach Gallery, 2003. *Teaching:* Instr painting, Hofstra Univ, Long Island, NY, 71-72, Pratt Inst, 74 & Skowhegen Art Sch, Maine, 75 & 76; vis critic, Grad Sch, Univ Pa, 77; vis artist, Syracuse Univ, NY, 79 & Centre Col, Ky, 92. *Awards:* Printmaking Grant, Nat Endowment Arts, 77; Threshold Foundation, 91. *Bibliog:* Helen Harrison (auth), Painterly Panels: Hybrid Art, NY Times, 8/23/87; Pat Van Gelder (auth), Animals as subjects in contemporary art, Am Artists Mag, 89; Gail Levin (auth), Arlene Slavin Screens (catalog essay), Yeshiva Univ, 91; Phyllis Braff (auth), Creatures, NY Times, 96; Carolee Thea (auth), Arlene Slavin Mediating Public Space, Sculpture Mag, 2001; Joyce Korotkin (auth), Arlene Slavin, NY Art World, 2003; City Art: NY % for Art Collections 2005, Merrell Publishers. *Mem:* Cent Women's Focus. *Media:* Metal sculpture, painting. *Interests:* Gardening. *Collection:* Metropolitan Mus of Art, New York, NY; Brooklyn mus of Art, Brooklyn, NY; Fogg Art Mus, Harvard Univ, Cambridge, MA; Allen Memorial Art Mus, Oberlin, OH; Readers Digest, Pleasantville, NY; Berkeley Univ Art Gallery, Berkeley, CA. *Mailing Add:* 119 E 18th St New York NY 10003

SLEMMONS, ROD
MUSEUM DIRECTOR, EDUCATOR
b Mar 5, 1941. *Study:* Univ Iowa, BA; Univ IA, MA in Eng; Rochester Inst Tech, MFA, 76-78. *Comn:* Cur Eye of the Mind/Mind of the Eye, 88, Water: The Renewable Metaphor, 97, Beyond Novelty: New Digital Art, 2000. *Pos:* Cur, prints and photog Seattle Art Mus, 82-96; dir, Mus of Contemp Photog, Columbia Col, Chicago, 2002-. *Teaching:* Teacher, hist photog and grad mus studies Univ Wash, Seattle; grad seminars, Sch Art Inst Chicago. *Awards:* Hon Educator, Soc Photog Educators. *Mailing Add:* Mus Contemp Photog Columbia Col Chgo 600 S Mich Ave Chicago IL 60605

SLETTEHAUGH, THOMAS CHESTER
PRINTMAKER, ASSEMBLAGE ARTIST
b Minneapolis, Minn, May 8, 1925. *Study:* Univ Minn, BS, 49, MEd, 50, with Walter Quint, Peter Lupori, Malcolm Myers & John Rood; Pa State Univ, DEd, 56, with Viktor Lowenfeld; spec study, Williams Coll, Univ SC, Univ Ga & Syracuse Univ, NY. *Work:* Bucharest Univ, Romania; Cult Ctr, Budapest, Hungary; Univ Belgrade, Yugoslavia; Univ Sao Paolo, Brazil; Cult Ctr Fjorde, Norway. *Comn:* Symbol of Excellence, Miss Univ Women, 70; Miss Univ Women Crest for Apollo 14, Alumni Asn, 71; Architectural Graphics, Newman Ctr, 86. *Exhib:* Taller Gallery, Barcelonia, Spain, 83-90; Centro Para Las Artes, Montevideo, Uruguay, 90; Arte Sella, Borgo Valsugana, Italy, 92 & 96; Mus de Arte Contemporanea, Sao Paulo, Brazil, 92; Culturehouse, Forde, Norway, 94; Acad Sci, Prague, Czech Repub, 96; Fine Arts Inst, Glasgow, Scotland, 97; La Sapienza, Mus Contemp Art, 1st Univ Rome, 98; New Sch Univ, NY, 2000; Reba & Dave Williams Collection, NY, 2003; and others. *Collection Arranged:* Max Klager--Printmaker, Heidelberg Univ, WGer; John Jackson--Drawings, Cambridge Univ, Eng; Charlotte Strobele Graphics, Univ Vienna, Austria; Zheng Sheng Tian Paintings, Hangzhou, PRC; Juan Carlos Ferreyra Santos-Acrylics, Punta del Este, Uruguay. *Teaching:* Prof fine arts, Slippery Rock State Univ, Pa, 56-62, Frostburg State Univ, Md, 62-68 & Miss Univ Women, 68-70; assoc prof grad studies art educ, Univ Minn, 70-, psychoaesthetician, emer prof, 87-; vis prof, Kenyatta Univ, Kenya, 86-88; Centro Paralas Artes, Montevideo, Uruguay, 90; Kossuth Univ, Debrecen, Hungary, 90, Univ Sao Paulo, Brazil 92, culturehouse, Forde Norway, 94; Casa Strobele Gallery, Borgo, Italy, 96, Intercultural Educ Through Art; prof emer, Empirical Aesthetician, Univ Minn. *Awards:* Minneapolis Arts Comn, 86-89; Minnesota Fine Arts, Color Photog, 88; Int Man of the Year Award for Aesthetics, Art & Educ, Int Biog Ctr, Cambridge, Eng, 97 & 98; Minneapolis Aquatennial Sculpture Award, 2002; 50 yr award, Minnesota State Fine Arts, 2003; 100 Distinguished Alumni Centennial Award, Coll Educ & Human Develop, Univ, Minn, 1905-2005; Minn's Greatest Generation Award, Minn Hist Soc, 2006; Laureate, Archimedes Medal of Honor, Oxford Univ, 2006. *Bibliog:* Hans Stumbauer (auth), Art education in Austria, Art Sch Linz, 71; Paul Cornel Chitic (auth), articles in Tribune & Art Rev, Bucharest, Romania, 72; Rajztanitas, Aradi jeno, Budapest, Hungary, 79. *Mem:* Int Soc Educ in Art; Int Soc Aesthet; Int Soc Art Hist; Int Soc Empirical Aesthet; Int Union Architects. *Media:* All Media, Serigraphs. *Res:* Visual, tactile stimuli and creative imagery, a life science statistical analysis. *Specialty:* Contemp-mixed media. *Interests:* The psychoaesthetics of the creative intellect, developmental aspects. *Collection:* Children's art, original works in various media. *Publ:* Auth, The analysis & synthesis of psychoaestheics, Cambridge Univ, 75; Southern Hemisphere Research, Aboriginals in Australia and Maori in New Zealand, 78 & Oriental Seminar

in People's Republic of China, Hong Kong, Japan and Philippines, Int Soc for Educ through Art, United Nations Educ, Sci & Cult Orgn, 79 & 81; Taller de la Flor, Centro Artistico Antesanal, Buenos Aires, Argentina, 84; Derivations of Psixel Modes of Visual Expression, Czech Acad Sci, Prague, Czech Repub, 96; Printworld Dir, 97; New University of Lisbon, Lisbon, Portugal, 2004; Univ Avignon, France, 2006. *Dealer:* The Picture Store 37 Clarendon St Boston MA 02116; North Shore Gallery 16 Hillview Est Rd Groveland MA 01834. *Mailing Add:* 49 Williams Ave SE Minneapolis MN 55414-3449

SLIDER, DORLA DEAN
PAINTER

b Tampa, Fla, Sept 9, 1929. *Study:* Study with Dr Walter Emerson Baum, 40-48. *Work:* Allentown Art Mus, Pa; Berman Art Mus, Collegeville, Pa; Lenfest Group Impressionist Am Artists; DuPont Corp, Del; Cedar Crest Coll, Pa; Brandywine River Mus, Chadds Ford, Pa; Fla Keys Mus, Marathon, Fla. *Exhib:* Allied Artists of Am, Nat Acad Design, 67-77; Pa Acad Fine Arts, Philadelphia, 69; William Penn Mus, Harrisburg, Pa, 75; Watercolor USA, Springfield, Ohio; Butler Inst of Am Art, Ohio; Nat Watercolor Soc, 2004; Adirondacks Nat, 2000-2011; San Diego Watercolor Soc, 2006-07; Mo Watercolor Soc, 2007; Am Watercolor Society, 72-, 2013. *Pos:* Bd dir, Philadelphia Watercolor Soc, 96-2003 & Nat Soc Painters Casein & Acrylic, 2006-; judge, juror, Nat & Regional Art Shows, currently; juror of selection, Am Watercolor Society, 2009; juror of selection, Nat Soc Painters in Casein & Accrylic, 92, 96, 2000, 2003, 2004, 2006, 2009; juror of selection & awards, Judge New Jersey Watercolor Soc, 2006, Berks Art Alliance, Reading, Pa, 2008; vpres, Nat League Am Pen Women, Chester Co Branch, Penn, 2006-; vice pres & sig mem, Am Watercolor Soc, NY, 2010-2012, 2013; juror of selection, Tewksbury Historical Soc, Oldwick, NJ, 2012. *Awards:* Old Forge Hardware Co Award, Adirondacks Nat of Am Watercolors, 2000; M Graham Award, Berman Art Mus, Pa, 2004; Bd Dir Award, PWCS, Widener Coll, Delaware, 2005; MF Kratz Award PWCS, Berman Art Mus, Pa, 2006; San Diego Watercolor Soc, 2006; Viewer's Choice Award PWCS, Wallingford, Pa, 2006; Joe Pikus Cash Award, P/S Yacht Sales, San Diego Watercolor Soc, 2007; Jack Richeson & Co Watercolor Award, Artists Equity, Berman Art Mus, Pa; Sallie & Gannon Kashiwa Award, Adirondacks Nat Am Watercolors, 2010; The Ralph Fabri Medal Merit, Nat Soc Painters in Casein & Acrylic, Salmagundi CLub, NY, 2011; George M Schmid Memorial award, Phila Watercolor Soc, 2012. *Bibliog:* Henry C Pitz (auth), Brandywine Tradition, Houghton Mifflin Co, Boston, 69; articles, Brandywine Bugle & Trade Mag, Pa, 71-74. *Mem:* Am Watercolor Soc & Nat Watercolor Soc; Nat Soc Painters Casein & Acrylic; Artists Equity Asn; Philadelphia Water Color Soc; Audubon Artists; Watercolor USA Hon Soc. *Media:* Watercolor, Acrylic. *Publ:* Artists Fla, 89-90; Pa Artists, 95-96; Best of Watercolor: Painting Light & Shadows, 97, The Best of Watercolor, 3rd ed, 99, Rockport Publ & Collected Best of Watercolor, 2002 & The Very Best of Watercolor, 2004; Daphne Landis (auth), Speaking for Themselves: The Artists of Southeastern Pennsylvania, 2005; Catherine Quillman (auth), Artists of the Brandywine Valley, 2011. *Dealer:* Chadds Ford Gallery Chadds Ford PA 19317; Hardcastles Gallery 5714 Kennet Pike Centerville Delaware 19807; Barnstone Gallery, Phoenixville Pa. *Mailing Add:* 268 Estate Rd Boyertown PA 19512

SLIGH, CLARISSA T
PHOTOGRAPHER, PAINTER

b Washington, DC, Aug 30, 1939. *Study:* Hampton Inst, BS, 61; Howard Univ, BFA, 72; Skowhegan Sch Art, Maine, 72; Univ Pa, MBA, 73; Int Ctr Photog, New York, 79-80; Howard Univ, MFA, 99. *Work:* Mus Mod Art, NY; Nat Mus Women in the Arts, Washington, DC; Victoria & Albert Mus, London; Australian Nat Gallery, Canberra; Corcoran Gallery Art, Washington, DC; Philadelphia Mus; Int Mus Photog, Rochester, NY. *Comn:* Who We Are: Autobiographies in Art Traveling Collection, Washington State, 90; Malcolm X: Man, Ideal, Icon Installation, Walker Art Ctr, 92. *Exhib:* Solo exhibs, Ctr for Photog in Woodstock, NY, 92, Art in General, NY, 92, Afro-Am Hist & Cult Mus, Philadelphia, 93, Toronto Photogrs Workshop, Toronto, 94, Univ Md, 2002; Malcolm X: Man, Ideal, Icon, Walker Art Ctr, Minneapolis & traveling, 92; The Subject of Rape (with catalog), Whitney Mus Am Art Film & Video Gallery, 93; The Visual Diary: Women's Own Stories, Houston Ctr for Photog & traveling, 94; Black Power Black Art: Political Imagery from the Black Arts Movement of the 1960s & 1970s, San Francisco State Univ, 94; History 101: The Re-Search for Family (with catalog), Installation at The Forum for Contemp Art, St Louis, 94; Imagining Families: Images & Voices (with catalog), Nat African Am Mus Project, Smithsonian Inst, Washington, DC, 94; Thinking Print: Books to Billboards, 1980-95, Mus Mod Art, NY, 96; Am Families in Photographs, Nat Mus Am History, Smithsonian Inst, Washington, DC, 97; Developing Illusions, 1873-1998, Photographs from the Collection, Corcoran Gallery Art, Washington, DC, 98; Reflections in Black: A History of Black Photogrs, Smithsonian Ctr for African-Am History & Cult, Wash DC, 2000; Photographers, Writers and the Am Scene: Visions of Passage, Mus Photog Arts, San Diego, 2000; Mus Art & Design, NY, 2003; Mus für Angewandte, Frankfurt, Ger, 2003; Screenings: Pub & Pvt, Noyes Mus Art, Oceanville, NJ, 2004. *Teaching:* Instr, City Col NY, 86-87; vis artist fac, Minn Col Art & Design, Minneapolis, Minn, spring term, 88-89; instr, Lower Eastside Printshop, NY, winter 88-90; distinguished vis artist/teacher, Carlton Col, Northfield, Minn, spring term, 92; artist-in-residence/teacher, Tisch Sch Arts, NY Univ, 2003-04; adj prof, Sch Vis Arts, NY, 2002-. *Awards:* Nat Endowment Arts, 88; NY State Coun Arts, 90; Artiste En France Award, Greater NY Links, French Govt, Moet & Chandon, 92; Ann President's Award, Nat Women's Caucus for Art, 94; Jerome Found Grant for Women Artists of Color Leadership Workshops, 94; NY Found for the Arts fel in Photog, 2000; grant, Andrea Frank Found, 2000; Anonymous was a Woman Award, 2001. *Bibliog:* Naomi Rosenblum (auth), A History of Women Photographers, Abbeville Press, 94; Arlene Raven (auth), Well healed, Village Voice, 3/1/94; Carla Williams (auth), Reading Deeper: The Legacy of Dick and Jane in the Work of Clarissa Sligh, Image, Vol 38, 1995; Deborah Wills (auth), Clarissa Sligh, Aperture, #138, Winter 1995. *Mem:* Coast to Coast Nat Women Artists Color; Women's Caucus Art Coll Art Asn. *Publ:* Auth, Reliving my Mother's Struggle, Liberating Memory: Our Work & Our Working Class Consciousness, Rutgers Univ Press, 94; The Plaintiff Speaks, Picturing Us: African American Identity in Photography, The New Press, 94; auth, Wrongly Bodied Two, Women's Studio Workshop Press, Rosendale, NY, 2004; auth, It Wasn't Little Rock, Vis Studies Workshop Press, 2005. *Dealer:* Robert Bain Joysmith Gallery 46 Huling Ave Memphis TN 38103

SLIM HELÚ, CARLOS
COLLECTOR

b Mex City, 1943. *Study:* Univ Nacional Autonoma de Mex, BA (civil engineering), 1961. *Pos:* Owner, Segumex, 1984-, Tabacos Mexicanos, Nayarit, 1990- & Prodigy Inc, 1997-; pres, bd dirs, Teléfonos de Mex, Mex City, 1990-, chmn bd, 1990-; co-owner & pres bd dirs, Sanborn's, 1992; co-owner, Condumex, 1992-; sr chmn bd & dir gen, Sanborn Hermanos; chmn bd, Carso Global Telecom, 1996-, Gropo Financiero Inbursa; hon lifetime chmn bd, América Movil, 2005-. *Awards:* Named one of Top 200 Collectors, ARTnews mag, 2004-13; named one of World's Richest People, Forbes mag, 2001-; named one of 25 Most Powerful People in Business, Fortune mag, 2007; named one of 100 Most Influential People in the World, TIME mag, 2008; Entrepreneurial Merit Medal of Honor, Mexico CofC; Leopold II Commander Medal, Belgium. *Collection:* Old Masters; pre-Columbian and colonial Mexican art; modern art, especially Rodin. *Mailing Add:* Telefonos Mex SA de CV Parque Via 198 Edifc 701 Mexico City Mexico 06500

SLIVE, SEYMOUR
HISTORIAN, MUSEUM DIRECTOR

b Chicago, Ill, Sept 15, 1920. *Study:* Univ Chicago, AB, 43, PhD, 52. *Pos:* Trustee, Solomon R Guggenheim Mus, New York, 78-2008; trustee, Norton Simon Mus, 89-91; emer, Elizabeth & John Moors Cabot & dir, Harvard Art Mus, 82. *Teaching:* Instr fine arts, Oberlin Coll, Ohio, 50-51; asst prof art & chmn dept, Pomona Coll, Calif, 52-54; mem fac, Harvard Univ, Cambridge, Mass, 54-, prof fine arts, 61-, Gleason prof fine arts, 73-91, emer & chmn dept fine arts, 68-71 & dir, Fogg Mus, 72-82. *Awards:* Off of Order of House of Orange-Nassau, 62; Charles Rufus Morey Prize, Coll Art Asn Am, 70; Award for Achievement in Art Hist, Art Dealers Asn Am, 79. *Mem:* Fel Am Acad Arts & Sci; hon mem Karel van Mander Soc; Coll Art Asn (dir, 58-62 & 65-69); Renaissance Soc; foreign mem Dutch Soc Sci; Corresp Fel Brit Acad. *Res:* Baroque art. *Publ:* Auth, Drawings of Rembrandt, 2 vols, Dover Publ, New York, 65; Frans Hals, 3 vols, Phaidon Press, London, 70-74; Jacob van Ruisdael, Abbeville Press, New York, 81; Frans Hals, Prestel Press, Munich, 89; Dutch Painting, Yale Press, New Haven, Conn, 95; Jacob van Ruisdael: A Complete Catalogue of His Paintings, Drawings and Etchings, Yale Press, 2001; Jacon Van Rusdael: Master of Landscape, Yale Univ Press, 2005; Rembrant Drawings, Getty Publ, 2009; Jacob van Ruisdael: Windmills and Water Mills, Getty Publ, 2011; Jacob Van Ruisdael: Windmills and Watermills, Getty, 2011; The Windmill at Wijk bij Duurstede: Jacob Van Ruisdael, Rijksmuseaum, 2013. *Mailing Add:* Harvard Univ Sackler Art Mus Cambridge MA 02138

SLOAN, JEANETTE PASIN
PAINTER, PRINTMAKER

b Chicago, Ill, Mar 18, 1946. *Study:* Marymount Coll, Tarrytown, NY, BFA, 67; Art Inst of Chicago; Univ Chicago, MFA, 69. *Work:* Nat Mus Am Art, Smithsonian Inst, Washington, DC; Cleveland Mus Fine Arts; Art Inst Chicago; Minneapolis Inst Art; Yale Univ Art Gallery; Metrop Mus Art, New York; and others. *Exhib:* Solo exhibs, G W Einstein co, New York, 77, 79-80, 83, 85, Tatischeff Gallery, New York, 95, 97, 99, Cline Fine Art, Santa Fe NMex, 98, Gierhard Wurzer Gallery, Houston, Tex, 98, 2001, Frederick Baker Fine Art, Chicago, 98, J Cacciola Gallery, 2004-2005 & Klaudia Marr Gallery, Santa Fe, 2007, Peltz Gallery, Milwaukee, 2011, William Havu Gallery, Denver, 2011, Lewallen Galleries, Santa Fe, 2011; group exhib, Cleveland Mus Art, 78; Toledo Mus Art, 79; Kent State Univ Gallery, 80; Trisolini Gallery, Ohio Univ, Athens, 81; Van Straaten Gallery, Chicago, 82; Print Club Gallery, Philadelphia, 83; Jerald Melberg Gallery, Charlotte, NC, 84; Art Inst Chicago, 85-87 & 99; Nat Mus Am Art, 87; Nelson-Atkins Mus Art, Kansas City, Mo, 88; Harbert Schoolhouse Gallery, Mich, 90; Nat Mus Women in Arts, Washington DC, 91; Callen McJunkin Gallery, Charleston, WVa, 92; Fletcher Gallery, Santa Fe, 94; Milwaukee Art Mus, 96; Portland Art Mus, 97; Yates Gallery, Chicago Cult Ctr, 2000; Saint John's Art Ctr, Alice R Rogers and Target Galleries, St John's Univ, Collegeville, Minn, 2003; Santa Fe Art Inst, 2004. *Teaching:* Instr, Northwestern Univ, Chicago, spring, 2000, Anderson Ranch Arts Ctr, Snowmass, Colo, summer, 2001. *Awards:* Ill Arts Coun Fel, 86. *Bibliog:* Michele Vishney (auth), Still-Life and the Art of Jeanette Pasin Sloan, Arts, 3/83; Am Artist, New York, 1/94; Gerritt Henry (auth), Jeanette Pasin Sloan, Hudson Hills Press, New York, 2000; James Yood (auth) The Prints of Jeanette Pasin Sloan, 2003. *Media:* Lithography, Oil. *Dealer:* Peltz Gallery 1119 E Knapp St Milwaukee WI 53202; J Cacciola Gallery 531 W 25th St New York NY 10001; William Havu Gallery 1040 Cherokee St Denver CO 80204; Llewellyn Gallery Santa Fe NM; Rarity Gallery Mykonos Greece. *Mailing Add:* 301 Loma Arisco Santa Fe NM 87501

SLOAN, JENNIFER
SCULPTOR

b New York, NY, Jan 20, 1958. *Study:* Empire State Col, State Univ NY, BA (photog, archeol), 78; Univ Paris, Nanterre, 79; Int Ctr Photog, New York, 83. *Work:* Brooklyn Mus, NY; Nat Mus Women Arts, Washington; NY Pub Libr, Media Libr, NY; Empire State Col, Saratoga Springs, NY; St Vincent's Med Ctr, NY. *Comn:* Photo Collages, Art on Film/Metrop Mus, NY, 89 & 90; photo sculpture, Francis Hauert, NY, 90; photo sculpture, Vasilli Kostoulas, Paris, France, 91; photo collage/sculpture, Julie Lipius/Steve Riskin, NY, 91; photo sculpture, Donna Cameron, NY, 92. *Exhib:* Solos exhibs, Photog Resource Ctr, Boston, NY, 89, Ctr Photog, Woodstock, NY, 91; Non-Traditional Photog, Robert Burge 20th Cent Photog, NY, 92; Earthly Virtues Window Installation, Art in Gen, NY, 92; Jennifer Sloan, Photo Sculpture, Kean Col, Union, NJ, 93; About Faces, Houston Ctr Photog, Tex, 94; AIDS Forum, Artists Space, NY, 94; Artist in the Marketplace, Bronx Mus Arts, NY, 94; Luminous Image,

Alternative Mus, 96; The Tree Truck installation, Downtown Arts Festival, NY, 97; Glass Photo Blocks, Robert Burge 20th Century Photographers, NY, 99. *Collection Arranged:* The Self-Portrait Show, Art Initiatives, NY, 94. *Pos:* Pub prog audio visual technician, Int Ctr Photog, New York, 81-83; exhib developer, Station Island Children's Mus, NY, 93-96, Children's Mus Manhattan, 96-97 & Web Master, WNYC radio, NY, 98-. *Teaching:* Artist/teacher art, Bronx Mus Arts, 93; artist/teacher art for kids, Franklin Furnace, New York, 94. *Awards:* Money for Women, Barbara Demming Mem Fund, 91; Artist Residency Program, Kean Coll Residency, Mid-Atlantic Arts Found, 93; Residency & Grant, Sculpture Space, 96. *Bibliog:* William Zimmer (auth), A religious spirit vies with fun, NY Times, 7/31/94; Holland Cotter (auth), A showcase for artists learning their business, NY Times, 8/19/94; Craig Kellog (auth), Galleries to Go, Metropolis Mag, 12/97 & 1/98. *Mem:* Int Sculpture Ctr; Art & Sci Collab Inc. *Media:* Mixed Media. *Publ:* Coauth, Its News To Me, teaching activities, Staten Island Children's Mus, 94. *Mailing Add:* 105 Duane St No 15C New York NY 10007

SLOAN, MARK
MUSEUM DIRECTOR, ARTIST
b Durham, NC, Nov 16, 1957. *Study:* Univ Richmond, BA, 80; Va Commonwealth Univ, MFA, 84. *Work:* High Mus Art, Atlanta; Nat Acad Sciences, Wash DC; Harvard Mus Nat History, Cambridge, Mass. *Exhib:* Photoglyphs: Rimma and Varleriy Gerlovin, 91; Intimate Technologies/Fictional Personas, 92; Dear Mr Ripley, 93; Self-Made Worlds: Visionary Folk Art Environments (with catalog), 97; PopLuxe: The Language of the Garment, (with catalog) 98; Right to Assemble (with catalog), 99; Palimpsest: Afghanisfan, 2002; Breath on a Mirror, 2002; No Man's Land, 2004; Alive Inside, 2005; Force of Nature; Site Installations by Ten Japanese Artists, 2006, Richard McMahan's Mini Mus, 2008; Mend: Love, Life, & Loss, 2008; Hair on Fire, 2009; Call & Response, Africa to Am, Art of Nick Cave & Phyllis Galembo; Leslie Wayne: Recent Work, 2011; Aggie Zed: Keeper's Keep, 2012; Return to the Sea: Saltworks by Moto Yamamoto, 2012; The Paternal Suit: Heirlooms from the F Scott Hess Family Found, The Pulse Dome Project: Art & Design by Don Fagna. *Collection Arranged:* Contemp Carolina Collection, Med Univ SC; Palmetto Portraits Project, State Mus Art, Columbia, SC. *Pos:* Assoc dir, San Francisco Camerawork, 86-89; dir, Roland Gibson Gallery, Potsdam, NY, 1992-1994, formerly & Halsey Inst Contemp Art, Col Charleston, SC, 1994, currently prof arts mgt. *Teaching:* Prof of Arts Mgt. *Awards:* Pres Theodore Stern Visionary Leadership Award, 2010; Elizabeth O'Neill Verner award, 2012. *Mem:* Soc Photog Educ; Coll Art Asn; Am Asn Mus. *Specialty:* Contemp Art in all Media. *Interests:* Adventurous international contemporary art. *Publ:* Auth, Spirit in the Land: Photographs from the Bible Belt, Southern Accents; Spectacular Photographs: Unforgettable Faces, Facts and Feats, 1989; Hoaxes, Humbugs and Spectacles, Villard/Random House, 1990; Dear Mr Ripley, Bulfinch/Little, Brown & Co, 1993; Self Made World's Visiononary Folk Art Environments (Aperture, 97); Wild, Weird and Wonderful: The American Circus 1901-1927 as Seen by F. W. Glasier, Quantuck Press, 2003; The Rarest of the Rare; Stories Behind the Treasures at the Harvard Mus of National History, Harper Collins, 2004; Aldwyth: Work v./Work N, Halsey Inst Contemp Art, 2009; No Man's Land: Comptemporary Photographers & Fragile Ecologies, 2004; Palmetto Portraits Project, 2010; Aggie Zed: Keepers Keep, 2012; Return to the Sea: Saltworks by Moto Yamamoto, 2012; The Paternal Suit: Heirlooms from the Fiscott Hess Farm Family Foundation, Pulse Dome Projects: Art & Design by Don Zan Fagna, Renee Stout; Tales of the Conjure Woman. *Mailing Add:* Col of Charleston Halsey Inst School of Arts Charleston SC 29424-0001

SLOAN, RONALD J
PAINTER
b Brooklyn, NY, Jan 8, 1932. *Study:* Central State Univ, Edmond, Okla, MA (art educ), 65; Univ Albany, NY, MA, 75; Univ Ky, Lexington, MFA (painting), 79. *Work:* Mattatuck, Waterbury, Conn; Provincetown Mus, Cape Cod, Mass; Chase Manhattan Bank, NY; Gen Elec Corp, Conn; Northwestern Community Col, Winsted, Conn. *Exhib:* Canton Gallery on the Green, Canton, Conn, 96; New Arts Gallery, Bantam, Conn, 96; Alexandria Mus Art, La, 96; Patterns of Perception, Conn Comn Arts Gallery, Hartford, 96; Provincetown Art Asn, 96. *Awards:* Provincetown Fine Arts Work Ctr Fel, 84-85; Nat Endowment Arts, 87-88; Conn Grant, 98. *Mem:* Conn Acad Fine Arts; New Haven Paint & Clay. *Media:* Acrylic. *Mailing Add:* PO Box 361 Norfolk CT 06058-0361

SLOANE, KIM
PAINTER
b May, 21, 1955. *Study:* Yale Univ, BA, 1977; Parsons Sch Design, MFA (Painting), 1993. *Exhib:* Solo exhibs include Painting Ctr, New York, 1999, Drawing Studio Art Exhib Prog, Dartmouth Coll, 2001, Cedar Crest Coll, Allentown, PA, 2005; Group exhibs include Artists Select Artists, Trenton City Mus, NJ, 1996; Kind of Drawing, Belk Gallery Western Carolina Univ, 1999; 177th Ann: Invitational Exhib Contemp Am Art, Nat Acad Mus, New York, 2002, 183rd Ann, 2008; Three Artist Exhib, Washington Art Asn, Washington Depot, Conn, 2004; All Terrain, RKL Gallery, Brooklyn, 2004; Body & Dangers, Painting Ctr, New York, 2005; Crossing Disciplines: Drawing, Pratt Inst, Brooklyn, 2005; 13th Anni Exhib, Painting Ctr, 2006. *Teaching:* Asst Prof Art, Cedar Crest Coll, Allentown, Pa; Vis Asst Prof, Pratt Inst, Found Drawing, 2000-03. *Awards:* Helena Rubenstein Found Sch, 1991-92; Ingram Merrill Found Award, 1992; Mikhail & Ekateryna Shatalov Prize, Nat Acad Design, 2002 & 2008 & Samuel FB Morse Medal. 2002. *Mailing Add:* 151 Driggs Ave Brooklyn NY 11222

SLOAT, RICHARD JOEL
PAINTER, PRINTMAKER
b Easton, Pa, Sept 18, 1945. *Study:* Univ Pa, BA, 69; Art Students League, 72. *Work:* Brit Mus, London; Israel Mus, Jerusalem; Fogg Mus, Cambridge, Mass; Mus City New York; Portland Art Mus, Oreg; Nat Acad Mus, New York; Libr Cong, Washington, DC; Nat Gallery Art, Washington, DC. *Comn:* 5 Print Eds, New York, Graphic Soc, Greenwich, 72-80. *Exhib:* Solo exhibs, Martin Sumers Gallery, New York, 87, Wood & Stone Gallery, Taipei, 90, FDR Gallery, New York, 93, Old Print Shop, New York, 95, Ottendoreer Libr, New York, 96, Howard Salon, Taiwan, 98 & 2001, Paul McCarron, New York, 2001, Safe-T-Gallery, New York, 2005; group exhibs, Mus City New York, 82 & 2002, Nat Acad Design, New York, 74, 86, 88, 94 & 99-2007, 2009, 2013, Michael Ingbar Gallery, New York, 93-94, 96, 98, 2000, 2006, 2008, Old Print Shop, NY 95-2012, NY Transit Mus, 97 & 2003, Springfield Art Mus, Mo, 2001, 2005 & 2007-08, Life of City, Mus Mod Art, 2002, UBS Paine Weber Art Gallery, 2002, Art Students League, 2002, 2005, & 2011, NY Hist Soc, New York, 2002, 2004, Susan Teller Gallery, New York, 2004, Int Print Ctr, New York, 2007, 2008, Arsenal Gallery, Central Parl, NY, 2011, The Old Print Gallery, Wash DC, 2011-2013, Univ New Orleans, La, 2012, Miss Mus Art, Jackson, Ms, 2013; Two person exhibs, Falkenstern Fine Art, New York, 90, Gate Gallery, Kaoshiung, Taiwan, 94, Old Print Shop, New York, 2004 & Michael Ingbar Gallery, New York, 2005, Clare Romano and Richard Sloat, Old Print Shop, New York, 2011, Su-Li Hung & Richard Sloat, 40 Yrs Together in Art, Old Print Gallery, Wash DC, 2012; Contemp Prints from the US, Nat Mus Fine Arts, Hanoi, Repub Vietnam, Macau Mus Art, 2000; Reveal Haromonize, Macau Mus Art, 2000; Noble Maritime Collection, New York, 2006; many others. *Pos:* Prog dir, Alliance Figurative Artist, 82-85; co-found, Sky Wheel Configurist Group, 84-90; cur, Contemp Block prints, Ten Worlds Gallery, New York, 88; cur, New York City Centennial Portfolio, The Old Print Shop, New York, 98; vpres, Soc Am Graphic Artists, 98-2002, pres, 2003-2006; rec secy & coun mem, Nat Acad Design, 2006-09, bd governors, 2009-2011. *Teaching:* Lectr drawing methods, Univ Calif, Berkeley, 96; adj instr printmaking, Fashion Inst Technol, New York & adj prof, 98-99; instr master drawing, Nat Acad Design Sch Fine Arts, 2003; critic, New York Studio Sch, NY, 2013. *Awards:* Leo Meisner Prize, Nat Acad Design, 86 & 94; Savoir Faire-Lana Paper Award, Audubon Artists, 96; Art Students League Award in Graphics, 98; Art Students League Award, Audubon Artists, 98 & 2002; AO Crimi Award, Audubon Artists, 99; JM Kaueney Award, Janet Turner Print Competition, 99; John Taylor Arms Award, Audubon Artists, 2001; Cash Award, Springfield Mus, Prints USA, 2005 & 2007-2008. *Bibliog:* Vivien Raynor (auth), Sunday NY Times, 3/6/88; Wu Jin Fa (auth), Min Chung Dailey News, Taiwan, 9/1/89; RJ Steiner (auth), Art Times, 3/98; Wendy Moonan (auth), NY Times, 5/3/2002; John Goodrich (auth), NY Times, 8/8/2006; James Garoner (auth), New York Sun, 5/31/2007; Martha Schwender (auth), article, NY Times, 6/1/2007; Peter Neofotis (auth), The Art Point, 2012. *Mem:* Soc Am Graphic Artists (coun mem, 95, vpres, 99-2002, pres 2003-2006); Found Mod Painters & Sculptors (exec comt mem, 96); Boston Printmakers; Nat Acad (acad, 97-, council, 2006-2009, recording sec, 2006-2010, bd gov, 2009-2011). *Media:* Etching; Watercolor, Oil. *Publ:* United Daily News Taipei, 89; Mythic City & Friends, Book by Artist, 91; article & illus, J Print World, 91, 98-2000; The Old Print Shop Portfolio, Vol LU, No 4, 95, Vol LXI, No 1, 2001 & Vol LXI, No 5, 2002, Vol LXIII #3, 2003, Vol LXV#3, 2005, Vol LXVIII #3, 2008, Vol LXIX#7, 2010, Clare Romano and Richard Sloat, Vol LXX#8; New York City Centennial Portfolio, Vol LVII, 6, 98; Marilyn Symmes (auth), Impressions of New York, Prints from the New York Hist Soc, 2004; auth, Forty Years Later, Print World, July 2012; Jour Print World, Vol 35 #3, 2012. *Dealer:* The Old Print Shop 150 Lexington Ave New York NY 10016; The Old Print Gallery Wash DC; Ebo Gallery Millwood NY. *Mailing Add:* 170 Second Ave No 7B New York NY 10003-5779

SLONE, SANDI
PAINTER, EDUCATOR
b Boston, Mass, Oct 1, 1939. *Study:* Mus Fine Arts Sch, Boston, diploma, 73; Wellesley Coll, BA, (art hist, Magna Cum Laude), 74; studied with Minor White, Mass Inst Technol. *Work:* Mus Mod Art, New York; Rose Art Mus, Brandeis Univ; Mus Contemp Art, Barcelona, Spain; Smithsonian Inst; Portland Art Mus, Ore; Fitzwilliam Mus, Cambridge, Eng; Boston Mus Fine Arts; Hirshhorn Mus; Edmonton Art Mus, Can; Corcoran Mus, Washington, DC; Harvard Univ; Hara Mus, Tokyo; Knoll Int; NY Times; Magazine Group; IBM; AT&T; Gen Electric. *Exhib:* solo exhibs, The Boston ICA, 77, Acquavella Gallery, 77, 79-82 & 84, Jersey City Mus, NJ, 95-96; Edmonton Art Mus, 80; The Uneasy Surface: Points of Turbulence, Univ RI, 96; Transfolk, Artists Mus, Lodz, Poland, 97; Ground Control, Lombard Freid Fine Arts, New York, 98; The 45th Corcoran Mus Biennial, 98; Masters of the Masters, Butler Inst Am Art, 98; Cristinerose Gallery, New York, 99; Savage Gallery, Portland, Ore, 2001; Santa Fe Art Inst, NMex, 2002; Tower Gallery, Hong Kong, 2004; Art In General, Through Our Eyes, 2004; The Transformer Room, Belfast, Ireland, 2006; Chang Hai Int, Beijing, 2008; Meredith Long Gallery, Houston, 2008; Epikur Gallery, Wuppertal, Germany, 2009; Gallery Forum Berlin Am Meer, Germany, 2010; Elizabeth Leach Gallery, Portland, Ore, 2010; Exit Art, New York, 2010. *Pos:* Dir & cofounder, Art/OMI Int Artists Found, 92; Bd of Dir, Fields Sculpture Park. *Teaching:* Prof painting grad fac, Sch Mus Fine Arts, Boston, 75-2004; instr, Harvard Univ, VES, Carpenter Ctr, 82--83; MFA fac, Sch Visual Arts, New York, 89-90; Santa Fe Art Inst, 92. *Awards:* Boston Mus Fine Arts traveling fel, 77, 79 & 81; Ford Found Grant, 81; Triangle Int Artists Colony, 82, 87 & 90; Artist-in-residence, City Hall, Barcelona, Spain, 87 & 89; Mus Fine Arts Sabbatical, China, 85-87. *Bibliog:* Art revs, NY Times Weekend Section, 84, 88 & 96; Raphael Rubinstein (auth), Sandi Slone at Jersey City Mus, Art in Am, 96; Karen Wilkin (auth), Partisan rev, 1/2000; Lilly Wei (auth), Sandi Slone at Cristinerose, ARTNEWS, 3/2000; Cristopher Chambers (auth), Sandi Slone at Cristinerose Gallery, FLASH Art, 2/2000; Art Bank, Belfast, Ireland, 2007; Architectural Digest, 2006; Van Der Heyt Mus, Wuppertal, Germany, 2009; Gallery Forum, Berlin, Germany, 2010. *Mem:* Coll Art Asn; Wellesley Coll Friends Art; bd dirs, Art OMI Int Arts Ctr The Fields Sculpture Park, Artists Exchange Int & Fine Arts Develop Laboratories Inc, New York. *Media:* All Media. *Dealer:* Cristinerose Gallery New York NY; Elizabeth Leach Gallery Portland OR. *Mailing Add:* 13 Worth St New York NY 10013

SLONEM, HUNT
PAINTER, MURALIST
b Kittery, Maine, July 18, 1951. *Study:* Skowhegan Sch Painting & Sculpture, 72; Tulane Univ, BA, 73. *Work:* Metrop Mus Art, NY; Birmingham Mus Art, Ala; Kemper Mus, Kans; Va Mus Fine Arts, Richmond; Solomon R Guggenheim Mus, NY; Whitney Mus. *Comn:* Fan Dance (mural), World Trade Port Authority Ctr, NY, 80;

Bryand Park Grill, NYC. *Exhib:* Figurative Drawings, Va Mus Art (with catalog), Richmond, 85; Feathers, Fur & Fin, Laguna Gloria Mus, Austin, Tex, 90; Menagerie, Mus Mod Art, 90; solo exhibs, Ben Shahn Galleries, William Paterson Col, Wayne, NJ, 90, Harcourts Contemp Art, San Francisco, Calif, 91 & Tenn State Univ Mus, Nashville; Marlborough Gallery, NY; Colby Mus, Waterville, Maine; plus many others. *Awards:* Fel, Millay Colony Arts, 82, 83, 84 & 86; Painting Grant, Nat Endowment Arts, 91; MacDowell Fel, Skowhegan Alumnae. *Bibliog:* Ken Johnson (auth), NY Times, 99; Brooks Adams (auth), Treasure Hunt, Elle Decor, 1/99; Vincent Katz (auth), Animal, Vegetable, Mystical, Art in Am, 99; Donald Kuspit (auth), Art Rich & Strange; Dominique Naiths (auth), Worlds of Hunt Slonem; Vincent Katz (auth), Pleasure Palaces. *Mem:* Art Committee New School, NYC; Skowhegan Alumni. *Media:* Oil on Canvas. *Interests:* collecting 19th Century houses. *Publ:* Illusr of three textbook. *Dealer:* Marlborough Gallery New York NY. *Mailing Add:* 87 E Houston New York NY 10012

SLOSBURG-ACKERMAN, JILL
SCULPTOR, JEWELER

b Omaha, Nebr, Aug 28, 1948. *Study:* Tufts Univ, BFA, 71, MFA, 83; Sch Boston Mus Fine Arts, dipl, 71. *Work:* Mass Coll Art, Boston; Boston Pub Libr; Cranbrook Acad Art Mus, Bloomfield Hills, Mich; Robert Lee Morris; Union Pac Railroad, NY; Daphne Farago; JL Brandeis & Sons, Omaha, Nebr; The Mary Ingraham Bunting Inst, Cambridge, Mass; Metropolitan Mus, NY; Re: the Squirrel, Squirrel Brand Park, City of Cambridge, Mass; Boston Mus Fine Arts; Worcester Art Mus, Worcester, Mass; Simmons Coll, Boston, Mass. *Exhib:* Solo exhibs, Harcus-Krakow Gallery, Boston, Mass, 78, 80 & 85, Helen Shlien Gallery, Boston, Mass, 80 & 82, Cohen Arts Ctr, Tufts Univ, Medford, Mass, 82, Van Buren/Brazelton/Cutting Gallery, Cambridge, Mass, 85, Genovese Gallery, Boston, 95, Conn Col, 95, Rose Art Mus, Brandis Univ, 96, Univ Mass, Dartmouth, 99, Judy Ann Goldman Fine Art, 99 & 2004 & Gallery at Green St, Jamaica Plain, Mass, 99; Amerricky Sperk, Mus Decorative Arts, Prague, 91; Of Power, Myth, and Memory, Bellevue Art Mus, Wash, 92; Crossroads, (with catalog), Artwear, NY, 92; Material Boundaries Between the Sexes, Genovese Gallery Albany, Boston, 92; Schmuckzene (with catalog), Munich, Ger, 93; Inside/Out (with catalog), Starr Gallery, Jewish Community Ctr, Newton, Mass, 93; Boston Mus Fine Arts, Traveling Scholars, 98; Annual Exhib, DeCordova Mus & Sculpture Park, Lincoln, Mass, 2000; Judy Ann Goldman Fine Art, Boston, 2002; Forest Hills Cemetery, Boston, 2002 & 2004; Mills Gallery, Boston, 2004; Fuller Craft Mus, Brocton, Mass, 2005; Cut, Paul Kotula Projects, Ferndale, Mich, 2007; Take Nine, N Am Costa Rica Cult Ctr, San Jose, 2007; One Line Drawing/Printmaking/Artist Books by award winning Mass Artists, Artspace Gallery, Maynard, Mass, 2007; Drawings that Work, Mills Gallery, Boston, 2009; Art and History, John Nicholas Brown House, Brown Univ, Providence, RI, 2009; Economies of Scale, Miller Block Gallery, Boston, 2009; Worcester Art Mus, Worcester, Mass, 2012. *Pos:* founder, mem, Boston Women's Action Coalition; bd dir, Cambridge Multi-Cult Ctr, Gallery at Green St, Mass, 93. *Teaching:* prof arts, Mass Col Art, 72-; artist-in-residence, Cranbrook Acad Art, 93. *Awards:* NEA Artists Grants, 74 & 86; Fel, Artist Found, 84 & 91; Prof Develop Grant, Mass Coll Art, 87; 20 x 24 Photog Grant, Polaroid Corp, 88; Boston Mus Fine Arts Traveling Scholar, 98; New Eng Found for the Arts Fel, 98; Mass Cult Coun Artist's Grant, 99 & 2006; Artist's Resource Trust, 01; New Eng Art Critics Asn Award, 2004 & 2006; Anonymous Was a Woman, 2007. *Bibliog:* Christine Temin (auth), Making Room for artworks, Boston Globe, 7/20/90; Cate McQuaid (auth) Boston Globe, 3/8/99, 12/16/2004, 8/19/2009; Ron Glowen (auth), These art works can be worn, be expressive & evocative, Herald, Seattle, Wash, 5/15/92; William Baran-Mickle (auth), Of Magic Power & Memory: Contemporary & International Jewelry, Metalsmith, fall 92; Lewin, Susan Grant (auth), One of a Kind: Art Jewelry Today, Abrams, 94; South End News, 6/1/95; Turner, Ralph (auth), Jewelry in Europe & Am: New Times New Thinking, Thames & Hudson Ltd, 96; Articles in Boston Globe & Boston Phoenix, 90, 98-2000, 2002 & 2004; Mary McCoy (auth), Art New England, 2004; Ann Wilson Lloyd (auth), Art in America (review), 6/2005; New American Painting, New England Ed, 2007; Eve Essex (auth), Big Red and Shiny, 8/11/2009. *Media:* Sculpture, Drawing. *Mailing Add:* C415 One Fitchburg St Apt C415 Somerville MA 02143-2128

SLOSHBERG, LEAH PHYFER
MUSEUM DIRECTOR

b New Albany, Miss, Feb 21, 1937. *Study:* Miss State Coll Women, BFA, 59; Tulane Univ, La, MA, 61; Univ Pa, Bryn Mawr, grad studies. *Pos:* Cur arts, NJ State Mus, Trenton, asst dir, 69-71, dir, 71-; bd mem, Conserv Ctr Art & Artifacts, 79 & Trenton Hist Soc, 87. *Mem:* Am Asn Mus; Conserv Ctr Art & Artifacts; Mid-Atlantic Asn Mus; NJ Asn Mus; Trenton Hist Soc. *Res:* American art; museum management. *Mailing Add:* New Jersey State Mus 205 W State St CN 530 Trenton NJ 08625

SLOTNICK, MORTIMER H
PAINTER, EDUCATOR

b New York, NY, Nov 7, 1920. *Study:* City Coll New York; Columbia Univ. *Work:* In pvt collections of Mrs Harry S Truman, Mrs Cordell Hull, Robert Merrill and others; New Brit Mus Am Art, Conn; Nat Mus Am Art, Smithsonian Inst; Johnson Art Mus, Cornell Univ; Nat Archives; and others. *Exhib:* Whitney Mus Am Art, Riverside Mus, Hudson River Mus, New Rochelle Pub Libr, Nat Acad Design, NY; solo exhib, Am Pastoral, Greenwich Art Soc, 2007; The Gallery at Kent, 2007; and others. *Teaching:* Adj prof art & art educ, City Col New York; supvr arts & humanities, City Sch Dist, New Rochelle, NY; adj prof art educ, Col New Rochelle; adj prof educ, Pace Univ; principal, Davis Elem Sch, New Rochelle, NY. *Mem:* Allied Artists Am; Am Artists Prof League; Artists Equity, NY; Am Vet Soc Artists; Knickerbocker Artists, NY; Salmagundi Club, NY. *Media:* Oil, Drawing. *Publ:* Works publ by Am Artists Group, Donald Art Co, Bernard Picture Co, Scafa-Tornabene Art Publ & McCleery-Cummings Co. *Mailing Add:* 43 Amherst Dr New Rochelle NY 10804

SLUSKY, JOSEPH
SCULPTOR, EDUCATOR

b Philadelphia, Pa, June 7, 1942. *Study:* Univ Calif, Berkeley, BA (archit), MA (art), studied with James Prestini, Ibram Lassaw, James Melchert, Wilfred Zogbaum, Sidney Gordin, Harold Paris, Richard O'Hanlon, William King & Robert Hudson. *Work:* Hayward Area Festival Arts, Calif; City San Francisco; San Francisco Dept Water; Civic Ctr Bldg, City of Orinda, Calif; Crocker Mus, Sacramento, Calif. *Comn:* Outdoor sculpture, City Berkeley, 81; interior lobby sculpture, San Francisco Dept Water, 84; interior lobby sculpture, Peerless Lighting Corp, Berkeley, Calif, 89; interior lobby sculpture, Ctr Middle Eastern Studies, Univ Calif, Berkeley, 2000; outdoor sculpture, Bayer Corp, Berkeley, Calif, 2002; Restoration, City Berkeley, 2004. *Exhib:* Outdoor Sculpture Exhib, Oakland Mus, Oakland, Calif, 94; Maquette Exhib, Mus Val'Aosta, Italy, 95; Interpretations of Light: Menorah Invitational, Jewish Mus, San Francisco, 95; Drawings & Sculpture, Galerie Johannestrasse, Erfurt, Ger, 96; Sculpture Survey 1978-1998, Oakland Mus Sculpture Ct, Calif, 99; Making Change: 100 Artists Interpret the Tzedakah Box, Jewish Mus, San Francisco, 2000; Steel Dreams, City Oakland Craft & Cult Arts Gallery, Oakland, Calif, 2001; Scents of Purpose: Artists Interpret The Spice Box, The Contemp Jewish Mus San Francisco, 2005; Sculpture Survey: 1973-2007, Sanchez Art Ctr, Pacifica, Calif, 2007; group exhib, Crocker Mus, Sacramento, Calif, 2007, 2010; Sculpture Survey: 1975-2008, Museo de Pueblo de Guanajuato, Guanajuato, Mex, 2008, Smith Andersen Editions, Palo Alto, Calif, 2008 & Art Foundry Gallery, Sacramento, Calif, 2008; Santa Cruz Mus, Calif, 2009; 20th Anniversary exhib, Sculpturesite Gallery, San Francisco, 2010; The Crocker Museum Unveiled, Sacamento, Calif, 2011-12; 75th Anniversary Exhib, Richmond Art Ctr, Richmond, Calif, 2011; Spectrum: Lar Landa and Joseph Slusky, Marin Moca, Novato, Calif, 2011; Interactions: Joe Slusky and Kaite Hawkinson, Sun Gallery, Hayward, Calif, 2012; Origins: Elemental Forms in Contemporary Sculpture, Berkeley Art Ctr, Calif, 2013. *Teaching:* Instr sculpture & drawing, Ohlone Coll, Fremont, Calif, 72-85; lectr sculpture, Calif State Univ, San Francisco, 78; sr lectr visual studies dept archit, Univ Calif, Berkeley, 80-2010. *Awards:* Purchase Award, Hayward Festival of the Arts, 75 & 79; First Place Award, Bay Arts, Belmont, Calif, 87 & 90; Sculpture Award, Calif State Fair, 85, 88, 91-96; and others. *Bibliog:* Victoria Powers (auth), Contrasts of concepts and form, Artweek, 3/29/86; Andy Brumer (auth), Joe Slusky: The fluidity of feeling & the solidity of form, Visions Art Quart, spring 94; Jack Foley (auth), Better Living Through Alchemy, The East Bay Express, 3/12/99; Philip Isaacson (auth), Pairing of Artists Provokes, Stimulates, Maine Sunday Telegraph, 11/19/2000; Jakob Schiller (auth), Calliope Shines Again at Marina Mall, Berkeley Daily Planet, 10/29/2005; Andy Brumer (auth), The Artist and the Dance, 360: Life From Every Angle, summer 2006; Rebecca Wallace (auth), Visual Jazz, Palo Alto Weekly, 1/18/2008; Benjamin Pacheco Lopez (auth), Slusky: Fosilizando la Imaginacion, AM, 6/5/2008; Kenneth Baker (auth), Richmond Exhib for it's 75th, San Francisco Chronicle, 04/14/2011; Dewitt Cheng (auth), Light/Dark: Hayward and Berkeley Shows Run Emotional Gamut, East Bay Express, 2011; Alex Bigman (auth), Festival of Form, East Bay Express, 2013. *Media:* Painted Steel; Drawing, Mixed Media. *Publ:* Art in The San Francisco Bay Area 1945-1980; Thomas Albright (auth), Univ Calif Press, 80; Joseph Slusky: Sculpture Survey 1978-1998; The Crocker Art Museum Unveiled (collection catalog), 2011; Joseph Slusky Sculpture 1965-1975, Norfolk Press, 2011; Joseph Slusky: Painted Metal Sculpture 1977-2012, Norfolk Press, 2012; Joseph Slusky: Postcard Drawings, 1997-2008, Norfolk Press, 2012; Earth: Joseph Slusky Drawings 1991-2001, Norfolk Press, 2012. *Dealer:* Smith Andersen Editions 440 Pepper Ave Palo Alto CA 94306; Norfolk Press Gallery 398 11th St 2nd Fl San Francisco Ca 94103. *Mailing Add:* 1727 8th St Berkeley CA 94710

SMALLEY, DAVID ALLAN
SCULPTOR, EDUCATOR

b New London, Conn, Dec 17, 1940. *Study:* RI Sch Design, 58-60; Univ Conn, with Antony Padovano, BFA, 63; Ind Univ with Jean-Paul Darriau, MFA, 65. *Work:* Lyman Allyn Mus & Conn Col, New London; State of Conn Superior Ct. *Comn:* Warlock III (cor-ten steel), Conn Commission Arts, New London, 73; State of Conn Ocean Clouds 35 ft suspended kinetic, Conn Comn on the Arts; Ad-Astra, stainless steel (10 ft), Conn Col. *Exhib:* Conn Painting, Drawing & Sculpture, Univ Bridgeport, New Britain Mus & Conn Col, 79; Penwith Gallery, Cornwall, Eng, 79; Kraushaar Galleries, NY, 80-81; Solo exhib, Lyman Allyn Mus, New London, Conn, 81 & Kraushaar Galleries, NY, 84, 87, 90 & 93; Vangarde Gallery, New London, Conn, 87 & 90. *Pos:* Bd dir, Art Resources Conn, 75-80; pres, Vangarde Co-op Gallery, 86; co-dir, Ctr Arts Technol, Conn Col. *Teaching:* Prof sculpture & Henry B Plant prof art, Conn Col, 65-. *Awards:* Ingram Merrill Found Grant, 69; Research Grant, Dana Found, 80. *Bibliog:* Barbara Zabel (auth), Profile, Art Voices, 7-8/81 & review, Arts Mag, 4/84, review Sculpture Mag, 9/87. *Mem:* Mystic Art Asn; Vangarde Co-op Gallery. *Media:* Stainless Steel, Brass. *Dealer:* Kraushaar Galleries 724 5th Ave New York NY

SMALLEY, STEPHEN FRANCIS
EDUCATOR, PAINTER

b Rockville, Conn, Apr 14, 1941. *Study:* Mass Coll Art, BS, 63; State Col, Boston, MEd, 65; Pa State Univ, DEd, 70. *Work:* Bridgewater State Coll, Mass; Mansfield State Coll, Pa; RI Coll. *Comn:* map of Can painting, Can Govt, 2008. *Exhib:* Mass Coll Art, Arnheim Gallery, 93; Touching All The Bases, Gallery 53, Cooperstown, NY, 96; The Word Is Art, Manchester Metrop Univ, 96; From Baseball Cards to Tutti Frutti, Univ Mass, Lowell, 98; Popular Celebrities & Personal Celebrations, Monmouth Univ, NJ, 2001; When I'm Sixty-four, Bridgewater State Coll, 2005; Henry VIII Series, Diehl Gallery, Bridgewater, Mass, 2011; Faculty and Friends, Monmouth Univ, NJ, 2012-2013; Mass Exhib, DiMattio Gallery, Monmouth Univ, NJ, 2013. *Teaching:* Fac art, Rindge Tech High Sch, Cambridge, Mass, 63-65; teaching asst design & printmaking, Pa State Univ, 65-67; assoc prof & chmn, Dept Art Educ, Tyler Sch Art, 67-72; chmn dept art, Bridgewater State Coll, Mass, 72-84, prof, 72-2005, vis lectr, 2005-, prof emer, currently; fac assoc, Wadham Coll, Bridgewater-at-Oxford, 96-2007. *Awards:* Outstanding Art Teacher Award, Mass Art Educ Asn, 85; Mass Higher Educ Art Educator of Yr, 2000; Outstanding Honors Fac

Award, Bridgewater State Coll, Mass, 2010. *Mem:* Nat Art Educ Asn; Mass Art Educ; Bridgewater State Univ Faculty Emeritus Club. *Media:* Acrylics, Pen & Ink, pencil, gouache. *Interests:* British art, popular culture, Pop art. *Publ:* Auth, Fungoes That Go Pop, A Teaching Compendium of Art Essays Tied to Pop Culture and the Classroom, 97; A Book of Yells (painting, poetry, & prose), 99; Lights Camera Cannes (painting, photog, poetry & prose); Coming Ashore (painting & prose), 2005; reproduction image, Canada, Bridgewater Rev, 6/2008; catalogue intro, Whole in the Wall Exhib, Galerie Helenbeck, New York; Voices of King Philip's War (cover illustration), Poems by Faye George, World Tech Editions, 2013. *Mailing Add:* 144 Atkinson Dr Bridgewater MA 02324

SMART, MARY-LEIGH
CONSULTANT, PATRON
b Springfield, Ill, Feb 27, 1917. *Study:* Oxford Univ, dipl Extra Mural Delegacy, 35; Wellesley Col, BA, 37; Columbia Univ, MA, 39; also with Bernard Karfiol, 38-39. *Collection Arranged:* Art: Ogunquit, A National Exhibition of Artists Who Have Worked in Ogunquit (auth, catalog), 67, Peggy Bacon, A Celebration (auth, catalog), 79 & three exhibitions each season, 80-86, Barn Gallery, Ogunquit, Maine. *Pos:* Founding secy & prog dir, Barn Gallery Assocs, Ogunquit, Maine, 58-78; cur, Hamilton Easter Field Art Found Collection, 66-79, pres, 69-70 & 82-87, hon dir, 71-78, cur exhibs, 79-86, chair exhib comt, 87-94, vpres, 94-; founding mem bd adv, Univ Art Galleries, Univ NH, 73-89, vpres, 75-81, pres, 81-89; mem coun adv, Farnsworth Art Mus, 86-98; mem mus panel, Maine Arts Comn, 83-86; mem collections comt, Payson Gallery, Westbrook Col, Portland, Maine, 87-90; founder, Surf Point Found, a non-profit art found, York, Maine, 88; Mem, Maine Women's Forum, 93-2008; corporator, Ogunquit Mus Am Art, 88-90 & 95-2000; Mem, Art Comt, York Public Library, Maine, 2002-2006. *Awards:* Deborah Morton Award, Westbrook Col, Portland, Me, 88; Friend of Arts Award, Maine Art Dealers Asn, 93. *Bibliog:* Louise Balch Hatfield (auth), Art Foundation, Wellesley, summer 92; Alice Giordano (auth), A Foundation for New England artists, Boston Sunday Globe, 1/7/98; Virginia L Woodwell (auth), Artists colony to be patron's legacy, York Weekly, 1/7/98; Jennifer McFarlend Flint (auth), The Long View on Life, Wellesley, Fall, 2007; Virginia Woodwell (auth), Surf Point: A Grand Vision, York Land Trust Newsletter, Fall, 2007; Lucky 7 (inside story), Portland Mag, 9/08. *Mem:* Fel Portland Mus Art, Maine; Nat Comt Friends Art, Wellesley Col. *Interests:* Contemporary art. *Collection:* Twentieth century New England painting and sculpture; American, European and Asian contemporary graphics; photography. *Publ:* Auth, Hamilton Easter Field Art Foundation Collection (catalog), 66; Ed, A Century of Color, Ogunquit, Maine's Art Colony, 1886-1986, Barn Gallery Assocs Pub, 87; J Scott Smart AKA, The Fat Man, pvt publ, 94; coauth (Beverly Hallam), Maine is their Mentor, Maine Arts Comn Mag, winter 2006. *Mailing Add:* 30 Surf Point Rd York ME 03909-5053

SMEDLEY, GEOFFREY
EDUCATOR, SCULPTOR
b London, Eng, Feb 24, 1927. *Study:* Camberwell Sch Art, London; Slade Sch Fine Arts, London, 54. *Work:* Victoria & Albert Mus & Arts Coun Gt Brit, London. *Comn:* Sculpture Garden, Commune Pirano, Istria, Yugoslavia, 72; Southern Arts Asn Eng, Portsmouth, 74; set design, Freddy Wood Theatre; Rowingbridge, a 50 foot high kinetic sculpture, Expo 86. *Exhib:* Whitechapel Art Gallery, 72; Arts Coun, traveling, 73 & 76; Agnes Etherington Art Ctr, Queen's Univ, Kingston, Ont, 78; Nature as Material, traveling, Eng, 80-81; solo exhib, Vancouver Art Gallery, BC, 82, Memory, Measure, Time and Numbers, Suncy inst Art & Design, Univ Col, UK; Vancouver Art & Artists, Vancouver Art Gallery (with catalog), 83; Canada Collects, Art Bank & traveling USA; Making Hist, Vancouver Art Gallery, 86; traveling show, Memory, Measure, Time and Numbers, 00; Pietro en tete: Meditation on Piero, 01; one man show, Memory, Measure, Time and Numbers, Suncy inst Art & Design, Univ Col, UK. *Teaching:* Prof fine arts, Univ BC, 78-, emer prof, 92-. *Awards:* Proj Art Award, Arts Coun Great Brit, 72; Sculpture award, West Gate Plaza Expo 86; Materials Grant, 85 & Sr Grant, 87, Can Coun; Can Coun Travel Grant, 00; Can Coun A Grant, 01; Fel Anni and Josef Albers Found, Conn, 01; Daniel Langois Found Award, 02. *Bibliog:* Memory, Measure, Time & Numbers, Suncy Inst Art & Design, Univ College, 69 pp; Piero en Tete-Canadian Ctr for Architecture, Montreal, 63 pp. *Mailing Add:* RR 3 Gambier Island Gibsons BC V0N 1V0 Canada

SMEDSTAD, DEBORAH BARLOW
LIBRARIAN
b Cooperstown, NY, Dec 14, 1958. *Study:* Univ San Diego, BA, 81; Simmons Coll Grad Sch Libr & Info Sci, MS, 84; Boston Univ Grad Sch Arts Sci, MA, 85. *Pos:* Visual resources librn, Cooper Union Libr, 85-87; art librn, asst prof & cur, Queens Coll, 87-90; reference librn, Univ S Calif, Archit Fine Arts Libr, 90-94; head librn, Los Angeles Co Mus Art, 95-2003 & Mus Fine Arts, Boston, 2003-. *Mem:* Art Libr Soc N Am. *Interests:* 17th to 20th century western art, general western art & American art. *Publ:* Contribr, Hendrick Goltzius and the Classical Tradition, Fisher Gallery, Univ S Calif, 92; Richard Diebenkorn: Prints from the Harry W and Mary Margaret Anderson Collection, Fisher Gallery, Univ SCalif, 93; Art Museum Library Collections & Collection Development, Art Mus Librs & Librarianship, Scarecrow Press, 2007. *Mailing Add:* William Morris Hunt Libr Mus Fine Arts 465 Huntington Ave Boston MA 02115

SMIDT, ERIC
COLLECTOR
Pos: Pres, Harbor Freight Tools USA. *Awards:* Named one of Top 200 Collectors, ARTnews mag, 2009-13. *Collection:* New York School; contemporary art. *Mailing Add:* Harbor Freight Tools USA 3491 Mission Oaks Blvd Camarillo CA 93011

SMIGOCKI, STEPHEN VINCENT
PAINTER, PRINTMAKER
b Washington, DC, Nov 20, 1942. *Study:* Univ Md, BA (fine arts), 64, MA (drawing), 68; Univ SFla, Tampa; Fla State Univ, painting with Karl Zerbe, PhD (art educ). *Work:* Ringling Mus, Sarasota, Fla; Huntington Gallery, WVa; WVa Sci & Cult Complex, Sunrise Gallery, Charleston. *Exhib:* Dallas Summer Arts Festival Nat Competition, Tex, 71; Biennial I Six-State Painting Competition, Va Commonwealth Univ, 73; Drawings '74 Nat Exhib, Wheaton Col, Norton, Mass; Thirteen State Regional Exhib, Appalachian Corridors, Charleston, WVa, 75; All WVa Exhib, Charleston, 79, 81, 83, 85 & 89; Huntington Galleries, 79, 83 & 88. *Pos:* Graphic artist, Univ Md Ctr Adult Educ, 64-66. *Teaching:* Prof art, Fairmont State Col, WVa, 72-. *Awards:* Purchase Awards, Huntington Galleries Exhib 280, WVa, 72 & Appalachian Corridors, 75; merit award, All WVa Exhib, Charleston, 79. *Bibliog:* Art Pedagogy of Paul Klee and Wassily Kandinsky (dissertation). *Mem:* Los Angeles Printmaking Soc. *Media:* Etching; woodcut. *Publ:* Contribr, Echo Without Sound, Northwoods Press, 80; illus, Perspectives Mag Fairmont State Col, Fall, 91. *Dealer:* Bill Tomlinson Garo Gallery Morgantown WV. *Mailing Add:* 1205 Peacock Ln Fairmont WV 26554

SMIRA, SHAOUL
PAINTER
b Oct 10, 1939. *Study:* Auni Art Inst, Tel-Aviv, 58-61; Acad Chomier, Paris, 65-66; Graphics study: etching & lythography, USA, 1969-72; The Art Paper Making, Belgium, 1975-79. *Work:* Tel-Aviv Mus, Israel; Rockefeller Art Ctr, NY; Fine Art Mus, Ostend, Belg; Fredrick Weisman Found, Los Angeles, Calif; Bank Paribas Collection, Bruselles, Belg. *Comn:* Sheraton Hotel, Tel-Aviv, 64; Beth Yeshuron Congregation, Houston, Tex 79; Collabr, Beth-El, Baltimore, Md, 82. *Exhib:* Contemp Israel Koninklijk, Belg, 85; The Concern Eyes, Port of Hist, Philadelphia, 86; Arbitrariness, Israeli Art, Ramat, Gan, 90; Collection, Skir Ball, Los Angeles, 91; solo exhib, Mus de la Nacion, Lima, Peru, 95, Gallereia et Museo, Bogota, Columbia, 2001, Gallery Guy Pieters, Knokke-Zoute, Belgium, 2003, July M Gallery, Tel-Aviv, Israel, 2003, Galerie Guy Pieters, Saint-Paul de Vence, France, 2004 & 05, De Latemse Galerij, Sint-Martens-Latem, Belgium, 2006; Cahn Gal, New York, 2000; Anne Frank, Syracuse Univ, New York, 2001. *Bibliog:* Kuspit Donald (auth), Art of Moral Mission, Flash Art, 86; The desire of Planet Earth, Kunst & Colture, 93; Gerard Goodrow (auth), Creative Chaos, Am House, 95. *Media:* Multi Media. *Dealer:* Alex Kahan Medison New York NY. *Mailing Add:* 451 Broome St New York NY 10013

SMITH, AJ
PRINTMAKER
b Jonestown, Miss, Mar 10, 1952. *Study:* Skowhogan Sch Painting & Sculpture, 73; Kansas City Art Inst, BFA, 74; Queens Col/CUNY, MFA, 77; Apprenticed with Robert Blackburn 77-82. *Hon Degrees:* Master Printer, Printmaking Workshop Inc, NYC. *Work:* Columbia Mus, SC; Philadelphia Mus of Art; Printmaking Workshop Inc, NY; Ark Arts Ctr Found Collection, Little Rock; Schomburg Res Ctr, New York City; Libr Congress, Washington, DC. *Comn:* Dream Microcosm Series, Henderson State Univ, Arkadelphia, Ark, 89; Dream Macrocosm Series, Southeast Ark Art Ctr, Pine Bluff, 90; Fellowship Edition, Brandywine Ctr Creative Arts, Philadelphia, 92; Life Series and Quiet Series, Cent Ark Pub Libr, Little Rock, 97; CALM Monoprint Series, Convention and Civic Ctr, Hot Springs, Ark, 98. *Exhib:* Impressive Expressions, Smithsonian Inst Traveling Exhib Series, 79-89; Prints of the City, Mus of the City of NY, 81; Way Down South Series, Ark Art Ctr, Little Rock, 83; In a Stream of Ink, Bronx Mus of Art, NY, 86; Acquisition Invitational, Philadelphia Mus Art, 94; Artist of Color, Albany Inst of History & Art, 95; 25th Anniversary Celebration, Longview Art Mus, Tex, 95; African-Am Artist, Carnegie Hall Mus, Lewisburg, WVa, 2000; 18th Southwest Comp Invitational, Mus African Am Art, Dallas, Tex; Black Romantic, Studio Mus, Harlem, NY, 02; Drawing VI, Koplin Gallery, Los Angeles, 02; In Print: The Language of Art, Fla State Univ Art Mus, Tallahassee, 03. *Pos:* Master printer Printmaking Workshop, Inc, NY, 78-82; Mentor Pratt Integrative Studies, Pratt Inst, Brooklyn, 79-80; Artist in Residence, Ark Arts Ctr, Little Rock, 82-83. *Teaching:* Adj prof art appreciation, Upper Montclair State Col, NJ, 79-82; Adj prof drawing, La Guardia Community Col, Long Island City, NY, 79-81; Prof drawing & printmaking, Univ Ark at Little Rock, 82-. *Awards:* Artist in Residence, Studio Mus in Harlem, 78-79; Mid-Am Arts Alliance/NEA, 84; Fel, Vt Studio Ctr, 97; Fel, Ark Arts Coun/NEA, 99. *Bibliog:* Xian Rang Yong (auth), Fine Art Society, Lu Xun Fine Art Inst Jour, 87; Xian Rang Yong (auth), Artist Anthology, Beijing Graphic Art Publishing House, 93; Halima Taha (auth) Collecting African American Art, Craven Publishing, Inc, 98. *Mem:* Ark Arts Ctr, Little Rock; Printmaking Workshop Inc, New York City; Kansas City Art Inst Alumni Asn; Skowhegah Sch of Painting and Sculpture Alumni Asn. *Media:* Drawing, Monoprint, Monotype, Lithography. *Res:* Traditional limestone lithography. *Dealer:* Mary Pauline 982 Broad St Augusta GA 30901; MCS Gallery 1110 Northampton St Easton PA 18042. *Mailing Add:* 1709 S Arch St Little Rock AR 72206

SMITH, ALBERT E
PAINTER
b San Francisco, Calif, 1929. *Study:* Univ Calif, Berkeley. *Work:* Achenbach Found, Calif Palace Legion of Hon, San Francisco; Stanford Univ Art Mus, Calif; Triton Mus, Santa Clara, Calif; Oakland Mus, Calif; Univ Calif, Davis. *Exhib:* Marunouchi Gallery, Tokyo, Japan, 84, 86, 91; Anthony Ralph Gallery, NY, 87, 89; Roger Ramsay Gallery, Chicago, 89; 871 Fine Arts, San Francisco, 91-93 & 98; retrospective 1954-1994, Triton Mus, Santa Clara, Calif, 95-2005; Kurt Lidtke Fine Art, Wash, 96; solo exhibs, Kurt Lidke Gallery, Seattle, Wash, 96 & 871 Fine Arts, San Francisco, 98; Perimeter Gallery, Chicago, 2000. *Publ:* Asteion, Japan, 88; Art of California, 3-4/93; California Vistas: 10 Paintings by Albert Smith, 95. *Dealer:* Perimeter Gallery Chicago IL; Anne Berthoud Gallery London Eng

SMITH, ALEXIS (PATRICIA ANNE)
COLLAGE ARTIST, SCULPTOR
b Los Angeles, Calif, Aug 24, 1949. *Study:* Univ Calif, Irvine, 66-70, BA (art), 70; study with Robert Irwin & Vija Celmins. *Hon Degrees:* Otis Coll Art & Design, Hon Dr, 2001. *Work:* Whitney Mus Am Art; Mus Contemp Art, Los Angeles; Walker Art Ctr, Minneapolis; Mus Mod Art, New York; La Co Mus OCMA, MCA, San Diego. *Comn:* Monuments, MacArthur Park Pub Art Prog, Los Angeles, 86; Snake Path, Stuart Collection, Univ Calif, San Diego, La Jolla; South & West Lobby Terrazzo

floors, Los Angeles Conv Ctr Expansion, 92; mixed media, murals, Getty Ctr Restaurant, 97; Terrazzo, Schottenstein Arena, Columbus, Ohio, 99; murals, CAEEP, Sacramento, 2005. *Exhib:* Lowe, Munger, Smith, Los Angeles Co Mus Art, 72; Four Los Angeles Artists, Corcoran Gallery Am Art, Washington, DC, 75; solo exhibs, Whitney Mus Am Art, 75, Rosamund Felsen Gallery, 78, 80 & 82, De Appel, Amsterdam, 79, Margo Leavin Gallery 82, 85, 88, 90, 95, 99, 2003, & 2009, Walker Art Ctr, 86, Inst Contemp Art, Boston, 86, Aspen Art Mus, 87, Brooklyn Mus, 87-88, Wexner Ctr Arts, Ohio State Univ, 97-98, Miami Art Mus, 2000, Lawrence Rubin Greenberg Van Doren Fine Art, New York, 2001, 2004 & 2011 & Mus Contemp Art, San Diego, 2001; Whitney Biennial, Whitney Mus Am Art, New York, 75, 79 & 81; Am Narrative/Story Art, Contemp Art Mus, Houston, Tex, 77, & J Paul Getty Mus, 97; Holly Solomon Gallery, 77-79, 81 & 83; Narration, Inst Contemp Art, Boston, 78; Mus as Site, Los Angeles Co Mus Art, 81; New Directions, Hirshhorn Mus & Sculpture Garden, 83; Verbally Charged Images, Independent Curators, 84-86; Mus Mod Art, New York, 84; Individuals, Mus Contemp Art, Los Angeles, 86-88; Josh Baer Gallery, 90; retrospective, Whitney Mus Am Art, Mus Cont Art, Los Angeles, 91-92; Whitney Mus Am Art, New York, 2001; Site Santa Fe Biennial, 2001; Japanese Am Nat Mus, 2002; Margo Leavin Gallery, Los Angeles, 2004 & 2009; Southern Exposure, MCASD, 2006; Art since 1960's, OCMA, 2007; Wack, Mus Contemp Art, Los Angeles, 2007, 2010; Tom Solomon Gallery, Los Angeles, 2009; Margo Leavin Gallery, 2009; Craig Knoll Gallery, 2013; Honor Fraser Gallery, 2013. *Teaching:* Instr, Calif Arts, 75, Univ Calif, Irvine & San Diego, 76-78, Los Angeles, 79-88, Skowhegan, 90, Southern Methodist Univ, Tex, 93, Univ Nev, Las Vegas, 2002 & Otis Art Inst, 2007-, Art Ctr, 2010. *Awards:* New Talent Award, Contemp Arts Coun, Los Angeles Co Mus Art, 74; Nat Endowment Arts Fel Grant, 76-77, 87-88; Residency, Rockefeller Found Study Ctr, Bellagio, Italy, 95; Terrazzo Job of the Year, Nat Terrazzo & Mosaic Asn, 99, Epoxy Terrazzo Job of the Century, 2000; COLA Individual Artist Fel, 2002. *Bibliog:* Nancy Marmer (auth), Alexis Smith: The narrative act, Artforum, 12/76; Leo Rubinfien, Through western eyes, Art in Am, 9-10/78; Hunter Drohojowska (auth), Alexis Smith: The Public Works, Artspace, summer 91; Richard Armstrong (auth), Alexis Smith (catalog Bk), Rizzoli publ, 91; Grace Glueck (auth), NY Times, B36, 4/6/2001; Art in Am, 11/2001. *Mem:* LA Inst Humanities; Skowhegan Sch. *Media:* Multimedia, Installation Sculpture, Collage. *Specialty:* Contemp Art. *Collection:* large collection of early works by LA artists owned with husband, artist Scott Grieger. *Publ:* Designer, misc media, 70's-; contribr centerfold, Avalanche, fall 75; auth, Alone, 77; contribr, Italics, Paris Rev, spring 79; Shanghai Express, Los Angeles Herald-Examiner, 11/81; coauth (with Amy Gerstler), Past Lives, 89. *Dealer:* Van Doren Waxter Gallery 23 East 73rd St New York NY 10021; Honor Fraser Gallery 2622 S La Cienaza Blvd Los Angeles Ca 90034. *Mailing Add:* 1625 Shell Ave Venice CA 90291

SMITH, ALLISON V
PHOTOGRAPHER

b Manassas, Va, 1972. *Study:* Eugene Lang Coll, New Sch Univ, BA, 1995; Parsons Sch Design, BFA, 1995; Yale Univ Sch Art, MFA, 1999; Independent Study Prog, Whitney Mus Am Art, 1999-2000. *Work:* Saatchi Gallery, London. *Exhib:* Solo exhibs include Barry Whistler Gallery, Dallas, 1998, 2002, 2004, 2006, Ty Stokes Gallery, Atlanta, 2005, Galveston Arts Ctr, Galveston, Tex, 2005; group exhibs include Pin Ups, Barry Whistler Gallery, Dallas, 2000; For the Birds, Galveston Arts Ctr, Texas, 2003; Four Walls, Displays Unlimited Inc, Fort Worth, 2003; Through the Lens, Arlington Mus Art, Arlington, Tex, 2005; Artists Among Us, Women's Mus, Dallas, Tex, 2005; Most Likely to Succeed, Art Prostitute, Dallas, 2006; One Up, Public Trust, Dallas, 2007; Reno07, Barry Whistler Gallery, Dallas, 2007. *Pos:* Photog intern, Dallas Times Herald, 1990, Los Angeles Times, 1993 & Albuquerque Journal, 1994; photog, Denton Record Chronicle, 1993-94; staff photog, Santa Fe New Mexican, 1995-96, Ft Worth Star-Telegram, 1996-98 & Dallas Morning News, 1998-2004; freelance photog, 2004-. *Awards:* Master Photog of Year, Tex Headliner Found, 1997; Found Contemp Awards Grant, 2008. *Dealer:* Barry Whistler Gallery 2909-B Canton St Dallas TX 75226. *Mailing Add:* 6026 Goliad Ave Dallas TX 75206

SMITH, ANDREA B
PAINTER

b Detroit, Mich, June 29, 1946. *Study:* Wayne State Univ, BA, 67. *Work:* Pearson Art Found Mus, Des Moines, Iowa; Pereslaul Mus, Russ; Univ Peace, San Jose, Costa Rica. *Comn:* Painting, Am Vet Vietnam War, NY, 87; Preuss Found, La Jolla, Calif, 88; Group Health Found, Seattle, 89; Writers Companion (painting), Prentice Hall, NY, 90; painting, Waokele Opuna-Rainforest, Hilo, Hawaii, 90. *Exhib:* Watercolor, Mich Watercolor Soc, Detroit, 79; 31st Ann Exhib, Knickerbocker Artists, NY, 81; Bakersfield Col, Calif, 83; Contemp Art, Am Mus, Williamsburg, Va, 86; Art for Peace, Women's Nat Bank, Washington, DC, 86, Irving Ctr Art Mus, 87 & Children's Russ Bibliotech, Moscow, 87. *Awards:* Best of Show, Mich Watercolor Soc, 79 & Musee de Duncan, 81. *Bibliog:* Jamie Forbes (auth), Sunstrom Mag, 86. *Media:* Watercolor, Acrylic. *Mailing Add:* 1590 Lokia St Lahaina HI 96761

SMITH, ANN Y
MUSEUM DIRECTOR, CURATOR

b Alma, Mich, Oct 7, 1950. *Study:* Univ Mich, BA, 72; State Univ NY, MA, 73; Univ Conn Law Sch, JD, 91. *Collection Arranged:* Fiddlebacks and Crooked-backs, 82; Connecticut Masters, 86; Brass Valley, 86. *Pos:* Asst cur, Hist Soc York Co, Pa, 73-74; dir, Lyme Hist Soc, Conn, 74-76; Mattatuck Mus, Waterbury, Conn, 76-. *Teaching:* Adj fac, Univ Conn, Archit Hist. *Mem:* Conn Comn Arts (art selection panel); New Eng Mus Asn; Am Asn Mus; Conn Mus Asn (chair); New Eng Found Arts (bd mem). *Publ:* Ed, Minds and Machines: Waterbury at Work, Mattatuck Hist Soc, 80; William Merit Post (essay), 97; auth, AT Van Laer, 98. *Mailing Add:* Mattatuck Mus 144 W Main St Waterbury CT 06702

SMITH, ANNA DEAVERE
PATRON

b Baltimore, Md, Sept 18, 1950. *Study:* Beaver Col, Pa, BA, 71; Am Conservatory Theatre, MFA, 77. *Hon Degrees:* Beaver Col, Pa, Hon Dr, 73; Univ NC, Hon Dr, 95; numerous hon degrees from US cols & univs, 95-97. *Pos:* Founding dir, Inst Arts & Civic Dialogue Harvard Univ, 98; trustee, Mus Modern Art, New York City. *Teaching:* artist-in-residence, Ford Found, 97; prof arts & drama, Ann O'Day Maples, Stanford Univ. *Awards:* Named One of Women of Year, Glamour Mag, 93; fel, Bunting Inst, Radcliffe Col; genius fel, The MacArthur Found, 96. *Publ:* Playwright, performer one-woman shows On the Road: A Search for American Character, 83, Aye, Aye, Aye, I'm Integrated, 84, Piano, 91, Fires in the Mirror, 89, Twilight: Los Angeles 92, House Arrest, 1997; writer, libretto for Judith Jamison, performer Hymn, 93; appeared in (films) Dave, 93, Philadelphia, 93, The American President, 95, Twilight: Los Angeles, 2000

SMITH, B J
MUSEUM DIRECTOR, INSTRUCTOR

b Beaver, Okla, Aug 22, 1931. *Study:* Okla State Univ, Stillwater, BFA, 55; Univ Okla, Norman, MFA, 59. *Work:* Joslyn Art Mus, Omaha, Nebr; Mus Art, Univ Okla, Norman; State Collection of Okla Artists & Craftsmen, Oklahoma City; Okla Art Ctr, Oklahoma City. *Exhib:* Ann Eight State Exhib, 63, 64, 68, 70 & 74, 13 Artists You Should Collect, 65, Okla Art Ctr, Oklahoma City; solo exhib, WNebr Arts Ctr, Scottsbluff, 83, Tex Wesleyan Col, Ft Worth, Tex, 86, WNebr Arts Ctr, Scottsbluff, 87, Western Okla Images, Pioneer Mus, Woodward, 87 & Ecent, Ada, Okla, 94; Pioneer Mus & Arts Ctr, Woodward, Okla, 83; Small Wonders, Kirkpatrick Ctr, Oklahoma City, 90; Okla Small Works 2, E Cent, Ada, 92; Tom Preston Mem Exhib, Alexandra, La, 92; 25th Ann, W Nebr Arts Ctr, Scottsbluff, 92; and others. *Pos:* Asst to dir, Okla Art Ctr, Oklahoma City, 61-65; dir, Gardiner Art Gallery, Okla State Univ, 65-94. *Teaching:* Assoc prof color & design, Okla State Univ, 65-81, assoc prof, 81-94; retired. *Awards:* Purchase Awards, Ninth Midwest Biennial, Joslyn Art Mus, Omaha, 66, Okla Biennial, Okla Art Ctr, Oklahoma City, 67 & Okla Artists Ann, Philbrook Art Ctr, Tulsa, 68. *Media:* Acrylic on Masonite. *Mailing Add:* 2132 W Sunset Dr Stillwater OK 74074

SMITH, BARBARA TURNER
VIDEO & PERFORMANCE ARTIST, EDUCATOR

b Pasadena, Calif, July 6, 1931. *Study:* Pomona Coll, BA, 53; Chouinard Art Inst, with Emerson Woelfer, 65; workshops with Alex Hay, 68 & Steve Paxton, 69; Univ Calif, Irvine, with Bob Irwin, Barbara Rose, Moira Roth & Larry Bell, MFA, 71. *Work:* Newport Harbor Art Mus, Newport Beach, Calif; Herbert F Johnson, Cornell Univ; Mus Mod Art; Frac des Pays De La Loire; Pomona Coll Mus Art; Pomona Coll Mus Art; and var pvt collections. *Comn:* Capp Street Proj, Installation/Performance 84; SPARC, Community-Wide Performance, 89; Kaprows Art as Life, Reinvention of Allan Kaprow's Push & Pull 1963, Moca, La, 2008. *Exhib:* People Who Should Be Seen, Los Angeles Co Art Mus, Los Angeles, 65; Performance Conf, Womanspace & Woman's Bldg, 73, 75, & 77; Retrospective (auth, catalog), Univ Calif, San Diego, 74; 60-80 Show Stedelijk Mus, Amsterdam, 82; Endurance, Exit Art, New York, 95; MAC galerie contemporaines des Musee de Marseilles l'art au Corpo, 96; Out of Action (with catalog), Mus Contemp Art, Los Angeles, 98, Between Performance & the Object: 1949-1979 (with catalog), 98; Centre Georges Pompidou, Paris, (Los Angeles 1955-1985), 2006; Wack: Art of the Feminist Revolution, Mus Contemp Art, Los Angeles, 2007; Art Since the 1960's: Calif Experiments, Orange Co Mus Art, 2007; Armory Ctr Arts, Pasadena, 2009; Galerie Parisa Kind, Frankfurt, Germany, 2008-09; The Box, Los Angeles, 2009; Maccarone allery, New York, 2008; Pomana Coll Mus Art, Calif, 2005; Orange Co Mus Art, 2009; Office for Contemp Art, Norway, 2008; Mus Contemp Art, LA, 2008. *Pos:* Co-founder, F-Space Gallery, Santa Ana, Calif, 70-72; founding mem, Grandview I & II Gallery & The Women's Bldg, Los Angeles, 73-75; organizer, New Dimensions in Sci series, Los Angeles Inst Contemp Art, 75; gallery dir, New Gallery, 18th St Arts Ctr, Santa Monica, Calif, 94-95; bd of dir, Highways Performance Space, 2007-2010; bd of dir, Los Angeles Poverty Dept, 2001-. *Teaching:* Fac fel art, Univ Redlands, Calif, 74-; vis performance artist, Univ Calif, San Diego, 77; vis artist, San Francisco Art Inst, 78 & Ohio State Univ, 90; lectr, Univ Calif, Los Angeles, 79-82 & Univ Calif, San Diego, 78, 86 & 93; vis artist design, Otis Coll Art, 96. *Awards:* Nat Endowment Arts Grant, 74, 79 & 85; Woman's Bldg Vista Award, Los Angeles, 83; Nat Hon Award, Women's Caucus Arts, 99; Durfe Grant, 2005, 2009; Elizeth Murray Oral Hist of Women in the Arts, Columbia Univ, New York, 2009; ARC/Durfee Grant, Cailf, 2009. *Bibliog:* Moira Roth (auth), The Amazing Decade: Women in Performance Art 1970-1980, 83; Linda Burnham (auth), Performance Art in Southern Calif: an overview, Vol 2, No 3, High Performance Mag; Tom Marioni (auth), l'Art corporel et ses Origines eo Caliponie Internationoules, l'Art au Corps, 96; Laura Cottingham (auth), Are You Experienced (catalog essay), l'Art au Corps, 96; 21st Century Odyssey Part II: The Performances of Barbara T Smith (catalog), Pomona Coll Mus Art; Remnants, Mara McCarthy & Barbara T Smith interview booklet, The Box, Los Angeles, 2008; LA Weekly, Christopher Miles Rev, Barbara T Smith: Old Shoes, 2010; Richarson, Issue A4 Herve, Class & Krafft, Eugenie, From Self Expression to Girls Gone Wild, 2009; Frieze, Carlson, Amanda, Barbara T Smith, 2009; Artforum, Ina Blom, Carnal Knowledge, 2009; Spike Quarterly, Vienna & Berlin, Baumann, Daniel, Body is Where it Happens, 2009; Catherine Taft, Barbara T Smith, Artforum, 2008; Roberta Smith, Art in Review, Barbara T Smith, NY Times, 2008; Charley 05, Deste Foundation, Athens, Greece, 2008; Wack! Catalogue, 2007. *Mem:* Los Angeles Contemp Exhibs; Women's Caucus Art; Mus Contemp Art; Santa Monica Mus Art; Highways; Performance Space; MOCA, Calif. *Media:* Body and Video. *Specialty:* The Box, Chinatown, Los Angeles, Perfromance, New Genre. *Interests:* Yoga, sci, photog, nature, reading. *Publ:* Auth, Rope, pvt publ, 71; Burden case tried, dismissed, Artweek, 73; Women in industry, Los Angeles Inst Contemp Art J, 74; contribr, Buddha mind performance, In: Vision, Crown, 75; auth, Rachel Rosenthal performs Charm, Artweek, 2/77; Notes on Allan Kaprow, Mus Am O St Wall, Dortmund, Fed Repub Ger, 87. *Dealer:* The Box Gallery Chinatown; Maccarone Galley NY. *Mailing Add:* 801 Coeur d'Alene Venice CA 90291

SMITH, BARRIE CALABRESE See Van Osdell, Barrie (Calabrese) Smith

SMITH, CARY
PAINTER
b Puerto Rico, 1955; US citizen. *Study:* Sir John Cass Art Sch, London, Eng, 76; Syracuse Abroad, Florence, Italy, 76; Syracuse Univ Art Sch, NY, BFA, 77. *Work:* Whitney Mus Am Art, NY; Brooklyn Mus, NY; Osaka Art Mus, Japan; Wadsworth Atheneum, Hartford, Conn. *Exhib:* Solo exhibs, Linda Cathcart Gallery, Santa Monica, 91, Stephen Wirtz Gallery, San Francisco, Calif, 91, Rubin Spangle Gallery, NY, 92, Roger Ramsay Gallery, Chicago, 93, Salvatore Ala Gallery, NY, 93-94, Galerie Paal, Munich, Ger, 95 & 97, Derek Eller, NY, 97, 99 & 2000; Whitney Biennial, Whitney Mus Am Art, NY, 89; Selection from the Collection: Art of the 80's, Whitney Mus Am Art, NY, 91; group exhibs, Wadsworth Atheneum, Hartford, Conn, 92, Rubin Spangle Gallery, NY, 92, August Confessions, Geoffrey Young Gallery, Great Barrington, MA, Boomerang, Collector's Choice, Exit Art, NY, 2001, Loss & Ardor, Geoffrey Young Gallery, Great Barrington, MA & Anna Appleby, Mala Breuer, Wes Mills, Cary Smith, Galerie Susan Albrecht, Munich, Ger, 2002; The Geometric Tradition in Am Art, Whitney Mus Am Art, NY, 93; The Uses of Geometry-Then and Now, Snyder Fine Arts, NY, 93; NY Abstract Painting, Salvatore Ala Gallery, NY, 94; Lawrence Markey Inc, NY, 96; Paol Gallery, Munich, Austria, 97. *Awards:* Nat Endowment Arts Fel, 91-92; Pollack Krasner Found Grant, 93-94; Artist Enhancement Prog, Wash Nat Airport, 94-97. *Bibliog:* Barry Schwabsky (auth), Carey Smith at Salvatore Ala, Art Forum, 4/94; Ken Johnson & Cary Smith (auths), Derek Eller, Art Guide, NY Times, 10/17/97; Faye Hirsch & Cary Smith (auths), Red Print Suite No 1, Rev of Prints, On Paper, 4/98; Holland Carter (auth), Bill De Lottie and Cary Smith at Derek Miller, New York Times, Art in Review, 6/18/99; Roberta Smith (auth), Cary Smith at Derek Miller, Art Guide, New York Times, 4/17/2000. *Dealer:* Lawrence Markey Inc 55 Van Dam New York NY

SMITH, CLIFFORD
PAINTER
b Passaic, NJ, July 8, 1951. *Study:* Southern Conn State Coll, BS, 73; Pratt Inst, MFA, 79. *Work:* Greenville Mus Art, Greenville, NC; Yale Univ, New Haven, Conn; Merrimack Coll, North Andover, Mass; Fairleigh Dickinson Univ, Teaneck, NJ; St Paul's Sch, Concord, NH. *Exhib:* Solo Exhib, Ten Years of Lanscape Painting, Greenville Mus Art, Greenville, NC, 95, Ocean Field- Clifford Smith Paintings, Alden B Dow Mus Sci & Art, Midland Ctr, Midland, Mich, 2010; Group exhib, Re-Presenting Representaion V, Arnot Mus Art, Elmira, NY, 2001-2002; Into the Eye of the Beholder, Boca Raton Mus Art, Fla, 2008; The Art of Fashion in the Hamptons, Guild Hall Mus, E Hampton, NY, 2009. *Teaching:* Southern Conn State Univ, New Haven, Conn, 86; New England Coll, NH, 93; Notre Dame Coll, NH, 92-94; NH Inst Art, NH, 2002-2003. *Awards:* NH Art Coun Fel, 2000. *Bibliog:* Clifford Smith pours oil on water, Martha's Vineyard Times, 2004; To the light house, Cape Island Home, 2003; The east ends natural beauty, Southampton Press, 2004; Design by degrees, Archit Digest, 2005; Oceans ten & sift series are worth sifting through, San Diego Union Tribune, 2006. *Mem:* Coll Art Asn. *Media:* Oil on Linen & Paper. *Dealer:* Spanierman Modern 53 E 58th St New York NY 10022; Rosenbaum Contemporary 608 Banyan Trl Boca Raton FL 33431; Scott White Contemporary 939 W Kalmia St San Diego CA 92101

SMITH, DAVID LOEFFLER
PAINTER, EDUCATOR
b New York, NY, May 1, 1928. *Study:* Bard Coll, BA; Cranbrook Acad Art, MFA; also with Hans Hofmann & Raphael Soyer. *Work:* Munson Williams Proctor Inst, Utica, NY; Crapo Gallery; Swain Sch Design; Paul Resikra; Leland Bell; Lennart Anderson. *Exhib:* Seligman Gallery, New York; solo exhibs, First St Gallery, New York, 72-73, 76-77, 79, 82 & 85; M13 Gallery, New York, 86-87 & 90; Water Street Gallery, Mass, 88; Nemasket Gallery, Fairhaven, Mass, 90; News as Muse, Baltimore, 91; Cherry Stone Gallery, 2004-2006; Crowell's Fine Art, New Bedford Art Mus, 2011; Retrospective: New Bedford Art Mus, Mass, 2011. *Teaching:* Dir Swain Sch Design, 62-66; chmn dept art, Chatham Coll; vis critic, New York Studio Sch, Md Art Inst, Queens Coll, State Univ NY, Grad Sch Painting & Parsons Sch Design; prof painting, Southeastern Mass Univ, North Dartmouth, Mass, formerly; retired. *Awards:* Henry Posner Prize, Carnegie Inst, 61. *Media:* Oil. *Publ:* Auth, articles, Am Artist, 59-62, Antiques Mag, 11/67, Arts Mag, 3/68 & Art & Artists, 1/70 & 5/71. *Mailing Add:* 7 Riverwoods Dr Apt P119 Exeter NH 03833-4397

SMITH, DINAH MAXWELL
PAINTER, PHOTOGRAPHER
b New York, NY. *Study:* L'Academie Julian; RI Sch Design, BFA (painting); Masters Prog, Santa Fe Inst Fine Arts, Wayne Thiebaud Workshop, 88. *Work:* Bank Rhode Island, RI; Bridgeport Mus Art, Science & Industry, CT; Chase Bank; O'Neals Lincoln Ctr, Rhode Island School of Design, RI; Union League Club. *Comn:* Dog portraits, comn by: Carolyn Rockafellow Lopez-Balboa, Mr & Mrs Kevin Cronin, Mssrs Peter Hallock & Craig Mowry, Mr & Mrs John Richey. *Exhib:* Solo Exhibs: Paradise Cafe, Sag Harbor, NY, 02; Hampton Road Gallery, 03; Union League Club, NY, 88 & 92; Gallery Wessel, Hamburg, Ger, 90-2001, 01; Lizan-Tops/AHI Gallery, NY, 95; Convent Sacred Heart, Greenwich, Conn, 95; Coach Gallery, E Hampton, NY, 96; New Light Arts, Water Mill, NY, 96; Mecox Gardens, Water Mill, NY, 98; Cook-Pony Farm, Sag Harbor, NY, 01; South Street Gallery, Greenport, NY, 2008; Thompson Community Center, Thompson, Conn, 2008; Hampton Road Gallery, Southampton, NY, 2009, Romany Kramores Gallery, Sag Harbor, NY, 2013, Chrysalis Gallery, Southampton, NY, 2013, Hail to the Beach!, Southampton Hist Mus, Southampton, NY, 2014, People and Other Four-Legged Friends, Southampton Hist Mus, Southampton, NY, 2014, Time and Again, Sag Harbor Whaling Mus, Sag Harbor, NY, 2015; Group shows, Local Color, Gallery North, Setauket, NY, 97-02, By-the-Sea, Lizan-Tops Gallery, E Hampton, NY, 96, 2000, Romany Kramoris Holiday Invitation, Sag Harbor, NY, 2014, Romany Kramoris (Group of 3), Sag Harbor, NY, 2015; Creatures, Elaine Benson Gallery, Bridgehampton, NY, 96; Potato Exhibit, Water Mill Mus, NY, 95 & Mem Show, 96; Artists' Registry, Dog Mus, St Louis, Mo, 92, 94, 96 & 98; Photog show, AKC/Dog Mus, St Louis, Mo; Ron Cavalier Gallery, Nantucket, Mass, 2008; Art Show at the Dog Show, Wichita Kans, 2006, 2007; TAOS Open. *Collection Arranged:* 65th Ann Conn Artists' Juried Invitational; Slater Mus, Norwich, Conn, 2007; East End Arts Arts Council, 2011; Color & Contrast, N Main Gallery, Southampton, NY, 2012. *Pos:* curator Art with a Heart Auction, Southampton, NY, 99. *Teaching:* Instr, Watercolor, Parrish Art Mus, Southampton, NY, 79; adult educ oil painting on paper, Southampton, NY, 97-98, pvt oil on paper, 99. *Awards:* Nat Arts Club Graphics Prize, 72 & Special Award, 74; Fourth Prize, Five Towns M&A Found, 85; Third Prize, Photog Show, 89, First Prize, Painting Show, 89, East End Arts Coun; Hon Men, Juried Show, Painting, 2011. *Bibliog:* James R Genovese (auth), Light at the end of the island, 5/28/83 & Phyllis Braff (auth), From the studio, 9/22/83, Hamptons Newspaper Mag; Helen Harrison (auth), NY Times; Karen Frankel (auth), Exposed Lines and Sunfilled Colors, Am Artist Mag, 3/98; Mary Cummings (auth), Images that capture moments in time, Arts & Living, Southampton Press, 8/31/00; Dan's Papers Covers & Write-Ups; Chenoa Pierce, Smith preserves photographs in oil paintings, Thompson Villager, A4, 9/5/2008; plus others; Dinah Maxwell Smith's Abstract Realism, Providence Mag, 9/2011. *Mem:* Artist Alliance East Hampton; Guild Hall, East Hampton; Parrish Art Mus, Southampton. *Media:* Oils; Black & White & Color Photography. *Specialty:* Fine Art. *Interests:* Photography, room-boxes (dioramas), tennis. *Publ:* Artists to Watch, Hamptons Real Estate Showcase, July 4, 2015; Hamptons Monthly: Artist Spotlight Interview, July, 2015. *Dealer:* South Street Gallery Greenport NY; Cavalier Galleries Nantucket MA & Greenwich CT; Hampton Road Gallery Southampton NY. *Mailing Add:* 59 Meeting House Lane Southampton NY 11968

SMITH, DONALD C
PAINTER, PRINTMAKER
b Dexter, Mo, July 10, 1935. *Study:* Univ Mo, BA & MA (painting, drawing & printmaking, Univ Fel), 53-58; Santa Reparata Ctr Graphic Art, Florence, Italy; also painting with Fred Conway & printmaking with Maricio Lasansky. *Work:* ABC Broadcasting Corp; Spiva Art Ctr, Joplin, Mo; Santa Reparata Stamperia d'Arte Grafica, Florence; Boston Pub Libr; Bank RI, Providence; Allan Stone Galleries, NY; RI Sch Design; Newport Mus Art, RI. *Exhib:* Big Eight Invitational, Univ Kansas, Lawrence, 57; group exhibs, Stephens Coll, Columbia, Mo, 57, Lily Iselin Gallery, Providence, 83, Cranston Public Gallery, Cranston, RI, 86 & Outstanding Alumni, Bingham Gallery, Univ Mo, Columbia, 90; Mo Show, City Art Mus St Louis, Mo, 58-60; solo exhibs, SW Mo State Univ, Springfield, 63, Trinity Theatre, Providence, RI, 64, RI Coll, 69 & 82, Wheelock Coll, Boston, 71, Lowell State Univ, 79, Bannister Gallery, RI Coll, Providence, 82, Wheeler Gallery, Providence, RI, 92, Full Circle Gallery, Providence, RI, 2000, Bromfield Gallery, Boston, Mass, 2001 & Newport Mus Art, New Work, 2005 ; SW Mo Ann, Mus Arts Springfield, Mo, 63; Univ Alumni Invitational, Columbia, Mo, 64; RI Arts Ann, 65 & 67 ; three-person exhib, Casdin Gallery, Worcester, Mass, 67 & Gallery 401 Jewish Community Ctr, Providence, 88; Tonoff Gallery, Drawing Group Show, 69; RI Coll, Providence, 73; Providence Art Club, 74 ; Boston Printmakers Ann (traveling exhib), 75-76; Davidson Nat Print & Drawing Competition, Davidson Coll, NC, 75; Alan Stone Gallery, Drawing, New York, 76; RI Painters Ann, RI Sch Design Mus, Providence, 81; Gallery 401, Lowell State Univ, Mass, 82; Bristol Art Mus, Bristol, RI, 84; Wheeler Gallery Opening, 87; Bannister Gallery, RI Coll, Providence, 89 ; retrospective, Bannister Gallery, RI Coll, Providence, 96; Attleboro Mus Art, Mass, 2000 & 2002; Bromfield Gallery, Boston, Mass, 2001; Ctr Arts, Sarasota, Fla, 2002; Two-person exhib, New Work, Wheeler Gallery, Providence, 2003; Univ Rhode Island, Providence, 2010; Ringling Sch Art, Shelby Gallery, Sarasota, Fla, 2013. *Pos:* Dir, Spiva Art Ctr, Joplin, Mo, 60-64; vis & guest lectr, Pittsburg Stage Coll, Kans, 63, RI Coll, 66 & 2003, Wheelock Coll, Boston, 70, RI Asn Librns, 74, Somerset Art Asn, NJ, 82, Brooklyn Coll, Student Artist's Union, 87, Yale Summer Sch Music & Art, 87 & Falmouth Art Asn, 93; vis artist, SW Mo State Coll, Springfield, 63, NW Mo State Coll, Maryville, 63, Springfield Watercolor Soc & Springfield Art Mus, Mo, 63, Harvard Univ Grad Sem, Carpenter Ctr, 71, RI Sch Design, 94 & Villa Cenci, Rome, Italy, 2000; consult, Federally Funded Art Prog for public schools, Fall River, Mass, 68; juror, Newport Art Festival, summer 70, Bristol Art Mus, summer 75 & Ann Painting Competition, Providence Art Club, 97; master printer, Estate of George A. Gale, 78. *Teaching:* Prof painting & drawing, RI Coll, 64-97, prof emer, 97-. *Awards:* Nat Art Award, Delta Phi Delta, 57; Faculty Res Grant, RI Coll, 89 & 91; Emerson Award, Wheeler Gallery, Providence, RI, 87. *Bibliog:* Don Smith: Painter (essay), Newport Mus, 2005. *Media:* Oil, Watercolor, Etching, Engraving. *Res:* Students of Edwin Dickinson: Archives of American Art. *Publ:* eleven proofs, Herbert Weiner (auth), Writers and Artist on the Sea, Abrams, 78; auth, Edwin Dickinson, draftsman/painter, Art New Eng, 7-8/82; papers and taped interviews of students and colleagues of Edwin Dickinson, Archs Am Art, Smithsonian Inst, 85; Edwin Dickinson: Notions of time and appearance, RI Sch Design Mus, 11/6/86; Edwin Dickenson: Dreams & Realities, Hudson Hills Press. *Mailing Add:* 12 Pine Hill Ave Johnston RI 02919

SMITH, E E
PHOTOGRAPHER, SCULPTOR
b 1956, Linton, Ind. *Study:* Rutgers Univ, NJ, BA (Studio Art); Hunter Coll, New York, MFA (Photography & Sculpture). *Exhib:* Solo exhibs include East Wing Gallery, Columbia Univ, New York, 1983, Matchmaker Gallery, Louisville, 1984, Amelie A Wallace Gallery, SUNY Coll Old Westbury, NY, 1993, Kim Foster Gallery, New York, 1995, 1996, 1998, 2000, 2002, 2003, 2006, 2008, 2011, 2013; Group exhibs include Big Little Show, Ammo Gallery, Brooklyn, 1988; Nat Juried Exhib, San Diego Art Inst, San Diego, 1989; Generations/Regenerations, Robin Rice Gallery, New York, 1990; Photo Alternatives, Rotunda Gallery, Brooklyn, 1991, Benefit Exhibition, 1995; Choice, AIR Gallery, New York, 1991; Photography=Art, Robin Rice Gallery, New York, 1992; Salon Exhib, Art in General, New York, 1992; The New Modernists, Robin Rice Gallery, New York, 1993; Beyond Photography, Foster Peet Gallery, New York, 1993; New Space: Group Show, Foster Peet Gallery, New York, 1994 ; Transferring Culture, La Mama Galleria, New York, 1997; Camera

Ready?, Kim Foster Gallery, New York, 1998, An Hors D'oeuvre, 2002, Selections from the Collection, 2003, A Tasting, 2005, 2006, 2011, 2012; Messages, Lower East Side Printshop, New York, 1999; Green Co Gallery, Catskill, NY, 2001; The Diversity Show, Credit Suisse, NY, 2005; Information Insight Interuption, Hallspace, Boston, 2006; 183rd Ann: Invitational Exhib Contemp Am Art, Nat Acad Mus, New York, 2008. *Awards:* William Graft Sch, Hunter Coll, 1981; Artists Space Individual Artists Grant, 1990; Special Editions Grant, Lower E Side Printshop, New York, 1995. *Media:* Photography. *Mailing Add:* Kim Foster Gallery 529 W 20th St New York NY 10011

SMITH, ELIZABETH ANGELE
CURATOR
Study: Columbia Univ, Degree art hist. *Work:* Mus Contemp Art, Los Angeles, 1989, Urban Revisions: Current Projects for the Pub Realm, 1994, Cindy Sherman: Retrospective, 1997, At the End of the Century: One Hundred Yrs of Archit, 1998, The Archit of RM Schindler, 2001 (Named Best Archit or Design Exhib of Yr, Int Asn Art Critics/USA, 2001), Matta in Am: Painting and Drawings of the 1940s, Mus Contemp Art, Chicago, 2001, Donald Moffett: What Barbara Jordan Wore, 2002, Lee Bontecou: A Retrospective, 2003 (Named Best Monographic Mus Show Nationally, Int Asn Art Critics/USA, 2004). *Pos:* Cur, Mus Contemp Art, Los Angeles, 83-99; James W Alsdorf Chief Cur, Mus Contemp Art, Chicago, 99-2010; exec dir curatorial affairs, Art Gallery Ontario, Can, 2010-; bd overseers, Sch Archit, Ill Inst Tech, Chicago. *Teaching:* Adj prof, pub art studies prog Univ Southern Calif, 92-98; bd adv, Independent Cur Int New York City. *Awards:* Named Woman of Yr, Chicago Soc Artists, 2004. *Publ:* auth, Techno Archit, 2000, Case Study Houses: The Complete CSH Prog 1945-66, 2002; co-ed, Lee Bontecou: A Retrospective of Sculpture and Drawing, 1958-2000, 2003

SMITH, ELLIOT
DEALER, HISTORIAN
b St Louis, Mo, Sept 22, 1942. *Study:* Washington Univ, St Louis, AB, 66; Univ Mo, MEd, 68. *Pos:* Founder & vpres, 87-88, St Louis Gallery Contemp Art; dir, Elliot Smith Gallery, St Louis, Mo & New York, NY, currently. *Teaching:* Assoc prof, English & speech, Washington Univ, St Louis, 68-73; assoc prof Am studies, St Louis Univ, 81-84. *Mem:* St Louis Gallery Asn (treas, 85-86 & vpres, 87); Friends Pub Art (founder & pres, 86-). *Res:* Early 20th century American architecture. *Specialty:* Paintings and sculpture of bold imagery and strong intellectual content. *Publ:* Auth, Louis Sullivan, The Last Romantic, St Louis Univ Press, 84

SMITH, FRANCES KATHLEEN
CURATOR, HISTORIAN
b Bolton, Eng, Nov 19, 1913; Can citizen. *Study:* London Univ, Eng; Queen's Univ, Kingston, Ont, BA, 56; Oxford Univ, Eng, with Pope Hennessey, Italian sculpture, 56-57. *Collection Arranged:* Andre Bieler: 50 Years (auth, catalog), Retrospective, traveled, Can, 70-71; Heritage Kingston (contribr, catalog), 73; Painting Now 1976/77 (auth, catalog); Henry Moore, Sculpture, Prints, Drawings, 78; Daniel Fowler of Amherst Island, (auth, catalog), traveled, Can, 79; The Brave New World of Fritz Brandtner Traveling Show (coauth, catalog), 81-82; Kathleen Moir Morris (auth, catalog), 83; John Herbert Caddy (auth, catalog), 85; Andre Bieler in Rural Quebec (auth, catalog), 88-89. *Pos:* Cur, Agnes Etherington Art Ctr, Kingston, Ont, Can, 57-79, cur emer, 79-. *Awards:* Merit Award, Ont Asn Art Galleries, 80; Merit Award, Can Mus Asn, 81; Distinguished Serv Award, Queen's Univ, 87; Celebration 88, Cert Merit, Olympic Comt, 88. *Mem:* Can Mus Asn (nominating comt, 78); Ont Asn Art Galleries (secy, 68-69). *Res:* Canadian artists: Daniel Fowler, Andre Bieler, Fritz Brandtner, John Herbert Caddy and others. *Specialty:* Canadian Art, European 16h and 17th Century paintings, African sculpture. *Interests:* Reading, Art History, Writing. *Publ:* Coauth, A Permanent Collection of the Agnes Etherington Art Centre, 68; auth, George Harlow White 1817-1887, 75 & Daniel Fowler of Amherst Island, 79, Art Ctr, Queens Univ, Kingston, Ont; Andre Bieler: An Artist's Life and Times, Merritt Publ Co, Toronto, 80, Re-printed French translation, new intro & epilogue, Philippe Baylaueg (ed), 9/2006. *Mailing Add:* 133-174 Ypres Green SW Calgary AB T2T 6M2 Canada

SMITH, FRANK ANTHONY
PAINTER
b Salt Lake City, Utah, Aug 4, 1939. *Study:* Univ Utah, BFA, 62, MFA, 64. *Work:* Univ Utah Mus Fine Art; Utah State Univ; Salt Lake Art Ctr; Nat Gallery, Washington, DC. *Comn:* design (dance pieces), Repertory Dance Theatre, 66, 71 & 73; stimuli sensory environ for children, Salt Lake Art Ctr, 70; mural, Univ Utah Biol Bldg, 72. *Exhib:* Look Again, Illusionist Painting, Taft Mus, Cincinnati, 76; Reality of Illusion, Univ Southern Calif, 79; Four Corners Biennial, Phoenix, Ariz, 81; Illusions, Faire Int D'art Contemp, Grand Palais, Paris, 82; solo exhib, Suellen Haber Gallery, NY, 82; and others. *Pos:* Illusr, Star Trek: The Movie, 77. *Teaching:* Prof painting & drawing, Univ Utah, 68-. *Awards:* San Francisco Art Dirs Gold Medal, 64; Purchase Award, 3rd Intermountain Biennial, 68. *Media:* Acrylic. *Dealer:* Osuna Gallery Washington DC; Phillips Gallery Salt Lake City UT

SMITH, GARY
SCULPTOR, GALLERY DIRECTOR
b Portland, Ore, Nov 25, 1949. *Study:* Lewis & Clark Col, Portland, Ore, BA, 71; Univ Calif, Santa Barbara, MFA, 75. *Work:* Art Mus Santa Cruz Co, Calif; St Mary's Col, Moraga, Calif; Calif Polytechnic Inst, San Luis Obispo. *Comn:* Large scale granite sculpture, Nanao, Japan, 96. *Exhib:* Large Scale Sculpture, Univ Calif, Davis, 79; Recent Sculpture, Quay Gallery, San Francisco, 80; Departure Gallery, NY, 83-86; Summer Int, Keramik Studio, Vienna, Austria, 84; Recent Sculpture, Cuesta Col, San Luis Obispo, Calif, 85. *Collection Arranged:* Hartnell Coll Farm Security Administration Photograph Collection (auth, catalog), 82; Leslie Fenton Netsuke Collection (auth, catalog), 85; Virginia Bacher Huichol Artifact Collection (auth, catalog), 86; Daniel Rhodes: The California Years (auth, catalog), 86. *Teaching:* Instr ceramics-art, Hartnell Col, Salinas, 76-, dir gallery, 76-. *Awards:* Harden Teaching Award, 92; Gleason Teaching award, 2004. *Mem:* Coll Art Asn. *Media:* Clay. *Mailing Add:* c/o Hartnell Col 156 Homestead Ave Salinas CA 93901

SMITH, GARY DOUGLAS
DRAFTSMAN, PAINTER
b San Francisco, Calif, July 29, 1948. *Study:* Calif Coll Arts & Crafts, BFA (scholar), 71; extensive study in Mexico; Atelier 17, Paris; etching with S W Hayter, also engraving with George Ball, also Mezzotint with Yozo Hamaguchi. *Work:* Palm Springs Mus Art, Calif; Achenbach Found Graphic Arts, San Francisco; De Saisset Mus, Santa Clara, Calif; Calif Acad Sciences, San Francisco; Calif Coll Arts & Crafts, Oakland. *Exhib:* San Francisco Mus Mod Art, 70 & 77; Anchorage Hist & Fine Arts Mus, Alaska, 77; El Paso Mus Art, Tex, 77; World Print Competition & Traveling Show, 79; Krannert Art Mus, Ill, 79; Toledo Mus Art, Ohio, 79; Achenbach Found Graphic Arts, San Francisco, 83; solo exhibs, Historic Olema Inn, Calif, 83, Vorpal Galleries, Soho, NY, 85, Laguna Beach, Calif, 85 & San Francisco, 86, Inverness Studio, Calif, 87-90, Robert Mondavi Winery, Oakmille, Calif, 90; Inverness Ridge Assoc, Calif, 87; San Francisco Arts Comn, Calif, 88; Concordia-Argonaut Club, San Francisco, 88 & 89. *Teaching:* Lectr/demonstration, Fine Art Mus San Francisco, 85; lectr, Calif Col Arts & Crafts, Oakland, 87 & 88. *Awards:* Silver Prize, Calif Coll Arts & Crafts, 69. *Bibliog:* Thomas Albright (auth), Landscapes in translation, San Francisco Chronicle, 7/7/71; John Marlowe (auth), interview, Currant Art Mag, 76; Carol A Hayes (auth), Profile of an artist, Bay View Mag, 9/81; Al Morch (auth), Too much of a good thing, San Francisco Chronicle, 11/9/81; Diana Freedman (auth), The catalyst in creation, Arts/Speak NY, 83. *Mem:* Graphic Arts Coun; World Print Coun. *Media:* Prismacolor Pencil, Silverpoint. *Publ:* Cover, Floating Island I, 76. *Dealer:* Claudia Chapline Gallery Stinson Beach CA; Waterworks Gallery Harbor Bay WA. *Mailing Add:* PO Box 244 Inverness CA 94937

SMITH, GARY HAVEN
SCULPTOR
b New Hampshire. *Study:* Univ NH, Durham, BFA, 1973. *Work:* Currier Gallery Art, Manchester, NH. *Exhib:* Solo exhibs include Hebron Acad, Hebron, Maine, 1975, Walt Kuhn Gallery, Cape Neddick, Maine, 1987, McGowan Fine Art, Concord, NH, 1989, 1991, 1994, 1996, 1998, 2000, 2003, Hynes Convention Ctr Boston, 1995; group exhibs include Frost Gully Gallery, Portland, Maine, 1976; Hobe Sound Galleries, Hobe Sound, Fla, 1987; Sculpture & Landscape, Maine Audubon Soc, Falmouth, 1994; Univ Mass Dartmouth Centennial Sculpture Exhib, 1995; Summer Group Show, Axel Raben Gallery, New York, 2001; Cairn Croft Sculpture Garden, Dover, Mass, 2002; Eye on Alumni, 6 Sculptors, Univ NH, Durham, 2003. *Awards:* David Campbell Scholar Award, Univ NH, Durham, 1973; Indian Head Nat Bank Award, Currier Gallery Art, Manchester, NH, 1984, Hitchner Award, 1984, Paul Costello Award, 1986; Enrichment Grant, Greater Piscataqua Found, Portsmouth, NH, 2002; Pollock-Krasner Found Grant, 2007. *Dealer:* Spheris Gallery 59 S Main St Hanover NH 03755; Thorne-Sagendorph Art Gallery 229 Main St Whyman Way Keene NH 03435; Reeves Contemp 535 W 24th New York NY 10011

SMITH, GIL R
ADMINISTRATOR, HISTORIAN
b Rochester, NY, Oct 18, 1952. *Study:* State Univ NY, BA (art hist), 75; Pa State Univ, PHD (art hist), 87. *Teaching:* asst prof art hist, State Univ, Fredonia, NY, 84-85; assoc prof archit, Ball State Univ, 85-95; prof art hist, Eastern Ky Univ, 95-. *Mem:* Coll Art Asn; SAH; NCAA; Am Soc 18th Century Studies; Mid-west Art Hists Soc. *Res:* 18th century architectural theory and practice, focusing on transition from baroque to neoclasssical. *Publ:* contribr, Projects & monuments in the Roman baroque, Penn State Press, 84; auth, Competitions Vol 2, Louisville, Ky, 92; auth, An architectural progress in the renaissance & baroque, Penn State Press, 92; auth, Architectural Diplomacy: Rome & Paris in the Late Baroque, Archit Hist Found, 93; contribr, The dictionary of art, Macmillan, London, 96. *Mailing Add:* 1104 Valley Run Dr Richmond KY 40475

SMITH, GREG
PAINTER, GRAPHIC ARTIST
b Easton, Pa, June 13, 1951. *Study:* Duke Univ, BFA, 73; Pa Acad Fine Arts, 73. *Work:* Chemical Bank Corp Collection, NY. *Exhib:* Reagan: Am Icon, Bucknell Univ, Lewisburg, Pa, 89; Scenic Views, Willoughby Sharp Gallery, NY, 90; New Landscape Paintings, Willoughby Sharp Gallery, NY, 91; 25th Juried Show, Allentown Art Mus, Pa, 96; Nat Soc Painters Casein & Acrylic, Salmagundi Club, NY, 96. *Pos:* Sr artist, Prodigy Videotex Servs, 87-93; graphic artist, Delphi Internet, 95. *Teaching:* 2D computer graphics, Pratt Inst, 92-95; visual founds, Muhlenberg Col, Allentown, Pa, 95-96. *Bibliog:* Patty Harris (auth), 4 summer art shows, Downtown, 9/90; Gary Azon (auth), Art Around Town, Downtown, 4/91; Geoff Gehman (auth), Juried show a vision of delights restored, Morning Call, Allentown, Pa, 1/96. *Mem:* Spec Interest Group Computer Graphics & Interactive Techniques, Asn Computer Machinery. *Media:* Oil, Acrylics; Computers

SMITH, GREGORY ALLGIRE
EDUCATOR, ADMINISTRATOR
b Washington, DC, Mar 31, 1951. *Study:* Johns Hopkins Univ, BA (art hist), 72; Williams Col-Clark Art Inst, MA (art hist), 74; Harvard Univ-Inst Arts Admin, cert, 74. *Exhib:* El Greco Toledo, Toledo Art Mus, 82-83; Impressionism & Post-Impressionism; The Courtauld Collection Nat Tour, Int Exhibs, 86-87; Malcolm Grear: The Art of Design (with catalog), Art Acad Cincinnati/Cincinnati Art Mus, 96. *Pos:* NEH intern, Walker Art Ctr, 75-76; asst dir, Akron Art Mus, 77-80; Asst dir admin, Toledo Mus Art, 80-86; exec vpres, Int Exhibs Fdn, 86-87; dir, Telfair Mus Art, 87-94; pres, Art Acad Cincinnati, 94-; adminstr asst, Washington Project for the Arts, 75. *Mem:* Asn Independent Cols Art & Design (trustee, 94-, exec comt mem, 99-); Greater Cincinnati Consortium Cols & Univs (exec comt mem, 96-99); Am Asn Mus. *Mailing Add:* Art Academy Cincinnati 1212 Jackson St Cincinnati OH 45202

SMITH, HARRY WILLIAM
ILLUSTRATOR, JEWELER
b Chicago, Ill, July 12, 1937. *Study:* Wash Univ, St Louis; Command Mgt Art Sch, Ft Belvoir, Va; Chicago Acad Fine Arts; Gemological Inst Am. *Work:* Yorktown Mus, NY; Gibbes Art Gallery, Charleston, SC; Miniature Mus, Kansas City, Mo; Mus Miniatures, Los Angeles, Calif; Ky Gateway Mus Ctr. *Comn:* Miniature Mus Kansas City, 89; Mus Miniatures, Los Angeles, 93; pair of torcheres, Mt Vernon miniature; Kentucky Gateway Mus, Maysville, Ky; Sterling Silver Exhib; corporate illustrations, 2009-2013. *Exhib:* Solo exhib, Brown Co Art Gallery, Nashville, Ind, 71; Colby Coll Mus Art, 76; Coe-Kerr Gallery, New York, 84; Mystic Seaport, Mystic, Conn, 84; Neiman Marcus, 87; Farnsworth Mus, 90; Landis Valley Mus; Abby Aldrich Rockefeller Art Ctr, Williamsburg, Va, 96; Naples Mus Art, 2000; Javits Ctr, New York, 2006-2008; Kokusai Art Galleries, Tokyo, Japan. *Pos:* Chmn, Maine Libr Comn, 79-83. *Teaching:* Lectr, nationwide. *Awards:* Early American Life Craftsman Award, Acad Honor; Am's Top 200 Traditional Craftsmen, CGA. *Bibliog:* Let it be wee, NY Mag, 83; articles in: Nutshell News, 90, Miniature Collector, 90 & 93-94, Forbes, Silver Mag, Collector Eds, Washington Univ Press, Traditional Homes, McCall's, Art in Auction; Traditional Crafts in America, Yankee Way with Wood, Random House; Crafts of America, Harper Row; Complete Book of Miniatures, Crown; American Period Interiors in Miniature, Scribner, Down East. *Mem:* Copley Soc; life mem, Brown Co Art Gallery Asn (bd dir, 70-71); Am Soc Marine Artists; Int Miniature Artists. *Media:* Watercolor; Precious Metals, Wood. *Collection:* Sterling silver Christmas ornaments. *Publ:* Auth & illusr, Michael and the Mary Day, 79, ABC's of Maine, 80, Windjammers of the Maine Coast, 82 & ABC's of New Hampshire, 84, Down East Bks; The Art of Making Furniture in Miniature, Dutton, 82, Kalmbach, 93 & Scott Publ, 98. *Dealer:* Barnstable Originals. *Mailing Add:* 50 Harden Ave Camden ME 04843

SMITH, JACK RICHARD
PAINTER, PRINTMAKER
b Fremont, Mich, Aug 3, 1950. *Study:* Columbus Coll Art & Design, 1968-69; Instituto Allende, San Miguel, Mex, 1969-70; Thomas Jefferson Col, 1970-71. *Work:* Muskegon Mus Art, Mich; De Pauw Univ, Indianapolis, Ind. *Comn:* Murals, comn by Thomas Worrell, at Dharma Holdings, 1997, at Milagroo, Taos, NMex, 1998 & at The Rectory, Delrey Beach, Fla, 1998; Robert D Morgan (portrait), De Pauw Univ, Indianapolis, Ind, 1998. *Exhib:* Solo exhibs include Univ Cincinnati, 1988, Sutton Bay Galleries, Mich, 1991, Muskegon Mus Art, Mich, 1992, Dennos Mus, Traverse City, Mich, 1992, The Print Gallery, Southfield, Mich, 1992, Mongerson Wunderlich Galleries, Chicago, 1998, 1999, Jacquelin Loyd Contemp, Rancho de Taos, 2000; group exhibs include La Fonda de Taos Gallery, 1981; Max Siegel Fine Art, Taos, 1983; Muskegon Mus Art, Mich, 1985, 1991; Perception Gallery, Grand Rapids, 1990, 1993; MCC Gallery, Muskegon, Mich, 1993; Bunting Gallery, Royal Oak, Mich, 1994; Sullivan Gross, Santa Barbara, Calif, 2003, 2004, 2005; Gerald Peters Gallery, 2006. *Media:* Oil. *Publ:* Tom Collins, Visual Fetishization, Albuquerque Jour, 2002; Las Casas de Los Valles, exhib catalog, Mongerson/Wunderlich Gallery. *Dealer:* Sullivan Goss Gallery 7 E Anapamu St Santa Barbara CA 93101. *Mailing Add:* 345 Vegas de Taos Taos NM 87571-4114

SMITH, JAMES MICHAEL
PAINTER, ASSEMBLAGE ARTIST
b Aug 18, 1949. *Study:* Univ Kans, Lawrence, BFA, 71, Univ Ill, Champaign-Urbana, MFA, 73. *Work:* Chase Manhattan Bank, NY; Univ Tex Collection, El Paso; Saks Fifth Avenue, NY; John W Hechinger Col, Largo, Md; Cedar Rapids Mus of Art, Cedar Rapids, Iowa. *Comn:* The Realty Co, St Louis, Mo; Renaissance Fin St Louis, Mo. *Exhib:* Solo exhibs, Festival Gallery, Krannert Ctr Performing Arts, Univ Ill, Urbana, 77, Joy Horwich Gallery, Chicago, Ill, 80, 81, 82, 83, 84 & 89, Locus Gallery, St Louis, MO, 85, 87, The City Series, Group Exch Cedar Rapids Mus of Art, Cedar Rapids, Iowa, 98, The Sheldon Art Galleries, St Louis, Mo, 2000, Cedar Rapids Mus of Art, 2000, plus others; The NY Connection, Florissant Valley Community Col, St Louis, MO, 89; Locus Gallery, St Louis, MO, 90; Flora '90, Chicago Botanical Gardens, Ill, 90; Painted constructions, Fassbender Gallery, Chicago, 95, 97, 97 & 98, & Duane Reed Gallery, St Louis, Mo, 96, 97, Bentley Gallery, Scottsdale, Ariz, 95, 96 & 97. *Pos:* Juror, Ill Small Painting Competition, Western Ill Univ, Macomb, 87; panelist, Careers in the Arts Seminar, St Louis Community Col, Florissant, 88. *Teaching:* Vis artist lectr, Nat Philosophical Soc, Joy Horwich Gallery, 83; vis artist, Sch of Ozarks, Lookout Point, MO, 88. *Awards:* Honorarium, Mo Vis Arts Biennial, Mo Arts Coun, 87; Cash Award, The Louis E Sieden Mem Award, Chautagua 27th Ann Nat Exhib, NY, 84; Honorarium, Five Choose Five Exhib, First Street Forum Gallery, St Louis, Mo, 82; Art Forms Nat Exhib, Philadelphia, 99; 49th Ann Art Competition, Nat Exhib, Ft Smith, Ark, 99; Dishman Competition, 99; Nat Exhib, Lamar Univ, Beaumont, Tex, 99. *Publ:* Tools as Art: The Hechinger Collection, Abrams; New American Painting, Open Studio Press, Boston, Mass; Art News, NY; New Art Examiner, Chicago, Ill; plus others. *Dealer:* Crows Ink PO Box 19842 St Louis MO 63144. *Mailing Add:* 436 Bismark Saint Louis MO 63119

SMITH, JAN
DIRECTOR, CURATOR
b Milwaukee, Wis, Aug 26, 1955. *Study:* Univ Wis, BFA, 76, MA, 89, Cert in Mus Studies, 89. *Exhib:* Solo Exhib: Monroe Arts and Activities Cen, Monroe, Wis, 85; Plymouth Arts Foundation, Plymouth, Wis, 2005; Group Exhib: Unique Arts & Craft Gallery, Shorewood, Wis, 82; Madison Art Cen, Sales & Rental Gallery, 83; Ave Art, Appleton Featured Exhib, 2010. *Collection Arranged:* Paul Joseph Stankard, 20 year Retrospective, 1990; Contemp Studio Glass, 40 pieces from pvt collection, 2000; Contemp Studio Glass, An Int Perspective, 2002; Kemper Insurance Group; Marc Chagall: Le Cerque, 2003; A Royal & Ancient Game: Presenting Golf, 2004; The Art of Assemblage. *Pos:* Wis Fedn of Mus, President; Convention Bur Bd, Chair Visitor. *Teaching:* Lakeland Coll. *Awards:* Best of Show, Wis Biennial, Edna Carlsten Gallery, 76. *Mem:* Wis Visual Artists; AAM; Wis Fedn of Mus; Rotary Int, Asn Midwest Mus. *Media:* Pastel, Watercolor. *Res:* Printmaking. *Specialty:* Coventry Glass Gallery, Appleton, WI; 19th & 20th Cen Am Art; Ave Art, The Hang Up. *Interests:* Reading, painting, hiking, biking, languages. *Publ:* Paperweight Bulletin, Paperweight Collectors Asn, 95; Brandwine River Mus Catalogue, 99; Paul Stankard Catalogue; Glass Art Mag, 2009. *Dealer:* Barry Sautner, Cameo Carved Glass, Wisconsin Glass Makers. *Mailing Add:* 9251 Bomar Ave Neenah WI 54956

SMITH, JEFFREY CHIPPS
HISTORIAN
b April 21, 1951. *Study:* Duke Univ, BA (art hist), 73; Columbia Univ, MA, 75, MPh, 77, PhD, 79. *Pos:* Co-ed, Journ of the Hist of Netherlandish Art, 2009-2013. *Teaching:* Vis asst prof, Univ Pittsburgh, 78; Ruth Head Centennial prof art hist, Univ Tex, Austin, 79-2000; Kay Fortson chair in Europ art, Univ Tex, Austin, 2000-. *Awards:* Alexander von Humbolt Stiftung Res Fel, Bonn, Ger, 85-86 & 92-93; Gordan Book Prize, Renaissance Soc Am, 96; John Simon Guggenheim Mem Found Fel, 98-99; NEH Fel, 2008; Berlin Prize, Am Acad in Berlin, 2010; Distinguished Int Fel, Australian Rsch Coun Ctr Excellence for the History of Emotions, Melbourne, 2012. *Bibliog:* co-ed, The Essential Dürer, 2010. *Mem:* Historians Netherlandish Art (bd dir, 89-94); Coll Art Asn, (bd dir, 96-2000); Renaissance Soc Am (exec bd 2000-2009, 2013-, counselor, 2013-); Sixteenth Century Soc and Conf (bd dir, 2004-07); Fruhe Neuzeit Interdisziplinan (pres, 2008-2012). *Res:* Northern Renaissance and Baroque art. *Publ:* Auth, Seventeenth-Century Landscape Drawings, Huntington Art Gallery, Austin, 82; Nuremberg A Renaissance City 1500-1618, Univ Tex Press, Austin, 83; ed, New Perspectives on the Art of Renaissance Nuremberg, Univ Tex Press, 85; auth, German Sculpture of the Later Renaissance, Princeton Univ Press, 94; Sensuous Worship: Jesuits and the Art of the Early Catholic Reformation in Germany, Princeton Univ Pres, 2002; The Northern Renaissance, 2004; contribr intro, Erwin Panofsky (auth), The Life and Art of Albrecht Durer, Princeton Univ Press, 2005; The Art of the Goldsmith in Late Fifteenth Century Germany: The Kimbell Virgin and Her Bishop, 2006; coed, The Essential Durer, 2010, Durer, Phaidon Press, 2012; over 180 revs & articles; ed, Visual Acuity and The Arts of Communication in Early Modern Germany, 2014. *Mailing Add:* University of Texas Dept Art & Art History 2301 San Jacinto Blvd, D 1300 Austin TX 78712

SMITH, JENNIE
ARTIST
b San Francisco, 1981. *Study:* Student, Burren Coll Art, Ireland, 2002; Mpls Coll Art & Design, BFA, 2004. *Exhib:* Migration, 2003; Animal Its Habitat, 2004; Animals Slumber, 2004; Kite Wars, 2004; We'll Never Tell You Where We Have Gone, 2004; Group exhibs, Made at MCAD, Mpls, 2005; Sr Exhib, Mpls Collection Art & Design, 2005; Drawing Show, Soo Vac Gallery, Mpls, 2005; Group Drawing Show, The Gen Store, Milwaukee, 2005; Four Color Drawing Show, Van Harrison Gallery, Chicago, 2005; Whitney Biennial: Day for Night, Whitney Mus Am Arts, 2006; Bull Bd Project 008, Calif, Collection Arts Wattis Inst Contemp Arts, San Francisco, 2006; Rena Bransten Gallery, San Francisco, 2006. *Mailing Add:* c/o Rena Bransten Gallery 77 Geary St San Francisco CA 94108

SMITH, JO-AN
PAINTER, GOLDSMITH
b Eugene, Ore, 1933. *Study:* Univ Wash, 50-52, Defense Lang Inst (span), 64; Indiana Univ, 65; Pvt studies in Buenos Aires, Arg, 66, San Salvador, El Salvador, 67, Panama, 68-70; Univ Tex, El Paso, BA (art), 71; NMex State Univ, MA (art), 75; Gemological Inst Am, 77; studied with Aleksander Titovets, 95-96, Albert Handel, 96, Cheng Khee Chee, 2000, Stephen Quiller, 2005, & Laura Robb, 2011. *Work:* Smithsonian Inst, Washington, DC; Mem Med Ctr, NMex State Univ; Mesilla Valley Hospice; Branigan Cult Complex Permanent Collection; NMex Capital Art Found, Permanent Collection, NMex Capitol Bldg, 2003; Gila Regional Medical Ctr Permanent Collection, Silver City, NMex; Jardin de los Niños. *Comn:* Roush Award Medallions, NMex State Univ, 85-2008; Borman necklace, 94; Lovell painting, 98; Medoff Jewelry, 99-2000; Pres's Medal, NMex State Univ, 2000; Betty & Bobby Merritt, 2001; Robert Jones, 2003; Senator Mary Kay Papen, 2007; Barbara Weaver Johnson, 2010-2011; Sallie Ritter Jacobs, 2009; Margaret Ritter, 1996-. *Exhib:* Sterling Silversmith's Guild, 74; Design Competition, New York 74; Biennale Int l'artemail, France, 75; Int Competition of Enamels & Glass, San Diego, 75; The Metalsmith, Phoenix & Seattle, 76-77; Soc N Am Goldsmiths Invitational, Carbondale, Ill, 84; Wearable Art, Potsdam Coll, New York, 89; Ancient Space, Las Cruces, NMex, 96; New Orleans Nat Exhib, 97; Pittsburg Aqueous Open, 97; Salmagundi Club Nat Exhib, New York, 97; Nightwalker 97, Ft Collins, Colo, 97; Solo exhibs, Emerging, NMex, 98, Up Close & Far Away, NMex, 99, Explorations, NMex, 2001, Inner Light, NMex, 2002; Sierra Med Int Exhib, Tex, 98-2000; Masterworks 2000, NMex, 2000; Sun Bowl Art Exhib 2000, Tex; NMex Watercolor Soc, Fall, 2000; Up Close & Far Away, NMex, 2001; Santa Fe Mus Art, 2004; New Harvest, NMex, 2004; Vibrant Rhythms, NMex, 2005; Bold Statements, 2007; Mexican Consulate (El Paso), 2008; Together 33 Years, 2008; The Cultivation of Art, Farm & Ranch Mus, NMex, 8/2009; Eclectic!, 2010, Intense Dialogue, 2010; Bienalle Grande, 2010; Intertwined, 2011; Tejido Fronterizo, 2012; Artist Orbit, 2012; Exciting Explorations, 2013; Botanica, 20113. *Pos:* Proprietor & designer, JOS Studio, 71-; designer & resident artist, Glenn Cutter Jeweler's 76-2008; dir citywide art tour, Las Cruces Artshop, 94-2003; designer & resident artist, Cutter Gallery, 2009-. *Teaching:* Instr design, NMex State Univ, 75-76 & 81 & Career Art Path, Las Cruces Sch (design), 94-97. *Awards:* Gamblin Merit Award, XVIII, New Orleans Nat Exhib, 97; Hon Mention, Nightwalker 97 Nat Exhib, 97; 1st Place, NMex Watercolor Soc, 2004; NMex Art Public Places Prog Award, 2007; Papen Family Award, Doña Ana Arts Council, 2008; Cert of Distinction, Paleozoic Trackaways Foundation, 2008. *Bibliog:* New Art Int, Book Art Press, 96-98; Artist Molds Dwelling Around Her Environment, NMex Mag, Santa Fe, 5/98; Jo-an Smith, An Artist and Jewelry Designer, Ventanas Del Valle, NMex Mountain Dreams Publ, Spring, 2001; Artist's Retreat, The Desert Home, Northland Press, 2002. *Mem:* Soc N Am Goldsmiths (distinguished mem); NMex Watercolor Soc (signature mem); Nat Oil & Acrylic Painter's Soc; Dona Ana Arts Coun; Border Artists; Shalam Colony Mus; Paleozoic Trackways Foundation.

Media: Gold; Watercolor, Oil, Cloisonné Enamel. *Interests:* Southwest landscapes & cliff dwellings hist; ancient civilizations, Spanish literature. *Publ:* Contribr, Bead J, Craftsman's Gallery, Design, Golddust, Goldsmith's J & Working Craftsman; ed & contribr, Cutters Comments, Las Cruces, 93-94; book cover illusr, Feroza Jussawala (auth), Chiffon Saris, Writer Workshop Publ, India, 2003 & Coach House Publ, Can, 2003. *Dealer:* Cutter Gallery 2640 El Paseo Rd Las Cruces NM 88001. *Mailing Add:* Box 786 Dona Ana NM 88032

SMITH, JOHN W
ADMINISTRATOR
Study: Southern Ill Univ, BA (eng), 1980. *Pos:* Founding cur special collections and archives, Chicago Park Dist, 1988-90; vis archivist, Royal Opera House, Covent Garden, London, 1991; chief archivist, Art Inst Chicago, 1990-94; cur archives, The Andy Warhol Mus, 1994-2000, dir, Archives Res Ctr, 1994-2000, interim dir, 1995-96, asst dir collections, exhibitions and rsch, 2000-06; dir, Archives of American Art, Smithsonian Inst, Washington, DC, 2006-. *Publ:* Auth, Strange Messenger: The Work of Patti Smith, 2002; auth, Andy Warhol's Time Capsule 21, 2003; auth, 365 Takes: The Andy Warhol Museum Collection, 2004; as well as others. *Mailing Add:* Archives American Art Smithsonian Inst PO Box 37012 Victor Bldg Ste 2200 MRC 937 Washington DC 20013-7012

SMITH, JOS(EPH) A(NTHONY)
ILLUSTRATOR, PAINTER
b Bellefonte, Pa, Sept 5, 1936. *Study:* Pa State Univ, with Hobson Pittman, 55-57 & 60; Pratt Inst, BFA. *Work:* Lauren Rogers Mus, Miss; Univ Miss, Oxford; Kassel Documenta Arch, Ger; Coeln Ludwig Mus, Ger; Stuttgart Staatsgalerie Grafische Sammlung, Ger; Univ Conn, Storrs; and others. *Exhib:* Pa Acad Fine Arts, 61, 67 & 69; solo exhib paintings, drawings & sculpture, Staten Island Inst Arts & Sci, 66; Bethel Gallery, Conn, 78; Newhouse Gallery, Staten Island Cult Ctr, NY, 82; Adirondak Community Col, NY, 87; Artists Select Artists, Trenton City Mus, NJ, 92; The Art of Drawing VII, Staemfli Gallery, NY, 92; The Esther Allen Greer Mus, Ohio, 2000; Martin Art Gallery, Muhlinberg Coll, Allentown, PA, 01; The Art Inst of Chicago, 01; Gallery 20, NY, 01; OHR-O'Keefe Mus, Biloxi, MS, 02. *Pos:* Design consult, Brooks Bros, 70-75; exhib designer & consult, Staten Island Inst Arts & Sci, 70-75; mem bd dir, Staten Island Coun Arts, 71-76. *Teaching:* Prof fine art, Pratt Inst, 61-; asst prof fine art, Richmond Col, London, Eng, 84. *Awards:* Mary S Litt Award for Watercolor, 100th Ann Am Watercolor Soc, 67; Merit Award, NY Soc Illusr, 73, 74, 79, 82 & 98; Merit Award, Nat Works on Paper, Univ Miss, Oxford; and others. *Bibliog:* Jane Cottingham (auth), The imaginary drawings of Joseph A Smith, Am Artist, 7/81; Albert, Seckler & Albert (auth), Figure Drawing Comes to Life, 2nd ed, Prentice Hall, 86; Suzi Galik (auth), The Reenchantment of Art, Thames & Hudson, 91; and others. *Mem:* NY Visionary Artists. *Media:* Oil, Pencil, Pen & Ink. *Publ:* Eric Jong (auth), Witches, Abrams, 80; Susan Cooper (auth), Matthew's Dragon, McElderry Bks, 91; auth, Pen & Ink Book, Watson-Guptill Publ, 92; illusr, Goblins in Green, Nicholas Heller, 95; Clay Boy, Mirra Ginsburg, 97; auth, Circus Trin, Abrams Pub, 01; The Yellow House, Susan Goldman Rubin, Abrams Pub, 01; Audubon, Jennifer Armstrong, Abrams Pub, 02; and others. *Mailing Add:* 381 Shawnee Dr Easton PA 18042

SMITH, JOSH
COLLAGE ARTIST
b Okinawa, Japan, 1976. *Study:* Univ Tenn, Knoxville, BFA, 1998. *Exhib:* Solo exhibs, Standard, Oslo, Norway, 2006, Galerie Catherine Bastide, Brussels, Belgium, 2006, Sketos Gabriele Gallery, Chicago, 2006, Abstraction, Luhring, Augustine, NY, 2007, Galerie Eva Presenhuber, Zurich, Switzerland, 2008, Mus Quartier, Vienna, Austria, 2008, Air de Paris, Paris, France, 2009, Hiromi Yoshii Gallery, Tokyo, Japan, 2009, Centre d'Art Cotemporain Geneve, Geneva, Switzerland, 2009, Deitch Studios, New York, NY, 2010, De Hallen Haarlem, The Netherlands, 2010; group exhibs, The Drawing Ctr, New York, NY, 2009, Comtemporary Mus, Baltimore, 2009, PSM Gallery, Berlin, Germany, 2009, Glendale Col Art Gallery, Calif, 2009, Altman Siegel, San Francisco, 2009, 54th Int Art Exhib Biennale, Venice, 2011. *Media:* Miscellaneous Media

SMITH, KEITH A
PHOTOGRAPHER, PRINTMAKER
b Tipton, Ind, May 20, 1938. *Study:* Art Inst of Chicago, BAE, with Aatis Lillstrom, Ken Josephson, Vera Berdich & Sonia Sheridan; Inst Design, Ill Inst Technol, MS (photog), with Aaron Siskind, Arthur Siegel & Misch Kohn; Guggenheim Fel in Photog, 72 & 80. *Work:* Mus Mod Art, NY; Art Inst of Chicago; Int Mus Photog, George Eastman House, Rochester, NY; Nat Gallery of Can, Ottawa, Ont; Houghton Rare Books Libr, Harvard Univ; and others. *Exhib:* Solo exhibs, Light Gallery, NY, 76, Chicago Ctr Contemp Photog, 78 & Stuart Wilber Inc, Chicago, 78, 79 & 80; Mirrors and Windows: Am Photog Since 1960, Mus Mod Art, 78 & traveling, 78-80; Am Photog of the Seventies, Art Inst Chicago, 79; Cliche Verre: 1939 to the Present, Detroit Inst Arts, 80; Hand-Colored Photographs, Philadelphia Coll Art, 80; and others. *Teaching:* Instr photog, Univ Calif, Los Angeles, 70; instr photog generative systems, Sch of Art Inst Chicago, 71-74; coordr of printmaking, Visual Studies Workshop, Rochester, 74-. *Awards:* Guggenheim Fel, 72 & 80; Nat Endowment Arts Grant, 78; NY Found Arts Grant, 85. *Media:* Photography; Etching with Photoetching. *Publ:* Auth, When I Was Two, Visual Studies Workshop, 77; auth, Book 91, 82 & Book 89 Patterned Apart, 83, Space Heater Multiples; coauth (with Jonathan Williams), Lexington Nocturne, A Poem by Jonathan Williams as Interpreted by Keith Smith, private publ, 83; auth, Book 95 Structure of the Visual Book, Visual Studies Workshop Press, 83. *Mailing Add:* 22 Cayuga St Rochester NY 14620

SMITH, KIKI
PAINTER, SCULPTOR
b Nuremberg, Ger, Jan 18, 1954. *Work:* Art Inst Chicago, Ill; Brooklyn Mus Art, Metrop Mus Art, Mus Mod Art, Whitney Mus Am Art & NY Pub Libr, NY; Corcoran Gallery Art, Washington, DC; Fogg Art Mus, Harvard Univ, Cambridge, Mass; plus many others. *Exhib:* Solo shows incl The Kitchen, New York, 82, Fawbush Gallery, 88, 92, 93, Galerie René Blouin, Montreal, 89, 91-92, 94, Dallas Mus Art, 89, Ezra and Cecile Zilkha Gallery Ctr for Arts, Wesleyan Univ, Conn, 89, Tyler Sch Art Temple Univ, Philadelphia, 90, Ctr d'Arte Contemporaine, Geneva, 90, Inst Art and Urban Resources The Clocktower, Long Island, NY, 90, Inst Contemp Art, Amsterdam, 90, Mus Mod Art, New York, 90-91, Shoshana Wayne Gallery, Santa Monica, 91-92, 92-93, MAK Galerie, Vienna, 91, Univ Art Mus, Berkeley, Calif, 91, Art Awareness, Inc, Lexington, NY, 91, Corcoran Gallery Art, Wash, DC, 91, Greg Kucera Gallery, Seattle, 91, Rose Art Mus, Brandeis Univ, Waltham, Mass, 92, Österreichisches Mus angewandte Kunst, Vienna, 92, Moderna Mus, Stockholm, 92, Bonner Kunstverein, Bonn, 92, Galerie M & R Fricke, Düsseldorf, Ger, 92-93, Williams Coll Mus Art, Williamstown, Mass, 92-93, Ohio State Univ, 92-93, Anthony d'Offay Gallery, London, 93, 95, Phoenix Art Mus, 93, Univ Art Mus, Santa Barbara, 94, La Mus Mod Art, Humlebaek, Denmark, 94, Israel Mus, Jerusalem, 94, Barbara Gross Galerie, Munich, 94, Laura Carpenter Fine Art, Santa Fe, 94, Pace Wildenstein, NY, 94, Royal LePage Gallery, Toronto, 94-95, Barbara Krakow Gallery, Boston, 94-96, Whitechapel Art Gallery, London, 95, Int Ctr for Photog, 2001, San Francisco Mus Mod Art, 2005, Contemp Art Mus, Houston, 2006; group shows incl Brooke Alexander Gallery, NY, 80, 91; White Columns, NY, 81, 83, 90; Artists Space, 81, 90; Barbara Gladstone Gallery, 82; Hallwalls, Buffalo, NY, 83; Susan Caldwel Gallery, NY, 84, 87; Galerie Engstrom, Stockholm, 84; Modern Masks, Whitney Mus Am Art, NY, 84; Moderna Mus, Stockholm, 85; Cincinnati Art Mus, 85; Art City, NY, 85; Brooklyn Mus, 86, 89; Curt Marcus Gallery, NY, 86; Fawbush Gallery, 87, 89, 90; Mus Mod Art, NY, 88, 92; IBM Gallery, NY, 88; Arch Gallery, Amsterdam 88; Tom Cugliani Gallery, 89; Simon Watson Gallery, NY, 90; Recent Acquisitions, Corcoran Gallery Art, Washington, DC, 90; Mus Fine Arts, Boston, 90, 95-96; The Interrupted Life, New Mus Contemp Art, NY, 91; Hunter Coll Art Gallery, 91; Milwaukee Art Mus, 92; Whitney Biennial, Whitney Mus Am Art, NY, 92 & 93, 2002; Corcoran Gallery Art, Washington, DC, 92, 97-98; Paula Cooper Gallery, 93; Serpentine Gallery, London, 94; The Material Imagination, Guggenheim Mus SoHo, NY, 95-96; Feminin-Masculin: le sex de l'art, Mus Nat D'Art Mod Ctr, Georges Pompidou, Paris, France, 95-96; Pace Wildenstein, NY, 95, 97, 98; Everything that's interesting is new: The Dakis Joannou Collection, DESTE Found, Athens, Greece, Mus Mod Art, Copenhagen & Guggenheim Mus SoHo, NY, 96-97; Am Acad Invitational Exhib Painting & Sculpture, Am Acad Arts & Letts, NY, 97; Ace Gallery, Mex, 97; Objects of Desire: The Modern Still Life, Mus Mod Art, NY, 97 & Hayward Gallery, London, 97-98; Beyond Belief: Modern Art and the Religious Imagination, Nat Gallery Victoria, Melbourne, Australia, 98; Giacometti to Judd: Prints by Sculptors, Mus Mod Art, NY, 98; Double Trouble: The Patchett Collection (traveling exhib), Mus Contemp Art, San Diego, Calif, 98; Yale Univ Art Gallery, New Haven, Conn, 98; As Above, So Below: The Body at Work, Fabric Workshop & Mus, Philadelphia, Pa, 99; My Nature: Works with Paper by Kiki Smith, St Louis Art Mus, 1999; John Berggruen Gallery, 2005; plus many others. *Awards:* Urban Glass Award, '96; Skowhegan Medal for Sculpture, 2000; Named one of 100 Most Influential People, Time Mag, 2006. *Bibliog:* Mercedes Vincente (auth), Un mundo natural, Lapiz, Spain, 2/98; Sarah Tanguy (auth), Kiki Smith: Night Sculpture, 9/98; Roberta Smith (auth), Galleries are labs of a sort, NY Times, 2/14/99. *Mem:* Nat Acad Design; AAAL

SMITH, LAWRY
DIRECTOR, CURATOR
b Cleveland, Ohio, Aug 29, 1952. *Study:* Baldwin Wallace Col, BA, 74; Cleveland State Univ, MFA, 77. *Collection Arranged:* Artist's Adopt, St Vincent Charity Hosp, 89; Ken Burgess (retrospective), La Mama La Galleria, 89, Danforth Mus, 90, Art Students League, 91. *Pos:* Dir & cur, Lamama Lagalleria, New York, 85-97, Citicorp Ctr, New York, 86-87, Cleveland Pub Theatre Ohio, 90; Nat Pub Radio, WBOE, 77-80; dir & cur, Marlen Gallery, NY, currently. *Awards:* Recipient Twyia M Conway Radio-TV Award; Hastings Grant. *Mem:* Screen Actors Guild; Am Fedn TV & Radio Artists. *Specialty:* Emerging artists. *Mailing Add:* La Mama La Galleria 74A East 4th St New York NY 10003

SMITH, LAWSON WENTWORTH
SCULPTOR, EDUCATOR
b Havana, Cuba, Apr 20, 1947; US citizen. *Study:* Okla State Univ, BFA, 70; Univ Nebr, MFA, 74. *Work:* Ctr Visual Arts Gallery, Ill State Univ, Bloomington & Normal; Sioux City Art Ctr, Sioux City, Iowa; and others. *Exhib:* Solo exhibs, Contemp Arts Found, Oklahoma City, 71, Henri Gallery, Washington, DC, 75, 77, 79 & 82, Schweinfurth Art Mus, Auburn, NY, 88, Rome Art Ctr, NY, 89, Bartlett Art Ctr, Stillwater, Okla, 93, Pooke Mus, Natick, Mass, 94 & OK Harris Gallery, NY, 98; Rutgers Nat Drawing Exhib, 79 & 81; OK Harris Gallery, NY, 82; Nat Works on Paper, Great Falls, NDak, 87. *Teaching:* Instr sculpture, Wichita State Univ, Kans, 74-75; assoc prof, Syracuse Univ, NY, 76, prof emeritus, currently. *Awards:* Purchase Award, 35th Ann Exhib, Sioux City Art Ctr, Iowa, 73; Purchase Award, Ball State Univ, 76; Sculpture Award, Fingerlakes Regional, Mem Art Gallery, Rochester, NY, 80; and others. *Media:* All

SMITH, LINDA KYSER
PAINTER, INSTRUCTOR
b Fort Worth, TX, Mar 16,1942. *Study:* Univ N Tex, BA & MA, 1966; Studied under: Everett Raymond Kinstler, Aaron Shikler, Burton Silverman, Bettina Steinke, William Reese, Ned Jacob, 1972. *Work:* Nat Cowgirl Hall of Fame, Fort Worth, Tex; Musée de la Grande Vigne, Dinan, Brittany; Montgomery Mus of Fine Art, Montgomery, Ala. *Comn:* Portrait of Fern Sawyer, Nat Cowgirl Hall of Fame, Fort Worth, 1998. *Exhib:* Allied Artists, Butler Mus, 1999. *Teaching:* instr, Scottsdale Artists' Sch, Ariz; instr, Andreeva Portrait Academy, Santa Fe, NMex. *Awards:* Gold. Medal for Oil, Knickerbocker Artists 45th Open, 2000; Everett Award, Allied Artists of Am, 2005. *Mem:* Nat Arts Club, NYC (artist mem); Salmagundi Club, NYC; Allied Artists of Am, NYC; Pastel Soc of Am, NYC; Artists Fel Inc, NYC. *Media:* Mixed Media. *Publ:* Coauth, Focus Santa Fe Cover & Feature Art, 1997, 2004; contribr (bk), Best of Portraits, Northlight Books, 1998; coauth, feature art, US Mag, 2002; coauth, Art Business News, 2002. *Mailing Add:* 233 Delgado St Santa Fe NM 87501

SMITH, LUTHER A
PHOTOGRAPHER
b Tishomingo, Miss, Mar 16, 1950. *Study:* Univ Ill, Urbana, with Art Singabaugh & Bart Parker, BA, 72; RI Sch Design, with Harry Callahan & Aaron Siskind, MFA (photog), 74. *Work:* Portland Mus Art, Maine; Mass Inst Technol; Ark Arts Ctr, Little Rock; Monmouth Col, Ill; La Grange Col, Ga; Chicago Art Inst, Ill; Houston Mus Fine Arts, Tex; Amon Carter Mus, Ft Worth, Tex; Dallas Mus Art. *Exhib:* Photog, Kansas City Art Inst, Mo, 78; Black & White & Color, Mass Inst Technol, 79; Contacts, Western Heritage Mus, Omaha, Nebr, 80; Invisible Light, Smithsonian Inst Traveling Exhib, 80-83; Second Sight, Carpenter Ctr, Harvard Univ, 81; Road & Roadside, Chicago Art Inst, 87; one person exhib, Waco Art Ctr, Tex, 87, Springfield Art Mus, Mo, 91 & Amarillo Art Mus, Tex, 94. *Teaching:* Vis lectr, Univ Ill, Urbana, 74-75, instr art, 75-78, asst prof, 78-81, assoc prof, 81-; assoc prof art dept, Tex Christian Univ, 83; prof art, Tex Christian Univ, 92-. *Awards:* Purchase Prizes, Allied Arts Asn, 79, Chattahoochi Art Asn, 80 & Ark Art Ctr, 80; Sesquicentennial Award, Tarrant Co Works on Paper, Ft Worth, Tex. *Mem:* Soc Photographic Educ. *Media:* Photography. *Res:* Landscape Photogr of Texas and the Am South. *Interests:* Landscape Photography. *Publ:* Illusr, Camera, 75, The Trinity River, TCU Press, 77; illusr, Chicago Mag, 78; illusr, Darkroom Dynamics, 78, Electronic Flash Photography, 80 & Photographing Indoors With Your Automatic Camera, 81, Curtin-London. *Dealer:* William Campbell Contemporary Art, Fort Worth, TX. *Mailing Add:* Art Dept Tex Christian Univ PO Box 298000 Fort Worth TX 76129

SMITH, MARK T
PAINTER, ILLUSTRATOR
b Wilimington, Del, Jan 12, 1968. *Study:* Pratt Inst, grad, 1990. *Work:* Walt Disney Co, IBM, MTV, ShowTime Networks, Nickelodeon, Harper Collins, Chrysler Motors, Pepsi-co. *Comn:* Absolut Smith nat ad campaign, comn by Absolut Vodka, 1996; painted Pt Cruisers, comn by Daimler-Chrysler, 2002; interior restaurant art, Taco Bell & Long John Silvers, Yum Brands, 2003. *Pos:* Official artist, US Olympic Comt, 2008. *Mailing Add:* Chase Contemporary 3176 MacArthur Blvd Northbrook IL 60062

SMITH, MICHAEL A
PHOTOGRAPHER, PUBLISHER
b Philadelphia, Pa, Feb 16, 1942. *Study:* Self-taught. *Work:* Mus Mod Art, Metrop Mus Art, New York; Art Inst Chicago; Mus Fine Arts, Boston; Philadelphia Mus Art; Victoria & Albert Mus, London; Cleveland Mus Art; Int Mus of Photographsm George Eastman House, Rochester, NY; Ctr for Creative Photography Tucson, Ariz; Int Ctr of Photography, New York; LA Co Mus Art; Mus Fine Arts, Houston; Nat Mus Mod Art, Kyoto, Japan; Mus Phtographic Arts, San Diego, Calif; San Francisco Mus Mod Art, Calif; Fogg Art Mus; Yale Univ Art Gallery; and many others. *Comn:* To Photograph Toledo, Toledo Mus Art, 80; Study of Princeton NJ, Princeton Gallery Fine Art, 84; To Photograph New Orleans, Hist New Orleans Collection, 85; Art in Pub Places, Broward Co, Fla, 89; To Photograph Chicago, US Equities Realty, 2008. *Exhib:* Solo exhibs, Sheldon Mem Art Gallery, 76, Del Art Mus, 78 & Ringling Mus Art, 80; Landscapes 75-79, Stanford Univ Mus Art, 81, Toledo Mus Art, 81 & Norton Gallery Fine Art, West Palm Beach, Fla, 82; Foto Biennal Enschede, The Neth, 84; Lowe Art Gallery, Syracuse Univ, 86; Loyola Coll, Baltimore, 87; Michael A Smith: A Visual Journey, Int Mus Photo at George Eastman House, 92; Fort Lauderdale Mus Art, 1995; Columbus Mus Art, Ohio, 1997; Mount Holyoke Coll Art Mus, South Hadley, Mass, 2000; Point Light Gallery, Sydney, Australia, 2007; Gallery 291, San Francisco, Calif, 2008. *Teaching:* Vis prof, Philadelphia Coll Art, 70-72, Bucks Co Community Coll, 71-73. *Awards:* Photogr Fel, Nat Endowment Arts, 77; Best Photog Bk of Yr, Le Grand Prix DuLivre, Recontres Int dela Photog, Arles, France, 81; Photogr Fel, Pa Coun Arts. *Bibliog:* Estelle Jussim (auth), A dead straight picture: The landscapes of Michael A Smith, Boston Rev, 2/77; James Enyeart (auth), Intro to Landscapes 1975-1979, Lodima Press, 81; Richard Trenner (auth), A portrait of the artist, Ont Rev, fall-winter 82-83; John Bratnober (auth), A Visual Journey, Lodima Press, 92. *Mem:* Soc Photog Educ. *Media:* Photography. *Publ:* Auth & illusr, Twelve Photographs 67-69, pvt publ, 70; auth, On teaching photography, Exposure, J Soc Photog Educ, 76; auth & illusr, Landscapes 1975-1979 (exhib catalog), Lehigh Univ, 81 & Landscapes 1975-1979 (monogr), Lodima Press, 81; Eight Landscape Photographs, Regnis Press, 83; illusr, Michael A Smith: A Visual Journey (monogr), Lodima Press, 92; auth & illusr, The Students of Deep Springs College, 2000 & Tuscany: Wandering the Backroads, 2004, Lodima Press; Chicago: Loop, Lodima Press, 2009; Iceland: A Personal View, Lodima Press, 2014; Ocean Variations, 2014. *Mailing Add:* PO Box 400 Ottsville PA 18942

SMITH, MIMI
SCULPTOR, CONCEPTUAL ARTIST
b Brookline, Mass, May 13, 1942. *Study:* Mass Coll Art, Boston, BFA, 63; Rutgers Univ, New Brunswick, NJ, MFA, 66. *Work:* Franklin Furnace, New York; The Getty Ctr, Santa Monica, Calif; The Inst Contemp Art, Tokyo; Mus Mod Art, New York; The Newark Mus; Spencer Art Mus, Lawrence, Kans; RI Sch Design, Providence; Fog Mus, Harvard Univ, Cambridge, Mass. *Exhib:* Committed to Print, Mus Modern Art, New York, 88; Television Apparatus, The New Mus, New York, 90; solo exhib, Inst Contemp Art, Univ Pa, 94; Div of Labor, Bronx Mus, La Mocha, 95-96; Art with Conscience, Newark Mus, NJ, 95-96; Addressing the Century, Hayward Gallery, London, 98-99; Representing a Show of Identities, Parish Art Mus, Southampton, NY, 2000; Gloria: Another Look at Feminist Art in the 1970's, White Columns, NY, Moore Coll, Philadelphia & RISD Mus, Providence, 2002-2003; Critical Mass, Mead Art Mus, Amherst Coll, Mass, 2003; Wack: Art & the Feminist Revolution (traveling exhib), Los Angeles Mus Contemp Art, Nat Mus Women Arts, PS1 & Vancouver Art gallery, 2007-2009; Dress, Codes, Katonah Mus, Katonah, NY, 2009; Building Blocks: Contemp Works from the Collection, Risd Mus, Providence, RI, 2011. *Awards:* Grant, Nat Educ Asn Artists Fel, 78; NYSCA Project Grant, Visual Studies Workshop, 82; Fel, NY Found Arts, 86; Grant, Joan Mitchell, 98. *Bibliog:* Roberta Smith (auth), Mimi Smith Knotted Thread Work from the 60's and 70's, 1/15/99, Helen Molesworth (auth), Frieze, Mimi Smith, Issue 46, 5/99, Gretchen Kurtz (auth), The Works Curators Covet, 11/18/2001, NY Times; Heinz-Norbert Jocks (auth), Mimi Smith: A Survey of Clothing, Kunstforum Int, p 150-163, June-July 2009; A Basic History of Western Art, Janson & Janson, Prentice Hall, p 621, 2006; Susan Earle (auth), Mimi Smith Fashioning Art and Life, Woman's Art Jour p. 13-21, 2011. *Publ:* Auth, This is a Test, Visual Studies Workshop. *Dealer:* Anna Kustera Gallery 520 W 21st St New York NY 10011. *Mailing Add:* 451 W Broadway New York NY 10012-5300

SMITH, NAN S(HELLEY)
SCULPTOR, CERAMIST
b Philadelphia, Pa, Nov 10, 1952. *Study:* Tyler Sch Art, Temple Univ, Philadelphia, BFA, 74; Ohio State Univ, Columbus, MFA, 77; Univ Ill, Japan House, with Shozo Sato, 79. *Work:* IDS/Am Express Corp Hq, Minneapolis, Minn; Lamar Dood Art Ctr, La Grange Col, Ga; Wocek Int Ceramics Collection; Ichon Ceramics Ctr, Korea. *Comn:* sculpture portraits, Gaston Family and John and Carol Koogler, Gainesville, Fla. *Exhib:* World Ceramics Exposition Korea, 2001; Taking Measure: Am Ceramic Art at the New Millennium, Yertu, Korea, 2001; Clay Body Rhetoric: Ceramic Figure of Speech, Marianna Kistler Beach Mus Art, Kans State Univ, Manhattan, 2002; Women Playing with Fire, Art Dept Gallery, Tex Women's Univ, Denton, 2003; Rawspace Gallery, Sofa Chicago, 2004; 21st Century Ceramics in the US and Can, Canzani Ctr, Gallery, Columbus, Ohio, 2003; Pygmalion's Gaze Reimagined: The Figure in Contemp Ceramics, Creative Alliance Gallery, Baltimore, MD, 2005; solo exhib, Series in White, The Tim Salon Gallery & The St Petersburg Clay Co, St Petersburg, Fla, 2006; Beyond Memisis, The Strecker Nelson Gallery, Manhattan, Kans, 2007; Form & Imagination: Women Ceramic Sculptors, The Am Mus Ceramic Art, Pomona, Calif, 2007; Mus Art, Fla Staet Univ, 2008; Armory Art Ctr, West Palm Beach, FlA, 2009; Body Perspectives, Tom Funke Gallery, Cincinnatti, 2009; Extraordinary Charators, Strecker, Nelson Gallery, Manhattan, Kansas, 2009; Earth Matters, Galleries at Moore Coll Art & Design, Philadelphia, 2010; Resonance, Studio at 620, 2011; The Florida Craftsman Gallery, 2011. *Pos:* Prof art, Univ Fla Ceramics Prog. *Teaching:* Vis instr design & ceramics, Univ Ill, Champaign-Urbana, 77-79; assoc prof ceramics, Univ Fla, Gainesville, 79-96, prof, 96-, res found prof, 2000. *Awards:* Fla Arts Coun Artist Fel, 81, 92, 98, 2010; SAF-NEA Fel, 93; Scholar Enhancement Fund Award, Univ Fla, 98-2002 & 2004-10. *Bibliog:* Potters of Northern Florida, The Studio Potter, vol 26, 6/98; Susan Peterson (auth), Contemporary Ceramics, Watson and Cuptill Pub, 2000; Glen Nelson and Richard Burkett (coauth), Ceramics: A Potter's Handbook, 6th edit, Harcourtt Coll Pub; Susan Peterson (auth), Working with Clay, Laurence King Pub, 2002; World Famous Ceramic Artists Studios, Hebei Fine Art Pub House, 2005; Mattias Ostormann (auth), The Ceramic Narrative, A & C Black Publ, London, 2006; Glen R Brown (auth), Evoking Nostalgia, Ceramics Monthly, July/Aug 2009; 500 Ceramic Sculptures, Sterling Pub Co, 2009; Body Perspectives, Ceramic Art & Perception, No. 81, 2010. *Mem:* Nat Coun Educ Ceramic Arts. *Media:* Clay; Gypsum Cement, Metal. *Res:* Figurative Installations. *Interests:* Innovative mold making using rubber molds for ceramics. *Publ:* Auth, Blending institution and logic, Ceramics Monthly Mag, fall 90; Flexible Molds for Ceramics, Ceramics Monthly Mag, 2/96; auth, Flexible Mold Making, The Studio Potter, 12/99; auth, Controlled Drying and Firing, Ceramics Monthly, 5/2000; auth, Color, Air, Illusions & Ceramics, Technical, No 11, 2000; auth, Through the Eye, in: The Figure in Clay, Lark Publ, Asheville, NC, 2005. *Mailing Add:* 2310 NW 142nd Ave Gainesville FL 32609-4022

SMITH, PAUL J
MUSEUM DIRECTOR
b Sept 8, 1931. *Study:* Art Inst Buffalo; Sch Am Craftsman. *Hon Degrees:* Parsons Sch Design; New Sch Social Res, Hon Dr Fine Arts, 87. *Collection Arranged:* Craft Today: Poetry of the Physical, 86; The Confectioner's Art; Designed for Production: The Craftmen's Approach; The Teapot, The Door; For the Body; Object for Preparing Food; Portable World; The Great Am Foot; Objects for Use: Handmade by Design; cur adv, Objects USA, 69; cur adv, Craft, Art & Religion, Vatican, Rome, Ital, 78; cur adv, In Praise of Hands, Toronto, Can, 74; plus over 200 other exhibs, 63-. *Pos:* Bd dir, Louis Comfort Tiffany Found, currently; former adv trustee, Haystack Mountain Sch Crafts, Deer Isle, Maine; Nat Coun adv bd, Atlantic Ctr Arts; dir emer, Am Craft Mus, currently; former bd trustees, Penland Sch Crafts; int adv bd, Friends Fiber Art Int; pres, LGT Foundation. *Awards:* Hon Degree, Fine Arts, Parsons Sch Design New Sch for Soc Res, 87; Aileen Osborn Webb Award for Philanthropy, In Recognition of Exceptional Support of the Craft Field, 2009; Legends Award, Watershed Center for Ceramic Arts, 2011. *Mem:* Hon Fel Am Craft Coun; Hon Intl Mem Can Craft Coun. *Publ:* Craft Today: Poetry of the Physical Am Craft Mus, Weidenfeld & Nicholson, 86; Objects for Use: Handmade by Design; served as general ed for a 336 book pub by Abrams, 2001. *Mailing Add:* 1349 Lexington Ave New York NY 10128

SMITH, RAE
PAINTER
b New York, NY. *Study:* Franklin Sch Prof Arts, New York, V K Jonynas. *Work:* China Mus Pastel Gallery, Suzhou, China; Noyes Mus, Oceanville, NJ; Shore Medical Ctr, Somers Point, NJ; Hackensack Univ Medical Ctr, Pascack Valley, NJ; Butler Inst Am Art, Youngstown, Oh. *Exhib:* Solo Exhibs: Galleria Prova, Tokyo, Japan; Lois Richards Gallery Greenwich, Conn; Accent Gallery, Ocean City, NJ; Greene Art Gallery, Guilford, Conn; Images Gallery, Briarcliff Manor, NY; Pen & Brush Inc, Gallery, New York; Emelin Theatre Gallery Inaugural Exhib, Mamaroneck, NY; Mussavi Art Ctr, New York; Butler Inst Am Art, Youngstown, Ohio; Charter Oak Gallery, Fairfield, Conn; Euro Pastel Exhib, St Petersburg, Russia; Xi'an Acad Fine Arts, China; SoHo Gallery 420, Nat Asn Women Artists, New York; Cork Gallery, Avery Fisher Hall, Lincoln Ctr, New York; Triton Mus Art, Santa Clara, Calif; Slater Mus, Norwich, Conn; Mus Contemp Masters, San Antonio; Noyes Mus, Oceanville, NJ; China Mus Art, Suzhou; Hammond Mus, North Salem, NY; Haggin Mus, Stockton, Calif; Bennington Art Center, Bennington, Vt; Mattatuck Mus, Waterbury, Conn. *Pos:* Pres, Pastel Society Am, NY, 2007-. *Teaching:* Instr pastel and oil painting, Katonah Art Ctr, NY; Brigantine Ctr, NJ. *Awards:* Gold Medal Hon,

Audubon Artists Inc; Pastel Soc Can Award, Pastel Soc Am; First Prize, Pastel, Mamaroneck Artists Guild, NY; Bd Dirs Award, Slater Mus, Norwich; Artistic Excellence in Oils Award, Mus Contemp Masters; Art du Pastel en France Award, Vernon; Cardman Award, CLWAC, Nat Arts Club, New York City; Atlantic Papers Award, PSWC, Haggin Mus, Stockton, Calif; Allied Artists of Am Award; PSWC Award, Triton Mus, Santa Clara, Calif; Hall of Fame Honoree, Pastel Soc Am, 2014. *Mem:* Pastel Soc Am, NYC (master pastelist); Fel Am Artists Prof League, New York; Catharine Lorillard Wolfe Art Club, NYC; Hudson Valley Art Asn, New York; Allied Artists Am New York; Audubon Artists New York; Noyes Mus Art, Oceanville, NJ (artist mem); Conn Pastel Soc (hon mem); Int Asn Pastel Soc (bd mem). *Media:* Pastels, Oils. *Publ:* Articles In: Mitsukoshi Mag, Publ Tokyo, Japan, 98, Best of Pastel 2, Rockport Publ Inc, 98, Pastel J Mag, 11-12/99 & Int Artists Mag, 5-6/2000 & 7-8/2002; Pastel Application Techniques, Nat Chiang Kai Shek Memorial Hall. *Dealer:* Accent Gallery Ocean City NJ; Lois Richards Gallery Greenwich Conn; Peter McPhee Gallery Stone Harbor NJ; Corporate Art Group Chicago IL. *Mailing Add:* 513 W Country Club Dr Egg Harbor City NJ 08215

SMITH, RALPH ALEXANDER
WRITER, EDUCATOR
b Ellwood City, Pa, June 12, 1929. *Study:* Columbia Univ, AB, Teachers Coll, MA & EdD. *Pos:* Ed, J Aesthetic Educ, 66-2000; exec secy, Coun Policy Studies Art Educ, 78-82; contrib ed, Arts Educ Policy Rev, 2000-. *Teaching:* Instr art hist & art educ, Kent State Univ, 59-61; asst prof art hist & art educ & chmn dept art, Wis State Univ-Oshkosh, 61-63; asst prof art hist & art educ, State Univ NY Coll New Paltz, 63-64; asst prof aesthet educ, Univ Ill, Urbana, 64-67, assoc prof, 67-71, prof cult and educ policy, 71-96, emer prof cult & educ policy, 96-. *Awards:* Distinguished Univ Vis Prof, Ohio State Univ; Distinguished Sr Scholar, Coll Educ, Univ Ill; Disting Lectr Studies in Art Edn Award, 91. *Mem:* Am Soc Aesthet; distinguished mem Ill Art Educ Asn; Nat Art Educ Asn. *Res:* Theoretical foundations of aesthetic and humanities education; cultural and educational policy analysis. *Publ:* Co-ed, Aesthetics and Arts Education, Univ Ill Press, 91; ed, The Sense of Art, 89, Cultural Literacy and Arts Education, Univ Ill Press, 91; coauth, Art Education: A Cultural Necessity, Univ Ill Press, 91; co-ed, The Arts, Education and Aesthetic Knowing, Univ Chicago Press, 92; Public Policy and the Aesthetic Interest, 92 & General Knowledge & Arts Educating, 94, Univ Ill Press; auth, Excellence II, Nat Art Educ Asn, 95; Culture Art the Art in Teachers Coll Educ, 2007. *Mailing Add:* 2909 Heathwood Ct Champaign IL 61822-7659

SMITH, RAYMOND WALTER
PHOTOGRAPHER, BOOK DEALER
b Newark, NJ, Oct 26, 1942. *Study:* Stetson Univ, BA, 64; Yale Univ, MA, 66, MPhil, 68. *Work:* Yale Univ Art Gallery, New Haven; Harry Ransom Center, Univ Tex, Austin; New Britain Mus of American Art, Conn; Mongomery Mus of Fine Arts, Alabama. *Exhib:* Conn Photography, Greater Hartford Arts Festival, Hartford, 74 & 75; Archetype Gallery, New Haven (with Paul Caponigro), 74; Am As Found Photos by Ray Smith, Yale Univ Libr, New Haven, 75; Photographs by Ray Smith, Stetson Univ Art Gallery, Deland, Fla, 75; Beyond Documentary Four Photographers, John Slade Ely House, New Haven, 77; In Time We Shall Know Ourselves (traveling exhib of photographs), Montgomery Mus Fine Arts, 2014, Hickory Mus Art, NC, 2014; Mus of Contemporary Art, Jacksonville, Fla, 2015; Georgia Mus Art, Athens, 2015; Ogden Mus of Southern Art, New Orleans, 2016. *Pos:* Cur, John Slade Ely House, New Haven, 85-95. *Mem:* Art Libr Soc-N Am; Antiquarian Booksellers Asn Am. *Publ:* American Art Review, 75, Chicago Review, 76, Photographic Rev, 79-80, Southern Cultures, 2013; ed, 15 Painters & Sculptors (exhib catalog), John Slade Ely House, 85; auth, Artists From People's Republic of China (exhib catalog), John Slade Ely House, 91, Architecture and Process (exhib catalog), 92; John OC McCrillis: 50 Years in Art & Design, John Slade Ely House, 94; book (52 photographs from 1974 road trip): In Time We Shall Know Ourselves, by Raymond Smith, with essays on the photographs by Alexander Nemerov and Richard H. King, Peter Hastings Falk Publisher, 2014. *Mailing Add:* c/o RW Smith Bookseller 130 Cold Spring St New Haven CT 06511

SMITH, RENE
PAINTER
b Philadelphia. *Study:* Bennington Coll, Bennington, Vt, BA (Painting), 1999; Tyler Sch Art, Philadelphia, MFA (Painting), 2002. *Exhib:* Solo exhibs include David Allen Gallery Brooklyn, 2005, Courthouse Gallery, Anthology Film Archives, New York, 2005, Deiglan Gallery, Akureyri, Iceland, 2007; Two person exhibs include Md Hall Creative Arts Annapolis, Md, 2005; Group exhibs include Windoworks Prog, Vt Arts Exchange, Bennington, Vt, 1999; Urban Cartography, Da Vinci Arts Alliance, Philadelphia, 2003; Composition in Hi-Fi, David Allen Gallery Brooklyn, 2004; Young Arts Alliance, Philadelphia Arts Alliance, 2005; Manager's Picks, Cooke Contemp, Jersey City, 2006; Out of Me, Out of You, Subdivision Long Island City, NY, 2007, Dreamer of Pictures, 2008. *Awards:* Bennington Scholars Fel, Bennington Coll, Vt, 1998-99; Proj Completion Grant, Temple Univ, Philadelphia, 2002; Artist's Grant, Vt Studio Ctr, Johnson, Vt, 2003; Director's Award, Halpert Biennial, Appalachian State Univ Boone, 2005; George Sugarman Found Grant, 2007

SMITH, ROBERT (BOB) CHARLES
DESIGNER, PAINTER
b Buffalo, NY, Jan 21, 1926. *Study:* Albright Art Sch, Univ Buffalo, BFA, 50; Univ Cincinnati. *Work:* Kemper Mus, Wash Univ, St Louis, Mo; Butler Inst Am Art; Laumeier, Sculpture Park, St Louis; Rutgers Univ Libr Spec Collections; Cleveland Art Inst Spec Collections. *Comn:* Fountain, Pub Libr Hamilton Co, Cincinnati, Ohio, 60; fountain, Temple Ark & Eternal Light, Glen Manor Temple, Cincinnati, 64; fountain, Munic Opera Asn Forest Park, St Louis, Mo, 74; fountain, Boone Co Nat Bank, Columbia, Mo, 75 & 86. *Exhib:* Fountains 69, Taft Mus, Cincinnati, 69; Multiples '80, Contemp Arts Ctr, New Orleans, La, 80; The Book, Peoria Art Guild, 98; Bookentics: Bob Smith, Book Artist, 98, Laumeier Sculpture Park; Beyond the Fold, Gallery at S Orange, NJ, 99; solo exhibs, Univ City Pub Libr, Bonsack Gallery, Art Acad Cincinnati, 95, Typoetica: Kinetic Books, Washington Univ, Special Coll, 2002; Bob Smith, Eclectic Vision, Turtle Gallery, Deer Isle, ME, 2008, 2011; Maturity and its Muse, Sheldon Art Galleries, 2011. *Teaching:* Instr design, Albright Art Sch, 50-52; instr design & drawing, Art Acad Cincinnati, 52-65; prof design, Sam Fox Coll Art & Design, Wash Univ, 65-94, prof emer, 95. *Awards:* Purchase Award, Ann Drawing Show, Ball State Univ Art Gallery, 74. *Bibliog:* K Hanna (auth), Fountains '69, Taft Mus, 69; S Pollack (auth), RC Smith--Waterworks, New Art Examiner, 81; Jan Garden Castro (auth), Bookonetics, Sculpture, 99. *Media:* All Media. *Publ:* Auth, Basic Graphic Design, Prentice-Hall, 86, 2nd ed, 92; Maine By Line, 91, Sunrise-Sunset, 91 & Master's Pieces, 92, Ocean Motion, Eclectic Press, 2009. *Dealer:* Turtle Gallery Deer Isle ME. *Mailing Add:* 6316 Washington Ave Saint Louis MO 63130

SMITH, ROBERT LEWIS
DESIGNER, EDUCATOR
b Salem, Ohio, Aug 5, 1940. *Study:* Univ Southern Calif; Univ Calif, Los Angeles, BA, 63, MFA, 66. *Collection Arranged:* Three Photographers--Bullock, Sommer, Teske, 68; Jud Fine, 72; Narrative Themes: Audio Works, 78; Sound, 79; Leroy Neiman-Andy Warhol, 81; Changing Trends: Content and Style, 82. *Pos:* Gallery dir, Calif State Univ, Northridge, 66-70 & Brand Lib Art Ctr, Glendale, Calif, 70-73; dir & founder, Los Angeles Inst Contemp Art, 74-86. *Teaching:* Prof & design, Calif State Univ, Northridge, 66-. *Awards:* DAAD Fel, 85. *Bibliog:* Michael Auping (auth), Interview with Bob Smith, La Mamelle, Berkeley, Calif, 75; plus others. *Publ:* Auth & designer numerous exhib catalogs. *Mailing Add:* Dept Art Calif State Univ 18111 Nordoff St Northridge CA 91330-8300

SMITH, ROWENA MARCUS
PAINTER, COLLAGE ARTIST
b Bethel, Vt, June 6, 1923. *Study:* Syracuse Univ, BFA, 43; Hofstra Univ, MS, 66; studied with Rex Brandt, Joan Irving, Miles G Batt, Charles Reid, Barbara Nechis, Don Andrews, 77-2000. *Work:* Broward Co Libr Found, Ft Lauderdale; Oakland Park Libr, Oakland Park, Fla; Coral Springs Libr, Fla; Nat Asn Women Artists Collection, Zimmerli Mus, Douglass Col, Rutgers Univ; Hollywood Art Culture Ctr, 94; Fla Atlantic Univ, Ft Lauderdale Ctr, Fla; City of Pembroke Pines, Fla; Hope Ctr, Miami, Fla; Childens' Center at Broward Gen Hospital, Ft Lauderdale, Fla; City of Tamarac. *Comn:* Ltd ed print 4-color lithography, Floyd L Wray Found, Davie, 88; 2-Ltd Ed Prints-4 Color Lithography, Smart Art Co, Boca Raton, Fla. *Exhib:* Allied Artists Am Ann, NY, 94; Soc Experimental Artists, Ft Worth, Tex, 94; Ga Watercolor Soc 15th Traveling Exhib, 94; All Fla, Boca Raton Mus Art, Fla; Taos Nat Exhib Am Watercolor II, NMex; Mentor to Mentor Traveling Exhib, Duneden Art Ctr, Coral Springs Mus Art, Fla, 99 & 2001; Under the Influence 2/3 Exhib, Fort Lauderdale Mus Art, 2000; Gross Innovations, Cynon Valley Mus, Aberdore, Wales, 2004-05; Bakers Dozen, Int Collage Exhib, New Zealand, 2007; NAWA Ann, Monroe Center Arts, 2007; Journeys (with Flamingo artists), Crest Theatre, Cornell Mus Art & Culture, Delray Beach, Fla, 8/2009; Solo exhib, Tour de Force, Glass Gallery, Pembroke Pines, Fla, 2009, Retrospective, Pembroke Pines City Center, Fla, 2/2009, Body Language, Rice Gallery, McDaniel Col, Westminister, MD, 10/2009; Body Language, Cornell Mus Art & American Culture, Delray Beach, Fla, 4/2011, New Lauderhill Art Ctr, 2013. *Pos:* Coordr, Masters Degree Prog in Creative Arts Therapy, Hofstra Univ, 75; exec secy, Gold Coast Watercolor Soc, 85-91; mem, co-chmn, 2 plus 3 Artists Orgn; exec dir, Gold Coast Watercolor Soc, 94-2003; dir & mentor, Flamingo Artists, S Fla; voting mem, Public Arts Comt, Tamarac, Fla, 2009-13. *Teaching:* Watercolor & collage, Broward Art Guild, 80-94, Floyd L Wray Found Flamingo Gardens, 87-; workshop leader painting & drawing, Art Adventures Inc, Ft Lauderdale, 84-89; Holiday Park Community Ctr, Ft Lauderdale, 91-93; figure workshop, Coral Springs Artists Guild, 93; Charlotte Maloney Workshops, 95-97; master workshop, Coral Springs Mus Art, 2001. *Awards:* Am Frame Award, Ga Watercolor Soc, 96; Am Artist Award, Western Colo Watercolor Soc 6th Nat Exhib, 96; Nautalus Fel, Int Soc Experimental Artists, 2000; and others. *Bibliog:* Joan Davenport (auth), Art Notes, Village Press, 3/92; City Link, Fort Lauderdale, Fla, 11/2000; Eastsider, Broward Co, Fla, 11/2000; Tamarac Forum, 3/21/03; Philip Volys (auth), Painter is Subject of Artist Retrospective, The Gazette, 2/2009; Cadace Russell (auth), Parklander Mag, 2011. *Mem:* Am Watercolor Soc; Nat Asn Women Artists; 2 + 3 Artists Asn, (co-chmn); signature mem Transparent Watercolor Soc Am; Nat Watercolor Soc (signature mem); Professional Artists Asn. *Media:* Watercolor, Acrylic; Collage. *Interests:* Artistic grooming of advanced artists for national competition, museum exhibitions and commercial galleries. *Publ:* Complete Guide to Creative Watercolor, Creative Art Publs, 88; Artists of Fla, vol I and vol II; XS Mag, Sun Sentinel, 6/93; Watercolor - A Step by Step Guide & Showcase, Rockport Press, 96; Bridging Time and Space Essays on Layered Art, Markowitz Publ, 98; Collage in all Dimensions, 2005. *Dealer:* Ganymede Gallery New York NY; Light House Gallery Tequesta FL; Gallery 421 Fort Lauderdale FL; Boca Raton Museum of Art Artists Guild; Artists Eye Fine Arts Gallery Dania Beach Fla. *Mailing Add:* 5313 Bayberry Ln Tamarac FL 33319

SMITH, RUTH REININGHAUS See Reininghaus, Ruth

SMITH, SHERRI
WEAVER, EDUCATOR
b Chicago, Ill, Mar 21, 1943. *Study:* Stanford Univ, Calif, BA, 65; Cranbrook Acad Art, Bloomfield Hills, Mich, MFA, 67. *Work:* Art Inst Chicago; Hackley Art Mus, Muskegon, Mich, Am Tel & Tel Co; Borg Warner Corp; Colorado Springs Fine Arts Ctr, Colo. *Comn:* Wall hangings, Detroit Plaza Hotel, 77; Fed Bldg, Ann Arbor, 78; Du Page Co Hosp, Ill, 78; Int Business Machines, Atlanta. *Exhib:* Mus Mod Art, NY, 69; Biennale of Tapestry, Lausanne, Switz, 71-77; Three-Dimensional Fibers, Govett-Brewster Art Gallery, New Plymouth, NZ, 74; Am Crafts 76, Mus Contemp Art, Chicago, 76; Fiberworks, Cleveland Mus Art, Ohio, 77; one-person show, Hadler Gallery, NY, 78; Mainstream, the Art Fabric Traveling Exhib; and others. *Teaching:*

Instr weaving & textile design, Colo State Univ, Ft Collins, 71-75; prof weaving & textile design, Sch Art, Univ Mich, Ann Arbor, 75-. *Bibliog:* Larson & Constantine, Beyond Crafts, The Art Fabric, Van Nostrand, 75; Kuenzi (auth), La nouvelle tapisserie, Bonvent, 75; Waller (auth), Textile sculptures, Studio Vista, 77. *Dealer:* Jacques Baruch Gallery 900 N Michigan Ave Chicago IL 60611; Modern Masters Tapestries 11 E 57th New York NY 10022. *Mailing Add:* 1733 Jackson Rd Ann Arbor MI 48103

SMITH, SHINIQUE AMIE
ASSEMBLAGE ARTIST
b Baltimore, 1972. *Study:* Md Inst Coll Art, BFA, 1992, MFA, 2003; Sch Mus Fine Arts, Boston, MAT, 2000. *Exhib:* Solo exhibs include Scuola dell'Arte dei Tiraoro e Battioro, Venice, 2002, Creative Alliance, Baltimore, 2002, The Proposition, New York, 2005, Boulder Mus Contemp Art, Colo, 2005, Cuchifritos Gallery, New York, 2006, Franklin Art Works, Minneapolis, 2007; group exhibs include 28, The Whole Gallery, Md, 2002, Black Russians, 2003; Upwardly Mobile, Ludwig Mus Contemp Art, Budapest, 2002 & Mus Mod Kunst, Frankfurt, Germany, 2002; Rising Voices, DC Arts Ctr Gallery, Washington, 2003; Veni Vidi Video II, Studio Mus Harlem, New York, 2004, African Queen, 2005, Frequency, 2005; Re: Source, Art in General, New York, 2004; WORD, Bronx River Art Ctr, New York, 2004; Drawn Out, Gallery 400, Chicago, 2005; Do You Think I'm Disco, Longwood Arts Gallery, Bronx, NY, 2006; I Feel You, Roebling Hall, Brooklyn, NY, 2006; Future Nomad, Vox Populi Gallery, Philadelphia, 2007; Unmonumental: The Object in the 21st Century, New Mus Contemp Art, New York, 2007

SMITH, SHIRLEY
PAINTER
b Wichita, Kans. *Study:* Kans State Univ, BFA; Provincetown Workshop Art Sch, Mass; Art Students League. *Work:* Whitney Mus Am Art, NY; Univ Calif Art Mus, Berkeley; Marianna Kistler Beach Mus, Kansas State Univ; Phoenix Art Mus, Ariz; Prudential Insurance Co Am, Newark, NJ; The Aldrich Mus Contemp Art, Conn; Ulrich Mus, Wichita State Univ; Everson Mus, NY; Telfair Mus, Savana, Ga; Chase Manhattan Bank Collection, New York; S Co Bank Collection, St Louis Mo; Emprize Bank Collection, Wichita, Kans; Bank of Whitewater, Whitewater, Kans; Prudential Life Insurance, Newark, NJ; King Features Syndicate, New York; Rodale Press Collection, Prevention Mag, Emmaus, Pa. *Exhib:* Am Painting 1970, Va Mus, Richmond; Lyrical Abstraction, Aldrich Mus Contemp Art, 70; Recent Acquisitions & Lyrical Abstraction, Whitney Mus Am Art, NY, 71; From the Mus Collection Art by Women, Univ Calif Art Mus, Berkeley, 73; Auditorium Installation Exhib, Everson Mus, Syracuse, NY, 76-79; Views by Women Artists, Women's Caucus Art, NY, 82; 161st Ann Exhib, Nat Acad Design, NY, 86; Animal Life, 87 & Nature in Art, 88, One Penn Plaza, NY; solo exhibs, Wichita Art Mus, 78, Art/EX Gallery, Stamford Mus & Nature Ctr, Conn, 87, Aaron Gallery, Washington, DC, 87, Joan Hodgell Gallery, 87, John Jay Gallery, New York, NY, 2000; Am Acad Inst Arts & Lett Invitational, NY, 90 & 91; solo retrospective (auth, catalog), Marianna Kistler Beach Mus Art, Kans State Univ, Manhattan, 99; East End Artists: Past & Present, Telfair Mus, Savanna, Ga, 2007-2008; The 183rd Ann: Invitational Exhib of Contemp Am Art, Nat Acad Mus & Sch, NY, 2008. *Teaching:* Instr painting, Teamsters Local 237, New York, 88-95. *Awards:* Grumbacher Artists Mat Cash Award Mixed Media, New Eng Exhib, Silvermine, 67; Acad Inst Award, Am Acad Arts & Lett, New York, 91; Richard Florsheim Art Fund Grant, 98; Retrospective Opening Grant, 99. *Bibliog:* Rosemary Mayer (auth), article, Arts, 2/73; April Kingsley (auth), article, Art Int; The Longboat Observer, Oct, Animals, Joan Hodgell Gallery, Sarasota, FL; The Wichita Eagle Beacon, Artists forms Muslim into Paintings, Dorothy Beldon (auth); Art in Focus, Two Viewpoints, Dorothy Grafly, Philadelphia, PA. *Mem:* Artists Equity. *Media:* All Media. *Publ:* American Painting 1970 (exhib catalog), Va Mus, Richmond, Va, 70; Lyrical Abstraction (exhib catalog), Whitney Mus Am Art & Aldrich Mus of Contemp Art, 70; New Accessions USA (exhib catalog), Colo Springs Fine Art Ctr, 72; Shirley Smith: A Retrospective (exhib catalog) Marianna Kistler Beach Mus, 99; East End Artists: Past & Present (exhib catalog), Telfair Mus, Ga, 2007; Invitational 183rd Ann Nat Acad Mus (exhib catalog), New York, 2008. *Mailing Add:* 141 Wooster St New York NY 10012

SMITH, SUSAN
PAINTER, COLLAGE ARTIST
b Greensburg, Pa. *Study:* Art Students League, 1955-57, with Edwin Dickinson; Briarcliff Col, BS, 1971; Hunter Col, New York, NY, MA, 1976. *Work:* Weatherspoon Art Gallery, Univ NC, Greensboro; Copenhagen Handelsbank, Denmark. *Exhib:* Solo Exhibs: Westmoreland Mus, Greensburg, Pa, 1986; Galerie Art In, Nürnberg, Ger, 1993; The Comerford Project, Karl Drerup Gallery, Plymouth State Univ, Plymouth, NH, 2006; group exhibs: Intericon 1986, Charlottenborg, Copenhagen, Denmark, 1986; After Matisse, Traveling Exhib, Worcester Art Mus, Mass, Portland Mus Art, Maine, Queens Mus, Flushing, NY, Chrysler Mus, Norfolk, Va, Dayton Art Inst, Ohio & Phillips Collection, Washington, DC, 1986-87; Invitational Exhib Visual Arts, Am Acad Arts & Letters, New York, 2008. *Teaching:* Lectr art & painting, Sch Visual Arts, New York, 1969-70; adj asst prof color, Pratt Inst, Brooklyn, NY, 1974; asst prof art, Wagner Col, Staten Island, NY, 1982-99; vis lectr, painting, Princeton Univ, Princeton, NJ, 1987. *Awards:* MacDowell Colony Fel, Peterboro, NH, 1969; New York Creative Artists Pub Serv Prog Fel, 1975-76; Artist Fel Grant, Nat Endowment Arts, Washington, DC, 1981; Acad Award in Art & Purchase Award, Am Acad Arts & Letters, 2008. *Bibliog:* Peggy Cyphers (auth), Susan Smith, Arts Mag, 9/91; Stephen Bann & William Allen (coauths), Interpreting Contemporary Art, 1991; Yve-Alain Bois (auth), Susan Smith's Archeology, Edinburgh: Reakton Books & New York: Harper Collins Inc, 1991; and others. *Media:* Oil. *Dealer:* Margarete Roeder Gallery 545 Broadway New York NY 10012. *Mailing Add:* 39 Bond St New York NY 10012

SMITH, TERRY
EDUCATOR, HISTORIAN
Pos: Art critic, Weekend Australian, Nation Rev & Times on Sunday, formerly; founder, Union Media Svcs, 1976-; bd dirs, Sydney Mus Contemp Art, 1988-2000 & Andy Warhol Mus, 2001; dir, Univ Sydney Power Inst Found for Art & Visual Cult, 1994-2001; ed bd, Univ Sydney Archit Theory Rev, 2005- & Coll Art Assn Art J, 2008-. *Teaching:* Power prof contemp art, Univ Sydney, 1994-2001 & vis prof archit, design & planning, currently; Andrew W Mellon prof contemp art history & theory, Univ Pitts, 2001-. *Awards:* Best Book on Mod Am Art prize, Georgia O'Keeffe Mus, 1993; Getty Scholar award, Getty Rsch Inst, 2001; Frank Jewett Mather award, Coll Art Asn, 2010. *Mem:* Sydney Mus Contemp Art (bd mem); Art Asn Australia & New Zealand (vpres, 1987-88 & 1995-97); Andy Warhol Mus (bd mem); Australian Acad Humanities (fel, 1996-, chmn, 1997-2000); Univ Sydney Asn Profs (vpres, 1999-2000, pres, 2000); Comite Int d'Histoire de l'Art (chmn Australian Nat Comt, 1999-2001, vpres, 2001-2003); Art & Language Group, New York; Nat Humanities Rsch Ctr (sr fel, 2007-2008); Int Asn Art Critics; Coll Art Asn; Asn Art Historians; Australian Mus Asn. *Publ:* Ed, Impossible Presence: Surface and Screen in the Photogenic Era, Univ Chicago Press, 2001; auth, Transformation in Australian Art, Volume 1: The 19th Century - Landscape, Colongy and Nation, Thames & Hudson, 2002; The Architecture of Aftermath, Univ Chicago Press, 2006; co-ed, Antinomies of Art and Culture: Modernity, Postmodernity, Contemporaneity, Duke Univ Press, 2008; auth, What is Contemporary Art, Univ Chicago Press, 2009. *Mailing Add:* Univ Pittsburgh Dept Art & Architecture 104 Frick Fine Arts Bldg Pittsburgh PA 15260

SMITH, TODD D
MUSEUM DIRECTOR
Study: Duke Univ, BA; Ind Univ, MA. *Pos:* with, Dayton Art Inst, Ohio, Mint Mus, Charlotte, NC; pres, Chief Exec Officer, Plains Art Mus, Fargo, Ndak; dir, Knoxville Mus of Art, Tenn, 2002-2006; dir, Gibbes Mus Art, 2006-2008. *Mailing Add:* Knoxville Mus Art 1050 World's Park Fair Park Knoxville TN 37916-1653

SMITH, TREVOR
CURATOR
Study: Univ BC. Grad. *Collection Arranged:* Andrea Zittel: Critical Space, New Mus Contemp Art, New York, 2003; Wrestle, Hessel Mus Art, Ctr Curatorial Studies, Bard Coll, Annandale-on-Hudson, NY, 2006, Martin Creed: Feelings, 2007. *Pos:* With Biennale of Sydney, formerly; cur contemp art, Art Gallery of Western Australia, formerly; sr cur, New Mus Contemp Art, New York, 2003-06; cur-in-residence, Ctr Curatorial Studies, Bard Coll, Annandale-on-Hudson, NY, 2006-08; cur contemp art, Peabody-Essex Mus, Salem, Mass, 2008-. *Mailing Add:* Peabody Essex Mus East India Sq Salem MA 01970-3783

SMITH-STEWART, AMY
GALLERY DIRECTOR, CURATOR
Pos: Cur, PS 1 Contemp Art Ctr/Mus Mod Art, Long Island City, NY, 2002-05; cur advisor, Mary Boone Gallery, New York, 2006; founder, Smith-Stewart Gallery, New York, 2007-; guest cur, Peter Norton Collection, Los Angeles, 2007-08. *Teaching:* Mem MFA prog faculty, Sch Visual Arts, New York, currently

SMITH-THEOBALD, SHARON A
CONSULTANT
b New Jersey, Feb 12, 1942. *Study:* State Coll NJ, BA; Hofstra Univ, MA. *Pos:* Dir, Bridgton Art Gallery, 69-75; exec dir, Greater Lafayette Mus Art, 78-89; bd mem, Ind State Coun, 82-92; pres, Theobald Co, West Lafayette, Ind, 92- & Appraisal Asn Int, 92-; ed, Am Soc Appraisers Quart; sr appraiser, fine art specialist. *Teaching:* Lectr commun, Wilfrid Laurier Univ Can, 75-77; instr art appreciation, Greater Lafayette Mus Art, 78-89. *Awards:* Estabrook Award, Hofstra Univ, 87. *Mem:* Am Asn Mus (chair, Small Mus Adminrs Comt, 87-89); Am Soc Appraisers, Ind Chap (pres, 92; state dir, 93, nat faculty mem); Contemporary Art Soc; Indianapolis Mus Art (personal property comt). *Res:* Women artists, specifically Laura Anne Fry and Alice Baber. *Publ:* Auth, Media, metaphor, manipulation, New Art Examiner, 81; Sculpture in the Space Age, 85 & Laura Anne Frye: Rookwood and Beyond, 86, Greater Lafayette Mus Art; Latin American Visions I, Am Express Found, 88; Arts Indiana, 88. *Mailing Add:* c/o Theobald Co 3746 Westlake Ct West Lafayette IN 47906-8612

SMITHER, EDWARD MURRAY
APPRAISER, CONSULTANT
b Huntsville, Tex, July 23, 1937. *Study:* Sam Houston State Univ, BS, 58; Dallas Mus Fine Arts Sch, 59. *Collection Arranged:* Collection of Tex Art, Dallas Country Club, 2012. *Pos:* Dir, Cranfill Gallery, Dallas, 70-72; owner & dir, Smither Gallery, Dallas, 72-74; co-owner, Delahunty Gallery, Dallas, 74-82; pvt dealer & consult, 83-; adv, AH Belo Corp, Estates of Otis Dozier, Jerry Bywaters, Charles Taylor Bowling, Dallas; consult, appraiser, currently. *Awards:* Legend Award, Dallas Visual Arts Ctr, 98. *Mem:* Dallas Mus Art. *Mailing Add:* 1934 Kessler Pkwy Dallas TX 75208

SMOKLER, STANLEY B
SCULPTOR, ASSEMBLAGE ARTIST
b Bronx, New York, Nov 27, 1944. *Study:* Univ Pittsburgh, studio art with Virgil Cantini, BFA, 67; Pratt Inst, with George McNeil & Calvin Albert, MFA, 75; also, study with Anthony Caro, 85. *Work:* Morgan Trust, NY; Minskoff Realty, 88; NY Sports Clubs. *Comn:* Steel sculpture (abstract), comn by Nitkin Alkalay-Robbins, NY, 82; steel sculpture abstractions, Edelman Pub Relations, 84, Patterson-Schwartz, Wilmington, Del, Krapf Assoc, Newark, NJ; wall-relief sculpture (steel), Tanenbaum-Haber Co, NY, 85; Dansko Manfacturing, Pa; Del Horticulture, Wilmington. *Exhib:* Sculpture Exhib, Stroud Water, PA, 79, Salmagundi Club, NY, 81, Tenn Tech Univ, 98, Albright Col, VA, 2000, Blue Streak, DC, 2001, West Chester Univ, PA, 2001, Mira Mar Gallery, Fla, 2001, Bloomsbury Univ, PA, 2002, Klein

Gallery, PA, 2002, Kim Foster Lines, NY, 2002, Dartmouth Col, Hanover, NH, 2003; Terminal Art Show, Brooklyn, NY, 83; In the Courtyard, PS 1, Long Island, NY, 83; Objects, Paulo Salvador, NY, 85; New Art in NY, Parsons Sch Design, NY, 85; Biennial, Everson Mus, Syracuse, NY, 85; Abstractions, Hudson Highland Mus, Cornwall, NY, 86; Case de Picos, Segovia, Spain, 86; one-person shows, Allegheny Col, 88 & Ledis Flam, NY, 89; Three Rivers Arts Festival, Pittsburgh, Pa; Bill Bace Gallery, NY, 91; Biennial, Delaware Art Mus, Wilmington, 93; one person exhib, Kim Foster Gallery, NY, 95. *Pos:* Artist-in-residence, Art Park, Nat Heritage Trust, Lewiston, NY, 85; guest lectr contemp art, IBM, NY, 85; fel, Triangle Artists, Pinc Plains, NY, 86. *Teaching:* Guest lectr mod art, NY Univ, 84 & other locations, 93-95; prof sculpture, Urban Ctr for the Performing Arts, 93-94; prof art, fundamentals 3D design, Del Col of Art & Design, 97-. *Awards:* NY Heritage Trust Grant, 85; City of NY Grant, 86. *Bibliog:* Susan Drew (auth), Art in public places (radio interview), WBAI, 8/83; The ladies mile, NY Times, 6/86; Vivian Raynor (auth), Blue Hill art exhibit, NY Times, 93; Koran Wilkin (auth), Partisan Rev. *Mem:* Found Community Artists; Coll Art Asn Am; Int Sculpture Ctr. *Media:* Steel, Fabricated. *Dealer:* Kim Foster Gallery, NYC. *Mailing Add:* 873 Broadway No 401 New York NY 10003

SMOLAREK, WALDEMAR
PAINTER, PRINTMAKER

b Warsaw, Poland, Sept 5, 1937; Can citizen. *Study:* Warsaw Sch Art, 52; Warsaw Acad Fine Arts, 57, with Zygmunt Tom-Kiewicz & Wincenty Sliwinski. *Work:* Miami Mus Mod Art; Mus Mod Art, Stockholm; Mus Nat, Warsaw, Poland; Artist Coop, San Francisco; Selected Artist Gallery, NY. *Exhib:* Langton Gallery, London, 77; group exhibs, Harrison Galleries, Vancouver, BC, 86; Osaka Found Cult, Japan, 91; 8th Int Graphic Exhib, Catania, Italy, 92; Montserret Gallery, NY, 92; Mus Historyczne m st, Warsaw, Poland, 99; Galerie d'Art, Nice, France, 99; Sharjah Art Mus, UAE, 2000; Gallery Forma & Color, Warsaw, 2001; Gallery Prezydenta, Warsaw, 2002; Melina Sztuki Artbrbakan, Warsaw, 2003 & 2004; Gallery Konfercyjna, Warsaw, 2005. *Teaching:* Instr form & color composition, Warsaw Sch Art, 57-60; instr continuing educ, Univ BC, 72. *Awards:* Man of Year, Am Biog Inst, 96; Men of Achievement, Int Biog Ctr, Cambridge, Eng. *Media:* Oil, Watercolor; Serigraphy, Woodcut. *Publ:* North Star News, (article), 8/18/76. *Dealer:* Artbarbakan Muzeum Historycznym Rynek Starego Miast 28 Warsaw 00-272 Poland. *Mailing Add:* 311-1564 SW Marine Dr Vancouver BC V6P 6R6 Canada

SMULKA, STEVE
PAINTER

b Detroit, Mich, 1949. *Study:* Sch Visual Arts, New York, BA, 1971; Univ Mass, Amherst, MFA, 1973. *Work:* Aldrich Mus; Mobil Oil; Oppenheimer & co; Conn Bank & Trust; Gen Instrument co; and var pvt collections. *Exhib:* Brunswick Upper Sch, Greenwich, Conn, 1994; Virtuosity Art Comm Int, New York, 1995; Art Miami '96 Int Art Exposition, Miami Beach, 1996; 7th Ann Realism Invitational, van de Griff Marr Gallery, Santa Fe, 2000. *Awards:* Pollock-Krasner Found Grant, 2008. *Media:* Oil. *Mailing Add:* c/o Klaudia Marr Gallery PMB 122 518 Old Santa Fe Trl Ste 1 Santa Fe NM 87505

SMUSKIEWICZ, TED
PAINTER, EDUCATOR

b Chicago, Ill, Sept 22, 1932. *Study:* Am Acad Art, AA, 56-60. *Work:* Northern Indiana Public Service Co, Hammond, Ind. *Exhib:* Solo exhib, Freeport Art Mus, Ill, 79; Denver Rotary Club's Artists of Am, Denver, Colo, 88 & 90; Butler Inst of Am Art, 88 & 89; Salmagundi 11th Ann Exhib, NY, 88; 4th Ann Arts for the Parks Nat Competition, 90; Oil Painters Am, 1st Nat Exhibit, Chicago, Ill, 92; Am Art in Miniature, Gilcrease Mus, Tulsa, Okla, 93 & 94; Miniatures Exhibs, Albuquerque Mus, NMex, 93, 94, 96, 97, 98, 99 & 2000. *Teaching:* Instr oil & pastel painting, Am Acad Art, Chicago, 79-, chair fine art dept, 93-. *Awards:* Diamond Medal, Palette & Chisel Acad, 70 & Gold Medal, 97; Finalist, Am Artist Mag Competition, 78; 1st Place Award, Municipal Art League Chicago, 90. *Bibliog:* Article, Back of the yards artist, Chicago Back Yards J, 70; article, Midwest Art Mag, 5/87. *Mem:* Palette & Chisel Acad Fine Arts, Chicago, Ill. *Media:* Oil, Pastel. *Publ:* Auth, Creative Painting of Everyday Subjects, Watson-Guptill, 86; Oil Painting Step By Step, North Light, 92; contribr, Basic Oil Painting Techniques, North Light Books, 93; Basic Portrait Techniques, North Light Books, 94; Basic Still Life Techniques, North Light Books, 94. *Dealer:* Ottinger Gallery 670 N Wells St Chicago IL 60610. *Mailing Add:* 1356 Whitcomb Des Plaines IL 60018

SNAPP, BRIAN
EDUCATOR, ADMINISTRATOR

Study: Calif State Univ, San Francisco, BA (Music); Calif State Univ, Los Angeles, MFA. *Exhib:* Internat Forum for Ceramics-China, Macsabal Woodfire Festival-Korea, 54th Premio Faenza: Internat Ceramic Art Competition-Italy, Feats of Clay XVIII-Calif, Rocky Mountain Biennial-Colorado, and CEBIKO 2nd World Ceramic Biennale-Korea. *Pos:* Presented lectures and workshops in Italy, Korea, China, Calif, Utah and New Zealand. *Teaching:* Assoc prof ceramics, Univ Utah, currently, chair dept art & art history, 2009-. *Mem:* Nat Council on Education for the Ceramic Arts; Internat Forum for Ceramics. *Publ:* Scope: Contemporary Research Topics; Selections of Ceramic Arts from International Masters; Macsabal International Woodfire Festival 2008; Clay TImes. *Mailing Add:* Department of Art & Art History University of Utah 375 S 1530 E Rm 161 Salt Lake City UT 84112-0380

SNEED, PATRICIA M
COLLECTOR, CONSULTANT

b Spencer, Iowa, Oct 24, 1922. *Study:* Drake Univ, 40-42; Univ Cincinnati, 45-46. *Collection Arranged:* Fifty Artists for Fifty States (nat art exhib), 65-; Art in Other Media, 70. *Pos:* Founder & mem women's bd, Rockford Art Mus, currently. *Mem:* Am Fedn Arts. *Collection:* Contemporary American art. *Mailing Add:* 1311 Parkview Ave Rockford IL 61107

SNIDOW, GORDON E
PAINTER, SCULPTOR

b Paris, Mo, Sept 30, 1936. *Study:* Art Ctr Coll Design, BA. *Work:* Nat Cowboy Hall Fame, Oklahoma City; Phoenix Mus, Ariz; Gilcrease Mus, Tulsa, Okla; Mont Hist Soc, Helena; Cowboy Artists Am Mus, Kerrville, Tex. *Exhib:* Cowboy Artist Am Ann Exhib, Nat Cowboy Hall Fame & Phoenix Art Mus, 65-75 & 78; two-man show, Nat Cowboy Hall Fame, 70; Solo exhib, C M Russell Gallery, Mont Hist Soc, 73; Cowboy Art Exhib, Grande Palais, Paris France, 80; Am Western Art Exhib, Beijing, China, 81; retrospective, Gilcrease Mus, Tulsa, Okla, 81; The American Cowboy, Libr Cong, 83; Hubbard's Mus of Am West, NMex; Smithsonian, Washington, DC. *Teaching:* Instr workshop, Cowboy Artists Am Mus, Kerrville, Tex, currently. *Awards:* Silver Medal for Watercolor, Cowboy Artist of Am, 74, Mem Award, 78; Gold Medal, 75, 77-79 & 81, Best of Show, 77, 78 & 82, Colt Award, 79, Silver, 84, Western Assoc, Phoenix Art Mus; and numerous other awards. *Bibliog:* Meigs (auth), The Cowboy in American Prints, Sage Swallow, 72; Broder (auth), Bronzes of the American West, Abrams, 74; Hassrick (auth), American Painting Today, Watson-Guptill, 75. *Mem:* Cowboy Artist Am (secy-treas, 67-68, vpres, 68-69, pres, 78-79 & 84-85). *Media:* Gouache. *Publ:* Contribr, Persimmon Hill, 70; auth, Gordon Snidow, Chronicler of the Contemporary West, 73; Hanging On: Gordon Snidow Portrays the Cowboy Heritage, Northland Press. *Mailing Add:* 1011 Hull Rd Ruidoso NM 88345-7703

SNIFFEN, FRANCES
SCULPTOR, PAINTER

b Greensboro, NC. *Study:* Corcoran College of Art & Design, BFA, 1996. *Exhib:* Solo Exhibs: Biennale Int Florence, Forte DeBaso, Italy, 2003 & Gallery K, Washington, DC, 2003; Bristol Art Museum, Bristol, RI, 2003; Attleboro Museum, Attleboro, MA, 2005; Art For Life, OAS Museum, Washington, DC, 2007; The Drawing Center, New York, NY, (auction), 2007. *Teaching:* instr summer workshop, Arlington Art Ctr, 2001. *Awards:* First Place, Regional Mixed Media Competition, Arlington Art Ctr, 2001; First Place, NAWA Inc, Tabak National Foundation Award, 2002; First Place, sculpture, International Gallery, Baltimore, MD, 2004. *Mem:* Int Sculpture Ctr; Wash Sculpture Group; Nat Assoc Women Artists; Arts Club of Wash; Nat Women's Mus, Wash, DC. *Media:* All Media; Installation Sculpture. *Publ:* coauth, Coloring Shadows, Dorriance Pub, 1994

SNODGRASS-KING, JEANNE OWEN (MRS M EUGENE KING)
CONSULTANT, WRITER

b Muskogee, Okla, Sept 12, 1927. *Study:* Art Instr, Inc; Northeastern State Col; Okla Univ. *Collection Arranged:* 214 exhibs of Indian art & artifacts, Philbrook Art Ctr, 55-68; Am Indian Artists Nat Competition Ann, Philbrook Art Ctr, 55-68; Beaver-McCombs Mem Exhib; Oscar Howe Retrospective, 1979-1982; The James Bialec Collection, Heard Mus, 99. *Pos:* Asst to dir & cur Am Indian Art, Philbrook Art Ctr, 55-68; admin asst to pres, Educ Dimensions, Inc, 69-71; registr, Gilcrease Mus, 73-90; assoc, Am Indian Affairs & mem Arts & Crafts Adv Comt; juror, many nat & regional Indian Art Exhibs. *Teaching:* Lectr, American Indian painting. *Awards:* Outstanding Contrib to Indian Art Award, US Dept Interior, 67. *Mem:* Okla Mus Asn (charter secy); Tulsa Hist Soc; Am Asn Mus; Life mem Gilcrease Mus. *Publ:* Ed, American Indian Basketry, 64; auth, American Indian Painters: A Biographical Directory, Heye Found, 68; American Indian Painting, Amarillo Art Ctr, Tex, 81; contribr, Oscar Howe, A Retrospective Exhibition, 82; auth, articles, Gilcrease Mag, 73-82, Southwestern Art Mag, 82-85 & Am Indian Art Mag, 85

SNOW, AGATHE
INSTALLATION SCULPTOR

b Corsica, France, 1976. *Exhib:* Solo exhibs include James Fuentes LLC, New York, 2007, 2008; Group exhibs include Follow Me, Follow You, Reena Spaulings Fine Arts, New York, 2003; Feed the Hering..., Canada Gallery, New York, 2005; Mid-Life Crisis, Salander-O'Reilly Galleries, New York, 2006; Kate Moss Show, Foam Museum, Amsterdam, 2006 ; Invasionistas, Kling and Bang Gallery, Iceland, 2006 ; The Perfect Man, White Columns, New York, 2007 ; Group Show, 303 Gallery, New York, 2007 ; Beneath the Underdog, Gagosian Gallery, New York, 2007; Whitney Biennial, Whitney Mus Am Art, 2008. *Teaching:* Assis Prof Film/Video, Mass Coll Arts & Design

SNOW, MARYLY A
LIBRARIAN, PRINTMAKER

b Oakland, Calif; Dec 1, 1944. *Study:* Univ Calif, Berkeley, BA, 66, MLIS, 73. *Work:* Fine Arts Mus San Francisco; Achenbach Found for Graphic Arts, San Francisco; Librn, archit slide & photograph libr, Univ Calif Berkeley, 76-96. *Exhib:* Recent Acquisitions, Fine Arts Mus, San Francisco, 81; Paper: A Survey of Bay Area Printmakers, Hatley Martin Gallery, Calif, 88; Sapporo Int Print Biennial Event Hall Marui Imai, Japan, 91; Current Trends in Printmaking, Art Works, Sacramento, Calif, 92; Pulp Fictions, Austin Mus Art, Tex, 96. *Mem:* Calif Soc Printmakers Art Libr Soc (secy 95-97). *Media:* Prints & Photographs. *Res:* Image management, intellectual property, data base standards. *Interests:* Architectural History, Urbanism & design. *Publ:* Auth, Visual Depictions and the Use of MARC & coauth, Access to Diverse Collections in University Settings, Beyond the Book, G K Hall, 90; auth, Spiro at the University of California, Computer & the History of Art, 95; auth, SPIRO FAQ, Visual Resources Association Bulletin, 96; auth, Pedagogical Consequences of Photo Mechanical Reproduction in the Visual Histories from Copy Photograph to Digital Mnemonics, Visual Resources, 96. *Dealer:* Suzy Locke & Assoc 4254 Piedmont Ave Oakland CA 94611

SNOW, MICHAEL
SCULPTOR, FILMMAKER

b Toronto, Ont, Dec 10, 1929. *Study:* Ont Coll Art, Toronto; Brock Univ, Ont, LLD, 75; Nova Scotia Coll Art & Design, Halifax, 90; Univ Victoria, 97; Univ Toronto, 99; Emily Carr Inst, Vancouver, 2004; Universite de Paris I, Pantheon-Sorbonne, 2004; UQAM, 2008. *Work:* Mus Mod Art & Albright-Knox Art Gallery, NY; Art Gallery of

Ont, Toronto; Montreal Mus Fine Arts; Nat Gallery Can, Ottawa; Univ Waterloo, Ont; many other pvt Am & Can Collections. *Comn:* Flightstop, Cadillac Fairview Comn, Toronto Eaton's Ctr, 79; Hologram Gallery, Round House, Expo '86, Vancouver, BC, 86; Audience, Skydome, Toronto, Ont, 88-89; photo mural, Reflections, Can Embassy, Wash, 89; Red, Orange & Green, Confederation Life, Toronto, 92; Lightline, Trump Tower, Toronto, Ontario, Canada. *Exhib:* Biennale of Can Painting, Nat Gallery Can, 57, 61 & 65; Walker Art Ctr, Minneapolis, Minn, 58, 75 & 90; Art Gallery of Ontario, Toronto, 59, 69, 70 & 83; JB Speed Art Mus, Louisville, Ky, 62; Gallery XII, Montreal Mus Fine Arts, Que, 63; Nat Gallery of Can Painting, Mus Mod Art, Paris, France, 67; Anti-Illusion: Procedures & Materials, 69 & Re-visions: Projects & Proposals in Film & Video, 79, Whitney Mus Am Art, NY; Another Dimension, Nat Gallery Can, 77-78; solo exhibs, Isaacs Gallery, 79, 82, 84, 86, 87, 88, 89 & 91, San Francisco Art Inst, Calif, 92, Galerie Claire Burrus, Paris, France, 92-93, SL Simpson Gallery, 93 & 94, Embodied Vision, The Power Plant, Toronto, Ont, 94, Art Gallery of Toronto, 94, Light, Surface & Sound, Presentation House Gallery, Vancouver, BC, 94, Michael Snow-Photo-Centric, Phila Mus Art, 2014; Photography & Art 1984-86, Los Angeles Co Mus Art, Calif, 87; Passages de l'image, Ctr Georges Pompidou, Paris, traveling, 90-92; SL Simpson Gallery, Toronto, Ont, 92; Crisis of Abstraction, Que Mus, traveling, 93; Wavelengths, 95; Whitney Biennial: Day for Night, Whitney Mus Am Art, NY, 2006; and many others; Nat Gallery, Wash DC, lectures and film screenings, 2014. *Teaching:* Prof advan film, Yale Univ, 70; vis artist, Nova Scotia Col Art & Design, Halifax, 70 & 74 & Ont Col Art, Toronto, 73, 74 & 76; vis prof, Princeton Univ, 88, vis prof, l'Ecole Nationale de la Photographic, Arles France, 96, vis artist, le Fresnoy, Tourcoing, Fr, 97-8, vis artist, Ecole Nationale superieure des Beaux-Arts, Paris, 2001, L'ecole Nationale superieure d'Art de Bourges, Fr, 2005, MAPS, Ecole Cantonale d'Art du Valais, Sierre, Switz, 2006. *Awards:* Guggenheim Fel, 72; Order of Can, 83; Best Independent Experimental Film, Los Angeles Film Critics' Asn, 83; Visual Arts Award, Toronto, 86; Chevalier de l'ordre des arts et des lettres, France, 95; Gov General's award in Visual & Media Arts, 2000; Queen's Golden Jubilee Medal, 2002; Prix Samuel-de-Champlain, 2006; Companion, 2007; Iskowitz prize, 2011. *Bibliog:* Adele Freedman (auth), Michael Snow: Forty Years of Achievement, Can Art, Spring, 94; Susan Walker (auth), Michael Snow Drawings at SLSG, Toronto Star, 3/12/94; Pamela Young (auth), Snow Storm, Maclean's Mag, 3/21/94; Almost Cover to Cover, Black Dog Publishing, London, 2001; Michael Snow: Photo-Centric, Philadelphia Mus Art, 2014. *Mem:* Royal Can Acad Arts. *Media:* Installation. *Specialty:* Contemporary Art. *Interests:* Music. *Publ:* Auth, Cover to Cover, Nova Scotia Series, NS Coll Art & Design, Halifax, 75; High School, Impulse Ed, Isaacs Gallery, 79; illustr, diacritics: A Review of Contemporary Criticism, fall 84; Scraps for the Soldiers, 2007. *Dealer:* Jack Shainman Gallery 513 W 20th St New York NY 10011. *Mailing Add:* 176 Cottingham St Toronto ON M4V 1Z5 Canada

SNOWDEN, GILDA
PAINTER, WRITER
b Detroit, Mich, July 29, 1954. *Study:* Wayne St Univ, BFA, 77, MA, 78, MFA, 79. *Work:* Art Ctr of Battle Creek, Mich; Dayton Hudson Corp, Post/Newsweek Corp, Mich Bell Tel & Edward F Duffy Co, Detroit; Detroit Inst Arts. *Comn:* Painting/construction, Post/Newsweek, Detroit, 83. *Exhib:* Group shows incl View Point-Out of Square, 84 & Detroit Artist Update, 86, Cranbrook Acad Art Mus, West Bloomfield, Mich; Transformations, 88 & Signature Images, 90, Detroit Inst Art; Black Creativity, Mus Sci & Indust, Chicago, Ill, 88; Coast to Coast, Univ Mich Mus Art, Ann Arbor, 89; and many others. *Pos:* Dir, Detroit Repertory Theater; contribr, Detroit Focus Quarterly, Focus Gallery & New Art Examiner, currently. *Teaching:* Instr fine arts, Wayne State Univ, Detroit, 79-85; assoc prof fine arts, Ctr Creative Studies, Detroit, 81-. *Awards:* Artists Grant, Mich Coun Arts, 82, 85, 88 & 90; Arts Midwest Award, Nat Endowment Arts, 90. *Bibliog:* Edsel Reid (dir) 15 Black Artists (video), 88; Jan Vander Marck (auth), Signature Images (exhib catalog), Detroit Inst Arts, 90. *Mem:* Nat Conf Artists; founders soc Detroit Inst Arts. *Media:* Painting, Drawing. *Publ:* Contribr, City Mag, Sutton Publ, 87; Detroit Artist Market J, 90; Chicago New Art Examiner, 92. *Dealer:* Paul Holoweski 430 N Washington Royal Oak MI 48067; Sherry Washington Gallery 1274 Library Detroit MI 48226. *Mailing Add:* c/o Fine Arts Ctr Creative Studies 201 E Kirby Detroit MI 48202-4048

SNYDER, DEAN
SCULPTOR
b Philadelphia, Pa, 1953. *Study:* Kans City Art Inst, BFA, 1975; Sch Art Inst Chicago, MFA, 1976. *Exhib:* Solo exhibs, Allrich Gallery, San Francisco, 1991, Zolla/Lieberman Gallery, Chicago, 1994, Miller Block Gallery, Boston, 1997, Jennjoy Gallery, San Francisco, 1998, Instituto Cultural Peruano Norteamericano, Lima, Peru, 1999, Coll St Rose Gallery, Albany, New York, 2004, Frances Young Tang Teaching Mus and Art Gallery, Skidmore Coll, 2008; Regional Selections, Hood Mus Art, Dartmouth College, 1997; On the Ball: The Sphere in Contemporary Sculpture, DeCordova Mus and Sculpture Park, Mass, 1999; Chain Reaction: Rube Goldberg and Contemporary Art, Williams Coll Mus Art, Mass, 2001; Obsessive Patterns, David Winton Bell Gallery, Brown Univ, 2003; 179th Annual: An Invitational Exhibition of Contemporary Art, Nat Acad Design, New York, 2004; Invitational Exhibition of Painting and Sculpture, Am Acad Arts & Letts, New York, 2006. *Bibliog:* Kenneth Baker (auth), Hint of the Grisly in Snyder's Sculpture, San Francisco Chronicle, 6/18/1998; Cate McQuaid (auth), Weird Science: Visions of a Mutant Future Grow out of Hieronymus Bosch's 'Garden' in MassArt's New Show, Boston Globe, 2/27/2004; Timothy Cahill (auth), Dean Snyder: Almost Blue, Sculpture, 10/2008

SNYDER, HILLS
SCULPTOR, WRITER
b Lubbock, Tex, Dec 1, 1950. *Study:* Univ Kans, Lawrence, 69-70; Tex Tech Univ, Lubbock, 70, 72-73; Univ Tex, San Antonio, MFA, 94. *Work:* Univ Tex, El Paso; Ucross Found, Ucross, Wyo; Austin Mus Art; Mont Arts Coun, Helena; Nicolaysen Mus Art, Casper, Wyo. *Exhib:* Solo exhibs, Tyler Mus Art (with catalog), Tex, 85, Custer Co Art Ctr, Miles City, Mont, 87, Patrick Gallery, Austin, Tex, 87, Nicolaysen Art Mus, Casper, Wyo, 92, ArtPace, San Antonio, Tex, 96, Austin Mus Art, Tex, 96, Hand Not Hand, ArtPace, San Antonio, Tex, 96, Representative Material, Rose Amarillo, San Antonio, Tex, 97, Gloville, Casino Luxembourg, 98, Suede Sandbox, DiverseWorks, Houston, Tex, 98, Neil Diamond's Greatest Hits, Sala Diaz, San Antonio, Tex, 98, The Incredible Shrinking Man, The Project Room, San Antonio, Tex, 99, Mercury Poisoning, Finesilver, San Antonio, Tex, 2000, The Wind Cries Mary, Project Space, Angstrom Gallery, Dallas, Tex, 2000, Tea For One, Three Walls, San Antonio, Tex, 2000, Jack, James Gallery, Houston, Tex, 2000. *Pos:* dir, Sala Diaz, San Antonio, Tex. *Teaching:* Artist-in-educ drawing & sculpture, Custer Co Art Ctr, Miles City, Mont, 86-87; Mont Arts Coun artist in Schs/Communities, 86-88; Lectr sculpture, Univ Tex, San Antonio, 92, 95-96. *Awards:* Fel, Art Matters Inc, 90 & 96; Fel (sculpture), Nat Endowment Arts, 95. *Bibliog:* Francis Colpitt (auth) Hills Snyder at The Austin Museum Art, Art in Am, 2/97; Michael Duncan (auth), Report from San Antonio, Artnet Mag, 8/2000; Dana Friis-Hansen (auth), Double Trouble: Mirrors/Pairs/Twins/Lovers, Blue Star Art Space, 96. *Media:* Mixed-media, Drawing. *Publ:* Auth, Predicaments: Elizabeth McGrath: Installations 94-96 (exhib catalog), Eugene Binder Gallery, Long Island City, NY, 96; Body and Site (exhib catalog), ArtPace, San Antonio, Tex, 96; Trajectory: How Am I? (exhib catalog), ArtPace, San Antonio, Tex, 96; Evidence of Play (exhib catalog), ArtPace, San Antonio, Tex, 96. *Mailing Add:* PO Box 831822 San Antonio TX 78283-1822

SNYDER, JILL
MUSEUM DIRECTOR
b Trenton, NJ, Jun 28, 1957. *Study:* Wesleyan Univ, Middletown, Conn, BA, 1979. *Pos:* Exec assoc, Guggenheim Mus, New York City, 1983-88, educ assoc, 1989-91; adj fac, NY Sch Interior Design, 1988-92, Mary Schiller Myers Sch Art, Univ Akron; staff lectr, Mus of Modern Art, New York City, 1989-94, Guggenheim Mus, 1988-92; dir, cur, Freedman Gallery, Albright Col, Reading, Pa 1993-95; dir, The Aldrich Mus of Contemp Art, Ridgefield, Conn, 1995-96; mem cur rev panel, Abington Art Ctr, Jenkintown, Pa, 1995; exec dir, Mus Contemp Art Cleveland, 1996-. *Awards:* Shelby and Leon Levy fel, 1988; Milton and Sally Avery Found fel, 1990. *Mem:* Art Table; Am Asn Mus; Coll Art Asn. *Mailing Add:* Cleveland Ctr Contemp Art 8501 Carnegie Ave Cleveland OH 44106

SNYDER, JOAN
PAINTER
b Highland Park, NJ, Apr 16, 1940. *Study:* Douglas Col, BA, 1962; Rutgers Univ, MFA, 1966. *Work:* Phillips Collection, Washington; Mus Fine Arts, Boston, Mass; Jewish Mus, NY; Mus Mod Art, NY; Whitney Mus Am Art; and others. *Exhib:* Solo exhibs, Wadsworth Atheneum, Conn, 1981, Nielsen Gallery, Boston, 1981, 1983, 1986, 1991, 1994 & 1997, Hirschl & Adler Mod, NY, 1985, 1988, 1990, 1992, 1994, 1996 & 1998, Allentown Art Mus, Pa, 1993, Rose Art Mus, Brandeis Univ, Waltham, Mass, 1994, Brooklyn Mus Art, NY, 1998, Betty Cunningham Gallery, NY, 2007, 2010; Group exhibs Whitney Ann, 1972, Whitney Biennial, 1974, 1980, Corcoran Biennial, 1975, 1987, Mus Modern Art, New York City, Ann Jaffe Gallery, Bay Harbor Island, Fla, 1991, Cynthia Mcallister Gallery, New York City, Bixler Gallery, New York City, Parrish Art Museum, Southampton, NY, Acad Arts and Letters, New York City, Tribeca 148 Gallery, New York City; Biennial exhib, Whitney Mus Am Art, NY, 1981 & Corcoran Gallery Art, 1987; Robert Miller Gallery, NY, 2001, Elena Zang Gallery, NY, 2003, Betty Cuningham Gallery, 2004. *Teaching:* Mem faculty SUNY, Stony Brook, 1967-69, Yale Univ, 1974, Univ Calif, Irvine, 1975, San Francisco Art Inst, 1976, Princeton Univ, 1975-77, Parsons, 1992, 1993 & Sch Visual Arts, NY, 1996. *Awards:* Nat Endowment Arts Grant, 1974; John Simon Guggenheim Fel, 1983; MacArthur Fellow, John D & Catherine T MacArthur Found, 2007. *Bibliog:* Donald Kuspit (auth), Joan Snyder at Hirschl & Adler Modern, Artforum, summer 94; Roberta Smith (auth), Building on the bare, bare bones, NY Times, 94; Ted Perl (auth), Seeing & Time, The New Republic, 8/3/98; Robert M Murdock (auth), Rev, 5/1/98. *Mem:* Nat Acad (acad, 1995-). *Media:* Oil, Acrylic

SNYDER, RICHARD
PAINTER
Study: Maryland Inst, Coll Art, BFA, 1975; New York Studio Sch Drawing, Painting & Sculpture, 1978; Alliance Francais/French Inst, 1985. *Exhib:* Solo exhibs include Leonarda Di Mauro Gallery, 1985, Maryland Gallery, Baltimore, 1987, 55 Mercer Street Gallery, 1988, 1992, 1995, 1997, Thompkins Coll Ctr Gallery, Cedar Crest Coll, Allentown, PA, 1999 ; Group exhibs include Thirty New York Painters, Hobart and Smith Coll, Geneva, NY, 1982; An Exhib Paintings By Four Young Am, Alliance Français/French Inst, New York, 1983; Ann Invitational Group Show, 55 Mercer St Gallery, New York, 1983; Leonarda Di Mauro Gallery, New York, 1983; Ann Invitational Exhib Contemp Am Art, Nat Acad Mus, New York, 1987, 2008; Painters Painting, Painting Ctr, New York, 1994; Pulp Friction, Artzon Gallery, Orefield, PA, 1997; Drawings on Paper & Off, Tompkins Coll Ctr Gallery, Cedar Crest Coll, Allentown, PA 1998. *Awards:* Creative Artists Pub Service Fel, New York, 1980. *Mailing Add:* Lohin Geduld Gallery 531 W 25th St #A New York NY 10001

SNYDER, RUTH (COZEN)
SCULPTOR, PAINTER
b Montreal, Que; US citizen. *Study:* Univ Calif, Los Angeles; Otis Art Inst. *Work:* Smithsonian Inst, Washington; Frederick S Wight Gallery, Univ Calif, Los Angeles; US State Dept, US Embassy, Lisbon, Portugal; US State Dept, US Embassy, Riyadh, Saudi Arabia; Coos Art Mus, Ore; Laguna Beach Mus; Brigham Young Univ, Provo, Utah; and others. *Comn:* The Three Muses (bronze sculpture), Los Angeles Co Mus Art, Nat Mus Women Art, Washington DC; Bone Jungle Gym (stainless steel), Orthopaedic Hosp, Los Angeles; Ghetto Wall (bronze), State Capitol Grounds, Sacramento, Calif; Emergence Structural Column, Santa Monica, Calif; Angel (bronze sculpture), Mark Taper Forum, Los Angeles, Calif; Fusion Dancers, Los Angeles, Calif; Mezuzahs, Jewish Home for the Aged, Reseda, Calif; Completing the Circle, State Capital Grounds, Sacramento, Calif; Emergence, Park Main Bldg, Santa

Monica, Calif; Runner, Frederick S Wight Gallery, UCLA, Los Angeles, Calif. *Exhib:* Armand Hammer Mus, Los Angeles; Palm Springs Desert Mus, Calif; Dept of Health & Human Serv, DC; Galleria Arcadia, Paris, France; Laguna Beach Mus Art, Calif; Butler Inst Am Art, Youngtown, Ohio; Tokyo Metrop Mus, Osaka, Japan; Coos Art Mus; Nat Mus Women Art, DC; Threshold Gallery Sculpture, Bergamont Station, Santa Monica, Calif; Chicago Cult Ctr; UN Hqrs, Nwe York; Anna Bondonio Camandona Gallery, Alba, Italy. *Collection Arranged:* Light, Illusion and Reality & Three from Los Angeles, Riverside Art Ctr & Mus, Calif; Merrill Lynch Corp, Newport Beach, Calif; First Beverly Bank, Beverly Hills, Calif; Dept State, US Embassy, Riyadh, Saudi Arabia; Lisbon, Portugal; Smithsonian Instn, Washington, DC; Frederick S Wight Galleries, Univ Calif, Los Angeles; Brigham Young Univ, Provo, Utah; Betty Ford Ctr, Eisenhower Hosp, Palm Springs, Calif; Coos Art Mus, Coos Bay, Oreg; Pacific Design Ctr, Los Angeles. *Pos:* Exec bd mem, Watercolor West, Riverside, Calif, 77-80; guest cur, Riverside Art Ctr, Calif, 85; juror, San Diego Int Water Color Soc, currently. *Teaching:* Lectr, Brigham Young Univ, Provo, Utah, 83, Southern Utah State Coll, Cedar City, 84 & Golden West Coll, Orange Co, Calif, 90. *Awards:* Walter Annenberg Award, Nat Watercolor Soc, 78; Scottsdale Ctr Arts Juror's Award; Sculpture & Watercolor Award, San Bernardino Mus Art; and others. *Bibliog:* Art in America, 9/84; Nancy Stapen (auth), Boston Globe, 7/93; Peter Frank (art critic), Ruth Snyder: Sculptor of the Human, 98. *Mem:* Nat Watercolor Soc; Artists Equity; Watercolor West; Womens Caucus Arts; Int Sculptor Soc. *Media:* Bronze; Watercolor. *Publ:* Contribr, Creative Seascape Painting, by Edward Betts, Watson-Guptill; and others. *Dealer:* Threshold Gallery Bergamot Station Santa Monica CA; Michael Himovitz Gallery Sacramento CA; Brenda Taylor Gallery New York NY; Anna Bondonio Camandona Gallery Alba Italy. *Mailing Add:* 550 Hanley Ave Los Angeles CA 90049

SOAVE, SERGIO
EDUCATOR, PRINTMAKER
Study: Univ Windsor, BFA; WVa Univ, MFA (printmaking and drawing), 1987. *Work:* Butler Mus Art, Southern Graphics Coun Achives, Centrum Frans Masereel, Royal Mus of Antwerpen. *Exhib:* Solo exhib, Carnival of Fun, Univ Del, Colorprint USA, Mesaros Galleries, Morgantown, WVa, 1995 Los Angeles Print Soc Int, Leband Art Gallery, Los Angeles, Diego Rivera Mus of Art, Guanajuato, Mexico; Exhibitions include Matrix, FSU Art Mus and Exploring Dreams, Arizona State Univ Mus. *Collection Arranged:* Works are included in collections of the Butler Mus of American Art, Royal Mus of Antwerpen, Ohio Univ, Bradley Univ, and others. *Pos:* established the Ohio State Univ Urban Arts Space. *Teaching:* Vis asst prof, WVa Univ, Morgantown, 1988-89, asst prof, 1989-95, assoc prof, 1995-2001, spl asst to dean rsch, 2000-01, chair, Div Art, 1997-2005, prof, 2001-05; prof, Ohio State Univ Dept of Art, 2005-, chair 2005-2012. *Awards:* WVa Arts and Crafts Fellowship; Artist Residency, Frans Masereel Centrum, Kasterlee, Belgium; Can Coun's Exploration Grant. *Mem:* Southern Graphics Council, pres, 1996-98; Nat Council Arts Administrators (bd dirs, 2012-)

SOBEL, DEAN
MUSEUM DIRECTOR, CURATOR
Pos: Cur, contemp art Milwaukee Art Mus; dir, chief cur, Aspen Art Mus, Colo, 2000-. *Publ:* Auth: One Hour Ahead: The Avant-Garde in Aspen, 1945-2004. *Mailing Add:* Aspen Art Mus 590 N Mill St Aspen CO 81611

SOBOL, JUDITH ELLEN
FOUNDATION DIRECTOR, CURATOR
b Washington, DC, June 1, 1946. *Study:* Univ Calif, Los Angeles, BA, 68; George Washington Univ, MA, 70. *Exhib:* Selected exhibs curaterd: Intaglio: An Appreciation, 82.; New Architecture-Maine Traditions (with catalog), Payson Gallery, 83.; Len Jenshel: Photographs, 10/83.; Guy Bourdin: Sighs & Whispers, 84.; Mainers Away, 85.; Sue Coe, Porkopolis, 90.; Fire, Air, Earth and Water, 94.; Rodin: A Magnificent Obsession, 2001.; Rodin: In His Own Words, 2004, Rodin: The Human Experience, 2014, Rodin: Portraits of a Lifetime, 2016. *Pos:* Asst cur Univ Collection, Georgetown Univ, 70-72; supvr interpretive serv, Minneapolis Inst Arts, 73-77; chair, div educ, Baltimore Mus Art, 77-78; exec dir, Don't Tear It Down, Washington, DC, 78-81; dir, Joan Whitney Payson Gallery Art, Westbrook Col, 81-91; dir Grand Rapids Art Mus, 91-95; dir Newport Art Mus, RI, 95-98; dir Ziegler Ctr, Los Angeles, Calif, 99-2001; exec dir, curator Iris & B Gerald Cantor Found, 2001-. *Teaching:* Lectr fine arts, Georgetown Univ, 70-72; instr Am art, Westbrook Col, 82-83, Elderhostel, Westbrook Col, 83-. *Mem:* Art Table; Am Asn Mus; LA Art Funders; Col Art Asn. *Res:* Contemporary art, impressionism and post-impressionism; American art and architecture, especially 1880-1920, art nouveau; Rodin sculpture. *Publ:* Auth, Gilbert Stuart Portrait, Bull, Minneapolis Inst Arts, 77; Neighborhood coalitions, Univ New Orleans, 82; Polly Brown: Drawings, Payson Gallery, 10/83; Land America Leaves Wild, Wilderness Society and Grand Rapids Art Mus, 99

SOCHYNSKY, ILONA
PAINTER, MURALIST
Study: Nat Acad Design, summer courses 63-66; RI Sch Design, BFA, 69; Yale Univ Sch Art, MFA, 72; Studied with William Bailey, Norman Ives (prominent instrs Yale). *Work:* Zimmerli Art Mus, Rutgers Univ, NB, NJ; Ukrainian Mus, New York, NY; Noyes Mus Art, Oceanville, NJ; Morris Propp Found, New York, NY; Daria Hoydysh Endowment Arts, New York, NY. *Comn:* The Fishing Pier Mural, City of Atlantic City, CRDA (Casino Reinvestment Develop Authority), SID (Special Improvement Dist), Atlantic City, NJ, 2001; Large scale mural & paintings, Bally's Atlantic City Casino, 2006-2007. *Exhib:* Bienale-Renewal, State Mus Kyiv, Ukraine, 91; Shades of Pastel, Md Pastel Soc, Baltimore, Md, 91; Journey into Abstraction & Retrospective, Atlantic Community Coll, Mays Landing, NJ, 96; Recent Acquisitions, Noyes Mus Art, Oceanville, NJ, 2003; Reflections & Permutations, Ukrainian Inst Am, New York, NY, 2003; Different Ways of Seeing, Noyes Mus Art, 2006; A Collection Revealed, Ukrainian Mus, 2008; solo exhib, Abstract Bitrigue, Noyes Mus Art, 2008. *Teaching:* Adj prof, arts & humanities, Atlantic Cape Community Coll, NJ, 93-96; Adj prof, Richard Stockton Coll NJ, 97-98. *Awards:* Merit Award Painting, Woman Artists Atlantic Co, Atlantic City Art Ctr, 2001; 2nd Prize, Miniature Art, Atlantic City Art Ctr, 2004 ; Paul Aiken Encore Award, S Jersey Cult Alliance, 2007. *Bibliog:* Sviatoslav Hordynsky (auth), Paintings of Ilona Sochynsky, Ukrainian Art Digest, 85; Penelope Bass Cope (auth), Paintings & More, Wilmington News J, Wilmington, Del, 89; Oksana Pelenska (auth), Bienale-Renewal Lviv (exhib catalogue), 91; Christina Saj (auth), A Journey into Abstraction, Creative Woman, 93; Robert Ayers (auth), Reviews: National, Art News, 2005. *Mem:* AIGA (Am Inst Graphic Arts), 1975-1985; Ukrainian Inst Am (exhib comt), 1985-; Ukrainian Mus (bd mem), 1992-1998; Atlantic City Arts Comn, 1995-; SJCA (S Jersey Cult Alliance), 1995-. *Media:* Oil, Pastel, Acrylic. *Publ:* Auth, Excerpts from a Conversation with Myself, Int Arts & Literary J, 92. *Dealer:* Zorya Fine Art 38 E Putnam Ave Greenwich CT 06830; Accent Gallery 956 Asbury Ave Ocean City NJ 08226. *Mailing Add:* PO Box 3271 Margate City NJ 08402

SOFFER, SASSON
ENVIRONMENTAL ARTIST, CONCEPTUAL ARTIST
b Baghdad, Iraq, June 1, 1925; US citizen. *Study:* Brooklyn Col, with Mark Rothko & others, 50-54. *Work:* Indianapolis Mus Fine Art; Albright-Knox Gallery, Buffalo; Rockefeller Inst, NY; Butler Inst Am Art, Youngstown, Ohio; Whitney Mus Am Art, NY. *Exhib:* Whitney Mus Am Art, NY; Solo exhibs, Betty Parsons Gallery, NY, 61-63, Corpus Christi Mus, Tex, 64, Portland Mus, Maine, 66, Montclair State Coll, NJ, 74, Battery Park, NY, 75 & 76 & Grandstreet, NY, 95-97; and others. *Pos:* Ford Found artist-in-residence, Portland Mus, 66. *Awards:* Ford Found Purchase Award, Whitney Mus Am Art, 62 & Portland Mus, Maine, 64; North Jersey Cult Coun, 74 & Nat Endowment Arts. *Bibliog:* Sasson Soffer in the City of New York, 85; Sasson Soffer, Metal Sculpture, 85; Art in Am, 96. *Media:* Stainless Steel, Glass. *Mailing Add:* 78 Grand St No 5 New York NY 10013

SOFTIC, TANJA
PAINTER, PRINTMAKER
Study: Acad Fine Arts, Univ Sarajevo, Bosnia & Herzegovina, BFA, 88; Old Dominion Univ/Norfolk State Univ, Va, MFA, 92. *Work:* Atlanta Coll Art & Design, Ga; Cornell Mus Fine Arts & Olin Libr, Rollins Col, Winter Park, Fla; Orlando City Hall & Valencia Community Col, Fla; Univ Dallas, Irving, Tex; Rutgers Archive Printmaking Studios, New Brunswick, NJ; and others. *Exhib:* Solo exhibs, Coker Coll Art Gallery, Hartsville, SC, 95, Kendall Gallery, Miami-Dade Community Col, 96, Allen R Hite Art Inst, Univ Louisville, Ky, 96, Catherine J Smith Gallery, Appalachian State Univ, Boone, NC, 97, Scuola Int Grafica Venezia, Venice, Italy, 99, Kathy Caraccio Studio Gallery, NY, 2000, Sarratt Gallery, Vanderbilt Univ, Nashville, Tenn, 2000, Miramar Gallery, Sarasota, Fla, 2001, Va Ctr Contemp Art, Virginia Beach, Va, 2001, Cervini Haas Gallery, Scottsdale, Ariz, 2001, New Harmony Gallery Contemp Art, Virginia Beach, Va, 2001 & Brad Cooper Gallery, Tampa, Fla, 2001; Ninth Nat Parkside Small Print Exhib, Parkside Gallery, Univ Wis, Kenosha, 95; Halpert Biennial, Catherine D Smith Gallery, Appalachian State Univ, NC, 95; Second Printmakers Renaissance Nat Exhib, Rolling Stone Press, Atlanta, Ga, 96; Eight States, Lamar Dodd Sch Art, Univ Ga, Athens, 96; Sapporo Int Print Bienalle, Hokkaido Mus Mod Art, Japan, 96 & 2000; Carroll Gallery, Tulane Univ, New Orleans, La, 97; 1st Northern Ireland Int Small Print Exhibition, Townhouse Gallery, Belfast, 98; You Cannot Go Home Again: Exiled Artists in the United States, Philadelphia Arts Alliance, Pa, 2000; International Print Triennial, World Award Winners Gallery, Katowice, Poland, 2000; Hyundai Art Gallery, Kwangju City, Korea, 2001; and many others. *Pos:* Printer, Kathy Caraccio Printmaking Workshop, New York, 91. *Teaching:* Asst, Old Dominion Univ, Norfolk, Va, 89-92; adj instr, Norfolk State Univ, Va, 91-92; asst prof art, Rollins Col, Winter Park, Fla, 92-98, assoc prof art, 98-2000; assoc prof art, Univ Richmond, Va, 2001-. *Awards:* Artist Scholar, Acad Arts & Scis, Bosnia & Herzegovina, 90-91; Visual Artist Grant, Southeastern Coll Art Conf, 92 & 94; Jack B Critchfield Grant Individual Fac Development, Rollins Col, 93-94; Individual Artist Fel, Fla Dept State, 96-97; Exhibition Support Grant, Open Soc Fund, 97; Residency Fel, Va Ctr Creative Arts, 98, Ucross Found, 98, McDowell Colony, 98, Pyramid Atlantic, 98, Scuola Int Grafica, 99 & Flemish Ministry Cult, 2001. *Bibliog:* Laura Stewart (auth), Tanja Softic at the Cornell Fine Arts Museum, Art Papers, 1/95; Elisa Turner (auth), Tanja Softic's Subtle Politics and Shadowy Pods, Miami Herald, 5/24/96; Lynne Allen, Phyllis McGibbon (auths), The Best of Printmaking, Rockport Publ, Inc; Mary Ann Marger (auth), Bicultural Identities, St Petersburg Times, 5/1/98; John Dorsey (auth), Collectors' at Evergreen, Baltimore Sun, 2/9/99; Deborah McLeod (auth), Tanja Softic at the Marsh Gallery, Art Papers, 2/2001. *Mailing Add:* Univ Richmond Modin Center Arts Dept Art and Art History Richmond VA 23173

SOKOL, DAVID MARTIN
ART HISTORIAN, MUSEOLOGIST
b New York, NY, Nov 3, 1942. *Study:* Hunter Col, AB, 63; Inst for Fine Arts, NY Univ, MA, 66, PhD, 70. *Pos:* Dir mus studies, Univ Ill, Chicago, 77-2006; cur, Terra Mus Am Art, 81-85; interim dir, Spertus Mus, 85-86; adj cur, Maier Mus Art, 88-90. *Teaching:* Instr art hist, Kingsborough Community Col, Brooklyn, NY, 66-68; asst prof art hist, Western Ill Univ, Macomb, 68-71; assoc prof art & archit hist, Univ Ill, Chicago, 71-82, chmn dept, 77-84 & 92-2002, prof, 82-, dir grad studies, 90-92; vis asst prof, New York Univ, 70; vis prof, Randolph-Macon Women's Col, 88-89; prof emeritus. *Awards:* Univ Scholar, New York Univ, 70; First Award for scholarship in contributions in the Arts in Ill, Ill Acad Fine Arts, 92. *Mem:* Coll Art Asn (placement comt, 77 & prof practices comt, 91-94, chair, 95-98; Am Studies Asn (nat coun, 76-78); Am Asn Univ Prof (comt treas, 75-78); Asn Historians Am Art (treas, 79-89); Am Cult Asn (gov bd mem, 95-99, vpres 2001-2003, pres 2003-2005); Art & Archit (area chmn, bd mem, 95-, sec, 99-); fel Inst Humanities (exec comt); Ill Hist Sties Adv Coun, 2008; chair, Oak Park Pub Art Comn 2009-; Oak Park Public Lib (trustee,

2011-); bd mem, Ill State Mus, 2012-. *Res:* American painting and decorative arts; relations between American and European art; history of art patronage in the US; F L Wright. *Publ:* Co-auth, Hist of Am Art, Abrams, 79; auth, Solitude, Terra Mus Am Art, 82; ed, Cambridge Monographs on Am Artists; co-auth, Am Art: American Vision, Maier Mus Art, 90; Six Prairie Artists, portfolio, State of Ill Art Gallery, 97; auth, Oak Park Illinois: Continuity and Change, Arcadia Publ, 2000; Engaging with the Present, Spertus Mus, 2004; auth, Otto Neumann, Prologue Press, 2006; The Noble Room, Frank Lloyd Wright's Unity Temple, Top Five Prss, 2008; Curt Frankenstein: Dream World and Real World, Koehline Mus Art, 2010; Oak Park: The Evolution of a Village, The History Press, 2011. *Mailing Add:* 222 N Marion St Oak Park IL 60302-1962

SOKOLOW, ISOBEL FOLB
SCULPTOR, EDUCATOR
b Brooklyn, NY. *Study:* Silvermine Coll Art, 65-68; Coll New Rochelle; Art Students League; Nat Acad Design; Educ Alliance Art Sch; Independent Study in Florence & Pietrasanta, Italy. *Work:* Westchester Community Col, Valhalla, NY, 85-88; Roosevelt High Sch, Yonkers, NY, 92-94. *Comn:* Private collections in US & Italy; Pan American Wall, Uruguay, SAm, 94. *Exhib:* Yonkers Art Asn, Hudson River Mus, Yonkers, NY, 80; solo exhibs, N Shore Sculpture Ctr, 80, Harkness House, 81, Musaui Gallery, 84, Atlanta Gallery, 88, 90, 92, 94 & 98; Sculptors Alliance, Lever House, NY 87; Am Soc Contemp Artists, Westbeth Gallery, NY, 88; Nat Asn Women Artists, Monmouth Mus, Red Bank, NJ, 88; Faustini Gallery, Florence, Italy, 2000; Bromme St Gallery, 2000; Atlantic Gallery, 2000. *Pos:* Dir, Westchester Art & Cult Asn, 80-92; co-dir fine arts in Venice, Pratt Sch Design, 85. *Teaching:* Instr art, Jewish Guild for the Blind, Home for the Aged Blind, Yonkers, NY, 74-76 & Clay & Marble Workshops, Pietrasanta, Italy, 84-86; producer & host, Art Scene through an Artists Eye (cable TV prog), 97-. *Awards:* Silver Medal, Audubon Artists; Best in Show, Am Soc Contemp Artists, 88 & 90; Tres Jolie des Arts, Nat Asn Women Artists. *Bibliog:* Enrico Moreti (critic), Il Progresso-An American Artist in Florence, 80; Malcom Preston (auth), Review, Newsday, 82; Angela Pegani (dir), Isobel Folb Sokolow (TV doc), 87; David Bourdon (critic), Art in America, Critics Diary, Sept, 92; Swiss/Italian TV, 87; State of the Art (TV series), 89; and others. *Mem:* Am Soc Contemp Artists (dir, 79-80, vpres, 94-98); NY Artists Equity (dir, 75-80, vpres, 80-84); Nat Asn Women Artists; Art Students League. *Media:* Welded Steel, Raku. *Dealer:* Atlantic Gallery 475 Broome St New York NY 10013. *Mailing Add:* 95 Lexington Ave Apt 3E New York NY 10016-8936

SOKOLOWSKI, LINDA ROBINSON
PRINTMAKER, PAINTER
b Utica, NY, May 20, 1943. *Study:* RI Sch Design, BFA (painting), 65; Univ Iowa, with Mauricio Lasansky & James Lechay, MA, 70 & MFA, 71. *Work:* State Univ NY, Potsdam; Libr Congress, Washington; Ball State Univ; Pepsico,; IBM. *Exhib:* Solo shows, Kraushaar Galleries, NY, 76, 79, 82, 86, 89, 91, 94 & 98; More than Land or Sky: Art from Appalachia, Nat Mus Am Art, Smithsonian Inst, 81; Realist Tradition in Central NY, Munson-Williams Proctor Inst; 43rd, 44th & 56th Ann Painting Exhib, Butler Inst Am Art; 154th, 161st & 165th Ann Exhib, Nat Acad Design; Artists Who Teach, Fed Reserve Bd, Washington, 87; Summer Pleasures, Kornbluth Gallery, Fairlawn, NJ, 89; The Art Show, Art Dealers Asn, NY, 89-2000; Works on Paper, Park Ave 7th Regiment Armory, 95-2000. *Teaching:* Prof Art, State Univ NY, Binghamton, 71-. *Awards:* Childe Hassam Purchase Award, Am Acad & Inst of Art & Lett, 78; Research grants, State Univ NY, Binghamton, 90. *Bibliog:* G Henry (auth), Art News (rev), 86; Wendy Beckett (auth), Contemporary Women Artists, Universe Bks, 88; John Driscoll & Arnold Skolnick (auths), The Artist and the American Landscape, Chameleon Bks. *Media:* Monotypes, Etching. *Publ:* Auth, The Original Prints and Restrikes from the Plates of Kaethe Kollwitz, Univ Iowa Press, 70. *Dealer:* Carole Pesner & Kathryn Kaplan Kraushaar Galleries 724 Fifth Ave New York NY 10028. *Mailing Add:* Binghamton Univ Art Dept Binghamton NY 13902-6000

SOKOLOWSKI, THOMAS
MUSEUM DIRECTOR
Study: Univ Chicago, BA (Art Hist), 1972; Inst Fine Arts, NY Univ, MA, 1974, PhD, 1976. *Pos:* Cur European painting & sculpture, Chrysler Mus, 1981-82, chief cur, 1982-84; dir, Grey Art Gallery & Study Ctr, NY Univ, 1984-96, Andy Warhol Mus, Pittsburgh, 1996-2011; bd dirs, Penny McCall Found, 1989-, Visual AIDS, 1990-94, MacDowell Colony, 1991-95, Artist & Homeless Collaborative, 1991-93, Dancy Alloy, Pittsburgh, 1996-, Pittsburgh AIDS Task Force, 1998-; ed bd, Art & Text, 1993-; TV arts correspondent, FX network, 1994-

SOKOV, LEONID
SCULPTOR, PAINTER
b Tver (Kalinin), USSR, Oct 11, 1941; US citizen. *Study:* Sch Art, Moscow, 56-61; Stroganov Coll Art & Design, Moscow, MFA, 69. *Work:* Metrop Mus part; Centre Gerges Pompidou, Paris; Guggenheim Mus; Pushkin Mus Fine Art, Moscow; Tretyakow Gallery, Moscow. *Comn:* 5 sculptures, comn by Pushino, 73; sculpture, Ashkhabad, Turkmenistan, 74. *Exhib:* La Biennale di Venezia la Nuova Arte Sovietica, Venezia, 77; Sots Art, New Mus contemp Art, NY, 86; Elvis & Marilyn 2 Immortal, traveling, 94-97; Art as Witness, Kwangju Beinnale Korea, 95; Russian Pavillion, 49th Venice Biennial (catalog), 2001. *Bibliog:* Margarita Tupitsyn (auth), Margins of Soviet art, Ginacarlo Politi Editore, 89; Tom Csasar (auth), Nonconformist vision, New Art Examiner, 96; Victor Tupitsyn, L'estetica della transparenza, Tema Celeste, 96; Victor and Ilva Kabakov, conversation with Leonid Sokov; Dan Cameron (auth), Comic Relief, Palace Editions. *Dealer:* Frediano Farsetti Via della repubblica Prato Italy. *Mailing Add:* 356 Broadway No 3A New York NY 10013-3927

SOLBERG, MORTEN EDWARD
PAINTER
b Cleveland, Ohio, Nov 8, 1935. *Study:* Cleveland Inst Art. *Work:* Nat Gallery Art, Washington, DC; Cleveland Mus Art; Nat Acad Design, NY; Hunt Wesson Foods, Home Savings & Loan, Calif; Leigh Yawkey Woodson Mus Art, Wausau, Wis; Dunnegan Mus, Springfield, Mo; Smithsonian; and others. *Comn:* Painting of hist fountain, Marriott Hotels, Newport Beach, Calif, 75; painting of hist settings, Irvine Co, Newport Beach, 75; collector print, Am Artist Mag, NY. *Exhib:* Nat Acad Design, NY, 66 & 76; Am Watercolor Soc, NY, 68 & 74-76; Nat Watercolor Soc, Los Angeles, 70-75; Soc Animal Artists, NY, 79-94; Birds In Art, Wausau, Wis, 87-94; and others. *Pos:* Art dir, Am Greeting Corp, Cleveland, 58-68 & Buzza Cardoza Corp, Anaheim, Calif, 68-71; pres, Calif Graphics, Design Studio, Orange, 71-73 & Graybear Publ, 92-93. *Teaching:* Instr, int workshops; art in Paris, 2005. *Awards:* San Bernardino Co Mus Award; Knickerbocker Artists, NY; Hall of Fame, US Art Mag, 93; Purchase Award, Calif Bicentennial; Master Artist, Wildlife Art Mag; Purchase Award, Nat Acad of Design; Master Artist, Soc Animal Artists; Calif Bicentennial Purchas Award; Grand Prize & Gold Medal, Arts for the Parks, 2005; Lifetime Master Mem Soc Master Impressionist, 2007; Robert Kuhn Award, Nat Mus Wildlife Art, 2009. *Bibliog:* Wildlife Art News, 5-6/87; Sporting Classic, 11-12/87 & 9-10/92; Southwest Art, 10/92; Wildlife Art, 5-6/2001, 2004, 2007, 2010; Peggy & Harold Samuels (auth), Contemp Wester Artists, 82; Exploring Color, Nita Leland, 91; Of Wings of Eagles, Col Springer, 94; Susan Rayfield (auth), More Wildlife Painting, 94; Natural Habitat, Spanierman Gallery, 98; Taverns of the Wild, 99; Joan Muyskens Pursley (auth), Wildlife Art, 60 Contemp Masters & Their Work, 2001; Denny Rogers (auth), Illustrated Owl, 2008. *Mem:* Soc Animal Artists, NY; Nat Watercolor Soc (ad hoc bd mem, 74, first vpres, 75); Knickerbocker Artists; Am Watercolor Soc; Artist Guild of The San Diego Mus of Art; Board Member Susan K Black Found. *Media:* All Media. *Collection:* Smithsonian; Cleveland Mus of Art; The White House; Hunt Wesson Foods; Wildlife Art Magazine; Dunnegan Mus of Art; Bennington Ctr for the Arts; The Irving Corp Commission; American Greetings Corp

SOLEM, (ELMO) JOHN
PAINTER
b St Paul, Minn, Aug 10, 1933. *Study:* Minn Sch Art, 51-53; Wartburg Col, Waverly, Iowa, BA, 59; Univ Calif, Los Angeles, MA, 62. *Work:* Santa Barbara Mus Art, Calif; Atlantic Richfield Corp Art Collection, Los Angeles; US Embassy, Embassy Residence, Oslo, Norway; Los Angeles Printmaking Soc; Tex Tech Univ, Lubbock. *Comn:* Chapel communion serving set, CA Lutheran Univ, Thousand Oaks, 1991. *Exhib:* 14th Nat Print Exhib, Brooklyn Mus, 64; Artists-Teachers in Southern Calif, Santa Barbara Mus Art, Calif, 75; Los Angeles Bicentennial Exhib, Mus Sci & Industry, 81; Ojai Art Ctr, 93; Conejo Valley Art Mus, 94; Calif Lutheran Univ, Thousand Oaks, 2000, 2003, 2005, & 2007; Northridge Hosp, 2004. *Pos:* Fac Emer, Calif Lutheran Univ, currently. *Teaching:* Sr extension teacher art, Univ Calif, Los Angeles, 1963-80; prof painting, printmaking & drawing, Calif Lutheran Univ, Thousand Oaks, 67-95. *Awards:* Purchase Awards, 5th Ann Colorprint, USA, Tex Tech Univ, 74 & Los Angeles Printmaking Soc 2nd Nat Exhib, 74; Best of Show, Int Soc Acrylic Painters, 13th Int Exhib, 2010. *Bibliog:* Louis Newman (auth), Recent works on paper, Monogr, 78; Betts Kimball (auth), John Solem: a portrait of the artist, Westlake Mag, 79; Sandy Roberts (auth), John Solem educator/artist...who looks for the challenge of climbing to the top, Conejo Mag, 1981. *Media:* Acrylic; Transparent watercolor. *Interests:* beauty in fractal quality of nature. *Publ:* Illus, Gethsemani Poems, Vanguard Press, 1994 & Voices and Echoes, CA Lutheran Univ, 1995; Blue Galaxy Iris, Van Guard Press, 2007. *Mailing Add:* 43070 Wild Flower Ct Coarsegold CA 93614

SOLIEN, TL
PAINTER
b Fargo, NDak, 1949. *Study:* Moorhead State Univ, Minn, BA, 1973; Univ Nebr, MFA, 1977. *Work:* Whitney Mus Am Art, New York; Walker Art Ctr, Minneapolis; Minneapolis Inst Arts; High Mus Art, Atlanta; Zimmerli Art Mus, NJ. *Exhib:* Solo exhibs include Barbara Toll Fine Arts, New York, 1987, Michael Walls Gallery, New York, 1990, Fassbender Gallery, Chicago, 2000, Clough-Hanson Gallery, Rhodes Coll, Tenn, 2005, Luis Ross Gallery, New York, 2006; Group exhibs include Game of Chance, Printworks Gallery, Chicago, 1998; 15 x 15 x 30, Fassbender Gallery, Chicago, 1999; Big Bang, Rochester Art Ctr, Minn, 2000; Strange Presences, Tory Folliard Gallery, Wis, 2005; New Location, Luise Ross Gallery, New York, 2006, Fun!, 2006, Rare Birds, 2007. *Awards:* McKnight "Mid-Career" Artist Fel, Minn, 1994; Fac Research Grant, Univ Wis-Madison, 1998, 1999; Joan Mitchell Found Grant, 2007. *Dealer:* Luise Ross Gallery 511 W 25th St #307 New York NY 10001

SOLINAS, RICO
PAINTER
b Berkeley, Calif, Sept 13, 1954. *Study:* Univ Calif, Santa Barbara, BA, 77; San Francisco Art Inst, MFA, 89. *Work:* Ft Worth Mus, Tex; Di Rosa Found, Peteluma, Calif; San Francisco Mus Modern Art. *Comn:* Illustrations, Richard Misrach, Emeryville, Calif, 90. *Exhib:* Hello Again, Oakland Mus, Calif, 97; Bravo 20, Ft Worth Mus, Tex, 98; Sawscapes, John Berggruen Gallery, 96; 100 Art Museums, Ariz State Univ Art Mus, 2011; 13 Art Museums, Gallery Paule Anglim, 2013. *Pos:* Installer, San Francisco Mus Modern Art, Calif, 87-2000. *Teaching:* Instr drawing, San Francisco Art Inst, Calif, 87; instr design, De Anza Coll, Cupertino, Calif, 94; prof drawing, Diablo Valley Coll, Calif, 96-98. *Bibliog:* A Ross (auth), Bravo 20, Documents, 92; Pete Hammil (auth), Tools As Art, Harry N. Abrams, 95; Mark Van Proyen (auth), New Issues, New Issues, 99; Sam Whiting (auth), San Francisco Chronicle, 2012; Kenneth Baker (aut), San Francisco Chronicle, 2013; Mark Van Proyen (auth) Art Practical, 2013. *Media:* Oil on Metal. *Publ:* Illusr, Bravo 20, The bombing of the Am west, Johns Hopkins, 90. *Dealer:* Gallery Paule Anglim 14 Geary St San Francisco 94108. *Mailing Add:* 2730 23rd St San Francisco CA 94110

SOLOCHEK, SYLVIA See Walters, Sylvia Solochek

SOLOMON, GERALD
ART DEALER, PAINTER
b Apr 3, 1930. *Exhib:* Tyringham Gallery, Mass, 96. *Pos:* Pres-dir, Solomon & Co Fine Art, New York, currently. *Specialty:* 20th century American and European paintings, graphics, drawing and sculpture. *Mailing Add:* 372 Central Park W New York NY 10025

SOLOMON, KEN
CONCEPTUAL ARTIST
b 1971. *Study:* Univ Syracuse, Florence, Italy, 1991; Univ Wis, Madison, BFA, 1993. *Exhib:* Solo exhibs, Still Moving: Video & Drawings, Josée Beinvenu Gallery, New York, Post Party, 2008; group exhibs include The Wig Project, Galapagos Art Space, Brooklyn, NY, 2002; The Will You Draw Me? Project, Brooklyn Mus Art, 2002; Troy Story, Hosfelt Gallery, San Francisco, 2004; Gwangju Biennial, Korea, 2004; Video Box, Centro Cult Reina Sofia, Madrid, 2005, Streetwise, 2008; RI Sch Design Mus, 2005; Opening of Lewis B & Dorothy Cullman Educ & Res Bldg, Mus Mod Art, New York, 2006, Micro & Soft on Macintosh Apple, 2006. *Mailing Add:* c/o Josée Bienvenu Gallery 2nd Fl 529 W 20th St New York NY 10011

SOLOMON, RICHARD H
PUBLISHER, ART DEALER
b Boston, Mass, May 12, 1934. *Study:* Harvard Col, AB, 56; Harvard Bus Sch, MBA, 58. *Pos:* Pres, Pace Editions Inc/Pace/Masterprints, Pace Primitive & Ancient Art, NY, currently; chmn, Pace/MacGill Inc 20th Century Photog Gallery, formerly; chmn, Overseers Vis Comt, Visual & Environ Studies Dept, Harvard Coll, formerly. *Mem:* Art Dealers Asn Am (pres, currently); Primitive Art Dealers Asn Am; Int Fine Print Dealers Asn (vpres); Art Dealers Asn Am (bd dir 1990-92, pres, currently); Int Fine Print Dealers Asn (pres, formerly 1989-2001). *Specialty:* Contemporary Amer & Chinese prints, modern master prints and drawings, contemporary modern photography, African, Oceanic and Nepalese; Japanese woodcut prints. *Collection:* Contemporary art and primitive art. *Mailing Add:* c/o Pace Editions Inc 32 E 57th St New York NY 10022

SOLWAY, CARL E
DEALER
b Chicago, Ill, Jan 12, 1935. *Pos:* Dir, Carl Solway Gallery, Cincinnati. *Mem:* Art Dealers Asn Am. *Specialty:* 20th century American and European painting, sculpture and graphics; video installations; publisher of graphic works by John Cage, Buckminster Fuller, Richard Hamilton, Nancy Graves, Nam June Paik, Matt Mullican, Peter Nagy, Julia Wachtel, Vito Acconci & Peter Saul. *Mailing Add:* 424 Findlay St Cincinnati OH 45214

SOMERS, FREDERICK D(UANE)
PAINTER, INSTRUCTOR
b Omaha, Nebr, Feb 26, 1942. *Study:* Univ Omaha, BFA, 65; Univ Iowa, MA (drawing), MFA (painting). *Work:* Univ Minn Hosp, Minneapolis; Nebr Mus Art, Kearny; Mayo Clinic, Rochester, Minn; Miller Art Mus, Sturgeon Bay, Wis Leigh Yawkey Woodson Mus, Wausau, Wis. *Comn:* Wausau Insurance, Wis; Radisson Hotels, Scottsdale, Ariz & Bloomington, Minn; Mayo Clinic, Rochester, Minn; Lutheran Brotherhood, Minneapolis; Grand Hotel, Mall of Am, 94. *Exhib:* Charles H MacNider Mus, 10th Ann Area Competition, Mason City, Iowa, 75; solo shows, Light in Tangent, Smoland Mus, Vaxjo, Sweden, 84, Am Swed Inst, Minneapolis, 84, Homeland, Am Swed Inst, 88 & Hyllningsfest, Birger Sandzén Mus, Lindsborg, Kans, 93; Contemp Realism, Nat Exhib, Yuma Art Ctr & Leslie Levy Gallery, Scottsdale, 85-86; Nebraska Artists Retrospective, Nebr Mus Art, Kearny, 90; Nat Wetlands Exhib, Yonkers, NY, 92; Birds in Art, Leigh Yawkey Woodson Mus, Wausau, Wis, 97; Int Pastel Soc, Kansas City, 97. *Teaching:* Instr drawing, painting & printmaking, Carleton Col, Northfield, Minn, 70 & 73 & St Olaf Col, 71, 72, 74, 75 & 80; Watercolor painting, Mus Folkhogskola, Sweden, 89 & pastel painting, 94. *Awards:* Various Peoples & Jurors Choice Awards. *Bibliog:* Article, US Art Mag, 3/89. *Mem:* Pastel Soc Am. *Media:* Pastels, Oils. *Mailing Add:* 9775 Dennison Blvd S Northfield MN 55057

SOMERVILLE, ROMAINE STEC
ADMINISTRATOR
b Scranton, Pa, May 24, 1930. *Study:* Marymount Col, BA, 51; Columbia Univ, MA, 53; Yale Univ, 58-60. *Collection Arranged:* The Peale Collection of the Maryland Historical Soc, 75 (coauth, catalog) & Life in Maryland in the 18th Century, Bicentennial Exhib, 76, Md Hist Soc; 200 Years of the Cath Church in Am, Md Hist Soc. *Pos:* Cur art, Everhart Mus, Scranton, Pa, 54-58; cur decorative art, Baltimore Mus Art, 60-63; exec dir, Baltimore City Comn Hist & Archit Preservation, 66-72; asst dir & chief cur, Md Hist Soc, 72-78, dir, 78-84; field consult, Nat Endowment Arts, 84-86; consult cur, Bicentennial Exhib, Roman Cath Archdiocese of Baltimore, 86-90; Admis Preserv Soc, Baltimore, 93-2000; pres, Baltimore Ci8ty Hist Soc Inc, 2002-05; chair, Peale Mus Restoration Coord Comt, 2002-; design consult, Baltimore City Main St Prog, 2009-. *Teaching:* Lectr art hist, Marywood Col, Scranton, Pa, 54-58; lectr Am decorative arts, Johns Hopkins Univ evening sch, 78-82, 2005. *Awards:* Douglas Gordon Award for distinguished hist preseruation accomplishment, Baltimore Heritage Inc, 2004. *Mem:* bd mem, Baltimore City Hist Soc Inc; Decorative Arts Accessions Comt & Friends of Am Wing (pres, 2007-2009), Baltimore Mus Art; gallery comt, Maryland Hist Soc; bd mem, develop comt chair & furnishings comt, Hist Hampton Inc; bd mem & preserv planning comt Baltimore Hert Inc; bd mem, preserv advocacy comt & archit design review comt, Federal Hill & Fell's Point Baltimore City Historic Districts; ad hoc comt, review ordinance governing Baltimore Com, Hist & Archit Preserv; adv bd, Garrett-Jacobs Mansion; pres, Friends of the Peale Mus, 2009-. *Res:* Nineteenth century American architecture, decorative arts and painting. *Publ:* The Perlman Bequest, BMA Quarterly, Fall 1961; Peale Collection at MHS, 11/75 & MHS Furniture Collection, 5/76, Antiques Mag; Contribr, Maryland Heritage, Five Baltimore Institutions Celebrate the American Bicentennial, Md Hist Soc, 76. *Mailing Add:* 118 W Lafayette Ave Baltimore MD 21217

SOMMER, SUSAN
PAINTER, PRINTMAKER
b Brooklyn, NY, 1950. *Study:* Art Students League NY, 65-70; Moore Coll Art & Design, BFA, 72; Studied Mathematical Basis of the Arts by Joseph Schillinger, with Bob Bianco, 75-83, studied with Calvin J Goodman. *Work:* Univ Santa Clara, de Saisset Mus, Calif; Children's Hosp, Vanderbilt Univ; Kimmel Ctr, Philadelphia; Govt House, St Vincent, West Indies; Albuquerque Mus Art & Hist, NMex. *Exhib:* Seven from the Seventies, Levy Gallery, Philadelphia, 97; 3d Ann Nat, Ceres Gallery, NY, 99; On-Line Exhib, Nat Arts Club, NY, 2004; Art Students League, NY, 2004; Susan Sommer's Improvisations, Kimmel Ctr, Philadelphia, Pa, 2005; Plein Air Abstraction, Riverside Art Mus, Riverside, Calif, 2008; Miniature & More, Albuquerque Mus, NM, 2009; Woodstock Artists Asn & Mus, 2010; Albany Inst Hist & Art, 2010; Nature Walk, Becket Art Mus, Becket, Mass, 2011; The Natural is Personal, Walter Wickiser Gallery, NY, 2012; Blue, SPAF, Saugerties, NY, 2012; Local Color, EB's Hudson Valley Finds, Rhinebeck, NY, 2013; Gallery Artists Part X, Walter Wickiser Gallery, NY, 2013; Women Artists of the Permanent Collection: Mid-Nineteenth Century to Present Day, Riverside Art Mus, Calif, 2013; Landscape of Abstraction, Mark Gruber Gallery, New Paltz, NY, 2014. *Bibliog:* Edward Feldman (auth), Two Ariel Soloists, Manhattan Arts, 97; Peter Frank (auth), Susan Sommer's Improvisations, Gee Tee Bee, 2005; The Week, US, Rev of Revs:Art, 4/30/2010. *Mem:* Art Students League of NY; Women's Studio Workshop; Woodstock Artist Asn. *Media:* Oil, Monotype. *Publ:* auth, Susan Sommer Oils, Charcoal & Pastels, Maiden Lane Publ, 90; auth, Mustique, Maiden Lane Publ, 94; coauth, Plein Air Abstraction, Maiden Lane Publ, 2007. *Dealer:* Walter Wickiser Gallery Inc 210 Eleventh Ave Ste 303 New York NY 10001. *Mailing Add:* 71 CHerry Hill Rd Accord NY 12404

SOMMESE, LANNY BEAL
EDUCATOR, DESIGNER
b East Moline, Ill, May 14, 1943. *Study:* Univ Fla, Gainesville, BD (graphics), 65, BFA (painting), 66; Univ Ill, Urbana, MFA (graphic design), 70. *Work:* Libr Cong; Zachata Art Gallery, Warsaw, Poland; Lahti Art Mus, Finland; Colo State Collection, Ft Collins; Moravian Gallery, Brno, Czech. *Exhib:* Warsaw Poster Biennale, Poland, 74, 76, 78, 80, 84, 86 & 88; NY Art Dirs Club, 76, 82 & 86; Colo State Biennale, Ft Collins, 79, 81, 83, 85 & 87; Lahti Poster Biennale, Finland, 79, 81, 83, 85 & 87; Brno Graphic Design Biennale, Czech, 80, 82, 84, 86 & 88; Toyama Triennial of Poster, Japan, 85. *Teaching:* Instr, Univ Ill, Urbana, 70; from instr to prof & head graphic design, Pa State Univ, 70-. *Awards:* Merit Award, New York Art Dirs Club, 76, 79 & 82; Gold Medal, Univ & Coll Design Asn, 79. *Bibliog:* Gibbons & Kinser (auths), article, Graphis 202, 78; Fukuda (auth), article, Idea 176, 83; Neumeier (auth), article, Communication Arts, 5-6/83; Von Conta (auth) article, Novum Gebrauchsgraphik, 7/88; article, Design J, 4/88. *Mem:* Am Inst Graphic Arts. *Publ:* Auth, James McMullan, Graphics 213, 82; Tom Carnase, Ligature, 82; McRay Magleby, Print, 82; Design and technology, 7/83 & coauth, Design training USA, 9/83, Novum Gebrauchgraphik; auth, On Campus: Personal Motives and Publis Interest, Am Inst Graphic Arts J, Vol VII, 88; Design Resource 7/88, Mobium Corp for Design & Commun, 10/88, Novum Gebrauchsgraphic. *Mailing Add:* Dept Art Penn State Univ 207 Visual Arts Bldg University Park PA 16802

SONDAY, MILTON FRANKLIN, JR
CURATOR
b Hamburg, Pa, Dec 18, 1939. *Study:* Wyomissing Inst Fine Arts, Pa, 55-61; Carnegie-Mellon Univ, Pittsburgh, Pa, 57-61, BFA(painting & design), 61; Penland Sch Crafts, NC, summer 66; ETenn State Univ (Penland Sch), summer 67; US Dept Agr Grad Sch, Washington, DC, fall 67; The Textile Mus (seminar), 67; The New Sch, New York, 68; Ctr Int d'Etude des Textiles Anciens, Lyon, France, 69. *Exhib:* Student Exhib, Carnegie Inst of Technol, 57-61; Reading Pub Mus & Art Gallery, Pa, 63; Gallery Mod Art, Fredricksburg, Va, 63. *Pos:* Mus asst & staff artist, Textile Mus, Washington, DC, 62-65, keeper of rugs, 65-67; asst cur textiles, Cooper Union Mus, New York, 67-68; cur textiles, Cooper-Hewitt Mus Design, Smithsonian Mus, New York, 68-. *Awards:* New York Home Fashion League Art Award, 72. *Mem:* Ctr Int d'Etudes des Textiles Anciens, Lyon, France. *Publ:* Illusr, Tiahnuaco Tapestry Design, 63 & Principles of Tixtile Conservation Science, 63-64, The Textile Mus; auth, Counterchange & New Color, Handweaver and Craftsman, summer, 69; coauth, with N Kajitani, A Type of Mughal Sash, 70 & A Second Type of Mughal Sash, 71, The Textile Mus J

SONG, SUZANNE
PAINTER
b Grand Rapids, Michigan, 1974. *Study:* Clemson Univ, Clemson, SC, BFA, 1997; Md Inst Coll Art, Baltimore, Post Baccalaureate, 1998; Yale Sch Art, MFA, 2000. *Exhib:* Solo exhibs include Caren Golden Fine Art, New York, 2003, Michael Steinberg Fine Art, New York, 2007; group exhibs include Red Door Gallery, Anderson, SC, 1997; MFA Exhib, Yale Sch Art, New Haven, Conn, 2000; Reconfigure, Richard Levy Gallery, Albuquerque, NMex, 2002; Winter Auction, Dumbo Arts Ctr, Brooklyn, NY, 2005; Site92, Smack Mellon Gallery, Brooklyn, NY, 2005, Emerging Artists Exhib, 2007; Space World Ctr Gallery, Long Island, NY, 2007. *Awards:* Fine Arts Undergrad Citation Award, Clemson Univ, SC, 1997; George R Bunker Award, Yale Sch Art, New Haven, Conn, 2000; New York Found Arts Fel, 2008

SONNABEND, JOAN
ART DEALER, COLLECTOR
b Boston, Mass, July 9, 1928. *Study:* Sarah Lawrence Col, BA, 50. *Specialty:* Contemporary American and European, drawings, painting, sculpture and prints. *Mailing Add:* 72 Mt Vernon St Boston MA 02114

SONNENBERG, FRANCES
SCULPTOR
b Brooklyn, NY, 1931. *Study:* With Prof Alfred Van Loen. *Work:* Hall of Fame. *Comn:* Five ft carved acrylic sculpture, Aquarius, Fla, 75. *Exhib:* Solo exhibs, Stephan Gallery, NY, Buyways Gallery, Fla, Shelter Rock Gallery, NY, Cedar Crest Col, Pa & Adelphi Univ, NY; and others. *Teaching:* Sculpture classes in own studio, 72-. *Mem:* Nat Asn Women Artists; NY Soc Women Artists (secy, 73-74, rec secy, 74-); Metrop Painters & Sculptors (rec secy, 73-, secy, 74-); Am Soc Contemp Artists; Artist Craftsman. *Media:* Acrylic

SONNENBERG, HENDRIKA
SCULPTOR
b Toronto, Canada, 1964. *Study:* Nova Scotia Coll Art & Design, Halifax, Canada, BFA, 1987; Sch Art Inst Chicago, MFA, 1995. *Work:* Mus Mod Art, New York; Mus Contemp Art, Chicago; Art Gallery Ontario, Toronto, Canada; Ernst & Young, London. *Exhib:* Solo exhibs include Vinyl Installation, Gallerie SKOL, Montreal, Canada, 1989, Thomas Blackman Exhib Space, Chicago, 1996, Windows, Brussels, 1998, Los Angeles Contemp Exhib, 1999, White Columns, New York, 2000, Cohan & Leslie, New York, 2001, 2004, 2005, Store, London, 2005, Suburban, Chicago, 2007, Friedrich Petzel Gallery, New York, 2008; group exhibs include Glom, Randolph Street Gallery, Chicago, 1995; Behind Closed Doors, Mus Contemp Art, Chicago, 1998; Greater New York, PS 1 Contemp Art Ctr (with Mus Mod Art), 2000, Building Structures, 2002; Promises, Contemp Art Gallery, Vancouver, Canada, 2001; Back in Black, Cohan & Leslie, New York, 2003; Interstate, Socrates Sculpture Park, New York, 2006; Lath Picture Show, Friedrich Petzel Gallery, 2007; Accident Blackspot, Markus Winter Gallery, Berlin, Germany, 2008; Arena, Art Gallery Nova Scotia, Canada, 2008; Invitational Exhib Visual Arts, AAAL, 2008. *Teaching:* Yale Univ Sch Art, Art & Labor, panel discussion, individual lect, critiques, 2004; Am Univ, Washington, Artist in Resident, lect & individual critiques. *Dealer:* Friedrich Petzel Gallery 535 & 537 W 22nd St New York NY 10011

SONNIER, KEITH
SCULPTOR, VIDEO ARTIST
b Mamou, La, July 31, 1941. *Study:* Rutgers Univ, NJ, MFA, 66. *Work:* Hara Mus Contemp Art, Tokyo; Mus Mod Art & Whitney Mus, NY; Australian Nat Gallery, Canberra; Sprengel Mus, Hannover, Ger; Mus Contemp Art, Los Angeles; Moderna Museet, Stockholm, Sweden; Dr Peter Ludwig Collection, Aachen, WGer; Mus Contemp Art, Los Angeles, Calif; Mus Haus Lange, Krefeld, WGer; Caltrans, Los Angeles; Kansas City Int Airport; Munich Passage; Miami Art Mus; Mus Mod Kunst Siftung Ludwig, Vienna; Halle Sud, Geneva; PS 122, New York; Tate Modern, London; Nat Gallery of Art, Australia. *Comn:* Lichtweg (permanent indoor neon installation), City of Munich, Ger, 89; Pro Eco (permanent outdoor neon installation), City of New Orleans, 91; Lecon en Bouge, Ja'une et Bleu (permanent indoor neon installation), City of Paris, 93; DeRouge a Bleu (permanent indoor neon installation), City of Rouen, France, 94; Miami Heliotrope (permanent outdoor neon installation), City of Miami, Fla, 96. *Exhib:* Solo exhibs, Hara Mus Contemp Art, Tokyo, 84, Mus Mod Art, NY, 86, Ceatre d'Art Contemporain du Kerguehennec, Rennes, 87, Chrysler Mus, Va, 88 & Hirshhorn Mus, Nat Gallery, Washington, 89, Marlborough Gallery, New York, 99, Nue Nat Galerie, Berlin, 2002, Pace Wildenstein, New York, 2005, 2008, The Arts Club of Chicago, 2005, Leo Castelli Gallery, New York, 2007, Mary Bonne Gallery, New York, 2008, Texas Gllery, Houston, Tex, 2008; Postminimalism, Aldridge Mus, Ridgefield, Conn, 82; Gravity & Grace, The Changing Condition Sculpture 1965-75; Galerie Montemy, Paris, 86 & 89; Blum-Helman Gallery, NY, 86 & 90; Tony Shafrazi Gallery, NY, 86 & 89; Domaine de Kerguehennec, Rennes, France, 87; Keith Sonnier/Lynda Benglis, Alexandria Mus, La, 87; solo exhibs Neon Sculpture, Chrysler Mus, Norfolk, Va, 88 & Expanded file series: 1969-1989, Stadtisches Mus, Abteiber; The New Sculpture 1965-75, Whitney Mus Am Art, 90; solo retrospective traveling exhib (with catalog), 93; Mary Boone Gallery, New York, 2006, 2008; Galerie Brandstrup, Oslo, Norway, 2007; Robert Miller Gallery, 2008. *Teaching:* Instr art & art hist, Rutgers Univ, NJ, 69-72, Sch Visual Arts, NY, 72-84 & Bard Col, Rhinebeck, NY, 84-86. *Awards:* Guggenheim Fel, 74; First Prize, Tokyo Prints Biennale, 74; Nat Endowment Arts, 86. *Bibliog:* Donald Kuspit (auth), Interim Shrines: The Sculptures of Keith Sonnier (catalog), 89; Lichtweg Keith Sonnier Lightway, Stuttgart Edition, Cantz, 93. *Dealer:* Leo Castelli Gallery 420 W Broadway New York NY 10012. *Mailing Add:* 145 Chambers St New York NY 10007

SONO, MASAYUKI
ARCHITECT
b Kobe, Japan, 1971. *Study:* Univ Wash, Seattle, MArch, 96; Kobe Univ, Japan, MArch, 98. *Work:* Asia Soc and Mus renovation and addition, NY City; Univ Va Art Mus, Charlottesville; LaGuardia Internat Airport Control Tower, Queens, NY; Aspen Residence, Colo; World Trade Ctr Site Perimeter Enclosure, NY City; Ashiya Art Gallery, Hyogo, Japan; Shofu-den renovation and addition, Sullivan County, NY; Postcards: The Staten Island Sept 11th Mem, NY (Merit award, Small Project, NY Construct News, 2004. *Exhib:* over 60 exhibs. *Pos:* Architect, Voorsanger & Assocs, NY City, 1998-2003; principle architect, Masayuki Sono Architects, 2003-. *Awards:* Achievement in the Arts award, Coun on the Arts & Humanities for Staten Island, 2004. *Mailing Add:* Masayuki Sono Architects 308 Mott St Suite 3F New York NY 10012

SOPPELSA, GEORGE
PAINTER, COLLAGE ARTIST
b Youngstown, Ohio, July 16, 1939. *Study:* Ohio State Univ, BFA, 61. *Work:* Mulvane Art Mus, Topeka, Kans; Conn Collection, Conn Comn Arts, Hartford. *Exhib:* Solo exhibs, Inter Art Galerie Reich, Cologne, 77, 81, 84, 87, 90, 94, 98, 2001 & 2007, Mulvane Art Mus, Topeka, 85, John Szoke Gallery, New York, 89, Univ Conn, 90-91 & Randall Tuttle Fine Arts, Woodbury, Conn, 96; Dreamscapes-Aspects of Surreality in Conn, Mattatuck Mus, Waterbury, 88; ARCHA Soc Touring Mus Exhib, Ger, 93; Surrealist Affinities, John Slade Ely House Gallery, New Haven, Conn, 94; Investing In Dreams, Mattatuck Mus, Waterbury, Conn, 95; Landscape as Inspiration, Aldrich Mus Contemp Art, Ridgefield, Conn, 96; 76th Nat Midyear show, Butler Inst Am Art, Youngstown, Ohio, 2012; New Brit Mus Am Art, Conn, 99; Greater Hartford Jewish Community Ctr, W Hartford, Conn, 99; Art in Embassies, US Dept State, US Embassy Res, 2011-2013. *Pos:* Vis Artist, Weir Farm Nat Hist Site, 95. *Teaching:* Instr, design theory, drawing, Fortman Studios, Florence, Italy, 78-80. *Awards:* Nat Endowment Arts Fel, 87; Vt Studio Colony Fel, 88; Conn Comn on the Arts, Individual Artist Grant, 91. *Bibliog:* Christine Smith (auth), Classical Balance within the New Realist Idiom: George Soppelsa Inter Art Galerie Reich, Koln, 81; Placido Torresi (auth) George Soppelsa Inter Art Galerie Reich, Koln, 84; Leo Forte (auth), Bridges Between Two Worlds of Light, Inter Art Galerie Reich, Köln, 89; Klaus Tippmann (auth), Domhofgalerie im Aufwind, Zwickauer Zeitung, Zwickau, 7/31/93; Annette Schroeder (auth), Sprung ins Blau Kolnishe Rundschau, 9/30/94; Raymond Tubbs (auth), How to See Through a Brick, The Work of George Soppelsa, Inter Art Galerie Reich, Cologne, Ger, 2007. *Media:* Acrylic. *Dealer:* Inter Art Galerie Reich Koln Cologne Germany; Brairton Tubbs Art Agents East Hartford CT. *Mailing Add:* 135 Central Ave Hartford CT 06108

SORCE, ANTHONY JOHN
PAINTER
b Chicago, Ill, Apr 30, 1937. *Study:* Am Acad Art, dipl, 57; Univ Notre Dame, BFA, 61, MFA, 62. *Work:* Allen & co, New York; AT&T, Long Vines, Va; British Airways, New York; Davis, Polk & Wardell, London, Eng; Pepiso, Purchase, NY; Wichita Art Mus, Wichita, Kans; The Speed Art Mus, Louisville, Ky; Snite Mus Art, Notre Dame, Ind; Newark Mus, Newark, NJ; Kalamazoo Inst Art, Kalamazoo, Mich; The Maslow Collection, Wilkes-Barre, Pa, Zales Corp, Dallas, Tex, Davis, Polk & Wardwell, London, and many more. *Comn:* Sculpture, Wichita Art Mus, Kans, 70; painting, TRW, Linhurst, Ohio, 84-85; painting, Arby's Inc, Atlanta, Ga, 90. *Exhib:* Midyear Exhib, Butler Inst, Youngstown, Ohio, 62; Watercolor USA, Springfield Art Mus, Mo, 63; solo exhibs, Kalamazoo Inst Art, Mich, 66, Nazareth Coll, Rochester, NY, 68, Jewish Mus, NY, 70, Wichita Art Mus, Kans, 70, OK Harris Works Art, NY, 77, 79, 80, 82, 84 & 86, Lance Fung Gallery, NY, Joan Prats Gallery, NY & Sordoni Art Gallery, Wilkes Univ, Pa, 98, 2nd Flint Int, Flint Inst Art, Mich, 70, NY Gallery Showcase, Okla Art Ctr, Oklahoma City, 81, Roy Boyd Gallery, Chicago, 2001-2006; OK Harris Works of Art, NY, 2005 & 2009; Wilson Adams Gallery, Denver, Colo, 2005. *Teaching:* Prof art, Nazareth Coll, Kalamazoo, Mich, 62-67; Nazareth Coll, Rochester, NY, 67-68; Manhattan Community Coll, City Univ NY, 71-. *Awards:* Guggenheim Fel, 68; Fac Res Award for Painting, City Univ, NY, 73-74, 96-98, 2003-04, State Univ, NY, 74-75; Rev Anthony J Lauck Award for Fine Arts & Visual Arts, Univ Notre Dame Alumni Asn, 2007. *Bibliog:* First Contemp Art Expo Tokyo, Isetan Gallery, Shinjuku, Tokyo, 85; Anthony John Sorce, Kalamazoo Inst Art, 68; Hilton Kramer (auth), Variety marks Three Exhibs at the Jewish Mus, NY Times, 3/18/70; NY Gallery Showcase, Okla City, Okla Art Ctr, 81. *Media:* Rhoplex, Acrylic. *Publ:* John Yau (auth), Anthony Sorce's Recent Work; Stanley I Grand (auth), Progress and Innovation: The Art of Anthony Sorce. *Dealer:* OK Harris Works of Art 383 West Broadway New York NY 10012; Roy Boyd Gallery 739 N Wells St Chicago IL 60610; Wilson Adams Gallery 1307 Bannock St Denver CO 80204. *Mailing Add:* 463 W St 939B New York NY 10014

SOREFF, STEPHEN
SCULPTOR, ASSEMBLAGE ARTIST
b New York, NY, Feb 2, 1931. *Study:* Brooklyn Coll, BA, 54; Pratt Inst, BA, 60. *Work:* Mus Mod Art Libr & Whitney Mus Libr, NY; Hirshhorn Mus Libr, Washington; Nat Mus, Stockholm Sweden. *Exhib:* Projects for a New Millennium, Peabody Mus, New Haven, Conn; Artists of the Springs E Hampton, NY; Artist's Woods, E Hampton, NY; AAEH, E Hampton, NY; Arlene Bujese gallery, E Hampton, NY; Williamsburg Ctr Arts, Brooklyn, NY; Solar Gallery, East Hampton, NY; Studio Show, New York, 2010. *Pos:* Staff reviewer, Artworld, 74, 57th Street Rev, 74-75, Art Economist, 80-81; ed & publ, Avant Garde Art Rev, 80-90; sr ed, Art & Artists, 81-83. *Teaching:* Prof art & design, Long Island Univ, Brookville, NY, 70-2000. *Awards:* Res grants, Long Island Univ Res Comt, 80, 83 & 90; Residency, MacDowell Colony, Peterborough, NH, 83; Residency, Va Colony Arts, Sweet Briar, Va, 87. *Bibliog:* In the art galleries, New York Post, 64; The big thing show?, Seattle Times, 69; Clifford Pickover (auth), Mazes for the Mind, Art News, 92. *Media:* All Media. *Mailing Add:* 79 Mercer St New York NY 10012

SORELL, VICTOR ALEXANDER
HISTORIAN, ADMINISTRATOR
b Mexico City, Mex, Oct 31, 1944. *Study:* Shimer Col, BA; Univ Chicago, with Joshua C Taylor and John Rewald, MA; Univ Chicago. *Collection Arranged:* Mexposicion I (with catalog in Eng & Span), 75 & Mexposicion II: Photographic Images of the Mex Revolution by Agustin Victor Casasola, 76, A Montgomery Ward Gallery, Univ Ill, Chicago Circle; Hispanic Am Art in Chicago & Chilean Arpilleras, Univ Galleries, Chicago State Univ, 80. *Pos:* Co-ed, Abrazo (Embrace) J, 76-; prog adminr, Park Forest Art Ctr, 78 & 79; coordr, Hispanic Am Cult Enrichment Progs, Chicago State Univ, 79-80 & 83; fac fel art hist & sr prog officer, Nat Endowment Humanities, 80-83. *Teaching:* Chmn art dept, Chicago State Univ, 75-80 & 83. *Awards:* Fac Scholar, Inst Bilingual Educ, Educ Prof Develop Act, 75; Grant, Ill Humanities Coun, 76; Grants, Ill Arts & Humanities Coun, 80. *Mem:* Coll Art Asn Am; el Movimiento Artistico Chicano (chmn, 79). *Res:* Documentary investigation of modern (1900-present) Canadian, Mexican & US mural art; Chilean arpilleras and subject of human rights as reflected in visual arts. *Publ:* Auth, Barrio murals in Chicago: Painting the Hispanic-American experience on our community walls, In: Revista Chicano--Riquena, Ind Univ-Northwest, 75; co-reviewer articles in American studies sect, Am Quart, 69-73; transl, Jose David Alfaro Siqueiros (auth), Como se Pinta un Mural (How to Paint a Mural), 78; ed, Guide to Chicago Murals: Yesterday and Today, 1st ed, 78, 2nd ed, 79; auth, Hispanic American Art in Chicago (catalog), 80. *Mailing Add:* 10420 S Wood St Chicago IL 60643

SORENSEN, LEE RICHARD
LIBRARIAN, WRITER
b Milwaukee, Wis, Nov 4, 1954. *Study:* Univ Chicago, AM (art hist), 83, AM (libr sci), 85; Art Libr Fel, Univ Calif, Los Angeles, 84. *Pos:* Catalog maintenance, Ryerson Libr, Art Inst Chicago, 84-86; art & reference librn, Univ Ariz, Tucson, 86-90; art librn & bibliographer, Duke Univ, Durham, NC, 90-. *Awards:* Libr Scholar, H W Wilson Found, 84. *Mem:* Coll Art Asn; Art Libr Soc N Am (exec bd, 89 & 97-, web adminr, 98-2000). *Res:* Art history, including bio-bibliographies of art historians. *Interests:* German expressionist art, Roman studies, art historiography. *Publ:* Auth,

Art bibliographies: their history 1595-1821, Libr Quart 56, 86; Determined Donor: T E Hanley, Univ Ariz, 89; ed, Cambridge Dictionary of American Biography, Cambridge Univ, 95; auth, Bibliography of art, MacMillan Groves, 96; Dictionary of Art Historians, Duke Univ, 97-. *Mailing Add:* Lilly Libr Duke Univ PO Box 90727 Durham NC 27708-0727

SORGE, WALTER
PAINTER, PRINTMAKER
b Forestberg, Alta, Oct 25, 1931. *Study:* Univ Calif, Los Angeles, BA, 54, MA, 55; Columbia Univ, EDD, 64; also with Stanley William Hayter, Paris, 61-62 & 68. *Work:* Victoria & Albert Mus, London, Eng; J B Speed Mus, Louisville, Ky; Sheldon Swope Art Gallery, Terre Haute, Ind. *Exhib:* Solo exhib, Inst Mex NAm Relationes Cult, Mexico City, 71; Sheldon Swope Art Gallery, Terre Haute, Ind, 71, Am Embassies, Ankara, Izmir & Istanbul, Turkey, 74-75; Second Can Biennial, 57 & Canadian Watercolors, Drawings & Prints, 66, Nat Gallery Can; Smithsonian Inst Traveling Exhib, Washington, DC, 67; and others. *Pos:* Chmn dept painting, drawing & printmaking, Ky Southern Col, 64-69 & Hardin-Simmons Univ, Tex, 69-70; chmn dept, Eastern Ill Univ, Charleston, 70-75, prof art, 75-; exchange prof, Portsmouth Polytech Inst, England, 77. *Awards:* C W Jefferys Award, 26th Ann Exhib, Can Soc Graphic Art, 59; Jr League Purchase Award, Mid-States Art Exhib, Evansville Mus Arts & Sci, Ind, 67; Helen Van Aken Purchase Award, Fifth Ann Gulf Coast Exhib, Mobile Art Gallery, 70. *Media:* Watercolor, Mixed Media; Intaglio. *Mailing Add:* Eastern Ill Univ Art Dept 600 Lincoln St Charleston IL 61920-3099

SORKIN, EMILY
ART DEALER, GALLERY DIRECTOR
b New York, NY. *Study:* New York Univ, BS (art): Hunter Col, NY, MA (fine arts). *Collection Arranged:* Richard Fergen Gallery, 71; New York to Bennington: Paintings (auth, catalog), 83 & Matter & Spirit, 85, Bennington Col, Vt; Seven Painters, State Univ NY, Purchase, 83; Ontogeny: Sculpture and Painting by 20th Century Am Sculptors, NY Studio Sch, 85; Portraits and Self-Portraits, Sorkin Gallery, NY, 86. *Pos:* Dir, Robert Freidus Gallery, 76-77, John Gibson Gallery, 79-81, Sorkin Gallery, 85-90, New York & K & E Gallery, New York, 93-95; private dealer, 96; cur, Art in Public Buildings, Monroe, Fla; cur, LKMC Gallery, Key West, Fla, Gato Building Gallery, Key West, Flas; consultant art, Key West Airport; head cur, Sculpture Key West Exhib, 2012-2013. *Bibliog:* Peter Gallo (auth), rev, Rutland Herald, Vt, 10/85; Barry Schwabsky (auth), rev, Arts Mag, 6/86; Vivien Raynor (auth), rev, New York Times, 4/86. *Mem:* Fla Keys Council of the Arts (Advisory bd mem, 2003-08, bd dirs, 2003-2011); Sculpture Key West (bd dirs 2012). *Specialty:* 20th century art. *Publ:* Auth, Intro to Bill Jensen Etching Portfolio, Universal Ed, 85; Matter & spirit, Bennington Col, Vt, 85; contribr, Bill Jensen Etchings (exhib catalog), Mus Mod Art, New York, 86; auth, The sculpture of Ronald Bladen, Arts Mag, 86; Introd to Margrit Lewczuk (exhib catalog), Heland Thorden Wetterling Galleries, Stockholm, Sweden, 87

SORKIN, MICHAEL
ARCHITECT
Pos: Archit critic, Village Voice; contrib ed, Architectural Record; pres, Inst Urban Design & Terreform; architect, Michael Sorkin Studio, New York. *Teaching:* Hyde chmn, Nebr; Saarinen chmn, Mich; prof, Pa, Tex, Minn, Ill, Harvard & Cooper Union; Gensler chmn, Cornell Univ; Davenport & Bishop chmn, Yale Univ; prof, dir Inst Urbanism, Acad Fine Arts, Vienna, 1993-2000; distinguished prof archit, dir Grad Prog Urban Design, City Coll NY. *Awards:* Archit award, Am Acad Arts & Letts, 2010. *Publ:* Auth, Variations on a Theme Park, Exquisite Corpse, Giving Ground, Wiggle, Local Code, Some Assembly Required, The Next Jerusalem, After the World Trade Center, Starting from Zero, Against the Wall & Indefensible Space. *Mailing Add:* Michael Sorkin Studio 180 Varick St Ste 1220 New York NY 10014

SORMAN, STEVEN
PAINTER, PRINTMAKER
b Minneapolis, Minn, June 14, 1948. *Study:* Univ Minn, BFA, 71. *Work:* Mus Mod Art, Whitney Mus Am Art, NY; Art Inst Chicago; Princeton Univ Art Mus; Walker Art Ctr, Minn; and others. *Comn:* Springhill Found, Minn; Prudential Insurance; IBM; Honeywell; Hyatt Regency. *Exhib:* Printmakers Midwest Invitational, Walker Art Ctr, Minn, 73; Corcoran Biennial, Corcoran Gallery Art, Washington, DC, 75; Paper as Medium, Smithsonian Inst, Washington, DC, 78; Painting and Sculpture Today, Indianapolis Mus Art, Ind, 78; 21st Nat Print Exhib, Brooklyn Mus, NY, 78; Artist and Printer, Walker Art Ctr, Minn, 80; Bienal Americana de Artes Graficas, Museo de Arte Moderno La Tertulia, Colombia, 81; 24th Nat Print Exhib, Brooklyn Mus, 86; First Impressions, Walker Art Ctr, 89; The 1980's: Prints from the Collection of Joshua P Smith, Nat Gallery, 89; Contemp Illus Books, Words & Image, 67-88, Independent Curators Inc, 90; Mind & Matter: New Am Abstract, World Print Coun, 90; 42nd Ann Acad Inst Purchase Exhib, Am Acad & Inst Arts & Lett, 90; 5th Int Biennial Print Exhib, Taipei, 91; Innovation in Collaborative Printmaking, Yokohama Mus Art, 92; Contemp Classics, The Illus Book Redefined, Minn Ctr Bk Arts, 93; Int Biennial Graphic Art, Ljubijana, 93 & 99; Printmaking in Am: Collaborative Prints & Presses, Zimmerli Art Mus, 95; Beyond Print, LaSalle, SIA Coll Arts, Singapore, 96; Singular Impressions: The Monotype in Am, Nat Mus Am Art, 97; Printed Abstraction: Prints from Tyler Graphics Arch Collection, CCGA, Fukushima, Japan, 97; Contemp Arts Ctr, Cincinnati, 98; 175th Ann Exhib, Nat Acad Design, NY; many others. *Awards:* Bush Found Artist's Fel, 79; Merit Award, San Francisco Mus Mod Art, 80; Rockefeller Found, Am Ctr Artist in Residence, Paris, 82. *Bibliog:* Bernard Toale (auth), Basic Printmaking Techniques, Worcester, 92; Joanne Moser (auth), Singular Impressions, The Monotype in America, Washington, DC, 97; Marjorie Devon, Tamarind Forty Years, Albuquerque, 2000. *Mailing Add:* 2201 Rt 82 Ancram NY 12502

SOROKIN, JANET
ARTIST, PAINTER
b Hartford, Conn, Apr 2, 1932. *Study:* Simmons Col, 50-52, Univ Hartford Art Sch, with Paul Zimmerman; courses at Trinity Coll & Wesleyan Univ, Conn. *Work:* Mass Mutual Insurance Co, Springfield; Metrop Fed Bank, Nashville; Dewey Ballantine, New York; Lourde's Hosp, Padukah, Ky; Peat, Marwick & Main, New York & Danbury, Conn; Univ Conn Health Ctr, Farmington, Conn; Harvard Pilgrim Health Care, Kenmore Facility, Boston, Mass; Prosser Public Library, Bloomfield, Conn; Mt Sinai Cancer Wing, New York; more than 100 corp & pub collections. *Comn:* 8 serigraphs chosen by Cesar Pelli & Assocs for the Cleveland Clinic, Ohio; cow, Cow Parade, New York, 2000. *Exhib:* Nat Acad Design, New York, 81, 84 & 90; Solo Exhibs: Slater Mus, Norwich, Conn, 73 & 89; Univ Conn, Storrs, 99; Univ Conn Health Ctr, 99 & 2006; Passages, Essex Art Asn, Essex, Ct, 2009, Essex Art Asn, Conn, 2009, Atticus Book Store, New Haven, Conn, 2011; Group Exhibs: Nat Asn Women Artists, 83-88 & 2007 & 2008; New Brit Mus Am Art, 93, 94, 2008, 2010-2012; Nat Soc Painters in Casein & Acrylic, 83-85 & 87; West Hartford Art League, 99-2008, Conn Women Artist Annual Mem, Mem Show, 2012; Nat Asn Women Artists, NJ, 2007; Ct Acad Fine Art, Mystic, Ct, 2008-13; Farmington Valley Arts Ctr, 2009; Variations, The Gallery at Theaterworks, Hartford, Conn, 2012; Slater Mus, Norwich, Conn, 92, 93 & 94; two-person exhib, Univ Minn at Morris, Humanities Fine Arts Gallery, 92; The Conn Vision 90, Mattatuck Mus, Waterbury, Conn; Glass, Textiles, Prints, San Francisco State Univ, 92; Horizon Series, 2000 & Small Work, 2002, Atrium Gallery, St Louis, Mo; featured artist, Serendipity, 2005-2006 & 10 at 20, Twentieth Celebration 20th Gallery anniversary; Work in Mini-Masterpieces, New Britian Mus Am Art, 2010, 2011, 2012, 2013; AA7 Los Angeles, Calif, 2012; Duncaster, Bloomfield, Conn, 2012. *Pos:* Bd mem, Conn Acad Fine Art, 82-90. *Awards:* First Prize, The Slater Mem Mus Ann Exhib, 81 & 88; Binney & Smith Award, 83; Janet Turner Award, Nat Asn Women Artists Ann Exhib, 85; Second Prize regional exhib, Mystic Art Asn, Conn, 2001; CT Watercolor Soc, Univ Hartford Award, 2004 & 2008; Univ Hartford award, Wintonbury Art League; Conn Watercolor Soc award, 2008; and over 58 other awards; Atrium Gallery, Los Angeles, Calif, 2012. *Mem:* Conn Watercolor Soc; Conn Women Artists; Conn Acad Fine Arts; Nat Asn Women Artists; Essex Art Asn. *Media:* Mixed Media, Serigraph, Acrylic. *Publ:* Illusr, The Other Side II (poster), Modern Art Ed, 85; poster, In: Room Design, House Beautiful, 6/85; Contemp Graphic Artists, Gale Res Co, New York, 88; greeting card, Glaucoma Res Found; Cover Artist, Hartford, 2008. *Dealer:* Atrium Gallery St Louis MO. *Mailing Add:* 101 Mohawk Dr West Hartford CT 06117

SOROKIN, MAXINE ANN
PAINTER, EDUCATOR
b Brooklyn, NY, Dec 15, 1948. *Study:* Kingsborough Community Coll, AA, 67; Brooklyn Coll, with Philip Pearlstein, Jimmy Ernst, Robert Wolff & Samuel Gelber, BA (cum laude), 70, MFA, 72. *Work:* Greeting Cards, Fuller Craft Mus Gift Shop, Mass. *Comn:* Window & portal paintings, Congregation of Kehillath Jacobs Synagogue, Newton, Mass, 73; paintings, Solomon Schechter Day Sch, Newton, Mass. *Exhib:* Invitational, Newton City Hall, Mass, 73-76; Meetinghouse Gallery, Boston, 73; Boston Visual Artists Union, 74 & 75; two-person exhibs, Goethe Inst, Boston, 80, Jewish Community Ctr Southern NJ, Cherry Hill, 80, Young Adult Ctr, Boston, 84 & Warner House Gallery, Univ Cincinnati, 86; 30 yr retrospective, Perkins Gallery, Stoughton, Mass, 95; group exhibs, Wells Pub Libr, Maine, 2004, Shore Gallery, Ogunquit, Maine, 2006-2012; Arnold Arboretum Gallery, Harvard Univ, May, 2008; 2 person show, Weston, Ma, 2014; Two Person Show, Wells Public Library, 2014. *Collection Arranged:* Hillel Collection, Univ Cincinnati. *Pos:* owner, 2Artistsandson. *Teaching:* Fel & grad asst painting, Brooklyn Coll, 71-72; lectr art, Univ Mass, Boston, 72-73; assoc prof, Art Inst of Boston, 87-; art specialist, Schecter Day Sch, 90-2003, Harvard Hillel Children's Sch, 90 & The Rashi Sch, 91-95; prog supv, Grad Sch Dept of Creative Arts in Learning, Lesley Univ; adj fac, grad sch, Lesley Univ, 2003-2007; designer & facilitator, Two Artists Workshop Program; after sch art instr, Needham Public Sch, 2005-. *Awards:* Eisler Award Painting Excellence, City Univ New York, 70. *Bibliog:* Lisa Taylor (producer), Woman 76, WBZ Television, 76; Jewish Perspective TV program on 2 artists, 2009, 2011. *Mem:* Boston Visual Artists Union; West Roxbury Artists Asn (vpres, 77-78); West Roxbury Hist Soc; Victorian Soc; Pomegranate Guild Judaic Needlework, (pres, 2007-). *Media:* Oil, Pen & Ink; Postal Stamp Collage. *Specialty:* Fine arts. *Interests:* antiques; needlework. *Collection:* USA; European. *Publ:* Auth, Harvard Hillel Children's Sch Curric, Cambridge, Mass, 90-91; cover illusr, Learning Disabilities, Houghton Mifflin Inc, 93; illusr, Burning Beds and Mermaids, Prentice-Hall, 93; It All Started in Kindergarten, Prentice-Hall, 93. *Dealer:* Shore Gallery Ogunquit ME. *Mailing Add:* 61 Perham St West Roxbury MA 02132

SOTH, ALEC
PHOTOGRAPHER
Study: Sarah Lawrence Col, NY, BA. *Work:* San Francisco Mus Modern Art; Los Angeles Co Mus Art; Mus Fine Arts, Houston; Walker Art Ctr, Minneapolis; Minneapolis Inst Arts; Odgen Mus Southern Art, New Orleans; Carleton Coll, Minn; NDak Mus Art. *Exhib:* Solo exhibs, The Middle Night, Minneapolis Photogr's Gallery, 93, Art at the Bar, Icebox Gallery, Minneapolis, 95-96, Minn Ctr Photog, 98, Portraits (From Here to There), Central Lakes Coll Gallery, 2001, Sleeping By the Miss, Weitman Gallery of Photog, Wash Univ, St Louis, Mo, 2003; group exhibs, at Campus as Place, Photog Carleton, Carleton Coll Art Gallery, Minn, 2002, Dog Days, Gallery T, Minneapolis, 2003, Summer Life, Alice Austen House Mus, Staten Island, NY, 2003, Picturing Bill - Portraits of William Eggleston, John Stinson Fine Arts, New Orleans, 2003, Sao Paulo Biennial, Sao Paulo, Brazil, 2004, Whitney Biennial, Whitney Mus Am Art, 2004. *Awards:* McKnight Photog Fel, 99 & 2004; Jerome Travel & Study Grant, 2001; Recipient Santa Fe Prize Photog, 2003. *Publ:* auth: (book) Sleeping by the Miss, 2004. *Mailing Add:* Alec Soth Photography 856 Raymond Ave Unit D Saint Paul MN 55114

SOTTUNG, GEORGE (K)
PAINTER, SCULPTOR
b Chicago, Ill. *Study:* Art Inst Chicago, grad; DePaul Univ; Brooklyn Mus Art, post grad study: apprentice to Haddon H Sundblom. *Work:* Bethesda Naval Hosp Rotunda, Washington; Princeton Univ, NJ; US Naval War Col, Newport, RI; US Military Acad, West Point; US Air Force Acad, Colorado Springs, 90; and others. *Comn:* First Atlantic Crossing, 75, Capt Healy, 78 & Invasion of Normandy, 79-80, US Govt; US Military History oil paintings series, United Technologies, 84-85; Hist Portrait, Lt Elmer Stone, 89; many portrait comns for pvt individuals and corps. *Exhib:* Grumbacher Exhib; Allied Artists Am Exhib, Nat Acad Galleries, NY, 75 & Am Watercolor Soc Exhib, ann; Am Painters in Paris Exhib, Palais des Cong, France, 75 & 76; Art Inst Chicago; Smithsonian Inst; Fogg Mus; Nat Acad Design, 167th Ann Exhib, 92. *Pos:* Illusr, Chicago Tribune Co, 54-62, Charles E Cooper Studios, New York, 62-64; freelance artist, painter & sculptor (style & technique, realism and abstraction), 64-. *Awards:* Art Students League Nat Sculpture Soc Award, New York, 83; Conn Watercolor Soc Award, 90; Seley Gold Medal & Abe Sharp Awards, Salmagundi Club NY; and others. *Bibliog:* US Navy Artists (film), US Govt, 74; Ellen Anderson (auth), Meet George Sottung, North Light/Fletcher Art Serv, 76; Creative Watercolor, 95 & Best of Watercolor, 97, Rockport Publ. *Mem:* Salmagundi Club; Am Watercolor Soc; Soc Illusr; Chicago Press Club; Conn Watercolor Soc. *Media:* All Media

SOUGSTAD, MIKE
GRAPHIC ARTIST, EDUCATOR
b Madison, SDak, June 18, 1939. *Study:* Dakota Wesleyan Univ, Mitchell, SDak, BA, 61; Univ Wyo, MFA, 85. *Work:* Pioneer Mus, Wyo State Fairgrounds, Douglas, Wyo; Univ Wyo Art Mus, Laramie; Friends of the Middle Border Mus & Dakota Wesleyan Univ Collection, Mitchell, SDak. *Comn:* Old West Cattle Trails (murals), High Plains Heritage Ctr, Spearfish, SDak; educational murals (3), Hopkins Elementary Sch, Littleton, Colo; History of the Region (mural), The West in Miniature, Spearfish, SDak; Fulton Area History (mural), Fulton State Bank, Mitchell, SDak; murals, The Country Store, Robb's, Inc, Belle Fourche, SDak; regional historic murals & paintings, Mid Border Mus, Mitchell SD. *Exhib:* Rushmore Insurance Prof Artist Invitational Art Show, Rapid City, SDak, 84-89; Railroads in the West, Oscar Howe Art Ctr, Mitchell, SDak, 87; Town Hall Art Ctr, Littleton, Colo, 88; Mus of Pioneer Life, Douglas, Wyo, 89; Dakota Prix, High Plains Heritage Ctr, Spearfish, SDak, 90-91; Douglas Invitational Art Show, Wyo, 91-94; The West in Miniature, Spearfish, SDak, 92-99; Fulton Art Show, 98-; Heartdreams & Legends, Int Tour of Lakota Sioux & Australian Aboriginal Art, 2000-03; Ctr Western Studies Juried Show, Sioux Falls, SDak, 2003. *Pos:* Freelance artist & illusr, 57-; ed, Dakota West (mag), SDak Cowboy & Western Heritage Hall of Fame, 75; mgr, Dakota Western Art Gallery, Lead, SDak, formerly; founder & dir, Dakota Inst, Spearfish, SDak, 91-98, Fulton, SDak, 98-; cofounder & dir, The West in Miniature, Spearfish, SDak, 92-99; curator art, Middle Border Mus, Mitchell, 2001-. *Teaching:* Vis lectr art, Univ Wyo, Laramie, 84-86; dept head & prof graphic design & illus, Arapahoe Community Col, Littleton, Colo, 87-91; adj fac, Metrop State Univ, Denver, Colo, 92, Black Hills State Univ, Spearfish, SDak, 94-, Dakota Wesleyan Univ, Mitchel, SDak, 2000-; instr graphic design, Platt Col, Aurora, Colo, 92-93; dir & instr art, Dakota Inst, Spearfish, SDak, 93--98, Dakota, Fulton, SD, 98- & Mobridge, SD, 2000-. *Awards:* Juried Award, Coors Corp Show, Adolf Coors Corp, 85, Oscar Howe Art Ctr, Mitchell, SD, 98, 2000; Purchase Award, Wyo State Fair, State of Wyo, 84. *Bibliog:* Ruth Brennan & Jan Nanman (auths), Sougstad's art mixes railroads with paint, Rapid City J, 1/27/84; Susan Lanneborg, Artist puts small-town life to canvas, Mitchell Daily Repub, 5/8/98; Jerry Wilson (auth), Fulton Artists, SDak Mag, Apr-May/2000. *Media:* Acrylics, Pencil. *Publ:* Navy UDT Handbook, US Navy, 66; Buffalo, 73-74; Old West Trail Vacation Guide, Old West Trail Found, 81-86, Visitor Mag, 83-84 & 96-97; Heart Dreams and Legends, 2000; History & Art of the Middle Border, 2002

SOUSA, JOHN PHILIP
PHOTOGRAPHER, PAINTER
b Detroit, Mich, 1960. *Study:* Bradley Univ, BFA, 82. *Exhib:* Photographs, Findlay Univ, Ohio, 97, John Philip Sousa at ACME Art Co, Columbus, Ohio, 97; Art Bytes, Freeport Art Mus, Ill, 95; 1996 Regional Biennial, Ft Wayne Mus Art, Ind, 96; Invitational Group Exhib, Carnegie Arts Ctr, Kans, 96; Members Show, Dayton Visual Arts Ctr, Dayton, Ohio, 97; Flirting at a Distance: New Abstraction, Del Ctr Contemp Arts, Wilmington, 97; Abstraction Two to Three, Cleveland State Univ, Ohio, 99; Transcending Limits: Moving Beyond Mainstream, Tex Fine Arts Asn, Austin, 99; ArtPrize, Grand Rapids, Mich, 2010; Latest Development: Focus on Regional Photographers, Huntington Mus Art, West Va, 2000; 20th Ann Dayton Works on Paper, Rosewood Gallery, Kettering, Ohio, 2010. *Awards:* Nat Scholastic Art Merit Scholar, 78; Individual Artist Fel, Montogomery Co Regional Arts & Cult Dist, 94 & 97; Art Prize, Grand Rapids, Mich, 2010; AIA Grant Award, Summerfair Found, 2014. *Bibliog:* Steven Litt (auth), Views on culture, The Plain Dealer, 12/10/94; Robert Schroeder (auth), 1996 Regional Biennial, Art Dialog, May/June 96; Scott Dowd (dir), Radio Interview with Artist, WFPK-WFPL, 1/96; Jennifer Borders (auth), Flirting at a Distance: New Abstraction, Dela Ctr Contemp Arts, 97; Michael Ray Charles & Don Bacigalupi, (auths), Transcending Limits, Moving Beyond Mainstream & Margin, Tex Fine Arts Asn, 99-2000; Robert Rowe (auth), Latest Develop: Focus on Regional Photographers, Huntington Mus Art, West Va, 2000. *Media:* Mixed Media, Abstract Photography. *Mailing Add:* 160 Village Dr Springboro OH 45066

SOUTH, JANE
SCULPTOR
Study: Central St Martins Sch Art, London, BA; Univ NC, Greensboro, MFA (painting & sculpture). *Exhib:* Escape Velocity, Socrates Sculpture Park, Long Island City, NY, 1998; solo exhibs, Alfred Univ, NY, 2000, Mass Mus Contemp Art, 2002, Nassauischer Kunstverein, Wiesbaden, Ger, 2003, Gallerie Pfriem, Lacoste, France, 2006, Weatherspoon Art Mus, 2007, Queens Mus, Bulova Ctr, 2009; 12 Views, Drawing Ctr, New York, 2001; Works on Paper, Weatherspoon Mus, Greensboro, 2002; Working it Through, Williams Coll Mus Art, Mass, 2003; Exquisite Corpse, Bowdoin Coll Mus Art, Maine, 2004; Drawing Narrative, Coll Wooster Art Mus, Ohio, 2005; Burgeoning Geometries: Constructed Abstractions, Whitney Mus Am Art, 2006; Collectors Gallery, Albright-Knox Art Gallery, Buffalo, 2007; New Directions in Am Drawing, Knoxville Mus Art, Tenn, 2008; Cut: The Makings of Removal, Wignall Mus, Rancho Cucamonga, 2009. *Pos:* Vis artist, Williams Coll, 1999, Univ NC, Greensboro, 2000, 2003, 2007, Pratt Inst, New York, 2004, Coll New Rochelle, NY, 2004, Univ Nev, Las Vegas, 2005, Coll Wooster, Ohio, 2005, Univ Houston, Tex, 2008, RI Sch Design, 2008; artist-in-residence, Sculpture Space, Utica, NY, 1999, Savannah Coll Art Design, 2006, Santa Fe Art Inst, NMex, 2007. *Awards:* Pollock Krasner Found Grant, 2001 & 2008; Develop Grant, Williams Coll Ctr for Technol, 2002; Mass Cult Coun Grant, 2003; NY Found Arts Fel, 2007; Pollock-Krasner Found Grant, 2008; Joan Mitchell Found Grant, 2009. *Bibliog:* Edith Newhall (auth), Talent, NY Mag, 7/28/2003; Louise Roug (auth), The Arty Circuit, Los Angeles Times, 6/24/2004; Kathleen Whitney (auth), Obsessed, Sculpture Mag, Vol 25, No 3, 46-47, 4/2006; Andrea K Scott (auth), Burgeoning Geometries: Constructed Abstractions, NY Times, 1/5/2007; Barbara A MacAdam (auth), SLASH: Paper Under the Knife, ARTNews, 1/2009. *Media:* Paper. *Dealer:* Spencer Brownstone Gallery 39 Wooster St New York NY 10013

SOUTHEY, TREVOR J T
PAINTER, SCULPTOR
b Zimbabwe, Jan 12, 1940; US citizen. *Study:* Brighton Coll Art, Eng, 59; Natal Technical Col, Durban, S Africa, 60; Brigham Young Univ, Provo, Utah, BFA, 67, MA, 69. *Work:* Utah State Mus, Salt Lake City & Springville Mus Art, Utah; Rhodes Nat, Zimbabwe; Brigham Young Univ; Mormon Mus, Salt Lake City. *Comn:* Painting, Brigham Young Univ, Provo, Utah, 75; mural, Salt Lake Int Airport, 81; life size sculpture, Univ Utah Medical Ctr, Salt Lake City, 81; Painter Freeze, Univ Scranton, Pa; Monumental Bronze, Trammell Crow Corp, Atlanta, Ga & Phoenix, Ariz; Nature Sunshine Prod Inc, Provo, Utah. *Exhib:* Utah State Mus, Salt Lake City, 79 & Ill Ctr, Chicago, 79; Twenty Utah Printmakers, traveling show, Utah Arts Coun, 82; solo exhibs, Salt Lake City Art Ctr, Utah, 97; Barbican Ctr, London, 89; Calif Soc Printmakers, San Francisco, 90; Kimball Arts Ctr, Park City, Utah, 91; Waterworks Gallery, Friday Harbor, Wash, 92; Salt Lake Art Ctr, Main Gallery, Utah, 92; Vorpal Gallery, San Francisco, 92; Belcher Street Gallery, San Francisco, 93 & 94; Alumni Exhib, Brigham Young Univ, Provo, Utah, 93; The Nude, Vorpal Gallery, San Francisco, 95; Richmond Art Ctr, Calif, 96; Beyond Boundaries Print Competition, 96; and others. *Teaching:* Asst prof drawing & painting, Brigham Young Univ, Provo, 69-76. *Bibliog:* Trevor Southey/Stephen Doherty, Images and Ideas, Am Artist, 80; Steven P Sondrup (auth), Trevor Southey - the art and the man, Artists of the Rockies and the Golden West, summer 82. *Mem:* North Mountain Artists Cooperative; Alpine Community Arts (chmn, 78-); Calif Print Makers Asn. *Media:* Oil, Etchings; Bronzes. *Publ:* Illusr, The Search, 69, Doubleday; The Growing Season, Bookcraft, 75; Marriage and Divorce, Deseret Book, 76; The Sex Book, Pelton, 78; A Widening View, Bookcraft, 83; and others. *Dealer:* Lowe Galleries Atlanta GA & Santa Monica CA. *Mailing Add:* 5366 Leona St Oakland CA 94619

SOWERS, RUSSELL FREDERIC
GALLERY DIRECTOR, MUSEUM DIRECTOR
b Kauai, Hawaii, Aug 1, 1934. *Pos:* Dir, Ramsay Mus, Honolulu. *Mem:* Honolulu Acad Arts. *Specialty:* Artists of Hawaii

SOWINSKI, STANISLAUS JOSEPH
PAINTER, ICONOGRAPHER
b Milwaukee, Wis, May 7, 1927. *Study:* San Diego Sch Arts, 48-49; San Diego State Univ, BA, 52. *Hon Degrees:* Dept Defense, Intelligence Sch, 65. *Work:* Dept Defense, Pentagon; Univ Calif, La Jolla; San Diego State Univ; City Escondido, Calif. *Comn:* 25 Major icons, Sts Constantine & Helen Church, Solana Beach, Calif, 82-90 & Corpus Christi Church, Bonita, Calif, 94-98; 3 large paintings, City Escondido, Calif, 88; full length portraits, City Escondido, Calif, 88; numerous large paintings, Univ Calif, La Jolla, 89-93, 5 large corp paintings, Poway, Calif, 90; designer altar, 5 large paintings, St Marys Ch, Escondido, Calif, 99-2000; Large painting, St Stephen's church, Valley Ctr, Calif & Wisconsin Polish Ctr, Franklin, Wis, 2005; 1 large painting & 1 large mosaic design, San Rafael Church, San Diego, Calif, 2009. *Exhib:* Royal Watercolour Soc, London, 65 & 66; solo exhibs, US Embassy, Gallery, London, 67 & Escondido Hist Mus, Calif, 83, A Huney Gallery & Thackeray Gallery, San Diego, Calif, 89-92, Brandon Gallery, Fallbrook, Calif, 2000, Santa Ysabel Gallery, Santa Yshbel, Calif, 2005, Bradley Fine Art, San Diego, Calif, 2004-2005, Wisconsin Polish Ctr, Franklin, Wis, 2006; Royal Soc Brit Artists, London, 67; Royal Acad, London, 67; Sparrow Fine Art Gallery, Solana Beach, Calif, 2002; Two Masters Exhiv, Poway Ctr Arts, Poway, Calif, 2008. *Pos:* Demonr watercolor, Grumbacher Inc, New York, 76-79 & Inveresk Paper Co, Bath, Eng, 79-86. *Teaching:* Instr watercolor workshops, Calif, Ore & SDak, 71-76; watercolor painting, San Diego Art Inst, 76-77. *Awards:* Int Friendship Festival Best of Show Award, El Cajon, Calif, 2000; ir, Calif, 2001. *Bibliog:* Brand Book IV, San Diego Corral-Westerners, Calif, 76; Land of Sunlight: Contemp Paintings of San Diego Co, San Diego Flora, 2007; video, Plein Air Painters of Santa Ysabel, Calif, 2008. *Mem:* San Diego Portrait Soc; San Diego Fine Arts Guild. *Media:* Oil, Watercolor, Acrylic, Tonal Impressionist. *Dealer:* Santa Ysabel Gallery PO Box 480 Santa Ysabel CA 92070; Kuhnly Fine Art 218 E Grand #4 Escondido CA 92025; Bradley Fine Art 2168 Chatsworth Blvd Sand Diego CA 92107. *Mailing Add:* 13040 Cedilla Pl San Diego CA 92128

SPAAR, LISA RUSS
WRITER, EDUCATOR
Study: Univ Va, BA (summa cum laude), 1978, MFA, 1982. *Teaching:* prof English poetry writing, Univ Va. *Awards:* Rona Jaffe Award for Emerging Women Writers, 2000; Emily Clark Balch Award, Va Quarterly Review, 2001; Guggenheim Fellowship, 2009-10; Libr of Va Award for Poetry, 2009. *Publ:* Auth, Cellar, 1983, Blind Boy on Skates, 1987, Glass Town, poems, 1999, Acquainted With the Night: Insomnia Poems, 1999, Blue Venus: Poems, 2004, All That Mighty Heart: London Poems, 2008. *Mailing Add:* University of Virginia 219 Bryan Hall PO Box 400121 Charlottesville VA 22904-4121

SPAFFORD, MICHAEL CHARLES
EDUCATOR, PAINTER
b Palm Springs, Calif, Nov 6, 1935. *Study:* Pomona Co, BA, 59; Harvard Univ, MA (art hist), 60. *Work:* Seattle Art Mus, Wash; Galeria de Inst Mexicano-Norte Americano, Mexico City; Tacoma Art Mus, Wash; Bellevue Art Mus, Wash; Henry Art Gallery, Univ Wash, Seattle. *Comn:* Mural, Kingdome, Seattle, Wash, 79; murals, House Chambers State Capitol Bldg, Olympia, Wash, 81; mural, Seattle Opera House, 85; Centrum Print, Ft Worden, Wash, 87. *Exhib:* Solo exhibs, Utah Mus Fine Arts, 75, Am Acad & Inst Arts & Letters Awards Selection Show, NY, 80 & 83 & Seattle Art Mus, 82 & 86; Focus Seattle, San Jose Mus Art, 87; Bellevue Art Mus, Wash, 91; Cheney Cowles Mus, Spokane, Wash, 94; Holter Mus Art, Helena, Mont, 97. *Teaching:* Instr painting, Mexico City Col, 61-62; assoc prof painting-drawing, Univ Wash, 63-78, prof, 78-95, retired. *Awards:* Award in Painting, Am Acad & Inst Arts & Lett, 83; The Neddy Artist Fel, Behnke Found, Seattle, 96. *Bibliog:* Bruce Guenther (auth), 50 Northwest Artists, San Francisco Chronicle Bks, 83; Barbara Johns (auth), Modern Art from the Pacific NW in the Collection of the Seattle Art Museum, Seattle, 90; Chris Bruce (auth), The Art of Microsoft, Henry Art Gallery, Seattle, 93. *Media:* Oil on Canvas. *Dealer:* Francine Seders Gallery 6701 Greenwood Ave N Seattle WA 98103. *Mailing Add:* 2418 E Interlaken Blvd Seattle WA 98112

SPAGNOLO, KATHLEEN MARY
PRINTMAKER, ILLUSTRATOR
b London, Eng, Sept 12, 1919. *Study:* Bromley Art Sch; Royal Coll Art, London, Royal scholar & Princess of Wales scholar, 39-42; Sch Design, with E W Tristram; Am Univ, with Robert Gates & Krishna Reddy. *Work:* Dept of Interior, Washington, DC; Univ Va, Charlottesville; George Washington Univ; Libr Cong, Washington, DC. *Comn:* Rendering (bench), Index Am Design, Nat Gallery Art, Washington, DC, 69. *Exhib:* Corcoran Gallery Art, Washington, DC, 62; Silvermine Guild Artists, 63; Soc Washington Printmakers, 69-75; Solo exhib, Va Mus Fine Arts, 78; All Hallows by the Tower, London, 82. *Mem:* Soc Washington Printmakers; Washington Watercolor Asn; Washington Print Club; Artist's Equity Asn. *Media:* Graphics. *Dealer:* Gallery 4 115 S Columbus Alexandria VA 22314. *Mailing Add:* 7401 Recard Ln Alexandria VA 22307

SPANDORFER, MERLE SUE
PAINTER, PRINTMAKER
b Baltimore, Md, Sept 4, 1934. *Study:* Syracuse Univ, 52-54; Univ Md, BS, 56. *Work:* Metrop Mus Art, Mus Mod Art & Whitney Mus Am Art, NY; Libr Cong, DC; Philadelphia Mus Art; Baltimore Mus; Israel Mus; Reading Mus; Pa Acad Fine Arts. *Comn:* Fifty-four graphics, Inland Steel Corp, Alexandria, Va, 75; graphics, Thiokol Corp, Newtown, Pa, 76; Mellon Bank, 83; Temple Univ, 84; Univ Pa, Inst Contemp Art, 91. *Exhib:* Md Regional, Baltimore Mus Art, 74; 30 solo exhibs incl RI Sch Design, Providence, 79, Yoseido Gallery, Tokyo, Japan, 81, Cabrini Coll, 99, Mangel Gallery, 2000, Sande Webster Gallery, 2010; Gov's Residence, Harrisburg, Pa, 87; Wennizer Graphics Gallery, Provincetown, Mass, 89; Philadelphia Mus Art, 90; Mangel Gallery, 92, 96 & 99; Widener Univ, 95; Mangel Gallery, 2006; Sandi Webster Gallery, 2010; Richard Rosenfeld Gallery, 2012. *Teaching:* Instr painting, Cheltenham Sch Fine Arts, 65-; instr printmaking, Tyler Sch Art, Philadelphia, 79-84 & Pratt Inst, New York, 85-86; lectr, Tokyo Nat Univ Fine Art & Sichuan Fine Arts Inst, China. *Awards:* Harry Rockower Mem Award, Cheltenham Ctr Arts, 88; Pa Coun Arts Grant Award, 89; Purchase Award, Berman Mus, 94; Outstanding Art Educ Award, Pa Educ Assoc; and others. *Bibliog:* Vivien Raynor (auth), NY Times, 9/13/92; Victoria Donohoe (auth), Philadelphia Inquirer, 5/10/92; Edward Sozanski (auth), Philadelphia Inquirer, 5/14/92, 12/19/93, 3/5/99 & 3/17/00, 2/14/2009, 6/5/2009, 6/10/2009, 1/17/2010. *Mem:* Artists Equity; Am Color Print Soc. *Media:* Acrylics, Water-based Printing Inks. *Interests:* Gardening, travel. *Publ:* Coauth, Making Art Safely, Van Nostrand Reinhold, 93. *Dealer:* Richard Rosenfeld Gallery. *Mailing Add:* 8012 Ellen Ln Cheltenham PA 19012

SPANGENBERG, KRISTIN L
CURATOR, HISTORIAN
b Palo Alto, Calif, June 3, 1944. *Study:* Univ Calif, Davis, AB, 68; Univ Mich, MA, 71. *Collection Arranged:* Cincinnati Collects Photographs (auth, catalog) & German Expressionist Prints (auth, catalog), Cincinnati Art Mus, 85. *Pos:* Asst cur prints, drawings & photographs, Cincinnati Art Mus, 71-73, cur, 74-. *Mem:* Print Coun Am. *Res:* prints of Paul Ashbrook; Stobridge lithography company posters. *Publ:* Auth, Eastern European Printmakers, 75, French Drawings, Watercolors & Pastels 1800-1950, 78, ed, Nineteenth Century Drawings from the Grand Duchy of Baden, 83 & auth, Photographic Treasures from the Cincinnati Art Mus, 89, Cincinnati Art Mus; Innovation & Tradition, Twentieth Century Japanese prints from The Howard & Caroline Porter Collection, 90; ed & contribr, Six centuries of master prints: Treasures from the Herbert Greer French collection, Cincinnati Art Mus, 1/93; compiled & organized, The Golden Age of Costume and Set Design, 2002; Public Spectacles, Personal Pleasures: Four Centuries of Japanese Prints from a Cincinnati Collection, 2006; Henry Farny Paints the Far East, 2007; Illusion and Reality: Prints by Jini Anderle, 2008. *Mailing Add:* c/o Cincinnati Art Mus 953 Eden Park Dr Cincinnati OH 45202-1596

SPANN, SUSANNA EVONNE
PAINTER, EDUCATOR
b Oakland, Calif, June 13, 1943. *Study:* Ariz State Univ, BFA, 67 & MA, 69; Art Ctr Coll Design, 74-77. *Work:* Tampa Electric Co, Tampa, Fla; Disney World, Orlando, Fla; Santa Fe Community col, Gainesville, Fla; City Miami Beach, Miami Beach, Fla; Nations Bank, Charlotte, NC; City of W Palm Beach, Fla; First Fed Bank of Fla. *Comn:* portrait, Judge Roberta Knowles Manatee Co Courthouse, Bradenton, Fla, 80. *Exhib:* Am Watercolor Soc, New York City, NY, 79, 86 & 97; Watercolor US, Springfield, Mo, 92; Nat Watercolor, Soc, Riverside, Calif, 97; and many others. *Pos:* Susanna Spann Studios, Bradenton, Fla, 77-; Workshop Instr, all over US, 94-. *Teaching:* instr, illus, Ringling Sch Art & Design, Sarasota, Fla, 81-95. *Awards:* Key Mem Award, Am Watercolor Soc, 79; Holbein Award, Fla Watercolor Soc, 2003; Kanuga Award, Fla Watercolor Soc, 2003; Am Artist Award, Fla Watercolor Soc, 2008; Award of Distinction, Tanpan Springs Art Festival, 2009; over 600 awards. *Bibliog:* Patrick Seslar (auth), Secrets of painting glass, The Artist's Mag, 3/93; Patrick Seslar (auth), Object lessons, The Artist's Mag, 11/98; Kristin Godsey (auth), Point-and-shoot sketchbook, Artist's Sketchbook, 7/2003. *Mem:* Am Watercolor Soc; Nat Watercolor Soc; Fla Watercolor Soc. *Media:* Watercolor. *Specialty:* outdoor art festivals. *Interests:* snow skiing; dancing. *Publ:* Splash I, America's Best Contemporary Watercolors, 91; Enliven Your Paintings with Light, F&W, 93; Splash II, Breakthroughs, 93; contribr, The Best of Flowers Painting I & II, F&W Publ, 97; auth, Painting Crystal and Flowers in Watercolor, F&W Publ, 2001; The One Hour Watercoloris, F&W, 2001; contribr, 100 Ways to Paint People & Figures, Int Artist, 2004; contribr, Painting Light & Shade, F&W Publ, 2004; Flowers & Bloom, F&W, 2005; contribr, Splash 9 - Watercolor Secrets, F&W Publ, 2006; Best of America Watercolod Artists, Kennedy Pubs, 2007. *Mailing Add:* 1729 8th Ave Bradenton FL 34205

SPARKS, JOHN EDWIN
PRINTMAKER, INSTRUCTOR
b Washington, DC, Sept 14, 1942. *Study:* Richmond Prof Inst; Yale-Norfolk Summer Sch Art & Music; Md Inst Coll Art, BFA; Univ Ill, Urbana, MFA. *Work:* Libr of Cong, Washington, DC. *Exhib:* 36th Int Exhib, Northwest Printmakers, Seattle, 65; Libr of Cong Print Exhib, Washington, DC, 66; 47th Exhib, Soc Am Graphic Artists, NY, 66; Maryland Artists Regional, Baltimore Mus Art, 68; Solo exhibs, L Katzenstein Gallery, Towson, Md, 69, Univ Md, Baltimore Co, Catonsville, 72, Watermark Gallery, Annapolis, Md, 81 & Catonsville Community Col, 83; 10th National Print Exhib, Silvermine Guild Artists, Conn, 74; Director's Choice, Albrecht Art Mus, St Joseph, Mo. *Pos:* Cataloger, George A Lucas Print Collection, Union of Independent Cols Art, 69; dir first restrike ed, Rodolphe Bresdin's etching Flight into Egypt, 70; art adv, Md Arts Coun, 70-71. *Teaching:* Instr lithography & intaglio, Md Inst Col Art, 66-, chmn, Printmaking Dept; instr intaglio & lithography, Lake Placid Summer Workshop, 71-75; instr intaglio, NS Col of Art & Design, 77. *Awards:* Printmaking Grant, Louis Comfort Tiffany Found, 67. *Media:* Intaglio, Lithography. *Mailing Add:* 2942 Guilford Baltimore MD 21218

SPEAR, LAURINDA HOPE
ARCHITECT
b Rochester, Minn, Aug 23, 1950. *Study:* Brown Univ, BA, 1972; Columbia Univ, 1975; Mass Inst Technol. *Work:* LA Entertainment Dist, Calif; Pan Am Games Study, Miami, Fla; Int Airport Terminal, Miami, Fla; Disney Cruise Terminal, Port Canaveral, Fla; Puerto Rico Trade & Convention Ctr Dist, San Juan. *Exhib:* Ctr for the Fine Arts, Miami, Fla, 1984; Inst Contemp Art, Philadelphia, 1986; Bass Mus, Miami Beach, Fla, 1988; Chicago Athenaeum Mus Archit and Design, 98, 2000; Urban Land Inst, Miami Beach, Fla, 2000; The Skyscraper Mus, NY, 2000; many others. *Pos:* Principal, Arquitectonica, Miami, Fla, 1977-; vis prof, Univ Miami, 1975-77, 1993-94, Harvard Univ, 1994. *Awards:* Excellence Award, Fla AIA, 2000; Am Architecture Award, Festival Walk, 2000, Philips Arena, 2000; Founder's Award, Salvadori Ctr, 2000. *Mem:* Archit Club Miami; Dade Co Historic Preservation Bd; Am Inst Architects; Int Interior Design Asn; Nat Acad (assoc, 93, acad, 94-)

SPEAR, RICHARD EDMUND
EDUCATOR
b Michigan City, Ind, Feb 3, 1940. *Study:* Univ Chicago, BA (art hist); Princeton Univ, MFA (art hist) & PhD (art hist). *Pos:* Dir, Allen Mem Art Mus, Oberlin Col, 72-83; pres, Intermuseum Conserv Asn, 75-77; ed-in-chief, Art Bulletin, 85-88. *Teaching:* Mildred C Jay prof art hist, Oberlin Col, 64-; distinguished vis prof, George Washington Univ, 83-84; Harn eminent scholar, Univ Fla, 97-98. *Awards:* Premio Daria Borghese Gold Medal, Rome, 72. *Mem:* Coll Art Asn. *Res:* Seventeenth century painting. *Publ:* Auth, Caravaggio and His Followers, Cleveland Mus Art, 71 & Harper & Row, rev ed 75; Renaissance and Baroque Paintings from the Sciarra and Fiano Collections, Pa State Univ Press & Ugo Bozzi, Rome, 72; Domenichino, Yale Univ Press, 82; The Divine Guido, Religion, Sex, Money & Art in the World of Guido Reni, Yale Univ Press, 97. *Mailing Add:* Oberlin Col Dept Art Oberlin OH 44074

SPECTOR, BUZZ (FRANKLIN MAC SPECTOR)
CONCEPTUAL ARTIST, CRITIC
b Chicago, Ill, Mar 13, 1948. *Study:* Southern Ill Univ, Carbondale, BA (studio art), 72; Univ Chicago, MFA, 78. *Work:* Mus Contemp Art, Chicago; Getty Res Inst, Malibu, Calif; Corcoran Gallery Art, Washington DC; Art Inst, Chicago; Los Angeles Co Mus Art; and others. *Comn:* Los Angeles Co Metrop Transportation Authority; Princeton Pub Libr. *Exhib:* Solo exhibs, Art Inst Chicago (with catalog), 88 & Spertus Mus of Judaica, Chicago, 88; Transgression (with Donald Lipski, with catalog), Corcoran Gallery Art, Washington, DC, 90; Newport Harbor Art Mus (with catalog), 90; Mattress Factory, Pittsburgh, Pa, 91; Cleveland Ctr Contemp Art (with catalog), 95; Cranbrook Art Mus (with catalog), Bloomfield Hills, Mich, 98; List Art Gallery (with catalog), Swarthmore Col, 2001; and others. *Pos:* Ed, WhiteWalls, 78-87; bd dir CAA, 2004-. *Teaching:* Vis lectr art hist & criticism, Art Inst Chicago, 83-88; vis lectr, Art Ctr Col Design, Pasadena, Calif, 89-94; prof, Univ Ill, Urbana-Champaign,

94-2001; Prof & Chair, Cornell Univ, 2001-2007; Dean, col & grad sch art, Sam Fox Sch Design & Vis Art, Wash Univ St Louis, 2009-. *Awards:* Fel for Drawing, Nat Endowment Arts, 82-83 & Fel for Artists Books, 85-86 & 91-92; Ill Arts Coun Fel, 88; Tiffany Fel, 91; NYFA Fel, 2005. *Bibliog:* Neal Benezra (auth), Buzz Spector: Library of Babel (exhib catalog), Art Inst Chicago, 88; Johanna Drucker (auth), The Century of Artists Books, Granary Bks, New York, 96; Renee Riese Hubert and Judd Hubert (auths), The Cutting Edge of Reading: Artists Books, Granary Bks, New York, 99. *Mem:* Coll Art Asn. *Publ:* Objects and Logotypes (exhib catalog), Renaissance Soc, Chicago, Ill, 80; Jo Ann Callis: Objects of Reverie (exhib catalog), Des Moines, Art Ctr, 90; Ann Hamilton: Sao Paulo-Seattle (exhib catalog), Henry Art Gallery, Univ Wash, 92; Book Maker's Desire (essays), Umbrella Press, Los Angeles, 95; Beautiful Scenes (exhib catalog), Cranbrook Art Mus, 98; Details; Closed to Open (artists' book), 2001; Between the Sheets (artists' bk), 2003. *Dealer:* Zolla-Lieberman Gallery Chicago IL; Marsha Mateyka Gallery Washington DC; Bruno David Gallery St Louis MO. *Mailing Add:* Washington University in St. Louis Sam Fox Sch Design & Visual Arts Campus Box 1031 One Brookings Dr Saint Louis MO 63130

SPECTOR, JACK J
HISTORIAN, EDUCATOR

b Bayonne, NJ, Oct 2, 1925. *Study:* City Coll New York, BS, 56; Columbia Univ, MA, 59, PhD, 64; Fulbright Fel, Paris, 60-61. *Pos:* Ed bd, Am Imag, 89-. *Teaching:* Prof art hist, Rutgers Univ, 62-79 & distinguished prof, 88; vis prof Romanticism, City Univ New York Grad Ctr, 79; vis distinguished prof, Columbian Col, George Washington Univ, Washington, DC, 85; vis scholar, Univ Queensland, Brisbane, Australia, 89. *Awards:* Am Coun Learned Socs Grant, 70; Sr Fel, Ctr Advanced Study Visual Arts, Nat Gallery Art, 85; Fel Rutgers Ctr Hist Analysis, 90-91. *Mem:* Coll Art Asn. *Res:* Nineteenth century French Romanticism, chiefly Eugene Delacroix; psychoanalytic approaches to 19th and 20th century art. *Publ:* Freud-Ferenczi Brief Wechsel, Vol I, Boler Verlag, Vienna, 93; ed, New Directions in Art History, Vol 53 No 1 & 2, Am Imago; Delacroixs Liberty on the Barricade in 1815 & 1830, Vol XV, No 3, Source, spring 96; Medusa on the Barricades, Vol 53, No 1, Am Imago, spring 96; Surrealist Art and Writing 1919-39, The Gold of Time, Cambridge Univ Press, 11/8/96. *Mailing Add:* 28 Spring St Somerset NJ 08873

SPECTOR, NAOMI
WRITER

b Lynn, Mass, Mar 6, 1939. *Study:* Brandeis Univ, BA, 60; NY Univ, MA, 66. *Pos:* Asst dir, Byron Gallery, New York, 63-64; mgr, Fischbach Gallery, New York, 67-70; dir, John Weber Gallery, New York, 73-75; pres, Greenwich Collection, Ltd, currently. *Res:* Contemporary art. *Specialty:* Minimal-conceptual. *Publ:* Auth, Robert Ryman (essay), Stedelijk Mus, Amsterdam, 2/74; Robert Ryman, Whitechapel Art Gallery, London, 9/77; Eva Hesse: anima and art, Galeries Mag, Int Ed, Paris, 12/92-1/93; Eva Hesse: the early years, 1960-1965, In: Eva Hesse: Drawing in Space - Paintings & Reliefs (catalog), Ulm Mus, Ger, 3/94; Forum: well defined enigmas/ordering chaos: an untitled drawing by Eva Hesse, Drawing, New York, 11/94. *Mailing Add:* 435 W Broadway New York NY 10012

SPEED, BONNIE ANNE
MUSEUM DIRECTOR

b Skowhegan, Maine, 1955. *Study:* Univ S Maine, BS, 1979; Univ Kans, MA, 1990. *Collection Arranged:* Treasures from Royal Tombs of Ur, Michael C Carlos Mus, Emory Univ, Atlanta, Ramesses I, Excavating Egypt; Radiant Colors, Trammel & Margaret Crow Collection Asian Art, Dallas, In the Shadow of Dragons. *Pos:* Editor, Patronage in Chinese Art, 1989; dir, Visual Arts Mitchell Mus Cedarhurst, Mt Vernon, Ill, 1991-2000, Trammel & Margaret Crow Collection Asian Art, Dallas, 2000-02, Michael C Carlos Mus, Emory Univ, Atlanta, 2002-Present. *Mem:* US Dressage Asn, Art Table, Am Asn Mus. *Mailing Add:* Michael C Carlos Mus At Emory Univ 571 S Kilgo Cir Atlanta GA 30322

SPEED, (ULYSSES) GRANT
SCULPTOR

b San Angelo, Tex, Jan 6, 1930. *Study:* Brigham Young Univ, BS; also with Soloman Aranda. *Work:* Whitney Mus, Cody, Wyo; Diamond M Mus, Snyder, Tex; Devonian Found, Calgary, Alta; Repub Nat Bank, Dallas. *Comn:* Sculpture, Brigham Young Univ Animal Sci Dept, 75-76, 76-77 & 77-78; monuments, Charlie Goodnight, Mesa Petrolium, Amarillo, Tex, 79, Buddy Holly, city of Lubbock, Tex, 79 & John Wayne, comn by Ron Chamnis, Dallas, 80. *Exhib:* Ann Preview Exhib, Tex Art Gallery, 71-78; Phoenix Art Mus, 73-75; two-man show, Tex Art Gallery, Dallas, 75; Spec Exhib, Whitney Mus, Cody, 75; Montrail Galleries, Scottsdale, Ariz, 77. *Awards:* Achievement Award Art, Brigham Young Univ Animal Sci Dept, 72; Purchase Award, Men's Art Coun Phoenix, 73; Gold Medal Award/Sculpture, Cowboy Artists of Am Ann, 76. *Bibliog:* Ed Ainsworth (auth), Cowboy in Art, World, 68; Pat Broder (auth), Bronzes of the American West, Abrams, 74; Don Hedgpeth (auth), From Broncs to Bronzes, 79. *Mem:* Cowboy Artists Am (pres, 72-73, bd dir, 73-74 & 76-78). *Media:* Bronze. *Publ:* Auth, Hooked on cowboyin', Western Horseman, 70. *Dealer:* Tex Art Gallery 1408 Main St Dallas TX 75202; Main Trail Galleries Jackson WY 83001. *Mailing Add:* 139 S 400 E Lindon UT 84042

SPEIGHT, JERRY BROOKS
EDUCATOR, WRITER

b Murray, Ky, Nov 27, 1942. *Study:* Murray State Univ, Ky, BS, 64, MA, 68; Memphis State Univ. *Comn:* YMCA Supergraphic, City of Somerset, Ky, 75. *Exhib:* Mid-States Art Exhib, Evansville Mus Arts & Sci, Ind, 70 & Mid-States Craft Exhib, 70 & 73; All Ky Drawing Competition, Univ Ky, Lexington, 78; Solo exhibs, Owensboro Mus Arts & Sci, Ky, 79, The Automobile in the Landscape, Watercolors, Evansville Indiana Street Rod Assoc Ann, Fairgrounds Exhib Ctr, Evansville, 97 & 98, Wyndham Resort, Nashville, Tenn, 97, Knoxville, Tenn, 98, Louisville Fairground Exhib Hall, Louisville, Ky, 98; Inaugural Faculty Exhib, Murray State Univ, 95; Five Kentucky Artists, Coconino Ctr for Arts, Flagstaff, Ariz, 96. *Pos:* Regional corresp for Art Voices South Mag, Art Voices Publ Co, West Palm Beach, Fla, 78-. *Teaching:* Art dept chmn, Brescia Col, Owensboro, Ky, 70-74; instr art educ, Univ Ky, Lexington, 74-75 & Murray State Univ, Ky, 75-, prof, 92-. *Awards:* Merit Award, All Ky Drawing Competition, 78; Ky Art Educator Year, 80. *Mem:* Ky Art Educ Asn (vpres, 77-78); Nat Art Educ Asn. *Media:* Watercolor, Graphite. *Res:* Artists' work from a technical and conceptual standpoint. *Publ:* Auth, John Thomas Bensing, Sch Arts, 11/80; Wear an original painting, Fiberarts, 1/81; Richard Abrams, Art Voices, 4-5/81; Basic photography experiences, Sch Arts, 5/81; A shoe recall, Sch Arts, 10/81; and many others. *Mailing Add:* 1601 Loch Lomond Dr Murray KY 42071-3704

SPEISER, STUART M
COLLECTOR, PATRON

b New York, NY, June 4, 1923. *Exhib:* Stuart M Speiser Collection of Photorealism, shown at 20 mus, incl, Addison Gallery Am Art, Andover, Mass, 74, Allentown Art Mus, Pa, 74, Witte Mem Mus, San Antonio, Tex, 74, Brooks Mem Mus, Memphis, Tenn, 75 & Krannert Mus, Champaign, Ill, 75; donated to Smithsonian Inst, 78. *Awards:* James Smithson Medal, Smithsonian Art Inst, 79. *Bibliog:* Judy Beardsall (auth), Stuart M Speiser Photo-Realist Collection, Art Gallery Mag, 10/73; Phyllis Derfner (auth), New York letter, Art Int Lugano Rev, 11/73; Gregory Battcock (auth), New York, Art & Artists, London, 3/74. *Interests:* Promoting new art movements and pioneering in law as it pertains to artists, in capacity as an attorney. *Collection:* Photorealism. *Mailing Add:* c/o Spelser Krause Madole & Nolan Two Grand Central Tower 140 E 45th St 34 New York NY 10017

SPELMAN, JILL SULLIVAN
PAINTER

b Chicago, Ill, Feb 17, 1937. *Study:* Hilton Leech Art Sch, Sarasota, Fla, 55-57; and with Paul Ninas, New Orleans, 56-58. *Work:* Univ Mass, Amherst. *Exhib:* Watercolor USA, Springfield Art Mus, Mo, 67; Mainstreams '70, Marietta Coll, Ohio, 70; Salon 72, Ward Nasse Gallery, NY, 72; Solo exhibs, Phoenix Gallery, NY, 73, 75 & 77 & Ward-Nasse Gallery, NY, 77; and others. *Pos:* Pres, Phoenix Coop Gallery, 72-74; assoc ed, Artists Rev Art, 77-78. *Teaching:* Lectr, Ringling Mus Art, Sarasota, 58-60. *Awards:* Sarasota Art Asn First Prize, Art Student Exhib, 57; Hamel Prize, Sarasota Art Asn Ann, 58; Grumbacher Oil Prize, Knickerbocker Artists Ann, 70. *Mem:* Asn Artist-Run Galleries. *Media:* Acrylic. *Dealer:* Rhodd Sande Gallery 61 E 57th St New York NY. *Mailing Add:* 22 W 96th St New York NY 10025

SPENCE, ANDREW
PAINTER

b Bryn Mawr, Pa, Oct 4, 1947. *Study:* Tyler Sch Art, Temple Univ, Philadelphia, BFA, 69; Univ Calif, Santa Barbara, MFA, 71. *Work:* Metrop Mus Art; Hirshhorn Mus Sculpture Garden; Whitney Mus Am Art; Smithsonian Inst, Washington, DC; Carnegie Mus, Pittsburgh; Phila Mus Art. *Exhib:* Solo exhibs, Barbara Toll Fine Arts, NY, 82, 83, 85, 87, 88 & 90, Compass Rose Gallery, Chicago, 90, James Corcoran Gallery, Los Angeles, 90, Insights: Ann Messner & Andrew Spence, Wooster Art Mus, Mass, 91, Max Protetch Gallery, NY, 92 & 93 & Morris Healy Gallery, 96, Art Resources Transfer, NY, 2000 & Edward Thorp Gallery, NY, 2001, 2002, 2006 & 2010; Jux: New Paintings, Storefront, Brooklyn, NY, 2011; group exhibs, Generations of Geometry, Whitney Mus Am Art at the Equitable Ctr, NY & The Fortieth Biennial Exhib Contemp Am Painting, Corcoran Gallery Art, Washington, DC, 87; Whitney Biennial, Whitney Mus of Am Art, New Acquisitions, Hirshhorn Mus & Sculpture Garden, Smithsonian Inst, Washington, DC, 89; The 1980s: Selections from the Permanent Collection, Whitney Mus Am Art, NY, 91; Metrop Mus of Art, NY, 93; Specifically Painting, Edward Thorp Gallery, NY, 2001; Painting by Design, Wayne State Univ, Detroit, MI, 2003; Ulrich Mus Art, Wichita, Kans, 2005; Two Friends and So On, Andrew Kreps Gallery, NY, 2006; Taking Form, Lennon Weinberg Gallery, NY, 2007; Invitational Exhib Visual Arts, AAAL, New York, 2008; Geometry As Image, Robert Miller Gallery, NY, 2008; Put it On Paper, Edward Thorp Gallery, NY, 2009; Geomtetric Progresson: Eleven Painter, Edward Thorp Gallery, NY, 2010; Cries & Whispers, Sam Lee Gallery, Los Angeles, Calif, 2011; All About Etching, Neptune Gallery, Wash DC, 2012; Painting Advanced, Edward Thorp Gallery, NY, 2013. *Teaching:* Prof painting, Bennington Coll, Vt, 94-. *Awards:* Painting, Nat Endowment Arts, 87; Guggenheim Fel Painting, 94; Hassam, Speicher, Betts & Symons Purchase Award, AAAL, 2008. *Bibliog:* Andrew Spence (monogr), Art Resources Transfer Inc, Los Angeles, 92; S Robert Orton (auth), Benevolence & Blasphemy, Turtle Point Press, 95; William S Bartman, Between Artists, Art Resources Transfer, Los Angeles, 96; Faye Hirsch (auth), The World in Brief, Art in Am, 9/2006; Lyn Kienholz (auth), L.A. Rising: SoCal Artists Before 1980. *Dealer:* Edward Thorp Gallery 210 W 26th St New York NY 10001. *Mailing Add:* Six Varick St New York NY 10013

SPENCER, DEIRDRE DIANE
LIBRARIAN

b Indianapolis, Ind, Sep 28, 1955. *Study:* Ind Univ, Bloomington, AB, 77, MLS, 85; Univ Chicago, MA, 84; Univ Mich, Ann Arbor, PhD candidate, 96. *Pos:* Asst art & archit librn, Univ Fla, Gainesville, 86-88; dir, Fine Arts Libr, Univ Mich, Ann Arbor, 88-; reference librn, Washteraw Community Coll, Libr, Ann Arbor, Mich, 2000. *Teaching:* Instr hist art, Martin Ctr Coll, Indianapolis, Ind, 83; adj instr hist art, Herron Sch Art, Ind Univ-Purdue Univ, Indianapolis, 84; Washtenaw Community Coll, Ann Arbor, 2002-2003; Concordia Coll, Ann Arbor Mich, 2003. *Awards:* Univ Mich Rackham Merit Fel Doctoral Study; Univ Mich Fel, Ctr Educ Women. *Bibliog:* Martha Keller (auth), Technology may radically alter the way art history is taught, Ann Arbor News, 2/12/89. *Mem:* Art Libr Soc N Am (chmn, Muehsam Award Comt, 90); Art Libr Soc Mich (pres, 90); Coll Art Asn. *Res:* African ethnicity in 19th century art and visual culture; ancient art; computer usage and digitized images in art libraries. *Interests:* 18th & 19th century French and American art; race & gender in 19th and early 20th century visual culture. *Publ:* Auth, Lockefield gardens, Ind Preservationist, 81; rev, Oliver Harrington's Why I Left America and Other Essays & Dark Laughter, pub-in Inks, Cartoon & Comic Art Studies, 94. *Mailing Add:* Univ Mich Fine Arts Libr 260 Tappan Hall Ann Arbor MI 48109

SPENCER, HAROLD EDWIN
HISTORIAN, PAINTER
b Corning, NY, Oct 1, 1920. *Study:* Art Students League, 1941-42; Univ Calif, BA (highest hon art), 1948 & James Phelan scholar, MA, 1949; Harvard Univ (summer scholar), 1958, Fac Arts & Sci Fel, 1960-61 & Frank Knox Fel, 1964, PhD, 1968. *Work:* William Benton Mus Art; New Haven Paint & Clay Club, Inc; Homer Babbidge Libr, Univ Conn. *Exhib:* Mo Exhib, St Louis Art Mus, 1952, 1955, 1959 & 1961; Ann Drawing & Print Exhib, San Francisco Art Mus, 1955-56; Washington Printmakers Soc, Smithsonian Inst, 1957 & 1962; Conn Acad Art Ann, Wadsworth Atheneum, Hartford, Conn, 1976; Monotypes Today I-XIII, 1977-96; Solo Exhib: Slater Mus, Norwich, Conn, 87; Benton Mus, Storrs, Conn, 1990; Jorgensen Gallery, Univ Conn, 1998, 1999, 2000; New Haven Paint & Clay Club Centennial Exhib, 2000; San Luis Art Center, 2005, 2006, 2007, 2008; Morro Bay Art Asn, 2008-2010; Studios on the Park, Paso Robles, 2009, 2010, 2011, 2012, 2013; Showroom Gallery, Paso Robles, 2012, 2013. *Collection Arranged:* The Am Earls, William Benton Mus, 1972; Connecticut and Am Impressionism, William Benton Mus, 1980; Wilson Irvine and The Poetry of Light, Florence Griswold Mus, 1998; A Connecticut Place: Weir Farm, An Am Painter's Rural Retreat, Nat Park Ser & Weir Farm Trust, 2000. *Pos:* coun overseers, Weir Farm Trust, 1989-93, 2002-, bd dir, vpres, 1995-2002; bd trustees, Lyme Acad Fine Arts, 1993-98; guest cur, Florence Griswold Mus, 1995-98 & Weir Farm Nat Hist Site, 1998-2000. *Teaching:* assoc prof, Occidental Col, Los Angeles, Calif, 1962-68, chmn art dept, 1963-68; assoc prof, Univ Conn, Storrs, 1968-69, prof, 1969-88, assoc dept head, 1977-79, prof emer, 1988-; Chmn art dept, Blackburn Col, Carlinville, Ill, 1949-62. *Awards:* First Prize, Conn Artists Ann, Slater Mus, 1987; Best in Show, San Luis Obispo Art Center, San Luis Obispo, 2007; 1st Prize, Showroom Gallery, Paso Robles, Calif, 2013. *Bibliog:* Roberta Capers (auth), Reviews of Readings in Art Hist, Art Bull, 1971; Henri Dorra (auth), article in Art J, summer 1978; William Zimmer (auth), Review of Wilson Irvine Exhib at Florence Griswold Mus, New York Times, 8/16/98. *Mem:* Coll Art Asn; Conn Acad of Arts & Sci; Weir Farm Arts Center; San Luis Obispo Art Mus; Studios on the Park. *Media:* Oil; Monotype, Watercolor. *Res:* Nineteenth Century European Painting and American Art. *Interests:* Poetry. *Collection:* Early 20th Century and Contemporary. *Publ:* Auth, Reflections on Impressionism: It's Genesis & American Phase, in Connecticut & American Impressionism (exhib catalog), William Benton Mus Art, 1980; ed, Readings in Art History, Scribner's 1969, 1976, 1982, 1983, Am Art, Scribner's, 80; coauth (with Elizabeth Kornhauser), Pride of Place: The Artistic Heritage of Connecticut, 1790-1920 (exhib catalog), Wadsworth Atheneum, 1989; auth, Wilson Henry Irvine and the Poetry of Light (exhib catalog), Florence Griswold Mus, 1998; auth, J Alden Weir and the Image of the American Farm, A Connecticut Place: Weir Farm, An American Painter's Rural Retreat (exhib catalog), Weir Farm Trust and National Park Service, 2000; and others

SPENCER, LINDA B
ENCAUSTIC ARTIST, JEWELER, COLLAGE, OIL
b Fl. *Study:* San Jose State Univ, BA, 1990; Inst Transpersonal Psychology, Palo Alto CA, MA, 1993; PhD, 1995. *Work:* Shark Project (Compaq Computer), Pub Art (sponsor), San Jose, CA; Volusia County Twenty Mile Road Project, Charter Artist, Daytona, FL. *Comn:* Painting, Mrs. C. Sewell, Lompoc CA, 1982; Retrospective piece indoor, Mr. & Mrs. Cooke, Los Gatos, CA, 1998; Landscape for City Hall, Tammy Rogers, Tavares, FL, 2006; 14 Paintings, Shamrock Homes, Eustis, FL, 2006. *Exhib:* Los Gatos Art Asn, Triton Art Mus, Los Gatos, CA, 1995-2001; Numerous exhibits, Forbes Mill Mus of Art, Los Gatos, CA, 1996-1998; Nat Mus of Women & the Arts, Eustis Mus of Art, Eustis, FL, 2003-2006; Mount Dora Center for the Arts Shows, Mt Dora, FL, 2003 & 2006; Nat League of Am Pen Women, Denver, Co, 2005; Orlando Mus Art, 2011; Gilmer Arts-Ellijay, Ga & Amicalola Falls Lodge, Ga, 2013. *Collection Arranged:* Becoming a Butterfly, (75 pieces done by 30 artists), FL State Conference, Gainesville, FL, 2005; Tavares City Hall, 2010; Nat League of Am Pen Women. *Pos:* Studio Artist. *Teaching:* Encaustic art instr & jewlery instr; private instr, 2005-2013; jewelry instr, 2013. *Awards:* First Place, Los Gatos Artists, Trinton Mus, 2000; Best of show, Perry, Ga, 2007; and many others. *Bibliog:* What a Feminist looks Like, Womens Vox, 1998; Roslyn Jennings (auth), Encaustic Artist, Orlando Sentinel, 2005. *Mem:* Nat League Am Pen Women (pres 2005-2013, & nat new member art chair 2008-2013, vp Orlando branch, 2012-13); Antique and Classic Boat Society; Nat League Am Pen Women, Wash, DC (art chair, 2013). *Media:* Collage & Oil painting; Fused glass & Jewelry making. *Res:* Art as it relates to healing. *Specialty:* Art and fine jewelry; fused glass jewelry, music collages. *Interests:* Symbols across cultures. *Collection:* shamrock home builders for model homes. *Publ:* Auth, Heal Abuse & Trauma Through Art (bk), CC Thomas, 1996; art, The Womens Vox Newspaper, Womens Vox, 1997-1999; art, Artist of the Month, Mountain Network News, 1999; art, Sentinel: Feminine Perspective Colors Tavares exhibit, 2007. *Dealer:* Amicalola Falls Lodge Dawsonville Ga; Gilmer Arts Dalton St Ellijay Ga; One Dane Place Eustis Fl. *Mailing Add:* PO Box 1707 Tavares FL 32778

SPENCER, MARK J
MUSEUM DIRECTOR, CURATOR
b Madison, Wis, June 8, 1957. *Study:* Univ Wis, Stevens Point, BS, 79; Madison MA (art hist), 83. *Collection Arranged:* Alan Rath, Johnson Co Community Col, 93; Johnny Naugahyde, Random Ranch, Kansas City, Mo, 93; Johnny Naugahyde & Mike Corgiat, Kansas City Artists Coalition, Mo, 94; William Christianberry Retrospective, Albrecht-Kemper Mus, (coauth, catalog), 94, Lorna Simpson Wigs, 95, Native Am Basketry-The Hartman Collection, (contribr, catalog), 96, William Wegmen Photographs & Paintings, 96 & William Wiley: 60 Prints for 60 Years, 97; Johnny Navgahyde, Dolphin Gallery, Kansas City, Mo, 99. *Pos:* Asst dir, Haggerty Mus Art, formerly; cur, Yellow Freight System, 89-94; dir, Albrecht-Kemper Mus Art, 94-. *Teaching:* Instr art hist, Univ Wis, Stevens Point, 84-86. *Mem:* Am Asn Mus; Midwest Mus Conf (gen co-chair, currently). *Res:* Contemporary art. *Publ:* Auth, Barry Moser: Original Wood Engravings, Exhibits USA, 90; Duane Hanson: Sculptures, Johnson Co Community Col, 91; Brininstool and Lynch: Architects, Inland Architect, 95. *Mailing Add:* c/o Albrecht-Kemper Mus Art 2818 Frederick Blvd Saint Joseph MO 64506

SPENCER, SUSAN ELIZABETH
PAINTER, INSTRUCTOR
b Buffalo, NY, Oct 31, 1954. *Study:* Sullivan Co Community Col, AA (graphic art), 74, Onondaga Community Col, 79-83. *Work:* Kidder-Peabody Inc, NY; Trustmark Nat Bank, Jackson, Miss; Neville Public Mus, Green Bay, Wis; Agway Corp; Peerless Insurance, Neth. *Comn:* Historical sites of Clay, NY, Marine Midland Bank, Syracuse, 85; painting of Crouse Col, King & King Architects, Syracuse, 86; 5 paintings, Zausmer & Frisch Archit Firm. *Exhib:* Pa Watercolor Soc, Port Hist Mus, Philadelphia, 87; 17th Int Exhib La Watercolor Soc, World Trade Ctr, New Orleans, 87; Audubon Artists Exhib, Nat Arts Club, NY, 88; Midwest Watercolor Soc, Neville Pub Mus, Green Bay, Wis, 88 & 89; Watercolor West, Brea Civic Ctr Gallery, Calif; Adirondack Nat Exhib Am Watercolors. *Teaching:* Pvt classes in watercolor, Syracuse, NY, 84-; instr, workshops for var organizations & institutes throughout central NY. *Awards:* Trustmark Purchase Award, Miss Watercolor Show, 86; Mary Garrison Award, Cooperstown Nat Exhib, 87; Outstanding Adirondack Painting, Central Adirondack Show, Enchanted Forest, 88; Award of Distinction, Syracuse Art Festival. *Bibliog:* Sherry Chayat (auth), rev, Syracuse Herald-Am, 85; Stephen Doherty, article, Am Artist, Watercolor, 90. *Mem:* Cent NY Watercolor Soc (secy, 87-89); Onondaga Art Guild. *Media:* Watercolor, Pencil. *Publ:* Security Mag, Security Mutual Insurance, 86; Nat Catalogue Arts, Assoc Arts Orgn, 87; Artists Mag, 5/93; The Best of Watercolor & Painting Composition, Rockport Publ. *Dealer:* Gallery Luna 7 Jordan St Skaneateles NY 13158

SPERAKIS, NICHOLAS GEORGE
PAINTER, PRINTMAKER
b New York, NY, June 8, 1943. *Study:* Pratt Inst, 1960; Nat Acad Design Sch Fine Art, New York; Art Students League, 1963; Pratt Graphic Art Ctr. *Work:* Kunst Mus, Fine Arts Mus Bern, Switz, Permanent Print Collection; The Ulmer Mus, ULM, WGer, Permanent Print Collection; The Australian Nat Gallery, Canberra, Australia, Permanent Print Collection; The Israel Mus, Jerusalem, Permanent Print Collection; Yale Univ Art Gallery, New Haven, Conn, Permanent Print Collection; Pratt Inst, The Schafler Gallery, Brooklyn, NY, Permanent Print Collection; The Stedman Art Gallery, Fine Arts Ctr State Univ NJ Rutgers, Camden, Permanent Print Collection; and many others. *Exhib:* Solo exhibs include Washington Irving Gallery, NY, 1982, Galerie Taub, Philadelphia, 1982-83, Arbitrage Gallery, NY, 1983 & Retrospective of Woodcuts, Museo Universitario Del Chopo, Mexico City, 1984, Univ Mass, Herter Art Gallery, 1987, Leonardo Di Mauro Gallery, 1988, Galerie Leopold, Hamburg, WGer, 1988, Alexander S Onassis Ctr for Hellenic Studies, NY, 1995, Stephen Gang Gallery, NY, 1998 & 2000, Andrew Edlin Gallery, NY, 2002; group exhibs include Brooklyn Mus Biennials, 1964, 1966 & 1970; Ann Print Exhib, Honolulu Acad Fine Arts, Hawaii, 1971; Reading & Bucks Co Collect, Reading Mus Art, Pa, 1977; Friends of Corcoran, Corcoran Gallery Art, 1981; Ann Acquisition Exhib, Midwest Mus Am Art, Elkart, Ind, 1981; Forum Gallery, NY, 1984; and others. *Teaching:* Instr painting, New Sch Social Res, New York, from 1972; teacher, Fashion Inst Technol, New York, 1972-, adj prof fine arts, currently; adj asst prof, Long Island Univ, Brooklyn Campus, 1985-86; adj asst lectr, Sch Painting & Sculpture of Columbia Univ, New York, from 1986; and others. *Awards:* Lawrence & Hinda Rosenthal Fel, Am Acad Arts & Lett & Nat Inst Arts & Lett, 1969; J S Guggenheim Mem Found Fel Graphics, 1970; MacDowell Colony Summer Residency, Peterborough, NH, 1976. *Bibliog:* Robert Henkes (auth), The crucifixion as depicted by contemporary artists, Nazarine Col, 1972; Barry Shwartz (auth), 20th Century Humanist Art, Praeger, 1973, The New Humanism: Art in a Time of Change, Praiger, 1974; articles, Arts Mag, 1975-78 & 1980; Raphael Soyer (auth), Nicholas Sperakis: Woodcuts, 1976. *Mem:* Am Fedn Modern Painters & Sculptors; Rhino Horn Orgn Humanist Art; Am Fedn Art; Soc Am Graphic Artists. *Dealer:* The Andrew Edlin Gallery 529 West 20th St 6th Fl New York NY 10011

SPERATH, ALBERT FRANK
MUSEUM DIRECTOR, SCULPTOR
b Philadelphia, PA, Feb 12, 1944. *Study:* Ohio Univ, BFA, 73; Univ Nebraska, Lincoln, MFA, 76. *Work:* Friedman Gallery, Louisville, Ky. *Comn:* Vietnam shrapnel sculpture, comn by Richard Lennon, Louisville, Ky, 96. *Collection Arranged:* The Art of Ellis Wilson, (painting retrospect; coauth, catalog), Univ Art Galleries, Murray, Ky, 2000. *Pos:* dir univ art galleries, Murray State Univ, Ky, 90-. *Awards:* Fel, Ky Arts Coun, 94. *Mem:* Coll Art Asn; Am Asn Mus; Asn Coll and Univ Mus and Galleries. *Media:* Mixed Media. *Res:* art of Ellis Wilson. *Publ:* coauth The Art of Ellis Wilson, Univ Press Ky, 2000. *Mailing Add:* Murray State Univ Art Galleries 604 Price Doyle Fine Arts Ctr Murray KY 42071-3342

SPEYER, JERRY I
COLLECTOR
b Milwaukee, Wis, Jun 23, 1940. *Study:* Columbia Coll, BA, 1962, MBA, 1964. *Pos:* Sr vpres, dir, Tishman Realty & Construction co, Inc, 1966-78; co-founder, pres, and chief exec officer, Tishman Speyer Properties, New York, 1978-, sr managing dir, Latin Am & Global Corp Marketing, 1984-; vchmn, Mus Mod Art, New York, New York Presbyterian Hosp; co-chmn, New York City Partnership; dept chair, Fed Reserve Bank of New York, formerly, chmn, 2007-. *Awards:* Named one of Top 200 Collectors, ARTnews mag, 2004-12. *Collection:* Contemporary art. *Mailing Add:* Tishman Speyer Properties 45 Rockefeller Plaza New York NY 10111

SPEYER, NORA
PAINTER
b Pittsburgh, Pa, Nov 24, 1922. *Study:* Tyler Coll Fine Art, Philadelphia, Pa. *Work:* Carnegie Inst, Philadelphia Mus Art, Pa; Corcoran Gallery, Washington, DC; Nelson Rockefeller Pvt Collection; Trees on Patience Brook, 2006. *Exhib:* Solo exhibs include Zena Gallery, Woodstock, NY, 54; Tanager Gallery, NY, 57; Galerie Faccheti, Paris, 59; Stable Gallery, NY, 62; Poindexter Gallery, NY, 66; Terza Karlis Gallery, Provincetown, Mass, 70, 72; Galerie Darthea Speyer, Paris, 70, 74, 89, 96, 2001; Landmark Gallery, NY, 73, 75, 78, 80, 82; Longpoint Gallery, Provincetown, 78, 80,

82, 85, 87, 91, 94; William & Mary Col, Williamsburg, Va, 80; Pa State Univ, 80; Brownstone Art Gallery, Manhattanville Col, Purchase, NY, 83; Gross McCleaf Gallery, Philadelphia, 83; Maurice M Pine Library, Fairlawn, NJ, 84; Ingber Gallery, NY, 87; Collage Drawings, Denise Bibro Fine Art Inc, NY, 96, Trees and Flowers, 98, Dream Sequences, 2000, Recent Landscape Paintings, 2002, Flowers in the Woods, 2004; Provincetown Art Asn and Mus, 2004; group exhibs include New Talent Exhib, Six Artists, Mus Modern Art, NY, 54; Four Young Americans, Poindexter Gallery, NY, 56; Stable Gallery, NY, 56, '57; Liverkusen Mus, Germany, 58; Carnegie Inst, Pittsburgh Pa, 58; Bradford Col, Mass, 65; Terza Karlis Gallery, Provincetown, Mass, 67, 68; The Obsessive Image, 1960-68, Inst Contemp Art, London, 68; Salon de Mai, Mus Modern Art, Paris, 69; L'Oeil Ecoute Festival, Avignon, France, 69; Certain Figure Trends Since the War, Mus d'Art, Saint-Etienne, France, 69; Philadelphia Civic Ctr, Pa, 72; Landmark Gallery, NY, 73, 77,; Fordham Univ, 73; Visual R & D at Corporations Collections, Univ Tex, Austin, 74; Women's Work, Mus Philadelphia Civic Ctr, 74; Works by Women, Kresge Art Ctr, Mich State Univ, 75; Butler Art Inst Am Art, Youngstown, Ohio, 78; Realist Drawing, Gross McCleaf Gallery, 81, Landscapes, 82; Weatherspoon Art Gallery, Greensboro, NC, 81; A Gray Day, Longpoint Gallery, 82, Works from the Collection, 98; Allentown Mus Art, Pa, 82; Pace Univ Art Gallery, 84; Ingber Gallery, NY, 85; Male Nude, Women Regard Men, Hudson Ctr Galleries, NY, 85; Cape Mus Fine Arts, Dennis, Mass, 91, 98; Nat Acad Design, NY, 92, 93, 98, 2000; Stuart Levy Gallery, NY, 93; Crayon, plum, fusain, Galerie Darthea Speyer, Paris, 94, Bestiaire, 95, 97; Tell Me a Story - Chapter 2, Cahoon Mus Art, Cotuit, Mass, 2001; Denise Bibro Fine Art, NY, 2002. *Bibliog:* Dore Ashton (auth), Nora Speyer, New York Times, 4/57; Judith Applegale (auth), Nora Speyer, Art Int, 10/70; William P Scott (auth), The Sensousness of Point-Nora Speyer, Am Artist, 5/84. *Mem:* Nat Acad (assoc, 91, 92). *Media:* Oil on Canvas. *Publ:* Auth, Painting the Landscape, Watson-Guptill, 86

SPICER, JEAN (DORIS) UHL
PAINTER, INSTRUCTOR, WRITER, AUTHOR
b Philadelphia, Pa, Nov 5, 1935. *Study:* Philadelphia Coll Art, dipl, 57; also with Domenic DiStefano, Charles Reid, Frank Webb, Judi Betts, Claude Crooney, 71 & Nita Engle. *Work:* Price Waterhouse, Pa; Haverford Sch Dist, Pa; Superior Models, Del; Stroemann Bread Co, Pa; John Sabatino Architects, Pa. *Comn:* Exhibitor/Flower Show, Philadelphia, 80; paintings, Havertown Sch Dist, Pa, 83. *Exhib:* Philadelphia Mus Art, 73; Bicentennial Cult Exchange Show, Wales, Gt Brit, 76; Salmagundi Club, NY, 79; Philadelphia Watercolor Club Ann, Pa, 89; Am Watercolor Soc, 95; Nat Watercolor Soc, 97. *Teaching:* Instr, Watercolor Workshop, Sydney, Australia, 86, Wayne Art Ctr, 86-2006, Naples & Ft Myers, Fla, 88 & 89, Bermuda & Cornwall, England, 1990-1994; instr, Wallingford Community Art Ctr, 2006, & Wayne Art Ctr, 87; instr, Somerset Art Asn, NJ, 2003, 2005; instr, Ocean Co, NJ, 2003, 2005; instr, Hudson River Valley, NY, 2003, 2006; instr, The Art Barn, Ind, 04; instr, Hawaii Watercolor Soc, Yosemite, Calif, 2006. *Awards:* Silver Medal, Art Dirs Club, 76; Gold Medal, Rittenhouse Sq, 83; Gold Medal, Philadelphia Sketch Club, 88; Gold Medal, Pa Watercolor Soc, 2005; Edgar Whitney Cash Award, Am Watercolor Soc, 95 & 2001; Watson-Guptill award, Pa Watercolor Soc, 02; Cash award, Philadelphia Watercolor Soc, 03; Cash award, Watercolor Mo, Nat, 04; Western Colo Watercolor Soc, 2006. *Bibliog:* Rachel Rubin Wolf (auth), The Best of Flower Painting #2, 99; Whyte (auth), Watercolor for the Serious Beginner, 97; Rachel Rubin Wolf (auth), Splash 5, 98. *Mem:* Pa Soc Watercolor Painters; Philadelphia Watercolor Soc; signature mem Am Watercolor Soc; signature mem Nat Watercolor Soc; Western Colo Water Soc; Catharine Lorillard Wolfe Art Club, NY. *Media:* Watercolor, Charcoal. *Res:* New Jersey Watercolor Soc, Juror, 2004; Jane Law Gallery, NJ, 2004; North East Watercolor Soc, Juror, 2005, NJ; Baltimore Watercolor Soc, Juror, 2010; Daylesford Abbey, Pa, Juror, 2011. *Specialty:* All painting media. *Interests:* Creates seashell designs for Sailor's Valentine's. *Publ:* Auth, Floral Painting-Watercolor, Am Artist Mag, Spring 94; auth, Landscape Painting, Int Artist Mag, 03; auth, Int Nat Artist Book (chap), 03; auth, Bright & Beautiful Flowers in Watercolor, for North Light Books, 04. *Dealer:* 11 Tenby Rd Havertown, PA 19083. *Mailing Add:* No 11 Tenby Rd Havertown PA 19083

SPIEGEL, LAURIE
COMPUTER ARTIST, COMPOSER
b Chicago, Ill, Sept 20, 1945. *Study:* Oxford Univ, 66-67; Shimer Coll, BA, 67; Julliard Sch, 69-72; City Univ New York, MA, 75. *Work:* Over 80 works in pub collections, incl: Unseen Worlds, Obsolete Systems & Music Mouse; The Expanding Universe. *Comn:* Waves, comn by Kathryn Posin Dance Co, Am Dance Festival Ballet, 75. *Exhib:* 2nd, 3rd & 4th Int Computer Arts Festival, New York, 74-76; Fur Augen und Ohren, Akademie der Kunst, Berlin, Fed Repub Ger, 79; Crossovers, Just Above Midtown Gallery, New York, 81; Space Probes, Nexus, Atlanta, Ga, 81; Art by Computer and Video, Mus Surreal & Fantastique, New York, 82; Location 1 Gallery, New York, 2006; 3LD Gallery, New York. *Collection Arranged:* A Harmonic Algorithm 2011, Museu d'Art Contemporani de Barcelona, 2011. *Pos:* Designer & programmer, var pioneering interactive computer progs for music & art, 73-; Film soundtrack composer & ed, audio special effects consultant on arts & tech. *Teaching:* instr, Aspen Music Festival Sch, 71-72; instr, Bucks Co Comm Coll, 71-75; Instr & dir computer music studio, Cooper Union, 80-82 & NY Univ, 82-83. *Awards:* ASCAP Standard awards, 75-; Creative Artists Pub Serv Fel, NY State Coun Arts, 75-76 & 79-80; Artist-in-residence Production Support Grant, Experimental TV Lab WNET-New York, 76; New York Found Arts Fel Award, 91-92. *Bibliog:* Evan Brubaker & Peter Wetzler (auths), Laurie Spiegel: technofolk, Ear Mag, 5/91; Cole Gagne (auth), Soundpieces 2: Interviews with American Composers, Scarecrow Press, 93; Vanessa Else (auth), EQ Mag, 5/94; Simon Reynolds (auth), Resident Visitor, Laurie Spiegels Music, Pitchfork Mag, 2012; Geeta Dayal (auth), An Interview with Laurie Spiegel, Frieze Mag, 2012; Francis Morgan (auth), She has the Technology, The Wire, 2012. *Mem:* ASCAP; ASCI; SEAMUS; ICMA. *Media:* Audio, Video, Digital Display Media, Pencil, Felt Tip Marker. *Res:* Interactive music, audio, video software, human interface design, interactive gnerative systems. *Specialty:* Human interface design, audio visual music/art. *Interests:* Compositional processes and structures, interactive systems. *Publ:* Auth, numerous articles on technol in the arts, Ear Mag, 78-86, Keyboard, Electronic Musician, Computer Music J & Organized Sound. *Dealer:* Unseen Worlds NY. *Mailing Add:* 175 Duane St New York NY 10013

SPIESS-FERRIS, ELEANOR
PAINTER
b Las Vegas, NMex, July 3, 1941. *Study:* Under Kenneth Adams, 59-60 & 64-67; Univ NMex, BFA, 60-62; Art Inst Chicago. *Work:* State of Ill Bldg, Chicago; Portland Art Mus, Ore; Ill State Mus, Springfield, Ill; Coll of Du Page, Ill; Kemper Group Art Collection, Long Grove, Ill; Block Mus, Northwestern Univ, Evanston, Ill; and others. *Comn:* Prints, Plucked Chicken Press, Evanston, Ill, 85. *Exhib:* New Horizons, Chicago Cult Ctr, 73-74, 80-82 & 85-86; Still and Not-So-Still Lives, Marianne Deson Gallery, Chicago, 77; Chicago Drawing, Columbia Univ, 79; Am Drawing IV, Portsmouth Mus, Va, 82; solo exhibs, Van Straaten Gallery, Chicago, 84, Univ Wis, Green Bay, Wustum Mus, Racine, Regeration, Zaks Gallery, Chicago, 99 & 2002, The Magpie Chronicles, Coll Lake Co, Fla, 2006 & Water (and otherwise), Aron Packer Gallery, Chicago, 2006; 80th and 81st Exhibition by Artists of Chicago and Vicinity, Art Inst Chicago, 84 & 85; Fetish Art, Rockford Art Mus, Ill, 86; Chicago Show, Chicago Cult Ctr; Sansker Kendra Mus, Ahmedebad, India; Watercolor '88, Springfield Arts Mus, Mo; Ill Women Artists, 2000-01; Evanston Art Ctr, Ill, 2002; Flights of Fancy, Printworks Gallery, Chicago, 2007; While all the Tribes of Birds Sang, Ill State Mus, Chicago Gallery & Lockport Gallery, Lockport, Ill; Sorrows of Swans, Chicago Cult Ctr, 2009, Printworks Gallery, Chicago, Ill. *Collection Arranged:* Shelters, 83, Chicago 1984 Contemporary Furniture, 84, Alter Egos-Masks, 85, Indoor-Outdoor Sculpture: An Overview, 85 & Vernal Woods, 86. *Pos:* Artist-in-residence, Anchor Graphics, Chicago. *Teaching:* Instr figure painting, Evanston Art Ctr, Ill, 86, 99-2000, 2005, 2008, 2011. *Awards:* Ill Arts Coun Artists Fel Grant, 89 & 2000; Arts Midwest Fel Grant, 91; Fel Grant, Ill Arts Coun, 99. *Bibliog:* James Bone (auth), Erotic dreams, The Reader, 84; Harry Boris, Art review, WTTW-FM Radio, 84; Estell Lauter (auth), Women as Mythmakers, Ind Univ Press; Stanely Marcus (auth), Exploring Imaginary Subjects, Am Artist Publ, 88; James Yood (auth), Eleanor Spiess-Ferris, Artforum, 91; and others. *Mem:* Arts Club Chicago; Art Inst Chicago (artists adv bd, 84-86). *Media:* Oil, Gouache. *Dealer:* Packer Schopf Gallery 942 W Lake St Chicago IL 60607; Printworks Gallery 311 W Superior St Ste 105 Chicago IL 60654. *Mailing Add:* 6551 N Ashland Ave Chicago IL 60626

SPINDELMAN, MARGOT
PAINTER
Study: Univ Mich, BFA; San Francisco Art Inst, MFA. *Exhib:* Solo exhibs include Katharina Rich Perlow Gallery, New York, 2005, 2007; Group exhibs include Talent at the Alan Stone Gallery, Alan Stone Gallery, New York, 1995, 1996, 1997, 1998; On the Wall, Compound Gallery, New York, 2001; Over Time Sq, Dept Cultural Affairs, New York, 2002; Merry Peace, Slideshow Gallery, Brooklyn, 2002, 2005; After Matisse Picasso, PS 1 Mus, Long Island City, NY, 2003; NY Collection, Albright Knox Gallery/Members Gallery, Buffalo, 2006, 2007; Brooklyn Footprints, Grand Space, Brooklyn, 2006; Art Now Fair, Miami, 2007. *Awards:* NY Found Art Fel, Painting, 2004; George Sugarman Found Grant, 2007. *Dealer:* Katharina Rich Perlow Gallery 41 E 57th St 13th floor New York NY 10022

SPINK, FRANK HENRY
PAINTER, CERAMIST, POTTER
b 1935. *Study:* Univ Ill, Urbana, BArch, 58; Univ Wash, MUP, 64. *Work:* Chung Cheng Art Gallery, St John's Univ, Jamaica, NY; Benihana of Tokyo & Va Bankshares. *Exhib:* Soc Western Artists, DeYoung Mus, San Francisco, 67; Palace Fine Arts Dedication, San Francisco, 67; 12th-45th Ann Sumie Soc Shows, 75-2013; Va Watercolor Soc Ann, 80-85, 91-92, 96, 2000, 2002 & 2008. *Pos:* Dir publ, Urban Land Inst, 72-88; dir, Non Residential Res, 83-88, vpres publ, 88-97; pub Urban Land Mag, 94-97, consultant 98-2009. *Awards:* Sketch Prize, Univ Ill, 55; Best of Show, Va Watercolor Soc, 81; Best of Show, Sumi-e Soc of Am, 91; First prize for Pottery, Northen Va Community Coll, 2008. *Mem:* Sumi-e Soc Am (treas, 2001-2012, 1st vp 2013-); Va Watercolor Soc; Potomac Valley Watercolorists; Kiln Club, Alexandria, Va; Lambda Alpha Int; Land Econ Soc (pres 98-99). *Media:* Watercolor, Somi-e, Clay. *Res:* Adaptive reuse of existing buildings, Shopping Centers, Suburban Activity Centers; Mixed Use Devel. *Interests:* Pottery, Community Svc Projects/Orgns. *Publ:* Ed, Community Builders Handbook Series, 75-96; contribr, Shopping Center Development Handbook, 1st ed, 77, 2nd ed, 85; Residential Develop Handbook, 78; Downtown Develop Handbook, 80; Shopping Centers USA, 81; Dollars and Cents of Shopping Centers, Series & Spl Reports, 78-87; Contbr auth Mixed Use Development Handbook, 2001; contribr, Business Pork Industrial Development, 2001; contrib auth, Professional Real Estate Development, 2009; contrib auth, Resort Development, 2006; contribr, Retail Development, 2008; plus others. *Mailing Add:* 5158 Piedmont Pl Annandale VA 22003

SPINK, WALTER M
EDUCATOR, ADMINISTRATOR
b Worcester, Mass, Feb 16, 1928. *Study:* Amherst Col, BA (summa cum laude), 49; Harvard Univ, MA (art hist), 50, PhD, 54; Fulbright grant, Dept Anthrop, Indian Mus, Calcutta 52-53. *Pos:* Cur, Brandeis Univ Art Collection, 56-61, acting chmn, Dept Fine Art, 59-60; dir, Asian Art Arch, Univ Mich, Ann Arbor, 62; dir, Photog Exped to India, 64-68. *Teaching:* Instr, Dept Fine Arts, Brandeis Univ, 56-61, assoc prof, 61-68; vis lectr, Dept Art, Brown Univ, 60; assoc prof art hist, Univ Mich, Ann Arbor, 61-70, prof, 70-2000, Emeritus, 2000-; vis lectr, Dept S Asian Studies, Univ Chicago, summer 72. *Awards:* Fulbright Grant, 90-91; Guggenheim Grant, 91-92; Am Inst Indian Studies Senior Grant for study at Ajanta, 2000; Research Fel, Nat Endowment for the Humanities, 2001; Rosenkranz Charitable Found Grant, 2003. *Bibliog:* K Khandalavala (auth), The Golden Age: Gupta Art, Mumbai, 91; A Jamkhedkar (auth), Discovery of Vakataka Temples at Ramtek, Shastri, 92; Pia Brancaccio (auth), Il

Complesso Repestre di Aurangabad, Naples, 95; Amina Okada (auth), Paris, 91, Delhi, 95; Benoy Behl (auth), The Ajanta Caves: Artistic Wonder, New York, 98; Donald Stadtner (auth), Vidarbha & Kosala, Bakker, p 157-166, 2004; Gregory Schopen, Figments & Fragments of Mahayana Buddhism in India, Honolulu, 2005; and many other. *Mem:* Am Inst Indian Studies (trustee, 62-65 & 72-73); Asn Asian Studies, Indian Asn Art Historians, Coll Art Asn, Am Comt S Asian Art (pres,72-76, dir color slide proj, 74-); An Univ Profs; Indian Nat Trust for Art & Cult Heritage (life mem); Asia Soc. *Publ:* Auth, Ajanta to Ellora, 67, Krishnamandala, 71, Ctr & Southeast Asian Studies, Univ Mich; The Axis of Eros, Schocken, 73 & Penguin, 75; Jogeswari, J Indian Soc of Oriental Art, 77; The Great Cave at Elephanta, with a study of sources, In: The Gupta Period, 77; The Journey of Siddhartha, Mumbai, 2000; Ajanta: History and Development (6 vol), Leiden, 2005-2007. *Mailing Add:* Dept Art Hist Univ Mich Main Campus 110 Tappan Hall Ann Arbor MI 48109

SPINKA, WILLIAM J
EDUCATOR, SCULPTOR
b Bridgeport, Conn, Oct 3, 1920. *Study:* City Coll New York, BS (art edn), 42, MS (art edn), 45. *Work:* Sharon Hosp, Sharon, Conn, Painting, 50. *Comn:* Coll seal, Baruch Coll, NY, 53, speaker stand, 53; MACE, 53; Pres chain and medal, City Coll NY, 54, student life lounges, 66-68. *Exhib:* Concoran Gallery, Painting and others - Sculpture, Washington, DC, 46; Jersey City Mus, NJ, 64; Nat Gallery, Nat Acad Arts Club, Salmagundi Club, 76-99; solo exhibs, Canton Artists' Guild, Conn, 79; Lever House Gallery, NY, 86, 95. *Pos:* Mem, Nat Soc Interior Designers, 60-75. *Teaching:* Instr, art hist, drawing, painting, design, metal & wood, City Coll NY, 46-60, asst prof, design, interior, 20th cent hist, ceramics & sculpture, 61-66, assoc prof, 2 & 3D design, sculpture & 20th cent art hist, 67-80, prof, design theory, interior & archit design, sculpture, grad archit proj, 81-85, prof emer, 86-. *Awards:* Gold Medal, Audubon Artists, Inc, 88 & Silver Medal, 92. *Bibliog:* Promotion To Full Prof-Critique-Louise Nevelson, 80. *Mem:* Audubon Artists, Inc (vpres sculpture, 87-93, sr vpres, 94-98), mem 80-present. *Media:* Mixed Media. *Res:* Methods of developing trusses for a unique roof design; Continued architecture research in space design with new forms and materials. *Interests:* Use of landscape design to present building forms. *Publ:* Auth, Wood Sculpture, Today's Art Mag, 11/62; contribr, Interiors, Contract Mag, 5/66; contribr, National Society of Interior Designers, Interior Design Mag, 3/66. *Mailing Add:* 4658 Grosvenor Ave Bronx NY 10471

SPINOSA, GARY PAUL
SCULPTOR
b Memphis, Tenn, Dec, 26, 1947. *Study:* Yale Univ Summer Sch Art & Music, 70; Cleveland Inst Art, BFA (Agnes Gund Mem Traveling Scholar), 72, Edinboro Univ, Pa, MFA, 88. *Work:* Southern Alleghenies Mus Art, Pa; Cleveland Art Asn, Ohio; Butler Inst Am Art; Lockhaven Univ, Pa. *Comn:* Public sculpture, Ohio Arts Coun, 78. *Exhib:* May Show, Cleveland Mus Art, 71-82; Eight State Ann, Speed Mus Art, Louisville, 74; Butler Inst Am Art, 74-75; European Triannual Sculpture Exhib, Paris, 78; Solo exhibs, Kent State Univ, 80, Ashland Col, 81 & Sandusky Cult Ctr, 82; Canton Art Inst, 89. *Awards:* Fel Grant, Ohio Arts Coun, 79; First Place for Sculpture, May Show, Cleveland Mus Art, 81; Pa Coun Arts Fel, 88. *Media:* Clay, Mixed Media. *Dealer:* Riley Hawk Galleries 642 N High St Columbus OH 43215; Riley Hawk Galleries 2026 Murray Hill Rd Cleveland OH 44106. *Mailing Add:* 22778 Blystone Rd Venango PA 16440

SPINSKI, VICTOR
SCULPTOR, EDUCATOR
b Newton, Kans, Oct 10, 1940. *Study:* Kans State Teachers Col, BSE, 63; Ind Univ, Bloomington, MFA, 67. *Work:* State Univ NY Potsdam; Haystack Mountain Sch Crafts, Deer Isle, Maine; Elmira Col, NY; Del Art Mus, Wilmington. *Exhib:* Coffee, Tea & Other Cups, Mus Contemp Crafts, NY, 71; Int Exhib Ceramics, Victoria & Albert Mus, London, Eng, 72; Soup Tureens, Campbell Mus, Camden, NJ, 76; Century of Ceramics in US, Everson Mus Art, Syracuse, NY, 79; Hot of the Press, The Craft Coun, London, Eng, 96 & 97; Food Glorious Food, Artists and Eating, Charles A Wustum Mus Fine Art, Nat Invitational Exhib, Racine, Wis, 97; Ceramic Still Life: The Common Object, Select Nat Exhib, Oakland, Calif, 97; Clay Realists, Nancy Margolis Gallery, NY, 98. *Teaching:* Grad teaching asst, Ind Univ, 67; prof ceramics, Univ Del, 67-; summer fac, Haystack Mountain Sch Crafts, 68 & 70, Brooklyn Mus Art Sch, 70 & Council Grove Craft Sch, Missoula, Mont, 74-76. *Bibliog:* Richard Zakin (auth), Ceramics: Mastering the Craft, Chilton Book Co, Radnor, Pa, 90; Paul Scott & Terry Bennett (auths), Hot of the press, Bellow Publ, 96; Robert Piepenburg (auth), The Spirit of Clay: A classical guide to ceramics, Pebble Press Inc, 98. *Mem:* Nat Coun Ceramic Arts; Am Crafts Coun; Int Acad Ceramics. *Media:* Ceramics; Photography. *Publ:* Auth, Ceramic Photo silk screening, Nat Coun Educ Ceramic Arts, 70; The New Yorker, New York, 87; The Craft and Art of Clay, Susan Peterson Prentice Hall, Englewood Cliffs, NJ, 92 & 95. *Dealer:* Theo Portnoy Gallery 56 W 57th St New York NY 10019. *Mailing Add:* Univ Del Art Dept Newark DE 19716

SPIRA, BILL
SCULPTOR, PHOTOGRAPHER
b Antwerp, Belg; US citizen. *Study:* Ill Inst Technology, with L Mies Van der Rohe, L Hillberseimer & Walter Peterhans, BS, 58. *Work:* Am Broadcasting Co, NY; Phillips Petroleum Co; also pvt collections of Richard Brown Baker, NY, Graham Gund, Boston & William King; Bauhaus, Ariv, Berlin. *Comn:* Sculpture, Sheraton, Manhattan & New York, 93, 97. *Exhib:* Penthouse Group, Mus Mod Art, NY, 65; Play Ball (with catalog), Queens Mus, NY, 78; On-Off the Wall, Va Beach Arts Ctr, 86. *Bibliog:* Ellen Lee Klein (auth), Bill Sprira, Arts, 1/84 & 4/87; Edmund Leites (auth), rev, Art in Am, 4/84. *Media:* Photography, Analogue B&W. *Publ:* Hasselblad Forum, Vol 35, no 2, 1999, no 4, 2001. *Dealer:* Robert Anderson Gallery 24 W 57th St NY 10019. *Mailing Add:* 30 Waterside Plaza Apt 28F New York NY 10010

SPITLER, CLARE BLACKFORD
ART DEALER
b Findlay, Ohio, Feb 2, 1923. *Study:* DePauw Univ; Univ Mich, AB, 44. *Pos:* Owner & dir, Gallery One, Findlay, Ohio, 65-76, Gallery One, Ann Arbor, Mich, 77-81 & Clare Spitler Works of Art, Ann Arbor, Mich, 81-, Clare Spitler Fine Art, 2000-; art writer, bi-weekly column, Art Dealings, Ann Arbor News, Mich, 82-83. *Specialty:* Contemporary American paintings, sculpture, graphics and selected crafts, often featuring Midwestern artists; additional European & Japanese artists. *Mailing Add:* Clare Spitler Fine Art 2007 Pauline Ct Ann Arbor MI 48103

SPITZ, BARBARA S
PRINTMAKER, PHOTOGRAPHER
b Chicago, Ill, Jan 8, 1926. *Study:* Art Inst Chicago; RI Sch Design; Brown Univ, AB. *Work:* Art Inst Chicago; Philadelphia Mus Art; Smart Gallery, Univ Chicago; DeCordova Mus, Lincoln, Mass; Los Angeles Co Mus, Calif; Mary & Leigh Block Collection, Northwestern Univ; pvt collections of Bank of Am, First Nat Bank of Boston, Price Waterhouse, Chase Manhattan Bank, IBM, Arthur Anderson & Co, Arthur Young & Co, Peat, Marwick & Mitchell, Std Oil of Ind, Union Nat Bank of Switzerland, others. *Comn:* First Ill Print Comn Prog, 73. *Exhib:* Libr Cong & Nat Collection Fine Arts, 73 & 74; Pratt Graphic Ctr, NY, 77; Nat Aperture, 86; Loyola Univ, Chicago, 88; Schneider Gallery, Chicago, 93; The Ctr Gallery, Southern Calif, 94; solo exhib incl Kunsthaus Buhler, Stuttgart, Ger, Elca London Studio, Montreal, Can, Tower Park Gallery, Peoria, Ill, Van Straaten Gallery, Chicago, Schneider-Bluhm-Loeb Gallery, Chicago, RST Galerie, Scottsdale, Ariz, Loyola Univ, Chicago, Ctr Gallery, Calif, Newport Beach Pub Libr, Benjamin Gallery, Chicago. *Teaching:* Studio demonstrations, Univ Irvine; instr, Highland Park, High Sch. *Awards:* Childe Hassam Purchase Award, Am Acad of Arts & Lett, 73; First Prize, 77 & Purchase Award, 78, Ill Regional Print Show; Stuart M Egnal Prize, Int Biennial Print Exhib, Print Club, Philadelphia, 77; Decordova Mus Purchase Awards, Boston Printmakers; George May Internat Award, New Horizons, Chicago; Municipal Art League Prize, Art Inst of Chicago; Purchase Award, Nat Exhib of Prints & Drawings, Okla Art Ctr; Ill Print Commn Program Grant. *Bibliog:* Article, Printmaker in Illinois, Ill Educ Asn, 72, Illinois Printmakers I Proj, Ill Arts Coun, 74 & others. *Mem:* Artist Equity Asn; Arts Club Chicago; Los Angeles Printmaking Soc; Boston Printmakers; Soc Am Graphic Artists; Print Club Philadelphia. *Media:* Intaglio; Photography. *Dealer:* Schneider Gallery Chicago IL

SPITZER, SERGE
INSTALLATION SCULPTOR, CONCEPTUAL ARTIST
b Bucharest, Romania, 1951. *Exhib:* Solo exhibs include Damon Brandt Gallery, New York, 1986, 1990, DAAD Galerie, Berlin, 1983, Mus Mod Art, Newe York, Kunstmuseum Bern, Switzerland, 1984, 2006, Hiram Butler Gallery, Houston, 1985, 1987, Burnett Miller Gallery, Los Angeles, 1986, 1987, 1990, Feigen Inc Gallery, Chicago, 1992, Galerie Aurel Scheibler, Cologne, Germany, 1993, 1994, Zoobrucke, Cologne, 2000, Am Fine Arts Co/Colin de Land Gallery, New York, 2002, Kunsthalle Bern, 2003, Mus Mod Kunst, Frankfurt, 2006, Nyehaus/Found 2021, New York, 2006, Aldrich Mus Contemp Art, Conn, 2008; group exhibs include Post Conteptualism after 1965, Mus Contemp Art, Chicago, 1993; Drawings by Sculptors, Brooklyn Mus, 1993; Painting Outside Painting, Biennial Exhib Contemp Am Art, Corcoran Gallery Art, Washington, 1995; Drawing is another kind of language, Fogg Art Mus, Harvard Univ, 1997; Venice Biennale, 1999; Lost & Found, Apex Art, New York, 2001; Chinese Aesthetics of Heterogeneity, Biennial, Mus Contemp Art Shanghai, 2006; No Leftovers, Kunsthalle Bern, Switzerland, 2008

SPOFFORD, SALLY
PAINTER, SCULPTOR
b New York, NY, Aug 20, 1929. *Study:* Swarthmore Col, BFA, 52; Art Students League, studied with Bernard Klonis & George Grosz, 53-54; The China Inst, New York, studied with Ya-Hung Wang, 53. *Work:* NJ State Mus, Trenton; Newark Mus, Newark, NJ; Owens Corning Fiber Glass, Corning, NY; AT&T Corp Hq, Basking Ridge, NJ; Morris Mus, Morristown, NJ; Bristol Myers, Squibb, Princeton, NJ; and others. *Exhib:* solo exhib, Morris Mus, Morristown, NJ, 89; Newark Acad, Livingston, NJ, 97; Monmouth Mus Art, Lincroft NJ, 98; Williams Gallery, 2000; Simon Gallery, Morristown, NJ, 2004. *Media:* Miscellaneous Media, Watercolor, Wood Sculpture. *Mailing Add:* 1123 Fellowship Rd Basking Ridge NJ 07920

SPOHN, FRANZ FREDERICK
PRINTMAKER, ILLUSTRATOR
b Columbus, Ohio, June 6, 1950. *Study:* Ohio State Univ, BFA, 73, MFA, 75. *Work:* Glenbow Mus, Calgary, Alta; Ohio State Univ. *Comn:* Print, Philadelphia Art Alliance, 88. *Exhib:* The Confectioner's Art, Am Craft Mus, New York City, (3 yr traveling exhib); Collaboration: Printmaking in Philadelphia, Glen Vivian Mus, Swansea, Wales & Strozzi Palace, Florance, Italy; solo exhib, Glenbow Mus, Calgary, Alta, 81; Collage & Assemblage Traveling Exhib, Miss Mus Art, Jackson, 81-83; Feast Your Eyes, Philadelphia Mus Art, 82; Material Illusions, Unlikely Materials, Taft Mus, Cincinnati, 83; and others. *Collection Arranged:* Eighteen Buys Twenty, Portico Gallery, Philadelphia, 83. *Awards:* Commissioned print by Philadelphia Art Alliance, Philadelphia, 88. *Bibliog:* Nancy Tousley (auth), Artist sweetens his biting satire, Calgary Herald, 2/12/81; Keith Morrison (auth), Realistic self portraits, New Art Examiner, 4/81; Jo Ann Lewis (auth), Artistic couples, Wash Post, 5/31/81. *Mem:* Coll Art Asn; Print Club Philadelphia. *Media:* Serigraphy, Silkscreen

SPONENBURGH, MARK
HISTORIAN, SCULPTOR
b Cadillac, Mich, June 15, 1916. *Study:* Cranbrook Acad Art, scholar, 40; Wayne Univ; Ecole Beaux-Arts, Paris, France; Univ London; Univ Cairo; Hon DFA, 70. *Work:* Detroit Inst Art; Portland Art Mus; Univ Ore; Willamette Univ; Ore State Univ. *Comn:* Architectural sculpture, McGruder Veterinary Hosp, 80; Fisherman's Mem, Newport, Ore, 88; Town & Gown, bronze group, Willamette Univ. *Exhib:* North Am

Sculpture, Paris Salon, France; Mus Mod Art, Cairo; Retrospective, 1940-1996, Triad Gallery, 96; and 35 solo sculpture exhibs. *Pos:* Consult, curator & museologist. *Teaching:* Assoc prof, Univ Ore, 46-56; vis prof, Royal Col Arts, 56-57; prof & dean, Nat Col Arts, Pakistan, 58-61; prof, Ore State Univ, 61-84, chmn art dept, 82-, emer prof, 84-. *Awards:* Distinguished Lectr, Phi Kappa Phi, 82; Distinguished Prof, Ore State Univ, 82. *Mem:* Int Asn Egyptologists; Royal Soc Arts; Royal Soc Antiquaries; Int Asn Art Historians; Am Res Ctr in Egypt; Oxford Soc. *Media:* Wood, Stone, Bronze. *Res:* Stylistic analogies in Coptic & Celtic; sculpture of Moukhtar; modular systems in Egyptian sculpture; the walking pose in Egyptian sculpture. *Publ:* Contribr, Arts Quart, J Inst Egypte, Rev Caire, Near E Bull & J Near E Studies; Royal Soc Antiquaries; and others. *Mailing Add:* PO Box 236 Monroe OR 97456

SPRATT, FREDERICK R
GALLERY DIRECTOR, PAINTER
b Cedar Rapids, Iowa, June 15, 1927. *Study:* Dallas Mus Fine Art, studied painting, 58; Iowa Wesleyan Col, BA, 51; Univ Iowa, MA, 56. *Work:* Iowa Wesleyan Col, Mt Pleasant; State Univ Iowa, Iowa City; De Saisset Mus, Univ Santa Clara, Calif; San Jose Mus Art; Coldwell-Banker Corp, Washington, DC. *Exhib:* Four Contemp Calif Artists, Calif Arts Comn, Humboldt, 68; California Landscape, Lytton Ctr Visual Arts, Los Angeles, 68; Biennial of Am Painting and Sculpture, Univ Ill, Urbana, 68; OK Harris Gallery, NY, 76; Janus Gallery, Los Angeles, 78; The Clocktower, Inst Art & Urban Res, NY, 79; Northern California Art of the Sixties, De Saisset Mus, Santa Clara Univ, San Jose, 82; Ten California Colorists, traveling exhib, Redding, San Jose & Palm Springs, Calif, 85-86. *Pos:* Owner/dir, Frederick Spratt Gallery, San Jose. *Teaching:* Prof art, San Jose State Univ, 56-; retired. *Bibliog:* Dorothy Burkhart (auth), Fred Spratt, Arts Mag, 78; Peter Frank (auth), Los Angeles Art, Art in Am, 78. *Specialty:* Contemporary American art with a focus on West Coast. *Publ:* Auth, Art Production in Discipline Based Art Education, J Paul Getty Educ Prog, 86

SPRICK, DANIEL
PAINTER
b May 1, 1953; US citizen. *Study:* Nat Acad Fine Arts with Harvey Dinnerstein, 76; Univ Northern Colo, BFA, 78. *Work:* Nat Mus Am Art, Smithsonian Inst, Washington, DC; Denver Art Mus, Colo; Hunter Mus Art, Chattanooga, Tenn; Evansville Mus Art & Sci, Ind; Williams Coll Mus Art, Williamsburg, Mass. *Comn:* Large triptych, Holme, Robert & Owens, Denver, Colo, 89; large diptych, US Govt, 94. *Exhib:* The Tradition of Vanitas in Contemp Painting, Noyes Mus, Univ Ala Mus, 87-89; solo shows, Aspen Art Mus, Colo, 90 & Hunter Mus Art, Chattanooga, Tenn, 93; Colorado 1990, Denver Art Mus, Colo; Love & Charity, Contemp Painting, State Univ NY, Cortland & Potsdam, 90; Am Still Life Painting, Minn Mus Art, Minneapolis, 91-92; Contemp Self Portraits, Nat Portrait Gallery, Washington, DC, 93. *Teaching:* Adj fac figure drawing, Colo Mountain Col, 83-94. *Awards:* Gold Medal, Allied Artists Am, 83. *Bibliog:* PD Douslin (auth), Daniel Sprick, Art Gallery Int, 86; Peter Eichner Dixon (auth), Daniel Sprick, Am Artist, 87; Michael & Patricia Coronel (auths), Daniel Sprick: Realism, Art Space, 91. *Media:* Oil. *Dealer:* Merrill Gallery of Fine Art 1401 17th St Denver CO 81601. *Mailing Add:* 1650 Fillmore St Apt 1606 Denver CO 80206

SPRINGER, BETHANY
SCULPTOR, EDUCATOR
b Washington, DC, 1975. *Study:* Va Tech, Blacksburg, BA; Univ Ga, Athens, MFA (sculpture). *Exhib:* Solo exhibs, Univ Tex, San Antonio, 1997, Univ Ga Main Gallery, Athens, 2000, Hudson D Walker Gallery, Fine Arts Work Ctr, Mass, 2002, UNO Art Gallery, Univ Nebr, 2004, Md Art Place, Baltimore, 2007, Fine Arts Ctr Gallery, Univ Ark, 2008; New American Talent 14, Tex Fine Art Asn, Austin, 2000; 10 x 10, Walker Gallery, Provincetown Art Asn, Mass, 2001; PFAWC!, Mills Gallery, Boston Ctr for the Arts, 2002; Building a Legacy, Bemis Ctr for Contemp Arts, Omaha, 2004; On the Street Gallery, Memphis Coll Art, 2007 . *Pos:* Artist-in-residence, Bemis Ctr for Contemp Arts, Omaha, 2002. *Teaching:* Vis artist, Sewannee Univ of the South, Tenn, 2000, Univ Nebr, Lincoln, 2002, Drake Univ, Des Moines, 2004, Univ SDak, 2006, Univ Ark, 2006, Univ S Fla, 2006 & Univ Tulsa, Okla, 2008; lectr, Dept Robotics & Automation Tech, Des Moines Area Community Coll, 2005 & Ind Univ, Bloomington, 2007; instr sculpture, Univ Ark, Fayetteville, currently. *Awards:* Visual Arts Fel, Fine Arts Work Ctr, 2001; Res Grant, Ctr for Digital Tech & Learning, Drake Univ, 2006; Travel Grant, Univ Ark, 2006-07; O'Connor Fel, Fulbright Coll Arts & Sciences, Univ Ark, 2007; Pollock-Krasner Found Grant, 2008. *Bibliog:* Jennifer Schultz (auth), Physical Physics, Flagpole Mag, 5/24/2000; William Zimmer (auth), When Humble Materials Interact, NY Times, 6/9/2002; Cate McQuaid (auth), Some Shining Moments at Mills Gallery, Boston Globe, 8/16/2002; Amanda Pierre (auth), Art Views Vague Faces as Seen From Satellite, Des Moines Sunday Register, 7/16/2006; Glenn McNatt (auth), Thousand Words, Baltimore Sun, 3/21/2007. *Mailing Add:* 116 Fine Arts Ctr Fayetteville AR 72701

SPROAT, CHRISTOPHER TOWNSEND
SCULPTOR, DESIGNER
b Boston, Mass, Sept 23, 1945. *Study:* Skowhegan Sch Painting & Sculpture, 69; Boston Univ; Boston Mus Sch Fine Arts; also with George Aarons. *Work:* US Govt; Hasbro; Hyatt Hotels; Bank of Am; Rayovac Corp; 600' Sculpture, Grand Cen Sta, NY Arts for Transit. *Comn:* Unibank Corp, San Francisco; Los Angeles Rapid Transit. *Exhib:* Solo exhib, Inst Contemp Art, Boston, 70; Elements of Art, Mus Fine Arts, Boston, 71-72 & Rohm/Sproat, 74; Whitney Mus Am Art Biennial, NY, 73; Hayden Gallery, Mass Inst Technol, Cambridge; Marian Goodman Gallery, NY, 80; Bette Stoler Gallery, NY, 83 & 85; Boston Athenaeum, Mass, 84; Barbara Krakow Gallery, Boston, Mass, 85, 95. *Awards:* Mass Arts & Humanities Found Fel, 75; Nat Endowment Arts Grant, 75, 80 & 84; Grant, Nat Endowment Arts, 84-85; Grant, NY Found Arts, 85. *Bibliog:* Kenneth Baker (auth), Sproat & Samaras, Boston Rev Arts, 4/72; Carl Belz (auth), Deliberating with color, drawing with light, Art in Am, 5-6/72; Robert Taplin (auth) Art in Am, 9/95; and others. *Media:* Light. *Dealer:* Barbara Krakow Gallery 10 Newbury St Boston MA 02116. *Mailing Add:* 467 Holland Hill Rd Putney VT 05346

SPROULS, DAVID
ADMINISTRATOR
Study: Rutgers Univ, Degree in Art History and American Studies; Fashion Inst of Technology, Degree in Restoration Decorative Arts. *Pos:* Admissions office, Albright Col, formerly, Fashion Inst of Technology, formerly; dir admissions, 2000-08, vpres enrollment management, 2008-2011, acting pres, NY Sch of Interior Design, 2012, pres, 2012-. *Mailing Add:* New York School of Interior Design 170 East 70th St New York NY 10021

SPROUT, FRANCIS
ARTIST, EDUCATOR
b Tucson, Ariz, Mar 5, 1940. *Study:* Univ Ariz, BFA, 67; Univ Calif, San Diego, MFA (Ford Found Fel), 72; Univ Calif, Los Angeles, MA (African Studies), 90. *Work:* Johnson Publ Co, Chicago, Ill, 73; Johns-Manville Corp, Atlanta, Ga, 76; Mountain Bell, Aurora, Colo, 78; Exxon Chemical, Linden, NJ, 80; Art Mus, Ariz State Univ, Tempe, Ariz, 86; Pfizer Learning Ctr, Rye Brook, 2000; Metro Media Corp, White Plains, NY, 2001; Neuberger Mus Art, Purchase, NY, 2002. *Exhib:* Emerging Southern California Artists, Pollock Gallery, Art Mus, Southern Methodist Univ, Dallas, 72; 74th Western Ann, 73 & 2nd, 3rd, 5th & 6th All-Colo, 74-80, Denver Art Mus; Colo-Nebr Exchange, Joslyn Mus Art, Omaha, 73; Remnant Transpositions, Fine Arts Ctr, Univ Colo, Boulder, 79; Aboriginal Transpositions, Patio Gallery, Univ Northern Colo, Greeley, 88; Animals in Art, Art Mus, Ariz State Univ, 88; Poetic License, Staller Gallery, State Univ NY, Stony Brook, 90; Fantasy in Form, Rye Arts Ctr, NY, 95; Millennium Box Exhib, Neuberger Mus Art, 2000; Beyond the Pale, Neuberger Mus Art, Purchase, NY, 2002; The Drawing Show, The Arts Exchange, White Plains, NY, 2003; Paintings, IRCC Gallery, Ft Pierce, Fla, 2006; New Painting, Admiralty Gallery, 2008; Musical Impressions, Admiralty Gallery, 2009; Holiday Exhib, Admiralty Gallery, 2011; Paper Jam, 2012; Neuberger Mus Art, 2012. *Teaching:* Asst prof painting, Univ Denver, 72-75; assoc prof painting, Metrop State Col, Denver, 76-87; adj prof, Ariz State Univ, West Campus, Phoenix, 87-90; adj prof, Purchase Coll, NY, 91-95; adj prof, Manhattanville Col, Purchase, NY, 93-2004; adj assoc prof drawing, Pratt Inst, Bklyn, 95-2004; adj prof, Indian River State Col, Fort Pierce, Fla, 2004-2012, Vero Beach Mus Art, 2004-. *Awards:* African Inst Fel, Hamline Univ, summer 78. *Bibliog:* Ellen Fisher (auth), On the Right Track, Vero Beach Mag, 3/2007. *Mem:* Coll Art Asn Am; Westchester Arts Coun; Indian River Cult Coun; and others. *Media:* Oil, Acrylic, Graphite, Mixed Media. *Dealer:* Ann McEvoy Admiralty Gallery Vero Beach FL. *Mailing Add:* 4132 N 16th Sq Vero Beach FL 32967

SPURGIN, JOHN EDWIN
ADMINISTRATOR, PAINTER
b Indianapolis, Ind, Dec 17, 1932. *Study:* Ind State Univ, BS & MA; Mich State Univ, with Angelo Ippolito; Univ Cincinnati, with Robert Knipschild, MFA. *Work:* Mich Educ Asn, East Lansing; Hubbard Milling Co, Mankato, Minn; Gustavus Adolphus Col, St Peter, Minn; Southwest State Univ, Marshall, Minn; Univ Cincinnati, Ohio. *Exhib:* Biennial of Painting & Sculpture, Walker Art Ctr, Minneapolis, 66; Okla Art Ctr, Oklahoma City, 67; Minn Mus, St Paul, 70; Miami Univ, Oxford, Ohio, 72; Northeast La Univ, Monroe, 74; Solo exhibs, Univ Wis, Marshfield, 75, Southwest State Univ, Marshall, 77 & Art Ctr, Minn, 83; Pillsbury Competitive Exhib, Minneapolis, 81; and others. *Collection Arranged:* Am National Bank Collection Exhibition, St Paul, Minn, 74; Mankato Clinic, Ltd, Minn, 81. *Pos:* Gallery dir, Gallery Five Hundred, Fine Arts, Inc, Mankato, 69-72 & Nichols Gallery, Mankato State Univ, 73-75. *Teaching:* Instr art educ, Flint Inst Art, Mich, 60-64; prof design, painting, Mankato State Univ, 65-, chmn art dept, 75-89; vpres acad affairs, Milwaukee Inst Art & Design, 89-. *Awards:* First Prize Painting, Rochester Area Artists, Rochester Art Ctr, Minn, 66; Best-in-Show, Southern Minn Art Exhib, Mankato Free Press, 67 & 72; Minn State Individual Artists Grant, 77-78. *Media:* Mixed Media. *Mailing Add:* 333 Pepperidge Ln Evansville IN 47711

SPURLOCK, WILLIAM
HISTORIAN, CRITIC
b Chicago, Ill, Oct 23, 1945. *Study:* Trinity Univ, San Antonio, Tex, BA; Univ NMex, Albuquerque, MA; Union Grad Sch, PhD. *Collection Arranged:* Vito Acconci (auth, catalog), Wright State Univ Art Gallery, 76; Barry Le Va (auth, catalog), Stephen Antonakos, Dennis Oppenheim, 77; Larry Bell (auth, catalog), Laurie Anderson, William Wegman, Alice Aycock & Pat Steir, 76; Photo-Realist Painting in Calif (auth, catalog), Santa Barbara Mus Art, 80; Herbert Bayer: Sited Sculpture and the Environment (auth, catalog), Roland Reiss, Sam Richardson, 81; and others. *Pos:* Fine art consult, Atlantic Richfield Co, Los Angeles, 79-84; cur exhibs & contemp art, Santa Barbara Mus Art, 78-81. *Teaching:* Asst dir educ in art hist & admin, Des Moines Art Ctr, Iowa, 72-74; asst prof art hist & dir, Fine Arts Galleries, Wright State Univ, Dayton, 74-78; assoc prof art hist, 82-, chair dept art, Univ Tex at Arlington, 82-86. *Mem:* Int Asn Art Critics; Coll Art Asn; Am Asn Mus; Int Coun Mus; Am Fedn Arts; Nat Coun Art Adminr; Nat Asn Sch Art & Design. *Res:* Modern and contemporary art forms; environmental arts; criticism & theory; museology. *Publ:* Auth, Social & Ecological Issues in Contemporary Art, National Arts Guide, 3-4/80; Cecile Abish, 78; Richard Fisher, Current Charts: Chosen Lands, 78; Federal Art Patronage in the State of New Mexico: 1933-1943 (catalog), Mus NMex, 78; Dialogue-Discourse-Research: Eleanor Antin, Helen and Newton Harrison, Fred Lonidier, Barbara Strasen, Santa Barbara Mus Art, 79; numerous articles & essays on contemp art & artists. *Mailing Add:* Dept Art & Art History Univ Tex Arlington TX 76019

SQUADRA, JOHN
PAINTER, RESTORER
b New York, NY, June 25, 1932. *Study:* RI Sch Design, BFA, 53. *Exhib:* Artist's Showcase, Mus Art, Bridgeport, Conn, 78; solo exhibs, Nonson Gallery, Soho, NY, 79, Gallery Lory, Norwalk, Conn, 88, Gallery-Musee des Duncan, Paris, 80 & Agape Ctr, Portland, Maine, 97; Vered Int Art Gallery, East Hampton, NY, 80; People 81, Hudson River Mus, Yonkers, NY; Athena Gallery, Chicago, 98. *Teaching:* Oils,

acrylics, watercolor, Rowayton Arts Ctr, Conn, 74-87. *Awards:* Top Ten, Irene Leache Mem, Norfolk Mus, Va, 55; Second Prize, Darien Art Show, 82; First Prize, Rowayton Arts Ctr, 85. *Bibliog:* Reviews in Le Nouveau J, Paris, 11/80 & Playboy Mag, 2/81; Hudson River Mus Show, New York Times, 10/81; and others. *Media:* Oil, Acrylic. *Publ:* Illusr, Songs from Silences, 76; auth & illusr, Dr Miraculous, 81; auth, This Ecstasy, 96; Compass Of The Rose (CD), 2000. *Mailing Add:* 9 Wexford Gardens Belfast ME 04915

SQUIER, JACK LESLIE
SCULPTOR, EDUCATOR
b Feb 27, 1927; US citizen. *Study:* Ind Univ, BS, 50; Cornell Univ, MFA, 52. *Work:* Mus Mod Art & Whitney Mus Am Art, NY; Houston Mus Fine Arts, Tex; Everson Mus, Syracuse, NY; Johnson Mus, Cornell Univ; Hirshhorn Mus, Washington, DC; Ithaca Col, NY; SUNY Potsdam Mus, NY; Castellani Mus, Niagara Univ, NY; Fogg Mus, Harvard, Univ,; Conn Conservancy. *Comn:* Disc (fiber glass & aluminum leaf sculpture), Ithaca Col, 68; Emerson Mus, Hamilton Col, NY. *Exhib:* Carnegie Inst, Pittsburgh; Brussels World's Fair; Recent Sculpture USA, Mus Mod Art; 30 Americans Under 35, Whitney Mus Am Art, 57; Hirshhorn Mus & Sculpture Garden, Washington; Los Angeles Co Mus Art; Art Inst Chicago; Denver Art Mus; Albright-Knox Art Gallery, Buffalo, NY; Addison Gallery, Phillips Acad, Andover, Mass; Houston Mus Fine Arts, Tex; Pa Acad Fine Arts, Philadelphia; St Louis Art Mus, Mo; Wadsworth Antheneum, Hartford, Conn; solo exhibs, Alan Gallery, NY, 56, 59, 62, 64, A D White Mus Art, Cornell Univ, 59, 64, 68, Inst de Arte Contemp, Lima, Peru, 63, Landau-Allan Gallery, NY, 66, 70 & 72; solo retrospective, Herbert F Johnson Mus Art, Cornell Univ, Ithaca, NY, 93. *Teaching:* From instr to asst prof, 52-64, prof sculpture, Cornell Univ, 65-. *Bibliog:* William Lipke (auth), Disc, by Jack Squier, Cornell Univ, 68. *Mem:* Int Asn Art; Sculptors Guild. *Media:* Bronze, Fiberglass. *Mailing Add:* 6217 Celadon Cir West Palm Beach FL 33418

SQUIERS, CAROL
WRITER, CRITIC
b Oak Park, Ill, 1948. *Study:* Univ Ill, Chicago, BA (art hist), 71; Hunter Col, NY. *Pos:* Cur photog, PS 1, Inst Art & Urban Resources, New York, 80-84; photog critic, Village Voice, New York, 82-83 & Vanity Fair, 83-84; assoc ed, Am Photogr Mag, 86-89; sr ed, Am Photog Mag, 89-. *Awards:* Nat Endowment Arts Fel, 81. *Bibliog:* Andy Grundberg (auth), Mixing art & commerce, NY Times, 5/81; Sharon Gill (auth), Curator as critic: Carol Squiers, New York Photo District News, 9/82; Brian Wallis (ed), Silvia Kolbowski, Discordant Voices, Blasted Allegories: An Anthology of Writings by Contemporary Artists, New Mus Contemp Art, New York & Mass Inst Technol Press, Cambridge, Mass, 87. *Res:* The politics of photographic representation. *Publ:* Diversionary (Syn)tactics: Barbara Kruger Has Her Way With Words, Art News, 87; Picturing Scandal: Iranscam, the Reagan White House, and the Photo Opportunity, The Critical Image: Essays on Contemporary Photography, Carol Squiers, ed, Bay Press, Seattle, 90; Entertainment and Distress: The Photographs of Sandy Skoglund, Sandy Skoglund: Reality Under Siege, Abrams/Smith Coll Mus Art, 98; Class Struggle: The Invention of Paparazzi Photography and the Death of Diana, Princess of Wales, Overexposed: Essays on Contemporary Photography, New Press, NY, 99. *Mailing Add:* 218 Thompson St No 15 New York NY 10012

SQUIRES, GERALD LEOPOLD
PAINTER, SCULPTOR, PRINTMAKER
b Nfld, Nov 17, 1937. *Study:* Danforth Tech Sch, graduate 1957; Ontario Coll of Art (night courses), 1958 & 1959; mainly self-taught. *Hon Degrees:* Mem Univ of NL, DLitt, 1992. *Work:* Saidye & Samuel Bronfman Collection, Montreal; Govt Nfld; Hibernia Corp; Art Gallery of Nfld & Labrador Permanent Collection; Confederation Art Gallery, Prince Edward Island. *Comn:* painting for Hibernia poster, Dept Mines & Energy, Govt Can, 88; St John the Baptist Cathedral, ceramic wall mural, "Portrait of Bishop Lampert", comn by Basilica Parish, St John's, 2005; Mary Queen of the World Church, Mt Pearl, Nfld, 27 paintings, drawings, 14 stained glass windows, comn by MQWC Parish, 1983-2004; St Clare's Hosp Foyer, St John's, "For Mercy Has A Human Heart" (history of St Clares), 16X16 raku ceramic wall mural comn by the Sisters of Mercy, 2004; St John's Airport, 6X10 oil on canvas, "Caribou on the Barrens", commissioned by St John's Airport Authority; Boyd's Cove Beothuk Interpretation Centre, life-size bronze sculpture, "Shanawdithit", comn by Beothuk Institute of Newfoundland & Labrador, 2002. *Exhib:* Solo exhibs, Portraits, 78, Ferryland Downs, 79-81, Cassandra Series, 83 (traveling exhib), Crucifixion-Resurrection, The Last Supper & St John's, Nfld, 87, Mem Univ, Nfld, Gerald Squires: A Retrospective, Atlantic Arts Gallery, St John's, Nfld, 81; No Fishing, RCA Gallery, St Johns, 1991; Cult Assets: Art From Newfoundland Corp Collections, AGNL, 1997; Gerald Squires: New Landscapes, RCA Gallery, St Johns, 1997; Gerald Squires: Journey - selections from 4 decades work, Art Gallery Newfoundland & Labrador, 1998; Whodunit, Ontario Coll of Art & Design, Toronto, 2004; A Showcase of Four Canadian Artists, St Jeromes 2nd Ann Festival of Art and Spirit, Waterloo Univ Art Gallery, Ont, 2004. *Pos:* Artistic dir, Breakwater Books Publishing Co, St John's; bd dir, Artist's Coalition Nfld & Labrador. *Teaching:* Instr art, Mem Univ Nfld, 70-88; workshops and lectrs in pub schs & art asns throughout Nfld & Labrador. *Awards:* Can Coun Arts B Award, 87; Royal Canadian Acad Arts Award, 1999; Her Majesty Queen Elizabeth 11, Golden Jubilee Medal, awarded 2003. *Bibliog:* Joan Marie Sullivan (auth), Nfld roots nurture Squires work, Globe & Mail, Toronto, 88; James Wade (auth), A medieval saint in a secular world, The Nfld Herald, 10/1/88; Arnold Bennett (auth, film) The Newfoundland Passion, 1998, Cine Terre-Neuve/Sleeping Giant, 60 minute doc film on Squires and his Mary Queen of the World Church paintings shown on Vision TV; Caroline Stone, Elizabeth Kidd (cur, auth) Gerald Squires, Journey, a 1998 Art Gallery of Newfoundland publication to commemorate the exhib by the same title, containing reproductions from the exhib, essays and articles; Sean J McGrath (auth), The Newfoundland Quarterly, Vol 96 #4, Transformative Imagery The Landscape Art of Gerald Squires, 2003 & 04. *Mem:* Great Northern AUK Workshop; founding mem Oshawa Art Gallery; Can Drawing Soc; Royal Can Acad. *Media:* All Media. *Dealer:* Emma Butler Gallery 111 George St St John's Nfld; Christine Parker Contemporary Graphics 127 Queen's Rd St John's Nfld; Gerald Squires Gallery Art St John's. *Mailing Add:* Bennetts Rd Box 361 Holyrood NL A0A 2R0 Canada

SQUIRES GANZ, SYLVIA (TYKIE)
PAINTER
b Southampton, NY, Oct 8, 1932. *Study:* Cortland State Univ, 51-53; also with Helen A Del Grosso, 70-71. *Work:* Smithsonian Inst Mus. *Comn:* Paintings, First Federal Savings Loan, Delray Beach, Fla, 79 & 81; poster, Isle Royale Nat Park, 96. *Exhib:* Nat Miniature Art Soc Fla Exhib, Clearwater, 77-2013; Nat Painters, Sculptors & Gravers Soc, Arts Club, Washington, DC, 78-2013; Nat Ann Miniature Art Exhib, Gallery La Luz, NMex, 79-2001; Miniature Art Asn traveling exhib; Mus Fine Arts, St Petersburg; Leigh, Yawkey Woodson Art Mus, 93; solo exhib, Hampton Bays Pub Libr, 2002; World Federation of Miniaturists, Smithsonian Int Gallery, Washington, DC, 2004; World Exhib of Miniatures, Tasmania, 2004; Benefit for the Bays-Reseeding with Artwork in Gallery Belage, West Hampton Beach, NY, 2011; World Exhib of Miniatures, Russia, 2012. *Pos:* Artist-in-residence, Isle Royale Nat Park, 96; jurist & judge for many nat shows, incl Miniature Art Soc Fla Int Show, 98-99; show judge Seacoast Gallery, Nags Head, NC, 2004, 2006, 2010; judge, Ridge Art Asn, Winter Haven, 2011. *Awards:* First Prize (acrylic), Arts for the Parks Nat Competition, 92-93, 96 & 99; Grumbacher Award, 96-99; Best in Show, Loxahatchee Nat Wildlife Refuge Yr Show, 2002 & 2003, 3rd Place, 2012; Palm Beach Community Coll First Nat Drawing, Painting & Printmaking Competition, Excellence Award; 1st Birds & Animals, Fla Int Miniature Show, 2007-2008; 1st Acrylic award, Fla Int Miniature Show, 2009; 2nd Pl Still Life, Miniature Paints, Sculptors, and Gravers Soc Wash DC, 2013; 2nd Pl award, Ridge Art Assn, Winter Haven, Fla, 2013. *Bibliog:* Timeless Treasures (video), Miniature Art Soc, Fla; Wildlife Art, Vol XIV, No 7, 96; Isle Royale (auth), The Island Within US, 97; Wes Segrist (auth), Modern Masters of Miniature Art in America, 2012. *Mem:* Assoc Miniature Painters, Sculptors & Gravers Soc, Washington, DC; Miniature Art Soc, Fla; Del Ray Art League; found mem, life mem, Miniature Artists Am, 85-; Hilliard Soc Miniaturists Wells, Somerset; Eng Soc Animal Artists; Artists for Conservation. *Media:* Acrylic. *Interests:* woodcarving, conservation, hiking, gardening. *Publ:* Contribr, Arts for the Parks, 91-93, 96 & 99; The Island within Us, 2000

STAAB, ROY
INSTALLATION SCULPTOR
b Milwaukee, Wis, 1941. *Study:* Layton Sch Art, Milwaukee, Wis, 1965; Milwaukee Inst Technol, Wis, 1966; Univ Wis, BFA, 1969. *Work:* Mus d'Art Mod, Paris; Le Fond National d'Art Contemp, Paris; Metrop Mus Art, New York; Milwaukee Art Mus, Milwaukee, Wis. *Exhib:* Exhibs include BWAC Open Studio Show, Brooklyn Mus, 1984; Mountains of the East, One Main, Brooklyn, 1992; Prairie Ring, Haggery Mus Art, Marquette Univ, Wis, 1992; Different Site Installations, Milwaukee Inst Art & Design, Milwaukee, Wis, 1997; Indoors & Out, Walker's Point Ctr Arts, Milwaukee, Wis, 1997; Swan's Tail, Long House, East Hampton, NY, 1997; Nature: Point of Departure, Del Arts Ctr Gallery, Narrowsburg, New York, 1998; Strong Willow, Klien Art Works, Chicago, 1998, Vaulted Arches, 2003; With the Environment, KM Fine Arts Gallery, Milwaukee, Wis, 1999; Wild Cyclic, Art St Windows, Milwaukee, Wis, 2001; Spring Ring, Charles Allis Art Mus, Milwaukee, Wis, 2002; Water, Land & Air, Ecoartspace, Garriso, NY, 2002; Clarity of Vision, Milwaukee Art Mus, 2002; River Surface "Imagine the River", Hudson River Mus, Yonkers, NY, 2003. *Awards:* Artist Space Exhib Grant, 1991; Puffin Found Grant, 1993; Gottlieb Found Award, 2000; Wis Arts Board Award, 2002; Artist-in-museum Yokohama Mus Art, 2005; Joan Mitchell Found Grant, 2007

STACH, JUDY
PAINTER, INSTRUCTOR
b Long Branch, NJ, Feb 25, 1947. *Study:* Mount Ida Chamberlain Coll, AA, 67; Art Students League with David LaFelle, 2000; Putney Painters with Richard Schmid, 2004. *Work:* Mount Ida Chamberlain Coll, Newton, Mass; Parker Clinic, Red Bank, NJ; Gateway Nat Park, Sandy Hook, NJ; Patricia Turchyn Interiors, Little Silver, NJ; Osprey Partners Investment Mgt, Shrewsbury, NJ. *Comn:* Kroon Family Home, Richard Kroon, Rumson, NJ, 2001; Family Home, Patrick Barovian, Coral Gables, Fla, 2003; Loveladies NJ Marina, Mr & Mrs Michael Tierney, Shrewsbury, NJ, 2004; Rogers Family, Kevin Rogers, Naples, Fla, 2005; Child on Beach with Dog, Adam Fazackerly, Reston, Va, 2005. *Exhib:* Three Unique Perspectives, Poricy Park Nature Ctr, Middletown, NJ, 96; Fla Invitational, Main St Gallery, Perry, Fla, 2002; two-person exhib, Guild Creative Art, Shrewsbury, NJ, 2002; Boulder Art Assoc Nat Juried Show, Boulder Art Assoc, Colo, 2003; Am Artists Prof League, Fla, NMex & New York, 2004-05; Am Impressionists Soc, Fla, NMex & New York, 2004-05; 19th Juried Show, Catherine Lorillard Wolf Art Club, New York, 2005; retrospective, Frederick Gallery, Allenhurst, NJ, 2006; Audubon Artists Nat Juried, Salmagundi Art Club, New York, 2006. *Collection Arranged:* Making Friends Around the World, Americorp Children's Expo, 2002; Sr Citizens Coun on Aging, Co Libr, Freehold, NJ, 2004. *Pos:* Vpres bd trustees, Guild of Creative Art, Shrewsbury, NJ, 96-2003; founder & pres, Plein Air Painters of the Jersey Coast, 2003-. *Teaching:* Instr plein air materials, Freehold, NJ Artists Soc, 2003 & Studio, Little Silver, NJ, 2003-; instr, Marketing Yourself, Guild Creative Art, 2006. *Awards:* Second Place Landscape Div, Ann Contest, The Artists Mag, 98; Hon Mention, The Best of Florida Art, Best Of Books, 2005-06; Inclusion in Volume, Long Beach Island Rhapsody, George Valenti (publ), 2006. *Bibliog:* Paul Soderburg (auth), Richard Schmid Interview, Art Talk Mag, 8-9/2004 & Gender Bias in the Arts, 8-9/2005; Kathy Collins (auth), Painting at Disney World, Vero Beach Mag, 2005; Linda DeNicola (auth), Living the Dream, The Hub, Monmouth Co, NJ, 6/2006; Painting on Sandy Hook NJ, Workshop Mag, fall 2006; Rebecca Minmeh (auth), Art Vs Cancer: The creative crusade of outdoor painter Judy Stach, Monmouth Health Life, 6/2007. *Mem:* Salmagundi Club; Plein Air Painters Fla (sig mem); Plein Air Painters of the Jersey Coast (founder & pres); Guild

Creative Art, Shrewsbury, NJ (exhib mem & bd mem, 96-2003); Am Impressionist Soc; Audubon Artists Inc, New York. *Media:* Oil, Acrylic. *Interests:* Boating, golf, tennis & gardening. *Publ:* Coauth, Living the Dream, Stinehour Wemyss, 2005; contribr, Long Beach Island Rhapsody, George Valenti, 2006; cover, Jersey Shore Home Garden, 5/2007. *Dealer:* Meghan Chandler/Findlay 1270 Hwy A1A Vero Beach FL 32963; Lambertville Gallery of Fine Art 20 Union St Lambertville NJ 08530; The Frederick Gallery 401 Spier Ave Allenhurst NJ 07760. *Mailing Add:* 15 Alwin Ter Little Silver NJ 07739

STACK, FRANK HUNTINGTON
PAINTER, PRINTMAKER
b Houston, Tex, Oct 31, 1937. *Study:* Univ Tex, Austin, BFA; Art Inst Chicago; Univ Wyo, Laramie, MFA; Acad Grande Chaumiere, Paris, Lakeside Studio Print Workshops. *Work:* Sheldon Mem Gallery, Univ of Nebr; Madison Art Ctr, Wis; Mo Hist Soc, Columbia; Kalamazoo Art Inst, Mich; Mus Art Archaeology, Columbia. *Comn:* Outdoor mural, First Nat Bank, Columbia, Mo. *Exhib:* Ten Missouri Painters, 69; solo exhibs, Etchings, US Info Serv, US Embassy, Turkey, Prints, Kalamazoo Art Inst, Mich, 76 & Watercolors, Va Tech Univ, 86, Harwell Mus, Poplar Bluff, Mo, 87 & Frye Art Mus, Seattle; From Zap to Zippy, San Francisco, 89; Misfit Lit Show, Seattle, 91; Bingham Gallery, Univ Mo, 2000; Paintings in France, Art Ker & Looney, Pakrs, 2008, 2010. *Pos:* Contrib ed, The Comics J, 88; ed bd, Inks. *Teaching:* prof art, Univ Mo-Columbia, 63-, Middlebush prof fine arts, 94-99, prof emeritus, 2000. *Awards:* Summer Res Fel, 68, 74 & 76 & Foreign Study Grant, 70 & 93, 98, Univ Mo Res Coun; Mo Arts Coun Awards, 86; The Artist We Like award, Gijon Comics Convention, 2007; Inkpot award, San Diego; Comic Con, 2011. *Bibliog:* Sidney Larson (auth), Etchings and Lithographs by Frank Stack, Singing Wind Publ, 76; exhib catalog, Watercolors by Frank Stack, Mo Arts Coun, 77; Naked Glory: Erotic Art of Frank Stack, Fantagraphics Book; 25 editions of lithographs, Galerie Item, Paris. *Mem:* Kans Watercolor Soc; Columbia Art League; Mo Watercolor Soc; Ms Contemp Ballet. *Media:* Oil, Watercolor; Etching, Cartoonist. *Res:* Comics History. *Interests:* Art History, English and Am Lit. *Collection:* European and Am Master Prints. *Publ:* assoc ed, Houston Chronicle, 59; Auth, A metal plate sketchbook, Am Artist, 10/75; New Adventures of Jesus, 69-73, Feelgood Funnies, 71, 84, Dorman's Doggie, Kitchen Sink Press, 90, Amazon, Fantagraphics, 90; ed, Alley Oop (4 Vols), 46-50, by V T Hamlin reprint of comic strip, 90-92; auth, Watercolor Wisdom, The Artist's Mag, 4/93; artist, Our Cancer Year, 93, American Spender 1988-2004; ed, Alley Oop Mag, 96-2007; artist/auth, The New Adventures of Jesus: The Second Coming, 2006; Les Nouvelle Aventures de Jesus, 2008; Adventures of Dirty Diana, Mineshaft, 2005-2010; Art of the Dance, 2010. *Dealer:* Denis Kitchen Art Agency, PO Box 2250, Northampton, MA 01004; Philip Slein Gallery, Washington Ave, St Louis, 63103. *Mailing Add:* 409 Thilly Ave Columbia MO 65203

STACK, GAEL Z
PAINTER, EDUCATOR
b Chicago, Ill, Apr 28, 1941. *Study:* Univ Ill, Champaign, BFA; Southern Ill Univ, MFA. *Work:* Mus Fine Art, Houston; Solomon R Guggenheim Mus, NY; Dallas Mus Art, Tex; Menil Collection, Houston Tex. *Exhib:* 19 Artists-Emergent Americans: 1981 (catalog), Solomon R Guggenheim Mus, NY, 81; solo exhibs, Hadler-Rodriguez Galleries, NY, 85, Brown-Lupton Gallery, Fort Worth, Tex, 85, Janie C Lee Gallery, Houston, Tex, 83, 85, 87 & 89, Beitzel Fine Arts, NY, 88, Sarah Campbell Blaffer Gallery, Univ Houston, Tex, 89, Univ Ark, Little Rock, 89, Moody Gallery, Houston, Tex, 90; Emerging Artists 1978-1986: Selections from the Exxon Series (catalog), Guggenheim Mus, NY, 87; The Artist's Eye: Fourteen Collections Diverse Works, Houston, Tex, 89; Women View Women, RGK Found Gallery, Austin, Tex, 90; Tradition and Innovation: A Mus Celebration of Texas Art, Mus Fine Arts, Houston, Tex, 90; Northwest X Southwest: Painted Fictions (catalog), Palm Springs Desert Mus, Calif, 90; Art from Houston in Norway, Stavanger Mus, 82; New Art from a New City, Frankfurter Kunstverein, Ger, 82; New Orleans Trienniale, New Orleans Mus Art, 83; Fresh Paint, The Houston Sch, Mus Fine Arts, 85; Texas Currents, San Antonio Art Inst, 85; and others. *Teaching:* Instr, Univ Wis, La Crosse, 72-73; from asst prof to assoc prof, Univ Houston, 74-85, prof, 85-. *Awards:* Nat Endowment Arts Artists Grant, 82, 89; Cult Arts Coun Houston Award Visual Arts, 85; Tiffany Found Award, 86. *Bibliog:* Michael Ennis (auth), Gael's Force, Domain, 5-6/89, 12, 14, 16; Elizabeth McBride (auth), Gael Stock, Artspace, 9-10/89, 65-65; Ann Holmes (auth), What artists collect, Houston Chronicle, 11/14/89, Sect D, 1, 4. *Dealer:* Condeso Lowler Gallery 524 Broadway New York NY 10012. *Mailing Add:* c/o Moody Gallery 2815 Colquitt Houston TX 77098

STACK, MICHAEL T
PAINTER, SCULPTOR
b Chicago, Ill, Oct 30, 1941. *Study:* Univ Ill, BFA, 64; Univ Fla, MFA, 66. *Work:* Okla Art Ctr; Olivet Univ; Nelson-Atkins Mus Art; Yellow Freight Corp, NCAA Headquarters, Overland Park, Kans; Hallmark Collection, Twentieth Century Investments, Dean Witter Reynolds, Kansas City, Mo; and others; Cindy Pritzker, San Diego, CA. *Comn:* Garden of Earthly Delights (painting), KCRF Inc, Hayworth, Ill, 69; painting, MLLJN Inc, Bloomington, Ill, 73; Tensegrity structure, Metrop Life Insurance, Overland Park, Kans, 83; Dancin' (serigraph), Kansas City Arts Coun & Crown Ctr Redevelopment Corp, Kansas City, Mo, 83; mural, Sharon & John Hoffman, Kansas City, 86; bronze sculpture, Pauline & Patrick Dolan, Kansas City, Mo; Gould Evans Goodman Architects, Kansas city, MO, 96; Cerner Corp, North Kansas city, MO, 97; sokkia Corp, Lenexa, KS, 2000; Blue Ridge Bank, Independence, MO, 2003. *Exhib:* Ultimate Concerns, Ohio Univ, Athens, 65; Art Across Am, Knoedler Gallery, NY & traveling, 65-66; Fla State Fair Fine Art Exhib, Tampa, 65 & 66; 72nd Chicago & Vicinity Exhib, Art Inst Chicago, 69; Nat Print & Drawing Exhib, Western Ill Univ, 70; Mid-Four Painting Exhib, Nelson-Atkins Mus Art, 80; Three Painters, Mulvane Art Ctr, Topeka, Kans, 83; Batz Gallery, Kansas City, MO, 83, 83, 89; Studio Sculpture Exhib, Kansas City, MO, 90; Mossa Ctr, Kansas City MO, 90; Park Coll, Parkville, MO, 93; Gruen Gallery, Chgo, Ill, 94; Leedy Voulkos Art Ctr, Kansas City, Mo, 2013; The Late Show, Kans City, MO, 2013; ARPS Gallery, Amsterdam, Netherlands, 2014. *Teaching:* Instr painting, Ill State Univ, 67-70; vis artist, NS Col Fine Arts, 69 & Kansas City Art Inst, 76, 87. *Awards:* Third Prize, Mid-Four Painting Exhib, 80; Award of Merit, Kansas City Artists Coalition Exhib, 88. *Bibliog:* Mary King (auth), Fishbowl taxicab, Stack-ed deck, St Louis Post Dispatch, 4/11/80; Mary Sprague (auth), article, New Art Examiner, 7/80; Donald Hoffmann (auth), 4 articles in Kansas City Star, 10/9/83 & 11/23/86; Ellen Goheen (auth), Parton Prompts painter, Forum, Vol 15, No 4, 90; Janet Majure (auth), Whirling dancers cast in bronze, Kansas City Star, 4/22/90. *Media:* Oil, Bronze. *Interests:* reading. *Dealer:* Leedy Volkous Art Ctr 2012 Baltimore Ave Kansas City MO 64108. *Mailing Add:* 3600 Roankoke Pkway Apt 3 Kansas City MO 64111-3867

STACY, JOHN RUSSELL
ILLUSTRATOR
b Denver, Colo, Mar 18, 1919. *Study:* Denver Art Inst, dipl, 39; Univ Wash, 47. *Work:* Boy Scouts Am Hq, Cimarron, NMex; Arches, Canyonlands, Yellowstone & Grand Teton Nat Parks, Wyo; Libr Cong, Washington. *Comn:* Painting, Izaac Walton League Am, Denver, Colo, 39; illusr, Colo Sch Mines, Golden, 60-70; illusr, Geological Soc Am, Boulder, Colo, 60-70. *Pos:* Illusr, US Geological Survey, Denver, Colo, 50-74; dir & illusr, Rocky Mountain Nature Asn, Estes Park, Colo, 74. *Awards:* O'Brien Faceting Trophy, Calif Fedn Mineralogical Soc, 84; Meritorious Serv Award, Dept Interior, 86. *Mem:* Life Santa Cruz Art League (bd dir, 81-82). *Media:* Oil, Acrylics. *Specialty:* Historical, portraiture. *Interests:* World travel, digital photo, computer tech, physical fitness. *Publ:* Auth & illusr, Terrain Diagrams in Isometric Projection--Simplified, Annals Asn Am Geographers, 58; co-auth & illusr, Philmont Country, Professional Paper 505, 64, Geologic Story of Yellowstone National Park, 73, Geologic Story of Canyonlands National Park, 74 & Geologic Story of Arches National Park, 75, US Geological Survey. *Mailing Add:* 12681 SW Peachvale St Portland OR 97224-2194

STAFFEL, DORIS
PAINTER, EDUCATOR
b New York, NY, 1921. *Study:* Tyler Sch Art, 39-44; Iowa Univ, MA, 45; Hans Hoffman Sch, 45-47. *Work:* Iowa Univ; Tylor Woodruff, London, Eng; Wills Eye Hosp; Cigna Mus. *Exhib:* Solo exhibs, Chatham Col, Pittsburgh, Pa, 65, Tyler Abroad, Rome Gallery, Italy, 68 & Gross McCleaf Gallery, Philadelphia, Pa, 79 & 82; Broad Spectrum, Allentown Art Mus, Pa, 81; Ann Drawing Exhib, Beaver Col, Glenside, Pa, 81. *Teaching:* Assoc prof painting, Philadelphia Col Art, 61-. *Awards:* Purchase Prize, Beaver Col, 78. *Media:* Oil, Watercolor. *Mailing Add:* 210 Locust St Apt 3A Philadelphia PA 19106

STAHANOVICH, KOLBA TAMARA See St Tamara

STAHL, ALAN M
CURATOR, HISTORIAN
b Providence, RI, Aug 7, 1947. *Study:* Univ Calif, Berkeley, BA, 68; Univ Pa, MA, PhD, 77. *Collection Arranged:* The Beaux-Arts Medal in Am, loan exhib, Am Numismatic Soc, NY, 87-88; USA Exhib, Int Fedn Medal, Helsinki, Finland, 90, British Mus, 92 & Budapest, Hungary, 94 & Neuchatel, Switz, 96. *Pos:* Cur medals, Am Numismatic Soc, 80-. *Mem:* Am Medallic Sculpture Asn (pres, 83-87); Fedn Int de la Medaille, (USA delgate, 85-); Nat Sculpture Soc (coun, 91-96). *Res:* History of the medal in USA & abroad; art of medieval coinage of Europe. *Publ:* Auth, The American Industrial Medal, The Numismatist, 84; Lauffer's Medal Cabinet, Medallic Sculpture, 85; coauth, The Beaux Art Medal in America, Am Numismatic Soc, 87; ed, The Medal in America, New York, 88; American Indian Peace Medals of the Colonial Period in Money of Pre-Federal America, New York, 92. *Mailing Add:* Am Numismatic Soc 75 Varick St 11th Fl New York NY 10013-1917

STAKE, PETER
EDUCATOR
Study: Arizona State Univ, BFA; Calif State Univ, Long Beach, MFA. *Exhib:* Ctr Art & Design, Univ Wales Inst. *Pos:* Chmn art & art hist dept Skidmore Col, Saratoga Springs, Calif. *Mem:* Bd trustees, Hyde Col. *Mailing Add:* Skidmore Col Art Dept 815 N Broadway Sasselin 200 Saratoga Springs NY 12866

STALLER, ERIC P
PHOTOGRAPHER, SCULPTOR
b Mineola, NY, Sept 14, 1947. *Study:* Univ of Mich, BArch, 71. *Work:* Mus Mod Art, NY; Everson Mus, Syracuse; Int Mus Photog, Rochester; Nat Acad Sci; State Univ NY, Stony Brook. *Comn:* lighting installations, Int Ctr of Photog, NY, 79, City Univ NY, 79 & Md Inst Coll Art, Baltimore, 79; light sculptures, Port Authority NY & NJ, 83; Three Rivers Art Festival, Pittsburgh, 85; Anchorage Performing Arts Ctr, Alaska, 86. *Exhib:* Biennials, Indianapolis Mus, 76 & Taft Mus, Cincinnati, 76; Samual Wagstaff Collection, Corcoran Gallery, Washington, DC, 79; Nat Acad Sci, Washington DC, 81; Lightmobile, City Univ Grad Ctr, NY, 85; City Lights, Int Ctr Photog, NY, 86. *Awards:* Creative Arts Pub Serv Prog Grant, 77; Nat Endowment Arts Grant, 78. *Bibliog:* Owen Edwards (auth), Tripping the light fantastic, Am Photog Mag, 4/78; article, The New York Times, 4/22/84; article, Wall St Jour, 8/8/85; article, Darkroom Mag, 11/85. *Media:* Light. *Mailing Add:* c/o Virginia Miller Galleries 169 Madeira Ave Coral Gables FL 33134

STALLWITZ, CAROLYN
PAINTER, PHOTOGRAPHER
b Abilene, Tex, Apr 27, 1936. *Study:* WTex State Univ, with Clarence Kincaid, Jr, BS (art); also with Emilio Caballero, Stefan Kramer, Lee Simpson & Chris Gikas. *Work:* Pioneer Natural Gas Co, First Nat Bank, Amarillo, Tex; Sun Bank, Dumas, Tex; Cliff Dwellers, Los Alamos, NMex. *Exhib:* Tex Watercolor Soc Exhib, 70; Wichita Centennial Nat Art Exhib, 70; Best Southwest, 71; Amarillo Fine Art Asn Citation Show, 73; Denver Audubon Wildlife Art Show, 77; African Wildlife, Crabb Art Ctr, Dumas, Tex. *Teaching:* Instr drawing, Amarillo Art Ctr, 73-74, instr watercolor, 74-75;

The Art Ctr, 99-2007. *Mem:* Moore Co Arts Asn (pres, 69-70 & 89-2008). *Media:* Watercolor, Pencil, Acrylics, Oils, Gouache. *Publ:* Window on the Prairie, Feather Press, 81. *Dealer:* Stallwitz Studio 5958 Stallwitz Rd Dumas TX 79029; The Art Center 234 W 1st Dumas TX. *Mailing Add:* PO Box 1225 Dumas TX 79029

STALOFF, FRED
PAINTER
b Jersey City, NJ, 1924. *Study:* Newark Sch Fine & Ind Art, Newark, NJ, 46-49; Acad de la Grande Chaumiere & Atelier Zadkine, Paris, 49-50. *Work:* Butler Inst Am Art, Youngstown, Ohio; James A Michener Art Mus, Doylestown, Pa; Kunstzall Polder Gallery, Holland; Atelier Decima, Paris, France. *Exhib:* solo exhib, Kunstzall Polder, Th Hague, Holland, 65; Bicentennial Exhib, Jersey City Mus, Jersey City, NJ, 76; Ann Exhib, Nat Acad Design, NY; 40 Years in Retrospect, Butler Inst Am Art, Youngstown Ohio, 96 & James A Michener Art Mus, Doylestown, Pa, 97; Allied Artists of America, Invitational Traveling Exhib, Tex, Ala, Wis, Va & Mich, 2003-2005; 65 Years: A Retrospective, Butler Inst American Art, Youngstown, Oh, 2012; Interiors and Landscapes, Trumbull Branch, the Butler Inst American Art, 2013. *Awards:* Allied Artists Gold Medal, Ann Allied Artist Am, Allied Artist Am, 97; Stefan Hirsh Mem Award, 97 & The Ralph Fabri Medal, 2000, Ann Audubon Artists, Gold Medal, Audubon Artists, 2006. *Mem:* Allied Artists Am (mem chmn, 94-97); Audubon Artists (treas, 70s); Artists' Fel. *Media:* Oil. *Mailing Add:* 2108 Harmon Cove Towers Secaucus NJ 07094

STAMATY, CLARA GEE KASTNER
PAINTER
b Piqua, Ohio, May 15, 1919. *Study:* Art Acad Cincinnati, 43; Art Students League, NY, 59; Pratt Graphic Workshop, NY, 69; Prints Div Libr, NY, 90. *Work:* Ford Times Collection Am Art, Detroit, Mich; Monmouth Reform Temple, Tinton Falls, NJ; United Methodist Church, Red Bank, NJ; Turbeville Collection, Emerson Coll, Boston, Mass; Libr Graphic Arts & Commun, Ohio State Univ, Columbus, Ohio. *Comn:* Paintings for windows & interior displays, Giddings, Cincinnati, Ohio, 42, Lawtons, 43, Rollman & Sons, and others. *Exhib:* Artists of Cincinnati & Vicinity, Cincinnati Art Mus, Ohio, 41; Ann New Year Show, Butler Art Inst, Youngstown, Ohio, 44 & 45; Artists of Dayton & Vicinity, Dayton Art Inst, Ohio, 45; NJ Watercolor Soc, Ann Juried Shows, Monmouth Mus, Lincroft, NJ 74-77; Am Watercolor Soc, 107th Ann Nat Acad Galleries, New York City, 74; solo exhibs, Guild of Creative Art, Shrewsbury, NJ, 99-2002; Art for Reflection, Avery Fisher Hall - Lincoln Ctr, New York City, 2000; Artists Studio, Monmouth Mus, Lincroft, NJ, 2001; and numerous group exhibs, 2003-2007; Solo Retrospective, Gallery on Grant, NJ, 2009. *Pos:* Artist, Air Serv Command/Paterson Field, Dayton, Ohio, 43-45; superv, art, Colony Surf Club, West End, NJ, 60-66. *Teaching:* Instr, Stamaty Studios, Elberon, 62-81; many seminars & workshops on printmaking, collage & mixed media, 60-2000. *Awards:* Recipient 8, 1st prize Awards Three Arts Club, 39-42; Special award, Dayton Art Inst, 45; Gold medal, Long Branch Community Ctr, 62; First Prize, Ann Exhib, Middletown, NJ, 72; First Prize, Mixed Media, Monmouth Arts Found, 74; and many others. *Bibliog:* Herman Landau (auth), Clara Gee Stamaty Exhibit is a Delight, Red Bank Register, 5/6/88; Kisha Ciabattari (auth), Tooned in Artist, Asbury Park Press, 5/15/89; Ronnie Gardstein (auth), Centerfold - No Title, State of Art, 7-8/2002. *Mem:* Monmouth Arts Found (bd mem, 65-80); Guild of Creative Art (secy, 67-68, vpres, 74-75); Nat Cartoonist Soc (honorary Lifetime mem, 79-); Monmouth Co Arts Coun (adv bd, 96-2001); Art Alliance NJ. *Media:* Watercolor, printmaking, monotype & Mixed Media. *Publ:* Freelance cartoonist & illustr for over 50 mags, 41-70; coauth, Life's Little Miracles, Am Mag, 48-50 & Budget Busters, Better Homes & Gardens, 50-51; auth & illustr, Sitter Sue, Christian Sci Monitor, 58-61; auth, Making the Rounds, NY Cartoon News, 3/59; auth & illustr, Ginny, Scholastic book Serv. *Dealer:* Guild of Creative Art 620 Broad St & Rt 35 Shrewsbury NJ 07702. *Mailing Add:* 1019 Woodgate Ave Long Branch NJ 07740-4631

STAMSTA, JEAN
PAINTER, WOVEN FIBER
b Sheboygan, Wis, Nov 2, 1936. *Study:* Univ Wis, Milwaukee, BS, 58; Haystack Mountain Sch Crafts, 66; Fiberworks Ctr Textile Research, 81; Banff Ctr, Alta, Can, 86; Leighton Artist Colony, Banff, Alta, Can, 87. *Work:* Cleveland Mus Art, Ohio; Am Craft Mus, New York; Milwaukee Art Mus, Wis; Mus Fine Arts, Columbus; US Vice President's House, Washington, DC; Racine Art Mus, Wis; Ark Art Ctr, Little Rock; Mus Wis Art, West Bend, Wis; Carroll Univ, Waukesha, Wis; Edgewood Collage, Madison, Wis. *Comn:* Woven panels, Bank of Commerce, Milwaukee, 78; wall hanging, Sentry Insurance, Wis, 78; wall hangings, Miller Brewing co, Milwaukee, 79; fiber sculpture, Ohio Bell, Cleveland, 84; painting, Johnson Hill Press, Ft Atkinson, Wis, 93; Painting, Kursel Family Collection, 2005. *Exhib:* Fiberworks (with catalog), Cleveland Mus Art, Ohio, 77; Fiber R/Evolution(with catalog), Milwaukee Art Mus, 86; Wis Triannual (with catalog), Madison Art Ctr, 87 & 90; Paper (with catalog), Fine Arts Mus, Budapest, Hungary, 92; USA-Today (with catalog), Textile Mus, Tilburg (with catalog), The Neth, 93; Spirit in the Land, Mem Union Gallery, Univ Wis, Madison, 94; solo exhibs, Univ Wis Ctr, Sheboygan, 98, Wis Luth Coll, Milwaukee, 99, Rendering Symbols and Codes, West Band Mus Art, Wis, 2000 & Carroll College, Waukesha, Wis, 2006; Paper Show, Bergtrom Mahler Mus, Neenah, Wis, 98; and others. *Pos:* Guest cur, Fiber R/Evolution exhib, 86. *Teaching:* Instr weaving, Alverno Coll, Milwaukee, Wis, 65-72, Mt Mary Coll, Milwaukee, Wis, 70-73, Univ Northern Mich, summer 77, Rochester Inst Technol, New York, summer 80 & Univ Wis, Milwaukee, 84. *Awards:* Nat Endowment Arts Craftsman Fel, 74; Lifetime Achievement award, Wis Visual Art, 2012. *Bibliog:* Elizabeth A Bard (auth), Great Lake series, Fiberarts, 4/83; Randy Bitter (auth), Papermaking using Wisconsin Effigies-The Art of Jean Stamsta, Progress in Paper Recycling, 5/94; Kevin Lynch (auth), Art show ties environment to human growth, The Capital Times, Madison, Wis, 6/30/94. *Media:* Paper, Fabric, acrylic paint on canvas. *Publ:* Coauth, Fiber R/Evolution (exhib catalog), 86. *Mailing Add:* W 299 N 9313 Center Oak Rd Hartland WI 53029

STANBRIDGE, HARRY ANDREW
PAINTER, PRINTMAKER
b Quesnel, BC, July 23, 1943. *Study:* Vancouver Sch Art, dipl (hons), 68; Univ BC, BA (art educ), 74, MA, 82. *Work:* City of Vancouver, BC; Seattle Art Mus; Nat Gallery Can Libr, Ottawa; Provincial Collection, Victoria, BC; Univ Alta Libr, Edmonton; Art Gallery of Greater Victoria; Can Coun Art Bank, Ottawa; Can Embassy, Australia. *Exhib:* Woman, Burnaby Art Gallery, BC, 72; Kinesis, Art Gallery Victoria, BC, 76; Victoria Artist, Art Gallery Victoria, BC, 86; Come Zion, Art Gallery of Greater Victoria, BC, 87; two-person exhib (with P Coupey), Surrey Arts Ctr, BC, 88; and others. *Teaching:* Instr drawing & painting, Spectrum Community Sch, Victoria, BC, 74-. *Awards:* Grant, Can Coun, 69; Purchase Award, Northwest Printmakers 40th Ann, Seattle Art Mus, 69. *Bibliog:* Charles Shere (auth), Four days from a diary, Arts Can, 75; Frank Nowasad (auth), Moments of cocksure bravado, Monday Mag, 86; N Tuele (auth), Come Zion, Recent Paintings by H Stanbridge (exhib catalog), Art Gallery of Greater Victoria. *Media:* Acrylic, Oil. *Publ:* Auth & illusr, Mirrored Barriers, Takao Tanabe (publ), 68; Great Works, Contemporary BC Artists, Melanie Gold, (publ), 96. *Dealer:* Bau-Xi Gallery 3045 Granville Vancouver BC V6H 3J9 Canada. *Mailing Add:* 4526 Hughes Rd Victoria BC V8X 3X1 Canada

STANCZAK, JULIAN
PAINTER, EDUCATOR
b Borownica, Poland, Nov 5, 1928; US citizen. *Study:* Uganda, Africa & London, Eng; Cleveland Inst Art, BFA, 54; Yale Univ, with Albers & Marca-Relli, MFA, 56. *Work:* Carnegie Mus Art, Pittsburgh; Albright-Knox Art Gallery, Buffalo; San Francisco Mus Art; Corcoran Art Mus, Washington, DC; Nat Gallery, Washington, DC; Tulsa Mus, Okla; Hirshhorn Mus, Washington, DC; Akron Art Mus; Butler Inst Am Art; Cincinnati Art Mus; Cleveland Art Mus; Hood Mus Art; Metrop Mus Art; Mus Fine Arts, Boston; Mus Mod Art, New York; Victoria & Albert Mus, London; and 54 other pvt & corp collections. *Comn:* Altar piece, St John's Unitarian Church, Cincinnati, 68; mural, Cleveland City Canvasses, 74; flag, City of Rottweil, Ger, 74; six paintings for atrium layout, Dracket Co, Cincinnati, 84; 4 paintings, Case Western Reserve Univ, Biomedical Bldg, Cleveland, Ohio, 93 & 94; outdoor facade 3d mural, 5/3rd Bank Hq, Cincinnati; and others. *Exhib:* Solo exhibs, Dayton Art Inst, 64, Akron Art Inst, 69, Concoran Art Gallery, Washington, DC, 72, Canton Art Inst, 74, Ohio State Univ, Columbus, 76, Int Monitary Fund, Washington, DC, 78, Butler Inst Am Art, 80, Nat Mus, Warsaw, Poland, 81, Standard Oil Co World Hq, Cleveland, Ohio, 87, Boca Raton Mus Art, 89 & Dennos Mus Ctr, Traverse City, Mich, 93, Columbus Mus Art, Ohio, 99, Asheville Mus Art, Ohio, 2000, Midland Ctr for the Arts, Midland, Mich, 2001, Eckert Fine Art Naples, Inc, Fla, 2002; retrospective, Butler Inst Am Art, Youngstown, Ohio, 98, Lowe Art Mus, Univ Miami, Coral Gables, Fla, 2001, Frederick R Weisman Mus Art, Pepperdine Univ, Malibu, Calif, 2001, Cleve Inst Art, Ohio, 2001, Washington State Univ Mus Art, Pullman, Wash, 2002, Naples Mus Art, Fla, 2002; Art in the Embassies, Madrid, 87; Galleria Zacheta, Warsaw, Poland, 91; Baum Gallery Art, Univ Ctrl Ark, Conway, 2000; Cleve Artists Found, Beck Ctr Arts, 2001; Bertha and Karl Leubsdorf Art Gallery, Hunter Coll, New York, 2003. *Teaching:* Instr, Art Acad Cincinnati, 57-64; prof painting, Cleveland Inst Art, 64-95; artist-in-residence, Dartmouth Coll, 68; prof emer, currently. *Awards:* Cleveland Fine Arts Award, Cleavland Found for the Arts, 68; Outstanding Educ Am, 70; Ohio Arts Coun Award, 72; Medal of Excellence Award, Cleveland Inst Art, 2001; Viktor Schreckengost Medal, Cleveland Inst Art, 2004. *Bibliog:* Art/Search & Self Discovery, 68; Jean Lipman (auth), Provocation Parallels: Naive Early American/International Sophisticates, Dutton Inc, New York, 75; Decades of Light, 40 years of works by Julian Stanczak, State Univ New York at Buffalo, 90; Elizabeth McClelland (auth), Julian Stanczak, Retrospective: 1948-1998, Butler Inst Am Art, 98; Annegreth T Nill (auth), Julian Stanczak, Columbus Mus Art, 99; MaLin Wilson-Powell (auth), Julian Stanczak: Op Art Painting, McNay Mus Art, 2003; Robert C Morgan (auth), Julian Stanczak, Construction and Color: Four Decades of Painting, Stefan Stux Gallery, 2005; Deedee Wigmore (auth), Freedom to Experiment: American Abstraction 1945-1975, Wigmore Fine Art, New York, 2007. *Mem:* Am Abstract Artists; Am Int Platform Asn. *Media:* Acrylic. *Res:* Pioneer in optical art. *Dealer:* McClain Gallery 2242 Richmond Ave Houston TX 77098; Renato Danese Gallery 535 W 24th St New York NY 10011. *Mailing Add:* 6229 Cabrini Ln Seven Hills OH 44131

STANFORD, GINNY C
PAINTER
b Lamar, Mo, Sept 3, 1950. *Study:* St Olaf Coll, Northfield, Minn, 67; Southwest Mo State Coll, 68. *Work:* Ft Smith Art Ctr, Ark; Nat Portrait Gallery, Smithsonian Inst, Washington, DC; Duke Univ, Durham, NC; Butler Ctr Arts, Little Rock. *Comn:* Two paintings, Kaiser Hosp, Santa Rosa, Calif, 89-90; three paintings, Kaiser Permanente Med Group, Santa Rosa, Calif, 89-91; painting, Bronson, Bronson & McKinnon, Santa Rosa, Calif, 91; five portraits, Duke Univ, Durham, NC, 96, 2003, 2007 & 2008; two portraits, Carolina Cent Bank, Durham, NC, 96; portrait, St Regis Sch, Denver, Colo, 2005; portrait, Hillary Rodham Clinton, Nat Portrait Gallery, Smithsonian Institution, Washington, DC, 2006; NASA Headquarters, Wash DC, 2008. *Exhib:* New Acquisitions, Nat Portrait Gallery, Washington, DC, 93; Chroma (with catalog), Fla State Univ, Tallahassee, 93; Emulations, Riverside Art Mus, Calif, 95; Recent Paintings, Saginaw Art Mus, Mich, 95; Recent Paintings, Pensacola Jr Coll, Fla, 95; A Brush With History: Notable Americans from the Collection of the Nat Portrait Gallery (with catalog), NC Mus Art, Raleigh, 2001; Tennessee State Mus, Nashville, 2001; Nat Mus Western Art, Tokyo, 2001; JB Speed Art Mus, Louisville, 2001-; Montgomery Mus Fine Arts, Ala, 2002-; A Brush with History, New Orleans Mus Art, La, 2002; Nat Portrait Gallery, London, Eng, 2002; Outwin Boochever Portrait Competition (with catalog), Nat Portrait Gallery, Washington, DC, 2006; Outwin Boochever Portrait Competition (with catalog), Nat Portrait Gallery, Wash DC, 2013. *Awards:* Western States Art Fedn Corp Collectors Project Award, Nat Endowment Arts, 90; Sonoma Co Found, Ind Artists Fel, Nat Endowment Arts, 90; Sonoma Found Grant, Individual Artist Fel, Sonoma Co Found & Nat Endowment Arts, 91. *Bibliog:* Laurie Cohn (auth), An American painter, KFTY Television, Santa Rosa, Calif, 4/91;

James Carroll (auth), The Paper, Study of an Assassination: Ginny Stanford's Poem Mourning John F Kennedy, 5/91; Julie Allen (auth), Studio View, KRBC Television, 92; Carolyn Kinder Carr & Ellen G Miles (auths), A Brush With History, Smithsonian Inst, 2001; Allys Paladino Craig (auth), Chroma: Contemp Luminist Painting, Florida State Univ, 94; Alison Guss (auth & producer), A Brush With History, History Channel, A&E Network, 2004. *Media:* Acrylic, Oil. *Publ:* Illusr, Victory Over Japan, Little Brown & co, 86; Mr Bridge/Mrs Bridge, N Point Press, 88; Remember Me, Mercury House, 91; The Light the Dead See, Univ Ark Press, 91; auth, Requiem: New Orleans Rev, Loyola Univ, 12/94. *Dealer:* Portrait Consultants 36 Brook Hills Circle White Plains NY 10605; Portraits Inc West 51st NY 10019. *Mailing Add:* 11 Mark Dr San Rafael CA 94903

STANFORTH, MELVIN SIDNEY
EDUCATOR, PAINTER
b Tuscaloosa, Ala, Sept 22, 1937. *Study:* Univ Ala, BFA; Wayne State Univ, MFA. *Work:* Duke Univ Med Ctr; R J Reynolds; Kaiser Permanente, Raleigh, NC; East Carolina Univ, Greenville, NC; Burroughs-Wellcome Corp; Bank Am; Rock Mt Art Ctr, NC; and others. *Exhib:* Regional Painting Exhib, 73-76 & Regional Drawing & Prints Exhib, 73-77, Southeastern Ctr Contemp Arts, Winston-Salem, NC; Ball State Univ Nat Drawing Exhib, Muncie, Ind, 74; Potsdam Nat Drawing Exhib, NY, 75; Piedmont Graphics, Greenville Co Mus, Greenville, SC, 77-78; Award Winners Exhib, NC Mus of Art, Raleigh, 79; NC Artists Exhibit, Rutgers Gallery, 80; Works on Paper, National-Weatherspoon Gallery, 87; Drawing/Photog, WVa Juried Show, 87; Outerbanks to Infinity (Nat Photog Show), 87-88; three man show, East Carolina Univ, 88, Boykin Gallery, Wilson, NC, 89; solo exhibs, Art Ctr, Goldsboro, 91, Greenville Mus Art, Spirit Sq Ctr, Charlotte, NC, 92, "Reunion" Rocky Mt Art Ctr, 2006, UNC Pembroke DA Gallery, 2007, Turchin Ctr Arts, Appalachian State Univ; Community Ctr for the Arts, Kinston, NC, 99; Coastal Bend Col, Beeville, Tex, 99; Nat Juried Exhib, Kinston, NC, 98-99 & 2007; Semi-Pub Gallery, Asheville, NC, 2001; Nat Juried Exhib, Rocky Mountain Art Ctr, 2002, 2005-2007. *Teaching:* Prof emer & painting, E Carolina Univ, Greenville, NC, 69-. *Awards:* Purchase Awards, Regional Painting Exhib, 73 & Regional Drawing & Prints Exhib, 73, Southeastern Ctr Contemp Arts, Winston-Salem, NC; NC Mus of Art Award, 74; NC Artists Fel, NC Arts Coun, 99; NC Art Fel, Weatherspoon Gallery, Greensboro, NC, 2000, Fayetteville Mus of Art, NC, 2000 & Platinum Gallery, Greenville, NC, 2000; Regional Artist Grant, NC Arts Coun, 2005 & 2007. *Media:* All Media. *Publ:* Contribr, Art Papers, 5-6/88, 8-9/90. *Mailing Add:* 2205 E Fifth St Greenville NC 27858

STANICH, NANCY JEAN
PHOTOGRAPHER, PRINTMAKER
b Pittsburgh, Pa, July 26, 1939. *Study:* Parsons Col, BA, 63; Ohio State Univ, MA, 67; State Univ NY, New Paltz, grad study printmaking, 82, 96. *Work:* Canal Lock Mus, High Falls, NY; Monhegan Mus, Monhegan Island, Maine; Pemiquid Point Mus, Maine; North Star Bank, Syracuse, NY. *Exhib:* Printmaking Traveling Exhib, Nat Asn Women Artists, 78-92; 155th Nat Acad Design Exhib, NY, 80; Audubon Artists Open Exhib, Audubon Artists Asn, NY, 86 & 89; Salmagundi Open Exhib, Salmagundi Club, NY, 86 & 89. *Teaching:* Instr serigraphy, Woodstock Sch Art, NY, 85 & Round Top Ctr Arts, Damarisotta, Maine, 93. *Awards:* First Place Graphics, Mt St Mary's Col, 83 & 85; Jeffery Childs Willis Mem Award, Nat Asn Women Artists, 92; First Place Graphics, Northeast Art Festival, Caldwell Col, 93. *Mem:* Nat Asn Women Artists; Woodstock Artist Asn; North Shore Artists Asn; Maine Coast Artists Asn. *Media:* All Media. *Dealer:* Nancy Starich 362 SR 32 N New Paltz NY 12561. *Mailing Add:* 362 Rte 32 N New Paltz NY 12561

STANKIEWICZ, MARY ANN
EDUCATOR
b Keene, NH, May 5, 1948. *Study:* Syracuse Univ, BFA (art educ), 70, MFA (art educ), 76; Ohio State Univ, PhD (art educ), 79. *Pos:* Consult, Getty Ctr Educ Arts, Los Angeles, 84-; servs at, Pa State Univ incl, adv, Pa Art Educ Asn student chap, 2000-01. *Teaching:* Prog off, Getty Ctr Educ Arts, Santa Monica, Calif, 90-92; asst vpres, acad affairs Ringling Sch Art and Design, Sarasota, Fla, 92-94; assoc prof, art educ, Sch Visual Arts Pa State Univ, Univ Park, Pa, 99-2000 & 2000-2004; prof, art educ, Penn State Univ, 2004; Nat Art Educator, Nat Art Education Assn, 2014. *Awards:* Grad Fel, 76-77, Grad Student Alumni Res award, 78; Grantee Nat Endowment of the Humanities, 86, Spencer Found, 87; recipient Kenneth Marantz Distinguished Alumni award Grad Students Dept Art Educ, Ohio State Univ, 92; summer res fel, Ore Ctr Humanities, Univ Ore, 99; June King McFee Award, NAEA Women's Caucus, 2003; Distinguised Fel, NAEA, 2007. *Mem:* Coun Policy Studies in Art Educ, Nat Art Educ Asn Women's Caucus (historian/archivist, 80-88, pres women's caucus 84-85, June King McFee award, 2003); Philos Educ Soc; Hist Educ Soc; Maine Art Educ Asn, (Maine Art Educator Yr, 83); Coun for Policy Studies in Art Educ; Nat Art Educ Asn (pres-elect 2001-2003, pres, 2003-2005, past pres, 2005-2007); Nat Art Educ Found (bd trustees). *Res:* History of art education. *Publ:* Co-ed, Framing the Past, 90; co-ed (with Patricia M Amburgy, Donald Soucy, Brent Wilson & Marjorie Wilson), History of Art Education: Proceedings from the Second Penn State Conference, Reston Va: Nat Art Educ Asn, 92; ed, Art Education, Nat Art Educ Asn, 95-98; auth, Roots of Art Education Practice, 2001; ed, books and monographs; contribr articles to prof jour & book chap. *Mailing Add:* Pa State Univ Art Educ Prog 30 D Barland Bldg State College PA 16802-2905

STANLEY, JOHN SLUSARSKI
MUSEUM ADMINISTRATOR
b Saginaw, Mich, July 23, 1956. *Study:* Univ Toledo, BBA, 1979; Bowling Green State Univ, MBA, 1988. *Pos:* Asst comptroller, Toledo Mus Art, 1982-84, asst to dir, 1984-88, asst dir, 1986-88, dep dir operations, asst sec treas, 1988-95; bd dirs, Ohio Mus Asn, 1986-88, Toledo Cult Arts Ctr, 1989-95; trustee, Intermus Conservation Asn, 1993; chief operating officer, dep dir programs & services, Mus Fine Arts, Boston, 1995-2008; dep dir, Whitney Mus Am Art, New York, 2008-. *Mem:* Ohio Mus Asn; Intermus Conservation Asn; AAM. *Mailing Add:* Whitney Mus Am Art 945 Madison Ave New York NY 10021

STANLEY, M LOUISE
PAINTER
b Charleston, WVa, Aug 28, 1942. *Study:* La Verne Col, BA, 64; Calif Coll Arts & Crafts, BFA, 67, MFA, 69. *Work:* Triptych, Oakland Mus; San Jose Mus Art; Triton Mus Art, Mills Coll; Yale Univ, de Saisset Art Mus. *Comn:* Neighborhood Convergence, Public Art Sculptures, I-80 Underpass, Emeryville, 2003. *Exhib:* Solo shows, Univ Art Mus, Univ Calif, Berkeley, 78, PS1, Queens, NY, 78, Quay Gallery, San Francisco, 83, Rena Bransten Gallery, 86, Calif State Hayward, 94, Cal State, Haywood, Calif, 96, SFMOMA Rental Gallery, San Francisco, 99, Dominican Univ, Ca, 07, Caffe Museo, SFMOMA, San Francisco, 08 & Sanchez Art Ctr, Pacifica, Calif, 09, Paintings that Matter, Lake Tahoe Community College, 2011, Paintings that Matter, Haldan Gallery, Solake, Tahoe, Calif, 2012; Group shows, Drawings by Painters, Long Beach Mus Art, Calif, 82; Second Sight: Biennail IV, San Francisco Mus Mod Art, 86; Myth and Magick, Fetterly Gallery, Vallejo, Calif, 98; Art the Other Industry, Emeryville, Calif, 99; Watercolor, City Col, San Francisco, 99; Wood St Gallery, Chicago, 99; "M Louise Stanley' San Francisco Mus Mod Art, 99; New Acquisitions: Permanent Collection, Triton Mus, Santa Clara, Calif, 2000; "M Louise Stanley: Classics Illustrated," Reese Bullen Gallery, Humboldt St Univ, Arcata, Ca, 2000; (group) "The Lighter Side of Bay Area Figuration," San Jose Mus of Art, 2000; Renegade Humor, San Jose Mus Art, 2012. *Pos:* Tour Leader, Art Lovers Tour of Italy, currently. *Teaching:* Instr painting & drawing, San Francisco State Univ, Calif, 77-78; asst prof painting, drawing & watercolor, La State Univ, Baton Rouge, 78-79; instr painting, San Francisco Art Inst, Calif, 82-; vis artist, Univ NC, Chapel Hill, 84; instr painting, Univ Calif, Berkeley, 85-86; prof art, Berkeley City Coll, Berkeley, 2002-. *Awards:* Nat Endowment Arts Grant, 83 & 89; Fleishhacker Grant S F; Adolph and Esther Gottlieb Found Grant, 97 & 2005; Pollock-Krasner Found Grant in Painting, 2014; John Simon Guggenheim Found Fellowship in Painting, 2015. *Bibliog:* Yasmin Anwar (auth), Mary, Mary quite contrary, Oakland Tribune, 4/1/97; Michelle Paisley (auth), The many faces of Mary, Contra Costa Sun, 3/26/97; Darwin Marable (auth), Mary exhib inspires and incites, Catholic Voice, 4/7/97; Peter Selz (auth, catalog), The Art of Engagement, San Jose Mus Art; Susan Landauer (auth, catalog), The Lighter Side of Bay Area Figuration, San Jose Mus Art. *Mem:* Charter mem Calif Fedn Art Teachers Local 1; Peralta Fedn Teachers. *Media:* Gouache, Acrylic. *Res:* Greco-Roman myth & history. *Interests:* Founder, dir, "Art Lovers Tours" to Italy, 1994-. *Publ:* Auth, portfolio, Paris Review, Winter 84; Modern Myths: Regarding Art: J of Exploration, Winter/Spring, 98. *Mailing Add:* 1420 45th St Apt 29 Emeryville CA 94608

STANLEY, ROBERT A
PAINTER, PRINTMAKER
b Defuniac Springs, Fla, Mar 10, 1942. *Study:* Univ Dayton, BA, 1964; Pratt Inst, MA, 1969. *Work:* Museum Mod Art, Chamalieres, France; World Print Coun, San Francisco, Calif; Koehnline Mus, Des Plaines, Ill; Brauer Mus, Valparaiso Univ, Ind; Ft Wayne Mus Art, Ft Wayne, Ind. *Comn:* Unity Found Mich City, Ind. *Exhib:* Man & the Urban Environment, Wm Penn Mus, Harrisburg, Pa, 1971; Current Visions: A Nat Survey, Germanow Art, Rochester, NY, 1985; Interface, Olympia & York, New York, NY, 1991; Solo exhibs: Mus Mod Art, Valery Larbeaud, Vichy, France, 2000; Oversoul, Lubeznik Ctr Arts, Michigan City, Ind, 2007; Int Digital Art Top 100, idaprojects.org/IDAA, 2001; Hooked Up, Columbia Coll Ctr Arts, Chicago, Ill, 2005; Sand, Steel, & Spirit, Ft Wayne Mus Art, Ft Wayne, Ind, 2006; Hyde Park Art Center, Chicago, Il, 2007; Beverly Arts Center, Chicagol, IL, 2008; Platform58_issue001, http://www.platform58.com; Univ Dayton, Ohio, 2009; Gallery Tundedal, Group Exhib, Manifestation Against Honorary Killings, Transgund, Sweden, 2009; Univ of Dayton Studio D Gallery, Group Exhib, Ohio, 2009; Solo Exhib Flow-Partial Count, Depot Gallery, Beverly Shores, Ind, 2009; Evanston Art Center, Evanston, Il, 2010; Substation #9, Invitational, The Stone Project, Hammond, Ind, 2011; Lakeside Gallery West, Two Person,Michigan City, Ind, 2012; Solo exhib: Brauer Mus Art, Valparaisio Univ, Ind, 2013; In recognition of Malala Yousafzai, Ostra Gymnasiet, Skogas, Sweden, 2015; Art in Dazzling Dimension Sculpture Group Exhib, SSAA Gallery, Michigan City, Ind, 2015. *Collection Arranged:* The Brauer Mus of Art, Valparaiso Univ, The Embassy of France, Washington, DC, Fort Wayne Mus of Art, Ind, IN FOCUS Systems, Lubeznik Art Center,Koehnline Mus, Asn Mouvement d'Art Contemporain, Chamalieres, France, NiSource, Rahabilitation Inst of Chgo, Telecomgroup, Palatine, Unity Found of LaPorte County, Ind, Univ Dayton, Ohio, World Print Council, and numerous personal collections. *Awards:* Gold Award, Art Ctr Show, Dayton Art Inst, Ohio, 1969; Award of Merit, Int All on Paper Exhib (AAOWNY), 1979; Prix de le ville de vichy, Chamalieres Triennial Int, Chamalieres, France, 1997; Award of Merit, 55th Ann Salon, Northern Ind Arts Ctr, 1998; Merit Award, Art Comp 2004, Chesterton Art Ctr, 2004. *Bibliog:* Une Breve et Ample Enonciation, Catalog Troisieme Mondiale d'Estampes, L'Association Musee D'Art Contemporair, 1994; Robin Nicols (auth), 2001 IDA Awards, Digital Photog & Design, 2001; Gregg Hertzlieb (auth), Robert Stanley, Catalog UF Gallery, 2004; Nathan Harpaz (auth), Artwalk at Oakton, Koehnline Mus Art, DesPlaines, Ill, 2005; Bruce Rimell (edit), Planet Earth Planet Art, Mirca Art Group, 2009; Neoteric Art Inteview, http://neotericart.com/2009/10/23/interview-with-robert-stanley/,10/23/2009; What Is Painting, Neoteric Art, http://neotericart.com/2014/06/13/the-wip-project-what-is-painting-featuring-robert-stanley/; BIG ART--2014 Neoteric Art, http://neotericart.com/2014/03/12/big-art-by-robert-stanley/. *Mem:* Ind Arts Comn (grants panel, 2007-2009). *Media:* Acrylic, Oil, Archival Computer Print. *Dealer:* Gallery 415 415 N LaSalle St Chicago IL 60610. *Mailing Add:* 23 E Stillwater Ave Box 922 Beverly Shores IN 46301

STANTON, HARRIET L
PAINTER
b New York, NY, Mar 27, 1924. *Study:* Cornell Univ, 41; Richmond Prof Inst, Coll William & Mary, Cert, 44; Art Student's League, 46-47. *Work:* Milwaukee Art Ctr, Wis; Yale Univ Art Gallery, New Haven, Conn; C W Post Coll Mus, Brookville, NY; US Embassy, Paris; Univ NC, Chapel Hill; Corp collections, Smith Barney, AT&T,

Xerox & IBM. *Exhib:* San Francisco Mus Art, Calif, 63; Artists Use of Paper, Suffolk Mus, Stony Brook, NY, 74; New Talent, Gimpel & Weitzenhuffer, New York, 74; Graphics, Albright-Knox Mus, Buffalo, NY, 78; Art in Bloom, Mem Art Mus, Univ Rochester, NY, 78; Am Printmakers, Tokyo Central Mus, Japan, 78; Elaine Benson Gallery, Bridgehampton, NY, 90 & 91; Gallery Emanuel, New York, 93; Adelphi Univ, Garden City, NY, 97; Nassau Co Mus Exhib, NY, Shelter Rock Libr, 97 & Great Neck Libr, 98. *Teaching:* Instr drawing & painting, Nassau Co Mus, Roslyn, NY; NY Univ, New York, 67-71 & Hofstra Univ, Hempstead, NY, 68-75. *Awards:* Art Hon Award, Richmond Prof Inst; Emily Lowe Found Award; Premier Prix Int, Cannes, France. *Mem:* Nat Drawing Asn; Nat Asn Women Artists. *Media:* Oil, Print. *Interests:* Photog & theatre. *Collection:* Sammlung Alison und Peter W Klein, Nussdorf, Ger. *Dealer:* Szoke Koo 164 Mercer St New York NY 10012. *Mailing Add:* 119 Malverne Ave Malverne NY 11565

STANTON, SYLVIA DOUCET
PAINTER
b New Orleans, La, Sept 21, 1935. *Study:* Newman, New Orleans, La, 52; Univ NMex, 62. *Work:* City of New Orleans, Permanent Collection, La; Sarah Gillespie Gallery, William Carey Col, Biloxi, Miss; Lucille Parker Gallery, William Carey Col, Hattiesburg, Miss. *Comn:* portrait of Gillian Hepburn, Great Niece of Catherine Hepburn. *Exhib:* group exhib, Montserrat Gallery, Broadway, NY, 2001; Solo exhib, Joye de Vie, Lucille Parker William Carrey Col, Hattiesburg, Miss, 2005, Artists Alley, San Fran, Calif, Maggie Mays Gallery, Bay St Louis, MO. *Pos:* pres, owner, Millbrook Art Gallery, Picayune, Miss, 2001-; pres, owner, French Salon Gallery, Bay St Luis, Miss, 2004-, Maggie Mays Fine Arts. *Teaching:* instr, oil painting, NMex Art League, 62-67; instr, oil painting, Millbrook Gallery, Picayune, Miss, 2001-; instr, oil painting, French Salon Gallery, Bay St Louis, Miss, 2004-; instr, Caboose Gallery, Long Beach, Miss. *Awards:* First Place Award, Pirates Alley Show, New Orleans Art League, 2002; First Place Award, Brew House Show, New Orleans Art League, 2003; First Place, Primate Center Show, St Tammy Art Assn. *Mem:* New Orleans Art League, La; Audubon Artists, NY; Allied Artists Am, NY; St Tammany Art League; Great Picayune Arts Council (dir). *Media:* Oil. *Specialty:* Show my own work; students work and New Orleans Artists; Realistic & impressionist. *Interests:* Art, interior design. *Collection:* City of New Orleans, James H Russell, Dr Herbert Marks, Dr Michael Sullivan, Mr Jacques Chavier. *Dealer:* French Salon In Serenity Place 126 N Main Bay St Louis, MS; Mont Serrat Gallery NY; Artists Alley San Francisco Ca. *Mailing Add:* 615 E Lakeshore Dr Carriere MS 39426

STAPEN, NANCY
CRITIC, WRITER
b New York, NY, Dec, 3, 1950. *Study:* Brandeis Univ, BA (fine art, magna cum laude), 72. *Collection Arranged:* Robert Henry Logan Retrospective, 84. *Pos:* Asst dir, Clark Gallery, Lincoln, Mass, 81-84; coordr, Mus Goers Month, var Boston mus, 83; sr art critic, Boston Herald, 84-90; exclusive Boston rep, Artforum, 85-88; feature writer, Christian Sci Monitor, Artnews & ELLE, 87-; Boston corresp, Artnews, 88-, Town & Country, 93-; art critic, Boston Globe, 90-. *Teaching:* Chmn fine arts, Belvoir Terrace Fine Arts, Lenox, Mass, summers 76-78; instr sculpture, Concord-Carlisle High Sch, Mass, 79-80; instr learning through art, De Cordova Mus, 81-83; lectr numerous univs & mus, 82-; dir, Docent Prog, DeCordova Mus, 83-84. *Awards:* Hon Mention Best Visual Arts Critic, Boston Mag, 86; Chemical Bank Award for Distinguished Newspaper Art Criticism, 87, 90 & 92. *Mem:* Am Asn Art Critics; Women's Caucus Art; PEN, New Eng; Nat Writers Union; Art Table; and others. *Res:* Visual arts; specializing in contemporary art. *Publ:* Auth, John Imber, Paintings, 78-89 (catalog essay), Fitchburg Art Mus, 9-11/90; Annette Lemieux, Recent Work, Paris Exhib, 9/91; Kiki Smith, Prints and Multiples 1985-1993, 1/94; Jake Berthot, Paintings (catalog essay), Dartmouth Col, 96

STAPRANS, RAIMONDS
PAINTER, SCULPTOR
b Riga, Latvia, Oct 13, 1926; US citizen. *Study:* Sch Art, Esslingen, Stuttgart, 46; Univ Wash, BA, 52; Univ Calif, MA, 55; also with Archipenko. *Work:* Calif Palace Legion Hon, San Francisco; Oakland Mus, Calif; Santa Barbara Mus, Calif; Los Angeles Co Mus; Phoenix Art Mus; Anderson Collection, San Francisco. *Exhib:* Portland Art Mus, Ore, 56 & 57; Oakland Art Mus, 57; Calif Palace Legion Hon Winter Invitational, 57, 59 & 60; Litton Industs, 62; Am Acad Arts & Lett, NY, 70; and many solo exhibs, in US, Can & Europe incl San Jose Mus of Art, Pasadena Mus Art, Calif, 2006, Latvian State Mus, 2006, Hackett-Freeman, 2006. *Teaching:* Instr, Univ Alaska, 78 & 81. *Awards:* San Francisco Art Festival. *Bibliog:* California Canvas (film), KRON, San Francisco, 66; Artists Eye (film), Motion Media, 67; Color in Contemporary Painting. *Mem:* Z Lazda Mem Found (past chmn). *Media:* Oil, Acrylic; Plastic. *Interests:* playwriting. *Publ:* Raimonos Staprans, Univ Washington Press. *Dealer:* Hackett-Mill Gallery 201 Post St Ste 1000 San Francisco CA 94108. *Mailing Add:* 2052 20th St San Francisco CA 94107

STARK, FRANCES
INSTALLATION SCULPTOR
b Newport Beach, Calif, 1967. *Study:* San Francisco State Univ, BA (Humanities), 1991; Art Ctr Coll Design, MFA, Pasadena, Calif, 1993. *Work:* Mus Contemp Art, Los Angeles; Los Angeles County Mus Art, CA; San Francisco Mus Mod Art; Judith Rothschild Found, New York; UCLA Hammer Mus, Los Angeles; Fonds Regional d'art Contemporain, Champagne-Ardenne. *Exhib:* Solo exhibs include CRG Gallery, New York, 1996, 2001, 2005, Greengrassi, London, 1998, 2002, 2004, Van Abbe Mus, Eindoven, The Netherlands; Group exhibs include Just Past: the Contemp & Permanent Collection 1975-1996, Mus Contemp Art at the Geffen Contemp, Los Angeles, 1996; The Power of Suggestion: Narrative & Notation in Contemp Drawing, Mus Contemp Art, Los Angeles, 1996; Made in Calif: Art, Image & Identity, 1900-2000, Los Angeles County Museum of Art, 2000; The Great Drawing Show: 1550-2003 AD, Michael Kohn Gallery, Los Angeles, 2003; For Nobody Knows Himself If He Is Only Himself & Not Another At the Same Time, Marc Foxx, Los Angeles, 2003; Post No Bills, White Columns, New York, 2005, Monuments for the USA, 2005; Looking at Words: The Formal Presence Of Text In Mod & Contemp Works On Paper, Andrea Rosen Gallery, New York, 2005; Whitney Biennial, Whitney Mus Am Art, New York, 2008; 54th Int Art Exhib Biennale, Venice, 2011. *Mailing Add:* 970 N Broadway St #216 Los Angeles CA 90012

STARK, KATHY
PAINTER
b Croton-on-Hudson, NY. *Study:* Univ NMex; NY Univ; Art Student's League, NY; Printmaking Workshop, NY. *Work:* Smithsonian Inst; Bibliotheque Nat; Neuberger Mus, Purchase, NY; Southeast Ark Art Ctr, Pine Bluffs; Chase Manhattan Bank; Chemical Bank; Bell Labs. *Comn:* Painting, comn by Mr R Kanofsky, NY 87; painting, Genesys Software Systems, Inc, 88; painting, comn by Dr & Mrs R Riechers, Mt Kisco, NY, 89; painting, comn by Mr D Masters, Nantucket, Mass, 90; painting, comn by Pamala Killen, Nantucket, Mass, 92. *Exhib:* Solo exhibs, Kenneth Taylor Gallery, Nantucket, Mass, 89, Sun Gallery, Nantucket, Mass, 90, 91 & 92, Art Source, Cleveland, Ohio, 91, Little Gallery, Nantucket, Mass, 91, de Havilland Gallery, Boston, 92 & New Hampton Gallery, NH, 93; Copley Soc, Boston, 91; Left Bank Gallery, Wellfleet, Mass, 93; Hooper Mus, Nyack, NY, 93; Nat Asn Women Artists Ann Exhib, Javits Ctr, NY, 93; Main Street Gallery, Nantucket, Mass, 93-99; West Branch Gallery, Vt, 2004-2006; SoHo 20, Chelsea, NY, 2006; Spheris Gallery, Vt, 2006. *Awards:* Target Presentations Grant, Found Community on Artists, 79-80; Independent Exhib Grant, Artists Space, 83 & 86; 1st Prize, Temple Arts Festival, 2005. *Mem:* Nat Asn Women Artists; Copley Soc; Artists' Asn Nantucket. *Media:* Acrylic. *Interests:* Gardening & reading. *Dealer:* SoHo 20 NY; West Branch Gallery Vt

STARK, LINDA
PAINTER
b San Diego, Calif, 1956. *Study:* San Diego State Univ, Calif, 75; Grossmont Col, El Cajon, Calif, 76; Univ Calif, Davis, BA, 78; Univ Calif, Irvine, Regents Fel, 83, Laguna Beach Arts Fel, 84, MFA, 85. *Exhib:* Newport Harbor Art Mus, 86; solo exhibs, Cirrus, Los Angeles, 90, 91 & 93, Jack Shainman Gallery, NY, 94 & 96, Feigen Inc, Chicago, 95, Marc Foxx, Santa Monica, Calif, 95, Runaway Love, Jack Shainman Gallery, NY, 96 & 97 & Angles Gallery, Santa Monica, Calif, 98; Aldrich Mus Contemp Art, 94; Skew: The Unruly Grid, Gallery 400, Sch Art & Design, Univ Ill, Chicago, 95; Sexy: Sensual Abstraction in California Art 1960s-1990s, Temporary Contemp Gallery, Las Vegas, 95; And the Verdict Is, Jack Shainman Gallery, NY, 95; Untitled, Jack Shainman Gallery, NY, 96; Pop Surrealism (catalog), Aldrich Mus Contemp Art, Ridgefield, Conn, 98; Precious, Jan Baum Gallery, Los Angeles, Calif, 98; Ecstasy, Jack Shainman Gallery, NY, 98. *Awards:* Vis Artist Fel Grant, Nat Endowment Arts, 95-96; Vis Artist Fel, Calif Arts Coun, Sacramento, Calif, 98. *Bibliog:* Michael Kimmelman (auth), In Los Angeles, the makings of a better mood, NY Times, 1/14/96; Michael Cohen (auth), Linda Stark at Mark Foxx, Flash Art, 1-2/96; Frederick Ted Castle (auth), Linda Stark at Jack Shainman, Rev, 4/1/96. *Dealer:* Jack Shainman Gallery 560 Broadway 2nd Floor New York NY 10012; Angles Gallery 2230 & 2222 Main St Santa Monica CA 90405

STARK, ROBERT
PAINTER, PHOTOGRAPHER
b Sidney, NY, Mar 27, 1939. *Study:* Studied photog with Minor White, 61-64; also painting restoration with Robert Scott Wiles, Corcoran Gallery of Art, 71-74. *Work:* Mus Modern Art, NY; Phillips Collection, Corcoran Gallery Art. *Comn:* Sullivan & Cromwell, Washington, DC, 89. *Exhib:* Solo exhibs, Corcoran Gallery, 69, Phillips Collection, Washington, DC, 79 & Cheekwood Fine Arts Ctr, Nashville, 82; retrospective, Southern Alleghenies Mus Art, Loretto, Pa, 94. *Pos:* Visual arts adv panel, Pa Coun on the Arts, 89-91. *Awards:* Belin Arts Scholar, 88. *Mem:* Cosmos Club, Washington, DC. *Media:* Oil. *Publ:* Am Arts Quart, fall 2005. *Mailing Add:* 518 Hermosa Dr SE Albuquerque NM 87108

STARK, RON
PAINTER, PHOTOGRAPHER
b Sidney, NY, June 27, 1944. *Study:* Univ Denver, Colo; NY State Univ, Oneonta, BA, 68; Int Inst Educ (Fulbright-Hayes Found fel), 74. *Work:* Baltimore Mus, Md; Smithsonian Inst, Phillips Collection, Corcoran Gallery Art, Washington, DC; Bibliot Nat, Paris; Mus Photog, Bievres, France; Metrop Mus Art Libr, New York; Am Art Mus, DC; Los Angeles Co Mus. *Comn:* Two portraits, comn by Leanne Rees, Bethesda, Md, 78; two portraits & painting, comn by J Forstmann, McLean, Va, 79; landscape painting, comn by Merceile Hayes, Mendocino, Calif, 82; eight still life works, Int Guitar Salon, Los Angeles, 2006; six pieces, Stepbridge Studios, Santa Fe, NMex, 2007. *Exhib:* Solo exhibs, Phillips Collection, Washington, DC, 73, San Francisco Mus Art, 74, Mus Art, Zurich, 76, Va Mus Art, Richmond, 80, Corcoran Gallery Art, Washington, DC, 81, Canyon Rd Fine Arts Studio, Santa Fe, 2005; Artists of America, Pompidou Ctr, Paris, 77; Harmon Gallery, Sarasota, Fla, 81; retrospective, Mus Photog, Bievres, France, 96; Rebis Galleries, Denver, 96-97; Summit of 8 Exhibition 97, 17 solo and group exhibs; Santa Fe, NMex Klebau Gallery, Chambrelain-Stark, Canyon Road Fine Art Studio, Gerald Peters Gallery, Shidoni & St Johns Coll, 96-2005; Ghost Ranch & Smithsonian Traveling Exhib, 2006; Albuquerque NMex Mus, Biennial; August Gallery, 2006; New Concept Gallery, 2007; Women's Shelter Benefit, Santa Fe, 2007; Art Feast, 2007; Farrell Gallery, Santa Fe, 2007; New Concept Gallery, Santa Fe, NM, 2008; Fine Arts Benefit, Santa Fe, NMex, 2009. *Pos:* Master printer, Reginald Marsh Photog, New York, 74; guest cur, Edward S Curtis Exhib, Corcoran Gallery Art, Washington, DC, 76; consult, Gallerie Die Brucke, Vienna, Austria & Nuance Gallery, Tampa, Fla. *Teaching:* Lectr art & photog, Smithsonian Inst, Washington, DC, 69-78. *Awards:* Va Mus Grant, 74. *Bibliog:* Werner Marz (auth), Collectable Photographers, pvt publ, Vienna, Austria, 74; Alan Porter (auth), Ron Stark - nudes, Camera Mag, 75; Mark Power (auth),

Washington photographers, Washingtonian Mag, 75; article, eight page featured article, Int Pastel Artist Mag, 2001. *Media:* Pastel, Landscape, Large Format Photography, Oil. *Interests:* concert flamenco guitar. *Publ:* Auth, Delicacies, William & Morrow, NY, 78; Logotypes, 94, 2nd ed, 95. *Mailing Add:* 715 Onate Pl #3 Santa Fe NM 87505

STARKWEATHER-NELSON, CYNTHIA LOUISE
PAINTER
b Moline, Ill, July 29, 1950. *Study:* Northern Ill Univ, BFA, 72; Univ Minn, Minneapolis, MFA, 76. *Work:* Gen Mills, NY; Bank Am, San Francisco; Prudential Insurance Co, Northwestern Life Insurance, Faegre & Benson Law Firm, Minneapolis; Champion Paper Co, Washington, DC. *Comn:* WCCO-TV, Minneapolis. *Exhib:* Solo exhib, Am Gallery, Bern, Switz, 81; Drawing, Minneapolis Inst Arts, 81; Works on Paper, Davis-McClain Gallery, St Louis, 82; Of, On, Or About Paper, USA Today, Arlington, Va, 82; New Am Paperworks, US & Far East, 82-84; and others. *Pos:* Printer, Vermillion Ed Ltd, Minneapolis, 76-79. *Teaching:* Instr drawing, St Thomas Acad, 95-97. *Awards:* Minn State Arts Bd Grants, 78 & 80. *Bibliog:* Mary A Martin (auth), Landscape portraiture, Twin Cities Mag, 80. *Dealer:* Peter M David Gallery 430 Oak Grove Minneapolis MN. *Mailing Add:* 666 Apache Ln Mendota Heights MN 55120

STARR, SUSANNA
SCULPTOR
Study: Md Inst Coll Art, Baltimore, BFA; Yale Sch Art, New Haven, MFA; Skowhegan Sch Painting & Sculpture. *Exhib:* Sculpture from the Permanent Collection, Harn Mus Art, Univ Fla, 1992; Make it Up, Wake Forest Univ Art Gallery, NC, 1999; solo exhibs, Visegelia Gallery, Caldwell Coll, NJ, 1999, Harwood Art Ctr, NMex, 2001, Mus Contemp Art, Ft Collins, Colo, 2002, Avram Art Gallery, Southampton Coll, NY, 2003, Long Island Univ, 2008; Checked, April 21, 2000 Coat Check Room, Mus Mod Art, 2000; Painting/Not Painting, White Columns, New York, 2001; Beyond the Pale, Neuberger Mus, NY, 2002; Form and Contents: Corporal Identity-Body Language, Mus Arts and Design, New York, 2004; Plastic Fantastic, Shore Inst Contemp Art, NJ, 2006; Washington Project for the Arts, Katzen Arts Ctr, Am Univ, Washington, DC, 2008. *Awards:* New York Found for Arts Fel, 1999 & 2009; Edward F Albee Found Fel, 2003

STARR, SYDNEY
LIBRARIAN, EDUCATOR
b Grand Rapids, Mich, Nov 12, 1939. *Study:* Wellesley Col, BA (art hist), 61; Simmons Col, MS (libr sci), 64; Rutgers Univ, PhD (libr & info sci), SLA Plenum Scholar, 83. *Pos:* Fine arts librn, Boston Pub Libr, Mass, 62-66. *Teaching:* Prof art & archit dept, Pratt Inst Libr, Brooklyn, NY, 66-91, lectr art info & picture resources, 68-80 & info resource for designers, 97, asst dean libr, 91-94, chmn, Libr Fac, 94-98, acting dean librs, 98-99, chmn libr fac, 99-. *Mem:* Special Libr Asn (pres, NY chap, 73-74); Art Librn Soc NAm; Art Librn Soc NY (chmn, 77); NY Libr Club (pres, 95-96); Am Libr Asn. *Res:* Methods in art and architecture research. *Interests:* Modern art, architecture and American art. *Publ:* Auth, American Painting: An Information Guide, 74 & ed, Art and Architecture Information Guide Series, 74-80, Detroit, 14 vols; Contemporary Art Documentation, Scarecrow Press, 86. *Mailing Add:* Pratt Inst Libr Brooklyn NY 11205

STASACK, EDWARD ARMEN
PAINTER, PRINTMAKER
b Chicago, Ill, Oct 1, 1929. *Study:* Univ Ill, BFA 55' with High Honors, MFA, 56. *Work:* Libr Cong, Washington, DC; Honolulu Acad Arts; Mus Mod Art, New York; Metrop Mus Art, New York; Art Inst Chicago. *Comn:* Precast concrete murals, City Honolulu, Fort St Mall, 68 & Honolulu Community Coll, 72; Captain Cook Series (print portfolio), Hawaii State Found Cult & Arts; outdoor sculpture & wall sculpture, Hawaii State Intake Serv Ctr, Honolulu. *Exhib:* Solo exhib, Honolulu Acad Arts, Hawaii, 76-78; Amfac Exhib Rm, Honolulu, 77; Ryan Gallery, Kailua, Hawaii, 81; Honolulu Acad Arts, 88; Volcano Art Ctr, 98; 79th Members Exhib, Society of American Graphic Artists, 2012; Addison Gallery Am Art, 61; Carnegie Biennial, 64; Paris Biennial Prints, 63; Smithsonian Inst, 66; Int Bieniale Grabados, Buenos Aires, Argentina, 70; Ann Soc Am Graphic Artists Exhibs, 2012. *Pos:* President & Founder, Rock Art Asn Hawaii, 88-90; principal investigator, Rock Art Hawaii, Volcanos Nat Park, 93-2014. *Teaching:* Prof art, Univ Hawaii, 69-88, chmn dept, 69-72 & prof emer, 88. *Awards:* Rockefeller Found Fel, 59; Award of Last Days of Capt Cook, Hawaii State and US Bicentennial Comn Grant, 76; Hawaii Community Found Grant, 2000; Crabtree award, Soc Am Archaeology, 2013. *Bibliog:* George Tahara (dir), Drawing-Painting-Stasack (film), 67; Neogy & Haar (auth), Artists of Hawaii, 74; Francis Haar, Artists of Hawaii (film), 75. *Mem:* Soc Am Graphic Artists; Am Rock Art Res Asn; Sharlot Hall Mus Asn; Soc Hawaiian Archeol. *Media:* Acrylic, Oil; Collagraph, Printmaking. *Res:* Recording reports on 30 rock art sites on Hawaii Island. *Publ:* coauth, Hawaiian petroglyphs, Bishop Mus, 70; Petroglyphs of Kahooawe, Hawaii, 93; Rock Art of Hawaii Volcanoes Nat Park, 95-2000; coauth, Spirit of Place, Easter Island Found, 99; coauth, Rock Art of Kona Village, Petroglyph Preserve, 2009; co-auth, Rock Art of Queen Liliuokalani trust, 2011. *Mailing Add:* 1623 Morning Stone Dr Prescott AZ 86305-1102

STASHKEVETCH, JOSEPH
PAINTER
b NJ, 1958. *Study:* RI Sch Design, Providence, 76-80. *Work:* Whitney Mus; Dallas Mus Art; Houston Mus of Art; San Francisco Mus Mod Art. *Exhib:* Solo exhibs, Morris-Healy Gallery, NY, 95, Road Work, John Berggruen Gallery, San Francisco, 98, New Works, Turner Runyon Gallery, Dallas, 98, Recent Drawings, Inman Gallery, Houston, Paul Morris Gallery, NY, 99, New Drawings; Clouds, Baldwin Gallery, Aspen, 2000, Quincunx, Von Lintel Gallery, NYC, 2003; Park II Exhib, Cooper-Hewitt Mus, NY, 86; Monnai de Paris, Quai de Conte, Paris, 94; Inaugural Exhib, Paul Morris Gallery, NY, 95; Brooklyn, New York, USA, Bonni Benrubi Gallery, NY, 96; A Show of Hands, George Adams Gallery, NY, 96; In Passing, Inman Gallery, Houston, 96; Bathroom, Thomas Healy Gallery, NY, 97; Pollution, Gian Ferrari Arte Contemporea, Milan, 98; The Great Drawing Show, Kohn Turner Gallery, Los Angeles, 99; Int Print Ctr, NY Fall/Winter Show, White Columns, NY, 2000; Int Print Ctr, Spring/Summer Show, NY, 2001; In Black and White, Forrest Scott Gallery, Millburn, NJ, 2002. *Media:* Crayon, Watercolor. *Mailing Add:* Von Lintel Gallery 520 W 23rd St Ground Fl New York NY 10011

STATMAN, JAN B
PAINTER, SCULPTOR
b New York, NY. *Study:* Hunter Coll, with William Baziotes, Bernard Klonis & Richard Lippold, AB. *Work:* Mus Mod Art Alto Aragon, Huesca, Spain; Civic Mus Contemp Art, Sasso Ferrato, Italy; Longview Mus Fine Arts, Tex. *Exhib:* Solo Exhibs: McAllen Int Mus, Tex, 85; Wichita Falls Art Asn, Tex, 90; Longview Art Mus, 94; Milam Gallery, Dallas, Tex, 95; Marshall Visual Art Ctr, Tex, 2007; Art Gallery 100, Tex, 2008, Greg Co Historical Mus, 2013, Tex Bank & Trust, Longview, Tex. 2013, Salon Verde, Tyler, Tex, 2014; Barnwell Art Ctr, Shreveport, La, 2002; 120th Juried Anniversay Exhib, Nat Asn Women Artist, Inc, Hub-Robeson Galleries, Penn State Univ, 2009. *Pos:* Auth, Art Notes (weekly column), Longview News, 65-70; Artists World (weekly column), Gtr Longview Post, 70-77; Final Word (weekly column), Dallas Morning News, 81-82; Artists World Column, Piney Woods Live Mag, 2012-. *Teaching:* Instr painting, Longview Mus & Arts Ctr, Tex, 72- & Kilgore Coll, 82-84; artist-in-residence, Tex Comn Arts, State of Tex, 85; instr Marshall Visual Art Ctr, Marshall, Tex, 99-. *Awards:* First Prize Painting, 33rd Ann Cedar City Nat Art Exhib, Utah, 73; Jr League Purchase Award, 25th Ann Exhib, Longview Mus & Arts Ctr, 83; Second Prize Painting, 19th Ann Juried Competition, Masur Mus Art, Monroe, La, 92; and others. *Bibliog:* Ruth Winegarten (auth), A New York Yankee in Longview Texas, Equal Times, Dallas, Tex, 76; Donna Berliner (auth), Jan B Statman, Art Voices-South, 12/78; Amanda Retallack (auth), The Surreal Life of Jan Statman, Piney Woods Live Mag, Longview, Tex, 2011. *Mem:* Nat Asn Women Artists New York. *Media:* Acrylic, Watercolor. *Interests:* Acrylic painting, watercolors, collage, drawings, printmaking, plexiglas sculpture, cur exhibs, writing, teaching. *Publ:* The Battered Woman's Survival Guide, Taylor Publ Co, Dallas, Tex, 90; coauth, Living With Environmental Illness, Taylor Publ Co, Dallas, 98; auth, Raisins & Almonds - and Texas Oil, Eakin Press, 2003 & 2004. *Dealer:* Art Gallery 100 100 W Tyler St Longview TX 75601. *Mailing Add:* PO Box 56 Judson TX 75660

STAUB, CAROL ANNE
PAINTER, INSTRUCTOR
b Milford, Del. *Study:* Self-taught. *Work:* Elliott Mus, Stuart, FL; Univ FL, Fort Pierce, FL; Artcolle Mus, Sergines, France; Associazione di Promozione Sociale Artetica, Rome, Italy; Museo de Collage, Cuernavaca, Mex; Co Arts Found, Ingram, Tex; Ctr Adult Educ, Melbourne, Australia; Amarillo Mus Art, Amarillo, Tex. *Exhib:* Garden State Watercolor 32nd Open, Trenton City Mus-Ellarslie, Trenton, NJ, 2001; Modernization, AE Bean Backus Mus, Ft Pierce, Fla, 2005; 2006 Biennial Artists Guild, Boca Raton Mus Art, Fla, 2006; 9th Annual Open, Coral Springs Mus Art, Fla; 9th Annual International Society of Acrylic Painters, Cornell Mus Art, Delray Beach, Fla, 2006; National Collage 22nd Annual Open, Berman Mus Art, Collegeville, PA, 2006; New Jersey Watercolor Annual Open, Monmouth Mus, Lincroft, NJ, 2006, 2010; 18th Annual Exhibit, Vero Beach Mus Art, Fla, 2006; Fla Watercolor Soc 37th Ann Exhib, Delray Beach, Fla, 2008; Catharine Lorillard Wolfe Art Club 112th Ann, Nat Arts Club, NY, 2008; Allied Artist Am 95th Ann Exhib, Nat Arts Club, NY, 2008; Pa Watercolor Soc 29th Ann Int Exhib, West Chester, Pa, 2008; Int Soc Acrylic Painters First Online Open Int Exhib, 2008; RI Watercolor Soc 15th Ann Nat Watermedia Competition, Pawtucket, RI, 2008; Nat Collage Soc 24th Ann Juried Exhib, Longmont Mus, Longmont, Colo, 2008; San Diego 29th Int Exhib, Int Soc of Experimental Artists, Calif, 2009; Catherine Lorrilard Wolfe Art Club, New York, 2009, 2010; Boca Raton Mus Art, Fla, 2009, 2010; Nat Arts Club, New York, 2009; Coral Springs Mus Art, Fla, 2009; Art Kudos 2010 Int Art Competition; Upstream People Gallery 10th Ann Summer All Media Exhib; Renaissance Art Gallery 3rd Ann Nat Spring Fine Arts Exhib, 2010; Nat Asn Women Artists, Fusion of Form, Content & Color Exhib, 2010. *Teaching:* Collage & Texture, instr, Elliott Mus, Stuart, FL, 2004 (winter), 2007, 2008 (winter); Collage & Texture, instr, Somerset Art Asn, Bedminster, NJ, 2006 (spring & fall); Collage & Texture, instr, Cornell Mus Art, Delray Beach, Fla, 2010 (spring). *Awards:* Savoir Faire Award, Int Soc Acrylic Painters, Savoir Faire Company, 1/2006; Best Abstract Design Award, Creative Catalyst Productions, Graham Paints, 10/2006; Nat Collage Soc Cash Award, Nat Collage Soc, 10/2006; 2nd Place Award, Boca Raton Mus Art Biennial Exhib, 2008; First Place Award, Vero Beach Mus Art Club 20th Ann Art by the Sea, 2008; Nat Soc Cash Award, Nat Soc Wish You Were Here Exhib, Glen Allen, Va, 2008; Wolfgang Amadeus Mozart Award, Art Ctr Contemp Art, Vienna, Austria, 2008; Premio Francisco de Goya Award, Vero Beach Mus Art, Art Club, spring 2008; 1st place, Boca Raton Mus Art Artist's Guild, Fla, 2009; 1st place, Artist's Mag All Media Online Competition, 2009; Jack Richeson & Company Merchandise Award, Witte Mus, San Antonio, Tex, 2009; Nummie Warqa Mem Award, NJ Watercolor 40th Ann Exhib, NJ, 2009; Merit, Renaissance Art Gallery, 2010; 1st Place Award, Boca Raton Mus Art Artists' Guild, 2010; 2nd place, Coral Springs Mus Art, 2010; Merit award, Vero Beach Mus Art, 2010; 2nd place, Nat Asn Women Artists, 2010; Honorable Mention, Boca Raton Mus Art Artists Guild, Delray Beach, Fla, 2011; 2nd place, Boca Mus Art Artists Guild, Delray Beach, Fla, 2011; Honorable Mention, Palm Beach Watercolor Soc 28th Exhib, Coral Springs Mus Art, Fla, 2011; 2nd place, Women in the Visual Arts, Creative Dimensions Exhib, Delray Beach, Fla, 2011; Special Recognition, Seascapes Exhib, Space and Time Gallery, 2012, All Women Exhib, 2012; 3rd Place award, 4th Exhib, Boca Mus Art Artists' Guild, Delray Beach, 2012; 1st Place award, Women in the Visual Arts, Artistic Adventures Exhib, Highland Beach, Fl, 2012; 1st Place, Nat Asn Women Artists Image Makers Exhib, Palm Beach Gardens, Fla, 2012; Hon Mention, Palm Beach Watercolor Society 29th Anniversary Exhib, Coral Springs Mus Art, Coral Springs, Fla, 2012; Blick Art Materials award,

Fla Artists Groud 62nd 2012 Exhib and Symposium, Ringling Sch Art and Design, Sarasota, Fla, 2012; Special Recognition in the Light, Space, & Time 4th Ann Abstracts Art Competition, 2013; Honorable Mention, Palm Beach Watercolor Soc, 30th Anniv Exhib, Coral Springs, Fla, 2013; Publishers Choice award, March/April Cover Competition for Art and Beyond Publication, 2013; Judges Recognition, Boca Raton Mus Art Artist's Guild, Delray Beach, Fla, 2013; 1st Place, Boca Raton Mus Art Artist's Guild, Coral Springs Art Exhib, Fla, 2013; Canson Fine Paper award, Southern Watercolor 36th Ann Exhib, Gadsden Art Ctr, Quincy, Fla, 2013; Outstanding Abstract, Bold Brush Painting Competition, 2013; Special Merit award, Light, Space, and Time Gallery, 2013; 2nd Place, Vero Beach Mus Art, Art by the Sea Exhib, 2013; Juror's Recognition, Boca Raton Mus Art Artists' Guild Exhib, Fla, 2013; Special Recognition award, Upstream People Gallery, 15th Ann All Media Exhib, 2013. *Bibliog:* Alcove Books, Carol Staub, Am Art Collector, Vol 2, bk 4, 2006, 2007, 2008, 2009, 2010; Maureen Bloomfield (auth), It's Never Too Late, Artists Mag, 1/2007 (issue); Book Art Press, Carol Staub, New Art int (bk), 1/2007; Art was featured in: Alcove Books, American Art Collector, 2008-2011; Art Buzz - The Book, 2008, 2009, 2010; 100 Contemporary International Artists, 2007, 2008, 2010; Best of America, 2007, 2008; New Art International, 2007, 2008; Masters of Today, 2009; Trends, 2009; 100 Mid Atlantic Artists, 2010; A Walk into Abstraction; Eyes on Abstracts, Blake Hill Press, 2012. *Mem:* Am Watercolor Soc,; Nat Asn Women Artists (treas, 2004-); Boca Raton Mus Art Artist's Guild (committee chair-nomination, 2005); Int Soc Acrylic Painters; Nat Watercolor Soc. *Media:* Acrylic; Collage; Watercolor. *Mailing Add:* 10316 Crosby Pl Port Saint Lucie FL 34986

STAUFFER, GEORGE B
ADMINISTRATOR, EDUCATOR
Study: Dartmouth Col, BA (music), 1969; Bryn Mawr Col, MA (musicology), 1971; Columbia Univ, MPh, 1974, PhD (musicology), 1978. *Teaching:* Humanitites instr, Columbia Univ, 1975-77, dir Chapel Music, 1977-1999; adj asst prof music, Yeshiva Univ, 1978-79; asst prof music, Hunter Col, City Univ of NY, 1978-83, assoc prof, 1984-1987, prof music, 1988-2000, chair Music Dept and Prog in Dance, 1994-2000; asst prof music, Grad Ctr, City Univ of NY, 1983, assoc prof, 1984-87, prof, 1988-2000; prof music history, Rutgers Univ, 2000-, dean Mason Gross Sch of Arts, 2000-. *Mailing Add:* Mason Gross School of Arts, Office of Dean Rutgers University 33 Livingston Ave New Brunswick NJ 08901

STAUTBERG, ANN
PHOTOGRAPHER
b Houston, Tex, 1949. *Study:* Tex Christian Univ, BFA, 71; Univ Dallas, MA, 72. *Work:* Metro Light Rail Station, Houston, 2001; Root Square Mem Park, Houston, 2003. *Exhib:* Solo shows incl Haggerty Art Ctr, Univ Dallas, 72, Laguna Gloria Art Mus, Austin, 75-76, Dallas Mus Fine Arts, 81, Tyler Mus Art, 87, Barry Whistler Gallery, Dallas, 90, 92, 94, 97, 98, 2001, 2002, 2003, 2004, 2005, Galveston Arts Ctr, Tex, 91, Art Pace, San Antonio, 98, James Gallery, Houston, 99, 2000, FotoFest 2000 exhib, Stephen L Clark Gallery, Austin, 2003, Barbara Davis Gallery, Austin, 2005; group shows incl Forth Worth Art Mus, 73, 75; Lamkin Camerawork Gallery, Fairfax, Calif, 75; Laguna Gloria Art Mus, Austin, 76; Allen Street Gallery, Dallas, 77; Dallas City Hall, 79, 80, 81; The Art Ctr, Waco, 83; Dallas Mus Art, 84; Barry Whistler Gallery, Dallas, 86, 87, 89, 93, 97, 98, 99, 2000, 2001, 2003, 2005; Nat Mus Women in Arts, Wash, DC, 88; Sewell Gallery, Houston, 91; Arlington Mus Art, Tex, 92; Houston Ctr Photog, 94; Contemp Arts Mus, Houston, 98; Mus Fine Arts Houston, 98, 99, 2000, 2001; Stephen F Austin Univ Gallery, 2001; Mod Art Mus, Fort Worth, 2001, 2002; Arlington Mus Art, Tex, 2005, 2006; Dallas Ctr Contemp Art, 2005; Barbara Davis Gallery, 2005. *Awards:* Fel, Houston Ctr Photog, 94; Otis and Velma Dozier Travel Grant, Dallas Mus Art, 96. *Media:* Oil. *Dealer:* Stephen L Clark Gallery 1101 W 6th St Austin TX 78703; Barbara Davis Gallery 4411 Montrose Houston TX 77006. *Mailing Add:* c/o Barry Whistler Gallery 2909B Canton St Dallas TX 75226

STAVANS, ISAAC
PAINTER
b Tampico, Mex, Aug 25, 1931. *Study:* Mexico City Col, BA, 52; Brooklyn Col, MA, 53; apprentice to Arnold Belkin, 56-60. *Work:* Pedagogical Mus, Mex Inst Cult Relations, Mexico City; Centro Asturiano de Mexico; CDI Gallery. *Exhib:* Solo exhibs, Recent Works, Misrachi Gallery, Mex City, 1979, Univ Ariz, 1981, Mus Art & Hist, Ciudad Juarez, Mex, 1983, Lourdes Chumacero Gallery, Estocolmo, Mex, 1986, Centro Asturiano, 2/1990 & Fragments, Gallery Torre del Reloj, 1991 & 2002, Centro Asturiano, 1997 & Lourdes Chumacero Gallery, Mex, 1999. *Teaching:* Instr painting, CDI Art Sch, 65-74, Hispanic-Mex Univ, 65-74 & privately, 74-. *Awards:* New Values Contest, Gallery CDI, 63; Artist of Yr, Mexico This Month Mag, 70. *Bibliog:* Alfonso de Neuvillate (auth), Stavans: Reminiscences and evolations, Novedades Newspaper, 2/5/76; Berta Taracena (auth), Art: Recent shows, Tiempo Mag, 7/19/76; Bryan Johnstone (auth), Stavans inner landscapes, Ariz Daily Wildcat Newspaper, 1/23/81; Alfonso de Neuvillate (auth), Stavans: An opalescent beauty, Novedades Newspaper, 4/4/86. *Mem:* Mex Soc Visual Artists. *Media:* Oil, Mixed Techniques. *Dealer:* Lourdes Chumacero Gallery Estocolmo 34 Mexico 6 DF 06600. *Mailing Add:* Bosque Minas 55B Apt 1104 Bosques Herradura Mexico 53920 Mexico

STAVEN, LELAND CARROLL
PAINTER
b Milwaukee, Wis, Dec 17, 1933. *Study:* Univ Wis-Milwaukee, BFA, 56; Layton Sch Art, 57; Calif Coll Arts & Crafts, MFA, 60; Ill Inst Technol, 63. *Work:* Univ Ga Art Mus; Ga Tech Univ Art Gallery; S DeKalb Col; LaGrange Col; State Mutual Insurance Co; Rome Area Coun Arts; Ga State Art Collection; and others. *Exhib:* 18th Southeastern Ann Exhib, Atlanta, Ga, 63; Contemp Southern Art Exhib, 64; 1st S Cent Exhib, Nashville, Tenn, 66; 1st Ann Greater Birmingham Arts Alliance Exhib, Ala, 75; 2nd Ann Nat Dogwood Festival Art Show, Atlanta, 75; Georgia Artists Show, 86; Carrollton Regional Exhibition, III, 86; Legacy of Arts, Cartersville, Ga, 2006. *Pos:* Vchmn, Ga Comn Arts, Atlanta, 67-72. *Teaching:* Chmn dept painting, drawing & printmaking, Berry Col, 60-68 & Mercer Univ Atlanta, 68-69; assoc prof painting, drawing & printmaking & cur, Dalton Galleries, Agnes Scott Col, 70-89; retired. *Awards:* Purchase Awards, Asn Ga Artists, 61 & Fourth Ann Callaway Gardens Art Exhib, 67; Achievement Award, Appalachian Corridors: Exhib I, 68; 3rd Place, Midwest Poetry Rev, 95. *Mem:* Southeastern Coll Art Conf; Southern Graphics Coun; Georgia Poetry Soc. *Media:* Acrylic. *Interests:* Prof jazz musician, trumpeter; golf, chess & poetry. *Publ:* Auth, poetry in: Motive, Discourse & Odessa Poetry Rev; Reach of Song, 86-2009, 2013. *Mailing Add:* 1 Etowah Ter SW Apt 1207 Rome GA 30161

STAVITSKY, GAIL BETH
CURATOR, WRITER
b Cleveland, Ohio, 1954. *Study:* Univ Mich, Ann Arbor, AB, 76; Inst Fine Arts, NY Univ, MA (cert curatorial studies), 78, PhD, 90. *Exhib:* Erie Carle: Animals and Friends, 2015; primary curator, catalogue contributor, Matisse and American Art, 2017. *Collection Arranged:* Precisionism in Am 1915-1941: Reordering Reality (auth, catalog), Montclair Art Mus, NJ & other venues, 94-; The Montclair Art Colony: Past and Present, 97; Steve Wheeler: The Oracle Visiting the Twentieth Century (auth, catalog), 97-98; Waxing Poetic: Encaustic Art in Am, (auth, catalog), Montclair Art Mus, 99; Paris 1900: The Am School, The Universal Exposition (project dir, catalog contribr), 1999-2000; Will Barnet: A Timeless World (curator, auth, catalog), 2000-01; Conversion to Modernism: The Early Works of Man Ray (co-cur, contbr catalog); The Unseen Cindy Sherman: Early Transformations 1975-1976, Montclair Art Mus, 2004; Roy Lichenstein: Am Indian Encounters (co-auth, catalog), Montclair Art Mus, 2005; Reflecting Culture: American Comic Book Superheroes, 2007; The Evolution of Will Barnet: Recent Work, 2007; Cézanne and American Modernism, 2009; Living for Art: the Dorothy & Herbert Vogel Collection, 2010; Warhol & Cars, Am Icons, 2011; Will Barnet: A Centennial Celebration, 2011; George Inness: Private Treasures, 2012; The New Spirit: Am Art in the Armory Show, 1913, 2013; co-curator, Robert Smithson's NJ, 2014. *Pos:* Supervisor docent progs, Carnegie Mus Art, Pittsburgh, Pa, 79-80, asst cur fine arts, 81-83; lectr, Mus Mod Art, 83-; contractual lectr, Metrop Mus Art, 84-; art critic, Arts, 85-87; independent cur & scholar, 90-94; cur collections & exhibs, Montclair Art Mus, NJ, 94, chief cur, 98-. *Awards:* Chester Dale Fel Twentieth Century Art, Metrop Mus Art, 87-88; Andrew W Mellon Fel Twentieth Century Art, Metrop Mus Art, 88-89. *Mem:* Coll Arts Asn; Am Asn Mus. *Res:* American modernism; private and public patronage of modern art; A E Gallatin; American abstract artists; Twentieth Century Art. *Publ:* auth, Waxing Poetic: Encaustic Art in America, 99; auth, Will Barnet: A Timeless World, 2000; auth, essay on Francis Criss in the 1930s: A Rare Synthesis of Realism and Abstraction, Corcoran Gallery of Art, 2001; co-auth, Montclair Art Mus Selected Works, 2002; auth, A Translation in Paris, 1918-39: Albert Eugene Gallatin The Paris-NY Connection, 2003; auth, Musee D'art 1927-1942, Am Giverny, Univ Calif Press, 2003; auth, The Unseen Cindy Sherman: Early Transformations 1975-1976, 2004; Primary auth, Roy Lichtenstein, American Indian Encounters, 2005; auth, Reflecting Culture: The Evolution of American Comic Book Superheroes, 2007; auth, Cezanne & American Modernism, 2009; auth, Warhol & Cars, Am Icons, 2011; co-auth, The New Spirit: American Art in the Armory Show, 1913, 2013; auth, Will Barnet (1911-2012), American Art, Summer, 2013; auth, Walt Kuhn: Underappreciated Artist and Armory Show, Organizer, NY: DC Moore Gallery, 2013; auth, Walt Kuhn: Armory Showman, The Armory Show at 100: Modernism and Revolution, Giles, NY Historical Soc, 2013. *Mailing Add:* 23 Macopin Rd Upper Montclair NJ 07043

STEADMAN, DAVID WILTON
MUSEUM DIRECTOR
b Honolulu, Hawaii, Oct 24, 1936. *Study:* Harvard Col, BA (magna cum laude), 60; Harvard Univ, MAT, 61; Univ Calif, Berkeley, MA (art hist), 66; Princeton Univ, PhD, 74. *Collection Arranged:* P P Rubens before 1620 (with catalog), Princeton Art Mus, 71; Selections from the Norton Simon, Inc Mus Art (with catalog), 73; Graphic Art of Francisco Goya (with catalog), Galleries of Claremont Cols, 75, 18th Century Drawing from California Collections (with catalog), 76 & Works on Paper 1900-1960 from Southern Calif Collections (with catalog), 77. *Pos:* Lectr, Frick Collection, New York, 70-71; asst dir, Art Mus, Princeton Univ, 71-72, actg dir, 72-73, assoc dir, 73; dir, Galleries of Claremont Cols, 74-80; res cur, Norton Simon Mus, Pasadena, Calif, 77-80; dir, Chrysler Mus, Norfolk, Va, 80-89; dir, Toledo Mus Art, 89-. *Teaching:* Asst prof 17th & 18th centuries art, Pomona Col, 74-78, assoc prof, 78-80. *Awards:* Nat Defense Educ Act fel, 66-69; Chester Dale Fel, Nat Gallery Art, 69-70. *Mem:* Am Asn Mus Dirs; Coll Art Asn; Art Mus Asn (trustee). *Res:* 17th and 18th century drawings. *Publ:* Auth, Abraham van Dipenbeeck, UMI Res Press, 82; coauth, A Tricentennial Celebration: Norfolk 1682-1982, 82. *Mailing Add:* Toledo Mus Art PO Box 1013 Toledo OH 43697

STEBBINS, THEODORE ELLIS, JR
HISTORIAN, ADMINISTRATOR
b New York, NY, Aug 11, 1938. *Study:* Yale Univ, BA, 60; Harvard Univ Law Sch, JD, 64, Harvard Univ, PhD, 71. *Collection Arranged:* Luminous Landscape, Fogg Art Mus, 66; Martin Johnson Heade, Whitney Mus Am Art, 69; New Haven Scene, New Haven Colony Hist Soc, 70; Richard Brown Baker Collects, Yale Univ, 75; Am Landscapes at the Wadsworth Atheneum, Hudson River Sch, 76; Am Master Drawings, Whitney Mus, 76. *Pos:* Assoc cur, Garvan Collections, Yale Univ Art Gallery, 68-77, cur Am painting & sculpture, 71-77; cur Am painting, Mus Fine Arts, Boston, Mass, 77-. *Teaching:* Instr hist art, Smith Col, 67; asst prof hist art, Yale Univ, 69-75, Morse fel, 72, assoc prof, 75-77; vis prof, Boston Univ, 78, prof art hist, 82-. *Awards:* Chester Dale Fel, Nat Gallery Art, Washington, 66; Joseph Coolidge Shaw Soc Medal, Boston Univ, 85; Minda Da Gunzberg Prize, 93; and others. *Mem:* Coll Art Asn Am; Am Fedn Arts. *Res:* American landscape painting of the nineteenth century; history of American drawings and watercolors. *Collection:* Nineteenth and twentieth century American art. *Publ:* Coauth, Boston Collects: Contemporary Painting and Sculpture, 86 & Charles Sheeler: The Photographs, Mus Fine Arts, Boston, 88; Introductory Essay in a Book by Anselm Kiefer, George Braziller Inc &

Mus Fine Arts, Boston, 88; auth, Weston's Westons: Portraits and Nudes, 89; The Lure of Italy: American Artists and the Italian Experience, 1760-1914, 92; Weston's Westons: California & the West, 94; coauth, John J Audubon: The Watercolors for The Birds of America, 94; John Singleton Copley in America, 95; The Lure of Italy: American Artists and the Halian Experience, 1760-1914, 92; Weston's Westons: California & the West, 94; coauth, John J Audubon: The Watercolors for The Birds of America, 94. *Mailing Add:* 74 Lillian St Ludlow MA 01056

STEBICH, STEPHANIE A
MUSEUM DIRECTOR
b Germany. *Study:* Columbia Univ, BA Art Hist; New York Univ, MA. *Pos:* Intern, Guggenheim Mus; asst, Am Fedn Arts Asn Art Mus Dirs; exec asst to dir, Brooklyn Mus, NY; asst dir, Cleveland Mus Art, 1995-2001, Minneapolis Inst Art, 2001-2005; exec dir, Tacoma Art Mus, Wash, 2005-Present. *Mailing Add:* Tacoma Art Mus 1701 Pacific Ave Tacoma WA 98402

STECHER, PAULINE
PAINTER, INSTRUCTOR
b Brooklyn, NY. *Study:* Studied painting with Paul Puzinas, 1961-63; Self taught. *Comn:* Oil paintings, Caesarea Gallery, Boca Raton, Fla. *Exhib:* Am Artists Prof League, Grand Nat, Salmagundi Club NY, 1991, 1994, 1997-2001, 2003, 2006-2008; Hudson Valley Art Asn Ann, Westchester Co Ctr, NY, 1991; Newington/Cropsey Found, Hastings-On-Hudson, NY, 1998, 2002, 2004, 2008; Salmagundi Club, NY, 2000; Art League Nassau Co Open Show, Nassau Co Mus Art, Roslyn, NY, 1993; Nat Arts Club, NY, 2005; also galleries throughout Long Island East End. *Teaching:* Instr oil painting, various adult educ ctrs, NY, 1960-85. *Awards:* American Artists Professional League: Dirs Award, 1991; Grabach Memorial Award, 1994; DeCozen Award, 1997; Pres Award, 1998, 2001; Raymond Chow Memorial Award, 2006; Alden Bryan Memorial Award for a Traditional Landscape in Oil, 2007; William P Lawrence Memorial Award for a Harbor Scene, 2008; Hudson Valley Asn: Steinschneider Memorial Award, 1991; First Prize Dumond Memorial Award, 1998; Spradling Memorial Award, 2000; Georgie Read Barton Memorial Award, 2002; Jane Peterson Still-Life Award, 2004; Gold Medal, Nat Art League, 1973; Coun Am Artists Socs Award, Art League of Nassau Co, 1993. *Mem:* Am Artists Prof League Inc (bd dir, 1985-2002); Hudson Valley Art Asn Inc; Art League of Nassau Co Inc; Nat Art League. *Media:* Oil. *Publ:* Auth, Teacher Feature, Grumbacher's Palette Talk, 1983, I'm Hooked on Oil Painting, 1987 & The Alluring but Elusive Aspects of Oil Painting, 1990; contrib, The Literary Cyclist, Auth Prof James E Starrs, Breakaway Books, 1997. *Dealer:* Karen Lynne Gallery Boca Raton FL; Gallery Matisse Naples FL. *Mailing Add:* 80-30 250th St Bellerose NY 11426

STECZYNSKI, JOHN MYRON
DRAFTSMAN, COLLECTOR, RETIRED EDUCATOR
b Chicago, Ill, June 22, 1936. *Study:* Art Inst Chicago; Craft Ctr, Worcester, Mass; Univ Notre Dame, BFA (magna cum laude), 58; Yale Univ, MFA, 61; Acad Fine Arts, Warsaw; and with Umberto Romano. *Work:* McMullen Mus Art, Boston Col; Marriott Corp; Hilton Corp; The Arts Visionary Col. *Comn:* Dossals for Easter, 71, Christmas, 71, Lent, 73, Pentecost, 75, & Easter, 93-94, Univ Lutheran Church, Cambridge, Mass; drawing, Hilton Hotel, West Palm Beach, Fla, 84; drawings, Marriott Corp, 86; Lithographs, NY Plaza Hotel, 94; Drawing, Eventide Arts Festival, Dennis, Mass, 97; and others. *Exhib:* Newport Art Mus, RI, 89; Kunsthalle Exnergasse, Vienna, 89; Greek Inst, Cambridge, Mass, 92; Fuller Art Mus, Brockton, Mass, 94; Fowler Gallery, Providencetown, Mass, 98; Univ Scranton Art Gallery, 00; Creighton Univ, Liet Gallery, 99 & 2007; Theological Union Gallery, 2010; St Louis Univ, Pius XII Memorial Libr, 2011; Marquette Univ, Raynor Memorial Libr, 2013; Fairfield Univ, DiMenna-Nysetlius Libr, 2014. *Teaching:* Instr studio art, Worcester Art Mus Sch, 61-64; instr art hist, Boston Mus Fine Arts Sch, 64-67 & Tufts in Italy, Naples, 67-68; asst prof & chmn dept studio art & art history, Newton Col Sacred Heart, 68-75; asst prof studio art, Boston Col, 75-79, asst chmn dept fine arts, 77-81, assoc prof, 79-88, acting chmn, 81-82, assoc chmn, 85-88, prof, 88-2011, chmn, 93-96, retired, 2011-present. *Awards:* Woodrow Wilson Found Fel, 58; Polish Gov Grant, 60-61; Mellon Found Grant, 82; Finalist Drawing, Artists Found, 87; and others. *Bibliog:* Pierrina Rohde (auth), John Steczynski: Artists Yes/Beatnick No, WORC Telegram, 4/26/64; Christine Temin (auth), John Steczynski: a figure outside the gallery scene, Boston Globe, 10/24/85; Christine Temin (auth), The Art of Resurrection: TWO Local Artists Find New Life in Easter Themes, Boston Sunday Globe, 4/7/96. *Media:* Pen & Ink, Acrylic. *Res:* the apocalypse, meditations on the crucifixion. *Interests:* gay sexuality and religion. *Collection:* skulls, stags, rams, elk, moose, religious, objects for home altars. *Publ:* Auth, Visual thinking in education, In: Inscape: Studies Presented to Charles F Donovan, SJ, 77; Tradition, Creativity and the Liturgical Artist, Religion Arts, Vol I, No 4, 98; Gay Archetypes: Visual Expression, White Crane J, summer 98; A Study of the Iconographic Program of Blessed Sacrament Church, Church of the Blessed Sacrament, Jamaica Plain: Historic Structure Report: Historic Boston Inc, 89; Pleasure, Sex and Salvation, White Crane Jour, 02; On Envisioning The Book of Revelation, Text, Context and Image, The Plume and The Palette, Essays in Honor of Josephine von Henneberg, 2001. *Dealer:* Ginsburg Hallowell & Assoc Fine Art 125 Newbury St Boston MA 02116; Dragonfly Gallery PO Box 2608 Oak Bluffs Martha's Vineyard MA 02557. *Mailing Add:* 109 Webster St #5 Boston MA 02128

STEEL, HILLARY
WEAVER, DESIGNER
b NY City, NY, 1959. *Study:* SUNY Buffalo, BA, 1980; MD Inst, Coll Art, Baltimore, MA, 1997. *Work:* Waterfront Ctr, Washington, DC; Renwick Gallery, Smithsonian Inst, Washington, DC; Duquesne, Univ, Pittsburgh, Pa. *Comn:* Wall Piece (handwoven, hand dyed), Mercer Meidinger & Hanson Inc, Pittsburgh, Pa, 1987. *Exhib:* Solo exhibs, Rosewood Ctr Arts Gallery, Kettering, Ohio, Hoyt Inst Fine Arts, New Castle, Pa, 1995, Glenview Mansion Art Gallery, Rockville, Md, 1999, 2002, 2007; Group exhibs, Snyderman/Works Gallery, Philadelphia, 2000, 2001, 2002, 2004, 2008, 2010 Int Fiber Biennial; Artists' Mus, Wash, DC, 2003; represented in permanent collections Smithsonian Am Art Mus Renwick Gallery, Wash, DC. *Pos:* US Consulate, Tijuana, Mex. *Teaching:* Instr, studio artist; US Embassy, Ouagadougou, Burkina Faso. *Awards:* Taegu Int Textile Design Competition, Merit Prize, Taegu, S Korea, 1998; Woven Works First Prize, Fitton Ctr/Ctr Arts, Ohio, 2006; Individual Artist Award, Md State Arts Coun, 2007. *Bibliog:* Art on the Edge, US Dept of State Bur Int Progs, 2005. *Mem:* Friends of Fiber Art Int. *Media:* Textiles. *Res:* Mexican Rebozos. *Interests:* Indigeneous textiles. *Publ:* VII Euro Americana Exposition of Visual Arts, Campeche, Mexico. *Mailing Add:* 1502 Sharon Dr Silver Spring MD 20910

STEEL, PHILIP S
PAINTER, INSTRUCTOR
b Lansdowne, Pa Nov 01, 1934. *Study:* Philadelphia Mus Sch, 1948; Pa State Univ (archit), 1957; Univ Calif, Berkeley (master of archit), 1963; Mus Art (special study), Vero Beach, Fla, 1992. *Work:* Smithsonian Inst Maritime Mus, Washington, DC; Vero Beach Mus Art, Vero Beach, Fla; Reedsville Maritime Mus, Reedsville, Va; Lighthouse Mus, Tequesta, Fla; Peddie Sch Marabo Mus, Hightstown, NJ. *Comn:* Glen Black (portrait), Glenda Black & Family, Fort Pierce, Fla, 2005; Mousehound (sailboat), Martha Davis, Littleton, Colo, 2005; Sailboat (art forms), John K P Stone III, Pompano Beach, Fla, 2005; Weatherbird (sailboat), John Isleib, SW Harbor, Maine, 2006; Mt Desert Island (seascape), Edward Madara, London, Eng, 2007; Causeway Golf Club, Southwest Harbor, Maine. *Exhib:* Nat George Gray Medal, Salmagundi Club, New York, NY, 2000; Northeast Watercolor Soc Nat Juried, Kent Mus, Kent, Conn, 2000; We Are the World, Vero Beach Mus Art, Vero Beach, Fla, 2001; Nat Am Marine Artist, Del River Mus, Wilmington, Del, 2001; Lemoyne Art Found Tri State, Lemoyne Mus, Tallahassee, Fla, 2003; Nat Am Marine Artist, Vero Beach Mus, Vero Beach, Fla, 2004; Coos Art Mus Ann Maritime, Coos Bay Mus, Coos Bay, Ore, 2004-2006; Steel Away, The Travels of Philip Steel, Lighthouse Mus, Tequesta, Fla, 2006. *Teaching:* Prof, archit/art, Univ Miami, Miami, Fla, 1970-1972; instr, advan watercolor, Vero Beach Mus Art, Vero Beach, Fla, 1992-; adj prof, archit, Indian River Community Coll, Ft Pierce, Fla, 2003. *Awards:* Gallery Award, Tri-State, Lemoyne Art Found, Fla, 1995; First Place Watercolor, Ann Four-Co Juried, Backus Gallery, Ft Pierce, Fla, 1996, 1997; Silver Brush Award, Fla Watercolor Soc, Melvin Gallery, Lakeland, Fla, 1997; First Place, Nat George Gray Medal Award, Salmagundi Gallery, NYC, 2000; First Place Oil, Ann Four-Co Juried, Backus Gallery, Ft Pierce, Fla, 2002; Merit Award, Coos Bay Nat Juried Show, Coos Bay, Ore, 2004, 2005; First Place, Watercolor, Vero Beach, Mus Art, Vero Beach Fla, 2008. *Bibliog:* Karyn Greep (auth), South Florida Galleries, Treasure Coastline, fall 1996; Beth Moulton (auth), Painting Ports of Call, Vero Beach Mag, summer 2001; Willi Miller (auth), Philip S Steel, Coastal Boating, Apr 2004; Carolanne G Roberts (auth), Painting the Fishermen, Southern Living Mag, 9/2006; Barbara O'Reilly (auth), Net Loss, Forum, July 2006. *Mem:* Am Soc Marine Artists (Signature Mem); Fla Watercolor Soc (Signature Mem); Am Artists Prof League (Fel); Am Watercolor Soc (Assoc Mem); Portrait Soc Am (Assoc Mem). *Media:* Oil, Watercolor. *Publ:* coauth with Evelyn Wilde Mayerson, Net Loss, Long Wind Publ LLC, 2004; illus, Net Loss (performance art, 20 locations in Fla), Fla Humanities Coun, 2005; coauth with Roger Vaughan, Finishing Gone, The Argian Press, 2009. *Dealer:* Salty Dog Gallery 323 Main St Southwest Harbor ME 04679; McBride Gallery 215 Main St Annapolis MD 21410. *Mailing Add:* PO Box 323 SW Southwest Harbor ME 04679

STEEL, VIRGINIA OBERLIN
GALLERY DIRECTOR, CURATOR
b Pa, Sept 27, 1950. *Study:* Carnegie-Mellon Univ; Univ Hartford, BA, 73; Univ Mass-Amherst, MA, 75. *Pos:* Dir, Stedman Art Gallery, Rutgers Univ, Camden, NJ, 76-. *Teaching:* Mus Studies Prog, Rutgers Univ, Camden, NJ, 79-. *Mem:* Am Asn Mus. *Mailing Add:* c/o Stedman Art Gallery Rutgers Univ The State Univ of NJ Camden NJ 08102

STEELE, BENJAMIN CHARLES
PAINTER, EDUCATOR
b Roundup, Mont, Nov 17, 1917. *Study:* Cleveland Inst Art, dipl; Kent State Univ, BS; Denver Univ, MA; Univ Ore; Ill State Univ; Mont State Univ. *Work:* Univ Mont; Mont Inst Arts, Permanent Collection; Brown Univ, Providence, RI; Mont State Univ, Billings; Ben Steele, WWII Japanese POW Collection; Mont Mus Art and Culture, Univ Mont. *Comn:* Arts of the West (mural), Denver Univ; Indoor and Outdoor Sports (mural), Mont State Univ, Billings; sculpture, Peter Yegen, Jr, Yellowstone Co Mus; and pvt collections. *Exhib:* Mont Arts & Crafts Exhib, Senate Caucus Room, Washington, DC; Mont Inst Arts Festivals; Stillwater Soc Shows; solo exhibs, CM Russell Mus & Minneapolis VA Med Ctr, WWII POW Collection, Mont State Univ, Billings, Univ Mont, 86-87, Truman Lib, 92 & US Air Force Acad, 96; Spirit of Modernism, Paris Gibson Ctr, Great Falls, Holter Mus, Helena, 87-88; Ctr for Arts, Scottsdale, Ariz; Meade Paper Co, Greater Southeastern Show, Atlanta Mus; Art in the Beartooths Shows, Main Stope Gallery, Butte, Mont, 2009, Western Heritage Ctr, Billings, Mont, 2009. *Pos:* Staff dir, Dept of Army Crafts, Military Dist of Washington, Third Army Area. *Teaching:* Art teacher, New London, Ohio High Sch, 51-52; crafts dir, Ft Riley, Kans, 53-54; staff crafts dir, Mil District Wash, 54-56 & Fort MacPherson, Ga, 54-59; prof art & head dept, Mont State Univ, Billings, 59-82, prof emer, 82-, chair art dept, retired. *Awards:* Ben Steele Day, Proc Gov, 77; Distinguished Prof Award, Mont State Univ, 80; Mont Governors Award, Outstanding Achievement Arts, 92; Heritage Montana Heroes award, 2012; Montana Cowboy Hall of Fame, 2012. *Bibliog:* Dorothy Larsen (auth), Man of gentle fiber & Nancy Olson (auth), Briefly biographical, Mont Arts Mag; Billings Gazette; also feature art in Washington Post, Atlanta Const, Kansas City Star; Wash Times; NY Times; Am Heritage Mag; Montana Mag, WWII Mag, Montana Quart, Army Mag. *Mem:* Am Defenders Bataan & Corregidor; Stillwater Soc; First United Methodist Church; Golden K Kiwanis Club; Am Ex Prisoners of War; Yellowstone Art Mus, Western Heritage Ctr; Order of Purple Heart Am Legion, VFW, Dav. *Media:* Oil, Watercolor. *Interests:* Art, travel & hist. *Publ:* Cover designs & illus, A Long March Home, 98,

Footprints of Courage, 2002, Silent Tears, 2002, Soldier of Bataan, Prisoner of Hope, Corregipor, Paradise to Hell, Cabanatuan Japanese Death Camp, WC Refused to Die, The Long March Home, Soochow of 4th Marines & Bataan Diary; illus, Tears in the Darkness. *Mailing Add:* 2425 Cascade Ave Billings MT 59102

STEELE, LISA
VIDEO ARTIST
b Kansas City, Mo, Sept 22, 1947. *Study:* Univ Mo, Kansas City, 65-68; Hon Dr, Ontario Coll Art & Design, 2003. *Work:* Art Gallery of Ont, Toronto; The Kitchen, NY; Mus Mod Art, New York City; National Gallery Can, Ottawa; Ctr Georges Pompidou, Paris. *Exhib:* A Response to the Environment, Rutgers Univ Art Gallery, New Brunswick, NJ, 75; Video Int, Aarhus Mus of Art, Denmark, 76; Videotapes, Mus of Mod Art, NY, 77; Southland Video Anthology, Part 4, Long Beach Mus of Art, Calif, 77; Kunsthalle, Basel, Switz, 78; Venice Biennale, 80; Documenta 8, Kassel, Ger, 87; Four hours & thirty-eight minutes, Art Gallery Ontario, Toronto, 89; The Enn, Chisenhale Gallery, London, 2000; Oberhausen Short Film Festival, 2001; Ctr Contemps de Basse, Normandie, France, 2003; Before I Wake..., Can Cult Ctr, Paris, 2003. *Pos:* Video coordr, A Space Gallery, Toronto, 72-74, creative dir, 80-. *Teaching:* lectr, Ontario Col Art & Design, 1981-2002; lectr, Univ Toronto, Dept Fine Art, 2002-. *Awards:* Award for Excellence in Video Art, Bell Can, 93; Gov Gerard's Award for Visual & Media Arts, Lifetime Achievement, 2005. *Bibliog:* Eric Cameron (auth), Structural videotape in Canada, In: Video Art, Harcourt, Brace & Jovanovich, 76. *Media:* Videotape. *Publ:* editor, UK/Canadian Video Exchange, 2003-04; auth, Persistence of Vision: Recent videoworks from the UK; guest editor, Felix: A Journal of Media & Culture, 2000. *Dealer:* Vtape 401 Richmond St W Suite 45 Toronto Canada M5V 3A8. *Mailing Add:* 287 Claremont Toronto ON M6J 2N1 Canada

STEELE, VALERIE FAHNESTOCK
MUSEUM DIRECTOR
b Boston, June 29, 1955. *Study:* Dartmouth Coll, BA (History), 1978; Yale Univ, MA, 1980, PhD (Mod European Cultural & Intellectual Hist), 1983. *Pos:* chief cur, Mus at the Fashion Inst Tech, 1997-2003, acting dir, 2000-2003, dir, 2003-. *Teaching:* Teacher, fashion hist, Fashion Inst Tech, Sch Grad Studies, 1985-1997. *Awards:* Iris Found; Bard Grad Ctr, 2002; Artistry of Fashion award, Am Apparel & Footwear Asn, 2003. *Mem:* bd dirs, Costume Soc Am, Int Asn for Costume; chair, Fashion Walk of Fame selection comt, Fashion Cr Bus Improvements Dist. *Mailing Add:* Museum at Fashion Institute of Technology Seventh Avenue at 27 Street New York NY 10001

STEEN, CAROL J
PAINTER, SCULPTOR
b Highland Park, Mich, Nov 6, 1943. *Study:* Mich State Univ, BA, 65; Cranbrook Acad Art, MFA, 71. *Work:* Printmaking Workshop, New York; Smithsonian Archives Am Art; Am Craft Mus, New York; Detroit Inst Arts; Robert McLaughlin Gallery, Oshawa, Ont; Libr Cong; Univ Waterloo, Ont, Can; Wayne State Univ, Detroit, Mich. *Exhib:* Solo exhibs, Detroit Inst Arts, Mich, 73, 55 Mercer Gallery, New York, 82, 85, 87, 89, 91, 95 & 97 & Cade Gallery, Royal Oak, Mich, 88; Brody's Gallery, Washington, DC, 88; Philadelphia Mus Art, 89-90; Cranbrook Acad Art, Bloomfield Hills, Mich, 90; B4A Gallery, New York, 91; C A Wustum Mus, Racine, Wis, 92; Cleveland Inst Art, Ohio, 92; Joel Starkman Gallery, Toronto, Ont, 92; La Frontera, New York, 93; Kouros Gallery, New York, 95; AIR Gallery, New York, 2000-2001; Rockefeller Univ, New York, 2003; Brookgreen Gardens, Pawleys Island, SC, 2007; Image Proj Room, New York, 2007; McMaster Mus, Hamilton, Ont, Can, 2008; Wayne State Univ, Detroit, Mich, 2009; 63rd Aldeburgh Festival of Music and the Arts, UK, 2010; Mus Modern Art Ukraine, Kiev, 2011; 03 Gallery, Oxford, 2013. *Pos:* Co-founder, Am Synesthesia Asn Inc, 95-, conf organizer, 99- & bd mem, 2000-. *Teaching:* Ford Found vis lectr, studio art, Univ Mich, 75; asst prof studio art, William Paterson Coll, 77-82 & Touro Coll, 83-; lectr, var univs, mus & colls, 97-. *Awards:* Founder's Soc Purchase Prize, Detroit Inst Arts, Mich, 71; Ford Found Grant, Univ Ann Arbor, Mich, 75; The MacDowell Colony Fel, Peterborough, NH, 80; Printmaking Workshop Fel, New York, 83-84; NY Found Arts Fel, 86-87; Materials for the Arts Grant, New York, 87. *Bibliog:* Doc films, Orange Sherbert Kisses, BBC, Eng, 12/94, Future Watch, CNN, 11/95, Seeing Things, 60 Minutes, Australian Broadcasting Co, 4/98, Beyond Human Senses, BBC, Eng, 7/2000, 6th Sense, 60 Minutes II, 1/2002 & 8/2002 & Super Senses, Asahi Television, Japan, 12/2006; Brad Lemley (auth), Do You See What They See, Discover Mag, 80-87, 12/99; Unmesh Kher (auth), Ah, the blue smell of it!, Time Mag, 64, 5/21/2001; Gabriella Boston (auth), Making sense of Synesthesia, The Wash Times, 9/4/2001; Sharon Begley (auth), Why George Gershwin, Wall St J, B1, 6/28/2002; The Infinite Mind, hosted by Fred Goodwin, Nat Pub Radio, 1/14/2002 & 1/12/2005; Anne Underwood (auth), Real rhapsody in blue, Newsweek, 67, 12/1/2003; Short Circuit, Radio Netherlands, 1/12/2003; Richard Schapiro (auth), Taste a concerto?, Chicago Tribune, 5/5/2005 & Kaleidoscope Eyes, New York Daily News, 6/2006; Michael Winter (auth), Picture a world where senses collide, The Tampa Tribune, 2/18/2007; ALC Mag, 8/2007; Eleection Strike, Synesthesia, radio broadcast, Studio 360, Show 905, 2/1/2008; Herve Pierre Lambert (auth), Representer les Formes Visuelles de la Synesthesie: Carol Steen, Le Trouble Recherches en Esthetique, No 17, pp. 113-126, 12/2011. *Mem:* Coll Art Asn, New York. *Media:* Oil; Metal. *Interests:* Hiking, canoeing. *Publ:* Auth, Visions Shared: A Firsthand Look Into Synesthesia and Art, Vol 34, Issue 3, Leonardo, The MIT Press, 6/2001; illus, Blue Cats and Chartreuse Kittens, Holt, New York, 2001 & State of the Art Synesthesia, Psychologist, 4/2003; illusr, book cover, Consciousness, Oxford Univ Press, 2004; auth, Von Klangen und Schmerzen: Nutzliche Farbe, chap 6, part II, 227-234, Synasthesien-roter Faden durchs Leben?, Die Blaue Eule, Essen, Ger, in prep; The hidden sense Synesthesia in Art and Science, Cretien van Campen, MIT Press, in prep; contribr, What a Synesthete Sees: On Why Tom Thomson Sends Me Over the Moon (in print); Synesthesia: Art and the Mind (exhib catalog), McMaster Mus, 2008; Evidence in Synesthetic Art (audio rec), Coll Art Asn, 2009; Sussex Conversations: Mind and Brain (online), London, UK, 2012; Synesthesia: Seeing the World Differently, Vol II, Automne, 2012. *Mailing Add:* 39 Bond St New York NY 10012

STEGLICH, DAVID M
MUSEUM ADMINISTRATOR
b Wis. *Study:* St Olaf Col, BA (math and philosophy), 1989; student in economics and political theory, Trinity Col, Dublin, Ireland, 1990; Yale Univ, JD, 1995. *Pos:* Law clerk for Chief Judge Paul A. Magnuson, US Dist Ct, St Paul, 1995-97; atty, Corp Law Dept, Dorsey & Whitney, Minn, 1997-2000; with McKinsey & Co, Minneapolis, 2000, assoc principal; chief operating officer, Walker Art Ctr, Minneapolis, 2006-. *Mailing Add:* Walker Art Ctr 1750 Hennepin Minneapolis MN 55403

STEGMAN, PATRICIA
PAINTER, PRINTMAKER
b San Antonio, Tex, Nov 27, 1929. *Study:* Kansas City Univ, Mo, 48-49; Kansas City Art Inst, Mo, BFA, 52; Art Students League, study with Reginald Marsh, Will Barnet, Vaclav Vytlacil & Morris Kantor, 54-57. *Work:* Paintings (Banners), Kansas City Art Inst, Kansas City, Mo. *Comn:* Paintings (Backdrops for plays, Him & Freud, Circle Repertory Company, NYC, 1974, 1975; Backdrop for play, Confrontation on Atlantic Avenue, Big Apple Theatre Company, Brooklyn, NY, 1975. *Exhib:* Drawings, Atlantic Gallery, NY, 77, 79, 84; Landmark Gallery, NY; Tenth St Days--Retrospective of Art of the 50s, Fourteen Sculptors Gallery, NY, 77; one-artist shows, paintings & drawings, Brata Gallery, NY, 61 & 63 & Gallery 91, Brooklyn, 75 & 76; Atlantic Gallery, NYC, 1988, 1993, 1995, 1997; Silk Rd Gallery, Brooklyn, NY, 2011; GO, Brooklyn Mus, NY, 2012. *Pos:* staff writer, Artists Review Art, New York & Phoenix (newspaper), Brooklyn, 76-80. *Teaching:* Instr painting & drawing, Kansas City Art Inst, 52. *Mem:* Art Students League, NYC; East End Arts Counc, Riverhead, NY. *Media:* Oil, Watercolor; Etching, Lithography. *Dealer:* East End Arts Coun Riverhead NY. *Mailing Add:* 245 Dean St Brooklyn NY 11217

STEIGMAN, MARGOT See Robinson, Margot Steigman

STEIN, CLAIRE A
ADMINISTRATOR
b New York, NY, Sept 19, 1923. *Study:* Art Students League; Adelphi Col, BA; sculpture with Robert Cronbach. *Collection Arranged:* Nat Sculpture Soc Ann, 68-86; North Shore Community Art Ctr Exhib, 60s. *Pos:* Bd dir, North Shore Community Art Ctr, 57-62; exec dir, Nat Sculpture Soc, retired. *Mem:* Art Table. *Publ:* Contribr, Nat Sculpture Rev, fall 73, winter 74 & 75 & spring 75; contribr sculpture suppl, Grolier Encyclopedia, 70-73. *Mailing Add:* 1755 York Ave Apt 4C New York NY 10128-0115

STEIN, JUDITH ELLEN
HISTORIAN, CURATOR
b New York, NY, June 27, 1943. *Study:* Barnard Col, Columbia Univ, BA (art hist), 65; Univ Pa, MA (art hist), 67, PhD (art hist), 81. *Collection Arranged:* Red Grooms: A Retrospective, 1956-1984, (auth, catalog), 85; Betye Saar: Sentimental Sojourn, 87; The Figurative Fifties: New York Figurative Expressionism, (auth catalog), 87; I Tell My Heart: Horace Pippin, (auth catalog), 94. *Pos:* Staff lectr, Philadelphia Mus Art, 66-71; arts reviewer, Art in Am, 74-99 & Nat Pub Radio, Philadelphia, 79-83; coordr, Morris Gallery, Pa Acad Fine Arts, 81-94; asst cur, Pa Acad Fine Arts, 83-85, assoc cur, 85-88, cur, 88-91, adjunct cur, 91-94. *Teaching:* Instr, Tyler Sch Art, Philadelphia, 71-78; Univ PA, 80; Md Inst Col Art, 90-93. *Awards:* Fel Literary Nonfiction, Pew, 94. *Mem:* Coll Art Asn (bd mem, 95-96); Int Art Critics Asn (treas, 96, pres, 98); Fabric Workshop. *Publ:* Collaboration, Power of Feminist Art, Abrams, 94; Space & place (Maya Lin), Art in Am, 12/94, The word made image (Hammond & Ashberry), 10/95 & Report on Australia: the Asia Pacific Triennial and the Sydney Biennale, 6/97, Art Am; John Kane(auth), Self-Taught Artists of the 20th Century: An American Anthology, Mus Am Folk Art & Chronicle Bks, 98. *Mailing Add:* 2400 Waverly St Philadelphia PA 19146

STEIN, LEWIS
CONCEPTUAL ARTIST
b New York, NY. *Study:* Mass Inst Technol, 64-66; Univ Calif, Berkeley, 66-68. *Work:* Ludwig Forum, Int Art, Aacheu, Germany; Ludwig Mus, Cologne, Ger; Yale Univ Art Mus, New Haven, Conn; Univ Art Mus, Berkeley, Calif; Mus Fur Modern Kunst, Frankfurt, Ger. *Exhib:* Whitney Biennial, Whitney Mus Am Art, NY, 69; Das Kapital-Blue Chips and Master Pieces, Mus Fur Moderne Kunst, Frankfurt, Ger, 2007; Lust for Life, Kunst Mus, Leichtenstein, Vapuz, 2007. *Bibliog:* Pratt J Archit, 88; Sammlung Rolf Rickie, 2008. *Media:* Photography, Mixed Media. *Dealer:* Projex MH Galerie 372 St Catherine W Number 212 Montreal H3b1A2. *Mailing Add:* 450 Broome St New York NY 10013

STEIN, LINDA
SCULPTOR, PAINTER
Study: Attended Sch Visual Art, NY, Art Students' League, NY, Pratt Graphics Ctr, NY; Queens Col, NY, BA (cum laude); Pratt Inst, NY, MA. *Work:* Portland State Univ, Ore; Adelphia Univ. *Comn:* Numerous comns. *Exhib:* Solo exhibs, Blades, Jamaica Arts Ctr, NY, 94, Musical Blades, Cortland Jessup Gallery, Mass, 96, Sounding Blades, Spiva Art Mus, Joplin, Miss, 98, Embedded Glyphs, The Art Club, NY, 2002, The Face: An Obsession, Morgan Gallery, Smith Col, Northampton, Mass, 2004, (K)night Watch, NY Univ, Broadway Windows, NY, 2005, Heroic Visions, Longstreth Goldberg Art, Naples, Fla, 2006, Wonder Woman Reborn, The Art Mission Gallery, Binghamton, NY, 2006, Sculpture of Heroic Woman, Anita Shapolsky Gallery, Pa, 2006, Knights, Flomenhaft Gallery, NY, 2006; group exhib, Constructions, Anita Shapolsky Gallery, NY, 94; Boxed and Bound, Arlene Bujese Gallery, East Hampton, NY, 95, A Matter of Synthesis, 95, Sacred and Profane, 95, Form as Function, 96, Dimensions: Drawings and Sculpture, 97, Methods & Materials, 99; To The End And Beyond, Nabi Gallery, Sag Harbor, NY, 97; Bridge: New York, Sakai City Mus, Japan, 98; Color, Millennium Gallery, East Hampton, NY, 99; Text: Word and Image, Firehouse Gallery, Nassau Community Col, NY, 2000; Overview, Blue Gallery, Santa Fe, 2001; Small Works, Gallery Merz, Sag Harbour, NY, 2004; Box Show, Concepto

Gallery, Brooklyn, NY, 2004; Wreath Interpretations, Arsenal Gallery, Ctrl Pk, NY, 2004; Outdoor Biennial, Adelphi Univ, New York, 2008. *Pos:* Artist-in-residence, America the Beautiful Fund, NY, 75; resident fellowship, Va Ctr Creative Arts, 87 and 89, Djerassi Found, Calif, 88. *Teaching:* Lectr in field. *Awards:* Guild Hall Mus Award, 99; Lower Manhattan Cultural Council Grant, 2005; NY City Dept Cultural Affairs Grant, 2005. *Bibliog:* Sallie Zimmerman (auth), exhib catalog, 2004; Joan Marter (auth), Linda Stein: Portraits in Mood, exhib catalog, 2004; Barbara J Love (auth), Feminists Who Changed America, 1963-1975, Urbana Champaign, Univ Ill Press, 443, 2006; Helen Hardacre (auth), Power and Protection: Japanese/American Crossroads and the Impact of 9/11, exhib catalog, 2006; and numerous mag, newspaper & J articles. *Dealer:* 547 W 27th St Suite 308 New York NY 10001. *Mailing Add:* 100 Reade St New York NY 10013

STEIN, LUDWIG
PAINTER, EDUCATOR
b Wyoming, Del, Mar 20, 1938. *Study:* Kutztown State Col, BFA, 64; Tyler Sch Art, with Steve Green, David Pease & Charles Schmitt, MFA, 69. *Work:* Sheldon Mem Gallery Art, Univ Nebr, Lincoln; Everson Mus Art, Syracuse, NY; Philadelphia Mus Art; Univ Belfast, Ireland; Long Beach Art Found, NJ. *Exhib:* One-man shows, Barbara Gillman, Miami, Fla, 86, Adele M Gallery, Dallas, Tex, 86, John Christian Gallery, NY, 86, Basel Art Fair, Switz, 87, Schoeneck Gallery, Basel, Switz, 90; and many others. *Teaching:* Instr, Wis State Univ, Eau Claire, 69-71; Univ Calif, Northridge, 71-72; prof, Syracuse Univ, NY, 72-. *Awards:* Best Show, Waterloo Regional, Iowa, 71; Jurors Award, Tyler Alumni, 76; Grant, Northern British Arts Coun, 77. *Mem:* Coll Art Asn. *Media:* Oil. *Mailing Add:* c/o Barbara Gilman Gallery 939 Lincoln Rd Miami Beach FL 33139

STEINBACH, HAIM
SCULPTOR, CONCEPTUAL ARTIST
b Israel, Feb 25, 1944; US citizen. *Study:* Pratt Inst, BA, 68; Yale Univ, MFA, 73. *Work:* Mus Contemp Art, Chicago, Ill; Los Angeles Co Mus Art, Calif; Israel Mus, Jerusalem; Centre Georges Pompidou, Paris, France; Milwaukee Art Mus, Wis. *Comn:* Coat of Arms, mixed media construct, Gruppo GFT, Torino, Italy, 88. *Exhib:* Brokerage of Desire, Otis Art Inst, Los Angeles, 86; Les Courtiers du Desir, Centre Georges Pompidou, Paris, 87; Documenta 8, Kassel, W Ger, 87; Solo exhib, Cape Mus D'Art Contemporain, Bordeaux, 88; Binational, Mus Fine Arts, Boston & Kunsthalle, Dusseldorf, W Ger, 88. *Teaching:* Instr, Middlebury Col, 73-77 & Cornell Univ, 77-80. *Awards:* CAPS Award, NY State Coun on the Arts, 83. *Bibliog:* Germano Celant (auth), Haim Steinbach's Wild Wild Wild West, Artforum, 87; John Miller (auth), The Consumption of everyday life, Artscribe, 88; Holland Cotter (auth), Haim Steinbach shelf life, Art in Am, 88. *Media:* Mixed. *Dealer:* Sonnabend Gallery 420 W Broadway New York NY 11222; Jay Gorney Modern Art 100 Greene St New York NY 10012. *Mailing Add:* 85 Quay St No 3A Brooklyn NY 11222

STEINBERG, BLEMA
COLLECTOR
Study: BA, McGill Univ, BA, 1955; Cornell Univ, MA; McGill Univ, PhD, 1961; cert psychoanalyst, 1989. *Teaching:* Assoc prof, McGill Univ, prof, 1996-2001, prof emer, 2001-. *Awards:* Named one of Top 200 Collectors, ARTnews mag, 2004-13. *Collection:* Modern and contemporary art. *Publ:* Auth, Shame & Humiliation: Pres Decision Making on Vietnam, 1996 (Quebec Writers Federation award, 1996, QSPELL First Book award, 1996); co-ed, Superpower Involvement in the Middle East, 1985; contribr articles to prof journals; auth, Women in Power: The Personalities and Leadership Styles of Indira Gandhi, Golda Meir, and Margaret Thatcher, McGill-Queen's Univ Press, 2008. *Mailing Add:* McGill Univ Political Sci Dept 855 Sherbrooke St W Montreal PQ H3A 2T7 Canada

STEINBERG, H ARNOLD
COLLECTOR
b Montreal, Canada, Oct 25, 1933. *Study:* McGill Univ, BA (commerce), 54; Harvard Univ, MBA, 57. *Hon Degrees:* McGill Univ, LLD. *Pos:* With Dominion Securities (now RBC Dominion Securities), Montreal, Canada; exec. v.p., CFO, dir. & mem. exec. com. Steinberg Inc., Montreal, Canada, 1958-89, chmn. Ivanhoe Inc.; prin. retail & investment banking, sr. officer Cleman Ludmer Steinberg Inc., Montreal, Canada, 1989-2009; chancellor McGill U., Montreal, Canada, 2009-. Former dir. Banque Nationale du Canada, Bell Canada Internat.; bd. dir. Almiria Capital Corp., Provigo Inc., Teleglobe Inc. Mem. Canada Coun., 1979-85, mem. exec. com., 1981-85; chmn. bd. gov. McGill U.-Montreal Children's Hosp. Rsch. Inst., 1972-91; mem. bd. gov. McGill U., 1980-90; chmn. interim bd. McGill U. Health Ctr., 1995-97, chmn. bd., 1997-2000; bd. mem. McGill U. Health Ctr. Found., 2000-; chmn. adv. bd. McGill U. Faculty of Medicine; chmn. Canada Health Infoway, 2003-. *Awards:* Named one of Top 200 Collectors, ARTnews mag, 2004-12. *Mem:* Order of Canada. *Collection:* Modern and contemporary art. *Mailing Add:* McGill University Office of Chancellor Rm 536 Bldg 845 Sherbrooke St W Montreal PQ H3A2T5 Canada

STEINER, CHARLES K
MUSEUM DIRECTOR, PAINTER
b Champaign, Ill, Apr 27, 1951. *Study:* Cornell Univ, BFA, 1973; George Wash Univ, MFA, 1976. *Work:* 3-M, Minneapolis, Minn; NY Health & Hosp Corp; Montgomery Co Md Govt, Rockville, Md; George Washington Univ, Washington, DC; Emprise Bank, Wichita, Kans; Gates Enterprises, Wichita, Kans. *Exhib:* Solo exhibs, 10 Downtown, NY, 1981, Educ Testing Serv, Princeton, NJ, 1993, Wichita Center for the Arts, Wichita, Kans, 2001 & 2006, Friends Univ, Wichita, Kans, 2008; Group exhibs, Coll Art Asn Drawing Show, Corcoran Mus, Washington, DC, 1975; The Working Process, Org of Independent Artists, NY Dept Cult Affairs, 1981; New Talent Outside of Calif, Delphine Gallery, Santa Barbara, Calif, 1987; Architecture; Artist Interpretations; Braithwaite Fine Arts Gallery, Southern Utah Univ, Cedar City, Utah, 1993; Wichita Ctr for the Arts, Wichita, Kans, 2001; 2006; Kans Masters Invitational Art Show, Strecker Nelson Gallery, Manhattan, Kans, 2007; Invitational, Kans Gov's Inaugural, Topeka, 2007; Hutchinson Art Ctr, Hutchinson, Kans, 2008. *Pos:* From asst mus educ to assoc, The Metropolitan Mus Art, NY, 1986; from asst dir to assoc, The Art Mus Princeton Univ, 1986-99; mus exec dir, Wichita Art Mus, 2000-. *Teaching:* Princeton Adult Sch, 1997-98, Drawing & Design. *Awards:* Vis Painter, Edward Albee Found, 1977 & 1978; Rockefeller Found Fel, Metrop, Mus of Art, 1977 & 1978; Metrop Mus Art travel grantee, Europe, 1981; Spears Travel Grants, Princeton Univ, 1995 & 1998. *Bibliog:* Meryl Secrest, Galleries: A Fusion of Sensibility, Washington Post, 1975; Artists Liaison Exhibitions, Santa Monica, Ca, 1987; Vivian Raynor, A Show by 28 Artists & A Solo Show By Their Judge, NY Times, 1993; Don Lambert (auth), Masters Invitational Art Show, Strecker Nelson Art Gallery, Manhattan, Kans, 2007, 114; and others; Art Story: Charles K Steiner (newsletter Trust Co Kans), 8/2008. *Mem:* Asn of Art Mus (dir, 2001-). *Media:* Acrylic. *Specialty:* American Art. *Publ:* Auth, Art museums & visually handicapped consumers, J Visual Impairment and Blindness, 1983; auth, Design comes to Whitney, Arts, Nat; auth, Extending a Welcome, Mastering Civic Engagement: A Challenge to Museums, AAM, Washington, DC, 1961-62; and others; 75 Years of American Art, Introduction, Wichita Art Mus, 2010. *Mailing Add:* Wichita Art Mus 1400 Museum Blvd Wichita KS 67203

STEINER, PAUL
WRITER, CRITIC
b Ger; US citizen. *Study:* NY Univ, BS. *Work:* Calif Mus Photogr; Mus Mod Art. *Exhib:* Reinhold & Brown, NY; Karl Junghans & Galerie Michael Schultz, Berlin; multiples show, Frankfurt, Berlin, Switz, Japan, Can, 90; MoMa, NY, 2007. *Pos:* Assoc ed, Esquire, Inc, 47-52; feature writer & columnist, NAm Newspaper Alliance, Women's News Serv, 60-80; writer, Pop Scene Serv (syndicated rev of NY mus exhibs), 67-72; contrib ed, Nat Jeweller, 76, 77 & 78; columnist, Murray Hill News, 77-79, NY Entertainer, 79-82, Stagebill, 81-, Artspeak, 81-, TV Today, 82-83, Jewish J, 83-86, Reuters, 83-, NY Sunday News, 84-, USA Today, 84-, Cable TV World, 84-, Theater Week, 87-90, Cover Arts & Jewish Herald, Greenwich Village Press, 92-95, 50-Plus Sr News, Forum of Queens, 99-; corresp, NY Post, 77-, NY Mag, Star Mag, US Mag, 78-82, People Mag, NY Daily News, 81-, Omni, 81-90, Broadway Mag, 85-86 & Metrop Home, 91, Ad Week, 94-96 & In Style Mag, 94-96; contrib ed, Metrop Jewish Life, Show Illus, 81-83; NY Business News, 89-90; media work, Clinton Chronicle, NY, 95-99, Crains NY, 96- & Modern Collage, 98-99; Jewish Post, 1985-2004; Jewish Voice, 2006 ; Zing Mag, New York, 2006. *Awards:* Columnist Award, 69 & Press Award, 70 & 94, Bk Author Award, 91, Beaux Arts Soc NY; Int Press Award, NY, 81; World Cult Prize, Italy Centro Studi Recherche dell Nazione, 85. *Bibliog:* Contemporary Authors. *Mem:* Alpha Delta Sigma; Alpha Epsilon Pi. *Publ:* Auth of 17 books; interviews with Chagall, Dali, Marisol, Warhol, LeRoy Neiman & O'Keefe, Artspeak, 81-96

STEINER, RAYMOND JOHN
CRITIC, WRITER
b Brooklyn, NY, May 1, 1933. *Study:* State Univ NY, New Paltz, BA, 66, MA, 71. *Exhib:* Natl Arts Club, Impressions: Oils by RJ Steiner; Hudson Valley Landscapes, Woodstock Artists Asn, 2006; Solo Exhib: Mezzaluna, Karpeles Mus. *Collection Arranged:* The League in Woodstock 1906-Present (cur), Woodstock sch Art, 7/2000. *Pos:* Ed, art critic & reviewer, Art Times, CSS Publ Inc, 84-. *Teaching:* Inst English, Kingston Schools, NY, 1994-. *Awards:* Award for Governors Office, 94. *Mem:* Int Asn Art Critics; Am Soc Aesthetics; Artists Fel Inc (vpres 89-92); Salmagundi Club NY; Woodstock Artists Asn Mus; Hudson Valley Art Asn. *Media:* Oil, Landscapes. *Interests:* Gardening, Painting, Landscapes. *Collection:* Extensive Art Times Art Collection. *Publ:* Heinrich J Jarczyk: Toward a Vision of Wholeness, Laumann Verlag, 92; Frank Mason (exhib catalog), Art Students League, 93; The Four Hearts of Chen Chi, Chen Chi Studio, 93; Feld-Am See: Etchings of Robert Angeloch, 96, Heinrich J Jarczyk: Etchings-1968-1998, 98, Phantom Press; The Art Students League of New York: Hist, CSS Publ, 99; The Mountain, CSS Publ, 2008. *Mailing Add:* c/o Art Times PO Box 730 Mount Marion NY 12456

STEINER, ROCHELLE
ADMINISTRATOR
b Los Angeles. *Study:* Syracuse Univ, BA (summa cum laude with honors); Univ Rochester, MA, PhD (Visual & Cult Studies). *Collection Arranged:* Takashi Murakami: Kaikai Kiki, 2002; Kutlug Ataman, 2003; Cindy Sherman, 2003; John Currin, 2003; Hiroshi Sugimoto, 2003; State of Play, 2004; Monika Sosnowska, 2004; Glenn Brown, 2004; Gabriel Orozco, 2004; Nick Relph & Oliver Payne, 2005; Rirkrit Tiravanija: A Retrospective, 2005; Ilya & Emilia Kabakov: The House of Dreams, 2005; Michael Elmgreen & Ingar Dragset: The Welfare Show, 2006; Ellsworth Kelly, 2006. *Pos:* Nat Endowment Arts intern, Walker Art Ctr, Minneapolis, 1994-96; assoc cur contemp art, St Louis Art Mus, 1996-2001; chief cur, Serpentine Gallery, London, 2001-06; dir, Pub Art Fund, New York, 2006-2009; dean, Univ Southern Calif Roski Sch Fine Arts, 2010-12

STEINER, SHERRY L
PAINTER, WRITER, INSTRUCTOR, GALLERY DIRECTOR
Bronx, NY. *Study:* Sch of Visual Arts, New York, 72. *Exhib:* Mobius, Boston, Berkshire Pub Theatre, Pittsfield, Mass, Ctr for the Arts, Northampton, Mass, 87; First Night, Pittsfield, Mass, 94-95; Front St Gallery, Housatonic Mus, Mass, 96-97; East West Fusion, Sharon, Conn, 97; Warehouse Gallery, Lee, Mass, 98; Norman Rockwell Mus, 99; Solo exhib, OK Harris, NY, 2013. *Pos:* Founder, Artists Action Group, Binghamton, NY, 74-76, The Mus of Teen Art, Housatonic, Mass, 99-; artist-in-residence, Cummington Community, Mass, 86, 92 & 93, Palenville Interarts Colony, Palenville, NY, 94 & Doset Writer's Colony, Vt, 96-2005; founder, owner, Le Petit Musee, Wild Sage, Pittsfield, Mass, 92-; owner, Albany Ctr Galleries, NY; Owner, Arts Moderne Gallery, 2008. *Teaching:* Hillel Acad, Vestal, NY, Riverbrook Sch, Stockbridge, Mass, 82-83, Acad for Myotherapy, Lenox, Mass, 85-86, Eden Hill Summer Prog, Stockbridge, Mass, 88-91,; instr, Private Studio Workshops,

Binghamton, Mass, 75-77, Housatonic, Mass, 86-88; instr, studio art & creative writing, Main Street Human Resources, Great Barrington, Mass, 80-85; instr, studio, drama, writing, music, film, & art history, John Dewey Acad, Great Barrington, Mass, 89-. *Awards:* Pittsfield & N Berkshire Arts Lottery, 91, 92, 95; Berkshire Taconic Foun, Mus of Teen Art, 99-2000; Mass Cult Coun Award, Finausr, Playwriting & New Theatre World, 2003 & 2005. *Mem:* Co-Chair, Great Cultural Coun; Berkshire Writers Room (pres of boads). *Specialty:* Eclectic Art. *Interests:* Music, The Written Word, Performance Poetry. *Publ:* profiled, WomanArt Mag, NY, 77 & 78, The Eagle, The Paper & Sp Union, 86-99; publ & ed, In The Arts, 89; Performance Poetry Publ in Imitation Fruit, 2009, Spokenwar, 2009, Berkshire Rev, 2003, 2005, Chronogram, 2009, Poets West, 2008, Physiognomy in Letters, 2009. *Dealer:* Self

STEINHARDT, ALICE
DRAFTSMAN, PAINTER - ACRYLIC, OIL
b New York, NY, Feb 9, 1950. *Study:* Univ Miami, Coral Gables, BA, 72; Int Ctr Photog, New York, 75. *Work:* Ctr Creative Photog, Tucson; Corcoran Gallery Art; Los Angeles Co Mus Art; Portland Mus Art, Ore; Santa Barbara Mus Art, Calif. *Exhib:* Solo exhib, Photog Gallery, La Jolla, Calif, 82, G Ray Hawkins Gallery, Los Angeles, Calif, 84, Leighton Gallery, Blue Hill, Maine, 88 & 89, Dean Velentgas Gallery, Portland, Maine, 89 & 92, Maine Coast Artists, Rockport, Maine, 93 & Icon Gallery, Maine, 96; Round Top Ctr Arts, Maine, 95; James A Michner Art Mus, Pa, 97; Portland Mus Art, Maine, 98; Bowdoin Col, Maine, 2001; June Fitzpatrick Gallery, Maine, 2005; Aucocisco Gallery, Maine, 2005. *Collection Arranged:* Bowdoin Coll Mus Art, Brunswick, Maine; Corcoran Gallery Art, Wash, DC; Los Angeles Co Mus Art, Calif; Santa Barbara Mus Art, Calif; Farnsworth Mus Art, Rockland, Maine. *Awards:* Purchase Prize, LaGrange III, 77; Millay Colony Arts Award, Austerlitz, NY, 94. *Bibliog:* Article, Photo Bulletin, 80. *Mem:* Friends Photog; Los Angeles Ctr Photog Studies. *Media:* Drawing & Painting. *Publ:* auth, Photography Yr 1982, Time Life Books; Suzette McAvoy (auth), Interstices, Farnsworth Mus, Rockland, 89; Edgar Allen Beem (auth), Maine Art Now, Dog Ear Press, Brunswick, 90; Liv Kristin Robinson (auth), Beyond Black and White, Farnsworth Mus, Rockland, 90; Wolff Theodore (auth), On the Edge: Forty Years of Maine Painting, Maine Coast Artists, Rockport, 92. *Dealer:* Aucocisco Galleries 157 High St Portland ME 014101; AIR Gallery 511 West 25th St New York NY 01001

STEINHARDT, JUDY
COLLECTOR
Awards: Named one of Top 200 Collectors, ARTnews mag, 2009-13. *Collection:* Classical antiquities; modern art, especially drawings; Judaica; Peruvian feathered textiles. *Mailing Add:* 1158 5th Ave New York NY 10029

STEINHARDT, MICHAEL H
COLLECTOR
b Brooklyn, 1940. *Study:* Univ Pa Wharton Sch Finance, BS, 1960. *Pos:* Founding partner, Steinhardt Partners LP, 1967-95; chmn, Jewish Life Network/Steinhardt Found, New York, 1994-, Jewish Media Renaissance, Birthright Israel; managing mem, Steinhardt Mgt LLC, 1996-; trustee & chmn investment comt, New York Univ, currently; trustee, Brandeis Univ, Brooklyn Botanical Garden, Mus Jewish Heritage, Wildlife Conservation Soc, currently; mem vis comt dept Greek & Roman art, Metrop Mus Art, New York, currently; chmn bd Israel Energy Initiatives Ltd, IDT Corp, 2010-. *Awards:* Named one of Top 200 Collectors, ARTnews mag, 2003-13; Medallion, Univ Albany, 2004. *Collection:* Classical antiquities; modern art, especially drawing; Judaica; Peruvian feathered textiles. *Publ:* Auth, No Bull: My Life In and Out of the Markets, Wiley, 2001. *Mailing Add:* Jewish Life Network 6 E 39th St 10th fl New York NY 10016

STEINHOFF, MONIKA
PAINTER, PRINTMAKER
b Swinemuende, Ger, Oct 19, 1941. *Study:* Univ Calif, Los Angeles, BA, 64, MA, 66, PhD Program Lit; Univ Munich, 67; Univ Calif, Berkeley; Master Class: Henriette Wyeth, 90; Monothon, 94-2002. *Work:* Smithsonian Inst, Washington, DC; IBM, New York; Mus NMex Fine Arts; Roswell M - Art Ctr, Albuquerque, NMex; pvt collections, Ricky Medlock, Dan Lynch, Sam Ballen, Daniel Schmalzer. *Comn:* Santa Fe Youth Mural Prog, May the Forest be with you (interior painting, mural exterior 24' x 15'), comn by Julian Heldman, 86; Denillos Garden, comn by Don Meredith; family portrait, comn by Eugene Talbert, Tyler, Tex; Old Mexico Grill, comn lg oil for hwy billboard; Last Supper after DaVinci, comn by Rob Weiland. *Exhib:* Solo exhibs, Dewey Gallery, 87, Zaplin-Lampert Gallery, Santa Fe, 88, Peyton Wright, 92, Turner Carroll, 94, Hand Artes, Truches, NMex, 96, Galerie am Havelufer, Berlin, 96, Roswell Mus, NMex, 99 & Univ NMex, Los Alamos Gallery, 2005, Leipzig, Germany, 2010, Galerie Esteban, Santa Fe, NMex, 2007, Jay Etkin Gallery, 2010, Sabine Nutt Galerie, Dresden, 2010, Peggy Lange Gallery, 2011, April Etchings, NMex, 2012; Fine Arts Mus SW, 90 & 96; Galerie Marstella, Mexico City, 94; Group shows, Gallery im Adlon, Berlin, Ger, 98; El Museo de Foca at Lewallen Gallery, 98 & 2005; Panacea on the Plaza, 10-11/2000; Austrian Biennal, 2002; Taos Mus, Water Media Soc, 2004; Berkley Art Ctr, mem Show, 2005; Masur Mus, Twin Cities, Monroe, La, 2006; Women in the Arts, Mus Fine Arts, Santa Fe, NM, 2005-2006. *Pos:* Cur, Sanctified and Censored Sanctuario de Gueadalupe, 7/2000; dir, ASEA Gallery, Santa Fe, NMex, 2010-. *Teaching:* Instr, Coll Santa Fe & Univ Calif, Berkeley, formerly; Santa Fe Community Coll, 2005-2012. *Bibliog:* Pase Tiempo, NMex, 10/97; Focus Mag, 12/96; Am Talk, 10/96; Santa Fe, NMex, 12/1/99 & 3/17/2000; ABQ J 3/23/2000; Austrian Bienale, 2002; Wemoon (2 images), 2012, 2014. *Mem:* Soc Egg Tempera Painters; Asn Socially Engaged Artists (founder, pres); NMex Print Makers (gallery mem); NMex Painters Exhib 2014, 2015, Highlands Univ, Las Vegas, NMex. *Media:* Egg Tempera; Etching Aquatint, Casein, Monoprints; Encaustic. *Specialty:* sociall concious works. *Interests:* Buddhism, swimming, skiing. *Collection:* Dan Lynch, Eric Lynch, Dr Rickey Medlock, Anna Lane, Margaret Amanda, Liz Robbins, Eileen Mandel, Roswell Mus Art, Albuquerque Mus Art, NMex Fine Arts Mus. *Dealer:* Hand Artes Truchas NMex; A Sea Gallery Sant Fe NMex; Asn of Socially Engaged Artists; Jay Etkin Gallery. *Mailing Add:* 513 Acequia Madre Santa Fe NM 87505

STEINHOUSE, TOBIE (THELMA)
PAINTER, PRINTMAKER
b Montreal, Que. *Study:* Sir George Williams Univ; Art Students League, NY, with Morris Kantor & Harry Sternberg, 46-47; Ecole Beaux-Arts, Paris; Atelier 17, Paris, France, with W S Hayter, 61-62. *Work:* Nat Gallery Can, Ottawa; Montreal Mus Fine Arts, PQ; Confederation Art Gallery, Charlottetown, PEI; Ministry of External Affairs of Can, Moscow Embassy, USSR; McMichael Conserv Collection, Kleinburg, Ont. *Comn:* Ed 250 prints, Carousel, Heuga Co, 81; ed 110 prints, Paysage de Rue, Sheraton Hotel, 82; ed 75 prints, Pastorale Quebecoise, Int Conf Opthamology-Sherbrooke, Que. *Exhib:* Solo exhibs, Galerie Lara Vincy, France, 57, Montreal Mus Fine Arts, 59, 63 & 78, Galerie du Parc, Trois-Riviellres, 83, 92, L'Equivoque Gallery, Ottawa, 80, 86, 90, Gallery Arts Sutton, Que, 91 & Galerie de la ville, Montreal, 96; Montreal Mus Fine Arts, 59 & 63; Japanese Calligraphy Exhibs, 65-99; 1st & 3rd Brit Int Print Biennial, Bradford, Eng, 68 & 72; 9th Int Biennial Art, Menton, France, 72; 50 Yr Retrospective of Atelier 17, Elvehem Art Centre, Wis, 77; Biennial de Grabado de Am, Venezuela, 82; Museo de la Estampa, Mex, 92; NY-Montreal Printcollectors Exhib, 97; Mus Que, Collection of Mus, 96-99; Royal Canadian Acad Arts Exhib, Mus Quebee, 98; Japanese Calligraphy, Los Angeles, 98. *Awards:* Sterling Trust Award, Soc Can Painter-Etchers & Engravers, 63; Jessie Dow First Prize Award, Montreal Mus Fine Arts, 63; Govt Can Centennial Medal of Honor, 67; and others. *Bibliog:* Guy Viau (auth), La Peinture Moderne au Canada Francais, Ministere Affaires Cult, PQ, 64; Guy Robert (auth), Ecole de Montreal, Collection Artistes Can, 65; V Nixon (auth), Tobie Steinhouse-artist, Vie des Arts Mag, summer 72; L'Estampe Originale au Québec - 1980-1990, Bibliotheque National du Québec, 91; and others. *Mem:* Royal Can Acad Arts; Can Group Painters (pres, 66-68); L'Atelier Libre Recherches Graphique; Soc Can Painter-Etchers & Engravers; life mem Art Students' League; and others. *Media:* Oils & Watercolours; Etching & Engraving. *Publ:* Songes et Limiére, portfolio of eight prints, La Guilde Graphique, Montreal, Que, 72; Into my Green World, portfolio of six prints, La Guilde Graphique, 75; and many other editions of prints, 70-92. *Dealer:* La Guilde Graphique 9 St Paul St W Montreal PQ H2Y 1Y6 Can; Galerie L'autre Equivoque 333 Cumberland Ottawa Can K1N 7J3. *Mailing Add:* 208 Cote St Antoine Rd Montreal PQ H3Y 2J3 Canada

STEINKAMP, JENNIFER
SCULPTOR, INSTALLATION ARTIST
Study: Calif Inst Arts, 84; Art Ctr Coll Design, Calif, BFA, 89, MFA, 91. *Work:* Hammer Mus, Los Angeles, Calif; Towada Art Center, Towada, Japan; Western Bridge, Seattle, Wash; Los Angeles County Mus Art, Los Angeles, Calif; Denver Art Mus, Denver, Colorado. *Exhib:* Solo exhibs include Santa Monica Mus Art, 89, FOOD HOUSE, Santa Monica, 93, Huntington Beach Art Ctr, Calif, 95, Mus Contemp Art, North Miami, 95, Ten in One Gallery, Chicago, 97, Henry Art Gallery, Seattle, 99, Williamson Gallery, Art Ctr Coll Design, 2000, Rice Univ Art Gallery, 2001, Experience Music Project, Seattle, 2002, Telfair Mus Art, Savannah, Ga, 2004, Lehmann Maupin, NY, 2004, Ulrich Mus Art, Wichita State Univ, 2005, Kemper Mus Contemp Art, Mo, 2006, Soledad Lorenzo, Madrid, 2006, Lehmann Maupin, 2006, Kemper Mus Contemp Art, Kansas City, 2007; group exhibs include Media/Metaphor, The Corcoran, Washington, DC, 2000; Parallels and Intersections, San Jose Mus Art, Calif, 2002, Collection Highlights, 2002; Animated Impulse, Cheekwood Mus Art, Nashville, Tenn, 2003; A Grain of Dust A Drop of Water, Gwangju Biennale, Korea, 2004; In Focus: Themes in Photography, Albright-Knox, Buffalo, NY, 2004; Visual Music, Hirshhorn Mus and Sculpture Garden, Washington, DC, 2005; Instanbul Modern, Istanbul, Turkey, 2005; Out There: Landscape in the New Millennium, Mus Contemp Art, Cleveland, 2005; Uneasy Nature, Weatherspoon Art Mus, Greensboro, NC, 2006; Looking Now, 21c Mus, Louisville, Ky, 2006; Taipei Biennial, China, 2006. *Teaching:* prof, Univ Calif Los Angeles. *Awards:* Seattle Art Comn Grant, 99; City Las Vegas Arts Comn Grant, 2000; Individual Artist Fellowship Award, City Los Angeles, 2001; LEF Found Award, 2002; NEA Mus Grant, Univ Wyoming Art Mus, 2006. *Res:* Digital projection. *Dealer:* Leamann Maupin NY

STEINMAN, BARBARA
CONCEPTUAL ARTIST, PHOTOGRAPHER
b Montreal, Que. *Work:* Nat Gallery Can, Ottawa, Ont; Art Gallery Ont, Toronto; Musee d'art Contemporain, Montreal; Vancouver Art Gallery, Ont; Maison Europeenne de la Photographie, Paris; Seoul Metropolitan Mus, Seoul. *Comn:* reflecting pool, sculpture & benches, Concord Pac Develop Corp, Vancouver, 96-97; urban park & walkway design, East of Bay Develop Corp, Toronto, 98-2003; Large Format Photographic Work, O & Y Properties, Inc, Toronto. *Exhib:* Mus Mod Art, NY, 90; Nat Gallery Can, Ottawa, 90; Biennale de la Imagen en Movimiento, Reina Sofia Centro de Arte, Madrid, 90; Places with a Past, Charleston, SC, 91; Setagaya Art Mus, Tokyo, 95; Recent Art of the Americas, Art Inst Chicago, 95; Notion of Conflict (with catalog), Stedelijk Mus, Amsterdam, The Neth, 95; ICA/VITA Brevis, Boston, Mass, 98; Mus Fine Art, Montreal, 2004. *Awards:* Governor General's Award in Visual and Media Arts, Can, 2002. *Bibliog:* Gillian Mackay (auth), Governor General's Awards, Visual & Media Arts, Ottawa 2002; Peggy Gale (auth), Toutle Temps, Le Biennale, Montreal, 2002; Jill Medvedow (ed) ICA/Vitra Brevis, 1998-2003: History, Landscape and Art, Boston, 2004. *Media:* Multimedia. *Dealer:* Olga Korper Gallery 17 Morrow Ave Toronto ON M6R 2H9 Canada

STEINWORTH, SKIP (WILLIAM) EUGENE, JR
GRAPHIC ARTIST
b St Paul, Minn, May 2, 1950. *Study:* St Cloud State Univ, Minn, BA, 74, MA, 79. *Work:* Springfield Civic Collection, Ill; Plains Mus, Moorhead, Minn; Minneapolis Inst Art; Kemper Insurance Corp Collection, Chicago; City of Winter Park, Fla. *Exhib:* Contemp Still Lifes, Riverside Art Mus, Calif, 91; Parkersburg Art Ctr, WVa, 95; Drawings Midwest, Minn Mus Art, St Paul, 97; Amarillo Mus Art, Tex, 98; Evansville Mus Art, Ind, 99. *Teaching:* St Columbia's Col, Melbourne, Australia, 74-77. *Awards:* Minn State Arts Bd Fel, 99. *Bibliog:* Betsy Goldman-Schein (auth),

Skip Steinworth, Am Artist, 6/89; Deborah Gimelson (auth), Contemporary realist drawings, Archit Dig, 7/95; Bill Lasarow (auth), Skip Steinworth, Art Scene, 5/98. *Media:* Pencil. *Dealer:* Hackett/Freedman Gallery 250 Sutter St San Francisco CA. *Mailing Add:* 13460 51st St N Stillwater MN 55082

STEIR, PAT
PAINTER
b Newark, NJ, April 10, 1940. *Study:* Boston Univ, 60; Pratt Inst, BFA, 62. *Hon Degrees:* Pratt Inst, DFA, 91. *Work:* Mus Mod Art, Metrop Mus Art, NY; Nat Gallery Art, Washington, DC; Walker Art Ctr, Minneapolis, Minn; Brooklyn Mus, NY; Tate Gallery, London; Phila Mus Art; Whitney Mus Am Art, NY; Albright-Knox Art Gallery, Buffalo, NY; The Art Mus, Princeton Univ; The Hirshhorn Mus, Washington, DC; Irish Mus Mod Art, Dublin; Lyon Mus d'Art Moderne, France; Malmo Mus, Sweden; Dallas Mus Fine Arts; and numerous others. *Exhib:* Solo exhibs, Galerie Franck & Schulte, Berlin, 93, Galleria Allessandra Bonomo, Rome, 93, Guild Hall Mus, East Hampton, NY, 93, Irish Mus Mod Art, Dublin, 94, Jaffe Baker Blau, Boca Raton, Fla, 94, Anders Thornberg Gallery, Lund, Sweden, 94, Kunstwerke Berlin, Ger, 95, Baldwin Gallery, Aspen, Colo, 96, Robert Miller Gallery, NY, 95, 97, Irish Mus Mod Art, Dublin, 96, Dorothy Blau Gallery, Bay Harbor Islands, Fla, 96, Brooklyn Gallery, 97, Galerie Deux Co Ltd, Japan, 97, Rhona Hoffman Gallery, Chicago, 98, 2000, Baumgartner Galleries, Washington, DC, 98, Whitney Mus Am Art, NY, 98, Weatherspoon Art Gallery, 99, Butler Inst Am Art, Youngstown, Ohio, 2000, Sherman Gallery, Boston U, 2001, Galleria Bonomo, Bari, Italy, 2001, Galerie Simonne Stern, New Orleans, 2001, Contemp Arts Mus, Honolulu, 2001, Rosenbaum Contemp, Fla, 2007, Cheim & Read Gallery, NY, 2007, Solway Gallery, Ohio, 2007 & many others; group exhib, Brooklyn Mus, NY, 84 & 92; Baltimore Mus Art, Md, 87; First Impressions (traveling exhib), Walker Art Ctr, Minneapolis, Minn, 89-90; Musee d'Art Contemporain, Lyon, 90; Nat Gallery Art, Washington, DC, 90; Inspired by Nature, Neuberger Mus, Purchase, NY, 94; Dialogue with the Other, Kunsthallen Brandts Klaedefabrik, Odense, Denmark, 94; A Room with Some Views, Sonnabend Gallery, NY, 94; Black & White & Read All Over, LaSalle Lobby Gallery, Nationsbank Plaza, Charlotte, NC, 95; American Art Today: Night Paintings, Art Mus, Int Univ, Miami, 95; Va Mus Fine Arts, 95; From Picasso to Woodrow, Suite of Prints, Long Vertical Falls, Tate Gallery, London, 95; Nuevas Abstracciones, Palacio de Velazquez, Museo Nacional Centro de Arte Reina Sofia, Madrid, Spain, 96; Museo de Arte Contemporaneo, Barcelona, Spain, 96; Original Visions: Women, Art and the Politics of Gender, Boston Coll Mus Art, 97; A Thought Intercepted, Calif Mus Art, Santa Rosa, 97; Mus Mod Art, 97; Likity Split Installation, Whitney Mus Art, NY, 98; The Am Century, Whitney Mus Am Art, 99; Nat Gallery of Art, 2000; Pat Steir, Brice Marden & Michael Mazur, Boston Univ, 2001; and numerous others. *Awards:* Nat Endowment Arts, 74, 76; Guggenheim Fel, 82; Boston Univ Sch for the Arts Disting Alumni Award, 2001; Clarice Smith Distinguished Lects in Am Art, Smithsonian Mus Am Art, Washington, DC, 2004. *Bibliog:* John Howell (auth), A Bloom of one's own, Elle Mag, 2/88; Pat McCoy (auth), Pat Steir: Knoedler, Artscribe, 2/88; Michael Kimmelman (auth), This American in Paris kept true to New York, New York Times, 4/17/88; Linda Yablonsky (auth), Artist in Residence, Elle Decor Mag, 5/2007; Roberta Smith (auth), Art Reviews Painting in the Heady Days After it was Proclaimed Dead, NY Times, 2/16/2007. *Mem:* Nat Acad Design. *Dealer:* Cheim and Read 547 West 25th Street New York NY 10001. *Mailing Add:* 80 MacDougal St New York NY 10012

STELLA, FRANK
PAINTER
b Malden, Mass, May 12, 1936. *Study:* Phillips Acad, with Patrick Morgan; Princeton Univ, with William Seitz & Stephen Greene; Princeton Univ, Hon DA, 84; Dartmouth Col, Hanover, NH, hon degree, 85. *Work:* Solomon R Guggenheim Mus, Metrop Mus Art & Whitney Mus Am Art, NY; Hirshhorn Mus & Sculpture Garden, Nat Collection Fine Art, Smithsonian Inst, Nat Gallery Art & Nat Mus Art, Washington, DC; Art Inst Chicago, Ill; Los Angeles Co Mus Art & Mus Contemp Art, Calif; Milwaukee Art Ctr, Wis; Walker Art Ctr, Minneapolis, Minn; Brooklyn Mus, NY; Musée d'Art Moderne, Paris; and many others. *Exhib:* Solo exhibs, Resource/Response/Reservoir: Stella Survey 1959-1982 (with catalog), San Francisco Mus Art, Calif, 83, Frank Stella 1970-1987 (with catalog), Mus Mod Art, NY, traveling, 87-89, Prints from the Collection, Hirshhorn Mus & Sculpture Garden, Smithsonian Inst, Washington, DC, 92, Arte e Architettura (with catalog), Palazzo della Esposizioni, Rome, Italy, 93, Moby Dick Series, Engravings, Domes & Deckle Edges (with catalog), Ulmer Mus, Stadthaus Ulm, Ger, 93, Space in Progress (with catalog), Kawamura Mem Mus Art, Sakura, Japan, 94 & Imaginary Places, New Work: Painting, Relief & Sculpture, Waddington Galleries, London, Eng, 94, Bernard Jacobson Gallery, London, Eng, 99, Sperone Westwater Gallery, NY, 99, Frank Stella at 2000: Changing the Rules, Mus of Contemp Art, N Miami, Fl, 2000, New Work, Paul Kasmin Gallery, NY, 2007, Barbara Mathes Gallery, 2007; Group exhibs, 30th Biennial Contemp Am Painting, 66 & 37th Ann Exhib Contemp Art Am Painting (with catalog), 81, Corcoran Gallery Art, Washington, DC, 66; Am Abstract Painting: Selections from the Whitney Mus Collection, 75 & Biennial Exhib, 79, Whitney Mus Am Art, NY, 75; Second Am Exhib, 76 & 73rd Am Exhib, 79, Art Inst Chicago, Ill; Acquisition Priorities: Aspects of Postwar Painting in Am, 76 & The NY Sch: Four Decades, Guggenheim Mus Collection, Major Loans, 82, Solomon R Guggenheim Mus, NY; Am Painting of the 1970's, Albright-Knox Art Gallery, Buffalo, NY, 78; Selections from the Meyerhoff Collection, Baltimore Mus Art, Md, 78; Stella Since 1970, Ft Worth Art Mus, Tex, 78; Emergence & Progression, Milwaukee Art Ctr, 79; Morton G Newmann Family Collection, Nat Gallery Art, Washington, DC, 80; Changes, Aldrich Mus Contemp Art, Ridgefield, Conn, 83; Selections from the Twentieth Century Art Collection, Los Angeles Co Mus Art, Calif, 83; Nine Printmakers & the Working Process, Whitney Mus Am Art Fairfield Co, Stamford, Conn, 85; Seven Master Printmakers: Innovations in the Eighties, Mus Mod Art, NY, 91; Four Centuries of Drawing 1593-1993, Kohn Abrams Gallery, Los Angeles, Calif, 93; Isamu Wakabayashi, Frank Stella, Jannis Kounellis, Richard Serra, Akira Ikeda Gallery, Nagoya, Japan, 94; Inaugural Exhib, Kemper Mus Contemp Art & Design Kansas City Art Inst, Mo, 94; and many others. *Pos:* vis critic, dept art, Cornell Univ, 1965. *Teaching:* Lectr, numerous cols, univs & orgns; Rep, by Leo Castelli Gallery, 1959; artist-in-residence, Dartmouth Coll, 1963; instr, art Univ Saskatchewan, 1967, Brandeis Univ, 1968; instr, Brandeis Univ, 1969; Charles Eliot Norton prof, poetry Harvard Univ, Cambridge, Mass, 1983. *Awards:* Charles Eliot Norton Professorship of Poetry, Harvard Univ, Cambridge, Mass, 83-84; NY Univ Resident Fel, Soc Fels; Award Am Art, Pa Acad Fine Arts, Philadelphia, 10/25/85; Hon Degree, Brandeis Univ, 86; Hon Degree, Dartmouth Col, 85; NH Award of Am Art, 85; NJ Bernard Medal of Distinction, 85; Nat Medal Arts award, Nat Endowment for the Arts, 2010; Lifetime Achievement award, Int Sculpture Ctr, 2011. *Bibliog:* Suzanne Stephens (auth), Portrait: Frank Stella, Blurring the Line Between Art & Architecture, Archit Digest, 7/94; Robert Smith (auth), Frank Stella (review: Knoedler), New York Times, 10/21/94; Judd Tully (auth), Art: Frank Stella at Knoedler Fine Arts in October, Cover, 10/94; and many others. *Mem:* Coun US and Italy; Fel Soc Fel (NY Univ); Nat Acad (assoc, 90, acad, 94-). *Publ:* Auth, On Caravaggio, New York Times Mag, 2/3/85; Working Space, Harvard Univ Press, 86. *Dealer:* Leo Castelli Gallery 420 W Broadway New York NY 10012. *Mailing Add:* Bernard Jacobson Gallery 6 Cork St London United Kingdom W1S 3EE

STELLA, HARRY
PAINTER, PHOTOGRAPHER
New York, NY, March, 21, 1925. *Study:* Studied with Mercedes Carles, 33; Phoenix Sch Art; Art Students League, instructor Miller and Macpherson, studied with Ben Dale, Cartoonist Illusr Sch, NY, Howard Arnold, 47. *Work:* Coral Springs Ctr Arts, Coral Springs, Fla; Bailey Hall, Davie, Fla; Schacknow Mus, Plantion, Fla; Chelsea Ctr, E Norwich, NY; David Posnack Ctr, Plantion, Fla. *Exhib:* Chelsea Ctr, E Norwich, NY, 99; Schacknow Mus, Plantation, NY, 2002; Coral Springs Ctr Arts, Coral Springs; Bailey Hall, Davie, Fla. *Collection Arranged:* Retrospective, Chelsea Ctr, 89. *Pos:* art studio, Cohama Decorative Fabrics, 56-84. *Awards:* Peacock Showcase award, Chelsea Ctr, 99; and many others. *Bibliog:* Betty Ommerman (auth), Artist Realizes Dream at 67, Newsday, Long Island, NY, 11/92; Lenny Della Rocca (auth), Dining & Entertaining, Parkland Forum, Coral Springs, Fla, 5/97; Amy Ward (auth), A Man with Art, Tamarac Forum, Fla, 8/2002. *Media:* Oil, Watercolor, Pastel. *Interests:* Art History, Photography. *Collection:* Paul Girol, Women in Mantilla, frama-surrealism. *Mailing Add:* 6040 NW 80th Ave Tamarac FL 33321

STELZER, MICHAEL NORMAN
SCULPTOR, INSTRUCTOR
b Brooklyn, NY, Jan 6, 1938. *Study:* Pratt Inst, 56; Art Students League, 60-62; Nat Acad Sch Fine Arts, Edward Mooney traveling scholar, 66 & Nat Sculpture Soc Joseph Nicolosi grant, 67; and with Nathaniel Choate, 64, Michael Lantz, 64-67 & Donald DeLue, 68 & 69. *Comn:* 12 ft relief, Worcester Polytech Inst, 64. *Exhib:* Am Artists Prof League Grand Nat, 63, 76 & 77; Nat Arts Club, 63-64; Nat Acad Design, 64-67, 70-71 & 74-77; Allied Artists Am, 67 & 71-81; Nat Sculpture Soc Ann Exhib, 68-81. *Pos:* Team mem, Restoration Leonardo Da Vincis 24 ft Horse Sculpture, 98. *Teaching:* Instr sculpture, Fashion Inst Technol, New York, 79. *Awards:* Helen Foster Barnett Prize, Nat Acad Design, 66; Gold Medal, Hudson Valley Art Asn, 76; Gold Medal, Grand Nat Exhib, Am Artists Pro Prof League, 76; Allied Artists Am Award, 81; Hudson Valley Art Asn Award, 85; Hudson Valley Art Asn Award, 2001, 2003, 2004, 2007, 2010. *Bibliog:* Article in, Pen & Brush, 66; Opportunities offered the young sculptor, 67 & Interpreting the human figure, 68, Nat Sculpture Rev. *Mem:* Nat Sculpture Soc; Hudson Valley Art Asn; Allied Artists Am; Am Artists Prof League. *Dealer:* James Cox Gallery 466 Route 212 Willow NY 12495. *Mailing Add:* 8 Everit St Brooklyn NY 11201

STENT, TERRY & MARGARET
COLLECTORS
Study: Yale Univ, BA, 61; Harvard Univ, MBA, 68. *Pos:* Pilot, Delta Air Lines, 70-97; dir, Callanwolde Fine Arts Ctr, Atlanta, 83-86; mem, Art Collectors group High Mus Art, Atlanta, 93—, dir, 97—, chmn, collections comt, 99-2001, bd chmn, 2001—; bd comnr & Art Forum Smithsonian Am Art Mus, Wash, chmn bd comnr, 99-2003. *Awards:* Decorated nine Air Combat medals; named one of Top 200 Collectors, ARTnews Mag, 2004. *Collection:* 19th & 20th century art, especially Hudson River Sch & Ashcan Sch; American Realism. *Mailing Add:* High Mus Art 1280 Peachtree St NE Atlanta GA 30309

STEPHANSON, LORAINE ANN
PAINTER
b Edmonton, Alta, Apr 19, 1950. *Study:* Univ Alta, BED & MVA, 78; Univ Sask, Emma Lake Workshops with Friedl Dzubas, John Elderfield & Kenworth Moffett, 79-80; Triangle Workshop, New York, with Larry Poons & Michael Fried, 86; Triangle Workshop, New York, NY, with Karen Wilkin, Willard Boepple, Michael Chisholm, Alexei Worth, 2000. *Work:* Univ Alta, Edmonton; Prov of BC Collection; Air Canada, Montreal; Royal Trust, Vancouver; Triangle Trust, NY. *Exhib:* Solo exhib, Univ Art Gallery & Mus, Edmonton, 78; Grand Forks Art Gallery, 92, Barton Leier Gallery, Victoria, 94 & CAC Gallery, Victoria, 2000; Emma Lake '79, 79-80, Alberta Now, 80 & Canadian Contemp Art, 83, Edmonton Art Gallery; The Joy of Form, Burnaby Art Gallery, Vancouver, 86; Celebrations, Univ Art Gallery, Edmonton, 87; 16X one, Gallery One, Toronto, 96; Arts 2000, Gallery Stratford, 2000. *Pos:* Illusr, Brit Inst Archeol-Univ Alta Classics Dept, Gravina, Italy, 70-71. *Teaching:* Lectr painting, Univ Alta, Edmonton, 78-80, asst prof, 85; extension fac, Univ Victoria, 90; Contemp Artforum, Victoria, 98. *Awards:* Univ Alta Prize Art & Design, 76; Heinz Jordan Mem Scholar, Heinz Jordan Co, Toronto, 77; Can Coun Grant, 80. *Bibliog:* R Lawrence (auth), Review, Vanguard Mag, 85; R. Amos (auth), Review, Victoria Times Colonist, 9/10/2000. *Media:* Acrylic on Canvas, Watercolor. *Dealer:* Virginia Christopher Galleries Ltd 1134 8th Ave SW Calgary Alberta T2P 1J5 Can; Art Placement Inc 228 3rd Ave S Saskatoon SK S7K 1L9. *Mailing Add:* 608 Oliver St Victoria BC V8S 4W3 Canada

STEPHEN, FRANCIS B
JEWELER, SCULPTOR
b Dublin, Tex, Mar 7, 1916. *Study:* Fine Art Ctr, Colorado Springs, Colo; Univ Okla, study with Jean Charlot & Robert von Neumann, MFA. *Work:* Witte Mem Mus, San Antonio, Tex; Okla Art Ctr; Hallmark Collection, Mo. *Exhib:* The Patron Church, Mus Contemp Crafts, NY, 61; 11th Mid-Am Exhib, Nelson Gallery, Kansas City, Mo, 61; Craft Exhib, Dallas Mus Fine Arts, 71-74 & 78; South Cent States Crafts Exhib, Denver Art Mus, Colo, 73; Contemp Crafts of The Americas, Denver Art Mus, 74; Lake Superior Int Crafts Exhib, Tweed Mus Art, Univ Minn, Duluth, 74-75; The Metalsmith, Phoenix Art Mus, Ariz, 77; Solo exhib, Mus of Art, Okla Univ, 79; and others. *Teaching:* Asst prof jewelry & sculpture, North Tex State Univ, Denton, 64-67; prof jewelry, Tex Tech Univ, Lubbock, 67-83. *Awards:* Swarovski Award, Great Designs in Jewelry, Swarovski & Co, 67; Grand Award, 15th Tex Crafts Exhib, 71; Purchase Award, Miniature Works, Tex Tech Mus Art, 75. *Mem:* Soc of NAm Goldsmiths. *Media:* Miscellaneous Media. *Dealer:* Schneider-Bluhm-Loeb Gallery Inc 230 W Superior St Chicago IL 60610. *Mailing Add:* 4610 29th St Lubbock TX 79410

STEPHENS, CURTIS
EDUCATOR, DESIGNER
b Athens, Ga, Dec 13, 1932. *Study:* Univ Ga, MFA. *Work:* Objects USA, Johnson's Wax Collection; Ill State Mus, Springfield. *Exhib:* Designed for Production, Mus Contemp Crafts, 64; Objects USA, Johnson's Wax Collection, Smithsonian Inst, 69; 24th & 25th Ill Exhib, Ill State Mus, 71 & 72. *Pos:* Designer, Callaway Mills, LaGrange, Ga, 63-66; photogr, 1960 Pandora (Popular Photog Award-Winning Yearbk, Univ Ga). *Teaching:* Asst prof art, LaGrange Col, 61-63 & Univ Northern Mich, 66-68; assoc prof art & design, Univ Ill, Champaign-Urbana, 68-, assoc dir sch, 75-90,emeritus assoc prof, 98. *Bibliog:* Lee Nordness (auth), Objects: USA, Viking Press, 70; Jay Hartley Newman & Lee Scott Newman (auth), Plastics for the Craftsman, Crown, 72. *Media:* Papers, Plastics. *Mailing Add:* 1909 Jane Ann Ct Urbana IL 61802-7055

STEPHENS, ELISA
ADMINISTRATOR
Study: Vassar Col, BA; Univ San Francisco Sch Law, JD. *Pos:* Law clerk, San Francisco Superior Ct, 1985-86, contrib editor, Barclays Law Publishers, 1986-88; in-house counsel, Cellular Holdings, Inc, San Francisco, 1987-88; in-house coun Acad of Art Univ (formerly Acad of Art Col), San Francisco, 89-92, pres, 92-. *Mem:* Young Pres's Orgn, San Francisco City Club, Metrop Club, University Club, San Francisco Rotary Club, San Francisco Jr League, Nob Hill Asn, Royal Arts Soc. *Mailing Add:* Academy of Art University School of Art & Design 79 New Montgomery St 2nd fl San Francisco CA 94105-3410

STEPHENS, THOMAS MICHAEL
KINETIC ARTIST, DESIGNER
b Elkins, Ark, Feb 21, 1941. *Study:* Univ Kans, 59-63; pvt study & travel. *Exhib:* New Tendencies 4 & 5, Galeria Grada Zagreba, Zagreb, Yugoslavia, 69 & 73; 20th Century Am Photog, Nelson-Atkins Mus, Kansas City, Mo, 74; Cybernetic Symbiosis, Lawrence Hall Sci, Berkeley, Calif, 79; Critica I, Mus Graphics, Terme, Italy, 81; Univ Ctr Gallery, Lawrence, Kans, 81; Solo exhibs, Lawrence Gallery, 81, Rockhurst Gallery, 82 & Batz Gallery, 83. *Pos:* Principal, T M Stephens Design Assoc, currently. *Teaching:* Instr sculpture, Kansas City Art Inst, 86-87. *Awards:* Proclamation of Commendation by Mayor of Kansas City, 85. *Bibliog:* Peter Von Ziegesar (auth), article, Kansas City Mag, 7/86; Virginia Hillix (auth), article, New Art Examiner, 10/86. *Mem:* Computer Art Soc; assoc Hypergraphics Int Alliance; Kansas City Art Gallery Asn

STEPHENS, WILLIAM BLAKELY
EDUCATOR, PAINTER
b Corpus Christi, Tex, June 8, 1930. *Study:* Univ Tex, BFA, 56, with Hiram Williams, MEd, 57, MFA, 66; Univ Fla, EdD, 72. *Work:* Mus ETex, Lufkin; Tyler Mus Art. *Exhib:* 23rd Ann Tex Painting & Sculpture, Dallas Mus Fine Arts, 61; Art on Paper, Weatherspoon Gallery, Greensboro, NC, 67; Super Graphics, Brooks Mem Art Mus, Memphis, Tenn, 74; Solo exhib, Emerging Figures, Univ Tex, Tyler, 82; Contemp Art of the USA, Hamburg, WGer, 89 & Bonn, WGer, 90; USAid Mission, Tegucigalpa, Honduras, 91; and others. *Pos:* Art ed, New Voices in Educ, 71-72. *Teaching:* Asst occup ther, Univ Fla, 70-71; assoc prof art educ, Memphis State Univ, 72-76; prof art, Univ Tex, Tyler, 76- & chmn dept, 76-84 650 Watercolors. *Awards:* Univ Tex at Tyler Fac Res Grants, 78, 80, 90 & 94. *Mem:* Life mem Tex Fine Arts Asn. *Media:* Watercolor. *Res:* Artists' personality types; monuments and myths; the family saga in the south. *Publ:* Auth, Blue Ridge Studies, Fac Publ, Appalachian State Univ, 5/69; On creativity and teaching: talk with Hiram Williams, Art J, summer 71; Relationship between selected personality characteristics, Studies in Art Educ, spring 73; University art departments and academies of art: The artists' psychological types to their specialties and interests, Bull of Res in Psychological Type, summer 77; Hiram Williams, Memphis State Univ, 78. *Mailing Add:* Univ Tex Tyler Dept Art 3900 Univ Blvd Tyler TX 75799

STEPHENSON, JOHN H
SCULPTOR, CERAMIST
b Waterloo, Iowa, Oct 27, 1929. *Study:* Univ Northern Iowa, BA; Cranbrook Acad Art, MFA. *Hon Degrees:* Grand Valley State Univ, Hon DFA, 92. *Work:* Int Mus Ceramics Faenza, Italy; Everson Mus, Syracuse, NY; Portland Art Mus; Detroit Inst Arts; Cranbrook Mus; Keramon, Frechen, Ger. *Comn:* Champion No 3 (sculpture), Mich Mall, Battle Cree, Mich, 76. *Exhib:* retrospective, Sustained Visions, Detroit, 88; Waterloo Mus Art, 90; Revolution Gallery, Ferndale, Mich, 96; Univ Mich Mus Art, 94; Detroit Mus Art, 9650; Nanfeng Mus, Foshan, China, 2000; World Ceramics Ctr, Icheon, Korea, 2004; Retrospective, Birmingham Bloomfield Art Ctr, Birmingham, Mich; In the Clay Birds Next, 2010; Crafting Modernism, Mus Art and Design, NY, 2012; New World Visions, IAC Biennale, Santa Fe Mus Art, 2012. *Teaching:* Instr ceramics, Cleveland Inst Art, 58-59; prof art, Univ Mich Sch Art, Catherine B Heller Distinguished prof, 89, interim dean, 91-93, prof art emer, 95. *Awards:* Artists Fel, NEA, 86; Artist Fel, Mich Coun, 89. *Bibliog:* Century of Ceramics in the USA, Objects USA; John H Stephenson: After the Fire, A Retrospective; Marcia Polenberg (auth), Retrospective, In the Clay Bird's Nest, Ceramics Art and Perception, Vol 21, No 2, 2011. *Mem:* Nat Coun Educ Ceramic Arts; Mich Potters Asn; Int Acad of Ceramics Asn (IAC); Founders Soc Detroit Inst Art; Friends, Mus Art, Univ Mich. *Media:* Ceramic, Mixed. *Res:* Chinese ceramic folk art. *Publ:* Perception/Inner & Outer Vision, Studio Potter, 88; Time, Place and a Taste of Clay, Studio Potter, 92. *Dealer:* Clay Gallery 335 Main St Ann Arbor MI 48104. *Mailing Add:* 4380 Waters Rd Ann Arbor MI 48103

STEPHENSON, SUSANNE G
CERAMIST, EDUCATOR
b Canton, Ohio, Nov 5, 1935. *Study:* Carnegie-Mellon Univ, BFA; Cranbrook Acad of Fine Art, Bloomfield Hills, Mich, MFA. *Hon Degrees:* D of Arts, Grand Valley State Univ, Allandale, Mich. *Work:* Victoria & Albert Mus, London; Everson Mus Art, Syracuse, NY; Detroit Inst Arts, Mich; Int Ceramics Mus, Bechyne, Czech Repub; Los Angeles Co Mus, Calif. *Comn:* Ceramic Planters, Burroughs Corp, Detroit, Mich, 70, Grosse Pointe Br, Nat Bank of Detroit, 72 & Harper Hosp, Detroit, 72; Liturgical Vessels, Lutheran Chapel, Eastern Mich Univ, Ypsilanti, 72. *Exhib:* Garth Clark Gallery, NY, 86; solo exhib, Carnegie Inst Mus Art, Pittsburgh, Pa, 85; Opening exhib, American Mus, Flican, Fuping, China, 2008; 4th Int Ceramic Competition, Mino, Japan, 95; Ist Ceramic Biennale Korean Int Competition, 2002, 03; Int Ceramic Exhib, Jingdezhen Ceramic Mus, Jingdezhen, China, 2009; New Worlds Timeless Vision, IAC Biennale, Santa Fe Mus Art, 2012. *Teaching:* Instr ceramics, Univ Mich, Ann Arbor, 60-61; prof ceramics, Eastern Mich Univ, 63-91. *Awards:* Mich Ceramics Award, 78, 81, 85, 88 & 2008; Best in Ceramics, Beaux Arts Designer Craftsmen Exhib, Columbus, Ohio; Regional Visual Arts Fel, 87; Mich Coun Arts Grant, 87. *Bibliog:* Garth Clark & Margie Hughto (coauths), Century of Ceramics, E P Dutton, 79; Garth Clark (auth), American Potters, Watson Guptill, 81; Janet Koplos (auth), Alternations--the ceramics of Susanne Stephenson, Am Crafts, 1/83; Marcia Polenberg (auth) Susanne Stephenson, Recycled Landscapes, Ceramics Art and Perception, Vol 21, No 2, 2011. *Mem:* Am Craftsmen's Coun; Mich Potters Asn; Nat Coun Educ for Ceramic Arts; Internat Acad Ceramics; Pewabic Soc. *Media:* Porcelain, Earthenware. *Dealer:* Pewabie Pottery Detroit MI; Clay Gallery Ann Arbor MI. *Mailing Add:* 4380 Waters Rd Ann Arbor MI 48103

STERLING, COLLEEN
PAINTER
b Sterling, Ill, Dec 17, 1951. *Study:* Mus Sch Art Inst, Chicago, Ill, 75-76; Massachusetts Coll Art, Boston, Mass, 85; John C Campbell Folk Sch, Brasstoun, NC, cert, 2003, 2009. *Work:* Hunter Mus Am Art, Chattanooga, Tenn; City Atlanta, Dept Aviation, Atlanta, Ga; City Atlanta, Rotating Art Collection, Atlanta, Ga. *Comn:* Site specific artwork (wall), Hyatt Roissy, Paris, France, 92; Site specific artwork (wall), Dept Aviation, City of Atlanta, Ga, 99; site specific artwork (wall) YMCA, Sterling, Ill, 2000; Fulton Co Arts Coun, public art prog, Sr Ctr, Palmetto, Ga, 2003. *Exhib:* Overlays, GSU Gallery, Boston Univ, Boston, Mass, 86; Works on Paper, Berkshire Art Mus, Pittsfield, Mass, 88; Basically Black & White, Riverside Art Mus, Riverside, Calif, 92; Inaugural Exhib, Contemp Mus of Art, Buford, Ga, 92; Urban Flashes, Amarillo Art Ctr & Mus, Amarillo, Tex, 93; Mapping the Self, Telfair Mus of Art, Savannah, Ga, 94; Nat Juried Exhib, Brenau Univ, Gainesville, Ga, 94; Intermix, Sarratt Gallery, Vanderbilt Univ, Nashville, Tenn, 95; Artstravaganza, Hunter Mus of Am Art, Chattanooga, Tenn, 98; Soho Gallery, Los Angeles, Calif, 2004; Silver Fox Gallery, NC, 2005. *Pos:* Freelance critic, Art Papers, Atlanta, Ga. *Teaching:* Instr art, private lessons in studio, 98- & Inst for Continuing Learning, Young Harris, Ga, 99- & Blue Ridge Mt Arts Assoc, Blue Ridge, Ga, 2006-. *Awards:* AVA II, nominee, SECCA, Winston Salem, 91; Ga Women in the Visual Arts, Nexus Contemp Art Ctr, State Rep Lewis Massey, 97; 2nd level award, Artstravaganza, Hunter, Mus, Donald Kuspit, 98. *Bibliog:* Bill Alexander (auth), Art Papers, Vol 18, No 5, 9-10/94; Donald Locke (auth), Creative Loafing, Vol 24, No 39, 2/17/96; Jerry Cullum (auth), Atlanta J & Constitution, 1/9/98. *Mem:* Blue Ridge Mt Arts Asn (mem at large). *Media:* Charcoal paste "drawing" with Plexiglas overlays; Mixed media. *Res:* Old masters oil glazing and egg tempera techniques. *Specialty:* Fine art. *Interests:* reading, research. *Publ:* Auth exhib catalogs, David Fraley, 93, Robert Rauschenberg, A Print Survey, 93, Charles Burchfield, 94 & Lee Bontecou, Sculpture & Drawings of the 60's, 94; William Dooley, rev, Art Papers Mag, 2001. *Dealer:* Bonnie Rash c/o Silver Fox Gallery, 508 North Main St Hendersonville, NC 28792. *Mailing Add:* 678 Mason Rd Blairsville GA 30512

STERLING, SUSAN FISHER
MUSEUM DIRECTOR
Study: Princeton Univ, PhD (Art Hist). *Pos:* Assoc cur, Nat Mus Women in the Arts, Washington, 1988-90, cur mod & contemp art, 1990-94, chief cur contemp art, 1994-2008, dep dir, 2001-08, dir, 2008-. *Awards:* Norwegian Royal Order of Merit; Order de Rio Branco, Brazil. *Mailing Add:* Nat Mus Women in the Arts 1250 New York Ave NW Washington DC 20005-3970

STERN, ARTHUR I
STAINED GLASS ARTIST, SCULPTOR
b June 18, 1950. *Study:* Dept Archit, Univ Ill, 68-72; Calif Coll Arts & Crafts, BFA (environ design), 73, MFA, 75. *Comn:* Las Vegas Temple, LDS Church, Las Vegas, Nev, 88; Leader glass, LDS Church, Bountiful, Utah, 94; sculpture & leaded glass windows, Fed Courthouse, Baton Rouge, 94; Christ Church Episcopal, Portola Gallery, Calif, 94; St Matthews Lutheran Church, Walnut Creek, Calif, 94; and others. *Exhib:* Solo exhibs, Bank Am Gallery, San Francisco, 83 & Calif Coll Arts Crafts Gallery, 83, Calif Coun Am Inst Archit Conv, San Diego, 83, Frank Lloyd Wright: In

the Realm of Ideas, Marin Co Civic Ctr, San Rafael, Calif, 90, Am Inst Archit Gallery, San Francisco, Calif, 94; Nat AIA Col, Phoenix, 84, San Francisco, 85 & NY, 88; Image, Light & Structure, Pontiac, Mich, 84; Nat Glass, Downy Art Mus, Los Angeles, 86; Design 1987, Galleria Design Ctr, San Francisco, 87; Calif Design 2000, San Francisco, 99. *Collection Arranged:* CCAIA, Arch Glass, 81; AIA Nat Conv, Arch Craft, 85. *Teaching:* Instr sculpture, Calif Col Arts & Crafts, Oakland, Calif, 87 & instr glass, 88. *Awards:* IFRAA, Art in Archit Award, 87 & 90; Am Inst Arts Design Award, 96. *Media:* Architectural Glass. *Publ:* Auth, Stained Glass, fall 94. *Mailing Add:* 1075 Jackson St Benicia CA 94510

STERN, H PETER
COLLECTOR, CHAIRMAN
b. Hamburg, Germany, June, 12, 1928. *Study:* Harvard Univ, AB (magna cum laude), 50; Columbia Univ, MA, 52; Yale Univ Law Sch, LLB, 54. *Collection Arranged:* co-founder, Storm King Art Ctr, Mountainville, NY. *Pos:* chmn, Storm King Art Ctr, Mountainville, NY; vchmn, World Monuments Fund, NY; chmn, Ralph Ogden Found, Mountainville, NY; hon dir, Friends of Vassar Art Gallery, Poughkeepsie, NY; chmn bd, Star Expansion Co, Mountainville, NY; advisory bd, Int Rescue Fund. *Awards:* Phi Beta Kappa, Harvard Univ; Cayaliere dell'Ordine, Republica Italiana; Eleanor Roosevelt Valkil Medal, NY; Ottaway Medal, Orange Co Citizens Found; World Monuments Hadrian Medal, 90; Spirit of the River award, Scenic Hudson, 99; Ogden Medal, 99. *Mem:* The Century, NY; University Club, NY; Harvard Club, NY. *Specialty:* modern & contemporary sculpture. *Interests:* Asian art, sculpture, music, travel, poetry. *Collection:* Indian & Turkish art, paintings, sculpture. *Mailing Add:* PO Box 330 Mountainville NY 10953

STERN, LOUIS
DEALER, CONSULTANT
b Jan 7, 1945; US citizen. *Study:* Calif State Univ, Northridge, BA, 1968. *Pos:* Pres, Wally Findlay Galleries, Beverly Hills, Calif, 1980-82; pres, Louis Stern Galleries, Beverly Hills, Calif, 1982-93, Louis Stern Fine Arts, Los Angeles, 1994-. *Awards:* Chevalier de l'ordre des Arts et des Lettres, French Ministry of Culture, 2001, Chevalier in the Ordre Nat de la Legion d'Honneur, Rep of France, 2007. *Bibliog:* Charlotte Chandler (auth), Nobody's Personal Biography, 2004; Ed Sikor (auth), One Sunset Boulevard: The Life & Times of Billy Wider, 2004. *Mem:* Los Angeles Co Mus Art; Los Angeles Art Coun; Int Found Art Res, NY; Friends of French Art; Am Friends of Blerancourt; Art Dealers Asn Calif; Fine Arts Dealers Asn (FADA); French Chamber Com, Los Angeles; Cedars Sinai Med Center (exec comt mem, bd govs); Am Society of French Legion of Honor; J Paul Getty Mus Photographic Arts Coun. *Res:* IRS commissioner's art advisory panel. *Specialty:* Impressionist, important Modern, Latin American, 19th and 20th century American and European painting and works on paper, 20th Century Hungarian Avant Garde; West Coast Hard Edge. *Publ:* Janos Mattis Teutsch and The Hungarian Avant Garde, 1910-1935, Louis Stern Fine Arts, 2002; Transmigrations, Sculpture by Cecilia Miguez, Louis Stern Fine Arts, 2002; Lorser Feitelson and the Invention of Hard Edge Painting, 1945-1965, Louis Stern Fine Arts, 2004; Frederick Wight, Visions of California, Louis Stern Fine Arts, 2005; Lorser Feitelson, The Kinetic Series - Works from 1916-1923, Louis Stern Fine Arts, 2005; Lucien Clergue, Fifty Years of Photography, Vintage & Recent Works, Louis Stern Fine Arts, 2006; Claire Falkenstein, Structure and Flow, Works from 1950-1980, Louis Stern Fine Arts, 2006; Frederick Wight, Seeing the Light: Postmodern Luminous Landscapes; Alfredo Ramo Martinez & Modernismo, Margarita Neito, PhD & Louis Stern, ed Marie Chambers, The Alfredo Ramos Martinez Research Proj, 2009; Karl Benjamin and the Evolution of Abstraction, 1950-1980, Louis Stern Fine Arts, 2011. *Mailing Add:* 9002 Melrose Ave West Hollywood CA 90069

STERN, LOUISE G
PRINTMAKER, PAINTER
b New Haven, Conn, Apr 24, 1921. *Study:* Syracuse Univ, 39-42; Boston Univ, BA, 43; Mus Mod Art, 60-62; Art Students League with Roberto DeLamonica & Edgar A Whitney (watercolor); study with Don Stacy & Reiji Kimura. *Work:* Gen Foods Corp, Tarrytown, NY; Cabrini Med Ctr, Dobbs Ferry, NY; Brown Chemical Corp, New York; Morani Art Gallery, Med Coll Pa, Philadelphia; Pfizer Collection, Westchester, NY; Westchester Metro Media Corp, White Plains, NY; pvt collections, Marjorie Isaac, Cathy & Walter Isaacson, Fay & Dennis Greenwald & Marion Stein; Tsanko Laurenov Nat High Sch Fine Arts, Plovdiv, Bulgaria, 2010; Art Coll, Mus Coll, Bretagne, France; Loft in the Red Zone, 9/11 Tribute Exhib, 23 Wall St, Moscow Mus Modern Art, 2011. *Comn:* Dr Barbara Melamed; Ellen Lazarus; Dr & Mrs Giancarlo Ginanangeli. *Exhib:* Prints Int, Silvermine Guild Artists, New Canaan, Conn, 90, 92 & 96; Heaton Gallery, Rockland Ctr Arts, West Nyack, NY; Adelphi Univ, Manhattan Ctr, 91; Grass Roots Alumni, Gallery Hastings, 91; Union Am Hebrew Congregations, New York, 92; The Printed Image, Gallery Hastings, 92; solo exhibs, Banco Popular, New York, 93, Silvermine Guild Arts Ctr, New Canaan, Conn, 94 & Broome St Gallery, Soho, New York, 96; Manhattan Borough Pres Off, Women's Hist Month, Working Artists Katonah Mus Artists, Mt Kisco, 2003-2007; Beauty & The Beast, Silvermine Guild Artists, 2005; Dynamic Synthesis, Mamaroneck Artists Guild, Iona Coll, 2007; Small Works Juried Show, 2007 & 09; The Female Gaze, Iona Coll, 2007 & Mamaroneck Artists Guild, 2008; Made in USA, Nat Asn Women Artists, Blue Hill Cult Ctr, Peal River, NY, 2007; Footprint Int, Ctr for Contemp Printmaking, Norwalk, Conn, 2008; Spring into Summer, Nat Asn Women Artists, NY, 2008; The 11th Int Collage Exhib and Exchange, New Plymouth, New Zealand, 2009; 12th Int Coll Exhib & Exchange New Plymouth, New Zealand; Open House to Benefit the Nat Mus Art, 2011; Loft in the Red Zone, Memorial to 9/11, 2011. *Collection Arranged:* Art Colle, Mus Collage, Bretagne, France, 2011; The Understudies I, Studio 26 Gallery, New York, NY, 2015; Gratitude, New Rochelle Coun on the Arts, New Rochelle, NY, 2015. *Teaching:* Children's class, Mamaroneck Artists Guild, 90; instr, watercolor, Learning in Retirement Inst, Iona Coll, 94-; instr, home studio, 95-2005; home studio, 2010. *Awards:* First Prize, Mixed Media, New Rochelle Art Asn, 97, 2000 & 2004; Louise H Renwick Mem Award, Graphics Art Show, Bedford, NY, 99; Dermont Gale Award, New Rochelle Art Asn, 2002; Third Place, Katonan Mus Artists Asn Juried Exhib; First Place, Active Members Award Show, MAG, 2004. *Bibliog:* Manhattan Arts Int, 96. *Mem:* Artist Equity NY; Nat Asn Women Artists, New York (chmn, print jury, 88-90 & chmn, nominating comt, 90-92); Silvermine Guild Artists, New Canaan, Conn; Mamaroneck Artists Guild, Larchmont, NY (exhib chmn); New Rochelle Art Asn, NY (exhib co-chmn); Am Asn Univ Women; New Rochelle Coun on the Arts. *Media:* Watercolor, Graphics; Mixed Media. *Interests:* playing the recorder. *Dealer:* Marla Passarelli 43 Irenhy Ave Port Chester NY 10573 web: www.m.p.artsales.com. *Mailing Add:* 120 Lakeshore Dr Eastchester NY 10707

STERRITT, COLEEN
SCULPTOR, EDUCATOR
b Morris, Ill, Jan 8, 1953. *Study:* Univ Ill, BFA, 76; Otis Art Inst, MFA, 79. *Work:* Mus Contemp Art, Los Angeles; Crocker Art Mus, Sacramento, Calif. *Exhib:* Solo exhibs, Karl Bornstein Gallery, 84 & 86, Seaver Coll Art Gallery, Pepperdine Univ, Malibu, Calif, 87, Santa Monica City Col, Santa Monica, Calif, 88, Cal State Univ, Los Angeles, 90, Claremont Grad Sch, Calif, 96 & Los Angeles Seoul Contemp Arts, 96, Riverside Art Mus, 2006, den Contemp Art, Los Angeles, 2006; Selections from the Permanent Collection: 75-91, MOCA, Los Angeles, 91; Sexy: Sensual Abstraction in California Art, 1950's-1990's, Contemp Artists Collective/Temporary Contemp, Las Vegas, Nev, 95; Armory Ctr Arts, Pasadena, Calif, 96; Drawn from LA, Armory Ctr Arts, 96; The Empowered Object, Hunsacker/Schlesinger Gallery, Santa Monica, Calif, 96; group exhibs: Group, Carl Berg Gallery, Los Angeles, 2005, Draw Paper Scissors, domestic setting, Los Angeles, 2006, Otis: Nine Decades of Los Angeles Art, LA Municipal Art Gallery, Barnsdall Park, Los Angeles, 2006, Themes & Variations: New Abstraction in Los Angeles, Torrance Mus Art, 2007,; and others. *Pos:* Bd dir, Los Angeles Contemp Exhibs, 86-92, treas, 88-90, chmn, 91-92. *Teaching:* Vis artist, Claremont Grad Sch, 85- 99, Calif State Univ, Fullerton, 86-87 & Pepperdine Univ, 87-88; instr drawing, Univ Southern Calif, 85-86, instr sculpture, 89; instr sculpture, Otis Art Inst, Parsons Sch Design, 87-93; Long Beach City Col, instr, sculpture, 96-98; head sculpture program, Long Beach City Coll, 98-. *Awards:* Fel, Nat Endowment Arts, 86; Artist Fel, Art Matters Inc, 94; Artist-in-Residence Grant, Roswell Mus & Art Ctr, NMex, 94; JP Getty Trust Fel, Calif Community Found, 96; COLA Fellowship, 2006-07. *Bibliog:* Charlotte Streifer Rubenstein (auth), American Women Sculptors, A History of Women Working in Three Dimension, GK Hall & Co, Boston, 90; Peter Frank (auth), Pick of the week, LA Weekly, 10/18/90; Michal Reed (auth), Coleen Sterritt at LASCA, Artweek, 12/96; Constance Mallinson (auth), Coleen Sterritt at d.e.n. contemporary art, Art in America, March 2007; Katherine Satorius (auth), Coleen Sterritt at d.e.n. contemporary art, Artweek, Feb 2007. *Mem:* Int Sculpture Ctr; Los Angeles Contemp Exhib; Coll Art Asn. *Media:* Mixed. *Publ:* Charlotte Streifer, Rubenstein, American Women Sculptors, A History of Women Working in Three Dimension, GK Hall & Co, Boston. *Dealer:* d e n Contemporary Art Culver City CA. *Mailing Add:* 3101 N Raymond Ave Altadena CA 91001

STETSON, DANIEL EVERETT
MUSEUM DIRECTOR, CURATOR
b Oneida, NY, Jan 3, 1956. *Study:* State Univ NY Coll Potsdam, BA, 1978; Syracuse Univ, NY, MFA (grad asst), 1981. *Collection Arranged:* Focus 1 Michael Boyd (auth, catalog), Focus 3 The Art of Haiti: A Sense of Wonder (auth, catalog), 1989, Focus 6 Contemp Developments in Glass (auth, catalog), 1990, Stieglitz and 40 other Photographers: The Development of a Collection (auth, catalog), 1991-92, New Works: Featuring Austin and Central Texas Artists (auth, catalog), 1992. *Pos:* Actg dir, Picker Art Gallery, Colgate Univ, Hamilton, NY, 1980-81; dir, Gallery Art & cataloger, Permanent Collection, Univ Northern Iowa, Cedar Falls, 1981-87, Davenport Mus Art, Iowa, 1987-91; exec dir, Austin Mus Art, Tex, 1991-96, Polk Mus, Lakeland, Fla, 1996-. *Teaching:* Museology, Colgate Univ, 1980-81; Univ Northern Iowa, 1981-87; Mem adv comt MBA Course of Study Styles & Strategies Non-Prof Orgn, St Ambrose Univ, 1989-91. *Awards:* Fel, Northeast Mus Conf, 1979; Scholar ALI-ABA, 1984. *Mem:* Am Asn Mus; Tex Asn Mus; Fla Art Dir Asn; Fla Asn Mus; and others. *Mailing Add:* Polk Mus Art 800 E Palmetto Lakeland FL 33801-5529

STETTNER, LOUIS
PHOTOGRAPHER
b New York, NY, Nov 7, 1922. *Study:* Princeton Univ, 42-44; Inst Hautes Etudes Cinematographiques, BA, 49. *Work:* Victoria & Albert Mus, London; Bibliotheque Nat, Paris; Mus Mod Art, Int Ctr Photog & Metrop Mus Art, NY; Nat Mus Am Art; Mus de Elysee, Switzerland; Chicago Art Inst; San Francisco Mus Art; Smithsonian Inst, Washington, DC; Carnaualet Mus, Paris; and others. *Exhib:* Bibliotheque Nat, Paris, 49; Photog in the Fine Arts, Chicago Inst Art, 61 & traveling exhib; Photo League, Int Ctr Photog, NY, 81; Critics Choice, Victoria & Albert Mus, London, 83; Subjective Photog, San Francisco Mus Mod Art, 84; Neikrug Gallery, NY, 85; Daniel Wolf Gallery, NY, 86; Ctr Photog, Geneva, 86; Retrospective Early Work Photofind Gallery, NY, 88; NY Trilogy, Union Sq Gallery, 88; Comptoir de la Photographie, Paris, 89; Kate Heller Gallery, London, 90; Vision Gallery, San Francisco, 90; Gallery Spectrum, Zaragoza, Spain, 90; Recent Work Howard Greenberg Gallery, 92 & 96; Bonni Benrubi Gallery, 96 & 2006; Suermondt Ludwig Mus Aachen, 97; Marion Mayer Gallery, 98; Mus Belle Artes, Santiago, Chile, 2000; Woerdsdoff Gallery, Paris, 2004 & 06; Camera Wovll Gallery, Berlin, 2006; Whitney Museum, NY, 2006. *Awards:* Photog Fel, Yaddo, 56; Creative Photog Grant, NY State Coun Arts, 73 & Nat Endowment Arts, 74. *Bibliog:* Norman Hall (auth), The Indestructible Image, Brit Photog, 67; Alan Porter (auth), monograph, Swiss Camera, 72; Ken Poli (auth), Delights of the Quiet Eye, Popular Photog, 83. *Media:* Black and White. *Publ:* Auth, Paris Street Scenes, Two Cities Publ, 49; Weegee the Famous, Knopf Publ, 78; Sur Le Tas, Cercle D'Art, 79; Streetwork, Symbax Inc, 81; photgr, Poster Series by Flammarion, Flammarion Publ, 86; Early Joys Photographs from 1947-72, J Iffland,

Pub, 86; Photo Poche #76 Louis Stettner, Nathan, 1994; Louis Stettner's New York, Rizzoli, 1996; Wisdom Cries Out in the Streets Editions, Flammarion, 1999; Edmund White (auth), Recent Work, Flammarion, 2000; Penn Station, Editions, Camera Work, 2006. *Dealer:* Howard Greenberg Gallery New York NY 10012. *Mailing Add:* 172 W 79th St No 6G New York NY 10024

STEVANOV, ZORAN
PAINTER, SCULPTOR
b Novi Sad, Yugoslavia, June 25, 1945; US citizen. *Study:* Fla Atlantic Univ, Boca Raton, BA, 68; Wichita State Univ, Kans, MFA, 70. *Work:* Wichita State Univ; Emporia State Univ, Kans; Ft Hays State Univ, Kans. *Comn:* Sculpture fountain, State Kans, Emporia State Univ Libr, 71-73. *Exhib:* Nat Exhib Drawing & Sculpture, Muncie, Ind, 67; Nat Ann Exhib, Monroe, La, 71; Kans Biennial Art Exhib, Lindsborg, 72; Eight State Ann Exhib, Oklahoma City, 74; three-man show, Lynn Kottler Gallery, NY, 75. *Teaching:* Instr sculpture & design, Emporia State Univ, 70-73; assoc prof design, Ft Hays State Univ, 73-, assoc prof art, currently. *Awards:* Second Prize Ann State Exhib, Fort Lauderdale, Fla, 67; First Prize Ann State Exhib, Hollywood, Fla, 68; Third Prize Nat Art Exhib, Winter Park, Fla, 68; and others. *Mem:* Coll Art Asn

STEVENS, ANDREW RICH
CURATOR, HISTORIAN
b Dubuque, Iowa, Feb 1, 1956. *Study:* Iowa State Univ, BA, 1978, MA, 1980; Univ Kans, MA (art hist), 1988. *Collection Arranged:* Am Color Woodcuts: Bounty from the Block, 1890s-1990s (with James Watrous, auth, catalog), 1993; Tandem Press Five Years of Collaboration and Experimentation (auth, catalog), 1994; Henry Moore: Prints and Maquettes from the William S Fairfield Collection (auth, catalog), 1995; Hogarth and The Shows of London (auth, catalog), 1996; 150 Years of Wisconsin Printmaking (auth, catalog), 1998. *Pos:* Cur of Prints, Drawings and Photographs, Elvehjem Mus Art; sr acad cur, L & S, Chazen Mus, Univ Wis, currently. *Mem:* Print Coun Am; Am Asn Mus. *Res:* History and aesthetic of printed art. *Publ:* Contribr, The World in Miniature: Engravings By the German Little Masters (exhib catalog), Spencer, 1988; Visions and Revisions: Works on Paper by Robert Cumming (exhib catalog), Elvehjem Mus, 1991. *Mailing Add:* Chazen Mus 272F Elvehjem Bldg Conrad A Madison WI 53706

STEVENS, ELISABETH GOSS
WRITER, PRINTMAKER
b Rome, NY, Aug 11, 1929. *Study:* Wellesley Coll, BA, 51; Columbia Univ, MA (high hons), 56. *Work:* Baltimore Mus of Art; Brown Univ; Cornell Univ; Harvard Univ; New York Public Libr; Princeton Univ; School of the Art Inst of Chicago; Univ of Texas at Austin; Hamilton Coll; Boston Public Lib. *Exhib:* Corcoran Gallery Art, Washington, DC; Towson State Univ, Baltimore; Atelier A/E, New York; solo exhib, Coll Notre Dame, Md, 97, Galerie Francoise, Lutherville, Md, 2000 & Univ Minn at Morris, 2001; Katharine Butler Gallery, Sarasota, Fla, 2004; Kirkland Libr, Clinton, NY, 2007; Art Center Sarasota, Fl; Stakenborg Fine Art, Sarasota, Fla; Bright Hill Literary Ctr, NY, 2012; Fukinsei Art Lab, Sarasota, Fla, 2013; Stakenberg Fine Art, Sarasota, Fla, 2013. *Pos:* Ed assoc, Art News, 64-65; art critic, Washington Post, 65; freelance art critic & writer, 65-78 & Sarasota Herald Tribune, 2005-2007, critic radio SR2, 2007-; columnist, The Gallery, Wall St J, 69-71; Sunday art columnist, Trenton Times, 74-77; art & archit critic, Baltimore Sun, 78-86; contrib writer, The Senses, 2006-2009; critic, Radio SRQ.com, 2007-. *Awards:* Prizewinner First Fiction Contest, Maryland Poetry Reviews, 93, Second Fiction Contest, 94; Prizewinner, Fiction Contest, Lite Circle, 94-96; Prizewinner, Playwriting Contest, Baltimore Writers Alliance, 95, Hon mention, 2011. *Mem:* Coll Art Asn; Soc Graphic Artists; Women Contemp Artists Sarasota, Fla; Towles Court Art Asn, Sarasota, Fla; SAGA; NY Society of Etchers. *Media:* Etching. *Specialty:* prints. *Publ:* Artist of Delight: A Retrospective of the Works of Keith M Martin, 1911-83 (exhib, catalog), Ciscle Gallery, 87; Horse and Cart: Stories from the Country, Wineberry Press, 90; The Night Lover, 94 & In Foreign Parts, Nine Stories, 97, Birch Brook Press; Household Words, Three Conditions Press, 2000, 2nd ed, 2009; Eranos, Goss Press, 2000; Cherry Pie and Other Stories, Lite Circle, 2001; auth, Long Trail Winding: New & Collected Upstate Stories (ragbag poems), Goss Press, 2008; Ragbag, Peppertree Press, 2010; Sirens' Songs, Goss Press, 2010; Impossible Interludes: Three Short Plays, Brick House Books, 2011; Ride a Bright and Shining Pony, Brick House Books, 2013; The Secret of Paintings of Elisabeth Stevens, Goss Press, 2013. *Dealer:* Stakenborg Fine Art 1545 Main St Sarasota Fl 34236. *Mailing Add:* Bards Castle 5353 Creekside Trail Sarasota FL 34243

STEVENS, JANE ALDEN
PHOTOGRAPHER, EDUCATOR
b Rochester, NY, 1952. *Study:* St Lawrence Univ, BA, 1974; Rochester Inst Technol, MFA, 1982. *Work:* Int Mus Photog, Rochester, NY; Mus de Arte Contemporanea, Sao Paulo, Brazil; Cincinnati Art Mus; Ctr Photog as Art Form, Bombay, India; Mus Fine Arts, Houston; Harry Ransom Res Ctr, Austin, Tex. *Exhib:* Solo exhibs, Ctr for Photog Woodstock, NY, 1990 & ARC Gallery Chicago, 1994, Blue Sky Gallery, Portland, Ore, 2002, Herbert F Johnson Mus Art, Ithaca, NY, 2004, Art Xchange Gallery, Seattle, Wash, 2012; Group exhibs, Int Mus Photog, Rochester, NY, 84; Photovisions, Contemp Arts Ctr, Cincinnati, 87; Pan Horama, Tampere, Finland, 91 & 97; Five Journeys, Cleveland State Univ Art Mus, Ohio, 2002; The Art of Caring, New Orleans Mus Art, La, 2009. *Teaching:* Asst prof photog, Univ Cincinnati, 83-88, assoc prof, 88-96, prof fine arts, 96-2013. *Awards:* Individual Artist Grant, Ohio Arts Coun, 1990, 1992, 2002; Travel/Res Grant, English-Speaking Union, 2000; Artists Projects Grant, Ohio Arts Coun, 2000. *Bibliog:* Adirondack Life Mag, 10/97; Jane Stevens Swing-Lens Photographs Absorbing, Arts & Entertainment section, Pittsburgh Post Gazette, 2/96; Why We Remember, Cincinnati Enquirer, Tempo Section, 5/31/2004. *Mem:* Coll Art Asn; Soc Photog Educ. *Media:* Photography. *Publ:* Contribr, www.fractionmagazine.com/janealdenstevens, 2010; Camerawork of Jane Alden Stevens, Adirondac Mag, 88; All-embracing camera, The World & I, 1/92, pp 282-287; The Elements of Photography, 2nd Ed, pp 128-133, Focal Press; auth, Tears of Stone: World War I Remembered, Cincinnati, Ohio, 2004; Popular Photography China, 2012. *Mailing Add:* 515 Terrace Ave Cincinnati OH 45220-1916

STEVENS, JANE M
PHOTOGRAPHER, ADMINISTRATOR
b Chicago, Ill, Oct 1, 1947. *Study:* Univ Ill Chicago, BA (anthropology), 72; Sch Art Inst Chicago; State Univ New York, Buffalo, MA (experimental video), 81; Univ Mass, Amherst, arts mgt cert, 94. *Work:* Visual Arts Collection Pensacola Col, Fla; Ill State Mus, Springfield; McCartney Award Portfolio, Women in Photography, London, Eng; Ill State Mus; Pensacola Coll Visual Arts Collection; pvt collections. *Exhib:* Positive/Negative, Coos Art Mus, Coos Bay, Ore, 89; 7th Nat Exhib, Alexandria Mus Art, La, 88; The Toronto/Chicago Exchange, Toronto, Canada, 92; Jane Stevens/Robert Walker, Univ Ariz, Tucson, 92; solo show, ARC Gallery, 93; and others. *Pos:* Asst cur, Chicago Hist Soc, 78-85; asst admin, Ill Art Gallery, Chicago, 85-. *Teaching:* Instr photogr, Morton Col, Cicero, Ill, 87-90 & 94-2005; coord, fine arts seminar, Chicago Metrop Ctr, 99-. *Awards:* Project Completion, Solitude, Ill Arts Coun, 81; Purchase Award, Pensacola Portrait Exhib, Pensacola Col, 84; Award Portfolio, McCartney Award, Women in Photography, 88; Rocke feller Fel Humanities, The Newberry Lib, Chicago, 2002. *Bibliog:* Catharine Reeves (auth), Jane Stevens, transformations, Chicago Tribune, 3/31/89; Abigail Foerstner (auth), Artists Residents Chicago Gallery, Burke/Stevens, Chicago Tribune, 4/12/91; Abigail Foerstner (auth), Array of images, Chicago Tribune, 3/12/93. *Mem:* Artists Residents Chicago (pres, 92-93, grants 91-92); Chicago Artists Coalition; Soc Photog Educ; Coll Art Asn; Am Asn Mus. *Res:* 50 years of Powwows at Newberry Library & Am Indian Ctr Chicago. *Publ:* Contribr, Zoom, Int Mag, 90; Computer Art: Pushing the Boundaries, Ill State Mus, 92; Camera & Darkroom Mag, 1/92; Visions From Within: Art from prison, Ill State Mus, 95; Artists using Science and Technology, YLEM, 9-10/96; From the Reservation to Urban Life, 2002; Chicago's 50years of Powwows, Arcadia publishing, 2004. *Dealer:* Artists Residents Chicago Gallery 1040 W Huron Chicago IL 60622; Ceres Gallery 584 Broadway New York NY 10011. *Mailing Add:* 1631 N Nagle Ave Chicago IL 60707

STEVENS, MICHAEL KEITH
SCULPTOR
b Gilroy, Calif, July 14, 1945. *Study:* Am River Col, 63-65; Calif State Univ, Sacramento, BA, 67, MA, 69; Univ Guadalajara, Mex, 66. *Work:* Squadron Press, Kansas City, Mo; Persis Corp, Honolulu, Hawaii; CSC Index, San Francisco; Livingston & Mattesich, Sacramento; Crocker Art Mus, Sacramento. *Comn:* Bronze sculpture, Cherry Island Golf Course. *Exhib:* Solo exhibs, Braunstein-Quay Gallery, NY, 78, Braunstein Gallery, San Francisco, 77, 79, 82, 84, 86, 89, 92, 94 & 97 & Betsy Rosenfield Gallery, Chicago, 81, 83, 85 & 88; Ovsey Gallery, Los Angeles, 90; Against The Grain: Contemp Wood Sculpture, Oliver Art Ctr, Calif Coll Arts & Crafts, Oakland, 90; Michael Stevens & Suzanne Adan: A Survey, Mem Union Gallery, Univ Calif, Davis, 90; California Eccentrics, Ill Union Art Gallery, Univ Ill, Urbana-Champagne, 90; Discovery Contemp Calif Narrations, Am Cult Ctr, Brussels, Belgium, 92; From The Studio: Recent Painting & Sculpture By 20 California Artists, Oakland Mus, 92; Mr & Mrs Michael Stevens & Suzanne Adan, Michael Himovitz Gallery, Sacramento, Calif, 93; The Michael Himovitz Gallery, Crocker Art Mus, Sacramento, Calif, 94; Here and Now: Bay Area Masterworks From The Di Rosa Collections, Great Hall High Bay, Oakland Mus, Calif, 94; The Art of Collecting: The Artist As Collector, Mem Union Gallery, Univ Calif, Davis, 94; and many others. *Awards:* Phelan Award, Sculpture, San Francisco Found, 82; Individual Fel Award, Calif Arts Coun. *Bibliog:* Albert Stewart (auth), Contemporary American Wood Sculpture, Crocker Art Mus, 84; Phil Linhares (auth), From the Studio: Recent Painting & Sculpture by 20 California Artists, Oakland Mus, 92; Phil Linhares (auth), Here & Now: Bay Area Masterworks From The Di Rosa Collections, 94. *Media:* Wood, Mixed Media. *Dealer:* Braunstein/Quay Gallery 250 Sutter St San Francisco CA 94108. *Mailing Add:* 3977 Rosemary Cir Sacramento CA 95821

STEVENS, THELMA K
EDUCATOR, DEALER
b New York, NY, Dec 4, 1932. *Study:* Pratt Inst, Brooklyn, NY, BS, 54; Queens Col, Flushing, NY, MS, 59; Fordham Univ, NY, PhD, 80. *Pos:* Owner & pres, Isis Gallery, 82-. *Teaching:* Art instructor, painting & sculpture, various NY State schs, grades K-12, 54-; instr reading & art, Fordham Univ Grad Sch, 79. *Awards:* Art Educator of the Year, NY State, 83; Award, Innovative curriculum design, Cromacyl Paint Co, 83. *Mem:* Nat Art Educ Asn (dir secondary educ, Eastern Region USA & Canada, 86-88); Int Soc Educ through Art (NY State Rep, 88-); US Soc Educ Art; NY State Art Teachers Asn; Long Island Art Teachers Asn. *Res:* Cognition and art. *Specialty:* Contemporary paintings and sculpture. *Publ:* Coauth, Super sculpture, Using Science and Technology, Van Nostrand Reinhold, 74; contribr, Art theory, In: Tapestry, Collegium Book Publ, Inc, 79; auth, articles in Clearing House, Sch Arts. *Mailing Add:* 17 Harriman Dr Sands Point NY 11050

STEVENSON, HAROLD
PAINTER
b Idabel, Okla, Mar 11, 1929. *Study:* Univ Okla, Norman; Univ Mex, Mexico City; Art Students League, New York. *Work:* Whitney Mus, New York; Ctr George Pompidou, Paris. *Comn:* Tennessee Williams gold medallion, comn by Nat Comt Literary Arts, 81; Stations of the Cross, Cathedral St John Divine, 90; mural, NY Eye & Ear Infirmary, 91. *Exhib:* Solo exhibs, San Francisco, 49, Univ Oklahoma, 49, Oklahoma Art Ctr, 49, Galerie Le Cour d'Ingres, Paris, 60, Le Sensuel Fantastique, Galerie Iris Clert, 62, Richard Feigen Galleries, New York, 64 & Sculptures in Crystal, Knoedler and Co, Murano, Italy, 70; Group exhibs, Ann Exhib, Whitney Mus Am Art, New York, 62 & New Realists, Sidney Janis Gallery, New York, 62; Galleria La Medusa, Rome, 73; Americans in Paris, Mus Nat Art Mod, 79; La Famille des Portraits, Louvre Mus Portrait of Francois de Menil, 79-80; and many others.

Teaching: Artist-in-residence, Austin Coll, Sherman, Tex, formerly. *Bibliog:* Andy Warhol (dir), Harold (film), New York, 64; Lucy Lippard (auth), Pop Art, New York, 66; Iris Clert (auth), Iris-Time l'artventure; Andre Morain (auth), Le Milieu de L'Art. *Media:* Oil. *Dealer:* Mitchell Algus Gallery511 W 25th St New York NY 10001

STEWARD, ALETA ROSSI
PAINTER
b Bethpage, NY, Dec 18, 1957. *Study:* Art Students League, W 57th St, New York, NY, with Frank Mason (figure painting), 76; Paul Wood Studios, Port Washington, NY, (abstract painting), 76; Lassen Coll, Susanville, Calif, with Sophie Sheppard, (drawing & compos), 86; Mass Audubon Birders Cert Prog, 2009-2010. *Work:* Modoc Med Ctr, Alturas, Calif; San Bernardino Co Mus, Redlands, Calif; Cape Cod Mus of Natural Hist, Brewster, Mass; Mass Audubon Soc, Marshfield, Mass. *Comn:* Wildlife mural, State of Calif, 34th Dist Agr Asn, Cedarville, 76. *Exhib:* The Still Wild West, Cape Cod Mus of Natural Hist, Brewster, Mass, 89; Ann Wildlife, San Bernardino Co Mus, Redlands, Calif, 90; Wyo Centennial, Wyo State Capitol Bldg, Cheyenne, 90; Ann Art in Nature, Vt Inst of Natural Sci, Woodstock, Vt, 92; Fac Exhib, Cape Mus of Fine Arts, Dennis, Mass, 93; Trees Place, 99, 2005, 2006, 2008, and 2010; Cahoon Mus Am Art, 2007; Thornton Burgess Soc, Sandwich, Mass, 2009; Highfield Hall, Mass, 2010; Priceless, Cape Cod Mus Art, Dennis, Mass, 2013; Impressions of New England, Bennington, Vt, 2013. *Teaching:* Instr wildlife drawing, Cape Cod Mus Art, summer, 94. *Awards:* 2nd Best in Show, Ann New Eng Woodcarving & Wildlife Art Show, 93, Best in Show, 97; Visitors Choice, Mass Audubon Soc, 94. *Bibliog:* Marcia Monbleau (auth), Ah Wilderness!, The Rev, 90; Member of the Issue, North Light Mag, 92; Emerging Artists of the Cape & Islands, Cape Cod Life, 96; Featured Artist, Cape Cod View, Mar/April 2010; Cape Cod Life Arts Ed, July 2010. *Mem:* Copley Soc Boston, 91-98; Soc Animal Artists, NY, 2004-. *Media:* Oil. *Publ:* Auth, Cape Cod Gems (series of 4 art), Cape Cod Oracle, 90; cover art, Dick Blick Art Supplies Catalog, 96. *Dealer:* Trees Place Julian Baird, Rt 6A at 28 Orleans MA 02653; Christina Cook Gallery PO Box 40 Edgartown MA. *Mailing Add:* 57 Colonial Way Harwich MA 02645

STEWARD, JAMES
MUSEUM DIRECTOR, EDUCATOR
b Nov 15, 1959. *Study:* Univ Va, BA, 1981; Inst Fine Arts, NY Univ, MA, 1988; Oxford Univ, England, DPhil, 1992. *Collection Arranged:* Edvard Munch and His Models: 1912-1944, 1992; Gertrude Jekyll: Private Gardens, Vanishing Arts, 1993; Innocence and Experience in German Expressionist Prints and Drawings, 1996; The Mask of Venice: Masking, Theater and Identity in the Art of Tiepolo and His Time, 1996; Masterworks of Greek & Roman Art from the Hearst Mus, 1996; Hogarth and His Times: Serious Comedy, 1998; When Time Began to Rant & Rage: Figurative Painting from Twentieth-Century Ireland, 1998; In Human Touch: Photographs by Ernestine Ruben, 2001; Donald Sultan: Smoke Rings, 2001; The Romanovs Collect: European Art for the Hermitage, 2003. *Pos:* Chief cur, Berkeley Art Mus, Calif, 1992-98; dir, Univ Mich Mus Art, 1998-2010, Princeton Univ Art Mus, 2009-. *Teaching:* Instr, Univ Va, 1981-83; adj asst prof, hist of art, Univ Calif, Berkeley, 1992-98; asst prof hist of art, Univ Mich, 1898-2001, assoc prof, 2001-2003, prof, 2003-2009; lectr, Princeton Univ, 2009-. *Awards:* Exhibition Grant, NEH, 1994 & 1997; Exhibition Grant, Am Ireland Fund, 1997; Exhibition Grant, Robert Gore Rifkin Found, 1996; Chancellor's Award Distinguished Service, Univ Calif, Berkeley, 1996; British Coun Res Fel, 1994 & 1995; Mellon Fund Fel, The Huntington Libr, San Marino, Calif, 1993-94; Art His Fel, Va Mus Found, 1990-91; Arnold, Bryce and Read Trust Award, Oxford Univ, 1991; Exhibition Grant, Samuel H Kress Found, 2002 & 2003. *Mem:* AAM; Asn Art Mus Dirs; Coll Art Asn; Mich Mus Asn (bd dir, 1999-, vpres 2001-); Asn Coll and Univ Mus and Galleries; Asn Art Historians; Am Soc Eighteenth-Century Studies; The Walpole Soc; The London Libr; Va Club of NY. *Res:* 18th and 19th century European art; Irish art 1900 to present; Contemporary photography; history of patronage; landscape history. *Publ:* The Mask of Venice, Univ Washington Press, 1996; When Time Began to Rant & Rage, Merrell Holberton, 1998; In Human Touch: Photographs by Ernestine Ruben, Nazraeli Press, 2001; The Romanovs Collect: European Art from the Hermitage, Merrell, 2003; Betye Soar: Extending the Frozen Moment, Univ Calif Press, 2005. *Mailing Add:* Princeton Univ Art Museum McCormick Hall Princeton NJ 08544

STEWART, BILL
SCULPTOR, CERAMIST
b Plattsburgh, NY, June 21, 1941. *Study:* State Univ NY Coll, Buffalo, BS (art educ), 63; Ohio Univ, MFA, 66. *Work:* San Angelo Mus Fine Arts, Tex; Mint Mus Art, Charlotte, NC; Ark Mus Art, Little Rock, Ark; Mus Am Crafts, New York; Mem Art Gallery, Rochester; Racine Art Mus, Racine Wis; Burchfield Penney Art Ctr, Buffalo, NY. *Comn:* Environmental sculpture, Greater Rochester Int Airport, NY, 91. *Exhib:* Clayworks--20 Americans, Mus Contemp Crafts, New York, 71; Figure and Fantasy, Renwick Gallery, 74; Clay, Whitney Mus, 74; Clay USA, Fendrick Gallery, Washington, DC, 75; Sculptureens USA, Campbell Mus, Camden, NJ, 76; Contemp Ceramic Sculpture, Achland Mem Art Ctr, Univ NC, Chapel Hill, 77; Tribute to Josiah Wedgewood, Philadelphia Mus Art, 80; Ancient Inspirations--Contemp Interpretations, Roberson Ctr, Binghamton, NY, 82; Solo exhibs, Dawson Gallery, Rochester, NY, 87, Munson Williams Proctor Mus Art, Utica, NY, 89, Bernice Steinbaum Gallery, Miami, 2005 & R Duane Reed Gallery, New York, 2005; Expressions in Color: Ceramics, NJ Ctr Visual Arts, Summit, NJ, 88; Contemp NY State Crafts, NY State Mus, 97; Okla City Mus Art, 97; Nancy Margolis Gallery, New York, 97; Western Heritage Mus, Omaha, Nebr, 97; Craft Alliance, St Louis, Mo, 98; John Elder Gallery, New York, 98; Works Gallery, Philadelphia, 98; Dorothy Weis Gallery, San Francisco, 98; Clockwork, Ctr Contemp Arts, Mo, 98; 12th San Angelo Nat Ceramic Competition, San Angelo Mus Fine Arts, Tex, 98. *Teaching:* Prof art, State Univ NY, Brockport, 66-, prof emer, currently. *Awards:* Nat Endowment Arts Res Grant, 76; Lillian Fairchild Award, Univ Rochester, 79; Chancellor's Award Excellence in Teaching, State Univ NY, 82; United Univ Prof Award, Outstanding Comm Serv, 90; Lillian Fairchild Award, Univ Rochester, NY, 90. *Bibliog:* Leon Nigrosh (auth), Sculpting Clay, Davis Publ Inc, Mass, 92; Richard Zakin (auth), Electric Kiln Ceramics, Chilton Bk Co, Radnor, Pa, 94; Johnathon & Angela Fina Fairbanks (auths), The Best of Pottery, Rockport Publ, Mass, 96; Suan Peterson (auth), Contemporary Ceramics, Watson Guptill, New York, 2000; 500 Figures in Clay Ceramic Artist Celebrate the Human Form, Lark Bks, 2004; Mathias Osterman (auth), The Ceramic Narrative, Univ Penn Press, Philadelphia, 2006; and many others. *Media:* Ceramics. *Mailing Add:* 245 Hinkleyville Rd Spencerport NY 14559

STEWART, DOROTHY S
PAINTER
b Brooklyn, NY. *Study:* Art Students League; Nat Acad Sch Fine Art, New York; NY Univ. *Comn:* In pvt collections. *Exhib:* Catharine Lorillard Wolfe Art Club 68-105th ann exhib, 65-2001, 2012; Allied Artists Am 56-89th Ann, 69-2002; Academic Artists, 88; Hudson Valley Art Asn, 89-91; Allied Artists Am, Butler Inst Am Art, 2001. *Teaching:* Instr art, Malverne Sr High Sch, New York, 65-66. *Awards:* Catharine Lorillard Wolfe Club Award, 74, 79, 83, 85, 87, 89, 94-95 & 99; Brookhaven Art Coun Award of Excellence, 98; Winsor & Newton Painting Award, Arts Coun East Islip, 2004 & 2006; OJS Award, Arts Coun, East Islip, 2008; First Prize, Art Coun East Islip, 2012. *Mem:* Catharine Lorillard Wolfe Art Club (dir, 70, 2nd vpres, 71-74); Allied Artists Am (asst corresp secy, 78-79); N Shore Art Asn; Kent Art Asn (pres, 77-78); life mem Art Students League; and others. *Media:* Oil, Watercolor. *Publ:* Contribr, Prize-winning art book 7, Allied Publ Inc, Ft Lauderdale, Fla, 67. *Dealer:* Phoenix Fine Arts Gallery 139 Main St Bellport NY 11713. *Mailing Add:* 39 Idle Hour Rd Oakdale NY 11769

STEWART, DUNCAN E
COLLAGE ARTIST
b St Paul, Minn, Sept 30, 1940. *Study:* Calif State Univ, San Diego, BA, 67, MA, 69; Fla State Univ, 74. *Work:* Pensacola Mus Art, Fla. *Exhib:* Solo exhibs, Fla State Univ-Florence Study Ctr, Italy, 82, LeMoyne Art Found, Fla, 84 & Univ New Orleans, 86; The Glove Invitational, Valencia Jr Col, Orlando, Fla, 87; The Box, SE Ctr Contemp Artists, Raleigh, 85; Pensacola Mus Art, Fla, 88; Fla A & M Univ, 89. *Pos:* Dir, Univ West Fla Art Gallery, Pensacola, currently. *Awards:* Fla Arts Coun Individual Artists Fel, 82. *Mem:* Coll Art Asn; Southeastern Coll Art Asn. *Dealer:* Mario Villa Gallery 3908 Magazine St New Orleans LA 70115. *Mailing Add:* 321 W DeSoto St Pensacola FL 32501

STEWART, F CLARK
DRAFTSMAN, PAINTER
b Evansville, Ind, July 18, 1942. *Study:* Univ Redlands, Calif, BA (art), 64; Claremont Grad Sch & Univ Ctr, Calif, MFA (painting), 66. *Work:* Mint Mus Art, Charlotte, NC; Tenn State Mus, Nashville; Knoxville Mus Art, Tenn; Austin Peay State Univ, Clarksville, Tenn; Clemson Univ, SC. *Exhib:* Solo exhibs, Hunter Mus, Chattanooga, 82, WVa Univ, Morgantown, 87 & Cheekwood Fine Arts Ctr, Nashville, 88; More Than Earth & Sky, Nat Mus Am Art, Washington, 81; Art Quest 86, Video Exhib, Los Angeles; Fact, Fiction, Fantasy-Recent Art in the Southeast, Touring Exhib, Univ Tenn, 87; Clemson Print & Drawing Show, Lee Hall Gallery, Clemson Univ, SC, 87; Festival Int de Louisiane, Lafayette Art Gallery, 91; and others. *Teaching:* Prof drawing, Univ Tenn, Knoxville, 66-. *Awards:* Purchase Prizes, Tenn Asn Mus, 76, Marietta Nat Print & Drawing Show, 81 & Clemson Nat Print & Drawing Exhib, 85; AAVW Prize, Northern Nat Art Exhib, Rhinelander, Wis, 90. *Bibliog:* Dale Cleaver (auth), illus rev, Art Express, Vols 1 & 2, 82; Fred Moffat (auth), illus rev, Art Papers, Vols 4 & 6; Susan Knowles (auth), rev, New Art Examiner, Vol 16, No 10, 6/89. *Mem:* Coll Art Asn. *Media:* Works on Paper; Mixed Media on Panels. *Publ:* Illusr, The Marriage of Heaven and Hell, Darkpool Press, Tenn, 72. *Mailing Add:* Dept Art Univ Tenn 1715 Volunteer Blvd Knoxville TN 37996

STEWART, JOHN LINCOLN
EDUCATOR, WRITER
b Alton, Ill, Jan 24, 1917. *Study:* Denison Univ, AB, 38; Ohio State Univ, MA, 39, PhD, 47. *Hon Degrees:* Denison Univ, Hon DA, 64. *Pos:* Assoc dir, Hopkins Art Ctr, Dartmouth Col, 62-64; dir, Mandeville Ctr for Arts, Univ Calif, San Diego, 75-76. *Teaching:* From asst prof to prof, Dartmouth Col, 49-64; prof Am lit & provost, John Muir Col, Univ Calif, San Diego, 64-87. *Awards:* Howard Found Fel, 53-54; Dartmouth Fac Fel, 62-63. *Res:* Contemporary American and British literature. *Publ:* Auth, John Crowe Ransom, Univ Minn, 62; Burden of Time, The Fugitives and Agrarians, Princeton Univ, 65; co-auth, Horizons Circled, Univ Calif, 74; Ernst Krenek, Calif Univ Press, 91. *Mailing Add:* 812 Carmel Ave Albany CA 94706

STEWART, JOHN P
PAINTER, PRINTMAKER
b Ft Leavenworth, Kans, Mar 11, 1945. *Study:* Univ Colo, with Roland Reiss & Wendel Black, BFA, 67; Univ Calif, Santa Barbara, MFA, 69. *Work:* Corcoran Gallery Art, Washington, DC; Whitney Mus Am Art, NY; Ponce Mus, PR; New Orleans Mus of Art, La; Mint Mus, NC; Cincinnati Art Mus. *Comn:* Painting, Rubloff Inc, Bicentennial, Cincinnati, 88; paintings, Wright Patterson Air Force Base, Dayton Ohio, 94. *Exhib:* Recent Acquisitions, Whitney Mus, NY, 72; Foire Int D'Art Contemporain, Grand Palais, Paris, 82; Carl Solway Gallery, Cincinnati, Ohio, 85; Works of the Figure, Allegheny Col, Pa, 86; Landscapes, Southern Ohio Art Mus, 91, An Infinite Adjustment, 2001; Atmospheres, AB Closson Co, Cincinnati, Ohio, 93; Art of the American West, Oglebay Institute, Wheeling, WVa, 2002; and others. *Teaching:* Prof, Univ Cincinnati, 73-. *Awards:* Individual Artist Grant, Ohio Arts Coun, 78 & 82; Prof of Yr, DAAP, 2000. *Media:* Oil. *Dealer:* A B Closson Art Gallery 401 Race St Cincinnati OH 45202. *Mailing Add:* 3836 Barker Rd Cincinnati OH 45229

STEWART, JOHN STEWART HOUSTON
DEALER
b Orange, NJ, Dec 24, 1945. *Study:* Miami Univ, BA, 68. *Collection Arranged:* Works by Van Selm, Barnwell Art Ctr, Shreveport, La, 78; Sculpture of Russell Jacques, Abilene Fine Arts Mus, 79; Watercolors by Jo Taylor, El Dorado Art Ctr, Ark, 80; Figurative Works by Charles Campbell, Univ Tex, Dallas, 81; Mardi Gras by Arie Van

Selm, Dallas City Hall, 81, Int House, New Orleans, 81 & touring in Europe; Nathan Jones Touring Exhib, Randall Gallery, NY, 81, Fed Reserve Bank, Cleveland, 81, Fed Reserve Bank, Cincinnati, 81, Univ Tex, Arlington, 81, Univ Calif, Los Angeles, 82 & Fisk Univ, 82; Landscapes by Jeff Tabor, Tex Women's Univ, 82; Artists from the Stewart Gallery, Abilene Christian Univ, 83; Black Heritage Today, Longview Mus, Tex, 83; Landscapes by Four Am Artists, Coninck Gallery, Holland. *Pos:* Designer & planner, Galleria des Bellas Artes, Phoenix, 71 & White Gallery, Westlake Village, Calif, 80; founder & dir, Stewart Gallery, Dallas, 72-; dir & mgr, Artists Courtyard, 76-; partner, Jones-Houston Graphics, currently. *Specialty:* Art by young, contemporary artists. *Mailing Add:* 7139 Azalea Ln Dallas TX 75230

STEWART, LORELEI
CURATOR, ADMINISTRATOR
b Hattiesburg, Miss, Sept 3, 1966. *Study:* Smith Coll, Mass, BA, 87; Corcoran Sch Art, Washington, DC, BFA, 92; Bard Col, Ctr for Cur Studies, NY, MA, 2000. *Collection Arranged:* At the Edge: Innovative Art in Chicago, 2008, 2009; Jenny Perlin: A Worry Free Life or Your Money, 2004; Impure Beauty: Ruben Ortiz to Torres, 2003; Revolutions Per Minute, 2001; Inside the City, 2001. *Pos:* Dir, Gallery 400, 2000-; intern, Mus Cont Art, Los Angeles, Calif, 99; prog dir, New Langton Arts, San Francisco, Calif, 94-98. *Teaching:* interim dir mus & exhib studies, Univ Ill at Chicago, 2010-2012; instr, Exhib and Display Practices, Mus Practices. *Specialty:* Contemporary Art. *Publ:* Contribr, New Langton Arts, 97; essayist, Edgar Arceneaux: The Alchemy of Comedy, Stupid, 2006

STEWART, NORMAN
PRINTMAKER, PUBLISHER
b Detroit, Mich, Mar 31, 1947. *Study:* Univ Mich, BFA, 69, MA, 72; Cranbrook Acad Art, studied with Irwin Hollander & Sewell Sillman, MFA, 77. *Work:* Brooklyn Mus, NY; Cleveland Mus Art, Ohio; Detroit Inst Art, Mich; Univ Ariz Mus Art, Tucson; Toledo Mus Art, Ohio; Kalamazoo Inst Arts, Mich. *Comn:* Print comn, PBS, WTVS, Detroit, Mich, 75; Creative Artist Grant, Mich Coun Arts, Detroit, 81; print comn, Detroit Inst Arts, Founders Soc, Detroit, Mich, 82 & 96; collaborative print comns, Univ Mich Sch Art, Ann Arbor, 84 & Mt Holyoke Col, South Hadley, Mass, 87; print comn, General Motors, Detroit, Mich, 98; Stewart & Stewart Screenprints, River Gallery, Chelsea, MI, 2002; Cranbrook Art Mus, Bloomfield Hills, MI, 2003. *Exhib:* 21st & 22nd Nat Invitational Print Exhib, Brooklyn Mus, NY, 78-79 & 81-82; 20th Century Prints & Drawings, Detroit Inst Arts, Mich, 81-82; New Am Graphics Two Invitational, Madison Arts Ctr, Wis, 82; Cabo Frio Int Print Biennial-82, Brazil, 82-83; Gene Baro Collects, Brooklyn Mus, 83; On the Leading Edge, Gen Elec Hq, Fairfield, Conn, 85; A Graphic Muse, Mt Holyoke Coll Art Mus, Mass, Yale Univ Art Gallery, Conn, Santa Barbara Mus Art, Calif, Va Mus Fine Arts, Nelson-Atkins Mus Art, Mo, 87-88; Collaboration in Print, Stewart & Stewart Prints, 1980-1990 (with catalog), touring 91-93; Print Fest, Milwaukee Art Mus, Wis, 93 & 95; IFPDA Print Fair, NY, 94-2015; Fine Print Fair, Cleveland Mus Art, Ohio, 96, 2007, 2010, 2011, 2015; solo exhib, Xochipilli Gallery, Mich, 75; Stewart & Stewart 25th Ann Exhib, Detroit Inst Arts, 2005; Flint Inst Arts, Fine Print Fair, Flint, Mich, 2009, 2010; Capital Fine Print Fair, Arlington, Va, 2010-2015; Boston Fine Print Fair, Boston, Mass, 2014, 2015; Works on Paper, Birmingham Bloomfield Art Ctr, Mich, 2007-2010; High Mus Art Print Fair, Atlanta, Ga, 2012, 2013. *Pos:* Partner & master printer, Stewart & Stewart, Bloomfield Hills, Mich, 80-. *Teaching:* Guest artist screenprinting, Wayne State Univ, Detroit, Mich, 79-80; adj asst prof screenprinting, Sch Art, Univ Mich, Ann Arbor, 79-85; guest artist & lectr screenprinting, numerous art schs & museums across USA, 79-. *Awards:* Disting Svc Award, Univ of Mich Sch of Art and Design, Ann Arbor, MI, 2000; Award of Special Recognition, Detroit Inst Arts Found Soc, Mich, 90; Creative Artist Grant, Mich Coun Arts, 81. *Bibliog:* Reviews, The Print Collector's Newsletter & Art On Paper, Stewart & Stewart Fine Print Publ, 84-96; reviews, J of the Print World, Stewart & Stewart Fine Print Publ, 91-2010; Janet Fish in Detroit, Printable News, Detroit Inst Arts, fall 96; Detroit Inst Arts Series, In the Frame: The Art of Screenprint, Pub Broadcasting Serv TV, Detroit, 2006. *Mem:* Int Fine Print Dealers Asn; Nat Educ Asn; Mich Educ Asn; Detroit Inst Arts Founders Soc. *Publ:* Contribr, Screenprint in the making: Sondra Freckleton collaborates with Norman Stewart (video), Stewart & Stewart Printer/Publisher of Fine Prints, 85; Collaboration in Print-Stewart & Stewart Prints; 1980-1990, Washtenaw Community Coll Found, Ann Arbor, Mich, 90; coauth, John Himmelfarb, Contemporary Impressions, The J of Am Print Alliance, fall 94; Ink on Paper, Quad/Collection, Milwaukee Art Mus, Wis, 96; Collaboration in Prints: Stewart & Stewart Screenprints 25th Ann Exhib, Detroit Inst Arts, 2005. *Dealer:* Stewart & Stewart 5571 Wing Lake Rd Bloomfield Hills MI 48301. *Mailing Add:* c/o Stewart & Stewart 5571 Wing Lake Rd Bloomfield Hills MI 48301-1250

STEWART, PAUL LEROY
PRINTMAKER, EDUCATOR
b Cleveland, Ohio, June 28, 1928. *Study:* Cleveland Inst Art, 46-48; Albion Col, BA, 53; Univ Mich, Ann Arbor, MA, 59. *Work:* Detroit Inst Art; Libr Cong; Metrop Mus Art, NY; Minneapolis Inst Art; Cleveland Mus Art, Ohio; Icon data WorldPrints 2005, Int Print Triennial, Krakow, Poland; Baltimore Mus Art, Baltimore, MD; Toldedo Mus Art, Toledo, Oh; Int Print Triennial Society, Krakow, Poland; Kyoto Seika Univ, Kyoto, Japan. *Comn:* Bicentennial print, Mich Workshop Fine Prints, Detroit, 75. *Exhib:* Solo exhibs, DeWaters Art Ctr, Flint, Mich, 79, Lill Street Gallery, Chicago, Ill, 87, Deutsch-Amerikanisches Inst, Tubingen, Ger, 87, Gallery Nishiazabu, Tokyo, Japan, 91, Fuji Cult Ctr, 94 & Gallery Otowa, Tokyo, 95 & 96, Univ Migh Residential Coll Gallery, Ann Arbor, Mich, 2011; Between Nature & Cult: Am Prints, Felix Jenewein Gallery, Czech Republic, 99; 14th Premio Int Biella Per L'Incisione, Italy, 99; Int Print Triennial-Cracow 2000-Bridge to the Future, Poland; Int Print Triennial Colour in Graphic Art, Torun, Poland, 2000; IconData WorldPrints, 2005, Triennial Cracow, Poland; Triennial 100 Cities, Intergraphia, Regional Mus, Ostreszow, Poland; 13th Int Biennial Print Exhib, ROC, 2008; Tyler Sch Art, Temple Univ, Phila, Pa, Southern Graphics Conf, 2010. *Teaching:* Assoc prof art, Albion Col, 59-72; Catherine C Heller prof art emer, Univ Mich, Ann Arbor, 73-2008; guest instr lithography, Univ NMex, Albuquerque, summer 79. *Awards:* Special Award, 13 Premio Int Biella Per L'Incisione, Italy, 96; 4th Prize, 3d Kochi Int Triennial Exhib of Prints, Japan, 99; Spl Prize, Int Print Triennial, Cracow, Poland, 2000; others. *Bibliog:* C Overvoorte (auth), article, For the Time Being Fine Arts Mag, Vol II, No 2, 73; Artists in Michigan of the 20th Century, Smithsonian Inst Arch Am Art; Artists in Michigan, 1900-1976, Wayne State Univ Press. *Media:* All Media. *Res:* Digital imaging. *Interests:* Photography. *Publ:* AXIS World Design J, No 44, Tokyo, Japan, summer 92; The Best of Printmaking, An International Collection, Allen & McGibbon, Rockport Publ, 97. *Dealer:* Art Search 717 W Huron Ann Arbor MI 48103. *Mailing Add:* 4040 Danford Rd Ann Arbor MI 48105

STEWART, REGINA
PAINTER, ADMINISTRATOR
b Passaic, NJ, 1942. *Study:* Cooper Union; Hunter Col. *Work:* Columbia Mus Art, SC; Greenville Co Mus, SC; Aldrich Mus of Contemp Art, Ridgefield, Conn; Mus Savannah Coll Art & Design, Ga; Jacqueline Casey Hudgens Ctr Arts, Duluth, Ga; SEMO Univ Mus, Cape Girardeau, Mo; Ogden Mus, New Orleans, LA; Crisp Mus, Cape Girardeau, Mo. *Exhib:* Collegeo Raffaello, Urbino, Italy, 73; Columbus Mus Art, Columbus, Ohio, 85; Ann Broome St Gallery Exhib, NY, 96-2009; Voices through Vision: Eight Women Artists, Gwinnett Fine Arts Ctr, Deluth, Ga, 97; Radford Art Mus, Va, 2000; SEMo Univ Mus, Cape Girardeau, Mo, 2002; solo exhib, 25 Yr Retrospective, NY, 2002, Jacqueline Casey Hudgens Ctr Arts, Duluth, Ga, 2005; 183rd Annual Invitational Exhibition of Contemp Art, Nat Acad, NY, 2008; Ogden Mus Southern Art, New Orleans, La, 2009; NY Hall of Sci, Queens, NY, 2012. *Pos:* Promotion for art & antiques, Channel 13 TV Sta, NY, 76; treas, NY Artists Equity, 90-91; pres, 91-93; exec dir, 93-; mem adv bd, Steffen Thomas Mus Art, 97-; mem adv bd, Fine Arts Fedn NY, 2000-. *Teaching:* Instr painting & drawing, NY Univ, 76-. *Awards:* First Prize/Painting, Ann John Roebling Exhib, John Roebling Found, 60; NEA Matching Purchase Funds Award; Certificate of Svc award, Fine Arts Federation NY, 97; appreciation award, Ogden Mus Southern Art, New Orleans, LA, 1/14/2009; cert appreciation, Loretan School of Creative Arts CS102, NY, 10/2008; statement of recognition, Congressional Record, Vol 119, No 199-1973, Vol 143, No 142, 1997, Vol 148, No 142, 2002, Vol 154, No 39, 2008. *Bibliog:* Regina Stewart: Women in Fine Arts, Manhattan Arts Int, 2000, The Sweep of History, Gallery & Studio, 2003; 25 Yrs of Artists Work, Artezine, #8, 5/10/2003; Regina Stewart Papers, Smithsonian Archives of Am Art, 2011. *Mem:* Art Spaces (adv, 60-); NY Artists Equity Asn; The Art Club, NY, 98; Steffen Thomas Mus of Art. *Media:* Acrylic. *Publ:* Auth, Richard Meier's building: The Athenaeum at New Harmony, USA Today, 1/84; co-auth, Golden Series of Books of Collectibles: American Stoneware, Kitchenware, Carnival Glass & Bottles, The Artists Proof News Mag, New York Artists Equity Asn, NY, 92-; auth, Henry Ryan McGinnis: American Impressionist 1875-1962, 2000; auth, Jack Stewart Drawings: Looking Into the 21st Century, 2000; auth, Broome Street Gallery, 15th Anniversary Exhib, 2005; NY Artist Equity Association Anniversary Journals, 50th (1997), 55th (2002), 60th (2008); ed, Graffiti Kings: Mass Transit Art, by Jack Stewart, Abrams Pub, 2009. *Mailing Add:* 31 E Seventh St New York NY 10003

STEWART, SHEILA L
DIRECTOR, CURATOR
Study: Ga Southern Col, BA, 76; Southern Ill Univ, MFA, 81. *Work:* Univ Mus, Carbondale, Ill; Alexandria Art Mus, La; Art Mus Southeast Tex, Beaumont. *Collection Arranged:* Laughing to Keep from Crying, Alexandria Mus, 85; Southeast Tex Collects Am Art (auth, catalog), 87; 500 Main: Installations (auth, catalog), Art Mus Southeast Tex, 85; Curator's Choice (auth, catalog), 88; James Surls, Art Mus Southeast Tex, 88. *Pos:* Cur, Alexandria Art Mus, 81-83, exec dir, 83-86; exec dir, Art Mus Southeast Tex, 86-. *Awards:* Alexandria Mus Art, 84; Special Exhib Award, Nat Endowment Arts, 85 & 87; Art Mus Southeast Tex, 89. *Publ:* Laughing to Keep from Crying (catalog), 85; Annual Report (catalog), 87-92; John Alexander (catalog), 90; Paths to Grace (catalog), 91; Paul Maness (catalog), 92. *Mailing Add:* Brevard Art Ctr 1463 Highland Ave Melbourne FL 32936

STEWART, WILLIAM
PAINTER, EDUCATOR
b Waco, Tex, Aug 18, 1938. *Study:* Univ Tex, BFA, 60, MFA, 62, int artists seminars, Fairleigh Dickinson Univ, Madison, NJ, summers 61 & 62. *Work:* Fordham Univ, Bronx, NY; Fairleigh Dickinson Univ, Madison, NJ; Mus Mod Art, Vienna, Austria; Harwood Mus; Univ NMex, Taos. *Exhib:* Solo exhibs, OK Harris Gallery, NY, 69, Rudolf Zwirner Gallery, Cologne, Ger, 70, Pergola Gallery, San Miguel de Allende, 78, Regional Mus, Oaxaca, Mex, 79, Bonnafont Gallery, San Francisco, Calif, 79, Old Jail Art Mus, Albany, Tex, 85, Taos Printings, Prince St Gallery, 2010, Legion Arts Cedar Rapids, Iowa, 2010; Thomas Moore Chapel, Fordham Univ, Bronx, NY, 76; Charles Furr Gallery, Santa Fe, Mex, 85; Munson Gallery, Santa Fe, NMex, 96; Collins Pettit Gallery, Taos, NMex, 96; Water Currents, Kouros Gallery, NY, 2005; Works on Paper, Prince Street Gallery, NY, 2007; On Board: Zeuxis & Guests, Lori Bookstein Gallery, NY, 2007. *Teaching:* Asst dir educ dept & instr, San Francisco Mus Art, Calif, 63-64; art instr, Baleares Int Sch, Palma de Mallorca, Spain, 66-67; instr, Dept Art, Fairleigh Dickinson Univ, Madison, NJ, 68-70, City Col NY, 71 & Ed Dept, Newark Mus, NJ, 73-74; instr drawing & painting, Instituto Allende, San Miguel de Allende, Guanajuato, Mex, 77-78; vis artist, dept art & art hist, Univ Iowa, Iowa City, 81; art instr, Taos Valley Sch, NMex, 85; instr, Dept Art, Northern NMex Community Col, 90-93 & Univ NMex, Taos, 93-; instr watercolor workshops, Taos Inst Arts, NMex, 93-97; instr drawing and painting, Univ NMex, currently; instr workshops, Taos Art Sch, summer, fall, 2000; instr, State Univ NY, Dutchess, Community Col, Poughkeepsie, NY, 2002; lectr, for art students, Relationship of Artist to Subject Matter, 2002; watercolor workshop, Georgia O'Keefe Museum, Santa Fe, NMex, 2012, 2014. *Bibliog:* Rosalind Constable (auth), New sites for new sights, NY Mag, 12/70; William Stewart at Zwirner Gallery, Kölner Kulturspiegel, 9/70; Colin Naylor (ed), Contemporary Artist, St James Press Ltd, London, 77; Eric Somers (auth), video documentary. *Media:* Oil, Watercolor, pastel, charcoal. *Dealer:* Hulse Warman Gallery Taos NMex; Laposada Gallery Santa Fe NMex

STEYNOVITZ, ZAMY
PAINTER
b Liegnitz, Poland, Jan 1, 1951; US citizen. *Study:* Avni Inst, Tel-Aviv, 70-72; Royal Acad, London, 72-75; Art League, New York, 76-80. *Work:* Museo Simon Bolivar, Caracas, Venezuela; Ana Frank Mus, Amsterdam, Holland; Nat Mus Art, San-Jose, Costa-Rica. *Comn:* Medal, Judaic Heritage Soc, NY, 79; mural, Mus Simon Bolivar, Caracas, Venezuela, 83. *Exhib:* One-man shows, Ramat-Gan, Israel, 70, Jewish Mus, Cleveland, Ohio, 80 & Nat Mus Art, San-Jose, Costa-Rica, 83; Tribute to John Lennon, Abraham-Goodman House, NY, 81; Homage to Bolivar, Simon Bolivar Mus, Caracas, Venezuela, 83; Centrum Judaica, Berlin, 95. *Bibliog:* Saul Mayzlish (auth), Zamy Steynovitz, Revivim Publ, 80; Alex Meilichson (auth), Zamy Steynovitz, Kshatot Arts, 92. *Media:* Oils, Lithograph. *Publ:* Auth, Peace Litographe between Israel & Egypt, NY Times & Harold Tribion Int, 79; Art Book of Steynovitz in Colors, Revivim Israel, 80 & Kshatot Israel, 92; Medal Ana Frank, NY Times, Sunday 80. *Mailing Add:* c/o ISART - Israeli Art Ctr 6721 N Corie Lane Canoga Park CA 91307

STICKER, ROBERT EDWARD
PAINTER
b Jersey City, NJ, Dec 26, 1922. *Study:* Art Students League, with Frank Reilly. *Work:* IBM Corp & AT&T. *Exhib:* Mystic Maritime Gallery; Grand Cent Art Gallery. *Pos:* Mem bd control, Art Students League, 59-. *Awards:* Gold Medal, Franklin Mint Nat Marine Competition, 74; Award of Excellence, Mystic Int, 89. *Media:* Oil, Watercolor. *Publ:* Illusr, Famous small boat voyages, 69-72 & Classical work boats of America, 73- (ser of paintings), Yachting Mag; Steam on the Rivers (prints), Janus Lithograph. *Dealer:* Mystic Maritime Gallery. *Mailing Add:* RD 1 Pleasant Mount PA 18453

STIEBEL, GERALD G
DEALER
b New York, NY, Sept 28, 1944. *Study:* CW Post Col, BA, 65; Courtauld Inst, London, 65-66; Study Centre Fine & Decorative Arts, London, dipl, 66; Columbia Univ, MA (art hist), 67. *Collection Arranged:* Grand Gallery Exhib, Metrop Mus Art, NY, 74-75; Experts Choice, Va Mus Art, 83; Chez Elle Chez Lui: At Home in 18th Century France, 87; Collecting at the top, 88; Of Knights & Spires: Gothic Renewal in France & Germany, 89; Louis XV and Madame de Pompadour: A Love Affair with Style, 90. *Pos:* Treas, Rosenberg & Stiebel Ltd, 68-71, vpres, 71-85, pres, 85-2000; Art Adv Panel, Internal Revenue Serv, 81-84; Pres's Cult Property Adv Comt, 94-99; pres, Stiebel Ltd, 2000-; dir, Diamond Point Theater Co, 2000. *Teaching:* Lectr, numerous universities & museums incl Guggenheim Mus & Metrop Mus Art, NY. *Mem:* Nat Antique & Art Dealers Asn Am (secy, 71-73, vpres, 73-77, pres, 77-79, bd dir, 71-84); La Confederation Int Negociants Oeuvres d'Art (permanent deleg, 72-, pres, 81-84, counr, 84-85, life councilor, 90-, bd dir, 97-, chmn internet com, 99-); Art Dealers Asn Am (bd dir, 80-89, 97-98, chmn pub rels com, 81-86, chmn internet com, 96-2000); Syndicat Nat des Antiquaires (France). *Specialty:* Old master paintings and drawings; important French 18th century furniture; renaissance bronzes. *Publ:* Auth, The Passionate Collector, Designer Mag, 72; Collector's Handbook, Cincinnati Art Mus, 78

STIEBEL, PENELOPE HUNTER See Hunter-Stiebel, Penelope

STILLMAN, DAMIE
HISTORIAN, EDUCATOR
b Dallas, Tex, July 27, 1933. *Study:* Northwestern Univ, BS, 54; Univ Del, MA, 56; Columbia Univ, PhD, 61. *Collection Arranged:* Architecture & Ornament in Late 19th Century Am (ed, catalog), 81. *Teaching:* Asst prof art hist, Oakland Univ, 61-65; assoc prof, Univ Wis, Milwaukee, 65-67, prof, 67-77, chmn dept, 75-77; prof, Univ Del, 77-2000, chmn dept, 81-86 & 93-98, John W Shirley prof emer, art hist, 2000-. *Awards:* Nat Endowment Humanities Fel, 70-71 & 86-87; Founders Award, Soc Archit Historians, 75; Gottschalk Prize, Am Soc for 18th Century Study, 88. *Mem:* Coll Art Asn Am; Soc Archit Historians (mem bd dir, 75-78 & 84-87, second vpres, 78-80, first vpres, 80-82, pres, 82-84); NE Am Soc for 18th Century Studies (exec bd, 87-93, vpres, 94-95 & pres, 95-96); Vernacular Architectural Forum; Soc Early Americanists. *Res:* American and British architecture with special emphasis on neo-classicism. *Publ:* Auth, The Decorative Work of Robert Adam, Tiranti, 67; ed, Architecture & Ornament in Late 19th Century America, Univ Del, 81; auth, English Neo-classical Architecture, Zwemmer, 88; auth, The United States Capitol: Icon of the Republic, In: Capital Drawings: Architectural Designs for Washington DC, Johns Hopkins Univ Press, 59-86, 2005; auth, Six Houses for the President, Pa Magazine of History & Biography, Vol 129, No 4, 411-431, 10/2005. *Mailing Add:* Dept Art Hist Univ Del Newark DE 19716

STILLMAN (MYERS), JOYCE L
PAINTER, LECTURER
b New York, NY, Jan 19, 1943. *Study:* New York Univ, BA, 64, Art Students League, 66; Pratt Inst, 72; Long Island Univ, MA, 75; Calif Inst Integral Studies; MFA, post grad studies. *Work:* Aldrich Mus Contemp Art, Ridgefield, Conn; Byer Mus Art, Evanston, Ill; Hillwood Gallery, C W Post Coll, Greenvale, NY; Randolf Macon Women's Coll, Lynchburg, Va; Greater Lafayette Mus, Indianapolis, Ind; Heckscher Mus, Huntington, NY. *Comn:* Time Life poster, Time Life Inc, New York, 77; Christmas card, Mus Mod Art, New York, 78 & 94. *Exhib:* Out of the House, Whitney Mus Downtown, New York, 76 & 78; Illusion and Reality, Australian Nat Gallery, Canberra, Australia, 77; Caps at the State Mus, NY State Mus, Albany, 81; What's New, Byer Mus, Evanston, Ill, 84; Holiday Show, New Mus, New York, 84; Art of Seventies and Eighties, Aldrich Mus, Ridgefield, Conn, 85; Traveling show Nassau Co Mus, NY, and others across US; 100 Women Artists, Arnot Art Mus, Elmira, NY, 91; Arts of the Southern Tier, Corning, NY, 2001. *Teaching:* Assoc prof painting, Towson Univ, 82-88; prof art hist, women in art, Tompkins-Cortland Community Coll, Dryden, NY, 88-90; lectr art, Cornell Univ, 90-. *Awards:* Creative Artist Pub Service Grant, 79; Distinctive Merit Award, Art Dir's Club, 79. *Mem:* Nat Asn Women Artists; Inst Noetic Sci; Arts Southern Tier, New York; Asn Univ Women. *Media:* Paint, Pastel. *Dealer:* Allan Stone Gallery E 96th St New York NY

STINNETT, HESTER A
PRINTMAKER
b Baltimore, Md, June 29, 1956. *Study:* Hartford Art Sch, Univ Hartford, Conn, BFA, 78; Tyler Sch Art, Temple Univ, Philadelphia, MFA, 82. *Work:* Walker Art Ctr, Minneapolis; West Chester Univ, Pa; Philadelphia Mus Art, Pa. *Exhib:* Fleisher Art Mem, Philadelphia, 82; 16th Nat, Potsdam State Univ, NY, 82; Rutgers Nat, Stedman Art Gallery, Camden, NJ, 84; Solo exhibs, Denison Univ, Ohio, 85 & Haverford Col, Pa, 86; Prints from Blocks: 1900-1985, Assoc Am Artists, NY, 85; Cassa di Risparmio di Biella, Biella, Italy, 87; Pertaining to Philadelphia, Philadelphia Mus Art, 92. *Pos:* Dir, Philadelphia Col Art printmaking workshop, 84-86. *Teaching:* Adj lectr printmaking, Philadelphia Col Art, 82-86; lectr printmaking, Bryn Mawr, Col Pa, 85-86; asst prof printmaking, Tyler Sch Art, Temple Univ, Philadelphia, 86-92, assoc prof & assoc dean, 92-. *Mem:* Coll Art Asn; Philadelphia Print Club. *Media:* Woodcut. *Publ:* Water-based Inks: A Screenprinting Manual for Studio and Classroom, Univ Arts, Philadelphia, Pa, 87

STIRNWEIS, SHANNON
PAINTER, ILLUSTRATOR
b Portland, Ore, Feb 26, 1931. *Study:* Univ Ore, 49-50; Art Ctr Coll Design with John Lagatta, BFA, 50-54; Study with Joseph Henniger & Reynold Brown, 56. *Work:* Parks Dept, US Dept Interior, US Air Force Hist & Mus Collection, US Army Hist Mus Collection, Washington, DC; Univ Wyo, Laramie; Calif Fed Savings Collection. *Comn:* Reindeer Being Loaded on Coast Guard Ship, US Coast Guard, 88; Jennings-All American (portrait), US Air Force Acad, Colo; portrait, US Air Force, Lt Gen De Cox, 2004. *Exhib:* Illustration of the 90s, Jeffrey Civic Ctr, Mus Am Illus, NY, 68-75; 200 Yrs of Am Illustration, Mus City NY, 76; Governors Show, Cheyenne, Wyo, 85; Hubbard Mus, NM, 2005 & 06. *Pos:* Pres, Have Brush Will Travel Inc. *Teaching:* instr, Western Conn State Col; instr, Sharon (NH) Arts Ctr. *Awards:* Best Dog Book of Year, Dog Writers Asn, 65; Award of Merit, Soc Illus Ann Exhib, 68-75 & 86. *Bibliog:* R Bolivar (auth), An artist who has returned to the West, SW Art, 10/77; Samuels (auth), Contemporary Western artists, SW Art; Walt Reed (auth), Illustrator in America 1880-1980, Madison Sq Press. *Mem:* Soc Illus, NY; Western Artists Am, Ariz; Have Brush Will Travel, Inc (pres); Sharon Arts Ctr, NH; New Ipswich Artists League, NH. *Media:* Oil. *Publ:* Illusr, Dogs of the World, Whitman, 65; Ah, Wilderness, Ltd Editions Club, 72; Auth, Art of Painting the Dog, 77, Art of Painting the Cat, 77 & Art of Painting the Wild West, 78, Grumbacher. *Dealer:* JW Art Gallery Hurley NM. *Mailing Add:* 116 Perry Rd New Ipswich NH 03071

STIRRATT, BETSY (ELIZABETH) ANNE
PAINTER, GALLERY DIRECTOR
b New Orleans, La, Sept 22, 1958. *Study:* La State Univ, BFA, 80; Ind Univ, MFA, 83. *Work:* Ind State Mus, Ind; Univ Art Mus, Ind. *Comn:* Milton Motels. *Exhib:* Dark Ages, Indianapolis Mus Art, 91; Language & Symbol in Contemp Art, Greater Lafayette Mus Art, Ind, 92; Salon Show, Art in General, NY, 92; Primarily Paint, Laguna Gloria Art Mus, Houston, Tex, 92; Gallery Artists, Carl Hammer Gallery, Chicago, Ill, 94; Solar Exhib; and others; Afterimage, Packer Schopf Gallery, Chicago. *Pos:* Dir, Sch of Fine Arts Gallery, Ind Univ, Bloomington. *Awards:* Master's Fel, Ind Arts Comn, 89; Fel, Arts Midwest, 89; Visual Arts Fel, Nat Endowment Arts, 90; Ind Arts Comn Masters Fel, 99. *Mailing Add:* 2504 Poplar Ct Bloomington IN 47401

STITT, SUSAN (MARGARET)
MUSEUM DIRECTOR, ADMINISTRATOR
b East Liverpool, Ohio, Jan 24, 1942. *Study:* Coll William & Mary, AB; Univ Pa, MA. *Pos:* Asst to dir, Hist Soc Pa; dir, Mus Albemarle; adminr, Mus Early Southern Decorative Arts; asst to dir, Brooklyn Mus; proj dir surv placement & training, Old Sturbridge Village, Mass; dir, Mus at Stony Brook, 74-88; consult, Mus Historical Gallery, 88; pres & chief exec officer, Hist Soc Pa, 90-98. *Teaching:* Adj assoc prof, State Univ NY, Stonybrook, 75-78. *Awards:* Women of the Year in Art, Village Times, 87; Kathleen Coffey Award, Mid-Atlantic Asn Mus, 87; Ward Melville Community Award, Three Village Historical Soc, 88. *Mem:* Am Asn Mus (vpres, 85-86); Mid-Atlantic Asn Mus, (vpres, 82-86); NY State Asn Mus (pres, 85-87); and others. *Publ:* Auth, The will of Stephen Charlton & Hungars Parish, Va Mag Hist & Biog, 7/69; Today's labor practices, the search for equality, Mus News, 9-10/75; Trustee orientation: A sound investment, Mus News, 5-6/81; Bryant F Tolles, Jr (ed), The Diamond Link: The Director as Internal Communicator and Human Resources Manager, in Leadership for the Future: Changing Directorial Roles in American History Museums and Historical Societies, 89; A Reference for Stewardship, Forum, Issue 11, May/June, 94. *Mailing Add:* c/o Historical Soc Pa 1300 Locust St Philadelphia PA 19107

STOCKHOLDER, JESSICA
SCULPTOR, ASSEMBLAGE ARTIST
b Seattle, 1959. *Study:* Univ Victoria, BFA, 1982; Yale Univ, New Haven, Conn, MFA, 1985. *Hon Degrees:* Emily Carr Col of Art, DFA (Hon), 2010; Columbia Coll, DFA (Hon), 2013. *Exhib:* Retrospectives include Kissing the Wall: Works, 1988-2003, Univ Houston, 2004, Weatherspoon Art Gallery, Univ NC, 2005 & Blaffer Art Gallery, Univ Tex, 2006; solo exhibs include Renaissance Soc, Univ Chicago, 1991, Weatherspoon Gallery, Univ NC, 1994, Jay Gorney Mod Art, New York, 1995, 1997, Dia Ctr Arts, New York, 1995, Galerie Nathalie Obadia, Paris, 1995, 1998, 2001, 2004, White Cube, London, 1998, Gorney Bravin + Lee, 2001, 2003, Rice Univ Art Gallery, Houston, 2004, PS1 Contemp Art Ctr, New York, 2006, 1301 PE, Los Angeles, 2007, Galerie Art & Essai, Rennes, France, Robischon Gallery, Denver, 2009, Carreras Mugica, Bibao, 2010, Aldrich Contemporary Art mus, Ridgefield, Conn, 2011; group exhibs include Making a Clean Edge, PS1 Contemp Art Ctr, 1989; Contingent Realms, Whitney Mus Am Art at Equitable Ctr, New York, 1990; Whitney Biennial, Whitney Mus Am Art, New York, 1991, 2004, Heart, Mind, Body, Soul: Am Art in the 1990s, 1997; As Long as It Lasts, Witte de With, Rotterdam, 1992; Simply Made in America, Aldrich Mus Contemp Art, Conn, 1993; Biennial Exhib Contemp

Am Painting, Corcoran Gallery Art, Washington, 1996; What I Did On My Summer Vacation, White Columns, New York, 1996; Colorflex, Apex Art, New York, 1997; Pop/Abstraction, Pa Acad Fine Arts, Philadelphia, 1998; Now and Later, Yale Univ Art Gallery, 1998, Objective Color, 2001; Beyond the Pale: Material Possibilities, Neuberger Mus Art, Purchase, NY, 2002; SiteLines, Addison Gallery Am Art, Andover, Mass, 2002; Under Pressure, Cooper Union Sch Art, New York, 2003; Painting on Sculpture, Tanya Bonakdar Gallery, New York, 2003; Ann Invitational Exhib Contemp Am Art, Nat Acad Mus, New York, 2004; Conn Contemp, Wadsworth Atheneum, Hartford, Conn, 2007; Denver Art Mus, Embrace!, 2009; Frances Young Tang Teaching Mus and Art Gallery, Skidmore Col, Saratoga Springs, NY, The Jewel Thief, 2010-2011. *Collection Arranged:* Corcoran Gallery of Art, Washington, DC, Ulrich Mus, Wichita State Univ, The British Mus, London England, Art Inst of Chicago, Addison Gallery of American Art, and sveral others. *Teaching:* Instr dept sculpture NY Univ, 1992, Bard Coll, 1993; prof, dir grad studies in sculpture, Yale Univ, 1999-2011; prof, chair, department of visual arts, Univ Chicago, 2011-. *Awards:* Nat Endowment Arts Award for Sculpture, 1988; NY Found Arts Grant in Painting, 1989; Guggenheim Fel, 1996; Lucelia Artist Award, Smithsonian Am Art Mus, 2007; Anonymous Was a Woman, 2012. *Mailing Add:* University of Chicago Department of Visual Arts Midway Studios 6016 S Ingleside Ave Chicago IL 60637

STOCKMAN, JENNIFER BLEI
PATRON
b Philadelphia, Dec 5, 1954. *Study:* Univ Md, BS, 1976; George Washington Univ, MBA in Finance, 1983. *Pos:* Systems engineer, IBM Corp, 1976-78, marketing rep, 1978-81, staff marketing mgr, 1981-83; dir tech trade, Sears World Trade, 1983-84, vpres tech investment, 1984-85; founder, Stockman & Associates Inc, Greenwich, Conn, 1985, past pres, chief exec officer; nat co-chair, Rep Majority for Choice (formerly Rep Pro-Choice Coalition); pres bd trustees, Solomon R Guggenheim Mus, 2003-

STODDARD, ELIZABETH JANE
PAINTER
b Buffalo, NY, June 20, 1940. *Study:* State Univ NY, Buffalo, 82-85; studied with Zoltan Szabo, 87, with Frank Webb, 90. *Work:* Albright Knox Art Gallery; Brea Cult Ctr Gallery, Calif; Broome Street Gallery, NY; Neville Mus, Green Bay; World Trade Ctr Gallery, New Orleans. *Comn:* Watercolor, Moog & Co, Buffalo, NY, 82; watercolor, Lockport Savings Bank Inst, Buffalo, 95; watercolor, Austin Develop, Erie, Pa, 98; watercolor, Roswell Park Mem, Buffalo, 98; watercolor, Henry & Henry Co, Buffalo, 98. *Exhib:* Adirondack Mus Nat Exhib, Old Forge, NY, 85; Grand Central Gallery, NY, 85; Albright-Knox Art Gallery Members Show, Buffalo, NY, 85-98; Midwest Watercolor Soc Exhib, Neville Mus, Green Bay, Wis, 96; La Int Show, World Trade Ctr, New Orleans, 96-98; Nat Watercolor Show, Brea Cult Ctr, Calif, 96; Realism, Parkersburg Art Mus, WVa, 97; Northeast Watercolor Soc, Harness Racing Mus, Goshen, NY, 97. *Awards:* Am Pen Women Award of Excellence, Lincoln Ctr Gallery, 93; Grumbacher Gold Medal, Pa Nat Watercolor Show, 95; William Roth Mem Award, Northwest Watercolor Show, 95. *Bibliog:* E Jane Stoddard (auth), From oil to water, Artist Mag, 97. *Mem:* Nat Watercolor Soc; Northwest Watercolor Soc; Am Artists Prof League; Pa Watercolor Soc; Ga Watercolor Soc. *Media:* Watercolor. *Mailing Add:* 123 Wellingwood Dr East Amherst NY 14051

STOEVEKEN, CHRISTEL E See Tucholke, Christel-Anthony

STOFFEL, GAYLE & PAUL T
COLLECTORS
Study: Harvard Bus Sch, MBA. *Pos:* Var positions; chmn, Triple S Capital Corp, Paul Stoffel Investments; bd dirs, Holly Corp, Dallas, Dallas Symphony Asn, Dallas Symphony Found; co-founder, Gayle and Paul Stoffel Found; bd mem, Dallas Symphony Orchestra, Southwestern Med Found, Aspen Art Mus, Dallas Art Mus, Dallas Ctr Performing Arts, Baylor Hosp. *Awards:* Named one of Top 200 Collectors, ARTnews mag, 2005-13 . *Collection:* Contemporary art. *Mailing Add:* 5949 Sherry Ln Suite 1465 Dallas TX 75225

STOFFLET, MARY
CURATOR, CRITIC
b Long Branch, NJ, Dec 23, 1942. *Study:* Skidmore Col, BA, 64; NY Univ, MA, 69; M H de Young Mem Mus, San Francisco, Rockefeller-Nat Endowment Arts Fel Mus Educ, 75-76, UCSD, AA, 98. *Collection Arranged:* International Rubber Stamp Art Exhibition, La Mamelle Arts Ctr, San Francisco, 76; Cityscapes, 77 & Yosemite, 79, Fine Arts Mus San Francisco, Downtown Ctr; Construction, San Francisco Int Airport, 82; Dr Seuss from Then to Now, 86, More Then Meets the Eye, 87, Cultural Currents, 88, San Diego Mus Art, 88; Faberge: The Imperial Eggs, 89, Li Huai: An Artist in Two Cultures, 89, Latin Am Drawings Today, 91, San Diego Mus Art; Calif Cityscapes, 91 & The Frederick R Weisman Collection of Contemporary California Art, 91, San Diego Mus Art; Silver/Clay/Wood/Gold, San Diego Crafts, San Diego, Mus Art, 93; Andy Goldsworthy Two Stones, San Diego, Mus Art, 94; Deborah Butterfield (auth, catalog), San Diego Mus Art, 95. *Pos:* Newsletter ed, Western Asn of Art Mus, Oakland, 74-77; contrib ed, Artweek, 74-81; assoc ed, La Mamelle, 75-77; ed, Front, 76-; coordr intern prog, M H de Young Mem Mus, 77-80; contrib ed, Images & Issues, 80-; asst cur, San Francisco Int Airport, 82-84; cur educ, San Diego Mus Art, 85-88, cur mod art, 88-97; asst dir, Education & Publications, San Francisco Airport Mus, 98-2005, retired. *Teaching:* Instr art hist, Oakland Mus, Calif, 77-; lectr art hist, San Francisco State Univ, 77 & 81, Univ Calif San Diego Extension, 87. *Mem:* Int Asn Art Critics. *Publ:* Auth, American Women Artists: 20th Century, Slides & Notes, 78 & Women Artists: Sculptors-Photographers, Slides & Notes, 79, Harper & Row; ed, Correspondence Art: Sourcebook for the Network of International Postal Art Activity, Contemp Arts Press, 84; auth, Dr Seuss From Then to Now, San Diego Mus Art, 86 & Random House, 87; essayist & coordr ed, Latin American Drawings Today, San Diego Mus Art & Univ Wash Press, 91; auth & coordr ed, California Cityscapes, San Diego Mus Art & Universe, 91. *Mailing Add:* 1520 California St No 9 San Francisco CA 94109

STOKES, LEONARD
COLLAGE ARTIST
Study: Yale Univ, BA 1966, MFA 1969 ; Allgemeine Gewerbeschule, Basel, Switzerland, 1977-78. *Work:* Newark Mus; Hospital Corp Am; Neuberger Mus. *Exhib:* Solo exhibs include Cordier & Ekstrom Gallery, New York, 1986, 1987, 1988, Jason McCoy Inc, 1991, 1992, 1994, 1997, Silicon Gallery Fine Art Prints, Philadelphia, 2003 ; Two Person exhibs include Cordier & Ekstrom Gallery(with Robert Ohnigian), New York, 1983, 1984, 1985, Washington Art Asn(with Jed Devine), Washington, Conn, 1988, Kiesendahl & Calhoun Gallery(with Laura Van Rosk), Beacon, NY, 2006, Union College (with Robert Kinsell), Schenectedy, NY, 2006 ; Group exhibs include Hudson River Mus Invitational, Yonkers, NY, 1976 ; Area Codes 914 & 203, Neuberger Mus, Purchase, NY, 1982 ; McNay Art Mus, San Antonio, TX, 1985; Collage: Made in Am, Rosenfeld Gallery, New York, 1995; Intimate Universe, Robert Steele Gallery, New York, 1997 ; Spaces Between, Contemp Art Ctr VA, 2004; The Medium: The Art Printmaking, Noel Fine Art, New York, 2004; 183rd Ann: Invitational Exhib Contemp Am Art, Nat Acad Mus, New York, 2008. *Awards:* Prof Visual Arts, Purchase Coll, NY, 1973-Present. *Dealer:* Noel Fine Arts, 80 Kraft Ave Bronxville NY 10708

STOKSTAD, MARILYN
HISTORIAN, WRITER
b Lansing, Mich, Feb 16, 1929. *Study:* Carleton Col, BA, 50; Mich State Univ, MA, 53; Univ Mich, PhD, 57; Hon LHD, Carleton Col, 97. *Hon Degrees:* Carleton Coll, Hon PhD, 1997. *Pos:* Cur, Spencer Mus Art, 67-95; res cur medieval art, Nelson-Atkins Mus Art, Kansas City, 69-2002. *Teaching:* Prof hist art, Univ Kans, 58-79, chmn dept, 61-72, dir, Mus Art, 61-67, assoc dean, Col Arts & Sci, 72-76, Univ Distinguished Prof, 79-2002 (retired). *Awards:* Dumbarton Oaks Fel, 81-82; Smithsonian Fel, 86, 90; Kans Gov's Arts Award, 97; Lifetime Achievement Award, WCA. *Mem:* Midwest Coll Art Conf (pres, 64-65); Coll Art Asn Am (vpres, 76-78, pres, 78-80); Am Asn Univ Prof; Soc Archit Historians; Int Ctr Medieval Art (vpres, 90-93, pres, 93-96). *Res:* Medieval art; Spanish art; art of the British Isles. *Interests:* Travel, mysteries. *Publ:* Auth, Santiago de Compostela in the Age of the Pilgrimages, Okla Univ, 79; Medieval Art, Harper & Row, 86; Art History, Abrams/Prentice Hall, 95, 98 & 2002; Art History: A View of the West, (3rd ed), Pearson/Prentice Hall, 2007-2008, 4th ed with Michael Cothren, 2010; Art a Brief History, Prentice Hall, 2000, 2004, 4th ed with Michael Cothren, Pearson/Prentice Hall, 2010; auth, Medieval Castles, Greenwood, 2005; auth, All About Art (trade ed), 2007. *Mailing Add:* 4703 Balmoral Dr Lawrence KS 66047

STOLOFF, CAROLYN
PAINTER, COLLAGE ARTIST
b New York, NY. *Study:* Univ Ill (drawing); Columbia Univ, BS (painting), 1949; Art Students League, with Harry Sternberg; Atelier 17, with Xavier Gonzalez, Eric Isenburger & Hans Hofmann; Dalton School, with Valclav Vitlacyl & Rufino Tamayo, 1944. *Work:* Norfolk Mus Arts & Scis; Canadian Imperial Bank Commerce; and others. *Exhib:* Whitney Mus Am Art, 51; Pa Acad Fine Arts; Audubon Artists; Oakland Art Mus; one-person shows, Dubin Gallery, Pa, Manhattanville Col, NY, Donnell Libr, 88, Open Studios, 84 & 87, Atlantic Gallery, 85, Pine Pub Libr, Fairlawn, NJ, 89 & Tom Kendall Gallery, 90; Silvermine Guild; ACA Gallery; Nat Asn Women Artists; City Ctr Gallery; Atlantic Gallery; Krasner Gallery; New Talent Show, Laurel Gallery; Knickerbocker Artists; Long Island League Painters & Sculptors; NJ Soc Painters & Sculptors; Arthur Brown Gallery; Bowery Gallery; Get Real Arts. *Pos:* Prof, 57-74 & chmn dept art, Manhattanville Col, 61-65. *Teaching:* Asst prof painting & drawing, Manhattanville Col, 57-74, lectr, Eng, 69-74; vis writer, Stephens Col, 75 & Hamilton Col, 85. *Awards:* Silver Anniversary Medal, Audubon Artists Annual, 67; Honorable Mention, Audubon Artists Annual, 72; Michael M Engel Sr Mem Award, Audubon Artists Annual, 82; Honorable Mention, L.I. League of Painters & Sculptors; Robert Phillips Mem Award for Painting, Audubon Artists Annual, 90; Daler-Rowney Award for Oil Painting, 94; Art Students League Award for Oil Painting, 95; Grumbacher Gold medal, 98; Emily Lowe Award for Oil Painting, 00; President's Award for Innovative Collage & Mixed Media, Audubon Artists Annual, 2008; Marquis Who's Who in American Art References Award in Collage & Mixed Media, Audubon Artists, New York, 2011; and others. *Bibliog:* Jean Gould (auth), Modern American Women Poets, Dodd Mead & Co, 85, 349; Robert Peters (auth), 2 collages reproduced, Caliban No 7; The Great Am Poetry BakeOff II; Robert Peters (interviewer), The Signal, Mag, Winter, 89-90. *Mem:* Poetry Soc Am; Audubon Artists. *Media:* Oil, Collage, Drawing. *Interests:* Animal behavior; Dance; Surrealism. *Collection:* Norfolk Mus; Can Imperial Bank of Com; Roslyn Willett; Lester Klepper; Sonya Hess; Ruth Unterberg; and others. *Publ:* Auth, Stepping Out, Unicorn Press, 71; Dying to Survive, Doubleday & Co, 73; Swiftly Now, Ohio Univ Press, 82; A Spool of Blue: New and Selected Poems, Scarecrow Press, 83; You Came to Meet Someone Else, Asylum Arts Press, 93; Reaching for Honey, Red Hen Press, 2003; Live Poets Society Anthology, three collages, 97, six drawings, 98; Ah Wind, Mad Hat Press, 2014. *Mailing Add:* 32 Union Sq E Ste 911 New York NY 10003

STOLPIN, WILLIAM ROGER
PRINTMAKER
b Flint, Mich, June 25, 1942. *Study:* Kettering Univ, Flint, Mich, BME, 65; Charles Stewart Mott Community Coll, Flint, Mich, AA, 78; Studied lithography with Emil Weddige, 69-70, Robert Nelson, 81 & Japanese woodblock with Akira Kurosaki, 86; Eastern Mich Univ, Ypsilanti, Mich, 92; Studied collaborative printmaking, New York Univ, 98; studied intaglio printmaking, Crown Point Press, San Francisco, 2000. *Work:* Smithsonian Inst Nat Air & Space Mus, Washington, DC; Flint Inst Arts, Mich; Detroit Inst Arts; Kettering Univ, Flint, Mich; Nat Trust, London, Eng; Brit Interplanetary Asn, London, Eng; Delta Coll, Midland, Mich. *Comn:* Serigraph, Genesys Corp, Flint, Mich, 94; serigraph, Mott Found, 2000; serigraph, Mass Transportation Asn, Flint, Mich, 2002; serigraph, Community Found Greater Flint, 2008, 2013. *Exhib:* Ann Print Competition, Ann Arbor Art Asn, Mich, 95 & 2003;

Ann Print Competition, Flora Beck Gallery, Mich, 96-2000, 2002-2004 & 2007; All Media Competition, Birmingham Bloomfield Art Asn, Mich, 96; Planetfest, Pasadena Convention Ctr, Calif, 97; Mich Asn printmakers, Left Bank Gallery, Flint, Mich, 2000 & 2003-2004; SAGA Nat Mems Exhib, Stephen Gang Gallery, New York, 2000 & 2002; Mich Directions, Flint Inst Arts, 2000; Scarab Club, Detroit, Mich, 2003; Festival of the Masters, Downtown Disney, Lake Buena Vista, Fla, 2006-2007; Am Color Print Soc, Art of Printmaking, Spring Bull Gallery, Newport, RI, 2006, Chestnut Hill Gallery, Phila, Pa, 2012; two-person exhib, Starkweather Gallery, Romeo, Mich, 2006; Members Exhib, Soc Am Graphic Artists, The Old Print Shop, New York, 2007, 2012; Fandangles, Flint, Mich, 2010, 2012; Shiawassee Arts Coun, Owosso, Mich, 2010; Mott Community Coll, Flint, Mich, 2010; Kettering Univ, Flint Mich, 2012. *Pos:* Art dept adv bd, Alma Coll, Mich, 98-2000; bd dir, adv & pub relations chmn, Greater Flint Art Coun, 98-2008; accessions & collections comt, Flint Inst Arts, Mich, 2000-. *Teaching:* Lectr color serigraphy, Cent Mich Univ, 99; lectr printmaking, Univ Mich, 99-2001 & Ctr Creative Studies, 2001; art dept, printmaking, Flint Inst Arts, Mich, 2006-. *Awards:* First in Graphics, Int Platform Asn, 69; Purchase Prize, Saginaw Art Mus, Mich, 98; Notable Mention, Friends Mod Art, 2001; First Prize, Flint Art Fair, 2004 & Third Prize, 2006, Hon mention, 2009, 2012; Second Prize, drawing, printmaking & graphics, Festival of the Masters, 2007; Materials award, Soc Am Graphic Artists, 2012. *Bibliog:* Michelle Harrison (auth), Art of the matter, On the Town/McVey Marketing, 94; Selma Smith (auth), William R Stolpin, Int Printworld Dir, 98-present; Rachelle Richert (auth), Michigan Directions, J Printworld, 2000. *Mem:* Soc Am Graphic Artists; Asn Sci Fiction & Fantasy Artists; Int Asn Astronomical Arts; Detroit Inst Arts; Guild Artists and Artisans; Flint Inst Arts; Greater Flint Arts Coun; Detroit Artists Market; Mich Renaissance Festival; Buckham Fine Arts Proj; Wood Engravers Network. *Media:* Printmaking. *Publ:* auth, Here There Be Dragons, 2011. *Dealer:* Detroit Artists Market 4719 Woodward Ave Detroit MI 48201; Blue Heron Gallery 133 Ames St Elk Rapids MI 49629. *Mailing Add:* 12201 Gage Rd Holly MI 48442-8339

STOLTENBERG, DONALD HUGO
PAINTER, PRINTMAKER
b Milwaukee, Wis, Oct 15, 1927. *Study:* Inst Design, Ill Inst Technol, BS (visual design). *Work:* Boston Mus Fine Art & Boston Nat Hist Park, Mass; Addison Gallery Am Art, Andover, Mass; DeCordova Mus, Lincoln, Mass; Portland Mus Art; Cape Mus Fine Arts, Dennis, Mass. *Exhib:* Venice Observed, Fogg Mus, Cambridge, Mass, 56; Boston Arts Festival, 56-61; Corcoran Gallery Art Exhib, Washington, 63; Landscape, DeCordova Mus, 71; Am Art Exhib, Art Inst Chicago; Mass Open, Worcester Art Mus, 77; Am Watercolor Soc, 90, 94, 98, 2000 & 05. *Teaching:* Instr painting & printmaking, DeCordova Mus Sch; vis critic, RI Sch Design; Instr drawing & printmaking, Cape Cod Conservatory. *Awards:* Grand Prize, Boston Arts Festival, 57, First Prize in Painting, 59; First Purchase Prize, Portland Mus Arts Festival; High Winds Medal, Am Watercolor Soc, Exhib, 2005; numerous others. *Bibliog:* Painting with the White of Your Paper, 94 & Splash #1, 2 & 4 Painting from Photographs, 99, North Light Bks, 94,; The Best of Watercolor, 95 & Abstracts in Watercolor, 96, Rockport Publ Inc; A Gallery of Marine Art, 98, Rockport Publ, Inc; Bound for Blue Water Contemp Am Marine Art, Greenwich Workshop Press, 2003. *Mem:* New Eng Watercolor Soc; Am Watercolor Soc; Fel Am Soc Marine Artists; Boston Printmakers (mem emer). *Media:* Oil, Watercolor. *Interests:* Maritime & Industrial History. *Publ:* Auth, Collagraph Printmaking, 75 & The Artist and the Built Environment, 80, Davis. *Dealer:* Mystic Maritime Gallery Mystic CT. *Mailing Add:* 947 Satucket Rd Brewster MA 02631

STOMPS, WALTER E, JR
EDUCATOR, PAINTER
b Hamilton, Ohio, July 13, 1929. *Study:* Miami Univ, BFA; Art Inst Chicago, with Boris Anisfeld, Paul Weighardt, Isabelle MacKinnon & Edgar Pillet, MFA; Syracuse Univ. *Work:* Cleveland Mus Art; Miami Univ; 4 works, TransFinancial Bank, Bowling Green, Ky. *Comn:* Ctr City Murals Proj, Nat Endowment Arts, Dayton, 72; Gen Motors (Frigidaire), Dayton; Bicentennial Poster Proj, Dayton. *Exhib:* Mid-States Exhib, Evansville, Ind, 77 & 79-80; Cent S Exhib, Nashville, Tenn, 77; 1st Ann Mid-Am Exhib Art, Owensboro Mus Art, Ky, 79; Eight States Exhib, Speed Mus Art, Louisville; Print Invitational, Univ Kans, Lawrence, 80; and others. *Teaching:* Prof painting & drawing, Western Ky Univ, 75-. *Awards:* James Nelson Raymond Award, Art Inst Chicago, 59; Purchase Awards, Dayton Art Inst, 66 & 68, Owensboro Mus Art, Ky, 79 & Evansville Mus Art & Sci, Ind, 86; and others. *Media:* Acrylic, Watercolor. *Publ:* Illusr, Dayton USA, 72. *Mailing Add:* 837 Nutwood St Bowling Green KY 42103

STONE, DON
PAINTER
b Council Bluffs, Iowa, Mar 27, 1929. *Study:* Vesper George Sch Art, Boston, 52. *Work:* Marietta Col, Ohio; Mobile Art Mus, Ala; Charles Greenshield Collection, Montreal; Peabody Maritime Mus, Salem, Mass. *Comn:* Large Egg Tempera, Univ NH, Durham, 79. *Exhib:* Nat Acad Design & Am Watercolor Soc, NY; Boston Soc Watercolor Painters, Boston Mus Fine Art, 71; Winter, 77 & New Eng Painters, 78, DeCordova Mus, Lincoln, Mass. *Pos:* Juror, of selection Am Water color Soc, New York City, 1977. *Teaching:* Instr art, Vesper George Sch Art, Boston, 60-65; instr, New Eng Sch Art, Boston, 60-65; Monhegan Island Workshop, Maine, 1970-. *Awards:* Gold Medals, Franklin Mint, 74 & 75 & Hudson Valley Art Asn, 80. *Mem:* Nat Acad (assoc, 68, acad, 94-); Am Watercolor Soc; Guild Boston Artists; New Eng Watercolor Soc; Hudson Valley Art Asn. *Media:* Egg Tempera, Watercolor. *Publ:* Auth, Watercolor page, Am Artist, 62. *Dealer:* Whistlers Daughter Art Gallery 88 S Finley Ave Basking Ridge NJ 07920. *Mailing Add:* 7 Hartman Pl Exeter NH 03833

STONE, JEREMY PATRICIA
ADVISOR, APPRAISER
b Boston, Mass, Nov 15, 1957. *Study:* Cooper Union, 1974-75; Univ San Francisco, Exec Cert in Nonprofit Orgn Mgmt, 1993, BS in Organization Behavior (summa cum laude), 1995; Appraisal Studies, Univ Calif, Irvine, 2005. *Exhib:* Curated over 90 exhibs. *Pos:* Spec activities coordr, Commonwealth Cult Preservation Trust, Boston, 79; res coordr, Anne Kohs Asn, San Francisco, 81-82; owner & dir, Jeremy Stone Gallery, San Francisco, 82-91; exec dir, Learning Through Educ in Arts Proj, 92; consult, Jewish Mus, San Francisco & Nestle Beverage Co, 93-94; dir career servs, San Francisco Arts Inst, Career Resources Prog, 94-97; founder & principal, Business Matters in the Visual Arts, San Francisco, 97-. *Teaching:* Vis lectr, Univ Wash, Pullman, 84, Calif Col Arts & Crafts, Oakland, 84-86, Univ Calif, Berkeley, 84 & 86, Sanford Univ Sch Law, 85, This Business of Art, Calif Lawyers for Arts, Hastings Col Law, 9/89; guest lectr, Calif Arts Coun, 96; vis fac, San Francisco Art Inst, 96-2000; Talking Art, The Players, San Jose Inst of Contemp Art, San Jose, Jan 11, 2005 panel; lectr, Metlife Found Nat Arts Forum Series, Yerba Buena Center Arts, San Francisco, Calif, 2007; lectr, Art & Conversation: Collectors & Collecting, Sonoma State Univ, 2007. *Awards:* Art Table Ann Award, Serv in the Visual Arts, 2008. *Bibliog:* Leah Garchik (auth), Pricing Yourself Into The Art market, San Francisco Chronicle, p 8, 8/10/97; Cay Lang (auth) Taking the Leap: Building a Career as a Visual Artist, 98; Andrea Siegel (auth), Open and Clothed, Agapanthus Books, Woodside, NY, 99; Linda Franklin (auth), Doing What Comes Naturally, The Calif Executive, 12/1988; Alice Marquis (auth), The Art Biz, Contemp Art Books, Inc, Chicago, 91; George Lauer, Eclectic Couple, The Press Democrat, Santa Rosa, CA, D1 & D6, 2/20/05; Catherine Bigelow, Swells, SF Chronicle, 11/7/04, p. D12; Ilana DeBare (auth), Artists mix business with pleasure, Seattle Post-Intelligencer, 1/16/2006; and many others. *Mem:* ArtTable, Inc (mem nat bd, co-chmn mem com No Calif chap 1995-97, mem exec com, 1995-2002, mem nat bd, 2000-02); Am Soc Appraisers (accredited senior mem); The Oxbow Sch, San Francisco Art Inst (bd trustees 87-2005). *Media:* Independent Curator. *Publ:* Auth, Honoring Ruth Asawa, Asake Bomani and Rudy Nothenberg, Bridging the Community Through Art (exhib catalog), Jewish Mus San Francisco, 93; Working artist: The purpose of work, Artweek, Vol 26, No 1, p 37, 1/95; Relationships are created and built, not bought, Artweek, Vol 26, No 6, p 32, 6/95; Thirty Years of Box Construction, Sunne Savage Gallery, Boston, MA, 11/79. *Mailing Add:* Business Matters in Visual Arts 2130 Fillmore St San Francisco CA 94115

STONE, JIM (JAMES) J
PHOTOGRAPHER, WRITER
b Los Angeles, Calif, Dec 2, 1947. *Study:* Mass Inst Technol, with Minor White, SB, 70; RI Sch Design, with Harry Callahan & Aaron Siskind, MFA, 75. *Work:* Corcoran Gallery Art & Nat Mus Am Art, Washington, DC; Fogg Art Mus, Harvard Univ, Cambridge, Mass; Int Mus Photog, Rochester, NY; Los Angeles Co Mus Art; Polaroid Collection, Offenbach, Ger & Cambridge, Mass; Mus Mod Art, NY; and others. *Exhib:* Photovision, Boston Ctr Arts, 72; New Eng Experience, De Cordova Mus, Lincoln, Mass, 72; Photog Unlimited, Fogg Art Mus, Harvard Univ, 74 & Contemp Photog, 76; Still Life, Corcoran Gallery Art, Washington, DC, 79; Venezia '79, Venice, Italy, 79; Boston Now: Photog, ICA, 85; Photographs Beget Photographs, Minn Inst Arts, 87; Twelve Photogs Look at US, Philadelphia Mus Art, 87; Future of Photog, Corcoran Gallery Art, Washington, DC, 87; Between Home and Heaven, Nat Mus Am Art, 92; Commodity Image, Int Ctr Photog, NY, 93; City of Las Vegas Cultural Ctr, 96; Innovation / Imagination, Friends of Photog, San Francisco, 99; Point of View, Silver Eye Ctr for Photog, Pittsburgh, 2000; Photog in Boston, DeCordova Mus, Lincoln, Nebr, 2000; Idea Photog, Mus Fine Arts, Santa Fe, NMex, 2002; Heartfelt, Fla State Univ Mus Fine Art, Tallahassee, Fla, 2005; Seeing Ourselves, George Eastman House, Rochester, NY, 2006; Water on the Edge, Univ N Tex, Denton, 2007. *Collection Arranged:* The Art of Polaroid, Musee de l'Elysee, Lausanne, Switz, 2010; Espace, Van Gogh, Arles, Fr, 2010; Westlicht Coll, Vienna, Austria, 2011; China Lishui Int Photograhpic Art Exhib, 2011. *Pos:* Artist-in-residence, Light Work, Syracuse, NY, 84, Visual Studies Workshop, Rochester, NY, 85, Nat Coll Arts, Lahore, Pakistan, 86 & Ariz Western Coll, Yuma, Ariz, 88; ed, PhotoEducation: A Polaroid Newsletter for Teachers of Photography, 88-; bd advs, Ctr (Santa Fe Ctr Photog), Santa Fe, NMex, 2005-; bd dirs, Soc Photographic Educ, 2007-2011. *Teaching:* Instr, Boston Coll, 73-88; instr, RI Sch Design, 75-78 & 93-98; asst prof, Univ NMex, 98-2002, assoc prof, 2002-2009, prof, 2010-. *Awards:* Mass Arts & Humanities Found photog fel, 76 & 88; New Eng Found Arts, 93; James D Phelan award in Photog, 2009. *Bibliog:* Channing (ed), Art of the State/State of the Art, Addison House, 78; Shamlian (auth), article in Philadelphia Photo Rev, 78; Hughes (ed), Photography Annuals, Popular Photog, 80 & 86; Photovision, Seville, Spain, 94; Riverstyx, 97; View Camera Mag, 2000. *Mem:* Boston Photog Resource Ctr (bd dir, 84-96, bd pres, 94-96); Soc Photog Educ (bd dirs, 2007-). *Media:* Photographs, Digital Prints. *Publ:* Ed, Darkroom Dynamics: A Guide to Creative Darkroom Techniques, Focal Press, 79; auth, A User's Guide to the View Camera, Harper Collins, 87, second ed, Addison Wesley Longman, 97, 3rd Prentice Hall, 2004; Stranger than Fiction, Light Work, 93; coauth, A Short Course in Photog, 3rd ed, Addison Wesley Longman, 96, Prentice Hall, 4th ed, 2000, 5th ed, 2003, 6th ed, 2006, 7th ed, 2009, 8th ed, 2012; Historiostomy, Piltdown Press, 2001; auth, Why My Photographs are Good, Nazraeli Press, 2005; Photography, Prentice Hall, 8th ed, 2005, 9th ed, 2008, 10th ed, 2011, 11th ed, 2014; Photography: The Essential Way, Prentice Hall, 2008; A Short Course in Digital Photography, Pearson Educ, 1st Ed, 2010, 2nd Ed, 2012. *Dealer:* Galerie Frank Schlag & Cie Meisenburgstrasse 173 D-45133 Essen Germany

STONE, JUDITH ELISE
ARTIST, ARCHITECTURAL HISTORIAN
b Boston, Mass, Sept 15, 1940. *Study:* Vassar Coll, BA (magna cum laude), 62; Harvard Univ, MAT, 65; Univ Colo, Boulder, MFA, 77. *Work:* Univ City Sci Ctr, St Joseph's Univ, Philadelphia; Baltimore Gulf & Electric; Toyoda Int Sales, The Design Studios, Tokyo; Idaho Nat Bank, Boise; Amazon Conservation Team, Washington, DC; Univ NH Mus Art; MacDowell Colony, Peterborough, NH. *Exhib:* Solo exhibs, All Colo Women in the Arts, 79, C Grimaldis Gallery, 85, Hinoki Gallery, Tokyo, 87, St Joseph's Univ Mem Exhib, 96, Lancaster Mus Art, 96, l'Espace 234, Montreal, 2002, Caelum Gallery, NY, 2003, 2005, Southern VT Art Ctr, 2003, Southern Vt Art Ctr, 2007; Art of the State, Pa State Mus, Harrisburg, 94; John Cage Retrospective, Philadelphia Mus Art, 95; Pa State Univ, Harrisburg, 98; Art on Campus, Southern Vt

Art Ctr, 2002; In Residence, MacDowell Colony Centennial (invitational), 2007 ; Caelum Gallery, 2009; Invitational Group Exhib, Palmer Gallery, Vassor Coll, 2012. *Teaching:* Adj prof humanities, Temple Univ, Philadelphia, 79-86; adj prof eng & drawing, St Joseph's Univ, Philadelphia, 83-96; asst prof humanities, Temple Univ, Japan, 86-87; vis instr, Middlebury Coll, 99; senior lectr, Univ Vt, Contemp Art Hist; lectr mod art hist, Univ Vermont; retired art hist, art, arch, and design prof. *Awards:* Resident Fel, MacDowell Colony, 92; Grand (first) Prize, San Diego 41st Int Juried Competition, 96. *Bibliog:* Edward Sozanski (auth), The art of drawing is thriving nicely, Philadelphia Inquirer, 84; Tom Weisser, Works Out, Baltimore Arts Newsletter, 85; Daina Savage (auth), Landscapes abloom in steel & grit, Intelligencer J, 96; Henry Lehmann, Books and Visual Arts, The Gazette, Montreal, 2002. *Mem:* AAUP; ACLU; UVM Ctr Holocaust Studies (faculty advisory bd). *Media:* Drawing, Collaged With Photo & Japanese Paper, transparent plexi & hardware. *Res:* German Satiric Art of the 1920's and 30's; Oxford Round Table, The Two Cultures: The Literary Moderns Revisited, 2006; Art Nouveau Masters: Henry van de Velde, Chs Rennie Mackintosh; Easel to Edifice: hs. Rennie MacKinstosh, Henry van de Velde, book contract, with Common Ground publishing, in progress. *Interests:* Holocaust Studies: International Film. *Collection:* Solomon and Barbara Wank; John Allen and Sheila Paulos; Michelle Addington; Eli and Chaya Passow. *Publ:* Auth, Part-time pathos, Temple Univ Fac Herald, 84; Discord in a Japanese sculpture garden, Vassar Quart, 89; Charlotte Solomon: Life or Theater, Holocaust Studies Bull, Univ Vt, 2001; The Two Cultures: The Literary Moderns Revisited, Forum on Pub Policy, Oxford Round Table; Interview with Miriam Kotzin (ed), Per Contra: The International Journal of the Arts, Literature & Ideas (interview), Winter 2009; Hindsight/Foresight: Two Art Nouveau Masters Wed Traditional Craft to Innovative Artistic and Industrial Innovation, Design Principles and Practices: An International Journal, Vol 5, No. 3, 2011; The Divine Sarah: Seeking Immortality through Film, Per Contra: The International Journal of the Arts, Literature, and Ideas, Spring 2015. *Mailing Add:* 68 Richardson St Burlington VT 05401

STONE, M LEE
ART DEALER

b Chicago, Ill, Apr 11, 1937. *Study:* Univ Ill, BS, 58; Univ Ill Coll Med, MD, 62. *Pos:* Pvt dealer, M Lee Stone Fine Prints, Inc 75. *Mem:* IFPDA. *Specialty:* American works of art on paper, 20th & 21st century; African American Art. *Interests:* African art. *Mailing Add:* 2101 Forest Ave Suite 130 San Jose CA 95128

STONE, NORAH
COLLECTOR

Awards: Named one of Top 200 Collectors, ARTnews mag, 2009, 2012, & 2013. *Collection:* Contemporary art. *Mailing Add:* 2790 Broadway San Francisco CA 94115

STONE, NORMAN CLEMENT
COLLECTOR

b Evanston, Ill, Apr 28, 1939. *Study:* Nichols Jr Coll, ABA, 1959; Stanford Univ, BA, 1962; Wright Inst, PhD, 1985. *Pos:* Founder, gen partner, San Francisco Venture Capital, 1970-76; co-founder, trustee, Nueva Day Sch & Learning Ctr, Hillsborough, Calif, 1976; therapist, Bay View Hunter's Point Found for Community Improvement, San Francisco, 1980-; trustee, San Francisco Mus Mod Art, currently; mem nat coun, Whitney Mus Art, New York, currently; mem, Tate Int Coun, London, currently; pres, W Clement & Jessie V Stone Found. *Awards:* Named one of Top 200 Collectors, ARTnews mag, 2008-13. *Collection:* Contemporary art. *Mailing Add:* 2790 Broadway St San Francisco CA 94115

STONEBARGER, VIRGINIA
PAINTER, INSTRUCTOR

b Ann Arbor, Mich, Mar 9, 1926. *Study:* Antioch Coll, BA, 50; Colorado Springs Fine Arts Ctr, 50-51; Art Students League, 51-52; Hans Hofmann Sch, 54; New York Univ, 54 & 56; Univ Wis-Milwaukee, MS, 72. *Work:* Mrs Harry Lynde Bradley, Milwaukee, Wis. *Comn:* Painting & reproduction, bldg, Nat Bank Tucson; two paintings, Arlington Race Course, Arlington Heights, Ill. *Exhib:* Univ Wis, 59; Milwaukee Art Ctr, 59-61; solo exhibs, Lakeland Coll, 69, Univ Wis, 71, Jewish Community Ctr, Milwaukee, 78 & Galleria Simon, 79; Tucson Int Airport, Ariz, 99; plus many others. *Teaching:* Instr art, Univ Lake Sch, Hartland, Wis, 59-62, Waukesha Co Tech Inst, 70-72 & Milwaukee Area Tech Coll, 73-77; instr painting, Univ Wis, Milwaukee Exten, 82- & Casas Adabes Fine Arts Acad, Tucson, AZ, 2000-2010; lectr art, Univ Ariz, 83-99. *Awards:* Danforth Found Fel, 69; Merit Award, Nat League Am Pen Women, Tucson; Awards, Southern Ariz Watercolor Guild, 86, 90 & 2006. *Mem:* Southern Ariz Watercolor Guild; Nat League Am Pen Women. *Media:* Watercolor, Acrylic. *Specialty:* Contemp art. *Dealer:* Cobalt Fine Arts 5 Camino Otero Tubac AZ 85646; Tansey Gallery 3001 E Skyline Dr #109 Tucson AZ 85718. *Mailing Add:* 855 E River #35 Tucson AZ 85718

STONEHOUSE, FRED A
PAINTER, COLLAGE ARTIST

b Milwaukee, Wis, June 30, 1960. *Study:* Univ Wis, Milwaukee, BFA, 82. *Work:* Tacoma Art Mus, Wash; Milwaukee Art Mus & Marquette Univ, Haggerty Mus Art, Wis; Madison Art Ctr, Wis; Univ Ariz, Tempe. *Exhib:* 10 Yr Survey, Madison Art Ctr, Wis, 92; In the Light of Goya, Univ Calif, Berkeley, 95; The Mythic Narrative, Palo Alto Cult Ctr, Calif, 96; Reality Bites, Kansas City Art Inst, Kemper Mus Contemp Art & Design, 96; Devotional Rescue, Contemp Arts Ctr, Cincinnati, Ohio, 97; Surreal Wisconsin, Madison Art Ctr, Wis, 98. *Awards:* Midwest Nat Endowment Arts Fel, 91; Penny McCall Found Fel, 92; Wis Arts Bd Fel, 93. *Bibliog:* Garret Holg (auth), Review, Art News, 9/94; David Ebony (auth), Fred Stonehouse at M-13, Art in Am, 12/95; Ken Johnson (auth), Review, NY Times, 4/24/98. *Publ:* Illusr, Playboy Mag, 90-97; Milwaukee Mag, 93. *Dealer:* Dean Jensen Gallery Milwaukee WI 53219. *Mailing Add:* 515 Kettle Moraine Dr S Slinger WI 53086-9705

STONER, JOYCE HILL
CONSERVATOR, EDUCATOR

b Washington, DC, Oct 9, 1946. *Study:* Coll William & Mary, BA (fine arts; summa cum laude); NY Univ, Inst Fine Arts, Conserv Ctr, MA (fine arts) & dipl conserv, spec grad study with Bernard Rabin (Metrop Mus) John Brealey; Getty Mus, with Mr Andrea Rothe; Univ Del, PhD (art hist), 95. *Work:* Freer Gallery Art; Winterthur Mus, Del; Va Mus Fine Arts, Richmond; Del Art Mus; and others. *Comn:* Edward Laning murals, NY Pub Libr; NC Wyeth mural treatments, WSFS, Wilmington, Del, 98. *Collection Arranged:* Know What You See, a traveling exhib organized by Louis Pomerantz, Found Am Inst Conserv & Smithsonian Inst Traveling Exhib Serv, 76; Flaking, Foxing and Fine Works, conserv exhib, Del Art Mus, 77; Factory Work: Warhol, Wyeth, and Basquiat, Brandywine River Mus, Farnsworth Art Mus, 2006; Wyeth Vertigo, Shelbourne Mus, 2013. *Pos:* Managing ed, Art & Archeol Technol Abstracts, 69-86; consult conserv paintings, Freer Gallery Art, 75-76 & 88-92; exec dir, Found Am Inst Conserv, 75-79; paintings conservator, Winterthur Mus, Del, 76-82, supv conserv section, 81-82; vis scholar painting conserv, Metrop Mus Art, 80; guest scholar, Getty Mus Painting Conserv, 85; trustee, Williamstown Regional Art conserv lab, 89-95; bd dir, Wyeth Found, 99-; chair, Edward F & Elizabeth Goodman Rosenberg Prof Material Cul Studies. *Teaching:* Assoc prof intro art conserv, Va Commonwealth Univ, 75-76; asst prof paintings conserv, Univ Del, 76-79, assoc prof, 79-, assoc dir, Art Conserv Prog, 80-82, dir, 82-97, chair, 90-97, prof, 96-; dir, Preserv Studies Doctoral Prog, Univ Del, 2005-. *Awards:* Getty Guest Scholar Grant, 85; Del Humanities Forum, 95 & 96; Am Inst for Conserv Lifetime Achievement Award, 2003; William Fishelis Book Award, Like a Breath on Glass: Painting Softly from James McNeill Whistler through Arthur B Davies, 2009; Frances Smyth-Ravenel Prize for Excellence in Publication Design, An Evolving Techniques: NC Wyeth's Methods & Materials, 2008; Award for Distinction in Scholarship and Conservation, Heritage Preservation, Coll Art Asn, 2011; Am Inst for Conservation for Outstanding Contributions to the Field of Painting Conservation. *Bibliog:* Andy Warhol and Jamie Wyeth, Interactions, America Art, Vol 12, No 3, fall 99; Are There Great Women Art Conservators, Int Inst for Conservation Bulletin, No 1, 2/2000; Climbing Toward an Ideal: Andrew Wyeth's Portrait of Henry Francis du Pont, Winterthur Mag, 12/2001; Hell vs. Ruhemann: The Metaphysical and the Physical, Controversies about the Cleaning of Paintings, Brit Mus, 12/2001; The Debate Over Cleaning Paintings: How Much is Too Much, Int Found Art Research Tour, Vol 5, No 3, 2002; Preservation of Bricks & Mortar, Era & Ambience: The Olson House & the Kuerner Farm, Studies in Conservation, Vol 48 No 4, 2003; The NC Wyeth Studio, Am Art, Spring 2005; An Evolving Techniques: NC Wyeth's Methods & Materials, 2008; Degrees of authenticity in the discourse between the original artist & the viewer, Art: Conservation & Authenticities, material, concept, context, 2009; Remembering Andrew Wyeth for American Art, Smithsonian Am Art Mus, 2010; co-ed with Rebecca Rushfield, Conservation of Easel Paintings (890 pg book), Routledge, 2012; Wyeth Vertigo, catalogue, Shelburne Mus, 2013. *Mem:* Fel Int Inst Conserv Historic & Artistic Works & Am Inst Conserv Historic & Artistic Works; Int Coun Mus; Nat Mus Act Adv Coun, 81-84; Nat Inst for Conserv Proj Dir; Coll Art Asn (bd 2000-04, vpres 2004-05). *Media:* Conservation of Oil & Tempera Paintings. *Res:* History of art conservation in America; the technique of contemporary artists Whistler, J McNeill, Andrew & Jamie Wyeth. *Interests:* Musical Theatre; Cabaret. *Publ:* co-ed, Conservation of Easel Paintings, Taylor and Francis, 2012; Book review for Daniel E Sutherland's book Whistler: A Life for Art's Sake, Nineteenth Century, Vol 34, No 2, fall 2014; Vignettes of Interdisciplinary Technical Art History Investigations Supplemented by the FAIC Oral History Archive in honor of Roger H Marijnissen, http://ceroart.revues.org/June, 2015; CAA Reviews on Looking Out, Looking In, NGA catalogue of the Andrew Wyeth Exhibition, article on the histiry of conservation training for the Burlington Mag essay on The Medium is the Message for a collection of essays about Andrew Wyeth, ed. David Cateforis and Wanda Corn, Rethinking Andrew Wyeth, Book Review for JAIC, Vol 53, No 3, 2014 of Andral, Jean-Louis; Raeburn, Micheal: Gautier, Gwenaelle et al, Picasso Express, Antibes: Musee Picasso, 2011. *Mailing Add:* Univ Del 303 Old College Newark DE 19716

STONES, MARGARET ALISON
EDUCATOR, HISTORIAN

b Eng, Mar 11, 1942. *Study:* Univ London, BA, 64, PhD (art hist), 70. *Teaching:* Assoc prof Medieval art, Univ Minn, 69-81, prof, 81-83; vis prof, Univ Reading, 75; prof, Univ Pittsburgh, 84-; vis fel, All Souls Col, Oxford, 99, Magdalen Col, Oxford, 2001 & Corpus Christi Col, Cambridge, 2002. *Awards:* APS Grant, 71, 79 & 93; Am Coun Learned Soc Grant, 73; Nat Endowment Humanities Grant, 73, 77, 78, 82, 85, 92-93 & 2001-; Andrew W Mellon Found Grant, 2001-2002. *Mem:* Medieval Acad Am; Brit Archaeol Asn; Int Arthurian Soc; Soc Nat des antiquaires de France; Fel Soc Antiquaries London. *Res:* Manuscript illumination. *Publ:* Auth, Images of Temptation, Seduction and Discovery in the Prose Lancelot: a Preliminary Note, Festschrift Gerhard Schmidt, Wiener Jahrbuch fur Kunstgeschichte, 46-47, pp 93-4; Les Manuscrits de Chriton de Troyes, ed, earth, 93; Madame Marie's Picture-Book: A Precursor of Flemish Painting around 1400, In: Flanders in a European Perspective, ed Maurits Smeyers, pp 429-43, Leuven: Peeters, 95; Qui a lu le Guide du plerin? (with Jeanne Krochalis), In: Plerinages et croisades, ed Leon Pressouyre 118e Colloque du Comite des travaux historiques et scientifiques, Pau, 93, Paris, pp 11-36, 95; Stylistic Associations, Evolution and Collaboration: Charting the Bute Painter's Career, The J Paul Getty Mus J, Vol 23, pp 11-29, 95; The Codex Calixtinus and the Iconography of Charlemagne, In: Roland and Charlemagne in Europe: Essays on the Reception and Transformation of a Legend, ed Karen Pratt King's Coll London Medieval Studies XII, London, pp 169-203, 96; The Pilgrims Guide to Santiago de Compostela, (with Jeanne Krochalis), ed, 98; Lelived Images de Madame Marie, Paris, 97; Seeing the Grail on the Grail: A Casebook (with D. Mahoney), ed, 2000; and others.

STOPPERT, MARY KAY
ADMINISTRATOR, GALLERY DIRECTOR
b Flint, Mich, Aug 19, 1941. *Study:* Western Mich Univ, Kalamazoo, BS, 64; Sch Art Inst Chicago, MFA, 68. *Work:* Mus Contemp Art & Northeastern Ill Univ, Chicago; Michael Rockefeller Art Ctr, State Univ NY, Fredonia; Northern Ill Univ, DeKalb; Kemper Insurance Co, Long Grove, Ill; Corcoran Gallery, Washington, DC. *Exhib:* Solo exhib (with catalog), New Mus Contemp Art, NY, 82; Painting and Sculpture Today, Indianapolis Mus Art, Ind, 76; Works on Paper, Art Inst Chicago, 78; Detroit and Chicago Art of the 70s, Detroit Inst Arts, 78; Art Inst Chicago, 74, 77 & 79; Museo de Arte Contemporanea, Sao Paolo, Brazil, 80; Chicago: Some Other Traditions, San Francisco Mus Art, 83; The Figure in Chicago Art, Mus Contemp Art, Chicago, 85. *Teaching:* Prof art, Northeastern Ill Univ, Chicago, 70-. *Awards:* Frank G Logan Award, 75th Chicago and Vicinity Show, 74, John G Curtis Jr Award, 77th Chicago and Vicinity Show, 78, Art Inst Chicago; President Merit Award, Northeastern Ill Univ, Chicago, 79; Nat Endowment of Arts Visual Artist Fel, 86. *Bibliog:* Grace Glueck (auth), rev, in: New York Times, 6/18/82; Christopher Lyon (auth), rev, in: Chicago Sun Times, 3/11/84. *Mem:* Coll Art Asn; Women's Caucus Art (bd adv 76-79, 81-85); Chicago Women's Caucus Art (pres, 79-83); Int Sculpture Ctr. *Dealer:* Phyllis Kind Gallery 136 Greene Street New York NY & W Superior Chicago IL 60610. *Mailing Add:* Northeastern Ill Univ Chicago IL 60625

STOREY, DAVID
PAINTER
b Madison, Wis, 1948. *Study:* Univ Calif-Berkeley, 66-68; Univ Calif-Davis, BA, 70 & MFA, 72. *Exhib:* Solo exhibs, Concord Contemp Art, 81, 83 & 84, Jay Gorney Mod Art, 85, Hirschl & Adler Mod, NY, 87, 91 & 92, Lino Silverstein Gallery, Barcelona, Spain, 89, Jorge Albero Arte Contemporaneo, Madrid, Spain & Davis-McClain Gallery, Houston, Tex, 90, Betsy Senior Contemp Prints, NY, 91; Surface Printing in the 80's, Zimmerli Art Mus, Rutgers Univ, NJ, 90; 42nd Ann Purchase Exhib, Am Acad & Inst Arts & Letts, NY, 90; The Unique Print 70s into 90s, Mus Fine Arts, Boston, 90; A Bestiary, Paula Cooper Gallery, NY, 91; Hirschl & Adler Gallery, NY, 92. *Awards:* NY State Found Arts Grant, 89; Nat Endowment Arts Fel, 91; Guggenheim Found Fel, 2010. *Bibliog:* Susan Tallman (auth), Many Monotypes, Arts Mag, 1/91; Peggy Cyphers (auth), review, Arts, 9/91; Lisa Liebmann (auth), review, Artforum, 10/91. *Publ:* Contribr, Bestiary, Brad Morrow (auth), 90. *Mailing Add:* 134 W Broadway New York NY 10013-3328

STORM, HOWARD
PAINTER, SCULPTOR
b Newton, Mass, Oct 26, 1946. *Study:* Denison Univ; J Ferguson Stained Glass Studio, Weston, Mass, apprenticeship; San Francisco Art Inst, BFA, 69; Univ Calif, Berkeley, MA, 70, MFA, 72. *Work:* Roswell Mus, NMex; Denison Univ; Mt St Joseph Col, Ohio; Ky Arts Comn, Frankfort; Baylor Univ. *Comn:* Pioneer Award, Northern KY Chamber Commerce. *Exhib:* Solo exhibs, Berkeley Mus, 72 & Baylor Univ, 73; Huntington Galleries, 72-74; Univ Cincinnati, 74; Cincinnati Art Mus, 75; plus others. *Pos:* Artist-in-residence, Roswell Mus, 71-72. *Teaching:* Prof art, Northern Ky Univ, 72-, chmn art dept, currently. *Awards:* Eisner Prize, Univ Calif, Berkeley, 72; Purchase Award, Preview '73; Purchase Award, Huntington Galleries. *Media:* Acrylic, Oil; Wood. *Publ:* Left Alone, Logan Elm Press, Ohio State Univ, 85. *Mailing Add:* 90 Hawthorne Ave Newport KY 41075

STORM, LARUE
PAINTER
b Pittsburgh, Pa. *Study:* Univ Miami, AB & MA; Art Students League, Woodstock; also printmaking with Calvaert Brun, Paris. *Work:* Lowe Mus, Coral Gables, Fla; Columbia Mus Art, Ga; Norton Gallery Art, West Palm Beach, Fla; Peabody Col, Nashville, Tenn. *Exhib:* Corcoran Gallery Art Biennial, Washington, DC, 57; Butler Inst Am Art, Youngstown, Ohio, 58-60; Miami Six, El Paso Mus, 65; Fla Creates, var mus Fla, 71-; Solo exhibs, Lowe Mus Art, Norton Gallery Art & Columbia Mus Art; and others. *Teaching:* Adj asst prof drawing & design, Univ Miami, 67-84. *Awards:* Purchase Award, Columbia Mus Art, SC. *Media:* Collage, Assemblage. *Publ:* Auth, Jose Guadalupe Posada: Guerrilla Fighter of the Throwaways, Carrell, 70

STORR, ROBERT
EDUCATOR, PAINTER
b Portland, Maine, Dec 28, 1949. *Study:* Swarthmore Col, BA, 1972; Sch Art Inst Chicago, postgrad, 1975-78; Skowhegan Sch Painting and Sculptor, MA, 1978. *Exhib:* Betty Cuningham Gallery; Andre Zarre Gallery; Jack Tilton Gallery; NY Studio Sch; Nelson Atkins Mus; Mus Modern Art, 1991, 93-96; Inst Contemp Art, Phila, 1991. *Pos:* Sr cur painting and sculptor, Mus Modern Art, NY City, 1991-2002; ed bd, Art Journal, 1985-95; consulting cur, mod & contemp art, Philadelphia Mus Art, currently; dir, Venice Biennial, Italy, 2007. *Teaching:* Assoc dean, NY Studio Sch, NYC, 1987-88; vis artist, critic, RI Sch Design, Providence, 1988; vis artist, Cooper Union, NY City, 1988-89; asst prof, Tyler Sch Art, Phila, 1989; Avery prof, Bard Col, Annandale on Hudson, NY, 1990-91; Rosalie Solow prof modern art, New York Univ Inst Fine Arts, 2002-06; prof painting/printmaking, dean, Yale Sch Art, 2006-; lectr art mus, univs and art schools in US and abroad. *Awards:* Penny McCall Found grantee, 1988; Peter Norton Family Found grantee, 1990. *Publ:* Auth, Philip Guston, 1986; co-auth Chuck Close, 1987; co-auth (with Lars Hitue), Susan Rothenberg 15 Years a Survey, 1990; co-auth (with Kirk Varnedoe) From Bauhaus to Pop: Masterworks Given by Phillip Johnson, 1996; contrib ed, Art in America, 1981-, Grand Street; bimonthly columnist, Frieze, London. *Mailing Add:* Art School & Graphic Design PO Box 208339 New Haven CT 06520-8339

STOTT, DEBORAH
HISTORIAN
b Minneapolis, Minn, June 11, 1942. *Study:* Wellesley Col, BA, 64; Columbia Univ, MA, 66, PhD, 75. *Pos:* Assoc dean undergrad studies, Sch Arts & Humanities, Univ Tex, Dallas, 94-. *Teaching:* Instr art hist, Wheaton Col, Mass, 70-75; asst prof, Intercollegiate Ctr Classical Studies, Rome, 75-76; assoc prof, Univ Tex, Dallas, 76-. *Awards:* Am Acad Rome Fel, 80-81; Delmas Found Grant, 80 & 82; Bunting Inst Fel, Radcliffe Col, 82-83. *Mem:* Coll Art Asn Am; Midwest Art Hist Asn; Soc Fels Am Acad (regional rep). *Res:* Style and theory in Italian Renaissance reliefs. *Publ:* Auth, Jacques Lipchitz and Cubism, Garland Publ, 78; auth, Jacopo Sansovino's Bronze Reliefs and Venetian Colorism, Hofstra Univ, 82; auth, Fatte a sembianza di pittura: Jacopo Sansovino's bronze reliefs in San Marco, Art Bulletin, spring 82. *Mailing Add:* Sch Arts & Humanities Univ Tex PO Box 830688 Richardson TX 75083-0688

STOUFFER, DANIEL HENRY, JR
PAINTER, DESIGNER
b Paulding, Ohio, Sept 26, 1937. *Study:* Ohio State Univ, BFA, 59. *Work:* Ohio State Univ, Columbus; Amoco Oil co, Houston; Pub Serv co, NMex; Sandia Fed Savings & Loan Bank, Albuquerque; Fed Reserve Bank, Denver; Univ NMex; Coutts Mus Art, El Dorado, Kans. *Comn:* Ann commemorative painting, Pub Serv co NMex, Albuquerque, 76; painting, Sandia Fed Savings, Albuquerque, 86; ann commemorative poster, NMex Arts & Crafts Fair, 88; ann commemorative poster, Weems Artfest, 90 & 94. *Exhib:* Albuquerque Mus, 82-83; Two Watercolorists, Carlsbad Mus, NMex, 84; Watercolor USA, 87, 93, 94, 98, 2000-2001, 2003-2004, 2007, 2009, 2012, 2013; Rocky Mt Nat Watermedia Exhib, 87-88, 93, 97, 2000, 2002-2006, 2009, 2010; Nature Conserv Show, Gingrass Gallery, Milwaukee, 90; Gov's Show, Albuquerque, 92; Arts for the Parks (Nat Traveling Show), Jackson Hole, Wyoming, 94, 96, 2000 & 2002-2006; Adirondacks Nat Exhib Watercolors, 2010. *Pos:* Artist & dir design, Charles Merrill Publ, Columbus, Ohio, 60-72; art dir, Univ NMex Press, Albuquerque, 72-79. *Teaching:* Ann workshop, White Sands Inst. *Awards:* Grumbacher Gold Medallion, NMex State Fair, 95; Award of Merit, Rocky Mt Nat, 97; Strathmore Award, Watercolor USA, 2004, Merit award, 2012; Region II Award, Arts for the Parks, 2004-2006; Region II Award, Paint Am, 2009; Grand Prize, Paint the Parks, 2010. *Bibliog:* Article, Watercolor Mag, summer 97; article, Southwest Art Mag, Feb 2003; article, Watercolor Magic, Dec, 2004. *Mem:* Rocky Mtn Nat Watercolor Soc; Watercolor USA Honor Soc. *Media:* Watercolor. *Publ:* The Great Taos Bank Robbery, 73; Acoma: Pueblo in the Sky, 76, This Shining Land, 82, Univ NMex Press; illusr & collabr, In Celebration of The Book, NMex Bk League, 82. *Dealer:* Weems Gallery 7200 Montgomery Blvd NE Ste D Albuquerque NM 87109. *Mailing Add:* 1190 Calle del Oro Bosque Farms NM 87068

STOUT, RENEE
SCULPTOR, PHOTOGRAPHER, PAINTER, INSTALLATION ARTIST
b 1958. *Study:* Carnegie Mellon Univ, BFA, 80. *Exhib:* Solo shows incl Mount Vernon Coll, Wash, DC, 87, BR Kornblatt Gallery, Wash, DC, 91, Pittsburgh Ctr for Arts, 92, Nat Mus African Art, Smithsonian Inst, Wash, DC, 93, Univ Art Mus, Univ Calif, Santa Barbara, 95, David Adamson Gallery, Wash, DC, 96, 98, Steinbaum Krauss Gallery, New York, 97, Morgan Gallery, Kans City, Mo, 99, Beach Mus, Kans State Univ, 2000, David Beitzel Gallery, New York, 2001, Belger Ctr for Arts, Kans City, Mo, 2002, Hemphill Fine Arts, Wash, DC, 2003, 2005 & 2007, Barrister's Gallery, New Orleans, 2004, Dennis Morgan Gallery, Kans City, Mo, 2005, Ogden Mus, New Orleans, 2005, Hammonds House Galleries, Atlanta, 2005, Arts Ctr, St Petersburg, Fla, 2006; group shows incl Smithsonian Inst, Wash, DC, 91; Whitney Mus Am Art Downtown, Fed Reserve Plz, New York, 91; LewAllen Gallery, Santa Fe, NMex, 92, 93; Nat Mus Am Art, Smithsonian Inst, 94; Nat Mus Women in Arts, Washington, 94, 2006; South Bank Ctr, London, 95; Coll Charleston, Halsey Gallery, 96; Neuberger Mus Art, State Univ NY, 97, 98; De Beyerd Mus, Holland, 98; Anacostia Mus, Smithsonian Inst, 98, 99; DC Moore Gallery, New York, 2000; Corcoran Gallery Art, 2003, 2005; Conner Fine Arts, Wash, DC, 2004; Washington Printmakers Gallery 2006 Invitational; Pyramid Atlantic Arts Ctr, Silver Spring, Md, 2006; She's So Articulate, Arlington Arts Ctr, Va, 2008. *Teaching:* Vis prof, Univ Ga, Athens, 95. *Awards:* Pollock Krasner Found Award, 91, 99; Louis Comfort Tiffany Found Award, 93; Regional Visual arts Fel, Mid-Atlantic Arts Found, Nat Endowment for Arts, 93; Mayor's Art Award, Wash, DC, 97; Anonymous Was A Woman Award, 99; Joan Mitchell Painter's and Sculptor's Grant Award, 2005; David C Driskell Prize, High Mus Art, Atlanta, 2010. *Bibliog:* MacGaffey Wyatt (auth), Michael D Harris (auth), Sylvia H Williams (auth), David C Driskell (auth), Astonishment & Power: The Eyes of Understanding: Kongo Minkisi/The Art of Renee Stout, Smithsonian, 93; Marla Berns (auth), George Lipsitz (auth), Dear Robert, I'll See You at the Crossroads: A Project by Renee Stout, Univ Calif Santa, 1996. *Media:* Mixed Media

STOUT, RICHARD GORDON
PAINTER, SCULPTOR
b Beaumont, Tex, Aug 21, 1934. *Study:* Cincinnati Art Acad, 52-53; Sch Art Inst Chicago, BFA, 57; Univ Tex, MFA, 69. *Work:* Mus Fine Arts, Houston; Dallas Mus Fine Arts; Marion Koogler McNay Art Mus, San Antonio; Rice Univ; Univ Houston; San Antonio Mus Art. *Exhib:* One Hundred Contemp Am Draftsmen, Univ Mich, 63; Marion Koogler McNay Art Inst, 64 & 71; Contemp Arts Mus, Houston, 75; Jurgen Schweinebroden, Berlin, 80; Fresh Paint, Mus Fine Art, Houston, 85; Barbara Davis Gallery, Houston, 94-96; Holly Johnson Gallery, Dallas, Tex, 2006; Beeville Mus Art, Beeville, Tex, 2009; William Reoves Fine Art, Houston, Tex, 2009, 2011, 2013. *Pos:* Mem adv bd, Mus Fine Arts, Houston, 73-. *Teaching:* Instr painting, Mus Fine Arts, Houston, 58-67; assoc prof drawing & painting, Univ Houston, 69-96. *Awards:* Longview Purchase Prize, Jr Serv League, 65 & 72; Tex Fine Arts Asn Awards, 66 & 71; Houston Area Exhib First Prize, Blaffer Gallery, Univ Houston, 75; and others. *Media:* Acrylic. *Dealer:* Graham Gallery 1431 W Alabama Houston TX 77006; Davis McLain Gallery 2627 Colqoitt Houston TX 77098. *Mailing Add:* 1213 Bonnie Brae Houston TX 77006

STOVALL, LUTHER MCKINLEY
PRINTMAKER
b Athens, Ga, Jan 1, 1937. *Study:* RI Sch Design; Howard Univ, BFA, 65. *Hon Degrees:* Corcoran Coll Art and Design, Hon DFA, 2001. *Work:* Corcoran Gallery Art, Nat Mus Am Art, Wash Post Co, Washington; Howrey & Simon; Ropes & Gray; Nat Gallery Art; Phillips Coll; Wash Post Co, Wash. *Comn:* Silkscreens, Smithsonian Inst

Resident Assoc Prog, 85, 87 & 88; silkscreens, Spalding-Amers, 86-; Right (silkscreen ed), Amnesty Int, 89; Breathing Hope (silkscreen ed), Howard Univ, 96; silkscreen ed Sam Gilliam's Think Tank, Joint Ctr Political & Econ Study, 96. *Exhib:* Impressionisms/Expressionisms: Black Am Graphic Exhibs (traveling), Smithsonian Inst, 80-81; Art in Washington & its Afro-Am Presence: 1940-1979, Washington Proj for Arts, 85; The Art of Black Americans in Japan, Tokyo, 87; Heroes and Teachers (auth, catalog), African-Am Atelier, Greensboro, NC, 91; Heroes, Teachers and Friends, Corcoran Gallery Art, 92; Art Silkscreen Printmaking, Howard Univ Gallery, 2001; Art, Strathmore Hall, 2004; Mormon Temple Visitors Ctr, Washington, DC, 2005; Kansas African Am Art Mus, Wichita, Kans, 2006; Gallery Cornelia, Charleston, SC, 2006; Prada Gallery, Washington, DC, 2007; Washington Printmakers Gallery, Washington, DC, 2007; African Am Mus, Dallas, Tex, 2007; Howard Univ, Washington, DC, 2007; Granary Gallery, West Tisbury, Mass, 2009; Addison/Ripley Fine Arts, 2010; Multiplicity, Smithsonian Am Art Mus, 2011; Am Univ Mus, 2012. *Pos:* Dir, Workshop, Inc, 68-; DC Comn Arts & Humanities, mem Georgetown Arts Comn, Pen Faulkner Bd Dir & Washington Nat Cathedral Arts Coun, Washington, currently. *Teaching:* Master printmaking & silkscreen, Workshop, Corcoran Gallery Art, 69-72. *Awards:* Stern Grant, 68-72; Individual Artist Grant, 72 & Workshop Grant, 72-76, Nat Endowment Arts; Fourth Ann Mayor's Art Award, Washington, DC, 85; Bd Dir Award, Source Theatre Co, Washington, DC, 88. *Bibliog:* Lou Stovall, Printmaker (film), Smithsonian Inst, 83; Patricia Dane Rogers (auth), A workshop atelier comes to life in NW Washington, Wash Post, 3/26/87; Ken Oda (auth), Lou Stovall, on how people make a difference, Koan, 3/93; Robin Tierney (auth), Printmaker Brings New Work Home, Examiner, 1/6/2007; Joanna Shaw-Eagle (auth), Lou Stovall: New Light of Color, Wash Times, 2/24/07. *Mem:* DC Comn Arts & Humanities. *Media:* Silkscreen. *Publ:* Auth, Of the Land, 73; conbr, Vertical Views: Silkscreen Monoprint Collage by Lou Stovall, 2012. *Dealer:* Prada Gallery 1031 Wisconsin Ave NW Washington DC 20007; Addison Ripley Fine Art 1670 Wisconsin Ave NW Wash DC 20007. *Mailing Add:* Workshop Inc 3145 Newark St NW Washington DC 20008

STOVER, DONALD LEWIS
CURATOR

b Staunton, Va, Jan 8, 1943. *Study:* Va Polytechnic Inst Coll Archit, 1961-65; St Marys Univ, BA, 1972; Univ Del Winterthur Prog, 1975-77. *Collection Arranged:* Early Texas Furniture and Decorative Arts (auth, catalog), 1972 & Tischlermeister Jahn (auth, catalog), 1975, San Antonio Mus Asn; Art of Louis C Tiffany (auth, catalog), 1981, Am Sculpture (auth, catalog), 1982 & Pennsylvania German, 1983, Fine Arts Mus San Francisco. *Pos:* Cur furniture, San Antonio Mus Asn, 1972-75; cur-in-charge, Decorative Arts & Sculpture, Fine Arts Mus San Francisco, 1981-83, cur-in-charge, Am Decorative Arts & Sculpture, 1983-. *Mem:* Soc Winterthur Grads; Decorative Arts Trust; Am Decorative Arts Forum Northern Calif; Western Region Arch Am Art (chmn, currently). *Res:* Nineteenth century Texas cabinetmakers; mid-19th century emigrant cabinetmakers, New York; Louis Comfort Tiffany; American sculpture. *Publ:* Coauth, Early Texas Furniture, Trinity Press, 1974; auth, American decorative arts: Recent acquisitions, Apollo Mag, 1980. *Mailing Add:* 880 Franklin St San Francisco CA 94102

STRACHAN, TAVARES
GLASS BLOWER

b Bahamas. *Study:* Coll Bahamas, Assocs Fine Arts, 1999; Rhode Island Sch Design, BFA (Glass), 2003; Yale Univ, MFA, 2006. *Work:* Cent Bank, Nassau Bahamas; Inter Am Develop Ban, Washington; Nassau Int Airport. *Exhib:* Solo exhibs include Cent Bank Gallery, Nassau Bahamas, 1999, Pro Gallery, Nassau Bahamas, 2001, Pierogi 2000, Brooklyn, 2006, Ronald Feldman Fine Arts, New York, 2006, Luggage Store, San Francisco, 2006; Group exhibs include On The Edge of Time, Contemp Art Caribbean, Washington, 2000; Shattered Fractions, Coll Gallery, Nassau, Bahamas, 2000; Glass Triennial, Woods Gerry Gallery, RI, 2000; Caribbean Biennial, Mus Mod Art, Santa Domingo, 2002; Meiosis, Sol Gallery, RI, 2002; Mine, Lombard Fried Fine Arts, New York, 2003; One on One, Pierogi, Brooklyn, 2003; School Days, Jack Tilton Gallery, New York, 2006; Black Part 2: An Exhib Drawing, Daniel Weinberg Gallery, Los Angeles, 2007; NY State of Mind, Queens Mus Art, New York, 2007; InnerOuterSpace, Mattress Factory, Pittsburgh, 2008, Armory Show, New York, 2008. *Awards:* Gov's Award, The Gov General Bahamas, 1998; Queen Elizabeth Arts/Poetry Award, 2000; Louis Comfort Tiffany Found Grants, 2008; Art Matters Found Grant, 2008. *Mailing Add:* Ronald Feldman Gallery 31 Mercer St New York NY 10013

STRAIGHT, ELSIE H
LIBRARIAN, SCULPTOR

b Cumberland, Eng. *Study:* Art Inst Pittsburgh, dipl (illus), 39; New York Sch of Applied Design for Women, with Kimon Nicholaides, dipl (des), 41; Roger Williams Col, BA, 66; Univ RI, MLS, 72. *Pos:* Librn, Ringling Sch Art Libr, 74-, retired; rare books & libr res, Univ So Fla. *Mem:* Art Libr Soc NAm, Southeastern Region (chmn, 80); Sch Libr Asn (secy, 70); Nat Sculpture Soc. *Media:* Stone, Clay. *Res:* John Simmons Collection of French Revolutionary Statesmen and military leaders; 17th century prints. *Interests:* Portrait artists, painters and sculptors; Pre-Columbian art. *Mailing Add:* 10604 Stradford Row Orlando FL 32817-2041

STRAND, SALLY ELLIS
PAINTER, INSTRUCTOR

b Denver, Colo, Oct 11, 1954. *Study:* Am Acad Art, Chicago, 75-77; Denver Univ, BFA, 78; Art Students League, New York, 81-82; MFA, Laguna Col Art and Design, Calif, 2014. *Work:* IDA, Am Express, Minneapolis; Goldman-Sachs, NY; Grand Hyatt Hotel, NY; Hunter Mus, Chattanooga, Tenn; Butler Inst Am Art, Youngstown, Ohio; Riverside Community Col, Calif. *Exhib:* Am Watercolor Soc, Salmagundi Club, NY, 83; All Media '83 Exhib, Laguna Beach Mus Art, Calif, 83; Pastel Soc Am, Nat Arts Club Gallery, NY, 1983-2013; Pastel Soc Am, Special Invitation, Hermitage Mus, Norfolk, Va, 85; Pastel Soc Am, Special Invitation, Monmouth Mus, NJ, 85; Pastel Soc W Coast, Sacramento Fine Arts Ctr, 92; J Cacciola Gallieries, NY, 99, 2000; Art Inst Southern Calif, Laguna Beach, 2002; Phoenix Airport Mus, 2006; Internat Asn of Pastel Societies, Brea, Calif, 2010, Youngstown, Ohio, 2010, Albuqueque, NMex, 2011, 2013; Laguna Art Mus, Calif, 2012-14; Telluride Gallery of Fine Arts, Colo, 2015; Oceanside Mus of Art, Calif, 2015-16; Solo Exhibs: Suzanne Brown Gallery, Scottsdale, Ariz, 87, 90, 91; J Cacciola Galleries, NY, 88, 90, 92, 99; Diane Nelson Fine Art, Laguna Beach, Calif, 2000; Telluride Gallery of Fine Art, Colo, 2004, 2006, 2009, 2016; Bakersfield Art Mus, Calif, 2006. *Teaching:* Fac color theory, Colo Inst Art, Denver, 78-79; fac pastel/mixed media, Scottsdale Artist's Sch, Ariz, 90-; Nat & Local workshops, The Color of Light. *Awards:* Master Pastellist Title, Pastel Soc of Am, 97, Hahnemuhle Pastel Award, 97 & Joseph V Giffuni Memorial Award, 98, 2001; Thomas & Margery Leighton Mem Award, Pastel Soc West Coast, 92; Bd Dirs Award, Pastel Soc Am, 93; Canson Talens Award, Pastel Soc Am, 95; Joseph V Giffuni Found Award, Pastel Soc Am, 99, Sauter-Margulies Award, 2000; Dick Blink Art Materials award, Pastel Soc Am, NY, 2002; Pastels Girault award, Pastel Soc Am, NY, 2004; Anita Kertzer award, Pastel Soc Canada, Pastel Soc Am, NY, 2005; Jack Richeson award, Pastel Soc Am, NY, 2006; Hall of Fame Honoree, Pastel Soc Am, NY, 2007; Pastel Soc NC, Pastel Soc Am, NY, 2008; Gold award, Internat Asn Pastel Societies, Calif, 2010, Bronze award, Ohio, 2010, Silver award, Masters Circle, NMex, 2011, Masters Circle Honoree, NMex, 2011, Award in Excellence, NMex, 2013; Kent award Asn award, Pastel Soc Am, NY, 2013; First Place Juror''s award, Pastel Soc Southern Calif Exhib, 2014; Savoir-Faire/Sennelier award, Pastel Soc Am, NY, 2015. *Bibliog:* Carole Katchen (auth), Ordinary people, great paintings, Artist's Mag, 9/87; Jacqueline M Pontello (auth), Sally Strand, Southwest Art Mag, 6/89; Martin Parsons (auth), The singular glory of pastel, Artspeak, 9/90; Georgina Kelnam (auth), Symbolic Gestures, Am Artists Mag, 9/99; Maggie Price (auth), Sally Strand, The Pastel Journal, May/2001, March/April, 2003; Susan Viebrock (auth), Artist Captures the Magical Interaction of Light Color, Telluride Daily Planet, 9/2004, Poster Embodies the Fun and Festivity, 6/2006; Jessica Canterbury (auth), The Best Advice I Ever Got, The Pastel Journal, 10/2012; Anne Hevener (auth), All Is Illuminated, Sally Strand, The Pastel Journal, 3/2014, Standing Out in the Crowd, 4/2014, Artists To Watch, Enid Wood by Sally Strand, 12/2015. *Mem:* Pastel Soc Am. *Media:* Pastel, Mixed Media. *Publ:* Auth, Pastels Masterclass, Harper Collins Publ, 93; Artist's Manual, Harper Collins Publ, 95; The Best of Pastel, 96 & The Best of Pastel 2, 98, Rockport Publ, Pure Color: Best of Pastel, North Light Publ, 2006; Guide to Materials and Techniques, Northlight, 96; The Artist's Guide, Darling Kindersley, 98; Barbara Benedetti Newton (auth), Pastel Drawing: Expert Answers to Questions Every Artist Asks (Art Answers), Barron's Educational Series, Hauppauge, NY, 2013; Katherine Tyrrell (auth), Sketching 365, Apple Press, London, UK, 2015, Drawing 365, North Light Books, Ohio, 2015; and others. *Dealer:* J Cacciola Galleries 501 W 23rd St New York NY 10011; Telluride Gallery of Fine Art 130 E Colorado Ave Telluride CO 81435; Diana Nelson Fine Art 435 Ocean Ave Laguna Beach CA 92651. *Mailing Add:* 33601 Moonsail Dr Dana Point CA 92629-4483

STRANGE, GEORGIA
EDUCATOR, SCULPTOR

Study: Ind Univ, BA (biological scis), 1973, MA (sci educ), 1977, MFA (sculpture), 1979. *Pos:* more than 100 juried and invitational exhibitions. *Teaching:* Chair, Art Dept, Centre Coll, Danville, Ky, 1979-83; interim dir, Henry Radford Hope Sch Fine Arts, Ind Univ, Bloomington, 2001, dir, 2002-06; prof art, Lamar Dodd Sch of Art, Univ Ga, Athens, 2006-, dir, 2006-2012; over 40 visiting lectures and presentations; national affiliate mem, SOHO20 Gallery, NY, 1990-. *Awards:* Ind Arts Comn Masters Fellowship; Sr Teaching Fellow, Ctr for Teaching and Learning, Univ Ga. *Mem:* Col Art Asn (bd dir 2011-). *Mailing Add:* University of Georgia Lamar Dodd School of Art - N301D 270 River Rd Athens GA 30602-7676

STRASEN, BARBARA ELAINE
PAINTER, CONCEPTUAL ARTIST

b Brooklyn, NY, Aug 12, 48. *Study:* Yale Univ Sch Art, summer 68; Carnegie-Mellon Univ, BFA, 69; Univ Calif, Berkeley, MFA, 71. *Work:* Nat Gallery Art, Washington; Best Products Collection, Richmond, Va; Callas, Powell, Rosenthal & Bloch Advert, Lafayette, Calif; Dorothy & Herman Vogel pvt collection, NY; Allen Mem Art Mus, Oberlin, Ohio. *Comn:* Visions LA 1992 (painting & videotape composite), Los Angeles Arts Recovery Grant. *Exhib:* Biennial Contemp Art, Whitney Mus Am Art, 75, AIR Gallery, 83, NY; About Face, Munic Art Gallery, Los Angeles, 96; Gallery Group, Adamar Fine Art, Miami, 96; Codpiece, Griffin Linton Gallery, Venice, Calif, 96; Light Abberations, Univ Tex San Antonio Art Gallery, 96; solo-exhibs, Angels Gate Cult Ctr, Los Angeles, 96, Forum Gallery, San Diego, Calif, 97, Galeria Soloblu, Milan, 98, Adamar Fine Art, Miami, Fla, 98 & Layers of Perception, Galerie Budapest, 98; Gallery Artists, Adamar Fine Art, Miami, Fla, 97; In Response, Marc Arranaga Contemp Art, Los Angeles, 97; New Art Los Angeles, Coast Contemp Art, Los Angeles, 97; Generations, AIR Gallery, NY, 97; House Party, Long Beach Mus Art, Calif, 98; Five Artists, Rico Gallery, Santa Monica, Calif, 98; Contempo-Italianate, Laband Gallery, Loyola Marymount Univ, Los Angeles, 98. *Pos:* Bd dir, Angels Gate Cult Ctr, San Pedro, 94-; asst cur, Hammer Mus, Univ Calif, Los Angeles, 98. *Teaching:* Instr visual arts, Cabrillo Col, Calif, 69-70, Southwestern Col, Calif, 72-75; asst prof visual arts, Univ Calif, San Diego, 75-80. *Awards:* Artist Fel Grant, Nat Endowment Arts, 75-76; Acad Senate Res Grant, Univ of Calif, San Diego, 76-77; Arts Recovery Grant, Los Angeles, 92-93. *Bibliog:* Lynn Crandell (auth), The Paintings of Barbara Strasen: Visual Metaphors for Leadership and the New Science, Southern Calif Bus J, 11/94; Peter Frank (auth), Solo Series: Works by Barbara Strasen, Marie Thiebault and Kathryn Tubbs, Long Beach Press-Telegram, 3/13/96; Robert L Pincus (auth), Layers on layers: Barbara Strasen, San Diego Union Tribune, 11/27/97. *Mem:* Inner City Arts (artist adv bd, currently); Angels Gate Cult Ctr, San Pedro, Calif (bd dir, 95-97); Los Angeles Cult Affairs Dept, Vis Art Div (panelist, 96). *Media:* Acrylic, Mixed; Photography. *Publ:* Auth, The Immigrants, J Los Angeles Inst Contemp Art, 75; Desert Notes, Santa Barbara Mus Art, 80; Women and Ecology, Heresies, winter, 82; Changing at Will Chapter of the Book Animal Art: The Animal as a conveyor and medium of art, Steirischer Herbst, Graz, Austria, 87. *Dealer:* Space Gallery 305 Main St Santa Monica CA. *Mailing Add:* 1724 S Pacific Ave San Pedro CA 90731

STRASSBERG, ROY I
CERAMIST, SCULPTOR
b Brooklyn, NY, Sept 18, 1950. *Study:* State Univ NY Col, Oswego, BA, 72; Univ Mich, MFA, 74. *Work:* Tenn State Mus, Nashville; SDak Mem Art Ctr, Brookings; Mint Mus Art, Charlotte, NC; Sourwood Regional Art Ctr, Jonesboro, Tenn. *Exhib:* J B Speed Mus, Louisville, Ky, 76; Mint Mus Art, Charlotte, NC, 76; Mus Contemp Crafts, NY, 78; Ft Wayne Mus Art, Ind, 80; Wichita Mus Art, Kans, 81; Plains Art Mus, Moorehead, Minn, 81; and others. *Teaching:* Fel ceramics, Univ Mich, 73-74; instr, Memphis State Univ, 74-76; asst prof, Minn State Univ, Mankato, 1976-2001, chair Art Dept, 1998-2001; prof art, Univ NC, Charlotte, 2001-, chair Art Dept, 2001-. *Awards:* Grand Prize, Miss River Crafts, Brooks Mem Art Gallery, 75; Second Prize, Midwest Craft Exhib, Rochester Art Ctr, Minn, 77; Purchase Award, Plains Art Mus, 79. *Mem:* Nat Coun Educ Ceramic Arts. *Media:* Clay. *Publ:* Contribr, Ceramics Monthly, 5/76-5/80 & Am Craft Mag, 8/76-12/81. *Dealer:* Cooper/Lynn Gallery 54 Seventh Ave S New York NY 10014; Robert L Kidd & Assocs 107 Townsend St Birmingham MI 48011

STRASSFIELD, CHRISTINA MOSSAIDES
MUSEUM DIRECTOR, CURATOR
b Bronx, NY, Nov 10, 1958. *Study:* Queens Col, BA (Art hist & Anthrop), 1980; Queens Col, MA (Art hist), 1985. *Collection Arranged:* Chuck Close: Up Close, Eric Fischl: A Cinematic View (curated). Guild Hall Mus, 1991; Roy Lichtenstein: Three Decades of Sculpture (curated), Guild Hall Mus, 1992; Lee Krasner, (curated), Guild Hall Mus, 1995; Cindy Sherman (curated), Guild Hall Mus, 2005; Elizabeth Peyton (curated), Guild Hall Mus, 2006. *Pos:* Cur, Guild Hall Mus, E Hampton, NY, 1990-1996; free lance art consultant/cur, 1996-2002; cur, Guild Hall Mus, E Hampton, NY, 2002-. *Teaching:* Adj assoc prof, Art Hist, Southampton Col, Long Island Univ, Southampton, NY, 1993-1989, Dowling Coll, 2010-. *Mem:* Art Table; Am Assoc of Mus; Long Island Mus Assoc (exec bd, 1990); Longhouse Found (art advisory bd). *Media:* Contemporary Artists. *Res:* Contemp Artists. *Publ:* Auth, Eric Fischl: A Cinematic View, Guild Hall Mus, 1991; auth, David Salle, Guild Hall Mus, 1994; auth, Dorothea Rockburne: The Transcendent Light of Geometry, Guild Hall Mus, 1995; auth, Lee Krasner: The Nature of the Body, Guild Hall Mus, 1995; auth, Audrey Flack: Daphne Speaks, Guild Hall Mus, 1996. *Mailing Add:* PO Box 1429 Water Mill NY 11976

STRASSHEIM, ANGELA
PHOTOGRAPHER
b Bloomfield, IA, 1969. *Study:* Mpls Coll Art & Design, BFA, 1995; Forensic & Biomedical Photog Cert, Metro-Dade Co, Forensic Imaging Bureau, Miami, Fla, 1997; Yale Univ, MFA, 2003. *Exhib:* Solo exhibs, Photog Thesis Exhib, Yale Univ, 2003; Black Milk, Marvelli Gallery, NYC, 2004; Factory Direct, Artspace Inc, New Haven, Conn, 2005; Traces & Omens, Noorderlicht Photofestival, Neth, 2005; Left Behind, Marvelli Gallery, 2005; reGeneration, Aperture Found, NYC, Marvelli Gallery, 2006; group exhibs, Whitney Biennial: Day for Night, Whitney Mus Am Art, NYC, 2006. *Pos:* Forensic photogr, Miami, Fla, NYC. *Awards:* Jerome Fel Emerging Artist Grant; Artist Initiative Grant, Minn State Arts Bd; Bush Found, Artist Fel, St Paul, Minn

STRATAKOS, STEVE JOHN
CRAFTSMAN, TAPESTRY ARTIST
b Chicago, Ill, Nov 26, 1954. *Study:* Italian Univ, Perugia, Italy, 74-75; Sch Art Inst Chicago, BFA, 77. *Work:* DuSable Mus African/American Art, Chicago, Ill; Chicago Public Libr, Chicago, Ill. *Comn:* Five banners, DeVry Tech Inst, Chicago, Ill, 85; 2 appliques, Brookfield Zoo, Brookfield, Ill, 87; bedspread, rug, wallpaper design, Univ Chicago, 87; 7 applique banners, Ruby Mem Hosp, Morgantown, WVa, 88. *Exhib:* New Horizons in Art, Chicago Pub Libr Cult Ctr, Chicago, Ill, 84; Artist as Quiltmaker, 84 & 86 and Fantasies in Fabric, 87, F A V A Gallery, Oberlin, Ohio; At the Table, Soc Arts & Crafts, Boston, Mass, 88; Manmade Quilts, Geneva Courthouse, Ill, 90. *Pos:* Banner designer & fabricator, Advert Flag & Banner, Chicago, Ill, 79-82; sr artist/designer, Brookfield Zoo, Ill, 83-90. *Bibliog:* Dimeta Karis (auth), First Prize Quilts, Simon & Schuster, 84; Roberick Kiracofe, The Quilt Digest 5, Quilt Digest Press, 87; The Guild, Sourcebook, Kraus Sikes, 87 & 88. *Media:* Fabric. *Dealer:* Sandy Friedman 107 Edinburgh South Cary NC 27511. *Mailing Add:* 1113 Robert E Lee Rd Austin TX 78704-2027

STRATMAN, DEBORAH
FILMMAKER
Study: Univ Ill, 1985-86; Sch of the Art Inst of Chicago, BFA, 1986-90; Calif Inst of the Arts, MFA, 1992-95. *Pos:* staff, audio visual dept, Mich & Adams, 1990-91; projectionist, The Film Ctr Art Inst Chicago, 1990-92; co-op & tech dir, Chicago Filmmakers, 1991-92; 35 mm projectionist, Cal Arts, Valencia, Calif, 1992-95; dir prodr, Ind Film/Video Production, Pythagoras Productions, 1995-2002. *Teaching:* vis instr, live action film/video Calif Inst Arts, Valencia, 2002; adj asst prof, dept film, video & new media Sch Art Inst, Chicago, 1998-2003; adj asst prof, art & archit dept Univ Ill, 2003-. *Awards:* Community Arts Assistance Grants, 1999, 2000, 2001; Cal Arts Deans Coun Grant, 2002; Guggenheim Fel, 2003. *Publ:* Prodr.: (films) My Alchemy, 1990, Upon a Time, 1991, A Letter, 1992, Possibilities, Dilemmas, 1992, the train from l.a. to l.a., 1992, In Flight: Day No. 2,128, 1993, Palimpsest, 1993, Waking, 1994, Iolanthe, 1995, On the Various Nature of Things, 1995 (Ann Arbor Film Festival, 1996), From Hetty to Nancy, 1997 (Athens International Film/Video Festival: best experimental, 1998), The BLVD, 1999 (Athens Inter Film/Video Festival: best documentary, 2000), Untied, 2001, In Order Not to Be Here, 2002 (THAW Film/Video Festival: best of festival, 2002, Chicago Underground Film Festival: best experimental, 2002, Film Festival: Gecko Award, 2002, Media City Film Festival: hon. mention, 2003, Ann Arbor Film Festival: best experimental & best narrative integrity, 2003), Meet Adiljan, 2003, Los Angeles Plays Itself, 2003, Kings of the Sky, 2004, The Magician's House, 2007. *Mailing Add:* 1958 Walnut St Chicago IL 60612-2406

STRATTON, JULIA
SCULPTOR
Study: Pa Acad Fine Arts, Philadelphia, Major: Sculpture, 1989-94; Johnson Atelier Sch & Technical Inst Sculpture, Mercerville, NJ, 1995-98; Int Cast Iron Conf, Mercerville, NJ, 1998-2002. *Exhib:* Solo exhibs include Woodmere Art Mus, Philadelphia, 1998, Fleisher Art Memorial, Philadelphia, 2002, Del Ctr Contemp Arts, Wilmington, Del, 2006-07; Group exhibs include In Her Voice: Self-Portraits by Women, Berman Mus Art, Collegeville, Pa, 1998-99; Exhibitions & Gallery Affiliation, Gallery 71, New York, 2001-04; Figurative Works from the Factory, John Michael Kohler Arts Ctr, Sheboygan, Wis, 2006; Size Matters, Woman Made Gallery, Chicago, 2006; Art of the State, State Mus Pa, Harrisburg, Pa, 2007; Invitational Exhib, Evearts Gallery, Haddonfield, NJ, 2007; Invitational Exhib, Gallery in the Garden, Orwigsburg, Pa, 2007. *Awards:* Purchase Prize, Fel Pa Acad Fine Arts, 2002-03; Independence Found Fel Arts, 2001, 2007; Dene M Louchheim Fel, 2002; Sculpture Award, State Mus Pa, 2007; Ludwig Vogelstein Found Grant, 2007; George Sugarman Found Grant, 2007; E Avery Draper Award, Del Ctr Contemp Arts, 2008

STRAUS, SANDY
PAINTER
b Omaha, Nebr, Mar 15, 48. *Study:* Art Inst Chicago, BFA, 76. *Comn:* Jessica Hahn (mural), The Tunnel, NY, 88; Billy Boggs (billboards), Mars Steel Corp, NY, 88; Clarence Darrow (billboard), D Fiedler, 89; Salmon Rushdie (poster), C Carson, NY, 90; Prejudice, Beat It Billboards, W Giles, NY, 93. *Exhib:* Nat Gallery Mod Art, New Delhi, India; NY State Mus, Albany; Documenta Kessel, Ger; Mus De Art Contemporanee, Sao Paulo, Brazil; Solo exhibs, Smart Gallery, Univ Chicago, 76, M Deson, Chicago, 80, 55 Mercer, NY, 82, Germans Van Eck, NY, 83, Sensory Evolution, 86-87, Air Gallery, NY, 95 & St Peter's Church, NY, 96; I Arose, Nat Arts Club, NY, 98; Rockford Mus, Ill; Mass Mus Contemp Art; Nat Arts Club, 2004-2005; Gallery 128, New York, NY, 2004-2010; Ellenville Mus & Libr, NY, 2006; Byrdcliff, Woodstock, NY, 2007. *Collection Arranged:* Nat Arts Club; Actors Inst; Mars Steel Corp; John Bergman, Jean Louis Bourgeois, Will & Elena Barnet, Jerry Wenzel, Anthony Cueto, Trudy Craney Germans, Blake Benton & Bretta Lundell. *Bibliog:* Newsweek Mag, 11/24/86; Sharon Churcher (auth), Art imitates death, Reuters Ltd, 1/14/88; Art & Artists Cover, Vol 17, 1/89. *Mem:* Artists Fel. *Media:* Oil, Charcoal, Pastel. *Publ:* (photos), France Soir, NY Post, NY Times Art Forum, Arts. *Mailing Add:* 124 Thompson St Apt C New York NY 10012-3131

STRAUSS, MATTHEW & IRIS
COLLECTORS
Pos: Co-founder, Dow Divas, 1996; mem, bd dirs, San Diego Opera, 1990-, pres, 2002-05, chmn, 2009- & life dir, 2009-; arts and cult liason, Mayor of San Diego; mem, exec comt, Comn Arts and Cult, San Diego. *Awards:* Named one of Top 200 Collectors, ARTnews mag, 2009-13; Gold Star Award, San Diego Performing Arts League; Champions of Opera Award, San Diego Opera; Living Legacy Award, Women's Int; Woman of Dedication Award, Salvation Army. *Collection:* Second-generation postwar and contemporary art. *Mailing Add:* San Diego Opera 18th Fl Civic Ctr Plz 1200 Third Ave San Diego CA 92101

STRAUSS, ZOE
PHOTOGRAPHER
b Philadelphia, Pa, 1970. *Work:* Philadelphia Mus Art. *Exhib:* One-women shows: Under I-95, S Philadelphia, 2001; The Ramp Project, Inst Contemp Art, Philadelphia, 2006; Whitney Biennial: Day for Night, Whitney Mus Am Art, NYC, 2006; This is America: Visions of the American Dream, Centraal Mus, Utrecht, Holland, 2006. *Pos:* Found, Philadelphia Pub Art Project, 1995; Mem advert comt, Leeway Found, Philadelphia. *Teaching:* Instr artist, Rosenbach Mus & Libr, Philadelphia. *Awards:* Pew Visual Arts Fel, 2005. *Mailing Add:* 1313 Dickinson St Philadelphia PA 19147-6217

STRAWN, BERNICE I
SCULPTOR
b Vallejo, Calif. *Study:* Univ Calif, Berkeley, BA, MA, 52. *Work:* Adrian Col, Mich; Western Mich Univ, Kalamazoo; McDonald's Corp, Chicago, Ill; Kaiser Permanente Corp. *Comn:* Bas relief, Christ on the Mountain Church, Denver, Colo, 81; crucifix, St Michael's Church, Aurora, Colo, 82; crucifix, Holy Family cast bronze, life size, St Francis & Mother Cabrini relief, St Joseph's Church, Golden, Colo, 85. *Exhib:* Nat Religious Art Exhib, Nat Cathedral, Washington, DC, 83; Colorado 3D Invitational, Arvada Ctr, Denver, 85; Kalamazoo Inst Art, Mich, 87; one-person shows, Mesa Coll Gallery, Grand Junction, Colo, 90 & Western State Col, Gunnison, Colo, 92; two-person show, Sangre de Cristo Art Ctr, Pueblo, Colo, 91, Western Mich Univ Space Gallery, Kalamazoo, 95; and others. *Teaching:* Art video instr, Adams City Sch Dist #12, Northglenn, Colo, 80- 87. *Media:* Wood, Bronze. *Publ:* New Lines, Portfolio of Drawings with Mel Strawn, Kalamazoo Press, 57. *Dealer:* Clay & Fiber Taos NM; Inkfish Denver CO. *Mailing Add:* c/o William Havu Gallery 1040 Cherokee St Denver CO 80204

STRAWN, MARTHA (A)
PHOTOGRAPHER, EDUCATOR
b Washington, Apr 29, 1945. *Study:* Fla State Univ, Tallahassee, BA, 67; Brooks Inst Photog, Santa Barbara, Calif, basic tech cert, 68; Ohio Univ, Athens, MFA, 70. *Work:* Indira Gandhi Nat Ctr Arts, New Delhi, India; Art Mus, Princeton Univ, NJ; Southeastern Ctr Contemp Art & RJ Reynolds Co, Winston-Salem, NC; St Petersburg Mus Art, Fla; Mint Mus Art, Charlotte, NC. *Comn:* Photog, NC Gov Bus Awards Comn, 82. *Exhib:* Fulbright Art Exhibition, Woodrow Wilson Ctr, Smithsonian Inst, Washington, 86; Southeast Seven 10, Southeastern Ctr Contemp Art, Winston-Salem, NC, 87; solo exhib, Sol Mednick Gallery, Univ Arts, Philadelphia, 87; Threshold Diagrams of India, Richard F Brush Art Gallery, St Lawrence Univ, Canton, NY, 96; Alligators, Prehistoric Presence in the Am Landscape, Mint Mus Art & Discovery Pl

Sci Mus, Charlotte, NC, 97; Artist as Activist: Ecological Concerns in the '90's, Wellington B Gray Gallery, Sch Art, East Carolina Univ, Greenville, NC, 97; The Swamp: On the Edge of Eden, The Samuel P Harn Mus Art, Univ Fla, Gainesville, Fla, 2000-2001; After the Dinosaurs, The Science Mus Minn, St Paul, 2000-2001; The Swamp: On the Edge of Eden, Cummer Mus Art & Gardens, Jacksonville, Fla, 2001; Peter C Bunnell Collection Exhib, Princeton Art Mus, NJ, 2002; When Crocodiles Ruled, The Milwaukee Co Zoo, WI, 2003, Carnegie Mus Nat History, Pittsburgh, PA, 2001-2002, San Diego Mus Nat History, Calif, 2002, Oregon Mus Sci and Indust, Portland, Ore, 2002, Nat Geographic Soc Mus, Washington, DC, 2001. *Pos:* Photogr, Goleta Gazette, Calif, 67-68. *Teaching:* Instr art, Fla State Univ, Tallahassee, 69-70; asst prof & mem grad fac, NE La Univ, Monroe, 70-71; courtesy prof, Univ Fla, Gainesville, 85; prof & women's studies fac, Univ NC, Charlotte, 71-2004. *Awards:* Photogr fel, Nat Endowment Arts, Washington, 80; Sr res fel, Fulbright, India, 84; Individual Artist Fel, 10th Ann SE7 Southeastern Ctr Contemp Art/RJ Reynolds, 86-87. *Bibliog:* The New York Art Review, Third Edition: Artist Profile, American References Publishing Corporation, Chicago, Ill, 88; Images from India Portfolio: Untitled, 1986, Chromogenic color print, 16x20 inches, Exploring Color Photography, Robert Hirsch, Brown, and Benchmark Publishers, page 109, 2nd ed, 89; Transient Acts and Permanent Records of Female Mark Making: Martha Strawn Documents the Art of Indian Threshold Drawing, English Knowles, ARTVU, pages 28-31, Vol 5, No 2, Fall, 91; Nicholas Drake (auth), Indian Culture Depicted in Halsey Gallery Exhibit (review), The Post and Courier, Charleston, SC, 9/1995; Alligators, Prehistoric Presence in the American Landscape, Forecasts, Publishers' Weekly, 3/1997; Peter N. Spotts, Know Your Neighbors Well, The Christian Science Monitor, books from University Presses, Section B1, page 1, 4/1997; Elaine Morgan (auth), Gators Lure Author Across the Country, The Tampa Tribune Newspaper, 1/1999; William E. Parker (auth), Martha Strawn, Alligators, Prehistoric Presence in the American Landscape, EXPOSURE (Photographic Arts Prof Jour), Vol 32.1, pages 90-91, 9/1999; and others. *Mem:* Ctr Am Places, Harrisonburg, Va (bd trustees, 93-); Friends Photog, San Francisco (bd trustees, 86-94 & exec bd mem, 88-90); Soc Photog, Educ (nat bd dir, 77-85, chmn, 82-83, 83-85 & adv bd liaison, 85-86); Light Factory, Inc (non-profit photog orgn), Charlotte, NC (co-founder, 73, dir, 74-76, 77-78, bd, 78-79, 82-85, chmn 84-85 & adv bd, 88-); Fulbright Alumni Asn, 84-. *Media:* Photography. *Specialty:* Contemporary Art. *Publ:* Coauth (with Jane Gibson, PhD, J Whitfield Gibbons PhD & LeRoy Overstreet), Alligators, Prehistoric Presence in the American Landscape, Johns Hopkins Univ Press (in prep), Baltimore, Md, 97; and others. *Dealer:* Hodges Taylor Gallery, Charlotte, NC. *Mailing Add:* PO Box 936 Davidson NC 28036-8792

STRAWN, MELVIN NICHOLAS
PAINTER, SCULPTOR
b Boise, Idaho, Aug 5, 1929. *Study:* Chouinard Art Inst; Los Angeles Co Art Inst; Jepson Art Inst; Calif Coll Arts & Crafts, BFA & MFA. *Work:* Columbus Mus Art; Antioch Col; Colo State Univ; Colo Springs Fine Arts Ctr; Western Mich Univ; Ohio State Univ; Ottowa Univ; Colo Hist Soc; Sangre de Cristo Community Center; Univ Denver; plus many corporate & pvt collections. *Comn:* Environ design (sculpture), Ottawa Col, Kans, 72. *Exhib:* Colo State Univ Centennial Exhib, 70; Cedar City Nat, Utah, 72; I-25 Artists Alliance, Colorado Springs Fine Arts Ctr, 72; Colorado Springs Biennial, Colorado Springs Fine Arts Ctr, 81; Major Retrospective, Denver Central Libr, Colo, 2006; and others. *Teaching:* Instr art, Midwestern Univ, Mich State Univ, Antioch Col & Univ Denver, 56-72; chmn dept art, Antioch Col, 66-69 & Western Mich Univ, 85-88; prof & dir, Sch Art, Univ Denver, 69-85, emer prof, 85-. *Awards:* First Purchase Award, Centennial Exhibs Colo State Univ, 70. *Bibliog:* Nathan Goldstein (auth), The Art of Responsive Drawing, third ed, Prentice Hall, 84; Harold Linton (auth), Color Consulting-A Survey of International Color Design, Van Nostrand Reinhold, New York, 91. *Media:* Oil, All; Computer-Direct Digital Prints. *Interests:* Art theory, digital technology & environmental studies. *Publ:* Transitions (Book-traditional to digital art), 98. *Dealer:* Sandra Phillips Gallery Denver Colo; Trembling Aspen Gallery Buena Vista Colo. *Mailing Add:* 8905 Hwy 285 Salida CO 81201

STREETER, TAL
SCULPTOR, WRITER
b Oklahoma City, Okla, Aug 1, 1934. *Study:* Univ Kans, BFA & MFA; Colorado Springs Fine Arts Ctr, with Robert Motherwell; Colo Col; with Seymour Lipton, 3 yrs. *Work:* Mus Mod Art, NY; San Francisco Mus Art; Corcoran Gallery Art, Washington; National Mus Contemp Art, Seoul, Korea; Newark Mus, NJ; Storm King Art Ctr, Mountainville, NY; Wadsworth Athenaeum, Hartford, Conn; Neuberger Mus, Purchase, NY; Smith Coll Mus, North Hampton, Mass; Hood Mus, Hanover, H; Milwaukee Art Ctr, Wis. *Comn:* High Mus Art, Mem Arts Ctr, Atlanta, Ga; Ark Art Ctr, Little Rock, 70; Hong-Ik Univ, Seoul, Korea, 74; Morris Col, Morristown, NJ, 81; Libr for the Blind, Trenton, NJ, 81-83; Kaywon Coll Art & Design, 91; Total Cont Art Mus, Seoul, Korea, 93; Il-San Lake Park Sculpture, Seoul, Korea, 96. *Exhib:* Whitney Ann, 65, NY World's Fair, 65; Cool Art & Highlights of the Season, Aldrich Mus, 68 & 70; Am Sculpture, Sheldon Art Mus, 70; Drawings by Sculptors, Corcoran Gallery, 78; Sky Art, Mass Inst Technol, 80 & 81; Bruckner Festival, Linz, Austria, 82; Minimal Line, Milton Avery Mus, Bard Coll, NY, 85; Dayton Art Inst, Ohio, 90; Total Mus, Seoul, Korea, 93; Like a Shadow on the Sky, Fairfield Art Ctr, Calif, 97-98; Indianapolis Art Mus, 98; Art Kites, Hudson River Mus, Yonkers, NY; Wiesman FA Mus, Minneapolis, Minn, 2004; Solo exhibs, Amel Gallery, NY, 66-67, Minami Gallery, Tokyo, 71, Neuberger Mus, Purchase, NY, 77, Univ Ky Mus Art, 82, Total Mus, Seoul, Korea, 93, Longhouse Reserve, East Hampton, NY, 2000, Am Craft Mus, NY, 2001, Crissy Field, San Francisco, Calif, 2001, Smithsonian Nat Air & Space Mus, Washington, DC, 2003, Streckler/Nelson Gallery, Manhattan, Kans, 2006, Beach Mus, State Univ Kans, 2011, and many others. *Collection Arranged:* cur, Art of the Japanese Kite, Japan Soc, NY, 80; co-cur, Art That Flies, Dayton Art Inst, OH, 90. *Pos:* Cur, Feather on the Wind, EPCOT Ctr, Orlando, Fla, 85; Ice & Air Show, Lake George, NY, 90; master artist & dir, Wind Art: Beyond Modern Kites, Atlantic Ctr Arts, New Smyrna, Fla, 2003. *Teaching:* vis artist-in-residence, Dartmouth Coll, Hanover, NH, 63 & Sun Valley Ctr for Arts, Idaho, 86; vis artist, Univ NC, Greensboro, 70 & 72-73 & Penland Sch Crafts, NC, 74-76; Fulbright prof, Seoul, Korea, 71; vis lectr, US Info Serv, Japan, 72; adj prof, Queen's Coll, 73; founder, prof Sculpture/III-D/media dept, Sch of Art & Design, State Univ NY Col Purchase, 71-2001, prof emer, 2001-; assoc fel & prof, Ctr Advan Visual Studies, Mass Inst Technol, 84-; Sun Valley Ctr Arts, Idaho, 86; prof, Univ NY, Purchase; assoc prof & fel, advan vis studies, Mass Inst Technol, 84-93. *Awards:* State Univ NY Int Studies Grant, Japan, 69; Collaborations in Art, Sci, & Technol, New State Coun Arts Grant, 78; Artpark Artist, Lewisboro, NY, 78; Kanaan of the Year, Art, Lawrence Joun World, 71. *Bibliog:* G A Ruda (auth), Kitesmanship: Tal Streeter, Craft Horizons, 74; Carter Ratcliff (auth), Tal Streeter: Beyond absolutes, Arts Mag, 77; article, Sky painting, Newsweek, 8/80; Nam Jun Palk (coauth), Sky, Moon, Dragons, Kites and Smiles: Am American Artist in Asia, 93; Susan Boetger (auth), Endless Columns, Sculpt Magazine, 94; Earth, Sky, and Sculpture, Storm King Art Ctr, Mountainville, NY, 2000; Large Scale Sculpture, Archit monographs, Princeton Univ, 2010. *Media:* Welded Metal, Photography, Glass, Paper. *Specialty:* Fine Art. *Interests:* Street photography. *Publ:* Heavenly Humors: The Modern Kite, Am Craft, 79; Art That Flys, Dayton Art Inst Press, 90; A Kite Journey Through India, Weatherhill, 96; The Philosopher's Kite, 2002; and others. *Dealer:* Gallerie Bhak, Seoul, Korea

STREETMAN, JOHN WILLIAM, III
ADMINISTRATOR
b Marion, NC, Jan 19, 1941. *Study:* Western Carolina Univ, AB; Lincoln Col, Oxford Univ, cert. *Collection Arranged:* The Eye and The Heart: Watercolors of John Stuart Ingle, 87-88; Two Am Realists: William Bailey and DeWitt Hardy, 73 & 74; Simplicity, A Grace: Jacob Maentel in Indiana, 89; Beverly Hallam: The Flower Paintings, 90. *Pos:* Founding dir, Jewett Creative Arts Ctr, South Berwick, Maine, 66-70; exec dir, Polk Pub Mus, Lakeland, Fla, 70-75; dir, Mus Arts & Sci, Evansville, Ind, 75-. *Awards:* Mayor's Arts Award, Evansville, Ind, 90. *Mem:* Am Asn Mus; Midwestern Mus Conf. *Mailing Add:* 411 SE Riverside Dr Evansville IN 47713

STREETT, TYLDEN WESTCOTT
SCULPTOR, INSTRUCTOR
b Baltimore, Md, Nov 28, 1922. *Study:* Johns Hopkins Univ; St John's Coll; Md Inst Coll Art, with Sidney Waugh & Cecil Howard, BFA & MFA; also asst to Lee Lawrie; Rinehart Sch Sculpture. *Work:* Bronze, John O'Donnel; bronze, Firefighter's Mem; incl the pvt collections of Mr & Mrs WM Downey, Mr & Mrs George Udel, Ms Jody Albright, Mr & Mrs Kurt Lederer, Mr & Mrs Lawrence Holdridge. *Comn:* Medal, Johns Hopkins Univ; Kuwait Embassy; Eisenhower's Class Mem; GBMC, Lifesize garden figure; Kirk in the Hills; Md State Courthouse; Nat Cathedral; portraits, St. John's Coll, Annapolis, Md. *Exhib:* Corcoran Gallery Art, Washington, DC, 60; Baltimore Mus Art, 69. *Teaching:* Figurative sculpture, Md Inst Coll Art, Baltimore, 59-, dir, Grad Studies, 66-72; instr sculpture, Jewish Community Ctr, Baltimore, 63-65; primary prof, Figurative Sculpture; prof of figurative sculpture, Maryland Inst Coll Art. *Awards:* John Gregory Award, 62; Union Independent Coll Art Grant, 71; Ford Found Grant, 80; Medal of Hon, Md Inst Coll Art, 2009. *Mem:* Fel, Nat Sculpture Soc; Artists Equity Asn; Sculptors Inc. *Media:* Bronze, Terracotta, Wood, Stone. *Interests:* history of sculpture, bronzes, carvings, plastics and flying, playing jazz music. *Publ:* Auth, Plaster Casting Using a Waste Mold (film), 70

STRICK, JEREMY
MUSEUM DIRECTOR, CURATOR
Study: Univ Calif, Santa Cruz, BA (hist art), 1977. *Collection Arranged:* Nat Gallery Art, Washington, DC, 1987 & 1990-96; NY Interpreted Joseph Stella and Alfred Stieglitz, Nat Gallery Art, 1987; A Century of Modern Sculpture The Patsy and Raymond Nasher Collection, 1987; Twentieth Century Art Selections for the Tenth Anniversary of the East Building, 1987; Mark Rothko The Spirit Myth, 1990-95; Milton Avery, 1990; St Louis Art Mus, Mo, 1993, 1994 & 1996; Brice Marden A Painting, Drawings, Prints, St Louis Art Mus, 1993; Currents 58 Susan Crile The Fires of War, 1994; Currents 60 Jerald Ieans, 1994; Masterworks from Stuttgar The Romantic Age in German Art, 1995; others. *Pos:* Asst cur 20th century art, Nat Gallery Art, Washington, 1986-89, assoc cur, 1989-93, acting cur, 1992-93; cur, Nat Sculpture Garden proj, 1989-93; cur mod art, St Louis Art Mus, Mo, 1993-96; Frances & Thomas Dittmer cur twentieth century painting & sculpture, Art Inst Chicago, 1996-99; dir, Los Angeles Mus Contemp Art, 1999-2008 & Nasher Sculpture Ctr, Dallas, 2008-. *Teaching:* Lectr, St Louis Art Mus, 1997, Allen Mem Art Mus, Oberlin Art Col, 1997, Art Club Chicago, 1997-1998, Art Inst Chicago, 1998. *Awards:* Samuel H Kress Found Instnl Fel, 1983-85; Mrs Giles Whiting Found Fel, 1985-86. *Bibliog:* James Bishop (auth), St Louis Post-Dispatch, 2/94. *Publ:* contrib auth Works by Antonie-Louis Barye in the Collection of the Fogg art Mus Vol IV, 1982. *Mailing Add:* Nasher Sculpture Center 2001 Flora St Dallas TX 75201

STRICKLER, SUSAN ELIZABETH
CURATOR, HISTORIAN
b Baltimore, Md, Jan 23, 1952. *Study:* Ecole du Louvre, Paris, 1st yr cert, 72; Mt Holyoke Col, BA, 73; Univ Del, MA, 77. *Collection Arranged:* John Ritto Penniman 1782-1841: An Ingenious New England Artist, 1982; John Frederick Kensett: An Am Master, 1985; Am Traditions in Watercolor: The Worcester Art Mus Collection (with catalog), 1987; Heritage of the Land: Contrasts in Native Am Art & Life, 1994; Impressionism Transformed: The Paintings of Edmund C Tasbell (with catalog), 2001; Andrew Wyeth: Early Watercolors (with catalog), 2004. *Pos:* Res assoc, Toledo Mus Art, Ohio, 1978-79; spec proj dir, Va Mus, Richmond, 1979-80; cur Am art, Worcester Art Mus, Mass, 1981-95, dir curatorial affairs, 1987-95; dir, Currier Mus Art, Manchester, NH, 1995-. *Mem:* Am Asn Mus Dirs; Am Asn Mus; New Eng Mus Asn. *Res:* American painting, especially eighteenth & nineteenth centuries. *Specialty:* American and European Art. *Publ:* auth, American paintings (catalog), Toledo Mus Art, 1979; ed, John Frederick Kensett; An American Master, Worcester Art Mus & W W Norton, 1985; auth, American Portrait Miniatures: The Worcester Art Mus

Collection, 1989; co-auth, The Second Wave: American Abstraction of the 1930s & 1940s: Selections from the Penny & Elton Yasuna Collection, 1991; auth, ed, Impressionism Transformed: The Paintings of Edmund C Tarbell, 2001; auth, Andrew Wyeth, Early Watercolors, 2004. *Mailing Add:* Currier Museum Art 201 Myrtle Way Manchester NH 03104

STRIKER, CECIL L
HISTORIAN, EDUCATOR
b July 15, 1932. *Study:* Oberlin Col, AB, 56; Inst Fine Arts, NY Univ, MA, 60, PhD, 68. *Hon Degrees:* Univ Pa, Hon MA, 73. *Pos:* Field archeologist, Dumbarton Oaks Ctr Byzantine Studies, 66-80; adj prof, Sabanci Univ, 2004-. *Teaching:* From instr to asst prof medieval art, Vassar Col, 62-68; from assoc prof to prof Byzantine & Medieval art & arch, Univ Pa, 68-2006, chmn dept art hist, 79-86, prof emeritus, 2006-. *Mem:* Coll Art Asn Am; Archeol Inst Am; Am Res Inst Turkey (pres, 78-84); Coun Am Overseas Res Ctrs (chmn, 81-84); corresp mem Ger Archaeol Inst; Koldewey Gesellschaft. *Res:* Byzantine architecture and archeology; medieval architecture. *Publ:* Coauth, Work at Kalenderhane Camii in Istanbul: Preliminary reports, Dumbarton Oaks Papers, 67-74; auth, The Myrelaion (Bodrum Camii) in Istanbul, Princeton Univ Press, 82; coauth, Tree ring dating in the Aegean & neighboring regions, J Field Archeol, 84 & 88; ed, Architectural Studies in Memory of Richard Krautheimer, Philipp-von-Zabern, Mainz, 96; coauth & ed, Kalenderhane in Istanbul: The Buildings, Philipp-von-Zabern, Mainz, 97; and others; The Excavations, Phillip-von-Zebern, Mainz, 2007; coauth, Quantitative Indications about Church Building in Constantinople, Architecture, 2008. *Mailing Add:* Univ Pa Dept Art Hist Philadelphia PA 19104-6208

STROKER, ROBERT T
ADMINISTRATOR, EDUCATOR
Study: Mich State Univ, BM (music performance), BM (music educ), PhD (music educ); Pa State Univ, MM (music performance); Harvard Univ, Certificate in LEadership and Management in Higher Educ. *Pos:* Prin percussionist, Lansing Mich Symphony, formerly; dir, Meadows Percussion Ensemble, 1993-2002; guest clinician, conductor, adjudicator, Percussive Arts Soc Internat Conf, World Asn of Symphonic Bands and Col Band Directors Nat Asn; guest conductor and consultant, Conservatory Band of Sao Paolo, Brazil. *Teaching:* Assoc dean, head music educ, interim chair Divisions of Music and Dance, Meadows Sch of Arts, Southern Methodist Univ, formerly; dean, Boyer Col Music and Dance, 2002-, prof music educ, 2002-, interim dean Tyler Sch Art, Temple Univ, 2009-2012, dean, 2012-, vice provost for the Arts, 2011-, dean, division of theater, film, and media arts, 2012-. *Awards:* Advocacy award, American Music Therapy Asn; Pa State Univ Outstanding Alumni Achievement award; Internat Musiktage Vocklabruck award; Singing City's 60th Year Celebration award. *Publ:* Published extensively on the topics of music education and pedagogy; co-auth, The Professional Music Educator, 2010. *Mailing Add:* Temple University Office of the Provost 1330 Polett Walk Philadelphia PA 19122

STROKOSCH, CAITLIN
DIRECTOR
Study: Columbia Coll of Chgo, BA (music performance); Roosevelt Univ, MA (musicology). *Pos:* Gen mgr, His Majesties Clerkes, formerly; exec dir, CUBE, Chgo, formerly; grants panelist, Nat Endowment for Arts, The Joyce Found, RI State Coun on the Arts; joined, Alliance of Artists Communities, 2002, exec dir, 2008-. *Mailing Add:* Alliance of Artists Communities 255 S Main St Providence RI 02903

STROMSDORFER, DEBORAH ANN
PAINTER, GRAPHIC ARTIST
b Aurora, Ill, Dec 18, 1961. *Study:* Northern Ill Univ, BFA (painting), 84, MFA (drawing), 89. *Work:* Arlington Heights Mem Libr, Ill; Schaumburg Township Libr, Ill; Kelley-Williamson Corp & Swed Am Hosp, Rockford, Ill; Sycamore Munic Hosp, Ill; Alexian Brothers Medical Ctr, Elk Grove Village, Ill. *Comn:* Triptych (44"h x 60"w) Lasalle Consult Ltd, 89; Growth (3 panels), Rockford Clinic, Ill, 91. *Exhib:* 25th Ann Exhib, San Bernardino Co Mus, Redlands, Calif, 90; Women Artists of Am, Chautauqua Art Asn Galleries, NY, 90; Inter Art Exhib, Helio Galleries, NY, 91; 6th Inter Small Works Exhib, Del Bello Gallery, Toronto, Can, 91; Nat Art Competition Winners, UND, Witmer Art Ctr, Grand Forks, NDak, 92; N Am Invitational, Mus Without Walls Inter, Bemus Point, NY, 92; Gray Gallery, Quincy Coll, Ill, 92; solo exhibs, Clack Art Ctr, Alma, Mich, 92, Schaumburg Prairie Ctr Arts, Ill, 93 & Tullibody Fine Arts Gallery, Ala State Univ, Montgomery, 93; Phoebus Abroad, Phoebus Gallery, Athens, Greece, 93; Stateline Vicinity Exhib, Rockford Art Mus, Ill, 94; Union League Club Chicago, 95; Village Gallery, Rockford, 96; Ill Artisans Shop Chicago, 2000; Wachovia Securities, Rockford, 2003; Sedona Arts Ctr, 2014. *Pos:* Graphic designer, Northern Ill Univ, DeKalb, Ill, 83-87 & Univ Ill Coll Med, Rockford, Ill, 87-90. *Teaching:* Art instr design/drawing, Rock Valley Coll, Rockford, Ill, 90-98 & 2001-2002. *Awards:* Best of Show, Rockford Vicinity Exhib, Gallery Ten, 88; Best of Show, Art Ctr '91, Elk Grove Village, IL, Talman Home Fed, 91; Best of Show, 2nd Ann Mem Juried Exhib, Colored Pencil Soc Am, Chicago, 96; People's Choice Award, Bernina Univ Fashion Show & Competition, Long Beach, Calif, 99. *Bibliog:* Bebe Raupe (auth), 1986 Floral Competition Winners (2nd place), Artist's Mag, 12/86; The Best of Colored Pencil Two, Rockport Publ, 94; Vicki Anderson (auth) Sew News Mag, 12/99. *Mem:* Colored Pencil Soc Am; Chicago Artists' Coalition; Nat Asn Women Artists; Sedona Arts Ctr. *Media:* Colored Pencil, Wearable Art. *Interests:* Theater, Landscape Design, & Sewing. *Mailing Add:* 765 E Cottontail Run Cottonwood AZ 86326

STRONG, BEVERLY JEAN See Jean, Beverly Strong

STRONG, LESLIE (SUTTER)
SCULPTOR, CERAMIST
b Newport News, Va, Dec 1, 1953. *Study:* Skidmore Col, Saratoga Springs, NY, BS(art), 76; Syracuse Univ, NY (Univ Fel), MFA, 85. *Work:* President's Collection, Skidmore Col, NY; Roland Gibson Collection, State Univ NY, Potsdam; Richard Brush Art Gallery, St Lawrence Univ, Canton, NY; North Ga Coll Art; also pvt collection of Dr Ralph Lillford, London. *Comn:* Exterior wall sculptures, State Univ NY, Cobleskill, 82. *Exhib:* Solo exhib, Work in Transition, St Lawrence Univ, NY, 85; Clay Nat, Upton Hall Gallery, State Univ NY, Buffalo, 85; Artist's Cent NY, 89 & 91; The Clay's the Thing, St Lawrence Univ, 93; Northern Clay Invitational, Potsdam Col, State Univ NY, 96. *Pos:* Consult & in-house conservator, Brush Gallery, St Lawrence Univ, Canton, NY, 85-88. *Teaching:* Art teacher, Burnt Hill Jr High Sch, NY, 81-83; instr, Skidmore Col, 84-88 & Potsdam High Sch, 87-. *Awards:* Hon Mention, AEIOU Exhib, Massena, NY, 86; Roland Gibson Award, N Co Regional Exhib, Gibson Gallery, Potsdam, NY, 88; First Prize, Small Sculpture Exhib, NGeorgia Col, Delongena, Ga, 90. *Mem:* Coll Art Asn. *Media:* Clay, Bronze. *Publ:* Auth, Handformed Ceramics, Zakin. *Dealer:* Sodarco Gallery Montreal PQ Can. *Mailing Add:* 11 New St Norwood NY 13668

STRONG-CUEVAS, ELIZABETH
SCULPTOR, KINETIC ARTIST
b St Germain en Laye, France, Jan 22, 1929; US citizen. *Study:* Vassar Coll, Sarah Lawrence Coll, AB, 52; Art Students League, 63-67 studied with John Hovannes, 63-73, with Toto Meylan, 75-83. *Work:* Bruce Mus, Greenwich, Conn; Heckscher Mus, Huntington, NY; Guild Hall Mus, East Hampton, NY; Grounds for Sculpture, Hamilton, NJ; Ann Norton Sculpture Garden, West Palm Beach, Fla; And others. *Comn:* Obelisk & Head V, comn by Evan Frankel, East Hampton, NY, 83; wall relief, comn by Mr & Mrs Lewis Cullman, New York. *Exhib:* Solo exhibs, Lee Ault Gallery, New York, 77-78, Tower Gallery, Southampton, NY, 80, Iolas Jackson Gallery, New York, 83-85, Guild Hall, East Hampton, NY, 85, Grounds for Sculpture, Hamilton, NJ, 99, Vassar Coll, Poughkeepsie, NY, 2006 & Island Weiss Gallery, New York, 2007, Premonitions in Retrospect, Guild Hall Mus, East Hampton, 2012; Group exhibs, The Art Show, Femgarten Galleries, New York, 90; Marisa del Re Biennale III & IV, Marisa del Re Gallery, Monte Carlo, Monaco, 91 & 93; Mirrors, Parrish Mus, Southampton, NY, 94; Fall/Winter 1994-95 Exhib, Grounds for Sculpture, Hamilton, NJ, 94-95; Arch I, Arch II, Set II, Shidoni, Tessaque, NMex, 95-96; Ann Norton Sculpture Gardens, West Palm Beach, Fla, 2006; Wyzwood Art Fair, Black and White Gallery, Miami, Fla, 2012; Southampton Cultural Ctr, 2012; and others. *Awards:* 1984 Award, 46th Ann Mem Exhib, William Woolfenden, with Guild Hall Mus, East Hampton, NY, 1984. *Bibliog:* Dorothy Kosinski (auth), Ancient Visions Through Modern Eyes (catalog) Bruce Mus, Greenwich, Conn, 84; Alexander Russo (auth), Profiles on Women Artists, Univ Publ Am Inc, 85; Robert Becker (dir), Ancient Visions Through Modern Eyes (video), 88; Christopher French (auth), The dichotomy of the profile (exhib catalog), Marisa del Re Gallery, 92; Lana Pih Jokel (video), 96; Brooke Barrie (auth), Contemporary Outdoor Sculpture, Rockport Publ Inc, Gloucester, Mass, 99; Strong-Cuevas Sculpture (video-DVD by Laura Jokel), 2002; Donald Kuspit (auth), Sculptural Dialectic, World Sculpture News, summer, 2003; plus others. *Mem:* Art Students League, NY; Nat Acad Design NY. *Media:* Bronze, Steel, Aluminum. *Interests:* Yoga. *Publ:* Auth, John Hovanes: A remarkable man, Art Students League, 73; A farewell to Michael Lekakis, Art Students League, 88. *Dealer:* Kouros Gallery 23 E 73d St New York NY 10021; Island Weiss Gallery 201 E 69th St New York NY 10021. *Mailing Add:* PO Box 7067 Amagansett NY 11930

STRONGHILOS, CAROL
PAINTER
b New York, NY. *Study:* Empire State, BFS, Art Students League; Brooklyn Mus Art Sch, study with Reuben Tam. *Exhib:* NJ State Mus, 72; Monmouth Col, 72; Brooklyn Mus, 74; Larry Aldrich Mus, 75; Women in the Arts, 76 & 77; Newark Mus, 77; Art in Pub Bldg, NY Orgn of Independent Artists, World Trade Ctr, 77; Women 78, Women's Caucus for the Arts, City Univ NY, 78; solo exhibs, Brooklyn Mus, 71, Whitney Mus, 75, Bernice Steinbaum Gallery, 83, Kingsborough Community Col, 88, Ctr Gallery, 2000; group exhibs, Madylon Jordon Gallery, 94. *Pos:* Founder, NY Feminist Art Inst, NY; consult, Am the Beautiful Fund, 76-77; dir, Art Sch-Mid Westchester, 83. *Teaching:* Instr painting, Brooklyn Mus Art Sch, 71-77 & Brooklyn House of Detention, 74-77; instr painting & drawing, Five Towns Music & Art Ctr, 74-76, Feminist Art Inst, 79-80, Old Church Cult Ctr, 86-2000. *Awards:* Fac & Alumni First Prize, Brooklyn Mus, 70; Grant, Adolph Gottlieb, 86. *Mem:* Women in the Arts; Woman's Caucus for Art, Coll Art Asn. *Media:* Acrylic, Oil

STROUD, BILLY
PAINTER, COLLECTOR
b Peoria, IL, Mar 23, 1969. *Study:* Univ Ill U-C, BFA (sculpture) 1994; MA (art educ) 2003. *Exhib:* Studio Show 2002; Gallery Studio 402, New York City, 2002; Skin Deep, I-Space, Chicago, Ill, 2005. *Pos:* Bd dir, McLean Co Art Ctr, 2005-. *Teaching:* Univ Ill, Urbana-Champaign, 2002-2003; instr, McLean Co Art Ctr, 2004-. *Awards:* Kotteman Sculpture Award, Bradley Univ, Peoria, Ill, 92-93. *Media:* Acrylic on Canvas & Paper. *Collection:* Karl Moehl, Ben Gardner & Tara McArthy. *Mailing Add:* 605 E Washington St Bloomington IL 61701

STROUD, PETER ANTHONY
PAINTER, EDUCATOR
b London, Eng, May 23, 1921. *Study:* Teacher Training Coll, London Univ, Central Hammersmith Schs Art, 48-53. *Hon Degrees:* East China, Normal Univ, hon Dr. *Work:* Tate Gallery, London; Guggenheim Mus, New York; Los Angeles Co Mus; Detroit Inst Fine Arts; Pasadena Art Mus; Mus Modern Art, New York; Whitney Mus, New York; Brooklyn Mus, New York; Metrop Mus, New York; San Francisco Mus Art; Brit Mus, London; Yale Univ Art Mus. *Comn:* Mural, Int Union Archit Congress Bldg, London, 61; mural, State Sch Leverkusen, Fed Repub Ger, 63; mural, Mfrs Hanover Trust co, New York, 69. *Exhib:* Nat Gallery Victoria, Melbourne, Australia, 70; Univ Calif, Santa Barbara, 70; Ulster Mus, Belfast, Northern Ireland, 71; Finch Coll, New York, 72; Retrospective New Jersey, State Mus, Trenton, NJ, 90; Cent Acad, Beijing, 92; East China, Normal Univ, Shang Hui, 94; Abstraction and Immanence, Hunter Coll, New York, 2002; Rider Univ, NJ, 2007. *Pos:* Ed bd, Am Abstr Artists & J, 92-2002, consult ed, 2002-. *Teaching:* Prof visual studies, Bennington Coll, 63-68; prof painting, Grad Sch, Rutgers Univ, New Brunswick, 68-,

prof emer, Rutgers Univ, 98. *Awards:* Pasadena Mus Fel, 64. *Bibliog:* Dore Ashton (auth), Peter Stroud's relief-paintings, Studio Int, 66; John Coplans (auth), Interview with Peter Stroud, Artforum, 66; Robert Storr (auth), retrospective interview, Art Am, 91. *Mem:* Am Abstr Artists. *Media:* Acrylic. *Res:* Philosophy & art. *Interests:* Critical writing. *Publ:* Paul Cumming (interview), Arch Am Art, 90; Chris Benencasor (tv interview), New Jersey on The Arts, 12/2004. *Mailing Add:* 59 Harriet Dr Princeton NJ 08540

STRUCK, NORMA JOHANSEN
PAINTER, ILLUSTRATOR
b West Englewood, NJ. *Study:* NY Phoenix Sch Design, 47-50; study with Paul Burns, 69; Art Students League, NY, 76-77; master class, John Sanden, 78. *Work:* Pentagon, Navy Hist Mus, USN Combat Mus, Coast Guard Art Collection, Washington, DC; Governor's Island, NY; Portrait of Sonja Henie, Henie-Onstad Mus, Oslo, Norway; Portrait of Sonja Henie, World Figure Skating Hall Fame, Colorado Springs, Colo. *Comn:* First Woman Line Admiral Fran McKee, Washington, 82, US Navy; Admiral Wayne Caldwell, 84 & Vice Admiral Paul Yost, Commandant, 86, US Coast Guard, Governor's Island, NY; Vice Admiral Donald C Thompson, US Coast Guard, 88; Vice Admiral James Irwin. *Exhib:* Navy Combat Art, Navy Combat Art Gallery, Washington, 77-86 & Salmagundi Club, NY, 77-82; Catherine Lorillard Wolfe, Nat Arts Club, NY, 78; Am Artist Prof League, World Trade Ctr, NY, 79; Coast Guard Traveling Art Show, 80-86; Belskiemus of Art & Sci, 2008. *Collection Arranged:* Navy Art Prog; Coast Guard Art Prog; Paintings Tour the Country, since 1970's, arranged by Hq in Washington, DC. *Pos:* Comt mem, Navy Art Coop & Liaison, 80-96; COGAP. 2000-. *Awards:* Louis E Seley Award, US Navy Art Prog, 79; George Gray Award, US Coast Guard, 82 & 89; Second Coast Guard Award, Governor's Island, 89. *Bibliog:* John Pangburn (auth), People, The Record, 82; Linda Bruhn (auth), Guard duty, Profile Mag, 83. *Mem:* Hudson Valley Art Asn (bd dir, 85-88); Am Artists Prof League; Art Students League (life mem); Coast Guard Art Prog (comt mem, 80-96); Soc Illustrators; Salmagundi Club; Nat Mus Women in Arts (charter mem). *Media:* Oil, Acrylic; Charcoal, Watercolor. *Interests:* Painting the natural beauty of all nationalities. *Publ:* Illusr, World Trade Ctr News, 79; Sea Power, Navy League USA, 82, 84; contribr, Profile: Art for Your Country, Am Portrait Soc, 83; illusr, Retiree News, US Coast Guard, 86. *Mailing Add:* 910 Midland Rd Oradell NJ 07649

STRUEKEN-BACHMANN, MARION
PAINTER, CURATOR
b Ger. *Study:* Nat Acad Design, (art), 70-74; New Sch of Social Res, cert, 76. *Exhib:* Am Painters in Paris, Palais Des Congres, Paris, 75; Pastel Soc, Hermitage Mus, 82; Pastel Soc, Copley Soc, Boston, 83; Pastel Paintings, Pen & Brush Club, NY, 85 & 87; Pastels, Nelson Rockefeller Art Ctr, NY, 86; Women in Art, Women Art Gallery, NY, 86. *Awards:* Blick Award, Pen & Brush Club, 90; Alice McReynolds Award, Salmagundi Club, 91; Hazel Witte Mem Award, Nat Asn Women Artists, 91; and others. *Bibliog:* Hamburger Abendblatt, Ger, 88; Artspeak, 9/92; Christel Vollmer (auth), Erfolgreiche Deutsche in New York, Ullstein Verlag, Berlin, Ger, 93; and others. *Mem:* Pastel Soc Am (bd dir); Salmagundi Club, NY; Nat Asn Women Artists; assoc mem Allied Artist Am; Nat Arts Club. *Media:* Pastel. *Publ:* Contribr, Contemporary Women Artists, 89. *Dealer:* Leader Assocs 66 Madison Ave New York NY 10003. *Mailing Add:* 444 E 86th St Apt 30G New York NY 10028

STRUNCK, JUERGEN
PRINTMAKER, PROFESSOR
b Ger, 1943. *Study:* Univ Munich, Germany, 64-65, 66-67; Wichita State Univ, Kans, 65-66; Univ Dallas, Tex, 67-70, MA, 68, MFA, 70. *Work:* Whitney Mus Am Art, New York; Mod Art Mus, Fort Worth, Tex; Calif Palace of the Legion of Hon; Honolulu Acad Arts; Univ N Dak; Univ Ill; Utah Mus Fine Arts; Univ Wis; Tex A&M Univ, Corpus Christi, Tex; Nat Ctr Fine Arts, Giza, Egypt; Mus Contemp Graphic Arts; Dallas Mus of Art; Nat Acad, NY; Lib Congress, Wash DC; Library of Congress, Wash DC; Notre Dame Univ, IN; over 80 more. *Comn:* Bank of the Southwest, Tex; Midwestern State Univ, Wichita Falls. *Exhib:* Solo exhibs, Martha Gault Art Gallery, Slippery Rock Univ, Pa, 90, Slocumb Galleries, Eastern Tenn State Univ, 93, Warehouse Living Arts Ctr, Corsicana, Tex, 93, Dutch Phillips & Co Fine Art, Fort Worth, Tex, 94, Univ Art Gallery, Baylor Univ, Waco, Tex, 94, Univ Tex, Tyler, 95, Museu Nacional de Bellas Artes, Rio de Janeiro, Brazil, 95, Spring Creek Gallery, Collin Co Community Col, Plano, Tex, 96, Stewart Ctr Gallery, Purdue Univ, Ind, 97, Mus Metrop de arte, Brazil, 98, The print Consortium, Southeast Mo State univ, 99, Ga Coll & State Univ, 2000, Tex Wesleyan Univ, 2002, Artcentre of Plano, Tex, 2003, Ctr Spirituality & Arts, San Antonio, 2004, Univ North Dakota, Grand Forks, 2006, Leslie Powell Found & Gallery, 2007, Univ Miami, Fla, 2009, Elle NOel Art Mus, Odessa, Tex, 2009, Art Mus Nat Taiwan Univ, Taipei, 2009, Univ Houston, Clear Lake, Tex, 2009, Galeri Magica, Ringsted, Denmark, 2010, Forum Gallery, 2011; Group exhibs, 10th Norwegian Int Print Triennale, Fredrikstad, Norway, 92, Southern Graphics Council, Univ Tenn, Knoxville, 92, Md Inst Coll of Art, Baltimore, 93, Nat Ctr for Fine Arts of Egypt, Giza, 93, 1st Int Print Triennale Colour in Graphic Art, District Mus, Old Town Hall, Torun, Poland, 94, San Angelo Mus Fine Arts, Tex, 94, 170th Ann Exhib, Nat Acad of Design, New York City, 95, La Societe Int des Beaux-arts, Trammell Crow Ctr, Dallas, 96, Bilkent, 96, ArtCentre of Plano, Tex, 2003, The Exchange Show, Bikent Univ, Turkey, 2004, Outside the Line 5, Bath House Cult Ctr, Tex, 2005, However the Hat Fits, Exhange Portfolio, MAPC Conf, Athens, Ohio, 2006, Mid Am Print Coun, Monoprint/Monotype exhib, Quincy Univ, Ill, 2008. Geometry in Dallas, Mus Geometric & Madi Art, Tex, 2009, Learning & Remembering: A Gift of Time, Portfolio Exhib, SGC Conf, Pa, 2010; others; workshop presenter, lectr, panelist, juror. *Collection Arranged:* Arlington Art Asn, Tex, 86; 17th Southwest Black Art Exhib, African Am Mus, Dallas, 75; Contemp Brazilian Prints, Haggar Gallery, Univ Dallas, 96; 18th Ann Nat Juried Art Exhib, Navarro Coun Arts, Tex, 2001; Hollywood Int Juried Print Exhib, Art & Cult Ctr, Fla, 2002; Upper Gallery Univ Dallas, 2002; You Should Know Them I, Haggar Univ Gallery, Univ Dallas, 2010. *Teaching:* Cistercian Prep Scho, Tex, 67-68; Univ Dallas, Irving, Tex, 68-; Southern Methodist Univ, Dallas, Tex, 73, 75-76; Univ Wash, Seattle, Wash, summer 76. *Awards:* Prize of Jury, 5th Norwegian Int Print Biennale, Norway; Best of Show, Purchase Award, Andy Turner Nat Print Comp, Calif State, Calif. *Bibliog:* Ross Romano Ross (auth), The Complete Printmaker, MacMillon, 90; EC Cunningham (auth), Printmaking: A Primary Form of Expression, Univ Press Colorado, 92; Jeffrey Snyder (auth), Printmakers Today, Schiffer, 2010. *Mem:* Southern Graphics Council; Midamerica Print Council. *Media:* Relief Prints

STRUNZ, KATJA
SCULPTOR, PAINTER
b Ottweiler, Ger, 1970. *Study:* Johannes Gutenberg Univ, Mainz, Germany, Philos Studies, Hist & Hist Art, 1989, Art & Philos, 1991; Staatliche Akademie Bildenden Künste, Karlsruhe, Germany, Fine Arts, 1993, Meisterschüler, 1998. *Work:* Carnegie Mus Art, Pittsburgh; Migros Mus Gegenwartskunst, Zurich, Switzerland; Fondazione Morra Greco, Naples; Sammlung Boros, Berlin; Daimler Contemp, Berlin. *Exhib:* Solo exhibs include Galerie Giti Nourbakhsch, Berlin, 2000, doggerfisher, Edinburgh, Scotland, 2003, whose garden was this, Gavin Brown's Enterprise GBE mod, New York, 2006, Mus Haus Esters, Krefeld, 2006, Mod Inst, Glasgow, Scotland, 2007, Guten Morgen Erwachen, Galerie Almine Rech, Paris, 2007; group exhibs include Landscape Galerie Giti Nourbakhsch, Berlin, 2000; waiting for the ice age, Georg Kargl Fine Arts, Vienna, Austria, 2002; Falling Angels, Greene Naftali Gallery, New York, 2003; On the Edge: Contemp Art from DaimlerChrysler Collection, Detroit Inst Arts, Detroit, 2003; It's All an Illusion: Sculpture Proj, Migros Mus Gegenwartskunst, Zurich, Switzerland, 2004; Dead/Undead, Galerie Six Friedrich Lisa Ungar, Munich, 2004; Conversation with Art, Tokyo Opera City Art Gallery, Tokyo, 2006; Music & Art, COMA Ctr Opinions in Music & Art, Berlin, 2006; inky toy affinitas, CerealArt, Philadelphia, 2007; Social Sculpture/Cult Design, Galerie Michael Hall, Vienna, Austria, 2007; Wenn ein Reisender in einer Winternacht, MARTa Herford, Herford, Germany, 2008; MAXImin, Fundación Juan March, Madrid, 2008; PORZADKI UROJONE, Städtisches Mus Abteiberg, Mönchengladbach, Germany, 2008. *Awards:* Promotion Prize Fine Arts Cult Circle, Fedn German Industs, 2004; Adolph-Luther-Preis, Adolph Luther Found, 2006. *Dealer:* ANDERSEN_S Contemp Art Klubiensvej 22 Copenhagen Denmark 2100; Galerie Almine Rech 19 rue de Saintonge Paris France 75003; Galerie Giti Nourbakhsch Kurfürstenstrasse 12 Berlin Germany 10785; Mod Inst 73 Robertson St Glasgow Scotland G2 8QD UK. *Mailing Add:* Gavin Brown's Enterprise GBE mod 620 Greenwich St New York NY 10014

STRYK, SUZANNE
PAINTER
b Chicago. *Study:* Northern Ill Univ, DeKalb, Ill, BA (Art History); E Tenn State Univ, Johnson City, Tenn, MA (Painting). *Work:* Art Mus Western Va, Roanoke, Va; Woodson Art Mus, Wausau, Wis; Nat Acad Sciences, Washington; Radford Hospital, Radford, Va; Johnson City Pub Libr, Johnson City, Tenn; Spirit Sq Ctr Arts, Charlotte, NC; Univ Va's Coll Wise, Wise, Va; Carroll Reece Mus, E Tenn State Univ, Johnson City, Tenn; Tenn State Mus, Nashville; Eleanor B Wilson Mus, Hollins Univ, Roanoke, Va; Smithsonian Inst, Nat Mus Air & Space, Washington. *Exhib:* Solo exhibs include Kingsport Renaissance Ctr, Kingsport, Tenn, 1992, McGuffey Art Ctr, Charlottesville, Va, 1993, Holden Gallery, Warren Wilson Coll, Asheville, NC 1997, Ralston Fine Art, Johnson City, Tenn, 1991, 1995, 1997, Peninsula Fine Arts Ctr, Newport News, Va, 1998, Carroll Reece Mus, Johnson City, Tenn, 1999, Nat Acad Sciences, Washington, 2000, Gescheidle Gallery, Chicago, 2002, Grover/Thurston Gallery, Seattle, 2003, McLean Proj Arts, McLean, Va, 2007, Morris Mus Art, Augusta, Ga, 2007, US Botanic Garden, Washington, 2007; Group exhibs include Ann Juried Exhib, Cooperstown Art Asn, Cooperstown, NY 1991; Primitive Origins, Sarratt Gallery, Vanderbilt Univ, Nashville, 1991; Mid Atlantic Exhib, D'Art Ctr, Norfolk, Va, 1991, 1992; Works on Paper, Marsh Art Gallery, Univ Richmond, Richmond, Va, 1992; Rutgers Nat, Stedman Art Gallery, Rutgers Univ, Camden, NJ, 1994; It's My Nature, Fredericksburg Ctr Arts, Fredericksburg, Va, 1998; Animals in Art, Blue Spiral I, Asheville, NC, 1998; Atlanta Art Exposition, Atlanta, 2002; Love, Second St Gallery, Charlottesville, Va, 2007. *Dealer:* Blue Spiral 1 38 Biltmore Ave Asheville NC 28801; Cumberland Gallery 4107 Hillsboro Circle Nashville TN 37215

STUART, JOSEPH MARTIN
PAINTER, MUSEUM DIRECTOR
b Seminole, Okla, Nov 9, 1932. *Study:* Univ NMex, BFA, 59, MA, 62. *Work:* Art Mus, Univ NMex, Albuquerque; Salt Lake Art Ctr, Salt Lake City; Coll Idaho, Caldwell; Sioux City Art Ctr, Iowa; Civic Fine Arts Ctr, Sioux Falls, SDak; SDak Art Mus, Brookings, SDak. *Exhib:* Northwest Artists 50th & 52nd Ann, Seattle Art Mus, 64 & 66; Midwest Biennial, Joslyn Art Mus, Omaha 74 & 76; Drawings USA, Minn Mus of Art, St Paul, 77; Nat Drawings, Rutgers Univ, Camden, NJ, 77; solo exhib, The Canyon Suite, W Tex State Univ, Canyon, 82; Ritz Gallery, SDak State Univ, Brookings, 92; Minimalist Painting, Ruhlen Gallery, Santa Fe, NMex, 97; Site Unseen, Site, Santa Fe, NMex, 2008. *Collection Arranged:* Jannis Spyropoulos: Paintings, Roswell Mus & Art Ctr, NMex, 62; Edward Kienholz: Sculpture, Boise Gallery Art, Idaho, 67; Art of South Dakota, 74, The Calligraphic Statement, 77, Berry Collection of Asian Arts & Crafts, 79, Sioux Art Collections, 86, Art for a New Century, 89 & Seiferle Collection of Am Art, 92, SDak Art Mus, Brookings; Utah painting & sculpture, Utah Mus Fine Arts, Salt Lake City, 90. *Pos:* Cur, Mus Art, Univ Ore, 62-63; dir, Boise Gallery Art, 64-68, Salt Lake Art Ctr, 68-71 & SDak Art Mus, 71-93. *Teaching:* Lectr art, Univ Utah, 69; prof art hist, SDak State Univ, 71-93; retired. *Awards:* First Prize in Painting, Cheney Cowles Mem Mus, Spokane, 65; Salt Lake Art Ctr Purchase Award, 67; Purchase Award, Sioux City Art Ctr, 73. *Media:* Acrylic. *Res:* Art history of South Dakota; Native American Tribal Art. *Specialty:* SDak Art. *Publ:* Auth, Stimuli, Utah Archit, fall 69; Art of South Dakota, SDak State Univ, 74; Architecture of Harold Spitznagel, Brookings, 75; South Dakota Collection, 88; The Legacy of South Dakota Art, Pierre, Robinson Mus, 90. *Mailing Add:* 18 Gavilan Rd Santa Fe NM 87508

STUART, MICHELLE
PAINTER, SCULPTOR
b Borrego Springs, Calif, Feb 10, 1940. *Study:* Chouinard Art Inst, Los Angeles; apprenticed to Diego Rivera, Mex; New Sch Social Res. *Work:* Mus Mod Art, Brooklyn Mus & Whitney Mus Am Art, NY; Walker Art Ctr, Minneapolis, Minn; Nat Collection Australia, Canberra; Mod Museet, Stockholm, Sweden; Kaiser-Wilhelm Mus, Krefeld, Ger; and others. *Comn:* Painting, Union Cent Life Insurance, Forest Park, Ohio, 1987; painting, Security Pac Nat Bank, 1987; bronze sculpture & corresponding painting, Coll Wooster, Ohio, 1987-88; Battery Park City, NY, 1992; Tochigi Ctr, Japan, 1996-97; and others. *Exhib:* Solo shows incl Haags Gemeentemuseum, Hague, The Neth, 1983, Walker Art Ctr, Minneapolis, Minn, 1983, Neuberger Mus, Purchase, NY, 1984, Brooklyn Mus, NY, 1986, Rose Art Mus, Waltham, Mass, 1988 & Wadsworth Atheneum, Hartford, Conn, 1988, Coll of Wooster Art Gallery, 1989, Fawbush Gallery, New York, 1992, Belles Artes, Santa Fe, 1993, 1996, Fawbush Gallery, New York, 1994, Anders Tornberg, Lund, Sweden, 1995, Glenn Horowitz, East Hampton, NY, 1998, Diane Villani Editions, NY, 1999, Leslie Tonkonow Artworks & Projects, NY, 2011, Salomon Contemp, NY, 2011; group shows incl Mus Mod Art, 1976, 1984, 1997; Nat Mus Mod Art, Kyoto, Japan, 1983; Mus Contemp Art, Chicago, Ill, 1984; Moderna Museet, Stockholm, Sweden, 1985; San Francisco Mus Mod Art, Calif, 1986; Cleveland Mus Art, Ohio, 1986; Biennial, US Pavilion, Cairo, Egypt, 1994; Rose Art Mus, Waltham, Mass, 1996; Neuberger Mus Art, Purchase, NY, 1997; Whitney Mus Am Art at Champion, Stamford, Conn, 1998; Radford Art Mus, Va, 1999; Nat Mus Women in Arts, Wash, DC, 1999; Montclair Art Mus, NJ, 1999; Mus Contemp Art, Los Angeles, 1999, 2012; Mus Modern Art, NY, 2010-2011; Mus Contemp Art, Chicago, 2011. *Awards:* Nat Endowment Arts Fel Individual Artists, 1974, 1977, 1980, & 1989; Award for Excellence in Design, Arts Comn, New York, 1990; Am Acad in Rome, 1995; Richard M Recchia Mem Prize, Nat Acad Mus, 97; Peter S Reed Found Grant for Painting, 2009. *Bibliog:* Carey Lovelace (auth), Michelle Stuart's silent gardens, Arts Mag, 9/1988; Susan L Stoops (auth), Michelle Stuart: Silent Gardens: The American Landscape (catalog), Rose Art Mus, Brandeis Univ, 1988; Joseph Ruzicka (auth), Essential Light: The Skyes of Michelle Stuart, Art in Am, 6/2000; Holland Cotter (auth), Michelle Stuart: Works from the 1960s-Present, The New York Times, 2011; Nancy Princenthal (auth), Michelle Stuart, Art in America, 2011; Lilly Wei (auth), Michelle Stuart, ArtNews, 2011; Chistine Filippone (auth), Cosmology and Transformation in the Work of Michelle Stuart, Woman's Art Jour, 2011. *Mem:* Nat Acad. *Media:* Encaustic; Bronze. *Publ:* Auth, The Fall, Printed Matter Inc, New York, 1976; A Complete Folk History of the United States at the End of the Century, Wright State Univ, Ohio, 1978; From the Silent Garden, Williams Col, Mass, 1979; I-80 Series: Michelle Stuart, Joslyn Art Mus, Omaha, Nebr, 1981; Sacred Precincts: From Dreamtime to the South China Sea, Neuberger Mus, State Univ, New York, 1984; auth, Natural Histories, Essay, Richard Foreman, NY, 1996; auth, Butterflies & Moths, Dadadog Press, NY, 2006; Michelle Stuart: Sculptural Objects-Journeys In & Out of the Studio, 2011. *Dealer:* Diane Villani Editions 271 Mulberry St #D New York New York 10012; Leslie Tonkonow Artworks & Projects 535 W 22nd St 6th Fl New York NY 10011. *Mailing Add:* 152 Wooster St New York NY 10012

STUART, NANCY
ADMINISTRATOR, PHOTOGRAPHER
Study: State Univ of NY, Buffalo's Graduate Sch of Educ in Educ Leadership and Policy, PhD, 1995. *Exhib:* Numerous solo and group exhibits. *Collection Arranged:* Photographic work is in the collection of The George Eastman House. *Pos:* Numerous administrative positions, founding faculty mem, Lansing Community Col Photographic Technology Program, Rochester Inst of Technology, 1975-84, faculty mem Sch of Photographic Arts & Sciences, 1984-2002, chair Applied Photography Department, 1991, assoc dir., Sch of Photographic Arts & Sciences, 1994, assoc dean, Col of Imaging Arts & Sciences, 1998; exec vpres, Chief Operating Officer, Cleveland Inst of Art, 2002-2005, provost, 2005-2011. *Bibliog:* DES Stories: Faces and Voices of People Exposed to Diethylstilbestrol, Visual Studies Workshop Press, 2001. *Mem:* Soc of Photographic Educators Nat Bd Dir (treasurer). *Publ:* (ed) Focal Press Encyclopedia of Photography, 2007. *Mailing Add:* University of Hartford Art School 200 Bloomfield Ave Hartford CT 06117

STUART, SHERRY BLANCHARD
PAINTER
b Newport, Ark, Feb 19, 1941. *Study:* Minneapolis Coll Art & Design, BFA, 64; studied painting with Richard Lack Atlier, 70; Scottsdale Artists Sch with Wilson Hurley, 89. *Work:* Tucson Mus Art, Ariz; Desert Caballeros Western Art Mus, Wickenburg, Ariz; 3M co; Bureau Engraving, Minneapolis, Minn; Phippen Mus, Prescot, Ariz; St George Art Mus, St George, Utah; Great Plains Art Mus, Lincoln, Nebr. *Comn:* Paintings comn by Mr & Mrs Graves, 89, Mr & Mrs Beede, 93, Mr & Mrs Rod Boggs, 97, Scottsdale, Ariz & Sharon Bracken, Scottsdale, 2002, 2012, Peter E Kump, La Quinta, Calif, 2011. *Exhib:* Mountain Oyster Club Exhib, Tucson, 93-2011; Women Artists of the West, Tucson Mus Art, 94-96; Oil Painters of Am, Long Grove Invitational, Ill, 94; Top 200 Arts for Parks, Nat Art Show, Jackson, Wyo, 94 & 98; Horses in Motion, Ky Derby Mus, Louisville, 96; Am Acad Women Artists, Ariz His Soc, 98; Am Plains Artists, 2002-2011; Oil Painters Am, 2003-2004, 2006-2011; Cowgirl Up!, Desert Caballeros Western Mus, Wickenburg, Ariz, 2005-2012. *Teaching:* Instr at various art schs, 64-2004. *Awards:* 1st Place Oil Painting & Gold Medal Purchase Award, Western Acad Women Artists, Desert Caballeros Western Art Mus, 97; Peoples Choice Award, Am Acad Women Artists, Cauley Gallery, 98; 1st Place Ariz Cowboy Classics, 2001; 1st Place Best of Show Award Am Plains Artists, 2002; Purchase Award, Great Plains Art Mus, 2006; Best in Show, Desert Caballeros Western Art Mus, 2008. *Bibliog:* A Contrad Posz (auth), Art of Sherry Blanchard Stuart, Illustrator, Vol 6, No 2, 83. *Mem:* Am Acad Women Artists (bd dir, 94-2003); juried mem Ariz Artists Guild; juried mem Western Artists Am; found mem Creative Women Pinnacle Peak (print dir, 98, found mem); sig mem Oil Painters Am; sign mem Am Plains Artists; Am Women Artist (master signature mem). *Media:* Oil on Linen. *Interests:* Photography, antiques, golf. *Publ:* Auth, articles in Midwest Art Mag, Dorn Commun Inc, 5-6/85; Equine Images Mag, Heartland Commun Group, 88; Am Artist Mag, 12/94; Cowboys & Indians Mag, 96; Art of West Mag, Duerr & Tierney, Ltd, 96; Southwest Art Mag (featured), March, 2005; Appaloosa J Mag (featured), 2006; The Illustrator, 2008; and many others. *Dealer:* Open Range Gallery Scottsdale AZ; Sherwoods Gallery Houston TX. *Mailing Add:* 8402 Country Club Tr Scottsdale AZ 85255

STUART, SIGNE NELSON See Nelson, Signe

STUBBS, LU
SCULPTOR
b New York, NY, Aug 16, 1925. *Study:* Sch Boston Mus Fine Arts, MA, 64, studied with Harold Tovish & Nathaniel Neujean; L'Acad di Belle Arti, Perugia, Italy, 71. *Work:* Brita (bronze), New Eng Med Ctr, Boston, Mass, 88; Happy Frog (bronze), Post Office Sq, Sharon, Mass, 96; US Eagle, Sharon high Sch, Mass, 99; life-sized bronze, Women's Div Greater Springfield Chamber Com, Mass, 77; Foxtale Family, Boyden Libr, Foxboro, Mass, 2000; Happy Frog, Northampton, Mass, 2008; Reaching Women II, Armoury Commons Park, Springfield, Mass, 2009. *Comn:* Three Women (bronze), Brookline, Mass, 75; Deborah Sampson, life-sized bronze, Sharon Pub Libr, Mass, 89; Sundial, with life-sized children (bronze), Browne Fund/City of Boston, Charlestown, Mass, 90-91; Pregnant Woman II (bronze), Cooley Dickinson Hosp, Northampton, Mass, 2001; Mary Lyon, Mt Holyoke Coll Libr, Mass, 2006; and others. *Exhib:* Solo exhibs, Attleboro Mus, Mass, 73, Brockton Art Mus, 73-74 & DeCordova Mus (with catalog), Lincoln, 77; Art in Transition-A Century of the Mus Sch, Mus Fine Arts, Boston, 77; Sculpture Outdoors, Schulman Sculpture Forum, White Plains, NY, 80-82; Nat Sculpture Soc Celebrates the Figure, Port Hist Mus, Philadelphia, 87; group exhibs, 100 yrs of Am Sculpture, America's Tower, NY, 93-94 & Sculpture in the Center, Stamford, Conn, 94; 2 person show, Forms & Views of Nature, Audubon Gallery, Sharon, Mass, 94. *Teaching:* Instr sculpture, Boston Ctr Adult Educ, 63-77, Milton Acad, 67-68 & Boston Univ, 76-77. *Awards:* Exhib grant, Nat Endowment Arts & Humanities, 77; First Prize, New Eng Artist Showcase, Univ Mass, 81; Best of Show, New Eng Sculptors Asn, 86. *Bibliog:* Marty Carlock (auth), A Guide to Public Art in Greater Boston, 93; Marty Carlock (auth), Nature adds form to art of sculptor, Boston Globe, 9/25/94; Pattie Hainer (auth), You gotta have art, Patriot Ledger, 9/7/96; Amy Guerrero (auth), Pulling up Stakes, Sharon Advocate, 8/25/2000. *Mem:* Nat Sculpture Soc; New Eng Sculptors Asn; Sharon Creative Arts Asn. *Media:* Bronze, Wood, Oil Painting, Marble. *Interests:* Creative writing. *Publ:* Auth, The Happy Frog Speaks, Sharon Advocate, 8/22/97 & Studying Language and Life in Italy, Boston Sunday Globe, 7/31/2000. *Mailing Add:* 11 Trumbull Rd Northampton MA 01060

STUCKEY, CHARLES F
HISTORIAN, CURATOR
b Teaneck, NJ, Mar 14, 1945. *Study:* Yale Univ, BA, 1967; Univ Pa, MA, 1970 & PhD, 1972. *Collection Arranged:* Georgia O'Keeffe, Art Inst Chicago, 1988, Andy Warhol: A Retrospective, 1989, Degenerate Art: The Fate of the Avant-Garde in Nazi Germany, 1991, Magritte, 1993, Max Ernst, Dada and the Dawn of Surrealism, 1993 & Claude Monet 1840-1926, 1995; The Art of Paul Gauguin, Nat Gallery Art, Washington, DC, Art Inst Chicago & Mus d'Orsay, Paris, 1988; Cezanne: The Early Years, London Royal Acad, Mus d'Orsay, Paris & Nat Gallery Art, Washington, DC, 1988-89; The Chicago Show, Chicago Cult Ctr, 1989; The Rudolf Staechelin Family Foundation Collection of Basel, Switzerland, Kimbell Art Mus, 97 & Renoirs Portraits: Impressions of an Age, 1998. *Pos:* Contrib ed, Art Am, 1980-; cur mod painting, Nat Gallery Art, Washington, DC, 1985-87; cur 20th century painting & sculpture, Art Inst Chicago, 1987-95; cur paintings & sculpture after 1800, Minneapolis Inst Arts, 1995-97; spec cur consult, Salvador Dali Mus, St Petersburg, Fla, 1995-98; sr cur, Kimbell Art Mus, Ft Worth, Tex, 1997-2001. *Teaching:* Asst prof art hist, The Johns Hopkins Univ, Baltimore, 1972-77; visiting prof, Sch Art Inst Chicago, 1979; visiting asst prof, Dept Visual Arts, State Univ, NY, 1980-81; adj prof fine arts, NY Univ, 1983; adj assoc prof Art Hist, Theory & Criticism, Sch Art Inst Chicago, 2002-. *Awards:* Outstanding Scholar, Ill Acad Fine Arts, 1993; Chevalier dans l'Ordre des Arts et des Lettres, 2000. *Mem:* The Turner Soc. *Res:* 19th and 20th century European and American art. *Publ:* Auth, Monet: Water Lilies, 1988 & French Painting, 1991, Hugh Lauter Levin Assocs Inc; contribr, Vance Kirkland 1904-1981: a Colorado painter without geographical boundaries, In: Vance Kirkland, Vance Kirkland Found & Mus, 1998; Love, money and Monet's debacle paintings of 1880, In: Monet at Vetheuil: The Turning Point, Univ Lithoprinters Inc & Univ Mich Mus Art, Ann Arbor, 1998

STULA, NANCY
MUSEUM DIRECTOR, CURATOR
b Hartford, Conn, Oct 10, 1961. *Study:* Univ Hartford, BA (summa cum laude), 1985; Columbia Univ, PhD (art hist), 1997. *Pos:* With Metrop Mus Art, New York, formerly; deputy dir & chief cur, Lyman Allyn Art Mus, New London, Conn, 2003-, interim dir, 2008-; trustee, Hartford Art Sch, West Hartford, Conn, 2005-; exec dir, Lyman Allyn Art Mus, 2009-. *Teaching:* Univ Hartford, formerly. *Mem:* AAM; Coll Art Asn. *Publ:* Auth, American Artists Abroad and their Inspiration: Selection from the Lyman Allyn Art Mus, New London, 2004; coauth (with Barbara Novak & David Miller Robinson), At Home and Abroad: The Transcendental Landscapes of Christopher Pearse Cranch 1813-1892, (exhib catalog), Lyman Allyn Art Mus, New London, 2007. *Mailing Add:* Benton Mus Art 245 Glenbrrok Rd #2140 Storrs Mansfield CT 06269

STULER, JACK
PHOTOGRAPHER, EDUCATOR
b Homestead, Pa, Aug 30, 1932. *Study:* Phoenix Col, 57; Ariz State Univ, BA, 60, with Van Deren Coke, MFA, 63; workshop with Ansel Adams, 66. *Work:* George Eastman House, Rochester, NY; Gen Aniline Films, NY; Univ Collections, Ariz State Univ, Tempe; Yuma Art Ctr, Ariz; Phoenix Col; Bibliotheque Nationale, Paris; San Francisco Mus Mod Art. *Exhib:* George Eastman House, 63; Photog In Twentieth

Century, Nat Gallery Can, 67; Am Photog: The Sixties, Sheldon Mem Art Gallery, Univ Nebr, Lincoln, 66; Photog USA, DeCordova Mus, Lincoln, Mass, 68; Celebrations, Hayden Gallery, Mass Inst Technol, 74; Ariz Arts Showcase, John F Kennedy Ctr for the Performing Arts, Washington, DC, 74; First Light, Focus Gallery, San Francisco, Calif, 75; Solo exhib, Univ of Ore, Eugene, 76. *Teaching:* Asst prof photog art, Ariz State Univ, 66-72, assoc prof, 73-75, prof, 75-, currently. *Awards:* First Award Biennial Photog, Phoenix Art Mus, 67; Southwestern Art Best of Show, Yuma Fine Arts Asn, 68; Summer Fel, Ariz State Univ, 68. *Bibliog:* Helmut Gernsheim (auth), A Concise History of Photography, Dover Publ Inc, New York, 86; Jack Stuler in the Nature of Things (monogr), Nazraeli Press, Munich, Ger, 90; Jack Stuler A Retrospective, 1962-1997 (monogr), Les Work Publ, Portland, Ore, 97. *Mem:* Soc Photog Educ; Inst Cult Exchange Through Photog (mem adv bd, 66-). *Publ:* Contribr, Photography in the Twentieth Century, Horizon, 67; Being without clothes, Aperture, 15:3, 70; Camera, Lucerne, Switz, 11/71; Concise History of Photography, Dover Publ. *Mailing Add:* Dept Art Arizona State Univ Tempe AZ 85287

STUMMER, HELEN M
PHOTOGRAPHER, WRITER

Newark, NJ, Jan, 8, 1936. *Study:* Kean Univ Studio Art, BA, 77, MA, 78; Norwich Univ, Vermont Coll Visual Sociology, MA, 87; Patt Blue Int Ctr Photog, studied Mary Ellen Mark, 76-95, 97. *Work:* Library of Congress, Wash DC; Rutgers Univ Special Collections Archive, New Brunswick, NJ; Int Ctr Photog, NY; Brooklyn Mus, NY; Mus of the City, NY. *Exhib:* East 6th St, Int Ctr Photog, NY, 80; No Easy Walk, NJ Arts Ann, Newark Mus, NJ, 85; NJ Arts Ann, NJ State Mus, Trenton, 99; Dressing for a NY City Childhood, Mus of the City, NY, 2001; Children at Risk, NY Historical Soc, NY, 2003; Turning Silver, Women in Photography Int Calif, 2006; Evoking the Spirit, Noyes Mus, 2009; No Easy Walk: A Lifetime of Concerned Photog Brookdale, CVA Gallery, NJ, 2011. *Teaching:* assoc prof photog, County Coll Morris, Randolph, NJ, 90-99; assoc prof photog, Kean Univ; instr photog, NJ Ctr Visual Arts, 90-2001. *Awards:* Fel, Geraldine Dodge & CCM Found, County Coll Morris, 92; Hon Mention, Traveling Exhib, Gordon Parks Competition, 96; Best in Show, Guggenheim Cur, NJ Ctr Visual Arts Int Show, 99; Two Grants, NJ Coun Arts, 95, 2003; George and Helen Segal Found grant, Segal Found, 2011-2012; Distinguished Alumni award, Kean Univ, 2012. *Bibliog:* Vivien Raynor (auth), Photographs of Lives Caught in Poverty, NY Times, 90; Helen Kohen (auth), Children Portraits Make for Powerful Exhibits, Miami Dade Comm Coll, 91; Seidel (auth), Portraits of the Inner City Provoke Thoughtful Comments, Star Ledger, 93; Miles Orvell (auth), American Photography, Oxford History of Art London, 2003; Bonnie Yokelson (auth), By Ending the Grid, Rest in Peace, Aijira Gallery, Newark, NJ, 2007. *Mem:* Women Artists Archives Nat Dir (2005-). *Publ:* auth, My Photographic Journey, Lens Work, Visual Sociology, Germany, 85; auth, No Easy Walk, Newark 1980-1993, Temple Univ Press, 94. *Mailing Add:* 171 High St Metuchen NJ 08840

STURGEON, JOHN FLOYD
VIDEO ARTIST

b Springfield, Ill, Jan 6, 1946. *Study:* Yale Univ, Yale-Norfolk fel, 67; Univ Ill, BFA, 68; Cornell Univ, MFA, 70. *Work:* Mus Mod Art, NY; Los Angeles Co Mus Art; Long Beach Mus Art; Kunstmuseum, Bonn, WGer; Biennale Venice, Italy; and others. *Comn:* No Earth-No Earth Station (video performance), Los Angeles Mus Art, 83; I Will Take You (video installation), Long Beach Mus Art, 84; Trap/bat (video installation), Mus Mod Art, NY, 93; Narkose (video installation), Contemp Art Ctr, Cincinnati, Ohio, 94; Blooming, While We Are Sinking (video installation), Braemen, Ger, 96. *Pos:* Video artist, Los Angeles Inst Contemp Art, 78-79; vis artist, Sch Art Inst Chicago, 80 & 83; Univ Iowa, 82. *Teaching:* Instr, Univ Calif, Los Angeles, 79-80; vis artist fac, Claremont Grad Sch, Calif, 80, Art Inst Chicago, 80, 82 & 83; assoc prof, Rensselaer Polytechnic Inst, 83-91; mem art fac, State Univ New York, at Purchase, 85-91; guest prof, Hochschule für Künste, Bremen, Ger; assoc prof art, Carnegie Mellon Univ Pittsburgh, Pa, 91-, assoc dept head, 96-. *Awards:* Nat Endowment Arts, Individual Artists Fels, 75, 77 & 80, Video Production Grant, 84; Guggenheim Found Fel, 81; Nat Endowment Arts Mid Atlantic Region Media Fel, 92 & 94; and others. *Bibliog:* Louise Lewis (auth), Art as alchemy, Artweek, 7/28/79; Barbara London (auth), Independent Video: The first fifteen years, Artforum, 9/80; Michael Nash (auth), Present tense rights of passage, Art-Com, fall 83; Kathy Huffman (auth), The Second Link (exhib catalog) & Video Art Personal Medium; Margot Lovejoy (auth), Postmodern Currents, Art & Artists in the Age of Electronic Media, UMI Press, 89, Prentice Hall, 2nd ed, 97. *Publ:* Contribr, Video Art, Harcourt Brace Jovanovich, 76; Two Video Installations, Long Beach Mus Art, 78; auth, Spinning dream, Dreamworks, fall 80; US Film & Video Festival (catalog), 83; Polulism--Report from the Field, Art-Com, spring 83; and others. *Dealer:* L A Louver Gallery 55 North Venice Blvd Venice CA 90291; Data Bank Sch of the Art Inst of Chicago Columbus at Jackson Blvd Chicago IL 60603. *Mailing Add:* Univ Maryland Dept Visual Art 1000 Hilltop Cir Baltimore MD 21250

STURGEON, MARY C
EDUCATOR, HISTORIAN

b Los Angeles, Calif, Dec 6, 1943. *Study:* Univ Minn, BA (summa cum laude), 65; Bryn Mawr Col, MA, 68, PhD (classical archaeol & Greek), 71; Am Sch Class Studies in Athens, 68-70 & 70-71. *Teaching:* Asst prof Greek & Roman Art, Oberlin Col, 72-77; assoc prof Greek art, Univ NC, Chapel Hill, 77-85, prof, 85-, chair, 93-; Whitehead Prof, Am Sch Classical Studies, Athens, 98-99. *Mem:* Archaeol Inst Am; Coll Art Asn; Am Sch Classical Studies in Athens; Am Philological Asn. *Res:* Greek sculpture. *Publ:* Auth, The reliefs of the Theatre of Dionysus in Athens, Am J Archaeol, 77; Corinth IX 2: Sculpture, The reliefs from the theater, Princeton-Am Sch, 77 & Isthmia IV; Sculpture I, 1952-1967, 87; The Corinth Amazon: Formation of a Roman Classical Sculpture, Am J Archaeol 99, 95; co-ed, Stephanos Studies in honor of Brunilde Sismondo Ridgeway, Philadelphia, 98; auth, A Peloponnesian Aphrodite, The Corinth Theater Type, Stephanos, 98

STURGES, HOLLISTER
CURATOR, HISTORIAN

b Kingston, NY. *Study:* Cornell Univ, BA, 62; Univ Calif, Berkeley, MA, 69. *Pos:* Dir, Univ Mo Art Gallery, Kansas City, 76-78, Springfield Mus Fine Arts & George Walter Vincent Smith Art Mus, Mass, 88-95 & Bruce Mus, Greenwich, Conn, 95-2000; cur European art, Joslyn Art Mus, 80-. *Teaching:* Instr, Univ Mo, Kansas City, 72-80 & Manhattan Coll, Riverdale, NY, 2003-2007; lectr, Univ Nebr, Lincoln, 83. *Mem:* Coll Art Asn; Asn Art Mus Dirs; Am Asn Mus. *Res:* 18th and 19th century French painting with emphasis on social themes; contemporary American. *Publ:* Auth, Chicago abstractionists: Romanticized structures, Univ Mo, Kansas City, 78; Angels and urchins: Images of children at the Joslyn, 80, I-80 series: Mario Merz, 81 & Jules Breton and the French Rural Tradition, 82, Joslyn Art Mus; coauth, Art of the Fantastic: Latin America, 1920-1987, 87; Collection Handbook, Indianapolis Mus Art, 88; auth, New Art from Puerto Rico, Springfield Mus Fine Arts, 90. *Mailing Add:* 91 Putnam Park Greenwich CT 06830

STURMAN, EUGENE
SCULPTOR, PAINTER

b New York, NY, Jan 28, 1945. *Study:* Alfred Univ, BFA, 67; Univ NMex, MFA, 69; Tamarind Lithograph Workshop, 70. *Work:* Metro Media Studios, Hollywood, Calif; Warner Bros Records, Universal City, Calif; Los Angeles Co Mus; Newport Harbor Mus. *Comn:* Pub sculpture, City of Los Angeles, 85. *Exhib:* LA Six 74, Los Angeles Co Mus, 74; 24 from Los Angeles, Barnsdall Munic Gallery, Los Angeles, 74; Basel Art Fair, Switz, 74 & 75; Whitney Mus Am Art Biennial, 75; Chicago Art Fair, 82; Los Angeles Co Mus, 83. *Teaching:* Instr printmaking, Long Beach State Univ, 72-74; lectr printmaking, painting & drawing, Univ Calif, Los Angeles, 73-78; instr, Otis-Parsons Sch Design, Los Angeles, 84-91; lectr, Pepperdine Univ, 92, 94-95. *Awards:* Michael Levins Award, Alfred Univ, 66; New Talent Award, Los Angeles Co Mus, 74; Nat Endowment Arts Grant, 75. *Media:* Copper, Lead. *Mailing Add:* 190 Loma Metisse St Malibu CA 90265

STURTZ-DAVIS, SHIRLEY ZAMPELLI
PAINTER, ARTS EDUCATOR

b Lewistown, Pa, 1937. *Study:* Penn State Univ, BS, 59, MA (studio art), 61. *Work:* Penn State, Univ Park, Pa; Pa Dept Educ, Harrisburg, Pa; Shriner Burn Inst, Boston; Wash Co Mus Fine Arts, Hagerstown, Md; Southern Alleghenies Mus, Loretto, Pa. *Comn:* Still Life Series, Mellon Bank, State Coll, Pa, 80s; watercolors, comn by private individuals, 80s-. *Exhib:* Solo exhibs, Mus Art, Indiana Univ Pa, 88 & Watercolor Still Lifes, Mus Fine Arts Wash Co, Hagerstown, Md, 2001-03; Art of State Juried Exhib, State Mus Pa, Harrisburg, 93-95, 97, 2000, 2003; Southern Alleghenies Trien Invitational, Southern Alleghenies Mus Art, Loretto, Pa, 93-94, 99-2000, 2008, 2010 & 2011-2013; San Diego Watercolor Soc Int, Poway Ctr Performing Arts, Calif, 94, 98 & 99; Watercolor USA Nat, Springfield Art Mus, Mo, 96, 2008-2011; Philadelphia Water color Soc Int, Berman Mus Art, Pa, 96-99; Miss Grand Nat Exhib, Miss Mus Art, Jackson, 98 & 99; Watercolor Hon Soc, 2003, 2008; Retrospective, Southern Alleghenies Mus Art, 2009, Things, Thoughts & Imagination, Visual Journeys of Soul Mates, 2010; Juried Nat Miniature Show, 2007-2011, Art Alliance Cent Pa, 2007-2012; 68th Nat Juried Exhib, Watercolor Soc of Ala, 2007-2013; WHS Invitational, Springfield, Mo, 2011-2013. *Collection Arranged:* Shippensburg Univ Fashion Archives Exhibs, 90-96; William D Davis Retrospective, 2004. *Pos:* Dir arts in educ, Cent Intermedia Unit 10, Penn State, 76-89; dir fashion archives, Shippensburg Univ, 90-96. *Teaching:* Instr art, pub sch Pa, 59-66; adj prof, Pa State Univ, 62-76 & Shippensburg Univ, 96-98. *Awards:* Grumbacker Gold Medal, 93 & 99; Jack Richeson Award, Jack Richeson Co, 94; First Place, Baltimore Watercolor Soc, 98; Gold Sable Award for Excellence in Watercolor, 2001; Hon mention, Art Alliance, 2007, 2009, 2012. *Bibliog:* Paula Banks Mitchell (auth), Portrait of an Organized Artist, State Coll Mag, 86; Stanley Marcus (auth), There's Always Time to Paint, Watercolor Mag of Am Arts, 96; Terry Di Domenico (auth), Passionate About Painting, VISTA, Shippensburg Univ, 99; Ctr Daily Times State Coll, Pa, April 2011. *Mem:* Watercolor Hon Soc USA (bd mem, 98-2003, signature mem); Tex Watercolor Soc; La Watercolor Soc; Ga Watercolor Soc; Pa Watercolor Soc; Ala Watercolor Soc; Baltimore Watercolor Soc; Philadelphia Watercolor Soc; Niagara Frontier Watercolor Soc. *Media:* Watercolor. *Interests:* Gardening, raising Bonsai trees, Ikebana, antiquing, reading, collecting, writing poetry. *Publ:* Contribr, Watercolor Sketching on the Move, Am Artists Mag, 98, Fifty Years of Excellence, Tex Watercolor Soc, 99, Watercolor Expressions & The Best of Watercolor Vol 3, Rockport Publ, 99; Things, Thoughts & Imagination, Visual Journeys of Soul Mates (catalogue), 2010. *Mailing Add:* 1427 Curtin St State College PA 16803

STUTESMAN, CEZANNE SLOUGH
PAINTER

b Bucks Co, Pa, Dec 25, 1956. *Study:* Univ State of NY, BS, 85; Pima Community Col, Ariz, AS; studied under Dr William Kuchler, Philadelphia, Pa. *Work:* BloodHorse Inc, Lexington; The Am Quarter Horse Asn, Amarillo, Tex; Nat Park Serv, Ariz; City of Beverly Hills; Univ Ariz, Tucson. *Comn:* SeaCove, GrandPrix horse, Belynda Bond; Clover Hills Trinity Champion horse, L MacMillan; Disco Lemonade champion horse, J Jensen; Paxton champion horse, K Herberger. *Exhib:* Solo exhibs, Military History of the SW, US Army Mus, Ft Huachuca, Az; Paradise Horses, Paradise Race Track, Phoenix; The Am Air Craft, Tucson Int Airport; 25 solo exhibs. *Pos:* Illustrative artist, Sears; textile designer, Quaker Lace; dir, Cezanne's Gallery, Ariz. *Awards:* Equine Artist of the Yr, NA Horsemens Asn, 03. *Mem:* USA Equestrian; British Horse Soc; Am Cattle Women; Az Cowbelles. *Publ:* PBS Feature, 95; Lisa Sheehy, CS Stutesman, Equine Images, 00; Lisa Sheehy, CS Stutesman, Polo Players Edition, 02; Gwen Rizzo (editor), Players Ed, 02; N Am Horsemen's Asn, 03

STUX, STEFAN VICTOR
ART DEALER, DIRECTOR
b Timisoara, Romania, Oct 28, 1942; US citizen. *Study:* New York Univ, PhD, 75. *Pos:* Pres & dir, Stux Gallery, Boston, 80-, Stux Gallery, New York, 86-, Stux Art Ltd, New York, 94 & Stefan Stux Gallery, 96. *Teaching:* Instr, Brandeis Univ, 75-78 & Harvard Univ, 79-84. *Specialty:* Contemporary, modern master, and impressionist. *Mailing Add:* 520 W End Ave Apt 9 New York NY 10024-3240

SUBA, SUSANNE (MRS BERTAM BLOCH)
PAINTER, ILLUSTRATOR
b Budapest, Hungary; US citizen. *Study:* Pratt Inst, grad. *Work:* Metrop Mus Art, NY; Brooklyn Mus, NY; Art Inst Chicago; Mus City of NY; Hyde Collection, Glen Falls, NY. *Exhib:* Ansdell Gallery, London, Eng; Hammer Gallery, NY; Kalamazoo Inst Art; Art Inst Chicago; Mus Mod Art, NY; Works on Paper, Weatherspoon Gallery, Chapel Hill, NC. *Pos:* Teacher, Nelson Univ, Nelson, BC & Community Col, NY. *Awards:* Awards, Am Inst Graphic Art, Art Dirs Club New York & Art Dirs Club Chicago. *Media:* Watercolor, Black Ink. *Publ:* A Rocket in My Pocket; The Monkeys and the Peddler; The Man with the Bushy Beard

SUBLETT, CARL CECIL
PAINTER
b Johnson Co, Ky, Feb 4, 1919. *Study:* Western Ky Univ, 1940; Univ Study Ctr, Florence, Italy, 1945; Univ Tenn, 1956. *Work:* Nat Acad Design, NY; Hunter Gallery Art, Chattanooga, Tenn; Mint Mus, Charlotte, NC; Springfield Art Mus, Mo; Tenn Arts Comn, Nashville; Knoxville Mus Art, Tenn. *Comn:* Five watercolor paintings, Kimberly Clark Corp Off, Knoxville, Tenn. *Exhib:* Southeastern Art Ann, Atlanta, Ga; Paintings of Yr, Atlanta; New Painters of South, Birmingham, Ala; Watercolor USA, Springfield, Mo, 1964-72; Am Watercolor Soc, NY, 1972; Solo retrospective, Tenn State Mus, Nashville, 83 & Knoxville Mus Art, Tenn, 91; A Visual Odyssey, Ewing Gallery, 2000-02; Greenville County Mus Art, SC, 2002-03. *Pos:* Indust eng, draftsman Enterprise Wheel & Car Corp, Bristol, Va, 1946-49; artist, asst mgr Bristol Art Engravers, 1952-54; art dir, Charles S Kane Co, Knoxville, Tenn, 1954-65; juror, Watercolor Soc Ala, Birmingham, 1979, Jacksonville Univ Ann, 1980; Juror, Bristol Art Guild 8th ann juried exhib, 1993; owner, Sublett Gallery, Knoxville, Tenn, 1984, Union, Maine, 2006-. *Teaching:* staff artist Bristol, Va-Tennessean & Herald Courier, 1950-52; asst prof art, Univ Tenn, 1966-67, prof, 1976-82. *Awards:* Art Embassies Prog State Dept, 68-83, 87-90, 90-; Lifetime Achievement Award, Mayor's Art Celebration, Knoxville Art Ctr; Inaugural Distinguished Fac/Alumni/Student Award, Univ Tenn Sch Art, 2000. *Bibliog:* Prize Winning Watercolors, Allied Publ, Inc, 1965; Invitational Carl Sublett Exhibition Catalog, Tenn State Mus, 1983; A Visual Odyssey: The Art of Carl Sublett, U T Ewing Gallery, 2000; Watercolor Expressions, Rockport Publ, 1999. *Mem:* Nat Acad (assoc, 1977, acad, 1994-); Knoxville Watercolor Soc; Tenn Watercolor Soc; Port Clyde Arts & Crafts Soc, Maine; Watercolor USA Hon Soc. *Media:* Watercolor, Oil. *Publ:* Illusr, (exhib catalog), Tenn State Mus, 1983. *Dealer:* Collector's Gallery Nashville TN; Bennett Galleries Knoxville TN. *Mailing Add:* Sublett Gallery 496 Wotton's Mill Union ME 04862

SUBOTSKY, MIKHAEL
PHOTOGRAPHER
b Cape Town, South Africa, 1981. *Work:* Mus Mod Art, New York. *Exhib:* Solo exhibs include Nelson Mandela Cell, Pollsmoor Prison, South Africa, 2005, Constitution Hill, Johannesburg, South Africa, Goodman Gallery, Johannesburg, 2006, Photog Mus Amsterdam, 2007, Goodman Gallery, Cape Town, South Africa, 2007; two-person exhib with Josephine Meckseper, Mus Mod Art, New York, 2008; group exhibs include Click, Goodman Gallery, Johannesburg, 2005; Snap Judgments: New Positions in Contemp African Photog, Int Ctr Photog, New York, 2006; Lift off II, Goodman Gallery, Cape Town, 2007, The Loaded Lens, 2007. *Awards:* Infinity Award for Young Photog, Int Ctr Photog, 2007. *Dealer:* Goodman Gallery 163 Jan Smuts Ave Parkwood Johannesburg Gauteng South Africa 2193

SUBRAMANIAM, RADHIKA
CURATOR, EDUCATOR
Collection Arranged: Cities, Art and Recovery, Lower Manhattan Cultural Coun, 2005-2006; Rods and Cones: Seeing from the Back of One's Head, 2008; Abecedarium for Our Times, Apexart, 2008. *Pos:* Dir cultural programs, Lower Manhattan Cult Coun; dir & chief cur, Sheila C Johnson Design Ctr; founding exec ed, Connect Art Jour. *Teaching:* Asst prof art & design hist & theory, Parsons New Sch. *Mailing Add:* 66 5th Ave New York NY 10011

SUDLOW, ROBERT N
PAINTER, PRINTMAKER, SCULPTOR
b Holton, Kans, Feb 25, 1920. *Study:* Univ Kans, BFA; Univ Calif, Berkeley; Calif Coll Arts & Crafts, Oakland, MFA; Acad Grande Chaumiere, Paris; Acad Andre L'Hote, Paris. *Work:* City Art Mus, St Louis, Mo; Yellow Freight Collection, Kansas City, Mo; Joslyn Art Mus, Omaha; Sheldon Art Mus, Lincoln, Nebr; Menninger Found, Topeka, Kans; Spencer Art Mus Univ of Kans, Lawrence, Kans; Beach Mus KS State Univ, Manhattan, Kans. *Comn:* Mural Com State Bank, Topeka, Kans. *Exhib:* Solo exhibs, Beauchamp Gallery, Topeka, 84-90, 94 & 2003, Am Legacy Gallery, Kansas City, Mo, 90-94 & 2003; Kansas Landscapes, traveling show, 85 & 87; solo Retrospective, Wichita Art Mus Kans, 94; Beyond the Horizon, Nat Traveling Show, 98; Spiritual Journeys Traveling Show Exhib, 2002-; retrospective, Lawrence Arts Ctr, Kansas, 2002. *Pos:* Prof Emer, 87. *Teaching:* Prof art, Univ Kans, 47-87; ret. *Awards:* Gov Artist, 76; Baker Univ Citation, 90; Native Son of Kans Award, 96. *Bibliog:* Sunflower Journey, Channel II KTWU. *Media:* Oil, Watercolor; Lithography; Wood. *Specialty:* Landscape Painting. *Interests:* Poetry. *Collection:* Spiritual Journeys The Art of Robert Sudlow. *Publ:* Landscapes in Kansas, Kans Univ Press, 87. *Dealer:* Am Legacy Gallery 5911 Main Kansas City MO 66103; Beauchamp Frame Shop 3113 Huntoon Topeka KS; Roy Gallery 1410 Kasold Dr Lawrence KS 66049. *Mailing Add:* 886 E 1050th Rd Lawrence KS 66047

SUFFOLK, RANDALL
MUSEUM DIRECTOR
Study: Conn Coll, BA (English); Columbia Univ, MA (higher ed admin); Bryn Mawr Coll, MA (Art History). *Pos:* Consult, Arts Corp, Ltd, Philadelphia, formerly; assoc, W Graham Arader III Galleries, Philadelphia, New York, formerly; cur, Hyde Collection, Glen Falls, NY, 1995-1998, deputy dir, 1998-1999, acting dir, 1999-2000, dir, 2000-2007; exec dir, chief exec officer, Philbrook Mus Art, Tulsa, Okla, 2007-. *Mem:* bd dirs, Adirondack/Lake George Regional Tourism Bd; bd dirs, Feeder Canal Alliance; mem, strategic planning comt, Univ Art Mus State Univ NY, Albany; rev panel mem, Special Opportunity Stipend Grants, NY State Coun on Arts. *Mailing Add:* Philbrook Museum of Art 2727 South Rockford Road Tulsa OK 74114

SUGGS, DON
PAINTER, PHOTOGRAPHER
b Ft Worth, Tex, Mar 16, 1945. *Study:* Univ Calif Los Angeles, MA, 71, MSA, 72. *Work:* San Diego Mus Contemp Art, Calif; Univ Calif, Los Angeles. *Exhib:* Clearing, Los Angeles Co Mus, Calif, 89. *Teaching:* Instr painting & drawing, Univ Calif Los Angeles, 83-. *Awards:* Artist Fel, Nat Endowment Arts, 91. *Mailing Add:* c/o LA Louver Gallery 45 N Venice Blvd Venice CA 90291

SUGGS, PAT(RICIA) ANN
PAINTER, INSTRUCTOR
b Reedley, Calif, Mar 17, 1936. *Study:* Old World Acad Training; Leighton Fine Art Acad, with Thomas & Margery Lester Leighton, San Francisco, 74-81; extensive travel & study at the great art centers of Europe, London, Paris, Rome, Florence, Dresden, Prague, Russia, Japan, China, Turkey, etc. *Comn:* Pastel portrait painting, comn by Melody Grey, Santa Rosa Calif, 86; Pastel floral painting, comn by Elaine Clarke, Grants Pass, Ore, 91; Pastel landscape painting, comn by James & Helen Riley, Saratoga, Calif, 92; Pastel rose floral, comn by Jean Afonso, 93 & 96. *Exhib:* Hayward Arts Coun, Calif, 98; Pure Pigment, Los Gatos, Calif, 98; Degas Pastel Soc Exhib, Lauren Rogers Mus Art, Miss; IAPS Open Exhib, Dartmouth St Gallery, Albuquerque, NMex, 99; Nat Exhib, Fort Walton Beach Mus Art, 2000-02; Pastel Soc of Am Thirteenth Ann Juried Exhib, 03 & Renaissance in Pastel, Slater Mem Mus, 2006; The Butler Inst of Am Art, Youngstown, Ohio, 03; Group exhibs, Gadabout Gallery, Los Gatos, Calif, 86, Pure Pigment, Los Gatos Mus of Art, 98; Leighton Studio Exhib, Triton Mus Fine Art, Santa Clara, Calif, 2001-2002; Binney & Smith Gallery, Banana Factory, Bethlehem, PA, 2004; Triton Mus Fine Art, Santa Clara, Calif, Allied Artists West, 2005; 4 Artists-4 Visions, Orinda Libr, Gallery Orinda, Calif, 2008; Triton Mus Fine Art, Santa Clara, Calif, 2008; 11th Exhib, IAPS Butler Inst Am Art, Ohio, 2008; Pastel by Invitation, Creative Arts Ctr, Chatham, Mass, 2009; Pastels Chicago, Koehnline Mus Art, 2009; 15th Juried exhib, IAPS, City of Brea Art Gallery, Calif, 2010; 24th Ann Int Open Exhib, Northwest Pastel Soc, America Art Co, Tacoma, Wash; The First Master Circle, Exhib Int Asn Pastel Societies, Hispanic Art Gallery, Albuquerque, NMex; Pastel by Invitation, Creative Arts Center, Chatham, Mass, 2011; Untamed Flora, Allied Artists West, Sent Sovi, Saratoga, Calif, 2011. *Pos:* Judge fine arts, Arts Clubs, The Peninsula, Northern Calif & San Joaquin Valley, 84-94 & 94-96 & Sonoma Co, Alameda Co & Santa Clara Co Fairs, 89-91; judge, SWA 50th Ann, 2000; judge, Santa Clara Co Fair, 2000 & Alameda Co Fair, 2003. *Teaching:* various workshops, Calif, NMex. *Awards:* Two Grumbacher Gold Medals, SWA Annual Show, 98; Award of Excellence, South Bay Fine Arts Festival, Santa Clara, Calif, 2000; Best Floral Award, Nat Pastel Art Show, Lone Star Pastel Soc, 2003; Canson Award, Pastel Soc Oreg, 2003; Master Circle Gold Medallion Award, Int Asn Pastel Soc, 2005; Daler Rowney Award (for pastel), Cape Cod, Mass, 2006; Great Am Art Works Pastel Award, Degas Pastel Soc, New Orleans, La, 2006; Merchandise award, Degas Pastel Soc, New Orleans, La, 2011. *Bibliog:* John Lehman (auth), Three Native Daughters' Show, The New Outlook, 6/6/83; Urania Tarbet (auth), Art Revue, winter 95/96; Pratt & Monato (auths), Best of Pastel, Rockport Publ, 96. *Mem:* Pastel Soc Am, NY; Pastel Soc W Coast, Carmichael, Calif (adv bd, 86-2010); Soc Western Artists (trustee, 86-96); Allied Artists West (dir, exhibs, 91-92); The Nat League Am Pen Women, Las Artes Br; Int Asn Pastel Soc (treas 94-2010). *Media:* Pastel, Oil, Plein-Air & Realistic Pastel. *Publ:* Luminous Translucence Mag, 50-57, 1/2000; Floral Inspiration, 72, 97 & Best of Pastel, 130, 96, Rockport Publ. *Dealer:* Carol A Dabb 41 Sunkist Lane Los Altos CA 94022. *Mailing Add:* 4127 Beebe Cir San Jose CA 95135-1010

SUGIMOTO, HIROSHI
PHOTOGRAPHER
b Tokyo, Japan, 1948. *Study:* St Pauls Univ, Tokyo, 1970; Art Ctr Coll Design, Los Angeles, 1972. *Exhib:* Solo exhibs, Nat Mus Art, Cleveland, Ohio, 89, Mus Contemp Art, La, 94-95, Mus Modern Art, NY City, Metrop Mus Art, 95, La Caixa, Madrid, Spain, 98, Beilefeld Mus, Ger, Kitakyushu Project Gallery, Moderna Museet, Sweden, Deutsche Guggenheim, Berlin, 2000, Soanbend Gallery, NY City, Robert Klein Gallery, Boston, Mass, 2006, Pace Gallery, 2010; Lion Biennale, Lion, France, 96; Palazzo delle esposioni, Rome, 96; Mus Contemp Art, Chicago, 96; Wexner Ctr Arts, 96; By Night, Found Caltier pour l'art contemporain, Paris, France, 96; Johannesburg Bienna, South Africa, 97; At the End of the Century: One Hundred Years of Architecture, Mus Brazil, 98; Terra Incognita, Neues Mus Weserburg, Bremen, Ger, 98; Photographer's Gallery, London, Eng, 98; Int Ctr Photography, NY City, 99; Portraits, Guggenheim Museum, Berlin, 2000; Noh Such Thing as Time, DIA Art Ctr, New York, 2001; The Architecture of Time, Fruit Market Gallery, Edinburgh, 2002; The Origins of Love, Yoshii Gallery, New York, 2004; History of History, Japan Soc Gallery, New York, 2005; Colors of Shadows, Marian Goodman Gallery, Paris, 2006; Leakage of Light, Gallery Koyanagi, Tokyo, 2007; 7Days / 7 Nights, Gagosian Gallery, New York, 2008. *Awards:* Hasselblad Award, 2001; Praemium Imperiale award for Painting, 2009. *Mailing Add:* c/o Robert Klein Gallery 4th Floor 38 Newbury St Boston MA 02116

SUGIURA, KUNIE
PHOTOGRAPHER, PAINTER
b Naqoya. *Study:* Art Inst Chicago, BFA, 67. *Work:* Mus Mod Art, NY; Mus Fine Arts, Boston; Denver Art Mus; George Eastman House, Rochester, NY; Va Mus Art, Richmond. *Comn:* photog, JGS, New York City, 03. *Exhib:* Selections From the Collection, Aldrich Mus Art, Ridgefield, Conn, 72; Painting & Sculpture Today, Indianapolis Mus Art, 72; Ann Exhib Painting, Whitney Mus Am Art, NY, 72; Fossilization: Imprinted Light, Mus Mod Art, Saltama, Japan, 97; New Photog 13, Mus Mod Art, NY, 97-98; Attractants: Kunie Sugiura, Aichi Prefectural Mus Art, Japan, 98. *Awards:* Robert Scull Found Grant, 85; Catalogue Project Grant, NY Found Arts, 97 & Artist Fel, 98. *Bibliog:* Julia Scully (auth), CKO, Mod Photog, 68; Janet Koplos (auth), Shadow Play, Art in Am, 4/02; Michael Klein (auth), Lucid Encounters, World Art, Spring 99. *Dealer:* Leslie Toukonow 535 W 22nd St 6th fl New York NY 10011. *Mailing Add:* 7 Doyers St 4th fl New York NY 10013

SUGIYAMA, AKIKO
CRAFTSMAN, ASSEMBLAGE ARTIST
b Noheji, Aomori Prefecture, Japan. *Study:* Joshibi Daigaku, Tokyo, BA, 74. *Work:* Fla Gulf Coast Art Ctr, Belleair, Fla; Polk Mus Art, Lakeland, Fla; Daytona Beach Arts & Scis Ctr, Daytona Beach, Fla; Deland Mus Art, Deland, Fla. *Comn:* Wall hangings, Holland & Knight Law Firm, Tampa, Fla, 88; wall hangings, Daytona Beach Int Airport, 93; wall hangings, Coca-Cola Co, Atlanta, Ga, 93; wall hangings, Bert Fish Med Ctr, New Smyrna Beach, Fla, 96; wall hangings, Volusia Co Courthouse, Deland, Fla, 2001. *Exhib:* Solo exhib, Tampa Mus Art, Tampa, Fla, 94, Paper Play, Gulf Coast Art Ctr, Belleair, Fla, 97, Polk Mus Art, Lakeland, Fla, 2009; Craft Show, Philadelphia Mus Art, 2000 & 2004-2009; Incarnations, Gayle Wilson Gallery, South Hampton, NY, 2001; Am Craft Expos, 2001-2009; Craft Show, Smithsonian, Washington, DC, 2002 & 2005-2009; Visual Art Fel Exhib, Lowe Art Mus, Coral Gables, Fla, 2004; Two-person exhib, Gallery Camino Real, Boca Raton, Fla, 2005. *Awards:* Grainger Best of Fiber award, American Craft Exposition, 2002; Visual Arts fellow, State of Fla, 2002; Exhibitors Choice Bronze Award, Smithsonian Craft Show, 2007; Award of Excellence, Palm Beach Fine Craft Show, 2004; Gold award, Smithsonian Craft Show, 2011. *Bibliog:* Paper Play, The Georgia Rev, spring 91; Portfolio, American Craft, 4/5/94; These Hands Tell a Story, Am Craft Expos, 4/2009. *Mem:* Am Craft Coun; Fla Craftsmen. *Media:* Paper; Fiber decorative. *Dealer:* Blue Spiral 1 38 Biltmore Ave Ashville NC 28801; Watson Macrae Gallery Sanibel Fla. *Mailing Add:* 5 Bay Hill Dr Ormond Beach FL 32174

SUJO, CLARA DIAMENT
GALLERY DIRECTOR, CURATOR, WRITER
b Argentina, 1921. *Study:* Studied with Jorge Romero Brest & Pierre Francastel. *Work:* 67 works in var mus, 2008-. *Exhib:* Vision of Venezuelan Art, Nat Gallery, Caracas, 95. *Collection Arranged:* 195 exhibs from 81-2008; Stanley Spencer, 92; Art & Psychoanalysis, 2006; J Torres-Garcia, 2007; Arshile Gorks, 2007; Latin Am Masters, 2008. *Pos:* cur New Acquisitions, Mus Bellas Artes Caracas, 58-63; dir, Documentary Films on Art, 63-67, dir, Estudio Actual, Caracas, 68-91 & CDS Gallery, New York, 81-2008. *Teaching:* Prof art hist & fine Arts, Cristobal Rojas Sch Fine Arts, Caracas, 58-65; prof art hist & art appreciation, Neumann Found Inst Design, 67-70. *Awards:* Order Andres Bello, Venezuelan Govt. *Mem:* Int Asn Art Critics; Art Table Inc; Art Dealers Asn Am. *Specialty:* International contemporary art, development of Latin Am Art. *Interests:* Showcasing Latin Am Art & sponsoring African Am & indigenous art. *Collection:* Duncan Family- Craig Duncan. *Publ:* Auth, Art in Latin America Today, Panamerican Union, 62; coauth, Joseph Albers, Kellar Velag, 67; contribr, The Emergent Decade, Cornell Univ, 65. *Dealer:* Beyever Switzerland

SULKOWSKI, ELIZABETH BRANDON
PAINTER
b Oct 09, 1952. *Study:* Calif Coll of Arts & Crafts, summer 1973; Univ of Ga, BFA Interior Design, 1974; Art Students League of NY, 1974-1979. *Exhib:* Women Artists, Cheekwood Mus, Nashville, Tenn, 1994; AAPL Grand Nat, Nat Arts Club, NYC, 1995; Women of the West, Tucson Mus of Art, Tucson, Ariz, 1996. *Media:* Oil. *Mailing Add:* 4685 Everal Ln Franklin TN 37064

SULKOWSKI, JAMES M
PAINTER, INSTRUCTOR
b Pittsburgh, PA, Dec 10, 1951. *Study:* Pa Acad Fine Arts, 69-71; Carnegie Mellon Univ, 71-72; Art Students League of NY with Frank Mason & Robert Beverlyhale, 74-79. *Work:* PNC Bank, Pittsburgh; Golden Eagle Resort, Stowe, Vt; Mercy Hosp, Pittsburgh; Metrop Opera, New York; George H W Bush Presidential Libr, Tex. *Comn:* Ikhwan Revolt of 1929, comn by King of Saudi Arabia, Jeddah, Saudi Arabia, 79-80; Court of Baghdad 9th Century, comn by King of Saudi Arabia, 79-80; 3 landscape murals, St Francis Health Sys, Pittsburgh, 86; Mural Gen Lafayette, Nemacolin Woodlands Resort, Pa, 2000; Portrait Richard White, Washington Fed Bank, Washington, Pa, 2006. *Exhib:* Art in Am, Denver Mus, 94-95; The Nude in Fine Art, Vanier & Roberts Fine Art, Scottsdale, Ariz, 94; Art in the Mountains, Nemacolin Woodlands Resort, Pittsburgh, 96; Art in the Garden, Washington Co Hist Soc, Washington, Pa, 2005. *Collection Arranged:* Opera Art, Chautauqua Inst, NY, 84; Opera Art of James Sulkowski, Metrop Opera of NY, 84; Art of James Sulkowski, Laroche Coll, Pa, 95; Opera Art, Stifel Fine Arts, Wheeling WVa, 2002; Beyond the Sea, Sulkowski Fine Art Gallery, 2005; Looking Back-A Retrospective 1966-2006, Sulkowski Fine Art Gallery, 2006. *Pos:* Artist in res, Pittsburgh Opera, Pittsburgh, 81-83; owner & inst, Sulkowski Acad of Fine Art, Houston, Pa, 94-2001; owner, Sulkowski Fine Art Gallery, Canonsburg, Pa, 2003-. *Teaching:* Classical still life painting, Sweetwater Art Ctr, Sewickley, Pa, 87-94; portrait painting, Sulkowski Acad Fine Art, Houston, Pa, 94-2001; figure drawing, Sulkowski Acad Fine Art, Canonsburg, Pa, 94-2001; and var nat workshops; painting & drawing, Point Park Univ, Pittsburgh, Pa. *Awards:* Helen de Cozen Award, Am Artists Prof League; Best of Show, 30th Ann Exhib of Printing Indus of Western Pa, 96; People's Choice Award, Art in the Mountains, US Art Magazine, 97. *Bibliog:* David Templeton (auth), A Fine Day for the Fine Arts, Pittsburgh Post Gazette, 94; Stephen Doherty (auth), Turning to Floral Still Lites, Am Artist Mag, 96; Kathryn Kipp (auth), The Best of Flower Painting, North Light Bks, 97; The Best of Flower Painting 2, North Light Bks, 97; M Stephen Doherty (auth), James M Sulkowski: Simplifying complex painting situations, Workshop Mag, Am Artist, winter, 2006. *Mem:* Nat Soc Mural Painters; Nat Arts Club NY; Am Artist Prof League; Art Students League NY. *Media:* Oil. *Specialty:* Original oil paintings and limited edition prints. *Interests:* Traveling, writing articles for art publications, painting & museums. *Publ:* Auth, Featuring original oil paintings, Xlibris, 2007; Dynamic Action in Floral Painting, Am Artist Mag, 1/2006; Mastering Oil Painting, Walter Foster Publications, 2013. *Mailing Add:* 329 Hawthorne St Canonsburg PA 15317

SULKOWSKI, JOSEPH H
PAINTER
b Pittsburgh, Pa Dec 10, 1951. *Study:* Pa Acad of the Fine Arts, 1969-1971; Art Students League of NY with Frank Mason, 1974-1979. *Work:* King Abdul Aziz Naval Mus, Jedda, Saudi Arabia; Tenn State Mus, Nashville, Tenn. *Comn:* The Ikhwan Revolt of 1929, The Court of Baghdad in the 9th Century, Saudi Arabian Royal Family, Jedda, Saudi Arabia, 1980. *Awards:* Grumbacher Gold Medallion, AAPL Show, 1990. *Bibliog:* Katherine A Sulkowski (auth), Master and Hands, Washington/Green, 2004. *Mem:* Art Students League of NY (life mem); Nat Arts club, NY; Nat Soc of Mural Painters; Am Artists Prof League; Artwatch Int. *Media:* Oil. *Publ:* A Joyous Process, Sporting Classics, 1997; The Sporting Art of Joseph Sulkowski, Canine Images, 2001. *Dealer:* Halcyon Gallery London England. *Mailing Add:* 4685 Everal Ln Franklin TN 37064

SULLIVAN, ANNE DOROTHY HEVNER
PAINTER, PRINTMAKER
b Boston, Mass, Mar 17, 1929. *Study:* Northeastern Univ, Boston, Mass, 72-74; Univ Lowell, Mass, BA (magna cum laude), 77; DeCordova Mus, with King Coffin, Carlton Plummer, Glen Bradshaw & K Chang Liu and others. *Work:* The New Eng Permanent Collection, Boston, Mass; Shawmut Bank, Boston, Mass; Bay Banks of New Eng, Boston, Mass; Sheraton Corp, Boston, Mass; Amoskeag Banks, Manchester, NH; and others. *Comn:* Painting, Enterprise Bank, Lowell, Mass, 2009. *Exhib:* Whistler House Mus (2 person invitational), Lowell, Mass, 95; Nat Asn Women Artists traveling graphics, 96, 120 years Celebration, 2009; Nat Asn Women Artists 107th Ann, NY, 96-98; NAm Open Competition, Boston, 92, 94, 96, 98, 2000, 2002, 2004; Catharine Lorillard Wolfe 100th Exhib, NY, 96; Int Soc of Experimental Artists, Sarasota, Fla, 98-99, 2002; Int Soc of Experimental Artists, Welch Exchange, Contemp Arts Soc for Wales, 2004; Cynon Valley Mus, Aberdare, Wales, 2004; DeVos Mus, N Mich Univ, New Bedford, Mass Mus, 2006; Attleboro Arts Mus, Nat Monotype Guild of New Eng, 2008; NAWA 120th Ann Exhib, Hub Robeson Gallery, Penn State, 2009; NAWA, Ann Exhib, Salmagundi Art Club, New York, 2009; Retrospective, Whistler House Mus Art, Lowell, Mass, 2009. *Collection Arranged:* Emerging Boston Artists, Brush Gallery, Urban Nat Park, Lowell, Mass, 90; Invitational Retrospective, Whistler House Mus Art, 2009. *Pos:* Vpres, Whistler Mus, 77-79; chmn, Lowell Arts Lottery Coun, 79-81; bd mem, Mass Arts & Humanities Adv Comt, 81-82; consult, pvt & pub collections, 88-90; dir, Abbey Art Gallery, Boston; pres, Monotype Guild New Eng, 92-93. *Teaching:* Dir & instr art prog, Whistler House Mus Art, Lowell, Mass, 75-76, instr, 96 & 98; dir & instr AID prog, Univ Lowell, Mass, 76-84; instr, Brush Gallery, Urban Nat Park Lowell, Mass, 96. *Awards:* MM Rines Award for outstanding contemporary painting, NAm Open Competition, Boston, 94; Am Artist Mag Award, Catharine Lorillard Wolfe Art Club, NY, 96; Hon Mention, Nat Open Competition, RI Watercolor Soc, 2002, 2008; Martha Reed Mem Award, 98; Hon Mention, 63rd Nat Open Competition, Exptl Artists Ala, 2004; Nautilus Fel Award, Int Soc Exptl Artists, 2007. *Bibliog:* Ann Schecter (auth), Sun Art critics review, Lowell Sun, Mass, 4/8/79 & 4/6/84; Marie Geary (auth), Art is, Chelmsford Weekly, Mass, 4/3/80; Boston Globe, 12/3/95; Nancy E Tuttle (auth), Art Review, Lowell Sun, Lowell, Mass, 5/14/09. *Mem:* New Eng Watercolor Soc (bd dir, 82-92); Nat League Penwomen, Washington, DC; Int Soc Experimental Artists, Fla; Monotype Guild of Northeast (pres, 92-93); Copley Soc Boston; Nat Asn Women Artists. *Media:* Mixed Media, Monotype. *Publ:* Contribr, Abstracts in Watercolor (cover & p 61), Rockport Publ, 96; Painting Composition, pg 56 & Best of Watercolor 2, pg 77, 97 Rockport Publ. *Mailing Add:* 44 Meadow Lakes Apt 8 East Windsor NJ 08520

SULLIVAN, BARBARA JEAN
PAINTER, INSTRUCTOR
b Indianapolis, Ind. *Study:* Howard Terpning, Cowboy Artists of Am, student. *Comn:* paintings (22), Virgins River Hotel / Casino. *Exhib:* Auction of Original Western Art, C M Russel Mus, Great Falls, Mont, 84; Mem Western Art Show, George Phippen Mus, Prescott, Ariz, 84; Women Artists Am West, PaJo's Gallery, Pinedale, Wyo, 85; 8th Ann Nat Western Art Show, Burk Gallery, Boulder City, Nev, 85; Artists Invitational Exhib, C M Russel Mus, Great Falls, Mont, 86; Native Am Indian Art Competition, Las Vegas Art Mus, Nev, 94; 43rd Ann Art Roundup, Las Vegas Art Mus, Nev, 95; Nat Fine Arts Competition, Braithwaite Fine Arts Gallery, Cedar City, Utah, 99; Navarro Gallery, Sedona, Ariz, 2002; Providence Gallery, Scottsdale, Ariz, 2006. *Collection Arranged:* White House, Washington, DC; Nev Nat Bank, Las Vegas; Virgin River Casino/Hotel, Mesquite, Nev. *Teaching:* instr oil painting, Las Vegas Art Mus, Nev, 83-85. *Awards:* Best of Show award, Native Am Indian Art Inst, Las Vegas, Nev, 94; Judges award, 43rd Ann Art Roundup, Las Vegas, Nev, 95; Gold Medal Award, Best Oil, Bosque Conservatory 16th Ann Art Competition, 2001. *Bibliog:* illusr, Winter Rage, 91 & The Horsemen, 92, Putnam Berkley. *Mem:* Oil Painters Am. *Media:* Oil. *Publ:* Vivian Woods (auth), Arts & Artists, Las Vegas Sun, 82; Vivian Woods (auth), Artist Thrives on Diet of Travel, Paint, Las Vegas, Review J, 86; Bill Hollis (auth), Emerging Artists, Southwest Art Mag, 96. *Dealer:* LMR Gallery 2470 Silver Sage Dr Pahrump NV 89060; Navarro Gallery Tlaquepaque Ste D103 336 Hwy 179 Sedona AZ 86336; Tribal Treasures Gallery Green Tree Inn 14173 Green Tree Blvd Victorville CA 92392; Inspirations Gallery 165 N Main St Lakeport CA 95453. *Mailing Add:* 2470 Silver Sage Dr Pahrump NV 89060

SULLIVAN, BILLY
ARTIST
b NYC, 1946. *Study:* Sch Vis Arts, NY, Ed, 1968. *Exhib:* Solo exhibs, Fischbach Gallery, NY, 1986, 1989, 1990, 1992, 1997; Rebecca Ibel Gallery, 1994, 1998, 2000, 2001; Photographs, New Mus Contemp Art, NY, 2002; New Work, Nicole Klagsbrun, NY, 2003; North Fork/South Fork: EastEnd Art Now, Parrish Art Mus South Hampton, 2004; Galleria Francesca Kaufmann, Milan, Italy, 2005; group exhibs, Face Value: Am Portraits, Parrish Art Mus, 1995; Summer 1996; Rebecca Ibel Gallery, 1996; Sex/Industry Stefan Stux Gallery, NY, 1997; Summer, Lennon, Weinberg, Inc, NY, 1998; Couples, Cheim & Read Gallery, NY, 2000; Reflection, 2001; Summertime, 2002; Ten Years in Columbus: Part 3, 2003; Fabulous, 2005; Whitney Biennial: Day for Night, Whitney Mus Am Art, NY, 2006. *Mailing Add:* c/o Rebecca Ibel Gallery 1055 N High St Columbus OH 43201

SULLIVAN, CATHERINE
VIDEO ARTIST
b in Los Angeles. *Study:* Calif Inst Arts, Valencia, BFA, 1992; Art Ctr Col Design, Pasadena, Calif, MFA, 1997. *Exhib:* Gander Mountain High, Room 10, Pasadena, 1995; SuperIntellectuals, Three Day Weekend, Calif State Univ, 1996; Margo Leavin Gallery, Los Angeles, 1998; Galerie Christian Nagel, Cologne, 1999; Museum Villa Stuck, Munich, 2000; Kunstverein Hamburg, 2001; solo exhibs, Galerie Christian Nagel, Cologne, 2001, Five Economies (big hunt/little hunt), Renaissance Soc, Univ Chicago, 2002, Metro Pictures, New York, 2003, Contemporain Fri-Art Kunsthalle, Fribourg, Switzlerand, 2003, Neuer Aachener Kunstverein, Germany, 2004, Richard Telles, Los Angeles, 2005, The Chittendens, Tate Modern, London, 2005, Whitney Mus Am Art Altria, New York, 2006, Triangle of Need, Walker Art Ctr, Minneapolis, Vizcaya Mus, Miami, Metro Pictures, New York, Smart Mus Art, Chicago, Galerie Christian Nagel, GSK Contemp, Royal Acad Arts, London, 2007-2008; Marianne Boesky Gallery, New York, 2002; Brightness, Mus Modern Art Dubrovnik, Croatia, 2003; Ice Flores of Franz Joseph Land, Whitney Biennial, New York, 2004, Prague Biennial, 2005; Whitechapel, London, 2006; Thyssen-Bornemisza Art Contemp, Vienna, 2007; Four Thursday Nights: Creative Imagination, Aspen Art Mus, 2008; Molten Stages, GSK Contemp, Royal Acad Arts, London, 2008; New Acquisitions, Miami Art Mus, 2009. *Awards:* Fel, Visual Arts, US Artists, 2008; Alpert Award in Arts, CalArts, 2004. *Bibliog:* Justin Hayford (auth), Dad's ham, Chicago Reader, 5/1997; Through the scattered glances, Spring J, 1999; James Yood (auth), Catherine Sullivan, Artforum, 9/2001; Uta Grosenick (ed) Art Now, Vol 2, 2005; Judy Radul (auth), I come to bury Ceasar: the image of theatre in the imagination of visual art, Art Lies, winter 2008; Alice Savorelli (auth), Americans in Milan, Artnet.com, 3/2009. *Publ:* Coauth (with Beatrix Ruf & Sebastian Egenhofer), Catherine Sullivan, JRP Ringier, 2005; auth, 1000 words, Artforum, 2/2006. *Mailing Add:* Metro Pictures Gallery 519 W 24th St New York NY 10011

SULLIVAN, DAVID FRANCIS
PAINTER, PRINTMAKER
b Stoughton, Mass, 1941. *Study:* Univ NH, 57-61; Chouinard Sch Fine Arts, Los Angeles, Calif; Boston Mus Fine Arts Sch. *Work:* Addison Gallery Am Art, Andover, Mass; Montreal Mus Art; Philadelphia Mus Art, Pa; Cleveland Mus, Ohio; Minn Mus Art, St Paul; Fogg Art Mus, Cambridge, Mass. *Exhib:* Twenty-Fifth Nat Exhib Prints, Smithsonian Inst, 77; Nat Print Exhib, Trenton State Col, NJ, 78; Art of the State, Hayden Gallery, Mass Inst Technol, Cambridge, 78; Printmaking Biennial, Brooklyn Mus, NY, 78; Recent Trends in Am Printmaking, Mitchell Mus, 79; New Am Still Life, Westmoreland Co Mus Art, Greensburg, Pa, 79; Genovese Gallery, Boston, 94. *Awards:* Purchase Awards, De Cordova Mus, 76 & Trenton State Col, 78; Stuart M Egnal Prize, Philadelphia Mus Art, 77; Blanche E Coleman Found Grants, 80, 81 & 82. *Bibliog:* Pamela Allara (auth), New Editions, Artnews, 9/82. *Media:* Oils; Silkscreens, Drawings. *Dealer:* Genovese/Sullivan Boston MA. *Mailing Add:* 94 N Main St Andover MA 01810-3515

SULLIVAN, FRANCOISE
PAINTER, SCULPTOR
b Montreal, Que, June 10, 1925. *Study:* Ecole des Beaux Arts de Montreal; modern Dance, New Dance Group, New York City. *Hon Degrees:* Hon Doctorate, York Univ, Toronto, 1998; Hon Doctorate UQAM, 2000. *Work:* Nat Gallery, Ottawa; Le Mus d'Art Contemporain, Montreal; La Banque d'Art du Can; Univ Sask; and others. *Comn:* Sculpture, Toronto City Hall, comn by City of Toronto, Ont, 67; sculpture, Expo '67, & Les Jeux Olympiques (artwork), 76, comn by City of Montreal; Corridart 1976-; UQAM 1995 for the Science Bldg. *Exhib:* Art and Engineering, Art Gallery Ont, Toronto, 65; 11th Biennial, Middleheim, Anvers, Belg, 71; Su Proust, Arte Studio, Brescia, Italy, 74; Chi E Pandora, Galleria Unimedia, Genova, Italy, 81; Retrospective (with catalog), Mus d'Art Contemporain, Montreal, 81; Montreal Painting, A Second Look, Mem Univ Art Gallery, St Johns, Nfld, 85; Le Musée Imaginaire, Saidye Bronfman Ctr, Montreal, 86; Station, Centre Int d'Art Contemp, 87, Consenses et Contestation, 92, L'Anarchie resplendissaute de la peinture, Galerie de l'UQAM, Montreal, 92; Kunst aus Canada, Galerie Clara Maria Sels, Dusseldorf, Ger, 92; Presence quebecoise, Chateau de Biron, Dordogne, France, 92; La Ferme du Buisson, Marne La Vallee, France, 92; Naissauce et persistance de la sculpture, Mus de Que, 92; Ten yrs of painting, traveling exhib, Quebec, 96; Solo exhibs, Univesite Libre de Brussels, Belg, 97 & Lillian Rodriquez Gallery, 98, UQAM Gallery, 98; Saint-Hilaire and the automatistes, Mus Mont Saint-Hilaire, 97; Epopee automatistle, Montreal Contemp Mus, 98; Ecstasy, Jack Shainman Gallery, NY, 98; Eclat de Rouge Gallery, UQAM, 1998; Sullivan/Ferron, Domaine Cataraqui, Quebec City, 99; Mirages Du Nord, Maisons Hamel-Bruneau, Quebec City, 99; Retrospective, Mus des Beaux Arts de Mtl, 2003; Le Touche de la Picture UQAM Gallery, 2004; Ron Moore Gallery, Toronto, 2004; Bruxelles Univ Libre, 2005. *Pos:* Instr; York Univ 1998, anniversary of the Refus Global Concordia & UQAM on the force of Painting; Goodby Monsieur Duchump, The Royal Soc, 2004. *Teaching:* Conf presenter, conceptual art, Univ Que, Montreal, 75; instr drawing & painting, Concordia Univ, Montreal, 77-. *Awards:* Maurice Cullen Prize 1943-Prixdu Que for sculpture 1963; Martin Lynch Staunten Award, Can Coun, 84; Prix Borduas, 87-; Royal Acad Arts, 92; The Governor General Prize, 2005. *Bibliog:* Manon Lapointe (auth), Francoise Sullivan: Renouer avec la presence du passe, ETC, spring, 88; Claire Gravel (auth), Francoise Sullivan: La parole retrouvee, Vie des Arts, 03/88; Gilles Daigneault (auth), L'Art au Quebec depuis Pellan-une histoire des prix Borduas, Mus du Que, 05/88; Les Femmes du Refus global Patricia Sniayt; Borduas, Sullivan, Riopelle, Louise Vignaut; From Automatism to Modern Dance, FS; With Franziska Boas in New York, 2003, by Allana Lindgren. *Mem:* Vehicule Art Inc; Montreal Art Coun-Beena Ellen Gallery Concordia Univ. *Media:* All media, Painting. *Specialty:* Painting. *Interests:* Art, Conversation, Friends, Swimming. *Publ:* Auth, Poeme, Da Vinci, Montreal, No 2, p 64, 74; Peiripheiries (exhib catalog), Mus d'Art Contemp-Vehicule Art Inc, Montreal, 74; Francoise Sullivan & David Moore (auths), Textes de F Sullivan et de D Moore, et Texte Commun des Deux Artistes (exhib catalog), Galerie Vehicule Art, Montreal, 77; Good by Monsieur Duchamp, Les Ecrits, 2005. *Dealer:* Ron Moore, Toronto. *Mailing Add:* 2358 Hingston Montreal PQ H4A 2J2 Canada

SULLIVAN, GRAEME
EDUCATOR, WRITER
Study: Ohio State Univ, MA, PhD, 1984. *Teaching:* Sr lectr, Col Fine Arts, Univ New South Wales, Kensington, Australia, 1988-98; assoc prof art educ, chair, Dept of Arts & Humanities, Teachers Col, Columbia Univ, 1999-2009; prof, dir, Sch Visual Arts, Pa State Univ, 2010-. *Awards:* Manual Barkan Meml Award, 1990; Lowenfeld Award, 2007. *Mem:* Nat Art Educ Asn; Univ Coun for Art Educ; Am Educ Rsch Asn; Int Soc Educ Through Art; Col Art Asn; Australian Inst Art Educ. *Publ:* Auth, Seeing Australia: Views of Artists and Artwriters, 1994, Art Practice as Research, 2005. *Mailing Add:* Penn State College of Arts and Architecture School of Visual Arts 210 Patterson Building State College PA 16802

SULLIVAN, JIM
PAINTER
b Providence, RI, Apr 1, 1939. *Study:* RI Sch Design, BFA, 61, Stanford Univ, 62-63. *Work:* Whitney Mus Am Art, New York; Wadsworth Atheneum, Hartford, Conn; Metrop Mus, New York; Amerado Hess, New York; Owens Corning, Toledo, Ohio; Phillip Morris, New York. *Exhib:* NY Painting Today, Three Rivers Festival, Pittsburgh, 83; Dart Gallery, Chicago, 84; Bayly Art Mus, Charlottesville, Va, 88; Queens Mus, New York, 88; Anne Jaffe Gallery, Bay Harbor Islands, Fla, 90; Nancy Hoffman Gallery, New York, 2004 & 2011; and others. *Teaching:* Prof painting, Bard Coll, 65-95, prof emer, currently. *Awards:* Fulbright Fel, Paris, 61-62; Guggenheim Award, 72; Rosenthal Award, Am Acad Arts & Lett, 73; Nat Endowment Arts Grant, 83. *Bibliog:* Kay Larson (auth), article, NY Mag, 1/19/81; Vivian Raynor (auth), article, NY Times, 1/9/81; Gerrit Henry (auth), rev, Art in America, 10/86; Ken Johnson (auth), rev NY Times, 12/24/04; and others. *Mem:* Schoharie Land Trust. *Media:* Oil on Canvas, wood panel & aluminum. *Publ:* Empire State Collection, Art for the Public, Tiffany Bell, 87; American Still Life, Linda Cathcart, 83; New York Painting Today, Donald Kuspit, 83; Diamonds are Forever, Peter Gordon, 87. *Dealer:* Nancy Hoffman 520 West 27 New York NY. *Mailing Add:* 59 Wooster St New York NY 10013

SULLIVAN, JUNEANN MARGARET
PAINTER, GALLERY OWNER
b Princeton, NJ. *Study:* Winthrop Col, BFA, 63; NY Univ, MFA, 65; studies with Betty Lou Schlemm, 74-76 & Frank Webb, 84-85. *Exhib:* Artworks, Ellarslie Mus, Trenton, NJ, 88; Nat Arts Club 89th Ann Open Watercolor, NY, 89; NW Pastel Soc Juried Exhib, Seattle, Wash, 90; Women History Month, Paterson Mus, NJ, 91; Nat Asn Women Artists Exhib, NY, 91 & 92; Catharine Lorillard Wolfe Ann Exhib, NY, 93; NE Watercolor Soc Ann Exhib, Goshen, NY, 94. *Pos:* Porcelain designer, Edward Marshall Boehm Co, Trenton, NJ, 64-68; chmn bd dir, Piermont Fine Arts Gallery, NY, 93-; co-founder & art consult, Cat Sullivan Gallery, Suffern, NY, 94-; owner, Watermark Gallery, Tuckerton, NJ, 99-. *Teaching:* Instr arts & crafts, Hopewell Valley Sch, Pennington, NJ, 75-78. *Awards:* Board of Directors Award, Catharine Lorillard Wolfe, 89; Irwin Zlowe Mem Award, Nat Asn Women Artists, 91; President's Award, Northeast Watercolor Soc, 91. *Bibliog:* Elizabeth Case (auth), June Sullivan translates life into art, Tuckerton Times-Beacon, 8/94. *Mem:* Nat Asn Women Artists; NE Watercolor Soc; Oil Pastel Asn Int; United Pastelists Am; Arts Coun Rockland Co, NY. *Media:* Watercolor, Monoprints. *Specialty:* Original fine art work. *Publ:* Contribr, The Encyclopedia of Printmaking Techniques, Quatro Publ, 93; cover artist, The Literary Review, Fairleigh Dickinson Univ, 95; contribr artist, The New Creative Artist (auth, Nita Leland), N Light Bks, 2006; Long Beach Island Rhapsody, Jersey Shore Publ, 2006. *Mailing Add:* 115 Water St Tuckerton NJ 08087

SULLIVAN, MARTIN E
MUSEUM DIRECTOR
b Troy, NY, 1944. *Study:* Siena Coll, BA, 65; Univ Notre Dame, MA, 70, PhD, 74. *Pos:* Exec dir, Indiana Comn Humanities, Indianapolis, 72-75; dir pub progs, Nat Endowment Humanities, Washington, 76-81; pres, Inst Man & Sci, Rensselaerville, NY, 81-83; dir, NY State Mus, Albany, 83-90, Heard Mus, Phoenix, 90-99, Hist St Mary City, Md, 99-2008, Smithsonian Nat Portrait Gallery, Washington, 2008-2012; trustee, Am Ritual Object Repatriation Found, New York, 92-98, AFM, 94-98; mem, Native Am Repatriation Act Adv Comt, 92-2005; chmn, US Govt Cult Property Adv Comt, 95-2003. *Awards:* AAM Centennial Honor Roll, 2006. *Mem:* AAM (vpres 1990-93, accreditation comn 1997-). *Publ:* Auth, Museums, Adults & the Humanities, 81; Inventing the Southwest: The Fred Harvey Company & Native Am Art, 96. *Mailing Add:* Nat Portrait Gallery Smithsonian Inst PO Box 37012 Washington DC 20013-7012

SULLIVAN, RONALD DEE
PAINTER, WRITER
b Norman, Okla, Feb 6, 1939. *Study:* Univ Okla, BFA, 63; Calif State Univ, Sacramento, MA, 69; E Tex State Univ, postgrad. *Work:* NY Pub Libr; Art Mus S Tex; Calif State Univ; Delmar Coll, Tex; Smithsonian Libr; The Witliff Collection, San Marcos, Tex. *Comn:* Ten oil paintings, K3 Cattle & Game Ranch, Beeville, Tex, 2010.

Exhib: Retrospective exhib, Joseph A Cain Gallery, 2000; Philbrook Art Inst, Temple Univ, 2000; Cheltenham Art Ctr, Philadelphia; Art Mus S Tex, Corpus Christi; Gallerie Rose Marie, Lille, France. *Pos:* cur, art Appraiser, conservator. *Teaching:* Prof sculpture, drawing, & design, Del Mar Coll & Tex AM, Corpus Christi, 69-2001. *Awards:* Outstanding Educator of Am, 74; Fac Develop Grant, Del Mar Coll, 89-92; NISOD Excellence Award, Univ Tex, Austin, 93; Master Teachers Seminar for Writers Award, 81. *Bibliog:* The Mystery and Magic of Glass, Channel 16, Corpus Christi, Tex, 78; Ron George (auth), Red Earth Images, Caller-Times, 92; Carey Rote (auth) Caller-Times, 93; Leakey Star (auth), Penny McGuire, 2005. *Media:* All Media. *Res:* Psychological & martial strategy of the 16th century as related to 20th century. *Publ:* contrbr, Contemp Plastics, Aplication in Sculpture, the Proceedings, Int Sculpture Publ, 71; featured, Queen of the Sea, Jane Beckman, Riviera ed, 95; auth, Projection into Imagery (film), Del Mar Coll, 80; auth, Hillabee to Weogfkee, Del Mar Coll, 98; featured, The Rotarian Mag, 92; auth, Sculpting a Portrait in Clay (video), Del Mar Coll, 98. *Dealer:* Rivers Edge Gallery. *Mailing Add:* 832 Water St Kerrville TX 78028

SULLIVAN, RUTH WILKINS
CURATOR, LECTURER

b Boston, Mass, Nov 20, 1926. *Study:* Wellesley Col, AB. *Collection Arranged:* Chinese Export Porcelain, 65; Am Painting from 1830 (with catalog), 65; Chinese Art from the Cloud Wampler Collection (with catalog), 68; Wealth of the Ancient World: The Nelson Bunker Hunter & William Herbert Hunt Collections (with catalog), 83. *Pos:* Admin asst, Everson Mus Art, 58-60, registr, 60-62, cur & ed publ, 63-70, cur collections, 66-70; consult, Mus Am China Trade, 71; cur educ, Kimbell Art Mus, 71-82, res cur, 83-2006, emer res cur. *Awards:* Woman Achievement Arts, Post Stand, 68. *Mem:* Coll Art Asn. *Res:* Cosimo I de' Medici: his court & his family in late Renaissance Florence; Coismo the Elder and his role as Art Patron: Donatello, Brunelleschi, Michelozzo, and Fra Angelico. *Publ:* Auth, Saints Peter & Paul: Some Ironic Aspects of Their Imaging, Art Hist, 94; Hospitality to the Divine Stranger in Jacopo Bassano's Supper to Emmaus, Source, 94; Cracking the Egg: Jacopo Bassano's Supper at Emmaus, Source, 95; Three Ferrarese panels on the theme of "Death Rather than Dishonor" and the Neapolitan connection, Zeitschrift fur Kunstgeschichte, Vol 57, No 4, 610-625, 94; The Wilton Diptych: mysteries, majesty, and a complex exchange of faith and power, Gazette des Beaux-Arts, 1-17, 1/97

SULLIVAN, SCOTT A
HISTORIAN, EDUCATOR

b Cleveland, Ohio, May 22, 1947. *Study:* John Carroll Univ, BA, 69; Case Western Reserve Univ, MA, 72, PhD, 78. *Teaching:* Asst prof art hist, Univ N Tex, 75-81, assoc prof, 81-87, prof, 87-96, chmn dept, 87-92, actg dean, 92-93, assoc dean, 93-96; dean fine arts, Kent State Univ, 96-99. *Mem:* Historians of Netherlandish Art; Coll Art Asn Am; Midwest Art Hist Soc (secy-treas, 85-87, pres, 87-89); Am Asn Netherlandic Studies; Nat Coun Art. *Res:* 17th century Flemish and Dutch painting, especially still life. *Publ:* In the Shadow of Caravaggio: Pietro Paolini's Bacchic Concert, Dallas Mus Art Bull, 85; Abraham van Beyeren's Visserij-bord at the Groote Kerk, Maassluis Oud Holland, 87; Auth, Still Life with a Dead Hore by Jan Weenix & Pantry Scene with a Serving Figure, 90; Dictionary of Art and Artists, Vol 2, St James Press, London, 90; Auth, Dictionary of Art, MacMillan Publ, Ltd, London, 96. *Mailing Add:* Kent State Univ Dean Fine & Prof Arts 204 Taylor Hall Kent OH 44242

SULTAN, ALTOON
PAINTER

b Brooklyn, NY, Sept 29, 1948. *Study:* Brooklyn Col, BFA, 1969, MFA, 1971, study with Phillip Pearlstein; Boston Univ at Tanglewood, 1969; Skowhegan Sch Painting & Sculpture, study with Gabriel Laderman, 1970. *Work:* Hunter Mus, Chattanooga, Tenn; Yale Univ Art Gallery; Metrop Mus Art, NY; Nat Acad Design, NY; Hunter Mus, Chattanooga, Tenn; Metrop Mus Art, NY; Mus Fine Arts, Boston; Nat Mus Women in the Arts, Washington, DC. *Exhib:* Solo exhibs include Marlborough Gallery, 1977, 1979, 1981, 1984, 1985, 1988, 1990, 1993, 1995, 1998, 1990, 1993, 1995, 1997 & 1998, Middendorf Gallery, Washington, 1987, Hokin-Kaufman Gallery, Chicago, 1990, Paris-NY-Kent Gallery, South Kent, Conn, 1991, DP Fong & Spratt Galleries, San Jose, Calif, 1992, Mary Ryan Gallery, NY, 1995 Pinnacle Gallery, Savannah Coll Art & Design, Ga, 1997, the Galleria Marieschi, Monza, Italy, 1999, Clarke Galleries, Stowe, Vt, 2000 & 2004, Tibor de Nagy Gallery, NY, 2001, 2004 & 2007; group exhibs include A Private View, Contemp Art from the Graham Gund Collection, Boston Mus Fine Arts, Mass, 1982; Lower Manhattan from Street to Sky, Whitney Mus Am Art, 1982; Small Pictures, New Brit Mus Am Art, 1982; Painted Light, Reading Pub Mus, Butler Inst Am Art, 1983; Am Realism: 20th Century Drawings & Watercolors, San Francisco Mus Mod Art, 1985; The Landscape in 20th Century Am Art: Selections from the Metrop Mus Art, Philbrook Mus Art, Tulsa, Okla; Community of Creativity: A Century of MacDowell Colory Artists, Wichita Art Mus, Nat Acad Design, 1996-97; Post-Pastoral: New Images of New Eng Landscape, Hood Mus Art, 1998; Invitational Exhib Painting & Sculpture, Am Acad Arts & Letts, NY, 1999; Green Woods and Crystal Waters: The Am Landscape Tradition, Philbrook Mus Art, Ringling Mus Art, Davenport Mus Art, 1999-2000; ReAppearance, Simmons Visual Arts Gallery (traveling), 2001; 178th Ann Exhib, Nat Acad Design, NY, 2003, The Artist's Eye, 2004; Things I Love, Boston Mus Fine Arts, 2005; Vistas & Visions, Nat Mus Women in the Arts, Washington, 2006. *Teaching:* Vis critic, Univ Pa, Philadelphia, 1985-88; Resident fac, Skowhegan Sch Painting & Sculpture, 1988; asst prof, San Jose State Univ, Calif, 1991-94; vis prof, Dartmouth Col, 1998-2001. *Awards:* Yaddo Fel, 1975 & 1976; Nat Endowment Arts Fel Grant, 1983 & 1989; Acad Award in Art, Am Acad Arts & Letters, 1999, Purchase Award, 1999; Duc Valverde d'Ayala Valva Prize, Found Monaco, 1999; J Sanford Saltus Gold Medal for Painting, Nat Acad Design, 2001. *Bibliog:* John Arthur (auth), The remembrance of tranquility: Altoon Sultan's new paintings, Arts Mag, 3/84; Articles and reviews in NY Times, Art News & Art Week, 1985-98. *Mem:* Nat Acad (acad, 95-). *Media:* Oil, Egg tempera. *Publ:* Culture/Cultivation: Thoughts on Painting the Landscape, Art Jour, 1998; The Luminous Brush: Painting with ESS Tempera, Watson-Guptill Pubs, 1999. *Dealer:* Tibor de Nagy 724 Fifth Ave New York NY 10019. *Mailing Add:* PO Box 2 Groton VT 05046

SULTAN, TERRIE FRANCES
MUSEUM DIRECTOR

b Asheville, NC. *Study:* Syracuse Univ, BFA, 1973; John F Kennedy Univ, MA, 1985. *Collection Arranged:* Corcoran Biennial 1991, 1993, 1995 & 1998; Ida Applebroog, 10 yr survey, 1898, DAP; Radcliffe Bailey: Tides, 2002; Chuck Close Prints, Retrospective of 30 yr career, Book PU Press, 2003; Angela Graverholz: Reading Room, 2003; Jessica Stockholder, 15 yr survey, DAP; Chantal Akerman: Moving Through Time & Space, 2008; Damaged Romanticism (book), D Giles Ltd, 2008; Jean Luc Mylayne (book), Twin Palms Pub, 2007; Jennifer Bartlett, 35 Yr Survey, Yale Univ Press, 2014. *Pos:* Cur contemp art, Corcoran Gallery Art, Washington, DC, 1988-99; dir, Blaffer Art Mus, Univ Houston, Tex, 2000-08, dir, Parrish Art Mus, Southampton NY, 2008-. *Teaching:* Critique, Md Inst, Baltimore, 1998. *Awards:* Chevalier Order Arts and Letters, 2003. *Mem:* AAM; Int Asn Art Critics; AAMD. *Res:* Preparation of survey of Chuck Close Photographs. *Publ:* Donald Lipski: Brief History of Twine, Madison Art Ctr/DAP, 2000; Seeing & Believing: Art of Nancy Burson, Twin Palms Press, 2002; Chuck Close Prints: Progress & Collaboration, Princeton Univ Press, 2003; Bob Knox: Non Fiction Paintings, Blaffer Gallery, 2003; Jessica Stockholder: Kissing the wall, Blaffer Gallery/DAP, 2004; James Surls: The Splendora Years, Univ Tex Press, 2005; Jean Luc Mylayne, Twin Palms Publ, 2007; Chantal Akerman: Moving through Time and Space, Blaffer Gallery, Art Mus of Univ of Houston, 2008; Damaged Romanticism: A Mirror of Modern Emotion, D Giles, Ltd, 2008; Rackstraw Downes: Onsite Paintings, 2010; Juliao Sarmento: Artist and Writers/House and Home, 2011. *Mailing Add:* Parrish Art Mus 279 Montauk Hwy Water Mill NY 11976

SUMMER, (EMILY) EUGENIA
PAINTER

b Newton, Miss, June 13, 1923. *Study:* Miss Univ for Women, BS; Columbia Univ, MA; Art Inst Chicago; Calif Coll Arts & Crafts; Penland Sch Crafts, NC; Seattle Univ. *Hon Degrees:* Hon Doc Art & Humane Letters, Miss Univ Women, 2005. *Work:* Miss Mus Art & First Nat Bank, Jackson; Nat Bank Commerce Collection, Columbus, Miss; First Nat Bank, Laurel, Miss; First Miss Nat Bank, Hattiesburg; Miss Mus Art, Jackson, Miss; pvt collection, Wilhelmina Cole Holladay, bd chair, Nat Mus Women Arts. *Exhib:* Delta Ann Exhib, Ark Art Ctr, Little Rock, 60, 62-63, 74 & 82; Art in Embassies Prog, US State Dept, Rio de Janeiro, Brazil, 66-67; Eighth Decade: Painters Choice, Ga Coll Milledgeville, 71; 5th Greater New Orleans Int Art Exhib, 75; Nat Asn Painters Acrylic & Casein, Nat Arts Club, New York, 80. *Pos:* Bd dir, Southeastern Coll Art Conf, 81-83. *Teaching:* Prof art, Miss Univ Women, 50-, head div fine & performing arts, 82-86, emer prof, 86-. *Awards:* Dumas Milner Purchase Award, Nat Watercolor Exhib, Jackson, 62 & Jurors Award, 68; Purchase Prizes, Lauren Rogers Mus Exhib & Miss Southern Univ Exhib; Award of Merit, Miss Mus Art, 83. *Bibliog:* Patti Carr Black (auth), Art in Mississippi, Heritage Miss series, Vol I, Univ Miss Press, 98; Robin Dietrick (ed), The Mississippi Story, Mississippi Mus Art, 2007. *Mem:* Coll Art Asn Am; Phi Kappa Phi; Miss State Comt; Nat Mus Women Arts. *Media:* Acrylic, Watercolor, Alkyd. *Mailing Add:* 915 5th Ave S Columbus MS 39701

SUMMER, EVAN D
ARTIST

b Buffalo, NY, Sept 26, 1948. *Study:* State Univ of NY, Cortland, BS in Chemistry, 70; State Univ of NY, Buffalo, BFA, 73; Yale Univ, MFA in Printmaking, 75. *Exhib:* Group exhibs, Chongqing and Tianjin Arts Coll, Tianjin, People's Republic of China, 1986, Pa Acad Fine Arts, 1987, Brooklyn Mus, 1989, Hewlett Gallery, Carnegie-Mellon Univ, Pittsburgh, 1991, Int Print Triennale and Intergrafia, Krakow, Poland, Katowice, Poland, 1991, 1st Egyptian Int Print Triennale, 1993, Corcoran Gallery of Art, Washington, DC, 2005; solo exhibs, Corcoran Gallery Art, Washington, DC, 99-2000, State Univ NY, Coll at Cortland, NY, 2000, Reading Public Mus, Reading, Pa, 2001 & 2005, The Arts Club of Washington, Washington, DC, 2003, Cosmos Club, Washington, DC, 2003; Rep in permanent collections Nat Gallery Art, Wash, Corcoran Gallery Art, Brooklyn Mus, Taipei City Mus Fine Arts, Nat Acad of Design, New York City, Metrop Mus Art, NY, Pa Acad Fine Arts, Philadelphia, Nat Mus Am Art, Washington, DC & many others. *Teaching:* Artist-in-residence, Univ Pa, Philadelphia, 1978-88; instr, State Univ NY, Buffalo, 77 & 79, Wesleyan Univ, Middletown, Conn, 78, Tyler Sch Art, Elkins Park, 1979, Pratt Graphics Ctr, New York City, 1983, Kutztown Univ, Pa, 1984-85, asst prof, 1987-91, assoc prof, 1991-94, prof, 1994-. *Awards:* Recipient Berthe von Moschzisker prize, 1982, Juror's award; Pacific States Nat Biennial Print Exhib, Univ Hawaii, 1992; Silver medal, 10th Norwegian Int Print Triennial, Fredrikstad, Norway, 1992; Tai-he Masterpiece Award, Int Print Biennial, Beijing, 2003; Henry Legrand Cannon Prize, 178th Ann Exhib, Nat Acad Design, 2003. *Mem:* Boston Printmakers, Inter print Triennial Soc, Nat Acad (assoc, 93, acad, 94-). *Media:* Printmaker - Etching, Engraving & Calligraphy. *Collection:* Metropolitan Museum of Art and Achenbach Foundation. *Mailing Add:* 108 S Whiteoak St Kutztown PA 19530

SUMMERS, CAROL
PRINTMAKER, WOODCUT

b Kingston, NY, Dec 26, 1925. *Study:* Bard Coll, BA, 51. *Hon Degrees:* PhD Fine Arts, Bard Coll, 74. *Work:* Corcoran Gallery Art, Libr Cong, Nat Gallery, Washington, DC; Metrop Mus Art & Mus Mod Art, New York; Kunstmuseum, Malmö, Sweden; and many others. *Comn:* Posters NY Film Festival, US Park Serv, Ojai Festival, Venice Biennial and many others. *Exhib:* Solo exhibs, Mus Mod Art, New York, 64-66, AAA Gallery, New York, 67 & Bard Coll, 68; Retrospective, San Francisco Mus Art, Calif, 67; 20th Nat Print Exhib, Brooklyn Mus, 77; ADI Gallery, 77; Bellas Artes, Saw Miguel de Allende, Mex, 93; 50 Year Rerospective, Artists Asn, Woodstock, NY, Mus Art Santa Cruz, Calif, 99; Indian Folk Textiles, Jean Byron Mus, Marfil, Mex, 2004; 57 Years Retrospective, Mus del Pub de Guarajuato, Mex, 2007; Notre Dame de Namur Univ, Belmont, Calif, 2009; Mus Quilts & Textiles, San Jose, Calif, 2013. *Pos:* Folk art and textiles tour leader, to Rajasthan, India, winters 93-2013. *Teaching:* Instr, Brooklyn Mus Sch Art, 54, Pratt Graphic Art Ctr, 62, Hunter

Coll, 63, Sch Visual Arts, New York, 65, Pa State Univ, 68, Columbia Univ, New York, 69 & San Francisco Art Inst, 73; US Info Serv tour of India, 74 & 79. *Awards:* Louis Comfort Tiffany Found Fels, 55 & 60; Guggenheim Found Fel, 59; Coun Int Exchange Scholars Grant, res India, 93-94; Artist of Yr, Santa Cruz Co Arts Comn, 2001; Outstanding Printmaker award, Mid Am Print Coun, 2004. *Mem:* Print Coun Am; Print Club Philadelphia; Calif Soc Printmakers; Nat Acad (assoc, 90, acad, 94-); Boston Printmakers. *Media:* Woodcuts. *Publ:* Carol Summers Catalogue Raisonne, 88; Carol Summers Woodcuts, 50 yr Retrospective, 99; A Treasury of Indian Folk Textiles, La Casa de Espiritus Alegres, 02; Another Treasury of Indian Folk Textiles, La Casa de Espiritus Alegres, 06; Yet Another Treasury of Indian Folk Textiles, La Casa de Espiritu s Alegres, 2012. *Dealer:* Davidson Galleries Seattle WA. *Mailing Add:* 2817 Smith Grade Santa Cruz CA 95060

SUMNER, STEPHEN CHARLES
ADMINISTRATOR, EDUCATOR
b New Haven, Conn, Sept 8, 1940. *Study:* Univ Mich, BS (design), 63; Univ Mass, MFA, 67. *Work:* Mills Col, Oakland, Calif; Colgate Univ, Hamilton, NY; Nelson Atkins Mus, Kansas City, Mo; Brooklyn Mus, NY; Potsdam Col, NY. *Exhib:* 15th Nat Print Exhib, Brooklyn Mus, NY, 66; Nat Print Exhib, Providence Art Club, RI, 69; Albright-Knox Graphic Ann, Albright-Knox Art Gallery, Buffalo, NY, 69; 31st Ann, Munson-Williams-Proctor Mus, Utica, NY, 72; Artist Space Gallery, NY, 77; Peripheral-Vision, Amarillo Fine Arts Ctr, Tex, 91; Philbrook Mus Art, Tulsa, Okla, 94. *Pos:* Dir, Sch Art, Univ Tulsa, 89-94 & Div Fine & Performing Art, 94-2001; Pres, Rocky Mountain Coll Art & Design, Co. *Teaching:* Prof photog, State Univ NY, Potsdam, 68-89; Provost, New World Sch Art, Miami, 2001-03. *Awards:* Fel, Orgn Am States, Guatemala, 74; Fulbright Fel, Peru & Bolivia, 80; The Makers Exhib, State Arts Coun Okla, 91. *Mem:* Found Art, Theory & Educ (pres, 84-93); Coll Art Asn Am; Nat Asn Art Adminr; Art Dirs Club Tulsa. *Mailing Add:* Rocky Mountain Coll Art & Design Off of Pre 1600 Pierce St Denver CO 80214

SUNDBERG, CARL GUSTAVE
ENAMELIST, DIRECTOR
b Erie, Pa, June 23, 1928. *Study:* Albright Art Sch, Univ Buffalo, grad; study with Joseph Plavcan, Virginia Cuthbert, Albert Blaustien, Letterio Calipia & Robert Bruce. *Work:* Butler Inst Am Art, Youngstown, Ohio; Tyler Mus Art, Tex; Erie Pub Libr; Erie Art Mus; Albright-Knox Rental Art Gallery; Metropolitan Mus Art, NY; Hunterian Art Gallery, Glasgow, Scotland. *Comn:* Six porcelain panels (mod motif with coins), Mellon Bank, Erie, 69; three porcelain enamel panels, Gannon Resource Ctr, Erie, 73; three enclosure set (Plexiglas-enamel), St Vincent Hosp, Erie, 74. *Exhib:* NPAA Exhibs, 1968-2005; The Cutting Edge, Frye Mus, Seattle, Wash, 92; Am, Can & Europ Enamelist, Kent State Univ & Glass & Ceramic Mus, Toronto, Can, 94; Int Enamel Exhib, Coburg Mus, Ger, 95; Enameling Art in Japan, Tokyo, 96; one-person shows, Hallwalls Contemp Art Ctr, Buffalo, NY, 90, Nina Freudenheim Gallery, Buffalo, NY, 94, Binghamton Univ Art Mus, NY, 97, Milton Weil Gallery, NY, 97, David Anderson Gallery, Buffalo, NY, 2004; group shows, Mona Bismark Found, Paris, 2003, Univ Alberta Print Ctr, Edmonton, Can, 2004, Vose Galleries, Boston, 2004, Susan Teller Gallery, NY, 2005. *Pos:* Art dir, Erie Ceramic Arts Co, 53-; dir, Galerie 8, Erie, 67-74. *Teaching:* Instr painting, Erie Art Ctr, 64-78; enamel screen print workshop, Kent State Univ, 90. *Awards:* Purchase Prize & Hon Mention, Butler Inst Am Art Mid Year Show, 70 & 81; Purchase Prize, Tyler Mus Art 7th Nat Exhib, 70 & Int Enamelist Exhib, Newport, KY, 80; Prize for Non-Traditional, Chautauqua Exhib, 72 & 76; Jurors' Choice Award, Pittsburgh North Hills Exhib, 87; Purchase Award, Int Enamelist Exhib, Newport, Ky, 89. *Bibliog:* Clyde Singer (auth), article, Youngstown Vindicator, 6/28/70; Ada C Turner (auth), article, Chautauqua Daily, 8/17/70; Peggy Krider (auth), Art Demonstration (film), Villa Maria Col, 70. *Mem:* Erie Art Ctr (pres, 67-69); Erie Arts Mus (vpres, 70-71); Pittsburgh Soc of Artists; Northwestern Pa Artist Asn (co-dir); Enamelist Soc, 88. *Media:* Porcelain Enamel, Graphic. *Mailing Add:* 5518 Bondy Dr Erie PA 16509

SUNDBERG, WILDA (REGELMAN)
PAINTER, INSTRUCTOR
b Erie, Pa, Oct 5, 1930. *Study:* Albright Art Sch, Univ Buffalo, 49-51; Gannon col, 64-66; Mercyhurst Col, Pa, 78-79; with Al Broulette, Harrisburg, 82; Edinboro Univ, 85 & 86; Tony Couch, Union Deposit, Pa, 86. *Work:* Thiel Col, Greenville, Pa; Erie Pub Libr; Erie Art Mus; Regional Cancer Res Ctr, Erie, Pa; Eat n Park Restaurant Chain, Pa; and others. *Exhib:* Albright-Knox Mem Gallery, Buffalo, 71-2000; one-women show, Waterford Community Ctr, Pa, Thiel Col, Pa, 77, Gannon Univ, Eric, Pa, 76,79,81, & Erie Art Mus, 84; Butler Inst Am Art, Ohio; Counterpoint II, Pittsburgh, Pa, 81; Pa Gov Mansion, Harrisburg, 81-82; McClelland Gallery, Melbourne, Australia, 83; La Roche Col, Pittsburgh, Pa, 85; Access to the Arts, Dunkirk, NY, 85; North Hills, 86-88; Jamestown Community Col, NY, 87; St Vincent Col, Latrobe, Pa 88; Blair Co Arts Festival, Altoona, Pa, 88 & 2000; Aqueous 89 & 91 Nat Watercolor; Lahaina Arts Soc, Maui, Hawaii, 90; one person exhibs, Erie Art Mus, 84 & 92, Gannon Univ, Erie, Pa, 76, 79, 81, Thiel Col, Greenvilla, Pa, 77; Northwest Pa Artist Asn Exhibs, 93-2000. *Teaching:* Instr art, Erie Art Mus, 64-90; instr drawing & painting, Mercyhurst Col, 79-90; Behrend, Pa State Instr Watercolor, Erie Art Mus, 64-2000; Harbor Creek Pub Sch, Enrichment Prog, 90. *Awards:* Chautauqua Nat Watercolor Award, Chautauqua Art Asn, 70; Nat Scholastic Scholar; Award Purchase, North Hills Pittsburgh, Pa. *Mem:* Pittsburgh Watercolor Soc; NW Pa Artist Asn; Watercolor Soc, Pa. *Media:* Transparent Watercolor. *Dealer:* Textures W 8th Erie PA 16503; Kada Gallery 2632 N 8th St Erie PA 16505. *Mailing Add:* 5518 Bondy Dr Erie PA 16509

SUNDBLAD, EMILY
ARTIST, DIRECTOR
Study: Parsons Sch Design, NYC, BFA, 2002. *Exhib:* One-women shows: 1000 Drawings, Artists Space, NYC, 2001; Fine Arts Thesis Exhib, Parsons Sch Design, 2002; Alicia McCarthy New Works, Rare Gallery, NYC, 2002; You're Just a Summer Love But I'll Remember You When Winter Comes, Priska Juschka Fine Art, Brooklyn, 2002; group shows: Whitney Biennial: Day for Night, Whitney Mus Am Art, NYC, 2006. *Pos:* Co-dir, Reena Spaulings Fine Art Gallery, NYC. *Mailing Add:* Reena Spaulings Fine Art 165 E Broadway 2nd Fl New York NY 10002

SUNDERLAND, NITA KATHLEEN
EDUCATOR, SCULPTOR
b Olney, Ill, Nov 9, 1927. *Study:* Duke Univ; Bradley Univ, BFA & MA. *Work:* Fed Plaza, Chicago; Civic Ctr, Peoria, Ill. *Comn:* Archit sculpture, Bradley Univ Bookstore, 64, monumental sculpture, Williams Hall Mall, 67; archit sculpture, St John's Cath Church, Woodhull, Ill, 69; stone and bronze sculpture, Ill State Univ, State Ill capital develop bd, 90. *Exhib:* Chicago Mus Without Walls, 78; 31st Ill Invitational, 79; Selections from the Collection of George M Irwin, 80; 30 Yrs of Pub Sculpture in Ill, 81; Eighteen Ill Sculptors, 83. *Teaching:* Prof art, Bradley Univ, 56-86, emer prof, 86-. *Bibliog:* Three Illinois Artists (film), Ill Arts Coun, WCBV-TV, Peoria, 79. *Mem:* Am Soc Testing & Materials. *Media:* Bronze, Stone. *Publ:* Contribr, Contemporary American Women Sculptors, Watson-Jones, Oryx Press, 86. *Mailing Add:* 22225 Grosenbach Rd Washington IL 61571

SURES, JACK
CERAMIST, EDUCATOR
b Brandon, Man, Nov 20, 1934. *Study:* Univ Man, BFA, 57; Mich State Univ, MA, 59. *Work:* Montreal Mus Fine Arts; Can Coun Art Bank, Ottawa; Sask Art Bd, Regina; Burlington Cult Ctr, Ont; Can Guild Potters, Toronto; Pecs Mus, Hungary; Norman Mackenzie Art Gallery; Tajimi Mus, Japan. *Comn:* Clay mural, Sch Archit, Winnipeg, Man, 64; clay mural, Coll Veterinary Med, Saskatoon, Sask, 69; 2900 square foot mural, Province Sask, Saskatoon, 79; clay wall, Waterloo Potters Workshop, Ont, 86; mural, Mus Civilization, Holl, Que, 89. *Exhib:* Nat Gallery, Ottawa, Ont, 67; Kunstnerforbundet, Oslo, Norway, 83; Rosemont Art Gallery, Regina, 85; Moose Jaw Art Mus, 87; Franklin Silverstone Gallery, Montreal, 87-89; Ashton's, Toronto, Il/91; and others; Hull Que Isnow Gatineau Qué. *Pos:* Chmn, Can Craftsman's Asn, 68-70; bd mem, Can Coun Arts, 69-71 & Sask Craft Coun. *Teaching:* Prof ceramics, Univ Regina, 65-98. *Awards:* Senior Award, Can Coun Arts, 72; Grand Prix Mino, Tajimi, Japan, 89; Order Can, 92; and others. *Mem:* Hon mem Waterloo Potters Guild; Nat Coun Educ Ceramic Arts; Ceramics Can; Saskatchewan Order of Merit (2003). *Media:* Clay. *Publ:* Coauth, Down to Earth, Nelson, 80; auth, Spirit of Place, In: Ceramic Art & Perception, No 14, CG Driscoll, 93

SUSSMAN, BARBARA J
ART APPRAISER, ARTIST
b Hackensack, NJ, Apr 14, 1955. *Study:* RI Sch Design, 72-73; Art Students League, study with Richard L Seyffert, 72-77; studies at George Washington Univ, 2002; Skowhegan Sch Painting & Sculpture, 76-77; Skidmore Coll, BS, 2005. *Work:* SIFMA, NY; Susan Blanchard Gallery, New York; Union Mutual, Portland, Maine; Hoglund & Pearce, Portland, Maine; Bond Market Asn, New York; Sloan Kettering, New York; Md Inst Coll Art; Meml Sloan Kettering; and pvt collections in Zurich, Switz, Elgin, Scotland & Singapore. *Exhib:* Solo exhibs, Hobe Sound Gallery, Maine, Hobe Sound, Fla, 85, Southern Vermont Artists, Highlands of Scotland, 2002; Group exhibs, Midtown Gallery, New York, NY, 82; Southern Vt Art Ctr, Manchester, 88 & 2004; Albany Biennial, 92; Pub Securities Asn, New York, 94; Kunstsalon Wolfsburg, Zürich, Switz, 96; Nat Acad Design, New York, 2000; Salander O'Reilly, New York, 2004; Newman Galleries, Philadelphia, Pa, 2006; N Bennington Arts, 2012. *Collection Arranged:* Columbia Presbyterian Hosp; Sidney Kimmel Ctr; Help USA, Genesis Clinton Hill, NJ. *Pos:* Art consult, McKinsey & Co Inc, New York & Covington & Burling, New York; pres, Am Soc Appraisers, Hudson Chap, 2008-2010; co curator, O'Silas Gallery, 2010; curator, Landscapes of Lansdale, 2011, ASA Greenwich, NY. *Awards:* Best Oils, State Show, Somerset, NJ, 78; Jay Hall Connoway Landscape Award SVA, 90. *Bibliog:* Rev, Art Critic, Maine Times, 12/16/83; Schenectady Gazette, 90; Manchester News, 7/22/92. *Mem:* Kent Art Asn; Life mem Art Students League; So Vt Art Ctr; Am Soc Appraisers, Designated Fine Arts (vpres, currently). *Dealer:* Newman Galleries, Philadelphia, Pa. *Mailing Add:* 173 Fog Hill Rd Hoosick Falls NY 12090

SUSSMAN, BONNIE KAUFMAN
DEALER, CONSULTANT
b Minneapolis, Minn. *Study:* Univ Minn, BS. *Pos:* Bd dir, Goldstein Gallery, Univ Minn, St Paul, formerly; dir & owner, Peter M David Gallery, Minneapolis, 70-. *Mem:* Arts Consortium (for religions art), Minneapolis/St Paul. *Media:* Works on paper. *Specialty:* Contemporary American and English paintings, sculpture, prints, drawings, watercolor, photography, handmade paper. *Dealer:* Pvt dealer. *Mailing Add:* 3412 Oak Ridge Rd #109 Minnetonka MN 55305

SUSSMAN, EVE
PAINTER
b London, England, 1961. *Study:* Robert Coll, Istanbul, Turkey, 1979; Univ Canterbury, Christchurch, New Zealand, 1983; Bennington Coll, BA Fine Arts, 1984; Skowhegan Sch, 1989. *Exhib:* Solo exhibs include Rice Univ Art Gallery, Houston, 2004, 2005, Reina Sofia, 2006; group exhibs include Wasserwerke, Berlin, Germany, 1991; Casa Tua è Casa Mia, Am Acad Rome, 1996; Whitney Biennial, Whitney Mus Am Art, New York, 2004; Re-Installation, Mus Mod Art, New York, 2004; Preview, Nasher Mus Art Duke, Durham, NC, 2006; Rape of Sabine Women, Athens Festival, 2007; Archaeology, Proj Space 176, London, 2007; La Mois de Photo a Montreal,

Montreal, Canada, 2007. *Awards:* Art Matters Inc Grant, 1995; Am Acad Rome Fel, 1995; John Simon Guggenheim Found Grant, 1995; Creative Capital Found Grant, 2008. *Dealer:* Creative Time 59 E 4th St 6E New York NY 10003; Lorena Ruiz de Villa Madrazo 107 2 2 Barcelona Catalonia Spain 08021; Roebling Hall 390 Wythe Ave Brooklyn NY 11211; Union 57 Ewer St London England SE1 0NR UK

SUSSMAN, GARY LAWRENCE
SCULPTOR, DIRECTOR
b New York, NY, Feb 15, 1952. *Study:* Art Students League, apprentice to Jose de Creeft, 71-75; Ecole des Beaux Arts, Paris, France, 74; Academy, Florence, Italy, 74. *Work:* Sunnyside State Park, Tarrytown, NY; Storm King Sch, Mountainville, NY; Mt Carmel Sch, Ridgewood, NJ; Art Students League, NY; Mus Art & Sci, Los Angeles, Calif. *Comn:* large relief sculpture, Rockefeller Ctr, 88; bronze cloisonne, Radio City Music Hall, NY, 88; temple doors, Bethel Synagogue, Bennington, Vt, 89; marble bust of Giomatti, Yale Univ, 91; Rainforest Steamroom, comn by Marlo Thomas, Gymnasium Westport, Conn, 96; bronze, victim violent crimes, Larry Mentich, Cascade Falls Mich, 2005; bronze, Dr George Hatsopoulos, Thermo Electron, Boston, Mass, 2006. *Exhib:* Solo exhibs, Art Students League, NY, 74, Bergen Co Mus, Paramus, NJ, 77 & St Gaudens Nat Hist Park, Cornish, NH, 87; Newark Mus Invitational, NJ, 78; Discovery, Rediscovery, 82, Toys by Artists, 84 & Drawings by Artists, 84, Sculpture Ctr, NY; Skowhegan Artists, Colby Mus, Waterville, Maine, 83 & 84; Portraits by Artists, Bethune Gallery, State Univ NY, Buffalo, 84. *Pos:* Pres, Fine Arts Studio, Hoosick Falls, NY, 76; dir, Sculpture Ctr Studio, Sculpture Ctr, Inc, New York, 79-88; exec dir, Art Students League, Vytlacil Campus, Sparkhill, NY, 2007. *Teaching:* Sculpture technician, Skowhegan Sch Painting & Sculpture, Maine, 76 & 77, dean, 83-84; prof sculpture, Sculpture Ctr, 79-89; adj lectr, City Col NY, 82-84; sculpture, Art Students League, NY, 92-. *Awards:* McDowell Fel, Art Students League, NY, 73; William Zorach Mem Scholar, NY, Bd Control Scholar, ASC, NY; Am Artist in Residence 90, Musie Roche, Fort en Terre, Brittany, France, 90. *Mem:* Life mem Art Students League, NY; Artists Equity; Nat Sculpture Soc (fel); Audubon Artists; Artist Fel Inc. *Media:* All Media. *Dealer:* Fog Hill & Co Inc. *Mailing Add:* Fine Arts Studio Fog Hill Rd Hoosick Falls NY 12090

SUSSMAN, JILL
GALLERY DIRECTOR
b New York, NY. *Study:* RI Sch Design, 75. *Pos:* Cur asst, Whitney Mus Am Art, New York, 77-81; dir, Marian Goodman Gallery, New York, 81-; partner/dir, Matthew Marks Gallery, New York, 2000-2005; pvt dealer, art adv, 2006-. *Specialty:* Contemporary American painting, sculpture, photography, video, & prints. *Mailing Add:* One Irving Pl No G324D New York NY 10003

SUTTENFIELD, DIANA
PAINTER
b Washington, DC, Nov 20, 1944. *Study:* Md Inst Coll Art, Baltimore, BFA (painting), 72. *Work:* Washington Co Mus Fine Arts, Hagerstown, Md; United Airlines; Fidelity Investments, Boston; Sunrise Mus, Charleston, WVa; Art in embassies Prog, US Dept State, 99 & 2001-2007; US Dept Interior, Nat Training Ctr, Shepherdstown, WVa, Chesapeake & Ohio Canal Nat Hist Park & Harpers Ferry Nat Hist Park; SAS, NC; Johns Hopkins Univ Hosp; AT&T, C&P Telephone, NJ; Marshall Univ, WVa; Univ Charleston, WVa; Univ WVa; McDonald's. *Comn:* Univ Md Hosp, Physicians Complex, Baltimore, 86; Peat Marwick Main & Co, Baltimore, 87; AT&T, Martinsburg, WVa, 89; Westfield Corp, Ohio, 93-94; Brunswick Corp, Chicago, 96; Nat Conserv Training Ctr, The Land Where We Were Dreaming, 2002. *Exhib:* Midyear Show, Butler Inst Am Art, Youngstown, Ohio, 81; USArtists 92 & Pa Acad Art, Philadelphia, Pa, 92; Pastel Soc Am, New York, 93-94; Md Pastel Soc, 94; Audubon Artists, New York, 2000; Md Fedn Art, Am Landscapes, 2001-; Retrospective Exhib, Washington County Mys Fine Arts (WCMFA), Hagerstown, Md, 2015; and others. *Awards:* Best Show, Wash Co Mus Fine Arts, Hagerstown, Md, 91 & 94; Carolyn Griffuni Award, Pastel Soc Am, 93-94; Perruso Emnance Award for Outstanding Painting, Washington County Mus Fine Arts, Hagerstown, Md, 2009. *Media:* Oil, Acrylic. *Publ:* Auth, Shepherdstown Sketchbook, 76; Martinsburg Sketchbook, 79; Pen & Ink Drawings of Harpers Ferry, 80; C and O Canal: An Illustrated History, 81; illusr, The Language of Literature & BlackBerry Cove Herbal, 2000; Elegy for Barns, 2002. *Dealer:* Mary Bell Galleries 714 N Franklin St Chicago IL; The Bridge Gallery Shepardton; McJunkin Gallery 219 Hale St Charleston WV 25301. *Mailing Add:* PO Box 832 Shepherdstown WV 25443

SUTTER, JAMES STEWART
SCULPTOR, EDUCATOR
b Milwaukee, Wis, Feb 12, 1940. *Study:* Univ Wis, BA (art educ), 64; Univ Iowa, MA (sculpture), 65; Univ Mass, univ fels, 65-67, MFA (sculpture), 67. *Work:* St Lawrence Univ, Canton, NY; Del Mar Col, Corpus Christi, Tex; Mus Fine Arts, Springfield, Mass; Hoyt Inst Fine Arts, New Castle, Pa; Millersville Univ, Pa; and others. *Exhib:* RK Parker Gallery, NY, 82 & 83; Peter Drew Gallery, Palm Beach, Boca Raton, Fla, 83-89; Tenth Anniversary Drawing Invitational, Artist Space Gallery, NY, 84; Sodarc Gallery, Montreal, Can, 94; La Grange Nat XIX, Ga, 96; and others. *Teaching:* Drawing asst, Univ Mass, 66-67; assoc prof sculpture, State Univ NY Col Potsdam, NY, 67-79, prof art, 79-; guest prof sculpture & drawing, Skidmore Col, Saratoga Springs, 79-88. *Awards:* First Prize, 5th Ann Arena Nat, Binghamton, NY, 78; Sculpture Prize, Cooperstown Nat, NY, 84; Prize, Nat Metal Sculpture Compt, Millersville Univ, Pa, 84; Prize for Sculpture, Nat Small Works Exhib, Schoharie Arts Coun, Cobleskill, NY, 85; Artist Fel, NY State Found Arts, 87. *Mem:* Coll Art Asn. *Media:* Bronze, Aluminum. *Publ:* Coauth, with Dr Frank Seiberling, The Role of Sculpture in Modern Architecture, Univ Iowa, 65. *Dealer:* Peter Drew Gallery Worth Crocke Ctr Boca Raton FL; Judith Posner Associates Milwaukee WI. *Mailing Add:* 11 New St Norwood NY 13668

SUTTON, CAROL (LORRAINE)
PAINTER
b Norfolk, Va, Sept 3, 1945. *Study:* Richmond Prof Inst, BFA (Va Mus fel), 67; Univ NC, MFA (Chancellors Purchase award), 69. *Work:* Mus Fine Arts, Boston; Nat Collection Fine Art & Am Art Mus, Smithsonian Inst; Can Coun Art Bank, Ottawa, Can; Agnes Etherington Art Ctr, Kingston, Ont; Art Gallery Alberta, Can; Mus Contemp Art Barcelona, Spain; Fitzwilliam Mus Cambridge, Eng; Weatherspoon Art Mus, Greensboro; Art Gallery Hamilton, Can. *Comn:* The Eye of the Oval, (painting 8 by 18) Cineplex Oleon Corp, Sand Lake Seven Cinemas, Orlando, Fla, 87. *Exhib:* Barcelona Triangle 1987 Exposicio, Centre de Creacio Contemporania, Inst NAm Studies, Brit Coun, Ambassador Can, Barcelona, Spain, 87; solo exhibs, Silhouette-Grill-Balcony, Gallery One, Toronto, Can, 89, A Spanner in The Works Ethos and Spirituality in Abstract Painting, Terrance Sulymko Fine Art & Oakham House, Ryerson Coll, Toronto, Can, 89, Ideas For A Collection-A Spanner in The Works, Randwood, Niagara Inst, Niagara-on-the-Lake, Can, 91, Recent Paintings, Kathleen Laverty Gallery Ltd, Edmonton, Can, 92, Gallery One, Toronto, Can, 2003; New Hall Art Collection Biennial Open Day, Cambridge, England, 2005; Art for Small Hearts: Neonatal Intensive Care Units, Mt Sinai Hospital, Toronto & Shaare Zedek Med Ctr, Jerusalem, 2006; Postcard Tombola, New Hall Collection, Cambridge, 2007; Sam & Adele Golden Found Arts, 10 Year Celebration & Art Auction Benefit, Golden Artists Colors, New Berlin, New York, 2007; Bright Colours, Big Canvas: Jack Bush, Agnes Etherington Art Ctr, Wueens Univ, Canada, 2009. *Teaching:* Instr, Mt Allison Owens Art Gallery, Sackville, Can, 1976, ABANA, 1991, Inst Farina Convitto, Vicenza, Italy, 1991, Kingston Univ, London, 1991. *Awards:* Blue Ribbon, 1st place in Junior Sections, Sears-Allstate Tidewater Arts Festival, 63; Va Mus Fel, 66, 67; Chancellors Purchase Award, Univ NC, 69; Ontario Arts Coun, 75-77; Can Coun, 79, 83, 88; Adolph & Esther Gottlieb Found Inc, 92. *Bibliog:* James Clark (auth), The Problem of Fundamental Ontology Book, Limits Bk Co, 81; Karen Wilkin (auth), Toronto: Fans, flickers & penny arcades, Art News, 2/82; David Burnett (auth), Cineplex Odeon, The First Ten Years A Celebration of Contemporary Canadian Art, 89; Roald Nasgaard (auth), Abstract Painting in Canada, 2008. *Media:* Acrylic on Canvas. *Dealer:* Gallery One Toronto 121 Scollard St Ont Can M5R 1G4. *Mailing Add:* 27 Davies Ave Toronto ON M4M 2A9 Canada

SUTTON, PETER C
CURATOR, HISTORIAN
b Mar 30, 1949. *Study:* The Gunnery, Washington, Conn, 68; Harvard Col, AB, 72 (Fel 72); Yale Univ, (Fel 73-76) MA, 75, PhD, 78. *Collection Arranged:* Masters of Seventeenth-Century Dutch Genre Painting (auth, catalog), Philadelphia Mus Art & tour to West Berlin & London, 84; Renoir, 85-86 & Manet to Matisse, 86, Mus Fine Arts, Boston; Masters of Seventeenth-Century Dutch Landscape Painting (auth, catalog), Rijksmus Amsterdam & tour to Boston & Philadelphia, 87-88; Prized Possessions: European Paintings from Private Collections, Mus Fine Arts, Boston, 92; Age of Rubens, Boston & Toledo, 93-94; The Golden Age of Dutch Landscape Painting, Thyssen-Bomemisza collection, Madrid, Spain, 94. *Pos:* Asst cur Europ paintings before 1900, Philadelphia Mus Art, 79-83, assoc cur, 83-85; Mrs Russell Baker cur Europ paintings, Mus Fine Arts, Boston, 85-94; sr dir, Old Master Paintings, Christies, New York, 94-96; dir, Wadsworth Atheneum, Hartford, Conn, 96. *Awards:* Kress Travel Grant Summer, 75; David E Finley Fel, Nat Gallery Art, 76-79; Alfred Barr Award Most Distinguished Mus Pub of 1984, Coll Art Asn, 86. *Publ:* Auth, Pieter de Hooch (1629-1684): Complete Edition, Phaidon Press 80; Masterpiece Paintings from the Museum of Fine Arts, Boston, Abrams Press, 86; Dutch Art in America, Eerdmans Publ Co, 86; Dutch & Flemish Seventeenth-Century Paintings, The Harold Samuel Collection, Cambridge Univ Press, 92. *Mailing Add:* Wadsworth Atheneum 600 Main St Hartford CT 06103-2990

SUZEN, SUSAN R RUBINSTEIN
PHOTOGRAPHER, DESIGNER
b New York, NY, May 17, 1946. *Study:* Brooklyn Mus Art Sch; Am Univ, BA (fine arts & graphic design); Art Ctr Coll Design, Los Angeles, with Todd Walker. *Work:* Denver Mus Art; Yale Univ Art Gallery; Exchange Nat Bank Chicago; Mus Art & Hist, Fribourg, Switz; Het Sterckhof Mus, Antwerp, Belg; Libr of Cong, Washington, DC; Santa Barbara Mus; Bibliotheque Nat, Paris. *Exhib:* Solo exhibs, Herbert F Johnson Mus, Ithaca, NY, 77, Bertha Urdang Gallery, NY, 80, Canon Photo Gallery, Geneva, Switz, 81, Galerie Karin Steins, Frankfurt, WGer, 82, Howard Univ, Washington, DC, 82 & Mus Ludwig, Cologne, WGer, 84; Fac Exhib, Int Ctr Photog, NY, 80; Independent Am Photog, Warsaw, 80; Live from NY, Lowe Gallery, Syracuse, NY, 82; Works in Progress, Heller Gallery, NY, 83; Spirit of Spring Festival of the Arts, Performance, at Port Authority, NY, 84. *Pos:* Founder/dir, Art for the People. *Teaching:* Instr photog, Hunter Col, 78-79, Marymount Manahattan Col, 78-, Int Ctr Photog, 79-82 & Asphalt Green/Murphy Ctr, 85-90, NY; artist-in-residence, Apeiron Workshops, Millerton, NY, 79, NY Found Art/Guggenheim Mus, 85. *Awards:* NY State Coun Arts grant, 84; Nat Endowment Arts/Inter Arts grant, 85. *Bibliog:* John Hunter (auth), Ironic reality, Art Week, 1/75; Jacques J Halber (auth), Brief vit Belge, Foto, 3/77; Arthur Secunda (auth), article, Visual Dialogue, winter 77-78; article, Kolner Stadt-Anseiger, WGer, 84; article, New York Daily News, 11-12/84. *Mem:* Soc Photog Educators; NY Mac User Group. *Media:* Light. *Publ:* Illusr, The Love Story of Sushi & Sashimi: A Cat Tale, Capra Press, 90. *Mailing Add:* 155 Banks St New York NY 10014-2010

SUZUKI, JAMES HIROSHI
PAINTER
b Yokohama, Japan, Sept 19, 1933. *Study:* Sch of Fine & Appl Art, Portland, Maine, 52; Corcoran Sch Art, 53-54; privately with Yoshio Markino. *Work:* Corcoran Gallery of Art, Washington, DC; Wadsworth Atheneum, Hartford, Conn; Rockefeller Inst, NY; Nat Mus Mod Art, Tokyo, Japan; Toledo Mus Art, Ohio. *Exhib:* Corcoran Gallery Art, 56, 58 & 60; Whitney Mus Am Art; Baltimore Mus Art, Md; Contemp Painters of Japanese Origin in Am, Inst Contemp Art, Boston; Everson Mus Art, Syracuse, NY, 58; Wadsworth Atheneum, 59; Waning Moon and Rising Sun, Mus Fine Arts of

Houston, 59; San Francisco Mus Art, 63 & 64; solo exhibs, Quay Gallery, 73, Braustein Quay Gallery, 76 & 78 & Sacramento State Univ, 78; Aesthetics of Graffiti, San Francisco Mus Mod Art, 78. *Teaching:* Instr, Univ Calif, Berkeley, 62-63 & Univ Ky, 66-68; assoc prof art, Sacramento State Univ, currently. *Awards:* Eugene Weiss Scholar, Corcoran Gallery Art, 54; John Hay Whitney Fel, 58; Larry Aldrich Prize, Silvermine Guild, 59. *Dealer:* Braunstein Quay Gallery 254 Sutter St San Francisco CA 94108. *Mailing Add:* 1319 Brown Dr Davis CA 95616

SUZUKI, TARO
SCULPTOR, PAINTER

b New York, NY, Nov 17, 1953. *Study:* Syracuse Univ, 71-72; Sch Visual Arts, 72-73; Cooper Union, BFA, 76. *Comn:* Installation, comn by Schorr, Aspen, Colo, 80; installation, comn by J Shore, Cincinnati, 82; installation, comn by M Sklar, NY, 82; installation, comn by C Cameron, NY, 83. *Exhib:* Marta Cerveras Gallery, NY, 90; White Columns, NY, 90; Fay Gold Gallery, Atlanta, 91; Rempire Gallery, NY, 91; Fogg Mus, Cambridge, Ma, 94; Rushmore Festival, Woodbury, NJ, 94; Fawbush Gallery, NY & Charles Cowles Gallery, NY, 94; Orange Co Mus Art, 2007; Mitchell Algus Gallery, 2008; Spanierman Mod, 2008. *Pos:* Dir, Space Force, NY, 80-84 & 92-; mem bd dir, Ocean Earth Construct & Develop, NY, 80-. *Teaching:* Teacher sculpture, RI Sch Design, 85. *Awards:* Nat Endowment Arts Grant, 82; Pollock Krasner Grant, 89 & 2006; Elizabeth Found for the Arts, Studio Award, 2006. *Bibliog:* Alan Jones (auth), article, Arts Mag, 89; Roberta Smith (auth), NY Times, 89 & 2008; R C Baker (auth), Village Voice, 2008; and others. *Mem:* White Columns; Bomb Mag. *Media:* All

SVEDLOW, ANDREW JAY
ADMINISTRATOR, PAINTER

b Stamford, Conn, Dec 9, 1955. *Study:* George Washington Univ, BA (fine arts), 77; Bank Street Col, MS, 82; Pa State Univ, PhD (art educ), 85. *Work:* Mus City New York; Whistler House Mus Art, Lowell, Mass; Mulvane Art Mus, Topeka, Kans; The Bruce Mus, Greenwich, Conn; NH Inst Art; Hallmark Collection, Kansas City, Mo; Ossorio Collection, Greenwich, Conn. *Exhib:* Realism Today, Stamford Mus, Conn, 80; Stamford Loft Artists, Stamford Mus, Conn, 83; Recent Prints, Washburn Univ Gallery, Topeka, Kans, 84; Fire & Air, Pa State Univ Gallery, 85; Voices of Poverty, Kans State Univ Gallery, 88; solo shows: Beowulf & Fragments, Dalton Gallery, Rock Hill, SC, 2001, Freedom, Gaston Coll Gallery, Gastonia, SC. *Pos:* Dir, Mulane Art Mus, Topeka, Kans, 86-89; asst dir, Mus City New York, 90-93; pres, NH Inst Art, 93-; Dean, Col Visual & Performing Arts, Winthrop Univ, 2000-2005; dean, Col Performing & Visual Arts, Univ Northern Colo, 2005-. *Teaching:* Vis assoc prof art educ, Univ Southern Miss, Hattisburg, 84; adv & adj fac mus leadership, Bank Street Col, New York, 89-; adj fac art educ, Parsons Sch Design, New York, 90-93. *Awards:* Fulbright Grant, 2010. *Mem:* NH Visual Arts Coalition (pres, 94-96); New York City Mus Educators Roundtable (chair, 92-94); Nat Art Educ Asn (task force chair, 87); Coll Art Asn; Int Soc Educ Through Art. *Publ:* Auth, Heartland of the here & now, New Art Examiner, 6/87; Reading Prints, Mulvane Art Mus, 87; Within the mask, Kans Quart, 88; Rare prints & drawings: A case study, Acume J, 88; A World Together: Korean Art, Korean Cult Serv, 92. *Mailing Add:* 3337 New Castle Dr Loveland CO 80538

SVENSON, JOHN EDWARD
SCULPTOR, MEDALIST

b Los Angeles, Calif, May 10, 1923. *Study:* Claremont Grad Sch, Calif. *Work:* Ahmandson Ctr, Los Angeles; San Bernardino Co Mus; Skagway, Alaska Sch Dist; Civic Ctr, Garden Grove, Calif; Smithsonian Air Mus; Foothill Ranch, Laguna Hills, Calif; and others. *Comn:* Gold portrait medallions of King Hussein, Jordan & Ibn Saud Saudi Arabia; bronze porpoise fountain, Ritz Carlton, Laguna Niguel, Calif; hist panels, San Gabriel Mission Chapel, Calif; bldg facade & sculpture, Purex Corp, Lakewood, Calif; Alaska Tlingit Medal, Soc Medalists An Issue; hist sculptures Anchorage, Valdez and Skagway, AK; Fleischer Mus, Scottsdale, Ariz; Brookgreen Gardens, NC; 22 Ft 17 Ton Redwood Sculpture, Ranchero, Pomona, CA; 8 Ft Bronze Sculpture, George Chaffey, City Hall, Uplano, CA. *Exhib:* Los Angeles Co Mus Art, 62; Newman Galleries, Philadelphia, 71; Kennedy Galleries, NY, 72; Alaska State Mus; Svenson Arts Gallery, Haines, Alaska; and others. *Pos:* Trustee, Alaska Indian Arts, Inc, Port Chilkoot, 67-. *Awards:* Awards for Excellence in Sculpture, Am Inst Archit, 57 & 61; Sculpture Award, City of Garden Grove, Calif, 80; Gold Medal & Hester Prize, Nat Sculpture Soc, New York, 96. *Bibliog:* Nat Sculpture Rev, 77; Inland Empire Mag, 8/82 & 10/98; Elan Mag, 3/90; Beautiful Things Art Book, 2000. *Mem:* Fel Nat Sculpture Soc; Soc Medalists, NY; Chaffey Art Asn (trustee); Calif Club. *Media:* Wood, Bronze. *Mailing Add:* c/o Svenson Arts Gallery 2480 Vista Dr Upland CA 91784

SWAIN, ROBERT
PAINTER

b Austin, Tex, Dec 7, 1940. *Study:* Am Univ, Washington, DC, BA. *Work:* Corcoran Gallery Art, Washington, DC; Walker Art Ctr, Minneapolis; Denver Art Mus, Colo; Albright-Knox Mus, Buffalo, NY; Everson Art Mus, Syracuse, NY. *Comn:* Painting (8 1/2ft x 20ft), Schering Labs, Bloomfield, NJ, comn by Skidmore, Owings & Merrill, New York, 70; painting (5ft x 10ft), Phillip Mallis, Kahn & Mallis Assocs, New York, 72; painting (4ft x 27ft), IBM, Charlotte, NC, 81; painting (5ft x 9ft), Tupperware World Headquarters, Kissimmee, Fla, 81. *Exhib:* The Art of the Real, Mus Mod Art, New York, 68; 31st Biennial, Corcoran Gallery Art, 69; The Structure of Color, Whitney Mus Am Art, 71; solo exhibs, Susan Caldwell Gallery, 74, 76, 78 & 81, Everson Art Mus, Syracuse, 74 & Columbus Gallery Fine Arts, Ohio, 76; Painting & Sculpture Today, Indianapolis Mus Art, Ind, 74; Color as Language (traveling exhib, Latin Am), Mus Mod Art, NY, 74-75; Nina Freudenheim Gallery, Buffalo, NY, 78; Toni Birckhead Gallery, Cincinnati, Ohio, 80. *Teaching:* Prof fine arts, Hunter Coll, NY. *Awards:* Guggenheim Fel, 69; Nat Endowment for Arts Grant, 76. *Bibliog:* Scott Burton (auth), Light from Aten to Laser, MacMillan co, 69; B Wasserman (auth), Modern Painting, Davis Publ, 70; Roberta Smith (auth), Artforum, 76. *Media:* Acrylic. *Mailing Add:* 57 Leonard St New York NY 10013

SWAIN, ROBERT FRANCIS
GALLERY DIRECTOR

b Halifax, NS, Oct 25, 1942. *Study:* Carleton Univ, BA. *Collection Arranged:* Joan Frick, 74; Robert Sinclair, 76; Made Glorious: 25 Years of Stratford Design, 76; A History of Children's Book Illustrations, 77; Fantastic Shakespeare; Coasts: The Sea and Canadian Art. *Pos:* Dir, Agnes Etherington Art Ctr, Kingston, Ont. *Mem:* Int Comt Mus; Ont Asn Art Galleries (dir); and others. *Publ:* Auth, many exhib catalogs. *Mailing Add:* 43 Jorene Dr Kingston ON K7M 3X5 Canada

SWANSON, CAROLINE
PAINTER

Work: Columbia Mus of Art, SC; Gertrude Herbert Inst Art, Augusta, Ga; Int Cult Ctr, Takarazuka, Japan; Nat Arts Club, NY; Deland Mus Art, Fla. *Collection Arranged:* Pvt and Corp Collections. *Awards:* Leila Gardin Sawyer Mem Award, AAPL, NY; Best in Watercolor, New Horizons Arts Festival, Augusta, Ga; Purchase Award, Visual Arts Ctr Mus, Panama City, Fla. *Mem:* Nat Asn Women Artists; Nat Watercolor Soc; Philadelphia Watercolor Soc; Tex Watercolor Soc; Western Colo Watercolor Soc. *Mailing Add:* 612 Brae Burn Dr Augusta GA 30907

SWANSON, J N
PAINTER, SCULPTOR

b Duluth, Minn, Feb 4, 1927. *Study:* Coll Arts & Crafts, Oakland, Calif; Carmel Art Inst; also with Donald Teague & Armin Hansen. *Work:* Read Mullin Collection, Phoenix; Sunset Mag Collection Art; Leaning Tree Mus, Boulder, Colo; Diamond M Mus, Tex; Cowboy Artist Am Mus, Kerrville, Tex; and others. *Comn:* Pvt comn only. *Exhib:* Monterey Co Fair Prof Div, Calif, 67; Springville Regional Show, Utah; Cowboy Artists Ann Show, Hall Fame, Okla, 70-75; Soc Western Artists, De Young Mus, San Francisco, 71. *Pos:* Co-founder, Stewards of the Range. *Teaching:* Horse anat, Cowboy Artist Mus, Kerrville, Tex. *Awards:* San Francisco Best of Show Award, Monterey Co Fair, 67; Soc Western Artists Atelier Award, De Young Mus, 71; Westerner of the Yr, Western Ranchero Beef Asn, 2001; Vquero Artist of the Yr, Santa Ynez Mus, Calif, 2008; Supporter of Monterey Art Award, 2008; Lifetime Achievement Award, Monterey Co, 2008. *Bibliog:* Ainsworth (auth), Cowboy in Art, World, 68; Paul Weaver (ed), Cowboy Artists Ann Exhib Bks, Northland, 69-75; Broder (auth), Bronzes of the American West, Abrams, 74; The Life & Times of a Western Artist: JN Swanson, autobiography, 2010. *Mem:* Cowboy Artists Am (vpres, 70). *Media:* Oil; Plastilene Clay. *Res:* Complete Western library for research into historical Western painting; first hand knowledge of the cowboy subject of present day. *Interests:* Training cows and horses. *Collection:* major western collections in US & England. *Publ:* Autobiography, Art Works Mag, Leanin Tree Publ, Carmel, Calif, 2010

SWANSON, RAY V
PAINTER

b Alcester, SDak, Oct 4, 1937. *Study:* Northrop Inst, BS, 60. *Work:* Indianapolis Mus Art; Riverside Art Collection Mus, Calif. *Exhib:* Wichita Nat Art Exhib, Kans, 70; Franklin Mint Gallery Am Art, 73-74; Capitol Bldg, Phoenix, Ariz, 75; Nat Acad Western Art, Cowboy Hall of Fame, 76. *Awards:* Silver Medal, Water Solubles, Cowboy Artists Am, 90 & Gold Medal, 92; Bronze Medal, Am Watercolor Soc, 91. *Bibliog:* J & J Ward (auth), Renaissance of Western Art, Franklin Mint Gallery, 74; Tom Cooper (auth), The Best of Arizona Highways, Ariz Hwys, 75; Royal B Hassrick (auth), Western Painting Today, Watson-Guptill Publ, 75. *Mem:* Prescott Fine Arts Asn; signature mem Am Watercolor Soc; Western Art Asn (bd mem, 91-92); Cowboy Artists Am (vpres, 92-93, pres, 93-94). *Media:* Oil; Watercolor. *Publ:* Contribr, Artist of the Rockies, Colo Publ, 75; contribr, Illuminator, Grand Cent Publ, 75. *Dealer:* Husberg Fine Arts Gallery 330 Hwy 179 Sedona AZ 86336

SWANSON, VERN GROSVENOR
MUSEUM DIRECTOR, HISTORIAN

b Central Point, Ore, Feb 4, 1945. *Study:* Brigham Young Univ, Provo, Utah, BA, 69; Univ Utah, Salt Lake City, MA (art hist), 75; Univ London, Courtauld Inst Art, PhD (art hist), 94. *Collection Arranged:* An Exhibition of British and Am Paintings (auth, catalog), 76, Auburn Univ; The Unknown Alma-Tadema (auth, catalog), Brigham Young Univ, Utah, 79; Permanent Collection (auth, catalog), 81 & National April Salon (auth, catalog), 81-89, Springville Mus Art; Soviet & Russian Impressionism, Fleischer Mus, 94; When Art Was Popular - European Masters of 19th Century Art, Springville Mus, 96; Retrospective - Art of John William Godward 1976-1997, Richard Green Fine Art, London, Eng, 97; over 65 other temporary exhibs at the Springville Mus Art. *Pos:* Mus aide supervisor, Nat Gallery Art, Washington, 69-70; gallery dir, House Fine Arts, Provo, Utah, 70-71; art consult British classical art, major auction houses, 73-; mus dir, Springville Mus Art, Utah, 80-; art hist, Brigham Young Univ, 87-88; art consult to Australian Collector. *Teaching:* Asst prof art hist, Auburn Univ, Ala, 71-75; guest lectr, Sotheby's, NY. *Awards:* Research grant, Paul Mellon Inst Studies Brit Art, 88 & Am Acad Art, 88; George S & Delores Dore' Eccles Found, 89; Gov Award, Dir Art Mus Utah, 94. *Mem:* Am Asn Mus; Victorian Soc Am; Art Mus Asn; Utah Mus Asn (vpres, 86-87); Grand Cent Art Galleries Educ Asn (bd dir, 88-92). *Res:* The fine arts among the Mormons in Utah; Catalogues Raisonnies on John William Godward & John Hafen; editing & preparation of volume on the Mormon theology of the 2011 expected atonement. *Publ:* The Life and Works of Sir Lawrence Alma-Tadema, Garton & Co, 90; The Biography & Catalogue Raisonne of the Paintings of Sir Lawrence Alma-Tadema, Garton & Co, 90; Utah Art, Peregrine-Smith, 91; Mormon art & belief movement, Southwest Art Mag, 12/91; Hidden Treasures: Russian & Soviet Impressionism 1930-1970's, 1/94; auth, Artists of Utah, 2000 & Soviet Working Class Impressionism, 9/2001; coauth, Utah Art - Utah Artists, 2001; Soviet Impressionist Painting, 2008; Dynasty of the Holy Grail: Mormonism's Sacred Bloodline, 2008; coauth, Painters of Utah's Canyons and Deserts, 2009. *Mailing Add:* Springville Museum of Art 1305 E Hobble Creek Dr Springville UT 84663

SWARD, ROBERT S
WRITER, EDITOR

b Chicago, Ill, June 23, 1933. *Study:* Univ Ill, BA (hons), 56; Univ Iowa, MA, 58; Univ Bristol, Eng, 60-61; post grad studies, Middlebury Col, 56-60; studies with Robert Frost & John Ciardi. *Work:* Archive Collection, City Hall, Toronto, Ont; Provincial Mus Collection, BC Provincial Govt; Santa Cruz Libr Archive; Wash Univ Libr Arch, St. Louis, Mo. *Comn:* Earthquake collage, loma Prieta, Santa Cruz, Calif, 89; Earthquake Cabrillo Col, Aptos, Calif, 89 & 2000. *Exhib:* Traveling Exhib, The Toronto Islands (auth, catalog), Toronto City Archive, Can, 80-83. *Pos:* Ed, Soft Press Publ, Victoria, BC, 70-79 & Business to Business Network, Santa Cruz, 86-88; ed-in-chief, Hancock House Publ, Vancouver, BC, 75-79; vis artist poetry & bk-making, Ont Arts Coun, Toronto, 81-85; vis artist poetry, bk-making & illus, Cult Coun Santa Cruz, 86-; freelance writer, ed & consult, currently; founder, Uncle Dog Audio, currently. *Teaching:* Instr creative writing, Univ Calif Ext, retired 2000; instr creative writing, Foothill Col; Eng prof, Monterey Peninsula Col, Calif, 85-87; instr, Univ Calif, Santa Cruz Extension, 86-; prof eng, Cabrillo Col, 87-2000, Esalen Inst autobiography/memoir workshop, spring 2010-. *Awards:* Guggenheim Fel Poetry, 65, 2000; D H Lawrence Fel Poetry, Univ NMex, 66; Grants, Can Coun, Ontario Arts Coun & Ontario Heritage Found, 81-84; Villa Montalvo Literary Arts Award, 90. *Bibliog:* John Malcolm Brinnin (auth), NY Times Book Review; Tina Barr (auth), Harvard Rev, 6/92; Contemporary Poets, ed by Janice Jorgenson, 6th ed, St. James Press, 94-95; Contemporary Authors: A Bio-Bibliographical Guide, Gale Thomson, vol 206, 2003; Collected Poems, 1957-2004, Black Moss Press; Robyn Sarah (auth), Globe & Mail, Toronto, 2004; The Muse, DVD Mag, Boss Productions, Calif, spring 2007. *Mem:* Nat Writer's Union; fel Yaddo, MacDowell Colony & Djerassi Found, 60-92; Poetry Santa Cruz; League of Canadian Poets. *Media:* Printmaker, Publisher. *Res:* Small Press Publications in the USA and Canada (bks & mags) Emily Carr: The Untold Story, 78 & The Art of the Haida, Argillite, 80, Hancock House. *Interests:* computers, multi-media, books, book making, documenting autobiography & memoir texts. *Publ:* Four Incarnations, New & Selected Poems, 1957-1991, Coffee House Press, 91; Contemp Authors Autobiography Series, Gale Research, vol 13, 90; CD-ROM, Discovering Authors Canada, ed by James Draper, 94; Family, Select Poet Series, 94; A Much-Married Man, A Novel, Ekstasis Eds, Can, 96; Rosicrucian in the Basement, New & Selected Poems, Black Moss Press, 2001; Heavenly Sex & Other Poems, Black Moss Press, 2002; Collected Poems: 1957-2004, Black Moss Press, 2004; God is in the Cracks, A Narrative in Voices, Black Moss Press, 2006; New & Selected Poems 1957-2010, Red New Press, 2010. *Mailing Add:* PO Box 7062 Santa Cruz CA 95061-7062

SWARTZ, BETH AMES
PAINTER

b New York, NY, Feb 5, 1936. *Study:* Art Students League; Cornell Univ, BS, 57; NY Univ, MA, 60. *Work:* Jewish Mus, NY; Nat Mus Am Art, Washington, DC; Phoenix Art Mus; San Francisco Mus Art; Mus Fine Art, Santa Fe, NMex. *Exhib:* Solo exhibs, Elaine Horwitch Galleries, Scottsdale, Ariz, 79, 80, 82, 84, 86 & 88, A Moving Point of Balance, traveling show, 85-92, Plaka Art Gallery, Athens, Greece, Nafplion Art Gallery, Greece, 89, Galeria Yolanda Rios, Sitges, Barcelona, Spain, 89, New Gallery, Houston, Tex, 89 & Elaine Horwitch Galleries, Palm Springs, 89; Paper: Surface and Image, Rutgers Univ, touring, 81-82; Artists in the Am Desert Touring Show, 81-82; Artist as Shaman, Women's Bldg, Los Angeles, 86; Artists of the Western States Biennial, Elaine Horwitch Galleries, Palm Springs, 87; New Sacred Art: Prayers for Peace, White Light Gallery, NY, 87; Newhouse Ctr Contemp Arts, Staten Island, NY, 88; The Transformative Vision, Phyllis Weil & Co, NY, 89; A Moving Point of Balance, Ariz Cancer Ctr, 98. *Teaching:* Assoc, Exten Dept, Ariz State Univ, 63-74. *Awards:* Nat Endowment Arts Grant, 75; Ariz Comn Arts & Humanities Educ Grant, 77. *Bibliog:* Lynn Pyne (auth), Artist approaches life from a different angle, Phoenix Gazette, 4/20/88; Victoria Beaudin (auth), Artist's work depicts heavenly inspiration, Scottsdale Progress Weekend Mag, 5/6/88; Jodie Snyder (auth), Valley Artist Hopes Work Helps Cancer Patients, Ariz Repub, A1 & A8, 1/12/98. *Mem:* Nat & Ariz Art Educ Asns. *Media:* Fire on Paper; Mixed-Media. *Publ:* Are we stifling our children's creativity?, Point West Mag, 63; Help your child create, Art Handbook for Parents, 65; auth, Inquiry into fire, Ariz Artist, fall 77. *Mailing Add:* 5346 E Sapphire Ln Scottsdale AZ 85253

SWARTZ, JULIANNE
ARTIST

b Phoenix, Ariz, Apr 29, 1967. *Study:* Univ Ariz, BA (photog & creative writing), 89; Skowhegan Sch for Painting and Sculpture, Postgrad, 99; Bard Col, MFA, 2002. *Work:* Brooklyn Mus Art, 1997 Bronx Mus for the Arts, 1999, Bellevue Art Mus, Seattle, 2000, Mus Contemp Art, Tucson, 2003, New Mus Contemp Art, New York City, 2004, Whitney Biennial, Whitney Mus Am Art, NY, 2004. *Exhib:* Solo exhibs, Numinious, Lombard Freid Fine Arts, NY, 97, NY Biennial Glass, Robert Lehman Gallery, Brooklyn, 99, Shadow House, Ricco/Maresca Gallery New York City 2000, Piot Brehmer Landing the Bubble, 123 Watts, New York City, 2001, Shroeder-Romero Gallery, Brooklyn, 2002; Group exhibs, Weatherspoon Art Gallery, Univ NC, Chapel Hill, 96, Robert Lehman Gallery at Urban Glass, Brooklyn, 98, Ellen Kim Murphy Gallery, Santa Monica, Calif, 99, Tulane Univ, New Orleans, 99, 123 Watts Gallery, New York City, 2000, Let's Get To Work, Univ Arts, Philadelphia, 2001, Plant Life, KS Art, New York City, 2001, clenchclutchflynch, Paul Rogers Gallery, New York City, 2001, Mixed Greens, Space 101, Brooklyn, 2001, Sculpture Ctr, New York City, 2001, Brooklyn!, Palm Beach (Fla) Inst Contemp Art, 2001, Periphera, Murray Guy Gallery, New York City, 2002, PS 1 Inst for Contemp Art, Queens, NY, 2000, Christinerose/Josee Bienvenu Gallery, New York City, 2003, Line Drawing, Artist's Space Project Room, New York City, 2003, Grant Selwyn Fine Art, Los Angeles, 2003, Still/Motion, Hosfelt Gallery, San Francisco, 2003, Muller Dechiara Gallery, Berlin, 2004, ARCO, Spain, 2004, Catharine Clark Gallery, San Francisco, 2004, Am Acad Arts & Letts Invitational, New York, 2010. *Awards:* Special Editions Grant, Lower East Side Printshop, 98; Richard Kelly Found Grant, 99; Cite Internationale des Arts, Paris, 2000. *Bibliog:* Barbara Macadams (auth), Magnetic Resonances, ARTnews, 2/2005; Benjamin Genocchio (auth), The Minds Eye, (It's all a Blur), The NY Times, 3/2006; Jerry Saltz (auth), Critics Pick, Julianne Swartz, NY Mag, 5/2007; Dominique Nahas (auth), Hope, Sculpture Mag, 5/2008 & Yulia Tikhonova (auth), Julianne Swartz at Josee Bienvenu, 1/2010. *Mailing Add:* c/o Josee Bienvenu Gallery 529 W 20th St New York NY 10011

SWARTZMAN, ROSLYN
PRINTMAKER, SCULPTOR

b Montreal, Que, Aug 17, 1931. *Study:* Montreal Artists Sch; Montreal Mus Fine Arts; Ecole des Beaux Arts, with Albert Dumouchez. *Work:* Nat Gallery Can, Ottawa, Ont; Montreal Mus Fine Arts, Que; DeCordova Mus, Boston; Brooklyn Mus, NY; NY Pub Libr; and many others. *Comn:* Aluminum bas-relief sculpture, Arctic Forms, Montreal, 83-84; aluminum wall sculpture, Oiseau de Feu, Place Bonaventure Entrance Lobby, St Antoine & Univ, Montreal, 90-91. *Exhib:* 2nd Int Graphics Biennial, Miami, 75; Jewish Experience in the 20th Century, Mt St Vincent Univ, Halifax, NS; Can Landscape through Drawings & Prints, Mus Fine Arts, Montreal; Boston Printmakers, 78; Solo exhib, Burnaby Art Gallery, BC, 80 & Saidye Bronfman Ctr, 81; and others. *Teaching:* Teacher & dir graphics dept, Sayde Bronfman Ctr, Montreal, 71-; printmaking instr, Univ Haifa, Israel, 88; art instr, Israel Painting Workshop Tour, 89; founder & coordr comprehensive art prog, Saidye Bronfman Centre, Montreal, Que, 90-. *Awards:* two patron selection awards, Boston Printmakers 30th Exhib; Thomas Moore Purchase Award, Montreal, 80; Travel Grant to Israel, Can-Israel Cult Found, 88; and others. *Bibliog:* Nicole Malenfant (auth), L'Estampe - La Documentation Québécoise, 79; Gilles Daigneault & Ginette Deslauriers (auths), La Gravure Au Québec - 1940-1980; Elyse (auth), Musée du Québec, 81; Marcel Broquet (auth), Musée du Québec, 86; Idea of North, Royal Can Acad Arts, 83. *Mem:* Royal Can Acad; Graphic Arts Coun Can; Print & Drawing Coun Can; Graphics Soc NH. *Media:* Intaglio; Bas-Relief. *Dealer:* La Guild Graphique 9 St Paul Ouest Montreal Can. *Mailing Add:* 4174 Oxford St Montreal PQ H4A 2Y4 Canada

SWEENEY, J GRAY
HISTORIAN, CURATOR

b Jacksonville, Fla, Nov 20, 1943. *Study:* Univ NMex, BA, 66; Ind Univ, MA, 69, PhD, 75. *Collection Arranged:* Themes in Am Painting (auth, catalog), Grand Rapids Art Mus, 77; Artists of Grand Rapids: 1840-1980 (auth, catalog), 81; Great Lakes Marine Painting of the 19th Century (auth, catalog), Muskegon Mus Art, 83, Artists of Michigan from the 19th Century (auth, catalog), Muskegan Mus Art, 87. *Pos:* Cur, Themes in Am Painting, Grand Rapids Art Mus, 75-77, Tweed Mus, 80, Grand Rapids Art Mus, Mich, 81 & Muskegon Mus Art, 83 & 86. *Teaching:* Asst prof 19th & 20th century Am painting, Grand Valley State Univ, 71-78, assoc prof, 78-85; assoc prof, Ariz State Univ, 86-88, prof, 89-. *Awards:* Fels, Carnegie Found, 67 & 70 & Samuel H Kress Found, 70-71; Senior fel, Smithsonian Inst, Nat Mus Am Art, 84-85. *Mem:* Coll Art Asn; Asn Hist Am Art. *Res:* Nineteenth century American landscape painting; influence of Thomas Cole; Regional and Western Am Art. *Publ:* The Nude of Landscape Painting: Emblematic Personification in the Art of the Hudson River School, Smithsonian Studies in Am Art, fall 89; A very peculiar picture: Martin J Heades Thunderstorm over Narragansett Bay, Archs Am Art J, #4, 88; Masterpieces of Western American Painting, 91; The Columbus of the Woods: Daniel Boone & Manifest Destiny (catalog), 92; Racism, Nationalism & Nostalgia in Cowboy Art, Oxford Art J, 92; and others. *Mailing Add:* c/o Sch of Art Ariz State Univ PO Box 871505 Tempe AZ 85287-1505

SWEENEY, SPENCER
ARTIST

Study: Pa Acad Fine Arts, BA, 1993-1997. *Exhib:* Free Coke, Greene Naftali Gallery, NYC, 1999; Legal Paper Work, Beyond Baroque, 2000; Paintings, Gavin Brown's Enterprise, 2002; Today's Man, John Connely, NY, 2003; Subway Series, Bronx Mus Arts, NY, 2004; Modern Inst, Glasgow, Eng, 2005; Whitney Biennial: Day for Night, Whitney Mus Am Art, NY, 2006. *Awards:* Lewis S Ware Mem prize exceptional work; Jimmy C Leuders painting prize; Angelo Pinto Mem prize exceptional work; Cuff/Sammack prize abstract art; Lucile Sorgenti scholar artistic excellence. *Mailing Add:* c/o Gavin Brown Enterprise 620 Greenwich St New York NY 10014

SWEET, FRANCIS EDWARD
PAINTER

b Watertown, NY, Oct 16, 1938. *Work:* Leigh Yawkey Woodson Art Mus, Wausau, Wis; Hirem Blauvelt Art Mus, Oradel, NJ; Roger Tory Peterson Inst, Jamestown, NY; Bennington Ctr for the Arts, Bennington, Vt; Joseph Hardy Collection, Farmington, Pa. *Comn:* Maryland Black Bear Stamp, MDNR, 97; Doves Unlimited Stamp, Doves Unlimited Nat, 99; 4 Nat Wildlife Fed Stamps, National Wildlife Fed. *Exhib:* SAA Exhibs, Cleveland Mus Nat Hist, Cleveland, Ohio, 91; SAA Exhibs, Witte Mus, San Antonio, Tex, 96; SAA Special Exhib, Nat Geographic Asn, Washington, DC, 2002; Nature Defined, Roger Tory Peterson Inst, Jamestown, NY, 2005. *Pos:* Pres, Soc of Animal Artist, NY, 2000-2003. *Awards:* Award of Excellence, SAA, 91-96 & 98-2004; Patricia Bott Award, Blauvelt Mus, SAA, 2003; Leonard Meiselman Mem Award, 91; 2nd Place, Animal category, Artists Mag, 2006. *Bibliog:* Kay Johnson (auth), How Sweet it is, Wildlife Art News Mag, 96; Dennis Gaffney (auth), A Late Bloomer, Wildlife Art Mag. *Mem:* Soc Animal Artists, New York (pres 2000-2003); World Wide Nature Artists Group, Can. *Media:* Oil & Scratchboard. *Publ:* Illusr, Ecology & Management of the Mourning Dove (bk), 93; Ecology & Management of the Woodduck (bk), 94; Best of Wildlife Art II (bk), 99. *Dealer:* Francis E Sweet Studios 1402 Port Echo La Bowie MD 20716. *Mailing Add:* 1402 Port Echo Ln Bowie MD 20716

SWEET, MARSHA (MARSHA SWEET WELCH)
PRINTMAKER, PAINTER

b Cleveland, Ohio, Dec 11, 1936. *Study:* Miami Univ, studied with Douglas Huebler, BFA, 58; Baldwin Wallace Coll, 70; Cleveland Inst Art; Case Western Reserve Univ, MA, 81. *Work:* Akron Art Mus Archive, Ohio; ADOGI, Cadaques Municipal Mus Art, Spain; Nat Mus Fine Arts, Hanoi, Vietnam; Artists Archive of the Western Reserve,

Cleveland; Chongqing Municipal Art Mus, Chongqing, China; Cadaques Municipal Mus Art, Cadaques, Girona, Spain; Dr. George Streeter Coll, Cleveland Metropolitan Hosp, Cleveland, Ohio; Xylon Argentina, Permanent Coll, Buenos Aires, Argentina. *Comn:* Limited ed patron print, Baycrafter Gallery Inc, Bay Village, Ohio, 75; Int traveling displays, Bruel & Kjaer, Copenhagen, Denmark, 79-80; Presentation print, Cleveland Arts Festival, Ohio, 83; Patron print, Am Print Alliance, 2006. *Exhib:* The May Show, Cleveland Mus Art, Ohio, 71, 75, 83 & 86; Print Int, ADOGI, Taller Gallerie Fort, Barcelona, Cadaques, Spain, 88-99; Int Prints, Mus Nat de la Estampa, Mex, 89; Boston Printmakers Nat Exhibs, Mass, 89-99 & 2003-2005; Saga 90, Grand Palais, Paris, France, 90; Indochina Arts Proj, Nat Mus Fine Arts, Hanoi, Vietnam, 91; Soc Wood Engravers 54th Exhib, various mus Eng, 91-92; Int Print Triennial, Contemp Art Gallery, Cracow, Poland, 94; Mid-Yr Painting Exhib, Butler Inst Am Art, Youngstown, Ohio, 99; Xylon Argentina, Buenos Aires, 2000; Chongqing Print Exhib, China, 2000; A Shared Journey, Greater Lafayette Mus Art, Lafayette, Ind; Cleveland Biennial, CSU, Cleveland, 2001; A Century of Portraiture, Cleveland Artists Found, 2002; Face to Face, FAVA Gallery, Oberlin, Ohio, 2003; We Just Met, AAWR Gallery, Cleveland, Ohio, 2003; Ohio Artists After Surrealism, Cleveland Artists Found Cleveland, Ohio, 2003; Buddha Proj, Cleveland State Univ Art Gallery, 2004; Sacred Images, Scarab Club Gallery, Detroit, Mich, 2004; A Selection of Contemp Prints, Studio 18 Gallery, New York, 2005; Solo show, Jewel Heart Tremont, Cleve, Ohio, 2010; Cinema Ol, Kenneth Paul Lesko Gallery, Cleveland, Ohio, 2010-2011; Looking Inward, AAWR Gallery, Cleveland, Ohio, 2011; Marsha Sweet: Retrospective and Recent Works, Sullivan Gallery, Bay Arts, Bay Village, Ohio, 2012; Cinema 3, Kenneth Paul Lesko Gallery, Cleveland, Ohio, 2012; Solo Show Portrait Prints: The Women, Intown Club, Cleveland, Ohio, 2013; The Archives Speak Exhib, Legacy Soc of AAWR, Cleveland, Ohio, 2014; Line & Life, Feinberg Gallery, Cain Park, Cleveland, Ohio, 2015; Majority Rising, AAWR Gallery, Cleveland, Ohio, 2015. *Pos:* Bd trustees, Baycrafter Gallery Inc, Ohio, 69-79, chmn, 77-78; asst dir visual arts, Interlochen Arts Acad Summer Prog, Mich, 78; juror, 10th Int Small Print Competition, Barcelona, Cadaques, Spain, 90. *Teaching:* instr Visual Arts, Bay Schools, Bay Village, Ohio, 71-98; Instr printmaking, Interlochen Arts Acad Summer, Mich, 76-78; lectr, Case Western Reserve Univ, Cleveland, Ohio, 86-87. *Awards:* May Show Spec Mention Graphics, Cleveland Mus Art, 83; 8th Mini Print Int Selection Award, ADOGI, Taller Gallery, Barcelona, Cadaques, Spain, 88-89; Boston Printmakers Show Award, Duxbury Art Complex, 89-90. *Bibliog:* Tisa, Empresa Editora, El Minigrabado Int, La Vanguardia, Barcelona, Spain, 1/7/89; Simon Brett (auth), An Engraver's Glove: Wood Engraving World-Wide in the Twenty-First Century, Primrose Hill Press, London, 2002; Elizabeth McClelland (auth), Marsha Sweet: Prints (Woodcuts and Wood Engravings), 2003; Nicole Hennessy (auth), Sweets Prints Show Womens' Strength, West Life News, Cleveland, Oh, 4/2012; The Archives Speak, Legacy Soc of the Artists Archives of the Western Reserve, Cleveland, Ohio, 2014. *Mem:* New Orgn Visual Arts; Wood Engravers Network; Boston Printmakers; Performers & Artists Nuclear Disarmament; Philadelphia Print Club. *Media:* Woodcut, Wood Engraving; Oil, Watercolor. *Publ:* With and Against the Grain, Contemp Impressions, J Am Print Alliance, fall 2006. *Mailing Add:* 29700 Osborn Rd Cleveland OH 44140-1852

SWEET, MARY (FRENCH)
PAINTER, PRINTMAKER
b Cincinnati, Ohio, Oct 10, 1937. *Study:* Stanford Univ, with Daniel Mendelowitz, AB (art), 59, MA (art), 60. *Work:* Carlsbad Art Mus, NMex; La Posada Hotel, Albuquerque NMex; First Nat Bank, Albuquerque, NMex; NMex Educ Credit Union; NMex Dept Transportation, Espanola Off. *Comn:* Painting, USS Barb Submarine, 63; NMex Educ Credit Union, Albuquerque, 88; Damsite, Elephant Butte State Park, NMex, 91 & 94. *Exhib:* Magnifico, Albuquerque, NMex, 91-97; Western Fedn Watercolor Soc 17 traveling exhib, Albuquerque Mus, NMex, 92; Main Street, Fort Worth, Tex, 93; Monothon, Coll Santa Fe NMex, 93, 95 & 96; 21st Ann San Antonio & Traveling Exhib, Western Fedn Watercolor Soc, 96; Moku Hanga Traveling Exhib: Contemp Japanese Woodcuts N Am, Walla Walla Coll, Wash, NW Print Coun Galleries, Portland, Ore, Columbia Arts Ctr, Vancouver & Wash & Japanese Cult Soc, San Francisco, Calif, 97; Handpulled Prints XI, Stone Metal Press, San Antonio, Tex, 97, 2003, & 09; Kyoto Int Woodprint Asn, Exhibits, Kyoto, Japan, 98-2000, 2003, 2007 & 2011; Janet Turner 4th Nat Print Competition, Chico, Calif, 2002; Western Fedn Watercolor Ann, Tex, 2004, Ariz, 2005 & Colo, 2007, 2011; Harwood Art Ctr, Albuquerque, NMex, 2005; WFS 22nd Ann, Tucson Mus Art, Ariz; Landscapes of NMex, Manitou Galleries, Santa Fe, 2006; Biennial Southwest, Albuquerque, NMex, 2008; Albuq Now, Albuq Art Mus, 2009; Solo exhibs, 30 Views of Mt Taylor, Harwood Art Ctr, 2010, Local Treature, Weyrich Gallery, Albuq, 2010; 36th Ann Western Federation of Watercolor Societies Exhib, Albuq, 2011; 18 Days, Ctr Contemp Art, Santa Fe, NMex, 2011. *Collection Arranged:* Art in the Embassies prog, US State Dept, 2000. *Teaching:* Teacher, watercolor & acrylics, YWCA, Greater Vallejo, CA, 67 & Albuquerque, NMex, 78; instr, Workshop in Traditional, Japanese & Experimental Woodblock Printing, State Fair Fine Arts Gallery, Albuquerque; instr, Japanese Style Woodblock Printing Without a Press, Harwood Art Center, Albuquerque, NMex. *Awards:* Lena Newcastle Award, Am Watercolor Soc, 88; Merit Award, Tubac Ctr Arts, 90; Best of Show, Western Fedn Watercolor Soc, 96; Yosemite Renaissance XIV, 99; Best of Show, NMex Watercolor Soc, fall 2005; Merchandise Award, Western Fedn Watercolor Soc, 2007; and others. *Bibliog:* SPLASH, America's Best Contemporary Watercolors, North Light Bks, 91; Phil Metzger (auth), Enliven Your Paintings with Light, North Light Bks, 93; Rachel Wolf (auth), The Acrylic Painter's Book of Styles & Techniques, North Light Bks, 97; Gary Greene (auth), Artist's Photo Reference Landscapes, North Light Bks, 2001; The Ultimate Guide to Painting from Photographs, North Light Bks, 2005; Douglas Bullis (auth), 100 Artists of the Southwest, 2006; Suzan Campbell & Suzanne Deats (coauths), Landscapes of New Mexico, UNM Press, 2006. *Mem:* NMex Watercolor Soc; Escribiente; Western Federation Watercolor Soc (signature mem); Libros, Book Arts. *Media:* Acrylics, Miscellaneous Media; Monotype, Woodcut, Watercolor, Artist Books. *Interests:* Hiking, backpacking, skiing, running & travel. *Publ:* Watercolor, Am Artist, fall 96. *Dealer:* Weyrich Gallery 2935D Louisiana NE Albuquerque NM 87059. *Mailing Add:* PO Box 280 Tijeras NM 87059

SWEET, STEVE (STEVEN) MARK
COLLAGE ARTIST, GRAPHIC ARTIST
b Boston, Mass, Mar 13, 1952. *Study:* Antioch Col, with Paul Sharits, Allan Jones & Tony Conrad, BA (visual arts), 74. *Work:* Pan-Am Life Insurance Corp, New Orleans; United Media Enterprises, NY; New Orleans Mus Art; Contemp Arts Ctr; Russel Wright Household Designs. *Comn:* The Appliance Giant Mural, comn by Tony Campo, New Orleans, 83; City of New Orleans, 89; New Orleans Int Airport, 90. *Exhib:* Louisiana Major Works, Contemp Arts Ctr, New Orleans, 79; New Orleans Triennial, New Orleans Mus Art, 80 & 86; Focus, Ft Worth Art Mus, 81; Art of New Orleans, Southeast Ctr Contemp Arts, Winston-Salem, NC, 84; New Music Am 83, Hirshhorn Mus & Sculpture Garden, 83; Birmingham Biennial, Birmingham Mus Art, 85; Corcoran Biennial, Corcoran Gallery, Washington, DC, 89. *Pos:* Artist-in-residence, La Superdome, 86; Webmaster, The Historic New Orleans Collection, 97. *Awards:* Services to the Field, Contemp Arts Ctr & Nat Endowment Arts, 80; Nat Endowment Arts Fel, 81 & Interarts grant, 85; Rockefeller Grant, Southeastern Interdisciplinary Fund, 89. *Bibliog:* Roger Green (auth), Flattened people: Portraits in depth, Times Picayune-States Item, 1/83; Jeff Zeldman (auth), Picture perfect, City Papers, Washington, DC, 10/14/83; David Rive (auth), SteveSweet, Art Papers, 5/87. *Mem:* Contemp Arts Ctr. *Mailing Add:* 16 S Park Pl New Orleans LA 70124

SWEITZER, CHARLES LEROY
MURALIST, PAINTER
b Brownsville, Pa, Mar 23, 1939. *Study:* Univ NC, BA, 76; NC Cent Univ, MA, 88; NC Cent Univ, MA (clin psychology), 91. *Comn:* History of North Carolina, comn by Dwight Phillips, Charlotte, NC, 68; Man's Relationship to God, Douglas MacArthur Acad, Tex Baptist, Brownwood, 72; Nashville Civil War Cyclorama, comn by Sam Fleming, Franklin, Tenn, 79; Place in Time, Othal Brand, Loma Linda, Calif, 85. *Pos:* pres, Educ Training Serv, Inc. *Teaching:* Instr visual art, Sweitzer Sch Art, 85-87 & Cent Piedmont Col, 80-82. *Bibliog:* Judith Sands (dir), Making a Mural (film), Media Consultants, 72; Carrol DeWhit (auth), The cyclorama at Franklin, Southern Living Mag, 79. *Mem:* Nat Soc Mural Painters, NY; NC Coun Arts; Wake Co Visual Artists. *Media:* Oil on Canvas. *Mailing Add:* 1302 Timber Dr Garner NC 27529-4730

SWENTZELL, ROXANNE
SCULPTOR
b 1962. *Study:* Inst Am Indian Art, Santa Fe, 78-80; Portland Mus Art Sch, Ore, 80-81. *Work:* Denver Art Mus, Santa Fe Convention Ctr, Smithsonian. *Comn:* Auditorium Wall Sculpture, Smithsonian Inst, Wash, DC, 2004. *Exhib:* Solo shows incl Inst Am Indian Arts, Santa Fe, 80, Arriot Gallery, Las Vegas, 82, St John's Coll Gallery, Santa Fe, 82, Gallery Studio 53, New York, 89, Praise Song Gallery, Fort Mason Ctr, San Francisco, 90, 98, Hahn Ross Gallery, Santa Fe, 2000; group shows incl Southwestern Asn Indian Arts Ann Indian Market, 85-88, 92-; Gorman Mus, Univ Calif Davis, 88; Mus of the Blackhawk, Calif, 93; Inst Am Indian Arts Mus, Santa Fe, 94; Heard Mus, Phoenix, 94; Mus Warm Springs, Ore, 94-95; Mus Mankind, London, 96; Soc Contemp Craft, Pittsburgh, 96-97; Robert F Nichols Gallery, Santa Fe, 97; Gallery 10, Carefree, Ariz, 98; Nat Mus Women in Arts, Wash, DC, 97-98; Heard Mus Guild Indian Fair and Market, 97, 2000-; Carnegie Mus Art, Pittsburgh, 98; Wheelwright Mus of Am Indian, Santa Fe, 99; Smithsonian Nat Mus Am Indian, 2000; Everson Mus Art, Syracuse, NY, 2000; Found Cartier pour l'art contemporain, Paris, 2001; Mus Indian Arts and Cult, Santa Fe, 2002; Poeh Mus, Pojoaque, NMex, 2003, 2004; Nat Mus Am Indian, Wash, DC, 2004; Roxanne Swentzell Tower Gallery, Pojoaque, NMex, 2006. *Pos:* Secy, treas, dir, Flowering Tree Permaculture Inst, Santa Fe, 89-. *Teaching:* Artist-in-residence, Santa Clara Puebl0 Elem Sch, San Juan Pueblo Elem Sch, Tesuque Pueblo Elem Sch, Santa Fe Indian Sch, NMex, 79-82. *Awards:* Bob Davis Mem Award, Southwestern Asn Indian Arts, 86, 1st Place Award, Bronze Category, 97,98, 99 & many others; Judges Choice Award, Heard Mus Guild Indian Fair and Market, 2000 & 2002; Native Treasures award, 2011. *Dealer:* Four Winds Gallery 5512 Walnut St Pittsburgh PA 15232; Hahn-Ross Gallery 409 Canyon Rd Santa Fe NM 87501; Faust Gallery 7103 E Main St Scottsdale AZ 85251; Berlin Gallery 2301 N Central Ave Phoenix AZ 85004. *Mailing Add:* Roxanne Swentzell Tower Gallery 78 Cities of Gold Rd Santa Fe NM 87506-0918

SWERGOLD, MARCELLE M
SCULPTOR
b Antwerp, Belg; US citizen. *Study:* NY Univ, painting with Aaron Berkman & Henry Kallem; sculpture at Art Students League, with John Hovanes & Jose deCreft; wax with Harold Caster. *Work:* Yad Vashem-Sculpture Garden & Shaare Zedek Med Ctr, Jerusalem, Israel; City Park Ma' Aleh Adumim, Israel; Fairlawn Jewish Ctr, Fairlawn, NJ; The Jewish Ctr, NY; Mudge, Rose, Guthrie, Alexander & Feldon, 82; and others. *Exhib:* Fairleigh Dickenson Univ, NJ, 72; Union Carbide Gallery, Park Ave, NY, 78; Cork Gallery, Lincoln Ctr, NY, 90, 91 & 94; Leaver House Gallery, Park Ave, NY, 80, 88, 90, 93, 94 & 98; Allied Artists of Am, Nat Acad Galleries, NY, Bankers Trust Co, Park Ave, NY; Broom St Gallery, 91, 92, 93, 94 & 95; Betty Barker Gallery, Carriage Barn Art Ctr, New Canaan, Conn, 98-. *Awards:* First Prize, Womanart Gallery, New York, 77 & Stanley Richter Asn Arts, Danbury, Conn, 85; Vincent Glinsky Mem Award, Audubon Artists, 86; Union Carbide, First Prize. *Bibliog:* Article, Museum collection grows again, The Herald, New Britain, Conn, 12/80; articles, Jerusalem Post, 10/90 & The News Times, Danbury, Conn; Mizrachi Magazine (Amit), 82. *Mem:* NY Soc Women Artists (corresp secy, 77-79, pres, 79-81, exec vpres, 81-); Artists Equity Asn, NY; Contemp Artist Guild. *Media:* Bronze, Stone. *Dealer:* 246 W 80th St New York NY 10024; 43 Paul St Danbury CT 06810. *Mailing Add:* 450 W End Ave New York NY 10024

SWETCHARNIK, SARA MORRIS
PAINTER, SCULPTOR
b Shelby, NC, May 21, 1955. *Study:* Schuler Sch Fine Art, 73-79; Art Students League, 80-82. *Work:* Haussners Restaurant & Mus, Baltimore, Md. *Comn:* Portrait sculpture, comn by Walter Finch Esq, 78. *Exhib:* Nat Sculpture Soc Gallery, NY, 95; Am Medallic Sculpture Asn Invitational Exhib, Am Numismatic Mus, Colorado Springs, 95; East Meets West: Old & New, Delaplaine Visual Arts Ctr, Frederick, Md, 95; Juried Exhib, Delaplaine Visual Arts Ctr, 96; Canine Art, Dog Mus, St Louis, Mo, 96; Exodus: An Installation of Figure Sculpture, Art in Embassies Exhib, Ambassador's Residence, Tegucigalpa, Honduras, 98-99; Delaplaine Visual Art Ctr, Frederick, Md, 2002; Down the Bridal Path: Historic Frederick County Weddings, The Historic Soc of Frederick County, Md, 2006. *Pos:* Juror, Nat Sculpture Exhib (V Concurso de Escultura y Ceramica Dante Lazzaroni Andino), Inst Honduren de Cult Interamericana, Tegucigalpa, Honduras, 95. *Teaching:* Monitor for Robert Beverly Hale, Art Students League, 79-80, fel, 81; instr, Frederick Acad Arts, Md, 81-82 & workshop, Landon Sch, Washington, DC, 91-96; lectr in field. *Awards:* Artist's Residency fel, Va Ctr Creative Arts, Sweet Briar, Va, 90, 2003; Artist's Residency fel, Am Numismatic Asn Conf, Am Numismatic Mus, Colorado Springs, 94 & 98; Juror: Biennial Nat Sculpture & Ceramics Exhib, V VI Concursos de Escultura y Ceramica, Instituto Hondureno de Cultura Interamericana, Tegucigalpa, Honduras, 95 & 97; Fulbright Grants to Spain, 88, 89; Distinguished Grad Award for Outstanding Achievement in Arts, Linganore Frederick County, Md, 2008. *Bibliog:* Dena Crosson (auth), Artists in residence, Frederick Mag, 6/94; Karen Gardner (auth), Sculptor gives life to zoo animals, Assoc Press, 94; George Baumann (interviewer), Interview of Sara Morris Swetcharnik on Maryland by George, Channel 7 News, Baltimore, 95. *Mem:* Fulbright Asn, Washington, DC; Delaplaine Visual Art Ctr, Frederick, Md. *Media:* Bronze, Terracotta. *Publ:* Portrait Medals of the Renaissance at the Nat Gallery, 94; Romeo's offering, 96; Spanish & English in Guacamaya: Revista Historico, Cultural de Honduros, 96; My Patriotic Primer, Lesson I: Patriotic Permissions, Swetcharnik Art Studio, Mt Airy, Md, 2008; Jungle Tails and Other Animal Stories, The Sun Vil IX, No 3. *Mailing Add:* National Capital Post Office Box 77794 Washington DC 20013

SWETCHARNIK, WILLIAM NORTON
PAINTER, SCULPTOR
b Philadelphia, Pa, Oct 18, 1951. *Study:* RI Sch Design, 69-71; Univ Calif, San Diego, 73-76; Towson State Univ, Md, BS, 77. *Work:* Art Mus, Fla Int Univ, Miami, Fla; Cintas Found, NY; Comm Cult Exchange between United States & Madrid, Spain; Salisbury St Hosp, Salisbury, Md. *Exhib:* Solo exhibs, Weinberg Ctr Arts, Frederick, Md, 80, Mt St Mary's Col, Emmitsburg, Md, 81, Harbor Gallery, NY, Cold Spring Harbor, Foxhall Gallery, Washington, DC, John Pence Gallery, San Francisco, Calif, Md Coll Art & Design, Silver Spring, Md, 86, Washington Co Mus Art, Hagerstown, Md, 93; Foxhall Gallery, Wash, DC, 82-84; Md Art Place, Baltimore, 90; Nat Acad Design, NY, 90. *Pos:* Resident artist, Hood Col, Fred, Md. *Awards:* Cintas Found Fel, Inst Int Educ, 85-86; Yaddo Residency, 87; Fulbright Int Fel, Spain, 87-89 & Honduras, 94-95. *Bibliog:* Robin Longman (auth), Emerging artists, Am Artist, 84. *Mem:* Delaplaine visual Art Ctr; Fulbright Asn. *Media:* Oils. *Mailing Add:* 7044 Woodville Rd Mount Airy MD 21771

SWICK, LINDA ANN
SCULPTOR
b Bedford, Ohio, Sept 9, 1948. *Study:* Kent State Univ, BA, 70; Fla State Univ, MFA, 77. *Exhib:* Solo show, Washington Proj Arts, Washington, DC, 79; Rutgers Univ, Camden, NJ, 79; Laguna Gloria Art Mus, Austin, 80; Middendorf Lane, Washington, DC, 80; Corcoran Gallery, Washington, DC, 81; Lawndale, Univ Houston, 82. *Pos:* Set designer for animated films, Broadcast Arts, Washington, DC, 80-. *Awards:* Fel, City Washington, DC, 82. *Bibliog:* Sylvia Shauck (auth), interview, Art & Craft Mag, 6/80; Charlotte Moser (auth), Washington art, Art News, 10/81. *Media:* Wood. *Dealer:* Gallery K 2032 P St Washington DC. *Mailing Add:* 1728 S St NW Washington DC 20009

SWIGART, LYNN S
PHOTOGRAPHER
b Kansas City, Mo, Aug 22, 1930. *Study:* Bradley Univ, Peoria, Ill, BS (psychol, philos); also photog with Minor White & George Tice. *Work:* Carpenter Ctr Visual Arts, Harvard Univ, Cambridge, Mass; Stanford Univ; Ill State Mus; Lakeview Mus; Petry Collection; Cape Ann Mus, Gloucester, Mass; Peoria Hist Soc Archives, Peoria, Ill; Peoria Riverfront Mus, Peoria, IL; Ctr Creative Photography, Univ Ariz, Tucson, Ariz. *Exhib:* Radius, 76, Burpee Art Mus, Rockford, Ill, 76; Solo Exhibs: Univ Conn, 77, Stanford Univ, 78, Univ Iowa, 78, Ill State Mus, 78, Art Inst, Chicago, 78, Lakeview Mus, Peoria, Ill, 80 & Cape Ann Hist Mus, Gloucester, Mass, 81; Twelfth Biennial Mich Regional, 82; Arts Works Nat Photog Exhib, Brattleboro, Vt, 82; Camera Movements, Moore Coll Art, Philadelphia, Pa, 82; Ill Photogr, 85; Ill State Mus, 85; Arts Ctr, Westport, Conn, 91-93; Retrospective, Cape Ann Mus, Gloucester, Mass, 2005; Rocky Neck Art Colony Ann Exhib, 2005-2007, Artspace, Gloucester, Mass, 2007; Peoria Art Guild and Hist Society, Peoria, Ill, 2008; Gallery Kayafas, Boston, Mass, 2009; On and Off Paper, Il State Mus, Chicago, 2010; The Rule of Four, Cape Ann Mus, 2012; Flatrocks Gallery, Gloucester, Mass; Trident Gallery, Gloucester, Mass, 2013, 2014. *Teaching:* Instr photog, Multimedia Arts Inst, Bradley Univ, summer, 73 & 74. *Awards:* Third Place Award, 2005, First Place Award, 2007, Rocky Neck Art Colony An Exhib. *Publ:* Contribr, Olson's Gloucester, LSU Press, 80, The Best of Photog Ann, 82 & NDak Quart, 85; 5th Wednesday Jour, Spring 2008; Lynn Swigart:Gloucester, Palm Press Portfolio, 2009. *Dealer:* Trident Gallery Gloucester Mass. *Mailing Add:* 13 Marble Rd Gloucester MA 01930

SWOFFORD, BETH
COLLECTOR
b Huntsville, AL. *Study:* Univ Southern Calif, BA. *Pos:* Motion picture agent, Creative Artists Agency, Los Angeles. *Awards:* Named one of Top 100 Collectors, Arts & Antiques, 2005 & 2008, 100 Most Powerful Women in Entertainment, Hollywood Reporter, 2004-2013, 50 Smartest People in Hollywood, Entertainment Weekly, 2008. *Mem:* MoMA/PS1 Bd Trustees; MoMA Media and Performance Art Com; MoMA Fund for the 21st Century; Am Friends of the Tate; Tate Americas Com. *Collection:* Contemporary art. *Mailing Add:* 2000 Avenue of the Stars Los Angeles CA 90067

SYJUCO, STEPHANIE
INSTALLATION SCULPTOR
b Manila, Philippines, 1974. *Study:* San Fransico Art Inst, BFA, 1995; Stanford Univ, MFA, 2005. *Work:* Contemporary Mus, Honolulu; Mills Coll Art Gallery, Oakland; New Mus, New York; San Francisco Mus Mod Art; Whitney Mus Am Art; and var corp collections. *Exhib:* Dare to be Different, Chinese Cult Ctr, San Franciso, 1996; To Be Real, Yerba Buena Ctr Arts, San Francisco, 1997; solo exhibs, John Berggruen Gallery, San Francisco, 1997, Haines Gallery, San Francisco, 1998, Del Ctr Contemp Arts, Wilmington, 1999, James Harris Gallery, Seattle, 2000, Contemp Arts Mus Houston, Tex, 2008, Wash State Univ, Pullman, 2010; At Home and Abroad: Twenty Contemporary Filipino Artists, Asian Art Mus, San Francisco, 1998; Fact/Fiction: Selections From the Permanent Collection, San Francisco Mus Mod Art, 2000; Eureka, Too!, San Jose Inst Contemp Art, 2001; California Biennial, Orange County Mus Art, Newport Beach, 2002; Subtle Sight, Mills Coll Art Gallery, Oakland, 2003; Botany 12, Sonoma County Art Mus, Calif, 2004; Political Nature, Whitney Mus Am Art, 2005; Fashion Hackers and Haute Couture Heretics, Garanti Gallery, Istanbul, 2007; Take Action! 83 Ways to Change the World, Mus World Culture, Goteborg, Sweden, 2008; 1969, Mus Mod Art, New York, 2009. *Pos:* Sr graphic designer, Exploratorium Mus, San Franciso, 1995-2000; artist comt mem, San Francisco Art Inst, 1999-2000; curatorial comt, Southern Exposure Gallery, San Francisco, 1997-2000, bd dirs, 2000-04. *Teaching:* Lectr, Calif Coll Arts, San Franciso, 2005-07, Univ Calif, Berkeley, 2008-09, Calif Coll Arts, San Franciso, 2009; vis asst prof, Carnegie Mellon Univ, Sch Fine Arts, Pa, 2008. *Awards:* Headlands Ctr for Arts Fel, 2001; Cantor Mus Fel, Stanford Univ, 2003; Murphy/Cadogan Fel, 2004; Creative Capital Profl Develop Fel, 2006; Joan Mitchell Found Grant, 2010. *Bibliog:* Peter Frank (auth), California Biennial, Los Angeles Weekly, 8/30/2002; Regina Hackett (auth), Photos Bridge a Culture Gap Uniquely, Seattle Post-Intelligencer, 9/16/2005; Stephanie Cash (auth), New and Now, Art in Am, 1/2006; Michael Leaverton (auth), Bag Ladies, San Francisco Weekly, 4/9/2008; Carol Vogel (auth), Cunning After Caution at London Art Fair, NY Times, 10/16/2009. *Dealer:* Catharine Clark Gallery 150 Minna St San Francisco CA 94105

SYLVESTER, ROBERT
EDUCATOR
b New York City, NY. *Pos:* dir, cult affairs Western Wash Univ; dean, Sch Fine & Performing Arts; pres, Portland State Univ, 1997-. *Mailing Add:* Portland State Univ Sch Fine & Performing Art 349 Lincoln Hall Portland OR 97207-0751

SZABO, JOSEPH GEORGE
CARTOONIST, EDITOR
b Budapest, Hungary, Feb 4, 1950; US citizen. *Study:* Sch Masters Typography, cert, 69; Hungarian Acad Journalism, BA (summa cum laude), 74; Sch Com, cert, 78. *Work:* Cult Ctr Scharpoord, Knokke-Heist, Belg; Yomiuri Shimbun, Tokyo; Cartoon Art Mus, San Francisco. *Exhib:* Humorfoto '82-'86, Cult Ctr Scharpoord, Kuokke Heist, Belg, 82-86; Man and His World, Int Salon Cartoons, Montreal, 84-86; Yomiuri Int Cartoon Contest, Tokyo, 85-86; Everything is Cabaret, World Cartoon Gallery, Skopje, Yugoslavia, 86; South Africa, Montevideo, Uruguay, 86; Int Simavi Cartoon Competition, Istanbul, Turkey, 86. *Pos:* Assoc art dir, Nôk Lapja (weekly), Budapest, Hungary, 75-78; managing graphics ed & ed cartoonist, Magyar Nemzet (daily), Budapest, Hungary, 78-80; art dir & cartoonist, Sting (satirical mag), Ctr Sq, Philadelphia, 84-85. *Awards:* Press Prize, Humorfoto '84, Belg, 84; Bronze Medals, Yomiuri Int Cartoon Contest, Tokyo, 85 & 86. *Bibliog:* Istvan Molnar (auth), article, Magyar Grafika, 2/80; Gloria Sipes Paleveda (auth), Hungarian political cartoonist, Philadelphia Inquirer, 6/23/85; Ann Whiteside (auth), Cartoonist's sketches span the globe, Montgomeryville Spirit, 4/30/86. *Mem:* Nat Cartoonists Soc; Asn Am Ed Cartoonists. *Media:* Coated Cardboard, Marker. *Publ:* Auth, Photo-Cartoon Calendar, self-publ, 83; Illus, Animal Farm, by George Orwell, Rainbow Publ, 84; auth, Never pointing a different way, Target, 85; ed, WittyWorld, Int Cartoon Mag, 87; Finest International Political Cartoons of our Time, 92, Witty World Books, 92. *Mailing Add:* 214 School St North Wales PA 19454

SZAKACS, DENNIS
MUSEUM DIRECTOR
Pos: Managing Dir, PS1 Contemp Art Ctr, New York,1994-97; deputy dir, New Mus Contemp Art, New York, 1997-2003; dir, Orange County Mus Art, 2003-Present; dir commun, Southeastern Ctr Contemp Art. *Mailing Add:* Orange County Mus Art 850 San Clemente Dr Newport Beach CA 92660

SZE, SARAH
INSTALLATION SCULPTOR
b Boston, Mass, 1969. *Study:* Yale Univ, BA, 91; Sch Visual Arts, MFA, 97. *Exhib:* Solo shows incl White Columns, NY, 97, Musée d'Art Mod de la Ville de Paris, 98, Inst Contemp Arts, London, 98, Mus Contemp Art, Chicago, 99, Marianne Boesky Gallery, New York, 2000, 2005, Mus Contemp Art, San Diego, 2001, Walker Art Ctr, 2002, Mus Fine Arts, Boston, 2002, Whitney Mus Am Art, 2003, Fondazione Davide Halevim, Milan, 2004, Doris C Freedman Plz, New York, 2006, Victoria Miro Gallery, London, 2007, Tanya Bonakdar, New York, 2010; group shows incl Pratt Artist's League, 96; Casey Kaplan Gallery, New York, 97; Marianne Boesky Gallery, New

York, 98, 2000, 2002, 2006; Whitney Mus Am Art, 98, 2000; Carnegie Mus Art, 99; Venice Biennale, 99; San Francisco Mus Mod Art, 2001; Barbican Ctr, London, 2001; Nat Acad Design, New York, 2002; Sculpture Ctr, 2003; 21st Century Mus Contemp Art, Japan, 2004; Mus Contemp Art, Chicago, 2005; Fabric Workshop Mus, Philadelphia, 2005. *Mailing Add:* 438 W 37th St New York NY 10018

SZEITZ, P RICHARD
EDUCATOR, SCULPTOR
b Budapest, Hungary, Jan 5, 1930; US citizen. *Study:* St Anselm Univ, Rome, 50-53; Layton Sch Art, BFA, 57; Univ Wis-Madison, MS & MFA, 59. *Work:* Dallas Mus Fine Arts, Tex; Herman Otto Mus, Miskole, Hungary; Minn Mus, St Paul; Rourke Gallery, Moorhead State Univ, Moorhead, Minn. *Comn:* St Albert (sculpture), Dominican Priory, Irving, Tex, 63; Fountain of Abundance (sculpture), W Acres Shopping Ctr, Fargo, NDak, 72; Assumption of the Virgin (sculpture), Assumption Church, Barnsville, Minn, 78; three-story fountain with 6 figures, First Bank, Robbinsdale, Minn, 83; Minnesota Flora and Fauna (six fountains series), Centennial Lakes Condominium Courtyards, Edina, Minn, 91. *Teaching:* From instr to assoc prof, Univ Dallas, 60-66; prof sculpture, art & law & dept chmn, Moorhead State Univ, 66-94. *Awards:* Fulbright Hayes Lectureship, US Govt, 65. *Media:* Metal, Cast Bronze. *Mailing Add:* 1220 S 12th Ave Moorhead MN 56560-3719

SZESKO, JUDITH CLARANN See Jaidinger, Judith Clarann Szesko

SZESKO, LENORE RUNDLE
PAINTER, PRINTMAKER
b Galesburg, Ill, Mar 13, 1933. *Study:* Art Inst Chicago, BFA (drawing, painting, illus), 61, MFA (painting), 66; wood engraving with Adrian Troy. *Work:* Standard Oil Co, Chicago; NJ State Mus; Jayell Publ House, Miami, Fla; Springfield Col; Kemper Ins Co Collection, Long Grove, Ill. *Exhib:* Conn Acad Fine Arts 62nd Ann, Wadsworth Atheneum, Hartford, Conn, 72; Cedar City Ann Fine Art Exhib, Utah, 72-75; Contemp Am Graphics, Old Bergen Art Guild, Bayonne, NJ (traveling exhib), 72-80; Soc Am Graphic Artists 52nd Nat Print Exhib, NY & Chicago, 73; NH Print Club 1st & 2nd Int, Nashua, 73-74. *Awards:* James R Marsh Mem Purchase Prize, Hunterdon Art Ctr 16th Print, Clinton, NJ, 72; Muth Award, Miniature Painters, Sculptors & Gravers Soc of Washington, DC, 73; Award Highest Merit-Drawing, Miniature Art Soc of Fla Nat Exhib, 76; and others. *Mem:* Audubon Artists, Inc, NY; Painters & Sculptors Soc NJ; Boston Printmakers, Mass; Miniature Art Soc NJ; La Watercolor Soc. *Media:* Multimedia. *Collection:* American Indian and Pre-Columbian, some African art; antique furniture and dolls. *Mailing Add:* 5728 N Austin Ave Chicago IL 60646-6231

SZILVASY, LINDA MARKULY
PAINTER, WRITER
b Granite City, Ill, Oct, 7, 1940. *Study:* Lindenwood Coll Women, St Charles, Mo, BA, 61; George Peabody Coll, Nashville, Tenn, MA, 62. *Work:* Eden Theol Sem, Webster Groves, Mo; US Army Chaplain Mus, Ft Hamilton, NY; Lindenwood Coll Women; George Peabody Coll. *Comn:* Paintings used for official Christmas cards, First Cavalry Div, Ft Hood, Tex, 72, III Corps, Ft Hood, 73 & 75 & Officer Wives Club, Ft Leonard Wood, Mo, 75; jeweled ostrich shells painted symbols of longevity, comn by Charlene Franz for Premier Sun Yun-hsuan & Pres Chiang Ching-kuo, Taiwan, 78; jeweled egg by Am Egg Board for First Lady Nancy Reagan, 80. *Exhib:* Solo exhib, Petite Pigalle Gallery, St Louis, Mo, 62; 10th Ann Arts & Crafts Festival, Killeen, Tex, 73; jeweled eggs, Galeria de las Artes, Las Cruces, NMex, 80; Centennial Mus, Univ Tex El Paso, 86; Glorietta's Gallery, El Paso, Tex, 86-90; Sun Bowl Exhib, juried show 3 paintings, Int Mus Art, El Paso, Tex, 2004 & 05; Fall Show, juried show 3 paintings, El Paso Art Asn, 2004; Arts Int Exhib, juried show, juror's recog award, Int Mus Art, El Paso, 2005; June Artistry, Rio Bravo Watercolorists, Int Mus Art, merit award, El Paso, 2005; Spring Show, El Paso Art Asn, juried show, third place, Basset Pl, 2005; The Arts of March, Rio Bravo Watercolorists, Int Mus Art, juried 3 paintings, 2006; Patriotic Art Exhib, El Paso Art Asn, merit award, Crossland Gallery, El Paso, 2006; El Paso Art Asn, Spring Show, 2007; Little Women exhib, Hal Marcus Gallery, 2008; Two men show, Multifaceted Images, Crossland Gallery, 2008; Living Under the Sun, Chamizal Nat Mem, 2009. *Pos:* Co-chmn Arts Comt, Metamora Woman's Club, 91-92; 1st vpres, Rio Bravo Watercolorists, El Paso, Tex, 2004-2008. *Teaching:* Art instr, Omaha Pub Sch System, Nebr, 63-66, Killeen Independent Sch Dist, Tex, 72-73 & var eggs-ibits, Dallas, Mich & Md, 75-. *Awards:* Best Depicting Texas History, Tex Guild Egg Shell Artists, 86. *Bibliog:* Barbra Brabec (auth), The jeweled egg, Artisan Crafts, 4/75; The egg and leather, Make It With Leather Mag, 1/77; Eggs $250 a dozen and up, El Paso Today Mag, 4/80. *Mem:* Tex Guild Egg Shell Artists (1st vpres, 85-86); Rio Brave Watercolors Asn; Woman's Club of El Paso; El Paso Art Asn; Rio Bravo Watercolorists (1st vpres, 2004-2008). *Media:* Jeweled Egg Shells, Paintings and Sculptures Inside; Paintings on Canvas. *Publ:* Illus, Dottie Miller's Around the World in 99 Beds, Eden Publ House, 73; contrib, A bit of the woods, Creative Crafts Mag, 6/75; auth, The Jeweled Egg: A Handbook for Beginning and Advanced Craftsmen, Assoc Press, 76; contrib, Barbara Brabec's Creative Cash: How to Sell Your Crafts, Countryside Bks, 79; Aline Becker (auth), Almost Everything about Heirloom Eggs, 80. *Mailing Add:* 9006 Belk St El Paso TX 79904

SZNAJDERMAN, MARIUS S
PRINTMAKER, PAINTER
b Paris, France, July 18, 1926; US citizen. *Study:* Sch Plastic Arts, Caracas, Venezuela, with Rafael Monasterios, Ramon Martin Durban & Ventrillon-Horber, 47-48; Columbia Univ, BS, with printmaker Hans Mueller, BS, 53; T C Colombia, MFA, 58. *Work:* Mus Mod Art, Jewish Heritage Mus, NY Pub Libr, Yeshiva Univ Mus, Yivo Inst, NY; Rayo Mus, Roldanillo, Colombia; Yad Washem Mus, Jerusalem, Israel; Nat Gallery, Mus Contemp Art, Caracas, Venezuela; B'nai B'rith Klutznick Mus, Washington, DC; Fine Arts Mus, Caracas, Venezuela; Libr Cong, Washington; N J State Mus, Trenton; Tel Aviv Univ, Ramataviv, Israel; Museo Del Barrio, NYC; Nat Mus Modern Art, Dublin, Ireland; Sugihara Mem Park, Yotsutown, Japan; Army Historical Found, Arlington, Va; NY Public Lib for Performing Arts; S Environmental Ctr, Birmingham Southern Coll, Ala; Inst Holocaust, Genocide, and Memory Studies, Univ Mass, Amherst; Fundacion Celarg, Caraas, Venezuela; Renee and Chaim Gross Foundation, NY; Statue of Liberty and Ellis Island Nat Park, NY; Joseph Hall, Notre Dame, Selshin Univ, Okayana, Japan. *Comn:* Prints, Agrupacion Grafica Pan Americana, 78-86; Carton de Venezuela, 86; Holocaust, brass monument, Temple Bethel, Hackensack, NJ. *Exhib:* Galeria Venezuela, NY, 76; solo exhibs, Estevez Vilas Gallery, Cincinnati, 82-84, Rayo Mus, Colombia, 82 & Galeria Borkas, Lima, 82, Mus Contemp Hispanic Arts, NY, 89 & Corinne Timsit Int Gallery, San Juan, PR, 90; Jewish Community Ctr Palisades, Tenafly, NJ, 90; Mus Contemp Art, Caracas, Venezuela, 91; The Venezuelan Ctr Gallery, NY, 99; Nat Yiddish Book Ctr, Amherst, Mass, 2005-06; Puffin Forum, Teaneck, NJ, 2007; Maurice M Pine Lib, Fairlawn, NJ, 2008; and others; Chashama Gallery Space, NY. *Pos:* Dir, Galeria Venezuela, New York, 74-83. *Teaching:* Instr art hist & painting, Sch Visual Arts, New York, 65-71; lectr, Fairleigh Dickinson Univ, Madison, NJ, 69-73; artist-in-residence, AIM Prog, NJ Pub Sch, 74-77. *Bibliog:* The Dictionary of Plastic Arts in Venezuela, 72, Dictionary of Visual Arts in Venezuela, Monte Avia, Caracas, 85; Hispanic Culture in New Jersey (film), NJ Pub TV, 78; Carlos Silva (auth), Historia De La Pintura en Venezuela, Tomo III, Caracas, 89; Printworld Directory of Contemporary Prints and Prices. *Media:* All. *Publ:* Illusr, Magicismos, Colleccion Rasgos Comunes, Caracas, 89; Who were the Precolombians, New World Art, Pinehurst, NC, 92; Scargot: Poems by Hugo Brett Figueroa, Maracaibo, Venezuela, 2005; Dali, Dumas, and Me, Matomi Press, Amherst, Mass, 2013. *Mailing Add:* 119 Spencer Dr Amherst MA 01002

SZOKE, JOHN
DEALER, PUBLISHER
Study: NY Univ, BS, 72; Grad Sch Bus Admin, MBA, 73. *Pos:* Owner, John Szoke Editions, NY. *Teaching:* Asst prof, Baruch Col, City Univ NY, 75-79; bus sem, Gallaudet Univ, Washington. *Awards:* Personal Citation, Int Olympic Comt, 66, 96; Recognition Award, Am Anorexia/Bulimia Asn, 93. *Bibliog:* There Are Miracles-Twelve American Careers, Bolgar-Fazekas, 93; The Life & times on an art dealer, SunStorm Fine Art Mag, winter 96. *Mem:* Fine Art Publ Asn; Gallaudet Univ, Washington (mem bd assoc). *Media:* Prints, Works on Paper

SZOLD, LAUREN G
PAINTER, SCULPTOR
b New York, NY, Nov 26, 1957. *Study:* RI Sch Design, 81. *Comn:* Ca-Ca Poo-Poo, Udo Kittelmann, Kolnischer Kunstverein, Koln, Ger, 97; Threshold/Recent American Sculpture, Serralves Found, Oporto, Portugal, 95; Heaven's in the Back Seat of My Cadillac, NAME, Chicago, Il, 95; Wild Friendzy, comn by Paula Hayes, NY, 94; Dyad, comn by Annie Herron, Sauce, Brooklyn, NY, 94. *Exhib:* Skin Deep, New Mus Contemp Art, NY, 93; Out Of Town: The Williamsburg Paradigm, Kranert Art Mus, Champaigne, Ill, 93; Pieces ou Sol, Le Consortium, Centre d'Art Contemporain, Dijon, France, 93; 44th Biennial Exhib Contemp Am Painting: Painting Outside Painting, The Corcoran Mus Art, Washington, DC; Sharpe Studios, Marie Walsh Sharpe Art Found, NY, 96; Show and Tell, Lauren Whittel Gallery, NY, 96; Bronwyn Keenan Gallery, NY, 96; Auto-Portrait: The Calligraphy of Power, Exit Art, NY, 97; Do Paintings Dream of Veronese Green?, Elga Wimmer Gallery, NY, 99; Artists to Artists, New York City, 02. *Awards:* award, Marie Walsh Sharpe Art Found, 96; award, Yado, Syracuse, NY, 93. *Bibliog:* Ynglingagaten1, Zapp Mag, Vol 4, 4-95; Gregory Volk (auth), Lauren Szold Transgressing Borders, Artnews, 105, 10/94; Roberta Smith (auth), Review, The NY Times, C22, 2/25/94. *Media:* All media. *Publ:* Artists to Artists, a Decade of the Space Prog. *Mailing Add:* 375 New Rochelle Rd Bronxville NY 10708

T

TABACK, SIMMS
ILLUSTRATOR, DESIGNER
b New York, NY, Feb 13, 1932. *Study:* Cooper Union, BFA; Sch Visual Arts. *Exhib:* Soc Illusr Ann Exhib, 63-86; Art Dir Club Show; Am Inst Graphic Arts; Soc Publ Designers; Type Dir Club. *Teaching:* Instr illus & design, Sch Visual Arts, New York, 67-82, Syracuse Univ Grad Program, 94. *Awards:* Cert of Merit, Soc Illusr Show, Ten Best Illus Children's Books, New York Times, 67 & 99; Louie Award, Greeting Card Asn; Caldecott Honor Bk, 98, Medal, 2000; Graphic Artists Guild Lifetime Achievement Award, 99; Cooper Union-Augustus St Gaudens Medal, 2000. *Mem:* Soc Illusr; Illusr Guild (pres, 75-76); Graphic Artists Guild (pres, 79-80 & 90-91). *Media:* Pen & Ink; Watercolor; Mixed Media. *Res:* Simms Taback; 2005 DVD & Video Weston Scholastic. *Publ:* Illusr, Ruggy Riddles, Dial, 86; Roadbuilders, Viking, 94; Sam's Wild West Show, Dial, 95; Two Little Witches, Candlewick Press, 96; There was an Old Lady Who Swallowed a Fly, Viking, 97; When I First Came to This Land, Putnam, 98; Joseph Had a Little Overcoat, Viking, 99; This is the House that Jack Built Putnam, 2002; Kibitzers & Fools, Viking, 2005

TABAK, CHAIM
PAINTER, SCULPTOR
b Bamberg, Ger, Nov 13, 1946; US citizen. *Study:* Brooklyn Coll, 70-71; Art Students League NY, cert, 75. *Work:* Brooklyn Mus; Wichita Art Mus, Kans; Weatherspoon Art Gallery, Univ NC; Samuel Dorsky Mus, State Univ NY, New Paltz; Fred F French Investment Corp; Nielson Corp. *Exhib:* On Radioactive Waste, Harvard Univ, 77 & Yale Univ, 78; Art and the Law, Landmark Ctr, Minneapolis, 82; HRCA 67th Ann, Hudson River Mus, Yonkers, NY, 82; The Radwaste and Stonehenge Series (with catalog), Wichita Art Mus, Carnegie Ctr Arts, Kans, Mulvane Art Ctr, Washburn Univ, Topeka, Pittsburg State Univ, Kans, Emporia State Univ, Kans, Samuel Dorksy Mus State Univ NY, New Paltz, Nelson Fosdick Gallery, State Univ NY & Alfred Tyler Art

Gallery, State Univ NY, Oswego, 85-89; solo exhib, Dorsky Galleries, NY, 86; Contemp Bestiary, Islip Art Mus, NY, 89; Recent Acquisitions, Samuel Dorsky Mus, State Univ NY, 92; Invitational, Collaborative Concepts Gallery, Beacon, NY, 2004; Apocalypse, Bau Gallery, Beacon, 2012. *Bibliog:* Anthony S Maulucci (auth), Radioactive waste as a subject of art, New Haven Register, 2/5/78; Nancy Pate (auth), Books are art with a message, Wichita Eagle Beacon, 4/7/85. *Media:* Mixed Media; Wood, Stone. *Mailing Add:* 509 Albany Post Rd New Paltz NY 12561

TABER, RYAN
SCULPTOR
b Fort Knox, Ky, 1978. *Study:* Univ Hartford, West Hartford, Conn, BFA, 2000; San Francisco Art Inst, PB, 2001; Calif Inst Arts, Valencia, Calif, MFA, 2004. *Exhib:* Solo exhibs include Mint Gallery, Cal-Arts, Valencia, Calif, 2002, 2004, Mark Moore Gallery, Santa Monica, Calif, 2004, 2006, Machine Gallery, Los Angeles, 2005; Group exhibs include The Way, Slipe Gallery, Univ Hartford, W Hartford, Conn, 2000; Lights Out, The Roxy Theater, San Francisco, 2000; A Night To Remember, Quotidian Gallery, San Francisco, 2000; Farallon Occupation, Detour Proj Space, 2001; Immergence, Track 16, Santa Monica, Calif, 2003; Field Trip, Swell Gallery, San Francisco, 2004; NADA Art Fair, Mark Moore Gallery, Miami, 2004; Terra Nullius, Shoshana Wayne Gallery, Santa Monica, Calif, 2005; Damaged Romanticism: A Mirror Mod Emotion, Blaffer Gallery, Univ Houston, Houston, 2008; Against the Grain, Los Angeles Contemp Exhib, Los Angeles, 2008. *Mailing Add:* c/o Mark Moore Gallery 5790 Washington Blvd Culver City CA 90232

TABOR, VIRGINIA S
PAINTER, PRINTMAKER
b Putnam, Conn, Mar 28, 1926. *Study:* Bethany Col, BA, 47; Cornell Univ, MA, 50; Pa Acad Fine Arts, 66-70; also critiques with Myron Barnstone, 88-92. *Exhib:* Boston Printmakers, 87; Provident Nat Bank, Philadelphia, Pa, 87; Philadelphia Art Show, Philadelphia, Pa, 90 & 91; Exhib of the Fel Pa Acad Fine Arts, 93; Barnstone Studio Group Show, Marywood Col, 94; and others. *Teaching:* Vis instr painting & design, Lehigh Univ, fall, 72 & 73; instr painting & drawing, Lehigh Co Community Col, 75-84. *Awards:* Pen & Brush Award, Salmagundi Club, New York, 83; Purchase Awards, Printmaking Coun NJ, Red Devil Corp, 83 & 85-87; 1st Place Pastels, Rittenhouse Sq Fine Arts Ann, 92. *Bibliog:* Jill Stewart Narrow (auth), Virginia Tabor-Artist & Printmaker, Theatrical Faces Mag. *Mem:* Lehigh Art Alliance (pres, 78-80); fel Pa Acad Fine Arts; Artists Equity; Philadelphia Watercolor Club. *Media:* Pastel; Silkscreen. *Dealer:* Tabor Studio 46 Covington Pl Catasauqua PA 18032. *Mailing Add:* 46 Covington Pl Catasauqua PA 18032

TACHA, ATHENA
SCULPTOR, CURATOR
b Larissa, Greece, Apr 23, 1936; nat US. *Study:* Nat Acad Fine Arts, Athens, MA (sculpture), 59; Oberlin Coll, Ohio, MA (art hist), 61; Univ Paris, PhD (aesthetics), 63. *Hon Degrees:* Coll Wooster, Ohio, FA, 90. *Work:* Mus Fine Arts, Houston; MOMA, NY; Smiths Mus Amer Art, Washington, DC; Albright-Knox Art Gallery, Buffalo, NY; J B Speed Art Mus, Louisville; Hirshhorn Mus, Washington, DC; Cleveland Mus Art; Nelson-Atkins Mus Art, Kansas City, MO; High Mus Art, Atlanta, Ga; Sheldon Mem Art Gallery, Univ Nebr, Lincoln, Nebr; Mus Modern Art, NY. *Comn:* sculpture, Dept Environ Protection, Trenton, NJ; sculpture, Case Western Reserve Univ, Cleveland, Ohio; sculpture, Low Water Dam Riverfront Park, Tulsa, Okla; sculpture, Dept Transportation, Hartford, Conn; sculpture, Strathmore Music Ctr, Bethesda, MD; sculpture, Am Airlines Plaza, Dallas, Tex; sculpture, Franklintown Park, Philadelphia, PA; sculpture, Metrorail, Miami; sculpture, Newark, NJ; Muhammad Ali Plaza, Louisville, Ky; Wis Pl, Friendship Heights, Md; and many others. *Exhib:* US Pavilion, Venice Biennale, 80; Land Marks, Bard Coll, NY, 1984; Solo exhibs, Zabriskie Gallery, NY, 79 & 81, Max Hutchinson Gallery, NY, 84, High Mus Art, Atlanta, 89, Franklin Furnace, NY, 94 & Beck Ctr, Cleveland, Ohio, 98-99, Kouros Gallery, NY, 2007; Found for Hellenic Cult, NY, 2001; M Mateyka Gallery, Washington, DC, 2004, 2008, 2013; Am Univ Mus/Katzen, Washington, DC, 2006; Retrospective, State Mus Contemp Art, Thessalonica, Larissa, Athens, Greece, 2010; Polyglossia, Onassis Cultural Ctr, Athens Greece, 2011; Grounds for Sculpture, 2013. *Pos:* Cur mod art, Allen Art Mus (as Athena Spear), Oberlin, Ohio, 63-73. *Teaching:* Prof art, Oberlin Coll, Ohio, 73-2000; adj prof art, Univ Md, College Park, 99-. *Awards:* Fel, Ctr Advan Visual Studies, Mass Inst Technol, 74; Artist's Grant, Nat Endowment Arts, 75; Artist's Grant, Ohio Arts Coun, 91; resident fel, Bogliasco Foundation, Genoa, 2003; resident fel, Bellagio Study Ctr, 2007. *Bibliog:* Articles, Landscape Architecture, 5/78 & 3/2007, Artforum, 1/81, Arts Mag, 10/88, Sculpture, 11/2000 & 10/2006; Catherine Howett (auth), Athena Tacha: Public Works, 1970-1988, 89; E McClelland (auth), Cosmic Rhythms: Athena Tacha's Public Sculpture, 98; Dancing in the Landscape: The Sculpture of Athena Tacha, 2000; Athena Tacha: Small Wonders, 2006; Syrago Tsiara (auth), Athena Tacha: Public to Private, 2010; Athena Tacha: Sculpting With/In Nature, 2013. *Mem:* Int Sculpture Asn; Coll Art Asn Am (dir, 73-76). *Media:* Sculpture, Photography. *Res:* Art. *Specialty:* Contemporary art when a museum curator (as A. Spear). *Interests:* Nature & science. *Publ:* auth, Rodin Sculpture in Cleveland Mus, 67; auth, Brancusi's Birds, 69; ed, Art in the Mind, 70; auth, Athena Tacha: Public Sculpture, 82; Forms of Chaos: Drawings by Athena Tacha, 88; Vulnerability: New Fashions, 94. *Dealer:* Marsha Mateyka Gallery Washington, DC; Kouros Gallery NY. *Mailing Add:* 3721 Huntington NW Washington DC 20015-1817

TACLA, JORGE
PAINTER, MURALIST
b Santiago, Chile, 1958. *Study:* Univ de Chile, Santiago, BFA, 79. *Work:* Archer M Huntington Art Gallery, Univ Tex, Austin; High Mus Art, Atlanta; Walker Hill Art Ctr, Seoul, South Korea; ECO Art, Rio de Janeiro, Brazil. *Comn:* Mural, Bronx Housing Ct, Percent Arts, NY, 91-92. *Exhib:* Myth & Magic in the Americas, Museo de Monterrey, Mex, 91; Cruciformed, Ctr Contemp Art & Travel, Cleveland, 91-92; solo exhibs, High Mus, Atlanta, 91 & Lehman Col, Bronx, 92; Migrations, RI Sch Design, Providence, 92; and others. *Awards:* Grant, NY Found Arts, 87 & 91; Grant, J S Guggenheim Found, 88. *Bibliog:* Donald Kuspit (auth), Jorge Tacla: Hemispheric Problem, 91 & Bruce Guenther (auth), Jorge Tacla-Borders, 92, Nohra Haime Gallery; Carrie Pryzbilla (auth), Art on the Edge: Tacla, High Mus Art, 91. *Media:* Oil on Canvas. *Mailing Add:* 245 E 50th St Apt 3A New York NY 10022-7752

TAFT, FRANCES PRINDLE
EDUCATOR, PAINTER - WATERCOLOR
b New Haven, Conn, 1921. *Study:* Vassar Col, AB 42; Yale Univ, grad sch, MA (art history), 48; with George Heard Hamilton, George Kubler & Sumner McKnight Crosby. *Exhib:* Print Club Exhib, Cleveland Artist Archives, 2004; South Wing Gallery St Paul's Church, Cleveland Heights, 2004. *Collection Arranged:* Collection of Artists of Northeast Ohio. *Pos:* Prof art hist, Cleveland Inst Art, 50-, actg dean, 73-74; trustee France Lehman Loeb Art Ctr, Eleanor Roosevelt Ctr, Val-Kill, NY, Laurel Sch, Cleveland Mus Art, Cleveland Arts Prize; Chmn liberal arts, 19th & 20th century art, Pre-Columbian art, Cleveland Inst Art, 50-. *Teaching:* instr, Cleveland Col, Case Western Reserve Univ, Cleveland Mus Art, Brandeis Univ; freelance lect, 20th century art, archit hist, Primitivism, Pre-Columbian art & European Megaliths. *Awards:* Medal of Excellence, Cleveland Inst Art, 94; Cleveland Arts Prize, 95; Smart Living Award, Judson at Univ Circle, 2007; Viktor Schreckengost Award for distinguished teaching, Cleveland Inst Art, 2010. *Mem:* Coll Art Asn Am; Western Reserve Archit Historians (pres, 71-72); Art Asn Cleveland; Cleveland Mus Art (prog chmn, 72, trustee, 72-); Women's Coun, Cleveland Mus Art; Cleveland Artist's Archives; Cleveland Archaeological Soc. *Media:* Watercolor. *Res:* Pre-Columbian art in Mesoamerica & Peru; study of Megaliths of Western Europe. *Collection:* Small pre-Columbian collection and collection of painting, sculpture & prints with a focus on northeastern Ohio artists

TAGUE, DAN
PHOTOGRAPHER, CONCEPTUAL ARTIST
Study: Univ New Orleans, MFA, 2000. *Work:* Whitney Mus Am Art; New Orleans Mus Art; Frederick R Weisman Art Found. *Exhib:* Emerging Artists, Here Gallery, New York, 2000; New Art, Arthur Roger Gallery, New Orleans, 2000; No Dead Artists, Jonathan Ferrara Gallery, New York, 2002, American Muscle, 2005; The Decline of Western Evolution, Barrister's Gallery, New Orleans, 2003, Unusual Suspects, 2007; America: Are We Drowning?, Art Murmur Gallery, Los Angeles, 2005; Katrina & the Waves, Bronx River Art Ctr, 2006; Paradise Lost, Frederieke Taylor Gallery, New York, 2006; Ultimate Destination, Dumbo Art Ctr, Brooklyn, 2006; South x East: Southeastern Contemp Art Biennial, Schmidt Gallery, Fla Atlantic Univ, 2008; Just What Are They Saying, Jonathan Ferrara Gallery, New Orleans, 2009; Soap Factory, Minn; Lost of War/Price of Freedom, Jonathan Ferrara Gallery, New Orleans, 2009. *Awards:* Pollock-Krasner Found Grant, 2007. *Dealer:* Good Children Gallery 4037 St Claude Ave New Orleans 70117; Jonathan Ferrara Gallery 400A Julia St New Orleans LA 70130. *Mailing Add:* c/o Jonathan Ferrara Gallery 400A Julia St New Orleans LA 70130

TAHEDL, ERNESTINE
STAINED GLASS ARTIST, PAINTER
b Vienna, Austria, Oct 12, 1940; Can citizen. *Study:* Acad for Appl Arts, Vienna, Austria, with Franz Herberth, MA in Graphic Arts, 61; with Prof Heinrich Tahedl, collab in design & execution of stained glass works, 61-63. *Work:* Paintings represented in public galleries in Vienna, Japan, Montpellier, France; Alberta Art Found; Art Gallery, Hamilton; Kanagawa Prefectural Gallery, Japan; Mus De Quebec; Publ Gallery City of Vienna, Austria; Musee de Quebec, Canada; Bowman Collection, Newmarket, Ont; Collection of External Affaire, Beijing, China, Ottawa, Ontario; Ecole de beaux-arts, Montpellier, France; Goethe Inst, Montreal, Quebec; Gov of Alberta; London Regional Art Gallery, Ontario; McGill Univ, Montreal, Quebec; Stewart Hall, Cultural Ctr, Pointe Claire, Quebec; Gov of Ontario Art Collection; Varley Art Gallery, Markham, Ont; Moderna Galarija, Zagreb, Croatia. *Comn:* Stained glass murals, Fed Revenue Bldg, Quebec, Que, 71, Bibiotheque Varennes, Quebec, 81, Greenfield Park Libr, Quebec, 82 & Ctr D'Accueil, St Bruno, Quebec, 82, Annunciation Church, Ottawa, 87, St Peters Church, Toronto, 90, 94 & Restoration, Chriskoenigs Church, Klagenfurt, Austria, 89-90. *Exhib:* Third & Fourth Int Print Biennale, Korea, 81 & 83; Solo Exhibs: Gallery Quan, Toronto, 83-93; Tudor Collection, Montreal, 83; Bugera Gallery, Edmonton, Alta, 90-2011; Trias Gallery, Toronto 97-2011; 15th Int Biennial Graphic Art, Ljubljana, Yugoslavia, 83; Hanga Int Print Exhib, Metrop Mus, Tokyo, Japan, 85-87; 3rd Int Biennial Print Exhib, Taipei, Taiwan; Agora Gallery, NY, 2006; Retrospective 1946-2006, Varley Art Gallery, Markham, Ontario, 2012; Opus Works 1946-2012, Niederosterrichisches Dokumentations Zentrum, 2012, Moderna Galeria, Zagreb, Croatia; Osterreichisches Kultur-Forum, Bratislava, Slovakia, 2013; Kunstebene Schloss Poggstall, Lower Australia, 2014. *Pos:* Vpres, Royal Can Acad Arts, formerly; Pres, Ontario Soc Artists, currently; pres bd dirs, currently; JB Aird Gallery Toronto, Ontario, 2001-2011. *Teaching:* Univ Alberta, Art Extension courses, 1964-1965; Stewart Hall Cult Center, Point-Claire, Que, 1968. *Awards:* Can Coun Arts Award, 67; 2000 Arts and Letters Award; In Celebration of Women, Arts, Long-Term Achievement Award, 2004; President's Medal, Ontario Soc Artists, 2006; Eleanor Besen award, 2014. *Bibliog:* Guy Robert (auth), Art Actuel au Quebec, Iconia, Quebec, 83; Joel Russ & Lou Lynn (auth), Contemporary Stained Glass, Doubleday, Toronto, 85; Guy Simard (auth), Verriers du Quebec, Ed Broquet, Ottawa, 89; Nancy Townshend (auth), A History of Art in Alberta 1905-1970, Bayeux Arts Inc, Calgary Can, 2005. *Mem:* Royal Can Acad Arts; Ont Soc Artists (past pres). *Media:* Acrylic Painting; Stained Glass; Printing. *Interests:* Music, traveling. *Publ:* Ltd ed portfolio etchings, Circle of Energy, Art World Int, 81; Contemporary Stained Glass Artists, ABC Black Publ Ltd, London, Eng, 2006. *Dealer:* Trias Gallery 11 Bronte Rd Oakville Ontario CA L6L3B6; Bugera Mathewson Gallery 10345 124th St NW Edmonton Alberta T5N IRI. *Mailing Add:* 79 Collard Dr King City ON L7B 1E4 Canada

TAHIR, ABE M, JR
CONSULTANT
b Greenwood, Miss, Feb 18, 1931. *Study:* Univ Miss, BBA; George Washington Univ, MBA. *Exhib:* With Nothing On: Prints and Drawings of the Nude by Am Artists, New Orleans Mus Art, 2-3/90; Gerald L Brockhurst: A Retrospective of Prints and Drawings, New Orleans Mus Art, 9-10/91. *Pos:* Dir, Tahir Fine Arts, currently. *Specialty:* Original prints & drawings. *Publ:* Auth, Jacques Hnizdovsky, Woodcuts and Etchings, 87

TAI, JANE S
ADMINISTRATOR
b Poughkeepsie, NY, May 14, 1944. *Study:* Syracuse Univ, BA, 67. *Pos:* Exhib coordr, Everson Mus Art, Syracuse, NY, 67-69; exhib coordr, Am Fedn Arts, New York, 70-75, asst dir, exhib dir, 75-78, assoc dir prog, 78-83, assoc dir & exhib prog dir, 83-87; owner, Tai Assoc, Int Inc, NY, Exhib Serv, currently. *Mailing Add:* 529 E 87th St No 1W New York NY 10028-1322

TAIRA, MASA MORIOKA
GALLERY DIRECTOR, CONSULTANT
b Kagoshima City, Japan, Nov 25, 1923; US citizen. *Study:* Studio Prog, Honolulu Acad Arts, with Joseph Feher & Ron Kowalke, studied gallery mgt with David Asherman & Tom M Klobe; materials tech, Univ Hawaii Art Dept with Don Dugal; painting with Helen Gilbert, Advanced Painting with John Wisnosky & intermediate & adv drawing with Ron Kowalke, Univ Hawaii; Life Drawing with Sara Frankel & Kenneth Bushnell; Sculpture with Rick Mills & David Landry. *Comn:* Human Form: From Egypt to the Renaissance, Queen's Med Ctr/Hawaii Med Libr. *Exhib:* Wu Shih Tung Tang, Five Generations in Hawaii, 87; Na Inoa Na Ali'i: First Homage to Manamana, 87-02. *Collection Arranged:* Human Form: From Egypt to the Renaissance, Queen Emma Gallery, 84, traveling, 84-86 & exhib, pub lecture & traveling, 97-98; Monouri: Street Vendors of Old Japan, Queen Emma Gallery, 85 & traveling, 86; Kumulipo: Hawaiian Chant of Creation, Visual Perspectives traveling, 88. *Pos:* Founder & chmn, Queen Emma Gallery, Honolulu, 76-85, dir, 85-02. *Mem:* Nat Mus Women Arts; Contemp Mus Art; Honolulu Acad Arts. *Publ:* Auth, Human Form: From Egypt to the Renaissance, Humanities News, 84

TAIT, WILL(IAM) H
PAINTER, SCULPTOR
b Edinburgh, Scotland, Apr 1, 1942; nat US. *Study:* Art Students League NY, 69-71; San Francisco Art Inst, 74. *Work:* Achenbach Found, Calif Palace Legion Honor, San Francisco. *Comn:* Painted mural, Mt Tamalpais State Park, Mill Valley, Calif, 93; expedition artist, The Giant Octopus Project, AK Pacific Univ, Ankorage AK, 2010. *Exhib:* Northwest Regional, Grants Pass, 76; Berkeley Nat Show, Berkeley Art Ctr, 84; Contemp Prints, Western NMex Univ, Silver City, 84; San Francisco Mus Mod Art Rental Gallery; Dow & Frosini Gallery, Berkeley, Calif; 5 over fifty group exhibs, Splady Gallery, Oakland, Calif, 2007; Solo exhibs, Float Gallery, Oakland, Calif; Group exhibs, Elemental Expressions, Pacific Grove Calif Art Ctr, 2009; Two person exhibs, Aldonza Gallery, Emeryville, Calif, 2010; Emeryville Ann Art Exhib, Emeryville, Calif; Olive Hyde Gallery, 2012. *Pos:* Coordr, Berkeley Art Ctr, Calif, 83-85; digital artist, Intuit. *Teaching:* Instr life drawing, painting, Rogue Community Col, Oreg, 76-77 & Monterey Peninsula Col, Calif, 81-82; instr interface design, San Francisco State Univ, 93-94; instr computer animation/multimedia develop, Ohlone Col, Fremont, Calif, 94; instr classical life drawing & anatomy, The Crucible, Oakland, Calif, 2000-2002; prosector, instr gross anatomy, UCSF Med Sch, San Francisco, Calif, 2002-2003. *Bibliog:* Feature article, Printing J, Mar/89. *Mem:* Int Soc Art, Sci & Tech; Asn Computing Machines; Siggraph; Surface Pattern Design Guild. *Media:* All Media. *Publ:* Coauth, Official Microsoft Image Composer Book & Photodraw by Design, Microsoft Press; auth, The Space Between: Fine Art and Technology, American Arts at the Turn of the Twentieth Century, American Studies Jour, Issue #43, 99. *Mailing Add:* 5950 Doyle St Ste 3 Oakland CA 94608

TAKAGI, MAYUMI
PAINTER, SCULPTOR, PRINTMAKER
b Fukuoka, Japan. *Work:* Williamsburg Art and Historical Ctr, NY. *Comn:* portrait of pres, Kyushu Gei Jutsu no Mori Art Mus, Japan. *Exhib:* Solo exhibs, Persona in New York, Ginza Bricks Gallery, Tokyo, Japan, 2004, Inner Vision & the Visual World, Brooklyn Pub Libr, NY, 2009, Threads of Life, OVED & OVED Gallery, New York, 2009; Group exhibs, New Era Fine Arts & Antiques Gallery, New York, 2001; The Walker Stage Gallery, New York, 2002; Salmagundi Club, New York, 2003, 2004, 2006, 2008; Kinokuniya Gallery, Tokyo, Japan, 2004; Chikyuudo Gallery, Tokyo, Japan, 2005; Asian Fusion Gallery, New York, 2005; The Kent Art Asn, Conn, 2005; Ringwood Barn Gallery, NJ, 2005, 2006; St John's Univ Art Gallery, 2005; O-Mus, Tokyo, Japan, 2006; Pen & Brush, New York, 2007; Nat Arts Club, New York, 2007; Art Students League, New York, 2008; Williamsburg Art & Hist Ctr, New York, 2008; Cooperstown Art Asn, NY, 2009; Tri State Artists Competition Winners Exhib, Hammond Mus, NY, 2010; 1st Nat Exhib of Intaglio Prints, NY Soc Etchers, NY, 2011. *Teaching:* tech instr plaster casting, Art Students League, NY. *Awards:* Hon Mention, 7th Ann Photog & Sculpture Exhib, 2003; Chief of Ota Award, 8th Ann Salon Du Blanc, 2004, Hon Mention, 9th Ann Salon Du Blanc, 2005; Award of Excellence for Any Medium, Kent Art Asn, 2005; Jean Gates Cash Award, 2006; Hon Mention, Ann Thumb-Box Exhib, Salmagundi Club, 2004, 2006; Ethel J Bowen Merit Award, Art Students League, New York, 2007; Michael Ponce de Leon Printmaking Award, Art Students League, New York, 2007, 2009; Jack Richeson & Co Gold Brush Award, Audubon Artists Ann Juried Exhib, 2008; Medal of Hon, 112th Ann Juried Exhib, Catharine Lorillard Wolfe Art Club, 2008; Hannibal DeBellis & Richman Sculpture Award, 125th Ann Mem Exhib, Salmagundi Culb, 2008; 2nd Place, Tri State Artists Competition, Hammond Mus, New York, 2009; Marquis Who's Who in Am References Award, Audubon Artists, 2009; Frank C Wright Medal of Honor, 82nd Grand Nat Exhib, Am Artists Professional League, 2010; Nessa Cohen Grant, Art Students League, NY, 2009. *Bibliog:* The Yomiuri Am, 12/13/2002, 8/29/2003; US Front Line, 12/20/2002; OCS News, Vol 29, No 693, 1/01/2003; Tokyo News Paper, 7/8/2004; Bijutsu no Mado, Japan, Sept 2004; Gallery & Studio, Vol 8, No 2, 2005; Shukan New York SeiKatsu, No 95, 12/17/2005, 10/11/2008; New York SeiKatsu, 12/17/2005, 10/11/2008, 10/17/2009; NHK (The Japanese Nat Pub Broadcasting Station) TV, Fukuoka Ichibanboshi, 7/23/2004. *Mem:* Salamagundi Club (2002-); Art Students League of NY (2001-); Soc Am Graphic Artists (2011-). *Media:* oil color, acrylic, etching, aquatint, lithograph, plaster, hydrocal & bronze. *Dealer:* Tolman Collection New York; The Old Print Shop 150 Lexington Ave New York NY 10016

TAKAHASHI, GINGER BROOKS
PHOTOGRAPHER
b 1977. *Study:* Oberlin Coll, BA, 1999. *Exhib:* group exhibs include 6 Degrees of Separation, Paul Sharpe Contemp Art, New York, 2007; Shared Women, Los Angeles Contemp Exhibs, 2007; Exile of Imaginary, Enerali Found, Vienna, Austria, 2007; Locally Localized Gravity, Inst Contemp Art, Philadelphia, 2007; Needles & Pens, Stencil Nation Budget Gallery, San Francisco, 2008; Pink & Bent, Leslie/Lohman Gallery, New York, 2008. *Awards:* New York Found Arts Fel, 2008; Art Matters Found Grant, 2009

TAKASHIMA, SHIZUYE VIOLET
ILLUSTRATOR, PAINTER
b Vancouver, BC, June 12, 1928. *Study:* Ont Coll Art, BA, 53; Fine Arts Inst, San Miguel, Mex (weaving), 65; Pratt Art Ctr Graphic Arts, New York, 66. *Work:* Nat Gallery, Ottawa, Can; Imperial Oil; Can Titanium Pigments Ltd, Montreal; Montreal Standard Publ Co, Montreal; Midland Computer Bldg, Syracuse, NY. *Comn:* Four Posters, Midwestern Regional Libr, Kitchener, Ont, 78. *Exhib:* Hamilton Art Gallery, Ont, 61; Hart House, Univ Toronto, 61; VI Biennial Exhib, Nat Gallery Ottawa, 65; Mystic Circle (traveling), Burnaby Art Gallery, 74; Five-man exhib, Montreal Mus Fine Arts, 65; Four-man exhib, Art Gallery Ont, Toronto, 60; Solo exhibs, Burnaby Art Gallery, BC, 65 & 78 & Japanese Can Cult Ctr, Toronto, 74. *Pos:* Assoc ed, Rika Mag, 76-79, Inner City Angels, Toronto, 79-84. *Teaching:* Instr drawing & painting, Forest Hill Learning & Ont Col Art, 71-94, Resources, 71 & Ont Col Art, Toronto, 76-95. *Awards:* Can Coun Grant, 71 & 73; Bronze Award, Can Asn Children's Libr Asn, 72; Sankai Shinbun Ann Literary Award, Tokyo, 74; VI Premio Europeo di Litteratura Gioranite Award, Padua, Italy, 76. *Bibliog:* Robin Mathews (auth), Young Artists, Can Forum, 61; David P Silcox (auth), Young Artists, Can Art Mag, 62. *Media:* Oils, Watercolor. *Publ:* A Child in Prison Camp, Tundra Books, Montreal, 71; illusr, Watercolors: Kenji and the Cricket, Adele Wiseman Porcupine & Quill Inc, 88. *Mailing Add:* 5438 Larch St Vancouver BC V6M 4C8 Canada

TAKAYAMA, MARTHA TEPPER
GALLERY DIRECTOR, PUBLISHER
b Cambridge, Mass. *Study:* Boston Univ, BA, 65; Boston Col, MAT, 74. *Exhib:* People and Landscape: Hiromi Tsuchida, Toshio Shibata, Fitchburg Art Mus, Mass, 97-98. *Pos:* Dir, Martha Tepper Fine Arts, 78-94 & Tepper Takayama Fine Arts, 94-; cur & co-publ no-print workshops. *Specialty:* Contemporary paintings, prints and photographs. *Interests:* Latin American and Japanese art. *Mailing Add:* 20 Park Plaza Suite 600 Boston MA 02116

TALABA, L (LINDA) TALABA CUMMENS
SCULPTOR, PAINTER
b Detroit, Mich, July 15, 1943. *Study:* Detroit Inst Technol, with Maxwell Wright; pvt instr with Lois Pety; Ill Wesleyan Univ, with Fred Brian, BFA; Southern Ill Univ, with David Folkman & Lewis Brent Kington, MFA; Phi Kappa Phi. *Work:* Henry Ford Found Print Collection, Detroit; Can Arts Coun Grant; Albion Univ Print Collection; Leopold Schepp Found Grant, New York; Detroit Art Inst Rental Collection; St John's Univ Prints; Burfon Title and Abstr co; Albion Univ, Ill; Wesleyan Univ; Roeper Found; Cranbrook Art Acad; and others. *Comn:* Painting, Waterford Twp Bd Educ, 61; Isaac E Crary Jr High Sch, 63; Burton Title & Abstract Co, Detroit, 67; bronze door ornaments, Little Grassy Mus, Southern Ill Univ, Grant, 70; bronze sculpture, Dir Budget, State of Ill, Springfield, 75; and other comn by individuals. *Exhib:* Solo Exhibs: Renee Gallery, Detroit, 68; Lewis Towers Gallery, Loyola Univ, 75; Deerfield Courts Gallery, 84-85; Kraft Corp Gallery, Cook Mem Libr & Highland Park City Hall Rotunda, 96, Siuslaw Bank Gallery, Springfield, Ore, 2009, 2012; Rotunda City Hall, Highland Park, 85 & 96; Cook Mem Libr Gallery, 88; Kraft Co Gallery, 89; Body Politic Gallery, Chicago, 93; Dittmar Gallery, 98; Group Exhibs: Koho Gallery, 2000-04; New Zone Gallery, 2010-2015, Emerald Art Ctr, 2006-08, 09, 2011-2015 (nat show); City Eugene, 2005-2007; Art Around Ore, 2006; Maude Kerns Group Shows, 2009-14; Mayors Show, Jacob Gallery, 2006, 2009; Sivslaw Bank Gallery, 2011 & 2012; One woman exhib: Siuslaw Bank Gallery, 2010 & 2013, City Eugene Courthouse, 2012-2014, Ophelia's Place Gallery, 2014-2015. *Pos:* Dir, sch art, Suburban Fine Art Ctr, 84-85, grant writer, Rose Children's Theatre, 98-2004. *Teaching:* Guest artist, sculpture, Springfield Art Asn, 74-78, Sangamon State Univ, 75-78, Coll Lake Co, 80-85, Suburban Fine Art Ctr, Highland Park, Ill, 83-86 & 96, Dist #113 Continuing Educ, 83-96 & Westmorebud Sch, 2000-05, Cesar Chavez Sch 2006-2008, Twin Oaks Sch, 2011; art fac, Park Dist Highland Park & Caruso Jr High, 86-96. *Awards:* Grants, Smithsonian Res, 76 & Cooper Hewett Mus; Chicago Women's Caucus Award, Beacon St Gallery, 90 & Northern Ill Art Mus, 90-91; Recent Works Award, Coll Lake Co, 91 & 93 & CLC Invitational Exhib; Dittmar Gallery-Parallel Visions, Northwestern Univ, 98; Awards Maude Kerns and Group Show 97-; Group Show Award, Florence, Ore, 2004; Drawing Award, Emerald Art Ctr, Eugene Mayor's Show, 2006, 2009, 2011; Award for poster, Chamber Music Amici, 2009, 2010, 2011. *Mem:* Symphony Guild; Left Coast Crime Writers; Sisters in Crime Writers; Willamette Writers Asn; Lifetime mem, AAUW; SCBWI Writers Asn; PNWA Writers Asn; Emerald Art Ctr; Opera Ambassadors. *Media:* Bronze, Graphics, Mixed Media. *Specialty:* sculpture, graphics, painting. *Interests:* Playing recorders, bass, tenor, alto & soprano, hiking, writing, poetry and mystery novels. *Publ:* Illusr, Lakeland's Paradise, Bd Educ Oakland Co, Pontiac, Mich, 61; art ed, Argus Newspaper, 62 & illusr, Black Book (literary mag), 63-65, Ill Wesleyan Univ;

illusr, Experimental Math Books, Cent Mid-Western Regional Educ Labs, 70; illusr & coauth, Helping Your Doctor - A Children's Self-Healing Guide, 84; Brochures, spot illusr, cartoon art, art from junk for kids & no budget art for teachers, 96-; art proj, Butterfly Pets in Oregon, YouTube, 2008-; Binnacle Journal, 2008; Passager Journal, 2008; Fortean Times, 2010; Frightmares Stories anthology, 2012. *Dealer:* Tom Talaba and Jim Cummens. *Mailing Add:* 3415 Timberline Dr Eugene OR 97405

TALASNIK, STEPHEN
PAINTER
b Philadelphia. *Study:* RI Sch Design; Tyler Sch Art. *Exhib:* Small Works on Paper, Newcastle Polytechnic, Eng, 1980; Int Drawing Biennial, Cleveland, Eng, 1981; Selections 27, The Drawing Ctr, New York, 1984; solo exhibs, Recent Drawings: Janet Fleisher Gallery, Philadelphia, 1985, Mythology: Recent Drawings, Pa Acad Fine Arts, 1987, Recent Drawings, INFORM Gallery, Kanazawa, Japan, 1993, Recent Drawings: Weatherspoon Art Gallery, Univ NC, 1995, Am Archit Found, Am Inst Architects Headquarters Gallery, Wash, DC, 1998, Davidson Galleries, Seattle, 1999 & 2002, Fictional Engineering II, Louis & Jeanette Brooks, Engineering Design Gallery, New York, 2001, Aeroparts Installation, Philadelphia Int Airport, 2003, Building Without a Net: Drawings & Sculpture, Marsha Mateyka Gallery, Wash, DC, 2005, Marlborough Gallery, New York, 2006 & Queens Mus Art, 2008; American Graphic Arts: Watercolors, Drawings and Prints, Collection of Pa Acad Fine Arts, Philadelphia, 1986; Achromatic Variations, Levy Gallery, Moore Col Art, Philadelphia, 1988; Exhib for China, Hillside Gallery, Tokyo, 1989; Works on Paper: Contemporary American Drawing, High Mus Art, Atlanta, 1990; Recent Acquisitions, Nat Mus Am Art, Smithsonian, Wash, DC, 1991; Nat Drawing Biennial, Ark Art Ctr, 1994; Recent Acquisitions: Drawings and Prints, Brit Mus, London, 1996; Nieuwe Aanwinsten - Recent Drawing Acquisitions, Teylers Mus, Haarlem, The Netherlands, 1997; Twenty Philadelphia Artists, Philadelphia Mus Art, 1998; Pattern, James Graham & Sons, New York, 1999; Blurry Lines: John Michael Kohler Arts Ctr, Sheboygan, Wis, 2000; Am Acad Arts and Letts Invitational, New York, 2001 & 2009; In the Details, Gallery Schlesinger, New York, 2002; Colored Pencil, KS Art, New York, 2004; USA, Hoy: Pintura y Escultura, Galeria Marlborough, Madrid, 2005; Nat Acad Design, New York, 2006; Galerie Bailly Contemporain, Paris, 2008; Recent Prints, Kido Press, Tokyo, 2009. *Teaching:* Instr art and drawing, Temple Univ, Japan, 1987. *Awards:* Purchase Prize, Am Acad Arts and Letts, 2009. *Media:* Oil. *Dealer:* Marlborough Gallery 4 W 57th St New York NY 10019-4069. *Mailing Add:* PO Box 1886 New York NY 10013

TALBERT, RICHARD HARRISON
PAINTER, ARCHITECT
b Rockville Centre, NY, Apr 23, 1957. *Study:* RI Sch Design, 75-77; Sarah Lawrence Col, BA (philos), 80; Inst for Archit & Urban Studies, 82-83; Univ Cambridge, cert, 86; Univ Miami, BA (archit), 92, MA (archit), 93. *Work:* Dana Roth Collection, Ft Lauderdale, Fla; Susie & Robert Lafer Collection, NY; Hyundai Motor Co, Seoul, Korea; Robert Scull Collection, NY; Michael & Katherine Karolyi Mus Collection, Vence, France. *Comn:* City Scapes Mural, Hoboken Arts Coun, NJ, 84; Water Tower Mural, 85, Banners, 85, Karolyi Found, Vence, France; mixed media/oil on canvas/neon, Mrs Dana Roth, Ft Lauderdale, Fla, 90; exterior mural, comn by Dr Harry Sanchez, Coral Gables, Fla, 95; Exterior Mural, EWALK, 42nd St Redevelopment, Times Sq, NY. *Exhib:* Solo exhibs, Michael Karolyi Found, Vence, France, 85, Esta Robinson Gallery, NY, 86, Gallery des Artiste, West Palm Beach, Fla, 90, Bonwit Teller's Atrium Gallery, Bal Harbor, Fla, 90, La Gallerie Presidence, Bordeaux, France, 91 & Santarella Mus & Gardens, Sky Gallery, Tyringham, Mass, 96; Summer Exhibition, Royal Acad Arts Mus, London, Eng, 86; Image Gallery, Stockbridge, Mass, 89; Berkshire Artisans, Pittsfield, Mass, 91; 80 Washington Sq E Galleries, NY, 93. *Pos:* Artist in Residence, Santarella Mus & Gardens, Studio of Sir Henry Hudson, Kitson, Tyringham, Mass, 2000. *Teaching:* Asst to Vincent Scully, hist of archit, Univ Miami, 92. *Awards:* Jane B W Whitney Award, Whitney Found, NY, 78; Michael Karolyi Fel, Karolyi Found, Vence, France, 85; Hon Travel Fel, Kettle's Yard Art Gallery, Univ Cambridge, Eng, 85. *Mem:* NY Artist Equity; Am Inst Archit. *Publ:* Auth, Art on Madison Avenue, Art Speak, 83; article in Views, RI Sch Design, 90; auth, Mural Maker, Sunday NY Times, 6/95. *Mailing Add:* 410 W End Ave New York NY 10024

TALBOT, CHRISTOPHER
ADMINISTRATOR, EDUCATOR, PHOTOGRAPHER
Study: Brigham Young Univ, BA; Univ Houston, MFA, 2004. *Work:* Mus Fine Arts Houston. *Pos:* working with Nat Park Svc to document El Camino Real de los Tejas Nat Historic Trail, 2009-; assoc prof photog, dir, Stephen F. Austin State Univ, currently. *Mailing Add:* Stephen F Austin State University College of Fine Arts, School of Arts Box 13001 SFA Station Nacogdoches TX 75962

TALBOT, JONATHAN
PAINTER, COLLAGE ARTIST
b New York, NY, Nov 14, 1939. *Study:* Brandeis Univ; New Sch Social Res; San Francisco Acad Art. *Work:* Smith Coll Mus, Northampton, Mass; Torun Mus, Torun, Poland; Everhart Mus, Scranton, Pa; Beach Mus Art, Manhattan, KS; Newark Mus, NJ; Musée Artcolle, Plemet, France; Montclair Art Mus, NJ; San Diego Mus Art; Housatonic Mus of Art, Bridgeport, Conn; Coos Art Mus, Oreg; Longview Mus of Fine Arts, Tex; Masterworks Mus Bermuda Art; and others; Weisman Art Mus, Univ Minnesota, Minneapolis, MN; Georgetown Univ Fine Print Coll, Wash DC. *Exhib:* Solo Exhibs: Res & Devel, Gallery Contemp Art, Sacred Heart Univ, Fairfield, Conn, 90; Jonathan Talbot: Collage Paintings 1980-2000; Housatonic Mus, Bridgeport, Conn, 2000; The Artist as an Explorer, Coos Art Mus, Ore, 2002; Mus Menagerie, Mus Mod Art, NY, 76; Recent Am Works on Paper, Smithsonian Inst Traveling Exhib Serv, 85-87; Surrealism After Surrealism, Ark Arts Ctr, Little Rock, Ark, 86; The Humanist Icon, Bayly Art Mus, Univ Va, Charlottesville, NY Acad Art, NY & Ulrich Mus Art, Wichita, Kans, 90; In This Time & Place, State Univ NY, New Paltz, 96; Art Collage, Brussels, Belg, 2008; Lost & Found: The Art of Collage, Northern Ky Univ, Highland Heights, Ky, 2010; and others. *Awards:* Ranger Fund Purchase Award, Nat Acad, 82; Audubon Artists Award, 41st Ann Exhib, Nat Arts Club, 83; C R Gibson Award, Art of Northeast USA, 83; and others. *Bibliog:* Ruth Bass (auth), Gimpel & Weitzenhoffer Gallery, NY, ARTnews, 86; Amy Goldberger (auth) Collage of Conscience, Orange Mag, 89; Gerald Brommer (auth), Collage Techniques, Watson-Guptill, 94; Pierre Jean Varet (auth), L'Art du Collage à l'Aube du Vingt et Unième Siècle, Editions Artcolle, Paris, 2006; Holly Harrison (auth), Mixed Media Collage, Quarry, 2007; Maureen Bloomfield (auth), Cut and Paste, The Artist's Mag, 2008; Benjamin Genacchio (auth), Piecing Things Together, NY Times, 10/18/2008; Randel Plowman (auth), Masters: Collage, Lark Books, 2010; Deborah K Snider (auth), The Collages of Jonathan Talbot, Royal Fireworks, 2014. *Publ:* Auth, Collage: A New Approach, 5th edit, Talbot Arts, 01; auth, Acrylic Image Transfer: A Handbook for Artists, 2012. *Mailing Add:* 7 Amity Rd Warwick NY 10990

TALBOTT, SUSAN LUBOWSKY
DIRECTOR
b Brooklyn, NY, Jan 16, 1949. *Study:* Pratt Inst, BFA, 1970, MFA, 1975. *Collection Arranged:* Constructivism and the Geometric Tradition, McCrory Corp, traveling exhib, 1977-80; Yasuo Kuniyoshi, 1986; George Ault (1891-1948), 1988; Artist and the Community, 1994-98; Heroic Painting, 1998; Vincent Desiderio, 1998; Almost Warm & Fuzzy: Childhood and Contemporary Art, 1999; My Reality: Contemporary Art and the Culture of Japanese Animation, 2001-02. *Pos:* Asst cur, McCrory Corp, NY, 1977-80; asst dir, Queens Mus, 1980-82; branch dir, Whitney Mus at Philip Morris, 1982-88 & Whitney Mus at Equitable Ctr, 1987-88; dir, Visual Arts, Nat Endowment Arts, 1989-92, Southeastern Ctr Contemp Art, Winston-Salem, NC, 1992-98; dir, Des Moines Art Ctr, 1998-2005; dir Smithsonian Arts, Smithsonian Inst, Washington, 2005-08; dir, Wadsworth Atheneum Mus Art, Hartford, Conn, 2008-. *Teaching:* Instr art hist & gallery dir, State Univ NY, Brockport, 1975-77; adj prof art, New York Univ, 1986-88. *Awards:* Distinguished Service Award, Nat Endowment Arts, 1991; Alumni Achievement Award, Pratt Inst, 1993. *Mem:* Asn Art Mus Dirs; Am Asn Mus; Int Coun Mus. *Res:* 20th century American art, specialization in the 1920s, 1930s and contemporary art. *Publ:* Auth, Figures of Mystery (exhib catalog), Queens Mus, 1982; Three American Families: A Tradition of Artistic Pursuit, 1983, Alexander Calder: Selections from the Permanent Collection, 1984, The Surreal City, 1930s-1950, 1985, coauth, Yasuo Kuniyoshi, 1986 (all exhib catalogs), Whitney Mus & auth, George Ault, Sculpture Since the 60's, 1988; Spaces '88, Mus d'Arte Contemporanea, Prato, Italy, 1988; coauth, Yasuo Kuniyoshi, Nat Mus Mod Art, Kyoto, Japan; Artist and Community Series: Donald Lipski, Tim Rollins, Fred Wilson, Hope Sandrow, Willie Birch, Eleanor Antin, Heroic Painting. *Mailing Add:* Wadsworth Atheneum 600 Main St Hartford CT 06103

TALIAFERRO, NANCY ELLEN TAYLOR
PAINTER
b Richmond, Va, Feb 16, 1937. *Study:* Va Commonwealth Univ, BFA, 59. *Work:* Portrait, Richmond Ct Clerk, Manchester Co Court House, Richmond, Va, 2000. *Comn:* Portraits pvt collections. *Exhib:* Charter Mem Uptown Gallery, Richmond, Va, 92; Nat Asn Women Artists Exhib, Du Pont Art Gallery, Washington & Lee Univ, Lexington, Va, 93; 32nd Irene Leache Mem Exhib, Chrysler Mus, Norfolk, Va, 94; Nat Asn Women Artists Traveling Exhib, Greater Lafayette Mus Art, Ind & Sordoni Art Gallery, Wilkes Univ, Wilkes Barre, Pa, 96, Midwest Mus Am Art, Elkhart, Ind, Gannon Gallery, Bismarck State Col, NDak & NW Art Ctr, Minot State Univ, NDak, 97, Charleston Heights Art Ctr & Reed Whipple Cult Ctr, Las Vegas, Nev & Longview Art Mus, Tex, 98; Va Portrait Painters, Peninsula Fine Arts Ctr, Newport News, Va, 97; Peninsula Fine Arts Ctr, Newport News, Va, 2002. *Awards:* Artists Mag Award, 92; Medal Honor & Audrey Hope Shirk Mem Award, Nat Asn Women Artists, 95; Doris Kreindler Mem Award, Nat Asn Women Artists, 2004. *Bibliog:* Mark St John Erickson, Grandmother of Juried Show is Back on Top, Daily Press, Northfolk, Va, June 5, 1994. *Mem:* Nat Asn Women Artists; James River Art League; Univ Painters. *Media:* Oil, Pastel, Charcoal. *Specialty:* Fine Arts. *Publ:* Photo of painting in The Artists Mag, 92. *Mailing Add:* 6724 Forest Hill Ave Richmond VA 23225

TALLEY, DAN R
WRITER, PHOTOGRAPHER
b Hogansville, Ga, Jan 6, 1951. *Study:* Atlanta Coll Art, BFA, 73; Univ Hartford, MFA (art), 76. *Pos:* Asst ed, Contemp Art-Southeast, Atlanta, 76-77; ed, Art Papers, 79-82, contrib ed, 98-; gallery dir, Nexus Contemp Art Ctr, Atlanta, 87-89; visual arts initiative, Forum Gallery, Jamestown, NY, 89-91, dir, 91-96; dir, Sharadin Art Gallery, Kutztown Univ, Pa, 96-. *Teaching:* Instr, Issues in contemp art, 92-96, Paris Its Art & People, 95-96, Jamestown Community Coll; instr, business art, 2005-, Digital Photog & Electronic media for Artist, 2006-, Kutztown Univ. *Mem:* Coll Art Asn. *Media:* Photography. *Res:* Socio-economic impact on specifically defined areas of domestic interiors. *Publ:* Color, Culture, Complexity, 2002 & Accelerating Sequence: Artists Consider Time and Aging, 2005, Mus Contemp Art Ga, Atlanta; Robert Raczka, Art Papers Mag, 2009; NCECA 2010: Earth Matters, Ceramics Monthly Mag, 2010; The Ineffable Conversation 1974-2012, 2012. *Mailing Add:* 496 W Walnut St # 2 Kutztown PA 19530

TALLMAN, AMI
PAINTER
b Calif, 1979. *Study:* San Francisco Art Inst, BFA, 1998; Art Ctr Coll Design, MFA, 2006. *Exhib:* Solo exhibs include Trudi Gallery, Los Angeles, 2007, See Line Gallery, 2008; Group exhibs include 17 artists, 35 works, 500 guests, 976 Valencia, San Francisco, 1998; Urban Birds, Balazo Gallery, San Francisco, 2004; Bedwetter Show, Paxico Gallery, Los Angeles, 2005; Supersonic 3, Barnsdall Art Park, Los Angeles, 2006; Boat Show, High Energy Constructs, Los Angeles, 2006; Naïve Set Theory, Cirrus Gallery, Los Angeles, 2006 ; Braveland, See Line Gallery, Los Angeles, 2006; Re Draw, Brooklyn Fireproof, Brooklyn, 2007; Paper Bombs, Jack Hanley Gallery, Los Angeles, 2007; Timeline, Seeline Gallery, Santa Monica, 2007 ; Rainbow Goblins, Advocate Gallery, Los Angeles, 2007; No Jerks Allowed, Rental Gallery, New York, 2007; Against the Grain, Los Angeles Contemp Exhib, Los Angeles, 2008

TALMOR, LIHIE
PRINTMAKER, SCULPTOR
b Tel-Aviv, Israel, Sept 9, 1944; Israeli & Venezuelan citizen. *Study:* Technion, Technol Inst Israel, BSc, 69; Tel-Aviv Univ, 71; Studio Luis Camnitzer, Italy, 89. *Work:* Nat Art Gallery, Caracas, Venezuela; NY Pub Libr; Cult Inst PR; Reina Sofia Ctr, Madrid, Spain; Nat Mus Prints, Mexico City. *Exhib:* Readings in National Art, Nat Art Gallery, Caracas, 87; Venezuelan Graphics, Nat Mus Mexico City, 90; Homage to Vladimir Horowitz, Robert Fisher Hall, Jerusalem, 92; La Habana Biennial, Wifredo Lam Prints Ctr, Havana, Cuba, 94 & 96; Estampa 95, Reina Sofia Mus, Madrid, Spain, 95; The Creativity of Evil, Sofia Imber Mus Contemp Art, Caracas, 96. *Awards:* Int Award for Printmaking, Biella, Italy, 93; Honorable Mention, Int Biennale Small Graphic Forms, Poland, 97; San Juan Biennale of Prints Honorary Prize, PR, 98; and others. *Mem:* Int Asn Art; Taller de Artistas Graficos Asociados; Painters & Sculptors Asn-Israel. *Mailing Add:* Bamco CCS-113-000 PO Box 025322 Miami FL 33102-5322

TAMBURINE, JEAN HELEN
PAINTER, SCULPTOR
b Meriden, Conn, Feb 20, 1930. *Study:* Traphagen Sch, New York, 48-49; Art Students League, New York, with Jon Corbino & John Groth, 48-50; also with Elizabeth Gordon Chandler, Harry R Ballinger. *Work:* Middletown Pub Libr & State Libr, Middletown, Conn; Nashville Pub Libr, Tenn; Strong Sch, Hartford, Conn; and others. *Comn:* Heritage (bronze sculpture), Wallingford Pub Libr, 86. *Exhib:* Town & Country Club Exhib, West Hartford, Conn, 69; George Walter Vincent Smith Art Mus, Springfield, Mass; Solo exhib, L'Heure Joyeux, Paris, France, 69; Pearl S Buck Found Exhib, Meriden Pub Libr, 72; Ellsworth Gallery, Simsbury, Conn, 76; and others. *Pos:* Comnr, Conn Comn on Arts, State Conn, 63-65; chmn & organizer, Cult Comn for Art Appointments to Pub Bldg, 66-70. *Awards:* Asn Members Prize, Academic Artists Asn, Inc, Springfield, Mass, 81; Martha Moore Mem Award for Excellence in Portrait, Rockport Art Asn, 83; Margaret Fitzhugh Brown Award Excellence in Painting, North Shore Arts Asn, 93. *Mem:* Acad Artists Asn; Am Artists Prof League; Salmagundi Club; Am Medallic Sculpture Asn; North Shore Arts Asn; Rockport Art Asn; FIDEM (int medallic sculpture orgn). *Publ:* Auth & illusr, How Now, Brown Cow, Abingdon Press, 67; illusr, It's Nice To Be Little, Rand-McNally, 65; The Complete Peddlers Pack, Univ Tenn Press, 67; Something Was Missing, Follett, 69; Five Busy Bears, Rand-McNally, 69; and others; auth & illusr, Almost Big Enough, Abingdon Press; auth & illusr, I Think I Will Go to the Hospital, Abingdon Press; illusr, The Five Busy Bears by Sterling North, Rand McNally. *Mailing Add:* c/o The Bertolli Studio 73 Reynolds Dr Meriden CT 06450

TAN, LIQIN
EDUCATOR
b Hengshan, Hunan, P.R. China, Feb 17, 1957. *Study:* Hengyang Teachers Coll Fine Arts, China - 1981; Central Acad Fine Arts, Beijing, China - 1984; Concordia Univ, Montreal, Can, MA, 1993. *Hon Degrees:* Sheridan Col, Computer Animation, Canada - 1996. *Work:* Shanghai Duolun Mus Mod Art Gal, China; Emin Hekimgil Art Gal, Turkish-Am Asn, Ankara, Turkey; Sing Tao Art Gal, Toronto, Can; The Noyes Mus Art, Oceanville, NJ; Beijing World Art Mus. *Exhib:* Nat Int Contemp Prints Exhib, Lancaster Mus Art, Pa, 2004; solo exhibs, Digital & Primitive, Shanghai Duolun Mus Mod Art, China, 2005 & Animation Permeates Rawhides, Stedman Art Gal, Rutgers Univ, Camden, NJ, 2004; 5th Dig Art & Anima Juried Competition, Beecher Ctr Art & Technol, Youngstown, OH, 2005; Threading Time, Digital Art Gal Siggraph, Los Angeles, Calif, 2005; Award Winning Artists, Gallery Int, Baltimore, MD, 2005; Path of Technol & Cosmology, Noyes Mus Art, Oceanville, NJ, 2006. *Pos:* exec art ed, Hunan Art Publ House, China, 1/1985-8/1987; art dir, 12 Sources Arts Inc., Mississauga, Can, 1/1991-12/1996; juror, Siggraph 2006 Art Gallery, Boston, 2/2006-8/2006; co-dir, Art Program, Rutgers Univ, 2007-. *Teaching:* art instr painting, Hengyang Teachers' Col, China, 1981-85; lectr 3D animation, Ngee Ann Polytechnic, Singapore, 1997-2000; asst prof 3D animation, Rutgers Univ, Camden, NJ, 2000-. *Awards:* Gold Medal, Ann Members Exhib, Da Vinci Art Alliance, 2004; Best of Show, Idea Int, Int Digital Media & Arts Asn, 2004; First Place, 5th Digital Art & Animation Competition, Beecher Ctr Art & Technol, Youngstown State Univ, 2006. *Bibliog:* Edward McCormack (auth), Uniting Nature & Technol, Gallery & Studio, New York City, 2005; Robert Baxter (auth), Revolutionary Artist, Courier-Post, 2005; William Zimmer (auth), The Collaboration Between Artists, The Noyes Mus Art, 2006; LiQin Tan, Digitalized Wonderland, NY, 2009; E Pearlman (auth), Digital Bllodless New Vision, 2009; Yuejin Zou (auth), Visual Archaeology World Art, 2010. *Mem:* ATC Asn Softimage/XSI, 1998-; Am Asn Univ Prof, 2000-; ACM Siggraph, 2000-; Asn Calligraphic Art, 2003-; Philadelphia Da Vinci Art Alliance, 2004-; Siggraph Digital Art Bd Committee. *Media:* Animation Installation, Digital Media. *Publ:* auth, A future Vision of China's Art (The Trend of Art Thought), Hubei Art & Littera Asn, 1985; auth, Art Criticism Approaches: A Scattered Sense & Theory, The Theory of Contemp Art, Hunan Art Publ House, 1988; coauth, Animating Art History for Teaching, Conf Abstracts & Applications, ACM Siggraph, 2002; coauth, Animating Art History-Building a Bridge Between Disciplines, Conf Select CD-ROM, ACM Siggraph, 2003; auth, Digital-Primitive Art: Animation Permeates Centuries Old Rawhides, IV04 Int Visualization, IEEE, 2004. *Dealer:* Yuan Fen New Media Art Space 798 Beijing; Dalat Gallery Philadelphia Pa. *Mailing Add:* 1712 Independence Ln Cherry Hill NJ 08003

TAN, NOELLE
PHOTOGRAPHER
b Manila, Philippines, 1969. *Study:* NY Univ, BFA, 1993; Calif Inst Arts, MFA, 2002. *Work:* Hirshhorn Mus & Sculpture Garden, Washington; Corcoran Mus Art, Washington; Ctr Photog at Woodstock, NY. *Exhib:* Solo exhibs include Creative Artists Agency, Beverly Hills, Calif, 2002, Ctr Photog at Woodstock, NY, 2004, Sch 33, Baltimore, 2004, DC Arts Ctr, Washington, 2005, Project 4 Gallery, Washington, 2006, Civilian Art Projects, Washington, 2007; group exhibs include AsianLens, Chambers Fine Art, New York, 2002, Group Photog Exhib, 2003; Am Photog, Rockefeller Arts Ctr, Fredonia, NY, 2002; Contrary Equilibriums, Asian Am Arts Ctr, New York, 2002; Close Calls, Headlands Ctr Arts, San Francisco, 2003; Memory, Salina Art Ctr, Kans, 2004; Made in Woodstock III, Ctr Photog at Woodstock, NY, 2006; Dear Diary: The Autobiographical Comic, Athens Inst Contemp Art, Ga, 2006; Currents: Recent Acquisitions, Hirshhorn Mus & Sculpture Garden, Washington, 2007-08. *Awards:* Creative Capital Grant, 2005. *Dealer:* Civilian Art Projects 406 7th St NW Washington DC 20004

TANANBAUM, LISA & STEVEN ANDREW
COLLECTORS
b New York, June 26, 1965. *Study:* Vassar Coll, BA, 1987. *Pos:* Analyst, Kidder, Peabody & co, New York, 1987-89; investment specialist, MacKay Shields, 1989-91, head high yield group, 1991-97, portfolio mgr hedge fund area, 1997; sr mng mem & founding partner, GoldenTree Asset Mgmt, LP, New York, 2000-, chief exec officer & chief investment officer. *Awards:* Named one of Top 200 Collectors, ARTnews mag, 2006-13. *Collection:* Postwar and contemporary art. *Mailing Add:* GoldenTree Asset Mgmt LP 300 Park Ave 21st Fl New York NY 10022

TANENBAUM, JOEY
COLLECTOR
Hon Degrees: Ryerson Univ, PhD (hon), 2003. *Pos:* Chmn & chief exec officer, Jay-M Enterprises Ltd, Jay-M Holdings Ltd; trustee, Royal Ontario Mus, Art Gallery Ontario, currently; hon chmn, Can Psychiatric Res Found, currently. *Awards:* Named one of Top 200 Collectors, ARTnews mag, 2003-13; Recipient Order of Can. *Collection:* African art; naive art

TANENBAUM, TOBY
COLLECTOR
Awards: Named one of Top 200 Collectors, ARTnews mag, 2009-13. *Collection:* African art; naive art

TANGER, SUSANNA
PAINTER, WRITER
b Boston, Mass, June 9, 1942. *Study:* Boston Mus Sch; Univ Colo; Univ Calif, Berkeley. *Exhib:* Post Washington NY Cent Hall Gallery, 75; City of Paris Mus Mod Art, 75; PS 1, NY, 76; Hal Bromm Gallery, NY, 76; Galerie Rencontres, Paris, France, 76; Moore Coll of Art Gallery, Philadelphia, 77; and others. *Mailing Add:* 141 Wooster St No 8C New York NY 10012

TANKSLEY, ANN
PAINTER, PRINTMAKER
b Pittsburgh, Pa, Jan 25, 1934. *Study:* Carnegie Inst Technol, with Samuel Rosenberg & Balcomb Green, BFA; Art Students League, with Norman Lewis; New Sch Social Res, with Robert Conover; Bob Blackburn Printmaking Workshop. *Work:* Johnson Publ Co, Chicago; Studio Mus In Harlem, NY; Maitland Art Ctr, Fla; City Coll NY; Medgar Evers Col, NY; Nat Mus Women Arts, Washington, DC. *Comn:* Book Jacket, The Power of the Porch (Trudier Harris, auth), Univ Ga Press; New Yorker Mag; Time-Life Bks Inc, Va; Pepsi Cola Co, NY; Coors Brewing Co. *Exhib:* Solo exhibs, Acts of Art, NY, 73-74, Dorsey Gallery, 86, Campbell Gallery, Sewickley, Pa, 87, Jamaica Arts Ctr, NY, 87, Spiral Gallery, NY, 88, Isobel Neal Gallery, Chicago, Ill, 90 & Maitland Art Ctr, 94; Carnegie Inst, Pa; Queens Mus, NY; Hudson River Mus, Yonkers, NY; Salmagundi Club, NY; Am Women in Art, Nairobi, Kenya; Indianapolis Mus Art; Langston Hughes Libr, Queens, NY; Christie's, NY; Savacou Galleries, NY. *Pos:* Consult, NY State Coun Arts. *Teaching:* Adj art instr, Suffolk Co Community Col, 73-75. *Awards:* Harlem Cult Coun Grant, 81. *Bibliog:* Arna Alexander Bontemps Stephenson (auth), Forever Free: Art by African-American Women, 1862-1980; Elton C Fax (auth), Black Artists of the New Generation, Dodd, Mead & Co, 77; Clara Heron (auth), In Celebration of Black History, Pittsburgh Post Gazette, 2/5/87; Robert Henks (auth), The Art of Black American Women-Works of Twenty-Four Artists of the Twentieth Century, McFarland & Co, 93; Leslie King-Hammon (intro), Gumbo Ya Ya: Anthology of Contemporary African American Women Artists, Mid March Arts Press, 95; Perspectives Authentic Voices of African Americans, Curriculum Assoc Inc, 96. *Mem:* Artists Equity Asn. *Media:* Oil, Charcoal. *Dealer:* Cinque Gallery 560 Broadway 5th Floor New York NY 10012; Sragrow Gallery 67-73 Spring St New York NY 10012. *Mailing Add:* 18 Carlton Rd Great Neck NY 11021

TANNENBAUM, BARBARA LEE
CURATOR, HISTORIAN
b Chicago, Ill, Aug 15, 1952. *Study:* Reed Col, Portland, Ore, BA, 75; Univ Mich, Ann Arbor, MA, 77, PhD, 93, Getty Leadership Inst Mus Mgt, 97. *Exhib:* The Art of Seymour Rosofsky, Krannert Art Mus, Champaign-Urbana, Ill, 84 & Cultural Ctr, Chicago, Ill, 85; Hollis Sigler, Akron Art Mus & Cult Ctr, Chicago, Ill, 87; Aminah Robinson: Painting and Sculpture, 87, Akron Art Mus (catalog), Akron Art Mus, 88-89; Ralph Eugene Meatyard: An American Visionary (co-cur), Akron Art Mus, San Francisco Mus Mod Art & Traveling, 91; A History of Women Photographers (co-cur), Akron Art Mus, New York Pub Libr & Traveling, 96; Chakaia Booker: Recent Sculpture, Akron Art Mus, 2000; John Heartfield vs Nazi Germany, Akron Art Mus, 2008; Lee Friedlander's Factory Valley, Akron Art Mus, 2009; Nuclear Enchantment, Photography by Patrick Nagatani, Akron Art Mus, 2009; Detroit Dissembles, Photographs by Andrew Moore, Akron Art Mus, 2010. *Pos:* Cur, Seymour Rosofsky Mem Found, 81-85; cur, Akron Art Mus, 85-96, chief cur, 96-, head pub prog, 97-; dir cur affairs, 2007-. *Teaching:* Vis instr art hist, Univ Ill, Chicago, 82; vis prof art hist, Univ Wyo, Laramie, 83; inst art hist, Oberlin Col, Ohio, 83-85; NE Ohio Univ Col Med, 88-96. *Awards:* Marion Talbot Endowed Fel, Am Asn Univ Women, 80; Henry Luce Found Grant, Univ Mich, 88; 100 Women of Distinction Award, Summit Co YWCA, 01. *Mem:* Nat Adv Bd of Photolucida Asn. *Res:* Contemporary art, photography, outsider art. *Publ:* Auth, Politics, economics and personality as media: the art of the Christos, Nat Arts Guide, 80; ed, The Edwin C Shaw Collection of American Impressionist and Tonalist Painting, Akron Art Mus, 86;

The soul cannot exist without the body: contemporary artists' books, In: Artists' books-Illinois: A Traveling Exhibition, 87; ed & contribr, Akron Art Mus: An Introduction to the Collection, 2001, Ralph Eugene Meatyard: An American Visionary, 91; ed, Detroit Dissembled, Photographs by andrew Moore. *Mailing Add:* c/o Akron Art Mus One S High Akron OH 44308

TANNENBAUM, JUDITH E
CURATOR, CRITIC
b Bronx, NY, Oct 26, 1944. *Study:* Douglass Col, Rutgers Univ, New Brunswick, NJ, BA (Eng), 66; Hunter Col, City Univ New York, MA (art hist), 73. *Collection Arranged:* Concept, Narrative, Document: Recent Photographic Works from the Morton Neumann Family Collection & Three Dimensional Painting, Mus Contemp Art, Chicago; Landscape in Sculpture, Day In/Day Out: Ordinary Life as a Source for Art, Art in Public Places & The Ceramics of Betty Woodman (auth, catalog), 81, Freedman Gallery, Albright Col; Peter Campus: Selected Works 1973-1987, Investigations, 86-89, Innst Contemp Art, Philadelphia. *Pos:* Ed-in-chief, Noyes Art Books, New York, 75-77; acting cur, Mus Contemp Art, Chicago, 78-79; contrib ed, Arts Mag, New York, 73-81; dir, Freedman Gallery, Albright Col, Reading, Pa, 81-86; asst dir, Inst of Contemp Art, Univ of Pa, 86-. *Mem:* Coll Art Asn Am. *Res:* European and American modern and contemporary art. *Publ:* Auth, Ilya Bolotowsky, 74, Arts Mag; auth, Blythe Bohnen: The kinesthetic of form, 77, Arts Mag; ed, New York Art Yearbook, Noyes Art Books, 76; contribr, Handbook of the Guggenheim Museum Collection, S R Guggenheim Mus, New York, 80. *Mailing Add:* 220 E 78th St New York NY 10021

TANNER, JAMES L
CRAFTSMAN
b Jacksonville, Fla, July 22, 1941. *Study:* Fla A&M Univ, BA, 64; Aspen Sch Contemp Art, summer 64; Univ Wis-Madison, MS, 66, MFA, 67; also studied with Harvey Littleton, Donald Reitz, Hal Lotterman & Amos White. *Work:* Renwick Gallery Nat Mus Am Art, Smithsonian Inst, Washington; Am Craft Mus, NY; Mus Contemp Crafts, NY; Everson Mus, Syracuse, NY; Charles A Wustum Mus Fine Arts, Racine, Wis; Frederish R Weisman Art Mus, Minneapolis, Minn; and others. *Exhib:* Objects USA, circulated by Smithsonian Inst, 69-70; Brooks Mem Art Gallery, Memphis, Tenn, 79; The Eloquent Object, circulated US & Japan, Philbrook Mus Art, Tulsa, Okla, 87-89; Craft Today - USA, circulated Europe, Am Craft Mus, NY, 89-91 & Breaking Barriers: Recent Am Craft, circulated US, 95-96; 28th Ceramic Nat Exhib, Everson Mus, NY, 90; Figures in Ceramics, La State Univ, Baton Rouge, 90; SDak Art Mus, Brookings, 90; Eight McKnight Artists, Minneapolis Coll Art & Design, 92; solo show, Minneapolis Inst Art, 95; plus many others. *Pos:* Bd Trustees, Am Craft Coun, 93-94; bd dir, Nat Coun Educ Ceramic Arts, 91-93 & 94-98. *Teaching:* Prof art ceramics, Mankato State Univ, Minn, 68-2003. *Awards:* Nat Endowment Arts Fel, 84 & 90; McKnight Found Fel, 91-92; Minn State Arts Bd Fel, 93. *Bibliog:* Lee Nordness (auth), Objects USA, 70; Ray Grover & Lee Grover (coauth), Contemporary Art Glass, Crown Publ Co Inc, 75; Paul Donhauser (auth), The History of American Ceramics--Studio Potter, WC Brown, Kendall/Hunt Publ, 78. *Mem:* Nat Coun Educ Ceramic Arts; Am Craftsman Coun; Minn Craftsman Coun (bd dir, 72-77); Am Craft Coun; Nat Coun Educ Ceramic Arts (pres, 96-98). *Media:* Ceramics, Mixed Media. *Dealer:* Maurine Littleton Gallery 1667 Wisconsin Ave NW Washington DC 20007. *Mailing Add:* 61449 185 St Janesville MN 56048

TANSEY, MARK
PAINTER
b San Jose, Calif, 1949. *Study:* Art Center Coll Design, LA, Calif, BA, 1972; grad studies in painting, Hunter Col, NY, 1975-78. *Exhib:* Solo exhibs, Grace Borgenicht, 1982, 1984, John Berggruen Gallery, San Francisco, 1984, Contemp Arts Mus, Houston, 1984, Curt Marcus Gallery, NY, 1986, 1990, 1993, 1997, 2000, Walker Art Center, Minn, 1990, Kohn/Abrams Gallery, Los Angeles, 1993, Mus Fine Arts, Boston, 1994, Galleri Faurschou, Copenhagen, 1995, Gagosian Gallery, NY 2004, Mus Kurhaus Kleve, Ger, 2005; Recent Acquisitions, Mus Modern Art, NY, 1983; Biennial Exhib, Whitney Mus Am Art, NY, 1983, 1991; Aperto 86, Venice Biennale, Italy, 1986; Color and/or Monochrome, Nat Mus Modern Art, Tokyo, 1989; 10+10: Contemp Soviet & Am Painters, Corcoran Gallery Art, Washington, DC, 1989; The Charade of Mastery: Deciphering Modernism in Contemp Art, Whitney Mus Am Art, 1990; Mountains of the Mind, Aspen Art Mus, Colo, 1994; Am Kaleidoscope, Nat Mus Am Art, Washington, DC, 1996; Double Trouble: The Patchett Collection, Mus Contemp Art, San Diego, 1998; Reality and Desire, J Miro Found, Barcelona, 1999; The Burbs, DFN Gallery, NY, 2003; Perspectivesat25: A Quarter Century of New Art in Houston, Contemp Arts Mus, 2004; Am Art of the 1980s, Washington Univ Gallery Art, St Louis, Mo, 2004. *Media:* Acrylic, Oil. *Mailing Add:* 80 Warren St New York NY 10007

TAPLEY, EMMA
PAINTER
b NY, 1967. *Study:* Pratt Inst, NY, 86-87; Sch Visual Arts, NY, BFA, 87-91; NY Acad Art, 95-97; Vt Studio Ctr, 97; Byrdcliffe Arts Colony, Woodstock, NY, 98. *Exhib:* Solo exhibs, Surfaces of Light, Small Gallery, NY, 94, archive of LIght, Fischbach Gallery, NY, 99, Streams, Sky Mountains, Trees, 2001, Elements, 2004, Nature Vivant, Hemphill Fine Arts, Washington, DC, 2001, Mountains and Rivers, Sykes Gallery, Millersville, Univ, Pa, 2001, Inversion, Village Zendo, NY, 2006; Group exhibs, Atlantic Gallery, NY, 95-96, 98; Small Matters of Great Importance, Hopper House, 98; East Meets West, Cooper Gallery, Jersey City, 98; Y2$ Artwork for the Millennium, Fischbach Gallery, NY, 2000, Gone Fisching, 2000, H20 '02: Paintings of Water, 2002, Light as Air, 2003, Gone Fisching: Paintings of Summer, 2004, Lost Art, 2006; Though As Place, Catholic Univ, Washington, DC, 2000; Contemporary American Realism III, MA Doran Gallery, Tulsa, 2000, Contemporary Realism V, 2002, Contemporary American Landscape, 2002; Take Home a Nude, Phillips de Pury & Co, 2005; Native Spirit, Brooklyn, 2006. *Awards:* Vt Studio Ctr Arts Grant, 97; ED Found Grant, NY, 2002. *Mailing Add:* 218 E 11th St #16 New York NY 10003

TARADASH, MERYL
ENVIRONMENTAL ARTIST, KINETIC ARTIST
b Passaic, NJ, Jan 25, 1953. *Study:* Conn Coll, New London, 70-71; Banff Sch Fine Arts, Alta, Can, 71; Pratt Inst, New York, BFA, 74, MFA, 78. *Work:* Newark Mus, NJ; Colgate-Palmolive co, New York; AT&T Longlines, Bedminster, NJ; Bellevue Hosp Ctr, New York; NY State Legislature, Albany; Cold Spring Harbor Labs, NY; The Long Island Children's Mus, Garden City, NY; Univ Va Sch Nursing, Charlottesville, Va; The Sculpture Foundation; Grounds for Sculpture, NJ; Stonybrook Hosp, NY. *Comn:* Light Dance (suspended installation), State NJ, Rutgers Med Sch, 84; Waves (suspended installation), ARAMARK Corp, Philadelphia, 89; Wind Dancing, (wind-driven outdoor sculpture), David Bermant Found, Santa Barbara, Calif, 92; Rhodes/Nadler Collection (suspended sculpture), McLean, Va, 2002; Music of Light (suspended installation), Music Ctr at Strathmore, North Bethesda, Md, 2004. *Exhib:* solo exhibs, James A Michener Art Mus, Doylestown, Pa, 97, Elaine Benson Gallery, Bridgehampton, NY, 98 & 2002 & Fordham Univ, Lincoln Ctr Campus, New York, 2001-02, Light, Wind and the Art of Meryl Taradash, Long Island Children's Mus, NY, 2010; Group exhibs, Kinetic Sculpture Show, Hastings Gallery, Hastings-on-Hudson, NY, 90-91; Wind Dancing, Art Mus Univ Calif, Santa Barbara, Calif, 92-93; Jacksonville Art Mus, Jacksonville, Fla, 93; Personal Patterns, Elaine Benson Gallery, Bridgehampton, NY, 89; Strokes of Genius, Artists' Miniature Golf Course, Montclair Art Mus, NJ, 98; New Additions Outdoors, Grounds for Sculpture, Hamilton, NJ, 2007; Wind Through the Trees, Jenkins Arboretum, Devon, Pa, 2010; Sideshow Gallery, Brooklyn, NY, 2012-15. *Teaching:* Vis specialist contemp art, Montclair State Univ, NJ, 88-2003, life drawing I-IV, 89, art & civilization I, 90, drawing II, 96 & 3D design, 2003-13; instr, Sch Visual Arts, Int Prog, New York, 97-2003 & Summer Residency Publ Art Prog, 2005-13; instr, NYC Coll of Tech (CUNY), 2008-15, 3D design, drawing. *Awards:* 1st Prize Int Kinetic Art Competition, 2015; Joan Mitchell Emergency Found Grant, 2014; Brooklyn Arts Coun Panelist, 2014, 2015; Ford Found Grant, 78; Post-Production Video Funds for Documentary Light Dance, NJ State Coun Arts, 85; Fel Panelist Sculpture, NJ State Coun Arts, 92. *Bibliog:* Vivien Raynor (auth), Art from state buildings, NY Times, 85; Kent Kiser (auth), Commissions, Int Sculpture, 86; Jessica Althoz (auth), Commissions, Sculpture Mag, 88; Erica-Lynn Gambino, Sculpture, Vol 18, No 2, 3/99; Mila Andre (auth), Sculptures Take to Great Outdoors, Daily News, 5/4/2001; Dickson Mercer (auth), Strathmore Hall, Frederick News Post, 2/3/2005; Deborah Dietsch (auth), Strathmore a Great Hall of Suburbia, Washington Times, 2/5/2005; Brooke Barrie (auth), New Additions Outdoors, Spring/Summer Exhibitions, Grounds for Sculpture, Hamilton, NJ, 2007; Maureen Korp (auth), Seeing What is Missing: Art, Artists, & September 11, Religion, Terror & Violence, 2008; Maureen Korp (auth), An Art Lover's Hallowed Ground, The Epoch Times, 7/17/2013. *Mem:* Int Sculpture Ctr; Coll Art Asn. *Media:* Rotating Lucite, Aluminum within Stainless Steel, Reflected Light

TARASIEWICZ, TAMARA
PAINTER
b Hajnowka, Poland, Feb 23, 50; US Citizen. *Work:* J K Kluk Agr Mus, Ciechanowiec, Poland; Grodno Mus Hist & Archeol, Belarus; St Nicholas Church, Bialowieza, Poland; Mus Belarusian Cult, Hajnowka, Poland; Metrop Bldg, Warsaw, Poland. *Exhib:* Fairytale World of Nature, J K Kluk Agr Mus, Ciechanowiec, Poland, 91; solo exhib, Mus Belarusian Cult, Hajnowka, Poland, 91; Melodies and Colors of Bialowieza, Grodno Mus Hist & Archeol, Belarus, 92; Beauty of Podlasie, Mus Bielsk Podlaski-Ratusz, Poland, 93; Freedom and Spirit of America, Larsen Fine Arts Ctr, Kankakee, Ill, 98; James R Thompson Ctr, Chicago, Ill, 2000; Pot Pourri, Cornell Mus Art & Hist, Delray Beach, Fla, 2007; I've Got Rhythm, Manhattan Borough President's Gallery, New York, 2008. *Pos:* Owner & dir, Forest Mus & Gallery, Bialowieza, Poland, 94-96. *Awards:* Mayor Bialowieza Award, Poland, 93; First Award, 2nd Rev Art, Hajnowka House Cult, Poland, 95; Cert Recognition, Cook Co Bldg, Maria Pappas, Chicago, 2005; Renee Denmark Mem Award, Indiana Arts Asn, 2005; Excellence Prize, 2nd Art Biennial, Medial Mus, London, 2007; Samuel Rosen Award, Am Soc Contemp Artists, New York, 2007. *Bibliog:* Danuta Peszczynska (auth), Malarstwo Tamary Tarasiewicz, Monitor, 88; Piotr Bajko (auth), Tamara Tarasiewicz - Talent Niezwykly, Gazeta Wspolczesna, 89; Teresa Zaniewska (auth), Wystawa T. Tarasiewicz, Tygodnik Podlaski, 91; W M (auth), article, Echa Lesne, 95; Kalina Jerzy (auth), Puszczanska Galeria, Czasopis, 96. *Mem:* Provincetown Art Asn & Mus, Mass; Chicago Artists Coalition; Nat Asn Women Artists; Art Asn Harrisburg, Pa; Am Soc Contemp Artists. *Media:* Acrylic & Oil. *Publ:* Contribr, New Art Int, Bk Art Press, 2002-2004 & 2006; Trends, 2008 & Masters of Today, 2008, Woa Bks. *Dealer:* Susanins Auctions 900 S Clinton Chicago IL 60607; Agra-Art Auction House ul Wilcza 55/63 Warsaw Poland

TARBET, URANIA CHRISTY
PAINTER, WRITER
b Dec 19, 1931. *Study:* Pasadena Col, 78; Otis Art Inst, 79-81; Sergei Bongart Sch Art, 81-83. *Work:* Loomis, Sayles Co Inc, Pasadena, Calif; South Gate Art Asn Collection, Calif; World Trade Ctr, San Francisco, Calif. *Comn:* pastel portraits, comn by Mr Lyn Nofziger, communication dir to Pres Reagan, Washington, DC, 90; pastel floral painting, comn by Ms M Burton, Casablanca Fan Corp, Newport Beach, Calif, 92; Unison Pastels, Jack Richesson, Kimberly, Wis; Prints from Pastel Original Paintings, Ronad Regan Pres Libr, Simi Valley; Ruth Cameron (portrait), Residential Living Senior Ctr, Cameron Park, Calif. *Exhib:* Pastel Society of Am, Ashland Art Mus, Ky, 90; Pastel Society of Am, Quincey Art Mus, Ill, 90; Degas Pastel Society, Lauren-Rogers Mus Art, Laurel, Miss, 90; Women Artists of the West, Chinese Cult Mus, Visallia, Calif, 92; Am Contemp Outstanding Masters, Dr Sun Yat Sen Mem Mus, Taiwan; Int Asn Pastel Soc Mus Exhib, Denver Hist Mus, Colo; Pastels by Invitation, Chatham, Mass, 2009. *Pos:* Co-founder & vpres, Pastel Soc West Coast, 84-85; pres & founder, Cassatt Pastel Soc/A Nat Soc Prof Artists, 88-90; co-found & pres, Int Asn Pastel Soc, 95-2009, IAPS Emeritus, 2009; ed, Pastel Artist Int Mag. *Teaching:* Instr oil, pastel, art marketing, art workshops throughout US, Mex & Europe, 83-92; instr, Hillcrest Art Ctr, 83-98; instr oil, pastel, St Mary's Art Ctr, 91-92

& St Mary's Art Ctr, 91-98. *Awards:* Fred & Mary Trump Award, Pastel Soc Am; Award Excellence, Degas Pastel Soc, 90; Award Excellence, Women Artists West, 91. *Bibliog:* Patricia Seligman (auth), Trees, Flowers and Foliage, Bastsford Publ; Hazel Harrison, Pastel Sch, Reader's Digest; 200 Painting Ideas for the Artist, Int Artists Mag, North Light, Australia, 12/98. *Mem:* Pastel Soc Am; Knickerbocker Artists; Calif Art Club; Soc Western Artists; pres Sacramento chap, Nat League Am Pen Women; Int Asn Pastel Soc (pres, 94-2001); Salmagundi Club. *Media:* Pastel, Oil. *Publ:* Auth, One artist's experience, Am Artist Mag, 7/89; Urania's Artistic Universe, The Mountain Democrat (weekly column), Placerville, Calif; auth, Flowers Always, Art Revue Mag, summer 95; Everett Raymond Kinstler, Art Revue Mag, Anniversary Issue, 95. *Dealer:* Helen Jones Gallery Sacramento CA; Gallerie Iona Stockton CA. *Mailing Add:* PO Box 567 Pollock Pines CA 95726-0567

TARBOX, GURDON LUCIUS, JR
MUSEUM DIRECTOR, ADMINISTRATOR
b Plainfield, NJ, Dec 25, 1927. *Study:* Mich State Col, BS, 52; Purdue Univ, MS, 54. *Pos:* Trustee, Brookgreen Gardens, Murrells Inlet, SC, 59-, dir, 63 & pres, 90. *Publ:* Contribr, A Century of American Sculpture - Treasures of Brookgreen Gardens, Abbeville Press, 81. *Mailing Add:* 186 Lakes at Litchfield Dr Pawleys Island SC 29585-5515

TARGAN, JUDY
PRINTMAKER, PAINTER
b New York, NY, Oct 12, 1931. *Study:* Smith Col, BA (magna cum laude, Ph Beta Kappa), 53; Rutgers Univ, 55; Fairleigh Dickinson Univ, 56-59. *Work:* State Mus, Trenton, NJ; Newark Mus, NJ; Libr Cong, Washington; Univ Pa, Philadelphia; Smith Coll Mus Art; Montclair Mus Art, NJ; Visual Arts Ctr NJ; and many corporate collections. *Comn:* Women's Div, Jewish Community Fedn, Metropolitan, NJ, 80; Nat Women's Div, Albert Einstein Coll Medicine, NJ, 81; UNICEF greeting cards. *Exhib:* State Mus, Trenton, NJ, 78; Boston Mus Fine Arts, Mass, 78; Newark Mus, NJ, 79; Outstanding Women Artists of NJ, YMHA & YWHA, 79; Unspoken Seasons, NJ Ctr Visual Arts, 95; Wood Works, Hutchins Gallery, Maplewood, NJ, 96; Earth Tapestries, Gallery South Orange, NJ, 98. *Pos:* Art comt, Montclair Mus, NJ; vis comt, Smith Mus Art. *Teaching:* docent, Newark Mus, 88-. *Awards:* Roth Award, Nat Asn Women Artists, 77; Purchase Award, Irvington Art Asn, NJ, 78; First Prize, Summit Art Ctr Regional Show, 79. *Bibliog:* Paintings from New Jersey Collections, The Judith Targan Collection, NJ Visual Arts Ctr; Edward J Nygren (auth), Smith Collects Contemporary, Smith Col, Northampton, Mass, 92. *Media:* Mixed Media, Oil on Wood. *Collection:* Contemporary painting and sculpture. *Publ:* Four commemorative stamps, United Synagogues Am, 76; UNICEF notecards, New York Botanical Garden, 78. *Mailing Add:* 40 Glenside Rd South Orange NJ 07079

TARK, SOONAE
PAINTER
b S Korea. *Study:* Dongduk Women's Univ, Seoul, BFA, 1990; Ecole Nat Superieure Beaux-Arts de Lyon, France, Diplôme Nat d'Art Pratique, 1993; Diplôme Nat Supérieur d'Expression Pratique, 1995. *Work:* NYC Dept Educ. *Comn:* mural work, NYC Percent Art Prog, NYC Public School PS 306, 2008; NYC MTA Art for Transit, Buhre Ave Station, Bronx, 2015. *Exhib:* Solo exhibs, AR Gallery, Lyon, France, 1995, Caffe Dell Artista, New York, 1998, New York Pub Libr, 1998, Hyundai Art Gallery, Seoul, Korea, 2000, David Allen Gallery, Brooklyn, NY, 2002 & 2003, Temple Univ Gallery, Philadelphia, 2002, Garmany, RedBank, NJ, 2009, Deffebach Gallery, Hudson, NY, 2009, Gallery 135, Hudson, NY, 2010, Yegam Art Space, Flushing, NY, 2012; Group exhibs, Katonah Mus Art, NY, 2001, Clifton Arts Ctr, NJ, 2002; Fla State Univ Mus Fine Art, Tallahassee, Fla, 2004; Lake George Art Proj, NY, 2007; OK Harris Works of Art, New York, 2008; Page Bond Gallery, Richmond, Va, 2009; Korean-Am Connections, US Embassy Seoul, Art in Embassies Prog, US Dept State, DC, 2009; Wash Project for the Arts, Wash DC, 2011. *Awards:* Revington Arthur Award, Silvermine Guild Arts Ctr, New Canaan, Conn, 2000; Susan & Phillip Allen Award, Allegheny Arts Coun, Cumberland, Md, 2001; Pollock-Krasner Found Grant, 2001 & 2007; Achievement Award, Long Beach Island Found Arts & Sciences, 2002; 3rd Place, Visions Int Competition, Art Ctr Waco, Tex, 2002; Astravaganza Award, Hunter Mus Am Art, Chattanooga, Tenn, 2002; Juror's Award, Oct Int Competition, Armory Art Ctr, West Palm Beach, Fla, 2002; Juror's Choice Award, Attleboro Mus, Mass, 2003; Beatrice Wofsey Award, Stamford Art Asn, Conn, 2004; 1st Place, Farmington Mus, NMex, 2004; 3rd Place, Kauffman Gallery, Shippensburg Univ, Pa, 2005; 1st Place, Art Ctr Plano, Tex, 2005; 1st Place, La State Univ, Baton Rouge, 2005; Individual Artist Initiative Award, Queens Coun Arts, Woodhaven, NY, 2007; Abbey Mural Painting Fund Fel, Nat Acad, 2008; Emergency Grant, Adolph & Esther Gottlieb Found, New York, 2009. *Bibliog:* D Dominick Lombardi (auth), Exploring the gamut of contemporary art, Katonah Mus Art, NY Times, 6/17/2001; Maya Kremen (auth), Different Strokes at Clifton Show, Herald News, 1/9/2002; Jin Hyae Kim (auth), article, The Korea Times, NY, 11/5/2003; Anne Price (auth), Bigger and better, but compact, The Advocate, Baton Rouge, 4/24/2005; Cover Artist, NYC Mayor's Management Report Mayor, Michael Bloomberg, 2009; US State Dept Desk Calendar, 2012. *Dealer:* James Yarosh Asn Fine Art Gallery 55 East Main St Holmdel NJ 07732; 135 Gallery 135 Warrant St Hudson NY 12534. *Mailing Add:* 4315 45th St #5C Long Island City NY 11104

TARRELL, ROBERT RAY
EDUCATOR, PAINTER
b Oct 18, 1956. *Study:* Univ Wis, Platteville, BS, 80; Univ Iowa, MA, 83; Univ Wis, MFA, 95. *Pos:* Ed, Art Times Newsletter, Wis Art Asn, 98-99. *Teaching:* Prof drawing & painting, Edgewood Coll, Madison, Wis, 90-. *Awards:* Wisconsin Art Educator of the Yr, 2003. *Mem:* Nat Art Educ Asn; Wis Art Educ Asn (pres, 99-2001); Wis Painters & Sculptors Inc; Wis Alliance Arts Educ; Nat Asn Schs Art & Design. *Media:* Oil. *Publ:* Coauth, Wisconsin Art Curriculum Guide, Wis Dept Pub Instr. *Mailing Add:* 4318 Tokay Blvd Madison WI 53711

TARSHIS, JEROME
WRITER
b New York, NY, June 27, 1936. *Study:* Columbia Col, AB, 57. *Awards:* Nat Endowment Arts Art Critic's Fel, 79. *Res:* Hist art mus & exhibs. *Publ:* Contribr, Am Heritage, Art in Am, Christian Sci Monitor, New Fillmore. *Mailing Add:* 25 Sanchez #424 San Francisco CA 94114-1142

TASCHEN, BENEDIKT
COLLECTOR
b Germany, 1962. *Pos:* Founder & mgr, Taschen Publ co, Cologne, 1980-, founder, mgr., publisher, Taschen, Cologne. *Awards:* Named one of Top 200 Collectors, ARTnews mag, 2005-09, 2012, & 2013. *Collection:* Contemporary art, especially American and German. *Mailing Add:* Taschen Hohenzollernring 53 Köln D-50672 Germany

TASENDE, JOSE MARIA
GALLERY DIRECTOR, DEALER
b Bilbao, Spain, 1932; US citizen. *Study:* Inst Bilbao, Basque Country, BA, 48. *Collection Arranged:* Francisco Zuniga: Exhibit of Drawings & Sculpture, Fine Arts Gallery San Diego, 71 & Everson Mus, 77; Jose Luis Cuevas: An Exhibition of Recent Works, Phoenix Art Mus, 75 & Calif Palace Legion Hon, 75; Jose Luis Cuevas Drawings, Brigham Young Univ, 77; Giacomo Manzu: Exhibition of Sculptures & Drawings, Springfield Mus Art, Mo, 78; Roberto Matta: Paintings & Drawings, Metrop Mus, Coral Gables, Fla, 81; Henry Moore Sculptures & Drawings, Blanden Mem Art Gallery, Ft Dodge, Iowa, 82; An Irreverent Approach (exhib), The Meadows Mus, Southern Methodist Univ, Dallas, 90; Pasadena City Col, Calif, 92; Univ Iowa Mus Art, Iowa City, 93. *Mem:* Art Mus Asn Am; Art Dealer Asn Am. *Publ:* Image and Specter (exhib catalog), Jose Luis Cuevas Letters, Tasende Gallery, 81; Personal Approach (exhib catalog), Figure, Space, Image, Tasende Gallery, 85; The American Factor (exhib catalog), Andres Nagel, Tasende Gallery, 90. *Mailing Add:* Tasende Gallery 820 Prospect St La Jolla CA 92037

TASSE, M JEANNE
HISTORIAN, CALLIGRAPHER
b Worcester, Mass, Mar 25, 1925. *Study:* Anna Maria Col, AB, 55; Univ Notre Dame, MA, 62; Boston Univ, PhD, 72, (Spec Study) with Sheila Waters, 87. *Work:* Hymn to the Sun; The Gospel According to Luke; An Old Irish Prayer; Dinner Customs on the Frontier; Psalm XCII, A Strong Insistent Music; Prayer for Animals. *Comn:* Calligraphy, comn by The Mountain State Co, Easter Seals and pvt comns; Marietta Col; Pyles Communs, Anna Maria Col. *Exhib:* By Women's Hands, ECC & MC Faculty Art Shows; All Calligraphy Exhib, Town House Gallery, Marietta Calligraphy; Letters at the Exhibition, 84, 86, 85, 92, 99, 2003, 2005, 2011, 2012. *Collection Arranged:* Marietta Coll Permanent Coll, By Women's Hands, Peoples Art Coll; Putnam-Houser House Gallery, Blennerhasset Island, 2007. *Pos:* Dir Inst Learning in Retirement; coordr Peoples Art Collection, Marietta, Ohio, 1992-2008; chair, Senior Arts Committee 2008-; chair, Winston Scholarships, 2002-2010. *Teaching:* Prof art & music, Anna Maria Col, 55-75; prof art, Marietta Col, 75-92; chmn, Art Dept, 77-82; instr & dir, Inst Learning in Retirement, 92-2010. *Awards:* Art Teacher Award, Artsbridge, 91; Outstanding Prof Achievement, Anna Maria Col, 2001; Zonta Int Woman of the Yr, 2006; Outstanding Educ Award, 2011. *Bibliog:* Calligraphy, The Marietta Times; Beautiful writing, Marietta Coll Mag; Ex-teacher promotes art in area, Parkersburg News. *Mem:* Nat Soc Arts & Lett (nat pres); founding mem Marietta Calligraphy Soc (pres formerly); Nat Mus for Women in the Arts; Parkersburg Art Ctr; Campus Martius Mus; The Castle. *Media:* Pen and Ink. *Res:* Medieval period; Sculpture, manuscripts. *Specialty:* calligraphy. *Interests:* Needlework; Music; Reading. *Collection:* Medieval manuscript folios; miniature prints and paintings. *Publ:* Career Award Winners for NSAL, 94, 2014. *Dealer:* Nat Soc Arts & letters. *Mailing Add:* 200 Timberline Dr #1218 Marietta OH 45750

TATE, BLAIR
TAPESTRY ARTIST, EDUCATOR
b New York, NY, Aug 28, 1952. *Study:* RI Sch Design, BFA, 74; Haystack Mountain Sch Crafts, studied with Jack Larsen, 78. *Work:* Mass Inst Technol, Cambridge; Boston Trade Bank. *Comn:* Inset (tapestry), Rocky Mountain Energy Co, Broomfield, Colo, 81; Crossover (tapestry in two parts), Conn Comn for Arts Stamford, Conn, 83-85; Revisions (tapestry), Southeastern Mass Univ, N Dartmouth, 89; Seton Hall Sch Law, Newark, 92. *Exhib:* Contemp Crafts Americas, Colo State Univ, Ft Collins & traveling, 75; Am Acad, Rome, 77; Three Dimensional Possibilities, Rose Art Mus, Brandeis Univ, Waltham, Mass, 79; National Miniature Textile Exhib, Textile Mus, Washington, DC & traveling, 79-81; Crafts of the Commonwealth, Berkshire Mus, Pittsfield, Mass & traveling, 80-81; Skidmore Coll Invitational, Saratoga Springs, NY, 84; Fiber R/Evolution, Univ Art Mus, Milwaukee & traveling, 86-87; one-person show, La Jolla Mus Contemp Art, 87, Am Craft Mus, NY, 91; 25 for the 25th, Browngrotta Arts, Wilton, Conn, 99. *Pos:* Studio artist, 75-. *Teaching:* Lectr textiles & weaving, Mass Col Art, Boston, 83 & RI Sch Design, 83-87; instr weaving, Sch Art Inst Chicago, 87. *Awards:* Fel, Mass Artists Found, Crafts, 80 & Project Completion Award, 82; Bunting Fel, Bunting Inst, Radcliffe Col, 83-84. *Bibliog:* Jack Larsen & Mildred Constantine (auths), The Art Fabric: Mainstream, Van Nostrand Reinhold, 81 & 85; Barbara Mayer (auth), Contemporary American Craft - A collectors guide, Peregrine Smith Bks, 88. *Mem:* Am Craft Coun. *Media:* Fiber. *Publ:* Auth, The Warp: A Weaving Reference, Van Nostrand Reinhold, 84. *Dealer:* Browngrotta Arts 276 Ridgefield Rd Wilton CT 06897. *Mailing Add:* 209 Clinton St Apt 2R Brooklyn NY 11201-6268

TATE, GAYLE BLAIR
PAINTER
b Abilene, Tex, Apr 3, 1944. *Study:* Univ Wyo, Laramie, 62-64; Fla State Univ, Tallahassee, BS, 67; Loch Haven Art Ctr, Orlando, Fla, 71-72. *Work:* Leigh Yawkey Woodson Mus, Wausau, Wis; Haggin Mus, Stockton, Calif; Huntsville Mus Art, Huntsville, Ala; Krasl Art Ctr, St Joseph, Mo; Montgomery Mus Fine Arts, Ala; Univ

Wyo, Heritage Art Ctr; Pensacola Mus Art, Fla; Portsmouth Mus, Va; Longmont Mus, Colo; Berstrom-Mahler Mus, Neenah, Wis; Lakeview Mus Arts & Sci, Peoria, Ill; Berman Mus Art, Collegeville, Pa. *Comn:* Trompe L'Oeil paintings, comn by Robert Smith, Tampa, Fla, 87 & 88 & Ken Allen, Hendersonville, NC, 88-90, 93-98; Ron Hall, Dallas, 90; Robert Griffin, Charlotte, NC, 91-92; Washburn Obenwager, elevator installation, Philadelphia, Pa, 2008. *Exhib:* Ann Jacob Gallery, Highlands, NC; S & S Dillon, Clayton, Ga; The Picture House, Charlotte, NC; M Kenneth Allen Fine Arts, Hendersonville, NC; Creighton Davis Gallery, Washington, DC, 93-94; and others; Vose Gallery, Boston, Mass; Eleanor Ettinger Gallery, New York; R H Ballard, Wash, Va, 2008. *Pos:* Pres, Tate Gallery, Tallahassee, 72-, Interarts Inc/Tate Galleries, Tampa, 73-83 & Southeast Prof Art Dealers Asn, 80-83; dir, Upper Room Gallery, Biltmore Village, NC, 93-98; Pres, GB Tate & Sons, Fine Art, Laramie, Wyo. *Teaching:* Lectr art & Christianity, 77-; guest lectr, Univ Tampa, 82; Biblical Principles, 85-; art & internet marketing, 98-. *Awards:* First & Third in Painting, Charlotte Spring Show, 91; Exhibitor's Award, Merrimon Galleries, Asheville, NC, 92; Prize, Ann Mus Show, Asheville Art Mus, 94. *Bibliog:* American Artists, Illustrated Survey 1986, New York Art Review, 89; Men of Achievement 1986, Internationale Biographie, 85; Eleanor Ettinger Presents -Trompe L'Oeil, 2003; Art for the New Collector, 2004; Artists Bluebook, 2005-2008; Davenport's Art Reference, 2005. *Mem:* Founding mem, The Seven, Artist Alliance, Asheville, NC (pres, 92-) & Trompe L'Oeil Soc Artists, 2002-2004. *Media:* Oil, Watercolor. *Specialty:* 19th & 20th Cent Amer and Europeean Paintings. *Interests:* Drawing. *Publ:* Auth, Miro, The Early Works, Interarts Inc, 78; Chapter One, Verse One, Living Waters Press, 89. *Dealer:* John Dupree Creighton-Navis Gallery 5501 Wilkins Ct Rockville MD 20852

TATHAM, DAVID FREDERIC
HISTORIAN
b Wellesley, Mass, Nov 29, 1932. *Study:* Univ Mass, AB; Syracuse Univ, MA & PhD. *Teaching:* Prof hist art, Syracuse Univ, 68-2002; Prof emer fine arts, Syracuse Univ. *Awards:* Am Art J Award, 84; H A Moe Prize, NY State Hist Asn, 91; J B Show Prize, 95; Newman Prize, Am Hist Print Soc, 2004. *Mem:* Coll Art Asn; Am Antiq Soc; life fel Athenaeum Philadelphia; Royal Soc Arts. *Res:* American painting and graphic arts of the nineteenth and twentieth centuries, contemporary art museum issues. *Publ:* Auth, Winslow Homer's Drawings, Lowe Art Gallery, 79; Winslow Homer in the 1880's, Everson Mus, 83; ed, Prints and Printmakers of New York State 1825-1940, Syracuse Univ Press, 86; Winslow Homer and the Illustrated Book, Syracuse Univ Press, 92; Fishing in the North Woods: Winslow Homer, Mus Fine Arts, Boston; Winslow Homer in the Adirondacks, 96 & Winslow Homer and the Pictoral Press, 2003, Syracuse Univ Press; North American Prints 1913-1947, Syracuse Univ Press, 2006; Winslow Homer at Houghton Farm, Syracuse Univ Art Gallery, 2009; Winslow Homer in London, Univ Press, Syracuse, 2010

TATRO, RONALD EDWARD
SCULPTOR, INSTRUCTOR
b Kankakee, Ill, Jan 12, 1943. *Study:* Southern Ill Univ, BA & MFA. *Work:* San Jose Mus Art, Calif; Southwestern Col; Fluor Corp, Irvine, Calif; Saddleback Col, Mission Viejo, Calif; Coleman Col, La Mesa, Calif. *Comn:* Shape Mountain No 4 (12' high), Co San Diego, Health Servs Complex, Calif, 89; Cube On Point (12' high), Paragon Gateway, Mariner Sq Loop, Alameda, Calif, 91; Shadows and Squiggles (8' h x 6' w x 18″ d wall sculpture), Technimed-Vernon, Calif, 92; Still Life No 3, Luce, Foward, Hamilton & Scripps, San Diego, Calif, 92; Laguna Sunrise (10' high), AT&T Global Information Solutions, San Diego, Calif, 94. *Exhib:* Fourteenth Ann Purchase Prize Competition, Riverside Art Ctr & Mus, Calif, 76; Calif Hawaii Biennial, San Diego Mus Art, 76; San Jose Mus Art, Permanent Collection Exhib, Calif, 85; New Art Forms-Chicago Int Expos, Nave Pier, Ill, 88; Art 17, 86, Art 19, 88, Art 20, 89, Art 21, 90, Basel Art Fair, Switz, 87; solo exhibs, Lever Meyerson Gallery, NY, 87, David Zapf Gallery, San Diego, Calif, 93 & Wylie & May Louis Jones Art Gallery, Bakersfield Col, Calif, 98; Erika Meyerovich Gallery, San Francisco, Calif, 93, 94, 95, 96, 97 & 98; Artwalk at the Paladion, San Diego, Calif, 94; Artwalk San Diego, David Zapf Gallery, Calif, 95 & 96; LA Current: The Fall Spectrum, Art Rental & Sales Gallery, Armand Hammer Mus Art & Cult Ctr, Calif, 96, Full Spectrum, 96, New View, 97, A Media Fusion, 97, Looking at the Light-3 Generations of Los Angeles Artists, 98; and others. *Teaching:* Instr basic art, Southern Ill Univ, Carbondale, 66-67; asst prof art, Va State Col, 67-68; instr sculpture, Grossmont Col, 68-95, instr art, 95-, dept chmn, 95-. *Awards:* Third Prize in Sculpture, San Diego Art Inst, 75; Juror's Award, Crafts-Sculpture-Painting-Graphics, Orange Co Art Asn, 76; Muckenthaler Cult Ctr, Fullerton, Calif, 79. *Media:* Steel. *Dealer:* Meyerovich Gallery San Francisco CA. *Mailing Add:* 202 Highline Tr El Cajon CA 92021

TAUBES, TIMOTHY EVAN
CRITIC, CURATOR
b New York, NY, June 6, 1955. *Study:* Ohio Univ, BA, 77; Hunter Col, art history with Rosalind Krauss & E C Goosens, MBA, 79. *Work:* Artists' Choice Mus, NY. *Exhib:* Abstractscapes, Longboat Key, Fla, 88. *Collection Arranged:* Frederic Taubes Memorial Retrospective, Butler Inst Am Art, Youngstown, Ohio, Canton Art Inst, Ohio & Westmoreland Mus, Greensberg, Pa, 83; Frederic Taubes-Paintings & Drawings, Marymount Manhattan Coll Art Gallery, NY, 84; Realist Antecedents, Artists' Choice Mus, NY, 85. *Pos:* Exec dir, Artists' Choice Mus, New York, 83-86; dir, Gallery Educ Ctr, Longboat Key, Fla, 87. *Teaching:* The Educ Ctr, Longboat Key, Fla, 87. *Bibliog:* Article in Art World Mag, 10/84, 3/85. *Res:* 20th century American painting. *Publ:* Contribr, J Artists' Choice Mus, Vols 5-8, 84-86; Chronicles, 3/93; Art & Philosophy, Prometheus Books, 93

TAVENNER, PATRICIA MAY
ARTIST
b Doster, Mich. *Study:* Mich State Univ, BA; Calif Coll Arts, San Francisco, Calif, MFA (painting & art hist). *Work:* San Francisco Mus Art; J Paul Getty Mus, Los Angeles; Royal Mus Fine Arts, Antwerp, Belgium; Sackner Mus, Miami, Fla; Mus Mod Art, New York. *Comn:* Facade, Mus Contemp Crafts, NY, 71; sect of wall, Can Nat Res Libr, Ottawa, 73; Univ Calif, San Francisco, 95 & 98. *Exhib:* Inst Environ, Paris, France, 74; solo exhibs, Mills Col, Oakland, 74, OHS Parsens, Los Angeles, Calif, 82, Atkins Mus Fine Arts, Kansas City, Mo, 85, Mus Mod Kunst, Weddel, Ger, 87, Univ Calif, Berkeley Exten, 85, 89, 92 & 97; Am Hist, Atlanta Coll of Art, 88; Davidson Gallery, Seattle, Wash, 89; Mus Fine Arts, Budapest, Hungary, 2007. *Collection Arranged:* Mus Mod Art, New York; J Paul Getty Mus, Los Angeles; San Francisco Mus Mod Art. *Teaching:* Univ Calif, Berkeley Exten, 67-2007, drawing, Photosilkscreen. *Awards:* Acquisitions, San Francisco Mus Mod Art; Residency, Centrum Frans, Belgium; Artist Stamps, Fine Arts Mus, Budapest, Hungary. *Bibliog:* Thomas Albright (auth), Bay Area Art, Univ Calif Press. *Mem:* Womens Caucus for Art; Calif Soc Printmakers; YLEM Art Tech; Coll Art Asn. *Media:* Collage, Prints, Photo & Mixed Media Collages. *Interests:* Drawing, art, travel, food. *Publ:* Contribr, Art: A Womans Sensibility, 75; A Point of View, D Balator, Nat Ctr Contemp Art, Moscow, 98; auth, Divine Inspiration: How to Release the Artist Within, Eternal Press, 2010; auth, 4 Years & Move, Eternal Press, 80; auth, How to Release the Artist within, Eternal Press, 2011; serial pub by Artist Sinee, 55, Appeditions, New York, 2009; Cont to Feminist Who Changed the World 65-75, Love Ed, Univ Ill Press. *Mailing Add:* PO Box 11032 Piedmont CA 94611

TAY, ENG
PAINTER
b Kedah, Malaysia, 1947. *Study:* Sch Visual Arts, NY, 67-72; Art Students League, NY, 68; Pratt Graphic Ctr, NY, 72-78. *Work:* Alor Seter Art Mus, Kedah, Malaysia; NY Univ; Pratt Graphics Ctr, NY; Singapore Develop Bank, Singapore; US Embassy Malaysia, Kuala Lumpur. *Exhib:* Solo exhibs, Nan Gallery, Taipei, Taiwan, 85, FAO Gallery, Fla, 86, Hsiung Shih Gallery, Taipei, 87, JRS Fine Art, RI, 87 & 90, Galerie Du Monde, Hong Kong, 88, Gallery Citra, Malaysia, 90 & Art Base Gallery, Singapore, 90; Multiple Impressions Gallery, NY, 91; Parkshore Gallery, Fla, 91; Premier Gallery, Va, 91; Portfolio Gallery, Eng, 91; Ginger Gallery, Eng, 91; John Sewell Fine Art, Eng, 91. *Publ:* Contribr, Eng Tay Illustrated Graphics, 87; Hsiung Shih, Art Mag, 11/87; Better Life Monthly, 1/88; The Works of Eng Tay, Sunstorm Arts Mag, 3/90; Eng Tay, World tour, Art Bus News, 10/90

TAYLOR, ALISON ELIZABETH
SCULPTOR
b Selma, Ala, 1973. *Study:* Art Ctr Coll Design, BFA, 2001; Columbia Univ, MFA, 2005. *Exhib:* High on Life, Am Visionary Art Mus, Baltimore, 2002; Hungry Eyes, Wallach Gallery, Columbia Univ, 2004; Other America, Exit Art, New York, 2005; Truly She Is None Other, New Image Art Gallery, Los Angeles, 2006; solo exhib, Coll Wooster Art Mus, Ohio, 2009; 85th Ann Invitational Exhib Contemp Am Art, Nat Acad Mus, New York, 2010. *Awards:* Louis Comfort Tiffany Found Grant, 2009. *Bibliog:* Blake Gopnik (auth), Going with the Grain to Convey Her Vision, Washington Post, 6/7/2008; Shi Jiu (auth), Portraying the Americans, Southern People Weekly, 9/2009; Karen Rosenberg (auth), Academy Gives Art Some Wiggle Room, NY Times, 2/28/2010. *Media:* Wood. *Mailing Add:* c/o James Cohan Gallery 533 W 26th St New York NY 10001

TAYLOR, ANN
PAINTER
b Rochester, NY, Mar 23, 1941. *Study:* Vassar Coll; New Sch Univ, BA (Eng), 62; self-taught painter; legal assisting prog, Phoenix Coll, 94-95. *Work:* Bank Am, Houston; Bausch & Lomb Inc & Xerox, Rochester; Palm Springs Desert Mus, Calif; Honeywell Inc, Minneapolis; and others. *Comn:* Paintings, Central Trust Co, Cincinnati, Ohio, 75; Third Nat Bank, Dayton, Ohio, 79; A C Neilson Corp, Northbrook, Ill, 85. *Exhib:* Butler Inst Am Art, Youngstown, Ohio, 66; Gallery Mod Art, NY, 67; Saginaw Art Mus, 68 & 84; Mem Art Gallery, Univ Rochester, 70; Scottsdale Ctr Arts, Ariz, 82 & 84; Rochester Mus & Sci Ctr, 84; Palm Springs Desert Mus, 84; Yuma Fine Arts Ctr, 84; Reed Whipple Cult Ctr, 84; Beaumont Art Mus, 85; CG Rein Galleries, Scottsdale; Gallery vander woude, Palm Springs, Calif, 86; Oxford Gallery, Rochester, NY, 87 & 95; Marilyn Butler Fine Art, Scottsdale, 87; Perry Sherwood Fine Art, Petoskey, 94; Solo exhibs, Scottsdale Ctr Arts, 85, Beaumont Art Mus, 85, Gallery Vander Woude, Palm Springs, Calif, 86, Oxford Gallery, Rochester, 87 & 95, Marilyn Butler Fine Arts, Scottsdale, 87, Rochester Mus & Sci Ctr, 92, Perry Sherwood Fine Art, Petoskey, 92; Indianapolis Ctr Contemp Art; Gallery Mod Art, NY; Everson Mus, Syracuse, NY; Janet Fleischer Gallery, Philadelphia; and others. *Pos:* Asst to com photogr, Jack Cowley Studios, NY, 66-70. *Teaching:* Pvt tutor English, NY, 65-70; pvt tutor, substitute teacher in language arts & humanities, creative writing, res, hist & social studies, grades 7-12, Scottsdale, Ariz, 95-98. *Awards:* Commemorative Lithograph Competition, Scottsdale Ctr for the Arts, 85. *Bibliog:* Donna Marxer (auth), Painting the very air, Southwest Art, 2/78; Carol Kotrozo (auth), Ann Taylor, Artspace, 4/81; Donald Locke (auth), Ann Taylor, Arts Mag, 2/83 & 3/84; Barbara Cortright (auth), The Reach of Solitude: The Paintings of Ann Taylor, Paul S Eriksson Publ, 83. *Mem:* Las Villas Homeowners Asn (property mgr, treas bd dir, 81-87, 94-98). *Media:* Oil, Lithographs. *Publ:* researcher, ed, designer, pub, documentary, All of Us: A Biographical History of John Jacob Bausch and his descendants, 1830 to 1978, 75-78; ed, co-designer, The Reach of Solitude: The Paintings of Ann Taylor, Paul S Erikson, pub, 1981-82; researcher, ed, designer, Rollie McKenna: A Life in Photography, Alfred A Knopf, Inc, 91; The Reach Beyond, 2011. *Mailing Add:* 7209 E McDonald Dr No 30 Scottsdale AZ 85250

TAYLOR, BRIAN DAVID
PHOTOGRAPHER, EDUCATOR
b Tucson, Ariz, June 14, 1954. *Study:* Univ Calif, San Diego, BA(visual arts, cum laude), 75; Stanford Univ, MA, 76; Univ NMex, studied with Beaumont Newhall, MFA(art), 79, Univ of New Mexico, MFA. *Work:* San Francisco Mus Mod Art, Calif; Bibliot Nat, Paris; Int Mus Photog, Rochester, NY; Australian Photog Soc, Victoria; Victor & Albert Mus, London, Eng. *Comn:* Logitech Corp, Silicon Valley, Calif. *Exhib:* Solo exhibs, Nagase Photo Salon, Tokyo, 85, Triton Mus, 90 & Ctr Photog Arts, 95; Facets of the Collection, San Francisco Mus Mod Art, 87; The Human

Vessel, Antwerp Mus Photog, Belg, 88; Picturim Calif, Oakland Mus, 89; Recent Acquisitions, Int Mus Photog, 89; Sneak Previews, Ansel Adams Ctr, 90; Gerald Peters Gallery, Dallas, Tex, 2006; Triton Mus, 2006; Modernbook Gallery, 2007; Gallery 291, San Francisco, 2010; Group exhibitions Jack Glenn Gallery, San Diego, 1974, Arizona State Univ, Tempe, 1978, 1989, Australian Mus, 1981, Catskill Center for Photography, NY, 1984, Vanderbilt Univ, 1986, Antwerp Mus of Photography, 1988, San Jose Inst for Contemporary Art, 1991, Triton Mus, 2001, Palo Alto Art Ctr, 2007, Ctr for Photographic Arts, 2008, Mentenkov Mus of Photography, Russia, 2011-12, Oakland Mus of Calif, 2011-12 and several others. *Collection Arranged:* Permanent collections Bibliotheque Nationale, Paris, Victoria and Albert Mus, London, San Francisco Mus of Modern Art, Los Angeles County Mus of Art, International Mus of Photography George Eastman House, Rochester, NY, San Jose Mus of Art, Calif, Oakland Mus, Calif, Smithsonian Institution Nat Mus of American Art, Calif State Univ Art Mus, Long Beach and several others. *Pos:* Pres, Bd Dir, Ctr for Photographic Art, Carmel, Calif, 2004-2006; Juror, Hawaii Photography Expo, 2010, Viewpoint Photography Contest, Sacremento, Calif, 2011; co-juror, Ctr for Photographic Art Exhibition, 2012; taught photography workshops for over 20 years at several institutions. *Teaching:* Prof Art & design, photog, Calif State Univ, San Jose, 79-, chair Department of Art and Art History, 2010-. *Awards:* Visual Arts Fel, Santa Clara Co, 90 & 96; Polaroid Artists Grant, New York Studio, 90; Regional Fel, Nat Endowment Arts, 91. *Bibliog:* Robert Hirsch (auth), Photographic Possibilities, Focal Press, 90, revised ed 2007, cover image, 2008; Stewart Tabori (auth), The Painted Photograph, Pa State Univ, 95; John P Schaefer (auth), The Ansel Adams Guide: Basic Techniques of Photography, Book 2, Little Brown Co Publ, 98. *Mem:* Soc Photog Educ (chair, West Coast region, 89-92, Honored educator, 2011); Coll Art Asn; Phi Kappa Phi. *Media:* Photography. *Publ:* Auth, Places of Magic, Darkroom Photog Mag, Vol 9, No 8, 12/87; work published in American Photographer, Photo Asia, and Exploring Color Photography. *Dealer:* Chris Winfield Gallery Carmel CA; Modernbook Gallery Palo Alto CA; Gerald Peters Gallery Dallas TX. *Mailing Add:* School of Art and Design San Jose State University One Washington Square Art Building 116 San Jose CA 95192-0089

TAYLOR, BRIE (BENJAMIN DE BRIE)
EDUCATOR, PAINTER
b Paris, France, Mar 5, 1923; US citizen. *Study:* Harvard Univ, BS, 47; Art Students League NY, dipl, 55. *Work:* Johnson Mus, Cornell Univ; Mus Mod Art Miami, Fla. *Exhib:* Butler Inst Biennial, 57; Am Artists, Dallas Mus Fine Arts, 57; Brooklyn and Long Island Artists, Brooklyn Mus, 58 & 60-62; solo exhib, Mus Mod Art Miami, Fla, 59; Contemp Am Painting, Whitney Mus, 60; Corcoran Gallery Biennial, 61; West Side Artists, Riverside Mus, NY, 66; Indiana Artists, Indianapolis Mus Art, 71. *Pos:* Dean, Parsons Sch Design, 68-70 & Herron Sch Art, Ind Univ, 70-73; dir, Inst Design, Ill Inst Technol, 73-75. *Teaching:* Instr painting & drawing, Pratt Inst, 60-68; instr drawing & visual communications, Parsons Sch Design, 67-70; prof drawing & art hist, Inst Design, Ill Inst Technol, 73-87, prof emer, 87-. *Awards:* Fels, MacDowell Colony, 62 & Yaddo, 62. *Bibliog:* James R Mellow (auth), In the galleries, Arts Mag, 10/58; Dore Ashton (auth), Art, NY Times, 10/3/58; Henry Butler (auth), New Herron dean, Indianapolis News, 10/30/70. *Mem:* Coll Art Asn; Art Students League; S Co Art Asn (pres, 92-96). *Media:* Oil, Watercolors. *Publ:* Auth, Towards a plastic revolution, Art News, 64; A problem in painting, Sch Arts, 67; John Heliker, Arts Mag, 68; articles, Art, Crowell-Collier, 62, 63, 64, 67, 68, 69 & 70; Design Lessons From Nature, Watson-Guptill, 74

TAYLOR, CHRISTOPHER
GLASS BLOWER
b Tehran, Iran, 1970. *Study:* Ohio State Univ, BFA, 1999; RI Sch Design, MFA, 2002. *Exhib:* Glass Triennial, Providence Art Club, RI, 2000; Reticello, The Glasmuseum, Ebeltoft, Denmark, 2003; solo exhibs, ArtSpace, New Haven, Conn, 2003, Artists Space, New York, 2006, Real Art Ways, Hartford, Conn, 2009; Exit Art Biennial 2006, Exit Art, New York, 2006; Ongoing Invention, Fullerton Mus, San Bernadino, Calif, 2007; Fac Exhib, RI Sch Design Mus, 2009. *Awards:* Louis Comfort Tiffany Found Grant, 2009. *Bibliog:* Dagmar Brendstrup (auth), Salut to an Old Technique, Neus Glass/New Glass, 4/2003; Bill van Syclen (auth), Glass 06, Providence J, 2/10/2006; Roger Catlin (auth), Cars, a Dinghy, a Skyscape at Real Art Ways, The Hartford Courant, 5/21/2009

TAYLOR, DAVID J
PHOTOGRAPHER
b 1968. *Study:* Tufts Univ & Sch Mus Fine Arts, BFA (Studio Art/Photog), 1989; Univ Ore, MFA (visual design/photog, David McCosh Mem Scholar), 1994. *Work:* Mus Contemp Photog, Columbia Coll, Chicago; Wash State Arts Comn, Olympia. *Comn:* Ryan & Sanders, LLP, 2003; US Gen Services Admin, 2004; Horak Develop/US Border Patrol, 2006. *Exhib:* Solo exhibs include Obscura Gallery, Portland, Ore, 1994, Univ Ore Mus Art, Eugene, 1995, Quartersaw Gallery, Portland, Ore, 1998, Soc Contemp Photog, Kansas City, Mo, 2001, Ironton Studios & Gallery, Denver, 2001, SPAS Gallery, Rochester Inst Tech, NY, 2008; group exhibs include Human Relationships with Place & Time, CUNY Lehman Coll, Bronx, NY, 1995; Nature & History, Renshaw Gallery Linfield Coll, McMinnville, Ore, 1995; Constructs, Benton County Historical Mus, Philomath, Ore, 1996; Harvesting the Land, Ball State Univ Mus Art, Muncie, Ind, 1997; From Tractors to Tornadoes, Whatcom Mus, Bellingham, Wash, 1999; Re-Imaging the West, SF Camerawork, San Francisco, 2001; Regarding Water in the West, Landmark Arts, Tex Tech Univ, Lubbock, 2004; Water, Northlight Gallery, Ariz State Univ, Tempe, 2004 ; Passing Through/Settling In, Stanlee & Gerald Rubin Ctr Vis Arts, Univ Tex El Paso, 2006. *Pos:* Gallery dir, Linfield Coll Renshaw Gallery, McMinnville, Ore, 1997-99. *Teaching:* Grad teaching fel, Univ Ore Dept Fine Art, 1993-94; adj fac, Ore Coll Art & Craft, 1995-97, Linfield Coll, Dept Art, McMinnville, Ore, 1995-99; asst prof, Dept Art, NMex State Univ, Las Cruces, 1999-2003, assoc prof, 2003-. *Awards:* Purchase Award, Evolving Medium: Biennial Photog Exhib, 1994; Fac Develop Grant, Linfield Coll, 1997; Merit Award for Current Works, 1998; Fac Minigrant, NMex State Univ, 2000, 2002, 2004; Nexus Press Proj Grant, Atlanta Contemp Art Ctr, 2001; John Simon Guggenheim Mem Found Fel, 2008. *Dealer:* Bonni Benrubi Gallery 52 E 76th St New York NY 10021

TAYLOR, DAVIS
EDUCATOR
Study: Sch Mus Fine Arts, Diploma in Fine Arts; Tufts Univ, BS (educ); Milton Avery Grad, Sch Arts Bard Col, MFA. *Exhib:* Whitney Biennial, Whitney Mus Am Art, 2004; Triple Candle, NY; Inst Contemp Art, Boston; Green Street Gallery, Boston; Chicago Arts Coun. *Teaching:* Asst prof, Mass Col Art, 99-; fac mem, Milton Avery Sch Arts Bard Col, 2003-. *Awards:* Recipient Artist Prize, Inst Contemp Art, 2001; Asn Int Arts Critics Award, 2002; grant St Botolph Found Grant, 2003

TAYLOR, HENRY
PAINTER
b Oxnard, Calif, 1958. *Study:* Calif Inst Arts, BFA, 1995. *Exhib:* Solo exhibs include Calif Inst Arts, Valencia, 1995, Georges, LA, 1999, 1234 Gallery, LA, 2000, Sister, LA, 2004, 2006, Daniel Reich Gallery, New York, 2005, Atelier Cardenas Bellanger, Paris, 2007, Studio Mus in Harlem, New York, 2007, Samson Projects, Boston, 2008, Santa Monica Mus, Calif, 2008; two-person exhib, Repeat After Me: I AM a Revolutionary, Rental Gallery, NY, 2007 & Peres Projects, Berlin, 2008; group exhibs include Nervous, Calif Inst Arts, 1994, Water & Power, 1995; Eccentric Abstraction II, 1234 Gallery, LA, 2000; Losing My Head, Sister, LA, 2004; Calif Earthquakes, Daniel Reich Gallery, New York, 2004; SPF: Self Portraits, Angles Gallery, LA, 2004; LAXed, Peres Projects, Berlin, 2006; Metro Pictures, Part 2, Mus Contemp Art, North Miami, 2006; Red Eye: LA Art from the Rubell Family Collection, Miami, 2006; Paper Bombs, Jack Hanley Gallery, LA, 2007

TAYLOR, JANET R
TAPESTRY ARTIST, WEAVER
b Lima, Ohio, Jan 19, 1941. *Study:* Cleveland Inst Art, BFA, 1963; Syracuse Univ Sch Art, MFA, 1965. *Comn:* Tapestries, Morris Knudson hq, Boise, Idaho, 1981; tapestries, Corpus Christi Bank, Tex, 1982; tapestry, Neshaminy Complex, Trevose, Pa, 1985; tapestries, The Boulders Resort, Carefree, Ariz, 1986; tapestries, Westcourt in the Buttes, Tempe, Ariz, 1986. *Exhib:* Solo exhibs, Swan Gallery, Philadelphia, 1983 & Willingheart Gallery, Austin, Tex, 1985; group exhibs, The Creative Spirit, Maier Mus Art, Lynchburg, Va, 1985; Woven Works, Univ Wis, Green Bay & traveling, 1985; Fiber and Clay, Augustana Col, Rock Island, Ill, 1985; The Hand and the Spirit Gallery, Scottsdale, Ariz. *Pos:* Dir Janet Taylor Studio, Asheville, NC, 1990-. *Teaching:* asst prof fiber art, Kent State Univ, Ohio, 1969-76; prof fiber art, Sch Art, Ariz State Univ, Tempe, 1977-2000, prof emer, 2000-; guest artists, instructor & bd trustees, Penland Sch Crafts, NC. *Bibliog:* Tapestries by Janet Taylor, Fiberarts Mag, 9-10/82; Contemporary tapestry, Interior Design, 11/85; Commissions, Am Craft Mag, 4-5/86. *Mem:* Am Craft Coun. *Media:* Tapestry

TAYLOR, MAGGIE
PHOTOGRAPHER
b Cleveland, Ohio, 1961. *Study:* Yale Univ, BA (philos), 83; Univ Fla, MFA, 87. *Work:* Fogg Art Mus, Harvard Univ, Cambridge, Mass; Mus Fine Arts, Houston, Tex; Princeton Univ Art Mus, NJ; Mobile Mus Art, Ala; Mus de la Photog, Charleroi, Belgium; High Mus, Atlanta, Ga; Santa Barbara Mus Art, Calif; Harn Mus Art, Gainesville, Fla; Ctr Creative Photog, Tucson; City Orlando, Fla; Davidson Coll Art Gallery, Davidson, NC; Museet Fotokunst, Odense, Denmark; Nations Bank, Charlotte, NC; Prudential Insurance co, Newark, NJ; Art Mus, Univ Nev, Las Vegas. *Exhib:* What Photographs Look Like, Art Mus, Princeton Univ, NJ, 95; Common Elements, Islip Art Mus, NY, 97; solo exhibs, Univ Ctr Gallery, Univ Ala, Huntsville, 98, Bassetti Fine Art Photogs, New Orleans, 98 & Space Gallery, W Mich Univ, Kalamazoo, 98, Lawrence Miller Gallery, NYC, 2005, Huntington Mus Art, WVa, 2005, Verve Fine Arts, Santa Fe, NMex, 2006, John Cleary Gallery, Houston, 2007, Mus Photog, Seoul, Korea, 2007; group exhibs, Jackson Fine Arts, Atla, 92, Creadle Sch Art, Fla, 94, Irvine Fine Arts, Calif, 97, The Equitable Gallery, NY, 99, Laurence Miller Gallery, NY, 2000, Halsey Gallery, Charleston, 2002, Critical Mass, Blue Sky Gallery, Portland, Ore, 2005, Through Others' Eyes, J Johnson Gallery, Jacksonville, Fla, 2006, Picturing Eden, George Eastman House, Rochester, NY, 2006; plus many others. *Awards:* Individual Artists Grant, State of Fla, 96, 2001; Grand Prize, Photo Dist News/PIX Mag Ann Digital Imaging Competition, 2000; Project Competition winner, Santa Fe Ctr Photog, 2004. *Bibliog:* Amy Standen (auth), Maggie Taylor's Landscapes of Dreams, Peachpit Press, Berkeley, Calif, 2005. *Mem:* Soc Photog Educ. *Media:* Photography, Digital Imagery. *Publ:* coauth, Solutions Beginning with A, Modernbook Ed, Palo Alto, Calif, 2007. *Mailing Add:* Verve Fine Arts 219 E Marcy St Santa Fe NM 87501

TAYLOR, MARILYN JORDAN
ADMINISTRATOR, EDUCATOR, ARCHITECT
Exhib: Radcliffe Col, BA, 1969; Univ Calif, Berkeley, MA (archit), 1974. *Pos:* Architect, Skidmore Owings & Merrill LLP, Washington, 1971, ptnr, Urban Design and Planning Practice, 1995, chmn, formerly, consulting ptnr, currently; chmn, NY Building Congress, 2002-03. *Teaching:* Dean, Sch of Design, Univ Pa, 2008-, Paley prof, currently. *Awards:* David Rockefeller Fellowship, Partnership for New York City, 1995. *Mailing Add:* University of Pennsylvania School of Design 102 Meyerson Hall 210 S 34th St Philadelphia PA 19104

TAYLOR, MICHAEL D
HISTORIAN
b Philadelphia, Pa. *Study:* Swarthmore Col, BA, 63; Princeton Univ, MFA, PhD, 70. *Teaching:* Asst prof art hist, Univ Chicago, 66-74; assoc prof & chmn, Univ Mo, St Louis, 74-84; prof & chmn, Univ Houston, 84-89; prof, Univ Mass, Dartmouth, 89- & dean, 89-98. *Mem:* Coll Art Asn; Nat Asn Schs Art & Design; Int Coun Fine Arts

Deans. *Res:* Medieval and early Renaissance imagery. *Publ:* Auth, Prophetic scenes at Orvieto, Art Bull, 72; A historiated tree of Jesse, Dumbarton Oaks Papers, 80-81; The Pentecost at Vezelay, Gesta, 80; Gentile la fabriano shame, J Family Hist, 82. *Mailing Add:* Univ Mass Col Visual & Performing Arts North Dartmouth MA 02747

TAYLOR, MICHAEL (ESTES)
INSTRUCTOR, SCULPTOR
b Lewisburg, Tenn, May 10, 1944. *Study:* Middle Tenn State Univ, BS, 1967; E Tenn State Univ, MA, 1968; Univ Wis, Post Grad Fel, 1970; E Tenn State Univ, MFA, 1977. *Work:* Corning Mus Glass, NY; Smithsonian Inst; Mus fur Kunsthandiwerk, Frankfurt, W Ger; Vanderbilt Univ, Tenn State Mus & Metrop Govt, Nashville; Speed Art Mus, Louisville, Ky; Chrysler Mus of Art, Norfolk, Va; and others. *Comn:* Sculpture, Bella Mare Towers, Miami, Fla; Awards, NY Gov Arts Awards, Albany; Sculpture, Nmseoul Univ, Seoul, Korea; Sculpture, Kanazawa Grand Hotel, Kanazawa, Japan; Sculpture, Seasons Hotel, Dobra, Qatar. *Exhib:* Boise Gallery of Art, Rosenthal Gallery Art, Caldwell, 80, Idaho; Contemp Art Glass Gallery, Toronto, Ont, 82; Elaine Potter Gallery, San Francisco, Calif, 84-85; Glass Now 85, Yamaha Nippon Gakki, Hamamatsu, World Glass Now '85, Hokkaido Mus Mod Art, Sapporo, Shimonoseki City Art Mus, 85, Japan; Sculptural Glass Invitational, Erie Art Mus, Pa, 85; Renwick Gallery, Smithsonian Inst, Washington, 94; The Studio, Corning Mus of Glass, Corning, NY; Resources Exhib, Bevier Gallery Art, RIT, Rochester, NY; Eighteenth Ann Int Invitational Glass Exhib, Habatat Galleries, Boca Raton, Fla; Glass Am '02, Heller Gallery, NY, 2001; Hodgell Gallery, Sarasota, Fla, The Furnace Found, Istanbul, Turkey, Gallery Artists, Sandra Ainsley Gallery, Toronto, Ontario, Can, 2002; Leo Kaplan Mod Gallery, NY; Clearly Influential Contemp Am Glass Art Educ; Tittot Mus Art, Taipei, Taiwan, Repub China; Contemp Glass, 20th Ann Int Invitational Habatat Galleries, Boca Raton, Fla; Racine Mus Art, Racine, Wis, 2003; Hodgell Gallery, Sarasota Fla; Sandra Ainsley Gallery, Toronto, Ontario, Can; Nat Liberty Mus, Philadelphia, Pa; Four Seasons Hotel, Dobra, Qatar, 2004; Prints & Glass Sculpture (solo), Ky Mus Art & Craft, Louisville, Ky, 2005; Cadence Sculptural Installation, WCI Bella Mare Communities, N Miami, Fla; Contemp Glass 22nd Ann Int Invitational, Habatat Galleries, Boca Raton, Fla & Berrington, Mass, 2005; and others. *Pos:* Chmn arts fac, George Peabody Col, 76-79; chmn art dept, Col Idaho, Caldwell, 80-81; bd gov's NY State Found for Arts; nat screening com, Inst Int Educ, 95-98; juror, New Glass Review, The Corning Mus Glass. *Teaching:* Assoc prof, Vanderbilt Univ, Nashville, 71-79, chairperson, 75-79; vis artist, glass, Konfax Skolen, Stockholm, Sweden, 74 & Gerrit Rietuield Akad, Amsterdam, Holland, 74; chmn art dept, Col Idaho, 79-81; prof, head of glass prog, Rochester Inst Technol, 81-; instr, Pilchuck Sch Glass, 96. *Awards:* Visual Artist Exhib Grant, NY State Coun Arts, 85-86; Visual Arts Fel, NY State Coun for the Arts, 86; Grand Prize, The Int Exhib Glass, Kanazawa, Japan, 88; Grand prize, Int Glass Exhib, Kanazawa, Japan, 89; Cultural Specialist Award Grant, US Dept Info Svcs, Monterey, Mexico, 95. *Bibliog:* Richard Skull (dir), Michael Taylor: Glass (film), Micki Colman, 68; Rusty Chapman (dir), Glass Craft (film); Glass Art Soc J, 88 & 90. *Mem:* Tenn Artists-Craftsmen Asn (pres, 70-71); Am Crafts Coun; Glass Art Soc (bd dir, 78-82); Am Asn Univ Prof; Asn Portugesa Vidizo. *Media:* Glass, Graphics. *Publ:* Auth, A Geometry of Meaning, Hudson Hills Press, NY, 2006. *Dealer:* Leo Kaplan Modern Gallery 41 E 57th St NY 10022; Habatat Gallery 608 Banyan Trail Boca Raton FL 33431; Hodgell Gallery 46 Palm Ave S Sarasota FL 34236; Holsten Gallery 1 Elm St Stockbridge MA 01262. *Mailing Add:* 41 French Road Rochester NY 14618-3825

TAYLOR, MICHAEL R
CURATOR
b London, Eng, 1966. *Study:* Univ Edinburgh, Scotland, MA; Courtauld Inst Art, London, MA & PhD. *Collection Arranged:* Giorgio de Chirico: The Ariadne Series, 2002 & The Alfred Stieglitz Coll Mod & African Art, 2003, Philadlephia Mus Art. *Pos:* Asst cur mod & contemp art, Philadelphia Mus Art, 1997-2003, acting cur mod art, 2003-2004, Muriel and Philip Berman cur mod art, 2004-. *Teaching:* Adj assoc prof hist art, Univ Pa. *Publ:* Coauth (with Ann Temkin & Susan Rosenberg), Twentieth Century Painting and Sculpture, Philadelphia Mus Art, 2000. *Mailing Add:* PO Box 7646 Philadelphia PA 19101-7646

TAYLOR, ROBERT
CRITIC, WRITER
b Newton, Mass, Jan 19, 1925. *Study:* Colgate Univ, AB, 47; Brown Univ Grad Sch, 48. *Pos:* Art critic, Boston Herald, 52-67; Boston corresp, Pictures on Exhib, 54-59; mem staff, Boston Globe Mag, 68-72, art critic, 72-, arts ed, 73-76, columnist, 76-82, chief bk & art critic, 82-. *Teaching:* Prof Eng, Wheaton Col, 60-; lectr art hist, Boston Univ, 72-74. *Mem:* St Botolph Club, Boston; Mass Hist Soc. *Publ:* Auth, In Red Weather, 61; ed, publs, Inst Contemp Art, Boston, 67; auth, Treasures of Massachusetts, 72; Saranac, 86; Fred Allen, 89. *Mailing Add:* 1 Thomas Cir Marblehead MA 01945

TAYLOR, ROSEMARY
CERAMIST, SCULPTOR
b Joseph, Ore. *Study:* Cleveland Inst Art; NY Univ; Greenwich House; Arrowmount Col. *Work:* Westchester Col. *Exhib:* Hudson River Gallery, NY, 81; Am Crafts, Cleveland, Ohio, 85-94; Guild Gallery, Princeton, NJ, 85-90; Sign of the Clef, Savannah, Ga, 91-94; James Michener Mus, Pa, 95-96; and others. *Pos:* pottery consult, McCall's Mag, 62-72; Juror, Fulbright Award & Grants, 81-82; standards chmn, NJ Designer-Craftsman, 92-94. *Teaching:* Instr, Rahway Art Ctr, 50-60. *Bibliog:* Arthur Williams (auth), Sculpture, Craft Report Mag. *Mem:* NJ Designer-Craftsman; Am Craft Coun. *Media:* Stoneware. *Publ:* Contribr, McCall's Needlework, Craft Mag & Craft Report; and others

TAYLOR, SAMUEL MCELROY
MUSEUM DIRECTOR
b Rochester, Minn, July 29, 1951. *Study:* Colo Coll, BA in Biology, 73; Univ Calif, Santa Barbara, MA in Zoology, 78; Univ Calif, Berkeley, PhD in Sci Educ, 86. *Pos:* Educ program specialist, Carnegie Mus Natural History, Pittsburgh, 83-86, dir, 2008-2012; biology dir, NY Hall of Sci, Flushing Meadows, 86-90; dir exhibs, Am Mus Natural History, NY, 90-96; chmn, curator educ dept, Calif Acad Sci, San Francisco, 96-2001; dir, mus advisor, Samuel L Taylor Mus Consulting, 2001-2008. *Mem:* Phi Beta Kappa. *Interests:* fly fishing, competitive, swimming, bicycling. *Publ:* Improving Exhibs Through Formative Evaluation, 91. *Mailing Add:* Carnegie Mus Natural History 4400 Forbes Ave Pittsburgh PA 15213

TAYLOR, SANDRA ORTIZ
ASSEMBLAGE ARTIST, COLLAGE ARTIST
b Los Angeles, Calif, Apr 27, 1936. *Study:* Univ Calif, with William Brice & Sam Amato, BA; Iowa State Univ, with Byron Burford, MA; Chicano & Latino Lit Studies Grad Prog, Univ Calif, Irvine. *Work:* Univ Iowa; Macy's Corp, NY; Univ Calif Res Libr, Los Angeles; Oakland Mus. *Comn:* wine series label, Imagery Winery, Glen Ellen, Calif, 2002. *Exhib:* Paper Stars: Nat Women's Exhib, San Francisco Artist Gallery, Calif, 94; Selections, Acad Art Coll Gallery, 96; Le Petit Three, Alder Gallery, Eugene, Ore, 96; Pulp Fiction Works on Paper, Tex Fine Arts Asn, 96; Works from Imaginary Parents (auth, catalog), Galeria Dos Damas, San Diego, Calif, 96; Glean, Four Walls, San Francisco, 96; solo exhibs, 871 Fine Arts, San Fran, 97, Oakland Int Airport, Calif, 2003, Sonoma Co Mus, Santa Rosa, Calif, 2003, San Francisco Main Libr, 2004, Motazabu Gallery, Tokyo, 2004, Nexus Gallery, Philadelphia, 2005, Glass Curtain Gallery, Columbia Col, Chicago, 2005; 6th Int Shoebox sculpture, Univ Hawaii Art Gallery, Honolulu; 19th Ann solo mujeres exhib, Mission Cultural Ctr Latino Arts, San Francisco, Calif, 2006; Artfully Reclaimed 2nd Ann Exhib, art League N Calif, Novato, 2006; 3rd ann nat juried exhib, Art League N Calif, Novato, 2006; Con(text) Koelsch Gallery, Houston, Tex, 2006; Terror Int Exhib, Intersection Arts, San Francisco, 2006; Recollections from 1987-2007 Exhib, Mus Fine Arts, Budapest, 2007; Solo Mujeres, Mission Cult Ctr Latino Arts, San Francisco & Galeria Tonantzin, San Juan Bautista, Calif, 2007; Wow: Women on War, Mission Cultural Center for Latino Arts, 2008; Food Show, Falkirk Cultural Center, San Rafael, Calif, 2008; Banned and Recovered Artists Respond to Cencorship, African American Mus, Oakland, Calif, 2008; Assemblage and Collage and Construction, The Mus Art History at the McPherson Center, 2009; Award and One Person Exhib, Arts on Fire, Sanchez Art Center, Pacifica, Calif; The Seduction of DuChamp, Bay Area Artists Resonse and Slaughter House Space, DuChamp Winery, Healdsburg, Calif, 2009, Art Zone 461 Gallery, San Francisco, Calif, 2010, Bay Area Artists Response, 2010, Mus Los Gatos, Calif, 2010; Excor: Revival of Exquisite Corpse, The Art of Chance, Firehouse North, Berkeley, Calif, 2011; Latin Arts in the Bay Area Now, Richmond Art Ctr, Calif, 2011-2012; The Seduction of Duchamp Installation, Fine Arts Fair, Fort Mason Art Ctr, San Francisco, Calif, 2011; Get Lucky: The Culture of Chance, Somarts Cultural Ctr, San Francsico, Calif, 2012; In Search of the Accidental Book, San Francisco Ctr for the Book, San Francisco, Calif, 2012; Altered Book Show/Benefit, Moca Marin Mus Contemporary Art Novato, Calif, 2012; Art Gallery, Online Exhib, Mama: Motherhood Around the Globe, Int Mus Women, 2012, Left Coast Ann, Sanchez Art Ctr, Pacifica, Calif, 2012. *Pos:* Gallery asst, John Bolles Gallery, 70-71; guest curator, Sonoma Mus Vis Arts, Santa Rosa, Calif, 2001. *Teaching:* Instr, San Francisco Community Col, 66-2001 & Indian Valley Col, Marin, Calif, 74. *Awards:* Jurors Award, Calif Small Works, 92; Barbara Deming Mem Fund Grant, 96; Individual Artist, Cult Equity Grant, San Francisco Arts Comn, 2007. *Bibliog:* Article in Art Monthly, 93; Randal Davis (auth), article, Artweek, 93; Chiori Santiago (auth), article, Oakland Tribune, 93; Timothy Don Adams (auth), Light Writing & Life Writing, Photography in Autobiography, Univ NC Press, 2000; Debra Castillo & Maria Socorro Tabuenca Cordoba (auths), Border Women, Writing From LA Frontera, Univ Minn Press (chap 4), 2003; Laura E Perez (auth), Altarities: Chicana Art, Politics & Spirituality, Duke Univ, 2006; Misplaced Objects, Migrating Collection & Recollections, Univ Tex Press, Austin, 2009. *Media:* Mixed Media; Found Objects. *Collection:* Peter Barglow, Berkeley, Calif, Geoffrey Beaumont, Las Vegas. *Publ:* Contribr, Imaginary Parents, Sheila Ortiz Taylor (auth), Univ Nex Mex Press, 1996. *Dealer:* Franny Koelsh Koelish Gallery Houston TX; Adrienne Fish 871 Fine Arts San Francisco, CA. *Mailing Add:* 2200 23rd St San Francisco CA 94107

TAYLOR, SUSAN M
MUSEUM DIRECTOR
Study: Vassar Coll, BA (Medieval & Renaissance studies); Inst Fine Arts, New York, grad degree. *Pos:* Cur, Solomon R Guggenheim Mus, New York, formerly; dir, Davis Mus & Cult Ctr, Wellesley Coll, Mass, 1988-2000, Princeton Univ Art Mus, NJ, 2000-08, New Orleans Mus Art, La, 2010-. *Mem:* Asn Art Mus Dirs. *Mailing Add:* NOMA PO Box 19123 New Orleans LA 70179

TAYOU, PASCALE MARTHINE
SCULPTOR
b Yaounde, Cameroon, 1967. *Exhib:* Exhibs Transgressions, Centre Cultural Francais, Yaounde, Cameroon, 1994, Beyond the Borders, International Biennale of Kwangju, South Korea, 1995, Galerie du jour, Agnès B Paris, France, 1996, Tokyshima Modern Art Mus, Tokyo, 1996, Biennale of Sante Fe, NMex, 1997, Le Tronconnage Performance, Paris, France, 1997, Galerie Bernard Dulon, Paris, France, 1998, The Bridge, Melbourne, Australia, 1998, Crazy Nomad, Gallery Lombard Freid, NY, 1999, Liverpool Biennal, 1999, Vancouver Art Gallery, Canada, 2000, Biennale Lyon, France, 2000, Castello di Rivoli, Torino, Italy, 2000, Berlin Biennale, Kunst-Werkin, Berlin, Germany, 2001, Institut of Visual Art, Milwaukee, 2001, Cameroon Embassy, The Short Century, NY, 2002, 8, Intanbul-Biennale, Turkey, 2003, Musterland Skulptur Biennial, Muster, Germany, 2003, Mus of Contemporary Art, Rome, Italy, 2004, Working Ethics, Krinzinger Projekte Vienna, Austria, 2004, Mus of Contemporary Art, Chgo, 2005, Mus of Fine Art, Houston, 2005, Venice Biennale, 2005, 2009, The Beautiful Game: Contemporary Art and Futbol, NYC, 2006, Habana Biennial, Habana, Cuba, 2006, Wherever We Go, Spazio Oberdan/Milan, Italy, 2006, San Francisco Art Inst, Calif, 2007, World Factory, 2007, Art Focus, Jerusalem Found, Israel, 2008, Prospect.1, New Orleans, 2008, Altermodern, Triennial, Tate Britain, Londres, 2009, Hypocricy, Mus of Contemporary Art, Oslo, 2009 and others. *Media:* All Media

TEACHOUT, DAVID DELANO
PAINTER
b Santa Monica, Calif, Nov 16, 1933. *Study:* NC State Univ, BA (landscape archit), 63. *Work:* Occidental Col, Los Angeles, Calif; Univ Calif, Santa Cruz. *Exhib:* James D Phelan Awards, Palace Legion Honor 65-67; 85th Ann Exhib San Francisco Art Inst, San Francisco Mus Art, 66; 15th Painting Ann, Richmond Art Ctr, 66; 30th Biennial Exhib Contemp Am Painting, Corcoran Gallery Art, Washington, 67; 14th Ann Exhib, Laguna Beach Mus Art, 68; Real Colorists, Richmond Art Ctr, Richmond, Calif, 69; Occidental Coll Centennial Exhib, Los Angeles, Calif, 87. *Bibliog:* Constance Perkins (auth), Critical Review of Teachout Painting Retrospective, Occidental Col, 75; Art Forum Mag, 75. *Media:* Acrylic, Oil. *Publ:* Co-auth, Jazz 4 Linguis, Jazz Press, 79; co-auth, Jazz 5, Jazz Press, 80; illusr, An Occasional Suite, Jazz Press, 81. *Mailing Add:* 315 McAmant Dr Santa Cruz CA 95060

TEALE, KATE
PAINTER
Study: Oxford Univ, England, MA (English Lit), 1984; City & Guilds London Art Sch, 1988; Hunter Coll, New York, MFA (Painting), 1998. *Work:* Russell Coats Mus, Bournemouth, England; Portsmouth City Art Gallery, England; Nat Libr Congress, Washington. *Exhib:* Solo exhibs include 1 Main St Gallery, Brooklyn, New York, 1992, Square Tower, Portsmouth, England, 1994, Yearsley Spring Gallery, Philadelphia, 1997, Kristen Frederickson Contemp Art, New York, 2003; group exhibs include Smith Gallery, London, 1991; Spring, Spring Gallery, SoHo, New York, 1996; London Art Fair, Contemp Art Ctr, London, 1999; Greer Art Mus, Rio Grande, Ohio, 2004; ID Check, LAB Gallery, New York, 2006; Keeping It Real, Richmond Ctr Arts, Kalamazoo, Mich, 2007. *Awards:* New York Found Arts Fel, 2008. *Mailing Add:* 99 State St 5E Brooklyn NY 11201

TECZAR, STEVEN W
EDUCATOR, PAINTER
b St Joseph, Mo, Aug 8, 1948. *Study:* Univ Mo, Columbia, AB, 70, AM, 72; Washington Univ, St Louis, MFA, 86. *Work:* Greenville Co Mus Art, SC; Southeastern Ctr Contemp Art, Winston-Salem, NC; Va Mus Fine Arts, Richmond; Suwa Munic Art Mus, Japan; Nanjing Sch Fine Arts, China. *Comn:* Sculpture, Southern Bankshares Inc & Va Commonwealth Univ Child Care Cooperative, Richmond, Va, 75; sculpture, RF&P RR Co, Richmond, Va, 76; play sculpture, Ethical Soc Nursery Sch, St Louis, Mo, 81. *Exhib:* 1940-80 Fellowship Recipients, Va Mus, Richmond, 80; The Next Juried Show, Va Mus, Richmond, 83; Currents 29: Drawing in St Louis, St Louis Art Mus, 85; Four Square Feet, Sazama/Brauer Gallery, Chicago, Ill, 88; New Work on Paper & Constructions, BZ Wagman Gallery, St Louis, 89; New Constructions and Drawings, Atrium Gallery, St Louis, 91; London Summer 94; Works on paper and Sculpture, Family resource Ctr, Gorham, NH, 2001; Autobiographical Fragments, A Gallery Installation, Maryville May Found Gallery, 2002; Drawings & Diversions, Bonsack Gallery, John Burroughs Sch, St Louis, Mo, 2003. *Pos:* Prin, Design Collaborative Richmond, Va, 74-78. *Teaching:* Asst prof drawing & design, Va Commonwealth Univ, Richmond, 72-79; instr, Southside Va Community Col, Alberta, 74; chair art & design, Maryville Univ St Louis, 79-99; prof art, Maryville Univ, St Louis, 99-; instr, all levels of Drawing (foundation through advanced including figure drawing). *Awards:* Prof Develop Grants, Maryville Univ, 95-2003; Sabbatical Sculpture and Mixed-Media Works, 2000; Emerson Excellence in Teaching Award, Emerson Electric, St Louis, Mo, 2006. *Bibliog:* Alexandra Bellos (auth), Sea Views, Riverfront Times, St Louis, 1/91; Karen Schmitendorf (auth), Teczar's Trailing Lines, St Louis Post-Dispatch, 2/2/91; Eddie Silva (auth), In the Realm of Possibility, Riverfront Times, St Louis, 1/98. *Mem:* Coll Art Asn Am. *Media:* All Media. *Res:* Self-reflective study. *Publ:* American Drawings, St Louis Art Mus, 76; Drawing in St Louis, 85; St Louis Contemporary Works: An International Exchange, 87; Art St Louis V, 89. *Mailing Add:* 315 S Gore Ave Saint Louis MO 63119-3603

TEFFT, ELDEN CECIL
SCULPTOR, EDUCATOR
b Hartford, Kans, Dec 22, 1919. *Study:* Univ Kans, BFA, 49, MFA, 50; Cranbrook Acad Art, 51-52; with Bernard Frazier, William McVey. *Comn:* Franklin D Murphy (bronze), Sculpture Garden, Univ Calif, Los Angeles, 69; Moses (bronze), Kans Sch Religion, Lawrence, Kans, 82; Ida B Wells (bronze bust), Wells Journalistic Ann Award, 83; Buddy Award, a bronze sculpture presented ann by the Kans Univ Dept Theatre & Media Arts & the Univ Theatre, 87-; Keepers of the Universe (limestone triptych), City of Lawrence, Kans, 88. *Exhib:* Solo exhibs, Philbrook Art Ctr, Tulsa, Okla, 48; San Francisco Mus Art, Calif, 50; Carnegie Mus, Philadelphia, Pa, 50; The Midwest Show, Joslyn Art Mus, Nebr, 52; 58th Ann Exhib for Western Artists, Denver Art Mus, Colo, 53; Mid-Am Invitational, William Rockhill Nelson Gallery Art, Kansas City, Mo, 55; Missouri Show, City Art Mus, St Louis Art Mus, 59; Kans Sculptors Asn Outdoor Ann Exhib, Lawrence, Kans, 88-89 & 91-92; two-man show with Kim T Tefft, Baker Univ, Baldwin, Kans, 92. *Pos:* Chmn, Nat-Int Sculpture Conf, 60-78; dir, Nat Sculpture Ctr, Lawrence, Kans, 67-77, Int Sculpture Ctr, Lawrence, Kans, 77-80, Sculpture Research Ctr, Univ Kansas, Lawrence, 80-90; dir emer, Int Sculptor Ctr, Washington, DC, 80-; prof emer, Univ Kans, 90-. *Teaching:* Prof sculpture, Univ Kans, 50-90; vis prof, Univ Philippines, Quezon City, 64, Univ Ore, Eugene, 64, Univ Costa Rica, San Jose, 71, Cent Inst Fine Art Beijing, Shanghai Jiao Tong Univ, China, 86 & Ateno Paraquayo, Asuncion, Paraguay, 88; workshop, Baker Univ, Baldwin, Kans, 92. *Awards:* 17th Mo Show, City Art Mus St Louis, 59; First Award Arch Sculpture Competition, Fidelity State Bank, Topeka, Kans, 67; Nat Sculpture Conf, Jonesboro, Ark, 77. *Bibliog:* Dennis Kowal & D Meilach (auths), Sculpture Casting, Crown Publ, Inc, NY, 72; Robert Rose (cinematographer), Moses, The Creation of a Heroic Sculpture, Sculpture Research Ctr, Lawrence, Kansas, 85. *Media:* Bronze, Stone. *Res:* World sculpture founding techniques and their effect on the creative process. *Publ:* Auth, Bronze Casting of Sculpture (film), Int Film Bureau, Chicago, 60; Lost Wax Sculpture Foundry Equipment & Design: Ceramic Shell Supplement, Sculpture Res Ctr, 83; Lost Wax Sculpture Founding, An Exploration, Sculpture Res Ctr, Univ Kans, 92. *Mailing Add:* Tefft Terra Studios 1333 E 1600 Rd Lawrence KS 66046

TEGEDER, DANNIELLE
PAINTER
b Peekskill, NY. *Study:* Amsterdam Sch Fine Arts, Netherlands, 1991; State Univ New York, Purchase Coll, BFA, 1994; Sch Art Inst Chicago, MFA, 1997. *Work:* Mus Mod Art. *Exhib:* Solo exhibs include ARC Gallery, Chicago, 1996, Contemp Arts Workshop, Chicago, 1996, Jan Cicero Gallery, Chicago, 1999, 2002, De Chiara Gallery, New York, 2002, Susanne Vielmetter Los Angeles Projs, Los Angeles, 2003, Gregory Lind Gallery, San Francisco, 2005, Bodybuilder & Sportsman Gallery, Chicago, 2005, Priska C Juschka Fine Art, New York, 2006; Group exhibs include Anatomy & Intellect, Silverstein Gallery, New York, 1996, Growing Into Space, 1997, Graves Supercomplication, 2001; Artist in the Marketplace Exhib, Bronx Mus Art, New York, 2001; Drawings, Mixture Gallery, Houston, Tex, 2001; Ten Years of Artists at the Marie Walsh Sharpe Found, Ace Gallery, New York, 2002; Out of Site, New Mus, New York, 2002; Selections, PS 1, New York, 2003; Open House, Brooklyn Mus Art, Brooklyn, 2004; New Found Land: An Inaugural Group Exhib, Priska C Juschka Fine Art, New York, 2005; Site 92, Smack Mellon, Brooklyn, 2006; Materiality, Caren Golden Fine Art, New York, 2006; 183rd Ann: Invitational Exhib Contemp Am Art, Nat Acad Mus, New York, 2008. *Awards:* Sch Art Inst Scholar Fund, 1999; Chicago Artists Assistance Grant, 2000 ; Ragdale Found, 2000; Pollock-Krasner Found Grant, 2000; Lower E Side Print Fel Edition Award, 2004 ; Elizabeth Found Studio Award, 2005; Ralph Fabri Prize, Nat Acad, 2008. *Dealer:* Priska C Juschka Fine Art 547 W 27th St 2nd Floor New York NY 10001

TEICHMAN, MARY MELINDA
PRINTMAKER, CALLIGRAPHER
b Newark, NJ, Sept 8, 1954. *Study:* Cooper Union, New York, BFA, 76. *Work:* Corcoran Gallery, Washington, DC; Brooklyn Mus, NY; Mus City NY; Mus Art Carnegie Inst, Pittsburgh; Duxbury Art Complex Mus; Nat Mus Women in Arts, Washington, DC; Jane Voorhees Zimmerli Art Mus, Rutgers Univ, N Brunswick, NJ; Newark Pub Libr, Newark, NJ. *Comn:* Recollection (ed 150 prints), Presentation Print Artist, Print Club Albany, 93. *Exhib:* Soc Am Graphics Artists Competition, NY, 79, 86, 88, 91-93 & 2002; Print Club, Philadelphia, 80-81; Brooklyn Mus, NY, 81; Hunterdon Art Ctr, NJ, 81, 83 & 85; Assoc Am Artists, NY, 82, 84-85, 87, 89, 92 & 96; Contemp Images, Mus City NY, 82-92; Boston Printmakers Int, De Cordova Mus, Lincoln, Mass, 82-84, 86, 89-91, 93 & 2005; Contemp Images of the City, Mus City NY, 92; Recent Acquisitions, Mus City NY, 94; Delta Nat Small Prints Exhib (auth catalog), Ark State Univ, 96 & 99-2001. *Awards:* Boston Printmakers Award, 88, 93 & 97; Chancellor's Purchase Award, 62nd Nat Print Exhib, Univ Wis, 89; Merit Award, Purdue Univ, Ind, 90; K Caraccio Color Intaglio Purchase Awards, SAGA, New York, 2000 & 2001, 2002, 2004; and others; Masscribes. *Bibliog:* Robin Longman (auth), Emerging artists-Mary Teichman, Am Artist Mag, 8/84; Nicole Plett (auth), The new Mexican, prints take you to...,Pasatiempo Mag, 7/85; Presentation print, Mary Teichman, the print club of Albany, Jour of print world, Vol 16, No 3, Summer 93; Mary Teichman, journal of the print world, Vol 28, No 1, Winter, 2005. *Mem:* Boston Printmakers; Soc Am Graphic Artists; Print Club Albany; Soc Scribes; Soc Egg Tempera Painters. *Media:* Color Etching. *Dealer:* The Old Print Shop New York. *Mailing Add:* PO Box 446 Easthampton MA 01027-0446

TEIGER, DAVID
COLLECTOR
b Newark, June 13, 1929. *Study:* Cornell Univ, BS, 51. *Pos:* served to lt, USA, 51-53; Partner, Samuel Teiger & Co, Newark, 53-59, Ira Haupt & Co, NY City, 59-64, Bache & Co, NY City, 64-65; exec vpres, Shearson, Hammill & Co, Inc, 65-73; chmn, Chief Exec Officer, United Res Co, Morristown, NJ, 73-90; chmn, Gemini Consulting, 90-95; hon trustee, Mus Modern Art, NY City. *Awards:* Named one of Top 200 Collectors, ARTnews mag, 2006, 2007. *Mem:* Meadowood; Mountain Ridge

TEJERA, ARIEL
PAINTER
b Matanzas, Cuba, Aug 1970. *Study:* Sch Art, Matanzas, Cuba, 1982-85; Escuela Nacional de Artes, Havana, Cuba, 1985-90. *Exhib:* Solo exhibs include Galeriea Arte, Sol y Mar, Varadero, Cuba, 1993 & 1994, Exhib Matanzas, Cuba, 1997, Ardex Gallery, Miami, 2006; group exhibs include Hidden Art of the Revolution, Sintiempo Cult Ctr, Toronto, 1997; Arte Cubano, West End Gallery, Hollywood, Fla, 2000; Encuentro Cubano, Art Ballery Am Leewasser, Brunnen, Switzerland, 2002; Cuba Nostalgia, Fla Int Univ, Miami, 2005; To the Ballet, Ardex Gallery, Miami, 2006; Cuban Art Expo, Latin Art Core Gallery, Miami, 2007, Arte América, 2008. *Awards:* Pollock-Krasner Found Grant, 2007. *Mailing Add:* 11850 SW 19th Ln #175 Miami FL 33175-8713

TELLIER, CASSANDRA LEE
MUSEUM DIRECTOR, EDUCATOR
Study: Ohio State Univ, MA, 79, PhD, 84. *Collection Arranged:* Ancient Art, 87; Petersburg/Perestroika: Contemp Russian Art from Ohio Collections, 90; Sakura in Buckeye Country: Japanese Artists in Ohio, 91; The Far North: Works of the Inuit & Northwest Indians, 95; African Art Revealed, 96; Selected Works by Modern Masters, 99; African Am Artists of WPA, 2001; African Am Artists of Central Ohio, 2003; Sioux Traditions: A Tribute to Oscar Howe, 2005; Sacred Legacy: Edward S Curtis & The North American Indian, 2006; Ansel Adams, 2008; Art on a String: Asian Kites, 2008; Carnaval!, 2009; Lee & Grant, 2009; Elliott Erwitt, 2010. *Pos:* Prog dir arts, Ga Tech, 80-81; dir, Schumacher Gallery, Capital Univ, Columbus, Ohio, 89-. *Teaching:* Vis asst prof art, Kent State Univ, 84-86; prof, Art Hist, Capital Univ, 89-. *Awards:* Marantz Distinguished Alumni Award, Ohio State Univ, 2006. *Mem:* Am Asn Mus; Ohio Mus Asn (bd trustees). *Res:* Egypt, Africa & the ancient Mediterranean world. *Publ:* Auth, What you see & what you get: frame of reference in museum exhibits, Curator, 86; auth, Imhotep, Cult of Isis, Anchient Ghana, Saharan Rock Art, Alwa & Makouria, in: Encyl Ancient World, Salem Press, 2001; auth, Warfare of African empires, Military Arts in the Cultures of African People, Moscow State Univ Press,

2001; auth, Ezana & the fourth century kingdom of Aksum, the Meroitic empire, rock art of the Sahara, Great Events From History: The Ancient World, Salem Press, 2003; auth, Founding of the Kingdom of Benin, Ife Cult Center of the Yoruba, Great Events from Hist: The Middle Ages, Salem Press, 2004; auth, Sofonisba Anguissola, Great Lives from History, Salem Press, 2005; auth, William Stukeley English Archaeologist & Antiquarian, Great Lives from History, Salem Press, 2006; auth, William Stukeley Studies, Stonehenge & Avebury, Great Events from History, Salem Press, 2006; auth, Sir Arthur Evans Excavations at Knossos, Great Lives from History, Salem Press, 2007; auth, Sir Anthony Van Dyck, Great Lives from Hist, Salem Press, 2005; auth, Jean-Michel Basquiat, The Eighties in America, Salem Press, 2008; auth, Jackson Pollock, The Forties in America, Salem Press, 2010. *Mailing Add:* c/o Capital Univ Schumacher Gallery 1 College & Main Columbus OH 43209

TEMKIN, ANN
CURATOR
b 1960. *Study:* Harvard Univ, AB (magna cum laude); Yale Univ, PhD (art history), 1987. *Collection Arranged:* Thinking is Form: The Drawings of Joseph Beuys, Phila Mus Art, 1993, Constantin Brancusi, 1995, Raymond Pettibon, 1998-99, Alice Neel, 2000-01, Barnett Newman, 2002; Color Chart: Reinventing Color, 1950 to Today, Mus Mod Art, New York, 2004-08, Against the Grain: Contemp Art from the Edward R Broida Collection, 2006. *Pos:* Cur asst, painting & sculpture dept, Mus Mod Art, New York, 1984-87, cur, 2003-2008, chief cur painting & sculpture, 2008-; asst cur 20th-cent art, Phila Mus Art, 1987-90, Muriel & Philip Berman cur mod & contemp art, 1990-2003. *Mailing Add:* Mus Mod Art 11 W 53rd St New York NY 10019-5497

TEMPEST, GERARD FRANCIS
PAINTER, SCULPTOR
b San Donato, Italy, Feb 23, 1918; US citizen. *Study:* Mass Sch Art (studio art), 39; Tufts Univ, Mus Sch, Boston, Mass, 45; pvt study with Giorgio de Chirico, Rome, 48; Univ NC, BA, 49. *Work:* Vatican Mus Art, Vatican City, Italy; Akiraniasaki Collection, Tokyo, Japan; NC Mus, Raleigh; La Fondation Michelange, Venaco, Corsica; Monte Cassino Mus, Cassino, Italy. *Comn:* Empress Farah Diba (HIM), comn by Shah of Iran, Teheran, 74. *Exhib:* Newport Art Soc Mus, 59; Salon D'Automne de Lyon, France, 67; Mus Fine Arts, Boston, 68; solo exhibs, Duke Mus Art, Durham, NC, 78 & Bergen Co, NJ, 91; NY Cult Ctr, 72. *Awards:* Purchase Award, NC Mus Art, Raleigh, 49; Gold Medal, II Biennale Azureen, Cannes, France, 67. *Bibliog:* Donald Kuspit (auth), Gerard Tempest: Abstract Spiritualism, Bergen Mus, 91; M Stephen Doherty (auth), Gerard Tempest: Giving form to spiritual notions, Vol 55, Am Artists, 10/91; Carol Volk (auth), On the Edge, Vol VIII, No 8, Art & Antiques, 10/91. *Media:* Oil on Canvas; Cast Metal. *Publ:* Illusr (cover), Vol 58, No 1, J Am Planning Asn, winter 92. *Mailing Add:* 132 E End St Durham NC 27703

TEMPLE, LESLIE ALCOTT (LESLIE JANE ATKINSON)
SCULPTOR, WRITER
b Oklahoma City, Okla, 1951. *Study:* Univ Denver, 69-70; Oklahoma City Univ, BS (ed & art), 73; grad work, Univ Central Okla, 73-74; studied with Bruno Lucchesi & Jon Zahourek. *Work:* Monumental Work, Mus Outdoor Art, Englewood, Colo; Denver Pub Libr Permanent Collection, Western Hist Dept, Colo; Founders Corp, NY; Serrano Corp, Mexico City; City & County of Denver Auditor's Office; Project Safeguard, Denver, Colo; Nat Jewish Medical & Research Ctr, Denver; Pvt collections of Dr Patricia Ellison, Denver, Colo, Denny LeRoux J Friedman, NY. *Comn:* Nude Female, marble statue, Mus Outdoor Art, Englewood, Colo; Mother & Child, bronze statue, Consortium for Community Centered Comprehensive Child Care, Tanzania, Africa; Bronze portrait, Child, comn by Dr David Clausen, Denver, Colo; Bronze portrait, Pres, Founders Corp, NY. *Exhib:* NAm Sculpture Exhib, Golden, Colo, 82, 83 & 84; Greeley Invitational, Greeley, Colo, 83; High Plains Sculpture Exhib, Loveland, 84, 86, 87 & 88; Catherine Lorillard Wolfe, 92nd Ann, Nat Arts Club, NY, 88; Am Artists Prof League, 60th Grand Nat Exhib, Salmagundi Club, NY, 88; Mus Outdoor Arts, Englewood, Colo, 2001; Denver Int Airport, 2001; Univ Denver, Mus Anthropology & Penrose Libr, 2002. *Pos:* Pres, SLA Arch/Couture Inc-An Environmental Enrichment Design Co, 90-; SLA Concrete Construction Inc, 90-93; adv comt, Colo Dept Transportation, 92-93; adv, Native Am, Denver Indian Ctr, 83-93; bd dir, Construction Women Owners & Exec, 90-93; bd trustees, Denver Art Mus, 92, mem marketing & ed, audience develop comt, 93; mem Artists Am Marketing Comt, Colo Hist Mus, Denver, Colo, 99. *Teaching:* Art, Oklahoma City Fin Arts Mus, 71-72; art & art hist, Our Lady of Lourdes Sch, Denver, 85-87. *Awards:* Drawing I, Best of Show, Greely Invitational, 83; Hon Mention, Sculpture, Nat Jewish Community Ctr, 86; Judges Merit Honor, Prof Fine Art Photog, Hayes Kans Art Coun, 15th Ann Nat Competition, 99. *Bibliog:* American Artists, An illustrated Survey of Leading Contemp, 90; Sculptor's Resistance Mirrors Her Withdrawal, Sunday Oklahoman, 7/8/84; The Mus Outdoor Arts(bk & film), Englewood, Colo. *Mem:* Denver Art Students League (82-94). *Media:* All Media. *Publ:* Coauth, with George Carlson, The Tarahumara, pvt publ, 76; auth, A Body of Work, pvt publ, 82; documentary film, Art in Process, produced by Mus of Outdoor Art, copyright, 90; Primitive Tarahumara Indian Tribe (5 bk series & photog exhib), in prep; Outstanding People of 20th Century, Biographical 2000 Data Ctr, Cambridge, Eng. *Dealer:* Belleli Antiques & Fine Art Gallery Denver CO. *Mailing Add:* 2088 S Pennsylvania Denver CO 80210-4034

TEMPLE, MARY
INSTALLATION SCULPTOR, PAINTER
b Ariz. *Study:* Ariz State Univ, BFA (painting), 1989; Ariz State Univ, MFA (painting & drawing), 1995; Skowhegan Sch Painting & Sculpture, Maine, 1999. *Exhib:* Solo exhibs include cherrydelosreyes, LA, 2003, ZieherSmith, New York, 2003, Mixed Greens, New York, 2003, 2004, 2006, Arts Club Washington, DC, 2004, Aldrich Mus Contemp Art, Conn, 2005, 2006, Martin Mus Art, Baylor Univ, Tex, 2006, Smack Mellon, Brooklyn, 2006, Sandroni Rey, LA, 2007, Trois Gallery, Savannah Coll Art & Design, Atlanta, 2007, Real Artways, Hartford, Conn, 2008; group exhibs include OnLine, Feigen Contemp, New York, 2003; Presence of Light, Berkshire Mus, Pittsfield, Mass, 2004; In Practice Project Series, Sculpture Ctr, Long Island City, NY, 2006; Light x 8: Light in Contemp Art, Jewish Mus, New York, 2006; New Prints, Int Print Ctr, New York, 2007; Double-Take: The Poetics of Illusion & Light, Contemp Mus, Baltimore, 2007; Inner & Outer Space, Mattress Factory, Pittsburgh, 2008; Badlands, Mass Mus Contemp Art, North Adams, 2008; New Work, San Francisco Mus Mod Art, 2008. *Awards:* Special Edition Fel, Lower East Side Print Shop, New York, 2006; Lily Auchincloss Fel in Painting, NY Found Arts, 2006; Dieu Donne Workspace Prog Grant, New York, 2006; Concordia Found Career Advancement Grant, 2007; Basil H Alkazzi Award for Excellence in Painting, 2010. *Mailing Add:* c/o Mixed Greens Gallery 531 W 26th St New York NY 10001

TEN,
PAINTER
b Marienberg, Neth, June 8, 1930. *Exhib:* Newark Mus, 61; Solo exhibs, Flemington Studio Arts, NJ, 71, Upstairs Gallery, Somerville, NJ, 72 & Papermill Playhouse, Milburn, NJ, 72; Plainfield Regional Art Mus, NJ, 79; Ctr Int D'Art Contemporain, Paris, France, 84; Mandragore Int Galerie D'Art, Paris, France, 86; Art Philadelphia, 2003; Int Festival Erotic Art, Montreal Calif, 2004; and others. *Pos:* Art dir, NJ Print Coun, 92-95. *Awards:* Tracy Long Mem Award, Summit Art Ctr, 66; Wally's Award, Plainfield Art Asn, 66, First Prize in Oils, 69. *Bibliog:* Doris Brown (auth), Surrealist's exhibit opens, 5/3/70, Franklin artist, 8/8/71 & Dutch-born artist, 6/25/72, Sunday Home News. *Mem:* Hunterdon Mus Art; NJ Print Coun; Ctr Contemp Art; Soc Art Imagination. *Media:* Oil, Ceramics. *Interests:* Enhanced natural phenomena. *Publ:* Erotic Art by Living Artists, Art Network Press, Renaissance, Calif. *Dealer:* Gallery of Surrealism 160 Bleecker St #10ME New York NY 10012 . *Mailing Add:* 2346 Amwell Rd Somerset NJ 08873-7217

TENENBAUM, ANN
ADMINISTRATOR, COLLECTOR
b Savannah, Ga, June, 1961. *Study:* Sarah Lawrence Coll, grad. *Pos:* Mem vis comt dept photog, Metrop Mus Art, 1996-2005, trustee, 2005-; vchmn bd trustees, Dia Art Found, New York, 1994-2006; co-pres bd trustees, Film Soc Lincoln Ctr for Performing Arts, currently; founding mem bd govs, Bard Coll Ctr Curatorial Studies; bd dirs, Sarah Lawrence Coll, Channel 13/WNET, Studio Mus, Harlem, NY, Second Stage Theatre, Guild Hall East Hampton; mem chmn coun, Mus Modern Art. *Awards:* Named one of Top 200 Collectors, ARTnews mag, 2003-13; Leo award, Independent Curs Int, 2003; Child Advocacy award, NY Univ Child Study Ctr, 2003. *Collection:* Contemporary & modern art; photography. *Mailing Add:* c/o Metrop Mus Art 1000 5th Ave New York NY 10028

TENNANT, DONNA KAY
WRITER, EDUCATOR
b Waynesburg, Pa, Nov 28, 1949. *Study:* Univ Rochester, NY, BA (art hist), 71; Univ NMex, Albuquerque, MA (art hist), 79; also with Beaumont Newhall; Tex teaching cert, 2008. *Pos:* Art critic, Houston Chronicle, Tex, 79-81; Jeremy Stone Gallery, San Francisco, 82-84 & 89-91, Sherry French Gallery, New York, 84-85; assoc ed, Mus Fine Arts, Houston, 85-86; adminr, Houston Art Dealers Asn, 87-89 & 91-; ed, Mus & Arts Mag, 93-94; managing ed, Houston Life Mag, 94-95; sr ed, Southwest Art, 96-98; ed, Polo Mag, 98-99; art reviewer, Visual Art Source, 2013-; art reviewer, Art Ltd Mag, 2014. *Teaching:* Adj lect, Art History, Univ of Houston, Downtown, 2001-2006; instr Eng and Journalism, Tex Pub Schs, 2007-2013. *Res:* Second-generation abstract expressionism thesis; 19th & 20th century art, history of photography, contemporary art. *Publ:* Benito Huerta, John Hernandez, Miami-Dade Coll, 88; Ibsen Espada (catalog), McMurtrey Gallery, 89; Nine in Fiber, Artspace, 90; Jacob Lawrence, Painter, Mus & Arts Mag, 92; Lydia Bodnar Balahutrak (catalog), Nave Mus, 95; Dianne L Reeves, Art Papers, 96; Chuck Russell (catalog) Art Mus SE Tex, 2004; Jeffrey Brailas, Lynn Randolph, Earl Staley (catalog), Scanlan Gallery, 2012. *Mailing Add:* 2603 Parana Houston TX 77080

TENZER, (DR & MRS) JONATHAN A
COLLECTORS
b New York, NY, May 21, 1940. *Study:* Dr Tenzer, Univ Vt, BA, 62; Univ Pa, DMD, 66. *Collection:* A Wyeth, Moses (Anna Robertson), Rockwell; Michele Delacroix

TEPFER, DIANE
EDUCATOR, HISTORIAN
Study: Brooklyn Col; Univ Wash, BA (art hist), 68, MA (art hist), 72; Univ Mich, PhD, 89. *Collection Arranged:* Am Artists Look at Chinese Culture, Beijing, Am Embassy, 96; A Vision of Am, (auth catalog) The Berlin Embassy, Berlin and Vienna, 99; Art from the Palouse and Beyond, The Cameroon Embassy Collection, Yaounde and Vienna, 99; Celebrating the Am Family, (auth catalog) The Copenhagen Embassy Collection, Denmark, 99; The Healing Spirit, (auth catalog) the Dar es Salaam Collection, Tanzania, 2000; Am Visions, the Ukraine Collection, Kiev, 2001; The Spirit of the Midwest, the Vilnius Embassy Collection, Latvia, 2001; From the Gulf States to the Caribbean, the Venezuela Embassy Collection, Caracas, 2001. *Pos:* asst cur prints and photographs div, Libr Congress, Washington, DC, 91-94; cur, Art in Embassies Program, US Dept State, 95-2001, curatorial cons, 2001-; coord, Islamic Art Symposium, Va Commonwealth Univ, Arts, Richmond, Va & Doha, Qatar, 2006-2008. *Teaching:* instr, Oberlin Coll, Ohio, 80-81; instr, Colby Coll, Waterville, Maine, 82-83; adj assoc prof humanities, Univ Md, Univ Col ONLINE, 2002-. *Awards:* Fel Am Art, Rockefeller Found, 77-78; Res Fel, Smithsonian Inst, Nat Mus Am Art, 81-82; Faculty Rsch grant, UMUC, 2011-2012. *Mem:* Coll Art Asn; Smithsonian Material Culture Forum; Wash Biog Group. *Res:* Am art patronage, dealers, crafts; Samuel and Edith Halpert; Christopher Columbus and Columbus Circle: Shifting Perspectives. *Publ:* Edith Gregor Halpert and the Downtown Gallery Downtown 1926-1940 & A Study in Am Art Patronage, UMI, 90; Edith Gregor Halpert, Impresario of Jacob Lawrence's Migration Series, The Phillips Collection,

Wash, 93; Times Square, Pont Neuf, Lake Mahopac, and More; the Art and Life of Samuel Halpert (1844-1930), 2001; Ukrainian Roots: American Visions: The Am Embassy Collection, Kyiv and Vienna, 2002; Janet Sobel 1894-1968, Art in America, 7/2002. *Mailing Add:* 1737 Willard St NW Apt 1 Washington DC 20009-1753

TEPPER, STEVEN J
ADMINISTRATOR, EDUCATOR
Study: Univ NC Chapel Hill, BA, 1989; Harvard Univ, MPP, 1996; Priceton Univ, PhD, 2001. *Pos:* Exec dir, U NC Chapel Hill Bicentennial Observance, 1989-1994; cons, Nat Humanities Ctr, Reseach Triangle Park, NC, 1996; dep dir, Ctr for Arts and Cultural Policy Studies, Woodrow Wilson Sch of Pub and Int Affairs, lectr sociology, pub policy, Princeton Univ, formerly; assoc dir, Curb Ctr for Art, Enterprise and Pub Policy, assoc prof of sociology, Vanderbilt Univ, 2004-2014; facilitator, Leadership Music, Nashville, 2012-; invited speaker in the field, currently; dean, Arizona State Univ, Herberger Inst for Design and the Arts, 2014-; NEH Distinguished Visiting Prof, Hartford Univ, 2013. *Awards:* Fulbright Scholar Finalist, 1989, Teaching Fellow, Harvard Univ, Kennedy Sch of Government, 1995, Andrew Mellon Found Affiliate in Cultural Policy, Princeton Univ, 2000, C Wright Mills Book award finalist, Soc for the Study of Social Problems, 2012. *Mem:* Adv bd mem, Poetics, 2006-; mem exec bd, Asn of Cultural Economics, Int, 2003, 2006; mem steering com, American Assembly, The Creative Campus, 2003-2004; mem research adv coun, League of American Orchestras, 2008-, task force Innovations in Orchestras Research, 2008-; mem task force on research and knowledge management, Asn of Performing Arts Presenters, 2008-; Nat Endowment for the Arts, working group, Survey of Pub Participation in the Arts, 2005-2010; mem research steering com, Ctr for Arts and Culture, George Mason Univ, 2006; advisor, Irvine Found Cultural Engagement Initiative, 2012-. *Publ:* Co-ed Engaging Art: The Next Great Transformations of America's Cultural Life, 2007; co-ed, Patterns and Pathways: Artists and Creative Work in a Changing Economy, Work & Occupations, 2013; auth, Not Here, Not Now, Not That!: Protest Over Art and Culture in America, 2011; contribr of several articles to prof publ. *Mailing Add:* Arizona State Univ Herberger Institute for Design and the Arts School of Arts PO Box 872102 Tempe AZ 85287-2102

TERMES, (DICK A)
PAINTER, SCULPTOR
b San Diego, Calif, Nov 7, 1941. *Study:* Black Hills State Coll, BS, 64; Univ Wyo, Laramie, MA (art), 69; Otis Art Inst, Los Angeles, MFA, 71. *Work:* Denver Art Mus; Sphere Mus, Tokyo, Japan; Coca Cola Corp, Atlanta, Ga; Doene Coll, Crete, Nebr; Univ Cent Fla, Orlando. *Comn:* 5 1/2 ft centennial sphere for State of SDak; Pull to the North (sphere), North Pole, Alaska; Order/Disorder (sphere), Law Enforcement Acad, Wyo; Univ Cent Fla, Orlando, 93; Against the Current, SDak Humanities Coun, 2003; Porthole to the Past, Deadwood SDak, 2002. *Exhib:* Spherical Thinking and Total Photos, Coll Archit Gallery, Ariz State Univ, 82 & Univ Ky, Lexington, 83; Mus of Fun (15 cities), Japan, 84; Air & Space Mus, Smithsonian Inst, 87; Montana Moon Gallery, Chicago, Ill, 88; Gallery on the Green, Lexington, Mass, 89; San Francisco State Univ, 90; Univ Ill; MS Escher Centennial Cong, Univ Rome, 98; Extrasensory Mus, Japan, 99. *Teaching:* Instr art, Henley High Sch, Klamath Falls, Ore, 64-66, Sheridan High Sch, 66-68 & Black Hills State Univ, 71-72. *Awards:* SDak Arts Coun Fel, 76, 80 & 94; Artistic Achievement Citation, SDak Mus Art, 86; Gov's Award for Creative Distinction, 99. *Bibliog:* Susan O'Neill (auth), Six point perspective--the total view, Denver Post, 77; David Miller (auth), Total photographer has whole world in his hands, Mod Photog, 80; Daralice Boles (auth), Termes total photo, Progressive Archit, 83; Shaping Space, 88; Rochelle Newman (auth), Malleable Matter and Stretchable Space, Pythagorean Press, 2000. *Media:* Lexan Plastic Globe Canvas, Acrylic. *Publ:* Art Gallery Int Mag, 8/89; Art & Man, MC Escher Scholastic, 92; The Visual Mind, Art and Math, Mass Inst Technol Press, 94; Psychological Perspectives, 92 & 96; Homage to Escher, Leonardo Mag, Vol 33, 1, 2000. *Mailing Add:* 1920 Christensen Dr Spearfish SD 57783

TERMINI, CHRISTINE See Genute, Christine Termini

TERRASSA, JACQUELINE
MUSEUM DIRECTOR
Study: MFA, Univ Chicago, 94. *Pos:* Staff mem, Columbia Col, Chicago; educ dir, Hyde Park Art Ctr, David and Alfred Smart Mus Art, Univ Chicago, 98-, interim dir, 2004-

TERRUSO, LUIGI LEONARDO
PAINTER, INSTRUCTOR
b New York, NY, Oct 19, 64. *Study:* City Univ New York, BS (honors), 87; Sch Art, Yale Univ, MFA, 94. *Exhib:* Invitational Exhib Painting & Sculpture, Am Acad Arts & Letters, New York, 2001; Together, Artforum-Jarfo, Kyoto, Japan, 2004; Century Asn Prof Painters, Century Asn, New York, 2005-2006; 183rd Ann Exhib Contemp Am Art, Nat Acad Mus, New York, 2008. *Teaching:* Instr abstract painting, Yale Univ, 92-93; pvt instr abstract painting, Santa Fe, 2007. *Awards:* Tenenbaum Scholar, 83-87; Vermont Studio Ctr Fel, 97 & 2005; Chautaugua Inst Scholar, New York, 90; Santa Fe Art Inst Residency Fel, 2005-2006; Joan Mitchell Found Residency Scholar, Santa Fe Art Inst, 2006; Edwin Austin Abbey Mural Fel, Nat Acad Mus, 2006. *Bibliog:* Michael Fressola (auth), Using the Past to Paint the Future, Staten Island Advance, 2003; Similar New Friends, Am Acad Rome Soc Fels News, 2004; interview by Mary Charlotte Domanoi, KSFR 90.7F Santa Fe Pub Radio, 2005; article, Mural Award Winners at Nat Acad Mus, Artnet News, 2006. *Mem:* Coll Art Asn; Hanoverian Found (bd dirs, 2006-); Artist Fel; Century Asn. *Media:* Acrylic & Oil. *Publ:* Auth, ed, illusr, contribr, 205, CSI Publ, 88. *Dealer:* Ober Gallery 14 Old Barn Rd Kent CT 06757. *Mailing Add:* 526 W 26th St #910 New York NY 10001

TERRY, CHRISTOPHER T
PAINTER, DRAFTSMAN
b Stamford, Conn, Jan 8, 1956. *Study:* RI Col, BA, 78; Univ Wis-Madison, MFA, 81. *Work:* Mus der Kreisstadt, Ahrweiler, Rheinland-Pfalz, Ger; Ger Fulbright Kommission, Berlin; Nora Eccles Harrison Mus Art, Logan, Utah; Springville Mus Art, Utah; Park Hyatt Corp Coll, San Francisco. *Exhib:* Solo exhibs, Hackett/Freedman Gallery, San Francisco, 2000, Enigmatic Ritual, Nicolaysen Mus, Casper, Wyo, 2000, Interior Landscapes, Plains Mus Am Art, Fargo, ND, 2000 & Marshall Art Gallery, Scottsdale, Ariz; Charlotte Int,Spirit Sq Ctr for Arts, NC, 93; Contemp Still Life, Riverside Mus Art, Calif, 94; Nachbar Am, Altes Synagogue, Ahrweiler, Rheinland Pfalz, Ger, 95; Still Life, Contemp Realist Gallery, San Francisco, 96; Utah Art, Utah Artists, Springfield Mus Art, Utah, 2001. *Teaching:* Lectr drawing & painting, Calif State Univ, Long Beach, 85-88; prof painting, Utah State, Univ, 88-; guest prof, Univ Essen NRW, Ger, 94-95; vis artist, Am Acad, Rome, Italy, 2000; guest prof, Univ Essen NRW, Germany, 2002-03. *Awards:* Westaf/Nat Endowment Arts Regional Fel in Painting, 95; Alumnus of Yr Award, RI Coll Art Dept, 2001; Fulbright Scholar, Univ Essen, Ger, 2003. *Bibliog:* Roberts Carasso (auth), Realism through a Modern Lens, Orange Co Register, 12/7/2000; Wesley Pulkka (auth), Contemporary Realism, Southwest Art, 3/2000; Bonnie Gangelhoff (auth), Contemporary Realism in California, Southwest Art, 1/2001; Amy Abrams (auth), Looking Beyond Oil, Canvas, Get Out Mag, Ariz Republican, 3/22/2001; Vern Swanson (auth), Utah Art, Utah Artists, Springville Mus of Art, 2002. *Media:* Oil on Canvas. *Dealer:* Hidell, Brooks Gallery 1910 South Blvd Charlotte NC 28203. *Mailing Add:* Utah State U Art Dept 4000 Old Main Hill Logan UT 84322

TERUYA, YUKEN
SCULPTOR
b Okinawa, Japan, 1973. *Study:* Tama Art Univ, Tokyo, Japan, BFA, 1996; Maryland Inst Coll Art, Post Baccalaureate, 1999; Sch Visual Arts, New York, MFA, 2001. *Work:* Mus Mod Art, New York; Altoids Collection, New Mus, New York; Guggenheim Mus, New York. *Exhib:* Solo exhibs include Aldrich Mus Contemp Arts, Conn, 2002, KS Art, New York, 2002, Shoshanawayne Gallery, Santa Monica, Calif, 2002, 2005, 2007, Diverse Works Art Space, Houston, Tex, 2004, Josee Bienvenu Gallery, New York, 2005, Asia Society, New York, 2007; Group exhibs include Retro Future Present, Magnifik Gallery, Brooklyn, 2001; Paper Cut, Islip Art Mus, E Islip, NY, 2002; Terrarium, Bronx River Art Ctr, NY, 2003; Internal Excess, Drawing Ctr, New York, 2003; A Stereoscopic Vision, Dumbo Arts Ctr, New York, 2004; Newspaper, Cristinerose/Joseebienvenu Gallery, New York, 2004; Greater New York, PS 1 Contemp Art Ctr, New York, 2005; The Altoids Curiously Strong Collection, New Mus Contemp Art, New York, 2005; The Shapes of Space, Guggenheim Mus, New York, 2007; Milk, David Castillo Gallery, Miami, 2007; Atomic Sunshine, Puff Room, New York, 2008; Transformed, Contemp Art Ctr VA, 2008; Second Life!, Mus Arts & Design, New York, 2008. *Awards:* Skowhegan Sch Painting & Sculpture Fel, Maine, 2001; Emerging Artist Award, Aldrich Mus Contemp Arts, Conn, 2002; NYFA Fel, Lily Auchincloss, 2005; Joan Mitchell Found Grant, 2007. *Mailing Add:* 1089 Willoughby Ave #203 Brooklyn NY 11221

TESFAGIORGIS, FREIDA
PRINTMAKER, EDUCATOR
b Starkville, Miss, Oct 21, 1946. *Study:* Graceland Col, Lamoni, Iowa, AA, 66; Northern Ill Univ, De Kalb, BS, 68; Univ Wis, Madison, with Ray Gloeckler & Robert Grilley, MA, 70, MFA, 71. *Work:* Grad Sch, Univ Wis, Madison; Du Sable Mus of African & Afro-Am Art, Chicago; S Side Community Art Ctr, Chicago; Afro-Am Ctr, Univ Wis. *Comn:* Mixed-media drawing, Afro-Am Arts Inst, Univ Ind, Bloomington, 76; prints & drawings, Wis Arts Bd, 78. *Exhib:* Sixth Concours Int de la Palme d'Or des Beaux Arts, Palmares, Monte Carlo, France, 74; Prints & Drawings, MAMA Gallery, Madison, Wis, 76; Beloit Vicinity Ann Exhib, Wright Art Ctr, Wis, 76; 15th Nat Print Exhib, Art Gallery, Bradley Univ, Peoria, Ill, 76; Midwestern Black Artist, Performing Arts Ctr, Milwaukee, Wis, 76. *Pos:* Artist-in-residence, Univ Wis, Madison, 71-72. *Teaching:* Asst prof African/Afro-Am art, Univ Wis, Madison, 72-77, assoc prof African/Afro-Am art, 77-. *Awards:* Wis Arts Bd Art Grant, 77; City Arts Grant, Prints & Drawings, Off of the Mayor, Madison, 77. *Bibliog:* Interest in African art is on the increase in US, Capital Times, 7/75; James Auer (auth), PAC surveys midwestern Black art, Milwaukee J, 2/76; Shirley Carley (auth), Starkville native making name in field of art, Starkville Daily News 3/76. *Mem:* Wis Women in the Arts; Nat Conf of Artists (regional coordr, 74); Nat Coun for Black Studies. *Media:* Woodcut. *Publ:* Illusr (cover), Ba Shiru, Univ Wis, 71 & 76-77; contribr, Center debut: A Black artist's view, Milwaukee J, 11/75. *Dealer:* Assoc Am Artist 663 Fifth Ave New York NY 10022. *Mailing Add:* 6109 Piping Rock Rd Madison WI 53711

THACHER, ANITA
INSTALLATION ARTIST, FILMMAKER
b New York, NY, Apr 4, 40. *Study:* Antioch Col; New Sch Social Res, BA, 64; New York Studio Sch Drawing, Painting & Sculpture, 65-66; Millennium Film Sch, 67. *Work:* Metrop Mus Art, NY; Chicago Art Inst; Neuberger Mus, State Univ NY, Purchase; SC Art Inst, Columbia; Inst Arts, Rice Univ Mus; Mus Mod Art. *Comn:* Painted Earth, The Art of the Mimbres Indians (Film), Metrop Mus Art & Getty Mus, 89. *Exhib:* Mus Mod Art, 91; Anthology Film Arch NY, 91; JM Kohler Arts Ctr, Sheboygan, Wis, 93; Los Angeles Co Mus, 93; Lumen-essence, Westbeth Gallery, NY, 96; The Luminous Image III Velan, Torino, Italy; Am Century 1950-1999, Whitney Mus Am Art, 2000; Arts for Transit, MTA, Greenpoint, NY, 20031. *Awards:* Nat Endowment Arts, 77, 78, 80 & 87; Martin E Segal Award, Lincoln Ctr, 88; Jerome Found; and others. *Bibliog:* Marion Boulton Stroud (auth), An Industrious Art, Innovation in Pattern and Print at the Fabric Workshop, WW Norton & Co, 91; Jill Conner (auth), Sculpture Mag, 10/2002; Hellen Harrison (auth), New York Times, 5/12/2002. *Mem:* NY Women in Film; Filmmakers Co-op (bd dir, 85-86); MacDowell

Colony (mem bd dir, 80-85); Civitelli Renigri, 2002. *Media:* Film, Video, Installation. *Publ:* Contribr, Frames, 78, Cover Mag, summer 80, Idiolects J, 83 & Film as Installation Catalog, 83; Millennium Film Jour, 2000. *Dealer:* Art Resources Transfer 511 W 33 St New York NY. *Mailing Add:* Cooper Sta PO Box 1625 New York NY 10276

THARP, STORM
PAINTER, SCULPTOR
b Ontario, Ore, 1971. *Work:* Whitney Mus Am Art, New York; Saatchi Gallery, London. *Exhib:* Pacific Northwest Annual Exhibition, Belleview Art Mus, 2001; War Drawings, Mount Hood Community Coll, Portland, 2005; Oregon Biennial, Portland Art Mus, 2006; Arm & Arm, PDX Contemp Art, Portland, 2008; Whitney Biennial, Whitney Mus Am Art, 2010. *Mailing Add:* PDX 3040 SE Yamhill Portland OR 97214

THATER, DIANA
VIDEO ARTIST, PAINTER
b San Francisco, Calif, 1962. *Study:* NY Univ, BA (art history), 84; Art Ctr Coll Design, MFA, 90. *Exhib:* Solo shows incl H&R Projects, Brussels, Belgium, 99, Carnegie Mus Art, Pittsburgh, 99, St Louis Art Mus, 99, Tensta Kontshall, Spain, 2000, 1301 PE, Los Angeles, 2000, 2001, 2004, 2005, Mus für Gegenwartskunst Siegen, 2000, 2004, Vienna Secession, 2000, DIA Ctr for Arts, New York, 2001, Galerie Ghislaine Hussenot, Paris, 2002, Galleria Emi Fontana, Milan, 2002, David Zwirner, New York, 2005, Zwirner & Wirth, New York, 2005; group shows incl Whitney Mus Am Art, New York, 2001; Harris Mus and Art Gallery, 2001; J Paul Getty Mus, Los Angeles, 2001; Kunsthalle Basel, 2002; Galerie Hauser & Wirth, Zurich, 2002; Guggenheim Mus Bilbao, 2003; Mus der Moderne, Salzburg, 2004; Contemp Jewish Mus, 2004; Whitney Biennial, 2006; Int Ctr Photog, 2006; Sammlung Falckenberg, Hamberg, Ger, 2006. *Dealer:* 1301PE 6150 Wilshire Blvd Los Angeles CA 90048; Galleria Emi Fontana Viale Bligny 42 20136 Milan Italy; Haunch of Venison 6 Brook St W1K 5ES London United Kingdom; Hauser & Wirth 196A Piccadilly London W1J 9DY United Kingdom; Parkett Editions 145 Avenue of the Americas New York NY 10013; Zwirner & Wirth 32 E 69th St New York NY 10021

THAW, EUGENE VICTOR
DEALER, COLLECTOR
b New York, NY, Oct 27, 1927. *Study:* St John's Col, BA, 47; Columbia Univ (art hist), 47-49. *Hon Degrees:* Hartwick Col, Oneonta, NY, Hon Dr Art, 90. *Exhib:* Pvt collection, Pierpont Morgan Libr, Cleveland Mus, Art Inst Chicago & Nat Gallery Can, 75-76; Part II, Thaw Collection, Pierpont Morgan Libr, 85 & Mus Fine Arts, Richmond, Va, 86; New Acquisitions, Pierpont Morgan Libr; Royal Acad, London, 96; Nomadic Art of the Eastern Eurasian Steppes, Eugene V Thaw and other NY Col, Metrop Mus Art, NY, 2002. *Pos:* Art dealer & pres, E V Thaw & Co, Inc, 50-; writer, Spectator, London, 76-77 & Times, London, 77-78; vchmn, Artemis, S A, 76-; contrib ed, New Republic, 83-; trustee, St John's Col, Annapolis & Santa Fe, 75-83, Glimmerglass Opera Theater, Cooperstown, NY, 83, Hartwick Col, Oneonta, NY, 86-89, Pierpont Morgan Libr, NY, 88 & World Monuments Fund, 90-96; pres, Pollock-Krasner Found Inc, NY; Trustee, Pierre & Maria-Gaetana Matisse Found, 2001-. *Teaching:* Vis lectr fine art, St John's Col, 73, Asn Art Mus Dirs, 83, Nat Gallery, Washington, DC, 83, Mus Fine Arts, Boston, 83, Pierpont Morgan Libr, 84-85 & Ft Worth Art Mus, 86. *Awards:* Gertrude Vanderbilt Whitney Award, Outstanding Patronage of the Arts, 2001; Medal for Distinguished Philanthropy, Asn Mus, 2002; Hadrian Award, World Monuments Fund, 2003. *Mem:* Art Dealers' Asn Am (bd dir, 64-, secy & treas, 66-68, vpres, 68-70 & pres, 70-72); IRS Art Adv Panel, 68-71; fel perpetuity, Pierpont Morgan Libr, NY; Grolier Club, NY; Century Asn, NY. *Collection:* Master drawings. *Publ:* Coauth, Jackson Pollock: A Catalogue Raisonne, Yale Univ Press, 78; auth, articles, New York Review of Books, 80, New Criterion, 83 & New Republic, 83; Am Scholar, 83-84 & New York Times Bk Rev, 84; The Abstract Expressionists, Metrop Mus Art, Bulletin, winter 86/87. *Mailing Add:* 726 Park Ave New York NY 10021

THENHAUS, PAULETTE ANN
PAINTER, WRITER
b St Louis, Mo, Nov 8, 1948. *Study:* Webster Univ, St Louis, Mo, BA, 71; San Francisco Art Inst, with Perkle Jones, Calif; Southern Ill Univ, Carbondale, Ill, MFA (Phi Kappa Phi), 87. *Work:* Tarble Art Ctr, Eastern Univ, Charleston, Ill; Woodstock Sch Art, NY; Granite City Steel Collection, Ill; Giant City State Park Ctr, Makanda, Ill; Fleming Collection, Peoria, Ill; Evansville Mus, Ind. *Comn:* Trailing the American Dream (painting), pvt collector, San Francisco, Calif, 84; Percent for Art (2 paintings), Ill State Grant City State Parklodge, 87. *Exhib:* One-woman shows, In the Field, Seghi Gallery St Louis, Mo, 86, The Land with Additions, Northeast Mo State, Kirksville, 90; Watercolor: Illinois '89, Tarble Art Ctr, Charleston, Ill, 87; Horizontal Traditions, New Harmony Contemp Gallery, Ind, 87; 44th Ann Wash Valley Exhib, Sheldon Swope Gallery, Terra Haute, Ind, 88; 20th Joslyn Biennial, Joslyn Mus, Omaha, Nebr, 88; Seven State Art in the Woods, Overland Park, Kans, 94; Thirteenth & Fifteenth Biennial Watercolor & Drawing Exhib, Eastern Ill Univ, Charleston; Seasons, Galesburg Civic Art Ctr, 2003; Buchanan Center Arts, Monmouth, Ill, 2006; New Directions, The Box, Galesburg, Ill, 2010; Up-Beat Paintings, Bick Gallery in Galesberg Civic Art Ctr, 2012; 64 Arts, 2013; Nat Juried Exhib, Buchanan Arts Ctr, Monmouth, Ill. *Collection Arranged:* Pressworks Ill Printmakers (catalog), 91; Collage/Assemblage (catalog), 92; cur & showed, Galesburg Artists Paint the "Burg", Galesburg Civic Art Ctr, 2009; Dorothea Tanning Davi, 2011. *Pos:* Asst dir, Peoria Art Guild, Ill, 87-88; mus ed, Blanden Mem Mus, Iowa, 89-90; dir, Galesburg Civic Art Ctr, Ill, 90-94; gallery/studio proprietor, Art, Naturally; owner, Studio T, 99-; art ed, Zephyr Journal, 93-2010. *Teaching:* Art educator studio art, Branson Sch, Marin, Calif, 78-84; artist-in-residence, Dorland Colony, Temecula, Calif, 85 & Woodstock Studio Space, NY, 87; instr painting, Carl Sandburg Community Col. *Awards:* Award, 20th Joslyn Biennial, 88; Best Show (purchase), Tarble Art Ctr, 89; 1st Pl Art Rev, Ill Press 2005, 2nd Pl, 2009. *Bibliog:* Celeste Rehm & Paulette Thenhaus (auths), New Art Examiner, 89; Suitcase is worth seeing, Peoria J Star, 91; Art Talks, Radio interview, 3/18/99; Exhibit focuses on two women, Register Mail, 2/6/2003; Artists Seek New Direction, Register Mail, 6/10/2010. *Mem:* Chic Artists Coalition. *Media:* Acrylic, Oil. *Res:* website creation, History of Public Art in Knox County; Dorothea Tanning. *Specialty:* contemporary art. *Interests:* art history. *Publ:* Auth, Form beyond function, New Art Examiner, Vol XIII, No 13, 6/86; Paul Flexner, 88 & James Fritz/Lisa Sheets, 89, New Art Examiner; Auth, Drawing From Life art column, Zephyr, 93-; Mark Barone, Southern Arts Fedn, 10/94; NewArt Examiner, 11/94; Art Review, The Zephyr; auth, A Century of Public Art in Knox County, pvt publ, 2006. *Dealer:* Studio T Galesburg Civic Art Ctr Galesburg, IL. *Mailing Add:* 1431 Maple Ave Galesburg IL 61401

THEOBALD, GILLIAN LEE
PAINTER, LITHOGRAPHER
b La Jolla, Calif, Nov 17, 1944. *Study:* Byam Shaw, Sch Art London, 64-65; San Diego State Univ, BA, 67, MA, 71. *Exhib:* Solo exhibs, Cirrus Gallery, Los Angeles, 83, 86, 88, 89, 90, 93, 94, 96, 99, 2001, 2005, 2010, Patty Aande Gallery, San Diego, 85, 87, Palomar Coll, San Marcos, 88, Mark Quint Gallery, La Jolla, 93, Linda Hodges Gallery, Seattle, 97, 98, 2000, 2001, 2002, 2003, 2006, 2008, 2010, 2013, Rocket Gallery, London, 98 & Polarities: A Retrospective, Port Angeles Fine Art Ctr, Port Angeles, Wash, 2002, Grossmont Coll Gallery, San Diego, Calif, 2009; Group exhibs, Spectrum Los Angeles (with catalog), Gallery Akmak, Berlin, Fed Ger Repub, 85; Scapes (with catalog), Univ Art Mus, Univ Calif, Santa Barbara, 85; Reaching the Summit: Mountain Landscape, Laguna Beach & Saddleback Coll, 86; On the Horizon: Emerging Art Calif, Fresno Mus, 87; Lines of Vision; Drawings by Contemp Women (with catalog), Long Island Univ, New York, 89 & Blum Helman, New York, 89; Waterfall as Image, Occidental Coll, Los Angeles, 90; Soul Survivors; The Courage to go Beyond (with catalog), Beacon St Gallery, Chicago, Ill, 90; The Contemp Drawing: Existence, Passage & the Dream (with catalog), Rose Art Mus, Brandeis Univ Mass, 91; The Spiritual Landscape, Biota Gallery, Los Angeles, 91; Eye of the Creator; Artist's Self Portraits, Bush Art Ctr, Salem, Ore, 92; Summer, 92, Cirrus Gallery, Los Angeles, Calif, 92; Made in LA (with catalog), Los Angeles Co Mus Art, Calif, 95; Utopian Visions, Port Angeles Fine Art Ctr, Wash, 96; Nine Painters Plus One, Emmanuel Gallery, Univ Colo, Denver, 97; In Over Our Heads: The Image of Water in Contemp, San Jose Mus Art, 98; Bumber Biennale Bumbershoot Festival Arts, Seattle, Wash, 2004; plus numerous others. *Bibliog:* Dr Judy Collischan Van Wagner (auth), Lines of Vision: Drawings by Contemporary Women, Hudson Hills Press, New York, 89; Nancy Stapen (auth), Drawings at Brandeis Ask Profound Questions, The Boston Globe, 3/91; Jan Butterfield (auth), The Art Collection of Pacific Enterprises, Pacific Enterprises, Los Angeles, Calif, 91; Bruce Davis (auth), Made in LA: The Prints of Cirrus Editions, Los Angeles Co Mus Art, 95; Robert Perine (auth), San Diego Artists, Artra Publ, 1988; Douglas Bullis (auth), 100 Artists of the West Coast, Schiffer Publ, 2003. *Media:* Oil, Mixed Media; Encaustic, Lithography, Acrylic on Canvas. *Dealer:* Cirrus Gallery 542 S Alameda St Los Angeles CA 90013; Linda Hodges Gallery Seattle WA. *Mailing Add:* 6041 Palatine Ave N Seattle WA 98103-5350

THEOFILES, GEORGE
HISTORIAN, DEALER
b Reading, Pa, July 28, 1947. *Study:* Md Inst Coll Art, BFA (graphics), 69. *Pos:* Owner, catalog publ & seller, Miscellaneous Man, Vintage Graphics, New Freedom, Pa, 70-. *Teaching:* Adj prof graphic design hist, York Coll, Pa. *Awards:* Gold Medal Poster Design, Baltimore Md Art Dir Club, 70-. *Mem:* Co Military Historians; Poster Soc (bd); Ephemera Soc; Manuscript Soc. *Specialty:* American and European poster art and communication graphics, 1850-1960. *Publ:* Publ, Catalog of Original Poster Art and Graphics (tri-ann), 71-; auth, American Posters of World War I, Dafran House, 73. *Mailing Add:* PO Box 191 New Freedom PA 17349-0191

THEROUX, CAROL
PAINTER
b Cardwell, Mo, Aug 10, 1930. *Study:* Cerritos Coll Calif, with Donald Putman, Gerome Grimmer, life teaching credential, 76; Scottsdale Art Sch, 90; Scholar Art Ctr Design, La, 48. *Work:* Northwestern Bell Corp, Omaha, Nebr. *Comn:* Drawing of Borglum Statue, Prescott C of C, Ariz, 86; Buffalo Child (painting to celebrate NE Indian Arts Show), State of Nebr, Omaha, 88. *Exhib:* Ten one-woman shows, Mammen Gallery, Scottsdale, Ariz, 81-91; Wilcox Gallery, Sedona, Ariz, 92-96; Classic-Am Art Show, Invitational, Beverly Hills, Calif, 89-94; C M Russel Art Show & Auction, Great Falls, Mont, 90-93; Pastel Soc Am, NY, 91; The Albuquerque Miniatures, Albuquerque Mus, NMex, 91-94; and others. *Teaching:* Artist, drawing & painting, S Calif Studios, 63-78; artist, demonstrations, All S Calif Art Asns, 70-80; artist, Bellflower High Sch, 75-77. *Bibliog:* Susan Vreeland (auth), Dancing the ancient steps, Southwest Art Mag, 4/83; Vicki Stavic (auth), One on One, 87 & Artists to watch, 89, Art West Mag. *Mem:* Charter mem Pastel Soc Am; Pastel Soc W Coast; Pastel Soc Southern Calif; Nat Mus Women Arts. *Media:* Pastel. *Interests:* Collectable dolls and porcelain plates. *Mailing Add:* 17825 Canehill Ave Bellflower CA 90076-7119

THERRIEN, ROBERT
SCULPTOR, PAINTER
b Chicago, Ill, Nov 17, 1947. *Work:* Mus Mod Art & Whitney Mus Am Art, NY; Walker Art Ctr, Minneapolis, Minn; Dallas Mus Art; High Mus Art, Atlanta; Los Angeles Co Mus Art, Mus Contemp Art, Los Angeles; Tate Gallery, London; Pompidou Mus, Paris; Kemper Mus, Kansas City. *Exhib:* Biennial Exhib, Whitney Biennial, 85; solo exhib, MOCA Los Angeles, Calif, 86 & Museo Nat Reina Sofia, Madrid, Spain, 91-92; Documenta Invitational, Kassel, Ger, 92 & San Diego, Calif, 94; Carnegie Int, Carnegie Mus Art, Pittsburgh, 95-96; Contemp Art Ctr, Cincinnati, Ohio, 97. *Bibliog:* Margit Rowell (auth), Robert Therrien, Nat Reina Sofia, 91;

William Hackman (auth), Sunshine & Noir, In: Art in Los Angeles, 97; Margit Rowell (auth), Objects of Desire: The Modern Still Life. *Media:* Miscellaneous Media. *Publ:* Illusr, 7 plus 6 (Michael Butor & Robert Creely, auths), Use Hoshour, 89; Mesa Verde (Evan Connell, auth), Whitney Mus, 93. *Mailing Add:* c/o Maureen Mahony 139 N 6th St Brooklyn NY 11211

THIBAULT, ANDRE (TEABO)
COLLAGIST
b Quebec, Can, 1948. *Study:* Boston Univ, BS, 72-76; pupil & asst, Romare Bearden, 80-88. *Work:* Owensboro Mus Fine Art, Ky; Kelly Springfield Tire Co, Great Falls, Va; Boston Univ, Mass; AT&T, Basking Ridge, NJ. *Exhib:* 22nd Nat Sun Carnival Art Exhib, El Paso Mus Art, Tex; 32nd New Eng Exhib Paintings, Drawings & Sculpture, Silvermine Ctr for Arts, New Canaan, Conn; Montclair Art Mus, NJ; Nat Gallery Art, Wash, DC, 2000; Solo exhib, Nabisco Hq, NJ, Warehouse Gallery, Lee, Mass, Seraphim Gallery, NJ, 85-91, Wycoff Gallery, NJ 96-99. *Pos:* Asst, to the famous African Am, Romare Bearden. *Awards:* 41st Nat Exhib Award, Salmagundi Club, NY; 32nd Silvermine New Eng Exhib Award, Conn; Mid Am Biennial Purchase Award. *Bibliog:* Myron Schwartzman (auth): A Bearden-Murray Interplay, Callaloo, Vol 11, No 3, John Hopkins Univ Press, 1988, Romare Bearden - His Life & Art, Harry N Abrams Publ, NY, 1990, Entering the World of Romare Bearden: Bostonia, Alumni Quart Boston Univ, spring 2001. *Mem:* NJ Artist Guild; Modern Artist Guild; NJ Art Coun. *Media:* mixed, collage. *Specialty:* Collages, landscapes, portraits & abstracts. *Interests:* Serious cyclist. *Mailing Add:* 453 Fort Lee Rd Leonia NJ 07605

THIBERT, PATRICK A
SCULPTOR, EDUCATOR
b Windsor, Ont, Feb 25, 1943. *Study:* Western Ontario Inst Tech, 61-65, Univ Windsor, Ont, BFA, 72; Fla State Univ, Tallahassee, MFA, 74. *Work:* McIntosh Art Gallery, Univ Western Ont, London; Can Coun Art Bank, Ottawa; London Regional Art & Hist Mus, Ont; Art Gallery of Ont, Toronto; Kitchener-Waterloo Art Gallery, Ont; Themes Art Gallery, Chatham; St Thomas, Eligen Pub Art Ctr; Gallery Lambton, On; Woodstock Art Gallery, On; The Roberk M Laughlin Gallery, On. *Exhib:* Solo exhibs, Art Gallery of Hamilton, Ont, 86, Kitchener-Waterloo Art Gallery, Ont, 86 & 95, Forest City Gallery, London, 87 & 94, London Regional Art & Hist Mus, London, Ont, 92, Locating Identity: Patrick Thibert, McIntosh Gallery, Univ West Ont, 93, Art Gallery At Windsor, Ont, 94 & Robert McLaughlin Gallery, Oshawa, Ont 95, In the Mind of the Viewer: An Epilogue, Thames Art Gallery, 2000, Gallery Lambton, Sarnia, Ont, 2000, Woodstock Art Gallery, Woodstock, Ont, 2001, Thielsen Art Gallery, 2003, Olga Korper Gallery, 2008, Abstraction to Abstraction, Mus London, 2014; Sculpture Tour, Univ Tenn, Knoxville, 83-85, 87-88; Outdoor sculpture exhib, Burlington Cult Ctr, Ont, 87; Artists & Portraits, McIntosh Gallery, Univ West Ont, London, 89; Open Doors, Centre Contemp Art, St Thomas, Ont, 92; Olga Korper Gallery, 2008; Thielsen Gallery, 2008. *Teaching:* Grad teaching asst, Fla State Univ, Tallahassee, 73-74; instr, St Clair Col Applied Art & Technol, Windsor, Ont, 74-75; prof, Fanshawe Coll Applied Art & Technol, London, Ont, 75-2003. *Awards:* Ont Arts Coun Mat Grants, 75-83,92, 2006. *Bibliog:* David Burnett (auth), Patrick Thibert-Sculpture, 86; Judith Maclean Rodger (auth), Patrick Thibert: Transitions 1979-1987, London Regional Art & Hist Mus, London, Ont, 92-93; Ihor Holubizky & Robert McKaskell (auths), Locating Identity: Patrick Thibert, 93; Ted Fraser, In the Mind of the Viewer: An Epilogue, 2000, plus others; Ray Cronin & Rick Nixon (coauths), New Work by Patrick Thibert, Patrick Landsley, 2006; Ron Shuebrook (auth), Abstraction to Abstraction, 2014. *Mem:* Forest City Gallery, London, Ont. *Media:* Metal, Mixed Materials. *Dealer:* Olga Korper Gallery 157 Morrow Ave Toronto ON Canada M6R 2H9; Thielsen Gallery 1038 Adelaide St London Ontario N5Y 2M9. *Mailing Add:* 8952 Irish Dr RR 1 Mount Brydges ON N0L 1W0 Canada

THIES, CHARLES HERMAN
PAINTER, PRINTMAKER
b Poplar Bluff, Mo, Aug 22, 1940. *Study:* SE Mo State Univ, BS (fine arts educ), 63; Kans State Univ, MA (drawing & painting), 70; also studied at Washington Univ, St Louis, Kans Univ, Lawrence & Univ Northern Colo, Greeley. *Work:* St Louis Art Mus; Nelson-Atkins Art Mus, Kansas City, Mo; Springfield Art Mus, Mo; Wichita Art Mus, Kans; Utah Mus Fine Arts; Minn Art Mus; Margaret Harwell Art Mus, Poplar Bluff, Mo. *Comn:* Exterior mural, Ford Found Sponsored Prog, Kans State Univ, 69; six canvases, Marriott Hotel, Ft Collins, Colo, 85. *Exhib:* Thirty Miles of Art, Nelson Gallery-Atkins Mus, Kansas City, Mo, 76; Western Ann Nat Drawing Exhib, Western Ill Univ, 76; Drawings/USA, Minn Art Mus, St Paul, 77; Joslyn Biennial, Joslyn Art Mus, Omaha, Nebr, 78; Solo exhibs, Margaret Harwell Art Mus, Popular Bluff, Mo, 82 & 88 & Univ Art Mus, Cape Girardeau, Mo, 87; All Colo Art Exhib, 86, 88, 91 & 92; Expo 93, Boston, Mass; CPCC, Charlotte, NC, 2002; and others. *Pos:* Asst dir admis, Kansas City Art Inst, Mo, 76-77. *Teaching:* Instr drawing, design & figure drawing, Florissant Valley Coll, St Louis, Mo, 69-76; instr 3-D design, Johnson Co Community Coll, Overland Parks, Kans, 76. *Awards:* Painting Award, Exhib 70, St Louis, N Co Art Asn, 70; Drawing Award, Quincy Ill Fine Arts Asn, 71; Purchase, Drawings/USA 1977, Minn Mus Art. *Bibliog:* Int Personalities, Parma, Italy, 81. *Media:* Oil; Etching, Lithography. *Interests:* Religious Art and Nostalgic Sports Art (by comn); painting, classical music. *Dealer:* Studio 37 20037 E Hanging J Ranch Pl Parker CO 80134. *Mailing Add:* 20037 E Hanging J Ranch Pl Parker CO 80134-5987

THISTLETHWAITE, MARK EDWARD
EDUCATOR, HISTORIAN
b Baton Rouge, La, Jan 26, 1948. *Study:* Univ Calif, Santa Barbara, BA, 70, MA, 72; Univ Pa, Kress Found Fel, PhD, 77. *Exhib:* A Band of Exiles on the Wild New England Shore: The Place of Rothermels Landing of the Pilgrims in America's National Memory & Lafayette Coll, 2014. *Collection Arranged:* The Artist as Interpreter of Am History (auth, catalog), Pa Acad Fine Arts, Philadelphia, 76; Ed Blackburn, Tex Christian Univ, Ft Worth, 82 & co-cur, Dan Rizzie, Kimbell Art Mus, 90; Peter Rothermel Exhib, Brandywine River Mus, 95; Ed & Linda Blackburn, Contemp Art Ctr, Ft Worth; Celebrating Early Texas Art, Fort Worth Arts Community Arts Ctr, Tex, 2005. *Pos:* Trustee, Mod Art Mus Ft Worth; Kay & Velma Kimbell chair art hist, Tex Christian Univ; Cardin Chair in Humanities, Loyola Coll, Md, 2000; trustee, African Am Mus, Dallas. *Teaching:* Lectr mod art, Univ Pa, Philadelphia, 74-75; lectr Am & mod art, Philadelphia Coll Art, 74-76; from asst prof to prof, Am & mod art & archit, Tex Christian Univ, Ft Worth, 77-; Larom Inst, Buffalo Bill Hist Ctr, 2006. *Awards:* Tex Christian Univ Grants, 79, 81, 84-85, 88-91, 95, 98-99 & 2003-04; NEH Summer Institute Fel, 85 & 95; Chancellor's Award Distinguished Teaching, 90. *Mem:* Coll Art Asn; Midwest Art Hist Soc; Southeastern Coll Art Conf. *Res:* American art and architecture, especially 19th century history painting and contemporary art. *Publ:* Coauth (with W Gerdts), Grand Illusions: History of Painting in America, 88; William Ranney: East of the Mississippi, Brandywine River Mus, 91; Painting in the Grand Manner: Art & PF Rothermel, 95; plus numerous articles, exhibition reviews and criticism. *Mailing Add:* Tex Christian Univ TCU Box 298000 Fort Worth TX 76129

THOMAS, C DAVID
PRINTMAKER
b July 15, 1946. *Study:* Portland Sch Art, Maine, dipl, 68; Tufts Univ, BFA, 72; RI Sch Design, MFA, 74. *Work:* Brooklyn Mus; Mus Fine Art, Boston; DeCordova Mus, Lincoln, Mass; Philadelphia Mus Art; Portland Mus, Maine. *Exhib:* Thirty Yrs of Am Printmaking, Brooklyn Mus, 78; Recent Prints, Gallery Nat Asn Graphic Artists, Boston, 83. *Teaching:* Asst prof art, Emmanuel Col, 78-. *Awards:* Bort Award, Boston Mus Sch, 72; Emmanuel Coll Fac Develop Grant, 83. *Mem:* Boston Printmakers (exec bd, 79-); Philadelphia Print Club; Los Angeles Print Soc; Nat Asn Graphic Artists (chair, 80-). *Media:* Lithography. *Dealer:* Gallery Nat Asn Graphic Artists 67 Newbury St Boston MA 02116. *Mailing Add:* Emmanuel College Dept Art 400 Fenway Boston MA 02115

THOMAS, CHERYL ANN
SCULPTOR, CERAMIST
b Santa Monica, Calif, Oct 16, 1943. *Study:* Art Ctr Coll of Design, BFA, 82. *Work:* Minneapolis Inst for Arts, Minneapolis, Minn; Gardiner Mus of Ceramic Art, Toronto, Can; Fuller Craft Mus, Brockton, Mass; Long Beach Mus ARt, Long Beach, Calif; Cranbrook Acad Art, Bloomfield Hills, Mich; Mus Fine Arts, Houston, Tex. *Exhib:* Overthrown, Denver Art Mus; Fables Contemporaines, Mouvements Modernes, Paris, France; Basins, Baskets, and Bowls, Minneapolis Inst Art; Adventures of the Fire, 5th World Ceramics Biennale, Korea, 2009; Fertile Groun,d Santa Fe Clay, Santa Fe, NMex, 2010; New Work, Frank Lloyd Gallery, Santa Monica, Calif, 2011; Soft, Frank Lloyd Gallery, Santa Monica, Calif, 2013. *Bibliog:* Donald Kuspit (auth), Overthrown: Clay Without Limits, Denver Art Mus, 2011; Michelle Plochere (auth), The Times Quotidian, Origin Stories, 2011; Nadine Vasseur (auth), Palace Costes, Creatives Ceramiques, 2011. *Media:* Clay. *Dealer:* Frank Lloyd Gallery 2525 Michigan Ave B5b Santa Monica CA 90404

THOMAS, ELAINE FREEMAN
EDUCATOR, ADMINISTRATOR
b Cleveland, Ohio, July 21, 1923. *Study:* Northwestern Univ, Evanston, 44; Tuskegee Inst, BS (magna cum laude), 45; Black Mountain Col, 45, with Josef Albers & Robert Motherwell; NY Univ, Bodden fel, MA, 49, with Hale Woodruff; Mexico City Col, 56; Berea Col, 61; Univ Paris, 66; Southern Univ Workshop, 68; Columbia Univ, 70. *Collection Arranged:* One-man exhib, Winston-Salem State Univ, 70; Discovery 70, Univ Cincinnati; George Washington Carver Exhib, White House, 71; Ala Black Artists Exhib, Birmingham Festival Art, 72; plus others. *Teaching:* Asst prof art & chmn dept, Tuskegee Inst, 45-89; retired. *Awards:* Distinguished Participation, Am Artists Prof League, 68; Beaux Arts Festival Award. *Mem:* Am Asn Mus; Coll Art Asn Am; Nat Art Educ Asn; Nat Conf Artists; Ala Art League

THOMAS, HANK WILLIS
PHOTOGRAPHER
b Plainfield, New Jersey, 1976. *Study:* NY Univ, BFA (Photog & Africana Studies), 1998; Calif Coll Arts, MA, 2004, MFA (Photog), 2004. *Work:* Int Ctr Photog, New York; Mus Fine Arts, Houston. *Exhib:* Solo exhibs include Tex Women's Univ, Danville, 2003, Long & Pollack Gallery, San Francisco, 2003, Diaspora Vibe Gallery, Miami, 2004, Light Factory, Charlotte, NC, 2005, African Am Mus Philadelphia, 2005, Jack Shainman Gallery, New York, 2006, 2008, Sesnon Art Gallery, Univ Calif Santa Cruz, 2006, de Saisset Mus, Santa Clara, Calif, 2008; two-person exhibs include Wadsworth Atheneum, Hartford, Conn, (with Willie Cole), 2008; group exhibs include Student Exhib, Smithsonian Inst, Nat Portrait Gallery, Washington, 1993; Images & Inspirations, Nat Mus Am Hist, Washington, 1994; Speak to my Heart, Smithsonian Inst, Anacostia Mus, Washington, 1999; Moments in Love, Grand Cent Sta, New York, 2001; Frequency, Studio Mus Harlem, New York, 2005; Sweet Sweetback's Baadasssss Song, Von Lintel Gallery, New York, 2007; We're All in this together, Swarm Gallery, Oakland, Calif, 2008; From Taboo to Icon, Ice Box Projs Space, Philadelphia, 2008; Global Africa, High Mus Art, Atlanta, 2008; Unchained Legacy, Williams Coll Mus Art, Williamstown, Mass, 2008. *Awards:* Creative Excellence Award, NY Univ Photog Dept, 1998; Barclay Simpson Award, Calif Coll Arts, San Francisco, 2003; Art Matters Grant, 2008. *Dealer:* Lisa Dent Gallery 660 Mission St 4th Floor San Francisco CA 94105; Jack Shainman Gallery 513 W 20th St New York NY 10011; Charles Guice Contemp PO Box 13433 Berkeley CA 94712; Wertz Contemp 264 Peters St Atlanta GA 30313

THOMAS, JEREMY
SCULPTOR
b Mt Vernon, Ohio, Oct 15, 1973. *Study:* Okla Summer Arts Inst, studied with Deloss McGraw & Robert Rahway, 1995; Coll Santa Fe, NMex, BFA (studio art, Outstanding Sophomore award, 1994, Outstanding Junior award, 1995), 1995. *Exhib:* Fine Arts Gallery, Coll Santa Fe, 1994-1996; Site Santa Fe, 1999-2000, 2002; Jett Gallery, Santa

Fe, 2001; James Kelly Fine Art, Santa Fe, 2004; Santa Fe Art Inst, 2004; Rocket Gallery, London, 2005; Mus Fine Art, Santa Fe, 2005; Ctr for Contemp Arts, Santa Fe, 2006; Charlotte Jacksone Fine Art, 2006-2007. *Awards:* Outstanding Junior Award, Visual Arts Adv Coun, 1995. *Mailing Add:* c/o Charlotte Jackson Fine Art 554 S Guadalupe St Santa Fe NM 87501

THOMAS, KATHLEEN K
SCULPTOR, ASSEMBLAGE ARTIST
b Jan 1, 1940; US citizen. *Study:* Wichita State Univ, BA (art educ), 75, BA (art hist, cum laude), 76; Ind Univ Masters Prog, 77; Helena Rubenstein Fel, Whitney Mus Am Art, 77; ISP (Independent Study Prog: Art Admin & Curational Studies). *Work:* Chase Bank, NY; Deste Found Contemp Art, Athens; pvt collections, Ms Anne Dayton, Mr & Mrs Saul Skolar & others; and others. *Exhib:* Solo exhibs, Barbara Gladstone Gallery, NY, 81 & 84, Fashion Moda Gallery, Bronx, NY, 81 & Civilian Warfare Gallery, NY, 86; The Times Square Show, NY, 80; Beelden/Sculpture 83 (with catalog), Rotterdam Arts Coun, The Neth, 83; Materialisms (with catalog), Visual Arts Gallery, State Univ NY, Purchase, 84; Preview: 1984 (with catalog), Ronald Feldman Gallery, NY, 84; Precious (with catalog), Grey Art Gallery & Study Ctr, NY Univ, 85; Int High Tech Art Festival (with catalog), Seibu Mus, Tokyo, 85; Solo exhib, Studio Bergemeinde, Frankfurt, W Ger, 88, Max Fish, NY, 90, 92, 96, 2000. *Pos:* Assoc cur, New Mus Contemp Art, NY, 78-80. *Awards:* Helena Rubenstein Fel, Whitney Mus Am Art, 77; Deste Found Contemp Art Fel, 86; Pajes PRize in Art Hist, Wichita State Univ, 75. *Bibliog:* Ronnie H Cohen (auth), rev, Artforum Mag, 9/80; Jamie Gambrell (auth), Kathleen Thomas, East Village Eye, 10/84; Annelle Pohlen (auth), Skulptur '85, Kunstforum, 5-6/85; Jamie Gambrell (auth), rev, Art in Am Mag, 5/86. *Media:* Electronic, industrial, military, automotive and unidentified machine-made components. *Collection:* JP Morgan Chase Bank, Anne Dayton, Sol & Laura Skolar, Deste Foundation, Athens. *Publ:* Co-cur, Outside New York (contribr, catalog), 78, Sustained Visions (contribr, catalog), 79, In a Pictorial Framework (contribr, catalog), 79, Ree Morton Retrospective: 1971-1977 (coauth, catalog), 77 & traveling, 80-81, New Mus Contemp Art; Coauth, The 1970's: New American Painting, US Info Agency, 80. *Mailing Add:* 198 E 7 St Apt 1 New York NY 10009

THOMAS, MICKALENE
PAINTER
Study: Pratt Inst, BFA (painting), 2000; Yale Univ Sch Art, MFA (painting), 2002. *Work:* Guggenheim Mus, New York; Mus Fine Arts Boston; Mus Mod Art, New York; Art Inst Chicago; San Francisco Mus Mod Art; Whitney Mus Am Art: New York Pub Libr; Nat Potrati Gallery, Smithsonian; Int Ctr for Photog; Akron Art Mus. *Exhib:* Maximum Flavor, Atlanta Coll Art Gallery, Ga, 2005; Wild Girls, Exit Art, New York, 2006; solo exhibs, Dust Gallery, Las Vegas, 2006, Rhona Hoffman Gallery, Chicago, 2006, Santa Barbara Contemp ArtS Forum, 2008, Lehmann Maupin Gallery, 2009, La Conservera Contemp Art Space, Spain, 2009, Susan Vielmetter Los Angeles Projects, 2010; Taking Aim, Rhodes Coll, Memphis, 2007; As Others See Us: The Contemporary Portrait, Brattleboro Mus Art Ctr, Vt, 2008; Posing Beauty, NYU Tisch Sc Arts, 2009; Pattern ID, Akron Art Mus, Ohio, 2010. *Pos:* Artist-in-residence, Vt Studios Ctr, Johnson, 2001, Studio Mus Harlem, New York, 2003, Versailles Found, Giverny, France, 2010. *Awards:* Rema Hort Mann Grant, 2007; Pratt Inst Alumni Achievement Award, 2009; Joan Mitchell Found Grant, 2010. *Bibliog:* Roberta Smith (auth), Where Issues of Black Identity Meet the Concerns of Every Artist, NY Times, 11/18/2005; Sarah Valdez (auth), Bling and Beyond, Art in Am, 4/2006; Karen Rosenberg (auth), An Afternoon in Chelsea, New York Mag, 5/7/2007; Lauren Weinberg (auth), Jet Set, Time Out Chicago, 11/20-26/2008; Dodie Kazanjian (auth), Dreaming the Landscape, Vogue, 216-223, 11/2009. *Mailing Add:* 20 Grand Ave Ste 507-508 Brooklyn NY 11205

THOMAS, W. RADFORD
EDUCATOR, PAINTER
b Waco, Tex. *Study:* Univ Tex at Austin, BFA, 1957; Highlands Univ, MA, 1962; Univ Tex at Austin, PhD, 1970. *Work:* Israel Mus, Jerusalem, Israel; Dallas Mus Art, Dallas, Tex; Oakland Mus, Oakland, Calif; Smith Col Mus Art, Northampton, Mass; Simon Fraser Univ Gallery, Burnaby, BC. *Comn:* Altar (oil & gold leaf), Holy Trinity Episcopal Church, Austin, Tex, 1957; Mosaic (mural), Fed Housing Proj, San Antonio, Tex, 1962; Lithograph, Elizabeth Arden Collection, New York, NY, 1963; Fiberglass Panels, Bank of the Southwest Bldg, Amarillo, Tex, 1964; Mural, Americana Motor Hotels Inc, Denver, Colo, 1967. *Exhib:* Men of Art Guild, Palacio de Bellas Artes, Mex DF, 1962; Contemp Work 82 Contemp Tex Artists, DD Feldman Found, Dallas, Tex, 1962; Our Land, Our Sky, Our Water, Expo '74 World's Fair Art Pavilion, Spokane, Wash, 1974; Biennial Exhib, Mint Mus Art, Charlotte, NC, 1975; Solo Exhib, Swiss Pavilion Invitational, Venice Biennial, Italy, 1976; Artists Stamps & Stamp Images, Glenow-Alberta Inst, Calgary, Alberta, 1979; Group Exhib, Mus Contemp Art, Utrecht/Neth, 1980; portrait, Judge Samuel Wilson, POFF Federal Bldg, Roanoke, Va, 2014. *Collection Arranged:* Ecce Homo, George Grosz Lithographs, 1971; Gallo, Works of Frank Gallo, 1972; Ken Friedman, Re: Omaha Flow Systems, 1973; Environmental Communications, Signage & Display, 1973; Chicano Art, Nat Invitational, 1974; Hertzberg Circus Collection, Poster, Photographs, 1989; Stamps from a Stamp Collector's Dream, 2008; Fabric and Fiber Through the Ages, 2014. *Pos:* Dir, Rockefeller Arts Ctr, Fredonia, NY, 1980-1982; dir, Noel Mus Art, Odessa, Tex, 1988-1990; chmn, E Washington Univ, Cheney, Wash, 1970-1974, Dept Art, E Tenn Univ, Johnson City, Tenn, 1974-1980. *Teaching:* Prof, Art Hist, Va Western Community Col, Roanoke, Va, 1998-2014; Prof, Radford Univ, Radford, Va, 2001-2005. *Awards:* Purchase Awards: Tex Ann, Dallas Mus Fine Arts, 1959; Witte Mem Mus, San Antonio, Tex, 1959. *Bibliog:* Cecile McCann (auth), Our Land, Our Sky, Our Water, Artweek, Vol 5, No 22, 1974; Ken Friedman (auth), Radford Thomas, Ecart Publs. Geneva, 1975. *Mem:* Men of Art Guild; Tex Fine Arts Soc. *Media:* Oil. *Specialty:* Portraits, landscapes, automotive fine art. *Interests:* Collecting Pre-Columbian artifacts. *Publ:* Ed, A Conceptual Design Statement for Ice Harbor Lock & Dam, US Army Corps Engineers, 1972; auth, Aeriel House, San Antonio Homes & Gardens, 1985; auth, Creating with Ideas, Trinity Univ, 1988; ed, Art Safety Workbook for Radford Univ, Thompson Educ, 2003. *Dealer:* Steele Thomas Studios Roanoke VA. *Mailing Add:* 4853 Hunting Hills Dr Roanoke VA 24018

THOMASON, MICHAEL VINCENT
PHOTOGRAPHER, CURATOR
b West Palm Beach, Fla, June 20, 1942. *Study:* Univ South, Sewanee, Tenn, BA, 64; Duke Univ, MA, 66, PhD, 68. *Exhib:* Work & Leisure in Turn Century Mobile, Fine Arts Mus South, Mobile, 80; Allied Arts Competition, 77, Mobile, 77; The Image of Progress: Alabama Photographs 1877-1917, Birmingham Mus Art, Ala, 81; Buildings Reborn: Adaptive Re-use Proposals, traveling exhib, Ala, 80. *Collection Arranged:* Work & Leisure Turn Century Mobile (auth, catalog), 80; The Image of Progress (auth, catalog), Birmingham, Ala, 81; Mobile's Black Heritage in Photographs, 83; Mardi Gras from the Gay Nineties to the Great Depression, 83; Trying Times: Alabama Photographs, 1917-1945 (auth, catalog), 85. *Pos:* Dir, Photo Archives, Univ South Ala, Mobile, 78-. *Teaching:* Prof, Univ S Ala, 78-. *Awards:* First Prize, Allied Arts Competition, 77. *Media:* Black & White. *Res:* Uses of photography in history; the photography as a historical source. *Publ:* Coauth, Mobile: American River City, Easter, Mobile, 75; coauth, Mobile: The Life and Times of a Great Southern Seaport, Windsor, Calif, 81. *Mailing Add:* 1548 Deerwood Dr E Mobile AL 36618-3073

THOMPSON, CAPPY (CATHERINE)
PAINTER
b Jan 22, 1952. *Study:* Fairhaven Col, Bellingham, Wash, 70-71; Factory Visual Arts, Seattle, Wash, 71-72; Evergreen State Col, Olympia, Wash, BA, 76. *Work:* Art Gallery W Australia, Perth; Chrysler Mus Art, Norfolk, Va; Hokkaido Mus Mod Art, Sapporo, Japan; Davis, Wright, Tremaine, Seattle, Wash; and others. *Comn:* Stained glass entryway, South Bay Elem Sch, Olympia, Wash, 84; stained glass panels, Mount Lake Terrace Pub Libr, Wash, 86. *Exhib:* Betsy Rosenfield Gallery, Chicago, Ill, 92; Leo Kaplan Gallery, NY, 93; Am Craft Mus, NY, 93; Hokkaido Mus Mod Art, Sapporo, Japan, 94; Seattle Art Mus, Wash, 95; Breaking the Mold: New Directions in Glass, Huntsville Mus Art, Ala, 96; Celebrating the Figure, Penland Gallery, Penland Sch Crafts, NC, 96; Solo shows, Leo Kaplan Mod, NY, 97, New Works, Grover/Thurston Gallery, Seattle, Wash, 97, Habatat Galleries, Boca Raton, Fla, 98, R Duane Reed Gallery, Chicago, 99, William Traver Gallery, Seattle, 02, Carnegie Mus Art, Pittsburgh, 02; Glass Today by Am Studio Artists, Mus Fine Art, Boston, Mass, 97; Telling Compelling Tales: The Narrative in Contemp Glass, Holter Mus Art, Helena, Mont, 98; The Dimensional Canvas: Painted Studio Glass, Dorothy Weiss Gallery, San Francisco, Calif, 98; Smithsonian Inst, 98-2000; Contemp Art Ctr Va, Va Beach, 99; Margo Jacobsen Gallery, Portland, Ore, 2000; Habatat Galleries, Boca Raton, Fla, 2000-01; Ky Art & Craft Found, 2000-01; Heller Gallery, NY, 2001; and others. *Collection Arranged:* Am Craft Mus, NY; Birmingham Mus Art, Ala; Hokkaido Mus Mod Art, Sapporo, Japan; Microsoft Corp, Redmond, Wash; Montgomery Mus Art, Ala; Nordstrom Inc, Seattle; Tacoma Art Mus, Wash; Wash State Arts Comn, Olympia; Toyama City Inst Glass Art, Japan. *Pos:* Studio coordr, Pilchuck Sch, Stanwood, Wash, 87, printmaker, 90; designer, Juanita Kreps Award, JC Penney Co, 95-00. *Teaching:* Artist-in-residence, Pilchuck Sch, Stanwood, Wash, 84, fac, 88, 89, 92, 96, Penland Sch Crafts, NC, 96; fac, Pratt Fine Arts Ctr, Seattle, Wash, 90, 91, master arts workshop, 01; Int Conf Workshop, Glass Art Soc, Monterey, Mex, 92; Int Conf Workshop, Auglass, Camberra, Australia, 93; workshop instr, Centro del Arte Vitro, Monterrey, Mex, 92 & Canberra Sch Art, Australia, 93; workshop, Toyana City Inst Glass Art, Japan, 95, Calif Col of Arts & Crafts, Oakland, 01, Sch Art, Rochester Inst Tech, NY, 01; Fac, Penland Sch Crafts, NC, 96 & Col Fine Arts, Jacksonville Univ, Fla, 97. *Awards:* Nat Endowment Arts Fel Visual Arts, 90; Artist in Res, Toyama City Inst Glass Art, Japan, 95; Fel, Artist Trust, Seattle, Wash, 97; John H Hauberg Fel, Pilchuck Glass Sch, Stanwood, Wash, 01; selected for a Univ Wash Artist Images Series Bookmark, 98. *Bibliog:* Tina Old Know (auth), Pilchuck: A Glass School, Univ Wash Press, 96; Cappy Thompson: Narrative, Mythopoesis and the Vessel Form, Glass Art, 1-2/97; Karen Chambers (auth), Cappy Thompson, Leo Kaplan Modern, through July 4, 1997, World Art Rev, 97; William S Ellis (auth), Glass: From the First Mirror to Fiber Optics, The Story of the Substance that Changed the World, 98; Geoffrey Wichert (auth), What Happened to Stained Glass?, Glass 86, 02. *Mem:* Glass Art Soc (bd dir, 89-92, secy, 90-92); Pilchuck Glass Sch (artistic adv comt, 92). *Media:* Blown Glass, Stained Glass. *Dealer:* Leo Kaplan Modern 965 Madison Ave New York NY 10021; Gover/Thurston Gallery 309 Occidental Ave S Seattle WA 98104. *Mailing Add:* 707 S Snoqualmie No 4A Seattle WA 98108

THOMPSON, DONALD ROY
PAINTER, EDUCATOR
b Fowler, Calif, Mar 2, 1936. *Study:* Calif State Univ, Sacramento, BA, 60, MA, 62. *Work:* Oakland Mus, Calif; Seattle First Nat Bank; Crocker Art Mus, Calif State Univ, Sacramento, Calif; Art Mus Santa Cruz Co, Calif; Santa Clara Univ Law Sch. *Exhib:* West '81/Art and the Law, Minn Mus Art, St Paul; Smith Andersen Gallery, Palo Alto, Calif, 86; D P Fong & Spratt Galleries, San Jose, Calif, 92, Frederick Spratt Gallery, San Jose, Calif, 02, 03; Composer's Choice: Selections from the Collection of Lou Harrison, Octagon Mus, Santa Cruz, Calif, 92; Frederick Spratt Gallery, San Jose, Calif, 93; solo show, Frederick Spratt Gallery, San Jose, Calif, 95, 98, 01 & Cabrillo Coll Gallery, Aptos, Calif, 00; and others. *Teaching:* emeritus Instr art, painting & drawing, Cabrillo Col, 71-2000. *Awards:* Purchase Award, West '81/Art & the Law, West Publ Co, 81. *Bibliog:* Mark Levy (auth), Vital fabrications, Artweek, 12/18/1982; Claude Lesuer (auth), Rare summer pleasures, Artspeak, 6/23/1983; Jack Fischer (auth), Artist Subverts Expectations, San Jose Mercury-News, 7/29/2001. *Media:* Acrylic. *Dealer:* Frederick Spratt Gallery San Jose CA

THOMPSON, ERNEST THORNE, JR
SILVERSMITH, PAINTER
b South Bend, Ind, Nov 9, 1928. *Study:* Huguenot Sch Art, with Courtney Allen, Charles R Kingnan, Ernest T Thompson, Sr, dipl; Sch Mus Fine Arts, Boston, with Joseph L Sharrock, Sr & Hazel Olsen Brown, dipl, independent study in Japan. *Work:* Mus Sci, Boston, Mass; USAF Chapel, Bien Hoe, Vietnam; Corp Plate, Boston, Gt

Brit. *Comn:* Industrial comns & pvt collections; chapel & altar pieces, Miles Mem Hosp Chapel. *Pos:* Trustee, Soc Arts & Crafts, 61-64; juror, Sterling Silver Design Competition, 75; owner & partner, Thompsons Studio Inc. *Teaching:* Dept head jewelry & silversmith, Boston Mus Sch, 61-70 & Portland Sch Art, 69-80. *Bibliog:* Bill Cauldwell (auth), Stop, silversmith at work, Ford Times Mag, 10/69; Richard Stilwell (auth), Ernest Thompson unselfish in silver, Maine Guide Dir, 74; article in House Beautiful Mag, 2/80; Damon Ripley & Lawrence Willard (auths), Thompson's silversmith studio, Yankee Mag, 12/81. *Mem:* Pemaquid Group of Artists; Am Legion (life mem). *Media:* Gold, Silver; Oils, Watercolor. *Res:* Japanese Sword Furniture. *Interests:* Wild Life Preservation. *Mailing Add:* 401 Back Meadow Rd Damariscotta ME 04951

THOMPSON, JACK
SCULPTOR, EDUCATOR
b Los Angeles, Calif, May 25, 1946. *Study:* Calif State Univ, Northridge, BA, 70; San Francisco Art Inst, 71; Tyler Sch Art, Temple Univ, MFA, 73. *Work:* Int Acad Ceramics, Calgary; John Michael Kohler Arts Ctr Mus, Sheboygan, Wis; Los Angeles Co Art Mus, Calif; Mint Mus, Charlotte, NC; Arizona State Univ, Phoenix; St Joseph's Univ, Philadelphia. *Comn:* Ltd ed teapots, Garth Clark Gallery, NY, 84 & 91; Sculpture, Caesars Palace, Las Vegas, Nev, 90; Sculpture, Riverwalk Piers 3 & 5, Philadelphia, Pa, 90. *Exhib:* Hot off the Press (auth catalog), Tulie House Mus, Carlisle, Eng; The Animal Image, Renwick Gallery, Smithsonian Inst, 81; Am Clay Artists, Port of Hist Mus, Philadelphia, Pa, 89; solo exhibs, Animal Love Sacred or Profane, Jasuta Gallery, Philadelphia, 94, Vision de Vida y Muerte, Casa de la Cultura, SCLC, Chiapas, Mex, Transmigrations, Works Gallery, Philadelphia, 99, Numina, St Joseph's Univ, Philadelphia, 2003, Reflections on the Zodiac, Projects Gallery, Philadelphia, 2005; Bucks Biennial, James Michener Mus, Doylestown, Pa, 94; Transformations, 4 Bucks Co Artists, James A Michener Art Mus, Doyelstown, Pa, 95; ICA: 1 Singular Sensation, Inst Contemp Art, Univ Pa, Philadelphia, 95; and others. *Teaching:* Prof fine arts, Moore Col Art & Design, Philadelphia, 74-; vis Lectr, Princeton Univ, 93-94. *Awards:* Fel, Pa State Coun Arts, 81, 83, 87 & 2007; Purchase Award, JM Kohler Art Mus, 89; Fulbright Fel, Mex, 96-97. *Bibliog:* Susan Peterson (auth), The Art & Craft of Clay, Prentice Hall, New York, 91; Arthur Williams (auth), Sculpture Technique form & Content, Davis Publ, Worcester, Mass, 91; Leon Nigrosh (auth), Sculpting Clay, Davis Publ, Worcester, Mass; Paul Mathieu (auth), Sexpots, Eroticism in Ceramics, Rutgers Univ Press, 2003; Suzanne Tourtillot (auth), The Figure in Clay, Lark Books, 2005, 500 Animals in Clay, 2006. *Mem:* Bucks Co Coun Arts; Int Sculpture Ctr; Nat Coun Educ Ceramic Arts. *Media:* Ceramic, Cement. *Dealer:* Projects Gallery Philadelphia PA. *Mailing Add:* 705 Almshouse Rd Doylestown PA 18901

THOMPSON, JEAN DANFORTH
PHOTOGRAPHER
b Baltimore, Md, May 3, 1933. *Study:* Md Inst Art, 50; Univ Md, BA, 54; Wright State Univ, MA, 72. *Work:* Univ Md; Am Embassy, Bonn, WGer; US Cent Intelligence Agency, McLean, Va; US Dept of State; Marriott Corp, Washington, DC; Sheraton Hotel, Baton Rouge, La. *Comn:* Xerox, Arlington, Va, 80, Nat Rural Electric Coop Asn, Washington DC, 80, McDonalds Corp, Fairfax, Va, 81, Am Apparel Asn, Rosslyn, Va, 83 & Paffrather Raiffeisen Bank, Cologne, WGer. *Exhib:* Solo exhib, Geilsdorfer Gallerie, Cologne, WGer, 82-84 & 86; Gayle Wilson Gallery, Southampton, NY, 83; Arverne Art Int, Ltd, NY, 83; Leighton-Richey Gallery, Columbia, 92; Bell-Atlantic, Washington, DC, 95; Regan Nat Airport Show, 2009; Art League, 2009-2010. *Collection Arranged:* Art USA, London, 80. *Mem:* Torpedo Factory Artists Asn (pres, 79-80, bd mem, 76-86); Fiber Workshop; Artists Equity. *Media:* Digital Photography. *Mailing Add:* Studio 16 Torpedo Factory Art Ctr 105 N Union St Alexandria VA 22314

THOMPSON, JOSEPH C
MUSEUM DIRECTOR
Study: Williams Coll, BA, 1981; Univ Pa, MA (art hist, Annenberg Fel), 1986, MBA (Morganthau Fel), 1987. *Pos:* Preparator, exhibs designer, Williams Coll Mus Art, 1982; James Webb Fel, Smithsonian Inst, Washington, 1984; founding dir, Mass Mus Contemp Art, North Adams, 1988-. *Teaching:* Lectr contemp art, Williams Coll, Univ Pa, 1988-90. *Mailing Add:* Mass Mus Contemp Art 1040 MASS MoCA Way North Adams MA 01247

THOMPSON, JUDITH KAY
PAINTER
b Kansas City, Kans, May 28, 1940. *Study:* William Jewell Col, Liberty, Mo, 60; Kans City Art Inst, Wilbur Neiwald, BFA, 65; Univ Cincinnati & Art Acad, MFA, 67. *Work:* Works purchased by private individuals throughout the US. *Exhib:* Nat Assoc of Women Artists, Millennium Collection, United Nations, Washington, DC, Works on Paper, Fairleigh Dickinson Univ, Hackensack, NJ, 75 & Brooklyn Mus, NY, 75; 96th Ann Nat Exhib Asn, Jacob K Javits Fed Bldg, NY, 85; Nat Asn Women Artists (traveling), 2000. *Pos:* Admin Asst (retired). *Teaching:* Instr drawing, Cincinnati Art Mus, 66; instr draw, 2-D & 3-D design, St Cloud State Univ, Minn, 69; instr painting & draw, St Benedict's Col, Minn, 69. *Awards:* Goldie Paley Award, Celebration Bicentennial, Nat Asn Women Arts, 76. *Bibliog:* Notable Women of Tex, 84; New York Art Review, 87; Who's Who in Am Art 78-2010; Who's Who in Am, Designer of the 20th Century, 2003; Biog Encyl Am Painters, Sculpt & Engravers of the US Colonial to 2002, Dealers Choice Books, Inc, Fla, 2002. *Mem:* Nat Asn of Women Artists, NY, 1975-2009; Nat Mus of Women in the Arts, Washington, DC, 1987-2006. *Media:* Oil. *Res:* 74-traveled to Europe to res women painters in hist. *Interests:* walking, pets. *Mailing Add:* 9337 Westwood Village Dr Houston TX 77036

THOMPSON, LYDIA
ADMINISTRATOR, EDUCATOR
Pos: head dept art, Mississippi State Univ, formerly; dir sch art, Tex Tech Univ, Lubbock, Tex, 2013-. *Mailing Add:* Texas Tech University School of Art 18th St and Flint Ave Lubbock TX 79409

THOMPSON, LYNN P
PAINTER, PHOTOGRAPHER
b Plainfield, NJ, July 22, 1922. *Study:* Bennett Jr Col, 39-40; Douglas Col, BA, 43; Cornell Med Col, MD, 46; Nat Acad Design; Art Students League, Maine Coast Workshops, Schlemm & Wagner, 97-98. *Work:* New York Hosp; Khanbegian Gallery, Sonogee, Bar Harbor, Maine; Inglemoor, Englewood, NJ; Kodak Artcart Collection, 86-. *Comn:* El Molino (oil), comn by George Moore, Sotogrande, Spain, 80; seascape, comn by Dr Eibl, Vienna, 80; Maine seascape, Drawing Room, Peninsula, Ohio, 81; painting (oil), New York Hosp, 83; Series Watercolors, David Elliott; plus many others. *Exhib:* Solo exhib, Bergen Mus, Paramus, NJ, 74 & El Molino, Spain, 79; Federated Art Asn, NJ State Mus, Trenton, 75; NY Physicians Art Asn Ann, Union Carbide, 76; NY Physicians Art Exhib, NY Acad Med, 76-79; Oil Painting & Watercolors Exhib, Coll Atlantic, Bar Harbor, Maine, 98. *Collection Arranged:* The David Elhots, Dean Lambertson, Anthony Swan; Collections with the George Moore Family of Spain and NYC, and Peter Thompson. *Pos:* Dir, New York Hosp Art Comn, 66-74 & 77-80 & Child Life Ctr, New York, 82-; dir & adv, Circulating Art Cart Prog, 78; coordr, Hosp Audiences, New York, 82-; 300 progs underway in 31 states, Que, Can & Am Hosp, Paris; exec comm assoc, Healthcare Art Admin, 89-. *Teaching:* Instr watercolor, Sonogee, Bar Harbor, Maine, 79-, Mainescape Gallery, Bar Harbor, Maine. *Awards:* Prix Etats-Unis, Duncan Gallery, New York & Paris, 75; First & Second Awards, New York Physicians Art Asn Ann, 76-79; Bocour Award, Orange Art Asn, 78; Volunteer of Yr Award for Art in Nursing Homes, Am Health Asn, 88. *Bibliog:* Marguerite Logan (auth), Circulating Art Program Brings New Vistas to Facility Life, Am Health Care Asn J, 85; Judy Haberek (auth), Nursing Home Volunteers Circulate Art & Heart in Bergen County, Voluntary Action Leadership, winter 86; Marian (auth), Doctor Finds Art the Best Medicine, Lancet, Art in Health care facilities, 12/88. *Mem:* Salmagundi Club; Catharine Lorillard Wolfe Club; Allied Artists Am; New York Physicians Art Asn (dir, 78-); Bergen Co Artists Guild. *Media:* Watercolor, Oil. *Res:* Cancer research with Dr. George Snell (Nobel Prize Winner) at the Jackson Lab in Bar Harbor, ME, 1940; Research on the development of Sanddollar embryos at MDIBL in Bar Harbor, ME, 1964. *Specialty:* Watercolors. *Interests:* Love to paint and facilitate a sense of well being at hospitals and nursing homes through work with the Circulating Art Program. *Publ:* Contribr, Cornell Medical College Alumni News, 81 & 84. *Dealer:* Mainescape Gallery 54 West St Bar Harbor ME 04609. *Mailing Add:* 8 Heritage Ln Cumberland Foreside ME 04110-1306

THOMPSON, MARK L
SCULPTOR
b Ft Sill, Okla, 1950. *Study:* Va Polytech Inst, 68-70; Univ Calif, Berkeley, BA, 72, MA, 73. *Work:* Berkeley Art Mus, Calif; Hartnell Col, Salinas, Calif; Newberger Berman Corp, San Francisco. *Exhib:* Invocations, Whitechapel Art Gallery, London, 90; Dance of the Honeybees: An Exploration of San Francisco's Mission District, Exploratorium, San Francisco, Calif, 92; Walk with Backpack I Live (performance), Japan-US friendship Comn, Kurobane, 92; Solo exhib, Hartnell Coll Art Gallery, Salinas, Calif, 93; Color in the Shadows: Bay Area Cyberart, Oliver Ctr, Calif Coll Arts & Crafts, Oakland, 94; Tiniest Show on Earth, Boulder Mus Contemp Art, Col, 96; Animalia, Stadtgalrie Wellerdeler, Berlin, Ger, 97; Out of Actions: Between Performance and the Object, 1949-1979, Los Angeles, 98-99; 25/25, Southern Exposure, San Francisco, 99; The Boy Mechanic, Yerba Buena Ctr for Arts, San Francisco, 99; Essence of Composition, Gallery Paule Anglim, San Francisco, 2001. *Pos:* Artist-in-residence, Hartnell Col, Salinas, Calif, 77; artist-in-residence proj mgr, Headlands Ctr Arts, Ft Barry, Calif, 86; panel mem, Going Public: Western Regional Pub Art Forum, San Francisco, 88, Earth Day: Artists Respond to the Environmental Crisis, Palo Alto Cult Ctr, Calif, 90 & Installation Art, Discussion with Chris Burden and Mark Thompson, Whitechapel Art Gallery, London, Eng, 90. *Teaching:* Var lect-film presentations, 77-92; lectr art-conceptual design, San Francisco State Univ, 88 & 89, lectr sculpture, 91-93, grad workshop, 92; vis lectr sculpture, Univ Col London, Slade Sch Fine Art, 90; grad workshop, Univ Colo, Boulder, 94; adj prof sculpture, Calif Col Arts & Crafts, 93-96, assoc prof, 96-2000, prof, 2000-. *Awards:* New Genre Artists Fel, Calif Arts Coun, 92; Creative Arts Fel, Cult Arts, City Oakland, Calif, 94; Visual Artists Award, Flintridge Found, 98; NEA Fel Grant, 89, 90; Civitella Ranieri Ctr Fel, Umbertide, Italy, 2001. *Bibliog:* George Gessert (auth), Notes on genetic art, Vol 26, No 3, Leonardo, 93; Barrett Watten (auth), Science Fair, Vol 25, No 4, Artweek, 2/17/94; Bill Berkson (auth), The Salon at Mission & Third, Art in Am, 6/94; and others. *Publ:* Animalia: Stellvertreter (catalog), Haus am Waldsee, Berlin, Ger, 90; Seven Obsessions (catalog), Whitechapel Art Gallery & Performance Mag, No 63, London, Eng, 11/90; Performance-Ritual-Process, Elisabeth Jappe, Prestel-Verlag, Munich, NY, 93; In Out of the Cold (catalog), Ctr Arts, Yerba Buena Gardens, San Francisco, Calif, 93; Visions of America: Landscape as Metaphor In The Late 20th Century (essays by Martin Friedman, et al), Denver Art Mus, 94; and others

THOMPSON, MICHAEL
ART DEALER
b Des Moines, Iowa, Aug 2, 51. *Study:* Univ Northern Iowa, BA magna cum laude in Econ, 73; Univ Iowa, JD cum laude in Econ, 76, MA in Econ, 77. *Pos:* Asst atty gen Iowa Dept Justice, Des Moines, Iowa, 76; econ Iowa Commerce Commn, Des Moines, Iowa, 76-77; spl asst NY Pub Svc Commn, Albany, NY, 77-80; commerce counsel Mo Pacific RR, St Louis, Mo, 1980-83; atty, Southwestern Bell Corp, St Louis, Mo, 83-86; exec vpres, gen. counsel SBC Int Devel Corp, 86-2000; pvt practice, Chicago, Ill, 2000-12; proprietor Boreas Fine Art, Evanston, Ill, 2011-. *Teaching:* adj instr corp fin Drake Univ, Des Moines, 1977; lectr Univ Chicago Law Sch, 2006-12. *Mem:* Am Printing History Asn (chmn. awards com 2014, 2015), Fellowship of Am Bibliophilic Socs (vpres 2012-, trustee 2014-), Univ Chicago Law Libraries (mem vis com 2013-), Chicago Bar Asn (co-chmn Entertainment and Art Law com 2003-04), Univ Chicago Libr Soc (chair 2014-), Newberry Libr, Chicago (trustee 2014-), Bibliographical Soc Am (chmn nominating com 2010, coun mem, chmn finance com 2012-), Nat Arts Club, Caxton Club of Chicago (pres 2003-05, coun mem 2012-15), Union League Club, Arts Club Chicago, Grolier Club, Houston

Yacht Club, Chicago Yacht Club. *Publ:* Dealers in Cultural Property: UNIDROIT and the UNESCO Code of Ethics, 3 ABAA Newsletter, Spring 2002; The Provenance of Fine Art and Cultural Property: Issues for Estate Planners and Trustees, presented to the private banking division, Bank of America, N.A., Chicago, 6/2003, Out of Print, presented before the Chicago Literary Club, Chicago, 11/2003, Five Things Every Lawyer Should Know About Entertainment and Art Law, Chicago Bar Asn Record, 01/2004 (co-auth), Holocaust Era Assets and the Extraterritorial Reach of US Law presented at Responsible Stewardship Towards Cultural Heritage Materials sponsored by the Int Fedn Libr Asns, Rare Books and Manuscripts Section, Kongelige Bibliotek, Copenhagen, Denmark, 8/2005, published in The Caxtonian, 12/2005; Organizer, moderator of the fifth ann Caxton Club / Bibliographical Soc of America Symposium on the Book, Bibliography, Collections, & the History of Science, The Pyle Ctr, Uni Wis, Madison, Wis, 04/26/2014 (in cooperation with the libraries at the Univ Wis, Madison), The 2014 Whitney Biennial: the Book as a Medium in Contemp Am Art, The Papers of the Bibliographical Soc of America, 06/2015, pp. 147-192 (Vol. 109, Issue 2), The Book as Medium in Contemp Am Art presented at The Ctr for Book Arts, New York, 10/09/2015, numerous other papers, publs and presentations. *Mailing Add:* Boreas Fine Art 1555 Sherman Ave Suite 362 Evanston IL 60201

THOMPSON, NANCY KUNKLE
JEWELER, EDUCATOR
b Marion, Ind, Dec 30, 1941. *Study:* Ball State Teachers Col, BS (art), 63; Ind Univ, MFA (jewelry design & metalsmithing), 68. *Work:* Ind Univ Mus Art, Bloomington; Greenville Co Mus Art, SC. *Exhib:* Extraordinary Vehicles, J M Kohler Arts Ctr, Sheboygan, Wis, 74; Southeastern Crafts, Greenville Co Mus Art, SC, 74; Bicentennial Craft Invitational, Ind Univ Art Mus, 76; Wearables, Renwick Gallery, DC, 79; The Next Juried Show, Va Mus Fine Arts, 83; New Art Forms: Virginia, Hand Workshop, 88. *Teaching:* Prof jewelry & metalwork, Va Commonwealth Univ, 73-. *Awards:* Exp Metalwork, Carnegie Found, 68; Slide Doc of Hist Jewelry-Ornamental Devices, Va Commonwealth Univ, 71, Fac Grant-in-Aid, 76. *Bibliog:* Geff Reed (auth), Thompson/Kerrigan, Craft Horizons, 72. *Mem:* Am Crafts Coun; Coll Art Asn; Soc NAm Goldsmiths. *Media:* Precious Metals, Nonmetallic Materials. *Mailing Add:* Dept Crafts Va Commonwealth Univ 325 N Harrison St Richmond VA 23284

THOMPSON, NATO
CURATOR
Collection Arranged: The Interventionists: Art in the Social Sphere, Mass Mus Contemp Art, 2004; Waiting for Godot in New Orleans, Creative Time, 2007; Democracy in America: The National Campaign, Creative Time, 2008. *Pos:* Cur, Mass Mus Contemp Art, formerly; chief cur, Creative Time, 2007-. *Awards:* Disting Writing in Art J award, Coll Art Asn, 2004. *Publ:* Auth, Experimental Geography: Radical Approaches to Landscape, Cartography, and Urbanism, Melville House Publ, 2009. *Mailing Add:* Creative Time 59 E 4th St Fl 6 New York NY 10003

THOMPSON, PAUL WARWICK
ADMINISTRATOR
b Aug 9, 1959. *Study:* Univ Bristol, BA, 80; Univ East Anglia, MA, 84, Doctorate, 87. *Pos:* Scriptwriter & researcher, Design Coun, Eng, 87-88; cur contemp design, Design Mus, London, 88-90, cur, 90-92, dir, 92-2001; dir, Cooper-Hewitt Nat Design Mus, Smithsonian Inst, New York, 2001-2009; pres, Royal Coll Art, London, 2009-; adv bd chmn, Fabrica, Italy. *Awards:* Hon fel, Royal Coll Art; City & Guilds of London Inst. *Mem:* Victoria & Albert Mus (trustee); Ashmolean Mus, Univ Oxford (trustee). *Mailing Add:* Royal College of Art Kensington Gore London SW7 2EU United Kingdom

THOMPSON, RICHARD CRAIG
PAINTER
b McMinnville, Ore, June 27, 1945. *Study:* Ore State Univ, 63-65; Univ NMex, BFA, 67, MA, 72; painting with John Kacere; also lithography with Garo Antresian. *Work:* San Antonio Mus Art, Tex; Roswell Mus, NMex. *Comn:* Twenty Sculpture Pieces, Univ Md, 69; Impermanent Sculpture, Mich Arts Coun, Detroit, 74; Cowboy Nights, Warehouse Living Arts Ctr, Corsicana, Tex. *Exhib:* Solo exhibs, Roswell Mus, NMex, 81, Monique Knowlton Gallery, NY, 81, 82 & 84, Art Mus STex, Corpus Christi, 84, Harris Gallery, Houston, 85; Biennial of Contemp Am Art, Whitney Mus, NY, 75; Space Gallery, Los Angeles, 80 & 84; Fresh Paint, Mus Fine Arts, Houston; Hill's Gallery, Santa Fe, NMex, 75-78; Scottish Arts Festival, Edinburgh, Scotland, 80; and others. *Teaching:* Lectr painting & drawing, Univ Albuquerque, 72-75; vis lectr color, Wayne State Univ, spring 74; instr design-color, Univ NMex, 75-78; vis prof, Univ Tex, San Antonio, 84; asst prof, Univ Tex, Austin, 84-. *Awards:* Nat Endowment Arts Fel, 78; Artist-in-residence, Australia Arts Coun, 82; Mid-Am Art Alliance Award, 86; artist-in-residence grant, Roswell Mus, NMex. *Bibliog:* Charlotte Moser, New Mexico, open land and psychic elbow room, ARTnews, 12/77; article in New America, Univ NMex, 79; Portfolio, Paris Review, Summer 79. *Mem:* Coll Art Asn; Nat Watercolor Honor Soc. *Media:* Acrylic, Oil. *Dealer:* Harris Gallery 1100 Bissonnet Houston TX 77005; Space Gallery 6015 Santa Monica Blvd Los Angeles CA 90038. *Mailing Add:* c/o Robischon Gallery 1740 Wazee St Denver CO 80202

THOMPSON, TAMARA See Bryant, Tamara Thompson

THOMPSON, VIRGINIA ABBATE
PAINTER, INSTRUCTOR
b Brooklyn, NY. *Study:* Univ Miami, BA, 60; Miami Dade Community Col, AS, 72. *Exhib:* Fla Watercolor Soc Ann, Mus Fine Arts, St Petersburg, 96; Audubon Artists Ann, Salmagundi Club, NY, 98; Lancaster Mus Art, Pa, 99; Magnificent Eleven, Schacknow Mus Fine Arts, Plantation, Fla, 2000; Int Watercolor Biennial, Lat Am Mus, Coral Gables, Fla, 2000. *Teaching:* instr, Miami Dade Community Col, 2001-02. *Awards:* Jane Peterson Mem Award, Audubon Artists, 95; Merit Award, Pa Watercolor Soc, 99; 2d Place Int Watercolor Biennial, Latin Am Mus, 2000. *Bibliog:* Mary Ann Beckwith (auth), Creative Watercolor, Rockport Publ, 95; Sara M Doherty (ed), Painting Light & Shadow, Rockport Publ, 97. *Mem:* Nat Watercolor Soc; Audubon Artists; Pa Watercolor Soc; Fla Watercolor Soc; Gold Coast Watercolor Soc. *Media:* Watercolor, Acrylics

THOMPSON, WADE S
PAINTER, EDUCATOR
b Moorhead, Minn, July 30, 1946. *Study:* Macalester Col, BA, 68; Bowling Green State Univ, MA, MFA, 72; Pratt Inst, 85. *Work:* IBM Corp, Kansas City, Mo; M-Bank Corp, Houston, Tex; Freeport-MacMahon Corp, New Orleans, La; Provincetown Art Asn, Mass; Hoyt Institute of Fine Arts, New Castle, Pa; Jena Int, Washington; Univ Art & Design, Helsinki, Finland. *Comn:* Aerialscape 2000 (painting), Springfield Branson Regional Airport, Springfield, Mo, 92. *Exhib:* Am Drawing 1976, Smithsonian Inst Traveling Exhib, Portsmouth Arts Ctr, Va, 76; solo exhibs, Hansen Galleries, NY, 77, Mary Bell Gallery, Chicago, 84, 85, 87, 88 & 89, Jack Meir Gallery, Houston, Tex, 85, 87, 88, 91, 93, 94 & 97, Martin Schweig Gallery, St Louis, 86, Still-Zinzel New Orleans, 90 & Parthenon Mus, Nashville, Tenn, 95; Washington Collectors: One Plus One, Watkins Gallery, Am Univ, 93; Gala '94 Nat, Brenau Univ, Gainesville, Ga, 94; Krasl Art Mus, St Joseph, Mich, 95; Millikin Univ, Decatur, Ill, 96; Keyes Gallery, Springfield, Mo, 99; Malton Gallery, Cincinnati, Ohio, 2001. *Collection Arranged:* Centennial Art Exhib; Springfield Art Mus, Feb 18-Mar 13, 2005. *Pos:* Designer, Assoc Design, St Paul, Minn, 70-71; co-chmn, Art, Design & Psychology Interest Group, Inter-Soc, Color Coun, 88-94, chmn, 94-96, bd dir, 96-98; organizing chmn, Color & Tech Conf, ISCC, Williamsburg, Va, 98. *Teaching:* Asst prof art, Tyler Sch Art, Temple Univ, 75-79; prof art and design, Mo State Univ, 79-91, distinguished scholar, 92-97, asst head dept art & design, 99-2001, acting dept head, 2001-2002 & 2007-, dept head, 2009-; vis prof, Summer Design Inst, Univ Minn, Minneapolis, 95. *Awards:* Award for Acrylic, 27th Ann Chautauqua Nat Exhib Am Art, 84; Best of Show, Brenau Univ Gala 94 Nat Invitational, Gainesville, Ga; Vis Arts Prog Grant, Miss Arts Coun, St Louis, 98. *Bibliog:* Camille Howell (auth), Artists Enjoy Their Work, Springfield News Leader, Mo, 4/7/94; Kay Dillon (auth), Two Worth While Exhibits, The Oaks Ridger, Tenn, 12/19/95; Christopher Willard (auth), How to set up a still-life, Am Artist Mag, NY, 11/97. *Mem:* Inter-Soc Color Coun (bd dir); Coll Art Asn; and others. *Media:* Acrylic, Oil, Mixed Media. *Res:* color theory and practice. *Publ:* Auth, Wade S Thompson, Color Light and Temperature: A General Studies Component for Fine Arts Painting; Aspects of Colour (ed by Harald Arnkil & Esa Hamalainen, Publ Series, Univ Art & Design, Helsinki, Finland, 95; Colour Illusion in Painting, Colour Anthology, Scandinavian Colour Inst, Stockholm, 97; Dimensional Form Through Color and Light, Colour Between Art and Science, Inst of Colour, Oslo, Norway, 98; Digitally Manipulated Images and Painting, 2001. *Dealer:* Malton Gallery, Cincinnati, OH. *Mailing Add:* Mo State Univ Springfield MO 65804

THOMSON, DAVID K R
COLLECTOR
Study: Upper Can Coll, BA; Selwyn Coll, Cambridge Univ, MA (hist), 1978. *Pos:* With Hudson's Bay co, formerly; pres, Zellers & Simpsons, 1980-90; dep chmn, Woodbridge co Ltd, 1990-; bd dirs, Thomson Corp, Toronto, 1988-, chmn, Thomson Reuters (formerly Thomson corp) 2002-. *Awards:* Named one of Top 200 Collectors, ARTnews mag, 2004-11, 2013; named one of World's Richest People (with family), Forbes mag, 2007. *Collection:* Old Masters; modern and contemporary art. *Mailing Add:* Thomson Reuters 3 Times Sq New York NY 10036

THORNE, JOAN
PAINTER, EDUCATOR
b New York, NY. *Study:* New York Univ, BS, 65; Hunter Col, MFA, 68. *Work:* Albright Knox Art Gallery, Buffalo, NY; Aldrich Mus Contemp Art, Ridgefield, Conn; Brooklyn Mus, NY; Dallas Mus Art; Krannert Mus, Univ Ill, Champaign. *Exhib:* Solo exhib, Corcoran Gallery of Art, Wash, DC, 73, Graham & Sons, NY, 90, Ramapo Col, NJ, Museo Voluntariado De Las Casas Reales (retrospective), Casa de Bastedas, Santo Domingo, Dominican Repub & Museo Patronato Plaza, de la Cultura (retrospective), Santiago Apostol, Dominican Repub, 98, Mus de Las Americas, San Juan, PR, 2000, Recent Paintings, Sideshow, New York, 2010; Whitney Annual, Whitney Mus Am Art, NY, 72, 1981 Biennial Exhib, 81; Spring Ann, Adrich Mus Contemp Art, Ridgefield, Conn, 72, Tenth Anniversary Exhib, 74, The Art of the 1970's & 1980's, 85; An Affair of the Heart, Albright-Knox Art Gallery, Buffalo, NY, 85; Graham Modern Selections, NY Stock Exchange, 91; Abstract Painting of the 90's, Andre Emmerich Gallery, 91; Altos de Chavon, Los Artislas Residentes (with catalog), Dominican Republic, 93; Through Thick & Thin, Andre Zarre Gallery, 94, The Exuberant 80's, 94. *Teaching:* assoc prof, Borough of Manhattan Community Col, NY. *Awards:* Painting Fel, Nat Endowment Arts, 79 & 83; Grant Painting, NY State Coun Arts, 80; Grant Painting, Prix de Rome, Am Acad Rome Pollock Krasner Found, 86. *Bibliog:* Richard Vine (auth), Art In America Mag, 6/98; Stephen Westfall (auth), Wild Beauty, essay in catalogue Mus de Las Americas, March/April 2000; Robert C Morgan (auth), PAINTED In New York City: The Presence of the Past, essay for catalogue Joe and Emily Lowe Art Gallery, 2001. *Mem:* Coll Art Asn; Am Acad in Rome (fellow). *Media:* Oil Paint on Linen. *Mailing Add:* 169 Mercer St New York NY 10012

THORNE, MARTHA
ADMINISTRATOR, CURATOR
Study: State Univ NY, Buffalo, BA (Urban Affairs); Univ Pa, Master of City Planning; London Sch Economics. *Exhib:* Unbuilt Chicago, Art Inst Chicago, Bilbao: The Transformation of a City, Modern Trains & Splendid Stations. *Pos:* Mem ed bd, Quaderns d'Arquitectura I Urbanisme, Barcelona, formerly; curator, Madrid, formerly; assoc cur & acting dept head, Dept Archit, Art Inst Chicago, 1995-2005; exec dir, Pritzker Archit Prize, 2005-; bd trustees, Graham Found Advanced Studies in Fine Arts, Chicago, currently; bd dirs, Internat Archive Women in Archit, currently. *Publ:* co-auth, Masterpieces of Chicago Archit; auth & ed, The Pritzker Archit Prize: The First Twenty Years; co-ed, Skyscrapers: The New Millennium. *Mailing Add:* Pritzker Archit Prize Hyatt Ctr 71 S Wacker Dr Chicago IL 60606

THORNE-THOMSEN, RUTH T
PHOTOGRAPHER, EDUCATOR
b New York, NY, May 13, 1943. *Study:* Columbia Coll, Mo, FA (dance), 63; Southern Ill Univ, Carbondale, BFA (painting), 70; Columbia Coll, Chicago, BA (photog), 73; Art Inst Chicago, MFA (photog, John Quincy Adams fel), 76. *Work:* Art Inst Chicago; San Francisco Mus Mod Art; Santa Barbara Mus Art, Calif; Walker Art Ctr, Minneapolis; Hallmark Photog Collection, St Louis; Mus Fine Arts, Houston. *Exhib:* Solo exhibs, Allan Frumkin Gallery, Chicago, 80, Art Inst Chicago, 81, Marcuse Pfeifer Gallery, NY, 83 & Jones Troyer Gallery, Washington, DC, 84, Cleveland Mus Art, 93, Within This Garden, Mus Contem Photog, Chicago, 93-95, Journey, Special Photographers Co, London, Eng, 95, Univ Wyoming Art Mus, 96, Mythologies, St Louis Art Mus, Mo, 97, Jackson Fine Art, Atlanta, Ga, 98, Schmidt Dean Gallery, Pa, 98, John Oulman Gallery, Minneapolis, 98, Orphans, Schmidt Dean Gallery, Philadelphia, 2000, Catherine Edelman Gallery, Chicago, 2002; The Photographer and the City, Mus Contemp Art, Chicago, 77; Landscape Images, La Jolla Mus Contemp Art, Calif, 80; Midwest Photog (with catalog), Walker Art Ctr, Minneapolis, 81; Timed and Spaced, Alchemic Gallery, Boston, 83; Extending the Perimeters of Twentieth Century Photog & Sign of the Times, San Francisco Mus Mod Art, 85; Photographs from the Getty Mus & City Light, Int Ctr Photog, NY, 85; Photog Fiction (with catalog), Whitney Mus Fairfield Co, Stamford, Conn, 86; Defining Eye: Women Photographers of the 20th Century, St Louis Art Mus, 97; Years Ending in Nine, Mus Fine Arts, Houston, Tex, 98; Resurrections, Brussels, Belgium, 98; Egypt of the Mind, Denver Art Mus, 98; The Cultured Tourist, Leslie Tonkonow Gallery, NY, 98; Fabulists: Fictions in Word Image by Philadelphia Artists, Levy Gallery, Moore Coll Art, Philadelphia, 99; Ancient History: Photographs of the Ancient World 1851-1997, Yancey Richardson Gallery, NY, 99; What's New: Recent Acquisitions in Photography, Sondra Gilman Gallery, Whitney Mus Am Art, NY, 2000. *Pos:* Staff photographer, Chicago Sun-Times, 78. *Teaching:* Instr photog, Columbia Col, Chicago, 74-83; asst prof, Univ Colo, Denver, 83-87, chair dept fine arts, 88, assoc prof, 87-89. *Awards:* Nat Endowment Humanities Fel, Paris, 79; Nat Endowment Arts Fel, 82; Lifetime Achievement Award, Columbia Col, Chicago, 95; Bessie Berman Award for Photography, Leeway Found, Philadelphia, 96; Fellowship, Pa Council on Arts, 2001. *Bibliog:* Discoveries, In: Photography Year 1980, Time-Life Bks, 80; Jon Cook, The marvelous journey: Photographs of Ruth Thorne-Thomsen, Nits & Wits Mag, 3-4/82; Owen Edwards (auth), Tripping the light fantastic, Am Photographr, 3/84; Lisbeth Morano (auth), Ruth Thorne-Thomsen at Marcuse Pfeifer, Art in Am, 4/84; Lauren Smith (auth), The Visionary Pinhole, Peregrine Smith Bks, Salt Lake City, 85. *Mem:* Soc Photog Educ

THORNS, JOHN CYRIL, JR
DESIGNER, PAINTER
b Denver, Colo, Apr 14, 1926. *Study:* Ft Hays State Univ, BA; Ind Univ, with Henry Hope & George Rickey, MA (art hist); Univ Iowa, with John Schulze & Lester Longman, MFA (archit design). *Work:* Hastings Coll, Nebr; Friends of Art Collection, Kans State Univ; Marian Coll, Wis; Hansen Mus, Logan, Kans; Ft Hays State Univ, Hays, Kans; Hadley Found Collection. *Comn:* Bldg design, First Presby Church, Hays, Kans, 74; campanile design, Campus, Ft Hays State Univ, 75. *Exhib:* Am Craftsman Coun Exhib, Mus Contemp Crafts, NY, 62 & 63; Watercolor USA, Springfield Art Mus, Mo, 63 & 64; Kans Watercolor Exhib, 71, 74, 76 & 85-88; Smoky Hill, 80, 83, 85-2012; Kans Nat Small Paintings, Drawings, Prints, 91-94; numerous solo exhibs; Kans Watercolor Mem Show, 90-95; Great Plains Nat, 95; Nat Collage Show, 2008; Solo show, B Sandlen Mus Art, 2013. *Pos:* Pres, Hays Arts Coun, Kans, 72-74; consult dir, Hadley Found Art Collection, 1990-2013; adminr, Hadley Found Art Collection. *Teaching:* Mem fac, Ft Hays State Univ, 54-72, prof art hist & design & chmn dept art, 72-90; consult, Hays Med Ctr, 93-2012. *Awards:* Governor's Artist, Kans, 85-86; Moss-Thorns Gallery Art, 87; Best Kans, Ft Hays State Names Art Gallery, 88; and others. *Bibliog:* Prairie Romantic: story of John C Thorns Jr, Kans Quart, Vol 24, No 1, Kans State Univ; Stories & Experiences of a PK. *Mem:* Coll Art Asn Am; Delta Phi Delta (pres, 70-73); Kans Watercolor Soc; Kans Art Educ Asn; Nat Coun Art Adminr; Cambridge Soc; and others. *Media:* Collage; Acrylic, Watercolor. *Res:* Kans Artists. *Specialty:* 2 dimensional work. *Interests:* collecting art. *Collection:* Artists of Kansas Represented. *Publ:* Illusr, Frontier Mag, 57-62; contribr, Ft Hays Studies, Ser 1 & 2, Ft Hays State Univ, 60 & 66; ed, Palette, spring 66-70 & 73; catalog, Hadley Art Collection, 2008; History of Hadley Art Collection, 2013. *Dealer:* History Dept of Art 75 Hays State Univ Madd Matter Gallery 112 E 11th St Hays KS 67601. *Mailing Add:* 500 W 36th St Hays KS 67601

THORNTON, RICHARD SAMUEL
EDUCATOR, WRITER
b Columbia, Mo, Aug 5, 1934. *Study:* Univ Mo, BA, 56; Cranbrook Acad Art, MFA, 57. *Collection Arranged:* cur, New Japanese Graphics, London Design Mus, 91. *Teaching:* Prof graphic design, Wash State Univ, 60-77, chmn art dept, 72-76; head art dept, Univ Conn, Storrs, 77-87, prof graphic design, 77-, interim dean, Sch Fine Arts, 89-90, interim head art dept, 97. *Awards:* Teacher of the Yr, Wash State Univ, 77-78; Fulbright Scholars Award, Japan, 90-91. *Mem:* Fulbright Assocs; Graphic Design Educ Asn; Conn Art Dirs Club; Conn Acad Arts & Sci. *Res:* Japanese graphic design history. *Publ:* Auth, Education of the Japanese designer, Graphis, 69; New generation Japanese graphic designers, Print Mag, 84; SEVEN, seven graphic designers, Grapha-Sha, 85; Japanese Posters: The First 100 Years, Design Issues J, 89; Essay, Best 100 Japanese Posters 1945-1989, Tokyo, Kodansha 90; Graphic Spirit of Japan, Van Nostrand Reinhold, 91. *Mailing Add:* Dept Art Univ Conn Storrs CT 06268

THORNYCROFT, ANN
PAINTER, PRINTMAKER
b Petersfield, Hampshire, Eng, Feb 29, 1944. *Study:* Central Sch Art, London, BA, 66; Chelsea Sch Art, London, Dipl (art), 68. *Work:* Los Angeles Co Mus Art, Calif; Pepsico, NY; Transamerica, Los Angeles, Calif; Boise Art Mus, Boise, Idaho; Cedars Sinai Med Ctr, Los Angeles. *Exhib:* Drawings by Painters, Long Beach Mus Art, Calif, 82; Michael & Dorothy Blankfort Collection, Los Angeles Co Mus Art, Calif, 82; Coastal Abstraction: Transcendence, Calif, Los Angeles, 98; Ruth Bachofner Gallery, Santa Monica, Calif, 2013. *Teaching:* Instr painting, Santa Monica Col Design, Art & Archit, 96-99, Brentwood Art Ctr, 96-2001. *Awards:* Individual Artist Grant, Nat Endowment Arts, 82. *Mem:* Los Angeles Printmaking Soc. *Media:* Oil, Watercolor, Etching, Monotypes. *Specialty:* Contemp Art. *Dealer:* Fresh Paint Art Advisors Culver City Calif; Ruth Bachofner Gallery Santa Monica Calif. *Mailing Add:* 12229 Palms Blvd Los Angeles CA 90066

THORPE, JAMES GEORGE
DESIGNER, ILLUSTRATOR
b Fort Dix, NJ, May 4, 1951. *Study:* Univ Md, College Park, BA, 73, MFA, 75; studied painting with Frank Bunts, sculpture & design with Claudia Demonte. *Work:* Poster Collection, Libr Cong, Washington, DC; Lahti Poster Mus, Finland; Warsaw Poster Mus, Poland; Musee de la Publicite, Paris, France; Hiroshima Mus Art, Japan. *Comn:* Hiroshima Appeals '85 (poster), Shoshin Soc Am, Washington, DC, 85. *Exhib:* 22nd Ann Irene Leache Exhib, Chrysler Mus, Norfolk, Va, 74; Maryland Biennial, Baltimore Mus Art, 76; 1st Triennial Toyama Poster Exhib, Toyama Mus Art, Japan, 85; Lahti Poster Biennale Int, Lahti Poster Mus, Findland, 85; Hiroshima Appeals '85 Invitational, Hiroshima Mus Art, Japan, 85; Colo Int Poster Biennial, Univ Colo Mus, Ft Collins, 85; 10 yr retrospective, Univ & Coll Designers Assoc, Chicago, Ill, 85; Warsaw Poster Biennale, Warsaw Poster Mus, Poland, 86; Lahti Poster Bienale, Lahti, Finalnd, 87; Moscow Int Peace Poster Exhib, USSR, 87; solo exhib, posters, Am Cult Ctr, Brussels, Belgium, 88. *Pos:* Designer-illusr, US Army European Command, 77-78 & Md Nat Capital Park & Planning Comt, 78; freelance designer-illusr, James Thorpe Graphic Design, 77. *Teaching:* Lectr graphic design-illus, Univ Md, College Park, 80-85, asst prof graphic design, 85-. *Awards:* Design Excellence Award, Nekoosa Paper Corp, 81. *Bibliog:* Walter Herdeg (auth), Graphis Posters, 84 & Glenn Beal (auth), Images for Survival, 12/85, Graphis Press; Ann & Ha Hanna (auths), the art of peace, ID Mag, 12/85. *Mem:* Univ & Coll Designers Assoc. *Media:* Montage, Posters. *Publ:* Contribr, Print Mag-Reg Design Ann, R C Publ, NY 83 & 84; American Illustration Ann, Abrams, NY, 84; Graphis Poster Ann, Graphis Press, Zurich, 84; ID Mag, 85. *Mailing Add:* Univ Md Art Dept Mount Hall College Park MD 20742

THORSON, ALICE R
EDITOR, CRITIC
b Hinsdale, Ill, Sept 22, 1953. *Study:* Western Ill Univ, BA, 75; Northern Ill Univ, MA, 81; Univ Chicago, PhD prog, 80-82. *Pos:* Managing ed, New Art Examiner, Chicago & Washington, DC, 82-90; Art Critic, Washington Times, Washington, DC, 87-90, Kansas City Star, Mo, 91-. *Teaching:* Adj Prof, Corcoran Sch Art, Washington, DC, 89-91 & Univ Mo, Kansas City, 98-99. *Res:* Contemporary visual art. *Publ:* Contribr, The Earthly Chimera & The Femme Fatale (exhib catalog), Univ Chicago, 81; auth, Hirshhorn's content swamps issues, 85 & 49th Carnegie International sets the record straight, 86, New Art Examiner; Morris Yarowsky: Paintings 1971-1991 (exhib catalog), McLean Project for the Arts, 91. *Mailing Add:* c/o Kansas City Star 1729 Grand Ave Kansas City MO 64108

THORSTON, LUDLOW
PAINTER
b Irvington, NJ, 1927. *Study:* Newark Sch Fine and Industrial Arts, 49; NY Univ, BA, MA, 59; student of Hans Weingartner, STanley Turnbull, Syd Browne & others. *Work:* Ludlow Thorston Galleries; Mural, US Army Comn. *Exhib:* Am Watercolor Soc; Ludlow Thorston Galleries. *Mem:* NJ Watercolor Soc (pres, formerly); Salmagundi Club, NY; others. *Media:* Watercolor, aquarelle. *Specialty:* Eastern US Figuratives. *Mailing Add:* PO Box 1047 10 Central Ave Island Heights NJ 08732

THRALL, ARTHUR
PRINTMAKER, PAINTER
b Milwaukee, Wis, Mar 18, 1926. *Study:* Univ Wis, Milwaukee, BS & MS; Univ Wis, Madison; Univ Ill, Urbana; Ohio State Univ. *Work:* Brit Mus, London; Libr Cong, Washington, DC; Art Inst Chicago; Brooklyn Mus, NY; Tate Gallery, London. *Comn:* 50 print ed, Wis Arts Found, 84. *Exhib:* Carnegie Inst Int Print Exhib, Pittsburgh, 51; Young Am Printmakers, Mus Mod Art, New York, 53; solo exhib, Smithsonian Inst, 60; 160th Ann, Pa Acad Art, Philadelphia, 64; 143rd Ann, Nat Acad Design, New York, 67; 43rd Ann, Audubon Artists, New York, 85. *Teaching:* Assoc prof art, Milwaukee-Downer Coll, 56-64; prof art, Lawrence Univ, 64-, chairperson, Art Dept, 81-86; vis prof art, Univ Wis-Madison, 66-67 (retired, 90). *Awards:* Louis Comfort Tiffany Found Fel Graphics, 63; Purchase Award, Brooklyn Mus 14th Ann, 63; Cannon Prize, Nat Acad Design 143rd Ann, 67. *Bibliog:* M Fish (auth), Arthur Thrall, Wis Architect, 65; D Anderson (auth), The Art of Written Forms, Holt Rinehart & Winston, 69; J Watrous (auth), A Century of American Printmaking, Univ Wis Press, 84. *Mem:* Soc Am Graphic Artists; Boston Printmakers; Audubon Artists. *Media:* Etching; Miscellaneous Media. *Mailing Add:* 4225 N Woodburn Shorewood WI 53211

THRELKELD, DALE
PAINTER
b Mo, Apr 11, 1944. *Study:* Northeast Mo State Col, BS, 66; Ball State Univ, MA, 70; Southern Ill Univ, Edwardsville, MFA, 75. *Work:* Brooklyn Mus Art, NY; Arco Collection Los Angeles; Ill State Mus; Northern Ill Univ Collection. *Exhib:* New Talent Exhib, Gimpel & Weitzenhoffer Gallery, NY, 74; Los Angeles Print Soc Nat Print Exhib, 74; 28th Ann Ill Invitational, Ill State Mus, 75; Unique Works on Paper, Frank Marino Gallery, NY, 75-79; Arco Collection, Los Angeles; Peoria Contemp Art Ctr, 96. *Teaching:* Prof drawing & painting, Belleville Area Col, Ill, 71-. *Awards:* Purchase Awards, Dulin Gallery Art, 70, Ark Arts Ctr, 71, Ill State Mus, 75 & Brooklyn Mus, 75. *Media:* Mixed, Oil on Canvas. *Mailing Add:* Dept Humanities & Soc Scis Belleville Area Col 2500 Carlyle Belleville IL 62221

THURMER, ROBERT
SCULPTOR, GALLERY DIRECTOR
b Vienna, Austria, Oct 8, 1953; US citizen. *Study:* Syracuse Univ, Coll Visual & Performing Arts, BFA, 77; Univ Nebr, Lincoln, RI Sch Design, MFA, 81. *Work:* Cleveland Mus Art, Ohio; Everson Mus Art, Syracuse, NY; RI Sch Design Mus, Providence; Annmary Brown Mem, Providence, RI; B K Smith Gallery, Lake Erie Col, Painesville, Ohio. *Comn:* Indoor monumental installations, numerous pvt individuals, Cleveland, NY, San Diego & Chicago, 86-92; indoor monumental installation, Jacobs/Visconci/Jacobs, Cleveland, 90. *Exhib:* May Show, Cleveland Mus Art, 86-88; Int Selected Group Show, Lucia Gallery, NY, 89; Int Art Horizons, Art 54 Gallery, NY, 89-90; Sculpture Survey, Metro Gallery (Tri-C), Cleveland, 92; Body and Soul, Beck Ctr Mus, Lakewood, Ohio, 93; and others. *Collection Arranged:* Nature in Art, Cleveland Mus Art, 85; North Coast-New Imagery, Beck Ctr Mus, 86; Sculpture Exposed essay, Everson Mus Art, 89; Metaphysical Vistas, Cleveland State Art Gallery, 91; Vision Quest, Cleveland State Art Gallery, 92; Celia Rabinovitch, The Grotto Cycle, Beck Ctr Mus, 92; GAIA Coughs, Cleveland State Art Gallery, 93; A Place in Time: Great Lakes Regional Painting 1913-1958 (auth, catalog), Cleveland State Art Gallery, Ctr Creative Studies, Detroit, Mich, 94; Body of Evidence: The Figure in Contemporary Photography, 95. *Pos:* Exhib specialist, Cleveland Mus Art, 83-83, gallery dir, 90-; cur educ, Everson Mus Art, Syracuse, 88-90; gallery dir, Cleveland State Univ Art Gallery, 90-; mem, visual arts & craft review panel, Ohio Arts Coun, 92. *Teaching:* Lectr 3-d design, State Univ NY, Oswego, 82-83; instr 3-d design, Cazenovia Col, NY, 88-90; acad appointment 3-d design & sculpture, Cleveland State Univ, 90-; exhib design, Univ Calif Berkeley Exten, San Francisco, 94; instr museology, Cleveland State Univ, 94-, drawing, 95-. *Mem:* Coll Art Asn; SPACES; New Organization Visual Arts; Am Asn Mus. *Media:* Miscellaneous. *Publ:* Auth, New World Folk Art 1492-1992, Cleveland State Univ, 92. *Mailing Add:* Cleveland State Univ Art Gallery 2307 Chester Ave Cleveland OH 44114

THURSTON, JACQUELINE BEVERLY
EDUCATOR, ARTIST, WRITER
b Cincinnati, Ohio, Jan 27, 1939. *Study:* Carnegie-Mellon Univ, BFA (painting), 61; Stanford Univ, MA (painting), 62. *Work:* Libr Cong; San Francisco Mus Mod Art; Oakland Mus, Calif; St Louis Mus Art; Henry Gallery, Univ Wash, Seattle; Los Angeles Co Art Mus, Calif; Carnegie Mus Art, Pittsburgh; Int Mus Photog, George Eastman House, Rochester, NY; Bibliotheque National; Biliotheque Alexandrina; and other pub & pvt collections; Bibliotheque Alexandrina. *Exhib:* Observations/Translations--Four Photogr, Oakland Mus, Calif, 72; Two Photogr, Oakland Mus, 75; Photog 2 (exhib catalog), Jack Glenn Gallery, Newport Beach, Calif, 75; Am Photogr: Past into Present (exhib catalog), Seattle Mus Art, Wash, 76; one-person show, Susan Spiritus Gallery, Newport Beach, 77, 80, 94, 95 & 2002; Graham Nash Collection (exhib catalog), Univ Santa Clara, Calif, 79, San Francisco Mus Mod Art, 80; La Photographie Creative (exhib catalog), Pavillon des Arts, Paris, France, 84; Univ NMex Mus Art, Albuquerque, 2002; San Jose Mus Thirty-Fifth Anniversary Exhib (catalogue), 2004; San Jose Mus of Art Vital Signs, One Person Show, 2005; One person show, Triangle Gallery, San Francisco, Calif, 2005; 3rd Int Book Biennale, Alexandria, Egypt, 2008; Time Will Tell, Triangle Gallery, Bibliotheca Alexandrina, 2008; The Artists of ZYZZYVA, Mina Dreden Gallery, San Francisco, 2009; Agenda 2010, Alexandria, Egyp, 2010. *Teaching:* Lectr, Stanford Univ, Calif; prof art, San Jose State Univ, Calif, 65-; lectr, CG Jung Inst, San Francisco, 89, San Francisco Psychoanalytic Inst, 92 & 94, Southern Calif Psychoanalytic Inst & Ctr Psychoanalytic Studies Creativity & Art, 96 & Am Inst Med Educ, Santa Fe, China, 98 & 2002, San Jose Mus Art, 2005, Psych Int Conference, San Francisco, 2008, CG Jung Inst, San Francisco, 2010; International Federation for Psychoanalytic Education, 2003; Dream Inst of Northern CA, 2004 & 2006; Visiting Scholars, Sonoma State Univ, 2004, 2006, 2007; lectr, Sacred Images from Ancient Egypt, Art & Psyche Int Coference, San Francisco, 2008; lectr, Sacred Deities from Ancient Egypt, CG Jung Inst, 2010. *Awards:* Nat Endowment Art Fel, 76 & 78; Fac Artist Residence, Arts Fac Inst, 88; Meritorius Performance & Prof Promise Award, San Jose State Univ, 89; CSU Summer Arts Exchange, 92; Fulbright Scholar, Egypt, 2006; and others. *Bibliog:* Thomas Albright (auth), Observations/translations - four photographers, 9/11/72 & Two photographers, 8/6/75, San Francisco Chronicle; Joan Murray (auth), Observations/translations - four photographers, 9/23/72, Dorothy Burkhardt (auth), rev, 76 & Rebecca Palmer (auth), Dioramas, 86, Artweek; Ann Elliott Sherman (auth), Don't squeeze the shaman, Metro, 1/99; Jack Fisher (auth), Exploring myth & metaphor through her art, San Jose Mercury News, 1/24/99; Shari Kaplan (auth), Montalvo exhibit features 10 years of expression, Los Gatos Weekly-Times, 1/20/99; Jack Fisher (auth), Man, Machine & Medicine, San Jose Mercury News, 7/5/2010. *Media:* All. *Res:* Nature of the creative process and artists' memories and dreams as sources for works of art. *Interests:* Hiking, Gardening. *Publ:* Coauth (with Ronald Carraherr), Optical Illusions and the Visual Arts, Van Nostrand Reinhold, 66; auth, Geoff Winningham & Jacqueline Thurston (exhib catalog), Calif Inst Technol, Pasadena, 78; Individual Visions (exhib catalog), 82 & A Show of Hands (exhib catalog), 82, San Francisco Mus Mod Art; contribr, The Voice of the Image, Cameraworks, 89. *Mailing Add:* 241 Creekside Dr Palo Alto CA 94306

THURSTON, ROY
PAINTER
b Huntington, NY, 1949. *Study:* Colo Coll, Colorado Springs, BA, 1971; Claremont Grad Sch, Calif, MFA, 1974. *Work:* Los Angeles Co Mus Art; Albright-Knox Art Gallery; Mus Contemp Art, San Diego; Weisman Art Found; Panza Collection, Milan. *Exhib:* Selected West Coast Painters, Miami-Daded Univ, 1975; solo exhibs, Madigan Gallery, Calif State Coll, Bakersfield, 1985, Kiyo Higashi Gallery, Los Angeles, 1989, 1991, Charlotte Jackson Fine Arts, Santa Fe, 1996, 2001, 2006, Los Angeles Harbor Coll, Wilmington, 2004; Quiet, Oakland Mus, Calif, 1989; Plane/Structures, Otis Gallery, Otis Coll Art & Design, Calif, 1994; 5 Easy Pieces, Nev Inst Contemp Art, Las Vegas, 1997; Panza: Legacy of a Collector, Mus Contemp Art, 2000; Natalie & Irving Forman Collection, Albright-Knox Art Gallery, Buffalo, 2005; SoCal: Southern California Art of the 1960's and 70's, Los Angeles Co Mus Art, 2007. *Awards:* Pollock-Krasner Found Grant, 2008. *Bibliog:* Franics Colpitt (auth), Palpable Surface/Elusive Death, Art Space, 1991; William Wilson (auth), Plane/Structures at Otis: Enriching Works, Los Angeles Times, 9/19/1994; Lis Bensley (auth), Roy Thurston Unlocks a Translucent Realm, The Santa Fe New Mexican, 9/13/1996; Mat Gleason (auth), Art Angelenos, Modern Painters, 2003. *Mailing Add:* 3039 E 12th St Los Angeles CA 90023

TICE, GEORGE (ANDREW)
PHOTOGRAPHER, AUTHOR
b Newark, NJ, Oct 13, 1938. *Study:* Newark Vocational & Tech High Sch, NJ, 55. *Hon Degrees:* William Paterson Univ, LHD, 2003. *Work:* Metrop Mus Art, NY; Mus Mod Art, NY; Art Inst Chicago; Bibliot Nat, Paris, France; Nihon Univ Art Mus, Japan; Getty Mus, Los Angeles; Newark Mus, NJ; Boston Mus Fine Art; High Mus Art, Atlanta, Ga; Chrysler Mus, Norfolk, Va. *Comn:* Two 55ft photog murals, Field Mus Natural Hist, Chicago, 75; photog, Liberty Park, Mus Mod Art, NY, 79; photog, Bank Archit, Mus Fine Arts, Houston, 90. *Exhib:* Solo exhibs, Metrop Mus Art, NY, 72, NJ State Mus, 76, Witkin Gallery, NY, 81 & Photo Gallery Int, Tokyo, 82, Nat Mus Photog, Film & Television, Bradford, Eng, 91, Newark Mus, 2006, The Poetry of the Everyday, See + Gallery, Beijing, China, 2011; Group exhibs, Photog in Am, Whitney Mus, 74; Mirrors & Windows, Mus Mod Art, 79; Where We Live, J Paul Getty Mus, 2006; George Tice: Urban Landscapes, Int Ctr Photography, New York, 2002; Out of the Dark Room, Irish Mus Mod Art, 2008; Seeing Beyond the Moment: The Photographic Legacy and Gifts of George Tice, Newark Mus, 2013; A Collective Invention: Photographs at Play, Morgan Library & Mus, 2014. *Teaching:* Instr master class photog, The New Sch Social Research, New York, 70-98. *Awards:* Grand Prix, Festival d'Arles, France, 73; Nat Endowment for Arts Fel, 73; Guggenheim fel, 73-74; Fel, Nat Mus Photog & Bradford & Ilkley Coll, Bradford, England, 90-91; NJ State Coun on the Arts Fel, 98. *Bibliog:* Gerry Badger (auth), Recent books, British J Photog, 3/77; Barbara Lobron, Romantic notions, Camera Arts, 6/83; Peggy Sealfon (auth), Meet the masters, Peterson's Photographic, 10/83; Larger Forces at Work, James Rhem Focus Mag, Feb 2008; Time Place memory, Dean Brierly, Black & White Mag, Dec 2008. *Media:* photography. *Specialty:* Photography. *Interests:* Genealogy. *Publ:* Auth, Artie Van Blarcum, Addison House, 77; Urban Romantic, The Photographs of George Tice, Godine, 82; Hometowns, Graphic Soc, 88; Stone Walls, Grey Skies, Nat Mus Photog Film & Television, Eng, 91; Fields of Peace, Godine, 98; George Tice: Selected Photographs, 1953-1999, Godine, 2001; George Tice: Urban Landscapes, W.W. Norton & Co, 2002; Common Mementos, Lodima Press, Revere, Pa, 2005; Quantuck Lane Press, 2006; Ticetown, Lodima Press, 2007; Seacoast Maine, Godine, 2009; Seeing Beyond the Moment, New Street Productions, 2013; Seldom Seen, Brilliant Press, 2013. *Dealer:* Peter Fetterman Gallery Santa Monica CA; Afterimage Dallas TX; Scott Nichols Gallery San Francisco; Nailya Alexander Gallery New York NY

TICHAVA, NINA
PAINTER, CONSULTANT
b Vallecitos, NMex, 1973. *Study:* Calif Coll Arts & Crafts, BFA. *Work:* Harlos/Huneke Collection. *Comn:* paintings, Jennifer Day Interior Design, Hawaii/Santa Fe, 2009; paintings, Richard and Virginia Ellenberg, Sante Fe, NMex, 2008; Numerous pvt commissions. *Exhib:* Solo Exhibs: include Tichava-Mills Fine Art, Santa Fe, 2008; Textile, Fabric and Paint: Function Inspires Fine Tichava-Mills Fine Art, Santa Fe; Foundations, Plant/Animal/Mineral, George Billis Gallery, Los Angeles, Calif, 2009; Group Exhibs: Catching the Blues, Hang Art, San Francisco, 2005; Originals 2005, Mus Fine Arts, Santa Fe, 2005; Affordable Art Fair, New York, 2009, 2010; Art Miami, Miami, Fla, 2009. *Pos:* Co-founder, Tichava-Mills Fine Art, Santa Fe, 2006-2010; found, Place Contemp, Seattle, Wash. *Teaching:* contract elementary teacher, Arts in Educ, Northern NMex, 2005, 2006. *Awards:* Pollock-Krasner Found Grant, 2007. *Mem:* Friends of Contemp Art (FOCA), Santa Fe, NMex. *Media:* Oil, Mixed Media, Metal Collage. *Specialty:* Orig Painting, Ceramic Sculpture. *Interests:* Abstract Expressionism, Print making, Asian and Mexican Art, fabric & textiles design, architecture. *Publ:* Originals 2005 (pg 41), NMex Comt Nat Mus Women Arts, 2005; 16 Artists You Should Know About/Artists to Watch in 2008 (pg. 29), Decor Mag, 2008; The Art Issue: Top Talent/Art For (and of) the Home (pg 45), Santa Fe Mag, 2008. *Dealer:* Bruce McGaw Graphics Publisher 389 West Nyack Road West Nyack NY 10994; Soho Myriad Art Consulting Services 1250 Menlo Dr Atlanta GA 30318; EA Gallery 18 Willett Ave Port Chester NY 10573; George Billis Gallery LA/NY 2716 La Cienega Blvd Los Angeles CA 90034; Tichava Mills Fine Art 667 Canyon Rd Santa Fe NM 87501. *Mailing Add:* 1255 Avenida Morelia Unit 103 Santa Fe NM 87506

TICHICH, RICHARD
EDUCATOR, ADMINISTRATOR
b Minneapolis, Minn, Jan 3, 1947. *Study:* Univ Iowa, MA, 71; Univ Tex, MFA, 79. *Work:* Ga Coun Art, Atlanta; Maine Photog Workshop, Rockport; Minneapolis Inst Art, Minn. *Exhib:* Cult Olympics, Ga Coun Art, Atlanta, 93; solo exhib, OK Harris Gallery, NY, 85. *Pos:* Photogr, Galveston Arts Ctr, 72-80, dir, 80-82; dept chmn, Ga Southern Univ, 82-. *Teaching:* Prof photog, Ga Southern Univ, 82-, dept chmn, 82-. *Awards:* Am Coun Educ Fel, 96. *Mem:* Coll Art Asn; Nat Coun Art Admn (bd, 94-97). *Mailing Add:* Dept of Art Ga Southern Univ PO Box 8032 Statesboro GA 30460

TIEGREEN, ALAN F
PAINTER, ILLUSTRATOR
b Boise, Idaho, July 6, 1935. *Study:* Univ Southern Miss, AB, 57; Art Ctr Coll Design, 61. *Work:* High Mus Art, Atlanta, Ga. *Comn:* Painting, Atlanta Bur Cult Affairs, Ga, 75; mural, Simmons Corp, Atlanta, 76; paintings, Hilton Hotels, Knoxville, Tenn, 81. *Exhib:* Nat Drawing Exhib, High Mus, Atlanta, 65; Prof Art Am, Smithsonian Inst, Washington, DC, 66; SEastern Ann Exhib, 67 & Ga Artists Exhib, 68, High Mus, Atlanta; SEastern Regional, Columbus, Ga, 70. *Teaching:* Prof, Ga State Univ, 65-. *Awards:* First Award, Nat Drawing Soc, 65; Purchase Prize, Atlanta Arts Festival, Ga, 68; 1st Award, Decatur Sesquicentennial, Ga, 72. *Bibliog:* Clyde Burnette (auth),

Charcoal drawings, Atlanta Newspapers, 2/80; article, Art Voices, 7/81; article, American Illustrators, Dell, 81. *Media:* Acrylic; Ink, Charcoal. *Publ:* Illusr, Doodle & the Go-Cart, Viking, 72; illusr, Ramona the Brave, Morrow, 75; illusr, Silver Woven in my Hair, Atheneum, 77; illusr, Kelly's Creek, Crowell, 77; illusr, Ramona Age 8, Morrow, 81. *Dealer:* Artists Assocs Gallery 3261 Roswell Rd Atlanta GA 30305. *Mailing Add:* 4279 Wieuca Rd NE Atlanta GA 30342

TIEMANN, ROBERT E
PAINTER, SCULPTOR

b Austin, Tex, Jan 12, 1936. *Study:* Univ Tex, Austin, BFA, 58; Univ Southern Calif, MFA, 60. *Work:* Los Angeles City Collection; San Antonio Mus Art, Tex; Am Tel & Tel Collection, NY; Univ Tex & Laguna Gloria Mus, Austin; Museo Cantonale d'Art, Lugano, Switz. *Comn:* Voyage to Cythera (mural), Charles Butt Found Hemisfair, San Antonio, Tex, 68; mural, Citizens Nat Bank, Austin, Tex, 74; Joffrey Ballet Program Cover, Soc Performing. *Exhib:* Invitational Texas Artists Show, Dallas Mus Fine Arts, 72; Laguna Gloria Art Mus, Austin, Tex, 74; San Antonio Mus Art, Tex, 82; Mus Dhond Dhgenens, Deurle, Belgium, 91; Panza DiBiumo: The Eighties & Nineties from the Collection, Mus Cantonale d'Arte, Lugano, Switz, 92. *Pos:* Art therapist, Audie Murphy Veterans Hosp, San Antonio, 75-77; design consult, Chumney-Urrutia Archit Firm, San Antonio, 85-. *Teaching:* Prof art, Trinity Univ, San Antonio, 65-, chmn dept, 82-88; prof art, Harvard Univ, summers, 82-85, Univ Tex, San Antonio, 81, Hanover Col, 86. *Awards:* Nat Endowment Arts Grant, 68; Fac Res & Develop Grant, Trinity Univ, San Antonio, 78. *Bibliog:* Susan Platt (auth), rev, Artforum, 4/80; Frances Colpitt (auth), Robert Tiemann/Annabelle & Robert Tiemann, A Survey: Twenty Years (catalog & essay), Blue Star Art Space, 92; Frances Colpitt (auth), article, Artspace, 9/92. *Mem:* Coll Art Asn; The Blue Star-Contemp Art for San Antonio (bd mem, 86 & 93-94). *Publ:* Auth, art criticism column, San Antonio Express-News, Tex, 78. *Mailing Add:* Dept Art Trinity Univ 715 Stadium Dr San Antonio TX 78212

TIERNEY, PATRICK LENNOX
HISTORIAN, EDUCATOR, LECTURER

b Weston, WVa, Jan 28, 1914. *Study:* Univ Calif, Los Angeles, EdB (cum laude), 36; Columbia Univ, New York, MA, 44; Sogetsu-Ryu, Tokyo, Japan, Seizan I, 52. *Pos:* Cur, Asian Art, San Diego Mus Art, 74-82; mem & cur Asian art, Mingei Mus, San Diego, 77-; Art Dir, Japanese Friendship Garden, San Diego. *Teaching:* Chmn arts fac, Pasadena City Col, Calif, 46-71; lectr, Univ Calif, Los Angeles & San Diego, 52-71; assoc dean col fine arts & prof hist Oriental art, Univ Utah, 71-94, emeritus, 94-; prof, Univ Pittsburgh, 89-90, 90-91. *Awards:* Emmy, Acad Television Arts & Sci, 67; Hons Citation, Resolution of Bd Trustees, Pasadena City Col, Calif, 71; Reischauer Int Educ Award, 2006; Order of the Rising Sun, bestowed by Emperor of Japan, Tokyo, 2007. *Bibliog:* Lennox Tierney Biog (2 vol), Oral Hist Dept, Marriot Libr, Univ Utah. *Mem:* Royal Asiatic Soc, Seoul, Korea; Pacificulture Found, Pasadena, Calif (dir, mus div, 61-70, mem bd dir, Asian Mus, 61-); Acad Television Arts & Sci; Salt Lake Art Ctr (mem bd dir, 71-); Japan-Am Soc, Southern Calif (dir, 72-); Asian Art Mus, San Francisco; and others. *Media:* Sumi-e. *Res:* Folk arts of Japan. *Collection:* Japanese Folk Arts, Painting, Prints, Ceramics and Textiles. *Publ:* Auth, Japan, Int Publ, 58; auth, Chanoyu, as a form of non literary art criticism, Chanoyu J, Kyoto, 76; auth, Cambodia, Khmer Remains, 79; auth, Wabi Sabi, A New Look at Japanese Design, 2000; auth, Shibui, 2007-10. *Mailing Add:* 3758 Adonis Dr Salt Lake City UT 84124

TIGERMAN, STANLEY
PAINTER, ARCHITECT

b Chicago, Ill, Sept, 20, 1930. *Study:* Mass Inst Technol, 48-49; Inst Design, 49-50; Yale Univ, BArch, 60 & MArch, 61. *Work:* Art Inst Chicago; Metrop Mus Art, NY; Mus Mod Art; Deutshes Arch Mus. *Comn:* Modular structure, Metrop Structures, Chicago, 71. *Exhib:* Eight Chicago Artists, Walker Art Ctr, Minneapolis, Minn, 65; Solo exhibs, Evanston Art Ctr, Ill, 69, Art Res Ctr, Kansas City, Mo, 69 & Springfield Arts Asn, Ill, 70; IBA, Deutches Architekus Mus, Frankfurt, WGerm, 86; Chicago Arch 1872-1922, Art Inst, Chicago, 89; Gulbenkian Found, Lisbon, Portugal, 89. *Pos:* Prin, Stanley Tigerman & Assocs, Chicago, 62-. *Teaching:* Prof archit & art, Univ Ill, Chicago Circle, 65-71, dir, Sch Arch, 80-; archit-in-residence, Am Acad in Rome, 80. *Awards:* AIA-DBA Suburban Village, 91; AIA Interior Archit Award Excellence, Am Standard, 92; AIA Int Archit Award, The Ernest Graham Study Ctr Art Inst Chicago, 92; AIA INT Archit Award, The Arts Club Chicago, Ill Acad Fine Arts, 92. *Bibliog:* R A M Stern (auth), New Directions in American Architecture, Braziller, 69; Faulkner & Ziegfield (auth), Art Today, Holt, Rinehart & Winston, 69; Dahinden (auth), Urban Structures of the Future, Praeger, 72. *Mem:* Am Inst Architects; Yale Art Asn; Ill Arts Coun; Yale Club NY; Arts Club Chicago. *Media:* Acrylic. *Publ:* VERSUS: An American Architect's Alternatives, 82; Chicago's Architectural Heritage: A Romantic Classical Image--Work of the Current Generation of Chicago Architects, Arquitectura, 79; Stanley Tigerman Architoons, 88; The Architecture of Exile, 88; Stanley Tigerman: Buildings & Projects 1966-1989. *Mailing Add:* 910 N Lakeshore Dr No 2916 Chicago IL 60611

TILESTON, JACKIE
ARTIST

b Manila, Philippines, 1960. *Study:* Yale Univ, BA in fine arts (painting), 83; Ind Univ, Bloomington, MFA (painting), 88. *Work:* Mus Fine Arts, Houston; Dallas Mus Art, Tex; JP Morgan Chase. *Exhib:* Solo Exhibs: Introductions, WA Graham Gallery, Houston, 90; New Work, 92; New Work, Lawing Gallery, Houston, 95; New Paintings, 97; Jackie Tileston: New Paintings, Satellite Space, Univ Tex, San Antonio, 98; Jackie Tileston, Univ NMex, Albuquerque, 2000; Empty and Full, Barbara Davis Gallery, Houston, 2003; Cures for Cosmophobia, Philadelphia Art Alliance, 2003; Heterotopia, Zg Gallery, Chicago, 2005, 2009; Not Always So, Barbara Davis Gallery, Houston, 2006; Everything in Your Favor, Pentimenti Gallery, Philadelphia, 2007; Chromotopia, Westby Gallery, Rowan Univ, NJ, 2007, 2009; Adventures of the Semionauts, Zg Gallery, Chicago, Ill, 2007; Phenomorama, Holly Johnson Gallery, Dallas, Tex, 2008; Mesocosmos, Zg Gallery, Chicago; Mesocosmos II, Pentimenti Gallery. *Teaching:* Univ Houston, Rice Univ; asst prof painting, Univ New Mex; from asst prof to assoc prof, fine arts, Univ Pa, 2000-. *Awards:* Mid-Am Arts Alliance/Nat Endowment for the Arts, 94; Pew Fel in the Arts, 2004; Bellagio Residency, Rockefeller Found, Italy, 2004; Guggenheim Fel, 2006. *Bibliog:* rev, Art in Am, 5/98; rev, Art News, 12/2003; Tema Celeste, 8/2005; New Am Painting, Vol 75, 2008; ArtForum, 12/2008. *Mem:* Coll Art Asn. *Media:* Painting, Drawing. *Dealer:* Zg Gallery 300 W Superior St Chicago IL 60610; Holly Johnson Gallery 1411 Dragon St Dallas TX 75207; Pentimenti Gallery 145 N 2nd St Philadelphia PA 19106

TILLENIUS, CLARENCE INGWALL
PAINTER, WRITER

b Sandridge, Man, Aug 31, 1913. *Study:* Teulon Col, with A J Musgrove; Univ Winnipeg, hon LLD, 70. *Work:* Pavilion Gallery, Winnipeg, Manitoba; Whyte Mus, Banff, Alta, Govt Manitoba. *Comn:* Collection of wildlife painting, North American Life Assurance Co, Winnipeg, 54-80; dioramas, habitat groups, Nat Mus Can, Ottawa, Ont, 60-72, BC Mus, Victoria, 65-70 & Mus Alta, Edmonton, 72-74; dioramas, paintings, Man Mus Man & Nature, Winnipeg, 69-79. *Exhib:* Two-person exhib, London Art Gallery, London Shute Inst, 54; Solo exhibs, Monarch Life Bldg, 62, Whitney Gallery Western Art, Cody, Wyo, 64, Man Mus Man & Nature, 74 & Glenbow-Alta Inst, 75; Soc Wildlife Art Nations Opening Exhib, Eng, 88; Retrospective, Mus Man & Nature, 98. *Pos:* Diorama dir, Nat Mus Can, Ottawa, 62-72. *Teaching:* Lectr art appreciation, Man, 50-52; lectr wildlife painters, Glenbow Inst, 70; dir wildlife drawings, Okanagan Summer Sch Arts, Penticton, BC, 73-82. *Awards:* Man Centennial Medal Honor, Gov Gen, Prov Man, 72; Seton Medal, 85. *Bibliog:* Peter Kelly & Paul Guyot (coauth), Tillenius on the Prairies (film), Can Broadcasting Corp, 63; Eric Mitchell (auth), Clarence Tillenius, Nature Can Mag, 73; Richard Savage (auth), Tokens of Myself--Tillenius, the Man and the Art (film), Wilderness Trail Motion Picture Co, 78, rev and copyrighted by artist, 84. *Mem:* Explorers Club, NY; Soc Animal Artists; life mem Man Naturalist Soc; Royal Geographical Soc, London, Eng; Soc Wildlife Art Nations, Eng. *Media:* Oil, Watercolor. *Res:* Lifetime study of wild animals, wilderness travels across North America into Yukon and the arctic. *Publ:* Illusr, Little Giant, 51, Orphan of the North, 58, Days of the Buffalo, 98; illusr & auth, Fur Bearers of Canada, 51, Buffalo, 92; Monarchs of the Canadian Wilds, 54-75; auth, Sketchpad Out of Doors, 56 & 62, Tillenius, 98. *Dealer:* Loch and Mayberry Fine Art Inc 306 St Marys Rd Winnipeg Manitoba Canada R2H 158. *Mailing Add:* 121 Parkside Dr Winnipeg MB R3J IMI Canada

TILLEY, LEWIS LEE
PAINTER, VIDEO ARTIST

b Parrott, Ga, May 17, 1921. *Study:* High Mus Sch Art, 37-39; Emory Univ, 37-39; Univ Ga, BFA, 42; Colorado Springs Fine Arts Ctr, with Boardman Robinson, Adolph Dehn & John Held, 42-45; Inst Allende, Mex, MFA, 68; British Film Inst, 72-75, Univ Ga, Cortona, Italy, 85. *Work:* Post Card No 2, Colorado Springs Fine Arts Ctr, Colo; Ga Art Asn; Southern States Art League; Cannon City Art Ctr, Colo. *Comn:* Mural, Broadmoor Cheyenne Mountain Zoo, Colorado Springs, 58; dragon wall mural, Victor Hornbein House, Denver, 59; mural, First Nat Bank, Colorado Springs, 59; four polyester resin sculptures, Colorado Springs Eye Clinic, 60; exterior wall mural, Horace Mann Jr High Sch, Colorado Springs, 62. *Exhib:* Am Fedn Arts; Graphic Arts Chicago; Denver Ann & Biennial; Artists West of Mississippi; Washington Cathedral Relig Exhib; Southern State Art League; Dallas Print & Drawing Show. *Pos:* Producer & dir, Alexander Film Co, 58-62; artist-in-residence, Univ Ga, Cotona, Italy, 85; columnist, Your Amiga, London. *Teaching:* Instr painting, life drawing & design, Colorado Springs Fine Arts Ctr, 45-51; prof art, Univ Southern Colo, 65-86, prof emer, currently. *Awards:* First Purchase Award for oil, Canon City Blossom Festival, 69; First Purchase Award for oil, Colo State Fair, 70. *Bibliog:* Discovery No 49, Mod Photog, 58; Info 64, 9/85. *Media:* All Media, Computer Graphics. *Publ:* Auth, History of writing and painting, 63; illusr, English with the twins, 63; History of medicine, 63; ed, The story of Nok culture, 63. *Mailing Add:* 241 Huckaby St NE Parrott GA 31777

TILLMANS, WOLFGANG
PHOTOGRAPHER

b Remscheid, Ger, 1968. *Study:* Bournemouth & Poole Coll Art & Design, Bournemouth, England (Photog), 1990-92. *Work:* Carnegie Mus Art, Pittsburgh; Guggenheim Mus, New York; Tate Britain, London; Mus d'Art Mod Grand-Duc Jean, Luxembourg; Los Angeles County Mus Art. *Exhib:* Solo exhibs, Andrea Rosen Gallery, New York, 1998, 2001, 2002, 2003, 2007, Regen Projs, Los Angeles, 1999, 2004, 2008, Wako Works of Art, Tokyo, 1999, 2001, 2004, if one thing matters everything matters, Tate Britain, London, 2003, Freischwimmer Neugerriemschneider, Berlin, 2004, Galería Juana de Aizpuru, Madrid, 2005, UCLA Hammer Mus, Los Angeles, 2006, Hirshhorn Mus & Sculpture Garden, Washington, 2007, Mus Tamayo, Mexico City, 2008 and others; Galerie Meyer Kainer, Vienna, (with Jochen Klein), 2000; Icons of a Mutinous Age, Three Photographers, Bournemouth & Poole Coll of Art & Design, Bournmouth, 1991, June, Galerie Thaddaeus Ropac, Paris, 1993, The Winter of Love, P.S. 1 Contemp Art Ctr, Long Island, 1994, The Enthusiast, Gavin Brown's Enterprise, NY, 1995, Everything That's Interesting is New, The Dakis Joannou Collection, Athens, 1996, Projects, Irish Mus Modern Art, Dublin, 1997, Zeitgeist Becomes Form-German Fashion Photography 1945-1995, Pat Hearn Gallery, NY, Morris Healy Gallery, NY, 1997, Fast Forward Image, Kunstverein, Hamburg, 1998, Still Life: 1900-1998, Marlborough Graphics, Marlborough Gallery, Inc, NY, 1998, Vision of the Body: Fashion or Invisible Corset, Kyoto Mus of Modern Art, Mus of Contemp Art, Tokyo, 1999, Protest and Survive, Whitechapel Art Gallery, London, 2000, Transform the World 2002, Wako Works of Art, Tokyo, 2001, Moving Pictures, Solomon R. Guggenheim Mus, NY; travelled to Guggenheim, Bilbao, 2002, Somewhere Better Than This Place: Alternative Social Experience in the Spaces of Contemp Art, Contemp Arts Ctr, Cincinatti, Ohio, 2003, Anniversary Exhib, Gavin Brown's Enterprise, NY, 2003, Atmosphere, Mus of Contemp Art, Chgo, 2004, 21st Century Mus for Contemp Art, Kanazawa, Japan, 2004, Growing Up Absurd, Herbert Read Gallery, Canterbury, 2005, Extreme Abstraction, Albright Knox Gallery, Buffalo,

NY, 2005, It's Not a Photo, Chelsea Art Mus, NY, 2006, Surprise Surprise, Inst Contemp Arts, London, 2006, Rebecca Camhi Gallery, Athens, 2007, At Home, Yvon Lambert, NY, 2007, Life on Mars: Carnegie International 2008, Carnegie Mus of Art, Pittsburgh, 2008, Ludlow 38, NY, 2008, Summer Show, Wako Works of Art, Tokyo, 2008, Venice Biennale, 2009, Form and Photo, Mus of Contemp Art, Los Angeles, 2009 and others; Grand Praemiere, Galleri Nicolai Wallner, Copenhagen, Denmark, 1999; British Art Show, 5 Ikon Gallery, Birmingham, England, 2000 Lost, 2000; Can You Hear Me?, Kunsthaus Dresden, Germany, 2000, Missing Link, 2001; Remix: Contemp art & pop, Tate Liverpool, England, 2002; Regen Projs, Los Angeles, 2003, 15 Year Anniv, 2004; COLECCIÓN TASCHEN, Reina Sofía, Madrid, 2004; Looking In Looking Out, Kunstmuseum Basel, Switzerland, 2003, Covering the Real, 2005; Visions of the Body, Seoul Mus Art, South Korea, 2005; Peintres de la vie moderne, Ctr Pompidou, Paris, 2006; Der Droste Effekt, Esther Schipper, Berlin, 2007; abstrakt, Mus Mod Kunst Kärnten, Klagenfurt, Austria, 2008; Konstellationen III, Städel Mus, Frankfurt/Main, Germany, 2008. *Pos:* runs exhib space, Between Bridges, London, 2006-. *Teaching:* Guest professorship, Hochschule für Bildende Künste, Hamburg 1998-99; Professor, Städelschule Frankfurt/Main, Germany, 2003. *Awards:* Ars Viva Prize, Kulturkreis der Deutschen Wirtschaft, 1995; Turner Prize, JMW Turner, 2000; Hon Fel, Arts Inst Bournemouth, 2001. *Dealer:* Andrea Rosen Gallery 525 W 24th St New York NY 10011; Ben Brown Fine Arts 21 Cork St First Floor London England W1S 3LZ UK; Wako Works of Art 3-18-2-101 Nishi-Shinjuku Shinjuku-ku Tokyo Japan 106-0023; Le Case d'Arte Via Circo 1 Milan Italy 20123. *Mailing Add:* c/o Regen Projects 6750 Santa Monica Blvd Los Angeles CA 90038

TILTON, JOHN ELLSWORTH
CERAMIST
b Red Bank, NJ, Nov 8, 1944. *Study:* Univ Fla, MS in Maths, 1970; Univ South Fla, MFA in Ceramics, 1972. *Work:* Lowe Art Mus, Miami; City of Winter Park, Fla; Cigna Corp, Philadelphia; Walt Disney Corp, Orlando; Blue Cross/Blue Shield NJ. *Mailing Add:* 16211 Northwest 88 Terr Alachua FL 32615-5012

TIMMAS, OSVALD
PAINTER, LECTURER
b Estonia, Sept 17, 1919; Can citizen. *Study:* Tartu State Univ; Atelier Sch Tartu & Tallinn, Estonia, with Nicholas Kummits & Gunther Reindorff. *Work:* London Art Mus, Ont; Art Gallery Hamilton; Art Gallery Windsor; Rodman Hall Art Ctr, St Catharines, Ont; Art Gallery Ont, Toronto. *Exhib:* Can Watercolors, Drawings & Prints, Nat Gallery Can, Ottawa, 66; Audubon Artists, 66-69, Am Watercolor Soc, 66, 67 & 69 & Nat Acad Design, 67, 68 & 71, NY; Royal Can Acad Arts, Nat Gallery Can, 70; OSA Image (circulating show), Ont Pub Galleries, 75-77 & 79; Watercolour Painting in Canada, A Survey, Univ Waterloo, 79; one-man shows, Pollock Gallery, Merton Gallery, Univ Toronto & St Mary's Univ; and others. *Awards:* CSPWC Hon Award, Sarnia Art Gallery, 81; Award, Adirondacks Nat Exhib, Am Watercolors, 82, 88, 91 & 92; Medal Hon, AWS Both Ann Int Exhib, NY, 97. *Bibliog:* Anthony Ferry (auth), A floating world, 2/20/65 & It's now time for Timmas, 11/11/65, Toronto Star; Stevens (auth), Osvald Timmas, La Rev Mod, 11/66. *Mem:* Royal Can Acad Arts; Am Watercolor Soc; Can Soc Painters Watercolor; Ont Soc Artists (vpres, 71-75). *Media:* Watercolor, Acrylic. *Dealer:* Harbour Gallery 1697 Lakeshore Rd West Mississauga Ontario LSJ 1J4. *Mailing Add:* 776 Marlee Ave Toronto ON M6B 3J9 Canada

TIMMS, PETER ROWLAND
MUSEUM DIRECTOR
b Philadelphia, Pa, Aug 26, 1942. *Study:* Brown Univ, Providence, RI, BA, 64; Harvard Univ, MA, 69 & PhD (anthrop), 76. *Pos:* Dir, Fitchburg Art Mus, Mass, 73-; trustee, Applewild Sch, Fitchburg, Mass, 82-92, Nashua Arts & Sci Ctr, 83-86 & Nat Plastics Mus, Leominster, Mass, 86-97. *Teaching:* Instr, Int Col, Beirut, Lebanon, 68; teaching fel, Harvard Univ & Mass Inst Technol, 69-73; vis lectr, Fitchburg State Col, 78; instr, Applewild Sch, 78-79. *Mem:* Am Asn Mus (chmn, State Comt Energy, 78); Applewild Sch (trustee, 82-); Nashua Arts & Sci Ctr (trustee, 83-). *Publ:* Auth, Flint Implements of the Old Stone Age, Shire Publ, United Kingdom, 74, 2nd ed, 79; consult ed & illusr, Human Biology & Ecology, Albert Damon, WW Norton & Co, New York, 77; auth, Accreditation and the small museum, Mus News, 7-8/80. *Mailing Add:* c/o Fitchburg Art Mus 185 Elm St Fitchburg MA 01420

TIMOTHY, GROVER See Whiten, Tim (Timothy) Grover

TIMPANO, ANNE
MUSEUM DIRECTOR, HISTORIAN
b Osaka, Japan; US citizen. *Study:* Coll William & Mary, Williamsburg, Va, BA, 72; George Washington Univ, Washington, DC, MA, 83. *Collection Arranged:* William Christenberry: A Southern Perspective, 87; A Select View: Am Paintings from Columbus Mus, (auth catalog), 87; Paintings and Sculpture from the Permanent Collection, 91; Starstruck: Images from Hollywood's Golden Age, (auth catalog), 92; Enriching the Future (auth, catalog), Univ Cincinnati Fine Arts Collection, Ohio, 95; A Different Drummer: Benny Andrews, the Music Series (auth, catalog), 99; Focus 2000: Juried Photography Exhib, 2000; William Christenberry: Architecture/Archetype (auth catalog), 2001; John Walker: Recent Painting and Prints, 2002; Katherine Kadish: Paintings and Monotypes, 2005; Univ Cincinnati Fine Arts Collection permanent installation, 2005; Making an Impression: Etchings & Engravings from Permanent Collection, 2006; The Saints at Penmarche: Watercolors by Elizabeth Nourse, 2006; The Queen City: Ann Artist's View, 2007. *Pos:* Docent prog coord, Nat Mus Am Art, Washington, DC, 77-80, res asst, 80-83 & prog mgt asst, 83-86; dir, Columbus Mus, Ga, 86-93; dir DAAP Galleries, Univ Cincinnati, 93-. *Teaching:* Adj prof Mus studies, Univ Cincinnati, 97-; dir Mus Studies Prog, Univ Cincinnati, 2000-. *Awards:* David Lloyd Kreeger Prize in the History of Art. *Mem:* Am Asn Mus; Coll Art Asn. *Res:* American art & architecture. *Mailing Add:* DAAP Galleries Univ Cincinnati PO Box 210016 Cincinnati OH 45221-0016

TIMS, MICHAEL WAYNE See Bronson, A A (Michael Wayne Tims)

TINSLEY, BARRY
SCULPTOR
b Roanoke, Va, Feb 19, 1942. *Study:* Coll William & Mary, Williamsburg, Va, BA, 64; Sch Art & Hist, Univ Iowa, Iowa City, MA, 67, MFA, 68. *Work:* S W & B M Koffler Found Collection, Nat Mus Am Art, Washington, DC; Lakeview Mus, Peoria, Ill; Ctr Visual Arts Gallery, Normal, Ill. *Comn:* Jetty (corten steel), comn by City of Chicago, Ill, 80; Silver Oak, (stainless steel & painted aluminum), Green Co, Miami, Fla, 85; Silver Blade (stainless steel relief), Borg Warner Corp, Chicago, Ill, 84; Urban Moraine, comn by State of Ill, Chicago, 84. *Exhib:* Solo exhibs, Ill State Mus, Springfield, 79, Piedmont Arts Asn, Martinsville, Va, 84 & Ordean Ct, Tweed Mus, Duluth, Minn, 86; Mayor Byrne's Mile of Sculpture, Int Art Expo, Navy Pier, Chicago, Ill, 82; Festival of the Arts, Arts Coun Oklahoma City, 85; Chicago Sculpture, Rockford Col, Ill, 85; Sculpture Campus Tour, Univ Tenn, Knoxville, 85-86; Traveling Exhib, New Traditions in Sculpture, Ill Grant, 86. *Pos:* Treas, Chicago Sculpture Soc, 82-; vis artist, Visual Arts Ctr Alaska, 83; bd mem, Sculpture Chicago, Burham Park Planning Asn, 84-. *Teaching:* Instr art & sculpture, Eastern Ky Univ, Richmond, 68-70; assoc prof art & sculpture, Ill State Univ, Normal, 70-78. *Awards:* Dick Blick Mem Award, Galex X, Galesburg, Ill, 76; Chicago Sculpture Syposium Award, 83. *Mem:* Ill Arts Coun (visual artist panel); Chicago Artists Coalition (adv bd, 86). *Mailing Add:* c/o Thomas McCormick Gallery 835 W Washington Blvd Chicago IL 60607

TINTEROW, GARY H
MUSEUM DIRECTOR
b 1954. *Study:* Brandeis Univ, BA, 76; Harvard Univ, MFA, 83; Columbia Univ, MBA, 2008. *Collection Arranged:* Degas, 88; Origins of Impression, 94; Manet/Velazquez: The French Taste for Spanish Painting, 2003; Francis Bacon: A Centenary Retrospective, 2009; Picasso in the Metropolitan Mus Art, 2010. *Pos:* chmn dept contemp art, Metropolitan Mus Art, 83-2011; dir, Mus Fine Art Houston, Tex, 2011-. *Awards:* Chevalier French Legion Hon, 2000; Officer of the French Order of Arts and Letters, 2003. *Mem:* Historic Preservation Comn Marbletown NY (chmn); Thomas Moran Trust; Asn Art Mus Curators (founding pres). *Mailing Add:* Museum of Fine Arts Houston 1001 Bissonnet Houston TX 77005

TIÓ, ADRIAN R
EDUCATOR, ADMINISTRATOR
Study: Temple Univ, BA, 1974; Tyler Sch of Art, Rome, Italy, Post Baccalaureate study, 1975-76; Univ Cincinnati, MFA, 1979. *Exhib:* Exhibited nationally as well as regionally in drawing, painting, and printmaking; Whitewater Valley Annual Competition, Ind Univ East Gallery, Richmond, 1979; Personal Mythology, Trinity House Gallery, Austin, Tex, 1983; Political Statements, Sarratt Gallery, Vanderbilt Univ, Nashville, 1986; Ohio Artists: The Human Figure, Canton Art Inst, Ohio, 1990; Graphic Works-Adrian Tio African-American Cultural Ctr, Univ Ill, 1995; 12th Mini Print International Exhibition, Studio Sch Art Gallery, Binghamton, NY, 1997; Artist's Books by Printmakers, Hayden Library, Arizona State Univ, Tempe, 1999; 16th Parkside Nat Small Print Exhibition, Univ of Wis-Parkside, 2003; Sun and Moon-International Ex Libris Competition, Museo Sempere, Buenos Aires, Argentina, 2004; Collaborations, solo exhibitions, Quad City Art Ctr, Rock Island, Ill, 2005; Day of the Dead Exhibition, Auburn Arts Ctr, Alabama, 2007; Crede Small Print Annual Exhibition, Fine Arts Ctr, Crede, Colo, 2008; and several others. *Collection Arranged:* Private and Public collections include Afro-American Mus and Cultural Ctr, Chicago, Ill, Ateneo Puertorriueno, San Juan, Puerto Rico, Rockefeller Found, NY, The White House, DC, Bradley Univ, Peoria, Ill, Univ Cincinnati, Ohio, Denver Public Library, Colo, Andy Warhol Found for the Visual Arts, NY, East Tennessee State Univ, Johnson City, Univ Buffalo, SUNY, NY, Elvehejm Mus, Univ Wisconsin, Madison, Villa Taverna Found, Washington, DC, Fort Hays State Univ, Kansas, Mexican Consulate Office, Chicago, Nat Endowment for the Arts, Washington, DC, Ohio Arts Coun, and Ohio State Univ. *Pos:* Maintains Hare of the Dog Press and Studio. *Teaching:* Conducted workshops on mural painting, papermaking and the book arts; Dean, Col of Visual and Performing Arts, Univ Mass, Dartmouth, currently. *Awards:* Recognition for work through exhibition awards and creative research grants from Arts Midwest/NEA, Indiana Arts Commission, Ohio Arts Coun, New Forms Regional Grant Program, and the Arts Commission of Greater Toledo. *Mem:* Col Art Asn; International Coun for Fine Arts Deans; Nat Coun of Arts Administrators; The Typophiles. *Dealer:* NAVIO Artist's Collaborative; Judith Klein Gallery. *Mailing Add:* University of Massachusetts Dartmouth CVPA Deans Office 285 Old Westport Rd Dartmouth MA 02747

TIRAVANIJA, RIRKRIT
SCULPTOR
b Buenos Aires, Arg, 1961. *Study:* Ont Coll Art, Toronto, 81; Banff Ctr Sch Fine Arts, Can, 84; Art Inst Chicago, 85; Whitney Independent Studies Prof, New York, 86. *Work:* Walker Art Ctr, Minn; Guggenheim Mus, New York; Migros Mus, Zurich, Switzerland; Mus Contemp Art, Los Angeles; Mus Mod Art, New York; Sammlung der BRD, Berlin, Ger; Carnegie Mus Arts, Pittsburgh; Bangkok Mus Contemp Art, Thailand; Astrup Fearnley Mus Mod Art, Oslo, Norway. *Exhib:* Solo exhibs, Paula Allen Gallery, NY, 90, Randy Alexander Gallery, NY, 91, 303 Gallery, NY, 92 & 95, Randolph St Gallery, Chicago, 93, Jack Hanley Gallery, San Francisco, 94, Schipper & Krome, Ger, 94, The Modern Inst, Glasgow, Eng, 99, The Land, Galerie Changtal Crousel, Paris, 2001, He Promised, Secession, Vienna, Austria, 2002, In the Future Everything Will Be Chrome, Gavin Brown's Enterprise, NY, 2003, Retrospective, Mus Bomans Van Beuningen, Rotterdam, Netherlands, 2004, ARC, Mus d'Art Moderne de la Ville de Paris, 2005, Galerie Chantal Crousel, Paris, 2006, Brychcy Bar, Gavin Brown's Enterprise, NY, 2006, Ontario Coll Art & Design, 2007, Stories Are Propaganda, Friedrich Petzel Gallery, NY with Philippe Parreno, 2007, Palm Pavillon, kurimanzutto, Mexico City, 2008, JG Reads, Gavin Brown's Enterprise, NY,

2008, Reflection, Nyehaus, NY, 2009, The House the Cat Built, Galeria Salvador Diaz, Madrid, Spain, 2009 and others; Simply Made in Am, Aldrich Mus Contemp Art, Conn, 93; Sleepless Nights, PS1 Mus, Queens, NY, 93; L'Hiver de l'Amour, Musee d'Art Moderne de la Ville de Paris, France, 94; Whitney Mus Am Art Biennial, NY, 95; Wexner Ctr, Columbus, Ohio, 99; Points of Departure, San Francisco Mus Modern Art, 2001; En Route, Serpentine Gallery, London, 2002; Elephant Juice, Kurimanzutto, Mexico City, 2003; Perfect Timeless Repetition, Alte Gerhardsen, Berlin, 2003; Big Nothing, Inst Contemp Art, Philadelphia, 2003; Small: The Object in Film, Video and Slide Installation, Whitney Mus Am Art, NY, 2004; Post No Bills, White Columns, NY, 2005; Looking at Words, Andrea Rosen Gallery, NY, 2005; universal experience. art, life and the tourist's eye, Hayward Gallery, London, 2005; Peace Tower, Day for Night, Whitney Biennial, 2006; Sao Paulo Biennial, Brazil, 2006; Open Ended (the art of engagement), Walker Art Ctr, Minn, 2006; Into Me/Out of Me, PS1 Contemporary Art Ctr, NY, 2006; The Shapes of Space, Guggenheim Mus, NY, 2007; Lyon Biennale, France, 2007; Show Me Thai, Mus Contemp Art, Tokyo, Japan, 2007; The Puppet Show, Santa Monica Mus Art, 2008; Yokohama Triennial, Japan, 2008; 1992009, D'Amelio Terras, NY, 2009; Venice Biennale, Italy, 2009; Brodno Sculpture Park, Mus Modern Art, Warsaw, Poland, 2009. *Pos:* Pres The Land Foundation; adv bd mem New Media Inst, Univ Chiang Mai, Thailand, 2003, Tokyo Wondersite Cultural Arts Center, Tokyo, 2003, Carnegie Int, 2002-04. *Teaching:* Guest prof and vis artist Nat Acad Fine Arts, Oslo, Norway, 2001; guest prof Stadelschule Staalich Hochschule Bildende Kunst, Frankfurt, 2001, Royal Danish Art Acad, 2001-02; adj asst prof Columbia Univ, 1999-2000; assoc prof professional practice, Columbia Univ, 2001-; assoc prof, graduate course in visual arts, IUAV Univ Venice, 2003-04. *Awards:* Hugo Boss Prize, 2004; Lucelia Artist Award, Smithsonian Am Art Mus; Goron Matta Clark Grant; Louis Comfort Tiffany Award; Silpathorn award, 2007; Central Kunst Prize. *Bibliog:* Rainald Schumacher (auth), Koln Kritik, Flash Art, 51, summer 94; Gavin Brown (auth), Otherthings Elsewhere, Flash Art, 102, summer 94; Bruce Hainley (auth), Reviews, Artforum, 86, 1/95. *Mem:* pres, The Land Found; adv bd mem, Carnegie Internat, 2002-04, Tokyo Wondersite Cultural Arts Ctr, Tokyo, 2003, CCA Kytakyshu, Japan, 2003, New Media Inst, Univ Chiang Mai, Thailand, 2003. *Mailing Add:* c/o Gavin Brown's Enterprise 820 Greenwich St New York NY 10014

TISCHLER, GARY
CRITIC
Study: Arts and entertainment critic Wash Diplomat, Wheaton, Md; art and entertainment critic Georgetowner, Wash. *Mailing Add:* Georgetowner 1054 Potomac St Washington DC 20007

TOBIA, BLAISE JOSEPH
PHOTOGRAPHER, EDUCATOR
b Brooklyn, NY, Jan 20, 1953. *Study:* Brooklyn Coll, with Walter Rosenblum, George Krause, Bob D'Allesandro & Philip Pearlstein, BA, 74; Univ Calif, San Diego, with David Antin, Allan Kaprow & Newton Harrison, MFA, 77. *Work:* City Archives, New York; Delaware Mus Art; World Lomographic Soc; Free Libr, Philadelphia; many pvt collections. *Comn:* Many commissioned photographic works as well as documentations of artist-performances. *Exhib:* Encampments, Randolph St Gallery, Chicago, 89; Biennial '91, Delaware Art Mus, 91; Surveillance: 6 Days, CEPA Gallery, Buffalo, 91; Am Pie: Myth Representation, Abington Arts Ctr, Philadelphia, 92; Crimes & Punishments, Philadelphia Art Alliance, 95; New Means, Silicon Gallery, Philadelphia, 96; Contemp-Italianate, Loyola Mary Mount Univ, Los Angeles, Calif, 98; Cult Syntax: Recent Work of Blaise Tobia, Drexel Univ, 2000, Tulane Univ, 2001; Blaise Tobia, Oskar Friedl Gallery, Chicago, 2002; Direct Objects, Delaware Ctr Contemp Art, 2005; Digital Space Object Painted Bride, Phila, 2007; Castle of Eufemio, Italian Am Mus, New York, 2008; Open Studio, Silicon Gallery, Phila, 2008; Plain & Fancy, Phila Int Airport Exhib, 2009; Close Views, Amos Eno Gallery, Brooklyn, 2009, Resilient Suspension, 2013; Conflation, Pearlstein Gallery, Drexel Univ, 2010; High/Low Density, Rowan Univ, 2012; 9, Mus Cafa, Beijing, 2012. *Pos:* Prof Art & Art Hist, Drexel Univ. *Teaching:* Vis photogr, Univ Calif, San Diego, 79 & Wayne State Univ, Detroit, 81; prof photog, Drexel Univ, 85-. *Awards:* Ford Found Grant, 77; Fac Res Award, Drexel Univ, Philadelphia, 86; Nat Endowment Humanities Res Fel, 88. *Bibliog:* Miles Orvell (auth), Democracy, Disorder, and the New Political Art, American Pie (exhib catalog), Abington/CEPA, 92; Wit on Wry: Humor in Photography, NY Times, 93; New Means, Philadelphia Inquirer, 96; Joseph Gregory (auth), Some Notes on Interpretation; exhib catalog, Design Arts Gallery, Drexel Univ; Joseph Gregory (auth), Dangerous Curves: Poetry and Politics in the work of Blaise Tobia, Afterimage, 2003. *Mem:* Coll Art Asn; Soc Photog Educ. *Media:* Photography, Digital. *Interests:* Image and text; panoramic imagery; social and political issues. *Publ:* Undermining Documentary, Afterimage, 90; auth, From Resistance to Embrace: Text/Image Relationships in 20th-Century Fine-Art Photographic Practice, Word & Image, fall 92; Art & Society- Monthly Colum (coauth with Virginia Maksymowicz), The Witness, 93-94; Change of Scenery, Silicon Gallery, 2000; Digital Printmaking, Photography, London, Eng, 2001; Digital Photography, Encyclopedia of 20th Century Photography, 2005; Castle of Eufemio, Achilles Press, 2007. *Dealer:* TandM Arts, Philadelphia PA. *Mailing Add:* c/o T and M Arts 3719 Lancaster Ave Philadelphia PA 19104-2334

TOBIAS, ROBERT PAUL
PAINTER, SCULPTOR
b Reading, Pa, Dec 14, 1933. *Study:* Ariz State Univ, BS (appl arts, ceramics), 64, MFA (sculpture), 69. *Work:* Matthews Ctr, Ariz State Univ, Tempe; Univ Ariz Mus Art, Tucson; Ariz Western Col, Yuma; Phoenix Art Mus, Ariz. *Comn:* Monumental sculpture, La Placita, City of Tucson, 74. *Exhib:* Painting, 1973 Four Corners Exhib, Phoenix & 1974 Mainstreams, Marietta Col, Ohio; sculpture, Nelson Art Mus, Kansas City, Mo, 70, Yuma Invitational, 73 & Arizona's Outlook '74, Tucson Art Ctr. *Teaching:* Instr design, Univ Kans, Lawrence, 69-71; assoc prof sculpture & design, Univ Ariz, Tucson, 71-. *Awards:* Sculpture Purchase Award, Wis State Univ, Platteville, 67; Painting Award, 1972 Yuma Invitational, Ariz Western Col; Sculpture Exhib Award, Tucson Art Mus, 74. *Bibliog:* Tobias show in Lawrence, Kansas City Star, 3/22/70; Darrell Dobraus (auth), Artists review, Desert Silhouette, Tucson, 10/75. *Dealer:* Gekas/Nicholas Gallery 6538 East Tangue Verde Rd Tucson AZ 85715. *Mailing Add:* 5600 W Moore Rd Marana AZ 85653-4109

TOBIN, STEVE ROBERT
SCULPTOR
b Philadelphia, Feb 10, 1957. *Study:* Tulane Univ, B (theoretical mathematics), 76-79. *Exhib:* Solo exhibs, Sculptured Glass, Bienville Gallery, New Orleans, 1979, Glasscapes, Spring Street Enamels Gallery, NY, 1980, Glass Portraits, Hanson Gallery, New Orleans, 1980, Glass Sculpture, Gallery 10, NY, 1982, Manhattan Bowls, Snyderman Gallery, Philadelphia, 1985, Wheaton Ware, LaVaggi Gallery, NY, 1986, Glass for Tea Ceremony, Tazawa Gallery, Kyoto, Japan, 1987, The Glass Garden, Coll Art & Design, Levy Gallery for Arts Philadelphia, 1988, Cocoons, Moore Coll Art & Design, Philadelphia, 1988, Transformations: Three Installations in Glass, Lehigh Univ, Wilson & Hall Gallery, Bethlehem, Pa, 1992, Retretti Art Centre, Punkaharju, Findland, 1993, Sanske Galerie, Zurich, Swit, 1994, Reconstructions, Philip and Muriel Berman Mus Art, Ursinus Col, Pa, 1995, Matzoh House, Gallery BAI, NY, 1996, Broadway River, NYU, 1997, Earth Bronzes, OK Harris, NY, 1998, Earth Bronze Trilogy-Part I, Buschlen-Mowatt Gallery, Vancouver, Can, 2001. *Pos:* res asst to Dr Campbell, Laird Univ, Pa, 1975. *Teaching:* teacher, glass sculpture, Tokyo Glass Art Inst, Japan, 1985-86. *Awards:* Fel, Wheaton Village, Millville, NJ, 1983-84. *Media:* glass

TOBLER, GISELA ERNA MARIA
PAINTER, ARCHITECT
b Hamburg, Ger, Mar 29, 1939; Swiss citizen. *Study:* Kunstgewerbeschule, Zurich, Switz, scholar grafique designer, 56-59. *Work:* Museo de Arte de La Universidad, Mexico City; Univ Tex, Austin. *Exhib:* 15 solo exhibs, 36 collective expositions; Museo de Arte dela Universidad, Mexico City, Los Colores en el Piensamento, Museo-Casa Diego Rivera, Guanajuato, Mex, 97; Mujeres y Sus Colores, Tallera-de Alfaro Sigueiros, Cuernavaca, Estado de Morelos, 98. *Media:* Oil. *Publ:* Contribr, Cien Mujeres en La Plastica Mexicana, UNAM-Muca, 97; Demos-Carta Demografica Sobre Mexico, UNAM-Raul Benitez Zenteno, 98 & Mujeres de Colores. *Mailing Add:* Otono 17 Col Merced Gomez Mexico DF Mexico

TODA, FUMIKO
PAINTER, PRINTMAKER
b Japan. *Study:* Kyoto Univ Art & Design, Assoc, 2000; Nat Adac Design, New York, 2001-07. *Comn:* Com de Shio, Art Glass Co, Japan. *Exhib:* Solo exhibs include Hisa Gallery, Mie, Japan, 1998, Art Expo, New York, 2004, Designers & Agents, New York, 2007, Cottage Place Gallery, Ridgewood, NJ, 2008; Group exhibs include Cork Gallery, Lincoln Ctr, New York, 2004, 2006; Lord Van's Gallery, New York, 2004; Ise Cultural Found, New York, 2006; Seed Proj, Winkleman Gallery, New York, 2007; Porj Benefit Auction, Rare Gallery, New York, 2007; Young Emerging Artists, Lana Santorelli Gallery, New York, 2008; 183rd Ann: Invitational Exhib Contemp Am Art, Nat Acad Mus, New York, 2008. *Awards:* Ralph Weiler Midyear Exhib Grant, 2002, 2004; Ogden Pleissner Scholar, 2002, 2005; Arthur & Melville Phillips Sch Scholar, 2003; Inga Denton Sch Scholar, 2006; Michal Jacobs Prize, 2006; Mural Workshop Scholar & Grant, Nat Acad Mus, 2007. *Media:* Drawing. *Publ:* Illus contribr: Am Illustration 26, Art Digest Mag, Studio Visit Molokot Mag

TODD, MICHAEL CULLEN
SCULPTOR, PAINTER
b Omaha, Nebr, June 20, 1935. *Study:* Univ Notre Dame, BFA, 57; Univ Calif, Los Angeles, MA, 59; Woodrow Wilson Fel, 59; Fulbright Fel, France, 61. *Work:* Whitney Mus Am Art, New York; Los Angeles Co Mus Art; Oakland Mus; Hirshhorn Mus & Sculpture Garden, Washington; Metrop Mus, New York; Sculpture Garden, City of Hope, Duarte, Calif; and others. *Comn:* Pac Mutual Insurance, Costa Mesa, Calif. *Exhib:* Whitney Mus Am Art Sculpture Ann, 64-70; Sculpture of 60's, Los Angeles Co Mus Art, 65 & Philadelphia Mus, 66; Living Am Art, Maeght Found, France, 71; Exhibs Large Scale Sculpture, Lippincott Corp; Charles Cowles Gallery, NY, 81; and others. *Teaching:* Instr sculpture, Bennington Col, 66-68; asst prof sculpture, Univ Calif, San Diego, 68-76. *Awards:* Nat Endowment Arts. *Media:* Steel, Aluminum, Bronze, Ceramics. *Publ:* 25 Year Survey (catalog), Palm Springs Desert Mus, Calif. *Dealer:* Stremmel Gallery Reno NV; Gremillion & Co Fine Art Houston TX; Sylvia White Gallery, Ventura, CA. *Mailing Add:* 2817 Clearwater Los Angeles CA 90039

TOGUO, BARTHÉLÉMY
PAINTER
b Cameroon, 1967. *Work:* Mus Contemp Art, Miami; Centre Georges Pompidou, Mus Nat d'Art Modern, Paris; Mus d'art moderne de la Ville de Paris; Fonds Nat d'Art Contemprain, Paris; Kunstamlungen der Stadt, Düsseldorf; Mus d'art contemprain du Val-de-Marne, Vitry; Frac Corse, Corte; Collection Antoin De Galbert, Maison Rouge, Paris; dakis Joannou Collection, Athens. *Exhib:* Solo exhibs, Carpe Diem Arte e Pesquis, Palace of Marquis de Pombal, Lisbon, Portugal, 94, Item Editions, Paris, 94, Goethe Inst, Yaoundé, Cameroon, 96, 2002, Centre d'Arts Plastiques, Saint-Fons, France, 98, Musée d'Art moderne de la Ville de Paris, 99, Düsseldorf in der Tonhalle, Düsseldorf, Germany, 99, La Criée centre d'Art contemporain, Rennes, France, 2000, The Box Associati Gallery, Turin, Italy, 2000, école régionale des Beaux-Arts de Dunkerque, France, 2001, CCC, Tours, France, 2002, Inst of Visual Art, Milwaukee, Wis, 2003, Palais de Tokyo, Paris, France, 2004, école supérieure d'Art, Lorient, France, 2005, Mario Marauner Contemp Art, Salzburg, Austria, 2006, 2008, 2009, Art Brussels, Bruxelles, Belgium, 2008, Galerie de la ville de Poitiers, 2010, Centre d"art Contemporain de Châtellerault, 2010, Biennale de Dakar, Inst Français de Dakar, 2010, Foto Mus Avers, Johannesburg Art Gallery, Cape Town, 2010, Galerie Lelong, Paris, 2010; Group exhibs, Int Art Meeting, Oviedo, Spain, 99, Aentre de'art, Marnay-sur-Seine, Farnce, 2000, ctr Nat de la Photographie, Paris, 2000, White Box, New York, 2001, Sudio Casoli, Milano, Italy, 2001, Mus Ludwig, Allemagne, 2002,

Mus für Gegenwartskunst, Zürich, Switzerland, 2003, Dolce Tocco, Napoli, Itlay, 2003, Forum Kunst Rottweil, Germany, 2003, Tri Postal, Lille, France, 2004, Biennale de Dakar, Senegal, 2004, Hayward Gallery, Londres, United Kingdom, 2005, Musée de Bamako, Mali, 2005, Palais de Tokyo, Paris, 2006, Mori Art Mus, Tokyo, 2006, Biennale de Shenzhen, China, 2006, Orangerie de Madame Elisabeth, Versailles, France, 2007, HE-Xiangning Mus, Chenzhen, China, 2007, Im Traklhaus, Salzburg, Vienna, 2008, Centro Atlantico de Arte Moderno, Canary Islands, Black Paris, 2008, Cornelius strasse, Düsseldorf, Germany,2009, Royal Mus Central Africa, Tervuren, Belgium, 2009, Cantor Arts Ctr, Stanford Univ, Calif, 2010, Mario Mauroner Cotnemp Art Vienna, 2010, Mus Mod Art, Saint-Etienne, France, 2010

TOKER, FRANKLIN
HISTORIAN, EDUCATOR

b Montreal, Que, Apr 29, 1944; US citizen. *Study:* McGill Univ, BA, 64; Oberlin Coll, AM, 66; Harvard Univ, PhD, 73. *Exhib:* Poussin en detail, Fogg Art Mus, Harvard Univ, 67. *Pos:* Archeol dir excavations, Cathedral of Florence, Italy, 69-74 & 80. *Teaching:* A W Mellon vis prof fine arts, Carnegie-Mellon Univ, Pittsburgh, 74-76, assoc prof, 76-80; assoc prof hist art & archit, Univ Pittsburgh, 80-87, prof, 87; vis prof hist art, Univ Florence, Italy, 89; vis prof hist archit, Univ Rome, Italy, 91 & Univ Reggio Calabria, Italy, 96. *Awards:* Interpretive Res Grant, Nat Endowment Humanities, 92-94; Residency, Bellagio Study Ctr, Italy, 94; Graham Found Advanced Studies in Visual Arts Fel, 95. *Bibliog:* Ada Louise Huxtable (auth), The current age of rediscovery, 11/27/77 & Henry Tanner (auth), Florence cathedral credited to sculptor, 5/7/80, NY Times; Brendan Gill (auth), Skyline, New Yorker, 1/9/89; Janet Maslin (auth), Review of Fallingwater Rising, NY Times, 9/28/2003. *Mem:* Life mem Medieval Acad Am; Inst Advan Study, Princeton; life mem Coll Art Asn; life mem Soc Archit Historian (dir, 85-88, vpres, 90-93, pres, 93-94); Archeol Inst Am. *Res:* Medieval art; American and 19th century architecture and urban design; Early Christian archaeology. *Publ:* Arnolfo's S Maria del Fiore, J Soc Archit Hist, 83; Alberti's ideal architect, Renaissance Studies honoring Craig Hugh Smyth, Florence, 85; auth, The Church of Notre-Dame in Montreal, McGill Univ Press, rev ed 91; Building on Paper: The Role of Architectural Drawings in Late-Medieval Italy, Actes du XVIIe congres International de l'Histoire de l'Art, Strasbourg, 92; auth, Pittsburgh: An Urban Portrait, Univ Pittsburgh Press, rev ed 95; Fallingwater Rising, Knoph publ, 2003; Buildings of Pittsburgh, Univ Va Press, 2007; On Holy Ground: Liturgy, Architecture and Urbanism in the Catheral and the streest of Medieval Florence, Brepols Publ, 2009; Pittsburgh: A New Portrait, Univ Pittsburgh Pressm 2009. *Mailing Add:* Dept Hist Art & Archit Univ Pittsburgh Pittsburgh PA 15260-7610

TOLL, BARBARA ELIZABETH
DEALER, CURATOR

b Philadelphia, Pa, June 8, 1945. *Study:* Goucher Coll, Towson, Md, AB, 67; Radcliffe Coll, 67; Pratt Inst, New York, MFA, 69. *Collection Arranged:* Focus: Donald Judd Furniture, Parrish Art Mus, 96; Curator David Rockefeller Col, 77-81; Friendships in Arcadia: Writers and Artists at Yaddo in the 90's, Art in General, MY; Follies: Fantasy in the Landscape, Parrish Art Mus, 01; Reconfiguring Space: Blueprints for Art in General, 03. *Pos:* Dir, Hundred Acres Gallery, New York, 70-77; freelance cur & dealer, 77-81 & 94-; owner & dir, Barbara Toll Fine Arts, New York, 81-94. *Teaching:* New York Univ Sch Continuing Educ, 79-81. *Mem:* Art Table; Corp Yaddo; Trustee, Independent Cur Int; Trustee, The Drawing Center, NY. *Specialty:* Contemporary works of art in all media. *Publ:* Covered in Dust, Bill Bollinger, Christine Meyer-Stoll (ed), Walther Konig, 2011; auth, Taking Aim! The Business of Being An Artist Today; The Journey from the Studio to the Collection: Six Interviews with Art Advisors, Corporate Curators, and Others, Fordham Univ Press & the Bronx Mus Art, 2011. *Mailing Add:* c/o Barbara Toll Fine Arts 138 Prince St New York NY 10012

TOLL, BRUCE E
COLLECTOR

Pos: Mem bd dirs, Toll Brothers, Inc, 1986-, chief operating officer & pres, 1986-1998; founder & pres, BET Investments; chmn, Philadelphia Media Holdings, LLC; mem bd dirs, Fifth St Fin Corp & UbiquiTel, Inc, 2000-06. *Awards:* Named one of Top 200 Collectors, ARTnews mag, 2009-13. *Collection:* Elizabethan and Jacobean painting; Impressionism; Post-Impressionism; 20th-century sculpture. *Mailing Add:* Toll Brothers Inc 250 Gibraltar Rd Horsham PA 19044

TOLLE, BRIAN
SCULPTOR

b Queens, NY, 1964. *Study:* SUNY Albany, BA (political sci), 1986; Parsons Sch Design, BFA, 1992; Yale Univ, MFA, 1994. *Exhib:* Real Art Ways, Hartford, Conn, 1994; Basilico Fine Arts, NY, 1995; Schloss Agathenburg, German, 1995; Bertha & Karl Leubdorf Art Gallery, New York, 1996; solo exhibs, Basilico Fine Arts, New York, 1996, 1998, Schmidt Contemp Art, St Louis, 1998, Parsons Sch Design, 1999, Shoshana Wayne Gallery, 2000, Cleveland Public Art, 2005, ICA, Philadelphia, 2006, Contemp Arts Ctr, Cincinnati, 2006 & CRG Gallery, New York, 2009; Galleri F15, Moss, Norway, 1997; Pusan Met Art Mus, Korea, 1998; Entwistle, London, 1999; Dee Glasoe, New York, 2000; Queens Mus Art, 2001; Whitney Biennial, New York, 2002; Kunsthalle Bern, 2003; Liverpool Biennial Int 06, 2006; Arsenal Gallery, 2007; Am Acad Arts and Letts Invitational, New York, 2009. *Awards:* Louis Comfort Tiffany Found Award, 2003; Irishman of Yr, Irish Am Heritage Comt, 2003; Irish Am Hist Soc Award, 2003. *Media:* Miscellaneous Media. *Mailing Add:* c/o CRG Gallery 535 West 22nd St New York NY 10011

TOLLES, BRYANT FRANKLIN, JR
EDUCATOR, HISTORIAN

b Hartford, Conn, Mar 14, 1939. *Study:* Yale Univ, BA, 61, MAT, 62; Boston Univ, PhD, 70. *Pos:* Asst dir & libr, NH Hist Soc, Concord, 72-74; exec dir & librn, Essex Inst, Salem, Mass, 74-84; dir, Mus Studies Prog, Univ Del, 84-2005. *Teaching:* Asst dean & instr hist, Tufts Univ, Medford, Mass 65-71; prof art history & hist, Univ Del, 84-2005, prof emeritus, 2005-. *Mem:* Orgn Am Historians; Soc Archit Historians; Nat Trust Hist Preserv; AAS. *Res:* New England architectural history, late 18th to early 20th century; White Mountain illustrators, 1820-1910; Architecture of tourism, 1800-1950. *Interests:* American architectural history; American portraiture, 1750-1900; American landscape art, 19th century. *Publ:* The Evolution of a Campus: Dartmouth Coll Archit Before 1860, Hist NH, 87; The Grand Resort Hotels of the White Mountains, David R Godine, Publ Inc, 98; Summer Cottages in the White Mountains, Univ Press of New Eng, 2000; Resort Hotels of the Adirondacks, Univ Press New England, 2003; NH Archit: A Guide, Univ Press of New Eng, 2004; Archit in Salem: An Illustrated Guide, Univ Press New England, 2004; Summer by the Seaside: The Architecture of New England Coastal Resort Hotels, 1820-1950, Univ Press New Eng, 2008; Architecture & Academe: Coll Bldg in New England Before 1860, Univ Press New England, 2011. *Mailing Add:* 39 Dwinell Drive Concord NH 03301

TOLPO, CAROLYN LEE
PAINTER, CERAMIC ARTIST

b Detroit, Mich, 1940. *Study:* Wayne State Univ, Detroit, BA, 62. *Work:* Highland Coll Art Collection, Freeport, Ill; Amaco Art Collection, Denver, Colo; Digital Corp, Denver, Colo; Joslyn Art Mus, Omaha, Nebr; Sheldon Art Gallery, Lincoln, Nebr; Cedar Rapids Art Mus. *Comn:* Alamo Ctr, Colorado Springs, 83; atrium fiber mural, Cumberland Bldg, Denver, 85; fiber mural, Mega Bank, 86 & Tishman West Inc, 89, Denver, Colo; fiber mural, Hamilton Standard Corp, Colorado Springs, 92; mural, Marina Hotel, Jacksonville, Fla, 93; sculpture, Mesa Co Libr, Grand Junction, Colo, 95. *Exhib:* Stanley Gallery, Muscatine, Iowa, 80; Women's Caucus Art Group Show, Western Ill Univ, Macomb, Ill, 81; Women's Caucus for Art Show, Quad City Arts Ctr, Rock Island, Ill, 81; Sculptour, Gunnison, Colo, 94-96; Art on the Corner Sculpture Exhib, Grand Junction, Colo, 94-96; Steam Plant Art Ctr, Salida, Colo, 99-2002; Convergence, World Fiber Conv, Exhib Shawnee Mt Gallery, 2004; Joslyn Art Mus Gallery, Omaha, Nebr, 2007; Sheldon Art Gallery, Lincoln Nebr; Molly Brown House, Denver, Colo; Nest Gallery, Winter Park, Colo, 2009; Creations Gallery, Louisville, Colo; Artifacts Gallery, Estes Park, Colo; Kaliedoscope Gallery, Denver, Colo. *Pos:* Gallery dir, Shawnee Mountain Gallery, Shawnee, Colo, 81-, owner, currently. *Teaching:* Art instr/coordr, Freeport Cath Sch, 71-76. *Awards:* Best Show Watercolor, Nat Orchid Soc Art Exhib, 81. *Bibliog:* Art Today Mag, 92; Fiberarts Mag, Nov/Dec, 92. *Mem:* Woman's Caucus Art, Midwest Chap (founding pres, 79-81); Cult Coun Park Co, Colo (founding bd mem); Rocky Mt Weavers Guild; Shawnee Hist Soc (founder). *Media:* Wrapped Fiber, Watercolor, Jewelry, Pottery. *Specialty:* contemporary art, jewelry, pottery. *Interests:* outdoor activities, swimming, reading, volunteering, gardening, history. *Publ:* The Guild 5, 6, 7 & 8: Artist Sourcebook, Krause Sikes Inc, Madison, Wis; Profiles in American Craft, Rosen Inc, Baltimore, Md; 93. *Dealer:* Stonehenge Gallery Georgetown CO; Campbell Steele Gallery Marion IA; Colo Hist Mus Shop, Denver, Colo; Molly Brown House Mus Shop Denver Colo; Nest Gallery Winter Park CO; Creations Gallery, Louisville, Colo; Grand Lake Art Gallery Grand Lake Colo; Nine Dot Arts Denver CO; Caboodle Gallery Denver CO; Kaliedoscope Gallery Littleton CO. *Mailing Add:* PO Box 134 Shawnee CO 80475

TOLPO, VINCENT CARL
PAINTER, SCULPTOR

b Chicago, Ill, Apr 26, 1950. *Study:* Univ Wyo, Laramie, 69-69, Am Acad Art, Chicago, 70-71; Ariz State Univ, Tempe, BFA, 74; studied with Carl & Lily Tolpo, 69-76. *Work:* Freeport Art Mus, Ill; Augustana Hosp Portrait Gallery, Chicago; Park Co Libr, Ft Carson, Colo; Joselyn Art Mus, Omaha Nebr. *Comn:* Fiber murals (collab with Carolyn L Tolpo), Alamo Ctr, Colorado Springs, Colo, 83; atrium metal sculpture, Glenarm Bldg, Denver, 92; metal wall sculpture, Regel Riverfront Hotel, St Louis, Mo, 93-; Moon Over Red Rocks (oil painting), Park Meadow Village, Denver, Colo, 96; Peaks & Valleys, metal & stoneware mural, Commercial Bank, Buena Vista, Colo, 97; metal wall sculpture, Elkhorn Conf Ctr, Colorado Springs, Colo, 2001; metal wall sculpture, Health Partners, Colorado Springs, Colo, 2004; Metal wall sculpture, Exempla Hosp Lafayette, Colo, 2005; metal wall sculpture, Woods Collection, Scottsdale, Ariz, 2007; Heatteor Stamm Mem, San Diego, 2009; Tom Spencer Collection, Boulder, Colo, 2008; Colo Medical Bldg, Denver, Colo, 2010; Seeling Coll, Buena Vista, Colo, 2012; McAlister Music Studio, Exhib Hall, Conifer, Colo; Bulsley Coll, Denver, Colo, 2014; Freeport Art Mus, Freeport Ill, 2014. *Exhib:* Scottsdale Ann, Scottsdale Fine Art Ctr, Ariz, 73; 14th Ann, Stanley Gallery, Muscatine, Iowa, 80; sculpture exhib, Art on the Corner, Grand Junction, Colo, 90-96; Sculpture, Gunnison, Colo, 93-96; Real West, Denver Art Mus, Colo, 96; Steamplant Art Ctr, Salida, Colo, 2000-03; Campbell Steel Gallery, Marion, Iowa, 2007; Mus Nebr Art, Kearney, Nebr; Stonehenge Gallery, Georgetown, Colo, 2009; Creations Gallery, Louisville, Colo, 2010; Artifacts Gallery, Estes Park, Colo, 2012; Kaleidoscope Gallery, Littleton, Colo. *Pos:* owner, Shawnee Mountain Gallery, Colo. *Teaching:* Ceramics, art appreciation, Highland Col, Freeport, Ill, 75-77. *Awards:* Co-visions, Colo Arts Coun, 92. *Bibliog:* Art Today Mag, 92; Fiber Arts Mag, Nov/Dec 92. *Mem:* Am Craft Coun; Park Co Cult Coun; Colo Metalsmith Asn; Rocky Mountain Weavers Guild. *Media:* Oil, Welded Metal, Ceramics, Fiber, Mixed Media. *Specialty:* Contemp Art; Ceramics; Jewelry. *Interests:* outdoor activities, local politics, cello, reading, workouts, poetry, swimming. *Publ:* Guild 5, 6, 7 & 8: Artist Sourcebook, Krause/Sikes Inc, Madison, Wisc; Profiles in American Craft, Rosen Inc, Baltimore, Md, 93. *Dealer:* Old Town Gallery Colorado Springs CO; Eartwoods Artisans Estes Park CO; Stonehenge Gallery, Georgetown CO; Campbell Steele Gallery Marion IA; Grand Lake Art Gallery Grand Lake Colo; Joselyn Art Mus Gallery Omaha Nebr; Nest Gallery Winter Park CO; Creation Gallery Louisville Co; Artifacts Gallery, Estes Park, Colo; Nine Dot Arts, Denver, CO; Kaleidoscope Gallery, Littleton, CO; Caboodle Gallery, Denver, CO; Firedworks Gallery, Alamosa. *Mailing Add:* c/o Shawnee Mountain Studios PO Box 134 Shawnee CO 80475

TOMASINI, WALLACE J
ADMINISTRATOR, HISTORIAN
b Brooklyn, NY, Oct 19, 1926. *Study:* Univ Mich, AB, 49, AM, 50, PhD, 53; Univ Florence, Fulbright grant, 51-52; NY Univ Inst Fine Arts, 54-57. *Teaching:* Instr hist of art, Finch Col, 54-57; asst prof art hist, Univ Iowa, 57-61, assoc prof, 61-64, prof, 64-, dir, Sch Art & Art Hist, 72-93. *Awards:* Am Numismatic Soc Grant, 57; Am Philos Soc Grant, 58. *Mem:* Am Numismatic Soc; Mid-Am Coll Art Conf; Int Exchange Scholars; Sixteenth Century Studies; Midwest Art Hist Soc; Haviland collectors int found pres. *Res:* Social and economic determinants of Italian Renaissance art; Late Imperial and Barbaric numismatics. *Publ:* Auth, Report on Visigothic Numismatic Research, 62; Exhibition Catalogue: Drawing & the Human Figure 1400-1964, 64; The Barbaric Tremissis in Spain & Southern France, Anastasius to Leovigild (numismatic notes & monogr 152), 64; contribr, 17th Century Art Essay (CIC Exhib Catalogue), 73; Paintings of Eve Drewelowe, 85; Catalogue of Haviland china: celebrating 150 yrs, 92. *Mailing Add:* 610 Beldon Ave Iowa City IA 52246

TOMCHUK, MARJORIE
PRINTMAKER, PAINTER
b Manitoba, Can, Oct 16, 1933; US citizen. *Study:* Univ Mich, BA, 57, MA, 61; Long Beach State Coll, 62; Sophia Univ, Japan; Pratt Graphics Ctr, NY. *Work:* Libr Congress, Print Collection, Wash DC, Poster Collection, Wash DC; Nat Air & Space Mus, Wash DC; Art in Embassies Program, State Dept, Wash DC; Mus City of NY, NY; Am Mus Papermaking, Atlanta, Ga; Ukranian Mus, NY; Newark Mus, NJ; DeCordova Mus, Lincoln, Mass; Nelson Gallery Art, Kans City, Mo; Denver Art Mus, Denver, Colo; Crane Mus Paper Making, Dalton, Mass; Lake Co Mus, Wauconda, Ill; Lake Co Mus, Wauconda, Ill; Davison Art Ctr, Middletown, Conn; Fayetteville Mus Art, Fayetteville, NC; Booth Western Art Mus, Cartersville, Ga; Nora Eccles Harrison Mus Art, Logan, Utah; Midwest Mus Am Art, Elkhart, In; Butler Inst Art, Youngstown, Oh; Mus Native Am Cultures, Spokane, Wash; Univ Club Chgo, Ill; Print Consortium, St Joseph, Mo; New Canann Libr, New Canaan, Conn; Baker Libr, Dartmouth Coll, Hanover, NH; Pan Asia Paper Mus, Jeonju, Korea; Mus Antiquities, Urumchi, China; Ebristan, Istanbul Ebri Evi, Uskudar, Istanbal, Turkey; Minato Mirai Concert Hall, Yokahama, Japan; Hall of Architect Associates of Muran City, Hokaido, Japan. *Comn:* Xerox Corp; General Electric; Northern Telecom; West Point Military Acad, NY. *Exhib:* World Art Exposition, Boston, 79; Solo exhibs, Art Expo NY, 79-98, Art Washington, 79-83 & Art Expo Calif, 81-93; Isetan Art Gallery, Tokyo, 86; Fayetteville Mus Art, NC, 89; West Point Military Acad, 93; Silvermine Guild Art Ctr, 99; Am Mus Papermaking, Atlanta, Ga; Carneage Barn Art Ctr, New Canaan, 2013. *Awards:* Boston Nat Print Show, Purchase Prizes, DeCordova Mus, 71 & 73; Best Print Award, Art Trends Mag, 2000; Hon Mention, Foot Print Exhib, Ctr Contemporary Printmaking, 2010, 2013. *Bibliog:* Ellen Kaplan (auth), A Collectors Guide, Prints, 83; Franz Geierhaas (auth), M Tomchuk Graphic Work, 1962-89, 89; Interview, PaintingsDirect.com, 12/21/99; Personal visions, the handmade look, Art Trends Mag, 8/2000; Marjorie Tomchuk, Printmaker, Embossings on Handmade Paper (video), Curtis/Cromwell Productions, 8/2000; Paper Art, 173 Int Artists, 2009; Homemade Paper, Embarkings, Journal of the Printworld, 11/2010. *Mem:* Silvermine Guild Artists (bd mem, 73-78); Int Artists & Papermakers Asn; NY Artists Equity; Friends Dard Hunter; Am Print Alliance; Mid Am Print Coun; Southern Graphics Coun. *Media:* Mixed Media, Etching, Miscellaneous Media. *Publ:* Contribr, article, J Print World, Vol 5, No 4 & Vol 17, No 4, 94; article, Prints, 7-8/2002; Printmakers Today, 2010; Journal of the Print World, Embossings, Article on M Tomchuck; Papier Global, Paper II, Deggendorf Mus, Ger; Paper Art, International Associatiion of Hand Papermakers and Paper Artists, 173 Artists. *Mailing Add:* 44 Horton Lane New Canaan CT 06840

TOMCIK, ANDREW MICHAEL
EDUCATOR, DESIGNER
b Cleveland, Ohio, June 18, 1938; Can citizen. *Study:* Cleveland Inst Art, Diploma, 60; Somerakadmie der Bildende Kunst, Salzburg, with Oskar Kokoschka, Cert, 61; Yale Univ Sch Art & Archit, BFA, MFA, 65. *Comn:* Loretto Coll Infirmary Chapel, 89. *Exhib:* Westlake Print Biennale, Zhejiang, China, 87; Sense of Place: Photographs, Founders Col, York Univ, Toronto, 88; Ekoplagat, Sch of Nature Protection, Gbel'any, Czechoslovakia, 90. *Pos:* Designer: The Carborundum Co, Niagara Falls, NY, 65-67; sr design assoc, Hauser Assoc Inc, Atlanta, Ga, 67-74; chmn, dept of visual arts, York Univ, Toronto, Ont, 81-84 & 90-91. *Teaching:* Assoc prof visual arts, Ga State Univ, Atlanta, 67-74; prof fine arts, York Univ, Toronto, 74-; master, Winters Col, 95-; prof emer, 2001. *Awards:* Fac Asn Award, Ont Coun Univ, 86; Gen Excellence Design Award, Can Church Press, 94. *Mem:* Soc Graphic Designers of Can (nat vpres educ, 85-87, secy, 87-90); Registered Graphic Designers, Ont. *Media:* Graphic Design, Print. *Res:* Design history, criticism. *Publ:* Auth, Art in Everyday Life: Aspects of Canadian Design, 67-87; Benchmarks, The Best of the Eighties, 85; From inspiration to imitation: How close can we come to our sources of inspiration before the work cannot be said to be ours?, Scan, summer 86; Exhib Rev, Ontario Craft, 88; Pol Posters, 89 & The Depreciation of Originality, Azure Mag, 90; Aspects of Color, Assorted art & design periodicals, Univ Art & Design, Helsinki, 1995. *Mailing Add:* 48 Parkhurst Blvd Toronto ON M4G 2C9 Canada

TOMKINS, CALVIN
WRITER
b Orange, NJ, Dec 17, 1925. *Study:* Princeton Univ, BA. *Pos:* Staff writer, The New Yorker, Mag, 61-. *Publ:* Auth, The Bride and the Bachelors, Viking Press, 65; Merchants and Masterpieces: The Story of the Metropolitan Museum of Art, EP Dutton, 70; Living Well Is the Best Revenge, 71 & auth, The Scene: Reports on Post-Modern Art, 76, Viking Press; Off the Wall: Robert Rauschenberg and the Art World of Our Time, Doubleday & Co, Inc, 80; Duchamp: A Biography, Henry Holt & Co, Inc, 96; Lives of the Artists, Heavy Holt & Co, 2008; Marcel Duchamp: The Afternoon Interviews, Badlands Unlimited, 2013. *Mailing Add:* c/o The New Yorker 4 Times Square New York NY 10036

TOMMERUP, METTE
PAINTER
b Kalundborg, Denmark, 1969. *Study:* Indiana Univ, Pa, BFA, 1990; Sch Visual Arts, New York, MFA, 1995. *Work:* Miami Art Mus; Four Seasons Hotel, Miami; Hallmark Print Collection, Mo; var pvt collections. *Exhib:* Space-Thinking Outside the Sphere, Miami Sci Mus, 2003; Surface Tension, Chelsea Art Mus, New York, 2004; ArtBasel Miami Beach, Fla, 2006; Recent Acquisitions, Miami Art Mus, 2009; Am Acad Arts & Letts, New York, 2010. *Teaching:* Asst prof painitng, Fla Int Univ, Miami, currently. *Awards:* Purchase Award, Am Acad Arts & Letts, 2010. *Mailing Add:* Florida International University Art & Art History UP VH 216 Miami FL 33199

TOMPKINS, BETTY (I)
PAINTER, PRINTMAKER
b Washington, DC, June 20, 1945. *Study:* Syracuse Univ, BFA, 66; Central Wash State Col, BEd, 69, MA, 69. *Work:* Aldrich Mus, Conn; Chase Bank, NY; Oberlin Col, Ohio; Marvin Sackner Archives, Miami Beach, Fla; Rutgers Univ; Stamford Mus, Conn; Zimmerli Mus, NJ; Paterson Mus, NJ; Mus of the City of New York, NYC; Islip Mus Art, East Islip, NY. *Exhib:* Solo exhibs, Fairleigh Dickenson Univ, NJ, 87, White Columns, NY, 91, Margulies Taplin Gallery, Boca Raton, Fla, 91, Fridholm Fine Arts, Asheville, NC, 91, Alan Brown Gallery, Hartsdale, NY, 91, Fridholm Fine Arts, NC, 93 & 94 & Drew Univ NJ Charleston Gallery, RI, 95, Juniata Mus, Huntingdon, Pa, 98, Egizio's Project, New York City, 2000, Mitchell Algus, New York City, 2002; Selections from the Collection, Aldrich Mus, Conn, 88; Lines of Vision (traveling show), US, Pan Am & Europe, 89-90; The Living Object: The Art Collection of Ellen H Johnson, Allen Mem Art Mus, Oberlin, Ohio, 92; Yale Univ, Conn, 95; Ctr Book Arts, NY; Berta Walker, Mass, 96; Juniata Mus Art, Huntington, Pa; Salvadore Park Mus, Miami, Fla, 2001; Mus Mod Art, New York City, 2002; Lyon Biennale, 2003. *Collection Arranged:* Animals in the Arsenal (auth, catalog), Central Park Zoo, 81. *Pos:* Contrib ed, Appearances Mag, 79-. *Teaching:* Painting, Sch Visual Arts, NY, 91-. *Awards:* NY Found Arts Grant, 88; Fel, MacDowell, 82, 83, 88 & 90; Artist in Residence, Weir Farm Heritage Trust, Branchville, Conn, 99. *Bibliog:* Joanne Barkan & Jon Friedman (auth), The beast in question, Arts Mag, 81; Sande Zorn (auth), Cows in the gallery, Holstein World, 82; Vivien Raynor (auth), Painter's work in a singular show, NY Times, 1/19/86; Robert Mahoney (auth), Betty Tompkins, Arts Mag, 88. *Media:* Acrylic, Watercolor; Etching. *Dealer:* Mitchell Algus NYC. *Mailing Add:* 101 Prince St New York NY 10012

TOMPKINS, MICHAEL
PAINTER
b Chester, Pa, 1955. *Study:* Cabrillo Col, Aptos, Calif, AA, 78; Univ Que, Montreal, 79; Univ Calif, Davis, BA (studio art), 81, MFA (painting) 83. *Work:* L Price Amerson, Deborah Born, Woodland, Calif; Gary Anderson, Carmichael, Calif; Dr Joseph Baird, San Francisco; Mr & Mrs Edward Grebitus, Sacramento, Calif; Robert Hudson, Cotati, Calif. *Exhib:* Solo exhibs, Richard L Nelson Gallery, Univ Calif, Davis, 83, Artworks Gallery, Fair Oaks, Calif, 85, Davis Art Ctr, Calif, 85, Artists Contemp Gallery, Sacramento, 86 & 88-90, William Sawyer Gallery, San Francisco, 87 & 89, Worden Gallery, San Francisco, 88 & Campbell-Thiebaud Gallery, San Francisco, 90, 91 & 93, Paul Thiebaud Gallery, San Francisco, 2010; California Figuration-Then and Now, Natsoulas/Novelozo Gallery, Davis, Calif, 90; Artists of Contra Costa Co, Hearst Gallery, St Mary's Col, Moraga, 90; Rodeo: A Contra Costa Studio Community, Bedford Gallery, Walnut Creek, 92; Landscapes: Paintings and Works on Paper, Wayne Thiebaud & Michael Tomkins, Artists Contemp Gallery, Sacramento, 92; and many others. *Teaching:* Teaching asst color, figure drawing & art appreciation, Univ Calif, Davis, 81-83; instr drawing, color theory, painting, printmaking & art hist, Sierra Col, Rocklin, Calif, 84-86; instr landscape painting, Am River Col, Placerville, 85; vis lectr drawing & descriptive drawing, Univ Calif, 86-88, painting, San Francisco Art Inst, 88-89. *Awards:* Fel, Nat Endowment Arts, 87 & 89; Am Acad & Inst Arts & Letts, 89; Richard & Hinda Rosenthal Found Award, 89; and others. *Bibliog:* Charles Shere (auth), Introductions '87, Oakland Tribune, 7/14/87; Victoria Dalkey (auth), Varying Visions, Sacramento Bee, 3/20/88; Teri Bachman (auth), Art at UC Davis, Univ Calif, Davis, Mag, summer 88; Ann Seymour (auth), Gallery reviews, Nob Hill Gazette, 4/89; Victoria Dalkey (auth), Invitation to contemplation, Sacramento Bee, 3/26/89; and others. *Dealer:* Campbell - Thiebaud Gallery San Francisco CA

TONELLI, EDITH ANN
MUSEUM DIRECTOR, HISTORIAN
b Westfield, Mass, May 20, 1949. *Study:* Vassar Col, NY, BA, 71, Helen Squier Townsend Fel, 71; Hunter Col, City Univ New York, with Vincent Longo & Robert Morris, MA (creative arts), 74; Boston Univ, Doctoral Fel, 74-79, with Patricia Hills, PhD, 81; Antioch Univ, MA (clinical psychology), 92. *Collection Arranged:* Homer to Hopper: 60 Years of Am Watercolor (auth, catalog), 76; By the People, For the People: New England (auth, catalog), 77; Non-Conformists: Contemporary Commentary from the Soviet Union (auth, catalog), 80; Louis Faurer: Photographs of Philadelphia & New York, 1937-1973 (auth, catalog), 81; Ralston Crawford: Photographs/Art and Process (auth, catalog), 82; Involvement: The Graphic Art of Antonio Frasconi (auth, catalogue), 88; Chicano Art: Resistance and Affirmation, 1965-1985, 89. *Pos:* Cur, DeCordova Mus, Mass, 76-78; dir, Univ Md Art Gallery, 79-; dir, Frederick S Wight Art Gallery, Univ Calif, Los Angeles, 82-91; dir, Art Mus, UCLA. *Teaching:* Instr Am material culture, Boston Univ, Mass, 76; asst prof, Univ Md, College Park, 80-82; adj asst prof, Univ Calif, Los Angeles, 82-92; adj instr art therapy, Antioch Univ, 93. *Awards:* Smithsonian Fel, 79. *Bibliog:* Jane Holtz Kay (auth), Boston, Art News, 12/77. *Mem:* Am Asn Mus; Coll Art Asn; Art Mus Asn; Am Asn Coll Univ Mus Galleries; Asn Art Mus Dirs (trustee, 87-); and others. *Res:* Twentieth century American art; American prints. *Publ:* Auth, The Avant-Garde in Boston: The WPA's federal art project, Archives Am Art J, 80; contribr, Frank Mechau, Aspen Ctr Visual Arts, 81 & City Life, Whitney Mus Amer Art, 86

TONEY, ANITA KAREN
PRINTMAKER
b New York City, NY. *Study:* Syracuse Univ, BFA; San Francisco State Univ, MA. *Exhib:* Group exhibs, Nancy Dodds Gallery, Carmel, Calif, Le Celle Gallery, San Anselmo, Calif, Andrea Schwartz Gallery, San Francisco, Images Gallery, Briarcliff, NY, exhibs incl with father, Anthony Toney, Coll of Marin, 2003. *Teaching:* Instr printmaking City Col San Francisco, 1979-. *Mem:* Calif Soc Printmakers; Nat Acad (acad, 95-). *Mailing Add:* City College of San Francisco Art Department 50 Phelan Ave San Francisco CA 94112

TOOGOOD, JAMES S
PAINTER, INSTRUCTOR
b Sept 26, 1954. *Study:* Pa Acad Fine Arts - 1973-76. *Work:* The Woodmere Art Mus, Philadelphia, Pa; The Noyes Mus, Oceanville, NJ; The Masterworks Mus Bermudian Art, Hamilton, Bermuda; Pa Acad Fine Arts Fellowship, Philadelphia; Naples Mus Art, Naples, Fla. *Comn:* Painting, Corp Hq, CIGNA, Philadelphia, Pa, 82; painting, Fireworks Over the City, Oceangate Twp, NJ, 94; painting, The Woodere Art Mus, Phila, Pa, 94; historic landmarks (paintings), Cherry Hill Twp, NJ, 96, 98 & 2000. *Exhib:* Dreams/Realities, Delaware Ctr Contemp Arts, Wilmington, 85; retrospective, Woodmere Art Mus, Philadelphia, Pa, 86; juried exhib, Nat Acad of Design, New York, 94; Two Centuries of Inspiration: Works from Recent Work, Masterwork Mus of Bermudian Art, Philadelphia, Pa, New York & Toronto, Can, 2000; juried exhib, Nat Watercolor Soc, Brea, Calif, 2003; A Collectors View, Noyes Mus, Oceanville, NJ, 2005; traveling juried exhib, Am Watercolor Soc, various cities, 2006-07; Philadelphia Sketch Mem from the permanent collection, Woodmere Art Mus, 2010. *Collection Arranged:* Co-cur, A Collectors View, Noyes Mus, Oceanside, NJ, 2005. *Teaching:* Instr, Pa Acad Fine Arts; instr, Nat Acad Design; instr, Perkins Ctr for the Arts, Moorestown, NJ. *Awards:* The Artist's Magazine Award, Am Watercolor Soc, 90; Dagmar Tribble Award Best in Show, Garden State Watercolor Soc, The Tribble Family, 92; Best in Show, Phila Sketch Club, 2005 & NJ Watercolor Soc, 2006. *Bibliog:* Lynn Kosek Brown (producer), The Art of James Toogood (film), State of the Arts, NJNTV, 90; Charles NiColl (auth), Toogood To Be True, Bermuda Mag, 96; Stephen Doherty (auth), Watercolor as a Personal Language, Am Artist Watercolor, 2001. *Mem:* Am Watercolor Soc; Nat Watercolor Soc; Pa Acad of Fine Arts Alumni & Fel; Northeast Watercolor Soc; NJ Watercolor Soc. *Media:* Watercolor. *Publ:* Auth, Behind The Scenes, The Artists Mag, 2001; coauth, Expressing the Visual Language of the Landscape, Int Artist Books, 2002; auth, Incredible Light & Texture in Watercolor, Northlight Books, 2004; The Simple Truth, Watercolor Magic, 2005, Five Techniques Every Watercolorist Should Know, 2006 & In a Minor Key, 10/2007; auth, Paint: Illustrated Techniques for Every Medium; Watercolor Secrets, North Light Books, 2009. *Dealer:* Rosenfeld Gallery Richard Rosenfeld 113 Arch St Phila PA 19106. *Mailing Add:* 920 Park Dr Cherry Hill NJ 08002

TOOLE, LOIS SALMON
PAINTER
b New Brunswick, NJ. *Study:* Douglass Coll, Rutgers Univ, BA (fine arts), 52; watercolor instr with Florian K Lawton, 77 & Claude Croney, 80. *Work:* Key Bank, Cleveland, Ohio; Brit Petroleum, Scotland; TRW, Cleveland, Ohio; Hi Techmetal Group, Cleveland, Ohio; Signal Financial Corp, Pittsburgh, Pa; Evans Printing co, Solon, Ohio. *Comn:* Dir covers-Collection regional, Chagrin Valley, Chamber Com, Ohio, 82, 90 & 2005; Pres off Greeting Card, Am Bar Asn, Cleveland, Ohio, 85; painting, EG Baldwin Corp, Cleveland, Ohio, 87; paintings, Antenna Specialists Allen Group, Solon, Ohio, 88. *Exhib:* Transparent Watercolor Soc Am, 78-79, 81, 87, 89-90, 92, 99, 2008, 2011; Ohio Watercolor Soc, 78-82, 84-85, 87-89, 93-95, 2001-2002, 2004, 2006-2008, 2010, 2013; Ky Watercolor Soc, Ky Mus, Bowling Green, 79-81, 84, 86, 88-89, 93-94, 97, 99, 2007, 2008; Rocky Mt Nat Watermedia Exhib, Foothills Art Ctr, Golden, Colo, 82, 85, 88, 90, 93-95, 99, 2003, 2006, 2011, 2013; Adirondacks Nat Exhib Am Watercolor 84, 88, 91; Allied Artists Am, Nat Arts Club, New York, 86, 89, 92, 97-99, 2002-2005, 2007, 2009, 2011; Watercolor USA, Springfield Mus, Mo, 87, 92 & 96, 2008; 50th Anniversary Signature Mem Invitational, NJ Watercolor Soc, Montclair Mus, 88; Butler Inst, 98 & 2000; Mary H Dana Women Artists Series, Douglass Coll Rutgers Univ, 99; World Fedn Miniature Art, London, Eng, 95, Tasmania, Australia, 2000, 2008, Moscow, Russia, 2012 & Smithsonian Inst, Washington, DC, 2004; Am Watercolor Soc, New York, 2001; Am Soc Marine Artist, 2001, 2004, 2011; plus 355 others. *Pos:* Trustee bd dir, Valley Art Ctr, 87-93, adv bd, 93-; coordr, Art in Park, Chagrin Valley CofC, 83-98; founding artist, Blue Moon Gallery, 93-; Awards Juror, 34th Int Exhib, Miniature Art Soc Fla, 2008; jury of selection, Catharine Lorillard Wolfe Art Club, 116th Nat Exhib, NYC, 2012; juror signature mems, Miniature Artists Am, 2013. *Teaching:* Pvt teacher, lectr in field, juror. *Awards:* M. Grumbacher Award, 83 & Lillian A Hart Mem Award, 87, Nat Watercolor Soc; Pearl Fine Arts Award, Rocky Mt Nat Watermedia Exhib, 93; Forbes Mag Award, NJWC Soc, 94; Catherine Lorillard Wolfe Art Club Corp and CLWAC Floral Award, NYC, 1994; NJ Water Color Soc Award, 96; Mark & Daphne Anderson Purchase Award, Watercolor USA, 96; M Grumbacher Award, Miniature Painters, Sculptors, Gravers Soc, Washington, DC, 97; Finalist Am Artist Realism Today Competition, 2000; Mary K Karasick Mem Award, 2002 & D Wu & Elsie Ject-Key Mem Award, 2005, Nat Asn Women Artists, 2010; Winsor & Newton Award, Allied Artists Am, 2005; Master Status Award, Transparent Watercolor Soc Am, 2011; Merchandise award, Pa Watercolor Soc, 2012; Best Watercolor, World Fedn Miniature Art, Moscow, Russia, 2012; Bronze Medal award, Ohio Watercolor Soc, 2013; and 128 others. *Bibliog:* Article, Am Soc Marine Artists, 2002; interview, Artist Mag, website, 2003; Verticle File, Smithsonian Am Art Mus Libr, 2006. *Mem:* Nat Watercolor Soc; Rocky Mt Nat Watermedia Soc; Transparent Watercolor Soc Am; Allied Artists Am, New York; Miniature Artists Am; Am Soc Marine Artists; Nat Asn Women Artists; Catharine Lorillard Wolfe Art Club; Ohio Watercolor Soc; NJ Water Color Soc; Ky Watercolor Soc, Pa Watercolor Soc; COGAP Artists; Salmagundi Club, NY. *Media:* Transparent Watercolor. *Publ:* Auth, NWS Conf Report, Ohio Watercolor Soc, 88; contribr, Splash III: Ideas & Inspirations, North Light Bks, 94; Best of Watercolor, Rockport Publ, 95; Painting Ships, Shores and the Sea, North Light Bks, 97; Landscape Inspiration, Rockport Publ, 97; Best of Watercolor III, Rockport Publ, 99; Splash 7: A Celebration of Light, North Light Bks, 2002; Watercolor Skies & Clouds Techniques of 23 International Artists, International Artist Publ, 2004; Modern Masters of Miniature Art in Am, 2010. *Dealer:* Imagery Fine Arts Inc North Main St Chagrin Falls OH 44022. *Mailing Add:* 16880 Knolls Way Chagrin Falls OH 44023

TOPALIS, DANIEL P
PAINTER, GALLERY OWNER
b Norwich, Conn, Sept 3, 1955. *Study:* Three Rivers Col; Univ Arts. *Work:* Slater Mem Mus, Norwich, Conn; Martin Luther King Ctr, Norwich, Ct; Quest Diagnostics, Teterborough, NJ; Westside Clinic, Norwich, Conn; Reliance House, Norwich, Conn; Otis Libr, Norwich, Conn. *Comn:* Peter Woodward, Caribbean Cruiseline, Heneley on The Thames, England; Dr and Mrs F Carter; Dr Shiela Tabakoff. *Exhib:* Conn Artist Show, Slater Mem Mus, 98, 99, 2000; 43rd Regional Exhib, Mystic Art Asn, 99, NAC Gallery 44th Regional Exhib, 2000; Conn Artist Show, 2001; Agora Gallery So Ho, NY; Solo Exhib: Slater Memorial Mus, John Slade Eli House, New Haven, Conn; Hunting House Mus, Windsor, Conn & Emporium Gallery, Mystic, Conn, Gallery at the Wauregan, Norwich, Conn; Agaat Salatte Gallery, Norwich, Conn; NAC Gallery, Norwich, Conn, 2007-8; Ct Commn Arts, Hartford, Conn; Artworks Gallery, Norwich, Conn, 2008; Artistic Wonderings, Norwich Arts Coun, Conn, 2009; Hygienic Galleries, New London, Conn, 2005, 2009, 2010, 2011, 2012, 2013; 114 Main St Gallery Norwich, Conn, 2010; Conn Artists Show, Slater Mus, Norwich, Conn, 2010; Reliance House Gallery, Norwich, Conn, 2010; Gallery at the Wauregan, Norwich, Conn, 2010-13; Rose City Gallery on Broadway, Norwich, Conn, 2010-11; Hammer & Nails, Hartford, Conn, 2011; Enabled Show, Norwich, Conn; Hygenic Annual Show, 2005-2014; Garde Theater, New London, Conn, 2014; Gallery at the Wauregan, 2014. *Pos:* mem bd, Norwich Arts Coun, 96-2001; mem bd, Agaat Salatte Gallery, Norwich, CT; assoc mem, Norwich Art Coun, 2010; mgr/owner, Gallery at the Wauregan, Norwich, Conn, 2011; mgr/owner, Rose City Gallery on Broadway, Norwich, Conn, 2011; mgr/owner, Gallery at the Wauregan, Norwich, Ct, 2011-2014. *Awards:* Artist Fel Award, Conn Comn of The Arts, 2000; Margaret Darrin Found Grant; Fel, Conn Comn Arts, 2004; Cash Award, 2nd Place, NAACP 100th Anniversary Juried Show, Norwich, Conn, 2009; 3rd prize, Enabled Show, 114 Main St Gallery, Norwich, Conn, 2011; 2nd prize, Artistic Wanderings, Norwich Arts Ctr, 2013. *Mem:* NAC Artist Co-Operative, Mystic Art Asn; Agaat Salatte Co-Operative. *Media:* Acrylic, Canvas, Painting on Bisque. *Specialty:* Work from local New England artists. *Publ:* Eleanor Charles (auth), Deadly Art, New York Times, 4/2001 & People in art, New York Times, 7/2002; "Salacious" Show (article), The Bulletin, Norwich, Conn, 2011; Norwich Mag, 2014; Adam Benson (auth), Artist Tries to Grow City Scene, 2014. *Dealer:* 114 Main St Gallery Norwich Conn; Reliance House Gallery Norwich Conn; Gallery at the Wauregan Norwich Conn; Rose City Gallery on Broadway Norwich Conn. *Mailing Add:* 72 Briar Hill Rd Norwich CT 06360

TOPERZER, THOMAS RAYMOND
MUSEUM DIRECTOR, PAINTER
b Homestead, Pa, Aug 12, 1939. *Study:* Sterling Col, 59-61; Southwestern Coll (Kans), BA, 63; Univ Nebr-Lincoln, Woods fel, 69-70, MFA, 70. *Work:* Des Moines Art Ctr, Iowa; Springfield Art Mus, Mo; Rochester Art Ctr, Minn; Blanden Art Mus, Iowa; Ill State Univ; Bethel Coll & Sem, Minn. *Exhib:* Iowa Artists, Des Moines Art Ctr; New Horizons, Chicago; Nat Drawing, San Francisco Mus Art; Nat Prints & Drawings, Okla Art Ctr, Mid-Am, Kansas City-St Louis, 74. *Pos:* Dir, Blanden Art Mus, 70-71, Rochester Art Ctr, 71-72; asst dir, Mus & Galleries, Ill State Univ, 72, dir, Univ Galleries, Ctr Visual Arts Gallery, 73-82, ed, Univ Mus Newslett, 75-76; coordr fine arts, Bethel Col, St Paul, Minn, 82-84 & Fred Jones Jr Mus Art, Univ Okla, 84-. *Mem:* Am Asn Mus; Coll Art Asn; Art Mus Asn. *Publ:* Auth, Current Issues in University Art Museums, Southern Ill Univ

TOPPER, DAVID R
EDUCATOR, HISTORIAN
b Pittsburgh, Pa, Jan 1, 1943. *Study:* Duquesne Univ, BS, 64; Case Inst Technol, MS, 66; Case Western Reserve Univ, MA, 68; & PhD, 70. *Pos:* Int co-ed, Leonardo Jour Arts, Sci & Technol, currently. *Teaching:* Prof art hist, Univ Winnipeg, Man, 70-. *Awards:* Clifford J Robson Mem Award for Excellence in Teaching, Univ Winnipeg, 81; 3M Teaching Fel, 87. *Mem:* Int Soc Arts, Sci & Technol. *Res:* Historical perspectives on visual perception of images and the interrelationship with science. *Publ:* Perspectives on perspective: Gombrich and his critics, Gombrich on Art & Psychology, 96; Trajectories of blood: Artemesia Genitleschi and Galileo's parabolic path, Woman's Art J, 96; The Neutrino and the Sydney Opera House, Leonardo, 97; On Anamorphosis, Leonardo, 2000; Visual Arts & Nat Sciences: Annotated Bibliography, Leonardo-online, 2003. *Mailing Add:* Univ Winnipeg Hist Dept Winnipeg MB R3B 2E9 Canada

TORAK, ELIZABETH
PAINTER
b NY City, April 12, 1959. *Study:* Art Students League, NY. *Exhib:* numerous solo, two person & group exhibs; Butler Inst Am Art; Sna Diego Art Inst; Arlington Mus Art, Tex. *Awards:* Honorable Mention, Butler Inst Am Art, Midyear Exhib; John Spiegel Mem Award, Am Artists Prof League; Marguerite Sinaly Mem Award, Salmagundi Club. *Bibliog:* Article Am Artist Mag, 8/94. *Media:* Oil. *Publ:* Contribr, Creative Oil Painting, Techniques from 15 Master Painters, Stephen Doherty (auth). *Dealer:* Helmholz Fine Art, New York, NY. *Mailing Add:* 360 Beaver Brook Rd Pawlet VT 05761

TORAK, THOMAS
PAINTER
b Pottstown, PA, Sept 17, 1953. *Study:* Art Students League New York, with Robert Beverly Hale & Frank Mason. *Work:* Masur Mus Art, Wallace Found; Art Students League, NY. *Exhib:* Butler Inst of Am Art; Nat Acad Mus; Springfield Mus Fine Art; Nat Arts Club; Bergstrom, Mahler Mus, Masur Mus Art, San Diego Art Inst,

Huntsville Mus Art, Krasl Art Ctr; and many others. *Teaching:* tchr, Painting from Life, Portraiture, Composition, Color, Art Students League of NY, 2008-. *Awards:* Medal of Honor, 66th Grand Nat Exhib, Am Artists Prof League; Gold Medal of Honor, 59th Ann Exhib, Audubon Artists; Silver Medal of Honor, 93rd Ann Exhib, Allied Artists Am; Marquis Who's Who in Am Art References award in Oils & Acrylics, Audubon Artists, NY, 2013. *Mem:* Salmagundi Club; Am Artists Prof League; Allied Artists of Am; Audubon Artists; Oil Painters of Am (signature mem). *Media:* Oil. *Dealer:* Anderson Fine Art St Simons Ga; Four India St Gallery Nantucket Ma; Principle Gallery Alexandria VA; Sloane-Merrill Boston Ma. *Mailing Add:* 360 Beaver Brook Rd Pawlet VT 05761

TORASSA, BETTY BROWN
PAINTER
b Coos Bay, Ore July 18, 1921. *Study:* Calif Coll Arts & Crafts, Summer scholar, 38; Univ Calif Berkeley, MA, 45; San Francisco Art Inst, MFA, 74; Studied with Julius Hatofsky, Fred Martin, Bruce McGaw, Timothy Clark, Calvin Goodman; 12 workshops with Timothy Clark to Spain, France, Italy, Hawaii, Maine, San Jaun Capistrano, Eng, UK, Calif. *Work:* Home Savings & Loan, Los Angeles, Calif; Omega Gallery, Davis, Calif; Vallejo Hist Mus, Vallejo, Calif; Still life painting, Virginia Rawson, Walnut Creek, Calif, 2008-2010; Watercolor of Japanese fountain, Delmer Brown, Walnut Creek, Calif, 2010. *Comn:* Japanese fountain, comn by Delmer Brown and Virginia Rawson. *Exhib:* MFA grad exhib, San Francisco Art Inst, 74; Print show, Graphic Art Inst, San Francisco, 80-85; Watercolor shows, Calif Watercolor Asn, Walnut Creek, Calif, Newport, RI, Omaha, Neb, San Ramon, Calif, Venice, Italy, 2004; Solo show, Bank of America, Walnut Creek, Calif, 2007; Punta Gordo, Fla; Two solo shows, Benicia Arts; Rutherford Grove Winery, Napa Valley, Calif, Danville, Calif. *Collection Arranged:* cur, 6 shows, Seasonal Topics, Rossmoor, Calif, 2009-2010. *Awards:* Hon Mention, Mario Andretti Winery, Napa Valley, Calif, 90. *Bibliog:* Calvin J Goodman (auth), Art Marketing Handbook, Gee Tee Bee, 2003. *Mem:* Valley Art Gallery, Walnut Creek, Calif, 2010; Benicia Arts, Benicia, Calif; Calif Watercolor Asn, Walnut Creek, Calif; The Transparent 12', Napa Valley, Calif. *Media:* Watercolor. *Specialty:* Landscapes, still life, wildlife, dogs, cats, ducks, geese, deer, Napa Vineyards, Calif. *Interests:* Plein air painting, floral still life. *Collection:* Florence Goodman, Martha Roub, Virginia Rawson, Maurice Mitchell, Barbara Ulbrect, Delmer Brown, Bob Bishop, Robert Torassa & Angela, George Torassa III, Glenna Torassa, Gregory Torassa, Arturo Rovo, Grady and Kristin Wright, Leslie McDevit, Jacqueline (Jackie), Mark Torassa. *Publ:* Benicia Herald (announcement of gallery opening in Benicia, Calif). *Dealer:* Valley Art Gallery 1661 Botelho Dr Suite 110 Walnut Creek CA 94596. *Mailing Add:* 1800 Atrium Pkwy #239 Napa CA 94559

TORBERT, STEPHANIE BIRCH
PHOTOGRAPHER, VISUAL ARTIST
b Wichita Falls, Tex, May 31, 1945. *Study:* Univ NMex, BFA, 68; Sch for Am Craftsman, Rochester Inst Technol, NY, 68; Visual Studies Workshop, State Univ NY, Buffalo, MFA, 71. *Work:* Weisman Mus Art, Minneapolis Inst Arts, Minn; Int Mus Photography, George Eastman House, Rochester; Ctr for Creative Photog, Tucson, Ariz; Mus NMex, Santa Fe. *Exhib:* Minn Survey: Six Photogrs, Minneapolis Inst Arts & Nat Endowment Arts, 78; one-person shows, Minneapolis Inst Arts, 70, Walker Art Ctr, Minneapolis, 73, Int Mus Photog, George Eastman House, Rochester, NY, 78 & Friends Photog, Carmel, Calif, 79; and others. *Collection Arranged:* Libr of Congress, Ctr for Creative Photog, Tuscon, Ariz, Walker Art Ctr, Minneapolis Inst of Art, Frederick R. Weisman Art Mus, Mus of NMex, Santa Fe, and others.; Minneapolis Inst Art. *Pos:* Visual arts panel, Minn State Arts Bd, 76-. *Teaching:* Asst prof, N Hennepin Community Col, Minneapolis, 74-75 & Minneapolis Col Art & Design, 77-78 & 88-89. *Awards:* Nat Endowment Arts Grant, Minn Survey: Six Photogr, 77; Artist Fel, 84; MacDowell Colony Fel, 83, 84, 92; Nadine Blacklock Mem Award for Women Photgr, 99; Hand Hallow Found, NY, 99; Bush Foundation Artists. *Mem:* Illinois Arts Council (photography panel). *Media:* Cibachrome, Pastel, Acrylic, Digital, Textile. *Interests:* Gardens of the World, Manikins, Dreams, Storytelling. *Publ:* The New Color Photography, Abbeville Press; Parks and Wildlands, Nodin Press; The Walk Book, Nodin Press; The Clay that Breathes, Milkweed Eds. *Dealer:* Alinder Gallery Gualala CA; Alan Klotz Photo Collect NY; B & W Color Mag; Thomas Barry Fine Art Minneapolis MN. *Mailing Add:* 3824 Harriet Ave Minneapolis MN 55409

TORCOLETTI, ENZO
SCULPTOR
b Fano, Italy, May 1, 1943; US citizen. *Study:* Inst Statale D'Arte A Apolloni, Fano, Italy, 54-58; Univ Windsor, Ont, BFA (sculpture), 69; Fla State Univ, MFA, 71. *Work:* Sculpture (40 ft site specific), Koger Properties, Jacksonville, Fla; Fla Nat Guard, Camp Blanding; Fla Artists Hall Fame, The Capital, Tallahassee; Waynesville Country Club, NC; Barnett Bank, Tampa, Fla. *Comn:* Aluminum wall relief, Fla Sch for Deaf, St Augustine, 90; granite site-specific sculpture, Kings' Hill, Kent, Eng, 92. *Exhib:* Solo exhibs, WGa Col, Carrollton, 73, Oklaloose-Walton Jr Col, Niceville, Fla, 76, Univ NFla, Jacksonville, 81 & 86, Sandestin, Destin Beach, Fla, 86, Embry-Riddle Aeronautical Univ, Daytona Beach, Fla, 88, Cummer Gallery Art, Jacksonville, 90-91; Brest Mus Gallery, Jacksonville Univ, 81, 82 & 84; Boca Raton Ctr Arts, Fla, 82; Jacksonville Collects, Jacksonville Art Mus, 84; Flagler Col, St Augustine, Fla, 90. *Teaching:* Asst, Fla State Univ, Tallahassee, 69-71; prof visual arts, Flagler Col, St Augustine, Fla, 71-; guest artist/lectr, Okaloosa-Walton Jr Col, Niceville, Fla, 72, Fla Jr Col & Univ NFla, Jacksonville, 80 & 81, Univ Fla, Gainesville, 81, Jacksonville Art Mus, 83, 84 & 87, Sandestin, Destin Beach, Fla, 86 & Douglas Anderson Sch Art, Jacksonville, 90. *Awards:* Purchase Award, Mint Mus Art, Charlotte, NC, 72; First Prize in Sculpture, Titusville Spring Art Show, Fla, 75; Hilton Leach Mem Award, Mus Arts & Sciences, Daytona Beach, 79. *Bibliog:* Susan Lynn Lester (auth), mag article, Jacksonville, 6/86; Diane Edwards (auth), mag article, 10/1/87; Arthur Williams (auth), Sculpture: Technique-Form-Content, 89. *Mem:* Fla Artists Group; Int Sculpture Ctr. *Media:* Stone, Bronze. *Dealer:* Agnes Gallery Birmingham AL; Moultrie Creek Studios Gallery St Augustine FL. *Mailing Add:* 120 W Genung Ave Saint Augustine FL 32086-7055

TORF, LOIS BEURMAN
COLLECTOR, PUBLISHER
b Boston, Mass, Sept 20, 1926. *Study:* Univ Mass, Amherst, BA, 46. *Hon Degrees:* Univ Mass, Hon DFA, 84; Art Inst Boston, Hon DFA, 95. *Exhib:* Two Women Collect, Wellesley Coll Mus Art, Mass, 76; The Modern Art of the Print, Williams Coll Mus Art, Williamstown, Mass & Mus Fine Arts, Boston, 84; 70's into 80's: Printmaking Now, Mus Fine Arts, Boston, 87; Faces & Figures in Contemp Art, Mus Fine Arts, Boston, 96; solo exhib, Univ Mass, 97; Photo Image Printmaking 60's-90's, Mus Fine Arts, 98, Des Moines Art Ctr, 99; Sets, Series & Suites: Contemp Prints (with catalog), 2005, David Hockney Portraits, 2006, Facets of Cubism, 2006, Degas to Picasso, 2006, Mus Fine Arts, Boston, Mass. *Pos:* VPres, Inst Contemp Art, 70-87. *Bibliog:* Deborah Menaker (auth), The Modern Art of the Print: Selections from the Collection of Lois & Michael Torf, Mus Fine Arts, Boston, 84; Pilgrims & Pioneers: New England Women in the Arts, Midmarch Arts Press, New York, 87. *Mem:* Int Coun Art, (trustee 70-); Mus Fine Arts, Boston (hon trustee 84-); Univ Mass Chancellor's Exec Comt, currently; hon mem Fine Arts Ctr, Univ Mass. *Collection:* 20th century graphic expressionism, pop & contemporary prints. *Mailing Add:* 15 Young Rd Weston MA 02193

TORLAKSON, JAMES DANIEL
PAINTER, FILMMAKER
b San Francisco, Calif, Feb 19, 1951. *Study:* Calif Coll Arts & Crafts, BFA, 73; San Francisco State Univ, MA, 74. *Work:* San Francisco Mus Mod Art; Oakland Mus, Calif; Brooklyn Mus; Carnegie Inst, Pittsburgh, Pa; Libr of Cong; Albright-Knox Mus; Chicago Art Inst. *Exhib:* Solo exhibs, Calif Palace Legion Hon, Achenbach Found, San Francisco, 76 & San Jose Mus Art, Calif, 79; VX Inst Sao Paul Biennial, Int Communications Agency, SAm, 79; Recent Trends in Am Printmaking, Mitchell Mus, Mt Vernon, Ill, 79; Am Realism, 20th Century Drawing & Watercolors, San Francisco Mus Mod Art, Calif, 85; Mainstream Am, The Collection of Phil Desind, Butler Inst Am Art, Youngstown, Ohio, 87; New Horizons in Am Realism, Flint Inst Arts, Mich, 91; and others. *Teaching:* Prof, City Col San Francisco, Calif. *Awards:* Airport Purchase Award, San Francisco Int Airport Painting Competition, 77; Purchase Awards, 17th Nat Print & Drawing Exhib, Bradley Univ, 79 & Boston Printmakers 31st Nat Exhib, 79. *Bibliog:* Peter Frank (auth), New York Reviews, Artnews, 10/75. *Media:* Watercolor; Oil. *Interests:* Guitar & surfing. *Publ:* Contemporary Am Realism, Since 1960, NY Graphics Soc, 81; Mendelowitz's Guide to Drawing, Holt Rinehart Winston, 82; Contrib, Am Realism, 20th Century Drawings & Watercolors, Abrams, 86; auth (with Judith Gordon), Deeping the third dimension, The Artist's Mag, 4/89. *Mailing Add:* 433 Rockaway Beach Ave Pacifica CA 94044

TORLEN, MICHAEL ARNOLD
PAINTER, EDUCATOR
b San Diego, Calif, Feb 28, 1940. *Study:* Cranbrook Acad Art, Bloomfield Hills, Mich, BFA, 62; Ohio State Univ, Columbus, fel 63-64, with Hoyt Sherman, MFA, 65. *Work:* Aldrich Mus, Ridgefield, Conn; Neuberger Mus & Roy Neuberger Collection, Purchase, NY; Prudential Insurance Co, Newark, NJ. *Comn:* Symbolic portraits, Arlene Sarapa, Wingafe Paine & Buford Pippin, NY, 76; Meditation Mandala, Growth Ctr, NY, 77 & Goldleaf Omega Cross, 78. *Exhib:* Weatherspoon Ann, Univ NC, Greensboro, 67, 69 & 83; Aldrich Mus, Ridgefield, Conn, 72 & 73; Solo exhibs, Neuberger Mus, Purchase, NY, 79 & Cathedral St John the Divine, NY, 83; Artists Space, NY, 83; Luise Ross Fine Art, NY, 83; and others. *Teaching:* Asst prof painting & drawing, Univ Ga, 65-70; assoc prof & dept head painting & drawing, State Univ NY Col, Purchase, 72-. *Awards:* Purchase Award, Ga Comn Arts, 69; State Univ NY Res Fel & Grant, 78; Visiting Artist Traveling Grant, Vis Arts Bd, Australia Coun, 82. *Bibliog:* Robert Yoskowitz (auth), article, Arts Mag, 9/81. *Mem:* Coll Art Asn; Lindisfarne Asn. *Dealer:* Luise Ross 162 56th St New York NY. *Mailing Add:* Purchase Col Suny Dept Visual Arts 735 Anderson Hill Rd Purchase NY 10577-1400

TORN, JERRY (GERALD J)
DRAFTSMAN, PHOTOGRAPHER
b Burlington, Iowa, Mar 16, 1933. *Study:* Univ Iowa, studied printmaking with Mauricio Lasansky, BA (fine arts), 58. *Work:* Art Inst Chicago, First Nat Bank Chicago, Ill; Ill State Mus, Springfield; Portland Art Mus, Ore; Kemper Insurance Co, Long Grove, Ill; Va Mus Fine Arts, Richmond; Mus Fine Art, Univ Iowa, Iowa City. *Comn:* Drawings for exec dining room, First Nat Bank Chicago, London Branch, 81; Lithograph Suite, Plucked Chicken Press, Chicago, 83. *Exhib:* New Figurative Work, Univ Ind, Gary, 80; Drawings of David, Univ Wis, Marshfield, 81; 62nd Ann Exhib, Arts Club Chicago, 82; Dancers, Univ Wis, Marinette, 82, Art Guild, Burlington, Iowa, 82 & 94 & Fairweather Hardin Gallery, Chicago, 82 & 85. *Teaching:* Instr design, Loyola Univ, Chicago, 70-71. *Bibliog:* Alan Artner (auth), Jerry Torn, Chicago Tribune, 7/25/80; Margaret Hawkins (auth), Jerry Torn, New Art Examiner, 11/80; Les Krantz (auth), The Chicago Art Review, Am References, 89. *Mem:* Arts Club Chicago. *Media:* Graphite. *Mailing Add:* 216 S Marshall Burlington IA 52601

TORNHEIM, NORMAN
SCULPTOR
b Chicago, Ill, Sept 16, 1942. *Study:* Art Ctr Coll Design, BS, 66; Calif State Univ, San Diego, MA, 75. *Work:* Las Vegas Art Mus, Nev; Marietta Col, Ohio; Smith Col, Northampton, Mass; Ind Univ. *Comn:* Sculpture, comn by Mr & Mrs Stern, Calif, 76; sculpture, comn by Mr & Mrs Lewis, Calif, 77; sculpture, comn by Dr I Mori, Calif, 77. *Exhib:* Mainstreams 76, Marietta Col, Ohio, 76; Calif Craftsmen, Monterey Mus Art, Calif, 76; Designer-Craftsmen 76, Richmond Art Ctr, Calif, 76; Nat Competition 77, Dahl Fine Arts Ctr, 77; Calif Craftsmen, E B Crocker Art Mus, Sacramento, 77; Goldsmiths USA, Univ Wash, Seattle, 77; Musical Instruments, The Smithsonian Inst, Washington, DC, 78-80. *Collection Arranged:* Golden West Coll Invitational, 78. *Teaching:* Instr wood, metal & leather, San Diego State Univ, Calif, 72-75; instr wood, metal, leather & clay, Golden West Col, Huntington Beach, Calif, 75-. *Awards:* Jurors

Award, Las Vegas Art Mus, 75; Purchase Award, Ark Art Ctr, 76; Merit Award, Nat Competition 77, Dahl Fine Arts Ctr, 77. *Bibliog:* Dona Z Meilach (auth), Wood Objects as Functional Sculpture, Crown, 76. *Media:* Clay, Porcelain. *Publ:* Contribr, Artweek, 76-77. *Mailing Add:* Golden W Coll Dept Art 15744 Golden W St Huntington Beach CA 92647

TORREANO, JOHN FRANCIS
PAINTER, SCULPTOR

b Flint, Mich, Aug 17, 1941. *Study:* Cranbrook Acad Art, BFA, 63; Ohio State Univ, MFA, 67; also with Robert King & Hoyt L Sherman. *Work:* Whitney Mus Am Art, NY; Aldrich Mus Contemp Art, Ridgefield, Conn; Michener Collection, Univ Tex; The Corcoran Gallery Art, Washington, DC; Denver Art Mus; Indpls Mus Art; Contemp Mus Fine Arts, Houston; Honolulu Mus Contemp Art. *Comn:* Found Villa Rufolo, Amalfi, Italy; Ghost Gems, McCarran Int Airport, Las Vegas, Nev, 92. *Exhib:* Solo exhibs, Scott Hanson Gallery, NY, 89, Shea & Beker Gallery, NY, 89 & 90, Corcoran Gallery, Washington, DC, 89, Susanne Hilberry Gallery, Birmingham, MI, 90 & 2000, Dart Gallery, Chicago, Ill, 90, Hypo Bank, NY, 92, Norton Gallery Art, Palm Beach, Fla, 93, Jean Albano Gallery, Chicago, 96 & 2000, 80 Washington Sq East Galleries, NY Univ, 97 & 99, Indianapolis Mus Art, 97, Butler Inst Am Art, Ohio, 99, Willoughby Sharpe Gallery, NY, 2000, Littlejohn Contemp Gallery, NY, 2000, Gerald Peters Gallery, Santa Fe, 2000, Feature Inc, NY, 2002 & 2004, Ctr Creative Studies, Detroit, 2003; group exhibs, Post Minimalism 1979-1990 An Extended Harvest, Genouese Gallery, Boston, MA, 90; Painting Between the Paradigms Part IV: A Category of Objects As Yet Unnamed, Penine Hart Gallery, NY; With the Grain: Contemp Panel Painting, Whitney Mus Am Art, Stamford, Conn, 90; group show, Margo Leavin Gallery, Los Angeles, Calif, 90; Laforet Mus, Havajuku, Japan; Pleasure, Hallwalls, Buffalo, NY, 91; Glass: Material in the Service of Meaning, Tacoma Art Mus, Wash, 91; Cruciformed: Images of the Cross Since 1980, Cleveland Ctr Contemp Art, Ohio, 91; Jean Albano Gallery, Chicago, 93, 95, 96, 2000, 2003, 2004-05; Corcoran Biennial Contemp Am Painting, Corcoran Gallery, Washington, 95-96, From Folk to Funk, 2004; Feature Gallery, NY, 98; SITE Santa Fe, 99; 9/11, Rochester Mus Art, Minn, 2002; Mus Contemp Art, Denver, 2002; Invitational Exhib Visual Arts, Am Acad Arts & Letters, New York, 2008. *Pos:* prog dir, NY Univ, 92-05. *Awards:* Nat Endowment Arts Grant & Creative Artists Pub Serv Grant, 78-79; Nat Endowments Arts Fel, 82-83 & 89-90; John Simon Guggenheim Mem Found Fel, 91; New York Found Arts Fel, 91; Nancy Graves Found Grant, 2002. *Bibliog:* Michael Welzenbach (auth), rev, The Washington Post, 89; Goings On About Town, The New Yorker, 5/21/90; Theodore F Wolff (auth), The Art of Painting Plywood, The Christian Science Monitor, 8/17/90; Brook Adams (auth), Scarred Diamonds, ArtNews, 2/91. *Media:* Plywood. *Dealer:* Jean Albano Art Gallery 215 W Superior Chicago IL 60610; Susanne Hilberry Gallery 700 Livernois Ferndale MI 48220. *Mailing Add:* 103 Franklin St New York NY 10013

TORRES, FRANCES
VIDEO ARTIST, SCULPTOR

b Barcelona, Spain, Aug 8, 1948. *Study:* Massana Art Inst, Barcelona, Spain (graphic design & painting), 64-67; Fine Arts Sch, Paris, France, cert (etching), 67-68. *Work:* Book Collection, Mus Mod Art, NY; Cooper-Hewitt Mus, NY; Everson Mus Art, Syracuse, NY; Mus Art, Carnegie Inst, Pittsburg, Pa; Museo Nacional Centro de Arte Reina Sofia, Madrid, Spain; Los Angeles Inst Contemp Art; Mus of Contemp Art, Sao Palo, Brazil. *Exhib:* This Is An Installation That Has A Title, Fundacio Joan Miro, Barcelona, 79; Residual Regions, Los Angeles Inst Contemp Art, Calif, 80; The Head of the Dragon, Whitney Mus Am Art, NY, 81; Field of Action, Herbert F Johnson Mus Art, Ithaca, NY, 82; Tough Limo, Mus Art, Carnegie Inst, Pittsburgh, Pa, 85; The Dictatorship of Swiftness, La Jolla Mus Contemp Art, Calif, 86; plus Ultra, Nat Galerie, Berlin, WGer, 88; La Cabeza del Dragon (with catalog), Muse Nacional Centro de Arte, Reina Sofia, Madrid, Spain, 91; Too Late for Goya (with catalog), Ariz State Univ Art Mus, Tempe, 93; solo exhibs: Gallery 21, St Petersburg, Russia, 95, MIT, List Visual Arts Ctr, Cambridge, Mass, 98, Univ Salamanca, Palacio de Maldonado, Spain, 99, Fundación Telefónica, Madrid, 00, Ctr Cult Tecla Sala, Hospitalet, Spain, 00, Rafael Inst Contemp Art, Barcelona, 01, Sala Metrónom, Barcelona, 01; Gallery 21, St Petersburg, Russia, 95; MIT List Visual Art Ctr, Cambridge, Mass, 98; Fundacio Rafael Tous d'Art Contemporani, Barcelona, Spain, 01; Garage: imágenes del automóvil en la pintura española del siglo XX, Ctr Gallego de Arte Contemp, Santiago de Compostela, Spain, 01; Darrera Escena, Casal Solleric, Ajuntament de Palma, Palma de Mallorca, Spain, 02; Fragments, Mus de la Univ d'Alacant, Alicante, Spain, 02; Desesculturas, Círculo de Bellas Artes de Madrid, 02; Granada de Fondo, Coleccíon de Arte Contemp de la Diputación de Granada, Ctr José Guerrero y Palacio de los Condes de Gabia, Granada, Spain, 03. *Collection Arranged:* NY Pub Libra Video Collection, Donnell Libr; LA Inst Contemp Art; Centro de Arte Reina Sofia, Madrid; La Jolla Mus Contemp Art; Mus Art, Carnegie Inst; Mus Mod Art; High Mus Art, Atlanta. *Teaching:* Instr mixed media & installations, Sch Visual Arts, NY, 86. *Awards:* Sponsored Projects Grant, NY State Coun Arts, 83-84; Spanish-Am Joint Com Cult & Educ Cooperation, 85; Individual Artist Fel, DAAD Berliner Kunstleprogramm, 86; NEA Video Prod Grant, 86-87, 93-94; NY Found for Arts, 1986-87; NEA Individual Artist Fel, 93-94; NY Found for the Arts, Individual Artist's Fellowship on Multidisciplinary Work, 01-02; Fundación Picasso, Casa Natal, Málaga, Spain, 02. *Media:* Mixed. *Dealer:* Elba Benitez Gallery, Madrid, Spain. *Mailing Add:* 38 N Moore St New York NY 10013

TORRES, MARIO GARCIA
CONCEPTUAL ARTIST

b Mex, 1975. *Study:* Univ de Monterrey, BFA, 1998; Calif Inst Arts, MFA, 2005. *Exhib:* Solo exhibs include Galeria de Arte Mex, Mex City, 2003, Jan Mot, Brussels,k 2004, 2005, 2006, Kadist Art Found, Paris, 2007; group exhibs include How to learn to love the bomb & stop worrying, Central de Art, Guadalajara, Mex City, 2004; Off the Record/Sound ARC, Mus d'Art Mod, Paris, 2004 & I still believe in miracles/Drawing Space, 2005; No Convenient Subway Stops, Art in General, New York, 2005; Saturday Live Actions & Interruptions, Tate Mod, London, 2007 & Learn to Read, 2007; Night at the Museum or What Betty Boop Saw, Centro de Arte Reina Sofia, Madrid, 2007; Escultura Social, Mus Contemp Art, Chicago, 2007; Venice Biennale, 2007. *Awards:* Colección Jumex Grant, 2003-05; Fulbright Grant, 2003-05; Cartier Award, 2007. *Mailing Add:* c/o Jan Mot rue Antoine Dansaertstraat 190 Brussels 1000 Belgium

TOSCAN, RICHARD ERIC
EDUCATOR

b New York, NY, Jul 1, 1941. *Pos:* Adv bd, Int Contemp Art Fair, Los Angeles, 89-91, Tygres Heart Shakespeare Co, Portland, 92-, Portland Ctr Performing Arts, 92-, Image Theatre Mask Ensemble, 94-; mem, theatre panel Cult Affairs Dept, Los Angeles, 90-92; mem, selection comt Javits fel US Dept Educ, Wash, 90-93; dean, sch fine and performing arts Portland (Ore) State Univ, 92-96; dean, sch arts Va Commonwealth Univ, Sch of Arts, Richmond, Va, 1996-2010. *Teaching:* Postdoctoral teaching resident Nat Endowment of the Humanities, 67-69. *Awards:* Woodrow Wilson Found fel, 63-64; Univ Ill fel, 64. *Mem:* Fel (Assoc) East Asian Study Ctr; Am Soc Theatre Res, Int Coun Fine Arts Deans. *Mailing Add:* Va Commonwealth Univ Sch of Arts 325 N Harrison St Richmond VA 23284

TOSCANO, DOLORES A
PAINTER, SCULPTOR

b Ft Worth, Tex. *Study:* Studied with Bruno Lucchesi (sculpture) & Daniel Green (pastel painting), 85. *Work:* San Juan Col, NMex; Benson Park, Loveland, Colo; and others. *Comn:* Life size bronze St Walburga, Walburga Convent, Boulder, Colo, 85-86; twelve ft marble figure of Christ, Risen Christ Church, Denver, Colo, 87; life size bronze Mary & Jesus, Blessed Heart Jesus, Boulder, Colo, 88. *Exhib:* Pioneer's Mus Show, Colorado Springs Mus, 85; Society de Pastellistes de France, Salon Int Du Pastel, Paris, 87; Miniature Show, Albuquerque Mus, 91 & 92; Women Who Paint the West, Tucson Mus, Ariz, 91-93; Rotary Invitational, Loveland, Colo, 92-95; and others. *Teaching:* Pastel instr portraits, Scottsdale Art Sch, Ariz, 87-88 & Denver, Colo Art Student League, 90-91. *Awards:* Gold Medal, Catherine L Wolfe, NY, 78-79; Gold Medal, Pastel Soc Southwest, 87; Master Pastelist, Flora Guffino, Pastel Soc Am, 87; and others. *Bibliog:* Toscano Southwest Art, 79-87; Mary C Nelson (auth), Pastels by Toscanco, Am Artist, 83; Vicki Stavig (auth), I had the want to's, Art West, 91; and others. *Mem:* Pastel Soc Am, NY; Catherine Lorrillard Wolfe Club, NY. *Media:* Pastel; Bronze. *Publ:* Contribr, American Artist of Renown, Wilson Pub, 81; Contemporary Western Artists, Harold Samuels, 82

TOSCHIK, LARRY
PAINTER, WRITER

b Milwaukee, Wis, July 17, 1922. *Study:* Wis Art Acad, scholar; Layton Art Sch, Milwaukee. *Work:* Ariz State Univ Coll Bus Admin; Riveredge Found, Calgary; US House of Rep; US Dept of Interior; Soc Wildlife Art Nations, London. *Comn:* Battlefield monument, 361st Inf 91st Div Mil Cemetery, Florence, Italy, 44; 30 paintings (wildlife), Hallmark Permanent Collection, 69-71; 20 silver medallions, Ducks Unlimited Inc, Chicago, 74; four wildlife lithographs, Franklin Mint; painting, 50th Anniversary of Ducks Unlimited, 86-87; two paintings for collector ed, Waterfowl of North Am, Can, 87. *Exhib:* Nat Cowboy Hall of Fame, Oklahoma City, 73; Waterfowl Festival, Easton, Md, 73; Pac Flyway Show, Santa Rosa, Calif, 75; Retrospective, Scottsdale Ctr for Arts, 78; Inaugural Exhib, Soc Wildlife Art for the Nations, London, Eng, 85; and others. *Awards:* 3M Co Design Award, 62; Ducks Unlimited Inc Artist of the Year, 75-76; two awards, Printing Indust Am, 77; Flyway Artist of Year, Ducks Unlimited, 92-93. *Mem:* Audubon Soc; Soc for Wildlife Art for the Nations, London, Eng (vpres). *Media:* Miscellaneous Media. *Publ:* Auth & illusr, Whispering skies of Arizona, 3/73, Shadowed trails, 2/76, Prowlers of the clouds, 2/79 & Shorebirds, 2/82, Ariz Highways Mag; illusr, Wildlife Techniques Manual; and thirty juvenile books on wildlife subjects. *Dealer:* Troys Gallery Main St Scottsdale AZ 85251. *Mailing Add:* 560 N Ash Dr Chandler AZ 85224

TOTH, CARYL
PHOTOGRAPHER

b Cleveland, Ohio, Dec 7, 1947. *Study:* Rochester Inst Technol, AAS, 68; State Univ NY, Buffalo, with Donald Blumberg, BA Eng, 70, MFA, 72. *Work:* Int Mus Photog at George Eastman House, Rochester, NY; Visual Studies Workshop, Rochester; Mus Mod Art, NY; Australian Nat Gallery, Canberra; San Francisco Mus Mod Art, Calif. *Exhib:* Ctr for Creative Photog, Tucson, 81; Northlight Gallery, Tempe, Ariz, 81; Corcoran Gallery Art, Washington, DC, 82; Cleveland Inst Art, 85; Los Angeles Ctr for Visual Studies Workshop, 85 & Photg Studies, 87; Mus Mod Art, Mexico City, 87; and others. *Teaching:* Head dept photog, Cranbrook Acad of Art, Bloomfield Hills, Mich, 72-; instr artistically gifted, Putnam Sch, WVa, 80-. *Awards:* Photogr Fel, Nat Endowment Arts, 75, 80 & 86; Mich Coun for the Arts, 83, 85 & 90. *Bibliog:* Photography Year, Time Life Books, 73; Exhibition Review, Artforum, 1/75 & 10/85. *Mem:* Soc Photog Educ; Coll Art Asn. *Publ:* Auth, Caryl Toth: Recent Works, Cranbrook Acad Art, 83; Latent Images: Great Lakes Arts Alliance, Nat Endowment Arts, 86; Under Construction: New Photomontage, Cranbrook Acad Art, 88. *Dealer:* MacGill Pace 32 E 57th New York NY; The Art Store Charleston WV. *Mailing Add:* c/o The Art Store 1013 Bridge Rd Charleston WV 25314

TOTH, GEORGINA GY
ART LIBRARIAN

b Budapest, Hungary, Aug 28, 1932; US citizen. *Study:* Eotvos Lorond Univ, Budapest, MA, 56; Case Western Reserve Univ, MSLS, 62. *Pos:* Cataloger, Cleveland Mus Art Libr, 62-69, reference librn, 69-75, assoc librn for reference, 75-; book reviewer, Art Documentation, 81-. *Mem:* Art Libr Soc NAm, Ohio chap, (vchmn, 88, chmn, 89). *Interests:* Art Research; Methodology; Collectors and Collecting; Bibliography

TOULIS, VASILIOS (APOSTOLOS)
PRINTMAKER, EDUCATOR
b Clewiston, Fla, Mar 24, 1931. *Study:* Univ Fla, with Fletcher Martin & Carl Holty, BDes; Pratt Inst, with Richard Lindner, Fritz Eichenberg, Jacob Landau & Walter Rogalski, BFA. *Work:* US State Dept, Washington, DC; Mus Arte Mod, Mexico City, Mex; Caravan House, NY. *Comn:* Portfolio of prints, Ctr for Contemp Printmaking, 68. *Exhib:* Brooklyn Mus, NY, 66; Fleishcer Mem, Philadelphia, 66; Mus Arte Mod, Mexico City, 67; Int Miniature Print Exhib, 68; New Paltz Nat Print Exhib, 68; and others. *Teaching:* Lectr serigraphic printmaking, Univ RI, 67 & Pratt Inst Seminar, 69; head graphic workshops, Pratt Inst, 66-, instr printmaking, 69-71, assoc prof & head undergrad printmaking, 71-; dir silk screen workshops, The Artists Collective, Hartford, Conn, 73-. *Awards:* Tiffany Found Grant in Printmaking, 67. *Mem:* Am Asn Univ Prof; United Fedn Coll Teachers; Screen Printers Asn. *Mailing Add:* 76 Oscawana Heights Rd Putnam Valley NY 10579

TOUSIGNANT, CLAUDE
PAINTER, SCULPTOR
b Montreal, Que, Dec 23, 1932. *Study:* Sch Art & Design, Montreal. *Work:* Nat Gallery Can; Phoenix Art Mus, Ariz; Larry Aldrich Mus, Ridgefield, Conn; York Univ; Mus Contemp Art, Montreal & Quebec; and others. *Exhib:* The Responsive Eye, traveling, 65; Biennale, Nat Gallery Can, Ottawa, 65 & 68; Trois cents ans de peinture Canadienne, Nat Gallery Can, Ottawa, 67; Panorama de la peinture au Québec, 1940-1966, Mus d'Art Contemporain, Montreal, 67; Forme-Couleur, Nat Gallery Can, Ottawa, 69; Panorama de la Sculpture au Québec 1945-1970, Mus d'Art Contemporain, Montreal & Mus Rodin, Paris, 70; Dix ans de Propositions Géométriques, Mus d'Art Contemporain & traveling, 79-81; Reflects, Nat Gallery Can, Ottawa, 84; Les vingt ans de Graff, Mus d'Art Contemporain, Montreal, 86; solo exhibs, 49th Parallel, NY, 87, Galerie Waddington Gorce, Montreal, 89, Vancouver Art Gallery, 90, Drabinsky Gallery, Toronto, 91, Mus de Québéc, traveling, 94, Galerie Christiane Chassay, Montreal & Christopher Cutts Gallery, Toronto, 95, and many more; La crise de l'abstraction au Canada, Les annéles 1950, traveling, 92-93; Recent Acquisitions, Montreal Mus Fine Arts, 95. *Awards:* Prize, Centennial Exhib, 67; Rome Prize, 73; Borduas Prize, 89. *Bibliog:* David Burnett & Marilyn Schiff, Contemporary Canadian Art, Edmonton: Hurtig, 83; James D Campbell, Abstract Practices (exhib catalog), Toronto, The Power Plant, 91; After Geometry: The Abstract Art of Claude Tousignant, Montreal: ECW Press, 95. *Mailing Add:* 181 Bourget Montreal PQ H4C 2M1 Canada

TOUSIGNANT, SERGE
PHOTOGRAPHER, CONCEPTUAL ARTIST
b Montreal, Que, May 28, 1942. *Study:* Ecole des Beaux-Arts de Montreal, dipl, 62; studied at Slade Sch Fine Art, London, Eng, 67. *Work:* Nat Gallery Can, Ottawa; Victoria & Albers Mus, London, Eng; Bridgestone Art Gallery, Tokyo, Japan; Mus d Art Contemporain, Montreal, Can; Conseil des Arts de Val-de-Marne, Credac, Paris, France; Musée des Beaux-Arts de Montreal, Can; Art Gallery Ontario, Toronto; Tate Gallery, London. *Exhib:* New Images, Que' Photog, 49 Parallel Gallery, NY, 83; Canadian Impressions, Contemp Art Ctr, Osaka, Japan, 84; Lumieres: Projections, Can Indian Artcrafts, Montreal, Can, 85; Les Temps Chauds, Mus Asn Can, Montreal, 88; Montreal/Berlin, Saydie Bronfman Ctr/TIP Berlin, Montreal, Can, 89; Constructed Spaces, Photog Resource Ctr, Boston Univ, 90; Phases in Photog (coauth catalog), Can Mus Contemp Photo, Ottawa, Can, 92-96; Cutting Edge, Arco, Madrid, 98; Art Paris, Carousel du Louvres, 2000; Le Cadres, Le Site, La Scene, Centro de La Imagen, Mexico City, 2000; Toronto Int Art Fair, Convention Ctr, Can, 2004; The Sixties in Can, The Sixties: The Question of Photog, Nat Gallery Can, Ottawa, 2005. *Teaching:* Prof art & photog, Univ Montreal, Que, Can, 78-2005. *Awards:* Tokyo Print Biennale Lithography Prize, Bridgestone Art Gallery, Mus Contemp Art, Japan, 65; 200th Anniversary, 1789-1989: Image Pour la Revolution (participant), Credac, Paris, 89; nominee, Royal Acad Arts Can, 2004. *Bibliog:* Sylvain Campeau (auth), Chambres Obscures, Ed Trois, Montreal, Can, 95; Indices, Études et Maquettes: Serge Tousignant, Eds Graff, Montreal, 2000. *Media:* Photography. *Specialty:* Contemp art. *Publ:* Auth, Monography of the Artist, Yvan Boulerice, Montreal, Can, 78. *Dealer:* Galerie Graf 963 ru Rachel est Montreal Quebec Canada H2J 2J4. *Mailing Add:* 4060 boul St Laurent App 606 Montreal PQ H2W 1Y9 Canada

TOWERS, JOEL
ARCHITECT, EDUCATOR
Study: Univ Mich, BS (archit); Columbia Univ, MS (archit). *Pos:* Founding ptnr, SR+T Architects, 1992; dir, Tishman Environment and Design Ctr, assoc provost environmental studies, The New Sch, formerly; dir sustainable design and ecology, Parsons The New Sch for Design, 2002, dean, Sch Design Strategies, assoc prof archit and sustainable design, 2007-2009, exec dean, 2009-. *Mailing Add:* Parsons The New School for Design 66 5th Ave, 600 New York NY 10011

TOWNER, MARK ANDREW
ADMINISTRATOR, PHOTOGRAPHER
b Evanston, Ill, 1956. *Study:* Visual Studies Workshop, Rochester, NY, 78; Columbia Coll, Chicago, BA, 78; Cranbrook Acad Art, MFA, 81; Int Ctr Photog, 82; Metrop Mus Art, New York, 88; Am Law Inst-Am Bar Asn, Boston, 2000. *Work:* Detroit Inst Arts; Ill State Mus; Cranbrook Acad Art Mus; Davenport Mus Art, Iowa; Univ Iowa. *Comn:* The Law Sch, Univ Mich. *Exhib:* Solo exhibs, Southeastern Ohio Series, Photog Gallery, Southern Ill Univ, Carbondale, 84, Anima/Animals: New Figurative Photographs, Photogr's Collective, South Bend, Ind, 85, Post Industrialization, P A C A Gallery, NY, 87, The Illuminated Ones, Trabia-MacAfee Gallery, NY, 89, Evolution of the Crucifix, Quad City Arts Gallery, Rock Island, Ill, 90, On Aesthetics, Mt Mercy Col, Cedar Rapids, Iowa, 93, Arresting Images From Popular Cult Arts, Iowa City, Iowa, 95, Oakland Co Arts Ctr, Pontiac, Mich, 95 & Quad City Arts Gallery, Rock Island, Ill, 95; 20/20 Vision, Cranbrook Acad Art, Bloomfield Hills, 92; The Search for Color, Detroit Inst Arts, Mich, 93; Iowa Artists 1994, Des Moines Art Ctr, 94; Art as Healing, Pyramid Arts Ctr, Rochester, NY, 94; Spirit In Art and Hist, Andover Hist Soc, Mass, 2001; Digital City, New Squirts for Now People, NESAD at Suffolk Univ, Boston, Mass, 2003; Endicott Faculty Reaches Out, Aberjona River Gallery, Winchester, Mass, 2004; Annual Spring Exhib, Small Works Gallery, Haverhill, Mass, 2004 & 06; Cranbrook to Lancaster and Back, Cranbrook Art Mus, Bloomfield Hills, Mich, 2005 & 06; Creative Arts, Dana-Farber Cancer Inst, Boston, Mass, 2006. *Collection Arranged:* Richard Bolton: Photographs, Gallery 681, Wayne State Univ, 82; Four Women Photographers, St Mary's Coll Photog Gallery, Notre Dame, Ind, 85; The Painted Spirit: Selected Works from the Permanent Collection, Davenport Mus Art, Iowa, 89; Three Decades of Midwestern Photography: 1960-1990, Davenport Mus Art; The Moving Wall: Vietnam War Mem, Frejervary Park, Davenport, Iowa, 91; Wellness Disease & Visual Art, Arts Iowa City, 97; Art By Healers, Broudo Gallery, 2004. *Pos:* Photogr, Metrop Mus Art, New York, 82-83; dir, Circlework Visions Ltd, New York, 85-87; chief preparator & exhib designer, Am Craft Mus, New York, 87-88; asst dir, Davenport Mus Art, Iowa, 89- & NE Doc Conserv Ctr, Andover, Mass; dir, proj art, Univ Iowa Hosp & Clinics, Iowa City, 94-98; Dean of Visual & Performing Art, Endicott Col, Beverly, Ma, 2000-. *Teaching:* Instr, senior art and design thesis, Endicott Coll, 2000-. *Bibliog:* Celeste Olalquiaga (auth), Megalopolis: Contemporary Cultural Sensibilities, 92; Arts In Healing, Butler Inst, 95; Sex Wars: Photography on the Frontlines, Exposure, 95. *Mem:* Am Asn Mus; Coll Art Asn; Am Art Therapy Asn. *Media:* Collage Art, Photography. *Publ:* Nathan Lerners Maxwell Street, River Cities Reader, 12/93; Featured Artist, ArtsBeat, 3/93; National Exposure, New City, Chicago, 6/10/93; Iowa Artists: 1994, Des Moines Art Ctr, 9/94; Offset: ARTS Iowa City, River Cities Reader, 10/95; Printed Pleasure: Published Pain, Iowa City Press, 9/95; Complex Collages Capture Culture, Moline Dispatch, 6/96; Iowa City: Views & Reviews, River Cities Readers, 2/94; Paper/Fiber XVII, Iowa City Press-Citizen, 4/20/94; Ralph Eugene Meatyard: An American Visionary, River Cities Reader, 5/94; Creating With Others, by Shaun Mcnitt, 2003. *Mailing Add:* Endicott College 376 Hale St Beverly MA 01915

TOWNSEND, GAVIN EDWARD
HISTORIAN, EDUCATOR
b Santa Monica, Calif, June 16, 1956. *Study:* Hamilton Coll, Clinton, NY, BA, 78; Univ Calif, Santa Barbara, MA, 81, PhD, 86. *Collection Arranged:* The Linens of R H Hunt: drawings by Chattanooga's Foremost Architect, Univ Art Gallery, Univ Tenn, 88. *Pos:* Asst cur archit drawing, Univ Calif, Santa Barbara, 82-86; gallery coordr, Univ Tenn, Chattanooga, 87-92, asst dir hons prog, 92 -97, dir hons prog, 97-2003. *Teaching:* Instr art hist, Univ Calif, Santa Barbara, 79-86; asst prof art hist, Univ Tenn, Chattanooga, 86-93, assoc prof, 93-2001, prof, 2001-. *Awards:* Kress Found Fel, 82-84. *Mem:* Soc Archit Hist; Hist Zoning Comn, Chattanooga, Tenn; Tenn State Hist Comn. *Res:* Anglo-American architecture 1865-1945. *Publ:* Auth, Airborne Toxins and the American House 1865-1895, Winterthur Portfolio, 89; The Tudor House of the Prairie Sch, Arris, 92; Frank Forster and the French Provincial Revival in America, Arris, 95; Lamb and Rich in Robert Mackay ed, Long Island Country Estates and Their Architects, 1860-1940, New York, Norton, 97; Reuben Harrison Hunt: A History of Tennessee Arts, Univ Tenn Press, 2004; contribr, Encyclopedia of 20th Century Architecture Chicago, Fitzray-Dearborn. *Mailing Add:* 1631 Rock Bluff Rd Hixson TN 37343

TOWNSEND, JOHN F
SCULPTOR, PAINTER
b La Crosse, Wis, 1929. *Study:* Carroll Col, Waukesha, Wis, BS, 51; Minneapolis Sch of Art, 53-55; Univ of Minn Grad Sch, MFA, 59. *Work:* Mus Fine Art, Boston, Mass; Rose Mus, Brandeis Univ, Waltham, Mass; Allentown Art Mus, Pa; Chase Manhattan Bank, NY; World Bank, Washington, DC. *Comn:* cast bronze sculpture of a Minuteman, Univ Mass, Amherst, 2002. *Exhib:* Art for US Embassies, Inst Contemp Art, Boston, 66; Optical Art Traveling Exhib, Mus Mod Art, NY, 66-68; Small Paintings for Mus Collections, Am Fedn of Art Traveling Exhib, 67-68; Solo exhibs, Eleanor Rigelhaupt Gallery, Boston, 67, Ward-Nasse Gallery, Boston, 70, Danco Gallery, Florence, 79, Berkshire Artisans, Pittsfield, 81 & Zone, Springfield, 85, Mass; and others. *Pos:* Dir art exhibs, 60-64 & dir grad art prog, 71-74, Univ Mass, Amherst; bd dir, Zone Art Ctr, Springfield, Mass, 86-. *Teaching:* Instr sculpture & painting, Eastern NMex Univ, Portales, 59-60; from instr to full prof sculpture, drawing & design, Univ of Mass, Amherst, 60-99; part-time instr painting, Mt Holyoke Col, South Hadley, Mass, 61-62. *Awards:* First Award Sculpture, Second Ann Univ Arts Faculty Exhib, Argus Gallery, Madison, NJ, 63; Crane Co Award, 17th Ann Exhib of Painting & Drawing, 68; President's Award, Springfield Art League 66th Nat Exhib, Mus Fine Arts, Mass, 85. *Bibliog:* Dona Z Meilach (auth), Contemporary Art with Wood, Crown Publ Inc, New York, 68; Gloria Russell (auth), review, The Sunday Republican, Springfield, Mass, 4/21/85. *Media:* Wood & Bronze; Acrylic. *Dealer:* Francis Frost Newport RI. *Mailing Add:* 118 Aubinwood Rd Amherst MA 01002-1690

TOWNSEND, STORM D
SCULPTOR, INSTRUCTOR
b London, Eng, Aug 31, 1937. *Study:* London Univ, NDD, ATC, Goldsmiths' Coll Art, 6 yrs, with Harold Parker & Ivor Roberts Jones. *Hon Degrees:* Nat Diploma in Design and Art Tchg Cert, NDD, ATC, London. *Work:* Fine Arts Mus NMex, Santa Fe; Genesee Co Mus, Rochester. *Comn:* Life-size portrait in bronze, David Cargo, Gov NMex, 67; To Serve & Protect (life-size bronze to honour the police force), comn by City of Albuquerque; Charlie Pride Int Sr Golf Classic (bronze trophy design), 87 & Tres Culturas del Rio Grande (bronze figures), 88, Sunwest Bank, Albuquerque, NMex. *Exhib:* One-person shows, Gallery Marquis, Denver, Colo, 75, Gallery Eleven, Lubbock, Tex, 77 & Am Inst Architects, Albuquerque, NMex, 90; Survey of Contemp NMex Sculpture, NMex Mus Fine Art, Santa Fe, 76; Santa Fe Festival Arts, 79; Great Garden Exhib, Sculptural Arts Mus, Atlanta, 82; Circle of Art Gallery, Scottsdale Village, Albuquerque, NMex, 97; State Fair, Fine Arts Gallery, Albuquerque, NMex, 2002, 2009; Acquiring Taste Gallery, Albuquerque, NMex, 2003; Corrales Fine Art Exhib, 2007. *Collection Arranged:* NMex Mus of Fine Art, Santa Fe; Sunwest Bank Albuquerque, NMex; Genesee Country Mus, Rochester, NY. *Pos:* Moulder/caster prep lab fossils, Mus Nat Hist, Albuquerque, NMex, 87-89. *Teaching:* Instr sculpture,

Pojoaque Art Ctr, Santa Fe, 65-66, Col of Santa Fe, 73-75, Univ Albuquerque, NMex & adult educ prog Univ NMex, currently. *Awards:* Jajasan Siswa Lokantara Resident Fel to study the arts in Indonesia, 60-61; Resident Fels, Huntington Hartford Found, Calif, 63 & Helene Wurlitzer Found, Taos, NMex, 64. *Bibliog:* Robert M Powers (auth), NMex Mag, 78; Mary Carroll Nelson (auth), articles, Am Artist, 79, Art Voices S, 80 & Southwest Art Mag, 86. *Mem:* Albuquerque Arts Alliance. *Media:* Clay to Cast Bronze, Concrete, Plaster, Fiberglass. *Interests:* Music, theatre, literature, opera, art, nature. *Dealer:* Occasions by Design 4223 Marshall Way Scottsdale AZ 85251. *Mailing Add:* PO Box 1165 Corrales NM 87048

TOWNSEND, TERYL
PAINTER, EDUCATOR
b Coronado, Calif, May 9, 1938. *Study:* Ray Froman Sch Art, Univ Tex, study with Millard Sheets, Chen Chi, Charles Reid, Edgar Whitney, Carl Molno & Glenn Bradshaw. *Work:* Foothills Art Ctr, Golden, Colo; US Navy; Riverside Theatre, Vero Beach, Fla; Community Church, Vero Beach, Fla. *Comn:* Painting, USN, US Bristol Co, 68; painting, Grumman Int Corp Off, 76; painting, Rawson Int Corp Off; 400 pvt collections. *Exhib:* Mus Albuquerque Western Fedn Group Show, 75; Watercolor Soc Group Show, Birmingham Mus Art, Ala, 76; Western Fedn Group Show, Tucson Mus Art, Ariz, 76; Butler Inst Am Art Mid-Yr Ann, Youngstown, Ohio, 77; Watercolor USA Ann, Springfield, Ill, 77; Southern Watercolor Soc Group Show, Tenn, 77; Solo exhib, Stephen F Austin State Univ, Tex, 78; Nat Watercolor Show, Nat Acad Design, Betty Barker Gallery, New Canaan. *Pos:* Art experience facilitator, Tex Inst Child Psychiat, 75-76. *Teaching:* Instr water media painting, Canary Hill Galleries, Houston, Tex, 74-77, Tex Art Supply Inc, Houston, 75-77 & pvt studio, Houston, 78-, Nantucket, Mass, 80-90. *Awards:* Director's Award, Southern Watercolor Ann Exhib, 77; Art League Houston Dimension Award, 82; Southwestern Watercolor Soc Award, 83; New Canaan Soc for the Arts Award, 96, 97. *Bibliog:* Pat Lasher (auth), Seeing the ordinary in a special way, Southwest Art Mag, 9/77; Naomi Brotherton (auth), Spotlight on the artist, The Scene, Southwestern Watercolor Soc, 1/78; Watercolor Energies, Frank Webb, 82. *Mem:* Am Watercolor Soc; Nat Watercolor Soc; Rocky Mountain Nat Watermedia Soc; Vero Beach Mus Art (bd trustees, exec comt, exibs comt chmn); New Canaan Soc Arts. *Media:* Acrylic, Watercolor. *Interests:* Philanthropy. *Mailing Add:* 913 Orchid Point Way Vero Beach FL 32963

TRACHTMAN, ARNOLD S
PAINTER
b Lynn, Mass, Oct 5, 1930. *Study:* Mass Sch Art, BFA; Sch Art Inst Chicago, MFA. *Work:* Fogg Art Mus, Harvard Univ, Cambridge, Mass; Addison Gallery Am Art, Andover, Mass; Wiggin Collection, Boston Pub Libr, Mass; Boston Mus Fine Arts; Mus Nat Ctr of Afro-American Artists, Roxbury, Mass; Lynn Mus, Lynn, MA; Decordova Mus, Lincoln, MA; Fla Holocaust Mus, St Petersburg. *Exhib:* Solo exhibs, Inst Contemp Art, Boston, 70 & Addison Gallery Am Art, Andover, Mass, 76, Brockton Art Ctr, Mass, 79, Montserrat Sch Visual Art, Beverly, Mass, 85; AAMARP Gallery, Boston, 81; Bradford Col, Mass, 82; Cambridge Mult Cult Art Ctr, Cambridge, Mass, 1999; Lynn Mus, Lynn Mass, 2000; group exhibs, Staatliche Kunsthalle, Berlin, WGer, 83, Royal Festival Hall, London, UK, 85, Gallery Naga, Boston, Mass, 88, Arvada Art Ctr, Colo, 90 & Boston Univ Art Gallery, Mass, 91; Newton Art Ctr, Newtonville, Mass, 92; Mus Am Art, St Paul, Minn, 95; Absence/Presente Univ of Minn, 99; 1850-1950 Lynn Mus, Lynn Mass, Lynn's Jewish Community, 2004; Galatea, 2012. *Teaching:* Instr art, Lynnfield High Sch, Mass, 71-80, Cambridge Sch, Weston, 80-81; assoc prof, Mass Col Art, 81-. *Bibliog:* Indochina Arts Proj Inc (auth), As Seen By Both Sides, Univ Mass Press, 91; Approaching a Horrible Truth: 2 Artists Painting the Holocaust, Newton Arts Ctr, 92; Witness & Legacy, Lerner Publ, 95; 100 Boston Painters, Schiffer Pub, 2012. *Mem:* Boston Visual Artist Union; Mass Cult Alliance. *Media:* Acrylic, Watercolor, Mixed Media. *Publ:* Alone Stands the Artist, Boston Globe, 72. *Dealer:* Howard Yezersky Gallery Boston Mass; Galatea Gallery Boston Ma. *Mailing Add:* 27 Dana St Cambridge MA 02138

TRACY, ROBERT H
EDUCATOR, CURATOR
b Alameda, Calif, March 14, 1948. *Study:* Calif State Univ, Hayward, BA, 70; Univ Calif, Los Angeles, MA, 77, PhD, 82. *Collection Arranged:* Palaces of Finance (co-cur), Spring St Hist Dist, 82; Architecture of Modern Olympiad: 1896 to Present (co-cur), 84; John & Donald Parkinson, Architects (auth, catalog), 89-90. *Pos:* Bd dir, Preservation Asn Clark Co, 84-, Las Vegas Neon Mus, 88- & Nev Inst Contemp Arts, 89-; Cur, Parkinson Arch, Los Angeles, 84-; chmn, dept art, Univ Nev, Las Vegas, 89-. *Teaching:* Assoc prof art hist, Chapman Col, Orange, Calif, 79-84 & Univ Nev, Las Vegas, 84-; cur, Parkinson Arch, Los Angeles, 84-; Univ London, spring, 93. *Awards:* Nevada Humanities Comt, 85-89 & 92; Las Vegas Chap Am Inst Architects, 85-89, 92 & 96; Nev State Coun Arts, 96. *Mem:* Soc Archit Historians; Coll Art Asn; Semiotic Soc Am. *Res:* Late 19th century to 20th century business architectural imagery. *Mailing Add:* Univ Nevada Las Vegas Dept of Art 4505 Maryland Pkwy Las Vegas NV 89154-5002

TRAGER, NEIL C
MUSEUM DIRECTOR, PHOTOGRAPHER
b Aug 14, 1947. *Study:* City Coll New York, BA, 69. *Work:* Mus Mod Art, New York; Neuberger Mus, Purchase, NY; Harry Ransom Humanities Res Ctr, Univ Tex, Austin; Ctr Photog, Woodstock, NY. *Comn:* Ok Harris Works Art; Brooklyn Mus Art; Ctr Photog, Woodstock, NY; Santa Fe Ctr Photog; Nikon House. *Exhib:* Hot Spots: America's Volcanic Landscape, Hudson Valley Artists Series. *Collection Arranged:* George Bellows Lithographs; A Kind of History; Mark Goodman; Ctr Photog, Woodstock, Permanent Print Collection; SDMA Historic & Contemp Metal Work. *Pos:* Assoc cur, Catskill Ctr Photog, Woodstock, NY, 78-81, mem bd dir, 86-; trustee, Klyne Esopus Mus, Port Ewen, NY, 82-84; dir, Samuel Dorsky Mus Art, State Univ NY, New Paltz, currently; adv bd, Ctr Photog Woodstock, currently. *Teaching:* Adj lectr photog & art, La Guardia Community Coll, Queens, NY, 76-78; lectr photog, State Univ NY, New Paltz, 79-81. *Awards:* Creative Artists Pub Serv Fel, NY State Coun Arts, 81; Chancellors Award for Excellence in Service, State Univ NY; United Univ Professions Award for Excellence. *Mem:* Gallery & Mus Asn, State Univ NY; Am Asn Mus. *Res:* Contemporary and historical photography. *Specialty:* AM Works on Paper; Hudson Valley-Caskill Mt. *Interests:* 19 & 20 Century Photographs, Metal works. *Publ:* Bolton Coit Brown; A Retrospective; Don Nice: The Nature of Art. *Mailing Add:* Samuel Dorksy Mus of Art Suny New 1 Hawk Dr New Paltz NY 12561

TRAGER, PHILIP
PHOTOGRAPHER
b Bridgeport, Conn, Feb 27, 1935. *Study:* Wesleyan Univ, BA, 56, DFA, 2008; Columbia Univ Sch Law, JD, 60. *Hon Degrees:* DFA, Wesleyan Univ, 2008. *Work:* Libr Cong, Washington DC; Mus Mod Art, Metrop Mus Art, NY; Brooklyn Mus, NY; Center for Creative Photog, Tucson; Bibliot Nat, Paris; Can Ctr Archit; Mus of the City NY; Musee Carnavalet, Paris; NY Public Libr; Baltimore Mus, Baltimore, Md; Brooklyn Mus. *Comn:* Photog study Wesleyan Univ, Bd Trustees, 80; Photog study Birmingham, Birmingham Mus Art, 88; Photog study Wave Hill, Bd Dirs, 90; Photog study, Saline Royale, Found Ledoux, 91; Photog Study, Aldrich Mus Contemp Art, 99. *Exhib:* Solo Exhibs: Davison Art Ctr, Middletown, Conn, 70, 74, 81, 92, 2000, 2006; Witkin Gallery, NY, 72, 77, 80 & 87; Baltimore Mus Art, Baltimore, Md, 1977; Mus of the City of NY, 1980-81; PhotographicResource Ctr, 96; Embassy of France, Washington, 2000; Mus Photog Arts, San Diego, Calif, 94; Les Recontres Internationales de la Photographie, Arles, France; Museo Nazionale di Villa Giulia, Rome, 2002; Allen Mem Art Mus, Oberlin Coll, Oberlin, Ohio, 2007; The Am Inst Architects, DC, 96; The Nat Building Mus, DC, 2009-2010; NY Public Libr, 2012; and others in the US and abroad. *Teaching:* Instr masterclasses & workshops. *Awards:* Distinguished Alumnus Award, 81; 1986, 1992, & 2000 Book Awards, Maine Photog Workshops; Finalist Grant Prix Award, Int Festival Photog, Arles, France; Book Award, Am Inst of Graphic Arts, 77. *Bibliog:* Barbara L Michael (auth), Art on Paper, Nov/Dec 2000; Ken Johnson (auth) The New York Times, 5/2000; Lee A Vedder (auth), Paris-New York aller-retour, 2002; John Stauffer (auth), 21st: Journal of Contemporary Photography, 2004; Reed Haslach Humphrey (auth), National Building Museum Online, 12/2009; Shawn O'Sullivan (auth), Black & White Mag, 4/2010; William Myers (auth), The Wall St Jour, 2012; Blake Gophik (auth), The Daily React, 2013; Parker Caitlin (auth), Artnet.com, 2013. *Media:* Silver, Platinum & Picment photographs. *Publ:* Echoes of Silence, Scroll Press, 1972; Photographs of Architecture, Wesleyan Univ Press, 1977; Philip Trager: New York, Wesleyan Univ Press, 1980; Wesleyan Photographs, Wesleyan Univ Press, 1982; The Villas of Palladio, NY Graphic Soc, 1986; Dancers, Bulfinch Press, 1992; Persephone, Wesleyan Univ Press with New Eng Found Arts, 1996; Changing Paris, Arena Eds, 2000; Faces Steidl, 2005; Philip Trager (Retrospective), Steidl, 2006; auth, Library of Congress: Webcast, 2009

TRAINES, ROSE WUNDERBAUM
SCULPTOR, LECTURER
b Monroeville, Ind, Sept 13, 1928. *Study:* Indiana State Teacher's Col, 1946-48; Mich State Univ, 1948-49; Central Mich Univ, BS, 1950-51. *Work:* Blake Libr Art Collection, Stuart, Fla; Alden Dow Science & Art Mus, Midland, Mich; Boston Coll Club Art Collection, Mass; Norman Cousins Office Art, Los Angeles, Calif; Park Libr, Cent Mich Univ, Mt Pleasant, Mich; Carnegie Libr, Montpelier, Ind; Pub Libr, Northville, Mich; Pub Libr, Alma, Mich; Garfield Pub Libr, Clare, Mich; Central Mich Comm Hosp, Mt Pleasant, Mich. *Comn:* Walt Kuhn Gallery, Ms. Kuhn, Cape Neddic, ME, 1988; Cent Mich Comm Hospital, 50th Anniversary, Bd Trustees, Mt Pleasant, Mich, 1999; "Donny" Hersee Collection, Mt Pleasant, Mich, 2000; 50th Anniv Rollie/Olga Denison, Detroit, Mich, 2001; Lewis Johnsons, Naples, Fla, 2002. *Exhib:* With This Torch I Thee Weld, Elliott Mus, Stuart, Fla, 1983-1988, 1993, 1998, 2006-2007; Self Family Performing Arts, Performing Arts Ctr, Hilton Head, SC, 1999; With This Torch I Thee Weld, Copley Soc of Boston, Mass, 2001; 2001 Ann Exhib, Allied Artists of Am, New York City, 2001; Photograph & Sculpture, Salmagundi Club, New York City, 2001; Comerica Bank Art Series, Palm Beach Gardens, Fla, 2001; Month-of-March, Gallery Five, Tequesta, Fla, 2002; Central Mich Art Exhib, Alden Dow Science Art, Midland, Mich, 2002; City Hall Exhib & Community Ctr Gallery, Palm Beach Gardens, Fla, 2003; With This Torch I Thee Weld, Glick Community Ctr, Indianapolis, Ind, 2004; This Torch I Thee Weld & All's Weld That Ends Weld, Art Reach of Mid-Michigan, Mt Pleasant, 2006; Orchid Island Beach Club, Orchid, Fla, 2007; Solo exhib with gallery talk to open new gallery on Broadway, Art Reach of Mid-Mich, Mt Pleasant, 2010; Dow Gardens Visitors Lounge, Midland, Mich, 2012. *Pos:* Guest presenter & teacher with majority of exhibitions/lectures at art galleries, museums, art centers, univ & school classes (gr 1-12), Indianapolis, Ind, Hiltonhead, SC, Mich, Fla & Ind cities, 1964-2007. *Teaching:* lectr & sculptor in res, Northwood Univ, W Palm, Fla & Midland, Mich, 1988; Elliott Mus, Stuart, Fla, Dec 2005-Jan 06 & Art Reach of mid-Mich, May-June 2006. *Awards:* Outstanding Alumni Recognition, Homecoming, Central Mich Univ, Mt Pleasant, 1991; Lifetime of Creative Excellence, Performing Arts Ctr, Hilton Head, SC Art League, 1998; Members Memorial, Ann Summer Exhib, Salmagundi Club, NYC, 2003; Art Reach Treasure, Art Reach of Mid-Mich, 2008. *Bibliog:* Videografic dept (dir), With This Torch I Thee Weld, CMU Media Ctr Publicity, 2002; Heitman Audio Visual (dir) With This Torch I Thee Weld, distrib to sculptor owners, schools, galleries, museums & art ctrs, 2003-2006; Junia Doan (interviewer), Uncommon Sense, PBS, 2008. *Mem:* The Salmagundi Club, NYC; Allied Artists of America Inc, NYC; The Copley Soc of Art, Boston, Mass; Alden Dow Science & Art Mus, Midland, Mich; Mus of Art, Vero Beach, Fla. *Media:* Metal, Welded, Brazed Oxygen/Acetylene Torch. *Specialty:* Indoor metal (welded/brazed), sculptures, original designs, multiple subjects. *Interests:* Family, friends, community activities, sculpting, presenting lectures, tennis & drums. *Publ:* Junkyard Junkie, Mich Journal, E. Berley, May/June 1981; contrib, Treasure Coastline - Coastal Currents, Dorothy

Yates, Stuart, Fla, Mar 1998; contrib, Mt Pleasant Magazine, Naseem Stecker, 1996; contrib, Niche, Magazine for Progressive Retailers, Susan York, Baltimore, Md, spring 2001; featured, Mt Pleasant Monthly Mag, 2009; Cent Life CMU, 2010; Time Out, Morning Sun, Mt Pleasant, Mich. *Mailing Add:* 1217 North Dr Mount Pleasant MI 48858-3226

TRAKAS, GEORGE
SCULPTOR
b Quebec, Que, May 11, 1944. *Study:* Brooklyn Mus Art Sch; Hunter Col, New York Univ, BS. *Hon Degrees:* Emory Univ, DHL, 2011. *Work:* Solomon R Guggenheim Mus. *Comn:* Omaha Opportunities Industrialization Ctr, 80; Nat Oceanic and Atmospheric Admin, Seattle, 83. *Exhib:* Projects: Pier 18, Mus Mod Art, NY, 71; Ten Young Artists: Theodoron Awards, Guggenheim Mus, NY, 71; Route Point, Scale and Environment: 10 Sculptors, Walker Art Ctr, Minneapolis, Minn, 77; El, 1979 Biennial, Whitney Mus Am Art, NY, 79; Pacific Union, San Diego Mus Contemp Art, La Jolla, Calif, 89; Routes from the Heart, La Mus, Humlebaek, Denmark, 89; Le Pont d'Epee au Creux de l'Enfer, Thiers, France, 89; Todd Terrace, Wash State Univ, Pullman, 90; Constructions, Wall Pieces and Drawings, Quint Krichman Projs, San Diego, Calif, 92; and others. *Teaching:* Lectr, Boston Mus, 72; lectr, Cooper Union, 78; lectr, Yale Univ, 80. *Awards:* Nat Endowment Arts Fel, 79; Guggenheim Fel, 83; Nat Acad Arts & Letts, 96. *Bibliog:* Paul Stimson (auth), article, Art Am, 9-10/75; Kate Linker (auth), George Trakas & the syntax of space, Arts Mag, 1/76; Sally Yard (aut), Drawings & Constructions, 93; Greux de l'Enfer Leauence Gateau, 2002. *Media:* Steel, Wood. *Publ:* Contribr, Outcrops, Avalanche, fall 71; catalogue essays, Projects in Nature, 75 & Artpark, 76; Structures for Behavior, 78; Fattoria di Celle, 82; Documenta, 87; Sitings, 89. *Mailing Add:* 55 St Marks Pl #2 New York NY 10003

TRAKIS, LOUIS
SCULPTOR, EDUCATOR
b New York, NY, June 22, 1927. *Study:* Cooper Union, BFA; Columbia Univ; Art Students League; Politechneion, Athens, Greece; Fulbright grants, Acad Fine Arts, Rome, Italy, 59-60 & 60-61. *Work:* Guild Hall Mus, East Hampton, NY; Village Kournas, Crete, Greece; Revco Corp, Southampton, NY. *Comn:* War hero monument (bronze), Crete, Greece, 88. *Exhib:* Pa Acad, Philadelphia; Corcoran Gallery, Washington, DC; Brooklyn Mus, NY; Feingarten Gallery, NY; Benson Gallery, Bridgehampton, LI, NY; Manhattanville Col, Purchase, NY; Benton Gallery, Southampton, NY; New Sch, Social Res, New York, NY; and others. *Pos:* Emer prof, Manhattanville Col, Artist's Equity Asn NY, Audubon Artists & Fulbright Asn. *Teaching:* Instr sculpture, Philadelphia Col of Art, Columbia Univ, New Sch for Social Res & Southhampton Col; prof ceramics & sculpture, Manhattanville Col, 65-, adminr, Summer in Crete Prog, 80-85. *Awards:* Sculpture Award, Parrish Art Mus, Southampton, NY; Sculpture Award, Guild Hall Mus, E Hampton, NY; Sculpture Award, Audubon Artists Exhib, NY; Tiffany Award, Louis Comfort, 61 & 63. *Bibliog:* Interview (TV prog), Carlson Int, 84. *Mem:* Artists Equity, NY; Am Asn Univ Profs; Audubon Artists. *Publ:* Contribr, Prize Winning Sculpture (bks I & II), Allied Publ. *Dealer:* Vorpal Gallery 459 West Broadway New York NY 10012. *Mailing Add:* 532 16th St Brooklyn NY 11215

TRAN, TAM VAN
PAINTER
b Kontum, Vietnam, 1966. *Study:* Pratt Film Inst, BFA, 1990; UCLA, Grad Film & TV Prog, 1996. *Work:* UCLA Hammer Mus; Whitney Mus Am Art, New York; Knoxville Mus Art, Tenn. *Exhib:* Solo exhibs, Turkey Diesel, Dirt Gallery, Los Angeles, 1999, Cold Frost, Irvine Fine Arts Ctr, Calif, 2000, Susanne Vielmetter Los Angeles Projects, 2000, 2001, Beetle Manifesto, 2002, Project Room: Lover of Air, Cohan Leslie & Browne, NY, 2002, Vegetarian Summer, 2003, Lord of Hot Butter, Anthony Meier Fine Arts, San Francisco, 2003; Kassel Ducumenta Archiv, Ludwig Mus, Cologne, 1990, House of Styles, Tri Gallery, Los Angeles, 1995, Asian Am Art Ctr, NY, 1998, Other Paintings, Huntington Beach Art Ctr, Calif, 1999, Pierogi 2000: Flat Files, Yerba Buena Ctr Arts, San Francisco, 2000, Luminous, Ikon Fine Art, Santa Monica, Calif, 2000, Radar Love, Gallery Marabini, Italy, 2000, Car Pooling from Los Angeles, Asian Am Art Ctr, NY, 2000; New Work: LA Painting, Hosfelt Gallery, San Francisco, 2001, Black Dragon Soc, Los Angeles, 2001, Panorama, Room Interior Products, 2002, Cohan Leslie & Browne, NY, 2002, Drawing Biennial, Weatherspoon Art Gallery, NC, 2002; In the Making: Drawings from a Pvt Collection, Univ Mass Amherst, 2003, Int Paper, Around About Abstraction, Weatherspoon Art Gallery, NC, 2005. *Awards:* Creative Fel Visual Arts, Colo Coun Arts & Humanities, 1991; Ucross Artists Residency, Ucross, Wyo, 1993; Pollock-Krasner Found Grant, 2000; Recipient Joan Mitchell Found Award, 2001; Art Matters Found Grant, 2008. *Mailing Add:* c/o Cohan Leslie & Browne 138 Tenth Ave New York NY 10011

TRAUB, CHARLES H
EDUCATOR, PHOTOGRAPHER
b Louisville, Ky, Apr 6, 1945. *Study:* Univ of Ill, Urbana, BA, 67; Inst of Design, Ill Inst of Technol, MS (photog), 71. *Work:* Int Ctr Photog, NY; Mus of Mod Art, NY; Art Inst of Chicago, Ill; Fogg Mus, Harvard Univ, Cambridge, Mass; Int Mus of Photog, Rochester, NY; and others. *Comn:* Olympic Arts Found, 84; New York City Parks Dept, 89. *Exhib:* Photographs of Charles Traub, Art Inst Chicago, 75; The City, Mus Contemp Art, Chicago, 77; Solo exhibs, Light Gallery, NY, 77, Looking in Color, Light Gallery, NY, 84, Nudes, Marcuse Pfeifer Gallery, NY, 84, In Decent Exposure, Van Straaten Gallery, Chicago, 83, Beach, Art Directors Guild of NY, 83, Recognitions, Faces and Places: Photographs by Charles Traub, Hudson River Mus, NY, 82; Contemp Photog, Fogg Mus, 77; Color in the Streets, Calif Mus Photog, Univ Calif, Riverside, 83; 10 Photographers: Olympic Photographs, LAOOC Mus Contemp Art, Los Angeles, Traveling, 85; Family Portraits (with catalog), Univ Art Gallery, Wright State Univ, Dayton, 87; Here is New York, 39 cities worldwide, 2001-2003; Taken by Design, Art Inst Chicago, 2002; Gitterman Gallery, New York, 2005-2007, 2011; Cajun Document, New Orleans, 2008; New York, New York, Vienna, 2009. *Pos:* Freelance photogr, 69-; pres, Photog Adv Group, Chicago, Ill, 75-77; dir, Light Gallery, NY, 77-80; sr ed, Matrix Publ; chmn, Sch visual arts, NY; partner, Wayfarer Photography Inc, 82-. *Teaching:* Vis artist, Franconia Col, NH, 73-74 & Tyler Sch Art, Philadelphia, Pa, 81; prof photog & chmn dept, Columbia Col, Chicago, Ill, 71-; instr, Sch Visual Art, NY, 85, dir grad dept photogr, 87-. *Awards:* Cornell Capa Infinity Award, ICP, 2002. *Mem:* Soc of Photog Educ; Coll Art Asn. *Media:* Photography. *Res:* In the Realm of the Circuit, Prentice Hall, 2003; Education of a Photographer, Alworth Press, 2007. *Publ:* Auth, Some Other Pictures of Italy, Portfolio Camera Int, No 11, Paris, France, 87; Nudes, Portfolio, Zoom, Paris, France, 12/87; Am Photography Annuals No 1 & 2, NY, 85-86; Italy Observed, Rizzoli, 88; An Angler's Album, Rizzoli, 90; In the Still Life, 2006; Still Life in Am, 2011. *Dealer:* Gitterman Gallery New York NY 10021. *Mailing Add:* 39 E 10th St New York NY 10003

TRAUSCH, THOMAS V
PAINTER, EDUCATOR
b Chicago, Ill, Sept 4, 1943. *Study:* Univ Ill, BFA, 66; Am Acad Art, with Irving Shapiro, 74-77, Art Study, Giverny, France with Gale Bennett, 97. *Work:* Elmhurst Fine Arts Mus, Ill; Smith-Barney, Chicago; Burlington Northern Railway, Ill; Nissei-Sanyo; Blue Cross-Blue Shield Ins co pvt collection; Northern Trust Bank; Oprah Winfrey pvt collection; McHenry Co Ill Gov Ctr. *Comn:* Oil mural, Home State Bank, Woodstock, Ill, 99; oil mural, 9 X 12, Holy Apostles Church, McHenry, Ill, 2007; oil mural, 9 X 16, City of Crystal Lake, Ill, 2007; over 200 commissioned original paintings, pvt collections & public collections. *Exhib:* Transparent Watercolor Soc Am, 90, 94, 97, 2000, 2003 & 2006; Am Watercolor Soc, New York, 86; Oil Painters of Am, 94, 98, 2004 & 2006; Bosque Conserv Art, Tex, 98 & 2003; Salon Int 2002, San Antonio; Visual Arts Ctr, Nat Art Exhib, Punta Gorda, Fla, 2012. *Pos:* Guest instr, Am Acad Art, 88-90 & Giverny & Normandy, France, 98; pvt instr, oil, watercolor, US currently; Gallery owner, 2006-. *Teaching:* Instr workshops, Giverny & Normandy, France, 98-2000, Great Smoky Mts Nat Park, 95-97 & 2004, & St Remy, Provence, France, 2001-2002; Ireland, 2006 & Rome & Tuscany, 2007 & 2009, Cape Cod, Mass, 2011, Brown Co Ind, 2013. *Awards:* Master Status Award, Transparent Watercolor Soc Am, 2006; 2nd Pl, Praire Plein Air, Schaumburg, Ill, 2011; 2nd Pl Prof, Nygren Juried Art Exhib, Burpee Mus, Rockford, Ill; Grand Prize, Edge of the Rock, Beloit, Wisc, 2011; Hon Mention, Pleinair, Pewaukee, Wisc, 2011; Best of Show, Tinker Art Exhib, Rockford, Ill, 2011; 3rd Pl Oil, 5th Ann Creative Arts Fesitival, Lovell Fed Healthcare Ctr, 2012; 2nd Pl, Celebration of Wild Flowers & Paint Out, 2012; Hon Mention, Edge of the Rock, Beloit, Wisc, 2012; 1st Pl, Bartlett, Int Art Show, 2012; 1st Pl, Chicago Botanic Gardens, Nature Theme, 2012; Outstanding Achievement award, Chicago Botanic Gardens, 2013; 3rd Pl, The Face of McHenry Countyill, 2013; 2nd Pl, Crabtree Nature Ctr, 2013; Honorable Mention, Cedarburg Wisc Plein Air, 2014. *Bibliog:* Danielle Aceto (auth), Couple finds painting adds to art of marriage, Northwest Herald, 88; William Stanek (auth), McHenry County artists, Chicago Tribune, 94; Artists Magazine (featured article), 2/2000; and many others. *Mem:* Transparent Watercolor Soc Am (sig mem, 88-, master, 2006); Oil Painters Am, 2009-. *Media:* Oil, Watercolor. *Interests:* Photography, travel, nature. *Publ:* Splash III, North Light Publ, Cincinnati, Ohio, 94; The Best of Watercolor, 96 & The Best of Watercolor II, 97, Rockport Publ; Portrait Inspirations, Rockport Publ; Plein Air Mag, 12/2005; Complete Photoguide to Creative Painting, 2010; Woodstock Plein Air Artist Enjoys the Journey, Northwest Quarterly Mag, 2012; and others. *Dealer:* Trausch Fine Arts 116 E Calhoun St (rear) Woodstock Il; State of Il Artisans Gallery Chicago Il; I love Chicago International Terminal O'hare Airport Chicao Il. *Mailing Add:* 2403 Mustang Trail Woodstock IL 60098-8423

TRAVANTI, LEON EMIDIO
PAINTER, DESIGNER
b Kenosha, Wis, Aug 5, 1936. *Study:* Cranbrook Acad Arts, MFA, 60; Layton Sch Art, BFA, 59. *Work:* Milwaukee Art Mus; Bergstrom Mus, Neenah, Wis; Rahr Art Ctr, La Crosse, Wis; Univ Mo; Univ Wis at Madison, Marinette, Milwaukee; Northern Ill Univ; Milwaukee Inst of Art & Design; Carroll Collage, Milwaukee; Strathmoe Paper Corp. *Comn:* Paintings & drawings, Ansul Int, Brussels, Belg, 74, Lane Ltd, Sydney, Australia, 74-75 & Malaysia Ancom, Kuala Lumpur, Malaysia, 75; painting, First Wis Nat Bank, 76; posters, comn by Wis Great Circus Parade, 88-92; Design House, Milwaukee Mural Comn, 91; Carroll collage, Milwaukee Inst Art & Design. *Exhib:* Detroit Inst Art, 60; Columbia Coll, Mo, 78; Pillsbury Nat, 81-82; West Art & The Law Nat, 83; solo exhibs, Charles Allis Art Mus, Milwaukee, 83, Posner Gallery, Milwaukee, 90, Michael Lord Gallery, Milwaukee, 2003 & Mt Mary Coll, Milwaukee, Wis, 2005; Technology in Art Invitational Exhib, Milwaukee Art Mus, 86; Rahr-West Mus, Manitowoc, Wis, 88. *Pos:* Art dir, Wis Archit & Milwaukee Mag, 60-64; dir graphic design, Sch Fine Arts, Univ Wis, 64-74; fellow, Vermont Studio Ctr, 2007; acquisitions com, Contemp Art Soc, Milwaukee Art Mus, 2011-. *Teaching:* Prof art & design, Univ Wis, Milwaukee, 64-, dir design prog; vis lectr graphic design, Parsons Sch Design, New York, summer, 77 & 79; vis lectr, Pratt Inst, Manhattan Campus, 78-79 & Parsons Sch Design, 79-80; instr, Adult Art Classes, Charles Allis Mus & Villa Terrace Mus. *Awards:* Purchase Prizes, Milwaukee Renaissance, 60, Wis Invitational, 65 & Pillsbury Co, Minneapolis; Int Artists & Writers Residency, Vt Studio Ctr, 2007. *Bibliog:* Walter Herdig (ed), Ann report paintings, Graphis Ann, 66-67 & 75-76; Paintings in reports, Print Mag, 76 & Current Am Paintings, La Revue Moderne, Paris, 60. *Mem:* Am Inst Graphic Arts; Graphic Arts Guild; Am Ctr Design; and others. *Media:* Acrylics & Collage. *Res:* On-site drawings/paintings and cultural backgrounds worldwide. *Interests:* Works with and directs children, teachers in annual art exhib at Villa Terrace Museum, Milwaukee. *Dealer:* Michael Lord Gallery Palm Springs Calif. *Mailing Add:* 1425 N Prospect Ave Milwaukee WI 53202

TRAVERS-SMITH, BRIAN JOHN
PAINTER, INSTRUCTOR
b Tangshan, North China, June 26, 1931; Can & UK citizen. *Study:* Ont Coll Art, Toronto, 49-50; self-taught in watercolor. *Work:* Art Gallery Greater Victoria, BC; Provincial Collection BC; Dofasco Collection, Hamilton, Ont; Chevron Standard Collection, Calgary, Alta; Hiram Walker Collection, BC; Royal Collection, Windsor, UK. *Exhib:* Solo exhib, Art Gallery Greater Victoria, BC, 62; Allied Artists Am, NY,

69, 71, 72 & 81; Am Watercolor Soc, ann & traveling, 71, 76, 77 & 81; Can Soc Painters Watercolour, Toronto, 76 & 77; BC Through the Eyes of Its Artists, Govt BC, traveling Europe, 79. *Pos:* Bd dir, Art Gallery Greater Victoria, BC, 63-70, pres, bd dir, 69-70; bd dir, Emily Carr Col Art & Design, 80-82. *Teaching:* Instr, Studios in Victoria, BC, 65-75. *Awards:* First Prize, Vancouver Island Ann, 62; Royal Jubilee Medal, Can, 77. *Bibliog:* Margaret Harold (auth), Brian Travers-Smith, Prize-Winning Watercolors, 63; R Ashwell (auth), Brian Travers-Smith, Westworld Mag, 4/78. *Mem:* Am Watercolor Soc; Allied Artists Am (hon). *Media:* Watercolor

TRAVIS, DAVID B
CURATOR, HISTORIAN
b Omaha, Nebr, Jan 31, 1948. *Study:* Univ of Chicago, BA (art hist), Smithsonian Inst, res fel, 72. *Collection Arranged:* Exhibitions of photography, Art Inst of Chicago, 73-; Starting with Atget (auth, catalog), 77; Photographs from the Andre Jammes Collection: Niepce to Atget (ed, catalog), 77; Photography Rediscovered: American Photographs 1900-1930 (auth, catalog), 79; Photographs in Chicago Collections (auth, catalog), 82. *Pos:* Asst cur photog, Art Inst of Chicago, 74-77, assoc cur photog, 77-78, cur photog, 79-. *Teaching:* Lectr hist of photog, Sch of the Art Inst of Chicago, 74. *Mailing Add:* Art Institute Chicago Michigan Ave and Adams St Chicago IL 60603

TRAYLOR, ANGELIKA
STAINED GLASS ARTIST
b Munich, Ger, Aug 24, 1942; US citizen. *Study:* Private Handelsschule Morawetz, Munich, WGer, 58; studied with Gil Reynolds & Tim McCreight. *Work:* Holmes Regional Med Ctr, Melbourne, Fla, 98; White House Christmas Ornament Collection, Washington, DC, 93 & 97; William Childs Hospice House, Palm Bay, Fla; Palm Bay Hospital, Palm Bay, Fla; Heartcenter of Health First, Melbourne, Fla. *Comn:* White House Christmas Ornament Collection, 93 & 97; Holmes Regional Med Ctr, Melbourne, Fla, 98; William Childs Hospice House, Palm Bay, Fla; and many others. *Exhib:* Fla Craftsmen Exhibit, 81, 83, 86, 87, 89 & 93; Ann Assoc Exhib, Stained Glass Asn Am, 84, 85, 89, 90, 91 & 94; Vitraux des USA, Chartes, France, 85; Ann Assoc Exhib, Stained Glass Asn Am, Nora Eckles Harrison Mus, Logan, Utah, 89; Artists Forum Ann Exhib, Brevard Art Ctr & Mus, Melbourne, Fla, 90, 91, 93 & 96. *Awards:* 2nd Place, Non-figurative Composition, Vitraux des USA, 85; Best of Show, Stained Glass Asn Am, 89; Historic Woman of Brevard, Brevard Cult Alliance, 91; One of 200 Best Craftsmen, Early Am Life Mag, 94, 95 & 97; and others. *Bibliog:* Melbourne Times, 94; The Orbiter, 96; Glass Collector's Digest, 96; Women's Day Mag, 99; Space Coast Press, 99; Sterling Publ, 00; Creative Stained Glass, Lark Books, 04; Florida Today, 2006; Florida Today, 2007; Geometry in Glass, Options Pub, 2008. *Mem:* Stained Glass Asn Am; Nat League Am Pen Women; Fla Craftsmen; Pa Guild of Craftsmen. *Media:* Stained Glass. *Dealer:* Dennison-Moran Gallery Naples FL; Nancy Markoe Gallery St Petersburg Beach Fla. *Mailing Add:* 100 Poinciana Dr Indian Harbor Beach FL 32937

TRAYNOR, JOHN C
PAINTER
b Morristown, NJ, 1961. *Study:* Paier Coll Art, New Haven, Conn, 77-80; Art Students League, NY; studied with Jerome Cox, Carol Jones & Frank Mason. *Work:* Sony Music Corp; Mural, Ironbound Cult Art Ctr, NJ. *Exhib:* Salmagundi Club, NY; Hudson Valley Art Asn; Noroton Gallery, Darien, Conn; many others 1984-2000; Copley Soc, 2001. *Awards:* Frank DuMond Award, Best Light & Atmospheric effect painting, Hudson Valley Asn; Frederick S Church Award, Salmagundi Club, NY; Award for Excellence, Franklin Mint. *Mem:* Salmagundi Club, NY; Copley Soc, Boston, Mass; Hudson Valley Art Asn; Nat Soc Mural Painters, NY. *Media:* Acrylic, Oil. *Specialty:* Landscapes, Still lifes, figures & portraits. *Dealer:* Carmel Fine Art Dolores & 6th Camel by the Sea Ca; The Christina Gallery 32 N Water St Edgartown Ma 02539; Haley & Steele Gallery 162 Newbury St 2nd Fl Boston Ma 02116; JM Stringer Gallery of Fine Art 21 Claremont Rd Bernardsville NJ 07924; JM Stringer Gallery of Fine Art 3465 Ocean Dr Vero Beach Fl; The Harison Gallery 39 Spring St Williamstown MA 01267; Lily Pad Gallery 124 Bay St Watch Hill RI 02891; Principle Gallery 125 Meeting St Charleston SC 29401; Whistle Pik Galleries 425 E Main St Fredericksburg TX 78624

TRECARTIN, RYAN
FILMMAKER
b Webster, Tex, 1981. *Study:* RI Sch Design, BFA, 2004. *Exhib:* Solo exhibs, I Smell Pregnant, QED, Los Angeles, Calif, 2006, Big Room Now, Crane Arts, Philadelphia, 2007; Group exhibs, Sympathetic Magic, 2005, Schindler House, Los Angeles, 2006, Whitney Biennial: Day for Night, Whitney Mus Am Art, NY, 2006, Metro Pictures, The Moore Space, Miami, 2006, USA Today, Royal Acad Arts, Burlington Gardens, London, 2006, Action Adventure, Canada Gallery, New York, 2006, Between Two Deaths, ZKM Karlsruhe, Ger, 2007, La Triennale di Milano, TIMER, Milan, 2007, 55th Int Art Exhib Biennale, Venice, 2013; Performances, Alternative Theatre Endings (with The Experimental People Band), New York Underground Film Festival, 2005, Nothing Wrong with August (with The Experimental People Band), Natural Disaster, New Orleans, 2005; Screenings, A Family Finds Entertainment, NY Underground Film Festival, 2005-2006, Big Muddy Film Festival, S Ill Univ, 2005, Chicago Underground Film Festival, 2005, Vox Pouli Gallery, Philadelphia, 2006, Madison Mus Contemp Art, Wis, 2006, Walker Art Ctr, Minneapolis, 2007; Valentine's Day Girl, Smack Mellon, Brooklyn, NY, 2005; Tommy Chat Just Emailed Me, The Getty Ctr, Los Angeles, 2006. *Awards:* Wolgin Fine Arts Prize, Temple Univ Tyler Sch Art, 2009; Pew Ctr for Arts Fel, 2009. *Dealer:* New Galerie Paris. *Mailing Add:* c/o Elizabeth Dee Gallery 545 W 20th St New York NY 10011

TRECHSEL, GAIL ANDREWS
DIRECTOR
b Washington, DC, Nov 4, 1953. *Study:* Coll William & Mary, Va, BA, 74; Cooperstown Grad Prog, NY, MA (mus studies), 76; Winterthur Summer Inst, 77; Attingham Summer Sch, 81. *Collection Arranged:* Black Belt to Hill Co: Ala Quilts, Birmingham Mus Art, 81; Alabama Quilts & Southern Quilts: A New View, Hunter Mus Art, 90. *Pos:* Nat Endowment Humanities Intern, Colonial Williamsburg, Va, 75-76; cur decorative arts, Birmingham Mus Art, Ala, 76-82, asst dir, 83-85, actg dir, 91-92, asst to dir, 92-. *Teaching:* Adj prof, Univ Ala, Birmingham, 83-87, dir, 96-. *Awards:* Nat Endowment Arts Fel, 86. *Publ:* Coauth, Index to American Coverlet Weavers, Univ Va Press, 78; auth, Lamprecht collection of cast iron art, 2/83 & Beeson collection of wedgwood in Birmingham Museum of Art, 6/83, Mag Antiques; Southern Quilts: A New View, EPM Press; contribr, Pictured in My Mind: Contemporary Self-Taught Art, Birmingham Mus Art, 96. *Mailing Add:* Birmingham Mus Art 2000 8th Ave Birmingham AL 35203-2278

TRECKER, STANLEY MATTHEW MATTHEW
ART COLLEGE PRESIDENT
b Manning, Iowa, July 15, 1944. *Study:* Ind Univ, Bloomington, MBA, 68; Columbia Col, Chicago, BA, 75; Sch Art Inst Chicago, MFA, 78. *Work:* Art Inst Chicago; George Eastman House. *Exhib:* Arles Festival, France, 75; Calif Inst Fine Arts, Valencia, 77; Moming Gallery, Chicago, 78; ARC Gallery, Chicago, 78; Art Inst Chicago, 78; Artist Coop, Toronto, Can, 79. *Pos:* Cur, Moming Gallery, Chicago, 77-80; dir, Photog Resource Ctr, Boston, 80-91; pres, Art Inst Boston, 92-. *Teaching:* Instr photog, Columbia Col, Chicago, 78-80. *Awards:* Ill Art Coun Grant, 79; Artists' Found Proj Grant, 83. *Mem:* Soc Photog Educators (bd dir, 83-87); Coll Art Asn. *Media:* Photography. *Mailing Add:* c/o Art Inst Boston 700 Beacon St Boston MA 02215

TREDENNICK, DOROTHY W
EDUCATOR, LECTURER
b Bristol, Conn, Oct 5, 1914. *Study:* Norwich Art Sch, 32-34; Berea Coll, AB, 46, Univ Mich, Gen Educ Bd fel, MA (art hist), 51. *Exhib:* Art by Women's Hands Berta Arts Coun. *Pos:* Assoc dir, Slater Mem Mus, 39-43. *Teaching:* Instr art, Norwich Art Sch, 33-34; prof art hist & humanities, Berea Col, 46-70, Morris Belknap prof art, 70-87, co-chmn dept art, 54-70, teaching consult, 85-87; lectr, US & Asia; Elderhostel Instr, 87-94. *Awards:* Seabury Award for Excellence in Teaching, Berea Col, 62; Fulbright Award, Chinese Civilization, 63; Nat Endowment Humanities Grant, Univ Calif, 77; Fel, Ctr Ecumenical & Cult Studies, St John's, Minn, 83-84. *Mem:* Southern Humanities Conf; Asn Gen & Liberal Studies; Interfaith Task Force for Peace; Berea Arts Coun. *Media:* Watercolor. *Publ:* Co-auth, This is Our Best, 55; Kress Study Collection, 61; auth, Living by Design, 63; Art & The Protestant Church Today, 66; Design for Living, 68; Two Worlds Meet: The Religious Dimensions of Art, 84

TREISTER, KENNETH
PAINTER, SCULPTOR, ARCHITECT
b New York, NY, Mar 5, 1930. *Study:* Univ Miami; Univ Fla, BArch, 53. *Hon Degrees:* Fel, Am Inst Architects; adj prof Archit, Univ Fla, Miami; Lifetime Achievement Award, AIA Miami. *Work:* Norton Gallery, Palm Beach, Fla; Miami Mus Mod Art, Fla; Fla Supreme Ct, Tallahassee; Bass Mus Art, Miami Beach, Fla; Lowe Art Mus, Coral Gables, Fla; Holocaust Memorial, Miami Beach, Fla; Miller Center Contemp Jewish Studies, Univ Miami, Bok Tower, Lake Wales, Fla; Polk Mus Art, Lakeland, Fla; Skirball Mus, Hebrew Union Coll, Cincinnati, Ohio. *Comn:* Family of God (limited ed bronze menorahs), 69 & six bronze plaques depicting hist of Jews, United Jewish Appeal; ten paintings depicting 4,000 yr hist of Jews, Temple Israel, Miami; Eternal Light, Great Miami Rabbinical Asn, 4/86; Niel Schiff Mem Bust, Univ Miami, 4/86; In Memory of the Six Million (sculpture), Mem Holocaust City of Miami, 4/86; bronze 30' sculpture, Dove of Peace, Temple Emanu-el, Miami Beach, Fla; produced 4 documentaries for TV, Holocaust Mem, Maya, Easter Island, Charleston, SC. *Exhib:* Greenwich Gallery, NY; Mus Fine Arts, Columbus, Ga; Lowe Art Gallery, Coral Gables, Fla; Contemp Art Mus, Houston, Tex; High Mus, Atlanta, Ga; Sirball Mus, Ohio; Metrop Mus Art, Coral Gables, Fla; Bass Mus Art, Miami Beach, Fla; Love Art Mus, Univ Miami; Harn Mus, Univ Fla; Polk Mus Art, Lackland, Fla; Polk State Coll, Winter Haven, Fla. *Pos:* fellow, American Inst Architecture. *Teaching:* Guest lectr art & archit, Mass Inst Technol, Univ Syracuse, Univ Pa, Fla Atlantic Univ, Dade Jr Col/South Campus, Univ Miami, Univ Fla, Jewish Fedn, Univ Chile & Qinghua Univ, Beijing, China, UNESCO Conf, Auburn Univ, Md Archit Bd & New Worlds Sch of the Arts; adj prof archit, Univ Fla & Univ Miami. *Awards:* First Prize for Four Conversations (sculpture), Nat Ceramic Exhib, Lowe Art Gallery, 53; Lifetime Achievement award & Silver medal, AIA, Miami, Fla, Gold medal, Fla, 2013. *Mem:* Blue Dome Soc, Miami; Fla Sculptural Soc; Southern Asn Sculptors; Real Academia de Belles Arts de Sant Jorge, Barcelona, Spain. *Media:* Bronze sculpture, Oil painting. *Publ:* Contribr, Fla Architecture (40th edition), Nat Mall Monitor, 10/81, FDQ-Design South, 5/85, Interiors, 12/85 & Fla Municipal Record, 2/86; A Sculpture of Love and Anguish, 93; auth, A Sculpture of Love and Anguish, 97; auth, Habaneros, 99; auth, Chapel of Light, 2001; auth, Cherubim & Palm Trees, The Judaic Art of Temple Emanu-el; auth, Havana Forever, A Pictorial & Cultural History of An Unforgettable City; auth, China Architecture: Urban Planning and Landscape Design; auth, Havau Forever, Univ Press, Fla, 2009; Maya Architecture, Temples in the Sky, Univ Press, Fla, 2013; Bok Tower Gardens, America's Taj Mahal, Rizzoli Rizzoli, 2013; Easter Island's Silent Sentinels, The Sculpture and Architecture of Rapa Nui, Univ NMex Press, 2013. *Mailing Add:* 1600 Island Way Winter Haven FL 33884-3606

TREITLER, RHODA CHAPRACK
PAINTER
b New York, NY. *Study:* Bennington Col, AB; Artists in America, studied with Paul Feeley, Moselsio, Eugene Goosen & Jerry Okimoto; Adelphi Univ, grad study in psychology. *Work:* Equitable Life, NY; private and corp collections. *Exhib:* First Open Exhib, Nassau Co Mus Fine Arts, Roslyn, NY, 88; Ten Bennington Graduates Exhib, Huntington Libr, NY, 88; Marbella Gallery, NY, 89; The Tree An Artist's Gift, Bergen Mus Art & Sci, NJ, 91; Gallery 395 Juried Show, NY, 94; Hutchins Gallery, CW Post Col, 1983, 1984, 1990; Federal Bldg, NY, 1982-1994; Concordia Gallery, NY, 1992; Adelphi Univ, 1993; Drake Co Ctr for the Arts, Ohio, 1993; Marcella Geltman Gallery, Art Center, NJ, 1995; Gallery Art 54, Soho, NY, 1997; New World Art Ctr,

Soho, NY, 1998-1999; Gallery, Boynton Beach, Fla, 1998; Wisser Mem Libr, NY Inst Tech, 1998; Chelsea Ctr for Cult Arts, NY, 1996-99; Atelier 14, NY, 2000; Elizabeth Found, NY, 2001; The Banana Factory, Bethlehem, Pa, 2002; Binney & Smith Gallery, 2002; NAWA Gallery, 2003; 88 Greenwich Street, NY, 2004; The Karpeles Libr Mus, 2006; Port of Call Gallery, Warwick, NY, 2006; Salmagundi Club, New York, 2009. *Pos:* Exec bd, Nat Asn Women Artists, 80- & Vaali, 96-98; pres, Aquarelle Watercolor Group, Long Island, 84-86; adv bd, Coun Celebration Arts, Nassau County Mus Fine Arts 84-86; juror, Long Island Arts League, 88-89. *Awards:* Nat League Am Pen Women Award, 97; Chelsea Ctr Peacock Showcase Award, 98; Sarah Winston Mem Award, 2002. *Mem:* Nat Asn Women Artists; Aquarelle Watercolor Group Long Island. *Media:* Watercolors, Acrylics on Canvas. *Mailing Add:* 81 Finch Dr Roslyn NY 11576

TREJOS, CHARLOTTE (CARLOTA) MARIE
PAINTER
b Trout Lake, Mich, Jul 5, 1920. *Study:* Hawthorne Christian Col, Calf, MA, 1975; No Light Art Sch, Cincinnati, Ohio, 1998-99. *Work:* Mus of Latin Am Art, Long Branch, Calif; Nat Mus of Women in the Arts, Washington, DC. *Comn:* Floral painting - Oil, BA Price, Bay City, 1986; Ukelele with Hibiscus, Eugenia Carpenter, Hemet, Calif, 1990. *Exhib:* So Bay Regional Art Show, Carson, Calif, 1980-87; Several Firsts, Redondo Beach Juried Art Show, Calif, 1985; Mus of Latin Am, Long Branch, Calif, 1986; Nat Mus of Women in Art, Washington, DC, 1990. *Awards:* Third prize, Am Legion, Prescott, Va, 2003. *Mem:* Nat Mus of Women in Arts, 10 yrs; Mus of Latin Am Art, 12 yrs. *Media:* Acrylic, Oil. *Mailing Add:* 3872 Roxbury Dr Hemet CA 92545

TREMBLAY, JOHN
PAINTER
b Mass, 1966. *Work:* Cabinet des Estampes du Musee d'Art et d'Histoire, Geneva, Switz; Collection Fonds National d'Art Contemporain, Puteaux, France; Fogg Art Mus, Harvard Univ; FRAC Poitou-Charentes, Angouleme, France. *Exhib:* Solo exhibs include Art Basel 25'94, Switzerland, 1994, Art & Public, Geneva, 1995, Sandra Gering Gallery, NY City, 1996, 1998, 1999, Galerie Jousse-Seguin, Paris, 1997, Richard Telles Fine Art, Los Angeles, 2000, Galerie Francesca Pia, Bern, Switzerland, 2001, 2002, Paula Cooper Gallery, NY City, 2003, 2005, Velan Ctr Fro Contemp Art, Turin, Italy, 2004, Emon Gallery, Tokyo, 2006, Paik Hae Young Gallery, Seoul Korea, 2007, Kunstmuseum, St Gallen, Switz, 2009, Gallery Side 2, Tokyo, Japan, 2009; group exhibs include Walter Bar, NY City, 1992; John Gibson Gallery, NY, 1993; Andrea Rosen Gallery, NY, 1994; Sandra Gering Gallery, NY City, 1995, 2001; Margarete Roeder Gallery, NY City, 1996; Thomas Healy Gallery, NY City, 1997; Richard Telles Fine Art, Los Angeles, 1999; Team Gallery, Ny City, 2000; Paula Cooper Gallery, NY City, 2002, 2008; Artists Space, NY City, 2002; Galeria Javier Lopez, Madrid, 2003; Anton Kern Gallery, NY City, 2003; Swiss Inst, NY City, 2004; Biennale d'art contemporain de Lyon, 2005; Salander-O'Reilly Galleries, 2006; Painting as Fact-Fact as Fiction, de Pury & Luxembourg, 2007; Centre d'art, la Chapelle Jenne d' art, Thouars, France, 2008; Deformalismes, Praza-Delavallade, Paris, France, 2008; I am by Birth a Genevese, Geneva & London, 2009; Portrait de l'artiste en motocycliste, Magasin, Ctr Nat d'Art Contemp n de Grenoble, France, 2009; Pictures About Pictures, Mumok, Vienna, Austria, 2010. *Bibliog:* Ken Johnson (auth), Painted World, NY Times, 11/11/2005; Konrad Bitterli (auth), rev, Fur Moderne Kunst Nurnberg, 86-87, 2009. *Media:* Acrylic. Mixed Media. *Dealer:* Galerie Francesca Pia Limmatstrasse 275 8005 Zurich Switzerland; Rago Arts and Auction Ctr 333 N Main St Lambertville NJ 08530; Galerie Almine Rech 19 rue de Saintonge 75003 Paris France; World House Editions 26 Wheeler Rd Middlebury CT 06762; Paula Cooper Gallery 534 W 21st St New York, 10011. *Mailing Add:* c/o Paula Cooper Gallery 534 W 21st St New York NY 10011

TRENTON, PATRICIA JEAN
HISTORIAN
b Los Angeles, Calif, 1927. *Study:* Univ Calif, Berkeley & Los Angeles, BA, MA (art hist), PhD, 80. *Exhib:* The Rocky Mountains: A Vision for Artists in the Nineteenth Century (auth, catalog), Buffalo Bill Hist Ctr, Cody, Wyo, 83; Native Faces: Indian Cultures in Am Art (coauth, catalog), Southwest Mus, Los Angeles, 84; California Light 1900-1930 (coauth, catalog), Laguna Art Mus, Laguna Beach, 90; Independent Spirits: Women Painters of the Am West 1890-1945 (with catalog), Autry Mus Western Heritage, Los Angeles, 95-97; Not-So-Still-Life, San Jose Mus Art, 2004. *Pos:* Cur Am art, Denver Art Mus, Colo, 69-74; art dir, The Los Angeles Athletic Club, 1982-2007. *Awards:* Nat Am Publ Award in Humanities, 83; Nat Hon Merit, Am Asn Mus, 84; Humanities Award, Nat Am Publ, 83; Western Heritage Wrangler Award, Nat Cowboy Hall of Fame & Heritage Ctr Outstanding Art Book, 95; Caroline Bancroft Award for Outstanding Book on Western Art, 97. *Bibliog:* Joseph Kleitsch (auth), A Kaleidoscope of Color, Irvine Mus, 2007. *Mem:* Coll Art Asn. *Res:* Feminist research. *Publ:* Coauth, The Rocky Mountains: A Vision for Artists in the Nineteenth Century, Univ Okla Press, Norman, 83; Native Faces: Indian Cultures in American Art, Southwest Mus in Asn with LAACO Ltd, 84; Native Americans: Five Centuries of Changing Images, Harry N Abrams Publ, 89; California Light, Laguna Art Mus, 90; The Not-So-Still-Life: a Century of California Painting and Sculpture, Univ Calif Press, 2004. *Mailing Add:* 10112 Empyrean No 303 Los Angeles CA 90067

TRESS, ARTHUR
PHOTOGRAPHER
b Brooklyn, NY, Nov 24, 1940. *Study:* Bard Col, NY, BA, 62. *Work:* Metrop Mus Art, NY; San Francisco Mus Mod Art; Los Angeles Co Mus Art; Art Inst Chicago; Ctr Nat D'Art Cult Georges Pompidou, Paris, France. *Exhib:* Talisman (auth, catalog), Mus Mod Art, Oxford, Eng, 86; Fish Tank Sonata, Santa Barbara Contemp Arts Forum, Calif, 94; Warlitzen Trilogy, Ctr Photog, Tucson, 95; Fantastic Voyage, Singapore Mus Art, 95; Requiem for a Paperweight, Univ Art Mus, Calif State Univ, Long Beach, 95; Retrospective, Taipei Mus Art, Taiwan, 97. *Bibliog:* A D Coleman (auth), A Grotesque in Photography, Summit Books, 77; Allen Ellenzweig (auth), Homoerotic Photograph, Columbia Univ Press, 92. *Publ:* Auth, Dream Collection, Avon Publ, 72; Theater of the Mind, Morgan & Morgan, 76; Facing Up, St Martin's Press, 80; Arthur Tress, Stemmle, 95. *Mailing Add:* 2705 Marlborough Ln Cambria CA 93428

TRIBE, KERRY
VIDEO ARTIST
b Boston, Mass, 1973. *Study:* Brown Univ, Providence, BA, 1997; Univ Calif, Los Angeles, MFA, 2002. *Exhib:* Solo exhibs, MWMWM Gallery, Brooklyn, 1998, Los Angeles Contemp Exhibs, 2003, SOuthern Exposure, San Francisco, 2005, Kunstlerhaus Bethanien, Berlin, 2006, Galerie Maisonneuve, Basel, 2007; Over Sight, Ctr for Curatorial Studies, Bard Coll, NY, 2005; Moment Making, Artspace, Auckland, New Zealand, 2007; Memory is Your Image of Perfection, Mus Contemp Art, San Diego, 2008; Closer, Beruit Art Ctr, Beruit, 2009; Whitney Biennial, Whitney Mus Am Art, New York, 2010. *Awards:* Artists Resource for Completion Grant, Durfee Found, 2003; Louis Comfort Tiffany Found Grant, 2005; Mundheim Fel, Am Acad in Berlin, 2005. *Bibliog:* Holly Willis (auth), In the Fast Lane, Los Angeles Weekly, 11/2004; Luke Heighton (auth), History Will Repeat Itself: Strategies of Re-Enactment in Contemporary Art, ArtReview, 2/2008; Holland Cotter (auth), At a Biennial On a Budget, Tweaking And Provoking, NY Times, 2/26/2010. *Mailing Add:* MAK Center 835 N Kings Rd West Hollywood CA 90069

TRIBE, LEE
SCULPTOR, INSTRUCTOR
b Danbury, Eng, Oct 3, 1945; arrived in US, 1977. *Study:* St Martins, London, BA (sculpture; 1st class honors), 1974, advanced course certification, 1975; Birmingham Sch Art, MA (sculpture), 1977; NY Studio Sch, Barnett Newman Scholar. *Work:* Storm King Sculpture Ctr, NY; Neuberger Mus Art; Arts Coun Great Britain; Weatherspoon Art Gallery, NC; Am Ornamental Metals Mus, Memphis, Tenn; City of Higashi, Hiroshima, Japan; Ctr Arts, Vero Beach, Fla; Madelein Carter Gallery, Boston. *Exhib:* Solo exhibs include Robert Steele Gallery, NY, JJ Brookings, Calif, Robert Morrison Gallery, NY, Victoria Monroe Gallery, NY; group exhibs include Weatherspoon Art Gallery, NC; Storm King Sculpture Ctr, NY; Arts Council Great Britain; Invitational Exhib Visual Arts, AAAL, New York, 2008. *Pos:* MFA seminar prof, City Univ New York, 2002. *Teaching:* prof, New York Studio Sch, 1980-2012; teacher, Columbia Univ, New York, 1980-81, Pratt Inst, Brooklyn, 1998-99; head sculpture dept, Bennington Coll, Vt, 1985-89; vis artist, Manchester Univ, Eng, 1992, Univ NC, Greensboro, 2003. *Awards:* Barnett Newman Scholar, 1977-78; Guggenheim Fel, 1987-88; Ingram Merrill Fel, 1982-83; Pollock Krasner Found Fel, 1991; Creative Capital Found Grant, 2008; Corange Ltd Fel; Ain award, Arts Coun Great Britain. *Bibliog:* Sculpture Featured in: Reginald Hudlin (dir), Boomerang (movie with Eddie Murphy), Alan Burns (dir), Something in Common (movie with Mary Tyler Moore); Judy Collischan (auth), Welded Sculpture of the Twentieth Century, Hudson Hill Press, NY, 2000; Ken Johnson (auth), Testing the Durability of Wedling as a Creative Form, NY Times, 2000; Robert Taplin (auth), Lee Tribe at Robert Steele, Art in Am, 11/2001; Mario Naves (auth), Gnarled Steel that Burlesques the Macho, New York Observer, 4/30/2001, Herculean Tribe Beats His Chest, 2002. *Mem:* Nat Acad. *Media:* Welded Steel, Charcoal on Paper. *Interests:* African art. *Publ:* Portfolio, The Paris Review (drawings), No 131, pp 134-140, 94. *Mailing Add:* 155 Wooster St Apt 7F New York NY 10012

TRIBE, MARK
VIDEO ARTIST, EDUCATOR
b San Francisco, Calif, 1966. *Study:* Brown Univ, Providence, BA (magna cum laude), 1990; Univ Calif, San Diego, MFA, 1994. *Exhib:* Day Jobs, New Langton Arts, San Francisco, 2002; Perpetual Art Machine: Video Art in the Age of the Internet, Chelsea Art Mus, New York, 2007; Democracy in America: The National Campaign, Park Avenue Armory, New York, 2008; Paradox Now, Arlington Arts Ctr, Va, 2009; DeCordova Biennial, DeCordova Mus & Sculpture Park, Mass, 2010. *Pos:* Designer, Pixelpark GmbH, Berlin, Ger, 1995; co-founder & chmn, StockObjects, New York, 1997-2000; founder & exec dir, Rhizome.org, New York, 1996-2003; adv bd, The Alternative Mus, New York, 2000-03, Calif Coll Arts & Crafts, San Francisco, 2001-03, Inst for Archit & Urban Studies, New York, 2002-; bd trustees, New Mus Contemp Art, New York, 2003-05. *Teaching:* Instr, Anderson Ranch Arts Ctr, Aspen, Colo, 2002 & 2004; dir art & technol, Sch Arts, Columbia Univ, New York, 2003-05; asst prof mod cult & media studies, Brown Univ, Providence, RI, 2005-. *Awards:* Creative Capital Grant, 2008; NY Found Arts Fel, 2009. *Bibliog:* Scarlet Cheng (auth), A Human Dimension to New Media, Los Angeles Times, 12/16/2001; Gabe Friedman (auth), To Err is Creative in Net Art, Wird Mag, 5/12/2003; Leora Falk (auth) Times, Faces Change; Struggle Remains, Chicago Tribune, 7/31/2007; Holland Cotter (auth), With Politics In The Air a Freedom Free-For-All Comes to Town, NY Times, 9/22/2008; Michael O'Sullivan (auth), Blurring the LIne Between Art and Truth, Washington Post, 8/7/2009. *Publ:* Coauth, New Media Art, Taschen, 2006; auth, The Port Huron Project: Reenactments of New Left Protest Speeches, Edizioni Charta, 2010. *Mailing Add:* 80 Perry St Apt 1E New York NY 10014

TRIBUSH, BRENDA
PAINTER, INSTRUCTOR
b New York, NY, Nov 5, 1939. *Study:* AAS, Fashion Inst Tech, NY; Adelphi Univ, NY, BA, 1981, MA, 1983; studied with Isaac Soyer & Ruben Tam, Brooklyn Mus of Art, NY; NY Art Students League, studied with Ernest Crichlow. *Exhib:* Ruth Harely Univ Ctr Gallery, Garden City, NY, 83; Union League Club, NY, 92; Pen & Brush Club, NY, 95; Louisa Melrose Gallery, Holicong, Pa, 99; Group Exhib: Butler Inst Am Art, Ohio; John Brown Univ, Alaska; Huntsville Mus Art, Ala; Dansville Mus Art, Va; Mus Tex Tech Univ; Tex A&M Univ; Peter Paul Fortress Mus; Russia, Nassau County Mus Fine Arts, NY; Allied Artist Am, NY, 1988-2006; Pastel Soc Am, NY, 87-2006; Centre Cultural, France, 2002-05 & 2006; Europastel, Italy, 2003; Xi'an Acad Fine Arts, China, 1997; Nat Taiwan Arts Center, Taiwan, 2007. *Collection Arranged:* Union League Club; DuPont Pharmaceutical Co. *Pos:* Juror, Alliance Queens Artist,

NY, 1994, Annual Fine Arts Show, Long Beach, NY, 2001 & 02. *Teaching:* instr, pvt classes, Studio Manhattan, NY & Long Island Arts Coun, Freeport, NY, 1993 & 94; instr workshop, Terence Cardinal Cooke Health Ctr, NY, 2003. *Awards:* William Alfred White Award, Salmagundi Club, NY & Jane Impastatd Award, 2002; Klimberger Meml Award, Pastel Soc Am, 2001; Pastel J Award, 2004. *Mem:* Allied Artists Am (bd dir, currently); NY Artists Equity (vpres); Pastel Soc Am (bd dir, currently); Salmagundi Club (lib comt). *Media:* Pastels. *Publ:* auth, Best of Pastels 2, 1998; Allied Artists Am, 2001; Butler Inst Am Art, Am Art Mag, 2001; Jour Pastello Contemporano en Europa, 2003; L'Art du Pastel, 2005; Taiwan Int Pastel Artists, 2007. *Mailing Add:* 41 Union Sq W Studio #711 New York NY 10003

TRIEFF, SELINA
PAINTER, INSTRUCTOR
b Brooklyn, NY, Jan 7, 1934. *Study:* Art Students League, study with Morris Kantor; Hans Hofmann Sch, study with Hofmann; Brooklyn Col, BA, study with Rothko & Reinhardt, 55. *Work:* Brooklyn Mus; NY Pub Libr; Inst for Human Develop; Prudential Life Insurance Co; Bayonne Jewish Ctr; Smite Mus, Norte Dame Univ; and others. *Comn:* Lithograph, Bayonne Jewish Ctr. *Exhib:* Contemp Am Figure Painting, Wadsworth Atheneum, 64; Work on Paper, Brooklyn Mus, 75; Butler Inst Ann, 77; Artes Gallery, Olso & Cassandra Gallery, Orobak, Norway, 84; Graham Modern Gallery, 86, 87 & 88; Ruth Bachofner Gallery, Santa Monica, 87, 90, 92 & 94; Katharina Rich Perlow Gallery, NY, 91, 93 & 94; Berta Walker Gallery, Provincetown, 92-93; and others. *Teaching:* Instr drawing, New York Inst of Technol, 75-; vis artist painting, Notre Dame Univ, Ind, 76; instr painting, New York Studio Sch, formerly; instr painting, Pratt Inst, formerly, Nat Acad Design. *Awards:* Second Prize, Goddard Coll Ann, 76; Purchase Prize, View from the Ctr, Bayonne Community Ctr, 78; Thomas B Clarke Prize, Nat Acad Design, 79; and others. *Bibliog:* Corinne Robins (auth), Selina Trieff, Arts, 78; Hilton Kramer (auth), article, New York Times, 82; Maureen Mullarky (auth), article, 84 & Joan Marter (auth), article, 6/86, Arts Mag; John Rusgell, New York Times; Vivian Raynol, New York Times. *Mem:* Women in the Arts; Womens Caucus Art; Coll Art Asn. *Media:* Oil, Charcoal. *Mailing Add:* c/o Ruth Bachofner Gallery 2525 Michigan Ave G2 Santa Monica CA 90404

TRIMM, H WAYNE
ILLUSTRATOR, PAINTER
b Albany, NY, Aug 16, 1922. *Study:* Cornell Univ, 40; Augustana Col, BS, 48; Kans State Univ, 49; Coll Forestry, Syracuse Univ, MS, 53. *Comn:* Dioramas, Springfield Mus Art; three eColl dioramas, Augustana Col, 67; World Wildlife Fund, Int Stamps for Congo, Bolivia, Bangladesh, 74; mural, Alley Pond Environ Ctr, Douglaston, NY, 80; mural of summer pond, 5 Rivers Environ Educ Ctr, Delmar, NY; and others. *Exhib:* Am Bird Artists Traveling Exhib, Audubon Artists; Joslyn Mus Art; Buffalo Mus Sci; Solo exhib, Remington Mus; SAA Show, San Francisco Acad Arts & Sci; Philadelphia Mus Art; and others. *Pos:* Art dir, Conservationist Mag, Div Educ Serv, NY State Dept Environ Conserv, 53-, sr ed, 53-73; ed, Outdoor Communicator Mag, formerly; vpres, Soc Animal Artists, NY, The Catasus (animal art), currently; ed, Catasus, Jour Soc Animal Artists, currently; leader Fed Duck Stamp workshops, 96, 97, 98; judge Fed Duck Stamp Competition, Washington, DC. *Teaching:* Lectr conserv & wildlife painting, currently; instr nature & sci illus, State Univ NY, Albany & Col St Rose, Nat Wildlife Fedn Summits, Sagamore Inst, Raguette Lake, New York, Adirondack Ctr Arts, Blue Mt Lake, New York, Asa Wright Ctr, Trinidad; Asa Wright Nature Ctr, 81; Fed Duck Stamp Workshop, Old Forge, NY; Outdoor World for Learning, Hoosick Falls, NY; art groups in Albany & Troy, NY; Peconic Dunes Environ Ctr, Peconic, NY. *Awards:* The Trad Award, NY State Dept Environmental Conservationist; The Golden Award, NYSOEA; Artist of the Year 1988, WNPE/WNPI, Watertown, NY; Purchase Award, Blauveld Mus. *Bibliog:* Glenn Goff (interviewer), Cabin Country, WNPE-TV, 87. *Mem:* Columbia Co Arts & Crafts; Soc Animal Artists (vpres); hon mem Tuscarora Indian Tribe; Am Ornithologists Union; Guild Nat Sci Illusr. *Media:* Watercolor, Acrylic, Oil; Marble, Wood. *Publ:* Illustr, The Guild Handbook of Scientific Illustration, Smithsonian Inst; Illustrators Annual--Nature Drawing, No 27 & Nature Sketching, Claire Leslie Walker; auth, Dr Phyllis Busch, Back Yard Satariis. *Mailing Add:* 64 High St Hoosick Falls NY 12090

TRIPLETT, RICHARD
ART DEALER, CONSULTANT
b Lenoir, NC. *Study:* Catawba Col, BA. *Pos:* Vpres, Louis Newman Galleries, Beverly Hills, Calif, 5/1977-11/1999; mgr, Anderson Galleries, Beverly Hills, Calif, 9/2003-3/2008; dir, Richard Triplett Fine Arts, West Hollywood, Calif, 4/2008-2013, Lenoir, NC, 2013. *Mem:* Los Angeles Co Mus Art; Caldwell Arts Coun; History Mus Art. *Specialty:* 20th Century Am & Comtemp. *Collection:* Paul Cadmus, David Aronson, Enrico Donati, Otto & Gertrude Natzler, Horace Bristol, Donald De Lue, Edith Carter, 20th Century Am & Contemp. *Mailing Add:* 318 Main St NW #607 Lenoir NC 28645

TRIPP, JAN PETER
PAINTER, PRINTMAKER
b Oberstdorf, Bavaria, Ger, May 15, 1945. *Study:* Acad Art, Stuttgart, sculpture, 68; Acad Art, Vienna, Austria, painting, 69-73; Masters class at Rudolf Hausner. *Work:* Staatsgalerie, Stuttgart, Ger; Kunsthalle, Hamburg, Ger; Albertina, Vienna, Austria; Frac, Strasbourg, France. *Exhib:* Graphic Biennales, Krakow, Ljubljana, Segovia, Bradford & Frechen, 72-90; 7 Ger Realists, Triennale, New Delhi, India, 78; 20 Ger Painters & Drawers, Warzowa, Poland, 79; Man and Landscape in Contemp Painting and Graphic in BRD, Moscow, Leningrad, Russ, 83; 25 Ger Painters, Lissabonn Iporto, Port, 84; and others. *Mem:* Deutscher Kunstlerbund. *Media:* Acrylic, Egg Tempera; Etching. *Publ:* Contribr, Die Kehrseite der Dinge, Gehring Gallery, Frankfurt, 85

TRIPP, SUSAN GERWE
MUSEUM DIRECTOR
b Baltimore, Md, Dec 28, 1945. *Study:* Univ Md, BS, 67. *Work:* Evergreen House, Johns Hopkins Univ; Homewood Mus, Baltimore, Md; Old Westbury Gardens, NY. *Pos:* Cur art, Johns Hopkins Univ, 74-79, dir univ collections, 79-91; exec dir, Old Westbury Gardens, 91-96; mus & hist restoration consult, 96-; trustee, Columbia Co Hist Soc, 96-2012, pres & bd dir, 97-2002, 2003-bd dir & secy, bd dir & vpres 2009; Judge Hist Hudson Preservation Awards, 2000-2005; Regional & Comty Hist Preservation Benefit 2002; chmn Vanderpael House restoration Columbia Co Hist Soc, 2002-2012; bd trustee AM Numismatic Soc, 2003-2007; Hornewood Mus Advisory Bd, Johns Hopkins Univ, 2010-; chair campaign comt, Evergreen Mus & Libr, 2012-. *Teaching:* Lectr art hist, Sch Continuing Educ, Johns Hopkins Univ, 78-91, Johns Hopkins Univ Campaign, Evergreen Mus & Libr chair, 2013-. *Awards:* Omicron Nu Hon Soc, 67; Hist Preserv Award, Baltimore, Heritage, 88 & 91. *Mem:* Am Numismatic Soc (mem, standing Comt, Libr & Archives, trustee, 2003-2007); Friends of the Am Wing, Baltimore Mus Art. *Res:* Japanese minor arts, emphasis on history of lacquer and adaptation of theater masks to netsuke; Leon Bakst; 18th and 19th century domestic economy; 19th century textiles and carpets; federal pd America. *Publ:* Auth, Bakst, Johns Hopkins Mag, 84; contribr, A Taste of Maryland, Walters Art Gallery, 85; auth, Chinese Collections in Evergreen House (exhib catalog), Baltimore Antiques Show, 85 & A Gentleman from Baltimore, Southeby's Great Sales, Barrie and Jenkins, Ltd, London, 89; coauth (with N K Davey), The Garrett Collection of Japanese Art, Dauphin Publ, 92; auth, Homewood in Baltimore, Maryland, Mag Antiques & Evergreen House, Baltimore, Md. *Mailing Add:* PO Box G Stuyvesant NY 12173

TRIPPI, PETER BRUCE
MUSEUM DIRECTOR
b Washington, DC, Aug 4, 1965. *Study:* Coll William and Mary, Williamsburg, Va, BA, 1987. *Pos:* Dir, Dahesh Mus Art, New York, 2003-06; ed, Fine Art Connoisseur Mag, 2006-. *Mem:* Assn Historians 19th Century Art (bd mem, 2006-)

TRIVIGNO, PAT
PAINTER, EDUCATOR
b New York, NY, Mar 13, 1922. *Study:* Tyler Sch Art; NY Univ; Columbia Univ, BA & MA. *Work:* Solomon R Guggenheim Mus, NY; New Orleans Mus Art, La; Everson Mus, Syracuse, NY; NY Times; Gen Elec Corp; Neuberger Mus, NY; AETNA Life Ins Co, New Orleans; Aquarium of Am, New Orleans; Brooklyn Mus; Los Angeles Land & Exploration Co; Canizaro Interests, New Orleans; Alton Ochnsner Medical Found; Touro Infirmary-Ogden Mus Southern Art. *Comn:* Murals, Lykes Steamship Lines & Cook Conv Ctr, Memphis, Sports Arena, New Orleans. *Exhib:* Whitney Mus Am Art Ann; Art Inst Chicago; Pa Acad Fine Arts; Am Acad Arts & Lett; Univ Ill Biennial; retrospective, (with catalog), New Orleans Mus Art; S Stern Gallery, New Orleans; Contemp Art Ctr, New Orleans. *Teaching:* Prof art, Tulane Univ La, 50-, chmn art dept. *Bibliog:* Articles in NY Times, 10/8/50 & 1/10/60; R Pearson (auth), Modern Renaissance in American Art, Harper; Retrospective Exhibit, catalog essay, New Orleans Mus Art, 94. *Media:* Acrylic, Oil. *Dealer:* Simone Stern Gallery New Orleans LA. *Mailing Add:* 1831 Marengo St New Orleans LA 70115

TROCKEL, ROSEMARIE
SCULPTOR, PAINTER
b Schwerte, Ger, 1952. *Study:* Art Sch Cologne (Painting), 1974-78. *Work:* Carnegie Mus Art, Pittsburgh. *Comn:* Frankfurt Engel memorial, Frankfurt am Main, Ger, 1995; large scale picture 176 sqm, Vienna State Opera, 2008, 2009; Concept Korea-Fashion Collective, 2010. *Exhib:* Solo exhibs include Plastics, Monika Sprüth Galerie, Cologne, Germany, 1983, Mus Mod Art, New York, 1988, Reina Sofia, Madrid, 1992, Venice Biennale, German Pavilion, Venice, 1999, Designs, Ctr Georges Pompidou, Paris, 2000, Knitted Works, Skarstedt Fine Art, New York, 2004, Menopause, Mus Nazionale Delle Arti Del XXI Secolo, Rome, 2006, Mus Paco das Artes São Paulo, Brazil, 2007, Keramiken und Collagen, Galerie Crone, Berlin, 2008, New Mus, NY, 2012; two-person exhibs include Donald Young Gallery, Seattle, (with Carsten Höller), 1997, And I found her bitter And I hurt her, Galerie Sprüth Magers, London, (with Thea Djordjadze), 2007; group exhibs include Licht bricht sich in den oberen Fenstern, Klapperhof 33, Cologne, Germany, 1982; Art from Europe, Tate Gallery, London, 1987; Carnegie Int, Carnegie Mus Art, Pittsburgh, 1988, 2008; Allegories of Modernism: Contemp Drawing, Mus Mod Art, New York, 1992; Féminin-Masculin: la sexe de l'art, Ctr Georges Pompidou, Paris, 1995, Dessins contemporains du Kunstmuseum de Bâle, 1996; Art/Fashion, Guggenheim Mus, New York, 1997; Beauty Now, Hirshhorn Mus & Sculpture Garden, Washington, 1999; Pattern language: Clothing as Communicator, Univ Art Mus, Univ Calif Santa Barbara, CA, 2006; Makers and Modelers: Works in Ceramic, Galerie Barbara Gladstone, New York, 2007; 54th Int Art Exhib Biennale, Venice, 2011, 55th Int Art Exhib Biennale, 2013. *Pos:* instr, Kunstakademie Dusseldorf. *Awards:* Scholarship, Kulturkreis der deutschen Wirtschaft, 1985; Fruhtrunk Award, Akademieverein München, 1991; Wolf Prize in Arts, 2011. *Dealer:* Regen Projs 629 N Almont Dr Los Angeles CA 90069; Skarstedt Fine Art 20 E 79th St New York City NY 10075; Monika Sprüth Philomene Magers 7A Grafton St London England W1S 4EJ UK; Niels Borch Jensen Galerie & Verlag Lindenstrasse 34 Berlin Germany 10969; Galerie Anne de Villepoix 43 rue de Montmorency Paris France 75003. *Mailing Add:* Donald Young Gallery 224 S Michigan Ave Suite 266 Chicago IL 60604

TROMBETTA, ANNAMARIE
PAINTER, PRINTMAKER
b Brooklyn, NY, Aug 5, 1963. *Study:* Parsons Sch Design; NY Acad Art, cert; Nat Acad Sch Fine Art, cert; Studies with Everett Raymond Kinstler, Wayne Thiebaud; Painting group, with Aaron Shikler & David Levine, Soho, NY. *Work:* Off Mayor R Guiliani, NY; Nat Acad Design, NY. *Comn:* Mural, State Island Mall Ctr, NY, 81; Croquet Game (painting), commn. by treas US Croquet Asn, NY, 94; Madonna of Maternity (painting), Daniel's Restaurant, NY, 95; portrait, commn by Dir Metrop

Mag, NY, 99; conservancy garden, commn by Mark Boyle, NY, 98; CEO Robert I Schulman, Tremont Group Holdings, 2007; Irsik Farms Manhattan, Kansas. *Exhib:* Solo exhibs, Liederkrantz Club, NY, 93, Historic Richmondtown Mus, 2001, Garibaldi-Meucci Mus, 2002, Dana Ctr Artworks of Cent Park NY, 2003, Wagner Col, 2003 & Junefest award, Citibank, Staten Island, NY, 2005, Italian Am Mus NYC, 2015, Union League Club Art Gallery NYC, 2015; 1st St Gallery Nat Competition Exhib, NY, 94; Catherine Lorillard Wolfe Art Club Competition Exhib, NY, 94; Am Artist Prof League Competition Exhib, NY, 94; Gallery on 2d Nat Juried Competition Figurative Art, NY, 96; PSA 25th Ann Exhib, NY, 97; Print exhib Pakistan Mission, NY, 98; Audubon Artists 58th Int Ann Exhib, NY, 2000; Godwin-Ternbach Mus Ital Am Women, 2001; Arnot Mus, 2003; Plain Air Painting, The Staten Island Mus, 2004; 64th Audubon Artists, NY, 2005 & 06; Bendheim Gallery, Greenwich, Conn, 2006; Yellow Gallery, Cross River, NY, 2006; Featured Paintings by A Trombetta, NY Left Bank-Art & Artist (off Washington Sq); Exhib at The Old Printshop, Soc Graphic Artists Group; group exhib, Packwood House Mus, Lewisburg, Pa, Contemp Am Realism Exhib, Ft Wayne Mus, Ind, 2008, Ormond Mus Soc of Graphic Artist Exhib, Fla, 2008, Soc Graphic Artists, Ormond Memorial Mus, Fla, 2008, Biennial Contemporary Am Realism, Fort Wayne Mus, 2008, Artist Fellowship 150th Anniversary Exhib, Nat Arts Club, NY, 2009, Cape House Group Exhib, Staten Island, 2009, Audubon Artists 66th Ann Group Exhib, 2009, Fort Wayne Mus Art 2010 Biennial Group Exhib, The Painting Group exhib featuring Aaron Shikler-Daniel Schwartz, Soho, NY, 2010, Landscape Invitational Group Exhib Art Lab Gallery, 2010, The Painting Group featuring Aaron Shikler Group Exhib Soho NY, 2011, Art Lab Gallery Group Exhib, 2011, Soc Graphic Artists Group Exhib Prince Street Gallery, NY, 2011, First Nat Exhib of Intaglio Prints Group Exhib, Nat Arts Club, NY, NY Soc Etchers, 2011, Audubon Artists 68th Ann Group Exhib, 2011, Sotheby's NY THaN Group Exhib, 2012, Catherine Lorillard Wolfe Art Club Juried Group Show, Nat Arts Club, 2012, Fort Wayne Mus Art Group Exhib Realism Biennial, 2012, Old Printshop NY Group Exhib for Soc Graphic Artists, 2012, Deck the Walls Group Exhib Wilkinson Galley NY Acad Art, 2013, The Painting Group Ann Exhib Chelsea, NY, 2013, Essex Gallery Group Exhib Conn, 2013, Six Summit Gallery Ivory Conn Food Fresco Farm, 2013, Delind Gallery Milw Wisc Group Exhib Soc Graphic Artists, 2013, Asian Influences & Dreams Group Exhib Sonia Gechtoff Gallery Nat Acad NYC, 2013, Fossatti Studio Turino Italy, 2014, Soc Graphic Artists The Old Print Shop, NYC, 2014, V Day Fourth Universalist Soc 160 Central Park West NYC, 2014, Soc Graphic Artists Centennial Nat Group Exhib, 2015; Auction at Sothey's Juried Exhib Take Home a Nude, 2009; Frye Art Gallery Australia Soc Graphic Artists Juried Exhib, 2010; Faculty Exhib Art Lab Staten Island, 2013; Nat Art Mus of Sport Third Ann Juried Exhib, 2013. *Teaching:* Instr, NY Acad Art, The Snug Harbor Cult Ctr. *Awards:* Inga Denton Award, 97; Milton Avery Award, 98; Ogden M Pleissner Award, 2000; Robert Lehman Award, 2001; Coashi Grant, 2001, 2003 & 2004; Pollack-Krasner Grant, 2004; Plein Air Painting Grant, 2005, Traveling Grant, 2006, Richmond Co Savings Bank; Ernest & Helen Adams Award, 2007; Stephen Sprouse Award, 2008; COASHI Grant, 2008; Coun of the Arts & Humanities for Staten Island Encore Grant, 2008; Lower Manhattan Cultural Ctr 2012 Artists Inst Scholarship Program Recipient, Nat Acad Sch Printmaking Scholarship, 2012, 2013; Full Scholarship to travel to Italy via Nat Acad 2014; Printmaking Scholarship award, 2014; Marquis Who's Who in American Art References award in Graphics, Audubon Artists, 2014. *Bibliog:* Raymond J Steiner (auth), profile, Art Times, 1/96; Frank Mazza (auth), The Artist Who Paints (video), CTV, Staten Island, NY, 98; Plain Air Painting Video, 2001; Cent Park to Staten Island, 2004 (video). *Mem:* Pastel Soc of Am; Nat Orgn of Italian Am Women; Soc Graphic Artists, (2007); Catherine Lorrilard Art Clus for Women (2007). *Media:* Oil, Watercolor. *Interests:* Running, Hindu Buddhist philos. *Publ:* Auth, Poetry in Pastel, Pastelagram, Spring 99; Future of Figurative Art, Art Times, July 99; Staten Island Advance, 2001- 2004; Italian Tribune, 2002; Wash Square News Artist Profile, 2007; Artist to Watch, Fine Art Connoisseur Mag, Nov Dec 2008, Three to Watch, April 2008, Artists in Our Parks, 2014; Sing For Hope, Public Art Program, 10th Anniversary Tribute to September 11th, Voice Interview featured with Peter Haskell, WCBS Local News, Artist at Work & Artwork featured in NY Mag by Wendy Goodman, In DNA.com Manhattan Local News, on Channel 7 Eyewitness News ABC Local News, 2011; Write up and photos, Outdoor Painter Mag, 2015, The Italian Tribune on Solo Exhib at the Italian Am Mus, 2015. *Mailing Add:* 175 E 96th St Apt 12 New York NY 10128

TROMEUR, ROBYN LORI
CURATOR, DIRECTOR

b Ridgewood, NJ, Oct 19, 1966. *Study:* Muhlenberg Col, BFA (art hist, summa cum laude), 88. *Hon Degrees:* Rutgers Univ, MFA, 92, cert mus studies, 92. *Collection Arranged:* The World of Faberge (Russian gems and jewels), Houston Mus Natural Sci, 94; Artifacts of an Assassination (hist manuscripts), Forbes Mag Galleries, 95; Treasures of the Czars, Mus Fine Arts, St Petersburg, Fla, 95; La Belle Epoque, Nassau Co Mus Art, Roslyn Harbor, NY, 95; Faberge: Juwelier des Zarenhofes, Mus fur Kunst und Gewerbe, Hamburg, Ger, 95; Small Wonders: The Fantastic Voyage into Miniature Worlds, Margaret Woodbury Strong Mus, Rochester, NY, 95-97; Faberge Silver from the Forbes Magazine Collection, Mus Natural Hist & Sci, Albuquerque, NMex, 95-96; First Families (hist manuscripts), Forbes Mag Galleries, 95-97; And If Elected...200 Years of Presidential Elections (hist manuscripts), San Diego Mus Art, 96; Faberge and Finland: Exquisite Objects, Corcoran Gallery Art, Washington DC, 96-97; Faberge in Am, Metrop Mus Art, NY, H.M. De Young Mem Mus, San Francisco, Mus Fine Art, Richmond, Va, New Orleans Mus Art, Cleveland Mus Art, 96-97; Philadelphia and the Am Revolution (hist manuscripts), Franklin Inst, 96-97; Faberge: Loistavaa Kultasepantaidetta, Lahti Art Mus, Finland, 97; Maryland Blossoms in the Arts, Govt House, Annapolis, Md, 97; Carl Faberge: Goldsmith tothe Tsar, Nat Mus, Stockholm, Sweden, 97; Highlights from the Forbes Magazine Collection, 97-2000; The Glitter and the Gold: Faberge at Biltmore Estate, Asheville, NC, 98; Peterhof: Treasures of Russia, Rio All-Suites Hotel and Casino, Las Vegas, 98-99; Regal Splendor: Masterpieces from the House of Faberge: Ronald Reagan Presidential Libr, Simi Valley, Calif, 98-99; Nicholas & Alexandra: The Last Imperial Family of Tsarist Russia, 1st USA Riverfront Arts Ctr, Wilmington, Del, 99. *Pos:* curator, Forbes Mag Collection, New York, 92-2000; exec dir, Somerset Art Asn, Bedminster, NJ, 2000-. *Mem:* Nat Asn Corp Art Mgt (newsletter ed). *Publ:* auth, Faberge Treasures, Harry N Abrams, 98; co-auth, Faberge: The Forbes Collection, 99. *Mailing Add:* Somerset Art Assn 2020 Burnt Mills Rd Bedminster NJ 07921

TROP, SANDRA
MUSEUM DIRECTOR

b Brooklyn, NY. *Study:* NY Univ, BS (cum laude); Everson Mus Art; Inst Arts Admin; Harvard Univ. *Pos:* Cur traveling exhibs, Everson Mus Art, Syracuse, NY, 72, asst to dir, 73, actg dir, 74, asst dir, 74-95, dir, 95-2007; prog auditor, NY State Coun Arts, 83-84, panelist, 89-90; field reviewer, Inst Mus Servs, 85-87. *Teaching:* Adj prof, Syracuse Univ Museology, 74. *Awards:* Women in Bus award, 2002; Spirit Women award; Northeast Baptist Scholarship award. *Mem:* Int Coun Mus (int comt mus & collections mod art); Am Asn Mus. *Specialty:* Ceramics, video, contemp art

TROUTMAN, JILL
PAINTER

b Newton, Iowa, July 20, 1938. *Study:* Univ Va, EdB (art hist), 69; Cleveland Inst Art, Lacoste, France, 83; Art Studios Int, Florence, Italy, 84. *Work:* NC Nat Bank, Charlotte, NC; R J Reynolds Collection, Winston-Salem, NC. *Comn:* Lobby collection, Guilford Neurological, Greensboro, NC; lobby collection, Cent Carolina Bank, Burlington, NC; lobby collection, York Properties, Raleigh, NC; lobby collection, WFMY-TV, Greensboro, NC; cancer unit, Duke Med Ctr, Durham, NC. *Exhib:* 37 solo exhibs, 72-94. *Teaching:* Instr painting, Ctr Creative Arts, Greensboro, NC, 81-86; instr, 50 adult art students, currently. *Mem:* High Point Fine Art Guild (pres, 78-79); NC Watercolor Soc (pres, 80-81); High Point Arts Coun; Alamance Co Arts Ctr. *Media:* Acrylic, Acrylic Collages. *Specialty:* Harrison's in Burlington, NC. *Interests:* Taking Jazz piano lessons. *Mailing Add:* 1089 Foxcliff Dr Mebane NC 27302

TROY, NANCY J
HISTORIAN, EDUCATOR

Study: Wesleyan Univ, BA (magna cum laude with Honors in Art), 74; Yale Univ, MA (twentieth century European art), 76, PhD (Kress Found Travel Grant, Fulbright-Hays Grant), 79. *Pos:* Mus training intern, Solomon R Guggenheim Mus, NY, 1972, curatorial and research asst, 1973, curatorial coordinator, special consultant to Ilya Bolotowsky, 1974; asst to curator of French painting, Nat Gallery of Art, Washington, DC, 1975; Guest cur, Yale Univ Art Gallery, New Haven, Conn, 79; mem fine arts accessions com, com collections, Baltimore Mus Art, Md, 79-82; cons, Walker Art Center, Minneapolis, Minn, 82 & Art Inst Chicago, Ill, 84-85; mem vis com, Harvard Univ Art Mus, Cambridge, Mass, 92-98; cons curator, High Mus of Art, Atlanta, Ga, 2004; series co-ed, Histories, Cultures, Contexts, Reaktion Books; editor-in-chief, The Art Bulletin, 94-97. *Teaching:* Asst prof, Johns Hopkins Univ, Baltimore, Md, 79-83; asst prof, Northwestern Univ, Department of Art History, 83-85, assoc prof, 85-92, acting chairperson, 88, chairperson, 90-92, prof, 92-93; vis prof, Univ Calif, Department of the History of Art, Los Angeles, 94; vis prof, Univ Southern Calif, Department of Art History, Los Angeles, 94-95, prof, 1994-2010, chairperson, 1997-2004; scholar-in-residence, Getty Res Inst for the Hist of Art & Humanities, 93-96; Victoria and Roger Sant Prof in Art, chair Dept Art & Art History, Stanford Univ, 2010-. *Awards:* Grant, Am Coun Learned Soc, 81, 91 & 98-99; Fel, John Simon Guggenheim Mem Found, 98-99; Zumberge Fac Res and Innovation Fund, Univ Southern Calif, 98-99; Distinguished Alumna Award, Wesleyan Univ, 99. *Bibliog:* Linda Dahlrymple (auth), The Fourth Dimension and Non-Euclidian Geometry in Modern Art, Design Bk Rev, fall 84; Kenneth E Silver (auth), Esprit de corps: The art of the Parisian avant garde and the first world war, Art Bulletin, LXXIII, 3/1/91. *Mem:* Nat Committee for the Hist of Art (bd dir, pres 2002-08). *Publ:* Auth, The De Stijl Environment, Mass Inst Technol Press, Cambridge, 83; Modernism and the Decorative Arts in France: Art Nouveau to Le Corbusier, Yale Univ Press, New Haven, 91; The logic of function, Decorative Arts Soc J, 95; Domesticity, Decoration and Consumer Culture: Selling Art and Design in Pre-World War I France, Not at Home the Suppression of Domesticity in Modern Art & Archit, Thames & Hudson, London & New York, 96; co-ed, Architecture and Cubism, Mass Inst Technol Press, Cambridge, Mass & London, 97; Couture Culture: A Study in Modern Art and Fashion, 2002. *Mailing Add:* Stanford University Department of Art and Art History 435 Lasuen Mall Stanford CA 94305

TRUBY, BETSY KIRBY
PAINTER, ILLUSTRATOR

b Winchester, Va, Nov 8, 1926. *Study:* Hiram Coll; Cleveland Sch Art; NMex Inst Mining & Technol; Univ NMex; also with David Moneypenny, Oden Hullenkramer & Joe Morello. *Work:* Int Moral Re-Armament Ctr, Mackinaw Island, Mich; Cancer Res & Treatment Ctr, Albuquerque; Truth or Consequences Geronimo Springs Art Mus, NMex; Sheraton Hotel, Santa Fe, NMex; La Quinta Mus, Albuquerque; First Presby Church, Albuquerque, NMex. *Comn:* Portrait, Congressman Albert G Simms, 64; Indian child portrait, NMex Easter Seal Soc, 69; paintings, First Presby Church, Albuquerque, 72-74; historical portrait, Synod Southwest, Presby Church, 75; paintings, Cystic Fibrosis Found, NMex, 76 & 77; paintings reproduced, Southwest Arts & Graphics, 84-90. *Exhib:* Fine Arts Gallery, Carnegie Inst, Pittsburgh, 46; NMex Fiesta Biennial, State Mus, Santa Fe, 64 & 68; Nat Art Show, Lawton, Okla, 74; Nat League Am Pen Women Mid-Ad Cong, Phoenix, Ariz, 75; 2 Women Show, Nat League Am Pen Women, Las Vegas, Nev, 77; solo exhibs, Gallery of South Western Art, Old Town, Albuquerque, 78 & Hiram Coll, Ohio, 87; Nat League Am Pen Women Nat Show, Kansas City, Mo, 90; Nat Pastel Show, Albuquerque, NMex, 94-99, 2007. *Pos:* exhib chmn, Yucca Art Gallery, Albuquerque, Old Town, NMex, 70-72; Photogr, Nat League Am Pen Women-Yucca Branch, 92-2009. *Teaching:* Instr ceramics, US Pub Health Hosp, 48-49, Ohio Pub Sch Syst, 49-50. *Awards:* Nat League Am Pen Women State Show, First Premium Pastel, Third Premium Oil, Secorro, NMex, 10/89; Third Premium-Pastel, Juried Exhib, Pastel Soc NMex,

Albuquerque, 91; Second Premium Pastel, Nat League Am Pen Women, NMex, 95, 99; Nat League Am Pen Women Show, Juried, Best of Show, Albuquerque, NMex, 2003; Nat Show, Master Works, 2nd award, Albuquerque, NMex, 2004; 2nd Place Pastel, Nat League Am Pen Woman State Show, Socorro, NMex, 2005; Outstanding Quality recognition, Am Nat Parks Juried Show, 2007. *Bibliog:* J Bonnette (auth), The Creative Process, KNME TV, Univ NMex, 73. *Mem:* Nat League Am Pen Women (charter mem); Pastel Soc NMex (charter mem). *Media:* Pastel, Watercolor. *Specialty:* Southwestern paintings. *Interests:* Boating & swimming. *Publ:* Cover illusr, Flags, 73 & Let Our Light Shine, 74. *Dealer:* Pastel Soc NMex Box 3571 Albuquerque NM 87190; Bardean Gallery PO Box 3055 Albuquerque NM 87190. *Mailing Add:* 6609 Loftus Ave NE Albuquerque NM 87109-2721

TRUE, RUTH & WILLIAM L
COLLECTORS
b Apr 1954. *Pos:* Chmn & chief exec officer, Gull Industries, Inc, Seattle; mem adv bd, Seattle Arts & Lectures; mem, Betty Bowen comt, Seattle Art Mus, 2004; co-founder, Western Bridge Gallery, Seattle; bd dirs, Pike Place Market Found, Seattle. *Awards:* Named one of Top 200 Collectors, ARTnews mag, 2003-11. *Collection:* Contemporary art. *Mailing Add:* 832 37th Ave E Seattle WA 98112-4326

TRUEBLOOD, EMILY HERRICK
PRINTMAKER
b Alexandria, Va, Aug 13, 1942. *Study:* Beloit Coll, Wis; Univ Wis, Madison, BA, 65; Columbia Univ Sch Libr Serv, MS, 69. *Work:* Mus Mod Art, Haifa, Israel; Portland Mus Art, Ore; Trenton State Coll, NJ; Newark Pub Lib, NJ; NY Pub Libr; Brit Mus; Cleveland Mus Art; New York Hist Soc; Detroit Inst Art. *Comn:* Pvt commissions. *Exhib:* Traveling exhib, Va Mus Fine Arts, Richmond, 86; Contemp Am Printmaker, Fairfield Univ, Conn, 94; Centennial Portfolio, Old Print Shop, NY, 98; Artists Revisit the Chrysler, Michael Ingbar Gallery, NY, 2000-2001, 2007; Xylon 13, 98, 2001; Up on the Roof, NY Hist Soc, NY, 2001; Miniprint Finland, 2001; 6th Int Miniature Art Biennial, Salle Augustin-Chenier, Ville-Marie, Que, 2002; two-person show, Old Print Shop, NY, 2003, 2009; Silvermine Guild, New Canaan, Conn, 2006; The Old Print Shop NY, 2010, Graphic Studio Gallery, Dublin, Ireland, 2006; Soc Am Graphic Artists, Hollar Soc Gallery, Prague, Czech Repub, 2006, Old Print Shop, 2012, Frye Gallery, Braidwood, Australia; Int Miniature Print Exhib, Conn Graphic Arts Ctr, New Canaan, 2009, 2011, 2013. *Pos:* vpres, Soc Am Graphic Artists, 2003-2006; bd mem, Catharine Lorillard Wolfe Art Club, 2006-2009; award jury, Salmagundi Club, 2009-2010. *Teaching:* Vis artist var classes. *Awards:* E Weyhe Gallery Purchase Award, SAGA 64th Nat, 91; Silver Medal of Honor for Graphics, Audubon Artists, 99, 2001; Catharine Lorillard Wolfe Art Club, Anna Hyatt Huntington Bronze Medal, 2002; Takayo Noda Award, Nat Arts Club, 2004; Alphaus P Cole Mem Award, Salmagundi Club, 2008; Speedball Art Purchase award, 2013. *Bibliog:* Helen Harrison (auth), Urban themes are a source for imagery in two shows, NY Times, 2/5/95; Eleanor Charles (auth), article, NY Times, 11/10/96; New York Centennial Exhibition at the Old Print Shop, Art Times, 3/98; William Zimmer (auth), A Commitment...to Good Things in Small., NY Times, 4/15/2001; Ariella Bodick (auth), Up on the Roof, Newsday, 7/10/2001; Mary Jane Fine (auth), Form & Function - Rooftop Water Tanks, Newsday, 11/8/2001; William Behnken & Emily Trueblood, Jour of the Print World, winter, 2003. *Mem:* Salmagundi Club; Special Libr Asn; Pen & Brush; Soc Am Graphic Artists; Nat Arts Club; Nat Asn Women Artists; Catharine Lorillard Wolfe Art Club. *Media:* Woodcut, Linocut. *Interests:* Swimming. *Dealer:* The Old Print Shop. *Mailing Add:* 20 E Ninth St No 18C New York NY 10003-5944

TRUEBLOOD, L'DEANE
SCULPTOR, PAINTER
b Norman, Okla, Dec 26, 1928. *Study:* Univ Okla, BFA, 45; Oklahoma City Univ, MA, 70; Scottsdale Artists' Sch, 86, 89, 91; Art Students League, 93; Studies with Richard Schmid, Charles Reid, Bruno Lucchesi & Sherrie McGraw. *Work:* City of Springville, Springville Art Mus, Utah; Dixie Coll Art Mus, St George, Utah; Latter Day Saints Church Art Mus, Salt Lake City; Birmingham Libr, Ala; Children's Art Mus, Pueblo, Colo; Friends Sch, Haverford, Pa; Aegis Ctr, Dana Point, Calif; pvt collection of Armand Hammer; St Anthony Church, Rockford, Ill. *Comn:* Pres Doug Alder (bust), Dixie Coll, St George, Utah, 89; Armand Hammer (bust), Huntsman Chem Corp, Salt Lake City, 90; Val Browning (bust), Browning Arms Corp, Odgen, Utah, 91; Sarah Sturdevant Leavitt (bronze monument), pvt comn by Leavitt family, Santa Clara, Utah, 98; Madonna (bronze monument), Mercy Hosp, Oshkosh, Wis, 2000; Children's fountain, Morinda Corp, 2002; Children's collection, Lake George Mem Hosp, Ill, 2002; Veteran's bronze monument, City of S Jordan, Utah, 2002; St Clare (bronze monument), Sisters of Mercy, Weston, Wis, 2004; Watermaster (bronze monument), City of St George, Utah, 2007. *Exhib:* Springville Salon Ann, Springville Mus Art, Utah, 80-2008; Sculptors of Utah, Springville Mus Art, Utah, 85; Int Latter Day Saints Church Ann Exhib, Latter Day Saints Church Art Mus, Salt Lake City, 89; Braithwaite Invitational, Braithwaite Mus Art, Cedar City, Utah, 90; Okla Watercolor Soc, Kirkpatrick Mus, Oklahoma City, 91; Utah Watercolor Soc, Pioneer Theatre Mus, Salt Lake City, 92; Pen & Brush Sculpture Ann, Pen & Brush Club, NY; solo exhibs, Braithwaite Mus, Utah, 92, Meyer Gallery, Santa Fe, NMex, 98-2007, St George Art Mus, 99, Hilligoss Gallery, Chicago, 2003; Sculptures in the Park Invitational, Loveland, Colo, 97-2006. *Pos:* Secy/pres, Southwest Utah Arts Coun, 85-86; bd dir, Utah Arts Coun, 85-97, Dixie Arts Found, 2000-2005 & Pioneer Arts Heritage Found, 2000-2001; founder & bd mem, Art Around the Corner, St George, Utah, 2004-2006. *Awards:* Religious Art Merit Award, 2000; Named Utah Top 100 Artists, 2002; Featured Artist, Governor's Invitational Show, 2003; Am 50 Most Successful Women, Feminine Fortunes Magazine, 2003. *Bibliog:* Cheryl Koeven (auth), Capturing the Inner Light, St George Mag, 92; Kimberly Perkins (dir), Images, KTVX TV, Salt Lake City, 92; Dianne Cauble (auth), Daydreams in the Sun, Focus/Santa Fe, 98; Oklahoma Living Mag, 99 & 2000; Emily Van Cleve (auth), Focus/Santa Fe, 2004; Brian Passey (auth), Fascination for Faces & People, St George Mag, 2007. *Mem:* Nat Sculpture Soc; Okla Sculpture Soc; Utah Watercolor Soc; Nev Watercolor Soc. *Media:* Metal, Cast; Watercolor. *Publ:* Illusr, cover, Am Mothers Mag, spring 94 & winter 94. *Dealer:* Meyer Gallery 225 Canyon Rd Santa Fe NM 87501; Coda Gallery 73-151 El Paseo Palm Desert CA 92260; Shaw Gallery 761 Fifth Ave S Naples FL 34102 ; and others

TRUETTNER, WILLIAM H
CURATOR
Pos: With Smithsonian American Art Mus, 1965-; sr cur eighteenth and nineteenth century painting & sculpture, currently. *Publ:* (auth) The West as America: Reinterpreting Images of the Frontier,1820-1920, 1991. *Mailing Add:* Smithsonian American Art Museum MRC 970 Box 37012 Washington DC 20013-7012

TRUJILLO, MARC
PAINTER
b Albuquerque, New Mexico, 1966. *Study:* Univ Texas, Austin, BA, 1991; Yale Univ Sch Art, MFA, 1994. *Work:* Long Beach Mus Art, Long Beach, Calif. *Exhib:* Solo exhibs include Tim Gleason Gallery, New York, 1994, Contemp Realist Gallery, San Francisco, 1994, 1995, Hackett-Freedman Gallery, San Francisco, 1997, 1998, You are here, 2007, Ruth Bachofner Gallery, Santa Monica, CA, 2000, 2001, The Plainness of Plain Things, 2003, Minor Works, Santa Monica Coll, CA, 2007; group exhibs include Mexicarte, Austin, TX, 1989; Flood Gallery, Univ Texas, Austin, 1990; Yale Grad Student Show, New Haven, CT, 1993; MFA Thesis Show, Yale Sch Art, New Haven, CT, 1994; 10th Anniv Exhib, Hackett-Freedman Gallery, San Francisco, 1997; Earl McGrath Gallery, New York, 1998, 1999; Speculative Terrain, Carnegie Art Mus, Oxnard, CA, 2004; Seeing & Reading, Art Gallery, Santa Monica, CA, 2004; A View From Here, Judson Gallery Contemp & Traditional Art, Los Angeles, 2008 ; Invitational Exhib Visual Arts, AAAL, 2008; Summer Show, Hirschl & Adler, NY, 2008. *Pos:* Cartoonist, The Daily Texan, 1989; Composed & Performed music for film El Mariachi, Columbia Pictures, 1992; Guest Speaker, Artforum Pac Art Found, Pac Club, Newport Beach, CA, 2004. *Teaching:* Instr in Drawing & Painting at Dougherty Arts Ctr, Austin, TX, 1995, Santa Monica Coll, CA, 2007 ; Printmaking & 2D Design Instr at Caldwell Coll, NJ, 1997-98; Painting Instr Art Ctr Coll Design, Pasadena, CA, 1999, 2003; Drawing Instr Pierce Coll, Woodland Hills, CA, 2000; Vis Artist Univ Calif Riverside, 2003. *Awards:* First place merit award painting, Univ Texas, Austin, 1990; Ellen Battell Stoeckel Trust Fel, Yale Univ Summer Sch Music & Art, 1993; Ely Harwood Schless Mem Fund Prize, Yale Univ, 1994; John Simon Guggenheim Fel, 2008; Rosenthal Family Found Award Painting, AAAL, 2008. *Bibliog:* Leah Ollman (auth), Art, Not Attitude, Los Angeles Times, Mar 2005; Michael Leaverton (auth), Suburban Slumber, SF Weekly, page 20, May 2, 2007; Johnny Huston (auth), Picks, San Francisco Bay Guardian, page 22, May 2, 2007; Joshua Rose (auth), Ordinary Into Extraordinary, Am Art Collector, pages 210-215, May 2007; Peter Frank (auth), Achille Perilli/Marc Trujillo, LA Weekly, 2007; Chris Ware (auth), Marc Trujillo: You Are Here, Hackett-Freedman Gallery, San Francisco, Calif, 2007; Yasmine Mohseni (auth), Mar Trujillo, Artworks Mag, pages 36-43, summer 2008. *Publ:* Auth, 6400 Laurel Canyon Boulevard (reproduction), Harper's Mag, Mar 2004. *Dealer:* Hackett-Freeman Gallery 250 Sutter St Ste 400 San Francisco CA 94108

TRUMBLE, BEVERLY (JANE)
PAINTER
b Milwaukee, Wis. *Study:* Univ Colo, 60; Art Students League, 76-83; Daniel E Greene Workshop, 84. *Work:* Nationwide Cellular Serv Inc, Valley Stream, NY; Strategic Resource Group Inc, East Norwalk, Conn. *Comn:* Terri & Jerry (oil portrait), Comn by Mr & Mrs Forrest Newton, Littleton, Colo, 86; 4 paintings, Comn by Mr & Mrs Thomas Keller, White Plains, 90; Brian (oil portrait), Comn by Lt Coll & Mrs Orville Hays, Breckenridge, Colo, 91; Taos Pueblo on Christmas Eve (oil painting), comn by Mrs William Webster, Taos, NMex, 98. *Exhib:* Solo exhib, Univ Denver, 93; Northern Ariz Univ Mus & Galleries, Flagstaff, 94; Western NMex Univ, Silver City, 96; Nightwalker Nat Juried Exhib, Colo State Univ, Ft Collins, 97; Great Plains Nat, Hays State Univ, Hays, Kans, 98; St Johns Coll, Santa Fe, NMex, 2000; La Chaleppe des Penitents, Gourdes, France, 2000. *Collection Arranged:* WSAC, Broadway Mall Gallery (coauth, catalog), 87-88; Riverside Arts Festival, City of NY, 88; Westside Arts Coalition (auth, catalog), Lever House Gallery, 88; Premiere Soho Exhib (auth, catalog), West Side Artists Pleiades, 88; Painting & Sculpture-WSAC, Pen & Brush, 89. *Pos:* Guided tours Artists Studios, NY, 88-90. *Teaching:* Drawing & pastel workshops, The Balance Sheet, Frisco, Colo, 91. *Awards:* Solo Exhib Award, Pen & Brush Inc, 85; Artist Guild Award, Mamaroneck Artist Guild, 88; First Prize, Summit Co Arts Coun, 92. *Bibliog:* T Alex Miller (auth), article, Summit Daily News, Colo, 4/20/93; Sonya Ellingboe (auth), article, Littleton Independent, Colo, 8/25/94; Ann Hartley, Susan McGarry, Mary Carroll Nelson (eds), Bridging Time & Space, Essays on Layered Art, Markowitza Publ, 11/98. *Mem:* Pastel Soc Am; Soc Layerists Multi Media; Art Students League NY; NY Artist's Equity; Taos Art Asn. *Media:* Oil, Pastel Aqua Media. *Mailing Add:* c/o Gail Newton 6851 S Forest St Centennial CO 80120

TRUPP, BARBARA LEE
PAINTER, DESIGNER
b Scottsbluff, Nebr, Nov 17, 1950. *Study:* Studied with Ilda Lubane, Banff Ctr Arts, Alta, Can, 68-70; John Paul Caponigro, Santa Fe Photog Workshops, 1999, 2000; Univ Puget Sound, Tacoma, Wash, 69-70; Univ Mich, Ann Arbor, BFA, 71-74, MAC Univ, 2000. *Work:* Ill State Mus, Springfield; Fermi Nat Accelorator Lab, US Dept Energy, Batavia, Ill; Ore State Mus, Portland; Am Mus, Bath, Eng; Banff Ctr Arts, Alta, Can; Mary & Leigh Block Gallery, NWestern Univ, Evanston, Ill; Krannert Mus, Univ Ill, Champaign; Ruttenberg Art Found, Chicago, Ill; Univ Nev, Reno. *Comn:* Ceramics, Paris Casino, Las Vegas, Nev; Prints, Plucked Chicken Press, Evanston, Ill, 88. *Exhib:* Selections from the Permanent Collection, Banff Ctr, traveling throughout Can, 75; 2nd Ann Great Lakes Show, Ill St Gallery, Chicago, Ill, 88; Chicago Int New Art Forms Expos, Navy Pier, Chicago, Ill, 88, 90 & 92; Selections from Permanent Collection, Ill State Mus, Springfield, Ill, 88-89; Am & Int Craft Exhib, World Trade Ctr, Boston, Mass, 90; Multiple Images, Ill State Mus, Springfield, 91; one-person

shows, Vignettes, 92, The New Collection, 94 & Prehistoire, 96, Citywoods, Highland Park, Ill; Fine Art of Fiber, Chicago Botanic Gardens, Glencoe, Ill, 97; Flights of Imagination, Chicago Cult Center, Ill, 2003; Alumni, Slusser Mus Gallery, Ann Arbur, Mich, 2007, 2008. *Pos:* Illusr, Designer, Art Dir. *Teaching:* Instr painting, Evanston Art Ctr, 87-96; Instr painting, digital media, art & design, 98-. *Bibliog:* Barbara Buchholz (auth), The tile revival, Chicago Tribune, 10/9/94. *Mem:* Nat Asn Photoshop Profs; Chicago Artists Coalition. *Media:* watercolor, digital media. *Mailing Add:* 2650 Hurd Ave Evanston IL 60201-1277

TRUTTY-COOHILL, PATRICIA
EDUCATOR, HISTORIAN
b Uniontown, Pa. *Study:* Univ Toronto, BA, 62, Pa State Univ, MA, 68, PhD, 82. *Pos:* Assoc prof art hist, Western Ky Univ, 83-. *Teaching:* Lectr, art dept, Western Ky Univ, 80-82, asst prof, 82-86, assoc prof, 86-. *Mem:* Coll Art Asn; Raccolta Vinciana; Leonardo Soc. *Res:* School of Leonardo da Vinci. *Publ:* Auth & illusr, La Eminentia in Antonello de Messina, Antichità viva vol XXI/4, 82; Narrative to Icon, Achademia Leonardi Vinci, vol 1, 88; The Drawings of Leonardo da Vinci and his Circle in America, Giunti, 93 with Carlo Pedretti; Visualizing Tymineniecka's Poetica nova, Analecta Hüserliana, 52, Jean-Claude Novaro, 96. *Mailing Add:* Western Ky Univ Art Dept Bowling Green KY 42101

TSAI, CHARWEI
CALLIGRAPHER, INSTALLATION SCULPTOR
b Taipei, Taiwan, Oct 1980. *Study:* RI Sch Design, BFA (industrial design), 2002. *Exhib:* Solo exhibs, Summer Hot, Taipei Econ & Cult Off, NY, 2006; Group exhibs, J'en rêve, Fondation Cartier, Paris, 2005; Poster, Hydra, Greece, 2006; Singapore Biennial, 2006. *Pos:* With Printed Matter, NY, 2002-04; asst to Cai Guo-Giang, NY, 2004-06; res artist, Cité Internat Univ, Paris, 2006. *Publ:* Editor & publ, Lovely Daze, 2006-. *Mailing Add:* c/o Printed Matter Artists Book 195 10th Ave New York NY 10011

TSAI, HSIAO HSIA
PAINTER, SCULPTOR
b China; US citizen. *Study:* Nat Coll Art China, BFA; Univ Okla, MFA (scholar); Hamilton State Univ, Hon PhD, 78. *Exhib:* White Mus, San Antonio, 65, 66 & 80; Jess Besser Mus, Pensacola Art Ctr, 75; Everhart Mus, Pa, 75; Dallas Mus Fine Arts, 76; Brick Stone Mus, 77; Corpus Christi Mus, 78-81; and many others. *Awards:* Gold Medal, Italy Competition, 83; Corpus Christi Mus Award, 86; Award, Art Mus S Tex, 91-94; and many others. *Mem:* Hon mem Int Asn Art. *Publ:* Principles Chinese Painting Adapted to Modern Needs and Treaties, Mustard Seed Garden Treaties; articles in Today's Art, Arts Mag, Art News, J Am, New York & Sund Mag, Houston

TSAI, WINNIE C
PAINTER, EDUCATOR, CALLIGRAPHER
b. China, Aug 15, 1946. *Study:* Providence Coll, BA (English Lit), Taichuang, Taiwan, 69; St John's Univ, MA, New York, 76; Fashion Inst, fashion design, New York, 80; Sch Visual Arts, graphic arts design, computer arts, 86-87, 95; Adelphi Univ, fine arts, New York, 94; studied pastel in Pastel Sch/Nat Arts Club, New York, 2003-2005; Frank Federico workshop, Pastel Sch/Nat Arts, Club, New York, 2005; Richard Pionk summer workshop, Art Student League, New York, 2003; Daniel Green workshop, Art Student League, New York, 2001. *Work:* Gallery of Amerasia Bank, Flushing, New York; 911 Mem Fundraising, World Journ, 2001; Fundraising for Indonesian Tsunami Disaster, World Journ, 2004; Cheng Huang Mus, Shanghai, China, 2002. *Exhib:* Solo exhibs, Bellport Lane Art Gallery, NY, 96, European Am Bank, Rockville, NY, 98, Amerasia Bank, Flushing, New York, 2000; Group exhibs, Gold Coast Art Ann Show, Brookville, NY, 97; 1st Int Open Juried Exhib, Taiwan Ctr Gallery, Flushing, New York, 2005; CPS Renaissance in Pastel, Slater Mem Mus Converse, Paris, 2005, 2008; Cheng Huang Mus, Shanghai, China, 2003; Nat Taiwan Arts Educ Ctr, Taiwan, 2005; Dr Sun Yei Shin Mem Hall, Taipei, Taiwan, 2004; Audubon Artists Inc, Salmagundi Club, New York, 2006-2010; Pastel Soc Taipei, Taiwan, 2007, 2008; Hung Zhou Nat Art Acad, Zhe Jiang, China, 2008; Church of St Elizabeth, Basel, Switzerland, 2010; Nat Taiwan Arts Educ Ctr, Taipei, 2010. *Pos:* Vpres, North Am Pastel Artists Asn, New York, 2010, exhib chair, 2005-2009; corresponding secy, Pastel Soc Taipei, Taiwan, 2008-2009; workshop chair, Village Art Club Rockville Ctr, New York, 98-99; office manager, Lucent Tech, New York, 98-2001; graphic art designer, AT&T, 87-97. *Teaching:* Adj prof, Chinese language, St John's Univ, New York, 2004-2010, Chinese calligraphy, 2004-2010, instr, summer prog arts, 2010; instr, adult educ prog, Mem High Sch, Valley Stream, New York, 2007-2010; instr, Plainview Cult Ctr, New York, 2000-2010. *Awards:* Best in Show, 2nd Ann Juried Art Show, Bellport Lane Art Gallery, New York, 96; Award of Excellence, 38th Ann Art Esxhib, Suburban Art League Asn, NY, 96; Best in Show & 1st Place, New Rochelle Art Asn, NY, 97; 2nd Place, Village Art Club, Rockville Ctr Art Show, NY, 98; Marquis Who's Who in Am Art References Award in pastels, Audubon Artists, New York, 2010. *Bibliog:* World Journ, 96, 98, 2000, 2001; The Epoch Time, 2000, 2010; New York Community Times, 2005, 2010. *Mem:* Pastel Soc Am (signature mem); Audubon Artists, Inc; North Am Pastel Artists Asn; Asn Chinese Calligraphy Am; Am Chinese Calligraphy Soc. *Media:* Pastel. *Publ:* auth, The Pastel World of Jason Chang, G & P Co/Marshall Wei, 96; Chung Wen Ya Ji, Yu Hua Wen Co, Inc, Shanghai, China, 2003; Chinese Am Artists, Ye Yan Tang Co, Inc, Taipei, Taiwan, 2004

TSARIKOVSKY, VALERY (TSAR)
PAINTER, MURALIST
b Kiev, Ukraine, May 29, 1952; US citizen. *Study:* Kiev Tech Coll Construct, Ukraine, diploma, 70. *Work:* Salmagundi Club Ctr Am Art, Metrop Opera Asn & Lincoln Ctr Performing Arts, NY; Contemp Mus Art, Atlanta, Ga; pvt collections, State House Pa, Lt Gov Catherine Baker Knoll, Sen Oran Hatch off, Washington, DC & var others; Hilde Gerst; World Economical Forum, Switz; Peter Arnot LLC, New York (Gallery Herbert Arnot Inc); Ukrainian Inst Am; State House, Pa. *Comn:* Ranch, Rockefeller Ctr Main off, New York, 97; Treehouse, mural (6 x 8), Rest, Cleveland, Ohio, 2006; var portraits, 2000-. *Exhib:* Salmagundi Art Club Ann Exhib, 87-91; Hilde Gerst Gallery, 91-; Miami Int Art Expos, Miami conv Ctr, 92-93; Palm Beach Int Art Antique Fair, 97; Fine Arts Dealers Asn, Univ Calif, Los Angeles, 97-98; Committed To Improving The State of the World, World Econ Forum, Davos, Switz, 98; Boston Int Fine Art Fair, 2006; solo exhibs, New York, New York, Hilde Gerst Art Gallery, 2006 & I Love NY, Marbella Gallery Inc, New York, 2007; Trinity Int Auction, NY, 2008; William J Jenack Auction, 2009; Trinity Int Auction, 2009; New York, New York, Ukrainian Inst Am, 2011. *Pos:* Archit asst, Kiev Tech Coll Construct, Ukraine, 75; designer, exhib group New York, 83-92; full-time artist, 92-. *Teaching:* Instr, pvt art lessons, 85-89 & Salmagundi Club, 89-92; pvt art lessons, 92-, 2008-2009. *Awards:* 1st Prize, Salmagundi Art Club, 87; Lee M Loeb Mem Award, Traditional Landscape, 91; Frank B Williams Found Award, 91; Donated painting, BEST & SFTT, 2008. *Bibliog:* Article, NY Times, 6/91; CNN Internet (TV doc), 1/98; CNN, Business Unusual (TV doc), 2/98; To Salute Our Troops, 5/9/2008; article and photo, NY Times, 6/26/2009. *Mem:* Salmagundi Art Club, New York, 85-92. *Media:* Oil. *Res:* How color & light interact during painting in oil. *Specialty:* impressionism, Renoir, Monet, Pissaro. *Interests:* Travel & paint on location with wife, Yelena, watch soccer & hockey. *Publ:* Marbella Art Gallery, New York Pub Libr Archives, 4/2007 & Frick Art Reference Libr, New York, 5/2007. *Dealer:* Marbella Gallery New York NY

TSCHUMI, BERNARD
ARCHITECT
b Lausanne, Switzerland, Jan 25, 1944. *Study:* Fed Inst Tech, MArch, Zurich, 1969. *Pos:* head firm, Bernard Tschumi Architects, Paris, 1983-, New York, 1983-. *Teaching:* tchr, Archit Asn, London, 1970-80; Inst Archit and Urban Studies, New York, 1976; Princeton Univ Sch Archit, NJ, 1980-91; Cooper Union, 1980-83; dean, Columbia Univ Grad Sch Archit, Planning & Preservation, New York, 1988-2003. *Awards:* 1st prize for design of Parc de la Villette, Paris, 1983; Grand Prix National d'Architecture, 1996; award for design of New Acropolis Mus, Athens, 2001; Ordre des Arts et Lettres. *Mem:* Nat Acad; Coll Int de Philosophie. *Publ:* contribr, The Manhattan Transcripts, 1981, Architecture and Disjunction, 1994, Event Cities, 1994, Bernard Tschumi: Architecture and Event, 1994. *Mailing Add:* Bernard Tschumi Architects 227 W 17th St 2nd Fl New York NY 10011

TSE, STEPHEN
PAINTER, EDUCATOR
b Hong Kong, Oct 20, 1938; US citizen. *Study:* Washburn Univ, Topeka, Kans, BFA; Univ Idaho, MFA; also with Jack Tworkov. *Work:* Wenatchee Valley Coll, Wash; Yakima Valley Coll, Wash; Spokane Falls Community Coll, Wash; Rainier Nat Bank, Olympia, Wash; First Nat Bank Idaho, Boise; Seattle First Nat Bank; Mus Art, Eugene, Ore; Univ Ore, Eugene, Ore; many others. *Comn:* Sculpture panels with painting, Student Union, Univ Idaho, 65. *Exhib:* Solo exhibs, Gallery-76, Wenatchee Valley Coll, Wash, 78 & Kirsten Gallery, Seattle, 77, 78, 80, 82 & 85, Prichard Art Gallery, Univ Idaho, 86 & Still Water Art Gallery, Seattle, 91; Nat Painting Exhib, Grover M Hermann Fine Art Ctr, Marietta Coll, Ohio, 79; Nat Small Painting Purchase Exhib, Western Ill Univ, Macomb, 79; Compton Gallery, Wash State Univ, Pullman, 83; Alcoa/Gallery 76 Art Exhib, Wenatchee, Wash, 84-86 & 89; Mus of Art, Univ Oreg, Eugene, Oreg; Big Bend Community Coll, Moses Lake, Wash; Watcom Mus History and Art, Bellingham, Wash; Yakima Valley Coll, Yakima, Wash; plus many others. *Teaching:* Prof emer, Big Bend Community Coll. *Awards:* Painting Award, 28th Ann Centennial Wash Artist Exhib, Larson Gallery, Yakima, 84; Merit Award, Carnegie Ctr, Walla Walla, Wash, 85 & 87; Painting Award, Carnegie Ctr, Walla Walla, Wash, 90, Third Painting Award, 93. *Mem:* Wash Art Asn; Oriental Ceramic Soc, London. *Media:* Oil and Watercolor; Clay. *Dealer:* Kirsten Gallery 5320 Roosevelt Way NE Seattle WA 98105. *Mailing Add:* 1302 Evergreen Point Rd Medina WA 98039

TSIEN, BILLIE
ARCHITECT
Study: Yale Univ, undergraduate degree in fine arts, 1971; UCLA, Masters in Arch, 1977. *Pos:* Worked with Tod Williams since 1977, ptnr Tod Williams Billie Tsien Architects, 1986-; advisory panel mem Wexner Prize; bd mem Public Art Fund, Architectural League, and the American Acad of Rome. *Teaching:* tchr Parsons, Yale Univ, Harvard Univ GSD, Univ Tex Austin, Univ Pa; Louis I Kahn co-chair, Yale Univ. *Awards:* co-recipient with Tod Williams, Brunner Award, American Acad Arts and, Medal of Honor from NYC AIA, Chrysler Award for Design Innovation, Cooper Hewitt Nat Design Award in Architecture, President's Medal, Architectural League. *Mem:* Nat Acad. *Mailing Add:* Tod Williams Billie Tsien Architects 222 Central Park South New York NY 10019

TUAZON, OSCAR
SCULPTOR
b Seattle, Wash, 1975. *Study:* Cooper Union Advancement Sci & Art, New York, 1995-99; Whitney Mus Am Art, independent study program, 2001-2003. *Exhib:* Landlords Instant Cash, PS1 Ctr for Contemp Art, New York, 2001; Strike, Wolverhampton Art Gallery, England, 2002; Wight Biennial, UCLA, Los Angeles, 2003; Urban Renewal: City Without a Ghetto, Princeton Sch Archit, NJ, 2004; Bridges, Univ Colo, Denver, 2005; Whitney Biennial, Whitney Mus Am Art, 2006, 2012; 54th Int Art Exhib Biennale, Venice, 2011; America is My Woman, 2011. *Pos:* Co-founder, Castillo/Corrales Gallery, Paris. *Awards:* Betty Bowen Award, 2007. *Bibliog:* Carly Berwick (auth), Civic Boosters, Metropolis, 2/2002; Holland Cotter, Body and the Archive, NY Times, 2/14/2003; Howard Halle (auth), Slouching Towards Bethlehem, Time Out New York, 2004. *Mailing Add:* Maccarone 630 Greenwich St New York NY 10014

TUCHMAN, MAURICE
MUSEUM CURATOR
b Jacksonville, Fla, Nov 30, 1936. *Study:* Nat Univ Mex; City Coll NY, BA (art hist), 57, Fel, 58; Columbia Univ, MA (art hist), 59, studies with Theodore Reff, George Collins & Julius Held; Fulbright Scholar, Freie Univ, Berlin, 60-61. *Collection Arranged:* Five Younger Calif Artists, 65; Edward Kienholz, 66; Irwin-Price, 66; John

Mason, 66; Am Sculpture of 60's (with catalog), 67; Soutine (with catalog), 68; Art & Technol (with catalog), 71; 11 Los Angeles Artists, 1971 Traveling Exhib (with catalog), Sidney Janis Gallery, 72; European Paintings in the 70's (with catalog), 75; Richard Diebenkorn: Paintings and Drawings, 77, Mus Mod Art, 89; Italo Scanga, 83; Susan Rothenberg, 83; The Artist as Social Designer: Aspects of Public Art Today, 85; in prep: Hidden Meanings in Modern Art: Abstract Painting and Mysticism, 1891-1986, 86; David Hockney A Retrospective, Metrop Mus Art, NY, 88 & Tate Gallery, London, 88; Chain Soutine Centenary Retrospective (with catalog), Odakyu Mus, Tokyo, 92. *Pos:* Art ed mod art sect, Columbia Encycl, 62; mem curatorial & lect staff, Guggenheim Mus, 62-64, organizer, summer 64; sr cur mod art, Los Angeles Co Mus Art, 64-94, emer sr cur, 94-; mem art adv panel to the comnr Internal Revenue Serv, 75-78; mem bd dir, Am Asn Mus/Inst Coun Mus, 79-83; mem adv comt & contribr, Random House Libr Painting & Sculpture, 81; mem adv comt, Skowhegan Sch Painting, New York, Archives Am Art, San Marino, Calif; mem int comt, Int Coun Mus & Collections of Mod Art, Int Coun Mus/CIMAM; mem int res & exhanges bd, Princeton Univ, NJ, 89; dir, Int Coun Artec Biennale, Nagoya, Japan, 92. *Awards:* Fulbright Scholar, 60-61. *Mem:* Am Arts Alliance, (bd dir, 77-80); Nat Endowment Arts, 77-79; Am Fedn Arts (nat exhib comt); Los Angeles Design Alliance, (bd gov, 84); Int Adv Comt, Mus Art Carnegie Inst, 85. *Publ:* Chaim Soutine (1893-1943) (essay, catalog), Kunstmuseum Lucerne, 82; The Avant-Garde in Russia, 1910-1930: New Perspectives, 82; Artists Look at Los Angeles, Am Illustrated, No 331, 6/84; The Spiritual in Art: Abstract Painting 1890-1985, Second Christensen Lect, Art Gallery Western Australia, 88; Chaim Soutine Catalogue Raisonné, Gay Loudmer & Perls Galleries Publ, Paris, 93

TUCHMAN, PHYLLIS
CRITIC, CURATOR

b Passaic, NJ, Jan 4, 1947. *Study:* Sarah Lawrence Coll Summer Session in Florence, 67; Boston Univ, BA (distinction in fine arts), 68; Inst of Fine Arts, NY Univ, MA, 73, with Robert Goldwater, Robert Rosenblum & William S Rubin. *Collection Arranged:* Six in Bronze, Williams Coll Mus Art, 84; Big Little Sculpture, Williams Coll Mus Art, 88; Venezuela: The Next Generation, Baruch Coll Gallery, 90; George Segal Retrospective, Caracas Mus Contemp Art, Imber 91-92; Drawing Redux, San Jose Mus Art, 92; Norte del Sur: Venezuelan Art Today, Philbrook Art Mus, 97; Robert Smithson's NJ, Montclair Art Mus, 2014; Robert Motherwell: The East Hampton Years, 1944-1952, Guild Hall, 2014. *Pos:* Mem ed bd, Marsyas, NY, 71-74; vpres, Art Table, 87-88; contribr, NY Newsday, 85-94, Town & Country, 95-2009, Smithsonian Mag 98-, artnet.com and mag, 2000-; pres, AICA USA, 86-90; art Comt, Long House Reserve, 2007, Art + Auction, 2007-2008, Obit-mag.com, 2007-; ed, IFA Alumni Newsletter, 2009-2014, New York Observer, 2010-2011. *Teaching:* Instr art hist, Sch of Visual Arts, NY, 72-75; adj lectr art hist, Hunter Coll, 76-79; vis prof art, Williams Coll, 81-83. *Awards:* Nat Endowment Arts art critic's grant, 78-79; Nat Endowment Humanities fel, 80. *Mem:* Inst Asn Art Critics (pres Am sect, 86-90, vpres Int parent body, 89-91); Art Table; Coll Art Asn; Art Committee, Long House Reserve. *Publ:* Auth, George Segal, Abbeville Press, 83; contribr, Town & Country, Smithsonian, Art in Am, Artnet, Bloomberg News, Art & Auction, Obit-mag.com; New York Observer; Artforum; Sculpture mag. *Mailing Add:* 340 E 80th St New York NY 10075

TUCHOLKE, CHRISTEL-ANTHONY
PAINTER, SCULPTOR

b Poland, Mar 2, 1941; US citizen. *Study:* Univ Wis, Milwaukee, BS, 65 & MS, 65; Tamarind Lithography Workshop, Los Angeles, 68. *Work:* Milwaukee Art Mus, Wis; Miller Brewing Co Hq, Milwaukee, Wis; Charles Wustum Mus Art, Racine, Wis; Bradley Univ, Peoria, Ill; Kans State Univ Art Mus, Manhattan; Wis Bell Co Hdqtrs, Milwaukee; plus others. *Comn:* Exterior mural, John Michael Kohler Art Ctr, Sheboygan, Wis, 77; four paintings, Northwestern Mutual Life Insurance Co, Milwaukee, Wis, 79; telephone bk cover, Wis Telephone Co, 81; mural, Percent for Art Prog, Wis Art Bd, 85; Artists Limited Editions, Kohler Co, Wis, 89. *Exhib:* 74th, 76th, 77th & 80th Exhibs by Artists of Chicago & Vicinity, Chicago Art Inst, Ill, 73, 77, 78 & 84; Wis Directions Two, Milwaukee Art Mus, 78; Wis Biennale, Madison Art Ctr, 80 & 82; State of the Art: Wisconsin Painting and Drawing, J Michael Kohler Art Ctr, Sheboygan, Wis, 82; Belk Gallery, Western Carolina Univ, NC, 85; Wis-Minn Interface, Minn Mus Art, St Paul, Minn & Milwaukee Art Mus, 86; Edgewood Orchard Gallery, Fish Creek, Wis, 98; Mount Mary College, Wauwatosa; and others. *Awards:* Top Award, Madison Art Ctr, 80; Purchase Award, Wright Art Ctr, 80; Purchase Award, Bradley Univ, 81; Purchase Award, Wustum Mus, 85 & 89. *Media:* Acrylic, Pastel, Wood. *Mailing Add:* 2005 Bayside Ave Mount Dora FL 32757

TUCKER, ANNE WILKES
CURATOR, HISTORIAN

b Baton Rouge, La, Oct 18, 1945. *Study:* Randolph-Macon Women's Col, Lynchburg Va, BA (art hist), 67; Rochester Inst of Technol, AAS (photog), 68; Visual Studies Workshop, SUNY Buffalo, NY, MFA, 72; photo hist and mus procedure with Nathan Lyons & Beaumont Newhall, 70. *Collection Arranged:* Am Prospects: The Photographs of Joel Sternfeld (traveling), 87, Evocative Presence: Twentieth-Century Photographs in the Mus Collection, 88, Am Classroom: The Photographs of Catherine Wagner (traveling), 88, The Private Eye, 89, Czeck Modernism 1900-1945 (traveling), 89 & Money Matters: A Critical Look at Bank Architecture (traveling), 90, Houston Mus Fine Arts, Tex; Martin Luther King and the Civil Rights Movement, Mus Fine Arts, Houston, 1991, travel to Baltimore Mus Art; Brassai, Mus Fine Arts, Houston, 1996; Myths, Dreams and Realities: Contemporary Argentine Photography, Pan Am Cultural Exchange Houston, 1996, toured US & Mexico, 1997-1999; Postwar Italian Photography, Mus Fine Arts Houston, 2002; Japanese Photography in the Manfred Heiting Collection, Lower Brown Gallery, Mus Fine Arts, Houston, 2003; Aaron Sisking: Centennial Celebration, Cameron Found Gallery, Mus Fine Arts, Houston, 2004; 94th Ann Exhib, Documenting Poetry: Contemporary Latin Am Photography, Maier Mus Art, Randolph Macon Women's Col, Lynchburg, Va, 2005; Where Rivers Join the Sea: Photographs by Robert Adams & Marcos Zimmermann, Mus Fine Arts, Houston, 2007; The Great Wall of China: Photographs by Chen Changfen, Mus Fine Arts, Houston, 2007; Photographs by Bill Brandt, A Sense of Wonder, Mus Fine Arts, Houston, 2008; Chaotic Harmony: Contemp Korean Photography, Mus Fine Arts, Houston, 2010. *Pos:* Res asst, Int Mus Photogr, George Eastman House, Rochester, NY, 68-70; res assoc, Gernsheim Collection, Univ Tex, Austin, 69 & 79; cur intern, NY State Coun Art Grant, Photogr Dept, Mus Mod Art, NY, 70-71; photogr consult, Creative Artists Pub Serv Prog, NY, 71-72; dir, Photo Lecture Series, Cooper Union Forum, NY, 72-75; cur photogr, Mus Fine Arts, Houston, Tex, 76-, Gus & Lyndall Wortham cur, 84-. *Teaching:* Vis lectr, New Sch Soc Research, NY, spring 73 & Philadelphia Col Art, 73-75; lectr, Cooper Union Advan Arts & Sci, NY, 72-75; affiliate artist, Univ Houston, Tex, 76-80; lectr, panelist numerous workshops, univs and confs, 1973-. *Awards:* Guggenheim Fel, 83; Nat Endowment Arts, 76, 86 & 90; Rsch Support Grant, Getty Center History of Art & the Humanities Resource Collections, 1995; Golden Light Awards Book of Yr, Maine Photogr Workshops, 1996; Selected Best Cur, Time mag, 9/17/2001; The 100 Most Important People in Photography, Am Photo Mag, 2005; Focus Award for Lifetime Achievement, Griffin Mus of Photography, 2006; Mellon Fel, Harry Ransom Humanities Res Ctr, Univ Tex Austin, 2007-2008; Recognized for design in the 2008 Asn Am Univ Presses Awards; Brown Found Fel, Dora Maar House, Menerbes, France, 2009. *Mem:* Soc Photog Educ (secy, nat bd 77-79); Coll Art Asn; Visual Studies Wkshp (bd trustees, 80-); Visual Arts Panel, Houston Fest, 81-83; Randolph-Macon Woman's Coll Art Gallery (adv bd, 82-84); Art Table, Inc, 83-; Houston Ctr for Photog (adv bd 1980-90, 1994-95, bd trustees 1990-93, sec 1990-93); Am Leadership Forum (bd trustees 1992-94, co-chair selection com 1993-94); others. *Res:* 20th century American photographs. *Interests:* Absences and gaps in current photographic history. *Publ:* The Blue Man'a Photographs, Rice Univ Press, 90; Czeck Modernism 1900-1945, Bolfinch Press & Mus Fine Arts, Houston, 90; Money Matters: A Critical Look at Bank Architecture, McGraw-Hill & Mus Fine Arts, Houston, 90; Carry Me Home, Smithsonian Press, 90; George Krause, Rice Univ Press, 92; Crimes and Splendors: The Desert Cantos of Richard Misrach, with essay by Rebecca Solnit, Bulfinch Press & Mus Fine Arts Houston, 1996; auth essay, When the Whole is Undecipherable, in: David Maisel: Terminal Image, Paul Kopeikin Gallery, Los Angeles, 2005; auth intro, Dave Anderson, Dewi Lewis Publ, Eng, 2006; auth, Rough Beauty: Photography by Dave Anderson, Dewi Lewis Publ, Stockport, England, 2006; auth, The Great Wall of China, Yale Univ Press, 2007; Habitat 7: Jeff Chien-Hsing Liao, Nazraeli Press, 2007; Looking in: Robert Frank's The Americans, Nat Gallery Art, DC, 2009. *Mailing Add:* Mus Fine Arts PO Box 6826 Houston TX 77265-6826

TUCKER, LEATRICE YVONNE See Edwards-Tucker, Yvonne Leatrice

TUCKER, WILLIAM EDWARD
PATRON

b Charlotte, NC, June 22, 1932. *Study:* Barton Col, BA, 1953. *Pos:* Ordained to ministry Disciples of Christ Church, 1956; prof, Barton Col, 1959-55, chmn dept religion & philosophy, 1961-66; mem fac, Brite Div Sch, Tex Christian Univ, 1966-76, prof church hist, 1969-76, dean 1971-76, chancellor 1979-98, chancellor emer, 1998-; pres, Bethany Col, WVa, 1976-79; dir, RadioShack Corp, 1985-2003, Brown and Lupton Found; mem gen bd, Christian Church (Disciples of Christ), 1971-74, 75-87, admin comt, 1975-81, chmn theological educ comn, 1972-73, mem exec comt, chmn bd higher educ, 1975-77; dir, Christian Church Found, 1980-83; moderator, Christian Church (Disciples of Christ), 1983-85; trustee, Amon Ctr Mus. *Mem:* Trustee, Amon Carter Mus; Phi Beta Kappa, Exchange Club; bd dir, Van Cliburn Found, 1981-, Ft Worth Symphony Orchestra. *Mailing Add:* 777 Taylor St Ste P2J Fort Worth TX 76102

TUCKERMAN, JANE BAYARD
PHOTOGRAPHER, EDUCATOR

b Boston, Mass, June 11, 1947. *Study:* Art Inst Boston, 68-71; RI Sch Design, MFA, 73-75. *Work:* Metrop Mus Art & Mus Mod Art, NY; Minneapolis Inst Art, Minn; Detroit Inst Arts; Boston Mus Fine Arts; RI Sch Design; Addison Gallery Am Art; Univ Mass. *Comn:* New Work's Portfolio, Boston Photog Resource Soc, 81. *Exhib:* Invisible Light, Smithsonian Inst Traveling Exhib, 80-84; solo exhibs, Addison Gallery Am Art, 76 & Photogalerie Pennings Edinhoven, The Neth, 81; Inst Contemp Art, Boston, 85; Ateneo de Caracas, Venezuela, 90; Photographers on Ellis Island, 1900-1990, Nat Park Ellis Island, 91; An Historical Preview 30 Woman Photographers, Silver Image Gallery, Seattle, 92; Looking at Death, Harvard Univ, 93; Mus de Chopo, Mexico City, 95; plus many others. *Collection Arranged:* Second Sight: Exhib of Infrared Photog (auth, catalog), traveling in US, Canada & Europe, 81-84. *Teaching:* Asst prof photog, Wellesley Col, 76-77; assoc prof & dir photog prog, Harvard Univ, 78-; guest instr & lectr, Maine Photog Workshop, Rockport, Factory Visual Arts, Seattle, 79; guest instr, Chulalongkoin Univ, Bangkok, 85, Yale Univ, 86; vis prof, Northeastern Univ, 90-91; Prof, Art Inst Boston, 90-; Harnish vis artist, Smith Col, 95-97. *Awards:* Polaroid Exhib Grant for Second Sight, 81; New Works Fel, Traveling Exhib in New England, Mass Coun Arts & Boston Photog Resource Ctr, 81-82; Individual Artists Fel, Nat Endowment Arts, 82-83; Smithsonian, Nat Endowment Arts, Benares proj, 85; Mass Artists Found Fel, 86. *Bibliog:* Allen Porter (auth), Camera Mag, 74, 80 & 81; Pamela Allara (auth), The scope of Boston art is much broader than it would appear, Art News, 11/81; Photography Year 1982, Time/Life Bks, 82. *Publ:* Contribr, Self Portrayal, Friends Photog, 78; Darkroom Dynamics, Curtain & London, 79; contribr & illusr, American photographer, CBS Publ, 82; contribr, Aperture Mag, 83; The Making of a Collection, Hartwell-Aperture, 85; auth, India: Ritual & the River, Aperture Mag, 87; Invisible Light, Univ Mass, 87. *Dealer:* Witkin Gallery 415 W Broadway New York NY; Pierce St Gallery 217 Pierce St Suite 206 Birmingham MI 48011. *Mailing Add:* Main St Box 399 Dublin NH 03444

TUEGEL, MICHELE BECKMAN
CRAFTSMAN, ADMINISTRATOR

b Pittsburgh, Pa, Sept 26, 1952. *Study:* Univ S Fla, Tampa, MFA, 77; Int Inst Experimental Printmaking, Calif, papermaking cert, 76; independent study at Dieu Donne Paper Mill, NY, 86. *Work:* Walt Disney World Productions, Orlando, Fla; Hyatt Regency Hotel, Aruba; Southern Progress Corp Birmingham Ala; City of St

Petersburg, Fla. *Comn:* Lobby installation (paper), AmeriFirst Bank, Boca Raton, Fla, 84; framed paperworks, SW Bell Telephone Co, St Louis, Mo, 86, Jewish Hosp, St Louis, 87; Landowne Conf Ctr, Washington DC, 90; Children's Presbyterian Hosp, Plano, Tex, 91; Fossil Park, City of St Petersburg Pub Art Comn, 97. *Exhib:* Paper As Medium, Smithsonian Inst, Washington, DC, 78-80; Papermaking & Paper Using, Southeastern Ctr Contemp Art, Winston-Salem, 79; Paper: New & Renewed Art, Tampa Mus, 87; A New Era of Paper, DeLand Mus Art, 90; Paper: US/Finland, WCarolina Univ, NC, 92-95. *Pos:* Spec proj coordr, Fla Gulf Coast Art Ctr, Belleair, 83-87; dir, Fla Craftsmen Inc, St Petersburg, 88-04; spec proj, Pinellas Co Cultural Affairs, 04-11; independent juror, cur, 2004-. *Teaching:* Asst design & silkscreen, Univ S Fla, Tampa, 76-77; workshop leader papermaking, Jacksonville Art Mus, Fla, and other cities, 79-; adj asst prof papermaking, Eckerd Col, St Petersburg, 84-85; lectr & juror papermaking workshops across US. *Awards:* Friends of the Arts Award, Pinellas Co Arts Coun, 87; Award of Excellence, Fla Craftsmen 36th Ann, Zelo Mag, 87; Distinguished Alumni Award Fine Arts, Univ of SFla, 93; Women Honoring Women Award, Soroptomist Int, 2005; Alumni Award for Distinguished Community Serv, Univ S Fla, 2006. *Bibliog:* MaryAnn Marger (auth), Fiber Arts, Fiber Arts Mag, 86; Heart on Paper, Creative Ideas for Living Mag, 87. *Mem:* Am Craft Coun; Fla Craftsmen; Fla Cult Action & Educ Alliance; Craft Org Dirs Asn. *Media:* Handmade Paper. *Mailing Add:* 433 Monte Cristo Blvd Tierra Verde FL 33715

TUER, DOT (DOROTHY) J
CRITIC, CURATOR
b Toronto, Ont, Aug 28, 1957. *Study:* Queen's Univ, BA, 81; Univ Toronto, MA, 94; Univ Toronto, PhD, 99. *Collection Arranged:* Perspectives of Women, Funnel Film Theatre, 88; Imaging Labor, Ont Ministry Cult, 91; Retrospective: Festival of Festivals, Can Cinema, 92; Images Film Spotlight: Retrospective of Vera Frekel, 97. *Pos:* Prog coordr, Funnel Experimental Film Ctr, 85-86; residency leader/consult, Banff Ctr Arts, 94; bd mem, Fuse Mag, 94-96 & The Power Plant, 91-95..*Teaching:* lectr art theory & hist, Ont Col Art & Design, 91-; lectr contemp art, Art Gallery Ont, 92. *Awards:* B Grants, Can Coun, 86, 87, 88, 91, 93 & 97; Best Curatorial Essay, Ont Art Gallery Asn, 94. *Mem:* Cinemateque Ont (bd mem, 91-97). *Res:* Contemp new media art; Latin Am art; issues of technol, identity & post colonialism. *Publ:* Contribr, Sightlines: Reading Contemporary Art, Artextes, 94; But is it Art? Spirit of Art as Activism, Bay Press, 94; Dara Birnbawn, Kuntshalle Vienna, 95; Robert Lehman Lectures in Contemporary Art, DIA Centre NY, 96; contribr, Ephemere: Char Davies, Nat Gallery Can, 98. *Mailing Add:* 143 Marlbourough Pl Toronto ON M5R 3J5 Canada

TULLIS, GARNER H
PUBLISHER, PRINTMAKER
b Cincinnati, Ohio, Dec 12, 1939. *Study:* Univ Pa, BFA, 64; Acad Di Belli Arte, Italy, Fulbright Scholar, 64-65; Stanford Univ, MA (Carnegie Fel), 67. *Work:* Cleveland Mus Art, Ohio; Philadelphia Mus Art, Pa; San Francisco Mus Mod Art, Calif; Mus Mod Art, NY; Brooklyn Mus Art, NY. *Exhib:* Ann Invitational, Pa Acad Fine Arts, 64; 49th Ann, Cleveland Mus Art, Ohio, 65; Nat Ann, San Francisco Mus Mod Art, Calif, 66; Albright-Knox Gallery, Buffalo, NY, 72; solo exhib, Cleveland Art Inst, Ohio, 75; Works in handmade paper, Mus Mod Art, NY, 76; 30 Yrs, 30 Printmakers, Nat Collection Fine Arts, Washington, DC, 78; Paper as Medium Traveling Exhib, Smithsonian, 78-82. *Pos:* Dir, Inst Experimental Printmaking, 73-; founder, Garner Tullis Workshop, New York, NY, Santa Barbara, Calif & Pietrarubbia, Italy, 86-. *Teaching:* Foundry supervisor sculpture, Univ Calif, Berkeley, 67-69; artist-in-residence papermaking, Bennington Col, 76; assoc prof printmaking, Univ Calif, Davis, 76-84; artist-in-residence, Harvard Univ, 92. *Awards:* Nat Endowment Arts Grant, 76. *Bibliog:* Jules Heller (auth), Papermaking Today, Watson-Guptill, 78; Paper: Art & Technology, World Print Coun, 79; Patricia Newman (auth), Experimental workshop of Garner Tullis, Smithsonian Mag, 8/80; Charles Millard (auth), Garner Tullis, Print Quart, 6/89. *Mem:* Life mem, The Print Club, Philadelphia; Calif Soc Printmakers; Coll Art Asn; Fulbright Alumni Asn. *Media:* Monotype. *Dealer:* Rosenberg & Kaufman Gallery 115 Wooser St New York NY 10012. *Mailing Add:* 200 E 10th St #302 New York NY 10003-7702

TULLOS, MARK A, JR
ADMINISTRATOR, CURATOR
b Baton Rouge, La, Jan 19, 1961. *Study:* La State Univ, Baton Rouge, BFA, 84; Stephen F Austin State Univ, Nacogdoches, Tex, 88-90. *Collection Arranged:* Some Past is Present, Janet Turner, 90; Nature in Ornament, Newcomb Pottery, 91; The Spiritual in Nature, Will Stevens/Walter Anderson, 92; Salvation on San Mountain: Jim Neel & Melissa Springer, 97; Louisiana Artist Alumni Retrospective, 98. *Pos:* Exec dir, Mus ETex, Lufkin, 87-90, Walter Anderson Mus Art, Ocean Springs, 91-92 & Alexandria Mus Art, La, 92-. *Awards:* Nancy Hanks Mem Award for Prof Excellence, Asn Mus, 95; Paul Harris Fel, Rotary Int. *Mem:* Am Asn Mus; SE Mus Asn; La Asn Mus (vpres, 96). *Mailing Add:* c/o Alexandria Mus Art 933 Main St PO Box 1028 Alexandria LA 71309

TULLY, JUDD
WRITER, CURATOR
b Chicago, Ill, Apr 13, 1947. *Study:* Am Univ, Washington, BA, 69; Univ Ore, Eugene. *Collection Arranged:* Vintage New York (auth, catalog), 83-84, One Penn Plaza, NY; Reuben Kadish Survey: 1935-1985 (auth, catalog), Artists' Choice Mus, NY, 86; The New Sculpture Group - A Look Back: 1957-1962 (auth, catalog), NY Studio Sch, 88; Made in NY: Encounters with contemp sculpture (auth, catalog), Williams Ctr for Arts, Easton, Pa, 89; Lost and Found (auth, catalog), Sculpture Ctr, NY, 91; The Convergence of Art & Poetry, Mus at Fashion Inst of Technology, 2003; Reuben Kadish: Monotypes & Sculpture, 55 Mercer Gallery, 2004. *Pos:* Lectr contemp art, NY Bd Educ, 84-; interviewer, Archives of Am Art, Smithsonian Inst, 88-; Editor at Large, Art & Auction Mag, 98; Chmn, The Reuben Kadish Art Found, 2000-. *Teaching:* NY Studio Sch Drawing, Painting & Sculpture, 95-. *Awards:* Arts & Cult reporting award, 98; Asn for Women in Commun 26th annual Clarion Awards, 98. *Mem:* Int Asn Art Critics; Nat Writers Union. *Res:* Cultural reportage on contemporary painting and sculpture. *Publ:* Auth, Red Grooms and Ruckus Manhattan, George Braziller, NY, 77; Troubled times for artists' foundations, Art & Auction, 11/94; Who owns NY mus old masters?, Wash Post, 1/12/95; Posthumous sculpture casts-the messiest subject alive, Artnews, 12/95; Outside, inside or somewhere in between, Artnews, 5/96; When is a Calder Not a Calder, Art News, 2/97; The Floor is Theirs, The NY Times Mag, 97; Michel Cohen: The Con & the Pros, Art & Auction, 3/2001; Special Report: The Taubman Trial, Art & Auction, 2/2002; High and Inside, Marlborough Chelsea, May, 2003; Reuben Kadish; Metaunorphosis, Pollock-Krasner House and Study Center, Aug, 2004; Market Spice; Modern Indian Art & Auction, April, 2005; Helmut Newton-Master of the Erotic Image, Cigar Aficionado, 2008. *Mailing Add:* 426 West Broadway Apt 2G New York NY 10012

TULUMELLO, PETER M
CONSULTANT, DESIGNER
b Welland, Ont, Apr 15, 1954. *Study:* Damaen Col, Buffalo, NY, 73-74; Univ Waterloo, Ont, BA (fine arts, hon), 78; Univ Regina, Sask, MFA, 80. *Work:* Univ Waterloo, Ont; Univ Regina. *Pos:* Dir & cur, Estevan Nat Exhib Ctr, 81-83, Mus Northern Hist, Ont, 84-85 & Art Gallery Northumberland, Cobourg, Ont, 85-89; pres, Corp Image Art & Design Consult Inc, 89-2000; pres, Wavelight Web Dimensions Inc, 2000-2009; exec dir, Atikokan Arts Ctr. *Teaching:* Lectr, Univ Regina, 79-83 & Niagara Col, 96. *Awards:* Prov Sask Grad Scholar, 79; Proj Cost Grant, Can Coun Award, 82. *Mem:* Can Mus Asn; Ont Mus Asn. *Collection:* University of Regina, University of Waterloo, Gazette Newspaper. *Publ:* 40 Years of Art in Kirkland Lake. *Mailing Add:* 66 State St Welland ON L3B 4K5 Canada

TUMAN, DONNA
EDUCATOR, ADMINISTRATOR
Study: Queen's Col, CUNY, BS, MS; Teachers Col, Columbia Univ, EdD. *Pos:* Pres, Univ Coun for Art Edn, 2003-2009. *Teaching:* Assoc prof, chair art dept, dir art edn program, CW Post Campus of Long Island Univ, currently. *Awards:* Recipient, Art Educator of the Year, CUNY, 1980, NYC "Apple for Education Honors", Queens Mus Education Dept, 1988, Citations from NY State Senate and Assembly, Nassau County and the Town of Hempstead for founding directorship of the Long Island Children's Mus, 1993, NY State Art Teachers Asn Special Citation/Leadership and Excellence, 2005, Annual award for Leadership, Art Supervisors Asn of Long Island, 2005; honoree Univ Coun for Art Education, 2009. *Mem:* Long Island Art Teachers Asn; NY State Art Teachers Asn; Subway Art Panel, NYC MTA, 1985-1988; Nat Art Education Asn (annual conf presenter, 1985-); Coun of the Arts for the North Shore (bd mem 1988-1991); Nassau County Office of Cultural Devlopment (mem adv bd, 1990-1992); Youth & Child Development Bd, Town of Oyster Bay, 1993-; Balanced Mind: Annual Arts Conf for Nassau County Educators (mem steering com, 1996-); Cultural Bd of Dirs, Nassau County, 1997-2002; Arts-in-Education Panelist, NY State Coun for the Arts, 1997-2002; Arts Supervisors Asn of Long Island (advisor, 2003-); NY State Alliance for Arts Education (bd mem 2004-2006); Achievement in Art and Music, NY State Education Dept (mem adv com 2004-); Univ Coun for Art Education (bd mem 2000-); Univ Coun for Art Education (pres 2003-2009); Art League of Long Island (bd mem 2006-). *Publ:* Works published in Visual Arts Research, Gender Issues in Art Education, Studies in Art Education and The Journal of Aesthetic Education. *Mailing Add:* CW Post Campus Long Island Univ Art Department 720 Northern Blvd Greenvale NY 11548

TUNIS, ROSLYN
CURATOR, GALLERY DIRECTOR
b Montreal, Que; US citizen. *Study:* State Univ NY, Binghamton, BA (studio art & art hist), 72, MA (art hist & anthrop), 80. *Collection Arranged:* Festival of Mexico (auth, catalog), 73; The Fine Art of Craftsmanship (auth, catalog), 74; William Bingham: Am a Good Investment (auth, catalog), 75; Artistic Spirit of the North Am Indian (auth, catalog), 76; Treasure House: Mus of the Empire State (auth, catalog), 79; Charles Eldred: Sculpture and Drawing (auth, catalog), 80; Fusing Traditions: Transformations in Glass, Native Am Artists Mus Craft and Folk Art, San Francisco (auth, catalog); The Art of Research: Nelson Graburn and the Aesthetics of Inuit Sculpture, Phoebe Hearst Mus Anthrop, UCLA Berkeley; Silent Voices Speak: Remembering the Holocaust, Paintings by Barbara Shilo, San Francisco Presidio (auth, catalog); The Pan Am Unity Multi-Media Exhib: An Exploration of the Mural by Diego Rivera, DeYoung Mus, San Francisco; Art As a Reflection of Eskimo / Inuit Culture: Tradition and Change in the 20th Century, Gallery Concord, Calif; The Artistic Spirit: Selections from the Phoebe A Hearst Mus Anthrop, UCLA Berkeley (auth, catalog), 90-93; and many others. *Pos:* Cur art, Roberson Ctr for Arts & Sci, Binghamton, NY, 72-84; dir, Carlyn Gallery, Madison Ave, New York, 84-89 & Danville, Calif, 90-93; chief cur & deputy dir curatorial servs, Univ Calif/Berkeley Mus, Blackhawk. *Teaching:* adj prof, John F Kennedy Univ, 94. *Mem:* Am Crafts Coun; Art Table Inc; Friends Ethnic Art (bd mem); Western Mus Asn (bd mem); Am Asn Mus. *Res:* Art of the Iroquois, contemporary American crafts; anthropology-Native American; Eskimo; ethnic art and folk art. *Mailing Add:* 5727 La Salle Ave Oakland CA 94611

TUPITSYN, MARGARITA
CRITIC, CURATOR
b Moscow, Russia, Mar 23, 1955; US citizen. *Study:* Grad Sch, City Univ New York, with Rosalind Krauss & R C Washton-Long; City Univ NY, PhD. *Collection Arranged:* SOTS Art (auth, catalog), New Mus, 86; Between Spring & Summer: Soviet Conceptual Art (auth, catalog), 90 & Montage & Modern Life (auth, catalog), 92, Inst Contemp Art, Boston; The Great Utopia (auth, catalog), Guggenheim Mus, 92. *Teaching:* Lectr Russ, Avanta-Garde New Sch, 87-87 & Avant-Garde State Univ NY, 87-88. *Mem:* Coll Art Asn. *Publ:* Auth, Margins of Soviet Art: Socialist Realism to the Present, Giancarlo Politi Editore, 89; Between art & politics: Gustave Klutsis, Art Am, 91

TUPPER, DANI
PAINTER, INSTRUCTOR

b Bloomington, Nebr, Jan, 26, 2013. *Study:* Hastings Coll, 1953-55; Eastern NMex Univ, 1973-74; workshops with various nationally known watercolorists. *Work:* St Mary's Memorial Hospital, Grand Juction, Colo; Pueblo Public Libr, Colo; Trinidad Public Libr, Colo; First State Bank, Tucson, Ariz; Tex State Bank, Muleshoe, Tex. *Comn:* portrait of family, Mary Kellerstraus, Ogden, Utah, 2002; religious mural, Central Christian Church, Pueblo, Colo, 2005; portrait of children, Melissa Webb, Delta, Colo, 2011; Colo Seasons mural, Delta Memorial Hospital, Delta, Colo, 2011; Italian Street Scene Mural, DiVitos Restaurant, Delta, Colo, 2013. *Exhib:* Western Co Watercolor Show, Grand Junction Art Ctr, 2006, 2008; ISEA Int, Seattle, Wash, 2010, 2013; Rockies West Nat Ctr Arts, Grand Juction, Colo, 2011, 2012, 2013. *Pos:* vpres, Aurora Artist Guild, 1994-95; founding pres, S Colo Watercolor Soc, 1998-2004; pres, Western Colo, 2009-2013. *Teaching:* pvt instr in own studios; instr watercolor, Eccles Art Ctr, Ogden, Utah, 1990-91, Art Ctr, Springfield, Ill, 1992-95. *Awards:* First Place, Ogden Art Guild, 91, Aurora Artist Guild, 94, Western Colo Watercolor Soc, 2007; Best of Show, Southern Colo Watercolor, 99, Second Place, 2008. *Mem:* Western Colo Watercolor Soc (pres, 2009-2013, vpres, 2013-); Southern Colo Watercolor Soc (founding pres, 1998-2004); Transparent Watercolor Soc Am (lifetime mem); Int Soc Experimental Artists; Colo Watercolor Soc (signature mem). *Media:* Watercolor, Mixed Media. *Publ:* contbr, Best of Flower Painting, Northlight, 1999; Memorial Cookbook, St Mary Corwin Medical Ctr, 2008; Splash 8 (book), Northlight, 2007, Splash II, 2010. *Mailing Add:* 960 Willow Wood Ln Delta CO 81416

TURCONI, SUE (SUSAN) KINDER
PAINTER, PHOTOGRAPHER

b Teaneck, NJ, Feb 26, 1939. *Study:* William Paterson Univ, Wayne, NJ, BA, 74; Pratt Inst, Brooklyn, MFA, 76. *Work:* NJ State Mus, Trenton; Newark Mus, NJ; Pratt Inst, Brooklyn; City Hall, Venice, Fla; Rutgers Univ, New Brunswick, NJ. *Comn:* Hackensack (photog pub), Hackensack CofC, NJ, 76. *Exhib:* Bergen Mus Art & Sci, Paramus, NJ, 90 & solo exhib, 92; Robeson Gallery, Rutgers Univ, Newark, NJ, 92; Barrier Island Ctr Arts, Big Arts Mus, Sanibel, Fla, 94; Nanjing Arts Coll, Nanjing, China, 97; Boca Raton Mus Art, Boca Raton, Fla, 98; Curator's Choice: Legacy II, Mus Art & Sci, Melbourne, Fla, 99; Jersey City Mus Exhib & Benefit Invitational, 2002; Tampa Mus Art, Tampa, Fla, 2004; Europ Coun Int Studies Ann Meeting, Conf & exhib, World Forum Convention Ctr, The Hague, Neth, 2005; ECIS, The Acropolis, Nice, France, 2006; Daytona Beach Mus Fine Arts, Daytona Beach, Fla; Mus South Fla, Bradenton, Fla; Highlands Mus of the Arts, Sebring, Fla, 2009; Leepa-Ratner Mus Art, St. Petersburg, Fla, 2009; Big Arts Mus, Sanibel, Fla, 2010; Tampa Mus Art, Tampa, Fla, 2012; Boca Raton Mus Art, Fla, 2013. *Pos:* Art critic, Suburban Trends, Riverside Publ Co, 74-80; writer column, Prof Women Photogrs Times, 81-82; NJ correspondent, Art Express, 82; print librn, Soho Photo, New York, 86-87. *Teaching:* Instr photog, Passaic Co Community Coll, Paterson, NJ, 84-86, Bergen Community Coll, Paramus, NJ, 85-93, Manatee Community Coll, Venice, Fla, 94- & Edison Community Coll, Ft Meyers, Fla, 96; instr, studio art, Vt Coll, Norwich Univ, Montpelier, 98, photography & printmaking, Venice Art Ctr, Fla, 99- & Manatee Community Coll, Venice, Fla, art history & art appreciation, 2007-9; instr art hist & art appreciation, State Coll Fla, Venice Fla, 2010-13. *Awards:* NJ State Coun Arts Fel, 85-85; Grumbacher Medal, Venice Art Ctr, Venice, Fla, 98; combined talents, Fla Int 2004, Fla State Univ Mus Fine Arts, Tallahassee. *Bibliog:* John Zeaman (auth), Fine Arts, Sunday Record, 92; Mitchell Siedel (auth), Photography, Sunday Star Ledger, 92; Joan Altabe (auth) Fine Arts, Sunday Sarasota Herald Tribune, 2000. *Mem:* Women Contemp Artists, Fla; Fla Artists' Group. *Media:* All Media. *Publ:* Auth, Getting started, 84 & Ghosts, 85, Strategies Mag; Historical Composition & Teaching & Learning Strategies, Ilford Photo Instructor Newsletter, 91; Notes on Photography, Sweet & Bitter Fruit, Bergen Community Coll, Paramus, NJ; A Walk into Abstracts (ebook), Vol 5. *Mailing Add:* 1220 Sleepy Hollow Rd Venice FL 34285-6441

TURK, RUDY H
MUSEUM DIRECTOR, PAINTER

b Sheboygan, Wis, June 24, 1927. *Study:* Univ Wis, 46-49; Univ Tenn, 49-51; Ind Univ, 52-56; Univ Paris, Fulbright Scholar, 56-57. *Work:* Bank One, Ariz. *Exhib:* Solo exhibs, The Store, Berkeley, Calif, 66, Udinotti Gallery, San Francisco, 79, Ariz Western Col, 81, Alwun House Found, Phoenix, 99; invitational group exhibs, Fac Art Exhibs, Ariz State Univ, 68, 69 & 70, Works by Wanda and Rudy Turk, Missoula Art Ctr, 75, Two Edges on a Line: A Comparative Migration of Images Between Ariz-NMex, ASA Gallery, Univ NMex, 77, Retributive Justice, Simms Art Ctr, Albuquerque, NMex, 77, Masks and Self-Portraits, Udinotti Gallery Scottsdale, 79-98, Valley Nat Bank (Tempe Off), Selected Works of Ariz State Univ Artists, 80 & Scholder Collects, Ariz State Univ Art Mus, 87; Spec Traveling Exhib, Scholder by Scholder and Others, Western Assoc Art Mus, 79; retrospective New Sch for the Arts, Scottsdale, Ariz, 98. *Collection Arranged:* The Works of John Roeder, Richmond Art Ctr, Calif, 61-62; Contemp Glass, San Diego Mus Fine Arts, 67; The World of David Gilhooly, Ariz State Univ, 69; Henry Strater Retrospective, 79; The World of Viola Frey, 82; Edward Jacobson collection of Am wood bowls, 85 & 90; Sculpture by John Paul Jones, 87; City Phoenix Ceramics Collection, 98. *Pos:* Art historian & dir art gallery, Univ Mont, 57-60; dir, Richmond Art Ctr, 60-65 & Univ Art Mus, Ariz State Univ, 67-; asst dir, San Diego Mus Fine Arts, 65-67; dir, Art Mus, Ariz State Univ, Tempe, 67-92, dir emer, 92-. *Teaching:* Prof art, Ariz State Univ, 67-77. *Awards:* Hon fel, Am Craftsman Coun, 88; Governor's Art Award, Arts of Ariz, 92. *Mem:* Friends Mex Art; Asn Am Mus; Coll Art Asn Am. *Media:* Oil, Acrylic. *Res:* Contemporary art; Eighteenth century French art; humanities; American history & contemporary ceramics. *Collection:* Eighteenth century French prints; contemporary American ceramics; New Guinea Sculpture. *Publ:* Auth, IL Udell, Univ Art Collections, 71; coauth, Scholder/Indians, Northland, 72; The Search for Personal Freedom, William C Brown, Vols I & II, 4th ed 72, 5th ed 77, 6th ed 81, 7th ed 84; auth, Monumental Landscapes of Merrill Mahaffey, Northland, 79; auth, Scholder, New York, Rizzoli Press, 266, 82; plus critical studies, art catalogues & art reviews. *Dealer:* Udinotti Gallery 4215 N Marshall Way Scottsdale AZ 85251

TURLINGTON, PATRICIA R
PAINTER, SCULPTOR

b Washington, DC, Sept 14, 1939. *Study:* Washburn Univ, 62-63; NC State Univ Sch Design, spec study with Joe Cox, 69-71; Atlantic Ctr Arts, spec study with Audrey Flack, 86. *Work:* Mint Mus, Charlotte, NC; Duke Univ Med Ctr, Durham, NC; Univ NC, Chapel Hill; Wachovia Bank & Trust co, Winston Salem, NC; Blue Cross-Blue Shield, Chapel Hill, NC. *Comn:* Brick sculpture murals, (first brick sculpture in a pub sch in the US), Goldsboro City Sch, NC, 75; brick sculpture mural, City of Sanford, NC, 80; brick sculpture mural, McDonald's Corp, Oak Brook, Ill, 90; brick sculpture mural, Rowan Mem Hosp, Salisbury, NC, 91; brick sculpture mural, New York City Transit Authority, 92. *Exhib:* Artist's Political Statements, Southeastern Ctr Contemp Art, Winston Salem, NC, 86; A Feminist Odyssey, Wake Forest Univ Fine Arts Ctr, Winston Salem, NC, 87; Am History, Atlanta Coll Art Gallery, Ga, 90; Women and Art: Creating the Feminine Icon, Winthrop Coll Fine Arts Ctr, Rock Hill, SC, 91; Women's Issues as Art, Salem Coll Fine Arts Ctr, Winston Salem, NC, 92. *Teaching:* Prof studio art & art hist, Wayne Community Coll, Goldsboro, NC, 86-2005. *Awards:* Collaborating Arts Award, NC Chap Am Inst Architects, 78; Cash Award, Tex Fine Arts Asn Nat Exhib, 84; First Prize: Works on Paper, Nat Asn Women Artists, Morris J Heiman, 85. *Bibliog:* Norman Farley (dir), Sculptured Brick (film), Brick Inst Am, 89; Kathryn Gleason (auth), Brick Added to McDonald's drive thru menu, BIA News Mag/Brick Inst Am, 1/90; Norman Farley (auth), Brick sculpture: art becomes architecture, Archit Mag, 12/90. *Mem:* Nat Asn Women Artists. *Media:* Watercolor, Acrylic, Oil. *Publ:* Auth, North Drive Elementary School Intaglio Brick Sculptures, NC Architect, 77. *Mailing Add:* 709 Park Ave Goldsboro NC 27530

TURNBULL, BETTY
CURATOR

b Hollywood, Calif, Aug 4, 1924. *Study:* Los Angeles Valley Coll (art hist, design, drawing & painting), 56-59. *Collection Arranged:* Art of the Northwest Indian & Alaska Eskimo, Fine Arts Patrons of Newport Harbor, 68; Directly Seen; New Realism, 70 & Art of the Indian Southwest, 71, Newport Harbor Art Mus & Pasadena Mus Art; Mary Cassatt (auth, catalog), 74; The Flute and the Brush: Indian Miniature Paintings, 76; The Last Time I Saw Ferus (auth, catalog), 76; David Park Retrospective (auth, catalog), 77; The Prometheus Archives-A Retrospective of the Work of George Herms, 79; Via Celmins Survey (intro catalog), 79; California, The State of Landscape 1827-1981 (auth, catalog), Newport Harbor Art Mus, 81; Perpetual Motion (auth, catalog), Santa Barbara Mus Art, 87-88; and others. *Pos:* cur art, Newport Harbor Art Mus, Calif, 69-72 & 73-77, actg dir, 72-73, cur exhibs & collections, 77-81; dir, Turnbull, Lutjeans, Kogan (TLK) Gallery, 81-85; speaker/adv, Art Forum Prog, Rancho Santiago Col, 83-85. *Teaching:* Asst prof, Mus Studies Prog, Calif State Univ, Long Beach, 86-87. *Specialty:* Contemporary painting, sculpture & graphics

TURNBULL, LUCY
MUSEUM DIRECTOR, EDUCATOR

b Lancaster, Ohio. *Study:* Bryn Mawr Col, Pa, AB, 52; Am Sch Classical Studies, Athens, Greece, 55-57; Radcliffe Col, Cambridge, Mass, AM, 54, PhD, 60. *Collection Arranged:* Yoknapatawpha Through Other Eyes, 83, O Look Heaven is Coming to Earth, paintings of Theora Hamblett (auth, catalog), 84, Three Southern Photographers, 84, Images of the Southern Woman, 85, Mr McCrady of La-Fay-Ette Co, 86, Univ Mus, Univ Miss, Treasures from Oxford Homes I & II, 87. *Pos:* Mus asst, Mus Fine Arts, Boston, 58-60; cur, classical antiq, Univ Mus, Univ Miss, 77-, dir, 85-90. *Teaching:* From asst prof classical archaeol, to assoc prof, Univ Miss, 61-66, prof classics, 74-81, prof classics & art, 81-90, emer prof, 90-. *Mem:* Am Asn Mus; Archaeol Inst Am; Asn Coll & Univ Mus & Galleries. *Res:* Iconography of Greek mythology, especially in vase-painting; influence of other arts on vase-painting; topical themes in iconography. *Publ:* Contribr, Art, Myth & Culture; Greek Vases from the Southern Collections, New Orleans Mus, 81; Poets and Heroes, Emory Univ, Atlanta, 86. *Mailing Add:* 714 S 8th St Oxford MS 38655

TURNER, ALAN
PAINTER, PRINTMAKER

b New York, NY, July 6, 1943. *Study:* City Coll New York, BA, 65; Univ Calif, Berkeley, MA (painting), 67. *Work:* Whitney Mus Am Art, Mus Mod Art, NY; Mus Fine Arts, Boston; Minneapolis Inst Fine Art; MIT. *Comn:* Lithograph, Kunstvereine, Hamburg, Ger, 71; Painting, Third Nat Bank, Toledo, Ohio, 79. *Exhib:* Whitney Mus Am Art Biennial, 75 & 95; The Am Artist as Printmaker, 23rd Nat Print Exhib, Brooklyn Mus, NY, 84; Mus Fine Arts, Boston, 84; solo exhibs, Jason McCoy Gallery, NY, 87, Everson Mus Art, 88, Koury Wingate Gallery, NY, 88, 90, Tyler Gallery, Temple Univ, Elkins Park, Pa, 89, Ealan Wingate Gallery, NY, 91, Allez Les Filles Gallery, Columbus, Ohio, 95, Lennon, Weinberg Gallery, NY, 96, 2000, 2003; Inst Contemp Art, Boston, 89; Who Chooses Who, The New Mus, NY, 94; Lennon Weinberg Inc, NY, 94, 98, 02; Oeuvres Choisis, Allez Les Filles Gallery, Columbus, Ohio, 94; Jay Gorney Mod Art, NY, 94; Barbara Gladstone Gallery, New York City, 2000; Mathew Marks Gallery, New York City, 2000; Islip Art Mus, East Islip, NY, 02; and many others. *Awards:* Nat Endowment Arts Fel Grant, 77, 81, 87; Spoleto Choice, Spoleto, USA, 80; John Simon Guggenheim Mem Found Fel, 88; Pollock-Krasner Found Grant, 01. *Bibliog:* Stuart Servetar (auth), Alan Turner: Recent paintings, NY Press, 1/17-23/96; Robert Mahoney (auth), Alan Turner, Time Out NY, 1/17-24/96; Pepe Karmel (auth), Alan Turner, NY Times, 2/2/96; and many others. *Media:* Oil. *Publ:* Auth, Etchings, Parasol Press, 78; Lithos & Etchings, Brooke Alexander, 80; Ilene Kurtz Editions, 90. *Mailing Add:* 114 Franklin St New York NY 10013

TURNER, (CHARLES) ARTHUR
PAINTER, INSTRUCTOR

b Houston, Tex, Nov 17, 1940. *Study:* N Tex State Univ, BA, 62; Cranbrook Acad Art, Bloomfield Hills, Mich, MFA, 66, with Zoltan Shepeshy. *Work:* Mus Fine Arts & Houston Ind Inc, Houston; McNay Art Inst, San Antonio; Art Mus SE Tex; McAllen Int Mus, McAllen, Tex; Lord Fairfax Community Coll, Middletown, Va; Art Mus S

Tex, Corpus Christi; Mus Texas Tech Univ, Lubbock, Tex. *Exhib:* Solo exhibs, Moody Gallery, Houston, 78, 82, 87, 92, 96, 99, 2004-06 & 09, 2010, 2011, Patricia Moore Gallery, Aspen, 83 & 86, Moody Gallery, 2013; Recent Acquisitions, Mus Fine Arts, Houston, 78, 2004, 2009; Kunst Fra Houston I Norge, Stavanger Mus, Norway, 82; Contemplating Translucence, Allen Ctr, Houston, 96; Flora Bella, Galveston Arts Ctr, Tex, 97; Watercolor USA, Springfield, Mo, 2000; Reserved Light, Mus Fine Arts, Houston, 2001; Spirit of the Planet, Residence of the US Amb to UN, Vienna, Austria, 2003; Recent Watercolors, Lew Allen Contemp, Santa Fe, 2002; Rocky Mt Nat Watermedia, Foothills Art Ctr, Golden, Colo, 2005; Retrospective, Jung Ctr Gallery, Houston, 2007; Legends, Williams Tower, Houston, Tex, 2009; People, Places, and Things, Walter Wickiser Gallery, NY, 2011; Gallery Artists Part IX, Walter Wickiser Gallery, NY, 2012; Totems and Roundels, Moody Gallery, Houston, Tex, 2013; Art Palm Beach, Palm Beach Convention Ctr, Palm Beach, Fla, 2013; Je Gallery, Shanghai, 2015-; Busan Int Art Fair, Busan, Korea, 2015. *Teaching:* Asst prof painting, Madison Col, Va, 66-68; instr painting, Glassell Sch Art, Mus Fine Arts, Houston, 69-; guest instr, Univ Houston, 73; instr, Hill Country Arts Found, Ingram, Tex, 84, 89 & 90 & Anderson Ranch Art Ctr, Snowmass, Colo, 85; instr watercolor workshop, James Madison Univ, Orkney Springs, Va, 90 & Malakad Schloss Goldegg, Austria, 96, 99, 2003; instr, watercolor workshop, Sue Barnum Studio, Tesuque, NMex, 2010, 2013. *Awards:* First Purchase Award, Beaumont Art Mus 20th Ann, 71; First Place, Clear Lake Arts Alliance, Tex, 2000. *Bibliog:* Edwy B Lee (auth), Arthur Turner, drawings, Art Voices/South, 3/78; Elanor Freed (auth), Texas roundup, Art Am, 11/68; Jana Vander Lee (auth), Arthur Turner, Grand Mesa Mask, ie Mag, summer 92; Charlie Bier (auth), Wing it! Houston Mag, 5/2011; Claudia Feldman (auth), Hooked on Watercolors, Houston Chronicle, 2011; Arthur Turner (auth), Big Watercolors, Houston Mag, 6/2013. *Mem:* Tex Watercolor Soc. *Media:* Acrylic, Watercolor, Collage, Ink. *Specialty:* contemporary art of the Southwest, Asian and American contemporary art. *Publ:* Color perception (video), Crystal Productions, Aspen, Colo; People, Places, and Things (exhib catalog), Walter Wickiser Gallery, NY, 2011; Gallery Artists Part IX, Walter Wickiser Gallery, NY, 2012. *Dealer:* Moody Gallery 2815 Colquitt Houston TX 77098; Walter Wickiser Gallery 210 Eleventh Ave Ste 303 New York NY 10001. *Mailing Add:* 2419 Julian Houston TX 77009

TURNER, BONESE COLLINS
PAINTER, DESIGNER

b Abilene, Kans. *Study:* Univ Idaho, BSEd, 53, MEd, 54; Univ Calif, Los Angeles, 67; Calif State Univ, Northridge, MA, 74. *Work:* Smithsonian Inst, Washington, DC; Nebr Libr, Lincoln; Home Savings & Loan; Ore Coun Arts, Newport; Hartung Performing Arts Ctr, Moscow, Idaho; Brand Libr Permanent Collection, Glendale, Calif, Robert Fulton Mus Art, Calif State Univ San Bernardino; San Bernardino Sun Telegram Newspapers, Calif; Springfield Art Mus, Springfield, Mo. *Comn:* Mural, mosaic, tile & glass, Indust Tile Corp, Lincoln, Nebr, 60-61; paintings & drawings, Harding Realty, Lincoln, Nebr, 60-61; paintings, Delta Gamma House, Moscow, Idaho, 69-70; paintings, Alsa Distributing co, Denver, Colo, 81-82; interior environment, Los Angeles Pierce Coll, Woodland Hills, Calif, 85-86. *Exhib:* Los Angeles Co Mus Art, 57 & 58; Va Mus Art, Richmond, 74 & 75; Traditional Concepts of Quilting in the US, Los Angeles Pierce Col, Woodland Hills, Calif, 76; Laguna Gloria Art Mus, Austin, Tex, 78; Birmingham Mus Art, Ala, 78-80; Solo exhibs, Brand Libr, 78, 88, 93 & 2000, Orlando Gallery, Sherman Oaks, Calif, 80, 86, 93, 98, 2002, 2005, 2010, Univ Nev, Reno, 87, Coos Art Mus, Coos Bay, Ore, 88, Angel's Gate Gallery, San Pedro, Calif, 89 & Village Square Gallery, Montrose, Calif, 2002 & 2005; Rocky Mt Nat Exhib, Golden, Colo, 81-82 & 85; National Egg Design Invitational, White House & Smithsonian Inst, Washington, DC, 84-85; Hollywood and the Muse, Olympic Arts Celebration, Palos Verdes Art Mus, Calif, 84; Art of the 80's, Calif State Univ, Northridge, 85; Burbank Creative Arts Ctr, Burbank Calif, 2005 & 2007; Birger Sandzen Galleries, Lindsborg, Kans, 2007; Springfield Art Mus, Springfield, MO, 2002, 4-5/2008. *Collection Arranged:* Traditional Concepts of Quilting in the US, Los Angeles Pierce Col, Woodland Hills, Calif, 76; Artists of the West, Brand Libr and Gallery, Glendale, Calif, 2006; Women of a Certain Age, Viva Gallery (co cur), Sherman Oaks, Calif, 2007. *Pos:* Lens consult, Warner Bros & 20th Century Fox, Calif, 67-68; coordr, Interior/Environ Design Prog, Los Angeles Pierce Coll, Woodland Hills, Calif, 68-; bd dir & consult, Preserve Bottle Village, Simi Valley, Calif, 84-. *Teaching:* Adj prof, art, Los Angeles Pierce Coll, Woodland Hills, Calif, 64-; instr, Interior/Environ Design Prog & drawing, watercolor, Los Angeles Pierce Coll, Woodland Hills, Calif, 68-; adj instr art structures, Fashion Inst, Los Angeles, 84; adj prof 3D art, design & interior design, Calif State Univ, Northridge, 86-88; adj prof, art hist & drawing, Los Angeles Valley Coll, Van Nuys, Calif, 87-89; adj prof, drawing, Moorpark Coll, Calif, 89-99. *Awards:* Cash Awards, 45th Ann Watercolor USA, 8 & 2002, Butler Inst 53rd Ann, 89, Nat Acrylic Painters Asn, Long Beach, Calif, 96 & Brand Libr Purchase Prize, 98, 2004, & 2006; First prize graphics, Pasadena Soc Artist Diamond Jubilee (catalog), 2002; Cash award, Springfield Art Mus, Mo, 2002. *Bibliog:* Louise Moore (auth), Celebrating women's art, Artweek, Vol 15, No 23, 6/4/84; Steve Harvey (auth), Only in LA, Los Angeles Times, 89; Shirle Gottlieb (auth), Press Telegram, 11/10/96; Tina Skinner (auth), 100 Artists of West Coast, Schiffer Publ, 2009. *Mem:* Life mem Nat Watercolor Soc (jury, 80, pres, 89-90, chmn: jury, 91); Pa Watercolor Soc; Univ Idaho Coll Art & Archit (adv bd); Watercolor West; Watercolor USA Honor Soc; Women Painters/West. *Media:* All Media, Mixed. *Specialty:* Contemp Art, Artists of the West. *Collection:* Native Am; Contemp such as Helen Lundeberg, Marvin Hardin, Irving Block, Ynez Johnston, & Kent Twitchell with Lita Albuquerque; Am folk art & quilts. *Publ:* Contrib, The great cover-up, Images & Issues, 7/8/83; TV interviews, The Sushi Series, Asahi Cable Systems, 89 & Multi-Media Works, Am Cable Systems, 89; Psychological Perspectives, Issue 23, 90; Best of Drawing & Sketching, Rockport Publ, 98; Josef Woodard (auth), Girls' Power, Valley B9, 5/19/2000 & 4Perspectives, B6 Gallery, 9/18/2000, Los Angeles Times; 100 Artists of the West Coast, Tina Skinner, Schiffer Pub Ltd, 2009-2010. *Dealer:* Orlando Gallery 14553 Ventura Blvd Sherman Oaks CA 91403; Galeria Gitana 120 N Maclay Ave Ste E San Fernando CA 91430. *Mailing Add:* 4808 Larkwood Ave Woodland Hills CA 91364

TURNER, BRUCE BACKMAN
PAINTER

b Worcester, Mass, Oct 28, 1941. *Work:* Sloan-Kettering Cancer Ctr, NY; Cheshire Pub Libr, Conn; also pvt collections throughout the US, Can, Eng, France, Belg, Swed, Saudi Arabia and Australia. *Exhib:* North Shore Arts Asn Ann, East Gloucester, Mass, 72-99; 2nd Greater New Orleans Nat Exhib, La, 72; Rockport Art Asn, 72-99; Attleboro Mus Ann, Mass, 75; Am Fortnight Exhib, Hong Kong, China, 75; Mainstreams, Marietta Col, Ohio, 76; Mid Yr Show, Butler Inst Am Art, Ohio, 78 & Hope Show, 80; A Tribute to Harry R Ballinger, Ellsworth Gallery, Simsbury, Conn, 80; New Eng Impressions, Painting From Life, Attleboro Mus, Mass, 80; Mary Bryan Mem Gallery, Jeffersonville, Vt, 96-98; and many others. *Teaching:* Pvt classes oil painting, Rockport, Mass, 71-72; workshops, Rockport, Mass, Carmel, Calif, Antigonish, NS, Knoxville, Tenn, Ridgewood, NJ, Cheshire, Conn, Sturbridge, Mass, Port Clyde, Maine. *Awards:* Shumaker Award, Rockport Art Asn, Mass, 76; Seley Purchase Prize, 76 & Arthur T Hill Mem, 79, Salmagundi Club, NY; Harriet Lumis Award, Acad Artists Asn, 78. *Mem:* Am Artists Prof League; Rockport Art Asn; North Shore Arts Asn; Acad Artists Asn; Salmagundi Club. *Media:* Oil. *Publ:* Contribr, Am Artist Mag, 1/86; Monhegan - The Artist Island, Down E Publ, 95; Best of Oil Painting, 96, Portrait Impressions, 97 & A Gallery of Marine Art, 98, Rockport Publ. *Mailing Add:* Four Story St Rockport MA 01966

TURNER, DAVID
MUSEUM DIRECTOR, EDUCATOR

b Houston, Tex, Dec 1, 1948. *Study:* Southern Methodist Univ, Dallas, BBA, 71; Univ Ore, Eugene, MA, 74. *Collection Arranged:* Approaches to Photography (auth, catalog), 79; Amarillo Earthworks, 81; Touring the World (auth, catalog), 81; Early French Moderns, (auth, catalog), 82. *Pos:* Asst registrar, Mus Fine Arts, Houston, Tex, 71-72; cur educ, Amarillo Art Ctr, Tex, 77-80, dir, 80-; dir, Mus Fine Arts, Mus NMex, formerly; dir, Colo Springs Fine Arts Ctr, currently. *Teaching:* Instr art hist & photog, Umpqua Community Col, Roseburg, Ore, 74-77; instr art history, Colorado Coll, 99. *Mem:* Am Asn Mus; Soc Photog Educ; Asn Art Mus Dirs. *Publ:* Auth & ed, American Images (video tape), 79 & auth, Amarillo Landmarks, 81, Amarillo Art Ctr; auth, Jack Boynton, Artspace, 81. *Mailing Add:* Colo Springs Fine Arts Ctr 30 W Dale St Colorado Springs CO 80903

TURNER, EVAN HOPKINS
MUSEUM DIRECTOR

b Orono, Maine, Nov 8, 1927. *Study:* Harvard Univ, AB, MA & PhD. *Hon Degrees:* Sir George Williams Univ, LHD, 65; Swarthmore Col, LHD, 67; Temple Univ, hon DL, 74l; Cleveland State Univ, hon DLA, 92. *Pos:* Lectr & res asst, Frick Collection, New York, 53-56; gen cur & asst dir, Wadsworth Atheneum, Hartford, Conn, 55-59; dir, Mont Mus Fine Arts, 59-64, Philadelphia Mus Art, 64-77, Ackland Art Mus, 78-83 & Cleveland Mus Art, 83-93. *Teaching:* Adj prof art hist, Univ Pa, 70-78 & Univ NC, Chapel Hill, 78-83; distinguished vis prof, Oberlin Col, Ohio, 91-94. *Bibliog:* Ray K Metclur (auth), Landscapes, Aperture, 2000. *Mem:* Am Asn Mus; Asn Art Mus Dirs (pres, 75-76); Benjamin Franklin fel Royal Soc Arts; Am Fedn Arts; Century Club. *Res:* Thomas Eakins; 19th century American sculpture

TURNER, JANET SULLIVAN
PAINTER, SCULPTOR

b Gardiner, Maine, Nov 15, 1935. *Study:* Chicago Acad Fine Arts (Scholarship), 53; Mich State Univ, BFA (cum laude), 56; Haystack Mountain Sch Arts & Crafts, Deer Isle, Maine, 64. *Work:* La Salle Univ Art Mus, Philadelphia; Noyes Mus, Oceanville, NJ; Nat Liberty Mus, Philadelphia; Kimmel Ctr, Philadelphia; Kresge Art Mus, Mich; American Album, Nat Mus Women in the Arts, Washington, DC; Bryn Mawr Coll, Pa; Villanova Univ, Pa; Rosemont Coll, Pa; State Mus Pa, Harrisburg; Scott Collection, Women Artists Works on Paper, Bryn Mawr Col; Penache Broadcasting, Charles Schwarts, Bala Cynwyd, Pa; First USA Bank, Wilmington, Del; Am Nat Bank & Trust Collection, Rockford, Ill; Blue Cross/Blue Shield, Philadelphia; ARA Services/ARA Towers, Philadelphia; Berman Mus, Ursinus Coll, Pa; Southern Alleghenies Mus Art, Pa; New Britain Mus Am Art, Conn. *Comn:* Painting, Univ Maine, Farmington, 80; painting, Systems & Computer Tech Corp, Malvern, Pa, 82; painting, Teradyne Cent Inc, Deerfield, Ill, 83; paintings, Del Investment Adv, Philadelphia, 86. *Exhib:* Solo exhibs, St Joseph's Univ, Philadelphia, 81, Villanova Univ, Villanova, 82, Pa State Univ, Middletown, 85, Temple Univ, Philadelphia, Pa, 86, Suzanne Gross Gallery, Philadelphia, 88, Gloucester Co Coll, NJ, 90, Newark Mus, Newark, NJ, 93, Rosemont Coll, Pa & Sande Webster Gallery, Philadelphia, 98, 2000; Am Women in Art, UN World Conf Women, Nairobi, Kenya, 85; Widener Univ Art Mus, Chester, Pa, 87 & 94; 4 person, Trenton City Mus, NJ, 90; 3 person, Del Ctr Contemp Arts, Wilmington, 92; Noyes Mus, NJ, 95, 97, 2000; 50 Year Retrospective, Widener Univ Art Gallery, Chester, Pa, 2005; West Chester Univ, Pa, 2008; Artists House Gallery, Penn, 2009; Southern Alleghenies Mus Art, Pa; and others. *Collection Arranged:* Per Collections State Mus of PA Harrisburg; Noyes Mus, NJ; Kresge Art Mus, Mich; Natl Liberty Mus; La Salle Univ Art Mus, Philadelphia, PA. *Pos:* Bd dir, Artists Equity, 85-86, 1st vpres, Philadelphia Chap, 86-, pres, 87-88. *Teaching:* Guest lectr, Cult Events Prog, Pa State Univ, 85, Rosemont Coll, Pa, 95 & Noyes Mus, NJ, 95. *Awards:* Hon Mention, Nat Artists Equity Traveling Show, Stedman Gallery, Rutgers Univ, 85; Third Prize, Katonah Art Mus, 92; Purchase Award, State Mus Pa, Harrisburg, 92. *Bibliog:* Victoria Donohoe (auth), critiques in Philadelphia Inquirer, 6/2/85, 1/10/86, 4/17/87, 5/14/88, 10/2/94 & 11/20/2005; Burton Wasserman (critic), article, Art Matters, 9/94, 9/95, 2/96, 2/98, 5/2000, 6/2000, 11/2005; Robin Rice (critic), Philadelphia City Paper, 8/2000; TV news, Dick Sheeran's World, Philadelphia, Channel 3, 5/1/2002; Dr Abraham Davidson (auth), critique, Art Matters, 2008. *Mem:* Philadelphia Watercolor Club (bd dir, 92); Artists Equity Philadelphia, Pa; Philadelphia Tri-State Artists Asn (life hon); Nat League Am Pen Women. *Media:* Oil, Acrylic; Sculpture. *Specialty:* Contemp Art. *Interests:* Art. *Publ:* Contemporary Women Artists, Cedco Publ, 92; Woodmere Art Museum, Philadelphia Sculptors 2000, Colorcraft Ltd, 2000. *Dealer:* Tyme Gallery PA; Artists House Gallery Philadelphia PA. *Mailing Add:* 88 Cambridge Dr Glen Mills PA 19342

TURNER, JUDITH ESTELLE
PHOTOGRAPHER, VIDEO ARTIST
b Atlantic City, NJ. *Study:* Boston Univ, Sch Fine Arts, BFA. *Work:* Libr Cong; J Paul Getty Mus, Santa Monica, Calif; Brooklyn Mus; Bibliot Nat, Paris, France; Tokyo Metrop Mus Photg, Japan; Whitney Mus, NY. *Comn:* Photogs, Philip Morris, Richmond, Va, 82; Becton Dickinson, Franklin Lakes, NJ, 86; Spiral, Tokyo, Japan, 87; Tepia, Tokyo, Japan, 89; Peoples Bank, Bridgeport, Conn, 89; Republic Nat Bank, NY, 90; Kajima Corp Tokyo, Japan, 91 & 94. *Exhib:* Solo exhibs, Sites/Insights, Int Ctr Photog, NY, 80, Int Cult Ctr, Antwerp, Belg, 81, Portland Mus Art, Maine, 83, White City (traveling exhib), Tel Aviv Mus, Israel, 84, Axis Gallery, Tokyo, Japan, 86 & City Arts Ctr, Oklahoma City, 95; Inside Spaces, Mus Mod Art, NY, 81; Site Work (traveling exhib), Photogrs' Gallery, London, Eng, 91; George Eastman House, Rochester, 93; Recontres Int de la Photographie, Arles, 94; Tokyo Metrop Mus Photog, 95; Marlborough Gallery, NY, 96; and others. *Awards:* Lila Acheson Wallace Fund, The Capitol in Albany, Reader's Digest Asn, 84; Asian Cult Coun Fel, 85; Honor Award, Am Inst Architects, 94. *Bibliog:* Albert Champeau (auth), Creatis, Publico, Paris, 79; A Busch (auth), The Photography of Architecture, Van Nostand, Reinhold Co, 86; William Kennedy (auth), The Capitol in Albany, Aperture, 86. *Publ:* Illusr, Judith Turner Photographs Five Architects, Rizzoli Int Publs, 80; White City, Tel Aviv Mus, 84; Annotations on Ambiguity, Axis Gallery, 86; Spiral Book, Wacoal Art Ctr, 88; Parables & Pieces, Kafka/Turner, After, Feingold/Turner V FitzGerald & Co, 91 & 93. *Dealer:* Vincent FitzGerald 11 E 78th St New York NY 10021. *Mailing Add:* 323 W 82nd St New York NY 10024

TURNER, NORMAN HUNTINGTON
PAINTER, WRITER
b Storm Lake, Iowa, July 11, 1939. *Study:* New York Studio Sch, 64-65; Empire State Col, BA, 79. *Work:* Samuel Dorsky Mus Art; Wright State Univ. *Exhib:* Drawing Each Other, Brooklyn Mus, 71; Solo exhibs, Green Mountain Gallery, 72-75 & Ingber Gallery, 77 & 79, NY, New Paintings from the Del Water Gap, Hopper House Nyak, 77, Bowery Gallery, NY, 89; Younger Artists', Artists Choice Mus, 83; Bowery Gallery, NY, 89-96; NY Studio Sch, 2003; Wash Art Asn, 2005; The Continuous Mark, NY Studio Sch, 2005; Normar Turner: A Survey, 2008-2009. *Teaching:* Adj lectr, Queens Col, 82-85, dir summer painting pro, 85-89 & adj asst prof, 86-; instr painting, NY Studio Sch, 82-84 & 94-2003. *Awards:* Painting Fel, NJ State Coun Arts, 80. *Bibliog:* Lawrence Campbell (auth), rev in Art News, 11/72; Laura Schwartz (auth), rev, 2/73, Ellen Lubell (auth), rev, 4/75 & Allen Ellenzweig (auth), rev, 4/77, Arts Mag; Jed Perl (auth), rev, Art in Am, 5-6/77; John Caldwell (auth), review, NY Sunday Times, 10/26/80. *Media:* Oil on Canvas, Drawing. *Publ:* Auth, Subjective Curvature in late Cezanne, Art Bull, 12/81; Stella on Caravaggio, Arts, summer 85; Some Questions About EH Gombrich on Perspective, J Aesthetics & Art Criticism, spring 92; The Semantic of Linear Perspective, Philosophical Forum, summer 96. *Mailing Add:* 71 Prospect St New Paltz NY 12561-1143

TURNER, RALPH JAMES
PAINTER, GRAPHIC ARTIST
b Ashland, Ore, Oct 24, 1935. *Study:* Reed Coll, with calligrapher, Lloyd Reynolds, BA, 58; Portland Art Mus Sch, with painter, Louis Bunce, dipl, 58; Portland State Coll, 59; Univ Ore, with Jan Zach & Gerald di Guisto, MFA (sculpture), 62; Univ Ariz, 65, 72 & 73. *Work:* Catalina Observatory, Univ Ariz, Tucson; Flandrau Planetarium, Tucson; Hayden Planetarium, New York; Nat Aeronautical & Space Admin-Ames, San Francisco; Phoenix (5 ft limestone), Syracuse Univ, NY, 66; also many pvt collections. *Comn:* Jupiter (two planetary models), NASA/Ames, Mt View, Calif, 74 & 76; Dr Gerard Kuiper (bronze bust), Univ Ariz, 75; Phobos (planetary model), Smithsonian Inst, 78; Seer (marble carving), M & J Shapiro, Beverly Hills, Calif, 80; mural of athletes, Multnomah Athletic Club, Portland, Ore, 81; four Northwest Indian motif wood carvings, Hyland Hills Ctr, Beaverton, Ore, 82; Athletic Figures (mural), Multnomah Athletic Club, Portland, Ore, 82; Factory Workers (mural), Norwest Publ Co, Greeley, Colo, 85; Athletic Figures Witham Oaks Recreation Ctr (mural), Corvallis, Ore, 87; Medieval Figures (mural), The Knight's Castle Apts, Wilsonville, Ore, 90; Brix Maritime Mural, Portland, Ore, 94; Mt Hood Community Coll Donor Wall, 99; The Columbia (mural), Tidewater Cove Condominiums, 2003. *Exhib:* Ralph J Turner, Sculpture, Tucson Art Ctr, 63 & Univ Ariz, Tucson, 64; three-man exhib, Space & Art, Rainbow Gallery, Cannon Beach, Ore, 76; Planets & Progs: A Retrospective, Delphian Found, Sheridan, Ore, 77 & Willamette Sci & Technol Ctr, Eugene, 77; Hexagon Galaxies, Delphian Found, 80; Electro Arts Gallery, San Francisco, 81. *Pos:* Res assoc planetary models, Lunar & Planetary Lab, Univ Ariz, Tucson, 64-73; co-dir/designer, Rock Creek Experimental Sta, 73-. *Teaching:* Instr sculpture, Univ Ariz, Tucson, 62-65; asst prof design & drawing, Syracuse Univ, NY, 66-69; art coordr graphics, humanities & sculpture, Pima Col, Tucson, 70-72; instr design & calligraphy, Chemekta Community Col, Salem, Ore, 75-78. *Awards:* Nat Endowment Humanities Fel, 72-73. *Bibliog:* Fred Crafts (auth), Is it art or science, Eugene Register Guard, 77; The Artists of Yamhill Co, McMinnville, Ore, 99, 2001 & 2002; Mary Rash (auth), Ralph Turner: Renaissance Man, The Sun, Sheridan, Ore, 12/5/2001. *Mem:* Int Sculpture Ctr; Int Soc Art & Technol; Oregon Art Inst. *Media:* Stone, Wood; Acrylic, Oil. *Interests:* photography; petroglyphs; genealogy. *Collection:* Randy Lieberman Collection; Marty & Judith Shapiro, NASA, Syracuse Univ. *Publ:* Auth, The Northeast Rim of Tycho, Lunar & Planetary Community, 70; Extraterrestrial landscapes through the eyes of a sculptor, Leonardo, 72; A model of the eastern portion of Schroter's Valley, Lunar & Planetary Community, 73; Modeling and mapping Phobos, Sky & Telescope, 77-78; A model of Phobos, Icarus, Cornell Univ, 78. *Mailing Add:* 14320 SW Rock Creek Rd Sheridan OR 97378

TURNER, WILLIAM EUGENE
PAINTER, EDUCATOR
b Dallas, Tex, Oct 15, 1928. *Study:* Southern Methodist Univ, BA, 52; Univ NMex, summer 53; La State Univ, MA, 54. *Work:* Portsmouth Arts Ctr, Va; Ark Arts Ctr, Little Rock; Atlantic Richfield Corp, Dallas, Tex & Anchorage, Alaska. *Comn:* Hallway murals, Dallas Middle & High Sch (with Bill Hendricks, archit), comn by STB Archit & Planners, Tex, 77. *Exhib:* Drawing Invitational, Emporia State Univ, Kans, 82; Smithsonian Inst traveling exhib, 82-83; Art in the Metroplex, Tex Christian Univ, Ft Worth, 83; Delta States Art Ann, Ark Art Ctr, Little Rock, 83; Works on Paper, SW Tex State Univ, San Marcos & Rutgers Univ, Camden, NJ, 83. *Teaching:* Prof painting & design, Univ Tex, Arlington, 59-92. *Awards:* Purchase Awards, Works on Paper, Portsmouth Art Ctr, 82 & Delta States Exhib, Ark Art Ctr, 83. *Mem:* Coll Art Asn. *Media:* Oil, Pencil. *Mailing Add:* 5600 Boaz St Dallas TX 75209-4302

TURNURE, JAMES HARVEY
EDUCATOR, HISTORIAN
b Yonkers, NY, July 8, 1924. *Study:* Princeton Univ, AB, MFA (art hist), PhD. *Teaching:* Instr, Cornell Univ, Ithaca, NY, 53-58, asst prof, 58-64, assoc prof, 64-68; prof, Bucknell Univ, Lewisburg, Pa, 69, Samuel H Kress Prof art hist, 74-92, prof emeritus; retired. *Mem:* Archeol Inst Am. *Res:* Interpretation of evidence in archaeology and art history. *Publ:* Auth, Statuette of Imhotep, Rec of Art Mus, 52 & Princeton's enigmatic relief, 63, Princeton Univ; auth, Late style of Ambrogio Figino, Art Bulletin, 65; contribr, Il Duomo di Milano, Edizioni La Rete, 69

TURRELL, JAMES ARCHIE
ENVIRONMENTAL ARTIST, SCULPTOR
b Los Angeles, Calif, May 6, 1943. *Study:* Pomona Col, BA, 65; Univ Calif, Irvine, 65-66; Claremont Grad Sch, MA, 73. *Work:* Guggenheim Mus, Brooklyn Mus, NY; Seattle Art Mus, Wash; Whitney Mus Am Art; Dallas Mus, Tex; Philadelphia Mus Art, Pa; Walker Art Ctr, Minneapolis, Minn; Three Gems, de Young Mus, San Francisco, 2005; Dear Shelter, Yorkshire Sculpture Park, Eng, 2006. *Comn:* Roden Crater, Ariz, Dia Art Found, New York, 77; Mattress Factory, Pittsburgh, Pa. *Exhib:* Solo exhibs, Muse d'Art Contemporain, Nimes, France, 89, Stein-Gladstone Gallery, NY, 90, Mus Mod Art, NY, 90, Turske & Turske, Zurich, Switzerland, 90, Ace Contemp Exhibs, NY, 90, Williams Coll Art Mus, Williamstown, Mass, 91 & Anthony D'Offay Gallery, London, Eng, 91, Knowing Light, Henry Art Gallery, Seattle, 2003-04, Light Leadings, PaceWildstein, NY, 2007; Group exhibs, Lichtprojecties En Lichtruimten, Stedelijk Mus, Amsterdam, 76; Light Space, Arco Ctr for Visual Art, Los Angeles, 76; Walker Art Ctr, Minneapolis, Minn, 87 & 89; St Louis Art Mus, 88; Guggenheim Mus, 89; Nat Gallery Art, Washington, DC, 89-90; Le Musee d'Art Contemporain de Montreal, Can, 90; Chateau de Rochechouart, France, 90; La Jolla Mus Contemp Art, La Jolla, Calif, 90; Musee d'Art Modernede la villa de Paris, France, 90; Karl Bornstein Gallery, Santa Monica, Calif, 90; 54th Int Art Exhib Biennale, Venice, 2011. *Awards:* Nat Endowment for the Arts, 68 & 75; Guggenheim, 74; Fel MacArthur Found, 84; Wolf Prize, 97. *Bibliog:* Calvin Tomkins (auth), The talk of the town-light, New Yorker, 12/15/80; Robert Hughes (auth), Poetry out of emptiness, Time Mag, 1/5/81; Nancy Marmer (auth), James Turrell: the art of deception, Art in Am, 5/81; and others. *Mailing Add:* 9000 Hutton Ranch Rd Flagstaff AZ 86004-8592

TUSKI, DONALD
ADMINISTRATOR, EDUCATOR
Study: Olivet Col, BA; Mich State Univ, MA, 1989, PhD (anthropology), 1998. *Pos:* Fac mem, asst vpres academic affairs, vpres academic affairs, Olivet Col, Mich, formerly, pres, 2001-2010; pres, assoc prof, Maine Col of Art, 2010-. *Mailing Add:* Maine College of Art Office of President 522 Congress St Portland ME 04101

TUSTIAN, BRENDA HARRIS
PAINTER, PUBLISHER
b Birmingham, Ala, Jan 20, 1943. *Study:* Univ Tenn, studied with Kermit Ewing, 63. *Work:* Coca-Cola Corp, Dow Chemical Corp, IBM Corp, Cox Broadcasting Corp, Atlanta; Reinhardt Col, Waleska, Ga. *Comn:* official 1996 poster, Semco Productions Inc, Atlanta, 96; official 1996 print, Atlanta Dogwood Festival, 96; 34″ x 42″ dogwood painting, Northside Hosp, Atlanta, 98. *Exhib:* Festival of the Masters, Walt Disney World, 80; Yellow Daisy Festival, Stone Mountain, Ga, 89-98; Cent Pa Art Asn Festival of Art, Pa State Univ, 91; City of Ann Arbor Art Festival, Mich, 96-98; solo exhib, Reinhardt Col, Waleska, Ga, 97. *Bibliog:* Christine Antolik & Mike Kendrick (auths), Art Trends, 96 & Watercolor Magic, 98. *Mem:* Southern Watercolor Soc; Am Watercolor Soc; juried mem Atlanta Artists Club; assoc mem Ga Watercolor Soc. *Media:* Watercolor. *Mailing Add:* 1579 Julius Bridge Rd Ball Ground GA 30107

TUTTLE, LISA
CONCEPTUAL ARTIST, CURATOR
b Little Rock, Ark, Sept 25, 1951. *Study:* New Col, Sarasota, Fla, BA, 74. *Work:* Mus Contemp Art, Ga; Dunbar Neighborhood Ctr, City of Atlanta Pub Art Prog; Hartsfield Jackson Atlanta Int Airport Art Prog, 94. *Comn:* Video installations, Memphis Contemp Art Ctr, Tenn, 88, New Visions Gallery, IMAGE Film/Video, Atlanta, Ga, 88, New South Group, NY, 89, Arts Festival, Atlanta, Ga, 90 & High Mus Art, 91; Landscape Poems, Art in Freedom Park, Atlanta, 2005; Fence, Agnes Scott Coll, Decatur, Ga, 2006-07. *Exhib:* Solo exhibs, Running Diana, Seven Stages, Atlanta, Ga, 88, Vindication of Lilith, Albany Mus Art, Ga, 89 & Ga Mus Art, Athens, Ga, 93, Sandler Hudson Gallery, Atlanta, 94, 96, 2001, 2008; Between Myth and Reality: New Southern Photog, Aperture Found, NY, 89; Rethinking the Sacred Image, Ga State Univ Gallery, 90; Artists on the Discovery of the New World, Agnes Scott Col, Decatur, Ga, 92; Constitutions, Spelman Col, Atlanta, Ga, 93; Retreat: Palimpsest of a Georgia Sea Island Plantation, City Hall E, Atlanta, 98, XChange Gallery, Atlanta, 2000, Clark Atlanta Univ Galleries, 2001, Atlanta Contemp Art Ctr, 2002; Poetic Pathway, Art on the Beltline, 2010; Harriet Rising, Underground Atlanta, 2011. *Collection Arranged:* Small scale sculpture, 87, 1938-88: The Work of Five Black Women Artists, 88, The Assembled Object, 89, Ecos del Espiritu, 90; New History: Buchanan/Edwards/Hassinger, 90, Oh, Those four white walls, Gallery as Context, 90; Contemporary Bronze: Process and Object, 91; Cross-Cultural Explorations, 92; The Metaphorical Machine, 93; Money Changes Everything, Or Seeking the Souk, 94; Pulse, 2010; The Painted Photography, 2011. *Pos:* Assoc cur, Nexus Contemp Art Ctr, Atlanta, Ga, 83-85; gallery dir, Nexus Contemp Art Ctr, Atlanta, 85-86; gallery dir, Atlanta Col Art, Ga, 86-93; visual arts dir, Arts Festival Atlanta, 93-; pub art adminr,

Arts Festival Atlanta, 93-97; public art consultant, 2010-. *Teaching:* Adj fac, Atlanta Col Art, 89-2006; Fulton County Arts and Culture, 2003-. *Awards:* Bur Cult Affairs, Artist Proj, Atlanta, 87; Fel Sculpture, Southern Arts Fedn, 91; Individual Artists Award, Ga Coun Arts, 93; Southern Arts Fedn, 95; Mayor's Fellowship in the Arts in Visual Arts, Atlanta, 99; Nexus Press Artist-Initiated Proj Award, 2000; Cavershwam Press Artist-in-Residence, S Africa, Fulton County Arts Coun, 2002; King Baudouin Found, Cult Exchange Fel, 2003; Soros Found/Open Soc Inst Doc Photography Grant, 2009. *Bibliog:* Jerry Cullum (auth), catalog essay, New S Group, 89; Peter Doroschenko (auth), essay, Albany Mus Art, 89; Carrie Przybilla (auth), Southern expressions: tales untold (catalog essay), 91. *Mem:* Nexus Studio Artist, 82-88; Atlanta Gallery Asn (adv bd, 85-86); Atlanta Arts Festival (adv bd, 89); Fulton Co Pub Art Committee; Arts Exchange Studio Artist (98-). *Media:* Mixed Media. *Interests:* Post-colonial studies, women's studies, hist, poetry & fiction, photography. *Dealer:* Sandler Hudson Gallery 1009-A Marietta St NW Atlanta GA 30318. *Mailing Add:* 1088 Amsterdam Ave NE Atlanta GA 30306

TUTTLE, RICHARD
PAINTER
b Rahway, NJ, July 12, 1941. *Study:* Trinity Col, Hartford, Conn, BA, 1963. *Hon Degrees:* Calif Coll Arts, DFA, 2006. *Work:* Fogg Art Mus, Harvard Univ, Cambridge, Mass; Metrop Mus Art, NY; Mus Mod Art, NY; Seattle Art Mus, Wash; Whitney Mus Am Art, NY; Stedekijk Mus, Amsterdam, Neth; City Art Mus, St Louis, Mo; and numerous pvt collections. *Exhib:* Solo exhibs incl Calif State Long Beach Art Mus, 1997, Art Gallery York Univ, Ont, 1997, Kunsthaus Zag, Switz, 1997, 1998-99, Fabric Workshop & Mus, Philadelphia, 1998, Ludwig Forum fur Int Kunst, Ger, 1998-99, Arts Club Chicago, Ill, 1999 & Stiftung Schleswig-Holsteinische Landesmuseum, Schloss Gottorf, 2000, Sperone Westwater Gallery, NY, 2007, Richard Tuttle: Walking on Air, Pace Gallery's 534 West 25th St Gallery, 2009, Dubner Moderne Gallery, Lausanne, Switzerland, 2010; group exhibs incl La Biennale di Venezia, XLVII Esposizione Int d'Art, Venice, 1997; Circa 1968, Museu de Serralves, Museu de Arte Contemp, Portugal, 1999; Landesmuseum, Schloss Gottorf, Schleswig-Holsteinische, 2000; Stiftung Schleswig, 2000; Sperone Westwater Gallery, NY, 2000, 2003; Extreme Connoisseurship, Fogg Art Mus, Cambridge, Mass, 2001; Andrea Rosen Gallery, New York, 2003; Mus Mod Art, New York, 2005; Stephen Friedman Gallery, London, 2006; PS1 Contemp Art Cent, Long Island City, NY, 2007. *Awards:* Fel, Nat Endowment Arts, 1968; Skowhegan Medal for Sculpture, NY, 1998; Aachen Prize, Ludwig Forum for Int Art, 1998; Acad Award in Art, Nat Acad Arts and Letters, NY, 2003. *Bibliog:* James Narwocki (auth), twistfoldlayerflake, New Art Examiner, 5/1999; Michael Kimmelman (auth), Richard Tuttle: Two with any to, NY Times, 1/28/2000; Kenneth Baker (auth), Great Art from Humble Means, San Francisco Chronicle, 1/20/2001. *Mem:* Nat Acad; American Acad Arts & Sciences. *Publ:* Contribr, Art Int. *Dealer:* Andrea Rosen Gallery 525 W 24th St New York NY 10011; Richard Levy Gallery 514 Cent Ave SW Albuquerque NM 87102; Barbara Krakow Gallery 10 Newbury St Boston MA 02116. *Mailing Add:* c/o Sperone Westwater 257 Bowery New York NY 10002

TWARDOWICZ, STANLEY JAN
PAINTER, PHOTOGRAPHER
b Detroit, Mich, July 8, 1917. *Study:* Meinzinger Art Sch, Detroit, 40-44; Skowhegan Sch Painting & Sculpture, Maine, summers 46 & 47. *Work:* Mus Mod Art, NY; Los Angeles Co Mus Art; NY Univ; Fogg Art Mus; Vassar Coll Art Gallery; Hirshhorn Mus. *Exhib:* Art Inst Chicago, 54, 55 & 61; Solo exhibs, Peridot Gallery, NY, 56-70; Five exhibs, Mus Mod Art, 57-69; Mus Fine Arts, Boston, 66; Retrospective, Heckscher Mus, Huntington, NY, 74; 30 Yr Retrospective Photog, Emily Lowe Gallery, Hempstead, NY, 79; Mitchell Algus Gallery, NY, 94, 96-2000. *Teaching:* Instr art, Ohio State Univ, 46-51; assoc prof, Hofstra Univ, 65-87. *Awards:* Guggenheim Found Fel, 56-57. *Mailing Add:* 133 Crooked Hill Rd Huntington NY 11743

TWAROGOWSKI, LEROY ANDREW
DRAFTSMAN, EDUCATOR
b Chicago, Ill, Sept 12, 1937. *Study:* Art Inst Chicago, 55-59; Univ Kans, Lawrence, BFA, 61, MFA, 65. *Work:* Denver Art Mus, Colo; Ft Hays State Univ, Hays, Kans; Hastings Col, Nebr; US Nat Bank, Omaha, Nebr; Mountain Bell Corp, Denver, Colo; Colo State Univ, Fort Collins. *Comn:* Colo Coun Arts & Humanities, 78. *Exhib:* Second All-Colo Competitive Exhib, Denver Art Mus, 74; 2nd Brit Int Drawing Biennale, Middlesbrough, Eng, 75; Drawings USA-75 Biennale, Minn Mus of Art, St Paul, 75; Spree-Colo Celebration of the Arts, Denver, 76; Rocky Mountain Drawing & Painting Exhib, Aspen Found for the Arts, Colo, 77; Denver Art Mus, 78. *Teaching:* Prof drawing, Colo State Univ, 67-. *Media:* Graphite. *Mailing Add:* Colorado State Univ Dept Art Bldg G100 Fort Collins CO 80523

TWIGGS, LEO FRANKLIN
PAINTER, EDUCATOR
b St Stephen, SC, Feb 13, 1934. *Study:* Claflin Univ. *Work:* Herbert F Johnson Mus, Cornell Univ; Gibbes Mus, Charleston, SC; Columbia Mus, SC; SC State Mus; Greenville Mus Art, SC. *Comn:* Winston Salem State Univ, NC; Nations Bank. *Exhib:* Salute to Black Artists, NJ State Mus, Trenton, 72; Directions in Afro-Am Art, Cornell Univ, 74; Studio Mus, New York, NY; US Art in Embassies Prog, Dakar, 84; Palazzo Venezia, Rome, Italy, 86; SC State Mus, 89; Uncommon Beauty Traveling Exhib, Am Craft Mus, Renwick Gallery, Wash, 94; Hampton III Gallery, Greenville, SC, 98; Milton Rhodes Gallery, Winston-Salem, NC, 98. *Pos:* Consult African Am art, Art Ed, currently. *Awards:* Award of Distinction, Smith Mason Gallery, 71; Merit Prize, Guild SC Artists, 75; Governor's Trophy, 80; Regional Award for Distinction, Nat Art Educ Asn, 81; Nat Distinguished Alumni, 86. *Bibliog:* M Carnell (auth), article in Art Craft Mag, 79; Rhoda McKinney (auth), Ebony mag, 88; African Am Lit, 92; Rosalina Ragin (auth), Art Talk, 94. *Mem:* Coll Art Asn Am; Nat Art Educ Asn; Nat Conf Artists; Guild SC Artists (vpres, 74); SC Mus Comn; African Am Mus Asn (vpres, 84). *Media:* Batik. *Publ:* Auth, articles in Design Mag, 72, Negro Educ Rev, 72, Sch Arts, 72, Mus News, 72, Hist News, 81, Arts in Educ, 86 & Art, Culture & Ethnicity, 90. *Dealer:* Hampton III Gallery Taylors SC 29678; Chuma Gallery Charleston SC 29403. *Mailing Add:* 420 Woodlawn Dr Orangeburg SC 29118

TYE, WILLIAM ROY
SCULPTOR
b Harlan, Ky, Jan 25, 1939. *Study:* Western Mich Univ, BS, 63, MFA, 77; Wayne State Univ, MA, 67. *Work:* Sturgis Coun Arts, Sturgis, Mich; Douglas Community Ctr & Western Mich Univ, Kalamazoo, Mich. *Comn:* Fighting Gamecock (bronze), Sr Class 1969, Univ SC, Columbia, 69; Cyclists (three bronze figures), City of Battle Creek, Mich, 76; J Fetzer (portrait relief), Western Mich Univ, 82; 10' Bronze Seal, Western Mich Univ, 93. *Exhib:* Solo exhib, Kalamazoo Inst Arts, 77; All State Competition, Battle Creek Art Ctr, 80 & 81; Mich Fine Arts, Birmingham Art Ctr, 83; Kalamazoo Bronzecasting Co, Krasl Art Ctr, St Joseph, Mich & Cain Gallery, Oak Park, Ill, 85; Mich Outdoor Sculpture, Southfield, 87; Sturges-Young Civic Ctr, 93; and others. *Pos:* Proprietor, Alchemist-Tye Studio (founder), Kalamazoo, 83-. *Teaching:* Teacher high sch art, South Redford Pub Sch, South Redford, Mich, 63-66, Clarenceville Schs, Livonia, Mich, 66-68 & Mattawan Conserv Sch, Mattawan, Mich, 70-78; art instr, Univ SC, Columbia, 68-70; head sculpture dept, Kalamazoo Inst Arts, Kalamazoo, Mich, 78-83. *Awards:* Hon Mention, All State Competition, Mich Nat Bank, 81. *Bibliog:* Linda Fortino (auth), Marriage of arts, Kalamazoo Gazette, 4/30/78. *Mem:* Int Sculpture Ctr; Chicago Artists' Coalition. *Media:* Bronze. *Dealer:* Cain Gallery 1016 North Blvd Oak Park IL 60301. *Mailing Add:* 701 N Berkeley Kalamazoo MI 49007

TYLER, RON C
ART HISTORIAN, MUSEUM DIRECTOR
b Temple, Tex, Dec 29, 1941. *Study:* Abilene Christian Coll, BS (educ), 64; Tex Christian Univ MA, 66, PhD, 68. *Hon Degrees:* Austin Coll, DHL, 86. *Collection Arranged:* The Wild West, Amon Carter Mus Western Art, 70; The Big Bend (auth, catalog), 75; The Image of Am in Caricature & Cartoon (auth, catalog), 75; Posada's Mexico (ed, catalog), Libr Cong, 79; Alfred Jacob Miller: Artist on the Oregon Trail (ed, catalog), 82; Views of Texas: Watercolors by Sarah Ann Lillian Hardings, Amon Carter Mus, 87; Nature's Classics: John James Audubon's Birds and Animals, Stark Mus Art, 92; Audubon's Great National Work: The Royal Octavo Edition of the Birds of Am, 93; Prints of the West, 94; Patterns of Progress, Birds-Eye View, 2006. *Pos:* Cur hist, dir publ & asst dir hist & publ, Amon Carter Mus, 69-84, asst dir collections & prog, 84-86, dir, 2006-2011; dir, Tex State Hist Asn, 86-2005. *Teaching:* Asst prof, Austin Coll, Sherman, Tex, 67-69; prof hist, Univ Tex, Austin, 86-2006. *Awards:* Scholar Inst Tecnologico Monterrey, Mex, 67; Am Philos Soc Grant, 70; H Bailey Carroll Award, 74; Coral H Tullis Award, 76; Alonso de León Medal, Sociedad Nuevoleonsa História Geografía y Estadistica, 2002. *Mem:* Am Antiquarian Society; Tex Inst of Letters; Philos Soc Tex (sec, 90); Phi Beta Kappa. *Res:* 19th century American & Western American art & prints; Mexican art & printmakers. *Publ:* Auth, The Mexican War: A Lithographic Record, Tex State Hist Asn, 73; The Rodeo Photographs of John A Stryker, Encino Press, 78; Visions of America: Pioneer Artists in a New Land, Thames & Hudson, 83; Nature's Classics: John James Audubon's Birds and Animals, 92; Prints of the West, 94

TYLER, VALTON
PRINTMAKER, PAINTER
b Texas City, Tex, Mar 30, 1944. *Study:* Dallas Art Inst, Tex, 67. *Work:* Tyler Mus Art, Tex. *Exhib:* First Fifty Prints, Pollock Galleries, Southern Methodist Univ, Dallas & Tyler Mus Art, 72; 8th Ann New Talent in Printmaking, Assoc Am Artists, NY, 72; Solo exhibs, Galerie Claude Jongen, Brussels, Belg, 77 & Vallery House Gallery, Dallas, 79; Rosa Esman Gallery, NY, 85. *Awards:* Second Place, Art in the Metroplex, 88. *Bibliog:* Reynolds (auth), The fifty prints--Valton Tyler, Southern Methodist Univ Press, 72. *Media:* Aquatint; Oil on Canvas. *Publ:* Auth, Jalons et Actualites des Arts, 1/77; Un Artiste de 33 Ans, Hebdomadaire, 2/24/77; Ultra, 12/81. *Mailing Add:* c/o Valley House Gallery 6616 Spring Valley Rd Dallas TX 75254

TYNG, ALEXANDRA STEVENS
PAINTER, INSTRUCTOR
b Rome Italy; US Citizen, Mar 22,1954. *Study:* Harvard Univ, BA, 1975; Univ Pa, MS (ed). *Work:* Drexel Collection, Drexel Univ, Philadelphia, Pa; Royal Inst British Architects, London, UK; Archit Archives Univ Pa, Philadelphia, Pa; Fed Court House US Dist Court, Philadelphia, Pa; Springfield Art Mus, Mo. *Comn:* Portrait (John Bogle), comn by John Bogle, Blairstown, NJ, 1996; Potrait (Hon Norma Shapiro), Hist Soc US Dist Court Eastern Dist Pa, 2003; Portrait (Louis I Kahn), Union Estonian Archits, Tallinn/Estonia, 2006; Portrait (Dr Constantine Papadakis), comn by Trustees Drexel Univ, Philadelphia, Pa, 2007; Portrait (George A Weymouth), Portrait Soc Am, Tallahassee, Fla, 2008. *Exhib:* Contemp Realism V, M A Doran Gallery, Tulsa, Okla, 2002; 71st Regional Exhib, Arnot Art Mus, Elmira, NY, 2005; Art of the Portrait, Portrait Soc Am, Dallas Tex, 2006; Ann Juried Exhib, Woodmere Art Mus, Philadelphia, Pa, 2005-2007; Allied Artists of Am 94th Ann, Nat Arts Club, New York, NY, 2007. *Pos:* Exhibs, Cecilia Beau Forum, Portrait Soc Am, 2006-2008. *Teaching:* Instr, portrait landscape, Wayne Art Ctr, Wayne, Pa, 2006-. *Awards:* 2nd Hons Award, Art of Portrait, Portrait Soc Am, 2006; Finalist, Int ARC Salon, Art Renewal Ctr, 2006, 2007; Certificate of Excellence, Art of the Portrait, Portrait Soc Am, 2007; Van Sciver Prize, Woodmere Art Mus, Pearl & Lloyd Van Sciver, 2007; Butler Inst Am Art Award, Allied Artists Am, Butler Inst, 2007; Top Ten Finalist, Cover Competition, Am Artist Mag, 2008. *Bibliog:* Carol Little (auth, ed), Art of Monhegan, Down East Books, 2004; Karen Heller (auth), Faces Forward for Art, Philadelphia Inquirer, 2007; Samuel Hughes (auth), Journey to Estonia, Pa Gazette, 2007; Suzette McAvoy (auth), Capturing the color of light, Maine Home & Design, 2008. *Mem:* Portrait Soc Am (exhib comt, Cecilia Beaux Forum, 2006); Philadelphia Sketch Club. *Media:* Oil. *Publ:* Auth, Beginnings: Louis I Kahns Philosophy of Architecture (bk), John Wiley & Sons, 1984; auth, A Tried & True Method of Achieving Atmosphere (art), Int Artist, 2006. *Dealer:* Fischbach Gallery Lawrence DiCarlo 210 11th Ave New York NY 10001; Gross McCleaf Gallery Sharon Ewing 127 S 16th St Philadelphia PA 19102; G Watson Gallery Ronald Watson 68 Main St Stonington ME 04681. *Mailing Add:* 117 Woodside Ave Narberth PA 19072

TYSER, PATRICIA ELLEN
STAINED GLASS ARTIST, ASSEMBLAGE ARTIST
b Rochester, NY, July 1, 1952. *Study:* St John Fisher Col, BA, 74; studies with Katay Bunnel & Dan Fenton, Oakland Calif, 83, Johannes Schreiter & Lutz Haufschild, Toronto, Ont, 84, Norm Dobbins, Albuquerque, NMex, 87, Kathy Bradford & Dan Fenton, Colo, 88, Ken von Roehn & Tim O'Neill, Toronto, Ont, Boyce Lundstrum, 91, 92, Virginia Gabaldo, Toas, NMex, 93, Newy Fagan, Cocoa, Fla, 95-96. *Work:* Rochester Lead Works; Collection of Paul DuFour, La State Univ Glass Dept. *Exhib:* Solo exhibs, Wilson Gallery, Rochester, 77-79, B Forman Invitational, Rochester, 83, Gallery at 15 Stops, Ithaca, NY, 84, Philadelphia Art Show, Pa, 85, Huntington Galleries, WVa, 86 & Philadelphia Port Hist Mus, Pa, 87; Street of Glass, NY, 83; Crafts Western, Burchfield Penney Gallery, Buffalo State Col, NY, 94; Earth, Sand & Fire, Niagara Community Col, 96; Guilford Glass Biennial, Conn, 96; and others. *Pos:* Mgr, Stained Glass Works, Rochester, NY, 74-78; prin, Patricia Tyser Glass Studio, Rochester, NY, 78-85; dir, Archit Glass Designs, Rochester, NY, 85-94. *Teaching:* Instr, State Univ NY, Brockport, 87-88, Norman Howard Sch, Rochester, 88-92. *Awards:* Best of Show Crafts, Quaker Arts Festival, 94; First Place Glass, Colden Valley Art Show, 96; Second Place Glass, Allentown Art Festival, Buffalo, NY, 96. *Mem:* Stained Glass Asn Am; Nat Asn Female Exec. *Publ:* Professional Stained Glass, 89, 90 & 91. *Mailing Add:* 1148 W Skyview Dr Prescott AZ 86303-5121

U

UBANS, JURIS K
PAINTER, EDUCATOR
b Riga, Latvia, July 12, 1938; US citizen. *Study:* Yale Univ, with William Bailey & Bernard Chaet, 65; Syracuse Univ, BFA, 66, with Ainslee Burke & Frederick Hauck; Pa State Univ, MFA, 68, with Enrique Montenegro & Eugenio Battisti. *Work:* Yale Univ; Syracuse Univ; Pa State Univ; Univ Southern Maine; and pvt collections. *Comn:* A Season in Hell (ballet visuals), Syracuse Univ, NY, 66; Good Woman of Setzuan (theater visuals), Univ Maine, Portland-Gorham, 72, Renascence (planetarium visuals), 75 & From Morn Till Midnight (theater visuals), 76; Photography Maine 1973 (poster, catalog & cert design), Maine State Comn on Arts & Humanities, 73. *Exhib:* Everson Mus Art, Syracuse, 66; Nat Exhib Prints & Drawings, Okla Art Ctr, Okla, 69-70; Statements in Media, Haystack Traveling Exhib, 72-73; solo shows, Univ Maine, Augusta, 74 & Univ of the South, Sewanee, Tenn, 78; First Light Traveling Show, Calif, 75-76; Grand Valley State Col, Allendale, Mich, 79; and others. *Collection Arranged:* As It Was (auth, ed, catalog), 74, Ben Shahn-Photographs (auth & ed, catalog), 76 & Walker-Evans-Photographs, 78, Univ Southern Maine. *Pos:* Dir art gallery, Univ Southern Maine, 68-, chmn art dept, 74-; pres bd dir, Film Study Ctr, Portland, 72-. *Teaching:* From asst prof to prof painting, film, photog & drawing, Univ Southern Maine, 68-; coordr Soleri sem, Haystack Mountain Sch, Deer Isle, Maine, summer 71. *Awards:* Helen B Stoeckel Fel, Yale Univ, 66; Hiram Gee Fel, Lowe Art Ctr, Syracuse, NY, 65; Greogry Batcock Prize, Independent Filmmakers, 68. *Mem:* Coll Art Asn; Nat Asn Sch Art; Am Film Inst; and others. *Media:* Oil, Mixed Media. *Mailing Add:* One Thomas St Portland ME 04102

UBOGY, JO
SCULPTOR
b Hartford, Conn, Mar 7, 1940. *Study:* Univ Wis, BS, 61; self-taught sculptor. *Work:* Bedford Executive Hotel, Stamford, Conn; Landmark Bldg, Stamford, Conn. *Exhib:* Silvermine Art of NE USA, Silvermine Galleries, New Canaan, Conn, 82, 86, 89 & 90; Pindo Gallery Invitational, Soho, NY, 83; Sidney Rothman, The Gallery, Barnegat Light, NJ, 79-90. *Mem:* Nat Asn Women Artists; Silvermine Guild Artists. *Media:* Welded Steel, Polyester Resins. *Publ:* Contribr, Encyclopedia of Gardening-Foliage Houseplants, Time-Life, 80. *Mailing Add:* 319 Cognewaugh Rd Cos Cob CT 06807

UCHELLO, PATRICIA MILLER
PAINTER
b New Orleans, La, Apr 19, 1954. *Study:* Tulane Univ, BFA, 76; Pratt Inst, MFA, 78. *Work:* IBM; IMF; HeathSouth. *Comn:* Catherine Gorham, Jane Slater, Jan Smith, Pam Merrill, Paul Doherty, Karen Summers, Wakefield Homes. *Exhib:* Juried Group Shows, Art League, 90-; Have a Seat, Nat Inst Health, Bethesda, Md, 94; solo exhib, Shenandoah Valley Art Ctr, Waynesboro, Va, 95; Twenty for Tea, Nat Inst Health, Bethesda, 96; Landscape Invitational, The Athenaeum, 97; Gallery West Juried Exhib, 99; LMI, McLean, Va, 2000; BTG, Fairfax, Va, 2000; Realism Invitational, The Athenaeum 2000; Wilson Art Gallery, DC; CSC, Alexandria, 2004; Words, Art & Poetry, Del Ray Artisans, 2007; Wish You Were Here, Del Ray Artisans, 2007; two-person exhib, Wide River Art Gallery, 2008; Bond for Life: Del Ray Artisans Gallery, 2009; Gallery Two: My Favorite Things, Leesburg, Va, 2010; A Show of Hands, Landscapes, Alexandria, Va, 2010; Green Springs Gardens, 2011; City Hall, Alexandria Va Art Exhib, Am Horticultural Soc, All Things Natural, 2012-2013; Young at Art, 2013; Art League, 2014. *Pos:* Visual arts panelist, Alexandria Comn Arts, Va, 89-92; artist, Winsor-Newton Demonstr, 96; mem bd dirs & 2nd vice pres, The Art League, Alexandria, Va, 2009-2012; Entrepreneurial Women, 2003-. *Teaching:* Instr art, Studio, 90-00, Northern Va Community Coll, Alexandria, Va, 94-95. *Awards:* First Prize Purchase Award, Am Ital Renaissance Found, 83; Equal Merit Award, Art League, 93; Curator's Award, Bond For Life: Del Ray Artisans, 2009; Honorable Mention, The Art League, 2013; Honorable Mention, Young at Art, 2014. *Mem:* Art League; The Twig; Md Art Place; Entrepreneurial Women; The Twig. *Media:* Oil on Canvas. *Specialty:* Realism. *Interests:* Gardening. *Publ:* Illusr, Seaport Savories, The Twig, 94; Illusr, Elan Mag (5 pg. article), Great Falls, VA, 4/2011. *Dealer:* The Art League 105 N Union St Alexandria VA 22314. *Mailing Add:* 2001 Shiver Dr Alexandria VA 22307

UDVARDY, JOHN WARREN
SCULPTOR, EDUCATOR
b Elyria, Ohio. *Study:* Skowhegan Sch Painting & Sculpture, scholar, summer 57; Cleveland Inst Art, scholar, 55-58, BFA, 63; Yale Univ, scholar, 64-65, MFA, 65. *Work:* Newport Art Mus, RI; Columbia Broadcasting Syst, New York; Fogg Mus, Cambridge, Mass; Mus Art, RI Sch Design; The Edmund Mauro Collection, Providence, RI; Wellesley Coll Mus, Mass; Cleveland Inst Art, Cleveland, Oh; Skowhagen Sch Painting and Sculpture, Skowhagen, Me; Am Fedn Arts, New York, NY; Pasadena Mus Art, Calif; Fidelity Investments, Boston, Mass; Blue Cross & Blue Shield of Rhode Island; Princeton Univ, Princeton, NJ. *Comn:* Outdoor site sculpture, Wellesley Coll, Mass, 86. *Exhib:* Addison Gallery Am Art, Andover, Mass, 84; Newport Art Mus, RI, 89, 2002, 2012, 2013; Clark Univ, Worcester, Mass, 91; Virginia Lynch Gallery, Tiverton, RI, 92, 96, 98, 2000-2006; Lenore Gray Gallery, Providence, RI, 96 & 2004-2007, 2009; Mus Art, RI Sch Design, 96 & 98-2001-; The Edmund Mauro Collection, Providence, RI; Wellesley Coll Mus, Wellesley, Mass; The Imago Gallery, Warren, RI, 2007, 2008, 2009, 2010, 2013; Big Town Gallery, Rochester, Vt, 2009, 2011 & 2012; Cade Tompkins Projects, 2012, 2013; Bristol Art Mus, Bristol, RI, 2007-2013; Jewett Art Gallery, Wellesley Coll, Mass, 2011; Univ Art Gallery, Univ Mass Dartmouth, New Bedforth, Mass, 2011. *Pos:* Artist-in-residence, Dartmouth Coll, Hanover, NH, fall 82; juror, Fel Awards, RI State Coun Arts, 85; vis artist, Wellesley Coll, Mass, fall 86; nat screening comt, Fulbright Awards, Inst Int Educ, New York, 91-93; cur, Contemp Am Folk Art, Bristol Art Mus, RI, 95; juror, Visual Arts Sea Grant, Fine Arts Ctr, Univ RI, 95; chmn bd dirs, Bristol Art Mus, Bristol, RI, 2008. *Teaching:* Instr drawing, Cleveland Inst Art, 62-63; asst printmaking, Yale Univ, 64-65; asst prof painting & design, Brown Univ, 65-73; chmn, Freshman Found Div, RI Sch Design, 73-77 & 79-82, prof design, 78-92, dir, summer transfer prog, 73-82; prof design (fac emer), RI Sch Design, 78-2008. *Awards:* Distinguished Alumnus Award, Cleveland Inst Art, Ohio, 70; First Prize, Silver Medal, Centennial Sculpture Show, Providence Art Club, 80; Silver Medal, RI Sch Design, Providence, 90; Gold Emeriti Medallion, RI Sch Design, 2008; First Prize, Bristol Art Mus, Bristol, RI, 2008, Second Prize, 2010, Best in Show, 2012. *Mem:* Warren Preservation Soc; Imago Gallery; Bristol Art Mus, RI, (chmn exhibs comt, bd dirs, currently). *Media:* Wood, Welded Iron, Natural Materials. *Publ:* Illusr, Los, fall 68 & spring 70, Art J, winter 73, Art in Am, 3-4/75 & Mich Quart Rev, spring 79; Networks, 2013. *Dealer:* Virginia Lynch Gallery 3883 Main Rd Rt 77 Tiverton RI 02878; Lenore Gray Gallery 15 Meeting St Providence RI 02903; Imago Gallery 16 Culter St Warren RI 02885; Cade Tompkins Projects 198 Hope St Providence RI 02906; Big Town Gallery 99 N Main St Rochester Vt. *Mailing Add:* 60 Croade St Warren RI 02885

UHL, PHILIP EDWARD
PAINTER, PHOTOGRAPHER
b Toledo, Ohio 1949. *Study:* Sch Dayton Art Inst, Dayton, Ohio, 67-69; Art Students League, New York, 76. *Work:* Hawaii Maritime Mus (Bishop Mus), Honolulu, Hawaii; UCLA Med Center (MAP Prog), Los Angeles, Calif; Newport Harbor Maritime Mus, Newport Beach, Calif; City & Co Honolulu, Honolulu, Hawaii; Transpacific Yacht Club Hist Arch, Long Beach, Calif; Wilikoch America's Cup Collection Exhib. *Comn:* Permanent display (mural & smaller works), James B Kilroy, Kilroy Airport Ctr, Long Beach, Calif, 88; Permanent display (10 works), Waikiki Yacht Club, Honolulu, Hawaii, 2000; Am's Cup Silver Jubilee (video prog), William I Koch, Osterville Mass, 2001; Transpac (100 yr commemorative poster design), Roy E Disney, Los Angeles, Calif, 2005; Am's Found (mus exhib video), William I Koch, Osterville, Mass, 2005. *Exhib:* Am Painters in Paris, Centre Int de Paris, Paris, France, 75; Digitally Charged Entities, Studio One, Honolulu, Hawaii, 2003; Honolulu Printmakers 75th Anniversary Exhib, Honolulu Acad Art Ctr, Honolulu, Hawaii, 2003; The Things I Love, Mus Fine Arts, Boston, Mass, 2005; Artists of Hawaii, Honolulu Acad Art, Honolulu, Hawaii, 2005; Upon the Sea, Soc Four Arts, Palm Beach, Fla, 2006; Natures Best Photography, Nat Mus Natural Hist, Smithsonian, Washington, DC, 2006-2007; An Exceptional Ocean Engineer, Mass Inst Technol Mus, Cambridge, Mass, 2007; Capturing the Sea, Mus Yachting, Newport, RI, 2008; Inaugural exhib, Mus Computer Art, Brooklyn, NY, 2008; Digital Fusion, Gallery on the Pali, Honolulu, 2010; Artists of Hawaii, Honolulu Mus Art, 2011. *Pos:* Creative Dir, Center Civic Initiative, Milwaukee, Wis, 69-71; producer, dir, cameraman, Am 3 Found, San Diego, Calif, 91-95; coord producer, Morning Light, Walt Disney Films, Burbank, Calif, 2007. *Awards:* Award Excellence, Soc Publ Designers Ann, SPD New York, NY, 83; Emmy, 1984 Emmy Awards, Acad Television Arts & Scis, 84; Golden Monitor, Racing the Winds of Paradise (PBS), Int TV & Video Asn, 89; Best Digita (traditional print), Honolulu Printmakers 75th Anniversary, 2003; First Place, Digitally Charged Entities, Video Life Honolulu, 2003; Highly Honored People in Nature, Natures Best Photog, Smithsonian, Windland Smith Rice Int Awards, 2006-2007; Gold Photography Annual, Graphis Pub, NY, 2012. *Bibliog:* William Robinson (auth), Hawaiian Eye, Yachting Mag, 78; Kimball Livingston (auth), Roving Eye for Sailboats, San Francisco Examiner, 82; Tim Jefferies (auth), Phil Uhl, Yachting World Mag (UK), 88; John Saimo (auth) Offshore Hawaii Marine Artist, Tokyo Broadcasting System, 93; John Watkin (auth), Rocking the Boat (One & Two), Lifetime TV Network, 2004-2005. *Mem:* Honolulu Printmakers; Asn Hawaii Artists; Int Yacht Restoration Sch (mus Yachting); Digital Art Soc Hawaii; Windward Artist Guild. *Media:* Digital, Mixed, Acrylic. *Publ:* Chapmans Piloting Seamanship & Boat Handling (contribr, bk), Hearst Bks, 79; auth (ed, illus), A Maritime History of Hawaii, Pan Am Clipper Cup Series, 80; Nautical Quarterly (contribr, bk), Donald C McGraw, 80; Stars & Stripes the Official Record (contribr, bk), Bruce Stannard, 88; To the Third Power (contribr, bk), Tillbury House Publ, 2004; contribr, What the Sea Teaches Us, Jeff Jurtti, Disney Publ, 2008; contbr, Kialoa, Dare to Win, by John Bkilroy, Sea Point Book. *Dealer:* Gallery Art Robe Ginza Tokyo; Uhl Studios Honolulu Hi. *Mailing Add:* UHL Enterprises 1750 Kalakaua Ave Ste 3-757 Honolulu HI 96826

UKLANSKI, PIOTR
SCULPTOR
b Warsaw, Poland, 1968. *Work:* Francois Pinault Found, Venice; Migros Mus fur Gegenwartskunst, Zurich; Tate Britain, London; Guggenheim Mus, New York. *Exhib:* Mirroring Evil: Nazi Imagery / Recent Art, Jewish Mus, New York, 2002; Art After Image, Neues Mus Weserburg Bremen, Ger, 2004; Experience de la duree, Lyon 8th Biennial Contemp Art, France, 2005; Shades of Space, Guggenheim Mus, New York, 2007; Whitney Biennial, Whitney Mus Am Art, New York, 2010. *Bibliog:* Roberta Smith (auth), Dear Gallery: It Was Fun, but I'm Moving Up, NY Times, 4/18/2008. *Mailing Add:* Galerie Emmanuel Perrotin 194 NW 30th St Miami FL 33127

ULLBERG, KENT
SCULPTOR
b Goteborg, Sweden, July 15, 1945. *Study:* Konstfack Univ Coll Art, cert (drawing & sculpture); Swedish Mus Natural Hist, anat, 4 yrs; Mus Des Sci Naturelles, Orleans, France. *Work:* Swedish Mus Natural Hist, Goteborg; Exhib Palace, Peking, China; Corpus Christi Mus, Tex; Los Angeles Co Mus; Denver Mus Natural Hist; City Ft Lauderdale, Fla; Island of Laeso, Denmark; Johnson C Smith Univ, Charlotte, NC; St Louis Zoo, Mo; Hiram Blauvelt Art Mus, Oradell, NJ; Brookgreen Gardens, Pawley's Island, SC. *Comn:* Monumental sculptures, Lincoln Ctr, Dallas, 81, Corpus Christi Nat Bank, Tex, 81, City Corpus Christi, 83, Corp Plaza, Boca Raton, Fla, 83, Lywam Art Mus, Wausau, Wis, 83, Genesee Mus, Rochester, NY, 84, Acad Natural Sci, Philadelphia, 87 & Nat Wildlife Fedn, Washington, DC, 89; First United Methodist Church, Corpus Christi, Tex, 95; Johnson C Smith Univ, Charlotte, NC, 2000; Fed Reserve Bank, Houston, Tex, 2005; First Nat Bank, Omaha, 2007; Laeso, Denmark, 2002. *Exhib:* Ann Exhib, Nat Acad Design, New York, 75-2008; Ann Exhib Nat Cowboy & Western Heritage Mus, Oklahoma City, 77-2008; Artists of Am, Colo Heritage Ctr Mus, 81-2000; Art Mus S Tex, 85; Biologiska Museet, Stockholm, Sweden, 89; Munic Art Gallery, Luxemburg, 89; Gilcrease Mus, Tulsa, Okla, 91; Fleischer Mus, Scottsdale, Ariz, 2000; STX Inst for Arts, Corpus Christi, Tex, 2002; Nat Geographic, Washington, DC, 2002; retrospective, Joslyn Art Mus, Omaha, 2002; Nat Mus Wildlife Art, Jackson Hole, Wyo, 2005. *Pos:* Cur, Nat Mus & Art Gallery, Botswana, Africa, 71-74; cur/consult, Denver Mus Natural Hist, 74-76. *Teaching:* Instr, Scottsdale Artists Sch, 86, Loveland Art Acad, 93. *Awards:* Gold Medal, Nat SC Soc, 83; Pres Award, Nat Arts Club, 91; H Hering Award, Nat SC Soc, 93-2008; Soc Animal Artists, 96; Rungius Medal, Am Wildlife Mus, 96; Prix De West Award, Nat Cowboy Hall Fame, 98. *Bibliog:* Article, Artists of the Rockies, winter 83; Kent Ullberg-Sculptor (film), PBS, 84; Kent Ullberg: Moments to Nature, 98; and others; American Wildlife Art, D Wagner PhD, Feb 2008. *Mem:* Nat Sculpture Soc; Nat Acad Western Art; Nat Cowboy Hall Fame; Nat Acad (assoc, 81, acad, 90-); Soc Animal Artists & Nat Arts Club, New York; Am Soc Marine Artists; and others; The Explorers Club, New York. *Media:* Bronze, Steel. *Interests:* Marine conservation, wildlife. *Dealer:* C C Art Connection 3850 S Alameda Corpus Christi TX 78411; Trailside Gallery Jackson Hole Wyoming 83001; Paderewski Fine Art Beaver Creek Co; Cavalier Gallery Nantucket Ma; Helena Fox Fine art Charleston SC; Whistle Pik Gallery Fredericksburg TX. *Mailing Add:* Padre Island 14337 Aquarius St Corpus Christi TX 78418

ULLENS DE SCHOOTEN, MYRIAM & GUY FRANCIS
COLLECTORS, ADMINISTRATORS
b San Francisco, Jan 31, 1935. *Study:* Leuven Univ, Belgium, Degree in law, 1958; Stanford Univ, MBA, 1960. *Pos:* Chief exec officer, Eurocan Packaging co, Mechelen, Belgium, 1965-73, Tiense Suikerraffinaderij, Tienen, Belgium, 1973-89, Artal Group SA, Luxembourg, 1989-2000; bd dirs, SEI Ctr Advanced Studies in Mgt; co-founder, Guy & Myriam Ullens Found, Switzerland, 2002, Ullens Sch, Lalitpur, Nepal, 2006, Ullens Ctr Contemp Art, Beijing, 2007. *Awards:* Named one of Top 200 Collectors, ARTnews mag, 2008-13. *Collection:* Contemporary Chinese art. *Mailing Add:* Karen Van Lorreinenlaan 34 Tervuren 3080 Belgium

ULLMAN, (MRS) GEORGE W
COLLECTOR
b Aug 23 1907, St Louis Mo, 1907. *Study:* Ariz State Univ, Hon PhD (humanities), 94. *Mem:* Costume Soc Am; Am Fedn Arts; Ariz Costume Inst; Desert Botanical Garden of Phoenix; Taliesin West. *Collection:* French furniture and paintings, Louis XV and Louis XVI periods; Haitian paintings; contemporary paintings of Philip Curtis; Spanish paintings, seventeenth and eighteenth century on painted furniture & glass

ULLRICH, POLLY
CRITIC
Study: Univ Wis, Madison, BA (jour), MA; Theory and Criticism, Sch Art Inst, Chicago, MA in Art History. *Teaching:* Lectr in field; served on panels and juried and cur exhib. *Mem:* Chicago Art Critics Asn. *Publ:* Independent art critic, freelance journalist for NY Times, Newsweek, Chicago Mag, Chicago Sun-Times and the Milwaukee Journal, written analyses and reviews on contemp art for Sculpture Mag, frieze, Am Craft, KeramikMagazin, Bridge, Metalsmith, Fiberarts, Surface Design Journal, New Art Examiner, Ceramics Art and Perception. *Mailing Add:* 852 W Wolfram St Chicago IL 60657

ULM-MAYHEW, MARY LOUISE
PAINTER, INSTRUCTOR
b Milwaukee, Wis. *Study:* Cardinal Stritch Univ, BFA, 81; workshops with Charles Movalli, Gregg Kreutz, Ann Templeton, 96, Matt Smith, Kevin McPherson, 99-2000, Dan Gerhartz, 2002-03. *Work:* Courtland Med Ctr & St Mary's (Seton Corp), Milwaukee, Wis; New Visions Gallery, Marshfield, Wis; West Bend Mutual, West Bend, Wis; Nature Conservancy, Madison, Wis; Wausau Ins & Northwestern Mut Ins; Acuity Ins, Kohler, WI. *Comn:* Oil painting, Univ Wisc, 98. *Exhib:* Northern Nat Art Competition, LRC Gallery Nicolet Col, Rhinelander, Wis, 93; two-person invitational, New Visions Gallery, 95; Six Counties, John Michael Kohler Art Mus, Sheboygan, Wis, 94; OPA 4th Nat, San Antonio, Tex, 95; Nightwalker 96, Colo State Univ, Ft Collins, 96; OPA Regional, Chicago, 2000; Best and Brightest, Scottsdale Artists Sch, Scottsdale, Ariz, 99-2000; Solo exhib Henderson Art Center, Farmington NMex; Birds in Art, Leigh Yawkey Woodson Art Mus, WI, 2004; Edna Carlston Gallery, UW Stevens point, WI. *Teaching:* Instr oil painting fundamentals, West Bend Art Mus, 89-; plein air painting workshops, San Juan Islands, Washington, 95 & Minocqua, Wis, 96-2000; instr, oil painting, Dillmans Art Found, 99. *Awards:* 1st Place, Artists Mag Cover Competition, 94; Second Nat Cover Award-First Place, North Light Mag, 95; Third Place - Far Europa Int Painting Competition, Stroncone, Italy, 98; Second Place - People Competition, Int Artist Mag; Cash Award, Flein Air Competition, Cedarburg, WI, 2000-2004. *Bibliog:* Glory McLaughlin (auth), First prize winner, North Light Mag, 3/95; Marsha Tuchscherer (auth), On site painter-teacher, Art Wis, 6-7/95; featured in Contemporary women artists, Cedco Publ, 96 & 99; Cynthia Marsh (auth), Painting nourishes artists soul, West Bend Daily News, 4/23/97; Prime Time, Sheboygan, 8/98. *Mem:* Wis Painters & Sculptors; Oil Painters Am; Alla Prima Int; Wis Women in the Arts; Tucson Plein Air Painters; Laguna Plein Air Painters. *Media:* Oil Paint. *Publ:* 100 Ways to Paint Florals, Intl Artists Pub, 2004. *Dealer:* Edgewood Orchard Galleries 4140 Peninsula Players Rd Fishcreek WI 54212. *Mailing Add:* 6871 Hickory Rd West Bend WI 53090

ULRICH, BRIAN
PHOTOGRAPHER
b Northport, NY, 1971. *Study:* Univ Akron, BFA (Photography), 1996; Columbia Coll, Chicago, MFA (Photography), 2004. *Work:* Art Inst Chicago; Mus Contemp Art, San Diego; Mus Fine Arts, Houston; Milwaukee Art Mus; Cleveland Mus Art; Mus Contemp Photography, Chicago,; DeCordova Mus & Sculpture Park, Lincoln, Mass. *Exhib:* Solo exhibs include Millworks Gallery, Akron, Ohio, 1996, Peter Miller Gallery, Chicago, 2004, Mus Contemp Art, Chicago, 2005, Robert Koch Gallery, San Francisco, 2006, Rhona Hoffman Gallery, Chicago, 2006-07, Mus Contemp Art, San Diego, 2006-07, Julie Saul Gallery, New York, 2007, Mississippi State Univ, 2007, Quality Pictures, Portland, Ore, 2008, Proj 4 Gallery, Washington, 2008; Group exhibs include Chicago Area Billboard Proj, ArtChicago, 2003; Ctr Awards, Ctr Photographic Arts, Carmel, Calif, 2003; FACT/FICTION, Creative Arts Workshop, New Haven, 2004; Unframed First Look, Sean Kelly Gallery, New York, 2004; Frozen in Light, Zolla Lieberman Gallery, Chicago, 2004; Manufactured Self, Mus Contemp Photography, Chicago, 2005; Servings, City Gallery, Chicago, 2005; Marcia Wood Gallery: Palm Beach 3 Contemp Art Fair, W Palm Beach, Fla, 2005; Point of Purchase, Dumbo Arts Ctr, Brooklyn, 2006; The Field, Jamaica Ctr for Arts, Jamaica, NY, 2007; Branded & On Display, Krannert Art Mus, Champaign, Ill, 2007; New Am Portrait, Jen Bekman Gallery, New York, 2007; Worlds Away: New Suburban Landscapes, Walker Art Ctr, Minneapolis, 2008. *Awards:* Follett Fel, 2001-02; Stuart & Iris Baum Grant, Chicago, 2003; City Chicago Dept Cultural Affairs Community Arts Assistance Grant, 2005; Finalist, Leica Oskar Barnack Award, 2005; Finalist, Critical Mass, 2005; Ill Arts Coun Artist Fel, 2007. *Dealer:* Julie Saul Gallery 535 W 22nd St 6th Floor New York NY 10011; Rhona Hoffman Gallery 118 N Peoria St Chicago IL 60607 ; Robert Koch Gallery 49 Geary Street 5th floor San Francisco CA 94108

ULRICH, DAVID ALAN
PHOTOGRAPHER, EDUCATOR
b Akron, Ohio, Apr 18, 1950. *Study:* Studied with Minor White, 70-76; Sch of Mus of Fine Arts, Tufts Univ, BFA, 74; RI Sch Design, MFA, 77. *Work:* Minor White Archives, Princeton Univ, NJ; Mass Inst Technol, Cambridge; RI Sch Design, Providence; The Photog Place, Philadelphia; Photogenesis, Columbus, Ohio; and others. *Comn:* Kahoolawe Proj, 93-95. *Exhib:* Recent Work of Twelve Photographers, Addison Gallery Am Art, Andover, 77; Second Sight-An Exploration Into Infrared Photog, Carpenter Ctr Visual Arts, Harvard Univ, 80; Solo exhibs, Hawaii: Landscape of Transformation, Gallery East, Boston, MA, 89, Bishop Mus, Honolulu, HI, 90, Hui No'eau Visual Arts Ctr, 91 & India Gandhi, Nat Ctr Arts, 94; Perspectival Multiples (catalog) Mus de Arte Contemp Gallery Caralas, Venezuela, 90; Image XVIII, Amfal Plaza, Honolulu, 91; Artists of Hawaii, Honolulu Acad Arts, 92; Contemp Mus, Honolulu, Hawaii, 93. *Pos:* Dir, Prospect Street Gallery, Cambridge, 73-74; exec dir, Hui No'eau Visual Arts Ctr, Maui, Hawaii, 91-93, Pacific Imaging Ctr, Honolulu, Hawaii, 93-. *Teaching:* Assoc prof photog, Art Inst Boston, 77-, co-chmn, photog dept, 80-84, chmn, 84-91. *Bibliog:* Fernando de Trazegnies G (auth), El sonido de una sola mano, El Comercio, Lima, Peru, 78; Stu Cohen (auth), The art of making a point, Boston Phoenix, 79. *Mem:* Soc Photog Educ; Photog Resource Ctr. *Publ:* Contribr, Aura, Mag of Contemp Photog, Buffalo, 76; Parabola vol XIV, No 3, 89, NY; Manoa vol 2, No 1, Univ Hawaii Press, 90; The Burning Island, Sierra Club Bks, 91; Parabola, Vol XVIII, No 2, 93. *Mailing Add:* 2841 Baldwin Ave Makawao HI 96768

UMLAUF, KARL A
PAINTER, SCULPTOR
b Chicago, Ill, May 16, 1939. *Study:* Univ Tex, Austin, BFA, 57-61; Yale Univ, fel, summer 60; Cornell Univ, MFA, 63. *Work:* New Orleans Mus Art, La; Everson Mus, Syracuse, NY; Joslyn Art Mus, Omaha; Mod Mus Art, NY; Dallas Mus Art; IBM Corp, New York, Austin & Dallas; Fogg Art Mus; Cornell Univ, New York; Okla Art Ctr, Oklahoma City; Ark Arts Ctr, Little Rock; El Paso Mus; Longview Mus; Metrop Mus & Mus Mod Art, New York; Philadelphia Mus Art; Hall Art Collection, Frisco, Tex; Midwestern State Univ, Wichita Falls, Tex; Tex A&M Univ, Commerce, Tex; Baylor Univ, Waco, Tex; Longview Mus, Longview, Tex; Wichita Falls Mus Art, Wichita Falls, Tex; Martin Mus Art, Waco, Tex; Tyler Mus Art, Tyler, Tex; Aldon B Dow Mus Art, Midland, Mich; Am Airlines, DFW Airport, Dallas. *Comn:* Painting (13 x 7), comn by Dillard College Admin Bldg, Midwestern Univ, Wichita Falls, Tex. *Exhib:* Ann Nat Painting & Sculpture Exhib, Longview Mus, Tex, 76, 79, 82, 84, 86-87 & 89-91; Longview Mus, Longview, Tex, 77, 86, 91 & 2003; Works on Paper Southwest '78, Dallas Mus Art, 78; The First 20 Yrs, Tyler Mus Art, Tex, 83; Tex Art Celebration, Houston, 86, 88, 90-91, & 2002-2010; Totally Tex, Dallas, 86; Univ Tex,

Permain Basin, 87; North East Mo Univ, 90; Martin Mus, Waco, Tex, 91, 96, 2002 & 2005; Harris Gallery, Houston, 94, 97, 2001, 2003 & 2006; Northwest Art Center, Minot, North Dakota, New York, 2010-11; Groft Gallery, Waco, Tex; solo exhibs Univ Tex, Tyler, 95, William Campbell Contemp Art Gallery, Fort Worth, 80, 83, 85, 90, 96, Martin Mus Art, Baylor Univ, Waco, Tex, 97, Okla State Univ, Stillwater, 98, Art Mus Southeast Tex, 99, Mus Southwest, Midland, Tex, 99, El Paso Mus Art, 99 & Imago Gallery, Palm Desert, Calif, 2000, Tyler Mus Art, Tyler, Tex, 08, Houston Baptist Univ, Houston, Tex, 2011; Art Ctr, Waco, Tex, 96 & 2002; Cline Gallery Santa Fe, Scottsdale, 2003-2005; Roswell Ctr Arts, 2004; Irving Arts Ctr, Irving Tex, 2004; TCU Art Mus, Fort Worth, Tex, 2006; Alden B Dow Mus Art & Sci, Midland Mich Dist Fine Arts, Washington, DC, 2007; Retrospectives (with catalogs), Wichita Falls Mus Art, Wichita Falls, Tex, 2008, Ft Worth Art Ctr, 2008; Tex Okla Biennial, 2010. *Collection Arranged:* Tyler Mus Art, Tex; Tex Sculpture Garden and Hall Coll, Frisco, Tex; John Belew Coll, Martin Mus Art, Waco, Tex; Midwestern State Univ Wichita Falls, Tex; Osu Mus Art, Stillwater, Okla; Longview Art Ctr, Tex; Masur Mus Art, Monro, La. *Pos:* Vis artist, Tex Tech Univ, 74, 85 & 87, Colo State Univ, 73, Austin Coll, Sherman, Tex, 74, Baylor Univ, Waco, Tex, 75 & 85, Ball State Univ, 75, Ariz State Univ, 79, Univ of Tex, Tyler, 86, Univ Tex, Arlington, 91, Emporia State Univ, Kans, 94, Okla State Univ, Stillwater, 98 & Midwestern Univ, Wichita Falls, Tex, 2001, 2004, 2006, Tex Christian Univ, Tyler, 2011. *Teaching:* Instr Art, Univ Pa, Philadelphia, 63-66; asst prof art, Univ Northern Iowa, 66-67; Prof art, E Tex State Univ, Commerce, 67-89; prof, Ind Univ, Bloomington, 74-75 & 80; artist-in-residence, Baylor Univ, Waco, Tex, 89-. *Awards:* 1st Prize Purchase, Everson Mus, Syracuse, NY, 63; Grants in fiberglass plastic & cast paper, A&M Univ, Commerce, 69, 71, 73, 75, 80 & 85; 1st Prize, Joslyn Mus, Omaha, Nebr, 74; Grants in Independent Res, Baylor Univ, 91, 93, 96, 98, 2001-2002 & 2005-2006; Third Prize, Tex Celebration, Houston, 91; First Prize 49th Ann Competition, Abilene Mus, Tex, 93; Purchase Prize, 23rd Prints Drawing Competition, Ark Art Ctr, 95; Pres Award & Purchase Prize, 28th & 30th Bradley Nat Drawing Exhib, Ill, 2001 & 2003; Special Award, Tex, Artist Celebration, Houston, 2005; Merit Award, 23rd Ann Dakota's Works on Paper Int, Vermillion, SDak; Allbritton Research Grants, 96, 98, 2001-02, 2004, 2006, & 2008-; 2nd Prize, Art Celeration of Tex, WIlliams Tower Art Ctr, Houston, 2008; Outstanding 2-D Texas Artist of 2012, Texas Commission on the Arts. *Bibliog:* Rev, Houston Chronicle, Art Scene, 86; Lifestyles, Perspective, Ft Worth Star Telegram, 88; Artists Turn Memories Into Reality, Waco Tribune, 91; Karl Umlauf at DUAC, Dallas Morning News, 93; Janice McCullagh (auth), Shrines, Mus Art, Waco, Tex, 94; Joe Kagle (auth), Salvage Series, Waco Art Ctr, 96; Art & Soul, Curatorial Review, Hall Art Collection, Frisco, Tex. *Mem:* Tex Sculpture Asn; Tex Fine Arts Asn; Tex Asn Coll Teachers; Coll Art Asn; Dallas Art Mus; The Mac, Dallas, Tex; Mod Art Mus, Fort Worth. *Media:* Mixed Media on wood & canvas. *Res:* 10 years of research in vacuum formed plasics, 1969-1979; research in deep relief cast paper forms, 1980-1990; research in creating industiral icons, walls, urban & geophysical facades, 1991-2004. *Specialty:* Landscapes & Industrial Reliefs. *Interests:* Taking trips to mountain regions. *Collection:* 19th & 20th Century Prints, Paintings & Drawings by 20th Century Artists. *Publ:* Auth, The First Twenty Years (catalog), Tyler Mus Art, 83; Karl Umlauf (catalog), 86; Karl Umlauf-Transitions (catalog), 89-91; The Journey: Life's Work Retrospective (monograph), pp 206, David Deming, Cleveland Art Inst, 2002; Recent Works in Cast Paper, Mark Thistle Waite (catalog); Transitions, William Wadley (catalog); Recent Works, Jan McCullagh, Longview Mus (catalog); Natural Evolution, Ft Worth Art Ctr (catalog); The Vacu Forms 1969-1980; Gene Binder Gallery, Marfa, Tex. *Dealer:* Imago Gallery Palm Desert CA; Harris Gallery Houston Tex; Gene Binder Gallery Marfa, Tex. *Mailing Add:* 307 S Borden St Lorena TX 76655-9778

UMLAUF, LYNN (CHARLOTTE)
SCULPTOR, PAINTER

b Austin, Tex, Jan 8, 1942. *Study:* Art Students League, 61-62; Acad Fine Arts, Florence, 65-66; Univ Tex, Austin, MFA, 68. *Work:* Chase Manhattan Bank; PS 1, Long Island City, NY; Fox & Horan, NY; Reading Pub Mus, Pa; Pacesetter Corp, Omaha; Carlton Fields, NY. *Comn:* installation sculpture on Tower of Prignano, Rifiutinart, Sculpture Symposium, Modena, Italy, 2013. *Exhib:* Whitney Mus Am Art Biennial Exhib, 75; Painting and Sculpture Today, Indianapolis Mus Art, 78 & 86; Seven Artists, Neuberger Mus, Purchase, NY, 85; solo exhibs, Hal Bromm Gallery, NY, 78-80 & Young & Hoffman Gallery, Chicago, 83; Oratorio Installation, Spinea (Ve), Italy, 92; Turchetto Plurima Gallery, 85-2000; Basanese Studio Art, 82, 90, 2000; Galerie Biedermann, Munich, Ger, 88, 92, 2003; Gallery Miralli, Chigi Palace, Viterbo, Italy, 2000; Revoltella Mus, Trieste, Italy, 2000; Eric Stark Gallery, NY, 2002; Installation, Libr, Sopra Tutto Libri, Prato, Italy, 2005. *Teaching:* Instr, Fairleigh-Dickinson Univ, 71-72, Philadelphia Col Art, 79, Kutztown State Col, 80-81 & Sch Visual Arts, NY, 81-2009; Ohio State Univ, 2004, Sch Visual Arts, NY, 81-2013; instr painting & sculpture. *Awards:* Artists residency, Villa Waldberta, Feldafing, Ger, 2002. *Bibliog:* Carmelo Strano (auth), Europe-USA Unimplosive Art, Osterio Magno Palace, 98; Serena Bellini (auth), Umlauf and Vecchiet: So Close, So Far, Il Piccolo, 6/15/2000; Robert C Morgan (auth), Local Papers-A Quick Look at Williamsburg, NY Arts, vol 5, 23, no 4; Robert C. Morgan (auth), Lynn Umlauf, Edition Peccolo, Livorno, Italy, 2001. *Media:* Acrylic, Wire, Plexiglas, Sheet Metal. *Publ:* Auth, The question of gender in art, Tema Celeste, autumn 92; auth, Transparency (bk), Libr Sopra Tutto Libri, Prato Italy, 2005. *Dealer:* Penine Hart Art & Antiques New York NY. *Mailing Add:* 222 Bowery Apt 6 New York NY 10012

UNTERSEHER, CHRIS CHRISTIAN
SCULPTOR

b Portland, Ore, May 14, 1943. *Study:* San Francisco State Col, BA, 65; Univ Calif, Davis, MA, 67. *Work:* Objects USA, Johnson Wax Collection, Racine, Wis; Allan Stone Galleries Collection, NY; Jim Newman Found, San Francisco, Calif; Oakland Mus, Calif; Smithsonian Collection, DC. *Comn:* Vet Admin Hosp, Reno, Nev. *Exhib:* Solo exhibs, Hansen-Fuller Gallery, San Francisco, 67-70 & De Young Mus, San Francisco, Calif, 68 & 77; Objects USA, Johnson Wax Collection, int traveling show, 69-73; 20 Americans, Mus Contemp Crafts, NY, 71; Clay, Whitney Mus, NY, 74; Quay Ceramics Gallery, San Francisco, 75 & 77; Los Angeles Co Mus Art, 2000; Cantor Arts Ctr, Stanford Univ, 2005-06. *Teaching:* Instr ceramics, Univ Calif, Davis, 68-69; instr ceramics, Univ Cincinnati, 69-70; chmn ceramics dept, Univ Nev, Reno, 70-90, prof art, currently; instr, Coll Marin, 91-; instr ceramics, City Coll San Francisco, 91-. *Awards:* Purchase Award, Mem Union Art Gallery, Univ Calif, Davis, 68; Sr Fel, Nat Endowment Arts, 81. *Bibliog:* Jo Lauria (auth), Color and Fire, Rizzoli Publs; Charlotte Speight and John Toki (auths), Make It in Clay, Mayfield Publ; Charlotte Speight (auth), Hands in Clay, Alfred Publ. *Mem:* Am Crafts Coun. *Mailing Add:* 1360 Burbank St Alameda CA 94501

UPTON, JOHN DAVID
EDUCATOR, CURATOR

b Des Moines, Iowa, May 4, 1932. *Study:* Calif Sch Fine Arts; Univ Rochester, with Minor White & Beaumont Newhall; Univ Calif, Berkeley; Calif State Univ Long Beach, BA & grad study art hist. *Work:* Mass Inst Technol Creative Photog Collection, Cambridge; Fine Arts Collection, Metrop Mus Art. *Exhib:* 15 Am Photogrs, Houston Mus Contemp Art, 64; solo exhibs, Mass Inst Technol Creative Photog Gallery, Cambridge, 65 & Camerawork Gallery, Costa Mesa, Calif, 68; Light 7, Mass Inst Technol Art Gallery, Cambridge, 68. *Collection Arranged:* The Photograph as: Metaphor, Object & Document of Concept (auth, catalog), 74 & The Photograph as Artifice (auth, catalog), 78, Calif State Univ Long Beach; Color as Form: A History of Color Photography, Corcoran Gallery Art, Washington, DC, 82. *Pos:* Chmn dept of photog & chmn div of fine arts, Orange Coast Col, Costa Mesa, Calif, 63-; vis cur, Int Mus Photog, George Eastman House, Rochester, NY, 79-82. *Teaching:* Prof hist of photog & creative photog, Orange Coast Col, Costa Mesa, Calif, 63-; vis lectr hist photog, Univ Calif, Los Angeles, 75, Calif Inst Arts, Valencia, 83-85; Calif State Univ Fullerton, 75-91. *Awards:* Ann Award for Contributions to Photog Ed and the Hist of Photog, Calif Mus Photog, Univ Calif, Riverside, 88. *Bibliog:* Minor White (auth), Photographers Northwest, Aperture, Vol 11, No 3, 64. *Mem:* Soc for Photog Educ (mem bd trustees, 75-79); Friends Photog (mem bd trustees, 74-80). *Res:* History of photography since 1900, especially Alfred Steiglitz, Minor White & Edward Neston. *Publ:* Contribr, New Vision of the 70's, Photographers Choice, Addison House, 75; coauth, Photography, Little, Brown & Co, 76, revised, 84, revised, 92 by Addison Wesley & Longman. *Mailing Add:* 3020 Via Buena Vis Unit N Laguna Woods CA 92637-3054

UPTON, RICHARD THOMAS
PAINTER, PRINTMAKER

b Hartford, Conn. *Study:* Univ Conn, BFA; Ind Univ, MFA; Ecole des Beaux Arts. *Work:* Nat Collection of Fine Arts, Smithsonian Inst, Washington; Mus Mod Art, NY; Victoria & Albert Mus, London, Eng; Bibliot Nat, Paris, France; Montreal Mus Fine Art, Can; and others; Metrop Mus of Art, New York City. *Comn:* Eros Thanatos Suite (German poem & woodcuts), Interlaken Corp, Providence, RI, 67; Salamovka Poster (limited ed silkscreen), Okla Art Ctr, Oklahoma City, 74; River Road Suite (lithographs), Salmagundi Mag for the Humanities, 76 & Robert Lowell at 66 (suite of drawings), 77; Ballingen Landscape, Rutgers Center for Innovative Print & Paper, NJ. *Exhib:* The Delaware Water Gap, Corcoran Gallery Art, Washington, 75; Nat Collection Prints & Poetry, Libr Cong, Washington, 76-77; Retrospective of prints from Elvehejm Art Ctr, Atelier 17, France, 77; Okla Art Ctr, 77; Weatherspoon Art Gallery, Greensboro, NC, 77; Tweed Mus Art, Duluth, Minn, 77; Paysage Demoralise--Landscape at the End of the Century, Grey Art Gallery, NY Univ; solo shows, List Gallery, Swarthmore Coll, Ben Shahn Gallery, William Patterson Univ, Georgia Mus f Art, Krannert Art Mus, Everson Mus Art, New Britain Mus Am Art & James A Michener Art Mus; The Artist in Rural Ireland: Images of North Mayo, Philadelphia Art Alliance; plus many others; Cooper Union, New York City; Nat Acad of Design, NY. *Collection Arranged:* Salamovka Series and Other New Paintings (auth, catalog), Oklahoma Art Ctr, Oklahoma City, 74; Bibliotheque Nationale, Paris; Metropolitan Mus Art, NYC; Nat Mus Art Inst, Washington, DC; Rose Art Mus, Brandes Univ; Montreal Mus Fine Art; Mus Mod Art, NYC; and others. *Awards:* Fulbright Fel; Nat Educ Asn Grant, Artists for Environ; Interlaken Corp Designer Award, Providence, RI, 67; Richard A Florsheim Foundation Award, Nat Acad Design, 95. *Bibliog:* Sherry Chayat (auth), Richard Upton: Museum American Art, Art News, 92; Kenneth E Silver (auth), Richard Upton: Ten Years of Italian; Landscapes/Michener Museum, Art in America, 94; David Shapiro (auth), Landscape as God: The New Drawings of Richard Upton, 96; Umbria Rediscovered-The Chronicles of Richard Upton, Everson Mus Art, Syracuse, NY, 91; Michael Brenson (auth), article, Defining nature by it's battle scars, Grey Art Gallery, NY; Paul Hayes Tucker (auth), Univ Wash Press, 91, Richard Upton and the Rhetoric of Landscape (monogr); Robert Boyers (auth), The Drawings of Richard Upton, David Shapiro (monogr), Skidmore Coll - Salmagundi, 97; Kim Smkapkh (auth), Landscape & Memory: The Tuscan Landscapes of Richard Upton, Cooper Union, 97; Richard Howard (auth), A Table of Green Fields: Richard Upton's Cortona Landscapes, Salmagundi, 2000; Fred Licht (auth), Richard Upton's Cortona Landscapes, Cur Peggy Guggenheim, Venice. *Mem:* Nat Acad (acad, 95-). *Media:* Oil, Water Based Media; Lithography, Intaglio. *Publ:* Auth, Impressions-A Paris Suite, 64, co-auth, Credo, 68 & Eros Thanatos, 68, Interlaken Corp; coauth & illusr, Models, 75 & River Road (with Stanley Kunitz), 75, Erebus Press

URAM, LAUREN MICHELLE
CONCEPTUAL ARTIST, ILLUSTRATOR

b Hartford, Conn, Nov, 9, 1957. *Study:* Pratt Inst, BFA, 80. *Work:* NBC & AT&T, New York, NY; Pacific Bell, San Francisco; Johnson & Johnson, New Brunswick, NJ. *Comn:* Collage of Golden Gate Bridge (pieces of ripped paper), Random House, Inc, NY, 85; relief portrait of Thomas Edison, Rupert Jensen Assocs, Atlanta, Ga, 85; collage of five portraits, Live for Life, Johnson & Johnson, New Brunswick, NJ, 85. *Exhib:* Student Scholarship Exhib (nat), 78 & 79 & 28th Ann Nat Exhib, 86, Mus Illus, NY. *Awards:* Art Directors Annual Award, 83; Commun Arts Illus Annual Award, 82 & 85; Print's Regional Design Annual Award, 86. *Mem:* Found Community Artists. *Media:* Paper. *Mailing Add:* 838 Carroll St No B Brooklyn NY 11215-1702

URBANELLI, LORA S
MUSEUM DIRECTOR
b Philadelphia, 1956. *Study:* Rutgers Univ, NJ, BA, 1980; Syracuse Univ, MFA, 1982. *Pos:* cur, prints drawings & photography, RI Sch Design Mus, Providence, RI, 1985-99, asst dir, 1999-2003, interim dir, 2003-2005; exec dir, Farnsworth Art Mus, Rockland, Maine, 2005-2008; dir, Montclair Art Mus, 2009-. *Teaching:* Dept Prints, Drawings & Photographs, Yale Univ Art Gallery, formerly. *Mem:* Penobscot Bay Regional Chamber of Commerce ; Diversity Comt, RI Sch Design, formerly; Technol Steering Comt, RI Sch Design, formerly; Am Asn Mus's Re-Accreditation Steering Comt. *Mailing Add:* Montclair Art Museum 3 South Mountain Ave Montclair NJ 07042

URICHTA, REY
COLLAGE ARTIST, PAINTER
b Glendolden, Pa, 70. *Study:* Univ Calif, BFA, 92, MFA magna cum laude, 2000. *Work:* Elliot Mus, Stuart, Fla; Benoma Sculpture Park; Mus Contemp Art; Shalom Public Works; Ackland Art Mus; Sackler Gallery; Walsh Gallery; Stone Mus. *Exhib:* Marian Goodman Gallery; Massimo Gallery; Children in Art, Kissala Galleria; Brighton Gallery; Ubalda Gallery; Peter Mott House; Rutherfurd Hall. *Pos:* artist-in-residence, Mosaic Masters, 2001, Color Perfection, 2002; designer, Meriks Mosaic Art, 2004-2012, vpres, 2012-2015, pres, 2016-. *Teaching:* adj prof, Univ Ga, Ga State Univ; instr, Atlanta High Sch, 2009-2010; instr, Middletown High Sch, NJ, 2010-2016; instr, Central High Sch, 2014-. *Awards:* Best in Show, Meriks Art Exhib, 2012. *Bibliog:* Janet James (auth), Mosaic in Bloom, Town Talk, 2000; David Syers (auth), Behind the Broken Glass, Gazette Galleria, 2002; Ian Dela (auth), The Method to the Madness: An Interview with the Mosaic Master, 2006; Alison Phoenix (auth), Smashed Glass Masterpiece, Monmouth Record, 2016. *Mem:* Am Mosaic Artists (pres 2015-); Collage Me Asn. *Media:* Acrylic, Oil, Mosaics. *Res:* the poetry of Lord Byron. *Interests:* Hot yoga, dog walking, Tai Chi. *Publ:* Auth, Breaking the Mold, UPA Press, 2006

URQUHART, TONY (ANTHONY) MORSE
SCULPTOR, PAINTER
b Niagara Falls, Ont, Apr 9, 1934. *Study:* Yale Univ, Norfolk, Conn, 55; Albright Art Sch, Buffalo, dipl, 56; Univ Buffalo, NY, BFA, 58. *Hon Degrees:* Order of Can, 1995. *Work:* Nat Gallery Can, Ottawa; Art Gallery Ont, Toronto; Mus Mod Art, NY; Victoria & Albert Mus, London; and others; Walker Art Center, Minneapolis, Minn. *Comn:* Mural, Govt Ont, 68, bas-relief, 78; Sculpture magic wood (site specific), Macdonald Stewart Art Ctr, Guelph, Ont, 86; Sculpture our house, Rim Park Waterloo, Ont, 2003. *Exhib:* Carnegie Int, Philadelphia, 58; Guggenheim Int, NY, 59; solo shows, Winnipeg Art Gallery, Man, 59 & Walker Art Ctr, Minneapolis, 60; Am Acad Arts & Lett, NY, 60; Nat Gallery Can, Ottawa, 75; Mus Mod Art, Paris, 76; retrospective, Kitchener-Waterloo Gallery, traveling, 78-80; Thematic Retrospective, Art Gallery Windsor traveling, 88-89; Power of Invention: Drawing in Seven Decades, Tour, 2003; Art of the 60's, National gallery of Can, 2005; Transforming Charonologies MOMA, 2006. *Collection Arranged:* Swinging London, 25 London Ont artists for Univ Waterloo Art Gallery, 1966; Vimy & After: The Drawings of Walter Allward 1910-1955, Ont, 2005-2006; Dark Bridges: Jane Hinton-Hugh Mackenzie. *Pos:* Artist-in-residence, Univ Western Ont, 60-65 & Kitchener-Waterloo Art Gallery, 81-83; Artist-in-residence, City of Kitchener, 2005. *Teaching:* Lectr, McMaster Univ, Hamilton, Ont, 1966; From asst prof to assoc prof, Univ Western Ont, London, 67-72; prof, Univ Waterloo, 72-, chmn, 77-79, 82-85 & 94-99; Retired, 99. *Awards:* First Prize, Albright-Knox Art Gallery, 58; Baxter Award, Art Gallery Ont, 60; Fel, Can Coun Sr Arts, 79-80; Gov General Award (visual arts), 2009. *Bibliog:* Dorothy Cameron (auth), Tony Urquhart: Reunion, 71, J Vastokas (auth), Archetypal imagery in the work of Tony Urquhart, 74 & Joe Bodelai (auth), Tony Urquhart: The story so far, 76, Artscanda; J Vastokas (auth), Worlds Apart: The Symbolic Landscapes of Tony Urquhart, Winsor Art Gallery, Ont, 88 & Dialogues of Reconciliation: The Imagination of Tony Urquhart, 91; Michael Ondaatje (ed), The Broken Ark: Book of Beasts, Oberon Press, Ont, 69, reprinted 78; Terrance Heath: Tony Urquhart Power of Invention: Drawings in Seven Decades, 2003; Joyce Zemans, The Revenants, Shadows, 2003; Off the Wall, Michael Phillips, 2009; Kirsten Greer/Joyce Miller, Ambiguous Geographies, 2010. *Mem:* foun mem Can Artists Rep/Front Artists Can (nat secy, 67-71), Honorary life mem, 1999; Jack Chambers Mem Found (chmn bd govs, 78-85); Can Conf Arts (vpres, 71-72). *Media:* Mixed Media; Oil. *Res:* French graveyards. *Interests:* Golf; Music. *Publ:* Auth, The Urquhart Sketchbook, Isaacs Gallery, Toronto, 62; auth, with Jane Urquhart, I Am Walking in the Garden of Your Imaginary Palace, AYA Press, Toronto, 82; Cells of Ourselves, 50 drawings chosen & annotated by G M Dault, Porcupines Quill Press, 89; Illustrator, special collectors edition of, The Scream, Rohinton Mistry, 2008, Lives of the Saints, Nino Ricci, 2010. *Dealer:* Thielsen Gallery 1038 Adelaide St London Ont Can; Galerie Jean Claude Bergeron 150 St Patrick St Ont Can. *Mailing Add:* 9 Church St PO Box 310 Colborne ON K0K 1S0 Canada

URSO, JOSETTE
PAINTER
b Tampa, Fla, June 5, 1959. *Study:* Univ S Fla, BFA, 80, MFA, 83. *Work:* Springfield Mus Art, Springfield, Ohio; Mint Mus Art, Charlotte, NC; Tampa Mus Art, Fla; GE Fairfield, Conn; US Dept of State, Washington, DC. *Comn:* Fabric collage: Hillsborough Co Courthouse, Plant City, Fla, 96; Community Mural Project, Ruskin, Fla, 2009. *Exhib:* The Drawing Ctr, NY, 88; Bronx Mus Arts, NY, 90; Bernice Steinbaum Gallery, NY, 92; Galerie A-16, Zurich, Switz, 94; Galerie Industria, Wuppertal, Ger, 2000; solo shows, Kathryn Markel Gallery, New York, 2000 & Museo de Las Americas, Old San Juan, PR, 2000, Lyons Wier Gallery, New York, 02, Gescheidle Gallery, Chicago, 03, Gulf Coast Mus Art, 2006, Young & Rubicam, New York, 2009; Leepa Rattner Mus of Art, Tarpon Springs, Fla, 2005; Mus Art & Design, New York, 2006; DFN Gallery, New York, 2006, 2007, 2009; Whitney Art Works, Portland, Maine, 2007; TAMPA Mus Art, 2008; Metaphor Contemp Art, New York, 2008; Allyn Gallup Contemp Art Gallery, Sarasota, NY, 2008; Projects Gallery, Philadelphia, 2009; Kenise Barnes Fine Art, Larchmont, NY, 2009; NY Public Lib, 2011; Two person show, NY Inst Tech, 2012. *Teaching:* Instr painting, Chautauqua Sch Art, NY, 84-90, 99, The 92nd St Y, New York, 88-90, Art New England, 99-2003 & Cooper Union, 98-; vis artist, Montclair State Univ, 2008. *Awards:* Grant, Pollock-Krasner Found Inc, 96 & 2008; Award Ballinglen Arts Found, Co Mayo, Ireland, 2000, 2002; Basil H Alkazzi Award, 2000; Grant, Lambent Fel Nominee, 2005; Residency, Yaddo, 2009; Loft Nota Bene, Cadaques, Spain, 2010. *Bibliog:* The Message in the Media, Phyllis Braff (auth), NY Times, April 95; City Focus, Chicago Cutting Edge Hip to Blue Chip, Magaret Hawkins, ARTNews, April 2003; One View/ Two Visions, Melissa Kuntz (catalog essays), 2005; Painting Paper (catalog essay), Univ Va, Charlottesville, Va, 2010. *Mem:* Col Art Asn. *Media:* Mixed Media. *Dealer:* Galerie Industria Wuppertal Ger; DFN New YorK NY

URSO, LEONARD A
SCULPTOR, PAINTER
b Rome, NY, May 21, 1953. *Study:* State Univ New York, New Paltz, BA, 75, MFA, 77. *Work:* Art Inst Chicago; Mem Art Gallery, Rochester, NY; Shanghai Univ Technol, Japan. *Comn:* MACE, Tri-State Univ, Angola, Ind, 90; 78 inch sculpture, Garth Fagan Dance, Rochester, NY, 90; 5 ft sculpture, Hansford Manufacturing, Rochester, NY, 91; Open Form, USA Today & Rochester Inst Technol, Rochester, NY, 92; Bauch & Lomb World Hq, 94. *Exhib:* Solo exhibs at Dawson Gallery, NY, 1989, 1991, Chelsea Gallery, Ohio, 1993, Switzer Gallery, Rochester, NY, 1994, Sonnenberg Gardens, Canandaigua, NY, 1995, Synaesthesia Gallery, Rochester, NY, 1998, Rome Art Ctr, NY, 1999, Bausch & Lomb World Headquarters, NY, 2000, Mellon Ctr, Soc of Contemp Art & Craft, Pittsburgh, Pa, 2001, Dyer Art Gallery, RI Inst Tech, 2002, Chosen Weston, Seoul, 2004; group exhibs include Posner Gallery, Birmingham, Mich, 2000; Priam & Eames Gallery, East Hampton, NY, 2001, 2004; Mokkumto Gallery, Seoul, 2002; Gallery Hyundai, Seoul, 2002; Montgomery Coll, Rockville, Md, 2003; Gyeongnam Art Mus, Int Sculpture Symposium, South Korea, 2003; Mus Art and Design, Frankfurt, Germany, 2004; Seoul Korea Int Art Exhib, 2004. *Teaching:* Assoc prof fine art, Rochester Inst Technol, NY, 83, Mowris-Mulligan Endowed Chair, Distinguished Prof, 99-. *Bibliog:* Ron Netsky (auth), Sculptor Shapes Flowing Figures, Democrat & Chronicle, 88. *Media:* Metal; Acrylic, Oil

US, VALTA
PAINTER
b Austria, 1944. *Exhib:* Solo exhibs include Harvard Law Libr, Cambridge, Mass, 1978, Harcus Gallery, Boston, 1984, Chapel Gallery, Newton, Mass, 1993, Creiger & Dane Gallery, Boston, 1999, Botanica Gallery, Bozeman, Mont, 2001; group exhibs include New Era/New World, Gallery Emanuel, Great Neck, NY, 2000; Virginia Lynch Gallery, Tiverton, RI, 2001; Evocations, Nabi Gallery, Sag Harbor, NY, 2001; Landscapes Seen & Imagined, Sense of Place, DeCordova Mus & Sculpture Park, Lincoln, Mass, 2001. *Awards:* Pollock-Krasner Found Grant, 2007. *Mailing Add:* 14 Rolling Hill Court E Sag Harbor NY 11963

UTKIN, ILYA See Brodsky, Alexander Ilya Utkin

UTTECH, THOMAS MARTIN
PAINTER, EDUCATOR
b Merrill, Wis, Oct 27, 1942. *Study:* Layton Sch Art, BFA; Univ Cincinnati, MFA. *Work:* Milwaukee Art Mus; Univ Wis-Madison; Philbrook Art Ctr, Tulsa, Okla; Mus Contemp Art, Honolulu. *Comn:* Milwaukee Athletic Club, Carron & Black, Milwaukee, Wis; Northwestern Mutual Life Insurance Co. *Exhib:* Directions, Milwaukee Art Ctr, 75; Whitney Mus Art Asn, 75, Monique Knowlton Gallery, 85, Maxwell Davidson Gallery, 88, Schmidt-Bingham Gallery, 88, 93, 95, 97 & 99, Sherry French Gallery, NY, 88; Visions from the Northwoods, Milwaukee Art Mus, 77; Arthur Rogers Gallery, New Orleans, La, 89; 100 yrs Wis Art, Milwaukee Art Mus, 82; Mind & Beast, Leigh Yankey Woodson Art Mus, Wausau, Wis, 93; Am Realism & Figurative Art, 1952-1990, Miyagi Mus Art, Sendai, Miyagi, Japan, 93; Am Realism & Figurative Art, Cline Fine Art Gallery, Santa Fe, NMex, 94; Tony Folliard Gallery, 94, 96 & 98; Recent Paintings, Alexandre Gallery, NY, 2006; Am Acad Arts & Letts Invitational, New York, 2010. *Awards:* Peninsula Sch Art Grant, Fish Creek, Wis, 73; Nat Endowment Arts, 88; Wis Arts Board, 89 & 94; Art Award, Am Acad Arts & Letts, 2010. *Bibliog:* Ellen Lee Klein, Arts, 12/85; Gerrit Henry, Art in Am, 3/86; John Arthur (auth), Spirit of Place: Contemp Landscape Painting & Am Tradition, 89. *Mem:* Am Acad Arts & Letts. *Media:* Oil, Photographs. *Publ:* Illusr, A roadless area revisited, Audubon Mag, 75; Earth Care, Sierra Club & Audubon Soc, 75. *Dealer:* Schmidt-Bingham New York; Struve Gallery Chicago IL. *Mailing Add:* 4305 Hwy O Saukville WI 53080

UTTERBACK, CAMILLE
DIGITAL AND VIDEO ARTIST
Study: Williams Coll, BA (magna cum laude), 1992; New York Univ, MPS, 1999. *Work:* La Caixa Found, Barcelona, Spain; Henderson Develop Corp, Hong Kong; Hewlett Packard, Houston; Itau Cult Inst, Sao Paulo, Brazil; Whitney Mus Am Art; Am Mus Natural History. *Exhib:* Solo exhibs, Goodrich Gallery, Williamstown, Mass, 1991, Cornwall Gallery, Boston, 1993, Dean's Gallery, MIT Sloan Sch Mgmt, 1996, Caren Golden Fine Arts, New York, 2001, Mass Mus Contemp Art, North Adams, 2002, Cummings Art Ctr, New Londong, Conn, 2005, El Paso Mus Art, Tex, 2007, Nelson Gallery, Davis, Calif, 2008, Contemp Art Ctr Va, 2009; TDC46, Fifth Avenue Gallery, Parson Sch Design, 2000; Digital Alice, Seoul Metrop Mus Art, Korea, 2000; The Genomic Revolution, Am Mus Natural History, New York, 2001; Labyrinths of Pleasure, Mus Contemp Art, Taipei, Taiwan, 2001; Self, Westport Art Ctr, Conn, 2002; Alt-Digital, Am Mus of the Moving Image, Queens, 2003; Surface Tension, Fabric Workshop & Mus, Philadelphia, 2003; Plays Well with Others, AIR Gallery, New York, 2004; Exquisite Electric, Grande Ctrl Art Ctr, Santa Ana, Calif, 2005; Brides of Frankenstein, San Jose Mus Art, Calif, 2005; Physical-Digital, Santa Cruz Mus Art & History, Calif, 2006; Impermanent Markings, Pratt Manhattan Gallery, New York,

2008. *Teaching:* Artist-in-residence, Tex A&M Univ, Coll Archit, 2004, Stanford Univ, Dept Art & Art History, 2007-2008, Atlantic Ctr for the Arts, NEw Smyrna Beach, Fla, 2008 & Headlands Ctr for the Arts, Sausalito, Calif, 2009. *Awards:* New Media Art Fel, Rockefeller Found, 2002; Transmediale Award, Int Media Art Festival, Berlin, 2005; IBM Innovation Merit Award, Boston Cyberats Festival, 2007; MacArthur Found fel, 2009. *Bibliog:* Mike Snider (auth), Artists getting into digital expression, USA Today, 7/31/2000; Nicholas Wade (auth), The Genome Gets to Meet the Family, NY Times, 5/25/2001; Cate McQuaid (auth), At this Gallery, Viewers Become Part of the Art, Boston Globe, 10/18/2002; Reena Jana (auth), The Ripple Effect, Wired Mag, Vol 12, 60, 2/2004; Susan Carpenter (auth), In touch with five very moving works of art, Los Angeles Times, 10/20/2005; Victoria Mather (auth), The Art of a Hotel Holiday, Vanity Fair, No 556, 156, 12/2006; Felicia R Lee (auth), For MacArthur grants, another set of geniuses, NY Times, 9/22/2009

UZILEVSKY, MARCUS
PAINTER, PRINTMAKER
US citizen. *Study:* Sch Art & Design, New York. *Work:* Bezalel Aca Art & Design, Jerusalem, Israel; New Britain Mus Art, Conn; Tucson Mus Art, Ariz; Washington Co Mus Fine Arts, Hagerstown, Md; Hood Mus Art, Dartmouth Coll, Hanover, NH; Cleveland Orchestra, Cleveland, Ohio; New Eng Ctr Contemp Art, Brooklyn, Conn; Portland Art Mus, Portland, Ore; Nat Wildlife Fedn, Washington, DC; Environ Protection Agency, San Francisco, Calif; Berlin Philharmonic Orchestra, Berlin, Ger; Nat Audubon Soc, New York. *Comn:* Musical Manuscripts, Chemers Gallery, Tustin, Calif. *Exhib:* Nat Print Competition, Edinboro, Pa, 83; Alexandria Mus, La, 84; 27th Nat Print Exhib, Hunterdon Art Ctr, Clinton, NJ, 86; Wesleyan Int Exhib Prints & Drawings, Wesleyan Coll, Macon, Ga, 87. *Awards:* Rapides Gen Hosp Purchase Award, Alexandria Mus, La; Purchase Award, Edinboro State Coll, Pa; Purchase Award, 19th Bradley Nat Print & Drawing Exhib. *Bibliog:* Marja Eloheimo (auth), Marcus Uzilevsky - where music and art meet, 11/1/84; Larry Sibley (auth), Uzilevsky's art, Eternity, 10/86; Ruth Thompson (auth), Screen Printing, Artist of Sight and Sound, 3/88. *Mem:* Marin Art Coun. *Media:* All. *Interests:* Music. *Dealer:* Oaksprings Impressions PO Box 572 Woodacre CA 94973. *Mailing Add:* PO Box 166 Woodacre CA 94973

V

VAADIA, BOAZ
SCULPTOR
b Israel, 1951. *Study:* Pratt Art Inst Brooklyn, NY, 76; Avni Inst Fine Arts, BFA, 71. *Work:* Metro Mus Art, Jewish Mus, NY; Tel Aviv Mus, Israel Mus, Israel; Mus Mod Art, San Francisco; Philharmonic Ctr Art; Ravinia Sculpture Garden, Chicago; Sculpture permanent installation Time Warner Bldg, New York, NY, 2004; and pvt collections; Mus Mod Art, San Francisco; Tokyo Metrop Teien Mus, Japan. *Comn:* Sculpture, Paine Webber, Puerto Rico, 87; Related Companies, NY, 88 & 93; LaSalle Partners, Roslyn, Va, 89. *Exhib:* Solo exhibs, OK Harris, NY, 86, 88, 89 & 92, Jewish Mus, NY, 88-89, Hokin Kaufman, Chicago, 89 & 90, Helander Gallery, Palm Beach, Fla, 91, Fay Gold Gallery, 93 & 97, Jaffe Baker Gallery, Fla, 96 & 97, Imago Gallery, Palm Desert, Calif, 97, Elaine Baker Gallery, Boca Raton, Fla, 2000, 02, Miriam Shiell Fine Art, Toronto, Can, 2004, Courcoux & Courcoux, Eng, 2005, Caldwell Snyder, San Francisco, Calif, 2005, Connaught Brown, London, Eng, 2006, Eckert Fine Art, Naples, Fla, 2006, Galerie Terminus, Munich, Ger, 2006, Eckert Fine Art, Kent, Conn, 2010; Utsukushi-ga-hara Open Air Mus, Japan, 92; Hakone Open-Air Mus, 94; First Lady's Sculpture Garden, White House, 95; Philharmonic Ctr Arts, Naples, Fla, 96; Connaugnt Brown, London, 2011; Jim Kempner Fine Art, NY, 2011; Gail Severn Gallery, Ketchum, Id, 2012; Elaine Baker Gallery, Boca Raton, Fla, 2012. *Awards:* Ariana Found Arts Grant, 86; Nat Endowment Arts Grant, 88; Utsukushi-ga-hara Open Air Mus Award, 92. *Bibliog:* Jan Sjostrom (auth), Sculptor draws from earth, Palm Beach Daily News; Bernie Gould (auth), Sculptor harvests Brooklyn boulders, NY Times, 7/2/2000. *Mem:* Int Sculpture Ctr. *Media:* Stone. *Publ:* Boaz Vaadia, Stone Sculpture, 92. *Dealer:* Elaine Baker Gallery 608 Banyan Tr Boca Raton FL 33431; Imago Galleries 45-450 Highway 74 Palm Desert CA 92260; Eckert Fine Art 27N Main St #1 Kent Ct 06757; Connaught Brown 2A Bermarle St London W1S 4HD England. *Mailing Add:* 104 Berry St Brooklyn NY 11249

VACCARINO, ROBIN
SCULPTOR
b Seattle, Wash, Aug 14, 1928. *Study:* Univ Calif, Los Angeles; Otis Art Inst, MFA (magna cum laude), 66. *Work:* Santa Barbara Mus; Library of Congress, Washington; De Cordova Mus; Los Angeles Co Mus. *Comn:* Hyatt Regency, Dallas, Tex, 78; Progressive Savings & Loan, Beverly Hills; Security Pac Nat Bank, Los Angeles; Koll Ctr, Irvine, Calif; IBM; Bank America; and others. *Exhib:* Otis Mus 50th Anniv Exhib, Los Angeles; Libr of Congress Nat Print Exhib, Washington; Univ of Calif, Santa Cruz; Santa Barbara Mus; Los Angeles Municipal Gallery, Barsdale Park: Los Angeles Bicentennial; Security Pacific Nat Bank Exhib. *Teaching:* Otis Art Inst, Parsons Sch Design, Los Angeles & Paris & Art Ctr Col Design; JP Getty Mus, Artists POV Series, Currently. *Awards:* Calif Arts Coun Grant, 79; Nat Endowment Arts Individual Fel, 80-81; and others. *Bibliog:* Joseph Mugaini (auth), Drawing, A Search for Form, Reinholt, 66; Innovative printmakers in Southern Calif, Southwest Art Mag, 73; article in Art Forum. *Media:* Metals, Resin, Concrete. *Mailing Add:* 3593 Berry Dr Studio City CA 91604

VACCARO, LUELLA GRACE
CERAMIST, PAINTER
b Miles City, Mont, June 2, 1934. *Study:* Univ Wash, Seattle; Univ Calif, Berkeley; workshops with Peter Voulkas. *Work:* Antonio Prieto Collection, Mills Coll, Oakland, Calif; Ceramics Monthly Collection, Columbus, Ohio; Spencer Art Mus Collection, Lawrence, Kans; Butler Mus Am Art, Youngstown, Ohio. *Exhib:* 32nd & 33rd Int Print Exhib, Seattle Art Mus, Wash, 61-62; Latitude 53 Gallery, Edmonton, Alta, 79; Mail Art Expo '80, Santa Cruz, Calif, 79; solo exhibs, Univ of Kans, 66 (125 pieces) & Lawrence City Libr, 67 (40 pieces), Percolator Gallery, Lawrence, Kans, 2010; Kellas Gallery, Lawrence, Kans, 81 & 82; two-person exhib, Lawrence Art Ctr, Kans, 86; Vaccaro Studio Shows 2011-2013; Ingredients, Lawrence, Kans, 2013; 5 Bar Ingredients, 2013-2014; 20 Painting Show, Alvamar Club, Lawrence, Kans, 2014. *Awards:* Laguna Gloria Award, Tex Fine Arts Asn, Austin, 61; Kans Designer Craftsman Award, Kans Univ Art Mus, Lawrence, 68; Ceramic Monthly Award, Ceramics Monthly, Columbus, Ohio, 71. *Bibliog:* Luella Vaccaro and Her Pottery, Sunflower Cablevision interview, 79; Lynn Bretz (auth), Nick and Lu: A Couple of Artists, Lawrence J World, Sunday Arts Section, 5/3/81; Come on Get GappyPodcast Lawrence.com, 2010. *Mem:* Lawrence Art Ctr, Spencer Mus Art, Kans; Mus Am Indian, DC. *Media:* Stoneware, Clay; Acrylic, Oil. *Interests:* Ebay, Etsy. *Mailing Add:* 535 Kansas St Lawrence KS 66046

VADIA, RAFAEL
PAINTER, LECTURER
b Havana, Cuba, Nov 27, 1950; US citizen. *Study:* Miami-Dade Jr Col, AA, 71; Ecole des Beaux Arts, Paris, France, 73; Fla Int Univ, BFA, 76. *Work:* Greater Miami Pub Librs; Mus Modern Art at the Orgn of Am States, Washington, DC; Metro-Dade Govt Ctr, Art in Pub Places Trust, Miami, Fla; Citibank Int; Visa Int; Fla Int Univ; Cintas Found. *Exhib:* 49th, 50th, 51st & 60th Ann Nat Competition Contemp Am Painting Soc Four Arts, Palm Beach, Fla, 87-89 & 98; Drawing 1990 Nat Competition, Harris Fine Arts Ctr, Brigham Young Univ, Provo, Utah, 90; Broward Community Coll, South Campus Art Gallery, Hollywood, Fla, 92; The Cult Resource Ctr/Metro Dade Govt Ctr, Miami, Fla, 93; Aqueous Open, Pittsburgh Ctr Arts, Penn, 95. *Pos:* Artist keynote speaker, Fla Art Educ Conf, Naples, 91; speaker, Miami Int Art Fair, 92; lectr, Broward Community Coll, Hollywood, Fla, 92; North South Ctr, Cuban Nat Heritage (panel head), Coral Gables, Fla, 95; adj fac, Acad Adv Miami-Dade Coll, 2002-. *Teaching:* Freshman Experience, Miami Dad Coll, 2007-2009. *Awards:* Judge's Recognition Award, 31st Competition & Exhib, Broward Art Guild, Ft Lauderdale, 83; John Gordon Mem Award, 49th Ann Nat Exhib Contemp Am Paintings, Soc Four Arts, Palm Beach, Fla, 87; Cintas Found Fel, Inst Int Educ, New York, 91-92; Miami Dade Coll Recognition of Excellence Award, 2007. *Bibliog:* Helen L Kohen (auth), Bright days for art in South Florida, 12/80 & The Nation, 6/81; Joanne Butcher (auth), Art Papers, Reviews, Art News, 1/88; Giulio V Blanc (auth), Arts Mag, 11/90; Elisa Turner (auth), Show Honors Artists from FIU, The Miami Herald, 10/97. *Media:* Mixed on Canvas and Paper. *Publ:* Modern & Colonial Latin American Paintings, Sotheby Parke-Bernet, New York, 80; Rafael Vadia: New Drawings, De Armas Publ, Miami; auth, Art of Cuba in Exile, Jose Gomez Sicre, Munder Press, Miami, 87; Selections From Art Bank, Metro-Dade Govt Ctr: 27 Artists from Collection of Art in Public Places Trust, North Miami Ctr Contemp Art, Fla, 89. *Mailing Add:* 3130 Center St Miami FL 33133

VAILLANCOURT, ARMAND
SCULPTOR, PAINTER
b Quebec, Can, Sept 3, 1929. *Study:* Ottawa Univ, 49-50; Ecole des Beaux Arts, Montreal, 51-55. *Work:* Banque d'oeuvres d'art du Can; Banque d'oeuvres d'art du Qué; Maison des Assemblées, Guernica, Espagne; Ville de Montréal; Ecole des Arts et Métiers, Asbestos; and others. *Comn:* Vaillancourt Fountain, Embarcadero Plaza, San Francisco, 67-71; Justice, Fountain, Palais de Justice de Qué; El Clamor, monumental sculpture-fountain, Santa Domingo, Dominican Repub, 85; Drapeau blanc, exterior monumental sculpture, Université Laval, Qué, 87; Passerelle Vaillancourt, pedestrian bridge (200 ft), Ville de Plessiville, 90; and many others. *Exhib:* Salon de mai, Musée d'Art Moderne, Paris, 62; First Ibero Am Symposium, Santo Domingo, Dominican Repub, 85; Contemp Outdoor Sculp at the Guild, Toronto, 82; Mus Fine Art Can, 90; La Sculpture au Québec (1946-61), Musée du Qué, 92; Collection au Musée, Musée d'Art Contemporain, Montréal, 92; Expos itinéiante a Travers le Canada, Musée des Beaux-Arts au Can, 92; solo shows, Galerie Maximum, Montréal, 84, Galerie Espace Global Montréal, 86, Caisse Pobulaire de Victoriaville, 87, Galerie d'Art Contemporain, Montréal, 90, Galerie Le Lieu et Mail Saint-Rock, Québec, 92; plus many others; and many other group & solo exhibs. *Awards:* First Prize, interior sculpture, 63 & exterior monumental sculpture, 63, Ecole des Arts & Métiers; First Prize, Int Competition for sculptural fountain, San Francisco, 69; and others. *Bibliog:* David Miller (auth), Vaillancourt sculptor (film), ONF, 63-64; Jean-Gaétan Séquin (auth), L'Univers d'Armand Vaillancourt (video), Radio Qué, Betacam, 84; Yvon Laurendeau (auth), Armand Vaillancourt, guercier de la paix (video), 92; Martial Lapointe (auth), Pierre et paix, J de Quebec, 7/24/87; A M Richard et C Robertson (auth), Performance in Canada, 1970-90, Inter ed, 91; Jocelyne Lepage (auth), A Vaillancourt, L'irréductible, La Presse, Montréal, 3/28/92; Pradel (auth), L'Art, la Résistance, L'Evénement du Jeudi, Paris, 10/23/86. *Mem:* Conseil de la Sculpture du Qué (founder); Conseil des Arts Visuels du Qué(founder). *Media:* All Media; Acrylic. *Mailing Add:* 4211 avenue del'Esplanade Montreal PQ H2W 1T1 Canada

VALADEZ, JOHN
PAINTER
b Los Angeles, Calif, 1951. *Study:* Calif State Univ, Long Beach, BFA, 76. *Comn:* Mural, Fed Bldg at border crossing, El Paso, Tex, 93; mural, Fed Bldg, downtown El Paso, Tex, 93; mural, Atrium at new Central Libr Bldg, Los Angeles, 93. *Exhib:* Solo Exhibs, John Valadez: Early/Recent Works, New Directions Gallery, Los Angeles, 83, Mark Taper Forum, 84, Simard Gallery, 84, Mus Contemp Hispanic Art, NY, 86, Lizardi/Harp Gallery, Pasadena, 87 & 89, Condenados, Saxon-Lee Gallery, Los Angeles, 90, New Visions & Ventures in Latino Art, Rancho Santiago Col, Santa Ana, Calif, 90, New Pastels, Daniel Saxon Gallery, Los Angeles, 90 & Domestic Allegories, Galeria de la Raza, San Francisco, 91; Only Los Angeles Contemp Variations, Munic Art Gallery, Los Angeles, 86; Made in Aztlan, Centro Cult de la Raza, San Diego, 86; Symbolic Realities: John Valadez/David Baze, Dominguez Hills, 86; Primer Espacio de Identidad Cult, El Barrio, Centro Cult Tijuana, Baja, 86; Hispanic Art in the United States: Thirty Contemp Painters & Sculptors, Corcoran Gallery Art, Washington, DC

and traveled, 87-89; From the Back Room, Saxon-Lee Gallery, Los Angeles, 88; Chicano Art/Resistance & Affirmation, 1965-85, Wight Art Gallery, UCLA, traveling through 1993 to Denver Art Mus, Albuquerque Mus, Nat Mus Am Art, San Francisco Mus Mod Art, Tucson Art Mus & Fresno Art Mus. *Bibliog:* Shauna Snow (auth), New Visions: Positive images through Latino art, Los Angeles Times, 3/11/90; Lynn Pyne (auth), Post-Chicano' art tries to 'break boundaries', Phoenix Gazette, 9/90; Susan Kandel (auth), LA in review, Arts Mag, 12/91

VALDES, KAREN W
DIRECTOR, EDUCATOR
b Los Angeles, Calif, May 25, 1945. *Study:* Univ Calif, Irvine, BFA, 68; Nat Univ Mex, Mexico City, 69; Univ Chicago, Ill, 72; Fla State Univ, Tallahassee, MFA, 74; NY Univ, 83. *Collection Arranged:* Lynda Benglis 1968-1978 (with catalog), Lowe Art Mus, Univ Miami, 80; Vito Acconci: Installation, Miami Dade Community Col, 83; A Separate Reality: Florida Eccentrics (with catalog), Mus Art, Ft Lauderdale, 87; Suzanne Giroux: Video Installation, Univ Fla, 89; The Great Am Lawnscape: Yard Art (with catalog), Univ Gallery Fla, 92. *Pos:* Cur exhibs, Art Mus STex, 75-76, Mus Art, Ft Lauderdale, Fla, 85-89; dir, Miami-Dade Community Col, Campu Art S Gallery, 76-85, Gloria Luria Gallery, Miami, 84-85, Univ Galleries, Univ Fla, 89-. *Teaching:* Assoc prof art & humanities, Miami-Dade Community Col, 76-84; assoc prof mus studies, Univ Fla, 89-. *Bibliog:* Elisa Turner (auth), A separate reality, Florida eccentric, Art News, 10/87. *Mem:* Coll Art Asn; Am Asn Mus; Fla Art Mus Dirs Asn; Hispanic Fac Asn, Univ Fla. *Res:* Contemporary art and outsider art. *Publ:* Contribr, The Eye of the Beholder: SFla Collects Essay (catalog), Mus Art, Ft Lauderdale, 86; Styles, Strands & Sequences: American Painters & Drawing (catalog), Univ Fla, 90; auth (article), Coral castle, Forecast: Pub Artworks J, 92. *Mailing Add:* 1130 Bayshore Dr Niceville FL 32578-3007

VALDEZ, VINCENT E
SCULPTOR
b Mora, NMex, Mar 15, 1940. *Study:* Univ Wyo, 67-70. *Work:* Nat Morgan Horse Asn Mus, Shellburn, NJ; Wyo State Mus, Cheyenne; Benson Park (outdoor sculpture), Loveland, Colo. *Comn:* Morgan Horse, comn by Anne Mears, Laramie, Wyo, 85; Monument of the Chase (bronze), Loveland High Plains Art Coun, Colo, 88; bas-relief, Tree of life, Ivinson Mem Hosp, Laramie, Wyo, 88. *Awards:* Best of Show, Western Regional Art Show, 87; Award of Merit, Anchorage Audubon Soc, 87; 2nd Place Bronze, George Phippen Mem Soc, 87. *Bibliog:* Anne Mears (auth), The magnificent Morgan, Today's Morgan, 5/85; Judy A Hughes (auth), Bronze: The rock of ages, Wildlife Art News, 1/88; Christina Leimer (auth), Metamorphic man, Art of the West, 11/88. *Mem:* Wyo Coun on the Arts. *Media:* Bronze. *Mailing Add:* PO Box 581 Laramie WY 82070

VALDEZ GONZALEZ, JULIO E
PAINTER, PRINTMAKER
b Santo Domingo, Dominican Republic, Jan 10, 1969. *Study:* Nat Sch Fine Arts, Dominican Repub, 84-86; Altos de Chavon/Parsons Sch Design, Dominican Repub, 86-88. *Work:* Museo Omar Rayo, Roldamillo, Columbia; Museo de Arte Moderno, Las Casas Reales Mus, Santo Domingo, Dominican Repub; Altos de Chavon Cult Ctr Found, Bob Blackburn's Printmaking Workshop, NY; The Robert Blackburn Print Collection, NY; Brandywine Workshop, Philadelphia, Pa. *Comn:* Wood mural, Batista-Morera-Valdez Arq, Santo Domingo, 89. *Exhib:* Solo show, Instituto de Cultura Puertorriquena, San Juan, PR, 93, La Era del Mito, Galeria San Juan Bautista, Casa Alcaldia, San Juan, PR, 95, Transpositions, Museo de las Americas, San Juan, PR, 97, Toomey Tourell Fine Arts, San Francisco, Calif, 98 & 99, Museo de las Casas Reales, Santa Domingo, Dominican Repub, 99, Maison des Arts et de la Cult, St-Jean-sur-Richellieu, Que, Can, 99; Artist in the Marketplace, Bronx Mus Arts, NY, 94; Int Triennial Graphic Art, Bitola, Repub Macedonia, 94; II Painting Biennial of Latin Am & Caribbean, Mus Mod Art, Santo Domingo, 94; A Tribute to Bob Blackburn, Wilmer Jennings Gallery, NY, 94; Shades of the Spirit: Contemp Explorations in Printmaking and Drawing, Painted Bride Art Ctr, Philadelphia, Pa, 95; Art in Transit: A Dominican Experience, Intar Latin Am Gallery, NY, 96; Artist In the Marketplace, Benefit Gala, Bronx Mus Art, NY, 96; Invitational Exhib, DNA Gallery, Provincetown, Mass, 96; Small, Gallery Juno, SoHo, NY, 96; Inaugural Exhib, Toomy Tourell Fine Arts, San Francisco, Calif, 97; Small Works '97, Studio Sch Asn Inc, NY, 97; From the Studio: Artist-in-residence Ann Exhib, Studio Mus Harlem, NY, 98; New Strokes, Taller Puertorriqueno, Philadelphia, Pa, 98; Caribbean Connections, Discovery Mus, Bridgeport, Conn, 98; Inter-Actions: Urena, Cofone, Valdez, Julia de Burgos Latino Cult Ctr, NY, 98; 22nd National Print Biennial, Silvermine Guild Art Ctr, New Canaan, Conn, 98; Onani: The African presence in Contemp Latin Am and Caribbean Visual Arts, Taller Puertorriqueno, Philadelphia, Pa, 99; Papeles Preciosos, Galeria Ada Balcacer, Santa Dominto, Dominican Repub, 99; The S Files, Site Specific Installation, El Museo del Barrio, NY, 99. *Pos:* Admissions comt mem, Parsons Sch Design, Dominican Repub, 90-93. *Teaching:* Instr printmaking, illus, drawing, two dimensional design, Altos de Chavon/Parsons Sch Design, 90-93. *Awards:* Fel, Bob Blackburn's Print Shop, NY, 94; Mus Mod Art First Prize Printmaking, XIX Nat Art Biennial, 94. *Bibliog:* Marianne de Tolentino (auth), Julio Valdez: fresh air, 8/89. *Media:* Acrylic, Silkscreen. *Publ:* Co-auth, Impresiones de la computadora, Royal Houses Mus, 93. *Mailing Add:* 176 E 106th Street 4th Fl New York NY 10029

VALDOVINO, LUIS HECTOR
VIDEO ARTIST, EDUCATOR
b Bahia Blanca, Arg, June 7, 1961. *Study:* Ohio Univ, with Arnold Gassan, BFA, 85; Univ Ill, Urbana, with Bea Nettles, MFA, 87. *Work:* Mus Mod Art, Rio de Janeiro, Brazil; Donnell Media Ctr, New York Pub Libr; APCLAI, Venice, Italy; Inst Cooperacion Iberoamericana, Buenos Aires, Arg; Univ San Diego, Calif; Mus Mod Art, NY. *Comn:* video, Cocteau Cento, Naropa Univ Audio Archive Preserv and Access Project, 2003. *Exhib:* II Cabo Frio Print Biennial, Mus Mod Art, Rio de Janeiro, 85; Dallas Video Festival, Dallas Mus Art, Tex, 90; Chicano Art: Resistance & Affirmation, San Francisco Mus Mod Art, Calif, 91; D'Ghetto Eyes, Kitchen, NY, 92; Committed Visions, Mus Mod Art, NY, 92; Black Maria Film Festival, Hirshhorn Mus, Washington, DC 93; Videonale Intermezzo, Kuntsmuseum, Bonn, Ger, 93; World Wide Video Festival, Stedelijk Mus, Amsterdam, The Neth, 97; Geme Biennale Int du Film surlant, Centre Georges Pompidou, Paris, France, 98; Third World Newsreel Retrospective, Mus Mod Art, NY, 98; Idea del Lugar, Museo Nacional Centros de Arte Reina Sofia, Madrid, Spain, 98; La Bienale di Venezia, Venice, Italy, 2000; BAC Int Film/Video Festival, Metrop Mus Art, NY, 2001. *Pos:* Assoc Prof, Art & Art History Dept, Univ of Colo, Boulder, Colo. *Teaching:* Prof video/computer, Carnegie Mellon Univ, Pittsburgh, Pa, 92-93; from asst prof to assoc prof video art, Univ Colo, Boulder, 93-. *Awards:* Individual Artist Fel, Nat Endowment Arts, 93; Film/Video Grant, Am Film Inst, 93; Ger Award Video Art, ZKM, Karlsruhe, Ger, 94. *Bibliog:* Coco Fusco (auth), Hybrid State Films, Anthology Film Arch, 91; Laura Marks (auth), Small pleasures in the dark, Afterimage, 93; Robert Koehler (auth), Society's outsiders get, Los Angeles Time, 93. *Mem:* Coll Art Asn; Independent Film & Video Asn; Univ Film/Video Asn; Friends of Photog; Film Arts Found. *Media:* video. *Res:* Latina/o video art. *Interests:* visual anthropology; video art. *Collection:* The mus of Modern Art, New York, NY. *Publ:* The Photo Review National Photographic Competition, The Photo Review, 85; contribr & illusr, Winners of Photographer Forum Photo Contest, 87 & Photographs Luis Valdovino, 88, Photographer's Forum; Dimensions of Discovery, Krannert Art Mus, 89; contribr, Festival Internacional de Video del Cono Sur, Mus Image & Sound, 93; Blanco y Negro y de Color, Mus Nacional Centro de Arte Reina Sofia, Madrid, 2001. *Dealer:* Video Data Bank 37 Wabash Ave Chicago IL 60603. *Mailing Add:* Univ Colo Campus Box 318 Fine Arts Dept Sibell-Wolle Bldg N196A Boulder CO 80309

VALENSTEIN, SUZANNE GEBHART
CURATOR
b Baltimore, Md, July 17, 1928. *Pos:* Assoc cur Far Eastern art, Metrop Mus Art, New York, formerly, res cur, Asian Art, currently. *Teaching:* Vis lectr Chinese ceramics, Princeton Univ, NJ, fall 76. *Mem:* Oriental Ceramic Soc London; Oriental Ceramic Soc Hong Kong. *Publ:* Auth, Ming Porcelains: a Retrospective, China Inst in Am, 70; A Handbook of Chinese Ceramics, 75, revised & enlarged, 89 & Highlights of Chinese Ceramics, 75, Metrop Mus Art; coauth, Oriental Ceramics: The World's Great Collections, Vol XII, The Metropolitan Museum, Kodansha Int, 77; auth, Chinese celadons reclaimed from the sea, Oriental Art Mag, spring 79; The Herzman Collection of Chinese Ceramics, 92. *Mailing Add:* Metrop Mus Art Fifth Ave at 82nd St New York NY 10028

VALENTI, THOMAS
PAINTER, INSTRUCTOR, ADMINISTRATOR
b New York, NY, May 5, 1953. *Study:* Newark Sch of Fine & Indust Art, Cert of Fine Art, 71-74. *Work:* Lipton Tea Co; Hoffman LaRoche Inc; Rutgers Univ; Bellemead Construct Co; Indian Head Corp. *Exhib:* Solo exhibs, Bergen Community Mus, Paramus, NJ, 80, Yard Sch Art, Montclair, NJ, 83; Group exhibs, Allied Artists Am Ann Juried Exhib, 98-99 & 2005-2006; Am Artists Prof League 71st Grand Nat Juried Exhib, Salmagundi Club, NY, 99, 77th Grand Nat Exhib, 2005, 78th Grand Nat Exhib, 2006; 32nd Ann Juried Exhib, Garden State Watercolor Soc, Trenton City Mus, NJ, 2001; 62nd Ann Open Juried Exhib, NJ Water Color Soc, Monmouth Mus, NJ, 2004 & 64th Ann Exhib, 2006; Am Watercolor Soc 137th Int Juried Exhib, 2004; 63rd Ann Juried Exhib, Audubon Artists of Am, Manhattan, NY, 2005 & 64th Ann Exhib, 2006; Contemp Realism 2005, Cavalier Gallery Int Juried Exhib, Manhattan, NY, 2005; Beijing World Art Mus, 2011; Am China Oil Painting Artists League, 2011; Allied Artists of Am 100 Yr Anniversary Juried Exhib, 2014. *Pos:* Juror Fort Lee Art Asn, NJ, 2000; pres, Allied Artists Am; juror, Salmagundi Club non-mem juried exhib, 2007-2008. *Teaching:* Instr, Ridgewood Sch Continuing educ, 2005. *Awards:* Am Artist's Prof League Award, Salmagundi Club, NY, 99; Forbes Mag Award, NJ Water Color Soc, Monmouth Mus, NJ, 2004; Traveling Exhib Award, Am Watercolor Soc, 2004; Best in Show Award, Ridgewood Art Inst 25th Regional Open Juried Show, 2005; 1st Place, Salmagundi Club, Mems Show, 2007; Best in Show, St Mark's Ann Juried Show, Mendham, NJ, 2007. *Bibliog:* The Tonal Technique in Watercolor, Thomas Valenti, Artist's Mag, 85; Bert Braham (auth), Design for Publishing, Graphic Arts Studio Manual, 86; Local Artist Finds Inspiration from City Streets, Community of Life, 2005; M Stephen Doherty (auth), Similar Procedures in Oil and Watercolor, Am Artist Mag 70 yr anniversary issue), 1/2007. *Mem:* Watercolor Club, NJ (pres, 80); NJ Watercolor Soc; Am Artist's Prof League, NY; Allied Artist's Am, NY (pres, 2007-); NE Watercolor Soc, NY; Salmagundi Club (hon mem); Audubon Artists Inc; Am China Oil Painting Artists League (founding mem & exec bd advisor). *Media:* Watercolor, Oil. *Interests:* Reading. *Publ:* Auth, The Tonal Technique for Watercolor, Artist's Mag; auth, Warren Chang: Narrative Paintings (introduction)

VALENTIN, JEAN-PIERRE
DEALER
b France, Jan 31, 1949; Can citizen. *Study:* Paris Business Sch, MBA (int trade), 71. *Bibliog:* A Gascon (auth), J P Valentin et galerie, Le Collectionneur, 78; G Robinson (auth), L' Art Francais Montreal, Can Art Investor's Guide, 80. *Mem:* Prof Art Dealers' Asn Can (pres, 81-85). *Specialty:* Prominent Quebec artists and Canadian artists; works by European masters of the 20th century

VALENTINE, DEAN
COLLECTOR
Study: Univ Chicago, AB, 1976. *Pos:* Pres, Walt Disney TV/Touchstone TV; pres & chief exec officer, United Paramount Network, Los Angeles, 1997-2002; with, Europlay Capital Adv, LLC, 2002-03; pres, First Family Entertainment, Beverly Hills, 2004. *Awards:* Named one of Top 200 Collectors, ARTnews mag, 2004-13. *Collection:* Contemporary art

VALENTINE, DEWAIN
SCULPTOR
b Ft Collins, Colo, Aug 27, 1936. *Study:* Univ Colo, BFA, 58, MFA, 60; Yale-Norfolk Art Sch, Yale Univ Fel, 58. *Work:* Whitney Mus Am Art, NY; Los Angeles Co Mus Art; Atlantic Richfield Corp, Washington, DC; Fed Reserve Bank, San Francisco; Stanford Univ Art Mus; Contemp Arts Ctr, Honolulu, Hawaii. *Comn:* Sky Gate (major outdoor work), comn by Frederick R Weisman; Open Diamond Double Diagonal (major outdoor work), comn by State Office Bldg, Van Nuys, Calif; Curved Waterwall (major indoor work), comn by Pacific Enterprises, Los Angeles; Diamond Waterwall (major outdoor work), comn by Metropolitan, Los Angeles. *Exhib:* Los Angeles Co Mus Art, 79; Pub Sch 1, Inst for Art & Urban Resources, NY, 81; Laumeier Int Sculpture Park, St Louis, Mo, 82; Madison Art Ctr, Wis, 83; Honolulu Acad Arts & the Contemp Arts Ctr, Hawaii, 85; Cartier Found for Contemp Art, France, 85-86. *Teaching:* Instr design & drawing, Univ Colo, 58-61 & 64-65; instr plastics, Univ Calif, Los Angeles, 65-67. *Awards:* John Simon Guggenheim Fel, 80; National Endowment for the Arts, 81. *Bibliog:* Peter Plagens (auth), Sunshine Muse, Praeger, 74; John Lloyd Taylor (auth), cover article in Art Int, Vol 17, No 7 & Jean Luc Bordeaux (auth), DeWain Valentine, Light Explored, Vol 67, No 8, 12/79, Art in Am; Jane Livingston, Artists Dialogue: DeWain Valentine, Archit Digest, 2/86. *Media:* Glass, Bronze, Steel, Stone. *Mailing Add:* 17921 S Western Ave Gardena CA 90248

VALERIO, JAMES ROBERT
PAINTER, EDUCATOR
b Chicago, Ill, Dec 2, 1938. *Study:* Art Inst Chicago, BFA, 66, & MFA (Anne Louis Raymond Fel), 68; spec study with Seymour Rosofsky. *Work:* Ill Bell Telephone Co; Univ Iowa Mus Art; Prudential Insurance Co; Albuquerque Mus Art; Metrop Mus Art; Guggenheim Mus Art; Whitney Mus. *Exhib:* Solo exhibs, Frumkin-Struve Gallery, Chicago, Ill, 81-84, Del Art Mus, Wilmington, 83, Allan Frumkin Gallery, NY, 87 & 90 & Frumkin/Adams Gallery, NY, 91, 93 & 95; Painting & Sculpture in California: The Mod Era, Nat Coll of Fine Arts of the Smithsonian Inst, Washington, DC & San Francisco Mus of Art, 76-77; Contemp Am Realism Since 1960, Pa Acad Fine Arts, 81; Drawings, Koplin Gallery, Santa Monica, Calif, 91; Am Narrative Painting & Sculpture: The 1980's, Nassau Co Mus Art, Roslyn Harbor, NY, 91; Am Realism & Figurative Art, 1955-1990 (traveling exhib), Miyagi Mus Art, Sendai, Japan, 92; Intimate Views (traveling), Glenn C Janss Collection of Am Realism; Recent Paintings, Univ Iowa Mus Art, 94; Art in Chicago 1945-1995, Mus Contemp Art, Chicago, 97; Still Life: The Object in Am Art 1915-1995 Traveling Exhib (auth, catalog), Metrop Mus Art, NY, 97-98; Twentieth Century Am Drawing from the Ark Arts Ctr Found Collection (traveling exhib), 1998-2000; Contemp Am Realist Drawing: The Jalane & Richard Davidson Collection, The Art Inst of Chicago, 11/6/00-1/2/00; Encyclopedia of LA Art Before 1980, Int Arts Found, Autumn, Calif, 2008; The Figure Revealed, Contemp Am Paintings and Drawings, Kalamazoo Inst Arts, 2008; George Adams Gallery, NY, 2008; Forum Gallery, NY, 2012. *Teaching:* Asst prof art, Rock Valley Col, Rockford, Ill, 68-70; assoc prof art, Univ Calif, Los Angeles, 70-79; assoc prof, Cornell Univ, 79-82; prof art, Northwestern Univ, Evanston, Ill, 85-2009, prof emer, 2009-. *Awards:* Purchase Award, Long Beach Mus of Art, 70; Creative Arts Award Fel, Univ Calif, Los Angeles, 76; Nat Endowment Arts Grant, 86; ULC Distinguished Artists Program, 2008. *Bibliog:* John Arthur (auth), Realists at Work, Watson-Guptill Publ, NY, 83; Charles Jencks (auth), Post-Modernism: The New Classicism in Art & Architecture, Rizzoli, 87; Edward Lucie-Smith (auth), Art Today, Phaidon Press, 95; and others. *Mem:* Union League Club of Chicago. *Dealer:* Forum gallery 745 5th Ave 5th Fl New York NY 10151. *Mailing Add:* 1308 Gregory Wilmette IL 60091

VALESCO, FRANCES
MURALIST, PRINTMAKER
b Los Angeles, Calif, Aug 3, 1941. *Study:* Univ Calif, Los Angeles, BA, 63; Sacramento State Univ, 64-65; Calif State Univ, Long Beach, MA, 72. *Work:* New York City Pub Libr; Oakland Mus, Calif; Readers Dig Corp; Clorox Corp; Boston Children's Hosp. *Comn:* Desert Mural, 82; Buffalo Sky Mural, 82; North Beach Fish Mural, 87; Quilt Mural, Dept Housing & Urban Develop, Off Community Develop, San Francisco, 93; Magic Carpet, Neighborhood Beautification Fund, San Francisco, 96. *Exhib:* 162nd Ann Exhib, Pa Acad Fine Arts, 67; Emerging Expression Biennial, Bronx Mus, 87; Recent Acquisitions, Achenbach Found, Fine Arts Mus, San Francisco, Calif, 91; Diversity & Vision of the Printed Image, Triton Mus Art, Santa Clara, Calif, 92; Miniatures, Bolinas Mus, 95; Clemson Nat Print Drawing Exhib, Clemson Univ, SC, 96; East/West Print Exchange (traveling), 96; Am Cult Ctr, Taipei, Taiwan, 99; McAllen Int Mus, Tex, 2000. *Pos:* Community artist, San Francisco Art Comn, 75-80; artist-in-residence in the community, Calif State Arts Coun, 80-85. *Teaching:* Lectr etching & screen printing, Univ Calif, Berkeley, 75-76 & 79; lectr screen printing, drawing & mural painting, Sonoma State Univ, 77-80; instr printmaking, Textiles & photog, San Francisco Acad Art, 82-96; lectr printmaking, San Francisco State Univ, 84 & 93-97 & San Francisco Art Inst, 93-96, San Francisco City Col, 97-. *Awards:* Print Purchase for Embassies, Beirut, Lebanon & Kuala Lumpur, Malaysia, US Info Agency, 67; Cert Hon, San Francisco City, 87; Proclamation, State of Calif, 94. *Bibliog:* Judith Anderson (auth), San Francisco's splashy outdoor art, San Francisco Chronicle, 82; Vivien Raynor (auth), Computer Reigns at Bronx Mus of Art, The NY Times, 87; William Zimmer (auth), East/West Print Exchange, NY Times, 96. *Mem:* Calif Soc Printmakers (historian, 78-80, pres, 94-96); San Francisco Mural (adv bd, 82-89); YLEM; Surface Design Asn; Am Print Alliance (vpres, bd dir, 95-97). *Media:* Mixed. *Publ:* Ed & illusr, Media Mixed, Joined Arts, 67; illusr, Music of the Whole Earth, Scribners, 76; coauth, Combining color xerography with the technique of silk screen and intaglio, Leonardo, 84; San Francisco Murals, Tim Drescher, 91; Zyzzva, 96. *Mailing Add:* 1901 Schiller St Alameda CA 94501

VALETTA
PAINTER
b Brooklyn, NY, Jan 17, 1940. *Study:* Pratt Inst, BS (art educ), 61; Tyler Sch Fine Art; Univ Pa. *Work:* Delaware Theatre Co, Wilmington; Widener Univ Mus, Chester, Pa; pvt collection, Pres Anwar Sadat Family, Egypt; Regional Ctr Women Arts; Independence Blue Cross, Philadelphia, Pa. *Exhib:* National Drawing Competition, Univ NDak, 80; Am Embassy, Brussels, Belg, 90; Italian Am Women Artists, Campagnia Del Paiolo-Galleria, Florence, Italy, 94; Syne, Beyond Language, Kalmar Mus Art, Sweden, 96; two-person exhibs, By Mutual Consent, Widener Univ Gallery, Chester, Pa, 98 & Five Times Two, Allentown Art Mus, Pa, 2001; In the Guise of Reality, West Chester Univ, Pa, 2000; Six Months Since September, Blue Streak Gallery, Wilmington, Del, 2002; Parallel Visions, traveling exhib, Del Ctr Contemp Arts, Wilmington, Del, 2005; Affinities, Freedman Gallery, Albright Coll, Reading, Pa, 2005; Craftforms, Wayne Art Ctr, 2005; Speaking Volumes-Transforming Hate, traveling exhib, The Holter Mus Art, Helena, Mont, 2007-; Kutztown Univ Gallery, Pa, 2010. *Pos:* Bd dir & co-chairperson collections comt, Afro Am Mus, Philadelphia, Pa, 82-88; Contemp Women Artists, Philadelphia Community Arts Ctr, Wallingford, Pa, 85-86; dir, Muse Gallery, Philadelphia, Pa, 89-90; cur, founder & dir, Regional Ctr Women Arts, West Chester, Pa, 98-; dir bd, The Art Trust Non-Profit Gallery, West Chester, Pa, 2006-2012; vice pres, Art on Avenue of the States, Chester, Pa, 2011-. *Teaching:* Instr, painting, Widener Univ, Life Long Learning Prog. *Awards:* Fisher Mem Award, 87; Harcum Jr Coll Award, Arts in Progress Gallery, Philadelphia, Pa, 87; Merit and Purchase awards, Reading Art Mus, Pa, 2001; Educator 500 Award, Inst Educ Excellence & Entrepreneurship, 2007. *Bibliog:* 100 Artists of the Brandywine Valley, 2011. *Mem:* Artists Equity Asn; Del Ctr Contemp Arts. *Media:* Oil, Pastel. *Interests:* screenwriting. *Mailing Add:* PO Box 510 Westtown PA 19395

VALIER, BIRON (FRANK)
PAINTER, PRINTMAKER
b W Palm Beach, Fla, Mar 13, 1943. *Study:* Art Student's League, Woodstock, NY, 63-65; Cranbrook Acad Art, BFA, 67; Yale Univ, MFA, 69. *Work:* Achenbach Found, Calif, Palace Legion Hon, San Francisco; Los Angeles Co Mus Art; Metrop Mus Art, NY; Mus Fine Arts, Boston; Norton Gallery Contemp Collection, West Palm Beach, Fla; Asheville Art Mus, NC. *Exhib:* 62nd Ann Int, Print Club, Philadelphia, Pa, 86; Brenau Nat Invitational, Brenau Col, Gainesville, Ga, 89; Acquisitions 1984-1990, Univ Art Mus, Univ of Queensland, Brisbane, Australia, 90; Urban Insights, Claremont Sch Art, Perth, West Australia, 92; Flagging The Republic, RMIT Gallery, Melbourne, Australia, 96; Along the Roadside, Stonemetal Press Gallery, San Antonio, Tex, 2002; Sulman Prize Finalists, Art Gallery of NSW, Sydney, Australia, 2008, 2012; Paris 1911-Sydney 2011, Alliance Francaise De Sydney, 2011. *Pos:* Artist-in-residence, Mass Arts & Humanities Found, 77; head found yr, Sch Art & Design, PCAE, Melbourne, 77-79; publs consult, Australian Bicentennial Authority, Sydney, 87-89. *Teaching:* Instr art, Wheelock Col, Boston, Mass, 69-72; instr printmaking, DeCordova Mus Sch, Mass, 74-77; lectr corp art collections, City Art Inst, Univ of NSW, Sydney, 87-90. *Awards:* Bicentennial Comn, Boston City Hall, Boston 200, 75; Mardsen's Open Acquisitive, Campbelltown City Festival, NSW, Marsden Solicitors, 88; Best of Show, Hand-Pulled Prints VI Int'l Exhib, San Antonio, Tex, 98; Six Months Gunnery Studio Grant for Printmaking, NSW Ministry for the Arts, 2006; First Place, Hand-Pulled Prints XIII Int Exhib, San Antonio, Tex, 2007. *Bibliog:* Bradford F Swan (auth), Valier at RI Coll exhibition, Providence Sunday J, 1/7/73; Robert Taylor (auth), Famous Boston potholes, Boston Globe, 3/14/78; Jennifer Moran (auth), Valier charts images of urban life, West Australian, 6/1/92. *Mem:* Coll Art Asn; Art Deco Soc Western Australia; 20th Century Heritage Soc NSW. *Publ:* Auth, Twenty Photographs, pvt publ, 67; Famous Boston Potholes, South Wind Graphics, 77; Luna and Metal, Namba Wan Arts, 82; Corporate sponsorship of the visual arts in Australia, Art Monthly Australia, 89; contribr, International Directory of Corporate Art Collections, ARTnews, NY, 90; Cinemas, Signs, and Marquees 1974-2013, 2014. *Dealer:* Wenniger Gallery 19 Mt Pleasant St Rockport MA 01966. *Mailing Add:* 303/12 Macleay St Potts Point NSW 2011 Australia

VALINCIUS, IRENE
PAINTER, PRINTMAKER
b Bonn, Ger, Feb 21, 1948. *Study:* Mass Coll Art, Boston, 75-77; Sch Mus Fine Arts, Boston, 78; Univ Mass, BA (magna cum laude), 78. *Work:* Mus Fine Arts, Boston Pub Libr; Rose Art Mus, Waltham, Mass; Huntsville Mus Art, Ala; Trenton State Col, NJ; DeCordova Mus Art, Lincoln, Mass; Graham Gund Collection, Cambridge Mass. *Comn:* Babson Col, Babson, MA, 99; Rose Art Mus, Visual Memories, 2000; DeCordova Mus, 2000, 2002; Gallery NAGA, 2002. *Exhib:* Restive Visions, Rose Art Mus, Waltham, Mass, 89; solo exhibs, Gallery NAGA, Boston, 89, 91, 93, 94 & 97, Scott Alan Gallery, NY, 91, Louis Newman Gallery, Beverly Hills, 92 & Horwitch Newman Gallery, Scottsdale, Ariz, 95; Metaphor as Reality, Danforth Mus Art, Framingham, Mass, 93; Timely and Timeless, Aldrich Mus Contemp Art, Ridgefield, Conn, 93; Landscape not Landscape, Gallery Camino Real, Boca Raton, Fla, 94; Manifest Destiny, Harns Mus Art, Gainesville, Fla, 96. *Pos:* Bd mem, Brickbottom Arts Asn, 91-94; adv bd mem, Somerville Arts Coun, 93-95. *Teaching:* Teacher art & printmaking, Rugg Rd, 91-93, Monserrat Sch Art, 93, Mass Col Art, 94-2005; Art New England Workshops, Bennington, Vt, 2003-2004. *Awards:* Dorchester Arts Coun Grant, 83; Somerville Arts Coun Grant, 90; Blanche Coleman Award, 94; Yaddo Visual Arts Fel, 82; Somerville Arts Grant, 99. *Bibliog:* Painting in Boston, 50-2000; DeCordova Mus, 2002; New Am Paintings VII, Open Studio Press; Basic Printmaking Techniques, Bernard toale, 92. *Mem:* Brickbottom Arts Asn; Somerville Arts Coun. *Media:* Oil Painting; Monotypes. *Specialty:* Contemp Art. *Interests:* Study of light. *Collection:* Au Bon Pain Corp, Boston, MA, NYC, NY; Bank of Lowell, Lowell, MA; Berkshire Partners, Boston, MA; The Boston Globe, Boston. *Publ:* Boston Globe, 94, 96, 97, 2002; Art New England, 91, 97, 81, 2002; Boston Phoenix, 91, 98; Bay Windows, 91, 89, 2002. *Dealer:* Gallery NAGA 67 Newbury St Boston MA 02116. *Mailing Add:* One Fitchburg St C107 Somerville MA 02143

VALLA, TERESSA MARIE
PAINTER, KINETIC SCULPTOR
b Lynchburg, VA. *Study:* Univ Vt, BS, 1979; NY Univ, Grad Studies, 1982; Art Students League, Leo Manso, Ponce de Leon, 1986-1989; Studio Art School of the Aegean, Samos Greece (Andrew Forge), 1987. *Work:* Mus of the City of NY; NY Pub Libr; Libr Cong, Washington, DC; New Eng Ctr Contemp Art, Brooklyn, Conn; Paterson Mus, Paterson, NJ; Mus Mod Art, New York; Siena Art Inst Lib, Italy; 911 Memorial Mus, 2014. *Comn:* Tree of Life, City Arts, NY, 94; NY Cares (Pub Figurative Mural), NY Cares, 96; Graffiti Alternative, NYC Housing Authority, 97; Celia Cruz Live in Miami, Art for DVD, 2014. *Exhib:* Women of the World: Diverse Perspectives, Am Mus of Natural Hist, New York, 99; Snapshot, Contemp Mus, Baltimore, Md, 2000; Life of the City, Mus of Mod Art, New York, 2002; Considering Peace, Sato Mus, Tokyo, Japan, 2003; War is Over, Sideshow Gallery, New York, 2006; Transforming Spaces, Messiah Col, 2007; Seed Project, Winkleman Gallery, New York, NY, 2008; Broad Thinking, ABC, New York, NY, 2008; It's Not Easy, Exit Art, New York, NY, 2008; Vital Symbols of Humanity, Governors Island, Figment, NY, 2008; It's A Wonderful Life, Sideshow Gallery, 2009; Reflections of Generosity, Katterbach, Germany, 2010; Art Around the Park, New York, 2010; Unquenched Life, What Matters Now, Aperture, 2011; Fracking: Art and Activism, Exit Art, Social Environmental Aesthetics, NY, 2011; Pomegranite Caretakers, Robert Blackburn Printmaking Workshop, NY, 2011; Oasis, Le Pave, Paris, 2012; Exposition de Pinas, Museo Dabawengo, Davao City, 2012; Interweave, Able Gallery, 2012; Ame Gallery, Provincetown, Mass, 2013; Sideshow Nation II at the Alamo, Sideshow Gallery, 2013; Postcards from the Edge, Sikkema Jenkins & Co, 2013; Luhring Augustine Gallery Visual Arts, 2014; Byrdcliffe Kement/James Ct for the Arts, 5x7 Show, 2014. *Pos:* Visiting Artist, Workshop (Abstraction of Art through Music, Nature & Mathematics), Carnegie Hall, New York, 94; coordr & workshop panelist, Int Arts Movement, Tribeca Performing Arts Ctr, New York, NY, 2007; founder, dir, Glow; visiting artist, LEAP. *Teaching:* Instr, Annenberg artist in res, 2000-01; lectr, Workshop, Experimental Drawing, Cooper Union, 2001; Jackson Pollock award residency, Byrdcliffe Colony, Woodstock, NY, 201. *Awards:* Ezra Jack Keats Mem Award, Lincoln Ctr, New York, 88-89 & 90; Recovery Grant, Gottlieb Found, 2002; Jackson Pollock Found, 2007-; Artist in Residence, Open Art Residency, Island of Dreams, Pezonis, Greece, 2008. *Bibliog:* Brazilian TV Global Network (Diario de Perambuco), 99; Dan Rather (auth, ABC News) Santa Fe Art Inst, Dan Rather 6PM News, 2001; Gary Shapiro (auth), The Pleasures of Urban Gardening, The NY Sun, 2005; Reflections of Generosity, 2010; Pomegranate Caretakers, Water based paint on wood; Roatan, Why We Travel, New York Times, 2011. *Mem:* Artists Circle; IslandsFirst.org. *Media:* Miscellaneous Media. *Interests:* Dance, poetry, rainforest-ecology, theology, music

VALLANCE, JEFFREY K R
SCULPTOR, PAINTER
b Torrance, Calif, Jan 25, 1955. *Study:* Calif State Univ, Northridge, BA, 79; Otis Inst Parsons Sch Design, MFA, 81. *Work:* Australian Nat Gallery, Canberra. *Comn:* Man and Dog (mural), Fallbrook Sq Mall, Woodland Hills, Calif, 73; Dinosaurs (mural), Powelle Butte Grocery, Ore, 77; Space (mural), Crippled Children's Soc, Woodland Hills, Calif, 77; Blinky (gravestone), Los Angeles Pet Cemetery, Calabasas, Calif, 78. *Exhib:* The Living Art Mus, Reykjavik, Iceland, 86; solo exhibs include The US Senate: A Survey on the Arts, Wash Project for Arts, 78, Daniel Sorano Hall Nat Treasure, Dakar, Senegal, 80, Machines and Other Articles, Rosamund Felsen Gallery, 81, Univ Art Mus, Santa Barbara, 82, Icelandic Women and the King of Tonga, 87, The Throne Room: Icelandic Women and the King of Tonga Part II, 98, The Nixon Mus, Galerie Praz-Delavallade, Paris, 94, Clown Stains, Univ Tex, 2002, The Shape of Tex, Majestic Ranch, Boerne, Tex, 2002, Relics from LBJ's 66 Visit to Australia, Tasmanian Mus and Art Gallery, 2002, Saami and Aboriginal Flags, Black Kettle Mus, 2002, exhibited in group shows at Faith, Dynamite Gallery, 2000, Off the Grid, Lehmann Maupin, 2002, Five by Seven by X, The Jones Ctr for Contemp Art, 2002, A Thousand Clowns, Robert Berman Gallery, 2002, To Whom it May Concern, Logan Galleries, Calif Coll Arts and Crafts, 2002. *Pos:* Art dir, Crippled Children's Soc, Woodland Hills, Calif, 76-77; host, Cutting Edge, MTV, Los Angeles, 83. *Teaching:* Prof, Univ Calif, Los Angeles, 84-85; Vis prof art; instructor Los Angeles, Pierce Col, Woodland Hills, Calif, 87, Parsons Sch Design, 87-92, Community Col of Southern Nev, Las Vegas, 96, Univ Nev, 95-98; prof inte contemp art Umea Univ, Sweden, 99-2002; vis artist Chicago Art Inst, 99, Cranbrook Acad of Art, Detroit, 2001; artist-in-residence Majestic Ranch, Univ Tex, San Antonio, 2002, Univ Tasmania, Australia, 2002. *Awards:* Grantee Guggenheim Memorial Foundation, 2004. *Bibliog:* Peter Schjeldahl (auth), Los Angeles demystified, Village Voice, 81; Howard Singerman (auth), article, 81 & Bob Pincus (auth), article, 84, Artforum. *Media:* Enamel, Electronics. *Res:* Polynesian myth of Tiki; Symbols of Iceland; The King of Tonga. *Publ:* Auth, Blinky the Friendly Hen, private publ, 79. *Dealer:* Rosamund Felsen Gallery 669 N La Cienega Los Angeles CA 90069. *Mailing Add:* UCLA Dept Art 11000 Kinross Ave Ste 245 Los Angeles CA 90095

VALLEE, WILLIAM OSCAR
PAINTER, GRAPHIC ARTIST
b South Paris, Maine, June 18, 1934. *Study:* Univ Alaska. *Work:* Many in pvt collections. *Exhib:* Anchorage Fur Rendezvous, 63; Easter Arts Festival, 63; Alaska Festival Music & Art, 63-64; Solo exhibs, Anchorage Petrol Club, 63 & Anchor Galleries, 63. *Pos:* Instituted (in coop with Am Artists Prof League), Am Art Wk, 63; treas, Soc Alaskan Arts, 63; co-founder, Alaska-Int Cult Arts Ctr; bd dir & co-founder, Anchorage Community Art Ctr, currently; pres & chmn bd, Alaska Map Serv, Inc, currently. *Awards:* Anchorage Fur Rendezvous, 63; Easter Art Festival, 63; Artist of the Month, Alaska Art Guild, 63. *Mem:* Alaska Art Guild (pres & chmn, 64); Alaska Watercolor Soc (pres, 63); Am Soc Photogrammetry; Am Artist Prof League. *Media:* Watercolor. *Mailing Add:* 4118 Irene Dr Anchorage AK 99504

VAN AKEN, SAM
INSTALLATION SCULPTOR, EDUCATOR
b Reading, Pa, 1972. *Study:* Slippery Rock Univ, BA (commun theory & Art), 1994; Univ NC, Chapel Hill, MFA, 2001; State Acad Fine Arts, Poznan, Poland. *Exhib:* Colby Coll Mus Art; Dallas Video Art Festival; Tacheles Art Ctr, Berlin, Ger; Portland Art Mus; Inst for Contemp Art, Maine Coll Art; Ctr for Maine Contemp Art; Blum Gallery, Coll Atlantic. *Teaching:* Assoc prof & prog coordr, Sch Art & Design, Coll Visual & Performting Arts, Syracuse Univ; vis artist, l'Ecole Nationale Superieure d'Arts de Cergy-Pointoise; asst prof art, sculpture, Univ Maine, Orono, 2001-. *Awards:* Good Idea Grant, Maine Arts Comn, 2005; Art Exhib Award, Asn Int Critics Art, 2006; Juror's Prize, Portland Mus Art Biennial, 2007; Grant for Emerging Fields, Creative Capital Found, 2009; Res & Develop Grant, Univ Maine. *Mailing Add:* College of Visual and Performing Arts Syracuse Univ ComArt Rm 013 Syracuse NY 13244-1010

VAN ALLEN, ADRIAN
DESIGNER, VIDEO ARTIST
Study: Sarah Lawrence Coll, BA, 1997; Calif Coll Arts & Crafts, MFA (photog), 1999, MFA (video & multimedia), 2000. *Exhib:* Solo exhibs, Door 3 Gallery, Oakland, 1999 & BioArts Gallery, Sausalito, Calif, 2002; Sunspot Laboratory Show, Calif State Los Angeles Fine Arts Gallery, 1999; Miniature Artist's Books, Mills Coll, Oakland, 2000; Freestyle, Southern Exposure Gallery, San Francisco, 2001; Interface Explorer: Shared Boundaries, Pub Netbase Media Ctr, Vienna, Austria, 2004; HandMade, Rock Paper Scissors Arts Collective, Oakland, 2007; Code-Switching, The LAB, San Francisco, 2008; Art in a Box, Compound Gallery, Oakland, 2009. *Pos:* Creative dir, ReadyMade Mag, 2000-2008; exhibit developer, Exploratorium, 2000-; designer & programmer, Archeol & Anthro Depts, Univ Calif, Berkeley, 2007-. *Awards:* Innovation award, Asn Sci & Technology Ctrs, 2000; Best award, Edn Network, 2001; Star award, Griffith Observatory, 2004; Sci & Technology for Astronomy award, Scientific Am, 2004; Cynthia Hazen & Leon Polsky Rome Prize, Am Acad in Rome, 2010. *Bibliog:* Katie Hafner (auth), At Museums, Computers Get Creative, NY Times, 12/2/2004. *Mailing Add:* c/o Exploratorium Museum 3601 Lyon St Oakland CA 94608

VAN ALSTINE, JOHN RICHARD
SCULPTOR
b Johnstown, NY, Aug 14, 1952. *Study:* St Lawrence Univ, 70-72; Kent State Univ, BFA, 74; Cornell Univ Sch Art & Archit, MFA, 76. *Work:* Nat Mus Am Art, Smithsonian Inst; Hirshhorn Mus & Sculpture Garden; Denver Mus; Carnegie Inst Mus Art; Mus Mod Art, Gulbenkian Found, Lisbon, Portugal; Baltimore Mus Art; Corcoran Mus Art, Washington; Del Mus Art, Wilmington; Herbert F Johnson Mus, Cornell Univ, Ithaca, NY; Newark Mus Art, NJ; and many others. *Comn:* Pub Comn, Billings, Mont, 82 & Luck Stone Corp, Richmond, Va, 83; outdoor public sculptures, Austin Col, Sherman, Tex, 86; Inst Defence Analyses, Washington, DC, 88-89. *Exhib:* Solo exhibs, Grimaldis Gallery, Baltimore, 84, 92, 95, 97 & 2000, Univ NH, Durham, 94, Troyer Fitzpatrick, Lassman Gallery, Washington, 94, Cleveland State Univ, Ohio, 94, Nohra Haime Gallery, NY, 94, 96, 98 & 2000, Dartmouth Col, Hanover, NH, 95 & DeCordova Mus & Sculpture Garden, Lincoln, Mass, 96-97; 2nd Fujisankei Biennale, Hakone Open-Air Mus, Ninotaira, Japan, 94; Semaphore, Art Initiatives, NY, 95; New Acquisitions, Phillips Collection, Washington, 95; Tudor Place Exhib, Int Sculpture Ctr, Washington, 95; Sculptors Drawings, NJ Ctr Visual Arts, 95; Cerrillos Cult Ctr, NMex, 96. *Teaching:* Asst, Cornell Univ, 74-76; asst prof, Univ Wyo, Laramie, 76-80 & Univ Md, College Park, 80-86; vis prof, Md Art Inst, Baltimore, 88. *Awards:* Yaddo Fel, 85; Individual Artist Fel, Nat Endowment Arts, 86; Individual Artists Fel, NJ State Coun Arts, 88. *Bibliog:* Christine Tenin (auth), Boston Globe (rev), 7/31/96; Miles Unger (auth), Sculpture Mag (rev), 10/96; Nick Capasso (auth), Bones of the Earth, Spirit of the Land, 2000. *Media:* Stone, Welded Metal. *Specialty:* Contemporary Art. *Dealer:* Nohra Haime Gallery New York NY. *Mailing Add:* Van Alstine Studios S Main St PO Box 526 Wells NY 12190

VAN BUREN, RICHARD
SCULPTOR
b Syracuse, NY, 1937. *Study:* Mexico City Coll; Univ Mex; San Francisco State Coll. *Work:* Mus Mod Art, New York; Walker Art Ctr, Minneapolis; Philadelphia Mus Art; Va Mus Fine Arts, Richmond; Nat Gallery, Washington, DC. *Comn:* Spirit Mold, Grand Arts, Kans City, Mo. *Exhib:* Solo exhibs, San Francisco Mus Art, 1962, Bennington Coll, Vt, 1970, Rice Univ, Houston, Tex, 1974, City Univ Grad Ctr, New York, 1975, Sculpture Ctr, Sydney, 1978, Md Inst, Baltimore, 1984, Maine Ctr for COntemp Arts, 2003; Whitney Sculpture Ann, Whitney Mus Am Art, New York, 68 & 70; Milwaukee Art Mus, 69 & 71; Art Inst Chicago, 69 & 72; Walker Art Ctr, Minneapolis, 71; Albright-Knox Art Gallery, Buffalo, NY, 71; Contemp Art Mus, Houston, 72; Harvard Univ, 73; Contemp Arts Ctr, Cincinnati, 73; Indianapolis Mus Art, Ind, 74; Va Mus Fine Arts, Richmond, 74; New York Cult Ctr, 74; PS1 Inst Contemp Art, Long Island City, New York, 1977; Madison Art Ctr, Madison, Wis, 1983; Parsons Sch Design, New York, 1988-89 & 91; Philadelphia Art Alliance, Pa, 1990; Brooklyn Children's Mus, New York, 1992; Degrees of Abstraction, Boston Mus Fine Arts, 1995; Afterimage: Drawing Through Process, Los Angeles Mus Contemp Art, 1999; Weatherspoon Mus, Greensboro, NC, 2006; Tamayo Mus, Mex City, 2007; Nat Gallery of Australia, Canbera, 2009. *Awards:* Adolph & Esther Gottlieb Award, 2007; Alex J Ettl Award for Sculpture, Nat Acad Invitational Exhib Contemp Art Awards, 2010. *Bibliog:* Barbara Rose (auth), Shall We Have a Renaissance, Art in Am, 3-4/67; Carter Ratcliff (auth), Solid Color, Art News, 5/72

VAN CALDENBORGH, JOOP
COLLECTOR
Awards: Named one of top 200 art collectors, ARTnews mag, 2004-13. *Collection:* Modern & contemporary art, photography, sculpture. *Publ:* Co-auth, Imagine You Are Standing Here In Front of Me, Caldic Collection, 2003. *Mailing Add:* c/o Rotterdam CofC Blaak 40 PO Box 450 Rotterdam 3000 Netherlands

VANCE, LESLEY
PAINTER
b Milwaukee, Wis, 1977. *Study:* Univ Wis, Madison, BFA, 2000; Calif Inst Arts, Valencia, MFA, 2003. *Exhib:* Making: WEEDS, LACMA, Calif, 2003; Drawn Out, Gallery 400, Univ Ill, Chicago, 2005; Imaginary Thing, Aspen Art Mus, Colo, 2008; The Front Room, Contemp Art Mus, St Louis, 2009; Whitney Biennial, Whitney Mus Am Art, New York, 2010. *Bibliog:* Amra Brooks (auth), Must See Art, Los Angeles Weekly, 9/26/2007; Carol Vogel (auth), Reality Leaves A Fingerprint On the Biennial, NY Times, 12/11/2009; Todd Levin (auth), Whitney Biennia: The Voices of Silence, Flash Art, 5-6/2010. *Mailing Add:* c/o David Kordansky Gallery 3143 S La Cienega Blvd Unit A Los Angeles CA 90016

VAN CLINE, MARY
GLASS BLOWER, SCULPTOR
Study: North Tex State Univ, BFA, 1971-76; Tex Women's Univ, 1976-77; Penland Sch Crafts, 1979-80; Mass Coll Art, MFA, 1980-82. *Exhib:* New Glass Review, Corning Mus Glass, 1984-93; Narrative Art in Clay & Glass, US Information Agency/Taft Mus, Cincinnati, traveling exhib, 1993-96; Maureen Littleton Gallery, Washington, 1995; 10 Yrs, Glasmuseum, Denmark, 1996; Recent Glass, Union of Ideas, Milwaukee Art Mus, 1997; Calido, Tucson Mus Art, 1997-99; Foster White Gallery, Seattle, 1998; Monumental Sculpture, Bryan Ohno Gallery, Seattle, 1998; Imago Gallery, Palm Desert, Calif, 1998 & 2007; Leo Kaplan Mod Gallery, New York, 1999; Veriiales 2000, Biot, France, 2000; Block Mus Art, Ill, 2005; Int Exhib, Habatat Galleries, Fla & Mich, 2006. *Pos:* Selection comt, Nat Endowment Arts, 1989; hon bd, James Renwick Alliance, Washington, 1990-93; bd dirs, Creative Glass Ctr, Wheaton, 1999. *Teaching:* Instr, Mass Coll Art, Boston, 1980-82, Pratt Sch Fine Arts, Seattle, 1986, Penland Sch Crafts, 1989, Pilchuck Sch Glass, 1993; lectr, Univ Ohio, Columbus, 1985, Univ Ill, Champaign-Urbana, 1988. *Awards:* Inaugural Award, Capitol Glass Invitational, 1982; Inaugural Fel, Creative Glass Ctr, Wheaton, 1983; Mass Arts & Humanities Fel, 1984; Cult Exchange Award, Japan-US Friendship Comn/Nat Endowment Arts, 1987; Masterworks Fel, Creative Glass Ctr Am, 1990; Visual Arts Fel, Wash State Arts Comn, 1992; Grand Prize, Glass Kanazawa 98, Japan, 1998. *Dealer:* Habatat Galleries 608 Banyan Trail Boca Raton FL 33431; Habatat Galleries 4400 Fernlee Ave Royal Oak MI 48073; Imago Galleries 45-450 Highway 74 Palm Desert CA 92260. *Mailing Add:* c/o Hawk Galleries 153 E Main St Columbus OH 43215

VANCO, JOHN LEROY
MUSEUM DIRECTOR, CURATOR
b Erie, Pa, Aug 21, 1945. *Study:* Allegheny Coll, BA (art hist); Whitney Mus Am Art. *Collection Arranged:* Teco: Art Pottery of the Prairie Sch; In Harmony with The Earth; Paperthick: Forms and Images in Cast Paper; Images of War and Artists Respond to the Gulf War; A Peculiar Vision: The Work of George Ohr, The Mad Potter of Biloxi; Loud & Clear: Resonator Guitars and the Dopyera Brothers Legacy to Am Music; Art & Life in Erie, Pa; From Mickey to the Grinch: Art of the Animated Film; Archaeology at the Dawn of History: the Khirbet Iskander Coll; Eva Zeisel: The Shape of Life; Kanga & Kitenge: Cloth & Culture in East Africa; Richard Anuszkiewicz: Painting...Sculpture, 1986-2012. *Pos:* Dir, Erie Art Mus, Pa, 1968-. *Awards:* Governor's Award for the Arts, 2010. *Mem:* Pa Humanities Coun; Am Asn Mus; Am Ceramic Cir. *Interests:* Photography, ceramics, folk art, popular culture. *Publ:* Auth, What Ever Happened to Louis Eilshemius?, 67; illusr, Roger Misiewicz: Wolfman of the Blues, 72; A Roycroft Desktop, 94; John Lysak: Multiples, 96; Structured Color: Kiyokatsu Matsumiya, 2003; Eva Zeisel: The Shape of Life, 2009. *Mailing Add:* Erie Art Mus 411 State St Erie PA 16501

VANDELINDER, DEBRA L
DIGITAL MEDIA ARTIST, EDUCATOR
b Troy, PA, Nov 9, 61. *Study:* Mansfield Univ, BA (Studio Art), 83, MEd (Art Educ), 86; Elmira Coll, digital imaging & photog with Jan Kather & Marc Dennis, 94-2011. *Work:* Macworld Digital Art Gallery, IDG Corp, San Francisco; St Josephs Hosp, Elmira, NY; Elmira City Sch Dist, Elmira, NY. *Comn:* Visual Treasures (triptych), Arts Southern Finger Lakes, Corning, NY, 2004. *Exhib:* 55th, 70th & 71st Northeast Regional, Arnot Art Mus, Elmira, NY, 88 & 2005-2006; Macworld Expo Art Gallery, Jacob Javits Ctr, New York & Moscone Ctr, San Francisco, 2002; Regional Biennial Photog Exhib, Gmeiner Art & Cultural Ctr, Wellsboro, Pa, 2006, 2012; Outside the Box, Art Space Juried Show, Corning, NY, 2006; Two Person Show: Full Bloom, Houghton Gallery, Cedar Arts Center, Corning, NY, 2008; Women in the Arts, CCC Workforce Develop Gallery, 2009; solo show, Between Gratitude & Regret, Exhibit A Contemp Art, Corning, NY, 2010; Gallery Gala, Arnot Art Mus, 2005, 2006 & 2012, Framed, 2011; Decadence, Evoke Contemp, John O'Hern, Santa Fe, NMex, 2011; Art of Art Educators, George Waters Gallery, Elmire Coll, Elmira, NY, 2010; Rochester Contemp Art Ctr, NY, 2011; Echo Art Fair, Central Terminal, Buffalo, NY, 2011, 2013; Making History, Chemung Valley History Mus, Elmira, NY, 2011; Represented Artists Show, Exhib A, Contemp Art, Corning, NY, 2011; State of the Art Gallery, Ithaca, NY, 2012, 2013; Gallery Gala, Artnot Art Mus, Elmira, NY, 2012; Art Takes Time Square, NASDAQ Tower, Broadway & 43rd St, NY, 2012; Solo exhib, Sticks and Stones and Bits of Bone, Mansfield Univ, Mansfield, Pa, 2012; 1930s Style: An Artistic Legacy, Nat Soaring Mus, Big Flats, NY, 2012; Agnes at 40: Personal Perspectives Comm Arts of Elmira, NY, 2012; Entomos, Exhibit A, Corning, NY, 2012; Forward, Exhibit A, Corning, NY, 2013; Photo Show, State of the Art Gallery, Ithaca, NY, 2013; 6x6x2013, Rochester Contemporary, NY, 2013. *Collection Arranged:* Altering Freud Collection, Arts of Southern Fingerlakes, Corning, NY, 2007. *Pos:* Freelance graphic designer, VanDelinder Graphic Design, Mansfield, Pa, 83-87; grad asst, Mansfield Univ, Pa, 84-85; principal graphic designer, Vandeli Art & Design, Elmira, NY, 99-2005. *Teaching:* Instr photog & computer art, Elmira City Sch Dist, Elmira, NY, 87-; prof computer art, Elmira Coll, NY, 2004-. *Awards:* Best of Show, Mansfield Univ Student Art Exhib, 83; Int Award, Macworld Expo Digital Art Gallery, 2002; Photog Biennial Viewers Choice Award, Gmeiner Art & Cultural Ctr, 2006; Strategic Opportunity Stipend, NY Found Arts, 2010. *Bibliog:* The Hand in Art, J Hand Therapy, 10 & 12/97; John O'Hern (auth), There is Art Beyond the Grid, Am Art Collector, 11/2006; Kim Hall (auth), Artist Spotlight: Debb Van Delinder, p. 40, Professional Artist Mag, 2012. *Mem:* Arnot Art Mus; Arts Southern Finger Lakes; Nat Art Educ Asn. *Media:* Digital Imaging, Scanography. *Interests:* running, travel. *Publ:* Illusr, Chemistry for Children, Nat Sci Found, 85; auth, A Study of Graphic Design Instruction in the Secondary, Mansfield Univ, 86; auth & illusr, Water Songs: Photography & Haiku, Elmira Coll, 98; Visual Sanctuary, Photoworks Inc, 2006. *Dealer:* Exhib A 22 East Market St Corning N 14830. *Mailing Add:* 416 Sharr Ave Elmira NY 14904

VANDEN BERGE, PETER WILLEM
SCULPTOR, MURALIST
b Voorburg, Zuid-Holland, Neth, Oct 16, 1935; US citizen. *Study:* Art Acad, The Hague, Neth; Calif State Univ, Sacramento, BA; Univ Calif, Davis, MA. *Work:* Henry Gallery, Univ Wash, Seattle; Mus Contemp Crafts, NY; Johnson Collection Am Crafts, Racine, Wis; Crocker Art Mus, Sacramento; Oakland Art Mus, Calif. *Comn:* Three glazed relief tile murals, San Francisco City Col, 71; pub murals, San Francisco Arts Comn, City of San Francisco; glazed tile relief, Contra Costa Jr Coll Dist Off, John F Gordon Educ Ctr, Martinez, Calif, 75; tile mural, Sacramento Metrop Arts Comn, 79. *Exhib:* Four Ceramic Sculptors from California, Alan Frumkin Gallery, NY, 73, Calif Ceramic Sculptors I & II, 74, Five Ceramic Sculptors from Calif, Chicago, 75; Clay, Whitney Mus Am Art, NY, 74; Fendrick's Gallery, Washington, DC, 76; Campbell Mus Contemp Crafts, Cranbrook Acad Art, Bloomfield Hills, Mich, 76; A Century of Ceramics in the United States, Everson Mus Art, Syracuse, NY, 79; Craft Today-USA, Mus Decorative Arts, Paris, France (traveling exhib through Europe); Poetry of the Physical, Am Craft Mus, NY; Contemp Am: 20 Americans, Newport Harbor Art Mus, Newport Beach, Calif; Tri Ann Int Craft Exhib, Art Gallery Western Australia, Perth. *Teaching:* Asst prof ceramics & sculpture, San Francisco State Univ, 66-73; prof ceramics & sculpture, Calif State Univ, Sacramento, 73-. *Awards:* Madeleine Cortese Williams Found Award, 63 & 66; Comn Awarded, Sacramento Metrop Arts Comn, Art in Pub Places Prog, 78-84; Nat Endowment for the Arts Fel Grant, 81. *Bibliog:* D Zack (auth), Mythology, California ceramics, Art & Artist Mag, London, 9/69, Nut art in quake time, Art News, 70 & Laugh in clay, Craft Horizon Mag, 71. *Media:* Stoneware, Porcelain; Clay, Terra Cotta. *Dealer:* Natsoulas/Novelozo Gallery 140 F St Davis CA 95616

VANDENBURGH, LAURA
EDUCATOR, ADMINISTRATOR
Study: Univ Calif Davis, BS (zoology), DVM; Hunter Col, NYC, MFA. *Exhib:* Exhibitions include Susan Hobbs Gallery, Toronto, Portland Art Mus, James Harris Gallery, Seattle, & Everson Mus, Syracuse, NY and others. *Teaching:* Academic appointments, Syracuse Univ and Hunter Col, CUNY; assoc prof, painting, Dept of Art, Univ of Oregon, 1998-, dept head, 2008-. *Mailing Add:* Department of Art 198 Lawrence 5232 University of Oregon Eugene OR 97403-5232

VANDERPOOL, KAREN
WEAVER, EDUCATOR
b Troy, NY, July 14, 1946. *Study:* State Univ NY, BS, 68; Tyler Sch Art, MFA, 70; Haystack Mt Sch Crafts; Sch Am Craftsmen. *Work:* Ball State Univ, Muncie, Ind; First Nat Bank, Boston. *Exhib:* Weaving Unlimited, De Cordova Mus, Lincoln, Mass, 71; Bodycraft, Portland Art Mus, Ore, 73; 3rd Int Exhib Miniature Textiles, Brit Craft Ctr, London, Eng, 78; Art in Crafts, Bronx Mus, NY, 78; Felting, Mus Am Craft, NY, 80; Art Fabric: Mainstream, San Francisco Mus Mod Art, 81; 30 Americans, Galveston Art Ctr, Tex, 81; Fiber Nat '85, Adams Mem Gallery, Dunkirk, NY, 85. *Teaching:* Asst prof weaving & fiber arts, Univ Wash, Seattle, 76-81; prof, Calif State Univ, Chico, 81-. *Awards:* First Award Fibers, Mass Artists-Craftsmen, 71 & Calif Works '84, 84; First Award Crafts, Pac Northwest Arts & Crafts, 72. *Bibliog:* Betty Scholossman (auth), Reviews: Clay, fiber, metal by women artists, Art J, Vol 37, No 4, summer 78; Betty Park (auth), Felting, Fiberarts, 11-12/80. *Mem:* Am Craft Coun; Handweavers Guild Am. *Media:* Papermaking, Computer Assisted Textile Design. *Dealer:* Dept Art & Art History. *Mailing Add:* Calif State Univ Dept Art Chico CA 95929-0820

VANDERSALL, AMY L
HISTORIAN, EDUCATOR
b West Newton, Pa, Oct 9, 1933. *Study:* Coll Wooster, Ohio, BA, 55; Mt Holyoke Col, South Hadley, Mass, MA, 58; Yale Univ, MA, 62, PhD, 65. *Teaching:* Asst prof medieval art hist, Smith Col, 66-72; assoc prof, Univ Colo, 73-81, prof, 81-95. *Mem:* Int Ctr Medieval Art (bd of dirs, 75-78 & 85-88); Coll Art Asn; Medieval Acad Am. *Res:* Carolingian ivory carving, Anglo-Saxon art and Romanesque sculpture. *Publ:* Auth, Two Carolingian ivories in the Metropolitan Museum of Art, 72 & Five Romanesque Portals: Questions of Attributions and Ornament, 83, New York, Metrop Mus J; Date and provenance of the Franks casket, Gesta, 73; Homeric myth in early medieval England: The lid of the Franks casket, Studies Iconography, 75; Relationship of sculptors and painters at the court of Charles the Bald, 76 & Romanesque sculpture in American museums: The west, 80, Gesta. *Mailing Add:* 360 20th St Boulder CO 80302-8011

VANDERWEG, PHILLIP DALE
ADMINISTRATOR, SCULPTOR
b Benton Harbor, Mich, Aug 16, 1943. *Study:* Albion Col, 61-63; Univ Mich, BS (design), 65, MFA, 68. *Work:* Tenn State Mus, Nashville; Butler Mus Art, Dayton, Ohio; NY State Univ, Potsdam; Kean Coll NJ, Union; Albion Col, Mich. *Comn:* Figure grouping (sculpture), Columbia State Univ, Tenn, 81; exterior sculpture, Pargos Restaurant, Nashville, Tenn, 87; seated figure (double sculpture), Vanderbilt Univ, Nashville, 87; Welcome site sculpture I-65, Tenn Arts Comn, Mitchelville, 88. *Pos:* Founding mem, Foundations in Art: Theory & Educ, 76; mem visual arts rev panel,

Tenn Arts Comn, 86-89; region 5 rep, Mich Artist Prog, Detroit Inst Arts, 90-92. *Teaching:* From instr to prof, Mid Tenn State Univ, 68-89; prof & chair, Western Mich Univ, 89-. *Mem:* Nat Asn Schs Art & Design; Nat Coun Art Adminrs; Coll Art Asn; Mid-Am Coll Art Conf. *Media:* All Media. *Mailing Add:* 6791 Penny Ln Kalamazoo MI 49009

VAN DUINWYK, GEORGE PAUL
GOLDSMITH, SILVERSMITH
b New York, NY, Sept 30, 1941. *Study:* Calif State Univ, Northridge, with Frederick Lauritzen, BA, 64; Calif State Univ, Long Beach, with Alvin A Pine, MA, 71; RI Sch of Design, with John A Prip, MFA, 72; Southern New Eng Sch Law, JD, 95. *Work:* Oakland Mus, Calif. *Exhib:* Mod Am Metalsmithing & Jewelry, Corcoran Gallery of Art, Washington, 72; Jewelry Invitational, Albright-Knox Mus, Buffalo, NY, 74; World Silver Fair, Mexico City, Mex, 74; Univ Colo, 74; 275 Yrs of Am Metalsmithing, Mus of Contemp Crafts, NY, 75; Goldsmiths 77, Phoenix Art Mus, Ariz, 77; Profiles of US Jewelry, Tex Tech Univ, Lubbock, 77; and others. *Pos:* Craftsman-in-residence, RI State Coun on the Arts, 76-77; dir tech resources, Jewelry Inst, Providence, RI, 77-79; dir, Southeast Asia Sch of Jewelry Arts, Bangkok, Thailand, 91, 92; freelance designer/craftsman; atty, Art Law. *Teaching:* Assoc prof metalsmithing, Calif State Univ, Long Beach, 72-73; adj prof metalsmithing, RI Sch of Design, 73-74; asst prof, Kent State Univ, 79-82. *Awards:* Purchase Award, The Metal Experience, Oakland Mus, 71; Design Award, Designer/Craftsman 77, Richmond Art Ctr, Calif, 76; Nat Endowment for the Arts Grant, Slide Jury Proj, 77. *Bibliog:* Ralph Turner (auth), Modern Jewelry, Eng publ, 76; Thelma Newman (auth), The Container Book, Chilton, 77; Oppi Untracht (auth), Jewelry Techniques, Doubleday 77. *Mem:* Soc NAm Goldsmiths; Am Crafts Coun; life mem Worshipful Co Goldsmiths, London, Eng; ABA; Mass Bar Asn; Federal Bar Assn. *Media:* Precious & Nonprecious Metals. *Publ:* Auth, Ralph Turner, Modern Jewelry, Crown Publ Jewelry, Oppi Untracht, Doubleday Publ. *Mailing Add:* 358 Boulevard 358 Boulevard Middletown RI 02842-5467

VAN DYKE, PETER
PAINTER
b Philadelphia, Pa, 1978. *Study:* Wesleyan Univ, 1997-98; The Florence Acad Art, 1998-2002. *Exhib:* Solo exhibs include The Cosmopolitan Club, Philadelphia, Pa, 2001, Artist's House Gallery, Philadelphia, 2002; group exhibs include Artist's House Gallery, 2001, 2002, 2004; The Friends of Select Sch, Philadelphia, 2002; Small Works, The More Gallery, Philadelphia, 2002, Drawings, 2003; Grenning Gallery, Sag Harbor, NY, 2003, Vanitas, 2003; Recent Works from Florentine Academies, Westbeth Gallery, NY, Providence, RI, Rome, Italy, Florence Italy, 2003; Int Summer Salon, Eleanor Ettinger Gallery, NY, 2003, Figure in American Art, 2004, 2005, 2006, In the Spirit of the Tradition: Masters of the Florence Academy, 2004, 2006, Int Autumn Salon, 2005; Self-Portraits, John Pence Gallery, San Francisco, Calif, 2003, Allegories, 2004, Introductions, 2004; Contemp Mid-Atlantic Painters, The Biggs Mus of Am Art, Dover, Del, 2004. *Teaching:* Instr drawing and painting, The Florence Acad Art, 2000-02; adj faculty, Pa Acad Fine Art, 2003-. *Dealer:* Grenning Gallery 90 Main St PO Boc 3049 Sag Harbor NY 11963; John Pence Gallery 750 Post St San Francisco CA 94109. *Mailing Add:* c/o Eleanor Ettinger Gallery 24 W 57th St Ste 609 New York NY 10019

VANESS, MARGARET HELEN
PHOTOGRAPHER, WRITER
b Seattle, Wash, Nov 6, 1919. *Study:* Univ Wash, BFA (painting), 70, BFA (printmaking), 71, MAT & MFA, 73; Drexel Univ, cert (prof educ women in bus), 75; spec study with Francis Cellentano, Glen Alps, George Tsutakawa, Freeman Patterson & Robert Stahl; Boeing Co, management training, 78-81; Soc Tech Commun, 81-83. *Work:* US Embassies in Athens, Bogata, Caracas, Copenhagen, Seoul, Managua, Lima, Lagos, Dar es Salaam & Tanzania; Cheney-Cowles Mus, Spokane, Wash; Pratt-Manhattan Ctr Gallery, NY; World Print Orgn, San Francisco, Calif; Evergreen State Coll Libr Collection, Olympia, Wash; and others. *Comn:* Two ed of ten prints each, US Info Agency, 73; mural, Med Ctr, Boeing Co, Philadelphia, Pa, 74; mural, Gem & Minerals Mag, 90. *Exhib:* Northwest Ann, Seattle Art Mus, Wash, 65 & 67; Judkin Mem Am Mus, Bath, Eng, Pratt Manhattan, NY, 72-74; 60th Ann, Del Art Mus, Wilmington, 74; Philadelphia Art Alliance, Pa, 75; one-person show, Greenhill-Lower Merion, Philadelphia, Pa, 76; Nat Print Exhib, Cheney-Cowles Mus, Spokane, Wash, 77; Gov Invitational, Olympia, Wash, 78; Gallery Soho, 2000; and others. *Collection Arranged:* Sari Robinson, Special Exhibit, Walnuts Gallery 73, Philadelphia, PA. *Pos:* Instr, Univ Washington, 71-73 & 84; audio-visual illusr, Boeing Co, Seattle, Wash, 72-73 & 78-84; tech illusr, Du Pont Co, Wilmington, Del, 73-74; consult, 80-; ed, Cable Releases, 85-90 & PSA Puget Soundoff (newsletter), 98; news ed & columnist, Photog Soc Am J, 96-98. *Teaching:* Instr painting & drawing, Burien Arts Gallery Sch, Seattle, Wash, 68-69; asst printmaking, Univ Wash, Seattle, 71-73; lectr, Abbotsford Can Photo-arts, 94; lectr at various other organizations 94-99. *Awards:* Progress/Serv Award for Advancement, Art & Photog, 89; Bronze Stars (4), Photogr Soc Am, Journalism, 91-95; Honor Award, Photog Soc Am, 93, Silver Star, 96 & 99; many others. *Bibliog:* Carolyn Wright (auth), Master of Fine Arts, Thesis exhibit at Henry Gallery, Univ Washington Daily, 6/73; Andrew Seraphin (auth), Four printmakers in Gallery F, Art Alliance Bull, 4/75; Karen Klamm (auth), Sound-Off, Soc Northwest Tech Commun, 12/83. *Mem:* charter mem Burien Arts Asn (trustee, 65-69); Photog Soc Am (zone dir, 94-98, dist rep, 88-94); charter mem Nat Mus Women in Arts, Washington, DC; Bellevue Art Mus; Boeing Employees Photog Soc (educ dir, 95-99). *Media:* Photography, Watercolor. *Res:* Visual Commun. *Specialty:* Painting; Photog (as painting); Natural Phenomena. *Interests:* Books; Gardens; Slide programs (Gemology, Geology & Gems); Visual Imagery. *Publ:* Contribr, Creativity, 4/91 & In pursuit of contemporary images, 7/92, Photog Am Soc J; Eye & mind/minds-eye, summer 91 & Abstraction, beginnings, summer 92, NWCCC Newletter; Articles, Photog Soc Am J, 91-96, 98, 99 & 2000; Try a New Angle-Make It Soft, Aesthetic Experience, 2001

VAN GINKEL, BLANCHE LEMCO
ARCHITECT, EDUCATOR
b Can. *Study:* McGill Univ, BArch; Harvard Univ, MCP. *Hon Degrees:* Univ Aix-Marseille, Hon Dr, 2005. *Work:* Can Ctr Archit, Montreal; Int Archive Women in Archit. *Exhib:* Costume Designs, Musee des Beaux Arts de Montreal, 1946; Plan for Old Montreal, Place Ville Marie, Montreal, Que, 63; Midtown Manhattan Plan Exhib, Art Dir Club & NY Cult Ctr, 72; Work of van Ginkel Assoc, Columbia Univ, NY, 73; Spectrum Can, Royal Can Acad Arts, Montreal, 76; Earthworks, JB Aird Gallery, Toronto, 98; Cur of exhib at Royal Canadian Acad of Arts, Ital Cult Inst, Toronto; Univ Toronto Sch of Archit; and others. *Pos:* Partner, van Ginkel Assocs, Montreal, Toronto, 57-; rep, Can Conf Arts, Ottawa, Royal Archit Inst Can, 71-74; mem adv comt on design, Nat Capital Planning Comn, 77-82; chmn, Massey Awards, Ottawa, Ont, 77-; bd, Asn Col Schs Archit, 81-84, vpres, 85-86, pres, 86-87. *Teaching:* Asst prof archit, Univ Pa, Philadelphia, 51-57; vis prof, Harvard Univ, Univ Montreal & McGill Univ; dean, Sch Archit, Univ Toronto, Ont, 77-82, prof archit, 77-. *Awards:* Asn Coll Schs Archit Distinguished Professor, 89; Citizenship Citation, Govt Can, 91; Alumni Award, 91; Hon Fel, Am Inst Architects, 95; Order of Can Mem, 2000. *Bibliog:* Article, New patterns for a metropolis, Archit Forum, 10/71; Les effets Reels--, Archit Concept, 5/73; Urbanite, Vol 2, No 3, Nov 2003. *Mem:* Royal Can Acad Arts (bd, 92-); Fel Royal Archit Inst Can. *Publ:* Auth, The form of the core, J Am Inst Planner, 2/61; ed & contribr, Automobile Issue Can Art, 62; Expo 67 Archit Design, 67; contribr, Phenomenon of Pollution, Harvest House, 68; contribr, Aesthetic Considerations, In: Urban Problems, Holt Rinehart & Winston, 71. *Mailing Add:* 38 Summerhill Gardens Toronto ON M4T 1B4 Canada

VAN HAAFTEN, JULIA
CURATOR, WRITER
b Lancaster, Pa, Nov 3, 1946. *Study:* Barnard Col, BA, 68; Columbia Univ, MLS, 70. *Collection Arranged:* Original Sun Pictures (with catalog), 77 & 96 Images: Talbot to Stieglitz (with catalog), 81, NY Pub Libr Col; Francis Frith in the Middle East, 84; Clarence Kennedy, 87; The View From Space (sites), 89; Berenice Abbott: Modern Vision (with catalog), 89; Yosemite: Photography's Landscape, 90; 400 Years of Native Am Portraits, 92; A J Russell and the Union, Pacific RR, 94. *Pos:* Contribr, Libr J, Portfolio Mag, Hist Photog, 73-; dir photog collections, New York Pub Libr, 79-. *Teaching:* Instr, Rare Book Sch, Columbia Univ, 86-87. *Awards:* Summer stipend, Nat Endowment Humanities, 94. *Bibliog:* Article, AB Bookmen's Weekly, 1/12/82, Darkroom Photogr, 1/83, Photography Year, Time-Life, 82 & Portfolio, 1/2/82. *Res:* Documentary photography; illustrated books, albums, other forms of publications of photographs. *Publ:* Contribr, Guide to the literature of art history, Am Libr Asn, 81; coauth, Egypt and the Holy Land: 77 Views by Francis Frith, Dover, 81; The View From Space: American Astronaut Photography, 88. *Mailing Add:* NY Pub Libr Fifth Ave at 42nd St New York NY 10018

VANHAERENTS, WALTER
COLLECTOR
Pos: former real estate and construction company executive; owner, Vanhaerents Art Collection, Brussels. *Awards:* Named one of Top 200 Collectors, ARTNews mag, 2011, 2012, 2013. *Collection:* Contemporary art. *Mailing Add:* Vanhaerents Art Collection 29 rue Annessens Brussels 1000 Belgium

VAN HARLINGEN, JEAN (ANN)
ENVIRONMENTAL ARTIST, PAINTER
b Dayton, Ohio, Feb 12, 1947. *Study:* Ohio State Univ, BS, 70; Tyler Sch Art (univ fel), MFA, 75. *Work:* Hallmark, Kansas City, Mo; Am Century Investments, Kansas City, Mo; AT&T, Kansas City; IBM, Detroit; Arrowmont's Sch of Arts and Crafts, 50th Ann Traveling Col, 97. *Comn:* Pet Inc, St Louis, Mo, 86; Laumeier Sculpture Park, St Louis, Mo, 95; Paper in the Millennium, Robert C Williams Am Mus of Papermaking, Atlanta, Ga, 2000. *Exhib:* 12th Int Biennial Tapestry, Mus Cantanol des Beaux Arts, Lausanne, Switz, 85; Int Biennial Paper Art, Leopold-Hoesch Mus, Duren, WGer; 13th Outdoor Sculpture Show, Shidoni Gallery, Santa Fe, NMex, 87; solo show, Leedy-Voulkos Gallery, Kansas City, 90 & 97, Western Mich Univ, Kalamazoo, 90, Park Col, Parkville, Mo, 98, Eastern Wash Univ, Chaney, 98; Liberties Expressions, 14th Int Sculpture Conf, Philadelphia, 92. *Pos:* Coordr, Visual Arts Pub Serv Prog, Brandywine Graphic Workshop, 78-80 & Women's Caucus Art, 80-81, Philadelphia, Pa. *Teaching:* Vis artist, Univ Mo, Kansas City, 86-94; adj prof, Park Univ, Parkville, Mo, 94-. *Awards:* Grant, Pa Coun Arts, 74; Second Prize, Paper Fiber XII, Iowa City/Johnson Co Arts Coun. *Bibliog:* Milena Lamarova (auth), Textile sculpture: The 12th international biennial of tapestry, Am Craft, 10-11/85; Greg Field (auth), Subtle Process Deserves a Second Look, 89; Susan Powers (auth), Pulp Art, Kansas City Mag, 6/96. *Mem:* Kansas City Artists Coalition (bd dir, 86); Int Sculpture Ctr; Int Asn Hand Papermakers; Robert C Williams Am Mus of Papermaking. *Media:* All. *Dealer:* Sherry Leedy Contemporary Art 2004 Baltimore Ave Kansas City MO

VAN HORN, DANA CARL
PAINTER, MURALIST
b San Diego, Calif, Nov 19, 1950. *Study:* Whitney Mus Am Art independent study prog, 70-71; San Diego State Univ, BFA, 72; Yale Univ, MFA, 74. *Work:* Metrop Mus Art, NY; Allentown Art Mus, Pa; Art Inst Chicago; Madison Art Ctr, Wis; US Dept of Labor, Washington, DC. *Comn:* Mural, Cathedral St Cath Siena, Allentown, Pa, 82; mural, Holy Ghost Church, Bethlehem, Pa, 90; portrait, MIT, 97; portrait, Lafayette Coll, 98; portrait, Penn State Univ, 2000. *Exhib:* Numerous solo & group exhibs in New York, 81-89; Perspectives on Contemp Realism, Pa Acad Fine Arts, 83; Landscape 1960-1985, Contemp Art Ctr, New Orleans; Local Heroes (retrospective), Allentown Art Mus, Pa, 88; Contemp Am Realist Drawings, Art Inst Chicago, 99. *Teaching:* Instr painting, SUNY, Oneonta, NY, 75-76; vis artist, Univ Wis, Madison, 89; instr painting, Baum Sch Art, Allentown, 93-; instr painting & drawing, Muhlenberg Coll & Moravian Coll, 99-2001. *Awards:* Allentown Arts Commission Award. *Bibliog:* Judd Tully (auth), article, Am Artist, 87; Tom Bolt (auth), article, Arts Mag, 87. *Media:* Oil on linen, Watercolor, Acrylic. *Mailing Add:* 1144 N 33rd St Allentown PA 18104-2674

VANIER, JERRE LYNN
ART DEALER, DIRECTOR
b Phoenix, Ariz, June 11, 1957. *Study:* Ariz State Univ, BA (art hist, magna cum laude), 78, MA (humanities); studied with Frederic G Renner. *Exhib:* Dan Namingha: Pueblo Symbolism & Landscapes, Vanier Galleries on Marshall, 2000, Scholder 2000: New Works by Fritz Scholder, 2000, Francoise Gilot: 60 Yrs of Her Art, 2000, The Art of Janet Fish, 2001 & The Art of Dale Chihuly, 2002. *Pos:* dir, Joy Tash Gallery, Scottsdale, Ariz, 96-97; dir Estate Art, Vanier Fine Art on Main, Scottsdale, Ariz, 98-99; dir, Vanier Galleries on Marshall, Scottsdale, Ariz, 99-2001; dir of Client Relations 2001-2004; pres, Jerre Lynn Vanier, Fine Arts Ltd, 2004-; dir, Cline Fine Art, 2005-2007. *Mem:* Nat Soc Arts & Letters (bd mem, 88-); Int Friends of Transformative Art (vchmn, 90-92 & chmn, 92-96); Scottsdale Cult Coun, Pub Arts Adv Bd; Adv bd, Friends of Sch Art, Ariz State Univ; Nat Art Chair for the Nat Soc of Arts and Letters 2001; Nat Art Competition 2001; Pres Elect for the Katherine Herberger Friends of the Sch of Art Ariz State Univ, 2004; Ariz Comt Nat Mus Women in the Arts (co-chmn, 2006-). *Specialty:* Contemp art; nineteenth & twentieth century estate art; Art of the Am West. *Interests:* Collector of Contemp Art

VAN LAAR, TIMOTHY
PAINTER, WRITER
b Ann Arbor, Mich, Mar 7, 1951. *Study:* Calvin Col, BA, 73; Wayne State Univ, MFA, 75. *Work:* Detroit Inst Art; Krannert Art Mus, Champaign, Ill; Herman Miller Inc, Zeeland, Mich; Valparaiso Univ, Ind; Steelcase Inc, Grand Rapids, Mich; Ill State Mus, Springfield. *Exhib:* Chinese Nat Fine Art Mus, Beijing, 87; Amalgama, Thessaloniki, Greece, 94; Fassbender Gallery, Chicago, 97, 2000; Univ Hertfordshire, Hatfield, Eng, 2000; Karl Gesellschaft, Berlin, Ger, 2002; Sheldon Memorial Gallery, Univ Nebraska, Lincoln, 2003; Grand Rapids, Art Mus, MI, 2004; Galerie Stella A, Berlin, Ger, 2006. *Pos:* Printer lithography, Mich Workshop Fine Prints, Detroit, 74-76; resident artist, Urban Inst Contemp Art, Grand Rapids, Mich, 78; ed bd, Art & Academe: A journal for the Humanities & Sciences in the Education of Artists, 88-; US Coordr, Burren Col Art, Ballyvaughn, Ireland, 94-99. *Teaching:* Instr painting & printmaking, Calvin Col, 77-81; asst prof painting, Univ Ill, Urbana-Champaign, 81-87, assoc prof, 87-97, prof, 97, painting program chair, 2000-2002; vis lectr, Glasgow Sch Art, 88-89. *Awards:* Yaddo Fel, 85; Ill Artists Fel, 87; Fulbright, 88; Arts Am Grant, 94; Howard Found Fel, 2001. *Bibliog:* Buzz Spector (auth), Natural Color Aerial Views (exhib catalog), Berlin, 1997; James Elkins (auth), The Exact Moment of Relaxation (exhib catalog), Chicago, 2001; Daniel A, Siedell (auth), Finding Our Way by Losing the Instructions (exhib catalog)., Lincoln, NE, 2003. *Media:* All Media. *Publ:* Coauth, Active Sights: Art as Social Interaction, Mayfield Press, 98; co-auth, Art with a Difference: Looking at Difficult and Unfamiliar Art, Mayfield Press, 2000. *Mailing Add:* Univ Ill Sch Art & Design Champaign IL 61820

VAN LEUNEN, ALICE LOUISE
ARTIST, SCULPTOR
b Evansville, Ind, Feb 7, 1943. *Study:* Smith Col, BA, 65; Ind Univ Fine Arts Dept, 66-67. *Work:* Seattle City Light Portable Works, 85; Atlantic Co Off Bldg, 85; Western Ore State Col, 89; Justice Servs Bldg, Hillsboro, Ore, 92; Napavine Wash Sch Dist, 2000; 8 NW 8th Bldg, Portland, Ore, 2004; and many others. *Comn:* Clackamas Community Col, Oregon City, 92; PT Mulia Bank Tower, Djakarta, Indonesia, 93 & 94; sculpture (in collab with Walter Gordinier), Nat Hig Magnetic Field Lab, Fla State Univ, Tallahassee, 95; sculpture (in collab with Walter Gordinier), Portland Community Col, Cascade Libr, 95; sculpture (in collab with Walter Gordinier), Minn High Security Hosp, St Peter; and others, 91-2000; Fairview Auditorium, Okla, 02; Paper Cuts, Nat'l Traveling Exhib under auspices of Exhibs USA, 2004-2007. *Exhib:* Two-person exhib, Univ Ore Mus Art, 78; Works in Fabric, Renshaw Gallery, Linfield Coll, Ore, 79; Group exhib, Seattle Pac Univ, 79; Solo exhibs, Contemp Crafts Gallery, Portland, 79 & The Lawrence Gallery Salishan, Gleneden Beach, Ore, 80; Smithsonian Inst, Washington DC, 80; Univ Evansville, Ind, 85; ECO Design, Yamhill, Ore, 2005; Golden Gallery, Beaverton, Ore, 2009; Sunriver Lodge, Bend, Ore, 2010; Pronghorn Bend, Ore, 2012. *Pos:* Asst dir, Delphian Gallery-Delphian Found, 77; exhib asst, Contemp Crafts Gallery, Portland, 78-79. *Teaching:* Seminar instr, Dept Fine Arts, Univ Ore, 78-; lectr textiles, Portland State Univ, 80-91. *Awards:* Honorable Mention, 6th Ann Exhib, Corvallis Art Ctr, 11/76; Individual Arts Fel, Ore Arts Comn, 94. *Bibliog:* The state of the crafts--a visual review, Frank Petock & Assoc, 1980, Interweave Mag, summer 80; The Guild, Kraus Sikes, Inc, NY, 86, 88, 89, 90, 91, 92, 94, 95, 96, 97, 2000-2010. *Mem:* Nexus; Surface Design Assn. *Media:* Mixed Media, Sculpture. *Publ:* Rental Sales Gallery, The First 50 Years, 1959-2009, Portland Art Mus, 2010. *Dealer:* Portland Art Mus Rental/Sales Gallery Portland OR; Billye Turner Bend OR; Art Commission Online; Art Resource. *Mailing Add:* 9025 SE Terrace View Ct Amity OR 97101

VANMOERKERKE, EDITH AND MARK
COLLECTORS
Study: Univ Denver, MBA. *Pos:* retail and real-estate investor, Belgium. *Awards:* Named one of Top 200 Collectors, ARTNews mag, 2011, 2012, 2013. *Collection:* European and American Contemporary Art. *Mailing Add:* Collection Vanmoerkerke Oud Vliegveld 10 Oostende 8400 Belgium

VANN, SAMUEL LEROY
PAINTER
b Ithaca, NY, Sept 16, 1952. *Study:* Ft Lewis Col, BA, 73; State Univ NY, Brockport, MS (educ). *Work:* Everson Mus Art; Menninger Fund, Topeka, Kans; Joan Kennedy; Dr Benjamin Spock; Corporate and private collections throughout the US. *Exhib:* Watercolors USA, Springfield Art Mus, Mo, 77; Chautauqua 20th Nat Show, CAA Gallery, NY, 78; Second Int All on Paper Show, Assoc Art Orgn Western NY, Buffalo, 80; Rivers, Gorges, Canyons Traveling Exhib, 82-82; Midwest Watercolor Soc First 100 Exhib, Tweed Mus Art; Butler Inst Am Art 82, Midyear Show, Youngstown, Ohio, 82; NMex Int Art Show, Clovis; solo exhibs, Prouty-Chew Mus, Geneva, NY, 82, Rome Art Ctr, NY, 82, Arnot Art Mus, Elmira, NY, 82, Schweinfurth Mem Art Gallery, Auburn, NY, 81, Sheldon Mem Art Gallery, Lincoln, Nebr, 82, Everson Mus Art, Syracuse, NY, 82, Albright-Knox Art Gallery, Buffalo, NY, 82. *Teaching:* Asst dir painting, Chautauqua Inst Ctr Arts, 79-80. *Awards:* First Prize Graphics, Twelfth Ann Western Art Show, 77 & Third Ann Nat Miniature Show, 77; First Prize Painting, Second Int All on Paper Show, 80. *Media:* Watercolor. *Dealer:* Bishop Gallery 7164 Main Scottsdale AZ 85251. *Mailing Add:* 5271 Cold Springs Rd Trumansburg NY 14886

VAN OSDELL, BARRIE (CALABRESE) SMITH
PAINTER, INSTRUCTOR
b Baton Rouge, La. *Study:* Self taught. *Work:* Pickens Co Art Mus, SC; SC Arts Comn. *Comn:* 17 pen & ink works, Am Bank Op Ctr, Baton Rouge, La, 82; 4 oil paintings, La Heritage Galleries, Baton Rouge, 85; 4 oil paintings of Clemson Univ, Campus Heritage Inc, Anderson, SC, 87; 22 oil paintings, Wachovia Bank, Winston-Salem & Charlotte, NC, 92-98. *Exhib:* Hudson Valley Art Asn, Hastings-on-Hudson, NY, 95 & 99; Nat Oil & Acrylic Painters Soc, Osage Beach, Mo, 95, 97 & 99; Am Artists Prof League, Salmagundi Club, NY, 95-2000; Oil Painters Am, Nat & Regional Exhib, 95-98, 2002 & 2006; Arts for the Parks Int Competition, Fed Nat Parks, Jackson, Wyo, 95-96 & 98; and others. *Teaching:* Pvt classes, 76-84; instr, painting workshops. *Awards:* Suppliers Award, Dick Blick Art Materials, 95; Award of Excellence, Oil Painters Am, 98; Medal Hon, Am Artists Prof League, 99. *Bibliog:* Don Marvine (auth), Design basics, Plate Collector Mag, 1/86; interview with Sumter Mus Art (TV doc), PBS, SC, 5/90. *Mem:* Oil Painters Am (signature mem); Am Artists Prof League (fel); Nat Oil & Acrylic Painters Soc (signature mem); Hudson Valley Art Asn (elected mem); Anderson Art League. *Media:* Acrylic, Oils. *Publ:* Art From the Parks, North Light Books, 9/2000; Painting North Carolina, Creative Pursuits, 2008. *Dealer:* Taylor Clark Gallery Baton Rouge LA 70806. *Mailing Add:* 609 Horseshoe Rd Honeapath SC 29654

VAN SANT, TOM R
SCULPTOR, PAINTER
b Los Angeles, Calif, Feb 26, 1931. *Study:* Stanford Univ, BA, 53; Otis Art Inst Los Angeles Co, MFA, 57; also studied with Herb Jepson, Peter Voulkos & Millard Sheets. *Work:* Davies Pac Ctr, Honolulu; Pac Design Ctr, Los Angeles; Libr Cong; Smithsonian Inst; Inst Contemp Art, London. *Comn:* Sculptured concrete walls, Irvine Co, Newport Beach, Calif, 68; sculptured concrete mural, Honolulu Int Airport, 73; mural, Taipei Int Airport, Taiwan, 74; fountain sculpture, City of Los Angeles, 75; bronze sculpture, Warmington Co, Newport Beach, Calif, 82. *Exhib:* Solo exhibs, Inst Contemp Art, London, 76, Myer Galleries, Melbourne & Sydney, Australia, 77, Stedelijk Mus, Amsterdam, The Neth, 77, Honolulu Hale, City Hall, 77 & Pac Design Ctr, Los Angeles, 80. *Teaching:* Instr design & drawing, Otis Art Inst Los Angeles Co, 60-66; instr creativity, Omega Sem, Fall City, Wash, 66-68; fel, Ctr Advan Visual Studies, Mass Inst Technol, 81-. *Awards:* Art in Architecture Award, Am Inst Archit, 56, 61 & 68; Award of Merit, First Ann Exhib Illus West, 59; Purchase Award, Int Sculpture Symposium, Calif State Univ, Long Beach, 74. *Bibliog:* Fundaburk (auth), Art in Public Places in the US, Popular Press, 75; Piene (auth), Sky Art Conf, Ctr Advan Visual Studies, Mass Inst Technol, 81-83. *Publ:* Co-dir, Flight Forms (film), Ed Spiegel Co, 76. *Mailing Add:* 146 Entrada Dr Santa Monica CA 90402

VAN SCHAACK, ERIC
HISTORIAN, EDUCATOR
b Evanston, Ill, June 10, 1931. *Study:* Dartmouth Col, AB, 53; Columbia Univ, PhD, 69. *Teaching:* Lectr & research asst, The Frick Collection, NY, 60-62; from asst prof to prof, Goucher Col, Baltimore, 64-76, chmn, Dept Visual Arts, 73-76; prof, Dept Art & Art Hist, Colgate Univ, 77-96, chmn, 77-83, prof emer, 96-. *Awards:* Italian Govt Grant & Fulbright Travel Grant, 62-63, Ford Found Grant Humanities, 72-73; Colgate Univ Humanities Fac Development Fund Grant, 79-80 & 93. *Mem:* Coll Art Asn Am; Soc Archit Historians. *Res:* Italian Renaissance & Baroque art; American architecture. *Publ:* An unpublished letter by Francesco Albani, Art Bull, 69; coauth, The music in Van Dyck's Rinaldo and Armida, Baltimore Mus Art Ann III, 69; contribr, Italian Paintings, Baltimore Mus Art, 81; Francesco Albani's Guida di Bologna, Acts of the 24th International Congress of the History of Art, Bologna, 82; other articles publ in Arte Antica e Moderna, Apollo and Picker Art Gallery Ann Report/Bull

VAN STEIN, THOMAS
PAINTER
b Pasadena, Calif, Aug 25, 1961. *Study:* Calif State Univ, BA, 1984; Pasadena Art Ctr Coll of Design, 1985; Calif State Univ, MA, 1997-99. *Exhib:* Solo exhibs include Moonlight Nocturnes, Montecito Art Gallery, Calif, 2000, Urban Nocturnes, Carnegie Art Mus, Oxnard, Calif, 2005; group exhibs include Art at Lotusland, Montecito, Calif, 1998; Small Images Show, Abend Gallery, Denver, Colo, 1998; Calif Collectors Gallery, Kentfield, Calif, 1998; Burning the Midnight Oil, Montecito Art Gallery, 1999; Historic Buildings of the San Gabriel Valley, Calif Art Club Gallery, Montecito, 2000; Spring Salon, Edenhurst Gallery, Los Angeles, 2000; Bottoms Sea Arts Gallery, Biltmore, Montecito, Santa Barbara, Calif, 2000; Elder Art Gallery, Santa Barbara, 2005; Waterhouse Gallery, Santa Barbara, 2006. *Dealer:* Edler Gallery 1427 South Blvd Ste 101 Charlotte NC 28203; Waterhouse Gallery 1114 State St Ste 9 Santa Barbara CA 93101. *Mailing Add:* Eleanor Ettinger Gallery 24 W 57th St Ste 609 New York NY 10019

VAN SUCHTELEN, ADRIAN
PRINTMAKER, EDUCATOR
b Semarang, Indonesia, June 18, 1941; US citizen. *Study:* El Camino Col, Calif; Otis Art Inst, Los Angeles, BFA, MFA, 66. *Work:* Indianapolis Mus Art; De Cordova Mus, Lincoln, Mass; Cleveland Mus Art; Riverside Mus, Calif; Milwaukee Art Ctr; and others. *Comn:* Art work on film Young Lovers, Samuel Goldwyn Studios, Los Angeles, 64. *Exhib:* Drawing Soc Nat Exhib, Am Fedn Arts, NY, 70-72; Colorprint USA, Tex, 74; Davidson Nat Print & Drawing Exhib, NC, 75; Pratt Graphics Ctr Int Print Exhib, NY, 75; Solo exhib, Northern State Coll, SDak, 83; and others. *Teaching:*

Prof drawing & grad dir, Utah State Univ, 67-. *Awards:* Purchase Award, NMex State Univ, 71; Ben & Abbey Grey Found Purchase Award, Salt Lake Art Ctr, 72; Purchase Prize, Boston Printmakers, 81. *Mem:* Graphics Soc; Boston Printmakers Soc. *Publ:* Contribr, Drawing A Search for Form, 65; auth & illusr, Lifetime Career Schools, Correspondence Art Course, 67; contribr, Oil Painting, Techniques and Materials, 69; The Hidden Elements of Drawing, 73. *Dealer:* Sylvesters Art Studio 61 E 320 S Salt Lake City UT 84111. *Mailing Add:* 655 E 1800 N Logan UT 84341

VAN VALKENBURGH, MICHAEL
ARCHITECT
Study: Cornell Univ, BS, 1973; Univ Ill Champaign-Urbana, M (landscape archit), 1977. *Pos:* principal, Michael Van Valkenburgh Assocs, Inc. *Teaching:* instr, Harvard Univ, Grad Sch Design Sch, 1982, chmn, Dept Landscape Archit, 1991-96, Charles Eliot Prof Landscape Archit and Prof in Practice. *Awards:* Nat Design Award in Environ Design, Cooper-Hewitt Nat Design Mus, 2003; Arnold W Brunner Mem Prize in Archit, Am Acad Arts & Letts, 2010. *Mem:* Fel Am Acad, Rome. *Mailing Add:* Michael Van Valkenburgh Assocs Inc 16 Court St 11th Fl Brooklyn NY 11241

VAN VLIET, CLAIRE
PRINTMAKER, BOOKMAKER
b Ottawa, Ont, Aug 9, 1933. *Study:* San Diego State Univ, AB, 52; Claremont Grad Sch, MFA, 54. *Hon Degrees:* Univ Arts, Hon Dr, 93; San Diego State Univ, Hon DFA, 2002. *Work:* Philadelphia Mus Art; Montreal Mus Fine Arts; Cleveland Mus Art; Victoria & Albert Mus, London; NDak Mus Art, Grand Forks; US Dept State; Nat Gallery Art, Washington, DC; Libr Cong; Winnipeg Art Gallery; Fleming Mus UVM, Burlington Vt; New Orleans Mus Art; Bates Coll Mus Art; Univ Maine Machias Gallery; Nat Mus the Philippines; Tate; Wiggin Gallery, Boston Pub Libr; Hood Mus Hanover NH. *Exhib:* Paper as Medium, Smithsonian Traveling Exhib, 78-80; The Janus Press 1975-80, Fleming Mus Traveling Exhib, 82-84; Dolan/Maxwell Gallery, Philadelphia, 84 & 91; Mary Ryan Gallery, NY, 86; Group exhibs, Brooklyn Nat, Philadelphia Arts Festival, Kunst zu Kafka, Germany, Paper as Medium, Smithsonian Inst, Washington, Paper Now, Cleveland Mus Art, 86, Boyle Arts Festival, Ireland, 93, Libr Congress, 97-, ND Mus Art, 99; Univ Arts, 89, 2001; Bates Coll Mus Art, Lewiston, Maine, 94 & 99; Victoria & Albert Mus, London, 94; NDak Mus of Art, 95; Wood Art Gallery, Vt, 2000; Rosenwald-Wolf Gallery Univ Arts Philadelphia 2001; Marlboro Coll Gallery, 2002; The Grolier Club New York City 2006; Nat Gallery Art Libr 2006; Humanities Gallery, Scripps Col, 2006; Janus Press, Fifty Yrs, Grolier Club, NY; LSU Libr; Sripps Coll Calif; Nat Gallery Libr, 2006; Smith Coll Libr; Univ Vt Libr; Boston Pub Libr, 2007; Brattleboro Mus, 2011; Janus 60, San Francisco Ctr for the Book, 2015; Castleton Downtown Gallery, Rutland, VT, 2015; Janus Press at Sixty, San Francisco Center for the Book, 2015. *Pos:* Proprietor, Janus Press, 54-. *Teaching:* Asst prof printmaking, Philadelphia Col Art, 59-65; vis lectr, Univ Wis, 65-66, Univ Vt, 74-75, Univ Ala, 83, US Info Agency, Arts Am Prog to NZ, 95. *Awards:* Ingram Merrill Fel, 89; Mac Arthur Prize, Fel, 89-94; Ballinglen Fel, Ireland, 93; Paton Prize, Nat Acad Design, 2001; Herb Lockwood Prize, 2015. *Bibliog:* Lehrer (auth), The Janus Press 1955-75 & Fine (auth), Claire Van Vliet: Landscape Paperworks, Dolan-Maxwell, Pa, 84; McLean (auth) In Black & White: Landscape prints by Claire Van Vliet, Maine, 99; Fine, Ruth (auth) The Janus Press - Fifty Years 2006. *Mem:* Soc Printers Boston; Nat Acad (acad, 95-); Vt Acad Arts and Scis. *Media:* Relief, Lithography; Paper, Book Arts. *Publ:* Illusr & ed, Sky and Earth-Variable Landscape, Janus Press, 70; auth & illusr, Satellite, Mus Mod Art, 71; designer, Aunt Sallies Lament, Chronicle Bks, 93; Woven and Interlocking Book Structures - Janus/Gefn Unlimited 2002. *Dealer:* Dolan-Maxwell 2046 Rittenhouse Sq Philadelphia PA 19103. *Mailing Add:* 101 Schoolhouse Rd Newark VT 05871

VAN WINKELEN, BARBARA
PAINTER, ILLUSTRATOR
b Waban, Mass. *Study:* Yale Univ Sch Fine Arts, BFA, 43. *Work:* Windsor Hist Soc; Nantucket Hist Soc; Shaker Mus, Hancock Shaker Village Inc, Mass. *Exhib:* 82nd Ann, Catharine Lorillard Wolfe Art Club, NY, 78; Conn Watercolor Soc, 78-86 & Conn Acad, 80-86, Wadsworth Atheneum, Hartford, Conn; Slater Mem Mus, Norwich, Conn, 78-81; Conn Acad Fine Arts, Olde State House, Hartford, Conn, 81; Springfield Acad Assoc & Springfield Art League Mus Show, 86; New Haven Paint & Clay Club; Nat Watercolor Soc Members Show, Colo; NAm Juried Shows, NE Watercolor Soc, 90, 92, 94, 96 & 98, Windsor Hist Soc, 98. *Pos:* Staff asst, Mus Mod Art, New York, 43-44; tech illusr, United Technol, 53-71. *Teaching:* Children's art, Wadsworth Atheneum, Hartford, Conn, 48-50. *Awards:* First Prize, Conn Watercolor Soc, 85 & 86; Best Show, Conn Women Artists, 83 & 84 & Acad Artists Assoc, 86. *Bibliog:* Maureen O'Sullivan (auth), Nantucket Artist Barbara van Winkelen (film), 79; J Merrick-Windsor (interviewer), On Camera (1 hour interviews), WWEU, 86 & 87. *Mem:* Conn Acad Fine Arts; Conn Watercolor Soc; Conn Women Artists (bd dir, 80-82); Nantucket Artists Asn; New Haven Paint & Clay Club; New Eng Watercolor Soc; Acad Artists Asn. *Media:* Egg Tempera; All Media. *Publ:* Illusr, Escape from the Chanticleer, Classic Collections Fine Arts Catalogues, 92-96; feature article, Nantucket Mag, autumn 93; Winds & Dragons Publ, 95. *Dealer:* Spindrift Gallery 11 Old S Wharf Nantucket MA 02554; Jay Whitney 405 Queen St Southington CT. *Mailing Add:* 1864 Poquonock Ave Poquonock CT 06064

VAN WINKLE, LESTER G
SCULPTOR, EDUCATOR
b Greenville, Tex, Jan 11, 1944. *Study:* ETex State Univ, BS; Univ Ky, MA; also sculpture with Michael D Hall. *Work:* Arrowmont Sch Arts & Crafts, Gatlinburg, Tenn; Dade Co Jr Col, Miami. *Exhib:* Sculpt 70, Corcoran Gallery Art, Washington, DC, 70; Whitney Biennial of Painting & Sculpture, Whitney Mus, NY, 73; Solo exhibs, Henry Gallery, Washington, 73-75 & Webb Parsons Gallery, Bedford, NY, 74-75; Waves Exhib, Cranbrook Acad Art Galleries, 74. *Teaching:* From asst prof to assoc prof sculpture, Va Commonwealth Univ, 69-. *Dealer:* Henri Gallery 1500 21st St NW Washington DC 20036. *Mailing Add:* VCU Sculpture Dept PO Box 843005 1000 W Broad St Richmond VA 23284-3005

VARGAS, JOSEPHINE
ILLUSTRATOR, PAINTER
b New York, NY, July 31, 1946. *Study:* Fashion Inst Technol, 64-65; Sch Visual Arts, 78-79. *Work:* Mus de la Historia, Ponce, PR. *Exhib:* Invitational, William Deford III Gallery, Citicorp, NY, 93; Fashion Inst Technol Mus, NY, 93-96; Flushing Coun on Arts, 93 & 94; Atelier 14, New York City, 2000; Gallery Emanuel, Great Neck, NY, 2000; Mus at the Fashion Inst Tech, New York City, 93-03; and others. *Pos:* Trustee, Nat Art League, Douglaston, NY, 87-. *Teaching:* adj, asst prof, Fashion Inst Tech, 92-; instr, Parsons Sch Design, 97-. *Awards:* Peacock Showcase Award, Visual Art Alliance of Long Island, 91; First Place Watercolor, Nat Art League, 91; Purchase Award Ponce Pinturoso Open Competition, Ponce, PR, 92. *Mem:* Nat Asn Women Artists (Marion de Sola Mendes award, 2000); Nat Art League (advisor). *Media:* Computer Artist; Watercolor, Mixed Media. *Publ:* contribr, Portfolio for Fashion Designers, 03

VARNAY JONES, THEODORA
PRINTMAKER, SCULPTOR
b Budapest, Hungary, Feb 26, 1942; US citizen. *Study:* Univ Fine Art, Budapest, BFA, 69, MFA, 70. *Work:* Achenbach Found Graphic Arts, Fine Arts Mus of San Francisco, Calif; Bank Am Corp Art Collection, San Francisco; New Canaan Libr Permanent Collection, Conn; Kyoto Seika Univ, Japan; Iris & B Gerard Cantor Ctr for Visual Arts, Stanford Univ, Calif; Crocker Art Mus, Sacramento, Calif; Fresno Art Mus, Fresno, Calif; Mus of Contemp Art, San Jose, Costa Rico. *Comn:* Color etching, Fine Arts Mus, San Francisco, 86; 12 large scale mixed media works, Sak's Fifth Ave, 89 & 90. *Exhib:* Contemp Calif Prints, San Jose Mus Art, Calif, 82; Mid Am Biennial, Mus Fine Art, Owensboro, Ky, 84; Prints USA, Nat Mus, Singapore, 84; Mini Print Int, Taller Galeria Fort, Cadoques, Spain, 84; Prints USA, Amerika Haus, Berlin, Ger, 85; The Hanga Ann, Metrop Art Mus, Tokyo, Japan, 85; Int Print Biennial, Mus de Arte Contemporanea, Cabo Frio, Brazil, 85; 3rd Biennial Exhib of Prints, Mus Mod Art, Wakayama, Japan, 89; Tamura Gallery, Tokyo, Japan, 90; Kieler Kloster, Kiel, Germany, 2000; Mem Union Art Gallery, UC Davis, 2004; Pacifica Ctr for the Arts, Calif, 2007; Fresno Art Mus, Fresno, Calif, 2008; San Jose Inst of Contemp Art, San Jose, Calif, 2009. *Pos:* artist-in-residence, Kyoto Seika Univ, Japan, 95. *Teaching:* Guest lectr on prints, Oakland Mus Asn, 85; Guest lectr on prints, Kyoto Seika Univ, Japan; Visiting lectr, UC Davis, Calif, 2002; Lectr, KALA Arts Inst, Berkeley, Calif, 2007-. *Awards:* Purchase Award, Prints USA, Pratt Graphics Ctr, 82; Fellowship Support Grant, Art Matters Inc, 92; Fellowship Grant, Calif Arts Coun, 99. *Bibliog:* Miyagi Television Rev, Japan, 90; interview article, Artcritical, 11/18/2008; interview article, ArtSlant, 2008. *Mem:* Calif Soc. *Media:* Mixed media. *Dealer:* Don Soker Contemporary 100 Montgomery St Suite 1430 San Fancisco CA 94104. *Mailing Add:* 2180 Bryant St San Francisco CA 94110

VARNEY, EDWIN
CONCEPTUAL ARTIST, PRINTMAKER
b New Rochelle, NY, Oct 16, 1944. *Study:* Syracuse Univ, BA, 65, MA, 66; Univ Vancouver, PhD, 76. *Work:* Vancouver Art Gallery, BC; Smith Coll Art Gallery, Northampton, Mass; Alta Coll Art, Calgary; Rotterdam Acad, Holland; Univ Colo, Boulder; Smithsonian, Washington DC: Art Bank, Ottawa; Allen Mus, Ohio; Nat Postal Mus, Ottawa; Art Pool, Budapest. *Comn:* Wood sculpture, Burnaby Art Coun, BC, 71; concrete sculpture, BC Sculptor's Soc, 77. *Exhib:* Space Window, RI Sch Design, Providence, 78; Artists' Stamps, Mus Art & Hist, Geneva, Switz, 79; Mail Etc, Univ Colo, Boulder, Tyler Sch Art, Philadelphia & Fla State Univ, Tallahassee, 79; Post-Art, San Diego Univ Art Gallery, 88; The Nude, Vancouver Art Gallery, 93; Searching For the Hidden, Queens Col, Cambridge, Eng, 94; Outpost Biennale, Venice Biennale, Italy, 95; Arte Correo, Mus de Bellas Artes, Argentina, 97; Cyclops Dreams, Access, Vancouver, BC, 2005; Surrealist Festival, Vancouver, BC, 2006; Parastamps, Mus Fine Arts, Budapest, 2007; and others. *Pos:* Artist/poet-in-residence, Intermedia, Vancouver, BC, 71-73, publ, ed & designer, 73-88; dir, Mus Int de Nuevo Art, 81-; pub art consult, Gibson & Varney, Vancouver, BC, 94-99; bd dir, Roundhouse Arts Ctr, 97-2001; cur, various inst, 1980-. *Awards:* Can Coun Grant, Environ Opera, 89. *Mem:* Cent Visual Arts Asn; Ave des Arts; West Coast Surrealists; Grupo des Artistes. *Media:* Conceptual Art, Printmaking, Sculpture, Collage. *Collection:* 5000 works by Canadian & Int Artists. *Publ:* Openings, 69; Human Nature, 74; ed, First, Second and Third International Artists' Stamp Edition, 76, 78 & 80; editor Contemporary Surrealist Prose, 79, Intermedia Bks; What the Wind Said, Caitlin Press, 91; Solar Eclipse, 93; Nothing Ever Changes, 95; Entering The World, 97; The Poem Factory; What is Poetry?, 99; Blue Skies, 2001; Sex Sells, 2008; Letter from Hell, 2009; Fast Grounded, 2010; Book of Nada, 2011; Tomorrow Never Comes, 2012; Walking the Dog, 2013. *Mailing Add:* 4426 Island Hwy S Courtenay BC V9N9TI Canada

VARNOT, ANNIE
SCULPTOR
b Barre, Mass, 1972. *Study:* Skidmore Coll, BS (studio art), 1994; Univ Mass, Amherst, MFA (painting), 2001. *Exhib:* Voices, Barre Hist Soc, Mass, 1994; One Step Forward, Two Steps Back, Saratoga Pub Libr, NY, 1997; Painters and Printmakers, Greenfield Community Coll, Mass, 2000; solo exhibs, Herter Art Gallery, Univ Mass, 2001, Galapagos Art Space, Brooklyn, 2001 & 2006, World Financial Ctr, New York, 2009; Site Specifics, Islip Art Mus, NY, 2001; Summer Six Fac Exhib, Schick Art Gallery, Skidmore Coll, NY, 2002; Hampden Gallery, Univ Mass, Amherst, 2003; EBayADay, Univ Mich, 2007; Four Artists in Four Galleries, Univ Conn at Avery Point, Groton, 2008. *Pos:* Designer & carpenter, Creativing Engineering Inc, Chalkline Studios, and Largent Studios, 2002-04; preparator & framer, Jewish Mus, Mus City New york, New Mus Contemp Art, Phillips de Pury & co, 2003-. *Teaching:* Instr fine arts, Univ Mass, Amherst, 1999, instr continuing educ, 2000, instr painting, 2000-01; instr studio art, Mount Wachusett Community Coll, Mass, 2001-02, instr studio design, 2002; instr painting, Skidmore Coll, NY, 2002-06. *Awards:* Pat Hearn & Colin De Land Found Grant, 2008; Gottlieb Found Grant, 2008; Artists' Fel Grant, 2008; Pollock-Krasner Found Grant, 2008. *Bibliog:* Helen Harrison (auth), Emerging Artists, Emerging Visions, NY Times, 7/15/2001. *Mailing Add:* 144 Spencer St #319 Brooklyn NY 11205

VARO, MARTON GEZA
SCULPTOR
b Szekelyudvarhely, Hungary, Mar 15, 1943. *Study:* Ion Andreescu Art Acad, univ grad, 60-66. *Work:* Stedelijk Mus, Amsterdam; Nat Gallery, Budapest; Deri Mus, Debrecen, Hungary; Mora Ferenc Muzeum, Szeged, Hungary; Muzeul Tarii Crisurilor, Oradea, Romania. *Comn:* Civic Ctr, City of Brea, Calif, 90; Pereira Sculpture Garden, Univ Calif, Irvine, 91; Peace Memorial, City of Palm Desert, Calif, 92; Plaza of the Americas, Dallas, 92; Angels, Performing Arts Hall, Ft Worth, Tex, 95. *Exhib:* Studio of Young Artists, Grand Palais, Paris, 78; 4th Int Exhib Small Sculpture, Budapest, 78; Mucsarnok Exhib Hall, Budapest, 81; Bronzetto Piccola Sculptura, Padua, Italy, 86; Muckenthaler Cult Ctr, Fullerton, Calif, 90. *Awards:* Studio of Young Artist Award, 76; Munkacsy Award, 84; Fulbright Scholar, 88-91. *Media:* Marble, Stone. *Mailing Add:* 2 Charity Irvine CA 92612

VASA
SCULPTOR, EDUCATOR
b Otocac, Yugoslavia, April 25, 1933; US citizen. *Study:* Sch Applied Arts, Belgrade, Yugoslavia, 47-51, Acad Applied Arts, Univ Belgrade, 51-54. *Work:* Hirshhorn Mus & Sculpture Garden, Smithsonian Inst, Washington; Mus Royaux des Beaux-Arts de Belgique, Art Mod, Brussels; Mus Mod Art, Belgrade; Phillips Collection, Washington; San Francisco Mus Mod Art, Calif. *Comn:* Sculpture, Toyota Auto Indus, Nagoya, Japan, 72; sculpture, Dallas Hyatt Regency, Tex, 78; sculpture, Cedars Sinai Med Ctr, Los Angeles, 79; sculpture, Tishman West Management Corp, Los Angeles, 86; sculpture, Olivetti, Ivrea, Italy, 86. *Exhib:* Solo exhibs, Palm Springs Desert Mus, Calif, 80, Mus Mod Art, Belgrade, 85 & 72, Gallery West, Los Angeles, 91, Hokin Gallery, Bay Harbor Islands, Fla, 91, John Mallon Gallery, Indianapolis, Ind, 92, Imago, Palm Springs, Calif, 92 & TR Yangle Gallery, Tokyo, 95. *Teaching:* Prof design, Univ Calif, Los Angeles, currently. *Media:* Laminated Acrylic. *Mailing Add:* 2243 Linnington Ave Los Angeles CA 90064-2339

VASELL, CHRIS
ARTIST, FILMMAKER
b Chicago, Ill, 1974. *Exhib:* Solo exhibs, It Puts the Lotion in the Basket, Boom, Oak Park, Ill, 2002; Don't go Outside they're waiting for you, Blum & Poe, Los Angeles, 2005, 2006; group exhibs, Whitecaps, Grand Rapids Art Mus, Mich, 1997; Nippon Steel, Chicago, 1999; Chicago Drawing, Forcefield Exhib Space, Chicago, 1999; Stray Show, Chicago, 2002; I See a Darkness, Blum & Poe, Los Angeles, 2003; On Paper, Nicole Klagsburn, NY, 2004; Trials & Terrors, Mus Contemp Art, Chicago, 2005; Having New Eyes, Aspen Art Mus, Colo, 2006; Whitney Biennial: Day for Night, Whitney Am Art Mus, NY, 2006. *Mailing Add:* Team Gallery 83 Grand St New York NY 10013

VASSDAL ELLIS, ELSI M
GRAPHIC ARTIST, EDUCATOR
b Fallon, Nev, June 9, 1952. *Study:* Western Wash State Col, BS, 74; Western Wash Univ, MEd, 77; Univ Wash, PhD, 83. *Work:* Hunt Libr, Carnegie-Mellon Univ; Moravian Gallery, Brno, Czech Repub; Nat Mus Women in Arts, Washington; St Bride Printing Libr, London; Musee de la Publicite, Paris. *Exhib:* Off the Shelf, Tempe, Ariz, 94; Books-Objects of Art, Somerville, Mass, 94; Inky Fingers, NY, 94; Shape-Shifting: Transformations, Greely, Colo, 96; Turning the Page, Honolulu, 96. *Teaching:* Prof book arts, Western Wash Univ, 94-. *Awards:* Best of Category-Offset Design, Bumbershoot, 90; Best of Category-Typographic Excellence, NC & Pa Ann, 91. *Mem:* Alliance Contemp Book Arts; Ctr Book Arts; Guild Book Workers; Pac Ctr Book Arts; Type Dir Club. *Media:* Offset, Letterpress. *Publ:* Auth, Type '87, J Für Drucksgesichichte, Pts 1 & 2, 88-89; contribr, An Introduction to Book Design, Writer's NW Handbk, 91; auth, Artist's statement, Artweek, 1/95. *Dealer:* Edwina Legget-Califia San Francisco CA. *Mailing Add:* Dept Art Col Performing Arts Western Wash Univ MS 9068 516 High St Bellingham WA 98225

VATANDOOST, NOSSI MALEK
EDUCATOR, PAINTER
b Teheran, Iran, May 22, 1935. *Study:* Persian Acad Art with Persian Miniatures Masters, 57-61; Western Ky Univ, BA, 70. *Work:* Wayland Baptist Col, Plainview, Tex; Nossi Coll Art, Goodlettsville, Tenn; Persian Acad Art, Tehran, Iran; Blue Field State Col, WVa. *Exhib:* Central South, Parthenon, Nashville, Tenn, 75; Greater Madison Arts & Crafts Festival, Madison CofC, Tenn, 76. *Teaching:* Educ dir com & fine arts, Nossi Col Art, Goodlettsville, Tenn, 73-; Pres, Art Resources of Tenn-Sumner. *Awards:* Outstanding Young Artist, Persian Acad Art, 60-61; Business of the Year, Goodlettsville CofC, 98. *Mem:* Int Coun Design Sch (pres, 96-97); Nat Asn Schs Art & Design; Nashville Advert Fedn; Goodlettsville CofC; Nat Mus Women Arts. *Media:* Acrylic, Oil. *Mailing Add:* Nossi College of Art 590 Cheron Rd Madison TN 37115

VATER, REGINA VATER LUNDBERG
CONCEPTUAL ARTIST, LECTURER
b Rio De Janeiro, Brazil, May 11, 1943. *Study:* Frank Schaeffer's Studio, Rio de Janeiro, 59; Sch Archit, Univ FED Rio de Janeiro, 60; Ibere Camargo's Studio, Rio de Janeiro, 62; Pratt Inst, Manhattan, NY, 74; Downtown Video Community Ctr, New York, 82. *Work:* Benson Latin Am Collection, Univ Tex, Austin; Video Annex, Long Beach Mus Art, Calif; Bibliotheque Nat Paris; Mus Contemp Arts, Univ Sao Paulo, Brazil; Jua Harfers, NY. *Comn:* Snake Nest, Laguna Gloria Arts Mus, Austin, 88; Light Poem, Women Studio Workshop, Rosendale, NY, 89; Amanaje, Clocktower Gallery, NY, 89; NikaUnikana, Ikon Gallery, Birmingham, Eng, 90; Mongarayba, Ctr Contemp Arts, Sante Fe, NMex, 90. *Exhib:* Biennale Des Jeunes, Paris, 67; Int Biennial Sao Paulo, 69; Venice Biennial, Italy, 76; solo show, Eugenia Cucalon Gallery, NY, 81; Montbeliard Int Video Festival, France, 84; Latin Am Women Artists, Bronx Mus, NY, 82; First Tex Triennial, Contemp Arts Mus, Houston, 88; The Revered Earth, Pratt Inst, NY, 90. *Collection Arranged:* Comtemp Brazil Works on Paper, 49 Artists, Nobe Gallery, NY, 79; Brazil Super-8 Films, Millennium, NY, 82; Latin Am Contemp Art, 83; Latin Am Visual Thinking, Art Awareness, Lexington, NY, 84. *Teaching:* Lectr, Univ Tex, Austin, 85, Mus Contemp Art, Univ Sao Paulo, 88 & S Eastern Mass Univ, 90. *Awards:* Travel abroad, Mod Art Nat Show, Ministery Cult Brazil, 72; Guggenheim Fel, 80; Fel on Film, NJ Coun Arts, 85. *Bibliog:* Robert C Morgan (auth), 3 South American women artists, High Performance-Astro Arts, Los Angeles, 86; Steve Kolpan (auth), The Amazon flows into--, Woodstock Times, 5/25/89; Guy Brett (auth), Transcontinental (exhib catalog), Ikon Gallery/Verso, London, 90. *Media:* Installation, Photography. *Publ:* Auth, Dreams That Money Can Buy, Artes Visuales Mus of Mod Art, Mexico City, 81; coauth, Latin American Contemporary Art Flue, Vol III, Now, Franklin Furnace, 83; auth Ecological art is alive and well in Los Angeles, High Performance Astro Artz, 88; Notes of ambition, High Performance Astroartz, 88; Women Artists Tell Her Own Stories-Regina Vater, Gallerie Publ, Vancouver, Can, 89. *Dealer:* Mexic-Arte Mus Austin TX. *Mailing Add:* 1908 Newning Ave Austin TX 78704

VAUGHN, MARY SUSAN
PAINTER, INSTRUCTOR
b Takoma Park, Md, Apr 27, 59. *Study:* Nova Southeastern Univ (Prof-Pre Law), 1989-1991; Georgetown Univ, BS, 1992-1994; Acad Art Coll (Prof-Fine Art), 2001-2003; Md Coll Art & Design (Prof-Drawing), 2003; Studied with Kevin MacPherson, Karin Wells, Peggy Baumgartner, Richard Schmid, Johnnie Liliedahl (workshops, personal commun, mentoring), 2003. *Comn:* Davis Family Home (oil painting), Ms Lisa Davis, Woodbine, Md, 2001; Olney House Inn (oil painting), Riccuittis Fine Italian Restaurant, Olney, Md, 2001; Greek Isles (oil painting), Mr & Mrs Chris Serdenes, Woodbine, Md, 2002; Young Girl Painting (Fragonard Reproduction), Dr Robert Fields, Olney, Md, 2003; St Andrews/At the Dock(oil painting), Mr & Mrs Daniel Barry, Weddington, NC, 2007. *Exhib:* Remembrance, Marshall Gallery, Greensboro, NC, 2002; Patriotism, Washington Gallery/Capitol Arts Network, Bethesda, Md, 2007. *Pos:* Art instr, Lake Providence Acad Art, 2005-; instr, NC Arts, Charlotte, NC, 2005-. *Awards:* Silver Kara Art Award, Kara Art, Geneva, Switz, 2007; America's Promise, First Place, Patriotism, Bethesda, Md, Capitol Arts Network, 2007; 2007 Paint the Parks Top 100 (hon position), Paint Am, 2007. *Mem:* NC Arts & Sci Coun (active mem); Christians in Portraiture (active mem),; Oil Painters Am (assoc mem); Union Co Community Arts Coun (active mem); Am Artists Prof League (assoc mem). *Media:* Oil & Pastel. *Res:* Through study of technique, impressionist masters of the 19th & 20th centuries. *Specialty:* Am Impressionist, vibrant color & composition, landscapes, seascapes, cityscapes, people & places, still life, architecture. *Interests:* Impressionists, composition, perspective, life events, patriotism, color theory, master painting study. *Collection:* Am Impressionist, landscapes, seascapes, cityscapes, people & places, still life, architecture, portraiture & comn works. *Mailing Add:* 8208 Lake Providence Dr Weddington NC 28104

VAUX, RICHARD
PAINTER, PRINTMAKER
b Greensburg, Pa, Sept 15, 1940. *Study:* Miami Univ, Ohio, BFA, 63; Northern Ill Univ, MFA, 69. *Work:* Wash Co Mus; Museu de Arte Contemporanea, Sao Paulo, Brazil; Gallery Robe, Ltd, Tokyo; NY State Mus Art, Albany, NY; Maier Mus, Lynchburg, Va; Heckscher Mus Art, Huntington, NY; Mary & Leigh Mus Art; European Inst Cultural Develop, Belgium. *Exhib:* Butler Inst Am Art, Youngstown, Ohio, 68; Minn Mus Art, St Paul, 71; James Yu Gallery, Soho, New York, 74-76; Guild Hall Mus, East Hampton, NY, 78; Hudson River Mus, 77 & 79; Long Beach Mus Art, 79; Silvermine Guild, Conn, 80; Heckscher Mus, Huntington, NY, 88; Nippon Int, Tokyo, 97; NY State Mus, 98; Phillips Gallery, Sanibel, Fla, 2001; Jain Marunouchi Gallery, 2002; Alpan Gallery, Huntington, NY, 2002; Exposicion Binacional Arte, Asuncion, Paraguay, 2002; Hafnarborg Inst Cult, Iceland, 2003. *Teaching:* Prof art, Adelphi Univ, 69, prof emer, 2006-. *Bibliog:* Irma B Jaffe (auth), Selected Silent Poems, Art News, 93; Jan Marunouchi (auth), Selected Silent Poems (catalog), 94; articles In: Asian Art News, 1/95 & Archit Digest, 5/96; Helen A Harrison (auth), Monumental landscapes, NY Times, 8/97; Europ 'Geneve Art, L'Arten Toute Liberté, 4/2001; Helen A Harrison (auth), Monumental Landscapes. *Mem:* Art League Long Island; Heckscher Mus Art. *Media:* Acrylic, Oil, Charcoal. *Publ:* The New York Art Rev, American References, 88. *Dealer:* Jain Marunouchi Gallery New York NY; Alpan Gallery Huntington NY. *Mailing Add:* 4 Lloyd Lane Huntington NY 11743

VAZQUEZ, PAUL
PAINTER
b Brooklyn, NY, Sept 19, 1933. *Study:* Ohio Wesleyan Univ, BFA, 56; Univ Ill, MFA (Kate Neal Kinley Fel), 57. *Work:* Univ Ill, Urbana; Ball State Teachers Col, Muncie, Ind; New Britain Mus, Conn; Butler Inst Am Art, Ohio. *Exhib:* Solo exhibs, Paley & Lowe Gallery, 71-73, shows in Koln Ger & Madrid, Spain, 75, David Findlay Gallery, NY, 76-80; Kipa Contemp Art (catalog), London Eng, 87-88; Galerie LaMaiginere, Paris, 90; Barnard-Biderman, NY, 96; Andre Zarre Gallery, New York City, 2004-05; and others. *Teaching:* Instr art hist, Bennett Col, 63-66; asst prof humanities, Western Conn State Col, 66-69; prof drawing & painting, Univ Bridgeport, 69-89. *Awards:* Purchase Award, Butler Inst Am Art, 58; Conn Comn Arts Grant for Painting, 74; Artist Sponsorship Prog, NY Found Arts, 92-05. *Bibliog:* Virginia Mann (auth), article, Arts Mag, 2/78; Robert Sievert (auth), article, Arts Mag, 2/80; Lilly Wei (auth), essay, exhib catalog, critic, Art Am, Art News. *Media:* Acrylic oil, Watercolor. *Publ:* From Irony to Laughter, An Art Book of Images and Poems, Upstream Press, 2005. *Mailing Add:* 100 Bank St Apt 3H New York NY 10014-2123

VECA, MARK DEAN
PAINTER
b Shreveport, Louisiana, 1963. *Study:* Otis Art Inst, Los Angeles, BFA, 1985. *Exhib:* Solo exhibs include Kravets/Wehby Gallery, New York, 1998, DiverseWorks Art Space, Houston, 1999, Daniel Silverstein Gallery, New York, 2002, Mars Gallery, Tokyo, 2003, Picturing Florida, Schmidt Ctr Gallery, Boca Raton, Fla, 2006; group exhibs include A Farewell to Bridal District, Los Angeles Contemp Exhibs, 1985;

Wall Drawings, Drawing Ctr, New York, 1997; Good Business is Best Art, Bronx Mus Arts, NY, 2000; Labor Day, RARE, New York, 2003; Open House, Brooklyn Mus Art, NY, 2004; Erotic Drawing, DiverseWorks, Houston, 2005; Otis, Los Angeles Munic Art Gallery, 2006. *Awards:* New York Found Arts Fel, 1998, 2002, 2008; Pollock-Krasner Found Grant, 2006. *Dealer:* Daniel Silverstein Gallery 520 W 21st St New York NY 10011; Merry Karnowsky Gallery 170 S La Brea Ave Los Angeles CA 90036

VEERKAMP, PATRICK BURKE
EDUCATOR, CERAMIST
b Joplin, Mo, Nov 22, 1943. *Study:* Adams State Col, BA, 66; Univ Denver, MA, 76; Colo State Univ, MFA, 81. *Work:* Colo State Univ, Ft Collins; E Tenn State Univ, Johnson City; Abilene Fine Art Mus; Southwestern Univ. *Exhib:* Rutgers National Drawing '79, Rutgers Univ, Camden, NJ, 79; 37th Ann Painting Competition, Abilene Fine Arts Mus, Tex, 81; Seventh Ann Ceramic Invitational, Weber State Col, Ogden, Utah, 81; Works on Paper, E Carolina State Univ, Greenville, NC, 81; Kansas Sixth National, Ft Hays State Univ, Kans, 81; two-person show, Univ Wis, Parkside, 83; Positive-Negative, Slocumb Gallery, E Tenn State Univ, 85; Marriage a la Mode: The Aesthetics of Mating, Wustum Mus Fine Art, Racine, Wis, 86; Form / Function Invitational, Univ Tex, 98; The Earthmen Vessel III, Baylor Univ, 99; Attachments 2000, San Angelo Mus; Northern Exposure: Texas Clay, Univ Dallas, 2002. *Pos:* Assoc dir, Spec Visual Arts Prog, Colo State Univ, Ft Collins, 81-82. *Teaching:* Instr art, Mesa Col, Grand Junction, Colo, 73-78 & N Idaho Col, Coeur d'Alene, 82-83; prof art, Southwestern Univ, Georgetown, Tex, 83-. *Mem:* Nat Coun Art Adminrs; Coll Art Asn. *Media:* Drawing; Ceramics. *Mailing Add:* Southwestern Univ Dept Art 1001 E University Ave Georgetown TX 78626

VEGA, CARLOS
PAINTER
Study: Univ Fine Arts, St Isabel of Hungary, Seville, Spain, 1983-86; Univ Fine Arts, San Fernando, Madrid, 1986-88; Summer Acad, Limpesberg, Luxembourg, European Parliament Fel (Engraving), 1986; Talleres de Arte Actual, Circulo de Bellas Artes, Madrid, 1988-90; Art Inst Chicago, 1990-91. *Work:* Pizzuti Co, Columbus, Oh; Rennie Coll, Vancouver, Can; Palacio de los Condes de Gabia, Grenada, Spain; Harvard Business Sch, Boston, Mass; Progressive Art Coll, Mayfield Village, Oh; Instituto Cervantes, NY; Columbia Business Sch, NY. *Exhib:* Solo exhibs include Lorenzo Rodriguez Gallery, Chicago, 1994, Jack Shainman Gallery, New York, 2001, 2003, 2004, 2008, 2011, 2012, Palacio de los Condes de Gabia, Granada, Spain, 2002, Lux Art Inst, Encinitas, Calif, 2013; group exhibs include Moving the Body Forward, Lorenzo Rodriguez Gallery, Chicago, 1991; The Curiosity Room, Jack Shainman Gallery, New York, 1997, Simultaneous, 2000, Starry Night, 2001, Untitled, 2002, A Charge to Keep, 2004, The Whole World is Rotten, 2005; Doman, Islip Art Mus, East Islip, NY, 1998, Travelers, 2003; Talavera Contemporanea, Ctr Cult San Francisco, Puebla, Mex, 1999; Realidad al Vacio, Salvador Diaz Gallery, Madrid, 2001; The City: Contemo Views of the Built Environment, Lehman Coll Art Gallery, Bronx, NY, 2005; The Whole World is Rotten, Contemp Arts Ctr, Cincinnati, 2006; Black Panther Rank & File, Yerba Buena Ctr Arts, San Francisco, 2006; Carlos Vega: If These Walls Could Speak, Palacio de los Condes de Gabia, Spain; Apocrifos, Instituto de América, Centro Damian Banyon, Granada, Spain, 2008; Lux Art Inst, Encinitas, Calif, 2013. *Pos:* artist in res, Lux Art Inst, Encinitas, Calif, 2013. *Bibliog:* Artist Carlos Vega: Fall Residency 2012, Flying Horse, 2013; Chicago Challenged Him to Think about Art, San Diego Union Tribune, 2013. *Mailing Add:* Jack Shainman Gallery 513 W 20th St New York NY 10011

VEGA, EDWARD
SCULPTOR, EDUCATOR
b Deming, NMex, Oct 13, 1938. *Study:* NMex State Univ, Las Cruces, BFA, 68; Univ NMex, Albuquerque, MA, 70; lithog with Garo Antreasian; drawing with Ilya Bolotowsky; sculpture with Charlie Mattox. *Work:* Eastern NMex Univ, Roswell; St Joseph Hosp, Albuquerque; Mus Albuquerque; Roswell Mus. *Comn:* City of Albuquerque, NMex. *Exhib:* Graphics '73, Western NMex Univ, Silver City; 50th Regional Art Exhib, Shreveport, La, 73; Goy Gallery, Santa Fe, NMex, 78; Roswell Mus, 79; Santa Fe Festival of the Arts, 79; and others. *Pos:* NMex Arts Comn chmn, 79. *Teaching:* Asst prof sculpture, drawing, Univ Albuquerque, 76-86. *Awards:* Third Place Purchase Award Sculpture, Univ NMex, 75; Res Grant Sculpture, NMex State Univ, 75; Artist-in-Residence Fel, Roswell Art Ctr; Finalist, five major sculpture comns, 85-86. *Media:* Steel, Wood. *Mailing Add:* 618 Roehl Rd NW Albuquerque NM 87107

VEGARA, CAMILO JOSE
PHOTOGRAPHER
Study: Univ Notre Dame, BA Sociology, 1968; Columbia Univ, MA Sociology, 1977. *Awards:* Nat Humanities medal, 2013; Revson fellow, Columbia Univ, 86-87, MacArthur Foundation Fellow, 2002, Berlin Prize Fellowship, 2010. *Publ:* Co-Auth Silent Cities: The Evolution of the American Cemetery, 1989; auth The New American Ghetto, 95 (Robert E Park award, Am Sociological Asn, 97), American Ruins, 99, Unexpected Chicagoland, 2001, Twin Towers Remembered, 2001, Subway Memories, 2004, How the Other Half Worships, 2005; contributor Loud Paper Magazine

VEKRIS, BABIS A
KINETIC ARTIST, SCULPTOR
b Tripolis, Greece, Aug 10, 1950; US citizen. *Study:* NY Studio Sch (Ford Found grant), 79-82; Studies in US and Europe, 87-88. *Work:* Reading Pub Mus, Pa; Goulandris Mus Art, Andros, Greece; Hunterdon Mus Art, Clinton, NJ; Mus Moderner Kunst, Passau, Ger; Egon Schiele Art Centrum, Krumlov, Czech Republic; sculpture, Haffmann La Roche, Basel, Switzerland, 96. *Comn:* sculpture, Leube Group, Gartenau, Austria, 95; monument, Sanyo-Carrefour Plaza, Athens, Greece, 99; monument, City of Athens, 2000. *Exhib:* The Digital Series, Museo Del Chopo, Mexico City, Mex, 91; Artec '95 Int Biennale, Mus Sci, Nagoya, Japan, 95; NJ Arts Ann, Newark Mus, 97; Forces, Contemp Art Mus Va, Virginia Beach, 97; Art for the End of the 20th Century, Bellevue Art Mus, Wash, 98; 9th Int Contemp Art Competition, Mydome Osaka, Japan, 98; The Kinetic Spectrum, Mus Moderner Kunst, Passau, Ger, 99; Modern Odysseys, Queens Mus, NY, 99. *Media:* Electronic components, Light sound; Metal

VELARDE, KUKULI
CERAMIST
Study: Hunter Coll, Univ New York, BFA (magna cum laude), 1992. *Exhib:* Solo exhibs, Inst Technol, New York, 1992, Univ Mich Mus Art, 1996, Long Island Univ, 1998, Int Biennial Lima, Peru, 1999, JOhn MIchael Kohler Arts Ctr, Wis, 2001; Remerica America, Leubsdorf Art Gallery, Hunter Coll, 1992; Testimonio, New Mus Contemp Art, New York, 1993; Beyond the Borders: Art by Recent Immigrants, Bronx Mus Arts, 1994; Hereos and Heroines, NJ Ctr for Visual Arts, 1995; Monsters and Wonders, De Cordoba Mus, Lincoln, Mass, 2001; Home/land: Artists, Immigration, and Identity, Soc for Contemp Craft, Pittsburgh, 2003; Uber Portraits, Bellevue Mus Arts, Wash, 2009. *Awards:* Joan Mithcell Found Grant, New York, 1997; Evelyn Shapiro Found Fel, Pa, 1998; Anonymous is a Woman award, 2000; Pew Ctr for Arts Fel, 2003; US Artists Knight Fel, 2009

VELASQUEZ, OSCAR
PAINTER, ILLUSTRATOR
b Pharr, Tex, Apr 5, 1945. *Study:* Cooper Sch Art, AA, 65. *Work:* Joslyn Art Mus, Omaha; Nat Acad Design-Henry Ward Ranger, NY; Erskine Col, Due West, SC; Opera House, Abbeville, SC. *Comn:* Lion & Lamb Peace Ctr, Bluffton, Ohio; Erskine Col, Due West, SC; BEMIS Art Ctr, Omaha, Nebr. *Exhib:* Ga Watercolor Soc, High Mus, Atlanta, 79; SC Watercolor Soc, Greenville Mus Art; Am Watercolor Soc, Columbia Mus Art, SC, 79; Camden Art Mus, SC, 83; Sumter Art Mus, SC, 83; Cannon Bldg, Capitol, Washington, DC, 83; and others. *Awards:* High Winds Medal, 75 & Silver Medal of Honor, 77, Am Watercolor Soc; Georgia Gold Award, Watercolor Soc, 81. *Mem:* Am Watercolor Soc; SC Watercolor Soc; Southern Watercolor Asn; Ga Watercolor Soc. *Media:* Watercolor, Acrylic; Oils. *Publ:* The New Spirit of Watercolor, Northlight Books; Exploring Color, Northlight Books

VELASQUEZ , ROXANA
MUSEUM DIRECTOR
Mex. *Study:* Universidad Iberoamericana, BA (art history); Ariz State Univ & Instituto Tecnologico Autonomo de Mexico, MBA. *Pos:* chief curator, European art collection, Museo Nacional de San Carlos, 1990-1997, dir, 1997, Museo Nacional de Arte, Museo del Palacio de Bellas Artes, Mexico City, 2007-2011; Maruja Baldwin exec dir, San Diego Mus Art, 2010-. *Mailing Add:* San Diego Museum of Art PO Box 122107 San Diego CA 92112-2107

VELDERS, DEBORAH
MUSEUM DIRECTOR
Study: Attended Univ Md, 1969-1971; Univ Houston, BA (Art Hist), MA (English & Am Lit). *Comn:* Melchin, 2008. *Exhib:* Five American Artists, 2006; William Ivey Long, 2007; Robert Delford Brown, 2008; Charles Gwathmey, 2009; Crafts in the 21st Century, 2010. *Pos:* Registrar Nat Collections Fine Arts, Smithsonian Inst, Washington, 1976-1978, mus specialist, Nat Collection Fine Arts, 1978-1980; exhibs/performance dir, Mus Temporary Art, Washington, 1977-1979; dir, Arlington Arts Ctr, Va, 1979-1980; conservation res assoc, Dept Conservation Menil Collection, Houston, 1985-1989; head, exhibs & pub progs, 1989-2005; dir, Cameron Art Mus, Wilmington, NC, 2005-. *Mem:* mem, adv bd, DiverseWorks Alternative Artspace, Houston, 1986-1989; mem, strategic planning comt, Cultural Arts Coun Houston & Harris Counties, 1998-1999; mem, curriculum adv bd, English Dept, Univ Houston, 2000-2005; bd dirs, Creative Wilmington, 2007-, *Res:* William Blake; Robt Delford Brown; Minnie Evans. *Interests:* Art, Literature, Dance. *Collection:* Fine Arts, Crafts, Design (18th-21st Century). *Mailing Add:* Cameron Art Mus 3201 S 17th St Wilmington NC 28412

VELEZ, EDIN
VIDEO ARTIST
b Arecibo, PR, Sept 3, 1951. *Study:* Univ PR, 69-70; Inst Bellas Artes, 70; Inst Puerto Rican Cult Sch Fine Arts. *Work:* Mus Mod Art, NY; Stedjelik Mus Art, Amsterdam, Neth; Ithaca Mus Art, NY. *Comn:* Oblique Strategist Too, 85 & Naruhodo (installation), 87, NY State Coun Arts, NY; AS IS (video essay), 85, Meaning of the Interval (video doc), 87 & Dance of Darkness (video doc), 88, Nat Endowment Arts, Washington, DC. *Exhib:* III Festival Int D'Art, Locarno, Switz, 82; Whitney Mus Am Art Biennial, NY, 83; Video Art: A History, 84 & Video Viewpoint, 86, Mus Mod Art, NY; Cinema Du Reel, Pompidou Ctr, Paris, France, 85; Arts for Television, Stedjelik Mus Art, Amsterdam, 87-88; Int Pub Television Conf, Granada, Spain, 87 & Philadelphia, Pa, 88; Image Forum Film & Video Festival, Tokyo, Japan, 89; Nagoya Mus, Japan, 89; Video and the Computer, Mus Mod Art, NY, 89; Louvre Mus, Paris, France, 90; Elected Affinities, Cronis Gallery, NY, 90; and others internationally. *Awards:* Fel, Guggenheim Found & US/Japan Friendship Comn; Grants, Nat Endowment Arts, Jerome Found & NY State Coun Arts; First Prize, First Latino Film & Video Festival, 88; Maya Deren Award, Am Film Inst, 90. *Bibliog:* Victor Ancona (auth), Edin Velez: In essence a romantic realist, Videography, 83; Image Forum (auth), Edin Velez, video artist, Video Culture, Japan, 86; John Wallace (auth), Innovation: It's a primary color on the video, NY Times, 87. *Mem:* Asn Independent Video & Filmmakers. *Dealer:* Electronic Arts Intermix 536 Broadway New York NY 10012; Tape Connection Via P Querini 3 Roma Italy

VELICK, BRUCE
CURATOR
b Los Angeles, Calif, Jan 29, 1949. *Study:* Univ Calif, Davis, BA (design), 71. *Pos:* Dir, Bruce Velick Eds, Mill Valley, Calif & New York, currently. *Specialty:* Contemporary art

VELICK, PAUL See Bob & Bob

VENA, DANTE
EDUCATOR, PRINTMAKER
b 1930. *Study:* Univ Wis, BS, 57, MS, 60; Univ Iowa, PhD, 76. *Work:* Milwaukee Art Ctr; Montgomery Mus, Ala; Bellarmine Col, Louisville; Nazareth Col, Ky; Ball State Univ, Ind. *Comn:* Wall mural (map), Customs House, New Orleans, 58; illus, Motive Mag, Nashville, 60; Keenland (illus), Ford Times Mag, 63; A Child is Born (cover illus), Companion Mag, 63; wall mural, Ohio Univ, Portsmouth, 68. *Exhib:* 14th Nat Exhib Prints, Libr Congress, Washington, DC, 56; 152nd Ann Exhib, Pa Acad Fine Arts, 57; 29th Int Exhib Northwest Printmakers, Seattle Art Mus, 57; 24th Ann Mid-Year Show, Butler Inst Am Art, 59; 65th Ann Western Artists, Denver Art Mus, 59; Nat Mus Wales, Cardiff, S Wales, 66; solo exhib, Bell Gallery, Belfast, N Ireland, 66; Southeastern Mass Univ Art Gallery, 72-91; group shows, Visual Images Gallery, New Bedford, 91 & 92; Hundred Languages of Children, Univ Mass, Dartmouth, 97. *Collection Arranged:* Alfred Sessler Retrospective Show, 61; A Town and its Artists, Portsmouth, 68; Artists Inmates, Portsmouth Gallery, 69. *Pos:* Framework curric comt, Mass Dept Educ, 93-96; exec coun, Mass Art Educ Asn, 94-95, Mass Alliance for Arts Educ; chairperson, Art, Music, Technol and Educ Conf, 94; dir, Art Educ Summer Inst, Nat Workshop Teachers, 98. *Teaching:* Art dir, Bellarmine Col, Louisville, Ky, 61-67; chmn art educ dept, Univ Mass, Dartmouth, 81-97. *Awards:* Fulbright to Italy, 53; Mrs Arthur Osborn Purchase Award, Ball State Univ, 63; New Bedford Arts Coun, 89; Research Fel, Edith Cowan Univ, Perth, Western Australia, 91. *Bibliog:* Cottie Burland (auth), Dante Vena-Artist Own Gallery, Arts Rev, 1/22/66. *Mem:* Nat Acad NY; Nat Art Educ Asn; Fairhaven Arts Coun (chmn, 81-83); Mass Asn Sch Comts; Bd Educ Fairhaven, Mass (chmn, 87-88). *Publ:* Auth, Contemporary Art, Irish-Am, 63; Learning Out There: A Program, Art Educ, 75; Integrated Arts in the Elementary Classroom, Charles Thomas Pub; Video Project, Integrated Arts in Schools, 91-92. *Mailing Add:* University of Massachusetts Dartmouth Dept Art Education 285 Old Westport Rd Dartmouth MA 02747

VENABLE, CHARLES L
MUSEUM DIRECTOR
Study: Rice Univ, Houston, BA (Am Hist & Art Hist); Univ Del, Newark, MA (Fine Arts & Decorative Arts); Boston Univ, PhD (Am Studies). *Pos:* Dallas Mus Art, 1986-2002, asst cur, dept dir; dept dir collections & progs, Cleveland Art Mus, 2002-2007; dir, CEO Speed Art Mus, Louisville, 2007-2012; Melvin & Bren Simon Dir, CEO, Indianapolis Mus Art, 2012-. *Publ:* Author, American Furniture in the Bybee Collection, 1989 (Charles F. Montgomery award), Silver in America, 1840-1940: A Century of Splendor, 1994 (Montgomery prize), China and Glass in America, 1880-1980, 2000

VENABLE, SUSAN C
SCULPTOR, PAINTER
b Calif, Dec 30, 1944. *Study:* Calif State Univ, BFA, 82; Univ Calif, Los Angeles, MFA, 85. *Work:* Horoko Nakamoto, Tokoyo, Japan; Payden & Rygel, Los Angeles, Calif; Bear Stearns & Co, Los Angeles, Calif; Sudler-Marlins, Chicago, Ill; US Army, Honolulu, Hawaii. *Comn:* Lobby installations, Pac Plaza, Walnut Creek, Calif, 87, Hotel Nikko, Chicago, Ill, 87, Metroplex Wilshire, Los Angeles, 89, Western Digital Corp, Irvine, Calif, 90; auditorium installation, IBM, Atlanta, Ga, 88. *Exhib:* Group shows, Fiber Revolution, Witchita Art Mus, 87, Boulder Ctr Art, 89, SITE, Los Angeles, 89, Off the Wall, Los Angeles Co Mus Art, 90, Monotypes, Ariz State Univ Mus, 90; solo shows, New Work, Tally Richards, NMex, Mahoney/Butler, Calif, 89, Square & Square, Scottsdale Ctr Arts, Ariz, 90 & Sun Art Mus, Phoenix, Ariz, 92. *Awards:* Dean's Discretionary, 82, Fishbaugh Mem, 83, Univ Calif, Los Angeles. *Bibliog:* Michel Thomas (auth), Textiles/Art/Language, Architecture 85, France; Michael Webb (auth), Poetry in Concrete, Inside Mag, Japan, 6/90; Cover & Feature Article: Seasons Mag, 8/2004; Feature Article, TRENDS Mag, 4/2005. *Media:* Mixed; Encaustic, Oil. *Dealer:* Sherwood Gallery, Laguna Beach, CA. *Mailing Add:* 2323 Foothill Ln Santa Barbara CA 93105

VENEGAS, HAYDEE E
CONSULTANT
b Arecibo, PR, Mar 4, 1950. *Study:* Univ PR, BA (art hist), 73; Fla State Univ, MA (mod art), 78. *Collection Arranged:* Francisco Oller: A Realist Impressionist, 83; La Moda en Puerto Rico, 85; Obra Uica sobre papel, 85; 25 anos de pintura Puertoriquena, 86; Quijano & Roche, 88; Irene Delano, 89; Antonio Nania, 92. *Pos:* Dir, Mus Fundacion Arqueologica, 76-79, Permanent Fund for Arts, 92-; asst dir, Ponce Art Mus, 80-88; pres, Concultura, 88-92. *Teaching:* Vis prof Puerto Rican art, Inter-Am Univ, summer 75, Escuelade Artes Plasticas, 90-91 & Escuela Hotelera, 92. *Awards:* Leon de Oro Award, 84. *Bibliog:* Connie Underhill (auth), The museum as a place, San Juan Star, Sunday Mag, 12/30/79; Mario Alegre (auth), Voluntades que Convergen, El Nuevo Dia, 4/14/90; Puerto Rican Art Phasing the End of the Century, Caribbean Art, Badajoz, Spain, 98. *Mem:* Int Comt Mus; Coll Art Asn; Asn of Latin-Am Historians; Int Asn Art Critics (bd dir, 92, 95-96, vpres, 97-). *Res:* Puerto Rican art; Francisco Oller, 19th century painter. *Publ:* Contribr, Juan Ramon Valazquez, El Mundo, 78; El Velorio: Propuesta para una reinterpretacion, Plastica, 79; auth, Francisco Oller: Profile of a Puerto Rican Painter, Mus Art Ponce, 83, Oller in Cuba: Horizontes, 85, Irene Delano, 89

VENET, BERNAR
SCULPTOR, CONCEPTUAL ARTIST
b France, Apr 20, 1941. *Study:* Sch Villa Thiole, Nice, France, 57-58. *Work:* Mus Nat Art Mod, Ctr Georges Pompidou, Paris; Neue Galerie Alten Kurhaus, Aachen, WGer; La Jolla Mus Contemp Art; Akron Art Inst, Ohio; Musee du Quebec, Can. *Comn:* tallest steel sculpture, France, 86; sculpture, Goodmann Gegar Hogan, Norfolk, Va, 87; sculpture, French Gout & Air France, Berlin, WGer, 88; Acropolis, Nice, France; Beijing Silver Tower Real Estate Develop Co, China; mural, ceiling of Galerie du Palais Cambon of the Cour des Comptes, Paris, 2007. *Teaching:* Instr, La Sorbonne, Paris, France, 73-75. *Awards:* Grand Prix des Arts de la Ville de Paris, 90; Commandeur dans l'ordre des Arts et Lettres, awarded by the Minister of Culture, France, 1996; Chevalier de la Légion d'honneur, France, 2005; Robert Jacobsen Prize in Sculpture, Wurth Stiftung Germany, 2006. *Bibliog:* Catherine Millet (auth), Bernar Venet, Chene, France & Prearo, Italy, 75; J Pierre Mirouze (producer), film, WDR, WGer, 75; Seth Schneidman (producer), film, Seven Hills Productions, 83. *Media:* Wood Reliefs, Corten Steel. *Dealer:* Robert Miller Gallery 524 West 26th St New York NY 10001

VENEZIA, MICHAEL
PAINTER
b Brooklyn, NY, July 23, 1935. *Study:* State Univ NY, Buffalo, BS, 63; Univ Mich, Ann Arbor, MFA, 68. *Work:* Mus Mod Art, NY; Nat Gallery Can, Ottawa; Mus Modbuer Kunst, Otterndorf, Ger; Solomon R Guggenheim Mus, NY; Detroit Inst Arts; Australian Nat Gallery, Canberra; Kunstmuseum Winterthur, Switz; Hartford Atheneum, Conn. *Exhib:* Works on Paper, Mus Mod Art, NY, 74; solo exhibs, Paintings, Bykert Gallery, NY, 73, Sperone Westwater Fisher Inc, NY, 79, Fred Hoffman Gallery, Santa Monica, Calif, 91, Umberg Rictveld, Ameusfoout, The Neth, 95, paintings 1970-1995 (with catalog), Kunstmuseum, Winterthur, Switz, 96 & Galericmeert-Rhioux, Brussels, 96; Two Artists: Dan Hill & Michael Venezia, Whitney Mus Art, NY, 77; Artists & Friends: Dan Flavin & Michael Venezia, Contemp Arts Ctr, Cincinnati, Ohio, 77; Drawings About Drawing Today, Acklund Art Mus, Chapel Hill, NC, 79; Selected Paintings 1969-1980, Detroit Inst Arts, 80; Carol Taylor-Art Inc, Dallas, Tex, 81 & 84; Paintings 1972-1983, Dia Found, Dan Flavin Art Inst, Bridgehampton, NY, 83; Biennale Artumbra, Foligno, Italy, 86; New Paintings, Margaret Roeder Gallery, NY, 87; Margaret Roeder Gallery, NY, 88; Frankfurt Art Fair, Ger, 89; Surface in Proportion, Margaret Roeder Gallery, NY, 90; Fred Hoffman Gallery, Santa Monica, Calif, 91; Michael Venezia, Rubin Spangle Gallery, NY, 92; Michael Venezia, Glan Enzo Sperone, Rome, Italy, 92; Westfalischeu Funstuenein, Munsten, Ger, 97; Heike Curtze, Dusseldorf, Ger, 98. *Teaching:* Vis lectr fine arts, Guildford Col, Surrey, Eng, 66-67, London Col Printing, 66-67; from asst prof to prof fine arts, Univ Rochester, NY 68-; prof art, Univ Rochester, 85-. *Awards:* Creative Artists Pub Serv Award, NY Coun Arts, State Univ NY, Fredonia, 75; Tiffany Found Award for Painting, 79; Artist Fel Painting, Nat Endowment Arts, 81-82. *Bibliog:* Helen A Harrison (auth), His paintings stress the paint, NY Times, Long Island Weekly, 11/27/83; David Carrier (auth), Michael Venezia, Tema Celeste, 80, spring 93; Alfred Corn (auth), Art in America, 1/97. *Media:* Powdered Metals, Glass and Pigments on Wood and Paper. *Dealer:* Stark Gallery 113 Crosby St New York NY 10012

VENN, BETH A
CURATOR
Study: Univ Del, MA (Am art hist), 1993. *Collection Arranged:* A Year from the Collection: Circa 1952, 1994; Edward Hopper and the American Imagination, 1995; Joseph Cornell: Cosmic Travels, 1995-96; Making Mischief: Dada Invades New York, 1996. *Pos:* Cur, Whitney Mus Am Art, 1993-2000; cur Mod & Contemp art & sr cur Am art, Newark Mus, 2000-. *Mailing Add:* 49 Washington St Newark NJ 07102

VENTIMIGLIA, JOHN THOMAS
SCULPTOR, EDUCATOR
b Augusta, Maine, Jan 12, 1943. *Study:* Skowhegan Sch Paint & Sculpture, 64, Sch Art, Syracuse Univ, BFA, 65; Rinehart Sch, Md Inst Art, MFA (sculpture), 67. *Work:* Portland Mus Art; Portland Pub Libr; Mt Holyoke Col; Chateau de Rochefort-en-Terre, France. *Comn:* Agavney Johnson Mem Sculpture, Portland Pub Libr, 81; The Cedars Home, Tree of Life, Portland, Maine, 91; Terzian Meml Sculpture, Mt Holyoke Coll Libr, South Hadley, Mass, 95. *Exhib:* Barn Gallery, Ogunquit, Maine, 77; Maine Coast Artists, Rockport; Barridoff Galleries; Round Top Ctr for Arts, Damariscotta, Maine; Icon Galleries, Brunswick, Maine. *Pos:* Chmn Sculpture Dept, Portland Sch Art, 1972-98; cur, Outdoor Sculpture Exhib Series, Portland Sch Art, 1973-78; adv panelist, Maine State Comn Arts & Humanities, 1981-85; restoration adv, Simmons Civil War Monument, Portland, Maine, 1997. *Teaching:* Prof sculpture, 3D design & drawing, Maine Col Art, Portland, 1972-. *Awards:* Scholar, Showhegan Sch Painting & Sculpture, 64; Artist Residency in Brittany, Klotz Found, Rochefort-en-Terre, France, 1997. *Bibliog:* 76 Maine Artists (exhib catalog), Maine State Bicentennial Comn, 76; Maine Art Now, Beam, 90. *Media:* Bronze, Mixed Materials, Wood. *Dealer:* Icon Gallery Brunswick ME. *Mailing Add:* 41 Pleasant Ave Portland ME 04103-3217

VENTURA, ANTHONY
PAINTER
b Southampton, NY, Jan 24, 1927. *Study:* Acad Arts, Newark NJ, BFA, 51; Pratt Inst, Brooklyn, NY, 52-53; Art Students League, NY, 54-55; studied with Robert Brackman, Ivan Olinsky, Edgar Whitney, Edmond Fitzgerald & Avery Johnson. *Work:* Ft Schlyer Maritime Mus, Bronx, NY; Am Can Co, Chicago, Ill; Hershey Corp, Pa; Winsor-Newton Co, Secaucus, NJ; Zhejiang Mus, China. *Exhib:* Tweed Mus, Duluth, Minn, 77; Am Watercolor Soc, NY, 82; Frye Mus, Seattle, 83; Am Artist Prof League, NJ, 87, 95-99, 2001-2010, 2011-2013; Salmagundi Club, NY, 96-99, 2001-2010; NJ Watercolor Soc, 96, 98, 99, 2001-2012; Am Watercolor Soc, 2012, 2013. *Pos:* Adv Comt Guild, Guild Creative Art, Shrewsbury, NJ, 80-84; pres, NJ Watercolor Soc, 86-87; off artist for US Coast Guard. *Teaching:* Workshops, demonstrations and lectures to art organizations throughout New Jersey and at own studio-gallery. *Awards:* Silver Medal Honor, NJ Watercolor Soc, 95, 98-2002; Am Artists Prof League Awards, 99-2006, 2007-2010, 2011, 2012, 2013, 2014; Salmagundi Club Awards, NY, 96, 98-2009; Am Watercolor Soc, Jury of Selection, 2014. *Bibliog:* Listed in-Judge and Jury Selector of Federated Art Asn, NJ; COGAP, Artist for US Coast Guard. *Mem:* NJ Watercolor Soc (pres, 86-87); Knickerbocker Artist; Salmagundi Club; N Shore Art Asn; Hudson Valley Art Asn; Am Artist Prof League; Garden State Watercolor Soc; Am Watercolor Society (Signature mem 2008). *Media:*

Watercolor, Oil. *Specialty:* Traditional landscapes, seascapes, still lifes. *Interests:* Reading, hiking, photography. *Collection:* Many private collections. *Publ:* Watercolor 95, 98, Am Artists Publ, fall ed; Best of Watercolor, Light & Shade, Rockport Publ, 97; Int Artist Pub, 99; 100 Artists of the Mid-Atlantic, Schiffer Pub, 2011. *Dealer:* Guild Creative Art 620 Broad St Rte 35 Shrewsbury NJ 07702; Lambertville Gallery of Fine Art 20 N Union St Lambertville NJ 08530; Anchor & Palette Gallery 40 Mount St Bay Head NJ 08742; Sea Holly Art Gallery 718 Union Ave Brielle NJ 08730. *Mailing Add:* 3430 Hwy 66 Neptune NJ 07753

VENTURI, ROBERT
ARCHITECT
b Philadelphia, Pa, June 25, 1925. *Study:* Princeton Univ, AB, 1947, MFA, 1950; Rome Prize Fel, Am Acad in Rome, 1954-56. *Hon Degrees:* Oberlin Col, Hon DFA, 1977; Yale Univ, Hon DFA, 1979; Univ Pa, Hon DFA, 1980; Princeton Univ, Hon DFA, 1983; NJ Inst Technol, Hon LHD, 1984; Philadelphia Coll Art, Hon DFA, 1985; Univ NC Chapel Hill, LHD, 1989; Philadelphia Coll Textiles & Sci, LHD, 1992; Laurea honoris causa in Architettura, Univ Rome, La Sapienza, 1994. *Comn:* Gordon & Virginia MacDonald Med Res Labs & UCLA, 86; Sainsbury Wing, Nat Gallery, London, Eng, 91; Hotel Midparque Resort Complex, Nikko, Kirifuri, Japan, 97; Hótel du Département de la Haute-Garonne, Toulouse, France, 99; and many others; First Campus Ctr, Princeton Univ, NJ, 2000; Anlyam Ctr, Yale Univ, 2003; Nano Systems Inst, UC Santa Barbaram 2006; Congregation Beth El Synagogue, Sunbury, Pa, 2007; Lehigh Valley Hosp, Muhlenberg, Bethlehem, Pa, 2008; Episcopal Acad Chapel, Newtown Square, Pa, 2008. *Exhib:* Work of Venturi & Rauch, Whitney Mus Am Art, NY, 71 & Pa Acad Fine Arts, Philadelphia, 75; Venturi, Rauch & Scott Brown, Acad delle Arti del Disegno, Firenze, Italy, 81; Buildings & Drawings, Max Protetch Gallery, NY, 82; A Generation of Architecture, Krannert Art Mus, Univ Ill & traveling, 84-86; High Styles: 20th Century Am Design, Whitney Mus Am Art, NY, 85-86; About Archit, Inst Contemp Art, Univ Pa, 93; Barnes Found Restoration & Renovation, Merion, Pa, 93; Disney Celebration Bank, Celebration, Fla, 93; Out of the Ordinary: Robert Venturi, Denise Scott Brown & Assoc-Architecture, Urbanism, Design, Philadelphia Mus Art, 2001. *Pos:* Partner, Venturi & Rauch, 1964-80; Venturi, Rauch & Scott Brown, 1980-89; Venturi, Scott Brown & Assoc, 1989-; architect-in-residence, Am Acad Rome, 66, trustee, 69-74. *Teaching:* From asst to assoc prof archit, Univ Pa, 57-65; Davenport Prof archit, Yale Univ, 66-70; bd adv, Princeton Univ, Dept Art & Archeol, 77-81; Walter Gropius lectr, Harvard Univ, Grad Sch Design, 82; Eero Saarinen vis prof archit design, Yale Univ, Sch Archit, 86-87. *Awards:* Pritzker Archit Prize, Hyatt Found, 91; US Presidential Award, Nat Medal Arts, 92; Commandeurde l'Oedre des Arts et Lettres, Republique Francaise, Minde la Cult and Commun, 2001; Vincent J Scully prize, Nat Bldg Mus (with Denise Scott Brown), 2002; Nat Design Mind award, Cooper-Hewitt, Nat Design Mus (with Denise Scott Brown), 2007; and others. *Bibliog:* Stanislaus von Moos (auth), Venturi, Scott Brown, and Associates: Buildings and Projects, 1986-1997, Monacelli, 2000; David Brownlee, David G. De Long & Kathryn B Hiesinger (coauths), Out of the Ordinary: Architecture/Urbanism/Design, Yale Univ Press, 2001; and many others. *Mem:* Fel Am Acad Rome; Fel Am Inst Archit; Fel Accademia Nazionale di San Luca; Fel Am Acad Arts & Sci; Hon Fel Royal Incorp Architects Scotland; and others. *Publ:* Complexity & Contradiction in Architecture, 66, 2nd ed, 77; coauth (with Denise Scott Brown & Steven Izenour), Learning from Las Vegas, 72, 2nd ed, 77; coauth (with Denise Scott Brown), A View from the Campidoglio: Selected Essays 1953-84, 84; Iconography & Electronics Upon a Generic Architecture, 96; Architecture as Signs & Systems for a Mannerist Time, 2004; and others. *Mailing Add:* Venturi Scott Brown & Assoc 4236 Main St Philadelphia PA 19127-1696

VERENE, CHRIS
MULTIMEDIA ARTIST
b Galesburg, Ill, Oct 29, 1969. *Study:* Ga State Univ, MFA, 96. *Work:* The Whitney Mus Am Art, NY; The High Mus Art, Atlanta, Ga; Metrop Mus Art; Walker Mus Art; Mus of Contemp Photog; San Francisco Mus Mod Art; Jewish Mus Art; Mus Contemporary Art Los Angeles. *Comn:* Jewish Mus, NY. *Exhib:* The Whitney Biennial, NY, 2000; Do You Hear What We Hear, Paul Morris Gallery, NY, 2000; Camera Club, Reflex Modern Art Gallery, Amsterdam, 2000; Uneasy, Howard Yezerski, Boston, 2001; A Way With Words, Whitney Mus Am Art at Phillip Morris, NY, 2001; Photographs, Cherry Street Temporary Gallery, Galesburg, Ill, 2001; What's New, Whitney Mus Am Art, NY, 2001; Vereni, Escapista!, Times Square, NY, 2001; Postmasters, New York, 2010. *Teaching:* adj prof, Atlanta Col Art, 98-99, MFA Photog and Related Media, Sch Visual Art, NY, 2001; prof, Int Ctr Photog, NY, 2001; guest lectr, Bard Col, NY, 2001. *Awards:* Jackson Pollock / Barbra Krasner award, 2002. *Bibliog:* Catherine St Louis (auth), What They Were Thinking, NY Times Mag, 6/17/01; Chris Verene, Monograph, Twin Palms Press, 2000; Rachel Kushner (auth), Openings: Chris Verene, Artforum, 2001; Johanna Lehan (auth), The Great Verene, Photo District News, 2001; Parkett, AM Homes (auth), 2002; Art Forum, 2004 & 2007. *Mem:* Soc for Photog Educ. *Media:* Narrative Photography, Costumes, video performance. *Dealer:* Paul Morris Gallery 530 W 25th St 5th Fl New York NY 10001; Deitch Projects 76 Grand St New York NY 10012 . *Mailing Add:* Box 118 442-D Lorimer St Brooklyn NY 11206

VERGANO, LYNN B
PAINTER, LECTURER
b New York, NY, Nov 14. *Study:* New York Univ, BA, MA; Pratt Inst; Studied with Kenneth Cushman & Dr David Kwo. *Work:* Hong Kong Arts Ctr; Am University Alumni, Bankok, Thailand; Princeton Univ, NJ; União Cultural Brasil, Estados Unidos, Brazil; St Sophia Mus, Istanbul, Turkey. *Exhib:* Solo exhibs, Hong Kong Art Ctr, 80, St Sophia Mus, Istanbul, Turkey, 88, American Univ Alumni, Bankok, Thailand, 80, União Cultural Brasil-Estados, Brazil, 82, Hudson River Mus, NY, 2006, Morris Mus, 2006, Venice Art Exhib, Galleria Fenice, Venice, 85, Macculloch Hall Hist Mus, 2006, Morris Mus, 2006, 2011, New York Acad Sci, World Trade Ctr, New York, 2010, UN Pan Pacific & Southeast Women's Asn, New York, 96, 2001, 2007, Delta Kappa Gamma Int, New York, 2010, Hon Soc Educ, Nat Arts Club, 89, Centreplace, Hamilton, New Zealand, 90, Chang Gung mem Hospital, Kaohsiung, Taiwan, 2002, Puebla, Mexico, 2003, Harvard Club, AAUW, NY, 2008, Delta Kappa Gamma Honor Soc for Professional Educ Conference, Stony Brook, NY, 2008; Groups exhibs, Nat Arts Club Mem Exhib, 81-2013, Audubon Soc, NJ State Capital Mus, Trenton, NJ, 79, Morris Mus, 77, 78, 88, 2003, 2009, 2010; Two person exhib, Pan Pacific & SE Asia Women's Asn, United Nations, NY, 2006; Monmouth Mus, Lincroft, 76, 77, 82; Bergen Mus, Paramus, 83; Salmagundi Club, 81, 2009; Macculloch Hall Hist Mus, Morristown, 84, 87, 89, 92, 96; Lincoln Ctr, New York, 87. *Pos:* Pres, trustee, chair of bd dir, Federated Art Asns of NJ, 82-88; mem of exec bd, NJ Chapter, Nat Soc Arts & Letters, 79-. *Teaching:* instr, Morris Co Coll. *Awards:* John H Miller Award, Morris Co Coll, 79; Grumbacher Gold Medallion, Fed Art Asns of NJ, 84; Torch Award, New York Univ, 93; Heydenryk Award, 108th Ann Exhib Artist, Nat Arts Club, 2007; Best in Show, 109th Ann Exhib Artist, Mem's Show, Nat Arts Club, 2008; Woman of Achievement Award, Harvard Club, AAUW, New York, 2008; Nat Arts Club Award, 2011, 2012. *Mem:* Exhib Artist Mem of the Nat Arts Club (81-); Nat Soc Arts & Letters, NJ Chapter (exec bd, 79-); Federated Art Asn of NJ (pres, trustee, chairman bd, 82-88); Nat League of Am Pen Women, New York City Branch; Millburn-Short Hills Art Ctr, NJ; Hudson River Mus (hon mem); Morris Mus Friends (hon mem); Delta Kappa Gamma Int (hon mem); Shanghai Tiffin Club (hon mem). *Media:* Watercolor. *Publ:* Paintings by Lynn Vergano, Franklin Press, 80, 88

VERGNE, PHILIPPE
MUSEUM DIRECTOR
b Troyes, France, 1966. *Study:* Sorbonne, Paris, Doctorate (art hist). *Collection Arranged:* Shake Rattle and Roll: Christian Marclay; How Latitudes Become Forms: Art in a Global Age, 2003; Walk Around Time: Selections from the Permanent Collection; Let's Entertain; Herzog & de Meuron: In Process; Art Performs Life: Merce Cunningham, Meredith Monk, Bill T Jones; Huang Yong Ping: A Retrospective, 2005; co-cur, Whitney Biennial, 2006. *Pos:* Dir, Mus d'Art Contemporain, Marseille, France, 1994-97; cur, visual arts, Walker Art Ctr, 1997-2003, sr cur, 2003-2004, dep dir and chief cur, 2005-2008; dir, François Pinault Found Contemp Art, Paris, 2004-2005, Dia Art Found, New York, 2008-. *Teaching:* Vis critic, Cranbrook Art Acad, Univ Ill, Sch of Art Inst, Chicago. *Awards:* Medal of Chevalier of Order of Arts and Letters, French Govt, 2004; AICA Award for Best Monographic Mus Show, 2008. *Publ:* Contribr to Artforum, Parkett, Asia Pacific mag, as well as other periodicals. *Mailing Add:* Dia Art Found 535 W 22nd St New York NY 10011

VERNON, KAREN
PAINTER, PRINTMAKER, GALLERY OWNER
b El Dorado, Ark, June 11, 1948. *Study:* Univ N Tex Denton, BFA, 72; private study with Robert Wood, 1985, Timothy Clark, 1999, Marilyn Hughey Phyllis, 2000; Art Marketing workshops with Calvin Goodman. *Work:* Corpus Christi Mus, Tex; Crete City Hall, Ill; Walt Disney Corp, Orlando, Fla; Delta Airlines Crown Club, Orlando, Tex; Amoco Corp, Chicago, Ill; Nat PGA Hdqtrs, Jacksonville, Fla; Gallery at Chateau de Vullievens, Switzerland; ECPI Tidewater, Virginia Beach, Va; Techmatics Inc, Fairfax, Va; plus others. *Comn:* Quilt Series (watercolor), Burd Clinic, Beaumont, Tex, 85 & comn by Frank Macher, Ann Arbor, Mich, 86 & 87; Palmestry (watercolor), ECPI Inc, Va Beach, 86; Oriental Suite (watercolor), comn by Gloria Young, Waco, Tex, 87 & Congressman Leath, Washington, DC, 88; 3 paintings (40X60), Royal Family, Saudi Arabia, 97; 3 paintings (48X60), Nat PGA HQ, Jacksonville, Fla, 98; 3 paintings (22X30), Delta Airlines, Orlando, Fla, 99; painting (48X60), Avatar, Orlando, Fla, 2000; 3 paintings (4X6), Moody Gardens Resort, Galveston, Tex, 2000. *Exhib:* Solo exhib, Corpus Christi Mus, Tex, 79, S Ark Art Ctr, El Dorado, 86 & Kershaw Co Art Ctr, Camden, 87; Watercolor Art Soc Houston, traveling exhib, 83; S Ark Art Ctr, El Dorado, 84; 65th Nat Springfield Exhib, 85; Art Alliance Int, El Paso Art Alliance, 85; WASH Int Spring Exhib, 2000; Nat Plein Air Competition, Miami, 2003; Water Media 2003, FWS Exhib, Houston, 2003; Sea to Shining Sea (traveling), Houston, Tex, 2003; Sea to Shining Sea, A Reflection of American, Haggin Mus, 2004; Int Water Media XIV, Colorado Springs, Colo, 2005; Red River Valley Mus, Vernon, Tex, 2006; Tex Watercolor Soc, Lubbock Art Ctr, 2006; ACT Int Exhib Invitational, 2010. *Pos:* Humble Art League, 84-86; sr bd mem, Tex Arts & Craft Found, 85-; dir, Coconut Grove Gallery, 2002-2005; consult & demonstr, Ampersand Art Supply, 2002-; bd dir, Art Guild Rural Tex, 2008, vice pres, 2011. *Teaching:* Art dept dir, Frisco ISD, Tex, 73-74, instr, 78-79; instr & art therapist, Corpus Christi, Tex, 79-84; instr painting, Watercolor Orgn, 80-; instr watercolor, Amarillo Art Ctr, Tex, 85; Hill Country Art Found, Ingram, Tex, 87-88; Toronto Watercolor Soc, 2009, Ore Watercolor Soc, 2010, Fallbrook Art Sch, 2010. *Awards:* Murt Hill Award, S Ark Art Ctr, Amarillo, Tex, 85; Best Floral, Vizcaya Days, Vizcaya Mus & City of Miami, 85; 1st Place Watercolor, Corsicana Nat Art Exhib, Corsicana Art Asn, 86; Best in Show, Boston Mills Art, 2005; 2nd Watercolor Soc, Houston Int, 2008, Tex Watercolor Soc, 2008; and others. *Bibliog:* Cover, Tallascope, 6-8/93; Cover, Metrop Woman, 7/95; Video, Unleashing Dynamic Color in Watercolor, Ampersand Art Supply, Austin, Tex; Beverly Fredericks (auth) Vernon Retrospective: The Art of Monotype (PBS Video). *Mem:* Tex Watercolor Soc (sig mem); Western Fedn Watercolorists; Watercolor Art Soc Houston (sig mem); Birmingham Watercolour Soc, Birmingham, UK (sig mem); Artists Changing Tomorrow (silver status sig mem). *Media:* Watercolor, Acrylic, Oil, Pastel. *Mailing Add:* 2251 FM 50 Rd Brenham TX 77833

VEROSTKO, ROMAN JOSEPH
PAINTER, HISTORIAN
b Tarrs, Pa, Sept 12, 1929. *Study:* Art Inst Pittsburgh, dipl; St Vincent Coll & Seminary, Latrobe, Pa, BA, 55; Pratt Inst, MFA, 61; New York Univ; Columbia Univ; Atelier 17, Paris. *Work:* Ariz State Univ, Tempe; Minneapolis Inst Art; Walker Art Ctr; Mus der Stadt Gladbeck, Ger; Minneapolis Coll Art & Design; Victoria & Albert Mus, London. *Comn:* Mural, Frey Sci & Eng Ctr, Univ St Thomas, St Paul, Minn, 97; Mural, Spalding Univ, Louisville, Ky, Fred Rogers Ctr, Latrobe, Pa, 2008. *Exhib:* Siggraph Art Shows, Dallas, 90, Chicago, 92 & 96, Los Angeles, 95 & 97, ComputerKunst, Gladbeck, Ger, 2000 & 2002, San Diego, 2003; Int Symp Elec Art,

Sydney, 92, Minneapolis, 93, Helsinki, 94 & Manchester, UK, 98; NY Digital Salon, 93, 95 & 96; Artec 95, Nagoya, Japan; Digital Art Mus, Gallery, Berlin, 2005, Algorithmic Revolution, Karlsruhe, Germany, 2010; Digital Pioneers, V & A Mus, London, 2009; Mus Contemp Art, Zagreb, Croatia, 2011; Northern Lights, Minneapolis, MN, 2011. *Pos:* Staff ed art & archit, New Catholic Encyclo, Catholic Univ, Washington, DC, 64-68; acad dean, Minneapolis Col Art & Design, 75-78; prog dir, Fourth Int Symp Electronic Art, 93. *Teaching:* Prof art hist, Minneapolis Col Art & Design, Minn, 68-94, emer prof, 94; Artist in Residence, Univ Bremen, Germany, 2010. *Awards:* Bush Fel, 69; Hon Mention, ars Electronica, 93; First Prize, Golden Plotter, 94; Siggraph Distinguished Artist Award, 2009. *Bibliog:* CJ McNaspy (auth), Art & the New Catholic Encyclo, Am, 3/67; F Debuyst (auth), Sculptures de Ciment, Roman Verostko, Art D'Eglise, 68; Roman Verostko in Visual Proceedings, Siggraph 97, ACM, Oxford, 52, 97; L Candy & E Edmonds (auths), Explorations in Art & Technology, 2002; Pearl Park Scriptures, Digital Art Mus (DAM), Berlin, 2005. *Mem:* Coll Art Asn; Am Asn Univ Prof; Asn Computing Machinery; Int Soc Elec Art. *Media:* Computer Code, Paper. *Res:* Changing roles of the artist in our society. *Publ:* Auth, Experience in Community: The New Art, Liturgical Arts, 72; Le Sacre et la Profane, Art D'Eglise, 75; A futures outlook on the role of artists and designers, Futurics, 80; Epigenetic Painting: Software As Genotype, Leonardo, 1/23/90; computer illus, Derivation of the Laws, St Sebastian Press, Minneapolis, 90; and others; Epigenetic Art Revisited In Code The Language of Our Time, Art Electronica, Linz Austria, 2004; WIM: The Upsidedown Book, Jewelweed Impressions, 2008. *Dealer:* Wolfgang Leiser, Gallery DAM, Berlin. *Mailing Add:* 5535 Clinton Ave S Minneapolis MN 55419

VERSTEEG, SIEBREN
CONCEPTUAL ARTIST
b New Haven, Conn. *Exhib:* Solo exhibs include The Stray Show Chicago, 2002, Beacon Project Space, Beacon, NY, 2003, Ten in One Gallery, New York, 2003, Mus Contemp Art, Chicago, 2003, Wexner Ctr Arts, Columbus, Ohio, 2004, Rhona Hoffman Gallery, Chicago, 2005, 2007, Bellwether, NY, 2006, Max Protetch, New York, 2007; group exhibs include Art Synthesis 97, Chicago Pub Libr, 1997; Sound, Video, Images, Objects, Donald Young Gallery, 2001; Watery, Domestic, Renaissance Soc, Chicago, 2002; Version 03, Mus Contemp Art, Chicago, 2003; The Paper Sculpture Show & POST-chicago, Gallery 400, Chicago, 2004; Public Execution, Exit Art, New York, 2004; Swarm, Fabric Workshop & Mus, Philadelphia, 2005; Broadcast, Contemp Mus, Baltimore, 2007; Lasso Project, ArtSpace, New Haven, 2007; The Cinema Effect: Illusion, Reality & the Moving Imag, Hirshhorn Mus & Sculpture Garden, Washington, 2008. *Awards:* Chicago Artists Assistance Prog Grant, 1998; Ill Arts Coun Fel, 2005

VERZAR, CHRISTINE B
EDUCATOR
b Basel, Switz, Sept 05, 1940; US citizen. *Study:* Courtauld Inst, London Univ, 63; Univ Florence, 63-64; Univ Basel, PhD, 66. *Teaching:* Asst prof hist art, Boston Univ, 66-69, Princeton Univ, 69-76; asst prof, Univ Mich, 73-84; prof/chmn hist art, Ohio State Univ, 84-94, prof hist Art, 9-. *Awards:* Phi Kappa Phi. *Mem:* Coll Art Asn; Int Ctr Medieval Art (bd dir, 85-89); Medieval Acad Am. *Res:* Italian medieval art; Connections East-West. *Publ:* Auth, Die Romanischen Skulpturen der Abtei Sagra San Michele, Bern, 68; coauth, The Meeting of Two Worlds, Ann Arbor, 81; Portal & Politics in the Early Italian City/State, Parma, 88. *Mailing Add:* Dept Hist Art Ohio State Univ 100 Hayes Hall 108 N Oval Hall Columbus OH 43210

VERZYL, JUNE CAROL
DEALER, COLLECTOR
b Huntington, NY, Feb 5, 1928. *Study:* Parsons Sch of Design. *Pos:* Co-dir, Verzyl Gallery, 66-. *Bibliog:* Jane Margold (auth), Galleries struggle with an image, Newsday, 3/31/67; Kevin Hayes (auth), Gallery almost set to re-open, Northport Observer, 10/29/81. *Mem:* Northport Hist Soc. *Specialty:* Contemporary American painting, graphics and sculpture. *Collection:* Contemporary American work, including Filmus, Refregier, Benda, Twardowicz, Clawson and Christopher; also a large collection of New England gravestone rubbings. *Mailing Add:* 25 Bevin Rd Northport NY 11768

VESCOLANI, BERT
MUSEUM ADMINISTRATOR
Study: Mich State Univ, BS (edn); Studied North Park Univ. *Pos:* sr vpres, John G Shedd Aquarium, Chicago, 1991-2005; dir, John Ball Zoological Gardens, Grand Rapids, Mich, 2005-11; pres, CEO, St Louis Science Ctr, 2011-; bd mem, Acad Sciences of St Louis, Forest Park Forever, St Louis Regional Chamber & Growth Asn, Founders Brewery, 2008-, Rock the Rapids, 2011-; vchmn, Experience Grand Rapids, 2008-11. *Mailing Add:* St Louis Science Center 5050 Oakland Ave Saint Louis MO 63110

VESTAL, DAVID
PHOTOGRAPHER, WRITER
b Menlo Park, Calif, 1924. *Study:* Art Inst Chicago, 41-44; studied photog with Sid Grossman, 47-55. *Work:* Mus Mod Art, NY Pub Libr, Metrop Mus & Whitney Mus Am Art, NY; Art Inst Chicago; George Eastman House, Rochester; Mus NMex, Santa Fe; High Mus Art, Atlanta; Nat Gallery, Ottawa; Univ Louisville, Ky; Mus Art, Columbus, Ohio; Nat Gallery, Wash, DC. *Exhib:* Solo exhib, Witkin Gallery, NY, 71, East Street Gallery, Grinnell, Iowa, 75, Tom Zimmermann Fine Arts, New Hope, Pa, 85, Galeria del Bosque, Guadalajara, Mex, 87 & Daytona Beach Community Col, Fla, 89; Photog Crossroads: The Photo League, Nat Gallery Can, Ottawa, Int Ctr Photog, NY Mus Fine Arts, Houston & Minneapolis Inst Arts, 78; The Great West: Real/Ideal, Univ Colo, Boulder, 79 & Smithsonian Inst Traveling Exhib; NY Sch, Corcoran Gallery, Washington, DC, 85; Robert Mann Gallery, NY, 1996, 2001; Univ Louisville, Ky, 96; Foto Riografia, Rio de Janeiro, Brazil, 96; others. *Pos:* Contrib ed, Popular Photog, 75-86 & Photo Tech, 89-2009. *Teaching:* Pvt instr photog, 56-; vis artist, Art Inst Chicago, 72-73; instr, Parsons Sch Design, 84-94, Sch Visual Arts, 86-93 & Pratt Inst, 87-01; B/W Workshop, Photogr Formulary, Condon, Mt, 2004-; Al Weber Workshops, Carmel, Calif, 2006-. *Awards:* Guggenheim Fel, 66 & 73-74; Fulbright Scholar Award, Brazil, 97. *Bibliog:* David Vestal, Photog Ann, 62; Vision and Expression, 69; David Vestal, Photog Ann, 76. *Media:* Silver halide, digital. *Res:* trips to Brazil to study the people & places. *Specialty:* Photography. *Publ:* ed, US Camera Annual 1971, 70; ed, Leica Manual, 72; auth, The Craft of Photography, 75 & The Art of Black-and-White Enlarging, Harper & Row, 84; non-newsletter, Grump, 88-2005, Finity, 2006-; column, Phot Techniques, 95-2009; auth, Picture Book, 2003; MCHNY, 2006: Easter Parade, 2007: Chicago, 2008; auth, Windows, Rooms, Stone Heads, 2009; auth, White, 2010. *Dealer:* Robert Mann Gallery 210 11th Ave New York NY 10001; Ann Cain, Chicago Ill. *Mailing Add:* PO Box 309 Bethlehem CT 06751

VETROCQ, MARCIA E
EDITOR
Study: Princeton Univ, NJ, BA; Stanford Univ, Calif, PhD. *Pos:* Prof, fine arts, Univ New Orleans, 82-98; sr ed, Art in Am Mag, New York City, 98-2011, Art & Auction, 2011-2013. *Awards:* Grantee, Andrew and Marian Heiskell Vis Fel in Criticism, Am Acad, Rome, 2004. *Publ:* Coauth, The Founders & the Architects: Design of Stanford Univ, 76; coauth, Domenico Tiepolo's Punchinello Drawings, 79

VEVERS, TABITHA
PAINTER
b New York. *Study:* Skowhegan Sch Painting & Sculpture, Maine, 78; Yale Univ, New Haven, Conn, BA (cum laude), 78. *Work:* LaSalle Univ Art Mus, Philadelphia; Provincetown Art Asn & Mus, Mass; Decordova Sculpture Park & Mus, Lincoln, Mass; Yale Univ Art Gallery, New Haven, Conn; New Britain Mus Am Art. *Exhib:* Art--Made in the USA (catalog), Stadtische Galerie Regensburg, Ger, 88; Contemp Provincetown (catalog), Pac Design Ctr, West Hollywood, Calif, 89; Crosscurrents: The New Generation (catalog), E Hampton Ctr Contemp Arts, NY, 90; solo exhibs, Kraushaar Galleries, New York, 92, 94, 97, 2000, 03; Tabitha Vevers: Narrative Bodies, DeCordova Mus, Lincoln, Mass, Provincetown Art Asn & Mus, Provincetown, Mass (retrospective, catalog), 2009, Lovers Eyes: The Gaze of Desire, Provincetown, Ma, 2012, Tabitha Vevers: Lover's Eyes, Lori Bookstein Fine Art, NY, 2013; DNA Gallery, 96, 97, 98, 99, 2000, 2001, 2002, 2003, 2004 & 2009; Immortalized (catalog), Art Complex Mus, Duxbury, Mass, 98; Painting in Boston 1950-2000 (book), DeCordova Mus, Lincoln, Mass, 2002-03; Pepper Gallery, Boston, 2004 & 2006; artSTRAND, Provincetown, Mass, 2005-08; Gold, Belvedere Mus, Vienna, Austria, 2012. *Collection Arranged:* Couples, Words and Pictures, 86, Laughter and Tears: a Show of Emotion, 88, Allegory, 89, Young Artists, 89, Provincetown Art Asn & Mus, Mass. *Pos:* Bd mem, Provincetown Art Asn & Mus, 85-91, mem exhib com, 86-91, 2004-08; juror, Va Ctr Creative Arts, 98-; mem artists' adv bd, Castle Hill Ctr for the Arts, 98-. *Teaching:* Instr, Castle Hill Ctr Arts, 95-2003; MFA mentor, Art Inst Boston, 2009; painting workshop, Mass Coll Art, Boston, Mass, 2010. *Awards:* VA Ctr Creative Arts Fel, Sweet Briar, Va, 86, 91 & 93; Oberpfaltzer Kunstlerhaus Painting Fel, Schwandorf, Ger, 93; fel, Fine Arts Work Ctr, Provincetown, Mass, 95-96; painting fel, MacDowell Colony, 83; grant, George & Helen Segal Found, 2005; Sea Grant, Univ RI, 2005; painting fel, Ballinglen Arts Found, Ireland, 2006; Pollack-Krasner Found Grant, 2013. *Bibliog:* Lise Motherwell (auth), The Eye of the Beholder: The Art of Tabitha Vevers, Provincetown Arts Magazine, 2004. *Mem:* Am Asn Mus; Provincetown Art Asn & Mus. *Media:* Oil, Gold Leaf, Mixed Media. *Publ:* Tabitha Vevers: Flying Dreams, DNA Editions, 2002; Painting in Boston: 1950-2000, DeCordova Mus & Sculpture Park, 2002; New American Painting, Open Studio Press, 2003 & 2005; Tabitha Vevers: Narrative Bodies, DeCordova Mus & Sculpture Park, 2009. *Dealer:* Clark Gallery 145 Lincoln Rd Lincoln MA 01773; Albert Merola Gallery 424 Commercial St Provincetown MA 02657; Lori Bookstein Fine Art 138 10th Ave New York NY 10011. *Mailing Add:* 75 Richdale Ave No 4 Cambridge MA 02140

VICK, CONNIE R
CONSULTANT
b Philadelphia, Pa, Oct 17, 1947. *Study:* Pa State Univ, BFA, 69; Cornell Univ, 70; Philadelphia Coll Art, 72. *Collection Arranged:* Am Express; Time Warner; Comcast; Mastercard Int; Deloitte. *Pos:* Owner & dir, Vick Gallery, Philadelphia, Pa, 73-79; lectr painting, Neumann Ctr, Philadelphia, 76-80 & Manor Jr Col, 80-84; asst to dir, Fischbach Gallery, New York, 82-84; corp art adv, Vick Corp Art Adv, 84-. *Mailing Add:* 210 11th Ave Suite 304 New York NY 10001

VIDAL, FRANCISCO
PAINTER, PRINTMAKER
b Barranquilla, Columbia, July 22, 1946. *Study:* Univ Altantico, Barranquilla, Columbia, 61-63, Art Students League, 69-71; printmaking workshop (scholarship), NY, 83-85. *Work:* Mus del Barrio, NY; Mus Modern Art, Cantagena, Columbia; Mus Contemp Art Monterrey, Marco, Monterrey, Mex; Adogi, Miniprint Intl, Cadaguez, Spain; Latin America Exhibit, Credit Swiss, NY. *Exhib:* Solo exhib, Mus Alternative, NY, 85, Gallery Frau, Soho, NY; Bass Art Mus, Miami, Fla, 88; Los Angeles Munic Art Gallery, Calif, 88; Centro Colombo Americano, Bogota, Colombia, 88; First Festival of Art, Barranquilla, Columbia, 89; E Hampton Ctr for Contemp Art, NY, 90; Mus Contemp Art, Monterrey; Int Contemp Art Biennial, Firenza, Italy, 2001; Ninth Anniversary Latin Am Mus, Coral Gables, Fla, 2002; Florence Biennal, Frienza, Italy; and others. *Teaching:* Prof drawing, Col Barranquilla for Ladies, 63-68. *Awards:* Selected for 84/86 Nat Studio Prog; Fel painting, Mid Atlantic Arts Found, Baltimore, Md, 92. *Bibliog:* Fred Stern (auth), Artists with Latin American Roots, Mizue Art Mag, Tokyo, Japan, 89; Susana Torreulla Leval (auth), Identity and Freedom, Decade Show, 90; Phyllis Braff (auth), Experimentation in the Still Life, NY Times, May 90. *Media:* Oil on Canvas, Miscellaneous Media. *Publ:* Contribr, Carnival on New York, 89 & En la brecha de la image, 90, El Tiempo, Columbia; article, Experimentation in still life, NY Times, 5/90; contribr, From the studio, East Hampton Star, 5/90; Miami Herald, 7/92; Ihalo mag, Bogota, Colombia, 10/94. *Mailing Add:* 143-16 Barclay Ave #2G Flushing NY 11355

VIDITZ-WARD, VERA LOUISE
PHOTOGRAPHER, HISTORIAN
b Buffalo, NY, May 24, 1952. *Study:* Hartford Art Sch, Univ Hartford, BFA, 75; Sch Fine Arts, Ind Univ, MFA (Fulbright Hayes Res Grant), 88. *Work:* Smithsonian Inst, Nat Mus African Art; Visual Studies Workshop; Nat Mus Sierra Leone, WAfrica; Ga Coastal Hist Mus, St Simons Island, Ga; Penn Ctr of Sea Islands, St Helena Island, SC. *Exhib:* Paramount Chiefs of Sierra Leone, Smithsonian Inst, 90-91; Recent Work, Avery Ctr African Am Cult, Charleston, SC, 92; Recent Work, Sierra Leone Nat Mus, Freetown, W Africa, 93; Other Africas, Photog Resource Ctr, Boston, 93; Paramount Chiefs, Newark Mus, NJ, 95; The Trans-Atlantic Linkage Traveling Exhib, Ga Coastal Hist Mus, 95-97. *Pos:* Photogr volunteer, US Peace Corps, Sierra Leone, 77-79; photogr/stringer, Assoc Press, WAfrica, 86-88. *Teaching:* Assoc prof photog, Bloomsburg Univ, Pa, 88-. *Awards:* WAfrica Res Asn Fel Photog, Howard Univ, 96. *Bibliog:* J Kaplan (auth), West African Gullah traditions alive, Los Angeles Trib & Chicago Tribune, 91; C Kratz (auth), Paramount chiefs of Sierra Leone, African Arts, 10/91; M Sidell (auth), Exhib rev, The Star Ledger, Newark, 2/95. *Mem:* Soc Photog Educ; Arts Coun of African Studies Asn; WAfrican Res Asn; Coll Art Asn. *Media:* Black & White Photography. *Res:* History of photography of Black Africa. *Publ:* Auth, Alphonso Lisk-Carew: Krio photographer, African Arts/Univ Calif Los Angeles, 85; Paramount chiefs of Sierra Leone: photographs by VV-W, Smithsonian, 91. *Mailing Add:* Bloomsburg Univ Dept Art Bloomsburg PA 17815

VIELEHR, BILL
SCULPTOR
b Chicago, Ill, Jan 6, 1945. *Study:* Univ Colo, 63-66; Colo State Univ, BFA, 69. *Work:* Crossroads Mall, Boulder, Colo; Byers Mus & Mus Contemp Art, Chicago; Prudential Bache, Boulder, Colo; Northern Ill Univ; Cherry Creek Plaza, Denver; City of Bellevue, Wash; Pikes Peak Community Coll, Colo Springs; Art on the Corner, Grand Junction, Colo; pvt collection, Mark & Polly Addison, Boulder. *Comn:* Interaction, Boulder Reservoir, Colo, 86; Digital, Colorado Springs, Colo, 86; Boulder Pub Libr, Colo, 91; Monument to Mining, Boulder Co Court House, Colo, 96; Pub Art, City of Flagstaff, Ariz, 99; Sch of Mines, Golden, Colo; Boulder Int Film Festival, 2005; Main Libr, Albuquerque, NMex, 2005; Fire Station #1, Aurora, Colo, 2006. *Exhib:* Denver Art Mus, 72; N Am Sculpture Exhib, 81 & 98; Art on the Corner, Grand Junction, Colo, 93-2008; Boulder Art Ctr Invitational, Colo 93; Boulder Flow, Univ Colo, 93; Sculpture in the Park, Littleton, Colo, 94; Artyard Show, Denver, Colo, 94, 2000; Dairy Ctr for Arts, Boulder, Colo, 99; Tadu Gallery, Santa Fe, 2005; Walker Fine Art, Denver, 2005; Blink Gallery, Boulder, 2006. *Collection Arranged:* Cur, Abstraction Examined, Dairy Ctr for the Arts, Boulder, Colo. *Pos:* Dir, Form Sculpture, 81-; juror, Leonardo Di Vinci Award, 84, 86, 88, 90, 92, 94, 96 & 98. *Teaching:* Vis artist sculpture workshop, Jefferson Co Schs, 71-72 & Colo State Univ, 73; speaker, Art Week, Univ Colo, Colorado Springs, 88 & Pub Art, CPRA Ann Conf, Vail, Colo, 95; workshops, Boulder Pub Schs, 89; instr sculpture, Rocky Mt Coll Art & Design, Denver, Colo, 2001-2003. *Awards:* City Arts Grant, Boulder, Colo, 81, 85, 88, 98 & 2001; Addison Grant, Neo Data, 98; Lou Wille Award for Excellence, Grand Junction, Colo, 2000; Best of Show, Firehouse 3D, Longmont, Colo, 2000; Cash Award, Firehouse 3D, Longmont, Colo, 2002; Best of Show, Art on the Commons, Lakewood, Colo, 2002; Purchase Award, Art on the Corner, Grand Junction, Colo, 2007. *Bibliog:* Art from the Soul, Taos Mag, 8/96; In Search of the Mark, Broomfield Enterprise, 4/97; Life of an Artist, Ariz Daily Sun, 6/99; Hot and Cool, Westword, 2/4/2004; Passion Takes 2 Forms, Rocky Mt News, 2/13/2004; Out and About, GJ Daily Sentinel, 2006 & 2007; Spotlight, Public Art's Open Secrets, Rocky Mt News, 3/3/2007. *Mem:* Bully Boys Beer Club (pres 77-); Loon Rafting (rear admiral 85-2001). *Media:* Cast & Fabricated Bronze & Aluminum. *Dealer:* Lumina Gallery 239 Movada Ln Taos NM 87571; Blink Gallery 1011 Pearl St Boulder CO 80302; Walker Fine Art 11th & Cherokee Denver CO 80204. *Mailing Add:* PO Box 19734 Boulder CO 80308-2734

VIERA, CHARLES DAVID
EDUCATOR, PAINTER
b Dartmouth, Mass, Feb 21, 1950. *Study:* Swain Sch Design, BFA, 72; Skowhegan Sch Painting & Sculpture; Brooklyn Coll Grad Sch, with Phillip Pearlstein, MFA, 74. *Work:* Pvt collection of A Hess, NY. *Comn:* Murals, Am Renaissance Festival, Brooklyn Mus, 79. *Exhib:* Brooklyn 1976, Brooklyn Mus; Nat Arts Club, NY, 77; 153 Ann, Nat Acad, NY, 78; solo shows, Animal Drawings, Long Island Univ, 80 & Paintings, Nassau Co Mus, 81; retrospective, Charles Viera 1972-1982, Brooklyn Mus Art Sch, 82; Works on Paper, Adam Gimbel Gallery, NY, 83. *Pos:* Coordr exhibs, Long Island Univ, Brooklyn, NY, 84 & 85, coordr fine arts, continuing educ prog, 86. *Teaching:* Instr painting & drawing, Brooklyn Mus Art Sch, 75- & Parsons Sch Design, 79-; assoc prof, Long Island Univ, 79-. *Bibliog:* Show of contrast, Phoenix, New York, 76; Inmates try art, 76 & Performers recreate art, 79, New York Times. *Media:* Mixed. *Mailing Add:* 10 Stacey Rd Flemington NJ 08822

VIERA, RICARDO
PAINTER, PRINTMAKER
b Ciego de Avila, Cuba, Dec 15, 1945; US citizen. *Study:* Sch of the Mus of Fine Arts, Boston, dipl, 72; Tufts Univ, BFA, 73; RI Sch of Design, Providence, MFA, 74. *Work:* Allentown Art Mus, Pa; Tel Aviv Mus, Israel; Canton Art Inst, Ohio; Cleveland Mus; Fed Soc Arts & Humanities, Lagos, Nigeria; and others. *Exhib:* Solo exhibs, Inst Contemp Art, Boston, 73 & Canton Art Inst, Ohio, 80; Transitions in Art, Boston Mus of Fine Arts, 77; The Kadishman Connection, Israel Mus, Jerusalem, 79; Instituto de Cultura Puertorriquena, San Juan, 81; Alfred O Deshong Mus, Chester, Pa, 82; and many others. *Collection Arranged:* Am Figure Drawing, Lehigh Univ & Victorian Coll of Art, Melbourne, Australia, 76; Intentions & Techniques (auth, catalog), 79, 26th Ann Contemp Am Art Exhib (auth, catalog), traveling, 81 & Computer Art (auth, catalog), 82, Wilson Gallery, Lehigh Univ, Bethlehem, Pa; Michael Smith, Landscape Photography (auth, catalog), traveling, 81; and others. *Pos:* dir & cur, Lehigh Univ Art Galleries, 74-, chmn pro-tempore, 77-78; community arts coordr & discussion leader, Baum Sch Art, Allentown, Pa, 79-; consult, Cuban Mus Art & Cult, Miami, 81-; bd dir, Pa Citizens Arts, 79-, ARTS, Washington, DC; bd dir, Valley Art Coun. *Teaching:* Instr, Lehigh Univ, 74-78, assoc prof, 78. *Awards:* Elizabeth H Bartol Scholarship, Boston Mus of Fine Arts Sch, 71-72; Cintas fel, Cintas Found, Inst of Int Educ, 74-75; Mellon Found Grant, 78-80; and others. *Bibliog:* Ricardo Viera/Illustraciones Enlace, Nueva Revista Hispanoamericana, 76; Keith Schneider (auth), Capturing the intensity of life, Times Leader, Wilkes-Barre, Pa, 9/13/79; Norma Niurka (auth), A box of surprises, Miami Herald, 10/7/81. *Mem:* Pa Counc Arts; Print Club Philadelphia; Am Asn of Mus; Am Asn Mus/NEastern Conf. *Media:* Oil, Acrylic; Enamel Spray, Oil Crayon. *Publ:* Illusr, Dr Fernando Ortiz, auth, Los Negros Brujos, Ed Universal, Miami, Fla, 73; illusr, Libro Quinto de Lectura Gramatica y Ortografia, Leal & Sanchez Boudy, Miami, 75; illusr, Introduccion al Estudio de la Civilizacion Espanola, Barroso, Miami, 76; auth, Arte Visual en la Palabra de Lydia Cabrera, Festschriften/Ed Universal, 77; auth, From Limestones to aluminum plate lithography, RI Sch of Design Bull, 77. *Dealer:* Forma Hispanic Arts Dealers 305 Alcazar Coral Gables FL 33134. *Mailing Add:* Art Gallery Lehigh Univ Zoellner Arts Ctr 420 E Packer Ave Bethlehem PA 18015

VIERTHALER, BONNIE
COLLAGE ARTIST, LECTURER
b Milwaukee, Wis, Sept 11, 1941. *Study:* Univ Wis-Madison, BS (art educ), 63; Univ Ga, MFA (fiber arts), 72. *Work:* City of Seattle, Seattle First Nat Bank, Wash; IBM, White Plains, NY; Prudential Insurance Co, NY. *Comn:* Fiber & dyed fabric hanging, comn by Richard Wimer, Atlanta, Ga, 71; works in rubber, Seattle Arts Comn, Wash, 76; Pollutius Conglomeratus (wearable art), Seattle Arts Comn & Seattle Aquarium, Wash, 79. *Exhib:* Solo exhibs, Polly Friedlander Gallery, Seattle, Wash, 74 & 76; Invitational, Seattle Art Mus, 76, Foster White Gallery, Seattle, 78; Works in Rubber (traveling), Smithsonian Inst, 79-80; The Joy of Smoking - A Spoof on Cigarette Advertising (traveling), Rotunda of Russell Senate Office Bldg, Washington, 86-90. *Pos:* Artist & pres, BADvertising Inst, Ithaca, NY, 86-; presenter, NJ Assist Prog, 88-. *Teaching:* Lectr hist fabrics, Emory Univ, Atlanta, 73-74; weaving teacher, Factory Visual Arts, Seattle, 76-77. *Awards:* Craftman's Fel, Nat Endowment Arts, 77 & Artist-in-Residence Grant, 78; Giraffe Award, Giraffe Proj, 90. *Publ:* Contrib articles in NJ J Med, 87. *Mailing Add:* 1216 State Hwy 235 Harpursville NY 13787

VIGTEL, GUDMUND
DIRECTOR
b July 9, 1925; US citizen. *Study:* Isaac Grunewald's Sch Art, Stockholm, 43-44; Univ Ga, BFA, 52, MFA, 53. *Hon Degrees:* Atlanta Coll Art, 91. *Collection Arranged:* The New Tradition, 63; The Beckoning Land, 71; The Modern Image, 72; The Dusseldorf Academy & the Am, 73; A Retrospective, Harvey K Littleton, 84; Art in Berlin, 1815-1989, 89-90; The Sacred Art of Russia, 95; 9 Women in Georgia, 96; Lamar Dodd, A Retrospective Exhib, 2008. *Pos:* Admin asst, Corcoran Gallery Art, 54-57, asst to dir, 57-61, asst dir, 61-63; dir, High Mus Art, 63-91. *Awards:* Chevalier des Arts et Lettres, 86; Order of Merit, First Class, Fed Repub Ger, 89; Lifetime Achievement Award, Ga Asn Mus & Galleries, 90. *Mem:* Am Asn Mus; Asn Art Mus Dirs. *Publ:* Auth, 100 Years of Painting in Georgia, Alston & Bird, Atlanta, 92; 9 Women in Georgia, 96; Art in Berlin, 1815-1989. *Mailing Add:* 2082 Golfview Dr NW Atlanta GA 30309-1210

VIKAN, GARY KENT
MUSEUM DIRECTOR
b Fosston, Minn, Nov 30, 1946. *Study:* Carleton Col, BA, 67; Princeton Univ, MA, 70; Princeton Univ, PhD, 76. *Collection Arranged:* Silver Treasure from Early Byzantium, 1986; Holy Image, Holy Space: Frescoes and Icons from Greece, 1988; Gates of Mystery: The Art of Holy Russia, 1992; African Zion: The Sacred Art of Ethiopia, 1993. *Pos:* Art mus admin, cur, Byzantine art Dumbarton Oaks, Wash, 75-84; asst dir cur, affairs, cur, medieval art Walters Art Mus, Baltimore, 85-94, exec dir, 94-2013; bd dirs, Md Citizens for the Arts, Greater Baltimore Cultural Alliance, MD Humanities Council, Baltimore Area Convention and Visitors' Assn; adv bd Getty Leadership Inst, dept art & archaeology Princeton U. *Teaching:* Adj prof, Johns Hopkins Univ. *Awards:* Woodrow Wilson Found fel, 1967-68; Chevalier de l'ordre des Arts et des Lettres, 2000. *Mem:* Byzantine Studies Counf (gov bd 89), US Nat Comt for Byzantine Studies (exec comt, 88-92). *Publ:* auth, Early Byzantine Pilgrimage Art, 2010

VILLA, THEODORE B
PAINTER
b Santa Barbara, Calif, Sept 28, 1936. *Study:* Santa Barbara City Col, AA, 61; Univ Calif, Santa Barbara, BA, 63, MFA, 74. *Work:* Inst Am Indian Mus, Santa Fe, NMex; Calif State Univ, Los Angeles; Univ Gallery, Univ Calif, Santa Barbara; Millicent Rogers Mus, Taos, NMex; Oakland Mus, Calif; Mus Northern Ariz, Flagstaff; Arco, Tulsa, Okla. *Comn:* Mus N Ariz, Flagstaff; Wigwam Resort & Country Club, Phoenix, Ariz; Desert Mountain Properties, Phoenix, Ariz; Phoenix Cardinals, Ariz; Stanford Univ Children's Hosp, Palo Alto, Calif; Sequoia Capitol Management, Menlo Park, Calif; and many pvt collections. *Exhib:* solo exhibs, Sun Valley Ctr Arts, Ketchum, Idaho, 83, Taylor Mus, Colorado Springs Fine Arts Ctr, Colo, 87 & Mus Inst Am Indian Art, Santa Fe, NMex, 88, Millicent Rogers Mus, Taos, NMex, 90; No Beads, No Trinkets, Palais De Nations, Geneva, Switz, 84; Visage Transcended, Am Indian Contemp Arts, San Francisco, 86; Four Sacred Mountains, 2 yr traveling exhib, Ariz Arts Comn, 88-90; Decolonizing The Mind: End of a 500 Yr Era, Ctr Contemp Art, Seattle, Wash, 92; Centro Wash Irving, USIS, Madrid, 93; Fenderson Collection, Heard Mus, Phoenix, 93; 3 Visions, 3 Missions, Mus NAriz, 95. *Collection Arranged:* Grupo Larios, Madrid, Spain; AT&T, San Francisco, Calif; Root Corp, Daytona Beach, Fla; US West, Denver, Colo; Wigwam Resort & Country Club, Phoenix, Ariz; Indian Wells Country Club, Los Angeles, Calif; Mus Inst Am Indian Arts; Calif State Univ, Los Angeles; Millicent Rogers Mus, Taos, NMex; many others. *Teaching:* Instr design-watercolor, life drawing, Santa Barbara City Col, 75-2000; lectr watercolor, Univ Calif, Santa Barbara, 83-86; Sun Valley Ctr Arts & Humanities; AHAA Sch, Telluride, Colo. *Bibliog:* Charles Clouse (auth), Doubletake, Southwest Art, 2/86.

Media: Watercolor. *Specialty:* American Art. *Interests:* Watercolor, fly fishing. *Publ:* Ya, Madrid, Spain & Valley Mag, Ketchum, ID, 2/8/93. *Dealer:* Broschofsky Galleries PO Box 1538 Ketchum ID 83340; Rare Gallery 60 East Broadway Jackson WY. *Mailing Add:* 1371 Santa Rita Cir Santa Barbara CA 93109

VILLARREAL-CASTELAZO, EDUARDO
ARCHITECT, PAINTER

b Mexico, DF, Mex, Apr 14, 1944. *Study:* Studied painting with Prof Alfredo Guati Rojo, 58 & Prof Carlos Medina, 63; Iberoamericana Univ, Archit, 68; Nat Univ Mex, MA, 78. *Work:* Mus Arzobispado Ministry Finance, Mex; Fla Mus Hispanic Latin Am Art, Miami; Mus Mod Art, Aquitaine, Lot et Garone, France; Gallery Mex Art, Seattle, Wash; Santa Cruz Parrish Complex XVI Century, Mex. *Comn:* Christmas decorations, Monterrey Insurance Corp Bldg, Monterrey Insurance Co, Mexico City, 65; Fountain Corp Bldg Proj, Mex Inst Social Security, Mexico City, 74; Fountain of Complex, Blessed Martyrs of Korea, Mexico City, 96; Mural Direction, Asuncion High Sch, Ixaltepec, Oaxaca, Mex, 87 & Corp Sculpture, 89. *Exhib:* Beams of Light, Salon Du Viex Colombier, Paris, France, 93; Winter Int Competition, Fla Mus Hispanic Latin Am Art, Miami, 93; 3rd Visual Dialogue, World Coun Visual Artists, Asis, Italy, 95; DAP 94, Pinacoteca Virreynal, Mex, 94; Museo Inconografico de Quijote, Guanajvato, VTO, 94; Top 70, Art 95, Gallery Art 54, NY, 95; Formalidades, Nat Univ Mex, Mexico, 96. *Pos:* Coordr cur, Nat Univ Mex, Acatlan Campus, 93-97; dir, Univ Exchanges World Coun Visual Artists, 95-97. *Teaching:* Archit contruct, Nat Univ Mex, Acatlan Campus, 80-98, precast in archit, 82-98, dipl art course coordr, 96-98. *Awards:* Jury Prize, Expos Flambouance, Paris, France, 93. *Bibliog:* Blanca Cecilia Puebla (auth), De Toro un Poco, Excelsior Newspaper, 11/29/93; Jorge Luis Berdeja (auth), El Centro Nacional de Las Artes, El Universal, 10/27/94; Maria Cecila Pontes (auth), Anniversary Enep Acatlan, El Universal Zona Norte, 10/20/95. *Mem:* World Coun Visual Artists; Colegio de Arquitectos de Mex; Sociedad de Arquitectos Mexicanos; Comn Univs (directorio de las artes plasticas, 96-). *Media:* Acrylic, Oil; Mixed Media. *Res:* application of construction materials in visual arts; quality in visual arts. *Publ:* Auth, Emergency Housing, CIDIV-INDECO, 81. *Mailing Add:* Jilquerds 39 Lomas Verdes Mexico 53120 Mexico

VILLINSKI, PAUL S
SCULPTOR, PAINTER

b York, Maine, May 28, 1960. *Study:* Mass Coll Art, 80-82, Cooper Union, 82-84, BFA, 84. *Work:* Mus Arts & Design, New York; Cleary, Gottlieb, Steen & Hamilton, Attys, Mound, Cotton & Wollan, Attys, Nomura Securities Int, Ctr Reinsurance, John A Levin co, New York; Brooklyn Union Gas co, New York; Ogunquit Mus Am Art, Maine; and others. *Comn:* McCann Erickson co, NY, 90; NY Life Insurance co, Parsippany, NJ. *Exhib:* Solo exhibs, St Peter's Church, Citicorp Ctr, New York, 89, Midtown Payson Galleries, New York, 89, Queens Mus Art, Bulova Corp Ctr, New York, 90, 3-D Lab, New York, 97, Three Rivers Arts Festival Gallery, Pittsburgh, Pa, 2000, Gallery 138, New York, 2005, Scope NY Art Fair, 2006, Jonathan Ferrara Gallery, New Orleans, La, 2006, Hillwood Art Mus, Brookville, NY, 2007 & Morgan Lehman Gallery, New York, 2007; group exhibs, Brookworld, Soho Arts Festival, New York, 96, A Large Show of Small Works, Cooper Union, NY, 96, Suture, Rotunda Gallery, Brooklyn, New York, 97, On Air, St Peter's Church, New York, 97, The Alternative Mus, New York, 97, Artspace, New Haven, Conn, 98, Zoon Gallery, New Haven, Conn, 98, Islip Art Mus, East Islip, NY, 99, Univ Wyo Art Mus, Laramie, 99, Miller Gallery, Carnegie Mellon Univ, Pittsburgh, 2001, Morgan Lehman Gallery, Lakeside, NY, 2002 & Scope, Miami, 2004; and many others. *Teaching:* Adj lectr, LaGuardia Community Coll, City Univ New York, Long Island City, 90-93. *Awards:* Michael S Vivo Prize for Excellence, Cooper Union, 84; Nat Endowment Arts Grant, 87; Agnes Bourne Fel Painting, Djerassi Found, Woodside, Calif, 88. *Bibliog:* Belle Elving (auth), The language of gloves, Washington Post, 10/16/97; Ellen Lubell (auth), Common threads, Newark Star Ledger, 2/3/97; Donimique Naas (auth), Review of On Air, Rev, 3/1/97; and others. *Mem:* St Peter's Church Art & Archit (rev comt, 91-98), New York. *Media:* All. *Dealer:* Morgan Lehman Gallery New York NY; Jonathan Ferrara Gallery New Orleans. *Mailing Add:* 9-01 44th Dr Long Island City NY 11101

VINCENT, CLARE
CURATOR, HISTORIAN

b Jersey City, NJ, Aug 30, 1935. *Study:* Coll William & Mary, AB, 58; Inst Fine Arts, NY Univ, MA, 63; Inst Fine Arts & Metrop Mus Art, cert, 63. *Collection Arranged:* A Sure Reckoning, 68, Northern European Clocks in NY Collections, 72, Nineteenth Century French Sculpture, 80, Rodin: The Gates of Hell, 82; Rodin: The B Gerald Cantor Collection, 86, Metrop Mus Art, NY; Rodin's Monument to Victor Hugo, 99; The Art of Time: European Clocks and Watches, Metrop Mus Art, NY, 2007. *Pos:* Asst to cur decorative arts, Cooper Union Mus, 60-61; curatorial asst western Europ arts, Metrop Mus Art, New York, 62-67, asst cur, 67-72, assoc cur Europ sculpture & decorative arts, 72-; consult to catalogue of antique sci instruments, Adler Planetarium, Chicago, 85-2005. *Teaching:* Curatorial Studies I, Metrop Mus Art & Inst Fine Arts, 95-96. *Mem:* Coll Art Asn; Antiquarian Horological Soc (vpres Am sect, 77-89). *Res:* European clocks and timekeeping instruments; European metalwork; European Renaissance enamels; 19th century European sculpture. *Interests:* Ballet, opera, concert going. *Publ:* auth, Rodin at the Metrop Mus Art: A Hist of the Collection, Metrop Mus Art, 81; Renaissance Decorative Arts, Leichtenstein: The Princely Collections, Metrop Mus Art, 85; A Beam Compass by Christoph Trechsler the Elder and the Origin of the Micrometer Screw, Metrop Mus J, Vol 24, 209-222, 89; coauth, A Watch for Monsieur Hesselin, Metrop Mus J, Vol 28, 103-119; coauth An Extravagant Jewel: The George Watch, Metro Mus J, Vol 35, 137-149; auth, Seventeenth Century French Painted Enamel Watchcases, Metrop Mus J, Vol 37, 89-106; auth, Seventeenth Century Limoges Enamel Watchcases and their Movements, Antiquarian Horology, Vol 30, 9/2007, 317-346. *Mailing Add:* 326 E 85th St New York NY 10028

VINE, MARLENE
PRINTMAKER, PAINTER

Study: Carnegie Inst Technol, BFA. *Work:* Deloitte & Touche, Dallas; Islip Art Mus, NY; King & Spalding, Inc; Progressive Insurance Corp, NY; York Cambridge Lab Cons, Mass. *Exhib:* Electrum XX, Holter Mus, Helena, Mont, 1991; America 500, City Coll New York, 1992; 34th Spring Exhib, Parrish Art Mus, Southampton, NY, 1994; Plateaus and Crossings: A View of Geometric Painting, Bard Coll, New York, 1997; solo exhibs, ART Resources Transfer, New York, 1998 & 2002, Saint Peter's Church, Citicorp, 1999, Deborah Berke & Partners, LLC, New York, 2001, Ok Harris Gallery, New York, 2009; Small Works, New York Univ, 2006. *Awards:* Pollock-Krasner Found Grant, 2008. *Bibliog:* John Dorsey (auth), Contemporary Art on Canvas, Baltimore Sun, 5/1993; Steven Psyllos (auth), Select Encounters, NY Arts Mag, 5-6/2006

VINELLA, RAY (RAIMONDO) JOHN
PAINTER, SCULPTOR

b Bari, Italy, April 6, 1933. *Study:* Art Ctr Coll Design, with Lorsor Fietleson, Harry Carmean, John Lagatta & Reynold Brown, BPA, 59, BFA, 68. *Work:* Diamond M Found Mus, Snyder, Tex; Mansato Int, NY; Carlsbad Mus, NMex. *Exhib:* First Exhib Southwest Art, People's Republic China, 81; Mus Native Am Cult, Spokane, Wash, 82; Colo Sch Mines. *Pos:* Art comt, Harvard Found Mus, Taos, NMex. *Teaching:* Instr painting, Taos Acad Fine Art, 71-72 & Taos Art Workshops, 82-; fac dean, Taos Sch Fine Art, 77-78. *Awards:* B Altman Award, 51; Prof Award, Painting Competition, NMex State Fair, 71 & 73. *Bibliog:* Peggi Ridgway (auth), Southwest Art, 3/84; Roberta McIntyre (auth), Western Art Digest, 1-2/86; Today Show, 7/31/87; Nancy Ellis (auth), Southwest Profile, 1/89; Southwest Profile, 9/96. *Mem:* Soc Am Impressionists; Monac Art Soc. *Media:* Oil, Egg Tempera; Watercolor. *Publ:* Auth, Masterworks of Impressionism: Arlene Doran Kirkpatrick. *Dealer:* Brazos Fine Art

VINOLY, RAFAEL
ARCHITECT

b Montevideo, Uruguay, 1944. *Study:* Univ Buenos Aires, Argentina, Grad in Archit, 1969. *Exhib:* Principal works incl John Jay Coll Criminal Justice, 1988, Tokyo Int Forum, 1996, Univ Chicago Grad Sch Bus, Howard Hughes Medical Inst Janelia Farm Research Campus, Virginia, Porter Neurosci, Research Ctr at Nat Inst of Health, Md, Cleveland Mus Art; author: Rafael Viñoly, 2003. *Pos:* Found partner, Estudio de Arquitectura, Argentina, 1964-78; found, prin Rafael Viñoly Archits PC, New York City, 1982-. *Teaching:* guest lectr, Univ Wash, Harvard Univ. *Awards:* Recipient Medal of Hon, Am Inst of Archit NY Chap, 1994. *Mem:* Fel: Am Inst of Archits; Nat Acad of Design (acad 1994-), Japan Inst Archit. *Mailing Add:* Rafael Vinoly Architects 50 Vandam St New York NY 10013

VIOLA, BILL
VIDEO ARTIST

b New York, NY, Jan 25, 1951. *Study:* Syracuse Univ, BFA (Experimental Studios), 73, Hon Dr Fine Arts, 95; Art Inst Chicago, 97; Calif Coll Arts & Crafts, 98. *Hon Degrees:* Syracuse Univ, DFA (hon), 95; Art Inst Chicago, 97; Calif Coll Art & Crafts, 98; Mass Coll Art, 99; Calif Inst Arts, 2000; Sunderland Univ, Eng, 2000; Royal Coll Art, London, 2004. *Work:* Mus Mod Art, NY; Ctr Georges Pompidou, Paris, France; San Francisco Mus Mod Art; Mus Fur Mod Kunst, Frankfurt, Ger; Mus Contemp Art, Los Angeles. *Comn:* The Stopping Mind (video/sound installation), Mus fur Mod Kunst, Frankfurt, Ger, 91; Nantes Triptych (video/sound installation), Ministry Cult, France, 92; Slowly Turning Narrative (video/sound installation), Inst Contemp Art, Va Mus Fine Art, 92; Tiny Deaths (video/sound installation), Biennale d'Art Contemporian de Lyon, France, 93; Deserts (film), ZDF/ARTE Television & VARA-VPRO, Vienna, 94; The World of Appearances (video/sound installation), Helaba Main Tower, Frankfort, 00. *Exhib:* Biennial Exhib, Whitney Mus Am Art, NY, 75-87; solo exhibs, Mus Mod Art, NY, 79, Mus Mod Art (with catalog), NY, 87, Mus d'Art Contemp de Montreal (catalogue), 93, Buried Secrets, 46th Venice Biennale, Venice, Italy, 95, Savannah Coll Art & Design, Ga, 96, Durham Cathedral, Eng, 96 & Chapelle Saint Louise de las Salpetriere, 96, Hatsu-Yume (First Dream) Mori Art Mus, Tokyo, Japan, 2006, Zahenta Nat Gallery of Art, Warsaw, 2007, Palazzo delle Esposizioni, Rome, 2008.; Video Spaces: Eight Installations, Mus Mod Art, NY, 95; Rites of Passage, Tate Gallery, London, 95; Mus d'art Contemp, Lyon, 95; By Night, Found Cartier pour l'art contemp, Paris, 96; Bill Viola, A 25 Yr Survey (with catalog), Whitney Mus Am Art, travels to seven venues in the US & Europ, 97-; Along the Frontier (traveling), Int Ctr Photog, NY, 96; Islands: Contemp Installations from Australia, Asia, Europe & Am, Nat Gallery Australia, Canberra, 96. *Teaching:* Scholar in residence, Getty Res Inst, Getty Ctr, Los Angeles, 98. *Awards:* Rockefeller Found Video Artist Fel, 82-83; John Simon Guggenheim Mem Fel Video Art, 85-86; John D & Catherine T MacArthur Found Award, 89-94; French Order Arts and Letters, 2006; Eugene McDermott Award in Arts, MIT, 2009; Praemium Imperiale award (painting category), Japan Soc, 2011. *Bibliog:* Barbara London (auth), Bill Viola: Installations and Videotapes, Mus Mod Art, New York, 87; Marie Luise Syring (auth), Bill Viola: Unseen Images, Stadtische Kunsthalle Dusseldorf, Ger, 92; Alexander Puhringer (auth), Bill Viola: Salzburger Kunstverein, Austria, 94; David A Ross (ed) Bill Viola, Whitney Mus of Am Art, NY, 97. *Mem:* Am Acad Arts and Scis; Nat Acad. *Media:* Videotapes, Video Installations. *Publ:* Auth, Sight Unseen-Enlightened squirrels & fatal experiments, No 4, spring 82 & Will there be condominiums in data space?, No 5, fall 82, Video 80; contribr, Video: A retrospective 1974-1984, Long Beach Mus Art, Calif, 84; Dan Lander & Micah Lexier (eds), Sound by Artists, The sound of one line scanning, Art Metropole, Toronto & Walter Phillips Gallery, Banff, 90; Video Black-The Mortality of the Image, Illuminating Video: An Essential Guide to Video Art, Aperture/Bay Area Video Coalition, 90; Reasons for Knocking at an Empty House: Writings 1973-95. *Dealer:* James Cohan Gallery 533 W 26th St, NY, 10001. *Mailing Add:* 282 Granada Ave Long Beach CA 90803

VIOLET, ULTRA
PAINTER, WRITER
b La Tronche, Isere, France, Sept 6, 1935; Fr & Am citizen. *Study:* Sacred Art Sch, La Tronche Isere, France. *Work:* Mus Mod Art, Medzilaborce, Czech; Petit Palais Collection, Paris, France; Mus Art, Paterson, NJ; Espace Giletta Mus, Nice, France; HRH Prince Albert of Monaco; Golden Pineapple, Spanish Inst. *Comn:* Portrait, Mr Toubon, French Minister of Cult. *Exhib:* Les Anges Apocalyptiques, French Inst, Bratislava, Czech, 92; L'art dams la Rue, La Rotonde, Beaulieu, France, 92; L'Art Influence les Artists, Found Sofia Lafitte, Antipolis, 92; Warhol et Moi, Inst Etudes Sup Arts, Paris, 92; Amherst Fine Arts Ctr, Mass Univ, 93; Galerie Olaf Clasen, Cologne, Allemagne, 93; Galerie Sabine Wachters, Knokke-Zoute, Belgium . *Pos:* Master of aprentis, Union Libre des Travailleurs Artistiques, 91-92; critic, New York Times. *Teaching:* Lectr, Arts Dept, Brigham Young Univ, currently & Del Univ; New Jersey City Univ. *Awards:* Award for best bookwriting, pictures & graphics, Frankfurt, Deutsh Bibliothek, 89. *Bibliog:* Grace Gluck (auth), We Threw Andy Out, NY Times, 88; Frederick Mitterand, du Cote' de Chez Fred (film), TV, French, 89; Pavel Vojir (auth), Fialovy Andel, Reflex, 92; Le Monde Mag, 4/2009. *Mem:* Union Libre des Travailleurs Artistiques (pres, 92); The Authors Guild. *Media:* All Media. *Res:* American pop art; Andy Warhol; Spiritual Christian belief, Scriptures; Angelogy (study of Angels). *Collection:* John Graham, Edward Ruschia, Andy Warhol, Salvador Dali, Ray Johnson. *Publ:* Auth & contrib ed, Diplomatic Corner, Diplomatic World Bulletin, 85; Famous for 15 Minutes, My Years with Andy Warhol, 88, 89, 90, 91 & 92; Kiki's Paris, J Art, 89; auth, Le Revers du Reve, Ancrage, 89; Goodbye Dali, It's Been Surreal, NY Times, 1/30/89; Tiffany, Warhol Christmas Boom, 2004; auth, Famous for Fifteen Minutes. *Dealer:* Galerie du Cirque Paris 8e France; Galerie Ferrero Nice France 06 300; Galerie Guy Peters St Paul France Vence; Stefan Stux New York; Sabine Wachters Fine Arts Belgium; Galerie Ferrero Nice France; Galery Stefan Stux, NY

VIOLETTE, BANKS
PAINTER, SCULPTOR
b Ithaca, NY, 1973. *Study:* Sch Visual Arts, NY, BFA, 98; Columbia Univ, MFA, 2000. *Work:* Rep in permanent collections, Whitney Mus Am Art, NY, Frederick R Weisman Art Found, Los Angeles, Mus OverHolland, Amsterdam, Mus Modern Art, NY, Mus Contemp Art, Los Angeles, Mus Art Moderne et Contemporain, Geneva; Diversity Plus: Emerging Artists in a Rapid World, Visual Arts Mus, NY, 2001; Whitney Biennial, Whitney Mus Am Art, NY, 2004. *Exhib:* Solo exhibs, Team Gallery, NY, 2000, 2002, 2004, 2007, LISTE, Basel, Switz, 2003, MW Projects, London, 2004, Galerie Rodolphe Janssen, Brussels, 2005, Maureen Paley, London, 2006, Standard, Oslo, 2006; Group exhibs, Two Friends and So On, Andrew Kreps Gallery, NY, 2000; Summer with Friends, Team Gallery, NY, 2000, The Ice Age, 2004; Learned American, PPOW, NY, 2001; Melvins, Anton Kern Gallery, NY, 2003; Back in Black, Cohan Leslie and Browne, NY, 2003; A Matter of Facts, Nicole Klagsbrun Gallery, NY, 2003; Flesh and Blood, Michael Steinberg, NY, 2003; Kult 48 Klubhouse, Deitch Projects, Brooklyn, NY, 2003; Beginning Here: 101 Ways, Visual Arts Gallery, NY, 2004; The Black Album, Maureen Paley, London, 2004; Bridge Freezes Before Road, Barbara Gladstone Gallery, NY, 2005; Blankness is Not a Void, Standard, Oslo, 2005; Thank You for the Music, Spruth Magers Projekte, Munich, 2005; The Image is Gone, Galerie Lisa Ruyter, Vienna, 2006; Cosmic Wonder, Yerba Buena Ctr for Arts, San Francisco, 2006. *Awards:* Rema Hort Mann Found Grant, 2000. *Dealer:* TEAM Gallery 83 Grand St New York NY 10013; Maureen Paley 21 Herald St London E2 6JT

VIRGONA, HANK (HENRY) P
PAINTER, PRINTMAKER
b Brooklyn, NY, Oct 24, 1929. *Study:* Pratt Inst Evening Sch, 54. *Work:* Metrop Mus Art, NY; Arch Am Art, Smithsonian Inst; Mus City New York; Wichita Mus, Kans; Pub Libr, NY; Samuel Dorsky Mus Art, State Univ NY. *Exhib:* New Am Still Life, Westmoreland Co Mus, Pa, 79; The Presidency: Relevant & Irrelevant Traveling Exhib, 80; West and the Law Traveling Exhib, 80-82; Prints USA, Pratt Inst, NY, 82; Subtle Observations-Subway Portraits by Hank Virgona, Transit Mus, Brooklyn, NY, 92; Satirical Prints of Hank Virgona, Samual Gorsky Mus of Art, New Paltz, NY, 2011. *Pos:* Co-founder, 41 Union Sq Open Studios, 80-. *Teaching:* Instr etching, pvt lessons, 82-; instr drawing, Pratt Graphic Ctr, NY. *Awards:* Purchase Prizes, Nat Acad Art, 79 & Prints USA, Pratt Inst, 82; Art Grant, NY Found Arts & Kanter-Plaut Found, 98. *Bibliog:* Ellyn Bloom (auth), Hank Virgona: The art of social satire, Am Artist Mag, 73; Paul Peter Piech (auth), Hank Virgona, Graphic Satirist, Idea Mag, 91; Unturned Corners, Recent Work by Hank Virgona, J Stefan Cole, 2002; Andrew French (auth), An Interlude with the Artist (short film), 2013. *Media:* Watercolor; Etching. *Specialty:* Modern and contemporary art. *Publ:* Auth, The System Works The Etchings and Random Notes of Hank Virgona, Da Capo Press, 77; illusr, Ivan the Terrible, Ivan the Fool, G Putnam Sons, 80. *Dealer:* Galerie Mourlot 16 East 79 St New York NY 10021; Weber Fine Art 17 Boniface Cir Scarsdale NY 10583; The Old Printshop 150 Lexington Ave NY NY 10016

VISCO, ANTHONY SALVATORE
EDUCATOR, SCULPTOR
b Philadelphia, Pa, Sept 13, 1948. *Study:* Fleischer Art Mem, Philadelphia, 64-66; Skowhegan Sch Painting & Sculpture, Maine, 69; Philadelphia Coll Art, BFA, 70; Acad delle Belle Art, Florence, Italy, 70-71; Univ Pa, archit studies, 83. *Comn:* Stations of the Cross, Old St Joseph's Nat Shrine, Philadelphia, 81, Religious Freedom, 85; Resurrection altarpiece & bronze Assumption relief, Church of Assumption, Atco, NJ, 86; Raredose relief panels, bronze, Bryn Mawr Presby, 87-89; Stations of the Cross, St Joseph's Univ Chapel, Philadelphia, 93; Sanctuary wall & relief sculpture with mosaic, Our Lady of Mt Carmel, Berlin, NJ, 94; and others. *Exhib:* Solo exhibs, First Street Gallery, NY, 80, Lace Gallery, Philadelphia, Pa, 81, Cabrini Col, Radnor, Pa, 81, Bourse Bldg, Philadelphia, 81, Pa Acad Fine Arts, 83 & Bryn Mawr Presby Church, 84 & 89; In the Religious Spirit, Nat Sculpture Soc, 90; In Conference, Fourteenth Int Sculpture Conv, Philadelphia, 92; Figurative Philadelphia, Woodmere Mus, Philadelphia, 93; Acad Artists, Contemp Realist Gallery, San Francisco, 93; and others. *Pos:* Art instr, Recreation Ctr for Older People, Philadelphia, summer 68; apprentice, Waler Erlbacher, Elkins Park, Pa, summer, 70; sculpture technician, Skowhegan Sch, Maine, summer, 75. *Teaching:* Instr sculpture, Philadelphia Col Art, 76-85 & Creuzberg Ctr, Radnor, Pa, 76-78; instr anat, Pa Acad Fine Arts, 85-, chmn, Sculpture Dept, 86-92. *Awards:* Greenshields Award, Pvt Studio Work, Can, 75-76; Arthur Ross Award for Sculpture, Classical Am, 84; Greater Harrisburg Arts Festival Drawing Award, State Mus Pa, 89. *Bibliog:* Anthony Apesos (auth), New Art Examiner, 1/84; Victoria Donohoe (auth), Philadelphia Inquirer, 8/17/84 & 6/21/86; Robin Longman (auth), Am Artist, 9/84. *Media:* Wax, Bronze. *Mailing Add:* 1426 Christian St Philadelphia PA 19146

VISO, OLGA
MUSEUM DIRECTOR
b Fla. *Study:* Emory Univ, MA (art hist), 92. *Collection Arranged:* Distemper: Dissonant Themes in the Art of the 1990s, 96; Regarding Beauty: A View of the Late Twentieth Century, 1999-2000; Juan Muñez, 2001. *Pos:* Positions in dept mod & contemp art, office registrar & office dir, High Mus Art, Atlanta, 89-93; asst cur Norton Mus Art, West Palm Beach, Fla, 93; asst cur, Hirshhorn Mus and Sculpture Garden, Washington, DC, 95, assoc cur, 98, cur contemp art, 2000-03, dep dir, 2003-2006, dir, 2006-07; mem Fed Adv Comt Int Exhibitions, Nat Endowment for Arts; co-comnr US Pavilion, Venice Biennial, 2001; dir, Walker Art Ctr, Minneapolis, 2008-. *Res:* contemporary Latin American Art. *Mailing Add:* Walker Art Ctr 1750 Hennepin Ave Minneapolis MN 55403

VITALE, MAGDA
PAINTER
b New York, NY, July 20, 1939. *Study:* Barnes Found, Marion, Pa, 77; Found Today's Art, Intern, Philadelphia, 78; Skowhegan Sch Painting & Sculpture, Maine, 79; Moore Coll Art, Philadelphia, BFA, 80. *Work:* Carnegie Ctr, Princeton, NJ; Best Products Inc, Richmond, Va; NJ Power & Light; Del Co Community Col, Media, Pa; Am Embassy, Dublin, Ireland; Wheat, First, Butcher, Singer, Philadelphia; Duane, Morris & Hecksher, Philadelphia; Islip Art Mus, NY; Ballinglen Art Foundation, Ballycastle, Ireland. *Exhib:* Solo exhibs, Paintings, Chambers Gallery, Penn State Univ, University Park, 84, Abstraction, Univ Pittsburgh Gallery, 87, New Paintings, Camden Col, Blackwood, NJ, 88 & Paintings, Henri Gallery, Washington, DC, 92 & 95, The Northern Indiana Arts Asn, Munster, 92, Leabharlann, Belmullet, Ireland, 99; New Am Talent 88, Laguna Gloria Art Mus, Austin, Tex, 88; Henri Gallery, Washington, DC; Biennial 89, Del Art Mus, Wilmington, 89; Am Embassy Cult Ctr, Brussels, Belg, 89; Nat Small Works Exhib, Schoharie Arts Coun Gallery, Cobleskill, NY, 90; Gallery Artists, J Lawrence Gallery, Melbourne, Fla, 90; Nat Works on Paper Exhib, Univ Tex, Tyler, 90; Metamorphosis of a Butterfly, Erie Art Mus, Pa, 92; group exhib, Moore Coll Art, Philadelphia, 89, Cabrini Col, Radnor, Pa, 89, Henri Gallery, Washington, DC, 89, Zenith Gallery, 89, Trenton City Mus, NJ, 89. *Awards:* Scholarship Award, Skowhegan Sch Painting & Sculpture, 79; Expo V Award Winner, Northport Galleries, NY, 86; Grant, Ballenglen Art Found Fel, Bally Castle, Ireland, 92. *Bibliog:* Mark Woodruff (auth), An Increase of Life, Paintings of Magda Vitale, Camden Co Col, Blackwood, NJ, 88; Francoises Andre (auth), Contemp Women Artists (exhib catalog), Am Embassy Cult Ctr, Brussels, Belg, 89; John Perreault & Jenine Culligan (coauths), Biennial 89 (exhib catalog), Del Art Mus, 89. *Res:* Gardening, reading. *Mailing Add:* 12 Springton Lake Rd Media PA 19063

VITALI, JULIUS M
PHOTOGRAPHER, PAINTER
b July 1, 1952. *Study:* Nassau Coll, Long Island, NY, 70-72; SUNY at Fredonia, BA, 74. *Work:* Bibliotheque Nationale, Paris, France; Polaroid Collection, Boston, Mass; Il Diaframma Galeria, Milan, Italy; Penn State Berks Campus, Reading, PA; Lehigh Univ Mus, Bethlehem, PA. *Comn:* Photo mural, Lawrence High Sch, Lawrence, NY, 85; mural, Weaversville Intensive Treatment Unit, Northampton, PA, 99. *Exhib:* Erronique, Crucial Gallery, London, Eng, 87; Fashion & Surrealism, Victoria & Albert Mus, London, Eng, 88; Tremplin Pour Les Images, Ctr Nationale de Photographie, Paris, France, 89; The Political Landscape, C W Post Mus, Greenvale, NY, 90; Hair Sculpture & Its Roots, Lehigh Univ Mus, Bethlehem, Pa, 91; Puddle Art: A Retrospective, Coll Misericordia, Dallas, Pa, 94; Perfecting Art of Errors, Open Space Gallery, Allentown, Pa, 97; solo exhib, Digital Photog, Eric Art Mus, Erie, Pa, 2000; Ground Zero, Mus of New Arts, Detroit, Mich, 2002; Celebrate New York City, Freyberger Gallery, Penn State Berks Campus, Reading, Pa, 2003; Awkwardology, Coll Misericordia, Dallas, Pa, 2010. *Collection Arranged:* From the Ashes, Open Space Gallery, Allentown, Pa, 2002. *Pos:* Gallery dir, Discovery Gallery, Glen Cove, NY, 82-85; exec dir, Open Space Gallery, Allentown, Pa, 96-02. *Teaching:* Instr photog, Pa Govt Sch Arts, Erie, 7-8/92; art instr, Weaversville Intensive Treatment Unit, Northampton, PA, 98-02. *Awards:* Nat Endowment Arts Forum Grant, Visuals & Music of Avante Disregarde, US Govt, 90; Spec Projs Award, At the Corner of Error & Perfection, Pa Coun Arts, 87, 91 & 93; Res Photog Award, Kodak Co, 92. *Bibliog:* Liana Bortolon (auth), The World in a Puddle, Grazia, Italy, 79; George Schaub (auth), Photography With a Splash, Photogrs Forum, 82; Lorenzo Santamaria (auth), Photography After the Rain, Fotopractica, Italy, 84. *Mem:* Lehigh Valley Writers Acad. *Media:* Digital & Experimental Photography. *Publ:* Illusr, feature article/cover, Brit J Photog Art, 86; auth, Erronique, L'ARCA, Italy, 88; illusr, Art Images & Ideas Book, Davis Publs, 92; auth, Puddle Art, Sch Arts; Fine Artists Guide to Marketing & Self-Promotion, Allworth Press, 96, rev ed, 2003. *Dealer:* Mistretta Galleries 394 Forest Ave Locust Valley NY 11560. *Mailing Add:* 612 Broad St Emmaus PA 18049

VITALI, UBALDO
CONSERVATOR, SILVERSMITH
b Italy, 1944; came to US, 1967. *Study:* studied at, Liceo Artistico Ripetta, Univ Rome, Acad di Belle Arti, Rome. *Exhib:* Newark Mus; Smithsonian Am Art Mus; Yale Univ Art Gallery; Mus Fine Arts Houston, Tex. *Pos:* silversmith, Ubaldo Vitali Inc, Maplewood, NJ. *Awards:* Named a MacArthur Fellow, John D & Catherine T MacArthur Found, 2011. *Publ:* featured on, The Next List, CNN, 1/29/2012. *Mailing Add:* Ubaldo Vitali Inc 188 Hilton Ave Maplewood NJ 07040-3507

VIZNER, NIKOLA
ART DEALER, GALLERY DIRECTOR
b Bezdan, Yugoslavia, Nov 9, 1945; US citizen. *Study:* Belgrade Univ, BA (art hist), 70, MA (hist mod art), 74; Univ of Zadar, Croatia, PhD, 05. *Pos:* Dir, Wiesner Gallery, Brooklyn & New York, NY, currently. *Teaching:* Prof art hist, Touro Coll, New York, currently. *Mem:* Nat Art Dealers Asn; Coll Art Assoc. *Specialty:* American and international contemporary art. *Dealer:* Art of Maxo Vanka The Mitchener Mus Bucks County PA. *Mailing Add:* 10 Clinton St Apt 10Q Brooklyn NY 11201

VO-DINH, MAI
PAINTER, PRINTMAKER
b Hue, Vietnam, Nov 14, 1933; US citizen. *Study:* Sorbonne, Fac Lett, 56; Acad Grande Chaumiere, 57; Ecole Nat Superieure Beaux-Arts, 59. *Work:* Mus d'Art Mod de la Ville de Paris; Mus Rouen; Schiedam Mus, Holland; Nashville Mus, Tenn; Wash Co Mus Fine Arts, Md. *Exhib:* Solo exhibs, Wash Co Mus Fine Arts, Md, 78 & Univ Md, 80; Arts Club Washington, Touchstone Gallery & Paul Rosen Gallery, Washington, 83; George Mason Univ, Va, 84 & 87; Les Jardins du Boise, Montreal, Can, 92; Pean Studio Savigny le Temple, Paris, 2000. *Teaching:* Instr watercolor painting, Hood Col, 78-79; artist-in-sch, Md State Coun, 86-87, 90 & 92. *Awards:* Christopher Award, Christopher Found, New York, NY, 75; Literature Prog Fel, Nat Endowment Arts, 84. *Bibliog:* Libbie Powell (auth), International recognized artist, The Daily Mail, Hagerstown, Md, 11/74; Henry Scarupa (auth), An artist's odyssey, Baltimore Sun, 7/80; Helen Hammond (auth), article, Diversions Mag, 3/90. *Media:* Oil, Acrylic; Woodblock. *Publ:* Sao Co Tieng Song; esssais, Van Nghe, 91; Sky Legends of Vietnam, Harper Collins, NY, 93; Lau Xep, Van Nghe, 97; Rung Mam, Van Nghe, 2000; Huyetuyet, Van Nghe, 2002; May Cho Thvdmd, 2004

VOGEL, (MR & MRS) HERBERT
COLLECTORS
b New York, NY, Aug 16, 1922 (Mr Vogel); b Elmira, NY, May 14, 1935 (Mrs Dorothy Vogel). *Study:* Mr Vogel, NY Univ Inst Fine Arts; Mrs Vogel, Syracuse Univ, BA, 57; Univ Denver, MA, 58. *Exhib:* Painting, Drawing & Sculpture of the 60's and 70's, from the Dorothy and Herbert Vogel Collection, Inst Contemp Art, Univ Pa & Contemp Arts Ctr, Cincinnati, 75-76; Drawings from the Collection of Dorothy and Herbert Vogel, Univ Ark, Little Rock, 86; Beyond the Picture, Works from the Collection of Dorothy & Herbert Vogel, Kunsthalle, Bielefeld, Ger, 87; From the Collection of Dorothy & Herbert Vogel, Arnot Art Mus, Elmira, NY, 88; Poetry of Form: Richard Tuttle Drawings from the Vogel Collection, Inst Valenciano de Arte Mod, Valencia, Spain, 92; Indianapolis Mus Art, 93; From Minimal to Conceptual Art Works from the Dorothy & Herbert Vogel Collection, Nat Gallery Art, Washington, 94; and others. *Awards:* Coll Art Asn; Centennial Award, Patronage in the Visual Arts. *Bibliog:* Paul Gardner (auth), Look It's the Vogels, Art News, 3/79; Meg Cox (auth), Postal clerk and wife amass art collection in a New York flat, Wall Street J, 1/30/86; Catherine Barnett (auth), A package deal, Art & Antiques, Summer 86; Paul Gardner (auth), Mesmerized by Minimalism, Contemporanea, 12/89; Sara Rimer (auth), Collecting priceless art, just for the love of it, NY Times, 2/11/92; and others. *Collection:* Contemporary drawing, sculpture and painting

VOGELSTEIN, BARBARA
COLLECTOR
Pos: Assoc & partner, Warburg Pincus, 1976-1992; partner, Apax Partners & co Ventures, London, 1992-2000; nat adv bd, Nat Mus Wildlife Art, Wyo; bd dirs & trustees, Vassar Coll, Brooklyn Mus, Sch Am Ballet, and Third Way; chmn & founder, ShareGift USA. *Awards:* Named one of Top 200 Collectors, ARTnews mag, 2010 & 2012. *Collection:* Modern and contemporar art

VOGELSTEIN, JOHN L
COLLECTOR
Pos: Partner, Lazard Freres & co, formerly; mng dir & sr adv, Warburg Pincus, currently, pres, formerly; dir, Flamel Technologies & Third Way, currently; chmn, New Providence Asset Mgmt & New York City Ballet; chmn & bd dirs, Prep for Prep; vice chmn bd overseers, New York Univ Leonard N Stern Sch Bus; trustee, New York Univ, Temple Emanu-El, and Jewish Mus. *Awards:* Named one of Top 200 Collectors, ARTnews mag, 2010-13. *Collection:* Modern and contemporary art

VOGT, ERIKA
VIDEO ARTIST
b NJ, 1973. *Study:* NYU, BFA, 1996; Calif Inst Arts, MFA, 2003. *Exhib:* Imaginer Los Angeles, Centre Pompidou, Paris, 2006; Bunch Alliance and Dissolve, Contemp Arts Ctr, Cincinnati, 2006; Films Around Photography, Hammer Mus, Los Angeles, 2007; California Biennial, Orange County Mus Art, Newport Beach, 2008; Whitney Biennial, Whitney Mus Am Art, New York, 2010. *Awards:* Prof Develop Fel, Coll Art Assn, 2002. *Bibliog:* Roberta Smith (auth), In These Shows, the Material Is the Message, NY Times, 8/10/2007; Holly Myers (auth), Around the Galleries, Los Angeles Times, 5/23/2008. *Mailing Add:* c/o Mesler & Hug 510 Bernard St Los Angeles CA 90012

VOISINE, DON
PAINTER
b Ft Kent, Maine, 1952. *Study:* Portland Sch Art, Maine, 1970-73; Concept Ctr Visual Studies, Portland, Maine, 1973-74; Haystack Mountain Sch Crafts, Deer Isle, Maine, 1974; Rochester Inst Technol, NY, 1976; Maine Coll of Art, Hon BFA, 2000. *Hon Degrees:* BFA, Maine Coll Art, 2000. *Work:* Joel & Lila Harnett Print Study Ctr, Univ Richmond Mus; Peabody Essex Mus, Salem, Mass; Missoula Art Mus, Mont; Cincinnati Art Mus. *Exhib:* Solo exhibs, Moming Arts Ctr, Chicago, 1982, Postmasters Gallery, New York, 1985, Marianne Deson Gallery, Chicago, 1987, Deson Saunders Gallery, Chicago, 1990, June Fitzpatrick Gallery, Portland, Maine, 1998, Margaret Thatcher Projs, New York, 1998, Icon Contemp Art, Brunswick, Maine, 2005, 2008, Metaphor Contemp Art, Brooklyn, NY, 2006, Abaton Garage, Jersey City, 2006, Gregory Lind Gallery, San Francisco, 2009, McKenzie Fine Arts, New York, 2009 & 2011, Reading Area Community Coll, Pa, 2010, Northampton Community Coll, pa, 2010, New Arts Program Exhibition Space, Pa, 2010, Icon Contemp Art, Brunswick, Maine, 2011; Salon of the Mating Siders, Herron Test Site, Brooklyn, 1992; The Passion/Passions Art, Richard Anderson Fine Arts, New York, 1999; An Homage to Albert Pinkham Ryder, State Art Gallery, Brooklyn, 2000; Significant Pursuits:Paint & Geometry, Smack Mellon Studios, Brooklyn, 2000; Toy Show, 41/2, Brooklyn, 2000; Repetition in Discourse, Painting Ctr, New York, 2001; Brooklyn Rail Presents: Made In Brooklyn, Whyte Studios, Brooklyn, 2002; Incredible Lightness of Being, Black & White Gallery, Brooklyn, 2003; Eccentric Spaces: Fiction of Place, N3 Proj Space, Brooklyn, 2003; Pierogi a Go-Go, Pierogi, Brooklyn, 2004; Paint it with Black, Betty Cunningham Gallery, New York, 2005; War Is Over, SideShow Gallery, Brooklyn, 2006; Orpheus Selection: In Search of Darkness, PS1 Contemp Art Ctr, Long Island City, NY, 2007; Unpainted, New Abstract Painting, Thomas Robertello Gallery, Chicago, 2008; Horror Vacui, McKenzie Fine Art, New York, 2008, Geometric Abstraction, 2008; 183rd Ann: Invitational Exhib Contemp Am Art, Nat Acad Mus, New York, 2008; Minus Space, MOMA PS1 Contemp Art Ctr, Long Island City, 2008-2009; Chunky Monkey, Coleman Burke Gallery, NY, 2009; Cooler heads Prevail, Gregory Lind Gallery, Calif, 2010, High-Def, 2010-11; Plane Speaking, Mckenzie Fine Art, NY, 2011; Ghost in the Machine, Lennon, Weinberg Gallery, NY, 2011. *Awards:* Edward Albee Fel, 2004; Artist's Fel, NY Found Arts, 2006; Henry Ward Ranger Fund Purchase Award, Nat Acad, 2008; Purchase Prize, portland Mus of Art, Maine, Hassam, Speicher, Betts and Symons Purhase Fund Award, American Acad of Arts and Letters, NY, 2011. *Mem:* Am Abstract Artists; American Abstract Artists (pres 2004-); Nat Acad. *Dealer:* McKenzie Fine Art 511 W 25th St New York NY 10001; Icon Contemporary Art 19 Mason St Brunswick ME 04011

VOLICER, NADYA
SCULPTOR
Study: Island Sch, Skopelos, Greece, Summer, 1998; Glasgow Sch Art, Scotland, 2000; Mass Coll Art, Boston, BFA (sculpture; with honors), 2001; Vt Studio Ctr, Resident, 2006, MacNamara Found, Maine, 2006, Millay Colony, 2006, Bemis Ctr Contemp Arts, Omaha, 2007, McColl Ctr Visual Arts, NC, 2008. *Exhib:* Beyond Walls, Little White Box, Boston, 2000; Ann Benefit Art Auction, Mass Coll Art, Boston, 2003-06; LocalMotive: Pub Art off the Beaten Path, Revolving Mus, Lowell, Mass, 2003, Subterranean Angels, 2004; The Next Step, Bedford Free Pub Libr, Mass, 2004; Ann Exhib, DeCordova Mus & Sculpture Park, Lincoln, Mass, 2005; Ann AIDS Benefit, Barbara Krakow Gallery, Boston, 2005 & 2006; Open, Real Art Ways, Hartford, Conn, 2007. *Awards:* Found Auction Award, Boston, 2001; Helen Blair Crosbie Sculpture Award, 2001; Vt Studio Ctr Fel, 2006; Lowell Cult Coun Grant, 2006; Technical Asst Grant, Haystack Mt Sch Crafts, Maine, 2006; St Botolph Club Found Grant-in-Aid Award, Boston, 2007; Pollock-Krasner Found Grant, 2007

VOLID, RUTH
DEALER, CONSULTANT
b Chicago, Ill. *Study:* Art Inst Chicago; Chouinard Art Sch, Los Angeles; Otis Art Inst; Univ Chicago; Am Acad Art. *Pos:* Pres, Ruth Volid Gallery Ltd, 70-91. *Teaching:* Corp Art Roundtable, 88. *Awards:* Am & Int Soc Interior Designers Distinguished Serv Award; Indust Found Award. *Bibliog:* Barbara Varro (auth), A new start at midlife, Sun Times, 10/77; Special places, special people, Chicago Tribune, 12/83; Rivernorth News, 8/86. *Mem:* Arch of Am Art; Arts Club Chicago; Am Soc Interior Designers (bd mem). *Collection:* Henry Moore, Rauschenberg, Thomas Hart Benton, George Segal, Robert Natkin, Matta & Lofstutter. *Publ:* Auth, Art/an added dimension, Designer, 10/79; Threads of tradition, Studio 40, 10/79 & Picking a corporate art curator, 10/80, Collector Investor; Great Poems of the Western World, Vol II. *Mailing Add:* 89 East Ct New Buffalo MI 49117

VOLK, GREGORY P
EDUCATOR, CURATOR
Study: Colgate Univ, BA; Columbia Univ, MA. *Collection Arranged:* Surface Charge, Anderson Gallery, Richmond, Va, 2005; Public Notice: Paintings in Laumeier Sculpture Park, St Louis, 2005-2006; Agitation and Repose, Tanya Bonakdar Gallery, New York, 2007; Carnival Within, UferHallen, Berlin, 2009. *Pos:* Assoc prof, Dept Painting & Printmaking, Va Commonwealth Univ Sch Arts; freelance cur & critic. *Awards:* Critic-in-residence, Art Omi Int, 1996. *Publ:* Auth, Bruce Nauman (exhib catalog), Milwaukee Art Mus, 2006; Joan Jonas (exhib catalog), Museu d'Art Contemporani de Barcelona, 2007; essay, In: Vito Acconci: Diary of a Body, 1969-1973, Charta, 2007; Ayse Erkmen (exhib catalog), Hamburger Bahnhof, 2008. *Mailing Add:* Va Commonwealth Univ Dept Painting & Printmaking 325 N Harrison St Box 842519 Richmond VA 23284

VOLKERSZ, WILLEM
SCULPTOR, PAINTER
b Amsterdam, Neth, Aug 3, 1939; US citizen. *Study:* Univ Washington, BA, 65; Mills Col, MFA, 67. *Work:* Seattle Art Mus, Seattle, Wash; Univ Arts, Osaka, Japan; Nanjing Coll Arts, China; Paris Gibson Sq Mus Art; Northwest Mus Arts & Cult; Nicolaysen Art Mus; Mus Neon Art; Booth Western Art Mus; Holter Mus Art; Univ Kans Hosp; Watertown Hotel. *Comn:* Paris Gibson Square Mus Art, Great Falls, Mont, 88. *Exhib:* Solo exhibs, Plains Art Mus, 94, Mont State Univ, 94, Salt Lake Art Ctr, 95, Nicolaysen Art Mus, 98, Mus Northwest Art, 99, Univ Puget Sound, 2000, Ind State Univ, 2001, Mus of Neon Art, 2002, Art Mus of Missoula, 2002, Beall Park Art Ctr, 2003, Mondak Heritage Ctr, 2004, Custer co Art Ctr, 2005, Holter Mus Art, 2006 & Paris Gibson Sq Mus of Art, 2008, Univ Mont/Western, 2009, Northwest Mo State Univ, 2010, Sherry Leedy Contemporary Art, 2010, Coconino Ctr Arts, 2011, Turman Larison Contemporary, 2011, Missoula Art Mus, 2011, Turman Larison Contemporary, 2013, Emerson Cultural Ctr, 2013; group exhibs, Bags & Baggage,

Arrowmont Sch Arts & Crafts, 96; Changing Horizons, Leedy Voulkos Gallery, 96; NW Neon (with catalog), Cheney Cowles Mus, 97; Pac NW Ann, Bellevue Art Mus, 98; The View From Here, Seafirst Gallery, 98; Drawing Retrospective, Mont State Univ, 99; Hsinchu Int Glass Art Festival, Taiwan, 99; Neon: Current (auth, catalog), Reed Whipple Cult Ctr, Las Vegas, 2000; Art Chicago, 2007; Sherry Leedy Contemp Art, 2007; Shack Up Gallery, 2007 ; Turman Larison Contemp, 2008; Missoula Art Mus, 2009, 2012; Holter Art Mus, 2010. *Collection Arranged:* Cur, Word & Image in Am Folk Art, Mid-Am Arts Alliance Traveling Exhib, 86-88 & The Radiant Object, Mont State Univ, Traveling Exhib, 94-98; Tell it Like it Is, Paris Gibson Sq Mus Art, 2012. *Pos:* Dir admiss, Kansas City Art Inst, 81-83; dir, Sch Art, Mont State Univ, 86-91 & 94-95; vis fel, Univ Kans, 86; vis scholar, Univ Kent, Eng, 91. *Teaching:* Prof found studies, Kansas City Art Inst, 68-86; prof art, Mont State Univ, 86-2001; Pilchuk Glass Sch, 99; prof emer, Mont State Univ, 2002-. *Awards:* Fulbright Award, Folk Art Res, Coun Int Exchange Scholars, 91; Anna Krueger Fridley Award, Mont State Univ, 96, Exceptional Opportunities Grant, 98, Wiley Fac Award for Meritorious Res, 98 & Provost's Award for Excellence, 99; Indiv Artists Fel, Mont Arts Coun, 98; George Sugarman Found Grant, 2007. *Bibliog:* Christian Schiess (auth), Willem Volkersz in The Light Artist Anthology, ST Publ, 93; Alan Goldman (dir), Glowing in the Dark (film), 97; Arthur Williams (auth), The Sculpture Ref, 2005. *Mem:* Phi Kappa Phi Hon Soc; Mus Am Folk Art; Folk Art Soc Am (nat bd, 90); Holter Mus Art (bd dirs, 2009-2013); Emerson Cult Ctr. *Media:* Neon, Wood, Mixed Media. *Res:* Outsider art and environments. *Interests:* American popular culture and folk art. *Collection:* Contemporary American folk and outsider art. *Publ:* Contribr, The Folk, Univ Kans, 89; auth (article), Private Spaces/Public Places, Pub Art Rev, 92; This is Art, This is Dream, This is Energy, Folk Art Messenger, 92; The Plastic Madonna, Phi Kappa Phi Nat Forum, 96; Roger Cardinal on Outsider Art, Raw Vision, 98. *Dealer:* Turman Larison Contemp Helena MT; Sherry Leedy Contemporary Art Kansas City Mo; NINE dot ARTS Denver. *Mailing Add:* 12299 Portnell Rd Bozeman MT 59718-9552

VOLKIN, HILDA APPEL
SCULPTOR
b Boston, Mass, Sept 24, 1933. *Study:* Mass Coll Art, BS, 54; Harvard Sch Educ, MA (teaching & fine arts), 56. *Work:* Cleveland Mus Art, Ohio; Univ NMex, Albuquerque Mus Art & Albuquerque Int Airport; Los Alamos Nat Lab, NMex; Massillon Mus, Ohio; Bernalillo Co Govt Auter, Albuquerque, NMex; Albuquerque Dept Labor, NMex; Univ Kans, 2014. *Comn:* Rose Med Ctr, Denver, Colo, 90; Gen Electric co, Pittsfield, Mass, 91; Lovelace Med Ctr, Albuquerque, NMex, 94; Penrose Hosp, Colorado Springs, Colo, 95; Morris View Nursing Home, Morris Plains, NJ, 95; Lehigh Valley Hosp, Allentown, Pa, 96; Los Alamos Med Ctr, NMex, 99; Percent Arts Comn, 2001; W Mesa Aquatic Ctr, Albuquerque, NMex, 2001; Los Padillas Aquatic Ctr, Albuquerque, NMex, 2005. *Exhib:* Here and Now: 35 Artists in New Mexico, Mus Albuquerque, 80 & 90 & Walton Art Ctr, Fayetteville, Ark, 94; Bergen Community Mus, Paramus, NJ, 83; retrospective, Mass Coll Art, Boston, 84; Exploring Multiple Dimensions, Albuquerque Mus, 2007; Traveling exhib, Lightworks, NMex Mus Natural History and Sci, NMex Tech, Socorro, NMex, Fuller Lodge Art Ctr, Los Alamos, NMex, 2012-2013, NMex Highlands Univ, Las Vegas, NMex, 2012, 2013. *Pos:* Dir, Fuller Lodge Art Ctr, 77-80 & Los Alamos Art Ctr, 77-80; art dir, EFA Studio, Albuquerque, NMex, 80-. *Teaching:* Instr painting, Univ NMex, Los Alamos, 74-. *Awards:* Purchase Award for Watercolor, Massillon Mus, 66; Percent for the Arts, NMex, 2001, 2005. *Bibliog:* Laurie Volkin (auth), Albuquerque artist produces first acrylic silkscreen sculpture, The Link 9/88; Mary Carroll Nelson (auth), Year of the woman brings five artists to public eye, Albuquerque J, 1/3/93; Woman's memorial a labor of love, Albuquerque J, 1/16/93; Wesley Pulkka (auth), American Artists, Ministry & Liturgy, 6-7/2003; Laurie Ann Volkin (auth), Aquatic Center Waterwave, Accent Albuquerque Mag, 7/2005; Wesley Pulkka (auth), Exploring Multiple Dimensions, Albuquerque J, 8/12/2007; Generations, Albuquerque Arts Mag, 1/2008; Wesley Pulkka (auth), Abstracts Prove Mastery, Albuquerque J Arts, 2/3/2008. *Mem:* Soc Layerists Multimedia, Albuquerque Mus. *Media:* Plexiglas LED Lighting, Metal, Mixed Media. *Publ:* Auth, Paper, the continuous thread, Cleveland Mus Art & Ind Univ Press, 82; Cover Artist of month, Take Five, 1/87; Bridging Time & Space, Markowitz Publ, 98; The Art of Layering Making Connections, Nelson & Dunaway, 2004. *Dealer:* Shidoni Gallery 1508 Bishops Lodge Rd Tesuque NM. *Mailing Add:* 14329 Skyline Rd NE Albuquerque NM 87123

VOLLMER, DAVID L
MUSEUM DIRECTOR
Pos: Dir, Janice Mason Art Mus, Cadiz, Kentucky, Swope Art Mus, Terre Haute, Ind, 2001-2008; deputy dir, Blaffer Gallery, Univ of Houston, 2008-. *Mailing Add:* Blaffer Gallery 120 Fine Arts Building Houston TX 77204

VON BARGHAN, BARBARA
EDUCATOR, WRITER
b Washington, DC, Feb 5, 1949. *Study:* Univ Iowa, BA, 70; New York Univ, with Jose Lopez-Rey & Charles Sterling, MA, 72, with Jonathan Brown, Egbert Haverkamp-Begemann & Colin Eisler, PhD, 79. *Collection Arranged:* Contributor to exhibition, Pre-Columbian Ceramics, Dimock Gallery, George Washington Univ, 81, among others. *Pos:* Dir, Von Braghahn Gallery, Washington, DC, 74-78; Lectr, Embassy of Spain & Smithsonian Inst. *Teaching:* Instr, Sweet Briar Col, 73-74; asst prof, George Washington Univ, 74-82, assoc prof, 83-. *Awards:* Research Grant, George Washington Univ, 78-86. *Mem:* Am Soc of Hispanic Historical Studies; Renaissance Soc of Am; Soc for Spanish & Portuguese Historical Studies; Coll Arts Asn. *Res:* Spanish, Portuguese and Latin American Art, Northern Baroque court art, architecture and gardens, Mannerism in the North, Primitive art. *Publ:* Auth, Philip IV and the Golden House of the Buen Retiro: In the Tradition of Caeser, 86; Age of Gold, Age of Iron: Renaissance Spain and Symbols of Monarchy, 86; co-auth (with Annemarie Jordan), The Torreao of the Lisbon Palace and the Escorial Library, 86; and many others. *Mailing Add:* Art Dept/George Washington Smith Hall Art Rm A 101 801 22nd St NW Washington DC 20052

VONBETZEN, VALERIE
PAINTER
b Providence, RI. *Study:* Studied, Art Students League, New York, Bard Coll, Annandale-on-Hudson, NY. *Exhib:* Solo exhibs, A Special Exhibit, NY Horticultural Soc, New York, 1989, Plant Drawings, NY Botanical Soc, Bronx, NY, 91, The Light of Day, Stover Mill Gallery, Erwinna, Pa, 92, Am Towns, Katharina Rich Perlow Gallery, New York, 97, Nocturnal Cityscapes, 2000, Urban Twilight Scenes, 2002 & A Limited Exhib of Recent Paintings, Morpeth Gallery, Hopewell, NJ, 2002; Fine Arts Inst San Bernardino Co Mus, Calif, 1995; Palm Springs Desert Mus, Calif, 97; Albright-Knox Art Gallery, Buffalo, NY, 98-99; Small Works Show, New York Univ, 1995, 1996; Allentown Art Mus, Allentown, Pa, 92 & 98; Palm Beach Art Fair, Fla, 99; Morpeth Gallery, Hopewell, NJ, 2000; Coryell Gallery, Lambertville, NJ, 2002; Butler Inst Am Art, 2003; Michener Art Mus, New Hope, Pa, 2005 & 2008; Butler Inst Am Art, Youngstown, Ohio, 2003, 2007; Hunterdon Mus Art, Clinton, NJ, 1991, 1995, 2007, 2010. *Awards:* Juror's award, Small Works at 50 Washington St E Galleries, New York City, 95, 96; Juror's award, Hunterdon Art Mus, Clinton, NJ, 95; The Artist Loofs at Hunterdon Co 91, 95; Spec patrons' award for painting, Phillips Mill Ann Fall Exhib, New Hope, Pa, 87, 92, 94, 96-97, 99, 2003; Vt's Studio Ctr Grant, Johnson, 97; Rauschenberg's Change Inc Grant, Captiva, Fla, 97; Elizabeth Greenshields Found Grant, Montreal, Can, 99; Millay Colony for the Arts Grant, Austerlitz, NY, 99; Art Comt award, Phillips Mill, 2009. *Bibliog:* Cathy Viksjo (auth), Gallery Hosts Classic Study in Contrasts, Times, Trenton, NJ, 12/12/1993; Doris Brandes (auth), Artist in Focus, New Hope Gazette, Pa, 11/1995; Doris Brandes (auth), Artists of the River Towns, River Arts Press, New Hope, Pa, 2000; Terry A McNealy (auth), Phillips Mill 75th Anniversary Retrospective. *Mem:* New York Artists Equity; Michener Art Mus; Hunterdon Mus Art. *Media:* Oil. *Dealer:* Coryell Gallery 8 Coryell St Lambertville NJ 08530

VON BRANDENBURG, ULLA
SCULPTOR, VIDEO ARTIST
b Karlsruhe, Ger, 1974. *Study:* Hochschule fur Gestaltung, Karlsruhe, 1995-1998; Hochschule fur Bildende Kunste, Hamburg, 1998-2004. *Exhib:* Neue Blicke, Neue Raume, Schauspielhaus, 2000; solo exhibs, Galerie Taubenstrasse, Hamburg, 2001, STudiogalerie Kunstverein Braunschweig, 2003, Palais fur aktuelle Kunst, Gluckstadt, 2004, Produzentengalerie, Hamburg, 2006, Palais de Tokyo, Paris, 2006, Kunsthalle, Zürich, 2006, Irish Mus Mod Art, Dublin, 2008, CCA, Wattis Inst Contemp Art, San Francisco, 2008 & Le Plateau/FRAC Iles-de-France, 2009; Slow, Shedhalle, Zurich, 2002; Deutschland Sucht, Cologne Kunstverein, 2004; I Still Believe in Miracles, ARC, Musee d'Art Moderne de la Ville de Paris, 2005; Neue Freunde, Galerie der Stadt Schwaz, Vienna, 2005; As if by Magic, Art Ctr-S Fla, Miami Beach, 2006; 2nd Turin Triennale, 2008; 53rd Int Art Exhib Biennale, Venice, 2009. *Awards:* Scholar, Dietze-Stiftung Found, 2003; Travel Scholar, Neue Kunst in Hamburg, 2004; Art Scholar, Künstlerstätte Schloß Bleckede, 2005

VON DER GOLZ, JAN See Mehn, Jan (Jan Von der Golz)

VON HABSBURG, FRANCESCA
COLLECTOR
b Lausanne, Switz, June 6, 1958. *Study:* Ctrl St Martins Coll Art & Design, London. *Pos:* Owner, Thyssen-Bornemisza Contemp Art, 2002-. *Awards:* Named one of Top 200 Collectors, ARTnews mag, 2009-13. *Collection:* Contemporary art

VON MERTENS, ANNA
TEXTILE ARTIST
b Boston, Mass, 1973. *Study:* Brown Univ, BA, 1995; Calif Coll Arts & Crafts, MFA, 2000. *Work:* Mus Art, RI Sch Design; Robert Hull Fleming Mus, Univ Vermont. *Exhib:* Solo exhibs include Southern Exposure, San Francisco, 2001, Proj Space, Headlands Ctr Arts, Calif, 2001, Gallery Paule Anglim, San Francisco, 2002, Berkeley Art Mus, Calif, 2003, Mills Coll Art Mus, Oakland, Calif, 2004, Lizabeth Oliveria Gallery, Los Angeles, 2005, Jack Hanley Gallery, San Francisco, 2006, OKOK Gallery, Seattle, 2008, Sara Meltzer Gallery, New York, 2008; Group exhibs include Mapping, Works gallery, San Jose, Calif, 2001; Body: Inner & Outer Landscapes, Balazo Gallery, San Francisco, 2001; Commission 02, San Francisco Arts Commission Gallery, 2002; Ag: Works, 25th Silver Anniversary Exhib, Works Gallery, San Jose, CA, 2002; Preservation, Artists Space, New York, 2003; Sewn Together, Gregory Lind Gallery, San Francisco, 2003; Topographies, Pasadena Mus Calif Art, Pasadena, CA, 2004; The Searchers, White Box, New York, 2006; Elizabeth Leach Gallery, Portland, Ore, 2007; In the Private Eye, Ise Cultural Found, New York, 2008; Works from the Permanent Collection, Mus Art, RI Sch Design, 2008; Making History, Jeff Bailey Gallery, New York, 2008. *Awards:* MFA Studio Award, Headlands Ctr Arts, 2000; Louis Comfort Tiffany Found Grant, 2007

VON RECKLINGHAUSEN, MARIANNE BOWLES
PAINTER, SCULPTOR
b Munich, Ger, Jan 24, 1929; US citizen. *Study:* Self taught. *Work:* Smithsonian Inst. *Exhib:* Solo exhibs, Hudson River Mus, Yonkers, 63 & 84 & Katonah Mus Art, 82, NY, Islip Mus Art, 87, NY, Univ Mass, Lowell, 90; 19th Area Exhib, Corcoran Gallery Art, Washington, DC, 74; The Animal Image, Renwick Gallery, Smithsonian Inst, Washington, DC, 81; Assemblage & Collage Traveling Exhib, Miss Mus Art, Jackson, 81-83; Germans in New Eng, Goethe House, Boston, 83; Catholic Univ Art Gallery, Washington, DC, 83. *Teaching:* Lectr, Katonah Gallery, 82 & 86, Univ Lowell, Mass, 83 & 90. *Awards:* Painting Award, Charles of the Ritz Found, New York & 16th Ann New England Exhib, 65; First in Painting Award, Westchester Art Soc, 65-66; First in Painting Award, Lowman Mem Award, Art of the Northeast, 34th Ann Exhib, Silvermine, 83. *Bibliog:* Les Krantz (auth), American Artists; an illustrated survey of leading contemporary Americans, Facts on File, New York & Oxford, England, 85; Virginia Watson-Jones (auth), Contemporary American Women Sculptors, Oryx Press,

86; Miles Under (auth), Darkness and Light Visible: Recklinghausen's Works, The Boston Globe, 12/90. *Mem:* Artists Equity; Silvermine Guild. *Media:* Acrylic on Wood; Sequential Painted Constructions. *Publ:* Dir, Mark Sadan & Lawrence Miller (film makers) Legends From Life: 12 Constructions from Paradise (film), Film & Video Workshop, NY, 86

VON RYDINGSVARD, URSULA
SCULPTOR
b Deensen, Ger, July 26, 1942. *Study:* Univ Miami, Coral Gables, Fla, BA, 64, MA, 65; Univ Calif, Berkeley, 69-70; Columbia Univ, New York, MFA, 75. *Work:* Metrop Mus Art & Whitney Mus Am Art, NY; Brooklyn Mus, NY; Walker Art Ctr, Minneapolis, Minn; Mus Mod Art, New York. *Comn:* Laumeier Sculpture Park, St Louis, Mo; Capp St Proj, San Francisco, Calif; Bloomberg Bldg, New York; Microsoft Corp, Redmond, Wash; NC Mus Art, Raleigh; Storm King Art Ctr, Mountainville, New York. *Exhib:* Solo exhibs, Univ Wyo Art Mus, Laramie, 95, Socks on My Spoons, Univ Gallery, Univ Mass, Amherst, 95, Mus Art, RI Sch Design, Providence, 96, Galerie Lelong, NY, 96, Yorkshire Sculpture Park, Wakefield Eng, 97, Madison Art Ctr, Wis, 98, Nelson-Atkins Mus Art, Kansas City, Mo, 98-99, Hood Mus Art, Dartmouth Col, NH, 98, Chicago Cult Ctr, 99, The Contemp Mus, Honolulu, 99, Barbara Krakow Gallery, Boston, 99, 2010, Indianapolis Mus Art, 99-2000, Galerie LeLong, Zurich & New York, 2000, 2010, Cranbrook Art Mus, Bloomfield Hills, Mich, 2000, Hill Gallery, Birmingham, 2000 & The Butler Gallery, Kilkenny, Ireland, 2001, Galerie Lelong, NY, 2006, Herbert F Johnson Mus Art, Cornell Univ, 2007 & Portland Art Mus, 2007, Patricia and Phillip Frost Art Mus, Miami, 2011, deCordova Sculpture Park and Mus, Lincoln, Mass, 2011; Group exhib, Corcoran Gallery, Washington, 75; Contemp Reflections, Aldrich Mus Contemp Art, Ridgefield, Conn, 76; Selections from the Collection, Aldrich Mus Contemp Art, Ridgefield, Conn, 85; Recent Acquisitions, Metrop Mus Art, NY, 89; New Acquisitions, Brooklyn Mus, NY, 89; Outdoor Sculpture, Walker Art Ctr, Minneapolis, Minn, 90-93; Woman's Mus, Washington; Out of Wood, Whitney Mus Contemp Art, NY, 90 & Landscape as Metaphor; Denver Art Mus, 94-95; Body As Metaphor, Procter Art Ctr, Bard Coll, Annandale-on-Hudson, NY, 95; Crossing State Lines: 20th Century Art from Pvt Collections in Westchester and Fairfield Counties, Neuberger Mus Art, Purchase Col, NY, 95 & New at the Neuberger, 2005; Am Sculpture: A Contemp Perspective, Univ Wyo Art Mus, Laramie, 95; Beyond Gender: In Three Dimensions; Women Sculptors of the Nineties Snug Harbor Art Ctr, Staten Island, NY, 95; The Shape of Sound, Exit Art, NY, 96 & The End: An Independent Vision of Contemp Cult, 1982-2000, 2000; A Moveable Feast, David Klein Gallery, Birmingham, Mich, 97; Wood Work, Fisher Landau Ctr, Long Island City, NY, 97; 20/20, Contemp Arts Forum, Santa Barbara, Calif, 97; Masters of the Masters: MFA Faculty Sch of Visual Arts, NY, 1983-98, Butler Inst Am Art, Youngstown, Ohio, 98; Sculptors and Their Environments, Pratt Inst, NY, 98; KolnSkulptur 2, Cologne, Ger, 99-2000; Doris C Freedman Plaza, Central Park, NY, 2000; Drip, Blow, Burn: Forces of Nature in Contemp Art, Hudson River Mus, Yonkers, NY, 99; City Art, Ctr for Archit, NY, 2005; Material Terrain: A Sculptural Exploration of Landscape & Place, Lowe Art Mus. *Teaching:* Asst prof, Pratt Inst, Brooklyn, NY, 78-82; instr, Sch Visual Arts, 81-82; asst prof, Fordham Univ, Bronx, NY, 80-82; assoc prof, Yale Univ, New Haven, Conn, 82-86; prof, Sch Visual Arts, Grad Div, New York, 86-2002. *Awards:* Sculpture Award, Am Acad Arts & Lett, 94; Joan Mitchell Award, 97; 2nd Prize, Best Show in a Commercial Gallery, Int Asn Critics, 2000; Rappaport Prize, DeCordova Mus and Sculpture Park, Lincoln, Mass, 2008; Skowhegan Medal for Sculpture, Skowhegan Sch of Painting & Sculpture, New York, 2011; Best Show in a Non-Profit Gallery or Space, American Sect of the Int Asn of Art Critics, 2011. *Bibliog:* Paul Zelanski & Mary Pat Fisher (auths), Shaping Space, Harcourt Brace Coll Publ, New York, 95; Arthur Williams (auth), Sculpture: Technique-Form-Content, Davis Publ Inc, Worcester, Mass, 95; Dore Ashton (auth), The Sculpture of Ursula von Rydingsvard, Hudson Hills Press, New York, 96; Ann Landi (auth), Prime Cuts, ARTnews, 106-109, 1/2007; Jan Garden Castro (auth), Draping and Shaping Wood, Sculpture, 30-35, 12/2010; Ken Johnson (auth), Weekend Arts: Artifacts of an Imagined Time, New York Times, 1/2011, he Week Ahead: Art, 1/2011, Galleries: Other: Ursula von Rydingsvard: Sculpture 1991-2009, 2/2011; Carlos Suarez de Jesus (auth), Ursula von Rydingsvard's Sculptures at the Frost Art Museum Through August 5, Miami New Times, 4/2012. *Mem:* Am Acad Arts & Letters; Nat Acad. *Media:* Wood. *Publ:* Review, Art Forum, Vol 33, No 2, 10/94; 15 Sacks for Cortazar (5 drawings), Point of Contact, fall/winter, 94; Studio Visits: Pleasure, Pain and Protocol, ARTnews, Vol 95, No 3, 3/96; articles, The New Yorker,4/3/2000 & New York Contemporary art Report, 3-4/2000; Ecology: Usularon Rydingsvard, Art 21, Art in the 21st Century, PBS Thirteen/WNET, New York, 11/2007. *Dealer:* Galerie LeLong New York NY Paris Zurich; Barbara Krakow Bartin Byron Conen Kansas City

VON ZUR MUEHLEN, BERNIS SUSAN
PHOTOGRAPHER
b Philadelphia, Pa, Apr 10, 1942. *Study:* Univ Pa, BA (lit), 63. *Work:* Corcoran Gallery Art, DC; Baltimore Mus Art, Md; B'nai B'rith Nat Jewish Mus, Washington, DC; Houston Mus Fine Arts, Tex; New Orleans Mus Art, La; Wesleyan Univ, Davidson Art Ctr, Middletown, Conn. *Exhib:* Va Mus Fine Arts, Richmond, 75 & Va Photogr, 75 & 78; Nation's Capital Photogr, Corcoran Gallery Art, DC, 76 & Recent Acquisitions, 79 & 80; Solo exhibs, Baily Mus Art, Univ Va, Charlottesville, 80, Del Mus Art, Wilmington, 81, Osuna Gallery, 81, 84 & 89, Photoworks Gallery, Richmond, Va, 84, Corcoran Gallery Art, Washington, DC, 90, B'nai B'rith Klutznick Nat Jewish Mus, 92, Narratives or Desire, Troyer, Fitzpatrick, Lassman Gallery, Washington, DC, 98, Troyer Gallery, Washington, 2001; Invisible Light: An Exhibition of Infrared Photog, Smithsonian Inst, Washington, DC, 80 & 82; 35th Anniversary Area Show, Corcoran Gallery Art, Washington, DC, 82; From the Collection, Photographs by Women, Corcoran Gallery Art, 82; Recent Acquisitions in Photog, Corcoran Gallery Art, 87; Image of the Male Nude, Frankfurter Kunstverein, Fed Rep Ger, 88; Behold the Man, Photog's Gallery, London, Eng & Stills Gallery, Scotland, 88; Landscape Photographs from the Permanent Collection, Corcoran Gallery Art, 89; Jones Troyer Fitzpatrick Gallery, Washington, DC, 91; Triennial Exhib, New Orleans Mus Art, La, 92; B'nai B'rith Nat Jewish Mus, 92; Transformations: Spirit and Icon, www.Mastersofphotography.com, 2000; Evanescence, Troyer Gallery, Washington, DC, 2001; WPA, Corcoran Curated Exhib & Auction, Washington, DC, 2006; Wash Women Artists, Osuna Gallery, Bethesda, Md, 2007, 2009; Go Artists, 2010; Beautiful: Va Women Artists and the Body, Greater Reston Arts Ctr, Reston, Va, 2010. *Teaching:* Lectr, Baltimore Mus Art, Md, 78, Cath Univ, Washington, DC, 78, Corcoran Sch Art, Washington, DC, 81 & Univ Va, 87-. *Awards:* Three Judges' Awards, Womansphere, Glen Echo, Md, 75; Purchase Award, Corcoran Gallery Art, 76. *Media:* Chrome, Silver, Digital, Ink Jet. *Publ:* Contribr, The Story of American Photography: an Illustrated History for Young People, Little Brown, 79; SX-70, Lustrum Press, 79; The Male Nude in Photography, Vermont Crossroads Press, 80; Frauen Sehen Manner, Frankurter Kunstverin, Verlag Photographie, 88; Male Nudes by Women: An Anthology, Eds Stemlag, AG, 95; Male Nude Now, Universe Publ, 2001; Male Bodies: A Photographic History of the Nude, Prestel, 2004; Male Nudes: Index, Feierabend Verlag, Berlin, 2006; The Nude Male: 21st Century Visions, Rizzoli/Universe, 2008. *Mailing Add:* 10435 Hunter View Rd Vienna VA 22181

VON ZUR MUEHLEN, PETER
PHOTOGRAPHER
b Berlin, Ger, Mar 10, 1939; US citizen. *Study:* Washington Univ, St Louis, BA, 61; Princeton Univ, PhD, 72. *Work:* Corcoran Gallery. *Exhib:* Solo exhibs, Va Mus Fine Arts, 75; Marcus Pfeffer Gallery, NY, 77; Wash Project of the Arts, Wash DC 79; Corcoran Gallery Art, 90; Baily Mus Art, Charlottesville, Va, 80. *Pos:* Economist, Fed Reserve Bd, Washington, DC; retired. *Awards:* Cert Distinction, Va Photographers, Va Mus Fine Arts, 75. *Bibliog:* David Tannous (auth), article, 7/78 & Capital art: in the major leagues?, 7/79, Art Am. *Media:* Chrome, Silver. *Publ:* Contribr, One of a Kind: Polaroid Photography, Polaroid Corp, 78. *Mailing Add:* 10435 Hunter View Rd Vienna VA 22181

VOORHEES, DONALD EDWARD
PAINTER, PRINTMAKER
b Neptune, NJ, May 6, 1926. *Study:* Acad Arts, Newark, NJ; Art Students League, New York, Studied with Ed Whitney, John Pike, Mario Cooper & Don Stone. *Work:* Am Int Group, New York; Metrop Life, New York; Pfizer Chem Co, New York; Sun Oil Co, Tulsa, Okla; USA Today, & US Air, Arlington, VA; Pfizer Pharmaceuticals; Chilean Embassy, Washington, DC; and others. *Comn:* Ed of prints, Sheraton Hotels, Tulsa, Okla, 84; ed of prints, Dallas Athletic Club, Dallas, Tex, 86; ed of prints, Buick Div Gen Motors, Flint, Mich, 88; ed of Prints, AIG, New York, 90; prints, Cambridge Sports Int, Washington, DC, 91; and numerous pvt comns. *Exhib:* Frye Mus, Seattle; Edward Dean Mus, Cherry Valley, Calif; Cent Mus Wyo; Martello Mus, Key West, Fla. *Teaching:* Instr watercolor, Guild Creative Art, 65-75, pvt instr, 2007-12. *Awards:* Hudson Valley Art Asn Award; NJ Watercolor Soc Award; Salmagundi Club Award; plus others. *Mem:* NJ Watercolor Soc (pres, 75-76, life fel); Artists Fel; Salmagundi Club. *Media:* Watercolor. *Publ:* Collectors Mart, 6/84, The Artist's Mag, 4/84, Gems of New Jersey, 86, Golf Week Mag, 10/88, PGA Mag, 1/91, US Art 5/91 & Art Business News 4/94; auth, Lessons from a Lifetime of Watercolor Painting, Northlight Publ, 2006. *Dealer:* Donald Voorhees Studio Box 182 Atlantic Highlands NJ 07716. *Mailing Add:* 10 Ocean Blvd 4E Atlantic Highlands NJ 07716

VOORSANGER, BARTHOLOMEW
ARCHITECT
b Detroit, Mich, Mar 23, 1937. *Study:* Princeton Univ, AB (cum laude), 1960; Diplome, Fontainebleau, 1960; Harvard Univ, MArch, 1964. *Hon Degrees:* Univ Archit & Urbanism, Romania, Hon Dr. *Work:* Le Cygne Restaurant; Neiman houseboat; New York Univ Midtown Ctr; New York Univ Business Sch Libr; La Grandeur housing; New York Univ dormitories; Hostos Community Col, NY; Wethersfield Carriage Mus, Amenia, NY; Riverdale Jewish Ctr, NY; Port Authority NY/NJ Air Traffic Control Towers; Univ Art Mus, Univ Va; Asia Soc & Mus, NY; Olana Mus, Hudson, NY; Elie Tahari Offices, NJ; numerous pvt residences in NY, Va, Calif, Ariz, Mont & Wyo. *Exhib:* New York Univ; Archit Asn, London; Harvard Grad Sch Design; Vacant Lots Housing Study, NY; Deutsches Architeckur Mus, Frankfurt; Mus Finnish Archit; Avery Libr, Centennial Exhib, Columbia Univ; Helsinki, Brooklyn Mus; Nat Acad Mus, NYC. *Pos:* Assoc, Vincent Ponte, Montreal, Can, 1964-67; IM Pei & Partners, 1968-78; dir, Iran, 1975-78; co-chmn, Voorsanger & Mills, NY, 1978-90; chmn bd advs, Study Am Archit, Columbia Univ, N, 1989-; founder & prin, Voorsanger & Assocs, 1990-; founder, Taylor/Voorsanger Urban Designers, 1991; pres, NY Found Archit, 2000-2001; mem archit rev panel, Port Authority NY & NJ; adv, Samsung Corp, Korea; chmn bd advs, Temple Hoyne Buell Ctr; adv bd, Parsons Sch Archit; bd dirs, Worldesign Found. *Teaching:* lectr, Bennington Col, Vt, Univ Pa, Columbia Univ & Harvard Univ; guest critic & lectr, Pratt Inst, CUNY, RI Sch Design, Univ Cincinnati, Syracuse Univ & Univ Tex, Arlington; mem adv bd, Parson Sch Archit. *Awards:* finalist, Brooklyn Masterplan Competition; winner, Pierpont Morgan Libr Masterplan; winner, competition for Nat WWII Mus, New Orleans; Cannon Prize, Nat Acad Design; and many others. *Bibliog:* Dinitia Smith (auth), Hallowed Ground Zero, New York Times, 2001; Craig Kellogg (auth), (Far) East Side Makeover, Oculus, 2002; Jill Hartz (auth), The Case for a New Univ Art Mus, Arhitext Design, 2002; Jason Kaufman (auth), Lest We Forget, The Art Newspaper, 2002; Livio Dimitriu (auth), Bartholomew Voorsanger: Montana House, Arhitext Design, 2004; Kathryn Harris (auth), Raising Arizona, House Beautiful,2005; Christopher Henderson (auth), York Observatory Comes into Focus, Queens Chronicle, 2006; Elaine Louie (auth), New Digs for Hip Pets to Help Others, New York Times, 2008; John Klingman (auth), The Years Best Archit: 6 Proj Worth Examining, 2010. *Mem:* NAD (fel); AIA (fel & former pres NYC chap); J Pierpont Morgan Libr, NY (fel); Harvard Grad Sch Design Alumni Coun; Wadawanuck Club; Century Asn; Sir John Soane Mus Found; Archit League, NY (bd dirs); Ellis Island Yacht Club (commodore, 2001-); Port Authority NY/NJ Ground Zero Archive; NY Hist Soc; NY State Regent's Comt Schs. *Mailing Add:* Voorsanger Archit PC 246 W 38th St Fl 14 New York NY 10018-5805

VOOS, WILLIAM JOHN
ADMINISTRATOR, PAINTER
b St Louis, Mo, July 2, 1930. *Study:* Wash Univ Sch Fine Arts, BFA, 52; Univ Kans, MFA, 53; NY Univ, US Arts & Humanities Art Admin fel, 67. *Work:* Rend Lake Coll Collection, Mt Vernon, Ill; Mus Contemp Art, Recife, Brazil; Ga Coun Arts. *Comn:* Mural, Army Educ Ctr, Ft Bragg, NC, 54; playground mural, Ferguson Park Comn, Mo, 60. *Exhib:* Solo exhibs, Lafayette Art Ctr, Ind, 66 & Northern State Coll, 74; Fac Shows, Steinberg Hall, Wash Univ, 68-72; Atlanta Coll Art Fac Show, High Mus Art, 75; Mus Contemp Art, Recife, Brazil, 75; Herron Gallery, 85-95. *Pos:* Dean, Atlanta Col Art, 73-75 & pres, 75-85; dean, Herron Sch Art, Indiana Univ-Purdue Univ, Indianapolis, 85-95, dean & prof emer, 95-. *Teaching:* Assoc prof art & chmn humanities div, Florissant Valley Community Col, 64-68; assoc prof art & assoc dean Sch Fine Arts, Wash Univ, 68-73. *Mem:* Indianapolis Mus of Art. *Media:* Acrylic, Watercolor. *Mailing Add:* 3899 Honey Creek Blvd Greenwood IN 46143-9316

VOS, CLAUDIA
PAINTER, PHOTOGRAPHER
b New York, NY, Mar 2, 1963. *Study:* Art Students League, 77-81; State Univ NY, Coll Purchase, BFA, 81-85; Copper Union, 90-92. *Work:* Libr Cong; Nat Mus Women Arts, Washington. *Comn:* Stage set, Residents Theatre Group, Cologne, Ger, 91; painting for book "The New Covanant", Outerlimits, NY, 93; painting, Japan Network Group, Inc, NY, 94. *Exhib:* Tower Gallery, NY, 93; Weapons and Shields (with catalog), Art Gallery Brocades, The Neth, 93; Claudia Puusep, Estonia House, NY, 95; Global Focus, Nat Mus Women Arts, Beijing, China, 95; Shifting Identities, CB's Gallery, NY, 96; Estonia House, 97; Artists Space, NY, 97, 98. *Awards:* Dealers Selectee, Art Initiatives, New York, 94. *Bibliog:* Susan Rutman (auth), All points bulletin, Photo District News, 8/91; Alfonso Manosalves (ed), Portfolio, Ark-Angel Rev, spring/summer 93; Delft Times (illus), p 15, sect A. *Mem:* Nat Mus Women in Arts; Art Students League, New York. *Media:* Oil, Acrylic. *Mailing Add:* 3340 81st St Apt 2 Jackson Heights NY 11372-1336

VOSS, GARY
SCULPTOR, EDUCATOR
Study: Univ Ill, Urbana-Champaign, BFA (Sculpture), 1974; Colo State Univ, MFA (Sculpture), 1978. *Comn:* Arts in Public Places, Colo Council on the Arts and Humanities, Denver, 1984, Perry Development Company, Denver, 1984, Sutherland Sculpture Green, Colo State Univ, Fort Collins, 1992, Willard Eddy Memorial Plaques, Colo State Univ, Fort Collins, 1994. *Exhib:* Invitational Exhibitions: Spree '76 Celebration, Denver, Colo, 1976, Art Partnership Exhibit, Selected Denver Galleries, 1988, One-West Art Ctr, Fort Collins, Colo, 1991, Hard Plat, Fort Collins Mus of Contemp Art, 1999, Reinventing Pleasure: Ornamentation and Experimentation in Contemporary Ceramics, Sangre de Christo Arts Ctr, Pueblo, Colo, 2004 and others; juried exhibitions: North American Sculpture Exhibit, Golden, Colo, 1979, 2006, Convergence of Art and Science, Fort Collins Mus of Centemp Art, 2005, Perspectives, Union Street Gallery, Chgo Heights, Ill, 2007 18th Annual Nat Juried Exhibition, Art Inst & Gallery, Salisbury, Md, 2009, Fusion, Kreft Juried Exhibition, Concordia Univ, Ann Arbor, Mich, 2011 and others; solo shows: Atwell Gallery, Colo Springs, 1985, Intimate Gallery, lincoln Ctr, Fort Collins, 1988, Fort Collins Mus of Contemp Art, 2000, Snook Gallery, Adams State Col, Alamosa, Colo, 2005, Hybrids, Mariani Gallery, Univ Northern Colo, Greenley, 2008 and others; group shows: Atwell Gallery, 1984, 1986, Inkfish Gallery, Denver, 1983-86, 1993, Art Faculty Show, Colo State U-Pueblo, 2003 and others. *Pos:* dir, Sculpturescape. *Teaching:* Co-dir Sch of the Arts, chair, department of art, Univ Center for the Arts, Colo State Univ, currently; teacher, undergraduate and graduate programs in sculpture, prof of art, Colo State Univ, currently. *Publ:* Critic's Choice, Mary Voelz Chandler, Rocky Mountain News, 2001. *Mailing Add:* University Center for the Arts 1778 Campus Delivery Fort Collins CO 80523-1778

VOTE, MELANIE
PAINTER
Study: Iowa State Univ, BFA (craft design), 1995; Grad Sch Figurative Art, NY Acad Art, MFA (painting, cum laude), 1998. *Exhib:* The Drawn Page, Aldrich Contemp Art Mus, 2004, Aldrich Undercover, 2006; 4 Artists/4 Walls, Interior Paintings, DFN Gallery, New York, 2004, 10th Anniversary Show, 2005, Wet, 2007, Works on Paper, 2008; Night & Day, Women's Caucus Art, Fairfield, Conn, 2005; The Beholder's Eye, Salmagundi Art Club, New York, 2006; Summer Exhib, NY Acad Art, 2007; Visions of Childhood, Bronfman Ctr Gallery, New York, 2008. *Teaching:* Instr, NY Acad Art, 2001; adj instr, Mohawk Valley Community Coll, Utica, NY, 2003; vis instr, Pratt, Manhattan Campus, New York, 2003; adj prof, Jersey City Univ, 2003-08; asst adj prof, Hofstra New Coll, Hempstead, NY, 2003-08; asst adj prof, York Coll, Jamaica, NY, 2008. *Awards:* Art & Design Chairperson Award, 1994; Anna Tohman Leadership Award, 1995; Dodge Found Fel, 2002; Rosenthal Found Best of Show Award, 2003; Pollock-Krasner Found Grant, 2007. *Mem:* Alumni Asn NY Acad Art; Coll Art Asn. *Dealer:* DFN Gallery 210 11th Ave 6th Floor NY 10001

VOURVOULIAS, JOYCE BUSH See De Guatemala, Joyce Bush Vourvoulias

W

WACHS, ETHEL
EDUCATOR, COLLECTOR
b New York, NY, Dec 26, 1923. *Study:* Brooklyn Coll, with Philip Pearlstein, A D Reinhardt & Jimmy Ernst, BS, MA & MS. *Exhib:* Nat Asn Women Artists, Federal Bldg, NY, 80-92; Nat Acad Design, NY, 80 & 82; Audubon Artists, Nat Arts Club, NY, 81-92; Bergen Community Mus, Paramus, NJ, 83; solo exhib, New Sch for Soc Res, 90-92; Marquet Patisserie, New York, 2003-09. *Teaching:* Teacher fine arts, High Sch Health Professions & Human Serv, New York, 58-2004, substitute teacher, 2004-09; instr adult educ, Brooklyn Coll, New York, 68-96. *Awards:* Martha Reed Mem Award, 91; Philip Isenberg Award, 96; Savoir Faire Paper Award, Audubon Artists, 99. *Mem:* New York Artists Equity; New York Soc Women Artists; Nat Asn Women Artists; Audubon Artists; Am Soc Contemp Artists. *Media:* Watercolor. *Interests:* Creating animal pins. *Collection:* Contemporary American art. *Mailing Add:* 20 E 9th St New York NY 10003

WACHTEL, JULIE
PAINTER
b New York, NY, July 24, 1956. *Study:* Middlebury Col, BA, 78; independent study prog, Whitney Mus, 79. *Work:* Brooklyn Mus, NY; Chase Manhattan Bank, NY; Progressive Corp, NY; Am Bar Asn, NY. *Exhib:* Solo exhib, Mus Contemp Art, Chicago, 91; Pittura Immedia, Neue Galerie am Landesmuseum Joanneum Graz, Graz, Ger, 95. *Bibliog:* Joshua Dechter (auth), Julia Wachtel, Mus Contemp Art, 91; Paul Ardenne (auth), Julia Wachtel: For an Ethics of Vision & Julia Wachtel: Expositions in France, Ondes de Pierre, Calif, 95. *Media:* Oil on canvas. *Dealer:* Sandra Gering Gallery Wooster St New York NY 10012. *Mailing Add:* 85 Quay Brooklyn NY 11222-2016

WADDELL, JOHN HENRY
SCULPTOR, PAINTER
b Des Moines, Iowa, Feb 14, 1921. *Study:* Art Inst Chicago, BFA, MFA, 48, BAE & MAE, 51; Univ Chicago; Eureka Col, Eureka, Ill. *Hon Degrees:* Nat Coll Educ, Evanston, Ill, Hon DFA & DAE, 79. *Work:* Phoenix Art Mus, Ariz; Univ Ariz Mus Art, Tucson; Kenyon Col, Gambier, Ohio; Ravinia Park, Highland Park, Ill; First Unitarian Universalist Congregation, Phoenix, Ariz; Flinn Found: "Compassion" bronze figure, Phoenix, 2000; US Tennis Assoc, Flushing Meadows, NY; Herberger Theater Center, Phoenix, Ariz; Detroit Med Ctr; West Valley Art Mus, Surprise, Ariz; Sedona Med Center, Sedona, Ariz; Robert Mondavi Winery, Oakville, Calif; Carver Mus & Cult Center, Phoenix, Ariz; Phoenix Pub Libr, Phoenix, Ariz. *Comn:* Dance (12 figure sculpture), City of Phoenix, Herberger Theater, 74; I Am That I Am (sculpture), Temple Beth Israel, Phoenix, 82; Backwalkover (sculpture), Ctr Sports Med & Orthopedics, Phoenix, 85; Touchstone (stone sculpture), Boswell Mem Hosp, Sun City, Ariz; Carver Mus, 98; Herberg Theater Center; Bust of Dr Anne Pittman, Hall of Fame Tennis Coach (sculpture), Ariz State Univ. *Exhib:* Northern Ariz Univ Art Mus & Gallery, 73, 82, 91-98; Coconino Ctr Arts, Flagstaff, 82 & 91, 2009; Robert Mondavi Winery, 82, 86 & 94; Scottsdale Ctr Arts, 84; Tempe Arts Ctr, Ariz, 90; Sun Cities Art Mus, 91-92; Retrospective Gallery, San Diego, Calif, 91; Phoenix Art Mus, 60, 62 & 64; Shrine of the Ages, Grand Canyon Nat Park, 2007; James A Michener Mus Art, Doylestown, Pa, 2010-2011; Trinity Cathedral, Phoenix, 2011; Painting Retrospective, Herberger Theater Ctr, 2013. *Pos:* Sculptor. *Teaching:* Instr art & art educ, Nat Col Educ, Evanston, Ill, 49-55; asst prof art, Inst Design, Chicago, 55-57; prof art, Ariz State Univ, 57-61 & 63-64; founder & dir, Master Apprentice Prog, Waddell Sculpture Fel, 72-92. *Awards:* Artist of the Year, Nat Soc Arts and Letters, 75; Artist of the Year, Ariz Gov Arts Awards, 95, Herberger Theater Hall of Fame, 2011; O'Connor House Nat award for Civic leadership, 2011. *Bibliog:* Alan Baker (dir), The Beauty of Individual Differences, Ariz State U; Amy Waddell (dir), The Reluctant Muse, 95; Michel F Sarda (auth), John Henry Waddell, the Art & the Artist, Bridgewood Press, Phoenix, Ariz, 96; Michael Sarda (auth), Faces of Arizona, 99; Univ Chgo Mag, 2005; Sedona Mag, 2003; Linda Freegard (auth), Living with Beauty, Playing with Fire (13 minute DVD); (DVD), Fall to the Sky (basedon Waddell Sculptural relief "Rising"), 8 minute dance, Choreography by Lisa Chow, Desert Dance Theatre, 2010; Marlo Bendau, Rising (film), 2010; (57 minute film), PBS, and film festivals. *Media:* Figurative Bronze, Stone; Pastel, Watercolor, oil. *Specialty:* Figurative Art. *Publ:* Dir, Discovering Sculpture, 58 & Discovering Drawing and Painting (films), 61; auth, The Beauty of Individual Differences, Master Apprentice Programs, 85. *Dealer:* John and Ruth Waddell 10050 E Waddell Rd Cornville AZ 86325-6010. *Mailing Add:* 10050 E Waddell Rd Cornville AZ 86325-6010

WADDELL, THEODORE
PAINTER
b Billings, Mont, Oct 6, 1941. *Study:* Brooklyn Mus Art Sch, 62; Eastern Mont Col, Billings, Mont, BS, 66; Wayne State Univ, Detroit, Mich, MFA, 68. *Work:* Eastern Mont Coll & Yellowstone Art Ctr, Billings, Mont; Sheldon Mem Art Gallery, Univ Nebr, Lincoln, Nebr; City of Great Falls, Mont; Dallas Mus Art; San Jose Mus, Calif. *Exhib:* 38th Corcoran Biennial, Corcoran Gallery, Washington, DC, 83; solo exhibs, Univ Calif, San Diego, 84, Cheney Cowles Mem Mus, Spokane, Wash, 85; The New West, Colorado Springs Fine Arts Ctr, Colorado Springs, 86; Bernice Stein Baum Gallery, NY, 92. *Bibliog:* Gordon McConnell (auth), Theodore Waddell, Yellowstone Art Ctr, 84. *Media:* Oil on Canvas. *Mailing Add:* c/o Stremmel Gallery 1400 S Virginia St Reno NV 89502

WADE, ROBERT SCHROPE
PAINTER, SCULPTOR
b Austin, Tex, Jan 6, 1943. *Study:* Univ Tex, Austin, BFA, 65; Univ Calif, Berkeley, MA, 66. *Work:* Menil Collection, Houston, Tex; Groningen Mus, Holland; Beaubourg Mus, Paris, France; NMex State Capitol; Royal Palace, Monaco; Nat Cowgirl Mus, Ft Worth, Tex; Dallas Mus, Austin Mus. *Comn:* Giant Iguana, Lone Star Cafe, NY, 78; Biggest Cowboy Boots, Washington Art Site, DC, 79; Giant Sax, Billy Blues, Houston, Tex, 93; Photo Canvas Murals; Torch Engery, Houston, 2001; photo canvas mural, Titos Vodka, Austin, Tex, 2011; Photo Canvas Series; Tex State Univ, 2012. *Exhib:* solo exhibs, Kornblee Gallery, NY, 71 & 74, Paris Biennale, Paris, France, 77, Jan Turner Gallery, Los Angeles, 78 & Elaine Horwitch Galleries, Santa Fe, NMex, 87, 90, 93 & 95; Biennial, Whitney Mus Am Art, New York, 69 & 73; Sky Art Festival, Anchorage, AK, 89; Stremmel Gallery, Reno, Nev, 95; M D Mod, Houston, Tex, 98; William Campbell Contemp Art, Ft Worth, Tex, 2000, 2003, 2008-2012; Nat Cowgirl Mus & Hall of Fame, Ft Worth, Tex, 2003; Am Pavilion Expo, Aichi, Japan

2005; Daddy-O's Texas Tales, Mus of the Southwest, Midland, Tex, 2008; 40 Yrs, South Austin Mus Popular Cult, Tex, 2009; Raising the Bar, Tex Lutheran Univ, Seguin, Tex, 2011; Art on the Green, La Guna Gloria Mus, Austin, Tex, 2012. *Teaching:* Instr, McLennan Col, 66-70; artist-in-residence & dir, Northwood Exp Art Inst, Dallas, 70-73; asst prof, NTex State Univ, Denton, 73-77; vis artist, Kansas City Art Inst, 79 & 92. *Awards:* Nat Endowment Grants, 73, 74 & 84; Career Achievement Medal, Austin Visual Arts. *Bibliog:* Kim Goad (auth), Bob Wade, A Portrait of the Artist as a Thoroughly Texas Icon, Dallas Morning News, 91; Jutta Feddersen (auth), Soft Sculpture (book), Gordon & Breach Int, London, NY, 93; Jeff Guinn (auth), Whats Up Daddy-o?, Ft Worth Star Telegram, 98; Karen Dinitz (dir) Too High Too Wide Too Long (documentary film), 99; Susie Kalil (auth), Bob Wade interview, Artlies Mag, Houston, Tex, Spring 2000; Vikki Loving (auth), Wildly Austin, Austin's Landmark Art, Wildly Austin Press, 2004; Jason Mellard (auth), Catalog Essay "40 Years", South Austin, Mus Pop Cult, 2009; Goetzmann and Goetsmann (auth), West of the Imagination, Univ Okla Press, 2009; Keith Oberman (host), Helicopter & Giant Iguana, MSNBC, 2010; Michael Brick (auth), Lizard as Big as Texas, New York Times, 2010; Roy Bragg (auth), Art for Big State, San Antonio Express News, 2012. *Media:* Miscellaneous Media. *Publ:* Article, Art Press Int, Paris, France, 10/77; coauth, Daddy-O: Iguana Heads and Texas Tales, St Martins Press, 95; Bob Wades Cowgirls, Gibbs Smith Pub, Salt Lake City, 2003; Ridin and Wreckin, Gibbs Smith Pub, 2006. *Dealer:* William Campbell Contemporary Art Fort Worth TX. *Mailing Add:* 3502 Winsome Ct Austin TX 78731

WADE, VALERIE
GALLERY DIRECTOR
Study: Va Commonwealth Univ, BFA (art history). *Pos:* Cons, Szoke Koo Assocs, NYC, 1984-87; sales rep, Crown Point Press, 1988, gallery dir, 1993-2006, dir, 2006-; adv bd, Southern Exposure. *Mem:* San Francisco Art Dealers Asn; ArtTable (Northern Calif chap). *Mailing Add:* Crown Point Press 20 Hawthorne St San Francisco CA 94105

WADLER, RONNI
PAINTER, ILLUSTRATOR
b New York, NY, Feb 26, 1946. *Study:* Queens Col, BA (fine arts), 67; Univ Wis-Madison, MA (painting), 69. *Work:* Queens Col. *Exhib:* 82nd Ann Exhib, Allied Artists Am, 95; 16th & 18th Ann Faber Birren, Nat Color Award Show, Mus Stamford, Conn, 96 & 98; Int Colored Pencil Exhib, San Diego, 95-97, 2001; Art Exhib, Athens, Greece, 96; 17th, 18th, 19th Ann Non-mems Exhib, Salmagundi Club, NY, 94-96; 56th Ann Exhib, Audubon Artists, 98; Realism Today, John Pence Gallery, San Francisco, Calif, 2000; Catherine Lorillard Wolfe Art Club, Int Exhib, New York City, 98, 2000. *Pos:* Film ed, Wis Bur Pub Instr, 68-69; freelance illusr with var publ, 88-96. *Teaching:* Asst instr drawing, Univ Wis, 68-69; teacher art, NY Pub Schs, 69-76; guest lectr Luoyang Univ Teachers Col, Luoyang, China, 99; instr Colored Pencil Painting, Greenwich, Conn, 98-99. *Awards:* Finalist, Realism Today, Am Artist, 2000; Yarka Art Materials Award, Audubon Artists, 98; and others. *Bibliog:* Contribr, The Best of Colored Pencil, 93, The Best of Colored Pencil 2, 94, Creative Colored Pencil, 95, The Best of Colored Pencil 3, 96, The Best of Colored Pencil 4, 97 & The Best of Colored Pencil 5, 99, Rockport Publ; illusr, Design Libr, Rockport Publ, 95. *Mem:* Nat Asn Women Artists; Colored Pencil Soc Am. *Media:* Colored Pencil, Pastel, Monotypes, Oil Painting. *Publ:* Sixtieth Ann Competition Finalists, American Artist, Oct, 97; Realism Today, American Artist Magazine, Oct 2000; Coping Through Art, American Artist Magazine, March 2005; Colorful Additions, Artists Mag, 93. *Dealer:* Steve Demus Bon a Tirer Gallery NY; Erlich Fine Arts Marblehead Mass. *Mailing Add:* 118 S La Jolla Ave Los Angeles CA 90048-3530

WAGNER, ELISE
PAINTER
b Jersey City, NJ, 1966. *Study:* Portland State Univ, Ore, BS (Richard Muller Meml Scholar, 1993, Lucille Welch Meml Scholar, 1994), 1995. *Work:* Portland State Univ; Univ Ore; LPL Financial Svcs; Kodiak Venture Ptnrs; Bulivant, Houser, Bailey PC; Saks Fifth Ave Nat Collection. *Exhib:* Solo exhibs, Quartersaw Gallery, Portland, 1997-99, Laura Russo Gallery, Portland, 2001 & 2003, Butters Gallery, Portland, 2006 & 2008, Chase Gallery, Boston, 2007 & 2009, Hallway Gallery, Bellevue, Wash, 2008; The Birds, Mark Whoolley Gallery, Portland, 1997; October Show, 333 Studios, Portland, 1998; Carrying On, Portland State Univ, 1999; San Francisco Int Art Exhib, Fort Mason, 2000; Unearthed: Contemporary Landscape, Davidson Galleries, Seattle, 2001; White Linen Night, Sylvia Schmidt Gallery, New Orleans, 2002; Encaustic Works, Biennial, Marist Coll Art Gallery, Poughkeepsie, 2003; Rouge Art Gallery, Medford, Ore, 2004; Butters Brand Abstraction, Butters Gallery, 2005; This Bountiful Place, Ore Hist Soc, 2006; Printmaking Currents, Pacific Northwest Coll Art, 2007; Sitka Art Invitational, World Forestry Ctr, Portland, 2008; Director's Choice, Chase Gallery, Boston, 2009. *Teaching:* Guest lectr, Portland Community Coll, 2001, Pacific Northwest Coll Art, 2002, Ore Coll Art & Craft, 2002; instr, Ore Coll Art & Craft, 2007 & Red Deer Coll, Alberta, Can, 2008; guest instr, Lewis & Clark Coll, Portland, 2009. *Awards:* Artist-in-residence, Vt Studio Ctr, 2001; Sue Lynn Thomas Juror's Honor award, 2004 & Univ Honda Award, 2006, Art About Agriculture, Ore State Univ; Best in Show, Pacific Northwest Art Ann, Ore Cult Trust, 2008. *Bibliog:* D K Row, All in the Name of Progress, The Oregonian, 1998; Pat Boas (auth), Elise Wagner at Laura Russo Gallery, Artweek, 7-8/2001; Jennifer Anderson (auth), Artist Find Kindred Spirits and Inspiration in NoPo, Portland Tribune, 2005. *Media:* Encaustic. *Mailing Add:* c/o Butters Gallery 520 NW Davis 2nd Fl Portland OR 97209

WAGNER, MERRILL
PAINTER
b Seattle, Wash, June 12, 1935. *Study:* Sarah Lawrence Col, BA, 57; Art Students League, NY, with Edwin Dickenson, George Grosz & Julian Levy, 59-63. *Work:* Chase Manhattan Bank, NY; Seattle Arts Comn, Wash; Tacoma Art Mus, Wash; Weatherspoon Art Gallery, Univ NC, Greensboro; Rose Art Mus, Brandeis Univ, MA; Gemeente Mus, The Hague, Holland; Richard Gluckman Archit, NYC; Microsoft Corp, Redmond, Wash. *Exhib:* Solo exhibs, The Clocktower, Inst Art & Urban Resources, NY, 79, Watson DeNagy Gallery, Houston, 82, Traver Gallery, Seattle, 87 & 2008, 89, 91, 96-97 & 99, Gemeente Mus, The Neth, 91, L Gray Gallery, Providence, RI, 91, Stark Gallery, NY, 92, Larry Becker Cont Art, Philadelphia, Pa, 2007, Patty Look Lewis Gallery, Santa Barbara, Calif, 2008, Lesley Heller Gallery, New York, 2008, Sundaram Tagore Gallery, New York, 2008, Lesley Haller Gallery, NY, 2008, Traver Gallery, Seattle, Wash, 2009, Larry Becker Contemp Art, Philadelphia, 2010; Larry Becker Gallery, Philadelphia, 93; Outdoor installation, CW Post Campus, Long Island Univ, 93; Impermanence, Aldrich Mus, Ridgefield, Conn, 93; Painting Outside Painting (with catalog), Corcoran Gallery Art 44th Biennial Exhib Contemp Am Painting, 95; Better Color through Chemistry, Islip Mus, NY, 97; Merrill Wagner & Scott Reynolds, Workspace Gallery, NY, 98; Painting with an Edge: Four Contemp Artists, Hunterdon Mus Art, Clinton, NJ, 98; Substance, Tricia Collins Contemp Art, NY, 98; Hands on Color, Bellevue Art Mus, Wash, 98; Copper Drawings, Garner Tullis Workshop, New York City, 98; Works on Slate, William Traver Gallery, Seattle, 99, Recent Paintings on Steel, 2001; Nicolaysen Art Mus, Caspar, Wis, 2000; Freedman Gallery, Reading, Pa, 2000; Univ of Wyo, Laramie, 2001; William Traver Gallery, Tacoma, Wash, 2001-03; group exhibs, Ann Messner & Merrill Wagner, Lenore Gray Gallery, Providence, RI, 2001, 25th Anniversary Exhib, William Traver Gallery, Seattle, Wash, 2002, Theories, Abstract NY Recent Paintings, LICK Lte, Fine Art, LI City, NY, 2003, Beyond the Surface, Sundaram Tagore Gallery, New York, 2004, New Arts Gallery, Litchfield, Conn, 2008, New Arts Prog, Kutztown, Pa, 2008; Univ of Puget Sound, Kitteridge Gallery, Tacoma, WA, 2002; Kiyo Higashi Gallery, Los Angeles, Calif, 2003; Sundaram Tagore Gallery, New York City, 2004; New Arts Program, Kutztown, Pa, 2005; Renate Bender, Munich, Ger, 2006; William Paterson Coll, Wayne, NJ, 2006; William Traver Gallery, Seattle, 2006; Univ RI, Kingston, 2007; Sundaram Tagore Gallery, New York, 2007. *Pos:* Lectr, William Paterson Coll, Wayne, NJ, 2006, Univ RI, Kingston, 2007, Lesley Heller Gallery, New York, 2007. *Teaching:* Vis lectr in the humanities, drawing & painting, Princeton Univ, 83-91, prof advan painting, 83-; instr drawing, Univ Puget Sound, summer 85 & 86 & Parson's, 92-97. *Awards:* Nat Endowment Arts Visual Artists Fel Grant, 89; Nat Endowment Arts Award Artists Bks, 90; AIGA Book Show Cert of Excellence, 91; Northwest Design Award, 92; Hassam Purchase Award, Am Acad of Arts & Lett, 2002; Acad Award in Art, Am Acad Arts and Letters, 2006. *Bibliog:* Edward Leffingwell (auth), Merrill Wagner, Art in Am, 12/2005; Ken Johnson (auth), For A Broad Landscape...', The NY Times, 5/31/2006; Lilly Wei (auth), Merrill Wagner, Art News, 5/2007; Carrie Lovelace (auth), Art in Am, 11/2007; Shane McAdams (auth), The Brooklyn Rail, 4/2007; Ben La Rocco (auth), The Brooklyn Rail, 2008. *Mem:* Am Abstract Artists (pres, 82-85). *Media:* Multi. *Specialty:* contemporary art. *Publ:* A Calendar, September 1982-December 1983, Magna Color Press, Inc, 82; auth, Notes on Paint, pvt publ, 90; Time and Materials, pvt publ, 95; Painted Sun Trails, pvt publ, 96; Oil & Water, pvt publ, 2001; Roger Boyce (auth), Art in Am, Merrill Wagner at Startk, 2002; ART Press, Merrill Wagner, 2003; Public and Private, pvt publ, 2004. *Dealer:* Traver Gallery Seattle WA; Larry Becker Contemporary Art Philadelphia PA; Sundaram Tagore Gallery New York NY. *Mailing Add:* 17 W 16th New York NY 10011

WAGNER, SARAH
INSTALLATION SCULPTOR
Study: Univ Tenn, Chattanooga, BFA (magna cum laude), 1994; Calif Coll Arts, MFA, 2005. *Exhib:* 12th Ann Mich Artists Exhib, Paint Creek Ctr for the Arts, Rochester, 1998; Auspicious Day, Mills Coll Concert Hall, Oakland, 2001; Sliv and Dulet Present:A Summer Line, New Langton Arts, San Francisco, 2003; solo exhibs, Asn for Visual Artis, Tenn, 2004, Yerba Buena Ctr for the Arts, San Francisco, 2006, George Ayers Cress Gallery, Univ Tenn, 2008, Santa Clara Univ, Calif, 2008; Perceptions, Calif Coll Arts, San Francisco, 2004; Small Works, Oakland Art Gallery, Calif, 2005; Everything but the Kitchen Sink, Flippo Gallery, Randolph-Macon Coll, Ashland, Va, 2007. *Pos:* Co-founder, Metro Art Gallery Collective, Tenn, 1993-94; apprentice, Faith/Works Pottery, Flintstone, Ga, 1994-95; freelance fabricator, Oakland, Calif & Pontiac, Mich, 1995-2007; preparator, Cranbrook Inst Sci, Cranbrook Art Mus, Bloomfield Hills, Mich, 1996-99, Revolution Gallery, Ferndale, Mich, 1997-99, Wattis Inst, Berkeley Art Mus, Jewish Art Mus, Calif, 1999-01; asst to Jack Lackey, Cranbrook Acad Art, 1997-99; milliner, San Francisco Opera, Calif, 2001; foreman, Batenburg & Assocs Home Remodeling, 2001-04; cur, PlaySpace Gallery, Calif Coll Art, 2004-05, Big Pagoda co, 2005-07. *Teaching:* Instr, West Bloomfield & Waterford Sch Dist, Mich, 1997-98 & Paint Creek Ctr for the Arts, Rochester, Mich, 1997-99, Piedmont Recreation Dept, 2005-06; instr art, Calif Coll Arts, Oakland, 2004-07, lectr, 2007; instr fiber and material studies, Sch Art Inst Chicago, 2007-08. *Awards:* Pollock-Krasner Found Grant, 2008. *Bibliog:* Silke Tudor (auth), Caught on Tape, San Francisco Weekly, 10/2002; Anne Nichols (auth), Crossover, Chattanooga Times Free Press, 4/18/2004; Ann Gordon (auth), Oh So Beautiful, Real Detroit Weekly, 5/18-24/2005

WAGONER, ROBERT B
PAINTER, SCULPTOR
b Marion, Ohio, July 13, 1928. *Study:* With Burt Procter & Olaf Weighorst. *Work:* Leanin' Tree Publ Mus, Boulder, Colo; Winthrop Rockefeller Collection. *Exhib:* Death Valley 49ers, Calif, 61; two-man shows, Scottsdale, Ariz, 72 & 73 & three-man show, 74; Mont Hist Soc, Helena, 74; Previews, Tex Gallery, Dallas, 75-79. *Pos:* Dir, Death Valley 49ers, 69-. *Awards:* First Award & Top Artists Award, Death Valley 49ers, 72 & 73 & First Award, 74, 75 & 76. *Bibliog:* James Serven (auth), Cattle, guns and cowboys, Ariz Hwys Mag, 70; Robert Wolenik (auth), Colorful west of Robert Wagoner, Westerner, 1-2/73; Portrait of a Westerner, Sierra Life Mag, 81. *Media:* Oil, Watercolor; Canvas, Masonite. *Dealer:* Texas Art Gallery Dallas TX; Saddleback Western Art Gallery Santa Ana CA. *Mailing Add:* 2710 Highland Dr Bishop CA 93514

WAHL, JONATHAN C
SCULPTOR
Study: Tyler Sch Art, Temple Univ, BFA, 1990; SUNY, New Paltz, MFA, 1994. *Work:* Samuel Dorsky Mus Art, New Paltz; Mus Arts & Design, New York. *Exhib:* Contemporary Crafts of New York State, NY State Mus, Albany, 1998; Defining Craft, Am Craft Mus, New York, 2000; Formed to Function, Kohler Arts Ctr, Wis, 2003; Art of Aging, Mus Hebrew Union Coll, Jewish Inst Religion, New York, 2004; Homomuseum, Exit Art, New York, 2005. *Awards:* Outstanding achievement award, Pa Soc Goldsmiths, 1990; Career Develop Grant, Empire State Craft Alliance, 1996; Biennial Award, Louis Comfort Tiffany Found, 1997; NY Found Arts Fel, 2009. *Bibliog:* Marjorie Simon (auth), Mikromegas, Metalsmith Mag, 2002; Grace Glueck (auth), The Art of Aging, NY Times, 1/16/2004; Suzanne Murray (auth), Keep Your Beauty in Balance, Organic Style Mag, 11/2005

WAHLING, JON B
SCULPTOR, WEAVER
b Council Bluffs, Iowa, Apr 14, 1938. *Study:* Kansas City Art Inst & Sch Design, BFA, 62; Haystack Mountain Sch Crafts, Deer Isle, Maine, summers 63-65; Cranbrook Acad Art, MFA, 64; also with Maija Grotell & Glen Kauffman. *Work:* Columbus Mus of Art, Ohio; Yager Gallery, Hartwick Col; Univ Art Mus, Univ Tex, Austin; Ohio Arts Coun; Huntington Mortgage Co, Columbus, Ohio. *Comn:* Fiber sculpture hanging, Merchants & Mechanics Fed Loan & Savings Bank, Springfield, Ohio, 79. *Exhib:* Packard Gallery, Columbus Mus Art, Ohio, 77; Fiber Directions, Grunnier Gallery & Mus, Iowa State Univ, Ames, 82; In the Round, Southern Ohio Mus & Cult Ctr, Portsmouth, 83; The Works, Statewide Touring Exhib, Ohio Found Arts, 83-84; Five Sculptors, Springfield Art Ctr, Main Gallery, Ohio, 87; solo shows, Fiber Art, Ells Gallery, Blossom/Kent Festival, Blossom Music Ctr, Ohio, 87 & Gallery 200, Columbus, Ohio, 88 & 90; Disciples of Reenchantment: Jon Wahling, Paulus Berenshn, Ted Hallman, Mel Someroski, Columbus Cult Arts Ctr, Columbus, Ohio, 97; Coming of Age: The Ohio Arts Coun Fellowship Recipients, Rife Gallery, Columbus, Ohio, 2001; Innovators & Legends: Generations in Textiles and Fiber, Muskegon Mus Art, Muskegon, Mich, 2012-2014. *Collection Arranged:* Lenone Davis and Bill Helwig: Surface Design and Enamels, Columbus Cultural Art Ctr, Ohio. *Pos:* Cur, artistic coordr, Garment Design: In Celebration of Body & Soul, Columbus Cult Arts Ctr, Ohio, 87. *Teaching:* Instr weaving, Columbus Cult Arts Ctr, Columbus Recreation & Parks Dept, Ohio, 64-; instr weaving, Penland Sch Crafts, NC, summers 66, 67 & 71; adjunct prof design, Columbus State Community Col, Col, Ohio. *Awards:* Craftsmen USA Nat Merit Award, Mus Contemp Crafts, New York, 66; Ten Outstanding Young Men Award, Columbus Jaycees, 72; Bordens Award for Outstanding Design in Fibre, 7th Beaux Arts Designer/Craftsmen Exhib, 73. *Bibliog:* Maryann Reilly (auth), Commissions opportunities for today's artists, Ohio Arts J, 7/80; Carla Peterson (auth), Technical virtuosity, Ohio Arts J, 1/85. *Mem:* Am Crafts Coun; hon mem Cent Ohio Weavers Guild; Ohio Designer Craftsmen; Ohio Designer Craftsmen (secy, 82-83); Surface Design Asn (North regional rep, Ohio rep). *Media:* Fiber, Metal, Pigments, Canvas. *Interests:* International travel. *Mailing Add:* 1794 E Broad St Columbus OH 43203

WAHLMAN, MAUDE SOUTHWELL
ADMINISTRATOR, HISTORIAN
b New York, NY. *Study:* Colo Col, BA (art), 69; Northwestern Univ, MA (anthrop), 69; Yale Univ, PhD (art hist, teaching fel), 80. *Collection Arranged:* Contemp African Arts, 73-75; Contemporary African Fabrics, Mus Contemp Art, Chicago, 75; Ten Afro-Am Quilters, 82-; Gifts of the Spirit, 84-85. *Pos:* Consult African ethnology, Field Mus Nat Hist, Chicago, 71-74. *Teaching:* Asst prof art hist & southern studies, Univ Miss, 80-85; assoc prof & chmn art dept, Univ Cent Fla, Orlando, 85-98; Dorothy & Dale Thompson, Missouri Endowed Prof Global Arts, Art & Art History Dept, Univ Mo, Kansas City, 98. *Awards:* Res Grant Southern Folk Arts, Nat Endowment Humanities, 81-84; Nat Endowment Arts Grant, 82; Resident Research Fel, Harvard Univ African Am Art, 98. *Mem:* African Studies Asn; Am Folklore Soc; Soc Folk Arts Preservation; Women's Caucus Art. *Media:* Photography. *Res:* Historical roots of Afro-American Folk. *Publ:* Auth, Ceremonial Art of West Africa, Mich State Univ, 79; Traditional Art of West Africa, Colby Col, 80; co-ed, Spirit of Africa, Memphis State Univ, 82; auth, Afro-American Quiltmaking, Ind Univ (in prep); Religious Symbols in Afro-American Folk Arts, New York Folklore, Philip Stevens, Vol 12, No 1-2. *Mailing Add:* 9700 Overbrook Rd Leawood KS 66206

WAHRHAFTIG, CLAIRE ISAACS
ADMINISTRATOR
b San Francisco, Calif, Feb 12, 1933. *Study:* Pomona Col, BA, 54; Ohio State Univ, 54-55; Univ Calif, Berkeley, 62-64; Univ Southern Calif, 71; Claremont Grad Sch, MA(20th century art hist), 75; Harvard Univ, cert art mgt, 77, Coro fel pub affairs for arts mgr, 79. *Collection Arranged:* Children's Book Illustrators (artmobile exhib), 67; Art of the African (traveling exhib), 69; Children's Art From Three Countries: Japan, Iran, USSR, 76; Int Child Art Collection, 1978-83 (auth, catalog), 83. *Pos:* Asst, Art Gallery, Univ Calif, Berkeley, 61-63; educ supvr, San Francisco Mus Mod Art, 63-66; asst dir & coordr, Visual Art Proj, PACE (Proj to Advance Creativity in Educ), San Bernardino, Inyo & Mono Co Sch, 66-69; dir, Jr Arts Ctr, Munic Arts Dept, Los Angeles, 70-83, Barnsdall Art Ctr, Los Angeles Affairs Dept, 80-83; dir cult affairs, City & Co, San Francisco Arts Comm, 83-90. *Teaching:* Lectr art for deaf, Univ Calif Exten, Los Angeles, 72. *Awards:* Golden Gate Award, Western Asn Art Mus, 78. *Mem:* Am Asn Mus; Am Asn Youth Mus; Nat Art Educ Asn. *Publ:* Auth, Paul Klee and Galka Scheyer, Artforum, 62; The Art of Borrowing and Distributing Art for the Small Community, Visual Arts Proj, 70; ed, Proceedings of the Conference on Art for the Deaf, Jr League Los Angeles, 75; contribr, The Museum and the Visitor Experience, Western Regional Conf Am Asn Mus, 77. *Mailing Add:* 56 Roble Rd Berkeley CA 94705

WAID, JIM (JAMES) E
PAINTER
b Elgin, Okla, Nov 2, 1942. *Study:* Univ NMex, with Morris Kantor & John Kacere, BFA, 65; Univ Ariz, MFA, 71. *Work:* Univ Ariz Mus Art; Metrop Mus Art, NY; Yuma Art Ctr, Ariz; IBM, Montvale, NJ; Chemical Bank, NY. *Comn:* Santa Cruz (mural), Tucson Pub Libr, 77. *Exhib:* 35th Biennial, Corcoran Gallery Art, 77; First Western States Biennial, Nat Collection Art, Washington, DC, 79-80; Four Corners States Biennial Exhib, Phoenix Art Mus, 81; Solo exhibs, Mus Art, Univ Ariz, Tucson, 85, Riva Yares Gallery, Scottsdale, Ariz, 86 & 88, Linda Durham Gallery, Santa Fe, NMex, 87, Southwest Tex State Univ, San Marcos, 87 & Shoshana Wayne Gallery, Santa Monica, Calif, 88; Phoenix Biennial, Phoenix Art Mus, 87; Large Scale Paintings, Riva Yares Gallery, Scottsdale, Ariz, 88; The New/Old Landscape, Mus Art, Univ Ariz, Tucson, 89. *Teaching:* Instr art, Pima Community Col, 71-80. *Awards:* Purchase Prizes, Arizona's Outlook, Tucson Mus Art, 80 & 14th Southwestern Invitational, Yuma Art Ctr, Ariz, 80; Nat Endowment Visual Arts Fel Grant, 85. *Mem:* Artists Equity; Dinnerware Artists Coop (treas, 79-82). *Dealer:* Riva Yares Gallery 3625 Bishop Lane Scottsdale AZ 85251. *Mailing Add:* c/o Riva Yares Gallery 3625 Bishop Ln Scottsdale AZ 85251

WAINWRIGHT, ROBERT BARRY
PAINTER, PRINTMAKER
b Chilliwack, BC, June 29, 1935. *Study:* Vancouver Sch Art, dipl, 62; Atelier 17, Paris, with S W Hayter, Emily Carr Travel Study Scholar, 62. *Work:* Nat Gallery Can; Art Gallery Ont; Mus Fine Arts, Mus Art Contemp, Montreal; Can Indust Ltd, Toronto. *Exhib:* Premio Int Biella L'Incisione, Italy, 71, 73 & 76; solo exhib, Galerie Martal, Montreal, 72, Concordia Univ, Montreal, 76 & 80 & Mazelow Gallery, Toronto, 77; Galerie Elca London, Montreal, 84. *Teaching:* Assoc prof printmaking, Concordia Univ, Montreal, 66-. *Awards:* Can Coun Grants, 63-64 & 67-68; Erindale Coll Purchase Prize, Int Exhib Graphics, Montreal, 71. *Mem:* Royal Can Acad Arts; Can Artists Rep. *Dealer:* Galerie Daniel 2159 Mackay St Montreal PQ H3G 2J2

WAISBROT, ANN M
ADMINISTRATOR, CURATOR
b Wausau, Wis, Oct 12, 1943. *Study:* Univ Wis, Stevens Point, BS (art educ), 70. *Collection Arranged:* New Visions' Culture & Agriculture, (Nat Invitational Exhib) 89-98; Tradition & Innovation: Japanese Prints from the Collection; Ira Moskowitz (original drawings, painting, prints), 91-92; India: A Sense of Form & Color (art artifacts from pvt collections), 92; Memories of New Guinea, Medicine & Art, 96; Wahid Nahle: The Vibrant Canvas, 98. *Pos:* Exec dir, New Visions Gallery Inc, Marshfield, Wis, 86-. *Mem:* Am Asn Mus; Midwest Mus Conf; Wis Fed Mus; Am Coun Arts; Am Crafts Coun. *Mailing Add:* New Visions Gallery 1000 N Oak Ave Marshfield WI 54449

WAKEHAM, DUANE ALLEN
PAINTER, WRITER
b Port Huron, Mich, May 2, 1931. *Study:* Mich State Univ, with Abraham Rattner, BA, 59; Stanford Univ, with Daniel Mendelowitz & Matt Kahn, MA, 61. *Work:* Galleries Claremont Coll, Calif; Port Huron Mus Art. *Exhib:* Artists of Hawaii, Honolulu Acad Art, Hawaii, 54; Mich Artists Ann, Detroit Inst Art, Mich, 59; Drawings of the Human Head (contribr, catalog), Metrop State Coll, Denver, Colo, 89; solo exhib, Triton Mus Art, Santa Clara, Calif, 90; Pastels Only, Pastel Soc Am, New York, 92-2007; Pastels USA, Pastel Soc W Coast, Sacramento, Calif, 93-2007. *Teaching:* Instr drawing & painting, Stanford Univ, Calif, 60-62 & 64-65; prof art hist & painting, Coll San Mateo, Calif, 65-87. *Awards:* Pastel Soc Am Hall of Fame, 2000; Master Pastellist, Pastel Soc Am, 95; Distinguished Pastellist, Pastel Soc W Coast, 95. *Bibliog:* Jean McCord (auth), Duane Wakeham: Sharing a way of seeing Am Artist, 11/77; Bruce Nixon (essay), Duane Wakeham-Recent Paintings, 97; Kristina Feliciano (ed), The Best of Pastel 2, Rockport Publ, 98; John Driscoll & Arnold Skolnick (auths), The Artist and the American Landscape, First Glance Bks, 98; Maggie Price (auth), Duane Wakeham, The Pastel J, 9-10/2000; Lynne Muss Perricelli (auth), Make Studies, Make Better Pictures, Am Artist, 9/2005. *Publ:* Auth, Joe Price: Serigraphs in light and tone, Am Artist, 10/77; coauth, Mendelowitz's Guide to Drawing, Harcourt Brace, rev eds, 82, 88, 92, 2003 & 2007; Contemporary landscape painting, Artweek, 9/3/92; auth, Arriving at representation through abstraction, Am Artist, 8/94. *Mailing Add:* 218 Hoffman Ave San Francisco CA 94114

WAKSBERG, NOMI
PAINTER, PHOTOGRAPHER
b Ger, July 16, 47; US citizen. *Study:* Ohio State Univ, Columbus, BFA & BSci, 69; Md Inst Art, Baltimore, 70; Rutgers Univ, New Brunswick, NJ, MA & MFA, 72. *Work:* Ohio State Univ, Columbus; Continental Life Insurance Co, NY; Continental Group Investors, New Haven, Conn; First Nat Bank, Chicago; Japanese Embassy, Washington, DC; Robert Wood Johnson Hospital, NJ; and others. *Exhib:* One-person show, Lehigh Univ, Bethlehem, Pa, 80, Morris Mus, Before Katrina, St John's Univ, New York, 2010; Artists Books, Philadelphia Art Alliance, 81; Rutgers Invitational, State Mus, Trenton, NJ, 82; Alternative Mus, NY, 82; Condeso/Lawler, NY, 82; Muse Found, Philadelphia, 83; State Mus, Trenton, NJ, 86; Lemieux Gallery, New Orleans, 2005; Robert Miller Gallery, New York, 2005; Islip Mus Contemp Art, NY, 2006; Artists Space, New York, 2006; Sikkema Jenkins & Co, New York, 2006; The Most Curatorial Biennial of the Universe, APEX ART, New York, 2007; Jersey Arts Ann, Noyes Mus Art, 2007; Summer, Jersey City Mus, 2008; and others. *Pos:* Coordr & cur, Women Artists Series, Douglass Col Libr, 72-76; project dir, Her Own Space, Muse Foud, 82. *Teaching:* Instr art hist, Trenton State Univ, NJ, 80-81. *Awards:* Bea Camhi Award, Hudson River Mus, 80; NJ Arts Fel, 82-83; NJ Arts Coun Award, 82 & 84; Nat Endowment Award, Her Own Space, 83. *Bibliog:* Kay Larson (auth), Small talk, Village Voice, 2/11/80; Victoria Donahue (auth), rev, Philadelphia Inquirer, 5/81; Judith Stein (auth), article, Art Express, 11-12/81; Benjamin Genocchio (auth), NY

Times, 7/23/2006. *Mem:* Women's Caucus Art (steering comt, 79-81); Coll Art Asn, 2005-. *Media:* All Media. *Publ:* Contribr, Lehigh University Fall Collections, Lehigh Univ, 80. *Dealer:* Condeso/Lawler 119 West 25th St New York NY; Van Straaten Gallery 646 N Michigan Ave Chicago IL. *Mailing Add:* PO Box 21 Flemington NJ 08822-0021

WALBURG, GERALD
SCULPTOR, EDUCATOR
b Berkeley, Calif, May 5, 1936. *Study:* Calif Coll Arts & Crafts, 54-56; Calif State Univ, San Francisco, BA, 65; Univ Calif, Davis, MA, 67. *Work:* Storm King Art Ctr, Mountainville, NY; San Francisco Mus Art, Calif; Oakland Mus; Metrop Mus Art, NY; City of San Francisco. *Comn:* Sculptor, City of Sacramento, McCven & Steele, Calif. *Exhib:* San Francisco Mus Art, 67 & 69; Joslyn Art Mus, Omaha, Nebr, 70; Oakland Mus, Calif, 71 & 74; Baltimore Mus Art, Md, 73; Storm King Art Ctr, Mountainville, NY, 73-74; Crocker Gallery, Sacramento, 73 & 79; Soc of the Four Arts, Palm Beach, Fla, 74; NY Cult Ctr, 75; Bank of Am World Hq, San Francisco, 82. *Teaching:* Prof art, Calif State Univ, Sacramento, 68-. *Bibliog:* Gerald Nordland (auth), Gerald Waldburg Recent Works, Oakland Mus, 79; David Collen & H Peter Stern (coauth), Sculpture at Storm King, NY, 80; Thomas Albright (auth), articles, San Francisco Chronicle, 4/17/76 & 12/19/78. *Mem:* Int Sculpture. *Media:* Metal, Welded. *Mailing Add:* Art Dept Cal State Univ Sacramento 6000 J St Sacramento CA 95819-6061

WALD, SYLVIA
PAINTER, SCULPTOR
b Philadelphia, Pa. *Study:* Moore Inst Art, Philadelphia. *Work:* Mus Mod Art, Metrop Mus Art & Whitney Mus Am Art, NY; Guggenheim Mus; Nat Gallery Art, Washington; Brooklyn Mus, NY; Aetna Oil co ; AAUW, Ball State Teachers Coll; Bibliotheque Nat Paris; Brooklyn Mus; Howard Univ; State Univ Iowa; Libr Cong; plus others. *Exhib:* Solo exhibs, Knoll Int, Munich, 79 & Construction & Sculpture, Aaron Berman Gallery, NY, 81, Tenri Cult Inst, 2004; Hirschl & Adler Gallery, NY, 93; New Brit Mus Am Art, 94; Dongah Art Gallery, Seoul, Korea, 95; Dong Shin Univ, Kwangiu, Korea, 96; Mus of Art, Chousun Univ, Kwangju, 2002; group exhib, Tenri Cult Inst, 2005; 2x13 Gallery, NY, 2006; Korea Gallery, NY, 2006; Celebration of Women Artists, Hirschl & Adler Gallery, New York, 2008; A Parallel Presence, Zimmerli Art Mus, Rutgers Univ, NJ, 2009; Two Artists Show, Sylvia Walk and Po Kim Art Gallery, NY, 2009; Sylvia Wald & Po Kim Art Gallery, New York, 2010. *Bibliog:* Zigrosser (auth), Prints and Their Creators-A World History, 74; Una E Johnson (auth), American Prints and Printmakers, 80; James Watrous (auth), A Century of American Printmaking 1880-1980, 84. *Mem:* Am Fedn Arts. *Media:* Miscellaneous. *Mailing Add:* 417 Lafayette St New York NY 10003

WALDMAN, LOUIS A
EDUCATOR
b Wyandotte, Mich, Oct 29, 1965. *Study:* Hunter Col, BA, 89; NY Univ, MA, 93, PhD, 99. *Hon Degrees:* Accademia delle Arti del Disegno, Florence, Ital, 2004. *Teaching:* Lectr renaissance art, Syracuse Univ, Florence, NY, 99; sr lectr renaissance art, Univ Tex, Austin, 2000, asst prof, 2000-2006, assoc prof, 2006-; acting asst dir, Villa I Tatti, Harvard Ctr for Ital Renaissance Studies, 2007-. *Awards:* Fel, Kunsth Inst, Fla, 95-97; Postdoctoral Fulbright, 99-200; I Tatti, 2005-2006. *Mem:* Coll Art Asn, Renaissance Soc Am. *Res:* Italian painting, sculpture, architecture, theory and criticism, 1400-1600. *Publ:* Auth, Baccio Bandinelli & Art at the Medici Court, Philadelphia, Am Philos Soc, 2004. *Mailing Add:* Univ Tex Dept Art & Art History Campus Mail Code D1300 Austin TX 78712-0337

WALES, KITTY
SCULPTOR
b 1957. *Study:* Boston Univ; Univ Ariz, MFA (sculpture). *Work:* Pine Sharks (sculptures), DeCordova Mus and Sculpture Park, Lincoln, Mass. *Exhib:* Represented in permanent collections Duxbury Art Complex Mus, Auburn Park, Cambridge, South Shore Conserv, Hingham, Mass. *Teaching:* Boston Univ, Dean Coll, Univ Ariz, Univ Mass Boston; vis artist, Gordon Sch, Waltham and Westboro High School, Commonwealth Sch, Boston. *Awards:* Award, Boston Found; Award, Elizabeth Found; Award, Mass Cult Coun; Award, Berkshire Taconic Community Found; Award, Virginia A Groot Found. *Mem:* Boston Sculptors Gallery. *Media:* Miscellaneous Media. *Mailing Add:* c/o Boston Sculptors Gallery 486 Harrison Ave Boston MA 02118

WALETZKY, TSIRL (CECELIA) GROBLA
ASSEMBLAGE ARTIST, STAINED GLASS ARTIST
b New York, NY, Feb 12, 1921. *Study:* Art Student League, NY, 42-43; Pratt Graphics, NY, 71; Parson's, 76-78. *Work:* Yeshiva Univ Mus, Cooper Hewitt Mus (Smithsonian), Jewish Mus, NY; Wolfson Mus, Jerusalem, Israel; Judaica Mus, Riverdale, NY. *Comn:* stained glass panel (with David Nulman), Hebrew Tabernacle, NY, 80; stained glass, 9 windows (with David Nulman), Cong Chofetz Chayim, Tucson, 88; stained glass scroll (with David Nulman), Cong Har Shalom, Potomac, Md, 89; cut-paper assemblage, Riverdale Temple, NY, 90; stained glass windows (with D Nulman), Cong B'nai Jacob, Phoenixville, Pa, 92-95, stained glass backlit panels (with D Nulman) Temple Emanuel, Lynbrook, NY, 96; Cut-paper Assemblage, Temple Shalom, Lawrence, NY, 98. *Exhib:* paper-cuts, Tower of David Mus, Jerusalem, Israel, 81; paper-cuts, Cooper Hewitt Mus, NY, 86; Stained glass (with David Nulman), Yeshiva Univ Mus, NY, 86; contemp paper-cuts, Judaica Mus, Riverdale, NY, 88; Expressions of Faith, Santuario de Guadalupe, Santa Fe, NMex, 90; Cut-paper Assemblage: Abrams Art Ctr Henry St, NY, 97; Castellani Mus, Niagara Falls, NY, 98; cut-paper and watch parts assemblage, Yeshiva Univ Mus, Ctr for Jewish Hist, 2004; plus others. *Teaching:* Judaic paper cutting, Hebrew Arts Sch, 85-87. *Bibliog:* From Editors, Papercuts by Tsirl Waletzky, Lilith, 78; Alice Greenwald (auth), The Mizrah, Hadassah Mag, 79; Lillian Wachtel (auth), Aus Kulturallem Interesse, Aufbau, 90. *Mem:* NY Artists Equity; Pomegranate Guild Judaic Needlework (bd mem, 76-94); Guild Am Papercutters. *Media:* Cut-Paper Assemblage; Stained Glass Design. *Publ:* illustr The New Book of Yiddish Songs, 72 & Pearls of Yiddish Songs, 88, Workmen's Circle; The Art of Judaic Needlework, Charles Scribners, 79; Eight Tales for Eight Nights, Jason Aronson, 90; The Jewish Wedding Book, Scripps Howard, 91; illustr, Yiddish Literature in America (two covers) 1870-2000, Vol 1, 99; Rememberings by Pauline, Wengeroff, Univ Md Press, 2000. *Mailing Add:* 11215 Seven Locks Rd #129 Potomac MD 20854-3250

WALFORD, E JOHN
HISTORIAN, EDUCATOR
b London, Eng, Feb 16, 1945. *Study:* Vrije Universiteit, Amsterdam, Kandidaats(hons), 76; Wolfson Col, Cambridge Speelman Fel (Dutch & Flemish art), 76-80; Univ Cambridge, Eng, PhD, 81. *Teaching:* Assoc prof & dept chmn art hist, Wheaton Col, Ill, 81-. *Mem:* Coll Art Asn; Historians Netherlandish Art; Asn Art Historians, Gt Brit. *Publ:* Auth, Art and the Christian today, Messiah Col, 85; Jacob Van Ruisdael and the Perception of Landscape, Yale Univ Press, New Haven, London, 91; also occasional paper series. *Mailing Add:* Wheaton Col 501 E College Ave Wheaton IL 60187

WALGREN, FRANCES J
APPRAISER
Study: Art Hist, Queens Col, NY, MA, 85; Attended, Parsons Sch Design, NY; Attended, Am Col, Paris. *Pos:* With Christie's, NYC, 91—, specialist in books and manuscripts, department head, North America. *Awards:* Catalogued and auctioned the Fox-Bute Set of Audubon's Birds of America (2000) for $8 million, a world auction record for any printed book. *Mailing Add:* Christies/NY 20 Rockefeller Plz New York NY 10020

WALKER, ANDREW J.
MUSEUM DIRECTOR, CURATOR
Study: Bowdoin Coll, AB (summa cum laude, art hist); Univ.Pa, PhD (history of art). *Pos:* rsch cons, Amon Carter Mus American Art, formerly, dir, 2011-; curator, Mo History Mus, formerly, Art Inst Chgo, formerly; asst dir curatorial affairs American art, Saint Louis Art Mus, formerly. *Awards:* Henry Luce Found / American Coun Learned Socities Dissertation Fellowship for Study American Art; Jacob Javits Found, US Dept Educ. *Mailing Add:* Amon Carter Museum of American Art 1305 Camp Bowie Blvd Fort Worth TX 76107

WALKER, BERTA
ART DEALER
b New York, NY. *Study:* Univ Colo, 59-61; Burdett Coll Bus, AA, 64. *Pos:* Founding dir mus progs, Opportunity Resources Arts, New York, 76-79; corp relations-spec events, Whitney Mus Am Art, New York, 79-81; assoc dir, Marisa del Re Gallery, New York, 81-83; founding dir, Graham Mod Gallery, New York, 84-89; owner, Berta Walker Gallery, Provincetown, Mass, 90- & Walkers Wonder Gallery. *Awards:* Community Serv Award, Provincetown Art Asn & Mus, 2008; Best Outer Cape Gallery, Cape Cod View, 2000. *Mem:* Fine Arts Work Ctr Artists Colony, Provincetown, Mass (chair, bd & trustee, formerly); Art Table, NY; Am Fedn Arts; Am Asn Mus; Provincetown Repertory Theatre, Mass (trustee, formerly); Provincetown Art Asn & Mus. *Specialty:* Provincetown affiliated art, folk, functional art and African art. *Mailing Add:* 208 Bradford St Provincetown MA 02657

WALKER, DANIEL
MUSEUM DIRECTOR
Study: Bowdoin Coll, BA; Harvard Univ, MA. *Collection Arranged:* Cur, Flowers Underfoot: Indian Carpets of the Mughal Era, Metrop Mus Art, 1998. *Pos:* Assoc cur to cur Ancient, Near Eastern & Far Eastern Art, Cincinnati Art Mus, 1975-1988; head Islamic Dept, Metrop Mus Art, New York, 1988-2005, Patti Cadby Birch Cur in Charge, Dept Islamic art, 1997-2005. *Mailing Add:* The Textile Museum 2320 S St NW Washington DC 20008

WALKER, JOHN SEIBELS
PAINTER
b Columbia, SC, Nov 12, 1960. *Study:* Univ South, BA (Studio Arts) 1983; apprentice study in classical realism, Atelier Lack, Minn, 1991. *Pos:* 19th and early 20th cent art dealer; instr, Charles Cecil Studios, Florence, Italy, 1991-; portraitist and fine artist, Charlotte, NC, 2000-. *Mem:* Am Soc Classical Realism; Am Soc Portrait Artists. *Media:* acrylic, oil

WALKER, KELLEY
PAINTER, SCULPTOR
b Columbus, Ga, 1969. *Study:* Univ Tenn, Knoxville, BFA, 1995. *Work:* Mus Mod Art, New York; Whitney Mus Am Art, New York; Capc Musée d'art Contemporain, Bordeaux, France; Carnegie Mus Art, Pittsburgh, Pa; Saatchi Collection, London, Eng; Rubell Collection, Miami, Fla. *Exhib:* Solo exhibs include Paula Cooper Gallery, New York, 2003, 2006 & 2008, Guyton/Walker, Midway Contemp Art, St Paul, Minn, 2004, La Salle de Bains, Lyon, France, 2005, Power House Memphis, 2006 & 2009, Gallerie Catherine Bustide, Brussels, Belgium, 2006, Capitain Petzel, Berlin, 2009, 2010, Thomas Pane Gallery, London, 2010; group exhibs include Andrew Kreps Gallery, New York, 1999; Ten in One Gallery, New York, 2001; Paula Cooper Gallery, New York, 2002, 2003, 2004; G Fine Art, Wash, DC, 2002; Anton Kern Gallery, New York, 2003; Exit Art, New York, 2004; Artists Space, New York, 2005; PS1 Contemp Art Ctr, Long Island City, NY, 2005; La Salle de Bains, Lyon, France, 2005; Serpentine Gallery, London, 2006; Whitney Biennial, 2006; Saatchi Gallery, London, 2006; PS1 Contemp Arts, Queens, NY, 2006; Thomas Dane Gallery, London, 2006; Mus de Hallen Haarlem, Haarlem, Netherlands, 2007; Modern Art Oxford, Oxford, England, 2007; Le Magasin Centre Nationál de'art Contemporain, Grenoble, France, 2007; Wiels Brussels, Belgium, 2007 & 2008; New Mus, NY, 2008; The Power Plant,

Toronto, Can, 2008; Biennale de Venezia, Venice, 2009; Galeria Massimo de Carb, Milan, Italy, 2009; Commentary, Paula Cooper Gallery, New York 2009; Cave Paintings, Gallery PSM, Berlin, 2009; Beg Borrow & Steal, Rubell Family Collection, Miami, 2010; Image Transfer, Henry Art Gallery, Seattle, Wash, 2010; Keeping It Real, Act 4, Material Intelligence, White Chapel Gallery, London, 2011. *Media:* Acrylic. Mixed Media. *Dealer:* Paula Cooper Gallery 534 W 21st St New York NY 10011. *Mailing Add:* c/o Paula Cooper Gallery 534 21st St New York NY 10011

WALKER, LARRY
PAINTER, EDUCATOR
b Franklin, Ga, Oct 22, 1935. *Study:* High Sch Music & Art, New York; Wayne State Univ, Detroit, BS, 58, MA, 63. *Work:* African Am Mus, Dallas, Tex; Mus Contemp Art Ga, Atlanta; LaGrange Art Mus, Ga; Clark Atlanta Univ, Atlanta; Huntsville Mus Art, Ala; Hammonds House Mus, Atlanta; The Studio Mus Harlem, New York; Fulton Cty Arts Coun, Atlanta; City of Atlanta; Contel Corp, Atlanta; Philadelphia Mus Art, Pa; Spelman Coll, Atlanta; Hartsfield-Jackson Int Airport, Atlanta; Hallmark Cards, Kansas City, Mo; Troutman & Sanders Law Firm, Atlanta; Univ Pacific; Haggin Art Mus, Stockton, Calif. *Exhib:* Solo exhibs, Mason Murer Fine Art, Atlanta, 2007, 2009, Sande Webster Gallery, Philadelphia, 2005, 2007, 2009, The Tubman African Am Mus, Macon, Ga, 2008, Mus Contemp Art of Ga, Atlanta, 2008, LaGrange Mus, 2007, Georgia Coll & State Univ, Milledgeville, Ga, 2004, Bank of Am Plaza, Atlanta, 2004, Huntsville Mus Art, Huntsville, Ala, 2003, Invitational/Group: Word, Peters Street Gallery, Atlanta, 2010, Drawing, Mason Murer Fine Art, Atlanta, 2010, Perception/Reality, K Cole & L Walker, Thelma Harris Art Gallery, Oakland, Calif, 2009, Tradition Redefined, The Larry & Brenda Thompson Collection of African Am Art, David Driskell Ctr, univ Md, 2009, City Gallery East, Atlanta, 2008, Univ Ark Art Gallery, 2007, Wayne State Univ, Detroit, Mich, 2007, The Birmingham Mus Art, Ala, 2005, and others. *Pos:* Prof emeritus, Sch Art & Design, Ga State Univ, 2000-. *Teaching:* Prof painting, drawing & art educ, Univ of the Pac, 64-83, chmn art dept, 73-80; dir, Sch Art & Design, 83-94, Ga State Univ, Atlanta, prof, 83-2000. *Awards:* Distinguished Faculty Award, Ga State Univ, 2000; Distinguished Alumni Award, Wayne State Univ, 2007; Working Artists Project, Charles Loridans Found, Mus Contemp Art, Ga, 2007-2008. *Bibliog:* Samella Lewis & Ruth Waddy (auths), The Black Artist on Art, Vol I, Contemp Crafts Publ, 69; article in Black Art, summer 77. *Mem:* Nat Coun Art Adminrs (bd dir, 76-79, 84-88, chmn, 78-79, 86-87); Nat Asn Sch Art & Design (bd dir, 89, 90-93); DeKalb Coun for the Arts (bd dir, 87-92, pres, 89-90); Hammonds House Mus, (bd dir, 10 years, pres, 6 years); Contemp Art Ctr (bd dir, 6 years); Mus Contemp Art Ga, 2009. *Media:* Acrylic, Charcoal. *Specialty:* Contemp Art. *Interests:* Photography, curating & judging art exhibs. *Publ:* Auth, The Visual Arts in the Ninth Decade, NCAA, 80; numerous revs of local & regional art exhibs, Stockton Record, Calif, 81-83; The State of the Arts in San Joaquin County, Walker & Watanabe, 81-82; Working Artist Proj, catalogue of Exhib, Mus Contemp Art, Ga, 2007-2008; Encounters, Larry Walker Exhib catalogue, Huntsville Mus, 2003; Body & Soul, Contemp Southern Art, Exhib Catalogue, Columbus Mus, 97. *Dealer:* Mason Murer Fine Art 199 Armour Dr Atlanta GA 30324; Sande Webster Gallery 2006 Walnut St Philadelphia PA 19103

WALKER, LARRY
PAINTER, EDUCATOR
b Newark, NJ, Mar 31, 1952. *Study:* Jersey City State Col, NJ, BA, 73; Denver Univ, Colo, grad study, 75-76; Montclair State Col, NJ, MA, 80. *Exhib:* New Jersey Parks & Recreation Comn, Newark, 80; Rutgers Univ, Newark, NJ, 81; Transport NY-NJ, 82; Prudential Insurance Co, Newark, NJ, 82; Emerging and Established, Newark Mus, NJ, 83; Jersey City Mus, NJ, 83; Metro Show, City Without Walls Gallery, Newark, NJ, 84; Atrium Gallery, Morristown, NJ, 95. *Pos:* Treas, Northern NJ Chap, Nat Coun Artists, 81-; district coordr, Union Teen Arts Festival, Union, NJ, 84-86. *Teaching:* Art teacher, Newark Bd Educ, 76-78, Elizabeth High Sch, NJ, 80-; adj instr art, Jersey City State Col, NJ, 83-. *Awards:* Grant, NJ State Coun Arts, 85; Geraldine R Dodge Found Artist/Educ Grant, 98. *Mem:* Nat Conf Artists; Art Educators NJ. *Media:* Mixed Media. *Mailing Add:* 55 Randolph Place No 101 South Orange NJ 07079

WALKER, LAURIE ANN
SCULPTOR, CONCEPTUAL ARTIST
b Montreal, Que, Feb 2, 1962. *Study:* Mount Allison Univ, BFA (distinction), 84; NS Coll Art & Design, MFA, 87. *Work:* Musée Dárt Contemporain de Montréal, Que; Can Coun Art Bank, Ottawa, Ont; Banque Nationale, Montreal, Que. *Exhib:* Eye of Nature, Walter Phillips Art Gallery, Banff, Alta, 89; solo shows, Southern Alta Art Gallery, Lethbridge, Alta, 90, Oakville Galleries, Oakville, Ont, 94, Musée Dart Contemporain, Montreal, Que, 94; Rise & Fall, MacDonald Stewart Art Ctr, Guelph, Ont, 96 & Agnes Etherington Art Ctr, Kingston, Ont, 96; Voir, Savoir, Croire, Musée Régional De Rimouski, Que, 97. *Awards:* Joseph F Stauffer Prize, Can Coun, 89. *Dealer:* Galerie Christiane Chassay Catherine St W Suite 372 Montreal PQ H3B1A2

WALKER, MARIE SHEEHY
PAINTER
b Glen Cove, NY, May 23, 1952. *Study:* Rosemont Col, BFA, 74; Art Students League, with Robert Brackman, 74-77. *Work:* Rosemont Col. *Comn:* Heffernan Hall (watercolor), Rosemont Col, 74. *Exhib:* Nat Acad Design Ann Exhib, NY, 82; Pastel Soc Am Ann Exhib Pastels Only, Nat Arts Club, NY, 82 & 83; Nassau Co Mus Ann Show, Roslyn, NY, 82 & 83; Nat Asn Women Artists Exhib, Bergen Community Mus, Paramus, NJ, 83; Nat Asn Women Artists Traveling Painting Exhib, 83-85; Huntington Libr, NY, 2003; 7x7 Seven Painters, Seven Sculptures, Hutchiars Gallery, CW Post, Long Island Univ. *Awards:* Pastel Soc Am Award, Salmagundi Show, 80; Charlotte Winston Mem Award, Nat Asn Women Artists Exhib, 83; Gold Medal Oil Painting, Nat Art League, 83; Pastel Society Award, Suburban Art League Open Juried Show, 2003; Silver Medal, National Arts League Members Show, 2003; Award of Excellence, Suburban Art League Open Show, 2004; Bronze Medal National Arts League, Members Show, 2004; Anna Hyatt Huntington Award, Catherine Lorillard Wolfe Art Club, 2011. *Mem:* Pastel Soc Am; Nat Asn Women Artists; Art Students League; Nat Art League; Catharine Lorillard Wolfe; Art League of Long Island; Suburban Art League of Long Island; Conn Pastel Soc; Audubon Artists; Am Artist Professional League; Salmagundi Club. *Media:* Pastel, Oil; Watercolor. *Dealer:* Huntington Art Gallery Main St Huntington. *Mailing Add:* 3 Huxley Dr Huntington NY 11743

WALKER, MARY CAROLYN
CRAFTSMAN, JEWELER
b Lancaster, Pa, Oct 24, 1938. *Study:* Pa State Univ, BS (home art); Rochester Inst Technol Sch for Am Craftsmen, with Don Drumm & Eleanor Moty. *Comn:* Maya Schock Award to Women in the Arts, Doshi, 85. *Exhib:* Young Americans, Mus Contemp Crafts, NY, 62; Southern Tier Arts & Crafts Show, Corning, NY, 73; First World Silver Fair, Mexico, 74; Spec Exhib for Nat Gov Conf, 76; one-person show, Pa Designer Craftsmen Gallery, Bushkill, 82; and others. *Pos:* Own, Tamcraft Products Co, Mechanicsburg, Pa, 60-. *Awards:* First Prize Metals, Harrisburg Arts Festival, 72; Best in Show, 73 & Fine Work in Precious Metals, 90, Pa Guild of Craftsman; and others. *Bibliog:* R Stevens (auth), Arts decoratifs, La Revue Mod des Arts et de la vie, France, 12/72. *Mem:* Am Crafts Coun (secy, Northeast Region, 71-74); Pa Guild Craftsman (treas, 70-71, pres, 72, vpres, 73); Harrisburg Craftsmen (pres, 70, secy, 72, treas, 73); Doshi Ctr Contemp Art (bd dir, 82-86). *Media:* Sterling Silver

WALKER, MORT
CARTOONIST
b El Dorado, Kans, Sept 3, 1923. *Study:* Wash Univ, Architecture. *Hon Degrees:* Univ Mo, BA; Wm Penn Col, Hon LLD, 81. *Work:* Bird Libr, Syracuse Univ; Boston Univ Libr; Kans State Univ; Montreal Humor Pavilion; Smithsonian Inst; Int Mus Cartoon Art; Ohio State Univ; and others. *Exhib:* Metrop Mus Art, NY, 52; Brussels Worlds Fair, 64; Mus Louvre, Paris, 65; NY Worlds Fair, 67; Expo, Montreal, 69; Int Mus Cartoon Art, 2000; Ohio State Univ, 2010. *Pos:* Creator of Beetle Bailey, King Features Syndicate, 50-, Hi & Lois, 54-, Sam's Strip, 61-63, Boner's Ark, 68-, Sam & Silo, 77, The Evermores, 82 & Gamin and Patches, 87; pres, Comicana Corp, currently. *Teaching:* Scholar-in-Residence, Univ Mo, 92. *Awards:* Inkpot Award, 79; Wordsmith Award, 90; Gold T-Square Award, Nat Cartoonists Soc, Lifetime Achievement, 99; and others; Purple Heart Award; NCS Ledgend Award; Reuben Award; Gold Key Hall of Fame; Adamson Award, Sweden. *Mem:* Nat Cartoonists Soc (pres, 60); Artists & Writers Asn (pres, 96-); Soc of Illustr. *Media:* Ink. *Publ:* Ed, Nat Cartoonists Soc Album, 61, 65 & 72; auth, Most, 71; Land of Lost Things, 72; auth & illusr, Backstage at the Strips, 76, Lexicon of Comicana, 81 & Best of Beetle Bailey, 84; The Coconut Crew, 96; ed, Inklings Magazine; auth, Mort Walker's Private Scrapbook, 2004; The Tallest Man in the World (novel); Mind Control; and 300 paperbacks, films & DVDS. *Mailing Add:* 61 Studio Rd Stamford CT 06903

WALKER, RANDY
SCULPTOR
b Tacoma, Wash, 1970. *Study:* Univ Ore, Eugene, BArch, 1994. *Comn:* Return Journey, George A Brackett Park, City of Minneapolis, 2005; Threaded wall, Sci Mus Minn, St Paul, 2006; Dream Elevator, City of St Louis Park, Minn, 2007; Woven Olla, City of Santa Fe, NMex, 2008. *Exhib:* Int Juried Exhib, NJ Ctr for Visual Arts, Summit, 1999; 26th Ann Juried Art Exhib, Bloomington Art Ctr, Minn, 2001; Art of Today: Artists from North Dakota and Minnesota, Plains Art Mus, Fargo, 2002; Transformations 5: Contemporary Works from Found Objects, Soc for Contemp Art, Pittsburgh, 2005; Paul Whitney Larson Gallery, Univ Minn, St Paul, 2007. *Awards:* Forecast Pub Artworks Grant, 2004; Minn State Arts Bd Grant, 2004, 2007; Pollock-Krasner Found Grant, 2008

WALKER, RONALD C
ARTIST
b Oxnard, Calif, Sept 3, 1958. *Study:* Cent Mo State Univ, MA; Univ Kans, MFA; studied with Gerd Koch, Margaret Peterson. *Work:* 11'x 14', Off the Deep End, Maturango Mus. *Exhib:* Solo Exhibs: Florence Events Ctr, Florence, Ore, July 2007; Pacific Grove Art Center, Pacific Grove, Calif, 2008; St Suppery Gallery, Napa, Calif, 2008; Grand Gallery, Tracy, Calif, 2008; Studio Channel Islands, Calif State Univ Channel Islands, Camarillo, 2009; Cedar Centre, Lancaster, Calif, 2009; Maturango Mus, Ridgecrest, Calif, 2011; Art Depot Gallery, Fontana, Calif, 2011, Goodkind Gallery, Glasgow, Montana, 2011, Lux Ctr Arts, Lincoln, Nebr, 2012, Twisted Fairy Tales, 2012, FE Gallery, Sacramento, Calif, 2013, Buenaventura Art Assn, Ventura, Calif, 2014, Merced Coll, Merced, Calif, 2014; Group exhibs, 12 Batavian Int Exhib, Richmond Meml Libr, Batavia, NY, 2001; 6th Nat, Cincinnati Art Club, Cincinnati, 2001; Sanchez Art Center, Pacifica, Calif, 2004; Brown & Scurlag Galleries, Beaumont, Tex, 2004; Upstream People Gallery, Omaha, 2005; Invitational Salon Exhib Small Works, New Arts Prog, Kutztown, Pa, 2006; Santa Cruz Art League, Santa Cruz, Calif, 2006; Featured Artist, Ghost Pony Gallery, Tuchas, NMex, July 2007; Chico Art Ctr, Chico, Calif, 2010; Ghost Pony Gallery, Truchas, NMex, 2010; 2 Person Show, Florence Events Ctr, Ore, 2014. *Collection Arranged:* Cent Mo State Univ, Warrensburg; Art City Gallery, Ventura, Calif; Learning Tree Univ, Thousand Oaks, Calif; Maturango Mus, Ridgecrest, Calif. *Teaching:* Art Instr, Tacoma Com Coll, Gig Harbor, Calif, 93-95; Art Instr, San Juan Sch Dist, 95-. *Awards:* Second Place, Internat Juried Competition, Pindar Gallery, NY, 92; Honorable Mention, 9th Internat Expo, Larado Ctr for the Arts, Tex, 2001; Hon Mention, Roseville Nat Open Expo, Calif, 2004. *Bibliog:* Leo Smith (auth), Lighter Side of Art, Los Angeles Times, 92. *Mem:* Calif Art Edn Asn; Northern Calif Artist Inc. *Media:* Gouache, acrylic. *Publ:* Lisa McKinnon, Deciphering Methods, Press Courier, 92; Leo Smith, No Drawbacks, Los Angeles Times, 92; Pomona Valley Review, Calif, 2012, 2013; Cool Art, Go and Do, Sacramento Mag, 2013; NYU Minetta Review, 2013; Gambling the Aisle, Denver, Colo, 2014; Pomona Valley Review, Calif, 2014. *Dealer:* Samantha Ridgeway Fine Art in Vegas Las Vegas NV; Ghost Pony Gallery Tuchas NM. *Mailing Add:* Smiling Carrot Gallery 9413 Bullion Way Orangevale CA 95662

WALKER, RUSTY (EDWARD D.)
PAINTER, EDUCATOR, WRITER
b Danville, Ill, Oct 31, 1946. *Study:* Queensland Inst Technol, Australia, BFA, 66; Greenwich Univ, MFA, 89, PhD (art educ), 91. *Work:* Pres Gerald R Ford, Calif; San Francisco Mus Mod Art; Charles & Emma Frye Art Mus, Seattle; Spec Collections, Stanford Univ, Calif; Harcourt Brace Jovanovich Publ, New York. *Comn:* Robert L Montgomery, Alta Bates Hosp, Calif, 83; Donald P McCullum, Superior Court Judge, Calif, 84; Posters, Leslie Levy Gallery Publ, 90-92; oil, comn by Bart Starr, 2000; Bella Redwineportrait, 2008; Dr Jonathan Coombs portrait, 2009. *Exhib:* Crocker Kingsley Ann, E B Crocker Art Mus, Sacramento, 76; Am Watercolor Soc, Nat Acad Design, New York, 77; Art and the Law, West Publ, 85; One Man Show, Hedden Art Gallery, Scottsdale, Ariz, 2008. *Pos:* Artist, US Air Force, Strategic Air Command Hq, Nebr, 67-71; artist, fine Arts, 71-; vpres, provost, Collins Coll, Ariz, 2005-2007 (retired). *Teaching:* Asilomar Watercolor Workshops, Monterey, Calif, 77-80 & Hewitt Workshops, San Miguel De Allende, Mexico, 83; instr illus, Collins Coll, Tempe, Ariz, 89-97. *Awards:* Emily Lowe Mem Award, Am Watercolor Soc, Nat Acad, New York, 77. *Bibliog:* Cover & feature article in Southwest Art, 6/80; feature article, Am Artist Mag, 10/80; feature article, Ariz Repub, 5/92; and others. *Mem:* Nat Watercolor Soc; Am Mensa. *Media:* Watercolor, Oils. *Interests:* Shuri-Ryu Karate Black Belt, 95, Am Karate Alliance; musician, blues harmonica player, book collecting. *Publ:* Auth, Transparent Watercolor, Northlight Publ, 85; Contemporary Western Artists, Southwest Art Publ. *Dealer:* www.walker-creative.com. *Mailing Add:* 3447 E Laurel Ln Phoenix AZ 85028

WALKER, SHARYNE ELAINE
PAINTER, SCULPTOR
b Vallejo, Calif, Sept 3, 1949. *Study:* Self-educated. *Work:* Williamsburg Art and Historical Society, NY. *Exhib:* Reve D'Artistes 90, Salon du Vieux Colombier Mus, Paris, 90; L'aura des Createurs, Chapelle de la Sorbonne Mus, Paris, 90; Women Artists of the West 1st Int, LJ Williams Theater Conv Ctr, Visala, Calif, 90; 17th Ann Non-Members Exhib, Salmagundi Club, 94; USA 1st Int, Nat Acrylic Painters Asn, 96; Seaside Gallery Int Christian Art Show, NC, 2000; 4th Nat Miniature & Small Works Show, Sulphur Springs Valley, Ariz, 2000; Int Miniature Art Exhib, Placerville, Calif, 2002; Louisville Art Festival, Nat Juried Fine Arts Show, Colo, 2002; Art of Imagination, Cork Street Gallery, London, 2003; Brave Destiny, Kirkcudbright, Scotland, 2003; Williamsburg Art Center Mus, 2003; Diego Victorio Gallery, Miami, Fla, 2004; Paradise Lost, Juried Art Competition, Williamsburg Art & Hist Ctr, NY, 2008; 11th Ann Int Exhibit, Int Soc Acrylic Painters, 2008. *Teaching:* private classes. *Awards:* Francesca Amato Kaulum Award, LRC Gallery, 89; City of Paris Laureat, Exposition Int d'Arts Plastiques, 90; Dorothy Roatz Myers Award, Salmagundi Club 17th Ann Non-Members Exhib, 94; Artists Mag Award, NAPA-USA 1st Int, 96; Award of Excellence, Manhattan Arts Int History Competition, 2000. *Mem:* Int Soc Acrylic Painters; Soc Art Imagination. *Media:* Acrylic; Paperclay, Resins. *Publ:* Contribr, The Calif Art Rev, 2nd ed, Am References Pub, 89; Le Petit Bleu, 10/90; Manhattan Arts, Renee Phillips, 90; The Best of Portrait Painting, Northlight Bks, 98; The Kali Guide, Zenprint, 2002; The Clay Palm Rev, 2000-2001; contribr, Best of America Watermedia, vol. II, Kennedy Pub, 2009. *Mailing Add:* 2575 S Willow Ave #14 Fresno CA 93725

WALKER, STEVEN EDMUND
PRINTMAKER, PAINTER
b Brooklyn, NY, Mar 1, 1955. *Study:* Wagner Col, New York, BA, 1978; Arts Students League of NY study under R Goetz & M Pellettieri - 1983-; Hunter Col, NY - 1998-2000; Landscape Workshop with Wolf Kahn -2000. *Work:* Housatonic Mus Art, Bridgeport, Conn; New York Hist Soc; Mus of City of New York; New York Public Library; Art Students League of NY; Brooklyn Mus, New York. *Comn:* paintings for pvt clients. *Exhib:* New York by New Yorkers, Mus of City of NY, 2002; 89th Annual Juried Exhib, Allied Artists of Am, New York City, 2002; Transit Views, NY Transit Mus Grand Cent Station, New York City, 2003; Trace 2003 Marie de 4ce, L'Hotel de Ville, Paris, France, 2003; Impressions of New York, NY Historical Soc, 2004; Hecho en New York, Instituto Cult Peruano N Americano, Lima Peru, 2005; Innovations in Contemp Printmaking, Housatonic Mus, Bridgeport, Conn, 2005; Tidelines, John A Noble Maritime Coll, Snug Harbor, Staten Is, NY, 2006; Light Realms, Shelter Rock Gallery, Manhasset, NY, 2007; Monmouth Mus, Lincroft, NJ, 2007; Art at First, NY, 2008; 2-person show, The Old Print Shop, NY, 2009; Audubon Artists, 2011; NY Soc Etchers 1st Nat Exhib, 2011; Four Etchers, Nat Arts Club, NY, 2011; Soc Am Graphic Artists Mems Exhib, 2011; Contemp Works on Paper Gallery, NY, 2011; Old Print Shop, 2011; Coo Gallery, NY, 2011; Allegra Viola Gallery, NY, 2011. *Pos:* graphic artist, CVS Graphics Inc, New York City, 1987-2000; art handler/matter, The Old Print Shop, New York City, 2004-; designer, Random House Inc, New York City, 2005-. *Teaching:* instr drawing & painting, Forest Hills High Sch Adult Ctr, NY, 2002-2006; instr drawing, painting, design, color & printmaking, Wagner Coll, Staten Island, NY, 2003-; private drawing & painting instr, currently. *Awards:* Tilden Award, 22nd Student Exhib, Nat Arts Club, New York City, 1997; Susan Teller Prize, Ringling School of Art and Design, Sarasota, Fla, 2006; Juror's Award (best in show), Wash Sq Outdoor Art Show, WSOAE Comt, New York, 2008 & 09. *Bibliog:* Helen A Harrison (auth), Winners Circle Review, The New York Times, 1/20/2002; Bernard Rittersporn (auth), New York by New Yorkers, Journal of the Print World, 2002, 2006, 2011; Marilyn Symmes (auth), Impressions of New York, Princeton Archit Press, NY, 2005. *Mem:* Soc of Am Graphic Artists (council mem 2007-); NY Soc of Etchers (bd mem 2004-); life mem Art Students League of NY. *Media:* Etching, Lithography, Oil, Woodcut. *Publ:* auth, It's Beyond Me, LINEA, Art Students League of NY, 2001; auth, Transit Views (catalog), The Evocative Power of the Railroad, NY Soc of Etchers, 2003. *Dealer:* The Old Print Shop Inc 150 Lexington Ave New York NY 10016; Gallery of Graphic Arts 1601 York Ave New York NY 10028. *Mailing Add:* 34-50 30th St #1F Long Island City NY 11106

WALKER, WILLIAM BOND
PAINTER, LIBRARIAN
b Brownsville, Tenn, 1930. *Study:* Bisttram Sch Fine Art, Taos, NMex & Los Angeles, with Emil Bisttram, 48-49; Univ Iowa, Iowa City, with Mauricio Lasansky, Howard Warshaw, James Lechay, Elliott R Twery & Stuart Edie, BA, 53; Rutgers Univ Grad Sch Libr Serv, MSLS, 58. *Work:* ABC-TV, New York; Heller Ehrman LLP, Washington, DC; also in numerous pvt collections. *Exhib:* Retrospective Exhib, Truffles & Such, Pittsfield, Mass, 96-97; solo exhibs, Brownsville, Tn, 82, Chatham, NY, 97-98, 2000 & 2005, Hudson, NY, 98, Old Chatham, NY, 2000, Becket, Mass, 2002, Rochester, NY, 2003, Lee, Mass, 2006, New Lebanon, NY, 2007-2008; group exhibs, Hudson, NY, 97, 2000-2007, 2009-2010, 2012, 2014, Pittsfield, Mass, 97, 2001 & 2005, Spencertown, NY, 97-98 & 2000, Canaan, NY, 98-99, West Stockbridge, Mass, 2000, Canaan, NY, 2012 & New Lebanon, NY, 2001, Philmont, NY, 2012. *Pos:* Cataloger & reference librn, Libr Metrop Mus Art, New York, 57-59; chief librn, Art Reference Libr, Brooklyn Mus, 59-64, Libr Nat Collection Fine Arts & Nat Portrait Gallery, Smithsonian Inst, 64-80 & Thomas J Watson Libr, Metrop Mus Art, New York, 80-94; retired, 94. *Teaching:* Art bibliog, Columbia Univ, Sch Libr Serv, 87-88. *Awards:* Distinguished Serv Award, Art Libr Soc N Am, 91. *Mem:* Am Libr Asn; Art Libr Soc N Am (pres, 75). *Media:* Acrylic; Casein. *Interests:* Twentieth century American prints and twentieth century painting. *Publ:* Bibliography on American Sculpture, Eighteenth to Twentieth Century, Washington, Smithsonian Inst Press, 80; co-publisher with Betty Jo Irvine, Tribute to The Late Wolfgang Freita G, Art Documentation, 2013. *Dealer:* Carrie Haddad 622 Warren St Hudson NY 12534; Park Row Art Gallery 2 Park Row Chatham NY 12037. *Mailing Add:* Kimball Farms 235 Walker St Apt 273 Lenox MA 01240

WALKER II, HERBERT BROOKS
SCULPTOR, DESIGNER
b Brooklyn, NY, Nov 30, 1927. *Study:* Art Students League, with Harry Sternberg & Robert B Hale, 43; Yale Sch Fine Arts, BFA, with R Eberhardt, R Zallinger, Graziani, J Albers & W De Konning. *Work:* Photographs of Antonio Gaudis Work, Mus Mod Art, NY; Barbados Mus, BWI; Walker Mus. *Comn:* Paintings, movie, photographs, Gahagan Dredging, Orinoco River, Venezuela, 53-54; paintings & photographs, US Steel, Cerro Bolivar, Venezuela; earth sculpture, Walker Mus, 60. *Exhib:* Solo exhibs, Stony Brook Mus, Long Island, NY, 52, Barbados Mus, 54 & IORC, Abadan, Iran, 58; Walker Mus, 60-; Rodin Mus, 70; Don Graziani Mem, Avesa, Italy, 94. *Collection Arranged:* Oil Exhibs, IORC, Abadan, Iran, 58 & 59; spec exhibs for pub schs, 60-72 & Walker Mus, Fairlee, Vt, 60-. *Pos:* Materials prod head, IROC, Abadan, Iran, 58-59; dir, Walker Mus, 59-. *Teaching:* Instr art, Thetford Acad, 64-. *Awards:* Gold Medal, ANCR, Verona, Italy, 74. *Bibliog:* H Brooks Walker, 1951, Eye Mag, Yale Univ, 67. *Mem:* Life mem Art Students League; Yale Arts Alumni Asn. *Media:* Sheet Metal, Bronze. *Res:* Arawak Carib, 54; Iran, 60; Italy, 70-. *Interests:* Writing, poetry, music. *Collection:* Justin Colin, Ted Leach, et alia in Japan Iran, Venezuela, France, Iceland, USA, Italy, Great Britain (private). *Publ:* Illusr, Gaudi, Mus Mod Art, 57. *Dealer:* Noel, Fairlee, VT 05045. *Mailing Add:* PO Box 6 Fairlee VT 05045

WALL, BRIAN
SCULPTOR
b London, Eng, Sept 5, 1931; US citizen. *Work:* Tate Gallery, London; Nat Gallery, Dublin; Art Gallery NSW, Sidney; Oakland Mus; Univ Art Mus, Berkeley; Seattle Art Mus; Sheldon Mem Art Gallery, Univ Nebr; Trition Mus Art, Santa Clara, Calif; San Antonio Mus Art; Crocker Art Mus, Sacramento, Calif; Gulbenkian Found, London, England. *Comn:* Thornaby (sculpture), New Town Ctr, Thornaby, Eng, 68; Ali (sculpture), Univ Houston, Tex, 78. *Exhib:* 2nd Paris Biennale, Mus Mod Art, 61; Sculpture of the Sixties, Tate Gallery, 65; Solo exhibs, Seattle Art Mus, 82, San Francisco Mus Mod Art, 83, Jon Berggruen Gallery, San Francisco, 83, Simon Lowinsky Gallery, NY, 87 & 98, Francis Graham-Dixon Gallery, London, 92, Sheldon Mem Art Gallery & Sculpture Garden, Univ Nebr, 95 & Jernigan Wicker Fine Art, San Francisco, 95; St Ives 1939-64, Tate Gallery, London, 85; The Mansion House, Ilkley, Eng, 94; Sixteen California Artists, Galerie Sho, Tokyo, 94; Iris Gallery, Eng, 95; Flowers East, London, 95 & 96. *Teaching:* Chmn sculpture dept, Cent Sch Art & Design, London, 64-72; prof sculpture, Univ Calif, Berkeley, formerly, emer prof, currently. *Bibliog:* Charles Spencer (auth), Brian Wall, sculptor of simplicity, Studio Int, 3/66; G S Whittet (auth), Question and artist: Brian Wall, Sculpture Int, 10/69; Hilton Kramer (auth), article, 5/13/77 & John Russell (auth), articles, 1/79 & 4/24/81, New York Times; Alan Bownes (auth), St. Ives 1939-64, Tate Gallery Pub, London, 85; Kenneth Baker (auth), San Francisco Chronicle, article, 4/86; Margaret Garlake (auth), Post-War British Abstract Art, Austin/Desmond Fine Art, London, 88; David Mellor (auth), The Sixties Art Scene in London, Phaidon, London, 93; Peter Davies (auth), World Sculpture News, article, 98; Peter Davies (auth), After Trewyn: St. Ives Sculptors Since Hepworth, Old Bakehouse Pub, Gwent, 01; Isabelle Anderson (auth), Art Week, article, 6/02; Suzanne Muchnic (auth), Los Angeles Times, article, 3/04. *Mem:* Int Sculpture Ctr, Washington, DC. *Media:* Steel. *Publ:* Christ Stephens (auth), Brian Wall, Momentum, London, 06. *Dealer:* Hacket Mill 201 Post St Ste 1000 San Francisco CA 94108. *Mailing Add:* 306 Lombard St San Francisco CA 94133

WALL, BRUCE C
PAINTER, INSTRUCTOR
b Dallas, Tex, Feb 14, 1954. *Study:* Univ Tex, Austin, BFA (with honors); RI Sch Design, Providence, RI, MFA; Fulbright-Hayes Grant, India, 79-80. *Work:* Aldrich Mus Contemp Art, Ridgefield, Conn; Best Products Corp, Richmond, Va; City Col, City Univ New York; Zale Products Corp, Dallas; Frederick R Weisman Found Art, Los Angeles, Calif; Ackland Art Mus; Univ North Carolina; Lehigh Valley Hospital, Allentown, Pa. *Exhib:* New York City New Work, Del Art Mus, Wilmington; East Village Artists, Va Mus Fine Art, Richmond; East Village Galleries, Saidyre Bronfman, Montreal, Can; Selection from Weisman Collection, Utah Mus Fine Arts, Salt Lake City; The Art of the 70s & 80s, Aldrich Mus Contemp Art, Ridgefield, Conn; This Way/This Way, Thorpe Intermedia Ctr, Sparkhill, NY; Cross Currents, Sande Webster Gallery, Philadelphia, Pa; Art & Ego, NY Acad Art, NY. *Teaching:*

Assoc prof art, Northampton Community Col, Bethlehem, Pa, 93-. *Awards:* Cecil and Eleanor Lipkin Award for Fine and Performing Arts, Northampton Community Col. *Bibliog:* John Howell (auth), Bruce Wall, Artforum, 11/85; Holland Cotter (auth), Bruce Wall, Arts Mag, 9/85; Yivian Raynor (auth), Bruce Wall, NY Times, 5/86. *Mem:* Coll Art Asn; New Arts Programs, Kutztown, PA (board member). *Media:* All Media. *Dealer:* Accola Contemporary, NY. *Mailing Add:* 509 Mixsell St Easton PA 18042-1611

WALL, JEFF
PHOTOGRAPHER
b Vancouver, 1946. *Study:* Univ BC, Vancouver, MA (Art Hist), 1970; Courtauld Inst, Univ London, 1970-73. *Exhib:* Solo exhibs include Inst Contemp Arts, London, 1984, Kunsthalle Basel, 1984, 1987, Marian Goodman Gallery, New York, 1989, 1990, 1992, 1995, 1998, 2001, 2002, 2004, 2007, Carnegie Mus Art, Pittsburgh, 1990, Vancouver Art Gallery, 1990, San Diego Mus Contemp Art, 1991, Foundation Cartier, France, 1993, Mus Nat Centro de Arte, Reina Sofia, Madrid, 1994, Jeu de Paume, Paris, 1995, Mus Contemp Art, Chicago, 1995, Mus Contemp Art, LA, 1997, Hirshhorn Mus & Sculpture Garden, Washington, 1997, Hammer Mus, Los Angeles, 2003, Galerie Marian Goodman, Paris, 2006, Mus Mod Art, New York, 2007, Art Inst Chicago, 2007, San Francisco Mus Art, 2007; group exhibs include About Place: Recent Art of the Americas, Art Inst Chicago, 1996; Public Information: Desire, Disaster, Document, San Francisco Mus Mod Art, 1995, Seeing Time, 1999; Whitney Biennial, Whitney Mus Am Art, New York, 1995; Hall of Mirrors: Art & Film Since 1945, Mus Contemp Art, LA, Wexner Ctr Arts, Columbus, Ohio & Mus Contemp Art, Chicago, 1996; The Time of Our Lives, New Mus Contemp Art, New York, 1999; The Museum as Muse: Artists Reflect, Mus Mod Art, New York, 1999; Carnegie Int, Carnegie Mus Art, Pittsburgh, 1999; Around 1984: A Look at Art in the Eighties, PS1 Ctr Contemp Art, New York, 2000; Open City: Aspects of Street Photography, Hirshhorn Mus & Sculpture Garden, Washington, 2002; The Last Picture Show: Artists Using Photography, 1960-1982, Walker Art Ctr, Minneapolis & Hammer Mus, Los Angeles, 2003-04; Shadowland: An Exhibition as Film, Walker Art Ctr, Minneapolis, 2005; Super Vision, Inst Contemp Art, Boston, 2006; Moscow Biennial, 2007. *Awards:* Paul de Hueck & Norman Walford Career Achievement Award for Art Photog, Ontario Arts Coun, 2001; Int Award Photog, Erna & Victor Hasselblad Found, 2002; Roswitha Haftmann Prize Visual Arts, 2003; Audain Prize for Lifetime Achievement in the Visual Arts, 2008; Named one of 10 Most Important Artists of Today, Newsweek mag, 2011. *Mem:* Fel, Royal Soc Can. *Mailing Add:* c/o Marian Goodman Gallery 24 W 57th St New York NY 10019

WALL, RHONDA
PAINTER, INSTRUCTOR
b Boston, Mass, Jan 26, 1956. *Study:* RI Sch Design, BFA, 78; Vt Col, Montpelier, MFA, 95. *Work:* Aldrich Mus Contemp Art, Ridgefield, Conn; City Col, Univ NY & Needham Harper Steers, NY. *Exhib:* UFO Show, Queens Mus, NY, 82; solo exhibs, Beulah Gallery, 84, Limbo Gallery, 84, Sensory Evolution Gallery, 84 & B Side Gallery, 85, NY; Art & Ego, NY Acad Art, NY, 84; Art of the 70's and 80's, Aldrich Mus Contemp Art, Ridgefield, Conn, 85; USA and then India, Lehigh Univ, Bethlehem, Pa, 96; Life Is a Dada Fashion Show at the Bauhaus, Cedar Crest Col, Allentown, Pa, 96; Mind and Machine, Allentown Art Mus, 99. *Teaching:* Instr painting, RI Sch Design, 90-92; instr painting, design & art hist, Northampton Community Col, Bethlehem, Pa, 96-; asst prof, 2D & 3D Design, Kutztown Univ, Pa, 97-2001. *Bibliog:* Mark Frisk (auth), Rhonda Wall (essay), Arts Mag, 1/85; Ken Sofer (auth), Present pop, Art News, 5/85; Vivian Raynor (auth), This way, this way, NY Times, 11/10/85. *Mem:* Coll Art Asn. *Media:* All Media. *Mailing Add:* 509 Mixsell St Easton PA 18042

WALL, SUE
PAINTER, PRINTMAKER
b Cleveland, Ohio, Feb 18, 1950. *Study:* Ohio Univ, BFA, 72, MFA, 74. *Hon Degrees:* hon degree Cleveland Institute Art, 1990. *Work:* Cleveland Mus Art; Canton Art Inst Mus, Ohio; Butler Inst Am Art, Youngstown, Ohio; Zanesville Art Ctr, Ohio; Kennedy Mus Am Art; The Hague, The Netherlands; Univ Iowa Mus Art; Ohio Nat Plaza Co Collection; Kenneth Beck Ctr for Cult Arts; Trisolini Gallery; Marie Selby Botanical Gardens Collection; Southwest Mus; George Streeter Circulating Collection; Nat Arts Club; Aurora Nat Bank Collection; Mondak Heritage Ctr; Richard Brown Baker Collection; Yale Univ Art Collection; Philip Desind Collection; The Zanger Collection; Clara Fritzsche Libr. *Exhib:* One-person shows, Gallery Madison 90, NY, 74, 76, 78, 80, 82, 84, 86, 88, 90 & 92, Zanesville Art Ctr, Ohio, 75, 86, 89 & 95, Strong's Gallery, Cleveland, 75, 77 & 79, Canton Art Inst, Ohio, 76, Gallery 200, Columbus, 75, 77, 84 & 86, Piccolo Mondo, Palm Beach, Fla, 76 & 78, Bonfoey's, Cleveland, 75, 77, 79, 81, 83, 85, 87, 89 & 91, Foster Harmon Gallery, Sarasota, Fla, 82, 84, 86, 89, 91 & 93, First Church Gallery, Springfield, Mass, 98, Cleveland Botanical Garden, Ohio, 99, Mondak Historical and Art Soc, Sidney, Mont, 99; Butler Ann Mid-Year Show, Youngstown, Ohio, 75-77; Sandusky Cult Ctr, Ohio, 78, 90 & 93; Holden Arboretum, 93, 97, 2000, 2004; Uptown Gallery, NY, 95, 2005; Loring Gallery, Sheffield, Mass, 94 & 95; Ziegonfuss Gallery, Sarasota, Fla, 95; Cleveland Inst Art, Ohio, 95; Capricorn Galleries, Bethesda, Md, 97; Gallery E, E Hampton, NY, 97; SW Mus, Los Angeles, Calif, 98; First Church Gallery, Springfield, Mass, 98; Gallery One, Mentor, Ohio, 2001 & 2005; Cleveland Ctr for Information and Technology, 2003; Clara Fritzsche Libr, S Euclid, Ohio, 2008. *Awards:* Nat Acad, 150th Annual Exhib, SJ Wallace Truman Award, NY, 75; 1st Place Award, painting, Zanesville Arts Ctr, Zanesville, Ohio, 97; Spec Mention Award, Jane Law's Long Beach Island Galley Miniature Exhib, Surf City, NJ, 2004; Women Artist Award, Butler Inst of Am Art, Youngstown, Ohio, 07 & 08; Special Recognition Award, Farmingham Mus, Farmingham, NMex, 2007; First Place Award, Int Miniature Show, Seaside Art Gallery, Nags Head, NC, 2007; Julia Castro Mem Award, Am Artists Prof League Nat Juried Exhib, NY, 2007; Merit Award, Nat Society of Painters in Casein and Acrylics, NY, 2007; 2nd Place Award (hon mention), Custer County Art and Heritage Center Mini Exhib, Miles City, Mont, 2007; 1st Place Award, acrylic, Miniature Art Society of Fla Ann Exhib, Gulf Coast Mus Art, Largo, Fla, 2008; 2nd Place Award, Sierra Artists Gallery Mini Exhib, Mariposa, Cali, 2008; 1st Place Award, Farmington Mus Nat Juried Exhib, Farmington, NMex, 2008; merit award, El Dorado Mini Exhib, Colo Springs, Colo, 2008; 2nd place, Manny Sullivan Award, Mini Society of Painters, Sculptors & Gravers Soc Wash DC, North Bethesda, Md, 2008; 1st place, Aurora Artists Guild, Aurora, Colo, 2008; Merit Award, Prairie Winds Mini Exhib, Grand Island, Nebr, 2008; Hon Mention, Gallery at Fell's Point N Am Mini Exhib, Baltimore, Md, 2008, 2014; Hon mention, Miniature int exhib, Miniature painters, sculptors, & gravins, Soc DC, 2009; People's Choice award, Renaissance Art Gallery, Ann Juried Miniature Exhib, Huntington, WVa, 2009; 1st place award, Gallery at Fel's Point North Am Miniature Exhib, Baltimore, Md, 2009; Hon Mention Award, Ice House Gallery, Miniature Painting Exhib, Wash, Va, 2010; Dorothy Barberis Mem Award, 2010, 1st place oil/acrylic, Catherine Lorillard Wolfe Art Club Exhib, NY, 2011; People's Choice Award, Sierra Artists Gallery Miniature Exhib, Mariposa, Calif, 2011; Special Mention Award, Sulpher Springs Valley Miniature Art Exhib, Willcox, Ariz, 2011; 1st Place Award, Casper Artists Guild Miniature Exhib, Casper, Wyoming, 2011, 2014, People's Choice Award, 2011; Hon Mention Award, Prairie Winds Art Ctr Annual Miniature Exhib, Grand Island, Nebr, 2011; Merit Award, Art and Antiques Fine Art Gallery, Melbourne, Fla, 2011; Hon Mention Award, Sulpher Springs Valley Miniature Exhib, Willcox, Ariz, 2012; 2nd place for Animals, Northern Calif Society of Arts in Miniature, Sierra Artists Gallery, Mariposa, Calif, 2012; Hon Mention Award, West Wind Gallery, Wyo, 2012; Prairie Winds Arts Ctr, Grand Island, Nebr, 2012; 2nd Place Award, Miniature Painters, Scultures, Gravers Soc, Wash DC; Award of Merit Still Life, Art and Antique Fine Art Gallery, Melbourne, Fla, 2012; People's Choice award, Renaissance Gallery, Huntington, NY, 2012, Gallery One, Mentor, Ohio, 2013, La State Univ Veterinary Med, Baton Rouge, La; 3rd Place Award, Sierra Artists Gallery, Mariposa, Calif, 2013; Hon Mention Award, Prairie Winds Art Ctr, Grand Island, Nebr, 2013; Hon Mention Award, Parklane Gallery, Kirkland, Va, 2013; Merit Award, La State Univ Int Exhib on Animals in Art, Baton Rouge, La, 2014; The Bill French Mem Award, Roswell Fine Arts League, NMex Miniature Art Soc, Roswell, NMex, 2014; 2nd Place Award, Sulphur Springs Valley Int Miniature Exhib, Wilcox, Ariz, 2015; 2nd Place Award and Hon Mention, Sierra Artists Gallery Elizabeth Specht Mem Miniatures in Mariposa, Mariposa, Calif, 2015; numerous other awards. *Bibliog:* American Artists: An Illustrated Survey of Leading Contemporary Americans, 85; The Painted Garden, 88; Victorian Homes Mag, 91 & 97; Archives of the Dutch Found of Miniature Art, The Netherlands, 98; Archives of the Int Miniature Art Res Ctr, The hague, The Netherlands, 98; Artists and Graphic Designer's Market, 98; Am Artist, Watercolor Mag, 2002; American Artist, Watercolor Magazine, 2002; 2000 Outstanding People, 2003-2010; Biog Encyl Am Painters, Sculptors, and Engravers, 2003-2010; Rifacimento Int, India, 2003-2010; Great Women of the 21st Century, 2004; Great Minds of the 21st Century, 2008; numerous others. *Mem:* New Orgn Visual Arts; Audubon Artists; Nat Soc Painters Casein & Acrylic; Miniature Art Soc NJ; Allied Artists Am Inc; Catharine Lorillard Wolfe Art Club; Nat Hist Preservation; Knickerbocker Artists; Am Artists Professional League; Am Craft Coun; Miniature Painters Sculptors & Gravers Soc Wash DC; Miniature Soc Fla; Garrison Art Ctr; Cider Painters Am; Victorian Soc Am; Am Asn Mus; Nt Asn Prof. *Media:* Acrylic on board. *Interests:* ballet; music; opera; theater; travel. *Publ:* Contribr, New York Art Rev. *Dealer:* Gallery One Mentor Ohio; Seaside Art Gallery 2716 Virginia Dare Trail Nags Head NC 27959; Cypress Fine Art Licensing 1500 Union County Pkwy Union NJ 07083; Snow Goose Gallery 470 Main St Bethlehem PA 18018. *Mailing Add:* 11 Riverside Dr Suite 8JE New York NY 10023-2304

WALLACE, CAROL ANN (BRUCKER)
PAINTER, ILLUSTRATOR
b Doylestown, Pa, Aug 2, 1944. *Work:* Posters & note cards (collected for research & educ purposes) Nat Mus of Am Hist, Smithsonian Inst, Washington, DC, 1997-2006; Country Stores of Vermont & Historic Bucks Co (posters), Libr of Cong, Washington, DC; US Coast Guard Permanent Traveling Art Collection, Washington, DC; Rhinestone Prancers, New England Carousel Mus, Bristol, Conn; Angel Delgadillo Hist Route 66. *Comn:* Eight drawings & paintings, James Biddle (past pres Nat Trust for Hist Preserv), Andalusia, Pa, 1997; The Lit Collection (watercolor painting & ltd ed prints), Univ of Conn, 1998; pen & ink drawings (20), Adirondack Mus, Blue Mountain Lake, NY, 1999; Ellis Island (painting), Statue of Liberty, Ellis Island Found, NY, 2001; Nat World War II Mem (pen & ink drawing & watercolor painting), Am Battle Monuments Comn, Washington, DC, 2004. *Pos:* Exec producer, Better Yet Connecticut; Gallery Artist, 1983; gubernatorial appointment, Conn Gov William O'Neill, Vacation & Travel Council, 83-85; founder & adminr, Preserve America (trademark in 3 int classes), 1997; designer (upscale stationery & giftware markets), 2003; consult, fine art print, 2007. *Awards:* Conn Tourism Award, 82; US Coast Guard Serv Award, 2002; Best NY Artists, Kennedy Promotions, 2005; Best Am Watercolor Artists, Kennedy Promotions, 2006. *Bibliog:* Rosemary Jette (auth), From Barns to Barbershops, History in a Small Format, NY Times, 2000; Pamela Graves (auth), Class of 2003, Giftware News, 2003; Pamela Bellows (auth) Carol Wallace on the Move, Pen Women Mag, 2006. *Mem:* Salmagundi Art Club (elected mem); Nat League of Am Pen Women (elected mem); Am Watercolor Soc (assoc mem); Nat Watercolor Soc (assoc mem). *Media:* Watercolor, Acrylic, Pen & Ink. *Res:* Independent research & extensive travels across America for Preserve America, 2000-2007. *Publ:* Illusr, Litchfield Co Times, 1984-1990; illusr, Litchfield Hills Touring Guides, Litchfield Hills Visitors & Conv Bur, 84-2006; illusr, The History of Pierce Pond, Knowlton & McLeary, 1992; contribr, The Artistic Touch 3, Creative Art Press, 1999; illusr (cover of sheet music), Cape May Preludes, SDG Press, 1999. *Dealer:* Nancy Cobean Gallery Direct; Rose Gallery 444 Warren St Hudson NY 12534; Omega Graphics Inc Digital Fine Art Reproductions 9 Tartan Ct Andover NJ 07821. *Mailing Add:* 48 W West Hill Rd Barkhamsted CT 06063

WALLACE, GAEL LYNN
PAINTER
b Ft Worth, Tex, Aug 5, 1941. *Study:* Okla State Univ, with Dale McKinney & David Allende, BA, 64; independent study with Don Fusco & Tom Owen. *Comn:* Old west storefront murals, Graden Elementary Sch, Kansas City, Mo, 78. *Exhib:* 60th Ann Nat Watercolor Soc, Laguna Beach Mus Art, Calif, 80 & 82; Rocky Mountain Nat Aquamedia, 82; Colorado 83 Biennial, Colo Springs Fine Art Mus, 83; San Diego Watercolor Soc Int Exhib, 85; State Watermedia Exhib, Colo Watercolor Soc, 93; Pike's Peak Watercolor Soc Invitational, 94; Contemp Art Exhib, Colo, 98. *Awards:* Purchase Awards, Nat Watercolor Soc, 80 & Glenwood Springs Fall Art Festival, Colo, 85; Honorable Mention, Colo State Fair, 80 & San Diego Watercolor Soc Int Exhib, 86. *Bibliog:* Diane Wengler (auth), The beauty of nature, Gazette Telegraph, 12/13/80. *Mem:* Nat Watercolor Soc. *Media:* Acrylic. *Mailing Add:* 23 Kris Ln Manitou Springs CO 80829

WALLACE, KENNETH WILLIAM
PAINTER, EDUCATOR
b Penticton, BC, July 7, 1945. *Study:* Calgary Coll Art, Alta, cert, 71; Vancouver Sch Art, BC, cert, 73; Banff Sch Fine Arts, 73. *Work:* Nat Art Gallery, Ottawa; Art Gallery Ont, Toronto; Vancouver Art Gallery, BC; Winnipeg Art Gallery, Man; Burnaby Art Gallery, BC; Surrey Art Gallery, Surrey, BC. *Exhib:* Solo exhibs, Alternate Space, Vancouver Art Gallery, 74, Burnaby Art Gallery, BC, 80, Lefebvre Gallery, Edmonton, Alta, 81, Robert Lawrence Int, Bellingham, Wash, 82, Teck Gallery, Simon Fraser Univ, Bau-Xi Gallery, Vancouver, BC, 92; Pac Northwest Ann, Seattle, Wash, 73; Current Energies, Saydie Bronfman Arts Centre, Montreal, Que, 74-75; Three Directions in Painting, Fine Arts Gallery, Univ BC, Vancouver, 75; Canadian Canvas, Time Exhib, 11 maj Can cities, 76; New Abstract Art in Am, Edmonton Art Gallery, Alta, 77; Affinities, 79, Vancouver Art & Artists, 1931-83, 83, Painted Gardens, Atilier Gallery, Vancouver, BC, 92; Canadian Painters, Can House, London, Eng, 79; Bienal De Arte Medellin, Columbia, SAm, 81; Current Concerns, Sarnia Art Gallery, Ont, 81; Living Nature 1987, Nat Mus Natural Sci, Ottawa, Ont, 87; Bau Xi Gallery, Vancouver, BC, 92, Image/ Mirage, Bau XI Gallery, Vancouver, BC, 2000; Wetlands Reclamation BauXi Gallery, Vancouver BC, 2001; BauXI Gallery, Toronto, Ont, 2002; Kimzeymillar Gallery, Seattle WA, USA, 2002; Aqua Illumine Bau-XI Gallery, Vancouver, BC, 2003; Agnes Bugera Gallery, Edmonton, AB, 2003; Faculty Exhib, Concourse Gallery, Emily Carr, Institute of Art and Design Toronto Air Fair, Toronto, Ont, 2004; Aqua Sanctum, Bau-XI Gallery, Vancouver, BC, 2005; Northwest Landscapes Kimzey Miller Gallery, Seattle, WA, 2005; Reflections: Bau-xi Gallery, Vancouver, BC, 2005; Agnes Bugera Gallery, Edmonton, Atla, 2005; Paint, Vancouver Art Gallery, Vancouver, BC, 2006; Sense of Place, Art Gallery of South Okanagan, 2008; Perspectives on Landscape, Agnes Bugera Gallery, Edmonton, AB, 2008; Patricia Rovzar Gallery, Kirkland, Wash, 2008. *Collection Arranged:* Images of Women (auth, catalog), Winnipeg Art Gallery, 75; Canadian Painters in Watercolor (auth, catalog), Glenbow Inst, Alta, 76; Olympic Exhibition of British Columbian Artists (auth, catalog), Montreal, Que, 76; West Coast on Canvas (auth, catalog), Birmingham Art Gallery, Ala, 79. *Teaching:* Instr painting & drawing, Univ BC, 76-78, instr painting, Dept Fine Arts, 77-80, Emily Carr Inst Art & Design, 80-2005 assoc Prof. *Awards:* Int Critics Award, Annecy Film Festival, France, 75; Can Coun Art Awards, 75-79. *Bibliog:* Mary Fox (auth), Images from the inside outside, Western Living, 76; Pat Fleisher (auth), interview in Arts Mag, Toronto, Ont, 76; Karen Wilken (auth), Vancouver scene, Art News, New York, 79. *Media:* Painting, Acrylic, Oil. *Dealer:* Agnes Bugera Gallery Edmonton Atla; Patricia Rovzar Gallery Kirkland Wash; Bau XI Gallery Vancouver BC. *Mailing Add:* 125 N Slocan St Vancouver BC V5K 3M3 Canada

WALLACE, PAULA S
ADMINISTRATOR
Study: Furman Univ, BA; Georgia State Univ, MEd; Georgia State Univ, EdS. *Hon Degrees:* Gonzage Univ, Honorary Doctor of Laws. *Pos:* Co-found, Savannah Col Art and Design, 79, pres, 2000-; founder, Savannah Film Festival; created shopSCAD and Working Class Studio. *Awards:* Recipient Oglethorpe Bus and Prof Women award, James T Deason Human Relations award, Sustainability award, Fashion Group Internat, Elle Decor Vision award Elle Decor magazine, Impact on Design Edn award, Style Atlanta awards; named Outstanding Young Woman of Am, Kentucky Colonel, Outstanding Georgia Citizen, Georgia Secretary of State Cathy Cox, Entrepreneur of the Year, Ernst & Young; named to Savannah Business Hall of Fame; named one of the 100 Most Influential Georgians-Georgia Trend Magazine. *Bibliog:* Co-auth of children's books, A House in the South and Perfect Porches. *Mem:* Fellow Royal Soc for the Encouragement of the Arts, Manufactures and Commerce (RSA, Great Britain); mem ArtTable, NY; mem nat adv bd Nat Mus of Women in the Arts, Washington, DC; internat art advisor, Chinese Red Sandalwood Mus Beijing, China. *Mailing Add:* Savannah College of Art and Design PO Box 3146 622 Drayton St Savannah GA 31402-3146

WALLACE, WILLIAM E
EDUCATOR, HISTORIAN
Study: Dickinson Coll, Carlisle, BA, 1974; Univ Ill, Urbana-Champaign, MA, 1976; Columbia Univ, PhD (art hist), 1983. *Pos:* Chmn, dept art hist & archaeol, Washington Univ, St Louis, 2000-. *Teaching:* Asst prof, Washington Univ, St Louis, 1983-90, assoc prof, 1990-99, prof, 1999-2000, Barbara Murphy Bryant Distinguished prof art hist, 2000-; fellow, Harvard Univ Ctr for Renaissance Studies, Florence, 1990-91 & Am Acad Rome, 1996-97; Robert Sterling Clark Distinguished vis prof, Williams Coll, Mass, 1999. *Awards:* Gov Award for Excellence in Teaching, Coord Bd for Higher Educ, 1995. *Publ:* Auth & ed, Michelangelo at San Lorenzo: the Genius as Entrepreneur, Cambridge, 1994; Michelangelo: Selected Scholarship in English, Garland, 1996; Michelangelo: The Complete Sculpture, Painting, and Architecture, Hugh Lauter Levin, 1998; Michelangelo: Selected Readings, Garland, 1999. *Mailing Add:* Dept of History & Archaeol Campus Box 1189 One Brookings Dr Saint Louis MO 63130-4899

WALLACE PATRUZIELLO, SARAH
PAINTER
b Athens, Ga, 1969. *Study:* Univ Ga, BFA (Drawing & Painting, Graphic Design), 1991, MFA (Painting), 1995. *Exhib:* Solo exhibs include Callanwolde Fine Arts Ctr, Atlanta, 1994, Thayer Gallery, Braintree, Mass, 2000, Pierro Gallery, South Orange, NJ, 2003, Westport Art Ctr, Westport, Conn, 2005, Azarian-McCullough Gallery, St Thomas Aquinas Coll, Sparkill, NY, 2006; Group exhibs include Spring Members Show, Copley Soc Boston, 2002; Women in the New Millennium: The Artists' Perspective, Walsh Libr Gallery, Seton Hall Univ, S Orange, NJ, 2003 ; Synopsis at 10, Pierro Gallery, S Orange, NJ, 2004; The Figure Now, Westport Arts Ctr, Westport, Conn, 2004; Drawing Conclusions, Md Fed Art, Baltimore, 2004; Catherine Lorillard Wolf Arts Club 109th Ann, Nat Art Club, New York, 2005; Artistic Fragments, Katonah Mus Art, Katonah, NY, 2005; NJ Fine Arts Ann, Noyes Mus Art, Oceanville, NJ, 2007; NJ State Coun Arts Fel Exhibit, Ben Shahn Galleries, William Patterson Univ, Wayne, NJ, 2007. *Awards:* George Sugarman Found Grant, 2007

WALLACH, ALAN
CRITIC, HISTORIAN
b Brooklyn, NY, June 8, 1942. *Study:* Columbia Col, BA, 63; Columbia Univ, PhD, 73. *Teaching:* Assoc prof art hist, Kean Col Union, NJ, 74-88; vis prof, Univ Calif, Los Angeles, 82-83, Stanford Univ, 86-87, Univ Mich, 89; Ralph H Wark prof art & art hist & Am studies, Col William & Mary, 89-. *Awards:* Smithsonian Sr Post-Doctoral Fel, 85-86; Distinguished Teaching Art Hist Award, Col Art asn, 2007; Robert Sterling Clark Award (prof), Clark Inst, Williamstown, Mass, fall 2008; Terra Vis Prof Am Art, Freie Univ, Berlin, Fall 2010. *Mem:* Coll Art Asn Am; Am Studies Asn; Am Soc Aesthetics; Art Historians Asn (Gt Brit). *Res:* Nineteenth century American art; history of museums; criticism of 20th century art. *Publ:* Coauth, Thomas Cole: Landscape into History, New Haven: Yale Univ Press, 94; auth, Exhibiting Contradiction: Essays on the Art Museum in the United States, Amherst: Univ Mass Press, 98; numerous articles. *Mailing Add:* 2009 Belmont Rd NW Suite 203 Washington DC 20009

WALLENSTEIN, ELLEN
PHOTOGRAPHER, EDUCATOR
b New York, NY, Oct 11, 1952. *Study:* Ctr Book Arts, New York; Visual Studies Workshop, Rochester, NY; State Univ NY, Stony Brook, BA (Art Hist), 1974; Pratt Inst, Brooklyn, NY, MFA (Photog), 1978. *Work:* Austin History Ctr; Brooklyn Mus; Ctr for Creative Photog; Ellis Island Mus; City of NY Mus; Performing Arts Lib, Lincoln Ctr; Humanities Research Ctr, Austin, Tex; Pfizer Inc Art Collec & Jaffee Collec, Fla Atlantic Univ; Russell Lee Collection, SW Tex State Univ. *Exhib:* Solo exhibs include Ew-Photographs, Alma Thomas Art Gallery, Southwestern Univ, Tex 80 Dream Images, Camera Club New York, 1989, Opus: Annes Windows, Creative Ctr Gallery, NYC, 2005, Director's Cut, Apeture Found online website, 2006, Opus for Anne: A Still Life, Abrons Art Ctr, Henry St Settlement, 2007; group exhibs include Fun & Games, Ctr Book Arts, New York, 1988, Signatures: Bookworks by Women, 1989, The Seven Deadly Sins, 1993, Mysterious Worlds, 1996, Broadsides: 30th Anniversary Mems Exhib, 2005; Ellis Island Photog Exhib, Ellis Island Mus, New York, 1990; Photog Book Art in the US, traveling, 1991-95; Women of the Book: Jewish Artists, Jewish Themes, traveling, 1998-2005; Group Show, Barbara Ann Levy Gallery, New York, 2000, DivRcity, 2003; Opus from 15K: Anne's Windows, Creative Ctr, New York, 2005; Opus for Anne: A Still Life, Abrons Arts Ctr, Henry St Settlement, New York, 2007; I Bienal de Arte Contemp, Circulo de Bellas Artes, Madrid, Spain, 2005; Artseen, Frederick Petzel Gallery, NY, 2009; The Photograph Unframed, Ctr for Book Arts, NY, 2011; El Mutanabbi Street Starts Here, Ctr Book Arts, NY, Manchester Libr, Eng, Columbia Univ Libr. *Collection Arranged:* The Nude, Pratt Inst Gallery, 1977; Looking Inward: Photographers Photograph Themselves, Photowork Gallery, Austin, Tex, 1983, Selected Portfolios, Tex, Photographic Soc, 1984; Now & Then: Camera Club of NY 1888-1988, City Gallery, New York, 1988; Winners, Arsenal Gallery & The Dairy, Central Park, New York, 1989; Picturing Brooklyn, Boathouse Gallery, Brooklyn, 1990; Photo Bookworks-A Selection, Visual Arts Gallery, New York, 2004; Black & White Delight, Sch Visual Arts Student Gallery, New York, 2006. *Pos:* Asst to W Eugene Smith, photog, New York, 1977; photog, Sharir Dance Co, Austin, Tex, 1982-83; photo acquisitions coord, Steck-Vaughn Publ, Austin, 1985-86; photo archivist, Mus City New York, 1986-88, New York City Dept Parks & Recreation, 1988-90; dep mgr & dir programs, Asser Levy Recreation Ctr, New York, 1990-94; Artist in residence, Creative Ctr, New York, 2003-2006. *Teaching:* Asst prof art, Univ Tex, 1978-85; adj prof photog, Sch Visual Arts, New York, 1986-; vis artist, Ellis Island Proj, Montclair State Coll, NJ, 1988; adj prof, Pratt Inst, 2013-; artist in residence, Creative Ctr, New York, 2003-06; instr, Int Ctr Photog, NY, 2011-. *Awards:* Fel, Pratt Inst, 1976, Faculty Develop Award, 2006, 2011; Ford Found Grant, Univ Tex, Austin, 1981, Innovative Teaching Grant, 1982-83; Women Studio Workshop Grant, 1986; NY Found Arts Fel, Photography, 2008; project artist, United States Artists, 2012; Faculty Development Grant, Pratt Univ Photog Dept, 2012. *Mem:* Ctr Book Arts, New York. *Media:* Photography, Book Arts. *Interests:* art history, portraiture, NY history, book art. *Publ:* Auth, Ties That Bind, Artweek, Vol 12, No 41, 12/1981; auth, Energy, Impulse & Yacov Sharir, Third Coast Mag, Vol 2, No 8, 3/1983; auth, Larry Clark Spot, Houston Ctr for Photo, Vol 3, No 3, fall 1984; auth, Fritz Henle, NY Photo District News, 5/1985; auth, Danny Lyon photos, After Image, Vol 15, No 8, 1988; auth, Looking Glass Lives, Metrosource Mag, Vol 10, No 4, 1999; auth, Review of M Chelbin Book, Black Eye, Fraction Mag, 2010; auth, Review of Regeneration 2, Fraction Mag, 2010; auth, PDNedu (book review), 2011; auth, The Bridge at Hoover Dam (book review), Jane Stillings, Fraction Mag, 2011; PDNedu, Project X, 2 articles, 2011, 1 article, 2012; My Dakota (book review), Fraction mag, 2012; Respecting My Elders: Age and the Creative Spin: Portraits by Ellen Wallenstein, 2013. *Mailing Add:* 1 University Pl Apt 16N New York NY 10003-4569

WALLER, AARON BRET
MUSEUM DIRECTOR, ART HISTORIAN
b Liberal, Kans, Dec 7, 1935. *Study:* Univ Kans, Lawrence, 53-56; Kansas City Art Inst & Sch of Design, BFA, 57; Univ Kans, Lawrence, MFA, 58; Univ Oslo, Norway, Fulbright Grant, 63-64; Univ Kans, 64-67. *Collection Arranged:* School for Scandal: Thomas Rowlandson's London (co-auth, catalog), 67 & The Waning Middle Ages (ed, catalog), 69, Univ Kans; Images of Love & Death in Late Medieval and Renaissance Art (ed, catalog), 75, Works from the Collection of Dorothy & Herbert Vogel (auth, catalog), 77, & The Crisis of Impressionism/1878-1882 (co-auth, catalog), 80, Univ Mich; The Fine Art of Funiture Maker (co-auth, catalog), 81 & Artists of La Revue Blanche, (co-auth, catalog), 84, Mem Art Gallery, Univ Rochester; South Bend Mus, Ind; Tucson Mus; Indianapolis Mus of Art, Ind. *Pos:* Dir, Mus Art, Univ Kans, Lawrence, 64-71; head, Dept Pub Educ & Higher Educ, Metrop Mus Art, NY, 71-73; dir, Univ Mich, Mus Art, 73-80; dir, Mem Art Gallery, Rochester, NY, 80-85; chmn mus educ comt, Col Art Mus, 81-82; assoc dir educ & pub affairs, J Paul Getty Mus, Malibu, Calif, 85-90; dir, Indianapolis Mus Art, Ind, 90-2001, dir emer, 2001; trustee, Asn Art Mus Dirs, 92-95. *Teaching:* Asst prof art hist, Univ Kans, Lawrence, 64-71; vis asst prof, Dept Art, City Col, 71-73; assoc prof art hist, Sch Art & chmn grad prog mus practice, Univ Mich, Ann Arbor, 73-80; adj assoc prof fine arts, Col Arts & Scis, Univ Rochester, 80-85. *Awards:* Nat Endowment Arts Prof Develop Grant, Int Art Market, 80; NY Governor's Award, Mem Art Gallery, 85; Int Citizen of the Yr, Int Ctr, Indianapolis, Ind, 98. *Mem:* Intermus Conserv Lab (vpres, 76-77, pres, 77-78); Am Asn Mus Dirs (treas, 80-81); NY State Asn Mus; Coll Art Asn; Asn Art Mus Dirs; Am Asn of Mus. *Res:* Graphic arts; 20th century art. *Publ:* Sowing the Dragon's Teeth, Bull, Mus Art & Archeol, Univ Mich, Vol III, 50-57, 80; Museums in the groves of academe, Mus News, 1-2/80; Contribr, Rouault's Abandonne: Transformations of an Image, Porticus, J Mem Art Gallery, Univ Rochester, 84; Auth, Aping their betters: art appreciation and social class, Penn State Univ, 10/89; Looking, but not seeing, J Mus Educ, spring 90. *Mailing Add:* 4035 N Pennsylvania St Indianapolis IN 46205

WALLER, SUSAN
GALLERY DIRECTOR, WRITER
b Newton, Mass, July 28, 48. *Study:* Brown Univ, BA, 70; Boston Univ, MA (art hist), 75. *Collection Arranged:* At Issue: Art and Advocacy, St Louis Gallery Art, 87; Artists' Books, Book Arts, 89, Swiss School: Late to Post Modern Graphic Design, Other Voices, Baxter Gallery, 91 & Imperiled Shores, 92, Baxter Gallery. *Pos:* Asst cur, Cranbrook Acad Art Mus, 81-84, cur, 84-86; asst dir, St Louis Gallery Contemp Art, 87-88; dir, Baxter Gallery, Maine Col Art. *Teaching:* Instr art hist, Ctr Creative Studies, 79-81 & Main Col Art, Maine, 89-. *Mem:* Coll Art Asn; Am Asn Mus. *Publ:* Auth, The artist, the writer and the queen, Women's Art J, 83; Strong-minded critics, Women Artists News, 85; Michael Hall: reasoned to believe (exhib catalog), St Louis Gallery, 88; Robert Stackhouse: St Louis bones (exhib, catalog), Laumeier Sculpture, 88; ed, Women Artists in the Modern Era, Scarecrow, 91. *Mailing Add:* c/o Horizons Unlimited 1636 Parkview Cir Salisbury NC 28144-2461

WALLIN, LAWRENCE BIER
PAINTER, PHOTOGRAPHER
b Norwalk, Conn, Apr 23, 1944. *Study:* Los Angeles City Col, 62; Otis Art Inst Los Angeles Co, BFA & MFA, 66. *Work:* Otis-Parsons Art Inst, Los Angeles. *Comn:* Rock Resorts, Maui, Hawaii, 79; Two cityscapes, Bank of Am, Long Beach, Calif, 82; western scene, Wells Fargo, Palm Desert, Calif, 81; skyscape mural, Northrup Corp, Hawthorn, Calif, 82. *Exhib:* Current Concerns, Part II, 75 & Imagination, 76, Los Angeles Inst Contemp Art; Book Show, Inst Mod Art Brisbane, Australia & traveling, 78; solo exhibs, Brand Libr Art Ctr, Glendale, Calif, 85, Peter Nahum, London, Eng, 87, Carnegie Art Mus, Oxnard, Calif, 89, Art Angles Gallery, Orange, 95, Oliver & Espig, Santa Barbara, 96, & Svit Ozor Studio Channel Art Ctr, 2nd Invitational, 2000 & 2001; Karpeles Manuscript, Libr Mus, Santa Barbara, Calif, 94. *Bibliog:* Calvin J Goodman (auth), Return to regional art, Am Artist, 6/82; A survey of contemporary art of the figure, Am Artist, 2/85; Best of Acrylic Painting, Rockport Publ, 6/96; Landscape Inspirations, Rockport Publications, 11/97; Portrait Inspirations, Rockport Publications, 11/97. *Mem:* Artist Equity Asn (vpres, bd dir, 81-82); Santa Barbara Studio Artist, 2002-2003. *Media:* Acrylic. *Publ:* Auth, The Adventure, 70 & The Model, 77, pvt publ; Lightfastness in colored pencils, Los Angeles Equity News, 82; contribr, Photographing your artwork, Am Artist, 84. *Dealer:* Corridan Gallery 125 N Milpas St Santa Barbara CA 93103; Chalk Gallery 963 Linden Ave Carpinteria CA 93013. *Mailing Add:* 895 Toro Canyon Rd Montecito CA 93108

WALLIN, LELAND (LEE) DEAN
PAINTER, DRAFTSMAN
b Sioux Falls, SDak, Oct 14, 1942. *Study:* Columbus Coll Art & Design, Ohio, 61; Kans City Art Inst, Mo, BFA, 65; Univ Cincinnati & Art Acad, Ohio, MFA fel, 67; Sabbatical Study, Philip Pearlstein's Studio, New York, 76. *Comn:* Numerous pvt collections. *Exhib:* 15th & 18th Ann Nat, El Paso Mus Art, 70, 74, Minneapolis Coll Art & Design, 77, Brooklyn 79, Brooklyn Mus, NY, 79; 20th Ann Vicinity Show, Cincinnati Art Mus, 66; Talent III, VI, VII, Minn Mus Art, 71, 83, 75; Toys Greenville Co Mus Art, SC, 83; Harold Reed Gallery, NY, 83; Gallery Henoch, NYC, 91; 30th Int Open Exhib, San Bernardino Co Mus, 95; Int Show, NJ Ctr Visual Arts, 95; Int Open Exhib, Sacramento Fine Arts Ctr, Calif, 97; Landscape and Still Life: A New Look, Downey Mus Art, Calif, 98; 30th Ann Palm Springs Desert Mus, 99; 44th Ann Int, San Diego Art Inst, 2000; Bellevue Art Mus, Wash, 2001; Morris Mus Art, Ga, 2001; Mississippi Mus Art, 2002; Art at Play, Huntsville Mus Art, 2002; New Directions, Barret Art Ctr Galleries, Poughkeepsie, NY, 2003, Myth, Magic, & Metaphor, Union St Gallery, Chgo, Ill, 2004; Childs Tables: Reflections on the Adult World (solo exhib), Greenville Mus Art, Greenville, NC, 2007; Fayetteville Mus of Art, NC, 2008; Contemp Realism Biennial, 2010; Fort Wayne Mus Art, Indiana, 2010; has exhibited in 36 states. *Collection Arranged:* Cur, New Realism 70 (auth, catalog), St Cloud State Univ, Minn, 70 & Philip Pearlstein Retrospective, Marywood Univ, Scranton, Pa, 88. *Pos:* Juror Panelist, F Lamont Belin Grant for Northeast Professionals, Pa, 86-89; juror, Northern Nat Art Competition, Wis, 94; lectr, Direct Observation-Realism, Minn Coll Art & Design 77, Ten Realist Views, Rutgers Univ, Newark, 81, NYC-Realism, Carnegie Mellon Univ, 88. *Teaching:* Prof emer, painting, E Carolina Univ, Greenville, NC, 92-2007; prof, St Cloud State Univ, Minn, 67-85; coordr, MFA Painting & prof, Mayrwood Univ, Pa, 85-90. *Awards:* Creative Leaves, 97, 2005; Int First Prize Oil Painting Awards, Laredo Ctr Arts, Tex, 97 & 99; Outstanding Research & Outstanding Teacher Awards, Sch Art & Design, 94, 95; Scholar-Teacher Award, Coll Fine Arts & Communs, E Carolina Univ, 2005. *Bibliog:* Vivien Raynor (auth), Realism exhib, New York Times, 81; Chuck Twardy (auth), Realism exhib, Raleigh News & Observer, 93; Gerrit Henry (auth), exhib catalog, Harold Reed Gallery, 83; Philip Pearlstein (auth), exhib catalog, Gallery Henoch, 91; Ralph Pomeroy (auth), exhib catalog, Gallery Henoch, 91; Realism Today, American Artist Mag, special issue, 2000; Stephen May (auth), exhib catalog, Greenville Mus of Art, NC, 2007; and others. *Media:* Oil on Canvas; Graphite Pencil on Paper. *Res:* Realism, as painter and writer. *Interests:* Still-life painting. *Publ:* Auth, The Evolution of Philip Pearlstein, Art Int Mag, Part I, summer 79, Part II, fall 79; A Twenty Year Cast of Nudes in Bronze: Richard McDermott Miller's Retrospective, Arts Mag, 5/84; Toys Take a Holiday, Play the Theater, and Travel Through Time, Arts Mag, 3/87; Rescuing Vermeer: Seeing Human Values and Virtues in Direct Observation, Am Arts Quart, Fall, 2002; Harnett's Hidden Constellation, Am Arts Quart, summer, 2004; Contribr, Art Elements Design Book, NC, 2011. *Dealer:* Harold Reed Gallery New York NY 78-85; Gallery Henoch New York NY 85-2000; and others. *Mailing Add:* 218 York Rd Greenville NC 27858

WALP, SUSAN JANE
PAINTER
b Allentown, Pa. *Study:* Mt Holyoke Coll, BA, 1970; Brooklyn Coll, MFA. *Exhib:* Met Show, Denver Art Mus, 1974; Artists Choose Artists, Lake George Arts Project, 1982; Texas Tech Lubbock, 1989-98; Nature Morte: A Current View, NY Studio Sch, 1993; solo exhibs, Victoria Munroe Fine Art, NY, 1994 Fischabach Gallery, 1996, Hackett Freedman Gallery, San Francisco, 1999, 2000; Objects of Personal Significance, Knoxville Mus Art, 1996-98; Hunter Mus Art, 1996-98; Tarble Art Center, 1996-98; Am Acad Arts and Letts Invitational, 1999 & 2009; Intimate Visions, State Univ NY, Cortland, 2001. *Teaching:* Fac mem painting, Int Sch Art, Montecastello di Vibio, Italy, 1979-99; vis asst prof, Dept Studio Art, Dartmouth Coll, Hanover, NH, 1998. *Awards:* Recipient Soc Illustrators Award, 1984; Am Illus Award, 1984; Guggenheim Found Fel, 2004; Skowhegan Purchase Prize; Acad Award, Am Acad Arts and Letts, 2009. *Media:* Oil. *Mailing Add:* c/o Tibor de Nagy Gallery 724 Fifth Ave New York NY 10019

WALSH, ANNE
PHOTOGRAPHER, LECTURER
Study: Univ Mich, BA (History of Art), 1985; Calif Inst Arts, Valencia, MFA, 1990. *Exhib:* Solo exhibs, Calif Inst Arts, Valencia, 1990, Casey Kaplan, New York, 1996, MUU Gallery, Helsinki, Finland, 1997, Gallery Video Program, Inst Visual Arts, Milwaukee, 1999, Huis a/d Werf, Utrecht, Netherlands, 2000, Pacific Film Archive, Berkeley, Calif, 2004, Mills Col Art Mus, Oakland, 2005 & Solway/Jones Gallery, Los Angeles, 2007; Art Wight Art Gallery, Univ Calif Los Angeles, 1994; Los Angeles County Mus Art, 1995; LACE, Los Angeles, 1996; Walter Phillips Gallery, Banff Centre Arts, AB, Can, 1997; Walter McBean Gallery, San Francisco, 1998; Antwerp, Belgium, 1999; New Mus Contemp Art, NY, 2000; Santa Monica Mus Art, 2001; Whitney Biennial, 2002; Anthony Wilkinson Gallery, London, 2003; Contemp Art Ctr, New Orleans, 2004; OR Gallery, Vancouver, 2004; Super Deluxe, Tokyo, 2005; Anne Reed Gallery, Ketchum, Idaho, 2006. *Teaching:* Lectr, Dept Art, Calif State Univ, Los Angeles, 1991 & Dept Studio Art, 1993; sr lectr, Dept Studio Art, Univ Calif, Irvine, 1991-2003; vis grad adv, Art Ctr Col Design, Pasadena, 1996-; vis lectr, Univ Calif, Riverside, 1999; vis asst prof, Univ Mich, Ann Arbor, 1999; asst prof, Dept Art Practice, Univ Calif, Berkeley, 2003-, chair, currently. *Awards:* Los Angeles Ctr Photographic Studies/Olson Grant, 1994; Faculty Career Develop Award, Univ Calif, Irvine, 1995, 1996 & 2003; Art Matters Found Grant, 1995 & 2008; Jr Faculty Enabling Grant, Univ Calif, Berkeley, 2003 & Jr Faculty Res Grant, 2004; Summer Rsch Grant, Univ Calif, Berkeley, 2004 & Res Fel, 2005-06. *Mailing Add:* Department of Art Practice 345 Kroeber Hall #3750 University of California Berkeley Berkeley CA 94720-3750

WALSH, DAN
PAINTER
b Philadelphia, Pa, 1960. *Study:* Hunter Coll, NY City; Philadelphia Coll Art. *Work:* Herbert F Johnson Mus Art, Cornell Univ, Itaca, NY; Jumex Collection, Mexico City, Mex; Saatchi Collection, London, Eng; Yale Univ Libr, New Haven, Conn; Maramotti Collection, Italy; Wasworth Atheneum, Hartford, Conn. *Exhib:* Solo exhibs include Daniel Newburg Gallery, 1991, Galerie Ludwig, Ger, 1993, Art & Public, Geneva, 1994, Paula Cooper Gallery, NY City, 1995, 1998, 2000, 2003, 2006, 2008, Galerie Bela Jarzyk, Ger, 1996, Petra Bungert Gallery, NY City, 1997, Barbara Flynn Gallery, Sydney, Australia, 1999, Forefront Gallery, Indianapolis Mus Art, 2001, Hazmat Gallery, Mus Contemp Art, Tucson, 2002, Galerie S65, Cologne, 2003, Chac Mool Gallery, Los Angeles, 2003, 192 Books, NY City, 2004, Galerie Xippas, Paris, 2004, Mario Diacono at ARS Libri, Boston, 2005, Galerie Tschudi, Zuoz, Switzerland, 2006, Galería Elvira Gonzáles, Madrid, Spain, 2007, Renos Xippas Gallery, Paris, France, 2007, Pace Prints, 2008, Stewe Gallery, Amsterdam, the Netherlands, 2008, Patric de Brook Gallery, Knokke, Belgium, 2009, Barbara Krakow Gallery, Boston, Mass, 2009, dAN wALSH: Dasy & Nights, Paula Cooper Gallery, New York, 2010, Dan Walsh, Galerie Xippas, Paris, France, 2010; group exhibs include Daniel Newberg Gallery, NY City, 1990; Hunter Coll Art Galleries, NY City, 1991; PS1 Contemp Art Ctr, NY City, 1992; Anthony Reynolds Gallery, London, 1992; Paula Cooper Gallery, NY City, 1993, 1994, 1996, 1998, 2000, 2002; New Mus Contemp Art, 1994, 1998; Galerie Sophia Ungers, Cologne, 1995; Sandra Gering Gallery, NY City, 1996; L'usine, Geneva, 1997; Galerie Tanya Rumpff, Haarlem, The Netherlands, 1998; Glassbox Open, Paris, 1998; Leslie Tonkonow Artworks + Projs, NY City, 1999;

Lawrence Rubin Greenberg Van Doren Fine Art, NY City, 2000; PS Gallery, Amsterdam, 2001; Dalhousie Art Gallery, Halifax, Nova Scotia, 2002; Currier Gallery Art, Manchester, NH, 2002; Ljubljana Biennial, Slovenia, 2003; Biennale D'Art Contemporain de Lyon, 2003; Open Studio Press, Boston, 2006; Patrick De Brock Gallery, Belgium, 2006; Renos Xippas Gallery, Paris, 2007; Paula Cooper Gallery, NY, 2007; Transitions, Painting at the (other) end of art, Colleziche Maramotti, Reggio Emilia, Italy, 2009; Abstract Vision 2010, Art & Art Gallery, Moscow, Russia, 2010; Once Removed, the Apartment, Athens, Greece, 2010. *Bibliog:* Dan Walsh: Paintings (illus), Paula Cooper Gallery, New York & Galerie Xippas, Paris, 2007; Dan Walsh & Poems by John Yao (illus), Architecture of Ink, New York, Garner Tullis, 99; Christophe Cherix, Dan Walsh Recycling (illus), Geneva: Cabinet des Estampes du Musée d'art etd' Histore, 2002. *Media:* Acrylic. *Dealer:* Art & Public 37 rue des Bains 1205 Geneva Switzerland; Patrick De Brock Gallery Strandstraat 11 B-8300 Knokke Belgium; Galeria Elvira Gonzalez General Castanos 3 28004 Madrid Spain; Pace Prints 32 East 57th Street NY City NY 10022; Galerie Xippas 108 rue Vieille du Temple 75003 Paris France; Paula Cooper Gallery New York. *Mailing Add:* c/o Paula Cooper Gallery 534 W 21st St New York NY 10011

WALSH, JAMES
PAINTER, SCULPTOR
b Newark, NJ, Aug 6, 1954. *Study:* Livingston Col, Rutgers Univ, NJ, BA, 76; Syracuse Univ, NY, MFA, 80. *Exhib:* First Biennial-New Jersey Artists, Newark Mus, 77; New Works in Clay III, Everson Mus Art, Syracuse, NY, 81-82; two-man show, Edmonton Art Gallery, Alberta, 85; Pre-Post Modern, Brush Art Gallery, St Laurence Univ, Canton, NY, 85; Assoc Am Artists, NY, 90. *Bibliog:* Valentin Tatransky (auth), The new avant-garde, Art Int, 4/84 & James Walsh, Arts Mag, 10/85; Russell Bingham (auth), James Walsh-John King, Update, 11-12/85. *Media:* Acrylic, Oil; Metal, Welded. *Dealer:* Galeria Joan Prats 24 W 57th St New York NY 10019; Associated American Artists 20 W 57th St New York NY 10019. *Mailing Add:* Four Great Jones St No 1 New York NY 10012

WALSH, JANET BARBARA
PAINTER
b Philadelphia, Pa, Aug 11, 1939. *Study:* Art Students League, with Mario Cooper, Daniel Greene, cert, 1969; Sch Visual Arts, with Francis Criss, Robert Frankenberg, Burton Silverman. *Work:* Progresso Corp; Mus de la Acuarela, Mex; Springmaid Found; St Antonin, Noble Val, France; Pfizer Corp. *Comn:* Avon Products Inc; Doran-Smith Adv Co. *Exhib:* Anchorage Hist & Fine Arts Mus, Alaska; Nat Acad Design, Salmagundi, Club, World Trade Ctr, Art Students League, Nat Arts Club, NY; Mus Arts & Hist, Port Huron, Mich; Columbus Mus Arts & Sci, Ga; Owensboro Mus Fine Arts, Ogunquit, Mass; Grants Pass Mus Art, Ore, 1980; Columbus Mus Art; Albrect Art Mus, St Joseph, Mo; Charles & Emma Frye Mus, Seattle; QE2, Maruzen Gallery, Tokyo; Mus de la Acuadrela, Mex; 1st Int Exhib Contemp Int Watermedia Masters, Nanjing, China, 2007. *Pos:* Pres & Dolphin fel, Am Watercolor Soc; nat vpres & dir, Knickerbocker Artists, New York, formerly. *Teaching:* Workshops throughout the US & Europe; New York Horticultural Soc; Salmagundi Club. *Awards:* Bronze Medal Hon, Am Watercolor Soc; Edgar A Whitney Award, 1992; Dixie Warehouse & Cartage Co Award, Ky Watercolor Soc, 1994; and others. *Mem:* Am Watercolor Soc (pres); Allied Artists; Catharine Lorillard Wolfe Art Club; Ky Watercolor Soc; Royal Soc Arts, London; Nat Arts Club; Salmagundi Club (hon mem). *Media:* Watercolor, Pastel, Printmaking. *Interests:* Gardening, Kayaking, travel. *Publ:* Auth, Watercolor Made Easy, Watson-Guptill; Works appearing in, Paint with the White of your Paper, The Best in Watercolor, Flowers in Watercolor, Fresh Flowers, Watercolor for the Serious Beginner and others. *Mailing Add:* 6140 Beverly Hills Rd Coopersburg PA 18036-1865

WALSH, NAN
PAINTER, SCULPTOR
b NY, Nov 4, 1932. *Study:* Fordham Univ, BS (elementary educ), 54; VK Jonynas, Long Island, NY, 88; Art Life Studio Inc, White Plains and Portchester, NY, 94; Art Ctr No NJ, 96-2002; Nat Acad Sch Fine Arts. *Work:* Sumner Mus, Washington, DC; Lehman Brothers, NY; Neiman Marcus, White Plains, NY; Pound Ridge Mus, NY; Westchester Beaux Arts Finale, NY; Katonah Mus Art. *Comn:* Central Park, Mayor & Mrs John Lindsay, NY, 72; Lazy Afternoon, Mr & Mrs Temple Buell, Denver Colo, 73; Still Life Impression, Dr & Mrs Austin Murphy, Mamaroneck, NY, 76; April Bouquet, Mr & Mrs Randolf Guggenheimer, NY, 78; Large Triptych, Mr & Mrs Ken Carlin, Weston, Conn, 85. *Exhib:* Gracie Mansion, Gracie Mansion for the Pub, 72; solo.exhibs, For Arts Sake, Hilton Hotel, NY, 73, Nan Walsh at Rockefeller Ctr, NY, 76, Nan Walsh says it with Flowers, Women's Club Bronxville, NY, 78, Abstract, Ward Nasse Gallery, NY, 80 & Semi Abstract Expressionism, MAG Gallery, Larchmont, NY, 84; Mamaroneck Artist Guild Nat Open Juried Exhib, White Plains, NY, 78, 81, 83, 84, 86-88, 91, 94 & 96; Studio XII Juried Exhib, Cork Room Gallery, Avery Fisher Hall, 78; Mamaroneck Artists' Guild, Nat Open Juried Exhib, 80; Studio XII, Art Show, Off of the Mayor, 80; Mag Gallery, 8 yrs 15 shows a year, 88-96; On the Cutting Edge, Broome Street Gallery, NY, 96; Nat League Am Pen Women, Sumner Mus, Washington, DC, 96; 33rd Ann Art Show (juried show), Bedford, NY, 2005; The Inner Eye, Harriman Krason Gallery, NYC, 2006; Best of the Jersey Shore. *Awards:* Award of Excellence, Sumner Mus, Wash, DC; First Prize, Beaux Arts Finale, Westchester, NY; Outstanding work, 11th Annual Sculpture Open, Salmagundi Club, NY. *Bibliog:* VK Jonynas (auth), About the Artist, The Villager Publ co, 78; Lorraine Lange, Nan Walsh, The Artist, The Villager Publ co, 78; Interview & Photos (Nan Walsh), Asbury Park Press, 8/31/2006. *Mem:* Nat Mus of Women in Arts; Mamaroneck Artists Guild Inc (vpres, 80-); Allied Artists Am; NY Artists Equity; Nat League Am Pen Women (mem chmn, 92-96). *Media:* Oil, Prrintmaking (monotypes), Clay & Metal. *Interests:* Jurying art shows, art consulting & helping legislate better laws for artists. *Collection:* Realistic painting, semi abstract paintings, expressionistic paintings, monotypes and sculptures. *Publ:* Auth, Hist of the Mamaroneck Artists Guild (article), Gannett Westchester Newspaper, 88; ed, Mamaroneck Artists Guild Publicity, Gannett Westchester Newspaper, Review Press Reporter, Soundview News, Art Times, 88-96

WALSH, PATRICIA RUTH
PAINTER
b Cleveland, Ohio. *Study:* Coll Mt St Joseph, Cincinnati, BA; Art Students League; Syracuse Univ, NY, MFA. *Comn:* Four paintings, St Timothy's Church, Trenton, Mich; design for altar furnishings, St Mary's Church, Oakland, Calif. *Exhib:* Northwest Printmakers Int, Seattle Art Mus, 65; Pollution Show, Oakland Mus, 70; Three Watercolorists, San Jose Civic Art Ctr, 73; Spaces & Places, Palo Alto Cult Ctr, 75; Walnut Creek Civic Arts Ctr, 80. *Pos:* Liturgical designer, Holy Names Col, Oakland, Calif & St Clement's Church, Hayward, Calif & Christ the King Catholic Community, Las Vegas, Nevada; consult, St Francis de Sales Cathedral, Oakland, Sacred Heart Cath Community, Hollester, St Jerome's Church, El Cerrito, Calif. *Teaching:* prof emer, Calif Coll Arts, 65-. *Awards:* Bene Award, Modern Liturgy Mag, 88; Hon Mention Mod Liturgy Mag, 92. *Mem:* Arch Mod Christian Art (bd mem). *Media:* Oil, Watercolor. *Mailing Add:* 1999 Gaspar Dr Oakland CA 94611

WALSH-PIPER, KATHY A
MUSEUM DIRECTOR, EDUCATOR
b Oak Park, Ill, Aug 17, 1947. *Study:* Washington Univ, St Louis, AB, 69, MA, 73. *Pos:* Mus Cons Dir, Univ Ky Art Mus, 2002-2013. *Teaching:* coordr resource ctr, St Louis Art Mus, 77-80; asst dir mus edn, Art Inst Chgo, 80-85; dir edn, Terra Mus Am Art, Chgo, 85-88; head dept teacher & sch programs, Nat Gallery Art, 88-95; dir edn public programs, Dallas Mus Art, 95-2002. *Awards:* Nat Mus Educator of Yr, NAEA, 84; Mus Guest Scholar, J Paul Getty Mus, 98; Robert Smith fel, Nat Gallery of Art, 96. *Mem:* Am Asn Mus (chair Midwest educ comt, 83-84); Mem Nat Art Educ Asn (reg mus educ 84, nat mus educ 85, dir mus division 92-). *Interests:* Inquiry teaching and creative writing, based on art. *Publ:* Image to Word: Art and Creative Writing, Scarecrow Press, 2002. *Mailing Add:* 307 Dudley Rd Lexington KY 40502

WALTEMATH, JOAN
PAINTER, EDUCATOR
b Nebr, Oct 6, 1953. *Study:* Rhode Island Sch Design, BFA, 76; Hunter Col, MFA, 93. *Work:* Fogg Mus, Harvard Univ, Boston, Mass; Muse de Beaux Arts, La Chaux De/Fonds, Switz; Sears Merchandise, Ill; Yale Univ Art Gallery, New Haven, Conn; Harvard Univ Art Mus, Cambridge, Mass; NY Pub Libr; Nat Gallery Art, Washington, DC; Mus Modern Art, NY; Seattle Mus Art, Wash; Mus Contemp Art, Tuscon, Ariz. *Comn:* Installation in lobby, Howco Investment Co, Metro Park, NJ, 87; St Canisius Ch, Berlin, 02. *Exhib:* Solo exhibs: White Skins, White-Out Studio, Knokke, Belgium, 2003; Two & Three, Victoria Munroe Fine Arts, Boston Mass, 2005; Infinity, notes on the sublime, Galerie Nivon, 2006; and others; Art on paper, Weatherspoon Gallery, Univ, NC, 2000; Fifteen Yrs of Painting, Stark Gallery, NY, 2001; Drawing, Victoria Munroe Fine Art, Boston, 2001; Immanance, Hunter Col, NY, 2001; Patient Process, Grinnell Col, Iowa, 2001; Math-Art Art-Math, Ringling Col, Sarasota, Fla, 2002; The Rhythm of Structure, Firehouse 5 Gallery, NY, 2003; Small Epiphonics, Victoria Munroe Fine Art, Boston; Paint it Black, B Cunningham Gallery, NY, 2006; Take Off, Basel Switz, 2006, Torso/Roots, Basel Switz, 2007, Passages/Passenger, Art on Bonn Germ, 2009, Contingencies, Peregrin Program, 2011; The Rhythm of Structure, Firehouse 5 Gallery, NY, 2003; Resonance, The Work Space, NY, 2003; The Incredible Lightness of Being, Black and White Gallery, Brooklyn, NY, 2003; Orpheus Selection, P.S. 1, NY, 2007; Dimensions in Nature, New Acquisitions, San Diego Mus Art, 2008; Group exhibs: Crossing Borders, Bjorn Ressle Gallery, NY, 2009, The Artist as Collector, Olivier Mosset La Magasin Ctr for Contemp Art, 2009, The Madame Eats, Frederico Seve Gallery, NY, 2010, Drawn/Taped/Burned: Abstraction on Paper, Katonah Mus Art, NY, 2011; and others. *Collection Arranged:* Nat Gallery Art, Washington, DC; NY Pub Libr; Fondation Leschot, Bern, Switzerland; Hood Mus, Dartmouth, NH; Yale Univ Art Gallery, New Haven, Conn; Harvard Univ Art Mus, Cambridge, Mass; S Moody Gallery, Univ Ala; Weatherspoon Art Gallery, Univ NC; Krannert Art Mus, Univ Ill; Mona, Univ Nebr. *Pos:* dir, Hoffberger Sch Painting, Md Inst Coll of Art, Baltimore. *Teaching:* vis lectr, I S Chanin Sch Archit, Cooper Union, New York, 97-2001, adj asst prof, 2001-; vis lectr, Princeton Univ, 00-02; instr, Sch Art, Cooper Union, 02-03. *Awards:* BRA Arch Award, City of Berlin, 2003; Edward Albee Found Award, 2003 & 2006; Jentel Found Award, 2005; Change Found Avard, 2006; Pollock-Krasner Found Grant, 2008. *Bibliog:* William Zimmer (auth), Matters of Scale, NY Times, 3/8/98; Michael Brennan (auth), Painters Journal; artnet.com, 10/29/99, 9/27/2000; Roberta Fallon (auth), Math Works, Philadelphia Weekly, 11/21/2001; Peter Frank (auth), Pick of the Week, LA Weekly Times, 10/2/1998, 2/1/2003; Kim Levin (auth), Art in Brief, The Village Voice, 79, 5/10/1994; Roberta Smith (auth), NY Times, C26, 7/7/1996; Stephen Westfall, Art in America, 108, 7/1992. *Mem:* AM Abstract Artists. *Media:* Oil on Canvas, Graphite or Mylar. *Publ:* Blast, X Art Found, 91; A Decade of Collecting, Harvard Univ Art Mus, Cambridge, Mass, 2000; Art on Paper (exhib catalog), Weatherspoon Art Gallery, Univ NC, Greensboro, 2000; Babel, babble..., Guggenheim pub, Venice, Italy, 3/2000; Patient Process, Grinell Col, Los Angeles, 2001; Thinking in Line, Univ Galleries, Univ Fla, 2003. *Dealer:* Niklas van Bartha London England; Gallery Joe Phila Pa. *Mailing Add:* 131 Bowery 4th Fl New York NY 10002

WALTERS, BILLIE
CERAMIST
b Colman, Tex, Mar 12, 1927. *Study:* Univ Colo; Univ NMex, BFA, 79, MA, 81. *Work:* Univ Calgary; Ariz State Univ; Southern Conn State Col; Western NMex Univ. *Exhib:* Ceramics Int, Calgary, Alta, 73; Mus Albuquerque, 79; Los Angeles Folk Art Mus, 79; Lange Gallery, Scripps Col, Claremont, Calif; and others. *Pos:* Crafts Rep, Bd NMex Arts & Crafts Fair, 74-; Southwest cur, Women's Caucus for Art Exhib, Bronx Mus, NY, 78. *Teaching:* Instr ceramics, Univ NMex, 79-81. *Awards:* Purchase Awards, Ceramics Int, 73 & Mus Albuquerque, NMex, 79. *Bibliog:* W R Mitchell (auth), Ceramic Art of the World 1973, Govt Can, Alta, 73; Elsbeth Woody (auth), Handbuilding Ceramic Forms, Farrar Straus Giroux, New York, 79. *Mem:* Albuquerque United Artists; NMex Potters Asn; Albuquerque Designer-Craftsman. *Mailing Add:* 3835 Rio Grande Blvd NW Albuquerque NM 87107-3093

WALTERS, ERNEST
PAINTER
b Elizabethtown, Ky, Nov 11, 1927. *Study:* Univ Louisville; Univ Miami; French Studio Schs. *Work:* Mus Mod Art, NY; Israel Mus, Jerusalem; Frankfurt Mus, Ger; Albertina, Vienna, Austria; Mus d'Art Mod, Brussels, Belg. *Exhib:* IFA Galleries, Washington, DC; Galerie Richter, Wiesbaden, Ger; Siemens, Overbeck Gallery, Lubeck; Galerie Kumar, Vienna, Austria; Daedal Fine Arts, Baltimore; and others. *Teaching:* teacher, Baltimore Pub Schs. *Mem:* Print Consortium; MD Writers Asn; Philadelphia Writers' Conf. *Media:* Oil. *Publ:* Auth, Wiener Schwarzweiss, 68; An Astonished Survivor, 73; The Beast Within; Thorns of Life. *Dealer:* IFA Galleries 2623 Connecticut Ave NW Washington DC 20008; Daedal Fine Arts Fallston Mall Fallston MD 21047. *Mailing Add:* 257 Foster Knoll Dr Joppa MD 21085

WALTERS, SYLVIA SOLOCHEK
PRINTMAKER, EDUCATOR
b Milwaukee, Wis, Aug 24, 1938. *Study:* Univ Wis, Madison, BS, MS, MFA, 62. *Work:* St. Louis Art Mus; Achenbach Found Graphic Arts; Oakland Mus; Milwaukee Art Mus; Magnes Mus; Chazen Art Mus; Libr Congress; Jewish Mus Milwaukee. *Exhib:* 3rd Graphics Biennial, Metrop Mus & Art Ctr, Miami, 77 & 80; 34th Ann Boston Printmakers, DeCordova Mus, 82; Prints from Blocks, Assoc Am Artists, New York, 85; California Prints in Japan, Tokyo Mus, 85; Drake Univ 8th Biennial PRWTA Symposium Exhibit; 150 Yrs of Wisconsin Printmakers, Elvejhem Mus Art; Cuts: Contemp Woodcuts, Kala Art Inst, 2003; Am Relief Prints, Univ Place Art Ctr, Lincoln, Nebr; 5th Minn Nat Print Biennial, 2004 & 2006; Boston Printmakers Biennial, 2005; Los Angeles Printmaking Soc 19th & 20th Nat Exhib; California in Relief: A History in Wood and Linocut Prints, Hearst Art Gallery, 2009; Turner 8th Nat Print Show, Janet Turner Print Mus, 2010; Colorprint USA, 40th Anniversary, Mus Tex Tech, 2010; Pacific States Biennial, Univ Hawaii, 2010; Contemp Am Woodcut, Morgan Conservatory, Cleveland, 2010; Boston Printmakers North Am Print Biennial, 2011; 75th Annual Exhib, Soc Wood Engravers, Bankside Art Gallery, 2012; Print Space, Pacific Design Ctr, Los Angeles, 2013. *Pos:* Graphic & bk designer, Univ Wis Press, 64-67; dir, Gallery 210, Univ Mo, 74-; chmn dept art, Univ Mo, 77-81; chmn, dept arts, San Francisco State Univ, 84-2004, prof emer, 2009, actg dean, Coll Creative Arts, 93-94 & 96-97. *Teaching:* Instr printmaking, Layton Sch Art, 63-64; instr drawing, Doane Coll, 67-68 & St Louis Univ, 68-69; prof printmaking & drawing, Univ Mo, St Louis & San Francisco State Univ, 84-2004. *Awards:* Colorprint USA, 88; 42nd N Am Boston Printmakers, 90; Prints USA Award, Springfield Art Mus, 2007; Purchase Award, Ink & Clay 35, 2009. *Bibliog:* Marlene Schiller (auth), article, Am Artist 10/79; Julia Ayres (auth), Printmaking Techniques, Watson-Guptill, 93; James Watrous & Steven Andrews (auths), American Color Woodcuts: Bounty From the Block 1890's-1990's, Univ Wis, 93. *Mem:* Boston Printmakers; Calif Soc Printmakers; Los Angeles Printmaking Soc. *Media:* Woodcut and Relief Prints, Watercolor. *Publ:* Auth, American Women Printmakers, Gallery 210, Univ Mo, St Louis, 75; Art on the Mississippi, 4/76 & Place, race & rights in St Louis, summer 76, Women Artist News; Calif Printmaker Quart J #3, 90; Sol Lewitt: Prints, Contemporary Impressions, Jour Am Print Alliance, Fall 97; Today: Seen Through the Artist's Eye, The California Printmaker News Brief, spring 2009; asst editor, Calif Soc Printmakers, One Hundred Years, 1913-2013. *Dealer:* Kala Art Inst Gallery; Peltz Gallery Milwaukee; Annex Galleries Santa Rosa. *Mailing Add:* 5217 Harbord Dr Oakland CA 94618

WALTNER, BEVERLY RULAND
PAINTER
b Kansas City, Mo. *Study:* Yale Univ, with Joseph Albers; Univ Miami, BA, 55; Kent State Univ, Blossom Kent Art Prog with Richard Anuszkiewicz, 68; Northern Ill Univ, MFA, 68. *Work:* Northern Ill Univ, De Kalb; also numerous pvt collections. *Comn:* Paintings, Alexander Muss & Sons, Equitable Life Assurance Soc, Zuckerman-Vernon Corp & Gen Development Corp. *Exhib:* Tenth Mid-Western Biennial, Joslyn Art Mus, Omaha, Nebr, 68; Chautauqua Exhib Am Art, Chautauqua Art Asn, NY, 68-73 & 78; Ann Exhib, Nat Soc Painters Casein & Acrylics, NY, 69, 70, 72 & 73; 35th Ann Mid Yr Show, Butler Inst Am Art, Youngstown, Ohio, 70; Ark Nat Art Exhib, Univ Ark, Little Rock, 70; Ann Exhib Am Painting, Soc Four Arts, Palm Beach, Fla, 71 & 74. *Teaching:* Instr art, Barry Col, Miami Shores, Fla, 69-70. *Awards:* Top Award, New Horizons in Painting, N Shore Art League, 66; First Place, 68 & Louis E Seldon Mem Award, 72, Chautauqua Art Asn. *Bibliog:* Donald L Hoffman (auth), The color image, Kansas City Star, 1/19/69; Bill van Mauer (auth), Colors get her vivid messages across, Miami News, 2/8/72. *Mem:* Chautauqua Art Asn; Prof Artist Guild (treas, Miami area, 77-78, vpres, 78); Artists Equity Asn; Visual Arts Coalition. *Media:* Acrylic, Oil. *Mailing Add:* 24500 142nd Ave SW Homestead FL 33032

WALTON, ALICE LOUISE
COLLECTOR
b Newport, Ark, Oct 7, 1949. *Study:* Trinity Univ, BBA, 1971. *Hon Degrees:* Southwest Baptist Univ, DBA, 1988. *Pos:* Investment analyst, First Commerce Corp, New Orleans, 1972-75; dir & vpres investments, Walton Enterprises, Bentonville, Ark, 1975; retail & investment broker, EF Hutton co, 1975-79; vice chmn & investment dir, Walton Bank Group, 1982-88; founder, former pres, chmn, and chief exec officer, Llama co/Llama Asset Mgt co; mem dean's adv coun, Univ Ark Coll Bus Adminstrn, 1989-90; bd trustees, Amon Carter Mus, Ft Worth, Tex; founder, exec dir Crystal Bridges Mus of American Art, Ark, 2011-. *Awards:* Named Distinguished Bus Lect Cent State Univ, Edmond, Okla, 1989; Arkansan of Yr, Ark Easter Seals Soc, 1990; named one of Top 100 Women in Ark, Ark Bus, 1995; #13 on Forbes' World's Richest People List, 2005; named one of Top 200 Collectors, ARTnews mag, 2006-13, Time Mag. 100 Most Influential People, 2012. *Mem:* Northwest Ark Coun. *Collection:* American art

WALTON, GUY E
WRITER, EDUCATOR
b New York, NY, Oct 18, 1935. *Study:* Wesleyan Univ, BA, 57; NY Univ, MA, 62, PhD, 67. *Collection Arranged:* Versailles a Stockholm (auth, catalog), Paris, 85. *Teaching:* Prof Baroque art & archit, NY Univ, 72-2002 & prof emer, 2002-. *Awards:* Nat Endowment Humanities Grant, 84-85; Pub Grant, J Paul Getty Trust, 85. *Mem:* Coll Art Asn; Soc Archit Historians; Soc l'Hist l'Art Francais. *Res:* Seventeenth century French and Italian sculpture; architecture and decor of palaces. *Publ:* Auth, Pierre Puget in Rome: 1662, Burlington Mag, 69; Lievin Cruyl, In: Essays for H W Hanson, Abrams, 81; The abduction of Helen, a 17th century French bronze, Bulletin Detroit Mus, 83; Louis XIV's Versailles, Univ Chicago Press, 86; ed, Gifts to the Tsars, Abrams, 2001. *Mailing Add:* 693 Route 519 Belvidere NJ 07823

WALTON, LEE
CONCEPTUAL ARTIST, DRAFTSMAN
Study: San Jose State Univ, Calif, BFA (printmaking and drawing), 97-98; Calif Coll Arts and Crafts, MFA (visual art), 1998-2000. *Exhib:* Solo exhibs, Red Ball, Silent Gallery, San Francisco, 2001; 50 Object, Project Space, Headlands Ctr for Arts, Marin, Calif, 2002; South Exposure, San Francisco, 2003, 2007; Lincoln Pk Golf Course, San Francisco, 2003; City Systems, Univ Fontenay-aux-Roses, France, 2004; Making Changes - Red vs Blue, 667 Shotwell, San Francisco, 2004; Writing a Song is Easy, Clubs Project Inc, Victoria, Australia, 2005; Following the Man in the Crowd, Spectropolis - Mobile Media, Art and the City, NY, 2005; Baseball and Drawings, Kraushaar Gallery, NY, 2005; 00130Gallery Helsinki, Finland, 2006, Organism, Portland, Ore, 2007; Group shows, Potrero Gardens, San Francisco, 2002; Solid Gold, Southern Exposure, San Francisco, 2003; Portland Film Festival, 2004; Out of Place, Indianapolis Mus Contemp Art, 2004; Dead Kids Do Nothing, 31 Grand, Williamsburg, NY, 2005; Rethinking the City, Reykjavik Art Mus, Iceland, 2005; Pratt Univ, 2006; Nat Acad Mus, 2006; Character Reference, Bryce Wolkowitz Gallery, NY, 2007; New Directions in Am Drawing, Columbus Mus, 2007. *Pos:* Artist in residence, Landmark, San Francisco Files, 2002, Socrates Park, Queens, NY, 2005. *Awards:* General Art Award, Emerge, San Francisco, 2002; Affiliate Artist Award, Headlands Ctr for Arts, 2002; The Bartlebooth Award, The Art Newspaper, London, 2006; SJ Truman Award, Nat Acad Mus, NY, 2006

WALTON, M DOUGLAS
PAINTER, INSTRUCTOR
b Alva, Okla, June 23, 1942. *Study:* Okla State Univ, BA, 65; study with Edgar Whitney, Robert E Wood & Milford Zornes; Tech Rome Prog, Italy. *Teaching:* Assoc prof archit & watercolors, La Tech Univ, Ruston, 72-84; instr workshops, throughout US; Watercolor Encounter & Journey Encounter, US and abroad, 77-. *Mem:* Southwestern Watercolor Soc (signature mem); La Watercolor Soc; Southern Watercolor Soc; Mid-Southern Watercolorists (signature mem); Watercolor Art Soc, Houston. *Media:* Watercolor. *Publ:* Auth, A Special Kind of Silence, in prep. *Mailing Add:* 150 Encounter Point Ruston LA 71270

WALTZER, STEWART PAUL
DEALER, PAINTER
b New York, NY, Mar 17, 1948. *Study:* NY Univ, BA, 69, MA, 70; Columbia Univ; New York Studio Sch; also with Irving Sandler, Audrey Flack, Chuck Close & Kenneth Noland. *Exhib:* City Univ NY; Gallery Don Stewart, Montreal; Waddington & Shiell, Toronto; Gallery 99, Miami, Fla; Eva Cohon Gallery, Chicago. *Pos:* Dir, Andre Emmerich Gallery Downtown, 72-74, Tibor de Nagy Gallery, 74-77 & Meredith Long Contemp, 77-79; pres, Waltzer & Assocs, 79-. *Specialty:* American 20th. *Dealer:* Galeria Joan Prats 29 W 57th St New York NY. *Mailing Add:* Stewart Waltzer Co 200 W Houston St New York NY 10014-4828

WAMBAUGH, MICHELE
FINE ART PHOTOGRAPHER
b Dayton, Ohio, Oct 12, 1943. *Study:* Sch of Art Inst Chicago, 61-64; Univ Calif Los Angeles, studied with Joyce Treiman, 69. *Work:* Mus Fine Arts Houston, Tex; Southland, Corp, Dallas, Tex; Vienna State Opera, Austria; Helen Johnston Mem Collection, San Francisco, Calif; Performing Arts Ctr, Dalton, Ga. *Exhib:* Backstage/Onstage, Oakland Mus, Oakland, Calif, 80; Exposed: The Performer Backstage, Morris Mus, Morristown, NJ 94-95, McNay Mus, San Antonio, Tex, 2001; Exposed: The Dancer Backstage, Nat Mus Dance, Saratoga Springs, NY, 94; Nutcracker & Friends, Monmouth Mus, Monmouth, NJ, 94; FotoFest, Houston, Tex, 2000, 2010, 2012; Backstage Around the World, Art Mus of S Tex, Corpus Christi, Tex, 2003; Faces of India, Tex State Mus Asian Cultures, Corpus Christi, Tex, 2006; Retrospective: 1978-2008, Chinese Int Cult Communication Ctr, Beijing, China, 2008; Fotofest, Houston, Tex. *Collection Arranged:* cur, assembled, & arr, Faces of Children, United Nations 40th Ann, San Francisco, Calif, 85. *Teaching:* Vis prof, Utkal Cul Univ, Bhubaneswar, India 2004; vis prof, Utkal Cultural Univ, Bhubaneswar, India, 2004, Sri Venkateshwara Coll Fine Arts, Hyderabad, India, 2009, Osmania Univ, Hyderabad, India, 2009. *Bibliog:* Lora W Jones (auth), Dancescape, Backstage, Dance Mag, 94, 95; Jay Jorgensen (auth), Career Profile, Petersen's Photographic, 98; Rosalind Smith, Women in Photography, Shutterbug, 98; JP Heller (auth), Career Profile, Rangefinder, 2000; Mathew Thottungal (auth), Feature Articles, Asian Photography, 2003, 2004, 2005. *Mem:* Civic Art Comn, City of Houston (mayoral appointee) (bd mem), 2003-2005. *Media:* Digital Photography. *Publ:* auth & illusr, Backstage in Ontario, Phto Life, 84; auth & illusr, Backstage, Canon Chonicle, Canon, 85; auth & illusr, Exposed: The Performer Backstage, the Ga Rev, 98; auth & illusr, Floating Portraits, Petersen's Photographic, 2002; auth & illusr, Backstage Around the World, Canon Chronicle, Canon, 94. *Dealer:* Thom Andriola New Gallery Houston Tex; Dorothy Moye Atlanta Ga

WANDEL, SHARON LEE
SCULPTOR, PAINTER
b Bemidji, Minnesota, Mar 19, 1940. *Study:* Gustavus Adolphus Coll, BA, 62; Columbia Univ, MSW, 65; State Univ NY, Purchase, Cert in Arts Mgt, 93. *Work:* Art Students League, 89; Westinghouse Corp Collection, Pittsburgh, 90; Nat Acad, 94; Housatonic Mus, Conn, 98; CofC, Toyamura, Japan, 99; Pfizer Corp Collection, Armonk, NY, 2000. *Comn:* two 8' bronze figures, Ihilani Resort, Kapolei, Hawaii, 93; two 5″ figures, Silvermine Galleries, 93. *Exhib:* Solo exhibs, Silvermine Guild of Artists, New Canaan, Conn, 93, 97 & 2001, Pen and Brush, New York, 94, Clark Whitney Gallery, Lenox, Mass, 94, James Cox Gallery, Woodstock, NY, 94 & 96, Cortland Jessup Gallery, Provincetown, Mass, 98, New York, 2000 & 02, Gallery Marya, Osaka, Japan, 99, Laura Barton Gallery, Westport, Conn, 2000, Firehouse Gallery, Damaviscotta, Maine, 2000 & Gallery Irohane, Osaka, Japan, 2001, Chace-Randall Gallery, Andes, NY, 2011; group exhibs, Nat Acad Design, New York, 88, 90, 92, 94, 95, 97-99, 2000, 2004, 2007 & 2009, Cortland Jessup Gallery, Provincetown & New York, 98-2002, Canyon Ranch, Lenox, Mass 99-2003, 2010, 2011, Chesterwood, Lenox, Mass, 2000 & 2001, Butler Inst Am Art, Youngstown, Ohio, 2000, Cavalier Gallery, Nantucket, Mass, 2001, Berkshires Botanical Garden, Mass, 2001, Paesaggio Gallery, W Hartford, Conn, 2001-04, Leighton Gallery, Blue Hill, ME, 2001-2011, Munson Gallery, Chatham, Mass, 2002-2012, Sakai (Japan) City Mus, 2002-06, Craven Gallery, Martha's Vineyard, Mass, 2002-2008, Berta Walker Gallery, Provincetown, Mass, 2002, Elan Fine Arts, Rockland, Maine, 2003-2007, Clarke Galleries, Stowe, Vt, 2003-2008, Palm Beach, Fla, 2003-2004, New York, 2003-2004, Westchester Arts Coun, White Plains, NY, 2004, Gallery Yellow, Cross River, NY, 2006-2007, Karin Sanders Gallery, Sag Harbor, NY, 2007 & Ctr Contemp Printmaking, Norwalk, Conn, 2007, 2009, & 2011, Millbrook Sculpture, Concord, NY, 2007-2008, Sculpture Barn, New Fairfield, Conn, 2007-2013, Wit Gallery, Lenox, Mass, 2008 & 2009, Landing Gallery, Rockland, Maine, 2007-2010, ACA Galleries, New York, 2008-2013, Chace Randal Gallery, Andes, NY, 2008-13, Harrison Gallery, Williamstown, Mass, 2010, Noelgallery.com, New York, 2009-2013, Ferrin Gallery, Canyon Ranch, Mass, 2011, Eriksson Fine Art, Boston & Vt, 2011-2013, Laura Barton Gallery, Westport, Conn, 2012-2013, Peter Lawrence Gallery, Gaylordsville, Conn, 2012-2013, Art Essex, Essex, Conn, 2012-2013, featured, 2012. *Pos:* Caseworker, Manhattan State Hosp, New York, 63-64; caseworker/researcher, Community Serv Soc, 65-67; mem adv, bd Lamia Inc, New York, 99-2003. *Teaching:* Teaching asst, dept med NY Univ Med Ctr, 67-70. *Awards:* Cleo Hartwig Award, Nat Acad Design, 90; 2nd place, Nat Am Sculpture Exhib, 91; Chaim Gross Found Award, 93; 1st place, Nat Competition Sundance Gallery, Bridgehampton, NY, 97; Ellin P Speyer Prize, Nat Acad Design, 2007; and others. *Mem:* Silvermine Guild of Artists; NY Soc Woman Artists (pres, formerly); Nat Acad of Design; Sculptors Guild. *Media:* Metal, Cast. *Dealer:* Munson Gallery Chatham NY; Laura Barton Gallery Westport Ct; Chace Randall Gallery Andes NY; Sculpture Barn New Fairfield CT; ACA Galleries NYC; Noelgallery.com, New York; Eriksson Fine Art Boston & VT; Laurence Clark Fine Art Houratonic NY; Peter Lawrence Gallery Gaylordsville Ct; George Billis NY. *Mailing Add:* PO Box 314 Croton On Hudson NY 10520-0314

WANDS, ROBERT JAMES
EDUCATOR, PAINTER
b Denver, Colo, June 24, 1939. *Study:* With Alfred Wands, 56-60; Univ Denver, BFA, 61, MA, 63; Cleveland Art Inst; Western Reserve Univ. *Work:* Univ Denver; Colo Women's Col; Western Colo Ctr Arts, Grand Junction; Univ Southern Colo; Colo State Fair Collection; Leanin Tree Mus, Boulder, Colo; Sangre de Cristo Art Ctr, Pueblo, Colo. *Comn:* Painting, Fine Am Art Calendar, Cleveland, 70; murals, Cleopatra Health Spa, Pueblo, Colo, 76 & YMCA, Estes Park, Colo, 77; paintings, United Bank, Pueblo, Colo, 78, Dain Bosworth, Pueblo, 84, Colo Nat Bank-Belmont, Pueblo, 86 & Pueblo Teachers Credit Union, Colo, 86; mural, Colo State Vet Ctr, Homelake, Colo, 95. *Exhib:* Solo exhib, Sangre de Cristo Art Ctr, Pueblo, Colo, 73 & 96, Western Colo Ctr Arts, Grand Junction, 74 & Univ Southern Colo, 81, Sabbatical Exhib, USC, 89 & Nemick Thompson Gallery, 2004; two-man exhibs, Sangre de Cristo Art Ctr, Pueblo, Colo, 84 & retrospective Exhib, Sangre de Cristo Art Ctr, 2001; Fac Exhib, S Colo Univ, 92, 93 & 94; Colo State Fair Art Exhib, 93; The Rockies Show, Sangre de Cristo Art Ctr, 94; Aqua Media Exhib 2000; Sangre de Cristo Art Ctr, 2000. *Pos:* Artist-in-residence, Asn Camp, Estes Park, Colo, summers 74-78. *Teaching:* Instr painting, Univ Denver, 63; assoc prof, Univ Southern Colo, 63-96. *Awards:* Purchase Prize, 65 & Meritorious Award, 72, Colo State Fair; Best of Show, Own Your Own Art Show, Sangre Cristo Art Ctr, 79 & Purchase Award, 96; Mayors Choice Award, Estes Park Plein Air Show, 2006. *Bibliog:* Carol Kronwitter (auth), Pueblo Chieftain, 2/28/81 & 9/30/84; Jeff Rennicke (auth), Colo Mountain Ranges, 86; Jane Ramsey & Marty Yochum Casey (auth), Early Estes Park Artists, 1970-1970, 2004. *Mem:* I-25 Artist Alliance; Oil Painters Am; Pike Peak Pleain Air Painters; bd mem, Cult Arts Coun of Estes Park, Colo. *Media:* Acrylic, Oil, Watercolor. *Dealer:* Wands Art Studio Gallery P O Box 2093 Estes Park CO 80517; Turf Exchange Art Ctr Pueblo CO; Steel City Art Works Pueblo CO

WANG, SAM
PHOTOGRAPHER
b Peking, China, Apr 4, 1939; US citizen. *Study:* Augustana Coll, Sioux Falls, BA, 64; Univ Iowa, MFA, 66. *Work:* SC State Collection; Chase Manhattan Collection & Metrop Mus Art, New York; Ctr For Creative Photog, Ariz; Herbert F Johnson Mus Art, Ithaca, NY; Lishui Mus Photography; and others. *Exhib:* Solo exhibs, Mint Mus Art, 70, Greenville Co Mus Art, 72, 77 & 81, Lishui Mus Photography, 2009, Shanghai Spring Gallery, 2010; Silver & Silk, Mus Hist & Technol, Smithsonian Inst, 75-77; Translations: Photog in New Forms, Herbert F Johnson Mus, 79; Counterparts, Metrop Mus Art, San Francisco Mus Mod Art & Corcoran Gallery Art, 83; Portrait of the South, Palazzo Vinizia, 84. *Pos:* Acquisitions adv panel, SC State Mus, 84-92; chmn, State Art Collections Comn, SC, 77-78; cur, Personal Visions, Pingyao Int Photog Festival, Pingyao, China, 2007. *Teaching:* Prof photog, Clemson Univ, SC, 66-2007; vis artist photog & computer graphics, Penland Sch Crafts, NC, summers 70, 74, 79, 89 & 91; vis artist printmaking workshop, Univ Notre Dame, 79; vis artist, Digital Imaging, Nanjing Arts Inst, 2004. *Awards:* SAF/NEA Photography Fel, 87; Alumni Distinguished Prof, 2000; Verner award, 2012. *Bibliog:* David Featherstone (auth), Art Week, 73. *Mem:* Soc Photog Educ (bd dir, 73-77). *Media:* Digital & Analog Photography. *Res:* Alternative printing process. *Publ:* Illusr, South Carolina Architecture 1670-1970, SC Tricentennial Comn, 70; New Am Nudes, Morgan & Morgan, 81; Beyond the Zone System, Focal Press, 88; auth, 4 Decades of Photographic Explorations, 2010. *Dealer:* Kiang Gallery, Atlanta

WANLASS, STANLEY GLEN
SCULPTOR, PAINTER
b American Fork, Utah, Apr 3, 1941. *Study:* Brigham Young Univ, BFA, 66, MA, 68. *Work:* Lewis & Clark Nat Monument, Ore; Mus'ee Nat De 'Automobile Raamsdonkveer, Holland; Hutchings Mus, Lehi, Utah; Mus Western Expansion, St Louis, Mo; Blackhawk Mus, Danville, Calif. *Comn:* Heroic sculpture, Wash State Arts Comn, Everett, 76; heroic bronze statue, Nat Park Serv, 83; heroic Lewis & Clark (bronze sculpture), City Seaside, Ore, 90; heroic sculpture, City Longbeach, Wash, 90; heroic bronze sculpture (founder), Muhlenberg Col, Allentown, Pa, 91. *Exhib:* Meadow Brook Concours D'Elegance, Rochester, Mich, 81-2003; Russo Bianco Mus, Aschaffenburg, Ger, 83-92; Los Angeles Co Mus, 85 & 94; Whitehouse, Wash, 88; Campbell (Soup) Mus, Philadelphia, 90; retrospective, Canton Art Inst, 90; Kodak-Japan, Tokyo, 92. *Teaching:* Instr, Brigham Young Univ, Provo, Utah, 65-70, Europ Art Acad, Paris, 65; prof, Univ Grenoble, France, 69-70, Medicine Hat Col, Univ Calgary, Alta, 70 & 71 & Clatsop Col, Astoria, Ore, 71-86. *Awards:* Best of Show, Ore Trail Nat, 81; Silver Medal, Springville Art Mus, Utah, 81; Blue Ribbon Concours d'Elegance, Oakland Univ, Detroit, Mich, 83; Grand Prize & First Place, Auburn-Cord, Duesenberg Mus, Auburn, Ind, 85. *Bibliog:* Articles, SW Art Mag, 82, Automania, 84, Automobile Quarterly, 84 & Forbes Mag, 90. *Mem:* Automotive Fine Arts Soc. *Media:* Bronze; Acrylic, Oil. *Publ:* Auth, Dictionary of American Automobiles 1900-1930, Dover Publ, 73; An Artist's Viewpoint, Knightsbridge Publ Inc, 94; auth, Se-Deuce-Ing (automotive Design Principles) Buckaroo Comn, 2005. *Mailing Add:* c/o Renaissance Int 10770 S Wasatch Blvd Sandy UT 84092

WARASHINA, M PATRICIA
CLAY SCULPTOR, EDUCATOR
b Spokane, Wash. *Study:* Univ Wash, Seattle, BFA, MFA. *Work:* Everson Art Mus, Syracuse, NY; Nelson Gallery Art, Kansas City, Mo; Detroit Art Inst, Mich; Henry Art Gallery, Seattle, Wash; John Michael Kohler Arts Ctr, Sheboygan, Wis. *Comn:* A Procession, Wash State Convention Ctr, Seattle, Wash, 1986; Mercurial Miss, Meydenbauer Convention Ctr, Bellevue, Wash, 1994; City Reflections, Tri-Met Public Art, Downtown Mall Public Art Program, Northwest Sculpture Collection, 2009. *Exhib:* Int Exhib of Ceramics, Victoria & Albert Mus, London, Eng, 72; Sensible Cup Int Exhib, Sea of Japan Expos, Kanazawa, Japan, 7; Clay, Whitney Mus Am Art, NY, 74; 1st World Crafts Exhib, Ont Sci Ctr, Toronto, 74; The Collector, Mus Contemp Crafts, NY, 74; NW 77 Exhib, Mod Art Pavilion, Seattle Ctr, Wash, 77; Contemporary Am Ceramiics (1950-1990), 2004; Yingge Ceramic Mus, Taipei Co, Taiwan, 2005; Human Form in Clay/The Mind's Eye, The Shigaraki Ceramic Cultural Park, Japan, 2006-2007; Retrospective Exhib, Am Mus Ceramic Art, Pomona, Calif, 2012; 50 Yr Retrospective Exhib, Bellevue Art Mus, Wash, 2013. *Teaching:* Instr art, Wis State Univ, Platteville, 64-65; instr art, Eastern Mich Univ, Ypsilanti, 66-68; prof art, Univ Wash, Seattle, 70-95, prof emeritus, currently. *Bibliog:* John Forsen (filmed by, prodr), Patti Warashina, Fidget TV, Seattle Channel, 2009. *Mem:* Am Mus Ceramic Art; Bellevue Art Mus; Seattle Art Mus; Wing Luke Mus. *Media:* Clay. *Publ:* Martha Kingsbury (auth), Patti Warashina: Wit and Wisdom, Am Mus Ceramic Art, Pomona, Calif, 2012. *Mailing Add:* 120 E Edgar St Seattle WA 98102

WARBURG, STEPHANIE WENNER
PAINTER, INSTRUCTOR
b Kalamazoo, Mich, Dec 29, 1941. *Study:* Univ Mich Coll Archit & Design, BS (drawing & design); and with Guy Palazzola & Milton Cohen; Columbia Univ Teachers Coll, MA (fine arts & fine arts educ). *Work:* Earthwatch, Atrium Schools, Watertown, Mass; Cancer Ctr, Mass Gen Hosp; Govt House, St Vincent; Renewal House & Advocates, Mass; Children's Hospital, Boston; Whidden Hospital, Boston; Somerville Hospital, Somerville, Mass. *Exhib:* Slater Mus, Norwich, Conn, 69; Gilman Gallery, Chicago, 72; Lord & Taylor Gallery, NY, 69-79; Flora & Fauna of Madeira, Funchal, Madeira, Portugal, 73; Bermuda Soc Arts, 84; St Botolph Club, Boston, 85; Gallery Nakazawa, Hiroshima, Japan, 86 & 2001; Oda Gallery, Hiroshima, Japan, 87; Nena's Choice Gallery, Bergdorf Goodman, NY, 90; Saks Fifth Avenue, 2002; Treasure Boutique, Mustique, West Indies, 2003; Marion Art Assoc Exhib, 2005; Lowarts Juried Show, 2006; Framingham Art Assoc Juried Show, 2006; Illuminations, Mass Gen Hosp, 2007; Cambridge Art Asn, 2010; L'Attitude Gallery, Boston, 2010-2011. *Pos:* vis artist Bermuda Soc Arts, 85. *Teaching:* Chmn, Dept Art, Latin Sch Chicago, 70-72; instr watercolor & freehand drawing, Chamberlayne Jr Coll, Boston, 75-81. *Awards:* Am Cancer Soc Art Awards, 67 & 68; Lyme Art Asn Second Prize for Painting, 68; 1st prize, Mass General Hosptial. *Bibliog:* Susan Croce Kelly (auth), It's all in the family: Sister artists display work here, St Louis Globe Dem, 70; On exhibit, Where Mag, 12/72. *Mem:* Bermuda Soc Arts; Art Connection, Boston; Cambridge Art Asn; Concord Art Asn; Marion Art Asn. *Media:* Oil Wash, Oil on canvas. *Specialty:* Magic realism. *Dealer:* L'Attitude Gallery Boston; Gingerbread Square Gallery Keywest Fl. *Mailing Add:* 360 Beacon St Boston MA 02116

WARCK MEISTER, LUCIA
INSTALLATION SCULPTOR, VIDEO ARTIST
Work: Museo Extremeno e Iberoamericano de Arte Contemporaneo, Spain; Deutsche Bank Art Found; Fundacion Telefonica de Argentina; Taplin Collection, Sagamore Hotel, Miami; and many pvt collections . *Exhib:* Solo exhibs, Centro Cultural Recoleta, Buenos Aires, 1997-98, Fondo Nacional de Las Artes, Buenos Aires, 2001, Haim Chanin Fine Arts, New York, 2003, Sara Zanin Gallery, Rome, 206, Pan Am Projects, Miami, 2007, CAMAC, Marnay-sur-Seine, France, 2008; Briggens Mus,

Bergen, 1999; Miura Mus Art, Matsuyama City, Japan, 2000; Sculpture in Four Dimensions, Mus of the Americas, Washington, DC, 2004; Plugged in Fest III, Ctr for Maine Contemp Art, Rockport, 2006; Project 59 Video Festival, Res Lab, Univ Tex, Austin, 2008. *Awards:* Sch Visual Arts Fel, 2005; First Prize, Palm Beach Biennale, Fla, 2006; Am Acad in Rome Fel, 2007; Pollock-Krasner Found Grant, 2008. *Bibliog:* Alfredo Cernadas Quesada (auth), Beauty and Vigour, Buenos Aires Herald, 6/1992; Sarah Schmerler (auth), Parsing the Line, Time Out, New York, 5/2-9/2002; Constance Wyndham (auth), DiVA, Art in Am, 4-5/2006

WARD, ELAINE
PAINTER
b Boston, Mass. *Study:* Ecole Des Beaux Arts, France, BA, 53; Art Students League, 57-61. *Hon Degrees:* Hon dipl, Asn des Beaux Arts de Cannes, 74. *Work:* New Eng Contemp Art Ctr, Brooklyn, Conn; Daytona Beach Mus, Fla; Ardan Asn, New York; Coastal Steel co, Carteret, NJ; Pandora co, Conway, NH; Zimmerli Mus, Rutgers Univ, New Brunswick, NJ; Daytona Beach Mus, Fla; Mus Roxbury, Conn. *Comn:* Portrait, comn by Barbara Andreadls, New York, 86; acrylic on canvas, Arthur Dann & co, New York, 88; acrylic on canvas, Design Decisions, New York, 89; mural on canvas, comn by Senor Louis Carraquillo Vieques, PR, 89. *Exhib:* Viewpoint Gallery, New York, 91; Phoenix Gallery, New York, 92; Elaine Benson Gallery, Bridgehampton, NY, 92; Barnes & Noble, Union Sq, New York; Guild Hall Mus, East Hampton, NY; solo exhib, Phoenix Gallery, New York, 2006; New Art Ctr, New York, 2010. *Teaching:* Instr & artist various schs, San Miguel de Allende, Mex. *Awards:* First Prize, Munic Casino Cannes, 77; Jeffrey Childs Willis Mem Award, 96; East End Arts Coun Award, 96; NAWA Award, recipient Muriel E Halpern Mem Award, 2003. *Bibliog:* Deanna Freedman (auth), Enlarging the viewers experience, Artspeak, 2/89; Mary Jo Godwin (auth), Exotic Star, Wilson Libr Bull, 4/89; Charles Ditlefsein (auth), Women Artists, Cedco Publ co, 90; John Austin (auth), Sirens & Mermaids, Dream & Play in the Work of Elaine Ward, 2010. *Mem:* Nat Asn Women Artist; Art Studio Club (treas, 88-90); Nat Art Club; New York Soc Illusr. *Media:* Watercolor, Acrylic. *Specialty:* Fine Arts. *Publ:* Illusr, cover, Wilson Libr Bull, 4/89; auth, articles in Manhattan Art Mag & Artspeak, 90; Art rev, NY Times, Helen A Harrison (cur), 9/29/2002. *Dealer:* Phoenix Gallery 568 Broadway New York NY 10012. *Mailing Add:* 175 E 62 St New York NY 10021

WARD, JOHN LAWRENCE
HISTORIAN, PAINTER
b East Orange, NJ, Feb 6, 1938. *Study:* Hamilton Col, BA, 60; Yale Univ, MA (art hist), 62; Univ NMex, MFA (painting), 66; Boston Univ, PhD (art hist), 84. *Work:* Univ NMex; Ala Power Co, Birmingham; Astronomy Dept, Univ Fla; McGraw-Hill Corp Headquarters, NY; Cornell Fine Arts Mus, Rollins Col. *Exhib:* The Human Presence, Jacksonville Art Mus, Fla, 74; Solo exhibs, Fla Tech Univ, Orlando, 76, Univ Fla, Gainesville, 76 & 86, Stetson Univ, DeLand, Fla, 92, & Univ N Fla, 01; Group exhibs, Southeastern Ctr for Contemp Art, Winston-Salem, NC, 79; Southern Realism, Miss Mus Art, traveling, 79, & Corporealities, Cornell Fine Arts Mus, Rollins Col, 2002; Southeast Juried Exhib, Fine Arts Mus S, Mobile, Ala, 87; 59th Ann Cooperstown Art Asn Nat, 94; Charlotte Co Nat Art Show, Punta Gorda, Fla, 98; and others. *Teaching:* Prof art hist and painting, Univ Fla, 62-64 & 66-. *Awards:* Best of Show, 5th Ann N Fla Art Competition, Fla State Univ, 90; First Prize, 59th Ann Cooperstown Art Asn Nat, 94; Best in Show, Charlotte Co Nat Art Show, Punta Gorda, Fla. *Mem:* Coll Art Asn; Hist Netherlandish Art. *Media:* Oil. *Res:* Flemish painting, American Realist painting. *Publ:* Auth, The criticism of photography as art: The photographs of Jerry Uelsmann, 70; Hidden symbols in Jan Van Eyck's Annunciations, Vol LVII, 75, Art Bulletin; The Perception of Pictorial Space in Perspective Pictures, Vol IX, Leonardo, 76; American Realist Painting, 1945-1980, UMI Res Press, 89; Disguised symbolism as enactive symbolism in Van Eyck's Paintings, Artibus et Historiae, 94; Edwin Dickinson: A Critical History of His Paintings, Univ Del Press, 2003

WARD, NARI
SCULPTOR
Exhib: One-person exhibs, Amazing Grace, Harlem Firehouse Space, New York & Carpet Angel, New Mus, New York, 93, Idle Drift, Le Magasin, Centre National d'Art Contemporain, Grenoble, France, 94 & Happy Smilers: Duty Free Shopping, Deitch Proj, New York, 96; Artists in Residence 1992-1993, Studio Mus, Harlem, NY, 93; Heart of Darkness, Kroller-Muller Mus, Neth, 94; Whitney Mus Am Art Biennial, New York, 95, 2006; Pursuit of the Sacred: Evocations of the Spiritual in Contemp African American Art, Betty Rymer Gallery, Art Inst Chicago, 97; Projects: How to Build and Maintain the Virgin Fertility in our Soul, PS1 Mus, Long Island, 97; Edge of Awareness, World Health Orgn, Geneva, Switz, 98; Am Acad Arts & Letts Exhib, New York, 98; and others. *Awards:* John Simon Guggenheim Fel, New York, 92; Nat Endowment Arts, Washington, DC, 94; Pollack Krasner Found, New York, 96; Willard L Metcalf Award, Am Acad Arts & Letters, 98; Joan Mitchell Found Grant, 2009. *Bibliog:* Jeffrey Deitch (auth), Nari Ward: Aperto, Flash Art, 97, summer 93; Holland Carter (auth), Bob Rivera, Michelle Talibah, and Nari Ward, NY Times, C12, 12/17/93; Leslie Camhi (auth), Other rooms, Village Voice, 83, 10/9/96; and others. *Mailing Add:* 307 W 141st St Apt 180 New York NY 10030

WARDEN, P GREGORY
ADMINISTRATOR, WRITER
b Florence, Italy, Nov 28, 1950; US Citizen. *Study:* Univ Pa, BA, 72; Bryn Mawr Col, MA, 76, PhD, 78. *Pos:* assoc dean, Meadows Sch Arts, 98-; interim dir, Meadows Mus, 2001-03. *Teaching:* prof, art hist, Southern Meth Univ, Dallas, 82-. *Interests:* Mediterranean Art & Archaeology. *Publ:* The Metal Finds from Poggio Eivitate (Murlo), Bretschneider, 85; Classical Near Eastern Bronzes in the Hilprecht Collection, Univ Pa, 97; Foru, Figure, and Narrative in Greek Vase Painting, Dallas, Ohio. *Mailing Add:* Southern Meth Univ Meadows Mus Meadows Sch of Arts Dallas TX 75275

WARDLAW, GEORGE MELVIN
PAINTER, SCULPTOR
b Baldwyn, Miss, Apr 9, 1927. *Study:* Memphis Acad Arts, BFA, 51; Univ Miss, with David Smith & Jack Tworkov, MFA, 55. *Work:* Milwaukee Art Mus, Wis; Wichita Art Mus, Kans; Mus Fine Arts, Springfield, Mass; Memphis Brooks Mus Art, Tenn; DeCordova Mus & Sculpture Park, Lincoln, Mass; Miss Mus Art, Jackson, Miss. *Comn:* Wall relief sculpture, 76 & sculpture, 76, Mt Sinai Med Ctr; site specific sculpture, Johnson Wax Corp, Racine, Wis, 86. *Exhib:* Yale Art Gallery, New Haven, Conn, 66; Abstract Paintings, DeCordova Mus, Lincoln, Mass, 71; solo exhib, DeCordova Mus, Lincoln, Mass, 78-79; Chicago Art Inst; Metrop Mus Art, New York; Nat Gallery, Washington, DC; Portland Mus Art, Maine; Yeshiva Univ Mus, New York, 2002. *Teaching:* Asst prof art, State Univ NY Coll, New Paltz, 56-63; assoc prof painting & exec off, Yale Univ, 64-68; prof painting & chmn dept, Univ Mass, 68-90, prof emer, 90-. *Awards:* Miss Inst Arts & Lett Award, 83; Univ Mass Fac Res Fel, 83. *Bibliog:* Auth, Hugh Davies, Paintings in the Round (exhib catalog), DeCordova Mus & Sculpture Park, Lincoln, Mass, 78-79; coauth, Transitions (exhib catalog), Memphis Brooks Mus Art, Tenn, 88. *Media:* Acrylic on canvas, Metal and wood. *Dealer:* Perimeter Gallery, Chicago, Ill. *Mailing Add:* 47 Morgan Cir Amherst MA 01002

WARDROPPER, IAN BRUCE
MUSEUM DIRECTOR
b Baltimore, Md, May 11, 1951. *Study:* Brown Univ, BA, 1973; NYU, MA, 1976, PhD, 1985. *Pos:* asst cur European sculpture, Art Inst Chicago, 1982-85, assoc cur European decorative arts and sculpture, 1985-89, Eloise W Martin cur European decorative arts and sculpture, and classical art, 1989-2001; Iris & B Gerald Cantor cur in charge dept European sculpture and decorative arts, Metrop Mus Art, NYC, 2001-05, chmn, 2005-11; dir, The Frick Collection, NYC, 2011-. *Teaching:* adj instr, Drew Univ, NJ, 1982; vis asst prof, Northwestern Univ, Evanston, Ill, 1986, Sch of Art Inst Chicago, 1988; guest scholar, J Paul Getty Mus, Malibu, Calif, 1995; Rhoades lectr, Univ Chicago, 1997. *Awards:* NEA fel, 1976-77; Chester Dale fel, Metrop Mus Art, 1978-79; Kress Found res grantee, Paris, 1979-81; Am Philos Soc grantee, 1991; Chicagoan of Yr in Arts, Chicago Tribune, 1994. *Mem:* Phi Beta Kappa. *Publ:* coauth, European Decorative Arts in the Art Institute of Chicago, 1991; Austrian Architecture and Design Beyond Tradition in the 1990s, 1991; News from a Radiant Future: Soviet Porcelain from the Collection of Craig H. & Kay A. Tuber, 1992; Chiseled with a Brush: Italian Sculpture, 1860-1925, from The Gilgore Collections, 1994; From the Sculptor's Hand: Italian Baroque Terracottas from the State Hermitage Museum, 1998; contribr articles to prof jours. *Mailing Add:* The Frick Collection 1 East 70th St New York NY 10021

WAREHALL, WILLIAM DONALD
GLASS BLOWER, CERAMIST
b Detroit, Mich, July 12, 1942. *Study:* Wayne State Univ, BFA, 68; Univ Wis, Madison, MFA, 71. *Work:* Chrysler Mus Art, Norfolk; Bergstrom Mahler Mus, Neenah, Wis; W Baton Rouge Hist Mus, Port Allen; La State Univ, Baton Rouge; Ariz State Univ, Tempe; and others. *Comn:* Reproduction of Ancient Maritime Glass Vessels, Tex A&M Univ, College Station, Tex, 90. *Exhib:* 20 Americans, Mus Contemp Art, NY, 71; Phases of New Realism, Lowe Art Mus, Coral Gables, Fla 72; California Design, Los Angeles Design Ctr, 76; Solo exhib, Anhalt Gallery, Los Angeles, 76; Tea Pot-24 Concepts, Rodell Gallery, Los Angeles, 82; New Glass, Heller Gallery, NY, 85; Southern Calif Glass, Scalar Gallery, Morristown, NJ 86; Calif, Elaine Potter Gallery, San Francisco, 86. *Teaching:* Instr art, Univ Minn, 71-73; from asst prof art to assoc prof, Calif State Univ, San Bernardino, 73-81, prof, 81-, chairperson, 88-90 & 95-97; asst prof, La State Univ, Baton Rouge, 78-79; exchange prof ceramics, Va Commonwealth Univ, Richmond, 86; Artist in residence, Buckingham Col Art & Design, UK, 94 & Southern Ill Univ, Edwardsville, 98-. *Bibliog:* Paul Donhauser (auth), History of Am Ceramics, Kendall & Hunt, 78. *Mem:* Am Craft Coun; Southern Calif Designer Craftsman; Glass Soc; Coll Art Asn; Nat Coun Art Adminr. *Media:* Cast Glass, Pate de Verre; Clay. *Dealer:* Sandy Webster Gallery Philadelphia PA; Craft Alliance Gallery St Louis MO. *Mailing Add:* Calif State Univ Art Dept 5500 State College Pkwy San Bernardino CA 92407

WARKOV, ESTHER
PAINTER
b Winnipeg, Man, Oct 12, 1941. *Study:* Winnipeg Sch Art, 58-61. *Work:* Nat Gallery, Ottawa; Mus Fine Arts, Montreal; Vancouver Art Gallery; Winnipeg Art Gallery; Beaver Brook Art Gallery, Fredrickton, NB. *Exhib:* Expo '67, Montreal; Marlborough Godard Exhib, 73; Mus Mod Art, Paris, 73; Albright-Knox Art Gallery, Buffalo, 74. *Awards:* Can Coun Bursaries, 67-72; Can Coun Grant, 73-74. *Bibliog:* Esther Warkov, Can Broadcasting Corp, 73. *Mem:* Royal Can Acad Arts. *Media:* Oil. *Dealer:* Marlborough Godard Ltd 1490 Sherbrooke W Montreal PQ Can. *Mailing Add:* 341 Matheson Ave Winnipeg MB R2W 0C9 Canada

WARLICK, M.E.
EDUCATOR, ADMINISTRATOR
Study: Univ NC, Greensboro, BSHE (Interior Design), 1968; Georgia State Univ, MA (Art History), 1976; Univ Md, College Park, PhD (Art History), 1984. *Pos:* Adv com mem, Acoma Theater, 2004. *Teaching:* Instructor of Art History, Georgia State Univ, 1977; Graduate Teaching Asst, Univ Md, College Park, 1979; instructor of Art History, Univ Col, Univ Md, College Park, 1980-82; instructor of Art History, Coe Col, Cedar Rapids, 1983, 1984; consultant, Department of Curatorial Records, National Gallery of Art, Washington, DC, 1983-85; National Gallery of Art Representative to the Mus Prototype Project, Getty Trust Art History Information Program, Los Angeles, 1985; vis lecturer of Art History, Univ Calif, Santa Barbara, 1984; vis asst prof of Art History, Univ Oregon, Eugene, 1985-86; vis asst prof of Art History, Univ Colo, Boulder, 1987; With Sch of Art and Art History, Univ Denver, 1986-, dir women's studies, 1987-90, asst prof European Modern Art, 1986-91, assoc prof, European Modern Art, formerly, prof European Modern Art, currently, dir Sch of

Art and Art History, currently, coordinator of Art History Records, 2007-, library liaison, 1992-99, 2000-, and several other service positions. *Awards:* Chester Dale Fellowship, National Gallery of Art, Washington, DC, 1982; Paul Mellon Visiting Senior Fellow, Ctr for Advanced Study in the Visual Arts, CASVA, National Gallery of Art, Washington, DC, 1990; Univ Denver, Distinguished Teaching award, 1991; Golden Key National Honor Soc, Outstanding Member of the Faculty, 1994; Stirling Maxwell Fellowship, Univ Glasgow, 1997; Univ Denver Professorship in the Arts and Humanities, 1997-2000. *Mem:* Col Art Asn; Denver Art Mus (mem col adv com, 1986-), Asn of Historians of Nineteenth Century Art; Soc for Literature and Science and the Arts; Friends of Early Modern Women. *Publ:* (auth) The Philosopher's Stones, 1997; (auth) The Alchemy Stones, 2002; (auth) Max Ernst and Alchemy: A Magician in Search of Myth, 2001; contributor of several journal articles, book chapters and conference proceedings. *Mailing Add:* 2940 S Marion Englewood CO 80113

WARNECKE, JOHN CARL
ARCHITECT
b Oakland, Ca, Feb 24, 1919. *Study:* Stanford Univ, AB, 41; Harvard Univ, MA 42. *Comn:* Works incl US Naval Acad Master Plan, Michelson and Chauvenet Halls, Annapolis, Md, Univ Calif at Santa Cruz Master Plan and Libr, Lafayette Sq, Wash, Georgetown Univ Libr, Wash, Kaiser Ctr for Technol, Pleasanton, Calif; bldgs, Stanford Univ, Hawaii State Capitol, Honolulu, Philip A. Hart Senate off bldg, USSR Embassy, Hennepin Govt Ctr, Minneapolis, JF Kennedy Mem Grave, Arlington Nat Cemetery, Va, Neiman Marcus and Bergdorf Goodman Stores, Logan Airport, Boston, Am Hosp, Paris, The Sun Co. Hdqrs, Radnor, Pa, King Abdulaziz Univ Med Ctr, Jedda, Saudi Arabia, Yanbu Town Ctr Master Plan, Hilton Hotel & Casino, Atlantic City. *Pos:* Assoc, Miller & Warnecke, archit, 44-46; partner, Warnecke & Warnecke, 54-62; pres, dir, design John Carl Warnecke & Assoc, 58-. *Awards:* Recipient Arnold Brunner prize in archit Nat Inst Arts and Letters, 57; also 70 nat, regional awards for excellence. *Mem:* Fel Am Inst of Archits; Nat Acad (assoc, 58-94, acad, 94-)

WARNER, HERBERT KELII, JR
PRINTMAKER
b Honolulu, Hawaii, July 29, 1943. *Study:* Univ Hawaii, BFA, 67; Pratt Inst, MFA, 72. *Work:* Rutgers Univ, Camden, NJ; Honolulu Acad Arts, Honolulu, Hawaii. *Exhib:* Purdue Univ, West Lafayette, Ind, 77; Okla Nat Drawing & Prints, Oklahoma City, 77; Asn Am Artists, NY, 77; Libr Cong, Washington, 77; Trenton State Mus, NJ, 80. *Pos:* Prod mgr, Philadelphia Forum, 96. *Teaching:* Asst prof, Rutgers Univ, Camden, NJ, 72-79; teacher design, Art Inst Philadelphia, 80-82. *Awards:* Purchase Awards, Purdue Univ, 77 & Honolulu Acad Arts, 77; Fel, State NJ, 78. *Media:* Etching, Lithography. *Mailing Add:* 5425 Walker St Philadelphia PA 19124

WARNER, MALCOLM
MUSEUM DIRECTOR, CURATOR
b Aldershot, England, May 17, 1953. *Study:* Univ London, BA, 1974, PhD, 1985. *Pos:* Assoc editor, Oxford Dictionary Nat Biography, Oxford Univ Press, England, 1997-2001; Res cur dept, European Painting Art Inst, Chicago, 1988-90; cur prints & drawings, San Diego Mus Art, 1990-92, cur, European art, 1992-96; cur paintings, Yale Ctr Brit Art, New Haven, 1996-2001; sr cur, Kimbell Art mus, Ft Worth, Tex, 2001-2007, deputy dir, 2007-, acting dir, 2007-2012; exec dir, Laguna Art Mus, Laguna Beach, Calif, 2012-. *Teaching:* vis asst prof, Univ Manchester, 1984-85. *Mem:* Asn Art Mus Cur; Print Coun Am; Assn Art Museum Dirs. *Mailing Add:* Laguna Art Mus 307 Cliff Dr Laguna Beach CA 92651

WARNER, MARINA
WRITER, CRITIC
b London, Eng, Nov 9, 1946. *Study:* Lady Margaret Hall, Oxford Univ, MA, 1967. *Hon Degrees:* Oxford Univ, Hon DLitt, 2006, Univ Exeter, Hon DLitt, 1995; Univ York, Hon DLitt, 1997; Univ St Andrews, Hon DLitt, 1998; Sheffield Hallam Univ, Hon Doc, 1995; Univ N London, Hon Doc, 1997; Tavistock Inst, Hon Doc, 1999; Royal Coll Art, Hon Doc, 2004, Univ Kent, Hon Doc, 2005; Univ Leicester, Hon DLitt, 2006, Two Year Fellowship, All Souls Coll, Oxford, 2013, Honorary Fellow, Mansfield Coll, Oxford, 2013, Honorary Fellow, St Cross Coll, Oxford, 2013. *Pos:* Vis scholar, Getty Ctr Hist Art & Humanities, 1987-88; lit panel, Arts Coun Great Brit, 1993-97; trustee, Artangel Trust, 1998-2004, George Orwell Soc, 2003-2007; pres, British Comparative Literature Assn, 2010-; chair, The Man Booker International Prize, 2015. *Teaching:* Tinbergen prof Erasmus, Univ Rotterdam; vis prof, Queen Mary & Westfield Coll, Univ London & Univ Ulster, 1995, Univ York, 1996, Birkbeck Coll, Univ London, 1999-2004, Stanford Univ, 2000, St Andrew's Univ, Scotland, 2000-, Univ Paris XIII, 2003, Royal Coll Art, 2008; Mellon prof art hist, Univ Pittsburgh, spring 1997; vis fel, Trinity Coll, Cambridge, 1998, Humanities Res Ctr, Warwick, 1999, All Souls Coll, Oxford, 2001, Italian Acad, Columbia Univ, New York, 2003; prof lit, film & theater studies, Univ Essex, 2004-2014; vpres, Inst Greece, Rome & Classical Studies, Univ Bristol, 2004; sr fel, Remarque Inst, NY Univ, 2006; Fel British Acad, 2005; distinguished vis prof, Univ London, 2009-; distinguished visiting prof, NYU, Abu Dhabi, 2014. *Awards:* Short Term Fel, Coun Humanities, Princeton, 1996; Harvey Darton Award, 1996; Mythopoeic Fantasy Award, 1996; Katharine Briggs Mem Prize, 1999; Chevalier de l'Ordre des Arts et des Lettres, 2000; Hon Fel, Lady Margaret Hall, Oxford, 2000; Rose Mary Crawshay Prize, Brit Acad, 2000; Aby Warburg Prize, 2004; Commendatore dell'Ordine della Stella di Solidareita, 2005; Commander, Order Brit Empire, 2008; Hon fel, Inst German & Romance Studies, Univ London, 2009; Nat Book Critics award for Criticism, 2012; Sheikh Zayed Book award, Arab Culture in Non-Arabic Languages, 2013; Truman Capote award for Literary Criticism, 2013. *Mem:* Fel Royal Soc Lit, Eng; Fel Brit Acad, 2005; Hon Fel London Inst Pataphysics, 2007; AICA, 2009; Nat Portrait Gallery, London (trustee). *Res:* Female symbols; the body as sign; the construction of female identity in imagery; fairy tales. *Publ:* Auth, Six Myths of Our Time, 1995; contribr, Zarina Bhimji (exhib catalog), Cambridge, 1995; Visual Display Culture Beyond Appearances (Lynne Cooke & Peter Wollen, eds), New York, 1995; Helen Chadwick Stilled Lives, Edinburgh, 1996; David Nash: Forms into Time, London, 1996; No Go the Bogeyman, 1998; Fantastic Metamorphoses, Other Worlds, 2002; Signs & Wonders, 2003; Phantasmagoria: Spirit Visions, Metaphors & Media, 2006; Stranger Magic: Charmed States & the Arabian Nights, Chatto & Windus, 2011, Harvard Univ Press, 2012; Scheherazae's Children: Global Encounters with the Arabian Nights, edited by Philip Kennedy and Marina Warner, NYU Press, 2013; The Symbol Gives Rise to Thought, Violette Editions, 2014; Once Upon a Time-A Shorty History of Fairy Tale, Oxford Univ Press, 2014. *Mailing Add:* 10 Dunollie Pl London NW5 2XR United Kingdom

WARREN, DAVID BOARDMAN
CURATOR
b Baltimore, Md, Mar 11, 1937. *Study:* Princeton Univ, AB (cum laude), 59; Univ Del, MA, 65. *Collection Arranged:* Bayou Bend Collection (auth, catalog), Mus Fine Arts, Houston, 65-, Southern Silver (auth, catalog), 68, Gothic Revival style in Am 1830-1870 (auth, catalog), 76, nineteenth century Am landscape: Selections from the Thyssen-Bornenisza Collection (auth, catalog), 82; Marks of Achievement: Four Centuries of Am Presentation Silver (auth, catalog), 87; The Masterpieces of Bayou Bend (1620-1870) and the Voyage of Life, Bayou Bend Mus Americana Tenneco, 91; The Grandeur of Viceregal Mexico: Treasures from the Museo Franz Mayer, 2002, Mus Fine Arts, Houston, 2002, Winterhven Mus, 2002-2003, San Diego Mus Art, 2003 (co-auth catalog). *Pos:* Cur, Bayou Bend Collection, Mus Fine Arts, Houston, 65-, assoc dir, 74-; trustee, Henry Francis Du Pont Winterthur Mus, 77-; dir, Bayou Bend Collections and Gardens, 87-. *Teaching:* Lectr, Am Decorative Arts, Rice Univ, 66-73. *Publ:* Coauth, Texas Furniture: The Cabinetmakers and Their Work 1840-1870, Univ Tex Press, 75; contribr, A Guide to the Collections, Mus Fine Arts, Houston, 81; Harry N Abrams (auth), Marks of Achievement: Four Centuries of American Presentation Silver, 87; American Decorative Arts and Paintings in the Bayou Bend Collection & Gardens, Princeton Univ Press, 98. *Mailing Add:* Mus Fine Arts Houston 1001 Bissonnet St PO Box 6826 Houston TX 77005

WARREN, JACQUELINE LOUISE
PAINTER, EDUCATOR
b National City, Calif, Nov 3, 1946. *Study:* Southwest Mo State Univ, BFA, 67; Ariz State Univ, MFA, 71; Stanford Univ, 89. *Work:* Hallmark Corp; Quaker Oats; IBM; Pepsi Cola; Blue Cross; Price Waterhouse; Seven Up Corp; May Corp. *Exhib:* Works of Paper Nat Competition, 80; Paper Nat Competitive, Columbia Col, Mo, 81; Watercolor, USA, Nelson-Atkins Mus Art, Kansas City; Morgan Gallery, Kansas City; Ruth Bachofner Gallery, Antsource Los Angeles, Calif; William Shearburn Gallery, St Louis. *Collection Arranged:* Art on Paper, Cox Gallery, Drury Col, 81. *Teaching:* Prof painting & drawing, Southwest Mo State Univ, Springfield, 75-79; prof design, Drury Col, Springfield, Mo, 79-; prof art & design, Drury Univ, currently. *Awards:* First Prize, Ariz State Fair, 70; Best of Show, Spiva Mus, Joplin, Mo, 78; First Prize, Sch Ozarks, Branson, Mo, 79; Best of Show, Mid Four Exhib, Nelson Alkins Art Mus, Kansas City; Fel painting, Nat Endowment Arts; Herword Cook Fel Painting. *Bibliog:* Edgar Albin (auth), Artist profile, Art Voices South Mag, 80; New Art Examiner. *Mem:* Coll Art Asn; Watercolor Nat Hon Soc. *Media:* Mixed Media. *Dealer:* Morgan Gallery Kansas City MO; Vanstraaten Gallery Chicago IL; William Shearburn St Louis. *Mailing Add:* 918 S Weller St Springfield MO 65802

WARREN, JULIANNE BUSSERT BAKER
PHOTOGRAPHER, HISTORIAN
b Lima, Ohio, May 8, 1916. *Work:* Pub Libr Cincinnati & Hamilton Co; Truman Libr & Johnson Libr, Austin, Tex; Smithsonian Inst. *Comn:* Photographs of eight US Presidents; Prime Minister Wilson, London; Princess Margaret. *Exhib:* Solo exhibs, Pub Libr Cincinnati & Hamilton Co, 67 & Exhib of Collection, 78; Cincinnati Art Mus, 59; Shillito's Dept Store, Cincinnati, 61; Jewish Community Ctr, Cincinnati, 70; Cincinnati Woman's Club, 74; Asn Am Ed Cartoonist Collection, Libr Commun Graphic Arts, Ohio State Univ, 84. *Pos:* Mgr, Photo-finishing Co, Cincinnati, 41-48; Photogr radio station, 50-52; news photogr, Cincinnati Post, 52-68; archivist, Asn Am Edit Cartoonist, Ohio State Univ, 84-. *Awards:* First Prize, Nat Heirloom Contest, 59; First Prize, Newspaper Guild's Page-One Ball, 61; Two Prizes, Best Women's Page Photog, Univ Mo, 65. *Mem:* Asn Am Edit Cartoonists (archivist 71-92, historian, 71-). *Publ:* Contribr & illusr, Press Photography, Macmillan, 61; coauth, Cincinnati in Color, Hastings House, 78. *Dealer:* B Alden Olson Corp Art Concepts The Loft Mt Adams St Cincinnati OH 45202

WARREN, LYNNE
CURATOR, WRITER
b Lowell, Mass, Mar 12, 1952. *Study:* Sch Art Inst Chicago, BFA, 76. *Collection Arranged:* Kenneth Josephson: Photographs (auth, catalog), 83; DOGS, 84; Alternative Spaces: A History in Chicago (auth, catalog), 84; Jon Kessler: Sculpture (auth, catalog), 86; Donald Sultan: Paintings (auth, catalog), 87; Starn Twins, 88; Julia Wachtel, 90; Art in Chicago, 1945-1995 (auth, catalog). *Pos:* Cur spec projs, Mus Contemp Art, Chicago, Ill, 90-95, cur, 95-. *Awards:* Catalog Auth Award, DOGS, Art Mus Asn, 84. *Publ:* Auth, Mies in Chicago (brochure), Mus Contemp Art, 86. *Mailing Add:* 1554 N Hoyne Ave Chicago IL 60622-8840

WARREN, PETER WHITSON See Whitson, Peter Whitson Warren

WARREN, RUSS
PAINTER
b Washington, DC, Dec 29, 1951. *Study:* Univ St Thomas, Houston, Tex, 69-71; Univ NMex, BFA, 73; Univ Tex, San Antonio, MFA, 77. *Work:* Chase Manhattan Bank, New York; Gen Elec co, Fairfield, Conn; Sydney & Francis Lewis Found, Richmond, Va; Princeton Univ, NJ; Gibbs Art Mus, Charleston, SC. *Exhib:* Biennial, Whitney Mus Am Art, New York, 81; Painting & Sculpture Today, Indianapolis Mus Art, Ind, 82; Painting in the South (with catalog), Va Mus Art, Richmond, 83; Southern Fictions, Contemp Art Mus, Houston, 83; USA Portrait of the South, Palazzo Venezia,

Rome, 84; Venice Biennale, Italy, 84; solo exhibs, Emblems of the Unseeable (with catalog), Knight Gallery, Charlotte, NC, 84 & NC Mus Art, Raleigh, 85; Looking South-A Different Dixie, Birmingham Mus Art, Birmingham, Ala, 88; 1989 Corcoran Biennial, Corcoran Mus, Washington, DC, 89. *Teaching:* Prof art, Davidson Coll, Davidson, NC, 78-. *Awards:* Southeast Cent Contemp Art Fel, 84; NC Artist Fel, 85. *Bibliog:* Richard Flood (auth), Russ Warren, Artforum, 9/81; Ronny Cohen (auth), Russ Warren, Art News, 2/83; Vivian Raynor (auth), Russ Warren, NY Times, 12/28/85; Barry Schwabsky (auth), Russ Warren's magic theater, Arts Mag, 85. *Media:* Acrylic, Oil. *Dealer:* Hodges-Taylor Gallery 227 N Tryon Charlotte NC 28202; Les Yeux du Monde Gallery 115 S First St Charlottesville VA 22902

WARREN, TOM
PHOTOGRAPHER, CONCEPTUAL ARTIST
b Cleveland, Ohio, Aug 23, 1954. *Study:* Kent State Univ, BS, 77. *Work:* Art Inst Chicago, Ill; Mus City New York; Fales Libr & Bobst Libr, NY Univ; Queens Mus Art, Flushing, New York. *Comn:* New Heritage Theater, Youth Portraits, Harlem, New York, 2005. *Exhib:* Portrait Studio, Semaphore Gallery, New York, 83; No Portraits, Greathouse Gallery, New York, 85; Portrait Studio, Spaces Gallery, Cleveland, 90; Flash, Willoughby Sharp Gallery, New York, 91; Lessons in Life, Art Inst Chicago, Ill, 94; East Village USA, New Mus Contemp Art, New York, 2004; Queens Int, Queens Mus Art, Flushing, New York, 2004 & 2006; Visual Journal #296, Project Room, Dinter Fine Art Gallery, New York, 2007; FoneCam & Test Projections, Abaton Garage, Jersey City, NJ, 2008; On a Few Years of the Eighties' Decade, Magasin Centre Nat D'art Contemp, Grenobce, France, 2008; Printed Matter, NY, 2011; Sideshow Gallery Ann, Brooklyn, NY, 2012, 2013. *Collection Arranged:* Dick & Nancy Taylor Collection, New York. *Pos:* Photogr, Sotheby's, 83-86 & freelance, 90-2003. *Teaching:* Instr photog, Case Western Reserve, Univ Cleveland, 88-90. *Bibliog:* Judd Tully (auth), No portraits review, East Village Eye, 6/85; Lynn Padwe (auth), Artistic endeavors, Photo Dist News, 9/86; Helen Cullinan (auth), Performance Artists Exposes Nuances of Photog, Cleveland Plain Dealer, 90; Walter Robinson (auth), Collaborative Projects, The Colab Conspiracy, Mag, 2011. *Mem:* Colab (Collaborative Projects), 80-. *Media:* Photography. *Res:* Music, sound, audio, film, statistics. *Specialty:* Contemp Art, music, performance. *Interests:* Art, music, literature. *Collection:* Small works by contemporary artists. *Publ:* ABC No Rio Dinero, Moore & Miller, 85; Contribr, East Village Guide, Portraits of Art Dealers, Roland Hagenberg, 86; Contribr, Just Another Asshole No 7, Thought Objects, Barbra Ess, 87; East Village USA, New Mus, Cameron, Kiwin, Moore, 2004; Espèces D'espace, the Eighties First Part, Magasin, France, 2008; The New Collectors Book, 2012. *Mailing Add:* 39-40 52nd St Apt 6D Woodside NY 11377

WARREN, WIN (WINTON) W
PAINTER, LECTURER
b Jakin, Ga, Nov 13, 1914. *Study:* Univ Ga, LLB & JD; US Dept Agr Grad Sch, 67; Cath Univ Am, 68 & 69; Univ Md Grad Sch, with Nicholas Krushenick, Jerry Clapsaddle & Helen Van Wyk, 77-82. *Work:* Univ Md; Sons of the Am Revolution Mus; Pioneers of Flight (painting), Hall of Fame Mus, 98; South Md Hosp Ctr; Airport Mus, Coll Park, Md. *Comn:* Equestrian portraits of George Washington & Lafayette, Johnston & Lemon Brokerage Firm, Washington, 76; mural, Community Ctr, Md-Nat Capital Park & Planning Comn, 79; portrait, Sons of the Am Revolution Mus, 92. *Exhib:* Solo exhibs, Montpelier Cult Arts Ctr, Laurel, 80 & Md Univ Club, 85; Artists Today Exhib, Md-Nat Capital Park & Planning Comn, 79; Art Barn Asn-Nat Park Serv Exhib, 83; Alpha Gallerie, Rockville, Md, 86. *Pos:* Lect & tours Am Art, Nat Mus Am Art, Smithsonian Inst, Washington, DC, 79-96; adv & selection bd, Montpelier Cult Arts Ctr, 79-93. *Awards:* Nat Capitol Area Artists Award, United Way, 85. *Bibliog:* article, Washington, DC Artists News, 3/84; article, Camilla Enterprise, 11/15/85 & 6/28/2000; article, College Park Gazette, Md, 3/18/99. *Mem:* Artists' Equity Asn; Coll Art Asn; Prince George's Art Asn; Washington Soc Landscape Painters. *Media:* Acrylic, Oils. *Mailing Add:* 324 E Main St Suite A Mechanicsburg PA 17055-6585

WARRINER, LAURA B
ASSEMBLAGE ARTIST, COLLAGE ARTIST
b Tulsa Okla, Jan 18, 1943. *Study:* Okla Baptist Univ; Oklahoma City Univ, 61-64 & 79-81. *Work:* Skidmore Coll Art Gallery, Saratoga Springs, NY; Henry Ward Ranger Fund Purchase through Smithsonian Inst Nat Gallery, Washington, DC; Okla Univ Found, Norman; Univ Okla Med Ctr, Okla City. *Exhib:* Solo exhibs, Firehouse Art Ctr, Norman, Okla, 86, Hulsey Gallery, Norick Art Ctr, Okla City Univ, Okla, 91; Dimensions '87: Lenexa's National 3-Dimensional Art Show, Lenexa, Kans, 87 & North Lake Col, Irving, Tex, 94; The Painted Photographs, Cent State Univ Mus Art, Edmond, Okla, 89; Flash Points, Goddard Art Ctr, Ardmore, Okla, 89; Small Works Invitational, M A Doran Gallery, Tulsa, Okla, 88 & 90; Okla Visual Arts Coalition Invitational 12 x 12 Exhib, Okla City, 91-94, 96-98; Woman's Work, Invitational Exhib, City Arts, Okla City, 94; Cafe City Art Invitational, City Arts Ctr, Okla City, 95 & 96; Continued renovation and documentation of 1920's warehouse, 97-99. *Pos:* Adv bd, Norick Art Ctr, Okla City Univ, 89-; bd trustees, 88-94. *Teaching:* Instr, Okla Mus Art, Okla City, 74-78; instr regional workshops, Norman, Okla, Stillwater, Okla, Okla City, Okla, Edmond, Okla & Red River, NMex, 75-; instr, Okla Arts Inst, Okla City, 77-81; instr artists-in-residence, Okla State Arts Coun, 81-85; instr, Goddard Art Ctr, Ardmore, Okla, 83. *Awards:* Award for Watercolor, Allied Artists Am 60th Ann Exhib, 74; Barbara Vassilieff Award for Flowers-Still Life, Allied Artists Am 61st Ann Exhib, 75; Century Award of Merit, Rocky Mountain Nat Watermedia Exhib, 75. *Bibliog:* Ralph Fabri (auth), Flower painting in all media, 2/74 & Can you succeed in art without really trying, 9/74, Today's Art; Barbara Nechis (auth), Watercolor the Creative Experience, Northlight; Flash Points (catalog), Central Univ, Edmond, Okla. *Mem:* Okla Visual Arts Coalition (vpres, 88- & bd trustee, 89-94). *Media:* Multimedia. *Mailing Add:* One NE Third St Oklahoma City OK 73104-2205

WARRIOR, DELLA C
ADMINISTRATOR
Study: Northeastern State Univ, BA (sociology); Harvard Univ, MA (educ). *Pos:* Pres, Inst Am Indian Arts, Santa Fe, develop dir; Chief Exec Officer, Otoe-Missouria Tribe, 89-92; exec bd mem, World Indigenous Nations Higher Educ Consortium; mem US Pres Bd Adv, on Tribal Col & Univ, 2002-

WARSHAW, ELAINE N
SCULPTOR, DIRECTOR
b New York, NY, Apr 11, 1924. *Study:* Pratt Inst, 41-44; Art Students League, 45; studied with Jose de Creeft, 70 and Elaine Rapp. *Comn:* Holocaust Mem, Limestone, Temple Israel, Jamaica, Queens, NY, 80, Long Beach, 82; Garden Sculpture, comn by Dr & Mrs S Pion, Md; 4 sculptures in coll, comn by Andy Allen, Nashville, Tenn, 2003. *Exhib:* Nat Asn Women Artists, Bergen Community Mus, NJ, 80, Equitable Galleries, New York, 82 & Lever House, NY, 82; Nat Acad Galleries, NY, 82; Family of Man, N Shore Sculpture Ctr, Great Neck, Long Island, NY, 85; Hecksher Mus, Long Island, 85; Big Bungalow Gallery, Nashville, Tenn, 2003; Prints-Golden Age of Haute Couture, Frist Mus Visual Arts Ctr, Nashville, Tenn, 2010. *Pos:* Dir sculptor, Merrick, NY, 72-90. *Teaching:* Instr stone carving, Sculpture Ctr, 70-72. *Mem:* Nat Asn Women Artists (lifetime hon mem). *Media:* Stone, Wood, Oil, Acrylic. *Dealer:* Ellen Warshaw 618 Fatherland St Nashville Tenn 37206. *Mailing Add:* 2164 Seneca Dr S Merrick NY 11566

WASCHEK, MATTHIAS
MUSEUM DIRECTOR
Study: Bonn Univ, PhD (art hist, archeology and mod hist). *Pos:* head acad programs, Louvre Mus, Paris, 1992-2003; exec dir Pulitzer Found, Arts in St Louis, Mo, 2003-11; dir, Worcester Art Mus, Mass, 2012-. *Teaching:* prof art hist, Parsons Paris, école du Louvre; guest lectr, Scuola Normale Superiore di Pisa, Univ de La Rochelle. *Publ:* auth, Brancusi and Serra in Dialogue (web catalog), 2004-05, Portrait/Hommage/Embodiment (web catalog), 2007, Ideal (Dis-)Placements: Old Masters at the Pulitzer (web catalog), 2009-10. *Mailing Add:* Worcester Art Museum 55 Salisbury St Worcester MA 01609

WASHBURN, JOAN T
ART DEALER
b New York, NY, Dec 26, 1929. *Study:* Middlebury Col, BA. *Pos:* Dir, Washburn Gallery, NY. *Awards:* RI Sch Design Fel. *Mem:* Art Dealers Asn Am. *Specialty:* Nineteenth and twentieth century American painting and sculpture. *Mailing Add:* 20 W 57th St New York NY 10019

WASHBURN, PHOEBE
SCULPTOR
b Poughkeepsie, NY, 1973. *Study:* Tulane Univ, BFA, 1996; Sch Visual Arts, MFA, 2002. *Exhib:* Family, Radiance Gallery, Greensboro, 1997; Breakout, Rosetree Gallery, New Orleans, 1997; Artist's Eye, Greensboro Artists' League, NC, 1998; Tree, Silverwood St, Philadelphia, 1999; Shape of Things to Come, Forma Gallery, NY, 1999; Integrated Aesthetics, SVA Satellite Gallery, Brooklyn, 2001; solo exhibs, LFL Gallery, NY, 2002, 2004, Rive Univ Gallery, Houston, Tex, 2003, Faulconer Gallery, Grinnell Univ, Iowa, 2003, Ierimonti Gallery, Milan, 2004, Kantor/Feuer Gallery, Los Angeles, 2005, UCLA Hammer Mus, 2005, Inst Contemp Art, Philadelphia, 2007, Deutsche Guggenheim, Gerlin, 2007; All You Can Eat, Visual Arts Gallery, NY, 2002, Slice and Dice, 2004, Beginning Here, 2004; Everyday Materials, Westside Gallery, NY, 2002; DNA @DNA, DNA Gallery, Mass, 2002; Ctr Curatorial Studies Mus, Bard Coll, 2003; Mixture Gallery, Houston, Tex, 2003; Rubbish, Cuchifritos, NY, 2004; Weatherspoon Art Gallery, Milan, 2004; PS1 Contemp Art Ctr, Long Island City, 2004-05; Strange Architecture, Catherine Clark Gallery, San Francisco, 2005; Greater NY, 2005; Makes for My Billionaire Status, Kantor Feuer Gallery, LA, 2005; Has No Secret Surprise, UCLA, Hammer Mus, 2005; Kemper Mus, Kansas City, 2006; Lipstick Bldg, 53rd and 3rd, NY, 2006; The Studio Visit, Exit Art, New York, 2006; Burgeoning Geometries, Whitney Mus at Altria, New York, 2006; Whitney Biennial, Whitney Mus Am Art, New York, 2008. *Awards:* Rusty Collier Meml Award in Studio Art, Tulane Univ, 1996; AAAL Award, 2005; Louis Comfort Tiffany Found Grant, 2009; NY Found Arts Alex Nason Fel, 2009. *Mailing Add:* c/o Zach Feuer Gallery 548 W 22nd St New York NY 10011

WASHBURN, STAN
PRINTMAKER, PAINTER
b New York, NY, Jan 2, 1943. *Study:* Calif Coll Arts & Crafts, Oakland, BFA, 67 & MFA, 68. *Work:* Chicago Art Inst; Brooklyn Mus, NY; Calif Palace of Legion of Honor, San Francisco; Libr Cong, Washington; Mus Fine Arts, Boston. *Exhib:* 24th Nat Exhib Prints, Libr Cong, Washington, 75; Hassam Fund Purchase Prize Exhib, Am Acad of Arts & Lett, NY, 75 & 76; Solo exhib, Achenbach Found for Graphic Arts, Calif Palace Legion Hon, 77; Boston Printmakers Ann, 77-79, 81 & 85; 7th Brit Int Print Biennale, Bradford, Eng, 82; Western States Print Invitational, Portland Art Mus, Ore, 85; and others. *Awards:* Pennell Fund Purchase, Libr 75; Purchase Award, Int Miniature Print Collection, Pratt Graphics Ctr, New York, 77. *Bibliog:* One-half hour spec, KQED-TV, San Francisco, 75; Matthew Gurewitsch (auth), Against the grain, Connoisseur Mag, 2/86. *Media:* Etching; Oil. *Publ:* Auth & illusr, True History of the Death by Violence of George's Dragon, 74; auth & illusr, The Moral Alphabet of Vice & Folly Arbor House, 86; Intent to Harm, Pocket Books, 93; Into Thin Air, Pocket Books, 96. *Dealer:* North Point Gallery 250 Sutter St San Francisco CA. *Mailing Add:* 2010 Virginia St Berkeley CA 94709

WASHINGTON, JAMES W, JR
SCULPTOR, PAINTER
b Gloster, Miss. *Study:* Nat Landscape Inst; also with Mark Tobey; Grad Theological Union Ctr Urban Black Studies, Berkeley, Calif, Hon DFA, 75. *Work:* Seattle Art Mus, Wash; San Francisco Art Mus. *Comn:* The Creation (series 7-10), Seattle First Nat Bank Main Br, 68; bust of hist men, Progress Plaza, Philadelphia, 69; the Creation

(series 5), Meany Jr High Sch, Seattle, 70; Woodchuck Sunning (sculpture), Frankfurt, WGer, 74; Children's Touchstone With Eagles (stone sculpture at Bailey Gatzert Elem), King Co Arts Comn, Seattle, Wash, 91; Bird From the Plane of Enlightenment (sculpture in stone), comn by John L & Dora E Smith, Seattle, Wash, 92; and others. *Exhib:* Solo exhibs, Foster-White Gallery, Seattle, Wash, 68, 78 & 80 & Mus Hist & Indust, Seattle, 80, Foster/White Gallery (with catalog), Seattle, Wash, 89; Expo '70, Osaka, Japan, 70; Art of the Pac Northwest, Nat Collection Fine Arts, Washington, 74; Retrospective, Frye Art Mus, Seattle, 80; Fest Sundiata, Seattle, 80; Portopia, 81, Kobe, Japan, 81; Retrospective (with catalog), Bellevue Art Mus, Wash, 89. *Pos:* Secy, Seattle Chap, Artists Equity Asn, 49-53, pres, 60-62; mem gov coun art, State of Wash, 59-60, state art comnr, 61-66. *Awards:* Gov Sculpture Award, 70; Wash State Centennial Hall Honor, Wash State Hist Soc, 84; Studio & Home of James W Washington Jr, Designated an Historic Landmark, Landmarks Preservation Bd, Seattle, Wash, 91; and others. *Bibliog:* Ann Faber (auth), James Washington's stone sculpture excellence, Seattle Post Intelligence, 56; Pauline Johnson (auth), James Washington speaks, Art Educ J, 68; Arch Am Art, Smithsonian Inst, 83. *Mem:* Int Platform Asn. *Media:* Oil, Tempera; Granite, Marble

WASHMON, GARY BRENT
PAINTER, PRINTMAKER
b Lake Charles, La, Nov 5, 1955. *Study:* Yale Summer Sch Music & Art, 75; Univ NMex, BFA, 76; Univ Ill, MFA, 78. *Work:* Yale Univ; Univ Dallas; Pa State Univ; Visual Art Ctr Alaska, Anchorage; Ark Art Ctr, Little Rock; Tex Woman's Univ. *Comn:* Art billboard, Patrick Billboard Co, Austin, Tex, 88. *Exhib:* Fort Worth Community Art Ctr, Tex, 2005; Cinema Gallery, Champaign, Ill, 2006; solo exhib, Tex A&M Univ, 94, Tarleton State Univ, 2003, Ross State Univ, 2004 & 416 West Gallery, 2005; New Orleans Triennial, 2006; Sept Juried Exhib, Alexandria, La, 2006; Art in the Metroplex, Tex Christian Univ, Ft Worth, Tex, 2007; Nat Compact Exhib, Louisiana State Univ, Baton Rouge, La, 2008; 28th Nat Print Exhib at ArtLink, ArtLink Gallery, Fort Wayne, In, 2008; Paper in, On, OfIV, Foundry Art Centre, St Charles, MO, 2008. *Pos:* Exhib comt, Denton Visual Arts Ctr, 89-; bd mem, Tex Asn Sch Art, 2002-05. *Teaching:* Asst prof painting & drawing, Univ Tex, Austin, 78-85; assoc prof, 86-94, Tex Womans' Univ, interim chmn, 97-2000, prof, 2001-. *Awards:* Res Enhancement Grant, Tex Womans' Univ, 92, Fac Develop Grant, 94; Fac Develop Leave, 2001. *Bibliog:* Edward Lucie-Smith (auth), American Art NOW, William Morrow & Co, 85; Edward Lucie-Smith (auth), Art of the Eighties, Phaidon Universe, New York, 90. *Media:* Acrylic, Oil, Etching. *Mailing Add:* 2297 Wood Hollow Rd Denton TX 76208

WASKO-FLOOD, SANDRA JEAN
PRINTMAKER, INSTALLATION SCULPTOR
b Flushing, NY, Mar 12, 1943. *Study:* Univ Calif, Los Angeles, Life Drawing with Gordon Nunes, Painting with Ray Brown & Charles Garabedian, BA, 65-69; UCLA, studied with Isabel Pons, Parque Lage, Rio de Janeiro, 72; Univ Wis, grad etching with Warrington Colescott, 77-78. *Work:* Mus de Arte Mod, Buenos Aires, Argentina; Nat Mus Women Arts & Libr Cong, Washington, DC; St Mary's Col, Md; Pushkin Mus, Moscow; Cult Found Russ; Corcoran Gallery Art, Washington, DC; and others. *Comn:* Labyrinth Meditation Wheel, Kinetic Sculpture, Potomac Hosp, Woodbridge, 2000. *Exhib:* Solo exhibs, St Peter's Church, NY, 89, Wash Printmakers Gallery, 86, 88 & 91, Mont Gallery, Alexandria, Va, 91, Montpelier Cult Arts Ctr, Laurel, Md, 92, Gallery 10 Ltd, Wash, 94 & 96, Sch 33 Installation Space, Baltimore, 96, Sch 22 Art Ctr, Baltimore, 97, Sub-basemment Studios, Baltimore, 2008-09, Harwood Mus Art, Taos, NMex, 2010, Millicent Rogers Mus, Taos, NMex, 2010, Optimysm Bookstore, Taos, NMex, 2011; group exhib, Boston Printmakers: 39th N Am Print Exhib, Danforth Mus, Framingham, Mass, 86, Printed Image 72nd Ann, Hudson River Mus, Yonkers, NY, 87, Seventh Ann Faber Birren Color Show Nat Juried Open Competition, Stamford, Conn, 87, Alternatives 88, Nat Juried Photog Competition, Univ Ohio, Athens, 88, Int Prints, 88, Silvermine Gallery, Stamford, Conn, 88, Stockton IV Prints & Drawings, Haggin Mus, Stockton, Calif, 88, Va Comn Arts Fel Winners, Peninsula Fine Arts Ctr, Newport News, Va, 95, Commonwealth Collects, Va Beach Ctr Contemp Arts, Va, 97, Cocoran Gallery Art, DC, 99, Artists Equity Coast to Coast, Harmony Hall Regional Art Ctr, Ft Washington, Md, 2001, Maryland Printmakers, Creative Partners Gallery, Bethesda, Md, 2002, Int Photography Competition, Fraser Gallery, Bethesda, Md, 2003, Foundry Gallery, DC, 2007, Light, Art Spirit Group, Metropolitan Memorial United Methodist Church, Wash DC, 2013, Pushkin Mus, Moscow, USSR, Museo de Arte Moderno, Buenos Aires, Argentina, Nat Mus Women in the Arts, Wash DC, Libr Congress, Wash DC. *Pos:* Pres, Wash Area Printmakers, 85-86; workshop coordr, Arlington Co Dept of Parks, Recreation & Community Resources, Lee Arts Ctr, 89-94; prog chmn, Women's Caucus for Art, Wash, 98-99; dir, Labyrinths for Peace, Exhib at Cannon Rotunda of House of Reps, 2000; cur, Common Ground: Labyrinth Designs, Past and Present, Charles Sumner Sch Mus, Washington, 2000; cur, Hist Part, Wash Women Artists Marching into the Millennium, Wash, 2001; founder/pres, Living Labyrinths for Peace Inc, 2005; dir, World Labyrinth Day event, Vietnam Memorial, Wash DC, Memorial Day Event at Vietnam Memorial, Angel Fire, NMex, 2013. *Teaching:* Instr printmaking, Wash Women's Arts Ctr, 83 & Arlington Co Art Prog, 89; artist-in-residence lithography, Univ Md, spring 84; prof printmaking, St Mary's Col, spring 85; printmaking instr, Alexandria Studio, 87-2005; Labyrinths for Creativity & Peace, workshops Elementary sch, Washington Performing Arts Soc, DC, 2002-09, 2011-2012, Kanchos Elementary, Taos, Public Schools, 2013. *Awards:* WPAS (Wash Performing Arts Soc), Artist Grant, Friends Torpedo Factory Art Gallery, Alexandria, Va, 1989, Friends, The Torpedo Factory Art Gallery, Alexandria, Va; Va Comn Arts Fel Grant, 95; Best Show Cash Prize, Artists Equity, Wash, DC, 97; Hon Mention, Artists Equity: Coast to Coast, Harmony Hall Regional Art Ctr, Ft Wash, Md, 2001; 1st Prize Printmaking, Taos Open Exhib, 2010; Honoring the Divine Feminine from Heal Humanity, Wash DC, 2012. *Bibliog:* Paul Franklin Pilato (auth), Printmakers: Cycles, Arlington Cable TV, 87; Lily Pond (auth), Yellow Silk Mag featured artist, Verygraphics, fall 87; Dance of the Labyrinth: An Installation by Sandra Wasko-Flood (video), Kelley Ellsworth Productions, 94; Al Kamen (auth), In the Loop: East Lawn, Right Brain, May Turns, Washington Post, 3/8; Julia Duin (auth), Spiritually Focused Labyrinth Coming to US Capitol Lawn, Washington Times, 3/3; Dash Robinson (auth), Labyrinth Camp, City Paper; Jessica Dawson (auth), Mus of the Muses, Washington Post, 2001; Mina Cheon (auth), NY Arts Mag, 2002; Mary Soloman (auth), Find Yourself in a Labyrinth: Give Inner Peace a Chance, The Washington Post Weekend, 2003; Ron Kipling Williams, Baltimore's Indypendent Reader, Living Labyrinths for Peace at Sub-basement Studios, Baltimore, 2008; Andy Stiny (auth), Meandering Path to Peace, Santa Fe Jour, 2010; Ariana Kramer (auth), One Step at a Time, Taos News, 2011; Joanne Lee (auth), Labyrinths Come Alive for Angel Fire Enthusiast, Sangue de Christo Chronicle, 2011; Ariana Kramer (auth), Centering in the Maze, Taos News, 2011. *Mem:* Wash Printmakers Gallery (1986-1991); Gallery 10, Wash, DC, 1992-1998; Southern Graphics Coun, Pensacola, Fla; Internat Labyrinth Soc (founding mem); Ylem, Artists Using Sci & Tech; ASCI (Art & Science Collaborations Inc, NYC; Washington Sculptors Group. *Media:* Installation Sculpture, Prints, Photo Etchings, Monotypes. *Res:* Nasca Tongue Iconography, El Dorado, Vol I, 77. *Interests:* Creative writing, classical music, hiking. *Publ:* Auth, The Role of Art in Feminist Spirituality, Women Artists News, spring 86; Unloose the Snake: One Artist's Labyrinth, Caerdroia, 94; Cultivating Curious and Creative Minds, Teachers Edn Yearbook XIX, Univ Houston. *Mailing Add:* 2229 Lake Ave Baltimore MD 21213

WASOW, OLIVER
PHOTOGRAPHER
b Madison, Wis, 1960. *Study:* Hunter Coll, New York, BA (Media Studies), 1983; Transart Inst, Krems, Austria, MFA, 2006. *Work:* Bayley Art Mus, Va; Chase Manhattan Bank, New York; Destre Found, Athens, Greece; Everson Mus, Syracuse, NY; Milwaukee Art Mus; Mus Mod Art, New York; Smith Coll Mus Art; Whitney Mus Am Art, New York. *Comn:* Somewhere Else, pub art prospect, City of Los Angeles and The Fremont St Experience. *Exhib:* Solo exhibs include Josh Baer Gallery, New York, 1986, White Columns, New York, 1987, Josh Baer Gallery, New York, 1988, 1990, 1991, 1993, Tom Solomon's Garage, Los Angeles, 1990, Glenn Dash Gallery, Los Angeles, 1991, Janet Borden Gallery, New York, 1993, 1995, 1997, 2000, Smallworks Gallery, Las Vegas, 1998, Sara Meltzer Gallery, New York, 2002, White Columns, NY, 2008; Group exhibs include Altered & Irrational, Whitney Mus Am Art, New York, 1996; What I Did On My Summer Vacation, White Columns, New York, 1996; Transmute, Mus Contemp Art, Chicago, 1999; Millenial Fever, Hudson Guild, New York, 1999; Winter Group Show, Jan Kesner Gallery, Los Angeles, 2000; Dreaming in Print, Fashion Inst Technol, New York, 2001; Drawings & Photographs, Mathew Marks Gallery, New York, 2001; Fast Forward, White Columns, New York, 2003; Drop Out, Julie Saul Gallery, New York, 2004. *Teaching:* Tchr, Bard Col, Sch Visual Arts, Art Inst Boston. *Awards:* NY State Coun Arts Grant, 1988; Louis Comfort Tiffany Found Award, 1995; NY Found Arts, 2000. *Interests:* New media and digital technol. *Mailing Add:* 15 Three Oaks Rd Rhinebeck NY 12572

WASSERMAN, ALBERT
PAINTER, INSTRUCTOR
b New York, NY, 1920. *Study:* Art Students League, with Charles Chapman, 37-39; Nat Acad Design, Pulitzer Prize scholar, 38-40; with Sidney Dickinson; Biarritz Am Univ, France, 45. *Work:* portrait, William R. Leigh, Traphagen Collection, Ariz; Aimee Ornstein Mem Libr, Adelphi Univ, NY, 83; Anne SK Brown Military Collection, Brown Univ, RI; Private collections Gibbs Smith, Utah, Frank J Oelshlager, Fla. *Comn:* Many private portrait commissions. *Exhib:* Nat Acad Design, NY, 40-42; Allied Artists Am, NY, 41-2007; NJ Painters & Sculptors Soc, 41-; Am Watercolor Soc, NY, 53-69 & 86; Audubon Artists, NY, 1960, 1990, 2000, 2002-2007; Am Masters Invitational, Salmagundi Club, 2007; Allied Artists of Am Invitational at Bennington Ctr Arts, Vt, 2007. *Pos:* Instr, painting & drawing (portrait painter). *Teaching:* Instr & lectr, Jackson Heights Art Asn, 55- & Nat Art League, 67-69; instr painting, Educational Alliance, 2003-. *Awards:* Obrig Prize, 41, Nat Acad Design; Grumbacher Award, Allied Artists, 85, Gilmore-Romans Award, 95; S.T. Shaw Mem Award, Salmagundi Club, 2005; Jack Richeson award, Salmagundi Club, 2010. *Bibliog:* Ethel Traphagen (auth), article, Fashion Digest, 54. *Mem:* Salmagundi Club; Allied Artists Am; Audubon Artists; assoc Am Watercolor Soc; Nat Art League; Jackson Heights Art Club. *Media:* Oil, Watercolor; Gouache. *Interests:* Painting, Music (classical & pop), cooking, animations & architecture. *Mailing Add:* 34-24 82nd St 4E Jackson Heights NY 11372

WASSERMAN, BURTON
PAINTER, EDUCATOR
b Brooklyn, NY, Mar 10, 1929. *Study:* Brooklyn Col, with Burgoyne Diller & Ad Reinhardt, BA; Columbia Univ, MA & EdD. *Work:* Philadelphia Mus Art, Pa; Del Mus Art, Wilmington; Montreal Mus Fine Arts; NJ State Mus, Trenton; Woodmere Art Mus, Philadelphia, Pa; and others. *Comn:* Relief triptych, comn by Mr & Mrs Herbert Kurtz, Melrose Park, Pa, 71; var indust & residential relief construction projs, Philadelphia area, 74-79. *Exhib:* 21st Am Drawing Biennial, Norfolk Mus Arts & Sci, 65; Art Alliance, Philadelphia, 66-80; USA Pavilion, Int Expos, Osaka, Japan, 70; Color Prints of the Americas, NJ State Mus, 70; Int Graphics Exhib, Montreal Mus Art, 71; Silkscreen: History of a Medium, Philadelphia Mus Art, 71-72; Benjamin Mangel Gallery, Philadelphia, Pa, 72-82; and others. *Teaching:* Prof emer art, Rowan Univ, Glassboro, NJ, 2004. *Awards:* Brickhouse Drawing Prize, 21st Am Drawing Biennial, Norfolk Mus Arts & Sci, 65; Ryan Purchase Prize, Art from NJ Ann Exhib, NJ State Mus, 67; Esther-Philip Klein Award, Am Color Print Soc Ann, 70; and others. *Mem:* Artists Equity Asn (nat pres, 71-73); Am Color Print Soc (mem exec coun, 65-81). *Media:* Oil. *Interests:* Travel. *Publ:* Auth articles in Leonardo, Am Artist, Art Educ, Sch Arts, & many more, 59-72; auth, Modern Painting: The Movements, the Artists, Their Work, 70 & co-auth, Basic Silkscreen Printmaking, 71, Davis, Mass; Bridges of Vision: The Art of Prints & the Craft of Printmaking; Exploring the Visual Arts, Davis, Mass, 76. *Dealer:* Francis Frost 36 Third St Newport RI 02840. *Mailing Add:* 204 Dubois Rd Glassboro NJ 08028

WASSERMAN, MURIEL
PAINTER
b New York, NY, May 27, 1935. *Study:* Queens Col, BFA & BA Art Hist, 78; Adelphi Univ, grad studies; Pratt Inst, MFA, 84; Studied at Brooklyn Mus, Five Town Music & Arts Found, New York, Newark Sch Art, NJ, Brookyln Coll; Studied with Phillip Guston, Rudolf Nakien, Richard Bove, Arhtur Coppedge & Jack Rabinowitz. *Comn:* many pvt commissions. *Exhib:* Brooklyn Mus Exhib, 78; Old Westbury Gardens, Long Island, 88-90; Bergen Co Mus, New York, 89; Sands Point Mus, New York, 90-91; East End Arts Coun, New York; and others. *Pos:* Craftsperson (potter), craft shows & exhibs, 70-91; docent & cataloger, Nassau Co Mus System, 75-77; monthly columnist, Sunstorm Long Island Arts Newspaper, 82-84. *Teaching:* Instr painting & drawing, Long Island Adult Prog, NY, 77-98, & St Johns Univ, Queens, NY, 79-98. *Awards:* Am Artists Mag, 77; Fed Plaza Exhibs, Nat Asn Women Artists, 80; Long Beach Art League (var awards). *Mem:* Nat Asn Women Artists; Long Beach Art League, NY; Palm Beach Watercolor Asn, Fla; Nat League Am Pen Women Inc; Tri-County Artists, NY. *Media:* Acrylic, Oil, Watercolors. *Interests:* Gardening, writing. *Publ:* Columnist, Sunstorm, Long Island Arts Newspaper. *Mailing Add:* 70 Brentwood Ln Valley Stream NY 11580

WASTROM, ERIKA
PAINTER
b South Orleans, Mass. *Study:* Alfred Univ, Sch Art & Design, NY, BFA, 2006. *Exhib:* Solo exhibs include Cell Space, Alfred, NY, 2003, Upcoming Kathleen Cullen Gallery, New York, 2006; Group exhibs include Best of SUNY Student Art Exhib, State Univ Plaza Gallery, Albany, NY, 2005 ; What Drives Me, Women's Leadership Ctr, Alfred, NY, 2005; Ordered Entropy, Turner Student Gallery, Alfred Sch Art & Design, Alfred, NY, 2006, Flavor, 2006; Landscaping, Lohin Geduld Gallery, New York, 2006; 183rd Ann: Invitational Exhib Contemp Am Art, Nat Acad Mus, New York, 2008. *Awards:* Stanley Z Koplik Certificate Mastery Award, Commonwealth of Mass Dept Educ, 2001; Ceramics Grant, Alfred Univ, Alfred, NY, 2002-06; Paint Scholar, GBH Paint, Buffalo, NY, 2006; Best in Show, Senior Show Award, Alfred Sch Art & Design, 2006; John Koch Award, Nat Acad, 2008

WATERHOUSE, RUSSELL RUTLEDGE
PAINTER, ILLUSTRATOR
b El Paso, Tex, Aug 11, 1928. *Study:* Tex A&M Univ, BS, 50; Art Ctr Coll Design, Pasadena, Calif, 54-56. *Work:* Tex Tech Univ Mus Art, Lubbock; El Paso Mus Art; Tex A&M Univ, College Station; Univ Tex, El Paso. *Exhib:* Solo exhibs, Wichita Falls Tex Cult Ctr & Mus Art, 72, Tex A&M Univ, 77, Dallas Safari Club, 83, Americana Mus, El Paso, 84 & 86 & Int Mus Art, El Paso, 2000, Univ Tex at El Paso, 12/2011; Game Conservation Int, San Antonio, 83, 85, 87, 89; El Paso Mus Int Art, 01; Univ Tex, El Paso Lib, 2011. *Pos:* Mem, Tex Comn Arts & Humanities, 70-75. *Awards:* El Paso's Mayor's Award, 89; Invitational Art Exhib, El Paso Mus Art, 89; Inductee El Paso Artists Hall of Fame, 2000. *Media:* Watercolor, Acrylic, Oil. *Publ:* Illusr, Goodbye to a River, Knopf, 60; The Legal Heritage of El Paso, 63 & Pass of the North, 68, Tex Western Press. *Dealer:* Mrs Adair W Margo PO Box 103 El Paso TX 79941. *Mailing Add:* PO Box 6 Lincoln NM 88338-9999

WATERS, JACK
FILMMAKER, CONCEPTUAL ARTIST
b Philadelphia, Pa, Oct 14, 1954. *Study:* Julliard Col, BFA, 79. *Work:* Libr Cong, Washington; New York Libr Performing Arts, Lincoln Ctr; Paterson Mus, NJ. *Exhib:* ABC No Rio, NY, 83-; Limbo Gallery; NYCDCA Gallery, 85; Whitney Mus, 94. *Collection Arranged:* ABC No Rio Archival (contribr, catalog), NYCDCA City Gallery, 85. *Pos:* Founder & pres, Allied Productions, Inc, NY, 82-; co-dir, ABC No Rio, New York, 83-; consult & mem, Collaborative Projs, Inc, 84-87; dir, Naked Eye Cinema, 87-. *Teaching:* Instr dance, Univ City Arts League, Philadelphia, Pa, 78 & Univ Settlement, New York, 84-. *Awards:* Louis Horst Award for Choreography, Julliard, 79. *Bibliog:* Robert Gautier (auth), New form on the Lower East Side, NY Times, 3/84; ABC No Rio Dinero: The story of a Lower East Side art gallery, 84. *Mem:* Film/Video Arts; Millennium Film Group. *Publ:* Auth, On notational methods, Ear Mag, 12/83; film critique, Jumpcut Mag, spring 91; Social comment, Color Life Mag, summer 91; film critique, Fuse Mag, fall 91. *Mailing Add:* PO Box 20260 New York NY 10009

WATERSTREET, KEN (JAMES KENT)
PAINTER, INSTRUCTOR
b Ogden, Utah, July 18, 1940. *Study:* Calif State Univ, Sacramento, BA, 63, MA, 69. *Work:* E B Crocker Art Mus, Sacramento; Southern Ill Univ; Stuart M Speiser Collection; San Francisco Mus Mod Art; Oakland Mus, Calif; Butler Inst Am Art; South Tex Mus Art; Yale Univ. *Exhib:* Human Concern-Personal Torment, Whitney Mus of Am Art, NY, 69; Solo exhibs, Louis K Meisel Gallery, NY, 74 & 77 & Zara Gallery, San Francisco, 79; Hue & Far Cry of Color, Ft Wayne Mus, Ind, 76; E B Crocker Art Mus, Sacramento, 80; Joseph Chowning Gallery, San Francisco, 81, 83, 86, 88, 91-92 & 96; Calif A-Z and Return, Butler Inst Am Art, Youngstown, Ohio, 90; Solomon Dubnick Gallery, Sacramento, Calif, 96, 98, 2000, 2003, 2006, 2009; Sierra Coll, Rocklin, Calif, 2009; Alex Bult Gallery, Sacramento, Calif, 2013. *Pos:* Comnr, Sacramento Metrop Arts Comn, 77 & 78; bd mem, Ctr Contemp Art, Sacramento, Calif, 94-2000. *Teaching:* Chmn, Dept Visual & Performing Art, Mira Loma, High Sch, Sacramento, Calif 65-96; instr summer session, Calif State Univ, Sacramento, 90, 91 & 96-98. *Awards:* Fulbright-Hayes Study Tour, China, 88; Tap Award, Marie Walsh Sharpe Art Found, 95; Calif Art Educator of the Year, 95-96. *Mem:* Nat Art Educ Asn; Calif Art Educ Asn. *Media:* Oil on Canvas. *Specialty:* contemporary. *Dealer:* Alex Bult Gallery Sacramento CA. *Mailing Add:* 3218 Tobari Ct Sacramento CA 95821

WATIA, TARMO
PAINTER, PRINTMAKER
b Detroit, Mich, May 11, 1938. *Study:* Univ Mich, BS (design), 60, MFA, 62. *Work:* Boise Cascade & Boise Art Mus, Idaho; Harrett Mus, Twin Falls, Idaho; Dennos Mus, Traverse City, Mich. *Exhib:* Boise State Coll, Idaho; Rogue Valley Art Asn, Medford, Ore; Southern Ore Coll, Ashland; Mont State Univ, Bozeman; Minot State Coll, NDak; Rackham Galleries, Ann Arbor; Mich State Univ, East Lansing; Detroit Inst Art; AAA Gallery, Detroit; Raven Gallery, Detroit. *Teaching:* Instr art, Southern Ore Coll, Ashland, 66-69; assoc prof, Boise State Univ, Idaho, 69-86. *Awards:* Purchase Award, Boise Art Gallery, Idaho, 74; Cash Award/Painting, Ninth Ann Arts & Crafts Festival, Coeur D'Alene, Idaho. *Media:* Oil; Woodcuts. *Collection:* Finnish American Heritage. *Mailing Add:* 1015 N Tenth St Boise ID 83702

WATKINS, EILEEN FRANCES
CRITIC
b Long Island, NY, Nov 22, 1950. *Study:* Marywood Col, BA. *Pos:* Art ed, Newark Star-Ledger, currently. *Awards:* Citation, NJ Soc of Architects. *Publ:* Auth, articles, Air brush Action, Am Artist & Equine Images. *Mailing Add:* Newark Star-Ledger One Star-Ledger Plaza Newark NJ 07101

WATKINS, LEWIS
SCULPTOR, PAINTER
b Beckley, WVa, July 24, 1945. *Study:* WVa State Col, BS (art educ), 78; Univ Southern Fla, MA, 82; St Leo Col, Fla, hon degree, 83. *Work:* Fla State Mus, Gainesville; WVa Fine Arts & Cult Ctr, Charleston; Vatican Mus, Rome, Italy; Leslie Stephens Fine Arts Ctr, Birmingham, Ala; Hyatt Regency Hotel, Atlanta, Ga. *Comn:* Limestone sculpture, Hernando Co, Brooksville, Fla, 81; Solidarity (steel sculpture), Brandon, Fla, 82; Crosses of Life (steel sculpture), City Atlanta, Ga, 83; Youth of Today (stone sculpture), Hernando Co, Fla, 83; St Leo (steel sculpture), St Leo Col, Fla, 83; Winning (steel sculpture), US Football League, 84; The National Memorial for the American Farmer (steel & bronze), 86. *Exhib:* Tools of Life, John W Davis Fine Art Gallery, Institute, WVa, 81; Leslie Stephens Fine Art Ctr, Samford Univ, Birmingham, Ala, 82; and others. *Teaching:* Vis artist series, Samford Univ, Birmingham, Ala, 82; vis artist, St Leo Col, Fla, 82, Univ Tampa, Fla, 83 & Univ SFla, Tampa, 83. *Awards:* Distinguished Serv Art Award, Atlanta, Ga, 83; Cert Recognition Art, State Ga, 83; Pub Serv Cult Award, Hernando Co, Fla, 83. *Bibliog:* Terry Misfeldt (auth), article, Future Mag, 6/83; Tom Kuennen (auth), article, Rock Products Mag, 6/83; John Levine (auth), article, Pit & Quarry Mag, 9/83; articles in: Agri- View, Country Today, Hog Farm Mgt, Western Art Digest, Art Papers, Kansas Square, Today's Farmer & Kansas City Corp Report, 86; and many others. *Media:* Watercolor, Acrylic; Marble, Steel. *Publ:* Coauth, Creating a year book, Instructor Mag, 80. *Mailing Add:* 22319 Powell Rd Brooksville FL 34602-5705

WATKINS, RAGLAND TOLK
CURATOR, DEALER
b San Francisco, Calif, Oct 31, 1948. *Study:* Lake Forest Col, BA, 72; NY Univ, MA, 82. *Collection Arranged:* Bochner, Le Va, Rockburne, Tuttle (ed & contribr, catalog) Contemp Arts Ctr, Cincinnati, 75. *Pos:* Cur, Contemp Arts Ctr, Cincinnati, 73-75; field rep, New York State Coun Arts, 76-77; assoc dir exhibs, Artists Space, New York, 77-81; dir, Concord Contemp Art, New York, 81-85; dir, Jason McCoy Inc, New York, 85-88, Blum Helman Gallery, New York, 90-91, Stux Gallery, New York, 91-92 & James Graham & Sons, New York, 92-93. *Mailing Add:* 169 Sullivan St New York NY 10012

WATKINSON, PATRICIA GRIEVE
MUSEUM DIRECTOR, CURATOR
b Surrey, Eng, Mar 28, 1946. *Study:* Bristol Univ, Eng, BA (hons), 68. *Collection Arranged:* A Partial View: Photographers in the Northwest (auth, catalog), 78; Contemporary Metals: Focus on Idea (auth, catalog), 81; British Prints: Highlights of Four Decades (auth, catalog), 81; Living with the Volcano: The Artists of Mount St Helens (auth, catalog), 85; Gaylen Hansen: The Paintings of a Decade (auth, catalog), 85; Patrick Siler: Recent Works (auth, catalog), 88; Facts of the Imagination, 89. *Pos:* Adminr, Mayfair Fine Arts, London, 69-71 & Bernard Jacobson Print Publ, 71-73; freelance cur & writer, Irish Arts Coun, Kilkenny Design Ctr & Trinity Col, Dublin, 75-76; cur, Mus Art, Wash State Univ, 76-83, dir, 84-. *Teaching:* Asst prof art hist, Wash State Univ, 78-79. *Bibliog:* Ron Glowen (auth), A partial view, 78 & Gaylen Hansen, 86, Artweek. *Mem:* Art Mus Asn Am (Wash State rep, 86-88); Wash Mus Asn (mem bd, 85-87); Int Coun Mus, CIMAM; Asn Coll & Univ Mus & Galleries (western rep, 86-89); Am Asn Mus. *Res:* 20th Century prints; contemporary art, Northwest & Am. *Publ:* Auth, Mount St Helens: An Artistic Aftermath, Art J, fall 84; A Decade Apart: A Curatorial View, Glass Art Soc J, 84-85; Drawing on the American Dream-Patrick Siler, Am Ceramics, summer 88 & Patti Warashina, spring 92. *Mailing Add:* Ft Wayne Mus Art 311 E Main St Fort Wayne IN 46802

WATSON, ALDREN A
DESIGNER, ILLUSTRATOR
b Brooklyn, NY, May 10, 1917. *Study:* Yale Univ, 35; Art Students League, with George Bridgman, Charles Chapman, Robert Brackman, William Auerbach-Levy & others. *Work:* Illus bks in libr, US, Can, Europe & pvt collections. *Comn:* Mural, SS Pres Hayes, Thomas Crowell Co Off, 64. *Exhib:* Fifty Bks Shows, Soc Illusr Ann; New Eng Textbk Shows. *Pos:* Textbk designer, D C Heath & Co, Boston, 65-66; chief ed curric oriented mat, Silver Burdett Co, Morristown NJ, 66-68; official NASA artist, Apollo 8, 68; consult art dir, Houghton Mifflin, Boston, 68-72. *Teaching:* Pvt instr, hand bookbinding. *Awards:* Prize, Domesday Bk Illus Competition, 45. *Bibliog:* Chap in Forty Illustrators & How They Work. *Mem:* Author's Guild. *Publ:* Auth & illusr, My Garden Grows, 62 & Maple Tree Begins, 70, Viking; auth & illusr, Hand Bookbinding, 63, 68 & 75; auth & illusr, Hand Tools: Their Ways and Workings, Norton, 82; coauth, Furniture Making Plain & Simple, Norton, 84; and others

WATSON, BETTY
PAINTER, INSTRUCTOR
b Passaic, NJ, Feb 19, 1928. *Study:* Pa Acad Fine Arts (Summer Sch), 1947; Art Students League, NYC, 1948, 1949, 1951; Wellesley Col, BA (art hist, Phi Beta Kappa), 1949; Univ NC, MFA, 1965; Studied art with: Margaret Fitzhugh Browne, Gloucester, Mass, 1944; Louis Bouche, Edwin Dickinson, Art Students League 1949,

1951; Francis Speight, Pa Acad Fine Arts, 1947. *Work:* Jackson Library, Univ NC, Greensboro, NC; Weatherspoon Mus, Greensboro, NC; Duke Univ Hosp, Durham, NC; Smithsonian Inst, Nat Portrait Gallery, Wash, DC; Cone Health Care Ctr, Greensboro, NC; Weaver Coll, Greensboro, NC. *Comn:* Portrait (comn by Randall & Mary Jarrell, 1959, 1960; Family Portrait, comn by Peter & Eleanor Ross Taylor, 1965; portrait, comn by Allen Tate. *Exhib:* Ann Exhib, Nat Acad Design, New York, NY, 1952; Ann Exhib, Montclair Art Mus, Montclair, NJ, 1954; Ann Exhib, SECCA, Winston-Salem, NC, 1960; NC Artists Exhib, NC Mus Art, Raleigh, NC, 1963; Award Winners Group Show, NC Mus Art, Raleigh, NC, 1964; Ann Exhib, Provincetown Art Asn, Provincetown, Mass, 1964; Young Artists Invitational, Grand Rapids Art Mus, Grand Rapids, Mich, 1965; Art on Paper Ann Exhib, Weatherspoon Art Mus, Greensboro, NC, 1970, 1980; Winter Shows, Green Hill Ctr, NC Art, Greensboro, NC, 1980-2004; Retrospective: Five Decades, Green Hill Center, 2006; Solo exhib, Francis Marion Univ, Darlington, SC, 95, Jackson Lib, Greensboro, NC, 1999; Artery Gallery, Greensboro, NC, 2014; Poetic Likeness, Smithsonian Nat Portrait Gallery, Wash DC, 2012, 2013. *Pos:* TV Artist (William Porth murder trial), ABC Television, High Point, NC, 1966. *Teaching:* Art Asst (art practice as adj Art Hist), Barnard Coll, New York, NY, 1949-1951; Instr (drawing), Calif State Univ at Northridge, 1968-1969. *Awards:* Award of Merit, Five State Festival Art in Philadelphia, Pa, 1945; Wash Sq Ann Outdoor Exhib (prize winner), 1953; Chancellor's Award for Best Graduate Work, Univ NC, Greensboro, 1965. *Bibliog:* Mary Jarrell (auth), The Artist in Her Studio, Greensboro Sun, 1977; Radio Interview, Nat Pub Radio, Winston-Salem, NC, 2006; Portrait of the Artist, UNCG Mag, Univ NC, 2007; Betty Watson Painting, Odalisque Press, 1999. *Mem:* Weatherspoon Mus Asn; Greenhill Ctr NC Art; Nat Mus Women Arts; Smithsonian Inst. *Media:* Oil, Watercolor. *Publ:* Cover, Southern Rev quarterly, 8 reproductions, 2009; cover, Night Blooming Cactus, Atheneum, 80; cover, The Conscious Reader, Macmillan, 92. *Mailing Add:* 4321 Galax Trail Greensboro NC 27410

WATSON, CLARISSA H
DEALER, WRITER
b Ashland, Wis. *Study:* Layton Art Sch, Milwaukee; Univ Wis-Milwaukee; Milwaukee-Downer Col, BA with spec hon; Country Art Sch, with Harry Sternberg. *Collection Arranged:* Long Island Artists Washington, DC, 67; The Collectors' Collections, Adelphi Univ, Garden City, Long Island, 68; Gabriel Spat (1890-1967) Retrospective, Fine Arts Asn Willoughby, Cleveland, Ohio, 70; Nobility of the Horse in Art--to Save America's Wild Horses, Washington, DC, 71; Salon de Normandie (50 Norman painters honoring 50th Anniversary D-Day), Locust Valley, NY, 94; and others. *Pos:* Dir-founder, Country Art Sch, Westbury, Long Island, 53-68; dir & co-founder, Country Art Gallery, Locust Valley, Long Island, 53-90; art consult, Adelphi Univ, 67-69; dir film festivals, 7 Village Arts Coun, Locust Valley, 69-71; dir-producer, Medieval Christmas Festival, Locust Valley, 70-73; trustee, Nassau Mus Fine Arts, 77-83, Roslyn & Hechsher Mus, Huntington, NY, 84-87. *Specialty:* Nineteenth and twentieth century American realism and American and European naifs. *Publ:* Auth, The art virus, This Wk Mag, 64; ed, The Artists' Cookbook, Stevenson, 71; auth, Fourth Stage of Gainsborough Brown, McKay, 77; The Bishop in the Back Seat, 80 & Runaway, 84, Atheneum; Last Plane from Nice, Atheneum, 87; Somebody Killed the Messenger, Atheneum, 88; and others

WATSON, HOWARD N(OEL)
PAINTER, PRINTMAKER
b Pottsville, Pa, May 19, 1929. *Study:* Pa State Univ, 47-49; Tyler Sch Fine Arts, 53-55; Mus Coll Art, dipl, 60. *Work:* White House, Art in Embassies, Washington, DC; Temple Univ; private collections of Richard Manogian & Walter Mondale; Pres Jimmy Carter. *Comn:* Logan Square (mural), Archdiocese Philadelphia, 75; Betsy Ross Making Flag, Upholsterer Int Union NAm, Philadelphia, 76; 50 watercolor painting Independence Blue Cross, Philadelphia, Pa; 10 large paintings pvt collection, ARCO Chemical. *Exhib:* Pa Acad Fine Arts, 62-68; Denver's Artists of Am, 81-82; Audubon Artist Show, NY; Am Watercolor Soc Exhibs, NY; Allied Artists Am Exhibs, NY; Knickerbocker Artists Exhibs, NY; Nat Acad, NY; Philadelphia Watercolor Club Shows. *Teaching:* Instr watercolor, Hussian Sch Fine Arts, 61-63, Philadelphia Col Art, 63-70 & Abington Art Ctr, 71-; int watercolor workshops, including Austria, Switz, & Can. *Awards:* Super Achiever Award Art, Juvenile Diabetes Found, 78; Distinguished Pennsylvanians Award Art, State Pa, 80; Thornton Oakley Mem Award, Philadelphia Watercolor Club, 92. *Bibliog:* Article, Forbes Mag, 80; TLC Mag, 87. *Mem:* Philadelphia Watercolor Club (pres, 82-93); Am Watercolor Soc; Allied Artists Am; Knickerbocker Artists. *Media:* Watercolor. *Publ:* Philadelphia Watercolors, Barre Publ, 70; Old Philadelphia Impressions, Heritage Publ, 76; Proud Past, 77. *Dealer:* Newman Art Gallery 1625 Walnut St Philadelphia PA. *Mailing Add:* 348 Sinkler Rd Wyncote PA 19095

WATSON, KATHARINE JOHNSON
HISTORIAN, CONSULTANT
b Providence, RI, Nov 11, 1942. *Study:* Duke Univ, BA, 64; Univ Pa, MA (art hist), 67, PhD (art hist), 73. *Pos:* Instr & cur exhibs, Univ Pittsburgh, Pa, 69-70; cur art before 1800, Allen Mem Art Mus; co-ed, Allen Mem Art Mus Bull, 74-77; dir, Peary-MacMillan Arctic Mus, Bowdoin Coll, Brunswick, Maine, 77-85 & Bowdoin Coll Mus Art, 77-98; trustee, Mus Art Ogunquit, 77-90, Williamstown Regional Art Conserv Laboratory Inc, 78-90 & Surf Point Found, Victoria Mansion, Me Coll Art. *Teaching:* Instr Ital sculpture & Europ Baroque art, Univ Pittsburgh, 69-70; lectr mus sem, Oberlin Coll, Ohio, 73-79; instr mus sem, Bowd. *Awards:* Kress Found fel, Univ Pa, 67-68; Fel, Harvard Univ Ctr Ital Renaissance Studies, 77-78; Nat Endowment Arts Grant, 81; and others. *Mem:* Asn Art Mus Dirs; Am Asn Mus. *Res:* Sixteenth and seventeenth century Italian sculpture; art patronage in eighteenth and nineteenth century America; Maine Archit & archit preservation. *Publ:* Auth, A Bronze Mercury after Giambologna, Allen Art Mus Bull, 75-76; Sculpture in the Allen Art Museum, Hellenistic to the Twentieth Century, Apollo, 76; Sugar sculpture for grand ducal weddings from the Giambologna Workshop, The Connoisseur, 78; contribr, Giambologna 1527-1608: Sculptor to the Medici, Arts Coun Gt Brit, 78; auth, Pietro Tacca, Garland Press, 83; coauth (with Anthea Brook), Pietro Tacca, In: Il Seicento Fiorentino, Vol III, Florence, 86; contribr, prof J & mus catalog. *Mailing Add:* 10 Boody St Brunswick ME 04011

WATSON, MARY ANNE
PRINTMAKER, PAINTER
b Can; US citizen. *Study:* Ont Coll Art; NY Univ, BSc, 71. *Exhib:* Catherine Lorillard Wolfe Show, Nat Arts Club, NY; Salmagundi Club; Audubon Show, Nat Arts Club, 89-91 & 93; Nat Asn Women Artists Show, ARC Gallery, Chicago, 92; Nat Asn Women Artists traveling print show, 92-93; Artists Equity Gallery, Soho, NY, Burr Artists Show, 92; Tom Thompson Mem Mus & Art Gallery, Owen Sound, Ont, 93, 95 & 96; Nat Asn Women Artists Ann Show, Soho, NY, 94, 97-98; solo show, Georgetown Art Ctr, Ont, 97, Safe Harbour Gallery, Owen Sound, Ont, 99, Hands to Work, Elora, Ont, 1999 & 2000; Southampton Mus, Southampton, Ont, 99; plus others. *Pos:* Printmaker, Bob Blackburn Workshops, NY, formerly. *Teaching:* instr art, Central YMCA, Toronto, Can, 60-61 & 66-. *Awards:* First Place, Individual Artists Showcase, 86; Warren E Bower Mem Award, Salmagundi Club, 88; Dr & Mrs IC Gaynor Award, Nat Asn Women Artists, 91; and others. *Bibliog:* Sun Times, Owen Sound, Ont, 3/14/98; Brucedale Family Reader, Brucedale Press, 99; Who's Who in Am Art, 90-present. *Mem:* Nat Asn of Am Women Artists; Nat Pen Women of Am; Bruce Peninsula Soc of Artists; Toronto Arts & Letters Club. *Media:* Acrylic, Oil, Etching, Watercolors. *Collection:* Nat Art Gallery, Ottawa; Rutgers Univ, New Brunswick, NJ; Nat Asn Women Artists Collection; Univ Toronto Libr, Univ Coll Art Collection, Univ Toronto, Art Inst Ont, Imperial Oil Awards Collection & Toronto Dominion Bank Collection; Printmaking Workshop Collection; pvt collections throughout US & Can; plus others. *Publ:* Brucedale Family Reader, Brucedale Press, 99. *Dealer:* Olga Domjan, 220 Smith St, Elora, Can, N0B 1S0; Bruce Peninsula Soc of Artists Co; Op Gallery. *Mailing Add:* 48 Spry Lake Rd Wiarton ON N0H 2T0 Canada

WATSON, MARY JO
EDUCATOR, ADMINISTRATOR
Study: Univ Oklahoma, BFA (art history), MLS (Seminole Aesthetics), PhD (Native American Art History). *Pos:* Native American art committees, including content committee for the Oklahoma History Ctr for the permanent Indian exhibition, content committee for the American Indian Cultural Ctr and Mus, serves on the Seminole Tribal Arts Council, curated the first Seminole Fine Arts exhibition; cons, State of Oklahoma Art in Public Places Program; honorary bd mem, Red Earth and Jacobson Found; with Native American and Fine Art Appraisals, Inc, 1990-. *Teaching:* Dir, Sch of Art and Art History, Univ of Oklahoma, currently, Regent's Prof Art History, currently, curator, Native American art, Fred Jones Jr Mus of Art, currently. *Awards:* Governor's Arts award for significant contribution to enhance the arts in Oklahoma, 1993; Oklahoma Regent's award for Superior Teaching, 2002; Governor's Art award for Outstanding Service, 2002; Special Recognition for Outstanding Service by Native American Women, 2003; Paseo Art Asn Lifetime Achievement award, 2010. *Mailing Add:* University of Oklahoma School of Art & Art History 520 Parrington Oval FJC Room 202 Norman OK 73019

WATSON, RONALD G
PAINTER, EDUCATOR
b Grand Island, Neb, Oct 9, 1941. *Study:* Univ Neb, Lincoln, BFA, 64, MFA (Woods Painting Fel), 67. *Work:* Grand Rapids Art Mus, Mich; Nat Collection Fine Arts, Washington, DC. *Comn:* Outdoor steel sculpture, City of Grand Rapids, Mich, 74; sculpture garden, Veterans Admin, Washington, DC, 81. *Exhib:* Solo exhibs, Grand Rapids Art Mus, Mich, 73, Ohio State Univ Art Gallery, 78, Dobrick Gallery, Chicago, 82, San Antonio Art Inst, 87, Tex Christian Univ, 91 & Midwestern Univ, Wichita Falls, Tex 99; Ft Worth Gallery, 83 & 86; Adams-Middleton Gallery, Dallas, 85; The Patrick Gallery, Austin, 86; William Campbell Contemp Art, Ft Worth, Tex, 88; and others. *Teaching:* Prof drawing & painting, Aquinas Col, Grand Rapids, Mich, 68-82, chmn dept art, 71-81; prof drawing & painting, Tex Christian Univ, 82-, chmn dept art & hist, 82-89, dir grad studies, Col Fine Arts & Commun, 91-94, Chmn, Dept Art & Art Hist, 94-. *Awards:* Artist Fel, Nat Endowment Arts, 75. *Bibliog:* Margaret Robinette (auth), Outdoor Sculpture, Watson-Guptill, 76; Fay L Hendry (auth), Outdoor Sculpture in Grand Rapids, Michigan, Iota Press, 76; Donald Thalacker (auth), Art in World of Architecture, Chelsea House, 80; Howard Smagula (auth), Currents: Contemporary Directions in the Visual Arts, Prentice-Hall, 83. *Mem:* Coll Art Asn. *Media:* Acrylic, Oil. *Publ:* Auth, The challenge of public sculpture, Mich Art J, 76; Art in public places, Ferris State Col, 79; Angels on High, Tex Christian Univ Press, 99. *Dealer:* William Campbell Contemp Art 4935 Byers Ave Ft Worth TX 76107. *Mailing Add:* 4712 Driskell Blvd Fort Worth TX 76107-7213

WATSON, ROSS
CURATOR
b Bangor, N Ireland, July 29, 1934. *Study:* Pembroke Col, Cambridge, BA(hist with hon), 56, MA, 59; Courtauld Inst Art, London, dipl (hist art, with distinction), 63. *Collection Arranged:* Brit Coun Exhib 18th Century English Watercolors (auth, catalog), Rijks Mus, Amsterdam, Albertina, Vienna, 66; J M W Turner from Mellon Collection, Nat Gallery Art, Washington, DC, 69; John Constable from Mellon Collection, 69; Joseph Wright Derby, from Mellon Collection, 69-70; William Hogarth from Mellon Collection, 70-71; Eye of Thomas Jefferson, Bicentennial Exhib, 76. *Pos:* Asst keeper, City Mus & Art Gallery, Birmingham, Eng, 63-66; asst cur, Paul Mellon Collection, Washington, DC, 66; cur, Nat Gallery Art, Washington, DC, 66-77; admin asst dir, Tudor Pl Found, Washington, DC, 88-. *Mem:* Walpole Soc; Asn Irish Art Hist; Palladian Soc Am, Decorative Arts Trust. *Res:* Eighteenth century European, particularly British painting. *Publ:* Coauth, Renaissance furniture, Antiques Int, 66; auth, Guardi and the visit of Pius VI to Venice in 1782, Nat Gallery Art Report & Studies Hist Art, 67; Irish portraits in American Collections, Irish Georgian Soc Bull, 69; National Gallery of Art, Washington, DC, 79

WATTLES, VIRGINIA
ARTIST
b Kearney, Nebr, 1939. *Study:* Univ Nebr, BA, MA. *Exhib:* Represented in permanent collection Mus Nebr Art. *Teaching:* Art educator. *Awards:* Nebr Artist / Educator of Yr, 1991; Grumbacher Silver Medal. *Mem:* Pastel Soc Am; Soc Portrait Artists. *Media:* Pastel

WATTS, R MICHAEL
MUSEUM DIRECTOR
b Quincy, Ill, July 2, 1951. *Study:* Western Ill Univ, BS, 73, BA (art hist), 75; Univ Tex Austin, MFA, 77. *Exhib:* Exhibs Curated: Vera Klement: Paintings, 2002; Burl Ives & Art of the 1930s & 40s, 2006; Stories of Folk Arts (with Dr Debra a Reid), 2007, Ruth Duckworth: Bronze and Ceramic Sculpture (with Thea Burger), 2008, Stephen Cartwright: Topographics, 2010, Harold Boyd: Works on Paper and Other Drawings, 2010, Bridging the Past: Paul Sargent's Coles County, 2011, Guit (art): Guitars from Mark Rubel's Collection, 2012, Looking at Lincoln 2013. *Collection Arranged:* Antique Quilts c 1830-1930, Paducah Art Guild Gallery, 82; New Wood/New Ways, with Paul Sasso co-curator, (with catalog), Southern Arts Fedn, 83; Am Scene Prints, Tarble Arts Ctr, Eastern Ill Univ, 87, Prints by the 20th Century Am Artists, 95, Landscapes by Paul T Sargent and Robert M Root, 95, Textiles from the Ill Folk Arts Coll, 98, Watercolors from the Coll, 2003, Modernist Art from the Coll, 2007, Peter Norton Family Christmas Project, 2011; Am Scene Prints, 87 & Illinois Traditions: Folk Arts, 90, Tarble Arts Ctr; Paul Sargent, Robert Root & the Brown Co Artist Colony (with Rachel Perry), Tarble Arts Ctr, 95. *Pos:* Dir, Paducah Art Guild, Ky; Eagle & Curris Galleries, Murray State Univ, Ky, 83-86; Tarble Arts Ctr, Eastern Ill Univ, 86-; Asst Dean, Pub Arts Prog, Col Arts & Humanities, Eastern Ill Univ, 2008; asst prof art, Eastern Ill Univ, 2008-. *Teaching:* Instr art, Paducah Community Col, Ky, 81-82; asst prof, Murray State Univ, Ky, 83-86; adj prof, Art Grad Prog, Eastern Ill Univ, 1990-. *Mem:* Am Asn Mus; Coll Art Asn; Asn Academic Mus Galleries; Ill Asn Mus; Asn Midwest Mus. *Res:* Twentieth century American art, particularly contemporary folk art. *Publ:* Contribr, James A Michener Collection: 20th Century American Painting, Univ Mus, Univ Tex, Austin, 77; ed, African Arts: Beauty In Utility (catalog), Eagle Gallery, Murray State Univ, Ky, 83; Collecting outside the mainstream (folk art), Dialogue, 88; Virgil Grotfeldt: Recent Paintings (catalog), 90 & American Scene Prints (catalog), 91, Tarble Arts Ctr, Eastern Ill Univ, 91; Ruth Duckworth: Bronze and Ceramic Sculpture (with Thea Burger), 2008. *Mailing Add:* Eastern Ill Univ Tarble Arts Ctr 600 Lincoln Ave Charleston IL 61920

WAUFLE, ALAN DUANE
MUSEUM DIRECTOR
b Hornell, NY, Feb 11, 1951. *Study:* Coll William & Mary, BA; Duke Univ, MA. *Collection Arranged:* Antique Quilts & Coverlets of Gaston Co, 77, Textile History of Gaston Co, 78, Frank Creach: Retrospective, 78, The Christmas Doll, 79, Wheels & Runners: 18th Century Am on the Move, 83, Gaston Co Mus Art & Hist. *Pos:* Dir, Gaston Co Mus Art & Hist, Dallas, NC, 76-. *Mem:* NC Mus Coun; Am Asn State & Local Hist; Am Asn of Mus; SE Mus Conf. *Res:* Iconography of works celebrating the 1571 Battle of Lepanto. *Publ:* Auth, Guide to mus, galleries & craft shops in NC. *Mailing Add:* 3308 Sherwood Cir Gastonia NC 28056

WAUGH, MICHAEL
DRAFTSMAN, PERFORMANCE ARTIST
Study: Univ Tex, Austin, BA (hist); New York Univ, MA; Tex State Univ, MFA. *Work:* Crystal Bridges Mus of Am Art. *Comn:* Tweets from Tahrir, TMagazine. *Exhib:* Exhibition Anthologie der Kunst, Akademie der Kunste, Berlin, 2004; Text Formed Drawing, Contemp Art Gallery, Univ Conn, 2006; Timeless, Morris Mus, NJ, 2008; Engagierte New Yorker Kunst in PRENNNG: The Next Step to Your Future, Villa Feuerloscher, Austria, 2009; Idee Fixe, Winkleman Gallery, 2011. *Pos:* Asst dir, Momenta Art, 2000-10. *Teaching:* Adj fac, Tex State Univ, 1995-96, LaGaurdia Cmty Coll, 2001-02, New Sch Univ, 2001-07, New York Univ, 2002-06. *Awards:* Joan Mitchell Found Fel, 2009; NY Found Arts Fel, 2009; Marie Walsh Sharpe Space Award, 2009; Sterling Clark Visaul Arts Award, 2009; Pollock-Krasner Found Grant, 2010. *Bibliog:* Calvid Reid (auth), Michael Waugh at Schroeder Romero, Art in AM, 6-7/2005; Holland Cotter (auth), Lead Me Astray, NY Times, 3/16/2007. *Mailing Add:* Schroeder Romero 173A N 3rd St #2 Brooklyn NY 11211

WAX, JACK
GLASS ARTIST, EDUACTOR
Study: Tyler Sch Art, Temple Univ, BFA (ceramics & glass), 1978; RI Sch Design, MFA (sculpture & glass), 1983. *Work:* Smithsonian Inst, Washington DC; Corning Mus Glass, NY; Speed Mus Art, Louisville; Los Angeles County Mus Art; Huntington Mus Art, WVa. *Comn:* Voice Stream, Phillip Morris Corp, Richmond, Va, 2004. *Exhib:* Solo exhibs, Fleischer gallery, Philadelphia Mus Art, 1991, Univ Gallery, Ill State Univ, 1997, Evanston Art Ctr, 2001, Anderson Gallery, Va Commonwealth Univ, 2003, Ga Southwestern Univ, 2005; The Glass Skin (traveling exhib), Hokkaido Mus Art, Sapporo, Japan, 1997; United States Artists, Tittot Mus, Taiwan, China, 2003; Instructors, Haystack Mountain Sch Crafts, 2004; Material Matters, Los Angeles County Mus Art, 2006; Am Acad Arts & Letts Invitational, New York, 2010. *Teaching:* Instr, RI Sch Design, 1987, Temple Univ Sch Art, Pa, 1987-90, Univ Arts, Philadelphia Coll Art, 1988-90, Cleveland Inst Art, 1990-91; prof, Toyama Inst Glass, Japan, 1991-96; assoc prof & head glass studies, Ill State Univ Sch Art, 1998-2002; assoc prof & head glass area, Va Commonwealth Univ, Ricmond, 2002-05, prof, 2005-. *Awards:* Individual Artist Fel, Nat Endowment for the Arts, 1986, 1988; Ill State Univ Res Grant, 1999, 2002; Individual Artists Grant, Ill State Coun on Arts, 2000

WAXTER, DORSEY
ART DEALER, GALLERY DIRECTOR
Pos: gallery dir, Nancy Hoffman Gallery, 1974-1977, Andre Emmerich Gallery, 1977-1992, Greenberg Van Doren, 1998-2012, Van Doren Waxter (formerly Greenberg Van Doren), 2012-; founder, gallery dir, eponymous art consultancy, 1991-1998; pres, Art Dealers Assn America, 2013-. *Mailing Add:* Art Dealers Association of America 205 Lexington Ave #901 New York NY 10016

WAYNE, CYNTHIA M
CURATOR, HISTORIAN
b St Louis, Mo, Aug 16, 1958. *Study:* Univ Mo, Columbia, BA, 80, MA, 83; Cornell Univ, Ithaca, NY, 86-87. *Collection Arranged:* Masters of Contemporary Art in Poland (co-auth, catalog), 86; Dreams, Lies & Exaggerations: Photomontage in Am (auth, catalog), 91; Masterworks from the Photography Collections, UMBC, 92; Alice Harold Murphy: Rediscovering the Female Perspective in Am Art 1920-1950, 93; Masters of Contemporary Art in Poland (coauth, catalog), Herbert F Johnson Mus Art, Cornell Univ, 86, New York State Artists V (with catalog), 86, Elements of Nature: Watercolors by Kenneth Evett, 87; Dreams, Lies and Exaggerations: Photomontage in Am (with catalog), Art Gallery, Univ Md, College Park, 91; Alice Harold Murphy: Rediscovering the Female Perspective in Am Art 1920-1950 (with catalog), Montpelier Cult Art Ctr, Laurel, Md, 93; Fields of Vision: Women in Photography (with catalog), Univ Md Baltimore Co, 95-96, Visual Groits: Works by Four African Am Photographers (with catalog), 96, Word & Image: Swiss Poster Design 1955-1997 (with catalog), 98, Imprints: Photographs by David Plowden, 98, Eye of the Storm, Photogs by Mildred Grossman (with catalog), 99. *Pos:* Actg dir/asst dir, Art Gallery, Univ Md, College Park, 87-92; exec dir, Pyramid Atlantic, 92-93; coordr exhib, Albin O Kuhn Libr & Gallery, Univ Md, Baltimore Co, 94-. *Mem:* Am Asn Mus; Coll Art Asn; Hist Photog Group. *Res:* History of photography, especially manipulated photography in Europe and United States. *Mailing Add:* Univ Maryland Albin O Kuhn Library & Gallery 1000 Hilltop Cir Baltimore MD 21250

WEARE, SHANE
PRINTMAKER
b Eng, Aug 29, 1936. *Study:* Royal Coll Art, London, Eng, ARCA (printmaking), 63; Univ Iowa, asst etching, 63-64. *Work:* Brit Mus, London; Lib Libr Cong, Washington, DC; Brooklyn Mus, NY; Art Inst Chicago; San Francisco Mus Art. *Exhib:* Int Exhib Graphic Art, Ljubliana, Yugoslavia, 66; Brit Int Print Biennale, 68; 22nd Ann Print Exhib, Boston Mus, 70; World Print Competition, San Francisco Mus Art, 73; Solo exhib, Calif Palace Legion Hon, San Francisco, 73; 20th Nat Print Exhib, Brooklyn Mus, NY, 77. *Pos:* prof art emeritus, Sonoma State Univ. *Awards:* Purchase Awards, Los Angeles Soc Printmakers, 68-74, City of San Francisco, 72, City of Palo Alto, 74 & Univ Colo, 74; Spaces Between Prog Award, KQED-TV, San Francisco, 75. *Bibliog:* John Brunsden (auth), Technique of Etching & Engraving, Batsford, 66. *Mem:* Calif Soc Printmakers (vchmn, 72-73). *Media:* Pastel. *Dealer:* Printworks 311 West Superior St Suite 105 Chicago IL 60610. *Mailing Add:* 2663 Bennett Ridge Rd Santa Rosa CA 95404

WEARING, GILLIAN
CONCEPTUAL ARTIST
b 1963. *Study:* Chelsea Sch Art; Godsmith Coll. *Exhib:* Okay Behavior, 303 Gallery, 93; Brilliant, Walker Art Ctr, 95; Sensation, London, 97; People, Tanya Bonakdar Gallery, 2011. *Awards:* Turner Prize, 1997; Named one of 10 Most Important Artists of Today, Newsweek mag, 2011. *Dealer:* Tanya Bonakdar Gallery 521 W 21st St New York NY 10011

WEAVER, AM
ADMINISTRATOR, HISTORIAN
b Philadelphia, Pa, Jul 31, 1954. *Study:* Univ Arts, Philadelphia, Pa, BFA; Md Inst Col, Hoffberger Sch Painting, MFA. *Exhib:* Retrospective (auth, catalog), Univ Pa, Contemp Inst Art, Philadelphia, Pa, James E Lewis Mus Art, Baltimore, Md, Lehigh Univ, Bethlehem, Pa, Ft Lauderdale Mus, Fla. *Pos:* fac, alternative art ctr, Philadelphia, Pa, formerly; dir, Visual & Media Arts, formerly; exec dir, Art Sanctuary, formerly; cur, exhibs & collections, Noyes Mus Art, NJ, currently; Independent Cur, currently. *Media:* Photography. *Interests:* African Aesthetics, traditional & contemporary; photography. *Publ:* auth, Black Artists, St James Press; many essays, catalog essays & jour. *Mailing Add:* Noyes Mus Art Lily Lake Rd Oceanville NJ 08231

WEAVER, CHEYENNE
SCULPTOR
Study: San Francisco Art Inst, San Francisco, 2000-02; Calif Inst Arts, Valencia, Calif, BFA, 2004. *Work:* Detroit Inst Arts. *Exhib:* Solo exhibs include Detour Gallery, San Francisco, 2002, Calif Inst Arts, Valencia, Calif, 2003, 2004, Machine Proj, Los Angeles, 2005, Pomona Mus, Pomona, Calif, 2006; Group exhibs include Light & Space, Office Space, Berkeley, Calif, 2001; Sea Level, Detour Gallery, San Francisco, 2002; Dark Days, Stevenson Blanch Gallery, Cal Arts, Valencia, Calif, 2003; Lodged In, Big Oaks Lodge, Los Angeles State Park, Saugus, Calif, 2003; Emergence, Track 16, Santa Monica, Calif, 2004; Girls Who Wear Glasses, Crazyspace, Santa Monica, Calif, 2004; Garden Lab, The Wind Tunnel, Pasadena, Calif, 2004; No Man's Land, Shoshana Wayne Gallery, Santa Monica, Calif, 2005; Fresh, Mus Contemp Art, Los Angeles, 2005; Bugology, Armory Ctr Arts, Pasadena, Calif, 2006. *Awards:* Gen-Art, Emergence Grant, Track 16, Los Angeles, 2002, 2003

WEAVER, MICHAEL K
ADMINISTRATOR, EDUCATOR
Study: Tenn Tech Univ, BA, 80; Univ Birmingham, MA, 81; Univ NC at Chapel Hill, PhD, 89. *Pos:* interim grad advisor, history MA program, Univ Tex Pan-Am, 92-93, grad advisor, 93-98, acting dept chair dept history and philosophy, 98-99, interim dept chair, 99-2000, dept chair, 2000-2001, interim dept chair dept english, 2000-2001,

interim dept head modern languages and lit dpet, 2001-2004, title V/Hispanic serving inst grant learning comm activity coordr, 2003-2005, asst dean coll arts and humanities, 2004, interim assoc dean, 2005-2006, co-dir, UTPA title V/HSI grant office, 2006-2008, interim chair dept art, 2008-2010, asst dean, Coll Arts & Humanities, 2010-. *Mailing Add:* 1100 Castile Ct Edinburg TX 78539

WEBB, ALEX(ANDER) (DWIGHT)
PHOTOGRAPHER
b San Francisco, Calif, May 5, 1952. *Study:* Harvard Univ, BA (hist and lit), 74; Apeiron Photog Workshop, with Charles Harbutt, 72. *Work:* Fogg Art Mus, Cambridge, Mass; Whitney Mus Am Art, NY; Int Ctr Photog, NY; Mus Photog Arts, San Diego, Calif; Brooklyn Mus, NY; Metrop Mus Art; Mus Fine Arts, Boston. *Comn:* Picturing the South, High Mus Art, Atlanta, Ga. *Exhib:* Contemp Photographers V, 75 & Color Photog, 80, Fogg Art Mus, Cambridge, Mass; 3 Color Photogrs, Amsterdam Photo 84, The Neth, 84; On the Line: The New Color Photojournalism (with catalog), Walker Art Ctr, Minneapolis, Minn, 86; solo exhibs, Calif Mus Photog, Riverside, 86 & Torino Fotografia, Torino, Italy, US-Mex Border, FotoMassan, Gothenburg, Sweden, 97, Leica Gallery, NY, 98, Zentrum fur Photog, Berlin, Ger, 98 Under a Grudging Sun and Beyond, Int Fototage Herten, 99 & Amazon, Sky Harbor Gallery, Phoenix, Ariz, 99; group exhibs, Masters of the Streets & Haiti: Revolution in Progress, Mus Photog Arts, San Diego, Calif, 89, This & Other Worlds, Mus Contemp Photog, Chicago, Ill, In Our Time, Magnum Photos, Int Ctr Photog, NY, 89, Palats de Tokyo, Paris, France, 89 (traveling) & Minneapolis Mus Art, 90; This & Other Worlds, Mus Contemp Photog, Chicago, Ill; Atrium Gallery, Univ Conn, Storrs, 91; Whitney Mus Am Art, NY Biennial Exhib, 91; Civilians in War, Art Inst Boston, 95; India: A Celebration of Independence, Philadelphia Mus Art, 97; World Views, Southeast Mus Photogr, Daytona Beach, Fla, 2000; Mus Contemp Art, San Diego, 2003; Benaki Mus, Athens, 2004; Sala de Exp, Canal de Isabel II, Madrid, 2007; Istanbul Mus Mod Art, Istanbul, 2007; Sepia Int, NY, 2007; Uinzavod Ctr, Moscow, 2008. *Pos:* Photogr, Magnum Photos, NY, 76-, vpres, 85-86. *Awards:* NY Found Arts Grant, 86; Nat Endowment Arts Grant, 90; Hasselblad Found Grant, 98; Leica Medal of Excellence, 2000; David Octavius Hill Medaille, 2002; John Simon Guggenheim Found Fel, 2007. *Bibliog:* Andy Grundberg (auth), Photojournalism: It's back with a new face, Mod Photog, 80; Gary Walther (auth), In the heat of the light, Camera Arts, 83; M Johnstone (auth), The active streets, Art Week, 83; Haiti, Photo Mag, France, 4/88; Max Kozloff (auth), Picturing the Killing Fields, Art in Am, 6/90; Aperture: 181, Istanbul, winter, 2008; Panorama Vol 26, No 2, Photog by Max Kozloff; Aperture: 40th Anniversary Issue. *Publ:* Auth, Hot Light/Half-Made Worlds: Photographs from the Tropics, 86 & Under a Grudging Sun: Photographs from Haiti Libere, 89, Thames & Hudson; From the Sunshine State: Photographs of Florida, 96 & Amazon: From the Floodplains to the Clouds, 97, Monacelli Press; Dislocations, Harvard Univ, 98-99; Crossings: Photographs from the US-Mexico Border, Monaalli Press; Istanbul: City of a Hundred Names, Aperture; I Grandi Fotografil Magnum: ALex Webb, Hacleffe; Alex Webb: Habla con Max Kozloff, La Fabvica. *Dealer:* Catherine Edelman Gallery Chicago IL; Ethenton Gallery Tucson AZ; Hasted Hurt Gallery NY; Joseph Bellows Gallery La Jolla CA; Stephen Bulger Gallery Chicago IL

WEBB, FRANK (FRANCIS) H
PAINTER, INSTRUCTOR
b North Versailles, Pa, Sept 14, 1927. *Study:* Art Inst Pittsburgh, with Edgar A Whitney. *Work:* Butler Inst Am Art, Youngstown, Ohio; PPG Found, Pittsburgh; Tweed Art Mus, Duluth, Mich; Ford Times Collection, Detroit; Taiwan Art Educ Inst; Palmer Mus Penn State Univ; Southern Alleghenies Art Mus; Portland Mus Art. *Comn:* Soc Naval Architects & Marine Engineers, 88. *Exhib:* Solo exhibs, Tweed Art Mus, Univ Minn, Duluth, 82, Purdue Univ, 84, LaRoach Coll, Pittsburgh, 91, Atelier Gallery, New York, 93, Chaffee Gallery, Rutland, Vt, 93, Glennville State Coll, WVa, 93, The Spotlight Gallery, Pittsburgh, 98, Va Southern Alleghenies Art Mus, Ligonier, 99, Southern Vt Art Ctr, 2004; Group exhibs, Am Watercolor Soc Ann, Nat Acad, NY, 71-80; Nat Arts Club, NY, 71-81; Butler Inst Am Art, Youngstown, Ohio, 73; Audubon Artists, Nat Arts Club, NY, 73-83; Allied Artists, Nat Arts Club, NY, 73-80; Nat Acad Ann, NY, 77; Midwest Watercolor Soc Ann, Rawr-West Mus, Manitowac, Wis, 79-83; and many others. *Pos:* Pres, Phillips Studio, Pittsburgh, 57-80. *Teaching:* Guest lectr painting throughout N Am, Cent Am & Europe, 73-. *Awards:* Sizek Award, Butler Midyear Ann, Butler Inst Am Art, Youngstown, Ohio, 73; Bronze Medal of Hon, Am Watercolor Soc, 76; Walser Greathouse Medal, Am Watercolor Soc, 89; Gold Medal of Hon, Audubon Artists, 95; Philadelphia Watercolor Soc Medal for Achievement in the Arts. *Bibliog:* Webb on Watercolor (film/video); Using your Head, Heart and Hand (film/DVD); Frank Webb's Painting by Design (film/DVD); Frank Webb's Expression in Painting (film/DVD); Frank Webb's Painting Enjoyable Color (film DVD). *Mem:* Am Watercolor Soc, Dolphin Fel, (chmn mems, 2001-2010); Rocky Mountain Nat Watermedia Asn; Allied Artists of Am; Audubon Artists; Jiangsu Watercolor Res Inst. *Media:* Watercolor. *Publ:* Auth, Watercolor Energies, 83, North Light Publ; Webb on Watercolor, 90; Strengthen Your Paintings with Dynamic Composition, 94. *Dealer:* Harbor Square Gallery 374 Main St Rockland ME 04841. *Mailing Add:* 5 Grandview Ave Apt 401 Pittsburgh PA 15211

WEBB, JEFFREY R
PAINTER, EDUCATOR
b Mineola, NY, Sept 29, 1952. *Study:* Pratt Inst, Brooklyn, NY, BFA, 74; studied with John Koch Nat Acad, 74-78; C W Post Col, Long Island Univ, Old Brookville, MA, 76. *Work:* Heckscher Mus, Huntington, NY; Bayville Mus, NY. *Comn:* portrait, Dr G Perry, Mercy Hosp, Rockville Centre, NY, 86; portrait, Dr Robbins, South Oaks Hosp, Amityville, 86; historical portrait, Capt T Cook, City Glen Cove, NY, 86; mural, Wizard of Oz, Village Green Golf, Lake Ronkonkoma, NY, 92; portrait, Maury Povitch and Connie Chung. *Exhib:* Pastel Soc Asn Ann Exhibs, Nat Arts Club, NY, 73-92; one-man show, Harbor Gallery, Cold Spring Harbor, NY, 78; Pastel Exposition Int, Maison Lafitte, Paris, France, 88; Master Pastellists, Quincy Art Mus, Ill, 90; Featured Show, Z Gallery, NY, 91; and others. *Pos:* Historian, bd dir, Pastel Soc Am, NY, 75-; vpres, Nat Drawing Asn, Garden City, NY, 88-90; art comt, Salmagundi Club, NY, 90-. *Teaching:* Instr painting, Huntington Township Art League, NY, 76-; instr pastel painting, Queensborough Community Col, Bayside, NY, 89-; instr art hist, Nassau Community Col, Garden City, NY, 88-; adj fac, SUNY, Farmingdale, NY. *Awards:* Knickerbocker Award for Oil, Knickerbocker Artists Ann, 78; Master Pastellist, Pastel Soc Am Exhib, 85; Grumbacher Gold Medal, Pastel Soc Am Ann Exhib, Grumbacher Artists Mats, 91. *Bibliog:* Domenique Sennelier (auth), The Sennelier Pastel Portrait Set, Sennelier Artists Mat, 91; Linda Price (auth) Creating Luminous Pastels The Paintings of Long Island Artist Jeff Webb, Am Artist Mag, 7/97; Kristina Feliciano (editor), The Best of Pastels 2, Rockport Press, 98. *Mem:* Pastel Soc Am (bd dir, 75-); Nat Drawing Asn (vpres, 88-90); Salmagundi Club (art comt, 90-); Nat Art League (exhib chmn, 92); Huntington Township Art League. *Media:* Pastel, Oil. *Publ:* Illusr, Introduction to Meditation, 78 & Fundamentals of Jain Meditation, 79, Dodd-Mead; auth, Artists and models, Encore Plus, 89. *Dealer:* Owl 57 Gallery Woodmere NY

WEBB, PATRICK
PAINTER, MURALIST
b New York, NY, July 20, 1955. *Study:* Md Inst/Coll Art, BFA, 76; Skowhegan Sch Painting & Sculpture, 77; Yale Univ, MFA, 79. *Work:* Fred Alger & Co & Chemical Bank, NY; Boston Pub Libr & Shearson Lehman, Boston, Mass; Univ Wis, Oshkosh; Housatonic Mus, Bridgeport, Conn; Queensboro Coll Mus, NY; Provincetown Art Asn & Mus; Zimmerli Art Mus, Rutgers, Univ. *Comn:* Painting, Glickenhaus & Co, NY, 86; paintings, Sharf Marketing Group 87 & 88; portraits, Art Matters 2 Lithographs; Landscapes, 99 & 2002. *Exhib:* Solo shows, Forum Gallery, Minneapolis, Minn, 90, Group Gallery, Provincetown, Mass, 92, Amos Eno Gallery, NY, 93, Figuring it out, Daniel Quinn Gallery, Long Island, NY, 92, Mercer Gallery, 95, Punchinello Goes West (with catalog), Julie Heller Gallery, Provincetown, Mass, Punchinello Works Out (PWO), Cortland Jessup Gallery, NY, 98, Punchinello Undressed, Julie Heller Gallery, 99, Punchinello Young, Julie Heller Gallery, Mass, 2001, Punchinello's City, CJG Projs, NY, 2002, Home, Julie Heller Gallery, Mass, 2003, Punchinello Inside and Out, CJG Projs, NY, 2004; Mementomori, Open Space Gallery, Allentown, Pa, 93; Unexpected Courage, Multimedia Gallery, NY, 94; Tongue 'n Cheek, 450 Gallery, NY, 94; group exhibs, Transformations, Sakia City Mus Gallery, Osaka, Japan, 2002, Pratt Responds to 9/11, Schaffler Gallery, Pratt Inst, NY, 2002, The Body and its Dangers, The Painting Ctr, NY, 2003; Chaet Julieheller Gallery, 2005; 25 Years of Work, Provincetown Art Asn & Mus, 2008. *Teaching:* Lectr, Univ Wis, 79-81; asst prof, Cornell Univ, 81-83; vis artist, Yale Univ, 85, Brandeis Univ, 88, Minneapolis Col Art & Design, 89, 90 & 92, Cranbook Acad, 92 & 94, NY Acad Art, 93-94, Fla Int Univ, 93 & RI Sch Design, 93, Pratt Inst, 95-; adj assoc prof, Pratt Inst, 2000-2004; assoc prof, Pratt Inst, 2004-. *Awards:* Fel, Nat Endowment Arts, 83, 85 & 87; Ingram Merrill Award, 89-90 & 95; Thomas B Clarke Award, Nat Acad, NY, 98. *Bibliog:* Phil Gambone (auth), Eros & Angst, Bay Windows; Nancy Grimes (auth), Punchinello Paintings (catalog), 93; and others; Stanley Kunitz (auth), Catalog, 2008. *Mem:* Coll Art Asn; NY Artists Equity; Provincetown Art Asn; Art Group Inc. *Media:* Oil & Miscellaneous Fresco, Etching. *Publ:* Cover, Public Speaking, Beebe Prentice Hall, 91; American Law Yearbook (reproduction & article by ed), 90; cover, Bar Asn J, Mass, 92; Punchinello Works Out, Weinsberg, Asn Am Mus; Male Desire: Homoerotic in American Art, Weinberg, Abrams, 2004. *Dealer:* Julie Heller Gallery Provincetown MA; Painting Ctr New York City NY. *Mailing Add:* Old Chelsea St PO Box 903 New York NY 10011

WEBB, SARAH A
PAINTER
b Nashville, Tenn, Feb 19, 1948. *Study:* Univ Tenn, Ba, 78; Vanderbilt Univ, 79-80. *Work:* Holiday Corp, Memphis, Tenn; First Tenn Bank, Gallatin, Tenn. *Exhib:* Ann Cent South Art Competition, Parthenon Gallery, Nashville, Tenn, 82, 87 & 92; solo exhibs, Leu Gallery, Belmont Univ, Nashville, 83, 99, Nashville Int Airport, Metro Arts Comn, 94; Am Artist Nat Art Competition, Grand Central Gallery, NY, 85; Ann Exhib, Soc Women Artists, Westminster Gallery, London, Eng, 89, 90, 91, 94, 98-01. *Awards:* Athena Award, 27th Central South Art Competition, 92. *Bibliog:* Clara Hieronymns (auth), Oh, how she loves Paris, 12/27/87 & Sarah Webb Works to Show in London, 5/17/89, Tennessean; Tennessee Crossroads: Profiling International Artist Sarah Webb in London (film), WDCN-PBS TV, Nashville, 94; Susan Chappell (auth), Nashville artist Sarah Webb breaks ground in Britain, Nashville Banner, 3/18/94; Alan Bostic (auth), Get real, Webb paints it like it is, The Tennessean, 9/12/99. *Media:* Oil. *Mailing Add:* PO Box 50134 Nashville TN 37205

WEBER, IDELLE LOIS
PAINTER, EDUCATOR
b Chicago, Ill, Mar 12, 1932. *Study:* Scripps Coll, 1951; Univ Calif, Los Angeles, BA & MA, 1954-55. *Work:* Art Inst, Chicago; Fogg Mus, Harvard Univ, Cambridge, Mass; Albright-Knox Art Gallery, Buffalo, NY; San Francisco Mus Art, Calif; Nelson Atkins Mus Art, Mo; Whitney Mus Art, New York; Skidmore Owens, Dallas, Tex; Archives of Am Art, Smithsonian, Wash, DC. *Comn:* Pac Bell, San Ramon, Calif. *Exhib:* Solo exhibs, Bertha Schaefer, New York, 63-64, Hundred Acres Gallery, New York, 73-77, OK Harris Gallery, New York, 79-82, Ruth Siegel Gallery, New York, 84-89, Anthony Ralph, New York, 89-92, Arts Club Chicago, 89, Gerald Peters Gallery, Santa Fe, NMex, 94 & Schmidt Bingham Gallery, 94-98, Nassau County Mus Art, NY, 2004; Group exhibs, Contemp Am Realism Since 60, Pa Acad Fine Arts, 81; Traveling Exhib, Woodson Art Mus, Wasau, Wis, 1995-97; Santa Barbara Mus Contemp Art, Calif, 1995; Harn Mus, Fla, 1996; Nat Acad mem exhib, 2003, 2005 & 2007; Nassau Co Mus Art, NY, 2004; Inaugural Exhib, Nelson Atkins Bloch Bldg, Kansas City, Mo, 2007; Seductive Subversion: Women Pop Artists 1958-1968, Univ Arts at Sheldon Mus Art, Lincoln, Neb, Elizabeth A. Sackler Ctr for Feminist Art, Brooklyn Mus Art, NY, Tufts Univ Gallery, Mass, 2010-2011. *Teaching:* Adj assoc prof art, NY Univ Grad Sch, 1974-89; asst prof art, Harvard Univ, 1989-91; master prog, Long Island Univ, Southampton, NY; Melbourne Univ, Australia, 1995 & Nat Acad, 2002 & 2005; retired. *Awards:* Distinguished Alumna Award, Scripps Coll; Artist-in-residence, Victoria Coll Art, Melbourne, Australia; Scholastic Arts mag

scholar, 1950; Nat Acad Art, 2002. *Bibliog:* Arts Mag, 1979, 1982, 1984 & 1986; L Meisel (auth), Photo Realism, 1980; L Nochlin (auth), San Antonio Mus Catalogue, 1981; CS Rubenstein (auth), Am Women Artists, 1982; Wall St J, 1985; Christian Sci Monitor, 1985-86; E Lubell (auth), Art in Am 1986; Wash Post, 1986-87; Chicago Tribune, 1986; Art Examiner, 1986; John L Ward (auth), Am Realist Painting, 1945-1980, 1989; Alloway, Jan Ernst, Idelle Weber, The, Oct, 1994; Grace Glueck (auth), article, NY Times, 1996; Whitney Chadwick, Women, Art and Society, Thames & Hudson, 1997; Gary Miles Chassman (auth), In the Spirit of Martin, the Living Legacy of Dr Martin Luther King, Jr, 2001; Jennifer New (auth), Drawing From Life: The J as Art, 2005. *Mem:* Coll Art Asn; Women's Caucus Art; Poets House; Nat Acad (coun). *Media:* Oil, Watercolor, Pastel & Photography. *Interests:* Poetry, Photography and Music. *Publ:* contribr, A Seductive Subversion: Women Pop Artists 1958-1968 (exhib catalog), 2010-2011. *Dealer:* Jean Albano Art Gallery 215 W Superior Chicago IL 60610. *Mailing Add:* 429 W Broadway New York NY 10012

WEBER, JOANNE PAGANO
PAINTER, WRITER
Exhib: Two-person exhibs include The Man From Brancheville, with Janice Mauro, Art 101, Brooklyn, NY, 2006; group exhibs include Transformations, Brooklyn Waterfront Artists Coalition Pier Show, Red Hook, NY, 2006; Ann Invitational Exhib Contemp Am Art, Nat Acad Mus, New York, 2008. *Pos:* Mem, Bruce Weber's No Chance Ensemble, 1996-. *Awards:* Richard H Recchia Mem Prize, Nat Acad, 2008. *Publ:* Co-auth, Poetic Justice, 2004. *Mailing Add:* 4801 42nd St Apt 4A Long Island City NY 11104

WEBER, JOHN PITMAN
MURALIST, PRINTMAKER, MOSAIC ARTIST
b Washington, DC, Dec 6, 1942. *Study:* Harvard Coll, BA (cum laude), 64; Atelier 17, Paris, with S Hayter & Jean Helion, Fulbright-Hays Scholar, 64-66; Ecole des Beaux Arts; Art Inst Chicago, with Yoshida & Halsted, MFA (painting), 68. *Hon Degrees:* Elmhurst Coll, DHL, 2011. *Work:* Cohen Libr, City Coll, City Univ NY; Valparaiso Univ Mus Art, Ind; Spertus Mus, Chicago; Elmhurst Coll, Ill; Art Inst Chicago; Ctr Study of Political Graphics, DePaul Mus, Chgo. *Comn:* Polychrome concrete relief mural, City Arts, NY, 84; mural, Valley Cities Jewish Community Ctr, Los Angeles, Calif, 93; mosaics (with N Cain), Beth-Anne Ctr, Chicago, 98-99; mosaic, The Gathering, Millennium Mosaic Plaza, Spencer, IA, 2000; play sculpture & mosaic (with Henri Marquet), A Place for Children, Sabin School, Chicago, 2005; Escus-Esku, Mosaic murals, Vitoria Spain, La Ciudad Pintada, 2010; Song of 47th St, Chicago, 2009. *Exhib:* Murals for the People, Mus Contemp Art, Chicago, 71; SubCult, Group Material, IRT Subway, NY, 83; Committed to Print, Mus Mod Art, NY, 88; Kunst und Krieg, Kongreshalle, Berlin, 90; solo retrospective, Valparaiso Univ Art Mus, Ind, 91; Chicago Crossings, Spertus Mus, Chicago, 94; Bridges & Boundaries (traveling), Jewish Mus, New York; solo exhibs, Night Scenes, Chicago State Univ Gallery, 97, 10 Yrs of Printmaking, Taller Mestizarte, Chicago, 98, A Shenere Velt Gallery, Los Angeles, 2002, Fences, A.R.C. Gallery, Chicago, 2005, Lamentation, St Xavier Univ Gallery, Chicago, 2005; and others. *Pos:* Dir & founder, Chicago Pub Art Group, Chicago, 70-81. *Teaching:* Prof art, Elmhurst Coll, Ill, 68-2011, prof emeritus; vis artist mural workshop, Univ NDak, Grand Forks, 75 & Dartington Coll Art, Eng, 80. *Awards:* Beautiful Chicago, City of Chicago donor, 73 & 76; Pub Art, Chicago Bar Asn, 91; Named Cultural Envoy, US State Dept Residency in Victoria, Spain, 2010. *Bibliog:* Shifra Goldman (auth), John Pitman Weber, (catalog), Valparaiso Univ, 91; Victor Sorell (auth), John Pitman Weber (catalog), Coll Dupage Art Ctr Gallery, 94; Harpaz & Piazza (co-auth), John Pitman Weber-Glancing Back, Oakton Coll, 2000; Paul Blum (auth), John Pitman Weber Returns to LA (catalog), 2002. *Mem:* Coll Art Asn; Chicago Pub Art Group; Community Built Asn; Chicago Artists Coalition; Piece Process Art Group. *Media:* Acrylic, Mosaic; Woodcut. *Publ:* Toward a People's Art, The Contemporary Mural Movement, Dutton, 77 & Univ NMex Press, rev 98; Community Sculpture, Art & Artists, Feb. 83; auth, Art in public spaces & public art, Art J, winter 90; Carlos Cortez, Catalog Essay, Dittmar Gallery, Northwestern Univ, 95; Murals as People's Art, Theories & Documents of Contemporary Art, Stiles & Selz, VCA, 96; Murals & Public Space, Mural Art 4, 2012. *Mailing Add:* 1726 W Cermak Rd Chicago IL 60608

WEBER, SUSAN
ADMINISTRATOR, COLLECTOR
b Brooklyn, New York, 1954. *Study:* Barnard Coll, BA (magna cum laude), 1977; Cooper-Hewitt Mus/Parsons Sch Design, MA, 1990; Royal Coll Art, PhD, 1998. *Pos:* Founder & dir, Bard Grad Ctr, New York, 1991-; founder & publ, Source: Notes in the History of Art; exec dir, Open Soc Fund. *Teaching:* Iris Horowitz prof hist decorative arts, Bard Grad Ctr, New York. *Awards:* Philip C Johnson Award, Soc Archit Historians, 2000 & 2005; Henry Russell Hitchcock Award, Victorian Soc in Am, 2000; George Wittenborn Meml Bk Award, 2000 & 2004; Bezalel Educator in the Arts Award, 2002; Cult Leadership Award, AFA, 2003; named one of Top 200 Collectors, ARTnews mag, 2010. *Mem:* Coll Art Asn; Am Asn State & Local Hist; Furniture Hist Soc; Am Asn Mus; Int Coun Mus; Metrop Mus Art (chmn coun). *Collection:* American art. *Publ:* Coauth, Thomas Jeckyll: Architect and Designer, Yale Univ Press, 2003; co-ed, The Castellani and Italian Archaeological Jewelry, Yale Univ Press, 2004; contribr, Georg Jensen Jewelry, Yale Univ Press, 2005; ed & contribr, James Athenian Stuart, Yale Univ Press, 2006. *Mailing Add:* Bard Graduate Center 18 W 86th St New York NY 10024

WEBER, SUZANNE OSTERWEIL
PAINTER
b Brooklyn, NY, June 22, 1940. *Study:* Pratt Inst, BS, 61, MFA, 64, with Richard Lindner, Jacob Landau, Fritz Eichenberg, Federico Castellon & Philip Pearlstein; Pratt Graphic Ctr, with Vasilios Toulis; NY Univ, with Lawrence Alloway; MS, Pace Univ. *Work:* US Info Agency (prints); Nat Art Mus Sport. *Comn:* Loral Corp, comn by Bernard Schwartz, NY, 75; Cent Rigging Corp, comn by Monroe Myerson, NY, 77; US Info Agency, Washington, DC, 78; portraits, comn by Dr Brian Torpey, Dr David Chalnick, Mr Spyros Niarchos; poster, Many Faces of Women, Monmouth Med Ctr; regular portrait comns since 98; Carolynn Ozon-Diakon, Resource Real Estate, Rumson, NJ. *Exhib:* Wagner Coll Gallery, Staten Island, NY, 92; Thompkins Park Visitors Ctr Gallery, Lincroft, 95; Monmouth Festival of the Arts, Tinton Falls, NJ, 95-; Owl 57 Gallery, Woodmere, NY, 95-; Art Forms Gallery, Red bank, NJ 2002-; Renée Fossmer Gallery, Millburn, NJ, 2003; Blue Bay Inn, Atlantic Highlands, NJ; Cooper Rehab & Sports, Middletown, NJ. *Pos:* Graphics juror, Nat Asn Women Artists, 68-; bd trustees, Nat Art Mus Sport; interviewer, Bennington Rev; juror, Pratt Inst Student Exhib. *Teaching:* Instr painting, Brooklyn Mus, NY (formerly); asst prin art, High Sch Art & Design, NY, 79-90; principal, Port Richmond High Sch, Staten Island, NY, 90-94 & Monmouth Regional High Sch, Tinton Falls, NJ, 94-98. *Awards:* Janet E Turner Prize, 74 & Dorothy Seligson Prize, 80, Nat Asn Women Artists; Leadership in Art Educ, NYCATA/UFT, 85; Fac Appreciation Award, HS of Art & Design, 90, Port Richmond HS, 94. *Bibliog:* 74-40 Jersey Mag, profile, Monmouth Co, 2011. *Media:* Acrylics on Canvas. *Interests:* photography, reading, writing. *Publ:* Contrib, Robert Henke (auth), Sport in Art, Prentice Hall & Statue of Liberty, Bernard A Weisberger (auth), Am Heritage; Sports in Am Art, Allen Guttman Amherst Univ Press, 2010. *Mailing Add:* 39 Stonehenge Dr Ocean NJ 07712

WEBSTER, MEG
SCULPTOR, PAINTER
b San Francisco, Calif, 1944. *Study:* Old Dominion Univ, Norfolk, Va, BFA, 1976; Yale Univ, New Haven, Conn, MFA, 1983. *Work:* Dallas Mus Art, Tex; Denver Art Mus, Colo; Rubell Family Collection, Miami; Solomon R Guggenheim Mus, New York. *Exhib:* Solo exhibs include Leavenworth St, San Francisco, 1980, Donald Judd's Exhib Space, NY City, 1983, Forecast Gallery, Peekskill, NY, 1986, 1987, Art Galaxy, NY City, 1986, Barbara Gladstone Gallery, NY City, 1988, 1990, Milwaukee Art Mus, 1990, Carnegie Mus Art, Pittsburgh, Pa, 1991, Contemp Arts Mus, Houston, 1992, Grand Salon, NY City, 1993, Hiram Butler Gallery, Houston, 1996, Morris-Healy Gallery, NY City, 1997, PS1 Contemp Arts Ctr, 1998, Thomas Healy Gallery, NY City, 1998, Paula Cooper Gallery, NY City, 2000, 2008, Meg Webster, Ark Art Ctr, Little Rock, Ark, 2009, Devor Borden hiram Butler Gallery, Houston, Tex, 2010, Paula Cooper Gallery New York, 2010, Hudson River Park, New York, 2010; group exhibs include Mus Fine Art, Roslyn Harbor, NY, 1984; Cable Gallery, NY City, 1986; Paula Cooper Gallery, NY City, 1987; Walker Art Ctr, Minneapolis, 1988; Inst Contemp Boston, 1988; Mus Fine Arts, Boston, 1988; Whitney Mus Am Art, NY City, 1989; Andrea Rosen Gallery, 1990; Barbara Gladstone Gallery, NY City, 1991; Solomon R Guggenheim Mus, NY City, 1992, 1994, 1995; Phillips Collection, Wash, DC, 1993; Denver Art Mus, 1994; Grand Salon, NY City, 1995; Hiram Butler Gallery, Houston, 1996; Barbara Krakow Gallery, Boston, 1997; Tricia Collins Grand Salon, NY City, 1998; Aspen Art Mus, 1999; Matthew Marks Gallery, 2000; Centro de Arte de Salamanca, 2001; Am Ctr for Wine Food & The Arts, Napa, Calif, 2003; Queens Mus Art, 2005; Andrew Kreps Gallery, 2006; Rhonda Hoffman Gallery, Chicago, 2008; The Hague Sculpture Center, Hague, Netherlands, 2008; Paula Cooper Gallery, New York, 2009; A Shot in the Dark, Walker Art Ctr, Minneapolis, Minn, 2010. *Media:* Copper, Steel, Wood, Mixed Media. *Dealer:* Paula Cooper Gallery 534 W 21st St New York, NY 10011. *Mailing Add:* c/o Paula Cooper Gallery 534 W 21st St New York NY 10011

WEBSTER, SALLY (SARA) B
HISTORIAN
b Hammond, Ind, May 24, 1938. *Study:* Barnard Col, BA, 59; Harvard-Radcliffe Prog in Business Admin, cert, 60; Univ Cincinnati, MA, 74; Grad Ctr, City Univ New York, PhD (Am art), 85. *Pos:* Dir educ, Taft Mus, Cincinnati, Ohio, 74-75; dir, AIR Gallery, NY, 79-81; partner, Rose Web Proj, NY. *Teaching:* Instr hist art, Col Staten Island, fall 83; instr hist art, Lehman Col, 83-85, asst prof, 85-90, assoc prof, 90-95, prof, 95-; fac, Grad Ctr, City Univ NY, 94. *Mem:* Heresies Collective, NY; Coll Art Asn; Arch Am Art; Asn Hist Am Art. *Publ:* Joyce Kozloft: Public decoration, Art America, 2/87; William Morris Hunt, Cambridge Univ Press, 91; co-ed, Critical Issues in Public Art: Content, Context and Controversy, Harper Collins, 92; Public Art in the Bronx, Lehman Coll Art Gallery, 93; Mary Cassatt & Mary Fairchild MacMonnies: The Search for Their Woman Building Murals, Am Art, Spring 94

WECHSLER, JUDITH GLATZER
ART HISTORIAN, FILMMAKER
b Chicago, Ill, Dec 28, 1940. *Study:* Brandeis Univ, BA, 62; Columbia Univ, MA, 67; Univ Calif, Los Angeles, PhD, 72. *Work:* Film, Daumier, Paris and the Spectator (with Charles Eames), 77, Pissarro, at the Heart of Impressionism, 81, Edouard Manet: Painter of Modern Life, 83, Cézanne: The Late Work, 78 (with Charles Eames), The Training of Painters, 87, Portraits, 88, The Arrested Moment, 88, Painting and the Public, 88, Abstraction, 89, Jasper Johns: Take an Object (with Hans Namuth), 90, Aaron Siskind,91, Harry Callahan, 93, Flora Natapof, 99 ; Rachel of the Comédie, Francaise, 2003; Nahum Glatzer and the German-Jewish Tradition, 2011. *Comn:* Titian: Venus & Adonis, Getty Mus, 94; Drawing: The Thinking Hand, Louvre, 96; Image and Enterprise: The Photography of Adolph Braun, RI Sch Design Mus, 98; Honoré Daumier, One Must be of One's Time, Reunion des Musees Nationaux, 99; Monet's Water Lillies, Vision & Design, 2007; Courbet, A Dream of the Modern, 2010. *Exhib:* Robert Moskowitz (cataloged), Mass Inst Technol Hayden Gallery, 71; Daumier: Parisian Types, Brandeis Univ, 79; Rachel, Une vie pour le théâtre, Mus d'art et d'hist du judaisme, Paris, 2004. *Pos:* Asst ed, Schocken Bks Inc, NY, 63-65; consult, off of Charles and Ray Eames, Venice, Calif, 76-78; res fel, Ctr for Advanced Visual Studies, Mass Inst Technol, 77-79. *Teaching:* asst prof, MIT, 70-78; Lectr, Harvard Univ, 81-82; from assoc prof to prof, RI Sch Design, 81-89; vis prof, Harvard Univ, spring 89; chmn, dept art & art hist, 90-95, NEH prof, Tufts Univ, 89-2010, prof emer, 2011-; vis prof, Hebrew Univ, Jerusalem, 94, 96, 2008; vis prof, Univ Paris, 98; vis prof, Ecole Normale Superieure, Paris, 2003. *Awards:* Nat Endowment for Humanities fel grants, 73, 75, 81, 83-84, 84-85, 85-86, 87-89 & 88-90; Nat Endowment for the Arts, 81, 87-89; Cine Golden Eagle Award for Manet Film, 84 & The Artist and the Nude, 85, The Arrested Moment, 89, and Portraits, 88; Am Film

Festival Red Ribbon Award for Portraits, 89; Chevalier de l'ordre des arts et des Lettres, 2007; Am Acad in Berlin fellow, 2010; Miller Reel award, 2011; Bugliasco fellowship, 2012; senior fellow, Van Leer Found, 2012. *Mem:* Coll Art Asn; 19th French Art Hist Asn; Int Coun Mus; SCAM. *Res:* 19th and 20th century art; Film; Video. *Publ:* Ed introd, Cézanne in Perspective, Prentice-Hall Inc, 75; auth, Gyorgy Kepes, 78, MIT Press & ed introd, On Aesthetics in Science, 78, Mass Inst Technol Press; The Interpretation of Cézanne, UMI res Press, 81; A Human Comedy: Physiognomy and Caricature in 19th Century Paris, Thames & Hudson Ltd, Univ Chicago Press, 82; Les Cabinets des Dessins, Daumier, Flammarion, 99; articles in Daedalus, Art Bulletin, Aperture, Artforum, Art J, Art News, Gazette des Beaux Arts & Studies in Visual Communications. *Mailing Add:* 993 Memorial Dr Cambridge MA 02138

WECHSLER, SUSAN
EDITOR, WRITER

b Neptune, NJ, Sept 15, 1943. *Study:* Douglass Col, Rutgers Univ, BA, 65; Teachers Col, Columbia Univ. *Exhib:* Marietta Crafts Nat, 75; solo exhib, Queens Mus, NY, 76; Women Artists: Clay, Fiber and Metal, Bronx Mus, 78 & traveling. *Collection Arranged:* Is Anybody Home? (auth, catalog), Esther Saks Gallery, Chicago, Ill, 85; The Raw Edge: Ceramics of the 80's (auth, catalog), Hillwood Art Gallery, CW Post College, Greenvale, NY. *Pos:* Photo ed, 66-; writer, 77-. *Teaching:* Instr ceramic hist, Cooper Hewitt Mus/Parsons Sch Design, New York, 85-86, thesis adv, 86-87; critic-in-residence, Sch Art, Univ Tasmania, Australia, 85; vis fac, Banff Centre Sch Fine Arts, Alta, Can, 86. *Awards:* Artpark Fel, Nat Heritage Trust, 77; Nat Endowment Arts Award, 81. *Bibliog:* Mikail Zakin (auth), New York clay, Craft Horizons, 76; Elisabeth Woody (auth), Hand Building Ceramic Forms, Farrar Straus, 78; Elaine Levin (auth), A History of American Ceramics, Abrams, 88. *Mem:* Int Asn Art Critics. *Res:* Contemporary & historical ceramics; design; photography. *Publ:* Auth, Low-Fire Ceramics: A New Direction in American Clay, Watson-Guptill, 81; Views on the figure, Am Ceramics, Vol 3, No 1, 84; New breed, Am Craft, 10-11/84; The new American ceramics, ID, 5/85; Power over the clay: American Studio Potters, Detroit Inst Arts, 89. *Mailing Add:* 420 W End Ave New York NY 10024

WEDDING, WALTER JOSEPH
CERAMIST, EDUCATOR

b Saginaw, Mich, Feb 17, 1952. *Study:* Arrowmount Sch Crafts, 69; Art Inst Chicago, 72; Mich State Univ, BFA, 76, MFA, 79. *Work:* Kresge Art Ctr, East Lansing; Mich Mus Asn, Detroit. *Comn:* Commemorative Pieces, Planters Bank, Salina, Kans, 82; Raku wall mural, City of Salina, Kans, 83. *Exhib:* Mid- Mich Arts, Midland Art Ctr, 79; Kansas Artists, Governor's Mansion, Topeka, 81. *Pos:* Coordr photog, Salina Arts Comn, Kans, 85. *Teaching:* Instr clay, Mich State Univ, East Lansing, 79-80; asst prof photog, Marymount Col, Kans, 80-86. *Mem:* Coll Art Asn; Nat Asn Ceramic Educ. *Media:* Clay. *Mailing Add:* 9130 NW Benson Ct Portland OR 97229

WEEDMAN, KENNETH RUSSELL
PAINTER, SCULPTOR

b Little Rock, Ark, Sept 26, 1939. *Study:* Memphis Acad Art; Univ Tulsa, BA & MA. *Work:* Cincinnati Mus Art, Ohio; Masur Mus Art, Monroe, La; Ark Art Ctr, Little Rock; Gilkey Ctr, Portland Art Mus, Ore; Mus de Arte Contemporanea Int, Salvador, Brazil; Internacional De Gravure Arte, Cabo Frio, Brazil. *Exhib:* Solo exhibs, Bienville Gallery, New Orleans, 71, Art & Drama Ctr Galleries, Baldwin-Wallace Coll, 73, Maryville Coll, Tenn, 98 & Gallery BAI, New York, 96, Janice Mason Art Mus, Cadiz, Ky, 2010, Fawick Galleries, Berea, Oh, 2013; Group exhibs, Prints: Made in Kentucky, Louisville Art Gallery, 83; Cabo Frio Int Print Biennial, Brazil, 85-86; Papelarte Int, Brazil, 86; Showcase '87, Water Tower Gallery, Louisville, Ky, 87; OIA Salon, NY, 94; Cumberland Coll Gallery, 2003; Mini Print Int, Cadaques, Spain, 2012; Jane Moore Gallery, Frankfort, Ky, 2013. *Pos:* Ed, Sculpture Quart, Southern Asn Sculptures, 74-75; cur, Cumberland Coll, 81-2003. *Teaching:* Instr sculpture, Sul Ross State Coll, Alpine, Tex, 65-66; prof sculpture, Cumberland Coll, Williamsburg, Ky, 68-2003; vis artist, Nicholls State Univ, Thiobodaux, La, 70-71. *Awards:* Award of Merit for Sculpture, Univ Tulsa, 64 & Nebr Wesleyan Univ, 66; Andrew Mellon Found Grant, 98; Lilly Found Grant, 89. *Bibliog:* Harold Cole, Kenneth Weedman, Baldwin-Wallace Coll, 73; Les Kantz (ed), Am Artists, Kantz Publ, 85; Miyako Yoshinaga (auth), Nikkei Art, Kenneth Weedman, 8/96; Vivien Raynor (auth), Kenneth Weedman, Gallery BAI, 96; James McCormick (auth), Dialogue, Kenneth Weedman, 5-6/97; Donald E Smith (auth), American Printmakers of the 20th Century, St Johann Press, 2004. *Mem:* Bluegrass Printmakers Coop. *Media:* Plastic, Steel; Acrylic, Oil. *Publ:* Contribr, Sculpture Quart, 74 & 75; Dialogue, 7-8/88. *Dealer:* Bluegrass Printmakers Lexington Ky. *Mailing Add:* 81 Man O' War Tr Corbin KY 40701

WEEGE, WILLIAM
PRINTMAKER, EDUCATOR

b Milwaukee, Wis. *Study:* Univ Wis-Milwaukee; Univ Wis-Madison, MA, 67, MFA, 68. *Work:* Akron Art Inst; Brooklyn Mus; Art Inst Chicago; Frankfurt Libr, Ger; Mus Mod Art, NY; plus many others. *Exhib:* Mechanics in Printmaking, 70 & Artist as Adversary, 70, Mus Mod Art, NY; Large Print Show, Whitney Mus Am Art, NY, 71; Works on Paper, Alice Simsar Gallery, Ann Arbor, Mich, 79, Inst for Experimental Printmaking, San Francisco, 79 & Circle Campus, Chicago, 79; Artrain, Mich Arts Coun, 79; Jones Road Print Shop, Univ of Mich, Kalamazoo, Mich, 79; Paper as Medium, Smithsonian Inst, 79-80; and many others. *Teaching:* From instr lettering to assoc prof art, Univ Wis-Madison, 67-80. *Bibliog:* Article, Arts, 1/78; article, Art News, 2/78. *Mailing Add:* 7046 Reiman Rd Arena WI 53503

WEEMS, CARRIE MAE
PHOTOGRAPHER

b Portland Ore, 1953. *Study:* Calif Inst Arts, Valencia, BA, 1981; Univ Calif, San Diego, MFA, 1984; Univ Calif, Berkeley, Grad Prog Folklore, 1984-87. *Exhib:* Solo shows incl Inst Contemp Art, 1991, Matrix Gallery, Wadsworth Atheneum, Hartford, Conn, 1991, Mus Mod Art, NY, 1995, J Paul Getty Mus Art, Malibu, Calif, 1995, Contemp Arts Mus, Houston, 1996, Whitney Mus Am Art, Philip Morris, NY, 1997, Va Mus Fine Arts, 1997, Rhona Hoffman Gallery, Chicago, 1999, Santa Barbara Mus Art, 1999, Williams Coll Mus Art, Williamstown, Mass, 2000-2002, Zora Neale Hurston Nat Mus Fine Arts, Etonville, Fla, 2001, Parrish Art Mus, Southampton, NY, 2001, Palmer Mus Art, Univ Park, Pa, 2002, SC State Univ, Orangeburg, 2002, Sheppard Fine Arts Gallery, Reno, Nev, 2002, Asheville Art Mus, 2003, Susanne Hilberry Gallery, Ferndale, Mich, 2004, Checkerboard Found, New York, 2005, Contemp Art Ctr of Va, 2006, Hampton Proj, Williams Coll Mus of Art, 2007, Hartnett Gallery, Univ of Rochester, 2007, Jack Shainman Gallery, New York, 2008, 2010, Galerie Pfriem, 2008, Red Gallery, 2008, Art Inst Chgo, Ill, 2011, Williams Coll Mus Art & Downstreet Art at the Lecacy, Legacy Gallery, North Adams, Mass, 2011, McNay Art Mus, San Antonio, Tex, 2012; group shows incl Inclusion/Exclusion, Steirischer Herbst, Graz, Austria, 1996; Nat Gallery Can, Calgary, 1999; Tretyakov Gallery, Moscow, 2000; UCLA Hammer Mus, 2001; Studio Mus in Harlem, NY, 2001; Jan Weiner Gallery, Kansas City, Mo, 2002; Tang Mus, Skidmore Col, Saratoga, NY, 2002; Mus Contemp Art, Chicago, 2003; Whitney Mus Am Art, New York, 2003; Beyond Compare: Women Photographers on Beauty, touring exhib, 2004; Perspectives at 25: A Quarter Century of New Art in Houston, Contemp Arts Mus, Houston, 2005; Common Ground: Discovering Community in 150 Years of Art, Corcoran Gallery, Washington, 2005; African Queen, The Studio Mus in Harlem, New York, 2005; Black Panther Rank & File, Yerba Buena Ctr for the Arts, San Francisco, 2006; Out of Time: A Contemp View, Mus of Mod Art, New York, 2006; Photography & the Self: The Legacy of F Holland Day, Whitney Mus of Am Art, New York, 2007; Black Womanhood, The Hood Mus, Hanover, NH, 2008; Bronx Mus Arts, NY, 2008, MoMA, NY, 2008, DePaul U, Chgo, Ill, 2009, Tate Liverpool, 2010, Edward Steichen Photography Galleries, MoMA, 2011, Irish Mus Modern Art, Dublin, Ire, 2012, Lyman Allyn Art Mus, Conn, 2013, Brown Found Gallery, Contemporary Arts Mus Houston, 2013, Memphis Brooks Mus, Tenn, 2013; retrospectives include Carrie Mae Weems: 3 Decades of Photography and Video, Frist Ctr Visual Arts, Nashville, 2012-2013. *Teaching:* San Diego City Coll, Calif, 1984; asst prof, Hampshire Coll, Amherst, Mass, 1987-91, Calif Coll Arts & Crafts, Oakland, 1991; vis prof, Hunter Coll, NY, 1988-89, Williams Coll, Williamstown, Mass, 2000, Harvard Univ, Cambridge, Mass, 2001; artist in res, Vis Studies Workshop, Rochester, NY, 1986, RI Sch Design, 1990, Art Inst Chicago, 1990, Atlantic Ctr for the Arts, New Smyrna, Fla, 2001, Wellesley Coll, Mass, 2001, Western Wash Univ, Bellingham, 2001. *Awards:* Engelhard Grant, 1990; Nat Endowment for the Arts Vis Arts Grant, 1994; Alpert Award for Vis Arts, 1996; Skowhegan Medal for Photography, 2008; Named a MacArthur Fellow, John D & Catherine MacArthur Found, 2013. *Bibliog:* Berta Sichel (auth), Carrie Mae Weems retrata a diáspora negra, Terra-Feira, Sao Paulo, Brazil, 1996; Grady T Turner (auth), rev, Art Am, 6/1996; Diane Neumaier (auth), Reframings: New American Feminist Photographies, Temple Univ Press, Philadelphia, 1996; and others. *Mem:* Women in Photog Int. *Mailing Add:* Jack Shainman Gallery 513 W 20th St New York NY 10011

WEERASETHAKUL, APICHATPONG
FILMMAKER

b Bangkok, Thailand, July 16, 1970. *Study:* Khon Kaen Univ, Thailand, BA (Architecture), 1994; Sch Art Inst Chicago, MA (Fine Arts in Film-making), 1997. *Work:* Carnegie Mus Art, Pittsburgh. *Exhib:* Films include Bullet, 1993, Kitchen & Bedroom, 1994, 0016643225059, 1994, Like the Relentless Fury of the Pounding Waves, 1996, Thirdworld, 1998, Malee & the Boy, 1999, Boys at Noon, 2000, Mysterious Object at Noon, 2000, Masumi is a PC Operator, 2001, Once Upon a Time, 2001, I-San Special, 2002, Blissfully Yours, 2002, Independence, 2002, Tropical Malady, 2004, Worldly Desires, 2005, Ghost of Asia, 2005, Syndromes and a Century, 2006, Luminous People, 2007; Solo exhibs include Beursschouwburg, Brussels, 2007, Replicas SCAI Bathhouse, Tokyo, 2008; group exhibs include Tirana Biennale, 2001; Alien generation, Art Ctr, Chulalongkorn Univ, Bangkok, 2002; Busan Biennale, 2004; Slow Rushes, Artspace, Auckland, New Zealand, 2005; Grey Flags, Sculpture Ctr, Long Island, NY, 2006; Drapeaux gris, Mus d'art contemp, Bordeaux, France, 2006; KunstFilmBiennale, Kunstmuseum Bonn, Germany, 2007; Comunismo da Forma, Galeria Vermelho, São Paulo, Brazil, 2007. *Pos:* Co-founder, Kick the Machine: Moving Image Studio, Bangkok, 1999-; juror, Cannes Film Festival, France, 2008. *Awards:* Silpatorn visual art award, Thai Ministry of Culture, 2005; Fine Prize, Carnegie Mus Art, 2008. *Dealer:* SCAI the Bathhouse Kashiwayu-Ato 6-1-23 Yanaka Taito-ku 110-0001 Tokyo Japan. *Mailing Add:* Kick the Machine Films Co Ltd 44/17 Ladprao Soi 15 Bangkok 10900 Thailand

WEGLARZ, LORRAINE D
INSTALLATION SCULPTOR, ENVIRONMENTAL ARTIST

Study: Wayne State Univ, Detroit, Mich, BA; San Francisco Art Inst, BFA. *Comn:* Addison St Windows, City of Berkeley Civic Arts Comn, 1993. *Exhib:* solo exhibs, Berekley Art Ctr, 1994 & Southern Exposure Gallery, Theater Artaud, 1997; San Jose Inst Contemp Art, 1994; Wiseman Gallery, Rogue Community Coll, Ore, 1995; Chavez Gallery, San Francisco State Univ, 1999; Cent Mich Univ Art Gallery, Mt Pleasant, 2000; Falkirk Cult Ctr, San Rafael, Calif, 2001; 1,000 Drawings Benefit, Artists Space, New York, 2007; Islip Art Mus, NY, 2008. *Awards:* Marin Co Arts Coun Grant, 1994, 2000; Pollock-Krasner Found Grant, 2000, 2008

WEGMAN, WILLIAM
PAINTER, PHOTOGRAPHER

b Holyoke, Mass, Dec 2, 1943. *Study:* Mass Coll Art, Boston, BFA, 1965; Univ Ill, Urbana-Champaign, MFA, 1967. *Work:* Brooklyn Mus, Mus Mod Art, Whitney Mus Am Art, Chrysler Mus, NY; Mus Mod Art, Paris; Los Angeles Co Mus Art; Int Mus Photog, Rochester, NY; Honolulu Acad Arts; Albright-Knox Gallery, Buffalo; Carnegie Inst, Mus Art, Pittsburgh; Corcoran Gallery Art, Washington, DC; Minneapolis Inst Art, Walker Art Ctr, Minneapolis; Mus Fine Art, De Meril Collection, Houston; Newport Harbor Mus, San Francisco Mus Mod Art, Stewart Collection, Univ Calif, San Diego, Calif; St Louis Mus Mod Art; and others. *Comn:* Semi-buffet color video tape, WGBH, Boston, 1974-75; video tape rev, Channel 13,

WNET, NY, 1975. *Exhib:* Solo exhibs, Honolulu Acad Arts, 1987, McIntosh/Drysdale Gallery, Washington, DC, 1987, Solo Gallery, NY 1988, San Francisco Mus Mod Art, 1988, Galerie Durand-Dessert, Paris, 1989, Neuberger Mus, State Univ NY, 1991, Galerie Andreas Binder, Munich, 1992, Mus Mod Art, NY, 1993, The Art Embodied, Musee de Marseilles, France, 1996 & Isetan Mus Art, Tokyo, 1997, Strange But True, Mass Coll Art, Boston & Springfield Mus, Mass, 1998, SOMA Gallery, La Jolla, Calif, 1999, Return of the Weimaraner, ACC Gallery, Weimar, Ger, 1999, William Wegman, Durant-Dessert Gallery, Paris, France, 1999, William Wegman: Fashion Photographs, Birmingham Mus Art, Ala, 1999, The MacKinney Ave Contemp, Dallas, Tex, 1999, Miami Art Mus, Fla, 1999, William Wegman, Orange Co Mus Art, Newport Beach, Calif, 2000, Pillbury & Peters Gallery, Washington, DC, 2000, Grant Selwyn Fine Art, Calif, 2003, David Adamson Gallery, Wash DC, 2003, Sperone Westwater, NY, 2003, Pace-Macgaill Gallery, NY, 2003, Imago Galleries, Calif, 2007, many others; Group exhibs, Animal Farm, James Corcoran Gallery Art, Santa Monica, Calif, 1994; Reconsidering the Object of Art: 1965-1975 (with catalogue), Los Angeles, Calif, 1995; A Century of Projection and More, Cinematheque Quebecoise, Montreal, Can, 1997; The Am Century, 1950-2000, The Whitney Mus Am Art, NY, 1999; PS 1, Long Island City, NY, 2003; The RISD Mus, 2003; Andrea Rosen Gallery, New York, 2005; Contemp Art Mus, St Louis, 2006. *Teaching:* Univ Wis, 1968-70; Cal State Univ, Long Beach, 1970. *Awards:* Guggenheim Fel, 1975 & 86; Nat Endowment Arts Grant, 1975-76 & 1982; Creative Artists Pub Serv, 1979; NY Found for the Arts Hon, 1999; Bailey House Key Hon, 1999. *Bibliog:* Christopher Knight (auth), William Wegman goes back to the future, Los Angeles Times, 4/11/1990; William Wegman, Pace Wildenstein MacGill, 1998; William Wegman: Fashion Photographs, Abrams, 1999. *Publ:* ABC, Hyperion, NY, 1994; What Do You Do?, Hyperion, 1999; Pups, Hyperion, 1999; The Night Before Christmas, Hyperion, 2000; Chip Wants a Dog, Hyperion, NY, 2003. *Dealer:* Holly Solomon Gallery 172 Mercer St New York NY 10012; Pace/MacGill Gallery 32 E 57th St New York NY 10022; Sperone Westwater Gallery 415 W 13 St New York NY 10014. *Mailing Add:* Adamson Gallery 1515 14th St NW Ste 202 Washington DC 20005

WEGNER, NADENE R
GOLDSMITH, CONSULTANT
b Sheboygan, Wis, Feb 18, 1950. *Study:* Univ Wis-Milwaukee, BFA, 72; Tyler Sch Art, Temple Univ, MFA, 75. *Work:* Tyler Sch Art, Temple Univ, Philadelphia, Pa; Kentucky Fried Chicken, Louisville, Ky. *Exhib:* Craftwork 76, Metrop Mus & Art Ctr, Miami, Fla, 76; Intent: Jewelry-Metal, Edinboro, Pa, 76; Women's Art Symp, Terre Haute, Ind, 77; Copper, Brass & Bronze Competition Tucson, Ariz, 77; Profiles of US Jewelry, Lubbock, Tex, 77; and others. *Teaching:* Asst prof metalsmithing & jewelry, Louisville Sch Art, Ky, 75-83; art dir, Bruce Fox, Inc, New Albany, Ind, currently. *Awards:* First Prize, Second & Third Nat Ring Show, Athens, Ga; Award, Copper II Exhib, 80. *Bibliog:* Metalsmithing USA, 75 & New York Metal, 76, Craft Horizons; Marcia Chamberlain (auth), Metal Jewelry Techniques, Watson-Guptill, 76. *Mem:* Am Crafts Coun; distinguished mem Soc NAm Goldsmiths. *Media:* Precious Metals, Precious Woods. *Mailing Add:* Bruce Fox Inc PO Box 89 New Albany IN 47150

WEIDA, DONNA LEE
PAINTER, PHOTOGRAPHER
b Logansport, Ind, Oct 29, 1939. *Study:* Calif Coast Univ, BS, 92. *Work:* Security Fed Savings Bank, Holiday Inn, Logansport, Ind; Bryant Products, Ixonia, Wis; Lewis Cass High Sch, Walton, Ind; Leading Edge Motor Sports, San Clemente, Calif. *Comn:* Portrait of Autumn, comn by David Smith, Springfield, Ill, 97; portrait of Emilee, comn by Deborah Delaplane, Logansport, Ind, 98; portrait of Torin, comn by Jill Jackson, Marco Island, Fla, 98; portrait of Christian, comn by Barb Mason, Springfield, Ill, 98; portrait of mother & child, comn by Deborah & Marla Spencer, Logansport, Ind, 98. *Exhib:* Niagara Frontier Nat Exhib, Kenan Ctr Gallery, Lockport, NY, 98; Aqueous '98, Actor's Theatre of Louisville, Ky, 98; Grand Exhib, Sheraton Suites, Cuyahoga Falls, Ohio, 98; Sixth Biennial NAm Open Show, Fed Reserve Bank of Boston, 98; Watercolor USA, Springfield Art Mus, 98; and others. *Awards:* Award of Excellence, Watercolor Soc Ind, 97; Edward Dupont Mem, La Watercolor Soc, 97; Merit Award, E Wash Watercolor Soc, 98; Outstanding Watercolor Award, Southside Art League, Greenwood, Ind, 2000. *Mem:* Hon life mem St Louis Watercolor Soc; Midwest Watercolor Soc; assoc mem Am Watercolor Soc; assoc mem Brown Co Art Guild; Ga Watercolor Soc; La Watercolor Soc; Watercolor Soc Ind. *Media:* Watercolor. *Specialty:* photography; investing; all arts. *Publ:* Best of Watercolor Series-People in Watercolor, Rockport Publ, Mass, 12/95; SPLASH 6, Northlight Books, 2000. *Dealer:* Hoosier Salon Gallery 6434 College Ave No C Indianapolis IN 46220; Reflections of the Heart-Tea Room 722 E Broadway Logansport IN 46947. *Mailing Add:* 625 Lakeview Dr Logansport IN 46947-2202

WEIDELL, CHARLEEN
METALSMITH, EDUCATOR, ADMINISTRATOR
Study: San Diego State Univ, MFA (Jewelry, Metalsmithing), 2002; Studied under renowned metal artists Helen Shirk and Arline Fisch. *Comn:* Ceremonial Medallion for President Roger Webb, Univ of Central Oklahoma. *Exhib:* Work in metal has been exhibited and collected on the international, national, and local levels. *Teaching:* With Univ Central Oklahoma, 2004-, chair art department, assoc prof jewelry & metalsmithing & head Jewelry/Metalsmithing program, currently. *Mailing Add:* The College of Fine Arts and Design University of Central Oklahoma 100 N University Dr Box 84 Edmond OK 73034

WEIDMAN, JEFFREY
LIBRARIAN, HISTORIAN
b New York, NY, Feb 17, 1945. *Study:* Hamilton Col, Clinton, NY, AB, 67; Ind Univ, Bloomington, with Albert Elsen & John Jacobus, MA (art hist), 69, with Louis Hawes, PhD (art hist, Samuel H Kress Fel), 82, MLS, 82. *Collection Arranged:* H P Lovecraft, Lilly Libr, Ind Univ, Bloomington, 82; William Rimmer: A Yankee Michelangelo (auth, catalog), Brockton Art Mus, Mass, 85-86; William Rimmer, Cleveland Mus Art & Brooklyn Mus, 86. *Pos:* Art librn, Clarence Ward Art Libr, Oberlin Col, Ohio, 83-97; assoc librn, Access Serv & Collection Develop, Spencer Art Reference Libr, Nelson-Atkins Mus Art, Mo, 98-2000, sr librn, 2000-2011. *Teaching:* Assoc instr art hist, Ind Univ, Bloomington, 68, 72-74 & 76; Art Dept, Oberlin Col, 93-96; adj prof art hist, UMO-KC, 2003-04. *Awards:* Gerd Muehsam Award, Art Libr Soc NAm, 83. *Bibliog:* Milo M Naeve (auth), A picture and sculpture by William Rimmer, Bull Art Inst Chicago, 77; Lewis Shepard (auth), American Art at Amherst, Wesleyan Univ Press, 78; Brockton's Artistic Heritage, Brockton Art Mus, 81. *Mem:* Art Libr Soc NAm; Asn Hist Am Art; Catalogue Raisonne Scholars Asn; Coll Art Asn. *Res:* Nineteenth century American art, especially the work of William Rimmer. *Interests:* Classical, Baroque, British and American eighteenth to twentieth century art, especially American painting and sculpture of the nineteenth century; art reference materials. *Publ:* Auth, Reclassification of the Hamilton College Portraits, Hamilton Col, 67; contribr, Seymour Lipton, Harry Abrams, 70; The Art Institute of Chicago Centennial Lectures, Contemp Bks, 83; (co-auth), William Rimmer: A Yankee Michelangelo, Univ Press New Eng, 85; Researching your art object, Personal Property J, 97-98. *Mailing Add:* Nelson-Atkins Mus Art Spencer Art Reference Libr 4525 Oak St Kansas City MO 64111

WEIDNER, MARILYN KEMP
CONSERVATOR, LECTURER
b Floral Park, NY, Jan 10, 1928. *Study:* Pratt Inst; Hofstra Univ, BA; Univ Pa; Metrop Mus Art; Freer Gallery Art. *Work:* Winterthur Mus, Wilmington. *Pos:* Asst registrar, Mus Mod Art, NY, 51-56; registrar, Brooklyn Mus, 56-58; conservator, pvt practice, Philadelphia, 60-79 & 84-2001; dir, Conserv Ctr Art & Hist Artifacts, Philadelphia, 77-84; adj conservator, Art Mus, Princeton Univ, 86-; chair, Conservators/Collections Care Network. *Teaching:* Adj prof conserv art on paper, NY State Univ, Cooperstown Grad Progs, 71-74; lectr, Univ Fine Arts & Music, Tokyo, Japan, Univ Del, Winterthur Mus & Am Inst Conserv Ann Meeting. *Awards:* Cert Conservator Hist & Artistic Works on Paper, 75; Rutherford John Gettens Merit Award, Am Inst Conserv, 90; Am Inst Conserv Univ Products Award Distinguished Achievement, 96. *Bibliog:* George W Cooke (auth), Marilyn Kemp Weidner pioneer paper conservator, Conserv Admin News, 7/92. *Mem:* Fel Int Inst Conserv Art & Hist Artifacts; Am Inst Conserv Art & Hist Artifacts (hon); Inst Paper Conserv, London; Mus Coun Philadelphia; Nat Inst Conserv Cult Property; Int Inst Conserv Art & Hist Artifacts (hon); Am Inst Conserv Art & Hist Artifacts (hon); Washington Conserv Guild (hon); The Ephrata Cloister, Ephrata, Pa. *Media:* Art on Paper. *Res:* Moisture Chamber/Suction Table System (patent) and related techniques for the conservation treatment of art on paper. *Publ:* Contribr, Damage and deterioration of art on paper, Studies in Conservation, Int Inst Conserv Art & Hist Artifacts, 67; Repair of Wall Charts from Cloister Edhrata, Pa Conserv & Restoration of Pictorial Art, Butterworth's, 76; Water Treatments and Their Uses with a Moisture Chamber on the Suction Table, Am Inst Conserv Arts & Hist Artifacts Preprints, 85; Conservation Management, Getty Conserv Inst, 88; Symposium 88, Conservation of Historic & Artistic Works on Paper, Can Conserv Inst, 94; auth, Roswell Theodore Weidner (1911-1999) Famed Artist of the Pine Barrens was Berks County native, Hist Soc of Berks Co, 27-31 Vol 7, No 1, 2004-2005. *Mailing Add:* 576 Brighton Way Phoenixville PA 19460-5718

WEIDNER, MARY ELIZABETH
PAINTER, EDUCATOR
b St Louis, Mo, June 10, 1950. *Study:* Sch Fine Arts, Washington Univ, St Louis, Mo, BFA (fel), 72, MFA, 75. *Work:* Papercraft Corp, F B Foster Corp & Carnegie-Mellon Univ, Pittsburgh. *Exhib:* Butler Inst Am Art, Youngstown, Ohio, 77, 79 & 80; William Penn Mem Mus, Harrisburg, Pa, 80; Broussard Mem Galleries, Baton Rouge, La, 80; Carnegie Inst Mus Art, Pittsburgh, 81; Coos Mus Art, Coos Bay, Ore, 81; Herman Fine Arts Ctr, Marietta, Ohio, 81; and many others. *Teaching:* Lectr, Grinnell Col, Iowa, 75-76; prof, Carnegie-Mellon Univ, Pittsburgh, 78-. *Bibliog:* The Art of Drawing, Purdue Univ, 79. *Mem:* Coll Art Asn; Women's Caucus Art; Assoc Artists Pittsburgh. *Media:* Oil, Colored Pencil. *Mailing Add:* Carnegie-Mellon Univ Sch Art Rm 312 5000 Forbes Ave Pittsburgh PA 15213

WEIL, MARIANNE
SCULPTOR
b Mt Kisco, NY, Aug 2, 1952. *Study:* Syracuse Univ, with Alan D'Arcangelo, 68; L'ecole des Beaux-Arts, Fontainebleau, France, 69; Goddard Col, BA, 74; Sch Visual Arts, MFA, 86. *Work:* Millhouse-Bundy Mus, Waitsfield, Vt; Commune di Pietrasanta "Mus dei Bozzetti", Pietrasanta, Italy. *Comn:* Bronze bust, comn by Frederick Ellwanger, Richmond, Va, 74; bronze sculpture, comn by Lawrence Lader, NY, 78; bronze sculpture, comn by Ed Weinberger, NY, 85 & 87; bronze sculpture, comn by Lenox Black, Philadelphia, Pa, 89 & 92; bronze sculpture, comn by Judy Woodard, NY, 91 & 96. *Exhib:* 12" x 12" x 12", Islip Art Mus, NY, 94; Goldstrom Gallery, NY, 97 & 98; Goodheart Fine Arts, Sag Harbor, NY, 98; solo exhib, Beatrice Conde Gallery, NY, 99; East End Arts Coun, Riverload, NY, 2000. *Pos:* artist-in-residence, US Dept Interior, Washington, 98. *Teaching:* Instr fine arts, Suffolk Community Col, NY, 90-; instr, Long Island Univ, CW Post, 93; prof sculpture, Univ Bridgeport, Conn, 94-95, State Univ NY, Stony Brook, 97-; vis prof, Haverford Col, 2006. *Awards:* Community Connection Grant, NYSCA, 2001; Individual Artist Grant, 2005-2006; Fundacion Valparaiso, Spain, 2007. *Bibliog:* Alistair Gordon (auth), Islip Mus, Newsday, 2/10/90; Helen Harrison (auth), NY Times, 9/96; Phyllis Braff (auth), NY Times, 4/19/98; Helen Harrison, NY Times, 6/4/00; Shari Narine, The Lethbridge Herald, 8/1/00; Cynthia Nadelman (auth), Sculpture Mag, 11/2004. *Mem:* Coll Art Asn; NY Artist Equity Asn; United Univ Prof. *Media:* Wax, Cast Bronze. *Res:* Sculpture. *Dealer:* Kouros Gallery 23 E 73rd St NYC; Arlene Bujese Gallery East Hampton NY. *Mailing Add:* PO Box 341 Orient NY 11957

WEIL, REX
CRITIC
Work: Art critic ARTnews. *Pos:* Dir, art program for handicapped children; instr Corcoran Col Art & Design, Wash. *Mailing Add:* ARTnews 48 W 38th St New York NY 10018

WEIL-GARRIS, KATHLEEN See Brandt, Kathleen Weil-Garris

WEILER, JOSEPH FLACK
PHOTOGRAPHER, WRITER
b Rockville Ctr, NY, 1943. *Study:* With Minor White, 65; Rochester Inst Technol, Sch Printing, AAS, 63, RIT Sch Photog, Syracuse Univ, BFA, 72. *Exhib:* Faces of Afghanistan, Berkshire Mus, Pittsfield, Mass, 81; 25-Year retrospective, Gordon Col, Wenham, Mass, 91. *Pos:* Dir, Flack Studio, Watertown, Mass, 68-. *Teaching:* Instr photog, NEng Sch Photog, Boston, Mass, 78 & Weiler Gallery, Gloucester, Mass, 92-. *Awards:* New Eng Book Show Award, Reprise, 75 & Encore, 76; First Place Award, 9th Open Photog, Salmagundi Club, 90. *Bibliog:* Photographer, Gloucester Times, 7/16/96; Faces of Afghanistan, Cambridge Chronicle, 12/26/2001. *Media:* Photographic Gelatin Silver Print. *Publ:* auth, Winslow Homer: Marine Painter, J Print World, 90; A Gift from Mr Alfred Stieglitz, J Print World, 91; Tarmarind Workshop at Thirty, J Print World, 91; The Tachach Press, J Print World, 92; Charles Sheeler: Photographer or Painter?, Jour Print World, 2003. *Dealer:* Weiler Gallery 77 Rocky Neck Ave East Gloucester MA 01930. *Mailing Add:* 288 Lexington St Watertown MA 02472

WEILER, MELODY M
ADMINISTRATOR, EDUCATOR
b Santa Monica, Calif, Mar 4, 1947. *Study:* State Univ NY, Buffalo, BFA; Ohio Univ, MFA; also with Harvey Breverman, Seymour Drumlevitch, Donald Roberts & Harvey Daniels; Kala Inst, Berkeley; Calif Coll Arts & Crafts, Oakland. *Work:* Ohio Univ, Athens; Kemper Gallery, Kansas City, Mo. *Comn:* Ceramic & screened mural, Ohio Univ, Athens, 70-71; cover design, Glass Eye Productions, Los Angeles, 76; posters, Hollins Col, Va & Murray State Univ, Ky, 76-77. *Exhib:* Western NY Art Exhib, Albright-Knox Art Gallery, Buffalo, 69; Nelson-Atkins Art Mus, Kansas City, Mo, 74; Huber Gallery, Washington, DC, 79; Lake Placid Sch Art, NY, 79; Imagery Gallery, Jacksonville, Fla, 79; Southeastern Ctr for Contemp Art, Winston-Salem, NC, 79; Appalachian Ctr for Crafts, Cookeville, Tenn, 80; and others. *Pos:* Pres-elect, Ky Arts Adminrs, 88-89, pres, 89-90; prog evaluator, Nat Asn Schs Art & Design, 92-. *Teaching:* Instr printmaking/design, Atlanta Sch of Art, Ga, 71-72; instr found design, Kansas City Art Inst, Mo, 72-73; asst prof printmaking, Murray State Univ, 75-78, assoc prof, 78-91; prof undergrad/grad sem, Tex Tech Univ, 91-. *Awards:* Res grant, Hand Papermaking, Murray State Univ, 76-77, 77-78, 90-91; Ky Arts Coun Grants, 77 & 78. *Mem:* Coll Art Asn; Nat Asn Schs Art & Design; Nat Coun Art Adminr (bd dir, 92-); Tex Asn Schs Art; Nat Art Educ Asn. *Media:* Papermaking; Serigraphy. *Publ:* Contribr, Exploring Printmaking for Young People, Van Nostrand Reinhold, 72; photogr, The Painted Vega, 75 & illusr, cover design, Southern Exposure, 76, Glass Eye Productions; contribr, Washingtonian Mag, 78 & Art Craft, 2-3/80. *Mailing Add:* Dept of Art Tex Tech Univ Box 42081 Lubbock TX 79409-2081

WEIMER, DAWN
SCULPTOR
b Denver, Colo, 1943. *Work:* Am Quarter Horse Mus, Amarillo, Tex; Westminster Munic Sculpture Garden, Colo; Fort Morgan Mus & Libr, Colo; Fort Collins Pub Libr, Colo; Colo State Univ, Fort Collins; Smithsonian Nat Mus Am History, Washington, DC, 2001. *Comn:* bronze sculpture, Colo State Univ, Fort Collins, 99, Loveland Good Samaritan, Colo, 2000, Shaner Hotel Group, Des Moines, Iowa, 2000 & Morgan Community Col, Fort Morgan, Colo, 2000, Univ of No Colo, 2004, The Ranch Larimer Co Fairgrounds and Event Ctr, 2004; sculpture, Mountain View High Sch, Loveland, Colo, 2000. *Exhib:* Am Artists Prof League, Salamagundi Club, NY, 93; Audubon Artists Exhib, Nat Arts Club, NY, 94; Catharine Lorillard Wolfe, Nat Arts Club, NY, 92-97; California Species, Oakland Mus, Calif, 97; Artists in Colorado, Colo Hist Mus, Denver, 97; two-person show, Old West Mus, Cheyenne, Wyo, 97; one-person show, Fort Morgan Mus, Colo, 98; Western Spirit Exhibit, Old West Mus, Cheyenne, Wyo, 95-2000. *Collection Arranged:* Map of 49 Public Installations. *Awards:* Leila Gardin Sawyer Award, Catharine Lorillard Wolfe Art Club, 92; Anna Hyatt Huntington Award, Am Artists Prof League, 93; Philip Isenberg Award, Pen & Brush Sculpture Show, 94. *Bibliog:* Judy L Stewart (auth), Caressing the bronze, Wildlife Art, 97; Coleman Cornilius (auth), Bronze ram stands proud, Denver Post, 8/17/99; Betty Harvey (auth), Gallery sect, Western Horseman, 12/99; Arlene Ahlbrandt (auth), Annie-The Railroad Dog, 1998; Karen Derrico (auth), Unforgettable Mutts, 1999; Ahlbrandt & Hagan (auths), Women to Remember, 2001; Art of the West Guidebook, 2001; Lonnie Pierson (ed), The Artists Bluebook, 2003; Arthur Williams (auth), The Sculpture Ref, 2005. *Mem:* Catharine Lorillard Wolfe Art Club; NSS; Women Artists of West; Nat Asn Women Artists; Nat Mus Women in Arts. *Media:* Bronze. *Interests:* Traditional, realistic animals. *Dealer:* Dawn Weimer Studios LLC Loveland CO. *Mailing Add:* 2727 Eldorado Springs Dr Loveland CO 80538-5321

WEINBAUM, JEAN
PAINTER, SCULPTOR
b Zurich, Switzerland, 1926. *Study:* Zurich Sch Fine Arts, 42-46; Acad Grande Chaumiere; Ecole Paul Colin; Acad Andre L'Hote, 47-48. *Work:* Mus Mod Art, Paris, France; Nat Collection Fine Arts, Washington; Univ Art Mus, Berkeley, Calif; Stanford Univ Mus, Calif; Calif Palace Legion Hon, San Francisco. *Comn:* Eleven stained glass windows, Chapelle de Mosloy, 51; rosette stained glass, Berne sur Oise, 55; 22 stained glass windows, St Pierre du Regard, 57; Wall of Light (monumental stained glass window), Escherange, 62; eight windows, Lycee de Jeunes Filles, Bayonne, France, 66. *Exhib:* Mus Mod Art, Paris, 62, 63 & 65; Solo exhibs, Galerie Smith-Andersen, Palo Alto, Calif, 70-73, 76 & 79, Calif Palace Legion Hon, 71, Mus Arts Decoratifs, Lausanne, Switz, 72, Bildungszentrum, Gelsenkirchen, Ger, 72 & San Francisco Mus Mod Art, 81; Michael Dunev Fine Arts, San Francisco, 86; Rado Int, Hong Kong, 87; Frank Bustamante Gallery, NY, 89; Fota Gallery, Old Town Alexandria, Va, 90 & 91; Alliance Francaise, San Francisco, 95; Kismet Gallery, San Jose, Calif, 96; Louvre Gallery, San Francisco, Calif, 2000; Rizzoli Gallery, San Francisco, Calif, 2000; Elizabeth Rice Fine Art, Sarasota, Fla, 2002 & 2003. *Awards:* Art Award, Inst for Aesthetic Develop, 87. *Bibliog:* Francois Mathey & others (auth), Vitrail Francais, In: Tendances Modernes, Ed Deux Mondes, Paris, 58; Robert Sowers (auth), Stained Glass: An Architectural Art, Universe Bks, New York, 65; Shuji Takashina (auth), Stained glass works by Jean Weinbaum, Space Design, Tokyo, 9/67. *Mem:* Mus of Modern Art Project Artaud. *Media:* Watercolor, Oil, Stained Glass, Mixed Media. *Dealer:* Elizabeth Rice Fine Art 1467 Main St Sarasota FL 34236

WEINBERG, ADAM D
MUSEUM DIRECTOR
b New York City, Dec 10, 1954. *Study:* Brandeis Univ, BA, 77; State Univ NY, Buffalo, MFA, 81. *Pos:* Dir educ, asst cur, Walker Art Ctr, Minneapolis, 81-88; dir equitable ctr, Whitney Mus Am Art, New York City, 88-90, sr cur permanent collection, 93-99, Alice Pratt Brown dir, 2003-; artistic & program dir, Am Ctr, Paris, 90-92; dir, Addison Gallery Am Art, Phillips Acad, Andover, MA, 99-2003; Alice Pratt Brown dir, bd trustees, Whitney Mus Am Art, 2003-. *Mem:* Am Asn Mus; Coll Art Asn. *Publ:* Auth, On the Line: The New Color Photojournalism, 86; Vanishing Presence, 89; Aldo Crommelynck: Master Prints with Am Artists, 89; Contingent Realms, 90. *Mailing Add:* Whitney Museum of American Art 945 Madison Ave New York NY 10021

WEINBERG, EPHRAIM
ADMINISTRATOR, PAINTER
b Philadelphia, Pa, Apr 28, 1938. *Study:* Philadelphia Coll Art; Univ Pa. *Exhib:* Philadelphia Coll Art; Moore Coll Art; Pa Acad Fine Arts; Philadelphia Mus Art; Westminster Coll; Cheltenham Art Ctr. *Pos:* Dean, Pa Acad Fine Arts, 77-82; dir, Schs, 82-84, Grand Rapids Art Mus, 84-86 & Nat Mus Am Jewish Hist, 86-88; pres, Art Sch & gallery mus consult, 88-. *Teaching:* Instr, Bournemouth Coll Art, Eng, 64-65, Bucks Co Coll, 67-68, Philadelphia Coll Art, 69-71 & Sch Art Inst Chicago, 71-77. *Awards:* Hon Fel, Nat Mus Am Jewish Hist. *Mem:* Cult Arts Found (chmn), Aventura; Urban Inst Contemp Art; Nat Asn Sch Art & Design (bd dir); Munic Arts Adv Comn, Grand Rapids (chmn); Abington Art Ctr, (bd mem, currently); and others; Art Ctr S Fla (vpres). *Publ:* Auth, Who teaches art, In: Art Educ: Junior High Sch, Nat Art Educ Asn, 73; co-auth, with Donald J Irving, The master of fine arts program, In: The Status of the Arts in Higher Education, Nat Coun Arts Adminr, 76; auth, Venerable institutions in an age of conservation, In: The Visual Arts in the Ninth Decade, Nat Coun Arts Adminr, 80; The school of the Pennsylvania Academy of the Fine Arts, Antiques, 3/81; School and Museum: The Pennsylvania Academy of the Fine Arts: A Case Study, Asn Art Mus Dirs, 82. *Mailing Add:* 19355 Turnberry Way Apt PHK Aventura FL 33180

WEINBERG, H BARBARA
CURATOR, EDUCATOR
b New York, NY. *Study:* Barnard Col, BA; Columbia Univ, MA, PhD (art hist, archeol). *Pos:* Alice Pratt Brown cur Am paintings & sculpture, Metrop Mus Art, NY. *Teaching:* Emer prof art hist, Queens Col, City Univ NY & Grad Sch. *Awards:* Lawrence A. Fleischman Award (Scholarly Excellence in Am Art Hist) Smithsonian Inst, 2007-. *Res:* Nineteenth century American painting. *Publ:* Auth, The Decorative Work of John La Farge, Garland, 77; The American Pupils of Jean-Leon Gerome, Amon Carter Mus, 84; The Lure of Paris: 19th Century American Painters & Their French Teachers, Abbeville, 91; (co-auth), American Impressionism & Realism: The Painting of Modern Life, 1885-1915, 94, Thomas Eakins and the Metropolitan Museum of Art, 94, Metrop Mus Art; (co-auth), Am Drawings and Watercolors in the Metrop Mus Art: John Singer Sargent, Met Mus Art, 2000; (co-auth), Am Impressionists Abroad and at Home, Am Fedn Arts, 2000; (co-auth), Child Hassam, Am Impressionist, Metrop Mus Art, 2004; Americans in Paris, 1860-1900, Nat Gallery, London, 2006; (co-auth), American Stories: Paintings of Everyday Life, 1765-1915, 2009. *Mailing Add:* Metropolitan Mus Art 1000 Fifth Ave New York NY 10028-0198

WEINBERG, JONATHAN EDMAN
PAINTER, HISTORIAN
b Passaic, NJ, Sept 10, 1957. *Study:* Yale Univ, BA, 78; Harvard Univ, PhD, 90. *Work:* Metrop Mus, NY; Montclair Art Mus, NJ; Jersey City, NJ. *Exhib:* 1980's: A New Generation, Metrop Mus Art, NY, 88; Divergenes, Montclair Art Mus, NJ, 90; Fun City, Jersey City Mus, NJ, 96; Still Life: The Object in Am Art, 1915-1955 (with catalog), Soc Four Arts, Palm Beach, Fla, 98; Later, Yale Univ Art Gallery, New Haven, Conn, 98; Alphabet, Nova Sch Fine Art, Vancouver, Can; Slifka Ctr, Yale Univ, 2007. *Pos:* fel, Vera List Ctr on Art & Politics, New School. *Teaching:* Assoc prof 20th century art, Yale Univ, 89-99. *Awards:* Guggenheim Mem Found, 2002. *Bibliog:* Vincent Scully (auth), Jonathan Weinberg, Cortland Jessup, 97; Robert Storr (auth), People: Recent Painting by Jonathan Weinberg, 2007. *Mem:* Coll Art Asn; Gay & Lesbian Caucus (co-chair, 95-96). *Media:* Oil on Canvas, Acrylic. *Res:* Gay & Lesbian studies, Stieglitz circle. *Publ:* Auth, Speaking for Vice: Homosexuality in the Art of Charles Demuth & Marsden Hartley & the First American Avant-Garde, Yale Univ, 93; Ambition & Love in American Art, Yale Univ Press, 2001; Male Desire: The Homoerotic in American Art, Abrams, 2005. *Mailing Add:* 251 Greene St New Haven CT 06511

WEINER, LAWRENCE CHARLES
SCULPTOR
b Bronx, NY, Feb 10, 42. *Work:* Mus Mod Art & Guggenheim Mus, NY; Vanabbe Mus, Eindhoven, Neth; Staatiches Mus Monchengladbach, Ger; Centre Georges Pompidou, Paris; Nat Gallery of Australia, Canberra; and others. *Comn:* Wexner Ctr, Columbus, Ohio; Pub Art Fund, NYC. *Exhib:* Solo exhibs, Hirshhorn Mus & Sculpture Garden, Washington, DC, 90, San Francisco Mus Mod Art, Calif, 92, Stadtische Galerie Chemnitz, Ger, 94, Philadelphia Mus Art, Pa, 94, Radio Dusseldorf, Ger, 94, Leo Castelli Gallery, NY, 94 & 95 & NY Pub Libr, 95, Marian Goodman Gallery, Paris, 2000, Kunstmus Wolfsburg, Ger, 2000-01, Mus Nat Ctr de Arte Reina Sofia, Madrid, 2001, Birmingham Mus Art, Ala, 2001-02, Galerie Roger Pailhas, Marseille, France, 2002, Wexner Ctr for the Arts, Columbus, 2002,

Synagogue Stommeln, Ger, 2003, Yvonne Lambert Gallery, Paris, 2003, The Wrong Gallery, 2004, Davis Mus Cult Ctr, 2004, Marian Goodman Gallery, NY, 2005, Regen Projects, LA, 2005, Whitney Mus Am Art, New York, 2007-08, In & Out of Amsterdam Mus of Mod Art, New York, 2009, Under the Sun, EACC, Castellon, Spain, 2009, Inclined Enough to Roll, Fondione Merz, Torino, Italy, 2009, Dicht Bu, Bak Utrecht, Netherlands, 2010, Taken from the Wind & Bulted to the Ground, House of Art, Budeveis, Czech Republic, 2010, A Syntax of Dependency, Mus Contemp Art Antwerp, 2011, & That was the Trouble with Aristotle, Festival du Peuple, Mairie du 2e Arrondissenment, Paris, 2011, Brought to Light, USA, Univ Calif, San Fran, 2011; group exhibs, Information, Mus Mod Art, NY, 70; Idea & Image in Recent Art, Art Inst Chicago, Ill, 74; Tate Gallery, London, Eng, 82; Mus Contemp Art, Los Angeles, Calif, 83; Fragments and Form: Conjunctions in the Permanent Collection, Mus Contemp Art, Los Angeles, 93; Rosebud, Kunstbau Lenbachhaus, Munich, 94-95; 10 Yrs Parkett 63 Artists' Editions, Peter Blum, NY, 94; For 25 Yrs-Brooke Alexander Editions, Mus Mod Art, NY, 94; The Tradition of the New: Postwar Masterpieces from the Guggenheim Collection, Guggenheim Mus, NY, 94; From Minimal to Conceptual Art: Works from the Dorothy and Herbert Vogel Collection, Nat Gallery Art, Washington, DC, 94; Visible Means of Support, Wadsworth Atheneum, 94; Installations: Selections from the Permanent Collection, Mus Contemp Art, Los Angeles, 94; Ars 95, Mus Contemp Art, Finnish Nat Gallery, Helsinki, 95; 1968 SMS, IC Editions Inc, NY, 95; Neuger Riemschneider, Berlin, 2000; Casino Luxembourg-Forum d'art Contemp, Luxembourg, 2000-2001; Northern Gallery for Contemp Art, Sunderland, Eng, 2001; Galeria André Viana, Porto, Port, 2001; Mus Contemp Art, LA, 2001; Mus d'Art Contemp, Bordeaux, France, 2002; New Sharjah Arat Mus, United Arab Emirates, 2002; Ctr de Arte de Salamanca, Spain, 2002-2003; Marian Goodman Gallery, New York City, 2003; Reykjavik Arts Festival, 2005; Venice Biennale, 2007; CAC, Malaga, Spain, 2008; Haunted: Contemp Photography/video/performance, Guggenheim Mus, New York, 2010; Mardin Biennial: Abboriakadabra, Turkey, 2010; Drawn, Taped, Burned: Abstraction on Paper, Kotonah Mus Art, Kotonah, 2011; 61st Berlin Int Film Festival, 2011; Observadores-Revelacoes, Transitos e Distancias, Lisbon, 2011. *Awards:* Nat Endowment Arts Fel, 76 & 83; Arthur Kopcke Prize, Copenhagen, Denmark, 91; John Simon Guggenheim Fel, 94; Skowhegan Medal for Painting/Conceptual Art, 99; Wolfgang Hahn Prize, Ludwig Mus, Cologne, Ger, 95; and others. *Dealer:* Marian Goodman Gallery New York NY. *Mailing Add:* 297 W Fourth New York NY 10014

WEINGARTEN, HILDE (KEVESS)
PAINTER, PRINTMAKER
b Berlin, Ger; US citizen. *Study:* Art Students League; Cooper Union Art Sch, with Morris Kantor, Robert Gwathmey & Will Barnet, cert, 47, BFA, 76; Pratt Graphics Ctr. *Work:* Brooklyn Mus; Herbert F Johnson Mus, Cornell Univ; Israel Mus, Jerusalem; NY Pub Libr Print Collection; Fogg Art Mus, Harvard Univ; and others. *Exhib:* Albright Art Gallery, Buffalo, 55; Dallas Mus of Fine Art, 56; Brooklyn Mus, NY, 58, 63, 71, 74, 76, 77 & 80; NY World's Fair, 65; Graphics 71 Print Exhib, Western NMex Univ, Silver City, 71; Audubon Artists, Nat Acad Design, NY, 71, 73, 75, 77-90; Palazzo Vecchio, Florence & Pompeiian Pavilion, Naples, Italy, 72; Pratt Graphics Ctr Ann, 72-79; plus many other group & six one-artist shows. *Awards:* Akston Found Prize, Nat Asn Women Artists, 80; Silver Medal Creative Graphics, Audubon Artists, 81; Doris Kreindler Memorial Award for Graphics, Am Soc Contemp Artists, 89; and many others. *Bibliog:* J L Collins (auth), Women Artists in America II & Contemporary Biography--Women, Vol I, Part II. *Mem:* Artists Equity Asn, NY (bd dir, 64-72, 90-92); Nat Asn Women Artists; Am Soc Contemp Artists (bd dir, 82-); Audubon Artists (bd dir, 85-87). *Media:* Oil, Acrylic; Etching, Collagraph. *Publ:* Illusr, Tune of the Calliope, 58; Collection of Poems by Aaron Kramer, Thomas Yoseloff Ltd; German folksongs, 68; 51 Songs, translated by Arthur Kevess, Oak Publ

WEINSTEIN, JOYCE
PAINTER
b New York, NY, June 7, 1931. *Study:* City Coll New York, 48-50; Art Students League, 48-50. *Work:* Mus Mod Art, NY; Pa Acad Fine Arts; Edmonton Art Gallery, Alta; NJ State Mus, Trenton; Weatherspoon Mus, Greensboro, NC; and many others. *Exhib:* Works on Paper, Women Artists, Brooklyn Mus, 75; New Abstract Art, Edmonton Art Gallery Mus, 83; New Acquisitions, Mus Mod Art, NY, 81; solo exhibs, Martin Gerard Gallery, Edmonton, Alta, 81-82, Gallerie Wentzel, Cologne, WGer, 82, Gallery One, Toronto, 83, 02, Haber Theodore Gallery, NY, 85, Flanders Contemp Art, Minneapolis, 99 & 2005, Harmon Meek Gallery, Naples, Fla, 2000, Ezair Gallery, New York, 2007, 2010, Hartwick Coll, Oreonta, NY, 2012; Meredith Long & Co Gallery, Houston, Tex & NY, 88 & 90; Alena Adlung Gallery, NY, 89; Spanierman Modern, NY, 2013; group exhibs Madelyn Jordon Fine Arts, Scarsdale, NY, 2014, Spanierman Modern, NY, 2014, Berry Campbell Gallery, NYC, 2015, Madelyn Jordon Fine Art, Scarsdale, 2015, At Wynwood, Booth of Berry Campbell Gallery, Art Fair Miami, 2015. *Awards:* Lambert Fund Award, Pa Acad Fine Arts, 53. *Bibliog:* Hilton Kramer-Review NY Times, 76; Grace Glueck (auth), article, New York Times, 12/14/79; Valentin Tatransky (auth), Joyce Weinstein at Haber Theodore Gallery, Arts Mag, 5/83; Nancy Tousley (auth), article, Calgary Herald, 5/85; Karen Wilkin (auth), rev, Partisan Rev, 2/90. *Mem:* Women Arts Found Inc (bd mem, 71-83, exec coordr, 78-82, exec bd mem, 83-90). *Media:* Oil & Mixed Media on Canvas, Monotypes. *Specialty:* paintings. *Dealer:* Flanders Contemporary Gallery Minneapolis MN; Gallery One Toronto Ont Can; Spanierman Modern NY; Ric Michel Fine Art NY. *Mailing Add:* 46 Fox Hill Rd Ancramdale NY 12503

WEINSTEIN, MARTIN
PAINTER
b New York, 1957. *Study:* Tayler Sch Art, NY, BFA, 1974. *Exhib:* Solo exhibs include List Gallery, Swarthmore Coll, Swarthmore, PA, 1994, MyungSook Lee Gallery, New York, 1996, Elliott Mus, Hutchinson Island, Stuart, Fla, 2003, Parthenon, Nashville, 2004, Anderson Fine Arts Ctr, Anderson, Ind, 2004, NY Hall Science, Queens NY, 2004, Wichita Art Mus, Wichita, Kans, 2005, 2006, Mus Southwest, Midland, Tex, 2005, Waterworks Visual Arts Ctr, Salisbury, NC, 2007, Gallery Henoch, New York, 2007; Group exhibs include Memory Images, Art in General, New York, 1987; To Enchant, Cynthia McCallister Gallery, Bixler Gallery, New York, 1994; The Small Painting, O'Hara Gallery, New York, 1995; Recollections & Reflections, MyungSook Lee Gallery, New York, 1997; Intimate Universe, Robert Steele Gallery, New York, 1997; Twelve Duets, Kouros Gallery, New York, 1999; Artists Choose Artists, Lake George Arts Proj, Lake George, NY, 2001; Travel, Gallery 100, Saratoga Springs, NY, 2002; Skies & Scapes, DFN Gallery, New York, 2004; 183rd Ann: Invitational Exhib Contemp Am Art, Nat Acad Mus, New York, 2008. *Mailing Add:* 80 White St 6th Floor New York NY 10013

WEINSTEIN, RAYMOND
ARTIST
b Alexandria, VA, Jan 6, 1920. *Study:* Pratt Inst - 1945-99; Educational Alliance Art Sch with Chaim Gross -1976-91. *Work:* Gallery One, New York City; Pace Coll, New York City; Educational Alliance, New York City. *Comn:* Sculptures, Michael Goodman, New York City, 2003. *Exhib:* Knickerbocker Artists, Nat Art Club, New York City, 1982; Audubon Artists, Salmagundi Club, New York City, 1989, 93, 94, 95; Den Invitational, Salmagundi Club, New York City; Ann Broome St Gallery Shows, Venezulean Embassay. *Pos:* master wood carver, Gallery One, NY; pres, Sculptors Alliance, 1989-1998; vpres ASCA. *Teaching:* asst instr wood sculp to Chaim Gross, Edu Alliance Art Sch, 1985-91. *Awards:* Alice McReynolds Award, 1990, Doris Kriendler Award, 2002, Leggieri Award, 2003, Salmagundi Club; and numerous other awards. *Bibliog:* Susan Josephs (auth), Model for Future, Jewish Week, 8/2/1996; Claude Leisuer (auth), Gallery One Artists, Art Speaks, 1/4/1994; Andrew Margolis (auth), Broome St Gallery, Manhattan Arts, 11/1999. *Mem:* Audubon Artists; Am Soc of Contemp Artists (dir 1998-); Sculptors Alliance (pres 1989-98). *Media:* Sculpture. *Interests:* Nature, travel, Italian & French art. *Collection:* Gallery One. NYC. *Mailing Add:* 453 FDR Dr Apt# 1805 New York NY 10002-5907

WEINSTOCK, ROSE
PAINTER
b New York, NY. *Study:* Wellesley Coll, BA; Nat Acad Design, with Harvey Dinnerstein; Queens Coll, with Charles Cajori; privately with Shirley Gorelick. *Work:* Larry Rivers Artist, D Porthault Inc, Clarion Partners, New York; Port Washington Pub Libr. *Exhib:* Solo exhibs, Recent Paintings, Art Upstairs Gallery, East Williston, NY, 87, Memories of Summer, Lakeside-Bloomfield Cult Ctr, NJ, 90, Archit Paintings, Pen & Brush Club, NY, 96, I Do Windows, Pen & Brush Club, 99, Windows, Mini/Maxi, Blue Mountain Gallery, New York, 2004, Mini Windows, Arts Club Washington, DC, 2001, Mini Windows Revisited, Interchurch Ctr, NY, 2002, Windows, a Retrospective, Port Washington Libr, NY, 2006, Loss & Memory, Blue Mountain Gallery, New York, 2007, Cloudscapes, Blue Mountain Gallery, New York, 2010, Additional Architectural Paintings, NY, 2013; Ann Long Island Exhib, Heckscher Mus, Huntington, NY, 85-87 & 90-93; 100 Yrs/100 Works, Traveling Exhib, India, 89; Longview Art Mus, Tex, 89; 171st Ann Exhib, Nat Acad Design, NY, 90 & 96; Queens Coll Art Ctr, Benjamin Rosenthal Libr, City Univ NY, 91; CW Post Coll, Brookville, NY, 93 & 98; Wellesley Coll, Mass, 93 & 98; State Univ NY, Stonybrook, 94; Traveling Painting Exhib, Sheldon Swope Mus Art, Terre Haute, Ind, Longview Art Mus, Texas, Greater Lafayette Mus Art, Ind, and others, 96-98; NJ Ctr Visual Arts; group exhibs, Fresh Paint, Flinn Gallery, Greenwich Libr, Conn, Made in the USA, Blue Hill Cult Ctr, Pearl River, NY, 2007; Art from New York, Gallerie Mani, Berlin, Germany, 2009; 30th Anniversary exhib, Blue Mountain Gallery, New York, 2010; Vernissage des Femmes Artistes, Armory Art Ctr, W Palm Beach, Fla, 2012. *Awards:* Gladys Serv Award, Heckscher Mus, 85 & 90; First Prize, Pindar Gallery, 87; Medal of Hon & Audrey Hope Shirk Mem Award, 91, Beatrice Jackson Mem Award, 95, Nat Asn Women Artists; Medal of Hon & Elizabeth Blake Stanton Blake Mem Awrd, Nat Asn Women Artists, May, NY, 2003; and others. *Bibliog:* Sean Simon (auth), Rose Weinstock: A realist master of light & shadow, Art Speak, 11/95; Steven Zevitas (ed), New American Paintings X, Open Studios Press, NY; Timothy Morrison (auth), The Poetry of Windows in the Paintings of Rose Weinstock, Gallery Studio, March/April, NY. *Mem:* Nat Asn Women Artists, NY; Audubon Artists, NY; Catharine Lorillard Wolfe Arts Club, NY; Artist's Equity, NY. *Media:* Oil, Pastel. *Dealer:* Blue Mountain Gallery 530 West 25th St 4th Fl New York New York 10001. *Mailing Add:* 35 E 75th St New York NY 10021

WEINTRAUB, ANNETTE
DIGITAL ARTIST, EDUCATOR
b New York, NY, July 2, 1946. *Study:* Cooper Union, BFA, 67; Univ Pa Grad Sch Fine Arts, MFA, 70. *Work:* Aldrich Mus Contemp Art, Ridgefield, Conn; Prudential Insurance Co; Cooper Union Sch Art, NY; WTex Mus Asn; Wichita Art Mus; Peat Marwick Inc; and others. *Comn:* Sampling Broadway (website), comn by Turbulance & Jerome Found Grant. *Exhib:* Solo exhbs, Annette Weintraub, Digital Composites: Disintegration/Reconstruction, Fine Arts Mus Long Island, 92; Group exhibs, Contemp Reflections, 1975-76, Aldrich Mus Contemp Art, 76; Members' Gallery, Albright-Knox Art Gallery, Columbus Art Mus, Ohio, 80; Third Int Symp Electronic Art, Gallery Arts Multiplicata, Sydney, Australia, 92; Picture Element Art Initiatives, NY Law Sch, 93; Night Light, Int Symp Elec Art, Mus Contemp Art, Helsinki, Finland, 94; The Art & Design Show, SIGGRAPH, Orlando, Fla, 94; Metamorphoses: Photog in the Electronic Age, Fashion Inst Technol Mus, 94; Image Electronic, Euphrat Mus Art, De Anza Col, Cupertino, Calif, 95; CODE, Ricco/Maresca Gallery, 95; Technoseduction, Cooper Union Sch Art, 97; Biennial, Whitney Mus Art, Bypaths, Moving Image Gallery, NY, 2000; plus others. *Collection Arranged:* Aldrich Mus; Best Products, FMC Corp; Peat Marwick; Prudential Ins; Wichita Mus; AT&T; Cooper Union; Euphrat Mus Art; Lehigh Univ; The West Texas Mus. *Teaching:* asst prof advert design & computer graphics, City Coll, City Univ NY, 83, assoc prof, 89; prof, City Coll, NY, 93; prof art, electronic design and multimedia, City Coll, NY. *Awards:* PSC-City Univ NY Res Found Grant, Visual Arts, 90, 93, 95, 97 & 98, 2000, 2001; NY Found Arts, Artists Fel, Printmaking/Drawing/Artists Bks, 91; ID Mag Silver Award, Interactive Media Rev, 98; and others. *Bibliog:* State of the art, Computer Graphics World, 3/93; Not painting by numbers, Newsweek, 7/25/94;

Psycho Geography, Intelligent Agent, Vol 2, No 2, spring 98; Bennial Angst, NY Mag, 3/2000; New York, Chaos Inspires Web Art, NY Times online, 7/2000; Whitney Biennial, ArtByte, May/June/2000. *Mem:* Women's Caucus Art (adv bd NY chap, 79-80); Spec Interest Group for Computer Graphics (bd dir, 88-90 & 90-92); Coll Art Asn; Int Symp Electronic Art. *Media:* Photography, Internet, Digital Media. *Res:* Multimedia narrative. *Publ:* Mapping the Learning Curve, Educators Tech Exchange, fall 94; Artice, Artifact: The Landscape of the Constructed Digital Environment, Leonardo 28:5, 95; When Worlds Collide: Live Action Footage & Computer-Generated Animation Sequences Learn to Get Along, FPS, Mag Computers & Animation, 96; Art on the Web, the Web as Art, Commun of one ACM, 10/92. *Mailing Add:* Two Bond St New York NY 10012

WEINZAPFEL, CONNIE A
GALLERY DIRECTOR, CURATOR
b Evansville, Ind, Aug 8, 1956. *Study:* Univ Southern Ind, BS, 78; Southern Ill Univ, MFA, 81. *Pos:* Coordr, Chicago Int Art Expo, Ill, 81-85; dir, New Harmony Gallery Contemp Art, Ind 85-. *Mailing Add:* Historic New Harmony PO Box 579 New Harmony IN 47631

WEISBERG, GABRIEL P
HISTORIAN, EDUCATOR
b New York, NY, May 4, 1942. *Study:* New York Univ, BA, 63; Johns Hopkins Univ, MA, PhD, 67. *Collection Arranged:* Against the Modern, Dagnan-Boureret and the Transformation of the Academic Tradition, 2002. *Pos:* Cur art hist, Cleveland Mus Art, 73-81; asst dir, Nat Endowment Humanities, 83-85. *Teaching:* Asst prof art hist, Univ NMex, 67-69; assoc prof art hist, Univ Cincinnati, 69-73; Mellon prof art hist, Univ Pittsburgh, 81-82; prof art hist, Univ Minn, 85-. *Awards:* Guggenheim Found Fel, 81-82; Advan Study Visual Arts, Nat Gallery Art, Washington, DC, 83; Regents Fel, Smithsonian Inst, Nat Mus Am Art, 92; Chevalier de l'ordre des Arts et des lettres, Republique Francaise, Le Ministre de La Culture, Paris, 95. *Mem:* Print Coun Am; Decorative Arts Soc; Coll Art Asn Am (bd dir, 80-). *Res:* Study of 19th century realism, Japonisme and art nouveau as a formalistic concern and as an example of social history. *Publ:* Art Nouveau Bing, 86; coauth, Japonisme Comes to America, 90; Beyond Impressionism: The Naturalist Impulse, 92; Collecting in the Gilded Age, Art Patronage in Pittsburgh, 1890-1910, 97; Art Nouveau Research Guide for Design Reform in France, Belg, Eng & US, 98; Overcoming All Obstacles: The Women of the Academic Julian, 2000. *Mailing Add:* Univ Minn Dept Art History 348 Heller Hall 271 19th Ave South Minneapolis MN 55455-0121

WEISBERG, RUTH ELLEN
PAINTER, EDUCATOR
b Chicago, Ill, July 31, 1942. *Study:* Acad di Belli Arte, Perugia, Italy, Laurea; Univ Mich, BS & MA; Atelier 17, Paris, with S W Hayter. *Hon Degrees:* DHL, Hebrew Union Col, 2001. *Work:* Bibliot Nat, France; Chicago Art Inst; Los Angeles Co Mus of Art; NY Pub Libr; Norwegian Nat Collection; Am Mus Art, Smithsonian; Oakland Mus, Calif. *Comn:* Together Again (ed of 150 lithographs), Midwest Regional Orgn for Rehabilitation & Training, 75; The Gift (ed of 60 lithographs), Univ Synagogue, Los Angeles, 75; Interlude, Los Angeles Co Mus of Art, 75; The Open Door Haggadal, Cen Conf of Am Rabbs. *Exhib:* Philadelphia Print Club, 85; Univ Richmond, Va, 85; Fisher Gallery, Univ Southern Calif, Los Angeles, 86; solo shows, Jack Rutberg Fine Arts, Los Angeles, 83, 85, 88, 91, 2006, The Scroll, Hebrew Union Col, NY, 87 & 88, Assoc Am Artists, NY, 87 & 90, Realms of Desire-A Print Retrospective, Fresno Art Mus, Calif, 90, Bethel Col, North Newton, Kans, 91 & Gwenda Jay Gallery, Chicago, Ill, 91 & 92; Her Story: Narrative Art by Contemp Calif Artists (catalog), Oakland Mus, 91; Passing Over, Sculptural Installation for, Passover and Passion, Leband Gallery, Loyola Marymount, Los Angeles, 91; 500 Yrs Since Columbus (catalog), Triton Mus, Santa Clara, Calif, 91; Presswork: The Art of Women Printmakers (traveling exhib, catalog), Nat Mus Women Arts, Washington, DC, Univ Art Mus, Univ Minn, Minneapolis, Elvehjem Mus Art, Univ Wis, Madison, Butler Inst Am Art, Youngstown, Ohio, 91-93. *Pos:* Dean, Univ Southern Calif, 74-77 & dept chmn, 86-2010; dir, Kelyn Press, currently; lectr, demonstr, juror, cur Univ Mich, 87, 88, Univ Hi, Honolulu, 88, Pa Acad, Philadelphia, 87, Queens Col, New York City, 87, City Col of NY, 87, Univ Iowa, 78, 87, Univ N Dakota, Grand forks, 87, Fresno (Calif) Arts Ctr and Mus, Carnegie Mellon Univ Pittsburgh, 86, 87, Univ Tenn, Knoxville, 86, Univ Calif, Santa Cruz, 85, Univ Wash, Seattle, Univ Kans, Lawrence Skirball Mus Hebrew Union Col, Los Angeles, Calif Inst Arts, Valencia, Otis Art Inst, Los Angeles, Mass Col Art, Boston, Norwegian Graphic Artists Asn, Oslo Col Art Asn Conference, Detroit, many others. *Teaching:* Asst prof fine arts, Eastern Mich Univ, Ypsilanti, 66-67; from assoc prof to prof fine arts, Univ Southern Calif, Los Angeles, 70-. *Awards:* Third Ann Vesta Award, Visual Arts, Women's Bldg, Los Angeles, 84. *Bibliog:* Lydia Matthews (auth), Stories history didn't tell us, Artweek, 2/14/91; Lisbet Nilson (auth), Loyola Gallery puts its faith in religious exhibit, Los Angeles Times/Calendar, 3/24/91; Suvan Geer (auth), Weisberg's family album, Los Angeles Times, 3/1/91. *Mem:* Coll Art Asn (bd dir & pres, 90-92); Western Regional Nat Women's Caucus Art (vpres & co-chair, 85); Nat Adv Bd Tamarind Inst; Los Angeles Artists Equity (adv bd). *Media:* Lithography. *Publ:* Illusr, Tom O'Bedlam's Song, 69 & auth & illusr, The Shtetl, A Journey and A Memorial, 72, Kelyn Press. *Dealer:* Assoc Am Artists New York NY; Gwenda Jay Gallery Chicago IL

WEISMAN, GARY MICHAEL
SCULPTOR, EDUCATOR
b Chicago, Ill, May 19, 1952. *Study:* Art Inst Chicago, 73-74; Leslie Posey student of Charles Grafley & A Polacheck, 73-78; Columbia Col, BFA, 76;. *Work:* Michael Reese Hosp, Union League Club, Chicago, Ill; Cigna Corp, Philadelphia, Pa; Ralph Lauren Corp, NY; Chicago Pub Libr, Ill. *Comn:* Lifesize sculpture, Burroughs Pharmaceut, Chicago, Ill, 89; outdoor sculpture plaza, City Duluth, Minn, 90; lifesize sculpture, Pepsico/Elmira Col, NY, 94; pub outdoor sculpture, City Chicago, Ill; outdoor pub sculpture, City Philadelphia, Pa. *Exhib:* Juried show, State Mus Pa, Harrisburg, Pa, 92, Nat Acad Design, NY, 92, Berman Mus, Collegeville, Pa, 93, Mus Am Art, Philadelphia, Pa, 94; invitational, Arnot Mus Art, Elmira, NY, 94; Solo exhibs, Prince Gallery, Chicago, Ill, 91, Sande Webster Gallery, Philadelphia, Pa, 93, 96, 98 & 2000, Berry-Hill Galleries, NY, 95, 97 & 98, Am Cult Ctr, Taipei, Taiwan, 98 & Alter & Gil Gallery, Los Angeles, 2000, Fred Baker Gallery, Chicago, Ill, 2003, Galerie Yoram, Los Angeles, Calif, 2003, Chen Gallery, Seoul, Korea, 2003; Arnot Art Mus, Elmira, NY, 93, 95 & 99; Sentec Int Ctr, Singapore, 96; many others. *Teaching:* Fac sculpture, Pa Acad Fine Arts, 86-. *Awards:* Sculpture Award, Nat Acad Design, 92; Purchase Award, Fel Pa Acad, 93; Pa Acad Fine Arts Fel, 93, 94, 96 & 97. *Mem:* Nat Sculpture Soc. *Media:* Bronze. *Mailing Add:* 376 Barnes Hill Rd Newfield NY 14867

WEISS, CLEMENS
CONCEPTUAL ARTIST, SCULPTOR
b Dusseldorf, Ger, Sept 26, 1955. *Study:* Studies in medizin, philos & art, Vienna & Düsseldorf, Ger, 73-78. *Work:* Anderson Gallery, Va Commonwealth Univ, Richmond; Mus Mod Art, Pub Libr, NY; Pushkin Mus, Moscow, Russia; Folkwang Mus, Essen, Ger. *Comn:* UN, Geneva, Switzerland, 98; stage set, Bochum, Ger, 96; stage design, Sylf, Bremen, Hamburg, Germany, 2002. *Exhib:* Buchstablich, Von der Heydt Mus, Wuppertal, Ger, 91; Transparenz/tranzendenz, Gainesville Samuel Pham Mus, 92; Transparenz/tranzendenz, Miami Art Ctr, Fla, 92; Transparenz/tranzendenz, Univ SFla Mus, Tampa, 92; Fdkwag Mus, Essen, Ger, 95; the XX Century, a century of art in Ger, Berlin; plus others. *Bibliog:* Uli Bohnen (auth), Quintessenz, Kunstforum, 89; Friedemann Malsch (auth), To the Art of C Weiss, Katalog Aachen, 90; Steven High (auth), Towards Knowledge, Katalog neuer Aachener Kunstverein, 90. *Media:* All Media. *Publ:* Auth, Konzepte, Objekte und Fragmente Inst No 1, Galerie Lohrl, 89; illusr, The Complaint of the Art, Juni Verlag, 90; auth, Installation & Logic-Fragment & Object, R Feldman Gallery, 91; auth & ed, Eighteen from New York (exhib catalog), Juni Verlag, 91; auth & illusr, Fragmentarische Logik-Logische Fragmente, Juni Verlag, 95; auth drawings-series 1990-1997. *Dealer:* Ronald Feldman Fine Arts 31 Mercer St New York NY 10013. *Mailing Add:* 31 E 31st St #9g New York NY 10023

WEISS, JEFFREY
CURATOR
Study: Dickinson Coll, BA, 80; Inst Fine Arts, NY, MA, 83, PhD, 91. *Collection Arranged:* Cur, Mark Rothko, 98; co-curator, Picasso: The Early Years, 1892-1906, 97; cur Pure Painting: Cubism - Furturism - Abstraction, 2002; cur, Jasper Johns: An Allegory of Painting, 1955-1965, 2007. *Pos:* Paul Mellon fellow, Ctr for Advanced Study in Visual Arts, Nat Gallery Art, Washington, DC, 87-90; res assoc & assoc res cur, Nat Gallery Art, 91-93, cur Dept Twentieth-century art, 99, head Dept Modern and Contemp Art, 2000-07; dir, Dia Art Found, New York, 2007-08; cur Panza collection, Guggenheim Mus, 2010-. *Teaching:* Kirk Varnedoe prof, Inst Fine Arts, NY, 2006-. *Publ:* Auth, The Popular Culture of Modern Art: Picasso, Duchamp, and Avant-Gardism, 94. *Mailing Add:* 1071 Fifth Ave New York NY 10128

WEISS, JEROME NATHAN
PAINTER, INSTRUCTOR
b NJ, Oct 21, 1959. *Study:* Metrop Art Ctr, Miami, study with Roberto Martinez, 78; Art Students League, study with Robert Beverly Hale, Ted Seth Jacobs & Jack Faragasso, 79-83; Nat Acad Design, New York, study with Harvey Dinnerstein & Mary Beth McKenzie, 81-83. *Work:* Abraham Art Found, Canadian, Tex; New Britain Mus Am Art, New Britain, Conn; Northeastern Univ, Boston, Mass; Boca Raton Mus, Fla; State Capitol Bldg, Hartford, Conn. *Comn:* Univ NC, Chapel Hill; Harvard Club of New York; Brigham and Women's Hosp, Boston, Mass; Debevoise and Plimpton, NY; Conn Superior Courthouse, New London, Conn. *Exhib:* 159th, 163rd & 167th Ann Exhibs, Nat Acad Design, NY, 84, 88 & 92; Fel Exhib, Monmouth Mus, Lincroft, NJ, 88; Amarillo Mus Art, Tex, 2000; Wayland Baptist Univ, Plainview, Tex, 2000; Tomasulo Gallery Union Co Coll, Cranford, NJ, 2001; Arnot Art Mus, Elmira, NY, 2005; Univ Bridgeport, Conn, 2005; United States Embassy, Kigali, Rwanda, 2006-08; Nicolaysen Art Mus, Casper, Wyo, 2008; Alexey von Schlippe Gallery, Univ Conn, Groton, Conn, 2009; Cornell Mus, Delray Beach, Fla, 2011; Mobile Mus Art, Mobile, Ala, 2012; Art Mus Southeast Tex, Beaumont, Tex, 2012; Art Mus South Texas, Corpus Christi, Tex, 2012; Mus Southwest, Midland, Tex, 2012; Haggin Mus, Stockton, Calif, 2012. *Collection Arranged:* Big as Life, curated for Lyme Art Asn; Coos Art Mus, Coos Bay, Ore, 2013; Minn Marine Art Mus, Winona, 2013. *Teaching:* Figure, Landscape Painting & Figure Drawing, Art Students League NY, Lyme Acad Fine Art, Old Lyme Conn; Silvermine Sch Art, New Canaan, Conn; Armory Art Center, West Palm Beach, Fla; Boca Raton Mus Art, Fla; Lyme Art Asn, Old Lyme Conn. *Awards:* Best in Show, Hortt Ann, Ft Lauderdale Mus, 85; Painting Fel, NJ Coun Arts, 88; Julius Hallgarten Prize, 167th Ann Exhib, Nat Acad Design, 92; and others. *Bibliog:* Theodore F Wolff (auth), Portrait of the artist as a young master, Christian Sci Monitor, 7/25/85; John A Parks (auth), Jerry Weiss; Observe, Think & Practice, Am Artist Workshop Mag, winter 2005; Maureen Bloomfield (auth), Light that stops time (cover), The Artists Mag, 6/2008. *Mem:* Am Soc Marine Artists. *Media:* Oil. *Publ:* auth, Master Class (continuing column & contrib ed), The Artists Mag, 7/2008-; Lockwood DeForest: The Perfect Medium, Cooley Gallery, 2010. *Dealer:* Portraits Inc New York NY; The Cooley Gallery Old Lyme CT; Ruggiero Gallery Madison CT. *Mailing Add:* 30 S Wig Hill Rd Chester CT 06412

WEISS, JOHN JOSEPH
PHOTOGRAPHER, EDITOR
b Philadelphia, Pa, Jan 31, 1941. *Study:* Temple Univ, BS, 63; Mass Inst Technol, 69-73; RI Sch Design, MFA, 73. *Work:* Mus Mod Art, NY; Addison Gallery Am Art, Andover, Mass; Princeton Univ, NJ; Del Art Mus, Wilmington; Photog Place, Philadelphia. *Exhib:* Addison Gallery Am Art, Andover, Mass, 73; Mass Inst Technol Creative Photog Gallery, Cambridge, 76; Photopia, Philadelphia, 79; G H Dalsheimer Gallery, Baltimore, 83; The Photographers' Gallery, London, 83; Andover Gallery,

Mass, 85; Book Trader Gallery, Philadelphia, 86. *Pos:* Coordr photog, Mass Inst Technol, 76-. *Teaching:* Instr photog, Mass Inst Technol, 69-73; asst prof photog, Univ Del, Newark, 75-79, assoc prof, 79-. *Publ:* Contribr, Portraits, Mod Photog, 77; auth, A darkroom philosophy, Camera 35, 77; ed, Venus, Jupiter and Mars--The Photographs of Frederick Sommer, Del Art Mus, 80; Philadelphia Photog Rev, 81; auth, Biography of Frederick Sommer, Collier's Encycl; article in Photo Review, 86. *Mailing Add:* Univ Del Dept Art Newark DE 19716

WEISS, LEE (ELYSE C)
PAINTER
b Inglewood, Calif, 1928. *Study:* Calif Coll Arts & Crafts, 46-47; also with N Eric Oback, 57 & Alexander Nepote, 58. *Work:* Nat Mus Am Art; Nat Mus Women in Arts, Wash; Phillips Collection, Wash; Exec Residence, State Wis; Springfield Mus Art, Mo; NASA Space Art Collection, Cape Canaveral, Fla; Davenport Munic Mus Art, Iowa; Hickory Mus, NC; US Dept of the Interior, Smithsonian Nat Air & Space Mus, Wash; Madison Mus Contemp Art, Wis; Milwaukee Mus Art, Wis; Chasen Mus Art, Madison, Wisc. *Comn:* Am Artist & Water Resources, one of 40 Am artists chosen for Bur Reclamation Art Proj, US Dept Interior, 71; artist for space shuttle launch, NASA, 84; comn artist, 2004 Gov's Awards, Support of Arts, Wis. *Exhib:* Solo exhibs, Walker Art Ctr, Minneapolis, 60, Calif Place Legion Hon, San Francisco, 62, Milwaukee Art Mus, 65, West Bend Gallery Fine Art, Wis, 88, Chicago Botanic Garden, 88 & 89 & Neville Publ Mus, Green Bay, Wis, 96, Uihliein Peters Gallery Milwaukee Wis 2004, 05; Wisconsin Painters & Sculptors, Milwaukee Art Mus; Oakland Art Mus; Penn Acad Fine Art, Philadelphia; San Francisco Art Mus; Setagaya Mus Art, Tokyo, Japan, 88, 89, 90 & 94; Nat Invitational Watercolor Exhib, Northern Ariz Univ, 89; State of the Art Nat Invitational Watercolor Exhib, Parkland Coll Art Gallery, Champagne, Ill, 89, 2009 & Biennial East/West Int Invitational, 97; Wis-Ill Art Exch, Art Asn, Springfield, Ill, 89; Meguro Mus, Tokyo, Japan, 91 & 92; Am Watercolor Invitational, Taipei Fine Arts Mus, Taiwan, 94; Shinjuku Cult Ctr, Tokyo, Japan, 95, 96 & 97; Charles Allis Art Mus, Milwaukee, 2003; Saitama Mus of Contemp Art, 2002, 2008; Reception Hall, Am Embassy, Prague, Czech Repub, 2007-; Contemporary International Watermedia Masters, Nanjing, China, 2007; First Invitational Exhib of Contemp Int Watermedia Masters, Nanjing, China, 11/2008-3/2008; Waterbourne: A Regional Exhibition of Watercolor Invitational, Katherine E Nash Gallery, Univ Minn, 2008; Retrospective: Watrous Gallery of the Wisconsin Acad Sciences, Arts, and Letters, Madison, Wisc, 2011. *Teaching:* Artist-in-residence, Rhinelander Sch Arts, 7/89; Dillman's Creative Workshops, Lac du Flambeau, Wis, 90, 92, 93 & 94, Arrowmont Sch Arts & Crafts, Gaitlinburg, Tenn, 95; Washington Studio Sch, DC, 98. *Awards:* First Award, Watercolor Wis, 82, 84, 87 & 2005; Adirondack Wilderness Award with Rouse Gold Medallion, Adirondack Nat Exhib Am Watercolors, 90; First Award, WASH 17th Ann, Houston, Tex, 93; 2nd award WASH, 2002; Governors Award in Support of the Arts, 2004; Honorary Reception, Am Embassy Residence, Prague, Czech Republic, 4/2008; Lifetime Achievement Award and Medal, Watercolor USA Hon Soc, 2009; Recognition Wall of five paintings, Springfield Art Mus, 2009; Lifetime Achievement Award, Wisconsin Acad Sciences, Arts, and Letters, 2011; Lifetime Achievement Award, Wisconsin Visual Artists, 2011; Lifetime Achievement Award, Mus Wisc Art, 2011. *Bibliog:* Watercolor 91 (feature article), Artist's Mag, 9/91; Watercolor Am Artist Publ, 94 & 96; featured interview, Watercolor, 2007; Artist to Artist (featured article), Am Artist Mag, 2007; Vignettes of AWS People: Lee Weiss, AWS-df, Am Watercolor Soc newsletter, Summer 2010. *Mem:* Dolphin fel, Am Watercolor Soc; Nat Watercolor Soc; life mem Wis Painters & Sculptors; Watercolor USA Hon Soc (vpres, 86, pres, 87-88); Rocky Mountain Water Media Soc; Fel Wis Acad Sci, Arts & Lett; hon mem, Jiangsu Watercolor Research Inst, Nanjing, China, Nov, 2007 & 2008. *Media:* Watercolor. *Publ:* Lee Weiss, Watercolors II, the Seventies, Am Printing & Publ Co, 81; Lee Weiss, Watercolors III, Straus Printing Co, 90; contribr, Creative Watercolor, Rockport Publ, 96; contribr, Cutting Across Time, Schroeder Hist Soc, 99; Famous Wisconsin Artists & Architects, Badger Books, Oct 2004; Lee Weiss, Madison Orginials Mag, vol 23, 2010. *Dealer:* Fanny Garver Gallery 230 State St Madison WI 53703. *Mailing Add:* 106 Vaughn Ct Madison WI 53705

WEISS, MADELINE
PAINTER
b New York, NY. *Study:* Studies with Lillian Orlowski and William Freed. *Work:* State of Fla, Cocoa; Palm Beach Co Home, West Palm Beach, Fla; Good Samaritan Hosp, West Palm Beach, Fla. *Comn:* Signage tubes installation, JFK Med Ctr, Edison, NJ, 91; tubular installation, Children's Rehabilitation Hosp, Tustin Health Fac, Calif, 92; tubular installation, Froedtert Mem Lutheran Hosp, Milwaukee, Wis, 98; tubular installation, Skywalk Restaurant, Milwaukee, Wis, 98; tubular installation, Devonshire Life Care, Palm Beach Gardens, Fla, 2000. *Exhib:* Solo exhibs, Bronx Mus Arts, NY, 85, State Capitol Bldg, Tallahassee, Fla, 86 & Palm Beach Co Coun Arts, West Palm Beach, Fla, 86; Art in Pub Places, West Palm Beach, Fla, 92; Northwood Univ, West Palm Beach, Fla, 95 & 96; Armory Art Ctr, West Palm Beach, Fla, 96; 45th Ann All Fla, Boca Mus, Fla, 96. *Pos:* Mem chair, Phoenix Gallery, New York, 84-90; mem prof artists comt, Palm Beach Co. *Teaching:* Instr fine arts, Jewish Community Ctr, West Palm Beach, 92-. *Awards:* First Place Acrylics, YWCA, 88; First Place, Artists Guild, 90; Merit Award, Jewish Community Ctr, 94. *Bibliog:* Kiki Arco (auth), Palm Beach Panorama, WPBT, Miami, 6/21/86; Betsy Hutton (auth), Catch that color, Sun-Sentinel/News, 8/28/88; Joseph Picconi (dir), Artist Scene WPB, Channel 20, 5/92; Candace Russell, City Link, 9/99. *Mem:* Nat Asn Women Artists (pres, Fla branch); Norton Artists' Guild (pres, 89-90 & 92-93); Nat Artists Equity; Boca Mus Artist Guild. *Media:* Acrylic. *Dealer:* Hodgell Gallery 46 Palm Ave S Sarasota FL 34236; Akontempo Gallery 508 E Atlantic Ave Delray Beach FL 33483

WEISS, MARILYN ACKERMAN
COLLAGE ARTIST, PAINTER
b Brooklyn, NY, Sept 4, 1932. *Study:* NY Univ, BS (magna cum laude), 53; Studied with Anthoney Toney, 66, Paul Margin, 67-72, Ruth Leaf, 78-79, Lynn Forgach, 92, Audrey Flack, 93 & Donna Karetsky, 95. *Work:* Mus Southwest, Midland, Tex; Fred Leighton Madison, Ltd, New York; CMF Colonial Inc, Hyannis, Mass; Bob Zimmerman Inc, Boca Raton, Fla; Sarah Lawrence Coll, Bronxville, NY; Sloan Kettering Art Collection, New York; Nat Mus Women Arts, Washington, DC. *Exhib:* Solo exhibs, Bodley Gallery, New York, 83, Discovery Gallery, Glen Cove, NY, 90, Z Gallery, New York, 95, Allen Sheppard Gallery, Piermont, NY, 95 & 97, Sundance Gallery, Bridge Hampton, NY, 98, West Hampton Libr, Westhampton Beach, NY, 99 & 2001, Downstairs Gallery, Hewlett, NY, 99-2000, Shelter Rock Art Gallery, Manhasset, NY, 2000, Omni Gallery, Uniondale, NY, 2003, Gayle Wilson Gallery, Southampton, NY, 2003-2005, Madelle Hegeler Semerjian Gallery, Southampton, NY, 2005, Interchurch Ctr, New York, 2005 & Harvest Gallery, Dennis, Mass, 2006-2007, Graphic Eye Gallery, Port Washington, NY, 2008, 2009, 2010, 2013; group exhibs, First Open Exhib, Fine Arts Mus Nassau Co, Roslyn, NY, 88; National Printmaking Exhib, Mus Southwest, Midland, Tex, 91; Quiet Reaction, Richmond Art Mus, Ind, 92; Global Focus-Women in Arts & Cult, Beijing, China & Women's Mus, Washington, DC, 95; Cork Gallery, Lincoln Ctr, New York, 99, 2003, 2009-2010; Broome St Gallery, New York, 99, 2002 & 2004-2008; Ise Art Found, New York, 2000; Elizabeth Found for Arts, New York, 2001; Frey Berger Gallery, Pa State Univ, Reading, 2002; Long Beach Art League, Long Beach, NY, 2003; Art-trium, Melville, NY; East End Art Coun Gallery, Riverhead, NY, 2004; Manhattan Boro Hall, New York, 2005; Google Works, Reading, Pa; Shelter Rock Art Gallery, Manhasset, NY, 2006; Made in the USA, Blue Hill Art & Cult Ctr, Pearl River, NY, 2007; Graphic Eye Gallery, Port Washington, NY, 2008-2012; Noyes Mus Art, Oceanville, NJ, 2009; Bel-Age Gallery, West Hampton Beach, NY, 2011; Guild Hall, East Hampton, NY, 2010, 2012, 2013. *Awards:* Miriam E Halpren Mem Award, 91; Canady-Karasik Mem Award, 97; Irving H Silver Award for Innovative Collage, 2000; Merit Award Long Beach Art League; Cleo Hartwig Award, Sculpture, NAWA Ann, 2004; Contemp Art Award, Bernard & Hortense Kassoy Am Soc Contemp Artists, New York, 2006. *Bibliog:* Salon des Femme Artists de NY, La Revue Moderne, France, 71; John & John Digby (auths), The Collage Handbook, Thames & Hudson Ltd, 85; Helen Harrison (auth), New York Times, 99; Pat Rogers (auth), Southampton Press, 2003; Valerie Kellogg (auth), Newsday, 2003; Marion Wolberg Weiss (auth), Dan's Paper, 2003-2004; Pola Rosen, ED.D (auth), Education Update, 2005; Q Review, 2010-2012, Q Review, Vol 18 (cover), Vol 16 & 17. *Mem:* Am Soc Contemp Artists; Artists Equity; Graphic Eye Gallery. *Media:* Hand Made Paper, Acrylic, Collage. *Dealer:* Graphic Eye Gallery 402 Main St Port Washington NY 11050 . *Mailing Add:* 1100 Park Ave Apt 14B New York NY 10128

WEISS, MONIKA
VIDEO ARTIST, INSTALLATION SCULPTOR
Study: Acad Fine Arts, Warsaw, Poland, MFA, 1989. *Exhib:* Solo exhibs, Nexus Contemp Art Ctr, Atlanta, 1996, Chelsea Art Mus, New York, 2004 & 2010, Lehman Coll Art Gallery, New York, 2005, Drawing Ctr, New York, 2006, Centre for Contemp Art, Elblag, Poland, 2009; OMNIART, Miami Basel Int Art Fair, Fla, 2005; Moment by Moment, NDak Mus Art, Grand Forks, 2006; Loneliness and Melancholy, Manchester Coll, Conn, 2007; Frauen bei Olympia, FrauenMus, Bonn, Denmark, 2008; The Prisoner's Dilemma, Cisneros Fontanals Art Found, Miami, 2009. *Pos:* Asst prof studio art, Dept Art & Art Hist, Washington Coll. *Awards:* Sch Art Inst Chicago Grant, 2002; Facto Found Grant, 2006; NY Found Arts Fel, 2009; Yaddo Fel, 2010

WEISS, RACHEL
CURATOR
b Paterson, NJ, Sept 22, 1954. *Study:* Marlboro Col, BA, 76; Mass Coll Art, MFA, 80. *Work:* Ctr Georges Pompidou, Paris; Nat Mus Sci & Technol, Ottawa, Ont. *Exhib:* The Nearest Edge of the World: Art and Cuba Now, var mus, 90-93; Ante Am, Biblioteca Luis Angel Arango, Bogota, Colombia; Among Africas/In Americas, Banff Ctr, 91. *Pos:* Coordr, Vis Artists Prog, Mass Col Art, 84-89; pres, Polarities, Inc, 85-; chairperson, Arts Inst, Chicago. *Teaching:* Asst instr holography, Mass Col Art, Boston, 79-80, spec prog asst, 78-81; asst instr holography, Brown Univ, Providence, RI, 80-81. *Awards:* Numerous pub & pvt grants in support of pub art prog organized since 1983. *Publ:* Auth, Boycotting the truth, Black New York Mag, 88; Creating freedom, Tres Mundo, 88; Necessity and Invention: New Cuban Art, Wolgan Misul Mag, Seoul, 90; ed, Being America, White Pine Press, 91; contribr, Territories of Difference (chapt), 92. *Mailing Add:* c/o Sch Arts Inst Chicago 37 S Warbash Chicago IL 60603-3103

WEISSMAN, JULIAN PAUL
DEALER
b New York, NY, June 28, 1943. *Study:* Hobart Col, Geneva, NY, BA. *Pos:* Art Critic, The Press, 73-77; ed assoc, writer & reviewer, Art News Mag, New York, 74-79; mgr, Susan Caldwell Gallery Inc, New York, 74-75; mgr, Gloria Cortella Inc (gallery), New York, 76-77; dir, Alexander F Milliken Inc (gallery), New York, 78-79; dir, Gruenebaum Gallery Inc, New York, 79-87; assoc dir, M Knoedler & Co, 87-89; dir, Mod Europ Art, Hirschl & Adler Galleries, New York, 89-91; dir & vpres, ACA Galleries, New York, 93-95; Owner, Jullian Weissman Fine Art, LLC, 95-Present. *Res:* Impressionism; German expressionism; the Bauhaus; 20th century sculpture; contemporary art and artists who live and work in New York; 20th Century European and Am and Contemp Art. *Specialty:* Contemporary American art and European modern. *Publ:* Auth, Standoff in Soho, Art News Mag, 74; What's wrong at the Whitney?, The Press, Vol 3, No 3, 75; Master Atget--& Portraits of the Artists, Art News Mag, 76; Here comes the taxman, Soho Weekly News, 76; Dazzling drawings are redefining the art, The Press, Vol 4, No 1, 76. *Mailing Add:* 26 Beaver St No 14 New York NY 10004

WEISSMAN, WALTER
PHOTOGRAPHER, SCULPTOR
b Brooklyn, NY, Dec 9, 1946. *Study:* Kingsborough Community Col, with Gregory Battcock, AA, 67; Brooklyn Coll, with Harry Holtzman, BA (hon; arts), 70; Hunter Coll, with Robert Morris, MA (fine arts), 75. *Work:* Mus Mod Art, Whitney Mus & Guggenheim Mus, New York; Tate Mus, London, Eng; Va Commonwealth Univ;

Franklin Furnace, New York. *Comn:* Alliance in the Park (outdoor/indoor collaborative work), Philadelphia Art Alliance, Pa, 87; Committed to Print, Mus Mod Art, New York, 88. *Exhib:* Contemp Reflections No 4, Aldrich Mus Contemp Art, 75; Open Studios at PS1, Queens, New York, 77; Centennial Exhib Sculpture, NJ Inst Technol, Newark, 81; Drawings, Models and Sculpture: A Re-Opening: Season's Premier, 14 Sculptors Gallery, 82; solo exhibs, Structures and Shelters, 83 & 87 & De-Archit, 84, 14 Sculptors Gallery, New York; Artists Call, Hudson Mem Church, NY, 84; Art Works: Three Dimensions, Beaver Coll, Glenside, Pa, 85; Art Against Apartheid, Boricua Coll, Brooklyn, 85; 13-state traveling exhib, 87-89; West Beth Ann Exhib, Drawing, NY, 2011. *Pos:* Sr ed, Art & Artists, New York, 78-89; adv, Artists Cert Cult Affairs, New York, 80-86; moderator, Artists Talk on Art, New York, 81-84; pres, 14 Sculptors Gallery, 85-88. *Teaching:* Asst instr photog, Yale Univ, 68; instr painting & drawing, Brooklyn Coll, 71; artist-in-residence, PS 1, Long Island City, New York, 77. *Awards:* New York FOund Arts, Fiscal Sponsorship, 2010. *Bibliog:* Burton Wasserman (auth), Exhibitions in sight, Art Matters, Pa, 6/85; Robert Metzger (auth), A 2nd Palette, In: Aldrich Mus catalog, 85; Michael Brenson (auth), article, NY Times, 12/28/86; Jennifer Landes (auth), Cultural History Through Weissman's Lens, East Hampton Star, 12/15/2011. *Mem:* Artists Meeting Cult Change (secy, 76-78); Found Community Arts (pres, 80-84); Graphic Artists Guild; Globe Photos Inc (93-2000); Corbis Photo Agency (2007-present). *Publ:* Coauth, An Anti-Catalog, Artists Meeting Cult Change, 77; auth, Interview with John Perreault, 4/80, Automata and autonomy: Sculpture now, 11/81 & ed, Special Supplement, 11/81, Artworkers News; ed, Special Supplement, 82, auth, The terror of bureaucracy, 5/85 & View from a coop, 3/86, Art & Artists Mag; coauth, The Village, 87. *Mailing Add:* 463 W St Ste B-332 New York NY 10014

WEITZMAN, EILEEN
SCULPTOR, DRAWER

b Chicago, Ill, Feb 28, 1951. *Study:* Self taught; Univ Minn, JD, Minneapolis. *Work:* Pierogi 2000, Brooklyn; Robert Chaney Collection, Houston, Tex. *Exhib:* 2-person show, 101 Wooster Gallery, NY, 1991; Monumental Propaganda (traveling), 1993; solo exhib, Jamaica Arts Ctr, NY, 1993, Kentler Int Drawing Space, Red Hook, NY, 1995, Tribes Gallery, NY, 1997, Boreas Gallery, Williamsburg, NY, 2005; Contemp Am Artists, Windows Gallery, Birobijan, Russia, 1994; Three Rivers Festival, Carnegie Mus Art, 1996; Holland Tunnel Gallery, Williamsburg, NY, 1998; N3 Project Space, Williamsburg, NY, 1999; 21st Suffragettes, Sideshow Gallery, Williamsburg, NY, 2001; Flat Files, Pierogi Gallery, Williamsburg, NY, 2003; Solstice, Boreas Gallery, Williamsburg, NY, 2004; Newark Between Us, Nat Newark Bldg, Newark, NJ, 2006; Sarah Bowen Gallery, Williamsburg, NY, 2007. *Teaching:* Instr, Jamaica Arts Center. *Awards:* Artist Grant, Artists Space, 1990; Artist Grant, Puffin Found, 1997; Full Fel, Vermont Studio Ctr, 1999. *Bibliog:* Basile Duodoumis (auth), Imagination and reality, The Reporters, 4/28/91; L Ulbyanenko (auth), 3 Americans at Windows Gallery, Press-fact, Birobijan, Russia, 12/21/94; Erin Kelly (auth), Using odds and ends to redefine clichés, NY Times, 3/5/95; Dan Bishoff, auth, Art stars align in Newark, The Star Ledger, NJ, 10/20/2006; Miriam Brumer, auth, Newark Between Us in Newark, Artcritical.com, 12/2006. *Media:* Textiles, Paper; Photographs, Found Objects. *Publ:* Auth, Tony Moore at Salena Gallery, Art Initiatives, 1992; Supermodern art, Art Initiatives, 1993. *Mailing Add:* 784 Manhattan Ave No 4L Brooklyn NY 11222

WEKUA, ANDRO
SCULPTOR, PAINTER

b Sochumi, Georgia, 1977. *Study:* Nat Art Sch, Sochumi, Georgia, 1986-91; Phil Inst Gogebaschwili, Tiblissi, Georgia, 1993-94; Visual Art Sch, Basel, Switzerland, 1995-99. *Work:* Carnegie Mus Art, Pittsburgh; Saatchi Gallery, London; Initial Access Frank Cohen Collection, Wolverhampton, England. *Exhib:* Solo exhibs include Galerie Peter Kilchmann, Zurich, Switzerland, 2004, 2005, 2007, Gladstone Gallery, New York, 2006, 2008, Wait to Wait, Mus Boijmans van Beuningen, Rotterdam, Netherlands, 2007; group exhibs include Persönliche Pläne, Kunsthalle Basel, Switzerland, 2002; It's in our hands, Migros Mus Gegenwartskunst, Zurich, Switzerland, 2003; Neue Kunsthalle St Gallen, Switzerland, 2004; ID Troubles, NurtureArt Gallery, Brooklyn, 2005; pose and sculpture, Casey Kaplan Gallery, New York, 2006; Kate Show, Foam Fotog mus, Amsterdam, 2006; Absent Without Leave, Victoria Miro Gallery, London, 2007; Like color in pictures, Aspen Art Mus, Aspen, 2007; Paintings 1936-2008, Approach, London, 2008; 54th Int Art Exhib Biennale, Venice, 2011. *Dealer:* Galerie Peter Kilchmann Limmatstraße 270 CH-8005 Zurich Switzerland. *Mailing Add:* Gladstone Gallery 515 W 24th St New York NY 10011

WELCH, CHARLES D
PAINTER, SCULPTOR

b Kearney, Nebr, Oct 5, 1948. *Study:* Kearney State Col, BA (art educ), 70, MS (art educ), 74; tuition fel, 84-87, Sch Mus Fine Arts, Boston, MFA, 87. *Work:* Chicago Art Inst; Tate Gallery, London; Mus Mod Art, NY; Arch Small Press & Commun, Antwerp, Belg; Nebr Art Collection; Getty Found Collection; Libr Congress. *Exhib:* Printmaking 1985, Northeastern Univ Gallery, Boston; Gallery II, Tufts Univ, Medford, Mass, 87; Paper Press Gallery, Chicago, 88; Int Stamp Invitational, Davidson Gallery, Seattle, 89; Aerial Gallery, NY, 89. *Pos:* Proprietor, Sandbar Willow Handmade Paper Mill, Omaha, 78-84, Lebanon, NH, 88-. *Teaching:* Chmn art dept, Bellevue Sr High Sch, 74-84 & Bellevue W High Sch, 77-84; instr, Bellevue Col, 78-80; teaching asst, Tufts Univ, 86-87; instr, AVA Gallery, 88-89. *Awards:* Fulbright Hayes Recipient, 76; Medal, Art 54 Gallery, 87; Special Artistic Excellence, Tokyo Metrop Mus, 90. *Bibliog:* Judith Hoffberg (auth), article, Umbrella Mag, 83; David Cole (auth), The Adventures of the Cracker Jack Kid, aka Chuck Welch, Lightworks Mag, 87. *Mem:* Nat Educ Asn; Bellevue Educ Asn; Int Soc Copier Artists; Friends Dard Hunter Soc. *Media:* Paper, Mail Art. *Publ:* Auth, Networking Currents, Sandbar Willow Press, 85; Whole Earth Review, Mail Art Glasnost, winter 89; ed, Eternal Network: A Mail Art Anthology, Univ Calgary Press, 95. *Dealer:* Benta West AVA Gallery Hanover NH; Rebecca McDonald Davidson Galleries Seattle WA. *Mailing Add:* 28 Evergreen Hill Rd Hancock NH 03449-5417

WELCH, JAMES EDWARD
PAINTER

b Nora, Va, July 14, 1943. *Study:* Art Sch Soc Arts Crafts, 63-64. *Work:* McLaren Regional Med Ctr, Flint, Mich; Marshfield Clinic, Wis; Saginaw Township City Hall, Mich; Bank of Com, Hamtramck, Mich; Old Kent Bank SW, Niles, Mich. *Comn:* Portrait founding pastor, Judson Baptist Church, Burton, Mich, 84; Children at Play (painting), McLaren Regional Med Ctr, 85 & pastel paintings, 98; portrait founding pastor, Grace Emmanuel Baptist Church, Flint, Mich, 86; Bankard Portraits, Sue and Miss Em, 86. *Exhib:* Midwest Regional Art Competition, Kendall Sch Design, Grand Rapids, 86; Five State Pastel Competition, Art Ctr Battle Creek, Mich, 86; Extended Media/Fresh Visions, Detroit Inst Arts, 87; Extended Media, Fresh Visions, Detroit Inst Arts, 87; Saginaw Art Mus, Mich, 88; Ella Sharp Mus, 90; Jackson Area Competition, Ella Sharp Mus, Mich, 90; 2-D 3-D Regional Art Competition, S Bend Art Ctr, Ind, 90; solo exhibs, Saginaw Twp City Hall, Mich, 93 & N E Acad Dance, 2007; All Media State Wide Competition, Left Bank Gallery, Flint, 95; Our Town, State Competition, Birmingham, Mich, 97; Holiday Exhib, Lansing Art Gallery, Mich, 98; All Area Exhib, Saginaw Art Mus, Mich, 98; Greater Flint Arts Coun Ann Mem Exhib, 99; NE Mich Artists Exhib, Jesse Besser Mus, 2004; Impromptu Exhib, East Shore Guild, 2007; N E Mich Artists Exhib, Jesse Besser Mus, 2007; Huron Shoreline Art Exhib, 2008; Mohave Coll Ann Art Exhib, Kingman, Ariz, 2007-2009; Degas Pastel Soc, 2010; 13th Biennial Exhib, Hammond Regional Art Ctr, La. *Awards:* Outstanding Award of Merit & Viewers Choice Award, Midland Ctr Arts, 95; Our Town Exhib Sponsor's Award, Chrysler Fund, 98; Citizens Banking Corp Sponsor Award, 2003; Best of Show Body of Work, Huron Shoreline Art Show, Tawas, Mich, 2007; Art prize, World Competition, Grand Rapids, Mich, 2012. *Bibliog:* Jean Spenner (auth), Artist portrays Bill Pless, Brighton Argus, 84; Cheryl Roof (auth), Tapping the surface in art, Independent, 86; An Illustrated Survey of Leading Contemp Am Reference Publ Corp, Chicago, 86; Marilyn Fosberg (auth), Hist of Mich Artists, 89. *Mem:* Saginaw Artists Guild (hon mem); Survivors Art Found NY. *Media:* Oil, Pastels, Acrylic, Watercolor, Poetry, Readings with Surreal Art. *Res:* Oil spill in the Gulf of Mexico. *Specialty:* The endangered planet earth series. *Interests:* Hiking in the endangered wetlands, mountains, forests, deserts, endangered species, dogs, cats, birds, and camping. *Collection:* landscapes, figurative, abstract, surealism with poetry reading. *Publ:* Contribr, Best of Pastel, Rockport Publs, 96 & Portrait Inspirations, 97; Biographical Encyclopedia of Am Painters, Sculptors, & Engravers of the US Colonial to 2002, Dealers Choice Books Inc, 2002

WELCH, MARSHA SWEET See Sweet, Marsha (Marsha Sweet Welch)

WELCH, ROGER
VIDEO ARTIST, INSTALLATION SCULPTOR

b Westfield, NJ, Feb 10, 1946. *Study:* Miami Univ, Ohio, BFA, 69; Whitney Mus Independent Study Prog, 70-71; Art Inst Chicago, MFA, 71. *Work:* Ga Mus Art, Athens; Rufino Tamayo Mus, Mexico City; Boston Mus Fine Arts; Mus Bellas Artes, Caracas, Venezuela; Chase Manhattan Collection, Mus Mod Art, NY; and other pvt and pub collections; Guggenheim Mus, NY; Reina Sofia Mus, Madrid. *Comn:* The OJ Simpson Project (multi-media work), Albright-Knox Art Gallery, 77; The Voice of Clint Eastwood (videotape), Process & Konstruktion, Munich, Ger, 85. *Exhib:* Solo exhibs, Milwaukee Art Ctr, 74, Albright-Knox Art Gallery, 77, Mus Nac, Havana, 81, Mus Bellas Artes, Caracas, Venezuela, 81, Whitney Mus Am Art, 82, Ted Greenwald Gallery, NY, 86 & 87, Ewing Gallery, Univ Tenn, 90, Liverpool Gallery, Brussels, Belg, 91 & Galerie Art Matters, Noerdwijk, The Neth, 93; The Solomon Collection, Sarah Lawrence Coll, 76; Am Narrative Art, 1967-77, Contemp Art Mus, Houston, Tex, 77; The Carter Collection, Ga Mus Art, 77; Photog & Art since 1946, Los Angeles Co Mus, 87; Specs, Annina Nosei Gallery, NY, 92; Site Seeing, Islip Art Mus, NY, 92; Concept Art, Mus D'Art Mod, Saint-Etinne, France, 93; Conceptual Art of the 70's, Boston Mus Fine Arts, 93; Galleria Milano, Milan, Italy, 2000; Neuberger Mus, Purchase, NY, 2001; Vicky Remy Collection, Mus Modern Art, St Etienne France; The Sports Show, Minneapolis Inst Arts, 2012; As the Eye is Formed, Parrish Art Mus, Southampton, NY, 2013. *Teaching:* Guest lectr many univs, 76-81; Sr instr, Univ Tex, Austin, 88 & 90; adj asst prof, SW Tex State Univ, 1998-99, assoc prof. *Awards:* Creative Artists Pub Serv Grant, 73 & 76; Nat Endowment Arts Grants, 74 & 80. *Bibliog:* William Zimmer (auth), A Genre comes into its own, New York Times, 8/2/92; Helen A Harrison (auth), For 12 artists, maps fill a role as raw material, NY Times, 10/18/92; Lucy Lippard (auth), Lure of the Local, The New Press, 97. *Mem:* Coll Art Asn; Artists Equity Asn. *Media:* Multi-media & Sculpture. *Publ:* Contribr, Tracks J, spring 75; Unbuilt America, McGraw-Hill, 76; The Big Jewish Book, Doubleday, 78; Wide Angle Film Quarterly, Vol 5, No 3, Ohio Univ Press, 83; Photography & Art since 1946, Abbeville Press, 87; Installation Art, Thames & Hudson, 94. *Dealer:* John Gibson Gallery New York NY; Galleria Milano Milan Italy; Galleria Tjerk Wiegersma Brussels. *Mailing Add:* 87 E Houston St New York NY 10012

WELD, ALISON GORDON
PAINTER, ASSEMBLAGE ARTIST, CONCEPTUAL ARTIST

b Ft Knox, KY, Jun 10,1953. *Study:* SUNY Coll of Art & Design Alfred Univ, BFA (painting) 75; Sch of the Art Inst of Chicago, MFA (painting). *Work:* New Jersey State Mus, Trenton, NJ; Jane Voorhees Zimmerli Art Mus, New Brunswick, NJ; Newark Pub Library, Newark, NJ; Springfield Mus Art, Springfield, Ohio; Radford Univ Art Mus, Va; Everson Mus Art, NY; William Paterson Univ, NJ; New Mex State Univ; Univ Memphis Art Mus; Eli and Edythe Broad Art Mus, Mich; Art Mus Univ Memphis. *Exhib:* New Painterly Abstraction, Jersey City Mus, NJ, 88; Hunterdon Mus of Art, Hunterdon, NJ, 98; Different Ways of Seeing, Noyes Mus of Art, Oceanville, NJ, 2005-06; Abstraction Now: Scratching the Surface, Delaware Ctr of Contemp Art, Wilmington, DE, 2005; Pattern & Pulse,Cazenovia College Art Gallery, Cazenovia, NY, 2005; Allegories of Strife: The Diptychs of Alison Weld 1990-2005, 2006; Alison Weld: The Figurative Impulse in Abstraction, Rider Univ Art Gallery, Lawrenceville, NJ, 2006; In the Abstract, Springfield Mus Art, Ohio, 2006; The Feminine Mystique, Jersey City Mus, NJ, 2007; Alison Weld: Let the Fur Fly, Radford

Univ Art Mus, Va, 2007; The Tenacious Gesture of Alison Weld, Paul Robeson Gallery, Rutgers Univ, 2008; Art is My Natural World, Alison Weld, 1980-2009, Art Mus, Univ Memphis, 2010; Striations and Silent Diaries, Atea Ring Gallery, Westport, NY; Alison Weld: A Necessary Convergence, Machias Art Gallery, Univ Maine. *Pos:* Asst cur, NJSM, 88-99. *Awards:* Stowells Trophy of England, 1975. *Bibliog:* Jonathan Goodman (auth), Marks and Materials, William Paterson Univ, 2003; Dominique Nahas (auth), The Emotional Life of Inanimate Things, Robert Steele Gallery, 2003; Donald Kuspit (auth), Discordia Concors, The Diptychs of Alison Weld, Springfield Mus of Art, 2006; Amanda Bell (auth), The Tenacious Gesture of Alison Weld, Rutgers Univ, 2008; Leslie Lubbers, AMUM, 2010; Leslie Luebbers (auth), I am Nature, She Said, Art as Biology. *Mem:* College Art Asn. *Media:* Acrylic, Oil. *Specialty:* Abstraction. *Publ:* Springfield Mus Art (exhib catalog), 2006; The Figurative Impulse in Abstraction (exhib catalog), Rider Univ, 2006; The Tenacious Gesture of Alison Weld (catalog), Rutgers Univ, 2008; PMUM, Univ Memphis (online catalog), 2010. *Dealer:* Atea Ring Gallery

WELDON, BARBARA MALTBY
PAINTER

b Yuma, Ariz. *Study:* San Diego State Univ, 50-52; Univ Calif, San Diego, 70-73. *Work:* Bank of San Francisco & Bank Am World Hq, San Francisco; San Diego Mus Art, Calif; Copley Mem Libr & Salk Inst, La Jolla, Calif; San Jose Mus Art, Calif; City of Santa Fe Springs, Calif; Utah State Univ; Gen-Probe, Inc, San Diego, CA; Oprah Winfrey; Saks Fifth Ave, New York, NY; Strauss Collections, Rancho Santa Fe, CA. *Comn:* Paintings, VRC Parkway Radiology Ctr, Escondido, Calif, 89; Peabody Hotel, Orlando, Fla, 88; Grossmont Hospital Women's Ctr, La Mesa, Calif, 90; Mason & Elizabeth Phelps Collection, La Jolla, Calif; Imperial Hotel, Tokyo, Japan, 96; Nikko Hotel, Tokyo, Japan, 96. *Exhib:* Solo exhibs, Thomas Babeor Gallery, La Jolla, 80-84, 86, 88, 90, 92, 96, 93 & 95, Ivory/Kimpton Gallery, San Francisco, 82, 83, 86 & 89, Patty Ande Gallery, San Diego, 84, Triangles, continuing rotation of artist's work, San Diego, 93-96, Tasende Gallery, Calif, 99, 2001, I Wolk Gallery, St Helena, Calif, 2003; Sheila Nussbaum Gallery, 84, 86, 92 & 96; Citizens Gallery, Yokohama, 92; Gallery 30, Calif, 96 & 97; Susan St Gallery, Calif, 97; Tasende Gallery, LaJolla, Calif, 99-01, Los Angeles, 2000-2001. *Pos:* Adv bd mem, Pub Arts, San Diego, Calif, 86 & 87; juror art exhibs (example: San Diego Del Mar Fair); commemorative artist for KPBS 25 yr Anniversary Poster, 92. *Teaching:* Guest Lecturer; Contemp Arts comt, SDMA, Feb, 2005. *Awards:* First Award, Nat Watercolor Soc, 74; Second Prize, San Diego Mus Art, 75; William A Paton Prize, Nat Acad Design, 79; Outstanding Achievement in the Arts Women Together Orgn, San Diego, 97. *Bibliog:* Les Krantz (auth), Calif Art Rev, 88 & 89; Robert Pincus (auth), rev, San Diego Union Tribune, 3/18/93, 12/23/93, 9/14/95; Johnathan Seville (auth), San Diego Reader, 8/95; and others. *Mem:* Mus of Contemp Art SD San Diego, Mus of Art; Mingei Int'l mus Kappa Alpha Theta (fraternity) Myeloma Research Found for a cure MRFC bd mem (Little Rock, AR); Children Home Soc of CA. *Media:* Oil, Encaustic, Acrylic. *Res:* Mythology; Medieval art; Symbolism; Ancient religious art pieces. *Specialty:* Tasende Gallery shows blue chip art with no specialty. *Interests:* Folk & Religious Art; my paintings are not restricted to religious art, Mythology, Symbolism, but are often influenced by music, I listen to classical & jazz while working & my work evolves from one series to another. Also influenced by my interest in world travel What I absorb from other cultures. *Collection:* David Copley, La Jolla; Mason & Elizabeth Phelps, La Jolla, Strauss Collection. *Publ:* Martin Petersen (profile), Applause Mag, 9/79; Phyllis Van Doren (profile), SD Home and Garden, 2/2002; Richard Reilly (rev), San Diego Union, 1/81; Robert McDonald (rev), Los Angeles Times, 4/15/86; Holly Myers (rev), LA Times, 10/2001; Robert Perine (bk, profiles of 40), San Diego Artists, Artra Publ, 88; Kathleen Mc Millen (profile) Decor and Style Mag, 2004. *Dealer:* Tasende Gallery La Jolla CA 92037

WELITOFF, SUARA
VIDEO ARTIST

b Jersey City, NJ, 1951. *Study:* Boston Univ, BA, 1973. *Exhib:* Transience & Sentimentality, Inst Contemp Art, Boston, 1998; Between Fantasy and Pleasure, Joseph Gross Gallery, Univ Ariz, Tucson, 2001; solo exhibs, Allston Skirt Gallery, Boston, 2005, Roger Williams Univ, RI, 2005, Inst Contemp Art, Boston, 2006, Mass Coll Art, Boston, 2006, Mass Inst Technol, Cambridge, 2007, Mus Fine Arts, Boston, 2010; War and Discontent, Mus Fine Arts, Boston, 2007; Worlds on Video, Centre for Contemp Cult Strozzina, Florence, 2008; Human Nature(s), Worcester Art Mus, Mass, 2009. *Awards:* Louis Comfort Tiffany Found Grant, 2009. *Bibliog:* Christine Temin (auth), In Mere Minutes, Her Fragmented Films Render Heartfelt Images, Boston Globe, 2002; Ken Johnson (auth), In Two Exhibits, Politics and War Are Held Up for Scrutiny, Boston Globe, 5/16/2007

WELLER, LAURIE JUNE
PAINTER

b Warsaw, NY, May 18, 1953. *Study:* Univ Ill, Urbana, BFA, 76; Tyler Sch Art, Philadelphia, MFA, 80. *Work:* Tambrands Inc, Lake Success, NY; Steak & Ale Corp, Dallas, Tex; Mischer Corp Collections, Houston, Tex; Prudential Insurance Co Am, Newark, NJ; Transco Corp Collection, Houston, Tex; Tex Woman's Univ, Houston & Dallas campuses. *Comn:* Sybaritica (watercolor on paper), comn by Thomas Wright, San Antonio, Tex, 84; Fiesta (watercolor on paper), comn by Dr Evelyn Hammon, Austin, Tex, 88; Rivulets Triptych (watercolor on paper), comn by Intellicall Corp, Dallas, Tex, 89; Grazioso Forza, acrylic on wood, Crossroads, Tex. *Exhib:* Elements and Environments, Univ Ark, Little Rock; Watercolor All-ways, Coll Mainland Gallery, Texas City, Tex; solo exhibs, Mountain View Coll, Dallas, Tex, 93, Tex Woman's Univ Gallery, 94, Richland Coll, Dallas, 95 & Univ Wis, Platteville, 96, Bimorphia, Oklahoma Univ, Norman, Okla, 2003, Eccentric Boundaries, Harris Coll, Houston, Tex, 2004, Ensemble, Hardin Simmons Univ, Albilene, Tex, 2006; Wood's Edge, Brookhaven Coll, Dallas, Tex, 93; Woods Edge II, North Lake Coll, Irving, Tex, 94; The Big Picture: Large Scale Watercolor, Meadows Gallery, Visual Arts Ctr, Denton, Tex, 94; Laurie Weller: Transformed by Nature, Nature Transformed (with catalog), Weil Gallery, Tex A & M, Corpus Christi, 97; Penrose Gallery, Tyler Sch Art, 2000; Scratching the Surface, Austin Coll, Sherman, Tex, 2001; Eccentric Boundaries, Tex Christian Univ, Ft Worth, 2002; Parallel Play, Cinema Gallery, Urbana, Ill, 2006. *Pos:* Vpres, Austin Contemp Visual Arts Asn, 84-84. *Teaching:* Lectr watercolor & drawing, SW Tex State Univ, San Marcos, 81-88; painting & drawing, Tex Woman's Univ, Denton, 88-90, adj asst prof, 90-2012, adj prof art emeritus, 2012; vis asst prof art, Tex A&M Univ, Corpus Christi, spring 97, Austin Coll, Sherman, Tex, spring 99 & 2006. *Awards:* Cash Award, Tex Fine Arts Asn Juried Exhib, 82; Plaque of Distinction, Marietta Nat 15th Ann Painting & Sculpture, 82; Resident Visual Artist Fel, Va Ctr Creative Arts, 82 & 84. *Bibliog:* Marcie J Inman (auth), Artists' works convey responses to nature, Artimes, 9/93. *Mem:* Greater Denton Arts Coun (exhib comt chmn). *Media:* Acrylic on wood. *Dealer:* William Campbell Contemp Art 4935 Byers Ft Worth TX 76107; Cinema Gallery 120 W Main Urbana IL 61801. *Mailing Add:* 2297 Wood Hollow Rd Denton TX 76208

WELLER, PAUL
PHOTOGRAPHER, PAINTER

b Boston, Mass, Dec 20, 1912. *Study:* Nat Acad Design, 32-33; Art Students League, 45. *Work:* Metrop Mus, NY; San Francisco Mus, Mod Art, Calif; Philadelphia Mus Art, Pa; Baltimore Mus Art, Md; Wolfson Found Mus, Miami, Fla. *Comn:* Mural, US Post Off, US Treasury Dept, Baldwinsville, NY, 41. *Exhib:* Ann Show, Chicago Art Inst, 39; Ann, Philadelphia Art Alliance, Pa, 40; Solo exhib, Paul Weller Photos, Brooklyn Mus, NY, 50; Ann, Univ Ky Mus, 86. *Mem:* Jimmy Ernst Artists Alliance, East Hampton, NY; Nat Arts Club, NY. *Media:* All Media. *Publ:* Illusr, Sci Am Mag, 50-75; Bantam Books, 60-77; Simon & Schuster, 65-77; Forbes Mag, 67-77; Woman's Day, 67-77. *Dealer:* Mary Ryan Gallery 452 Columbus Ave New York NY 10024. *Mailing Add:* 281 Old Stone Hwy East Hampton NY 11937

WELLS, BETTY CHILDS
PAINTER, ILLUSTRATOR

b Baltimore, Md, Dec 7, 1926. *Study:* Johns Hopkins Univ, 46; Md Inst Art, grad, 48, scholar, 49. *Hon Degrees:* Md Inst Coll Art, Hon BFA, 96. *Work:* Peale Mus, Baltimore; White House & Supreme Court, Washington, DC; NZ Nat Gallery Art; Ariz State Univ Art Mus, Ariz, 2005; Maryland Inst Coll of Art; Towson State Univ, Holtzman Art Gallery, MD; Toronto Pub Libr, Can; Colo State Univ; Provident Savings Bank; pvt collection, Arthur Houghton Jr; Piper Rudnick Convention Center, Philadelphia. *Comn:* Interior murals (plaster & mosaic), Taylor Manor Psychiat Ctr, Ellicott City, Md, 69; interior murals (mosaic), Lake Clifton Sch, Baltimore, 71; exterior mural (mosaic), Templeton Sch, Baltimore, 73; Chief Justice Warren E Burger (portrait sketch), 76; Mrs Warren E Burger (portrait), Coll William & Mary, 83. *Exhib:* Solo exhibs, Betty Wells, Pen & Inks & Collages, Int Gallery, Baltimore, 66, Baltimore Mus Art, 74, US Supreme Ct, Washington, DC, 78-79, Fla State Univ, 80, Supreme Court Odyssey, Grinter Galleries, Univ Fla, 80, Art of Betty Wells, Va Beach Arts Ctr, 87, Watergate Drawings by Betty Wells, Newseum, Arlington, Va, 97, Mad Hatter Gallery, Farmville, Va, 2007, Promega, 3 month show, Fitchburg, Wisc, 2011; Audubon Artist Ann, Nat Acad Art, New York; An Am Album: Images from women artists, Nairobi, Kenya, 85; and others. *Collection Arranged:* Ariz State Univ Art Mus, 2005; Harry Ransom Ctr, Univ Tex, 2005. *Pos:* Freelance courtroom illusr, Washington Post, 72-77 & WTOP, Washington, 73-74; courtroom illusr, NBC, 74-; comnr, Va Beach Resort Area Adv Comn, 84-88 & 94-; juror, Chesapeake Bay Watercolorists, 2003 & Chesapeake Bay Art Asn, 2003. *Teaching:* Instr basic drawing, Md Inst Art, 46-48. *Awards:* Henry Walters Award for First Place in Fine Arts, Md Inst Col Art, 48; Best in Show, Easton Acad Arts, Md, 66; Two Emmy Awards, 78; Distinguished Alumni Award, Md Inst, Col Art, 96. *Bibliog:* Robert Leslie (auth), Walls designed by Betty Wells, Idea, Japan, Vol 23, No 130; cover story, Am Bar Asn J, 7/79; Patricia Paul Newsom (auth), Betty Wells: Veteran Washington Reporter, Am Artist, 11/84. *Mem:* Artists Equity Asn (pres, Md Chap, 66-68); Arts and Humanities Comn, Virginia Beach, Va; Nat Acad TV Arts & Sci; Tidewater Artists Asn. *Media:* Multimedia, Oil. *Res:* Working on new style in oils. *Specialty:* Fine art and illustration. *Interests:* Swimming, ballroom dancing, biking, news. *Collection:* news and courtroom illustrations, acrylic paintings of the Burger Court, oil paintings including florals, landscapes, portraits, abstract/art deco. *Publ:* Contribr, Designing and Making Mosaics, Davis, 71; Arts for Architecture, Dept Housing & Urban Develop, 73; illusr, Supreme Court on Nixon Tapes, NY Times, US News & World Report, 74 & Newsweek, 10/77 & 12/77; cover, Am Bar Asn J, 3/77; cover design & illusr, Bryson B Rash's Footnote Washington, EPM Publ Inc, 83; co-auth with Vicki Gentri, Illustrating Justice for NBC News, 2014. *Dealer:* Mickey and Arlene Sego The Art-Cade Gallery 1321 Jamestown Rd 204 Williamsburg VA 23185; Vickie 1312 Egret Ct Little Elm TX 75068; Keri Douglas 19 Logan Cir Wash DC 20005. *Mailing Add:* 2180 Rosewell Dr Virginia Beach VA 23454

WELLS, CHARLES
SCULPTOR, PRINTMAKER

b New York, NY, Dec 24, 1935. *Study:* Student, George Sch, Newton, Pa; Student, Amherst Col; Apprentice, Leonard Baskin, 61—64. *Work:* Represented in permanent collections Nat Mus Am Art, Wash, Whitney Mus, New York City, James A Michener Art Mus, La Salle Univ Art Mus, 2004. *Exhib:* Represented in permanent collections, Nat Portrait Gallery, Libr Congress, Mass Inst of Technol, Nat Acad of Design, New York City; group shows, at Brooklyn Mus Art, Whitney Mus, Spoleto Festival, Italy, Macedonian Mus of Modern Art, Thessaloniki, Greece, Amsterdam Concertgebouw, Corcoran Gallery. *Teaching:* With Am Sch, Rome, 1964-1965. *Awards:* Recipient Prix de Rome, 64, 3 gold medals, Nat Acad of Design Annual. *Mem:* Fel Am Acad, Rome; Nat Acad (assoc, 88, acad 94-)

WELLS, KARIN CHRISTENSEN
PAINTER, INSTRUCTOR

b Chicago, Ill, Nov 24, 1943. *Study:* New Eng Sch Art & Design, Suffolk Univ, Boston, Dip, 1965; Butera Sch Art, Boston, Dip, 1987; Studied with Numael Pulido, Hancock, NH, 1992-1994; Calvin Goodman, 2008-. *Work:* James Gelly, Sr VP & CFO, Ingersoll Rand Co LTD; David D'Alessandro (former Pres & Ceo), John

Hancock. *Exhib:* Thorne-Sagendorf Gallery, Keene, NH, 1997; Am Soc Portrait Artists, Montgomery, Ala, 1997; Wash Soc Portrait Artists, Senate Rotunda, Washington, DC, 1998; Portrait Soc Am, Washington, DC, 1999; Copley Soc Boston, Boston, Mass, 2002; Portrait Soc Am, Philadelphia, Pa, 2008. *Pos:* Artist Member, Sharon Art Ctr, Peterborough, NH, 1995-; Copley Soc, Boston, Mass, 1997-; Founding Member, Portrait Soc Am, Tallahassee, Fla, 1998-. *Teaching:* Instr, Master Class, Karin Wells Studio, Peterborough, NH, 2004-. *Awards:* People's Choice Award, Jurors' Choice Competition, Thorne-Sagendorf, Keene, NH, 1997 ; First Prize, Int Portrait Arts Festival, Am Soc Portrait Artists, Montgomery, Ala, 1997; Special Recognition, Int Juried Competition, Washington, Soc Portrait Artists, Washington, DC, 1997; First Prize Ann Int Portrait Competition, Portrait Soc Am, Washington, DC, 1999; Winner, Richard & Mary Schroeder Portrait Award, Copley Soc Boston, Mass, 2002; Award Excellence, Ann Int Portrait Competition, Portrait Soc Am, Philadelphia, Pa, 2008. *Bibliog:* Joni Hullinghorst (auth), Challenging the Odds: Wells Settles the Nature VS Nurture Debate, Keene Sentinel, 2003; Planet Luxury TV Series, Episode 5: Feature Karin Wells, Can Broadcasting, 2007; Award winning paintings reported in: Int Artist Mag; Artist's Mag; Am Artist Mag; Boston Globe; Manchester Union Leader. *Mem:* Portrait Soc Am; Copley Soc Boston; Monadnock Art, Friends of the Dublin Art Colony; Sharon Art Center. *Media:* Oil. *Publ:* Auth, Achieving Traditional Lighting with New Technology, Portrait Signature, 1997; auth, Master Showcase, Int Artist Mag, issue 12, 2000; auth, Building Art Beyond the Image, Text of Speech, PSOA Convention, 2001. *Dealer:* Copley Society of Boston 158 Newbury St Boston MA 02116; Twinhouse Art Gallery 2815 Peachtree Rd Atlanta GA 30305; Art 3 Gallery 44 W Brook St Manchester NH 03101. *Mailing Add:* 408 Middle Hancock Rd Peterborough NH 03458

WELLS, LYNTON
PAINTER
b Baltimore, Md, Oct 21, 1940. *Study:* RI Sch Design, Providence, BFA, 62; Cranbrook Acad Art, Bloomfield Hills, Mich, MFA, 65. *Work:* Mus Mod Art, NY; Dallas Mus Fine Art, Tex; Henry Gallery, Washington; Walker Art Ctr, Minneapolis; Indianapolis Mus Art. *Exhib:* Solo exhibs, Andre Emmerich Gallery, NY, 75, Clair Copley, Los Angeles, 76, Droll/Kolbert Gallery, 78, Univ Wis-Eau Claire, 79, Sable-Castelli, Can, 85 & Mary Delahoyd Gallery, NY, 94, Post Gallery, Los Angeles, 2001; retrospective, Princeton Univ Art Mus, 79; Baron/Boisanté, NY, 92; Univ Nev, Las Vegas, 95; 109 Crosby St, NY, 2005; Jonathan Shorr Gallery, 2006; Rebecca 1Bel Gallery, Columbus, Ohio, 2008; Christopher Henry Gallery, 2008. *Teaching:* Instr, Sch Visual Arts, 1976-. *Awards:* NY State Coun Arts, 73 & 77; Nat Endowment Arts Grant, 75. *Bibliog:* Bruce Boice (auth), article, Artforum, 5/73; Peter Bunnell (auth), catalogue, Princeton Univ, 79; Dave Hickey (auth), catalogue, Univ Nev, Las Vegas, 95; Dave Hickey (auth), catalog, Post Gallery, Los Angles, 2001. *Media:* Raw Pigment, Acrylic Resin & Ink. *Interests:* Japanese art, Edo & Momoyama eras. *Dealer:* Rory Bertifiaume NY. *Mailing Add:* 307 W Broadway New York NY 10013

WELLS, MENTHE
PAINTER, SCULPTOR
b New York, NY, July 3, 1942. *Study:* Univ Bridgeport, BS Art and Psychology, 63; Rutgers Univ, MA in Fine Art, 64; Univ Conn, DpED, 81; Univ Conn, PhD (synaesthetics, PhD (art/psychology), 84. *Work:* Jane Voorhees Zimmerli Art Mus, NJ painting; Eastern Conn State Univ painting; Univ Calif, Riverside painting; Univ Conn; Univ Bridgeport, Conn; and others paintings in public collections; Roundabout, NYC Event and Exhib solo 80 animated sculptures FM Fine Art Gallery solo 2015 (50 paintings/sculpture). *Comn:* public and pvt collections Includes: Europe, England, Thailand, Australia, Poland, Thirty-two ft mural, Windsor Bd of Educ, Conn; Impressions (first sight-sound intermedia in an art mus 1970-71); Impressions (sight-sound intermedia), Wadsworth Atheneum Art Mus & Enfield Bd of Educ. *Exhib:* Solo exhib, Animated sculpture, Lutz Mus, (35 animated sculptures), Manchester, Conn, 79; Crespi NYC Paintings; Winter juried exhib, Bushnell Gallery, 80; invitational show, Bosham Gallery, Sussex, Eng, 84 & 85; Carlson Gallery, Arnold Bernhard Arts & Humanities Ctr, 88; Zimmerli Art Mus; Wadsworth Atheneum Art Mus; Fac Gallery; Sculpture, (ECOARTS) EcoArts Mus, 2002-08; Three Elements Gallery, 2007; Chiang Mai, Thailand, Seoul, Korea, Okinawa, Japan, 2012; LA Art Core, Historic Brewery Art Ctr, Los Angeles, 2012-2013 tandem solo (40 paintings/sculptures), Chiang Mai Univ Mus Art, Thailand, 2012 (28 artworks 25 paintings and 3 projection studies); Philharmonic Design House, 2012; Calif Home Mag Selected Design House, 2012; Shintaro Akatsu Sch Design; The Schelfhaudt Gallery, 2013; Hugo Rivera Gallery 3, 2013; San Luis Obispo Mus Art, 2013 painting; HangUp 2012 SAE Internat Publication of 20 photgraphic studies Gallery (52 paintings/sculpture); filmed artist Art World; KSBR radio 88.5 Featured Famous Artist, April, 2013; KSBR radio 88.5 Featured Artist interview Dec, 2013; Laguna Design Ctr 2014-15 sculpture; Gallery 104 (78 paintings/sculpture); San Luis Obispo Mus of Art tandem solo (29 paintings/sculpture), spring, 2014; San Luis Obispo Mus of Art fall, 2014 painting; Shintaro Akatsu Sch Design, Schelfhaudt Gallery 2015 painting/sculptures; European Tour 2014 65 paintings/sculptures in solo exhibs; Lublin Marii-Curie Sklodowskiej Univ; solo Mus Zajezdnia Galley (65 paintings/sculptures) public art acquisitions; Muncipal Contemporary Gallery Mus Zamosc Poland (65 Paintings/Sculpture). *Pos:* Dir, Acad Assoc, Beverly Hills. *Teaching:* Instr, synaesthetics, Wadsworth Atheneum, Art Mus, 69-76; instr sculpture, drawing & art hist, Manchester, Greater Hartford & Tunxis Col, 77-79; instr animated sculpture, Trinity Col & Skidmore Col. *Bibliog:* L Guica (auth), Animated sculpture-puppets lead the class, Hartford Courant, 8/14/77; L Margolies (auth), Carol Menthe soft sculpturist extraordinaire, Farmington Valley Herald, 3/39/79; Gene Feist (auth), Menthe Wells: A Retrospective, scintillating works, Chelsea Arts Newsletter (publ), 2006; J Maes Zepada (auth), El Aviso (review), 2011; Cassone Mag Art, 2013; Cassone, 2013, Cassone 2014 European Tour; Art Wall, 2013. *Media:* Oil, Enamels, Acrylic, Granite Installation, Mixed, Welded Steel. *Res:* Synaesthesia. *Collection:* 493 current pvt collections, hold paintings, and sculpture. *Publ:* Impressions Workshop, Sight Sound Intermedia, Arts in Soc. *Dealer:* Academic Assoc; AAI; aaintec@gmail.com. *Mailing Add:* 751 Weir Canyon Rd Suite 157-124 Anaheim CA 92808

WELTER, COLE H
PAINTER, EDUCATOR
b Watertown, SDak, July 26, 1952. *Study:* Univ Tex, Austin, with Bob Levers & Everett Spruce, BFA, 74, MFA, 76; Tex Tech Univ, with Gene Mittler & Bill Lockhart, PhD,89. *Work:* Huntington Gallery, Univ Tex, Austin; Anchorage Mus Hist Art, Alaska; San Antonio Mus Mod Art, Tex; Abilene Fine Arts Mus, Tex; Univ Alaska Anchorage Permanent Collection. *Comn:* Windows, First Christian Church, Anchorage, Alaska, 92. *Exhib:* 39th Ann Midyear Show, Butler Inst Am Art, Youngstown, Ohio, 75; 69th Ann Am Exhib, Newport Fine Arts Asn, RI, 76; 34th Ann Competition, Abilene Fine Arts Mus, Abilene, Tex, 76; 43rd Ann Competition, Abilene Fine Arts Mus, Tex, 87; 10th Ann Regional Exhib, McCormick Gallery, Midland Col, Tex, 87; Alaska '92, Alaska Visual Arts Ctr, 92; and others. *Pos:* Exec bd dir, Anchorage Mus Asn, 88-92; ed, Alaska J Art, 88-95; mem, NASAD comn on accreditation, 2001-2006. *Teaching:* Instr, design, Univ Tex, Austin, 75-76, Tex Tech Univ, 86-88; Chmn, Dept Art, painting, Univ Alaska Anchorage, 88-95; prof & dir, James Madison Univ, Sch Art & Art Hist, 95-2004, prof Art, James Madison Univ, 2004-. *Awards:* Fel, Ford Found, 75 & 76; Reston Prize, Nat Asn Schs Art & Design, 87; Distinguished Art Alumni Award, Tex Tech, 91 & 2004. *Bibliog:* Jan Ingram (auth), Exhibits make happy partners, 9/10/89 & Alaska 92 offers a fresh, bold view of state arts scene, 7/26/92, Anchorage Daily News. *Mem:* Coll Art Asn. *Media:* Mixed-Media. *Publ:* Auth, Discipline based art education: not if, but where?, Design Arts Educ, 87; Art and Computers: is there room in the studio for both?, Design Arts Educ, 89; ed, Technological segregation: A peek through the looking glass at the rich and poor in an information age, Arts Educ Policy Review, 97. *Mailing Add:* James Madison Univ Sch Art & Art History Duke Hall MSC7101 Harrisonburg VA 22807

WELTY, JENNIFER ROTH
PAINTER, INSTRUCTOR
b San Jose, Calif, Jun 14, 1958. *Study:* Int Fine Arts Coll (interior design, valedictorian), AA, 79; studied with Daniel Green, 2001, Richard Schmid, Nancy Guzik, Casey Baugh, Sherrie McGraw, CW Mundy, Jeremy Lipking, Frank Serrano. *Work:* Bradford Exchange, Chicago, Ill. *Comn:* Julie Inkster Hall of Fame, LPGA Champion, Calif, 82; Mr & Mrs Proulx, found & inventor Intuit, Calif, 92; Maria Bartiromo, CNBC Anchorwoman Wall St Managing Ed, New York, 2003; Tony Holbrook, Advanced Micro Devices CEO, Calif, 2003; Roy Nichols, Huntsville Bus Hall of Fame, Ala, 2004. *Teaching:* Head Instr portraiture, Pvt Attelier, Santa Cruz, Calif, 97-99; mentor, Cecelia Beaux Soc mentoring Prog, 2010. *Awards:* Finalist winner, Portraits, The Artists 20th Ann Art Competition, Artist's Mag, 2002; Certificate Recognition, Int Portrait Competition, Portrait Soc Am, 2002, Certificate of Excellence, 2004, 2008, Top Ten Finalist Hon Award, 2003, 2005; Award of Exceptional Merit, Int Portrait Compeitions, Portrait Soc Am, 2010. *Bibliog:* Int Artist, Master Portrait Artist Showcase, Int Artist Mag Vol 28, Dec 2003; Johanna Spinks, Masters in the Making, Folio Mag, Portrait Soc Atlanta, Vol 25, 2005; M Stephen Doherty, A Top Agency Answers Your Questions, Am Artist Mag, Nov 2007; Veranda, July-Aug 2010. *Mem:* Portrait Soc Am, 99-2009; Cecelia Beaux Soc, 2007-2009. *Media:* Oil on linen. *Dealer:* Portraits Inc 7 W 51st St New York NY 10019; Beverly McNeil Gallery 2801 6th Ave S Birmingham AL 35233

WELTZHEIMER, MARIE KASH See Kash, Marie (Marie Kash Weltzheimer)

WELU, JAMES A
MUSEUM DIRECTOR
b Dubuque, IA, Dec 15, 1943. *Study:* Loras Coll, BA, 1966; Univ Notre Dame, MA, 1967, MFA, 1968; Boston Univ, PhD, 1977, Coll of the Holy Cross, 2008, Loras Univ, 2009, Clark Univ, 2010, Assumption Coll, 2012. *Pos:* Asst cur, Worcester Art Mu, Mass, 1974-76, assoc cur, 1976-80, instr, 1977-78, 80-81, chief cur, 1980-86 & dir, 1986-2011, dir emeritus, 2011-. *Teaching:* Instr, St Mary-of-the-Woods (Ind) Coll, 1968-70 & Clark Univ, Worcester, 1980, Worcester Art Mus, 1977-. *Awards:* Boston Univ grantee, 1973, Nat Educ Asn Mus' Prof grantee, 1976-81; Samuel H Kress Found fel, 1973; recipient Netherland-Am Found award Nether Found, 1973, Distinguished Alumni award Boston Univ Grad Sch, 1986. *Mem:* Historians Netherlandish Art, Northeast Mus Assoc, Am All Mus (accreditation comnr 2000-2012), Coll Art Asn Am, Am Fedn Arts (trustee), Asn Art Mus Dirs (pres, 1999-2000, trustee). *Publ:* Vermeer: His Cartographic Sources, The Art Bulletin, 1975; 17th Century Dutch Painting: Raising the Curtain on New England Private Collections, 1979; The Collector's Cabinet: Flemish Painting from New England Private Collections, 1983; Judith Leyster & Pieter Biesboer et al (co-auths), A Dutch Master and Her World, 1993. *Mailing Add:* 10 Massachussets Ave Worcester MA 01609-1649

WENGER, BRUCE EDWARD
PRINTMAKER, GRAPHIC ARTIST
b Grand Rapids, Mich, Mar 10, 1948. *Study:* Western Mich Univ, BA, 70; Ohio Univ, MFA, 73. *Work:* Grand Rapids Art Mus, Mich; US Info Agency, Washington, DC; Western Mich Univ Print Collection, Kalamazoo; Chicago Gallery, Univ Ill; Ohio Univ Print Collection, Athens. *Exhib:* 6th Biennial Paper & Clay Exhib, Memphis State Univ, Tenn, 87; LaGrange Nat XII, Chattahoochee Valley Art Asn, Ga, 87; 7th Ann Faber Birren Color Award Show, Stamford, Conn, 87; 2nd Nat Juried Exhib, Viridian Gallery, New York, 88; 20th Nat Works on Paper Exhib, Minot State Col, NDak, 90; LaGrange Nat XVII, Chattahoochee Valley Art Asn, Ga, 92; 10th Ann Maine/Maritime Flatworks Exhib, Univ Maine, Presque Isle, 92. *Teaching:* Asst prof studio art & art hist, Houghton Coll, NY, 78-86, head dept art, 82-86; lectr in drawing & printmaking, Rochester Inst Technol, NY, 86-92 & asst prof 2D design, 92-2007, instr computer graphics & drawing, 2010. *Awards:* Purchase Award, Fourth Ann Maine Maritime Flat Work Exhib, Univ Presque Isle Maine, 86. *Mem:* Coll Art Asn; The Print Club. *Media:* Computer Graphics. *Publ:* Coauth, Design Dynamics: Integrating Design and Technology, Prentice-Hall, 2003. *Mailing Add:* PO Box 21 Fillmore NY 14735-0021

WENGER, JANE (B)
PHOTOGRAPHER, CONCEPTUAL ARTIST
b New York, NY, Jan 24, 1944. *Study:* Alfred Univ, NY, BFA, 66; Ill Inst Technol, Chicago, 69; Univ Ill, Chicago, MFA, 80. *Work:* Mus Mod Art, NY; Mus Contemp Art, Chicago, Ill; Milwaukee Art Mus, Wis; Lehigh Univ, Bethlehem, Pa; Southern Ill Univ, Edwardsville. *Exhib:* One-person shows, Artemisia Gallery, Chicago, Ill, 76, Foto Gallery, NY, 78 & 80, Allen Frumkin Photographs, Chicago, Ill, 80, Mus Contemp Art, Chicago, Ill, 81, Milwaukee Art Mus, Wis, 82 & PS 1, NY, 82; Art in Chicago, 1945-1995, Mus Contemp Art, Chicago. *Teaching:* Instr photog, Univ Ill at Chicago, 75-90. *Awards:* Project Completion Grants, Ill Arts Coun, 79-83. *Bibliog:* Carole Harmel (auth), The dialectics of sexuality, New Art Examiner, 79; Lynne Warren (auth), Jane Wenger, Arts Mag, 3/81; Mary Jane Jacob (auth), Options 7, Jane Wenger: An Environmental Installation, Mus Contemp Art, 81. *Mem:* Soc Photog Educ. *Mailing Add:* 1509 N Wicker Park Chicago IL 60622

WENGLOWSKI, JOYCE
PAINTER
b Sept 2, 1943. *Study:* Rochester Inst Technology, 1962-63; Manhattanville Coll, BFA cum laude, 80; Haystack Sch Crafts, 90, 91. *Work:* Hudson Valley Hospital, Cortland Manor, NY; Northern Westchester Hospital, Mt Kisco, NY; Pfizer Corp, Rye Brook, NY; Pepsi Co, Purchase, NY; Goldman Sachs and Co, New York, NY; Westchester Medical Ctr, Valhalla, NY. *Comn:* 18 ft interactive painting, Hope Soars Over All, Northern Westchester Hospital, Mt Kisco, NY. *Exhib:* KMAA Featured Artist, Katonah Mus, NY, 2002; Real to Unreal, The Hammond Mus, North Salem, NY, 2004; Paper Jam 1, 2, 3, 4, Neuberger Mus, Purchase, NY, 2009, 2010, 2011, 2012; Womens Work, Morgan Stanley Smith Barney, Purchase, NY, 2008; g Watson Gallery, Stonington, ME, 2014; LaGianna Bldg, White Plains, NY, 2015. *Collection Arranged:* Joyce Wenglowski Gallery, Blue Hill, Me, 96-99; co-curator, From the Painters' Perspective, The Studio, Armonk, NY. *Pos:* adv bd mem, Deer Isle Artists Assn, Maine, 1993-1997, The Katonah Mus Artists Assn, NY, 1995-2015, The Katonah Mus Artists Assn NY, adv bd mem, 1995-, The Studio, An Alternative Space for Art, Armonk, NY, 2002-2010; pres, The Katonah Mus Artists Assn, NY, 2002-2003. *Teaching:* grantee, visiting artist, Westchester Magnet Acad, Purchase, NY, Empire State Partership, Council of the Arts between Westchester and Greenburg Central School District, 2005. *Awards:* Mixed Media award, Stamford Art Assn, 1996, KMAA at Northern Westchester Center for the Arts, Katonah Mus Arts, 2001. *Bibliog:* Gillian Greenhill Hannum (auth), Somewhere Between Sea and Sky, 1992, Seduced by Color: Joyce Wenglowski and the Painterly Tradition, 2007; Dominick Lombardi (auth), Between Places, NY Times, 2002; Kim Daley (auth), Wenglowski Exhib on View at the Studio in Armonk, White Plains, NY, 2007; GG Kopilak, Maria Hale, Pleasantville Connects to the Visual Arts, PCTV Channel 76, 2008. *Mem:* Katonah Museum Artists Assn (pres, 2003, chair visiting artists program, 2003-2007, chair featured artist at the Katonah Mus Art, 2009-2015, chair online gallery artist of the month, 2011-2015); Arts Westchester (1982-present); Deer Isle Artists Assn (adv bd mem, 1993-97). *Media:* Acrylic. *Collection:* Jason Moran, Toby and Lee Cooperman, Rayanne and Eduard Kleiner, pvt collectors 15 US states, England and Italy. *Publ:* auth, The Re-Emergence of the Creative Self: Teaching Art in a Nursing Home, MCA Newsletter, 1994; auth, Making a Difference, Teaching Art in a Nursing Home, Art Calendar, The Business Magazine for Visual Artists, 1995. *Dealer:* g Watson Gallery 68 Maine St Stonington ME 04681; Deer Isle Artists Assn 15 Main St Deer Isle ME 04627. *Mailing Add:* 32 Partridge Rd Katonah NY 10536

WENGROVITZ, JUDITH
PAINTER, INSTRUCTOR
b Brooklyn, NY, Jan 3, 1931. *Study:* Hunter Coll, New York, with Dong Kingman, BA (art educ), 52; workshops with Frank Webb, Millard Sheets and Carlton Plummer. *Work:* Pen Arts Bldg, Washington, DC; NIH, Bethesda, Md. *Comn:* Series of Drawings, PMA Properties, Alex, Va; Nat Bus Educator's Asn, Reston, Va, 82; IBM, Washington, DC, 83; painting, comm by Judge Stanley Sporkin, Washington, DC, 87 & 88; NIH Children's Inn, Bethesda, Md, 92 & 98. *Exhib:* Va Watercolor Soc, 80-2012; Solo exhibs, 20th Century Gallery, Williamsburg, Va, 91 & Nat Inst Health Bethesda, Md, 94; Allied Artists Am 76 exhib; Int Exhib of Miniature Painters, Sculptors & Gravers Soc, Washington, DC, 96-2013; Southern Watercolor Soc, Colquitt Co Arts Ctr, Moulfrie, Ga, 2007; Ratner Mus, Bethesda, Md, 2013; Goodwin House, Falls Church, Va, 2012, 2013; Frame Factory, 2014. *Pos:* Layout artist, Woodward & Lothrop, Washington, DC, 52-54; judge, Arts on the Lawn at Bellgrade, Richmond, Va, 96. *Teaching:* Instr drawing, design & painting, Judy Wengrovitz Sch Art, 62-2014; guest lectr painting, George Mason Univ, 94, Manassas Art Guild & Springfield Art Guild, 96-2003 & Brush & Pallete Club, Sanford, NC, 2003, Jewish Community Ctr, Fairfax, Va, 2013. *Awards:* Excellence award, NLPW, Washington, DC, 2004; Mid Atlantic Watercolor Exhib, 2008; Windsor Newton Award, Southern Watercolor 30th Exhib, 2007; Award of Excellence, Va Watercolor Soc, 2010. *Bibliog:* Kathryn Evans (auth), Springfield artist details in watercolor, Springfield Connection, 87; Daniel Seligson (auth), Wengrovitz: Matron of the Arts, The Connection, 4/98; Alice Ross (auth), Elan Mag, 4/2003. *Mem:* Nat League Am Pen Women (NLAPW) (prog chmn, 2004-09, 2013, pres, 74-76, 2013); Va Watercolor Soc (pres, 88-2009); Washington Watercolor Soc; Southern Watercolor Soc; Springfield Art Guild (pres & founder, 97-2014). *Media:* Watercolor, Mixed Media, Acrylic. *Publ:* Best of Watercolor Places, 97 & Best of Watercolor Textures, 98, Rockport Publ; The Artists Mag, 9/98; illusr book cover design Vital Signs of Poetry, NIH, Bethesda, Md, 99; Int Artist Mag, 4-5/2000; The Collected Best of Watercolor selected by Betty Lou Schlemm, 2002. *Dealer:* The Art League 105 N Union St Alexandria VA 22314. *Mailing Add:* 5220 Cather Rd Springfield VA 22151

WENTWORTH, JANET
PAINTER
b Norwell, Mass, May 5, 1957. *Study:* Parsons Sch Design, New York, BFA, 80; Nat Acad Sch Fine Arts, New York, with Harvy Dinnerstein, 81-82; Art Students League, New York, with Harvy Dinnerstein, Ted Seth Jacobs & Frank Mason, 83-87; La Napoule Arts Found, France & Durham, NH, with Jack Beal, 85-86; Brooklyn Col, New York, with Philip Pearlstein & Lennert Anderson, MFA, 91; Sch Visual Arts, New York, cert (art educ), 92. *Work:* Art Students League Permanent Collection, NY. *Exhib:* Am Watercolor Soc Ann Exhib, Nat Acad Fine Arts, NY, 76; Pastel Soc Am Ann Exhib, Nat Arts Club, NY, 85; League Am Pen Women Ann Exhib, Copley Soc, Boston, 87; Choice, AIR Gallery, NY, 91; Nat Acad Design 167th Ann, Nat Acad Fine Arts, NY, 92. *Awards:* Bd Dirs Award, Pastel Soc Am, 84; Gold Medal Honor, Knickerbocker Artists, NY, 85; Cert Merit, Nat Acad Design 167th Ann, 92. *Mem:* Nat Asn Women Artists; Pastel Soc Am; NY Arts Group; Coll Art Asn. *Media:* Pastel, Oil. *Dealer:* Harris Peel Box 1 Peel Gallery Rd Danby VT 05739. *Mailing Add:* 665 Kortwright Church Rd East Meredith NY 13757-1055

WENZEL, JOAN ELLEN
ASSEMBLAGE ARTIST, SCULPTOR
b 1944. *Study:* Syracuse Univ, 62-64; NY Univ, BS (painting), 66 & MA (painting), 76; Harvard Univ 66-67. *Work:* Skirball Mus Jewish Art, Los Angeles; Aldrich Mus Contemp Art, Ridgefield, Conn; City of Orlando, Fla. *Comn:* Multi-section wall structures, Prudential Life, Newark, NJ, 89, Citibank, NY, 87, Peerless Corp, Greenpoint, NY, 87, Nevele Hotel, Ellenville, NY, 88 & IBM Corp, NY, 90. *Exhib:* Approach, Avoidance Art in the Obsessive Idiom (with catalog), 81 & Off the Wall (with catalog), 85, Queens Mus, NY; solo exhibs, Gallery Yves Arman, NY, 82 & Helander Gallery, Palm Beach, Fla, 89 & 94; Kisch & Wenzel, SoHo Crt Visual Art, NY, 86; 10 Yrs of Collecting, Aldrich Mus Contemp Art, 86; Solo exhib, Albertson Peterson, Orlando, Fla, 92, Univ Jacksonville Art Mus, Fla, 93 & Admar Fine Art; and others. *Media:* Wood and Metal. *Dealer:* Albertson Peterson Gallery 329 Park Ave S Winter Park FL 32789; Helander Gallery 350 S County Rd Palm Beach FL 33480. *Mailing Add:* 2275 Ibis Isles Dr E Palm Beach FL 33480-5367

WERFEL, GINA S
PAINTER, EDUCATOR
b Brooklyn, NY, July 1, 1951. *Study:* Kirkland Col, NY, with Elias Friedensohn, BA, 74; New York Studio Sch, with Mercedes Matter, Leland Bell & Andrew Forge, cert, 76; Columbia Univ, with David Lund, Leon Goldin & Jane Wilson, MFA, 79. *Exhib:* Solo exhibs, Prince Street Gallery, NY, 80, 82, 85, 86, 89, 92, 94 & 98, Coll Mus Art, Waterville, Maine, 89 & Maier Mus Art, Randolph-Macon Woman's Col, Lynchburg, Va, 92 & Monty Stabler Gallery, Birmingham, Ala, 93; two-person exhibs, Cong Sq Gallery, Portland, Maine & Colby Coll Mus Art, Waterville, Maine, 81, 83 & 84 & Second St Gallery, Charlotteville, Va, 94 & Monty Stabler Gallery, Birmingham, Ala, 95; Drawings from Nature, Joan Whitney Payson Mus, Portland, Maine, 82; Maine Coast Artists Gallery, Rockport, 83, 87, & 90; Jersey City Mus, NJ, 86; Personal Views: Four Painters & Landscape, Plymouth State Col, NH; 30 Years of Drawing, NY Studio Sch; Contemp Landscape, Art Inst Boston, Mass; 3 Landscape Painters: Armstrong, Lewis & Werfel, Washington Art Asn, Conn, 99. *Pos:* Co-dir, NY Studio Sch, Paris, France, summers, 74 & 75; artist-in-residence, Va Ctr Creative Arts, Sweetbriar, 81, Rockefeller Found Ctr, Bellagio, Italy, 84 & Djerassi Found, Woodside, Calif, 86; vis artist, Washington & Lee Univ, Lexington, Va, 94 & Fairbanks Art Asn, Alaska, 94. *Teaching:* Assoc prof art, Colby Col; Waterville, Maine, 80-91; chair & prof, Randolph-Macon Woman's Col, Lynchburg, Va, 91-97; head & prof, Dept Art & Art Hist, Univ Conn, Storrs. *Bibliog:* Carl Little (auth), Gina Werfel at the Colby Mus, Art in Am, 10/89; David Little & Arnold Skolnick (auth), Paintings of Maine, NY, 91; John Driscoll & Arnold Skolnick (auth), The Artist & the American Landscape, First Glance Bks, 98. *Mem:* Coll Art Asn. *Media:* Oil. *Dealer:* Prince Street Gallery 121 Wooster St New York NY 10012. *Mailing Add:* 2855 Mallorca Ln Davis CA 95616-6579

WERGER, ART(HUR) LAWRENCE
PRINTMAKER, EDUCATOR
b Ridgewood, NJ, Dec, 4, 1955. *Study:* RI Sch Design, BFA, 78; Univ Wis, Madison, with Warrington Colescott, MFA, 82. *Work:* High Mus Art, Atlanta, Ga; Boston Pub Libr; Brooklyn Mus, NY; Philadelphia Mus Art, Pa; Mus Fine Arts, Boston. *Exhib:* Southeast Seven 9, Southeastern Ctr Contemp Art, Winston-Salem, NC, 86; Georgia Printmakers (with catalog), High Mus Art, Atlanta, 86; 10 Yrs of Southeast Seven, Southeastern Ctr Contemp Art, 87-88; Fact/Fiction/Fantasy: Recent Narrative Art in the Southeast, Univ Tenn, Knoxville, 87-88; Colorprint USA Update 88, Mus of Tex Tech Univ, 88; Art Werger: In Print, Macon Mus Arts & Sci, 88; Technique is not always cheap: Extraordinary Printmaking, Art & Sci Ctr, Statesville, NC, 89; Solo exhibs, Peterson Hall Gallery, SGa Col, Douglas, 90, Overview, Gertrude Herbert Inst Art, Augusta, Ga, 91, The Graphic Narrative, Alexander Best Gallery, Jacksonville State Univ, Fla, 92, Chattahoochee Valley Art Mus, La Grange, Ga, 92, Middle Tenn State Univ, Murfreesboro, 92 & Prints, The Theater Arts Gallery, Greenville, NC, 97; Southern Printmakers 90, Southern Graphic Coun, Traveling Exhib, 90-91; The Graphic Narrative, Shelton State Community Col, Tuscaloosa, Ala, 90; Overview, NGa Col, Dahlonega, 91, Carriage Wks Gallery, Ga Coun Arts, Atlanta, 93 & Davidson Gallery, Seattle, Wash, 96; Man/Woman: Different Perspectives, N Arts Ctr, Atlanta, Ga, 91; Images 1990: A Portfolio of Thirty Six Prints, Davis Gallery, Idaho State Univ, Pocatello, 91, Merwin Gallery, Ill & Wesleyan Univ, 92; Temporary Positions, E Gallery, Porter Auditorium, Wesleyan Col, Macon, Ga, 92; Combined Talents, Fla Nat Exhib, Fla State Univ, Tallahassee, 92; Consumenta '91, Nuremberg, Ger, 92; Casual Observations, John Marlor Arts Ctr, Milledgeville, Ga, 93, Madison/Morgan Cult Ctr, Ga, 94 & Stephen F Austin Univ, Nacogdoches, Tex, 96; Recent Works, S Vt Art Ctr, Manchester, Vermont, 94, Halsey Gallery, Coll Charleston, SC, 94, Stone & Press Gallery, New Orleans, La, 94 & Columbia Col, SC, 94; Recent Works on Paper, Fanny Garver Gallery, Madison, Wis, 95 & 96; Printmaking Invitational, Ball State Mus Art, Ball State Univ, Muncie, Ind, 98-99; Beneath the Surface, Five Am Printmakers, St Mary's Univ, Winona, Minn, 98; Common Ground, Am Print Alliance, Roanoke Col, Salem, Va, Univ SColo, Pueblo, Lankershim Arts Ctr, Gallery N Hollywood, Calif & Iowa Wesleyan Col, Mt Pleasant, 99; 12th Norwegian Int Print Trienale, Fredrikstad, Norway, 99; Recent Impressions, Wesleyan Col, Macon, Ga, 96. *Teaching:* Assoc prof graphics & print, Wesleyan Col, 82-, chmn, Visual Art Area, 85-, Fine Art Dept, 82- & prof art, 82-. *Awards:* Southern

Arts Fed/Nat Endowment Arts Regional Fel, 92; Grant, State of Ga, 93; 2nd Place Award, 17th Ann Hoyt Nat Art Show, Hoyt Inst Fine Arts, New Castle, Pa, 98. *Bibliog:* Patrick E White (auth), Passionate Attention, Southeast Seven 9, 86. *Mem:* Coll Art Asn; Southern Graphics Coun; Los Angeles Printmaking Soc; Philadelphia Print Club. *Media:* Etching. *Dealer:* Eve Mannes Gallery Atlanta GA; Wenninger Graphics Boston MA. *Mailing Add:* 8245 Rock Riffle Rd Athens OH 45701-8823

WERNER, HOWARD
SCULPTOR

b Deal, NJ, July 27, 1951. *Study:* Rochester Inst Technol, BFA, 77; Sch Am Craftsmen. *Work:* Sch Am Craftsmen, Rochester, NY; Ariz State Univ Mus Fine Art, Tempe; Am Craft Mus, NY. *Exhib:* Okun Gallery, Santa Fe, 92; Sybarus Gallery, Royal Oak, Mich, 92; Joann Rapp Gallery, Scottsdale, 93; Snyderman Gallery, 93; solo shows, Sneiderman Gallery, Philadelphia, 96 & Rapp Gallery, Scottsdale, Ariz, 96-97; Expressions in Wood, Oakland Mus, Calif, 97; Oakland Mus Art, Calif, 97; Expressions in Wood: The Wornick Collection, Am Craft Mus, NY, 98. *Pos:* Resident, Art Park, Lewiston, NY, 75-77; traveling residency, NY State Parks & Recreation Cult Program, 76; vis artist, Nat Endowment Arts Omni Int, Atlanta, Ga, 77; resident, Peters Valley, Layton, NJ, 77-78. *Teaching:* Instr sculpture & furniture design, Peters Valley, Layton, NJ, 77-82; instr sculpture, Haywood Tech Inst, NC, 78; instr sculpture, Keane Col, NJ, 81; instr workshop, State Univ NY, New Paltz, 83; adj prof, Ariz State Univ, Tempe, 86-88. *Awards:* NY State Fel Grant, 87 & 93; Nat Endowment Arts, 88; Fel for the Arts, NY State, 92. *Bibliog:* Review, Craft Horizons, 78; John Kelsey (auth), New Handmade Furniture, Fine Woodworking, 79; Michael Stone (auth), review, New York Times, 10/81. *Mem:* Am Craft Coun; Peters Valley. *Media:* Wood. *Publ:* Coauth, Carving, Fine Woodworking, 77. *Dealer:* Gebert Contemporary Scottsdale & Santa Fe; Pritam Eames, E Hampton NY; Reform Gallery Los Angeles; Rakova Brecker Ft Lauderdale FL. *Mailing Add:* PO Box 430 Shokan NY 12481

WERNER-VAUGHN, SALLE
PAINTER, ILLUMINATOR

b 1939. *Study:* Tex Woman's Univ, BA, 61; Sacramento State Univ, 63; Rice Univ, host-grad, 78; Studied with William Hayter, Atelier Dix-Sept, Paris, 79; Am Acad in Rome, vis artist/scholar, 99-2000. *Work:* San Francisco Mus Mod Art, Calif; Akron Art Inst, Ohio; Bridwell Libr, Southern Methodist Univ, Dallas; Mus Fine Art, Boston; Mus Fine Art, Houston; Metrop Mus Art, NY; Mus Modern Art, Moscow; and others. *Exhib:* Solo exhib, Tyler Mus Art, Tex, 73, Helen Serger, La Boetie, New York, 82, 83, 84, Twilight, Unveiling, Choral Recital Hall, Moores Sch Music, Univ Houston, Tex, 1997-, Beauty Unforsaken, Meadows Gallery, Univ Tex, Tyler, Tex, 99, Salle Werner Vaughn: Parallel Universes, Meredith Long Gallery, 2004, Symbol: Coda to the Unseen, House of Redeemer, New York, 2007, CG Boerner, New York, 2008; Biennial Exhib Painting & Sculpture Show, Whitney Mus, NY, 73; Contemp Watercolors, Akron Art Inst, Ohio, Indianapolis, Ind & Rochester, NY, 76; Helen Serger, La Boetie Inc, NY, 77; Carus Gallery, NY, 79. *Teaching:* Founder experimental art, Art Involvement & Motivation, 70-; founder, Crystal Press, 79. *Bibliog:* Patsy Swank (auth), Salle Werner (film), Dallas Educ TV, 72; Arch Am Art, Smithsonian Inst; Lowery & Hopps (auths), Beauty Unforsaken, Univ Tex, Tyler, Tex, 99; Christine Pittel, Great Style, House Beautiful/Hearst Books, New York, 96; Holly Moore, Bob Brinkley & Laurann Claridge, Domestic Art: Curated Interiors, Assouline, New York, 2008; Elizabeth Milleker (auth), Songs from Elsewhere, Crystal Press, 94; Allison de Lima Green, Texas 150 Works from the Mus Fine Arts, Houston, Harry N Abrams, New York, 2000; Denison, Herrmann, Kunz & E Milliker, Collected Affinities Salle Werner-Vaughn, Artist & Collector, CG Boerner, New York, 2008. *Media:* Watercolor, Oil, tempera, installation. *Publ:* William Kelly Simpson, Werner-Vaughn, & Helen Serger, La Boetie, New York, 83. *Dealer:* Meredith Long Gallery Houston TX; CG Boerner New York. *Mailing Add:* 4618 Blossom St Houston TX 77007

WERNESS, HOPE B
HISTORIAN

b Del Rio, Tex, Feb 10, 1943. *Pos:* Dir, Univ Gallery, 82-87. *Teaching:* Vis lectr art hist, San Jose State Univ, Calif, 76-77; asst prof art hist, Calif State Col, Stanislaus, Turlock, Calif, 77-81, assoc prof & chair, 81-86, prof, 86-. *Awards:* Nat Endowment Humanities Summer Seminar, 80. *Mem:* Coll Art Asn. *Res:* Nineteenth century art history, specializing in Van Gogh, twentieth century art history; pre-Columbian and primitive art. *Mailing Add:* 913 Dianne Dr Turlock CA 95380

WERT, NED OLIVER
EDUCATOR, PAINTER

b Millersburg, Pa, May 26, 1936. *Study:* Indiana Univ of Pa, BS (art educ), 58; Pa State Univ, MEd (art), 64; Kent State Univ, with Alex Katz, Jim Melchert & Jack Tworkov, 70. *Work:* Southern Alleghenies Mus Art, Loretto, Pa; Pittsburgh Plate Glass Corp, Alcoa Corp, Pittsburgh, Pa; Am Int Sch, Dusseldorf, Ger; Pa State Mus, Harrisburg, Pa; Blue Cross, Blue Shield; IUP Mus, Indiana, Pa. *Exhib:* Assoc Artists Pittsburgh, Carnegie Mus Art; Butler Inst Art; Three Rivers Festival, Pittsburgh, Pa; La Mostra CAS, Lucca, Italy; Triennial Invitational, Southern Alleghenies Mus Art, Loretto, Pa; Noho Gallery, NY; Six Am Painters, Nancy, France; Lynden Gallery, Elizabethtown, Pa. *Collection Arranged:* 25 Exhibs, Univ Mus, Indiana, Pa. *Pos:* Dir, Univ Mus, Indiana, Pa, 88-96, retired; Eastern vpres, Nat Art Educ Asn; pres, Pa Art Educ Asn. *Teaching:* Art, Elizabethtown Area Sch Dist, Pa, 58-70; prof emer painting, Ind Univ Pa, 70-88. *Awards:* Best of Show, Fourth Ann Exhib, Westmoreland Mus, 82; Jurors Award, Assoc Artists Pittsburgh, Carnegie Mus Art, Pittsburgh, Pa, 82 & 97; Outstanding Educator, Nat Art Educ Asn, 86; Distinguished Alumnus, Indiana Univ of Pa, 88. *Mem:* Associated Artists Pittsburgh; Found IUP Presidents Coun; Allied Artists Johnstown; Millersburg Hist Soc; Ned Smith Ctr Nature & Art. *Media:* Acrylic, pastel. *Specialty:* Fine art. *Interests:* Travel, folk art, theater. *Collection:* Contemp artists in Western Pa; Folk Art, Am Mex origins, circa 1850 to present; Latin Am & South African Folk Art. *Publ:* Coauth, Multiple image and sound: Motivation for creative activity, Art Teacher Mag, fall 74; Colored light and shadow: A stimulus for creative movement, Pa J Physical Educ, winter 74; Multi-media: Motivation for the arts and basic education, Learning Resources Mag, 4/75; Readings: Developing arts programs for handicapped students, Pa Dept Educ, 82; cover art, If You Live By the Sword: Politics in the Making and Unmaking of a University President by Lawrence K Pettit. *Dealer:* Lynden Gallery Elizabethtown PA. *Mailing Add:* PO Box 1 Brush Valley PA 15720

WERTHEIMER, ALAIN
COLLECTOR

Pos: Chmn, Chanel Inc, 1974-; co-owner, Chateau Canon, Margaux, 1994-, Chateau Rausan Segla. *Awards:* Named one of World's Richest People, Forbes Mag, 1999-2004; named one of Top 200 Collectors, ARTnews mag, 2004-12. *Collection:* Modern art. *Mailing Add:* Chanel SA 135 Ave Charles de Gaulle 92521 Neuilly-sur-Seine France

WERTHEIMER, ESTHER
SCULPTOR

b Poland. *Study:* studies, Montreal Mus Fine Arts, Quebec, Can, 1958-63; studies, Int Acad, Austria; studies, Acad Belle Arte, Florence; Loyola Montreal, BA, 1973; Goddard Col, MA, 1975. *Work:* Reaching & Melee/Football (bronze), Douglas Hosp, Verdun, Can; Airborn & Family, City Place, West Palm Beach, Fla; Airborn (bronze), Civic Ctr Lib, Livermore, Calif; Water Babies, Royal Palm Plaza; Democracy/Primavera (bronze), city hall, Fukuoka, Japan; Hakone Open Air Mus, Tokyo; Celebration, Washington DC E Gate Condominium, 2008. *Comn:* Merle with Ribbon II (bronze), comn by Govt of Quebec, Montreal Casino; monumental sculpture of Count & Countess de Hoernle (corten steel, in progress), comn by Countess Henrietta de Hoernle, Mizner Park, Boca Raton, Fla; bust of Rita Hobbs (bronze). *Exhib:* J & W Gallery, New Hope, Pa, 1998 & 99; Boca-Pointe Country Club, Boca Raton, Fla, 2000 & 2001; Yvan Methot Gallery, Sydney, Australia; solo exhib, Ritz-Carlton Hotel, Sydney, Australia, 2000; D'Adamo/Hill Gallery, Seattle, 2001; Log Van Gallery, Singapore, 2008; Shanghai Space Mus, Shanghai, China, 2008; Art Fair, Shangai, China, 2009; Biennale, Florence, Italy, 2009. *Teaching:* prof drawing, painting & sculpture, Loyola Col, Montreal, 70-74. *Awards:* Govt of Can grant for exhib, Singapore, 1994; B'nai B'rith Int Arts award, 1997; best sculpture for Expressions 4, Mountain Lake PBS show, 1999; Shanghai Sculpture Space Cert; numerous others. *Bibliog:* Sandra Giannahasio (auth), Forma e crescita nella scultura di Wertheimer, Trevi Editori, 76; film, Achievers, CBC, 90; Roberta Sandler (auth), Sculpting life's energy, Simply the Best, 12/2000; Arlene Rodman (auth), Boca Pointe News. *Mem:* Int Sculpture Ctr; Canadian Sculpture Soc; Mus Art (Fort Lauderdale); Norton Mus (West Palm Beach); Boca Raton Mus Art; Nat Soc Arts & Letters; ArtistsRegistry.com. *Media:* Bronze, Steel, Metal, Cast. *Res:* Research with epoxy and bronze powder; Thixatropic application on wire armature; Larger than life size. *Interests:* Music; theatre; dance; travel. *Publ:* contribr articles to, Peak Mag, 95, "B" Mag, 5/2002, Simply Best Mag, 12/2002, Boca Life Mag, 2003. *Dealer:* Sher Gallery Miami FL; Klimantiris Gallery Montreal PQ; Lamoureux Gallery Montreal PQ; Lawrence Gallery Portland OR; Norolstrom Gallery Bellevue WA; Galerie Michel de Kerdour Quebec City CA. *Mailing Add:* 145 Radcliffe Montreal PQ H4X1C1 Canada

WESLEY, JOHN
PAINTER

b Los Angeles, Calif, Nov 25, 1928. *Work:* Albright-Knox Art Gallery, Buffalo, NY; Mus Mod Art, Whitney Mus Am Art, NY; Portland Art Mus, Ore; Univ Ky, Lexington; Chinati Found, Marfa, Tex; Speed Mus, Louisville, Ky; Detroit Inst Arts; Fogg Art Mus, Cambridge, Mass; Hirshhorn Mus and Sculpture Garden, Washington; and others. *Exhib:* Solo exhibs include (13) Robert Elkon Gallery, NY, 63-83, Univ Rochester, 74, Carl Solway, Cincinnati, 74, 84 & 89, Reinhard Onnasch Galerie, West Berlin, 82, 101 Spring Street Gallery, 87 & 93, Chinati Found, Marfa, Tex, 90 & 98, Drew Gallery, Canterbury, eng, 90, fiction/nonfiction (catalogue), NY, 91, Galerie Marc Jancou, Zurch, 93, Jose Freire Fine Art, NY, 94, Galerie Haus Schneider, Karlsruhe, Ger, 96, Jessica Fredericks Gallery, NY, 96, 98 & 99, Danese Gallery, NY, 98, Daniel Weinberg Gallery, Los Angeles, 2000, Tex Gallery, Houston, 2000, PSI Contemp Art Ctr, Long Island City, 2000 & Fogg Art Mus, Harvard Univ, Cambridge, Mass, 2001, Fredericks & Freiser, NY, 2007 & many others; group exhibs include Kunstverein, Ludwisburg, Ger, 93; Mus Am Art Pa Acad Fine Arts, Philadelphia, 98; Galerie Nacht St Stephen, Vienna, 99; Newhouse Ctr Contemp Art, NY, 2000; Ludwig Gallery, Houston, 2001; The Menil Collection, Houston, 2001; New Paintings, Gagosian Gallery, London, 2002; The Big Nothing, Inst Contemp Art, Philadelphia, 2004; After Cezanne, Mus Contemp Art, Los Angeles, 2005; Waddington Galleries, London, 2008; Cheep!, El Sourdog Hex, Berlin, 2009; Am Acad Arts & Letts Invitational, New York, 2010. *Teaching:* Instr, Sch Visual Arts, New York, 70-73. *Awards:* Guggenheim Fel, 76; Nat Endowment Arts, 89. *Bibliog:* Hannah Green (auth), A journal in praise of the art of John Wesley, In: The Unmuzzled Ox, spring 74; Ken Johnson (auth), Troubled toons, Art in Am, 2/93; Martin Hentschel, John Yau & Hannah Green (auths), John Wesley Paintings 1963-1992 (catalog essays), Daad Galerie, 93; Wayne Koestenbaum, Best of 2000, Artforum, 12/2000; Michael Kimmelman (auth), Comforting funny outlandishness that sticks to its own logic, The New York Times, 12/2000

WESSEL, FRED W
PAINTER, PRINTMAKER

b Amityville, NY, June 14, 1946. *Study:* Syracuse Univ, BFA, 68; Univ Mass, MFA, 76. *Work:* Mus Mod Art, NY; Brooklyn Mus, NY; Philadelphia Mus Art, Pa; Libr Cong, Washington; De Cordova Mus Art, Lincoln, Mass. *Comn:* Watercolor with tempera painting, Marriott Hotels, Washington, 86; gold leaf prints, Cutter Financial Ctr, Hartford, Conn, 87; watercolor with tempera painting, Univ Mass Fine Arts Ctr Theater, 90; portrait, Pres Univ Hartford, 98. *Exhib:* Hanga Print Ann, Tokyo Metrop Mus Art, Tokyo, Japan, 86; Int Prints, Fine Arts Ctr, Seoul, Korea, 87; Philadelphia Coll Art, 87; Schneider Mus Art, Ashland, Ore, 87; one-person show, Printworks Gallery, Chicago, Ill, 88, Stonepress Gallery, Seattle, Wash, 88, Arden Gallery, Boston, Mass, 93, 95, 97 & 98 Springfield Mus Fine Arts, 94; Sherry French Gallery,

97 & 98. *Pos:* Artist advisory bd, Offset Inst, 85-. *Teaching:* Instr printmaking, Univ Mass, 76-77; prof printmaking, Hartford Art Sch, Univ Hartford, 77-. *Awards:* Purchase Award, Gallery Tolbuchin, Bulgaria, 85; Juror's Award, Boston Printmaking 39th Ann, Strathmore Paper, 86; Color Print USA, Tex Tech Univ, 86. *Bibliog:* Feature article, Am Artist Mag, 4/95. *Mem:* Philadelphia Print Club. *Media:* Tempera; Lithography. *Publ:* Auth, Hartford print workshop, Print News, 80; illusr, Motherlode of gamefish, Country J, 86; North America's Freshwater Fishing Book, Charles Scribners & Sons, 88. *Dealer:* Arden Gallery Newbury St Boston MA 02115; Sherry French Gallery 57th St New York NY. *Mailing Add:* 4 Edgewood Terr Northampton MA 01060

WESSEL, HENRY
PHOTOGRAPHER
b Teaneck, NJ, July 28, 1942. *Study:* Pa State Univ, BA, 66; State Univ NY, Buffalo, Visual Studies Workshop, MFA, 72. *Work:* Mus Mod Art, Metrop Mus Art, NY; Nat Gallery Can, Ottawa; Int Mus Photog, George Eastman House, Rochester, NY; Philadelphia Mus Art; Los Angeles Co Mus Art, Mus Contemp Art, Los Angeles. *Exhib:* Mus Mod Art, NY; Nat Gallery Can, Ottawa; Contemp Photog V, 70 & New Topographics, 75, George Eastman House Traveling Exhibs; Solo exhibs, Mus Mod Art, NY, 73, Pa State Univ, 74, Fraenkel Gallery, San Francisco, 81, Charles Cowles Gallery, NY, 81 & Mus Contemp Art, Los Angeles, Calif, 98, San Fran Mus Modern Art, 2007; and many others. *Teaching:* Instr, Pa State Univ, 67-69, Ctr Eye, Aspen, Colo, 73, Univ Calif, Berkeley, 73 & San Francisco Art Inst, 73-; asst prof, San Francisco State Univ, Calif, 74; vis artist, Univ Calif, Davis, 77; vis lectr, Calif Col Arts & Crafts, 77. *Awards:* Guggenheim Fel, 71 & 78; Nat Endowment Arts Grant, 75, 77 & 78. *Bibliog:* Articles, Art News, 9/73, Camera, Lucerne, Switz, 5/74 & Art in Am, 1/76; Artforum, 2/90; Art News, 5/92. *Publ:* Contribr, Looking at Photographs, 73 & Mirrors and windows, 79, Mus Mod Art, New York, 79; Nude, Harper & Row, 80; Pleasures & Terrors of Domestic Comfort, Moma, NY. *Dealer:* Rena Bransten Gallery 77 Geary St San Francisco CA 94108; Pace/MacGill Gallery New York. *Mailing Add:* PO Box 475 Richmond CA 94807

WEST, ALICE CLARE
PAINTER
b Detroit, Mich, Oct 5, 1951. *Study:* San Francisco State Univ, with Robert Bechtle & Richard Mclean, BA, 75; Univ Calif, Berkeley, with Joan Brown, Chris Brown, Elmer Bischoff, David Simpson & Anne Healy, MFA, 86. *Work:* Levinson Brothers Inc, San Francisco; SAP Am, San Jose, Calif; Del Mondo LLC, San Francisco. *Exhib:* Recipients of MFA Show, Univ Art Mus, Berkeley, Calif, 87; 5th Int Exhibition, Rolando Castellon Contemp Art Gallery, San Francisco, 87; Art & the Woman Artist, Clary-Miner Gallery, Buffalo, NY, 89; Registered, Installed & Nailed, Calif Mus Art, Santa Rose, Calif, 91; Sixty-Eighth Crocker Kingsley Ann, Crocker Art Mus, Sacramento, 94; Print & Draw: Biennial, Triton Mus Art, Santa Clara, Calif, 95; California Small Works, Calif Mus Art, Santa Rosa, Calif, 96; Drawing Exhib, Galeria Nacional, San Jose, Costa Rica, 2008; Temenos, SomArts Main Gallery, San Francisco, 2007; Traveling, Text-o-&-Figura, Galeria Nacional, San Jose, Costa Rica, Meridian Gallery, San Francisco, Calif, & Fabula-Urbis, Lisbon, Portugal, 2010, Centro Alfredo Pinheiro, Cascais, Portugal, 2011, Sienna Art Inst, Sienna, Italy, 2012; 50/50, Sanchez Art Ctr, Pacifica Calif, 2010, 2012; Feira Do Livro de Artista, Fabula Urbis, Lisbon, Portugal, 2011; Art Book Faire, Fabula Urbis, Lisboa, Portugal, 2011; Drawing Connections, Siena Art Inst, Siena, Italy, 2011; Libro Arte 2012, Galeria Alternativa, San Jose, Costa Rica, 2012; Int Art Book Fair, Palo Alto, Calif, 2013. *Pos:* libr asst, UC Berkeley, 84-86; libr asst, Acad Art Col Libr, 89-90. *Teaching:* instr, Art Sch, 88-89; artist-in-residence, Exploratorium, 76-78; teaching asst, UC Berkeley, 85. *Awards:* Richmond Art Ctr for Juror's Prize, 83; John Michael Welcome Prize, Univ Calif, Berkeley, 85; Calif Small Works Exhib for Juror's Prize, 96. *Bibliog:* Mark Van Proyen (auth), Drama of Space and Surface, Artweek, 4/2/88; Mary Hull-Webster (auth), Primarily Paint, Artweek, 3/4/93; Michael Schwager (auth), Registered, Installed and Nailed, Art Muse, summer 97. *Media:* Works on Paper, Acrylic, Digital Prints. *Publ:* Contribr Univ Art Mus Calendar, Univ Calif Berkeley, 87; contribr Contemporary Women Artists, Bo-Tree Press, 87; contribr Five Fingers Review, McNaughton & Gunn, spring 98. *Dealer:* San Francisco Mus Modern Art Artists Gallery Bldg Fort Mason Center San Francisco CA 94123. *Mailing Add:* 4047 Cesar Chavez St San Francisco CA 94131

WEST, CHRISTINA A
CERAMIST
Study: Santa Reparata Int Sch Arts, Florence, Italy, 2002; NY State Coll Cèramics at Alfred Univ, Alfred, NY (Grad Fel), 2003-04, MFA (ceramic sculpture), 2006. *Exhib:* Solo exhibs, Refiguring the Ordinary, Klemm Gallery, Adrian, Mich, 2003, Allen Priebe Gallery, Univ Wis-Osh-Kosh, 2008, Hallwalls Contemp Art Ctr, Buffalo, 2008; group exhibs, Mich Mud, Mich Ceramic Artists Asn, Dearborn, 2003; Toledo Area Artists Exhib, Toledo Mus Art, 2003; San Angelo Mus Fine Arts Nat Ceramic Competition, Tex, 2004; New Art from Alfred Univ, Loupe Gallery, Prattsburgh, NY, 2004; Alfred on 25th, J Cacciola Gallery, New York, 2006; Mastery in Clay, Clay Studio, Philadelphia, 2006; The Interpreted Figure, Schein-Joseph Int Mus Art, Alfred, NY, 2007; Ceramics...On the Edge, Umlauf Sculpture Garden & Mus, Dallas, 2007; Renegade Clay: 5 Views from the West, Ariz State Univ Art Mus, Tempe, 2007, Ceram*A*Rama: Soul on Fire, 2008. *Pos:* Resident artist, Archie Bray Found, Helena, Mont, 2006-07; vis artist, Univ Wis-Madison, 2007-08. *Awards:* 3rd Place, Nat Ceramic Competition, San Angelo, Tex, 2004; Lilian Fel, Archie Bray Found, 2006; George Sugarman Found Grant, 2007; NY Found Arts Fel, 2007

WEST, E GORDON
PAINTER
b Salt Lake City, Utah, June 1, 1933. *Study:* Art Inst Chicago; Univ Louisville, BS, 55. *Work:* McNay Art Mus, San Antonio, Univ Louisville, Ky; Tex A&M Univ, College Station, Tex. *Exhib:* Watercolor USA; Tex Watercolor Soc; Am Watercolor Soc; Nat Watercolor Soc; and many others. *Awards:* Artist of Year, San Antonio Art League, 85; and many others. *Mem:* Signature mem Am Watercolor Soc; signature mem Tex Watercolor Soc; signature mem Nat Watercolor Soc; signature mem Western Fedn Watercolor. *Media:* Watercolor. *Publ:* Tex Hill Country, 81, Pecos to Rio Grande, 83, Tex A & M Press; Watercolor Magic, 3/95 & 10/95; The Artists' Mag, 4/95 & 6/96; The Best of Watercolor, 95 & No 2, 97; When Relative Value is the Galy Issue in Watercolor, Am Artist Mag, 2010. *Mailing Add:* 2910 Briarcroft St San Antonio TX 78217-3801

WEST, JENNIFER
GRAPHIC ARTIST
b Topanga Canyon, Calif. *Study:* Art Ctr, Pasadena, Calif, MFA, 2004. *Work:* Henry Art Gallery, Seattle; Tacoma Art Mus, Wash. *Exhib:* Solo exhibs include Proj Room, Sandroni Rey, Los Angeles, 2007, White Room, White Columns, New York, 2007, Marc Foxx, Los Angeles, 2007, Art Basel, 2008, Vilma Gold, London, 2008; two-person exhib, Transmission Gallery, Glasgow, Scotland, 2007; group exhibs include Celine & Julie Go Boating, Anna Helwing Gallery, Los Angeles, 2005; Pacing, Marc Foxx, Los Angeles, 2006; Yeah Film, Sandroni Rey, Los Angeles, 2007; When Language Fails, Mus Contemp Art, Detroit, 2007, When Words Fail, 2007; Viewfinder, Henry Art Gallery, Seattle, 2007; Drawing on Film, Drawing Ctr, New York, 2008; Come Forth! Eat, Drink, and Look..., Gavin Brown at Passerby, New York, 2008; Video Show, Blum & Poe, Los Angeles, 2008. *Teaching:* Adj faculty, Univ Southern Calif, Roski Sch Fine Arts. *Dealer:* Vilma Gold 6 Minerva St London E2 9EH England UK. *Mailing Add:* USC Roski Sch Fine Arts Watt Hall 104 Univ Park Campus Los Angeles CA 90089-0292

WEST, JORDAN
PAINTER
b 1969. *Study:* Univ Idaho, 1987-88; Hunter Coll, 1994-96; New York Univ, 2001-02. *Exhib:* Solo exhib, Inside/Outside, Ctr for Contemp Art, Santa Fe, 2003; Richard Levy Gallery, Scope Art Fair, Los Angeles, 2004; Push Pin, Mus NMex Stuart L Udall Ctr, 2005; Scenic Overlook, Ctr for Contemp Art, Santa Fe, 2006; Pulse Art Fair, Miami, 2007; Drawing from the West Collection, SEI Gallery, SEI Investments, Pa, 2008. *Awards:* Pollock-Krasner Found Grant, 2008. *Bibliog:* Sara S King (auth), Santa Fe Summer Preview, Art in Am, 6-7/2006; Michael Abatemarco (auth), Silent, decaying tributes, Jordan West, The New Mexican-Pasatiempo, 2/12-18/2010. *Mailing Add:* 214 Griffin St Santa Fe NM 87501

WEST, RICHARD VINCENT
MUSEUM DIRECTOR, HISTORIAN
b Prague, Czech, Nov 26, 1934; US citizen. *Study:* Univ Calif, Santa Barbara, BA (with highest honors), 61; Akad Bildenden Kuenste, Vienna, with Wotruba, 61-62; Univ Calif, Berkeley, MA (art hist), 65; Mus Mgt Inst, 81. *Collection Arranged:* Section d'Or (auth, catalog), 67-68; Language of the Print (auth, catalog), 68-69; Rockwell Kent: The Early Years (auth, catalog), 69; Howard Warshaw: A Decade of Murals (auth, catalog), 72; Pre-Rembrandtists (auth, catalog), 74; Munich & Am Realism (auth, catalog), 78; An Enkindled Eye: The Paintings of Rockwell Kent (auth, catalog), 85; Orbis Pictus: The Prints of Oskar Kokoschka (ed catalog) 87; Standing in the Tempest: Painters of the Hungarian Avant-Garde, 1908-1930 (auth, catalog), 91; Am in Art (auth, catalog), 91; A Significant Story: Am Painting and Decorative Arts from the MXM Karolik Collections, 93; A Bounty of Flowers: Masterpieces of Am Floral Painting, 94; Rounding the Mark: 150 Years of Treasures from the NY Yacht Club, 1844-1994, Newport Art Mus, RI, 94; Old Master Existentialism: Recent Paintings by Odd Nerdrum, Frye Art Mus, Seattle, 97; Contemporary Am Marine Art: Am Soc of Marine Artists, Frye Art Mus & Cummer Mus Art & Gardens, 97; Circle of Lyon: 7 French Painters of Reality, Frye Art Mus, 98; Children of the Yellow Kid: The Evolution of the Am Comic Strip, Frye Art Mus & San Francisco Cartoon Art Mus, 98-99; Representing LA: Contemp Pictorial Art from Southern California, Frye Art Mus & Art Mus of S Tex, 2000-2001. *Pos:* Cur, Cleveland Art Mus, 65-66; Albright-Knox Art Gallery, 66-67; dir, Bowdoin Col Mus Art, 67-72, Crocker Art Mus, 73-83, Santa Barbara Mus Art, 83-91, Newport Art Mus, 92-94, Frye Art Mus, 95-. *Teaching:* Lectr, Bowdoin Col, Univ Calif, Davis & Calif State Univ, Sacramento. *Awards:* Ford Fel, 65-67; Smithsonian Fel, 71. *Mem:* Am Asn Mus; Western Asn Art Mus (pres, 75-77); Calif Asn Mus (vpres, 86-91); Coll Art Asn; Int Coun Mus. *Publ:* Coauth, Language of the Print, Random House, 68; Walker Art Building Murals, 72; Rockwell Kent Reconsidered, Am Art Rev, 12/77; An enkindled eye: Paintings of Rockwell Kent, 85; auth, Rockwell Kent (monograph), Abrams (in prep). *Mailing Add:* c/o Frye Art Mus 704 Terry Ave Seattle WA 98104

WEST, VIRGINIA M
FIBER ARTIST, WRITER
b Boston, Mass. *Study:* Goucher Coll; Philadelphia Coll Textiles; Md Inst Coll Art. *Work:* Baltimore Mus Art; Del Art Mus; Hilton Hotel, Baltimore, Md; Goucher Coll Kraushaar Gallery, Baltimore; Peterson Howell & Heather, Hunt Valley, Md. *Comn:* Ark curtain, Shaarei Zion Synagogue, Baltimore, Md, 68; tapestry, The Center Club, Baltimore, 80; fiber artwork, Community Ctr, Baltimore, 80; fiber murals, Lucayan Beach Hotel, Freeport, The Bahamas, 82; other comns for pvt collections. *Exhib:* Contemp Crafts Exhib, Del Art Mus, Wilmington, 70-75; Md Artists Exhib, Baltimore Mus Art, 70 & 75; Fibre Art Am Artists, Ball State Univ, 72; Mus Contemp Crafts, NY, 72; Galleria d'Assisi, Italy, 79; Handwoven Altar Frontals, First Lutheran Church, Baltimore, Md. *Pos:* Conference keynote speaker; writer, Shuttle, Spindle & Dyepot, 72-, Fiber Arts, 78-81, Handwoven, 80- & Weavers, 85-. *Teaching:* Instr weaving, fiber sculpture & textile design, Md Inst Coll Art, 69-; instr sem & workshops, US, Can, NZ & Australia. *Awards:* First Award, Creative Crafts Biennial, 68; Purchase Award, Baltimore Mus Art, 70; Purchase Award, Del Art Mus, 75; and others. *Mem:* Baltimore Weavers Guild (pre, 59-61); Md Crafts Coun (pres, 62-64); Am Crafts Coun (secy, 69-72). *Media:* Fiber. *Res:* Basketry styles & techniques, original designs for handwoven clothing. *Publ:* Auth, The Virginia West Swatch Book, 85-86; Finishing Touches for the Handweaver (rev ed), 87; Designer Diagonals, A Portfolio of Patterns for Bias Clothing, 88; A Cut Above, 92. *Mailing Add:* 1055 W Joppa Rd #640 Baltimore MD 21204

WESTERMANN, MARIËT
FORMER MUSEUM DIRECTOR, ADMINISTRATOR
Study: Williams Coll, BA (history, magna cum laude with highest honors, Phi Beta Kappa), 84; New York Univ, Inst Fine Arts, MA, 89, PhD, 97. *Collection Arranged:* guest cur, Jan Steen: Painter & Storyteller, Nat Gallery Art, Washington, 94-96; cur consultant, Art & Home: Dutch Interiors in the Age of Rembrandt, 2001-02. *Pos:* Res asst, Metrop Mus Art, New York, 89, grad asst, 89-92, vis comt for European paintings & Watson Libr, 2002-; cur consultant, Nat Gallery Art, Washington, 94-96; bd mem, Historians Netherlandish Art, 98-2002; co-ed, Nederlands Kunsthistorisch Jaarboek, 98-2005; assoc dir res & acad programs, Clark Art Inst, Williamstown, Mass, 2001-02; dir, Inst Fine Arts, New York Univ, 2002-2007, Robert Lehman Collection scholarly catalogue exec, 2002-, provost, Abu Dhabi, 2007-; rev ed & ed bd mem, Art Bulletin, 2002-06; trustee, ARTstor, 2006-. *Teaching:* Asst prof art hist, Rutgers Univ, 95-2000, assoc prof art hist, 2000-02; prof fine arts, Inst Fine Arts, New York Univ, 2002-. *Awards:* Morse Fel, New York Univ, Inst Fine Arts, 88 & 91; Lehman Fel, New York Univ & Metrop Mus Art, 89; Finley Fel, Nat Gallery Art, Washington, 92; Mellon Found Grant, 97 & 2005; Rutgers Univ Res Coun Grant, 97 & 98, Bd Trustees Fel, 2000; Am Philos Soc Res Grant, 98; Nat Endowment for the Humanities Grant, 98 & 2001; Clark Art Inst Fel, 2001. *Publ:* Auth, A Worldly Art: The Dutch Republic, 1985-1700, Abrams & Prentice-Hall, 96; The Amusements of Jan Steen: Comic Painting in the Seventeenth Century, Waanders, 97; co-ed, Art for the Market, Nederlands Kunsthistorisch Jaarboek, 99, The Culture of Home in the Early Mod Netherlands, 2000, Print Work, 2002, Virtue & Virtuosity in the Netherlands, 1400-1700, 2003, Rubens & the North, 2004; auth, Rembrandt, Art & Ideas, Phaidon, 2000; Art & Home: Dutch Interiors in the Age of Rembrandt, Newark Mus & Denver Art Mus, 2001; Johannes Vermeer (1632-1675): Rijksmuseum Dossier, Waanders, 2004; ed, Anthropologies of Art, Yale Univ Press, 2005. *Mailing Add:* Inst Fine Arts New York Univ 1 E 78th St #118 New York NY 10012

WESTERVELT, ROBERT F
HISTORIAN, CERAMIST
b New York, NY, Apr 6, 1928. *Study:* Williams Coll, AB; Claremont Grad Sch, MFA; Emory Univ, PhD. *Work:* Delgado Mus, New Orleans; High Mus of Atlanta, Ga; Frank Wingate Collection of Contemp Am Ceramics, Syracuse Univ; Scripps Coll Collection, Claremont, Calif. *Comn:* Ceramic decoration (with Joseph Amisano, archit), Visual Arts Bldg, Univ Ga, 59. *Exhib:* Georgia Artists, Smithsonian Inst, Washington, DC, 64; Scripps Coll Invitational, Claremont, 69. *Pos:* Consult, Ctr Study Southern Cult, Univ Miss, 81-85. *Teaching:* Assoc prof hist Am art, Agnes Scott Coll, Decatur, Ga, 57-81; prof art, Gainesville Coll, Ga, 83-96. *Awards:* Cash grant, Atlanta Arts Festival, 64; Purchase Awards, Delgado Mus & Arts Festival of Atlanta; Ga Coun Arts Grant, 81-82. *Mem:* Ga Designer Craftsman; Southeastern Coll Art Asn; Ga Mountain Crafts. *Media:* Stoneware, Porcelain. *Res:* 19th-20th century American painting and demotic culture. *Publ:* Auth, The Whig painter of Missouri, Am Art J, Kennedy Gallery, 70; illusr, Morphology of Artistic Style (website), 2011

WESTFALL, CAROL D
ARTIST, EDUCATOR
b Everett, Pa, Sept 7, 1938. *Study:* RI Sch of Design, BFA; Maryland Inst, Coll of Art, MFA. *Work:* Del Mus of Art, Wilmington; NJ State Mus, Trenton; Michael Carson Productions, NY; PD 100, Architects, Mexico City; Zimmerli Mus, Newark Pub Libr; and others. *Comn:* Nine batiks, R F Kennedy Family Collection, 70 & three batiks, L B Johnson Family Collection, 70, Washington Gallery of Art, DC. *Exhib:* Washington Co Mus, Hagerstown, Md, 72; Del Mus Art, Wilmington, 73; Baltimore Mus Art, Md, 74; Auditorium Gallery, NJ State Mus, Trenton, 75; 7th Biennial of Tapestry, Mus Contonal des Beaux Arts, Lausanne, Switz, 76; Mus of Art, Carnegie Inst Int, Pittsburgh, Pa, 76; Mus Contemp Crafts, NY, 76 & 87; Textile Mus, Washington, DC, 86; Bermuda Arts Centre, 87; Gryphon Gallery, Melbourne, Australia, 88; Solo exhibs, Conde Gallery, Inst Allende, Mex, 75, NJ State Mus, 76, Florence Duhl Gallery, NY, 76, Am Ctr, New Delhi, India, 8a, Ruth Kaufman Gallery, NY, 81; Gallery/Gallery, Kyoto, Japan, 92. *Teaching:* Instr fibers & fabrics, Md Inst, Baltimore, 68-73; asst prof fibres & fabrics, Montclair State Col, NJ, 73-79, assoc prof, 79-88, prof, 88-; guest assoc prof, Teachers Col, Columbia Univ, NY, 77-87 & Sch Am Craftsmen, Rochester Inst Technol, 77 & 86. *Awards:* Morton & Sophie Macht Found Award, Baltimore Mus of Art, 72; Levi Sculpture Award, Baltimore Mus of Art, 74; Governor's Purchase Award, NJ Biennial, State of NJ, 75; Indo-Am Fel, 80-81; Master Print Award, Rutgers Ctr Innovative Printmaking, 88; and others. *Bibliog:* Articles in Crafts Horizons, 69-77; Shuttle, Spindle & Dyepot, 77-85; Ars Textrina, 86-96. *Mem:* Handweavers Guild of Am; Am Crafts Coun; NJ State Coun on the Arts, Artists in Schs Prog; NY Rug Soc; Ars Textrina (bd mem). *Media:* Mixed. *Publ:* Coauth, Plaiting Step by Step, Watson-Guptill, 76. *Mailing Add:* Montclair State Univ Dept Fine Arts Upper Montclair NJ 07043

WESTIN, ROBERT H
HISTORIAN
b St Paul, Minn, Jan 11, 1946. *Study:* Univ Minn, BA, 68; Pa State Univ, MA, 70, PhD, 78; Birbeck Col, Univ London, with Sir Nikolas Pevsner & Sir John Summerson. *Collection Arranged:* Figurative Drawings from Windsor Castle of the Roman Baroque; Collection of Her Majesty the Queen; Carlo Maratti and His Contemporaries (coauth, catalog), Mus Art, Pa State Univ, 75. *Teaching:* Asst prof Renaissance-Baroque art hist, Ariz State Univ, Tempe, 73-78; assoc prof art, Univ Fla, Gainesville, 78-. *Awards:* Nat Defense Educ Art Title IV, US Govt, 71-72; Ariz State Univ Fac Fel, 74. *Mem:* Coll Art Asn; Mid-Am Coll Art; Nat Coun Art Adminr; SE Coll Art Conf; Southeastern Am Soc Eighteenth Century Studies. *Res:* Collections of Metropolitan Museum of New York, Philadelphia Museum of Art and the collection of Janos Scholz, Cooper-Hewitt Union; Roman Baroque sculpture and Michelangelo. *Publ:* Auth, Antonio Raggi's Death of St Cecilia, Art Bull 74; co auth, Contributions to the late chronology of Giuseppe Mazzuoli, Burlington Mag, 74; auth, Ars Mohendi tradition and the visualization of death in Seventeenth Century Roman Baroque sculpture, Int J Death Educ, 80; coauth, Carlo Maratti and Camillo Rusconi: Two new portrait medallions, Burlington Mag, 80. *Mailing Add:* Univ Fla Dept Art 302 FAC Gainesville FL 32611

WESTLUND, HARRY E
PUBLISHER, DEALER
b Chicago, Ill, Nov 20, 1941. *Study:* Calif State Col, Long Beach, BA, 67; Tamarind Inst, Albuquerque, Master Printer cert, 70. *Work:* Pasadena Mus, Calif; Gruenwald Found, Univ Calif, Los Angeles; Mus Mod Art, NY, Los Angeles Co Mus Art, Los Angeles; Tamarind Inst Collection, Univ NMex. *Exhib:* Eight Tamarind Printers, Motel Gallery, Albuquerque, NMex; New Multiples, San Diego; Art of the Master Printer, Robinson Galleries, Houston, Tex; Collectors Exhib, Starline Gallery, Albuquerque, 78; Bramante Gallery, Walla Walla, Wash, 80. *Pos:* Shop mgr, Lakeside Studios, Mich, 71; mgr, Tamarind Publ, Tamarind Inst, 72-75; litho/silkscreen staff printer, Cirrue Ed, Hollywood, Calif, 75-76; dir, Serigraphics Custom Silkscreen Workshop, Albuquerque, 76-84; gallery mgr, Rie Munoz Ltd, Juneau, Alaska, 84-85; owner, Halibut Fine Arts, Juneau, Alaska, 85-87; picture framer, Legacy Framing, Albuquerque, NMex, 87-88; owner, Centipede Custom Serigraph, Albuquerque, NMex, 88-91, Westlund Arts, 93-. *Teaching:* Instr silkscreen, Univ NMex, 78; numerous workshops at many univ from 74-87. *Specialty:* Publishing, custom printing, silkscreen process. *Collection:* Contemporary; Old Master. *Publ:* Auth, Polymer Reversal Technique as Applied to Zinc Plates, Tamarind, 71. *Mailing Add:* PO Box 486 Angel Fire NM 87710-0486

WESTMORELAND, TERESA D
DESIGNER
b Comanche, Tex, Feb 1, 1970. *Study:* Tarlton State Univ, BS, 96. *Exhib:* Solo show, Colletiva Works, Tarlton State Univ Longdon Cult & Educ Ctr, Grandbury, Tex, 98. *Pos:* Dir & cur, Bernards Mill Art Mus, 93-96. *Media:* Jewelry. *Collection:* Western art & bronzes; works by Amy Miers Jackson, Robert Summers & Jack Bryant. *Publ:* Anthologies, Vol I, 95. *Mailing Add:* c/o Shimmer Jewelry 1313 Paluxy Rd Granbury TX 76048-5663

WESTWATER, ANGELA KING
ART DEALER, EDITOR
b Columbus, Ohio, July 6, 1942. *Study:* Smith Col, BA; NY Univ, MA. *Pos:* Asst dir, Ctr Int Studies, NY Univ, 67-69; res assoc, Inst Govt & ed, Ga Govt Rev, Univ Ga, 69-71; managing ed, Artforum, 72-75; trustee, Louis Comfort Tiffany Found, pres, 80-; vis comt, Smith Col, Mus Art; partner, Sperone Westwater Inc, NY, 75-. *Mem:* Art Dealers Asn Am (vp 2000-). *Specialty:* Contemporary painting and sculpture. *Mailing Add:* Sperone Westwater 257 Bowery New York NY 10002

WETENHALL, JOHN
MUSEUM DIRECTOR
b Jun 1, 1957. *Study:* Dartmouth Col, AB (cum laude), 1979; Williams Col, MA (Clark Fel), 1982, Williamstown, Mass; Stanford Univ, MA, 1985, PhD, 1988; Vanderbilt Univ, MBA, 1999. *Pos:* cur, painting & sculpture Birmingham Mus Art, Ala, 1989-95; dir, Checkwood Mus Art, Nashville, 1995-2001; exec dir, John and Mable Ringling Mus Art, Sarasota, Fla, 2001-09; interim dir, Miami Art Mus, 2009-10; pres, Carnegie Mus Pittsburgh, 2011-13; dir, George Washington Univ Mus & The Textile Mus, 2013-. *Teaching:* Lectr, Santa Clara Univ, Calif, 1985, Univ Minn, Minneapolis, 1988; George Washington Mus Studies Program, 2013-; fac admin, Fla State Univ, 2001-09. *Awards:* Lyndon Baines Johnson Found Moody Travel grantee, 1986; John F Kennedy Libr Found grantee, 1986, Inst Mus and Libr Servs grantee; B Gerald Cantor fel, 1986; Nat Endowment for the Arts grantee, 1991; Recipient Award of Excellence Tenn Asn Mus, 1996, 2001; Gold & Silver medals for educ prog Southeastern Mus Conf, 1999; Lifetime Achievement Award, Fla Asn Mus, 2010; Mus Service Award, Southeastern Mus Conf, 2010; DC Excellence in Hist Preservation Award, 2015. *Mem:* Am Teachers Asn of the Martial Arts (sensei); Rotary (Paul Harris fel); Kiwanis; Beta Gamma Sigma; Asn Art Mus Dir; Sarasota CofC; Sarasota Conv & Visitors Bureau (bd); Am Asn Mus (bd); ICOM, US Board. *Publ:* Auth: (with Karal Ann Marling) Iwo Jima: Monuments, Memories and the Am Hero, 1991, (with David Cass) (catalogue) Italian Paintings, 1850-1910, 1982; editor: (catalogue) Splendors of the Am West, 1990; contribr articles to prof jours.; appearance in Am. Masters: Alexander Calder, PBS, 1998; A Museum Once Forgotten: Rebirth of the Ringling Museum, 2007. *Mailing Add:* George Washington University Museum 701 21st St NW Washington DC 20052

WETHINGTON, WILMA
PAINTER, INSTRUCTOR
b Clinton, Iowa, Apr 15, 1918. *Study:* Marshall Univ, Huntington, WVa; Wichita State Univ; also with Mario Cooper, John Pike, Dale Meyers, Charles R Kinghan, Tom Hill, Clayton Henri Staples, Robert E Wood, Robert Wade, Joe Bohler, Jim Wilcox & others. *Work:* Wichita State Univ, Kans; Episcopal Diocese Kans, Topeka; Smithsonian Inst, Washington; US Fed Bldg, Wichita, Kans; Off Secy Transportation, Washington; US Fed Bldg, Kans City; Emprise Bank, Wichita, Kans; Wichita Ctr for the Arts; Air Capitol Mus, Wichita; Lonestar Community Coll, Spring, Tex; US Federal Bldg, Topeka, Kans; Wichita Ctr Arts. *Comn:* Portrait, Hon Richard Rogers, 90; portrait, Hon Dale Saffels, 91; portrait, Hon Earl E O'Conner, 92; portrait, Miss Am (Debbie Bryant), Gov Kans; portrait, Miss USA (Kelly McCarthy), City Wichita, 92; Hon John Pearson, 99, and others; Barbara Bush Lib, Houston, Tex; Lonestar Community Coll, Tex; and many others. *Exhib:* Salmagundi Club, NY, 85, 86, 2000; Air & Space Mus, Washington; Southern Watercolor Soc; Am Watercolor Soc; Pastel Soc West Coast; Nat Watercolor Soc, Okla; Wichita Ctr for Arts. *Pos:* Owner, Accent Frames & Gallery, 74-79; com artist & illustr, Boeing Airplane Co & McCormick-Armstrong Printing Co, Wichita; pres, Wichita State Univ. *Teaching:* Pvt art instr, Wichita, Kans, 50-; instr painting, McConnell Air Base, Wichita, spring 73;

instr painting, portraiture & drawing, Wichita Center for the Arts, 81-; painting workshops, Kans, Colo & NMex. *Awards:* First Award in Watercolor, Okla Mus Art, 75; Best of Show, 2nd Scottsdale Artist Ann Show, Scottsdale Artist League, 93; Best Show, Kingman, Kans, 93; and 75 other awards; Best of Show, NLAPW, Fayetteville, Ark, 98. *Mem:* Am Watercolor Soc (assoc mem); Pastel Soc Kans; Kans Watercolor Soc (found, sig mem); Southern Watercolor Soc; Nat Asn Am Pen Women; Pastel Soc Am (sig mem); Oil Painters Am; Kans Acad Oil Painters; Watercolor Art Soc, Houston, Tex. *Media:* Pastel, Watercolor. *Interests:* Gardening, music. *Publ:* Wichita pizzazz, 84: Smithsonian Book of Flight & The Best of Oil Paintings, Rockport Press; Watercolor Expressions, Rockport, Publ, Inc; Int Artist, North Light Mag; featured articles, Wichita Eagle Newspaper, Houston Chronicle. *Mailing Add:* 4111 Cypress Lake Dr Spring TX 77388-9702

WEXLER, ALICE
PAINTER, ADMINISTRATOR
Study: Boston Univ, BFA; Royal Col of Art, MFA; Teachers Col, Columbia Univ, EdD. *Teaching:* Prof, Dir, Art Educ, State University of NY, New Paltz, currently. *Awards:* Nat Arts Club, 1995; Faculty Development award to support research on the art of exceptional adults at the G.R.A.C.E. facility, Vermont, 2001. *Publ:* Writings have been published in Studies in Art Education and Art Education. *Mailing Add:* State University of New York SUNY New Paltz School Fine & Performing Arts SAB 108A 1 Hawk Dr New Paltz NY 12561

WEXLER, ALLAN
DESIGNER
b 1962. *Study:* RI Sch Design, BFA, 71, BA (archit), 72; Pratt Inst, MA (archit), 76. *Comn:* Park and plaza entrance, New York City Bd of Educ, NY, 99; Tool shed/sukkah, Aldrich Mus Contemp Art, 2000; Walking paths, pavilions, study classrooms for park, Chastain Park, Atlanta, Ga, 2000; Picnic tables Douglas Park, Santa Monica Dept Cult Affairs, Calif, 2000; Permanent picnic park, Expo 2000, Hanover, Ger, 2000, many others. *Exhib:* Too Jewish?, Jewish Mus, NY, 96; Subversive Domesticity, Edwin A Ulrich Mus Art, Wichita State Univ, 96; Art Auction at MCA in La Jolla, Mus Contemp Art, San Diego, 96; Home Show II (with catalog), Santa Barbara Contemp Arts Forum, 96; People in Glass Houses, Robert Lehman Gallery Urban Glass, NY, 96; Inside (with catalog), Calif Ctr Arts Mus, Escondido, 96; Sit On This: The Chair as Art, Palm Beach Community Coll Mus Art, Lake Worth, Fla, 97; Gallery Joe, Chicago Art Fair, 97; Pub Pvt Landscapes, Union Brauerei/Dortmunder Univ, Dortmund, Ger, 98; Solo exhibs, Custom Built: A Twenty-Year Survey of Work by Allan Wexler, Atlanta Coll of Art Gallery, City Gallery at Chastain, Atlanta, Ga, 3/19-4/25/99, Travel to Contemp Arts Ctr, Cincinnati, Ohio, 11/99-1/2000, Forum for Contemp Art, St Louis, Mo, 3/2000-5/2000, Custom Built: A Twenty-Year Survey of Work, San Francisco Mus Art, Calif, 3/30-6/24/2001, Travel to Space One Eleven and Visual Art Gallery, Univ Ala at Birmingham, Ala, 10/12-1/2002, WORKS, Ronald Feldman Fine Arts, NY, 3/23-4/20/2002 & Allan Wexler: Recent Works, Parrish Art Mus, Southampton, NY, 10/20-1/5/2003, and many others; Group exhibs, Unquiet Urbanism, White Box, NY, 4/99-5/99, Faith: The Impact of Judeo Christian Religion on Art at the millennium, Aldrich Mus Contemp Art, Ridgefield, Ct, 1/2000-5/2000, Wave Hill Glyndor Gallery, Bronx, NY, 5/2000-8/2000, Multiformity: Multiples from the MCA Collection, Mus Contemp Art, Chicago, Ill, 7/5/2002-7/28/2002, Neuberger Mus Biennial Mus Pub Art, Neuberger Mus, 6/22/2003-10/19/2003 & many others; Investigations 30, Inst Contemp Art, 89; Dining Rooms and Furniture for the Typical House, Univ of Mass, Amherst, Mass, 89. *Teaching:* Asst prof, NJ Inst Technol, Sch Archit, 74-83; fac, Brown Univ Sch Art, 86, Environ Design, Parsons Sch Design, 83-94, sculpture, Tyler Col Art, Temple Univ, 89 & Cooper Union Sch Fine Arts, 89; vis prof, Sch Archit, RI Sch Design, 92 & Hochschule der Kunste, Berlin, Ger, 94; vis critic sculpture, State Univ NY, Purchase, 93; assoc adj prof, Sch Archit, Pratt Inst, 94-; workshop leader, Bauhaus Sch Architecture, Weimar, Ger, 99. *Awards:* Chrysler Award for Design Innovation, 97; Expo 2000, Hannover, Ger, 98; George Nelson Design Award, 99; Sponsored Project Award, NY State Coun on the Arts, 89; Fel Award, NY Found for the Arts, 90; Henry J Leir Prize, Jewish Mus, New York, 2009. *Bibliog:* William Zimmer (auth), Pieces of Domesticity And Links to Nature, The NY Times, 6/11/2000; Grace Glueck (auth), Creative Souls Who Keep the Faith or Challenge its Influence, NY Times, 4/21/2000; Sonnenwende wird am Windrad groB gefeiert, Calenberger Zeitung, Germany, 5/19/2000; Allan Wexler: custom built, The Art Newspaper, 5/2001; The Aldrich Museum, Tema Celeste 92, 7/8/2002. *Mailing Add:* c/o Ronald Feldman Fine Arts 31 Mercer St New York NY 10013

WEXLER, JEROME LEROY
PHOTOGRAPHER, ILLUSTRATOR
b New York, NY, Feb 6, 1923. *Study:* Self-taught; student, Univ of Conn, Pratt Inst Bklyn. *Awards:* Twelve Outstanding Sci Books Children awards, Nat Sci Teachers Asn & Childrens Book Coun, Joint Comt. *Publ:* 50 bks publ to date. *Mailing Add:* 8 North Ave North Haven CT 06473-2708

WEXLER, PETER J
SCULPTOR, PHOTOGRAPHER
b New York, NY, Oct 31, 1936. *Study:* Art Students League, New York; Univ Mich, BS (design), 58; Yale Sch Drama, 58. *Hon Degrees:* Furman Univ, Greenville, SC, 2013. *Work:* Univ Libr, Univ Ariz, Tucson, Ariz; The Tobin Collection, McNay Art Mus, San Antonio, Tex; Harvard Theatre Collection, Harvard Univ, Mass; Smithsonian Inst, Cooper Hewitt & Nat Design Mus, New York; NY Pub Libr Performing Arts, Lincoln Ctr, Billy Rose Theatre Collection, New York; State Univ NY, Binghamton, New York; Digital Mus, Wexler's Work, Furman Univ, Greenville, Sc. *Comn:* Stage Designs for Metrop Opera, Lincoln Ctr, New York, 73-2005; NY Philharmonic, Lincoln Ctr, NY, 65-2005; Ctr Theatre Group Mus Ctr, Los Angeles, 66-2003, NY Shakespears Festival, 59, Boston Symphy Orchestra, Boston, 95-2000; Plaza sculpture, Am Life & Accident Insurance Co, Louisville, Ky, 2011. *Exhib:* Kennedy Ctr Exhib Gallery, Washington, DC, 70's; Libr Mus Performing Arts, New York, 75; The Look of Music, Avery Fisher Hall, New York, 78; Reflections, Photography of Venice, Cult Ctr, Chicago, Ill, 2007; Univ Mich Sch Art & Design, summer 2007; Schoenherr Gallery, N Central Coll, 2009; Lincoln Ctr Celebrating 50 Years, NY Pub Lib of the performing Arts, 2009-2010; Schoenherr Gallery, N Central Coll, 2011. *Pos:* Consult, Peace Ctr & Furman Univ, Greenville, SC, 2011. *Teaching:* Lect prog, N Cent Coll, Naperville, Ill & Wellesley Coll, 2011. *Awards:* Maharam Award, Maharam Corp, 67; LA Drama Critics Circle, LA Drama Critics, 70's; 28th Bard Award for Excellence in Archit & Urban Design, City Club New York, 96. *Bibliog:* Dorle Soria (auth), Artist Life, Musical Am, 11/73; Laurie Shulman (auth), The Meyerson Symphony Center, Univ N Tex Press, 2000; Ari Teplitz (auth), Profile: Peter Wexler, Yale Sch Drama Alumni Mag, 2003. *Media:* Large Scale Digitally Manipulated Photography, Large Scale Steel, Sculpture & Site Spec. *Specialty:* Galleria Bugno, Venice - Modern. *Publ:* Illusr, White House Stage, NY Times, 10/5/61; Peter Wexler's War & Peace, Theatre Design & Technol, 1968; A Win for The Trojans, Time Mag, 3/25/74; Theatre in the Raw, Progressive Archit, 75; auth, Photos, Reflections, US Equities Chicago, 2006; var revs & articles, NY Times & others, 60-2000. *Dealer:* Massimiliano Bugno Galleria Bugno 1996/A San Marco 30124 Venezia Italia. *Mailing Add:* 277 West End Ave New York NY 10023

WEXNER, ABIGAIL
COLLECTOR
Pos: Dir, Ltd Brands, Inc, Columbus, Ohio, 1997-; founder & chmn, Columbus Coalition Against Family Violence; chmn, Ctr for Child & Family Advocacy, currently. *Awards:* Named one of Top 200 Collectors, ARTnews mag, 2004-12. *Mem:* Columbus Found (chmn, formerly, governing comt); Children's Hosp, Inc, The Columbus Acad, The Wexner Ctr Found (mem bd trustees, currently). *Collection:* Modern and contemporary art; British sporting pictures. *Mailing Add:* LTD Brands Inc Three Limited Pkwy Columbus OH 43216

WEXNER, LESLIE HERBERT
COLLECTOR
b Dayton, Ohio, 1937. *Study:* Ohio State Univ, BSBA, 1959, HHD, 1986; Jewish Theological Seminary, PhD. *Hon Degrees:* Hofstra Univ, LLD, 1987; Brandeis Univ, LHD, 1990. *Pos:* Trustee, Columbus Mus Art, Columbus Symphony Orchestra, Whitney Mus Am Art, Capitol S Community Urban Redevel Corp, formerly, Columbus Jewish Fedn, 1972, Columbus Jewish Found, Aspen Inst, Ohio State Univ, Columbus Capital Corp for Civic Improvement; memr gov comt, Columbus Found, formerly; founder, pres, and chmn bd, The Limited, Inc, Columbus, 1963-; bd dirs, Columbus Urban League, 1982-84, Hebrew Immigrant Aid Soc, New York, 1982-; mem bus admin adv, Ohio State Univ; co-chmn, Int United Jewish Appeal Comt; nat vchmn & treas, United Jewish Appeal; chmn, Retail Industry Trade Action Coalition; dir & mem exec comt, Banc One Corp, Sotheby's Holdings Inc; vis comt, Grad Sch Design Harvard Univ; bd dirs & mem exec comt, Am Jewish Joint Distrib Comt, Inc; founding mem & first chmn, The Ohio State Univ Found; exec comt, Am Israel Pub Affairs Comt. *Awards:* Decorated Cavalier Republic of Italy; named Man of Yr, Am Marketing Asn, 1974; named one of Top 200 Collectors, ARTnews mag, 2004-13. *Mem:* Young Pres's Orgn & Sigma Alpha Mus Clubs. *Collection:* Modern and contemporary art; British sporting pictures. *Mailing Add:* Limited Inc PO Box 16000 3 Limited Pkwy Columbus OH 43230-1450

WEYHE, ARTHUR
SCULPTOR
b New York, NY. *Work:* Everson Mus Art, Syracuse, NY; Herbert F Johnson Mus Art, Cornell Univ; Neuberger Mus, Purchase, NY; William Benton Mus of Art, Storrs, Conn; Storm King Art Ctr, Mountainville, NY. *Exhib:* NY Sculpture Selected by Ivan Karp, William Paterson Col, Wayne, NJ, 74; 55 Mercer Gallery, NY, 75 & 77; O K Harris Gallery, NY, 76; Waterside Plaza, NY, 78; PS1, Long Island City, 79; and others. *Mailing Add:* 477 Spillway Rd West Hurley NY 12491-5144

WHARTON, ANNABEL JANE
ART HISTORIAN
b New Rochelle, NY. *Study:* Univ Wis, Madison, BSc, 66; Univ Chicago, MA, 69; Courtauld Inst, London Univ, PhD, 75. *Pos:* Ed bd, CAA Reviews; ed, J Medieval & Early Modern Studies. *Teaching:* Res fel Byzantine art, Barber Inst, Univ Birmingham, Eng, 71-75; asst prof Medieval art, Oberlin Col, 75-78; asst prof Medieval art, Duke Univ, 79-86, assoc prof, 86-95, prof, 95-; prof (William B Hamilton), Art Hist, 2002. *Awards:* Dumbarton Oaks Fel, 78-79; ACLS Fel, 81-84; Nat Humanities Ctr Fel, 85-86; Fel CASVA, Nat Gallery, Washington, DC, 91-92; Nat Humanities Ctr Fel, 2002-03. *Mem:* Byzantine Studies Conf (bd pres); Art Bulletin (ed bd mem); Int Ctr Medieval Art (bd mem). *Res:* art and architecture of the Late Ancient and Byzantine periods; modern architecture. *Publ:* Tokali Kilise, Dumbarton Oaks Ctr of Byzantine Studies Press, 87; Art of Empire, Penn State Univ Press, 88; Change in Byzantine culture in the 11th and 12th century, Univ Calif Press, 84; Refiguring the Post Classical City, Cambridge Univ Press, 95; Building the Cold War: Hilton International Holds and Modern Architecture, Univ Chicago Press, 2001; Selling Jerusalem: Relics Replicas, Theme Parks, Univ of Chicago Press, 2006. *Mailing Add:* 3624 Carlisle Dr Durham NC 27707

WHARTON, DAVID W
PRINTMAKER, PAINTER
b Wichita Falls, Tex, Nov 19, 1951. *Study:* Univ Okla, BFA, 74; Cranbrook Acad Art, MFA, 77. *Work:* Pacific Nat Bank, Guadeloupe, WI; Levi Strauss Corp, San Francisco, Calif; Cranbrook Acad Art, Bloomfield Hills, Mich; Coll Southern Idaho, Caldwell; Univ Lethbridge, Alta; Inst N Am West; Boise Gallery Art. *Comn:* Rocky Mountain Mag, comn by Leslie Sielko, Boulder, Colo, 79; Seattle Art Comn; First Security Bank, Idaho. *Exhib:* Los Angeles Printmaking Soc, Los Angeles Co Mus, Calif, 80; Regional Printmakers, Blue Door Too, Denver, Colo, 80; Cranbrook Printmakers, St Mary's Col, Notre Dame, 81; Denver Art Mus, Colo, 81; Northwest Printmakers, Mont State Univ, Bozevian, 81; Recent Decents, Colo Mountain Co,

Breckenridge, 81; Mint Mus, Charlotte, NC; Schneider Mus, Ashland, Ore; Kunstsammlungen Der Veste Coburg, Fed Repub Ger; Pilchuck Glass Sch; Lorinda Knight Gallery, Spokane, Wash; Pendleton Ctr for the Arts; Univ Colo Gallery Contemp Art. *Collection Arranged:* Boise Art Mus, Mint Mus, Windsor Art Mus; Rockwell Mus. *Pos:* Dir printmaking, Sun Valley Ctr Art, 77-86; exec dir, Mus AK Transportation & Industry, currently. *Teaching:* Prof printmaking, Univ Wash & Humboldt State Univ, 81; Pilchuck Glass Sch, Wash, formerly; Univ Windsor, Ont, Can, formerly; asst prof, Whitman Col, Walla Walla, Wash; vis asst prof book arts, Colo Col. *Awards:* Ford Found Fel, 76; Western States Arts Found Fel, 79; Art Pub Places Award, Wash State, 83. *Bibliog:* Leslie Silka (auth), Storyteller, Rocky Mountain Mag, 79; James Mills (auth), Printmakers, Denver Post, 80; What's western about western art, Milkweed Chronicle, 80; Luminous Impressions, Mint Mus; The Primal Plastic Pool, Missoula Mus Art, Mont; Northern Lights, Missoula, Mont; Peter Hasspick (auth), Drawn to Yellowstone, An Accidental Assemblage, Sun Valley Mag. *Mem:* Coll Art Asn. *Media:* Printmaking, Digital Media; Watercolor. *Interests:* Digital media. *Publ:* Auth, Suite Southern Prints, Cranbrook Acad Art, Bloomfield Hills, Mich, 77; The Rain Baby, Univ Wash Press, 81; Indian Self Rule, Inst Am West, 82; Potters and Prints, Sun Valley Ctr Publ, 83. *Dealer:* Lorinda Knight Spokane Wash. *Mailing Add:* Whitman Coll Art Dept 345 Boyer Ave Walla Walla WA 99362

WHEADON, NICO
CURATOR, PHOTOGRAPHER
b San Francisco, Calif. *Study:* Acad Performing Arts, Film & Television Sch, Prague, Czech Rep, 2005; Brown Univ, BA (art semiotics), 2006. *Exhib:* Roma Independent Film Festival, Rome, 2005; Art Semiotics Exhib, List Art Ctr, 2006; Ivy Film Festival, Providence, 2006; in Transit: From Objectto Site, David Winton Bell Gallery, 2006; ShapeShifting: Reinventing Heritage, Division of Human Works, Brooklyn, New York, 2009; Nightshift III, Hudson Guild, New York, 2009. *Collection Arranged:* Nothing is Missing: Mieke Bal, Cogut Ctr for Humanities, 2006; Art for Life Miami Beach, Rush Philanthropic Arts Found, 2008; Satellite, Scope Int Art Fair, Miami, 2008; The Happening: Kinesics as Art Object, Rush Arts Gallery, New York, 2009; Comet Fever, PPOW Gallery, New York, 2009. *Pos:* Gallery mgr, The Space at Alice, Providence, RI, 2004-2005; multimedia lab consult, List Art Ctr, Providence, 2005-2006; cur & installation dir, The Cogut Ctr for Humanities, Providence, 2006; art consult & studio mgr, Marylyn Dintenfass Studio, New York, 2006; curatorial asst, Studio Mus, Harlem, New York, 2006-2007; curatorial dir, Rush Arts Gallery, New York, 2007-. *Teaching:* Teaching asst, Mod Cult & Media Dept, Brown Univ, 2005-2006. *Bibliog:* Allissa Wickham (auth), Installation Explores Art within Space, Brown Daily Herald, 9/11/2006; Marina Cashdan (auth), Design for Loving, V Mag, 12/22/2008; Karen Rosenberg (auth), Toplessness and Taxidermy in a Bottoming Market, NY Times, 3/6/2009; Charlie Schultz (auth), Separate but Equal, Art Slant, 8/16/2009; Kim Levin (auth), Young Curators, New Ideas II, ARTnews Mag, 10/2009. *Publ:* Auth, Lorna Simpson: Duet, spring 2007, A Conversation with Joshua Darden, The Map Office: Mapping a New Graphic Landscape & Glen Ligon: Give Us a Poem, summer, 2007, Studio Mag; Cacy Forgenie: Live! from New York (exhib catalog), Rush Arts Gallery, New York, 2008; Decades, Archaeology of Wonder (exhib catalog), Real Arts Way, Hartford, 2009; Noise Culture and the Tenor of Rupture, NuktaArt, Karachi, Pakistan, 2009

WHEELER, AMY
PAINTER
b Los Angeles, Calif, 1968. *Study:* Reed Col, Portland, Ore, BA, 1991; Hochschule der Kunste, Berlin, 1994; Sch Art Inst Chicago, MFA, 1996. *Exhib:* Solo exhibs include AOK, Chicago, 1996, Chicago Proj Room, 1997, Ten in One Gallery, Chicago, 1997, Bronwyn Keenan, NY City, 1999, Post, Los Angeles, 1999, Bruning + Zischke, Dusseldorf, Germany, 1999, Shoshana Wayne Gallery, Santa Monica, Calif, 2001, 2003; group exhibs include Randolph Street Gallery, Chicago, 1994; Collier Gallery, Macon, Ga, 1996; Dottie Space, Chicago, 1996; David and Alfred Smart Mus, Chicago, 1997; Rhona Hoffman Gallery, Chicago, 1997; Post, Los Angeles, 1998; Rocket Gallery, London, 1998; Otis Gallery, Los Angeles, 2000; UCLA Hammer Mus, Los Angeles, 2001; Mus Contemp Art, Tucson, Ariz, 2002. *Teaching:* vis lectr, Sch Art Inst Chicago, 1997, Univ Ill Chicago, 1997; instr, advanced painting, Univ Calif Irvine. *Mailing Add:* c/o Shoshana Wayne Gallery 2525 Michigan Ave B1 Santa Monica CA 90404

WHEELER, JANET B
ASSEMBLAGE ARTIST, COLLAGE ARTIST,
b Poughkeepsie, NY, Feb 12, 1936. *Study:* Antioch Col, 54-57; Stanford Univ, BA, 57-59; Corcoran Sch Art, with James Twitty, 64-66. *Work:* Stanford Univ, Calif; Johns Hopkins Univ, Baltimore; Gettysburg Col, Pa. *Comn:* Paper collage (3' x 5'), Standard Oil of Ohio, Washington, 83; paper collage, triptych (each 3' x 4'), Marriott Hotel, Oklahoma City, 84; paper collage (3' x 5'), Georgetown Univ Fac Club, Washington, 85; paper collage (3' x 5'), TIAA, NY, 85. *Exhib:* New Acquisitions, Rosenfeld Gallery, 91; 2nd Ann Invitational Show, Perry House Galleries, Alexandria, Va, 93; Art on Paper, Md Fedn Art, Annapolis, 96; Greater Reston Arts Ctr, Va, 2000; Contemp Md Artists, Govt House, Annapolis, Md, 2000; Touchstone Gallery, Wash, DC, 2003, 2005, 2008, 2011, & 2013; Montpelier Cult Arts Ctr, Laurel, MD, 2005; Glenview Mansion Art Gallery, Rockville, Md, 2009, 2013; The Object: Found, Multiplied, Manipulated, Univ Mary Wash Galleries, Fredericksburg, Va, 2009; GAPS, Greater Reston Art Ctr, Reston, Va, 2010; Galerie Myrtis, Baltimore, Md, 2013. *Pos:* Bd dir, Artists Equity Asn, 85-. *Awards:* Best in Show, Perry House Galleries, 93; Individual Artist Award in Visual Arts, Md State Arts Coun, 96; Best in Show, Artists Equity Asn, 2000; Best in Show Award, Greater Reston Art Ctr, 02. *Bibliog:* Lenore D Miller (auth), Mythric worlds, parallel pathways, Washington Rev, 90; Hobart Rowland (auth), A jury's search for the best, Gazette Packet, 93; Mark Jenkins (auth), Galleries-Natural Selections, The Washington Post, 4/29/2011. *Mem:* Touchstone Gallery (pres, 76-77, treas, 78); Artists Equity Asn (vpres, 85-); Nat Asn Women Artists. *Media:* Collage, Assemblage, Mixed Media. *Dealer:* Touchstone Gallery 901 New York Ave NW Wash DC 20001. *Mailing Add:* 10019 Reddick Dr Silver Spring MD 20901

WHEELER, LAWRENCE JEFFERSON
MUSEUM DIRECTOR
Study: Pfeiffer Coll, BA (Hist & French, cum laude), 1965; Univ Ga, MA (European Hist), 1969, PhD (European Hist), 1972; Fed Execs Inst, Charlottesville, Va, cert, 1977; Univ NC, cert, 1982. *Pos:* Dep sec, NC Dept Cult Resources, Raleigh, 1977-85; staff liaison for building & staffing, NC Mus Art, Raleigh, 1977-83, dir, 1994-; coord, 400th anniversary celebration of Sir Walter Raleigh's voyages festival, 1984; asst dir mus & dir develop, Cleveland Mus Art, 1985-1994; bd dirs, Am Arts Alliance, 1991-92. *Teaching:* Asst prof European hist, Pfeiffer Coll, Misenheimer, NC, 1970-74. *Awards:* Man of Yr, News & Observer, Raleigh, NC. *Mem:* AAM (chmn, develop & membership prof comt, 1990-92, sr reviewer, mus assessment prog, 1992-); Asn Art Mus Dirs; Inst Mus Services (reviewer, 1988-); Art Mus Develop Asn (pres, 1987-88). *Mailing Add:* NC Mus Art 4630 Mail Services Ctr Raleigh NC 27699-4639

WHEELOCK, ARTHUR KINGSLAND, JR
CURATOR, EDUCATOR
b Worcester, Mass, May 13, 1943. *Study:* Williams Col, BA, 65; Harvard Univ, PhD, 73. *Pos:* Cur Northern Baroque painting, Nat Gallery Art, Washington, DC, 76-. *Teaching:* Prof Northern Baroque art, Univ Md, College Park, 74-. *Awards:* Johannes Vermeer Prize for outstanding achievement in Dutch art, The Hague, 96; Bicentennial Medal, Williams Col, 96; Dutch Am Achievement Award, Neth-Am Amity Trust, 96. *Mem:* Coll Art Asn. *Res:* Dutch and Flemish art of the seventeenth century, primarily Vermeer and Rembrandt; artists' techniques; problems of optics and perspective. *Publ:* Co-ed, Van Dyck 350, Nat Gallery Art, 94; Dutch Paintings of the 17th Century, Nat Gallery Art & Oxford, 95; Vermeer & the Art of Painting, Yale, 95; ed & coauth, Johannes Vermeer, (exhib, catalog), Yale, 95; coauth, Jan Steen, Painter & Storyteller, Yale, 96; Saint Praxedis: New light on the early career of Vermeer, Artibus et Historiae, 86; Masterworks from Munich: 16th to 18th Century Paintings from the Alte Pinakothek, (exhib, catalog), Nat Gallery Art, 88; and others. *Mailing Add:* 3418 Rodman St NW Washington DC 20008

WHEELWRIGHT, JOSEPH STORER
SCULPTOR
b 1948. *Study:* Yale Univ, BA, 70; RI Sch Design, MFA, 75. *Work:* Charlestown Navy Yard; DeCordova Sculpture Park; St Paul's Sch, Concord, NH. *Comn:* Large works in stone, bronze & wood. *Exhib:* Allan Stone Galleries, NY, 78, 81, 83, 86 & 96; Hall Gallery, Wash, 85; Zoe Gallery, Boston, 87, 88; Boston Sculptors Gallery, 92, 94, 96, 98 & 00; De Cordova Mus & Sculpture Park, Lincoln, WA, 2003-2004. *Pos:* Asst prof, Wellesley Col. *Teaching:* Pvt lessons wood & stone carving in own studio, 75-; De Cordova Mus Sch. *Awards:* Nat Endowment Arts Grant, 81; Fund for Arts Award, WBZ Radio Station, Boston, 84. *Bibliog:* Numerous articles in Boston Globe, Boston Herald, ArtSpeaks & New Art Examiner. *Mem:* Founding mem Boston Sculptors Gallery. *Media:* Stone, Wood. *Dealer:* Allan Stone Galleries 48 E 86th St New York NY 10028; Boston Sculptors at Chapel Gallery Newton MA. *Mailing Add:* 1 Waldorf St Boston MA 02124

WHITAKER, WILLIAM
PAINTER, ILLUSTRATOR
b Chicago, Ill, Mar 5, 1943. *Study:* Univ Utah, BA; Otis Art Inst. *Work:* Brigham Young Univ; Weber State Univ; Nat Cowboy Hall of Fame; Utah State Univ, Logan; Springville Mus Art, Utah. *Comn:* Many portraits, 67-2001. *Exhib:* Utah Inst Arts, 72-73 & 76; Nat Acad Western Art, Oklahoma City, 75-2000; Am Western Art Exhib, Beijing, China, 81; Artists Am, Denver, 80-2000; Am Embassy, Australia, 94-2000. *Pos:* Advert mgr, Capital Records Inc, Hollywood, Calif, 68-69. *Teaching:* Assoc prof art & design, Brigham Young Univ, 69-81. *Awards:* Gold Medal, 76 & Silver Medal, 77, Nat Acad Western Art; Press Award, Western Rendezvous Art, 82. *Bibliog:* Articles, Ariz Hwy, 4/74 & 7/75; article, SW Art, 3/82; Stratos, 6/97. *Mem:* Nat Acad Western Art; Prix de West Soc; AOA master; Oil Painters Am (master signature mem). *Media:* Oil, Pastel. *Dealer:* Nedra Matteucci Gallery 1075 Paseo de Peralta Santa Fe NM 87501. *Mailing Add:* 4662 BRookshire Cir Provo UT 84604

WHITCHURCH, CHARLES A
ART DEALER, EDUCATOR
b Long Beach, Calif, Sept 29, 1940. *Study:* Studies with Ben Messick, 57; Santa Clara Univ, BA, 62; Univ Calif, Irvine, MA, 70. *Collection Arranged:* Prints '85, Golden West Coll, 85; Rufino Tamayo (auth, catalog), Mod Mus Art, Santa Ana, 87; Rufino Tamayo, Riverside Mus, 89; Rauschenberg (auth, catalog), Pyo Gallery, Seoul, 90; Peter Alexander, Charles Whitchurch Gallery, 92. *Pos:* Owner, Charles Whitchurch Fine Arts, 79-. *Teaching:* Teaching assoc & fel, Univ Calif, Irvine, 68-70; prof humanities, Golden West Coll, Huntington Beach, Calif, 72-2010, prof appreciating fine art, 82-85. *Awards:* Hayward Award Excellence in Educ, 2003; Teacher of the Year, Golden West Coll, 2003. *Bibliog:* Charles Whitchurch, Mizue, Tokyo. *Mem:* Art Dealer Asn Calif (secy, 88-89, pres, 90-92, member, currently); founding mem Huntington Beach Art Asn; Found Creative Arts (member, 2007); Robert Gumbiner Found (bd dir, 94-95). *Specialty:* Modern and contemporary art. *Interests:* US, European, and Latin American art. *Publ:* Contribr, Art is hot, but buy it cautiously (interview), USA Today, 88; auth, Meaning in the Art of Tamayo, Mizue, Tokyo, 89; Discontinuities: Nam June Paik and Ku-Lim Kim, Charles Whitchurch Gallery, 92. *Mailing Add:* 16172 Brent Cir Huntington Beach CA 92647

WHITCOMB, KAY
ENAMELIST, MURALIST
b Arlington, Mass, May 20, 1921. *Study:* RI Sch Design, 39-42, Hon BFA, 90; Cambridge Sch Art, 40-41; apprentice in enameling to Doris Hall, 46-47, studied with Aldro Hibbard & Fred Hocks. *Comn:* Creche (needlepoint), Better Homes & Gardens, Des Moines, 75; Infinite Wisdom (enamel on steel), Univ Hosp, San Diego, 76; Arab Transportation, Int Airport, Dubai, United Arab Emirates, 81; Baranof, Russian Alaska Kodiak, Alaska High Sch, 86; Niles Col, Chicago, 92; and many other pvt comns.

Exhib: Solo show, San Diego Mus Art, 65, 80, 84 & 87; Int Biennale, Art Enamel, Limoges, France, 75-84; Int Festival Enamel, Laguna Beach Mus Art, Calif, 86; Int Shippo, Cent Mus, Tokyo, 81, 85 & 96; Enamels 50-80, New Eng, 81; Int Enamel II & III, Coburg, Ger, 87 & 95; Boston Publ Libr, Mass; and many others. *Pos:* Cur & dir, Int Festival of Enamel, Laguna Beach Mus, Calif, 76; ed, Cloison, 80-, prof, 89. *Teaching:* Instr design & enameling, San Diego Community Col, 74-81; workshop dir enameling, 91-96. *Awards:* Prix Syndicat d'Initiative, Int Biennale, Art Enamel, Limoges, France, 78; Int Shippo Prize, Tokyo, 81 & 85; Grand Prize, Int Cloisonné, Tokyo, 94. *Bibliog:* Wayne Endicott (auth), Artist turns enameling paste into art, Ceramic Industry, 10/81; Susan Vreeland (auth), Enamelles of Kay Whitcomb, Hill Courier, 5/84; Calif Art Rev, 89; Shippo Mag, 89; Archit Design Collaborators, 92; and others. *Mem:* founder Enamel Guild West (pres, 76-78); Allied Craftsmen San Diego (vpres, 72-73); San Diego Art Guild (chmn, 68-69); USA-Int Comt Enamel Creators, Limoges, France (vpres, 85-89); Cloisonné Collectors Club (ed, 80-, vpres, 85, pres, 89); Enamel Guild NE (bd, 94). *Media:* Enamel. *Res:* Byzantine to turn of century golden era enameling; American enameling 1940 to 1970; Japanese Meiji Cloisonné; liturgical enamels. *Publ:* Auth, Germany Stuttgart: International handcraft, Craft Horizons, 71; Shippo Yaki excursion--enamel tour of Japan, 78, First international Shippo exhibition May 1978, Tokyo, Japan, 78 & Multi techniques of enamel, 78, Goldsmith J. *Mailing Add:* 115 S St Box 96 Rockport MA 01966

WHITCOMB, MILO W SKIP
PAINTER, PRINTMAKER

b Sterling, Colo, 1946. *Study:* Art Ctr Coll Design, Los Angeles, Calif, BFA, 71; studied with Ned Jacob, 73, Colo State Univ, Fort Collins, 64-67. *Work:* Fine Arts Coll, Cambell Co Libr, Gillette, Wyo; Bank One Collection; Merrill Lynch, New York, NY; Solomon Smith Barney, Casper, Wyo; Sen & Mrs Alan K Simpson; Sen John Warner; Santa Fe Railroad, Chicago, Ill; Fine Arts Coll, Sublette Co Lib, Pine Dale, NY. *Exhib:* Allied Artists Am, Nat Acad Art, NY, 74 & 76; Am Watercolor Soc, Nat Acad Gallery, NY, 75; Western Visions, Wildlife of Am West Mus, Jackson, Wyo, 88-2009; Govs Invitational, Colo 94-2002; Am Art Invitational, Gilcrease Mus, Tulsa, Okla, 92-94, 96-98; Coors Western Art Exhib (Ann Invitational), Nat Western Exhib Ctr, Denver, Colo, 99-; From Sea to Shining Sea (with catalog), Traveling Mus Exhib, Haggin Mus, Stockton, Calif, 2004-; Variations on a Theme (with catalog), Gerald Peters Gallery, Santa Fe, NMex, 2005; American Legacy (with catalog), Haggin Mus, Stockton, Calif, 2009; Allure of Water (with catalog), Haggin Mus, Stockton, Calif, 2011; Prix de West Invitational (with catalog), Okla City, Okla, 2010-2012. *Awards:* Best of Show, Western Visions, Nat Wildlife Mus, 91 & 2000; Best of Show, Buffalo Bill Hist Ctr Mus, Cody, Wyo, 98-2000; Grand Award, Pastel Journal Int Juried Exhib, 2000; Elliot Award for Excellence in Landscape Art, Colo Mountain Club, Golden, Colo, 2003; Award of Excellence, Northwest Rendevous Group, Helena, Mont, 2008; Best of Show, Coors Western Art Exhib, Denver, Colo, 2011. *Bibliog:* Elizabeth Clair Flood (auth), feature, SW Art Mag, 9/94; Ken Schuster (auth), feature, SW Art Mag, 8/96; Karen Frankel (auth), feature, Am Artist Mag, 96; Jean Stern, Roy C Rose & Molly Siple (auths), Enchanted Isle, A History of Plein Air Painting in Santa Catalina Island, Soc for Advancement of Plein Air Painting, Avalon, Calif, 2003; Jennifer King (auth), feature, Fine Art Connoisseur Mag, 9/2005; Todd Wilkenson (auth), feature, Southwest Art Mag, 8/2005; Emily Van Cleve (auth), Art of the West Mag, 9/2007. *Mem:* Plein Air Painters Am, 2003. *Media:* Oil, Pastel; Etching, Watercolor. *Publ:* Auth, Figures in Watercolor, Am Artist Mag, 76. *Dealer:* Simpson-Gallagher Gallery 1161 Sheridan Ave Cody WY 81414; Gerald Peters Galleries 1011 Paseo De Peralta Santa Fe NM 87501; In Sight Gallery 244 W Main Fredericksburg TX 78624; Astoria Gallery 35 E Deloney Jackson NY 83001. *Mailing Add:* PO Box 271940 Fort Collins CO 80527-1940

WHITE, AMOS, IV
CERAMIST, PHOTOGRAPHER

b Montgomery, Ala. *Study:* Ala State Univ, BS, 58; Sculpture Studio, with Isaac S Hathaway, 58; Univ Southern Calif, MFA, 61; Long Island Univ, 66; Univ Md, PhD, 82. *Work:* Quinn Gallery, Univ Southern Calif; Lemoyne Art Found, Tallahassee, Fla. *Exhib:* Designer-Craftsmen USA, 60 & Young Americans, 62, Mus Contemp Crafts, NY; Am Fedn Arts Traveling Exhib, 63; 18th Nat Decorative Arts & Ceramics Exhib, Wichita, 64; Outstanding Atlantic Seaboard Artists, Jacksonville, Fla, 73; Black Artists South, Huntsville Mus Art, 79; plus many others. *Pos:* Md Conf pres, Am Asn Univ Prof, 78-79. *Teaching:* Assoc prof ceramics, Fla A&M Univ, Tallahassee, 61-69; prof & chmn art dept, Bowie State Col, Bowie, Md, 69-77, prof photog, 70-, chmn dept fine & performing arts, 83-86, chmn dept humanities & fine arts, 86-. *Awards:* Design West, Los Angeles Mus Sci & Indust, 60; Merit Award, Am Craftsmen's Coun, 61; Ceramic Award, Fla State Fair Fine Arts Comn, 65; Outstanding Alumnus, Univ Southern Calif, 82. *Bibliog:* Lewis & Waddy (auths), Black artists-art, Contemp Crafts, 69; J W Chase (auth), Afro-American Art & Crafts, Von Nostrand-Reinhold, 71. *Mem:* Am Craftsmen's Coun NY (Fla state councilman, 68-69); Fla Craftsmen (pres, 69); Md Fedn Art; Nat Coun Art Adminr; Coll Art Asn Am. *Media:* Clay. *Mailing Add:* Fine & Performing Arts Dept Bowie State Univ 14000 Jericho Park Rd Bowie MD 20715

WHITE, B J (BEVERLY)
PAINTER, PRINTMAKER

b Hobart, Okla, 1946. *Study:* Oklahoma City Univ, BS, 69; Phillips Univ, 74-76; La Tech Univ, 80, 82, 84 & 85; Univ Okla MFA, 96. *Work:* Arts Coun Okla City, Okla Health Care Corp, Fred Jones Jr Mus Art, State Collection of OK Kirkpatrick Ctr Museum Complex & Okla Christian Coll; Tex Educ Corp, CESSNA Inc; Okla City Mus Art. *Comn:* Painting, Arts Coun Okla City, 93; paintings and sculpture, City of Edmond, Okla, 2005. *Exhib:* Goddard Ctr for Visual Arts, Ardmore, Okla, 91; Nat WC Muckenthaler Cult Ctr, Fullerton, Calif, 92; Kirkpatrick Ctr Mus Complex, Oklahoma City, 99; Fred Jones Mus Art, Norman, Okla, 96; Norick Art Ctr, Okla City Univ, 98; Untitled Gallery, Oklahoma City, Okla, 2000; Spiva Ctr for the Arts, Joplin, Mo, 2001; plus others. *Teaching:* Instr drawing & painting, City Arts Ctr, 98; studio class, Fine Arts Inst, Edmond, Okla, 98 & 99; instr mixed media and collage workshop, 2000. *Awards:* Grumbacher Gold Medallion/Cash Award, Kans Watercolor Soc Five-State Competition, 89; Hederman Brothers Printers Award, Southern Watercolor Soc, 85; Third, Nat Watercolor Okla Exhib, 89. *Bibliog:* Marcia Lionberger (auth), The nature of her art, Art Gallery, 5-6/83; Lynne Jones (producer), BJ White, Artist in Okla, Okla Educ Television Authority Inc, 93; George Lange (auth) BJ White, Hist Living, Vol 1, 7/2000. *Mem:* Okla Visual Arts Coalition; Nat Watercolor Soc; Individual Artists of Okla; Okla Watercolor Asn. *Media:* All Media. *Dealer:* JRB Art 2810 N Walker Oklahoma City OK 73103-1329. *Mailing Add:* 7874 Pleasant Oaks Dr Edmond OK 73034

WHITE, BROOK FORREST, JR
GLASS BLOWER

b Columbus, Ga, June 25, 1969. *Study:* Centre Col, BA, 91, with Lino Tagliapietra & Marvin Lipofsky, 2000; Appalachian Center Crafts, with Curtiss Brock, 93. *Work:* Owensboro Mus Fine Art, Ky; Ky History Ctr, Frankfort; Centre Col, Danville, Ky; CINergy, Cincinnati, Ohio; Trans Financial Bank, Bowling Green, Ky. *Comn:* Recognition Awards, Cent Ky Cancer Prog, Danville, Ky, 99; Real Hero Awards, Am Red Cross, Owensboro, Ky, 2000; Vice-Presidential Debate Paperweight, Centre Coll, Danville, Ky 2000. *Exhib:* A Kentucky Cycle, Kennedy Ctr, Washington, DC, 93; Southeast Glass, Asheville Art Mus, NC, 95; Exhibition 280, Huntington Mus Art, WVa, 97; 36th Mid-State Exhibition, Evansville Mus Arts & Sci, Ind, 99; solo exhib, Owensboro Mus Fine Art, Ky, 2000; Am Craft Council Spotlight 2000, Kennesaw State Univ, Ga, 2000. *Pos:* grad fel art, Centre Col, Danville, Ky, 91-92. *Bibliog:* Keith Lawrence (auth), Glass work, Owensboro Messenger-Inquirer, 4/98; Susan Gosselin (auth), Through glass, brightly, Louisville Mag, 10/1998; Jennifer King (auth), Over the moon, Cincinnati City Beat, 4/99. *Mem:* Glass Art Soc; Am Craft Coun; Ky Guild Artists & Craftsmen. *Dealer:* Marta Hewett Gallery 815 W Market St Louisville KY 40202

WHITE, BRUCE HILDING
SCULPTOR, EDUCATOR

b Bay Shore, NY, July 11, 1933. *Study:* Univ Md, BA; Columbia Univ, MA & EdD. *Work:* Revenue Bldg, Springfield, Ill; Ill State Mus, Springfield; Indianapolis Mus Art, Ind; Rogers Libr & Mus Art, Laurel, Miss; Ill Ctr, Chicago. *Comn:* Mellerud, Sweden, 92; Ill Acad Math & Sci, 92; Fla Solar Energy Ctr, Cocoa, Fla, 96; Appalachian State Univ, NC, 97; Millennium sculpture, City of Woodlands, Tex, 2000; Peter Melendy Park, Cedar Falls, Iowa, 2000; The Farallon, Chicago, 2001; Jacksonville, Fla, 2002; Wilmette, Ill, 2003; Harper Col, Palatine, Ill, 2004; Wiley Post Skate Park, Oklahoma City, 2006; Oklahoma City, 2006; Newport News Int Airport, Newport News, Va, 2008; Fla State Univ, 2008; Four Winds, New Coll, Sarasota, Fla, 2011; sculpture, Chromosphere Garden, Princeton, NJ, 2013. *Exhib:* Solo exhibs, Boyd Gallery, Chicago, Ill, 81, 82, 85 & 90, Sears/Willis Tower, Chicago, 2009-2010; Festival of Arts, Oklahoma City, 85; Outdoor Sculpture Invitational, Appalachian Summer Festival, NC, 87-88; Sculpture in the Landscape, Paine Art Ctr & Arboretum, Oshkosh, Wis, 88; Pierwalk '96, 97, 98, 99, 2001; Pub Sculpture Proj Univ Notre Dame, 96; Sarasota Seasons of Sculpture, 2001, 2003, 2005, 2007-2008; 7th Odyssey Conf Sculpture, Purdue Univ, 2005; Krasl Mus, 2007; Sculpture 360 Invitational, Clearwater, Fla, 2008; Bruce White Sch of Sculpture, Hon Exhib Ctr of Excellence, Austin Peay State Univ, 2010. *Teaching:* Distinguished res prof, emer sculpture, Northern Ill Univ, 68-. *Awards:* Percent for Art, Ill, 81, 83, 92 & 98, Iowa 86 & 91, Wis, 94, Fla, 96, Minn, 96; First Prize, sculpture, Appalachian Summer Festival, Boone, NC, 87. *Media:* Sheet Metal, Cast Metal. *Dealer:* West Branch Gallery 17 Town Farm Ln Stowe VT; Art Rouge 46 NW 36th St Miami FL 33127. *Mailing Add:* 521 E Locust St Dekalb IL 60115

WHITE, DEBORAH
DEALER

b Toronto, Ont. *Study:* Univ Toronto, BA; Univ Florence, spec cert. *Pos:* Dir, Albert White Gallery, currently. *Mem:* Can Prof Art Dealers Asn. *Specialty:* Modern art, international artists, Moore, Chagall, Picasso, Leger, Miro, Lichtenstein, and others; primitive and pre-Columbian art

WHITE, E ALAN
ADMINISTRATOR, PAINTER

b Rutherglen, Lanarkshire, Scotland, Sept 13, 46. *Study:* La State Univ, New Orleans, BA (art), 70; Univ Cincinnati, MFA, 72. *Work:* Hunter Mus Art, Chattanooga, Tenn; Univ Cincinnati. *Exhib:* Tennessee Painting, Cheekwood Gallery, Nashville, 73; Nat Drawing Exhib, Southern Ill Univ, Carbondale, 74; Two by Two in Wuxi, At Mus, China, 83; A White Still Life: An Installation, George Cress Gallery, Chattanooga, Tenn, 91; White Houses: An Installation, George Cress Gallery, Univ Tenn, Chattanooga, 92. *Teaching:* Prof painting & dept head, Univ Tenn, Chattanooga, 72-. *Awards:* Outstanding Teacher Award, 86 & 88 & Distinguished Service Award, Univ Tenn, Chattanooga, 93; Outstanding Prof, Univ Tenn Alumni Asn, 95. *Mem:* Nat Asn Schs Art & Design; Coll Art Asn; Charles Rennie Mackintosh Soc, Glasgow, Scotland; Found Art: Theory & Educ; Southeastern Coll Art Conf. *Publ:* Auth, Hilda Gilkeson: A Critical Review, 86, Genuflections at Misogynist Altars, 91, Art Papers; 15th Ann Tenn Watercolor Soc Exhib, Chattanooga Times, 87; George Cress: 50 Yrs Painting, Hunter Mus Art, 90. *Mailing Add:* Dept Art Univ Tenn 615 McCallie Ave No 1301 Chattanooga TN 37403

WHITE, FRANKLIN
PAINTER, DRAFTSMAN

b Richmond, Va, 1943. *Study:* Skowhegan Sch Painting & Sculpture, Maine, 66; Brooklyn Mus Art Sch, 67-68; Nat Collection Fine Arts Internship, 69-70; Howard Univ, BFA, 69, MFA, 71. *Work:* Woodward Found, Washington, DC; Am Fedn Arts; Stern Found, Washington, DC; Washington Post; Corcoran Gallery Art. *Comn:* Three multi-color serigraphs, The Workshop, Washington, DC, 72 & 78. *Exhib:* Contemp Black Artists in Am, Whitney Mus Am Art, NY, 71; 2nd Ann Exhib Washington Artists, Phillips Collection, 72; Corcoran Mus Art, 72 & 75; Directions in Afro-Am

Art, Johnson Mus, Cornell Univ, Ithaca, NY, 74; 77 Artists, Wash Project for the Arts, 77; Solo exhibs, Corcoran Gallery, Washington, DC, 72, Jefferson Pl Gallery, 72 & 74 & Gallery Rebecca Cooper, Washington, DC, 75 & 77; and others. *Pos:* Info guide intern, Nat Collection Fine Arts, 69-70. *Teaching:* Instr painting & drawing, Georgetown Univ & Md Sch of Arts & Design; artist-in-residence, DC Pub Sch & DC Comn on the Arts, 70-71; instr, Corcoran Gallery Art Sch, 75-. *Awards:* Painting Award, Skowhegan Sch Arts & Design; Nat Endowment Arts Grant, 70-71. *Bibliog:* Roberta Smith (auth), Directions in Afro-American art, Artforum, 75; Henri Ghent (auth), article, Art in Am, 1-2/75; Benjamin Forgery (auth), Washington DC round-up, Artnews, 2/75. *Mailing Add:* 1413 Swann St NW Washington DC 20009

WHITE, JACK
PAINTER
b Raleigh, NC, July 23, 1931. *Study:* Morgan State Univ, Baltimore, with James Lewis & Albert Sangiamo BS, 58; Syracuse Univ, mus studies with Richard Porter, 86-87. *Work:* Schomberg Cult Ctr, NY; Ark Arts Ctr, Little Rock; Munson-Williams-Proctor Inst, Utica, NY; Everson Mus, Syracuse, NY; John Mulroy Civic Ctr, Syracuse, NY, 76; Urban League, Niagara Mohawk Power, Syracuse, NY, 89; Stephen's Collection, Stephen's Inc, Little Rock, Ark, 2001; Geometric Madi Mus, Dallas, Tex, 2012. *Exhib:* Solo exhibs, Asheville Art Mus, NC, 77, Whittaker Gallery, SC State Coll, Orangeburg, 77, NC Mus Art, Raleigh, 80, Colgate Univ, Hamilton, NY, 80, Ark Arts Ctr, Little Rock, 82, Danville Mus Art, Va, 87 & NC State Univ, Greensboro, 90, Beach Inst, Savannah, Ga, 2000, Galerie Zygos, Athens, Greece, 2005 & 06, Onondaga Com Coll, Onondaga Hill, NY, 2005; Collage/Assemblage Nat Traveling Exhib, 81-83; The Side Show, Chapman Cult Ctr, Cazenovia, NY, 88; Dedicated Exhib, James E Lewis Mus Art, Morgan State Univ, Baltimore, 90; In Our Own Voices, Bevier Gallery, Rochester Inst Technol, 91; Group shows, Pantazidis Art Ctr, Athens, Greece, 2003; George Washintong Carver Mus, Austin, Tex, 2009; Mckinney Ave Contemp, Dallas, 2010; Geometricmadi Mus, Dallas, Tex, 2012; Contemporary Arts Mus, Houston, Tex, 2013. *Awards:* Agusta Savage Spirit Award, Community Folk Art Ctr, Syracuse, NY, 2009; Presidents award for Excellence, 2012; AVAA, Austin, Tex. *Bibliog:* Mary Schmidt Campbell (auth), American art with African roots, Syracuse New Times, 9/29/74; Ruth Ann Appelhof (auth), The Flight Genesis, Cat Essay, 77; John Dorsey (auth), Artist uses computer cards to create collage, Evening Sun, Baltimore, 5/18/90; Katherine Rushworth (auth), Tapping into Ancestry, The Post Standard, Syracuse, NY, 10/30/2005. *Mem:* Austin Visual Art Asn, Austin, Tex. *Media:* Mixed Media, Acrylics. *Publ:* Stephen's Collection, Stephen's Inc, Little Rock, Ark, 2001; Convergence, James E Lewis Mus Art, 12/14/2002-4/19/2003; Stone Canoe, J Arts & Ideas from Upstate NY, Syracuse Univ, 2007. *Mailing Add:* 3307 Helms St Austin TX 78705-2425

WHITE, JAMES RICHARD
SCULPTOR, EDUCATOR
b Dayton, Ohio, Jan 14, 1950. *Study:* Ohio Univ, BFA (painting), 72, MFA (sculpture), 74. *Work:* USAF, Dayton, Ohio. *Comn:* Murray State Univ, Ky. *Exhib:* Solo exhibs, Wright State Univ, Dayton, Ohio, 79 & SE Mo State Univ, Cape Girardeau, 79; Evansville Mus Arts & Sci, Ind, 79 & 80. *Teaching:* Asst prof, Murray State Univ, Ky, 74-81; assoc prof, Ariz State Univ, Tempe, 81-. *Awards:* Ind Found Arts & Sci Award, 80. *Bibliog:* Jerry Speight (auth), Shelter skelter, Ky Art Educ J, 12/79, Air city, free air, air fair affair, School Arts/Davis, 9/80 & James R White, sculptor, Art Voices S/Davis, 7/80. *Mem:* Coll Art Asn. *Media:* Metal, Wood. *Mailing Add:* 5504 S Heather Dr Tempe AZ 85283

WHITE, KAREN J
SCULPTOR, ASSEMBLAGE ARTIST
b Coshocton, Ohio, Jan, 1943. *Study:* Ohio State Univ, BFA, 69; Metrop State Coll 74-75; Univ Colo, 85. *Work:* Mus du pays et Val de Charmey, Switz; Imadate Art Hall, Japan. *Exhib:* Triennale Int Du Papier, Switz, 93; Int Exhib Contemp Paper Imadate, Fukai, Japan, 95; Nat Assoc Women Artists, NY, 2000; Gallery Cont Art, Univ Colo, Colorado Springs, 2001; Mus Outdoor Art, Littleton, Colo, 2002; Ridge Art Asn Fine Art Show, Fla, 2011; and others. *Collection Arranged:* Musee Du Pays Charmey, Switzerland; Imadate Art Fukui, Japan; Community Col, Denver. *Pos:* co-founder Womens Art Ctr & Gallery, Denver, Colo, 1997, Bus Corridor Arts Alliance, Denver, 96; nat juror NEA Pres Com on Arts, 99, NEA for Youth, 2001. *Teaching:* Workshop handmade paper, Univ Northern Colo, 88, Arvado Ctr Arts, Colo, 90, Colo Inst Art, 91- & Front Range Community Col, 96. *Awards:* Colo Coun on Arts Grant, 2000; Neighborhood Cult of Denoer Pub Art Grant, 95. *Bibliog:* Int Women Artists, 2001; Rocky Mountain News, Art Column, 2002; The Art of Layering (book feature), 2004. *Mem:* Nat Asn Women Artists Inc; Polk Art Alliance; Ridge Art Asn; Nat Mus Women in the Arts. *Media:* Miscellaneous Media; Handmade Paper. *Specialty:* Contemporary mixed media dimensional art. *Interests:* creating, politics. *Dealer:* KW Studio/Galleries. *Mailing Add:* 235 6th St NW Winter Haven FL 33881

WHITE, MARY BAYARD
SCULPTOR, EDUCATOR
Study: Calif Coll Arts, BFA (ceramics), 1970, MFA (glass & painting), 1982. *Work:* Munic Art Mus Glass, Spain; Corning Mus Glass, NY; Notojima Mus Glass, Japan; Oakland Mus Calif; Wheaton Village Am Glass Mus, NJ; var pvt & corp collections. *Comn:* Phantom Canyon (glass paintings), Colo, 1987. *Exhib:* AM Design in Iceland, Kjarvalsstadir Mus, Iceland, 1983; Crafts Traditions, Calif Crafts Mus, 1984; Perspectives in Glass: Present Tense, Craft & Folk Art Mus, Los Angeles, 1986; Elegant Vessels, Bannaker Gallery, Calif, 1989; Art from the Ashes, Ctr for Visual Arts, Oakland, 1992; solo exhibs, Grohe Gallery, Boston, 1992, Margaret Douglas Gallery, Sonoma, 1995, Portia Gallery, Chicago, 1997-98 & 2000, John Natsoulas Gallery, Davis, 1999; Issues and Objects, Richmond Art Ctr, Calif, 1993; Slumped and Fused Glass, Los Gatos Mus, Calif, 1994; Glass as Sculpture, Boston Mus Fine Arts, 1997; California Glass Today, Fresno Mus Art, 1998; The Quality of Glass: Heat and Light, Mus Art & Hist, Santa Cruz, 1999; American Glass Educators, Tittot Glass Art Mus, Taipei, 2002; Carpe Lumen, Univ San Francisco Thatcher Gallery, 2005; Eco Art Matters, Oakland Zoo Educ Ctr Gallery, 2007; Passover Plates, Jewish Contemp Mus, San Francisco, 2009. *Pos:* Treas, Bay Area Studio Art Glass, Oakland, 1989-93. *Teaching:* Instr ceramics, Berekely Adult Sch, Calif, 1970-72; instr design, graphics & screen printing, Oakland High Sch, 1971-79; instr, Calif Coll Arts & Craft, Oakland, 1981-82 & 95; head Glass Prog & prof, San Jose State Univ Sch Art Design, 1986-2005; co-coodr, Crucible Glass Ctr, 2004-. *Awards:* Lottery Grant, San Jose State Univ, 1993-96, 2001 & 2004; Jurors Choice Award, Bay Area Glass Inst, 2007; Fulbright Grant, 2010. *Bibliog:* Melinda Levine (auth), Bay Area Stuido Art Glass, Am Craft, 8-9/1985; Shawn Waggoner (auth), The Glass Canvas: Cold and Reverse Glass, Glass Art, 5-6/1989; Mary Fortney (auth), Clearly, this is art, San Jose Mercury News, 3/12/1994. *Mem:* Women Environmental Art Discovery (bd mem, 1988-); Glass Art Soc (bd mem, 1990-94). *Media:* Glass

WHITE, MICHAEL
ARCHITECT, ADMINISTRATOR
Study: Degrees from Mississippi State Univ and Ga Inst of Technology. *Pos:* NCARB and NCIDQ certified and is a registered architect and interior designer, State of Ga; Studio dir, Gensier, Atlanta, formerly. *Teaching:* Joined Ga State Univ in 2002, tenured in 2008, dir, Ernest G Welch Sch of Art and Design, 2012-. *Mailing Add:* Georgia State Univ Ernest G Welch School of Art and Design PO Box 4107 Atlanta GA 30302-4107

WHITE, NORMAN TRIPLETT
SCULPTOR, KINETIC ARTIST
b San Antonio, Tex, Jan 7, 1938. *Study:* Harvard Col, with T Lux Feininger, 55-59, BA (biol), 59. *Work:* Nat Gallery Can & Art Bank, Ottawa; Vancouver Art Gallery. *Comn:* Light mural, CBC Bldg, Vancouver, BC, 75. *Exhib:* Some More Beginnings, Exp in Art & Technol Show, Brooklyn Mus, NY, 68; Norm White at the Electric Gallery, Toronto, 71; retrospective, Vancouver Art Gallery, BC, 75; New Directions, Nat Gallery of Can, 77; Hearsay, Global Telecommun Event, 85; Ubiqua, Venice Biennale, 86; Like Life, Europ Conf Artificial Life, 97. *Teaching:* Instr, Ont Col Art, Toronto, 78-99. *Awards:* La Villette, Paris, 85; Prix Ars Electronica-Interactive Sculpture, 90; Petro Can Award, 95. *Bibliog:* John Turnbull (auth), article, Vanguard, 9/75; Joe Bodolai (auth), article, Artscanada, 5/76; Brian Reffin Smith (auth), Soft Computing, Addison-Wesley, 84. *Mem:* Artex-IPSA Telecommun Group; Inter-Access. *Media:* Multi. *Mailing Add:* PO Box 1032 Durham ON N0G 1R0 Canada

WHITE, PAE
SCULPTOR, COLLAGE ARTIST
b Pasadena, Calif, 1963. *Study:* Scripps Coll, Claremont, Calif, BA, 1985; Skowhegan Sch Painting & Sculpture, Maine, 1990; Art Ctr Coll Design, Pasadena, Calif, MFA, 1991. *Exhib:* Solo exhibs, Bliss Gallery, Pasadena, Calif, 1989, WC Gallery, Art Ctr Coll Design, Pasadena, 1990, Shoshana Wayne Gallery, Santa Monica, 1993, I-20 Gallery, New York, 1997, Finesilver Gallery, San Antonio, 1999, China Art Objects Galleries, Los Angeles, 2000, Galleria Francesca Kaufmann, Milan, Italy, 2001, Govett-Brewster Art Gallery, New Plymouth, New Zealand, 2002, Richard Telles Fine Art, Los Angeles, 2003, Le Salle de Bains, Lyon, France, 2004, Milton Keyes Gallery, UK, 2005, Manchester Art Gallery, UK, 2006,; Mixed Media, Mixed Messages, Lang Art Gallery, Scripps Coll, 1990; Detour, Int House, New York, 1992; TIMES, Anderson O'Day Gallery, London, 1993; Bad Girls, The New Mus, New York, 1994; Smells Like Vinyl, Roger Merians Gallery, New York, 1995; Mus Contemp Art, Los Angeles, 1996; New Grounds, Univ S Fla Contemp Art Mus, Tampa, 1997; The Unreal Person, Huntington Beach Art Ctr, Calif, 1998; OldNewTown, Casey Kaplan, New York, 1999; Works on Paper, Studio Guenzani, Milan, Italy, 2000; Featherweight, Susan Hobbs Gallery, Toronto, Can, 2001; Center of Attraction, Contemp Art Centre, Vilnius, Lithuania, 2002; Hover, The Henry Art Gallery, Seattle, 2003; The Raw and the Cooked, Claremont Grad Univ, Calif, 2004; Extreme Abstraction, Albright-Knox Gallery, Buffalo, 2005; Domestique, Gallery Standard, Oslo, Norway, 2006; Skulpture Projekte Munster, Ger, 2007; 53rd Int Art Exhib Biennale, Venice, 2009; Whitney Biennial, Whitney Mus Am Art, New York, 2010. *Teaching:* Instr, Art Ctr Coll Design, 1995, 1998 & 2006, Claremont Grad Univ, 2002 & USC, 2004-2005. *Awards:* Individual Artist Grant, Pasadena Cultural Affairs, 1995; COLA Artist's Grant, 2003; Durfee ARC Grant, 2003. *Bibliog:* Ralph Rugoff (auth), Missing Persons, LA Weekly, 27, 8/2/1991; Lane Relyea (auth), Politically Correct/Incorrect, Artspace, 28-30, 7-8/1992; Cathy Curtis (auth), Nice n Subversive, LA Times, Orange co ed, 4, 3/18/1993; Lane Barden (auth), In the Eye of the Beholders, Artweek, 10, 11/17/1994; Roberta Smith (auth), Testing Limits at the Corcoran, NYTimes, 1/6/1996; Lauri Mendenhall (auth), Digital Deception, Coast Mag, 33, 6/4/1998; Edward J Sozanski (auth), Along the fuzzy boundary between design and art, Philadelphia Inquirer, 2/13/2000; Suzaan Boettger (auth), Report from Beacon, Art in Am, 39, 6/2003; Leslie Camhi (auth), People are Talking about Art, Vogue, 11/2004; David Moos (auth), Extreme Abstraction, ArtUS, No 10, 33, 10-11/2005; Alan G Artner (auth), An old way of playing with light, new results, Chicago Tribune, 27, 5/19/2006. *Dealer:* 1301PE Los Angeles Santa Monica CA; Artware Editions New York NY; Xavier Hufkens Brussels Belgium; Skestos Gabriele Gallery Chicago IL . *Mailing Add:* 1301PE 6150 Wilshire Blvd Los Angeles CA 90048

WHITE, ROBERT RANKIN
HISTORIAN, WRITER
b Houston, Tex, Feb 8, 1942. *Study:* Univ Tex, Austin, BA, 64; Univ Ariz, MS, 71; Univ NMex, PhD, 93. *Res:* Nineteenth and early twentieth century New Mexico art. *Publ:* Auth, The Taos Society of Artists, Univ NMex Press, 83 & 98; coauth, Pioneer Artists of Taos, Old West Publ Co, 83; coauth, The New Mexico Painters, Gerald Peters Gallery, 99; coauth, Bert Geer Phillips and the Taos art colony, Univ NMex Press, 94; auth, The Southwestern Etchings of Peter Moran, Imprint, 94. *Mailing Add:* 1409 Las Lomas Rd NE Albuquerque NM 87106

WHITE, STEPHEN LEON
COLLECTOR, ART DEALER
b Jacksonville Fla, May 4, 1938. *Study:* San Francisco State Coll, BA (hist), 62; Univ Calif Los Angeles, MFA (motion pictures), 68. *Collection Arranged:* A Window to the Orient, GEH Photographs, John Thomson, 85; Parallels and Contrasts (auth, catalog), New Orleans Mus Art, 88; Industry in California, Laguna Art Mus, 94; The Photograph and The Am Dream, Van Gogh Mus, Amsterdam (catalog), 2001. *Pos:* Founding pres, Asn Int Photog Art Dealers, 79-80; vpres photog coun, Mus Contemp Art, Los Angeles, 90-91; bd mem, Mus Photog Arts, San Diego, 92-94; adv bd & chair photog comt, Ransom Humanities Res Ctr, Univ Tex, 93-99. *Teaching:* Instr history photog, Orange Coast Coll, 76. *Mem:* Getty Photog Coun; Lacma Photo Art Coun. *Specialty:* 19th & 20th Century photography. *Collection:* Collection of over 10,000 photographs, subjects: Alaska, American West, 20th century Russia, industrial history, aviation & others. *Publ:* Auth & ed, Harry Smith: Magic Moments, pvt publ, 82; auth, John Thomson, Life and Times, Thames & Hudson, 85; The far east, Image Mad, 91; The Photograph & The American Dream, Van Gogh Mus, 2001; ed, Stephen White Ed, 2006. *Mailing Add:* c/o Stephen White Assocs PO Box 1664 Studio City CA 91614

WHITE, STUART JAMES
PAINTER, ASSEMBLAGE ARTIST
b Salisbury, Md, May 31, 1944. *Study:* Carnegie-Mellon Univ, BFA, 68, MFA, 70, DA, 78. *Work:* Newark Mus, NJ; NJ State Mus, Trenton; Crawford Art Gallery, Cork, Eire; Univ Salisbury & Peninsula Gen Hosp, Salisbury, Md; pvt collections of Peter Homitzky, Hoboken, NJ, Bruce Arnold, critic, Dublin, Ireland, Deirdre Carroll, dealer, Dublin, Ireland, Paddy McEntee, collector & Daniel Whealton, Salisbury, Md. *Comn:* Construction (wall piece), Tanners Coun Am, Washington, DC, 79. *Exhib:* Solo exhibs, NJ Biennial, Newark Mus, 82, figurative work, NJ State Mus, Trenton, 83, Crawford Art Gallery, Cork, Ireland, 89, Proj Art Ctr, Dublin, 89 & Wyvern Gallery, Dublin, 91 & 93; Scottish Sculpture Open, Kildrummie Castle, Scotland, 85; Sculpture Biennale Int, Invitational Ctr d'Arts du Normandie, Jouy sur Eure, France, 86; Wyvern Gallery, 95-96; Bridge Gallery, 99-2000; and others. *Collection Arranged:* Melnick, Conn; Cooper, Jersey City; Wealton, Salsbury, Md. *Pos:* Dir, Robeson Gallery, Rutgers Univ, Newark, 79-; Head fine art & ceramic design, Crawford Coll Art & Design, Cork, Ireland, 87-2007, retired, currently. *Teaching:* Intern drawing, Carnegie-Mellon Univ, 72-73; asst prof art hist, Mt Union Coll, 74-78; dept head resins, Johnson Atelier, Princeton, 78-79; vis specialist, Montclair State Coll, 79-; asst prof sculpture, Rutgers Univ, Newark, 79-. *Awards:* Grant, Newark: Genesis of a City, NJ Comt Humanities, 80; Sculpture Fel, NJ State Coun Arts, 83 & 87; Res Fel, Scottish Sculpture Workshop, Rutgers Univ, Lumsden, Scotland, 84. *Bibliog:* Hildreth York (auth), Stuart White: The Figurative Work, NJ State Mus, 83; Peter Murray (auth), Stuart White: Corpus, Crawford Art Gallery, Cork, Ireland. *Mem:* Coll Art Asn Am; Assoc Irish Artists. *Media:* Egg-tempera, Oil, Miscellaneous Media, Collage, Assemblage, Tableaux. *Res:* Proto-Renaissance imagery, Japanese Ukiyo-e. *Specialty:* Fine Art. *Interests:* Piano. *Publ:* Auth, Calvin Albert, 78 & Dennis Oppenheim, 79, Sculpture News Exchange; coauth, Stalking the post office mural: An artful odyssey, NY Sunday Times, 80; foreword, catalog, Talk Less, 2005. *Dealer:* Deirdre Carroll Bridge Gallery Dublin Ireland

WHITE, SUSANNE E.
PAINTER
b Conn, 1959. *Study:* Md Inst Coll Art, BFA (painting), 82. *Exhib:* Solo exhib, Unitarian Universalist Soc Rockport, Mass, 2009, Catherine Lorillard Wolf Art Club, 2012, National Oceanic and Atmospheric Admin Nat Marine Fisheries Svc, Gloucester, Ma, 2012, Rockport Art Assn, 2012, Soo Rye Art Gallery, Rye, NH, 2012, North Valley Art League, Redding, Calif, 2012, North Shore Art Asn, Gloucester, Ma, 2013; Group exhibs, 17th Ann ISAP Open exhib, Santa Cruz, Calif, 2014, Soo Rye Art Gallery, Rye, NH, 2012, Catharine Lorillard Wolf Art Club 116th Ann Open Exhib, NY, 2012, North Valley Art League, Redding, Calif, 2012, Laumeister Fine Art Competition, Bennington, Vt, 2013, 16th Ann ISAP Open Exhib, Santa Cruz, Calif, 2013; Silvermine Guild Arts Ctr Art Northeast, New Canaan, Conn, 2004; New England Exhib, Cape Cod Art Asn, Mass, 2006; Blanche Ames Nat Art Exhib, Borderland State Park, North Easton, Mass, 2006; Gallery 181, Lawrence, Mass, 2007; 41st Ann Mother Lode Nat Art Exhib, Placerville, Calif, 2007; Open Painting Juried Exhib, Providence Art Club, 2008; Audubon Artists, 2008, 2011; Artists Asn Northern Colo, 2009; Emerald Spring Exhib, Emerald Spring Art Ctr Gallery, 2009; 59th Ann Nat Exhib, Academic Artists Asn, Mass, 2009; 32nd Ann Juried Painting & Sculpture Exhib for Non Mem, Salmagundi Art Club, 2009; 12nd Ann Int Exhib, Int Soc Acrylic Painters, 2009; 43rd Ann Mother Lode Art Exhib, Placerville Arts Asn, Placerville Calif, 2009; 67th Ann Juried Exhib, Salmagundi Club, Audubon Artists, 2009; 68th Ann Juried Exhib, Salmagundi Art Club, Audubon Artists, 2010; 82nd Grand Nat Exhib, Am Artists Prof League, Salmagundi Art Club, 2010; Am Artists Prof League, 2011; Int Soc Acrylic Painters, 2011; Oak Park Art League, 2011. *Awards:* Ford Found Grant, 81; Excellence in Innovative Painting, Rockport Art Asn, 2003; Best in Show, Francis N Roddy Open Competition, Concord Art Asn, Concord Mass, 2005; Award, Int Soc Acrylic Painters, 2007; Art Students League New York Award, Audubon Artists, 2008; J Tweed Hill & Josephine Petrus Award, North Shore Art Asn, 2009; Elias & Lillian Judith Newman Award in Oils, Audubon Artists, 2009; Marquis Who's Who in American Art Reference Award in oils/acrylics, Audubon Artists, New York, 2010. *Mem:* Int Soc Acrylic Painters (signature mem); Rockport Art Asn; North Shore Art Asn, Mass; Copley Soc Art; Nat Asn Women Artists. *Media:* Hemp Canvas, Acrylic. *Publ:* Art New England Mag. *Dealer:* White Seagull Gallery 59 Main St Rockport MA 01966. *Mailing Add:* PO Box 787 Rockport MA 01966

WHITELEY, ELIZABETH
PAINTER, SCULPTOR
b Erie, Pa, Sept 6, 1945. *Study:* Carnegie Mellon Univ, BA, 68; Case Western Reserve Univ, MS, 69; Sch Art Inst Chicago, BFA, 76; Am Univ, studied with Luciano Penay, 2001-03. *Work:* Carnegie Mus Art, Pittsburgh, PA; Mus Mod Art, New York; Nat Mus Women Arts, Washington, DC; Smithsonian Mus Am Art & Libr, Washington, DC; Victoria & Albert Mus, London; Erie Art Mus, Erie, Pa; Nat Gallery Art Libr, Wash, DC. *Comn:* Painting, Linowes & Blocher, Washington, DC, 88; painting, Montgomery Co exec off, Md, 2001; painting, Sch Art Inst Chicago, 2001; painting, The Connecticut, 2003; paintings, Embassy Suites, 2005. *Exhib:* Founding: The Pouring of Hot Metal, Art Inst Chicago, 75; solo exhib, Arnold & Porter, Washington, DC, 93; 10,000 Plus Alumni Show, Sch of Art Inst Chicago, 94; Am Ctr Physics, College Park, Md, 96 & 2003; The Ralls Collection, Washington, DC, 2002; London Univ Inst Educ, London, 2006; McLean Project Arts, Va, 2013. *Pos:* Ed, Eye Wash Peer Revs, 89-93; moderator & speaker, Smithsonian Inst sem, 96; presenter, Art & Mathematics, State Univ NY, Albany, 94-2000, ISAMA/CTI, Chicago, IL, 2004 & ISAMA, Tex A&M, 2007, Chicago, Ill, 2010, JMM 2014, Balt, Md, JMM 2015, San Antonio, Tex; ed bd, J Mathematics & Arts, 2007-2010, assoc ed, 2010-2011. *Teaching:* Instr drawing & etching, Ivy Sch Prof Art, Pa, 78-79. *Awards:* Asn Artists Painting Purchase Award, Carnegie Inst Mus Art, 80; Jurors Award, Sculpture Now, Wash DC, 2008. *Bibliog:* Johanna Drucker (auth), The Century of Artists Books, 95; Nicole Miller (auth), WPA/Corcoran Open Studios, Wash Post 10/27/2002; Claudia Rousseau (auth), Stones and Water, Rockville Gazette, 2008; Serena Kovalsoky (auth), The Mathematical Artist Interview, Artful Vagabond, blog. *Mem:* Intl Soc of the Arts, Mathematics and Architecture (ISAMA); Mathematical Asn Am. *Media:* Acrylic; Wood; Metalpoint Drawing. *Publ:* Visually Transforming Square Root Rectangles in Symmetry, Culture and Science, Vol 6, No 3, 95; Lines and Spaces: Dynamic Symmetry in 2-D Art, Proceedings, ISAMA/CTI, 2004; Folding Screens: An Interaction of Sculpture and Geometry, Proceedings, ISAMA, 2007; A Process for Generating 2D Paintings and Drawings from Geometric Diagrams, J Mathematics and the Arts, Vol 2, Number 1, 2008; Curved Plane Sculpture: Triangles, Proceedings, ISAMA, 2010

WHITEMAN, EDWARD RUSSELL
PAINTER
b Buffalo, NY, Dec 16, 1938. *Study:* Univ Buffalo Albright Art Sch, AD. *Work:* Nat Collection Fine Arts, Washington, DC; Albright-Knox Art Gallery, Buffalo; New Orleans Mus Art, La; Montgomery Mus Fine Arts, Ala; Chrysler Mus Art, Mass. *Exhib:* Whitney Biennial Contemp Am Art, NY, 75; Eight State Exhib Paintings & Sculpture, Okla Art Ctr, 75; Pratt Graphic Ctr, 75; La Jolla Mus Contemp Art, Calif, 79; Columbia Mus Art, SC; Paper Making & Paper Using, Southeastern Ctr Contemp Art, Winston-Salem, NC; Edward Whiteman: Works on Treated Paper, 1975-1982, Mus Art, Carnegie Inst, 82; Corcoran Biennial, Corcoran Gallery Art, Washington, DC, 88. *Awards:* Artist Fels, Nat Endowment for the Arts & Southeastern Ctr Contemp Art, 78-79; Ford Found Grant, 80; Grant, Penny McCall Found, 90. *Bibliog:* Jean Nathan (auth), Newswatch Art, Channel 6 News, 75; Calas & Terrington (coauths), Edward Whiteman and the unlovely metaphor, Arts Quarterly New Orleans, Vol 4, No 3, 82. *Media:* Liquitex, Pastel. *Dealer:* Arthur Roger Gallery. *Mailing Add:* c/o Arthur Roger Gallery 432 Julia St New Orleans LA 70130

WHITEN, COLETTE
SCULPTOR, INSTRUCTOR
b Birmingham, Eng, Feb 7, 1945; Can citizen. *Study:* Ont Coll of Art, AOCA. *Work:* Nat Gallery of Can, Ottawa; Art Gallery of Ont, Toronto; Art Bank, Ottawa; Oakville Galleries, Ont, Can; Art Gallery Hamilton, Ont, Can. *Comn:* sculpture, Mental Health Ctr, Toronto, 78; Manufacturer's Life Insurance Bldg, Toronto, 85-86; sculpture, Bankers Hall, Calgary, Alberta, Can. *Exhib:* En Scene, Amsterdam; The Power Plant, Toronto, Ont, Can, 92; Susan Hobbs Gallery, Toronto, 94, 96, 98, 2000; Trayecto Galeria, Vitoria, Spain, 97; Museu d'Art de Girona, Spain, 97. *Teaching:* Instr concept develop, Ont Col of Art, Toronto, 74-; resident artist, Univ Western Ont, London, 78-79. *Awards:* Toronto Arts Award, 90; Can Coun Sr Grant, 93, 94, 96; Ont Arts Coun Sr Grant, 97. *Bibliog:* David Burnett & Marilyn Schiff, Contemporary Canadian Art, Hurtig Publ, Edmonton, 83; Elke Town (auth), Prince Charming and the Associated Press: The Needlepoint Work of Colette Whiten, Descant, 80-98, winter 87; Carol Laing (auth), Colette Whiten, Parachute, 42-43, 6-8/87. *Media:* Plaster, Wood; Mixed Media. *Publ:* Contribr, Carmen Lamanna Gallery at Owens Art Gallery, Owens Art Gallery, Sackville, NB, 75; auth, Photographic Inscription: Kunst Aus Toronto (exhib catalog), 90, Denunciation (exhib Catalog), 91, Power Plant Catalogue, 92, Seducing the Receiver (exhib catalog), 96. *Dealer:* Susan Hobbs Gallery, Toronto, Ont, Can

WHITEN, TIM (TIMOTHY) GROVER
SCULPTOR, ENVIRONMENTAL ARTIST
b Inkster, Mich, Aug 13, 1941. *Study:* Cent Mich Univ, BS, 64; Univ Ore, creative arts grant, 65, MFA, 66. *Work:* Nat Gallery Can, Can Coun Art Bank & Ministry External Affairs, Ottawa, Ont, Can; Art Gallery Ont, Toronto; Ingalls Stone Co, Bedford, Ind. *Comn:* Cast concrete walls, Dept Parks & Recreation, Jasper, Ore, 64; monumental sculpture, Lane Co Parks Comn, Orchard Lake, Eugene, Ore, 66; Earth Work Ritual Installation, Art Park, Lewiston, NY, 77; Ritual Installation, Cent Park, Art Across the Park, NY, 82. *Exhib:* Solo exhibs, Art Gallery York Univ, North York, Ont, 72, Morris Gallery, Toronto, Ont, 72 & 74; York Univ, Zacks Gallery, Stong Col, North York, Ont, 74, St Lawrence Coll Appl Arts & Technol, Kingston, Ont, 74 & 79, Univ Waterloo, Ont, 76, Bau-Xi Gallery, Toronto, Ont, 76, 77, 78, 79, 81, 82, 83 & 85 & Olga Korper Gallery, Toronto, Ont, 86, 90 & 93; Maquette Auction, Harbourfront Art Gallery, Toronto, 85; Cult Exchange Exhib, Zhejlang Acad, Hangzhou, People's Repub China, 86; York Work I, Art Gallery York Univ, NY, 86; Membership Sales, Art Gallery Ont, Toronto, 87 & 88; Int Art Fair, Chicago, 87; Int Art Fair, Cologne, Ger, 88; Day of the Dead, York Quay Gallery, Harbourfront, Toronto, 88. *Teaching:* Assoc prof fine arts, York Univ, Downsview, Ont, 68-; vis lectr, univs & arts schs, Can, 70-; chmn, Fine Arts Coun; chmn visual arts dept, York Univ, 84-87 & assoc prof, 87-; instr, Atlin Ctr Arts, BC, 86. *Awards:* O'Connell Purchase Award, 63. *Bibliog:* Numerous articles in periodicals & newspapers including, Artpost 24, Harpers, Artscanada, Arts Mag & Village Voice. *Media:* Human Skulls, Mud; Found Objects, Paper. *Res:* Investigation of consciousness as it manifests in a variety of cultures, historically and contemporarily

WHITESELL, JOHN D
PRINTMAKER
b Hamilton, Ohio, Dec 1, 1942. *Study:* Earlham Col, Richmond, Ind, BA; Miami Univ, Ohio, with Robert Wolfe, Jr; Ind Univ with Rudy Pozzatti & Marvin Lowe, MFA. *Work:* Bradford City Art Gallery, Yorkshire, Eng; Libr Cong, Washington, DC; Miami Art Ctr, Fla; US Info Agency, Prints in Embassies Prog. *Comn:* Vermillion Seven (suite of prints), comn & publ by Univ SDak, 75. *Exhib:* Nat Print, Libr Cong, 71 & 73; 5th Ann Nat Exhib Prints, San Diego, Calif, 72; 1st Int Graphics Biennial, Miami, Fla, 73; Nat Print Los Angeles, 73; Bradley Nat Print Show, Peoria, Ill, 75. *Teaching:* Assoc prof printmaking, Univ Louisville, Ky, 73-. *Awards:* Third Award, Miami Print Int, 73; Purchase Awards, Libr Cong, 73 & Bradley Univ, 75. *Media:* Silkscreen, Lithographs. *Mailing Add:* Dept of Art Rm 104 Univ of Louisville Schnider Hall Louisville KY 40292

WHITESIDE, WILLIAM ALBERT, II
PAINTER, ART DEALER
b Bradenton, Fla, Aug 1, 1925. *Study:* Ringling Sch Art, 48-51; Fla State Univ, Tallahassee, with Karl Zerbe & Arthur Deshaies, BS (art educ), 58, MFA (painting), 66. *Work:* Marine Corps Mus, Washington, DC, Quantico, Va; New Eng Air Mus, Windsor Locks, Conn; Marine Corps Mus, Quantico, Va; Marine Corps Air Mus, MCAS, El Toro, Calif; Marine Corp Mus, Washington, DC; Marine Corps Air Mus, MCAS, El Toro, CA; North Carolina Aviation Mu, Ashboro, NC; Burt Reynolds Mus, Jupiter, FL; Marine Corps Mus, San Diego, CA; Nat Mus Naval Aviation, Pensacola, Fla; Military Mus, Palmetto, Fla; Heard Mus, McKinney, Tex; Fla State Univ, Tallahassee, Fla; Fla State Capitol, Tallahassee, Fla; Nat WWII Mus, New Orleans, La; Marine Heritage Mus, Quantico, Va; Oconee Vet Mus, Walhalla, SC; Southern Mus Flight, Birmingham, Ala. *Comn:* Portrait-riverscape, Burt Reynolds, Jupiter, Fla, 81; Portrait, Charles Coody, Augusta Masters. *Exhib:* First Miami Nat Painting Exhib, 62; Am Watercolor Soc Ann Exhib, New York, 65; NY World's Fair, Fla Pavilion, 65; Ala Watercolor Soc Ann Exhib, 65; Third Monroe Ann, Masur Mus Art, La, 66; Midyear Show, Butler Inst Am Art, 66 & 67; Seventh Ann Nat Western Art Show, San Antonio, Tex, 69; solo exhibs, Gallery 210, Chattanooga, Tenn, 82, Baker Gallery Fine Art, Lubbock, Tex, 83, N Fla Union Coll, Madison, Fla, 85, Louise Bascom Barrett Art Gallery, Highlands, NC, 87, Carolinian Art Gallery, Greenville SC, 87, Depot Art Gallery, Mooresville, NC, 2003 and others; NC Watercolor Soc, Asheville Art Mus, NC, 76; and others. *Teaching:* Instr art, Fla State Univ, 64-65; instr painting, N Tex State Univ, 66-68 & Western Carolina Univ, 73-75; artist-in-residence, High Hampton Inn & Country Club, 69-74. *Awards:* Transparent Watercolor Award, 73 & Purchase Award, 74, Tex Watercolor Soc; NC Watercolor Soc Purchase Award, 76; Acrylic Best of Show, Anderson Artists Guild, 2005 & 2006; Best of Show, Anderson Co Fair, 2005 (and 3rd prize, 1st prize & Merit award). *Mem:* NC Watercolor Soc. *Media:* Acrylic, Watercolor, Egg Tempura. *Dealer:* Whiteside Art Gallery. *Mailing Add:* PO Box 522 Cashiers NC 28717

WHITMAN, KAREN
PRINTMAKER
b Bronx, NY, Feb 22, 1953. *Study:* State Univ NY, Buffalo, with Harvey Breverman, BFA, 75; Parsons Sch Design, cert graphic design, 90; studied at Woodstock Sch Art, 91, Art Students League NY, with Peter Homitzky, 92-94. *Work:* NY Pub Libr; Mus of the City of New York; NY Transit Mus; NY Historical Soc; The British Mus, London; Taiwan Univ Inst of Fine Arts, Taipei, Taiwan; Jane Voorhees Zimmerli Art Mus, New Brunswick, NJ; Hofstra Mus, Hofstra Univ, Hempstead, NY; Samuel Dorsky Mus Art, New Paltz, NY. *Exhib:* Solo exhibs, The Old Print Shop, NY, 2002, 2007, The Pen & Brush, Inc, 2004, St Thomas Aquinas Coll, 2004 ; Schenectady Mus, NY, 95 & 98 ; A Century on Paper; Prints by Art Students League Artists, UBS/Paine Webber Gallery, 2002; Zimmerli Art Mus, New Acquisitions, 2002; Hofstra Mus at 40, Works on Paper, 2003; Trans Views, NY Transit Mus, 2003; NY Hist Soc, 2004; Allied Artists of Am Ann Exhib, 2003-2007; NY by New Yorkers: Artist Views in Prints, Mus of the City of NY, 2002; Noble Maritime Mus, Staten Island, NY, 2006; Belskie Mus Art, Closter, NJ, 2007-2008; Wagner Coll Art Gallery, Staten Island, NY, 2008; The Interchurch Ctr, New York, 2008. *Pos:* Coun mem, Soc Am Graphic Artists, 94; Artists Coun, Nat Asn Women Artists, 2003-2007; juror, Allied Artists Am Ann, 2007 & Audubon Artists Ann, 2008. *Teaching:* Guest lectr, Woodstock Sch Art, 99, instr, 2003. *Awards:* Medal of Honor for Graphics Award, Nat Asn Women Artists, 2002; Gold Medal of Hon, Allied Artists Am, 2006; Gold Medal Hon, Audubon Artists, 2006, 2007. *Bibliog:* Antiques and the Arts Weekly, 12/7/2001; Journal of the Print World, fall 2002; Am Artist Mag, 12/2002; Impressions of NY-Prints from the NY Historical Soc by Marilynn Symmes, Illus, 2004; Ray Steiner (auth), Art Times, 12/2005-1/2006. *Mem:* Soc Am Graphic Artists; Allied Artists Am; Catharine Lorillard Wolfe Art Club; Nat Asn Women Artist; Audubon Artists. *Media:* Linoleum Cut, Etching. *Dealer:* Old Print Shop 150 Lexington Ave New York NY 10016; Platt Fine Art 561 W Diversey Pkwy Ste 213 Chicago IL 60614. *Mailing Add:* PO Box 550 Bearsville NY 12409

WHITMAN-ARSENAULT, KATE
PAINTER
b Camden, NJ, Oct 25, 1922. *Study:* Wellesley Col, BA, 44; Univ Bridgeport, MS, 77; Silvermine Sch Art, Conn, studied with Don Stone, Charles Reid, Herb Olsen & Ed Whitney, MA in Art Therapy. *Work:* Union Trust Co, Darien, Conn; Darien Libr, Conn. *Comn:* Long Island Sound House, comn by Eliz Lucas, Darien, Conn, 78; Vt pitcher & bowl, St Lukes Church, Darien Conn, 79; Cape Cod House, comn by Barbara Moyes, Vero Beach, Fla, 81; Wellfleet House, comn by Stephen Ambler, Peterborough, Ont, 83; shells, comn by Jeanne Rich, Dallas, Tex, 87. *Exhib:* Wellesley Col-Jewett M Wellesley, Mass, 70; solo exhibs, Salmagundi Club, NY, 80, Copley Soc, Boston, Mass, 85-86, New Eng Gallery Art & Cape Cod Art Asn, Heritage Plantation, Sandwich, 94 & Cataumet Art Ctr, Mass, 94; Boston Univ Art Gallery, Mass, 80; Cape Cod Conserv, Barnstable, Mass, 87; Monotype Guild New Eng Inc, Clyde Gallery, Mosman Park, Boston, Mass, 88; two-woman show, Creations of Cap Artists, Osterville, Mass, 90; Cahoon Mus Am Art, Cotuit, Mass; Gallery of Creations, Nokomis, Fla. *Pos:* News ed, Darien News, 70-80. *Teaching:* Instr, Darien Art Gallery, Conn, 74-76; instr, Darien Adult Educ, 76-77; art therapist, Darien Convalescent Ctr, 77-80; art therapist, Pocasset Mental Health Ctr, 87-; instr, Catamet Art Ctr, Mass, formerly. *Awards:* Award Falmouth Artist Guild-Cape Cod Art Asn. *Bibliog:* Peter Konig (auth), Dir Duxbury, Mass Art Asn, 87. *Mem:* Salmagundi Club; Am Watercolor Soc; Copley Soc; Guild of Boston Artists; Cape Cod Art Asn; assoc mem New Eng Watercolor Soc; fel Roy Soc Arts, London, Eng. *Media:* Watercolor, Oil. *Publ:* Illusr, Print-Nantucket, Globe Press, 87; L and Art, Cape Cod Life, Nantucket, Cape Cod Life, 88. *Dealer:* Arlene Hecht Gallery 333 North Falmouth, MA

WHITNEY, RICHARD WHEELER
PAINTER, INSTRUCTOR
b Burlington, Vt, Jan 22, 1946. *Study:* Univ NH, Durham, BA, 68; with Sidney F Willis, Bennington, NH, 65; with R H Ives Gammell, Boston, 66-71. *Hon Degrees:* Univ NH, DFA, 2015. *Work:* Harvard Univ; Univ Chicago; Anchorage Hist & Fine Arts Mus; Newark Mus Art, NJ; Anderson House Mus, Washington, DC; Mass State Capital; NH State Capital; Ohio State Univ Sch of Law; Northeastern Univ; Mt Sinai Hosp; Stanford Univ, MIT; and others. *Comn:* portrait of Cardinal Humberto Medeiros, Cath Univ Portugal, 88; portrait of James H Webb, Jr, Secy of Navy, Pentagon, Washington, DC, 89; mural, comn by Frederick Hart Family, Hume, Va, 91-93; portrait of Lane Kirkland, president AFL-CIO, Washington, DC, 93; Robert Reich, Sec of Labor, Washington, DC, 98; portrait of Gov Mitt Rommey, Mass State House, 2009; Portrait of Nobel Laureate Economist, Paul Samuelson, Mass Inst Tech. *Exhib:* Allied Artists Am Nat Exhibs, NY, 76-77, 80-81 & 83; solo exhibs, Guild Boston Artists, 80 & 82; Maryhill Mus, Wash; Springfield Mus, Utah; Amarillo Art Ctr, Tex, 83; and others. *Collection Arranged:* Allied Artists Am, New Eng Exhib, 82. *Pos:* Bd mem Am Renaissance of the Twenty First Century, NY, Art Renewal Ctr, NYC; Chairman emeritus Am Soc Portrait Artists Found. *Teaching:* Instr painting, Sharon Arts Ctr, NH, 71-77; instr art, Cushing Acad, Ashburnham, 71-80; pvt instr & workshops, 81-. *Awards:* 3 Grants, Elizabeth T Greenshields Found, Montreal, Can, 70-72; Gold Medal, Guild Boston Artists Competition, 83 & 87; Medal Hon, Am Artist Prof League, 84 & 91; Silver Medal, Soc Illusr, New York, 87. *Bibliog:* Charles Movalli (auth), A conversation with Richard Whitney, Am Artist Mag, 82; Alexandra York (auth), Richard Whitney, neoclassical impressionist, Am Arts Quart, winter 92; Colin Berry (auth), A Sensitive Eye, Am Artist Mag, 2000. *Mem:* Portraits Inc; Guild Boston Artists; Portraits South, Raleigh, NC; and others. *Media:* Oil, Pastel. *Interests:* Boating, Hiking; Classical Pianist, specializing in the works of Scriabin. *Publ:* Auth, Return to Excellence, Profile, fall 83; coauth, Realism in Revolution: The Art of the Boston School, Taylor Publ Co, 86; auth, Painting the Visual Impression, 2005. *Dealer:* Studios at Crescent Pond 100 Chalet Dr Stoddard NH 03464. *Mailing Add:* 100 Chalet Dr Stoddard NH 03464

WHITNEY (STEVENS), CHARLOTTE
PAINTER, JEWELER
b New York, NY, Dec 13, 1923. *Study:* Corcoran Sch Art, George Washington Univ, with Eugen Weiscz & Peggy Bacon, BFA, 45; Cranbrook Acad Art, with Zoltan Sepeshy, MFA, 46. *Work:* Series of 24 wild plant watercolors & series of 32 tree flower watercolors Kingman Mus, Battle Creek, Mich. *Comn:* over 50 house watercolors in Marshall, Mich since 1990. *Exhib:* Solo exhibs, Pasghetti's, Kalamazoo, 88, Triola Gallery, Lansing, Mich, 92, Olivet Coll Art Gallery, Saginaw Art Mus, Mich, 95, Northwood Univ, Midland, Mich, 97, The Gallery, Battle Creek, Mich, 2000, Surveying Mus, Lansing, Mich, 2000, Milbridge Hist Mus, Maine, 2000, Charlotte Community Libr, Mich, 2001 & 2008-9, New Scenes of Maine, Milbridge Hist Soc, Maine, 2003 & 2007, Pub Art Gallery, East Lansing, Mich, 2005, Art Studio Tours of Artwork, Harrington, ME, 2008-9, Drawings & Paintings, Charlotte Community Libr, Mich, 2008-2011, Milbridge Historical Mus Art Gallery, 2014; Paintings of Miami and Mich Art Deco Archit, CompuServe's Fine Art Forum, 93; two-person retrospective 1992-1993, Battle Creek Art Ctr, 94; Mich Art Deco Archit Exhib, Mich Touring Arts Directory, Mich Coun Arts & Cult Affairs, 96-98; Group Exhibs: Barn Again, Eaton Co Hist Comn Courthouse Sq Asn, Charlotte, Mich, 99; The Eclectic Gallery, Battle Creek, Mich, 2000; Pierce Cedar Creek Inst, Hastings, Mich, 2008; Pierce Cedar Creek Inst, Hastings, Mich, 2006; Battle Creek Art Ctr, 2007; Carnegie Ctr Arts, Three Rivers, Mich, 2007; 41 paintings (continuously shown), Silver and Pewter Gifts, Easton, Md; Kellogg Community Coll, Battle Creek, Mich, 2009; Mich Artists Comp Art Ctr Battle Creek, Mich, 2012; Carnegie Ctr Arts, Three Rivers, Mich, 2012; Milbridge Historical Mus, Me, Tidal Arts Group, 2012; Pierce Cedar Creek East, Hastings, Mich, 2013; Kresge Found Gallery, Olivet Coll, Mich, 2013; Battle Creek Art Ctr, Battle Creek, Mich, 2014. *Collection Arranged:* Battle Creek Art Ctr, Mich. *Pos:* Co-dir, Whitney Galleries, Birmingham, Mich, 50-59; dir traveling exhib Olivet Restoration Drawings, Mich Coun Arts & Olivet, Mich City Hall, 74-75. *Teaching:* Art, Roeper City & Country Sch, Bloomfield Hills, Mich, 50-59, Olivet Col, Mich, 65-70, 87 & 90 & Olivet Schs, Mich, 72-89. *Awards:* Olivet Downtown Storefronts Restoration Award, Keep Mich Beautiful, 73; Graham Found Grant, 93. *Bibliog:* Virginia Gust (auth), Olivet woman sketches youth into old buildings, Enquirer & News, Battle Creek, Mich, 2/4/73; Linda Scott (auth), A Most Retiring Journey, Battle Creek Enquirer, 3/21/95; Patty Maher (auth), for the Love of Art and Architecture, Battle Creek Enquirer, 2/6/2000. *Mem:* Southwest Michigan Watercolor Soc; Eaton Art League; Tidal Arts, Milbridge, ME. *Media:* Watercolor, Acrylic; Metalcraft, Oil Pastel. *Specialty:* watercolors. *Publ:* Auth, Children's Art, Olivet Coll Press, 65. *Dealer:* Woodwind Gallery Machias ME 23 Main St 04654. *Mailing Add:* PO Box 305 Olivet MI 49076

WHITSON, ANGIE
SCULPTOR, PAINTER
b San Jose, Calif, 1932. *Study:* Pasadena Mus Art, 74; Art League, Los Angeles, Calif, 74-78; Northridge Univ, Calif. *Work:* Ore Hist Soc; Xerox Corp; Virginia City CofC; Paper Source Mus, Los Angeles, Calif; Television Acad Arts & Scis; and others. *Comn:* Sculptures, Golden Nugget, Atlantic City, NJ, McDonald's, Greenville, NC,

Lozano, Mexico City & Sterns, Nevada; Television Acad Arts & Sci, Joyce Hall of Hallmark Cards; Leonard Goldenson, Exec Paramount Films & ABC TV; Ernie Kovacs, Comedian. *Exhib:* Art Festival Laguna, Laguna Beach, Calif, 77-95; Miniature Soc NJ, Nutley Gallery, NJ, 79; Miniature Soc Washington, Archit Inst, 79; Cody Mus Art, Wyo, 79; La Luz, NMex, 83; Paramount Invitational, 86-91. *Pos:* Founder, Ume Publ, 86. *Teaching:* Instr sculpture, Pierce Coll, Woodland Hills, Calif, 78-80 & Univ Judaism, Belair, Calif, 95-96. *Awards:* Gold Medals, San Gabriel Fine Art Asn, 79-81; Miniature Soc Washington; two Gold Medals, Paramount Invitational, 87, 90 & 91. *Bibliog:* Article, Nevada Sun, Las Vegas, 82; This Week in Laguna, 84-86. *Mem:* Women Artists Am West; Golden State Sculpture Soc. *Media:* Etching, Sculpting. *Publ:* The Sophistiguins, Cartoon Serial Penguins, Warner Ctr News. *Mailing Add:* 5105 Tendilla Ave Woodland Hills CA 91364

WHITSON, PETER WHITSON WARREN
COLLAGE ARTIST, EDUCATOR

b Concord, Mass, Sept 7, 1941. *Study:* Univ NH, BA, 63; Univ Iowa, MA & MFA, 67; Eastern Montana Col, 83-84. *Work:* Univ NH; Univ Iowa; Kansas City Art Inst; Mod Museet, Stockholm, Sweden; Galeria Teatru Studio, Warsaw, Poland. *Exhib:* Solo exhibs, Univ Iowa, 65 & 67, Univ Buffalo, NY, 70, Scalping Gallery, Regina, Sask, 75, Eastern Mont Col, 79, Yellow Art Ctr, Billings, Mont, 80; Nat Art Gallery, Wellington, NZ, 76; San Francisco Art Inst, 84; Idaho State Univ, Pocatello, 86; Eastern Mont Col, 92; The Dead School Show, 96; Kaleidoscope, Billings, Mont, 96; Anderson Gallery, Billings, Mont, 98; Faculty Show, Mont State Univ, Billings, 2005; plus many others. *Pos:* Pres, founder, Western Dakota Junk Co, Billings, Mont, 69-; founder & pres, Acad Neodada, 74-79; pres, Nat Acad Conceptualists, 79-80; ed & publr, SLUJ Press, 75-; gallery dir, Eastern Mont Col, 78-79, slide librn, 79-80; art ed, Alkali Flats Mag, 81-; bd dir, Photog Inst Billings, 84-86; publ & ed, The Dead School Epitaph, currently. *Teaching:* Asst drawing, Univ Iowa, 65-67; from instr to prof drawing, design, photog & art hist, Eastern Mont Col, formerly; chmn art dept, 86, 87 & 92-96; prof, Mont State Univ, Billings, currently. *Awards:* Third Place Black & White Print, Photog Inst Billings 9th Ann Competition, Yellowstone Art Ctr, Mont, 85; Two Honorable Mentions, Artists Valentines, HG Merriam Gallery, Billings, 86; Cash Award, Big Sky Biennal IV, Idaho State Univ, 86. *Bibliog:* Ronny Cohen (auth), Please Mr Postman look & see-Is there a work of art in your bag for me?, Art News, 12/81; Michael Crane & May Stofflet (auths), Correspondence art, Contemp Arts Press, San Francisco, 84. *Mem:* Yellowstone Art Mus; Photographic Hist Soc, New Eng; MNO; AANR. *Media:* Oil Stick, Pencil & Oil; Photomontage, Gelatin Silver Prints. *Res:* Photographic documentation. *Interests:* Figure photography, The Dead School, Postcards. *Publ:* Auth, Al's Ham 'n' Egger & Body Shop Again, Basilisk Press, 74; The SLUJ Book, 76, SLUJ Press; ed, The Dead School Epitaph, The Jour of the Dead Sch, 1996-2006. *Mailing Add:* Mont State Univ Art Dept 1500 University Dr Billings MT 59101-0298

WHITTEN, JACK
PAINTER

b Bessemer, Alabama, 1939. *Study:* Tuskegee Inst, Alabama, 1959; Southern Univ, Baton Rouge, 1960; Cooper Union, New York, BFA, 1964. *Work:* Columbia Univ; Metrop Mus Art, New York; Mus Mod Art, New York; Price Waterhouse & Company; Princeton Art Mus, NJ. *Exhib:* Solo exhibs include Allan Stone Gallery, New York, 1968, 1970, Whitney Mus Am Art, New York, 1974, Studio Mus Harlem, New York, 1983, Onyx Gallery, New York, 1984, Cure Gallery, Los Angeles, 1990, Horodner Romley Gallery, New York, 1992, 1994, PS1 Contemp Arts Ctr, Long Island City, NY, 2007, Alexander Gray Assocs, New York, 2007, Mem Paintings, Atlanta Contemp Art Ctr, 2008; group exhibs include Four Men-One Theme, Allan Stone Gallery, New York, 1965; Annual Exhib Contemp Am Painting, Whitney Mus Am Art, New York, 1969, 1972, Art at End of 20th Century, 1996; Jr Coun Art Lending Serv, Mus Mod Art, New York, 1971, Reinstallation of 3rd Floor Galleries, 1990, Directions in Art, 2007; Reinstallation of 20th Century Art Galleries, Metrop Mus Art, New York, 1977; Since Harlem Renaissance, Ctr Gallery Bucknell Univ, Lewisburg, PA, 1986, Off the Record, 2000; Chemistry of Color, PA Acad Fine Arts, Philadelphia, 2005; Nat Acad Mus, New York, 2006; Short Distance To Now, Galerie Thomas Flor, Dusseldorf, Germany, 2007; Invitational Exhib Visual Arts, AAAL, 2008; High Times Hard Times, Ctr Art & Media Karlsruhe, Karlsruhe, Germany, 2008. *Mailing Add:* Alexander Gray Associates 525 W 26th St Rm 215 New York NY 10001

WHITTINGTON, JON HAMMON
EDUCATOR, PAINTER

b Jackson, Miss, Oct 20, 1938. *Study:* Belhaven Col, BA (art), 64; Miss Col, MEd, 66; Univ Miss, MA (art), 73. *Work:* Belhaven Coll Permanent Collection, Jackson, Miss. *Exhib:* Ark Art Ctr, Little Rock, 73 & 74; Miss Art Asn Gallery, Jackson, 73 & 74; Images on Paper, Jackson, 74; solo exhibs, Meridian Mus, Miss, 74 & 75, Belhaven Col, 83 & 84 & Miss Art Asn Gallery, Jackson, 73 & 74; Miss Arts Festival, Jackson, 81. *Pos:* Mem, Governor's Comt Arts, Miss & Bd Regents, Miss Mus Art. *Teaching:* Chmn, art dept, East Miss Jr Col, 66-76; prof & chmn art dept, Belhaven Col, 76-86. *Awards:* First Place Award, Miss Medal Design for 1976 US Bicentennial, Franklin Mint, 76; Phil Hardin Found Grant; Inducted into Legacy of Learning, Belhaven Col, Jackson, Miss. *Mem:* Southeastern Coll Art Conf; Nat Asn Schs Art & Design. *Media:* Watercolor. *Res:* Silver point drawing. *Mailing Add:* 1815 Howard St Jackson MS 39202

WHITTINGTON, MICHAEL E
MUSEUM DIRECTOR

Pos: Cur, Pre-Columbian & African Art, Mint Mus Art, Charlotte, NC, formerly; exec dir, Monterey Mus Art, Calif, 2005-. *Mailing Add:* Monterey Museum of Art 559 Pacific Street Monterey CA 93940

WHITTOME, IRENE F
SCULPTOR, PAINTER

b Vancouver, BC, Mar 4, 1942; Can citizen. *Study:* Vancouver Sch Art, BFA, 63. *Work:* Nat Gallery Can; Montreal Mus Fine Arts; Bibliot Nat, Paris; Mus Art Mod, Buenos Aires; Munic Mus, Birmingham, England. *Comn:* Print, Art Bank Can, 78; installation, Can Coun, NY, 79; sculpture, Hakone Open-Air Mus, Tokyo, 84. *Exhib:* Int Grafik-Bienale, Frenchen, Ger, 72; Paperworks, Nat Gallery Can, 78; solo exhibs, Montreal Mus Fine Arts, 80, Vancouver Art Gallery, 81, Winnnipeg Art Gallery, 81 & Hamilton Art Gallery, 81, Galerie Yajima, Montreal, Que, 82, Alberta Coll Art Gallery, 83, Galerie du Mus du Que, 84, Walter Philips Gallery, Alberta, 86, Galerie Christiane Chassay, Montreal, 87, Musée des Traces, Montreal, Que, 89, Galerie Samuel Lallouz, Montreal, Que, 90 & Musée des Traces, Art Gallery Ont, Toronto, 90-91; Mus des beaux-arts du Can, Ottawa, 84; Mus d'Art Contemp de Montreal, Que, 85; Art Gallery Acadia Univ, Welpville, 85; Ctr Saidye Bronfman, Montreal, 86; Galerie 13, Montreal, 87; Mus d'Art Contemp de Montreal, Que, 87; Centre int d'art contemporain (CIAC), Montreal, Que, 89; and others. *Collection Arranged:* The Second Dalhousie Drawing Exhibition (auth, catalog), Dalhousie Art Gallery, Halifax, NS, 77. *Teaching:* Assoc prof art, Concordia Univ, Montreal, 68-. *Awards:* Medal Hon, Int Grafik-Biennale, Frechen, Ger, 72. *Bibliog:* Monique Brunet Weinmann (auth), L'Eternité transitoire d'Irene Whittome, Vie des Arts, Montreal, 3/91; Linda Genereux (auth), Irene F Whittome, Artforum, New York 3/91; John K Grande (auth), Vice Versa, Montreal, No 32, 2/91. *Mem:* Royal Can Acad Arts; Jack Chambers Found. *Publ:* Auth, Book of Insects, Vancouver Art Gallery, 63; Reproduction de quatre oeuvres, Rebirth 1987, dans C Mag, No 13, 87; and many others. *Mailing Add:* 1245 Chemin Beaudoin Ogden PQ J0B3E3 Canada

WHYTE, BRUCE LINCOLN
CONSULTANT, ADMINISTRATOR

b New York, NY, Mar 13, 1941. *Study:* Fordham Univ, BS, 62; NY Univ, MS, 63; San Francisco Univ, PhD, 2005. *Pos:* Founder & chmn, Original Print Collectors Group, Ltd, 72-84; gov, Nat Arts Club, 73-76 & 86-, chmn graphic arts, 73-, treas, 86-; expert art witness, US Treas Dept, 83-; founder & pres, Bruce Whyte Art Bus Develop Enterprises Inc, 84-; managing consult, Knoedler-Modarco Galleries, 84-88; Am art liaison, Found Mitterand, Declaration of Human Rights on behalf of United Nations, UNESCO, Heads of State, Nat Mus, 89; consult, Mystic Seaport Mus Stores, 91; Am art liaison, Doctors of the World, Paris, 92; chmn, Mus Arts & Technol, 93-94; pres, Ulster Arts Alliance, 93-95; tech assistance prog consult, NY State Coun Arts, 96-; marketing consult, Evercolor Fine Art, 98-; to Chief Exec Officer of Conceptual Art and Beyond, 2003-. *Teaching:* Lectr advan OMNA, NY Univ, 82. *Awards:* Best in Art Catalogs USA, Maxwell Sroge Publ; Nat Arts Club Award, 86; Fel Int Biographical Centre, Cambridge, Eng, 2002-; Int Order of Merit, Univ Eng, Cambridge, 2003; Deputy Dir Gen Americas, Cambridge, 2003. *Bibliog:* Leo Lloyd (auth), Graphic art by mail, United Press Int, 6/4/79; Sandra Salmans (auth), Good buys in fine art, NY Times, 1/25/81; Maxwell Sroge (auth & publ), Inside the 250 US Leading Mail Order Houses, 88. *Mem:* Soc Am Graphic Artists; Fine Arts Publ Asn (dir); Artist Fel; Greenwich Village Soc Hist Preserv (trustee); Nat Arts Club. *Specialty:* Contemporary original prints and fine old master prints. *Interests:* Photography and study of cultures. *Publ:* Auth, The Original Print Collectors Newsletter (bi-monthly), 72-90; publ, The Multiple Image: A Guide to Collecting Original Prints, 83. *Mailing Add:* 195 Wards Terrace 2B Fairfield CT 06825

WIBLE, MARY GRACE
PAINTER, EDUCATOR

b Three Springs, Pa, Apr 27, 1911. *Study:* Pa State, BS, 38 & MEd, 42; Denver Univ, 54; Tyler Sch Art, Temple Univ, 67-68. *Work:* Kutztown Univ Gallery, Pa; Brandywine Sch, Topton, Pa; Reading Community Coll, Pa; Kutztown Univ, Pa. *Exhib:* Ann Exhib, Reading Pub Mus, 58, 61-63, 74 & 88; Harrisburg State Juried, William Penn Mem Mus, 74; Juried Ann Regional, Reading Pub Mus, 82, 84 & 88; 50th Ann Exhib, Muhlenberg Coll Art Ctr, Allentown, 85. *Teaching:* Art supervisor, State Coll Pa & Bradford, 38-46; asst prof art, Lock Haven Univ, 46-54; assoc prof art, Kutztown Univ, 54-68, prof emer, 68-. *Awards:* Lehigh Art Alliance, 50th Anniversary Exhib, 85; 1st Place Watercolor, Allentown Coll St Frances, 86; Award Excellence, Pa Watercolor Show, 93. *Mem:* Pastel Soc. *Media:* Watercolor. *Publ:* Contribr, several articles, Design Mag, 46; illusr, Lock Haven Express Newspaper, 10/24/53. *Mailing Add:* 700 N Franklin St #R209 West Chester PA 19380-2334

WICKLANDER, EDWARD A
SCULPTOR

b Puyallup, Wash, 1952. *Study:* Cent Wash Univ, BA, 75, MA, 77; Univ Ill, MFA, 80. *Work:* Sage Co, Minneapolis; Wash State Arts Comn; Seattle Arts Comn; Univ Georgia, Athens; Frederick R Weisman Found of Art, Los Angeles. *Exhib:* One-man shows, Louisville Sch Art, 79, Northlight Gallery, Everett Community Col, 81, Sarah Spurgeon Gallery, 82, Glass Eye Gallery, Seattle, 84, Window Installation & Nine One One, Seattle, 85, Greg Kucera Gallery, Seattle, 85, 87, 88, 92 & 94 & Greg Kucera Gallery, Seattle, Wash, 96; Wunderkammer, Rena Bransten Gallery, San Francisco, Calif, 94; Musical Variations: Contemp Sound and Vision, Port Angeles Fine Art Ctr, Wash, 94; Fallen Timber, Tacoma Art Mus, Wash, 94; Off the Wall, Phyllis Kind Gallery, Chicago, 95. *Pos:* Instr sculpture, Cornish Col Arts, Seattle. *Awards:* Nat Endowment Arts, 88; Artist Trust Fel Award, Seattle, 90; Art Matters Grant, 94; and others

WICKS, ROBERT S
MUSEUM DIRECTOR, EDUCATOR

Study: Univ Wash, Seattle, BA (Hist of Art), 1975; Cornell Univ, PhD, 1983. *Pos:* dir, Miami Univ Art Mus, currently. *Teaching:* Fulbrigth lectr, Silpakorn Univ, Bangkok, 1987; vis prof, Asian Studies, Kansai Gaidai Univ, Osaka, Japan, 1992; prof art hist, Miami Univ, Oxford, Ohio, 1983-. *Mailing Add:* Miami University Art Museum 801 S Patterson Ave Oxford OH 45056

WIDING, ERIC P
FINE ART AUCTIONEER
b 1959, Pittsburgh, Pa. *Study:* Williams Col, BA (art hist and Am studies), 81; Phi Beta Kappa. *Pos:* Deputy Chmn, Christie's, New York City, currently. *Awards:* Karl E Weston Prize in Art History, Williams Coll, 81. *Publ:* Contribr, articles to art journals. *Mailing Add:* Christie's NY 20 Rockefeller Plaza New York NY 10020

WIDMER, GWEN ELLEN
PHOTOGRAPHER, EDUCATOR
b Chicago, Ill, Mar 10, 1945. *Study:* Goshen Col, Ind, BA, 67; Art Inst Chicago, MFA, 73. *Work:* J B Speed Art Mus, Louisville, Ky; Madison Art Ctr, Wis; Kalamazoo Inst Arts, Mich. *Exhib:* Photogr Midwest, Walker Art Ctr, Minneapolis, 73; The Invented Landscape, New Mus, NY, 79; The Hand Colored Photograph, Philadelphia Coll Art, Pa, 79; Attitudes: Photog in the 1970's, Santa Barbara Mus Art, Calif, 79; one-person show, Camerawork Gallery, San Francisco, Calif, 80, & Ctr Contemp Arts, Santa Fe, NMex, 82; Playing It Again: Strategies of Appropriation, traveling 85-86, Santa Fe, NMex, Boulder, Colo, Los Angeles Ctr Photo Studies, Camerawork, San Francisco, Diverse Works, Houston, Photo Resource Ctr, Boston, Univ RI, Kinston; Am Photog today, Univ Denver, 82 & 84; Sights Unseen, AIR Gallery NY, traveling to Bard Col. *Teaching:* Instr photog, Univ Ill, Urbana/Champaign, 72-74; instr photog, Univ Northern Iowa, Cedar Falls, 76-; Univ NMex, Albuquerque, 80-86; Kansas City Art Inst, Kansas, 87-. *Awards:* Photog Fel, Nat Endowment Arts, 75 & 80; Third Prize, Bicentennial Exhib of Photog, Andromeda Gallery, Buffalo, NY, 77; Purchase Award, Light II, Humboldt State Univ, 77. *Mem:* Soc for Photog Educ. *Publ:* Contribr, Popular Photography, Vol 75 (2), Ziff-Davis, 74; Self--Portrayal, Friends of Photog, Carmel, Calif, 78; Darkroom Dynamics, Curtin & London, Marblehead, Mass, 79; Color, Life Libr of Photography, Time-Life Bks, 80; and others. *Mailing Add:* 6 E 62nd Terr Kansas City MO 64113

WIEBE, CHARLES M
DEALER, HISTORIAN
b Morgantown, WVa, Oct 8, 1949. *Study:* Carnegie Mellon Univ, with Robert Lepper, 66; W Va Univ, Morgantown, BA (painting), 72; Univ Florence, Italy, with Eugenio Battisti, 74-75; Pa State Univ, MA (art hist), 79. *Collection Arranged:* Bijutsu, The Fine Arts Japan (co-cur), Southern Alleghenies Mus Art, Hollidaysburg, Pa, 87; Changing Lives, Ill Col, Jacksonville, 98. *Pos:* Gallery rep, Marson Ltd, Baltimore, 78-80; owner & dir, Wiebe Gallery, Pittsburgh, 80-87; dir exhibs, Int Images Gallery, Sewickley, Pa, 87-2002; Development Office, Carnegie Mus, Pittsburgh, 2004; film reviewer, DVD movies examiner, www.examnier.com, 2009-. *Teaching:* Lectr, Vatican Mus, Rome, 75; lectr Japanese prints, Univ Pittsburgh, 84-; lectr, Point Park Col, Pittsburgh, 85-87, 2005; faculty mem humanities & film studies, Univ Phoenix, Pittsburgh; adj prof art hist, Art Inst Pittsburgh, 2010-. *Mem:* Coll Art Asn Am; Am Mus Asn; Am Film Inst. *Res:* Italian Renaissance Art; Early American. *Specialty:* Japanese woodblock prints; old master prints; contemporary paintings and sculpture, Eastern European Art. *Publ:* Auth, Meaning in Hokusai's art, J Print World, winter 88; The New Soviet Avant-Garde, Int House, New York, 89; Women Between Times (catalogue), 93; Ed, The Mezzotint: Joop Vegter, Antwerp, Belgium, 98. *Mailing Add:* 315 Joseph's Ln Pittsburgh PA 15237

WIGGINS, GUY A
PAINTER, LECTURER
b New London, Conn, Aug 23, 1920. *Study:* Univ Calif, Los Angeles, BA, 50; Harvard Univ, MA, 51; London Univ, Msc, 56; Corcoran Mus Sch, 68-69; Art Students League & Nat Acad Sch, 75-78. *Work:* Trenton Mus Art, NJ; Florence Griswold Mus, Old Lyme, Conn; City Hall, New York; New Britain Mus Am Art, Conn; US Embassy, London; permanent collection, Joan Whalen Fine Art. *Comn:* Cartier (painting), Caspari Inc, 2005 & 2007. *Exhib:* Three Generations of Wiggins, New Britain Mus Am Art, 79; solo exhibs, Marbella Gallery, New York, 81, Reyn Gallery, New York, 84, Optique Gallery, Lambertville, NJ, 87, Lyme Acad Gallery, Old Lyme, Conn, 88, Caroline Hill Gallery, New York, 91 & Elizabeth Bartholet Gallery, New York, 92; Winter Exhibs, Salmagund Club, New York, 87-88 & 94-96 & 98-2011; Landscape Painters of the Delaware Valley, Trenton Mus Art, NJ, 88; Paintings of Food, Grand Central Galleries, New York, 89; 150 Yrs of Painting: The Wiggins Tradition, Lyme Acad Gallery, Old Lyme, Conn, 96; Wiggins, Wiggins & Wiggins, Joan Whalen Fine Art, New York, 98; Salmagundi Club, 98-2012; Joan Whalen Fine Art, 2002-10; Wiggins Tradition: Painting by John Carleton, Guy C and Guy A Wiggins, Salmagundi Club, 2011. *Bibliog:* Richard T Boyle (auth), Guy A Wiggins--painter (catalog), 87; Alexander Cokos (auth), Guy A Wiggins (catalog), 88; Shirley C Lally (auth), Guy A Wiggins-The third generation, Fine Arts Trader, Oct 96; Joan Whalen (auth), Wiggins, Wiggins & Wiggins (catalog), 98; Anne Cohen DePietro (auth), Wiggins, Wiggins, & Wiggins, 2011; Antiques and Fine Art, 2011; A Family of Painters is Having its Moment, New York Times, 2011. *Mem:* Art Students League; Salmagundi Club; Nat Arts Club; hon mem, Allied Artists. *Media:* Oil, Acrylic. *Specialty:* Am art. *Dealer:* Joan Whalen Fine Art 954 Third Ave New York NY 20022; Lambertville Gallery of Fine Art 20 N Union St Lambertville NJ 08530; The Cooley Gallery Lyme St Old Lyme CT 06371. *Mailing Add:* 258 W Fourth St New York NY 10014

WIGGINS, K DOUGLAS
PAINTER, ART DEALER
b Roswell, NMex, Apr 8, 1959. *Study:* San Antonio Col, Tex, 78-79; Independent Baptist Col, Dallas, Tex, 82-83; Eastern NMex Univ, Roswell, 83-85; Santa Fe Inst Fine Arts, 89. *Work:* Jon R Stuart Collection, Tulsa, Okla; Charles Geneux Collection, Epalingers, Switz; Mus Fine Arts; Mus NMex, Santa Fe; and many others. *Comn:* Painting, Powell Adams Co, Kansas City; painting, Park 39 Consult, NY; paintings, Hilbert Partnership, Newport Beach, Calif; paintings, Four Sixes Ranch, Guthrie, Tex; painting, Anschutz Collection, Denver, Colo. *Exhib:* Solo exhibs, Johnson-Kraynick Galleries, Dallas, Tex, 84, Geoffrey Cline Gallery, Santa Fe, NMex, 86-96 & Altermann & Morris, Houston, Tex, 92, 93, 94 & 95; Gov Gallery Exhib, Santa Fe NMex, 88, 89 & 90; RD Hubbard Mus, Ruidoso, NMex, 92, 93 & 94; Pa Acad Fine Art, Philadelphia, 92-96; MH DeYoung Mem Mus, San Francisco, 93-96; Mus NMex, Santa Fe, 94-95; and others. *Pos:* Mgr, Wiggins Galleries, Santa Fe, NMex, 83-; owner, Print & Promise, Roswell, NMex, 96. *Bibliog:* Les Krantz (auth), American Artists, Am Ref Publ Corp; Peggy & Harold Samuels (coauths), The New American Impressionism, Castle; Sandra D'Emilio (auth), Douglas Wiggins-A Sense of Spirit. *Mem:* Soc Am Impressionists; Int Platform Asn. *Media:* Oil. *Specialty:* 19th century American and European, Hudson River, Taos founders and regional masters. *Publ:* Southwest Art, 3/91; Int Fine Art Col, 5/91; Archit Dig, 6/92. *Mailing Add:* Altermann Galleries 225 Canyon Rd Santa Fe NM 87501

WIGHTMAN, WILLIAM
EDUCATOR, ADMINISTRATOR
Study: Va Wesleyan Col, BA; Radford Univ, MFA; Ohio State Univ, PhD. *Teaching:* Taught art educ courses at the univ level; additionally teaching positions at Adams State Col, Morehead State Univ, and Northern Kentucky Univ, formerly; Prof art and art educ, dir Sch Art, Design and Art History, James Madison Univ, currently. *Awards:* Distinguished Serv award for the Col of Visual and Performing Arts; Va Higher Educ Educator of the Yr. *Mem:* Nat Art Educ Asn; Va Art Educ Asn; Caucus for Social Theory in Art Educ. *Mailing Add:* School of Art Design & Art History James Madison University Montpelier Hall Room 375/377 235 Cantrell Ave MSC7101 Harrisonburg VA 22807

WIITASALO, SHIRLEY
PAINTER
b Toronto, Ont, 1949. *Study:* Ont Coll Art, Toronto, 67-78. *Work:* Can Coun Art Bank & Nat Gallery Can, Ottawa; Owens Art Gallery, Mt Allison Univ, Sackville, NB; Mem Univ Art Gallery, St John's, Nfld; Art Gallery Ont, Toronto. *Exhib:* Solo exhibs, Carmen Lamanna Gallery, 74, 76, 78, 80-82, 87, 89 & 90, Art Gallery Ont, traveling, London Regional Gallery, London, Can, Thunder Bay Art Gallery, Can, Winnipeg Art Gallery, Can, 87; Contemp Ont Art, Art Gallery Ont, Toronto, 74; Carmen Lamanna at Owens Art Gallery, Mt Allison Univ, Sackville, NB, 75; Some Canadian Women Artists, Nat Gallery Can, Ottawa, 75; Ont Now-A Survey of Contemp Art, Kitchener-Waterloo Gallery, Art Gallery of Hamilton, Ont, 76; 17 Canadian Artists-A Protean View, Vancouver Art Gallery, BC, 76; Kanadische Künstler Kunsthalle, Basel, Switz, 78; 20th Century Can Painting, Nat Gallery Can, 81; Canadian Horizon, Can Coun, 82; Fiction (with catalog), Art Gallery Ont, 82; Toronto Painting (with catalog), traveling exhib, 84; Six Toronto Artists in Amsterdam, Fodor Mus, Amsterdam, 84; Late Capitalism, Art Gallery at Harbourfront, 85; Canadian-Swiss Art Connection, Toronto, 85; Canadian Biennial Contemp Art, Nat Gallery Can, 89; and many others. *Awards:* Can Coun Grants, 69, 70, 72 & 73, Sr Grant, 82; Ont Arts Coun Grant, 75-76. *Media:* Oil on Canvas. *Mailing Add:* 57 Pemberton Ave Willowdale ON M2M 1Y2 Canada

WILBERT, ROBERT JOHN
PAINTER, EDUCATOR
b Chicago, Ill, Oct 9, 1929. *Study:* Univ Ill, BFA, 51, MFA, 54. *Work:* Saginaw Mus, Mich; South Bend Art Ctr, Ind; Kresge Art Ctr, Mich State Univ; Detroit Inst Arts; Wayne State Univ, Detroit. *Comn:* Design, Mich Statehood Stamp, US Postal Serv, 87. *Exhib:* Am Watercolors, Drawings & Prints, Metrop Mus Art, 52; Butler Inst Am Art Midyear Ann, 60, 62, 63 & 68; Pa Acad Fine Arts Ann, 61 & 63; J B Speed Art Mus, Louisville, Ky, 65 & 75; Kalamazoo Art Ctr, Mich, 73; Slusser Art Ctr, Univ Mich, Ann Arbor, 74 & 76; Detroit Inst Arts, 76 & 82; Muskegon Mus Art, 82. *Teaching:* Instr painting, Flint Inst Arts, Mich, 54-56; prof painting, Wayne State Univ, 56-. *Awards:* 57th Exhib Mich Artists Werbe Award, Detroit Inst Arts, 69; Nat Endowment Arts Fel, 77; Mich Found Arts Award, 80. *Mem:* Detroit Artists Market; Detroit Focus. *Media:* Oil, Watercolor. *Mailing Add:* c/o Donald Morris Gallery PO Box 1508 Birmingham MI 48012-1508

WILCOX, LESLIE
SCULPTOR
Study: Sch Mus Fine Arts. *Exhib:* Installations incl Decordrova Mus, Lincoln, Mass, Fuller Mus, Brockton, Mass, Deering Oaks Park, Portland, Maine; group shows incl Barbara Krakow Gallery, Boston; Boston Sculptors, Chapel Gallery, Newtown, Mass; Prudential Tower Lobby; Office Environments of Boston; Boston Corp Art; represented in permanent collections Mus Fine Arts, Boston, Brandeis Univ & Harvard Univ. *Media:* Aluminum, Bronze, Copper, Brass Screen. *Mailing Add:* c/o United South End Artists Inc 524 Harrison Ave Studio #A Boston MA 02118

WILCOXON, HEATHER
PAINTER
b Los Angeles, California, 1947. *Study:* San Francisco Art Inst (Painting), BFA, 1986, MFA, 1988. *Work:* Rene Di Rosa Preserve, Napa, Calif. *Exhib:* Solo exhibs include Patricia Sweetow Gallery, Napa, Calif, 1995, Brenda Taylor Gallery, New York, 2001, 2006, 2007, Chebithes Gallery, Laguna Beach, Calif, 2005, Marin Mus Contemp Art, Marin County, Calif, 2008; two-person exhibs include Back lot, Donna Seager Gallery, San Rafael, Calif, (With Inez Storer), 2007, Kindred Spirits, Bank Am, San Francisco, (With Inez Storer), 2007; group exhibs include Sacred Images Sacred Space, Bolinas Mus, Calif, 1994; Who We Are, Triton Mus Art, Santa Clara, Calif, 2002; New Space, Brenda Taylor Gallery, New York, 2005, Surface, 2006, Red Dot Art Fair, 2007, 2008; Books, Donna Seager Gallery, San Rafael, Calif, 2006, Book Show, 2008; Art Fair, Anna Bondonio Art Gallery, Alba, Italy, 2008; Thomas Paul Fine Art, Los Angeles, 2008; Show & Tell, Zimmer Childrens Mus, Los Angeles, 2008. *Awards:* Bronze Discovery Award Painting, Art of Calif, 1993; Pollock-Krasner Found Fel, 1999, Grant, 2007. *Dealer:* Brenda Taylor Gallery 511 West 25th St 401 New York NY 10001; Toomey Tourell Fine Art 49 Geary St San Francisco Ca 94108; Donna Seager Gallery 851 4th St San Rafael Ca 94901. *Mailing Add:* Heather Wilcoxon Studio 300 Napa St Sausalito CA 94965-1961

WILDA, STEVEN A
PAINTER, FILMMAKER
b Northampton, Mass, June 3, 1955. *Work:* Farnsworth Art Mus, Rockland, Maine; Leigh Yawkey Woodson Art Mus, Wausau, Wis. *Exhib:* Solo exhibs, Drawn to the Essence, Mus Fine Arts, Springfield, Mass, 2003; Group exhibs, Birds in Art, Leigh Yawkey Woodson Art Mus, Wausaw, Wis, 2004; Black & White, Copley Soc, Boston, Mass, 2005; Audubon Artists Ann Exhib, Salmagundi Club, New York, 2005, 2008; Allied Artists of Am, Inc, Invitational, Bennington Ctr for the Arts, Bennington, Vt, 2007; Birds in Am (Invitational), Francesca Anderson Fine Arts, Lexington, Mass, 2007; Hudson Valley Art Asn, Inc, Lyme Art Asn, Old Lyme, Conn, 2008. *Awards:* President's Award, Springfield Art League, Springfield, Mass, 2001, 2003, 2004; Finalist Award, The Artist's Mag, Cincinnati, Ohio, 2000, 2003, 2015; Best in Show, Mem Juried Exhib 2, Concord, Mass, 2002, 2004, 2010; Conn Acad of Fine Arts Award, Allied Artists of Am, Inc, New York, 2008, 2009; 3rd Place, Conn Acad of Fine Arts, Mystic, Conn, 2008, Top Drawing Award, 2003, 2007, 2010; Best in Show, Am Artists Prof League, New York, 2009; Hon Award, Acad Artists Asn, 2001, 2007, 2009, 2011, 2012; Best in Show, Nat Soc Painters in Casein and Acrylic Inc, NY, 2011; Int Grand Prize, Artist Portfolio Mag Anniversary II, 2013; Finalist, Art Renewal Center (online), 2013; Gerry Lenfest award for American Art, Nat Soc of Painters in Casein and Acrylic, NY, 2013; Best in Show, Academic Artists Asn, Vernon, Conn, 2013; Honorable mention, Art Renewal Center (online), 2014; Outstanding Acrylic award, Bold Brush (online), 2014; Honorable mention, International Soc of Acrylic Painters (online), 2015; Mark Freeman Memorial award, Nat Soc of Painters in Casein and Acrylic, NY, 2015. *Mem:* Allied Artists of Am, New York, 2006-; Conn Acad of Fine Arts, Mystic, Conn, 2005-; Acad Artists Asn, Springfield, Mass, 2003-; Conn River Valley Artist, Somers, Conn, 2006-. *Media:* Graphite. *Publ:* contribr, Int Artist Mag, Elladrent Pty, Ltd, 2003; contribr, Drawing Board Mag, Artist Mag Specials, 2004; contribr, The Pegmatite Mines Knows as Palermo, Friends of Palermo Mines, 2004; contribr, Am Artist Drawing Mag, VNU Business Media, 2006; contribr, Strokes of Genuis II, North Light Books, 2009; contribr, Splash 11, North Light Books, 2010; contribr, Splash 12, North Light Books, 2011; contribr, Stokes of Genius 6, North Light Books, 2014; contribr, Stokes of Genius 7, North Light Books, 2015; contribr, AcrylicWorks, North Light Books, 2014; contribr, AcrylicWorks 2, North Light Books, 2015. *Mailing Add:* 53 Rocky Hill Rd Hadley MA 01035

WILDE, STEPHANIE
CONCEPTUAL ARTIST, PRINTMAKER
b Coalville, Utah, July 1, 1952. *Work:* Harris Fine Art Mus, Provo, Utah; Boise Art Mus, Idaho; Marriott Libr, Univ Utah. *Comn:* Pen & ink drawing, Springville Mus, Utah, 87 & Boise State Univ, Idaho, 88. *Exhib:* 3rd Biennial Juried Show, Boise Art Mus, 83; Solo exhibs, Harris Fine Art Mus, Provo, 86 & Herrett Art Mus, Twin Falls, 86; Critic Collects, Art Attack Gallery, Boise, 86; 2nd Biennial, Maryhill Mus, Glendale, Wash, 87; 64th Nat Spring Salon, Springville Mus, 87-88; Works on Paper, Springville Mus Art, 88; Stewart Gallery, Boise, Idaho, 89; Aids, Mus Fine Art, Montana, 89; Long Beach Art Mus, 93; Boise Art Mus, 98; Salt Lake Art Ctr, 99; Evolving Space, 98; and others. *Awards:* Visual Arts, Fel Idaho Art Asn, 88. *Bibliog:* Jeanette Ross (auth), Women of visible power, Boise Mag, 88. *Media:* Ink. *Publ:* Coauth, The Wilde Birds, private publ, 86. *Dealer:* Lane Stewart Bune 426 North 8th St Boise ID 83702; Evolving Space San Francisco CA. *Mailing Add:* 406 E Crestline Dr Boise ID 83702

WILES, STEPHANIE
MUSEUM DIRECTOR
Study: Hunter Coll, New York, MA (Art Hist); City Univ New York, PhD. *Collection Arranged:* Jim Dine: The Photographs, 2000-05. *Pos:* With John Pierpont Morgan Libr, New York, 1981-98, asst drawing & prints dept, cur drawings & prints; cur, Davison Art Ctr, Wesleyan Univ, 1998-2004; John GW Cowles dir, Allen Mem Art Mus, Oberlin Coll, Ohio, 2004-. *Teaching:* Asst prof art, Oberlin Coll, 2004-. *Mailing Add:* Allen Mem Art Mus Oberlin Coll 87 N Main St Oberlin OH 44074

WILEY, KEHINDE
PAINTER
b Los Angeles, 1977. *Study:* San Francisco Art Inst, BFA, 1999; Yale Univ Sch Art, MFA, 2001. *Work:* Studio Mus Harlem, New York; Walker Art Ctr, Minneapolis; Brooklyn Mus Art; Hammer Mus, Los Angeles; Miami Art Mus. *Comn:* Portraits of VH1 Hip Hop Awards Honorees, 2005; Nike Billboard Project, LA, 2006. *Exhib:* Solo exhibs include Roberts & Tilton, LA, 2003, 2006, Deitch Projects, New York, 2003, 2005, 2008, Rhona Hoffman Gallery, Chicago, 2004, 2006, 2008, Brooklyn Mus Art, 2004, Franklin Art Works, Minneapolis, 2005, Conner Contemp, Washington, 2005, Sorrywereclosed, Brussels, 2006, Columbus Mus Art, Ohio, 2006, John Michael Kohler Arts Ctr, Wis, 2007, Portland Art Mus, 2007, Studio Mus Harlem, New York, 2008; group exhibs include It's Bigger Than Hip Hop, Rush Arts, New York, 2001; Black Romantic, Studio Mus Harlem, New York, 2002, Ironic/Iconic, 2002; Painting as Paradox, Artists Space, New York, 2002; The New York Mets & Our National Pastime, Queens Mus Art, New York, 2004; Maximum Flavor, ACA Gallery, Atlanta Coll Art, 2005; Redefined: Mod & Contemp Art from the Collection, Corcoran Gallery Art, Washington, 2006; Down by Law, Whitney Mus Am Art, New York, 2006; Down, Mus Contemp Art, Detroit, 2008; Selected Drawings, Mus Contemp Art, Cleveland, 2008; Recognize! Hip Hop & Contemp Portraiture, Nat Portrait Gallery, Smithsonian Inst, Washington, 2008. *Awards:* Rema Hort Mann Found Grant, 2002. *Dealer:* Rhona Hoffman Gallery 118 N Peoria St Chicago IL 60607; Roberts & Tilton Gallery 6150 Wilshire Blvd Los Angeles CA 90048; Deitch Projects 76 Grand St New York NY 10013. *Mailing Add:* Roberts & Tilton Gallery 5801 Washington Blvd Culver City CA 90232

WILEY, LOIS JEAN
PAINTER, WRITER
b West Mifflin, Pa, Sept 17, 1928. *Study:* Allegheny Coll, BA, 50; studies with Andrew Sanders, Art Sch, Erie, Pa, 64-74; Edinboro Univ Pa, MFA, 79. *Work:* Oil Painting, Orange on Antiques Box, Erie Art Mus; Oil Painting, Onions on Silver Tray, Butler Inst Am Art, Youngstown, Ohio. *Comn:* Portraits of individuals and pets for pvt collections; Portrait, Works on Children, Mr. and Mrs. Chris Walker, 96; Portrait, Lady and the Cat, Mr. and Mrs. Jim Graves, 99; Portrait, Cavalier King Charles, Mr. and Mrs. Jim Graves, 2001; Portraits, Princess, Mr. and Mrs. Don Monroe, 2011. *Exhib:* Audubon Artists Ann, Nat Acad Galleries, NY, 73; Butler Midyear Show, Butler Inst Am Art, 76-78 & 80; Silvermine Guild of Artists, New Canaan, Conn, 78; Salmagundi Club 1st Open Exhib, Salmagundi Club Galleries, NY, 78; Allied Artists 61st Ann, Nat Acad Galleries, NY, 80; Grand Exhib, Akron Soc Artists Juried Exhib, Ohio, 96; 23rd Ann October Evenings Exhib, Meadville, Pa, 97, 2000-2001; Erie Art Mus Spring Show, 2002; Nat Asn of Women Artists Ann, 2002; solo exhibition, Homage to the Orange, Kada Gallery, Erie, PA, 2004; Regional Invitational, Meadville Council on the Arts, 2004; Waterford Artists Biannual, 2004, 2006; Erie Festival's Panorama, 2007-2008; Lily Festival, 2007-2008, 2012; Multinational contrib of a pastel landscape, Presque Isle Audubon Soc Fund Lottery, 2008; Summers Bounty, Kada Gallery, Erie, Penn, 2009; NPAA Mem Shows, 2011, 2012. *Pos:* Dir publicity, Cur Exhib Series, 75-77; publicity chairperson, Northwestern Pa Artists Asn, 81-82; freelance writer-art rev, Times Publ-Showcase, 88-2011; asst producer, Heart of the Arts of Series, PBS, 95; mem, Collections Comt, Erie Art Mus, 95-2002; organizer, dir, Drawing From Life, 2002-; examiner, Int Baccalaureate Org, 2004. *Teaching:* Pub sch tchr, 59-89. *Awards:* Berta N Briggs Mem Award, 77 & Elizabeth Stanton, Blake Prize for Portrait in Oil, 81, Nat Asn Women Artists; Muriel Ritchie Mem, Acad Artists Asn, 78; Second prize, Campbell Pottery Lily Ann, 2001; Juror's Choice award, Eric Festival of Art: Panorama, 2010; Third Prize, Campbell Pottery Lily Ann, 2012. *Mem:* Nat Asn Women Artists (hon lifetime mem, 2009); Northwestern Pa Artists Asn. *Media:* Oil, Colored Pencil, Watercolor. *Interests:* Conservation, Animal Rights. *Publ:* Auth, Shuttle spindle and dyepot, Handweavers Guild Am Inc, fall 78; Fiberarts, Fiberarts Mag, 1-2/79. *Dealer:* Kada Gallery Erie PA; Glass Growers Gallery Erie PA; Bayfront Gallery Erie PA. *Mailing Add:* 917 High St PO Box 816 Waterford PA 16441-0816

WILEY, WILLIAM T
PAINTER
b Bedford, Ind, Oct 21, 1937. *Study:* San Francisco Art Inst, BFA, 61, MFA, 62. *Work:* Philadelphia Mus Art, Pa Acad Fine Arts, Philadelphia, Pa; Seattle Art Mus, Wash; Mus Mod Art, Whitney Mus Am Art, NY; Art Inst Chicago; San Francisco Mus Mod Art, City of San Francisco, San Francisco Art Inst; Los Angeles Co Mus Art; Nat Mus Am Art, Hirshhorn Mus & Sculpture Garden, Corcoran Gallery Art, Washington, DC; Brooklyn Mus, NY. *Comn:* 75 ft bronze sculpture, Lippincott Inc. *Exhib:* Solo exhibs, LA Louver, Venice, Calif, 84, 87, 91 & 92, Max Protetch Gallery, NY, 91 & 94, Marsha Mateyka Gallery, Washington, DC, 91 & 93, Corcoran Gallery Art traveling show, Washington, DC, 91, Marian Locks Gallery, Philadelphia, Pa, 92 & 94, Ind State Univ, Bloomington, 93 & Rena Bransten Gallery, San Francisco, 93, Charles Cowles Gallery, NY, 2007, Crown Point Press, San Francisco, 2007, Punball: Only One Earth, Electric Works, San Francisco, 2008, Fear Rules, John Berggruen Gallery, San Francisco, Calif, 2008, Whats it all Mean: William T Wiley in Retrospect, Smithsonian Am Art Mus, 2009, Berkeley Art Mus, Calif, Pacific Film Festival, Calif, 2010, Ventura Rocks, Sylvia White Gallery, Ventura, Calif, 2010, I Keep Foolin' Around, Anderson Gallery of Graphic Art, Fine Arts Mus San Francisco, 2010, A Seek Wince of Evince, Project Space, Electric Woods, San Francisco, Calif, 2010, 5 Decades, Ochi Gallery, Lewis St, Ketchum, Id, Wally Hendrick and William T Wiley, James Mayor Gallery, London, Eng, Abstraction with Leaky Wicks, Max Davidson Gallery, NY, The Desperate Ours, Sarah Moody Gallery Arts, Univ Ala, Tuscaloosa, 2011; Group exhibs, The Making of a Legend: Chief Seattle's Reply, Hatley Martin Gallery, San Francisco, 90; Rain of Talent: Umbrella Art, The Fabric Workshop, Philadelphia, Pa, Traveling, 89-94; Selections from the Anderson Collection, San Jose Mus Art, Calif, 92; Directions in Bay Area Printmaking: Three Decades, Palo Alto Cult Ctr, Calif, 92-93; Clearly Art, Whatcom Mus Hist & Art, Bellingham, Wash, traveling, 92-95; Here and Now: Bay Area Masterworks from the di Rosa Collections (with catalog), Oakland Mus, Calif, 94; Advice and Dissent: Collaborative Work, William Allan, Robert Hudson, William T Wiley, John Berggruen Gallery, San Francisco, Calif, 94; Altered and Irrational: Selections from the Permanent Collection, Whitney Mus Am Art, NY, 95; Form & Function of Drawing Today-90s, Meese Frankfurt, Frankurtam Main, Germany, 97; William Allan, Robert Hudson, and William T Wiley, Palm Springs Desert Mus, Calif, Art Mus, Fla, Int Univ, Miami, Fla, Mus Art, Wash State Univ, Pullman, Wash, Scottsdale Mus Contemp Art, Scottsdale, Ariz, 98-99; 25th Anniv Exhib, Hirshorn Mus and Sculpture Garden, Wash DC, 99; Crossroads of Am Sculpture, Indianapolis Mus Art, Indianapolis In, New Orleans Mus Art, La, 2000; Tamarind, 40 Yrs, 2002; Aftershock: The Legacy of the Readymade in Post-War and Contemporary American Art, Dickinson Roundell, NY, Eng, 2003; 100 Artists See Satan, Grand Central Art Ctr, Santa Ana, Calif, 2004; The Corcoran 2005 Print Portfolio: Drawn to Representation, Corcoran Gallery Art, Wash DC, 2005; Twice Drawn, The Frances Young Tang Teaching Mus and Art Gallery, Skidmore Coll, Saratoga Springs, NY, 2006; Ways of Seeing: John Baldessari Explores the Collection, Smithsonian Mus, Lower Level Gallery, Wash DC, 2007; Looking for Mushrooms, San Francisco and the Bay Area in the Sixties, Mus Ludwig, Cologne, Germany, 2008; Instruments, Solway/Jones Gallery, Los Angeles, Calif, 2009; Image and Text, Donna Seeger Gallery, San Rafael, Calif, 2010; Re-imagining Don Quixote or Don Quixote in New York, Queen Sofia Spanish Inst, NY, 2011; and many more. *Teaching:* Assoc prof art, Univ Calif, Davis, 62-73; instr, San Francisco Art Inst, 63, 66-67, Univ Nev, Reno, 67, Wash State Col, Pullman, 67, Univ Calif, Berkeley, 67, Sch Visual Art, New York, 68, Univ Colo, Boulder, 68. *Awards:* Purchase Prize, Whitney Mus Am Art, 68; Nealie Sullivan Award, San Francisco Art Inst, 68; Bartels Prize, 72nd Am Exhib, Art Inst Chicago, 76; Traveling Grant, Australian Arts Coun, 80; Guggenheim Fel, 2004; Life Work award, Marin Arts Coun, 2004; Robert &

Happy Doran Artist in Res Fel, Yale Univ Art Gallery, New Haven, Conn, 2004; Lifetime Achievement award in Printmaking, S Graphics Art Coun, 2005. *Bibliog:* Lee Fleming (auth), Talents that brush into each other, The Washington Post, 5/15/93 & San Francisco Examiner, 3/23/93; Three Artists Collaborative Riddles, San Francisco Chronicle, 1/15/94; Holland Cotter (auth), William T Wiley, New York Times, 2/4/94. *Mem:* Nat Acad; Calif Soc Printmakers (hon mem). *Publ:* Contribr, Over Evident Falls (theater event), Sacramento State Col, 68; auth, Man's Nature (film), shown Hansen Fuller Gallery, 71; Wiley Mind, tricycle, The Buddhist Review, fall 91. *Mailing Add:* c/o Wanda Hansen 615 Main St Sausalito CA 94965-1317

WILHELMI, WILLIAM MERLE
CERAMIST, SCULPTOR
b Garwin, Iowa, Feb 4, 1939. *Study:* San Diego State Col, BA, 60; Univ Calif, Los Angeles, MFA, 69. *Work:* Long Beach Mus Art, Calif; Everson Art Mus, Syracuse, NY; Tweed Mus Art, Duluth, Minn; Libr Cong; Renwick Gallery, Smithsonian Inst, Washington, DC; Gene Autry Western Heritage Mus, Los Angeles, Calif. *Comn:* Tile mural, Whataburger Nat Hq, Corpus Christi, 79; planters & tile murals, Corpus Christi State Univ, 79; Corpus Christi Nat Bank, 82; tile floor mosaic, Corpus Christi City Hall rotunda, 88; mosaic design, Six-Points Station (RTA-CC), 92. *Exhib:* Renwick Gallery, Washington, DC, 76, 80 & 82; 20th Century Ornament, Cooper-Hewitt Mus, New York, 78; Contemp Am, S Tex Art Mobile, Corpus Christi, 79; Hill's Gallery, Santa Fe, 81; Marilyn Butler Gallery, Scottsdale, Ariz, 81; Libr Cong, 83; Emily Edwards Gallery, Southwest Craft Ctr, San Antonio, Tex, 89; Twenty-five Yr Survey Show, Art Mus S Tex, 96; Musee de la Civilisation, Quebec, Canada, 2002-2003; Fuller Craft Mus, Brookton, Mass, 2010-2011. *Pos:* Resident potter, Richard Colley, architect, Corpus Christi, 69-76, Kaffie Gallery, Corpus Christi, 76-83 & Carancahua Gallery, 83-86; bd trustees, Art Mus S Tex, 80-87; Wilhelm/Holland Gallery, Corpus Christi, 86-. *Awards:* Two Purchase Awards, San Mateo Coll, 69; First Place & One-Man Show Art Found Award, Art Mus S Tex, 73; Tex Arts Comn, 81; Dirs Award, CC Carts Coun, 92. *Bibliog:* Lon Taylor & Ingrid Maar (auths), The American Cowboy, Libr Congress, 83; Jan E Adlmann, William Wilhelmi (auth), Prodigal Potter, Art Mus S Tex, 96; Ben Holland (auth), The Potte from Dos Patos, The Clay's the Thing, Art Mus S Tex, 96; Lynda Jones (auth), Wilhelmi-Holland has Monsters and More, Corpus Christi Caller Times, 2012. *Mem:* Am Crafts Coun; Tex Designer Craftsmen; Tex Potters Guild; Art Found. *Media:* Clay. *Res:* Color. *Specialty:* Ceramics. *Collection:* Ceramic Work 1969-present. *Publ:* Contribr, Studio Potter, Daniel Clark Found, 78; Tex Monthly, 12/80; New York Art Rev, 88-89; Chicago Art Rev, 90; American Ceramics, Rizzoli, New York, 92; ARTODAY, Phaidon, 96. *Dealer:* Wilhelmi & Holland Gallery Corpus Christi TX; Ben Holland. *Mailing Add:* 300 S Chaparral Corpus Christi TX 78401-2806

WILKIN, KAREN
CURATOR, CRITIC
b New York, NY. *Study:* Barnard Col, BA (cum laude); Columbia Univ, MFA. *Collection Arranged:* Sculpture in Steel: Gonzalez, Caro, Steiner & Scott (with catalog), 74; The Collective Unconscious: US/Canada 1940s (with catalog), 75; Adolph Gottlieb: The Pictographs Touring Exhib (with catalog), 77-78; David Smith: The Formative Years Touring Exhib (with catalog), 81-82; Frankenthaler: Works on Paper 1949-1984 Touring Exhib (with catalog), 85-86; Stuart Davis Drawing Retrospective, touring exhib (with catalog), 92-93; Judith Rothschild (with catalog), 2002; Hans Hofmann Retrospective (with catalog), 2004; Jules Olitski: Six Decades (with catalog), 2005. *Pos:* Chief cur, Edmonton Art Gallery, Alta, 71-78. *Teaching:* Lectr art hist, Univ Alta, Edmonton, 67-70; adj prof, Trent Univ, Peterborough, Ont, 79-85, SUNY, Purchase, NY, 86; vis prof, Univ Toronto, 91-97; New York Studio Sch, 97-. *Awards:* Woodrow Wilson Fel; Fulbright Fel, Rome, 64-65; Can Coun Sr Arts Grant, 81. *Mem:* Int Asn Art Critics; PEN. *Res:* 20th Century Art. *Publ:* Stuart Davis, Abbeville Press, 87; Kenneth Noland, Rizzoli, 90; Anthony Caro, Prestel, 91; Georges Braque, 92 & Cézanne, 96, Abbeville, 92. *Mailing Add:* 28 W 38th St New York NY 10018

WILKINS, DAVID GEORGE
HISTORIAN
b Battle Creek, Mich, Sept 12, 1939. *Study:* Oberlin Coll, BA, 61; Univ Mich, MA, 63 & PhD, 69. *Pos:* Dir, Univ Art Gallery, Univ Pittsburgh, 76-92. *Teaching:* Prof art hist, Dept Hist Art & Archit, Univ Pittsburgh, 67-2004, chmn, 89-92, & 98-2004. *Awards:* Chancellor's Distinguished Teaching Award, 87; Coll Art Asn Award for Distinguished Teaching of Art Hist, 2005. *Mem:* Coll Art Asn; Renaissance Soc Am; Italian Art Soc. *Res:* Florentine painting and sculpture; American painting; World art. *Publ:* Coauth, Illustrated Bartsch, Vol 53, 85; coauth, Hartt, History of Italian Renaissance Art, 4th ed, 94, 5th ed, 2004, 6th ed, 2008,7th ed, 2010; coed, The Search for a Patron in the Middle Ages and the Renaissance, 96; Art of Duquesne Club, 2001; coauth, Art Past/Art Present, 5th ed, 2003, 6th ed, 2007; ed, A Reflection of Faith: St Paul Cathedral, Pittsburgh, 1906-2006, St Paul Cathedral Centennial Book Committee, 2007. *Mailing Add:* 1005 E Shore Dr Silver Lake NH 03875

WILL, JOHN A
PAINTER, VIDEO ARTIST
b Waterloo, Iowa, June 30, 1939. *Study:* Univ Iowa, MFA, 64; Rijsacadamie von Beeldende Kunston, Amsterdam, 64-65; Tamarind, Albuquerque, NMex, 70-71. *Work:* NY Pub Libr; Art Inst Chicago; Libr Cong; Art Gallery Nova Scotia; Glenbow Mus; Univ Lethbridge; Art Gallery Ontario. *Exhib:* Glenbow Mus, Calgary, 80; 49th Parallel Gallery, NY, 88; Dunlop Art Gallery, Regina, 88; The Miracle of OJ as Revealed By the Man they once called Prince, OWW, Calgary; Ain't Paralyzed Yet, Nickle Arts Mus, 91; Mendal Art Gallery, Saskatoon, 91; Kitchener Waterloo Art Gallery, 91; Walter Phillips Gallery, Banff, 91; White Columns Gallery, NY, 2007; YYZ, Toronto, 2007; Oh Canada, MASSmoca, North Adams, Mass. *Teaching:* Univ Wis-Stout, 65-70; resident artist, Yale Univ, summer 66 & Peninsula Sch Art, Fish Creek, Wis, summer 68; Univ Calgary, 71-97; instr, Nova Scotia Col Art & Design, summers 73-75, 77, 79 & 84, Baniff Ctr, summers 80 & 81 & Emily Carr Sch Design, 85. *Awards:* Fulbright Fel, Holland, 64-65; Ford Found Grant, 70-71; Can Coun A Grant. *Bibliog:* John Will-Triple Threat Artist (exhib catalog), Dunlop Art Gallery, 88; Atomic Haiku (exhib catalog), Truck Gallery, 95; John & Lou's 1923 Voyage (exhib catalog), Banff Ctr, 2000; Willagio, (exhib catalog), Art Gallery of Calgary, 2001; Ain't Paralysed Yet (exhib catalog), Nickle Art Mus, 2001; Firsty & Lastly, YYZine, 2007. *Mem:* RCA. *Media:* Painting; Video. *Dealer:* Jarvis Hall Fine Arts Calgary Angela Brayham Toronto. *Mailing Add:* 1818 18A St SW Calgary AB T2T 4V9 Canada

WILLARD, GARCIA LOU
GRAPHIC ARTIST, PAINTER
b Apr 15, 1944. *Study:* Marshall Univ, with George Bobby Jones, 78-83; studied with Ben Konis, 89; WVa Univ, 93; Univ NDak, 94. *Comn:* The honorable Russell Daughtery (oil portrait), Cabell Co Bar Asn, Huntington, WVa, 78; Figurative (fresco mural), Vanco Park, Loganville, Ga, 78; fresco mural, Western Savings & Loan, Phoenix, 91; fresco mural, Silverton & Williams, Durango, Colo, 93; oil mural, Franklin Enterprises, Phoenix, 93. *Exhib:* Am Artist Prof League, 60th Grand Nat Exhib, Salmagundi Club, NY, 88; Catharine Lorillard Wolfe Art Club 92nd Grand Nat Exhib, Gramercy Park, NY, 88; Eighth Ann Exhib Pastel Soc Southwest, D'Art Visual Art Ctr, Dallas, 88; Hermitage Found Mus, Va, 88; 20th W & J Nat Painting Show, Olin Fine Arts Ctr, Washington, Pa, 88; 2nd Biennial Nat Exhib, Degas Pastel Soc, New Orleans, 88; Sonoran Gallery, 88; Two Flags Int Exhib, Little Gallery, Ariz, 89; Ariel Gallery, New York City, 88; Pen & Brush Club, New York City, 88; and others. *Pos:* Exhib juror for numerous art orgns, 87; lectr for numerous art orgns, 88. *Teaching:* Instr figure drawing, pastel & portraitures, Stifel Fine Art Ctr, Oglebay Inst, 84-87; instr portraiture in pastel & graphics, Ohio Univ, 87. *Awards:* Grumbacher Silver Award for Pastel Excellence, Degas Pastel Soc, 88; Molly Guion Mem Graphic Award, Catharine Lorillard Wolfe Art Club, 88; Pastel Award, Am Artists Prof League, 88. *Bibliog:* Jack Hardin (auth), Huntington artist, Herald-Dispatch, 85; Kitty Doepken (auth), Nationally recognized artist, Family-News, 86; Gladys Van Horne (auth), Museum reception, News Register, 87. *Mem:* Fel Am Artists Prof League; signature mem Pastel Soc Am; Catharine Lorillard Wolfe Art Club; Nat Drawing Asn; Acad Artists Asn. *Media:* Pastel, Oil; Silverpoint. *Publ:* Illusr, Dr Horton on African Art, Carnegie-Mellon, 85; contribr, The California Art Review, Am References, 89. *Dealer:* Sonoran Gallery; Roger Willard. *Mailing Add:* 8819 W Corrine Dr Peoria AZ 85381-8166

WILLENBECHER, JOHN
SCULPTOR, PAINTER
b Macungie, Pa, May 5, 1936. *Study:* Brown Univ, BA, 58; NY Univ Inst Fine Arts, 58-61. *Work:* Whitney Mus Am Art, NY; Albright-Knox Art Gallery, Buffalo, NY; James A Michener Found Collection, Univ Tex, Austin; Hirshhorn Mus & Sculpture Garden, Washington, DC; Solomon R Guggenheim Mus, NY. *Comn:* US Fed Bldg & Court House, Providence, RI, 82; Republic Bank, Houston, 83; Minneapolis Inst Arts, Minn, 93. *Exhib:* Mixed Media & Pop Art, Albright-Knox Art Gallery, Buffalo, 63; Young Americans, Whitney Mus Am Art, NY, 65; Arts Club, Chicago, 76; Allentown Art Mus, Pa, 79; Neuberger Mus, Purchase, NY, 79; Minneapolis Inst Art, Minn, 93; Univ NMex Mus Art, Albuquerque, NMex, 96. *Teaching:* Lectr painting, Philadelphia Coll Art, 72-73; artist-in-residence, Dartmouth Coll, 77 & Univ Wis, Milwaukee, 83. *Awards:* Nat Endowment Arts Fel, 76; Esther & Adolph Gottlieb Found Grant, 94. *Bibliog:* Joseph McElroy (auth), Through the labyrinth: The art of John Willenbecher, Art Int, 3/75; William Wilson (auth), John Willenbecher: Pyramids, spheres & labyrinths, 3/75; Daniel Cameron (auth), John Willenbecher & the riddle of Grandeur, Arts Mag, 9/83. *Mem:* Art Comn New York. *Media:* Acrylic. *Mailing Add:* 145 W Broadway New York NY 10013

WILLIAMS, BENJAMIN FORREST
CURATOR, HISTORIAN
b Lumberton, NC, Dec 24, 1925. *Study:* Corcoran Sch Art, with Eugene Weisz; George Washington Univ, AA; Univ NC, AB; Columbia Univ, Paris Exten, Ecole du Louvre; Netherlands Inst Art Hist; Art Students League New York. *Exhib:* Va Intermont, Bristol; Weatherspoon Gallery, Greensboro; Person Hall Gallery, Chapel Hill, NC; Asheville Art Mus; Traveling Exhib, Am Fedn Arts; and others. *Collection Arranged:* Retrospectives for Josef Albers, Hobson Pittman, Jacob Marling, Victor Hammer, Fedor Zakharcv, Henry Pearson & the collections of the NC Mus Art; Atlanta Art Asn; NC Mus Art; Duke Univ; Greenville Civic Art Gallery, NC; Knoll Assoc, NY; and many others. *Pos:* Retired curator, art. *Teaching:* Lectr, art criticism, City of Raleigh, NC. *Awards:* Ronsheim Mem Award, Corcoran Sch Art, 46; Washington Soc Arts, 47; Prizes, Southeastern Ann, 47. *Mem:* Am Asn Mus; Southeastern Mus Conf; Coll Art Asn Am. *Res:* 19th Century Art. *Publ:* Contribr articles on 19th century American painting & sculpture to NC Mus Art Bull & NC Hist Rev. *Mailing Add:* 2813 Mayview Rd Raleigh NC 27607

WILLIAMS, CHESTER LEE
SCULPTOR
b Durham, NC, July 24, 1944. *Study:* NC Cent Univ, BA, 68; Univ Mich, MFA, 71. *Work:* Student Union Gallery, NC Cent Univ, Durham; Art Dept Gallery, Univ Mich, Ann Arbor; Univ Gallery, Appalachian State Univ, Boone, NC; Black Arch Mus & Res Ctr, Fla A&M Univ, Tallahassee; Voorhees Coll Libr, Denmark, SC. *Comn:* Sculpture, bronze casting, comn by Dr Oscar Cole, NY, 71 & Dr & Mrs Robert Zakarin, Tallahassee, 77; painting & sculpture, Fla A&M Univ, 77-78; bronze bust of Johnathan Gibbs, Fine Arts Coun of Fla, Div Cult Affairs, State of Fla, Tallahassee, 77-78; and others. *Exhib:* Solo exhibs, Spec Exhib, Div Cult Affairs, State Fla, 77, Fla House Rep, Ms Gwendolyn S Cherry, 106th Dist, 77, Fla Dept Com, Tallahassee, Fla, 77, Bainbridge Jr Coll, Ga, 80, Winston-Salem State Univ, NC, 82, Elizabeth City State Univ, NC, 84, OMNI Gallery, Greenville, NC, 90; Fla A&M Univ, 75, 78, 84 & 91, LeMoyne Art Found, 77, 79 & 83 & Fla Ctr Prof Develop, Fla State Univ, Tallahassee, Fla, 84; Smith-Mason Gallery, 80, Power Objects: Ancient and to the Future, Howard Univ, Washington, DC, 80; Dimensions and Directions: Black Artists

of the South, Miss Mus Art, Jackson, Miss, 80; The Harmon Gallery, 80, Fine Arts Exhib, Naples, Fla, 80; Atlanta Life Ins Co, Ann Afro-Am Nat Art Competition & Exhib, 80, 87, 89, 90 & 91; NC Cent Univ, Durham, 85, Waterways Visual Arts Ctr, Salisbury, 88, Greensboro Artists' League, Greensboro, 89, Rocky Mt Arts Ctr, NC, 89; Beaufort Co Arts Ctr, 89 & 90, African-Am Art Extravaganza, 89, Greenville Mus Art, 91, Ubiquitous Gallery, Charlotte, 90, Onslow Co Coun Arts, Jacksonville, NC, 90; ABC Art Buyers Caravan, Orlando, Fla, 90; Third World Art Gallery, Cincinnati, Ohio, 92; Phillip Cult Ctr Gallery, Albany, Ga, 92. *Pos:* Illusr, Nat Air Pollution Control Ctr, Durham, NC, 69-70; mem, Arts Selection Comt, Tallahassee City Comn, 77-79; mem bd, LeMoyne Art Found, Tallahassee, 79-84; pres, Williams Foundry, Tallahassee & Durham, NC, 79-; dir, Fla A&M Univ Art Gallery, Tallahassee, Fla, 74-78, 83-84 & 92-. *Teaching:* Instr creative woodwork, Sch Design, Durham, NC, 68-69; asst prof sculpture & art appreciation, Voorhees Col, Denmark, SC, 71-74; assoc prof sculpture & painting, Fla A&M Univ, 74-84; assoc prof sculpture & design drawing, NC Cent Univ, Durham, 84-; vis artist at numerous universities and institutions since 69. *Awards:* Sculpture Award, Harmon Gallery, Naples, Fla, 80; Purchase Award, Summer of 80 Fine Art Exhib, Naples, Fla, 80; Prince Hall Grand Lodge Econ Grant Prog, Durham, NC, 91. *Bibliog:* Joy McIlwain (auth), Sculptor with a message of hope, Tallahassee Mag, fall 84; Chris Redd (auth), Four Artists at Waterworks, Contemp Southeastern Vis Arts, Vol 2, 88; Kathy McQuaid (auth), Area exhibit shows black artists' work, The Daily News, 2/8/90. *Mem:* Coll Art Asn Am; Nat Conf Artists; LeMoyne Art Found; Tri-State Sculptors. *Media:* Bronze Casting. *Dealer:* LeMoyne Art Found Tallahassee FL; Gallery of Art Panama City FL

WILLIAMS, CHRISTOPHER
PHOTOGRAPHER
b Los Angeles, 1956. *Work:* Carnegie Mus, Pittsburgh, Pa; Mus Boijmans Van Beuningen, Rotterdam; Lenbachhaus, Munich; Mus Contemp Art, Los Angeles; The UBS Corp Art Collection. *Exhib:* Whitney Biennial, Whitney Mus Art, NY, 2006; David Zwirner Gallery, NY; 55th Int Art Exhib Biennale, Venice, 2013. *Mailing Add:* c/o David Zwirner Gallery 525 W 19th St New York NY 10002

WILLIAMS, CLARA A
SCULPTOR
b Nashville, Sept 16, 1972. *Study:* School Visual Arts, BFA, 1995; Yale Univ, MFA (Sculpture), 2000. *Exhib:* Solo exhibs include Temporary-Contemp Gallery, Cheekwood Mus Art, Nashville, 2000, Something Like This, Nicole Klagsbrun Gallery, NY City, 2002, The Price (Giving in Gets You Nowhere), Pub Art Fund, 2003; group exhibs include Some Young New Yorkers, PS1 Mus Contemp Art, 1997, Greater New York, 2000; Wood, Lombard/Freid Fine Arts, 1998, Urban Romantics, 1998; True West, PPOW Gallery, 1999, Impact: New Mural Projects, 2004; Minty, Richard Tells Gallery, 1999; All-Terrain, Friedrich Petzel Gallery, 1999; Small World, Mus Contemp Art, San Diego, 2000; Zobeide & Man With Bags, Nicole Klagsbrun Gallery, 2000, 2001; Fresh: The Altoids Curiously Strong Collection, New Mus, 2001 & 2004; The Armory Show, Int Fair of New Art, NY, 2001; Beyond City Limits, Socrates Sculpture Park, 2001; Past Tense, Brigham Young Univ, 2002; Into the Woods, Julie Saul Gallery, 2002; Escape from New York, NJ Ctr Visual Arts, 2003; Fellowship Artists Exhib, Conn Comn on the Arts, 2003; Unnaturally, traveling, 2003-2005; Starting Here, Sch Visual Arts Gallery, NY City, 2004. *Awards:* Blair Dickinson Award, Yale Univ, 2000; Rena Hort Mann Found Award, 2000; Fel Conn Comn on Arts, 2001; Bronx Recognizes Its Own Award, 2003; Guggenheim Mem Fel, 2004; NY Found Arts Fel, 2004. *Bibliog:* Jerry Salz (auth), Greater Expectations, Village Voice, 3/00; Katy Siegal (auth) Greater NY, Artforum, 5/00; Origin of Mary Replica a Mystery, New Haven Register, 3/20/00; Roberta Smith (auth), Weekend Rev, NY Times, 1/25/02; Kim Levin (auth), Recommended Show, Village Voice, 1/23/02; TV interview, NY1, 9/03; Sculpture Mag, 3/04

WILLIAMS, DAVE HARRELL
COLLECTOR, PATRON
b Beaumont, Tex, Oct 5, 1932. *Study:* Univ Tex, BS (chemical eng), 1956; Harvard Univ, MBA, 1961. *Pos:* Trustee, USS Intrepid Mus Found Serv with US Naval Res, 1956-59; financial analyst & chemical eng, Exxon Corp, Baton Rouge, 1959; security analyst, deVegh & co, New York, 1961-64; dir res, Waddell & Reed, Kansas City, Mo, 1964-67; exec vpres, Mitchell Hutchins, Inc, New York, 1967-77; chmn bd, Alliance Capital Mgt Corp, 1977-2001, chmn emer, 2001-2004; trustee, Skyscraper Mus & USS Intrepid Mus Found, currently. *Awards:* Named one of Top 200 Collectors, ARTnews mag, 2004-10. *Mem:* NY Soc Security Analysts (pres, formerly); Financial Analysts Fedn (officer & dir, formerly); Bond Club NY, Econ Club NY, Knickerbocker Club, Grolier Club. *Collection:* American prints. *Publ:* Contribr, articles in Print Quart

WILLIAMS, DAVID JON
MEDICAL ILLUSTRATOR, HISTORIAN
b Muskegon, Mich, June 21, 1944. *Study:* Muskegon Community Col, AA, 64; Mich State Univ, BA, 66, MA, 73; studied medical illus with Prof Mary Maciel, Univ Cincinnati Sch Med, 68-70; anatomical art with Franz Batke, Innsbruck, Austria, 80. *Pos:* Med illusr, Mich State Univ, East Lansing, Mich, 70-73. *Teaching:* From asst prof to prof med art, Purdue Univ, West Lafayette, Ind, 73-. *Awards:* First Award, 11th Eaton-Student Am Med Asn Competition, 69, Third Award, 17th Competition, 75 & Third Award, 18th Competition, 76; First Place, Med Illus, Cent Ind Chap, Biol Photog Asn, 84; Literary Award, Asn Med Illustrators, 89, 94 & 2005; 23rd Charles H Hackley Distinguished Lecture in The Humanities Award, 2004. *Mem:* Asn Med Illusr (archivist, parliamentarian & mem, bd dir); Guild Natural Sci Illusr; Am Asn Hist Med; World Asn Hist Vet Med; Am Vet Med Hist Soc; Med Artists Asn of Gt Britain. *Media:* Carbon Dust on Media Paper, Transparent Watercolor. *Res:* History of Wilhelm Ellenberger's Handbuch der Anatomie der Tiere fur Kunstler, pub in Leipzig 1898, others. *Publ:* Coauth, Fundamental Techniques in Veterinary Surgery, W B Saunders Co, 75, rev ed, 81 & 87; contribr, Anatomy of the Rat, Williams & Wilkins, 76; Atlas of Human Anatomy, Urban & Schwarzenberg, 81; illusr, Intervertebral Disk Diseases, J B Lippincott Co, 85; Natural Voltage Gradients in Limb Regeneration and Development, Oxford Univ Press, 85; The History of Eduard Pernkoof's 'Topographische Anatomie des Menschen,' J Biocommunication, spring 88; Art Anatomy and Medi; The Evolution of Medical Illustration, Helix, 92; The History of Werner Spalteholz's Handatalas der Anatomie des Menschen J Biocommunication 2003; Vet Med An Illustrated History, 96. *Mailing Add:* 824 Carrolton Blvd West Lafayette IN 47906

WILLIAMS, FRANKLIN JOHN
PAINTER
b Ogden, Utah, Feb 5, 1940. *Study:* Carbon Coll, 58-60; Calif Coll Arts & Crafts, BFA, 60-64, MFA (Spencer Mackey Scholarship), 64-66. *Work:* Oakland Art Mus, Calif; Univ Calif, Berkeley Mus; Corcoran Mus, Washington, DC; San Francisco Mus Mod Art; Sheldon Mem Mus, Lincoln, Nebr; San Jose Mus Art; Noru Eccles Harrison Mus Art; DeRosa Preserve, Napa, Calif; Crocker Art Mus, Sacramento, Calif. *Comn:* Painting, comn by Marc Moyens, Washington, DC, 83; Lizabeth Oliveria Gallery, Oakland, Calif. *Exhib:* Seattle Art Mus, Washington, 66; 1967 Painting Ann, 1968 Sculpture Ann, Whitney Mus Am Art, NY; New Zealand Mus, Auckland, 71; Nat Mus, Washington, DC, 72; On and Off the Wall, Oakland Mus, Calif, 83; solo exhibs, San Jose Mus Art, Calif, 83 & Utah Mus Fine Art, Salt Lake City, 84; San Francisco Bay Area Painting, Calif, 84; Formative Acts, San Francisco, 98. *Collection Arranged:* DeRosa Preserve, Napa, Calif. *Teaching:* Prof painting & drawing, San Francisco Art Inst, 66-; Calif Coll Arts & Crafts, 69-; Tutor painting & drawing, Ruskin Sch, Oxford, Eng, 90. *Awards:* Grant Ford Found, 66; Nat Endowment Arts, 68; Conference on World Affairs, 98-2000. *Bibliog:* Fred Martin (auth), article, Art Int, 63 & 76; Thomas Albright (auth), Art in the San Francisco Bay Area 1945-1980, 85, The American Painting Collection Sheldon Memorial Art Gallery, The Painting & Sculpture Collection, San Francisco Mus Art. *Media:* Oil, Acrylic. *Publ:* Contribr, Soft as Cotton, Centered and Hard, 97. *Mailing Add:* 713 Elm Dr Petaluma CA 94952

WILLIAMS, IDAHERMA
PRINTMAKER, PAINTER
b New York, NY. *Study:* Philadelphia Coll Art, BFA (scholar) 59; Pa Acad Fine Art, 59-63; Univ Pa, MFA, 63. *Work:* Bristol-Myers Squibb Co, NJ; Zimmerli Art Mus, Rutgers Univ, NJ, 66; Kyoto Int Woodblock Asn; Graphic Arts Libr, Princeton Univ; Print Consortium, Kansas City, Mo; Newark Pub Libr, Special Collection, Newark, NJ; Kendall at Hanover, NH; Zimmerli Art Mus, NJ; Lucis Trust, London, Eng; Free Libr Philadelphia, Print Collection, Philadelphia, Pa; Rider Univ Collection, Lawrenceville, NJ; Franklin Twp, Council Chambers, Franklin, NJ; R Moriyon, Spain; Villanova Univ, Pa; Frye Gallery, Braidswood, Australia; Parkway Ctr Libr, Pa; Mus Am Hungarian Found, New Brunswick, NJ; Michener Mus, Doylestown, Pa; Ursinus Col, Collegeville, Pa; Phila Sketch Club, Phila, Pa; Villanova Univ, Pa; Mus Am Hungarian Found; Villanova Univ; The Mishener Mus. *Comn:* Woodblock prints, Society Am Graphic Artists, 2008. *Exhib:* Solo exhibs, NJ State Mus, Trenton, 75, Ursinus Coll, Collegeville, Pa, 83, Johnson & Johnson Corp World Hq, New Brunswick, NJ, 92, Gloucester Co Coll, Sewell, NJ, 98 & Café Gallery, NJ State Mus, Trenton, 2002, Idaherma: Joy in Watercolor and Woodblock Prints Mus Am Hungarian Found, New Brunswick, NJ, 2011, A Discovery of Woodblock Prints in Color, Villanova Univ, Pa, 2012; group exhib, TAWA in the USSR, the Soviet Union, 90; 3rd Biennial Int Print Exhib, Somerstown Gallery, Somers, NY, 90; FRRIC Int, Salon de Peinture et d'Estampe de Montreal, Montreal, Quebec, 90; The Francis Witherspoon Ann Printmakers Award Exhib, An Int Juried Exhib, Dome Gallery, New York, 91; Philadelphia Int Contemp Art Competition of Old City, 479 Gallery Inc, Rodger LaPelle Galleries, Pentimenti Gallery & Convergence Ctr, Philadelphia, Pa, 94; Mangum Opus VIII, 8th Int Open Exhib, Sacramento Fine Arts Ctr, Carmichael, Calif, 95; The May Exhibitions, Kyoto Int Woodprint Asn, Kyoto, Japan, 98; World Artists for Tibet, 1860 House Montgomery, Skillman, NJ, 98; 102nd Ann Exhib, Catharine Lorillard Wolfe Art Club, Nat Arts Club, NY, 98; Members' Exhib, Catharine Lorillard Wolfe Art Club, Broome St Gallery, New York, 98; Ann Fleisher Fac Exhib, Philadelphia, Pa, 98; Realism 98, Parkersburg Art Ctr 10th Ann Nat Exhib, Parkersburg, WVa, 98; Digital Print Exhib, AIR Gallery, New York, 98; TAWA Invitational, NJ; In the Tracks of Hercules (Lucis Trust), Lennox Gallery (Fulham), London, Eng, 2005; S A G A Prague, Hallar Soc Gallery, Ceska Republica, 2006; Labors of Hercules, Princeton Theological Soc, Princeton, NJ, 1-2 & 6-7/2007; 6th Ann Lessandra Print Exhib, Sofia, Bulgaria, 6/2007; 7th Ann Lessandra Print Exhib, Sofia, Bulgaria, 2008; Am Color Paint Soc, Villanova Univ, Pa, 2009; Lessendra Print Exhib, 2009; Mini Print Int Cadaques, Barcelona, Spain, 2009; Philadelphia Sketch Club, 2009; Frye Gallery, Braidwood, Australia, 2009; Art & Soul of Bucks Crenay, James A Michener Art Mus, Pa, 2010; Mini Print Int Cadaques Spain, 2011; 10th Lessendra World Art Print Ann, Bulgaria, 2011, 2012. *Pos:* Bd trustees, Catherine Lorillard Wolfe Art Club, New York, 98; Past Pres, Am Color Print Soc, Soc Am Graphic Artists, 2001-; artist & found, Ann Clothesline Exhib, Franklin, NJ, 2001-2010. *Awards:* Frank B & Mary Anderson Cassidy Mem Award, 100th Annual Catharine Lorillard Wolfe Art Club, New York, 96; Stella Drabkin Mem Award, 2d prize, Am Color Print Soc, Am Coll Bryn Mawr, Pa, 2001; 18 Nat Gallery 76; Antonio Frasconi award for woodblock print, Soc Am Graphic Artists, New York, 2002; 1st prize, Kyoto Int Wood Block Asn exhib, 2003; 1st prize for printmaking, Ellarslie Open, Trenton City Mus, NJ, 2003; Silver Medal, Audubon Artists 62nd Ann, New York, 2004; Medal of Honor, Nat Asn Women Artists, 2004; Printmaking Award, Eliza Morse Genius Found, 2004; May Audubon Post Award Fel, Philadelphia, Pa, 2005; and many others; Ziegler Award (medals show), Philadelphia Plastic Club, Philadelphia, Pa; Best in Show, Printmaking & Pres Award, Ellarslie Open XXVII, Ternton City Mus, NJ, 2009; Carolyn Howard Mem Awards, Philadealphia Watercolor Soc, 2009; Best in Show printmaking & president award, Ellarslie Open, Trenton, NJ, 2009; 69th Ann Audubon Soc, Salmagundi Art Club, 2011; Adozi, 33 mini prints, Spain, 2013. *Bibliog:* Patrick Monaghan (auth), All the Plants that are Fit to Print, Time Off, Princeton Packet, 15 & 31, 92; Laurie Granieri (auth), Going with the Grain, On the Go, Home News Tribune, 9, 11/3/2000; Susan Van Dongen (auth), Listening to the Wood, Time Off, Princeton Packet, 4/19/2002, Labors of Hercules,

2007; Victoria Donohoe (auth), 49 Artists Show Prints at Villanova; Philadelphia Inquirer, Pa, 6/19/2009; Tyler Burton Wasserman (auth), From Purple Orchids to Multicolor Dreamscapes, Icon mag, 2011; Jour of the Print World, Vol 34, 2011; P Fazekas (auth), Idaherma Williams Joy in Water Color and Woodblock Prints; Victoria Donahue (auth), A Printmaker Goes her Own Way, Phila Inquirer, 2012. *Mem:* Audubon Artists Inc, NY; Am Color Print Soc (vpres, 88-95 & 2000, bd trustees, 96, pres 2003-2010); Philadelphia Watercolor Club; Soc Am Graphic Artists, New York; The Print Consortium, St Joseph, Mo; Los Angeles Printmaking Soc; Cult Heritage Comn Somerset Co NJ (adv bd, artistic dir); Franklin Twp (NJ) Coun Chambers; Hist Comn, Franklin Twp, NJ. *Media:* Woodblock Prints; Watercolor, Acrylics, Digital. *Specialty:* Hand-printed original prints. *Interests:* archival pigment prints, nature study, photography. *Publ:* interview, Kyoto Int Woodprint Asn, 2001; cover, On the Go, Home News Tribune, 9/20/2002; Newark Pub Libr, Print Collection; Quotable Women: A Celebration, Courage Books, Running Press, Condin, Philadelphia; Idaherma, The Scroll Series of Woodblock Prints, 2011; Idaherma: A Discovery of Woodblock Prints in Color, 2012; Idaherma: Joy in Watercolor, 2013. *Dealer:* Old Print Shop NYC. *Mailing Add:* 61 Coppermine Rd Princeton NJ 08540

WILLIAMS, JOHN ALDEN
HISTORIAN
b Ft Smith, Ark, Sept 6, 1928. *Study:* Am Univ Beirut, 50-51; Univ Munich, with Hans Sedlmayer, 51-52; Univ Ark, BA (hist & philos), 53; Princeton Univ, MA & PhD, 53-57; further work under Sir K A C Creswell in Cairo on hist of Islamic art & archit, 57-59. *Pos:* Asst field dir, Am Ctr for Res in Egypt, 57-59; sr res fel, Ctr Middle East Studies, Harvard Univ, 71-72. *Teaching:* Asst & assoc prof Islamic studies, McGill Univ, Montreal, Que, Can, 59-66; dir & prof, Ctr for Arabic Studies, Am Univ Cairo, 66/69; prof art hist & Middle East studies, Prof Ctr for Arabic Studies, Univ Cairo, 69-72; prof art hist & Islamic study, Univ Tex, Austin & Univ Cairo, alternate yrs, 72-88; Wm R Kenan Jr prof humanities, Col William & Mary, Williamsburg, Va, 88-. *Mem:* Coll Art Asn Am. *Res:* History of Islamic art and architecture, Islamic inst(s). *Publ:* Coauth, Architecture of Muslim India (400 slides with commentary), Art and Architecture of Ancient Egypt (400 slides with commentary) & Timurid Monuments of Central Asia (40 slides with commentary), Visual Educ Inc, 77; auth, The Khanqah of Siryaqus, In: Towards an Islamic Humanism, Cairo, 83; Urbanization and Monument Construction in Mamluk Cairo, In: Muqarnas II, 84; and others. *Mailing Add:* 6 Coventry Rd Williamsburg VA 23188

WILLIAMS, JOHN WESLEY
HISTORIAN, EDUCATOR
b Memphis, Tenn, Feb 25, 1928. *Study:* Duke Univ; Yale Univ, BA; Univ Mich, PhD. *Teaching:* From instr to assoc prof Medieval art, Swarthmore Col, Pa, 60-72, chmn fine arts dept, 71-72; prof, Univ Pittsburgh, retired, chmn fine arts dept, 79-84, retired. *Awards:* Fulbright-Hays Res Grant, Spain, 64 & 69; Nat Endowment Humanities Project Grant, 71-73; Guggenheim Fel, 84-85. *Mem:* Medieval Acad Am; Int Ctr Medieval Art. *Res:* Spanish Medieval art. *Publ:* Auth, Romanesque Bible of San Millan, JWCI, 65; auth, Valeranica and the Scribe Florentus, Madrider Mitteilungen, 70; auth, San Isidoro: Evidence for a new history, Art Bulletin, 73; auth, Early Spanish Manuscript Illumination, George Braziller, 77; ed, Actas del Simposio sobre Beato de Liebana, Vol II, Madrid, 80; and others. *Mailing Add:* 749 Linden Ave S Pittsburgh PA 15208

WILLIAMS, KATHERINE
COLLECTOR, PAINTER
b Trinidad, W Indies, Sept 7, 1941; US citizen. *Study:* Harvard Univ, EdM, 84, EdD, 87. *Exhib:* Solo exhib, (photographs) Mus Mod Art Latin Am, Washington, 81, (paintings) Another Look, Touchstone Gallery, Washington, 98, In the Cosmos II, Gutman Libr, Harvard Univ, 98 & In the Cosmos, Summer Sch Mus & Archives, Washington, 98, Space Telescope Sci Inst, Johns Hopkins Univ and Nat Ctr Gallery, US Geol Survey, 99, Another Look, Gutman Libr, 99, Fitting Them Together, Gutman Libr, Harvard Univ, 2000; (photographs), Give Me Your Tired, Your Poor, Schomberg Ctr, NY, 86; Group shows, Trinidad and Tobago Week at the Orgn of Am States, Wash, DC, 98 & 2002; Art Soc Int Monetary Fund, Washington, DC, 98; Exhibicion de Pinturas: Mujer Y Arte en las Americas, OAS, Washington, DC, 98; Art for Life - Hope for Our Children, Mus Americas, Washington, DC, 98; White Columns Gallery, New York City, 2000; Women of the World: A Global Collection of Art, Tucson Mus Art, Ariz, 2001; Univ of New Eng, Portland, Maine, 2001; In The Cosmos, NASA, Greenbelt, Md, 2001; Womens Art Gallery, Ohio, 2002. *Media:* Watercolor, Acrylic. *Collection:* Nineteenth century American & European oils & watercolors, nineteenth century American prints, twentieth century European prints. *Publ:* Auth, Where Else But America?, Fishergate Pub, Annapolis, MD, 77; Computers: Our Road to the Future, DC Pub Sch System, Washington, 82; Fitting Them Together, DC ABC, Inc Washington, 2000. *Mailing Add:* 628 Wilderness Trail Dr Charlotte NC 28214-5005

WILLIAMS, MELISSA
ART DEALER
b Kansas City, Mo, June 1, 1951. *Study:* Univ Mo, BA & MA (summa cum laude), 78; Phi Beta Kappa, 73. *Pos:* Owner, Antiques at Greenwood, 73-86, Williams & McCormick, 83-89, & Melissa Williams, Am Arts, 89-. *Specialty:* American paintings 1840-1940. *Publ:* Auth, Portrait of a Lady, Muse, 72. *Mailing Add:* 11 S 9th St Columbia MO 65203-2863

WILLIAMS, PAUL ALAN
PAINTER, ILLUSTRATOR
b Detroit, Mich, Sept 10, 1934. *Study:* Chadsey Art Sch, Detroit, 48-49; Meinzinger Arts, 50-51; Art Ctr Sch, Los Angeles, BPA, 59. *Hon Degrees:* SSI, New York, 70-85. *Work:* Jack McCormack & Co Inc, NY; Radio City Music Hall Mus; Readers' Digest Col; La Maison du Temps, Conn; Stadtisches Mus Leipzig. *Comn:* Production & prom, ABC & NBC TV, NY, 80's; space illus, United Tech-Norden, 80's; St Mary's, 98; Sandi Oliver, 2007. *Exhib:* Connolly & Alterman Gallery, Tex, 85; Eagles Lair Gallery, Conn, 86; Int Show, Waveny Park Mus, Conn, 86-88; Cath Charity Show, Bruce Mus, Greenwich, Conn, 87; Doyle Gallery, NY, 87 & 88; Litchfield Auction Gallery, Conn, 87, 88, 89, 90, 91 & 92; Wilton Historical, Soc Am Craftsmanship Show, Conn, 91 & 92; Westport Merchants Show, Conn, 92-98; Gracie Mansion Park Show, NY, 92; West Point Art Show, 92-2001; Westport Art Ctr, 2007-2008. *Pos:* Art cur, SSI, 80-83; art consultant, Casa Oliver - Special, 91-2004. *Teaching:* Art prof, Va Art Asn, 79; Oliver & Williams Studio, 98 & 2004. *Awards:* Best in Show, Casa D'Oliver Garden Show, Conn, 91 & 2004. *Bibliog:* Vision of flowers (article), Your Family, 3/90; Sandi Oliver (auth), American Impressionist Paul Alan Williams: His Garden & His Oil Paintings, (catalog raissone), 91, 92 & 93. *Mem:* Soc Am Impressionists; Soc Illus (special honors). *Media:* Oil. *Interests:* Collecting antiques & antique restoration, raising dogs, walking. *Publ:* Paul A Williams' His Garden & His Oil Paintings, Am Impressionist, 91, 92, 93-98. *Dealer:* Sandi Oliver. *Mailing Add:* c/o Sandi Oliver Fine Art PO Box 1203 Weston CT 06883-0203

WILLIAMS, RAYMOND LESTER
PAINTER, INSTRUCTOR
b Lenoir City, Tenn, Nov 10, 1926. *Study:* Chicago Acad Fine Arts, study with Edgar Whitney, John Pellew, Edmound Fitzgerald & Zolton Zabo, cert. *Work:* United Tel co, Bristol, Tenn; Dobyns-Bennett High Sch & Tenn Eastman Co, Kingsport; Carrol Reese Mus & Tipton-Haynes Mus, Johnson City, Tenn; Old Derry Inn Mus, Blountville, Tenn. *Comn:* Highlands of Roan, Southern Appalachian Highlands Conservancy, 77; Church Circle, City of Kingsport, Tenn, 79; Four Homecoming '86 Print-Tri Cities Radio, 86; Directory Covers, United Tel System, 86; and others. *Exhib:* Abingdon Highlands Fest, 70-2006; Covered Bridges of Tenn, Tenn State Mus, Nashville, 73; World's Fair, Knoxville, Tenn, 80; Emory & Henry Univ, Emory, Va, 86; Mount Dora Art Festival, Mount Dora, Fla, 88; Lenox Square Fine Art, Atlanta, 87; Wilkes Art Gallery, North Wilkesboro, NC, 88; and many others. *Collection Arranged:* DKA of Kingsport, Tenn, United Tel Co, Bristol Tenn & Va. *Pos:* Graphic artist, Tenn Eastman Co, 50-74; painter & gallery owner, 74-. *Teaching:* Instr watercolor, oil painting & drawing, 74-2009. *Awards:* Best of Show, Jonesboro Days, Jonesboro, Tenn, 75 & 81; Award, Tenn Watercolor Soc, 79; Best of Show, Dunwoody Fine Arts Asn, Atlanta, Ga, 87; and others. *Bibliog:* Artist of the Tennessee, Vol I & II; United Inter-Mt Tel Co; Tri-Cities Living Mag. *Mem:* Tenn Watercolor Soc (dist dir, 74-75); Tenn Artists; Kingsport Art Guild (pres, 75-76). *Media:* Watercolor, Oils. *Res:* Light fastness of watercolor paint and durability. *Specialty:* Watercolor, oil paintings and limited edition prints, glasses. *Interests:* Sports, Travel. *Collection:* Zolton Zabo, Edgar Whitney, John Pellew, Edmound Fitzgerald and artist friends. *Publ:* Historical Collectors Calendar, 12 paintings, 76; 18 limited ed prints. *Dealer:* Gallery 81. *Mailing Add:* 3322 Roller Dr Kingsport TN 37663

WILLIAMS, REBA WHITE
COLLECTOR, WRITER
b Gulfport, Miss, May 21, 1936. *Study:* Duke Univ, BA; Harvard Grad Sch Bus Admin, MBA, 1970; Hunter Coll, MA (art hist), 1988; Grad Ctr, CUNY, PhD (art hist), 1996. *Pos:* Res, McKinsey & co, Inc, formerly; mem, New York Art Comn, 1995-98, pres, 1997-98, NY State Coun Arts, 1996-99, vchmn, 1999, Manhattan Community Bd 8, 1999-2000; vchmn, White Williams Holdings, Ltd, 2001-; hon keeper of Am prints, The Fitzwilliam Mus, Cambridge, Eng; dir spl projects & mem bd dirs, Alliance Capital Mgt; securities analyst, Mitchell Hutchins, Inc. *Awards:* Distinguished Cult Leadership award, NY Rep Co Cot, 1999; Woman of Distinction award, NY State Senate, 2000; named one of Top 200 Collectors, ARTnews mag, 2004, 2006-07 & 2009-10; The Augustus Medal, Brooklyn Mus Art. *Mem:* Munic Art Soc. *Collection:* American prints. *Mailing Add:* 654 Madison Ave Suite 703 New York NY 10065

WILLIAMS, ROBERT
CARTOONIST, PAINTER
b March 2, 1943. *Exhib:* It's Only Rock and Roll: Rock and Roll Currents in Contemporary Art, Contemp Arts Ctr, Cincinnati, 1995; Huntington Beach Art Ctr, Calif, 1998; Hollywood Art Ctr, Miami, Fla, 1999; Customized: Art Inspired by Hot Rods, Low Riders and American Car Culture, Inst Contemp Art, Boston, 2000; Whitney Biennial, Whitney Mus Am Art, New York, 2010. *Pos:* Founder, Juxtapoz Art & Culture Mag. *Mailing Add:* Tony Shafrazi Gallery 544 West 26th St New York NY 10001

WILLIAMS, SUE
PAINTER, SCULPTOR
b Chicago Heights, Ill, 1954. *Study:* Calif Inst Arts, BFA, 76. *Exhib:* Connections, Contradictions, Emory Univ, 98; Pop Surrealism (with catalog), Aldrich Mus Contemp Art, Conn, 98; Submit, Bricks & Kicks, Austria, 98; Skulptur Figur Weiblich, Landesgalerie, Oberosterreich, Austria, 98; Unbearable Laughter, Ctr Curatorial Studies, Bard Col, NY, 98; Whitney Biennial, Whitney Mus Am Art, NY, 97. *Awards:* Joan Mitchell Found Grant, 2009. *Bibliog:* Roberta smith (auth), rev, NY Times, 10/30/98; rev, New Yorker, 10/26/98-11/2/98; Under the influence, New Yorker, 11/2/98

WILLIAMS, TOD
ARCHITECT
Detroit, Michigan. *Study:* Princeton Univ, 1965, MFA (archit), 1967; Cambridge Univ, 1966. *Pos:* archit, Richard Meier, 1967-73; principle, partner, Tod Williams Billie Tsien Architects, 1986-. *Teaching:* teacher, Cooper Union, 1974-89; vis prof, various archit schs; Ruth Carter Stevenson Chair, Univ Tex, Austin, 1995; Eliel Saarinen Chair, Univ Mich, 2002; Louis I Kahn Chair, Yale Univ, 2003 & 2005; Thomas Jefferson Chair, Univ Va, 2004. *Awards:* Nat Award, Am Inst Architects, 1988, 1989, 1992 & 2002, fellow, 1992; Nat Hon Award, Neurosciences Inst, 1997; Advanced Fellowship, Am Acad in Rome, 1982. *Mem:* Fel Am Inst Architects, 1992; Am Acad Arts and Letts, 2009; Nat Acad. *Mailing Add:* Tod Williams Billie Tsien Architects 222 Central Park South New York NY 10019

WILLIAMS, TODD
SCULPTOR, PAINTER
b Savannah, Ga. *Study:* City Col New York; Sch Visual Arts, New York, cert & scholar, 1964. *Work:* Smithsonian Inst, Washington, DC. *Comn:* sculpture, Mary Bethune Towers, New York, 1970; wall painting, New York Parks Dept, Livingston & Bond Sts, Brooklyn, 1970; sculptures, New York Bd Educ, I S 167, Bronx, 1973 & Boys & Girls High Sch, Brooklyn, 1975; 83rd Precenct Station House, New York Police Dept, 1983. *Exhib:* Colored Sculpture, Oakland Art Mus, 1965; Witte Mem Mus, Madison, Wis, 1966; Cranbrook Acad of Art, Bloomfield Hills, Mich, 1966; Books, Boxes & Things, Jewish Mus, New York, 1969; Contemp Black Artists, Whitney Mus Am Art, New York, 1971; Banners, Nat Mus, Singapore, 1976 & Hirshhorn Mus, Washington, DC, 1976. *Collection Arranged:* Colored Sculpture, Am Fedn Art, 1965; Ten Negro Artists from the United States Dakar, Senegal, US State Dept, 1965; Small Sculpture from the United States, 1971 & Bicentennial Banners, 1976, Smithsonian Inst. *Pos:* Bd mem, City Walls Inc, New York. *Teaching:* Adj instr sculpture, Brooklyn Col, NY, 1973-76; asst prof sculpture, Columbia Univ, New York, 1976-. *Awards:* John Hay Whitney Found Fel, 1965; J Clawson Mills Fel, Archit League of New York, 1966. *Media:* Mixed-Media

WILLIAMS, WILLIAM EARLE
PHOTOGRAPHER, CURATOR
b Vicksburg, Miss, Apr 19, 1950. *Study:* Hamilton Col, BA, 73; Yale Univ, MFA, 78. *Work:* Philadelphia Mus Art; Lehigh Univ, Bethlehem, Pa; Metrop Mus & Brooklyn Mus, NY; Univ Md & Baltimore Mus Art, Baltimore; Allentown Art Mus; Princeton Univ Mus, Princeton, NJ; Cleveland Mus Art; Chrysler Mus Art; Philadelphia Mus Art; Princeton Univ Mus; Minneapolis Art Inst.; Mus Fine Arts, Houston; Nelson Atkins Mus Art. *Comn:* Philadelphia Conv Ctr, Pa, 93; Chester Springs Art Ctr, Pa, 97; Philadelphia Print Collaborative, 2002. *Exhib:* Solo Exhibs: Butler Inst Am Arts, Youngstown, Ohio, 80, Party Photographs, Univ Md, Baltimore, 86, Trumbull Art Gallery, Warren, Ohio, 90, Sol Mednick Gallery, Univ Arts, Philadelphia, Pa, 94, Smith Col, Northampton, Mass, 95, W Moreland Mus, Greensburg, Pa, 96 & Esther Klein Art Gallery, Philadelphia, Pa, 97; Am Photog, 1910-1983 (with catalog), Tampa Mus, Fla, 83; Contemp Photogrs, Pa Acad Fine Arts, Philadelphia, 84; Pa Photographers IV, Allentown Art Mus, Pa, 85; 61st Int Print Club Competition, Philadelphia, 85; Contemp Philadelphia Artists (catalog), Philadelphia Mus Art, 90; Baltimore Mus Art, Md, 90; Allentown Art Mus, Pa, 95; Chrysler Mus Art, Norfolk, Va, 98; S Eastern Mus Photog, Daytona Beach Community Col, Fla, 98; Canady Libr, Bryn Mawr Col, 2002; Princeton Univ Mus Art, African Am Mus Art, Philadelphia, 2005; Unsung Heroes: Af Am Soldiers in the Civil War (lightwork), Syracuse, NY, 2007; Af Am Battlefields of the Civil War (contemp photographs), Mus Fine Arts, Houston, 2008. *Collection Arranged:* Lewis Hine: Child Labor Photographs, 79, Muybridge and Eakins, Photographers of Motion, 80, Walker Evans: A Retrospective, 81, Arbus, Weegee and Model Photographers, 82, Masterpieces of Photography from the Collection, 84, & Adolphe Brown, Walker Evans, Andre Kertesz: Photographers of Sculpture, 88, Comfort Gallery, Haverford Col, Pa, Paul Strand Prints in Ink, 2000, Remembering September 11, 2001, Cantor-Fitzgerald Gallery, Haverford Col; Sol Mednick Remembered, Mcgill Libr, Haverford Col, 2005; W Eugene Smith, Mcgill Libr, Haverford Col, 2006; A Haverford Sampler: A Selection of Masterworks from the Collection, 2010; George Eastman House, Rochester, NY, 2011. *Pos:* Cur photog, Haverford Col, 79- & gallery dir, 81-93. *Teaching:* Prof fine arts photog, Haverford Col, Pa, 78-; Prof, Audrey A & John L Dusseau Prof in Humanities, Haverford Col, Pa, 2008. *Awards:* Purchase Award, 61st Ann Int Competition, The Print Club, Philadelphia, 85; Pa Individual Arts fel, 85 & 87; Pew Charitable Trusts Individual Artist Fel Award, 97; Pa Individual Artists fel, 85, 97, 2003; Guggenheim fel, 2003. *Bibliog:* Porter Aichele (auth), William Earle Williams, Party Photographs, Comfort Gallery, Haverford Col, Pa, 85; William Southwell (auth), Documentary revival, Lens on Campus, Hearst, New York, 86; Deborah Willis-Thomas (auth), Black Photographers, 1940-1988: An Illustrated Bio-Bibliography, Garland Press, NY, NY, 88. *Mem:* Coll Art Asn; Soc Photog Educ; Am Studies Asn; Soc Photographic Educ (Nat bd dir, 96-03); Civil War Preservation Trust (Nat bd dir, 97-00). *Media:* Medium & large format photography. *Res:* Walker Evans, Robert Frank, Paul Strand, 19th century landscape photog. *Specialty:* Slave Culture in North America. *Publ:* Illusr, William Williams Portfolio, Philadelphia Photo Rev, Perloff, 82; Party Pictures, Aronis Press, 85; auth Gettysburg a Journey in Time, Klein Gallery, Philadelphia, 97; Deborah Willis Reflections in Black: A History of Black Photographers 1840 to the Present, Norton, NY, 2000; auth, Unsung Heroes: African American Soldiers and the Civil War (contact sheet 140), 2007; Uncovering the Path to Freedom: Photographs of the Am Underground Railroad, 2008. *Mailing Add:* Dept Fine Arts Haverford Col Haverford PA 19041

WILLIAMSON, PHILEMONA
PAINTER
b New York, NY. *Study:* Bennington Col, Vt, BA, 73; NY Univ, MA, 79. *Work:* Mint Mus Art, Charlotte, SC; AT&T, NJ; Reader's Digest, Pleasantville, NY. *Exhib:* ArtSounds, Nohra Haime Gallery, NY, 86; Artist in the Marketplace, Bronx Mus Arts, NY, 88 & 90; Alice and Look Who Else Through the Looking-Glass, Bernice Steinbaum Gallery, NY, 88; Introductions, June Kelly Gallery, NY, 89; Five from Bennington, Krasdale Foods Art Gallery, Bronx, NY, 90; solo shows, June Kelly Gallery, NY, 90, 92, 95 & 98, African Am Mus, Hempstead, NY, 91, Powers Art Gallery, E Stroudsburg Univ, Pa, 92, Pa State Univ, Univ Park, 93, Flushing Coun Cult & Arts, NY, 93, Hypo-Bank, NY, 94 & John Michael Kohler Arts Ctr, Sheboygan, Wis, 99, June Kelly Gallery, NY, 00, Amelie A Wallace Gallery, SUNY Coll, Old Westbury, NY, 01; Visions of Life, Nat Conference Women's Caucus Art, Islip Art Mus, E Islip, NY, 91; The Children Among Us, Krasdale Foods Gallery, White Plains, NY, 91; Selections from Artists in the Marketplace, PepsiCo Gallery, Purchase, NY, 91; In the Looking Glass: Contemp Narrative Painting (with catalog), Mint Mus Art, Charlotte, NC, 91; Present Tense, Univ Wis Fine Arts Gallery, Milwaukee, 92; Child's Play, Art in General, NY, 93; Empowerment: The Art of African-Am Artists, Coll Art Gallery & Krasdale Foods Art Gallery, Bronx, NY, 94; June Kelly: A Particular Vision, Anderson Gallery, Buffalo, NY, 94; Current Identities: Recent Painting in the United States (with catalog), IV Int de Pintura, Cuenca, Ecuador & Ctr Contemp Art, Newark, NJ, 94; Other Agendas, Kingsborough Community Coll Art Gallery, City Univ NY, Brooklyn, 96; The Boat, Object and Metaphor, Pratt Manhattan Gallery, NY & Rubelle & Norman Schafler Gallery, Pratt Inst, Brooklyn, NY, 96; Real: Figurative Narratives in Contemp African-Am Art, Bass Mus Art, Miami Beach, Fla, 96; Bearing Witness: Contemp Works by African Am Women Artists, Spelman Coll Mus Fine Art, Atlanta, Ga, Fort Wayne Mus Art, Ind, Polk Mus Art, Lakeland, Fla, Columbus Mus, Ga, African Am Mus, Dallas, Tex, Minn Mus Am Art, St Paul & Ulrich Mus Art, Wichita, Kans, 96; Women in Full Effect, RUSH Philanthropic Art Found, NY, 97; Walk the Walk, Forum Contemp Art, St Louis, Mo, 98; Postcards from Black Am (with catalog), Ctr Contemp Art, Breda, The Neth & Frans Hals Mus, Haarlem, The Neth, 98; June Kelly Gallery, 2010. *Pos:* Vis artist, Norfolk State Univ, Va, 82, Ctr d'Art, Port-Au-Prince, Haiti, 87, Univ NC, Chapel Hill, 92 & Parsons Sch Design, 94. *Teaching:* Instr, Harlem Sch Arts, 78-83, Metrop Mus Art, 83; adj fac, RI Sch Design, 89-90, Parsons Sch Design, 91-92 & Cooper Union, 91-92; fac painting, Milton Avery Grad Sch Arts, Bard Col, 91. *Awards:* Nat Endowment Arts Fel Painting, 87-88; Ludwig Vogelstein Grant, New York, 93-94; Joan Mitchell Found Award Painting, 97. *Bibliog:* Grady T Turner (auth), article, ARTnews, 9/98; Halima Taha (auth), Collecting African American Art: Works on Paper and Canvas, Crown Publ, New York, 98; Susan Osmond (auth), Philemona Williamson: half-remembered dreams, World & I Mag, Washington, DC, 2/99. *Dealer:* Kelly Gallery New York NY. *Mailing Add:* 11 LaSalle Rd Upper Montclair NJ 07043

WILLIAMS WHITING, JANICE E
PAINTER, SCULPTOR
b Augusta, Ga, Dec 12, 1954. *Study:* Univ Ga, BFA (cum laude), 77; Ind State Univ, MFA (drawing & painting), 79; Ohio State Univ; Western Carolina Univ. *Work:* Morris Mus Art. *Exhib:* Solo exhibs, Lander Col, SC, 86, Etherridge Ctr Gallery, Univ SC, Aiken, 87, Quinlan Art Ctr, Augusta Col, Ga, 89, N Ga Coll Gallery, Dahlonega, 89, Wasteland Series, Hon Conf, Washington, DC, 2000, Firehouse Gallery, Ga, 2007; Southdown Fine Arts Exhib, Houma, La, 88; La Grange Nat XIV, Ga, 89; Augusta Coll Fac Exhib, Istituto D'Arte Dosso Dossi, Ferrara, Italy, 90; two-person exhib, Vanderbilt Univ, Sarratt Gallery, 92; three-person exhib, Univ Dayton, 92; Elvis & Marilyn: 2 X Immortal Traveling Exhib, 95-97; two-person exhib, Mary Pauline Gallery, 2000-08; Morris Mus Art, 2005. *Pos:* artist-in-residence, Baiaid Gallery, St John's, Newfoundland, Can, 96; artist-in-residence, CApe Pine, Can, 2006, 08. *Teaching:* Instr art, Augusta State Univ, 81-85, asst prof, 87-90, assoc prof, 91-, dir Italian studies abroadm 92-2007. *Awards:* Fel, Soc Art Religion & Contemp Cult; Asian Studies Bd Grant, Madras Christian Col, India, 96. *Mem:* Coll Art Asn. *Media:* Oil. *Interests:* travel. *Publ:* Auth, Icon Series: Graces Under Fire in Elvis and Marilyn 2 X Immortal (ed by Geri DePaoli), Rizzoli Int, New York, 94. *Mailing Add:* 1218 Troupe St Augusta GA 30904

WILLIFORD, HOLLIS R
PAINTER, SCULPTOR
b Hill Co, Tex, Oct 31, 1940. *Study:* Univ Tex, Arlington, 59-63; N Tex State, 63-64; Art Ctr Coll Design, BA, 71. *Work:* Denver Art Mus, Colo; Nat Cowboy and Western Heritage Mus, Oklahoma City; Lacrosse Hall of Fame, John Hopkins Univ; Buffalo Bill Hist Center, Cody, Wyo; Gunesse Contry Mus, Rochester, NY; Thomas Gilcrease Mus, Tulsa. *Exhib:* Nat Acad Western Art, Nat Cowboy Hall Fame, Oklahoma City, Okla, 80-88; Nabisco Invitational, Nabisco Brands World Hq, E Hanover, NJ, 84; Gilcrease Rendezvous, Thomas Gilcrease Mus, Tulsa, Okla, 88; Prix de West Collection, Wildlife Am W Mus, Jackson, Wyo, 88. *Teaching:* Drawing, Art Ctr Col Design, Los Angeles, 69 & 70; drawing & illus, Rocky Mountain Sch Art, Denver, 71-72; sculpture, Fechin Inst, Taos, NMex, 97; drawing, Loveland Acad Fine Art, Colo. *Awards:* Prix de West, Nat Acad Western Art, Cowboy Hall Fame, 80 & 88 & Gold Medals, 80 & 86. *Bibliog:* John Jellico (auth), Hollis Williford, Artist Rockies & Golden West, 80; Carol Dickinson (auth), Facing the Challenge of Nature, SW Art, 87; Fred Myers (auth), Hollis Williford, Gilcrease Mag, 88. *Media:* Bronze, Oil. *Dealer:* Williford Arts Ltd Loveland CO; Simpson Gallagher Gallery Cody WY; Ernest Fuller Fine Art, Denver

WILLIS, BARBARA FLORENCE
PAINTER
b Bronx, NY, Dec 17, 1932. *Study:* Vesper George Sch Art, with Robert Douglas Hunter & Robert Cummings. *Exhib:* Solo exhibs, Peel Gallery, Danby, Vt, 88 & Cumeo Mus, Vernon Hills, Ill, 92; Pastel Soc Am 20th Nat Show, 92; joint show, Peel Gallery, Danby, Vt; Ringmaster, Pastel Soc Am, 94; Grandmother's Doll, Am Artists Prof League, 94; 23rd Nat Pastel Soc Am Show, 95 (Catherine Lorillard Wolf Art Club Award & Master Pastelist Designation); 46th Nat Show Acad Artists Asn, 96 (Gulluip Watson Award); 68th Grand Nat Exhib of Am Artists Prof League, 97 (Michael Werwolf Mem Award); Peel Gallery, Danby, 2002; 3-person show of pastels, Love Gallery, Chicago. *Awards:* First Prize, Conn Pastel Soc, 92; Nat Arts Club Award, 94; Master Pastelist, Pastel Soc Am, 95. *Bibliog:* Hazel Harrison (auth), Pastel School, Readers Digest. *Mem:* Charter mem Conn Pastel Soc; Am Artists Prof League; Pastel Soc Am; Copley Soc, formerly; Guild Boston Artists. *Media:* Oils, Pastels, Acrylics. *Publ:* Encyclopedia of Oil Painting Techniques, Quartro Pub Co, London, Eng; Hardcover, Boston Sch Publ Blue Tree, Postsmouth, NH. *Dealer:* Quidley and Co 26 Main St Nantucket MA 02554 38 Newbury St Boston MA 02116. *Mailing Add:* 64 State Rte 202 Bennington NH 03442

WILLIS, JANE B(ROOME)
GRAPHIC ARTIST, PAINTER
b New Orleans, La, July 25, 1937. *Study:* Louisiana State Univ, BS, 59; Burlington Co Col, NJ, with Merton Howe, 78; Camden Co Col, NJ, with Bill Marlin, 80-82; Univ New Orleans, 83; New Orleans Acad Fine Arts, with Auseklis Ozols, 92. *Work:* World Trade Ctr, New Orleans; Curray & Co, Monroe, La; Wood Treating Inc, Picayune,

Miss. *Exhib:* New Orleans Art Asn Fine Arts Fest, World Trade Ctr, New Orleans, 92-93; A Shared Element - Artists Work on Paper, Slidell Cult Ctr, La, 92; Southeastern Exhib, Fine Arts Mus South, Mobile, Ala, 93; Salon Int, Jackson, Miss, 94; Catharine Lorillard Wolfe's 100 Yr Traveling Exhib, 96 & 97. *Pos:* Mem oper comt, Slidell Cult Ctr, 89-95. *Awards:* Nellie Evans Mem Award, Artwave's 7th Ann 93; Artists Mag Award Merit, Westbank Art Guilds Nat, 94; Second Place, New Orleans Art Asn, 94. *Mem:* Nat League Am Pen Women; Artwave; Catharine Lorillard Wolfe Art Club; New Orleans Art Asn; Slidell Art League Inc. *Media:* Graphite, Oil. *Publ:* Contribr, The Best of Colored Pencil 2, Rockport Publ, 93; illusr, cover, Art Calendar Mag, 9/96. *Mailing Add:* 859 Cross Gates Blvd Slidell LA 70461

WILLIS, JAY STEWART
SCULPTOR, EDUCATOR

b Fort Wayne, Ind, Oct 22, 1940. *Study:* Univ Ill, Urbana, BFA (sculpture), 63; Univ Calif, Berkeley, MA (sculpture), 66. *Work:* Hirshhorn Mus, Washington; Del Mar Col, Corpus Christi, Tex; Am Tel & Tel, Chicago; Metrop Mus Art, NY; Calif State Univ, Fullerton; Walker Hill Art Mus, Seoul, Korea. *Comn:* Multiple Structures, Cirus Ed, 73; ALCOA, Univ Southern Calif sculpture garden, Los Angeles, 78; sculpture, comn by Ernesto W Hahn & Charles Kober Assocs, Pasadena, Calif, 80; Bankers Trust, Los Angeles; Pac Enterprises, Los Angeles. *Exhib:* One-person exhibs, Cirrus Gallery, Los Angeles, 81, 83, 85, 86, 88 & 91; A Broad Spectrum: Contemp Los Angeles Painters, Design Ctr Los Angeles, 84; Olympic Project, Los Angeles Co Mus Art, Calif, 84; Sculpture Installation, Fisher Art Gallery, Univ Southern Calif, Los Angeles, 85; Los Angeles Int Art Fair, 86-89; Beverly Hills Sculpture Garden, Calif, 87; Calif Artist in Educ, San Francisco, 89; Monumental Sculpture, Calif State Univ, San Bernardino, 89; Made in LA: The Prints of Cirrus Editions, Los Angeles Co Mus Art, 95; Blessings and Beginnings, Skinball Cult Ctr, Hebrew Union Col, Los Angeles, 96; plus many others. *Teaching:* Instr sculpture, Univ Ariz, Tucson, 66-69; asst prof fine arts, Univ Southern Calif, Los Angeles, 69-73, prof fine arts (sculpture), 74-, chmn studio arts, 88-89, dir pub art studies, 92-. *Awards:* Purchase Award, Los Angeles Art Ann, Barnsdall Park, Calif, 76; Runner-Up, Los Angeles Int Airport Sculpture, Calif, 76; Univ Southern Calif Fac Innovation & Res Grant, Color & Structure, 85-86; Art in Pub Places Award, Calif Arts Coun, 90; and others. *Bibliog:* Suzanne Muchnic (auth), Los Angeles Time, 5/5/81 & 3/1/85; Kathy Zimmer-McKelvie, Images & Issues, spring 82; Betty Brown (auth), Artweek, 11/12/83; Sandy Nelson (auth), Images & Issues, 7-8/84; Stephen Grossman (auth), Artweek, 3/23/85; Colin Gardner (auth), Los Angeles Times, 10/10/86; Marlene Donahue (auth), Los Angeles Times, 5/13/88; and many others. *Mailing Add:* c/o School of Fine Arts USC Watt Hall Rm 103 Los Angeles CA 90089-0292

WILLIS, SIDNEY F
PAINTER

b Newark, NJ, Dec 14, 1930. *Study:* Vesper George Sch Art, grad, continued study with Robert D Hunter. *Work:* over 1,000 works sold to various collectors. *Exhib:* Southern Vt Artists, 72; Jordan Show, Boston, Mass, 73; Ogunquit Art Ctr, Maine, 74; Am Artists Prof League, NY, 74; Coun Am Artists Show, NY. *Teaching:* Instr painting & drawing, Vesper George Art Sch, Boston, Mass, 67-69 & Sharon Art Ctr, Peterborough, NH, 65-75. *Awards:* Grand Prize, Jordan Show, Boston, 58 & 62; First Prize, Ogunquit Art Ctr, Maine, 61; Gold Medal, Heritage Salon, 88; and many others. *Bibliog:* Classical Realism (video). *Mem:* Guild Boston Artists; NH Art Asn; Am Artists Prof League; Paste Soc Am. *Media:* Oil, Pastel, Acrylic. *Publ:* Contribr, New York Graphic Soc, Yankee Mag; Techniques in Oil Painting, Quartro Pub, London, Eng; Hardcover, Boston Sch Publ Blue Tree, Portsmouth, NH, 2006. *Dealer:* Quidley & Co 26 Main St Nantucket MA 02554 118 Newbrry St Boston MA 02116; Fox Gallery Woodstock VT. *Mailing Add:* 64 Rte 202 Bennington NH 03442

WILLIS, THORNTON
PAINTER

b Pensacola, Fla, May 25, 1936. *Study:* Auburn Univ, Ala; Univ Southern Miss, Hattiesburg, BS; Univ Ala, MA. *Work:* Mus Modern Art, New York; Solomon Guggenheim Mus, New York; Whitney Mus Am Art, New York; Mus Art, Carnegie Mellon Pittsburgh, Pa; Albright-Knox Gallery, New York; New Orleans Mus Fine Art, New Orleans, La; Power Inst Fine Arts, Sydney, Australia; Phillips Collection, Washington, DC; Rose Art Mus, Brandeis Univ; Denver Mus Fine Art, Denver, Colo, Maslow Coll, Marywood Univ, Scranton, Pa, High Mus, Atlanta, Ga, Weatherspoon Art Gallery, Univ NC, Milwaukee Art Mus, Wisc. *Exhib:* Group exhibs, Lyrical Abstraction, Aldrich Mus, 69 & Whitney Mus, 71; solo exhibs, Andre Zarre Gallery New York, 80-92, Oscarsson-Hood Gallery, New York, 80-81 & 84, Marianne Deson Gallery, Chicago, 81, Nina Freudenheim Gallery, Buffalo, NY, Galerie Nordenhake, Stockholm & Pensacola Mus, Fla, 88, Elizabeth Harris Gallery, New York, 2006, 2008, 2009, 2011, Sideshow Gallery, New York, 2007, Rider Univ, Lawrenceville, NJ, 2009; Mus Mod Art, New York, 81 & 84; Galerie Gonet, Lausanne, Switz, 82; Art Mus Ateneum, Helsinki, Finland, 83; Gloria Luria, Miami, Fla, 85; Univ Southern Miss, Hattiesburg, 85; Twining Gallery, New York, 88-91; Andre Emmerich Gallery, New York, 92; Andre Zarre Gallery, New York 92; Abstraction and Immanence, Hunter Coll, 2001; NY Artists, Emily Lowe Gallery, Hofstra Mus, 2001; Musee Cantonal Des Beaux-Arts De Lausanne, Switz, 2000; Am Abstract Artists 2000, Hillwood Art Mus, 2000; Sideshow Gallery, 2005-2007; Elizabeth Harris Gallery, NY, 2008, 2009, 2011, 2013; Univ Ala, 2012; Works of the Jenney Archive, Gagosian Gallery, NY, 2013. *Teaching:* Wagner Coll & La State Univ; grad lectr, Pratt Inst, 74, 77 & 80; lectr, Art Inst Chicago, Ill, 81; assoc prof art, Univ La, Baton Rouge, 83 & State Univ NY, Purchase, 86; Univ Ala, 2013; Marywood Univ, Scranton, Pa, 2013. *Awards:* Fel Award, John Simon Guggenheim Found, 78-79; Nat Endowment Arts Painting Fel, 80; Adolph & Esther Gottlieb Found, 91; Fel, The Pollock-Krasner Found, 2001. *Bibliog:* Peter Bellamy (auth), The Artist Project: Portraits of the Real Art World, New York Artists, 91; Reviews in Art in Am, Arts Mag, ArtForum Mag & Art News, 79-94, New Criterion, 93, New Republic, 2003, NY Times, 2003; The Brooklyn Rail, 2005-2007; Art in Am, 2005-2007; The NY Sun, 2006-2008; Gallery Chronical, The New Criterion, 2012, 2013; James Panero; Two Approaches to Abstraction, Xico Greenwald, The Sun, 2013; Lance Esplund (auth), Thornton Willis, Elizabeth Harris Gallery, 2011. *Mem:* Am Abstract Artists Asn, NY. *Media:* Oil, Acrylic. *Publ:* Joseph Masheck (auth), Historical Present: Essays of the 1970's, Contemporary Am Art Critics, Univ Mich Press, 84; Tom Armstrong, A Singular Vision: Architecture, Art Landscape, 2011. *Dealer:* Elizabeth Harris Gallery 529 W 20th St New York NY 10011. *Mailing Add:* 85-87 Mercer St New York NY 10012

WILLMOTT, ELIZABETH ANN
SCULPTOR, PHOTOGRAPHER

b Indianapolis, Ind, June 18, 1928. *Study:* Oberlin Coll, Ohio, BA, 50; Univ Mich, Ann Arbor, MA, 52; Univ Saskatchewan with Eli Bornstein, 59-62. *Work:* Erindale Col, Univ Toronto; Glendon Col, York Univ, Toronto, Ont; Kenderdine Gallery, Univ Saskatchewan, Saskatoon, Sask, CA; Mondriaanhuis, Amersfort, Neth; Gallery One, Univ Manitoba, Winnipeg, Manitoba, Ca; Tom Thomson Mem Art Gallery, Owen Sound, ON; Robert McLaughlen Gallery, Oshawa, ON; Winnipeg Art Gallery, Winnipeg, MB. *Exhib:* Solo shows: Inaugural Exhib, McLaughlin Coll, York Univ, Downsview, Ont, 1969; Dunkleman Gallery, Toronto, Ont, 1970; Lattice, Light, and Landscape, Durham Art Gallery, Durham, Ont, 1998; The Scanner as a Camera, The Gallery Rm, Collingwood Pub Libr, Collingwood, Ont, 2002; Jewelry 71, Art Gallery of Ont, Toronto, 1971; Structurist Reliefs with Dave Barr, Marianne Friedland Gallery, Toronto, 1975; The Constructivist Heritage, Harbourfront Gallery, Toronto, 1981; Global Echoes, Mondriaanhuis, Amersfort, Neth, 2000, 2001; Glendon Coll York Univ, Toronto; Erindale Coll Univ Toronto; Univ Saskatchewan; Univ Manitoba; Munic Gallery, Cholet, France; Mondrianhuis, Amersfort, the Netherlands; Tom Thomson Mem Art Gallery, Owen Sound, Ont; Winnipeg Art Gallery, Manitoba. *Bibliog:* Harold Hayden (auth), Structurist Movement, Chicago Omnibus, 5/67; Jim Purdie (auth), The Structurists, Globe & Mail, 7/75; Michael Greenwood (auth), Relief Structures: Elizabeth Willmott & Dave Barr, Arts Can, 75-76. *Media:* Relief Constructions; Photography. *Publ:* Auth & illustr, the Structurist Art Ann, Univ Saskatchewan, 65-; Lattice, Light and Landscape, New Circle Publ, 1/95; contribr, Blank Page 3, B4 Publ, London, 90. *Mailing Add:* 267 8th St W Owen Sound ON N4K3M3 Canada

WILLOUGHBY, JANE BAKER
COLLAGE ARTIST, PAINTER

b Toledo, Ohio, 1923. *Study:* Smith Col, Mass, BA, 43; Art Students League with George Grosz, 45-49; New Sch Social Res, New York, 50-51. *Work:* Lyman Allyn Mus, New London, Conn; Discovery Mus, Bridgeport, Conn; The Robert Benjamin Collection, NY; Conn Bank & Trust Co, New Haven; Sen & Mrs George McGovern, Washington, DC; Pres & Mrs Ronald Reagan, Washington, DC. *Exhib:* Solo exhibs, Silvermine Guild Artists, New Canaan, Conn, 63 & 76, Slater Mem Mus, Norwich, Conn, 76, Lyman Allyn Mus, New London, Conn, 80, Bridgeport Mus Art, Sci, Conn, 80 & Whitney Mus Am Art, New Haven, Conn, 81; The Benjamin Collection, Yale Univ Art Gallery; Viridian Gallery, NY, 83 & 86; Albertus Magnus Col, 90; Fairfield Univ, 85. *Teaching:* Instr, Silvermine Guild Artists. *Awards:* Munson Award & Purchase Prize, New Haven Paint-Clay Club, 75; Arches Paper, Nat Asn Painters in Casein & Acrylic, 78; Audubon Medal Honor, Audubon Artists Am, 78; Conn Women Artists, 90; Best in Show, Conn Women Artists, New Brit Mus Am Art, 92. *Bibliog:* Shirley Gonzales (auth), New Haven Register, 9/16/83; Shirley Sandler (auth), Manhattan Arts, 11/16/83; Amy Friedman (auth), Artspeak, 11/16/83; and others. *Mem:* Silvermine Guild Artists; Conn Acad Fine Arts; Conn Watercolor Soc; Audubon Artists Inc; Conn Women Artists Asn. *Media:* Monotype. *Mailing Add:* 261 Ridgewood Ave New Haven CT 06517

WILLUMSON, GLENN GARDNER
EDUCATOR, CURATOR

b Glendale, Calif, June 22, 1949. *Study:* St Mary's Col, BA, 71; Univ Calif, Davis, MA, 84; Univ Calif, Santa Barbara, PhD, 88. *Collection Arranged:* Masterpieces of the Rubel Collection, Crocker Mus Art, 82; Collecting with a Passion (auth, catalog), Palmer Mus Art, 93; Double Plots, Palmer Mus Art, 94; Wayne Miller: Tokyo, Hiroshima, Palmer Mus Art, 95; Capturing the Light, Palmer Mus Art, 96; History Past, History Present: Am Daguerreotypes, 01; Double Exposure, Calif State Railroad Mus, 2013-2014. *Pos:* Curator, Getty Inst, Santa Monica, Calif, 88-92; cur, Palmer Mus Art, State College, Pa, 92-96, sr cur, 97-2001. *Teaching:* Adj prof, Univ Calif, Santa Barbara, 86-87; vis prof mod art, Univ Calif, Irvine, 89-90; affil prof contemp art & theory, history of photography, Pa State Univ, 94-2000; Prof Art history, Univ Fla, 01-; dir grad program in Mus Studies. *Awards:* Getty Publ Grant, Getty Found, 91; John Randolph & Dora Hayes Fel, Huntington Libr, 95; Univ Teacher's Fel, Nat Endowment Humanities, 97-98; NEH Summer Fel, 2005; Fla Humanities Grant, 2005-2006; Beinecke Fel, 2007; Smithsonian Fel, 2007-2008; Fel, Bill Lane Ctr, Stanford Univ; Found Rsch Prof, 2013-16; Getty Project Fellow, 2014; Ansel Adams Fellow, CCP, 2014; vis fellow, Univ Glasgow, 2015. *Bibliog:* P Palmquist (auth), Thesis review, Stereo World, 85; J Carson (auth), review, Winterthur Portfolio, 92; A Ellenzweig (auth), Life and Eugene Smith, Times Lit Suppl (London), 93; F Brunet (auth), review, Hist of Photo, 2014; J Watts (auth), review, Pac Hist Rev, 2014; R Grant (auth), Am Hist Rev, 2014. *Mem:* Soc Photog Educ (regional bd, 92-97); Coll Art Asn; Am Studies Asn; Asn Historians Am Art; Am Alliance Mus; (comt bd, 2004-); Southeast Mus Assn. *Publ:* Auth, AA Hart: Photographer of the transcontinental railroad, Hist Photo Mag, 88; contribr, Anthony Van Dyck's Antwerp, Sedelijk Prenteenkab, 91; auth, W Eugene Smith and the Photographic Essay, Cambridge Univ Press, 92; The Getty Research Inst; Materials for a New Photo-History, Hist Photo, Mag 98; The Shifting Audience of the Univ Mus, Mus International, 2000; contribr, Photos Objects Histories, Rutledge, 04; contribr, From Perifery to Center, NAEA, 2007; contribr, Framing the West, Yale Univ, 2010; contribr, Crocker Mus Collection Unveiled, CAM, 2010; Iron Muse, Univ Calif Press, 2013; El Album fortograficocmoartefacto cultural, Papel Alpha, 2013. *Mailing Add:* Univ Fla PO Box 115801 Gainesville FL 32611-5801

WILMERDING, JOHN
EDUCATOR, HISTORIAN
b Boston, Mass, Apr 28, 1938. *Study:* Harvard Col, AB, 60; Harvard Univ, AM, 61 & PhD, 65; also Am art with Benjamin Rowland. *Hon Degrees:* Univ Vt, DLitt, 90. *Collection Arranged:* Fitz Hugh Lane, De Cordova Mus, Lincoln, Nebr, 66 & Robert Salmon, 67; Am Marine Painting, Va Mus Fine Arts, Richmond, 76; 100 Am Drawings from the JD Hatch Collection, Nat Gallery Ireland, 76; Am Light: The Luminist Movement (auth, catalog), Nat Gallery Art, Washington, DC, 80, An Am Perspective: The Ganz Collection, 81, Important Information Inside: The Art of John F Peto (auth, catalog), 83 & The Paintings of Fitz Hugh Lane (coauth, catalog), 88; Winslow Homer in the 1870s (coauth, catalog), Art Mus, Princeton Univ, 90; Thomas Eakins (coauth, catalog), Nat Portrait Gallery, London, 93; Roy Lichtenstein (coauth) catalog, Still Lifes, Gagosian Gallery, 2010; Wayne Thieboud (auth), Acquavella Galleries, 2012. *Pos:* Cur Am art & sr cur, Nat Gallery Art, Wash, 77-82, deputy dir, 83-88; trustee, Solomon R Guggenheim Mus, New York City, currently; sr cur, Am Art Nat Gallery Art, 77-83, dept dir, 83-88; vis cur, Metrop Mus, 98-2006; hon cur, painting Peabody Mus, Salem, Mass. *Teaching:* prof, Am art, Leon E Williams, Dartmouth Col, 65-77; vis lectr art, Yale Univ, 72; vis prof fine arts, Harvard Univ, 76, Univ Md, 79 & Univ Del, 82; Sarofim prof Am art, Princeton Univ, 88-2007, chmn dept art & archaeol, 92-99; asst prof, Dartmouth Col, 65-68, assoc prof, 68-73, Leon E Williams prof, 73-77, chmn dept art, 68-72, chmn humanities div, 71-72. *Awards:* Guggenheim Found Fel, 73-74; Comt for Preservation of White House (Presidential app); Fleischman Award for Scholarly Excellence in Am Art Hist, Archives Am Art, 98; Maine in Am Award, Farnsworth Art Mus, 2006. *Bibliog:* The Pop Object: The Still Life, Tradition in Pop Art, Rizzoli, 2013. *Mem:* Coll Art Asn; Am Studies Asn; Am Philosophic Soc. *Res:* American 19th century art and culture, pop art. *Publ:* American Art, Pelican-Penguin, 76; Important Information Inside, Harper & Row, 83; American Marine Painting, Abrams, 87; American Views: Essays on American Art, Princeton, 91; The Artist's Mount Desert: American Painters on the Maine Coast, Princeton, 94; Compass & Clock: Defining Moments in Am Cult, 99; Signs of the Artist, Signatures and Self Expression in American Paintings, 2003; auth, West to Wesselmann: American Drawings and Watercolors in the Princeton Univ & Mus, 2004 (catalog) Princeton Univ.; auth, Richard Estes, Rizzoli, 2006; Tom Wesselmann: His Voice & Vision, Rizzoli, 2008. *Mailing Add:* Dept Art & Archaeol Princeton Univ 105 McCormick Hall Princeton NJ 08544-1018

WILMETH, ERNEST, II
COLLAGE ARTIST, POTTER
b Perryton, Tex, Dec 21, 1952. *Study:* Northern Ariz Univ, BFA, 76. *Work:* Bowne Corp, Nashville; Brownstein, Hyatt, and Farber, Albuquerque, NMex; Delancy Street Found, San Francisco; First State Bank & First Nat Bank, Spearman, Tex; pvt collections of Gov and Mrs Bruce King, Ms. Nancy Langwiser, Mr. James Muir, Mr. Gary Needle, Mr. Mark Ricketts, and many others; UNM Health Sci Ctr. *Exhib:* two person shows, Coupland/Jackson Fine Art, Taos, NMex, 91, Cone 10 Gallery, Albuquerque, 92 & First State Bank, Spearman, Tex, 92; Sixteen Squared, Nina Bean Gallery, 96, Impressions: Works on Paper, 2000, NMex Clay, 2000, Contemp Clay, Dearing Gallery, Taos, 2000; Abstract Art, Anderson Contemp Gallery, Santa Fe, NMex, 2003; Less is More, A Perspective, Harwood Art Ctr, Albuquerque, NMex, 2004; From the Ground Up, Mus of Fine Arts, Las Cruces, NMex, 2004; Paper in Particular, Columbia Col, Columbia, MO, 2004; Fusion Form Function, Union St Gallery, Chicago, Ill, 2004; Dimensions, Artspace 116, Albuquerque NMex, 2005; 8th National Juried Show, Gallery West, Alexandria, Va; 33rd Annual Juried Competition, Masur Mus Art, Monroe, La; 38th Annual National Juried Exhibition, Palm Springs Art Mus, Calif, 2007; 38th Annual Visual Arts Exhibition, Meadows Gallery, Denton, Tex, 2006; FFCS 6th International Juried Exhibition, Austin, Tex, 2005. *Awards:* Standard's Choice, SWAF, 97; Juror's Award, Impressions: Works on Paper, 2000; Best of Show, Arts Int, El Paso, 2004; Award of Achievement, From the Ground Up, Las Cruces, 2004; VNU Business Publications Award, 37th Annual Visual Arts Exhib, 2005. *Bibliog:* Mary Alice Hines (auth), article, in: Accent W, 7/78; articles in Albuquerque Monthly, 96, Albuquerque Jour, 96, Phoenix Gazette, 91, Ceramics Monthly, 89. *Mem:* Fel Royal Soc Arts; life mem Royal Soc Encouragement Arts Manufactures & Com; Southwest Arts and Crafts Festival (bd mem, 90, 91 & 97); MAGNIFICO The Art Albuquerque (visual comt mem, 92-96, chair & bd mem, 95-97). *Media:* Collage; Clay. *Publ:* Stuart Ashman & Suzanne Deats (auth), Abstract Art, 7/03; Albuquerque J, Art Review, Wesley Pulka, 9/04. *Mailing Add:* PO Box 3104 Albuquerque NM 87190

WILSON, BLENDA JACQUELINE
PATRON
b Woodbridge, NJ, Jan 28, 1941. *Study:* Cedar Crest Col, AB, 62; Seton Hall Univ, AM, 65; Boston Col, PhD, 79. *Hon Degrees:* Numerous US cols & univs, 87-2003. *Pos:* sr assoc, dean Grad Sch Educ Harvard Univ, Cambridge, Mass, 72-82; vpres, effective sector mgt Ind Sector, Wash, 82-84; exec dir, Colo Comn Higher Educ, Denver, 84-88; chancellor and prof, pub admin & educ Univ Mich, Dearborn, 88-92; pres, Calif State Univ, Northridge, 92-99; Northridge Hosp Med Ctr, 93-99; James Irvine Found, 96-99; mem bd trustees, J Paul Getty Trust, currently; dir, Univ Detroit Jesuit High Sch; Arab Community Ctr for Econ & Social Serv's; Int Found Educ & Self-Help, Achievement Coun, LA; dir, vchmn, Metrop Affairs Corp; exec bd, Detroit area coun Boy Scouts Am; bd dir, Commonwealth Fund, Henry Ford Hosp-Fairlane Ctr, Henry Ford Health System, Metrop Ctr for High Tech, United Way Southeastern Mich; mem Nat Coalition 100 Black Women, Detroit, Race Relations Coun Metrop Detroit, Women & Found, Greater Detroit Interfaith Round Table Nat Conf of Christians & Jews, Adv. Bd Valley Cult Ctr, Woodland Hills; trustee assoc, Boston Col; trustee emer, bd dir, Found Ctr; trustee emer, Cambridge Col; trustee, Henry Ford Mus & Greenfield Village; Sammy Davis Jr Nat Liver Inst. *Teaching:* Teacher, Woodbridge Township Pub Sch, 62-66. *Mem:* Am Asn of Univ Women; Asn Gov Boards (adv coun of pres, currently); Asn Black Women in Higher Educ; Am Asn State Cols & Univ (comt, on policies & purposes, acad leadership fel selection comt). *Mailing Add:* Nellie Mae Educ Found 1250 Hancock St 205N Quincy MA 02169-4331

WILSON, CARRIE LOIS
LECTURER
b Philadelphia, Pa, Sept 15, 1944. *Study:* Barnard Col, Columbia Univ, BA (art hist), 66; Neighborhood Playhouse School of the Theatre, Sanford Meisner, 68; philosophy of Aesthetic Realism with its founder, Eli Siegel, 69-78, with chmn, Ellen Reiss, 78-. *Collection Arranged:* Art as Criticism, 1976; The Arts, They're Here!; Ten Arts & the Opposites, 77; Couples Closeness & Clash in Art & Life, 83; Lasting Impressions: Opposites in the Art of the Print, 2004; The Drama in Things: Three Photographers-Amy Dienes, Steve Poleskie, Perry Hall, 2009; Chaim Koppelman: A Memorial Exhib, 2010. *Pos:* Co-dir, Terrain Gallery, 72-84, dir, 84-88, Co-Dir 88-; lectr, 84-. *Teaching:* Consult & instr, Aesthetic Realism Found, 72-. *Mem:* The Kindest Art; Int Soc Educ Through Art; Aesthetic Realism Theatre Co; Nat Asn Teachers of Singing. *Specialty:* contemporary American & European Art. *Publ:* auth, Aesthetic Realism Shows How Art Answers the Questions of Your Life, Columbia Univ, 2003; Surprising and Abiding Opposites, Jour Print World, Winter/2002; A Brief History of the Terrain Gallery, 2005; Terrain Gallery Celebrates 50th Anniversary, Printmaking Today, 2006; coauth, Chaim Koppelman: Pioneering Printmaker & Teacher, Jour Print Wald, Winter 2010. *Mailing Add:* Aesthetic Realism Found 141 Greene St New York NY 10012

WILSON, CHARLES
ADMINISTRATOR
Study: Univ West Ga, BA, 82; NC State Univ, MA, 84; Univ Ga, PhD, 88. *Pos:* chair dept English, Old Dominion Univ, Norfolk, Va, 2001-2004, acting assoc dir grad studies, Coll Arts & Letts, 2005, vice provost undergrad studies, 2006-2010, dean Coll Arts & Letts, 2010-. *Mailing Add:* Old Dominion University College of Arts & Letters 9000 Batten Arts and Letters Norfolk VA 23529

WILSON, CLARENCE S, JR
CONSULTANT, PATRON
b Brooklyn, NY, Oct 22, 1945. *Study:* Williams Col, Williamstown, Mass, BA, 67; Northwestern Univ Sch Law, Chicago, JD, 74. *Pos:* Trustee, Chicago Symphony Orchestra, 87-96, Art Inst Chicago, 90- & MERIT Music Prog, 91-96; pres, Lawyers for Creative Arts, 87 & 88; outside gen coun, DuSable Mus African Am Hist, Chicago, Ill, 88-95 & 98-; gov, Sch Art Inst Chicago, 94-; vchmn, Jazz Mus Chicago, 94-97; vis comt on visual arts & dept of music, Univ Chicago, 95-. *Teaching:* Adj prof Law, Chicago-Kent Col Law, 81-94; lectr, Columbia Col Chicago, 95-97 & 99-. *Mem:* Ill Arts Coun, 83-89; Arts Midwest, 83-89. *Interests:* Masterworks by Americans of African Descent, Latin America, Chicago. *Publ:* Contribr, Visual Arts & the Law, in the book, Law & the Arts-Art & the Law, 79

WILSON, CYNTHIA LINDSAY
PAINTER
b Washington, DC, May 3, 1945. *Study:* Auburn Univ, BFA, 67; Conn Graphic Art Ctr, 97; Penland School, 2002. *Work:* Housatonic Mus Art; Ga Tech Coll, Atlanta; US Tobacco Co, Conn; Fairfield Univ, Conn; Westport Sch Permanent Art Collection; and many others. *Comn:* Kitchen Interiors, 2002. *Exhib:* Pa Watercolor Soc Ann Exhib, Mechanicsburg, 89, 90 & 92; Adirondack's Nat Exhib Am Watercolors, Old Forge, NY, 89; Am Artists Prof League Exhib, Salmagundi Club, NY, 89, 90 & 94; 1990 Am Realism Competition, Parkersburg Art Ctr, WVa, 90; Salmagundi Non Member Exhib, Salmagundi Club, NY, 90, 91, & 93; New Eng Watercolor Soc N Am Open Exhib, Boston, 90, 94 & 95; Springfield Art League Nat Exhib, Springfield Mus Fine Arts, Mass, 92; Nat Acad Design Ann Exhib, NY, 92; Nat Soc Painters in Casein & Acrylic, 91, 93-96, 98-2006; Am Watercolor Soc Ann Exhib, Salmagundi Club, NY, 96; Spartanburg Mus Biennial Juried Art exhib, SC, 2003; South Carolina Watercolor Soc, 2004-2006; New Eng Watercolor Soc, Masters of Watercolor, New Bedford Art Mus, 2006. *Pos:* chmn, Artists Open Studio Tour, Hendersonville, NC, 2013. *Teaching:* Watermedia painting, Ridgefield Guild Artists, Conn, 95-96 & Mooresville Art Guild, Mooresville, NC, 97-98; tchr Process & Possibilities Workshops, NC, 98-2006; Acrylics wth Attitude Workshops, NC, 2012-2013. *Awards:* Margaret Hamlin Mem Award, Acad Artists, 92; Joseph Cain Award, nat Soc Painters in Casein & Acrylic, 98; Elsie Ject Key award, Nat Soc Painters in Casin & Acrylic, 2001, Liquitex award, 2002; Regional Projects grant, 2001; Nat'l soc Painters in Casein & Acrylic Glenn Bradshaw Award, 2004; Best in Show Award, Wickwire Gallery City of Four Seasons, 2004; M Graham & Co Award, SC Watercolor Soc, 2005; Arches Paper Co Award, SC Watercolor Soc, 2006. *Mem:* New Eng Watercolor Soc; Pa Watercolor Soc; Am Artists Prof League; Nat Soc Painters in Casein & Acrylic; SC Watercolor Soc. *Media:* Acrylic, Watercolor, Multi-Media Constructions. *Publ:* Auth, Steps to painterly acrylics, Artist's Mag, 3/93; The Best of Watercolor, Flowers in Watercolor & Floral Inspirations, Rockport Publ. *Dealer:* Grovewood Gallery Asheville NC; Design Gallery Bakersville NC. *Mailing Add:* 521 Orchard Circle Hendersonville NC 28739

WILSON, DOUGLAS FENN
PAINTER, SCULPTOR
b Orinda, Calif, July, 18, 1953. *Study:* Dartmouth Col, Hanover, NH, BA, 75. *Work:* Fine Arts Mus San Francisco, Calif; Worcester Art Mus, Mass; Minneapolis Mus Art, Minn; Tucson Mus Art; Hood Mus Art, Dartmouth Col. *Comn:* Constructed paintings, The Hibernia Bank, 79, Dean Witter Reynolds, 83 & Bay West Development Co, 85, San Francisco, Calif; constructed painting, Deloitte, Haskins & Sells, New York, NY, 86. *Exhib:* 30 Watercolors & Pastels, Worcester Art Mus, Mass, 76; 20 Watercolors & Pastels, Dartmouth Col, Hanover, NH, 76; Recent Acquisitions, Fine Arts Mus San Francisco, 77; Fishabach Gallery, NY, 82; Contemp Images, Univ Wis, Oshkosh, 83; John Pence Gallery, San Francisco, 84; Jan Cicero Gallery, Chicago, Ill, 85. *Awards:* Marcus Hieman Achievement Award, Dartmouth Col, 75, Marcus Hieman Proj Grant, 75 & Dartmouth Gen Fel, 79. *Media:* Watercolor, Acrylic. *Mailing Add:* PO Box 848 Glen Ellen CA 95442

WILSON, ELIZABETH (JANE)
PAINTER, EDUCATOR
b Philadelphia, Pa, June 24, 1959. *Study:* Corcoran Sch Art, Wash, 78-79; Pa Acad Fine Arts, Philadelphia, 80-84; Univ Pa, Philadelphia, 85. *Work:* Bryn Mawr Col, Pa; E I DuPont de Nemours Co, Wilmington, Del; Robert Half Assoc, Pa; Johnson & Johnson, NJ; Price Waterhouse, Pa. *Comn:* Portrait, Joseph Paradise, Pennsauken, NJ, 83; Portrait, Lee & Rosie Hymerling, Haddonfield, NJ, 90; Portrait, Michael & Betina Bernstein, Bala Cynwd, NJ, 90. *Exhib:* Solo exhibs, Pa State Univ, Middletown, 88, Gross McCleaf Gallery, Philadelphia, 90, 92 & FAN Gallery, Philadelphia, 94, 96 & 98; Contemp Philadelphia Artists, Philadelphia Mus Art, 90; Award Winners - Fel Exhib, Mus Am Art Pa Acad Fine Arts, Philadelphia, 94; Women: Object/Subject, Rosemont Col, Pa, 96; 171st Nat Acad Design, NY, 96. *Teaching:* Adj assoc prof, drawing & design, Temple Univ, Philadelphia, 88-95; adj asst prof, drawing, Univ Arts, Philadelphia, Pa, 94-97; adj prof 2D-3D design & drawing, Philadelphia Col Textiles & Sci, 96-. *Awards:* First Prize, Rutgers Univ, 88; Catherine Gibbons Granger, Pa Acad Fine Arts, 93; First Prize, Am Col, 98. *Bibliog:* Karen Heller (auth), Contemporary Philadelphia Artists, Philadelphia Inquirer Mag, 5/90; Victoria Donohoe (auth), Philadelphia Inquirer, 4/96; Edward Suzanski (auth), Philadelphia Inquirer, 5/96. *Mem:* Fel Pa Acad Fine Arts, 82-. *Media:* Oil. *Dealer:* FAN Gallery 311 Cherry St Philadelphia PA 19106; Mulligan Shanoski Gallery 747 Post St San Francisco CA 94109. *Mailing Add:* 340 Oxford Rd Havertown PA 19083

WILSON, EVAN CARTER
PAINTER
b Tuscaloosa, Ala, Oct 31, 1953. *Study:* NC Sch Arts, 70-73; Md Inst, Coll Art, with Joseph Sheppard, 72-75; Schuler Sch Fine Art, 75-76. *Work:* Altos de Chavon, La Romana, Dominican Republic; Gulf States Paper Corp, Tuscaloosa, Ala; Greenville Co Mus Art, SC. *Comn:* Oil portraits, Congressman Walter Flowers, Ala, 75, George A LeMaistre (chmn, FDIC), 84 & Vahakn Hovnanian, Red Bank, NJ, 84; interior paintings, Mildred Warner House, Tuscaloosa, Ala, 91; landscape paintings, comn by Jack Warner, Tuscaloosa, Ala, 92; oil portraits, comn by Arthur & Holly MaGill, Greenville, SC. *Exhib:* Mid-Year Show, Butler Mus Art, Youngstown, Ohio, 74 & 90; Impressions of Am: The Warner Collection, Montgomery Mus Fine Art, Ala, 91; Robert M Hicklin Jr Inc Fine Arts of the Am South, 94 & 95; Southern Vt Arts Ctr, Manchester, 94; Alabama Impact: Contemp Artists with Ala Ties, Fine Arts Mus South, Huntsville Mus Art, 95; Gracious Plenty: Still Life Paintings from Southern Collections, 95-96; Morris Mus Art, Augusta, Ga; Hunter Mus Art, Chattanooga, Tenn; Telfair Acad, Savannah, Ga, 96; Parson's Sch Design, NY, 97; Solo exhibs incl JR Leigh Gallery, Tuscaloosa, Ala, 80-87, 92-98, 2000, Il Punto Gallery, Florence, Italy, 79, Huntsville Mus Art, Huntsville, Ala, 2001, plus others; John Pence Gallery, San Francisco, Calif, 1988-2000; plus others. *Awards:* Gold Medal, Knickerbocker Artists, 86; Macowin Tuttle Award, Ann Mem Exhib, Salmagundi Club, 87; Ala Arts Award, Soc Fine Arts/Univ Ala, 99; plus others. *Bibliog:* Ben Windham (auth), Ransom and Evan Wilson, Arts Review, Univ Ala, summer 84; Sonny Tiedeman (auth), Festival Brushstrokes, Horizon Mag, 1-2/86; Martha R Severens (auth), Greenville County Museum of Art: The Southern Collection, 95; Ben Windham (auth) Local man's painting takes viewers "down to the river", The Tuscaloosa News, 2/13/2000; plus others. *Mem:* Salmagundi Club; Southern Vt Art Ctr, Manchester; Portraits, Inc, NY. *Media:* Oil, Watercolor. *Publ:* Auth, Sizing up a portrait, 86 & The Italian lesson, 86, Artists Mag; Create a World Inside a Painting, Am Artist, 11/90. *Dealer:* Robert M Hicklin Jr Inc Spartanburg SC; Robert Wilson Galleries Nantucket MA. *Mailing Add:* 601 S St PO Box 159 Hoosick NY 12089

WILSON, HELENA CHAPELLIN WILSON
PHOTOGRAPHER
b Caracas, Venezuela. *Study:* Inst de Dibujo Tecnico y Arquitectura; Columbia Col, Chicago, BA, 76. *Work:* New Orleans Mus Art, La; Ill State Mus, Springfield; Art Inst Chicago, Mus Contemp Photog, Chicago, Ill; Galeria de Arte Nacional & Museo de Bellas Arts, Caracas, Venezuela. *Exhib:* Hecho en Venezuela, Mus Arte Contemp, Caracas, 78; solo exhibs, Marianne Deson Gallery, Chicago, Ill, 81, Hewlitt Gallery, Carnegie-Melon Univ, 83, Galeria de Art Nacional, Caracas, Venezuela, 90; Illinois Photographers 1985, Ill State Mus, Springfield, 85; Clarence John Laughlin Collection, New Orleans Mus Art, La, 89; Under the Spell of Dreams, Rachel Adler Gallery, NY, 93-94; Aldo Castillo Gallery, Chicago, 99 & 2001. *Pos:* Artist and designer, 60-; mem, comt on photog, Art Inst Chicago, currently; trustee, Columbia Col, Chicago, currently; mem, comt on acquisitions, Mus Contemp Photog, currently. *Awards:* Photography Award, Univ Iowa, 75. *Bibliog:* Hans Neumann (auth), Fotografias, El Nacional, Caracas, Venezuela, 7/29/90; rev, Art in Am, 7/94. *Publ:* Contribr, Women Photograph Men, William Morrow, 77; auth, Basic gum bichromate printing, Darkroom Techniques, 6/81; Out of the Darkroom (didactic mats), Art Inst Chicago, 95. *Dealer:* Rachel Adler Fine Art 1200 Broadway New York NY 10001; Castillo Gallery 233 Witturon Chicago IL 60610

WILSON, J KEITH
CURATOR
Study: Williams Coll, BA (Chinese studies); Univ Mich, MA (Far Eastern art); Princeton Univ, MFA (Chinese & Japanese art & archaeol). *Pos:* Cur Chinese art, Cleveland Mus Art, 1988-1996; head Far Eastern art & chief cur Asian art, Los Angeles County Mus, 1996-2006; assoc dir & cur ancient Chinese art, Freer Sackler Gallery, 2006-. *Teaching:* Vis research scholar archaeol, etymology & philology, Tokyo Univ. *Mailing Add:* Office Public Affairs & Marketing Freer & Sackler Art Gallery PO Box 37012 MRC 707 Washington DC 20013-7012

WILSON, JEAN S
MUSEUM DIRECTOR, HISTORIAN
b Lakeland, Fla. *Study:* Metrop State Col, Denver, Colo, BA, 79; Univ Denver, Colo, MA, 82. *Collection Arranged:* Personal Landscapes; Art Quilts and Wearable Art, FACET, 90; Third Wyoming Biennial, 89; Paper Innovations, Am Mus Asn, 87. *Pos:* Educ dept, Denver Art Mus, 81-82; asst cur, Colo Gallery Arts, 83-85, dir/cur, 85-92; exhib & educ dir, Foothills Art Ctr, Golden, Colo, 92-. *Mem:* Colo Art Educ Asn (currently, state bd); Am Asn Mus; Small Mus Asn. *Res:* Renaissance and early modern art. *Mailing Add:* 300 Remington St Apt 512 Fort Collins CO 80524

WILSON, JOHN DAVID
ADMINISTRATOR, ART DEALER
b Flint, Mich, Aug 30, 1934. *Study:* Mich State Univ, BA, 60; Univ Notre Dame, MA, 67. *Pos:* Dir, Lakeside Studio, formerly; pres, Chicago Int Art Exposition, currently; pres, Lakeside Group, Shanghai Int Art and Antique Exposition; Consultant, Art Caucasus, 2004. *Awards:* Chevalier De L'Ordre Des Arts et Des Lettres, City Milan, Milan CofC; Moscow Arts Award. *Bibliog:* David & Cecile Shapiro (coauth), Lakeside Studio: conserving the printmaking tradition, Art News, 3/77; Charlotte Moser (auth), John Wilson brings art world to Chicago, Chicago Sun-Times, 9-11/83; 20 people who changed Chicago, Chicago Mag (20th anniversary issue). *Mem:* Artist Union Republic of Ga (bd dir); The Cliff Dwellers Club; The Tavern Club. *Specialty:* Original graphics, old masters, modern and contemporary; ceramics

WILSON, JUNE
PAINTER, EDUCATOR
b Somerville, NJ, July 12, 1946. *Study:* Ithaca Coll, NY, 64-65; Monmouth Coll, West Long Branch, NJ, BA (hons), 68; Pratt Inst, Brooklyn, NY, MFA, 72. *Work:* The Newark Mus, NJ; Aldrich Mus Contemp Art, Ridgefield, Conn; Franklin Furnace, & Jewish Mus, NY; Art & Cult Ctr, Hollywood, Fla; Michael Grainger Collection, Tyler Mus, Tex; Prudential Ins Co, Newark, NJ; Johnson & Johnson, New Brunswick, NJ; XTO Energy, Fortworth, Tex. *Comn:* Lobby painting, Sheraton Meadowlands Hotel, NJ, 86; Weather Vanes, NJ Transit, Exchange Place Station, Jersey City, NJ, 99; Hyatt Regency, New Orleans, La, 2011. *Exhib:* Solo exhibs, Newark Mus, NJ, 90, Johnson & Johnson Hq, New Brunswick, NJ, 93, Seton Hall Univ Sch Law, Newark, 94, Mercer Co Coll, W Windsor, NJ, 95, Georgian Court Coll, Lakewood, NJ, 97 & Aljira at the Academy, Montclair, NJ, 2000, Brodsky Gallery, Princeton, NJ, 2009; Drawing into the 90's (catalog & tour), Laguna Gloria Mus, Austin, Tex, 93; Made to Order, The Alternative Mus, New York, 95; Colors, Contrasts, Cultures, Discovery Mus, Conn, 97; Paintings with an Edge, Hunterdon Mus, Clinton, NJ, 98, Gifts, 2004; New Am Talent 13, Jones Ctr, Austin, Tex, 98; Simon Gallery, Morristown, NJ, 2000; Michael Granger Collection, Tyler Mus, Tex, 2002; Art of Collecting Fine Art, Morris Mus, NJ, 2002; Reality & Artifice, NJ State Mus, Trenton, NJ, 2006-2010. *Collection Arranged:* The Punch Line: Humor in Art, Tweed Arts Group, Plainfield, NJ, 83; Urban Spirit, City Without Walls (co-cur with G Graupe-Pillard), Newark, NJ, 85; cur, Dolores Murasky Mem Show, The Guild, Island Heights, NJ, Aug 2010. *Teaching:* Adj asst prof, painting & drawing, Ocean Co Coll, Toms River, NJ, 76-; spec projs, NJ Sch Arts, Trenton, 98-2002; adj prof, Kean Univ, NJ, 73-76; instr printmaking, Monmouth Univ, NJ, 76-82. *Awards:* NJ State Coun Arts Fel, 81 & 85; Fel, Rutger's Ctr for Innovative Print & Paper, 2003; Fel (painting), NJ State Coun Arts, 2004. *Bibliog:* Robert Mahoney (auth), New York in Review, Arts Mag, 3/91; Barry Schwabsky (auth), Borrowing from Nature, NY Times, 1/18/98; Grace Graupe Pillard, Tasting Shape (video), June Wilson at the Brodsky Gallery, 2009. *Media:* Oil and Acrylic on Canvas, Wood, & Paper. *Publ:* New American Paintings No 69, The Open Studios Press, 2007; New American Paintings, Open Studios Press, 2009. *Mailing Add:* 47 Brandywine Way Middletown NJ 07748

WILSON, KAREN LEE
CONSULTANT
b Somerville, NJ, Apr 2, 1949. *Study:* Harvard Univ, AB, 71; Inst Fine Arts, NY Univ, MA, 73, PhD, 85. *Exhib:* Vanished Kingdoms of the Nile: The Rediscovery of Ancient Nubia, 92; Faces of Ancient Egypt, Smart Mus Art, 96-97; In the Presence of the Gods: Art from Ancient Sumer, Smart Mus Art, 97-98; Mary and Joseph Grimshaw Egyptian Gallery, 99; Persian Gallery, 2000; Treasures from the Royal Tombs of Ur, 2000-01; Edgar & Deborah Jannotta Mesopotamian Gallery, 2003. *Pos:* Cur & dir, Oriental Inst Mus, 88-96, dir, 96-2003; adminr cataloguer, Jewish Mus, New York, 82-83, coordr curatorial affairs, 84-86; res assoc, Oriental Inst, 88-; proj coordr, Kish Field Mus, 2004-. *Teaching:* Instr various courses, 90-2001. *Mem:* AAM; Am Oriental Soc; Archeol Inst Am; Coll Art Asn. *Publ:* Auth & ed, Mendes, ARCE, 82; Preliminary Report Excavations at Tell Genj, Sumer, 85; auth, Definition & Relative Chronology of the Jamdat Nasr Period, NY Univ, 85; Nippur: The Definition of a Mesopotamian Jamdat Nasr Assemblage, TAVO, 86; Oriental Institute Discoveries at Khorsabad, 95; The Temple Mound at Bismaya, in: Leaving No Stone Unturned: Essays on the Ancient Near East and Egypt in honor of Donald P Hansen, Erica Ehrenberg (ed), 279-299, Eisenbrauns, 2002; Bismaya Recovering the Lost City of Adab, 2012; and others. *Mailing Add:* Oriental Institute Museum 1155 E 58th St Chicago IL 60637

WILSON, KAY E
CURATOR, DIRECTOR
b Rockford, Ill. *Study:* Rockford Col, BA, 72; Art Inst Chicago, Collection Mgt, Cert, 88. *Exhib:* Art in Exile; Contemp Iraqi Art; Contemp Estonian Art. *Collection Arranged:* Jiri Anderle: The Grant Lawrence Collection, Grinnell Coll Print & Drawing Study Room, 97. *Pos:* Dir, Print & Drawing Study Room, Grinnell Col, 86-, Cur Art Collection. *Media:* Paper. *Publ:* Coauth, Jan Krejci: The Werksman Collection, Grinnell Col, 87. *Mailing Add:* Grinnell College Print and Drawing Study Room Grinnell IA 50112-0811

WILSON, MARC FRASER
CONSULTANT
b Akron, Ohio, Sept 12, 1941. *Study:* Yale Col, BA, 63; Case Western Univ, Cleveland Mus Art, 63-64; Yale Univ, MA, 67; Fel, Ford Found Mus Training Prog, Nelson Gallery-Atkins Mus, Kansas City, 67-69; Study Grant, Ford Found, Japan, Taiwan, Hong Kong, 69-71; Univ Kans, 68. *Pos:* Dept asst prints & drawings, Cleveland Mus Art, 64; translr & project consult, Nat Palace Mus, Taipei, Taiwan, 68-71; assoc cur Chinese Art, dept Oriental art, Nelson Gallery-Atkins Mus, 71-73, cur Oriental art, 73-82, Menefee D & Mary Louise Blackwell dir & chief exec officer, 82-2010; mem ad hoc comt, Munic Art Comn Urban Sculpture, 84-; mem, China Inst Am Adv Comt, 85-, Asia Soc Galleries Adv Comt, 85- & K C Planning Comt Sister City, Xian, China 86-; chmn works of art comt, Asn Art Mus Dirs, 86-88, arts & artifacts indemnity adv panel, Fedn Coun Arts & Humanities 86-89 & Am subcomt Mus Exchanges of CULCON, 86-88; Am panel, Joint Comt Japan-US Cult & Educ Coop, 86-88; indemnity panel, Washington, 93-. *Teaching:* Grad teaching asst, Dept Hist Art, Yale Univ, 65-66. *Mem:* Asn Art Mus Dirs (treas, trustee 1988-90, chmn works of art comt 1986-90); Missouri China Coun; Fed Coun Arts and Humanities (chmn arts and artifacts indemnity adv panel 1986-89, 1995-98). *Publ:* Auth, The Chinese painter and his vision, Apollo, No 97, 3/73; coauth, Friends of Wen Cheng-ming, 74; auth, Potter's choice, Am Craft, Vol 40, No 4, 8-9/80; coauth, Eight Dynasties of Chinese Painting, Ind Univ Press, 80; auth, Identification of the subject of an important scroll painting by Ma Yuan, Museum, 11/82

WILSON, MARTHA
MUSEUM DIRECTOR
b Philadelphia, Dec 18, 1974. *Study:* Wilmington Coll, BA (cum laude), 69; Dalhousie Univ, MA (Eng Lit), 71, Postgrad, 72. *Pos:* Asst to mng ed, Harry N Abrams, Inc, New York, 74-75; founder & dir, Franklin Furnace Archive, Inc, Brooklyn, NY, 76-. *Teaching:* Adj lectr, Nova Scotia Coll Art & Design, Halifax, Can, 72-74, Brooklyn Coll, 75-76, Sch Visual Arts, New York, 78, New Sch, New York, 93. *Awards:* Nat Endowment Arts Fel, 78 & 83; Gov's Award for Serv to Arts, Skowhegan Sch, 91; Bessie award for commitment to artists' freedom of expression, 92; Obie award for commitment to artists' freedom of expression, 92; Citation for Commitment to Principle of Freedom of Expression, Robert S Clark, Nathan Cummings, Joyce Mertz-Gilmore, Rockefeller & Andy Warhol Founds, 93; NY Found Arts Fel, Performance Art, 2001. *Mailing Add:* Franklin Furnace Archive Inc James E Davis Arts Bldg 80 Hanson Place Ste 301 Brooklyn NY 11217-1596

WILSON, MELISSA ANNE
SCULPTOR
b New Rochelle, NY, July 9, 1968. *Study:* Silvermine Sch Art, 86-89; Wooster Art Ctr, 87-90. *Hon Degrees:* Stanley Bleifield sculpture degree, 89-2000. *Work:* Lever House, New York, NY; New Britain Mus, Conn; Hillsberg Mus Collection, Indian Wells, Calif; Lever House Collection; Bleifield Collection. *Comn:* Georgetown Saloon Gallery, 98. *Exhib:* Waveny Barn Mus, New Canaan, Conn, 87, 88 & 89; All New Eng Show, 89 & 90; Pietrasanta, Italy, 89 & 90; Int Sculpture Show, Roxensteins, Helsingborg, Sweden, 90; Chicago Int Art Show, 90; Stanley Bleifield Asn of Fairfield, Lever House, NY, 90; Bliefield Sculpture Asn, 92; group show, Waveny Park Carriage Barn Mus, New Canaan, Conn, 92; Westport Art Ctr, 2007-2008. *Pos:* Art agent, Sandi River, 91-2007. *Teaching:* Var galleries. *Awards:* First in Show, Sandi Oliver Fine Art, Weston, Conn; Best Sculpture, Casa D'Oliver, Conn, 91 & 98 & 2004. *Bibliog:* Stanley Bleifield Asn, Fairfield County Sculptors. *Mem:* Int Sculpture Asn; Bleifield Sculpture Asn. *Media:* Bronze, Clay & Oil Painting. *Interests:* Running, Writing. *Publ:* Bleifield Sculpture Group Catalog Raissone, Bleifield, 92; Casa D' Oliver, CT, 2004. *Dealer:* Sandi Oliver Box 1203 Weston CT 06883. *Mailing Add:* c/o Sandi Oliver Fine Art PO Box 1203 Weston CT 06883

WILSON, MILLIE
CONCEPTUAL ARTIST
b Hot Springs, Ark, Nov 26, 1948. *Study:* Yale Summer Sch Music & Art; Univ Tex, Austin, BFA, 71; Univ Houston, MFA, 83. *Work:* San Francisco Mus Mod Art; Orange Co Art Mus; Hammer Mus Art, Univ S Calif; Henry Art Gallery, Seattle. *Comn:* Thresholds, Servales Found, Oporto, Port, 95. *Exhib:* Solo exhibs, Fauve Semblant: Peter (A Young Eng Girl), San Francisco Camerawork, 90, Sweet Thursday, Meyers, Bloom Gallery, Santa Monica, 91, Living in Someone Else's Paradise, New Langton Arts, San Francisco, 92, A Disturbing Emotional Coloring, White Columns, NY, 92, Wolf in the Garden, Ruth Bloom Gallery, Santa Monica, Calif, 93, Not a Serial Killer, Jose Freire Fine Art, NY, 94 & Monster Girls, Ruth Bloom Gallery, 95; Something Borrowed, Mus Fine Arts, Santa Fe, NMex, 95; Addressing the Century: 100 Yrs Art & Fashion, Hayward Gallery, London, 98; Cola, Hammer Mus, 2000; Laguna Art Mus, 2004; Univ of Va Mus, 2005; Threshold/Recent Am Sculpture, Serrabes Found, Oporto, Port; Showdown, Mak Ctr, Los Angeles. *Pos:* Reg fac, program art, Calif Inst Arts, 85-2007. *Teaching:* Fel drawing, Univ Houston, 81-83; asst prof painting, Univ Ill, Urbana-Champaign, 83-85; fac, Calif Inst Arts, 85-, fac develop grants, 86-2007. *Awards:* Nat Endowment Arts Fel, 93; Pollock-Drasner Found Grant, 96; Individual Artist Fel, Los Angeles Cult Affairs, 98. *Bibliog:* Tania Guha (auth), Disrupted borders, Time Out, London, 7/20/94-7/27/94; David A Greene (auth), A feast for the eyes, Los Angeles Reader, 7/29/94; PC Smith (auth), Millie Wilson at Jose Freire, Art in Am, 9/94; Whiteness, A Wayward Construction (catalog), 2003; Hair, Untangling A Social History (catalog), 2004; and others. *Mem:* Coll Art Asn. *Media:* New Genres, Conceptual. *Publ:* Facing the Finish (exhibition catalog), San Francisco Mus Mod Art, 91-92; Errors of Nature, 92; Longing & Belonging, Site Santa Fe, 95; Pipe, Pulp, Pony, Nothing Momements Proj, MOCA, Pac Design Ctr, Los Angeles, 2007. *Mailing Add:* Art Dept Calif Inst Arts 24700 McBean Valencia CA 91355

WILSON, PATRICK
PAINTER
b Redding, Calif, 1970. *Study:* Univ Calif, Davis, BA, 1993; Claremont Coll Grad Sch, MFA, 1995. *Exhib:* Drawn Conclusion, Riverside Art Mus, Calif, 1996; Art Auction 6, Long Beach Mus Art, Calif, 1997; Richard L Nelson Gallery, Univ Calif, Davis, 1998; Gabriel Stux Gallery, Dusseldorf, Ger, 1999; Maximal-Minimal, Feigen Contemp, New York, 2000; Florence Lynch Gallery, New York, 2001; solo exhibs, Susan Vielmetter Los Angeles Projects, Calif, 2004, Brian Gross Fine Art, San Francisco, 2004 & Fusebox, Washington, DC, 2005; Gyroscope, Hirshhorn Mus & Sculpture Garden, 2005. *Mailing Add:* c/o Brian Gross Fine Art 49 Geary St 5th Fl San Francisco CA 94108

WILSON, ROBERT
GRAPHIC ARTIST, DESIGNER
b Waco, Tex, 1941. *Study:* Univ Tex, Austin, 1959-62; Painting with George McNeil, Paris, France, 1962; Pratt Inst, NY, BFA, 1965; apprenticed to Paolo Soleri, Phoenix, Ariz, 1966; Calif Coll Arts & Crafts, Hon Dr, 1994. *Work:* Mus Mod Art, NY; Mus Mod Art, Paris, France; Australian Nat Gallery, Canberra; Stedelijk Mus, Amsterdam; Menil Collection, Houston; and others. *Exhib:* Solo Exhibs: include Inst Contemp Art, Boston, 1985; Paula Cooper Gallery, NY, 1993, 1994, 1996, 2000, & 2007; Galerie Biedermann, Munchen, Ger, 1994; Galerie Lehmann, Lausanne, Switz, 1996; Modernism, San Francisco, 1996; Fotouhi Cramer Gallery, East Hampton, NY, 1996; Robert Wilson, Mus Villa Stuck, Munich, 1997; Robert Wilson, Installation Galeria Luis Serpe, Lisboarte Contemporanea, Lisbon, Portugal, 1998; Hiram Butler Gallery, 1999; Galerie Fred Jahn, Munich, 2000; Reina Sofia Mus, Madrid, 2001; La Galerie des Galeries, Paris, 2002; Rena Bransten Gallery, San Francisco, 2004; Phillips de Parey & Co, NY, 2007; Joslyn Art Mus, Omaha, Nebr, 2008, Bernice Stienbaum Gallery, Miami, Fla, 2009; Palazzo Reale, Milan, Italy, 2009; Hydra School Proj, Hydra, Greece, 2009; Phoenix Hallen & Hamburger Kunsthalle, Hamburger, Germany, 2009; Group exhibs, Whitney Biennial, Whitney Mus Am Art, 1980, 1997; An Int Survey of Contemp Painting & Sculpture Mus Mod Art, NY, 1984, New Works on Paper 3, 1985, Special Relationships in Video, 1985; The New Figure, Birmingham Mus Art, 1985; High Style, Whitney Mus Am Art, 1985; Passge de L'image Traveling Exhib, Mus Nat d'Art Mod, Paris, 1991; Die Muse?, Galerie Thaddaeus Ropac, 1995; Alice, Brooklyn Acad Music, 1995; Breaking the Frame, The Drawing Legion, Cedar Rapids, Iowa, 1995; Prints: To Benefit the Found for Contemp Performance Arts, Brooke Alexander, NY, 1995; Link, Gerald Peters Gallery, Dallas, Tex, 1996; Graphit Auf Papier, Galerie Thomas Von Lintel, Munich, 1997; Tableaux Contemp Art Mus, Houston, Tex, 1997; Paine Webber Art Gallery, NY City, 1999; Curt Marcus Gallery, NY, 2000; Contemp Arts Mus, Houston, 2001; Exit Art, NY, 2002; Cooper-Hewitt Nat Design Mus, NY City, 2004; Annemarie Verna Galerie, Zurich, Switzerland, 2005; The Third Mind: Am Artists Contemplate Asia, 1860-1989, Guggenheim Mus Art, New York, 2009; Scene-Quadro Caporossi, Kantor, Santasangre, Wilch, La nuova Pesa Cenne for Contemp Art, Rome, Italy, 2010. *Pos:* Artistic dir, Byrd Hoffman Found, 1970-. *Awards:* First Prize, Venice Biennale 45th Int Art Exhib, 1993; Tadeusz Kantor Prize, Crakow, Poland, 1997; Harvard Excellence in Design, Harvard Design Sch, Cambridge, Mass, 1998; Pushkin Prize, Taganka Theater, Moscow, 1999; Wilhelm Hansen Honorable Prize, Copenhagen, 1999; Nat Design Award, Smithsonian Inst, Nat Design Mus, 2001; Thomas Jefferson Award, Am Inst Architects, Houston, 2002; Trophée des Arts Gala 2009, French Inst Alliance Française, New York, 2009. *Bibliog:* Howard Brookner (dir), A Minute with Bob Wilson (film), BBC, London, 1985; Bice Curiger (ed), Collaboration Robert Wilson Parkett, 1988; Mel Gussow (auth), Conjuring works of art that live mostly in memory, NY Times, 10/22/1998. *Mem:* Hon mem Am Repertory Theater; PEN Am Ctr; Dramatist Guild; trustee Nat Int Music Theater; Soc des Auteurs et Compositeurs Dramatiques; Hon mem Am Acad Arts and Letters. *Publ:* Contribr, Swan Song (play), Kammerspiele Theater, Munich, 1990; Konig Lear (play), Schauspiel, Frankfurt, 1990; The Black Rider: The Casting of the Magic Bullets (play), Theatre Musical de Paris, Le Chatelet; When We Dead Awake (play), Am Repertory Theatre, Boston, 1991. *Dealer:* Paula Cooper Gallery 534 W 21st St New York NY 10011. *Mailing Add:* c/o Paula Cooper Gallery 534 W 21st St New York NY 10011

WILSON, STEVE
MUSEUM DIRECTOR
Study: Univ Southern Calif, BFA; Nat Theatre Conservatory, Denver, MFA in acting. *Pos:* artist-in-residence Cherry Creek and Denver Pub Sch Dists; Denver Sch Arts; exec artistic dir, acting dir, Mizel Ctr for Arts and Cult; dir, Wolf Theatre Acad. *Teaching:* Teacher, performing arts chmn St. Mary's Acad, Colo; fac mem, Wolf Theatre Acad and Stage Eleven. *Mailing Add:* Mizel Ctr Arts and Cult 350 S Dahlia St Denver CO 80246

WILSON, TOM MUIR
DESIGNER
b Bellaire, Ohio, Dec 6, 1930. *Study:* WVa Inst Technol; Cranbrook Acad Art, BFA; Rochester Inst Technol, MFA. *Exhib:* Solo exhibs, Rochester, NY & Wheeling, WVa, 57, 59 & 61; Boston Art Festival, 61; Photog Exhib, George Eastman House, Rochester, 63; Western NY Ann, Buffalo, 63 & 64; Art of Two Cities, Minneapolis, 65; and others. *Pos:* Designer exhib galleries, George Eastman House Mus Photog, 61-62; freelance photogr & graphic designer, New York, Rochester & Minneapolis, 61-. *Teaching:* Prof art & instr photog & graphic design, Minneapolis Sch Art, formerly; instr photog, Rochester Inst Technol, assoc prof photog arts, 77-; instr sculpture & design, Nazareth Col, Rochester. *Awards:* Award for Sculpture, Art Inst Am Inst Architects, 56; Prize, Philadelphia Print Club, 61. *Media:* Graphic. *Mailing Add:* 6776 Warboys Rd Byron NY 14422

WILSON, WALLACE
PHOTOGRAPHER, EDUCATOR
b Dallas, Tex, June 10, 1947. *Study:* Univ Tex, Austin, BA, 70; pvt study with Ralph Eugene Meatyeard, Lexington, Ky, 71-72; Art Inst Chicago, MFA, 75. *Work:* Mus Mod Art, NY; Art Inst Chicago; Baltimore Mus Art, Md; Bibliotheque Nationale, Paris; Brooklyn Mus, NY. *Exhib:* Solo exhibs, Baltimore Mus Art, 76, OK Harris, NY, 77 & 87, Photogalerie Lange-Irschl, Munich, WGer, 79, Marcuse Pfeifer Gallery, NY, 87 & 89, The Tartt Gallery, Washington, DC, 87, 90 & 92, The Photographers Gallery, London, 89, Robert Klein Gallery, Boston, 91, Southeast Mus Photog, Daytona Beach, Fla, 93. *Teaching:* Asst prof photog & design, Univ Del, 75-79; prof art & contemp criticism, Univ Fla, 79-94; prof & chair art dept, Univ SFla, Tampa, 94-. *Awards:* Individual Artists Fel, State Fla, 82 & 88. *Bibliog:* Fred McDarrah (auth), Voice Choices, Village Voice, 10/10/77; Vince Aletti (auth), Voice Choices, Village Voice, 11/10/87 & 12/12/89; Pamela Kessler (auth), The Washington Post, 9/19/89. *Mem:* Soc Photog Educ. *Publ:* Contribr, Camera, Bucher Press, Zurich, Switz, 73; Fifteen Photographs in Color, Mancini Gallery, 78; Artwords and Bookworks, Los Angeles Inst Contemp Art, 78; Victims of Paradox, by Alison Nordstrom, Southeast Mus Photog, 92. *Dealer:* The Tartt Gallery Washington DC. *Mailing Add:* 1725 Ryan Dr Lutz FL 33549

WILSON-HAMMOND, CHARLOTTE
VISUAL ARTIST, PAINTER
b Montreal, Que, Nov 19, 1941. *Study:* Ind Univ, 64-65; 3 schs of art, Toronto, 66-68; Royal Canadian Acad Arts, 2006. *Work:* Art Gallery NS & Royal Trust Corp, Halifax; Confederation Ctr Arts, Charlottetown, PEI; Shell Energy Sources Can, Calgary, Alta; Norcen Energy Corp, Toronto; Dalhousie Art Gallery, St Mary's Univ Art Gallery, Nova Scotia; St Francis Xavier Univ Art Gallery, Nova Scotia; Mt St Vincent Art Gallery, Nova Scotia. *Comn:* Drawings for feature film, Life Classes, William MacGillivrey, producer, 87. *Exhib:* Osaka World's Fair, Japan, 79; Confederation Ctr Arts, Charlottetown, PEI, 80-81; Centre Art Tapes, Halifax, 88; Naked/Nude, A Twenty Yr Survey, Art Gallery NS, 90; Intimate Communion, St Marys Art Gallery, 94; Millenium Flag Show, Art Gallery of Nova Scotia, Halifax, Nova Scotia, 2000; VANS Eastern Shore, Alderney Gate Gallery, Dartmouth, Nova Scotia, 2000; Cats: an exibition, Art Gallery of Nova Scotia, Halifax, Nova Scotia, 2004; States of Being, Dalhousie Art Gallery, Halifax, Nova Scotia, 2005; Solo exibs: rtü, Arts Place, Annapolis Royal, Nova Scotia, 2000 (spring), Saint Frances Xavier Univ Art Gallery, Nova Scotia, 2000 (fall), Alderney Gate Gallery, Nova Scotia, 2001 (winter); Landscape with Thighs, Art Gallery of Nova Scotia, Halifax, Nova Scotia, 2002; In/finite, Zwickers Gallery, Halifax, Nova Scotia, 2004, Inverness Ctr for the Arts, Inverness, Nova Scotia, 2005, ARTsPLACE, Annapolis Royal, Nova Scotia, 2006; Craig Gallery, Dartmouth, Nova Scotia, 2009; Anna Leon Owens Gallery, NCAD, HFX, 2009; St Mary's Univ Art Gallery, Halifax, 2011. *Pos:* Bd mem, NS Col Arts & Design, Halifax, 87-; bd dir, Vis Art Copyright Inc; bd govs, Nova Scotia College of Art & Design, currently; past chair, Nova Scotia Talent Trust; bd, Cultural Federations NS. *Teaching:* Artist-in-residence, Holland Col, PEI, 80. *Awards:* NS Dept Cult Grant, 76, 77, 83, 85, 89, 94 & 95; Can Coun Visiting Artists Grant, 79-80; Cultural Life Award, NS Dept Cult, 81; Can Coun Explorations Grant, 85; Can Cou A Grant, 98; Portia White Award, 2004. *Bibliog:* Maria Tippett (auth), Three Centuries of Canadian Women Artists, Penguin, 10/92; The Creators, WTN Television, 94; review, Arts Atlantic, 95. *Mem:* Can Artists Representation; Visual Arts NS (chmn, 78-79, bd); Women Arts (organizer, 80-); Can Conf Arts-Coun of Canadians; NS Coll Art & Design (life mem); Royan Canadians Acad of the Arts; NS Talent Trust; Cult Fedn NS (bd). *Media:* Oil, Conte, Multimedia, Digital Images. *Publ:* By a Lady, Three Centuries of Canadian Art, Maria Tippet, Viking. *Dealer:* The Artist 33 Beach Road Clam HBR NS BOJ 1YO

WILTRAUT, DOUGLAS SCOTT
PAINTER
b Allentown, Pa, July 12, 1951. *Study:* Kutztown Univ, Pa, BFA (painting), 73. *Work:* Philip & Muriel Berman Mus Art, Collegeville, Pa; Yale Law Sch Libr, New Haven, Conn; Binney & Smith Corp, Easton, Pa; Pentamation Corp, Bethlehem, Pa; Pa Dept Educ, Harrisburg; Raymond Holland Collection; Jack Richeson Collection; Sacred Heart Hosp, Allentown, Pa. *Comn:* Portrait, Myres McDougal, Yale Law Sch, New Haven, Conn, 76; portrait, Philip I Berman, chmn bd trustees, Philadelphia Mus Art, 80; Still Life, Lehigh Valley Hospital, 2001-. *Exhib:* Nat Acad Design, 88; Inaugural Exhib, Philip & Muriel Berman Mus Art, Collegeville, Pa, 90; Am Watercolor Soc, 93 & 2004-2005 & 2007; The Face of Am: Contemp Portraits in Watercolor, Arts Guild Old Forge, NY, 94; Aim for Arts Int Exhib, Vancouver, Can, 2000; Butler Am Art, 2001 & 2003-2004; plus others. *Collection Arranged:* Philip & Muriel Berman Collection, Raymond Holland Collection, Jack Richeson Collection. *Awards:* Ralph Fabri Medal, 72nd & 74th Ann Exhibs, Allied Artists Am, 85-87; Butler Inst Am Art Award, 50th Anniversary Midyr, 86; Gold Medal Hon, 38th Ann Knickerbocker Artists, 88; Rouse Gold Medallion, Adirondacks Nat Exchange Am Watercolors, 99; Crest Medal, Philadelphia Watercolor Soc, 99; Trails & Streams Medal, Adirondacks, Nat Exhib Am Watercolors, 2000; Keystone Medallion, Pa Watercolor Soc 25th Ann Exhib, 2004; Sylan Grouse Guild Medal, Pa Watercolor Soc, 2002; Rothermel Award, Kutztown Univ Alumni Assoc; Gerry Lenfest Award for Am Art, NSPC & A, 2004. *Bibliog:* Ralph Fabri (auth), Youngest medal winner, Today's Art Mag, 75; Valerie R Rivers (auth), Douglas Wiltraut, Am Artist Mag, 88; Walter Garver (auth), Enrich the familiar with egg tempera, Artist's Mag, 91; Marilyn Fox (auth) Douglas Wiltraut, Lehigh Valley Mag, 98; Cathy Bennett (auth), A Most Versatile Paint, Artist Mag, 2004; plus others. *Mem:* Nat Soc Painters Casein & Acrylic (dir, 77-86, exhib chmn, 87-90 & pres, 89-); Allied Artists Am; Audubon Artists Inc (exhib chmn, 88-90 & sr vpres, 89-92); Knickerbocker Artists; Pa Watercolor Soc; Philadelphia Watercolor Soc; Salmagundi Club (hon); Am Watercolor Soc; Hudson Valley Art Asn. *Media:* Egg Tempera, Watercolor. *Publ:* Contribr & illusr, How to Discover Your Personal Painting Style, David P Richards (auth), N Light Bks; Best of Acrylic Paintings, Alfred M Duca & Lynn Loscutoff (eds), Rockport Publ; auth, article, Ultra realism in the unorthodox way, Palette Talk, 79; illusr, cover, Prevention Mag, Rodale Press, 83; contribr & illusr, The Artist Illustrated Encyl, Phil Metzger (auth), N Light Bks; coauth (with Richard Meryman), Andrew Wyeth: A secret life, rev, Am Artist Mag, 97; auth, Crack open your shell, Artists Mag, 2005; Shedding light on a marvelous medium that has been kept in the shadows, Artists Mag, 2005; contrib, My Friends, Today's Great Masters, Jack Richeson (auth). *Dealer:* Somerville Manning Gallery Greenville DE. *Mailing Add:* 969 Catasauqua Rd Whitehall PA 18052

WIMAN, BILL
PAINTER, EDUCATOR
b Roscoe, Tex, Nov 12, 1940. *Study:* E Tex State Univ, BS, 62; Univ Fla, MFA, 64. *Work:* Butler Inst Am Art, Youngstown, Ohio; Okla Art Ctr, Oklahoma City; San Antonio Mus Art; AT&T, New York; Mus Arts & Sci, Evansville, Ind. *Exhib:* Real, Really Real, Super Real, San Antonio Mus Art, 81; New Works, Laguna Gloria Art Mus, Austin, 85; one person exhib, Adams-Middleton Gallery, Dallas, 85, 90; Five Figurative Painters, Abilene Fine Arts Mus, 86; Accurate Depictions? Figurative Realist Paintings, Bowling Green State Univ, 86; Waco Art Center, 2002; 511 Gallery, NYC, 2005; Davis Gallery, Austin, Tex, 2007. *Teaching:* Instr, Frank Phillips Col, 64-66; asst prof painting, E Tex State Univ, 66-71; guest prof, Central Washington State Univ, fall 70; prof, Murray State Univ, 71-72; prof painting, Univ Tex, Austin, 72-2005. *Awards:* Ford Found Grant, 79; Teaching Excellence Award, Univ Texas, 87; Univ Res Inst Grant, Univ Texas, 89. *Bibliog:* 50 Texas Artists: A Critical Selection, Chronicle Books, 86; articles, Arts Mag, 10/85 & ArtNews, 5/86. *Media:* Watercolor. *Dealer:* Davis Gallery Austin TX

WIMBERLEY, FRANK WALDEN
PAINTER, COLLAGE ARTIST
b Pleasantville, NJ, Aug 31, 1926. *Study:* Howard Univ, with Lois M Jones, James Wells & James Porter. *Work:* Mus Mod Art, Metrop Mus, NY; Art Inst Chicago; Pitney Bowes, Stamford, Conn; Islip Art Mus, East Islip, NY; Brooklyn Union Community Gallery, Brooklyn, NY. *Comn:* Clearly, Gottlieb, Steen & Hamilton, NY, 86; Crown Plaza Hotel, E Elmhurst, NY, 89; Bruce Llewellyn, Coca Cola Bottling, Philadelphia, 91; Don Anderson, Time Warner, NY, 92. *Exhib:* Albright-Knox, Buffalo, NY, 86; Jamaica Arts Ctr, Jamaica, NY, 92; Brooklyn Union Community Gallery, NY, 92; Russel Sage Col, Albany, NY, 93; Adelphi Univ, Garden City, NY, 94; Gallery Authentique, Roslyn, NY, 94; Cinque Gallery, NY, 94; Arlene Bujese Gallery, East Hampton, NY, 94; From Here to There, June Kelly Gallery, NY, 2007. *Awards:* Best Work on Paper, 79, Best Abstract, 83, Best Mixed Media, 87, The Guild, NY. *Mem:* Guild Hall, East Hampton, NY. *Media:* Collage. *Dealer:* Arlene Bujese Gallery East Hampton, NY; June Kelly Gallery 591 Broadway New York NY. *Mailing Add:* 99-11 35th Ave Flushing NY 11368-1834

WIMMER, GAYLE
SCULPTOR, EDUCATOR
b Pittsburgh, Pa, Oct 2, 1943. *Study:* Pratt Inst, Brooklyn, NY, BFA, 67; Tyler Sch Art, Philadelphia, Pa, MFA, 70; Acad Fine Art, Warsaw, Poland, with Wojclech Sadley, 71. *Work:* Cent Mus Textiles, Lodz, Poland; Stedman Gallery, Rutgers Univ, Camden, NJ; Nat Mus Mod Art, Sofia, Bulgaria; Nelson Ctr Mus Art, Tempe, Ariz; Arrowmont Sch, Gatlinburg, Tenn. *Comn:* US Nat Park Serv, Harper's Ferry, WVa, 77; Nat Steel Corp Serv Ctr, Wayne, NJ, 77; Pittsburgh Glove Mfg Co, Pa, 82; Roda Machine S A, Ticino, Switz, 86; Ctr for English as a Second Language, Tucson, Ariz, 89. *Exhib:* Solo exhibs, Annenberg Ctr, Philadelphia, 82, Mandell Theatre, Philadelphia, 83, Galerie Rzezby, Warsaw, Poland, 86, Galerie Faust, Geneva, Switz, 86 Am Cult Ctrs, Jerusalem & Tel Aviv, Israel, 88, Univ Mus Art, Tucson, Ariz, 89, Allersnaweg Castle, The Neth, 94, Women of the Book, The Finegood Gallery, Los Angeles, 97 & Int Biennial of Textile Art, Cite des Arts, Paris, France, 98; Ariz Biennial, Tucson Mus Art, Ariz, 88, 92 & 97; Contemp Ariz Textiles, Ariz State Univ Mus Art, Tempe, 91; Black & White, Ariz Mus Youth, Mesa, 92; 2eme Biennale Int Tapisserie Contemp, Beauvais, France, 96. *Collection Arranged:* Head curator, Contemp Polish Fiber Art, Mus Ein Harod, Israel, 91; cur, contemp Israeli Textile Art, Lodz, Poland, 93. *Teaching:* Lectr textile art, Hunter Col, NY, 72-77; instr fiber sculpture, The New Sch, NY, 73-77; prof art & initiator Fiber Prog, Sch Art, Univ Ariz, Tucson, 77-. *Awards:* Individual Artist's Grant, Nat Endowment Arts, 73; Grant Research in Poland, Int Research & Exchanges Bd, New York, 82, 82-83, 99; Fulbright Fel, Artist-in-Residence, Israel, 87-88; Visual Artists' Fel, Tucson/Pima Arts Coun, Ariz, 90, 99. *Bibliog:* Irena Huml (auth), The Sphere of Time-Memory Transience: Gayle Wimmer, Projekt Mag, 2/91; Suzanne McCormick (auth), The Woven Word, Ariz Daily Star, 5/11/92. *Mem:* Textile Soc Am; Fulbright Asn. *Media:* Mixed Media, Fiber. *Publ:* Auth, Seasonal Marks, 10-11/84 & Polish Textile Art: Photorealism in the second generation, 2-3/86, Am Craft Mag; Contemporary Polish fiber (essay), Modan Publ House Ltd, Tel Aviv, Israel, 91; Contemporary Israeli fiber art (essay), Cent Mus Textiles, Lodz, Poland, 93. *Mailing Add:* Schenley Gardens #516 3890 Bigelow Blvd Pittsburgh PA 15213

WIND, DINA
SCULPTOR
b Haifa, Israel, Jan 15, 1938; US citizen. *Study:* Hebrew Univ, Jerusalem, BA, 61; Barnes Found, Merion, Pa, cert art appreciation, 72; Univ Pa, MA, 74. *Work:* Field Assocs, Tokyo, Japan; Hechinger Collection, Landover, Md; Interdisciplinary Ctr, Herzlia, Israel; Morgan Lewis & Bockius & Venturi Scott Brown & Assocs, Philadelphia. *Exhib:* Scatterpins (sculpture), Nexus Gallery, Philadelphia, 96; Chain Reactions, Viridian Gallery, NY, 97; Art of the State: Penn '97, State Mus Pa, Harrisburg, 97; Sculptors' Terrain, Philadelphia Sculptors Washington Square, Washington, DC, 98; Philadelphia Sculptors: a Group Exhibition, Grounds for Sculptor, Hamilton, NJ, 98. *Pos:* Bd mem & comn chmn, Fleisher Art Mem, 91-; assocs adv bd, Philadelphia Mus Art, 95-; bd mem, treas, Nexus-Found Today's Art, 96-. *Awards:* Merit Award Sculpture, Visual Arts Exhib, Three Rivers Art Festival, 98. *Bibliog:* Alexandra Shaw (auth), Dina Wind - Viridian Gallery, Manhattan Arts, 1/89; Diana Roberts (auth), Dina Wind breaking new ground, Manhattan Arts, 3-4/92; Ann Sargent Wooster (auth), Dina Wind - metal sculpture, Mid-Career Catalogue, 97. *Media:* Metal. *Dealer:* Contemp Artists Services 560 Broadway No 206 New York NY 10012. *Mailing Add:* 1041 Waverly Rd Gladwyne PA 19035

WINFIELD, RODNEY M
EDUCATOR
b New York, NY, Feb 6, 1925. *Study:* Univ Miami, Sch Music, Coral Gables, Fla, 42-43; Cooper Union, 43-45; Atlier 17of William Stanley Hayter, New York, 45-46; Wash Univ, St Louis, 70-71; Maryville Univ, St Louis, Mo, 92-93. *Work:* Nat Basilica of the Little Flower, San Antonio, Tex, Stained glass windows 52-2009, Shaare Zedek, St Louis, First 3D windows in USA churches, 53-54, Keileth Israel, Kansas City, Mo, Tabernacle doors baked enamel on gold plated background, 58-59, Temple Israel, Ladue, Mo, 3D sculptured wall of wood, steel, bronze, Arch HOK 59-60, Our Lady of Snows, 4 cast bronze chapel doors, altar & facade mosaics, Arch R Cummings 59-60, St Louis Univ Hosp Chapel, Christ the Crucified King windows & altar, 83-87, Wash Nat Cathedral, The Space Window, 70-72, Grace Cathedral, San Francisco, United Nations Brotherhood Man plaque, Original concept by Meri Jaye & Assoc Commissioned by Ralph K Davis, 65, Christ the King Church, Littel Rock, Ark, round silver & brass repousse alter piece, 69, 2008. *Exhib:* Solo exhibs, Galerie Creuze, Paris, 50, Martin Schweig Gallery, St Louis, Craft Alliance, St Louis, Mo, 80, Soroban Gallery, Wellfleet, Mass, 86, Matrix Gallery, Provincetown, Mass, 94, Fresno Art Mus, 95; Pope Pius Libr, St Louis Univ; Pallette Bleau, Paris; City Art Mus, St Louis. *Pos:* Stained glass designer, Emil Frei Assocs, St Louis, 53-; designer, Winfield Jewelry, St Louis, 70-. *Teaching:* Prof emer, Maryville Univ, St Louis, 64-90. *Awards:* Outstanding Educators of Am, Washington, DC, 74-75; Outstanding Tchr Award, Marysville Univ, 90; Teaching Excellence & Campus Leadership Award, Sears-Roebuck Found, 90. *Media:* Acrylic; Stained Glass, Brass and Silver Repousse. *Dealer:* Winfield Gallery Dolores between Ocean & 7th Carmel CA 93921. *Mailing Add:* 3483 Ocean Ave Carmel CA 93923

WINGATE, GEORGE B
PAINTER
b Mt Holly, NJ, Oct 13, 1941. *Study:* Univ Rochester, BA, 63; Syracuse Univ Sch Archit, 65; New Sch, with Henry Pearson, 72-76; Art Students League, with Frank Mason, 73-78; Vt Col, MFA, 93 with Will Barnet. *Work:* Everson Mus; Mus City New York. *Exhib:* Butler Art Inst Ann, 80 & 83; Foxhall Gallery, Washington, DC, 82-; solo exhibs, Everson Mus, 82, Katonah Gallery, NY, 83 & John Pence Gallery, San Francisco, 83; Painting NY, Mus City NY, 83; New York City Anthology, Grace Borgenicht Gallery, 88; Century Asn, NY, 90; Cooley Gallery, Old Lyme, Conn, 90-95; Nat Acad, 94. *Teaching:* Instr drawing, Parsons Sch Design, NY, 85-88; instr printmaking & drawing, Gordon Col, 89-2001. *Awards:* Emil Carlsen Prize for Best Still Life, 173rd Ann Exhib, Nat Acad; Emil Carlsen Prize 179th Annual Exhib, Nat Acad, 2004. *Bibliog:* Gordon Muck (auth), Wingate's Cazenovia, Syracuse Post Standard, 9/15/80; Vivien Raynor (auth), article, NY Times, 10/16/83; Stephen Doherty (auth), article, Am Artist Mag, 10/83; Bruce Herman Image Mag Looking again, The Art of George Wingate, Fall 2004. *Mem:* Art Students League; CIVA. *Media:* Oil, Sculpture. *Publ:* The World Below the Window A Poem by William Jay Smith; Stone House Press, Morris Gelfand (pub), 98; Broadside Illustrated by George Wingate; Paintings by George Wingate poems by Mark Stevick: The language of Objects, Gordon College, 99. *Mailing Add:* 72 Dodges Row Wenham MA 01984

WINGO, MICHAEL B
PAINTER, DRAFTSMAN
b Los Angeles, Calif, Nov 21, 1944. *Study:* Art Ctr Coll Design, 60-62; Claremont McKenna Coll, BA, 64; Otis Art Inst (scholar), BFA, 65, MFA, 67. *Work:* Santa Barbara Mus Art, Calif; Oakland Mus, Calif; Manatt, Phelps, Rothenberg & Phillips, Los Angeles; Security Pac Nat Bank, Los Angeles; IBM, Crocker Ctr, Los Angeles; Munger, Tolles & Olsen, Los Angeles; and numerous pvt collections. *Exhib:* Solo exhibs, Santa Barbara Mus Art, 70, Newport Harbor Art Mus, Newport Beach, 76, Turnbull Lutjeans Kogan Gallery, Costa Mesa, 83, Janet Steinberg Gallery, San Francisco, 83 & Terry DeLapp Gallery, Los Angeles, 84, Resende Ctr, Porto Portugal, 2001, Townsend Gallery, Los Angeles, (Cache Contemp), 2005, Gallery KM, Santa Monica, 2011; Art & Archit Tour, Los Angeles Co Mus Art, 85; New Art: Paintings from NY, Tex, Calif, Laguna Gloria Art Mus, Austin, Tex, 89; Feitelson, Artist & Teacher, Long Beach City Coll, 89; Contemp Abstractions, Weingart Ctr, Occidental Coll, 90; LA Current: Armand Hammer Mus Rental & Sales Gallery, Los Angeles; The New Minimalism, Gensler, Santa Monica, Calif, 2000; Flix, Ricon Gallery, Dublin, Ireland, 2003; Death, Arts & Consciousness Gallery, John F Kennedy Univ, Berkeley, Calif, 2004. *Pos:* vis artist, School Fine Arts, Porto, Portugal, 2001. *Teaching:* Instr painting & drawing, Pasadena Art Mus, 68-72; guest lectr, San Francisco Art Inst, 84 & vis artist, 87; instr drawing & painting, Otis Art Inst, Parsons Sch Design, Los Angeles, 85-95; inaugural fac, Calif State Summer Sch Arts, 87; vis lectr, Royal Academy Art, London, 2001. *Awards:* Visual Artists Fel Grant in Painting, Nat Endowment Art, 89-90; Who's Who in the West, 23rd ed, Marquis Who's Who, 91; Individual Support Grant in Painting, Adolph & Esther Gottlieb Found, 92. *Bibliog:* Fidel Danieli (Monogr), Los Angeles Valley Coll Art Gallery, 85; Joseph Mugnaini (auth), Expressive Drawing Through the Schematic Approach, Davis, 88; Les Krantz (ed), The California Art Review, Am References Inc, 88; Mark Van Proyen (auth), Dissonant Abstractions Catalogue, San Jose Inst of Contemp Art, 86; Henry T Hopkins (auth), California Painters: New Work, Chronicle Bks, San Francisco, page 7, 89; Michael Wingo Catalogue Essay, Resende Center, 2001; Lyn Kienholz (auth), Encyclopedia of the Art of Southern California, Calif Int Arts Found, 2009; Leah Ollman (auth) Review, Los Angeles Times, 2011. *Media:* Oil. *Publ:* Mark Van Proyen (auth), Artweek; Review, Vol 15, No 36, 10/27/84; Debra Koppman (auth), Artweek: Previews, Vol 35, No 6, 7-8/2004; Mark Van Proyen (auth), Art in America Reviews, 11/2005. *Dealer:* Gallery KM 2903 Santa Monica CA 90404. *Mailing Add:* Gallery KM 2903 Santa Monica Santa Monica CA 90404

WINIARSKI, DEBORAH
PAINTER, EDUCATOR
b Ft Meade, Md, Dec 22, 1959. *Study:* Queens Coll, Flushing, NY, MS, 95; Arte Sch Art & Photography, Florence, Italy, 2001; Art Students League NY, 2003. *Exhib:* Solo Exhibs: St Peter's Church, New York, 2009; Small Works, 27th Ann, 80 Wash Sq E Galleries, NY, 2004; Sources, Int Group Exhib, Roseline Koener Atelier, Westhampton, NY, 2005; Monmouth Festival Arts, NJ, 2006; Summer Invitational, Denise Bibro Fine Art, NY, 2006; 18th Nat Juried Exhib, Viridian Artists Inc, New York, 2007; Accrochage, New Artists at Kouros Gallery, New York, 2007; Accrochage New and Established Talent, Kouros Gallery, NY, 2008; Summer Exhib, Kouros Gallery, New York, 2009; Accrochage 2010, Kouros Gallery, New York, 2010; Winter Salon 2010-2011m Denise Bibro Fine Art Inc, NY, 2010-2011; Color Speaks: Five Artists from the Art Students Leagueof NY, Heather James Fine Art, Palm Desert, Calif & Jackson, Wyo, 2011; Wax: Contemporary Encaustic Works, Pajaro Arts Council, Watsonville, Calif, 2012; The Wax Book: Altered, Repurposed, Remade, Truro Ctr Arts at Castle Hill, 2012; Truro Ctr Arts at Castle Hill, Truro, Mass, 2013; Red, A Gallery, Provincetown, Mass, 2013; Instructors Exhib, 7th Internat Encaustic Conf, The Schoolhouse Gallery, Provincetown, Mass, 2013; WAXING, Denise Bibro Fine Art, NY, 2014; FAR & WIDE, 6th Ann Woodstock Regional, Woodstock Artists Assoc and Mus, Woodstock, NY, 2014; BIG BAD WAX, Nat Juried Encaustic Exhib, Mount Dora Ctr for the Arts, Mount Dora, Fla, 2014; Spring Group Exhib, Broadhurst Gallery, Pinehurst, NC, 2015; One + One, A gallery Art, Provincetown, Mass, 2015. *Collection Arranged:* Curator: Casting Shadows: Work in Dimension and Relief, Julie Heller East, Provincetown, Mass, 2015. *Pos:* Featured Artworks Editor, ProWax Jour; Residencies: The Studios at Key West, Key West, Fla, 2014. *Teaching:* Instr, Mixed Media, Collage, Painting, Dimensional Art, Art Students League NY, 2003-2004; instr, Contemporary Uses of Wax and Encaustic, Encaustic Monotypes Printmaking, Encaustic in Three Dimensions, Art Students League New York, 2009-Present; instr, Beginning Encaustic, Truro Ctr Arts at Castlehill, Truro, Mass, 2013-Present; Presenter: Encaustic Painting Basics, Int Encaustic Conf, Provincetown, Mass, 2013-Present. *Awards:* Painting Award, Annual Concours, ASL of NY, 2004. *Bibliog:* Maureen Mullarkey (auth), Winter Salon 2010-2011, New York's Review of Culture, Vol 3 Issue 1, Jan 2011; Katy Niner (auth), Art League Shows Off Some of its True Colors (reveiw), Jackson Hole News & Guide, 6/29/12. *Mem:* Art Students League of NY; NY Artists Equity Asn Inc; Artists Fel Inc. *Media:* Encaustic, Mixed Media, Acrylic. *Publ:* Contribr, Broadhurst Gallery Artists, 2005; contribr, Linea, Vol 9, No 2, fall/winter 2005, 21; contribr, A Juried Selection of International Artists, Studio Visit Mag, The Open Studio Press, Vol 3, 2008; Nancy Natale (ed), The Wax Book: Altered, Repurposed, Remade (catalog, curator Supria Karmaker), 2012; The Studio Project: Deborah Winiarski, Online Journal of the Art Students League of NY, 2013; Video: Deoborah Winiarski: RED at a Gallery, 2013; contribr, A Juried Selection of International Artists, Studio Visit Mag, The Open Studios Press, Vol 24, 2013; contbr, Embracing Encaustic Mixing Media, 3rd ed, Linda Womack, 2015; contrib., ProWax Journal, issues 7-9, 2014-Present; contribr, exhib catalog, One + One, A gallery press, 2015; Editor, exhib catalog, Casting Shadows Work in Dimension and Relief, 2015;. *Dealer:* Denise Bibro Fine Art Inc New York NY 10011; Broadhurst Gallery 2212 Midland Rd Pinehurst NC 28374. *Mailing Add:* c/o 215 W 57th St New York NY 10019

WINICK, BERNYCE ALPERT
PAINTER, PHOTOGRAPHER
b Brooklyn, NY, Oct 20, 1922. *Study:* NY Univ, BA (fine arts & music), 43; Art Students League with Mario Cooper, 61-64; Nat Acad Sch Fine Arts, 68-72 & additional studies at Brooklyn Mus Art Sch, Traphagen Sch Fashion & Nat Acad Design Sch. *Comn:* Large watercolor, comn by Dr & Mrs Marcel Weinberger, Woodmere, NY, 84; 2 large watercolors, comn by Pittway Corp, Syosset, NY, 89. *Exhib:* Am Watercolor Soc, Salmagundi Club, NY, 92; Nat Asn Women Artists, Jacob Javits Fgd Bldg, NY, 92; Nat Asn Women Artists, Washington & Lee Univ, Lexington, Va, 93; Discovery Gallery, Glen Cove, NY, 93 & 94; Soho, Z Gallery, NY, 94; Fine Arts Mus Long Island, 97; Discovery Art Gallery, Sea Cliff, NY, 98; Town Hall, Town of Hempstead, NY, 2000; NY Inst Tech, 2003; Mem Libr, 2003-04; Carnegie Hall, 2006; Julliard, 2006; Solo exhibs, Salmagundi Club, NY, 1982, Discovery Art Gallery, Sea Cliff, NY, 1989, 96, 98, Glen Cove, NY, 1991, Chelsea Ctr, East Norwich, NY, 1993, 96, 98 & 2000, Z Gallery, Soho, NY, 1994, Fine Arts Mus Long Island, NY, 1997, NY Inst Technol, Wisser Mem Libr, 2001, 2003, 2006 & 2007, Nat Arts Club, NY, 2002, New York Inst Tech, Wisser Memorial Lib, Old Westbury, NY, 2008, 2010, Winners Exhib, Molloy Coll Art Gallery, Rockville Centre, NY, 2009. *Awards:* First Prize, Nat Arts Club-86th Ann, 85; First Prize, Salmagundi Club, 90, Salmagundi Club Award, 2004; Showcase Award Chelsea Ctr, NY, 2000; First Prize Photog, Nat Arts Club, NY, 2001; Thomas Moran Mem Award for Watercolor, First Prize, Salmagundi Club, NY, 2002; Salmagundi Club Award, 2004; First Prize, Mills Pond House, St. James, NY, 2005; Fabian Adler Mem Award, Long Island Council, Freeport, NY, 2006; Wisser Libr Int, NY Inst Technol Award, 2007; Nat Soc Painters in Casein & Acrylic Prize, NY, 2007; Peter Jones Mem Award (innovative watercolor), Audubon Artists, NY, 2007; First prize in Black & Whtie Photography, Long Island Arts Coun, Freeport, NY, 2009; 3 Winners Exhib, Rockville Ctr, Molloy Coll, NY, 2009. *Bibliog:* Robin Earl (auth), Artist with an everchanging palate, Nassau Herald, 12/85; Roberta Graff (auth), A symphony of paintings by Bernyce Winick, South-Shore Record, 5/89; Chris Jonny (auth), A Stroke of Genius, Nassau Herald, 10/94; Helen Harrison (auth), 19th ann juried photography in show, NY Times, 4/25/99; Herbert Keppler (auth), Me and my shadows, Popular Photography, 2/99, Keep it simple, 5/2000; Chris Unwin (auth), The Artistic Touch 4, West Bloomfield, Michigan: Creative Art Press, 99; Phylis Braff (auth), Capturing the Seen & Unseen in Photographs, NY Times, 2001; 39 Musical Photographs, Juilliard Bookstore, 2003; Town & Country & Opening Night (Carnegie Hall), Gala Jour, 2003; Putting Together What Aint, Popular Photog, 2004. *Mem:* Am Watercolor Soc; Nat Asn Women Artists; Harvard Club Arts Group; Audubon Artists; Artist's Fellowship, New York. *Media:* Aquamedia, Art Photography, Oil Stick on Canvas. *Interests:* Classical piano, poetry, fashion design, published poetry, patent pending on face cream. *Publ:* Auth, The Encyclopedia of Watercolour Landscape Techniques, Headline Publ Ltd, Gt Brit, 96; Curated Collection III (CD-Rom), ACI Art Communication Int, 96; Abstracts in Watercolor, Rockport Publ, 96; auth, My Lifestyle, 88 Years of Nutrition Exercise and the Arts; Life's Rhythms, 60 Wedded Years in Poetry. *Mailing Add:* 923 Beth Lane Woodmere NY 11598-1507

WINIGRAD, ETTA
SCULPTOR
Study: Univ Penn, BA. *Work:* Holocaust Ctr, Kean Univ, Union, NJ. *Comn:* J. Blank Coll, New York, 1997; Nat Liberty Mus, Philadelphia, 2004. *Exhib:* New Hope Arts Group, New Hope, PA, 2005-07; DUMBO, Glorida Kennedy Gallery, Brooklyn, NY, 2007; Hunterdon Art Mus, Clinton, NJ, 2011; Muse Gallery, Philadelphia, 2011. *Awards:* Holocaust Mem Comp, 81. *Bibliog:* Leon Nigrosh (auth), Sculpting Clay, 92; Susan Peterson (auth), Working with Clay, 2002. *Media:* Clay. *Publ:* contribr, Upfront, Ceramics Monthly, 1996-98; contribr, Politics and Clay, Studio Potter, 6/2001; contribr, Singularities, Ceramics Monthly, 2/2001; contribr, 500 Animals in Clay, Lark Books, 11/2006

WINK, CHRIS
CONCEPTUAL ARTIST, KINETIC ARTIST
b New York, NY, Jan 24, 1961. *Study:* Wesleyan, Am Studies, 84. *Work:* New Mus Contemp Art (performance), NY; Milwaukee Art Mus (performance), Wis; Contemp Art Ctr New Orleans (performance), Fla. *Awards:* Obie, Tubes, Village Voice, 91; Drama Desk, Tubes, 92; Lucille Lortel Found Award, Tubes, 92. *Bibliog:* Alisa Soloman (auth), Pissing on propriety, Village Voice, 1/15/91; Vicki Goldberg (auth), Hi tech meets God with Blue Man Group, NY Times, 1/17/91; Thomas M Disch (auth), Blue Man Group: Tubes, Nation, 1/20/92. *Media:* Performance. *Mailing Add:* c/o The Astor Place Theater 434 Lafayette St New York NY 10003

WINK, DON (JON DONNEL)
PAINTER, EDUCATOR
b San Angelo, Tex, July 13, 1938. *Study:* Univ Tex, BFA, 60; Ohio Univ, 61-62; Univ Wash, MFA, 63. *Exhib:* The Texas General, Dallas Mus Fine Arts, 61; two-man exhib, Witte Mus, San Antonio, 66; Texas Painting & Sculpture, Dallas Mus Fine Arts, 68; Associated Artist, Carnegie Mus, Pittsburgh, 71-75; Westmoreland Co Mus, Greensburg, Pa, 72-75; Mus STex Ann, Corpus Christi, 82; Recent Works from East Texas, Tyler Mus Art, 82. *Teaching:* Instr painting & drawing, Southwestern Univ, Tex, 65-69; prof & chmn dept art, Slippery Rock State Col, 69-76 & Stephen F Austin State Univ, 76-. *Awards:* First Prize, 13th Ann 180, Huntington Galleries, WVa, 65 & 30th Ann Allied Artist, 65; Jury Award, Asn Artist, 72. *Mem:* Nat Coun Art Adminr; Tex Asn Schs Art (secy, 79-80). *Media:* Acrylic, Oil. *Mailing Add:* Box 13001 Stephen F Austin State Univ Nacogdoches TX 75962

WINKFIELD, TREVOR
PAINTER
b Leeds, Eng, 1944. *Study:* Leeds Coll Art, Intermediate Cert Art, 1960-64; Royal Coll Art, London, MFA, 1964-67. *Exhib:* Solo exhibs include Fischbach Gallery, New York, 1977, Coracle Gallery, London, 1978, Blue Mountain Gallery, New York, 1980, Inst Contemp Art, Boston, 1985, Edward Thorp Gallery, New York, 1986, 1989, EM Donahue Gallery, New York, 1995, 1996, Tibor de Nagy Gallery, New York, 1997, 1999, 2002, 2004, 2006, Barbara Ann Levy Gallery, New York, 1999; group exhibs include Yale Ctr for Brit Art, New Haven, Conn, 1989; Washburn Gallery, New York, 1990; Edward Thorp Gallery, New York, 1990; Paula Cooper Gallery, New York, 1991; Marlborough Gallery, New York, 1992; Baxter Gallery, Portland, Maine, 1993; Phyllis Kind Gallery, Chicago, 1994; Bergamot Station Arts Ctr, Santa Monica, 1995; Whitney Mus Am Art at Champion, Stamford, Conn, 1997; Tibor de Nagy Gallery, New York, 1999, 2001; Am Acad Arts & Letters, New York, 2000, 2008; Geoffrey Young Gallery, Great Barrington, Mass, 2000; DC Moore Gallery, New York, 2001, 2004; Brit Consul-General's Residence, New York, 2001; Nat Acad Design, New York, 2002, 2006; Westbeth Gallery, New York, 2003; NY Acad Sci, 2004; Painting Ctr, New York, 2006. *Awards:* Engelhard Award, 1986; Pollock-Krasner Award, 1989; John Simon Guggenheim Mem Found Fel, 1990; Hillwood Fel, 1993; Acad Award in Art, Am Acad Arts & Letters, 2000 & Hassam, Speicher, Betts & Symons Purchase Award, 2008; Chevalier dans l'Ordre des Arts et des Lettre, 2003. *Media:* Acrylic. *Publ:* auth, In the Scissors' Courtyard, 1994 & Trevor Winkfield's Drawings, 2004, Bamberger Books; auth, Pageant, Hard Press Inc, 1997; ed, How I Wrote Certain of My Books, Exact Change, 2005. *Dealer:* Tibor de Nagy Gallery 724 Fifth Ave New York NY 10019. *Mailing Add:* 256 W 15th St Apt 5FE New York NY 10011

WINKLER, MARIA PAULA
PAINTER, EDUCATOR
b Krakow, Poland, Oct 24, 1945; US citizen. *Study:* Univ Pa, study with Karl Umlauf, BA (art & art hist); Pa State Univ, study with Enrique Montenegro, MFA (painting & drawing) & study with Kenneth Beittel, PhD (art educ). *Work:* Pa State Univ, State Col; Boise Art Mus, Idaho; Univ Calif Med Ctr, Sacramento; Sutter Mem Hosp, Sacramento; Kaiser Permanente, N Calif. *Comn:* Two paintings, Raley's Corporate Offices, Sacramento, Calif; two paintings, Kronick, Moskovitz, Tiedemann and Girard, Prof Corporation, Sacramento, Calif; two paintings, TCSI Commun Corp, San Francisco, Calif; painting, El Dorado Hills Develop Co. *Exhib:* Nat Drawing & Small Sculpture Exhib, Ball State Univ, Muncie, Ind, 70; NY Exhib of Paintings, Sculpture & Graphics, Avanti Galleries, NY, 71; New Generation Drawing, Cheney-Cowles Mem State Mus, Spokane, Wash, 73; Contemp Watercolor Paintings, Pence Gallery, Davis, Calif, 88; Contemp Realists, Gump's Gallery, San Francisco, 91; 69th Ann Crocker-Kingsley Open Exhib, Crocker Art Mus, Sacramento, Calif, 94. *Pos:* Tech illusr, Aerojet Gen Corp, Sacramento, 63. *Teaching:* Asst prof art & art educ, Boise State Univ, Idaho, 73-75; asst prof art educ, Univ BC, Vancouver, 75-77; prof art, Calif State Univ, Sacramento, 77-. *Awards:* First Place & William Harrington Mem Award, Northern Calif Arts 26th Ann Open Show, Sacramento, 80; Mixed Media, Second Place, Northern Calif Arts 36th Ann Open Exhib, Carmichael, 91; Gold Discovery Award, Works on Paper, Art Calif Mag, 93 & 94. *Bibliog:* A Survey of Contemporary Art of the Figure, Am Artist, 2/85. *Mem:* Nat Art Educ Asn. *Media:* Watercolor, Pastels. *Res:* Research and writings on techniques of teaching art appreciation to teachers and museum volunteers; curriculum development in art. *Publ:* Illusr, Art: Magic, Impulse and Control, A Guide to Viewing, Prentice-Hall, 73; Eight Posters, Editions Limited, San Francisco, 90-91; Two Artists Cards, Allport Editions Artist Cards, Portland, 90; Four Mini-Prints, Portal Publications, Corte Madera, 91. *Dealer:* Susan Willoughby Art Consult 73 Starlit Cir Sacramento CA 95831. *Mailing Add:* c/o Art Dept Calif State Univ Sacramento CA 95819

WINKLER, MAX-KARL
EDUCATOR, ILLUSTRATOR
b New Braunfels, Tex, May 14, 1938. *Study:* Univ Tex, Austin, BA, 59, BFA, 63, MFA, 68. *Pos:* Illusr & graphic designer, Washington, DC, 84-88; illusr, Nat Sci Resources Ctr, Washington, DC, 88-94. *Teaching:* Instr studio art & art hist, Col Mainland, Texas City, Tex, 68-73; asst prof, Colo Mountain Col, Glenwood Springs, Colo, 73-76; instr studio art, Smithsonian Resident Assoc Prog, Washington, DC, 86-. *Mem:* Guild Natural Sci Illustrators. *Media:* Pen, Ink. *Publ:* Illusr, Science & Technology for Children: Teachers' Guides & Student Activity Books, Nat Sci Resources Ctr, 88-; Almanac Edition, Chronicle of Higher Education, 89-. *Mailing Add:* 10309 Drumm Ave Kensington MD 20895

WINKLER, MICHAEL
CONCEPTUAL ARTIST
b Lima, Ohio, Feb 28, 52. *Work:* Mus Mod Art, NY; Stanford Univ, Calif; Staatsgalerie, Stuttgart, WGer; King Stephen Mus, Szekesfehervar; Sackner Archive, Miami Beach, Fla. *Comn:* Spoke of the Wheel, Intermedia Dance Proj, Portland Ballet Co, 2006. *Exhib:* Solo exhibs, Kunstraum Kunoldstrasse 34, Kassel, WGer, 84, Univ Md, Baltimore, 85, Kansas City Art Inst, 88 & Univ Mass, Lowell, 94; Text Out of Context, Soho Ctr, NY, 91; Univ of Penn, 2004; Poetic Positions, Kasseler Kunstverein, 2004; Lessons in Learning, Mus Contemporary Art, Chgo, 2007; Cryptograph, Spencer Mus Art, Univ Kans, 2012. *Pos:* NY Correspondent, Rampike Mag, Toronto, 85-93. *Awards:* Spec Proj Fel, Pa Coun Arts, 84; Visual Artists Fel, Nat Endowment Arts, 85; LINE Grant, Line II Asn, NY, 85. *Bibliog:* Sue Scott (auth), Alphastructures, Art Res Ctr, 84; Skuta Helgason (auth), Regular words, Afterimage, 84; Rasula & McCaffery (auth), Imagining Language, MIT Press, 98. *Media:* Mixed Media. *Publ:* Auth, Word Art/Art Words, 85, An Artist's Statement, 86 & Equivalents, 87, Extreme Measures, 89, Printed Matter. *Mailing Add:* 370 1st Ave Apt 9H New York NY 10010

WINOKUR, NEIL
PHOTOGRAPHER
b New York, NY, June 28, 1945. *Study:* Hunter Col, City Univ NY, BA, 67. *Work:* Mus Mod Art, Metrop Mus Art, Jewish Mus & Chase Manhattan Bank, NY; Los Angeles Co Mus Art; Centro Cult Arte Contemporaneo, Mex City, Mex; Philadelphia Mus Art, Pa; Denver Mus Art, Colo. *Comn:* New York Food, Columbia Univ Sch Arts, Metrop Transp Authority, Arts for Transit, LIRR Pa Station, NY; Movie Portraits, 42nd St Art proj, NY; Progressive People (10 multiple portraits), Progressive Ins Co, Cleveland, Ohio, 93; Dynamics of an Insurance Giant, Caroon/Black Plaza, Nashville, Tenn; Transit Art: LIRR Workers and Objects, Pub Art Fund, Pa Station, NY. *Exhib:* Commission a Portrait, PS 122 Gallery, NY, 91; Artist's Choice: Chuck Close, Head-On The Modern Portrait, Mus Mod Art, NY, 91 & The Pleasures and Terrors of Domestic Comfort (auth, catalog), 91; Special Collections, The Photog Order from Pop to Now, Int Ctr Photog Midtown, NY, 92; Persona, Mus Photogr Arts, San Diego, Calif, 92; Solo exhibs, Portraits, Barbara Toll Fine Arts, NY, 92, Progressive People: Photographs by Neil Winokor, Cleveland Contemp, Ohio, 93, Neil Winokur: Photographs, Denver Mus Art, Colo, 93, For Bill, A Memorial, Janet Borden Inc, NY, 93, Galerie du jour Agnes b, Paris, France, 95, Daily Life, Janet Borden Inc, NY, 97 & NY Food, LIRR Pa Station Lightboxes, NY, 98; Multiple Images: Photographs Since 1965 from the Collection, Mus Mod Art, NY, 93; Autour de Rogier Vivier (auth, catalog), Galerie Enrico Navarra, Paris, France, 95; The Dead (auth, catalog), Nat Mus Photog, Film & TV, Bradford, Eng, 95; New in the Nineties, Katonah Mus Art, NY, 96; Portrait Paintings, Bernard Toale Gallery, Boston, Mass, 96; New Art on Paper (auth, catalog), Philadelphia Mus Art, Pa, 96; Bathrooms, Thomas Healy Gallery, NY, 98; Food, SF Camerawork, San Francisco, Calif, 98; NY Photographs, Janet Borden Inc, 2000; Double Vision, Univ Art Mus, Calif State Univ, Santa Barbara, 2001; Monochromes, Janet Borden Inc, 2002; Great Inventions, Thief Burden, 2005. *Awards:* Fel in Photography from Art Matters Mc, 84, Nat Endowment Arts, 84 & Guggenheim Found, 87; Grant, Art Matters Inc, 86 & 88. *Bibliog:* Pepe Karmel (auth), Out of the Ghetto?, ARTnews, 4/94; Charles Hagen (auth), Review-Neil Winokou, 7/1/94 & 2/2/96, NY Times; Edith Newhall (auth), Portrait Parts-Neil Winokur, NY Mag, 1/15/96; Charles Hogen (auth), Neil Winokar-Barbara Tull Fine Arts, Vol XXVI, Arttorum, 88; Vince Aletti (auth), Choices-Neil Winnkur, Village Voice, 1/3/89; Carter Radcliff (auth), Elle, 11/89; Max Kozloff, Hapless Figures in an Artificial Storm, Artforum, 11/89. *Media:* Photography. *Specialty:* Photography-Contemporary. *Interests:* Cooking, gardening. *Publ:* The Dog in Art from Rococo to Post-Modernism, Robert Rosenblum & Harry N Abrams, New York, 88; New Art, Phyllis Freeman, Mark Greenberg, Eric Himmel, Andreas Landshoff, Charles Miers & Harry N Abrams, New York, 90; How to Look at Modern Art, Philip Yenawine & Harry N Abrams, 91; Everyday Things, Smithsonian Press, Washington, DC, 5/94; Album, Gabriel Bauret, L'Ecole des loisirs, Paris, France, 95. *Dealer:* Janet Borden 560 Broadway New York NY 10012. *Mailing Add:* 16 Hudson St No 2A New York NY 10013

WINOKUR, PAULA COLTON
CERAMIST, CRAFTSMAN
b Philadelphia, Pa, 1935. *Study:* Temple Univ, BFA, BSEd, 58, with Rudolf Staffel; Alfred Univ, New York, summer 58. *Work:* Montreal Mus Decorative Arts; Philadelphia Mus of Art; Nat Mus Am Art, Washington, DC; Mint Mus Crafts/Design, Charlotte, NC; Los Angeles Co Mus Art; Houston Mus of Fine Arts; Palisades Pinnacle, Gifts from America, Hermitage, St Petersburg. *Comn:* Ed patrons plates (60), Nat Mus Am Jewish Hist, 83; fireplace installations, pvt residences, Philadelphia, 84, 85 & 86; lintel (A view of Diamond Head), Hawaii Sch for Girls, Honolulu, 88; fireplaces, comn by Mr & Mrs Robert Coon, Montclair, NJ, 89 & Mr & Mrs William

Harris, Lynchburg, Va, 90; large wall installation, Pa Convention Ctr, 93. *Exhib:* 100 Artists Celebrate 100 Yrs, Fairtree Gallery & Xerox Gallery, 76; Inaugural Exhib, Am Crafts Mus, 86; Solo show, Helen Drutt Gallery, NY, 90, Helsinki, Finland, 2005; First Yixing Ceramic Invitational, Yixing & Jingdezen, China; Int Biennial, Khon, Korea; Color & Fire: Defining Moments in Studio Ceramics, Los Angeles Co Mus, Calif; Contemp Mus, Honolulu, 2004; Alchemy: From Dust to Form, Harn Mus Art, Gainesville, Texas; Lancaster Art Mus, Pa; Michener Art Mus, Pa. *Teaching:* Asst prof ceramics, Philadelphia Col Art, 67; prof, Arcadia Univ, Glenside, Pa, 73- & Tyler Sch Art, 83; prof emer, Arcadia Univ, 2003. *Awards:* Merit Award, Craftsmen USA, Am Crafts Coun, 66; Prize, Ceramics Int 73, Calgary, Alta, 73; Nat Endowment for the Arts Craftsmen's Fel, 76 & 88; PA Coun Craftmen's Fel, 86 & 2005; Leeway Grant, 2003. *Bibliog:* Robin Rice (auth) American Craft Mag, 2000; Ed Sozanski (auth) The Philadelphia Inquirer, 2000; Ivy Barsky (auth), Art & Perception #13, Winokur Landmarks; Gerald Brown (auth), Paula Winokur's Poetic Earth. *Mem:* Fel Am Crafts Coun; Fel Nat Coun Educ Ceramic Arts (bd dir, 79-82); Int Acad Ceramics; Int Acad Ceramics. *Media:* Porcelain. *Specialty:* Fine arts. *Interests:* Geology, The landscape. *Collection:* Montreal Mus of Decorative Arts; Mus Art & Design, NY; Philadelphia Mus Art; L.A. Co Mus; Mus Design, Helsinki, Finland; Houston Mus Fine Arts; Fuller Craft Mus; Racine Art Mus. *Publ:* Coauth, The light of Rudolph Staffel, Craft Horizons, 77. *Mailing Add:* 435 Norristown Rd Horsham PA 19044

WINOKUR, ROBERT
CERAMIC ARTIST

b Brooklyn, NY, Dec 24, 1933. *Study:* Tyler Sch Art, Temple Univ, with Rudolph Staffel, BFA, 56; NY State Coll Ceramics, Alfred, MFA, 58. *Hon Degrees:* Am Craft Coun Coll Fel. *Work:* Houston Mus Fine Arts, Tex; Contemp Mus, Honolulu, HI; Los Angeles Co Mus Art, Calif; Mus Boymans von Beuningen, Rotterdam, Neth; Philadelphia Mus Art, Pa; Am Mus Ceramic Art, Pomona, Calif; State Cult Mus, Riga, Latvia; Smithsonian Mus Am Art, Renwick Collection, Washington, DC; The Mercer Mus, Doylestown, Pa; Nerman Mus Contemporary Art, Kansas City, Kans; R Hawk, Wash DC; The Smithsonian Archive of American Art: Oral History Coll, Wash DC. *Comn:* Pvt comn by Helen Drutt; Trammel-Crowe corp; Ford & Earl Archit, First Nat Bank Chicago. *Exhib:* 300 Yrs of Am Art, Philadelphia Mus Art, 76; Philadelphia Contemp Artists, Philadelphia Mus Art, 90; Haldane Connections Exhib, Int Acad Ceramics with Glasgow Sch Art, Glasgow, Scotland, 90; Furniture Philadelphia, Morris Gallery Pa, Acad Fine Art, Philadelphia, 91; Three In Clay-Three Points of View, Nat Mus Ceramic Art, Baltimore, Md, 92; From the Ground Up, Ten Philadelphia Artists Invitational, Levy Gallery, Moore Coll Art & Design, 92; retrospective, The Philadelphia Yrs, 1962 to 1992, Helen Drutt Gallery, Philadelphia, Pa, 92; Chinese & Foreign Ceramic Artists Works Invitational Show, Yixing Int Ceramics Symposium, Yixing, China; Color and Fire: Defining Moments in Studio Ceramics 1950-2000, Los Angeles Co Mus Art, Calif; solo-exhibs, Dorothy McRae Gallery, Atlanta, Ga, Helen Drutt Gallery, Philadelphia, 2001, Ceramics 1950-1990: A Survey of Contemp Am Ceramics, Nat Mus Modern Art, Kyoto, 2002, Setaquya Art Mus, Tokyo, 2002, Poetics of Clay: An Int Perspective, Philadelphia Art Alliance, Mus Art & Design, Helsinki, Finland, 2002, Houston Ctr Contemp Crafts, 2003, The Aileen Osborn Webb Awards Exhib, Contemp Crafts Gallery, Portland, Ore, 2003, The Schein-Joseph Int Mus Ceramic Art, NY State Coll Ceramics, Alfred, NY & Rosenfeld Gallery, Philadelphia, 2010; Rose Lehrman Art Ctr, Harrisburg Area Community Coll, Harrisburg, Pa, 2012; 21st Century Ceramics, Cahzahi Ctr Gallery, Columbus Coll Art & Design, Columbus, Ohio; In Our Own Backyard, Pa Coun Arts, Fel Traveling Exhib, 2004-2006; Standing Room Only, Invitational, 60th Scripps Ann, Scripps Coll, Claremont, Calif, 2004; Archit/Structure in Contemp Craft, Soc Arts & Crafts, Boston, 2007; Cross/Mackenzie, Washington, DC, 2007; Architectural Ceramics, Northern Clay Ctr, Minneapolis, Minn; Three Ceramic Artists, Pace Univ, Pleasantville, NY, 2008; The Dealers Eye: Artists of Helen Drott Gallery, Clay Studio, Philadelphia, 2009; 3 one-person shows, Rosenfeld Gallery, Philadelphia, 2010; 20th Ann Exhib, Northern Clay Ctr, Minneapolis, 2010; The Michener Mus Paton, Smith, Della Penna Galleries, Doylestown, Pa, 2012; Int Acad Ceramics, New World, Timeless Vision, NMex Mus Art, Santa Fe, NMex, 2012; Value Refuge: Berard Ave Found, France, 2012; Musee du Serre, Paris, France, 2013; Robert and Paula Winofur: Lancaster Mus Art, Lancaster, Pa, 2013. *Pos:* Proj dir, Philadelphia Ceramic Consortium, currently; on-site prog chmn, Nat Coun Educ Ceramic Arts, 75 & 92; adv bd, Clay Studio, Philadelphia, currently; invited participant, Symp Contemp Ceramics, Int Ceramic Studio, Kecskemet, Hungary, 93. *Teaching:* Coordr two-dimensional visual design dept, N Tex State Univ, Denton, 58-63; area chmn ceramics, Tyler Sch Art, Temple Univ, 66-, prof emer & area head ceramics, 66-2005, chmn craft dept, 79-82 & 88-91; vis artist & guest lectr, Glasgow Sch Art, Scotland, 87. *Awards:* Nat Endowment Arts Fel, 79; Nat Coun Educ Ceramic Arts Fel, 83; Pa Coun Arts Fel, 88 & crafts, 2003. *Bibliog:* Elaine Levin (auth), American Ceramics, Abrams; Jack Troy (auth), Salt Glazed Ceramics, Watson Guptill; Susan Peterson (auth), The Craft & Art of Clay, Prentice Hall & Contemporary Ceramics, Watson-Guptill; Richard Polsky (auth), the Columbia University Oral History Collection, Columbia Univ Archives; Daniel Rhodes (auth), Clay and Glaze for the Potter, Krouse Pub; Emanuel Cooper (auth) Ten Thousand Years of Pottery, 4th ed, Univ Pa Press; Suzanne Ramljak (auth), Crafting: A Legacy of Contemporary American Crafts for the Philadelphia Mus of Art, Philadelphia Mus Art Publ; Janet Kaplos (auth), At Helen Drutt, Art in Am, 10/2001; Bai Ming (auth), Oversea Contemporary Ceramic Art Classics, Hubei Fine Art Publ House, China; Robin Hopper (auth), Making Marks, Kraus Pub; Roald Hoffman (auth), Robert Winokurs Houses, New Ceramics, Ger, 5-6/2007; Glen R. Brown (juried by), 500 Ceramic Sculptures, Lark Books, 2009; Emanuel Cooper (auth) Contemporary Ceramics, Thames and Hudson, 2009; Ceramic Bible & Louisa Taylor, RetroVision/Chronicle, London, 2011; The Best of 500 Ceramics, Celebrating a Decade in Clay, Lark Books, Ashville, NC. *Mem:* Am Crafts Coun; Nat Coun Educ Ceramic Arts (br dir, 69-70, vpres, 72-73); Philadelphia Coun Prof Craftsmen; adv bd, The Clay Studio, Philadelphia, Pa, 85; Int Acad Ceramics, Geneva, Switz, (hon mem, 2005). *Media:* Salt Glazed Stoneware. *Publ:* Auth, The Tyler School of Art of Temple University, Ceramics Mo, 75; coauth, The light of Rudolph Staffel, Craft Horizons, 77. *Mailing Add:* 435 Norristown Rd Horsham PA 19044

WINSOR, JACKIE
SCULPTOR

b St John's, Nfld, Oct 20, 1941; US citizen. *Study:* Yale Summer Sch Art & Music, 1964; Mass Coll Art, BFA, 1965; Rutgers Univ, MFA, 1967; Univ Nfld, LHD, 1994. *Work:* Mus Mod Art, NY; Whitney Mus Am Art, NY; Australia Nat Gallery, Canberra; Detroit Inst Arts, Mich; Mus d'Arte Mod, Paris, France; Tehran Mus Contemp Art, Iran; Albright-Knox Art Gallery, Buffalo. *Exhib:* Solo exhibs, Paula Cooper Gallery, NY, 73, 76, 82-83, 86, 89, 92, 95, Mus Mod Art, NY, traveling, 79, Va Mus, Richmond, 81, Margarete Roeder Fine Arts, NY, 85, Margo Leavin Gallery, Los Angeles, Calif, 87, Ctr d'Art du Domaine de Kerguehennec Bignan, Locmine, France, 88, Milwaukee Art Mus (traveling), Wis, 91-92; Whitney Mus Am Art, NY, 70, 73-74, 77-79, 82-85, 88-89, 94; Aldrich Mus Contemp Art, Ridgefield, Conn, 71, 79, 82, 88, 94; Mus Mod Art, NY, 73-74, 79, 84, 86; 8th Biennial Paris, Mus Mod Art, Paris, 73; 71st Am Exhib, Art Inst Chicago, 74; Four for the Fourth, Albright-Knox Art Gallery, Buffalo, NY, 76; Art in Our Time, HHK Found, Va Mus, Richmond, 81; Mus Fine Arts, Boston, 85; San Francisco Mus Mod Art, 85; Transformations in Sculpture, Solomon R Guggenheim Mus, NY, 85; 1988: The World of Art Today, Milwaukee Art Mus, 88; In Three Dimensions: Women Sculptors of the 90's, Newhouse Ctr Contemp Art, Harbor Cult Ctr, Staten Island, 95; The Material Imaginations, Solomon R Guggenheim Mus, 95; 25 Yrs: An Exhibition of Selected Works, Margo Leavin Gallery, Los Angeles, 95; 15 Degrees from Rutgers, Mason Gross Sch Arts, Rutgers, State Univ NJ, 96; More Than Minimal: Feminism & Abstraction in the 70's, Rose Art Mus, Brandeis Univ, 96; Masters of the Masters, Butler Inst Am Art, NY, 98; Sculpture: Donald Judd, Sherrie Levine, Sol Lewitt, Tony Smith, Jackie Winsor, Paula Cooper Gallery, NY, 98; Crossroad, Groninger Mus, The Neth, 98; Aspen Art Mus, 99; Ceres Gallery, NY City, 2000; D'Amelio Terras, NY, 2001; Palazzo Zorzi, Venice, 2003; CU Art Mus, Univ Colo, Boulder, 2005; Multiplex: Direction in Art 1970 to Now, Monia, NY, 11/21/07-7/28/08; Decoys, Complexes, and Triggers: Feminism and Land Art in the 1970s, Sculpture Center, Long Island City, NY, 5/4-7/31/08. *Teaching:* Instr art introd & ceramics, Douglass Col, 1967; instr art introd, Middlesex Co Col & Newark State Teachers' Col, 1968, 1969; instr ceramics, Mills Col Educ, 1968, 1971, Greenwich House Pottery Sch, NY, 1969-72; instr graphics, Loyola Univ, New Orleans, summer 1969; instr sculpture, Sch Visual Arts, NY, 1971, 1975; instr art introd, Hunter Col, 1972-75; lectr, NY Studio Sch Drawing, Painting & Sculpture, fall 1987. *Awards:* Nat Endowment Arts Grant, 1974, 1977, 1984; Guggenheim Fel, 1978; Creative Artist Award, Brandeis Univ, 1979; and others. *Bibliog:* Robert Pincus-Written (auth), Entries maximalism, Out of London Press, 1983; Craig Gholson (auth), Jackie Winsor, Bomb, winter 1986; Tobine Siebers (auth), The subject and other subjects: On ethical, aesthetic and political identity, Univ Mich Press, 1998. *Media:* All. *Dealer:* Paula Cooper Gallery 534 W 21st St New York NY 10011. *Mailing Add:* c/o Paula Cooper Gallery 534 W 21st St New York NY 10011

WINT, DENNIS MICHAEL
MUSEUM DIRECTOR

b Macon, Ga, March 17, 1943. *Study:* Univ Mich, BS, 65; Case Western Univ, PhD, 77. *Pos:* dir environ educ, Wiloughby Eastlake City Sch, Ohio, 68-70; dir, Ctr Develop Environment Curriculum, 70-75; cons Ohio Dept Educ, 75-77; dir mus and educ, Acad Natural Scis, Phila, 77-79; vice pres, dir, Natural History Mus, 79-82; dir, Cranbrook Inst Sci, Bloomfield Hills, Mich, 82-86; pres, St Louis Sci Ctr, 86-95; pres, CEO, The Franklin Inst, Phila, 95-2014, pres, CEO emeritus, 2014-. *Teaching:* Mem mus leadership graduate degree program, Antoinette Westphal Col of Media Arts and Design, Drexel Univ, 2014-. *Awards:* Fellow Award for Outstanding Contribution, Asn Sci Tech Ctrs, 2008. *Mem:* Asn Sci-Tech Ctrs (vp, 93-95, pres, 95-97, strategic planning comn, 2002-2005); Am Asn Museums (chmn int comn, 2000-2005, bd dirs, 2003-, vice chair, 2006-). *Mailing Add:* Drexel University URBN Center 136 3501 Market St Philadelphia PA 19104

WINT, FLORENCE EDYTHE
PAINTER, SCULPTOR

b Newark, NJ, 1928. *Study:* NY Univ, BS, 51; Teachers Coll, Columbia Univ, MEA, 68; Art Students League, 69-71; Pratt Graphic Ctr, 72-77. *Work:* Exxon NJ, Linden; Johnson & Johnson, New Brunswick, NJ; The Collective Portfolio II, Somerville, NJ; Rabbet Gallery, New Brunswick, NJ; Noyes Mus, Oceanville, NJ; pvt collection, Law Offices of Neal Brickan, New York; Bristle Meyers. *Exhib:* Flower Show, Gallery at Squib, Princeton, NJ, 94; solo exhib, Fantasy Mania, Woodcuts and Sculptures, Kent Place Sch, 2000; Grounds for Sculpture, NAWA, 2001; Northeast Prints, Ben Shahn Gallery, William Patterson Univ, 2002; Women in the New Millennium, Seton Hall Univ, 2003; Point of View, Poughkeepsie Art Mus, Bernardsville, NJ, 2004; Pfeiser, Morris Plains, NJ, 2005; Montclair State Univ, NJ, 2005; WOW Small Works Show 1978, Maplewood, NJ, 2006; The Cube 1978, Maplewood, NJ, 2007; Forces of Nature, Gallery Borough Pres Manhattan, 2007; Close to the Edge, City Walls, Seton Univ Sch Law, Newark, NJ, 2008; Belski Mus Art, Closter, NJ, 2008; Seven Visions, Newark Acad, Livingston, NJ, 2008; Menagrie, Arts Guild of Rahway, Rahway, NJ, 2008; Close to the Edge, City Without Walls, Seton Hall Univ Sch Law, Newark, NJ, 2008; Evolution 20@10, Arts Guild of Rahway, Rahway, NJ, 2009; Artscopes, Summit Medical Group, Berkley Heights, NJ, 2009; Cross Sections, Bergen Community Coll, Hackensack, NJ, 2009; 11th Gorlen Juried show, Whippany, NJ; Sculpture affiliates, Art Ctr Northern NJ; Celebration of Heart, Summit Med Group, Berkeley Heights, NJ; The Cube, JCC, West Orange, NJ; Art Connections-7 George Segal Gallery, Montclair, NJ, 2011; Ann Gaelen Juried Art Show, Whippany, NJ, 2011; Two Person Show: 14 Sculptures, East Leon and Toby Cooperman, JCC, West Orange, NJ; Nexus, Art Guild of NJ, Rahway, 2011; Art Connections, George Segal Gallery, Montclair State Univ, Sculpture Affiliates, West Orange, NJ, 2012; The Retreat, East Hampton, NY, 2013; Peter Louis Salon Gallery, NY, 2013; Conceptual

Confluence, Passaic Co Coll, Patterson, NY, 2013; Celebrating Women Through Art, Zufall Health Ctr, Dover, NJ. *Teaching:* Teacher ceramic sculpture, Greenwich House Pottery, 79-2003. *Awards:* V Johnson Graphic Prize, NJ Show, Ctr Visual Arts, 87; First Prize, Printmaking Coun, NJ, 91; First Prize, Sculpture's Affiliates Show, 98; Merit Award, Heart of The Artist; Fel, NJ Coun Arts, 2002. *Bibliog:* Gene Kleinsmith (auth), Twenty Americans in Clay, Multi-Visual Sound Prod, 84. *Mem:* Printmaking Coun NJ; Salute to Women in the Arts; Nat Asn Women Artists Inc; Contemp Artists Guild; Sculpture Affil NJ. *Media:* All Media. *Publ:* Illusr, Cowboy Ed, Harper Collins, 93. *Dealer:* Mona Lisa Gallery NJ. *Mailing Add:* 93 Hillcrest Rd Maplewood NJ 07040

WINTER, GERALD GLEN
PAINTER, EDUCATOR
b Milwaukee, Wis, Sept 1, 1936. *Study:* Univ Wis-Milwaukee, BFA, Madison, MS & MFA. *Work:* Milwaukee Art Ctr; Lowe Mus, Univ Miami, Coral Gables, Fla; Ringling Mus, Sarasota, Fla; Dade Co Pub Libr, Miami. *Exhib:* 39th, 40th, 43rd, 44th & 53rd Exhib Contemp Am Painting, Palm Beach; solo exhibs, Miami-Dade Community Col, 75, Lowe Mus, Univ Miami, 75 & 87 Univ Miami Art Dept Gallery, 79; Metrop Mus & Art Ctr, Coral Gables, Fla, 83; Galerie Helene Grubair, Miami, Fla, 90; Lowe Mus, Univ Miami, 94; Sarasota Biennial 2000, Ringling Mus Art, 2000; Miami Pub Libr, 2006; and others. *Teaching:* Prof art, Univ Miami, 65-99, prof emeritus, 99, chmn dept, 75-79. *Awards:* Ford Found Purchase Award, 62; Third Prize, Corcoran Gallery of Art Biennial, 62; Honorable Mentions, Hortt Mem Exhib, 69, 80 & 81. *Media:* Oil, Beadwork. *Mailing Add:* 6629 SW 62nd Terr Miami FL 33143

WINTER, HOPE MELAMED
COLLECTOR, PATRON
b May 2, 1921. *Study:* Univ Wis, Madison, 38-40; Goodman School, Art Inst Chicago, 40-42. *Pos:* Trustee, Milwaukee Art Mus, Wis, 74-83 & 92-; coun, Elvehjem Art Mus, Univ Wis, Madison. *Bibliog:* Cubist Prints in Collection of Dr and Mrs Abraham Melamed, Univ Wis, 72; Selections from Collection of Hope and Abraham Melamed, Milwaukee Art Mus, 83. *Mem:* Art Inst Chicago; Am Asn Mus; Arch Am Art. *Collection:* Principally cubist prints, drawings & paintings; Cubism, primarily French between 1909-1914, including Picasso, Braque, Gleizes, Metzinger, Jacques Villon, Duchamp, Marcoussis, Gris, Severini, Chagall and others

WINTER, ROGER
PAINTER
b Denison, Tex, Aug 17, 1934. *Study:* Univ Tex, BFA, 56; Univ Iowa, MFA, 60; Brooklyn Mus Sch, Beckmann scholar, 60. *Work:* Mus Art, Univ Okla, Norman; Southern Methodist Univ & Dallas Mus Fine Arts, Dallas; Longview Mus & Art Ctr, Tex; El Paso Mus Art, Tex; Portland Mus Art, Maine; Dallas Mus Art, Tex; many others. *Comn:* Fed Reserve Bank of Dallas, 83. *Exhib:* Tex Painting & Sculpture, 20th Century Dallas, 71-62; two-man show, Whitte Mus, San Antonio, Tex, 67; solo exhibs, Pollock Gallery, 68 & 79, One i at a Time, 71, Southern Methodist Univ, Dallas, Delgado Mus, New Orleans, La, 68 & Fischbach Gallery, NY, 84, 86, 88 & 89, Eugene Binder Gallery, Dallas, Tex, 92, Maine Coll Art, Baxter Gallery, Portland, Maine, 96, Maine Coast Artists, Rockport, Maine, 96, Greenville Co Mus Art, SC, 96, El Paso Mus Art, Tex, 96, The McKinney Ave Contemp, Dallas, Tex, 96, Art Gallery, Univ Tex, San Antonio, Tex, 97, Edith Baker Gallery, Dallas, Tex, 98, 2000, Fishbach Gallery, New York City, 98, Artist's Gallery, San Antonio, Tex, 2000; group exhibs, Behold, Narrative Visions, 55 Mercer Gallery, New York City, 99, Outward Bound, Meridian Corp, Washington, DC, 99, Y2$, Fishbach Gallery, NY, 2000, Animals in Art, Bates Mus, Henkley, Maine, 2000, many others. *Pos:* Installation asst, Dallas Mus Contemp Arts, 62-63; gallery tours & lectr, Dallas Mus Fine Arts, 63-76; guest critic, many various orgs, 89-2000. *Teaching:* Instr painting, Ft Worth Art Ctr, 61 & Dallas Mus Fine Arts, 62-68; prof painting, Southern Methodist Univ, 65-89; instr painting, Washington Univ, St Louis, 89, Univ Pa, Philadelphia, 90, Brooklyn Col, NY, 91 & Vermont Studio Ctr, 90 & 92, 95, 2000. *Awards:* Top Award, Dallas Ann, Dallas Mus Fine Arts, 64; Nat Endowment Arts Grant, 88; Painting Fel Award Mid-Am Arts Alliance/NEA, 88. *Bibliog:* Film on work produced on KERA-TV, Dallas, 71; Maine Light: The Ambassador's Residence, US State Dept Santiago, Chile, 99; Outward Bound: American Art at the Brink of the 20th Century (catalogue), Meridian Int Ctr, 99. *Media:* Oil. *Publ:* Auth, Introduction to Drawing, Prentice Hall, 83; On Drawing, Collegiate Books, 91, 2d edition, 97. *Mailing Add:* 35 W 92nd Apt 9D New York NY 10025

WINTERBERGER, SUZANNE
PHOTOGRAPHER, ASSEMBLAGE ARTIST
b Binghamton, NY, June 23, 1952. *Study:* Rochester Inst Technol, NY, BFA, 75; Cranbrook Acad Art Bloomfield Hills, Mich, MFA, 78. *Work:* Visual Studies Workshop, Rochester, NY; Franklin Furnace Archives, NY; Cranbrook Acad Art, Bloomfield Hills, Mich; Erie Art Mus, Pa; WGBH-TV, Boston, Mass. *Exhib:* Solo exhibs, Ideas About Life, Color Servs, Santa Barbara, Calif, 81, Maxims, Rutger Gallery, Utica, NY, 82, Aging Barbies, New Art Ctr, Washington, DC, 87 & Prisoner of the Pedestal, Bayfront Gallery, Erie, Pa, 90; Bookworks Invitational, Erie Art Mus, Erie, Pa, 86; NoNeo, Zoller Gallery Invitational, State Col, Pa, 89; Pennsylvania Photo Educators Invitational, Pittsburgh, Pa, 91; 20 Yrs of Cranbrook Photog, Juried Invitational, Cranbrook Art Mus, Bloomfield Hills, Mich, 92; Everyday Gothic, Sandford Gallery, Clarion, Pa, 94; and others. *Collection Arranged:* Photo Collaborations, Bruce Gallery, Edinboro, Pa, 86; Neighboring Novellas, Sandford Gallery, Clarion, Pa, 94. *Pos:* Collabr, Aunt Marion & Cousin Mimi photog postcards series, Enthusiastic Enterprises, Edinboro, Pa, 82-86, Edinboro Bookarts Collective, 86-. *Teaching:* Asst prof photog, Edinboro Univ, 82-. *Awards:* Nat Endowment Arts Fel, 85; Pa Coun Arts Fel, 86. *Bibliog:* Julie Moran (auth), Women artists on women, Pulse, 10/13/87; Gary Wykoff (auth), Heart of a humanist, Erie, Pa Times-News, 4/90; Richard Briggs (filmmaker), Suzanne Winterberger - A Portrait, PBS Documentary, WVIA-TV, Pittston, Pa, 90; PhotoPaper, Blatent Image/Silver Eye Quarterly, Pittsburgh, Pa, 91. *Mem:* Soc Photog Educ. *Publ:* Contribr, In-Sights, Godine, 79; How To Spot a Patriarch, 90; Go Ask Elvis, 91; Fat Girl Meditations, 93. *Mailing Add:* Art Dept Edinboro Univ Edinboro PA 16444

WINTERS, SANDY L
PAINTER
b Arcadia, Calif, Feb 10, 1949. *Study:* Univ Kans, Lawrence, 67; Univ NH, Durham, BSc (art educ), 71; Cornell Univ, MFA, 77. *Work:* Prudential Insurance Co Am & Manufacturers Hanover Trust Co, NY; Bank of Boston, Mass; Southeast Banking Corp, Miami, Fla; Arnot Art Mus, Elmira, NY; Metro-Dade Art in Public Places, NY. *Comn:* 50 prints for Graymoore, Comn by Rollins Found Tex, Garrison, NY. *Exhib:* Selections 14, Drawing Ctr, NY, 81 & 82; Everson Mus Art, Syracuse, NY, 82; Soc Four Arts, Palm Beach, Fla, 84; The Art of Miami, Southeastern Ctr Contemp Art, Winston-Salem, NC, 86; Pensacola Mus Art, 88; Jacksonville Mus Art, Fla, 89; Fresh Cuts: Large Scale Installation, George Adams Gallery, NY, 98; Ann Collector's Show, Ark Arts Ctr, Little Rock, 98; Recent Works, Frederic Snitzer Gallery, Miami, Fl, 99; Sarasota Biennial 2000, The John and Mable Ringling Mus, 2000; Move, Barbara Gillman Gallery, Miami, Fla, 2002; Collector's Show, Ark Art Ctr, Little Rock, 2003; Under the Influence Of, George Adams Gallery, NY, 2004, In My Backyard, 2007; The Body and Its Dangers, Painting Ctr, NY, 2005. *Teaching:* Asst prof printmaking & drawing, Univ Tulsa, Okla, 78-80; vis asst prof drawing, printmaking & painting, Cornell Univ, Ithaca, NY, 82-86; assoc prof painting & drawing, Fla Int Univ, Miami, 84-97; prof painting, Mus Fine Arts, 97-. *Awards:* Fla State Visual Art Fel; SAF/Nat Endowment Arts Fel; Fac Res Develop Grant, Fla Int Univ, Miami. *Bibliog:* Vivien Raynor (auth), Selections 14, NY Times, 7/17/81; Helen Kohen (auth), Gallery salutes, Miami Herald, 7/5/85; Ronny Cohen (auth), Sandy Winters, (exhib catalog), Frances Wolfson Gallery, 11/86; Stephen Westfall (auth), The Art Mus at Fla Int Univ, Miami. *Mem:* Coll Art Asn; Women's Caucus Arts. *Media:* All. *Publ:* Auth, Human Ecology Forum (cover), Vol 9, No 2, Cornell Univ, fall 78; New Directions in American Drawing, Catalog Drawing Ctr, 82; contribr, Art in Bloom, Jacksonville Mus Art Catalog; The Art of Miami, (exhib catalog), Southeastern Ctr Contemp Art, Winston, Salem, 86. *Dealer:* George Adams Gallery 41 W 57th St New York NY 10019

WIRSUM, KARL
PAINTER, SCULPTOR
b Chicago, Ill, Sept 27, 1939. *Study:* Sch Art Inst, Chicago, BFA, 61. *Work:* AT&T, Chase Manhattan, Citibank & Whitney Mus Am Art, NY; Art Inst Chicago, First Nat Bank, Smart Gallery/Univ Chicago & Mus Contemp Art, Chicago; Nat Mus Am Art, Smithsonian Inst, Washington, DC; Mus des 20, Jahrhunderts, Vienna; Weatherspoon Art Gallery, Univ NC, Greensboro. *Comn:* First Nat Bank, Chicago, Ill; Harold Washington Libr, Chicago, Ill. *Exhib:* Solo exhibs, Hare Toddy Kong Tamari, Mus Contemp Art, Chicago, 81, Southeastern Ctr Contemp Art, Winston-Salem, NC, 82, Du Page Col, Glen Ellyn, Ill, 88, and many others; Made in USA: An Americanization in Mod Art, the 50's & 60's Traveling Show, 87; Friday Diego: Una Pareja, Prairie Ave Gallery, Chicago, 87; Contemp Cutouts: Figurative Sculpture in Two Dimensions, Whitney Mus Am Art, NY, 87-88; Diamonds are Forever: Artists & Writers on Baseball, Traveling Show, 87-90; Seymour Rosofsky & the Chicago Imagist Tradition, Milwaukee Art Mus, Univ Wis, 88; Birthday Cake, Hyde Park Art Ctr, Chicago, 89; Chicago Painters in Print, Landfall Press, 89-90; and many others. *Teaching:* Part-time instr painting & drawing, Sch Art Inst, Chicago, 74-. *Awards:* Logan Medal, Chicago and Vicinity Show, Chicago Art Inst, 69; Nat Endowment Arts Fel, 71, 77 & 83; Ill Arts Coun Fel, 86. *Bibliog:* Comic Iconoclasm, Inst Contemp Arts, London, Eng, 87; A broad brush colors Terra's exhib of Chicago Art, Chicago Tribune, 9/11/87; The Import of Imagism, Dialogue Mag, 5/6/88. *Media:* Acrylic; Wood. *Dealer:* Phyllis Kind Gallery 313 W Superior Chicago IL 60610 & 136 Greene St New York NY 10012. *Mailing Add:* Jean Albano Gallery 215 W Superior St Chicago IL 60610

WIRTZ, STEPHEN CARL
GALLERY DIRECTOR
b Peoria, Ill, Apr 9, 1945. *Study:* Occidental Col, 63; Univ Calif, Berkeley, BA, 67; Antioch Col, Ohio, MA, 68. *Specialty:* Contemporary American and European sculpture & photography. *Mailing Add:* c/o Stephen Wirtz Gallery 49 Geary St San Francisco CA 94108

WISCHER, WENDY
INSTALLATION SCULPTOR
Study: Univ Wis, Madison, BFA, 1993; Fla Stat Univ, Tallahassee, MFA, 1995; LED Inst, Lighting Res Ctr, Troy, NY, 2002; Basic Digital Audio Series for Artists, iSAW, Miami, 2003-05 & Desktop Video Prodn Series, 2003-04. *Work:* Miami Art Mus; Miami Dade Coll; Arthur & Mata Jaffe Collection, Fla Atlantic Univ, Boca Raton. *Exhib:* Solo exhibs include The Warehouse, Miami, 1999-2000, Dorsch Gallery, Miami, 2001-02, Kimberly Venardos & Co, New York, 2002, Bernice Steinbaum Gallery, Miami, 2002, Miami Herald Bldg, 2002-03, J Johnson Gallery, Jacksonville Beach, Fla, 2003, Soap Factory, Minneapolis, 2004, Diana Lowenstein Fine Arts, Miami, 2004, David Castillo Gallery, Miami, 2006 & 2008, Freedom Tower, Miami, 2007; group exhibs include The Cat's Away, Sara Meltzer Gallery, New York, 2001; Art Basel Miami Beach, 2002 & 2004; Space: Thinking Outside the Sphere, Miami Sci Mus, 2003; Transitory Patterns: Fla Women Artists, Nat Mus Women Arts, Washington, Ft Lauderdale Mus Art, Deland Mus Art & Bary Brogan Mus Art & Sci, 2004-06; Light & Atmosphere, Miami Art Mus, 2004, Marking Time: Moving Images, 2005, Disappearances: Shadows & Illusions, 2008; Native Seeds, South Fla Art Ctr, Miami Beach, 2006; Polymer Video Show, Hunter Mus Am Art, Chattanooga, Tenn, 2006; SCOPE Miami 2007. *Awards:* Art Ctr South Fla Fel, 1999; New Forms Grant, Miami-Dade Div Cult Affairs, 2000-01, 2001-02, Artist Enhancement Grant, 2004, South Fla Cult Consortium Fel, 2008; Artist Access Grant, TigerTail Prodns, Miami, 2002, 2003, 2004, 2005; Alberta Prize Visual Art, Alberta duPont Bonsal Found, 2003; Artist Enhancement Grant, Fla Div Cult Affairs, 2007; Pollock-Krasner Found Grant, 2007

WISDOM, JOYCE
PAINTER
b Los Angeles, Calif, 1940. *Study:* Pasadena City Coll, 58-59; Univ Calif, Los Angeles, 59-61; Univ Southern Calif, BFA, 62. *Work:* Los Angeles Inst Contemp Art; pvt collections, Peter Plagens, New York, Brooke Alderson & Peter Scheldahl. *Exhib:* Solo exhib, Municipal Art Gallery, 78 & Barnsdall Art Center Gallery, 90, Los Angeles, Calif,; Directions, Mt San Antonio Coll Art Gallery, Calif, 95; Korean Cult Ctr, Los Angeles, 98; Shock of the New, Gallery 825, Los Angeles, 2000; Los Angeles Nat Juried Art Exhibit, Ruth Bachotner Gallery, 2000; Black & White, BGH Gallery, Los Angeles, Calif, 2003; Group show, I 5 Gallery, Brewery Art colony, Los Angeles, 2006. *Teaching:* Instr drawing & design, Calif State Univ, Northridge, 78-80; instr, Junior Art Ctr, Los Angeles, 78-95; instr, life drawing & painting, Barnsdall Art Ctr, 81-97; instr, landscape painting, Univ Calif, Los Angeles, 91-97. *Awards:* Silver Mat Award, Oil Pastel Asn, 88; Lucille Julia Award, Oil Pastel Asn, 90; First Prize Juried Exhib, Long Beach Art Asn, 90. *Bibliog:* Louise Lewis (auth), Desert moods & sensuality, Artweek, 6/1/78; Suzanne Muchnic (auth), Wisdom's world in landscape, Los Angeles Times, 6/8/78; S Muchnic (auth), The Galleries, Los Angeles Times, 83. *Mem:* Gallery 825, Los Angeles, Calif; Los Angeles Art Asn. *Media:* Oil, Watercolor. *Dealer:* Artpic, Marina Kieser, North Hollywood. *Mailing Add:* 21144 Hillside Dr W Topanga CA 90290

WISE, GERALD LEE
GRAPHIC ARTIST, PRINTMAKER
b Pittsburgh, Pa, Dec 15, 1941. *Study:* Wheaton Col, Ill, BA, 63; Northern Ill Univ, MA (design), 67, MFA (printmaking), 69. *Work:* Mankato State Univ; Ball State Univ; St Lawrence Col. *Exhib:* Drawings USA, Minn Mus Art, 73; Ball State Drawing & Sculpture, 73 & 82; 24th Nat Prints & Drawing Exhib, Okla Art Ctr, 82; Springfield Nat Exhib, Mus Fine Arts, Mass, 82 & 83; West 82--Art and the Law Traveling Exhib, 82 & 83; Tex Fine Arts Nat, Laguna Gloria Mus, Austin, 83; 17th Nat Drawing & Sculpture Exhib, Del Mar Coll Gallery, Tex, 83. *Teaching:* Asst prof art, Mankato State Univ, 69-74 & Westfield State Col, 82-; instr, G Walter V Smith Art Mus, Springfield, Mass, 80-82. *Awards:* Purchase Awards, 24th Nat Drawing & Print Exhib, Okla Art Ctr, 82, 63rd & 64th Springfield Nat Exhib, Holyoke Community Savings Bank, Mass, 82 & 83 & Mattoon Art Festival, Bank Boston, 83. *Bibliog:* Robert Girouard (auth), Wiser yet, Mankato Free Press, 4/4/74; Mary Kronholm (auth), Wise makes living an art, Country J, 6/82; Sally Robinson (auth), A profile: Gerald Wise, Westfield Sunday News, 9/82. *Mem:* Coll Art Asn; Springfield Artists League. *Media:* Ink, Pen and Brush. *Dealer:* Hill Gallery Worthington MA 01098. *Mailing Add:* Dept Art Westfield State Col Western Ave Westfield MA 01086

WISE, JOSEPH STEPHEN
PAINTER
b Seattle, Wash, 1939. *Study:* Purdue Univ, 57-58; West Point, 58-59; Univ Puget Sound, 59-60; Indiana Univ, BS, 63; San Jose State Univ, MA, 66. *Work:* San Jose Art Mus, Calif; De Saisset Art Mus, Santa Clara, Calif; IBM Corp; twi paintings, San Jose Art Mus; DeSaisset Art Mus, Santa Clara Univ. *Comn:* Abstract, Owens/Corning Fiberglass Corp, Sunnyvale, Calif, 70; five paintings (abstract), Amdahl Corp, Sunnyvale, Calif, 79; abstract, IBM Corp, San Jose, Calif, 82; abstract, San Jose Pub Libr, Calif. *Exhib:* Solo exhibs, Triton Art Mus, San Jose, Calif, 67, Idaho State Coll, Moscow, Idaho, 69, Wash State Coll, Pullman, 69, Cabrillo Jr Coll Art Gallery, Aptos, Calif, 74, Toll House, Los Gatos, 92, Gallery Morgan Hill, 2006; 85th Ann Nat Exhib, Mus Art, San Francisco, 67; Greenleaf Gallery, Saratoga, Calif, 81. *Teaching:* Instr art, W Valley Jr Coll, 64-67 & San Jose Pub Schs, 68-2000. *Awards:* Award for Oil Painting, San Jose Art League, 71; Award for Oil Painting, Los Gatos Art Asn, 94, 96, 99 & 2003; Plein Air painting contest winner, Hidden Villa, Los Altos, Calif, 2005; Honorable mention, Paint the Adobes Plein Air, Monterey, Cal, 2012. *Mem:* Nat Educ Asn; Calif Teachers Asn; Life mem West Point Alumni Asn; Calif Art Educ Asn; Los Gatos Art Asn; Valle del Sur Plein Air Painters, Morgan Hill, Calif (pres). *Media:* Oil, Canvas. *Specialty:* Creatively interpreting the Am landscape. *Interests:* writing; poetry; reading; hiking; golf. *Collection:* Original artwork By Boucher, M Logan, H Richter & more. *Dealer:* The Affordable Masterworks Gallery

WISE, KELLY
PHOTOGRAPHER, CRITIC
b New Castle, Ind, 1932. *Study:* Purdue Univ, BS, 55; Columbia Univ, MA, 59. *Hon Degrees:* Purdue Univ, LHD, 2009. *Work:* Int Mus Photog; Nat Portrait Gallery; Mus Fine Arts, Houston; Libr Cong, Washington, DC; Baltimore Art Mus; Biblioteque Nationale, Paris; Mus Fine Arts, Boston; Polaroid Int; Fogg Art Mus. *Exhib:* Solo exhibs, Fogg Art Mus, 73, Addison Gallery Am Art, Andover, Mass, 85, Art Ctr, Delaware Univ, 86, Art Gallery, Con Coll, 86, Yuen Lui Gallery, Seattle, 86, Kresge Art Mus, Mich State Univ, 87 & Brockton Art Mus, 87; Private Realities, Mus Fine Arts, Boston, 74; Recent Photographs, Il Diaframma, Milan, Italy, 77; Warm Truths & Cool Deceits, Sidney Janis Gallery, NY, 78; Color Photographs, Snite Art Mus, Univ Notre Dame, 81; Still Points, Rose Art Mus, Brandeis Univ, 81; Portraits: Men & Women of Letters, Vision Gallery, Boston, 83; Iisalmon Kamera, Helsinki, Finland, 84; Archive Gallery, New York, 87. *Pos:* Photog consult, Nat Humanities Fac, Concord, Mass, 70-74 & Polaroid Corp, Cambridge, Mass, 74-77; photog critic, Boston Globe, 82-93; art commentator, Nat Pub Radio 87-89. *Teaching:* Phillips Acad, Andover, Mass, 66-2000. *Awards:* City Limits Proj Grant, Polaroid Corp, 85-87; Distinguished Alumnus Award, Purdue Univ, 96. *Bibliog:* Max Kozloff (auth), Photography & Fascination, Addison House Publ, 79. *Mem:* Soc Photog Educ; Photog Resource Ctr, Boston. *Publ:* Ed, The Photographers Choice, 75, auth, Still Points, 77 & ed, Lotte Jacobi, 78, Addison House; assoc ed, Views Jour Photog, 80-81; ed, Portrait: Theory, Lustrum Press, 81; ed, Photo Facts and Opinions, Addison Gallery Am Art, 81; ed & auth, Photog, City Limits, 87. *Mailing Add:* 427 B Pond St Jamaica Plain MA 02130

WISE, SUE
PAINTER
b Bronx, NY, Mar 22, 1921. *Study:* Univ Colo with Gene Mathews & Frank Sampson; special study with Thomas Currey, William Schimmel, and Herb Thompson. *Work:* Nat State Bank, Boulder, Colo; US Bank Art Collection, St Paul, Minn; Geille Associates, Boulder, Colo; First Nat Bank, Denver, Colo; United Bank, Denver, Colo; and others. *Comn:* Sinage, Coot Lake Interpretive Trail, City of Boulder Parks and Recreation, 2003. *Exhib:* Own Your Own Exhib, Denver Art Mus, Colo, 67, 68; Watercolor USA, Springfield Art Mus, Mo, 71; 59th Ann Exhib, Nat Watercolor Soc, Palm Spring Desert Mus, Calif, 79; 60th Ann Exhib, Nat Watercolor Soc, Laguna Beach, Calif, 80; 155th Ann Exhib, Nat Acad Design, NY, 80; Fine Arts Exhib, State Fair, Pueblo, Colo, 81; Rocky Mt Nat, Foothills Art Ctr, Colo, 81; 114th Ann Exhib, Am Watercolor Soc, Nat Acad Galleries, New York, 81; Rocky Mountain Nat Watermedia Exhib, Foothills Art Ctr, Golden, Colo, 84; and others. *Awards:* Bronze Medal of Honor, Am Watercolor Soc, 74; Foothills Art Ctr Award, 78; Mary Pleissner Mem Award, Am Watercolor Soc, 82. *Bibliog:* Edward Betts (auth) Creative Seascape Painting, pp 50, 105, NY, 81; Gerald F Brommer and Nancy K Kinne (coauths), Exploring Painting, pp 30, 132, 214, Worcester, Mass, 88; Gerald F Brommer (auth), College Techniques: A Guide for Artists and Illustrators, pp 66, 67, 138, 139, NY, 94. *Mem:* Am Watercolor Soc; Dolphin Fel; Nat Watercolor Soc; Rocky Mountain Nat Watermedia Soc; Longmont Artists Guild, Colo (hon mem). *Media:* Mixed Watermedia, Collage, Watercolor. *Publ:* Auth, The watercolor page, Am Artist Mag, 2/77; contribr, Easy Living Mag, The Webb co, 78. *Dealer:* Red Canyon Art Gallery Lyons Co; Fine Print Imaging Fort Collins Co. *Mailing Add:* 2424 9th Ave Apt 2110 Longmont CO 80503

WISE, SUZANNE TANDERUP
ADMINISTRATOR, HISTORIAN
b Great Lakes, Ill, Jan 31, 1952. *Study:* Univ Nebr, Lincoln, BA, 1974; Univ Kans, MA, 1980. *Pos:* Cur, Mary & Leigh Block Gallery, Northwestern Univ, 1982-84; educ specialist, Sheldon Art Gallery, Univ Nebr, Lincoln, 1984-; visual arts mgr, Nebr Arts Coun, 1988, exec dir. *Teaching:* Instr art hist, Univ Nebr, 1979-82 & 1985- & Creighton Univ, 1980. *Mem:* Coll Art Asn; Am Asn Mus; Midwest Art Hist Soc; Nat Art Educ Asn. *Res:* Nineteenth and twentieth century American painting and photography. *Publ:* Contribr, Jules Breton and the French Rural Tradition, 1982 & Joslyn Art Museum Handbook of the Permanent Collection, 1983, Joslyn Art Mus; Alice Aycock: The Machine That Makes the World, Nouveau and Deco Art Glass, 1985; American Impressionism from the Sheldon Collection, Sheldon Art Gallery, 1986. *Mailing Add:* Nebr Arts Coun 1004 Farnam St Plaza Level Omaha NE 68102

WISE, TAKOUHY
GALLERY DIRECTOR, ART DEALER
b Teheran, Iran; US citizen. *Study:* Univ Lausanne, Switz, 61-63; Int Ctr Photog, 77-80. *Collection Arranged:* Hollywood Fashion, 83, Nudes by Fashion Photographers, 83, Portraits of Artists, 84, Louise Dahl Wolfe, 84 & Horst: His Work and World, 85, Staley-Wise Gallery, NY. *Pos:* Fashion & photog ed, Seventeen Mag, 67-70; co-dir, Staley-Wise Gallery, New York, currently. *Specialty:* 20th century photography. *Mailing Add:* Staley-Wise Gallery 560 Broadway New York NY 10012

WISEMAN, ARI
MUSEUM DIRECTOR
Study: Courtauld Inst Art, London, MA (art hist). *Pos:* Sr asst acquisitions, Metrop Mus Art, New York, formerly; dep dir, Mus Contemp Art Los Angeles, 2001-2010 & Solomon R Guggenheim Found, 2010-. *Mem:* PS Arts (bd mem). *Mailing Add:* Guggenheim Foundation 345 Hudson St New York NY 10014-4502

WISEMAN, DEANNA LYNN
PAINTER, INSTRUCTOR
b Sunbury, Pa, Nov 12, 1959. *Study:* York Acad Arts, 1980; Studied with Am Soc Portrait Artists, Metropolitan Mus & Art Students League, with John Howard Sanden, Richard Schmid, and Martha Orozco, NY, 2001; Studied with Mike Heid, Lewisburg, Pa, 2009. *Work:* Line Mtn Animal Hospital, Herndon, Pa; Gratz Nat Bank, Gratz, Pa; Polk Found, Millersburg Pa; Hut Restaurant, Herndon, Pa; St John's Church, Berrysburg, Pa; Grace Community Church, Herndon, Pa. *Comn:* A Late Afternoon Hunt, comn by Dr Steve Rebuck, Rebuck, Pa, 1997; Lacey, comn by Dr Carole J Patton, Millersburg, Pa, 2001; Hawaiian Honeymoon, comn by Dr Poonan Strivastava, Selinsgrove, Pa, 2002; Winter Shadows Along Fishers Ridge, comn by Bryant Troutman, Klingerstown, Pa, 2006; Loading Hay (hist mem), comn by Dr John A Romberger, Elizabethville, Pa, 2008; Gathering Wheat (hist mem), comm by Dr. John A Romberger, Elizabethville, Pa, 2011; If my People, comn by Bryant Troutman, Klingerstown, Pa, 2012; Bryants's Hidden Paradise, comn by Shirley Troutman, Klingerstwon, Pa. *Exhib:* Lewisburg Art Festival, Packwood House Mus, Lewisburg, Pa, 2000, 2002-2009; Lewisburg, Stroll through the Arts, 2000; Portrait Arts Festival, Metrop Mus, New York, NY, 2001; Art Educators Exhib, Gallery on the Square, Millersburg, Pa, 2003; Judged Juried Art Show, Packwood House Mus, Lewisburg, Pa, 2006; Sun, Sand & Surf, Wiseman Graphics Gallery & Frame Shop, Herndon, Pa, 2006; Sea Lore Art Show, Art Asn Harrisburg, Harrisburg, Pa, 2007; Susquehanna Bank Show, Millersburg, Pa, 2000-2013; Susquehanna Art Soc, 2013; Susquehanna Bank Art Show, 2013. *Collection Arranged:* Sun Sand & Surf, 2004, 2006, Fall Hunt, 2004, The Messiah, 2005, Frame Your Sweetheart Photography, 2006, Mahanocy & Mahantango Hist Preservation Soc Holiday Art Tour, 2006, Wiseman Graphics Gallery, Herndon, Pa. *Pos:* Art instr, Gallery on the Sq, Millersburg, Pa, 1994-2007; pvt art classes, Wiseman Graphics, Herndon, Pa, 2006-; art instr, Northern Dauphin Christian Sch, 2012, 2013. *Teaching:* Instr, drawing & Painting, Millersburg Area Art Asn, 1993-2007; instr (pvt classes), basic drawing, Found painting, Wiseman Graphics & Frame Shop, 1995-; found drawing, Northern Dauphin Christian Sch, Millersburg, Pa, 2013, painting, 2013. *Awards:* Scholastic Art Award, Nat High Sch Art Exhib, Harrisburg Patriot News, 1972; A I Watts Award, York Acad Arts, Founder York Acad Arts, York, Pa, 1980; Award for Excellence in Portraiture, Portrait Exhib, York Acad

Arts, York, Pa, 1980; Best of Show, Community Banks Art Show, Community Banks, Millersburg, Pa, 1999; Best of Show, Dauphin Co Gratz Fair, Gratz Fair Asn, 2006; Second Place, Juried Sea Lore Art Show, Art Asn Harrisburg, 2007; Best of show, Dauphin Co Grtz Fair, Gratz Fair Asn, 2009, 2010; 2nd place, Susquehanna Art Soc, Sunbury, Pa, 2009; 1st place, Dauphin Co Gratz Fair, Gratz Fair Asn, 2012. *Bibliog:* Julie L Blizzard (auth), The Picture of Generosity, Daily Item, Susquehanna Today, April 2000; Michelle Adams, Klingerstown Bicentennial Album, Huele & Gordon, May 2007; Steve Troutman (auth), Bridge Over Pine Creek, Susquehanna Life, 2008; Lauren Hackenberg (auth), Memories in Art, The News Item Repulican & Herald, Feb 2008. *Mem:* Millersburg Area Art Asn (art instr, 1993-2007); Lewisburg Arts Coun (judge, 2006); Am Soc Portrait Artists (signature mem 1999-); Art Asn Harrisburg (artist mem, 2005-); Lewisburg Art Coun (1998-); Susquehanna Art Soc (2008-) ; Pastel Soc Am (2012-). *Media:* Pastel, pencil, charcoal, oil, acrylic. *Res:* Hist res with Dr John Romberger, Steve Troutman, Clair Troutman, Bryant Troutman on hist of Klingerstown Landmarks & Homesteads. *Specialty:* Hist Art, local landmarks, portraiture. *Interests:* Preserving History with commissioned art and prints; Horseback riding, traveling, photog, res & copy writing, publ. *Publ:* Many advert illus & logos. *Dealer:* Carrie Whisler Thomas Art Asn of Harrisburg 21 N Front St Harrisburg PA 17101; Owen Mahon Open Door Gallery 430 Market St Lewisburg PA 17837; Jim Stutsman Gallery on the Square 226 Union St Millersburg PA 17061. *Mailing Add:* PO Box 383 Herndon PA 17830

WISNESKI, KURT
PRINTMAKER
Study: Syracuse Univ, NY, MFA, 1974; Univ of Mass, Amhurst, BFA, 1972. *Exhib:* Miami Int Print Biennial Exhib, Metrop Mus, Miami Fla, 1982; Int Exhib of Smaller Prints, Taller Galeria, Barcelona, Spain, 1985-1987; Works on Paper, Fine Arts Acad, Warsaw, Poland, 1988. *Pos:* Printmaking Lab Demonstrator, Univ of Mich, Ann Arbor, 1975-76; printmaking staff asst, Univ of Mass, Amherst, 1976-80. *Teaching:* Vis Lectr, Univ of Mass, Dartmouth, 1980-86; asst prof, Univ of Mass, Dartmouth, 1986-91; prof, Univ of Mass Dartmouth, 1996-. *Awards:* Group Exhib at Art Adv/Boston, 2000; One person Exhib at Brown Univ Art Gallery, 2000; NH Inst of Art Print Exhib, 2001; Photo Into Art, Bridgewater State Univ, 2001; South Coast New Eng Printmaking, Univ of Mass Dartmouth Art Gallery, 2003. *Publ:* Auth: Monotype/Monoprint, Hist and Tecn, Bullbrier Press, Ithaca, NY, 1995. *Mailing Add:* Univ of Mass Dartmouth 285 Old Westport Rd Dartmouth MA 02747-2300

WISSEMANN-WIDRIG, NANCY
PAINTER
b Jamestown, NY. *Study:* Syracuse Univ, NY, BFA; Ohio Univ, Athens, MFA. *Work:* Canton Art Inst, Ohio; Univ Kans Mus Fine Arts; Port Authority of NY; Univ Tulsa, Okla; Farnsworth Mus Art, Rockland, Maine; American Telephone & Telegraph Co; Amerada Hess Corp; Bank of Boston, MA; Conde Nast Publications; DeLoitte and Touche; ICI Americas; Mony Corp, NY; Port Authority, NY; Portland Mus Art, Portland, Me. *Exhib:* Farnsworth Art Mus, Maine, 1996; Flowers, Heckscher Mus, Huntington, NY, 1996; solo exhibs, Gleason Fine Arts, Boothbay Harbor, Maine, 1996, Gold/Smith, Boothbay Harbor, Maine, 2007 & Caldbeck Gallery, Rockland, Maine, 2008; Roundtop Ctr Arts, Damariscotta, Maine, 1996; G Watson Gallery, Stonington, Maine; New O'Farrell Gallery, Brunswick, Maine, 2001; Caldbeck Gallery, Rockland, Maine, 2003; Whitney Artworks, Portland, Maine, 2004; Water Paintings, Caldbeck Gallery, Rockland, Maine, 2005; The Sea Garden, Gallery North, Setauket, NY, 2006; Am Acad Arts and Letts Invitational, New York, 2009; The Drawing Room, St George, Maine, 2009; Percent for Art, Litchfield Sc, Litchfield, Maine; Am Acad Arts & Letters, 2009; Caldbeck Gallery, 2010, 2012; Water Gallery West, Michael J Grant Campus, Suffolk County Community Coll, Brentwood, NY, 2010; Caldbeck Gallery, Rockland, Me, 2012. *Teaching:* Instr, Oysterponds Sch, 1969-85 & Laurel Sch, 1977-85. *Awards:* Outstanding Realist, Western New York Artists, Albright-Knox Art Gallery, 1964; Purchase Award, Am Acad Arts and Letts, Childe Hassam Fund, 1969. *Bibliog:* Carl Little & Arnold Skolnick (coauths), Painting of Maine, Potter, 1991; Bernice Steinbaum (auth), The Rocking Chair, Rizzoli, 1992; Theodore Wolfe (auth), On The Edge 40 Years of Maine Painting, 1992; C. Little & A. Akolnick (coauths), The Art of Maine in Winter; Stephen May (auth), Painting the Sea, Maine's Moving Target, Portland Mag; Philip Isaacson (auth), Visit to the Peaks, Three Artists Currently Residing There, Maine Sunday Telegram, 2001; Liz Wood (auth), A Moveable Feast, Liz Wood, The Suffolk Times; Suzette Mac Avoy (auth), Maine Home Design, 8/2008; Carl Little (auth), Maine Home, Boats, and Harbors (article), 2012; Britta Konav (auth), Fresh from the Studio, Maine Home Design, 2014. *Mem:* E End Arts & Humanities Long Island; Ctr Maine Contemp Art, Portland Mus Art. *Media:* Acrylic, Oil. *Dealer:* Calbeck Gallery 12 Elm St Rockland ME 04841

WITHAM, VERNON CLINT
PAINTER, PRINTMAKER
b Eugene, Ore, Dec 6, 1925. *Study:* Univ Ore; Calif Sch Fine Arts, San Francisco. *Work:* Univ Ore Mus Art, Eugene; Univ Wyo Mus Art, Laramie. *Comn:* Murals, Multnomah Athletic Club, Portland, Ore. *Exhib:* Under 25, Seligmann Gallery, NY, 49; Artists of Oregon, Portland Art Mus, 53; Solo exhibs, Calif Palace Legion Hon, San Francisco, 60 & Univ Ore Mus Art, 80; Maxwell Gallery, San Francisco, 61; Am Landscape, Peridot Gallery, NY, 68. *Teaching:* Resident artist, Univ Wyo, 71-. *Awards:* Purchase Award, Northwest Painting Ann, 72. *Media:* Oil; All. *Collection:* Antique primitive art from around the world. *Publ:* Coauth, 12 new painters (serigraph folio), 53; contribr, insert 4, Written Palette, 62. *Dealer:* Tiqua Gallery 812 Canyon Rd Santa Fe NM 87501

WITHERS, JOSEPHINE
HISTORIAN, WRITER
b Cambridge, Mass, July 3, 1938. *Study:* Oberlin Col, BA (art hist), 60; Columbia Univ, MA, 65, PhD, 71. *Collection Arranged:* Julio Gonzalez, Sculpture and Drawings, Mus Mod Art, NY, 68; 350 Years of Art in Maryland, 20th Century Section (auth, catalog), Univ Md Art; Women Artists in Washington Collections (auth, catalog), Univ Md Art Gallery, 79. *Pos:* Assoc dir, Univ Md Art Gallery, 70-73; chief reader art hist, Advan Placement Educ Testing Serv, 79-83; art consult, Feminist Studies, 78-. *Teaching:* Asst prof art hist, Temple Univ, Philadelphia, Pa, 68-69; assoc dir, Art Gallery, Univ Md, 70-73, asst prof art hist, 71-78, actg dir women's studies prog, 82-84, assoc prof art hist, 78-. *Awards:* Aelioian Fel, Oberlin Col, 64; Gen Res Bd, Univ Md, 72, 77 & 85; fel, Nat Endowment Arts, 72 & 78. *Mem:* Coll Art Asn; Women's Caucus Art (nat bd dir, 80-83); Washington Women's Art Ctr (bd dir, 76-77); Conf of Women in the Visual Arts (steering comt, 72); Wash New Art Asn (bd mem, 87-91). *Res:* Twentieth century art; American women artists of the nineteenth and twentieth centuries. *Publ:* Auth, Artistic women and women artists, summer 76 & The artistic collaboration of Picasso and Gonzales, winter 76, Art J; auth, The Famous Fur-Lined Teacup and The Anonymous Meret Oppenheim, Arts Mag, 11/77; Julio Gonzalez, Sculpture in Iron, New York Univ Press, 77; In search of the magic kingdom, New Art Examiner, 10/81; Musing about the muse, Feminist Studies, spring 83. *Mailing Add:* Art History Dept-Art/Sociology Bldg Univ Maryland Rm 4212 College Park MD 20742

WITKIN, JEROME
PAINTER, DRAFTSMAN
b Brooklyn, NY, Sept 13, 1939. *Study:* Cooper Union Art Sch, 57-60; Skowhegan Sch Painting & Sculpture; Berlin Acad, WGer, Pulitzer traveling fel, 60; Univ Pa, MFA, 70. *Work:* Hirshhorn Mus; Uffizi Gallery, Florence, Italy; Butler Inst Am Art, Youngstown, Ohio; Am Acad Arts & Letters; Everson Mus Art, Syracuse; Nat Acad Design; Metrop Mus Art, NY; Minn Mus, St Paul, Minn; Nat Acad Design, NY; Ark Art Ctr, Little Rock, Ark; Achenback Found Graphic Arts, San Francisco, Calif; numerous others. *Comn:* Portraits, Flower Veterinary Library, NY State Coll Veterinary Medicine. *Exhib:* Drawings USA, Minn Mus Art, 71; Sherry French Gallery, NY; Drawings, Kraushaar Gallery, NY, 71; Pa State Mus, 78; Religion into Art, nat traveling exhib, 81; Real, Really Real, Super Real, San Antonio Mus, 81-82; traveling show, West '85 Art & the Law; Morality Tales: Hist Painting in the 80's, Independent Curators Inc, NY, 87-88; Nocturnes & Nightmares, Fla State Univ Gallery & Mus, 87; Life Stories, Henry Art Gallery, Univ Wash, Seattle, 88; Jack Rutberg Fine Arts, LA, Calif, 2007. *Teaching:* Instr drawing, Md Inst Art, Baltimore, 63-65; lectr painting, Manchester Col Art, Eng, 65-67; vis prof design, drawing & painting, Moore Col, 68-71; assoc prof art, Syracuse Univ, 71-81, prof, 82-; lectr, Columbia Mus Art, SC, 83, Ark Art Ctr, Little Rock, 83; vis artist, Univ Utah, 86, Univ Wis, 88 & Univ Wash, 88. *Awards:* Guggenheim Found Fel Painting, 63-64; Paul Puzinas Award, Nat Acad Design, 80; Fund Purchase Prize, Am Acad Arts & Letters, 81; Chancellor's Citation for Excellence in Teaching, Syracuse Univ, 83. *Bibliog:* Theodore F Wolff (auth), The excellence of the work of Jerome Witkin, 4/28/83 & A master storyteller on the threshold of great art, 11/6/85, Christian Sci Monitor; Kenneth Baker (auth), Paintings not to miss: Jerome Witkin in Santa Clara, San Francisco Chronicle, 87; W S Di Piero (auth), Force & witness: on Jerome Witkin, Arts Mag, 11/87. *Mem:* Nat Acad Design; Nat Acad (assoc, 83, acad, 90-). *Media:* Oil on Linen. *Publ:* Life Lessons: The Art of Jerome Witkin, SU Press, 94. *Dealer:* Jack Rutberg Fine Arts 357 N La Brea Ave Los Angeles CA. *Mailing Add:* 201 Whitestone Dr Syracuse NY 13215

WITKIN, JOEL-PETER
PHOTOGRAPHER
b Brooklyn, NY, Sept 13, 1939. *Study:* Cooper Union, New York, BFA, 75; Univ NMex, MA, 77, MFA, 86. *Work:* Metrop Mus Art & Mus Mod Art, NY; Nat Gallery Art & Nat Mus Am Art, Smithsonian Inst, Washington; San Francisco Mus Mod Art, Calif; Boston Mus Fine Arts, Mass; Victoria & Albert Mus, London, Eng; Walker Art Ctr, Minneapolis, Minn; MEP, Paris; Philadelphia Mus; Art Inst Chicago; Whitney Mus; Guggenheim Mus; Mus d'Arte Contemp; Biblioteche Nationale Paris, MOMA, NY. *Comn:* photograph, The Plague Years, New York Times, History of the First Millenium, 2000; Raft of George W Bush, Galerie Boudoin, Lebon, Paris. *Exhib:* Great Photographs from the Museum Collection, Mus Modern Art, NY, 59 & Paintings from City Walls, 69, Mus Mod Art, NY; Contemp Photogrs of NMex, Art Inst Chicago, Ill, 80; Form, Freud & Feeling, 82, Biennial Exhib, 84 & Signs of the Times (with catalog), 86, San Francisco Mus Mod Art, Calif; Mois de la Photo, Mus Mod Art, Paris, France, 82; Personal Choice, Victoria & Albert Mus, London, Eng, 83; Whitney Biennial, 85 & Sacred Images in Secular Art, 86, Whitney Mus Am Art, NY; solo exhibs, Forty Photographs (with catalog), San Francisco Mus Mod Art, traveling, 85, Brooklyn Mus Art, NY, 86, Pace/MacGill Gallery, NY, 87, 89, 91, 93 & 95, Fraenkel Gallery, San Francisco, 91, 93 & 95, Mus de Cahors, France, 93, Galerie Mokka, Rayjkavik, Ireland, 94, Solomon Guggenheim Mus, 95 & Castello Di Rivoli, Mus d'Arte Contemp, Torino, Italy, 95, Palves di Tokyo, Paris, 95, Mus of Fine Arts, Mus of NM, 98, Biblioteque Nationale, Paris, 2011, Lust Gallery, Vienna, 2012, Santiago Mus, Chile, 2013; Crosscurrents, Forty Yrs of Photog Art (with catalog), Los Angeles Co Mus Art, Calif, 87; The Photog of Invention, Nat Mus Am Art, Washington, 89; Ojects O Trouves d'Artiste, Galerie Urbi et Orbi, Paris, France, 92; Magicians of Light, Nat Gallery Can, 93; Mexico Through Foreign Eyes, Mus Art Contemp, Mexico City, 93; Photo Dessin/Dessin Photo, Espace Van Gogh, Arles, France, 94; Still Pictures/Still Life, Univ RI, 94; Interkamera Photo Festival, Prague, 95; The Mythic Image, David Adamson Gallery, Washington, 97; Presence of Greek Myth, Univ di Palermo, Sicily, 98; MEP Paris, Bibliotheque, Nationale de France, 2012; Gallery Vienna, 2012; Vol de Nuits, Galerie Marseilles, 2013; JB Gallery, Geneva, 2013; Topographie del'art, Paris, 2013; Museo Alinari, Florence, 2013; Pan Mus, Naples, 2013; Santiago Mus Modern Art, Chile, 2013. *Awards:* Nat Endowment Arts Fel Photog, 80, 81, 86 & 92; Int Ctr Photog Award in Art Photog, 88; Cooper Union Distinguished Alumni Citation, 88; Decorated Chevalier Des Arts et de Lettres, France, 90; Augustus Saint Gaudens Medal, Cooper Union Sch Art, 96; Decorated Comdr Arts and Letters, France, 2000. *Bibliog:* Hofman (auth), Physical prodigies of all kinds, The Times Literary Supplement, London, 3/1/96; William Messer (auth), A tale of two festivals, World Art, 97; Hubert Fisher (auth), Spiel mit der asthetik des schrecklichen, Munchner Kultur, 6/97. *Media:* Photography. *Publ:* Auth, Forty Photographs, San Francisco Mus Mod Art, 87; Photovision, Madrid, Spain, 88; Gods

of Earth & Heaven, Twelvetrees Press, 91; Joel-Peter Witkin, Twelve Photographs in Gravure, Kevin Begos, 94; ed, Harms Way, Twelvetrees Press, Santa Fe, NMex, 94; auth, Disciple and Master, Marval, Paris, 95; auth, Photographs, Phaidon, 98; auth, Maestro, Delpire, Paris, 2012; Bibliotheque Nat de France, Heaven or Hell, 2012; Heaven & Hell, Biblioteque Nat De Fr, 2012; Joel-Peter Witkin, Maestro, Delpire, Paris, 2012. *Dealer:* Galerie Boudoin Lebon Paris; Silverstein Photography NY; Catherine Edelman Gallery Chicago

WITKOVSKY, MATTHEW
CURATOR
Study: Yale Univ, BA (lit); Univ Pa, MA & PhD (hist art). *Collection Arranged:* Dada: Zurich, Berlin, Hannover, Cologne, New York, Paris, 2006; Foto: Modernity in Central Europe, 1918-1945, Nat Gallery Art, Washington, 2007; The Art of the American Snapshop: From the Collection of Robert E Jackson, 2007. *Pos:* Vis fel, Sterling & Frances Clark Art Inst, formerly; Andrew W Mellon curatorial fel, Nat Gallery Art, Washington, formerly, res assoc, dept mod & contemp art, formerly, asst cur photog, formerly, assoc cur photog, 2003-09; with Solomon R Guggenheim Mus, New York & Philadelphia Mus Art, formerly; chair photog, Art Inst Chicago, 2009-. *Awards:* Am Asn Mus Curs Award, 2006; Kraszna-Krausz Award, 2007; Alfred H Barr, Jr Award, Coll Art Asn, 2007. *Mailing Add:* Art Inst Chicago 111 S Michigan Ave Chicago IL 60603

WITMEYER, STANLEY HERBERT
PAINTER, CONSULTANT
b Palmyra, Pa, Feb 14, 1913. *Study:* Sch Art & Design, Rochester Inst Technol, dipl; State Univ NY Coll Buffalo, BS; Syracuse Univ, MFA; Univ Hawaii, with Ben Norris. *Exhib:* Rochester Mem Art Gallery; Albright-Knox Gallery, Buffalo; Honolulu Acad Fine Arts; Everson Mus, Syracuse. *Pos:* Dir sch art & design, Rochester Inst Technol, 52-68, assoc dean Coll Fine & Appl Arts, 68-82. *Teaching:* Instr art, Cuba Pub Schs, NY, 39-44; prof painting & design, Sch Art Design, Rochester Inst Technol, 46-52. *Awards:* Distinguished Alumni Award, Rochester Inst Technol, 72; Distinguished State Art Teachers Award, NY, 78; Distinguished Alumni Award, State Univ NY, Buffalo, 80. *Mem:* Rochester Torch Club (pres, 52); Nat Art Educ Asn; Rochester Art Club (pres, 56); NY State Art Teachers Asn. *Media:* Mixed. *Collection:* American printmakers and painters. *Publ:* Auth, articles in, Everyday Art, Design Mag, Sch Arts, Nat Art Educ J & NY Art Teachers Bull

WITOLD, KACZANOWSKI
PAINTER, SCULPTOR
b Warsaw, Poland, May 15, 1932; US citizen. *Study:* Acad Fine Arts, Warsaw, with W Fangor & H Tomaszerski, dipl, 56. *Work:* Mus NMex, Santa Fe; Phoenix Art Mus, Ariz; Nat Libr, Paris, France; Conoco Oil Co, Houston, Tex; United Calif Bank. *Comn:* Mural, Polish Exhib, Moscow, USSR, 60; Auschwitz (mural), Govt Poland, 61; painting, United Bank Calif, Beverly Hills, 71; painting, Conoco Oil Co, Houston, Tex, 74; mural, Mainstreet Art Festival, Houston, 75; Colo Symphony Orchestra, 2004. *Exhib:* Solo exhibs, Keystone Ctr, Colo, 77, Anneke Whatley Gallery, Keystone, Colo, 78, Gallery 400, Aspen, Colo, 79, J Houston Gallery, Vail, Colo, 81 & Richtofen Castle, Denver, 81; Solo Retrospective, Sothebys, Amsterdam, Netherlands, 2007; Gallery Arte, Denver, Colo, 86; Classic Century Sq Gallery, NMex, 87; From Man to Black Holes, Tyle Swiatow Gallery; Music in Art, Anchorage Mus History and Art, 2004; From Little People to Black Holes, Royal Lazienski Nat Gallery, Warsaw, 2011; Close to 50 solo and group exhibs in Europe and the United States. *Teaching:* Lectr, Seton Hall Univ, 71, Cranbrook Acad Art, 78, Univ Detroit, 78, Wedgewood Soc, Chicago, 79 & Alliance Francaise Soc, Calif, 87. *Awards:* Medal of Esteem, Pagart, Polish Artists Agency, 90; Medal of Achievement and Honor, Republic of Poland,97. *Bibliog:* Michel Casse (ed), Le Crevasses du Ciel, Paris, 67. *Media:* Oil, Acrylic; Metal. *Mailing Add:* 329 Detroit St Denver CO 80206

WITT, DAVID L
WRITER, CURATOR
b Kansas City, Mo, Nov 3, 1951. *Study:* Kans State Univ, BS, 74; Univ Okla, MA, 2000. *Collection Arranged:* Emil Bisttram, 83; True Fresco: The Artistic Descendants of Diego Rivers, 86; Larry Calcagno, 87; Joe Waldrum, 88; Earl Stroh, Paintings 1953-1990, 90-91; Ken Price, Ceramic Sculpture and Drawings, 94; Agnes Martin, Recent Paintings, 94; Linda Benglis, Ceramic Sculpture, 94; Patroriño Barela, 96; Michio Takayama, 99; Three Taos Pueblo Painters, 2003; Wild at Heart: Ernest Thompson Seton, NMex Hist Mus, 2010-2011; and numerous others. *Pos:* Curatorial asst, Seton Mus, Cimarron, NMex, 72-74; cur, Gaspard House Mus, Taos, NMex, 78-79, Harwood Found Mus, Taos, NMex, 79-2005 & Acad for the Love of Learning, 2005-. *Awards:* SW Bk Award, Border Reg Libr Asn, 93, 98 & 2003; Ralph Emerson Twitchell Award, Hist Soc NMex, 2003. *Mem:* NMex Asn Mus (pres, 86-88); NMex Art Hist Conf (founder, 86). *Res:* Artists and art history of twentieth century New Mexico; contemporary art. *Collection:* Artwork of Ernest Thompson Seton. *Publ:* Auth, The Taos Artists - A Historical Narrative and Biographical Dictionary, Ewell Publ, 84; contribr, The Transcendental Art of Emil Bisttram, Pintores Press, 88; Taos Moderns: Art of the New, Red Crane Bks, 92; The Harwood Foundation of the University of New Mexico, Taos 1923-1993, History and Collection, Harwood Found, 93; coauth, Spirit Ascendant, The Art and Life of Patrocino Barela, Red Crane Bks, 96; publ & contribr, New Mexico Art History Conference Abstracts, SWAHC, 96; contribr, Taos Artists and their Patrons, UNM Press, 99, The New Mexico Millennium Collection, NMMC, Ltd; Ernest Thompson Seton, The Life & Legacy of an Artist & Conservationist, Gibbs Smith Publ, 2010 (Ralph Emerson Twitchell award, 2011). *Mailing Add:* PO Box 317 Taos NM 87571

WITT, JOHN
PAINTER, PRINTMAKER
b Wilmington, Del, Jan 30, 1940. *Study:* Philadelphia Coll Art, BFA, 62; Univ Md Grad Sch; Brooklyn Mus Sch Art. *Work:* New Britain Mus Am Art; Smithsonian Inst, USMC Combat Art Collections, US Navy Combat Art Collection, Pentagon & US Army, Off Chief Mil Hist, Washington, DC; USAF Art Program. *Comn:* Oil Painting, Ida Lewis Rescue 1869, US Coast Guard 200th Anniversary Moments in History Collection; oil painting, CMSGT Etchberger, Air Force Cross, A1C Pitsenbarger; Medal of Honor, USAF Heritage Hall, 2000; Ssgt Henry Erwin Medal of Honor; USAF Res Libr, Ala, 2003; USAF Documentation of "Enduring Freedom" Pacific Theater, 2001; Iraqi Freedom, 2003; Tsunami Relief, 2005; Afghanistan, 2009, 2012. *Exhib:* Smithsonian Inst Vietnam Exhib, Washington, DC, 69; Nat Arts Club, NY, 72; Hudson Valley Art Asn Ann, White Plains, NY, 72; Audubon Artists Ann, NY, 73; Am Artists Prof League Ann, NY, 73; Iraq War, 2003; Tsunami Relief, 2005; Afghanistan, 2009, 2012. *Pos:* Combat artist, USMC Civilian Comn, 68-69 & US Navy, 73 & 76; courtroom trial artist, ABC News, 74; chmn, Soc Illusrs Mus Am Illus, 88-. *Teaching:* Instr illus, State Univ NY, 84-. *Awards:* Gold Medal, Hudson Valley Art Asn, 72; Best in Show, Nat Arts Club, New York, 72; Gold Medal, Louis E Seley NACAL Award, 78; Dean Cornwell Award, Soc of Illustr, 90. *Bibliog:* US Army, Executive Corridor Section of the Army, USGPO, 66; Mark Goodman (auth), Trial of art, New Times Mag, 5/17/74; Coll Raymond Henri (auth), Combat art since 1775, Marine Corps Gazette, 74; US Coast Guard Moments in History, 90. *Mem:* Soc Illusr (pres, 80-83). *Media:* Multimedia. *Publ:* Auth & illusr, Vietnam, Sterling, 72; illusr, Mitchell-Stans Trial, Newsweek Mag, Mitchell-Stans Trial Courtroom Drawings, ABC News, 74, Marine Corps Gazette, 74 & Portraits of Valor, USMC, 74. *Mailing Add:* 1450 Baptist Church Rd Yorktown Heights NY 10598

WITTE, JUSTIN
PAINTER
Study: Student, Lacoste Sch Fine Art, France, 1997; Student, NY Studio Prog 1998; Milwaukee Inst Art and Design, BfA, 1999; Univ Ill, Chicago, MFA, 2007. *Work:* Contemp Mus, Baltimore, 2000. *Exhib:* Solo exhibs, Ontploffing, Vox Populi, Philadelphia, 2002, Lurk, 2004, work has also been exhib at, NY Studio Prog, 1998, Vox Populi, 2001, 2002, 2004, 2005, Nexus Found for Today's Art, Philadelphia, 2003, Abington Art Ctr, Jenkintown, Pa, 2003, Space 1026, Philadelphia, 2003, Basekamp, Philadelphia, 2004, Cheltenham Ctr for the Arts, Beaver Coll Art Gallery, Artists Space, New York City, Milwaukee Int Art Fair, Art Ledge, 2006, Gallery 400, Chicago, 2006, 2007. *Awards:* Pew Fel in the Arts, 2004; Independence Found Fel in the Arts, 2004

WITTKOPP, GREGORY
MUSEUM DIRECTOR
Study: Wayne State Univ, Detroit, MA (art hist), 1994. *Pos:* Archit intern, William O Prine, Saginaw, 1981, Wigen, Tincknell & Meyer, Saginaw, 1983; asst to cur, Hist Mus Bay County, Bay City, Mich, 1982-83; exhibs cur, Saginaw Art Mus, 1983-85; asst cur, Cranbrook Art Mus, Bloomfield Hills, Mich, 1985-86, assoc cur, 1986-89, collections cur, 1989-91, collections cur & mus adminr, 1991-94, dir, 1994-; mem dir's search com, Mus Contemp Art, Detroit, 2007-. *Awards:* Pres's Award for Excellence, Cranbrook Educ Community, 1994. *Mem:* Soc Archit Historians; Coll Art Asn; Midwest Mus Asn; Mich Asn Mus (bd dirs 1998-2006, vpres programs 2001-03, pres 2003-05, co-chair annual Southeast conf 2005, pres 2005-06); AAM. *Publ:* Auth, Saarinen House & Garden: A Total Work of Art, 1995; ed, A Life Without Beauty is Only Half Lived: A Brief History of Cranbrook, 1999. *Mailing Add:* Cranbrook Art Mus 39221 Woodward Ave Bloomfield Hills MI 48303

WIZON, TOD
PAINTER
b Newark, NJ, June 1, 1952. *Study:* Sch Visual Arts, New York, BFA, 74-76. *Work:* Metrop Mus Art, NY; Mus Contemp Art, Los Angeles; Minneapolis Mus Art. *Exhib:* Solo exhibs, PPOW Gallery, NY & Willard Gallery, NY, 84, Phyllis Kind Gallery, Chicago, 85 & Annina Nosei Gallery, NY, 87, Hot Suite & Recent Paintings, Nicholas Robinson Gallery, New York, 2004, Little Darknesses, Small Nocturnes, 96-2010, Homespun Peregrinations, Nicholas Robinson Gallery, NY, 2010; A Contemp View of Nature, Aldrich Mus Contemp Art, 86 & State of the Artists, 87; Bischofberger, Switz, 91 & 96; Galeria Ramis Barquet, Mex, 93; Galerie Daniel Templon, Paris, 94; Earl McGrath Gallery, NY, 95; Briggs Robinson, NY City, 2004; Frenzy and Aftermath, Nicholas Robinson Gallery, NY, 2009. *Bibliog:* Michael Krugman (auth), Tod Wizon at Willard, Art in Am, 3/81; Ronnie Cohen (auth), article, Art News, 9/84; Laura DeCoppet &Alan Jones (auths), The Art Dealers, Clarkson Potter, New York, 84; Theodore Wolff (auth), Many masks of modern art, Christian Sci Monitor, 11/84. *Media:* Acrylic, All. *Interests:* music, poetry, film, literature. *Publ:* Contribr, Appearance Mag, 77; Interview by Anney Benney (text by David Rattray), Bruno Bischofberger Gallery, Zurich, 91; contribr, Selected Paintings 1995-1998 (by Luca Marenzi), Remis Barquet Gallery, NY, 99. *Dealer:* Briggs Robinson New York City; Luca Marenzi London England; Nicholas Robinson New York. *Mailing Add:* 25 Monroe Pl Apt 10F Brooklyn NY 11201

WODICZKO, KRZYSZTOF
EDUCATOR, SCULPTOR
b Warsaw, Poland, 1943. *Study:* Acad Fine Arts, Warsaw, Poland, MFA, 1968. *Work:* Personal Instruments, Warsaw, Poland; First Vehicle; Homeless Vehicle; plus more than 70 public projs in Australia, Austria, Can, Eng, Ger, Holland, Ireland, Israel, Italy, Mex, Poland, Spain, Switz, United States & Poland, 1981-92. *Exhib:* Life-Size, A Sense of the Real in Recent Art, Israel Mus, Jerusalem, 1990; The Projected Image, Mus Mod Art, San Francisco, 1991; Pour la suite du Monde, Mus d'Art Contemporain, Montreal, 1992; In and Out of Place: Contemp Art and the Am Social Landscape, Mus Fine Arts, Boston, 1993-94; The Decade Show, Rhetorical Image, New Mus Contemp Art, NY, 1993; Europa-Europa, Kunstmuseum, Bonn, 1994; Contemp Canadian Art: Beyond (National) Identities, Setagaya Mus Art, Tokyo, 1995; Retrospective, De Appel Found, Amsterdam, 1995 & Centrum Sztuki, Warsaw, 1995; Horizons, 14 Polish Artists, Sonje Mus Contemp Art, Seoul, Korea, 1996; NowHere, Walking and Thinking, La Mus, Denmark, 1996; Project for Survival, Nat Mus Mod Art, Kyoto, Japan, 1996; Face a l'histoire, Ctr Georges Pompidou, Paris, France, 1996-97; Xenology: Immigrant Instruments, Univ of N Tex Art Gallery, 1997; The

Hanukkah Proj: A Festival in Lights, Jewish Mus, New York, 1998 ; The Hiroshima Proj, Galerie Lelong, New York, 2000 ; Whitney Biennial, Whitney Mus Am Art, New York, 2000 ; Strangers: The First ICP Triennial of Photography & Video, Int Ctr of Photography, New York, 2003; Designs for the Real World, Generali Found, Vienna, 2002; IF YOU SEE SOMETHING, Galerie Lelong, New York, 2005; The Freedom Salon, Deitch Projs, New York, 2005; The Message is the Medium, Jim Kempner Fine Art, New York, 2006; Open City: Tools for Public Action, Eyebeam, New York, 2007. *Pos:* Dir, Ctr Advan Visual Studies, Mass Inst Technol, 1994-96 & Interrogative Design Work Group, 1994-; dir, Ctr Advanced Visual Studies (CAVS), 1994-1996, 2003-. *Teaching:* Adj prof, Warsaw Polytech Inst, 1970-75 & Indus Design, Ont Col Art, 1979; vis prof, Nova Scotia Col Art & Design, 1977-79 & Calif Inst Arts, 1988; asst prof, Nova Scotia Col Art & Design, 1980-81, Univ Hartford, 1988-89 & Calif Inst Technol, 1991; guest prof sculpture, Cooper Union Sch Art, 1987, 1989; prof, Ecole Nat Sup rieure des Beaux Arts, 1991-95; prof visual arts Mass Inst Tech, 1997-. *Awards:* Recipient Hiroshima Art Prize, 1998; Kepes Art Prize, Coun for Arts, Mass Inst of Technol, 2004; Artist Award for Distinguished Body of Work, Coll Art Asn, 2004; Skowhegan Medal for Sculpture, 2008. *Publ:* Auth, Art Public, Art Critique: The Collected Writings of Krzysztof Wodiczko, Ecole Nat Superieure des Beaux Arts, 1995; Assemblage, Ctr Advan Visual Studies, Mass Inst Technol, No 23, 1995. *Mailing Add:* 116 E Seventh St New York NY 10009

WOGSTAD, JAMES EVERET
EDUCATOR, ILLUSTRATOR
b Lordsburg, NMex, Sept 24, 1939. *Study:* San Antonio Col, cert, 59; Univ Tex, Austin, BFA, 61, MFA, 68. *Comn:* Original graphics prog, Univ Tex Med Sch, San Antonio, 68-69; dioramic backgrounds & natural hist graphic displays, Witte Mus, San Antonio, 70-74. *Pos:* Lead illusr, Creative Commun, Houston, 62-63; chief illusr, Finger Contract Supply, Houston, 63-65; preparator-cur, Witte Mus, 70-74; ed-illusr, Replica in Scale, 72-76 & Aerophile, 76-. *Teaching:* Prof art, San Antonio Col, 68-, chmn dept, 73-77, graphic arts prog coordr, 73-95. *Mem:* Coll Art Asn Am; Tex Asn Schs Art (bd dir, 94-); Tex Jr Coll Teachers Asn. *Media:* Acrylic on Canvas; Black Ink on Paper. *Publ:* Illusr, Any Time is Party Time, 67, Auschuitz, 67 & Belsen, 67, Naylor; auth/illusr, AV-8 Harrier, Aerophile, 82; EA-6 Prowler/Intruder, Aerophile, 85

WOIT, BONNIE FORD
PAINTER
b New York, NY, Jan 19, 1931. *Study:* Allegheny Coll, BA (cum laude), 53; Harvard Univ exten, 54-55; Westchester Workshop, 60-61; Silvermine Sch Art, 70-73; photog graphics workshop, 75. *Work:* Bankers Trust Co, NY; Sapolin Co, Danbury, Conn; IBM, Green Castle, Ind; Sea Containers, NY. *Exhib:* Silvermine Guild Artists, New Canaan, Conn, 74; Munson Gallery, 90; Kohn Pederson & Fox Gallery, NY, 94; Hastings Art Gallery, 94; Hammond Mus, North Salem, NY, 94; Stamford Mus, 97; Gallery BAI, NY, 99 & Barcelona, 2000; solo exhib, Bowman Gallery, Allegheny Coll, 2002. *Pos:* Chmn & founder, Inst Visual Artists, 85-88; bd trustees, Silvermine Guild Artists, 94. *Awards:* William Lowman Award, 78 & New Eng Award, 79, New Eng Exhib. *Bibliog:* Rev, Profile Mag, 3/89; Abstract Expressionism (rev), NY Times, 11/27/94; Zimmer (auth), rev, NY Times, 4/14/96. *Mem:* Silvermine Guild Artists (secy, 74-75, vpres, 75-80 & 83-84). *Media:* Acrylic on Canvas, Paper and Wood. *Mailing Add:* 55 W 16th St 5th Floor New York NY 10011

WOITENA, BEN S
SCULPTOR, EDUCATOR
b San Antonio, Tex, Mar 24, 1942. *Study:* Univ Tex, Austin, BFA, 64; Univ Southern Calif, MFA, 70. *Work:* Houston Mus Fine Arts, Tex; City of Houston, Tex; Trammell Crow Co, Tex; San Antonio Mus Art, Tex; Jack Kerouac Commemorative Park. *Comn:* Sculpture, Jack Kerouac Commemorative Park, Lowell, Mass, 88; sculpture, Mayor Emmett F Lowry Commemorative, Texas City, Tex, 90; sculpture, Alley Theatre, Danton's Death, Robert Wilson, Dir, Houston, Tex, 92; sculpture, Amarillo Mus Art Archway Amarillo, Tex, 94. *Exhib:* Collector's Exhib, Houston Mus Fine Arts, 75; A Century of Sculpture in Tex, 1989-1990, Archer M Huntington Art Gallery, Austin, Tex, 89; 64 Beds, Blue Star Art Gallery, San Antonio, Tex, 91; Politics as usual, Lawndale Art and Performance Ctr, Houston, Tex, 92; Artistic Views on Cult Diversity, Tex A&M Univ Art Galleries, Coll Station, Tex, 93; Afterimages, The Omni Houston, Solo Exhib, Houston, Tex, 94; Amarillo Mus of Art, Ben Woitena: Related Works, Amarillo, Tex, 94; Dana Campbell/Paul McCoy/Ben Woitena, Waco Crative Art Ctr, Waco, Tex, 94; and others. *Teaching:* Instr sculpture, Glassell Sch Art, 71-. *Bibliog:* George F Will (auth), Daddy who was Kerouac, Newsweek, 88; staff writer (auth), The talk of the town, The New Yorker, 88; Sculpture on the Green (film), The Omni Houston, 94. *Mem:* Nat Arts Club, NY. *Media:* Welded Steel, Cast Bronze. *Dealer:* Ben S Woitena, 1547 Waverly Houston TX 77008. *Mailing Add:* 1547 Waverly Houston TX 77008

WOJTYLA, HAASE (WALTER) JOSEPH
PAINTER, DRAFTSMAN
b Chicago, Ill, Feb 10, 1933. *Study:* Art Inst of Chicago; Univ of Ill, BFA (painting); Univ Cincinnati, MFA; Brooklyn Mus Art Sch. *Work:* Scripps Mem Hosp, Mus Contemp Art, San Diego, Calif. *Exhib:* Int Drawing Competition, State Univ of Educ, Potsdam, NY, 60; Tenth Ann Nat Exhib of Painting & Sculpture, Ringling Mus Art, Sarasota, Fla, 60; Brooklyn & Long Island Artists Biennial Exhib, Brooklyn Mus Art, 60; Art in Am Exhib, NY, 62; All Ohio Painting & Sculpture Exhib, Dayton Art Inst, 66; solo exhibs, Recent Paintings, Fine Arts Gallery San Diego, 75 & A Coincidence of Paintings (with catalog), Oceanside Mus Art, Calif, 2006; Calif-Hawaii Biennial, Fine Arts Gallery San Diego, 76 & 78. *Teaching:* Instr, San Diego State Univ, Calif, 76 & 80. *Awards:* Singer & Sons Prize, Artists of Chicago & Vicinity, Art Inst Chicago, 56; Painting Award, All Calif Juried Exhib, Laguna Beach Mus Art, 76; Painting Award, Calif Ann Award Show, Jewish Community Ctr, San Diego, 77. *Bibliog:* Artist-in-Residence, KPBS-TV, San Diego, 82; The black comic art of Walter Wojtyla, Hill Courier, 9/83. *Mem:* San Diego Art Inst; Art Guild, San Diego Mus Art. *Media:* Oil, Mixed Media; Ink, Charcoal. *Publ:* Auth, San Diego Artists, Atra Publ Inc, 88. *Dealer:* Oneiros Gallery 711 Eight Ave Studio A San Diego CA 92101; Perry Meyer Fine Art 2400 Kettner Blvd Ste 104 San Diego CA 92102. *Mailing Add:* 2102 C St San Diego CA 92101

WOLANIC, SUSAN SESESKE
PAINTER, GRAPHIC ARTIST
b Hartford, Conn, Mar 25, 1947. *Study:* Paier Sch Art, 69; Univ Hartford. *Work:* Yale New Haven Hosp, Conn; Constitution Nat Bank, Hartford, Conn; Storer Cable, New Haven, Conn; Carriage House, Guilford, Conn. *Comn:* Family portrait-impressionism, Expressions Furniture, Milford/Cheshire, Conn, 89; illus of house for mag, comn by Lois & Vicent La Bonia, Palm Springs, Calif, 90; logo & stationery, Bethany Community sch, 92; Watercolor, Assumption Church, Woodbridge, Conn, 94; pewter Christmas Ornaments, Bethany Volunteer Fire Dept Womens Auxilliary, 93, 94, & 95; Picnic in the Park (poster), 94. *Exhib:* St Raphaels Hosp, art corridor, 92. *Pos:* Archit secy (draftsperson), off of John Damico, AIA, Waterbury, Conn, 76-; art dir, Marketing Serv Corp, Waterbury, Conn. *Teaching:* Instr, lectr, demonstrator, watercolor, various art organizations, Conn & adult educ prog, Watertown, 75-; instr watercolor, Arts Alive Studio, Cheshire, Conn & Thomaston Adult Ed, Prospect, Conn; instr adult ed, orange arts & crafts. *Awards:* Picador, Ligoa Duncan Gallery, New York & Paris, 79. *Bibliog:* Vincent & Lois La Bonia (auths), Illustrations of California house, Palm Springs Life Mag, 90; Yale Art Gallery & Hosp, American Artists Publication, Yale Art Library, 90; Joyce Zimmerman (auth), Easy Line II, (article). *Mem:* Conn Watercolor Soc; Cheshire Art League (vpres, pres, 80's); Conn Classic Artists; Watertown Art League; Mt Carmel Art Asn. *Media:* Watercolor. *Publ:* Auth, 5 cookbooks: Vegetables, Ethic Artistry, Cookies, HorDoevres, Seafood, Private Publ, 89; illusr, 2 Views of a Palm Springs California Home (watercolors), Palm Springs Life Mag, 90 (in prep); The Day of the Fish, 90; ann report cover, Meridan-Wallingford Hosp, 92; cover & illus, Bethany Cookbook. *Mailing Add:* 219 Carrington Rd Bethany CT 06524

WOLANIN, BARBARA A
HISTORIAN, CURATOR
b Dayton, Ohio, Dec 12, 1943. *Study:* Oberlin Col, BA, 66, MA (art hist, Woodrow Wilson Fel), 69; Harvard Univ Grad Sch Educ, MAT (fine arts), 67; Univ Wis, Madison, PhD (art hist), 81. *Collection Arranged:* Arthur B Carles Collection (auth, catalog), Hirshhorn Mus, 77; Arthur B Carles, Painting with Color (auth, catalog), Pa Acad Fine Arts, Corcoran Gallery Art & Nat Acad Design, 83-84; Jane Piper Retrospective: Paintings 1940-1985 (auth, catalog), James Madison Univ, Pa Acad Fine Arts & State Univ NY, Oswego, 86-87; Arthur B Carles Prints (auth, catalog), Print Club, Philadelphia, 89. *Pos:* Cur for arch of US Capitol, 85. *Teaching:* Asst prof art hist, Trinity Col, Washington, 78-83 & James Madison Univ, 83-85; pub lectures, Jurying Art Exhib. *Awards:* Kress Fel, 74; Smithsonian Fel, 76; James Madison Univ Fac Develop Award, 85; Woodrow Wilson Fel, 1966; Architect of the Capitol Spl Contribution, 1998. *Mem:* Coll Art Asn; Asn Historians Am Art; Women's Caucus Art; Am Asn Mus; Phi Beta Kappa; Am Inst Conservation: Art Table. *Res:* Arthur B Carles, pioneer American modernist, Constantino Brumidi. *Publ:* Auth, The Advent of Modernism, 86; revs, Art Am, 92, 93 & 96; Constantino Brumidi: Artist of the Capitol, 98; The Orchestration of Color: The Paintings of Arthur B Carles, 2000. *Mailing Add:* 7807 Hamilton Spring Rd Bethesda MD 20817

WOLBER, PAUL J
PAINTER, EDUCATOR
b Deer Creek, Ill, June 23, 1935. *Study:* Ill State Univ; Southern Ill Univ, Edwardsville; Bob Jones Univ, BS & MA. *Work:* Evansville Mus Art, Ind; Franklin Life Ins Co, Springfield, Ill; Mitchell Mus Art, Mt Vernon, Ill; Calumet Nat Bank, Ill; Ill State Mus, Springfield. *Comn:* Mural, Spring Arbor Free Methodist Church, 80; mural, Ingham Co Correctional Ctr, Ingham Co Arts Comn, 81. *Exhib:* Ill State Mus, Springfield, 74; Grand Galleria Nat Ann, Seattle, 74; Gov Exhib, 30 Ill Artists, Springfield, 75; Marietta Nat, Ohio, 78. *Pos:* Art educ consult, State Off Pub Instr, Springfield, Ill, 74-75. *Teaching:* Assoc prof art, Spring Arbor Col, Mich, 76-81, prof, 81-. *Awards:* Nat Small Painting Award, NMex Art League, Albuquerque, 74 & 75; Illinois-Indiana Bicentennial Purchase Award, Hammond, Ind, 77. *Bibliog:* Glen P Ives (auth), Museum object of the week, Sunday Courier, Evansville, Ind, 10/6/74; Abner Hershberger (ed), Mennonite Artists Contemporary, Goshen Coll Art Gallery, 75; Howard Derrickson (auth), article, The Advocate, Greenville, 1/28/75. *Mem:* Mid Am Coll Art Asn; Nat Art Educ Asn; Bond Co Art & Cult Asn (vpres, 73-74). *Media:* Oil, Acrylic. *Mailing Add:* 2812 Trudy Ln Unit 17 Lansing MI 48910

WOLF, PATRICIA B
MUSEUM DIRECTOR
Pos: Dir, exec dir, Anchorage Mus Hist and Art, 1989-. *Mem:* Arctic Studies Ctr (steering comt, currently). *Mailing Add:* Anchorage Mus History and Art 121 W Seventh Ave Anchorage AK 99501

WOLF, SYLVIA
GALLERY DIRECTOR, CURATOR
b 1958. *Study:* Northwestern Univ, BA; RI Sch Design, MFA(Photog); Amsterdam Sch Cult Analysis, Univ Amsterdam. *Pos:* Cur contemp art, Art Inst Chicago, formerly; endowed chmn & head photog dept, Whitney Mus Am Art, New York, 1999-2004, adj cur, 2004-08; dir, Henry Art Gallery, Univ Wash, 2008-. *Teaching:* Vis prof, Sch Visual Arts, New York; adj prof art history, Tisch Sch Art, New York Univ; prof cur studies, Columbia Univ. *Awards:* Chevalier de l'Ordre des Arts et des Lettres. *Publ:* Auth, Visions from America: Photographs from the Whitney Mus Am Art, 1940-2001, Michal Rovner: The Space Between, Ed Ruscha & Photog, The Kids Are Alright: Photographs by Ryan McGinley, Polaroids: Mapplethorpe. *Mailing Add:* Henry Art Gallery Univ Wash Box 351410 Seattle WA 98195-1410

WOLFE, JAMES
SCULPTOR
b New York, NY, Apr 28, 1944. *Work:* Mus Fine Arts, Houston; Whitney Mus, NY; Mus Fine Arts, Boston; Kresge Art Ctr, Mich State Univ; Storm King Art Ctr; Hirshhorn Mus & Sculpture Garden, Washington, DC; Ft Worth Art Mus, Tex; Portland Mus Art, Portland, OR; Ackland Art Mus, Chapel Hill, NC; Huntington Mus Art, Huntington, WV; Art Mus Western Va, Roanoke, VA. *Comn:* Ten painted steel sculptures, comn by Johnstown Flood Mus, Centennial Comt & Bethlehem Steel for James Wolfe Sculpture Trail, Johnstown, Pa, 89; steel sculpture, comn by Harold Kant, Reno, NV. *Exhib:* Solo exhibs, Don Stewart Gallery, Montreal, Can, 88, Andre Emmerich Gallery, NY, 88, Huntington Mus Art, Huntington, WVa, Galarie Am Tiergarten 62, Ger, 89, Lucy Berman Gallery, Palo Alto, Calif, 90, 93, Palazzetti Gallery, Los Angeles, 92, Civic Ctr Plaza, Palo Alto, 93, Marion Meyer Gallery, Laguna Beach, Calif, 99, 2002, James A Michener Art Mus, Doylestown, Pa, 2007; Andre Emmerich Gallery, NY, NY, 73, 74, 75, 76, 77, 85, 86, 88; Monumenta, Newport, RI, 74; Clayworks Studio Workshop, NY, 81; Stephen Roseberg Gallery, 83 & 84; Lucy Berman Gallery, Palo Alto, Calif, 93; Marion Meyer Gallery, Laguna Beach, Calif, 99, 2002; and others. *Pos:* Tech dir, Theater Dept & tech asst, Sculpture Dept, Bennington Col; fac mem, Va Polytechnic & State Univ, 78, Sch Visual Arts, 79 & Boston Mus Sch, 80. *Awards:* Nat Endowment Arts, 74; Saint Gaudens Found Prize, 84. *Bibliog:* Karen Wilkin (article), James Wolfe Sculpture Trail, Sculpture Mag, 5-6/90; Karen Wilkin (auth), James Wolfe's New Sculpture, Arts, 4/85; Karen Wilkin (auth), James Wolfe Sculpture Trail, 5-6/90; and others. *Dealer:* Andre Emmerich 41 E 57 St New York NY 10022; Marion Meyer Contemporary Art 354 N Coast Hwy Laguna Beach CA 92651. *Mailing Add:* 35 Cobe Rd Northport ME 04849

WOLFE, LYNN ROBERT
PAINTER, EDUCATOR
b Red Cloud, Nebr, Sept 11, 1917. *Study:* Univ Nebr, BFA; Univ Colo, with Max Beckman, MFA; Paris Atelier with Ossip Zadkine. *Work:* Univ Nebr State Mus, Lincoln; Univ Colo, Boulder. *Comn:* Copper doors, Danforth Chapel, Colo State Univ, Ft Collins, 54; mosaic (stained glass), McPherson Chapel, Durango, Colo, 60; stained glass window, Norgren Chapel, Denver, 65; stained glass windows, St Aidans Episcopal Church, Boulder, 70; sculpture, St Johns Episcopal Church, Boulder, 93; bronze sculpture, Yampa River Botanic Park, Steamboat Springs, Colo, 99; bronze sculpture and painting, Univ Colo Boulder; painting US Ambassador's residence, Athens, Greece; Sculpture in Cemetery, Boulder Colo, Red Cloud Nebr; aluminum sculpture, Boulder Colo Cemetary, 53; bronze sculpture, Redeland Nebr Cemetary, 2011. *Exhib:* Nat Watercolor & Drawing, Metrop Mus, New York, 52; Nat Drawing & Small Sculpture, Muncie, Ind, 58; Mus Contemp Crafts, New York, 59; Western Artists, Denver Art Mus, 72. *Pos:* Cur collections, Univ Colo, Boulder, 64-74. *Teaching:* Instr sculpture, Univ Nebr, Lincoln, 45-46; vis artist watercolor, Univ Alaska, summer 46; prof painting, Univ Colo, Boulder, 47-, chmn dept fine arts, 72-74; vis artist, Univ Hawaii, 82. *Awards:* Sculpture Award, Ball State Teachers Coll, 58; Univ Colo Fac Fel, 67; Award, Outstanding Educators Am, 75. *Media:* Acrylic, Canvas; Stained Glass, Faceted Dalles, Bronze. *Mailing Add:* 701 Euclid Boulder CO 80302

WOLFE, MAURICE RAYMOND
CONSULTANT
b Paris, France, Oct 13, 1924; US citizen. *Study:* Univ Calif, Berkeley, BA, 48, MA, 52, grad study; Fr Govt fel to Univ Paris at Sorbonne. *Work:* Carmel Valley History Mus. *Collection Arranged:* Art from Mobilier of the Djukas of Surinam, Pacific Northwest & Eskimo Material Culture, Meso-Am Prehistory, Mohave Desert Culture, African Musical Instruments & Domestic Objects & The Art of New Guinea, 74-75, The Cuna of Panama--Arts & Crafts, West Africa, Aboriginal Australian Art from Expo 74 & California Gatherers & Hunters, Circa 1776 (Bicentennial celebration), 75-76, Oceanic Cultures: Emphasis on Am Trust Territories, Folk Art of Mexico & Archaeology, 77-78, Merritt Coll Anthrop Mus; Carmel Valley Hist Soc Exhib, Carmel Valley Centennial Celebration, 89. *Pos:* Dir, Merritt Col Anthrop Mus, 73-87, consult, currently; mem, CVHS Bd Exhibs, EsselEix, 2013. *Teaching:* Instr, Merritt Col, Oakland, formerly, prof prehist art, formerly; adj prof, Golden Gate Univ, Monterey, 94-. *Awards:* Fel, French Govt, 66. *Mem:* Am Asn Mus; Western Art Asn; Calif Archaeol Soc; Carmel Valley Historical Society Mus (bd mem). *Res:* Prehistoric Art. *Mailing Add:* 33751 Carmel Valley Rd Carmel Valley CA 93924

WOLFE, ROBERT, JR
PRINTMAKER, PAINTER
b Oxford, Ohio, May 15, 1930. *Study:* Miami Univ, BFA, 52; Cincinnati Art Acad, 55; Univ Iowa, scholar, 59, with M Lasansky, MFA (printmaking), 60; Tamarind Inst Workshops, 75 & 79. *Work:* Ohio State Univ; Univ Wis-Madison; Sheldon Mem Art Gallery, Univ Nebr, Lincoln; Casa da Gravura, State Collection, Curitiba, Parana, Brazil; Rajasthan Sch Art, Jaipur, India; and others; Cincinnati Art Mus; The Dayton Art Inst, Ohio; Ball State Univ. *Comn:* Five color intaglios, Miami Univ, 71; color lithograph, Sch Fine Arts Folio, 2011. *Exhib:* Nine Midwest Printmakers, Mt St Joseph Col, Cincinnati, Ohio, 77; Rutger's Drawing, Camden, 79; Honolulu Acad Arts 5th Nat, Hawaii, 80; Intaglio Printmakers 81, Univ Louisville, Ky; Rajasthan Sch Art, Jaipur, India, 88; 40 Am Printmakers, Bratislava, Slovakia, 94; Artists Books, Ball State Univ, Ind, 2005; Miami Univ Art Mus, 2013. *Collection Arranged:* Cinn Art Mus, Ohio; Dayton Art Inst, Ohio; Hunt Botanical Libr, Pa; New York City Pub Libr. *Pos:* Artist-illusr, US Army, 52-54. *Teaching:* Instr design, Clarion Col, Pa, 61-62; prof printmaking, Miami Univ, 62-93, emer prof, 96-; vis artist, Univ Nebr, Grinnell Col, Ohio State Univ, Fed Univ Parana, Brazil & Western Kentucky Univ. *Awards:* Award for Contribution to the Arts in Ohio, Ohio Arts Council, Governor of Ohio, 72; Purchase Award, Intaglio Printmakers 81, Univ Louisville, Ky, 81, Ball State Univ, Ind, 2006; Alumni Award for Painting, Miami Univ, 82; and others; Effective Educator Award, Miami Univ, 91; and others. *Media:* Mixed, Oil, Engraving, Etching. *Interests:* historic preservation. *Publ:* Contribr, Voiles Before Regatta, Finial Press, 84; The Miami Portfolio, Faculty Prints, 2012. *Mailing Add:* 418 Bouden Ln Oxford OH 45056

WOLFF, ROBERT W, JR
DEALER
b Monroe, La, Feb 18, 1947. *Study:* Troy State Univ, Ala, BS, 74. *Pos:* Art dealer, Ashland Gallery, Mobile, Ala, currently. *Mailing Add:* 32 S Section St Fairhope AL 36532-2212

WOLFSON, JORDAN
PAINTER
b Calif, 1960. *Study:* Univ Calif, Santa Cruz, Calif 1986; Yale Univ Sch Art, New Haven, Conn, MFA, 1991. *Exhib:* One-man shows: Hudson D Walker Gallery, Provincetown, Mass, 1992, Contemp Realist Gallery (Hackett-Freedman Gallery, San Francisco, 1992, Artspace Gallery, 1995, 1996, 1998, 2000, 2001, Univ Haifa Art Gallery, Haifa, 1999, Sara Kishon Gallery, Tel Aviv, 2002, Drue Chryst Gallery, Sparta, NJ, 2003, DFN Gallery, NY, 2005 & 2008, Seraphin Gallery, Phila, 2006; group exhibs, Traces Contemp Drawing in Israel, Artist's House, Jerusalem, 2001, Common Threads, Artspace Gallery, Jerusalem, 2002, Ballinglen: The Artist in Rural Ireland, May Coun Ctr, Castlebar, 2003, Images from North May, Ballinglen, Ireland, 2004, Hirschl & Adler Modern, NY, 2004, Masters & Mavericks, Seraphin Gallery, Phila, 2004, New Works, Artspace, Jerusalem, 2004, Interior Paintings, DFN Gallery, NY, 2004, Masters & Mavericks Nudes, Seraphin Gallery, Phila, Enchanted Place, Ba-sis Gallery, Beit Yanai, Israel, 2005, Tenth Anniversary Show, DFN Gallery, NY, 2005, Woods, DFN Gallery, NY, 2005, Amer Artists in Rural Ireland: The Ballinglen Experience, Concord Art Assoc, Mass, 2006, Hidell Brooks Gallery, Charlotte, NC, 2007, Works on Paper, DFN Gallery, NY, 2007. *Teaching:* Private instr, painting & drawing, 1992-2005; instr, Emunah Col Arts & Tech, Jerusalem, 1992-1997; instr, Bezalel Acad Art & Design, Jerusalem, 1999-2002; vis artist, Boston Univ, MFA Prog, 2003; instr, Sussex Coun Community Col, Newton, NJ, 2003-2005; instr, vis artist, Univ Wash, 2006; instr, Woodstock Sch Art, NY, 2006; Omega Inst, Rhinebeck, NY, 2006; Western Conn State Univ, Danbury, Conn, 2005-2006; RI Col, Providence RI, 2007; Univ Mass, Dartmouth, Mass, 2007-2008. *Awards:* Ingram Merrill Found Grant, 1992; Ish-Shalom Fel, 1993; Pollock-Krasner Found Grant, 1993-94; Purchase Award, Am Acad Arts & Letters, 1998; Israel-Tennessee Artists Exchange Prog, 1998; Ballinglen Arts Found Fel, 2002. *Bibliog:* Irene Tseitlin (auth), Enchanted Place, Ba-sis Gallery, 2005; Marion Weiss (auth), Dan's Papers, 2/2006; Concord Art Assoc, American Artists in Ireland: The Ballinglen Experience, 2006; Am Art Collector, States of Being, 5/2008; Maureen Mullarkey (auth), Shimmer and Shadow, NY Sun, 5/22/2008. *Dealer:* Seraphin Gallery 1108 Pine St Philadelphia PA 19107; Artspace 5 Hazefira German Colony Jerusalem Israel 93102. *Mailing Add:* c/o DFN Gallery 46 W 85th St Apt A New York NY 10023

WOLPERT, ETTA
PAINTER, PRINTMAKER
b Dec 6, 1930. *Study:* Univ Minn, BA MA (magna cum laude), 54; Columbia Grad Sch, 53; DeCordova Mod Art Sch, 68. *Exhib:* Walker Art Ctr, Minneapolis, 47; one-women shows, Cary Libr, Lexington, Mass, 62, Int Student Center, Cambridge, Mass, 62, Lexington Theatre, 72 & Lexington Trust Co, 74; Fourth Ann Int Exhib Miniature Art, Toronto, Can, 89; Cambridge Pub Libr, North Branch, 92. *Teaching:* Asst prof, Northern Essex Community Col, Mass, 65. *Awards:* First & Third Prize, drawing, Minn State Fair, 49. *Media:* Acrylic, Oil; Silkscreen. *Publ:* Contribr, Harvard Advocate, 64; auth, Selections from her writings, 73. *Mailing Add:* 4 Revere St Lexington MA 02173-6876

WOLSKY, JACK
PAINTER, EDUCATOR
b Rochester, NY, Aug 5, 1930. *Study:* Rochester Inst Technol, AS, 51; State Univ NY Col, Buffalo, BS, 55, MS, 57. *Work:* Rochester Mem Art Gallery, NY; New Britain Mus Am Art, Conn; Munson-Williams-Proctor Inst, Utica, NY; Rochester Inst Technol; State Univ NY Col, Brockport. *Exhib:* Am Fedn Arts Exhib, Turkey, Iran & Pakistan; 154th Exhib, Pa Acad Fine Arts; State Univ NY Arts Convocation Exhib, Albright-Knox Gallery; Chautauqua Exhib Am Art; Univ Omaha Nat Exhib; State Capital Bldg, Albany, NY; NY Ten Exhib, Ithaca Col; Bellair Gallery Int Art, Toronto, Can; Corning Glass Center; Pioneer Gallery, Cooperstown, NY; DE Kendall Galleries, Wellfleet, Mass; Rochester Inst Technol, NY; Robert Wesleyan Coll, Rochester, NY; solo shows, Zenith Gallery, Washington, DC, Galerie Int, New York, NY & Mem Art Gallery, Rochester, NY. *Teaching:* Prof studio art, State Univ NY Col, Brockport, 59-85, prof emeritus, 85-. *Awards:* Fac Exchange Scholar, State Univ NY, 74; Civic Award in Culture & Arts, Rochester Chamber of Commerce, 1999; Visual Artist award, Arts & Cult Coun Greater Rochester, 2002. *Bibliog:* Talis Bergmanis (auth), Exuberant art of Jack Wolsky, Dem & Chronicle Publ, 12/13/70; Karen Ibrahim (auth), Abstract art of Jack Wolsky, News & Rev, Rochester Inst Technol, 71; Evolution of a moment, Channel 21 TV, Rochester, NY, 74; Robert Henkes (auth), Themes in American Painting: A Reference Work to Common Styles & Genres, McFarland & Co Publ, 92. *Media:* Acrylic, Encaustics. *Publ:* Memory and Mastery: Primo Levi as Writer & Witness ed by Roberta S. Kremer, Pub, by State Univ of NY Press. *Dealer:* Oxford Gallery 267 Oxford St Rochester NY 14607. *Mailing Add:* 80 Saint Paul St Apt 3B Rochester NY 14604-1333

WOMACK, ROB (ROBERT) ROBINSON
PAINTER
b Norfolk, Va, July 3, 1957. *Study:* Va Commonwealth Univ, BFA (painting), 80. *Work:* Renwick Gallery, Smithsonian Am Art Mus. *Comn:* The Woman's Place (mural), Univ Va Hosp, Charlottesville, 93; Landmark Theatre (mural), City of Richmond Percent for Art, 95. *Exhib:* Bravura Coloratura, Anderson Gallery, Va Commonwealth Univ, 85; Furniture as Art/Room as Allusion, Md Art Place, Baltimore, 86; Dream House, Peninsula Fine Arts Ctr, Newport News, Va, 92; Coloratura: Sories & Scenarios (with catalog), Hand Workshop Art Ctr, Richmond, Va, 92; Coloratura, Spirit Square Ctr Arts, Charlotte, NC, 93; By Heart and Hand - Collecting Southern Decorative Art, Art Mus W Va, Roanoke, Va, 98; Commonwealth Collects - 1998, Contemp Art Ctr, Va Beach, Va, 98; Residency Va Ctr Creative Arts,

2001, 2002, 2004, 2007, 2010, H Scott November Gallery, Richmond, Va, 2010, Rivermont Gallery, Lynchburg, Va, 2010; group shows, Cudahy Gallery, 2001; Sleight of Hand, McDonough Mus Art, Youngtown, Ohio, 2004; Right at Home: Am Studio Furniture, Renwick Gallery, Smithsonian Am Art Mus, Washington, DC, 2004. *Pos:* Mem bd dir, Folk Art Soc Am, 86-90. *Awards:* Visual Artists Fel, Nat Endowment for the Arts, 94; Individual Artist Fel, Va Comn Arts, 94 & 2000; Theresa Pollak Prize in Applied Arts, 2010. *Bibliog:* Dan Tranberg (auth), Sleight of Hand (catalog), McDonough Mus, Youngstown State Univ, Youngstown, OH, 2004; Oscar P. Fitzgerald (auth), Studio Furniture of the Renwick Gallery, Smithsonian Am Art Mus, 2008; Bue Harwood (auth), Architecture & Interior Design from the 19th Century: an Integrated Hist, vol 2, 2009; Deborah Rockman (auth), Drawing Essentials, 2011. *Media:* Miscellaneous Media. *Publ:* Illusr of article, J Am Planning Asn, 94. *Mailing Add:* 3810 Thimble Lane Richmond VA 23222

WONG, ALBERT Y
PAINTER
Study: Columbus Coll Art & Design, BFA, 1970; Kent State Univ, MFA, 1974. *Work:* Chase Manhattan Bank, NY City; Akron Art Mus, Ohio; Rutgers Univ Art Mus, Camden, NJ; Brit-Am Tobacco Co Ltd, Hong Kong; Coca-Cola Bottling Co, Elizabethtown, Ky; Evansville Mus Arts & Sci, Ind; Ill State Mus, Springfield, Ill; Univ Evansville, Ind. *Exhib:* Solo exhibs include Millikin Univ, Decatur, Ill, 1981, Quincy Col, Ill, 1982, Evansville Mus, Ind, 1986, Auburn Univ, Ala, 1991, Dept Art Resources, City of El Paso, Tex, 1992, Deming Art Ctr, NMex, 1993, Gallery V, Columbus, Ohio, 1996, 1998, 2002; group exhibs include 38th Ann Mid-Yr Exhib, Butler Inst Am Art, Youngstown, Ohio, 1974; Springfield and Vicinities, Ill State Mus, 1981; Watercolor USA 2002, Springfield Art Mus, Mo, 2002. *Collection Arranged:* Off the Wall, Fox Fine Arts Ctr, Main Gallery, El Paso, Tex, 1999; Graphic Design of Mex Today, 2000. *Teaching:* assoc prof of graphic design & chmn art dept, Univ Tex, El Paso. *Awards:* Visual Artists Award, Flintridge Found, 1998; Juror's Award, Springfield Art Mus, Mo, 2002. *Mailing Add:* Univ Tex at El Paso Dept of Art FOXA 351 500 W University El Paso TX 79968

WONG, AUDREY E(LIZABETH)
PAINTER, GRAPHIC ARTIST
b Kingston, Jamaica, Sept 2, 1950. *Study:* Jamaica Sch Art, BFA, 72: Sch Visual Arts, painting with George Rodney, graphic design with Werner Starzman & painting with Colin Garland. *Work:* Cult Ctr Collection, Univ West Indies, Creative Arts Ctr, Kingston, Jamaica. *Comn:* Urban Pollution (no I ecology series), comn by Dr Allison Charles, Kingston, Jamaica, 77; Solitude, Yan Yan Restaurant, Kingston, 78; When the Tide Comes In, comn by G Woon Choy, Kingston, 78; Target, comn by Louis Marriott, Kingston, 78; Writings on the Wall, comn by Audley St John Vaughan, London, 79. *Exhib:* Inst Jamaica Ann, Kingston, 72-74; 2nd Caribbean Festival of the Arts, Nat Gallery Jamaica, Kingston, 76; solo exhib, John Peartree Gallery, Kingston, 77, Mutual Life Gallery, Kingston, 78 & Bolivar Gallery, Kingston, 80; 3rd Caribbean Festival of the Arts, Havana, Cuba, 78; Artist in the Market Place XIV, Bronx Mus Arts, NY, 94. *Collection Arranged:* The Jamaican Artist & Craftsmen Guild (with catalog), Mutual Life Inaugural, 77; Three Women Artists (with catalog), Mutual Life Gallery, 77; Protest '78, Mutual Life Gallery, 78; Seven Plus One, Mutual Life Gallery; International Year of the Child, Mutual Life Gallery, 79. *Pos:* Graphic designer, New York Urban Coalition, 81-86 & Matthew-Lawrence-Pelletier Inc, 83-86; creative dir/artistic dir, Caribbean-Am Enterprises, 86-89. *Teaching:* Art instr book & art/creative writing, Pub Sch 198, Bronx, NY, 93-; art instr interpretive day sch, Bronx Mus Art, 94-. *Awards:* Honorable Mention, Govt of Jamaica, 73. *Bibliog:* Andrew Hope (auth), Images of protest, Jamaican Daily Gleaner, 5/14/78; Sandy McIntosh (auth), An angry artist, Jamaican Daily News, 5/19/78; William Doyle-Marshall, From the heart of Jamaica, Jamaican Daily Gleaner, 11/18/80. *Mem:* Artist Marketplace XIV Group. *Media:* Acrylic Polymer Paint, Watercolor; Collage, Assemblage. *Publ:* Illusr, Through A Child's Eye, Pat Persaud, Roman Catholic Church, 79. *Dealer:* Loris Crawford 249 E 13th St New York NY 10003. *Mailing Add:* c/o Bronx Mus Arts 1040 Grand Concourse Bronx NY 10456

WONG, FREDERICK
PAINTER, GRAPHIC ARTIST
b Buffalo, NY, May 31, 1929. *Study:* Univ NMex, BFA & MA. *Work:* Butler Inst Am Art, Youngstown, Ohio; Reading Mus Art, Pa; Philbrook Art Ctr, Tulsa, Okla; Neuberger Collection, Purchase, NY; Smithsonian Inst, Washington, DC. *Exhib:* Los Angeles Co Mus Art, 59; Butler Inst Am Art, Youngstown, 60; Am Watercolor Soc, NY, 60-69; Watercolor USA, Springfield, Mo, 63; Mainstreams '69, Marietta, Ohio, 69. *Teaching:* Instr form & structure, Pratt Inst, 66-69; instr painting, drawing, calligraphy & design, Hofstra Univ; Watercolor, Art Students League. *Awards:* Butler Midyear Ann Bronze Medal, Butler Inst Am Art, 60; Gold Medal, Nat Arts Club, 61; Mainstreams '69 Award of Excellence, Marietta Col, 69. *Mem:* Am Watercolor Soc; Allied Artists Am; Audubon Artists Inc. *Media:* Watercolor. *Publ:* Auth, Oriental Watercolor Techniques, 77 & The Complete Calligrapher, 80, Watson-Guptill; The Zen of Watercolor, Watercolor '90, Am Artist Publ. *Dealer:* Self 77 Chambers St New York NY 10007. *Mailing Add:* 315 Riverside Dr New York NY 10025

WONG, LUCILLE (LUCILA) GUERRA WONG
PAINTER, PRINTMAKER
b Mex City, Mex, Oct 20, 1949. *Study:* Univ Nac Autonoma Mex, BA, 74; Univ Kent, Eng, MA, 76; studied art with Robin Bond, ARCA, London, 79. *Work:* Mus Escuela Nac Preparatoria, Inst Nat Nutricion, Facultad Veterinaria Univ Nac, Acervo Patrimonial y Bibliotecas, Mex City; Mus Art Mod, Toluca, Mex; Cent Cult Vito Alessio Robles. *Comn:* Caballos, Univ Nac, Mex, 89. *Exhib:* LaMujer en la Plastica, Mus Acuarela, Mex, 89; Grabadores Mexicanos, Mus Metrop, Tokyo, 91; Primera Bienal Monterrey, Mus Monterrey, Mex, 92; Arte Mexicano Hoy, Maison Am Latine, Monaco, 94; Ofrendo de Muertos, Mus Casas Aguila, Santillana, Spain, 94; Presencia de Arte Mexicano, Univ Cantabria, Spain, 94; Romances del Viento, Mus de Yucatan, 97 & Corceles que cabalja ealma, Mus de Queretaro, 2000; Perfume Quequeda, Cent Cult Vito Alessio Robles, 2003; Tiempo Abrasado, Mus de Bellas Artes de Toluca, 2005; Desnudos, CC Vito Alessio Robles, Mex, 2007. *Bibliog:* La Magia de Lucille Wong, Mex, 95; Daniel Higuera (auth), Corceles de Viento, Estudio, San Angel, Mex, 96; El Silencio y la Luz, 98; Leonora Martin del Campo (auth), Corceles que cabalga el alma, DAP, 2000; ER Blackaller (auth), EL Libro de las Celebraciones, 2004; Julieta Ortiz (auth), Guia de Murales, 2004; Aflonso S Arteche (auth), La Piel de la Memoria, 2005. *Mem:* Ideas Artisticas (pres, 91-94); Consejo Mundial Artistas Visuales, 92; Asn Int Artistes Plastiques, Unesco, 92; Asn Ex-Alumnos Coll Aleman Comn Cult (dir, 95); Fedn Mex de Univ Rias, 2002-2006; Int Fedn Univ Women, 2002-2006. *Publ:* Coauth, Presencia de Arte Mexicano, Fomento Cult, 90; auth, Carpeta Serigrafica, Universidad Nac, 91; coauth, Ayer, Hoy y Mañano, 91 & Arte Mexicano en Europa, 93, Fomento Cult; Lucille Wong, 37 Formas de describir la Luz, poesia, 2000; E R Blackaller (auth), 24 Invenciones y Preludios Según imágeres de Lucille Wong, Inst Politechnico Nac, 2000. *Mailing Add:* Calle de la Otra Banda 80-14 San Angel DF CP 01090 Mexico DF Mexico

WONG, PAUL KAN
PAINTER, SCULPTOR
b Fargo, NDak, Oct 30, 1951. *Study:* Moorhead State Univ, BA, 73; Univ Wis, Madison, MFA, 76. *Work:* Madison Art Ctr; New York Pub Libr. *Comn:* Suspended sculpture installation, Hudson River Mus, Yonkers, NY, 83. *Exhib:* 21st Ann Print Exhib, Brooklyn Mus, 78; 77th Vicinity Exhib, Chicago Art Inst, 78; Shaped Field, Eccentric Formats, PS1, Long Island City, 81; Making Paper, Am Craft Mus, 82; Paper as Image Traveling Exhib, Brit Art Coun, UK, 82; Solo exhibs, Air Space: Projection, Hudson River Mus, Yonkers, NY, 83 & Condeso-Lawler Gallery, NY, 83 & 85. *Pos:* Dir, Dieu Donne Press & Paper, NY; cur, Paper as Paint, Fashion Inst Technol, NY. *Teaching:* Instr hand papermaking, The New Sch, NY, 80-86. *Awards:* Apprenticeship Grants, Louis Comfort Tiffany Found, 78 & Nat Endowment Arts, 80; Graphics Grant, Creative Artists Pub Serv, 83. *Bibliog:* Judd Tully (auth), Paper chase, Portfolio Mag, 83; Ronny Cohen (auth), Paper routes, 83 & rev, 84, Art News; rev, Artforum, 85. *Publ:* Illusr, Our Lady of the Three Pronged Devil, Red Ozier Press, 81. *Dealer:* Condeso-Lawler Gallery 76 Greene St New York NY 10013. *Mailing Add:* 40 N Moore St 2W New York NY 10013

WOOBY, WILLIAM JOSEPH
ART DEALER, CURATOR
b Kearny, NJ, Sept 25, 1947. *Exhib:* official presidential inaugural exhibs, 93,97,2001. *Collection Arranged:* Official Arkansas Inaugural Exhib, 93; Freedom Quilt Exhib for 1996 Olympics, Afro-Am History in Quilts, 96. *Pos:* Mus Dir, Millennium Arts Ctr. *Awards:* Washington Art Coalition Award, 89; Nominated DC Mayor's Arts Award, 92 & 94; Ark Traveler Award, 94; Vision Award, Committee of 100 on the Federal City, 2002. *Mem:* Life Skills Ctr; Friends of Alice Pike Barney; Kearny NJ Hist Soc. *Specialty:* Nat and Internat artists, performing and visual. *Mailing Add:* 1327 Corcoran St Washington DC 20009-4310

WOOD, ALAN
PAINTER
b Widnes, Lancashire, Eng, Aug 3, 1935; Can citizen. *Study:* Liverpool Coll Art, Eng, Nat Dipl Design, 58; Liverpool Univ, Inst Educ, Eng, Art Teachers Dipl, 59. *Work:* Seattle Art Mus, Wash; Art Gallery Greater Victoria, BC; Art Gallery South Australia, Adelaide; Tate Gallery, London; Nat Mus Wales, Cardiff; Vancouver Art Gallery, BC; and others. *Comn:* Mural, Leeds Univ, Yorks, 65; mural, BC Govt, Victoria, 77; mural, Fed Govt Can, Calgary, Alta, 81; Cineplex, Vancouver, BC, 85. *Exhib:* New Abstract Art, Edmonton Art Gallery, 86; Land/Scape, Vancouver Art Gallery, 86; solo exhibs, Galerie Franklin Silverstone, Montreal, 88, Kelowna Art Gallery, 89, Heffel Gallery, Vancouver, 89 & 93, Franklin Silverstone Gallery at Olga Korper, Toronto, 90, Gillian Jason Gallery, London, Eng, 90, John Ramsay Contemp Art, Vancouver, 92 & Project Gallery, Vancouver, 93; Recent Acquisitions, Vancouver Art Gallery, 90, 91 & 92; The First Five Yrs, Art Gallery of Southern Alta, Lethbridge, 93; Contemp Landscape, Project Gallery, Vancouver, 94; and others. *Awards:* Sr Can Coun Grant, 78; Can Coun Proj Cost Grant, 81; Can Coun A Grant, 82 & 85-86; and others. *Bibliog:* John Beardsley (auth), Earthworks and Beyond, Abbeville Modern Art Movements, New York, 84; Steven Denure & Christopher Lowry (dirs), Ranch: The Alan Wood Ranch Proj (film), 86; The Octagon Expedition (film), Pacific Report, CBC, 88. *Media:* Acrylic; Wood Constructions. *Mailing Add:* c/o Jenkins Showler Gallery 15735 Croydon Dr Surrey BC V3S0C5 Canada

WOOD, BETTY J
PRINTMAKER, PAINTER
b Pittsboro, Ind, Mar 2, 1942. *Study:* Penn State Univ, BA, 1984; Univ Okla, MFA, 1992; Studied printmaking (Okla State Univ), with Rudy Pozatti, Cert, 2003. *Work:* Sch Art Gallery, Penn State Univ, Univ Park, Pa; Fred Jones Jr Mus Art, Norman Okla; Sch Art/ Art Hist, Univ Okla, Norman, Okla; Okla City Mus Art, Okla City; Collection: Pres Bill Clinton, Vpres Al Gore, NY, Tenn, Pres Barack Obama, Wash DC; V.P. Joe Biden, Univ Sci & Arts Okla, Chickasha, Okla. *Comn:* Mosaic Fountain, Firehouse Art Ctr, Norman, Okla, 2001; Landscape mural (painted), Firehouse Art Ctr, 2002. *Exhib:* Juried exhibs: 60 Square Inches (juried), Purdue Univ Mus, West Lafayette, Ind, 2004; 19th Ann Parkside Print Exhib, Univ Wis Mus, Kenosha, Wis, 2006; Exhib ROC, Taiwan Mus Fine Arts, Taiwan, ROC, 2007; 26th Mini Print Int Exhib, Wingfield, Eng, 2008-2010; Paseo Print Exhib, Paseo Art Asn Gallery, Okla City, (juried), 35th Mini Print Internat Exhib, Wingfield Arts & Music Festival, Wingfield, Eng; Taller Galeria, Fort Gadaques, Girona, Spain; Invitational exhibs: Int Vision Exhib, Individual Artists of Okla, Oklahoma City, 2007; Artist's Exhib, Julia & David White Mus, Ciudad Colon, Costa Rica, 2007; Sixty Years of Printmaking Univ Okla, Lightwell, Norman, Okla, 2007; Suite Oklahoma (22 printmakers), Leslie Powell Mus, Lawton, Okla, 2008, Two Voices; Painter and Poet, Group Exhib, USAO Univ, Nesbitt Gallery, Chickasha, Okla; 26th Invitational Salon Exhib of Small Works, New Artists Program, Inc, Kutztown, Pa; Women of Norma Who Paint, Group Exhib,

Depot Gallery, Norman, Okla; Legend's Times Two, Group Exhib, Legend's Gallery, Norman, Okla; 450 exhibs, nat & int. *Collection Arranged:* Paintings & Prints (prints, paintings), 1987; 5-9 Exhibs (collection of 5-9 art group), 2005. *Pos:* Pres, Univ Okla Alumni Asn, 1994-1999. *Teaching:* Instr (foundations/art), Univ Okla, 1997-1998; instr (glass etching), Oklahoma City Art Mus, 2002; instr (etching process), Univ Okla, 2004-2005, 2010-2012; adjunct prof printmaking & drawing, Univ Okla, Oklahoma City, 2010-2011. *Awards:* Juror's Mention, Individual Artist Okla, 2004; Purchase Award, Okla Centerfold, Univ Sci & Arts Okla, 2006; other awards include: Graphics Award; Best of Show; Merit Award; Hon Mention; Juror's Award, Okla Art Guild Exhib. *Bibliog:* Julia Kirt (auth), 12x12 Exhibit, Art Focus, 2007; John Brandenburg (auth), Oklahoma Exhibition (traveling), Daily Oklahoman, 2007; Cecil Lee (auth), Internal Vision, Crosstimbers, 8/2007; Ron Shira (auth), Small Works Discover Big Ideas, Reading Eagle Pa, 6/15/2008; Allison Meier (auth), Life's Visual Arts, Okla Gazette, 8/20/2008; Kent Anderson (auth), Norman Living Mag, 2009. *Mem:* Okla Visual Arts Coalition (comt mem, 2007); Am Print Coun (2007); Southern Graphics Coun (2007 & 2009); School of Art Art-History Alliance (2010); Oklahoma City Art Mus (2008-9); Fred Jones, Jr Mus Art, 2009; Okla Art Guild, 2010. *Media:* All Media, Mix Media. *Specialty:* contemporary art. *Interests:* Antiques, theatre, art production, movies, reading. *Collection:* etchings, lithographs, woodcuts, collagraph, monotype, monoprint, mixed media, serigraph. *Publ:* Ed, Manuscript (article), Mid-Atlantic Mus Asn, 1985-1986; Article, Somerset Studio Mag, 2010. *Dealer:* Mainsite Contemporary Art Gallery 122 E Main St Norman OK 73069; JRB Art Gallery 2810 N Walker Ave Oklahoma City, OK 73103

WOOD, JOHN AUGUST
WRITER, HISTORIAN
b Jan 2, 1947; US citizen. *Study:* Univ Ark, MFA, 72, PhD, 77. *Collection Arranged:* Secrets of the Dark Chamber: The Art of the Am Daguerreotype, Nat Mus Am Art, 95. *Pos:* Ed, Journal of Contemp Photography, currently. *Teaching:* Prof photog hist, McNeese Univ, 76-. *Awards:* Outstanding Book of Yr, Am Photog Hist Soc, 89; Choice Outstanding Academic Book, Am Libr Asn, 92; Best Photobook of Yr, New York Times, 95. *Res:* All aspects of photographic history from 1839 to the present. *Publ:* Auth, The Art of the Autochrome, Univ Iowa Press, 92, In Primary Light, 94, The Scenic Daguerreotype: Romanticism & Early Photography, 95; Secrets of the Dark Chamber, Smithsonian Inst Press, 95; The Photographic Arts, Univ Iowa Press, 97; Songs of Innocence and Experience, Joel-Peter Witkin, 2003. *Mailing Add:* PO Box 218 Saxtons River VT 05154-0218

WOOD, MCCRYSTLE
EDUCATOR, ADMINISTRATOR
b Cincinnati, Ohio, Sept 20, 1947. *Study:* Kansas City Art Inst, with Ron Slowinski, BFA, 73; Ind Univ, with Rudy Pozzatti, MFA, 76. *Work:* Cincinnati Art Mus; Atlantic Richfield Corp, Columbus, Ohio; Hyatt Hotels, Washington; AT&T, Cincinnati; Proctor & Gamble Co, Cincinnati. *Comn:* Litton Ind. *Exhib:* Centennial Invitational, Cincinnati Art Mus, 81; Gifts, Contemp Art Ctr, Cincinnati, 88; Prevailing Light, Portsmouth Mus, Ohio, 90; Siggraph, 95. *Pos:* Dir, sch design, Univ Cincinnati, 89-90; assoc dean, Col DAAP, Univ Cincinnati, 96-. *Teaching:* Prof design/art, Univ Cincinnati, 82-. *Awards:* Individual Artist Fel, Ohio Arts Coun, 86; Grant, Ky Found Women, 87. *Mem:* Coll Art Asn; Siggraph; Am Asn Univ Prof. *Media:* Electronic Media. *Dealer:* Toni Birckhead Gallery W 4th St Cincinnati OH 45202. *Mailing Add:* 3662 Grandin Rd Cincinnati OH 45226-1117

WOOD, MELISSA ANN
PAINTER, ASSEMBLAGE ARTIST
b Little Rock, Ark, Dec 7, 1957. *Study:* Sch Fine Art, Washington Univ, St Louis, Mo, BFA, 80; Visual Art Access, San Francisco, Calif, cert, 92; studied with Edward Stanton & Carol Levy, Coll Marin, Kentfield, Calif, 98; studied with Raymond Saunders, Calif, 98, L'Atelier, L'Ecole d'Art, Aix-en-Provence, France, 99, mixed media printmaking studies, 2002 & 2005 & alt photog, 2006, Kala Art Inst, Berkeley, Calif. *Comn:* Set design, Luther Coll, Decorah, Iowa, 89. *Exhib:* solo exhibs, Liquid What it is, What you do with it & Why, Artist Studio Residency, Exhib/Demonstrations, de Young Art Ctr and Legion of Honor, San Francisco Fine Arts Mus, Calif, 2003, Looking Back, Looking Here, Looking Ahead, Collector's Gallery, Oakland Mus, Calif, 2003 & Hive, installation exhib, Davis Art Ctr, Davis, Calif, 2006, Hive 2: Sweet Layers, Firehouse Gallery, Grants Pass, Ore, Geographic Layers: Melissa Wood Works on Paper, Int House, Davis, Calif, 2010; Group exhibs, 3rd Ann Warehouse Sale, San Francisco Mus Mod Art Rental Gallery, San Francisco, Calif, 96; Carving the Forces of Change, Women's Caucus Art, Artemisia Gallery, Chicago, Ill, 97; Alternative Interpretations, Cox Gallery, Drury Coll, Springfield, Mo, 98; Animals in Art, Anchorage Mus His & Art, Alaska, 2000; Hang Gallery, San Francisco, 2002; Cliché-Verre, Ark State Univ Gallery, Jonesboro, Ark, 95 & San Francisco Mus Mod Art Artists Gallery, 95; Introductions South 2003, San Jose Inst Contemp Art, San Jose, Calif, 2003; ICA Ann Fall Art Auction San Jose Inst of Contemp Art, San Jose, Calif, 2004; New Photography, San Francisco Mus Mod Art Artists Gallery, Calif, 2005; Abstraction-The Poetic Visual Image, Bolinas Mus Art, Bolinas, Calif, 2005; The Crocker-Kingsley Biennial Crocker Art Mus, Sacamento, Calif, 2005; Invitational Salon Exhib Small Works, New Arts Prog, Kutztown, Pa, 2005; Gallery Artists, Julie Baker Fine Art, Grass Valley, Calif, 2005; Uncommon Object, Pence Gallery, Davis, Calif, 2009. *Teaching:* Extended educ instr, Coll Marin, Kentfield, Calif, 92-95, Univ Calif, Berkeley, 93 & Tamalpais Union High Sch Dist, 93; art workshops, de Young Art Ctr, Fine Arts Mus of San Francisco, 2003 & 2004. *Awards:* Fel, Women Studio Workshop, New York, 93; Third Place Award, North Coast Collage Soc 9th Ann Exhib, 93; Artreach Grant, Nelson Art Friends, Davis, Calif, 2000 & SADVC, Yolo Co, Calif, 2000; Artist Studio Residency, de Young Art Ctr and Legion of Honor, San Francisco Fine Arts Mus, 2003. *Bibliog:* David J Brown (auth), The San Francisco Jung Inst Libr J, Prints by Melissa Wood, A mind prepare for chance, Vol 3, No 4, summer, 82; Melissa Wood (auth), Gallery Town Meeting, Art Calendar, Vol 10, No 4, 2/96; Ryan Kim (auth), National Show Exhibits at Gallery in Concord, Ledger Dispatch, 7/11/96; Anita Creamer (auth), The Sacramento Bee, Art Showcases Mending Lives, 8/7/2000; Alix Williams (auth), Healing Power of Art, The Davis Enterprise, 4/11/2000; Dewitt Cheng, Artweek, Introductions South at the San Jose Institute of Contemporary Art, 17, 10/2003 & Art For Real-Art Revs, Abstraction: The poetic visual image, 2/24/2005; Brown Turtle Series #2, with Aries Corridor, Spring Newsletter, San Jose Inst. of Contemporary Art, 2003; Here's Series #3 Gate, Jardins a Versailes, France with Rain and France, The Greater Sacramento Arts Reporter, 6, 7-8/2003; Suzanne Munich (auth), The Davis Enterprise, Spotlight: It's the whole ball of wax, C8, 10/5/2006. *Mem:* Nat Women's Caucus Art; Calif Lawyers Arts; Pac Rim Sculptors Group. *Media:* Mixed Media. *Publ:* Palace Chain, 1996 Contemp Women Artists Datebook, Cedco Publ, San Rafael, Calif, 96; House of Apples, Women Artists Wall Calendar, 97, House of Rain, Women Artists Datebook, 99 & Arched Door, Fallow Deer, 2001, Cedco Publ; ed, People in the News, Mill Valley Herald, 11/3-10/97. *Dealer:* San Francisco Mus Mod Art Artists Gallery Ft Mason Bldg A San Francisco CA 94123. *Mailing Add:* PO Box 567 Davis CA 95617

WOOD, NICHOLAS WHEELER
SCULPTOR, PAINTER
b San Francisco, Calif, Sept 21, 1946. *Study:* San Francisco State Univ, BA, 72; Alfred Univ, NY, MFA, 77. *Work:* Lannan Found, Palm Beach, Fla; Arts Comn, San Francisco; Atlantic Richfield Co, Dallas, Tex; Southwestern Bell Telephone, Dallas; NY State Coll Ceramics, Alfred; Veronica & Rene di Rosa Found, Napa, Calif; Palm Beach Coll Found, Mus Contemp Art, Palm Beach, Fla; Nora Eccles Mus Art, Utah State Univ, Logan, UT. *Comn:* Sculpture, Criswell Develop Corp, 84; St Paul's Med Ctr, Dallas, 85. *Exhib:* Oakland Mus Art, Calif, 74; Dallas Mus Fine Arts, 79; solo shows, Ft Worth Art Mus, 79, 500X Gallery, Dallas, Tex, 84; Showdown, Alternative Mus, NY, and traveling, 83; Sculpture on the Wall, San Antonio Art Inst, Tex, 83; American Ceramics Now, Everson Mus Art, 87; At the Edge, Laguna Gloria Art Mus, Austin, Tex, 90; Holga in Germany, Vorgeschicts/Archaologischen Mus, Bad Konigshofen, Ger, 2002; Strata, Am Inst of Archit, D/AIA Gallery, Dallas, 2003; Capsulated...Mostly, Langdon Arts & Cultural Ctr, Granburg, Tex, 2008; Nicholas Wood, Creative Arts Ctr, New Haven, Conn, 2008; Skulpturen und Zeichnung, Galerie Palais Walderdorff, Trier, Germany, 2009; Tangents & Adjustments, FW Community Arts Ctr, 2011. *Collection Arranged:* Drawing by Sculptors, 500X Gallery, Dallas, 85; Presence (with catalog), Center for Research in Contemp Art, Arlington, Tex, 92; OBJECTification (with catalog), The Gallery at Univ Tex, Arlington, 04; Layered, Stacked, Assembled (with catalog), Arlington Mus Art, Tex, 2005. *Teaching:* Assoc prof, Univ Tex, Arlington, 77-. *Awards:* Grant for Sculpture, Nat Endowment Arts, 81; Individual Res Grant, Univ Tex, Arlington, 81; Grumbacher Gold Medallion Award, Drawing, 90; Artist Grant Sculpture, Connemara Conservancy Found, 92; Millennium Award Art, Hawn Mem Found, 2000. *Bibliog:* Ned Rifkin (auth), Tablets and grids: Clay by Wood, 6/2/79 & Robert Raczka (auth), Nicholas Wood: Evolution of a theme, 3/21/81, Artweek; Kathryn Shields (auth), Nicholas Wood - Strata, Artiles, 9/2004; Anthony Mariani (auth), Jewels, Kulthr, Fort Worth Star Telegram, 4/2009; Anna Caplan (auth), Nicholas Wood, A&C DFW, 7/2011. *Mem:* Int Sculpture Ctr; Mod Art Mus, Fort Worth, Tex; Dallas Mus Art; Arlington Mus Art, Tex; Dallas Ctr Contemp Art; McKinney Ave Contemp, Dallas. *Media:* Wood, Paint, Clay, Mixed Media. *Interests:* Curating Exhibitions & Photography. *Dealer:* William Campbell Contemporary Art Gallery 4935 Byers Ave Fort Worth TX 76107

WOOD, ROBERT L
SCULPTOR, CERAMIST
b 1960. *Study:* St Joseph Univ; Univ Dallas, BA, 83; Ind State Univ, MFA, 87. *Work:* Burchfield-Penny Art Ctr & M&T Bank Permanent Collection, Buffalo, NY; Univ Indianapolis, Ind; Kanazawa Coll Art, Japan. *Exhib:* 1995 Ceramics USA Exhib, Meadows Gallery, Denton, Tex, 95 & 2003; 10th Rosen Nat Outdoor Sculpture Exhib, Appalachian State Univ, Boone, NC, 96; Contemp NY State Crafts, NY State Mus, 97; Sculpture in Clay, Rockefeller Arts Ctr Gallery, Fredonia, NY, 2000; Rendezvous 2001, Mus Nebr Art, Kearney, 2001; ESP Writing on the Wall Exhib, Castellani Art Mus, Lewistown, NY, 2002; 14th San Angelo Nat, San Angelo Mus Fine Arts, San Angelo, Tex, 2002; Creating Old & New Ceramics, Ind Hist Soc, Indianapolis, 2004; Materials: Hard & Soft, Ctr Visual Arts, Denton, Tex, 2005-2006; Solo exhib, Concord Univ, Athens, WV, 2007; Univ Dallas: Clay Nucleus, Wichita Falls Mus Art, Kans, 2013; Solo retrospective exhib, Kenan Ctr Gallery, Lockport, NY, 2015. *Teaching:* Assoc prof ceramics & coordr of ceramics prog, Buffalo State Coll, 87-, prof, coordr ceramics program, 96-, chair design, 97-99, asst to dean of arts & humanities, 2000, chair design dept, SUNY Buffalo State, 2010-2013. *Awards:* Sylvia Rosen Purchase Award, Craft Art, 96; First Place Award, ceramics, Guildford Handcraft Ctr, 2003. *Bibliog:* Robert A Ellison Jr (auth), Judgement call: the 29th Ceramics National, Am Craft Mag, 10-11/93; Gerry Williams (auth), Rollerblading along the Erie Canal, Studio Potter Mag, 12/95; Susan Peterson (auth), Ceramics 2003, Ceramics Monthly, 10/2003. *Mem:* Nat Coun Educ Ceramic Arts; Burchfield-Penney Art Ctr. *Media:* Clay, glass. *Publ:* Contribr, The Ceramic Glaze Handbook, 2001, Lark Bks; Ceramics: Mastering the Craft, Kraus Pub, 2001; Surface Design for Ceramics, 500 Plates & Chargers; 500 Ceramic Sculptures, Lark Bks, 2009. *Mailing Add:* 135 Stillwell Ave Kenmore NY 14217

WOOD, RON
GLASS ARTIST, SCULPTOR
b Miami, Fla, Sept 16, 1939. *Study:* Long Beach State Col, BA (rhetorical theory & sociology), 66, postgrad (fine arts, studio), 70-72. *Work:* Laguna Beach Mus Fine Art, Calif; Four Seasons Hotel, San Francisco. *Comn:* dome, Boyd Jeffires, Laguna Beach, Calif, 72; glass piece, Steigenberger Hotel, Berlin, Ger, 83; bent glass doors, comn by Joan Borinstine, Beverly Hills, Calif, 89; sculptures, Sheaton Waikiki Hotel, Honolulu, 96; glass pieces, St Vincent de Paul Catholic Church, Houston, 2000. *Exhib:* Festival Fine Arts, Festival Arts Pageant Masters, Laguna Beach, Calif, 72-75; Calif Artist Exhibit, Laguna Beach Mus Fine Art, Calif, 75; solo exhib, Nat Galerie Mus, Berlin, 83-84. *Teaching:* instr multimedia, Mt San Jacinto Coll, Meniffe, Calif,

97-99. *Awards:* Pacific Northwest Photo Exhibition for Best Still Life Blue Ribbon, Ocean Shores, Wash, 89. *Bibliog:* Horst Hartman (auth), Galleriest, Kunstler/Art in Berlin, 83; Beverly Inskeep (auth), Fine Arts Commissioner, Orange Co Mag, 85; Angela Geiser (auth), Editor, The Californian, 99/2000. *Mem:* Sigraph. *Mailing Add:* 25801 Roanoke Rd Sun City CA 92586

WOODARD, CATHERINE
PATRON

Study: History magna cum laude, Wake Forest Univ, BA, 81; Journalism, Columbia Univ, MS, 82. *Pos:* Reporter, Ft Worth Star-Telegram, Tex, 82-84, NY Newsday, 84-94; deputy ed, Newsday Direct, 94-95; news ed, iGuide News Corp, New York City, 95-96. *Awards:* Recipient James Wright Brown Pub. Svc. award, Deadline Club, NY Newspaper Pub. award, Soc. of Silurians award; named one of Top 200 Collectors, ARTnews Mag., 2004, 2012, 2013; fellow Va Ctr Creative Arts, 2011, Hambidge Ctr Creative Arts & Sci, 2012. *Mem:* Mus Modern Art Print Assoc, Artists Space (board dir, coordinator new media), Phi Beta Kappa. *Collection:* Germen expressionism, modern & contemporary art, Wiener Werkstatte metalwork and furniture

WOODFORD, DON (DONALD) PAUL
PAINTER, EDUCATOR

b Kansas City, Kans, June 16, 1941. *Study:* Cornell Col, BA, 63; Ill State Univ, MA, 64; Univ Wis, MFA, 65. *Work:* Cedar Rapids Art Ctr Mus, Coe Coll Gallery, Iowa; Davenport Munic Mus, Iowa; Wright State Univ Mus, Dayton, Ohio; Western Ill Univ Gallery, Macomb. *Exhib:* Sixty-ninth Ann Exhib Chicago & Vicinity, Art Inst Chicago, 66; 6th Nat Drawing Exhib, Erie Art Ctr, Pa, 66; Northwest Ann, Seattle Mus, 70; Solo exhibs, Tacoma Art Mus, Wash, 71 & Univ Redlands, Calif, 80; Calif Artist-Works on Paper, Int Art Fair, Basel, Switz, 77. *Teaching:* Asst prof art-painting, Cornell Col, Mt Vernon, Iowa, 65-68; asst prof art-painting, Reed Col, Portland, Ore, 68-72; prof art-painting, Calif State Univ, San Bernardino, 72-. *Awards:* Arts & Riverwoods Prize, Riverside Art Ctr, 74. *Bibliog:* Thomas Albright (auth), Paintings on paper, San Francisco Chronicle, 6/7/75; Louis Fox (auth), Roplex and assemblage in relief, Artweek, 4/15/78; Julous Kaplin (auth), Don Woodford's Recent Constructions, Univ Redlands, 80. *Mem:* Coll Art Asn Am. *Dealer:* Hank Baum Gallery 2140 Bush San Francisco CA 94115; Getler/Paul Gallery 50 W 57th St New York NY 10019. *Mailing Add:* 3334 N Arrowhead Ave San Bernardino CA 92405

WOODHAM, DERRICK JAMES
SCULPTOR, DIGITAL ARTIST

b Blackburn, Eng, Nov 5, 1940. *Study:* SE Essex Tech Coll Sch Art, intermediate dipl design; Hornsey Coll Arts & Crafts, nat dipl design; Royal Coll Art, dipl. *Work:* Tate Gallery, London, Eng; Mus Contemp Art, Nagaoka, Japan; Radford Univ Collection, Radford, Va; Calouste Gulbenkian Foundation. *Comn:* Sculpture, Gates, comn by North Jersey Cult Coun, Paramus, NJ, 74; C G and E Atrium Sculptures, Moire Screen, 88 & Emerging Cube, Cincinnati, Ohio, 89. *Exhib:* Paris Biennale, Mus Art Mod, 65; Solo exhib, Jewish Mus, 69; Der Geist Surrealismus, Baukunst Galerie, Koln, WGer, 71; Sculpture in the Park, Paramus, NJ, 71 & 74; Wright State Univ Gallery, 76; Nat Sculpture Exhib traveling exhib, 76-77; Artists Choose Artists, Tweed Mus, Duluth, 77; Twister, Alice & Harris Weston Gallery, Cincinnati, Ohio, 97-98; Intersculpt, Biennial Symposia & online exhib, Paris, France, 97, 99, 2001, 2005, 2007, 2009; Int Rapid Prototyping Sculpture Exhib, South Western Univ, Tex & tour, 2003; Computer Art, Mus der Stadt Gladbeck, Germany, 2002; Abstraction & The Human Figure in CAM's Brifish Art Collection, Gulbenbian Ctr od Art, Portugal; Aisi Font Les Reveurs/As Dreamers Do, Qulbenkion Cult Ctr, Paris, France. *Pos:* prof emer Fine Arts, Univ Cinn. *Teaching:* Instr sculpture, Philadelphia Col Art, 68-70; asst prof art forms found, Univ Iowa Sch Art, 70-73; assoc prof, Dept Art, Univ Ky, Lexington, 73-80; prof & dir, Sch Art, Univ Cincinnati, 80, prof emer. *Awards:* Univ Cincinnati Fac Achievement Award, 1996; Univ Cincinnati Fac Develop Award for Sculpture Production & Exhib, 1996-1999. *Bibliog:* Otto Kulturman (auth), The New Sculpture, Praeger, 69; Teruo Fujieda (auth), Form and Structure, Kodansha Ltd, 72; Michael Findlay (auth), Contemporary Artists, St James Press, 77, 88 & 96; plus others. *Mem:* Int Sculpture Conf. *Media:* Mixed Media, Digital Modeling. *Res:* Modeling for multi-user virtual environments on the internet. *Interests:* Model making, playing violin, running. *Mailing Add:* 1910 Bluebell Dr Cincinnati OH 45224

WOODHAM, JEAN
SCULPTOR

b Midland City, Ala, Aug 16, 1925. *Study:* Auburn Univ, BA; Sculpture Ctr, New York; Univ Ill, Kate Neal Kinley Mem fel. *Work:* Massillon Mus Permanent Collection, Ohio; US Merchant Marine Mus, NY; Telfair Acad Arts & Sci, Savannah, Ga; Alfred Khouri Mem Collection, Norfolk Mus Arts & Sci, Va; Westport Permanent Collection, Conn; 20th Century American Painting & Sculpture, Foreign Mus, Sophia, Bulgaria; Spinoff acquired by The Jule Collins Smith Mus Art, Auburn Univ, Ala. *Comn:* Fountain pieces, Gen Elec Credit Corp, Stamford, Conn, 71-72; Scholars' Sphere (four and one-half ton sculpture), Harry S Truman High Sch, NY, 77; Monody (welded bronze sculpture), Goodwin Hall, Archit & Fine Arts Ctr, Auburn Univ, Ala, 79; Cent Conn State Univ, New Britain, Conn, 87; Conn State Comn Arts, Comn Med Examiner's Off, Farmington, Conn, 89. *Exhib:* Master Sculptors of Conn, Conn State Comn Arts Showcase, Bradley Int Airport, Conn, 90, within 12″ x 12″, Cast Iron Gallery, NY, 91; The Coming of Age of Am Sculpture: The First Decades of the Sculptors Guild, 1930s-1950s, Hofstra Mus, Hofstra Univ, Hempstead, NY, 90, traveling, 92; solo exhibs, Conn State Comn Arts Showcase, Bradley Int Airport, Conn, 91, Jean Woodham Fifty Years of Sculpture, Foy Union Gallery, Auburn Univ, Ala & Jean Woodham Fifty Yrs of Sculpture (with catalog), Stamford Mus, Conn, 98, Borglum Gallery, Silvermine Guild Galleries, New Caanan, Conn 2000, PMW Gallery, Stamford, Conn, 2001, Art/Place, Southport, Conn Art/Place, 2003, plus others; Collaborative Exhib of Sculptors, Kyoto Gallery, Kyoto, Japan, 93; The Sculptors Guild at PPG Wintergarden, Three Rivers Arts Festival, Pittsburgh, Pa, 94; Chesterwood Mus, Stockbridge, Mass, 2000; Dialogues in Abstraction, Univ of Conn, Stamford Art Gallery, 2004. *Pos:* Charter mem, Fine Arts Adv Coun, Liberal Arts Col, Auburn Univ, 88-94; adv bd Julie Collins Smith Mus Art, Auburn Univ, Ala, 2000. *Teaching:* Head dept sculpture, Silvermine Guild Artists, 55-56; instr sculpture, Stamford Mus, Conn, 67-69; vis asst prof sculpture, Auburn Univ, 70, assoc prof, 74-75; vis critic, Cornell Univ, Col Archit, Art & Planning, 80. *Awards:* Audubon Artists Medal for Creative Sculpture, 62; Medals of Honor for Sculpture, Nat Asn Women Artists, 66 & 74; Djerassi Found Grant, Woodside, Calif, 83; Finch Award, Art of the Northeast USA, 85; Citation for Contribution to Arts, Conn Gen Assembly & Gov Conn, 86; Citation for Contribution to Arts, Gov Ala, 89; Franklin Lectr, John & Mary Franklin Found, Auburn Univ, 96; Lifetime Achievement Award Westport Arts, Ct, 99; Malvina Hoffman Artists Fund Prize for Best Sculpture in Exhib, Nat Acad 175th Ann Exhib, NY, 2000; Artist of the Year, Art/Place, Southport, Conn, 2003. *Bibliog:* Dolly Curtis (dir), Jean Woodham, Sculptor, Extraordinaire (film), Curtis/Cromwell Productions, 89; Phillipe Clerin (auth), La Sculpture En Acier, Dessain et Tolra, Paris, 93; Jean Woodham, Franklin Lecture Series, Auburn Television (film), 96; Monograph on the Jule Collins Smith, Mus of Finearts, Lethander Family foundation, 2003; and others. *Mem:* Sculptors Guild (treas, 60-65, exec bd, 66-68 & 77-82, secy, 72-74, vpres for mem, 82-83, pres, 90-93, bd adv, 94; Sculptor's Guild (exec bd mem, 88, 89 & 95-96); Westport-Weston Arts Coun (bd dir, 82-83); Artists Equity Asn; Sculptors Guild (pres, 90); Silvermine Guild Artists (bd mgrs, 58-60, bd trustees, 81-83, chmn admissions, 83). *Media:* Metal, Welded, All Media. *Publ:* Alabama-Bound for New York, The Guild Reporter, Vol 7 no 1. *Mailing Add:* 26 Pin Oak Ct Westport CT 06880-1022

WOODLOCK, CAROLE
INSTRUCTOR

Exhib: Work has been exhibited in both one person and group exhibitions regionally and internationally; videos and films have been exhibited internationally at over 50 festivals. *Teaching:* Prof, chair, Sch of Art, Rochester Inst of Technology, currently; dir, Art Educ Graduate Program, Rochester Inst of Technology, currently. *Mailing Add:* Rochester Institute of Technology College of Imaging Arts and Sciences 73 Lomb Memorial Dr Rochester NY 14623-5603

WOODS, BURTON ARTHUR
PAINTER

b Brooklyn, NY, Sept 3, 1935. *Study:* Studied painting with Charles Sovek & Dan Gilhooley, portrait painting with Bob Behrens & drawing with Dan Gilhooley. *Work:* Clayton Liberatore Gallery, Bridgehampton, NY; Suffolk Co Court Bldg, Riverhead, NY; Tuthill House, Easthampton, NY; Goodman Gallery, South Hampton; Sailors Valentine Gallery, NY; Clayton Liberatore Gallery, Bridgehampton, NY; MRK Gallery, Port Jefferson, NY; Christopher Gallery, Stony Brook, NY. *Comn:* Reitano House, Setauket, NY, 93; Randall House, Mt Sinai, NY, 93; Tooker House, Port Jefferson, NY, 94; Infant Jesus Church, Port Jefferson, NY, 94. *Exhib:* 41st Ann Open Juried Exhib, Heckser Mus, Huntington, NY; 24th Ann Open Juried Exhib, Pastel Soc Ann, NY; Mills Pond House, Smithtown, NY, 93; Carriage House Mus, Philadelphia, Pa, 93; 2nd Ann Pastel Show, Paul Mellon Art Inst, Wallingford, Conn, 94; Long Island Artists Show, Bald Hill Cult Ctr, Farmingville, NY, 94; Vanderbilt Mus, Centerport, NY, 94; Water Mill Mus, NY, 94; Open Juried shows, Paul Melton Art Ctr, Wallingford, Conn, 95, 97, & 98, Duck Decoy Mus, Havre de Grace, Md, 96, Nat Art League, Dougleston, NY, 96, Ridgewood Art Inst, NJ, 97, Brookhaven Arts, Conn, 97 & 98; Int Juried Exhib, NJ Ctr Visual Arts, Summit, 96. *Awards:* First Place Pastels, North Shore Art Guild, Bald Hill Cult Ctr, 94; Best in Show, First Place & Second Place, Brookhaven Art Coun. *Bibliog:* K Mandracchia (auth), Harvest Times Mag; Carol Paquette (auth), Gatehouse critique, Port Jefferson Record, 93; article in North Light, 10/95. *Mem:* Wet Paint Soc, Sayville, NY; East End Arts Coun, Riverhead, NY; Allied Artists Am, NY; Conn Pastel Soc. *Media:* Pastel, Oil. *Collection:* Don Burridge, Va, Frank and Theresa Maglio, Sag Harbor, NY, William Hulse, Greenport, NY, Al and Honer Kopienski, Mount Sinai, NY, Dr Mia Carayanopolis, Corpus Christi, Tex, North Shore Cadiologist, Port Jefferson, NY, Dr. James Carlson, Port Jefferson, NY, Frame that Art Inc, Miller Place, NY. *Dealer:* Champlain Collection Fine Art Publs Highgate Commons 223 Swanton Rd Saint Albans VT 05478; Frame That Art Inc Reggie Andre Miller Place NY. *Mailing Add:* 27 Ridgeview Pl Mount Sinai NY 11766

WOODS, JAN
SCULPTOR

b 1945. *Study:* Univ Okla; Univ Ark. *Comn:* Awards, Nat Grand Prix League; monuments, Oaklawn Jockey Club. *Exhib:* Group shows incl St Huberts Giralda; Catharine Lorillard Wolfe Art Club; Kentucky Derby Mus; Headley-Whitney Mus; Equifest; Morven Park Mus of Sporting Art; Gideon Putnam Hotel, Saratoga Springs. *Awards:* Arts Fest Award for Artistic Excellence, Am Artist Profl League, 1989; Award of Excellence, Am Acad Equine Art, 2001. *Media:* Bronze

WOODS, LAUREN
FILMMAKER

b Kansas City, Missouri, 1979. *Study:* St Louis Univ, Mo, 1997-99, Madrid, 1999-2000; Univ N Tex, Denton, BA Radio TV & Film/BA Spanish/Minor Sociology, 2000-02; Univ Sagrado Corazon, San Juan, Puerto Rico, 2002; San Francisco Art Inst, MFA (Film), 2006. *Work:* Natl Taiwan Univ Arts, Taipei. *Exhib:* group exhibs include Experimental Film & Video Fest, Univ N Tex, Denton, 2002; Ephemeral Feminism, Crucible Steel Gallery, San Francisco, 2005; Athens Int Film & Video Festival, Ohio, 2005 ; Short Film Market, Clermont-Ferrand, France, 2006; Int Women of Color Film Festival, Yerba Buena Ctr Arts, San Francisco, 2006; Efface, Steve Tuner Gallery, Los Angeles, 2006; Ethno-fictive, Swarm Gallery, Oakland, Calif, 2006; She's So Articulate, Arlington Arts Ctr, Va, 2008. *Awards:* Creative Capital Found Grant, 2008

WOODSON, SHIRLEY ANN
PAINTER, COLLAGE ARTIST
b Pulaski, Tenn, Mar 3, 1936. *Study:* Wayne State Univ, BFA, MA; Grad Study, Art Inst Chicago. *Work:* Detroit Inst Arts, Detroit, Mich; Studio Mus Harlem, NY; United Am Health Care, Detroit, Mich; Mus Nat Ctr Afro Am Artist, Boston, Mass; Mus African Am History, Detroit, Mich. *Comn:* Site installation, Chene Park, City of Detroit, 86; mural, Fairlane Town Ctr, Dearborn, Mich, 90; Detroit Rigers, Comerica Park, Mich, 2000; Cobo Convention Ctr, Detroit, Mich, 2004. *Exhib:* Share the Memories, Detroit Inst Arts, 87; Coast to Coast, Nat Women Color Bookworks (with catalog), Radford Univ, Va, 90; Ancestors Known and Unknown, Box Works, Islip Art Mus, Islip, NY, 91; solo show, Sherry Wash Gallery, Detroit, Mich, 92; I Remember--30 Yrs After March on Washington, Concoran Gallery, Washington, DC, 93; Contemp African Am Artists 1980-1994, Nat Arts Club, NY, 94; 20th Century DIA Collection of Drawings & Graphics, Detroit Inst Arts, 2001; Seasons: Paintings & Collages by Shirley Woodson, Ft Valley State Univ, Ga. *Collection Arranged:* Detroit Inst Arts Fabric Workshop & Mus, Phila, Pa; Florida A & M Univ, Tallahassee; Wayne State Univ, Detroit, Mich. *Pos:* Dir exhibs, Arts Extended Gallery, 63-71; pres, Nat Conf Artists, Mich, 96-2000. *Teaching:* Instr painting, design, drawing & art hist, Highland Park Community Col, 66-78; consult, Highland Park Schs, Mich, 78-; vis prof, Eastern Mich Univ, 87-88; adminr & supervisor fine arts, Detroit Pub Schs, 92-; adj prof, Wayne State Univ, 96-. *Awards:* Fel, MacDowell Colony, 66-67; Mich Coun Arts Grant, 83-84 & 87-88; Arts Achievement Award, Wayne State Univ, Detroit, 95; New Initiatives for Arts Exhib Grants, 1994-96. *Bibliog:* Bamidele Demerson (auth), The Nile as vivifying power: Art of Shirley Woodson, Int Quart African-Am Art, 90; Anthony Murphy (auth), Portfolio/Shirley Woodson, American Visions, 92; Robert Henkes (auth), Art of Black American Women: Works by 24 Artists of the 20th Century, MacFarland & Co Publ, 93. *Mem:* Nat Conf Artists; Coll Art Asn. *Media:* Painting, Collage, Assemblage. *Publ:* Auth, African American Women Artists in Michigan (study guide), Detroit Hist Mus, 85; contribr, Walter O Evans Collection of African American Art (catalogue), King Tisdell Cottage Mus, 91. *Dealer:* Sherry Washington 1274 Library St Detroit MI 48226. *Mailing Add:* 5656 Oakman Blvd Detroit MI 48204

WOODWARD, KESLER EDWARD
PAINTER, CURATOR
b Aiken, SC, Oct 7, 1951. *Study:* Davidson Col, NC, BA, 73; Idaho State Univ, Pocatello, MFA, 77. *Work:* Alaska State Mus, Juneau; Univ Alaska Mus, Fairbanks; Atlantic Richfield Co, Los Angeles; Anchorage Hist & Fine Arts Mus & Alaska Contemp Art Bank, Anchorage; Morris Mus Art, Augusta, Ga; Tacoma Art Mus, Wash; Juneau City Mus, Alaska; Pratt Mus, Homer, Alaska; Ted Stevens Internat Airport, Anchorage, Alaska. *Comn:* Pacific Rim Hospital, Fort Richardson, Alaska; Morris Communications Corp Offices, Anchorage, Alaska; Holy Family Chapel, Fairbanks, Alaska; Alaska Airlines Corp Offices, Seattle. *Exhib:* Solo exhibs, Univ Alaska Mus & Alaska State Mus, 85, Jerald Melberg Gallery, NC, 86, Davidson Coll Art Gallery, 86, Univ Ala, Huntsville, 90, Anchorage Mus Hist & Art, 91 & Univ Alaska, Anchorage Art Gallery, 91, Univ Alaska Fine Arts Gallery, 2000, Well St Gallery, Fairbanks, 2001, Decker/Morris Gallery, Anchorage, 02, Univ Alaska Anchorage Kenai Campus Gallery, 2003, Aikea Ctr for the Arts, 2009, Chirate Fault Gallery, 2011, Beaux des Ameriques, Montreal, Can, 2013; Terra Borealis, Visual Art Ctr Alaska, Anchorage, 91; Contemp Art from Alaska, Magadan, Art Gallery, Russia, 92; SC Artists, Greenville Mus Art, SC, 91; True North, Anchorage Mus Hist & Art, 96; Morris Mus of Art, Augusta, Ga, 2001. *Collection Arranged:* New Possibilities: Works from the Canadian Art Bank (auth, catalog), Alaska State Mus, 78; A Celebration of Tradition, Visual Arts Ctr of Alaska, 78 & National Invitational, 78-79; Canadian Horizons (with catalog), 81-82; Sydney Laurence Retrospective (with catalog), Anchorage Mus Hist & Art, 90 & Eustace Ziegler Retrospective (with catalog), 98; Fred Machetanz Retrospective, Anchorage Mus of History & Art, 04. *Pos:* Cur temp exhib, Alaska State Mus, Juneau, 77-78, cur visual arts, 79-81; artistic dir, Visual Arts Ctr of Alaska, Anchorage, 78-79; dir, Univ Alaska Fine Arts Gallery, 82-88; dir, Fine Arts & Humanities Proj, Inst Canada, Dartmouth Col, 88-91; chair, Dept Art & Div Arts & Communications, Univ Alaska, 96-. *Teaching:* Asst prof painting, Univ Alaska, 81-88, assoc prof, 88-96, prof, 96-, prof emeritus, 2000-. *Awards:* Alaska State Coun Arts Fel, 82; Vis Res Fel, Dartmouth Col, 88-91; Alaska Governors award for Lifetime Achievement in the Arts, 2004; Rasmuson Found Distinguished Artist Fellowship, 2012; Artsmith Artist of the Year award, 2012. *Bibliog:* Julie Decker (auth), Kesler Woodward, In: Icebreakers: Alaska's Most Innovative Artists, 99; Kesler Woodward, Alaska Home, 2009; Frank Soss (auth), Kesler Woodward: North and South (catalog essay), Morris Mus Art, Augusta, Ga, 2002. *Mem:* Coll Art Asn. *Media:* Acrylic, Oil. *Res:* Early pictorial material pertaining to polar regions and little-known Alaskan historical artists. *Publ:* Sydney Laurence, Painter of the North, 90; Painting in the North, 93; A Sense of Wonder, Art from Alaska, 95; Spirit of the North: The Art of Eustace Paul Ziegler, 98; Painting Alaska, 00; Modernist Mind and Mystical Spirit: The Art of Oscar Gluemner, 02; exhib catalog Frank Soos, Morris Mus of Art, 01; exhib review Art News, 01; color reproduction, Harpers, 02. *Dealer:* Beaux Arts des Ameriques Montreal Canada. *Mailing Add:* PO Box 70892 Fairbanks AK 99707

WOODWARD, STEVEN P
SCULPTOR
b Little Falls, Minn, 1953. *Study:* St Cloud State Univ, BA, 76. *Work:* Walker Art Ctr, Minneapolis; Tweed Mus, Duluth, Minn; First Bank System, Minneapolis; Minn State Arts Bd, St Paul. *Comn:* Univ Upper Iowa, Fayette; One Percent for Arts program, Univ Minn, Duluth, 96; One Percent for Arts program, Univ Minn, Minneapolis, 96; The St Paul Cos, Inc, St Paul, 97; US Gen Svcs Administration Art and Arch Program US-Can border crossing Sta, Pembina, ND, 97; Percent for Arts Comn, Univ Wis, Madison, 97; Percent for Arts Comn Minn Dept Revenue Bldg, St Paul; Percent for Arts Commn, Kirchbak Gardens, Richfield, Minn. *Exhib:* Ann Juried Exhib, Queen's Mus, NY, 84; Bim Bam Botterham, Stokker Stikker Gallery, NY, 85; Bockley Gallery, Minneapolis, 88; Thomas Barry Fine Arts, Minneapolis, 90, 91 & 92; Kiehle Gallery, St Cloud State Univ, Minn, 91; one person shows, Recent Sculpture, Thomas Barry Gallery, Minneapolis, 88 & 90, New Sculpture, Thoms Barry Gallery, 92, Open Studio, 233 Park Avenue, Minneapolis, 96 & 2000; Forms '92, 13th Ann Invitational Sculpture show, Hennepin Avenue United Meth Ch, Minneapolis, 92; Landscape as Object, Thomas Barry Gallery, 93; The Key to the Garden (installation with David Culver and Kate Hunt), Walker Art Ctr Educ Dept, 94; Six McKnight Artists, Minneapolis Coll Art and Design, 96; Cast Metal Invitation Exhib, Humanities Fine Arts Ctr, Univ Minn, Morris, 96; and others. *Awards:* Juror's Award, Small Works Show, New York Univ, 84; Nat Endowment Arts, 88; Jerome Travel and Study Grant, 94 & 98; McKnight Found Fel, 94; Minn State Arts Bd Fel, 95

WOODWARD, WILLIAM
PAINTER, MURALIST
b Washington, DC, Mar 11, 1935. *Study:* Abbott Sch Art, Corcoran Sch Art, Am Univ, BA & MA, Washington, DC; Acad de Belli Arti, Florence, Italy. *Work:* Corcoran Gallery; Speed Mus, Louisville; Washington Co Mus Fine Art; Ogunquit Mus Fine Art, Ogunquit, Maine; Payson Col, Delaplans, Va; and others. *Comn:* Drawing, The White House, DC, 68; mural, Clydes Inc, Tysons Corner, Va, 80; mural, City Hall Rockville, Md, 82; mural, History of Medicine, Fairfax Hosp, Va, 97; US Army Mus, Washington, DC. *Exhib:* Solo exhibs, Mickelson Gallery, Washington, DC, 66-74, Hirschl & Adler Gallery, NY, 71, John State Col, Vt, 74 & Int Monetary Fund, Washington, DC, 75; Fendrick Gallery, Washington, DC, 82 & 89; Marin-Price Galleries, 2000. *Teaching:* Instr painting, Corcoran Sch Art, DC, 65-; from asst prof painting to prof & program dir, George Washington Univ, DC, 69-; dir, Summer Fine Arts Prog, Brittany, France, 76-79. *Awards:* Painting Fel in Italy, Leopold Schepp Found, 57-59; Mary Graydon Scholar, Am Univ, 53-57 & Teaching Fel, 58-61; Design Prize, Silver Dollar Cong Commemorative Coin, 89; First Prize, 49th Ann Contemp Am Painting, Soc of the Four Arts, Palm Beach, Fla, 97. *Bibliog:* Rafael Sqirru (auth), The Washington mannerists: the foresight to look backwards, Americas, Vol 19, No 1; Legrace N Benson (auth), The Washington scene, Art Int, Vol 13, No 10; Jill Weschsler (auth), William Woodward: Traditional themes, modern methods, Am Artist, 12/76; D Bowers (auth), Commemorative Coins of the US, Bowers & Merena, 91; M Shwartz (auth), The Greatest Mural on Earth, Am Artist, 3/92. *Publ:* Contribr, Art in America, 1760-1860, 69; contribr, Leonardo da Vinci, 70 & Dreamers of Decadence, 72, Washington Post. *Dealer:* Marin-Price Galleries 7022 Wisconsin Ave Chevy Chase MD 20815

WOODY, (THOMAS) HOWARD
SCULPTOR, ENVIRONMENTAL ARTIST
b Salisbury, Md, Sept 26, 1935. *Study:* Richmond Prof Inst, BFA; ECarolina Univ, MA; Univ Iowa; Art Inst Chicago; Kalamazoo Art Ctr; Univ Ky. *Work:* SC State Art Collection, Columbia; Gibbes Art Gallery, Charleston, SC; Mus Art, Charlotte, NC; Birmingham Mus Art, Ala; Columbus Mus Arts & Crafts, Ga; and others. *Exhib:* Tenth Int Sculpture Conf, Toronto, 78; Arcosanti Conf, 78; 11th Int Sculpture Conf, Washington DC, 80; Coll Art Conf, New Orleans, La, 80; Sky Art Conferences, Mass Inst Technol, Cambridge, 81 & 86, Linze, Austria, 82 & Munich, Ger, 83. *Teaching:* Instr sculpture, Roanoke Fine Art Ctr, Va, 59-61; assoc prof sculpture, Pembroke State Univ, 62-67; prof sculpture, Univ SC, 67-. *Awards:* Spec Citation Award, Atlanta Festival Sculpture, 68; SC State Art Collection Award, 71 & 74 & Fel grants, 73 & 77, SC Arts Comn. *Bibliog:* Ann Weinstein (auth), The sky's no limit, Art Voices, 7/81; L G Redstone (auth), Public Art: New Directions, McGraw-Hill, 81. *Mem:* Southern Asn Sculptors (pres, 65-70); Nat Sculpture Ctr (adv, 66-80); Guild SC Artists (mem bd, 69); SC Craftsmen (mem bd, 68); Southeastern Coll Art Conf. *Media:* Plastic. *Publ:* Auth, Atmospheric sculpture: An event, not an object, Vol 7, No 1 & Atmospheric concepts, Vol 6, No 2, Southeastern Coll Art Conf Rev; Workshops in environmental sky art, Design for Arts in Educ, 3-4/79; Environmental art, Sculptor's News Exchange, Princeton, NJ, 9-10-11/79; and others. *Mailing Add:* 433 Arrowwood Rd Columbia SC 29210

WOOF, MAIJA GEGERIS ZACK See Peeples-Bright, Maija Gegeris Zack Woof

WOOL, CHRISTOPHER
PAINTER
b 1955. *Exhib:* Boymans-Van Beuningen, Rotterdam, 91; Kolnischer Kunstverein, Koln, 91; Kunsthalle Bern, Bern, 91; Galerie Max Hetzler, Koln, 93; Brandl/Oehlen/Wool, Nat Gallery, Prague, 94; The Whitney Mus, NY, 95, 97; Mus of Modern Art, NY, 96, 97, 98; Ctr d'Art Contemporain, Geneva, 99; Skarstedt Fine Art, NY, 00; Eleni Koroneou Gallery, Athens, 2000; Galerie Micheline Szwajcer, Antwerp, 2001; Luhring Augustine NY, London, 2001; Le Consortium, Dijon, 2002; group exhibs, Aspen Art Mus, 99, Angles Gallery, Santa Monica, Calif, 99, Greene Naftali, NY, 99, Mus Modern Art, 2000, New Mus Art Lucerne, Switz, 2000, Barbara Gladstone Gallery, New York City, 2000, Alexander Gallery, New York City, 2000, Whitney Mus Am Art, 2001, Sabine Knust, Munich, 2001, Mus des Beaux Arts, Dole, France, 2001, Paine Webber Art Gallery, NY, 2002, Norton Mus Art, West Palm Beach, Fla, 2002; 54th Int Art Exhib Biennale, Venice, 2011; and others. *Awards:* Fel, Nat Endowment Arts, 87. *Bibliog:* Gray Indiana (auth), Chronicle in black & white, The Village Voice, 3/31/87; Jerry Saltz (auth), This is the end, Art Mag, 9/20/88; Parkett, No 33, 92. *Mailing Add:* c/o Luhring Augustine & Hodes Gallery 531 W 24th St New York NY 10011

WOOLF-PETTYJOHN, NANCY ANNE
PAINTER, COLLECTOR
Exhib: Solo exhib, Honiton Laces, Allhallows Mus, Honiton, Devon, England, 2009. *Bibliog:* appeared in the Lexington News, The Odessan, Piecework Mag, Interweave Press, Am Art Collector Mag, Int Artists's Pub, 2011; KCTV5 Morning News (TV interview); Kans City Star. *Media:* Acrylic. *Res:* Historical places, historical portraiture, figurative art, legal & medical, natural botanicals, American slavery. *Specialty:* history, art, people. *Interests:* advocate for helping the aged poor & those who can not help themselves. *Collection:* laces and linens

WOOLSCHLAGER, LAURA TOTTEN
PAINTER, PRINTMAKER
b Dallas, Tex, Sept 1, 1932. *Study:* Syracuse Univ, BFA (magna cum laude), 54; Southern Ore Col, with Robert Alston, 65. *Work:* Carnegie Libr, Lewiston, Idaho; Mus Native Am Cult, Spokane, Wash; Favell Mus Western Art, Klamath Falls, Ore. *Exhib:* Southwest Rendezvous, Oro Valley Country Club, Tucson, Ariz, 79-81; C M Russell Show, Heritage Inn, Great Falls, Mont, 79-81; Western Experience, Stewart Anderson Ranch, Ellensburg, Wash, 80; Artist in Residence, Mus Native Am Cult, Spokane, Wash, 80; Ceres Western Art Show, 92-95. *Pos:* bd mem, Robert Graves Gallery, Wenatchee Valley Community Coll, 2014. *Awards:* Best of Show, Artists of the Old West, 79 & Nat Western Art Show, Western Art Asn, 79. *Bibliog:* Dr Darwin Goodey (auth), An inner view, Art West Mag, 1/80; Paula Hartwig (auth), Northwest Originals, Washington Women & Their Art, Ann 90. *Mem:* Western Art Asn; Larson Gallery Guild, Yakima Community Coll, Yakima, Wash. *Media:* Acrylic, Watercolor; Intaglio, Monoprint; Assemblages; Mixed Media. *Interests:* Native Am hist, gardening, creative writing & poetry. *Mailing Add:* 1221 Poe St Wenatchee WA 98801

WOOSTER, ANN-SARGENT
PAINTER
b Chicago, Ill, Jan 19, 1946. *Study:* Bard Col, AB, 68; Hunter Coll, with Robert Morris, MFA, 73, and Leo Steinberg, Rosalind Krauss & Ray Parker, MA (art hist), 78. *Exhib:* Anthology Film Archives; Black Maria Festival; Contemp Arts Ctr, Cincinnati; New Arts Ctr, Kutztown, 94. *Pos:* Ed educ dept, Shorewood Publ, New York, 69-72; free lance writer, Art Am, New York, 73-; staff writer, Art Forum, 75-76, Village Voice, 79-83 & Afterimage, 81-92; contrib ed, East Village Eye, 83-86, Amtrak Express, 87-91 & High Performance, 88-. *Teaching:* Instr, Sch Visual Arts, New York, 75-, Kean Coll, Union, NJ, 79-83, New York Univ, 85; New York Sch Interior Design, 89-2011; instr, MFA Prog, Pa Acad Fine Arts, 94-. *Awards:* Helen Rubenstein Fel, Whitney Mus Am Art, 75; Award, 82, Grant for Media Production, 85, NY State Coun Arts; Logan Grant for New Writing on Photography, 88; Video Fel, New York Found of the Arts, 88. *Bibliog:* Jean Sousa (auth), NAME events, NAME Gallery, 80; Charlene Spretnak (auth), Politics of Women's Spirituality, Anchor Doubleday, 82. *Mem:* Int Art Critics Asn; Women's Caucus; Int Art Critics Asn (secy Am Sect, 92-96); New Arts Prog, Kutztown, Pa (bd dirs, 89-). *Media:* Miscellaneous Media. *Publ:* Auth, Moving to dance, 12/80 & Yvonne Rainer: Journeys to Berlin 1971, 5/81, Drama Rev; Making Their Mark: Women Artists Move Into The Mainstream (catalog essay), 89; essay, Reach Out & Touch Someone: The Romance of Interactivity (book), Illuminating Video, New York, Aperture Press, 91; chapters in American Painting, Goodman Publ, 91; The First Generation: Women and Video (catalog essay), 93. *Mailing Add:* 170 Second Ave New York NY 10003-5754

WORDELL, EDWIN HOWLAND
PAINTER
b Philadelphia, Pa, Aug 27, 1927. *Hon Degrees:* San Diego State Univ, dipl (hon), 61. *Work:* San Diego Zoological Soc; NASA; Tex Instruments; Transco Energy co, Houston, Tex; Scripps Clinic & Res Found, The Burnham Inst & Univ Calif San Diego Burn Ctr, La Jolla, Calif; Utah State Univ; San Bernardino Valley Coll; pvt collections, Millard Sheets, Nat Acad, George Gibson, Nat Acad, Robert E Wood, Walter Wojtyla & Richard A Morris. *Comn:* Triptych (watercolor), Zoological Soc, San Diego; three watercolor paintings, San Diego Trust & Savings Bank; two watercolor paintings, Great Am Develop co, San Diego; US Coast Guard; Borden Chemical, N Am Terminals Inc; NASA. *Exhib:* Butler Inst Am Art, Youngstown, Ohio, 92, 95 & 2002; Sangre de Cristo Arts Ctr, Pueblo, Colo, 99; Van Vechton-Lineberry Taos Art Mus, NMex, 2000; Winston Churchill Mem & Lib, Fulton, Mo, 2001; Segreto Contemp Art, Santa Fe, NMex, 2002; Aesthetics, Inc, San Diego, 2003; CSG Dominquez Hills, Carson, Calif, 2005; Pentagon, 2007-2008. *Pos:* Juror, Nat Watercolor Soc, 94, Carlsbad/Oceanside Art League, Calif, 96, Southbay Watercolor Soc, San Pedro, Calif, 96 & local art orgs, 2000-03; Int Soc Experimental Artist, 2007. *Teaching:* Instr watercolor workshop, Greece, 85, NZ, Fiji & Australia, 86, Mex, 88-89, 93 & 96-97, Port, 90, Guatemala, 91, Turkey, 92 & Bora Bora Moorea, 99, Hendersonville, NC, 99 & 2003 & local workshops. *Awards:* Merit award, La Watercolor Nat Exhib, 2001; Award of Merit, Internat Soc Exptl Artist, 2002 & 2003; Donor's Award Taos, Hist Mus NMex, 2004; Mem Award San Diego Watercolor Soc, Int Exhib, 2005; Gold Pallet award, Nat Watercolor Soc, 2012. *Mem:* Nat Watercolor Soc; Watercolor West; San Diego Art Guild (pres, 90-91); Taos Soc Watercolorists; Rocky Mt Watermedia Soc, Boulder, Colo; San Diego Watercolor Soc (pres 75-76). *Media:* Watermedia, Mixed. *Interests:* Reading, music. *Collection:* Walter Wytila, Richard Allan Morris, Robert E Woods, and others. *Publ:* First issue cover, San Diego Metro Mag, 85 & 90; Creative Collage Techniques, 94, Creative Watercolor, 96 & Exploring Color (rev ed), 98, Northlight Bks; NC & Ga State Bar J, 96; Watercolor, Abstract 96, Artists Mag, 9/2000; Watercolor Mag, winter 2001; Creative Computer Tools for the Artist, J Pollard & J Little, 2001; James Lightner (auth), Land of Sunlight, 2007. *Dealer:* Aesthetics Inc 301 Spruce St San Diego CA 92103. *Mailing Add:* 6251 Lorca Dr San Diego CA 92115

WORKMAN, ROBERT P
PAINTER, ILLUSTRATOR
b Chicago, Ill, Jan 27, 1961. *Study:* Sch Art Inst Chicago; Roosevelt Univ (Belg, Europe), PhD, 86; Pac Western Univ, BA, 87, MA, 92; Ecole du Louvre, Doctorate, 97. *Work:* Libr Nat Mus Am Art Portrait Gallery, Nat Arch, Washington, DC; Ridge Hist Soc Mus, Chicago; The Vatican, Rome, Italy; Ill State Mus, Springfield; Musee de Louvre; and others. *Comn:* Portrait, Mayor Richard J Daley, Daley Branch Libr, Chicago Pub Libr, Ill, 89; Mt Greenwood Br Libr, Chicago; Walker Br Libr, Chicago. *Exhib:* Nat Vet For War Conv, Chicago, 87; Int Cartoon Festival, Europe, 87; Sch Art Inst, Nat Reunion Alumni, Chicago, 91; Ridge Hist Soc Mus, Chicago, 92; Expo 92, Seville Worlds Fair, US Pavilion, Spain, 92; Nat Exhib, Sch Art Inst Chicago; Royal Acad Arts, London, 95 & 96; Expo 98, Lisbon, Portugal, US Pavilion, 98; Kennedy Park Libr/Mus; and others. *Collection Arranged:* Kennedy Park Libr, Chicago; National 911 Memorial (digital artists registry). *Pos:* Graphic artist/cartoonist, Village View Publs, 83-88; artist, Villager (newspaper), 91-; founder, Kennedy Park Libr, Chicago. *Teaching:* Instr art/writing, St Xavier Coll, 85; artist-in-residence, Chicago Pub Libr, 91-; adj lectr, Univ Ariz, 96; Maitre de Conf, Paris, 97; prof, Mus Nat d'Histoire Naturelle France. *Awards:* Plaque, Ill Dept Conserv; Chicago, 150th cert, City of Chicago, 87; Plaque/Cert Appreciation, Vet For War, Post 5220; First American Artist Accepted into Louvve for 21st Century; Placed in Congressional record, March 4, 2010. *Bibliog:* Stan Barker (auth), Home grown, Artists Mag, 90; Dan Rafter (auth), Seville expo, Beverly Rev, 92; Steve Metsch (auth), Artist wins spot at worlds fair, 92. *Mem:* Assoc mem Am Watercolor Soc; Ridge Art Asn; Sch Art Inst Chicago; Artists Resource Inst, Ft Wayne Mus Art; Reader, Oxford Univ, Eng. *Media:* Watercolor, Acrylic. *Res:* Egyptian hieroglyphics and cult; Mayan hieroglyphics and culture and the possible influences and similarities between the two since 1997. *Interests:* Chess, reading, movies. *Collection:* Musee du Louvre, Paris. *Publ:* Auth & illusr, Angels of Doom; Sesqui Squirrel, Hist Mt Greenwood, Ill; Sesqui Squirrel Meets George Washington; Sesqui Squirrel presents the Wright Brothers First Flight; Sesqui Squirrel Tours the Art Inst Chicago. *Dealer:* The American Society of Portrait Artists 2781 Zelda Rd Montgomery AL 36106. *Mailing Add:* 2509 W 111th St Chicago IL 60655

WORTH, ALEXI
PAINTER
Study: Yale Univ, BA, 86; Skowhegan Sch Art, 89; Boston Univ, MFA, 93. *Exhib:* The Cave, Mills Gallery, Boston Ctr for the Arts, 90, Boston Drawing Show, 90; New Narratives, Clark Gallery, Lincoln, Mass, 91, Social Life, 95; Two Painters, Union League Club, NY, 91; Locate, Leubsdorf Gallery, Hunter Col, NY, 96; Group Show, Virginia Lynch Gallery, Tiverton, RI, 96; About Drawing, Hilles Library, Radcliffe Col, Cambridge, Mass, 97; Nude and Narrative, PPOW, NY, 2000; The Mylar Portraits, Elizabeth Harris Gallery, NY, 2001; Alter Ego, RB Stevenson Gallery, San Diego, 2001; Double Vision, Adam Baumgold Gallery, NY, 2001; Focal Points, Univ Pa, 2002; Gerberman at Large, Bill Maynes Gallery, NY, 2002; Salon Portraiture, Diamantina Gallery, NY, 2003; Endless Love, DC Moore Gallery, NY, 2004; Am Acad Arts & Letts Invitational, New York, 2010. *Collection Arranged:* Cur, The Figure, Snug Harbor Cultural Ctr, Staten Island; cur, Self-Made men, DC Moore Gallery, NY, 2006. *Teaching:* Teacher, Univ NH, formerly, Yale Univ, formerly; sr critic, Univ Pa, currently. *Awards:* Regional Fellowship, New England Found for Arts, 94; Tiffany Found Award, 99

WORTH, KAREN
SCULPTOR
b Philadelphia, Pa, Mar 9, 1924. *Study:* Tyler Art Sch, Temple Univ; Pa Acad Fine Arts; Acad Grande Chaumiere, Paris. *Work:* Smithsonian Inst; West Point Acad, NY; Am Jewish Hist Asn, Boston; Jewish Mus, NY; Israel Govt Coins & Medals Div, Jerusalem. *Comn:* Space Age (medal), Soc Medalists, 63; Hist Jews of Am, Judaic Heritage Soc, 69; Presidents USA, Whittnauer Precious Metals Guild, 74; Bicentennial Presidents (medal), Galaxies Unlimited Inc, 75. *Exhib:* Nat Acad, NY, 65; Lever House, NY, 66-; Ceramic Sculpture of Western Hemisphere. *Teaching:* Pvt sculpture classes, 72-73. *Awards:* Saltus Award, 80, Numismatics Lifetime Achievement Award; Lindsey Morris Award (for a portrait), 86. *Bibliog:* Ed Trautman (auth), Almanac, Franklin Mint, 68. *Mem:* Fel Nat Sculpture Soc (coun, 69-); Fine Arts Fedn New York. *Media:* Clay, Bronze. *Mailing Add:* 19 Henry St Orangeburg NY 10962

WORTHEN, AMY NAMOWITZ
PRINTMAKER, HISTORIAN
b New York, NY, Aug 13, 1946. *Study:* Smith Col, with Leonard Baskin, BA, 67; Univ Iowa, with Mauricio Lasansky, MA, 69; Sir John Cass Col, City London Polytechnic, 86- 87. *Work:* Metrop Mus Art, NY; Cooper-Hewitt Mus, NY; Des Moines Art Ctr, Iowa; Nat Mus Am Art, Washington; Mus Fine Arts, Boston. *Comn:* Two engravings, Terrace Hill Soc, Des Moines, Iowa, 79; Patron's Print, Univ Iowa, 82; Aida in Des Moines (engraving), Des Moines Metrop Opera; Centro Internazionale di Grafica, Venice, 92. *Exhib:* World Print III, San Francisco, Mus Mod Art, 80; Smithsonian Touring Exhib, II Int Mus, 80-83; solo exhibs, Brunnier Gallery, Iowa State Univ, Ames, 81, Selected Prints and Drawings, 1979-84 (with catalog), Sioux City Art Ctr, 84, State Univ NY, Binghamton, 89, Grinnell Col, Iowa, 90, Louise Noun Collection: Art by Women, Des Moines Art Ctr, Iowa, École des Beaux-Arts, Saint-Étienne, France, 92, Scuola Int di Grafica, Venice, Italy, 94 & Associazione Int Incisori, Rome, Italy, 94; Boston Printmakers 33rd, 35th, 36th & 38th Nat Exhibs, 81, 83, 84 & 86; Print Club Philadelphia, 82 & 83; Playing Cards, Cooper Hewitt Mus, NY, 86; Art Quest 88, CW Post Col, NY, Beaver Coll Pa & Univ Calif, Irvine, 88; plus many others. *Collection Arranged:* The Etchings of Jacques Bellange (com auth, catalog), Des Moines Art Ctr, Mus Fine Arts, Metrop Mus, 75-76; Benton, Curry, Wood--Lithographs, Iowa Arts Coun touring exhib (auth, catalog), 78; Giorgio Morandi (auth, catalog), Des Moines Art Ctr, San Francisco Mus Mod Art, Guggenheim Mus, 81; Etchings of JN Darling (auth, catalog), Brunnier Gallery, Iowa State Univ, 84; Centro Internazionale di Grafica (Iowa Printmakers), Venice, 89; Maestri della Scuola Internazionale di Grafica di Venezia, Drake Univ, 89 & Sioux City Art Ctr, 90; Des Moines Art Center (manuscripts & early printed book pages), 91. *Teaching:* Instr printmaking hist prints, Des Moines Art Ctr, Iowa, 71-; lectr, Drake Univ, Iowa, 72-74, 81, 83, 85, 92 & 94; Instr drawing & engraving, Scuola Int di Grafica, Venice, Italy, 93-99. *Awards:* Iowa Arts Coun Touring Exhib Grant, 78; Art Quest Printmaking, 88. *Mem:* Print Coun Am; Women Caucus Art; Boston Printmakers; Mid Am Print Coun; Coll Art Asn. *Media:* Engraving. *Res:* History of prints. *Dealer:* Olson-Larson Galleries 203 Fifth St W Des Moines IA 50265. *Mailing Add:* 5130 Shriver Ave Des Moines IA 50312

WORTZ, MELINDA FARRIS
GALLERY DIRECTOR, CRITIC
b Ann Arbor, Mich, Apr 30, 1940. *Study:* Radcliffe Col, BA (cum laude), 62; Otis Art Inst, 62-63; Univ Calif, Los Angeles, MA, 70; also with John Altoon. *Pos:* Gallery dir, Univ Calif, Riverside, 72-74 & Univ Calif, Irvine, currently; Southern Calif ed, Artweek, currently; contrib ed, Arts Mag, Art Gallery, Art News & Archit Dig, currently. *Teaching:* Asst prof issues in art, Calif State Univ, Long Beach, 72-75 & Calif State Univ, Los Angeles, 74-75; lectr, Univ Calif, Irvine, currently. *Res:* Contemporary American art. *Publ:* Auth, Seven Southern California Artists (catalog), Cirrus Gallery, Los Angeles, 74; auth, Dewain Valentine (exhib catalog), Long Beach Mus Art, 75; auth, Ludwig Redl (catalog essay), 75. *Mailing Add:* 1725 Cedar St Santa Monica CA 90405-2723

WORTZEL, ADRIANNE
PAINTER, PRINTMAKER
b Brooklyn, NY, Oct 7, 1941. *Study:* Brooklyn Mus Art Sch, NY, 57-65; Brooklyn Col, with Ad Reinhardt, Burgoyne Diller & Louise Bourgeois, BA (with honors fine art), 63; Hunter Col, New York, with Mark Rothko, MA, 69. *Work:* Moderna Museet, Stockholm Sweden; Citibank, NY; City of Lund, Sweden; pvt collection of Mr & Mrs Larry Hagman, Malibu, Calif. *Comn:* Landmark Systems, Philip Johnson Bldg, Vienna, Va. *Exhib:* Galleriet, Sweden, 79 & 82; New Acquisitions, Moderna Museet, Stockholm, Sweden, 80; one-person show, Scottsdale Ctr Arts, Ariz, 80 & Bernice Steinbaum Gallery, NY, 81 & 83; Graphic Plus, Herbert F Johnson Mus, Ithaca, NY, 81; Stamford Mus, Conn, 89. *Teaching:* Lectr contemp art, Great Neck Adult Educ Program, 70-73; guest artist, printmaking workshop, 89. *Awards:* Creative Artists Pub Serv Grant, NY State Coun Arts, 81. *Bibliog:* Patricia Ensworth, Adrianne Wortzel, Arts Mag, 3/80; Sarah Cecil (auth), article, Artnews, 3/82; Donna Harkavy (auth), Adrianne Wortzel, Arts Mag, 9/83. *Media:* Acrylic on Canvas; Etchings

WRAY, DICK
PAINTER
b Houston, Tex, Dec 5, 1933. *Study:* Univ Houston. *Work:* Albright-Knox Art Gallery, Buffalo; Mus Fine Arts, Houston. *Exhib:* Mus Contemp Art, Houston, 61; Southwest Painting & Sculpture, Houston, 62; Hemisfair, Houston, 68; Homage to Lithography Temp Art, Houston, 61; Response, Tyler Mus, Tex, 80; Houston Artists Exhibition, Stavanger Mus, Norway; In Our Time: Houston's Contemp Arts Mus 1948-1982, Contemp Arts Mus, Houston, 82; Fresh Paint: The Houston Sch, Mus of Fine Arts, Houston (catalog), traveling exhib, 85; Third Western States Exhib, The Brooklyn Mus, NY, (catalog), traveling exhib, 86; Line and Form: Contemp Tex Figurative Drawing, Art Mus of S Tex, Corpus Christi, 87; Texas Art: An Exhibition Selected from the Menil Collection, The Mus of the Menil Collection-Richmond Hall, Houston, 88; Wade Wilson Art, Tex, 2007. *Teaching:* Glassell Sch of Art, Mus Fine Arts, Houston, Tex, 68-82. *Awards:* Purchase Prize, Ford Found, 62; Purchase Prize, Mus Fine Arts, Houston, 63. *Media:* Painting, Works on Paper. *Mailing Add:* c/o Moody Gallery 2815 Colquitt Houston TX 77098

WRIGHT, BAGLEY
COLLECTOR
Study: Princeton Univ, BA, 46. *Pos:* With Daily Mirror, Newsweek; real estate developer Pentagram Corp, Harbor Properties; chmn Physio Control Corp, 68-80; Developer Space Needle, Seattle. *Awards:* Named one of Top 200 Collectors, ARTnews Magazine, 2004, 2006. *Collection:* Contemporary Art; Japanese Art. *Mailing Add:* 407 Dexter Ave Seattle WA 98109

WRIGHT, BARTON ALLEN
WRITER, GRAPHIC ARTIST
b Bisbee, Ariz, Dec 21, 1920. *Study:* Univ Ariz, BA, MA (anthropology & geology). *Work:* Ariz Bank (now Bank of Am); Mus N Ariz; pvt collections. *Comn:* Wupatki Nat Monument, Ft Union Nat Monument, Babbitt Stores; Great Sand Dunes Nat Monument; Montezuma Castle Nat Monument. *Exhib:* La Jolla Art Asn, Calif, 69; The Athenaeum, La Jolla, 70; Festival of Arts, Lake Oswego, 71; Solo exhibs, San Diego, 71-75; Thorne Gallery, Scottsdale, 74 & 75; Indian Summer Gallery, Estes Park, Colo; Blaire Gallery, Santa Fe; and others. *Collection Arranged:* M R F Colton, 58; G E Burr, 59; Indian Artists, 60; Western Artists, 62; Paul Dyck, 64; Am Art, 65; Frederick Sommers, 67; Southwest Art, 68; Widforss, 69; Santa Fe Indian Art, 70; Nat Park Illustrated, 71; N Fechin, 72; and others; History of Hopi Kachinas. *Pos:* Cur arts & exhib, Mus Northern Ariz, 55-58, cur, Mus, 58-77; sci dir, Mus of Man, 77-82; res anthropologist, Heard Mus, 83; sci lect & guide, Sierra Club, Stanford Alumni, Canyonlands. *Teaching:* Vis instr, Univ Calif, Riverside, 77, Univ Calif, San Diego, spring 83, Pitzer Col, spring 83. *Awards:* Anisfield Wolf-Cleveland Found, 86; Rounce & Coffin, 86; Border Regional Libr Asn, 86. *Mem:* Am Asn Mus; Indian Arts & Crafts Asn; Ariz/Nev Acad Sci; Westerners, San Diego & Phoenix. *Media:* Acrylic, Scratchboard, carvings. *Res:* Hopi Kachinas. *Interests:* Western Art; Indian Art. *Publ:* Auth, Hopi Clowns, 94, Kachinas, a Hopi Artist's Documentary, 73, Unchanging Hopi, 75, Pueblo Shields, 76, Hopi Kachinas, The Complete Guide, 77; Mythic World of the Zuni, 88; Hallmarks of the Southwest, rev 2, 2000; auth catalog, Kachinas, Flak Galerie, Paris, 2003; Spirits of the Past, Vendome Press, in press; coauth (with Andrea Portago), Classic Hopi & Zuni Figures, 2006; Cateclaw Cave, Lower Colorado River, 2008. *Mailing Add:* 4143 Gelding Dr Phoenix AZ 85023

WRIGHT, BING
PHOTOGRAPHER
b Seattle, 1958. *Study:* Columbia Coll, NY City, BA (art hist). *Work:* Mus Mod Art, New York; Portland Art Mus, Ore; Seattle Mus Art, Wash. *Exhib:* Solo exhibs include Linda Fariis Gallery, Seattle, 1986, Julian Pretto Gallery, NY City, 1988, Berland Hall Gallery, NY City, 1991, Pace Wildenstein McGill, NY City, 1993, Lipton Owens Com, NY City, 1994, Tricia Collins, NY City, 1998, Rena Bransten Gallery, 1999, Lucas Schoormans Gallery, NY City, 2000, 2003, Paula Cooper Gallery, NY City, 2004, James Harris Gallery, Seatle, Wash, 2007, Paula Cooper Gallery, New York, NY, 2008, 2010; group exhibs include Queens Mus, NY City, 1986; White Columns Gallery, NY City, 1987, 1990; Linda Farris Gallery Seattle, 1988; New Mus, NY City, 1991; Berland Hall Gallery; Amy Lipton Gallery, NY City, 1993; Lucas Schoormans, NY City, 1996; Rena Bransten, San Francisco, 1998; Julie Saul Gallery, NY City, 1999; Soc for Contemp Photog, Kans City, Mo, 2000; Western Bridge, Seattle, 2005; Abington Art Ctr, Jenkintown, Pa, 2006; James Harris Gallery, Seattle, Wash, 2007; Lucas Shoorman Gallery, 2007; Tang Mus & Art Gallery, Saratoga Springs, NY, 2007. *Dealer:* Ochi Fine Art 119 Lewis St Ketchum ID 83340; Lucas Schoorman Gallery 508 W 26th St NY City NY 10001; Paula Cooper Gallery New York. *Mailing Add:* c/o Paula Cooper Gallery 534 W 21st St New York NY 10011

WRIGHT, FRANK
PAINTER, EDUCATOR
b Washington, DC, Oct 10, 1932. *Study:* Am Univ, BA, 54; Univ Ill, Urbana, MA, 60; Fogg Mus, Harvard Univ, fel, 60-61; Villa i tatti, with Bernard Berenson, Florence, Italy, 56-58; Atelier 17, Paris, 61-64. *Work:* Bibliot Nat, Paris; Nat Collections Fine Arts, Washington, DC; Univ Seattle Law Sch, Wash; Nat Gallery Art, Rosenwald Collection, Washington, DC; Tucson Mus Art, Tucson, Ariz; Am Univ & Georgetown Univ, Washington, DC; Guilford Col, Greensboro, NC; Morris Mus Art, Augusta, Ga; Sallie Mae, Washington; Deloitte and Touche, Washington. *Comn:* Deepbite etching demonstration plate & ed, Lessing J Rosenwald, Jenkintown, Pa, 68; oil painting - Cityscapes, WC Bradley Co, Columbus, Ga, 85; oil painting - Hist, Pershing Assoc, Washington, DC, 86; oil painting - Washington Scene & Washington Hist, Perpetual Am Bank, Washington, DC, 87; oil painting 18 x 7' Mural for Lobby of Rep PL, Oliver Carr Co, Washington, DC, 88; portrait - US House of Rep Speaker Thomas Foley, US Capitol; painting, Pennsylvania Ave in 1890, Chevy Chase Bank, Bethesda, Md, 2003; painting, Harpers Ferry, WVa, Capital One Bank, Tyson's Corner, Va, 2005. *Exhib:* West 83/Art & The Law, Woodruff Arts Ctr, Atlanta, 83; Allentown Art Mus, Pa, 83; Frank Wright: Painting 1968-1980, Corcoran Gallery of Art, Washington, DC, 81; Frank Wright: Washington Past & Present, Int Monetary Fund Visitors' Ctr, Washington, DC, 86; Paintings, Covington & Burling, Washington, DC, 93; Paintings, Susquehanna Art Mus, Harrisburg, Pa, 93; Remembering Times Past; Savoring Times Present, George Washington Univ, 94; Frank Wright: A Look Back, Paintings and Prints 1963-1998, Strathmore Hall Arts Ctr, North Bethesda, Md, 98, Frank Wright: Annapolis and the Bay Paintings 1989-1996, Md Hall for the Creative Arts, Annapolis, Md, 98; Pulse 2006, Hillyer Art Space, 2006. *Pos:* Prof drawing & graphics & fine arts, George Washington Univ, 70-. *Teaching:* Instr master drawings, Corcoran Sch Art, Washington, DC, 66-70; asst prof design & graphics, George Washington Univ, 70-78, assoc prof drawing & graphics, 79-83, prof, 83-. *Awards:* Schepp Found Fel, 56-58; Paul J Sachs Fel, Nat Gallery Art, 59-60; Fel, Fogg Mus Harvard, 60-61. *Bibliog:* Jill Wechsler (auth), Frank Wright an artist with a sense of history, Am Artist, 9/82; Ruth Palombo (auth), DC Artist is Historian with a Paint Brush, Chevy Chase Gazette, 12/21/89; Sandra Martin (auth), Frank Wright's Ideal America, The New Bay Times Vol II, No 15, 6/30/94-7/6/94; and others. *Mem:* Cosmos Club of Washington; Columbia Historical Soc; Omicron Delta Kappa; Nat Soc Arts & Letters (Wash chap). *Media:* Oil; Graphics (Engraving, Deep-bite Etching). *Res:* Civil War in Washington. *Publ:* Auth, Why I love to engrave, GW Forum, Vol 7, No 1 (winter 77). *Mailing Add:* Dept Art George Washington Univ 801 22nd St NW Washington DC 20052

WRIGHT, JESSE GRAHAM, JR
DIRECTOR
b Sidney, Ohio, July 29, 1939. *Study:* Loyola Univ, Chicago, BA, 64, MA, 65; Univ Notre Dame, Ind, MFA (painting & sculpture), 69; Univ Tulsa, Okla, 84. *Pos:* Dir, South Bend Art Ctr, Michael C Rockefeller Art Ctr Gallery, Fredonia, NY, 68-71, Canton Art Inst Ohio, 74-77, Philbrook Art Ctr, Tulsa, Okla, 77-84, J B Speed Art Mus, Louisville, Ky, 84-86 & Mus of the Horse, NMex, 94-96; pres, Wright Group, 86-90; develop dir, Buffalo Bill Hist Ctr, Cody, Wyo, 91-94. *Teaching:* Fac mem, St Mary's Col, Notre Dame, Ind, 68-77; asst prof, State Univ NY, Fredonia, 68-77; dean, Col Fine Arts, Jacksonville, Fla, 96-. *Mem:* Am Asn Mus

WRIGHT, JIMMY
PAINTER, PRINTMAKER
b Ky, July 8, 1944. *Study:* Art Inst Chicago, BFA (George D Brown Fel), 67; Southern Ill Univ, Carbondale, MFA, 71; student, Murray State Univ, Ky, 62, 63; Aspen School of Contemp Art, Co, 63. *Work:* St Paul Art Ctr, Minn; Okla City Art Ctr; Univ Ohio, Athens; Yeiser Art Ctr, Paducah, Ky; Sch Art Inst Chicago, Ill; Metrop Mus Art, NY; Springfield Mus Art, Springfield, MO; Lower East Side Print Shop, NY; Center for Book and Paper arts, Chicago Columbia College, Chicago, Ill; W Libr State Col, W Liberty, WV; Art Inst Chicago. *Comn:* Sets & Costumes, Stan Dancers Ballet, Tokyo, Japan, 79; cover painting, Readers Digest, Pleasantville, NY, 98; four screenprint eds, AFA Press, Lakeside, Mich, 98. *Exhib:* Nat Drawing Exhib, San Francisco Art Mus, 70; L Atelier de L Artiste, Maison Natale Gustave Courbet, Ornans, France, 87; An Artists Ode to Flowers, Nassau Co Mus Art, Roslyn, NY, 92; The Flower Show, Portland Mus Art, 92; Self Portrait: the changing self, NJ Ctr Visual Arts, Summit, 93; Painting After Nature (with catalog), Mus Contemp Art, N Miami, Fla, 94; In Bloom, NJ Ctr Visual Arts, Summit, NJ, 96; Solo Exhibs: Eagle Art Gallery, Murray State Univ, Ky, 74; Tochigi Fine Arts Mus, Japan, 79; Tavelli Gallery, Aspen, Colo, 92; DC Moore Gallery, New York City, 97; Roger Ramsay Gallery, Chicago, 97; Wild Flowers Katonah Mus Art, Katonah, NY, 99; Fen Way Gallery, Chicago, Ill, 2001; DC Moore Gallery, NY, 2001; Eagle Art Gallery, Murray State Univ, Murray, Ky, 2005; Nutting Gallery, W Liberty State Col, W Lib, WV, 2005; Argazzi Art, Lakeville Ct, 2005; Corbett vs Dempsey, Chicago, Il, 2007; Selections, Giffuni Gallery of American Pastels, Butler Inst of Am Art, Youngstown, Ohio, 2004; Brainstorm, Lolapoloza Gallery, Oxford, Great Britain, 2005; The Body and Its Dangers, The Painting Center, NY, 2005; 181st Annual: An International Exhibition of Contemp Art, Nat Academy, NY, 2006; Jimmy Wright, Argazzi Art, Lakeville, Ct, 2006; Lost Women, Corbett vs. Dempsey, Chicago, Ill, 2007; The Lens and the Mirror: Modern Self-Portraits From the Collection, Metropolitan Mus Art, 2009; Jimmy Wright: Twenty Years of Painting

and Pastels, Springfield Mus Art, 2009; Chicago Stories: Prints, Art Inst of Chic, 2010; Gram and Ox-Bow: Joint Centennial Celebration Exhib, Grand Rapids, Mich, 2010; Pastels by Invitation, 2010, 2011; Creative Arts Center, Chatham, Mass, 2010; 7th Anniv Show, Argazzi Art, Lakeville, Ct, 2010; Pastel Soc Am, 39th Exhib, Nat Arts Club, NY, 2011. *Teaching:* instr, Skidmore Coll, 2010; instr, Ox-Bow, Mich, 2011; instr, 92Y, NY, 2012. *Awards:* Jurors Award, NY Univ, 87; Grant, Lower E Side Printshop, 90. *Bibliog:* Donna Gustafson (auth), Jimmy Wright, Arts Mag, 97; Grace Glueck (auth), NY Times, 2001; Contemp Am Art, Art in Embassies Prog, Embassy of US, Vienna, Austria, 2002. *Mem:* Pastel Soc Am (treas, 2008); Int Asn Pastel Societies (bd of dir, 2008). *Publ:* illusr, BOMB, Vol XVII, 84-95, winter 87, BOMB, New York, 87 & Vol XXXX, No 1, 73-79, fall 92; Kaleidoscope, Vol 6, No 1, 1-3, Cornell Univ, 8/97; Readers Digest, 98; illustr, Architectural Digest, 97; contribr, Journal of the Print World, XXII, no.1, Winter, 99; illustr, Am Artist (p.72), 2002; Bowery Artists Tribute (bio and photos), New Mus Contemp Art, NY, 2008. *Dealer:* DC Moore Gallery 724 Fifth Ave New York NY 10019; Corbett vs Dempsey 1120 N Ashland Ave Chicago Il 60622

WRIGHT, VICKI C
MUSEUM DIRECTOR, MUSEOLOGIST
b Willard, Ohio, Apr 13, 1956. *Study:* Ohio Wesleyan Univ, BFA, 77; Ariz State Univ, MA, 86. *Collection Arranged:* Proj dir, 350 Years of Art & Architecture in Md (with catalog), 84; proj co-dir, New Hampshire Folk Art (with catalog), 89; cur, Prints by Honoré Daumier, 91; co-cur & coordr, Artists & Environment: NH, 91; proj dir, Hyman Bloom: Paintings & Drawings, 92; proj dir, Realism & Invention in the Prints of Albrecht Durer (with catalog), 95; NH Traditions in Wood (with catalog), 97; Art & Architecture: The Vision of Graham Gund, 98; Against the Grain: The 2d Generation of Boston Expressionism, 2000; On Great Bay: Paintings by C Cook and A Mambro, 2001; co-cur, Art of Samuel Bak: Memory and Metaphor (catalog), 2006; proj dir, The Simple Art: Printed Images in an Age of Magnificence (catalog), 2006. *Pos:* Asst dir, 82-84 & acting dir, 84-86, Art Gallery, Univ Md, College Park; dir, Art Gallery, Univ NH, Durham, 86-2009; dir collections & exhibs, Kalamazoo Inst Arts, 2009-. *Teaching:* Adj asst prof mus studies, Univ NH, Durham, 87-. *Mem:* Am Asn Mus; NH Visual Arts Coalition (co-pres, 91-92, secy, 97-99). *Publ:* Auth, La Reunion des Plus Celebres Monuments Antiques de la France, Phoebus III, Ariz State Univ, 79; ed & contribr, Portfolios: Artists' Series from the Collection of Univ of Md, Art Gallery, Univ Md, 86; auth, The Artists Revealed, Art Gallery, Univ NH, 89. *Mailing Add:* The Art Gallery Paul Creative Arts Ctr Univ NH 30 Coll Rd Durham NH 03824-3538

WRIGHT, VIRGINIA
COLLECTOR, CURATOR
Study: Barnard Col, BA, 51. *Pos:* Asst Sidney Janis Gallery; trustee Virginia Wright Fund, Seattle Art Mus; Cur Color Field Paintings and Related Abstractions, 2005. *Awards:* Named one of Top 200 Collectors, ARTnews Magazine, 2004, 2006. *Mailing Add:* 407 Dexter Ave Seattle WA 98109

WRIGLEY, RICK
DESIGNER, CRAFTSMAN
b Arlington, Va, Dec 9, 1955. *Study:* Rochester Inst Tech, Sch Am Craftsmen, BFA, 81. *Work:* Contemp Crafts Asn, Portland, Ore. *Comn:* Boardroom table (with Kohn Pedersen, Fox Conway Asn), Home Box Office Inc, NY, 84; 22 hearing room doors, Conn Comn on Arts, Hartsford, 88; mantlepiece, Babson Coll Ctr Educ, Wellesley, Mass, 88; dining-conference tables, Time Inc, NY, 88. *Exhib:* Material Evidence, Renwick Gallery, Nat Mus Am Art, Washington, DC, Fine Arts Mus South, Mobile, Ala & Mus des Art Decoratifs, Montreal, Can, 84; Artist Designed Furniture, Norton Gallery Art, W Palm Beach, 86; World of Art Today, Milwaukee Art Mus, 88; Architectural Art, Am Craft Mus, NY, 88. *Pos:* Artist-in-residence, Art Park, Lewiston, NY, 79. *Awards:* Daphne Award for Residential Furniture Design, Hardwood Inst, 86. *Bibliog:* Pamela Scheinman (auth), Dialogue with architecture, Am Craft, 6/88; Robert Jensen (auth), Angels in the architecture, Metrop Home, 5/88; Clair Whitcomb (auth),article in: House Beautiful Today, 4/88. *Mem:* Am Craft Coun; Soc Arts & Crafts. *Mailing Add:* c/o Meredith Gallery 805 N Charles St Baltimore MD 21201

WRISTON, BARBARA
HISTORIAN, LECTURER
b Middletown, Conn, June 29, 1917. *Study:* Oberlin Coll, AB; Brown Univ, AM. *Hon Degrees:* Lawrence Univ, DLitt. *Work:* Rare Doings at Bath. *Pos:* Exec dir, formerly, mus ed, Art Inst Chicago, 61-78; trustee, secy & antiqn, Conn; mem adv comm, Hist Am Bldgs Survey, 72-78. *Teaching:* Lectr, State Univ NY, Stonybrook, formerly. *Mem:* Benjamin Franklin fel Royal Soc Arts; Soc Archit Historians (pres, 60-61); Furniture Hist Soc. *Res:* Seventeenth and eighteenth century English and American architecture and furniture. *Interests:* Architectural history and decorative arts. *Publ:* Auth, Who was the Architect of the Indiana Cotton Mill, 1848-1850?, J Soc Archit Historians, 5/65; Joiner's tools in The Art Institute of Chicago, 67 & The Howard Van Doren Shaw Memorial Collection in the Art Institute of Chicago, 69, Mus Studies; Visual Arts in Illinois, 68; Rare Doings at Bath, 78 & 79; and many articles on architectural history in decorative arts and art museums education. *Mailing Add:* 455 E 86th St New York NY 10028

WROBLEWSKI, JENNIFER
DRAFTSMAN
Study: Univ Pa, BA (magna cum laude), 1994; New York Acad Art, MFA (cum laude), 2003. *Exhib:* Human Form: Oregon Coast Coun for the Arts 9th Ann Juried Exhib, Newport Art Ctr, 2000; Movement on the Static Page, Hudson Guild Gallery, New York, 2005; SCALE: A National Drawing Invitational, Tower Fine Arts Gallery, SUNY Brockport, 2006; Timeless: The Art of DRawing, Morris Mus, NJ, 2008; Radius 11, Ridgefield Arts Guild, Conn, 2009; solo exhib, AIR Gallery, 2009. *Teaching:* Instr, Women's Studio Ctr, Long Island City; asst prof drawing, Univ Arts, Philadelphia, 2005-08; adj lectr, Sch Art & Design, Purchase Coll, 2006. *Awards:* Ed Found Grant, 2001; AIR Gallery Fel, 2008; NY Found Arts Fel, 2009. *Bibliog:* Sharon Butler (auth), Neo-Maternalism: Contemporary Artists' Approach to Motherhood, The Brooklyn Rail, 12/2009; Benjamin Genocchio (auth), Blurring Boundaries in Words and Swirls, NY Times, 12/18/2009

WU, WAYNE WEN-YAU
PAINTER
b Tachia, Taiwan, Oct 5, 1935; US citizen. *Study:* Taiwan Normal Univ, BA (fine arts), 59; Art Students' League, New York, 75. *Work:* Nat Mus Hist, Taipei, Taiwan; Nat Taiwan Arts Ctr, Taipei; Hunter Mus Am Art, Tenn; Taiwan Mus Art; Asian Studies Ctr, St John's Univ, Jamaica, NY; Taichung Seaport Art Center,; Taichung Co Cult Center. *Comn:* Chattanooga Shines, Carter St Corp, Tenn, 85; Chattanooga-Yesterday & Today, Arthur Andersen & Co, Chattanooga, Tenn, 85; Daufuskie Island No 1 & No 2, Melrose Club, Daufuskie Island, SC, 86; The Clubhouse, Chattanooga Golf & Country Club, Tenn, 90; Baylor Sch, Chattanooga, Tenn, 92. *Exhib:* solo shows, Taiwan Mus Art, 95 & Hunter Mus Art, Chattanooga, 80 & 98; East Gallery, Taipei, Taiwan, 99; East Gallery, Taipei, Taiwan, 01; Taipei Int Art Fair, 2001, & 2004; Korea Int Art Fair, 2004; East Gallery, Taipei, 2004; Taichung Seaport Art Center, 2006; Nat Galleries, Nat Mus Hist, Taipei, Taiwan, 2010; Taiwan Gallery Week, East Gallery, 2013. *Pos:* Supervisor, Fine Arts Ctr, Taichung Libr, Taiwan, 70-74. *Teaching:* Instr, oil painting, watercolor, Taiwan Normal Univ, 73-74, Hunter Mus Art, Chattanooga, 80-92 & Wayne Wu's Art Studio, Atlanta, Ga, 94-2000; instr, San Jose, Calif, 2000; instr, Salinas, Calif, 2000-2004; instr, Gilroy, Calif, 2004-. *Mem:* Am Watercolor Soc. *Media:* Oil, Watercolor. *Mailing Add:* 7440 Carnoustie Ct Gilroy CA 95020-3004

WUJCIK, THEO
PAINTER, PRINTMAKER
b Jan 29, 1936; US citizen. *Study:* Ctr Creative Studies, dipl, 62; Tamarind Lithography Workshop, TMP, 68. *Work:* Mus Mod Art, NY; Los Angeles Co Mus Art, Calif; Mus Fine Arts, Boston; Libr Cong, Washington; Nat Gallery Art, Washington. *Comn:* 40th anniversary poster, Univ SFla Contemp Art Mus, Tampa, 95; First Night St Pete, Mus Fine Arts, St Petersburg, Fla, 99; 90 X 40' bldg wrap, Outdoor Art Found, Tampa, Fla, 2003; official portraits, Moffitt Cancer Center, Tampa, 2003. *Exhib:* Drawings of the 70's, Art Inst Chicago, 77; Recent Acquisitions, Drawings, Mus Mod Art, NY, 77; Am Drawings in Black & White, 1970-80, Brooklyn Mus, NY, 80; Richard Brown Baker Collection, Mus Art, RI, 85; Mus Mod Art, NY, 91; Artists Choice, Chuck Close, Head-On/The Mod Portrait; Silverpoint Etcetera-Contemp Am Metalpoint Drawings, Huntsville Mus Art, Farnsworth Art Mus & Philadelphia Art Alliance, 93; Omni Gallery, NY, 96; Three Levels of Abstraction, Indigo Galleries, Boca Raton, 96; 30-yr retrospective, Gulf Coast Mus Art, Largo, Fla, 2000; Fla Fel exhib, Lowe Mus Art, Miami, 2002, Gulf Coast Mus Art, Largo, 2003; Global Warming, Tampa Mus Art, Fla, 2006; United Nations World Environ Day Exhib, Envisioning Change, Noble Peace Ctr, Oslo, Norway, 2007; Bozar Ctr Arts, Brussels, 2007; Transformative Influences, St Petersburg Art Ctr, 2010; and others; Visual Unity II, Polk Mus Art, Lakeland, Fla, 2010; Recent Painting, Midy solomon Gallery, St Petersburg Fla, 2010. *Pos:* Mgr, Graphicstudio, Tampa, Fla, 70-72. *Teaching:* Instr printmaking, Ctr Creative Studies, 64-70; assoc prof printmaking & drawing, Univ South Fla, Tampa, 72-2003. *Awards:* Louis Comfort Tiffany Found, 64; Grant Lithography, Ford Found, 67; Award Drawing, Nat Endowment Arts, 77; Individual Artist Fel, Div Cult Affairs, Fla Dept State, 2001-2002; Fel, Edwin Austin Abbey Mem Fund for Mural Painting in Am, Nat Acad Design, New York, 2004. *Bibliog:* Marvin Sadik & Harold Pfister (coauth), American Portrait Drawings, Smithsonian Inst Press, 80; Frank H Goodyear (auth), Contemporary American Realism Since 1960, New York Graphic Soc, 80; Hilarie Faberman (auth), Modern Master Drawings (catalog), 86; 60 Years of North American Prints, with essays by David Acton. *Media:* Acrylic; Lithography, Etching. *Publ:* Auth, Robert Rauschenberg Etching, Brooke Alexander Inc, New York, 77; Tatyna Grosman, Self-Portrait, Chiseled Engravings, Brooke Alexander Inc, New York, 79; Jasper Johns Etching, Graphicstudio, Tampa, Fla, 85; Ed Ruscha Etching, Graphicstudio, 96; Paradiso Etching, Graphicstudio, 2000. *Dealer:* Mindy Solomon Gallery 124 2nd Ave NE Petersburg FL 33701. *Mailing Add:* PO Box 5571 Tampa FL 33675-5571

WUNDERLICH, PAUL
PAINTER, PRINTMAKER
b Eberswalde, Brandenburg, Ger, Mar 10, 1927. *Study:* Hamburg Coll Art Develop, Landeskunstschule, 47-51; Hochschule fur Bildende Kunste, Hamburg, 63-68. *Exhib:* Mus Goteborg, Sweden, 70; Kunsthalle Kiel, Ger, 80; Seibu Mus, Tokyo, Japan, '80; Schleswig-Holsteinisches Landesmuseum, Ger, 87; Schleswig, Schloss Gottorf, Ger, 87. *Teaching:* Etchings & lithograph, Hamburg Col Art Develop, 51-60; lectr free graphics & painting, Col Creative Arts, 63-68. *Awards:* M S Collins Prize, Er wird alt, Philadelphia, Pa, 62; Edwin Scharff Prize, 65; Gold Medal, Florence, Italy, 70. *Bibliog:* Volker Zielke (dir), Portrait of Paul Wunderlich (film), 73; Notizen (sketches 66-74), Volker Huber, 74; Homo sum, Volker Huber, 78; and others. *Media:* Gouach, Oil; Original Lithograph. *Mailing Add:* c/o Davidson Galleries 313 Occidental Ave South Seattle WA 98104

WUNDERLICH, SUSAN CLAY
ART DEALER
b Indianapolis, Ind, Jan 30, 1942. *Study:* Colby Col. *Pos:* Dir, Mongerson Wunderlich Gallery, currently. *Mem:* Chicago Art Dealers Asn. *Specialty:* Nineteenth and 20th century American art, such as: Frederic Remington, C M Russell, Nicolai Fechin, Leon Gaspard, Taos Founders and the American impressionists; illustrators, N C Wyeth and Howard Pyle; sporting art; sculpture. *Mailing Add:* 704 N Wells St Chicago IL 60610-3310

WUNDERMAN, JAN (LILJAN) DARCOURT
PAINTER, PRINTMAKER
b Winnipeg, Man, Jan 22, 1921; US citizen. *Study:* Otis Art Inst, Los Angeles, BFA, 42; Studied with Reuben Tam, Brooklyn Mus Art Sch, 54-56. *Work:* Alfred Khouri Collection, Norfolk Mus, Va; Ball State Univ Art Gallery, Muncie, Ind; Univ SC Art Gallery, Columbia; CW Post Coll, Long Island & Brookville, NY; Nat Asn Women Artists Permanent Collection, Zimmerli Mus, Rutgers, NJ; Skidmore Print Collection; NYU Loeb Coll, New York; Norfolk Mus, Va; Harry N Abrams Coll, New York; Daimler Chrysler Collection, Ger; Northwest Airlines; Dillingham Corp, Honolulu; and others. *Comn:* Painting, New York off, Bank Am, 76; painting, New York off, The Boston Co, 77; Warner Lambert, New York; Bank One, Columbus, Ohio; Freeport Mac-Moran Corp, New Orleans, La; and others. *Exhib:* Solo exhibs, Pasadena Art Inst, Calif, 43, Dabney Hall, Calif Inst Tech, 43, Gastine Gallery, Los Angeles, Calif, 45, Golde Gallery, Great Neck, NY, 57-60, Angeleski Gallery, NY, 61-62, Roko Gallery, NY, 63, 66, 68, 71, 73, 76, East Hampton Guild Gallery, NY, 65, 66, Talisman Gallery, Bartlesville, Okla, 75, 77, Voltaire Gallery, New Milford, Conn, 69-83, Les Mouches, NY, 80 & Denise Bibro Fine Arts, New York, NY, 96-98, 2002, 2006, 2007; Pasadena Mus, Calif, 45; Los Angeles Co Mus Art, 45; Brooklyn Mus, NY, 56; Philadelphia Mus Art, 56-62; Pa Acad Fine Arts, Philadelphia, 59-65; Butler Inst Am Art, Youngstown, Ohio, 59-66; Va Mus Fine Arts, Richmond, 67; traveling show, 100 Yrs-100 Works, Nat Asn Women Artists; Plaides Gallery Invitational, NY, 88; Nat Acad Design, NY, 94 & 96; Sarah Lawrence Col, 2002. *Collection Arranged:* Zimmerli Mus, Rutgers Univ, NJ; Prints, Skidmore Coll; Loeb Collection, NY Univ; Norfolk Mus, Va; Harry N Abrams Collection, New York; Bank Am, New York; Cameron Corp, Houson, Tex; Northwest Airlines, Detroit. *Teaching:* Great Neck Art Ctr, NY, 59-63. *Awards:* Ohaski Award, Pan Pac Exhib, Tokyo & Osaka, Japan, 62; Marcia Brady Tucker Award, Nat Asn Women Artists, 65, Medal of Honor, 66, Joseph J Akstone Prize, 76, Jane C Stanley Award, 77, Canaday Mem Prize, 79, De Solo Mendes Prize, 81, Charles Hormon Mem Prize, 83, Bertha P Greenblatt Award, 86, Moore Greenblatt Award, 90, Amelia Peabody Award, 91, Grumbacher Gold Medal of Honor, 92 & Florence B Andresen Award, 94; Emily Lowe Award, NY, 65; Int Women's Year Art Festival Award, Ford Found Auditorium, 75; Bocour Award, Am Soc Contemp Artists, 80, Elizabeth Erlanger Mem Award, 89 & Kreindler Award, 92. *Mem:* Nat Asn Women Artists; Artists Equity; Am Soc Contemp Artists; Soc Am Painters and Sculptors; Soc Painters Casein and Acrylic; Contemp Artists Guild. *Media:* Oil, Acrylic; Black & White Intaglio Prints. *Interests:* Travel and music. *Publ:* Contribr, My background & intent as an abstract painter, Leonardo Publ, 8/81. *Dealer:* Denise Bibro Fine Arts 529 W 29th St NY. *Mailing Add:* 131 E 19th St New York NY 10003

WURM, JAN
PAINTER, EDUCATOR
New York, NY. *Study:* Univ Calif Los Angeles, BA, 72; Royal Coll Art, MARCA, 75. *Work:* Fine Arts Mus San Francisco; NY Public Libr; Universitat Fur Angewandte Kunst, Vienna, Austria; Tiroler Landesmuseen Moderne Galerie, Innsbruck, Austria; Univ Calif Santa Barbara Libr; Judith A Hoffberg Archive. *Exhib:* Jan Wurm & Milano Kazanjian, Los Angeles Municipal Art Gallery, 78; Figurative Art, Univ Calif, San Diego Mandeville Art Gallery, 1980; Jan Wurm & John Hannaford, Palo Alto Cultural Ctr, Palo Alto, Calif, 1985; Broken Vows, Morris Graves Mus, Eureka, Calif, 2000; Banned & Recovered, African Am Mus & Libr, Oakland, Calif, 2008-2013; The Seduction of Duchamp, Los Gatos Mus, Calif, 2009-2010. *Pos:* lectr series coordinator, Berkeley Art Ctr, Calif, 2009-2012. *Teaching:* instr, ASUC Art Studio, UC Berkeley, Calif, 1995-2004, instr, 1996-2010; instr, Painting Sommer Akademie Kunstler Dorf, 2013. *Bibliog:* Victoria Hogan (auth), Shooting Straight from the Hip: Jan Wurm's Recent Episodes from the American Dream, Foothill Coll, 1979; Susan Boettger (auth), Jan Wurm's Social Arts Situations (catalog), 1985; Robert Reese (auth), The Art of Gaming, Lisa Esherick and Jan Wurm (catalog essay), Carl Cherry Ctr, 2009; Joyce Nishioka (auth), Jan Wurm-Time Traveler (film), Curly Tail Prodns, 2008. *Mem:* VC Art Alumni Steering Comt (vice pres, 2010-2013); Coll Art Assn; Art Table. *Media:* All Media. *Publ:* auth, Drawn in Dust, Folly Mag, 2007, 2013; A Cut Glass, Steel-Heeled Dance, WS Jour, Routledge, 2008; No Naked Nudes, WS Jour, Routledge, 2009; contbr, paintings, Catamaran Literary Reader, 2013. *Dealer:* Stephen Rosenberg 115 Wooster St New York NY 10012; Neo Images 924 Olive St Santa Barbara CA 93101; EM Galerie Heideanjer 8B Drachten Netherlands 9202 PG. *Mailing Add:* 1308 Fourth St Berkeley CA 94710

WURMFELD, SANFORD
PAINTER, EDUCATOR
b New York, NY, Dec 6, 1942. *Study:* Dartmouth Col, BA, 64; Independent study Rome, Italy, 64-65; Hunter Col, 66. *Exhib:* Art of the Real, Mus Mod Art, NY, 68, Grand Palais, Paris, 68, Kunsthaus, Zurich, 68 & Tate Gallery, London, 69; Contemp Painting Review, Lehigh Univ, Pa, 76; Susan Caldwell Gallery, NY, 76 & 78; Patterns Plus, Art Mus, Dayton, 79; Carnegie Int, Mus Art, Pittsburgh, Pa, 82; Labor Intensive Abstraction, Clocktower, NY, 84; Approaches to Abstraction, Shanghai, 86; A Debate on Abstraction, Hunter Col, 89; Choices, Long Beach Mus Art, Calif, 89; The Grid, Ben Shahn Galleries, William Paterson Col, NJ, 90; Red, Karl Ernst Osthaus-Mus, Ger, 99, Cyclorama, 2000-; and others. *Pos:* Dir, Hunter Galleries, Hunter Col, City Univ NY, 78-; external examiner, Acad Minerva, Groningen, Netherlands, 98, Glasgow Sch Art, 99-. *Teaching:* From lectr to prof art, Hunter Col, 67-, chmn dept, 78-; visiting artist, Calif State Col, 70; visiting instr in color theory, Cooper Union, NY, 71-72. *Awards:* Ames Award, Dartmouth Col, 64; Guggenheim Fel, 74-75; Nat Endowment Arts Individual Artist Fel, 87-88; City Univ NY Fac Res Award, 79-81, 84, 85, 87, 91, 93 & 97. *Publ:* Auth, Color documents: A presentational theory, Hunter Coll Art Gallery, 4/85; Approaches to Abstraction, City Univ New York, 86; On Color Charts and Painting, Color Order and Aesthetics: The Oeuvre of Dr Amelius Muller, Hunter Coll Art Gallery, NY, 87; From Surface to Luminous from Color in Abstract Painting, Wake Forest Univ, 96; Color in Abstract Painting, Elsevier Press, Amsterdam, 98; and others. *Mailing Add:* 18 Warren St No 5 New York NY 10007-1066

WÜRTH, REINHOLD
COLLECTOR
b Ohringen, Ger, Apr 20, 1935. *Hon Degrees:* Univ Tubingen, Hon Doctorate, Hon Senator. *Pos:* First apprentice screw trade, Wurth Group, Kunzelsau, 1949, head bus & mgt, 1954, chmn adv bd, 1994-; head Interfacultative, Inst Entrepreneurship Univ Karlsruhe, 1999-2003; mem supervisory bd, IKB Deutsche Industriebank AG, Dusseldorf; shareholder & mem bd trustees, Robert-Bosch Found; chmn adv bd, Entrepreneurs Soc Int Cooperation Baden-Wurttemberg. *Awards:* Named one of World's Richest People, Forbes Mag, 1999-2007; Chevalier dans l'Ordre des Arts et des Lettres, French Ministry Cult, 2000; Ludwig-Erhard Medal, Ludwig-Erhard Found, 2004; named one of Top 200 Collectors, ARTnews mag, 2004-12; Distinguished Serv Cross, 1st Class, Order of Merit, Germany; Medal Economic Merits, Baden-Wurttemberg. *Collection:* Medieval, postwar, modern and contemporary art. *Mailing Add:* A Wurth GmbH & Co KG Reinhold-Wurth Str 12-17 Kunzelsau Germany

WYATT, GREG ALAN
SCULPTOR
b Nyack, NY, Oct 16, 1949. *Study:* Columbia Col, BA, 71, MA, 74; Nat Acad Sch Design, 72-74; Columbia Univ, EdD, 74-76. *Work:* Brookgreen Gardens, Murrells Inlet, SC; Nat Arts Club, Gramercy Park, NY; Princeton Univ Libr, NJ; Bergen Mus Art, NJ. *Comn:* Fantasy Fountain, Gramercy Park, NY, 83; Standing portrait James Cash Penney, Tex, 92; Life Forces, Am Cynamid, 93; Soul of the Arts, Newington-Cropsey Found, 94; Olympic Woman, Avon Products, NY, 96; Victory Eagle and Hippomenes, Hofstra Univ, 98-99; Tree of Learning, Vanderbilt Univ, 99; and others. *Exhib:* Harvard Univ, Cambridge, Mass, 91; Bronze Casting Exhib (in conj with Paul Manship Retrospective), Metrop Mus Art, NY, 91; US Cong, Washington, 92; Nat Acad Design, NY, 92; US Senate, Russell Rotunda, 93; Newington-Cropsey Found, 94; Kennedy Gallery, NY, 94; US Supreme Ct, 95; NY State Govs Mansion (Red Room), 1998-2000. *Pos:* sculpture in residence, Cathedral St John the Devine. *Teaching:* Instr, NY Univ, 73-75 & Gallitin Sch, San Marino, Italy, 91-2000; Newington-Cropsey Found Acad Art, currently; Fantasy Fountain Fund, currently. *Awards:* Helen Foster Barnett Award, Nat Acad Design Nat Ann, 79; Walter Lantz Award, Nat Sculpture Soc Young Sculptors Ann, 79; Citation, US Cong, 92; Nat Arts Club Pres Award, 85. *Bibliog:* Michael Lantz (ed), Woman, the sculptor's vision, Nat Sculpture Rev, spring 79; Pam Lambert (auth), The eagle has landed off lower Broadway, Columbia Univ Mag, winter 79; Greg Wyatt & His Work, Charles Kuralt, CBS-TV, 12/90 & 94. *Mem:* Nat Arts Club; Nat Sculpture Soc. *Media:* Bronze, Marble. *Publ:* Manhattan Guide to Public Sculpture, Municipal Art Soc; Guide to Collection, Brookgreen Gardens. *Mailing Add:* 320 W 86th St Penthouse S New York NY 10024

WYCKOFF, SYLVIA SPENCER
EDUCATOR, PAINTER
b Pittsburgh, Pa, Nov 14, 1915. *Study:* Coll Fine Arts, Syracuse Univ, BFA, 37, MFA, 44. *Work:* Radio Sta WSYR, Syracuse, NY; R E Dietz Co, Syracuse; Marquardt Switches, Cazenovia, NY; Marine Midland Bank, Syracuse, NY; in pvt collections. *Exhib:* Mem Art Gallery, Rochester, NY; Everson Mus Art, Syracuse; Cooperstown Art Asn, NY; Nat Asn Women Artists, NY; Nat League Am Pen Women, Wash, DC; Solo shows, Nationally with Eight Syracuse Water Colorists, NY, 42-45, Coleman Hall, Cazenoviz Col, 75, Chancellor's Off, Syracuse Univ, Oneida, NY, 76, Opening of New Coll Art Bldg, Cazenovia Col, 2004. *Teaching:* Prof watercolor & drawing & chmn, Freshman Core Progs Dept, Syracuse Univ, 42-81; prof, art, painter chmn, Prog in London, 71-71; retired. *Awards:* Outstanding Am Educ, 74; Spec Citation, NY State Art Teachers Asn, 81; Priscilla Hancock Award, Serv to the Arts, Cazenovia Watercolor Soc, 92. *Mem:* Cazenovia Watercolor Soc (pres & founder), 76-; Women in the Arts (charter mem); Stone Quarry Art Park, Cazenovia, NY. *Media:* Watercolor, Drawing. *Interests:* Painting, drawing, bridge and knitting. *Mailing Add:* PO Box 423 Cazenovia NY 13035

WYLAN, BARBARA
PAINTER
b Providence, RI, Oct 23, 1933. *Study:* RI Sch Design, BFA, 55. *Work:* Mobile Mus Art, Ala; Cahoon Mus Am Art, Cotuit, Mass; Cape Cod Mus Art, Dennis, Mass; Springfield Art Mus, Mo. *Exhib:* Solo exhibs, Small Abstracts, Market Barn Gallery, Mass, 80, Barbara Wylan at the Spectrum, Spectrum of Am Artists & Craftsmen, Brewster, Mass,83, 84, 86, 87, 88, 90, 92, 95, 2000, 2003, China, Cape Cod Conservatory, W Barnstable, Mass, 84, Dawn & Dusk, Cahoon Mus Am Art, Cotuit, Mass, 98, Three Visions/Swiss & Am Landscapes, Main Gallery, Boston City Hall, Mass, 83; Group exhibs, Watercolor USA, Springfield Art Mus, Mo, 82; 21 in Truro, Cape Cod Mus Nat Hist, Brewster, Mass, 87; Women Creating, Cape Mus Fine Arts, Dennis, Mass, 2002; 21 in Truro, Cape Mus Fine Arts, Dennis, Mass, 2005; Visions & Voices of the Outer Cape, Provincetown Art Assoc & Mus, 2007; 21 in Truro, Truro Hist Mus, Mass, 2002, 2003m 2004m 2006m 2008m 2009; Between Sea and Sky, 21 in Truro, Cultural Center of Cape Cod, Mass, 2010; Outermost Embrace, 21 in Truro, Cotuit Center for the Arts, Cotuit, Mass, 2011; Cape Cod Visions/21 in Truro, Downtown Art Gallery, Westfield State Univ, Mass, 2013; 21 Reflections/21 in Truro, SRD Gallery, SO Dennis, Mass, 2013; Standing Tall/Lighthouses in Cape & Islands Art, Cape Cod Mus Art, Dennis, Mass, 2013; Two person exhib, The Field Gallery, W Tisbury, Mass, 2006, 2007, 2009, 2010. *Teaching:* instr watercolor, Falmouth Artists' Guild, 78-9. *Awards:* Best Cape Cod Art, Chatham Festival Arts, 80; Springfield Award, Watercolor USA, Springfield Art Mus, Mo, 82; Dr David Soloway Mem, Nat Soc Painters Casein & Acrylic, 91. *Bibliog:* China at Cape Cod Conservatory, The Register, 84; Carol Dumas (auth), Simple Beauty, The Cape Codder, 93; The Best Sunsets on Cape Cod, Spyglass, 98. *Mem:* Nat Soc Painters in Casein and Acrylic; Watercolor USA Honor Soc (signature mem); New England Watercolor Soc (signature mem); 21 in Truro; The Copley Soc Art, Boston, MA. *Media:* Watercolor, Acrylic. *Dealer:* The Spectrum of Am Artists and Craftsmen Inc 369 Old King's Hwy Brewster MA 02631; Eastaway Inc 20 Circuit Avenue, Oak Bluffs, MA, 02557. *Mailing Add:* PO Box 548 Barnstable MA 02630

WYLAND, STEVE CREECH
ENVIRONMENTAL ARTIST, PAINTER
b Detroit, Mich, July 9, 1956. *Study:* Ctr for Creative Studies, Detroit, 76-77, study with Jay Holland (sculpture), Russel Ketter (painting) & Bill Girrard (painting). *Hon Degrees:* Am Int Univ, Atlanta, Ga, LHD, 2001. *Work:* Provincial Mus, Victoria, BC; Ellis Island Mus, NY; Whaling Mus, Taiti, Japan; USA Today, Gannette, Cocoa Beach, Fla; Royal Ont Mus, Toronto. *Comn:* Whaling Wall XXII (ceiling), comn by Mr Kawada, Yamagata, Japan, 90; Planet Ocean, City Long Beach, Calif, 92; Art in Public Place (mural), Smithsonian Inst Nat Zoo, Washington, DC, 93; Whaling Wall 50, The Underground, Atlanta, 93; 91 Life-size Whaling Wall Murals, 1981-2004. *Exhib:* Solo exhibs, Nat Zoo, Wash, DC, 83, Nice Exhib, France, 89, Exhib, Sydney, Australia, 90 & Tokyo, Japan, 91; East Coast Whaling Wall Tour, 93; West Coast Whaling Wall Tour, 94; Midwest Whaling Wall Tour, 97; Wyland Ocean Challenge of Am Tour-50 States in 50 Days, Reaching out to 120,000 pub and pvt sch and 67 million students, Fall 1998-; celebrating the United Nations "Int Year of the Oceans"; Wyland Ocean Challenge, "Clean Water for the 21st Century" Underwater Village 11-city Aquarium Tour, 2003; Wyland Ocean Challenge16-City East Coast Clean Water Tour, 2004. *Pos:* Founder, Dir, Wyland Found, a 501 c3 non-profit orgn, devoted to marine conservation & educ, currently; hon chmn, Orange Co March of Dimes, WalkAmerica, 2002; adv bd, The Cousteau Soc, Artist in Residence, Acad of Underwater Arts & Sci, 2002; developed, Wyland Ocean Challenge "Clean Water for the 21st Century and Beyond" with Scripps Inst of Oceanography and the Birch Aquarium; created, Wyland Ocean Challenge, "Clean Water for the 21st Century" 5-year Int Clean Up Tour Series. *Awards:* Congressional Tribute to Wyland-103rd Congress of the US; John M Olguin Marine Environ Award, Cabrillo Marine Aquarium, San Pedro, Calif, 2002; Hon Chief, Repub of Palau, 2003. *Bibliog:* The Art of Wyland (video), 97; Wyland's Ocean World (13 part series), Animal Planet, 98; Wyland's Ocean Planet, The Quest to Paint 100 Whaling Walls (video), 98. *Mem:* Founding mem, Wyland Found; founding artist, The Very Spec Arts. *Media:* Oil, Watercolor; Sculpture, Mural. *Publ:* Co-auth, The Art of Wyland, Wyland Studios, 92; Whale Tales, Wyland Studios, 94; Celebrating 50 Wyland Whaling Walls, Wyland Studios, 94; Undersea World of Wyland, Time Life Bks. *Mailing Add:* c/o Wyland Galleries 5 Columbia Aliso Viejo CA 92656-1460

WYNGAARD, SUSAN ELIZABETH
LIBRARIAN
b 1947. *Study:* Univ Wis, Madison, BA & MLS; Univ Per Stranieri, Siena, Italy, cert; Taos Valley Weaving Sch, with Kristina Wilson; Univ NMex. *Pos:* Assoc librn, Univ Calif, Santa Barbara, 74-79; dir archives, Int Mus Photog, George Eastman House, 80-81; head, Fine Arts Libr, Ohio State Univ, currently. *Mem:* Art Libr Soc NAm (midwest rep exec bd, 85-87); Am Libr Asn. *Interests:* History of photography; art librarianship; library management. *Publ:* Coauth, Printed catalogues of the Art Exhibition Catalogue Collection of the Arts Library, Univ Calif, Santa Barbara, Somerset House, Cambridge, Eng & Teaneck, NJ, 77; The Humanities and the Library, Am Libr Asn, Chicago, 93. *Mailing Add:* Ohio State Univ Fine Arts Libr Wexner Ctr for the Visual Arts Columbus OH 43210

WYNN, GAINES CLORE
PAINTER, CURATOR
b Lamesa, Tex, Jan 13, 1946. *Study:* Tex Tech, with Hugh Gibbons, BA, 68; Ariz State Univ, with Rip Woods & Eugene Grigsby, MFA (summa cum laude), 71, PhD (art educ). *Work:* Nat Mus Women Arts, Washington; pvt collection of Queen Elizabeth the Queen Mother, Clarence House, London; Ariz State Fine Arts Collection; Ten Years of Painting Retrospective Gaines Clore Wynn, Bradley School of the Arts, York Penn, 2001; Jerry Samet Found, 2007. *Comn:* Portrait of A L Stamper, Calvert Co Bd Educ, Prince Frederick, Md, 81; portrait of Karen, Al Bird Assoc, Annapolis, Md, 90; Hewlett Packard, 98; portrait, Dorothy Ford, 2007. *Exhib:* Four States Invitational, Phoenix Art Mus, 73; Realists of Washington, Arlington Arts Ctr, Va, 80; Mus Invitational, Nat Mus Women Arts, Washington, 88; Bright Visions: The Making of Myth, Rahr-West Mus, Manitowoc, Wis, 90, Charles Allis Art Mus, Milwaukee, Wis, 91; Ann Juried Exhib, Montpelier Arts Ctr, Laurel, Md, 95. *Collection Arranged:* Nat Hons Exhib (auth, catalog), Nat Mus Women Arts, 91; A Glimpse of Joy: Corrine Mitchell (auth, catalog), Nat Mus Women Arts, 92; Pulse Points: Transforming Tradition (auth, catalog), Harvard Univ, 96. *Pos:* Educ prog consult, Nat Mus Women Arts, 88-; Currently Adv on African Am Women Artist Collectors in US for Nat Mus Women in the Arts Chair Fine Art Dept, Charles Herbert Flowers Sch, 2000-; Nat Adv Bd-NMWA; co-admin chair, Visual & Performing Arts Dept, Flowers High Sch, 2000-. *Teaching:* Chmn, art dept, Calvert High Sch, 75-81 & 90-; adj prof Fine Arts, Bowie State Univ; instr landscape painting, Montorno Studio, Tuscany, Italy, 2009. *Awards:* Presidential Award, Nat Art Educ Asn, Houston, 95; Founder for the Nat Art Honor Soc 1975 Calvert Co, MD; 1500 Chap in Secondary Sch in US 2005. *Mem:* Women's Caucus for Art (nat bd dir, 90-94); Nat Art Educ Asn; Nat Dem Spouse Org (2001-); Nat Congressional Black Caucus Spouse Org, CBCS (chair, 2001-); Md State Arts Council 2 terms 2001-Present (Appointed by Gov Md); Celebration of Leadership Fine Arts (2006-); Nat Inst Health (bd mem, 2006-). *Media:* Oil, Pastel. *Interests:* Gardening, reading, journal writing. *Collection:* Hewlett-Packard. *Publ:* Coauth, Gumba Ya Ya: An Anthology of African Women Artists, Mid March Press, NY, 95; Violence Against Women: Breaking the Silence Greenbelt Art Center; Greenbelt, Maryland, wrote exhib catalogue as well as curated exhib, 2003; Seven Artist of St Martins VI The Influence of Romare Bearden, Parish Gallery, Georgetown, Wash DC, 2004. *Dealer:* Soho 20 469 Broome St NY 10013; Parish Gallery Georgetown Washington DC Present; The Gaines Clore Wynn Studio/Gallery 3711 Rhode Isl Ave Mt Rainier MD. *Mailing Add:* 2410 Enterprise Rd Bowie MD 20721-2529

WYNN, STEPHEN A
COLLECTOR
b New Haven, Conn, Jan 27, 1942. *Study:* Univ Pa, BA, 1963. *Pos:* Pres & chief exec officer, Best Brands, Inc, 1969-72; chmn bd dir, pres, and chief exec officer, Mirage Resorts Inc (formerly Golden Nugget Inc), 1973-2000; managing mem, Valvino Lamore, LLC, 2000-02; chmn & chief exec officer, Wynn Resorts Ltd, 2002-, owner, Wynn Las Vegas Resort, 2005-, Wynn Macau, 2006-; bd trustees, John F Kennedy Ctr Performing Arts, 2006-. *Awards:* Named one of Top 200 Collectors, ARTnews mag, 2004-13; named one of 100 Most Influential People, Time Mag, 2006; named one of Forbes' Richest Americans, 2003-, World's Richest People, 2004-. *Collection:* French Impressionism; modern and contemporary art. *Mailing Add:* Wynn Resorts Ltd 3145 Las Vegas Blvd S Las Vegas NV 89109

WYNNE, ROB
CONCEPTUAL ARTIST, PAINTER, SCULPTOR
b New York, NY, Nov 28, 1948. *Study:* Pratt Inst, Brooklyn NY, BFA, 70. *Work:* Chase Manhattan Bank, NY; Arthur Anderson & Co, Chicago; Prudential Life Insurance, Newark, NJ; Guerlain Found, Les Mesnuls, France. *Comn:* Silk screen on enamel panels, Allianz, Munich, Ger, 98. *Exhib:* The Unique Print, Mus Fine Arts, Boston, 90; Slow Art, PS 1, Mus Contemp Art, Long Island City, NY; Window Shopping, Grey Art Gallery, NY Univ, 94; A Dress, Winnipeg Art Gallery, Can, 95; Le Corps du Livre, Carre d'Art, Niemes, France, 98. *Awards:* Pollack Krashner Found Award, 92. *Bibliog:* Ed Leffingwell (auth), The paintings of Rob Wynne, Arts Mag, 88; Nancy Princenthal (auth), Review, Art Am, 96; Naumann & Rimanelli (co-auths), Afterglow, Oliver Schweden, Munich, 97. *Dealer:* Holly Solomon 172 Mercer Ct New York NY 10012

WYRICK, CHARLES LLOYD, JR
PUBLISHER, EDITOR
b Greensboro, NC, May 5, 1939. *Study:* Davidson Coll, BA; Univ NC, MFA; Univ Mo. *Exhib:* Corcoran Biennial Exhib Am Painting, 67; Assoc Artists NC Ann, 68; Univ Va Print Exhib, 68; Va Mus Fine Arts; Weatherspoon Art Gallery; Carspecken-Scott Gallery. *Collection Arranged:* Art from the Ancient World, The Human Figure in Art, A Wyeth Portrait & Light as a Creative Medium, Va Mus Fine Arts, 66-68; Contemporary Am Paintings from the Lewis Collection, Del Art Mus, 74; Louise Nevelson, Spoleto Festival USA, 83; and others. *Pos:* Artmobile coordr, Va Mus Fine Arts, Richmond, 66-68; exec dir, Asn Preservation Va Antiq, 68-70; pres, Fine Arts Consults, Richmond, 71-73; art critic, Richmond News Leader, 71-73; dir, Del Art Mus, 73-79 & Gibbes Art Gallery, 80-86; pres, Wyrick & Co, 86- & Dixie Media, Inc, 89-; ed dir, Wyrick & Co, 2005-. *Teaching:* Instr, Stephens Coll, 64-66. *Awards:* First for Column, Va Press Asn, 72. *Mem:* Am Asn Mus; Halsey Inst Contemp Art (bd mem, 2008-); Gibbes Mus Art (bd mem, 2010-). *Media:* Photography. *Res:* Contemporary American painting; 18th to 20th century American architecture; 20th century American photography. *Publ:* Auth, Art & urban aesthetics (weekly column), Richmond News Leader; A Wyeth Portrait, 67 & Contemporary Art at the Virginia Mus, 72, Arts in Va; ed, Oystering: A Way of Life, 83; Nets & Doors: Shrimping in Southern Waters, 89; The A B Frost Book, 93; ed of numerous mus catalogs and bks. *Mailing Add:* Wyrick & Co PO Box 89 Charleston SC 29402-0089

X

XIE, XIAOZE
PAINTER, EDUCATOR
b Guangdong, China, June 26, 1966. *Study:* Tsinghua Univ, Beijing, BArch, 1988; Ctrl Acad Arts & Design, Beijing, MA, 1991; Univ North Tex, Sch Visual Arts, MFA, 1996. *Work:* Mus Fine Art, Houston; Scottsdale Mus Contemp Art; Eastfield Coll, Dallas; Univ Seattle; Ariz State Univ Art Mus, Tempe, Ariz. *Comn:* Art in Archit Prog Comn for the Fed Bldg and US Courthouse, Daveport, Iowa. *Exhib:* Building for the Millennium: Recent Acquisitions, Scottsdale (Ariz) Mus Contemp Art, 1998; Solo exhibs: Devin Borden Hiram Butler Gallery, Houston, 1998 & 99; The Blinding Light: Paintings and Photographs by Xiaoze Xie, Davidson Galleries, Seattle, 1999; The Gold Paintings, 2000; Order: An Installation and Paintings by Xiaze Xie, Scottsdale Mus Contemp Art, 2000; Charles Cowles Gallery, NY, 2002-2004; History; A Microscopic View China Art Archives and Warehouse, Beijing, 2003; Mod Chinese Art Found, gent, Belg, 2007; Rosalyn Richards & Xiaoze Xie, Bucknell Univ Art Gallery, Lewisburg, Pa, 2000; Recipients of 1999 Arizona Artists Materials Fund Grants, Contemp Forum, Phoenix Art Mus, 2000; Guangdong Mus Art, Guangzhou, China, 2000; Allentown (Pa) Art Mus, 2001; Sally Packard and Xiaoze Xie, Art League Houston, 2001; Nat Forces; Earth, Air, Fire and Water, Boise Art Mus, Boise, ID, 2003-2004; The Meadows Mus, Southern Methodist Univ, Dallas, 2004; Regeneration: Contemp Chinese Art from China and the US, Samek Art Gallery, Bucknell Univ, PA, 2004-2006; One Man show, Nicholas Metivier Gallery, Toronto, Canada, 2005; The Daily News, Salt Lake Art Ctr, Salt Lake City, UT, 2005-2006; numerous others; Danish Art Exchange, Beijing, China, 2007. *Teaching:* asst prof, dept arts & design, Shantou Univ, Guangdong, China, 91-92; tchg fellow, Sch Visual Arts, Univ North Tex, Denton, 94-96, adj instr, 96; vis artist, The Evergreen State Col, Olympia, Wash, 96-97; asst prof, Bucknell Univ, Lewisburg, Pa, 99-; numerous lectr positions. *Awards:* Kimborough Fund award, Dallas Mus Art, 1996; Ariz Artists Materials Fund grant, Phoenix Art Mus, 1999; Minority Jr Faculty award, Christian R & Mary F Lindback Found, 2001; Pollock-Krasner Found Grant, 2003. *Bibliog:* Robin Updike (auth), Show wrestles with reality, books dominate Xie's haunting, ambiguous work, Seattle Times, Wash, 2/25/99; Ted Loos, Fish Wrap, Bird CageLiner, Still Life, The New York Times, 3/21/2004; Matthew Guy Nichols, Xiaoze Xie at Charles Cowles, Art in America, June/July 2004. *Media:* Oil

XING, DANWEN
PHOTOGRAPHER
b Xi'an China. *Study:* BFA, Central Acad Fine Arts, Beijing, 1992; MFA, Sch Visual Arts, New York, 2001. *Work:* Whitney Mus Am Art, New York; Santa Barbara Mus Art; Internat Ctr Photography; San Francisco Mus Mod Art; J Paul Getty Mus, Los Angeles; Metrop Mus Art, New York; George Pompidou Ctr, France; Fonds Nat d'art Contemp, France; Victoria & Albert Mus, London; Groninger Mus, Netherlands; Guangdong Mus Art. *Exhib:* Solo exhibs, Urban Fiction, TPW, Toronto, 2006, The City Fairy, Korea Art Ctr, Busan, Korea, 2008, In a Perfect World, Ooi Botos Gallery, Hong Kong, 2009, Seeing Utopia, Past and Future Wang Di & Xing Danwen, Fairbank Ctr Chinese Studies, Harvard Univ, 2010, Chinese Modernism and US Vernacular, Xing Danwen & Jim Vecchi, arCH-Architecture Ctr Houston Foudn, 2010, A Personal Diary, Haines Gallery, San Francisco, 2010, disCONNEXION, ABBT PROJ, Zurich, Switzerland, 2010; group exhibs, Transience-Chinese Experimental Art at the end of 20th entury, Smart Mus Art, Chicago, 1999; 1st Tirana Biennale, Albania, 2001; Re-interpretation, A Decade of Experimental Chiense Art, 1st Guangzhou Triennial, Guangdong Mus Art, 2002; Alors, la Chine? Ctr Pompidou, Paris, 2003; Am Effects, Whitney Mus Am Art, 2003; Between Past & Future, Internat Ctr Photography & Asian Soc, New York, 2004; Reason & Emotion, Biennale of Sydney, Mus Contemp Sydney, 2004; Reason & Emotion, Biennale of Sydney, Mus Contemp Art, Australia, 2004; Gravity, Maap, the Singapore Art Mus, Singapore, 2004; Grotesque Reality, Nat Mus Contemp Art, Seoul, Korea, 2004; re-VIEWING the City, 1st Guangzhou Photo Biennale, Guangdong Mus Art, 2005; Between Past & Future, Victoria & Albert Mus, London, 2005; On the Edge, Cantor Ctr Visual Arts, Stanford Univ, 2005; MADE in CHINA, Mus Contemp Photography, Chicago, 2006; New Urban Realities, Mus Boijmans Van Beuningen & NAi, Rotterdam, Netherlands, 2006; C on Cities, 10th Venice Archit Biennale, Venice, 2006; Stairway to Heaven, H&R Block Artpace at Kans City Art Inst, Kans, 2009; imPOSSIBLE, San Francisco Arts Com & Mission 17, San Francisco, 2009. *Awards:* grant & fel, Asian Cult Coun, New York, 1998-2001; Best Pub Proj Award, Les Recontres d'Arles Festival, France, 2003; finalist, ING Real Photo Award, Netherlands, 2008

XIUZHEN, YIN
INSTALLATION & ENVIRONMENTAL ARTIST
b Beijing, China, 1963. *Study:* Fine Arts Dept, Capital Normal Univ, Beijing, BA, 89. *Work:* Capital Normal Univ Mus, Beijing; COM-ART Mus, Korea; Asian Art Mus, Fukuoka, Japan. *Exhib:* New Time Painting Exhib, China Nat Gallery, Beijing, 88; 1st Biennial of Chinese Oil Painting, China Nat Gallery, 93; Post October 1st, Zhao Yao Gallery, 94; solo exhibs, Beijing Contemp Art Mus, 95, Capital Normal Univ Mus, 96, Ruine for Arts, Berlin, Ger, 97, Hua Yan Li, Beijing, 97, Manchester Craft Ctr, 98, 200 Gertrude Front Gallery, Melbourne, 2000, Asian Fine Arts Berlin Gallery, Ger, 2001, Chambers Fine Art, New York, 2002 & 2006, ISE Found, New York, 2003 & Town Hall, Friedrichshafen, Ger, 2004; Displacement, Capital Normal Univ Mus, 95; 2nd United Art Project with Am Artists, Tibet, 96; Another Long March: Chinese Contemp Art Show, Chasse Kazerne-Breda, The Neth, 97; Between Ego & Society: An Exhib of Contemp Female Artists in China, Artcmisia Gallery, Chicago, 97; Cities on the move (traveling exhib), Mus Contemp Art, Helsinki, Finland, Mus d'Art Contemp, Bordeaux, France & PS1 Contemp Art Ctr, New York, 97-99; Half of the Sky: Contemp Chinese Women Artists, Frauen Mus, Bonn, Ger, 98; Transience: Chinese Art at the end of the 20th century, The Smart Mus Art, Chicago, 99; Virtual and Real, Wan Fung Art Gallery, Beijing, 2000; Text & Subtext (traveling exhib), Earl lu Gallery & Lasalle Gallery, Singapore, 2000-2003; Chronicles of Women: Illness as Metaphor, Shatin Town Hall Concert Hall, Hong Kong, 2001; Crossroads, Chen Du Contemp Art Mus, China, 2001; Here and Now, BueroFriedrich Fine Arts, New York, 2002; Time After Time; Asian a Moment, Yerba Buena Ctr for Arts, San Francisco, 2002; How Latitudes Become Forms: Art in a Global Age, Walker Art Ctr, Minneapolis, 2003; Home and Away: The New Globalism, Vancouver Art Gallery, Can, 2003; Future Cities, Contemp Art Mus, Hamilton, Can, 2004; Follow Me, Mori Art Mus, Tokyo, 2005; News, Beijing Commune, Beijing 798, 2006. *Pos:* Artist-in-residence, Visiting Arts South East Asian Prog, London, 98. *Awards:* Scholarship, Kuenstlerhaus Schloss Balmoral Bad Ems, Ger, 99; Laureate, UNESCO/ASCHBERG, 2000; Art Award, China Contemp Art Asn, 2000

XU, BING
PRINTMAKER, CALLIGRAPHER
b Congqing, China, 1955. *Study:* Central Accad Fine Arts, Beijing, grad, 81, MFA, 87. *Exhib:* Solo exhibs include Nat Fine Art Mus, Beijing, 88, Tokyo Gallery, 90, & 97, DF Fong & Spratt Galleries, San Jose, Calif, 91, NDak Mus Art, Grand Forks, 92 & 95, Han Mo Art Center, Beijing, 93, Bronx Mus Arts, NY, 94, Inst Contemp Arts, London, 97, Calif Inst Arts, 98, New Mus Contemp Art, New York, 98, Nat Gallery Prague, 2000, Arthur M Sackler Gallery, Smithsonian Inst, Washington, 2001, Hong Kong Arts Centre, 2003, Shanghai Gallery Art, 2004; group exhibs include Brit Mus, London, 86; China Avant-Garde, Nat Fine Art Mus, Beijing, 89; The Book as an Objet d'art, Hong Kong Arts Center, 91, Desire for Words, 92; Venice Biennial, 93; Cocido y Crudo, Reina Sofia Nat Mus Art, Madrid, 94; Beyond the Form, Lincoln Center Gallery, New York, 98; Inside-Out, Asia Soc Mus & PS1, New York, 98; Fukuoka Asian Art Triennale, Japan, 99; Banner Project, Mus Mod Art, New York, 99; Give and Take, Serpentine Gallery & Victoria & Albert Mus, London, 2001; Contemp Art Cmns, Asia Soc & Mus, New York, 2001; Guangzhou Triennial, China, 2002; Shanghai Biennial, 2002; Beijing Int Art Bienale, 2003; Chinese Printmaking Today, Brit Libr, London, 2003; Crossroads, Shanghai Art Gallery, 2004; Brush & Ink, Met Mus Art, New York, 2006. *Pos:* Dir, Chinese Artists Assn, formerly. *Teaching:* Instr, Central Accad Arts, Beijing, 88; lectr, La State Univ Sch Design, formerly, Princeton Univ, formerly, McGill Univ, formerly. *Awards:* Pollock-Krasner Found Grant, 98; MacArthur Genius Grant, 99; Fukuoka Asian Cult Prize, 2003; Coca-Cola Fel, 2004. *Mailing Add:* Xu Bing Studio Inc 540 Metropolitan Ave Brooklyn NY 11211

XU, JAY JIE
MUSEUM DIRECTOR
Study: Shanghai Univ; Princeton Univ, MA, 1993. *Collection Arranged:* Treasures from a Lost Civilization: Ancient Chinese Art from Sichuan (auth, catalog), touring, 2001; Japanese Art from the Alsdorf Collection, Art Inst Chicago, 2004, & Perpetual Glory: Medieval Islamic Ceramics from the Harvey B Plotnick Collection, 2007. *Pos:* Asst cur, Shanghai Mus, 1988-90; fellow Asian art dept, Metrop Mus Art, New York, 1994-96; dir Asian art dept, cur Chinese art, Seattle Art Mus, 1996-2003; Pritzker cur Asian art, Art Inst Chicago, 2003-06, Pritzker chmn Asian and Ancient art dept, 2006-08; mem selection comt, Mellon Prog Chinese Mus Professionals, 2003-, mng dir, 2007-; dir, Asian Art Mus San Francisco, 2008-. *Awards:* Outstanding Merit Award, Shanghai Mus, 1989; Hon Marc Haas '29 Mem Fel, 1993; Jane & Morgan Whitney Fel, 1994; Ittleson Fel, 1996; Smithsonian Inst Fel, 1996; Patterson Sims Fel, 2001. *Mailing Add:* Asian Art Mus 200 Larkin St San Francisco CA 94102

XU, JINYI See Chee, Cheng-Khee (Jinyi Xu)

Y

YAGER, DAVID
PHOTOGRAPHER, PRINTMAKER
b Bronx, NY, Mar 16, 1949. *Study:* Univ Conn, BA, 71; Fla State Univ, MFA, 74, DeMontfort Univ, United Kingdom, HDD, 96. *Hon Degrees:* DeMontfort Univ, Dr Design. *Work:* Mus Mod Art, NY; Art Inst Chicago & Columbia Col, Chicago; Univ S Fla, Tampa; Boston Mus Fine Arts. *Comn:* Photographic mural, Bell Tel Co, Atlanta. *Exhib:* Light, Loch Haven Mus, Orlando, Fla; New Photographers, Ellenburg, Wash, 79-81; Magic Silver Show, Washington, DC, 80; Sch Art Inst Chicago, 81; Daytona Beach Gallery, Fla, 81; Tampa Mus, Fla, 82; Silver Int, Univ S Fla, Tampa, 82; Univ S Fla, Tampa, 83 & 85. *Teaching:* Prof art & chmn dept, Univ Md, Baltimore, 86-, distinguished prof art. *Awards:* Grant, State of Fla, 82, Warhol Found & Streurr Found. *Mem:* Soc Photog Educ; Coll Art Asn. *Res:* digital imagery. *Publ:* Contribr, Bomb Mag, Winter, 98. *Mailing Add:* Visual Art Dept Univ Md Baltimore Co Catonsville MD 21228

YAGI, SANDRA S
PAINTER
b Long Beach, Calif, Mar 5, 1955. *Study:* Univ Colo at Denver, BS (Business Admin), 80, MBA (Finance), 85; Otis Parsons, Los Angeles. *Exhib:* Solo exhibs, Univ Tenn, Knoxville, Tenn, 99, Opposing Forces, Pima Comm Coll, Tucson, Ariz, 2004; Group exhibs, Bay Area Art III, Juried Exhib, Napa Valley Coll, Calif, 2000; Collector-Curator, Catherine Clark Gallery, San Francsico, Calif, 99; Statewide Exhib, Santa Cruz Art League, Santa Cruz, Calif, 2000; Dia de los Muertos, Oakland Mus of Calif, 2006; Columbia Coll, Chicago, Ill, 2009. *Bibliog:* Displaced Passion: The Melodrama of Love, Loss & Transformation at Circle Elephant Art, by Shana Nys Dambrot, Artweek, 2001; Illusion by Intent - The appeal of Sandra Yagi's painting is their resistance to easy interpretation, by Josef Woodard, Los Angeles Times, 3/12/98.; Kittredge Cherry (auth), Art That Dares, Gay Jesus, Woman Christ and More, Apocryphile Press, 2007; Paul Ruscha, Full Moon, the Collection of Paul Ruscha, Steidl, 2006; CD cover, Gun 'N Roses, Chinese Democracy Special Ed Getty Records, 2009. *Mem:* Watercolor West (signature mem). *Media:* Oil painting. *Dealer:* Bert Green Fine Art 102 W 5th St Los Angeles CA 90013; Brad Cooper Gallery 1712 E 7th Ave Tampa FL 33605

YAHOOZER, PAUL
GRAPHIC ARTIST, WEAVER
b Philadelphia, Pa, Dec 15, 70. *Study:* Philadelphia Coll Art, BFA, 91; Univ Ariz; Yale Univ, MFA, 95. *Hon Degrees:* Hon DFA. *Work:* Gardiner Art Gallery; Okla State Univ; Agawam Pub Libr, Mass; Neilson Libr; Dept Art, Ga Coll; Kent State Univ. *Exhib:* Yale Univ; Edward Thorp Gallery; Philadelphia Art Alliance, Pa; Whitney Art Mus; Leo Castelli Gallery; Colby Coll Mus Art; Nat Mus of Graphical Art; Visual Arts Feel Mus; Cleveland Mus Art; Funk Heritage Ctr; Meadow Garden. *Pos:* artist, Melina Arts Ctr, 96-2000; graphics artist, Lucky You, 2000-2008; graphics artist, Meriks Graphic Arts, 2009-. *Teaching:* adj prof, Leona High Sch. *Bibliog:* Penelope San Giovani (auth), Paul Yahoozer Masters the Weave, 2013. *Mem:* Mericks Weaving Soc; GoodWeave. *Res:* World War II. *Collection:* Beatrice Potter. *Publ:* Auth, The Inner Working of a Weaver, 2001; auth, Men and Basket Weaving, 2004; auth, Conveying Your Work in the Weave, 2009; auth, Weave Your Way to the Top, 2014; coauth, Grafika, 2016

YAMAGUCHI, YURIKO
SCULPTOR
b Osaka, Japan, 1948. *Study:* Univ Calif Berkeley, BA, 75; Univ Md, MFA, 79. *Comn:* Wall mural, JBG Assocs, Wis Ave, Bethesda, Md, 88; wall mural, City of Atlanta, Dept Aviation, Hartsfield Int Airport, 99; wall mural, New Wash Conv Ctr, 2003. *Exhib:* Solo shows incl Japanese Cult Ctr, San Francisco, 75, Foundry Gallery, 81, Gallery 10, Wash, DC, 82, Wash Proj for Arts, 82, Southeastern Ctr Contemp Art, Winston-Salem, NC, 86, Middendorf Gallery, Wash, DC, 87, 89, 90, Penine Hart Gallery, NY, 89, Koplin Gallery, Santa Monica, 91, 94, 96, 99, 2002, 2007, Inax Gallery, Tokyo, 92, Middle Tenn Univ, 93, Baumgartner Gallery, Wash, DC, 95, Emon Gallery, Nagoya, Japan, 97, 2000, Numark Gallery, Wash, DC, 99, Del Ctr Contemp Art, 2001, Sheehan Gallery, Whitman Coll, Walla Walla, Wash, 2002, Howard Scott Gallery, New York, 2004, 2005, Univ Md Gallery, 2007; group shows incl San Francisco Juried Art Fair, 72, 73, 74; Gallery & Atelier Momyo, Tokyo, 82; Middendorf Gallery, Wash, DC, 82, 88, 89; Gallery K, 83, 84; Md Art Inst, Baltimore, 84; Hokin/Kaufman Gallery, Chicago, 85, 89; Arlington Art Ctr, 87; Gallery K, Wash, DC, 88; Phillippe Staib Gallery, NY, 91; Corcoran Gallery Art, Wash, DC, 93, 99,

2002, 2003; Art Mus of Am Org Am States, Wash, DC, 93; Va Mus Fine Arts, Richmond, 93; Rosenberg Gallery, Baltimore, 94; Milwaukee Inst Art & Design, 96; Longwood Ctr Visual Arts, Wa, 97; Univ Art Gallery, Sonoma State Univ, 2000; Art Gallery Univ Md, 2001; Worth Ryder Gallery, Berkeley, Calif, 2002; Southern Ore Univ, Ashland, 2004; Towson Univ Art Ctr, Md, 2005; Am Acad Arts and Letters, 2006. *Teaching:* Univ Md, 82, 83; prof, sculpture, Md Inst Coll Art, Baltimore, 91, 95, fine art, Corcoran Coll Art & Design, Wash, DC, 88-97; vis asst prof, sculpture & ceramics, George Wash Univ. *Awards:* Fel, Va Ctr Creative Arts, 82, Salzburg Kunstlerhaus Artist-Residency Grant, 93; Prof Fel, Va Mus, 85, 88, 2001; Grant, Va Comn of Arts, 94, 2000; Benesse Award, Japan, 2005; Joan Mitchell Found Award, 2005; Am Acad Arts & Letters, 2006. *Media:* Resin, Miscellaneous Media. *Dealer:* Koplin del Rio Gallery 464 N Robertson Blvd W Hollywood CA 90048. *Mailing Add:* Dept Fine Arts & Art Hist George Wash Univ 801 22nd St NW Washington DC 20052

YAMAMOTO, NAMI
INSTALLATION SCULPTOR

b 1968. *Study:* Aichi Prefectural Univ Fine Arts, Japan, BFA, 1994; Mt Royal Grad Sch Art, Md Inst, Baltimore, MFA, 2001 . *Exhib:* Solo exhibs, Vt Studio Ctr, 1998, Vox Populi Gallery, Pa, 2003-05, Spaces, Cleveland, 2005, Philadelphia Int Airport, 2005, Painted Bride Art Ctr, Pa, 2006, Del Ctr for Contemp Arts, Wilmington, 2006, Samuel S Fleisher Art Meml, Pa, 2007; Tracks, Mayer Gallery, Akron, Ohio, 1998; Nine Lives, Lake Erie Coll, Painesville, Ohio, 1999; This is Nanotechnology, Whole Gallery, Baltimore, 2001; DeLux, Penrose Gallery, Tyler Sch Art, Pa, 2002; Joan Mitchell Found Exhib, CUE Art Found, New York, 2003; O, Shore Inst Contemp Arts, Long Branch, NJ, 2005; MicroBIOPHILIA, Hicks Art Ctr, Bucks County Cmty Coll, Pa, 2007; Paper[space], Philadelphia Art Alliance, 2008; Amicale, Mus Contemp Arts, Siegen, Ger, 2009. *Pos:* Designer, Richard Felber Designs, Inc, Cleveland, 2001-03; studio asst & printer, Fabric Workshop & Mus, Philadelphia, 2004-05, proj tech & printer, 2005-07, proj coordr & master printer, //, 2007-09. *Teaching:* Adj fac, Philadelphia Univ, Pa, 2007-09 . *Awards:* Pola Art Found Award, Tokyo, Japan, 1999; Joan Mitchell Found Grant, 2001; Individual Creative Artist Fel, Pa Coun Arts, 2005 & 2008; Independence Found Fel in Arts, Pa, 2005; Pew Ctr for Arts Fel, 2009. *Bibliog:* Robin Rice (auth), Hot and New, Philadelphia Citypaper, 8/2002; Rboerta Fallon (auth), Thinking Outside the Vox, Philadelphia Weekly, 10/2004; Benjamin Genocchio (auth), Exploring the Circle from Every Angle, NY Times, 1/1/2006; Edith Newhall (auth), Pleasant Uncertainty, Philadlephia Inquirer, 1/5/2007

YAMASHIRO, TAD
PHOTOGRAPHER

b Calif, Nov 24, 1930. *Study:* Cooper Union, 54-58. *Work:* George Eastman House Int Mus Photog, Rochester, NY; Mus Mod Art, NY. *Exhib:* Tad Yamashiro, George Eastman House, Rochester, NY, 83; Big Picture Show, Mus Mod Art, NY, 83; Photog Moma, Univ Hawaii Mus Art, Honolulu, 83; 20th Century Photog from Moma, Seibu Mus Art, Tokyo, 84; Treasure from the Collection, George Eastman House, Rochester, NY, 85. *Teaching:* Instr, seminar & thesis, Sch Visual Arts, 63-84. *Mailing Add:* 24 Strong Pl Apt 4 Brooklyn NY 11231-3757

YAMIN, MARTINA (SCHAAP)
CONSERVATOR

b Amsterdam, Neth. *Study:* Wellesley Col, Mass, BA (art hist), 58; Fogg Art Mus, Harvard Univ Conserv Dept, Lab Asst & Study, 58-61. *Comn:* Mus, pvt collections & galleries. *Exhib:* Davis Art Mus, Wellesley Coll, Mass, 2007. *Pos:* Conservator, pvt practice, Paper Studio, New York, 61-; vis, paper conservator, Philadelphia Mus, 64-79; Whitney Mus, Guggenheim Mus, Albers Found, Woodner Collection, David Smith Estate. *Awards:* Hon, Int Print Ctr, New York. *Bibliog:* D Brewer (auth), The Delicate Art Restoring Paper, New York Times, 5/4/89; T Trucco (auth), Saving Old Documents, New York Times, 9/5/91; Drawing Collection, Catalogue Davis Art Mus; Friend of Contemp Drawings, Mus Mod Art. *Mem:* Fel Int Inst Conserv; fel Am Inst Conserv; Nat Arts Club (curatorial comt mem); Wellesley Coll Friends of Art, NY (comt mem); Art Table, NY; Mus Modern Art; Morgan Lib. *Media:* Works on Paper. *Publ:* Auth, Report on the Inst of Paper Conserv Conf, Drawing, 92

YAMIN, STEVEN EDWARD
PRINTMAKER

b New York, NY, Apr 5, 1946. *Study:* Olivet Col, BA, 68; Pratt Inst, MFA, 71. *Work:* Victoria & Albert Mus, London, Eng; Libr Congress, DC; Mary Armstrong Print Collection, Olivet Col, Mich; NJ State Mus, Trenton; NY Pub Libr. *Exhib:* New Printmakers, Victoria & Albert Mus, London, Eng, 74, 19th Nat Print Exhib, Brooklyn Mus, 75; 5th British Int, Bradford Mus, Eng, 75; 55th Soc Am Graphic Artists Nat, AAA Gallery, NY, 77; 12th Nat Print Exhib, Silvermine Guild, New Canaan, Conn, 78; 7th Int Miniature Print, Pratt Graphics Ctr, NY, 79; Sense of Scale III, Univ Albuquerque Mus, 79; Davidson Galleries, Seattle, Wash, 2004; 5th Biennial Int Miniature Print Exhib, Norwalk, Conn, 2005; Contemp Printmakers, The Old Printshop, NY, 2005. *Collection Arranged:* Prints from Fitch-Febvrel Gallery, NY; Cantor-Lemberg, Birmingham, Mich. *Pos:* Guest instr, Pratt Graphics Ctr, NY, Feb-Mar 75 tech asst, Am Atelier, NY, 76-. *Teaching:* Lectr printmaking, Brooklyn Col, 74-76; Pratt Manhattan Ctr, 81. *Awards:* Purchase Awards, 16th Ann Nat Print Exhib, Okla Art Ctr, Oklahoma City, 74 & Potsdam '78, State Univ NY Potsdam, 78; Graphic Chemical & Ink Co Award, 7th Miniature Print Exhib, 79; Purchase Award, 5th Biennial Int Miniature Print Exhib, 2005. *Bibliog:* W A S Hatch (auth), The European Graphic Biennale; Matthew Kangas (auth), Seattle Times, 4/2/2004; Journal of the Print World, Vol 28, No 4, fall 2005. *Mem:* Print Club, Philadelphia; Exec Coun Soc Am Graphic Artists; Visual Artists & Galleries Asn. *Media:* All. *Dealer:* The Old Print Shop 150 Lexington Ave New York NY 10016. *Mailing Add:* 3903 Ave I Brooklyn NY 11210

YAMPOLSKY, PHYLLIS
CONCEPTUAL ARTIST, PAINTER

b Philadelphia, Pa, Aug 23, 1932. *Study:* Philadelphia Coll Art, 50-52; Inst Allende, 54-55; Hans Hoffman Sch, New York, 56-58; Ecole de Beaux Arts, Fontainbleau, France, 56. *Work:* Dallas Mus Fine Arts; Mus Erotic Art, Stockholm, Swed; Nat Archives, Washington, DC; Pvt collections of Marcel Duchamp, Robert Graham, Sr, JP Lannin & Herbert Mayer. *Comn:* Mural, Concord Hotel, Kiamesha Lake, NY, 56; mural, Monticello Raceway, NY, 65; collective mural, Pathfinder Press, NY, 89. *Exhib:* Philadelphia Mus Art, 57; Dallas Mus Fine Arts, 76; McNay Inst, San Antonio, Tex, 77-78; one-man show, OK Harris & Susan Caldwell Galleries, NY, 78; Teilhard & Metamorphosis, Arcosanti, Ariz, 81; Women in our Midst, Peter David Galleries, Minneapolis, Minn, 85; Town Hall Wall, America's Reunion on the Mall, Clinton Inaugural Comt, Wash, 93; The March Against Cancer, Washington, DC, 97-98; The Hague Appeal Peace Conference, The Hague, The Neth, 99; Main St Millennium, Washington, DC Millennium Celebration, 99-2000; Williamsburg Art & Hist Ctr, 2000-2004; 1st Anniversary of 9/11, Union Sq, NY & Am Constitution Ctr, Philadelphia, 2002. *Pos:* New York City's 1st artist-in-residence, New York City Parks, Recreation & Cult Affairs, 66-67; consult, NY State Coun Arts, 67-70; founder & pres, Independent Friends of McCarren Park & The McCarren Park Conservancy, 82-. *Teaching:* Dir, founder & instr drawing & painting, Workshop Yampolsky, NY, 56-66; instr, 92nd St YMHA, NY, 58-60; founder & dir Hall of Issues, Judson Church, NY, 60-61; dir, Portrait of Ten Towns, NY State Coun Arts, 67-70; instr, Impact, Marylerose Acad, Albany, NY, 69; instr, The New Millennium, Bennett Col, Millbrook, NY, 76; founder & officer, Northeast Windham Coun Arts, Vt, 78-79; instr, Vermont Acad, Saxton's River, 79-81; co-founder & instr, New Vt Sch Arts, Putney, 81-82. *Awards:* Walter Damrosch Award, Ecole de Beaux Arts, Fontainbleau, France, 56; Ann Valentine Awards, Cue Mag, 67; Betsy Barlow Rogers Environmental Award, 95. *Bibliog:* Grace Glueck (auth), The reports were greatly exaggerated, NY Times, 7/9/67; Feast of Connections for the First 50 Strangers, Woodstock, NY, 67; Philip Hyde (auth), Festival Program, NY State Coun Arts Ann Report, 69; Matthew Naythons (auth), An American Reunion, The 52nd Presidential Inauguration, Warner Books, 93; New York, WW Norton, 98; The New Amazon, The New Mus, New York, 2000; Hilary Ballon & Kenneth T Jackson (eds), Robert Moses and the Modern City: The Transformation of New York, WW Norton, NY, 2007. *Mem:* The Brooklyn Accent; Greenpoint Coun Arts; Windham Co Coun Arts, Vt (founder); Commun Coord Comt United Nations (adv bd). *Media:* Visual Arts, Public Event and Program Design. *Res:* The rescue of McCarren Pool from threatened demolition to a $50 million dollar restoration project, Brooklyn, NY, 88-. *Specialty:* Painting, sculpture, mixed media. *Interests:* The Participatory Agenda; Yoga. *Publ:* Auth, Multiples, Art News 40th Ann, 67; contribr, Erotic Art, 1st ed, Bell/Grove Press, 68; auth & illusr, The American diner, Country J, 81; auth, The 10,000 things: Aesthetics as a system of morality, Breakthrough Mag, Global Educ Asn, 90; coauth & illusr, Sculpting With the Environment, Van Nostrand-Reinhold, 95; illusr, Poems From 42nd Street, Educare Press, Seattle, 2002. *Dealer:* Stephen Gang Gallery 529 W 20 New York NY 10111

YAMRUS, FRANK
PHOTOGRAPHER

b Kingston, Pa, Nov 23, 1958. *Study:* Wilkes Univ, Pa, BA, 80; Drexel Univ, Pa, MBA, 86. *Work:* Mus Fine Arts, Houston; Victoria & Albert Mus, London. *Exhib:* Orange Co Ctr Contemp Arts, Santa Cruz, Calif, 93; Falkirk Cult Ctr, San Rafael, Calif, 93; Alexandria Mus Art, La, 95; Provincetown Art Mus, Ma, 95-97; Soc Contemp Photog, Kansas City, Mo, 95-97; Mus Fine Arts, Houston, Tex, 97; Discoveries of the Fotoplace, Fotofest 98, Houston, 98; San Francisco Cameraworks, Calif, 98. *Awards:* Bronze, Calif Discovery Awards, 94 & 95; Purchase Award, Soc Contemp Photog, 95 & Merit Award, 97. *Bibliog:* Portfolio, Paris Rev, 97; J A Hager (auth), Ferral portraiture, Provincetown Mag, 8/96. *Publ:* Contribr, Full Exposed: The Male Nude in Photography, Routledge, 95; Whitman's Men, Universe/Rizzoli, 96; One Thousand Male Nudes, Taschen Publ, 97; articles in Paris Rev, 97 & Not Only Blue Mag, 98. *Dealer:* Sara Morthland 225 Tenth Ave New York NY 10011

YANAI, TADASHI
COLLECTOR

b Feb 7, 1949. *Study:* Waseda Univ, BA. *Pos:* Founder & pres, Fast Retailing co, Ltd, (Uniqlo co Ltd), Yamaguchi, Japan, 1984-2002, chmn, pres, and chief exec officer, 2002-, chmn. Link Theory Japan Co., Ltd, 2004-, Cabin Co. Ltd, 2007-, Gov Retaling Co, Ltd, 2008-, dir Nippon Venture Capital Co., Ltd, 2009-. *Awards:* Named one of World's Richest People, Forbes mag, 2000-; named one of Top 200 Collectors, ARTnews mag, 2010-13. *Collection:* Modern and contemporary art. *Mailing Add:* Fast Retailing Co Ltd 717-1 Sayama Yamaguchi City Japan 754-0894

YANG, ANDERSON
PAINTER, INSTRUCTOR

b Hua-Lian, Taiwan, Feb 20, 1956. *Study:* Nat Taiwan Normal Univ, Fine Art Dept, MA, 1985. *Work:* Nat Mus Hist, Taipei, Taiwan; Leigh Yawkey Woodson Art Mus, WI; Taipei Munic Fine Arts Mus, Taipei, Taiwan; Nat Fine Arts Mus, Taichung, Taiwan. *Comn:* Postage stamps (5 sets), Postal Bur, Taiwan, 1991-1995. *Exhib:* The Beauty of Yangtze River, Taipei Munic Fine Arts Mus, Taipei, Taiwan, 1992; Bird Paintings of Anderson Yang, Nat Fine Arts Mus, Taichung, Taiwan, 1993; Birds in Art (group), Leigh Yawkey Woodson Art Mus, WI, 1998-2000; Ecoart Exhibition Taipei (group), Nat Mus Hist, Taipei, Taiwan, 1999-2000; Cranes of the World (solo), Nat Mus Hist, Taipei, Taiwan, 2005. *Collection Arranged:* The Beauty of Mt Jude-An Epitome of Taiwan, 2004; Masterpiece of Watercolor, Nat Mus Hist, 2006. *Pos:* Art Consultant, Chine Time, Taiwan, 2006-2007; exec dir, Chinese-Asia Watercolor Artist Asn, 1/2006-; exec supervisor, Taipei Ecoart Asn, Taiwan, 12/2006-. *Teaching:* Instr, watercolor, drawing, Fu-Zen Catholic Univ, Taipei, Taiwan, 8/1985-7/1990; guest prof, Eco-Art, Nat Taiwan Normal Univ, Taiwan, 2/2006-6/2007; guest prof, watercolor, Qin-Dau Univ, Art Acad, China, 5/2006-7/2006. *Awards:* Award of Excellence, Ann Exhib of the Society of Animal Artist, 1998-2000; Leonard

Meiselman Memorial Award, Ann Exhib of the Soc of animal Artist, 1999. *Mem:* Taipei Eco-Art Asn, 1995-2007; Soc Animal Artist, 1998-2005; Chinese-Asia Watercolor Artist Soc, 2006-2007. *Media:* Watercolor. *Publ:* Auth, Illusr, Fossil Birds of China, Yun-Nan Sciences Technol (Chinese), 2003; auth, The British Watercolor Masters, Victoria Albert Mus (Chinese), 2004; auth, Swans of the World, a travel sketch of the artist (Chinese), 2005; auth, Follow the Footsteps of Darwin-The Galapagos Islands, Sun-Moon (Chinese version), 2006

YANG, HAEGUE
INSTALLATION SCULPTOR
b Seoul, South Korea, 1971. *Study:* Seoul Nat Univ, S Korea, BFA, 1995; Cooper Union New York, Exchange prog grant, 1997 ; Städelschule, Frankfurt, Germany, Meisterschüler, 1999. *Work:* Carnegie Mus Art, Pittsburgh; Sammlung Haubrock, Berlin; Galerie für Zeitgenössische Kunst, Leipzig, Germany. *Exhib:* Solo exhibs, Galerie Barbara Wien, Berlin, 2000, 2004, 2007, unfolding, Dépendance, Brussels, 2004, Kasse, Shop, Kino & Weiteres, Hessisches Landesmuseum Darmstadt, Germany, 2004, Cremer-Preis, Westfälisches Landesmuseum Kunst & Kulturgeschichte Münster, Germany, 2005, Unevenly, Basis voor Actuele Kunst, Utrecht, Netherlands, 2006, Les Indepliables, galerie ColletPark, Paris, 2006, Lethal Love, CUBITT, Artists, London, 2008, Haegue Yang-Integrity of the Insider, Walker Art Ctr, Minn, 2009, Condensation, Korean Pavilion; Tirana Biennale, 2001; The Fall, Galleri Christina Wilson, Copenhagen, Denmark, 2002; Hermes Korea Awards, Artsonje Ctr, Seoul, S Korea, 2003; Black Friday - Exercises in Hermetics, Galerie Kamm, Berlin, 2004; E-Flux Video Rental, Arthouse Jones Ctr, Austin, 2006; Prague Biennale 3, 2007; Brave New Worlds, Walker Art Ctr, Minneapolis, 2007; Wessen Geschichte, Kunstverein Hamburg, Germany, 2008; Interfacing Practices, Magnusmuller, Berlin, 2008; Der grosse Wurf, Kaiser Wilhelm Mus, Krefeld, Germany, 2008; 53rd Int Art Exhib, Venice Biennale, Italy, 2009. *Awards:* Maria-Sibylla-Merian-Prize, Hessisches Ministerium fur Kunst und Wissenschaft, 2001; Baloise Art Prize, Art Statements, Art 38 Basel, Switzerland, 2007. *Dealer:* Dépendance Rue du marché aux porcs 4 Brussels Belgium 1000; Galerie ColletPark 203bis rue saint martin Paris France 75003. *Mailing Add:* Manteuffelstr 112 Berlin D-10997 Germany

YANG, MIMI
PAINTER
b Taipei, Taiwan, Oct 2, 1952. *Study:* Taiwan Nat Art Coll, BA, 75; Studied with Jack Liang, Taiwan & Edison, NJ, 2008. *Awards:* 3rd Place, NRAA 92nd Ann Exhib, 2007; Honorable Mention, NRAA 94th Ann Exhib, 2009; Gold Brush Award, Audubon Artists 68th Ann, 2010; 3rd Place, NRAA 96th Ann Exhib, 2011; Marquis Who's Who in American Art Reference Award in Pastels, Audubon Artists, New York, 2011. *Media:* Pastel, Oil. *Mailing Add:* 39 Rieder Rd Edison NJ 08817

YANISH, ELIZABETH SHWAYDER
SCULPTOR, LECTURER
b St Louis, Mo, 1922. *Study:* Wash Univ; Denver Univ; also with Frank Varra, Wilbur Verhelst, Edgar Britton, Marian Buchan & Angelo DiBenedetto. *Work:* Tyler Mus, Tex; Colo State Bank, Denver, Martin-Marietta Co, Denver; Colo Women's Col; Ball State Col; and numerous pvt collections. *Comn:* Carved doors, eternal light, Menorah, BMH Synagogue, Denver, 72-74; complete interior, Har Ha Shem Congregation, Boulder, 74; Relief Tree (bronze), Beth Israel Hosp, Denver, 74; mem relief, Denver Gen Hosp, 75. *Exhib:* Denver Art Mus Exhib, 61-75 & Western Ann, 65; Midwest Biennial, Joslyn Mus, Omaha, Nebr, 68; Int Exhib, Lucca, Italy, 71; solo exhibs, Woodstock Gallery, London, 73, Randi's Art Gallery, Denver, Colo Women's Coll Honor Exhib, Denver, Northeaster Jr Col, Sterling, Colo, The Denver, Denver, Brass Cheque Gallery, Denver, Beaux Arts Gallery, Denver, International House, Denver, Contemporaries, Sante Fe, NMex, 7th Red Door, Pueblo, Colo, Rubenstein, Serkez Gallery, Denver, Southern Colo State College, Pueblo, Colo, Neusteters, Denver, Littledale, Littleton, Colo; Artrain, Mich Fine Arts Coun, 74; Univ No Colo, Greeley; Fine Arts Ctr, Canon City, Colo; City Mus; Sangro de Cristo Gallery, Pueblo, Colo; Kirkand Mus, 2009; and numerous others. *Pos:* Trustee, Denver Ctr Performing Arts, 73-75; chmn, Visual Arts Festival, Bicentennial, 76; bd educ, Arts in Elem Educ, 77-78; bd mem, Mizel Mus, Denver, 88; mem, Denver Cult Action Steering Comt, 88; pres, Beth Israel Hosp Auxiliary. *Teaching:* Lectr contemp sculpture, var cols & univs; resource artist, Denver Public Sch. *Awards:* 1st Place Award Airspace Exhib; 1st Place Award Air Force Acad; Minori Yasui Award for Community Service, 90; 500 Notable Women, 98; Service to Mankind, Mile Hi Sertoma Club, 94; Woman of Yr, Eng, 2010. *Bibliog:* Article in Artforum, 63; Jim Mills (auth), var feature stories, Denver Post Art Ed, 64-75; John Manson (auth), Artists of the Rockies, 74; Artists of Colorado. *Mem:* Artists Equity Asn (nat vpres, 63); Rocky Mountain Liturgical Arts; Allied Sculptors Colo; Denver Coun Arts & Humanities (pres, 73-75); Colo Artists Equity Asn (pres, 79-80); Eden Theatrical Workshop; Rose Hosp Auxiliary; Nat Coun Jewish Women (bd mem); Asian Arts Asn (bd mem); Am Medical Ctr; Am Women Sculptors; Colo Painter and Sculptors. *Media:* Welded Steel, Bronze. *Dealer:* Elizabeth Schlosser Fine Art 311 Detroit St Denver CO 80206. *Mailing Add:* 2400 Cherry Creek S Dr Unit 503 Denver CO 80209-3259

YANOFF, ARTHUR (SAMUEL)
PAINTER
b Boston, Mass, May 9, 1939. *Study:* Mus Sch Fine Arts, Boston, 58-61; studied with Jason Berger, 62-65. *Work:* Mus Fine Arts, Santa Fe, NMex; Congregation Ahavath Chesed, Jacksonville, Fla; Rose Art Mus, Brandeis Univ, Waltham, Mass; Mus Fine Arts, Boston, Mass; Detroit Inst Arts, Detroit, Mich; Yeshiva Univ Mus, NY; Currier Mus Art, Manchester, NH; Addison Gallery Am Art, Andover, Mass; Chabad House, Lubavitch of NH, Manchester, NH; Le Centre D'Art, Baie-St-Paul, Quebec, Can; Berkshire Mus, Pittsfield, Mass; Beth Menachem Chabad Synagogue, Newton, Mass; Sam and Adele Golden Found for the Arts, New Berlin, NY. *Comn:* Portrait (Gil Williams), Bellevue Gallery, Binghamton, NY, 73; charcoal studies, NH Composition, Concord, 74 & Mrs Gerard Derepentigny, Manchester, NH, 74; portrait (Paul Metcalf), Lillabulero Press, Northwood, NH; portrait (Mrs Charles Gordon), comn by Charles Gordon, Concord, NH; Paintings (Carolyn Dorfman Dance Co), the Legacyy Proj, New York Univ Tisch Sch of Arts, 2009; Development Corp for Israel State of Israel Bonds, New York, 2007. *Exhib:* solo exhibs, Mus Fine Arts, Boston, 83, New Images in Watercolor, Currier Gallery Art, Manchester, NH, 85, Concordia Coll, Bronxville, NY, 86, Babson Coll, Wellesley, Mass, 88, New Eng Coll Gallery, NH, 95, Yeshiva Univ Mus, NY, 96 & 97, Lingo Fine Arts Gallery, West Stockbridge, Mass, 99 & Steerage to Ellis Island, Gallery at Stageworks, 2006, Berkshire Mus, Pittsfield, Mass, 2009; Drawings from Holst's Sculpture, Addison Gallery Am Art, 74; Group exhibs, Collectors Show, Va Mus Fine Arts, 70; Wade Gallery, Los Angeles, 87; Sound Shore Gallery, Stamford, Conn, 89; New Eng Coll Gallery, 94; New Directions, Contemp Art from the Currier Collection, Manchester, NH, 94; The Luria Series, Cline Fine Art Gallery, 95; Koussevitzky Arts Festival, Berkshire Community Coll, Pittsfield, Mass, 97; Eastern Spirit in Contemp Art & Made in the Americas, Creative Projs, Warehouse Gallery, Lee, Mass, 97; Sarah Y Rentschler Gallery, Hudson, NY, 2000; Western Wall Project, Deborah Davis Fine Art, Hudson, 2002-03; Rural Artists with Urban Sensibilities, Perrala Gallery, Fulton Montgomery Community Coll, Johnstown, NY, 2003; CW White Gallery, Portland, Maine, 2003; Abstraction Now, Gallery at Stageworks, Hudson NY & Rensselaer Polytech Inst, Troy, NY, 2004; Drawings, Deborah Davis Gallery, Hudson, NY, 2005; ADD Gallery, Group Show, Hudson, NY, 2005; They Should See Us Now: Six Abstract Painters Look at the Hudson River School Through the Lens of Photog, Gallery at Stageworks, Hudson, NY, 2006-2007; Drawn To The Edge, Greene Co Coun on the Arts, Catskill Gallery, Catskill, NY, 2008; Clyde Forth Visual Theatre (multi media proj), New York, 2009; Local Self Portraits, Hudson Opera House, NY, 2010; Mixed Media, Brill Gallery, N Adams, Mass, 2010; Warren Street, Hudson, NY, 2011; Reflections on Melville, With Kay Canavino, Herman Melville's Arrowhead, Pittsfield, Mass, Eclipse Mill Gallery, North Adams, Mass, 2011; Summer Landscapes, Berkshire Art Gallery, Great Barrington, Mass, 2013. *Pos:* Art design consult, Lillabulero Press, Northwood Narrows, NH, 67-74; art therapist, NH Hosp, 70-71 & pvt clinic, 75-. *Teaching:* Instr, pvt students, 67-, Manchester Inst Art, NH, 73-74, painting workshops, Berkshire Community Coll, S Co Campus, Great Barrington, Mass, 97 & Coun Creative Proj, Lee, Mass, 98; art instr, Adult Educ Prog, Coe-Brown Acad, Northwood, NH, 72; Berkshire Community Coll, South Coun Campus, 1997-; workshop instr, IS183 Sch Art, Stockbridge, Mass, 98- & Hudson Opera House, 2005-. *Awards:* Direct Vision Exhib Awards, Mass Coun Arts, 73 & 75; Priy Pene Richard, Symposium, 88; Mem Found for Jewish Culture Award, New York, NY, 89-90; Grant, Max and Anna Levinson Found, Santa Fe, NMex, 99; Development Corporation for Israel State of Israel Bonds, NYC, work on paper: The Western Wall Menorah reproduced in honor of Chabad of the Berkshires in coop w/Deborah Davis Fine Art, Hudson, NY, 2007; Jewish Artist of the Year, Develop Corp for Israel, State of Israel Bonds, Wash DC, 2010. *Bibliog:* Piri Halasz (auth), From the Mayor's Doorstep, Electronic Edition, no 43, 12/1/02; Richard Roth (auth), Making Memory Come Alive, The Independent, 11/29/02; The Western Wall Project, Register Star, 12/6/02; Menachem Wecker (auth), The esthetic of mishegaas: Tom Baron & Arthur Yanoff at Stageworks, The Jewish Press, NY, 11/26/2004; Vicky Perry (auth), Abstract Painting: Concepts & Techniques, Perry Watson-Guptil Publ, 2005; Marcia Stamell (auth), Am Space, Contemporary abstract painters take on the Hudson River School, The Independent, 10/20/2006; Piri Halasz (auth), If they could see us now, From the Mayor's Doorstep, 12/2006; Kevin Murphy (auth), Art New England, Hudson River: Abstract Revision, Feb & Mar 2008; French Clements (auth), The Independent, on Warren Street visual rambles through time & space, 3/21/2008; Owen Orel (auth), Looking Backward, Dancing Forward, The Forward, New York, May 29, 2009; The Country & Abroad, Great Barrington Artist Arthur Yanoff, Berkshire Mus, 2009; Local Self Portraits, Hudson Opera house catalog, forward by cur Richard Roth, poem by John Asbery, Columbia Hist Soc, NY, 2010; Ambassador's Ball Catalog, designed by Shirley Berman, Wash C Comt, State of Israel Bonds; Andrew Boiter (auth), Artists Reflect on Melville & Hawthorne, The Berkshire Eagle: Berkshire Week, 2011; Allison Sheardy (auth), Reflections on Melville, Berkshire Record, 2011; Charles Giuliano (auth), Reflections on Melville: Arthur Yanoff and Kay Canavino, Berkshire Fine Arts, 2011; Piri Halasz (auth), Inspiration at Arrowhead, Mayors Doorstep, No 96, 2011; Delora Gilbert (auth), Opera House Show Paves Way for View of Warren St, Columbia Paper, 2011; Bess Hochstein (auth), Rural Intelligence, Reflections on Melville Opens at Arrrowhead, 2011. *Mem:* Boston Painters & Sculptors; NH Art Asn; Am Art Therapy Asn. *Media:* Acrylics, Watercolor. *Publ:* Illusr, Broken Syllables, 67 & Waiting to Freeze, 69, Lillabulero Press; auth, The paste-up autobiography: Collage in the treatment of disturbed adolescents, Am J Art Therapy, 73; illusr, Raw Honey, Alice James Books, 75. *Dealer:* Berkshire Art Gallery 80 Railroad St Great Barrington Ma 01230. *Mailing Add:* 624 S Egremont Rd Great Barrington MA 01230

YANOW, RHODA MAE
PAINTER, INSTRUCTOR
b Newark, NJ. *Study:* Newark Arts Club; Parsons Sch Design; Heritage Art Sch, with Henry Gasser; Nat Acad Design, with Henry Gasser, Daniel Greene, Harvey Dinnerstein, John Grabach, & Burt Silverman. *Work:* Newark Pub Libr; West Orange Town Hall; NJ Ballet; Prince Albert Mus; Jack Richardson; Pastel Soc Am; Pegasus Meadowlands; Butler Inst Am Arts; Morris Mus; Noyes, Mus; Kean Univ; Township of Hunderdon Co. *Comn:* Portraits, comn by Thuryoung Family, 92-94; Nat Acad Design, 79-81; Rensselaer Univ. *Exhib:* Nat Arts Club Pastel Show,74; Am Artists Prof League Grand Nat Exhib, 75; Salmagundi Club Watercolor Show, 75; Nat Acad Design, 78-80; Solo Exhibs: Nathan's Art Gallery, West Patterson, NJ; Swain's Art Gallery, Plainfield, NJ; Hait Gallery, Maplewood, NJ; Gallery of South Orange & Maplewood, NJ; Butler Inst Am Art and many others; Int Mus Cartoon Art, 2000; Int Pastel Artists Invitational Exhib (contrib artist), Taipei, Taiwan, 2007; Kean Univ, 2009. *Collection Arranged:* Butler Institute of Am Art; First Pastel Mus, China. *Pos:* Instr, Figure Painting, Visual Arts Center, Summit, NJ. *Teaching:* Instr pastel painting & life drawing, Du Cret Sch Arts & Newark Mus, 93-94; instr figure painting in pastel, PSA Nat Arts Sch, NY; instr drawing, Newark Mus, NJ. *Awards:* Gold Medal, Nat Asn Women Artists, 89; Bronze Medal Hon, Pastel Soc Am, 90; Pen & Brush

Award, Gene Alder Walker, 96; Knickerbocker Artists Silver & Gold Medal Honor, Catharine Lorillard Wolfe Art Club, 87; Ladies Auxiliary Award, Columbus Club, 90; Best in Show, Conn Pastel Soc, 2003 & 2009; Artsbridge Award, Works on Paper, 2008; Prallsville Mills Award, Hunterdon, Inside Out, 2008; Marquis Who's Who in Am Art References award in Pastels, Audubon Artists, NY, 2013. *Bibliog:* Ruthann Williams (auth), Graven images, NJ Music & Arts, 6/74; Jack Richeson (auth), My Friends, Today's Great Masters. *Mem:* Am Artists Prof League; Nat Asn Women Artists; Catharine Lorillard Wolfe Art Club; Pen & Brush; Pastel Soc Am; Am Women Artists; Noyes Mus (signature mem). *Media:* Pastels, Pen & Ink; Lithography. *Res:* Observing human behavior. *Specialty:* Ballet paintings, people. *Interests:* People, Books, Movies. *Publ:* Illusr, The Art of Pastel Portraiture, Watson-Guptill Publ; contribr, Star Ledger & other local newspapers; Am Artist Mag, 2/89; cover, NJ Goodlife, 10/89; illusr, The Best of Pastel I & II, Rockport Publ, 96; Ron Lister (auth) Drawing With Pastels; Pastel Application Techniques for Beginners. *Dealer:* Connoisseur Gallery 52 Bernards Ave Bernardsville NJ. *Mailing Add:* 19 Springtown Road Whitehouse Station NJ 08889

YARBER, ROBERT
PAINTER
b Dallas, Tex, 1948. *Study:* Cooper Union Col, NY, BFA, 71; La State Univ, Baton Rouge, MFA, 74. *Comn:* Created a medal commemorating the millennium for the Vatican's Jubilee Campaign, 2001. *Exhib:* Oakland Mus, 79, (with catalog), 83 & 91 (with catalog); San Francisco Mus Mod Art (with catalog), 84; Whitney Mus Am Art (with catalog), 85-86; Mus Fine Arts, Boston (with catalog), 86; Walker Arts Ctr, 87; Pa Acad Fine Arts, 87; Baltimore Mus Art, 87; Nat Mus Mod Art, Kyoto, Japan, 88; Galleria Naz Roma, Italy, 88; Stedelijk Mus (with catalog), Amsterdam, The Neth, 89; solo exhibs, Va Mus Fine Arts, 89, Sonnabend Gallery, NY, 93 & 95, Galerie Lehmann, Lausanne, Switz, 94, Nev Inst Contemp Art, Las Vegas, 95, Patricia Faure Gallery, Los Angeles, 95 & Marella Arte Contemp, Italy, 96, Milan, Rome, Florence, and Prato; Butler Inst Am Art (with catalog), 90; Mint Mus Art, 91; The World Tomorrow, Thomas Solomon's Garage, Los Angeles, 94; In the Field, Margo Leavin Gallery, Los Angeles, 94; Go Figure, Patricia Faure Gallery, Los Angeles, 95; 16 Artists, Patricia Faure Gallery, Santa Monica, Calif, 96. *Teaching:* Vis instr painting, Univ Calif, Berkeley, 82 & vis lectr, 83; vis lectr, Univ Tex, Austin, 82 & lectr, 84; vis artist, Univ Calif, Santa Barbara, 88; asst to full prof art, Pa State Univ, 94-, named distinguished prof, 2003. *Awards:* Nat Endowment Arts Fel Grant, 83 & 85. *Bibliog:* Ivana Mulatero (auth), Robert Yarber, Juliet Art Mag, No 61, 2-3/93; The horror: Robert Yarber (artist)-All around esthetes, Artforum, Vol 32, No 8, 94; David Pagel (auth), Taking a glimpse into the world of tomorrow, Los Angeles Times, 2/24/94; and others. *Dealer:* Patricia Faure Gallery Bergamot Sta 2525 Michigan Ave B7 Santa Monica CA 90404. *Mailing Add:* 725 Unionville Pike Julian PA 16844

YARBROUGH, LEILA KEPERT
PRINTMAKER, PAINTER
b Katoomba, NSW, Australia, Mar 23, 1932; US citizen. *Study:* Univ Fla; Atlanta Coll Art, Ga. *Work:* Augusta Mus Art, Ga; Agnes Scott Coll, Decatur, Ga; Loch Haven Art Ctr, Orlando, Fla; Piedmont Coll, Demorest, Ga; Piedmont Hosp, Atlanta, Ga; and others. *Comn:* Sen Paul Coverdell & US Senate off; inspirational landscapes, Prayer Room, Tanner Medical Ctr, Douglasville, GA. *Exhib:* Eastern US Drawing Competition, Cummer Gallery Art, Jacksonville, Fla, 70; Contemp Am Drawing V: Norfolk, Smithsonian Inst Travel Exhib, 71-73; 34th Ann Contemp Am Painting, Soc Four Arts, Palm Beach, Fla, 72; 1st Nat Monoprint-Monotype, Oglethorpe Univ, Atlanta, Ga, 73; 64th Ann, Conn Acad Fine Arts, Hartford, 74; Am Drawings, Portsmouth Community Art Ctr, Va, 76; 12th Nat Print Exhib, Silvermine Guild Artists, New Canaan, Conn, 77; Salute to Louis XIV, Miriam Perlman Gallery, Chicago, Ill, 91; Drawing Soc Nat Travel Exhib, Am Fedn Arts, New York; Norman Wagner and his Students-34 yrs, Chattahoochee Valley Art Mus, LaGrange, Ga, 97; Colors, Exhib, Roswell, GA, 2005. *Teaching:* Printmaking workshop, Yarbrough Graphics, 74; demonstr viscosity etching, Southern Graphics Coun, Atlanta Coll Art, 86; instr art workshop, etchings, Atlanta Artists Club, 96. *Awards:* Am Drawing Purchase Award, Norfolk Mus, 71; First Prize, The Single Impression, Oglethorpe Univ, Atlanta, 73; Great Smoky Mts Nat Park Purchase Award, US Govt Art Purchase Prog, 74. *Bibliog:* Martin Sharter (auth), Art, Atlanta Mag, 12/73; Selma Smith (ed), Printworld Directory of Contemporary Prints and Prices, Printworld Inc, 88-2008. *Media:* Etchings, Monoprints; Watercolor, Oil. *Interests:* Travel; Tennis; Swimming; Writing. *Dealer:* Monty Stabler Gallery Birmingham AL; Lola Roswell GA

YARD, SALLY ELIZABETH
HISTORIAN, CURATOR
b Trenton, NJ, Sept 24, 1951. *Study:* Harvard Univ, AB, 73; Princeton Univ, MFA, 75, PhD, 80. *Collection Arranged:* Christo: Oceanfront (auth, catalog), Princeton Univ, 75; John Roy, Christopher Sproat (auth, catalog), Vincent Smith Art Mus, 78; Images of the Self (auth, catalog), 79 & A Sense of Place--The Am Landscape in Recent Art (auth, catalog), 80, Hampshire Coll Gallery; The Shadow of the Bomb (auth, catalog) Mt Holyoke Coll Art Mus, S Hadley, Mass & Univ Gallery, Univ Mass, Amherst, 84; An Architect's Eye: Selections from the Collection of Graham Gund (auth, catalog), Mt Holyoke Coll Art Mus, South Hadley, Mass, 85; Place and Preference - Studies of San Diego's Art in Public Spaces Since 1980 (auth, catalog), Univ San Diego, 91. *Pos:* Acting cur, Univ Gallery, Univ Mass, Amherst, 80; ed dir, inSITE 97, San Diego/Tijuana, 94-97 & co-cur, 96-97. *Teaching:* Instr mod art, Mt Holyoke Col, Mass, 78-79, lectr mod art, 80-81, asst prof mod art, 81-83; vis asst prof mod art, Amherst Col, Mass, 81-83; lectr mod art, vis asst prof & vis assoc prof, Univ of Calif, San Diego, 87-96; asst assoc prof art, Univ San Diego, 89-. *Mem:* Coll Art Asn. *Res:* Abstract expressionism, especially Willem de Kooning; contemporary painting & sculpture; public space; popular culture. *Publ:* Auth, Deep Time, Mus Contemp Art, Los Angeles, 93; Tagged Turf in the Public Sphere (exhib catalog), inSITE 94, San Diego/Tijuana, 95; Willem de Kooning, Poligrafa, Barcelona & Rizzoli, New York, 97; coauth, Francis Baum, Abrams, New York, 99; Private Time in Public Space, Installation, San Diego, 98. *Mailing Add:* PO Box 12985 La Jolla CA 92039

YARINSKY, ADAM
ARCHITECT
Study: Univ Va, BS (archit), 1984; Princeton Univ, MA (archit), 1987. *Exhib:* Architecture Research Office: Work, Princeton Univ Sch Archit, 2000; Forever Modern: 50 Years of Record Houses, Archit Record and Pratt Inst, 2005; From the Ground Up, Van Alen Inst, 2009. *Pos:* Architect, Michael Graves Architect, Princeton, NJ, 1985 & 1986, Deborah Berke Architect & Assocs, New York, 1987-88 & Steven Holl Architects, New York, 1988-92; founding partner, Archit Res Off LLC, 1993-. *Teaching:* Walter B Sanders tchg fel, Univ Mich Coll Archit and Urban Planning, 1992-93; asst prof, Univ Va Sch Archit, 1993-94 & Harry S Shure prof, 2001; visiting prof, Yale Univ Sch Archit, 1995, Harvard Univ Grad Sch Design, 1996, 1998 & 2004, Parsons Sch Constructed Environments, 2007 & Syracuse Univ Sch Archit, 2008. *Awards:* Henry Adams Medal, Am Inst Architects, 1987, Nat Hon Award for Interior Archit, 2001 & 2002; Merit Award, Am Inst Architects NY State Chap, 1998 & 2006, Archit Award, 2000 & 2001 & Hon Award, 2008; Independent Projects Award, NY State Coun on Arts, 1998; Award for Design Excellence, Art Comn City of NY, 1999; Emerging Voices Award, Archit League, New York, 2001; Hon Award, Am Inst Architects, NJ Chap, 2008; Archit Award, Am Acad Arts & Letts, 2010. *Mailing Add:* Archit Res Office 170 Varick St New York NY 10013

YAROS, CONSTANCE G
PAINTER, SCULPTOR
b Philadelphia, Pa. *Study:* Tyler Sch Art, Temple Univ, Philadelphia, 57-60; Boris Blai Studio, 76-81; Pa Acad Fine Arts, 78, 79, 87 & 88; Schuler Sch Art, Baltimore, 90, 91. *Work:* Tyler Sch Libr, Elkins Park, Pa; Temple Univ-Paley Libr, Philadelphia; Jefferson Park Hospital, Pa Board of City Trusts Philadelphia, Pa; Fed Court House, Philadelphia, Pa. *Comn:* Portraits, comn by Mr & Mrs Herbert Pincus, Glenside, Pa, 80, Mr & Mrs Mark Hankin, Erwinna, Pa, 88, Mr & Mrs Francis Strawbridge III, Merion, Pa, 89, Mr & Mrs William Silverman, Lafayette Hill, Pa, 94 & Mr William Austin Meehan, Philadelphia, Pa, 92; many other commissions including portraits, landscapes, equines, ballet & still lifes; Fed Judge Joseph L McGlynn, 2000. *Exhib:* Old York Rd Art Guild, 75; Artists Equity Triennial, Port of History Mus, Philadelphia, 84 & 88; Sketch Club, Philadelphia, 87; Catharine Lorillard Wolfe Art Club, NY, 88; Salmagundi Art Club, NY, 88; Allied Artists Am, NY, 88; Art at Amory, Philadelphia, 90-92; Solo exhibs, Tyler Alumni Gallery, Diamond Club, Temple Univ, Philadelphia, 92, Allied Artists Prof League, NY, 93 & Oil Painters of Am, Chicago, Ill, 94; Woodmere Art Mus, Philadelphia Pa. *Awards:* Len G Everett Painting Award, Allied Artists Am, 88. *Bibliog:* Denise Breslin Kachin (auth), Artist achieves recognition hoped for, Philadelphia Evening Bulletin, 81. *Mem:* Artists Equity (bd mem 76-90); Pa Acad Fine Arts; Philadelphia Art Alliance; Am Soc Portrait Artists; Plastic Art Club; Women's Mus Art Archives; Allied Artists of Am; Am Soc Classic Realism; Oil Painter Am; Portrait Soc Am. *Media:* Pastel, Oil; Metal (Bronze), Hydrocal. *Mailing Add:* c/o Portraits Philadelphia 2401 Pennsylvania Ave 4A5 Philadelphia PA 19130

YAROTSKY, LORI
ART DEALER, CURATOR
b Houston, Tex. *Study:* Haystack-Hinckley Sch Crafts, Hinckley, Maine, studied weaving, 72-73; Sam Houston State Univ, BFA (painting & drawing), 76, Tex A&M Univ, MFA (painting), 80; NY Univ, studied fine art conserve & old master paintings, 93-94; NYS Summer Writers Inst, Skidmore Col, Saratoga Springs, NY, 2007. *Work:* La State Mus, New Orleans; Univ St Thomas, Houston. *Collection Arranged:* Wemco (textile-related artworks), New York, 93; Granite Capital (19th-20th century photographs), New York, 94; Rubenstein Assoc (paintings and works on paper), New York, 94-; Ramius Capital (vintage & contemp photogs), NY, 97-98; Gerard Huber (paintings & drawings) (with catalog), Grace Cult Ctr & Mus Abilene, Tex, 98. *Pos:* Consult, Grad Sem Elem Art Educ, 80; dir, Tilden-Foley Gallery, New Orleans, La, 83-88 & Lori Yarotsky Gallery, 96-; proprietor, Res Nova Gallery, New Orleans, La, 88-, dir, 91-96; adv bd, Curric Rev, Dept Fine Art, Delgado Coll, New Orleans; bd dir, Red Bass Lit Mag; adv bd, Sac-O-Lait Found, Mamou, La; head specialist, Mod and Contemp Art Specialist, Artnet Worldwide Corp, NY, 2007-; dir, Strategic Art Management Alliance, New York, NY. *Teaching:* Fel, East Tex State Univ, 77; lectr, Grad Studies Arts Admin, Univ New Orleans, 84; Dept Fine Arts, Sch Visual Arts, New York, 2007-. *Awards:* Scholar, Haystack-Hinckley Sch Crafts, Maine, 73; Fel, E Tex State Univ, 77; Scholars, Houston Northwest Art League, Tex, 77; Elizabeth George Found Fel Grant (independent writing), 2007. *Bibliog:* Errol Laborde (auth), Gallery growth, Gambit, 12/15/87; Roger Green (auth), New gallery will open in warehouse district, Times-Picayune, 12/23/87; Roger Green (auth), 1987: Warehouse district renaissance, Times-Picayune, Lagniappe, 1/1/88; George Jordon (auth), Critics choice: New Orleans art community, GO: New Orleans, 5/88; John Kemp (auth), Art mecca in the warehouse district, New Orleans Mag, 9/88; Georgina Adam (auth), Bidding in Pajamas, Financial Times, 2010. *Mem:* Friends Contemp Art, New Orleans Mus Art (adv bd); La Composers Guild; Jr Comt New Orleans Opera Asn; ArtTable, New York; ArtWalk (Coalition for the Homeless), NY; Valatie Free Libr, Kinderhook, NY (co-chair, co- capital campaign). *Res:* Louisiana Purchase; French and American Revolutions. *Specialty:* Contemporary fine art (paintings, sculpture, photographs, drawings, site-specific installations and video); 19th century American and European paintings; French Barbizon School paintings; Old Master paintings; 19th Century French Papier Peints Panoramiques; Vintage and Modern Photographs. *Publ:* Auth, Garden notes, Blackjack J, 79-80; île des cartes, 99; Words 73, 2011, Words 25, 2012. *Mailing Add:* PO Box 2028 New York NY 10021

YASKO, CARYL A(NNE)
MURALIST, SCULPTOR
b Racine, Wis, Mar 11, 1941. *Study:* Dominican Col, Wis, sculpture with Monica Gabriel & painting with Branislov Bak, grad, 63. *Work:* Fulbright Off, Tokyo, Japan; Prairie Wave, McKenzie Environ Ctr, Poynette, Wis; The Inland Sea, Prairie Wave II, Palmyra, Wis Elem Sch Libr; Wind Prairie, Evansville, Wis. *Comn:* The Stonecutters,

Lemont, Ill, 75 & 93; The Wind Whistlers of Ixonia, Rise to the Sky, sculpture of 57 giant pole's with airplane beacon and flags, Wis Arts Bd, Oconomowoc Sch Dist, Wis Elec Power Co; Unity with Yasko, Catch a Turtle, concrete fresco, Municipal Pool, Monona, Wis Arts Bd, Monona City, Monona Sch Dist, 93 & 94; Cup of Light, mural, Evansville, Wis Elem Sch, Wis Arts Bd, Evansville Sch Dist; Reach, mural, Very Special Arts Wis & City of Sun Prairie, 94; Forest Mem Sculpture, McKenzie Environ Ctr, Poynette, Wis; Rainbow, mural, Madison, Wis, 2002; Pride, mural, Manitowoc City Hall, Wis, 2003; Brainstorm, rotunda mural, Manitowoc Pub Libr, 2002. *Exhib:* On Chicago Walls, Chicago State Univ, 74; Civic Sculpture, Appleton, Neenah & Menasha, Wis, 77; Levi Strauss & Co, Europ Exhib of US Murals, Mus Royal d'Art, Ancien, Brussels, 78; Chicago, The City & Its Artists, 1945-1978, Univ Mich, Ann Arbor, 78; French Ministry Foreign Affairs, traveling exhib, Caen, Normandy, 81; Working Together: Forms of Collaboration, Montgomery Ward Gallery, Univ Ill, Chicago, 81; Healing Walls, Ill Art Gallery, Chicago, 95 & Springfield, 96. *Pos:* Panelist, Chicago Art Asn, Chicago & Nat Conf Mural Artists, 76 & State Arts Conf, 78-92; guest speaker, Chicago State Univ, 76, Univ Mich, Ann Arbor, 78, Waterloo, Wis, 79, Waupan State Prison, 79, UW Parkside, 80, Kamakura, Kanazawa & Tokyo, Japan, 82 & The Community Develop Wis, 86; artist-in-residence, Wis & Midwest, 78-92; visual arts panel, Wis Arts Bd, 79; guest artist, Brigada L'Eteiller Mural Proj, Chicago, 79, Artists for Peace Proj, Chicago, 80, State of Wis, Arts World, 82-91 & Chicago Pub Art Group, 90; speaker, Community Built Asn, 95, 97 & CBA Conf, Phoenix, Ariz, 2000; keynote speaker, Line Drawing WEA Conf, Madison, Wis, 97 & Mich Asn Community Arts Agency, E Lansing, 2001. *Teaching:* Instr, Art Inst Chicago, 75 & 76, Oakton Community Col, Morton Grove, Ill, 77 & Carthage Col, 81-; lectr murals, Loop Jr Col, Valparaiso Univ, 76; lectr, Univ Wis, River Falls, 81 & mural instr, 82; concrete fresco instr, Joseph Art Sch, Joseph, Ore, 94. *Awards:* Chicago Beautiful Award, Mayor Daley, 75 & 76; Hon Citizen, Lemont, Ill, 75 & 94; Key to the City of Manitowoc, 2003; First Generation Muralist Award, Chicago Public Art Group, 10/27/2005. *Bibliog:* John & Eva Corckroft, John Weber (coauth), Towards a People Art, Dutton, NY, rev ed, 97; Phyllis Berg Pagorsch (dir), The Great Wall of Waunakee (film), Yahara Films, Madison, Wis, 78; Alan Barnett (auth), Community Murals, Art Alliance Press, Philadelphia & Cornwall Books, NY, London, 83; Mary Gray (auth), A Guide to Chicago's Murals, 2000; and others. *Mem:* Chicago Pub Art Group; Community Built Asn, Ithaca, NY. *Media:* Oil, Watercolor, Fresco, Mixed Media. *Publ:* Contribr, Art Workers News, 73, New Art Examiner, 74 & 80 & Nat Murals Newsletter, 78. *Mailing Add:* 136 Whiton St Whitewater WI 53190

YASSIN, ROBERT ALAN
RETIRED MUSEUM DIRECTOR, CURATOR
b Malden, Mass, May 22, 1941. *Study:* Dartmouth Col, BA (Rufus Choate Scholar), 62; Boston Univ, 62-63; Univ Mich, MA (hist art, Teaching Fel), 65, PhD (Samuel H Kress Found Fel), 70. *Collection Arranged:* Am Art from Alumni Collections (auth, catalog), Yale Univ Art Gallery, 68; Art & the Excited Spirit (with catalog), Yale Univ Art Gallery, 72; Victor Higgins Retrospective (auth, catalog), Notre Dame Univ Art Gallery & Indianapolis Mus Art, 75; Eiteljorg Collection of Western Am Art, 76; Leonard Baskin (auth, catalog), Indianapolis Mus Art, 76; Painting & Sculpture Today (auth, catalog), Indianapolis Mus Art, 76, 78, 80, 82, 84 & 86; Art in Business and Corporate Collections (auth, catalog), Indianapolis Mus Art, 77; Ind Artists Show, 77-79, 81, 83 & 85; Enrico Baj (auth, catalog), Indianapolis Mus Art, 78; George Carlson, Sculptures and Drawings (auth, catalog), Indianapolis Mus Art & Grand Cent Art Galleries, NY, 79; Batuz: Works in Paper (auth, catalog), Indianapolis Mus Art, 82; Sasson Soffer Sculpture (auth, catalog), Indianapolis Mus Art, 84; Masks (auth, catalog), Tucson Mus Art, 90; Fine Art for Fine Causes (auth, catalog), Tucson Mus Art, 91; Am Primitive Paintings and Drawings: The Dr Paul Schiffman Collection (auth, catalog), Tucson Mus Art, 91; Women Artists and the West (auth, catalog), Tucson Mus Art, 91-96; James Cook: New Paintings (auth, catalog), Tucson Mus Art, 92; Harmony Hammond: Ghost Farms (auth, catalog), Tucson Mus Art, 93; Rebecca Davis & Roger Asay, Tucson Mus Art, 95; Jim Ward, Tucson Mus Art, 96; Dave Asay (with catalog), Tucson Mus Art, 99; Miriam Shapiro: Works on Paper (with catalog), Tucson Mus Art, 99; Joanne Kerrihard (with catalog), Tucson Mus Art, 2000; About Van Gogh, Palos Verde Art Ctr, 2010. *Pos:* Asst to dir, Mus Art, Univ Mich, Ann Arbor, 65-66, instr, History of Art Dept, co-dir joint prog mus training, Univ Mich, ed Art Bull, 70-73, from asst dir to actg dir Mus Art, 70-73; asst to dir, Yale Univ Art Gallery, 66-68, ed, Bull, 66-68; chief cur, Indianapolis Mus Art, 73-75, actg dir, 75, dir, 75-89; exec dir, Tucson Mus Art, Ariz, 90-2001 & Palos Verdes Art Ctr, 2002-2012. *Teaching:* Instr graphic arts & mus practice & co-dir joint mus training prog, Univ Mich, Ann Arbor, 70-73; adj prof, Herron Sch Art, Purdue Univ, Indianapolis, 76-88. *Awards:* Ford Found Fel, Yale Univ, 66-68; Horace Rackham Felo, Univ Much, 68-69, 69-70; Sagamore of the Wabash, State of Ind, 85. *Mem:* Coll Art Asn Am; Am Asn Mus (sr accreditation examiner, 80-, co-chmn, ann meeting, 81, int coun mus, bd dir, 86-89); Asn Art Mus (dir, 75-89); Nat Trust Hist Preservation; Am Asn State and Local Hist; Ariz Hist soc; Asn Art Mus Dirs (mem prof ethics and standards comt, 75-89, mem nominating com, 78-89); Intermuseum Conserv Asn (trustee, 73-89, mem exec comt, 75-77, chmn, 77-79, mem int comt exhib exchange); Mus Asn Ariz; Midwest Coll Art Asn; Tucson Arts Coalition; Tucson Asn Mus; Calif Asn Mus. *Res:* Late 19th and 20th century American art; contemporary art. *Specialty:* Contemporary art. *Mailing Add:* 7321 Marina Pacifica Dr Long Beach CA 90803

YASUDA, ROBERT
PAINTER, EDUCATOR
b Lihue, Kauai, Hawaii, Nov 14, 1940. *Study:* Pratt Inst, Brooklyn, NY, BFA, 62, MFA, 64. *Work:* Brooklyn Mus, NY; Libr Cong, Washington, DC; State of Hawaii Found Arts; Hillwood Mus, Long Island Univ, NY; NY Pub Libr. *Exhib:* Solo exhibs include Sculpture at the Coliseum, NY Coliseum, 1980, Albuquerque Sight-Line, Hoshour Gallery, NMex, 1981, Koplin Gallery, Los Angeles, 1982, 1987, Marianne Deson Gallery, Chicago, Ill, 1982, Betty Parsons Gallery, New York, 1984, Hanalei Gallery, Kauai, Hawaii, 1984, Julian Pretto Gallery, New York, 1990, Elizabeth Harris Gallery, New York, 1993, 1996, 1998, 2002, 2004, 2006, Ledbetter Lusk Gallery, Memphis, 1997, New Arts Prog, Kutztown, Pa, 1999, David Lusk Gallery, Memphis, 2000, 2003, 2005, 2008; two-person exhib (with Judith Murray), Galleria Miralli, Viterbo, Italy, 2005; group exhibs include A More Store, Jack Tilton Gallery, New York, 1984; The Anchorage Exhib, Large Scale Painting Installations, Brooklyn Bridge Anchorage, New York, 1985; 8x10, Washington Co Mus Fine Arts, Hagerstown, Md, 1986; Opening exhib, Cutler-Schreiber Gallery, NY, 1986; Reveal, Koplin Gallery, Los Angeles, Calif, 1988; Small Scale Works, Julian Pretto Gallery, New York 1991; Stark Gallery, New York, 1992; Slow Art: Painting in New York Now, PS1 Mus, Inst Contemp Art, NY, 1992; Six Abstract Artists, Elizabeth Harris Gallery, New York, 1993, 1995, 1998, Summer Color, 2003; After the Fall, Newhouse Ctr Contemp Art, Snug Harbor Cult Ctr, New York, 1997; Monochrome/Monochrome?, Florence Lynch Gallery, New York, 2001; Honolulu to New York, Contemp Mus, Honolulu, 2005; Invitational Exhib Visual Arts, Am Acad Arts & Letters, New York, 2008. *Teaching:* Prof art, Long Island Univ, C W Post, painting & drawing, 69-92. *Awards:* J H Whitney Found Grant, 62-63; Nat Endowment for the Arts Fel Grant, Washington, DC, 81; Purchase Award, Am Acad Arts & Letters, 2008. *Bibliog:* Kathleen Shields (auth), Robert Yasuda-Albuquerque sight line, Art Space, spring 82; Alan Artner (auth), Best solo shows, art 1982, Chicago Tribune, 1/2/83; Kim Levin (auth), Art in the Anchorage, Village Voice, 5/21/85; Susan Fleminger (auth), Inside the Bridge, Art in the Depths of the Anchorage, Prospect Press, 5/30/85. *Media:* Acrylic, Oil. *Dealer:* David Lusk Gallery 4540 Poplar Ave Memphis TN 38117. *Mailing Add:* c/o Elizabeth Harris Gallery 529 W 20th St New York NY 10001

YATES, MARVIN
PAINTER, INSTRUCTOR
b Jackson, Tenn, Sept 22, 1943. *Study:* Memphis Acad Art, BFA, 66. *Exhib:* Am Watercolor Soc, Nat Acad Gallery, NY, 73-79; Watercolor USA, Springfield Art Mus, Mo, 75 & 76; Mainstreams, Grover Hermann Mus, Marietta, Ohio, 76; Southern Watercolor Soc, Cheekwood Gallery, Nashville, 77-79; Rocky Mountain Nat Water Media, Foothills Art Ctr, Golden, Colo, 78; Real Show, Grand Cent Art Gallery, NY, 79. *Pos:* Art dir, Memphis Publ Co, currently. *Teaching:* Instr watercolor, Memphis State Univ, 75-. *Awards:* Rechenbach Award, Rechenbach Gallery, 73 & 80; Washington Sch of Art Award, 74; Second Place Watercolor, Sterling Regal Inc, 79. *Bibliog:* Susan Meyer (auth), Watercolor Page, Am Artist Mag, 75; Ralph Fabri (auth), Watercolor Page, Today's Art, 75. *Mem:* Am Watercolor Soc; Southern Watercolor Soc; Tenn Watercolor Soc; Memphis Watercolor Group. *Media:* Watercolor, Pencil. *Publ:* Contribr, 40 Watercolorists and How They Work, Watson-Guptill, 76. *Mailing Add:* 1457 Hwy 304 Hernando MS 38632

YATES, SHARON
EDUCATOR
b Rochester, NY, 1942. *Study:* Syracuse Univ, Sch Art, BFA, 1964; Tulane Univ, MFA, 1966. *Work:* exhib in group shows at Nat Acad of Design Mus, New York City, 1997, Bates Coll Mus Art, Maine, 2000, LC Bates Mus, Hinkley, Maine, 2000, Bates Coll Mus Univ Louisville, Oklahoma City Art Mus. *Exhib:* Solo exhibs incl Fishbach Gallery, New York City, 1976, Univ Maine, Macias, 1991, 1997, Maine Coast Artists Exec Gallery, Rockport, 1993; exhib in group exhibs at Turtle Gallery, Deer Isle, Maine, 1997, Maine Coast Artists Gallery, Rockport, 1999, Va Hist Soc, Richmond, 2000, Rep in permanent collections Nat Acad of Design, New York City, United Technol, Conn, Lucent Technol, Univ Louisville. *Teaching:* Fac Maryland Inst Col Art, Baltimore, 1968—. *Awards:* Recipient Prix de Rome, 1972-74; grantee Ingram-Merrill Found fel, France, 1977-78, Ludwig Vogelstein Found, 1996. *Mem:* Nat Acad (acad, 95-, Shatalov award)

YATES, STEVEN A
CURATOR, SCHOLAR, PHOTOGRAPHIC ARTIST
b Chicago, Ill. *Study:* Univ Nebr, with dir Norman Geske, Sheldon Art Mus, Jim Alinder, Jim Eisentrager, BFA, 72; Univ NMex, with Beaumont Newhall & Van Deren Coke, MA, 75, MFA doctoral degree with Ford Found Fel, 78, Fulbright Scholar, USSR, Russia, Ukraine, Lithuania, Latvia, Belarus, 1991, Russia, 1995 & 2007. *Work:* Pushkin Mus Fine Arts, Moscow; Multimedia Mus, Moscow; San Francisco Mus Mod Art; Univ NMex Art Mus; Ctr for Creative Photog, Tucson; Sheldon Mem Art Gallery, Univ Neb; Mint Mus Art, NC; Hist Collection, Russian Union Art Photographers, Moscow; Latvian Mus Photog; Moscow House Photog; Polaroid Collection; Raymond Jonson Collection, Univ NMex. *Comn:* numerous pvt collections internationally. *Exhib:* Steve Yates, Sheldon Mem Art Gallery, Univ, Neb, 78; The Markers (with catalog), San Francisco Mus Mod Art, 80; Extending the Perimeters of 20th Century Photog (with catalog), San Francisco Mus Mod Art, 85; 21 NMex Photogrs, Vision Gallery, San Francisco, 91; Contemp Am Photog Masters, Cinema Inst, Moscow, 91; NMex Impressions: Printmaking, 1880-1990, (traveling), 91-92; Solo exhibs, Cent Photog Gallery, Minsk, Belarus, 94, New Contemp Art Gallery, Minsk, Belarus, 95, Gallery A3, Moscow, 95 & Coll Fine & Performing Arts, Univ Nebr, 96; The Painted Photograph: A Survey of Hand Colored Photog, 1839 to the Present (traveling), Art Mus, Univ Wyo, 96; Experimental Gallery Up-Down, Kharkov, Ukraine, 96; Empires, collaborative installation, Irving Arts Ctr, Irving, Tex, 98-99; Photographic Icons: Film Form and Montage, homage to Sergei Eisenstein and Gustav Klucis, Mus Photog, Riga, Latvia, 98; 9 Photog Reconstructions from Moscow, Prague, St Petersburg, Nikolaevsk, Paris, River Amur, Gallery A3, Moscow, 2002; Site-specific installation for Freedom: Being Aware of the Big Picture, M'ARS Ctr Contemporary Arts, 2013; VIII Moscow Int Biennale, 2013; Site-specific installation for Pagamintos Buti Fotografija, Constructed to be Photographic, Galerija Meno Parkas, Kaunas, Lithuania, 2014. *Collection Arranged:* as curator, Mus NMex, Snta Fe, after 1991: To collect the Art of Women: The Jane Reese Williams Photography Collection, Mus Fine Arts, NMex Mus, 91; Contemporary Am Masters, Cinema Inst, Moscow, 91; Proto-Modern Photography (auth, catalog), co-cur Beaumont Newhall, Mus Fine Arts, NMex Mus, 92; 4+4, Late Modern: Photography Between the Mediums (auth, catalog, essay), Mus Fine Arts, NMex Mus, 94; Early Modern Photography: Selections from the Collection of the Russian Union of Art Photographers, Union Gallery, Moscow, 94; Betty Hahn: Photography or Maybe Not:

30 Yr Retrospective, traveling 95, State Russian Art Mus, St Petersburg, Marble Palace and Spain; Georgia O'Keeffe: From 291 to New Mexico, Mus Fine Arts, Mus NMex, 96-97; New Histories in Photography, Mus Fine Art, NMex Mus, 97; Joel Peter Witkin: Unpublished & Unseen, Mus Fine Art, NMex Mus, 98 traveling Portugal, Greece, US; Theatre as Memory, Photographic Installation Works by Laurent Millet, Musée Nicephore Niepce, Chalon-sur-Saone, France and Santa Fe Ctr for Visual Arts, 99-2000; 20/20 Twentieth Century Acquisitions by Twenty Leading Patrons, Mus Fine Arts, Mus NMex, 2000; Classic Russian Photog 1900 to WWII, Russian Art Photographers Union, Press Photo 2000, Moscow; In His Native Land: Early Modern Photog John Candelario, 2000-01; Avant-Garde Document: Photogs by Aleksandras Macijauskas, Mus Fine Arts, Mus NMex 2001-02; Alexander Rodchenko: Photomontage, Modern Photog and Film, Curatorial Assistance, Pasadena Art Mus, Univ NMex, 2001-2004 traveling exhib with trilingual publ, Bilbao, Spain, Vancouver, British Columbia, UA museums; Brett Weston, From the Collection: New Hists of Photog, pvt collection Erica Weston, 2002-03; Idea Photographic: After Modernism (and collection website: www.museumofnewmexico.org/idea), Mus Fine Arts, with loans, San Francisco Mus Modern Art, Princeton U Art Mus, 2002; Georgi Zelma, Documentary Photographs of Eastern Europe, 1924-1944, Modernity & Change: New Histories of Photography, Coll Mus Fine Arts, 2003-04; Selected lectures from 2006: Early Modern Photography, Historical Parallels in Russia & Am, Kazan State Univ, Russsia, 2006; Self as art, Identity as cult, Art Mus, Rostov on Don, 2007; Joel-Peter Witkin: Icons of Modernity, Nat Photography Ctr Russian Fed, St Petersburg, 2007; Modern & Contemp Photography in Russia, The Early 20th & 21st Centuries, Albuquerque Mus, 2008; Birth of Mod Photography in Am & Russia, Art & Art Hist Dept, Lake Forest Coll, 2008; Proto Modern Photography: Paradigm of Diversity for Art in the New Century, Nat Ctr Contemp Art, Nizhny Novgorod, Russia, 2009; From Dada to Surrealism: Photography's Primary Role in Mod Art, Int Fotografie Forum Frankfurt, 2010; Portraiture Redefined in Early Modern Photography, Latvian Photographers Asn and US Embassy, Riga, Latvia, 2011; Proto Modern Photography, Early Innovators of Modernist Discourse, Univ Daugavpils, Latvia, 2011, Proto Modern Photography, Art History with Russia and Eastern Europe, Fulbright Conf, 2012, London; Mod Art History in Photography, Keynote Lecture, 40th Anniversary Fulbright Conf, Moscow, 2013, S. Yates After Modernism, M'ARS Contemp Arts Ctr, Moscow with site-specific installation, 2013, Proto Mod Photography, Russian Avant-garde, Moholy-Nagy, Nat Gallery of Art, Canberra, Australia, 2013, Three contemp lectures series, Guest Artist-Scholar with site-specific installation, Photography Asn and Meno Parkas Galerija, Kaunas, Lithuania, 2014, two early modern history lectures, G. Oprescu Inst Art History, Romanian Acad and Fine Arts Univ, Bucharest, Romania, Photographic Inceptions, seven contemp lectures series, St. Thomas Inst with last at Lumiere Brothers Centre for Photog, Moscow, 2015. *Pos:* Cur asst, Sheldon Mem Art Gallery, Univ Nebr, 72-73 & Univ Art Mus, Univ NMex, 73-75; cur photog, Mus Fine Arts, Mus NMex, 80-2007, independent scholar, cur, photographic artist, author, & intern lectr, 2007-. *Teaching:* Instr part-time, Univ NMex, Albuquerque, 75-78; vis instr, Pomona Col, Claremont Col, 76-; vis instr art dept, Summer Exten Prog, Univ Calif, Los Angeles, 76; lectr, Humboldt State Univ Workshop, 86; assoc adj prof, Art Dept, Univ NMex, 94-; pub lect in Am & Eastern Europe (former USSR); lectr hist photog and contemp courses, Santa Fe Community Coll, 98-2002; lectr, master seminars US, eastern/central Europe, Russia, Asia; vis prof, British Higher Sch Art & Design, Moscow, 2006-07; lectr series, Libr Foreign Literature, Moscow, 2007; lectr, Nat Gallery of Art, Parkes Place, Canberra, Australia, 2013; lectr, Marriott Courtyard Conf Ctr, Russia, 2013. *Awards:* Photographers Fel, Nat Endowment for the Arts, 80; Guest Artist, Taramind Inst, Albuquerque, 88; Guest Artist, 20x24 Polaroid Camera Proj, 88; Sr Fulbright Scholars Award to USSR, 91 & Russ, 95, 2006-2007; Outstanding Alumni Achievement Award, Coll Fine & Performing Arts, Univ Nebr, Lincoln, 94. *Bibliog:* Steve Yates, History: The Birth of Modern Photography, Origins of Artistic & Documentary Style from Russia & America, ZOOM Photog Jour, MediaPUB Publ House & Editrice Progresso, Moscow, 7-8/2007; Idea Photographic: After Modernism, Santa Fe: Mus Fine Arts, Mus NMex, 2002; Poetics of Space, Hungarian ed, Typotex Publ, Hungarian Nat Fund, Budapest, 2009; Poeticas del Espacio, Barcelona: Editorial Gustavo Gili, FotoGGrafia, Spanish edit, 2002; Poetics of Space: A Critical Photographic Anthology, Albuquerque, Univ NMex Press, 1995; The Avant-Garde Document: Photographs by Aleksandras Macijauskas, Santa Fe: Mus Fine Arts, Mus NMex, 2001; Theatre of Memory, Photographic Installation Works by Laurent Millet, Santa Fe: Mus Fine Arts, Mus NMex, 1999; 4 + 4, Late Modern: Photography Between the Mediums, Santa Fe: Mus Fine Arts, Mus NMex, 94; Threads of Culture: Pinewood Collection of Farm Security Administration Photographs in New Mexico, 1939-43, Santa Fe: Mus Fine Arts, Mus NMex, 93; expanded edit, Far from Main Street, New Mexico Farm Security Administration (FSA), 94; Beaumont Newhall: Colleagues and Friends, Santa Fe: Mus Fine Arts, Mus NMex, 93; Proto Modern Photography, Santa Fe: Mus Fine Arts, Mus NMex, 92; Betty Hahn: Photography or Maybe Not (30-yr retrospective), Albuquerque: Univ NMex Press, 95; The Essential Landscape: The New Mexico Photographic Survey with Essays by JB Jackson, Albuquerque: Univ NMex Press, 85; Curator to Curator, Critical Role of Concept, Research and Collaborations, Mus Jour, Moscow, 2/2010; Photographic Diversity from Hungary: Global Lessons for the New Century Without East or West, Photographic Work of Gabor Kerekes, Hungarian Nat Mus Photog, 2012. *Media:* Photographic arts. *Res:* The photographic contributions of the avant-garde and first modern photographers during the early Soviet era (1917-1933); early and late modern photography into the 21st century; contemporary multimedia photographic arts after modernism; curatorial projects; in progress: Proto Modern Photography of the Russian Avant garde, Int traveling exhib & publ, in progress with Curatorial Assistance and; László Moholy-Nagy thematic retrospective, guest cur with Foundation for the exhibition of Photography and multilingual publication. *Collection:* individual photographic works from 69 to present; site-specific installations; black and white photomontages and collages with drawing, painting, and photograms; photographic installation works and digital color photographic works with drawing and painting. *Publ:* and many others

YAU, JOHN
WRITER, CURATOR
b Lynn, Mass, June 5, 1950. *Study:* Bard Col, BA, 69-72; Brooklyn Col, MFA, 76-78. *Pos:* Freelance writer, 77-; freelance cur, 82-; dir, Poetry Reading Series, Md Inst, Col Art; Pupl, Black Square Eds, 2000-. *Teaching:* Instr, Pratt Inst, 85-90 & Sch Visual Arts, NY, 88-90; vis writer, Brown Univ, 92; instr, Univ Berkeley, Calif, 93-94; Grad Art Dept Instr, Yale, 2003-. *Awards:* Chevalier in Order of Arts and Letters by Fr Govt; Peter S Reed Found Grant, 2002; NY Found for the Arts, Grant, 2003; Found for the Performance of Contemp Art, Grant, 2002-03. *Publ:* Auth, Giant Wall, Limestone Press, 91; Flee Advice, Collectif Generation, 91; Postcards from Trakl, Universal Ltd Art Eds, 92; Edificio Sayonara, Black Sparrow Press, 92; Genghis Chan: Private Eye, Art Inst Chicago, 93; ed, Four Walls Eight Windows, 98. *Mailing Add:* 1200 Broadway Apt 3C New York NY 10001-4316

YBARRA , MARIO, JR
INSTALLATION SCULPTOR
b Los Angeles, Calif, 1973. *Study:* Art Ctr Coll Art, Pasadena, CA, 1996; Otis Coll Art & Design, Los Angeles, BFA, 1999; Univ Calif, Irvine, MFA (Studio Art), 2001. *Exhib:* Solo exhibs include Art Basel Miami Beach, Art Positions, Miami, 2006, Anna Helwing Gallery, Los Angeles, 2007; Group exhibs include Democracy When?, Los Angeles Contemp Exhibs, Los Angeles, 2002, The Rebirth Wonder, 2003; 100 Artists See God, Contemp Art Ctr VA, Va Beach, 2005; 2006 Calif Biennial, Orange County Mus Art, Newport Beach, 2006; The World as a Stage, Tate Mod, London, 2007; Whitney Biennial, Whitney Mus Am Art, 2008. *Awards:* Creative Capital Found Grant, 2008

YEAGER, SYDNEY PHILEN
PAINTER, PRINTMAKER
b Lufkin, Tex, Feb 12,1945. *Study:* Univ Tex, Austin, BA, 67, BFA, 87, MFA, 87. *Work:* Belo Corp Collection & Barrett Collection, Dallas; Austin Mus Art & Samsung Corp Collection, Austin. *Exhib:* Dual Intention, Amarillo Art Mus, 94. *Pos:* Artist adv coun, women & Their Work, Austin, 93-95. *Awards:* Cultural Arts Grant, City of Austin, 90; Nat Endowment Arts Fel/Mid Am Arts Alliance, 96. *Bibliog:* Sandra Goldman (auth), Review New Art Examiner, 93; Mark Smith (auth), Review Art Lies, 98. *Mem:* Tex Fine Arts Asn. *Media:* Oil. *Dealer:* McMurtrey Gallery 3508 Lake St Houston TX 78705. *Mailing Add:* 1310 Ardenwood Austin TX 78722

YEDIDSION, MEIRA
PAINTER, INSTALLATION ARTIST
Study: Univ Fine Arts, Tehran, MFA, 72-76; Acad Fine Arts, Rome, Italy, MFA, 77-81. *Work:* Israel Mus, Jerusalem; Hebrew Union Col, Skirball Mus, Los Angeles; Mus Modern Art, NY; Detroit's Mus New Art, Mich; Fuller Mus, Brockton, Mass; Creative Flag, a cult official event of 2002 FIFA World Cup Korea/Japan, Seoul, Korea, 21st Century New Generation Artists Asn, Seoul Metrop Gov. *Comn:* Detroit Mus New Art; Fuller Mus Art. *Exhib:* Solo exhibs: Palazzo Valentini, Rome, Italy, 85; Nat Mus Villa Pisani, Stra, Venice, Italy, 96; Mus Palazzo Ducale, Isabella D'Este Apartment in Santa Croce, Mantua, Italy, 96; Suspended Room, Italian Cult Inst, Los Angeles, 1998; Ark of the Covenant, Bank of am Main, Beverly Hills, 2002-2007; Seville Universal Expo 92, Art Pavilion; Israel Mus, Jerusalem, 1992; Hebrew Union Coll Skirball Mus, Los Angeles, 96-97; Baltimore Mus Art, Baltimore, MD, 2002; Mus Fine Arts, Boston, 2002; Smith Cols, Mus Fine Art, Northampton, Mass, 2002; Walker Libr, Minneapolis, MN, 2002; Chicago Cult Center, 2002; Calif Inst Arts, Valencia, Calif, 2002; Univ Mass at Amherst Hampden Gallery, Amherst, 2002; Maine Coll Art, Portland, 2002; Int Flag Art Festival, 2002; Open 2003, Art & Cinema in Conjunction with the 60th Venice Film Festival, Venice Biennial, Italy, 2003; FIFA World Cup Korea/Japan, Seoul, Nanjicheon Park, Seoul; Zendai Mus Mod Art, Shanghai Intrude 366, Arch Cae, 2008; Boston Ctr Arts, 2002; Open Studio Press, Boston, 2002; Ft Collins Mus Art, Colo, 2002; Detroit Mus New Art, MONA, 2002; Hameenlinna Art Mus, Finland, 2002; Museo De La Ciudad, Mex, 2002; Mus Nat Ctr African Am Artists, Roxbury, 2002; Mus ChungHakDae, Korea, 2002; Southeast Mus, Brewster, New York, 2002; Inner Mongolia Mus Fine Arts, China, 2002; Foyer Gallery Gray Sch Art, Aberdeen, Scotland, 2002; List Art Ctr, Brown Univ, Providence, RI, 2002; Judy Saslow Gallery, Chicago, 2002; Barbara Krakow Gallery, Boston, 2002; Oskar Friedl Gallery, Chicago, 2002; Bernard Toale Gallery, Boston, 2002; Andreas Bumgartl Gallerie, Munich, 2002; Florence Lynch Gallery, New York, 2002; Art Ctr, Jamestown, NDak, 2002; North Eastern Northampton Univ, Bsoton, 2002; Univ Mass Boston, 2002; New England Sch Art & Design, Gallery 28, Boston, 2002. *Awards:* La Mimosa, Pres Regional Coun Rome & Lazio, Italy, 92; Sagra Del Mandorlo, City Province Region Agrigento, Italy, 93; Gold Medal Award, Intl Biographical Ctr, Cambridge, England, 2003; Woman of the Year (medal), Am Biog Inst, 2004; Proclamation of City of Los Angeles, award by Mayor Richard J Riordan & Councilman Michael Feuer, 98. *Bibliog:* RAI, Italian Nat State Television & Radio, Meira Yedidsion, 83-98; Costanzo Costantini (auth), Meira Yedidsion, Mus Palazzo Ducale Mantova, 96; One Thousand Greats-Meira Yedidsion, 2003; Great Lives of the 21st Century, Intl Biographical Ctr, Cambridge, England, 2003-2005; 2000 Outstanding Intellectuals of the 21st Century: Int Biog Ctr, Cambridge, Eng, 2004 & 2005 ed; Cambridge Blue Book of Foremost Int Intellectuals, Meira Yedidsion, Int Biog Ctr, 2008. *Media:* Oil, All Media, Multimedia, Installation Sculpture. *Publ:* Auth, Enrico Crispolti, Meira Yedidsion, Palazzo Valentini, 85; Achille Bonito Oliva, Giovanni Carandente, ARIE, 91-93; Laura Cherubini: Meira Yedidsion, Giancarlo Politi Editore, Flash Art, 92; Paolo Balmas, Meira Yedidsion, D'oro, 1993; Meira Yedidsión, Laura Cherubini (text), Fontanella Borghese Cult Ctr, 92; auth, Meira Yedidsion Flash Art, 92, 96, 98; auth, Poetry of the Winds, 2002; auth, Art & Cinema, Meira Yedidsion, 2003; Constanzo Costantini (text), Meira Yedidsion, catalogue of solo exhib, Palazzo Ducale of Mantova, 96

YEGUL, FIKRET KUTLU
EDUCATOR, ARCHITECT
b Themiscyra, Turkey, Oct 27, 1941. *Study:* Middle East Technical Univ, BA (archit), 64; Univ Pa, MA (archit), 66; Harvard Univ, PhD (art hist), 75. *Exhib:* Mamluk Architecture of Cairo (photographs), Fogg Art Mus, 74. *Teaching:* Asst prof art hist, Wellesley Col, 75-76; asst prof, Univ Calif, Santa Barbara, 76-82, assoc prof, 82-88, prof, 88-. *Awards:* Fulbright Fel, 64-66; Senior fel, CASVA, Nat Gallery Art, 85-86; Alice Davis Hitchock Award, 94. *Mem:* Sardis Archaeol Expedition; Am Inst Archaeol. *Res:* Roman art and architecture. *Publ:* Auth, A reconstruction study of Lucian's Baths of Hippias, Archaeol Classica, Vol 31, 79; Kaisersaal and the Imperial Cult, Art Bulletin, 3/82; Bath-Gymnasium Complex in Sardis (Report 3), Harvard Univ, 86; Gentlemen of Instinct & Breeding: Architecture at the American Academy in Rome 1894-1940, Oxford Univ, 91; Baths & Bathing in Classical Antiquity, Mass Inst Technol, 92. *Mailing Add:* Univ Calif Art Hist Dept Santa Barbara CA 93106

YEISER, CHARLES WILLIAM
PAINTER, ART DEALER
b Womelsdorf, Pa, Nov 20, 1925. *Study:* Kutztown State Teachers' Col, 43; Pratt Inst Art Sch, cert, 49; New York Univ, 49-51. *Work:* Westmoreland Mus Art, Greensburg, Pa; Southern Alleghenies Mus Art, Loretto, Pa; Tulpehocken Settlement Hist Soc, Womelsdorf, Pa. *Comn:* The Good Shepherd (panel), Dutch Reformed Church, West Nyack, NY, 60. *Exhib:* Bd Dirs Exhib, Hopper House, Nyack, NY, 76; The New Am Still Life, 80, Small Works for the Armchair Collector, 82 & Regional Artists Salute the Mus 25th Anniversary, 83, Westmoreland Mus Art, Greensburg, Pa; The Am Still Life Tradition 1955-1985, Montgomery Gallery, San Francisco, Calif; Recent Paintings, Westmoreland Mus Art, Greensburg, Pa, 86, O'Hara Gallery, NY, 93 & Owen Gallery, NY, 96. *Pos:* Asst dir, FAR Gallery, New York, 51-70, dir, 71-80. *Teaching:* Workshop, Rockland Ctr Arts, 94. *Awards:* First Prize Watercolor, Rahway Pub Libr, Rahway, NJ, 48. *Bibliog:* Martha B Scott (auth), Charles Yeiser: A painter of still life, Westmoreland Mus Art, 86; Muriel Hitzig (auth), Art works by Hopper House trustees, Rockland J News, 1/30/77; Nancy Cacioppo (auth), Realities, the Rockland Center for the Arts presents 8 area realists, Rockland J News, 3/14/93; Richard Gutwillig (auth), Artist captures the moment, Rockland J News, 1/30/96. *Mem:* Hopper House (bd dir, 75-78); Rockland Ctr Arts (bd dir), West Nyack, NY. *Media:* Oil on Canvas or Panel. *Mailing Add:* 11 Wheeler Pl West Nyack NY 10994

YEKTAI, MANOUCHER
PAINTER
b Tehran, Iran, Dec 22, 1922; US citizen. *Study:* Univ Tehran; Ecole Superior Beaux Arts, Paris, 45, 46 & 47; studied with Ozenfant in New York, 45-47; Art Students League, 47-48. *Work:* Baltimore Mus Art, Md; Mus Mod Art, NY; Everson Mus, Syracuse, NY; Hirshhorn Mus, Washington, DC; and others. *Exhib:* Solo exhibs, Grace Borgenicht Gallery, NY, 51-53; Robert Elkon Gallery, NY, 56; Poindexter Gallery, NY, 57-58, 61-62, 64; Felix Landau Gallery, Los Angeles, 59; Gumps, San Francisco, 59, 64; Piccadilly Gallery, London, 61, 69-70; Anderson-Meyer Gallery, Paris, 62; Feingarten Gallery, Chicago, 62; Semiha Huber Gallery, Zurich, 65; Gertrude Kasle Gallery, Detroit, 65-68 & 70; Benson Gallery, Bridgehampton, NY, 66, 72-73, 75, 84, 96 & 2004; USIS Teheran, Iran, 70; Teheran Galerie Zand, 77-78; Alex Rosenberg Gallery, NY, 81, 84 & 86; Watershed Yrs, Frumkin Gallery, NY, 74; Alex Rosenberg Gallery, NY, 86; NY Joseph Lubin Gallery, 85; Guild Hall Mus, East Hampton, NY, 88; and others. *Media:* Oil. *Publ:* Auth, Hooye Cagaxe Sfid, 94. *Mailing Add:* 225 W 86th St New York NY 10024

YENAWINE, PHILIP
EDUCATOR
b Athens, Ga, July 12, 1942. *Study:* Govern State Univ, BA, 77; Goddard Col, MA, 79. *Hon Degrees:* Doctorate of Fine Arts Honoris Causa, Kansas City Art Inst, 2003. *Pos:* Dir educ, Mus Contemp Art, Chicago, Ill, 77-78; dir, Aspen Art Mus, Colo, 78-82; curatorial consult, Aspen, Colo & Santa Fe, NMex, 82-83; dir educ, Mus Mod Art, NY, 83-93; vis cur, Inst Contemp Art, Boston, 92-94; partner, Development Through Art, NY & Cambridge, Mass, 94-97; co-dir, Visual Understanding in Educ (non-profit educ research orgn), Projects in Russ, Eastern Europe, Cent Asia & four US sites, 97-. *Teaching:* Vis fac, Univ Ill, Chicago, 76-77; vis prof, Mass Coll Art, 93-94; George A Miller vis scholar, Univ Ill, 96. *Awards:* Gov's Award, Prog People with Hearing Disabilities, Mus Mod Art, 84 & Visual Aids & Day Without Art, NY, 90; Mus Educ Yr, Eastern Div, 87 & Mus Educ Yr, 91, Nat Art Educ Asn; Distinguished Serv Award, Nat Art Educ Asn, 93. *Mem:* Mus Educ Consortium (chmn, 86-89). *Publ:* Auth, Looking Books: Colors; Lines; Shapes; Stories, Mus Mod Art & Abrams, 90; How to Look at Modern Art, Harry N Abrams, 90; Inheriting the theory: new voices and multiple perspectives on discipline based art education, Univ Tex, 90; Visual Thinking Strategies Starter Lessons, 98; Art Matters: How the Culture Wars Changed America, New York Univ Press, 99; plus others. *Mailing Add:* Box 677 Wellfleet MA 02667

YES, PHYLLIS A
PAINTER, SCULPTOR
b Red Wing, Minn, May 15, 1941. *Study:* Luther Coll, BA, 63; Univ Minn, MFA, 68; Univ Ore, PhD, 78. *Work:* Levi-Strauss, San Francisco; Microsoft Art Collection, Redmond & Seattle, Wash; Portland Art Mus; Security Pacific Nat Bank, Los Angeles; Univ Wash Med Ctr, Seattle; US Embassy, Addis Ababa, Ethiopia; Nat Pectin Co, Chicago; Lutheran Brotherhood Co, Minn; Whitwort Coll, Spokane, Wash; Banco de Brasil, Ceara, Brazil. *Comn:* many pvt collections. *Exhib:* Solo exhibs, Recent Work, John Edward Hughes Gallery, Dallas, 84, Tables, etc, Linda Rhodes Gallery, Winterpark, Fla, 84, Paintings and Lacquered Work, Elizabeth Leach Gallery, Portland, Ore, 84 & Nishiazabu Gallery, Tokyo, Japan, 93; Lace/War, Bernice Steinbaum Gallery, New York, 86; Northwest Biennial, Brooklyn Mus, New York, 86; mini retrospective, Seattle, Wash, 94; Tools & Flowers, Hanson-Howard Gallery, Ashland, Ore, 94; retrospective, Freed Gallery, Lincoln City, Ore, 95; Tool Show, Portland Inst for Contemp Art, Lewis-Clark, Lewiston, Idaho, 96. *Pos:* Juror of Nat, Regional Exhibs. *Teaching:* Asst prof, Ore State Univ, 76-79; prof, Lewis & Clark Coll, 79-, dean arts & humanities & chair, Art Dept. *Awards:* Barbara Deming Grant, 87; Distinguished Alumni Award, Luther Coll, Decorah, Iowa, 88, State of Ore, 95; Burlington Northern Achievement Award, 91. *Bibliog:* Focus: Phyllis Yes, NW Gallery Mag, fall 90; Paintings have grace of lace, Japan Times, 3/31/91; Phyllis Yes, Styling Mag, 7/91; and numerous other articles in nat periodicals. *Mem:* Artists Equity Asn; Coll Art Asn Am; Women's Caucus Arts; Contemp Arts Coun. *Media:* Acrylic, Mixed. *Interests:* mushroom hunting, sports, gardening. *Collection:* T and K Hensley Collection; Ore State Univ; Microsoft Coll; Banco do Brasil. *Publ:* Auth, History of lace, Art & Antiques Mag, 12/87. *Dealer:* Lee Freed Gallery Hwy 101 Lincoln City OR 97367; Lisa Harris Gallery, Seattle WA. *Mailing Add:* 23 SW Boundary St Portland OR 97239

YIADOM-BOAKYE, LYNETTE
PAINTER
b 1977, London, England. *Study:* Central St Martins Sch Art & Design, 1996-1997; Falmouth Col Art, 1997-2000; Royal Acad Sch, 2000-2003. *Work:* Kunsthalle Mannheim, Germany; Saatchi Collection, London; Studio Mus in Harlem, New York; Zabludowicz Collection, London; and others. *Exhib:* Solo exhibs include Prowler Proj Space, London, 2004, ARQUEBUSE, Geneva, 2007, Gasworks, London, 2007, Faye Fleming & Partner, Geneva, 2009, Michael Stevenson Gallery, Cape Town, 2009, 2010, Armory Show, New York, 2010, Jack Shainman Gallery, New York, 2010, 2012, Studio Mus in Harlem, New York, 2010, Corvi-Mora, London, 2011, 2013, Utah Mus Fine Arts, Salt Lake City, Utah, 2012, Chisenhale Gallery, London, 2012, Pinchuk Art Ctr, Kiev, Ukraine, 2013; Group exhibs, Blackout, Brixton Art Gallery, London, 2001; Work Ethic, Gone Tomorrow Gallery, London, 2003; John Moores 23, Liverpool Biennal, 2004; 100 Years Kunsthalle, Kunsthalle Mannheim, 2007; Flow, Studio Mus in Harlem, New York, 2008; Newspeak, Saatchi Gallery, London, 2010; Biennale de Lyon, France, 2011; The Ungovernables, New Mus, NY, 2012; Restless: Recent Acquisitions fromt he MAM Collection, Miami Art Mus, Fla, 2012; Breadbox, ZieherSmith at the Icon, Nashville, Tenn, 2012; A World Away, Dyrham Park, Gloucheстershire, UK, 2012; Prose/Re-Prose: Figurative Works Then and Now, SCAD Mus Art, Savannah, 2012; Future Generation Art Prize Exhib, Pinchuk Art Ctr, Kiev, Ukraine, 2013; Fiction as Fiction, Stevenson Gallery, Capetown, 2013; The Progress of Love, Menil Coll, Houston, 2013; 55th Int Art Exhib Biennale, Venice, 2013. *Awards:* deciBel Award for Visual Arts, 2006; Arts Found Awards for Painting, 2006. *Bibliog:* Adrian Searle (auth), Picture Perfect, The Guardian 2004; Sally O'Reilly, Lynette Yiadom-Boakye, Gasworks, Time Out, 2007; Chika Okeke-Agulu, Arise Mag, 2009; Newspeak, British Art Now, Booth-Clibborn Editions, 2010; Okwui Enwezor (auth), Lynette Yiadom-Boakye, Studio Mus in Harlem, 2010. *Mailing Add:* 513 W 20th St New York NY 10011

YODER, JANICA
PHOTOGRAPHER, EDUCATOR
b Milwaukee, Wis, June 21, 1950. *Study:* Univ Wis, Madison, BS (art), 74, MA (photog), 76, MFA (photog), 77. *Work:* Corcoran Gallery, Washington, DC; J Paul Getty Mus, Malibu, Calif; Madison Art Ctr, Wis; Milwaukee Art Mus, Wis. *Exhib:* Solo exhibs, Michael H Lord Gallery, Milwaukee, 91 & 94, New Work, The Pain Mus, Oshkosh, Wis, 92-93, Honolulu Acad Art, 93, Contemp Art Mus, Honolulu, Hawaii, 95, Wis Acad Gallery, Wis Acad Arts & Scis, Madison, 97; Woman Photographers, Corcoran Gallery Art, Washington, DC, 82; Multiple Exposure: 5 Contemp Photogrs, Milwaukee Art Mus, Wis, 88; A Decade of Exhibitions, Madison Art Ctr, Wis, 90; Recent Acquisitions in Photog, Corcoran Gallery Art, Washington, DC, 83, 86 & 90; May 1992, Betsy Rosenfield Gallery, Chicago Int Art Expo, 92; Color Photog Invitational, Crossman Gallery, Univ Wis, Whitewater, 92; The Wisconsin Triennial, Madison Art Ctr, 93 & 96; Regarding Beauty, Halsey Gallery, Sch Arts, Coll Charleston, SC, 93; Highlights from the Permanent Collection, Madison Art Ctr, Wis, 94; Gallery Artists, Michael Lord Gallery, Milwaukee, Wis, 98. *Teaching:* Instr photog, Int Ctr Photog, New York, 78-80; asst prof, Herron Sch Art-Ind Univ, 80-86; instr, Milwaukee Inst Art & Design, 89-; lectr, Madison Art Ctr, Wis, 96; guest lectr photog, Milwaukee, Wis, 97; vis lectr, art dept, Waukesha, Wis, 97. *Bibliog:* Popular Photog, winter 78; AfterImage, spring 79; Photography Ann, Popular Photography, 86. *Media:* Color and black & white photography. *Mailing Add:* c/o Tory Folliard Gallery 233 N Milwaukee St Milwaukee WI 53202

YODER, ROBERT EDWARD
ARTIST
b Danville, Va, May 22, 1962. *Study:* James Madison Univ, BFA, 84; Univ Washington, Seattle, MFA, 87. *Work:* Mus of Fine Arts, Houston; Seattle Tacoma Int Airport, WA; Microsoft, Redmond, WA; City of Seattle Pub Art Collection. *Comn:* Four Paintings, Portland Bureau of Gen Service, 2000; Integrated Installation, Seahawks Stadium, Seattle, 2000. *Exhib:* New Am Talent, Centerspace, Austin, 2001; The End, Tacoma Art Mus, 99; Material Process and Object, Univ Idaho, 2000. *Awards:* Pollack Krasner, Pollock Krasner Found, 2001; Artists Trust Fel, Artist Trust, 2000. *Bibliog:* Rhonda Lane Howard, Holly A. Getch Clarke, (auth), Abfall (essays), Thread for Art. *Media:* Mixed Media Painting, Collage. *Publ:* Fionn Meade, Courting the Off Modern, FISURA, 2002; Joyce Korotkin, Yoder, Kurten and Greenfield, NY Arts, 2002. *Dealer:* Charles Cowles Gallery Inc 537 W 24th St NY 10011; Howard House 2017 2nd Ave Seattle WA 98121. *Mailing Add:* 1222 NE Ravenna Blvd Seattle WA 98105

YORDANOV, PLAMEN
INSTALLATION SCULPTOR
b Assenovo, Bulgaria, 1961. *Study:* Sts Cyril & Methodius Univ, Turnovo, Bulgaria, Certs (Dept Fine Arts), 1982-1985; Nat Accad Fine Arts (Dept Painting), Sofia Bulgaria, MFA, 1985-1990; Vermont Studio Ctr, 1992; Ratti Foundation, Como, Italy (advan course Visual Arts), with Prof Joseph Kosuth, Cert, 1995; Int Summer Accad Fine Arts, Salzburg, Austria, with Prof Agnes Denes, Cert, 1997. *Work:* Microsoft Corp, Chicago, Ill; Queens Mus Art, New York, NY; San Fernando Mus, Madrid,

Spain; Nat Palace Cult, Sofia, Bulgaria; The Nat Art Mus China. *Comn:* Suite Home Chicago (Pub Art furniture set), Microsoft Corp, Chicago, Ill, 2001; Village Orland Park, Orland Park, Ill, 2008; Scenes of Chicago Ave (12x24 mural), West Town, Chicago, 2008; Green Office Challenge Awards, Local Governments for Sustainability, 2010; Guggenheim Partners, 2011. *Exhib:* Installations & Assemblages, Nat Palace of Cult, Sofia, Bulgaria, 1994; VideoHart, project by Soros Ctr Arts, Nat Archeol Mus, Sofia, Bulgaria, 1995; T E S '95, 4th European Sculpture Triennial, Paris, France, 1995; Located Work (project by Joseph Kosuth), Antonio Ratti Foundation, Como, Italy, 1995; Stedelijk Mus Hof Van Busleyden, Meechelen, Belgien, 1997; Recent Paintings & Paper Works, Ill Inst Art, Chicago, Ill, 2000; Peace Tower (project by Mark di Suvero), Chicago Cult Ctr, Chicago, Ill, 2007; Beyond Borders, Richard J Daley Ctr, Chicago, Ill, 2007-2009; Chicago Art Ctr, 2008, 2009, 2010, Mus Mod Art, New York, 2008, Art Inst Chicago, 2009; Architrouve Gallery, Chicago, 2009; Design It: Shelter Competition, Guggenheim Mus, New York, 2009; Manifest Creative Res Gallery & Drawing Ctr, Cincinnati, Ohio, 2009; Arts Horizons LeRoy Neiman Art Ctr, New York, 2009; Immigration Journeys Jukebox Project, Queens Mus Art, New York, 2009; South London Gallery, London, 2009; 4th Beijing Int Art Biennale, Nat Art Mus China, 2010; Mus Mod Art Chicago, 2010; RE: Contemplating the Void, Guggenheim Mus, New York, 2010; Mass Mus Contemp Art, North Adams, Ma, 2011; Kyoto Municipal Mus, Kyoto, 2011; Kic Kunst in Der Carl Skutte, Budelsdorf, Germany, 2011; 4th Moscow Biennale Contemp Art, Parallel Program, Moscow, Russia, 2011; Daley Ctr, Chgo, 2011; Siena Art Institute, Siena, Italy, 2011; Cheim & Read Gallery, NY, 2012; ARC Gallery, Chicago, 2012; Olson Gallery, DeKalb, Ill, 2012; Visions of Death, Queens Mus Art, NY, 2012; Sikkema Jenkins & Co, NY, 2012; Personal Structures, 55th Venice Biennale, Italy, 2013. *Pos:* Founder & Art Dir, Chicago Art Ctr, 2007-; Founder, Art Dir, Mus Mod Art, Chicago, 2008. *Awards:* Hon Mention, 3rd Int Competition Drawing, Ell Ferrol, Spain, 1989; Dipl, 2nd place pub & jury, 5th Int Woodcarving Symposium, Brienz, Switz, 1998; Guggenheim Partners Sculpture award, 2011. *Bibliog:* Aleksander Stanev (auth), Drawing: Some Methodical & Creative Processes in the Nat Accad Fine Arts, Sofia Press, Sofia, Bulgaria, 1992; Svilen Stefanov (auth), Balance of the Eclectic Time, Duma Nat Newspaper, #30, 1994; Svilen Stefanov (auth), Plastic Image of the 90's, Art in Bulgaria Mag, #32, 1997; Dimiter Nedev (auth), Voyage: Plamen Yordanov, Artec N1 Gallery, Mannheim, Ger, 1998; The 4th Beijing Int Art Biennale, China. *Media:* All Media. *Dealer:* Chicago Art Center. *Mailing Add:* 6540 N Washtenaw Ave Chicago IL 60645

YORK, SUSAN
INSTALLATION SCULPTOR
b Newport RI. *Study:* Cranbrook Acad Art, Mich, MFA, 1995. *Work:* Lannan Found; Panza Collection, Switzerland; Mus Fine Arts New Mex. *Exhib:* Solo exhibs include van de Griff Gallery, Santa Fe, NMex, 1999, Braunstein/Quay Gallery, San Francisco, 2000, 2005, Klaudia Marr Gallery, Santa Fe, NMex, 2003, Exhib 2d, Marfa, Tex, 2006, 2007, Lannan Found, Santa Fe, NMex, 2008; Group exhibs include Color/Form/Texture, Freehand Gallery, Los Angeles, 1988; CCA Invitational, Ctr Contemp Arts, Santa Fe, NMex, 1989; Golden Mean Constructions, Janus Gallery, Santa Fe, NMex, 1992; Silicate, Baltimore Works, Baltimore, 2001; Rendezvous, Mus Nebr Art, 2002; Steel Girrrls, Jonson Gallery, Albuquerque, NMex, 2002; Minimal, The Clay Studio, Philadelphia, 2004; Dorsky Projects, Long Island City, New York, 2008. *Teaching:* Asst Prof, Sculpture, Coll Santa Fe, NMex, 1998-Present. *Awards:* Fulbright Fel, Finalist, 1996; Joan Mitchell Found Grant, 2007

YOST, ERMA MARTIN
FIBER ARTIST, INSTRUCTOR
b Goshen, Ind, Jan 12, 1947. *Study:* James Madison Univ, Harrisonburg, Va, BA (art educ), 69, MA (painting), 75. *Work:* Pace Univ Art Mus & Am Craft Mus, NY; James Madison Univ, Va; East Tenn State Univ, Johnson City; Bethel Col, North Newton, Kans; Bristol-Meyers Squibb, Princeton, NJ; Mus Art & Design, New York; Va Art Inst, Charlottesville, Va; Goshen Coll, Goshen, Ind. *Comn:* Painting & quilt assemblage, Rockingham Mem Hosp, Harrisonburg, Va, 82 & Philhaven Hosp, Mt Gretna, Pa, 85, Chicopee, Inc, New Brunswick, NJ, 90. *Exhib:* Solo exhibs, Noho Gallery, NY, 75-2013 & Int Embroidery Exhib, Japan (6 cities), 94; Desert Images, Jersey City Mus, NJ, 79; Invitational, Southwestern Exposure, Gayle Willson Gallery, Southampton, NY, 89; Contemp Quilts, Perimeter Gallery, Chicago, Ill, 89; New Jersey Arts Ann, NJ State Mus, Trenton, 92, 96 & 97; New Acquisitions, Am Craft Mus, NY, 94 & 9 x 3 x 9, 98; Invention & Diversity, Trenton City Mus, NJ, 98; and others; Art of the State, State Mus Pa, 2009, 2012. *Pos:* Illusr, Simplicity Pattern Co, NY, 72-73; Greer fine arts endowment vis artist, Bethel Col, Kans, 91; exchange teacher, Abbotsleigh Sch, NSW, Australia, 93. *Teaching:* Instr art, Eastern Mennonite Univ, 69-70; instr art, Spence Sch, 77-2000 & St Peter's Prep Sch, 2002-08. *Awards:* NJ State Coun Arts Fel, 92 & 99. *Bibliog:* Jean Ray Laury (auth), Imagery on Fabric, ed No 1, C & T Publ, 92 & ed No 2, 97; The Surface Designer's Art, Lark Books, 93; Robert Shaw (auth), The Art Quilt, Levin Assoc, 97; Object Lessons, The Guild, 2001. *Mem:* Textile Study Group of New York; Pro Arts; Ind Sch Art Instr Asn (co-pres, 96-98); Am Crafts Coun; CALC (bd dirs); Surface Design Asn. *Media:* Fiber, Stitched Construction, Felt. *Dealer:* Noho Gallery Inc 530 W 25th St New York NY 10001. *Mailing Add:* 274 Belvedere Carlisle PA 17013

YOST, LEON C
PHOTOGRAPHER
b Atglen, Pa, July 7, 1943. *Study:* Eastern Mennonite Univ, 63-65; Pace Univ, 72-77. *Work:* Pace Univ, NY; Cenlar Corp, NJ; E Tenn State Univ; Goshen Coll, Ind; Chikapee Corp, Princeton, NJ. *Exhib:* Solo exhibs, Noho Gallery, NY, 77, 83, 85, 87, 90, 92, 95, 97, 2000, 2002, 2006, & 2009 CEU Prehistoric Mus, Price, Utah, 95 & San Diego Mus Man, 97; Fel Exhib, Monmouth Mus, NJ, 88; NJ Arts Ann, NJ State Mus, 89. *Pos:* Mem bd, Printmaking Coun NJ, 88-89; mem, Artist's Certification Bd, Jersey City, NJ, 96-2006; mem adv comt, Jersey City Mus, 2000. *Awards:* Fel, NJ State Coun Arts, 86. *Bibliog:* Peter Fingesten (auth), article, Arts Mag, 2/83; Vivian Raynor (auth), review, New York Times, 12/9/89; Ed McCormack (auth), Leon Yost's Stunning Images from the Outback, Artspeak, 1/95. *Mem:* Am Rock Art Res Asn; Australian Rock Art Res Asn; Utah Rock Art Res Asn. *Publ:* Contribr, The depiction of sexuality in art, from premodern awe to postmodern envy, The World I, 1/93 & Art and Intimacy, Univ Wash Press, 2000; coauth, Changing Jersey City: A History in Photographs, Schiffer, 2009. *Dealer:* Noho Gallery 530 W 25th St New York NY 10001. *Mailing Add:* 274 Belvedere St Carlisle PA 17013

YOUDELMAN, NANCY
SCULPTOR
b New York, New York, 1948. *Study:* Calif Inst Arts, BFA, 1973; Univ Calif, Los Angeles, MFA, 1976. *Exhib:* Solo exhibs include Grandview Gallery, Los Angeles, 1974, Loyola Marymount Univ, Westchester, Calif, 1981, Fresno Art Mus, Calif, 1994, Gallery 25, Fresno, Calif, 2006, Mohr Art Gallery Finn Ctr, Mountain View, Calif, 2006, 8 Mod, Santa Fe, NMex, 2008; group exhibs include Assemblage & Collage, Los Angeles Inst Contemp Art, Century City, Calif, 1975; 500 Years Since Columbus, Triton Art Mus, Santa Clara, Calif, 1992; 4 Generations of Armenian Artists, Fresno Art Mus, Calif, 2002; Assemblage, Merced Art Ctr, Merced, Calif, 2005; Where Truth Lies, Anne Reed Gallery, Ketchum, Idaho, 2006; Exquisite Acts & Everyday Rebellions, Calif Inst Arts, Valencia, 2007; Calif Sculpture, San Francisco Mus Mod Art Gallery, 2007. *Awards:* Pollock-Krasner Found Grant, 2005; Gottlieb Found Grant, 2007. *Dealer:* SFMOMA Artists Gallery Fort Mason Building A San Francisco CA 94123. *Mailing Add:* Eight Modern 231 Delgado St Santa Fe NM 87501

YOUENS, RACHEL P
PAINTER
Study: Oxbow Sch Painting, 1980; Sch Art Inst Chicago, BFA, 1980; Brooklyn Coll, NY, MFA, 1993. *Exhib:* Solo exhibs include Verso Books, New York, 1996; two-person exhibs include Sideshow Gallery, Brooklyn, (with Victor Pesce), 2006; three-person exhibs include Gallerythe.com, Brooklyn, NY, (with Daphne Cummings & Susan Hamburger) 2005, Theater Actors Inst, New York, (with Karen Schmauk & Wendy Waxman), 1994; group exhibs include UNScene, ARC Gallery, Chicago, 1987; Found Fac Exhib, Pratt Inst, Brooklyn, NY, 2003; Zeuxis at LIU, Long Island Univ Gallery, Brooklyn, NY, 2003; MERRY PEACE, Sideshow Gallery, Brooklyn, NY, 2003, 2004, War is Over, 2004; Annual Benefit, Kentler Int Drawing Space, Brooklyn, NY, 2004; Facets, Snug Harbor Cultural Ctr, Staten Island, NY, 2006. *Pos:* Artist in residence, Ragdale Found, Winnetka, Ill, 1989. *Teaching:* Assoc adj prof, St Francis Coll, Brooklyn, 1997-2003, vis lectr, 2001; vis lectr, New Sch Social Res, New York, 1997, CAA, 2005; adj asst prof, City Coll Technology, Brooklyn, 2003-2006, LaGuardia Community Coll, Queens, 2007; adj prof, Parsons Sch Art & Design, New York, 2002-07. *Awards:* Chicago Neighborhood Coalition, 1985; Charles H Shaw Mem Award for Painting, Brooklyn Coll, 1991 & 1992; Pollock-Krasner Found Grant, 2004; John Simon Guggenheim Mem Found Fel, 2008

YOUKELES, ANNE
PAINTER, PRINTMAKER
b Bad Ischl, Austria; US citizen. *Study:* Kunstgewerbeschule Vienna, Austria; Acad de la Grande Chaumiere, Paris; Ohio State Univ; painting with Alexander Dobkin & Rudolf Baranik; printmaking with Sidney Chafetz & Carol Summers. *Work:* Philadelphia Mus Art; Rosenwald Collection, Smithsonian Inst; Bibliotheque Nat, Paris; Lehman Collection; Atlantic Richfield Co; DeCordova Mus, Lincoln, Mass; Minneapolis Mus Art. *Comn:* Editions of prints, Int Graphic Arts Soc, 72, Jewish Mus, 73 & Print Club, Philadelphia, 75; acrylic triptych, Guaranty Bank, Milwaukee, 79. *Exhib:* Ann Print Exhibs, Brooklyn Mus, 70 & 72; Art Today USA II, Mod Art Mus, Tehran, Iran, 77; one-person shows, Marion Locks Gallery, Philadelphia, 73 & 77, Dubins Gallery, Los Angeles, 78 & 80, Posner Gallery, Milwaukee, 79, 84 & 86; Benjamin Mangel Gallery, Philadelphia, 82 & 86; and others. *Awards:* Purchase Prizes, Pratt Miniature Show, Boston Printmakers Ann & Philadelphia Print Club. *Bibliog:* Gabor Peterdi (auth), Printmaking, Macmillan Publ Co, New York, 72; Ross & Romano (auths), Techniques in Printmaking, 74. *Mem:* Soc Am Graphic Artists; Boston Printmakers; Silvermine Guild Artists; Am Colorprint Soc; Print Club, Philadelphia. *Media:* Acrylic, Work in Handmade Paper. *Mailing Add:* 118 Del Pond Dr Canton MA 02021-2748

YOUNG, ANDREW
PAINTER
b Mt Kisco, NY, Nov 23, 1962. *Study:* Univ Calif, Berkeley, BA, 87; Sch Art Inst Chicago, MFA, 89. *Work:* Arthur Anderson & Co, Detroit, Mich; Ill State Mus, Springfield; Jones, Day, Revas & Poge, Los Angeles; Proskauer, Rose, Goetz & Mendelsohn, NY; Prudential Insurance Co, Newark, NJ. *Comn:* Harbor (triptych), McKinsey & Co Inc, NY. *Exhib:* Solo Exhibs, Betsy Rosenfield Gallery, Chicago, 90 & 92, Chicago Int Art Expo, Ill, 90, David Beitzel Gallery, NY, 91 & 92, Dorothy Goldeen Gallery, Santa Monica, Calif, 91en Gallery, Santa Monica, Calif, 91; two-person exhib, Bilder uber dem Wasser (traveled), USIS, Bonn, Ger, 91-92; four-artists show, Haines Gallery, San Francisco, Calif, 92; Paper Houses, David Beitzel Gallery, NY, 92; Betsy Rosenfield Gallery, Chicago, Ill, 92; Art Fair/Seattle, Betsy Rosenfield Gallery, 92; and others. *Awards:* Maybelle M Toombs Prize, Univ Calif, Berkeley, 86-87; Competitive Scholar, 87-89 & Fred J Forster Fel, 90, Sch Art Inst Chicago; Community Arts Assistance Grant, Chicago Office Fine Arts, 91. *Bibliog:* Justin Spring (auth), Andrew Young, ArtForum, 11/91; Eileen Myles (auth), Andrew Young at David Beitzel, Art Am, 12/91; Amerikanische Kunstler in Koln, Deutsche Welle PBS/Europ J, 12/30/91. *Media:* Egg Tempera on Panel

YOUNG, BARBARA
PHOTOGRAPHER
b Chicago, Ill, Oct 27, 1920. *Study:* Knox Coll, Galesburg, Ill, AB, 42; Johns Hopkins Univ Med Sch, MD, 45; Baltimore Psychoanal Inst, grad, 55. *Work:* Mus Mod Art, New York; Baltimore Mus Art; Eastman House, Rochester, NY; Santa Barbara Mus Art, Calif; Yale Univ Gallery; Johns Hopkins Sch Medicine, Nelson/Harvey Bldg.

Exhib: solo exhibs, Butler Inst Am Art, Youngstown, Ohio, 74, Santa Barbara Mus Art, Calif, 78; 2nd Generation Pioneers: Blance DeBra & Harvey Young, Baltimore Mus Art, 76 & Timberlane, A Sculpture Garden, 77; Am Vision, Nat Artists Alliance, New York Univ Galleries, 79; Maryland Artscape, 86; retrospective, The Passage of Time, Univ Md, Baltimore Co, 87 & Coll Notre Dame, Baltimore, 96; Francoise Gallery, Baltimore, 94; A Photographer's Vision: Gifts to the Collection from Barbara Young, Baltimore Mus Art, 96; Paradoxes of Modernism, Univ Md Baltimore County, 2008. *Awards:* First Prize, Nat Artists Alliance, 79; First Prize, Md Mag, 12/82. *Publ:* Auth, Our garden in the city, Horticulture, 70; Hunting for the ostrich, Hasselblad, Mag, 71; Getting acquainted with Maine, Am Forests Mag, 72; The Coleman's vegetable garden at Cape Rosier, Downeast Mag, 75; The Plop-A-Lop Tree, photographic study of a Bahama Community, 93; Tales of Courage: Recovering Life After Catastrophe Articles, 2003; Mamma and Me, The Awakenings Review, an Outreach Program for People with Psychiatric Disabilities, Univ Chicago, 2003; Yale J Humanities Med; Virginia Woolf: Her Cries of Joy and Longing, 2003; Perspectives in Biology and Medicine: Vignettes from Medical school during the war, 2002, Vignettes from Psychiatric training, 2004, A Psychiatrist's life & the emerging of her creative eye, 2005 & Building blocks that make a doctor, 2006; Efficacy of Psychoanalysis and the analytic therapies, J Acad Psychoanalysis & Dynamic Psychiatry, 2006; Integrative Power of the Creative Spirit, Psychoanalytic Inquiry; The Persona of Ingmar Bergman: Conquering Demons Through Film, 2015. *Dealer:* Princess Street Gallery Harbour Island Bahamas. *Mailing Add:* 5307 Herring Run Dr Baltimore MD 21214

YOUNG, BARBARA NEIL
LIBRARIAN, CURATOR

b Bristol, Va, July 18, 1943. *Study:* Fla State Univ, Tallahassee, BA, 65; Drexel Univ, Philadelphia, MLS, 75. *Exhib:* Sabores y Lenguas: Miralda-Food Cult Mus, Miami, 2006. *Collection Arranged:* Books & Pages, South Florida Artists Books, 87; Purvis Young, Me and My People, (with Cesar Trasobares), 89; Miami Thriving in Change/Fifty Years of Photography, 90; Miami Thriving in Change 1940-1990/Fifty Years of Collecting, 90; Narratives from the Diaspora, Willie Birch, Kabuya Pamela Bowens, Gary Moore, 90; Flora and Fauna in Illustration, 91; Miami/Clay/5, 92; Something About Libraries (3" x 5"), 94; Becalmed in Miami, South Florida Artists Made Boats, 95; Drums of Steel, 96; 100 Years of Architecture, 96; The Artful Book, 98; Touched by AIDS (with Helen Kohen & Margarita Cano), 98; A Declaration of Place African Influences in Vernacular Architecture of South FL, 2002; Young at Sixty: Paintings, Drawings & Artist's books by Purvis Young, 2003; Dog Tales: Words & Images, Fact & Fiction from Miami Artists & Collectors, 2009; pvt collections, Ruth & Richard Shack & Margarita Cano. *Pos:* Artmobile librn, Miami-Dade Pub Libr, Fla, 76-81, art & music reference librn, 81-85 & art serv coordr, 85-2005; Vasari Project Coord 2000-2005. *Mem:* Art Table. *Res:* Afro-American, Hispanic and South Florida artists Library System, Fla Assoc Newsletter, 77. *Mailing Add:* 7231 SW 61st St Miami FL 33143

YOUNG, CHARLES E
ADMINISTRATOR, MUSEUM DIRECTOR

b Highland, Calif. *Study:* Univ Calif, Riverside, BA (political sci), 1955; Univ Calif, Los Angeles, MA, 1957, PhD, 1960. *Pos:* chancellor, UCLA, 1968-1997; pres, Univ Fla, 1999-2008 & Qatar Found, 2004-2006; chief exec officer, Los Angeles Mus Contemp Art, 2008-; bd mem, Intel Corp, Nicholas-Applegate Capital Mgmt, Acad TV Arts & Sci Found, Los Angeles World Affairs Coun. *Mem:* Assn Am Univ (former chmn); Nat Assn State Univ & Land Grant Coll; Am Coun on Educ. *Mailing Add:* Museum of Contemporary Art 250 S Grand Ave Los Angeles CA 90012

YOUNG, CYNTHIA M
PAINTER

b Ravenna, Ohio, May 20, 1933. *Study:* RI Sch Design, 54; Corcoran Sch Art, with G Davis & Leon Berkowitz, 78-79; Conn Coll Women, BA, 55; Univ Hawaii, 75; George Washington Univ, MFA, 79. *Work:* Gibbes Art Mus, Charleston, SC; Gettysburg Col, Gettysburg, Pa; Nat Park Serv, DC Superior Court, George Washington Univ, Washington, DC; DC Superior Court, Washington, DC; Kass Skallet Law Firm, Washington, DC. *Comn:* Abstr & oil painting, Overseas Priv Investment Corp, Washington, DC, 89; watercolor renderings (of proposed structure), Northern Va Sci Ctr, 95. *Exhib:* At the Crosshairs, Westbeth Gallery, NY, 91; Water: A Group Show of Five Washington Artists, Mahler Gallery, Washington, DC, 92; National Works on Paper, Marsh Gallery, Richmond, Va, 93; For the Love of Children, Mus Americas, OAS, Washington, DC, 94; Global Focus 4th Ann World Conf, Women in Art & Cult, Beijing, China & Nat Mus Women Arts, Washington, 95; solo exhibs, Archaic Mirrors, McLean Project for the Arts, McLean, Va, 2001, Grid Scapes, 2002, Tidepools, 2004, & Sun & Shadows, 2008, Touchstone Gallery, Washington, DC & Meditations on Nature, Ozmosis Gallery, Bethesda, Md, 2004. *Pos:* Bd, Artist Equity, DC Chap, 89-91; Vpres, Touchtone Gallery, 93, bd, 93-96. *Teaching:* Adj fac drawing & watercolor, Northern Va Community Col, 79-94. *Awards:* Award of Merit, Ninth Ann Artist Equity Exhib; David Lloyd Kreeger First Prize for Painting, Grad Awards Show, 79; Fel, Va Ctr for the Creative Arts, Sweet Briar, Va, 81. *Bibliog:* Linda Joyce (auth), Memories of La Napoule, Freelance Star, 91; Michael Welzenbach (auth), Water paintings at Mahler, Washington Post, 92; Bill Dunlop (auth), Around Town, WETA CPBS, 2/5/95. *Mem:* Artists Equity, Washington, DC; Coll Art Asn. *Media:* Oil, Mixed Media. *Specialty:* Contemporary art. *Interests:* Opera, theater, literature. *Collection:* McGraw Hill Publishing. *Publ:* A French connection, Washington Artist News, 90. *Dealer:* Touchstone Gallery 901 New York Ave NW Washington DC. *Mailing Add:* 6903 Southridge Dr Mc Lean VA 22101

YOUNG, JANIE CHESTER
MUSEUM DIRECTOR, EDUCATOR

b Port Huron, Mich, Apr 19, 1949. *Study:* Univ Mich, BA (Eng lit & art hist), 71, MA (mus practice), 75; Toledo Mus Art, Nettie Poe Ketcham Fel Mus Educ, 72-73. *Collection Arranged:* Art, Ann Arbor, 71; Decorative Arts of New Brunswick, 76 & What's It To You? (auth, catalog for children), 77, Rutgers Univ Art Gallery; Patrick Thibert: Young Canadian Sculpture, 77, Young New York Painting, 79 & Helen Frankenthaler: The Artist in three Media, Saginaw Art Mus; The Queen's Choice: Burmese, 1885-1985, (auth, catalog) New Bedford Glass Mus. *Pos:* Fel coordr, Toledo Mus Art, Ohio, 73-75; cur educ, Rutgers Univ Art Gallery, 75-77; dir, Saginaw Art Mus, Mich, 77- & New Bedford Glass Mus, Mass, 82-. *Teaching:* Instr mus arts & educ, Grad Sch Educ, Rutgers Univ, New Brunswick, NJ, 76; Pairpoint Cup Plate Collector's Am, 85; Nat Early Am Glass Club, 86. *Mem:* Nat Early Am Glass Club, 82-; Glass Asn (G B), 88-. *Res:* First interdisciplinary, professional bibliography of museum education; 19th century American and English art glass. *Publ:* Auth, An Annotated Bibliography of Museum Education, Univ Mich Mis Pract Prog, 75; Evolution of Burnage Glass, Bull, Nat Early Am Glass Club, spring 89. *Mailing Add:* 8 W Seminary St Brandon VT 05733-1159

YOUNG, KENNETH VICTOR
PAINTER, DESIGNER

b Louisville, Ky, Dec 12, 1933. *Study:* Ind Univ; Univ Louisville, BS (design, painting & humanities), 62; Art Workshop, Assis, Italy 2000; Studied at George Washington Univ. *Work:* Corcoran Gallery Art, Washington, DC; Va Nat Bank, Alexandria; Johnson Publ Co, Chicago; Am Tel & Tel, NY; Fisk Univ, Nashville; Univ of Louisville, KY; Univ District of Columbia, Washington. *Comn:* DC Com of Art & Humanity. *Exhib:* Solo exhibs, Univ of Louisville, Ky, 60-63, 85, Bellarmine Col, Louisville, Ky, 63, Frame House Gallery, Louisville, 63, Franz Bader Gallery, Washington, DC, 68-71, 75, AM Saks Gallery, New York City, 72, Studio Gallery, Washington, Ed, 72-74, Fisk Univ, Nashville, Tenn, 73, Corcoran Gallery Art, Washington, DC, 74, St Mary's Col, Md, 76, Gallery K, DC, 78, 79, 84, 88 & 91, Grimaldis Gallery, Balt, 78, C Grimaldis Gallery, Baltimore, 80, Owensboro Mus, Ky, 83, & Howard Univ, Washington, DC, 86; Inst Contemp Arts, Washington, DC, 67; Baltimore Mus, 69; Indianapolis Mus, 72; Corcoran Gallery Art, 74; Black Artist from the South, Huntsville Mus, Ala, 79; Gallery K Washington, DC, 79-89, 99 & 2001; Owensboro Mus, Kent, 84; African Am Exhib, Gibellina Museo Civico D'Arte Contemporanea, Italy, Washington, DC, 90; Gallery K, 92, 94, 95; Roads to Liberty: Bicentennial on Constitution, Africans-Am Mus Asn; Group Show: Perish Gallery, 2005; Parish Gallery, 2012; Mus Am Art, Smithsonian, 2012. *Collection Arranged:* Music Machines, Hall of Graphic Arts, Women & Politics, Gandhi Centennial Exhib, Explorers NZ, Black Wings traveling exhib & Egyptian Antiquities; Mel Fisher Heritage Soc; Henrietta Marie Exhib; Arts Am Program to Eritrea; Mus of Beni-Senf Cairo Egypt. *Pos:* Designer, Smithsonian Inst, 64-94; Washington artist, Health, Educ & Welfare Dept, DC, 79; acad specialist, Egyptian Mus, Cairo, currently; mus consult, currently. *Teaching:* Instr painting, Louisville Pub Sch, 62-63; instr design & painting, Corcoran Sch Art, 70-, Duke Ellington Sch Art, studies prog. *Awards:* Arts Am Grant, 97 & 98. *Bibliog:* B Rose (auth), Black artist in America, Art in Am, 70. *Mem:* AMA. *Media:* Watercolor, Acrylic. *Collection:* Univ Louiseville Libr Art. *Dealer:* Parish Gallery 1054 31st NW Wash DC 2007. *Mailing Add:* 1930 Columbia Rd NW No 303 Washington DC 20009

YOUNG, LEEMEI
PAINTER

b Taiwan, Mar 28, 1951. *Study:* Sch for Pastel Only Nat Arts Club, with Jason Cheng, 99; The Ridgewood Art Inst, with Betty Kaytes, 2001; The Art Students League of NY, with Barbara Adrian, 2002. *Hon Degrees:* Univ China-Nan Sch Pharmacy, BS, 73; Univ North Carolina, Charlotte, 83. *Work:* Yi-Yeh Art Gallery, Chiba, Japan; Gallery of First Am Int Bank, Flushing, NY; Gallery of Taipei Econ & Cult Ctr, New York City; DSA Gallery, Tainan, Taiwan; Feng Ming Art Gallery, Chung Shan, China. *Comn:* Still Life with Fruits, Pastel Soc of Am, New York City, 2000; Spring, Sou Clinic, Chiba, Japan, 2003; Forever Love, Gallery of Amerasia Bank, Tom & Liz Mao, Flushing, NY, 2004; Autumn, Taiwanese Women Asn, Irene & Mike Lee, Flushing, NY, 2005; Sunflowers, Taiwanese Women Asn, Tom & Liz Mao, Flushing, NY, 2005. *Exhib:* CPS Renaissance in Pastel, Slater Mem Mus Converse, Norwich, Conn, 2000-02; Pastel Soc of Am Ann, National Arts Club, New York City, 2001; Hawaii Pastel Soc, Hawaii Art Ctr, Honolulu, Hawaii, 2002; Audubon Artists Inc Ann, Salmagundi Club, New York City, 2002-05; Am Artists Prof League, Salmagundi Club, New York City, 2001-03 & 2005; Taiwanese Am Pastel Artists Asn, Gallery of Taipei Cultural Ctr, New York City, 2005; Taiwan Ctr 1st Int Open Juried Exhib, Taiwan Ctr Gallery, Flushing, NY, 2005; Taiwan Ctr 2nd Int Open Juried Exhib, Taiwan Ctr Gallery, Flushing, NY, 2006. *Pos:* Vpres, North Am Pastel Artists Asn, 2004-; exhib chair, Taiwan Ctr Int Open Juried Exhib, 2005-. *Teaching:* Pastel instr, Tzu-Chi Cultural Dev Ctr, 2002. *Awards:* Pastel Painter Cape Cod, Conn Pastel Soc 7th Ann, 2000; Myra Biggerstaff, Pastel Soc of Am 29th Ann, 2001; Paul Bransom, Am Artists Prof League 77th Grand Nat, 2005. *Bibliog:* Kevin Shih (auth), Lee Mei Young's Pastel World, NY Community Time, 12/2004; Sonia Shi (auth), Donation to Tsunami, The Epoch Time, 2/2005; Shirly Chiu (auth), Nat Competition Winner, World Jour, 11/2005. *Mem:* North Am Pastel Artists Asn (99-); Chinese Calligraphy Arts Soc (2000-); The Am Artists Prof League (2002-); Pastel Soc of Am (signature mem, 2004-); Audubon Artists Inc (2005-). *Media:* Pastel. *Publ:* Auth, Pastel World of Jason Chang, G&P Co/Marshall Wei, 99; auth, Chinese Artists, Chinese Calligraphy Arts/City King, 2003 & 2005; auth, L'Art du Pastel, Art Du Pastel En France/Sylvie Cabal, 2005. *Dealer:* Sone Co Ltd 738-2 Dainichi Yotsukaido Chiba Japan 284-0001. *Mailing Add:* 136-24 Maple Ave #9D Flushing NY 11355

YOUNG, LESLIE (MCCLURE)
PAINTER, MURALIST

b Greensboro, NC, 1954. *Study:* Univ NC, Greensboro, BFA (studio painting), 76, MFA (studio painting), 79. *Work:* Flower Mound CofC, Tex. *Comn:* portrait, comn by Dr Matthew Harden, Highland Village, Tex, 96; portrait, comn by Mr & Mrs Allen Hoggatt, Double Oak, Tex, 96; portrait, comn by Dr Rita Sherbenou, Denton, Tex, 96; interior with figures, comn by Dr Jane Chihal, Carrollton, Tex, 96; murals, comn by developer Ken Hodge, Flower Mound, Tex, 98. *Exhib:* Arlington Art Asn Regional, Arlington Mus Art, Tex, 90; Members Exhib, Arlington Mus Art, Tex, 93; 27th Ann Regional Painting Exhib, Richardson Civic Arts Ctr, Richardson, Tex, 93; The

Kempinski, Dallas, Tex, 95; Silver Gala, Lewisville, Tex, 96; Women's Asn, Denton, Tex, 96; Univ N Tex, Dept Cognition & Technol, Denton, 98. *Awards:* Gold Ltd & Merrill Award, Arlington Art Asn Regional, 90; Oil Painting Honorary, Richardson 27th Ann Regional, Grumbacher Co, 93. *Bibliog:* Greensboro Daily News, 72 & 79; Liberty News, 79; Denton Record-Chronicle, 96. *Mem:* Women in Arts, Washington. *Media:* Alkyd Oil. *Res:* Development of teaching program for very young children - piano performance and signt-reading. *Publ:* Auth & illusr, Progressive Piano, 90; Garden Gate, Garden Pond, Iris and Water Lilies I & II, pvt publ, 3/96. *Dealer:* O'Delle Abney Abney Galleries 591 Broadway 3rd Flr New York NY 10012; Margie Art 5111 Winewood Lane Milford MI 48382-1543. *Mailing Add:* 211 Valley View Double Oak TX 75077-8432

YOUNG, RICHARD ALAN
PAINTER, ADMINISTRATOR
Study: Northern Mich Univ, BFA with honors;Boise State Univ, MA in Art; Washington State Univ, MFA, 1986; Northern Mich Univ, BFA, 1975; Boise State Univ, MAEd, 1978, Washington State Univ, MFA, 1986. *Exhib:* Paintings and drawings have been included in numerous exhibitions throughout the country. *Collection Arranged:* Boise Art Mus, Herrett Ctr for Art and History, Twin Falls, Idaho, US West Telephone Co, Denver, Colo, Ford Motor Co, Mich and several private collections. *Pos:* Co-taught in service and master teacher workshops for elementary teachers throughout Idaho; artist-in-Residence at over 60 elementary schools in Southwest Idaho; special lecturer, Boise State Univ, 1977-78; asst dir, Art Attack Gallery, Boise, 1987-88; dir Art Reach Bus Outreach Program, Boise Gallery of Art, 1987-89; curator of edn, Boise Art Mus, 1988-91; adj faculty, art dept, Northwest Nazarene Col, 1989, adj faculty, art dept, Boise State Univ, 1990-94; commissioner, City of Boise, Dept of Arts and History; mem-at-large, Idaho Commission on the Arts, 1995-99; mem Boise City Arts Commission, 1997-99; juror: Art in the Park, Boise Art Mus: Best in Show, 1999-2002. *Teaching:* Asst prof, gallery dir, art dept, Boise State Univ, 1994-2000, gallery dir Boise State Univ Graduate Faculty, art dept, 1995-2003, assoc prof, chair, art dept, 2003-. *Publ:* Ford Times Magazine, 1974-75, Boise State Univ Alumni Magazine/Focus, 1996, High Ground/Limited Edition Artist's Book Two Studio: One Bed, 1997, Front and Back cover art, Idaho Review, Literary Journal of Boise State Univ, 2009. *Mailing Add:* Art Department Boise State University 1910 University Drive LA 262-F Boise ID 83725-1510

YOUNG, ROBERT JOHN
PAINTER
b Vancouver, BC, Aug 8, 1938. *Study:* Univ BC, BA (art hist); City & Guilds London Sch Art, Eng; Vancouver Sch Art, dipl (graphics). *Work:* Can Coun Art Bank, Ottawa; Govt BC Prov Collection; Art Gallery Ont; Montreal Mus Fine Arts; and others; The Tate Collection. *Comn:* Christmas card Clothworkers Guild, London, 63; portrait, comn by Paul William White, London, 73; portrait, comn by Donna MacDonald, London, 76. *Exhib:* Solo exhibs, Redfern Gallery, London, 71, 73, 75, 79 & 82 & Vancouver Art Gallery, 74; Realismus und Realitat, Darmstadt, WGer, 75; Time Mag, Can Canvas, Across Can, 75-76; Can Cult Ctr, Embassy, Paris, 76; Vancouver Art Gallery, BC, 76-77; Marlborough-Godard, Toronto & Montreal, 76-77, 80 & 82; 10-Year Retrospective, Charles M Scott Gallery, Vancouver, 84; Vancouver Art Gallery, 88; Simon Frazer Univ, 2011. *Teaching:* Instr painting, Banff Sch Fine Arts, Alta, 75 & 81; vis artist, Royal Col Art, London, 76, Vancouver Sch Art, 77 & 81 & Alta Col Art, 78; assoc prof, Univ BC, 82-98. *Bibliog:* Doris Shadbolt (auth), Robert Young, The Implacable Image, Vanguard, Vancouver Art Gallery, 77; Fenella Crichton (auth), A juggler of styles, Art & Artists, 4/79. *Media:* Oil; Intaglio Printmaking. *Dealer:* Atelier Gallery Vancouver; Redfern Gallery 20 Cork St London ON Can. *Mailing Add:* 3940 Quebec St Vancouver BC V5V 3K8 Canada

YOUNG, ROBERT S W
SCULPTOR
b Honolulu, Hawaii, Nov 24, 1948. *Study:* Univ Hawaii, BFA, 76, MFA, 80. *Work:* Honolulu Acad Art; Contemp Arts Ctr, Honolulu; Hawaii State Found Culture & Arts. *Exhib:* Artist of Hawaii, 77-80 & 82 & Art Flora, 84, Honolulu Acad Art; Clay-Form, Function & Fantasy, Long Beach Gallery, 79; We're Talking About 3 Artists, 81 & Sculpture Syntaxis: Best Shot, 84, Contemp Arts Ctr; 30th Ann Drawing & Sculpture Exhib, Ball State Univ, Muncie, Ind, 84. *Pos:* Chmn, Raku Ho'olaulea, Hawaii Craftmen, Honolulu, 80-82. *Teaching:* Instr pottery, Hickam Air Force Base, Honolulu, 76-82; instr ceramics, Univ Hawaii, Honolulu, 80-81. *Awards:* Coll Art Award, Coll Art Comt, 79 & 80; Crafts Excellence Award, Hawaii Craftsmen, 81; First Place Sculpture, Art Flora '84, Honolulu Garden Club, 84. *Mem:* Hawaii Artist League. *Media:* Clay. *Mailing Add:* 1056 Brandon Ave Norfolk VA 23507

YOUNG, TOM (THOMAS) WILLIAM
PAINTER, PHOTOGRAPHER
b Huntington, WVa, Oct, 7, 1924. *Study:* John Herron Art Inst; Cincinnati Art Acad, Univ Cincinnati; Univ Ala, BFA & MA (fine arts); Ohio State Univ; Chouinard Art Inst; Univ Southern Calif; Columbia Univ, EdD; also with Hans Hofmann, New York. *Work:* Mus Mod Art; Univ Southern Ill; Victoria & Albert Mus; New Orleans Mus Art; Pan American Life Insurance Bldg, New Orleans. *Comn:* Mural, US Air Base, Altus, Okla, 43. *Exhib:* After Twenty Yrs, Birmingham Mus Art, 71; Ft Wayne Ind Art Mus, 84; Independent Curators 10th Anniversary Exhibition, Puck Bldg, NY, 85; solo exhib, Malton Gallery, Cincinnati, Ohio, 86-88; Still-Zinsell Gallery, New Orleans, 88; Mus Folkwang Essen, Ger, 92; John Stinson Fine Arts and Ogden Mus of Southern Art, New Orleans, La, 2004; solo exhibs, Ogden Mus Southern Art, New Orleans, La, 2008; and others. *Pos:* Illusr exp aircraft, Douglas Aircraft Corp, Los Angeles, 52-53; art dir, Good Health Mag, New York, 53-57; cover designer, Electronic Design Mag, New York, 55-56; design & color consult, Royal Metal Mfg co, 56-57; color consult, New Orleans Dock Bd, 71-72. *Teaching:* Prof fine arts & chmn dept, Wagner Coll, 53-69; head prof art, Auburn Univ, 69-70; prof fine arts & mem grad fac, Univ New Orleans, 70-, chmn dept, 70-78, prof emer, 92. *Awards:* Weissglass Award, Staten Island Mus, 55; Hon Mention, New York City Ctr Gallery, 56; Winner, Nat Exhib, Contemp Arts Ctr, New Orleans, 82. *Mem:* New Orleans Mus Art (bd trustees, 73-); Coll Art Asn Am. *Media:* All Media; Color Film; Oil, Watercolor. *Collection:* Mary-Franz Kline, William Eggleston. *Mailing Add:* 5605 W Esplanade Ave Metairie LA 70003

YOUNGBLOOD, DAISY
SCULPTOR
b Asheville, NC, Sept 14, 1945. *Study:* Va Commonwealth Univ, 66; Am Acad Arts and Letters, Hon Degree, 1989. *Exhib:* Sculpture Now, Va Mus Fine Arts, Richmond, 83; Modern Masks, Whitney Mus Am Art, NY, 84; Standing Ground: Sculpture by Am Women, Contemp Arts Ctr, Cincinnati, Ohio, 87; solo exhibs, Beaver Coll Art Gallery, Glenside, Pa, 92; Next of Kin, List Visual Arts Ctr, Mass Inst Technol, Cambridge, 95; A Labor of Love, New Mus Contemp Art, NY, 96; Mint Mus Craft & Design, Charlotte, NC, 2000. *Awards:* grantee fellow, MacArthur Foundation, 2003. *Bibliog:* Regina Coppola (auth), Daisy Youngblood, Univ Mass, 96; Eleanor Heartney (auth), Daisy Youngblood at David McKee, Art Am, 11/99. *Media:* Clay. *Mailing Add:* McKee Gallery 745 Fifth Ave New York NY 10151

YOUNGBLOOD, JUDY
PRINTMAKER, PAINTER
b El Paso, Tex. *Study:* Univ Wis, Madison, BS, 71, MFA, 74; Hayter's Atelier 17, Paris, Fulbright Scholar, 79. *Work:* DeCordova Mus, Boston; Boston Mus Fine Arts, Mass; Ark Art Ctr, Little Rock; Mus Fine Arts, Houston, Tex; Mus Mod Art, Ft Worth, Tex; Elvehjem Mus Art, Madison, Wis. *Comn:* Presentation print, Madison Print Club, 83; Centennial Print, Univ N Tex, 90. *Exhib:* Mini Print Int, Galeria Taller Fort, 88, 90 & 92; William Campbell Fine Art, Ft Worth, Tex, 90-92; Edith Baker Gallery, Dallas, Tex, 90-92; Printmaking in Texas: The 1980's, Mod Art Mus Ft Worth, 91; Flatbed Press, Austin, Tex, 96; solo exhibs, Transitions, Art Mus SE Tex, Beaumont, 97, Human Presence, William Campbell Contemp Art, Ft Worth, Tex, 98, Recent Works, Edith Baker Gallery, Dallas, Tex, 98, Univ Tex Tyler, 99; Across the Grain, Am Woodcut Portfolio, Univ Del, Newark & Univ Tex, Tyler, 98; Texas Roots, Ctr Visual Arts, Denton, 98; In Relief: Contemp Am Relief Prints, Neb Art Asn, Lincoln & Hastings Col, Nebr, 98; Ashland Univ Printmaking Invitational Exhib, Ohio, 99; 27th Ann Bradley Univ Print & Drawing Exhib, Peoria, Ill, 99; The Boston Printmakers Biennial 1999, Boston Univ, Mass, 99. *Pos:* Fel residency, MacDowell Colony, Peterborough, NH, 82 & 85. *Teaching:* Prof printmaking, Univ N Tex, 76-98, prof emer, 98-. *Awards:* Artistic Achievement Award, Okla State Univ, 82; Award, 22nd Bradley Nat Print & Drawing Exhib, 89; Award, 42nd North Am Print Exhib, 90; Award, Am Miniature Printmakers Exhib, 88. *Bibliog:* Scott Gordon (auth), Judy Youngblood: New Work, New Art Examiner, 11/81; Andrew Stasik (auth), Toward a broader view, 81 & Betti & Sale (auths), Print Rev, 81, Drawing: A contemporary approach, 91; Lynne Allen & Phyllis McGibbon (auths), The Best of Printmaking: An International Collection, Rockport Publ, Gloucester, Mass, 97. *Mem:* Philadelphia Print Club; Women's Caucus Art; Southern Graphics Coun. *Media:* Miscellaneous Media. *Publ:* Auths, Lynne Allen & Phyllis McGibbon, The Best of Printmaking: An International Collection, Rockport Publ, Gloucester, Mass, 97; Hayden's Ferry Review, Ariz State Univ, Tempe, Ariz, 99. *Mailing Add:* Univ N Tex Sch Visual Arts PO Box 5098 Denton TX 76203

YOUNGBLOOD, NAT
PAINTER, ILLUSTRATOR
b Evansville, Ind, Dec 28, 1916. *Study:* Univ NMex, Albuquerque, with Millard Sheets; Am Acad Art, Chicago; also with Barse Miller, Raymond Johnson, Ralph Douglass & Howard Mosby. *Hon Degrees:* Washington and Jefferson Col, Hon DFA, 1999. *Work:* Indiana Univ Pa; Calif State Col, Pa; Rockwell Int Col, Ft Pitt Mus, Pa. *Comn:* Oil portraits (indust leaders), Pittsburgh Press, Pa, 56; portrait President Kennedy, Metro News Service, 61; ten hist paintings (pioneer life), Ft Pitt Mus, Pittsburgh, Pa; Duquesne Club, Pittsburgh, Pa; numerous works in pvt collections. *Exhib:* Artist of the Yr, Pittsburgh Ctr Arts, 76; Am Painters in Paris, 76; solo exhibs, Atheneum, New Harmony, Ind, 84 & Main Trail Galleries, Scottsdale, Ariz, 85, Dewey Galleries, Santa Fe, 91, Albuquerque Mus Art, 91, 92 & 95, Wash & Jefferson Col, 95; Four-man show, Dewey Galleries, Santa Fe, NMex, 85; Pioneer Mus, Colorado Springs, Colo, 85 & 86; Artists of Am, 86-2000; Arts for the Parks Top 100, 98. *Pos:* Art dir, cartoonist, illusr & painter, Pittsburgh Press, 46-79. *Teaching:* Instr painting & design, LaRoche Col & Art Inst Pittsburgh, 74. *Awards:* First Place, Pennational Exhib, 66; First Prize Alcoa Award, Aqueous Open, 86; Best Show, Art in the Mountains, 96. *Bibliog:* Nancy Ellis (auth), Nat Youngblood, Focus, Santa Fe, NMex, 1-2/89; Rita Simmons (auth), Nat Youngblood, Southwest Art, 8/90; Santa Fe Focus, 8/9/94. *Mem:* Pittsburgh Experiment; Fortnightly Wash Jefferson Univ. *Media:* Watercolor, Oil. *Publ:* Ed, 101st Airborne Division Picture History, 45; auth, Watercolor page, Am Artist Mag, 59; Western Art Digest, 85. *Dealer:* Dewey Galleries Ltd 74 E San Francisco St Santa Fe NM 87501. *Mailing Add:* PO Box 73 West Middletown PA 15379

YOUNGER, DAN FORREST
PAINTER, PRINTMAKER
b Denver, Colo, Sept 14, 1954. *Study:* Kansas City Art Inst, BFA, 76. *Work:* Am Express, Salt Lake City; Nat Mus, Brazil; Continental Insurance Co, NY; AT&T, Kansas City, Mo; Dean Witter Reynolds, Kansas City; and others. *Comn:* Mural, Dixons Inc, Independence, Mo, 78. *Exhib:* Atkins Mus Fine Arts, Kansas City, Mo, 76-81; Univ Dallas, Irving, 77; Sheldon Mus, Lincoln, Nebr, 81; Univ Mo, Kansas City, 81; and others. *Pos:* Originator & dir, Squadron Press Fine Art Printing, 79-84. *Teaching:* Print technician, Kansas City Art Inst, Mo, 76-83. *Awards:* Best Show, Dixie Ann, Montgomery Mus, Ala, 78; Purchase Prize, Mid Four Ann, 79 & 81; 2nd Place, William Rockhill Nelson Gallery Art, 80. *Bibliog:* Elizabeth Kirsch (auth), Squadron Press, Kansas City, 2/80; Vicki Melcher (auth), Kansas City, Art News, 10/80; Barbara Westerfield (auth), Dan Younger, New Art Examiner Vol 13 No 3, 11/85. *Mem:* Print Soc Kansas City; Friends Art, Kansas City. *Mailing Add:* 5911 McGee Kansas City MO 64113

YOUNGER, ROBERT M
SCULPTOR
b Philadelphia, Pa, 1947. *Study:* Philadelphia Coll Art, BFA, 69; Fulbright-Hayes Grant, Italy, 69-70; Yale Univ Grad Sch Fine Arts, 71-72. *Exhib:* Solo exhibs, Pa Acad Fine Arts, 80, Craig Cornelius Gallery, NY, 89, Drexel Univ, Philadelphia, 90, Kees Schouten Gallery, Haarlem, The Neth, 93, Univ Arts, Philadelphia, 94, InterArt Gallery, NY, 94 & De Etalage, Haarlem, The Neth, 95; The Gift Show, Dooley Le Cappellaine, NY, 92; Brides and Topiaries, Flamingos East, NY, 92; The Return of the Cadavre Exquis, Drawing Ctr, NY, 93; Souvenirs, Rosenwald/Wolf Gallery, Univ of Arts, Philadelphia, 94; Drexel Univ Gallery, Philadelphia, 99; and others. *Awards:* Nat Endowment Arts Grant, 82 & 90; NY State Coun Arts Sponsored Proj Award, 86

YOURITZIN, VICTOR KOSHKIN
EDUCATOR, HISTORIAN
b New York, NY, Dec 20, 1942. *Study:* Trinity Sch (valedictorian), New York, 60; Williams Coll, BA (cum laude with honors), 64; Sch Archit, Int Fels Prog cert, Columbia Univ, 64-65; Inst Fine Arts, NY Univ, MA, 67; Cert Mus Training, Inst Fine Arts & Metrop Mus Art, New York, 69. *Work:* Bibliothèque nationale de France, Paris; NY Pub Libr; Wadsworth Atheneum Mus Art, Hartford; Nat Mus Am History, Smithsonian Inst; The State Russ Mus, St Petersburg. *Exhib:* 27th Ann La State Art Exhib Prof Artists, 71; and others. *Pos:* Mem bd trustees, Okla City Mus Art, 78-84, collections mgt comt, 92-96; regional corresp, Art Voices-South, 78-79, contrib ed, 79-82; mem exhibs & collections comt, Philbrook Art Ctr, Tulsa, Okla, 83-85; mem exhib comt, Okla Art Ctr, 84-87; panelist, Nat Endowment Humanities, 84 & Prog for Art on Film, Getty Trust, Metrop Mus Art, 87; co-cur, Am Watercolors, Metrop Mus Art, 91-92; coun adv mem, Ogden Mus Southern Art, Univ New Orleans, 95-2003; chmn bd trustees, Mabee-Gerrer Mus Art, Shawnee, 96-99. *Teaching:* Instr art hist, Vanderbilt Univ, Nashville, Tenn, 68-69 & Newcomb Coll, Tulane Univ, New Orleans, 69-72; asst prof art hist, Univ Okla, Norman, 72-80, assoc prof, 80-94, prof, 94-97 & David Ross Boyd distinguished prof, 97-. *Awards:* Ford Found Fel, Dept Am Painting & Sculpture, Metrop Mus Art, New York, 67-68; Gov's Arts & Educ Award, State Okla, 92; Honorable Citation, House Reps, State Okla, 93; Award Winning Author, Book-of-the-Month Club, American Watercolors from the Metropolitan Museum of Art, Abrams, 91. *Mem:* Koussevitzky Recordings Soc Inc (vpres, 92-). *Res:* Nineteenth and twentieth century art; museology. *Publ:* Auth, The Irony of Degas, Gazette des Beaux-Arts, 1/76; Thomas Hart Benton: Bathers rediscovered, Arts Mag, 5/80; coauth, American Watercolors from the Metropolitan Museum of Art, Abrams, 91; auth, Pavel Tchelitchew, Fred Jones Jr Mus Art, Univ of Okla, 2002; Photographs by Charles Henri Ford, Fred Jones Jr Mus Art, Univ Okla, 2006; co-auth, From Vernet to Villion: 19th Century French Master Drawings from the National Gallery of Art, 2012. *Mailing Add:* 1721 Oakwood Dr Norman OK 73069

YU, SHAN
ARTIST
b Fuzhou, China, Oct 24, 1949. *Study:* Fujian Art Sch, China, BA, 80; Shanghai Theater Acad, grad study, 85-86; Boston Univ, MFA, 89. *Work:* National Great River Mus, Indiana State Mus, Angel Mounds Historic Site, Evansville, Ind, Mus Sci, Boston. *Comn:* Murals, Ind State Mus, Indianapolis; Murals, Mus Ctr, Cincinnati, OH; Mural, Mus of Sci, Boston; Mural, Childrens Mus, Boston; panoramic mural, Nat Great River, Mus, Alton Ill; 2 murals, Seacoast Sci Ctr, Rye, NH, 2004; 3 murals, exhib Sci Mus Minn, St. Paul, 2005; Painting for Hollywood film Ocean 13 (mural), Los Angeles, Calif, 2006; Ink Paintings & Calligraphy for Disney film, Pirates of the Caribbean, Los Angeles, Calif, 2007; Mural Series for Genghis Kahn Exhib, Mus affiliated to Smithsonian, 2008. *Exhib:* Solo Exhibs: Hong Kong Arts Ctr, 89; CCI Gallery, Boston, 98; Hong Kong Art & Design Gallery, 03; Shanghai Theatre Accad, China, 2006; Poetry with a Nature, ART50 Gallery, Shanghai, China, 2007; Group exhibs, Creative Arts Workshop Gallery, New Haven, Conn, 92; Hewlett Packard HQ, Mass, 94; Kane Gallery, Boston, 95; Juried Ann Exhib, Am Watercolor Soc, NY, 99; Salmagundi Club Gallery, New York City, 99; Shanghai Theater Acad Gallery, China, 01; murals, Ind State Mus, 01, 02, Royal BC Mus, Victoria, Can, 03; Fugian Art Mus, China, 2009; Light of Art, Int Artists Joint Exhib, Shanghai Waitum Mus Art, 2010; Reconnection with Hong Kong Contemp Arts, Hong Kong City Hall, 2010. *Pos:* sr set designer, VDA Inc, 89-99; pres, Eastern Decor & Art Co, 98-. *Teaching:* Teacher, Fujian Art Sch, 80-85; Vis Prof, Shanghai Theater Accad, 2001. *Awards:* Fel, Asian Cult Coun, 86; Outstanding Int Scholar, Boston U, 89; Am Citizenship, 98. *Bibliog:* Christine Temin (auth), Watercolors on a Pleasing Scale, The Boston Globe, 93; Zhu Weiyi (auth), Yushans Mural in Mus, World Jour, No. 872, 00. *Mem:* Nat Mural Painters Soc. *Media:* Acrylic, Watercolor, Oil. *Publ:* Watercolor Painting, Silent Night, The Boston Globe, 93; Landscape Painting by Yu Shan, Kiaoning Art Press, 97; Painting with Article, Am Artist Mag, 7/92; Landscape Paintings (with art), Art Guide Mag, 5/2007. *Dealer:* Art of Nature Int. *Mailing Add:* 45 Robinson St Somerville MA 02145

YU-HO, TSENG
PAINTER, HISTORIAN
b Peking, China, Nov 29, 24; US citizen. *Study:* Fu-jen Univ, Peking, BA, 42; Univ Hawaii, MA, 66; Inst Fine Arts, NY Univ, PhD, 72. *Work:* Honolulu Acad Arts, Hawaii; Walker Art Ctr, Minneapolis; Nat Mus Mod Art, Stockholm, Sweden; Mus Cernuschi, Paris, France; Stanford Art Gallery, Calif. *Comn:* Mural, St Katherine's Church, Kaui, Hawaii, 57; mural, Manoa Chinese Pavilion, Honolulu, 68; mural, Golden West Savings & Loan, San Francisco, Calif, 64; wall painting, Castle & Cooke Co, Ltd, Honolulu, 68; wall painting, Honolulu Int Airport, 72. *Exhib:* Contemp Am Painting & Sculpture, Univ Ill, Urbana, 58, 61 & 65; Carnegie Inst Painting & Sculpture Int, Pittsburgh, Pa, 61 & 65; Kunstverein, Munich & Frankfurt, Ger; Walker Art Ctr; San Francisco Mus Art, Calif; and others. *Teaching:* Instr studio art, Honolulu Acad Art, 50-63, consult Chinese art, 53-; assoc prof Chinese art hist, Univ Hawaii, 63-66; prog chmn art hist, Univ Hawaii, 71-, prof art, 73-. *Awards:* Am Artists of the Western States Award, Stanford Art Gallery; NY Univ Founders Day Award for Outstanding Scholarship, 72. *Bibliog:* Article, Time Mag, 1/19/62; Seldis (auth), Pacific heritage, Art in Am, 65. *Mem:* Am Coll Art Asn; Asian Soc; Asian & Pacific Art Asn Hawaii (organizer, 72). *Media:* Watercolor, Collage. *Res:* Chinese art; the Art of Chinese folding fan; folk art. *Publ:* Contribr, four articles, Studies of 16th Century Chinese Artists, 54-63; contribr, Encyclopedia World Art, Rome, 64; auth, Some Contemporary Elements on Chinese Classic Pictorial Art, 65 & 71; illusr, The Analects of Confucius, 70. *Mailing Add:* c/o Robyn Buntin of Honolulu 848 S Beretania St Honolulu HI 96813

YUEN, KEE-HO
SILVERSMITH, SCULPTOR
b Hong Kong, China, Aug 7, 1956; US citizen. *Study:* Chinese Univ Hong Kong, BA (fine arts), 83; Sch Art & Art Hist, Univ Iowa, MA (metalsmithing & jewelry), 88, MFA, 89. *Work:* Am Craft Mus, NY; Univ Iowa Mus Art, Iowa City; Univ Mus, Chinese Univ Hong Kong; Waterloo Mus, Iowa. *Comn:* flatware, comn by BS Rabinovitch, Seattle, Wash, 96; sculpture, comn by Todd & Jennifer Duncan, St Louis, Mo, 2000; sculpture, comn by Ivan Jacklin & Alison Weianstein, Richmond, Va, 2000; flatware & sculpture, comn by Lois Jecklin, Davenport, Iowa, 2001. *Exhib:* Nat Fortunoff's Silver Design Competition, NY, 92; Born with a Silver Spoon, Nat Ornamental Metal Mus, Memphis, Tenn; solo exhibs, Pivoine Gallery, Taipei, Taiwan, 95 & Waterloo Mus Art, Iowa, 98; British and Am Contemp Server, Goldsmith Hall of Worshipfull Co of Goldsmith, London, Eng, 96; Guests of USA, Mus fur Kunst und Gewerbe, Hamburg, Ger, 97; Contemp Silver Servers, Seattle Art Mus, 98; The Teapot Redefined, Mobilia Gallery, Cambridge, Mass, 2001. *Teaching:* head art area, Hong Kong Salesian Sec Sch, 83-86; prof metalsmithing & jewelry, Univ Northern Iowa, Cedar Falls, 89-2000; assoc prof metalsmithing & jewelry, Univ Iowa, Iowa City, 2000-. *Awards:* First Place, Nat Crafts Competition, Pa, 87; Third Place, Fortunoff's, 89; Certificate of Excellence & Outstanding Achievement in Metalwork, Artitude Int, 89. *Bibliog:* Helen Clifford & Seymour Rabinovitch (auths), Slices of Silver, American Craft, 97 & Contemporary Silver: Commissioning, Designing Creating, Merrell Halberton Publ, 2000; Jean Sampel, Forging Ahead: Contemporary Metalwork in Iowa, Metalsmith, 97; CJ Hines, Exhibit a study in Contrast, Waterloo Courier, 5/7/98. *Mem:* SNAG; Soc Am Silversmiths. *Media:* Metal, All Media. *Publ:* contrib, The Metalsmith's Books of Boxes and Lockets, 99; auth, Seen and Unseen, 99. *Dealer:* 167 E 61st St New York NY 10021. *Mailing Add:* 2106 13th St Coralville IA 52241

YUH, SUN-KOO
CERAMIST
Study: Hong Ik Univ, Seoul, Korea, BFA, 1988; NY State Coll Ceramics at Alfred, MFA, 1997. *Work:* Renwick Gallery, Nat Mus Am Art, Smithsonian Inst, Washington; Int Mus Ceramic Art, Alfred, NY; Philadelphia Mus Art; Houston Ctr Contemp Craft; Soc Contemp Crafts, Pittsburgh. *Exhib:* Solo exhibs include To-Art Space, Seoul, 1995, Helen Drutt Gallery, Philadelphia, 1997, 1999, Navy Pier, Chicago, 2000, Western Ill Univ Art Gallery, 2001, Univ Ill, Springfield, 2002, Len G Everett Gallery, Monmouth, Ill, 2003, Tho Art, Seoul, 2003, Parkland Coll Gallery, Champaign, Ill, 2005, Roswell Art Ctr West, Ga, 2006, Nancy Margolis Gallery, New York, 2007; group exhibs include Seoul Contemp Ceramic Show, 1997, 1998; Cloth & Clay, Pacific Asia Mus, Pasadena, Calif, 1999; Life from Clay, San Jose Inst Contemp Art, Calif, 2000; Regeneration, LA Folk & Craft Mus, 2000; Poetics of Clay: An Int Perspective, Philadelphia Art Alliance, 2001; Expressing the Human Form: The Figure in Contemp Ceramic Sculpture, Baltimore Clayworks, 2001; Ceramic Master Works, 1962-2002, Moderne Gallery, Philadelphia, 2002; Hundreds of Cups, Santa Fe Clay, 2003, Nature/Culture, 2006; Mastery of Clay, Clay Studio, Philadelphia, 2003, 30th Anniversary Exhib, 2004, Excess, 2005; A Tale to Tell, John Michael Kohler Arts Ctr, Sheboygan, Wis, 2005. *Teaching:* Lectr, Calif State Univ, Long Beach, 1997-2000; asst prof, Western Ill Univ, Macomb, 2000-04, assoc prof, 2004-05; assoc prof, Univ Ga, Athens, 2005-06. *Awards:* Virginia A Groot Found Recognition Award, 2003; Elizabeth R Raphael Founder's Prize, 2003; Artists Fel Award, Ill Arts Coun, 2004; Joan Mitchell Found Grant, 2005. *Mailing Add:* c/o Nancy Margolis Gallery 523 W 25th St New York NY 10001

YUNICH, BEVERLY B
COLLAGE ARTIST, JEWELER
b New York, NY, Nov 11, 1920. *Study:* Studied at Parsons Sch Design; Skidmore Col, BA, 42; studied with Moses Soyer & Robert Kulicke. *Work:* Albany Inst Hist & Art, Albany, NY; Meade Collection, Amherst Col, Mass; Hudson River Mus, Yonkers, NY; Ringling Mus, Sarasota, Fla; Skidmore Coll Art Gallery, Saratoga Springs, NY. *Exhib:* Solo show, Albany Inst Hist & Art, NY, 72-80; Paper Works, Hudson River Mus, NY, 80; Jewelry-original, Rochester Mem Art Gallery, NY, 80-94; Skidmore Alumni Invitational, Skidmore Art Coll & Gallery, 92; Painters & Sculptors Soc NJ, Newark Mus; Selected Artists Gallery, Ringling Mus, Sarasota, Fla. *Teaching:* Instr collage-mixed media, Westchester Art Workshop, 78-84. *Awards:* Purchase Award, Yonkers & Hudson River Mus, 88; Pen & Brush Club Solo Awards for Oil & Pastel Mixed Media; Best in Show, Mamaroneck Artists Guild. *Mem:* Nat Asn Women Artists; Audubon Artists Nat Acad; Scarsdale Art Asn. *Media:* Collage, Mixed Media; Gold on Silver. *Specialty:* Well known Contemp Artist, Lee Weber Gallery, Westchester, Greenwich. *Publ:* Jewelry Designs, jewelers cir Vogue Mag, NY Times. *Dealer:* Lee Weber Fine Arts. *Mailing Add:* 26 Cooper Rd Scarsdale NY 10583

YUST, DAVID E
PAINTER, PRINTMAKER
b Wichita, Kans, Apr 3, 1939. *Study:* Birger Sandzen, Lindsborg, Kans; Wichita State Univ; Kans State Univ; Univ Kans, BFA, 63; Univ Ore, MFA, 69. *Work:* Denver Art Mus; Indianapolis Mus Art; Rockford Art Mus, Ill; Minnesota Mus Art, St Paul; Butler Inst Art, Youngstown, Ohio; Kirkland Mus Fine and Decorative Arts, Denver; Colo Springs Fine Art Ctr; 2 paintings, Ambassador Ralph Frank's Residence, USA Art in Embassies Prog, Zagreb, Croatia, 2003-2006; Manama, Bahrain, 2008-2010; Loveland Mus & Gallery, Loveland, 2013; Colo St Univ Art Mus, Ft Collins, Colo,

2013; Emprise Bank, Wichita, Kans. *Exhib:* Solo Exhibs: Purdue Univ, West Lafayette, 99: Colo State Univ, Fort Collins, 99, 2012; Rourke Art Mus, Moorhead, Minn, 2003; Ft Collins Mus Contemp Art, Colo, 2003; Regis Univ, Denver, 2004; Gallery 72; Omaha, 2005; Plus Gallery, Denver, 2006; Arvada Center, Arvada Co, 2008; Colo Abstract (with catalog), Ctr for Visual Arts, Denver, Colo, 2009; St Paul Gallery, Minn, 2010; Loveland Mus & Gallery, Loveland, Colo, 2012; Colo State Univ, Ft Collins, Colo, 2012; Plus Gallery, Denver, 2013. *Teaching:* Prof painting, drawing & grad painting coord, Colo State Univ, 65-, John N Stern distinguished prof, 2005, prof emer, 2012. *Awards:* Purchase Awards, 11th Biennial, Kans State Univ, 70, Colo State Univ, 70, Okla Art Ctr, 73, Rourke Gallery, Moorhead, Minn, 89, Binney and Smith, Easton, Pa, 90; AFKEY Award, Alliance for Contemp Art/Denver Art Mus, 2000; First Place Award, Foothills Art Ctr, Golden, 2001; Art Educ of the Year, Colo Higher Educ, 2003; Art Educ of the Year, Pac Region Higher Educ, 2004. *Bibliog:* Charles Parson (videotape), 90 & 2004; Yust/Arvada Exhib, (DVD), 2009; Yust/Loveland Mus/Gallery Print Retrospective, Loveland, Colo, 2013. *Mem:* Denver Art Mus. *Media:* Acrylic, Lithography. *Dealer:* Ivar Zeile PLUS Gallery 2501 Larimer St Denver CO 80205. *Mailing Add:* 1301 Patton St Fort Collins CO 80524-4231

Z

ZABARSKY, MELVIN JOEL
PAINTER, EDUCATOR
b Worcester, Mass, Aug 21, 1932. *Study:* Sch Worcester Art Mus; Ruskin Sch Drawing & Fine Arts, Univ Oxford; Sch Fine & Appl Arts, Boston Univ, BFA; Univ Cincinnati, MFA. *Work:* Mus Mod Art, NY; De Cordova Mus, Lincoln, Mass; Addison Gallery Am Art, Andover, Mass; Wiggins Collection, Boston Pub Libr; Currier Gallery Art, Manchester, NH. *Exhib:* Solo exhibs, Boris Mirski Gallery, Boston, 62, Tragos Gallery, Boston, 66, De Cordova Mus, 70, Circulo Bellas Artes, 82 & Salones Berkowitoch, Madrid, 83; Surreal Images, De Cordova Mus, 68; New Eng Painters Traveling Exhib, Ringling Mus, Sarasota, Fla, 69. *Teaching:* Instr painting, Swain Sch Design, New Bedford, Mass, 60-64; asst prof painting, Wheaton Col, 64-69; prof painting, Univ NH, 69-. *Awards:* Painting Prize, Boston Arts Festival, 62; Ford Found Grant in humanities, 68. *Bibliog:* B Schwartz (auth), Humanism in 20th Century Art, Praeger, 73. *Media:* Oil. *Mailing Add:* Dept of Art Univ NH Durham NH 03824

ZABEL, CYNTHIA
PUBLISHER
Study: Tulane Univ, BA Art History. *Pos:* adminr, Sothebys, 1996-1999; advert dir, Artnet, 1998-2005; owner, Cynthia Zabel Fine Art, NYC; advertising dir, Art in America, 2005-2008, publ, 2008-. *Mailing Add:* BMP Media Holdings LLC 575 Broadway New York NY 10012

ZABLUDOWICZ, ANITA
COLLECTOR
b Gateshead, UK. *Pos:* Trustee, Tate Modern & Camden Arts Centre; sponsor, Whitechapel & Zoo Art Fair; owner, 176 Gallery, London, 2007-. *Awards:* Named one of Top 200 Collectors, ARTnews mag, 2009-13. *Collection:* Contemporary art

ZABLUDOWICZ, POJU
COLLECTOR
b Helsinki, Apr 6, 1953. *Study:* Tel Aviv Univ, grad (econ & social sci). *Pos:* Chmn & chief exec officer, Tamares Group, 1990-; co-founder & trustee, Zabludowicz Art Projects, London, Zabludowicz Collection, London, 1995-; co-founder & sponsor, Zoo Art Fair, London, 2004-; co-founder, 176 (exhib space), London, 2007-. *Awards:* Named one of Top 200 Collectors, ARTnews mag, 2005-13. *Collection:* Contemporary art. *Mailing Add:* Zabludowicz Art Projects 41 Dover St London United Kingdom W1S 4NS

ZABOROWSKI, DENNIS J
PAINTER, EDUCATOR
b Cleveland, Ohio, Jan 31, 1943. *Study:* Cleveland Inst Art, cert, 61-65; Yale Univ, BFA, 65 & MFA, 68 with Jack Tworkov & Bernard Chaet. *Work:* Mint Mus of Art, Charlotte, NC; NC Nat Bank, NC Collection; Rauch Indust Inc, Gastonia, NC; Ackland Art Mus, Chapel Hill, NC; NC Mus Art, Raleigh. *Comn:* Youth Ctr mural, New Haven Redevlop Agency, 68. *Exhib:* Arts Festival of Atlanta, Ga, 69; 4th Ann James River Art Exhib, Mariners Mus, Newport News, Va, 70; 3rd Am Exhib, Washington & Lee Univ Mus, Lexington, Va, 71; solo exhibs, Gallery Contemp Art, Winston-Salem, NC, 72, NC Mus Art, Raleigh, 86 & Mint Mus, Charlotte, NC, 90; 39th Triannual NC Artists Exhib, NC Mus of Art, Raleigh, 90; and others. *Collection Arranged:* Fac Choice Exhib, Va Polytech Inst, Blacksburg, Va, 71; New Talent Show, Allan Stone Gallery, NY, 75; 200 Yrs of the Visual Arts in NC, NC Mus of Art, Raleigh, 76. *Teaching:* Prof painting, drawing & design, Univ of NC, Chapel Hill, 68-; asst prof design, Duke Univ, Durham, NC, 72. *Awards:* Purchase Awards, NC Artists Exhib, Rauch Indust, 73 & Realism in NC, Mint Mus of Art, Charlotte, 74; Best Oil Painting, Spring Mills Exhib, Spring Mills Corp, 75; Honor Award, Durham Art Guild Exhib, 87. *Mem:* Nat Asn Schs Art. *Media:* Mixed Media. *Mailing Add:* 100 Birchcrest Pl Chapel Hill NC 27516

ZACHARIAS, ATHOS
PAINTER
b Marlborough, Mass, June 17, 1927. *Study:* Art Students League, summer 52; RI Sch Design, BFA, 52; Cranbrook Acad Art, MFA, 53. *Work:* Mus Art, Providence, RI; Inst Contemp Art, Boston; Kalamazoo Inst Art, Mich; Phoenix Art Mus, Ariz; Westinghouse Corp, Pittsburgh; Corcoran Gallery Art, Washington, DC. *Comn:* Decor for Manhattan Festival Dancers, comn by Robert Ossorio, NY, 63; designed & executed opaque Projections for Edith Stephan Dance Co. *Exhib:* Joachim Gallery, Chicago, Ill, 61; solo exhibs, Gallery Mayer, 61, Louis Alexander Gallery, 63, Landmark Gallery, 73 & James Yu Gallery, NY, 77, Owl 57, Woodmere, NY, 88-93, Ann Harper Gallery, Amagansett, NY, 95, Nabi Gallery, Sag Harbor, NY, 99 and many others; Bologna Landi Gallery, East Hampton, NY, 86; Benton Gallery, Benton Plaza, Southampton, NY, 86; Galerie Kwartijin Amsterdam, The Neth, 86; Nat Acad Design, NY, 86; mus exhibs, NC Mus Art, Raleigh, NC, 59, Riverside Mus, NY, 62, Guild Hall Mus, East Hampton, NY, 79, Hempstead Mus, Hempstead, NY, 86 & Laforet Mus, Tokyo, Japan, 87; group exhibs, Boston Arts Festival, 54, Image Gallery, Stockbridge, Mass, 71, Lehigh Univ, Bethlehem, PA, 74, Object of Artists, Guild Hall, East Hampton, NY, 84, Jaski Art Gallery, Amsterdam, The Neth, 96, Fed Reserve Bank, NY, 97 and many others. *Teaching:* Instr painting, Brown Univ, 53-55 & Parsons Sch Design, 63-66; assoc prof painting, Wagner Col, 67-88; instr, SUNY New Paltz, NY, 71. *Awards:* Best in Show Award, Guild Hall, 61; Longview Found Grant, 62; Festival Arts Purchase Award, Southampton Col, 68; Best Show Award, Guild Hall, East Hampton, NY, 79; First Prize, Am Inst for Creative Living, Staten Island, NY, 87. *Bibliog:* reviews, Nancy Reynolds (auth), Pembroke Record, 1955, Gordon Brown (auth), Arts Mag, 1973, Phyllis Braff (auth), The E.H. Star, 1983, Rose C.S. Slivka (auth), The E.H. Star, 1986-1988, 1994-1995, 1998 & 1999 and many others. *Media:* Oil. *Publ:* Illusr cover, Sci & Technol, 63. *Dealer:* Owl 57 Galleries 1074 Broadway Woodmere Long Island 11598. *Mailing Add:* 141 Copeces Lane East Hampton NY 11937-1707

ZACK, BADANNA BERNICE
SCULPTOR, WRITER
b Montreal, Que, Can, 1933. *Study:* Concordia Univ, Montreal, BA, 64; Rutgers Univ, MFA, 67. *Work:* Concordia Univ, Montreal; Rutgers Univ, Douglass Col, New Brunswick, NJ; Art Gallery Hamilton, Ont; and pvt collections. *Comn:* Cambridge Gallery & Libr, Ont, 94. *Exhib:* Reflecting a Rural Consciousness, traveling in US, Can & France, 78-80; Home Sweet Home, Toronto, Ont, 85; Eighteenth Sculpture Biennial, Antwerp, Belg, 86; Twelfth Int Biennial of Tapestry, Lausanne, Switz, 86; solo exhibs, Tom Thompson Gallery, Owen Sound, Ont, 87, Lynnwood Arts Ctr Simcoe, Ont, 90, Homage to My Grandfather Sculpture Installation Exhib, Justina Barnicke Gallery, Hart House, Univ Toronto, Ont, 91, Art Gallery Algoma, Sault Ste Marie, Ont, 91, Cambridge Libr & Art Gallery, Ont, 94, Cast Offs, Art Gallery of Mississauga, Ont, 99 & The Pool Room, Justina Barnicke Gallery, Hart House, Univ Toronto, Ont, 99; Perfect Fit, Oakville, Ont, 88; Wild Life Exhib, Koffler Gallery, Toronto, Ont, 96; The Tree Mus, Gravenhurst, Ont, 98; and many others. *Awards:* Arts Grants, Can Coun, 68-69, 74-75 & 78 & Ont Arts Coun, 75-83; Gottlieb Found Grant, 96. *Bibliog:* William Fabrycki (auth), Badanna Zack: L'Enfant terrible, Artmag, 81; Jim Tiley (auth), Badanna Zack at Studio Gallery Nine, Artmag, 83; John Bentley Mays (auth), Hand stitched visions cut from fabric of life, Globe & Mail, 86. *Mem:* Royal Can Acad. *Media:* Miscellaneous. *Publ:* Auth, Toronto: A look back at sculpture during the sculpture conference, 78, Paul Dempsey at the art gallery of Hamilton, 79, Deiter Hastenteufel at Factory 77, 81-82 & The dinner party by Judy Chicago, 82, Artmag; co-producer, Horse to Horsepower (videotape), 83

ZAFRAN, ERIC MYLES
CURATOR, HISTORIAN
b Malden, Mass, Apr 19, 1946. *Study:* Tilton Sch, NH, 63; Brandeis Univ, BA, 67; Inst Fine Arts, NY Univ, MA, 70, PhD, 73. *Collection Arranged:* Master Paintings from the Hermitage (coauth & ed, catalog), Nat Gallery, 75; One Hundred Drawings in the Chrysler Mus (auth catalog), 79; French Salon Paintings from Southern Collections (auth, catalog), High Mus, 82; The Rococo Age (auth, catalog), High Mus, 83; Master Drawings from Titian to Picasso in The Curtis O Baer Collection (auth, catalog), Nat Gallery, 85; Cavaliers and Cardinals: Nineteenth-Century French Anecdotal Paintings (auth, catalog), Taft Mus, 92. *Pos:* Curatorial asst, Rose Art Mus, Waltham, Mass, 65-67; print cataloguer, Parke-Bernet Galleries, New York, 68-71; res asst, Metrop Mus Art, New York, 72-75; chief cur, Chrysler Mus at Norfolk, 76-79; cur Europ art, High Mus, Atlanta, 79-84; cur, Renaissance & Baroque Art, Walters Art Gallery, Baltimore, Md, 84-89; cur, Europ Painting, Mus Fine Art, Boston, formerly; dept dir curatorial affairs, Jewish Mus, New York, 95-97; cur, European Painting, Wadsworth Atheneum, Hartford. *Teaching:* Assoc prof Rembrandt, City Col New York, 75-76; assoc adj, Northern Paintings, Old Dominion Univ, 77-78; assoc prof, French 19th Century Acad Art, Emory Univ, 81 & 83; adj prof, Renaissance & Baroque Art, Johns Hopkins SCE, 86 & 87; sem, French 18th Century Painting, Mus Fine Arts, Boston, 90. *Mem:* Coll Art Asn; Am Asn Mus. *Publ:* European Art in the High Museum, Atlanta, 84; Fifty Old Master Paintings in the Walters Art Gallery, 88; The Forsyth Wickes Collection of Paintings and Drawings in the Museum of Fine Arts, 92; Collecting Italian Baroque Painting in America, 94; French Paintings in the MFA, Boston, 98. *Mailing Add:* 600 Main St Hartford CT 06103

ZAGO, TINO (AGOSTINO) C
PAINTER
b Crespano del Grappa, Italy, 1937; US citizen. *Study:* Lawrence Inst Technol, Mich, BS (archit), 60; Cranbrook Acad Art, MFA (painting), 66; Yale Univ, 69. *Work:* Cranbrook Acad Art, Bloomfield Hills, Mich; State Univ New York at Buffalo; Tucson Mus Art, Tucson, Ariz; Flint Inst Art, Flint, Mich; Erie Art Mus, Erie, Pa; Butler Mus Art, Youngstown, Ohio; St Roock & St Roock, Lavan, New York; AT&T Long Lines, Va. *Comn:* Painting, comn by Hyatt Regency Hotel, Aruba, 90; painting, comn by New York Hilton Hotels, 92; painting, comn by Benesch Friedlander Coplan & Aranoff, Cleveland, Ohio, 95. *Exhib:* OK Harris Gallery East, Scottsdale, Ariz, 1981; OK Harris Gallery, NY, 81, 83-87, 89, 91, 93-95, 98, 2000, 2003, 2006, 2009, 2011; McIntosh Gallery, Atlanta, Ga, 86 & 89; OK Harris Gallery South, Miami, Fla, 1987; Tortue Gallery, Santa Monica, Calif, 88; Jaffe Baker Gallery, Boca Raton, Fla, 92; Robert Kidd Gallery, Birmingham, Mich, 96. *Teaching:* Vis artist, Mich State Univ, East Lansing, Yale Univ, New Haven, Conn & Summit Art Ctr, Summit, NJ. *Awards:* Emerging Artist Grant, Nat Endowment Arts, 82; Nat Endowment Arts Grant, 85.

Bibliog: M H Stolback (auth), Tino Zago, Arts Mag, 81; Theodore F Wolff (auth), Zago's American Vision, The Christian Sci Monitor, 83; Suzanne Muchnic (auth), At the Galleries--Tino Zago, Los Angeles Times, 88. *Media:* Acrylic. *Dealer:* OK Harris Gallery 383 W Broadway New York NY 10012. *Mailing Add:* 376 Broome St 2nd Flr New York NY 10013

ZAHAYKEVICH, TAMARA
SCULPTOR
b Maplewood, New Jersey, 1971. *Study:* Tyler Sch Art Rome, 1991; Tyler Sch Art, Elkins Park, Pa, BFA (Sculpture), 1995. *Exhib:* Solo exhibs include He Said She Said, Oak Park, Ill, 2008; group exhibs include L C Bates Mus, Hinckley, Maine, 1995; A Special Place, Arena, Brooklyn, NY, 2002; End of the Rainbow, Bellwether Gallery, Brooklyn, NY, 2002; You, Lisa Kirk Projs, New York, 2003; Love Apples, Morsel, Brooklyn, NY, 2005; Brooklyn Fire Proof Inc, Brooklyn, NY, 2004; You have to be almost gifted to do what I do, Alexander & Bonin, New York, 2006; packedsockdrawer, Feature Inc, New York, 2007, Shit: Found Stuff Used, 2008; Accident Black Spot, ATM Gallery, New York, 2008. *Awards:* Pollock-Krasner Found Grant, 2007

ZAHEDI, CAVEH
FILMMAKER, VIDEO ARTIST
b Washington, DC, Apr 29, 1960. *Study:* Yale Univ, BA (philos), 81; Sch Film & Television, Univ Calif, Los Angeles, MFA (film production), 91. *Work:* I Was Possessed by God (film); I Don't Hate Las Vegas Anymore (film); A Little Stiff (with Greg Watkins). *Comn:* Worm (with Jay Rosenblatt), comn by Con Works, Seattle. *Exhib:* Sundance Film Festival, Sundance Inst, Park City, Utah, 91; New Directors/New Films, Mus Mod Art, NY, 91; Pesaro Film Festival, Lincoln Ctr, Pesaro, Italy, 91; Am Independents Ser, WDR Television, Koln, Ger, 92; Towards a New Narrator, Centro Galego Arte Contemporanea, Santiago, Spain, 96. *Teaching:* San Francisco State Univ, 99-2000; Acad Art Col, San Francisco, 99; City Col, San Francisco, 2000. *Awards:* Rotterdam Film Festival Critics Award, Asn Dutch Critics, 94; Atlanta Film Festival Best Feature, Image Film & Video Ctr, 97; Guggenheim Fel, 97. *Bibliog:* Elizabeth Royle (auth), The Sundance Kids, Details Mag, 91; Jonathan Rosenbaum (auth), A few things well, Chicago Reader, 91; Janet Maslin (auth), The awkward appeal of a young man's chase, NY Times, 91. *Mem:* Independent Feature Project; Film Arts Found. *Media:* Film. *Publ:* Contribr, Treize Facons De Regarder un Merle, Babylone, 84; On Recent Cinema, Passion, 86; Wanting to say thank you, thank you, thank you, The Voyeur, 89; I Love Kath Bloom With Platonic Love, Dear CMJ, 96

ZAHOUREK, JON GAIL
PAINTER, SCULPTOR
b Oklahoma City, Okla, Jan 5, 1940. *Study:* Univ Northern Colo, 58-59; Colo Inst Art, with Charles Dye & John Jellico, cert, 61; New Sch Social Res, 79-81. *Work:* Ariz State Univ Matthews Ctr; City & Co Denver; Oklahoma City Chamber Commerce. *Exhib:* Missouri Valley Drawing, Mulvane Art Ctr, Topeka, Kans, 67; Changing Image of the Indian, Mus NMex, Santa Fe, 70; Colo Biennial, Denver Art Mus, 75; Mainstreams of Am Art, Marietta Col, 76; Am Bronzes, Ariz State Univ, 81; Drawing Defined, Nat Arts Club, NY, 82; solo exhib, Newhouse Gallery, NY, 84. *Teaching:* Instr graphics, Univ Denver, 67; Instr drawing & anatomy, Parsons Sch Design, 78-; instr anatomy, New York Acad, 82- & Art Students League, 84. *Awards:* Second Prize, Black & White on Paper, Nat Arts Club, 82. *Bibliog:* John Jellico (auth), Jon Zahourek--draughtsman, Am Artist, 67. *Mem:* Soc Artists & Anatomists (chmn, 82-84). *Media:* Oil. *Publ:* Auth, Drawings I, pvt publ, 75; Maniken--A Comprehensive Educational System for the Study of Human & Comparative Gross Anatomy, Zahourek Systems Inc, 82. *Mailing Add:* 2198 W 15th St Loveland CO 80538

ZAIKINE, VICTOR (ZAK) EUGENE
SCULPTOR, PAINTER
b Queens, NY, Sept 7, 1941. *Study:* Pratt Inst, NY, 59-64, sculpture with Charles Ginnever, 63, also painting with Nicholas Buhalis, 81-83. *Work:* Wright State Univ Mus, Dayton, Ohio; Brooklyn Automotive High Sch, NY; Laguna Gloria Art Mus, Austin, Tex; Hecksher Mus, Huntington, NY; Woodstock Mus & Hist Soc, NY; Sonoma County Art Mus; Multiple Choice: A Multimedia Exhibit, Sebastopol Center for the Arts, Sebastopol, Calif, 2007; Small Things Considered, Sebastopol Center for the Arts, 7/19/2007-8/19/2007; The Galleria, Occidental, Calif, 2008; White House, 2010. *Comn:* Sculpture, Midwood High Sch, Brooklyn, NY. *Exhib:* Solo exhibs, The Woodstock Yrs and Beyond, 93, Sebastopol Ctr Arts 20 X 1, Calif, 95, New Works, Franki Waters Gallery, Bodega Bay, Calif, 96, Tribute to Landscape, Impressions Gallery, Healdsburg, Calif, 97, The Joyful Feeling Again, Santa Rosa, Calif, 98, A Survey of Studio Ceramics: 1998-2002, C Street Gallery, Davis, Calif & And the River Flows Etcetera, Etcetera, Guerneville, Calif; 1st Ann Woodstock Guild-Members Show, Kleinert Art Ctr, 85; Form & Line, Woodstock Artist Asn, Woodstock, NY, 88; Big Fruit and Big Flowers, State of Calif Bldg, Santa Rosa, Calif, 96; The Joyful Feeling Again, Mendocino, Calif, 97; Raining Cats and Dogs, Studio Gallery, Alameda, Calif, 98; Magical Lillies, New Ceramics Wimberly, Sable V Fine Art Gallery, Tex, 98; Art Full Living at Home and with Art, Sebastopol, Calif, 98; Getting the Pearls and New Sprit, Bodega, Calif, 98; The Human Form, Juried Exhib, Sebastopol Ctr Arts, Calif, 2004; Feeding the Earth & Ourselves, Saga Art Gallery, Cotati, Calif, 2005; 60 Yrs of Fire, Form & Function, Juried Group Exhib, Falkirk Cult Ctr, San Rafael, Calif, 2005; New Spirit, Mayhew Gallery, Tubac, Ariz, 2006-; Multiple Choice, Juried Exhib, Sebastopol, Calif, 2007; New Bronze Sculpture...Ceramics & Representational Sculpture also Mixed Media, 1992-2007, Bodega Landmark Studio, Calif; and many others; Crossing the Line Juried Group exhib, San Rafael, Calif, 2009; New Works on Canvas, Featured Artist, Madison, Wis, 2009; That Joyeous Feeling Again, Featured Artist, Bodega, Calif, 2009; The Quicksilver mine6, Forestville, Calif, 2010; Featured Artist Bodega Land March Studio, Bodega, Calif, 2010; Small Works, Artworks, San Rafael, 2009; Out of the Fire, Clay & Glass from ACGA, 2009-2010; Magical Earth with John O Hanses, Rick Press Gallery, 2011. *Pos:* Adjudicator, State Grants, Mich Coun Arts, 88; cur, Working in Woodstock, Six contemp artists, Pittsfield Arts Ctr, Pittsfield, Mass; art consult, currently. *Teaching:* instr workshops, Selling Your Art, Not Your Soul, currently. *Awards:* First Place, Fiesta de Artes, Los Gatos, Calif, 76; Distinction Award, State Univ NY, Albany, 85; Best of Show, Laquinta Arts Found, 86; Grant, Adolph & Esther Gottlieb Found, 2006; Grant, Pollack-Krasner Found, 2007; Grant, Artist Fel Found, 2007; Best in Show, Beverly Hills, Calif, 85; Artist Fel Grant, 2005, 2009; Visual Aid Grant, San Francisco, 2010. *Bibliog:* Tram Combs (auth), Zak Zaikine's drypoints, 12/23/82 & Zaikine's tribute to the landscape, 6/1/83, Woodstock Times; Bernard Bovasso (auth), Zaikine's works defy morality, Daily Freeman, 5/31/83; Rebecca Daniels (auth), Zak Zaikine, Woodstock Times, Vol 14, No 25, NY, 85; Olivia Casey (auth), Zak's magic, Sonoma Index-Tribune, Calif, 2/21/86; Mark Dorrity, Man of Steel, New Art International, Vol XII, 2007-2008; Polychrome welded steel sculptures (10 page spread), 1983-2007; Ceramics Today, Schiffer Publ, Atglen, Pa, 2009; Barbara Shola (auth), Artist Profile, Zak Zaikine, Sonoma County, 2010; A New Era New Beginnings, The upbeat Times, Santa Rosa, Calif, 2010. *Mem:* Sonoma Co Arts Coun; Woodstock Arts Asn Inc; Cooperstown Art Asn Inc; Woodstock Guild Craftsmen Inc; Sebastopol Ctr for Arts; Asn Clay and Glass; Art Collecting Network Group; Am Asn Mus; Art Dealer Network; Russian Am Prof Assn. *Media:* Steel, Bronze, Mixed Media, Ceramics. *Interests:* Creating art that reflects introspection; joyeous, happy & colorful images. *Collection:* Warren + Susie Buffett, Charles Ginnever, Red Grooms, Dorothy Dehner & EP Draper, Betty Asher, Barack & Michelle Obama, Paul Taylor, Dr Michael Ross, Dennis & Zeplyr Sweeny, Shayne Cook. *Publ:* auth & illusr, numerous children's books, 2003-; auth, I love you (poetry book); auth, I love you too (poetry book); auth, Love inside (poetry book); auth, Thinking of You (poetry book); Karin O'Keefe (co-auth) Eugene & His Magical Dreams, 2009-2010; Karin O'Keefe (co-auth), The Magic of Hanalei Bay, 2006; Karin O'Keefe, A Mother's Love, 2006; Karin O'Keefe (co-auth), Eugene & the Magical Carrot Tree, 2006; Karin O'Keefe (co-auth), Dreams; Karin O'Keefe (co-auth), Dancing by the Light of the Moon, 2012. *Dealer:* Landmark Gallery Bodega CA. *Mailing Add:* 8885 Oak Grove Ave Sebastopol CA 95472

ZAIMA, STEPHEN GYO
PAINTER, SCULPTOR
b San Jose, Calif, Jan 3, 1947. *Study:* Pratt Inst, 68; Sch Visual Arts, New York, 68; Calif State Univ, San Jose, BA, 69; Univ Calif, Davis, MFA, 71. *Work:* Univ Calif, Davis & Veterans Mem Bldg, Long Beach. *Comn:* Long Beach Mural, Calif Arts Coun, 83. *Exhib:* Gallery Tamura, Tokyo, Japan, 74; Queens Mus, NY, 85; Everson Mus Art, Syracuse, NY, 85; City Univ NY Grad Ctr, 86; Stephen Rosenberg Gallery, 86; McNay Found, 87; One Penn Plaza, NY, 87. *Teaching:* Syracuse Univ, 80-. *Awards:* Fel, Nat Endowment Arts, 74; Grant, Ford Found, 80 & 81; Fel, Edward Albee Found, 81. *Bibliog:* Peter Morrin (auth), article, Atlanta Art Papers, 3/80; Vered Lieb (auth), A study of scale, Arts Mag, 2/87; Kenneth Baker (auth), catalog essay, Everson Mus Art, 85. *Media:* Oil; Mixed. *Publ:* Contribr, Contesting the Boundaries Between Liberal & Professional Educ, Syracuse Univ Press, 88

ZAJAC, JACK
SCULPTOR
b Youngstown, Ohio, Dec 13, 1929. *Study:* Scripps Col, 49-53; also with Millard Sheets, Henry McFee & Sueo Serisawa; Am Acad in Rome. *Work:* Whitney Mus Am Art, Mus Mod Art, NY; Los Angeles Mus Art; Pa Acad Fine Arts, Philadelphia; Israel Mus, Jerusalem; Hirshhorn Mus & Sculpture Garden, Washington; plus others. *Comn:* Reynolds Metals Co, 68; Wells Fargo Bank Plaza, Beverly Hills, Calif; Univ Calif, Santa Cruz; Civic Ctr Mall, Inglewood, Calif; Civic Ctr Plaza, Huntington Beach, Calif. *Exhib:* Whitney Mus Ann, 59; Recent Sculpture USA, Mus Mod Art, 59; Am Painting, Va Mus Fine Arts, Richmond, 62; Fifty California Artists, Whitney Mus Mod Art, NY, 62-63; Pittsburgh Int, Carnegie Inst, 65; retrospectives, Newport Harbor Art Mus, Balboa, Calif, 65, Temple Univ, Rome, 69, Santa Barbara Mus, 75 & Fine Arts Gallery San Diego, 75; Stephen Wirtz Gallery, San Francisco, Calif, 84 & 87; Monterey Peninsula Mus Art, Calif, 88; Palo Alto Cult Ctr, Calif, 88; Jack Zajac Sculpture: 1954-1987, Art Special Gallery, Oakland Mus, Calif, 90; Art Mus Santa Cruz Coun, Calif, 93; solo exhibs, Art Mus Santa Cruz Co, Calif, 93, Acad Art Col, San Francisco, 96 & Meditations on Falling Water & Other Works, Frederick Spratt, Calif, 97; Sculptor Exhib, Acad Art Col, San Francisco, 94; Still Working, Former IBM Gallery, NY, 95; Lost Wax Foundry Friends III, Conley Art Gallery, Calif State Univ, Fresno, 96. *Teaching:* Instr, Pomona Col, 59; prof, Univ Calif, Santa Cruz, retired. *Awards:* Artist-in-residence, Am Acad in Rome, 68; artist-in-residence, Dartmouth Col, 70; artist in residence, Univ Calif, Santa Cruz, 69-70. *Bibliog:* Kenneth Baker (auth), San Francisco Chronicle, 3/31/88; Mary Ann Toal (auth), Jack Zajac, Art Calif, 10-11/89; Susan Greer (auth), Un-Sitely specific, Artweek, 11/30/89. *Mem:* Nat Acad (assoc, 81, acad, 02-). *Media:* Bronze, Marble. *Mailing Add:* c/o Stephen Wirtz Gallery 49 Geary St 3rd Flr San Francisco CA 94108

ZAKANITCH, ROBERT RAHWAY
PAINTER
b Elizabeth, NJ. *Study:* Newark Sch Fine & Indust Art. *Work:* Whitney Mus Am Art, New York; Munich Mus Mod Art, Ger; Philadelphia Mus, Pa; Wadsworth Atheneum, Hartford, Conn; Phoenix Mus, Ariz; Hirshhorn Mus & Sculpture Garden, Washington, DC; Rothschild Bank, Zurich, Switz; AT&T, New York; High Mus, Atlanta, Ga. *Exhib:* The Expressionist Image: Am Art from Pollock to Today, Sidney Janis Gallery, New York, 82; The Restoration of Painterly Figuration, Kitakyushu Munic Mus Art, Japan, 84; Works on Paper, Robert Miller Gallery, New York, 85; An Am Renaissance: Painting and Sculpture Since 1940 (with catalog), Mus Art, Ft Lauderdale, Fla, 86; solo exhib, Sidney Janis Gallery, New York, 90, Jason McCoy Gallery, New York, 94, Hirschl/Adler Modern, New York, 97 & Spike Gallery, New York, 2003; Patricia Faure Gallery, Los Angeles, 97 & 2003; Spike Gallery, 2005; Samuel Freeman Gallery, Los Angeles, 2010. *Teaching:* Painting, Univ Calif, San Diego, 73; vis artist, Chicago Art Inst, 78; instr drawing & painting, Okla Summer Arts Inst, 89-. *Awards:*

Guggenheim Fel, 95. *Bibliog:* John Perreault (auth), Patterning, Artforum, 11/78; John Ashbery (auth), Climbing the wallpaper, NY Mag, 1/29/79; Cover review, Art in Am, 10/94; Arthur Danto (auth), Colossal canvases, Nation, 3/94; Carter Ratcliff (auth), Art in Am, The Politics of Ornamentation, 4/98. *Mailing Add:* PO Box 1954 New York NY 10156

ZAKIAN, MICHAEL
MUSEUM DIRECTOR, CURATOR
b New York, NY, April 7, 1957. *Study:* Columbia Univ, BA, 79; Rutgers Univ, MA, 84, PhD, 94. *Collection Arranged:* Agnes Pelton: Poet of Nature, 95; Nathan Oliveira: The Wind Hover, 96; Sam Francis: The Archetypes Image, 97; Historical Landscapes of Malibu, 98; Sanoro Chia: New Paintings, 99; Peter Lodato: From Installation to Painting, 2000. *Pos:* assoc cur, Palm Springs Desert Mus, 86-95; dir, Pepperdine Univ Federick Weisman Mus of Art, 95-. *Teaching:* instr modern art Rutgers Univ, NJ, 85; instr American art Calif State Univ, San Bernardino, 89; instr modern art, Univ of the Redlands, Calif. *Mem:* Art Historians of Southern Calif (vp 2000, pres 2001). *Interests:* abstract expressionism, modern American art. *Publ:* Auth, Barnett Newmon and the Sublime, Arts Mag, 2/88; Barnett Newmon: Paintings and a Sense of Place, Arts Mag, 3/88. *Mailing Add:* Pepperdine Univ Frederick R Weisman Mus of Art 24255 Pacific Coast Hwy Malibu CA 90263

ZAKIN, MIKHAIL
SCULPTOR, EDUCATOR
b Brooklyn, NY, June 23, 1920. *Study:* Sch Mus Fine Arts, Boston, Mass; Art Students League, sculpture with William Zorach & Albino Manca; also ceramics with Karen Karnes & David Weinrib. *Work:* Peat Marwick Art Collection, Montvale, NJ; Brooklyn Mus; Nagamatso Collection, Japan; Mobach Potten Bakker, Holland; Epstein Collection, Paris, France; Mus Art & Science, Salt Lake City, Ia. *Exhib:* Am Potters, Mus Arts & Sci, Salt Lake City, 75; Four US Potters, Fair Tree Gallery, 75; Pratt Grad Sch, NY, 75-77; Brooklyn Col, 75-77; Baruch Col, NY, 75-77; Retrospective, Sarah Lawrence Col, 91; Retrospective, Worcester Ctr Craft, 2002; Hunterdon Mus, 2008; Dennis Mus, Mass. *Pos:* Founder & dir, Sch Art at Old Church Cult Ctr, Demarest, NJ, 74-; potters sem leader, England, 76, Japan, 77, Mexico, 78, Italy, 79, China, 81, Holland, 82 & Korea, 83; co-founder, Scotland-North Coast Continuum, 78-; co-founder, East-West Inst Arts & Sch Art, Old Church Cult Ctr, Demarest, NJ. *Teaching:* Advan ceramics instr, Greenwich House Pottery, 71-75; head ceramics dept, Brooklyn Mus Art Sch, 72-75 & Sarah Lawrence Col, 76-90; instr, Castle Hill Ctr Arts, Mass, 76-; instr, Art Sch at Old Church; Mendocino Ctr for the Arts, Calif. *Awards:* Lebensburger Found Grant, 74; Craftsmen's Fel, NJ Coun Arts, 75 & Nat Endowment Arts, 76; NJ State Coun, 89. *Bibliog:* Elsbeth Woody (auth), Hand Building Ceramics, Farrar Strauss Giroux, 79; Anthony Padovano (auth), Sculpture Practice, Doubleday, 81; Nino Caruso (auth), Ceramica Raku, Hoepli-Milano, 82. *Mem:* Am Crafts Coun; World Crafts Coun; Nat Conf Ceramic Educators; NY Artist Craftsman; Korea Cult Coun (video documentation grant, project dir Korean pottery making 82, 83, 84). *Media:* Clay. *Interests:* Visual commun in the arts. *Collection:* Halpert Collection, Mass, Utrecht Holland, Greenwich Collection, NY. *Publ:* Contribr, Poletechnic Design, Korea, 84, Keranos-Madrid, 86; Jack Troy & Watson-Guptill (auth), Salt Glaze Ceramics, 77; Padovano (auth), Process of Sculpture, Double Day, 81; Hand Built Ceramics, Lark Book Tripplet. *Mailing Add:* 37 County Rd Closter NJ 07624

ZALLINGER, JEAN DAY
ILLUSTRATOR, EDUCATOR
b Boston, Mass, Feb 15, 1918. *Study:* Mass Coll of Art, cert (drawing & painting), 35-39; Yale Sch Fine Arts, BFA, 42. *Work:* Kerlan Found; Univ Minn; Rutgers Univ; Univ Southern Miss; De Grummond, permanent collection, Paint & Clay Club, NH; Univ Conn Collection. *Exhib:* Dinosaurs Past & Present, Los Angeles Co Mus Natural Hist (travel US & Europe), 86-90; Aetna Gallery, Hartford; Mass Coll Art, 92; Mellon Gallery, Cheshire, Conn, 94. *Pos:* Tech illus draftsman, Applied Physics Lab, Univ Wash, Seattle, 51-53. *Teaching:* Prof drawing & illusr, Paier Col Art, Hamden, Conn. *Awards:* Nat Sci Teachers Awards for Biography of a Fish Hawk & I Watch Flies, 77; Alumna of the Year, 92; Mass Coll Art, 92. *Bibliog:* NH Register, 1/83; Rocks & Minerals, Heldref Publ, 3-4/92. *Mem:* Paint & Clay Club, New Haven, Conn; Arts Coun New Haven; Artspace, New Haven; Soc Children's Book Writers. *Publ:* Biography of a Fish Hawk, Putnam Bk, 77; Nature's Champions, 80, Dinosaurs, Asteroids & Super Stars, 82, Baby Dinosaurs, 84, Sharks, 86, Whales, 87 & Eagles, 88, Lothrop Lee Shepard; Sesame St Q & A Book About Animals, 83; Monsters of the Sea, Little Brown, 90-; The Earliest Americans, Clarion, 93. *Mailing Add:* c/o Paier Col 20 Gorham Ave Hamden CT 06514

ZALOUDEK, DUANE
PAINTER
b Texhoma, Tex, Jan 15, 1931. *Study:* Portland Mus Art Sch, Ore, cert, 56. *Work:* Portland Art Mus, Ore; Dallas Mus Fine Arts, Tex; Aargauer Kunsthaus, Aarau, Switz; Schweizerische Landesbibliothek, Bern, Switz. *Exhib:* Various exhib, Portland Art Mus, 49-86; Northwest Ann, Seattle Art Mus, 59-68; W Coast Ann, San Francisco Art Mus, 60-61; W Coast Now, Los Angeles City Mus, 68; Whitney Mus Am Art, 69; Watercolors, Akron Art Inst, Ohio, 76; Radikal Auf Papier, Aargauer Kunsthaus, Aarau, Switz, 90; 3Ness, Mus Dhondt-Dhaenes, Deurle, Belgium, 2000; Das Gedachtnis Der Malerei, Aargauer Kunsthaus, Aarau, Switz, 2000; 29 solo exhibs, 55-2013; Boden und Wand/Wand Und Fenster, Helmhaus, Zurich. *Teaching:* Artist-in-residence, Portland Univ, 62-65; vis artist, Univ Calif, Davis, 70-73. *Awards:* Adolph Gottlieb Found Award, 78; Mark Rothko Found Award, 86; Nat Endowment Arts, 87; fellow, Radcliffe Inst Advanced Study, Harvard Univ, 2011-2012. *Bibliog:* Charlotte Hughes (auth), A profile, Univ Portland Rev, 65; Tiffany Bell (auth), article, Arts Mag, 4/78. *Media:* Acrylic, Oil, Watercolor. *Specialty:* Contemp Art. *Publ:* Duane Zaloudek, Nomad Songs, Lars Muller, 2010. *Dealer:* Galerie Mark Muller Hafnerstrasse 44 CH 8005 Zurich; Akira Ikeda Gallery Nagoya Japan & New York NY. *Mailing Add:* 431 E 12th St New York NY 10009

ZALUCHA, PEGGY FLORA
PAINTER
b Peoria, Ill, Sept 18, 1948. *Work:* Lakeview Mus Arts & Scis, Peoria, Ill; Hoyt Inst Fine Art, New Castle, Pa; Brea Mus Fine Art, Calif; Paine Mus Art, Oshkosh, Wis; Charles A Wustum Mus Fine Art, Racine, Wis. *Comn:* Seventeen paintings, Wis Chamber Orchestra, Madison, 83-2000; six paintings, 84 & two mem paintings, 88 & 93, Dane Co, Madison, Wis, 88; painting, Madison Civic Ctr, Wis, 87. *Exhib:* Nat Watercolor Soc Exhibs, Brea Cult Ctr, Calif, 82, 83, 87, 89-92; Nat Soc Painters Casein & Acrylic Exhib, Nat Arts Club, NY, 83, 84, 89, 92; Rocky Mountain Nat Watermedia Exhib, Foothills Art Ctr, Golden, Colo, 85, 88, 89, 92, 93 & 94; solo exhibs, West Bend Gallery Fine Art, Wis, 86, Lakeview Mus (exhib catalog), Peoria, Ill, 90, Neville Mus, Green Bay, Wis, 91 & Wis Acad Fine Arts, Madison, 91. *Awards:* Best of Show, Nat Watercolor Soc Exhib, 87; Century Merit Award, Rocky Mountain Nat Watermedia Exhib, Foothills Art Ctr, 88 & 92; Nat Galleries Award, Nat Watercolor Soc Exhib, Nat Galleries, 91. *Bibliog:* Bebe Raupe (auth), Award winning watercolorists, Artists Mag, 7/88; William C Landwehr (auth), Defining light with tight control, Am Artist Mag, 9/90; Gerald Brommer (auth), Understanding Transparent Watercolor, Davis Publ Inc, 93. *Mem:* Am Watercolor Soc; Nat Watercolor Soc; Nat Soc Painters Casein & Acrylic; Midwest Watercolor Soc; Wis Painters & Sculptors/Artists All Media, (chap bd 88-). *Media:* Transparent Watercolor, Acrylic on Paper. *Mailing Add:* 109 Sunset Lane Mount Horeb WI 53572-1865

ZAMORA, HECTOR
INSTALLATION SCULPTOR
b Mexico City, Mex, Nov 19, 1974. *Study:* Universidad Autonoma Metropolitana Xochimilco, BA (graphic design), 1998. *Exhib:* Fission/Fusion, Mexican Cult Inst, Washington DC, 2003; Dialogues, Indian Int Ctr, New Delhi, India, 2005; 27th Bienal de Sao Paulo, Sao Paulo, Brazil, 2006; Viva Mexico, Zacheta Nat Gallery Art, Warsaw, Poland, 2007; 53rd Int Venice Biennale, Venice, Italy, 2009. *Awards:* Pollock-Krasner Found Grant, 2007. *Mailing Add:* Rua Catequese 100 Sao Paulo Brazil 05502-020

ZANE, JOE
SCULPTOR
b Utica, NY, 1971. *Study:* Alfred Univ, BFA, 1992; Cornell Univ, MFA, 2003. *Exhib:* Solo exhibs, Experimental Gallery, Cornell Univ, 2001, Herbert F Johnson Mus, Cornell Univ, 2003, Allston Skirty Gallery, Boston, 2004, 2006, Carroll & Sons, Boston, 2009; Look What Washed Ashore, Experimental Gallery, Cornell Univ, 2001; small & UGLY, Univ Md, Baltimore, 2002; Just Stand There!, MIT List Visual Art Ctr, 2003; Likeness: Portraits of Artists by Other Artists, Inst Contemp Art, Boston, 2005; Don't Know Much About History, ArtSpace New Haven, COnn, 2006; This Is Killing Me, Mass Mus Contemp Art, 2009. *Teaching:* Lectr, MIT Visual Arts Ctr, currently. *Awards:* Louis Comfort Tiffany Found Grant, 2009. *Bibliog:* Christine Temin (auth), Here's Looking at You, Boston Globe, 2005; Ben Genocchio (auth), Show Gives Art History New Meaning, NY Times, 12/31/2006; Keith Powers, Four Eyes, Boston Herald, 11/20/2008. *Mailing Add:* MIT Visual Arts Ctr 265 Massachusetts Ave Rm N52-396 Cambridge MA 02139

ZANISNIK, BRYAN
VIDEO ARTIST, PHOTOGRAPHER
b Union, NJ, June 25, 1979. *Study:* Drew Univ, BA, 2001; Skowhegan Sch Painting & Sculpture, 2008; Hunter Coll, MFA, 2009. *Work:* Hudson Valley Ctr Contemp Art, Peekskill, NY. *Exhib:* Washing Crossing the Meadowlands, Jersey City Mus, NJ, 2006; High Roads & Low Roads, Mus Fine Arts, Tallahasse, Fla, 2006; Sprawl, Jersey City Mus, NJ, 2008; This Land is Your Land, Mus Contemp Photography, Chicago, 2008; T.error= Your Fear is an External Object, Mus Kunsthalle, Hungary, 2008; Kurye Int Video Festival, Istanbul Mus Mod Art, Istanbul, Turkey, 2010; Now Playing, PS1 Contemp Art Ctr, New York, 2010. *Awards:* Artist Grant, Puffin Found, 2005; Graf Travel Grant, Hunter Coll, New York, 2007; Artist Fel, Geralding R Dodge Found, 2007; Artist Fel, Skowhegan Sch Painting & Sculpture, 2008; Artist in Residence, Acad Fine Art, Poznan, Poland, 2010; Artist in Residence, The Aldrich Contemp Art Mus, 2010. *Bibliog:* Joseph R Wolin (auth), Young Cur, New Ideas II, Time Out New York, 2009; Kim Levin (auth), Young Cur, New Ideas II, ARTnews, 2009; Joseph R Wolin (auth), Critics Pick, Artforum.com, 2009; David Duncan (auth), Bryan Zanisnik at Sunday LES, Art in Am, 2010; Kate Stone Lombardi, 13 Artists, & Just as many Themes, NY Times, 2010. *Media:* Video

ZANSKY, MICHAEL
PAINTER, SCULPTOR, PHOTOGRAPHER
b New York City, 1947. *Study:* Boston Univ, Sch Fine Arts, BFA, 69. *Work:* Brooklyn Mus, New York; De Cordova Mus, Lincoln, Mass; Neuberger Mus, Purchase, NY; Prudential Life, New York; Whitney Mus, New York; Berkeley Art Mus, Berkeley, Calif; Biocraft Laboratories; Inter-Am Develop Bank; Tremaine Found; Wadsworth Athenaeum; Krannert Art Mus; Dallas Mus Art. *Exhib:* Solo exhibs, Cavin-Morris Gallery, New York, Gallery Camino Real, Boca Raton, Fla & Universal Concepts Unlimited, New York, 2000, Lab Gallery for Installation & Performance Art, New York, 2009, Ice Box Gallery, Philadelphia, Pa, 2010, GAGA Arts Ctr, Garnerville, NY, 2010; John Michael Kohler Art Ctr, Sheboygan, Wis, 2000; Norton Mus, West Palm Beach, Fla, 2001; Briggs Robinson Gallery, NY, 2003; Slought Found, Philadelphia, Pa, 2003; Am Panopticon, Gigantic Art Space (GAS), 2005; Aldrich Mus Contemp Art, Ridgefield, Conn, 2006; Nassau Mus, NY, 2007; Fieldgate Gallery, London, 2007; Nicholas Robinson Gallery, New York, 2007 & 09; Sandy Carson Gallery, Denver, 2008; Corn xchange Gallery, Edinburgh, Scotland, 2008; Dorsky Gallery Cur Prog, Long Island City, NY, 2008; Schmidt Ctr Gallery/ Fla Atlantic Univ, Boca Raton, Fla, 2009; Housatonic Mus, Bridgeport, Conn, 2011; Artjail, New York, 2010; SICA, Long Branch, NJ, 2010; Rodger La Pelle Galleries, Philadelphia, Pa, 2010; Exit Art, New York, 2011; Hampden Gallery, UMass Amherst, Am Panopticon, Amherst, Mass, 2012; Yellowstone Mus, Billings, Montana, 2013; Boca Raton Mus Art, Boca Raton, Fla, 2013; Univ Tenn, Ewing Gallery, Knoxville, Tenn, 2013; Mana

Contemporary, Jersey City, NJ, 2013. *Pos:* Production designer, master set painter. *Awards:* Fulbright-Hayes Fel, Peru; Louis Comfort Tiffany Award, 78; Fel, Creative Artists Pub Serv. *Bibliog:* Gerrit Henry (auth), Art in Am, 2000; Christopher Chambers (auth), Sculpture Mag, 2003; Raymond Jon (auth), Artforum, 2004; Jay Murphy (auth), Contemp Mag, Vol 21, 2007; D Dominick Lombardi (auth), NY Arts Mag, 2008; Michael Wilson (auth), Time Out New York, 2009; Mary Hrbacek (auth), The M Mag, 2009; and others. *Mem:* Sculpture Guild, NY; United Scenic Artists, NY; Rockland Ctr Arts (bd dirs). *Media:* Painting, optics, sculpture. *Publ:* Michael Zansky: of Giants and Dwarfs, Ewing Gallery of Art & Architecture, Univ Tenn, Knoxville, 2013; Insomnia: Works by Michael Zansky, Yellowstone Mus Art, 2013; American Panoptican, Hampden Gallery, Univ Mass, Amherst, 2012. *Dealer:* Berry Hill Gallery 11 E 70th St NY; Nicholas Robinson Gallery 535 W 20th St NY; Gigantic Art Space 59 Franklin St NY. *Mailing Add:* 67 Demarest Ave West Nyack NY 10994

ZAPEL, ARTHUR LEWIS
ILLUSTRATOR-CHILDREN'S BOOKS, PAINTER

b Chicago, Ill, Nov 17, 1921. *Study:* Columbia Coll Radio & Theatrical Arts, 40; Univ Wis, BA, 46. *Work:* Pikes Peak Ctr, Colorado Springs, Colo; Koshare Indian Mus, La Junta, Colo. *Comn:* Off mural, Meriwether Pub Ltd, Colorado Springs, 84. *Exhib:* Artists of the West, Pioneer Mus, Colorado Springs, 92; Rotary Art Show, Pioneer Mus, Colorado Springs, 93; Colorado Springs Opera Festival Exhib, Pikes Peak Ctr, 94, 95, 96 & 97; Arts Students League Exhib, Smoke Brush Ctr Arts, Colorado Springs, 94; Country Club Colo, 2000; Colorado Springs Open Festival, 94-2000. *Pos:* Creative dir, Kling Studios, Chicago, 52-54; writer & producer, J Walter Thompson Advert, Chicago, 54-70; pres, Arthur Meriwether Inc, 70-83, chmn, exec; chmn, exec ed, Meriwether Publ Ltd. *Awards:* DuKane Gold Camera Award, US Indust Film Festival, 83; Gold Award, Houston Int Film Festival, 84. *Mem:* Arts Students League (pres, 92-93). *Media:* Oil, Alkyds. *Publ:* Illusr, 'Twas the Night Before, Meriwether Publ, 93; ed, Theatre Alive, Meriwether Publ, 93; illusr, The Jabberwocky, Meriwether Publ, 94; auth, Sweet Uncertainty (novel). *Dealer:* Ravens Gallery, Westcliffe, CO. *Mailing Add:* 228 Cobblestone Dr Colorado Springs CO 80906-4803

ZARAND, JULIUS JOHN
PAINTER, RESTORER

b Nagyvarad, Hungary, June 27, 1913; Can citizen. *Study:* Royal Acad, dipl & dipl (educ); also with Oskar Kokoschka, Salzburg, Austria; Acad Ital, Dipl Hon Causa Maestro Pittura, 83. *Work:* City Hall, Halifax, NS; Yokahama Univ Gallery, Japan; Art Bank Nova Scotia; Govt House, PEI. *Comn:* Portrait of Pope Pius XII, comn by Prime Cardinal of Hungary, 38; portrait, comn by Lord Thompson, Toronto, 54; murals, St Bridgid Church, Toronto, 55; portrait of Sir John Thompson, City of Halifax, NS, 68; portraits of all presidents of the co, Maritime Telegraph & Telephone Co, Halifax, NS; murals, Veterans Mem Hosp, Halifax, 88; and others. *Exhib:* Solo exhibs, Halifax Libr, 64, Lafayette Art Ctr, Ind, 69, Purdue Univ Gallery, 69, Zwicker's Gallery, Halifax, 70, Lunenburg Art Gallery, Lunenburg, NS, 89 & Annapolis Valley MacDonald Mus, Middleton, NS, 94, St Mary's Univ Art Gallery, 2009. *Teaching:* Asst prof fine arts, St Mary's Univ, Halifax, 56-65. *Awards:* Gold Medal, Acad Italy, 81; Primo Oscar D'italia, 85; Centauro d'Oro, Acad Italy, 88. *Mem:* Acad Ital; Lunenburg Co, Art Coun; Art Gallery NS; Art Gallery, Lunenburg. *Media:* Oil, Egg Tempera

ZAUFT, RICHARD
ADMINISTRATOR, PHOTOGRAPHER

Study: Univ Wis Madison, BS, 1977, MFA, 1979; Management Development Program, Harvard Univ, Certificate, 2000. *Comn:* California Door Company, Identity Design, Wis, 1990-1992, Kettering Found, Website design, Ohio, 1995-1996, Peck School of the Arts, Univ Wis Milwaukee, Redesign format for all printed matter, 1998, Studio Z, Identity Design, Madison, Wis, 2006, Council of Graduate Schools, Identity Design, Washington, DC, 2011 and several others. *Exhib:* Refocus International Photographic Exhibition, Univ Iowa, 1976, 1977, National Photography Juried Exhibition, Kansas City Art Inst, 1979, Books and Broadsides, North Texas State Univ, 1980, Photography/Xerography National Exhibition, Pinnacle Gallery, Rochester, NY, 1984, National Collegiate Book Arts Exhibition (traveling exhibition to nine US States), 1986-1988, Image-Text, Univ Art Mus, Univ Wis Milwaukee, 1994,, Beautiful Beasts, Ctr for Book Arts, NYC, 1997, The Interaction Between Visual, Literary, and Performing Artists, Crossman Gallery, Ctr for the Arts, Univ Wis Whitewater, 1998, Wood Type Prints From the Hamilton Wood Type Mus, Carey Collection Gallery, Rochester Inst Technology, 2000, Col Book Art Mem Exhibition, Univ Iowa, 2010 and several others. *Collection Arranged:* John D Rockefeller, Jr Library, Rare Book Collection, Brown Univ, Neilson Library Smith Coll, NY Public Library Rare Book Collection, National Gallery of Canada, Scottsdale Community Coll, Ariz, Inst for the Book Arts Univ Alabama and several others. *Pos:* coordinator, arts industry program, John Michael Kohler Art Ctr, Sheyboygan, Wis, 1987-1988; mem artistic board, Hamilton Wood Type and Printing Mus, Two Rivers Wis, 2009-. *Teaching:* Instructor, photography, Madison Arts Ctr, 1976-1977, Univ Wis Extension, 1977-1980; asst to assoc prof art, Univ South Dakota, 1980-1989, chair art dept, 1984-1988; assoc prof art, Peck School of the Arts, Univ Wis-Milwaukee, 1990-1999, head, graphic design program, 1991-1998, chair visual art dept, 1994-1999, assoc dean, 1998-2004, prof art, 1999-2004; assoc vp academic affairs, Emerson Col, Boston, Mass, 2004-2014, exec dir Inst of Interdisciplinary Studies, 2008-2010, interim dean liberal arts, 2008-2010, dean graduate studies, 2009-2014; dean, Lesley Univ Col of Art and Design, 2014-; several visiting artists and lectureships. *Mem:* Soc of Printers (mem exec council, 2007-, vp, 2008-2010, pres, 2010-2012); Col Book Art Asn (vp membership, 2008-2011, bd dirs 2009-, pres 2011-2014). *Mailing Add:* 58 Pantry Rd Sudbury MA 01776

ZAUSNER, TOBI
PAINTER

b New York, NY, Oct 8, 1942. *Study:* Hunter Col, BFA (studio art & art hist), 63; NY Univ, MA (studio art & art theory, Int Ctr Advan Studies Art Fel), 83, Icasa Fel, Int Art Symp, 83, PhD (art & psychology), 93. *Work:* Mus Stony Brook, NY; Williams Ctr Arts, Rutherford, NJ; Art Students League, Mus City New York, NY; Bellevue Hosp, NY; Armenian Archdiocese, Venice, Italy; Mus City of New York; Am Mus Natural Hist; NY Pub Libr Print Collection; Bancroft Pub Libr, Univ Calif, Berkeley; numerous private collections. *Comn:* Lena Albert, Santa Fe, Iris and Stanley Ashkinoz, NY, Leslie Bauman, NY, Charles Biderman, Santa Rosa, Calif. *Exhib:* Solo exhibs: Ronald Feldman Fine Arts, 73, Vision Quest, William Carlos Williams Ctr Arts, 93, Adobe Gallery, NJ, 95, Nat Asn Women Ann Exhib, NY, 96, 2002, 2003, 2009, Small Works Show, Gallery Art 54, NY, 1997, Johnson Gallery, Bedminster, NJ, 1998, Nat Asn Women Artists, NY, 1999, Fragments: Collage and Assemblage, ISE Art Found, NY, 2000, Small Things Considered: A Large Show of Small Works, Elizabeth Found, NY, 2001, Meditations on War, NAWA Gallery, 2004, Small Works Exhib, 2005, Artrageous, 2009, Women & Spirituality, Interchurch Ctr, New York, 2006, Women of Color-Personal Totems, Univ Ctr Gallery, Adelphi Univ, Garden City, NY, 2007, Art Envisions Science, NY Hall of Sci, Queens, NY, 2008, Nat Assn Women Artists, 120th Exhib, Salamagundi Club, NY, 2009, It Started with Eve, Hamilton Fish Park Lib, NY, 2010, Small Works Exhib, NAWA, Gallery, NY, 2011, American Artists, Guilin Mus, China, 2012; Heresies Show, Grey Art Gallery, NY, 81; Figure in Landscape, Artists' Choice Mus, NY, 85; In Her Own Image, Philadelphia Mus Art, Fleischer Mem, 73; The Big Picture, Javits Fed Bldg, NY, 94; Nat Asn Women Ann Exhib, NY, 96; Small Works Show, Gallery Art 54, NY, 97; Continuity and Change, New World Art Ctr, NY, 98; Johnson Gallery, Bedminster, NJ, 98; Nati Asn of Women Artists, New York City, 99; Fragments: Collage and Assemblage, ISE Art Found, New York City, 2000; Small Things Considered: A Large Show of Small Works, Elizabeth Found, New York City, 2001; Ann Exhib, Nat Assoc of Women Artists, New York City, 2002-2003; Meditations on War, NAWA, New York City, 2004, Small Works Exhib, NAWA Gallery, NY, 2005, Women & Spirituality, Interchurch Center, NY, 2006; Women of Color, Personal Totems, Univ Ctr Gallery, Adelponi Univ, 2007; Art Envisions Science, NY Hall Science, Queens, NY, 2008; Spring Into Summer, NAWA Gallery, NY, 2008; Artrageous, NAWA Gallery, New York, 2009; It Started with Eve, Hamilton Fish Park Lib, NY, 2010; Small Works Exhib, NAWA Gallery, NY, 2011; 123rd Ann Mem Exhib, NAWA, Sylvia Wald and Po Kim Gallery, NY, 2012; American Artists, Guilin Mus, China, 2013. *Collection Arranged:* The Mus of the City of NY; The Am Mus of Natural History; The NY Public Library Print Collection; The Bancroft Library, Univ of California, Berkeley; Williams Ctr for the Arts, Rutherford, NJ; The Long Island Mus, Stony Brook, NY, The Guilin Art Mus, Guilin, China. *Pos:* Chair art/art hist, Soc for Chaos Theory in Psychology & the Life Sci, 93; moderator/chair, Symp on Chaos Theory & the Creative Process, Johns Hopkins Univ, 94; chair, Symp Challenges and Creativity, 113 ann Conv of Am Psychological Assoc, Wash, DC, 2005; officer bd, Arts, Crafts and Theatre Safety, 2006. *Teaching:* Guest lectr psychology art, NY Univ, 85, 90, 91 & 93; instr psychology art/art theory, New Sch Social Res, NY Col, 94-99; instr psychology art, CG Jung Found, NY, 96-2008; adjunct prof, psychology creativity, Saybrook Univ, 1997-2013; lectr, participant symposia in field; instr psychology art, Long Island Univ, CW Post Campus, 2007-8. *Awards:* Fel, Int Ctr for Advanced Studies in Art, New York Univ, 1983; Gottlieb Award, A & E Gottlieb Found, 90; Susan Kahn Award, Nat Asn Women Artists, 92; Drawing reproduced in Parabola, 2002-2003; chair, Symp Challenges and Creativity, 113th ann Conv of the Am Psychological Assoc in Wash, DC; featured artist, Nonlinear Dynamics, Psychology, and Life Sciences, 2007; advisory bd appoint, Mind-Body Medicine, Greenwood Pub Group, 2007; Rose Biller Scholarship, Rose Biller Endowment Fund, UJA Fed New York, 2009; Jacob Goldfein Award for Excellence & Creativity in Clinical Res, 2010; co-chair symposium, Creative Expression and Healing, 119th Ann Convention, Am Psychological Asn, Orlando, Fla, 2012; consulting mem, organizing comt, Humanistic Psychology Inst under auspices of Society of Humanistic Psychology, 2012; Johnson Memorial award for Works on Canvas, 2012. *Bibliog:* Peter Frank (auth), Where is New York, Art News, 11/79; Art centers around Native Americans, Twin-Boro News, NJ, 7/23/93; Eileen Watkins (auth), Art, Sunday Star Ledger, NJ, 7/25/93; ArtForum, The Village Voice, Newark Star Ledger, Christian Sci Monitor, The New York Post, The Philadelphia Bull, The New Yorker, Newsday, The Wall Street Journal; Transforming Illness, Encyclopedia of Creativity, 2nd Ed, Academic Press, San Diego, 2011. *Mem:* Nat Asn Women Artists; Soc Chaos Theory Psychology & Life Sci; Archive Res Archetypal Symbolism; Am Psychological Asn, Div Psychology & Arts & Div Humanistic Psychology (chmn symposium film on art & disabilities). *Media:* Oil, Acrylic. *Res:* Psychology of art; research in creativity; non-linear dynamics; psychology of art in the Renaissance; altered states of conciousness in the creative process. *Interests:* physics, non-linear dynamics, cosmology. *Publ:* Georgia O'Keefe, Encyl Creativity, Acad Press, San Diego, Calif, 98; Chaos, Dict Symbols, Arch Res Archetypal Symbolism, 98; When Walls Become Doorways: Creativity, Chaos, Theory and Physical Illness, Creativity Res J, Vol II, 1, 98; Utke's Rainbow: Phenomenology, Mythology, and Physical Science in Dialogues, summer 99; contribr, Trembling-Trembling Patients in Panic-Patients in Awe, 99; Psychological revelations: the outsider artists of hospital audiences, inc, Bull Div 10 Psychology & Arts, Am Psychol Asn, 2000; Trembling and Transcendence: chaos theory, panic attacks, and awe, Psychotherapy Patient vol 11, no 1-2, 1999, & chpt in Trembling-Trembling, Patients in Panic-Patients in Awe, 2000; The Transcendent profane: recognizing the hidden self, in Psychotherapy Patient, 2002; The Mind's mirror: visual art, in Bull Psychology and Arts Div 10, Am Psychol Asn, 2002; When Walls Become Doorways: Creativity and the Transforming Illness, Harmony, 2007; The Effects of Aging on Creativity: A Study of Lindauer's Investigations into the Visual Arts, Creativity Research Journal, 2009; Transcending the Self Through Art: Altered States of Consciousness and Anomalous Events during the Creative Process, Jour

Consciousness and Exploration and Rsch, 2011; Chaos, Creativity, and Substance Abuse: The Nonlinear Dynamics of Choice, Nonlinear Dynamics, Psychology, and Life Sciences, 2011; Mary Cassatt, Encyclopedia of Creativity, 2nd Ed, Academic Press, San Diego, 2011; Creativity, Resilience, and Chaos Theory, Dance Therapy Asn Australia Jour, pp 39-41, 2012

ZAVADA, BARBARA JOHANNA
PAINTER, PRINTMAKER

b June 20, 1938. *Study:* Traphagen Sch Fashions, Cert, 1959; Rochester Inst Tech, Assoc, 1966; Art Students League, Studied with George Grosz, 1960; Theodoros Stamos, 1970-1971; Hochschule fuer Bildende Kuenste, Karl Bobeck, Berlin, 1962. *Work:* Mus Art, Sci & Indust, Bridgeport, Conn; Concordia Hist Soc, St Louis, Mo; Greenwich Acad, Greenwich, Conn; Moab Grand Ctr, Utah. *Comn:* Repose at Zion (painting), comn by Mrs Ruth McAlpine, Summit, NJ, 1992; Illus poem, Hopi, comn by Dr Sally Cargill, Castle Valley, Utah, 1999. *Exhib:* Artist's Showcase, Mus Art Sci & Indust, Bridgeport, Conn, 1974; Illus & Paintings, Bruce Mus, Greenwich, Conn, 1976; Images & Illusions, Stamford Tower Rotunda, Stamford, Conn, 1985; Conn Artists, Stamford Mus, Stamford, Conn, 1989-1990; Canyon Song, Edge of the Cedars Mus, Blanding, Utah, 1999-2001; Beaver St Gallery, Flagstaff, Ariz, 2005; Group exhib, St John's Col, Santa Fe, NMex, 2005; Mayo Clinic, Scottsdale, Ariz, 2009. *Pos:* Artist-in-residence, Monument Valley High Sch, Utah, 1998-2000; lectr, Western Colo Art Ctr, Grand Junction, Colo, 2002; lectr, Art Ctr Fuller Lodge, Los Alamos, NMex, 2003. *Teaching:* teacher, Senior High Sch, Art Ctr, Children's Mus, Santa Fe, NMex, 2003-2004. *Awards:* Fashion Award, NYC, Allen Knitting Mills, 1960; Images & Illusions, Stamford Art Assoc,, 1980; Faber Birren Color Award, Stamford Art Asn, 1981; Southwest Abstract, Art Gallery Stamford, Marina Materazu, 1987; Nat League Am Pen Women, A & E Gottlieb Found, 1990; Santa Fe Sunset, Sedona Art Ctr, 1992. *Bibliog:* Paul Weideman (auth), Memories of Canyon Country, The Santa Fe New Mexican, 1999. *Mem:* Nat Mus Women Arts (2004-2008); Nat Women's Hist Mus (charter mem, 2005-2008). *Media:* Acrylic, Pastel, Printmaker, Lithography. *Specialty:* Abstract expressionism. *Interests:* golf; wine making; travel. *Publ:* Auth, Creativity in Abstract Expressionism (Dick Martin product), 1998; The Immigrant, Living on the Cutting Edge (autobiography), 2014. *Dealer:* PMW Gallery Eastern National International 530 Roxbury Rd Stamford CT 06902; Art Price BP 69 Domaine de la Source 69270 Saint Romain au Mont d'Or France; Concordia Historical Society 801 DeMun Ave St Louis MO 63105. *Mailing Add:* HC 64 Box 3001 Castle Valley UT 84532

ZEGART KETT, MAR(GARET) JEAN KETTUNEN
ARTIST, EDUCATOR

b Lansing, Mich, Aug 19, 1926. *Study:* Univ Calif, Berkeley, MA, 54; Arts Admin Credential, UC Berkeley Prog, 81; Mich State Univ, BA (cum laude), Crown Point Press Workshop, 2010. *Work:* Usher Gallery, Lincoln; The Brit Mus, London; Whitney Mus; Mus of Modern Art; NY Pub Libr; Guggenheim Mus, New York; The Achenbach Graphic Arts Collection, Palace of the Legion of Honor, San Francisco; Museo de Arte Moderna, Sao Paolo, Brazil. *Comn:* Watercolors of Home, Outdoor Art Club of Mill Valley-Gardens, 2005-2007. *Exhib:* Works on Paper, Met Mus, 48; Pastel Drawing, Metrop Mus, 48; Invitational Painting Shows, Palace of the legion of Honor, San Francisco, 55-60; solo exhibs, Wittenborne Schultz Inc, New York; Mus of Modern Art, San Francisco; Marin Co Civic Ctr; Kings Gallery; many others; Ann Juried Exhib, Pasadena Art Mus, 80; Marinscapes, Escalle, Greenbrae, Calif, 95-98; and many other group exhibs of copper engravings. *Pos:* Ast to art ed, Glamour Mag, New York, 47-53; Smith Tepper Sundberg, Designers, San Francisco, 53-54. *Teaching:* Laserna High Sch, East Whittier, 60-61; Coll of Marin, 60; art tnstr, Tamalpais Union High Sch Dist, 61-91; instr, Fulbright Exchange Teacher, 79-80, Testwood, Winchester Dist, Eng. *Awards:* Rockefeller Purchase Award, Brooklyn Mus Print Juried & Invitational Ann, Brazil, 50; Smith Coll Purchase Award; Stanford Univ Global Educ Project; Korea and Hong Kong Arts Instruction and Visual Arts Consultant. *Mem:* Calif Teachers' Asn (life mem); Marin Retired Teachers Asn; Nat Educator's Asn (life mem); Fine Arts Mus, San Francisco, Calif; Asian Art Mus; Graphic Arts Coun; San Francisco Legion of Honor. *Media:* Copper Engraving; Painting Oil and Acrylic. *Interests:* Poetry and graphics to accompany text folios, community planning, development advocacy. *Dealer:* Susan Teller Gallery 568 Broadway 502A New York NY 10012; Dolan Maxwell 2046 Rittenhouse Sq Philadelphia Pa 19103. *Mailing Add:* 118 Highland Lane Mill Valley CA 94941

ZEIDLER, EBERHARD HEINRICH
ARCHITECT, DESIGNER

b Braunsdorf, Ger, Jan 11, 1926; Can citizen. *Study:* Bauhaus Weimar, Cand Arch, 45-48; Karlsruhe Univ, Dipl Ing, 49; McMaster Univ, LLD, 82; Tech Univ NS, DEng 87; Univ Toronto, DArch, 89; York Univ, LLD, 92. *Hon Degrees:* Hon FAIA. *Comn:* Designer, Eaton Ctr, Toronto, 73-79, Can Place, Vancouver, 86; MediaPark, Cologne, 88; Raymond F Kravis Ctr Performing Arts, W Palm Beach, 92-96; Hosp for Sick Children, Toronto, 93. *Pos:* Guest speaker, var world confs; sr partner, Zeidler Partnership/Architects, 80-. *Teaching:* Lectr archit design, Univ Toronto, 53-55; adj prof, Univ Toronto, 83-. *Awards:* Order of Can, 84; 75 national and international design awards; Gold Medal, Royal Archit Inst Can, 86. *Bibliog:* Robert Fulford (auth), The rise and fall of modern architecture, Saturday Night Mag, 80; Geoffrey Simmons (auth), Eberhard Zeidler, City & Country Home, spring 83; Christian W Thomsen (auth), Eberhard Zeidler: In Search of Human Space, Ernst & Sohn, 92. *Mem:* Academician Royal Can Acad Arts; fel Royal Archit Inst Can; Ont Asn Architects; hon fel Am Inst Archits; Archit Inst BC; and others. *Publ:* Auth, Healing the Hospital-McMaster Health Science Centre: Its Conception & Evolution, 74; Multi-Use Architecture in the Urban Context, Karl Kramer Verlag, 83; and many articles in leading prof mags; Buildings, Cities, Life, Dundurn, Eberhard, 2 vols. *Mailing Add:* 315 Queen St W Toronto ON M5V 2X2 Canada

ZEIGLER, GEORGE GAVIN
PAINTER, SCULPTOR

b Nashville, Tenn, 1962. *Study:* Atlanta Coll Art; Pratt Inst, Cert Prog Graphic Arts, NY, 88; Fordham Univ, NY, BA (art hist), 94; Center for Furniture Craftsmanship, Rockland, Maine, 2007. *Work:* Peat, Marwick & Mitchell, Loews Vanderbilt Plaza, Nashville; Cramer Berkowitz & Co, Freedom Mgt Asn, Inc, NY; Victory Systems Inc, Southport, Conn; Southern Energy Corp HQ, Atlanta; Honorable Michael R. Bloomberg, New York City; Judge Phyllis Kravitch, Ark, Ga; The Ritz Carlton, South Beach, Fla; Mr & Mrs William Scharf; Telfair Mus, Savannah, Ga; W Hotel, San Diego, Calif; Kempinski Hotel; Accra Ghana. *Comn:* W Hotel, San Diego, Calif. *Exhib:* Solo Exhibs: Kenneth Winslow Gallery, 97 & Chuck Levitan Gallery, NY, 97; The Altered Image, Islip Art Mus, East Islip, NY, 97; 11th Ann Art Exhib, Hunter Mus Am Art, Chattanooga, Tenn, 98; Savannah Coll Art & Design, Savannah, Ga, 99; Lizan Tops Gallery, NY, 2002; Anita Shapolsky Gallery, New York City, 2003; Springfield Art Mus, Mo, 2004; Red Dot Fine Art, Santa Fe, 2005; World's Exhibition Aichi, Japan, 2005; Telfair Mus, Savannah, Ga; Peter J Marcelle Gallery, 2012; Silas Marner Gallery, 2012; 30 Yr Retrospective, Peter Marcelle Gallery, 2013. *Pos:* Admin asst, Hilde Gerst Gallery Inc, NY, 94-95. *Teaching:* guest lectr, Fordham Univ, NY. *Awards:* First Place Ivan Karp of Okla Harris Gallery, 95; Exhib Award for Donald Kuspit, 98; Artist of Month, Liquitex, 2002; David Houston, Alexandria Mus Art, 2005; Curator Recognition award, Palm Beach Int Biennale, 2006. *Bibliog:* Erica Weitzman (auth), Illustrations, William & Mary Rev, 97; H I Gliick (auth), Illustrations, New Am Paintings, 97; Phyllis Braff (auth), Subjective & abstract flow in many directions, NY Times, 98; Emerging artist, Art & Antiques Mag, 4/2003; Marilyn Noble (auth), Gavin Zeigler: Basic Elements in Bronze, Sculptural Pursuit Mag, 2007; Thom Filicia (auth), Thom Filicia Style, Atria Books, New York, 2008; Sara Evans (auth), Vox Hamptons, Out of the Ordinary, the Art of Gavin Zeigler, East Hampton, NY, 2008; Eric Ernst (auth), Illustrations, The Southampton Press, 2009; Annette Hinkle (auth), Sag Harbor Express (newspaper), 2013. *Mem:* Soc Illustrators. *Media:* Acrylic, Metal, Wood, Mixed Media, Glass. *Specialty:* Modern Contemporary. *Interests:* Contemporary and modern painting and sculpture. *Collection:* E Vicente; W Scharf; Warner Wildner; Garry Beals; Richard Kalina; Robert Dash; Howard Newman; Sandor Bodo; Bunn Gray; Valorie Jardon; Carl Sublett. *Publ:* New American Paintings, H I Glick, Book # 10, 97; Living Artists, Constance Smith, ed. 13th Ed, 2003; Jamie Drake, New Am Glamour, 2005; Thom Filicia, The Franklin Room, 2005; Acquisition Highlights, Telfair Mag, 2008; Gavin Ziegler, A Thirty Year Retrospective of Paintings and Sculpture, 2013-1983. *Dealer:* www.GavinZeigler.com; Peter J Marcelle Gallery. *Mailing Add:* PO Box 137 Shelter Island NY 11964

ZEITLIN, HARRIET
PAINTER, SCULPTOR

b Philadelphia, Pa, Feb 12, 1929. *Study:* Pa Acad Fine Arts, Univ Pa, BFA, 46-50; Barnes Found, 49 & 50; Univ Calif, Los Angeles, 63-69. *Work:* Libr Cong; Am Embassy, New Delhi, India; Los Angeles Co Mus Art, Los Angeles Athletic Asn & Grunwald Ctr Graphic Arts, Univ Calif, Los Angeles; Pa Acad Fine Arts. *Comn:* Mixed media painting, comn by City Los Angeles Cult Affairs Dept, 91. *Exhib:* Los Angeles Co Mus Art; Weyhe Gallery, NY; Bernice Steinbaum Gallery, NY; Lobby Gallery/Am Craft Mus, NY; Biblioteque Forney, Paris; Women Artists of Southern Calif, Track 16 Gallery, Santa Monica, 2007; Salon d'Automne, Paris. *Pos:* Exec bd mem, Los Angeles Printmaking Soc, 64-69; artist/community relations & exec bd mem, Graphic Arts Coun Los Angeles Co Mus Art, 73-75; corresp secy, Artists for Economic Action, 73-74, vpres, 75-76, pres, 77-78 & exec dir CETA Title VI, Art in Pub Places, 77-78. *Teaching:* Mirman Sch Gifted Children, Los Angeles, 80-82; UCLA Exten Artsreach, Univ Calif, Los Angeles, 86; Los Angeles High Sch Music & Art, 88. *Awards:* Calif Arts Coun Grant, 77; Los Angeles City Cult Grant, 90-91; JL City Exhib, 2009; Los Angeles Period Exhib, 2009. *Bibliog:* Barbara Wilson (auth), Interview, Currant Art Mag, 75; Kathy Zimmerer-McKelvie (auth), Three from Los Angeles, Art Scene, 85; Eleanor Tufts (auth), Am Women Artists, Vol II, 89. *Mem:* Int Sculpture Ctr; Arelis Fiber Soc, Paris, France; Pen Ctr West. *Media:* Fiber, Sculpture, Mixed Media. *Publ:* Auth, A community of artists, Graphic Arts Coun Newsletter, Vol IX, No 4, Los Angeles Co Mus, 74; President's report, Artists for Econ Action Newsletter, 77-78; Calif Art Rev, Am References, 89; Los Angeles Times, 2000; Art of the Fiber, Biblioteque Forney, Paris, 2004; Salon d'Automne, 2007. *Mailing Add:* 202 S Saltair Ave Los Angeles CA 90049

ZEITLIN, HARRY LEON
PHOTOGRAPHER

b Denver, Colo, 1952. *Study:* Yale Univ, BA, 74; pvt studies with Hisashi Ohta, Los Angeles, 80-82; Univ Calif, Los Angeles, with Robert Heinecken & Edmund Teske, 77-79. *Hon Degrees:* Rabbinic Ordination, 1998. *Work:* Israel Mus, Jerusalem; Fogg Art Mus Harvard Univ; Bibliotheque Nationalé, Paris, France; Denver Art Mus, Colo; Yale Univ Art Gallery; Hallie Ford Mus, Salem Ore; Tel Aviv Mus Art; NY Pub Libr; Mizel Mus, Denver, Col. *Comn:* Aaron Copland (portrait), comn by Aaron Copland, NY, 78; Elliot Carter (portrait), comn by Elliot Carter, NY, 78; Eugene Ionesco (portrait), comn by Eugene Ionesco, Los Angeles, 79; Bob Marley (portrait), comn by Bob Marley, Los Angeles, 80; Hisashi Ohta (portrait), comn by Hisashi Ohta, Los Angeles, 82. *Exhib:* One-man shows, Am Cult Ctr, Jerusalem, 86, Bezalel Acad Art, Jerusalem, 86, Bertha Urdang Gallery, NY, 88 & 91, Henry Art Gallery, Univ Wash, Seattle, 91, Silver Image Gallery, Seattle, 91 & 93, CG Jung Soc Chicago, Evanston, Ill, 93, Anigrafix, Jerusalem & Goldwasser & Wilkinson, San Francisco, 96; Skyline, Tel Aviv Mus, Israel, 88; Art-Cubic, Barcelona, Spain, 2003; La State Univ, Baton Rouge, La, 2005; Cafe Flora, Seattle, Wash, 2006; Hadash, Jerusalem, Israel, 2006; Benhan Studio Gallery, Seattle, 2007; Madison Park, Seattle, 2007; Slifka Center, Yale University, 2009; and others. *Teaching:* Photog, Art is the Spiritual, Seattle, Wash, 92- & The Evergreen Sch, Seattle, 96. *Media:* Black and White Photography, Digital color photography. *Interests:* interconnectedness of reality, transcendence via visual. *Publ:* Houston Photofest Laser Disc, 92; cover photo, Musica de Sobrevivencia, Egberto Gismonti Group, ECM Records, 93; cover photo, Reflections, Bobo Stenson Trio,

ECM Records, 96; Harvester, Geffen Records, 96; Pathways, Richard Greenberg, Jason Aronson Books, 96; Songs to an Invisible God, Ruth Weider Magan, Sounds True Records. *Dealer:* Art is the Spiritual 6523 39th Ave NE Seattle WA; Silver Image Gallery 300 Queen Anne Ave N No 701 Seattle WA 98109. *Mailing Add:* 6523 39th Ave NE Seattle WA 98115

ZEITLIN, MARILYN A
CURATOR, WRITER, MUSEUM DIRECTOR
b Newark, NJ, July 14, 1941. *Study:* Harvard Univ, AB, 66 MAT, 67; Cornell Univ, 74. *Collection Arranged:* Messages: Words & Images (auth, catalog), 79 & 80, Freedman Gallery, Reading, Pa; Masters of Contemporary Drawing (auth, catalog), 83-85 & As if the Universe were an object: Larry Miller Retrospective (coauth, catalog), Anderson Gallery, Richmond, Va, 86; Happy Families: Works by Ida Applebroog (coauth, catalog), 89, S Bronx Hall of Fame: Sculpture by John Ahearn & Rigoberto Torres (coauth, catalog), Houston, 90; Too Late for Goya: Works by Francese Torres (auth, catalog), Tempe, Ariz, 94; Art Under Duress: El Salvador 1980-Present (auth, catalog), Tempe, Ariz, 94; Contemporary Art from Cuba: Irony and Survival on the Utopian Island, 98. *Pos:* Dir, Ctr Gallery, Bucknell Univ, Lewisburg, 76-79, Freedman Gallery, Albright Col, Reading, 79-82, Anderson Gallery, Va Commonwealth Univ, Richmond, 82-87, Contemp Arts Mus, Houston, 87-90, WPA, Washington, DC, 90-92 & Univ Art Mus, Ariz State Univ, 92-; comnr, US to Venice Biennale, 95. *Teaching:* Instr, Bucknell Univ, Albright Col & Va Commonwealth Univ, formerly. *Awards:* Samuel H Kress Fel, 71-72. *Mem:* Am Asn Mus; Asn Coll & Univ Mus & Galleries (vpres, 84-86). *Res:* Contemporary art, chiefly video, painting & sculpture; political art. *Publ:* Auth, Magic & Medicine: Chinese Ceramics in Southeast Asia, Pac Press, 78; Small is Beautiful, Bucknell Univ, 79; Jo Sandman: Work in process, Anyart, 80; Attemped, Not Known, Paintings by Benito Huerta, Artspace, 89. *Mailing Add:* Ariz State Univ Art Mus PO Box 872911 Tempe AZ 85287-2911

ZELANSKI, PAUL JOHN
PAINTER
b Hartford, Conn, Apr 13, 1931. *Study:* Cooper Union, cert, 55; Yale Univ, BFA, 57; Bowling Green State Univ, MFA, 58. *Work:* Univ Mass, Amherst; Slater Mus, Norwich, Conn; The Leonard Bacour Collection, NY; Hampshire Col, Northampton, Mass; Yale Univ Print Collection; Benton Mus, Storrs, Conn. *Exhib:* New Eng in Five Parts, De Cordova Mus, Lincoln, Mass; Harvard Univ Carpenter Ctr, Boston; New Directions in Painting, Univ Mass, Amherst; The Peterdi Yrs, Yale Univ, New Haven; Acad Fine Arts, Krakow, Poland; Amel Gallery, New York City; Amon Carter Mus, Fort Worth, Tex; Benton Mus, Storrs, Conn; Boston Mus Contemp Art; Bowling Green State Univ, Ohio; Dallas Mus Fine Art; ETC Collection, Hartford, Conn; Grand Street Gallery, New York City; Hampshire Col, Mass; Maastricht Acad, The Neth; Nexus Gallery, Boston; North Tex State Univ, Denton; Shippensburg Univ, Pa; Slater Memorial Mus, Norwich; Smith Col, Northampton, Mass; Cooper Union, New York City; The Gallery, Provincetown, Mass; Trinity Col, Hartford; Wadsworth Mus, Hartford; Mr & Mrs Booma, Boston; Wyman, Kraskow, Poland; Silver Gallery, Putnam, Conn; Gallery One, Old Saybrook, Conn; Essex Art Assn. *Collection Arranged:* Academy Fine Arts, Krakow; Calmann & King Collection, London; John Slade Ely House Collection, New Haven; Mr & Mrs Chaplin, Hartford, Conn; Forth Worth Art Ctr, Ft. Worth; Hampshire Coll Collection, Mass; Harcourt Brace Collection, Tex; Housatonic Mus, Norwalk, Conn; IBM Collection; Kearns Collection, Guilford, Conn; La Corrie Collection, NY; Univ Mass Drawing Collection, Amherst; Univ North Tex, Denton; Leonard Bocour Collection, NYC; Cooper Union Collection, NYC; Dodd Ctr, Storrs, Conn; Slater Memorial Mus, Norwich, Conn; Takenaga Collection, Japan; Verda Am, Japan; Yale Univ Art Mus, New Haven; Alan K Bingham, Portland, ore; The Tood Tood, Chester, Conn; The Fawcell, Waldobararo, Maine; Univ Conn, Storrs, Conn; Mr & Mrs Lambert, Williamsberg Penn; Mr Michael Gordon, Brooklyn, NY; Mr Russell Connor, NY; Mr Morgan Powell, Champaign, Ill. *Pos:* Vis Art, Acad Fine Arts, Kraskow, Poland, 90 & Acad Visual Arts, Maastsricht, Holland, 94. *Teaching:* Instr painting, drawing & design, N Tex State Univ, 58-61; instr painting, Ft Worth, Tex, 61-62; assoc prof art, Univ Conn, 62-76, prof, 76-95, prof emeritus, 95-. *Awards:* Painting Prize, New Haven Art Asn, 94, 95 & 96; Painting Prize, Guliford Art Asn, 94, 95 & 96; Painting Prize, Mystic Art Asn, 95 & 96; Painting Prize, Essex Art Asn, 2005-2013; Hall of Fame, Conn Art Dirs Club. *Bibliog:* Alan Graham Collier (auth), Form, Space and Vision, Prentice-Hall; Barnard Chaet (auth), Artists at work, Webb, Studio Talk; B. Chate (auth), Studio Talk, Prentice Hall; B. Chate (auth), Drawing, Prentice Hall; Albers (auth), Interaction of Color, Yale Press. *Mem:* Silvermine Guild Artists; Conn Acad Fine Arts; Berkshire Art League; Munsell Group; Computer Art & Design Educ; Essex Art Asn Gallery; Guilford Art Asn. *Media:* Acrylic, Collage. *Res:* Study of Color. *Publ:* Auth, Design Principles and Problems, 2 edits, Harcourt Brace; The Art of Seeing, 8 edits, Prentice Hall; Auth, Shaping Space, 3 edits, Harcourt Brace; Color, 6 edits, Prentice Hall. *Dealer:* Francis Frost Rd; Noemi Kerus. *Mailing Add:* Cowles Rd West Willington CT 06279

ZELENAK, EDWARD J
SCULPTOR
b St Thomas, Ont, Nov 9, 1940. *Study:* Meinszinger Sch Art, Detroit, Mich; Ft Worth Art Ctr, Tex; Ont Coll Art, Toronto. *Work:* Cantonal Mus, Lausanne, Switz; Nat Gallery Can, Ottawa; Ont Art Gallery, Toronto; Rothman's Ltd, Stratford, Ont; Dept Pub Works, Toronto. *Comn:* Major outdoor sculpture, Nat Gallery Can, 72, Dept Pub Works, Toronto, 73 & North York, 76, Rothman's Art Gallery, 73 & Northfield Minn, Carleton Col, 73; major sculpture, Prov Dept Pub Works, Kitchener, Ont, 77; Forest City Gallery, London, Ont, 85-86. *Exhib:* Solo exhib, Maj Outdoor Sculpture, Nat Art Ctr, Ottawa, 69, Carleton Coll, 72, Christopher Cutts Gallery, Toronto, 97 & Two Sculptors Inc, NY, 98; Tendence Actuelles, Galerie de France, Paris, 69; 3rd Int Pioneer Galleries Exhib, Cantonnal Mus, Lausanne & Mus Mod Art, Paris, 70; 49th Parallels, Ringling Mus, Sarasota, Fla & Mus Contemp Art, Chicago, 71; Washington, Northfield, Milwaukee major touring sculpture, Minn State Art Coun & Henry Gallery, 73-74; Mt Allison Univ, 75; Art Fiera, Bologna, Italy, 77; Chicago Atheneum, Chicago, 98; Art Forum, Berlin, 98. *Teaching:* Instr, Univ Western Ont, 79-88. *Awards:* Can Coun Jr Arts Grant, 68-71, Sr Arts Grant, 73-75; Prov Ont Coun Arts Grant in Aid, 74. *Bibliog:* Jean Noel Chandler (auth), article in Artscanada, 4/69; Barry Lord (auth), articles in Art in Am, 1-2/69; R Naasgard (auth), article in Artscanada, 6/73. *Mem:* Royal Can Acad Acad Arts. *Media:* Metal, Fiberglas. *Specialty:* Contemporary painting and sculpture. *Dealer:* Christopher Cutts Gallery 21 Morrow Ave Toronto Ont Canada MGR 2H9. *Mailing Add:* RR 1 West Lorne ON N0L 2P0 Canada

ZELEVANSKY, LYNN
MUSEUM DIRECTOR
Study: Carnegie Mellon Univ, Pittsburgh; Pratt Inst, New York, BFA, 1970; NY Univ Sch Fine Arts, MA (photog). *Work:* Cur (exhibs) Sense and Sensibility: Women Artists and Minimalism in the 90s, 94, Love Forever: Yayoi Kusama 1958-68, 98-99, Robert Therrian retrospective, 2000, Jasper Johns to Jeff Koons: Four Decades of Art from the Broad Collections, 2001, Keith Edmier and Farah Fawcett, 2002, Beyond Geometry: Experiments in Form, 1940s-70s, 2004 (Award for Best Thematic Mus Show Nationally, Inter Asn Art Critics/USA, 2005), many others. *Pos:* Cur, Mus Modern Art, New York, 87-1995; assoc cur, dept 20th century painting Los Angeles Co Mus Art, 95, assoc cur modern and contemp art, Terri and Michael Smooke cur, dept head mod and contemp art; Henry J Heintz dir, Carnegie Mus Art, Pittsburgh, 2009-. *Mailing Add:* Carnegie Mus Art 4400 Forbes Ave Pittsburgh PA 15213-4080

ZELIN, ELAINE
SCULPTOR
b New York, NY, Dec 13, 1931. *Study:* Stephens Col, AA, 51; Fairleigh Dickinson Univ, BA, 80; Art Students League; New School; studied with J Hovannes, Tony Paderano & Minouri Niizuma. *Work:* New England Ctr Contemp Art, Brookline, Conn. *Comn:* Marble seal, Dart Indust, Paramus, NJ, 81; Windswept (marble sculpture), Accurate Box Co, Newark, NJ, 82; Pinnacle, Ft Lee Marketing Co, NY, 84; Citiscape, Cosmetic Scenting Co, NY, 85. *Exhib:* Stone Sculpture Soc NY, Lever House, 81, 86, 90; Nat Asn Women Artists, Jacob Javits Plaza, NY, 82, 83, 85; Tri Co, Bergen Co Mus, Paramus, NJ, 84; Norton Artists Guild, Norton Mus, West Palm Beach, 92; NAWA Cornell Mus, Delray Beach, Fla, 2001-02; Boca Mus Artists Guild, Boca Raton, Fla, 2002, 03; Rosetta Stone Fine Art Gallery, Juno Beach, Fla. *Awards:* Anonymous Members Prize, Nat Asn Women Artists, 82 & 83. *Bibliog:* NY Art Yearbook, 76. *Mem:* NY Artists Equity; Nat Asn Women Artists; Norton Artists Guild; Boca Raton Mus Artists Guild; Alabaster; Acrylics. *Media:* Marble. *Mailing Add:* 7847 Lakeside Blvd Apt 1052 Boca Raton FL 33434

ZELLER, FREDERIC
SCULPTOR
b Ger, May 20, 1924. *Study:* Univ London, BA, 55; Art Students League, NY, studied with Stephen Green, 59-61; The Greenwich House, studied with Paul Frazier, 61-64; Educ Alliance Art Sch, studied with Licio Isolani, 65-70. *Exhib:* Vorpal Gallery, NY, 82; Centre Articule, Montreal, Quebec, 83; Sarah Y Rentschler Gallery, Bridgehampton, NY, 85; Clark Whitney Gallery, Lenox, Mass, 85; Elaine Benson Gallery, Bridgehampton, 86; Benton Gallery, Southampton, NY, 86, 87 & 88; solo shows, Pace Univ Art Gallery, NY, 80, Vorpal Gallery, 82 & 83, Studio 99, Westhampton Beach, 82, Benton Hallery, 88. *Mailing Add:* 775 Ave of the Americas No 5 New York NY 10001

ZELLER, JOSEPH R
EDUCATOR, CERAMIST
b Chicago, IL, Aug 8, 1945. *Study:* Univ Ill, Urbana, BFA, 68; State Univ NY, Alfred, MFA, 70. *Pos:* Trustee design div, Am Ceramic Soc, 92-96. *Teaching:* Instr art, Cleveland Inst Art, 70-77; assoc prof art, Ohio Univ, 77-88; prof & chmn design, Univ Kans, 88-. *Mem:* Am Ceramic Soc; Nat Coun Educ Ceramic Arts; Tile Heritage Found; Am Craft Coun; Ohio Designer Craftsman. *Media:* Ceramics. *Mailing Add:* Univ Kans 300 Art & Design Lawrence KS 66045

ZELLER, ROBERT
PAINTER
Study: Boston Mus Sch Fine Arts/Tufts Univ, Boston, BFA, 1993; Water Street Atelier/Jacob Collins, June 2001-Oct 2003; NY Acad Art, New York, MFA, 2001. *Work:* Gettysburg Winery, Pa; Forbes Gallery, New York. *Exhib:* Solo exhibs include 511 Gallery, New York, 2006; group exhibs include NY Acad Art, New York, 2001; More Gallery, Philadelphia, 2003; Alumni Show, Stricoff Gallery, New York, 2004, Summer Group Show, 2004; The Narrative, Century Gallery, Alexandria, Va, 2005; Contemp Realism, Grey McGear Mod, Santa Monica, Calif, 2006; Water St Exhib, John Pence Gallery, San Francisco, 2006; Water St Atelier, Meredith Long, Houston, 2008. *Teaching:* Prof, NY Acad Art, New York, 2007-2008, Stevenson Acad Art, Oyster Bay, NY, 2008, Long Island Acad Fine Art, Glen Cove, NY, 2008. *Awards:* Boit Competition Award, Boston Mus Sch, 1992; Posey Found Grant, 1998, 2000; Pollock-Krasner Found Grant, 2007. *Mailing Add:* 115 Irving Ave Apt 2L Brooklyn NY 11237

ZEMANS, JOYCE L
EDUCATOR, ART HISTORIAN
b Toronto, Can, Apr 21, 1940. *Study:* Univ Toronto, BA, 62, MA, 66. *Hon Degrees:* Nova Scotia Coll Art & Design (hon doctorate), 1995; Ontario Coll Art & Design (hon fel), 1997; Univ Waterloo (hon doctorate), 2004. *Exhib:* Curated Exhibs: The Inner Landscape: Jock Macdonald, Art Gallery, Ont, Toronto, 1981; Alexandra Luke: The Watercolours, Robert McLaughlin Gallery, Oshawa, 1984; Christopher Pratt: A Retrospective, Vancouver Art Gallery, Vancouver, 1986; Kathleen Munn & Edna Tacon: New Perspectives on Modernism in Can, Art Gallery of York Univ, Toronto, 1988; Tony Urquhart, The Revenants: Long Shadows, Univ Waterloo Art Gallery,

Waterloo, Ont, 2002. *Pos:* Dir grad prog art hist, York Univ, 94-95, co-dir prog MBA arts & media admin, Schulich Sch Bus, York Univ, 94-2000, acting dir MBA prog in non-profit mgt and leadership, 2000-2001, 2008-2009; dir, MBA Prog Art & Media Admin Schulich Sch Bus, 2000-. *Teaching:* Art historian, Ont Col Art, Toronto, 66-75, chmn, Art Hist Dept, 69-71, chmn, Liberal Arts Studies, 72-75; prof art hist, York Univ, Toronto, 75-95, chmn, Dept Visual Arts, 75-81, dean, fac fine arts, 85-88; dir, Can Coun, 89-92; prof emer, Senior Sch & Univ, 2005. *Awards:* Queens Jubilee Medal Serv, 2000. *Mem:* Int Asn Art Critics; Nat Coun Arts Admins; Can Asn Fine Arts Deans (bd mem); Int Coun Fine Arts Deans (bd mem). *Res:* art history (20th century, North American); cultural policy. *Publ:* Contribr, Bertram Brooker & Emergent Modernism, Vol 7, 89; Free Expression, Public Support & Censorship: Examining Government's Role in the Arts in Canada and the United States, Univ Press Am, Lanham, Md, 94; Beyond Quebec: Taking Stock of Canada, McGill-Queen's Press, 95; auth, Establishing the canon: The early history of reproductions at the National Gallery of Canada, J Can Art Hist, spring 95, Where is Here? Canadian Cultural Policy in a Globalized World, 96, Comparing Cultural Policy: A Study of Japan & the United States, 99; And the lion shall lie down with the lamb: US-Canada cultural relations in a free trade environment, Am Rev Can Studies, Vol 24, No 4, 95; coauth with Griselda Pollock, Museums after Modernism: Strategies of Engagement, 2007. *Mailing Add:* York Univ N318 Schulich Sch Bus 4700 Keele St Toronto ON M3J 1P3 Canada

ZERNER, HENRI THOMAS
HISTORIAN, CURATOR

b Suresnes, France, May 15, 1939. *Study:* Univ Paris, Lic es Lett, 61, Dr (fine arts), 69; Ecole Pratique des Hautes Etudes, Paris, dipl (fine arts), 63. *Collection Arranged:* Venice in the Eighteenth Century (cataloged), Mus Art, RI Sch Design, 67 & J J J Tissot (cataloged), 67; The School of Fontainebleau (cataloged), Grand Palais, Paris, 72-73. *Pos:* Cur, Painting & Graphic Arts Mus, RI Sch Design, 65-66 & Prints & Drawing Mus, 66-72; cur prints, Fogg Mus, Harvard Univ, presently. *Teaching:* From asst prof to assoc prof fine arts, Brown Univ, Providence, RI, 66-72; prof fine arts, Harvard Univ, Cambridge, Mass, 72-. *Awards:* Guggenheim Fel, Paris, 71; Prix Achille Fould, Acad des Inscriptions et Belles Lett, 71; Medal of Order of Arts and Letters, French Ministry Culture, 2006; as well as many others. *Publ:* auth, Tout l'oeuvre peint de Raphael, Flammarion, 69; auth, L'Ecole de Fontainebleau-Gravures, Abrams, 70; auth, Illustrated Bartsch, Vol XVI, In: Sixteenth Century Italian Etchings, 79; coauth (with Charles Rosen), Romanticism and Realism: The Mythology of 19th Century Art, Viking, 84; L'Art de Le Renaissance in France, L'invention du classicisure, Paris, Flammarion, 96. *Mailing Add:* Fogg Art Mus 32 Quincy St Cambridge MA 02138

ZGODA, LARRY
STAINED GLASS ARTIST, DESIGNER

b Chicago, Ill, Oct 27, 1950. *Study:* Columbia Col, Ill, BA, 75. *Work:* City Chicago Public Art Collection; Ill State Mus. *Comn:* Archit stained glass, 90, stained glass entry, 95, City of Chicago, Chicago Pub Libr, Ill; archit stained glass, AARP, Washington, DC, 91; clerestory panels, American Family Insurance Int Hq, Madison, Wis, 93; Wall of Glass, TCF Tower, Minneapolis, Minn, 97; ten windows, Our Lady of Angels Chapel, Marian Village, Homer, Ill, 2000; lighted wall of glass, Woodsin Suites, Emeryville, Calif, 2000; stained glass for partitioning wall, Huron Pub Libr, Huron, Ohio, 2002; 5 stained glass entries, Sacred Heart of Jesus Chapel, Our Lady of Victory Convent, Lemont, Ill, 2002; Windows & decorative inserts, Craig Hall, Grad School Social Work, Univ Denver, 2005; Windows & Doors, VIA Christi Health, Wichita, Kans, 2010. *Exhib:* 1st Int Stained Glass Exhib, Corning Mus Glass, NY, 87. *Teaching:* stained glass instr, Chgo Mosaic Sch. *Awards:* Guild Am Craft Awards, Guild, 87; Graham Found grant. *Bibliog:* Article, Contemporary Crafts for the Home, Kraus Sikes Inc, 90; Chris Peterson (auth), The Art Stained Glass, Quarry Bks, 98; Beautiful Things, Guild.com, 2000; Object Lesson, Guild.com, 2001; Glass House, Hearst Books, 2006; Kevin Nance (auth), Through a Glass, Glass Art, 9/10/2006; The Artful Home, Lark Books, 2007; Built for Learning, A Unified Architectural Vision for the Univ Denver, 2008; Perspectives on Design, Chicago Pnacke Parners, 2010. *Mem:* Friends of Kebyar; Chicago Mosaic Sch (bd of dir); Stained Glass Asn Am; Am Glass Guild. *Media:* Stained Glass, Wood, Tile, Mosaic, Metals. *Res:* Art and life of Edgar Miller (1899-1993). *Interests:* Architectural Ornament, history of crafts in architecture, organic architecture. *Publ:* Auth, Beauty of stainless glass, Professional Stained Glass, 5/90; article, Am Craft, 8-9/90; Lines of Poetry, Prof Stained Glass, 8/91; auth, A Renaissance of Ornament in Architecture; auth, Edgar Miller, 20th Century Renaissance Artist both in Friends of Kebyar Journal, 2008; auth, The Stained Glass Renaissance: A Multitude of Glass Techniques, Glass Art, 2011. *Dealer:* Vale Craft Gallery Chicago. *Mailing Add:* Larry Zgoda Studio 3932 N Oakley Ave Chicago IL 60618

ZHAO, HONGBIN
PAINTER

b Shanghai, China, Aug 15, 1952. *Study:* Shanghai Jiao Tong Univ (fine art res), 84. *Hon Degrees:* Doc Fine Arts, The Yorker Int Univ, 2006. *Work:* Tsinghua Univ Art Ctr, Taiwan; Chen Liu Mus, Taiwan; 77 Bank, Miyagi City, Japan; City of Brighton Town Hall, Birghton VIC, Australia; City of Camberwell Town Hall, Canberwell VIC, Australia. *Comn:* Traveling Topic with figures, Australian Traveling & Hospitality Coll, Melbourne, 92; Portrait Chief gen mgr, Ansett Airline, Melbourne, 90; Portrait of pincipal, Australian Acad Bus Studies, Melbourne, 89; painting, Baillieu Knight Frank Residential, Melbourne, 89. *Exhib:* Nat Popular Sci Fine Art exhib, China Art Mus, Beijing, 79, 81; 6th Nat Fine Art Exhib, Shanghai Art Mus, Shanghai, 84; ACTA Australian Maritime Art Award Nat Tour, Australian Nat Maritime Mus, 91; Old Sills in New Cult, Nat Gallery Victoria, Australia, 92, 94; Archibald Award Finalist Exhib, Art Gallery of New S Wales, New S Wales, 94; Mary MacKillop: a tribute, S Australian Art Gallery, 95; China Famous Figure works Exhib of the Art Circle, Chinese War Mem Mus, Beijing, 95; First Global Art Exhib, Dr Sun Yat-Sen Mem Mus, Taipei, Taiwan, 97. *Pos:* Art ed & designer, Sci Life Mag, Munic Sci & Tech Asn, SHanghai, China, 79-85; chief ed, Modern New Products Pictorial, Shanghai Univ Tech, China, 85-88; judge, Nat Ann Art Competition, Toorak Coll, Australia, 96; dir of Oil Painting Comt, China Artists (HK) Asn, 2008-. *Awards:* Mulcahy Mazda Award, Rotary Club of Ringwood Ann Art Exhib, 91; First Prize, Victor Harbor Nat Oil Award, Rotary Club of Victor Harbor, 91; 24th Earnest Henry Mem Portrait First Prize & Landscape First Prize, Cloncurr Arts Soc, 92; Omega Contemp Art Award, Royal Overseas League 22nd Ann Art Exhib, United Kingdom, 93; Top four finalist Award, Doug Moran Nat portrait prize, Doug Moran Group, 92; Bronze Metal, China Famous Figure Works Exhib of the Art Circle, China Int Celebrity Res Inst, 95. *Bibliog:* Yu Qing Wang (auth), Monet of the Orient, All Fine Art Mag, China, 2007; Wang Ming Qin (host), Famous Artist, Asia TV, Hong Kong, 2007; Li Hui (host), Talk with the Angel, Phoenix TV, Hong Kong, 2007; Rong Chung Ruan, Hongbin Zhao's Artwork, Art Observation Mag, China Art Inst Publ House, 2008; Chief edit, Light & Color- Painter of Children, Japan Monthly Fine Art Mag, 99, Impressionist of Color & Life Intensity, 2000. *Mem:* Chinese Celebrity's Assoc, 92; Adv, Chinese Poetry, Calligraphy & Painting Inst, 92; Hon adv, Am Biographical Inst, 94; Life Fellow: Int Biography Assoc, United Kingdom, 94; Chinese Cult Celebrity's Assoc, 2007. *Publ:* contrbr, 50 Australian Artist, Artists Ink Australia, 94; auth, Painting of Zhao Hongbin, Chen Liu Publ, 97; contribr, Famous Teacher in Modern Times, China Cult Celebrity Assoc, Chinese Lit & Art Publ House, 2008; auth, the Oil Painting of Hongbin Zhao, Tian Jin People's Fine Arts Publ House, 2008; contribr, New Leader Figures: The Most Influential Masters in China's Contemporary Art, China Cult Hist Publ House, 2008; contribr, Sixty Years Six Masters, China Int Cult Publ House, 2009; contribr, Three Masters of Chinese Oil Painting- Hou Yimin, Zhan Jianjun, Zhao Hongbin, Beijing Craft Art Publ House, 2009; contribr, Ten of China's Most Influential Figures in Calligraphy & Painting, Jiuzhou Press, 2010; contribr, Eight Contemporary Great Masters in Fine Art, China Asia Pacific Economy Cooperation Ctr, 2010. *Dealer:* HZ Int Fine Arts 772 Central Ave Westfield NJ 07090; Wan Fung Art Gallery Hong Kong China; Silkland Art Gallery Ginza Tokyo Japan

ZHEUTLIN, DALE R
PAINTER, EDUCATOR

b Newark, NJ, July 27, 1948. *Study:* RI Sch Design, BFA, 70; Columbia Univ, MFA, 72. *Work:* The Robert Martin Co, White Plains, NY; Wang Laboratories Inc, NY; IBM Collection, NY; Chase Manhattan Bank, NY; Pfizer Corp, NY; and others. *Comn:* Kramer, Levin, Nessen, Kamin & Frankel, 86; Peat, Marwick & Main, Indianapolis, Ind, 88; Citibank Tower, Phoenix, Ariz, 90; Am Int Group, NY, 90; Aetna, Hartford, Conn, 90; and others. *Exhib:* Aldrich Mus, Trustees Choice, Ridgefield, Conn, 83; 46th Concorso Int della Ceramica a'arte, Faenza, Italy, 89; Katonah Mus Art, NY, 90; 2nd Int Ceramics Competition, Mino, Japan, 90; San Angelo Mus Art, Tex, 90; Wheeler Seidel Gallery, NY, 92; and others. *Teaching:* Art fac, New Rochelle High Sch, NY, 74-84, Mamaroneck High Sch, 84-2007; adj prof ceramics, Col New Rochelle, NY, 77-; guest lectr, NY Univ, 86. *Awards:* Award Merit, Mamaroneck Artists Guild, 79; Pauline Law Prize, Nat Asn Women Artists, NY, 80; Sculpture Award, Hudson River Mus, NY, 81. *Bibliog:* Jennifer Dunning (auth), A chance to find if the art of women in special, 86, Vivian Raynor (auth), Four artists at gallery shows, 1/89, NY Times; Bill Kraus (auth), Contemporary Crafts for the Home, Kraus Sikes Inc, 90; Leon Nigrosh (auth), Sculpting Clay, Davis Publ Inc, 91; and others. *Mem:* Nat Asn Women Artists Inc; Artists Equity Asn; Empire State Crafts Alliance (bd dir). *Media:* Acrylic, Oil. *Publ:* Contribr, Apprenticeship in Craft, Daniel Clark Bks, 81. *Dealer:* Wheeler Seidel Gallery New York NY. *Mailing Add:* 71 Glenwood Ave New Rochelle NY 10801-3126

ZHUKOVA, DASHA
COLLECTOR

b Moscow, June 8, 1981. *Study:* Univ Calif, Santa Barbara, BA (Slavic Studies and Lit). *Pos:* Founder, IRIS Found; co-founder, Garage Ctr for Contemporary Culture, Moscow; co-founder, Kova & T; editor-in-chief, Pop, 2009-10; bd trustees, Los Angeles Mus Art. *Awards:* named one of Top 200 Collectors, ARTnews mag, 2011, 2012, 2013. *Mem:* Los Angeles Co Mus Art (bd trustees). *Interests:* philanthropy. *Collection:* Modern and contemporary art. *Mailing Add:* Garage Center for Contemporary Culture 19A Ulitsa Obraztsova Moscow Russia

ZIB, TOM (THOMAS) A ZIBELLI
CARTOONIST

b Mt Vernon, NY. *Study:* Grand Cent Sch Art; Com Illus Studios. *Publ:* Contribr, Saturday Rev & Weight Watchers, 1972, Saturday Evening Post, Nat Enquirer, Reader's Digest, 1973-81, Wall Street J, 1981, Good Housekeeping & Woman's World, Cosmopolitan, Better Homes & Gardens. *Mailing Add:* 167 E Devonia Ave Mount Vernon NY 10552

ZIEGLER, DOLORES ANN
PAINTER, CONCEPTUAL ARTIST

b Northampton, MA, Sept 6, 1930. *Study:* Dean Jr Col, AA, 1949; Northampton Com Col, 1950. *Work:* St Clair Hosp, Denville, NJ; Norton Hosp, Louisville, Ky; Ryder Trucking, Harrisburg, Pa; Dominion Bank, Montreal, Can; Hershey Medical Ctr; Bell Lakes; Ricoh, Norton Medical, KY; Sealand, Squibb, Merck, Dominion Bank, Canada; Liberty Dialysis Ctr, Flagstaff, Ariz; The Perks, Coconino Coll, Ariz. *Comn:* Holiday Inn, Penns Grove, NJ, 1989; St Claire Hosp, Denville, NJ, 1990. *Exhib:* Traveling show, Nat Watercolor Soc, 2005; Northeast Watercolor Int Exhib, Conn, 2002; Am Watercolor Soc, Salmagundi Club, NY, 2004-2006; Am Watercolor Soc, Traveling Show, 2005-2006; Lincroft Monmouth Mus, Lincroft Mus, Monmouth, NY, 2006; High Country Conference Ctr, Flagstaff, 2013, 2014. *Collection Arranged:* Atrium Art Gallery, Morris Records Bldg, 1991; Morris Co Art Asn, Morris Co Libr, 2002; Ocean County Artist Guild,stated Juried Show, 2010; Artist Coalition of Flagstaff, 2011; Mt Oasis, Flagstaff. *Pos:* Jury of selection, NJ Watercolor Soc, Guild Creative Art, Shrewsbury, NJ, 2005; Judge, Pasacat Show Outdoor, 2006, Coconino Co Fair, Flagstaff, Ariz, 2012; chmn, Artist Trading Card Show Celebration of 100 Yr Statehood; docent, Mus Northern Ariz; mgr, Artist Coaltion, Flagstaff, Ariz, 2013.

Teaching: Instr, Morris Co Art Asn, 85-2004; instr, Guild Creative Arts, Shrewsbury, NJ, 2004-05; instr acrylic collage, Somerset Art Asn; instr, Markham Art Ctr, Haddonfield, NJ, 2006; instr, Ctr Visual Arts, Summit, NJ, 2006-2009; instr, Ocean County Artist Guild, Island Heights, NJ, 2006-2010, Coconino Ctr Arts, Flagstaff; Hozoni Sch. *Awards:* Endico Award Excellence, North East Watercolor Soc, 2002; Art Competition, Artist Magazine, 2003; Ocean County Artist Guild State Juried Show, 2008; Southern Ctr Arts, NJ, Garden State Watercolor Soc, 2008-2009; NJ Watercolor Assn, 2011-2012; Northern Univ Ariz Highpoint Art Selection, 2013, 2014; Selected for Juried Auction, Coconino Coll. *Bibliog:* Greg Schaber (auth), Take Command College, Artist Mag, 1998; Joanne Moore (auth), Starting Points, Artist Sketch Book, 2003; Rachel Hunter (auth), Holiday Windows, Splash 6, 2003. *Mem:* Int Soc of Acrylic Painters,; NJ Watercolor Soc (juror, workshop organizer, signature mem); Baltimore Watercolor Soc (signature mem); North East Watercolor Soc (juror); Am Watercolor Soc; Nat Watercolor Soc; Artist Coalition of Flagstaff (bd mem, 2011-). *Media:* Acrylic/Collage. *Specialty:* Artist Coalition of flagstaff AZ, crafts & fine art. *Interests:* reading. *Collection:* Coll Paintings of New Arizona Aspens. *Publ:* Walk into Abstracts; Splash 6; Bridging Time and Space; Noise Newspaper, Flagstaff. *Mailing Add:* 3134 E Mt Elden Dr Flagstaff AZ 86004

ZIFF, JERROLD
HISTORIAN, COLLECTOR

b Los Angeles, Calif, Dec 20, 1928. *Study:* Occidental Col, BA, 51; Univ Southern Calif, MA, 54; Harvard Univ, PhD, 59. *Collection Arranged:* French Masters: Rocco to Romanticism (coauth, catalog), Univ Calif, Los Angeles, 60-61; George F Mc Murray Collection of 19th century Am Paintings, Trinity Col, Hartford, Conn, 68; Drawings from Four Collections (co-auth, catalog), 73 & II (auth, catalog), Univ Ill. *Pos:* Asst prof 19th century art, Univ Calif, Los Angeles, 58-66; prof 18th & 19th century art, Trinity Col, Hartford, 66-69; prof 18th & 19th century art & drawings, Univ Ill, Champaign, 69-94. *Mem:* Coll Art Asn; Midwest Art Hist Soc; Turner Soc. *Res:* Art of J M W Turner; old master drawings. *Collection:* Old master and 19th century drawings. *Mailing Add:* 930 Curtiss St Unit 205 Downers Grove IL 60515-4886

ZILCZER, JUDITH KATY
CURATOR, HISTORIAN

b Waterbury, Conn, Nov 6, 1948. *Study:* George Washington Univ, BA, 69 & MA, 71; Univ Del, PhD, 75. *Collection Arranged:* Willem de Kooning: Hirshhorn Mus Collection (auth, catalog), 93; The Noble Buyer: John Quinn, Patron of the Avant-Garde (auth, Catalog), Hirshhorn Mus & Sculpture Garden, 78; Joseph Stella: The Hirshhorn Mus Collection (auth, catalog), 83; The Advent of Modernism: Post-Impressionism and North Am Art 1900-1918 (coauth, catalog), High Mus Art, Atlanta, Ga, 86; Keith Sonnier: Neon (auth, catalog), Hirshhorn Mus, 89; Richard Lindner: Paintings and Watercolors, 1948-1977 (auth, catalog), Hirshhorn Mus, 96; Directions: Cecily Brown, 02; Visual Music, Mus Contemp Art & Hirshhorn Mus (auth, catalog), 05. *Pos:* Historian, Hirshhorn Mus & Sculpture Garden, 74-88; assoc cur painting, 88-92, cur paintings, 92-2003; cur Emeritas, 2003-; editorial bd, Womans Art Jour. *Teaching:* Asst professorial lectr Am studies & art hist, George Washington Univ, 75-76, assoc professorial lectr, 80-86 & 91. *Awards:* Penrose Fund res grant, Am Philos Soc, 76-77; Award Exceptional Serv, Smithsonian Inst, 86, 92, 93, 94-98; Smithsonian Scholarly Studies Grant, 2003-04; Best Exhib of Time Based Art, Int Assn Art Critics, US Section, 2004-2005; George Wittenborn Mem Book Award, 2006. *Mem:* Asn of Historians Am Art; Am Asn Mus; Archives Am Art; Coll Art Asn. *Res:* Nineteenth and twentieth century art; history of patronage, visual music. *Publ:* The Face of War: The Last Works of Raymond Duchamp-Villon, Art Bulletin, 3/83; Synaesthesia and popular culture: Arthur Dove, George Gershwin and the rhapsody in blue, Art J, winter 84; Color Music: Synaesthesia and Nineteenth-century sources for Abstract Art, Artibus et historiae 16, 87; De-coding John Covert's Time, 1919, Art Bull, 12/93; A Not So Peaceable Kindon, Horace Pippin's Holy Mountain, Archives Am, Art, 01; Away of Living: The Art of Willem de Kooning, Phaidon, 2014. *Mailing Add:* 2351 N Quantico St Arlington VA 22205-2045

ZILIUS, VLADAS
PAINTER

b Silale, Lithuania, May 13, 1939; US citizen. *Study:* Vilnius Art Acad, DFA, 59-65. *Work:* Vilnius State Mus & Vilnius State Gallery, Lithuania. *Exhib:* Int Biennial, Cracow, Poland, 68; Barcelona Mus, Spain, 70; Graphic Arts from USSR, State Mus, Sophia, Bulgaria, 72; solo exhib, Drawing Center, Queens Col, NY, 84. *Teaching:* Instr drawing, Archit Inst, Vilnius, Lithuania, 74-75. *Media:* Miscellaneous Media. *Dealer:* Galerie Aldonna 215 E 79th St New York NY 10021

ZIMILES, MURRAY
PAINTER, EDUCATOR

b New York, NY, Nov 30, 1941. *Study:* Univ Ill, BFA, 63; Cornell Univ, MFA, 65; Ecole Nat Superieure Beaux-Arts, Paris, 66-67. *Work:* Brooklyn Mus, NY; Neuberger Mus, NY; Mus Mod Art, NY; Nat Collection Fine Arts; NY Pub Libr; Nat Acad Design, New York. *Comn:* Civic Ctr, Dutchess Co Arts Coun, Poughkeepsie, NY, 81. *Exhib:* Prints from Portfolios, Brooklyn Mus, 70; Solo exhibs, Kunstnerforbundet Gallery, Oslo, Norway, 72, Vassar Coll Gallery, 77, Neuberger Mus, NY, 80-81 & Johnson Mus, Cornell Univ, Ithaca, NY, 81; Cathedral St John the Divine, NY, 92; Suffolk Co Community Col, Selden, NY, 93; Holocaust Mem Mus, Madeira Beach, Fla, 94; Sydney Jewish Mus, Australia, 96; BMG Gallery, Adelaide, Australia, 98; DFN Gallery. *Pos:* Guest cur, Mus Am Folk Art, NY, 2007-08. *Teaching:* Instr printmaking, Pratt Graphics Ctr, NY, 68-71; asst prof drawing & printmaking, Silvermine Col Art, New Canaan, Conn, 68-71; asst prof drawing & printmaking, State Univ NY, New Paltz, 72-77; prof drawing & printmaking, State Univ NY, Purchase, 77-; Kempner Distinguished prof, State Univ NY, Purchase, 98-. *Awards:* Dorot Found Grant, 93-94; NY State Coun Arts Grant, Artists' Books Fel, 95-96; Smart Found Grant, 95 & 96; Nat Jewish Book award, 2008; Elected, Nat Acad Design, New York, 2009. *Bibliog:* Review, NY Times, 1/4/81; Article, Art News, 4/92; Article, NY Newsday, 2/93. *Mem:* Soc Am Graphic Artists; Nat Acad Design, NY. *Media:* Oil, Lithography, digital prints. *Specialty:* Morrison Gallery, Kent, Conn. *Collection:* Brooklyn Mus; Jewish Mus; Mus Modern Art; NY Pub Libr; Neuberger Mus; Purchase, Johnson Mus, Ithaca; Portland Mus. Ore. *Publ:* Coauth, The Technique of Fine Art Lithography, Van Nostrand Reinhold, 70; Early American Mills, Clarkson Potter, 73; The Lithographic Workshop Around the World, Van Nostrand Reinhold, 74; Boris Margo, A Retrospective (exhib catalog), Provincetown Art Asn; review, The book of Fire at the Sydeny Jewish Mus, Australian Mag, 3/96; Guilded Lions and Jeweled Horses, Brandeis Univ Press, 2007. *Dealer:* BMG Gallery 94-98 Melbourne St North Adelaide S Australia 5006; Morrison Gallery Kent CT. *Mailing Add:* Visual Arts Dept SUNY Col Purchase Purchase NY 10577

ZIMMERMAN, ALICE A
COLLECTOR, ART DEALER

b Chicago, Ill, June 6, 1939. *Study:* Univ Wis, Madison, 57-58; Emory Univ, BA, 77; Vanderbilt Univ, MA, 79. *Pos:* Mem, adv comt, Southeastern Ctr Contemp Art, Winston-Salem, NC, 78-; exec dir, Metrop Nashville Arts Comn, 81-83; trustee, Am Craft Coun, NY, 83-; dir, Zimmerman-Saturn Gallery, Nashville, Tenn, formerly. *Specialty:* Emerging artists; fine crafts; contemporary art. *Collection:* Photo-realists; painters and sculptors; contemporary Europeans; handmade furniture and crafts. *Mailing Add:* 6004 Dunham Springs Rd Nashville TN 37205

ZIMMERMAN, ELYN
SCULPTOR, PHOTOGRAPHER

b Philadelphia, Pa, Dec 16, 1945. *Study:* Univ Calif, Los Angeles, BA, 68, MFA, 72. *Work:* Los Angeles Co Mus Art; Whitney Mus Am Art; Mus Mod Art, NY; General Mills Corp, Minneapolis, Minn; Birmingham Mus Art, Ala; Chase Manhatten Bank, NY; Addison Gallery, Andover, Ma; Telfair Mus Art, Savannah, Ga. *Comn:* Keystone Island, Dade Co Art Pub Places, Miami, Fla, 89; CRA Art Prog, Los Angeles, 90; Plaza Design, 525 Market St, San Francisco, 90; Sanctuary, Univ S Fla, Tampa, 90; World Trade Ctr Mem, NY, 95; Conn Art Commision, Bridgeport, Conn; US Embassy, Dar es Salem, Tanzania; IAS, Princeton NJ, 2005; Vancouver, BC, Can, 2007; Olympic Park, Beijing Olympics, China, 2008; Canal St Park, NY, 2010. *Exhib:* Palisades Project, Hudson River Mus, Yonkers, NY, 82; Directions 1983, Hirshhorn Mus, Washington, DC, 83; Art & Archit & Landscape, San Francisco Mus Mod Art, 85; Artist As Social Designer, Los Angeles Co Mus Art, 85; solo exhib, Projects Wave Hill, Riverdale, NY, 88; Art Mus Univ S Fla, Tampa, 91; Hoffman Gallery, Los Angeles, Calif, 92; 65 Thompson Gallery, NY, 92; Gagosian Gallery, NY, 93, 96, 98, 2001, 2003, & 2004. *Pos:* Appointed mem, Comn Fine Arts, Wash DC, 2003-2008. *Awards:* New Talent Award, Los Angeles Co Art Mus, 76; Artist Fel Grant, Nat Endowment Arts, 76, 80 & 82; CAPS Grant, NY State, 80. *Bibliog:* Marc Treib (auth), Elyn Zimmerman: A decade of projects (exhib catalog), Wavehill, Riverdale, NY, 88; John Beardsley (auth), Earth works & beyond, Abbeville Press, 89; John Beardsley (auth), Elyn Zimmerman (exhib catalog), Art Mus Univ S Fla, 91; Robert Pincus Witten (auth), Elyn Zimmerman (exhib catalog), Gagosian Gallery; Pepe Karnel (auth), New Drawings (exhib catalogue), 01. *Mem:* Creative Time Inc (bd dir, 85-92); Int Sculpture Ctr (bd dir, 89-95); Columbia Land Conserv (bd dir, 93-2006); Century Association, 2008. *Media:* Mixed Media. *Mailing Add:* 140 Greene St New York NY 10012

ZIMMERMAN, PAUL WARREN
PAINTER, INSTRUCTOR

b Toledo, Ohio, Apr 29, 1921. *Study:* John Herron Art Sch, BFA. *Work:* Pa Acad Fine Arts, Philadelphia; Houston Mus Fine Art; Butler Inst Am Art, Youngstown, Ohio; Springfield Mus Fine Art, Mass; Wadsworth Atheneum, Hartford, Conn. *Comn:* Mural, First New Haven Nat Bank, Conn, 65. *Exhib:* Indiana Artists Exhibition, John Herron Art Mus, Indianapolis, 57; Am Painting & Sculpture, Univ Ill, 61; Pa Acad Fine Arts, Philadelphia, 62; 144th Ann Exhib, Nat Acad Design, NY, 69; Midyear Show, Butler Inst Am Art, Youngstown, 70. *Teaching:* Prof painting & design, Univ Hartford Art Sch, 47-. *Awards:* First Prize, Conn Watercolor Soc, 64; Altman Landscape Prize for Second Place, 67 & First Place, 69, Nat Acad Design. *Bibliog:* Henry Pitz (auth), Paintings of Paul Zimmerman, Am Artist Mag, 1/60. *Mem:* Nat Acad (assoc, 70, acad, 72-); Conn Acad Fine Arts; Conn Watercolor Soc (pres, 52-53). *Media:* Oil. *Dealer:* Munson Gallery New Haven CT; Korn Bluth Gallery Fair Lawn NJ. *Mailing Add:* PO Box 780 Granby CT 06035-0780

ZIMON, KATHY ELIZABETH
LIBRARIAN

b Szeged, Hungary, Feb 20, 1941; Can citizen. *Study:* Univ BC, BA (art hist), 66, BLS, 69, MA (art hist), 70. *Pos:* Fine arts librn, Univ Calgary Libr, Alta, 69-; cur, Can Archit Arch. *Mem:* Can Libr Asn; Can Asn of Spec Libr & Info Serv (newsletter ed, 75-78, chmn art sect, 79-80); Art Libr Soc North Am. *Res:* Alberta artists: currently working on an index. *Mailing Add:* Fine Arts Libr 9LT Univ Calgary 2500 University Dr NW Calgary AB T2N 1N4 Canada

ZINC, RUTA See Dean, Nat

ZINGALE, LAWRENCE
PAINTER

b Florida, NY, Aug 12, 1938. *Work:* Int Mus Folk Art, Santa Fe, NMex; Chase Manhattan Bank, NY; Silvermine Guild Ctr Arts, New Canaan, Conn. *Exhib:* Int Mus of Folk Art, Santa Fe, 76; The All-Am Dog, Mus of Folk Art, NY, 77-78; The Am Game, Wilson Art Ctr, Rochester, NY, 78; solo exhibs, Am Hurrah Antiques, NY, 78, Jay Johnson Gallery, NY, 81 & 88 & Frank Miele Gallery, 93; Jay Johnson Gallery, NY, 88-91; Frank Miele Gallery, NY, 93; Fenimore House, Cooperstown, NY, 92. *Bibliog:* Robert Bishop (auth), The All-American Dog, Avon Publ, New York, 77; Ellen Stern (auth), article, New York Mag, 10/78; article, Attenzione Mag, 12/81; Jay Johnson & William Ketchum (auths), American Folk Art of the Twentieth Century, Rizzoli Publ; and others. *Media:* Oil, Acrylic

ZIRKER, JOSEPH
PRINTMAKER, LECTURER
b Los Angeles, Calif, Aug 13, 1924. *Study:* Univ Calif, Los Angeles, 43-44, 46-47; Univ Denver, BFA, 49; with Jules Heller & Francis de Erdely, Univ Southern Calif, MFA, 51; Tamarind Lithography Workshop, printer fel, 62-63 & res fel, 64. *Work:* Achenbach Found Graphic Arts, Calif Palace Legion Honor, San Francisco; Portland Art Mus, Ore; La Art Mus, Denmark; Koninklijk Mus voor Schone Kunsten, Antwerp, Belgium; Stanford Univ Art Museum; The de Saisset Mus; Oakland Art Mus; Graham Gund Collectioni, Los Angeles; Univ Art Collection, Ariz State Univ; Centrum Frans Masereel, Kasterlee, Belgium; La Art Mus, Denmark; Nat Acad Design, New York; Nat Gallery, DC; Fine Art Mus San Francisco; Charles Randall Dean Colection, New York. *Exhib:* Solo exhibs, Calif Palace Legion of Honor, San Francisco, 74, De Saisset Art Gallery & Mus, Univ Santa Clara, Calif, 75, Univ Art Collection, Ariz State Univ, Tempe, 83, Portland State Univ, Ore, 84, Espace Latino Americain, Paris, France, 87, Centrum Frans Masereel, Kasterlee, Belg, 89, Galerie Witteveen, Amsterdam, The Neth, 90, Smith Andersen Editions, Palo Alto, 91, 93, 95, 97, 99, 2001, 2003, 2004, 2005, 2006, 2007, & 2010, de Saisset Mus, Univ of Santa Clara, 2005, Nev Mus Art, Reno, 2005-06, Santa Cruz Mus Art and History, 2010, Peninsula Art Mus, Belmont, Calif, 2010, Smith Andersen Editions, 2010, 2012; New Ways With Paper, Nat Collection of Fine Arts, Smithsonian Inst, Wash, DC, 77-78; New Am Monotypes & Paper as Medium, Smithsonian Traveling Exhib, 78-80; Paper-Art, Crocker Art Mus, Sacramento, Calif, 81; New Am Paperworks, Orient & United States, 82-86; Calif Palace of Legion of Honor, San Francisco, 2000; Nat Acad Design, NY, 92, 93, 95, 97, 99, 2001, 2003, 2005, 2007; The Abstract Impulse: 50 Years of Abstraction at the Nat Acad, 1956-2006; Nat Acad Design, NY, 2008, 2009. *Pos:* Dir, Joseph Press, Venice, Calif, 63-64. *Teaching:* Lectr printmaking, Univ Southern Calif, 63; instr drawing, San Jose City Col, 66-82; lectr printmaking, Stanford Univ, Calif. *Awards:* Nat Acad Design, 92; Pollock-Krasner Grant, 2003-04; Pollock-Krasner Grant, 2010-2011. *Bibliog:* Jules Heller (auth), Papermaking, Watson-Guptill Publ, NY, 78. *Mem:* Nat Acad (assoc, 92, acad, 94-); Achenbach Found Graphic Arts. *Media:* Monotype, Paper Art, Sculpture. *Res:* invented: the Cast Acrylic Print method. *Specialty:* works on paper. *Interests:* Music, literature, physics and evolution. *Publ:* Auth, Survey Exhibition 1962-82 (exhib catalog), Smith-Andersen Gallery, Palo Alto, 82; Innovations in monotype and paper art, Arte Grafika, Antwerp, Belg, spring 90; The Cast Acrylic Print, (manual), Joseph Zirker, 2002; Translucent Transformations (catalog), de Saisset Mus, 2005; The Cast Acrylic Print, 2005; Machines of Memory catalog. *Dealer:* Smith Andersen Editions 440 Pepper Ave Palo Alto CA 94306; Smith Andersen North 2240 Fourth St San Rafael CA 94901. *Mailing Add:* 451 O'Connor St Menlo Park CA 94025

ZISLA, HAROLD
PAINTER, GRAPHIC ARTIST
b Cleveland, Ohio, June 28, 1925. *Study:* Cleveland Inst Art; Western Reserve Univ, BS (educ) & AM. *Work:* South Bend Regional Mus Art; Midwest Mus Am Art; Snite Mus Art, Notre Dame. *Exhib:* Cleveland Mus Art; South Bend Michiana; John Herron Art Mus; Ft Wayne Art Mus; Kalamazoo Art Inst; and others. *Pos:* Dir & bd mem, South Bend Art Ctr, 57-. *Teaching:* Instr, South Bend Art Ctr, 53-89; prof emer fine arts, Ind Univ, South Bend. *Awards:* Amoco Found Award; All Univ Teaching Award, 79; First Eldon Lundquist Fac Fel, Ind Univ South Bend, 85; Arts Midwest Fel Award, 86. *Dealer:* Blue Gallery Three Oaks Mich. *Mailing Add:* 1230 Dennis Dr South Bend IN 46614

ZITO, JOSEPH (PHILLIP)
SCULPTOR, CONCEPTUAL ARTIST
b Brooklyn, NY, June 6, 1957. *Study:* Sch Visual Arts, BFA, 79. *Work:* Harvard Univ Art Mus. *Exhib:* Solo exhibs, Il Ponte Gallery, Rome, Italy, 88 & 91, Greenberg Gallery, St Louis, Mo, 89, Resa Esman Gallery, NY, 88, 89 & 91; Oltreluce, Claudio Bottello Arte, Turin, Italy, 90; Joseph Zito & Gerald Giamportone, Blumhelman Gallery, Los Angeles, Calif, 90. *Bibliog:* Walter Thompson (auth), Joseph Zito, Art in America, 10/88; William Zimmer (auth), 7 Days Mag, 4/6/88; Michael Welzenbach (auth), Washington Post, 2/17/90. *Mailing Add:* 57 Cheever Pl Brooklyn NY 11231

ZITTEL, ANDREA
PRINTMAKER, SCULPTOR
b Escondido, Calif, 1965. *Study:* San Diego State Univ, BFA (painting & sculpture), 1988; RI Sch Design, MFA (sculpture), 1990. *Work:* Carnegie Mus Art, Pittsburgh, 1994, New Work, San Francisco Mus Mod Art, 1995, Sch Mus Fine Arts, Boston, 1996, New Art 6, Cincinnati Art Mus, 1996, Mus Mod Art, Humlebaek, Denmark, 1996, Mus Mod Art, NY, 1994, Whitney Biennial, Whitney Mus Am Art, NY, 1995, 2004, Just Past, Mus Contemp Art, Los Angeles, 1996, Mus Contemp Art, San Diego, Calif, 2001, Tempo, Mus Mod Art, NY, 2002, Just Love Me, Bergen Art Mus, 2003. *Exhib:* Solo exhibs, Purity, Andrea Rosen Gallery, NY, 1993, A-Z Living Units, Jack Hanley Gallery, San Francisco, 1993, A-Z Carpet Furniture, Christopher Grimes Gallery, Santa Monica, Calif, 1993, Comfort, Anthony d'Offay Gallery, London, 1994, Three Living Systems, A Series of Rotating Installations, Andrea Rosen Gallery, NY, 1994, 1995, New Work, Social Fictions, Barbara & Steven Grossman Gallery, A-Z Escape Vehicles, Andrea Rosen Gallery, NY, 1996, RAUGH, 1998, A-Z Personal Panels, Saide Coles Hq, London, 1999, Point of Interest, Pub Art Fund, Central Park, NY, 1999, A-Z Time Trials: Free Running Rhythms, Regen Projects, Los Angeles, 2002, Philomene Magers Projekte, Munich, Ger, 2003, Sammlung Goetz, Munich, Ger, 2003, Small Liberties, Whitney Mus Am Art, 2006, Galleria Massimo De Carlo, Milan, 2007, Smock Shop, 2008, Single Strand, Forward Motion, Andrea Rose Gallery, 2009, Between Art & Life, Palazzo Pitti, 2010, Spruth Magers, Berlin, 2011; Group exhibs, Ornament: Ho Hum All Ye Faithfull, John Post Lee Gallery, NY, 1991, One Leading to Another, 303 Gallery, NY, 1992, Writing on the Wall, 1992, Radio Show, Artist's Space, NY, 1992, Add Hot Water, Sandra Gering Gallery, NY, 1993, Don't Look Now, Thread Waxing Space, NY, 1994, Sense & Sensibility, Light for the Dark Days of Winter, A/D Gallery, NY, 1995, About Place: Recent Art of Am, Art Inst Chicago, 1995, Staging Realism, Wexner Ctr Arts, Ohio, 1997, Patrick Painter Editions, Lehmann-Maupin Gallery, NY, 1997, Travel & Leisure, Paula Cooper Gallery, NY, 1998, Inglenook, Feigen Contemp, NY, 1998, Art in Pub Places at Miami Design District, Dacra Companies, Miami Beach, 1999, Elysian Fields, Ctr Georges Pompidou, Paris, 2000, Threshold: Invoking Domestic in Contemp Art, Contemp Art Ctr, Va, 2000, Drawings, Regen Projects, LA, 2001, Everything Can Be Different, Calif Ctr Arts, 2002, Living Units, Triple Candie, Harlem, NY, 2003, Whitney Biennial, 2004, Mus Mod Art, New York, 2005, Van Abbemuseum, Eindhoven, The Netherlands, 2006, Guggenheim Mus, New York, 2007, Californial Biennial, Orange County Mus Art, 2008, Julia Stoscheck Found, Dusseldorf, 2009, Tanya Bonakdar Gallery, 2010, Royal Acad Arts, London, 2010, Patrick Painter, Santa Monica, 2011. *Awards:* Recipient Distinction Art, San Diego State Univ, 1988, Award Excellence, RI Sch Design, 1989, 1990, catalogue support prize, Alfried Krupp Von Bohlen und Halbach Found, 1999; Deutschen Akademischen Austauschdienst Grant, Berlin, Ger, 1995, Coutts Contemp Arts Found, Zurich, Switz, 1996; Lucelia Artist Award, Smithsonian Am Art Mus, 2005; Distinguished Body of Work Award, Coll Art Asn, 2006; Best Archit or Design Show Award, Int Asn Art Critics, 2007; Frederick Kiesler Prize for Architecture & the Arts, 2013. *Media:* Lithograph, Etching. *Dealer:* Editions Fawbush 448 W 19th St New York NY 10011; Richard Levy Gallery 514 Central Ave SW Albuquerque NMex 87102; Monika Sprüth Philomene Magers Schellingstrasse 48 80799 Munich Ger; Patrick Painter Editions 8415 Granville St Vancouver British Columbia Can; Regen Projects 633 N Almont Dr Los Angeles CA 90069; Andrea Rosen Gallery 525 W 24th St New York NY 10011; Galerie Thomas Schulte Charlottenstrabe 24 10117 Berlin Ger; SOLO Impression Inc 601 West 26th St New York NY 10001; Kornelia Tamm Fine Arts 1012 Marquez Pl Santa Fe NM 87505. *Mailing Add:* c/o MOCA Grand Ave 250 S Grand Ave Los Angeles CA 90012

ZIVIC, WILLIAM THOMAS
PAINTER, SCULPTOR
b Ironwood, Mich, Aug 31, 1930. *Work:* City of Tucson; Univ Ariz; Pima Col; Lockheed Aircraft, Los Angeles; Grissmer Corp, Indianapolis, Ind; Toyota Corp, Tokyo, Japan; Rodeo Cowboy Hall of Fame; Roy Rogers Mus; White House Archives; plus over 1,000 pvt collections, US, Europe, Africa & Asia. *Comn:* Paintings, Great Western Bank, Phoenix, 73; painting, Ariz Bank, Tucson, 75; painting, US Postal Serv, 75. *Exhib:* Tucson Art Ctr Ann, 74; Alamo Kiwanis Art Show, San Antonio, 74; Casa Grande Art Fiesta, Ariz, 75; Tubac Art Festival, Ariz, 75. *Awards:* Best of Show, Int Fine Arts; 1st place sculpture, Palm Springs, Calif. *Mem:* Tucson Art Ctr; Casa Grande Art Asn; Santa Cruz Valley Art Asn; SW League Fine Arts. *Media:* Bronze; Multimedia. *Collection:* John Wayne, Bob Hope, James Garner, Wayne Gretzky, James Caan, Roy Rogers. *Publ:* Illusr, Tucson Bi-Centennial Mag, 75; Southwest Memories, 75. *Dealer:* Sonoita Creek Gallery Box 159 Sonoita AZ 85637. *Mailing Add:* 1778 E Bishop Pl Casa Grande AZ 85222-6324

ZIVKOVICH, KAY PICK
ADMINISTRATOR, EDUCATOR, PRINTMAKER
Study: Southern Ill Univ, BA, 1971, MFA, 1973, MS, 1979. *Exhib:* Essential Journay, Olive Tjaden Gallery, Cornell Univ, Ithaca, NY; Earth and Sky, the Closeness, Componere Gallery, St Louis, MO; Earth to Sky and Back, Northeastern Univ Sch Law, Boston, Mass; Body Scapes, Castle Gallery, Christianholm Festening Kristiansand, Norway; Natural Impressions, Rosette Studio, Cincinnati, OH. *Pos:* prof comm design, associate dir, Southern Ill Univ, currently. *Interests:* design process, critical and creative thinking, design consulting, design curriculum, and environmental graphic design. *Dealer:* Componere Gallery St Louis MO. *Mailing Add:* 10162 Old Hwy 13 Murphysboro IL 62966

ZLAMANY, BRENDA
PAINTER
Study: Yale Coll, Pre-Coll Prog, 1976-77; Tyler Sch Art, Rome, 1981; SW Hayter's Atelier 17, Paris, 1981; Wesleyan Univ, BA (Johnson Trust Scholar), 1981; Skowhegan Sch Painting & Sculpture, 1984. *Work:* Cincinnati Art Mus; Mem Sloan-Kettering Cancer Ctr, New York; Mus Mod Art, Houston; Neuberger Mus Art, Purchase, NY; World Bank, Washington; Deutsche Bank. *Comn:* Dr Martini (portrait), Martini Libr, Sloan-Kettering Cancer Ctr, 1995; Jeffrey Dahmer (portrait), NY Times Mag, June 1995, Marian Anderson (portrait), Nov 1996, Slobodon Milosevic & Mira Markovic (portrait), Jan 2002 & Osama bin Laden (portrait), Sept 2005; James D Wolfensohn (portrait), World Bank, Washington, 2007. *Exhib:* Solo exhibs include South Gallery, Wesleyan Univ, 1981, Hallwalls Contemp Arts Ctr, Buffalo, 1989, EM Donahue Gallery, New York, 1991, 1992 & 1994, Sabine Wachters Fine Art, Belgium, 1993 & 1995, Galerie Quintessens, Utrecht, Netherlands, 1994, Jessica Fredericks Gallery, New York, 1996, Stux Gallery, 1998, Galapagos Art & Performance Space, New York, 1999, Fine Arts Ctr, Univ Mass, Amherst, 2001, Art Upstairs @ GHB, East Hampton, NY, 2002, Jonathan O'Hara Gallery, New York, 2007; group exhibs include Dumb Animals?, White Columns, New York, 1990; Detritus: Transformation & Reconstruction, Jack Tilton Gallery, New York, 1990; Chords & Discord, Hudson River Mus, Yonkers, NY, 1991; Close Scrutiny, Art in General, New York, 1991; Neurotic Art: Return of the Repressed, Artists Space, New York, 1992, Painting as Paradox, 2002; Flesh, Four Walls Gallery, Brooklyn, 1992; Summer Review, Stux Gallery, New York, 1994, Inaugural Exhib, 1996, Sex/Industry, 1997; Crossing State Lines, Neuberger Mus Art, Purchase, NY, 1995; Anima Mundi, James Graham & Sons, New York, 1996, Portraits, 1996; Ceremonial, Apex Art, New York, 1996; Sans Tire, Boulder Mus Contemp Art, Colo, 1999; The Figure: Another Side of Modernism, New House Ctr Contemp Art, Snug Harbor Cult Ctr, Staten Island, NY, 2000; The Swamp: On the Edge of Eden, Samuel P Harn Mus Art, Gainesville, Fla, 2000; Tribeca Works on Paper Show, DFN Gallery, New York, 2002, People Places & Things, 2004, Animal Tales, 2004, The Woods, 2005; POPjack: Warhol to Murakami, Mus Contemp Art, Denver, 2002; Outwin Boochever Portait Competition Exhib, Nat Portrait Gallery, Washington, 2006-07; Contemp Art Invitational, Salmagundi Club New York, 2007. *Awards:* Jerome Found Fel, Printmaking Workshop, New York, 1981; Vt Studio Colony Fel, 1987; NY Found Arts Fel, 1994; Pollock-Krasner Found Grant, 2007. *Mailing Add:* 119 N 11th St Apt 4C Brooklyn NY 11211-1168

ZLATKOFF, CHARLES
PAINTER, SCULPTOR
b Chicago, Ill, Feb 24, 1935. *Study:* Univ Ill, Champaign-Urbana, BFA, 1957; Art Inst Chicago, student; Royal Coll Art, London, student. *Work:* Art Inst Archit Chicago; Mus NMex, Santa Fe; The Albuquerque Mus; Crocker Art Mus, Sacramento; NMex Capitol Art Found, Santa Fe. *Exhib:* Munic Art Gallery, Los Angeles, 63-66; Long Beach Mus Art, Calif, 64; Fine Arts Mus, San Diego, 65; 161st Ann, Pa Acad Fine Arts, Philadelphia, 66; Am Now-A Look at 70's, Belgrade & Zagreb, Yugoslavia, Budapest, Hungary, 80-81; Alternative Media, Downey Art Mus, Downey, Calif, 82; The Joyful Vision, Craft & Folk Art Mus, Los Angeles, 86; Skirball Mus, Bellair, Calif, 92; Capitol Art Collection, NMex Capitol Art Found, Santa Fe, 03; Pasadena Mus of Calif Art, Pasadena, Calif, 2003; Weisman Art Mus, Malibu, Calif, 2003, 2006. *Teaching:* lectr art & design, UCLA, 67-70; lectr art & design, Univ Calif, ext, LA, 67-90; instr art, Santa Barbara Arts Inst, Santa Barbara, Calif, 71-72. *Bibliog:* William Wilson (auth), Potpourri of work - Art Festival Calendar, Los Angeles Times, 7/18/65; Jason Silverman (auth), Zlatkoff's paintings embrace spirit - Pasatiempo, Santa Fe New Mexican, 94. *Mem:* Calif Art Club. *Media:* Watercolor; All Media. *Dealer:* Owings Duey North Gallery 120 E Marcy St Santa Fe NM 87501. *Mailing Add:* c/o California Art Club 75 S Grand Ave Pasadena CA 91105-1602

ZMIJEWSKI, ARTUR
VISUAL ARTIST, FILMAKER
b May 26, 1966. *Exhib:* Solo exhibs: Repetition, 51st Venice Biennale, 2005; Projects 91, Projects Gallery, Mus Modern Art, 2010; Group exhibs: Documenta, Kassel, Germany, 2007; Double Agent, Inst Contemp Arts, London, 2008; 11th Int Istanbul Biennial, 2009; 55th Int Art Exhib Biennale, Venice, 2013. *Awards:* Named one of 10 Most Important Artists of Today, Newsweek mag, 2011. *Publ:* dir, Them (film), 2007; dir, Democracies (film), 2009; and others

ZOLLWEG, AILEEN BOULES
ARTIST, WRITER
b East St Louis, Ill. *Study:* Sch Art Inst, Chicago, Ill; Carnegie Mellon Univ, Pittsburgh, Pa. *Work:* Carnegie Mus Art, Corning Glass Corp & Mellon Bank Collections, Pittsburgh; Dressler Ctr Arts; Southern Alleghenies Mus of Art. *Comn:* Moat tracing, Three Rivers Arts Festival, Pittsburgh, 83; Swimming Pool Mural, San Diego, Calif, 88; Greater Pittsburgh Comn for Women, 1995. *Exhib:* Solo exhibs, Washington & Jefferson Univ, Washington, Pa, 84, Pittsburgh Ctr Arts, 90, 2002-03, 2005-06, Dressler Arts Ctr, Somerset, Pa, 92, Gallery 937, Pittsburgh, 96, Southern Alleghenies Mus Art, 99, 2002-0009, AAP Ann, Carnegie Mus Art, 2001, Westmoreland Mus Art Southwestern Artists Exhibit, 2001 & 2004, Southern Allegheny Mus Arts Biennial, 2002, 2005 & 2007, Gallery Chiz, 2002, 2005, AAP Ann, Warhol Mus, 2002; Westmoreland Art Mus, Greensburg, Pa, 85 & 2003; New Technol Invitational, Carnegie Mellon Univ Gallery, 85; Butler Inst Am Art, Youngstown, Ohio, 88, 2001 & 2005; Univ Pittsburgh Gallery, 2003; Carnegie Mus Art, Pittsburgh, Pa; Seton Hill Col, 2003; Three Rivers Gallery, 2004; Regina Gouger Miller Gallery, 2004; Expressions of Color, Southern Allegheny Mus Art, 2008; Pittsburgh Gifted Ctr, 2010; The Greatest Generation, Southern Allegheny Mus Art, 2011; Art from the Carnegie Mus Collection at Conroy, 2012. *Pos:* organized exhibs, established Gallery Space, Monroeville, Pa, 79-84; bd mem, Three Rivers Art Festival. *Awards:* Purchase Award, 83 & 84, Juror's Award, 84 & 91, AAP Carnegie Mus; Jurors Award, Pittsburgh Soc Artist, 97 & 98; Purchase Award, AAP, Warhol Mus, 2002. *Bibliog:* TV prog, Women in Art, Monroeville Cable, 83; tv prog, Pittsburgh Women Artists, Pub TV, 92; article, Successful-Women-96. *Mem:* Asn Artists Pittsburgh; Pittsburgh Soc Artist; Nat League of Am Pen Women. *Media:* Acrylic; Miscellaneous Media. *Publ:* Fabulous Fanny Defeats the South (novel); Airbrushing Angels (poetry); Myth of the Given (novel). *Dealer:* Boules/Zollweg. *Mailing Add:* 5850 Meridian Rd Apt 504B Gibsonia PA 15044-9688

ZOMBEK, W See Lamantia, Paul Christopher

ZONA, LOUIS A
MUSEUM DIRECTOR, EDUCATOR
b New Castle, Pa, June 28, 1944. *Study:* Youngstown State Univ, BS (art educ), 1966; Univ Pittsburgh, MS (art educ), 1969; Carnegie-Mellon Univ, doctorate, 1973. *Collection Arranged:* Patrick Ireland, Blue Room Exhib, 1983; Alfred Leslie, 100 Views Along the Road, 1985; George Segal: The Drawings, 1985; Fireworks: Am Celebrate the Eighth Art, 1986; Ray Parker: A Retrospective Exhibition, 1986; Anatomy of a Cloud: The Collage Paintings of Paul Jenkins, Butler Inst Am Art, 1986; Leo Castelli: A Tribute (auth, catalog), 1987; Jasper Johns: Drawings and Prints from the collection of Leo Castelli, 1989; Gregory Arnenoff: Monotypes/Prints, 1989; Michael Hardesty: Polar Event & Vigil II, 1989; Chuck Close: Editions, 1989; Philip Pearlstein: The Abstract Landscapes, 1992; The Artist at Ringside, 1992; Nassas Daphnis: Color & Form: A Retrospective, 1993; Patrick Ireland: Gestures, 1994; Robert Motherwell: The Elegy Series, 1994; The Complete Prints of Alfred Leslie, 1994; Norman Bluhm: A Tribute Exhibition (auth, catalog), 1999; Robert Passchenberg & Darryl Pottorf, 1999; Chuck Close: The Photographic Work, 2000; Joseph Nechvatal: Contamination, 2006; Ronald Davis: Digital Prints, 2006; K K Smith: Works on Paper, 2006; Sally Weber: Strata Series Holograms, 2006; Stephen Hannock, A Survey, 2006, Three Video Artists, 2007; Ken Noland, 2007; James Rosati, 2007; Stephen Knapp: Light Paintings, 2007; Ron Amstutz: Right Roads & Wrong Way, 2008; Tom Christopher: Metropolis, 2008; Grace Hartigan: A Survey of Six Decades, 2008. *Pos:* exec dir & chief cur, Butler Inst Am Art, Youngstown, Ohio, 1981-. *Teaching:* Adj prof art & mus studies, Westminster Col, Pa, 1976-80; prof art hist & museology, Youngstown State Univ, 1970-; chmn, Dept Art, Youngstown State Univ, 1978-82. *Awards:* Distinguished Prof Award, Youngstown State Univ, 1978; Gov Award Arts (Admin Category), Ohio, 90; Gary Melcher Mem Award for Contribution to Am Fine Arts, Nat Arts Club, 96; Friends of Pastels Award, Pastel Soc Am, NYC, 2005; Leadership in the Fine Arts, Portrait Soc Am, 2009. *Mem:* Hoyt Inst Fine Arts, Pa (trustee); Ohio Mus Asn (chmn ann meeting, 89); Asn Art Mus Dir; Portrait Soc Am. *Publ:* Auth, Anatomy of a cloud: the collages of Paul Jenkins, Dialogue Mag, 1986; Leo Castelli, interview, Dialogue Mag, 1987; Jasper Johns: Drawings & Prints from the Collection of Leo Castelli, 1989; Nassos Daphis, Color and Form: A Retrospective (catalog) monograph), 1993; auth, cat essay on Paintings of Joseph Raffael for Nancy Hoffman Gallery, 2006. *Mailing Add:* Butler Inst Am Art 524 Wick Ave Youngstown OH 44502

ZONIA, DHIMITRI
PAINTER, GRAPHIC ARTIST, SCULPTOR
b St Louis, Mo, June 12, 1921. *Study:* Independent study in England & India. *Work:* I Gallerise Kombetare Te Arteva, Tirana, Albania; Ark Art Ctr; Albrecht Mus, St Joseph, Mo; Planetarium Prague, Czech Republic; Jewish Community Ctr, St Louis; Institute of Sacred Art, NMex; Meramec Community College, St Louis; Butler Inst American Art, Youngstown, OH; Concordia Publishing Co, St Louis; William Woods Univ, Fulton, Mo; William Woods Univ, Fulton, Md; Oklahoma Art Center; Litte Rock Ark Art Center; St Joseph Art Mus, Mo; Yamaha Corp, Tokyo, Japan; Galeria De Arte, Tirane, Albania; Catholic House of Prayer, Wash DC; Concordia Publishing Co, St. Louis, Mo. *Comn:* Poster, McDonnell Planetarium, St Louis; murals, St Cyril and Methody Ch, Granite City, Ill; Political Cartoons, The Scene, Forest Park Community Coll; St Bernadette Inst Art, Albuquerque; Arber Restaurant, St Louis; and others. *Exhib:* Midyear Show, Butler Inst Am Art, Youngstown, Ohio, 74; Western Ill Univ, 79; Nat Traveling Exhib, Minn Mus Art, 80; Ariz State Univ, 80; Univ Mo, Cape Girardeau, 85; Concordia Publishing co, 87; St Louis Community Coll Ctr, 2007, 2008; William Woods Univ, Fulton, MO, 2009; Forest Park College, St Louis, 2009. *Teaching:* Instr painting & drawing, Crestwood Community Ctr & Parkway Unitarian Church, Educ Ctr, currently; lectr & demonstration, computer graphics, St Louis Community Coll; staff, Louis Community Coll; staff, Forest Park Community Coll; lectr, William Woods Univ, 2008. *Awards:* Catholic Press Assoc, 76; Printing Inst America, 76; Second Prize Painting, Spiva Art Ctr, Joplin, Mo, 85; Popular Choice Award, Dakota Art Ctr, Rapid City, SDak, 85; 1st Prize Painting, Aesthetics 2000, Linsborg, Kansas; Best of Show, Arcon, Collinville, Ill; 3rd Prize Ed cartoon, Mo State Coll Media Asn; 1st Prize Editorial Art, Am Civil Liberties Union (ACLU),; 1st Prize, Mo State Col Media Asn; 1st Prize Donor, Dr Walter Jones Award, Fort Hayes-Lindsborg, Kansas, 2000; Am Civil Liberties Union, Political Cartoon. *Mem:* St Louis Artists Guild (bd gov, 79-81); Albanian Asn Fine Art; Soc Independent Artists (lifetime mem); Catholic Fine Arts Soc. *Media:* Animation, Painting, Computer Art. *Res:* Church Fresco Restoration, Albania; Art Restoration. *Specialty:* Phoenix Pottery, Ceramics. *Interests:* Digital animation, three dimensional modeling. *Publ:* Air and Space Mag; Step by Step; Am Artist Mag; Song of Solomon; The Scene Newspaper, Concordia Publ co, Forest Park Coll; and others; contribr, Columbia Tribune, Christian Bd of Publ, Fulton, Mo, 09. *Dealer:* Phoenix Potteries St Louis MO; Mus Sacred Art Albuquerque NMex. *Mailing Add:* 4680 Karamar Dr Saint Louis MO 63128

ZOOK, MAURINE JOYCE
PAINTER, ILLUSTRATOR
b July 17, 1929. *Study:* Univ Kans, 47-50; studies with William F Reese, 85-87; El Camino Col, studies with Willy Suzuki, 87-88; Calif State Univ, Long Beach, studies with Steven Warlick, 89-90, Charles Reid, 2000. *Comn:* Red Lilies at Sunset (painting), Clayton Morgan. *Exhib:* Sol Del Rio Gallery, San Antonio, Tex, 77-98; Los Angeles Int Art Fair 1989, Calif, 89; Feingarten Gallery, 89-98; Chain Reaction (with catalog), Franklin Plaza, Austin, Tex, 91; Watercolor USA 1994, Springfield Art Mus, Mo, 94; Western Fedn Watercolor Soc Ann Exhib, Sun City Art Mus, Ariz, 94 & Lubbock, Tex, 98; Watercolor USA, Springfield, Mo, 2006. *Teaching:* Drawing with children, Dougherty Arts Ctr, 87-88; drawing & watercolor & children at risk, Austin Schs, Tex, 91-94. *Awards:* Best of Show, KLRU 96 Auction; Art Patron Award, Waterloo Watercolor Show, 97. *Bibliog:* John Hay (auth), Book displays artist talents, Pittsburgh Sun, 80; Pete Szilagyi (auth), Review show, Austin Statesman, 91; Dian Covey Birdwell (auth), Austin watercolor artist, Austin Mag, 2000. *Mem:* Nat Watercolor Soc. *Media:* Watercolor, Oil. *Res:* Large watercolor collage-landscapes and waterscapes. *Specialty:* large oil landscapes. *Interests:* Gardening, reading, running. *Publ:* Illusr, Gabbys Christmas Wish, Shoal Creek Publ, 80. *Dealer:* Art Inc 9401 San Pedro San Antonio TX 78216

ZOPP, DUDLEY
PAINTER, INSTALLATION ARTIST
b Lexington, Ky, Apr 12, 1941. *Study:* Univ Ky, BA, 1963, MA, 1964; postgraduate studies, Allen R Hite Art Inst, Univ Louisville, 1986-91. *Work:* Farnsworth Art Mus, Rockland, Maine; Portland Mus Art, Maine; Boston Athenaem, Boston; Univ Chicago Libr; Univ Ky, Lexington; Univ Maine, Presque Isle, Maine. *Exhib:* one-person shows: Erratics, Maine Coast Artists, Rockport, Maine, 1997; Reading the Landscape, Univ Maine at Farmington, 1998; Ctr for Maine Contemp Art, 2004; Univ Maine, Presque Isle, Maine, 2004; Univ Southern Maine/Lewiston-Auburn, 2006; Waterfall Arts, Belfast, Maine, 2007, Coleman Burke Gallery, NY, 2011, 12 Gallagher Ln, San Fran, 2012, Univ Maine, Orono, 2014; group shows: Exhibition 280, Huntington Mus Art, Huntington, 1992; Portland Mus Art, Portland, Maine, 1998; Paper New England, Hartford, Conn, 2007, George Marshall Store Gallery, York, Me, 2013; Art of Northeast USA, Silvermine Guild Arts Ctr, New Canaan, Conn, 1999, 2010; Maine in Am, Farnsworth Art Mus, Rockland, Maine, 2000-02; Univ Maine Mus Art, 2009; Am Drawing Biennial, Muscarelle Mus Art, Williamsburg, Va, 1992; June Fitzpatrick Gallery, 2011, 2014. *Pos:* studio resident, Pouch Cove Found, Saint Johns, Newfoundland, Can, 97; resident, Art in Nature, Arts Ctr Kingdom Falls, 2001; res, Can Serrat Centro de Actividades Artisticas, El Bruc, Spain, 2011. *Teaching:* instr drawing, Water Fall Arts, Belfast, Maine, 2001; painting instr, Vt Col, Montpelier, Vt, 2002, 2008. *Awards:* fel, Eleven Artists, Maine Arts Comn, 2002; Good Ideas Grant, Maine Arts Comm, 2003; visibility Grant, Maine Arts Comm, 2009; Grant, Maine Arts Council, 2014. *Bibliog:* Sarh R Maline (auth), Eleven Artists, Univ Maine, 2002;

Jeremy Antworth (auth), Dudley Zopp, Installation Artist, Univ So Maine (video), 2001; Edgar A Beem & Verzosa Andres, Maine Art New, 2013. *Media:* Oil, Installations. *Publ:* CoAuth, A Butterfly Careless, Stinehour Press, 2002. *Dealer:* June Fitzpatrick Gallery 522 Congress St Portland ME 04101. *Mailing Add:* PO Box 207 Lincolnville ME 04849-0207

ZUCCARELLI, FRANK EDWARD
PAINTER, INSTRUCTOR
b Pa, Oct 23, 1921. *Study:* Newark Sch Fine & Indust Art, with William J Aylward & John Grabach; Art Students League, with Robert Philip; Kean Univ, NJ, BA, 75. *Work:* Marine Corps Base, Barstow, Calif; Egan Corp, Bridgewater, NJ; Malcolm Forbes Collection, NY; US Navy Mus, Washington, DC; MCC Corp, Murray Hill, NJ. *Comn:* Paintings for US Navy, Newport RI, 71 & US Coast Guard, Washington, DC, 75; Dahlgren Weapons Lab, Va, 71 & Mediterranean Sixth Fleet, 72; Recovery of Astronauts in Pacific, Apollo-Soyuz Test Proj, 75; Carrier Flight Qualifications, USS Kennedy, 82. *Exhib:* Combat Art Collection, Washington, DC; Essex Fine Arts, Montclair, NJ; Miller Gallery, Cincinnati, Ohio; Palais Rameau, Lille, France; and others. *Teaching:* Pvt instr oils, pastels & watercolor. *Awards:* Hall of Fame, Pastel Soc, 96; Grand Nat Award, Am Artist Prof League, 2000-02; Liskin Mem Award Salmagundi Club, Salmagundi Prize, 2003-2005; and many others. *Bibliog:* Somerset Artist, Painter of all Seasons, 88; Magic of Pastel (video), Pastel Soc New York; Dedication & hard work, Courier News, 93. *Mem:* Pastel Soc Am, NY; Salmagundi Club, NY; Am Artist Prof League; Hudson Valley Art Asn; Allied Artists, NY; and others. *Media:* Oil, Pastel. *Interests:* Photography & Gardening. *Publ:* Am Artist Mag, 11/96; Best of Pastel-Best of Oils, Rockport Publ, 96; Art with Element of Mystery, Pastel Jous, 5-6/2002; Pastelagram, winter 2003; Pastel Artists of the World, Int Artist, 12/2003. *Dealer:* Swain Gallery Plainfield NJ; Swerdlow Gallery Bound Brook NJ; Miller Gallery Cincinnati OH; Louise Melrose Gallery Frenchtown NJ

ZUCCARINI, DAVID ANTHONY
PAINTER, INSTRUCTOR
b Baltimore, Md, 1953. *Study:* Corcoran Sch Art, 69-71; Md Inst, BFA (painting), 71-76. *Work:* Univ Md, Md Artists Col, College Park; Howard Community Col; Nat Inst Health Libr. *Exhib:* Mid-Year, Butler Inst, Youngstown, Ohio, 76-82 & 85-90; Int Pastels, Soc Des Pastellistes, Paris, France, 87; Nat Works on Paper, Univ Tex, Tyler, 88; African Influences, Md Mus African Art, Columbia, 90; Drawing 1990, Brigham Young Univ, Provo, Utah; Contemp Self Portraits from the James Goode Collection (with catalog), Nat Portrait Gallery, 93; Legacy, Univ Md; Legacy (traveling exhib), 2006-08. *Teaching:* Instr drawing & painting, pvt studio, 76-. *Awards:* Artists Fel, Md State Arts Coun, 85; Distinguished Teacher, White House, 87; Juror Award, Drawing 1990, Brigham Young Univ. *Bibliog:* Pearl Oxorn (auth), Narrow world/wide vision, Baltimore Sun, 81; Pamela Kessler (auth), Zuccarini's curious studio, Washington Post, 87; Fran Fanshel (auth), Columbia's realist, Columbia Flier, 87; Wayward Passions, Art News, summer 96; E Lynne Moss (auth), Self Portraits Public and Private Collections, Am Artist, 9/97. *Mem:* Pastel Soc Am, 78-; Acad Artists Asn, 78-. *Media:* Oil, Charcoal, Pastel. *Publ:* Auth, Painting figure compositions, Am Artist, 84. *Dealer:* Foxhall Gallery 3301 New Mexico Ave NW Washington DC 20016. *Mailing Add:* 9402 Mellenbrook Rd Columbia MD 21045

ZUCKER, BOB
PHOTOGRAPHER
b New York, NY, Dec 10, 1946. *Study:* Hunter Col, BA; and with Philippe Halsman, NY. *Work:* Libr of Cong; J P Morgan libr; Soc Preservation Long Island Antiquities; Nat Trust Hist Preservation; Sotheby's Int Realty. *Comn:* Photos, 19th Century Pub Sculpture, Metrop Mus, 73; Sculpture of Isodor Konti, Hudson River Mus, 74; Historic Architectural Documentation of Old Westchester Co Courthouse Complex, Co of Westchester, 74; Bicentennial Exhib, Venturi & Rauch AIA & Whitney Mus, 75; Am Bicentennial: Signs of Life in the City, Renwick Gallery, Smithsonian Inst, 75; and others. *Exhib:* 19th Century Pub Sculpture in NY Parks, 73; Life in Am in the 18th Century, Nat Mus Am Hist, 85. *Teaching:* Farmingdale State Col, SUNY. *Publ:* Auth, American Architecture: Westchester Co, 77; Architectural Guide to Nassau & Suffolk Counties, Am Inst Architects, Long Island. *Mailing Add:* 3 Burbank Ct Greenlawn NY 11740

ZUCKER, JOSEPH I
PAINTER
b Chicago, Ill, May 21, 1941. *Study:* Miami Univ, 59-60; Art Inst Chicago, BFA & MFA. *Work:* Walker Art Ctr, Minneapolis; Whitney Mus Am Art; Albright-Knox Gallery, Buffalo; Metrop Mus, NY; Philadelphia Mus Art; and others. *Exhib:* Art Inst Chicago, 64 & 81; Walker Art Ctr, 68; New Am Abstract Painting, Madison Art Ctr, 72; Prospect, Dusseldorf, Ger, 73; Bykert Gallery, NY, 74; Whitney Biennial, Whitney Mus, 79, 92 & 83; Venice Biennale, 80; Surfacing Images, The Paintings of Joe Zucker 1969-82, Albright-Knox Gallery, Buffalo, 82; Queens Mus Traveling Exhib, 85-86; Arts Club Chicago, 88; Guild Hall, East Hampton, NY, 99. *Teaching:* Instr painting, Minneapolis Sch Art, 66-68, Sch Visual Arts, NY, 68-71 & NY Univ, 71-74. *Bibliog:* Edward Lucie-Smith (auth), Art in the Seventies, Cornell Univ Press, 81;. *Mem:* Nat Acad (acad, 95-). *Dealer:* Hirschl & Adler Mod 851 Madison Ave New York NY 10021. *Mailing Add:* PO Box 553 Wainscott NY 11975-0553

ZUCKER, MURRAY HARVEY
SCULPTOR, COLLAGE ARTIST
b New York, NY, Dec 14, 1920. *Work:* AFL-CIO Hq, Washington; Community Blood Coun, NY; Omaha Nat Bank, Nebr; Slater Mem Mus, Norwich, Conn; Butler Inst Am Art, Ohio. *Comn:* Paintings, Atlantic Richfield Co, NY, 68, Technicon Corp, Ardsley, NY, 69 & Police Benevolent Asn, NY, 70. *Exhib:* Gallery Carron, NY, 79; Lever House, NY, 80; Salmagundi Club, NY, 81; Springs Invitational, 96; Seven Sculptors, 96; and others. *Awards:* First Prize Graphics, Am Soc Contemp Artists, 76; Kulicke Award for Graphics, 78; Feigin Award Graphics, 81; and others. *Bibliog:* C Crane (auth), Contemporary collages, Interiors, 5/70; Gerald F Brommer (auth), The Art of Collage, Davis Publ, Inc, 78; and others; Gerald F Brommer (auth), Collage Techniques, Watson-Guptill Publ, 94. *Mem:* Artists Equity Asn; Am Soc Contemp Artists; Metrop Painters & Sculptors; Jimmy Ernst Artists Alliance; and others. *Media:* Wax for Bronze; Paper on Paper. *Mailing Add:* 54 Cosdrew Ln East Hampton NY 11937

ZUGAZAGOITIA, JULIAN
MUSEUM DIRECTOR
b Mexico City, Mex. *Study:* L'Ecole du Louvre, MA; Sorbonne Paris IV, France, PhD. *Pos:* Cultural corresp, Excélsior newspaper, Mexico City, formerly; cons, Getty Conservation Inst, Paris & Rome, 1991-99; dir visual arts, Spoleto Festival, Italy, 1997-99; cur & exec asst to the dir, Guggenheim Mus, New York, 1999-2002; exec dir, El Museo del Barrio, 2002-2010; dir & CEO, Nelson-Atkins Mus Art, 2010-; vchmn, Cult Inst Group, currently; chmn, NYC & co, currently. *Awards:* Chevalier des Arts et des Lettres, 2003. *Mem:* Asn Art Mus Dirs (bd mem, 2007-). *Mailing Add:* Nelson-Atkins Museum Art 4525 Oak St Kansas City MO 64111

ZURIER, JOHN
PAINTER
b Santa Monica, Calif, 1956. *Study:* Univ Calif, Berkeley, BA, 1979, MFA, 1984. *Work:* Berkeley Art Mus, Calif; Colby Coll Mus Art; Farnsworth Mus, Maine; Oakland Mus Calif; San Francisco Mus Mod Art. *Exhib:* Painting and Drawings, Philippe Bonnafont Gallery, San Francisco, 1980; Hayward Area Forum of the Arts Ann, Centennial Hall, Hayward, 1983; solo exhibs, Dana Reich Gallery, San Francisco, 1984, Pamela Auchincloss Gallery, Santa Barbara, 1985, Gallery Paule Anglim, San Francisco, 1986, Concourse Gallery, Bank Am World HQ, San Francisco, 1990, Aurobora Press, San Francisco, 1999, Larry Becker Contemp Art, Philadelphia, 2001, Galeria Javier López, Madrid, 2007; Three Pick Four, Univ Calif, San Francisco, 1984; Sixteen Young Bay Area Artists, Colo State Univ Art Gallery, Fort Collins, 1988; Chain Reaction Six, San Francisco Arts Comn Gallery, 1990; Practice and Process: New Painterly Abstraction in California, Armory Ctr Arts, Richmond, 1998; Minimalism: Then and Now, Berkeley Art Mus, 2001; Whitney Biennial, Whitney Mus Am Art, 2002; Specific Light, Eugene Binder Gallery, Marfa, Tex, 2004; Motion Picture: Videos by 18 Artists, De Young Mus, San Francisco, 2005; CCA: 100 Years in the Making, Oakland Mus Calif, 2007; Evergreen: Green Paintings, George Lawson Gallery, San Francisco, 2009. *Bibliog:* Jamie Brunson (auth), A Sense of Spiritual Metaphor, Artweek, Vol 17, No 40, 11/29/1986; David Bonetti (auth), Return of the Abstract at Mills College, San Francisco Examiner, 12/6/1996; Peter Frank (auth), Essence in Purity, Practice and Process, LA Weekly, 4/2/98; Roberta Smith (auth), Bad News for Art at the Whitney Biennial, NY Times, 3/31/2002; Edith Newhall (auth), Paint in a Bottle, Philadelphia Enquirer, 4/15/2005. *Mailing Add:* 3246 Ettie St #22 Oakland CA 94608

ZWEERTS, ARNOLD
PAINTER, MOSAIC ARTIST
b Bussum, Neth, 1918; US citizen. *Study:* Sch for Arts & Crafts & Sch for Art Teacher Training, Royal Acad Art, Amsterdam; Royal Acad Art, Copenhagen, Denmark; Acad Belli Arti, Ravenna, Italy; Inst Allende, Univ Guanajunto, Mex, MFA; also study with Jos Rovers, Riseby, Orselli, Signoriny & Kortlang. *Work:* Stedelijk Mus, Amsterdam; Collection of the State, The Hague, Neth; and others. *Comn:* Mosaics, Hengelo, Neth, 54, Lockhorst, Koldewyn, Van Eyck, Rotterdam Architects, 55-56, Chicago Process Gear Co, 61, Boulder Med Arts Bldg, Colo, 63-64, Lombard Dental Med Bldg, 72, 73 & 74 & Postville Sch House, Wis, 76-77; 220' mosaic, comn by US Dept Agr, Multnomah Falls Pedestrian Tunnel, Ore, 84; First Hood River Mosaic Wall, 88; Second Hood River Mosaic Wall, 89; Third Hood River Mosaic Wall, 92. *Exhib:* Art Inst Chicago, 66; Gallery Margaret Huisman, The Neth, 80; Mosaic Proposals, Mt Hood Col, Gresham, Ore, 86; Giverny Gallery, Gresham, Ore, 87; The Dalles Art Gallery, The Dalles, Ore, 88; two-man show, Columbia Gorge Arts Asn & Gallery, Hood River, 91; and others. *Teaching:* Instr mosaic & color, Kingston Upon Thames, Surrey, Eng, 51-53; instr appreciation of art, Stedelijk Mus, Rijksmus, Amsterdam, 54-57; asst prof drawing & painting, Art Inst Chicago, 57-73; lectr, dept fine arts, Loyola Univ Chicago, 68-78. *Awards:* First Prize-Printmaking, Civic Fine Arts Asn, Sioux Falls, 76; Award of Hon, 63 Salon, Madison Art Mus, 77. *Bibliog:* Pieter Scheen (auth), Lexicon Nederlandse Beeldende Kunstenaars 1750-1950, Part II, Kunsthandel P Scheen N V, The Hague, 70. *Mem:* Columbia Gorge Creative Arts League. *Media:* Oil; Mosaic Glass. *Publ:* Delphian Quart, Vol 43, No 4, A Renaissance in Architectural Art. *Dealer:* Ricciardi Gallery 108 Tenth St Astoria OR 97103

ZWERLING, LISA
PAINTER
Study: Sarah Lawrence Coll, BA; Cooper Union, BFA; New York Univ, MFA (painting). *Work:* Frye Art Mus, Seattle; Bayly Mus, Va; New York Univ; Dong Ah Exim Corp, Seoul; La Salle Univ Art Mus, Pa. *Exhib:* Postcard Size Art, PS1 Contemp Art, New York, 1978; Bayly Mus, Charlottesville, Va, 1979; Hudson Highlands Mus, New York, 1984; Fruits de la Passion, Witzenhausen Meijerink, Amsterdam, Neth, 1992; Trenton City Mus, NJ, 1993; 175th Ann, Nat Acad Design, New York, 2000; solo exhib, Frye Art Mus, Seattle, 2000. *Pos:* Artist-in-residence, Va Ctr for Creative Arts, 1993, 1995 & 2009, Vt Studio Ctr, 1994, Am Acad in Rome, 1998, Banff Centre for the Arts, 2000 & 2006. *Teaching:* Instr art hist, Staten Island Coll, New York, 1974, London Am Art Studies Centre, Stowe, England, 1977, Bloomfield Coll, NJ, 1979; adj prof painting, drawing & art hist, New York Univ, 1979-85 & 1988-; instr drawing, Princeton Univ, NJ, 1986, Pratt Inst, Brooklyn, 1986-87. *Awards:* Pollock-Krasner Found Grant, 1995, 1997, 2008; Travel Grant, Nat Endowment for the Arts, 1996; Individual Suport Grant, Gottlieb Found, 2003. *Bibliog:* Amei Wallach (auth), History Painting Revived, Newsday, 10/1982; Jed Perl (auth), Getting Emotional, New Criterion, 2/1993; Grace Glueck (auth), rev, NY Times, 4/1997

ZWIETNIG-ROTTERDAM, PAUL See Rotterdam, Paul Zwietnig

ZWIRNER, DAVID
GALLERY OWNER, ART DEALER
b Cologne, Germany, Oct 23, 1964. *Pos:* owner, dir, David Zwirner Gallery, NY, 93-; partner with Iwan Wirth, Zwirner and Wirth Gallery, NY, 2000-2009. *Interests:* philanthropy. *Mailing Add:* David Zwirner Gallery 525 W 19th St New York NY 10003

ZYNSKY, TOOTS
SCULPTOR
b Boston, Mass, 1951. *Study:* RI Sch Design, Providence, BFA, 73. *Work:* Mus Mod Art, Cooper-Hewitt Mus, NY; Corning Mus Glass, Corning, NY; High Mus Art, Atlanta, Ga; Hokkaido Mus Mod Art, Sapporo, Japan; Musee des Arts Decoratifs, Paris, France; Philadelphia Mus Art; and many others. *Exhib:* Solo shows incl Stedelijk Mus, Amsterdam, The Neth, 89, Clara Scremini Gallery, Paris, France, 90, Snyderman Gallery, Philadelphia, Pa, 91, 92, 94, Elliott Brown Gallery, Seattle, 95, 97, 99, 2000, Galerie L, Hamburg, Ger, 96, Glasmuseet, Ebeltoft, Denmark, 2001, Barry Friedman Ltd, New York, 2003, Woodside/Braseth Gallery, Seattle, 2004; group shows incl Glass Now '89, Yamaha Corp, Tokyo, Japan, 89, 90, 91, 92, 94, 95; Masterpieces of Glass from the Corning Collection, Nat Gallery Art, Washington, DC, 90; Gaste aus Frankreich, Kunstmuseum, Hamburg, Ger, 90; Betsy Rosenfield Gallery, Chicago, 94; Boston Mus Fine Arts, 97; Mus Am Art, Greensburg, Pa, 2000; Corning Mus Glass, 2001; Carnegie Mus Art, Pittsburgh, 2002. *Pos:* Asst dir, NY Experimental Glass Workshop, 80-81 & dept head, 81-82. *Teaching:* Instr, RI Sch Design. *Awards:* Visual Arts Fel, Nat Endowment Arts, 82 & 86; Grant, Stiching Klanschap, Amsterdam, 84; Innovation in Glassworking Tech, UrbanGlass Ann Award, 99. *Media:* Glass. *Publ:* Auth, International Crafts, Am Craft Mag, 91; auth, (article), Thames & Hudson, London & New York Times, 12/93. *Dealer:* Elliot Brown Gallery PO Box 1489 North Bend WA 98045-1489. *Mailing Add:* c/o Snyderman Gallery 303 Cherry St Philadelphia PA 19106

Geographic Index

ALABAMA

Auburn

Coe, Henry   Painter
Furr, Jim   Painter, Printmaker
Gluhman, Margaret A   Graphic Artist, Photographer
Hatfield, Donald Gene   Painter, Educator
Lewis, Jeffrey   Painter, Educator
Olson, Douglas John   Educator, Collector
Ross, Conrad H   Painter, Printmaker
Ross, Janice Koenig   Painter

Birmingham

Andrews, Gail   Museum Director
Chapman, Gary Howard   Painter
Crouse, Michael Glenn   Educator, Printmaker
Finley, Donny Lamenda   Painter, Illustrator
Lewis, Ronald Walter   Painter, Educator
Liles, Raeford Bailey   Painter, Sculptor
Livingston, Margaret Gresham   Administrator, Patron
Medenica, Branko   Sculptor, Restorer
Nordan, Antoinette Spanos Johnson   Curator, Consultant, Historian
Rankin, Don   Painter, Instructor
Shelton, Robert Lee   Designer, Educator
Trechsel, Gail Andrews   Director

Coffee Springs

Raeburn, Carrie R.   Painter

Fairhope

Wolff, Robert W, Jr   Dealer

Hartselle

Howell-Coon, Elizabeth (Mitch)   Painter, Illustrator

Huntsville

Baldaia, Peter Joseph   Curator, Director
Bass, Clayton   Director
Boyd, Lakin   Educator, Printmaker
Fleming, Frank   Sculptor
Parrish, David Buchanan   Painter
Parsons, Cynthia Massey   Painter, Writer
Pope, Mary Ann Irwin   Painter
Reeves, James Franklin   Historian, Collector
Robb, David Metheny, Jr   Historian, Consultant

Mobile

Conlon, James Edward   Sculptor, Historian
Kennedy, James Edward   Painter, Sculptor
Rathle, Henri (Amin)   Painter
Thomason, Michael Vincent   Photographer, Curator

Montgomery

Johnson, Mark M   Museum Director

Tuscaloosa

Kakas, Christopher A   Printmaker, Painter
Pagani, Catherine   Educator, Administrator
Sella, Alvin Conrad   Painter, Educator

ALASKA

Anchorage

Appel, Keith Kenneth   Sculptor, Muralist
Birdsall, Byron   Painter
Conaway, Gerald   Sculptor, Painter
Erikson, Christine   Educator
Hedman, Teri Jo   Printmaker, Painter
Henry, James Pepper   Museum Director
Jaeger, Brenda Kay   Painter
Kaulitz, Garry Charles   Printmaker, Painter
Owens, Tennys Bowers   Dealer
Redmond, Rosemary   Painter
Regat, Jean-Jacques Albert   Sculptor, Muralist
Regat, Mary E   Sculptor, Muralist
Shadrach, Jean H   Painter, Educator
Vallee, William Oscar   Painter, Graphic Artist
Wolf, Patricia B   Museum Director

Cordova

Bugbee-Jackson, Joan (Mrs John M Jackson)   Sculptor, Educator, Painter

Fairbanks

Amason, Alvin Eli   Painter
Freer, Fred-Christian   Painter, Illustrator
Jonaitis, Aldona   Historian, Administrator
Woodward, Kesler Edward   Painter, Curator

Juneau

Munoz, Rie   Painter, Printmaker

Sitka

Joseph, Tommy   Sculptor, Craftsman

ARIZONA

Apache Junction

Coe, Anne Elizabeth   Painter

Carefree

Lawrence, Jaye A   Sculptor, Craftsman

Casa Grande

Zivic, William Thomas   Painter, Sculptor

Chandler

Toschik, Larry   Painter, Writer

Cornville

Mion, Pierre Riccardo   Illustrator, Painter
Waddell, John Henry   Sculptor, Painter

Cottonwood

Stromsdorfer, Deborah Ann   Painter, Graphic Artist

Douglas

Dusard, Jay   Photographer, Writer

Flagstaff

Edgerton, Debra   Painter, Educator
Horn, Bruce   Painter, Educator
Turrell, James Archie   Environmental Artist, Sculptor
ZiegLer, Dolores Ann   Painter, Conceptual Artist

Globe

Kilb, Jenny   Painter, Muralist

Gold Canyon

Braig, Betty Lou   Painter, Educator

Lake Montezuma

Carpenter, Earl L   Painter

Marana

Tobias, Robert Paul   Painter, Sculptor

Mesa

Dawson, John Allan   Painter, Sculptor
Hulick, Diana Emery   Sculptor, Photographer
Missal, Joshua M   Art Dealer, Consultant
Schultz, Marilou   Weaver, Instructor
Slater, Gary Lee   Sculptor

Oracle

Davis, James Granberry   Painter
McGrew, Bruce Elwin   Painter
Rush, Andrew   Printmaker, Sculptor

Paradise Valley

Gale, Nessa   Sculptor, Painter
Harnett, Lila   Collector, Critic
Kipp, Lyman   Sculptor
Rothschild, John D   Dealer

Pearce

Dredge, Jill Ann   Painter

Peoria

Charles, Larry   Painter, Lecturer
Hillis, Richard K   Painter, Printmaker
Willard, Garcia Lou   Graphic Artist, Painter

Phoenix

Ballinger, James K   Museum Director, Historian
Dignac, Geny (Eugenia) M Bermudez   Sculptor, Environmental Artist
Frerichs, Ruth Colcord   Painter, Lithographer
Grigsby, Jefferson Eugene, Jr   Educator, Painter
Mahaffey, Merrill Dean   Painter, Instructor
McGuire, Maureen   Designer, Stained Glass Artist
Moore, Ina May   Painter, Educator
Richter, Hank   Painter, Sculptor
Rider Berry, Tarah J   Photographer, Instructor
Walker, Rusty (Edward D.)   Painter, Educator, Writer
Wright, Barton Allen   Writer, Graphic Artist

Prescott

Dutton, Allen A   Photographer, Painter
McClure, Thomas F   Sculptor, Educator
Stasack, Edward Armen   Painter, Printmaker
Tyser, Patricia Ellen   Stained Glass Artist, Assemblage Artist

Scottsdale

Afsary, Cyrus   Painter
Cawley, Joan Mae   Art Dealer, Publisher
Collins, Dan (Daniel) McClellan   Painter
DeLoyht-Arendt, Mary   Painter
Gentry, Warren Miller   Painter
Hack, Phillip S & Patricia Y   Collectors
Halle, Diane & Bruce T   Collectors
Haverty, Grace   Painter
Hill, John Conner   Art Dealer, Designer
Jacobson, Frank   Administrator
Kroll, David   Painter
Magenta, Muriel   Computer Artist, Video Artist
Missal, Stephen J   Educator, Illustrator
Moore, Matthew   Environmental Sculptor
Ortiz, Virgil   Ceramist, Designer
Pritzlaff, (Mr & Mrs) John, Jr   Collectors
Simmons, Julie Lutz   Painter, Restorer
Stuart, Sherry Blanchard   Painter
Swartz, Beth Ames   Painter
Taylor, Ann   Painter
Waid, Jim (James) E   Painter

Sedona

Coleman, M L (Michael Lee)   Painter, Instructor
De Mille, Leslie B.   Painter, Sculptor
Garrison, Gene K   Painter, Writer
Hull, Gregory Stewart   Painter
Mahoney, Joella Jean   Educator, Painter

Sonoita

Copenhaver-Fellows, Deborah Lynne Fellows   Sculptor, Painter

CALIFORNIA (cont)

Canoga Park

Rosenfeld, Sarena Painter
Steynovitz, Zamy Painter

Capistrano Beach

Clark, Timothy John Painter, Educator

Capitola

Reding, Barbara Endicott Artist

Carlsbad

Asaro, John Painter, Illustrator
Capps, Kenneth P Sculptor

Carmel

Clark, Robert Charles Painter, Lecturer
Cook, Joseph Stewart Painter
Crispo, Dick Painter, Printmaker
Jacobs, Ralph, Jr Painter
Johnson, Barbara Louise Painter, Printmaker
Kenna, Michael Photographer
Millea, Tom (Thomas) Francis Photographer
Winfield, Rodney M Educator

Carmel Valley

Sexton, John (William) Photographer
Wolfe, Maurice Raymond Consultant

Carpinteria

Hansen, Robert Painter, Sculptor
Kelm, Bonnie G Museologist, Assemblage Artist

Carson

Hirsch, Gilah Yelin Painter, Writer
Ivers, Louise H Historian

Castro Valley

Estabrook, Reed Photographer, Instructor

Cathedral City

Lupper, Edward Painter, Publisher

Cayucos

McIntosh, Gregory Stephen Painter

Cazadero

Beall, Dennis Ray Printmaker, Educator

Cerritos

Anderson, Robert Dale Painter, Draftsman, Printmaker

Chico

Cotner, Teresa Educator
Epting, Marion Austin Printmaker, Educator
Herhusky, Robert Sculptor, Administrator
Lucero, Manuel F Ceramist
Pierce, Ann Trucksess Painter, Educator
VanDerpool, Karen Weaver, Educator

Claremont

Ackerman, Gerald Martin Historian, Educator
Blizzard, Alan Painter, Educator
Hueter, James Warren Sculptor, Painter
MacNaughton, Mary Davis Museum Director, Educator
Pagel, David Educator, Critic
Rankaitis, Susan Mixed Media Artist, Photographer
Reiss, Roland Sculptor, Painter
Simon, Leonard Ronald Administrator, Writer

Coarsegold

Solem, (Elmo) John Painter

Coleville

Petterson, Margo Painter

Corona

Hargis, Barbara Picasso Gallery Director

Corona Del Mar

DeLap, Tony Sculptor, Painter

Costa Mesa

Muller, Jerome Kenneth Art Director, Photographer
Romans, Van Anthony Sculptor, Designer

Cotati

Hudson, Robert H Painter, Sculptor
Schwager, Michael R Educator, Curator

Cruz

Anderson, David Kimball Sculptor

Culver City

Bosman, Richard Painter, Printmaker
Coolidge, Matthew Director, Educator
De Larios, Dora Sculptor
De La Torre, Jamex Glass Blower
Fisher, Vernon Painter, Conceptual Artist
McMillian, Rodney Sculptor, Painter
McMillian, Rodney Painter, Installation Artist
Taber, Ryan Sculptor
Wiley, Kehinde Painter

Cupertino

Rindfleisch, Jan Director, Curator

Cypress

George, Patricia Painter

Dana Point

Strand, Sally Ellis Painter, Instructor

Davenport

Deutsch, Richard Sculptor

Davis

Gefter, Judith Michelman Photographer
Kaltenbach, Stephen Sculptor
Pardee, Hearne Educator, Painter
Pardee, William Hearne Painter, Educator
Pritikin, Renny Gallery Director, Educator
Suzuki, James Hiroshi Painter
Werfel, Gina S Painter, Educator
Wood, Melissa Ann Painter, Assemblage Artist

Del Mar

Antin, David A Art Critic, Writer
Antin, Eleanor Conceptual Artist, Photographer
Kittredge, Nancy (Elizabeth) Painter

Desert Hot Springs

Daniels, Martha K Sculptor, Ceramist

Eagle Rock

Andrews, Charleen Kohl Sculptor

El Cajon

House, Suda Kay Photographer, Video Artist
Lawrence, Les Ceramist, Sculptor
Markarian, Alexia (Mitrus) Painter, Sculptor, Designer
Tatro, Ronald Edward Sculptor, Instructor

Elmira

Montoya, Malaquias art educator, artist

Emeryville

Grafton, Rick (Frederick) Wellington Painter
Jensen, Clay Easton Sculptor, Educator
Misrach, Richard Laurence Photographer
Stanley, M Louise Painter

Encinitas

Patterson, Patricia Film Critic, Painter
Provder, Carl Painter, Instructor

Encino

LaCom, Wayne Carl Painter, Graphic Artist

Escondido

Bryce, Mark Adams Painter, Printmaker
Ecker, Robert Rodgers Painter, Printmaker

Eureka

Marak, Louis Bernard Ceramic Sculptor, Educator

Fair Oaks

Barrios, Benny Perez Painter, Art Dealer
Potter, (George) Kenneth Painter, Printmaker

Fairfax

Dern, F Carl Sculptor
McCormick, Daniel Environmental Sculptor
Shaw, Richard Blake Sculptor

Fallbrook

Perhacs, Les Sculptor, Industrial Designer
Ragland, Jack Whitney Painter, Printmaker

Felton

Shaffer, Richard Painter, Printmaker

Fort Bragg

Downie, Romana Anzi Sculptor

Fresno

Curreri-Ermatinger, Dyana M Director, Curator
Martinez, Carlos Director
Maughelli, Mary L Painter, Printmaker
Walker, Sharyne Elaine Painter, Sculptor

Fullerton

Macaray, Lawrence Richard Painter, Educator

Gardena

Valentine, DeWain Sculptor

Gilroy

Wu, Wayne Wen-Yau Painter

Glen Ellen

Wilson, Douglas Fenn Painter, Sculptor

Glendale

Burchett, Debra Administrator, Curator
Ganz, Julian, Jr Patron
Pekar, Ronald Walter Painter, Sculptor

Graeagle

Halbach, David Allen Painter, Historian

Gualala

Alinder, James Gilbert Gallery Owner, Photographer
Alinder, Mary Street Writer, Curator
Romeu, Joost A Conceptual Artist, Designer

Harbor City

Kwak, Hoon Painter

Hayward

Graham, Lanier Art Historian, Curator, Artist, Poet
McLean, Richard Painter

Hemet

Trejos, Charlotte (Carlota) Marie Painter

Hillsborough

Siberell, Anne Hicks Painter, Sculptor

Huntington Beach

Anderson, Bill (William) Maxwell Painter, Printmaker
Hitchcock, Howard Gilbert Educator, Sculptor
Tornheim, Norman Sculptor
Whitchurch, Charles A Art Dealer, Educator

Inglewood

Antrim, Craig Keith Painter, Draftsman
Lebejoara, Ovidiu Painter, Sculptor

Inverness

Smith, Gary Douglas Draftsman, Painter

Irvine

Bolen, John E Art Dealer, Collector
Bolen, Lynne N Art Dealer, Collector
Leung, Simon Conceptual Artist
Martinez, Daniel Joseph Conceptual Artist
Silverman, Ronald H Educator, Writer
Varo, Marton Geza Sculptor

Joshua Tree

Downer, Spelman Evans Painter, Photographer

Kelseyville

Fletcher, Leland Vernon Painter, Sculptor

Kingsburg

Olson, Maxine Painter, Instructor

La Crescenta

Injeyan, Seta L Painter

La Jolla

Adams, Robert McCormick Administrator, Writer
Beebe, Mary Livingstone Art Administrator
Cohen, Harold Artist, Theorist, Educator
Crandall, Jordan Video Artist, Administrator, Educator
Cuevas, Jose Luis Draftsman
Davies, Hugh Marlais Museum Director, Historian
Fredman, Faiya R Sculptor, Painter
Hawkinson, Tim Sculptor
Imana, Jorge Garron Painter, Muralist
Karlen, Peter H Educator, Writer
Kester, Grant Educator, Historian
Lonidier, Fred Spencer Photographer, Educator
Marcus, Angelo P Dealer, Collector

CALIFORNIA (cont)

Napa

Chase-Bien, Gail Painter
Torassa, Betty Brown Painter

Nevada City

McCauley, Gardiner Rae Administrator, Painter

Newport Beach

Armstrong, Elizabeth Neilson Curator
Bren, Donald L Collector
Glenn, Constance White Museum Director, Writer, Curator
Pergola, Linnea Painter, Printmaker
Szakacs, Dennis Museum Director

North Hollywood

Easterson, Sam Peter Video Artist, Conceptual Artist

North Palm Springs

Houston, Bruce Sculptor, Assemblage Artist

North San Juan

Acton, Arlo C Sculptor

Northridge

Alfano, Edward C Photographer, Educator, Administrator
Bordeaux, Jean-Luc Art Historian, Curator, Art Expert
Brown, Betty Ann Educator, Critic
Elder, David Morton Sculptor
Fricano, Tom S Painter, Printmaker
Lewis, Louise Miller Gallery Director, Educator
Smith, Robert Lewis Designer, Educator

Oakland

Andrews, Lawrence Video Artist, Sculptor
Baczek, Peter Gerard Painter, Printmaker
Beasley, Bruce Sculptor
Beldner, Lynn Karen Sculptor
Byrne, Charles Joseph Designer
Carnwath, Squeak Painter
Ciriclio, S(usan) E (Fay) Photographer, Educator
Crum, Katherine B Museum Director, Educator
Doyle, Joe Painter, Educator
Fogarty, Lori Museum Director
Hardy, David Whittaker, III Painter, Instructor
Hartman, Robert Leroy Photographer, Educator
Kagemoto, Haro Filmmaker, Photographer
Kagemoto, Patricia Jow Photographer, Painter
Kelso, David William Printmaker, Art Dealer
Kimpton, Laura painter
Kirk, Jerome Sculptor, Kinetic Artist
Kraft, Steve Designer
Levy, Mark Writer, Historian
Linhares, Philip E Curator
MacGregor, Gregory Allen Photographer
Martin, Fred Thomas Painter, Educator
Melchert, James Frederick Sculptor, Educator
Meyers, Michael Sculptor, Painter
Miyasaki, George Joji Printmaker, Painter
O'Banion, Nance Assemblage Artist
Perez, Vincent Painter, Illustrator
Porges, Maria Franziska Sculptor, Printmaker
Ramos, (Mel) Melvin John Painter, Educator
Rath, Alan T Sculptor
Ritchey, Rik Painter, Sculptor
Roloff, John (Scott) Sculptor, Environmental Artist
Roth, Moira Educator, Historian, Curator, Poet, Playwright
Russell, Christopher Ryan Painter
St John, Terry N Painter, Curator
Saunders, Raymond Jennings Painter, Educator
Southey, Trevor J T Painter, Sculptor
Tait, Will(iam) H Painter, Sculptor
Tunis, Roslyn Curator, Gallery Director
Van Allen, Adrian Designer, Video Artist
Walsh, Patricia Ruth Painter
Walters, Sylvia Solochek Printmaker, Educator
Zurier, John Painter

Oceanside

Reynolds, Wade Painter

Ojai

Martin, Lys Photographer, Curator
Pastine, Ruth Painter, Lecturer

Ontario

Hanner, Jean Patricia Painter, Muralist

Orange

Felisky, Barbara Rosbe Painter, Printmaker

Orangevale

Walker, Ronald C Artist

Orinda

Brody, Blanche Painter, Printmaker
Light, Ken Photographer, Educator

Oro Grande

Bender, Bill Painter

Pacific Grove

Downs, Douglas Walker Sculptor

Pacific Palisades

Chesney, Lee R, Jr Painter, Printmaker
Laskin, Myron, Jr Curator, Historian
Perloff, Marjorie G Critic, Historian
Sherman, Z Charlotte Painter, Gallery Director

Pacifica

Petersen, Roland Conrad Painter, Printmaker
Torlakson, James Daniel Painter, Filmmaker

Palm Desert

Kilian, Austin Farland Painter, Educator

Palm Springs

Henry, David Eugene Painter, Sculptor
Lewin, Bernard Dealer, Collector
Lord, Michael Harry Dealer, Curator
Nash, Steven Alan Museum Director, Curator, Historian

Palo Alto

Acebo, Davis Terry printmaker
Bergstrom, Edith Harrod Painter
Ford, Rochelle Sculptor
Smith, Anna Deavere Patron
Thurston, Jacqueline Beverly Educator, Artist, Writer

Palos Verdes Peninsula

Mac Innes, David Harold Painter, Printmaker

Paradise

McManus, James William Sculptor, Gallery Director

Pasadena

Adams, Peter Painter
Bieltvedt, Arnor G Painter, Instructor
Buchman, Lorne M Administrator
Dreiband, Laurence Painter, Lecturer
Gill, Gene Painter, Craftsman
Hertz, Richard A Educator, Critic
Jones, Ronald Warren Artist, Critic
Lamensdorf, Joan Painter, Designer
Monk, Nancy Mixed Media Artist
Murdoch, John Museum Director
Sakoguchi, Ben Painter
Zlatkoff, Charles Painter, Sculptor

Pebble Beach

Mortensen, Gordon Louis Printmaker, Painter

Petaluma

Fuller, Mary (Mary Fuller McChesney) Sculptor, Writer
Skalagard, Hans Painter, Lecturer
Williams, Franklin John Painter

Piedmont

Dhaemers, Robert August Sculptor, Educator
Gunn, Ellen Painter, Printmaker
Mendenhall, Jack Painter, Instructor
Murray, Joan Critic, Photographer
Tavenner, Patricia May Artist

Pinole

Gerbracht, Bob (Robert) Thomas Painter, Instructor

Placerville

Davis, Thelma Ellen Painter
Gruver, Mary Emmett Painter, Instructor

Point Reyes Station

Hall, Susan Painter, Ceramist
Quinn, Thomas Patrick, Jr Painter
Rogers, Art Photographer

Pollock Pines

Tarbet, Urania Christy Painter, Writer

Pomona

Hannibal, Joseph Harry Educator, Painter

Portola Valley

Jackson, Oliver Lee Painter, Sculptor
Neri, Manuel Sculptor

Ramona

Dani Sculptor, Painter

Rancho Palos Verdes

Palko Kolosvary, Paul Collage Artist, Printmaker

Rancho Santa Fe

Jacobs, Scott E Painter, Illustrator

Redlands

Johnston, Richard M Sculptor, Educator
Slatkin, Wendy Historian

Redondo Beach

Saar, Lezley Painter

Redway

Holbrook, Peter Greene Painter, Printmaker

Redwood City

Shukman, Solomon Painter, Printmaker

Reseda

Gialanella, Donald G Sculptor, Graphic Artist

Richmond

Wessel, Henry Photographer

Riverside

Divola, John Manford, Jr Photographer
Earle, Edward W Curator, Historian
Green, Jonathan (William) Museum Director, Photographer, Filmmaker
Medel, Rebecca Rosalie Sculptor, Environmental Artist
Reeves, Esther May Painter

Rocklin

Peeples-Bright, Maija Gegeris Zack Woof Painter

Rohnert Park

Moulton, Susan Gene Historian, Painter

Rolling Hills

Agid, Lucy Bradanovic Sculptor

Roseville

Euren, Barry A Painter, Illustrator

Sacramento

Adan, Suzanne Painter
Drachnik (Cay), Catherine Meldyn Painter, Educator
Jones, Lial A Museum Director
Marcus, Irving E Painter, Educator
Moment, Joan Instructor, Painter
Parker, Olivia Photographer
Piskoti, James Printmaker, Painter
Rippon, Ruth Margaret Sculptor, Ceramist
Roberts, Randy Museum Director
Stevens, Michael Keith Sculptor
Walburg, Gerald Sculptor, Educator
Waterstreet, Ken (James Kent) Painter, Instructor
Winkler, Maria Paula Painter, Educator

Saint Helena

Frederick, Robilee Painter, Sculptor

Salinas

Puckett, Richard Edward Painter, Administrator
Smith, Gary Sculptor, Gallery Director

San Bernardino

Budicin, John Painter
Civitello, John Patrick Painter
Kaplan, Julius David Historian
Lintault, Roger Paul Administrator, Educator
Warehall, William Donald Glass Blower, Ceramist
Woodford, Don (Donald) Paul Painter, Educator

San Clemente

Garbutt, Janice Lovoos Painter, Writer
Lopina, Louise Carol Painter, Printmaker

San Diego

Cordy-Collins, Alana (Kathleen) Curator, Educator
Cottone-Kolthoff, Carol Painter, Illustrator
Criss, Cheryl Lynn Painter
Cutler-Shaw, Joyce Conceptual Artist, Sculptor
Esser, Janet Brody Historian

CALIFORNIA (cont)

Sausalito

Anderson, Margaret Pomeroy   Appraiser, Collection Manager
Maisel, David   Photographer, Environmental Artist
Oda, Mayumi   Painter, Printmaker
Rector, Marge (Lee)   Painter, Graphic Artist
Wilcoxon, Heather   Painter
Wiley, William T   Painter

Sebastopol

Black, Lisa   Painter, Photographer
Caswell, Helen Rayburn   Painter, Writer
Hasegawa, Noriko   Painter
Lipzin, Janis Crystal   Filmmaker, Photographer
Mills, Agnes   Printmaker, Sculptor
Zaikine, Victor (Zak) Eugene   Sculptor, Painter

Sherman Oaks

Burg, Patricia Jean   Painter, Printmaker
Carl, Joan   Sculptor, Painter
Manders, Susan Kay   Artist

Sierra Madre

Converse, Elizabeth   Painter, Writer
De Kansky, Igor   Painter, Sculptor

Solana Beach

Gronborg, Erik   Sculptor, Ceramist

Sonoma

Anderson, Gunnar Donald   Painter, Illustrator
Moquin, Richard Attilio   Painter, Sculptor
Nottebohm, Andreas   Painter

Sonora

Popovac, Gwynn   Painter, Sculptor

Soquel

McClellan, Douglas Eugene   Painter

Soulsbyville

Hartwig, Heinie   Painter, Instructor

South Pasadena

Askin, Walter Miller   Painter, Printmaker

Stanford

Bryan, Sukey   Painter
Eisner, Elliot Wayne   Educator
Seligman, Thomas Knowles   Director
Troy, Nancy J   Historian, Educator

Stinson Beach

Chapline, Claudia Beechum   Painter, Writer, Curator, Assemblage Artist
Schwarm, Harold Chambers   Painter, Instructor

Stockton

Gyermek, Stephen A   Educator
Pecchenino, J Ronald   Painter, Educator

Studio City

Brommer, Gerald F   Painter, Writer
Vaccarino, Robin   Sculptor
White, Stephen Leon   Collector, Art Dealer

Suisun City

Schmaltz, Roy Edgar   Painter, Educator

Sun City

Guest, Richard G   Painter, Consultant
Wood, Ron   Glass Artist, Sculptor

Tiburon

Parker, Gertrud Valerie   Sculptor

Toluca Lake

de Musée, Moran   Sculptor

Tomales

Foote, Howard Reed   Artist, Painter

Topanga

Wisdom, Joyce   Painter

Turlock

Camarata, Martin L   Artist, Educator
Werness, Hope B   Historian

Upland

Svenson, John Edward   Sculptor, Medalist

Valencia

Buchanan, Nancy   Video Artist, Conceptual Artist
Fiskin, Judy   Photographer, Video Artist
Gaines, Charles   Educator, Conceptual Artist
Hatch, Connie   Photographer, Educator
Mandel, John   Painter
Preston, Ann L   Sculptor
Wilson, Millie   Conceptual Artist

Vallejo

Fried, Howard Lee   Sculptor
Salmon, Donna Elaine   Illustrator
Salmon, Raymond Merle   Illustrator, Cartoonist, Educator

Valley Glen

Reed, Dennis James   Curator, Designer

Van Nuys

Davis, L Clarice   Book Dealer, Art Librarian
Irmas, Audrey Menein   Collector

Venice

Alf, Martha Joanne   Painter, Writer
Arnoldi, Charles Arthur   Sculptor, Painter
Baca, Judith   Muralist
Baldessari, John Anthony   Conceptual Artist
Brewster, Michael   Installation Sculptor, Educator
Byrd, Jerry   Painter
Campbell, Rebecca   Artist, Instructor
Cheng, Fu-Ding   Filmmaker, Painter
Colson, Greg J   Sculpture, Conceptual Artist
Davis, Kimberly Brooke   Gallery Director, Art Dealer
Davy, Woods   Sculptor
Dill, Guy   Sculptor, Educator
Edge, Douglas Benjamin   Sculptor, Painter
Fine, Jud   Sculptor, Educator
Kossoff, Leon   Painter
Kraal, Lies   Painter
Leaf, Ruth   Printmaker, Instructor
McMillen, Michael C(halmers)   Environmental Artist, Sculptor
Richards, Bruce Michael   Painter, Printmaker
Scheer, Sherie (Hood)   Photographer, Painter
Smith, Alexis (Patricia Anne)   Collage Artist, Sculptor
Smith, Barbara Turner   Video & Performance Artist, Educator
Suggs, Don   Painter, Photographer

Ventura

Koch, Gerd Herman   Painter, Educator

Walnut Creek

Esaki, Yasuhiro   Painter, Printmaker
Kuhlman, Walter Egel   Painter, Educator
Parton, Ralf   Sculptor, Educator
Reimann, Arline Lynn   Printmaker, Painter

Watsonville

Hernandez, Jo Farb   Museum Director, Curator
Hernandez, Sam   Sculptor, Educator

West Hills

Duzy, Merrilyn Jeanne   Painter, Lecturer

West Hollywood

Stern, Louis   Dealer, Consultant
Tribe, Kerry   Video Artist

Westlake Village

Liu, Katherine Chang   Painter, Curator

Woodacre

Uzilevsky, Marcus   Painter, Printmaker

Woodland Hills

Ebin, Cynthia   Sculpture, Painting
Price, Joe (Allen)   Serigrapher, Watercolorist
Turner, Bonese Collins   Painter, Designer
Whitson, Angie   Sculptor, Painter

Woodside

Concannon, George Robert   Painter
Hogle, Ann Meilstrup   Painter

Yountville

Gillen, John   Sculptor, Painter

COLORADO

Arvada

Jones, Jane   Painter
Pech, Arleta   Painter, Instructor

Aspen

Farver, Suzanne   Administrator, Collector
Hurst, Robert Jay   Patron
Jacobson, Heidi Zuckerman   Curator
Lord, Andrew   Sculptor
Magoon, Nancy & Robert   Collector
Sobel, Dean   Museum Director, Curator

Aurora

Hughes, Paul Lucien   Dealer, Consultant

Bayfield

Gummersall, C Gregory   Painter

Berthoud

Balas, Jack J   Painter, Photographer

Boulder

Ambrose, Kirk   Educator, Administrator
Barnes, Carole D   Painter
Chong, Albert Valentine   Photographer, Educator
Foley, David E   Painter
Iwamasa, Ken   Educator, Printmaker
Johnson, James Alan   Graphic Artist, Educator
Kuczun, Ann-Marie   Painter, Illustrator
Sampson, Frank   Painter, Printmaker
Valdovino, Luis Hector   Video Artist, Educator
Vandersall, Amy L   Historian, Educator
Vielehr, Bill   Sculptor
Wolfe, Lynn Robert   Painter, Educator

Brighton

Shaklee, Kim   Sculptor

Buena Vista

McCoy, Katherine Braden   Designer, Educator
McCoy, Michael Dale   Designer, Educator
Silva, Jude Hutton   Artist

Carbondale

Powers, John & Kimiko   Collector

Centennial

Trumble, Beverly (Jane)   Painter

Colorado Springs

Bransby, Eric James   Muralist, Educator
Broome, Rick (Richard) Raymond   Painter
Hoge, Robert Wilson   Curator, Educator
Kinnee, Sandy   Painter, Papermaker
Raintree, Shawn   Director
Rubin, Donald Vincent   Sculptor
Turner, David   Museum Director, Educator
Zapel, Arthur Lewis   Illustrator-Children's Books, Painter

Creede

Quiller, Stephen Frederick   Painter, Printmaker

Delta

Tupper, Dani   Painter, Instructor

Denver

Cline, Clinton C   Printmaker, Educator
Cole, Jean (Dahl)   Painter, Watercolor
Cunningham, E C (Eldon) Lloyd   Printmaker, Educator
Encinias, John Orlando   Painter
Graese, Judy (Judith) Ann   Painter, Illustrator
Heinrich, Christoph   Museum Director
Hempel, Wes   Artist
Kremers, David   Conceptual Artist
Maytham, Thomas Northrup   Fine Arts Consultant
Michael, Gary   Painter, Writer
Morper, Daniel   Painter, Printmaker
O'Hagan, Desmond Brian   Painter
Ortega, Tony (Anthony) David   Painter, Printmaker
Payton, Cydney M   Museum Director, Curator
Ragland, Bob   Painter, Instructor
Saylors, Jo An   Sculptor, Instructor
Scott, Sandy (Sandra) Lynn   Sculptor
Sprick, Daniel   Painter
Strawn, Bernice I   Sculptor
Sumner, Stephen Charles   Administrator, Educator
Temple, Leslie Alcott (Leslie Jane Atkinson) Sculptor, Writer
Thompson, Richard Craig   Painter

COLORADO (cont)
Wilson, Steve Museum Director
Witold, Kaczanowski Painter, Sculptor
Yanish, Elizabeth Shwayder Sculptor, Lecturer

Elizabeth
Kaplinski, Buffalo Painter, Watercolorist

Englewood
Cooper, Susan Sculptor, Painter
Kaplan, Sandra Painter, Printmaker
Lamb, Darlis Carol Sculptor, Painter
Warlick, M.E. Educator, Administrator

Evergreen
Kastner, Barbara H Painter

Fort Collins
De Vore, Richard E Ceramist
Getty, Nilda Fernandez Educator, Silversmith
Jacobs, Peter Alan Sculptor, Educator
Lundberg, Thomas Roy Artist
Marander, Carol Jean Painter, Graphic Artist
Risbeck, Philip Edward Graphic Artist, Educator
Twarogowski, Leroy Andrew Draftsman, Educator
Voss, Gary sculptor, educator
Whitcomb, Milo W Skip Painter, Printmaker
Wilson, Jean S Museum Director, Historian
Yust, David E Painter, Printmaker

Gardner
Cocchiarelli-Berger, Maria Giovanna Painter, Muralist

Greeley
Cole, Julie Kramer Painter
Ruyle, Lydia Miller Printmaker, Educator

Gunnison
Johnson, Lee Painter, Educator
Julio, Pat T Educator, Craftsman

Hotchkiss
Blackstock, Virginia Harriett Painter, Juror

La Veta
Schneider, Kenny Sculptor, Painter, Filmmaker

Lakewood
Cadillac, Louise Roman Painter, Instructor

Littleton
Poduska, T F Lecturer, Painter

Longmont
Roots, Garrison Sculptor, Educator
Wise, Sue Painter

Loveland
Lundeen, George Wayne Sculptor
Maior, Philip Sculptor
Marston, JD Photographer
Ostermiller, Dan Sculptor
Svedlow, Andrew Jay Administrator, Painter
Weimer, Dawn Sculptor
Zahourek, Jon Gail Painter, Sculptor

Lyons
Gordon, Coco Environmental Artist, Writer

Manitou Springs
Wallace, Gael Lynn Painter

Mesa
Fritzler, Gerald J Painter, Watercolor

Monument
Bohler, Joseph Stephen Painter

Nathrop
Schmidt, Frederick Lee Painter

Ouray
Carlile, Janet (Hildebrand) Painter, Educator

Parker
Balciar, Gerald George Sculptor
Thies, Charles Herman Painter, Printmaker

Pueblo
Divelbiss, Maggie Director

Pueblo West
Fisher, Philip C Painter, Art Dealer

Salida
Strawn, Melvin Nicholas Painter, Sculptor

Shawnee
Tolpo, Carolyn Lee Painter, Ceramic Artist
Tolpo, Vincent Carl Painter, Sculptor

Vail
Cotter, James Edward Sculptor, Designer
Milhoan, Randall Bell Painter, Designer

Westcliffe
Merfeld, Gerald Lydon Painter, Sculptor

Wheat Ridge
Dawson, Doug Painter, Instructor

CONNECTICUT

Avon
Atkinson, Tracy Consultant, Museologist

Barkhamsted
Wallace, Carol Ann (Brucker) Painter, Illustrator

Bethany
Bills, Mitchell Designer, Video Artist
Hauer, Erwin Franz Sculptor, Educator, Designer
Wolanic, Susan Seseske Painter, Graphic Artist

Bethlehem
Vestal, David Photographer, Writer

Bloomfield
Ferguson, Charles B Museum Director, Painter

Branford
Morrison, Edith Borax Collage Artist, Painter

Bridgeport
Jordan, George Edwin Historian, Consultant
Reed, James M Printmaker

Bridgewater
Abbett, Robert Kennedy Painter, Writer
Gilbert, Albert Earl Painter, Illustrator
Macdonald, Carroll Painter

Brooklyn
McIlvane, Edward James Stained Glass Artist, Glassblower

Chester
Nilsson, Katherine Ellen Painter
Weiss, Jerome Nathan Painter, Instructor

Colchester
Liverant, Gigi Horr Painter

Cornwall Bridge
Bolton-Smith, Robin Lee Curator, Historian

Cos Cob
Ubogy, Jo Sculptor

Coventry
Doudera, Gerard Painter, Educator

Danbury
Kan, Michael Historian, Administrator
Mann, Jean (Adah) Ceramist, Sculptor
Renee, Paula Painter, Tapestry Artist

East Haddam
Conant, Jan Royce Painter, Illustrator

Easton
Bogart, Richard Jerome Painter
Curtis, Dolly Powers Sculptor, Weaver
Sharp, Susan S Painter

Enfield
Gerich, Betty A. Sculptor

Essex
Lenker, Marlene N Painter, Collage Artist

Fairfield
Eliasoph, Philip Historian, Critic
Glaser, Bruce Historian, Educator
Khachian, Elisa A Painter

Reinker, Nancy Clayton Cooke Painter, Sculptor
Whyte, Bruce Lincoln Consultant, Administrator

Falls Village
Cronin, Robert (Lawrence) Painter, Draftsman

Farmington
Cormier, Cindy Museum Director
Dalton-Meyer, Marie Museum Director

Glastonbury
Bailey, Marcia Mead Painter

Goshen
Federico, Frank Painter

Granby
Zimmerman, Paul Warren Painter, Instructor

Greenwich
Arguimbau, Peter L Painter, Lecturer
Brant, Peter M Patron
Moonie, Liana Painter, Lecturer
Parker, Robert Andrew Painter
Perless, Robert Sculptor
Sturges, Hollister Curator, Historian

Guilford
Pease, David G Administrator, Painter

Hamden
de Bretteville, Sheila Levrant Designer, Educator
MacClintock, Dorcas Sculptor, Writer
Zallinger, Jean Day Illustrator, Educator

Hartford
Banks, Anne Johnson Painter, Educator
Boothe, Power Painter, Administrator
Cartin, Mickey Collector
Frey, Mary E Photographer
Gaddis, Eugene Richard Curator, Historian
Kornhauser, Elizabeth Mankin Museum Director, Curator
Mahoney, Michael R T Historian, Educator
Samuels (Joesam), Joe Sculptor
Soppelsa, George Painter, Collage Artist
Stuart, Nancy Administrator, Photographer
Sutton, Peter C Curator, Historian
Talbott, Susan Lubowsky Director
Zafran, Eric Myles Curator, Historian

Ivoryton
Jensen, Leo Sculptor, Painter
Ramanauskas, Dalia Irena Painter, Draftsman

Kent
Randall, Colleen Painter

Lakeville
Close, Mary Painter

Litchfield
McKnight, Thomas Frederick Painter, Printmaker

Madison
Davies, Kenneth Southworth Painter, Instructor

Meriden
Bertolli, Eugene Emil Sculptor, Designer
Ivers, Christine D Painter, Instructor
Tamburine, Jean Helen Painter, Sculptor

Middletown
Frazer, John Thatcher Filmmaker, Painter
Imlah, Rachel Crawford Painter, Photographer
Ottmann, Klaus Curator, Critic
Roth, Michael S Administrator, Educator
Schiff, Jeffrey Allen Sculptor, Installation Artist

Milford
Fagan, Alanna Painter, Printmaker
Maier, Maryanne E Painter
Quinn, William Painter, Sculptor

Mystic
De Vore, Sadie Davidson Printmaker, Painter

New Britain
Cipriano, Michael R Painter, Educator
Hyland, Douglas K S Museum Director

New Canaan
Tomchuk, Marjorie Printmaker, Painter

CONNECTICUT (cont)

New Fairfield

Carlson, Jane C Painter

New Hartford

Gill, Bryan Nash Sculptor, Printmaker

New Haven

Carter, David Giles Museum Director, Curator
Gross, Jennifer R Curator, Critic
LaPalombara, Constance Painter, Draftsman
Lindroth, Linda Photographic Artist, Curator
Meyers, Amy Museum Director
Newick, Craig D Architect
Papageorge, Tod Photographer
Pollitt, Jerome Jordan Historian, Educator
Pronin, Anatoly Photographer
Prown, Jules David Art Historian
Reynolds, John (Jock) M Director, Writer
Roche, (Eamonn) Kevin Architect
Rolland, Peter George Architect
Scully, Vincent Joseph, Jr Architect, Educator, Writer
Smith, Raymond Walter Photographer, Book Dealer
Storr, Robert Educator, Painter
Weinberg, Jonathan Edman Painter, Historian
Willoughby, Jane Baker Collage Artist, Painter

New London

Hendricks, Barkley Leonnard Painter, Photographer
Leibert, Peter R Ceramist, Sculptor
Patnode, Mark William Painter, Designer

New Milford

Crawford, Rainie Painter
Kepets, Hugh Michael Painter, Printmaker

Newtown

Christensen, Betty (Elizabeth) Illustrator, Painter
Cottingham, Robert Painter, Printmaker
Purdy, Donald R Painter

Norfolk

Sloan, Ronald J Painter

North Grosvenordale

Kornbluth, Frances Painter, Assemblage Artist

North Haven

Field, Richard Sampson Curator, Historian
Wexler, Jerome LeRoy Photographer, Illustrator

North Stonington

Gregoropoulos, John Painter

Norwalk

Bohnen, Blythe Conceptual Artist, Photographer
Gevas, Sophia Director, Painter
Landau, Jon Collector
Meagher, Sandra Krebs Painter, Photographer

Norwich

Gualtieri, Joseph P Museum Director, Painter
Topalis, Daniel P Painter, Gallery Owner

Old Lyme

Andersen, Jeffrey W Museum Director

Oxford

Baldassano, Vincent Painter

Pawcatuck

Gordley, Scott Matthew Educator, Administrator, Illustrator

Plainville

Brzozowski, Richard Joseph Artist, Painter

Poquonock

Van Winkelen, Barbara Painter, Illustrator

Quaker Hill

Braunstein, Mark Mathew Curator, Photographer
McCabe, Maureen M Collage Artist

Redding

Bloch, Babette Artist, Sculptor
Mellon, Marc Richard Sculptor, Medalist

Redding Ridge

Morton, Robert Alan Editor

Ridgefield

Benton, Suzanne E Sculptor, Art Writer
Businо, Orlando Francis Cartoonist
Calle, Paul Painter, Writer
Giordano, Greg Joe Painter, Photographer
Hopkins, Julie Painter
Klein, Richard Director, Curator
Ramírez-Montagut, Mónica Curator
Sanden, John Howard Painter, Instructor
Schaffer, Debra S Collage Artist, Sculptor

Roxbury

Komarin, Gary Painter

Salisbury

Blagden, Allen Painter, Printmaker
Boyle, Richard J Art Historian, Writer

Sharon

Griesedieck, Ellen Muralist
Johns, Jasper Painter
Learsy, Raymond J Collector

Simsbury

Ford, John Painter, Sculptor

South Kent

Kaplan, Jacques Collector, Dealer

South Norwalk

Kavanagh, Cornelia Kubler Sculptor, Designer

South Windsor

Patterson, Shirley Abbott Painter, Instructor

Southbury

Rorick, William Calvin Painter, Instructor

Southington

Deckert, Clinton A Painter, Assemblage Artist

Southport

Sill, Gertrude Grace Curator, Writer

Stamford

Cohen, Steven A Collector
Graham, Robert C, Jr Art Dealer
Heston, Joan Painter, Instructor
Hollinger, Morton Painter
Rudman, Joan (Combs) Painter, Instructor
Sissman, Liron Painter
Walker, Mort Cartoonist

Stonington

Fix, John Robert Sculptor, Silversmith

Storrs

Crossgrove, Roger Lynn Printmaker, Educator
Thornton, Richard Samuel Educator, Writer

Storrs Mansfield

Stula, Nancy Museum Director, Curator

Stratford

Eisinger, Harry Painter
Passantino, George Christopher Painter, Instructor

Trumbull

Kozlowski, Edward C Painter, Designer

Unionville

Dublac, Robert Revak Painter

Vernon

Groff, Barbara S Painter

Voluntown

Caddell, Foster Painter, Writer

Wallingford

Lauttenbach, Carol L Painter
Neff, John A Painter, Designer

Washington

Grimes, Margaret W Painter, Educator
Poskas, Peter Edward Painter

Waterbury

Smith, Ann Y Museum Director, Curator

Watertown

Grossman, Barbara Painter, Educator

West Hartford

Bronner, Felix Painter, Collage Artist, Editor
Faude, Wilson Hinsdale Director, Curator
Lyle, Charles Thomas Administrator
Sorokin, Janet Artist, Painter

West Haven

Leka, Derek Painter

West Willington

Zelanski, Paul John Painter

Weston

Oliver, Sandra (Sandi) Art Dealer, Painter
Williams, Paul Alan Painter, Illustrator
Wilson, Melissa Anne Sculptor

Westport

Bloom, Martha Collage Artist, Photographer, Educator
Chernow, Ann Painter, Printmaker
Cifolelli, Alberta Painter, Printmaker
Fisher, Leonard Everett Painter, Illustrator
Hall, Christine & Andrew J Collectors
Heyman, Ronnie Feuerstein Collector
Kovatch, Jak Painter, Sculptor
Madan-Shotkin, Rhoda Painter
Minkowitz, Norma Sculptor
Neilson, Mary Ann Painter
Reilly, Nancy Painter
Rothenberg, Barbara Painter, Educator
Sallick, Lucy Ellen Painter, Instructor
Siff, Marlene Ida Painter, Sculptor
Woodham, Jean Sculptor

Woodbridge

Lytle, Richard Painter, Educator

Woodbury

Odate, Toshio Conceptual Artist, Educator
Seltzer, Peter Lawrence Painter

DELAWARE

Bear

Lane, Rosemary Louise Printmaker, Sculptor

Dover

Bailey, Richard H Sculptor
Danko, Linda AK Museum Director

Laurel

Blaine, Frederick Matthew Sculptor, Educator

Lewes

Costigan, Constance Frances Painter, Educator

Newark

Breslin, Wynn (Winifred) Painter, Sculptor
Craven, Wayne Art Historian, Writer
Hethom, Janet Designer, Educator, Administrator, Writer
Matsumoto, Roger Photographer
Moss, Joe (Francis) Sculptor, Painter
Nees, Lawrence Educator, Historian
Rowe, Charles Alfred Painter, Educator
Spinski, Victor Sculptor, Educator
Stillman, Damie Historian, Educator
Stoner, Joyce Hill Conservator, Educator
Weiss, John Joseph Photographer, Editor

Rockland

Harvey, Andre Sculptor

Seaford

Jurney, Donald (Benson) Painter

Wilmington

Allmond, Charles Sculptor
Brown, Hilton Painter, Educator
Bruni, Stephen Thomas Museum Director
Gaiber, Maxine Oliansky Museum Director
Gore, David Alan Painter, Photographer
Hatch, W A S Painter, Educator
Hayes, Tua Painter
Homer, William Innes Historian, Educator
Hummel, Charles Frederick Administrator
Messina, Charles artist
Mowry, Elizabeth M Painter, Writer
Rice, Danielle Museum Director

Winterthur

Bowman, Leslie Greene Museum Director

DISTRICT OF COLUMBIA

Washington

Abbott, Rebecca Phillips Curator, Photographer
Bloomfield, Sara J Museum Director
Bollerer, Fred L Museum Director
Breslin, Nancy Photographer
Broude, Norma Freedman Historian, Educator
Brougher, Kerry Museum Director, Curator
Broun, Elizabeth Gibson Museum Director, Historian
Brown, David Alan Historian, Curator
Caldwell, Graham Artist
Carr, Carolyn K Curator, Historian
Chiu, Melissa Museum Director
Christenberry, William Painter, Sculptor, Photographer
Cikovsky, Nicolai, Jr Curator, Historian
Clark, Michael Museum Director
Cogswell, Margaret Price Instructor
Cooper, Theodore A Dealer, Art Appraiser
Cowart, Jack Museum Director, Curator
Cropper, M Elizabeth Historian, Lecturer
Dailey, John Revell Director
Danziger, Joan Sculptor
De Andino, Jean-Pierre M Dealer, Collector
Demetrion, James Thomas Museum Director
Doumato, Lamia Librarian, Historian
Edwards, Gary Maxwell Art Dealer, Writer
Eisenstein, (Mr & Mrs) Julian Collectors
Escallon, Ana Maria Museum Curator
Falchook, Jason Photographer
Faubion, S Michael Administrator
Fetting, Rainer Painter
Fine, Ruth E Curator, Printmaker
Fisher, Sarah Lisbeth Conservator
Fleischman, Aaron I Collector
Fletcher, Valerie J Curator, Historian
Forgey, Benjamin Franklin Architect, Critic
Garrard, Mary DuBose Historian, Educator
Glass, Brent D. Museum Director
Goodman, Janis G Painter, Draftsman
Gossage, John Ralph Photographer
Gover, Kevin Museum Director
Green, Tom Instructor, Sculptor
Grossman, Sheldon Museum Curator, Historian
Grossman, Wendy A Curator, Historian
Grundberg, Andy Critic, Curator
Gumpert, Gunther Painter
Hall, Robert L Museologist, Painter
Haslem, Jane N Dealer
Hay, (George) Austin Painter, Filmmaker
Hogan, Felicity Museum Director
Holladay, Wilhelmina Cole Collector, Patron
Ishaq, Ashfaq Administrator
Jacobsen, Hugh Newell Architect
Jurovics, Toby Curator
Kaskey, Raymond John Sculptor, Architect
Katz, Jonathan G Administrator
Kennedy, Robyn L Gallery Director
Kessmann, Dean educator, administrator
Kloss, William Historian, Writer
Koshalek, Richard Former Museum Director
Kosinski, Dorothy M Museum Director
Kraft, Craig Allan Sculptor, Curator
Krate, Nat Painter
Kravitz, Walter Sculptor, Painter
Laiou, Angeliki E Educator
Lawrence, Sidney S Painter, Writer
Leigh, Simone Sculptor
Leithauser, Mark Alan Painter, Designer
Leven, Ann R Administrator
Lewton, Val Edwin Painter, Designer
Lowe, Harry Administrator, Designer
Lynch, Robert L Art Association Administrator
Margo, Adair Administrator, Gallery Owner
Maria, Levya Curator
Markowski, Eugene David Painter, Sculptor
Maxwell, David Ogden Patron
McCoubrey, Sarah Painter
Miller, Nicole Writer
Millie, Elena Gonzalez Curator
Pachter, Marc Museum Director
Paige, Wayne Leo Painter, Draftsman
Patton, Sharon Frances Museum Director, Art Historian
Perlin, Ruth Rudolph Educator, Art Historian
Polan, Annette Painter, Draftsman
Raby , Julian Gallery Director
Rales, Emily and Mitchell P Collector
Rales, Steven M Collector
Rathbone, Eliza Euretta Curator, Art Consultant
Revri, Anil Painter, Graphic Artist
Richard, Paul Critic
Roberts, Steven K Sculptor, Printmaker
Robertson, Charles J Administrator
Robinson, Lilien Filipovitch Historian, Educator
Rockefeller, John (Jay) D, IV Collector
Rode, Meredith Eagon Printmaker, Educator
Rose, Robin Carlise Painter, Sculptor
Rosenzweig, Phyllis D Curator
Sajet, Kim Museum Director
Sant, Victoria P Museum Director
Schneider, Julie Saecker Painter, Draftsman
Schottland, M Illustrator, Painter
Shaw-Eagle, Joanna Critic
Sherman, Claire Richter Historian, Educator
Smith, John W Administrator
Sterling, Susan Fisher Museum Director
Stovall, Luther McKinley Printmaker
Sullivan, Martin E Museum Director
Swetcharnik, Sara Morris Painter, Sculptor
Swick, Linda Ann Sculptor
Tacha, Athena Sculptor, Curator
Tepfer, Diane Educator, Historian
Tischler, Gary Critic
Truettner, William H Curator
Von Barghan, Barbara Educator, Writer
Walker, Daniel Museum Director
Wallach, Alan Critic, Historian
Wegman, William Painter, Photographer
Wetenhall, John Museum Director
Wheelock, Arthur Kingsland, Jr Curator, Educator
White, Franklin Painter, Draftsman
Wilson, J Keith Curator
Wooby, William Joseph Art Dealer, Curator
Wright, Frank Painter, Educator
Yahoozer, Paul Graphic Artist, Weaver
Yamaguchi, Yuriko Sculptor
Young, Kenneth Victor Painter, Designer

FLORIDA

Alachua

Tilton, John Ellsworth Ceramist

Aventura

Weinberg, Ephraim Administrator, Painter

Bal Harbour

Elias, Sheila Painter

Big Pine Key

Fleischer, Roland Edward Historian, Educator

Boca Raton

Bolge, George S Museum Director
Coleman, Gayle Lecturer, Conservator
De St Croix, Blane Sculptor, Educator
Dorst, Mary Crowe Graphic Artist, Craftsman
Keeler, David Boughton Painter
McConnell, Brian E Educator, Administrator
Orze, Joseph John Administrator, Sculptor
Rivo, Shirley Winthrope Painter
Zelin, Elaine Sculptor

Boynton Beach

Baumel-Harwood, Bernice Painter, Printmaker, Sculptor
Faulds, W Rod Administrator, Designer
LaFogg-Docherty, Deborah Painter
Ludman, Joan Hurwitz Writer, Researcher

Bradenton

Collins, Harvey Arnold Muralist, Educator, Painter
Flackman, David J Painter
Howard, Linda Sculptor
Jerdon, William Harlan Painter, Instructor
Spann, Susanna Evonne Painter, Educator

Brooksville

Watkins, Lewis Sculptor, Painter

Casselberry

Renee, Lisabeth Sculptor, Assemblage Artist

Cedar Key

Gernhardt, Henry Kendall Sculptor, Ceramist

Clearwater

Bansemer, Roger L Painter, Writer

Cocoa Beach

Blum, June Painter, Sculptor

Coral Gables

Bannard, Walter Darby Painter, Art Writer
Gerlach, Christopher S Painter
Staller, Eric P Photographer, Sculptor

Coral Springs

Mason, Lauris Lapidos Art Dealer, Writer

Crawfordville

Siamis, Janet Neal Painter

Daytona Beach

Biferie, Dan (Daniel) Anthony, Jr Photographer, Educator
Libby, Gary Russell Museum Director, Author

Deland

Bolding, Gary Wilson Painter, Curator
Messersmith, Harry Lee Sculptor, Museum Director

Delray Beach

Kalisher, Simpson Photographer

Doral

Oyuela, Raul M Museum Director, Curator

Enterprise

Abernethy-Baldwin, Judith Ann Painter

Fort Lauderdale

Bulkin Siegel, Wilma Painter
Duaiv Painter
Gianguzzi, Joseph Custode Sculptor, Painter
Goldszer, Bath-Sheba Painter, Graphic Artist
Johnson, Linda K art educator, administrator, writer
Krause, Dorothy Simpson Painter, Collage Artist
Liebowitz, Janet Painter, Sculptor
Lippman, Irvin M Museum Director

Fort Myers

Biolchini, Gregory Phillip Painter
Clemente, Joann P Painter, Consultant
Picciano, Lana Painter

Fort Pierce

Kamm, Dorothy Lila Painter, Writer
Martin, Mary Finch Painter, Gallery Director

Gainesville

Calluori Holcombe, Anna Ceramist
Isaacson, Marcia Jean Artist, Educator
Janowich, Ronald Painter
Lavelli, Lucinda Administrator
Mesches, Arnold Painter, Educator
Nagy, Rebecca Martin Museum Director, Historian
O'Connor, John Arthur Painter, Consultant
Smith, Nan S(helley) Sculptor, Ceramist
Westin, Robert H Historian
Willumson, Glenn Gardner Educator, Curator

Hallandale

Beltran, Elio (Francisco) Painter
Geller, Bunny Zelda Writer, Sculptor

Hobe Sound

Coheleach, Guy Joseph Painter, Sculptor
Payson, John Whitney Art Dealer, Collector

Hollywood

Laguna, Mariella Painter, Printmaker
Sadowski, Carol (Louise) Johnson Painter

Homestead

Waltner, Beverly Ruland Painter

Hudson

Angelini, John Michael Painter, Writer

Indialantic

Plankey, Ellen J Painter

Indian Harbor Beach

Traylor, Angelika Stained Glass Artist

Jacksonville

Arbitman, Kahren Jones Director, Historian
Banas, Anne Painter, Educator
Dempsey, Bruce Harvey Museum Director
Hoffman, Helen Bacon Painter
Kobaslija, Amer Painter
Koscielny, Margaret Sculptor, Draftsman

Jupiter

Sadow, Harvey S, Jr Ceramist, Sculptor

Key Biscayne

Margulies, Martin Z Collector

Key Largo

Fundora, Thomas Painter

FLORIDA (cont)

Key West

Burnside, Madeleine Hilding Critic, Museum Director
Marks, Roberta Barbara Sculptor, Collage Painter
Pennington, Claudia Museum Director

Lake Worth

Sanchez, Thorvald Painter

Lakeland

Hardee, Rodney Charles Painter, Patron
Stetson, Daniel Everett Museum Director, Curator

Longboat Key

Rowan, Frances Physioc Painter, Woodcutter

Lutz

Wilson, Wallace Photographer, Educator

Mary Esther

Simpson, Marilyn Jean Painter, Instructor

Matlacha

Belan, Kyra Artist, Writer

Melbourne

Stewart, Sheila L Director, Curator

Merritt Island

Neal, Irene Painter, Sculptor

Miami

Alquilar, Maria Painter, Ceramist
Anderson, Craig Painter, Sculptor
Bernay, Betti Painter
Braman, Irma Collector
Braman, Norman Collector
Brito, Maria Sculptor, Painter
Buchanan, Beverly Sculptor, Painter
Buergel, Roger M Curator, Historian
Cano, Margarita Painter
Cano, Pablo D Sculptor, Educator
Carulla, Ramon Painter, Printmaker
Cianfoni, Emilio F Conservator, Painter
Cisneros, Ella Fontanals Collector, Director
Collins, Thom Museum Director
Couper, James M Painter, Educator
Cubiñá, Silvia Karman Museum Director, Curator
De La Cruz, Carlos Collector
De La Cruz, Rosa Collector
Delehanty, Suzanne Museum Director
Duncan, Richard (Hurley) Draftsman, Printmaker
Duque, Adonay Painter, Draftsman
Dursum, Brian A Museum Director
Duval Carrie, Edouard Painter, Sculptor
Fleming, Erika Administrator
Fontanals-Cisneros, Ella Patron
Friedman, Marvin Ross Dealer
Gillman, Barbara Seitlin Dealer
Huff, Robert Sculptor, Painter
Kaplan, Betsy Hess Educator
Kolasinski, Jacek J new media artist, educator
Larraz, Julio F Painter
Leff, Cathy Director
Levenson, Rustin S Conservator, Restorer
Lizama, Silvia Administrator. educator, photographer
Martinez-Canas, Maria Photographer
Miller, Virginia Irene Gallery Director
Morgan, Dahlia Museum Director, Educator
Morin, James Corcoran Cartoonist, Editor
Poon, Hung Wah Michael Painter
Poon, Yi-Chong Sarina Chow Painter, Calligrapher
Presser, Elena Assemblage Artist
Ripstein, Jacqueline Painter, Writer
Rodriguez, Bert Installation Sculptor
Romney, Hervin A R Architect
Roselione-Valadez, Juan Museum Director
Rubell, Donald Collector
Rudman, Betty & Isaac Collector
Salinas, Baruj Painter, Printmaker
Schein, Eugenie Educator, Graphic Artist
Shack, Richard Collector, Patron
Talmor, Lihie Printmaker, Sculptor
Tejera, Ariel Painter
Tommerup, Mette Painter
Uklanski, Piotr Sculptor
Vadia, Rafael Painter, Lecturer
Winter, Gerald Glen Painter, Educator
Young, Barbara Neil Librarian, Curator

Miami Beach

Balas, Irene Painter
Chiarlone, Rosemarie Conceptual Artist
Findlay, James Allen Librarian
Lehr, Mira T(ager) Painter
Stein, Ludwig Painter, Educator

Micanopy

Arbuckle, Linda J Ceramist, Educator

Mount Dora

Kirton, Jennifer Myers Graphic Artist, Juror
Salter, Richard Mackintire Painter
Tucholke, Christel-Anthony Painter, Sculptor

Naples

Brown, Alan M, Jr Dealer, Consultant
Meek, J William, III Dealer, Consultant

Navarre

Few, James Cecil Painter

Niceville

Valdes, Karen W Director, Educator

Ocala

James, Bill (William) Frederick Painter, Illustrator

Orange Park

Hunt, Courtenay Painter, Instructor

Orlando

Gentele, Glen Museum Director, Curator
Lotz, Steven Darryl Painter, Gallery Director
Morrisey, Marena Grant Museum Director
Straight, Elsie H Librarian, Sculptor

Ormond Beach

Patton, Karen Ann Painter
Perrotti, Barbara Painter, Instructor
Roberson, Sang Craftsman
Sugiyama, Akiko Craftsman, Assemblage Artist

Osprey

Gross, Marilyn A Painter, Printmaker
Koenig, Peter Laszlo Painter, Curator, Educator

Oviedo

Francis, Madison Ke, Jr Sculptor, Printmaker

Palm Beach

Gardiner, Henry Gilbert Art Appraiser, Museum Director
Gilbertson, Charlotte Painter, Lecturer
Luntz, Irving Dealer
Marcus, Robert (Mrs) P Collector, Patron
Wenzel, Joan Ellen Assemblage Artist, Sculptor

Palm Beach Gardens

Kaplan, Muriel S Sculptor, Collector

Parkland

Kroll, Lynne Francine Painter, Collage Artist

Pensacola

Burke-Fanning, Madeleine Painter, Educator
Maki, Countess Hope Marie Painter
Stewart, Duncan E Collage Artist

Poiniana

Mastrangelo, Bobbi Sculptor, Environmental Artist

Pompano Beach

Lis, Janet Painter, Illustrator

Port Saint Lucie

Brody, Arthur William Printmaker, Painter
Castile, Rand Museum Director
Staub, Carol Anne Painter, Instructor

Quincy

Lindquist, Mark Sculptor, Photographer

Roseland

Segal, Mary Graphic Artist, Printmaker

Safety Harbor

Banks, Allan R Painter
Banks, Holly Hope Painter

Saint Augustine

Torcoletti, Enzo Sculptor

Saint Petersburg

Crane, Jim (James) G Painter, Cartoonist
Grastorf, Jean H Painter, Instructor
Harte, John Painter
Kropf, Joan R Curator, Lecturer
Nyren, Edward A Painter
Schloder, John E Director

Sarasota

Ahlander, Leslie Judd Critic, Consultant
Bilodeau, Daniel Alain Painter, Draftsman
Capes, Richard Edward Graphic Artist, Instructor
Chambers, Park A, Jr Educator, Photographer
Chase, Jeanne Norman Painter, Printmaker
Christ-Janer, Arland F Painter, Printmaker
Clement, Shirley Painter
Corbino, Marcia Norcross Critic, Writer
Dabbert, Patricia Ann Ceramist, Sculptor
Dean, Kevin Lee Gallery Director, Educator
DeCaprio, Alice Photographer, Collage Artist
Dowd, Jack Sculptor
Ebitz, David MacKinnon Museum Director, Historian
Freund, Pepsi Painter, Collage Artist
Gelinas, Robert William Painter, Educator
Gerstein, David Steven Filmmaker
Goodacre, Glenna Sculptor
Kessler, Leonard H Illustrator of Children's Books
Kowal, Dennis J Sculptor, Writer
Masterfield, Maxine Painter
Pappas, George Painter
Petersen, Franklin G Painter
Rice, Anthony Hopkins Historian, Artist
Rosenzweig, Daphne Lange Historian, Museum Consultant
Savenor, Betty Carmell Painter, Printmaker
Seyler, Monique G Painter
Stevens, Elisabeth Goss Writer, Printmaker

Seminole

Scalzo, Joyce Ann Ceramist, Curator

Summerfield

Shaw, Nancy (Rivard) Art Historian, Independent Scholar

Summerland Key

Anthony, Lawrence Kenneth Sculptor, Painter

Sun City Center

Johnston, Roy Painter, Historian

Tallahassee

Bell, Trevor Painter
Burggraf, Ray Lowell Painter, Educator
Eden, F(lorence) Brown Collage Artist, Painter
Edwards-Tucker, Yvonne Leatrice Ceramist, Educator
Fichter, Robert W Educator
Henne, Carolyn Sculptor, Administrator
Palladino-Craig, Allys Director, Curator

Tamarac

Pravda, Muriel Instructor, Restorer
Smith, Rowena Marcus Painter, Collage Artist
Stella, Harry Painter, Photographer

Tampa

Covington, Harrison Wall Painter, Sculptor
de Lama, Alberto Painter
Gurbacs, John Joseph Painter, Restorer
Kronsnoble, Jeffrey Michael Painter, Educator
Mitchell, Dean Lamont Painter
Moy, James S Administrator, Educator
Nazarenko, Bonnie Coe Painter
Pachner, William Painter
Santiago, Richard E Sculptor, Educator
Schofield, Roberta Painter, Photographer
Wujcik, Theo Painter, Printmaker

Tavares

Spencer, Linda B Encaustic Artist, Jeweler, Collage, Oil

The Villages

Deremer, Susan René Painter, Illustrator

Tierra Verde

Tuegel, Michele Beckman Craftsman, Administrator

University Park

Scalera, Michelle Ann Conservator, Educator

Venice

Bateman, Robert McLellan Painter
Turconi, Sue (Susan) Kinder Painter, Photographer

Venice Park

Lacktman, Michael Craftsman, Jeweler

FLORIDA (cont)

Vero Beach

Christman, Reid August   Painter
David, Ivo   Painter, Writer
Ferguson, Alice C   Painter
Ferrell, Catherine (Klemann)   Sculptor
Gedeon, Lucinda Heyel   Museum Director, Administrator
Hoffman, Martin   Painter, Illustrator
Krupp, Barbara D   Conceptual Artist, Painter
Sprout, Francis   Artist, Educator
Townsend, Teryl   Painter, Educator

Wellington

Brody, Carol Z   Painter, Collage Artist

West Palm Beach

Baker, Dina Gustin   Painter
Brutvan, Cheryl   Curator
Cowan, Ralph Wolfe   Painter
Elliot, John   Painter, Filmmaker
Elliot, Sheila   Writer, Administrator
Gaudieri, Alexander V J   Museum Director
Gruss, Martin David   Patron
Orr-Cahall, Anona Christina   Museum Director, Curator
Schwartz, Ruth   Painter, Instructor
Squier, Jack Leslie   Sculptor, Educator

Windermere

Hubert, Anne M   Curator, Collector
Lewis, Joseph   Collector

Winter Haven

Schepis, Anthony Joseph   Instructor, Painter
Treister, Kenneth   Painter, Sculptor, Architect
White, Karen J   Sculptor, Assemblage Artist

Winter Park

Blumenthal, Arthur R   Museum Director Emeritus, Consultant
Booth, Dot   Painter, Printmaker
Fager, Charles J   Ceramist, Sculptor
Haxton, David   Photographer, Filmmaker
Lemon, Robert S, Jr   Educator, Historian
Ruggiero, Laurence J   Museum Director

GEORGIA

Alpharetta

Sirlin, Deanna Louise   Painter, Environmental Artist

Athens

Arnholm, Ronald Fisher   Designer, Educator
Barsness, Jim   Painter, Cartoonist
Clements, Robert Donald   Sculptor, Educator
Colangelo, Carmon   Administrator, Printmaker
Eiland, William U   Museum Director
Feldman, Edmund Burke   Educator, Critic
Firestone, Evan R   Administrator, Historian
Goldsleger, Cheryl   Painter, Draftsman
Hammond, Gale Thomas   Printmaker, Educator
Hammond, Mary Sayer   Educator, Photographer
Herbert, James Arthur   Painter, Filmmaker
Lukasiewicz, Nancy Bechtold   Administrator, Tapestry Artist
Lukasiewicz, Ronald Joseph   Printmaker, Administrator
Meyers, Ronald G   Educator, Ceramist
Nasisse, Andy S   Sculptor, Writer
Paul, William D, Jr   Painter, Collector
Sapp, William Rothwell   Sculptor, Educator
Siegesmund, Richard   Educator
Simon, Michael J   Ceramist
Strange, Georgia   Educator, Sculptor

Atlanta

Artemis, Maria   Sculptor, Educator
Bunnen, Lucinda Weil   Photographer, Collector
Carlstrom, Lucinda   Painter, Printmaker
Chandler, Angelyn Sanders   Museum Director
Creecy, Herbert Lee   Painter, Sculptor
Cullum, Jerry   Editor
Fortin, Sylvie   Editor
Frabel, Hans Godo   Sculptor
Galina, Brenda Moss   Museum Director
Gibson, Michael   Painter
Gleim-Jonas, Lisa   Painter, Writer
Gromala, Diane   Video Artist, Critic
Guberman, Sidney   Painter, Sculptor
Harkins, Dennis Richter   Administrator, Photographer
Heath, David C   Dealer
Laxson, Ruth   Conceptual Artist, Printmaker
Longobardi, Pam   Painter, Photographer
Malone, James Hiram   Painter, Writer
Mari, M   Painter, Printmaker
McLean, James Albert   Educator, Printmaker
McPhee, Sarah Collyer   Historian, Educator
Meyer, James Sampson   Writer, Historian
Mills, Lev Timothy   Printmaker, Designer
Mitchell, Katherine   Painter
Nick, Lloyd   Museum Director, Painter
Paschall, Jo Anne   Printmaker, Librarian
Patterson, Curtis Ray   Sculptor, Instructor
Portman, John C, Jr   Architect, Collector
Pressly, Nancy Lee   Curator, Administrator
Pressly, William Laurens   Historian, Educator
Riddle, John Thomas, Jr   Sculptor, Painter
Rooks, Michael   Curator
Rothwell, Junko Ono   Painter
Scogin, Mack   Architect, Educator
Seaberg, Steve (Stevens)   Assemblage Artist, Performance Artist
Shapiro, Michael Edward   Museum Director, Curator
Speed, Bonnie Anne   Museum Director
Stent, Terry & Margaret   Collectors
Tiegreen, Alan F   Painter, Illustrator
Tuttle, Lisa   Conceptual Artist, Curator
Vigtel, Gudmund   Director
White, Michael   architect, administrator

Augusta

Engler, Kathleen Girdler   Sculptor
Grogan, Kevin   Museum Director
Gruber, J Richard   Administrator, Historian
Swanson, Caroline   Painter
Williams Whiting, Janice E   Painter, Sculptor

Ball Ground

Tustian, Brenda Harris   Painter, Publisher

Blairsville

Sterling, Colleen   Painter

Carrollton

Bobick, J Bruce   Educator, Painter

Cartersville

Hopkins, Seth M   Museum Director

Columbus

Butler, Charles Thomas   Museum Director, Curator

Decatur

Bleser, Katherine Alice   Painter
Greco, Anthony Joseph   Painter, Administrator
Lindsay, Arturo   Sculptor, Painter
Loehle, Betty Barnes   Painter
Loehle, Richard E   Painter, Illustrator
Moore, Wayland D   Painter, Printmaker
Shaw, Louise E   Director

Douglasville

Lieberman, Laura Crowell   Administrator, Critic

Fayetteville

Rosser, Donna King   Photographer, Consultant

Gainesville

Shead, S Ray   Painter, Printmaker

Hahira

Penny, Donald Charles   Craftsman, Sculptor

Lookout Mountain

Lynch, Mary Britten   Painter, Collage Artist

Macon

Ambrose, Andy   Museum Director
Gray, Elise Norris   Sculptor
Ivey-Weaver, Jacquelyn Kunkel   Painter, Sculptor
Liles, Catharine (Burns)   Painter, Patron

Marietta

Eden, Glenn   Draftsman, Painter
Lahtinen, Silja (Liisa) Talikka   Painter, Printmaker
Slaughter, Kwabena   Photographer

Newnan

Harless, Carol P   Sculptor

Parrott

Tilley, Lewis Lee   Painter, Video Artist

Rome

Staven, Leland Carroll   Painter

Roswell

Cabot, Mary A. Booth   Painter, Printmaker
Rayburn, Boyd (Dale)   Painter, Printmaker

Saint Simons Island

Rensch, Roslyn   Historian, Collector

Sandy Springs

Urichta, Rey   Collage Artist, Painter

Savannah

Fischer, Thomas Jeffrey   Photographer, Educator
Francis, Tom   Painter
Gabeler, Jo   Painter
High, Steven S   Museum Director, Curator
Hsu, Pang-Chieh   Educator, Printmaker
Jackson, Suzanne   Painter, Printmaker
Joseph, Stefani A   Painter, Educator
Lesko, Diane   Museum Director, Curator
Miller, Kathryn   Painter, Printmaker
Norgard, Karen-Sam   Sculptor, Educator
Wallace, Paula S   Administrator

Snellville

Fenton, Julia Ann   Curator, Conceptual Artist

Statesboro

Carter, Patricia   printmaker, educator, administrator
Hines, Jessica   Photographer
Tichich, Richard   Educator, Administrator

Stone Mountain

Mickish, Verle L   Educator, Illustrator

Thomasville

Powers, Donald T   Painter

Tybee Island

Burr, Tricia   Painter

Valdosta

Dodd, M(ary) Irene   Painter, Educator
Lahr, J(ohn) Stephen   Painter, Educator

Waleska

Mathis, Billie Fritz   Painter, Conceptual Artist

HAWAII

Hilo

Miyamoto, Wayne Akira   Painter, Printmaker

Honolulu

Bushnell, Kenneth Wayne   Painter, Educator
Chan, Gaye   Educator, Administrator, Conceptual Artist
De la Torre, David Joseph   Museum Director
Ellis, George Richard   Museum Director
Haar, Tom   Photographer, Filmmaker
Johnson, Bruce (James)   Painter
Klobe, Tom   Gallery Director, Educator
Lagoria, Georgianna Marie M   Museum Director, Curator
Little, Stephen   Museum Director
Morse, Marcia Roberts   Printmaker, Writer
Nagano, Paul Tatsumi   Painter, Picture Maker
Preiss, Alexandru Petre   Designer, Illustrator
Roster, Fred Howard   Sculptor, Educator
Ruby, Laura   Sculptor, Printmaker
Uhl, Philip Edward   Painter, Photographer
Yu-ho, Tseng   Painter, Historian

Kailua

Kowalke, Ronald Leroy   Painter, Printmaker

Kapaau

Jankowski, Theodore Andrew   Painter, Muralist

Lahaina

Smith, Andrea B   Painter

Lihue

Lai, Waihang   Painter, Educator

Makawao

Adams, Loren Dean, Jr   Painter, Sculptor
Ulrich, David Alan   Photographer, Educator

Volcano

Morrison, Boone M   Architect, Photographer

Waialua

Goodwill, Margaret   Painter, Designer

IDAHO

Bellevue

Bennett, Don Bemco Painter, Printmaker

Boise

Jessup, Wesley Museum Director
Kober, Alfred John Educator, Sculptor
Neil, J M Writer
Watia, Tarmo Painter, Printmaker
Wilde, Stephanie Conceptual Artist, Printmaker
Young, Richard Alan Painter, Administrator

Coeur D Alene

Johnstone, Mark Conceptual Artist, Curator

Harrison

Carlson, George Arthur Sculptor, Painter

Middleton

Killmaster, John H Enamelist, Painter

Moscow

Machlis, Sally Graves Educator, Administrator, Painter

Pocatello

Dial, Gail Metalsmith, Educator

Sandpoint

Schultz, Stephen Warren Painter, Educator

ILLINOIS

Arlington Heights

Chambers, William Thomas Painter

Belleville

Threlkeld, Dale Painter

Bloomington

Finch, Richard Dean Printmaker, Educator
Gregor, Harold Laurence Painter, Educator
Hobbs, Jack Arthur Educator, Writer
Stroud, Billy Painter, Collector

Buffalo Grove

Kipervaser, Anna Painter

Buncombe

Edgren, Gary Robert Painter, Craftsman

Carbondale

Deller, Harris Administrator, Ceramist
Logan, Fern H Photographer, Graphic Artist
Plochmann, Carolyn Gassan Painter, Graphic Artist
Shay, Ed Painter

Carterville

Mavigliano, George Jerome Administrator, Educator

Champaign

Breen, Harry Frederick, Jr Painter, Sculptor
Gammon, Juanita L Art Educator, Graphic Artist
Goggin, Nan Elizabeth Educator, Graphic Artist
Harleman, Kathleen Towe Museum Director
Smith, Ralph Alexander Writer, Educator
Van Laar, Timothy Painter, Writer

Charleston

Hubschmitt, William E Educator, Administrator
Sorge, Walter Painter, Printmaker
Watts, R Michael Museum Director

Chicago

Alvarez, Candida Painter, Educator
Anderson, Scott Painter, Graphic Artist
Artner, Alan Gustav Critic
Aubin, Barbara Painter, Collage artist
Balzekas, Stanley, Jr Museum Director, Collector
Barter, Judith A Curator, Historian
Berns, Pamela Kari Painter, Administrator
Blackman, Thomas Patrick Director, Printmaker
Blackmon, Julie painter
Bluhm, Neil Gary Patron, Collector
Boardman, Deborah Painter, Conceptual Artist
Bramson, Phyllis Halperin Painter, Educator
Caporael, Suzanne Painter
Castillo, Mario Enrique Painter, Muralist, Educator
Chavez, Juan Angel Educator
Christiansen, Diane Painter, Cartoonist
Cohen, Charles E Historian, Educator
Conger, William Painter, Educator
Crane, Arnold H Photographer
Crane, Barbara Bachmann Photographer, Educator
Czarnopys, Thomas J Sculptor
Donmez, Yucel Painter, Sculptor
Druick, Douglas Wesley Curator, Museum Director
Duffy, Michael John Painter, Printmaker
Edlis, Stefan T Collector
Facey, Martin Kerr Painter, Educator
Feinman, Stephen E Dealer, Publisher
Ferrari, Virginio Luigi Sculptor, Educator
Fish, Julia A Painter
Gang, Jeanne Architect
Garofalo, Chris Sculptor
Gerber, Gaylen Conceptual Artist, Painter
Giuffre, Hector Painter, Graphic Artist
Godfrey, Winnie (Winifred) M Painter, Instructor
Gordon, James A Patron
Gray, Richard Dealer
Griffin, Anne & Kenneth C Collector
Grynsztejn, Madeleine Museum Director
Hannum, Terence J Critic, Director
Hansen, James Lee Sculptor
Hanson, Philip Holton Painter
Herzberg, Thomas Illustrator, Educator
Hill, Gary Video Artist
Himmelfarb, John David Painter, Sculptor
Hirschel, Anthony G Museum Director
Hormuth, Jo Sculptor, Printmaker
Hunt, Richard Howard Sculptor
Jaidinger, Judith Clarann Szesko Printmaker, Painter
Jashinsky, Judy Painter, Curator
Kahn, Katie (Kathryn) Anna Painter
Kearney, John (W) Sculptor
Kearney, Lynn Haigh Curator
Kenney, Estelle Koval Art Therapist, Painter
Kim, Kwang-Wu Administrator, Educator
Kirshner, Judith Russi Curator, Critic
Klamen, David Painter
Klement, Vera Painter, Writer, Graphic Artist, Photographer
Kochman, Alexandra D Sculptor, Painter
Kolisnyk, Peter Painter, Sculptor
Krantz, Claire Wolf Mixed Media Artists, Writer
Lamantia, Paul Christopher Painter
Lamb, Matt Painter, Sculptor
Lausen, Marcia Educator, Designer
Lee, Li Lin Painter
Lehrer, Leonard Painter, Printmaker
Lennon, Timothy Painting Conservator
Leopold, Susan Sculptor, Muralist
Lincoln, Louise Museum Director, Educator
Luecking, Stephen Joseph Sculptor, Educator
Lutes, Jim (James) Painter
Maldre, Mati Photographer, Educator
Mann, Curtis Photographer
Marshall, Kerry James Designer, Painter
Massey, Walter E Administrator, Educator
McCarter, John Wilbur, Jr Retired Museum Director
McElheny, Josiah sculptor
Meyers, Michael K Performance Artist, Painter
Miller, Denise Museum Director, Educator
Miller, Michael Stephen Printmaker, Painter
Morishita, Joyce Chizuko Historian, Painter
Mosena, David Museum Director
Myers, Terry R Critic, Curator
Neeson, H Gael Collector
Neimanas, Joyce Photographer
Nordland, Gerald John Gallery Director, Critic
Nourse, Mike Video Artist, Instructor
Parfenoff, Michael S Educator, Lithographer
Paul, Art(hur) Designer, Painter
Peart, Jerry Linn Sculptor
Perelman, Jeffrey E Collector
Phillips, Bertrand D Painter, Photographer
Phillips, Tony Painter, Draftsman
Piatek, Francis John Painter, Educator
Postiglione, Corey M Painter, Educator, Critic
Preciado, Pamela Painter, Illustrator
Pritzker, Penny S Collector
Pruitt, Robert A Assemblage Artist
Puryear, Martin Sculptor
Rabb, Madeline M Consultant
Reddington, Charles Leonard Painter, Educator
Reilly, Bernard Francis Historian, Curator
Roberts, Darrell Keith Painter
Rupprecht, Elizabeth Instructor, Professor, Painter
Salomon, Lawrence Sculptor, Educator
Schnackenberg, Roy Painter, Sculptor
Schupp, Ronald Irving Social Justice Artist, Writer
Seed, Suzanne Liddell Photographer, Writer
Sensemann, Susan Painter, Educator
Shaffer, Fern Painter, Lecturer
Silverman, Lanny Harris Director, Curator
Slemmons, Rod Museum Director, Educator
Sorell, Victor Alexander Historian, Administrator
Spiess-Ferris, Eleanor Painter
Stevens, Jane M Photographer, Administrator
Stockholder, Jessica Sculptor, Assemblage Artist
Stoppert, Mary Kay Administrator, Gallery Director
Stratman, Deborah Filmmaker
Stuckey, Charles F Historian, Curator
Szesko, Lenore Rundle Painter, Printmaker
Thorne, Martha Administrator, Curator
Tigerman, Stanley Painter, Architect
Tinsley, Barry Sculptor
Travis, David B Curator, Historian
Trockel, Rosemarie Sculptor, Painter
Ullrich, Polly Critic
Warren, Lynne Curator, Writer
Weber, John Pitman Muralist, Printmaker, Mosaic Artist
Weiss, Rachel Curator
Wenger, Jane (B) Photographer, Conceptual Artist
Wilson, Karen Lee Consultant
Wirsum, Karl Painter, Sculptor
Witkovsky, Matthew Curator
Workman, Robert P Painter, Illustrator
Wunderlich, Susan Clay Art Dealer
Yordanov, Plamen Installation Sculptor
Zgoda, Larry Stained Glass Artist, Designer

Cicero

Mehn, Jan (Jan Von der Golz) Printmaker

Cissna Park

McCullough, Edward L Sculptor; Instructor

Crystal Lake

Pike, Joyce Lee Painter, Writer

Decatur

Cunningham, Sue Painter, Illustrator
Klaven, Marvin L Painter, Educator

Deerfield

Price, Rita F Painter, Printmaker

Dekalb

Bilder, Dorothea A Printmaker, Painter
Boughton, Doug Administrator, Educator
Carp, Richard M Administrator, Educator
Doherty, Peggy M Museum Director, Curator
Even, Robert Lawrence Educator
Maxfield, Roberta Masur Silversmith
Meyer, Jerry Don Historian, Educator
White, Bruce Hilding Sculptor, Educator

Des Plaines

Schildknecht, Dorothy E Painter
Smuskiewicz, Ted Painter, Educator

Downers Grove

Kind, Joshua B Educator, Critic
Ziff, Jerrold Historian, Collector

Edwardsville

Anderson, Daniel J Ceramist, Educator
Hampton, Phillip Jewel Painter, Educator
Harroff, William Charles Brent Conceptual Artist, Illustrator
Malone, Robert R Painter, Printmaker

Elmwood Park

Hofmann, Kay Sculptor

Elwood

Bartels, Phyllis Elaine Painter

Evanston

Altman, Edith Sculptor, Conceptual Artist
Archer, Cynthia Printmaker, Painter
Clayson, S Hollis Art Historian
Corrin, Lisa G Museum Director
Groot, Candice Beth Ceramist
Hausman, Jerome Joseph Educator
Hirshfield, Pearl Painter, Sculptor
Hurtig, Martin Russell Painter, Sculptor
Nakoneczny, Michael Painter
Relyea, Lane Administrator, Educator
Rush, John Painter, Illustrator, Printmaker
Schiff, Molly Jeanette Painter, Printmaker
Thompson, Michael Art Dealer
Trupp, Barbara Lee Painter, Designer

Forest Park

Rogovin, Mark Muralist, Museum Director

Galena

Narkiewicz-Laine, Christian K Museum Director, Writer
Robertson, David Alan Museum Director

ILLINOIS (cont)

Galesburg

Thenhaus, Paulette Ann   Painter, Writer

Geneva

Buitron, Robert C   Photographer, Video Artist

Glenview

Halliday, Nancy R   Illustrator, Instructor
Hough, Winston   Painter, Draftsman

Highland Park

Feldman, Arthur Mitchell   Museum Director, Art and Antiques Dealer
Hawkins, Margaret   Critic, Educator, Writer

Homewood

Heller, Reinhold August   Historian

Joliet

Brulc, Lillian G   Painter, Sculptor

Lake Forest

Brewer, Paul   Painter, Illustrator
Schulze, Franz   Historian, Critic

Lawrenceville

Dooley, David I   Painter, Educator

Lombard

Ahlstrom, Ronald Gustin   Collage Artist, Painter

Long Grove

Robertson, Joan Elizabeth Mitchell   Graphic Artist

Macomb

Jones, Frederick   Printmaker
Parker, Samuel Murray   Painter

Makanda

Kington, Louis Brent   Sculptor

Mount Auburn

Schietinger, James Frederick   Sculptor, Educator

Murphysboro

Zivkovich, Kay Pick   Administrator, Educator, Printmaker

Naperville

Skurkis, Barry A   Painter, Sculptor

Normal

Crowley, Tony   administrator
Justis, Gary   Sculptor, Kinetic Artist
Mai, James L   Painter, Educator
Major, James   administrator

Northbrook

Davidson, David Isaac   Painter
Smith, Mark T   Painter, Illustrator

Oak Lawn

Jachna, Joseph David   Photographer, Educator

Oak Park

Hugunin, James Richard   Critic
Sokol, David Martin   Art Historian, Museologist

Oakbrook Terrace

McGrail, Jeane Kathryn   Painter, Photographer

Palatine

Fortunato, Nancy   Painter, Instructor
Pirnat-Dressler, Nia   Painter, Administrator

Park Ridge

Fornelli, Joseph   Sculptor, Painter

Payson

St Maur, Kirk   Sculptor, Painter

Peoria

Gillespie, Oscar Jay   Printmaker
Krainak, Paul   painter, critic, art school administrator

Petersburg

Hallmark, Donald   Retired Museum Director, Lecturer

Quincy

Irwin, George M   Patron, Collector
Mejer, Robert Lee   Painter, Educator

Ringwood

Pearson, James Eugene   Instructor, Sculptor

River Forest

Powell, Gordon   Sculptor

Rockford

Apgar, Jean E   Painter
Heflin, Tom Pat   Painter, Designer
Sneed, Patricia M   Collector, Consultant

Rolling Meadows

Rebbeck, Lester James, Jr   Gallery Director, Painter

Saint Charles

Darling, Sharon Sandling   Historian, Museum Director

Schaumburg

Martyl,   Painter, Muralist

Sidney

Rowan, Dennis Michael   Printmaker, Educator

Springfield

Dunbar, Michael Austin   Sculptor, Administrator
Hodge, R Garey   Painter
Madden-Work, Betty I   Painter, Historian
Madura, Jack Joseph   Painter, Instructor

Sycamore

Rollman, Charlotte   Painter

Urbana

Bodnar, Peter   Painter, Educator
Replinger, Dot (Dorothy Thiele)   Weaver, Designer
Stephens, Curtis   Educator, Designer

Washington

Sunderland, Nita Kathleen   Educator, Sculptor

Wauconda

Czach, Marie   Historian, Curator

Wheaton

Das, Ratindra   Painter, Instructor
Driesbach, David Fraiser   Printmaker
Walford, E John   Historian, Educator

Wilmette

Drower, Sara Ruth   Painter, Craftsman
Nilsson, Gladys   Painter
Nutt, Jim   Painter, Draftsman
Valerio, James Robert   Painter, Educator

Winnetka

Kramer, Linda Lewis   Painter, Collector
Plowden, David   Photographer, Writer

Woodstock

Trausch, Thomas V   Painter, Educator

INDIANA

Albany

Davis, James Robert   Cartoonist
Patrick, Alan K   Ceramist, Painter

Anderson

Ryden, Kenneth Glenn   Sculptor

Beverly Shores

Stanley, Robert A   Painter, Printmaker

Bloomington

Boger, Christyl   Ceramist, Educator
Brubaker, Jack   Sculptor, Blacksmith, Designer, Painter
Calman, W(endy) L   Printmaker, Photographer
Gealt, Adelheid Medicus   Museum Director, Historian
Irvine, Betty Jo   Librarian, Instructor
Jacquard, Jerald (Wayne)   Sculptor
Kleinbauer, W Eugene   Historian, Writer
Mather, Timothy Wayne   Educator, Sculptor
Pozzatti, Rudy O   Printmaker, Painter
Stirratt, Betsy (Elizabeth) Anne   Painter, Gallery Director

Brazil

Hay, Dick   Sculptor, Educator

Crawfordsville

Sabol, Frank Robert   Administrator, Educator

Evansville

Blevins, James Richard   Art Administrator, Educator
Miley, Les   Ceramist, Sculptor
Spurgin, John Edwin   Administrator, Painter
Streetman, John William, III   Administrator

Fort Wayne

De Santo, Stephen C   Painter
Papier, Maurice Anthony   Educator, Painter
Watkinson, Patricia Grieve   Museum Director, Curator

Granger

Langland, Tuck   Sculptor, Educator

Greencastle

Johnson, Kaytie   Curator

Greenwood

Voos, William John   Administrator, Painter

Hammond

Berrier, Wesley Dorwin   Painter, Conservator

Indianapolis

Anderson, Maxwell L   Museum Director, Educator
Day, Holliday T   Curator, Critic
Dooley Waller, M L   Painter
Eagerton, Robert Pierce   Painter
Eickmeier, Valerie   Educator
Faust, James Wille   Painter, Sculptor
Goodine, Linda Adele   Photographer, Sculptor
Lee, Ellen Wardwell   Curator
Orr, Leah   Sculptor
Patchen, Jeffrey H   Museum Director
Schaad, Dee   Educator, Ceramist
Waller, Aaron Bret   Museum Director, Art Historian

Logansport

Weida, Donna Lee   Painter, Photographer

Madison

Gunter, Frank Elliott   Painter, Educator

Michigan City

Saxton, Carolyn Virginia   Director

Muncie

Blume, Peter F   Museum Director
Griner, Ned H   Educator, Craftsman

Munster

Meeker, Barbara Miller   Educator, Painter

Nashville

Brown, Peggy Ann   Painter, Instructor

New Albany

Wegner, Nadene R   Goldsmith, Consultant

New Harmony

Weinzapfel, Connie A   Gallery Director, Curator

Notre Dame

Gray, Richard   Administrator, Educator
Loving, Charles R   Museum Director, Curator
Sandusky, Billy Ray   Painter, Printmaker

Purdue University

Paul, Rick W   Sculptor

South Bend

Gnott, Jacqueline   Painter
Larkin, Eugene   Designer, Educator
Rosenberg, Charles Michael   Historian, Educator
Zisla, Harold   Painter, Graphic Artist

Terre Haute

Benjamin, Lloyd William, III   Historian, Administrator
Engeran, Whitney John, Jr   Painter, Educator
Evans, Robert Graves   Educator, Sculptor
Ganis, William V   Educator, Administrator, Writer
Lattanzio, Frances   Photographer, Educator
McDaniel, Craig Milton   Educator, Painter

INDIANA (cont)

Vincennes

Jendrzejewski, Andrew John Sculptor, Administrator

West Lafayette

Berg, Mona Lea Museum Director
Smith-Theobald, Sharon A Consultant
Williams, David Jon Medical Illustrator, Historian

IOWA

Ames

Pohlman, Lynette Museum Director, Curator
Rico-Gutierrez, Luis architect, educator, administrator

Burlington

Garrison, David Earl Painter, Muralist
Koehler-Trickler, Sally Jo Retired Illustrator
Middaugh, Robert Burton Painter
Torn, Jerry (Gerald J) Draftsman, Photographer

Cedar Falls

Behrens, Roy R Editor, Designer, Curator

Cedar Rapids

Barth, Charles John Educator, Printmaker
Gilmor, Jane E Sculptor, Educator
Kocher, Robert Lee Painter, Educator

Coralville

Yuen, Kee-ho Silversmith, Sculptor

Davenport

O'Harrow, Sean Museum Director

Decorah

Kamm, David Robert Printmaker, Educator

Des Moines

Beam, Patrice K Administrator, Museum Director
Fleming, Jeff Museum Director
Gaskell, Anna Photographer
Pappajohn, John & Mary Collectors, Patrons
Reece, Maynard Painter, Illustrator
Worthen, Amy Namowitz Printmaker, Historian

Dubuque

Gibbs, Tom Sculptor

Dysart

Behrens, Mary Snyder Painter, Assemblage Artist

Grinnell

Hettmansperger, Sue Painter
Wilson, Kay E Curator, Director

Indianola

Heinicke, Janet L Hart Painter, Educator

Iowa City

Barrett, Timothy D Educator, Craftsman
Breder, Hans Dieter Sculptor, Video Artist
Choo, Chunghi Silversmith, Fiber Artist, Educator
Cuttler, Charles David Historian, Lecturer
De Puma, Richard Daniel Historian, Lecturer
Foster, Stephen C Historian, Writer
Monroe, Betty Iverson Educator
Patrick, Genie Hudson Painter, Instructor
Patrick, Joseph Alexander Painter, Educator
Rorex, Robert Albright Educator, Historian
Schmidt, Julius Sculptor
Scott, John Beldon Historian, Educator, Writer
Tomasini, Wallace J Administrator, Historian

Marion

Prall, Barbara Jones Painter, Instructor

Mason City

Leet, Richard (Eugene) Retired Museum Director, Painter

Mount Vernon

Lifson, Hugh Anthony Painter, Educator

Orange City

Kaericher, John Conrad Printmaker, Educator

Solon

Myers, Virginia Anne Printmaker, Educator

KANSAS

Baldwin City

Graber, Steven Brian Graphic Artist, Painter

Emporia

Perry, Donald Dean Painter, Educator

Great Bend

Nuss, Joanne Ruth Sculptor, Painter

Hays

Jilg, Michael Florian Painter, Printmaker
Nichols, Francis N, II Printmaker, Educator
Thorns, John Cyril, Jr Designer, Painter

Lawrence

Bangert, Colette Stuebe Painter
Brejcha, Vernon Lee Glass Blower, Photographer
Craig, Susan V Librarian
Eldredge, Charles C, III Historian
Hardy, Saralyn Reece Museum Director
Iversen, Earl Harvey Photographer, Educator
Jordan, Mary Anne Educator, Administrator
Katz, Cima Printmaker
Satz, Janet Painter, Educator
Shimomura, Roger Painter, Performance Artist
Stokstad, Marilyn Historian, Writer
Sudlow, Robert N Painter, Printmaker, Sculptor
Tefft, Elden Cecil Sculptor, Educator
Vaccaro, Luella Grace Ceramist, Painter
Zeller, Joseph R Educator, Ceramist

Leavenworth

Melby, David A Painter, Photographer

Leawood

Wahlman, Maude Southwell Administrator, Historian

Lecompton

Copt, Louis J Painter

Manhattan

Craig, Gerry Educator, Administrator, Writer
Garzio, Angelo C Potter, Craftsman
Kren, Margo Painter, Educator
Larmer, Oscar Vance Painter, Educator
Munce, James Charles Printmaker, Draftsman
Ohno, Mitsugi Glassblower
Pujol, Elliott Educator, Medalist
Schmidt, Teresa Tempero Printmaker, Draftsman

McPherson

Robinson, Mary Ann Painter, Educator

Pittsburg

Krug, Harry Elno Printmaker, Educator

Shawnee Mission

Goheen, Ellen Rozanne Historian, Curator
Kuemmerlein, Janet Fiber Artist

Spring Hill

Sipho, Ella Painter

Topeka

Merrill, Hugh Jordan Printmaker, Painter
Peters, Larry Dean Ceramist, Collage Artist

Wichita

McDonnell, Patricia Joan Museum Director
Miller, Rodney E Administrator
Plott, Paula Plott Amos Painter, Sculptor
Riegle, Robert Mack Art Dealer, Collector
Scott, B Nibbelink (Barbara Gae Scott) Painter, Sculptor
Steiner, Charles K Museum Director, Painter

KENTUCKY

Alexandria

Douthat, Anita S Photographer

Ashland

Richmond, Rebekah Printmaker, Painter

Berea

Caudill, Dave Sculptor
Pross, Lester Fred Educator, Painter

Bowling Green

Klein, Michael Eugene Historian, Writer
Oakes, John Warren Educator, Painter
Schieferdecker, Ivan E Printmaker, Painter
Stomps, Walter E, Jr Educator, Painter
Trutty-Coohill, Patricia Educator, Historian

Burlington

Enstice, Wayne Assemblage Artist, Writer

Corbin

Weedman, Kenneth Russell Painter, Sculptor

Farmington

Merida, Frederick A Art Dealer, Printmaker

Florence

Goodridge, Lawrence Wayne Painter, Sculptor

Goshen

Saborsky, Teresa Sculptor, Director

Highland Heights

Houghton, Barbara Jean Photographer, Video Artist
Knight, David J Gallery Director, Educator

Lexington

Carpenter, Dennis (Bones) Wilkinson Photographer, Educator
Close, Frank Stained Glass Artist, Sculptor
Feldman, Joel Benet Printmaker, Educator
Girard, (Charles) Jack Painter, Educator
Hamann, Marilyn D Educator, Painter
Henrich, Sarah E Museum Director
Jensen, Robert Educator, Administrator
Piwinski, Carl B Artist
Sandoval, Arturo Alonzo Educator, Weaver
Shannon, R Michael Painter
Singh, Carolyn Painter, Ceramist
Walsh-Piper, Kathy A Museum Director, Educator

Louisville

Baker, Jill Withrow Painter, Writer
Begley, J (John) Phillip Museum Director
Blake, Jane Salley Publisher, Editor
Bratcher, Collen Dale Painter
Chodkowski, Henry, Jr Painter, Educator
Cloudman, Ruth Howard Curator
Coates, Ann S Curator, Photographer
Covi, Dario A Historian
Hackett, Mickey Painter, Educator
Henry, John Raymond Sculptor
Morrin, Peter Patrick Administrator, Critic
O'Brien, Kevin James Museum Director
Rapp, M Yvonne Art Dealer, Lecturer
Whitesell, John D Printmaker

Murray

Head, Robert William Painter, Educator
Leys, Dale Daniel Educator, Draftsman
Speight, Jerry Brooks Educator, Writer
Sperath, Albert Frank Museum Director, Sculptor

Newport

Storm, Howard Painter, Sculptor

Owensboro

Hood, Mary Bryan Museum Director, Painter

Paducah

Beattie, Elise Meredith Painter, Educator

Princeton

Granstaff, William Boyd Painter, Illustrator

Prospect

Garner, Joyce (Craig) Painter

Richmond

Isaacs, Ron Painter, Sculptor
Smith, Gil R Administrator, Historian

Shelbyville

McCardwell, Michael Thomas Graphic Artist, Painter

Union

Akers, Gary Painter, Writer

Wickliffe

Frueh, Deborah K. (Debi) Painter, Sculptor

LOUISIANA

Alexandria

Tullos, Mark A, Jr   Administrator, Curator

Baton Rouge

Andry, Keith Anthony   Painter, Instructor
Betts, Judi Polivka   Painter, Instructor
Corso, Samuel (Joseph)   Stained Glass Artist, Painter
Cox, Richard William   Historian, Writer
Crespo, Michael Lowe   Writer, Painter
Goodell, Rosemary W   Painter, Educator
Hamblen, Karen A   Educator, Writer
Livesay, Thomas Andrew   Museum Director, Educator
Parker, Ron   Educator, Administrator
Price, Anne Kirkendall   Critic

Covington

Dautreuil, Linda Trappey   Painter
Dufour, Paul Arthur   Painter, Designer
Flattmann, Alan Raymond   Painter, Instructor

Lafayette

Caffery, Debbie Fleming   Photographer
Lafaye, Bryan F   Museum Director, Educator
Mhire, Herman P   Museum Director, Curator
Miller, Joan Vita   Museum Director, Administrator

Lake Charles

Fourcard, Inez Garey   Painter
Kelley, Heather Ryan   Painter, Draftsman

Mandeville

Clark, Emery Ann   Painter, Environmental Artist

Metairie

Casselli, Henry Calvin, Jr   Painter
Young, Tom (Thomas) William   Painter, Photographer

New Iberia

Harrington, Chestee Marie   Painter, Sculptor, Printmaker

New Orleans

Allen, Jere Hardy   Painter, Educator
Amoss, Berthe   Illustrator, Painter
Bishop, Jacqueline K   Painter
Bourgeois, Douglas   Painter
Brumfield, William Craft   Photographer, Writer
Bullard, Edgar John, III   Museum Director
Cameron, Dan   Curator
Casellas, Joachim   Painter, Director
Derby, Mark   Ceramist, Instructor
Drummer, William Richard   Gallery Director
Dunlop, Anne   Administrator
Emery, Lin   Kinetic Artist, Sculptor
Fagaly, William Arthur   Curator, Historian
Glasgow, Vaughn Leslie   Curator, Historian
Harris, Ronna S   Painter, Educator
Hayes, Cheryl   Administrator, Educator
Kern, Arthur (Edward)   Educator, Sculptor
Koss, Gene H   Sculptor, Educator
Lamantia, James   Architect, Painter
Lucas, Charlie   Painter, Sculptor
Maklansky, Steven V   Curator
Muniot, Barbara King   Collector
Reddix, Roscoe Chester   Painter, Educator
Reese, Thomas Ford   Historian, Administrator
Simons, Dona   Painter, Video Artist
Sweet, Steve (Steven) Mark   Collage Artist, Graphic Artist
Tague, Dan   Photographer, Conceptual Artist
Taylor, Susan M   Museum Director
Trivigno, Pat   Painter, Educator
Whiteman, Edward Russell   Painter

Ruston

Dablow, Dean Clint   Photographer, Educator
Donehoo, Jonathan   Administrator, Educator
Walton, M Douglas   Painter, Instructor

Shreveport

Allen, Bruce Wayne   Educator, Sculptor

Slidell

Boyd, Blake   Painter, Installation Sculptor
Willis, Jane B(roome)   Graphic Artist, Painter

Youngsville

Savoy, Chyrl Lenore   Sculptor, Educator

MAINE

Belfast

Mays, Victor   Painter, Illustrator
Squadra, John   Painter, Restorer

Blue Hill

Muir, Emily Lansingh   Painter, Sculptor

Boothbay Harbor

Mellor, Mark Adams   Painter, Gallery Director

Brunswick

Bearce, Jeana Dale   Painter, Printmaker
Davies, Harry Clayton   Painter, Photographer
Rakovan, Lawrence Francis   Printmaker, Painter
Scanga, Carrie   Installation Sculptor, Educator
Watson, Katharine Johnson   Historian, Consultant

Camden

Smith, Harry William   Illustrator, Jeweler

Castine

Mancuso, Leni   Painter, Graphic Artist, Collage Artist, Writer

Cumberland Foreside

Thompson, Lynn P   Painter, Photographer

Cushing

Caponigro, Paul   Photographer
Magee, Alan   Painter, Sculptor

Damariscotta

Thompson, Ernest Thorne, Jr   Silversmith, Painter

Deer Isle

Gilchrist, E. Brenda   Writer, Editor

East Boothbay

Plummer, Carlton B   Painter, Art Educator

Falmouth

Kellar, Jeff   Sculptor

Freeport

Knock, Sarah   Painter

Friendship

Cady, Samuel Lincoln   Painter, Instructor

Georgetown

Palazzolo, Carl   Painter

Gorham

Franklin, Patt   Painter, Sculptor

Hollis Center

Hewitt, Duncan Adams   Sculptor, Educator

Kittery

Cutler, Bess   Art Dealer
Sauter, Gail E   Painter

Lewiston

Bessire, Mark HC   Museum Director
Isaacson, Philip Marshal   Critic, Writer

Lincolnville

Zopp, Dudley   Painter, Installation Artist

Monhegan

Chappell, Kate Cheney   Printmaker, Painter

New Harbor

Lyford, Cabot   Sculptor, Painter

Northport

Wolfe, James   Sculptor

Ogunquit

Culver, Michael L   Painter, Curator

Orono

Lewis, Michael H   Painter, Educator

Port Clyde

Lewis, Nat Brush   Painter, Instructor

Portland

Douglas, Edwin Perry   Painter, Instructor
DuBack, Charles S   Painter, Printmaker
Elowitch, Annette   Dealer
Holverson, John   Curator, Museum Director, Art Dealer
O'Gorman, James Francis   Lecturer, Writer
O'Leary, Daniel   Administrator
Tuski, Donald   Administrator, Educator
Ubans, Juris K   Painter, Educator
Ventimiglia, John Thomas   Sculptor, Educator

Readfield

Péladeau, Marius Beaudoin   Writer, Museum Director

Rockland

Brownawell, Christopher J   Museum Director
Crosman, Christopher Byron   Museum Director, Writer
Fasoldt, Sarah Lowry   Administrator, Curator
Larsen, Susan C   Curator, Historian

Rockport

Altschul, Charles   Administrator

Round Pond

MacDougall, Peter Steven   Artist, Sculptor

Saint George

Pearlman, George L   Ceramist

Searsport

Barnes, Robert M   Painter, Educator

Solon

Shahn, Abby   Painter

South Berwick

Hardy, (Clarion) Dewitt   Painter, Instructor, Printmakers

Southwest Harbor

Steel, Philip S   Painter, Instructor

Steuben

Haroutunian, Joseph Halsey   Painter

Trevett

Bettinson, Brenda   Painter, Printmaker

Truro

Craig, Nancy Ellen   Painter

Union

Sublett, Carl Cecil   Painter

Waterville

Simon, David L   Historian, Educator

York

Davison, Nancy R   Printmaker
Smart, Mary-Leigh   Consultant, Patron

MARYLAND

Annapolis

Alderdice, Cynthia Lou   Painter, Jeweler
Chaplin, George Edwin   Painter, Educator
Gurlik, Philip John   Painter, Printmaker
Markman, Ronald   Painter

Baltimore

Carlberg, Norman Kenneth   Graphic Artist, Photographer
Ciscle, George   Curator, Educator
Cleaver, Richard Bruce   Sculptor
Cohen, Jean R   Ceramist, Collector
Ford, John Gilmore   Collector
Grabill, Vin (E Vincent, Jr)   Video Artist, Environmental Artist, Educator
Hammond, Leslie King   Art Historian, Writer
Hanson, JB   Sculptor, Weaver
Hofmann, Douglas William   Painter, Printmaker
Hoi, Samuel Chuen-Tsung   Educator, Administrator
Johnston, William Ralph   Administrator, Curator
Jones, James Edward   Painter, Printmaker
Karnes, Mark   Educator, Painter
Kelbaugh, Ross J   Collector, Historian
Kessler, Herbert Leon   Educator
Koch, Philip   Painter, Draftsman
Kornblatt, Barbara Rodbell   Dealer
Lippman, Judith   Gallery Director, Educator
Marciari-Alexander, Julia   Museum Director
Middleman, Raoul Fink   Painter
Printz, Bonnie Allen   Painter, Photographer
Richardson, Frank, Jr   Muralist

MARYLAND (cont)

Sangiamo, Albert Educator, Painter
Segal, Thomas H Art Dealer
Sheppard, Joseph Sherly Painter, Sculptor
Somerville, Romaine Stec Administrator
Sparks, John Edwin Printmaker, Instructor
Sturgeon, John Floyd Video Artist
Wasko-Flood, Sandra Jean Printmaker, Installation Sculptor
Wayne, Cynthia M Curator, Historian
West, Virginia M Fiber Artist, Writer
Wrigley, Rick Designer, Craftsman
Young, Barbara Photographer

Bethesda

Cable, Maxine Roth Sculptor
Fraser, Catriona Trafford Gallery Director, Photographer
Kan, Kit-Keung Painter
King, Elaine A Curator, Historian
Koenig, Elizabeth Sculptor
Maddox, Jerald Curtis Curator, Historian
Moir, Alfred Collector, Curator
Moser, Joann Curator, Historian
Plattner, Phyllis Painter
Siegel, Barbara Painter, Architect
Wolanin, Barbara A Historian, Curator

Bowie

Dasenbrock, Doris (Nancy) Voss Designer, Painter
Sweet, Francis Edward Painter
White, Amos, IV Ceramist, Photographer
Wynn, Gaines Clore Painter, Curator

Bozman

Cox, Ernest Lee Sculptor, Educator
Krestensen, Ann M Ceramist, Painter

Catonsville

Yager, David Photographer, Printmaker

Chevy Chase

Asher, Lila Oliver Printmaker, Painter
Curtis, Robert D Sculptor
Curtis, Verna P Curator
Fern, Alan Maxwell Museum Director
Freeman, Kathryn Painter, Instructor
Friend, Patricia M Painter
Greene, Louise Weaver Tapestry Artist, Librarian
Hutchison, Jane Campbell Educator, Historian
Kranking, Margaret Graham Painter, Lecturer
Levy, Phyllis Painter
Rand, Harry Historian, Educator
Shuler, Thomas H, Jr Photographer, Educator

Cockeysville

Bartlett, Christopher E Gallery Director, Illustrator

College Park

Carrico, Anita Librarian
Richardson, W C Painter, Educator
Thorpe, James George Designer, Illustrator
Withers, Josephine Historian, Writer

Columbia

Feldman, Aline M Printmaker, Painter
Kurlander, Honey W Painter, Instructor
Lok, Joan M Painter
Morgan, Roberta Marie Painter, Writer
Zuccarini, David Anthony Painter, Instructor

Crownsville

Keck, Jeanne Gentry Painter

Cumberland

Llewellyn, Robert Printmaker, Educator

Drayden

Egeli, Peter Even Painter, Illustrator

Easton

Plumb, James Douglas Painter, Educator

Edgewater

Egeli, Cedric Baldwin Painter, Instructor

Fort Washington

Grady, Ruby McLain Painter, Sculptor

Gaithersburg

Gigliotti, Joanne Marie Administrator, Painter
Huff, Laura Weaver Printmaker, Instructor

Gwynn Oak

Johnston, Barry Woods Sculptor

Hyattsville

Driskell, David Clyde Painter, Educator
Nevia, Joseph Shepperd Rogers Painter
Powell, Earl Alexander, III Museum Director, Historian

Joppa

Walters, Ernest Painter

Kensington

Murray, Richard Newton Museum Director, Curator
Winkler, Max-Karl Educator, Illustrator

Landover

Greenough, Sarah Curator
Hand, John Oliver Historian, Curator
Kelly, Franklin Wood Curator, Historian
Luchs, Alison Curator, Historian
Robison, Andrew Museum Curator, Writer

Lanham Seabrook

Chapin, Deborah Jane Painter, Instructor

Mount Airy

Swetcharnik, William Norton Painter, Sculptor

Phoenix

Meyerhoff, Robert E Collector

Potomac

Waletzky, Tsirl (Cecelia) Grobla Assemblage Artist, Stained Glass Artist

Rockville

Chen, Hsin-Hsi Graphic Artist
Desmidt, Thomas H Painter, Educator
Goldstein, Charles Barry Art Dealer, Appraiser
Kraus, (Ersilia) Zili Sculptor, Jeweler
Lippman, Mandy Consultant, Writer

Royal Oak

McNamara-Ringewald, Mary Ann Therese Painter, Illustrator
Saff, Donald Jay Painter, Educator

Salisbury

Gillie, Phyllis I Danielson Administrator, Tapestry Artist
Richards, David Patrick Painter, Writer

Sandy Spring

Murphy, Susan Avis Painter, Art Dealer

Savage

George, Sylvia James Painter, Illustrator

Shady Side

Nadolski, Stephanie Lucille Painter, Printmaker

Silver Spring

Allen, Henry Southworth Critic
Carter, Jerry Williams Sculptor, Architect, Video Artist, Mosaic Artist
Coleman, Floyd Willis Educator, Painter
Cusick, Nancy Taylor Collage Artist, Assemblage Artist
Daniels, David Robert Painter, Educator
Edelman, Ann Painter, Lecturer
Fink, Lois Marie Historian, Curator
Fitzgerald, Joe Painter, Printmaker
Folsom, Rose Calligrapher, Writer
Frederick, Helen C Printmaker, Conceptual Artist
Gresser, Seymour Gerald Sculptor, Writer
Lapinski, Tadeusz (A) Printmaker, Educator
Peiperl, Adam Video Artist, Kinetic Sculptor
Pruitt, Lynn Sculptor, Assemblage Artist
Ritchie, Charles Morton, Jr Painter, Printmaker
Silver, Rawley A Writer, Painter
Singletary, Michael James Painter
Slate, Joseph Frank Writer, Painter
Steel, Hillary Weaver, Designer
Wheeler, Janet B Assemblage Artist, Collage Artist,

Takoma Park

Jewell, Joyce Painter, Printmaker

Wheaton

Folsom, Fred Gorham, III Painter, Conservator, Writer

MASSACHUSETTS

Amherst

Barker, Elizabeth E Museum Director, Curator
Barnhill, Georgia Brady Curator, Historian
Campbell, Nancy B Printmaker
Clark, Carol Art Historian, Curator
Grant, Daniel Howard Writer, Critic
Hendricks, James (Powell) Sculptor, Painter
Liebling, Jerome Photographer, Filmmaker
Richardson, Trevor J Gallery Director, Curator
Sandweiss, Martha Ann Museum Director
Sznajderman, Marius S Printmaker, Painter
Townsend, John F Sculptor, Painter
Wardlaw, George Melvin Painter, Sculptor

Andover

Allen, Brian Museum Director
Harle, Matt Sculptor
Sullivan, David Francis Painter, Printmaker

Arlington

Ainslie, Sophia Painter, Installation Sculptor
Dahill, Thomas Henry, Jr Painter, Illustrator

Ashfield

Lund, Jane Painter

Ashland

Jorgensen, Bob (Robert A) Painter, Instructor

Barnstable

Lummus, Carol Travers Printmaker, Etching
Wylan, Barbara Painter

Beverly

Bartnick, Harry William Painter, Photographer, Educator
Bauer, Ruth Kruse Painter
Bodin, Kate Educator
Broudo, Joseph David Educator, Painter
Towner, Mark Andrew Administrator, Photographer

Boston

Amalfitano, Lelia Curator, Gallery Director
Barrett, Dawn Administrator, Educator
Beck, Ken Painter, Instructor
Bosworth, Barbara Photographer, Educator
Bourque, Louise Filmmaker
Bratton, Christopher Alan Administrator, Video Artist
Carlhian, Jean Paul architect
Chamberlain, David (Allen) Sculptor, Painter
Cheney, Liana De Girolami Art Historian, Curator
Crump, Walter Moore, Jr Printmaker, Painter
Dluhy, Deborah Haigh Educator, Administrator
Faulkner, Frank Painter
Fink, Alan Art Dealer
Fink, Joanna Elizabeth Art Dealer, Gallery Director
Fletcher, Stephen L Appraiser
Folman, Liza Printmaker, Painter
Fox, Judith Hoos Curator
Freeman, Robert Painter
Fresko, Colleene Appraiser
Gaither, Edmund B Museum Director, Historian
Ghikas, Panos George Painter, Educator
Grippe, Florence (Berg) Painter, Instructor
Harcus, Portia Gwen Dealer, Consultant
Harris, Conley Painter, Printmaker
Hawley, Anne Museum Director
Headley, David Allen Painter
Hills, Patricia Historian, Curator
Howlett, D(onald) Roger Art Dealer, Historian
James, Christopher P Photographer, Painter
Johnson, Edward C, III Collector
Juarez, Benjamin Educator
Keough, Jeffrey Director
Krakow, Barbara L Dealer
Liotta, Jeanne Film Director
Locke, Steve Painter
Malo, Teri (A) Painter, Printmaker
McCauley, Elizabeth Anne Historian, Writer
Medvedow, Jill Museum Director
Meister, Mark J Institute Director, Art Historian
Mergel, Jen Curator
Miaoulis, Ioannis Nikolaos Museum Director
Michaux, Ronald Robert Art Dealer, Gallery Director
Mineo, Jean Gallery Director
Moe, Kiel K Architect
Moses, Jennifer Educator, Administrator
Picker, Sebastián Painter
Pinckney, Stanley Painter, Tapestry Artist
Pucker, Bernard H Art Dealer
Rogers, Malcolm Austin Museum Director
Rolly, Ronald Joseph Art Dealer, Gallery Director
St George, William (M) Painter, Instructor

MASSACHUSETTS (cont)
Serenyi, Peter Historian, Administrator
Shackelford, George T M Curator
Shibata, Toshio Photographer
Simms, Jeannie Visual Artist
Simpson, Bennett Curator, Critic
Smedstad, Deborah Barlow Librarian
Sonnabend, Joan Art Dealer, Collector
Steczynski, John Myron Draftsman, Collector, Retired Educator
Sugimoto, Hiroshi photographer
Takayama, Martha Tepper Gallery Director, Publisher
Thomas, C David Printmaker
Trecker, Stanley Matthew Matthew Art College President
Wales, Kitty Sculptor
Warburg, Stephanie Wenner Painter, Instructor
Wheelwright, Joseph Storer Sculptor
Wilcox, Leslie Sculptor

Brewster
Stoltenberg, Donald Hugo Painter, Printmaker

Bridgewater
Hausrath, Joan W Printmaker, Weaver
Smalley, Stephen Francis Educator, Painter

Brookline
Ablow, Roselyn Karol (Roz Karol Ablow) Painter, Instructor
Barron, Thomas Painter
Kay, Reed Painter, Writer
Moss, Karen Canner Painter, Educator
Papo, Iso Painter
Sina, Alejandro Kinetic Artist

Brookline Village
Barron, Ros Painter, Video Artist

Cambridge
Ackerman, James S Historian, Educator
Bapst, Sarah Artist
Buchloh, Benjamin Historian, Critic
Callahan, Aileen Loughlin Painter, Muralist
Cohn, Marjorie B Curator, Historian
Denker, Susan A Historian, Critic
Dorfman, Elsa Photographer, Writer
Farver, Jane Curator, Museum Director
Fleming, Ronald Lee Designer, Administrator
Gibbons, Joe Filmmaker
Goldring, Elizabeth Writer, Environmental Artist
Harries, Mags (Margaret) L Sculptor, Educator
Jacob, Wendy Educator
Janowitz, Joel Painter
Jonas, Joan Video Artist, Conceptual Artist
Katayama, Toshihiro Painter, Designer
Kelsey, Robin E Educator
Lee, Barbara Collector
Lee, Jae Rhim Environmental Artist, Designer
Marran, Elizabeth Painter, Educator
McKie, Todd Stoddard Painter
Mitchnick, Nancy Painter, Educator
Molesworth, Helen Curator
Norfleet, Barbara Pugh Curator, Educator
Ranalli, Daniel Artist, Educator
Reimann, William P Sculptor, Educator
Ribas, Joao Curator, Educator
Rosenfield, John M Educator, Curator
Rosenthal, Donald A Historian, Critic
Scher, Julia Conceptual Artist, Video Artist
Slive, Seymour Historian, Museum Director
Trachtman, Arnold S Painter
Vevers, Tabitha Painter
Wechsler, Judith Glatzer Art Historian, Filmmaker
Zane, Joe Sculptor
Zerner, Henri Thomas Historian, Curator

Canton
Kaiser, Diane Collage Artist, Photographer
Youkeles, Anne Painter, Printmaker

Carlisle
Amenoff, Gregory Painter
Nielsen, Nina I M Dealer

Charlestown
Kelley, Donald Castell Gallery Director

Chatham
O'Connell, Ann Brown Printmaker, Collector
Reid, Charles Clark Writer, Painter

Chestnut Hill
Netzer, Nancy Museum Director, Educator
Shepard, Lewis Albert Dealer, Historian

Concord
Awalt, Elizabeth Grace Painter
Ihara, Michio Sculptor
MacNeill, Frederick Douglas Painter
Nick, George Painter, Educator

Cotuit
Hemmerdinger, William John, III Painter, Critic

Dartmouth
Anderson, Robert Alexander Painter, Illustrator
McCoy, T Frank Painter, Educator
Miraglia, Anthony J Educator, Painter
Tió, Adrian R Educator, Administrator
Vena, Dante Educator, Printmaker
Wisneski, Kurt Printmaker

Dennis
Harper, Gregory Franklin Director, Curator
Hunter, Elizabeth Ives-Valsam Museum Director

East Falmouth
Lincoln, Jane Lockwood Painter, Printmaker

East Longmeadow
Grigely, Joseph Installation Sculptor

Easthampton
Teichman, Mary Melinda Printmaker, Calligrapher

Edgartown
Furino, Nancy V Painter

Fitchburg
Timms, Peter Rowland Museum Director

Florence
Ravett, Abraham Filmmaker, Photographer

Framingham
Evans, Bob Painter, Photographer
Lipton, Leah Historian, Curator

Gloucester
Crane, Bonnie Loyd Private Dealer, Appraiser
Crowley, Charles A Craftsman
Movalli, Charles Joseph Painter, Writer
Pettibone, John Wolcott Curator, Administrator
Swigart, Lynn S Photographer

Great Barrington
Agar, Eunice Jane Painter, Writer
Filmus, Michael Roy Painter
Filmus, Stephen I Painter
Yanoff, Arthur (Samuel) Painter

Greenfield
Anthony, Amy Ellen Craftsman, Jeweler

Hadley
Edelman, Rita Painter
Norton, Paul Foote Historian, Educator
Wilda, Steven A Painter, Filmmaker

Harwich
Steward, Aleta Rossi Painter

Haydenville
Rupp, Sheron Photographer

Hingham
Dunn, Roger Terry Historian
Giovanni Painter, Printmaker
Pierce, Patricia Jobe Art Dealer, Historian
Rose, Samuel Painter, Muralist

Holliston
Harrington, William Charles Sculptor

Hyannis
Devine, Nancy Painter

Hyannis Port
Barber, Sam Painter, Sculptor

Hyde Park
Pinardi, Enrico Vittorio Sculptor, Painter

Jamaica Plain
Apesos, Anthony Painter, Critic
Cantor, Mira Painter, Draftsman
Wise, Kelly Photographer, Critic

Lee
Arnold, Gloria Malcolm Painter, Instructor

Lenox
Ginzel, Roland Painter, Printmaker
Walker, William Bond Painter, Librarian

Lexington
Berman, Vivian Printmaker, Educator
Havelock, Christine Mitchell Historian, Educator
Janney, Christopher Draper Environmental Artist, Designer
Rieber, Ruth B Printmaker, Painter
Wolpert, Etta Painter, Printmaker

Lincoln
Kois, Dennis Museum Director
Kumler, Kipton (Cornelius) Photographer, Lecturer
Master-Karnik, Paul Museum Director, Critic
Parks, Addison Painter, Sculptor

Lowell
Edmonds, Tom Museum Director, Painter
Faudie, Fred Painter, Illustrator

Ludlow
Stebbins, Theodore Ellis, Jr Historian, Administrator

Lynn
Fioravanti, Jeffrey Paul artist

Marblehead
Seamans, Beverly Benson Sculptor
Taylor, Robert Critic, Writer

Marion
Bidstrup, Wendy administrator

Marshfield
Greenamyer, George Mossman Sculptor, Educator

Mashpee
Searle, William Ross Painter

Mattapoisett
Mazer, Mike Painter, Artist

Medford
Raguin, Virginia C Historian, Consultant

Melrose
Hahn, Charles Sculptor

Millis
D'Onofrio, Bernard Michael Glass Blower, Sculptor

Milton
Jans, Candace Painter, Printmaker

Montague
Coughlin, Jack Printmaker, Sculptor

Nantucket
Cocker, Barbara Joan Painter, Gallery Director
Harris, Lily Marjorie Art Dealer, Administrator

Natick
Abany, Albert Charles Painter, Printmaker
Geller, Esther Geller Shapero Painter, Printmaker

Needham
Branfman, Steven Ceramist, Instructor
Gribin, Liz Painter, Printmaker

Newton
Baratz, Robin Painter
Hurwitz, Sidney J Painter, Printmaker
Korzenik, Diana Historian, Writer
MacDonald, Bruce K Artist, Historian
Maxwell, Jane Hoffman Artist
Raiselis, Richard Painter, Educator
Schon, Nancy Quint Sculptor

Newtonville
Polonsky, Arthur Painter, Educator

North Adams
Demartis, James J Painter
Graving, Brandon Printmaker
Thompson, Joseph C Museum Director

MASSACHUSETTS (cont)

North Brookfield
Neal, (Minor) Avon Writer, Publisher
Parker, Ann (Ann Parker Neal) Photographer, Writer

North Dartmouth
Lindenberg, Mary K Painter, Instructor
Taylor, Michael D Historian

Northampton
Fabing, Suzannah J Director
Gibson, John Stuart Painter, Printmaker
Kopf, Silas Craftsman
Meyersohn, Elizabeth Painter, Educator
Nettler, Lydia Kann Painter
Nicoll, Jessica F Curator
Nigrosh, Leon Isaac Ceramist, Writer
Ritz, Lorna J Painter, Sculptor
Stubbs, Lu Sculptor
Wessel, Fred W Painter, Printmaker

Orleans
Minear, Beth Weaver, Tapestry Artist

Osterville
Bowman, George Leo Painter

Pelham
Cohen, Michael S Ceramist, Photographer
Kindahl, Connie Weaver, Craftsman

Pittsfield
Adams, Shelby Lee Photographer
O'Connell, Daniel Moylan Muralist, Administrator
Patti, Tom Sculptor

Plainville
Dverin, Anatoly Painter

Provincetown
Barooshian, Martin Painter, Printmaker
Collins, Larry Richard Painter, Photographer
de Groot, Pat Painter
Evaul, William H, Jr Painter, Printmaker, Curator
Fabbris, Vico Painter, Environmental Artist
Hutchinson, Peter Arthur Conceptual Artist, Environmental Artist
Maynard, William Painter, Educator
McCarthy, Christine M Director
Walker, Berta Art Dealer

Quincy
Wilson, Blenda Jacqueline Patron

Rehoboth
Carpenter, Joseph Allan Graphic Artist, Cartoonist

Rockport
Bissell, Phil Cartoonist, Illustrator
Colao, Rudolph Painter
Martin, Roger Painter, Writer
Morrell, Wayne (Beam) Painter
Nicholas, Thomas Andrew Painter, Gallery Owner
Ramsey, Dorothy J Painter, Writer
Schlemm, Betty Lou Painter, Instructor
Turner, Bruce Backman Painter
Whitcomb, Kay Enamelist, Muralist
White, Susanne E. Painter

Sagamore Beach
Corn, Wanda M Historian, Educator

Salem
Corrigan, Karina Curator
Hartigan, Lynda Roscoe Curator, Historian
Monroe, Dan L Museum Director
Prodger, Phillip Curator, Historian
Smith, Trevor Curator

Scituate
Beale, Arthur C Filmmaker, Consultant

Seekonk
Backes, Joan Painter, Artist
Klitzke, Theodore Elmer Educator, Historian

Sharon
Avakian, John Printmaker, Instructor

Shelburne Falls
Simpson, Josh (Josiah) J L Simpson Glass Blower

Somerville
Campbell, David Paul Painter, Instructor
Cooper, Mark F Sculptor, Collage Artist
Gabin, George Joseph Painter, Instructor
Halevi, Marcus Photographer
Sandman, Jo Photographer, Conceptual Artist
Slosburg-Ackerman, Jill Sculptor, Jeweler
Valincius, Irene Painter, Printmaker
Yu, Shan Artist

South Chatham
Quidley, Peter Taylor Painter, Photographer

South Egremont
Parker, June Painter

South Hadley
Doezema, Marianne Museum Director, Historian
Herbert, Robert L Historian, Educator
Hutt, Lee Sculptor, Photographer

Springfield
Haskell, Heather Director
McCurdy, Michael Charles Illustrator, Writer

Stockbridge
Norton-Moffatt, Laurie Museum Director

Stoneham
Cleave, Marcie Van Museum Director

Sudbury
Nyman, Georgianna Beatrice Painter
Zauft, Richard Administrator, Photographer

Sunderland
Kamys, Walter Painter, Educator

Swansea
Caswell, Sally (Caswell-Linhares) Painter, Printmaker

Tewksbury
Kaufman, Mico Sculptor

Truro
Cicero, Carmen Louis Painter, Educator
Dunigan, Breon Nina Sculptor
Johnson, Joyce Writer, Sculptor
Peters, Jim (James) Stephen Painter, Sculptor

Vineyard Haven
Bramhall, Kib Painter

Walpole
Hunter, Robert Douglas Painter, Instructor

Waltham
Allara, Pamela Edwards Educator
Bedford, Christopher Curator
Bohlen, Nina (Celestine Eustis Bohlen) Painter, Draftsman, Prints
Campbell, Graham B Painter
Edminston, Scott Director, Educator
Hodes, Suzanne Painter, Printmaker

Watertown
Mandel, Mike Photographer, Artist
Schwalb, Susan Draftsman, Painter
Weiler, Joseph Flack Photographer, Writer

Wellesley
Fineberg, Gerald S Collector
Moser, Barry Graphic Artist, Printmaker
Perkinson, Roy L Conservator, Historian
Rayen, James Wilson Painter, Educator

Wellesley Hills
Fischman, Lisa Curator
Law, Jan Painter, Art Dealer

Wellfleet
Grillo, John Painter, Printmaker
Yenawine, Philip Educator

Wenham
Wingate, George B Painter

West Brookfield
Higgins, Brian Alton Painter, Gallery Director

West Hyannisport
Lynch-Nakache, Margaret Painter, Sculptor

West Roxbury
Altmann, Henry S Painter, Educator
Driscoll, Edgar Joseph, Jr Critic
Sorokin, Maxine Ann Painter, Educator

West Stockbridge
Ripps, Rodney Painter

Westfield
Wise, Gerald Lee Graphic Artist, Printmaker

Weston
Torf, Lois Beurman Collector, Publisher

Westport Point
Sexton, Janice Louise Painter, Sculptor

Westwood
Fairbanks, Jonathan Leo Curator, Painter

Whately
Cumming, Robert H Artist, Photographer

Williamstown
Burger, Gary C Museum Director
Conforti, Michael Peter Museum Director, Historian
Glier, Mike Draftsman, Painter
Johnson, Eugene Joseph Historian
Mathews, Nancy Mowll Historian, Curator

Winchester
Fitch, Blake Museum Director, Photographer, Curator
Lee, Mack Art Dealer
Neuman, Robert S Painter

Worcester
Bailey, Gauvin Alexander Historian, Educator
Hovsepian, Leon Painter, Designer
Priest, Terri Khoury Painter
Waschek, Matthias Museum Director
Welu, James A Museum Director

Yarmouth Port
Hitch, Jean Leason Painter

MICHIGAN

Allen Park
Mandziuk, Michael Dennis Computer Artist

Allendale
McGee, J David Director, Educator

Alma
Parks, Carrie Anne Sculptor, Educator
Rozier, Robert L Painter

Alpena
Bodem, Dennis Richard Consultant

Ann Arbor
Blakely, Colin photographer, administrator
Busard, Roberta Ann Painter, Sculptor
Cassara, Frank Painter, Printmaker
Cervenka, Barbara Educator, Painter
Eisenberg, Marvin Educator, Historian
Forsyth, Ilene H(aering) Educator, Historian
Glasser, Norma Penchansky Sculptor
Gloeckner, Phoebe Louise Cartoonist, Illustrator
Guastella, C Dennis Painter, Instructor
Kirkpatrick, Diane Historian
Kumao, Heidi Elizabeth Photographer, Kinetic Artist
Kusnerz, Peggy Ann F Editor, Historian
Leonard, Joanne Photographer, Educator
Lewis, William Arthur Painter, Educator
Nadarajan, Gunalan Curator, Educator, Administrator
Pijanowski, Eugene M Educator, Craftsman
Sears, Elizabeth L Educator, Historian
Smith, Sherri Weaver, Educator
Spencer, Deirdre Diane Librarian
Spink, Walter M Educator, Administrator
Spitler, Clare Blackford Art Dealer
Stephenson, John H Sculptor, Ceramist
Stephenson, Susanne G Ceramist, Educator
Stewart, Paul LeRoy Printmaker, Educator

Berrien Center
Constantine, Greg John Painter, Educator

MINNESOTA (cont)
Verostko, Roman Joseph Painter, Historian
Viso, Olga Museum Director
Weisberg, Gabriel P Historian, Educator

Minnetonka
Morin, Thomas Edward Sculptor, Educator
Sussman, Bonnie Kaufman Dealer, Consultant

Moorhead
Szeitz, P Richard Educator, Sculptor

Morris
Nellis, Jennifred Gene Sculptor

Nevis
Laske, Lyle F Sculptor, Educator

Northfield
Arneson, Wendell H Painter
Somers, Frederick D(uane) Painter, Instructor

Park Rapids
Shilson, Wayne Stuart Painter, Illustrator

Rochester
Onofrio, Judy Sculptor

Saint Cloud
Hendershot, J L Printmaker, Educator
Petheo, Bela Francis Painter, Printmaker

Saint Joseph
Gordin, Misha Photographer, Video Artist

Saint Paul
Cummings, Mary T Administrator, Consultant
Czarniecki, M J, III Museum Director, Consultant
Gorski, Richard Kenny Educator, Graphic Artist
Jolly, Eric J Museum Administrator
Kielkopf, James Robert Painter
Koplos, Janet Critic, Editor
Lasansky, Leonardo Draftsman, Printmaker
Michels, Eileen Manning Educator, Art Historian
Olson, Bettye Johnson Painter, Educator, Lecturer
Palmgren, Donald Gene Painter, Photographer
Rich, David Painter, Educator
Sears, Stanton Gray Painter, Sculptor
Shambroom, Paul D Photographer
Soth, Alec Photographer

Saint Peter
Basset, Gene Political Cartoonist

Stillwater
Steinworth, Skip (William) Eugene, Jr Graphic Artist

White Bear Lake
Larkin, John E, Jr MD Collector, Patron

Winona
Curmano, Billy X Conceptual Artist, Sculptor

MISSISSIPPI

Belzoni
Halbrook, Rita Robertshaw Papermaker, Painter

Carriere
Stanton, Sylvia Doucet Painter

Cleveland
Britt, Sam Glenn Educator, Painter
Koehler, Ronald Gene Sculptor

Clinton
Gore, Samuel Marshall Painter, Sculptor
Miley, Randolph Benton Educator, Administrator, Papermaking

Collinsville
Marshall, John Painter, Instructor

Columbus
Ambrose, Charles Edward Painter, Educator
Nawrocki, Thomas Dennis Printmaker, Educator
Summer, (Emily) Eugenia Painter

Courtland
Lindgren, Carl Edwin Photographer, Historian

Diamondhead
Bannister, Pati (Patricia) Brown Bannister Painter, Sculptor

Gautier
Shepard, Steven L Painter

Hattiesburg
House, John C Educator, Administrator

Hernando
Yates, Marvin Painter, Instructor

Jackson
Bradley, Betsy Museum Director
Cook, Stephen D Printmaker, Draftsman
Whittington, Jon Hammon Educator, Painter

Liberty
Lewis, Douglas Historian, Consultant

Natchez
Golden, Rolland Harve Painter, Printmaker

Oxford
Dale, Ron G Ceramist, Sculptor
Turnbull, Lucy Museum Director, Educator

Starkville
Scucchi, Robie (Peter), Jr Educator, Painter

Tupelo
Francis, Jean Thickens Assemblage Artist, Painter

University
Rieth, Sheri Fleck Educator, Administrator

MISSOURI

Bolivar
Douglas, Tom Howard Painter, Sculptor

Cape Girardeau
Holladay, Harlan H Historian, Painter
Parker, James Varner Designer

Charleston
Robbins, Joan Nash Painter, Collage Artist

Chesterfield
Beckner, Joy Kroeger Sculptor
Kagan, Andrew Aaron Historian, Consultant

Columbia
Boyer, Nathan P Video Artist, Educator
Cameron, Brooke Bulovsky Educator, Printmaker
Jackson, Paul C Painter
Larson, Sidney Educator, Muralist
Peckham, Nicholas Architect, Educator
Platt, Melvin Administrator
Revington Burdick, Elizabeth Collector
Rugolo, Lawrence Printmaker, Educator
Stack, Frank Huntington Painter, Printmaker
Williams, Melissa Art Dealer

Jackson
Riley, Sarah A Painter, Printmaker

Joplin
Christensen, Val Alan Printmaker, Gallery Director

Kansas City
Bennett, Philomene Dosek Painter, Ceramist
Bloch, Henry Wollman Collector
Cadieux, Michael Eugene Educator, Painter
Crist, William Gary Visual Artist, Educator
Davis, Keith F Curator, Historian
Dikeman, Deanna Photographer
Eaton, Tom Cartoonist, Writer
Ehrlich, George Historian
Eickhorst, William Sigurd Educator, Curator
Fowle, Geraldine Elizabeth Historian
Lawrence, Susan Art Dealer, Consultant
Lighton, Linda Sculptor
O'Brien, Barbara Museum Director
Stack, Michael T Painter, Sculptor
Thorson, Alice R Editor, Critic
Weidman, Jeffrey Librarian, Historian
Widmer, Gwen Ellen Photographer, Educator
Younger, Dan Forrest Painter, Printmaker
Zugazagoitia, Julian Museum Director

Kirksville
Jorgenson, Dale Alfred Educator, Administrator

Labadie
Haynes, R (Richard) Thomas Painter, Illustrator

Lamar
Bowling, Gary Robert Painter

Maryville
Hageman, Charles Lee Educator, Jeweler

Osage Beach
Orr, Joseph Charles Painter

Saint Joseph
Oldman, Terry L Museum Director
Spencer, Mark J Museum Director, Curator

Saint Louis
Benjamin, Brent R Museum Director
Bohan, Ruth L Educator, Historian
Bryant, Donald L, Jr Collector
Byron, Michael Painter
Childs, Elizabeth Catharine Art Historian, Educator
Crane, Michael Patrick Museum Director, Curator
Eastman, Michael Douglas Photographer
Engelhardt, Thomas Alexander Editorial Cartoonist
Fondaw, Ron Sculptor
Glines, Karen Writer
Grannon, Katy Photographer
Greenberg, Ronald K Dealer, Collector
Huberman, Anthony Curator
Hunt, Michael Director
Kennon, Arthur Bruce Educator, Editor
Knode, Marilu Curator, Administrator
Kornblum, Myrtle Painter, Printmaker
Magel, Catharine Anne Sculptor, Painter
Newman-Rice, Nancy Painter, Critic
Olynyk, Patricia J Painter, Educator
Patton, Tom Photographer, Curator
Schultz, Saunders Sculptor
Sigala, Stephanie Childs Librarian, Educator
Smith, James Michael Painter, Assemblage Artist
Smith, Robert (Bob) Charles Designer, Painter
Spector, Buzz (Franklin Mac Spector) Conceptual Artist, Critic
Teczar, Steven W Educator, Painter
Vescolani, Bert Museum Administrator
Wallace, William E Educator, Historian
Zonia, Dhimitri Painter, Graphic Artist, Sculptor

Sedalia
Freed, Douglass Lynn Painter, Retired Museum Director

Springfield
Armstrong, Bill Howard Painter, Educator
Murphy, Dudley C Educator, Graphic Designer
Simmons, John Herbert Educator, Historian
Thompson, Wade S Painter, Educator
Warren, Jacqueline Louise Painter, Educator

Webster Groves
Boccia, Edward Eugene Painter, Writer

Wildwood
Addison, Byron Kent Painter, Educator

MONTANA

Arlee
Boussard, Dana Painter, Stained Glass Artist

Bigfork
Fellows, Fred Painter, Sculptor

Billings
Forbes, Donna Marie Museum Director
Fritz, Charles John Painter
Morrison, Robert Clifton Painter, Calligrapher
Peterson, Robyn G Curator, Director
Steele, Benjamin Charles Painter, Educator
Whitson, Peter Whitson Warren Collage Artist, Educator

Bozeman
Anacker, John William Gallery Director, Painter
Butterfield, Deborah Kay Sculptor
Helzer, Richard Brian Metalsmith, Sculptor
Judge, Vaughan Educator, Administrator, Photographer
Volkersz, Willem Sculptor, Painter

NEW JERSEY (cont)

Bordentown
Barker, Al C   Painter, Printmaker

Brick
Riccio, Louis Nicholas   Painter, Curator
Schaeffer, S(tanley) Allyn   Painter, Instructor, Author

Bridgewater
Glesmann, Sylvia Maria   Painter

Brielle
Punia, Constance Edith   Painter

Burlington
Knight, William   Sculptor, Painter

Caldwell
Mueller, OP, (Sister) Gerardine   Calligrapher, Stained Glass Artist
Palombo, Lisa   Painter

Califon
Reilly, John Joseph   Painter, Instructor

Camden
Dowell, John E, Jr   Educator, Printmaker
Steel, Virginia Oberlin   Gallery Director, Curator

Cherry Hill
Appelson, Herbert J   Educator, Printmaker
Tan, LiQin   Educator
Toogood, James S   Painter, Instructor

Chester
Duerwald, Carol   Painter, Illustrator

Cliffside Park
LaMarca, Howard J   Designer, Educator

Clifton
Dinc, Alev Necile   Painter, Designer
Kanter, Lorna J   Painter, Printmaker
Kostecka, Gloria   Painter

Closter
Zakin, Mikhail   Sculptor, Educator

Colts Neck
Rogers, Muriel I   Painter, Instructor

Cranford
Gatto, Rose Marie   Painter
Lowe, Joe Hing   Painter

Denville
Rafferty, Joanne Miller   Painter, Collage Artist

Dover
Kearns, James Joseph   Sculptor, Painter

East Brunswick
Bloom, Donald S   Painter, Illustrator

East Windsor
Sullivan, Anne Dorothy Hevner   Painter, Printmaker

Eatontown
Preede, Nydia   Painter, Illustrator

Edison
Phillips, Robert J   Filmmaker, Photographer
Robinson, Donald Warren   Painter, Instructor
Yang, Mimi   Painter

Egg Harbor City
Ahlsted, David R   Painter
Smith, Rae   Painter

Egg Harbor Township
Robbins, Hulda D   Painter, Printmaker

Emerson
Salomon, Johanna   Painter, Instructor

Englewood
Bremer, Marlene   Painter, Sculptor
Grom, Bogdan   Sculptor, Painter
Ringgold, Faith   Painter, Sculptor

Englewood Cliffs
Liao, Shiou-Ping   Painter, Printmaker

Ewing
Brooks, Wendell T   Printmaker, Educator

Fair Haven
Quon, Michael George   Designer, Painter

Fairfield
de Smet, Lorraine   Painter

Far Hills
Folk, Tom C   Art Dealer, Historian

Farmingdale
Anastasia, Susanna   Painter, Instructor

Flemington
Viera, Charles David   Educator, Painter
Waksberg, Nomi   Painter, Photographer

Florham Park
Debarry, Christina   Painter

Fort Lee
Morenon, Elise   Painter, Instructor

Franklin Lakes
Ghahary, Zia Edin   Consultant, Art Historian
Janjigian, Lucy Elizabeth   Painter, Muralist
Reinkraut, Ellen Susan   Painter

Freehold
Kunz, Sandra Thurber   Painter

Gillette
Merkl, Elissa Frances   Printmaker, Painter

Glassboro
Wasserman, Burton   Painter, Educator

Glen Ridge
Konopka, Joseph   Painter

Haworth
Bernstein, Saralinda   Art Dealer, Historian

Highland Lakes
Ross, Joan M   Painter, Instructor

Highland Park
Kolodzei, Natalia   Administrator, Curator
Puniello, Françoise Sara   Librarian

Highlands
Egan, Laury Agnes   Photographer, Instructor

Hightstown
Rivera, Frank   Painter

Hoboken
Rose, Roslyn   Digital Photographer, Collage Artist

Hopewell
Hein, John   Craftsman

Howell
Culver, Margaret Victoria   Administrator, Artist

Island Heights
Thorston, Ludlow   Painter

Jersey City
Besante, John L, Jr   Painter
Bruso, Arthur   Curator, Sculptor
Cummings, David William   Painter
Gluck, Heidi   Painter, Educator
Gurevich, Grigory   Sculptor, Painter, Graphic artist, Printmaker, Inventor
Harrison, Tony   Painter, Educator
Jones, Ben   Painter, Sculptor
Lay, Patricia Anne   Sculptor
Mady, Beatrice M   Painter, Artist
Magnan, Oscar Gustav   Painter, Sculptor
McCarron, Paul   Art Dealer, Art Appraiser
Mount, Marshall Ward   Educator, Art Historian
Palaia, Franc (Dominic)   Photographer, Muralist
Rosenberg, Herb   Sculptor, Educator, Administrator
Russell, Robert S   Sculptor

Keyport
Graupe-Pillard, Grace   Painter, Photographer

Lakewood
Hutter, Jean M   Painter, Jeweler

Lambertville
Cusworth, Christyl   Painter, Conservator
Goodyear, John L   Sculptor, Painter

Lawrenceville
Naar, Harry I   Painter, Educator
Saretzky, Gary Daniel   Photographer, Historian

Leonia
Dickerson, Daniel Jay   Painter, Instructor
Thibault, Andre (Teabo)   Collagist

Little Falls
Cochran, Dorothy Parcells   Printmaker, Curator

Little Silver
Clark, Roberta Carter   Painter, Illustrator
Stach, Judy   Painter, Instructor

Long Branch
Migliaccio, Anthony J   Painter, Educator
Stamaty, Clara Gee Kastner   Painter

Madison
Henry, Sara Corrington   Historian, Critic
Pranger, Ben   Sculptor
Rodeiro, Jose Manuel   Painter, Muralist

Mahwah
Genute, Christine Termini   Painter, Sculptor
Peck, Judith   Sculptor, Writer

Manasquan
Collinson, Janice   Painter, Gallery Director

Maplewood
Vitali, Ubaldo   Conservator, Silversmith
Wint, Florence Edythe   Painter, Sculptor

Margate City
Sochynsky, Ilona   Painter, Muralist

Metuchen
Arbeiter, Joan   Artist, Educator
Stummer, Helen M   Photographer, Writer

Middletown
Wilson, June   Painter, Educator

Milford
Ciardiello, Joseph G   Illustrator

Millville
Gavin, Ellen A   Painter

Montclair
Bushnell, Kenneth Wayne   Painter
Chavooshian, Nora   Sculptor, Designer
Culbreth, Carl R   Sculptor
Kawecki, Jean Mary   Sculptor, Gallery Director
Pickett, Janet Taylor   Artist
Urbanelli, Lora S   Museum Director

Morganville
Dyshlov, Valeriy   Painter, Instructor

Morris Plains
Ferris, (Carlisle) Keith   Illustrator, Painter

Morristown
Harrison, Alice   Painter, Collage Artist
Klindt, Steven   Administrator

Mount Arlington
Grodsky, Sheila Taylor   Painter, Collage Artist

Neptune
Ventura, Anthony   Painter

Neshanic Station
Allen, E Douglas   Painter, Writer, Sculptor

New Brunswick
Brodsky, Judith Kapstein   Printmaker, Educator
Frazier, LaToya Ruby   Photographer, Curator
McHam, Sarah Blake Wilk   Historian, Educator
Nozkowski, Thomas   painter
Ortiz, Raphael Montanez   Conceptual Artist, Educator
Rusak, Halina R   Librarian, Painter
St Tamara   Painter, Printmaker
Stauffer, George B   Administrator, Educator

NEW MEXICO (cont)
Sbarge, Suzanne Director, Painter
Stark, Robert Painter, Photographer
Truby, Betsy Kirby Painter, Illustrator
Vega, Edward Sculptor, Educator
Volkin, Hilda Appel Sculptor
Walters, Billie Ceramist
White, Robert Rankin Historian, Writer
Wilmeth, Ernest, II Collage Artist, Potter

Angel Fire
Westlund, Harry E Publisher, Dealer

Anthony
Grissom, Freda Gill Painter, Goldsmith

Arroyo Hondo
Barsano, Ron (Ronald) James Painter, Sculptor
Davis, Ronald Painter, Printmaker

Belen
Chicago, Judy Painter, Sculptor

Bosque Farms
Stouffer, Daniel Henry, Jr Painter, Designer

Carlsbad
Johanningmeier, Robert Alan Painter, Writer

Carson
Ross, Jaime Graphic Artist, Painter

Cerrillos
Gilbert, Bill Educator, Ceramist
Parry, Eugenia Writer
Pedersen, Carolyn H Painter, Collage Artist

Corrales
Barry, Steve Sculptor
Conley, Zeb Bristol, Jr Collector, Gallery Director
Townsend, Storm D Sculptor, Instructor

Coyote
Johnson, Douglas Walter Painter, Ceramist, Publisher
Olsen Bergman, Ciel (Cheryl) Bowers Painter, Environmental Artist

Dona Ana
Smith, Jo-an Painter, Goldsmith

Farmington
Cogan, John D(ennis) Painter
Farm, Gerald E Painter, Sculptor
Mayhew, Timothy David Painter, Draftsman

Galisteo
Lippard, Lucy Rowland Writer

Gallup
Cattaneo, (Jacquelyn A) Kammerer Painter, Instructor

Guadalupita
Shaw, Donald Edward Sculptor, Painter

Hanover
Renner, Eric Painter, Photographer

La Luz
Kellar, Martha Robbins Painter, Instructor

Lamy
Housewright, Artemis Skevakis Jegart Painter, Sculptor

Las Cruces
Barello, Julia M Administrator, Educator
Boler, John Alfred Art Dealer, Collector
Chilton, Fred Painter
Coker, Carl David Painter, Educator, Sculptor
Fidler, Spencer D Printmaker
Guzevich-Sommers, Kreszenz (Cynthia) Painter, Instructor
Hutchins, Robin Art Dealer, Gallery Director
Ocepek, Lou (Louis) David Printmaker, Painter
Oliver, Julie Ford Painter, Instructor

Lincoln
Waterhouse, Russell Rutledge Painter, Illustrator

Mountainair
Jaffe, Ira S Educator, Critic

Pena Blanca
Fitch, Steve (Steven) Ralph Photographer, Instructor

Ranchos De Taos
Lerner, Alexandria Sandra Painter

Rio Rancho
Arnold, Jack Art Dealer, Publisher

Roswell
Dopp, Susan Marie Painter
Du Jardin, Gussie Painter, Printmaker
Peterson, Dorothy (Hawkins) Painter, Educator

Ruidoso
Snidow, Gordon E Painter, Sculptor

San Patricio
Rogers, Peter Wilfrid Painter, Writer

Sandia Park
Brody, J(acob) J (erome) Historian, Museologist
Perez-Zapata, Guilloume Painter, Publisher

Santa Fe
Adams, Phoebe Sculptor
Altermann, Tony Art Dealer
Arnett, Joe Anna Painter, Sculptor
Barger, M Susan Consultant, Conservator
Bass, David Loren Painter
Bauer, Betsy (Elizabeth) Painter, Printmaker
Beall, Karen Friedmann Curator, Writer
Berg, Tom Painter
Berry, Carolyn B Painter, Illustrator
Bol, Marsha C Museum Director, Historian
Bradbury-Reid, Ellen A Administrator, Educator
Brady, Robert D Sculptor
Brooks, Jan Sculptor, Lecturer
Brycelea, Clifford Painter, Illustrator
Burgess, Joseph James, Jr Painter, Educator
Clark, Garth Reginald Dealer, Historian
Clift, William Brooks Photographer
Coffin, J Douglas Sculptor, Painter
Cook, Richard L Administrator, Sculptor
Coulter, Lane Silversmith, Historian
Dailey, Chuck (Charles) Andrew Museologist, Painter
Deaderick, Joseph Painter, Educator
De Amaral, Olga Tapestry Artist
Dean, Nat Painter, Educator, Administrator
Dodds, Robert J, III Collector
Dominguez, Eddie Ceramist
Enyeart, James Lyle Historian, Director
Ettenberg, Franklin Joseph Painter, Printmaker
Evans, Dick Painter, Sculptor
Fincher, John H Painter, Assemblage Artist
Gandert, Miguel Adrian Photographer, Lecturer
Gildzen, Alex Writer, Collector
Hackett, Dwight Vernon Publisher, Director
Handell, Albert George Painter
Harrison, Jimmie Jeweler, Craftsman
Harroun, Dorothy Sumner Painter, Graphic Artist
Ice, Joyce Museum Director
Jean, Beverly Strong Painter, Art Dealer
Kawashima, Shigeo Bamboo Artist
Kelley, Ramon Painter
Kessler, Alan Painter, Sculptor
Kurtz, Richard Painter
Lamuniere, Carolyn Parker Painter
LaPlantz, David Jeweler, Sculptor
Laurence, Geoffrey F Painter
Lehman, Max Sculptor
Lomahaftewa, Linda Joyce Painter, Instructor
Lutz, Marjorie Brunhoff Painter, Sculptor
Mathias, Thelma Conceptual Artist, Sculptor
Miles, Sheila Lee Painter, Instructor
Moses, Forrest (Lee), Jr Painter, Printmaker
Nagakura, Kenichi Artist
Nelson, Signe Painter
Newberg, Deborah Painter, Printmaker
Niblett, Gary Lawrence Painter
Nieto, John W Painter, Sculptor
Orduno, Robert Daniel Painter, Sculptor
Palmer, Kate (Katharine) A Painter
Pena, Amado Maurilio, Jr Painter, Illustrator
Pletka, Paul Painter, Printmaker
Relkin, Michele Weston Painter, Instructor
Rivera, Elias J Painter
Romero, Megan H Painter, Dealer
Roybal, James Richard Sculptor, Painter
Ruthling, Ford Painter, Sculptor
Sauer, Jane Gottlieb Sculptor, Curator
Schenck, William Clinton Painter, Printmaker
Scott, Sam Painter
Shepherd, William Fritz Painter
Sky, Carol Veth Painter, Photographer
Sloan, Jeanette Pasin Painter, Printmaker
Smith, Linda Kyser Painter, Instructor
Smulka, Steve Painter
Stark, Ron Painter, Photographer
Steinhoff, Monika Painter, Printmaker
Stuart, Joseph Martin Painter, Museum Director
Swentzell, Roxanne Sculptor
Taylor, Maggie Photographer
Thomas, Jeremy Sculptor
Tichava, Nina Painter, Consultant
West, Jordan Painter
Wiggins, K Douglas Painter, Art Dealer
Youdelman, Nancy Sculptor

Silver City
McCray, Dorothy Westaby Painter, Printmaker

Taos
Bell, Larry Stuart Sculptor
Harmon, Barbara Sayre Painter, Book Artist
Harmon, Cliff Franklin Painter
Hensley, Jackson Morey Painter
Macpherson, Kevin Painter
Nes, Margaret Isabel Painter
Smith, Jack Richard Painter, Printmaker
Witt, David L Writer, Curator

Tesuque
Gagan, Jamie L. Painter, Printmaker
Haozous, Bob Sculptor

Tijeras
Sweet, Mary (French) Painter, Printmaker

NEW YORK

Accord
Arum, Barbara Sculptor
Massie, Lorna Printmaker
Sommer, Susan Painter, Printmaker

Afton
Schwartz, Aubrey E Printmaker, Sculptor

Albany
Marlowe, Willie Painter, Educator
Mayer, Edward Albert Sculptor, Educator
Miles, Christine M Museum Director, Administrator
Mooney, Michael J Painter, Assemblage Artist
Shankman, Gary Charles Painter, Educator

Alfred
Bellavance, Leslie Administrator, Educator
McConnell, Walter Ceramist

Alfred Station
Gill, John P Sculptor
Higby, (Donald) Wayne Painter, Sculptor

Altamont
Cowley, Edward P Painter, Educator
Frinta, Mojmir Svatopluk Art Historian, Educator

Amagansett
Durham, William Painter, Sculptor
Gussow, Sue Ferguson Painter, Educator
Strong-Cuevas, Elizabeth Sculptor, Kinetic Artist

Amenia
Hale, Nathan Cabot Sculptor, Writer, Painter

Ancram
Schweninger, Ann Rozzelle Illustrator
Sorman, Steven Painter, Printmaker

Ancramdale
Weinstein, Joyce Painter

Annandale On Hudson
Battle, Laura Painter

Ardsley
Lysun, Gregory Painter, Restorer

Ardsley On Hudson
Kipniss, Robert Painter, Printmaker

Astoria
Pellettieri, Michael Joseph Printmaker, Painter

Athens
Homitzky, Peter Painter

NEW YORK (cont)

Callicoon
Bastian, Linda Painter, Educator

Callicoon Center
Hilson, Douglas Painter, Educator
Kreznar, Richard J Painter, Sculptor

Cambria Heights
Brown, James Painter, Graphic Artist

Campbell Hall
Greenly, Colin Environmental Artist, Conceptual Artist

Canaan
Juarez, Roberto Painter

Catskill
Milbourn, Patrick D Painter, Illustrator, Portrait Painter

Cazenovia
Ridlon, James A Sculptor, Assemblage Artist
Wyckoff, Sylvia Spencer Educator, Painter

Chappaqua
Asoma, Tadashi Painter
Hecht, Irene Painter

Chatham
Andell, Nancy Painter
Bartlett, Barry Thomas Sculptor
Noyes, Sandy Photographer

Chautauqua
Kimes, Don Painter, Educator

Chestertown
Longhurst, Robert E Sculptor

Chestnut Ridge
Mesibov, Hugh Painter, Printmaker

Claverack
Schneier, Donna Frances Dealer

Clinton
Loy, John Sheridan Painter

Cold Spring
Marzollo, Claudio Sculptor
Murphy, Hass Sculptor, Draftsman

Corning
Dowler, David P Sculptor, Designer

Cortlandt Manor
Obrant, Susan Elizabeth Painter, Fiber Artist
Rosenberg, Marilyn R Visual Poet, Graphic Artist

Coxsackie
Morrill, Rowena Illustrator

Croton On Hudson
Pinkney, Jerry Illustrator
Wandel, Sharon Lee Sculptor, Painter

Cutchogue
Dank, Leonard D Illustrator, Consultant
Penney, Jacqueline Painter, Instructor

Delmar
Goodwin, Daniel Educator, Administrator, Photographer

Dix Hills
Fouladvand, Hengameh Painter, Critic

Dobbs Ferry
Eisner, Gail Leon Painter, Sculptor
Hart, Allen M Painter, Educator

East Amherst
Garver, Walter Raymond Painter, Writer
Reedy, Susan Painter, Collage Artist
Stoddard, Elizabeth Jane Painter

East Chatham
Egleston, Truman G Painter

East Elmhurst
Langer, Sandra Lois (Cassandra) Art Appraiser, Historian, Critic, Author
O'Connor, John Jerome Painter
Ruda, Edwin Painter

East Hampton
Appelhof, Ruth A Curator
Barons, Richard Irwin Museum Director, Historian
Bujese, Arlene Curator, Art Dealer
Chase, Louisa L Painter
Daskaloff, Gyorgy Painter
DeMartis, James Michael Sculptor
Gordon, Joy L Curator, Director
Hammond, Phyllis Baker Sculptor
Hoie, Claus Painter
Leiber, Gerson August Printmaker
Mim, Adrienne Claire Schwartz Sculptor, Painter
Roth, Frank Painter
Schlesinger, Christina Painter, Muralist
Weller, Paul Photographer, Painter
Zacharias, Athos Painter
Zucker, Murray Harvey Sculptor, Collage Artist

East Meadow
Herman, David H Painter

East Meredith
Wentworth, Janet Painter

East Northport
Cohen, George Michael Educator

East Norwich
Germano, Thomas Painter, Educator

East Quogue
Setlow, Neva C (Delihas) Sculptor, Painter

East Setauket
Remsen, John Painter, Consultant

Eastchester
Alfano, Angel Painter
Stern, Louise G Printmaker, Painter

Edmeston
Catania, Philip Painter, Sculptor

Ellenville
Berhang, Mattie Sculptor, Lecturer

Elmira
Macdonell, Cameron Painter, Muralist
VanDelinder, Debra L Digital Media Artist, Educator

Endicott
Kotasek, P Michael Painter, Lecturer

Far Rockaway
Grillo, Esther Angela Sculptor, Printmaker

Farmingdale
Gatto, Paul Anthony Painter, Instructor

Fillmore
Wenger, Bruce Edward Printmaker, Graphic Artist

Fishers Island
Menil, Georges & Lois de Patron, Collector

Fishkill
Schulz, Charlotte Draftsman, Educator

Flushing
Chang, Jason Painter
Clark, William W Historian
de Luise, Alexandra Curator, Librarian
Feng, Ying Painter, Photographer
Gonzalez, Tony photographer, educator, administrator
Hammerman, Pat Jo Painter, Printmaker
Kam, Mei K Painter, Instructor
Murrell, Carlton D Painter
Petrulis, Alan Joseph Printmaker, Photographer
Schneider, Janet M Museum Director, Painter
Vidal, Francisco Painter, Printmaker
Wimberley, Frank Walden Painter, Collage Artist
Young, LeeMei Painter

Fly Creek
Dusenbery, Walter Sculptor

Forest Hills
Ashvil-Bibi, Sigalit Painter
Baer, Norbert S Educator
Balka, Sigmund Ronell Gallery Director, Curator
Raviv, Ilana Painter, Printmaker

Franklin Square
Indiviglia, Salvatore Joseph Painter, Instructor

Fredonia
Booth, Robert Alan Sculptor

Freehold
Maltzman, Stanley Painter, Printmaker

Garden City
Fleming, Margaret Nielsen Graphic Artist, Illustrator
Mattick, Paul Educator, Critic
Myron, Robert Historian

Gardiner
Oshita, Kazuma Sculptor

Garnerville
Harvey, Dermot Kinetic Artist, Sculptor

Germantown
Drummond, Sally Hazelet Painter
Gladstone, M J Publisher
Saul, Peter Painter
Shahly, Jehan Painter

Glen Cove
Beckhard, Ellie (Eleanor) Painter, Photographer

Glen Head
Brown, Edith Rae Sculptor, Medalist, Painter
Newmark, Marilyn Sculptor

Glenfield
Carter, (Charles) Bruce Printmaker, Educator

Glens Falls
Lyons, Francis E, Jr Art Dealer, Lecturer
Setford, David F Gallery Director

Goshen
Bleach, Bruce R Printmaker, Painter, Sculptor
Digby, Lynne Painter, Writer

Great Neck
Dellis, Arlene B Museologist, Craftsman
Dennett, Lissy W Sculptor
Eisenberg, Marc S Painter, Sculptor
Gorbaty, Norman Painter, Sculptor
Harnick, Sylvia Painter
Mayer, Sondra Elster Art Dealer, Art Appraiser
Meyer, Seymour W Sculptor
Obler, Geri Printmaker, Collage Artist
Tanksley, Ann Painter, Printmaker

Greenlawn
Fludd, Reginald Joseph Painter, Craftsman
Zucker, Bob Photographer

Greenvale
Tuman, Donna Educator, Administrator

Greenwich
Lorber, Stephen Neil Painter, Photographer
Nunnelley, Robert B Painter

Greenwood Lake
Ingber, Barbara Dealer, Curator

Groton
Colby, Victor E Sculptor, Educator

Hamburg
Johnson, Anita Louise Painter, Graphic Artist

Hamilton
Knecht, John Filmmaker, Video Artist

Harpursville
Vierthaler, Bonnie Collage Artist, Lecturer

Hartsdale
Glanz, Andrea E Administrator, Curator
McMann, Edith Brozak Painter, Sculptor

NEW YORK (cont)

New Hartford

MacDonald, Scott Critic, Educator

New Hyde Park

London, Anna Graphic Artist, Sculptor

New Paltz

Adair, Jim R Painter, Designer
Atlas, Nava Writer, Book Arts
Azank, Roberto Painter
Bender, Leslie Marilyn Painter, Muralist
Miller, (Richard) Guy Sculptor
Raleigh, Henry Patrick Painter, Writer
Stanich, Nancy Jean Photographer, Printmaker
Tabak, Chaim Painter, Sculptor
Trager, Neil C Museum Director, Photographer
Turner, Norman Huntington Painter, Writer
Wexler, Alice Painter, Administrator

New Rochelle

Canning, Susan M Historian, Critic
Goldfinger, Eliot Sculptor
Liebman, Sarah Educator, Painter
Livingston, Constance Kellner Collage Artist, Sculptor
Nikkal, Nancy Egol Collage Artist
Perlmutter, Merle Printmaker
Schlanger, Jeff Sculptor, Painter
Slotnick, Mortimer H Painter, Educator
Zheutlin, Dale R Painter, Educator

New Suffolk

Biggers, Sanford Sculptor
Diaz, Alejandro Installation Sculptor
Schulze, Paul Designer

New Woodstock

Scala, Joseph A Sculptor, Painter

New York

Abram, Ruth J Writer
Abramowicz, Janet Painter, Printmaker
Abrams, Joyce Diana Painter, Sculptor
Abts, Tomma Painter
Abularach, Rodolfo Marco Painter, Printmaker
Ackerman, Andy Museum Director
Adams, Dennis Paul Sculptor, Conceptual Artist
Adams, Laurie Schneider Historian, Editor
Adamson, Glenn Museum Director
Adrian, Barbara Tramutola Painter, Collector
Ahearn, John Sculptor
Ahrens, Hanno D Sculptor
Akin, Gwen Photographer
Akutsu, Shoichi Painter, Instructor
Al-Hadid, Diana Sculptor
Alberti, Donald Wesley Painter
Albrecht, Donald Curator, Educator
Alden, Todd Critic, Conceptual Artist
Alexander, Edmund Brooke Art Dealer, Publisher
Alexis, Michael painter
Allain, Rene Pierre Painter, Sculptor
Allen, Roberta Conceptual Artist, Photographer
Allen, Stan Architect, Educator
Allyn, Jerri Conceptual Artist, Educator
Alpert, Bill (William) H Painter, Sculptor
Althoff, Kai Painter, Installation Sculptor
Altshuler, Bruce J Educator, Writer
Alvarado-Juárez, Francisco Painter, Photographer
Alys, Francis Conceptual Artist, Performance Artist, Painter
Amano, Taka Painter
Amoros, Grimanesa Painter, Sculptor, Video Artist
Amos, Emma Painter, Printmaker
Anatsui, El Sculptor
Andersen, Leif (Werner) Painter
Anderson, Laurie Conceptual Artist
Andre, Carl Sculptor
Andres, Holly Photographer, Filmmaker
Anker, Suzanne C Sculptor, Painter
Anthony, William Graham Painter, Draftsman
Antoni, Janine Sculptor
Aoki, Carole I Ceramist
Apfelbaum, Polly Artist
Appel, Eric A Sculptor, Painter
Arai, Tomie Printmaker, Muralist
Arakawa, Ei Sculptor, Director
Arcangel, Cory Graphic Artist
Arcilesi, Vincent J Painter, Draftsman
Arcuri, Frank Painter
Arias, Soledad M Curator
Armajani, Siah Sculptor
Armstrong, L C Painter
Armstrong, Martha (Allen) Painter, Photographer
Armstrong, Richard Curator, Museum Director
Arnold, Ann Illustrator
Arnot, Andrew H Gallery Director
Aronson, Sanda Assemblage Artist, Sculptor
Aschheim, Eve Michele Painter
Ashcraft, Eve Painter
Ashton, Dore Art Critic, Writer, Educator
Atkinson, Conrad Sculptor, Painter
Atlas, Charles Filmmaker
Audean Painter, Illustrator
Avlon-Daphnis, Helen Basilea Painter, Sculptor
Aylon, Helène Painter, Conceptual Artist
Azaceta, Luis Cruz Painter
Azara, Nancy J Sculptor, Painter
Bachner, Barbara L Painter, Installation Sculptor
Backström, Fia Conceptual Artist
Baer, Jo Painter, Writer
Baker, Elizabeth C Art Editor, Critic
Baker, Richard Painter
Bakoian, Lauren Director
Ballard, James A Painter, Architect
Bandy, Gary Painter, Educator
Bandy, Mary Lea Editor, Administrator
Banerjee, (Bimal) Painter, Sculptor
Bankowsky, Jack Critic, Curator
Bardazzi, Peter Painter, Filmmaker
Barnes, Curt (Curtis) Edward Painter, Instructor
Barnes, Kitt Painter
Barnett, Emily Painter, Printmaker
Barnett, Vivian Endicott Curator, Historian
Barney, Matthew Sculptor, Filmmaker
Barowitz, Elliott Painter
Barr-Sharrar, Beryl Art Historian, Painter
Barrett, Bill Sculptor
Bartelik, Marek Art Historian, Art Critic
Barth, Jack Alexander Painter
Barton, Nancy Educator, Photographer
Baruch, Barbara Gallery Director
Basquin, Kit (Mary Smyth) Writer, Educator
Bass, Ruth Educator, Critic
Bates, David Painter
Battis, Nicholas Painter, Gallery Director
Baum, Erica Photographer
Baum, Jayne H Art Dealer
Baumann, Caroline Museum Director
Baume, Nicholas Curator, Director
Baxter, Douglas W Art Dealer
Bayer, Arlyne Painter, Printmaker
Beallor, Fran Painter, Printmaker
Beatty, Frances Fielding Lewis Art Dealer, Collector
Beaumont, Betty Environmental Artist
Beck, Doreen Writer, Fiber Artist
Becker, Carol Dean, Educator, Writer
Beckman, Ericka Filmmaker, Photographer
Bedia, Jose Painter, Sculptor
Behnke, Leigh Painter
Beilin, Howard Art Dealer
Beirne, Bill Video Artist, Conceptual Artist
Bekman, Jen Gallery Director
Belag, Andrea Painter, Graphic Artist
Bell, Dozier Painter
Beloff, Zoe Video Artist
Ben-Haim, Zigi Sculptor, Painter
Ben-Tor, Tamy Performance Artist
Benarcik, Susan Installation Sculptor
Berg, Siri Collage Artist, Painter
Bergdoll, Barry historian, educator
Bergen, Jeffrey B Art Dealer, Director
Berger, Emily Painter
Berger, Maurice Cultural Historian, Critic
Berkowitz, Terry Installation Artist, Photographer
Berlind, Robert Painter, Educator
Berman, Nina Photographer
Bernhard, Dianne Barbee Painter, Director
Bernstein, Judith Painter, Educator
Beshty, Walead Photographer
Bialobroda, Anna Painter
Bidlo, Mike Conceptual Artist
Biesenbach, Klaus Curator, Museum Director
Billian, Cathey R Environmental Artist, Educator
Birchler, Alexander Filmmaker
Birnbaum, Dara Video Artist
Blagg, Daniel Painter
Blaugrund, Annette Museum Director, Art Historian
Bleckner, Ross Painter
Blessing, Jennifer curator
Blodgett, Anne Washington B. Painter
Blum, Andrea Sculptor
Bonino, Fernanda Art Dealer
Bontecou, Lee Artist, Sculptor
Booker, Chakaia Sculptor, Painter
Bordes, Adrienne Painter, Instructor
Bordo, Robert Painter
Borgatta, Isabel Case Sculptor, Educator
Botero, Fernando Sculptor
Boursier-Mougenot, Céleste Installation Sculptor
Boutis, Tom Painter, Printmaker
Bowman, John Painter
Boyd, (David) Michael Painter, Graphic Artist
Bradford, Mark Collage Artist
Bradshaw, Ellen Painter
Braff, Phyllis Critic, Curator
Brandt, Kathleen Weil-Garris Educator, Art Historian
Brannon, Matthew Printmaker
Bratsch, Kerstin Painter, Installation Sculptor
Braun, Emily Educator, Curator, Writer
Breen, Susan Painter
Brett, Nancy Artist
Brodsky, Alexander Ilya Utkin Architect, Sculptor
Brodsky, Beverly Painter, Illustrator
Brodsky, Eugene V Painter
Brody-Lederman, Stephanie Painter, Drawings
Bronson, A A (Michael Wayne Tims) Post-Conceptual Artist, Writer
Brookner, Jackie Environmental Artist, Sculptor
Brooks, Ellen Photographer
Brosk, Jeffrey Sculptor
Brower, Steven Graphic Designer, Educator
Brown, Cecily Artist
Brown, Eric L Gallery Director
Brown, Jonathan Historian
Brown, Julia Administrator
Brown, Larry Painter
Brown, Robert K Dealer
Bruder, Harold Jacob Painter, Educator
Brumer, Miriam Painter
Bruno, Phillip A Director
Brunswick, Cecile R Painter
Bruskin, Grisha Painter, Sculptor
Bryant, Linda Goode Art Dealer, Gallery Director
Buckingham, Matthew Video Artist
Budny, Virginia Sculptor, Writer
Buecker, Robert Gallery Director, Painter
Buist, Kathy Painter
Bunts, Frank Painter, Educator
Burdin, Anthony Installation Sculptor
Burdock, Harriet Historian, Printmaker
Burns, Ian Sculptor, Kinetic Artist
Burton, Richmond Painter
Bush, Martin H Museum Director, Historian
Buszko, Irene J Painter
Butterly, Kathy sculptor
Cabrera, Margarita Sculptor
Caivano, Ernesto Artist
Calatrava, Santiago Architect
Calibey, Gregory Painter
Calle, Sophie Photographer
Campbell, Thomas P Museum Director
Cardillo, Rimer Angel Printmaker, Sculptor
Carey, Ellen Photographer
Carlson, Cynthia J Painter, Educator
Carr, Simon Painter
Carter, Mary Painter, Printmaker
Carter, Nanette Carolyn Painter, Printmaker
Carvalho, Josely Printmaker, Painter
Casey, Tim (Timothy) William Painter, Educator
Caspe, Lynda Painter, Sculptor
Cassell, Stephen Architect
Castrucci, Andrew Painter, Sculptor
Cateura, Patty Painter
Cattelan, Maurizio Artist
Cavaliere, Barbara Critic, Historian
Cecil-Wishing, Devin Painter, Illustrator
Celmins, Vija Painter
Cembalest, Robin Editor
Cemin, Saint Clair Sculptor
Censor, Therese Sculptor
Cesarco, Alejandro Installation Artist, Painter
Chaiklin, Amy Painter
Chalif, Ronnie Sculptor
Chamberlain, Beau Painter
Chambers, William McWillie Painter, Art Dealer
Champlin, Andrea Painter
Chan, Eric Painter
Chan, Paul Video Artist
Chase-Riboud, Barbara Sculptor, Writer
Cheim, John Gallery Director
Chemeche, George Painter, Sculptor
Cheng, Emily Painter
Chermayeff, Ivan Designer, Graphic Artist
Chernick, Myrel Video Artist
Chevins, Christopher M Painter, Draftsman
Chin, Mel Sculptor
Cho, Y(eou) J(ui) Painter
Chong, Ping Director, Video Artist, Choreographer, Visual Artist
Chu, Anne Sculptor
Ciarrocchi, Ray Painter, Educator
Citron, Harvey Lewis Sculptor
Clark, Edward Painter
Clark, Michael Vinson Painter, Printmaker
Clarke, John Clem Painter
Clough, Charles Sidney Painter
Clutz, William Painter
Codding, Mitchell Allan Museum Director, Administrator
Code, Audrey Painter
Coe, Sue Painter
Coffin, Anne Gagnebin Arts Administrator
Cohan, James Gallery Director
Cohen, Joan Lebold Art Historian, Photographer

NEW YORK (cont)

NEW YORK (cont)

NEW YORK (cont)

Rosen, Andrea Gallery Director
Rosenbaum, Allen Museum Director
Rosenberg, Alex Jacob Art Dealer, Consultant, Appraiser
Rosenberg, Carole Halsband Art Dealer, Philanthropist
Rosenberg, Terry Painter, Sculptor
Rosenfeld, Samuel L Art Dealer, Appraiser
Rosenfeld, Sharon Painter
Rosensaft, Jean Bloch Curator, Museum Director
Rosenthal, Deborah Maly Painter, Educator
Rosenthal, Mark L Curator, Historian
Roser, Ce (Cecilia) Painter, Video Artist
Ross, John T Printmaker, Educator
Ross, Rhoda Honore Painter, Instructor
Ross, Wilbur Louis, Jr Collector
Rosser, Phyllis F Sculptor, Painter
Rothenberg, Susan Painter, Printmaker
Rothkopf, Scott Curator, Critic
Rotter, Alex Art Appraiser
Row, David Painter
Rowe, Heather Installation Sculptor
Rowland, Anne Photographer
Roy, Rajendra Curator
Rubell, Mera Collector
Rubenstein, Ephraim Painter
Rubin, Lawrence Art Dealer, Collector
Rubin, Patricia Historian, Administrator
Rubinstein, Raphael Critic
Ruby, Sterling Sculptor
Ruehlicke, Cornelia Iris Painter, Printmaker
Ruilova, Aida Video Artist
Ruscha, Edward Joseph Painter, Photographer
Russell, Jeff Painter, Photographer
Russotto, Paul Painter, Educator
Rychlak, Bonnie L Sculptor, Curator
Ryman, Will Sculptor
Saar, Betye Assemblage Artist, Collage Artist
Saccoccio, Jacqueline Artist
Sachs, Tom Painter, Sculptor
Sacks, Beverly Art Dealer, Consultant
Sager, Anne Photographer
Sal, Jack Photographer, Painter
Salt, John Painter
Salvest, John Sculptor, Educator
Sanders, Rhea Painter, Writer
Sandler, Barbara Painter
Sanin, Fanny Painter
Saphire, Lawrence M Writer, Art Dealer
Sarabia, Eduardo Installation Sculptor
Saraceno, Tomas Installation Sculptor
Sasnal, Wilhelm Painter
Sato, Masaaki Painter
Saul, Andrew M Collector
Saul, Denise Collector
Schab, Margo Pollins Art Dealer
Schaefer, Robert Arnold, Jr Photographer, Director
Scharf, William Painter
Schatz, Heather Painter
Schenning, Matthew Photographer
Schjeldahl, Peter Critic, Editor
Schneider, Jo Anne Painter
Schneider, Lisa Dawn Dealer, Critic
Schnitger, Lara Sculptor
Schorr, Collier artist
Schulson, Susan Painter, Silversmith
Schulte, Arthur D Collector
Schuselka, Elfi Painter, Sculptor
Schutz, Dana Painter
Schwartz, Lillian (Feldman) Filmmaker
Schwartz, Marvin D Historian
Scribner, Charles, III Historian, Lecturer
Segall-Marx, Madeleine (Maddy Marx) Sculptor, Painter
Seidl, Claire Painter, Printmaker
Selldorf, Annabelle M Architect
Seltzer, Joanne Lynn Painter, Printmaker
Semmel, Joan Painter
Seplowin, Charles Joseph Sculptor
Sera, Assunta Painter, Instructor
Serra, Richard Sculptor, Video Artist
Serra, Rudy Sculptor
Shainman, Jack S Art Dealer, Gallery Director
Shalala, Edward Graphic Artist
Shapiro, Babe Painter
Shapiro, David Painter, Printmaker
Sharp, Anne Catherine Painter
Shashaty, Yolanda Victoria Painter
Shaw, Paul Jefferson Calligrapher, Designer, Historian
Shechet, Arlene J Artist
Sheikh, Fazal Photographer
Sheirr, Olga (Krolik) Painter
Shemesh, Lorraine R Painter, Sculptor
Sherman, Cindy Photographer
Sherman, Sarai Painter, Sculptor
Sherrod, Philip Lawrence Artist, Poet, Composer
Shettar, Ranjani Sculptor
Shorr, Harriet Painter
Shotz, Alyson Assemblage Artist, Sculptor
Sibony, Gedi Sculptor
Sigal-Ibsen, Rose Calligrapher, Painter
Sikander, Shahzia Painter
Siler, Todd (Lael) Painter, Sculptor
Silver, Shelly Andrea Video Artist, Filmmaker
Silverberg, June Roselyn Painter, Graphic Artist
Silverman, Burton Philip Painter
Simmons, Laurie Photographer
Simonian, Judith Painter, Collage Artist
Sims, Lowery Stokes Art Historian, Curator
Singerman, Howard Educator, Administrator
Sira, Victor Photographer
Skogerson, Gretchen Video Artist, Installation Sculptor
Skupinski, Bogdan Kazimierz Printmaker, Painter
Sky, Alison Environmental Artist
Slavin, Arlene Sculptor
Sloan, Jennifer Sculptor
Sloat, Richard Joel Painter, Printmaker
Slone, Sandi Painter, Educator
Slonem, Hunt Painter, Muralist
Smira, Shaoul Painter
Smith, E E Photographer, Sculptor
Smith, Lawry Director, Curator
Smith, Mimi Sculptor, Conceptual Artist
Smith, Paul J Museum Director
Smith, Shirley Painter
Smith, Susan Painter, Collage Artist
Smokler, Stanley B Sculptor, Assemblage Artist
Snyder, Richard Painter
Soffer, Sasson Environmental Artist, Conceptual Artist
Sokolow, Isobel Folb Sculptor, Educator
Sokov, Leonid Sculptor, Painter
Solomon, Gerald Art Dealer, Painter
Solomon, Ken Conceptual Artist
Solomon, Richard H Publisher, Art Dealer
Sonnier, Keith Sculptor, Video Artist
Sono, Masayuki Architect
Sorce, Anthony John Painter
Soreff, Stephen Sculptor, Assemblage Artist
Sorkin, Michael Architect
Spector, Naomi Writer
Speiser, Stuart M Collector, Patron
Spelman, Jill Sullivan Painter
Spence, Andrew Painter
Speyer, Jerry I Collector
Spiegel, Laurie Computer Artist, Composer
Spira, Bill Sculptor, Photographer
Sprouls, David Administrator
Squiers, Carol Writer, Critic
Stahl, Alan M Curator, Historian
Stanley, John Slusarski Museum Administrator
Stashkevetch, Joseph Painter
Steele, Valerie Fahnestock Museum Director
Steen, Carol J Painter, Sculptor
Stein, Claire A Administrator
Stein, Lewis Conceptual Artist
Stein, Linda Sculptor, Painter
Steinhardt, Judy Collector
Steinhardt, Michael H Collector
Steir, Pat Painter
Stettner, Louis Photographer
Stewart, Regina Painter, Administrator
Stoloff, Carolyn Painter, Collage Artist
Storey, David Painter
Strachan, Tavares Glass Blower
Straus, Sandy Painter
Strueken-Bachmann, Marion Painter, Curator
Strunz, Katja Sculptor, Painter
Stuart, Michelle Painter, Sculptor
Stux, Stefan Victor Art Dealer, Director
Subramaniam, Radhika Curator, Educator
Sugiura, Kunie Photographer, Painter
Sullivan, Catherine Video Artist
Sullivan, Jim Painter
Sundblad, Emily Artist, Director
Sussman, Jill Gallery Director
SuZen, Susan R Rubinstein Photographer, Designer
Swain, Robert Painter
Swartz, Julianne Artist
Sweeney, Spencer Artist
Swergold, Marcelle M Sculptor
Sze, Sarah Installation Sculptor
Tacla, Jorge Painter, Muralist
Tai, Jane S Administrator
Talasnik, Stephen Painter
Talbert, Richard Harrison Painter, Architect
Tananbaum, Lisa & Steven Andrew Collectors
Tanger, Susanna Painter, Writer
Tannenbaum, Judith E Curator, Critic
Tansey, Mark Painter
Tapley, Emma Painter
Taylor, Alison Elizabeth Sculptor
Temkin, Ann Curator
Temple, Mary Installation Sculptor, Painter
Tenenbaum, Ann Administrator, Collector
Terruso, Luigi Leonardo Painter, Instructor
Thacher, Anita Installation Artist, Filmmaker
Thaw, Eugene Victor Dealer, Collector
Thomas, Kathleen K Sculptor, Assemblage Artist
Thompson, Nato Curator
Thomson, David K R Collector
Thorne, Joan Painter, Educator
Tiravanija, Rirkrit Sculptor
Toll, Barbara Elizabeth Dealer, Curator
Tolle, Brian Sculptor
Tomkins, Calvin Writer
Tompkins, Betty (I) Painter, Printmaker
Torreano, John Francis Painter, Sculptor
Torres, Frances Video Artist, Sculptor
Towers, Joel Architect, Educator
Trakas, George Sculptor
Tran, Tam Van Painter
Traub, Charles H Educator, Photographer
Trecartin, Ryan Filmmaker
Tremblay, John Painter
Tribe, Lee Sculptor, Instructor
Tribe, Mark Video Artist, Educator
Tribush, Brenda Painter, Instructor
Trombetta, Annamarie Painter, Printmaker
Trueblood, Emily Herrick Printmaker
Tsai, Charwei Calligrapher, Installation Sculptor
Tschumi, Bernard Architect
Tsien, Billie Architect
Tuazon, Oscar Sculptor
Tuchman, Phyllis Critic, Curator
Tullis, Garner H Publisher, Printmaker
Tully, Judd Writer, Curator
Turner, Alan Painter, Printmaker
Turner, Judith Estelle Photographer, Video Artist
Tuttle, Richard Painter
Umlauf, Lynn (Charlotte) Sculptor, Painter
Valdez Gonzalez, Julio E Painter, Printmaker
Valenstein, Suzanne Gebhart Curator
Van Dyke, Peter Painter
Van Haaften, Julia Curator, Writer
Van Stein, Thomas Painter
Vasell, Chris Artist, Filmmaker
Vazquez, Paul Painter
Vega, Carlos Painter
Vergne, Philippe Museum Director
Vick, Connie R Consultant
Vincent, Clare Curator, Historian
Vinoly, Rafael Architect
Voorsanger, Bartholomew Architect
Wachs, Ethel Educator, Collector
Wagner, Merrill Painter
Wald, Sylvia Painter, Sculptor
Walgren, Frances J Appraiser
Walker, Kelley Painter, Sculptor
Wall, Jeff Photographer
Wall, Sue Painter, Printmaker
Wallenstein, Ellen Photographer, Educator
Walp, Susan Jane Painter
Walsh, Dan Painter
Walsh, James Painter, Sculptor
Waltemath, Joan Painter, Educator
Waltzer, Stewart Paul Dealer, Painter
Ward, Elaine Painter
Ward, Nari Sculptor
Wardropper, Ian Bruce Museum Director
Washburn, Joan T Art Dealer
Washburn, Phoebe Sculptor
Waters, Jack Filmmaker, Conceptual Artist
Watkins, Ragland Tolk Curator, Dealer
Waxter, Dorsey Art Dealer, Gallery Director
Webb, Patrick Painter, Muralist
Weber, Idelle Lois Painter, Educator
Weber, Susan Administrator, Collector
Webster, Meg Sculptor, Painter
Wechsler, Susan Editor, Writer
Weems, Carrie Mae Photographer
Weil, Rex Critic
Weinberg, Adam D Museum Director
Weinberg, H Barbara Curator, Educator
Weiner, Lawrence Charles Sculptor
Weinstein, Martin Painter
Weinstein, Raymond Artist
Weinstock, Rose Painter
Weintraub, Annette Digital Artist, Educator
Weiss, Clemens Conceptual Artist, Sculptor
Weiss, Jeffrey Curator
Weiss, Marilyn Ackerman Collage Artist, Painter
Weiss, Monika Video Artist, Installation Sculptor
Weissman, Julian Paul Dealer
Weissman, Walter Photographer, Sculptor
Wekua, Andro Sculptor, Painter
Welch, Roger Video Artist, Installation Sculptor
Wells, Lynton Painter
Westermann, Mariët Former Museum Director, Administrator
Westwater, Angela King Art Dealer, Editor
Wexler, Allan Designer
Wexler, Peter J Sculptor, Photographer
Whitten, Jack Painter
Widing, Eric P Fine Art Auctioneer
Wiggins, Guy A Painter, Lecturer
Wilkin, Karen Curator, Critic

NEW YORK (cont)

Scarsdale

Mannor, Margalit Photographer, Conceptual Artist
Ries, Martin Painter, Printmaker
Roda, Rhoda Lillian Sablow Painter, Tapestry Artist
Yunich, Beverly B Collage Artist, Jeweler

Schenectady

Gilson, Giles Sculptor, Designer
Hatke, Walter Joseph Painter, Educator
Shaheen, Gary Edward Administrator, Collage Artist

Scottsville

Castle, Wendell Keith Sculptor

Sea Cliff

Jacobs, David (Theodore) Sculptor, Kinetic Artist
Seiden, Katie Sculptor, Assemblage Artist

Searingtown

Chichura, Diane B Administrator, Art Dealer

Setauket

Badalamenti, Fred L Painter, Educator
Guilmain, Jacques Historian, Painter
Kemp, Flo Printmaking

Shelter Island

Gage, Beau Sculptor, Photographer
Zeigler, George Gavin Painter, Sculptor

Shelter Island Heights

Culbertson, Janet Lynn (Mrs Douglas Kaften) Painter, Environmental Artist

Shirley

Cohen, Jean Painter

Shokan

Werner, Howard Sculptor

Sleepy Hollow

Perlmutter, Linda M Painter, Instructor

South Nyack

Churchill, Diane Painter

Southampton

Brown, David Lee Sculptor
Koehler, Henry Painter
Martine, David Bunn Painter
Smith, Dinah Maxwell Painter, Photographer

Spencerport

Stewart, Bill Sculptor, Ceramist

Staatsburg

Fujita, Kenji Sculptor

Stanfordville

Froman, Ann Sculptor, Designer

Staten Island

Butti, Linda Painter, Educator
Coleman, A(llan) D(ouglass) Critic, Curator
Gear, Emily Museum Director, Curator
Grabel, Susan Sculptor, Printmaker
Greenfield, Amy Filmmaker, Video Artist
Hermus, Lance Jay Art Appraiser, Art Dealer
Mailman, Cynthia Painter, Educator
Matyas, Diane C Author, Printmaker
Moakley, Paul Photographer, Curator
Moore, Alan Willard Art Critic, Historian
Newhouse, Victoria & Samuel I, Jr Collector

Stephentown

Gordon, Albert F Art Dealer
Pentak, Stephen Painter, Educator

Stony Brook

Bogart, Michele Helene Historian, Curator
Cooper, Rhonda H Gallery Director, Curator
Dinkins, Stephanie Sculptor
Ellinger, Ilona E Painter, Educator
Levine, Martin Printmaker, Educator
Pekarsky, Mel(vin) Hirsch Painter, Educator
Pindell, Howardena Doreen Painter, Educator

Stuyvesant

Tripp, Susan Gerwe Museum Director

Suffern

Leigh, Harry E Sculptor, Painter

Surprise

Fintz, Jeanette Painter

Syosset

Greene, Chris (Christine) E Caricaturist, Illustrator

Syracuse

Bakke, Karen Lee Assemblage Artist, Calligrapher
Belfort-Chalat, Jacqueline Sculptor, Painter
Clarke, Ann Educator
DuBois, Douglas Photographer
Harootunian, Claire M Sculptor, Educator
Jerry, Michael John Educator, Craftsman
Orentlicher, John Video Artist, Sculptor
Reed, Cleota Historian, Lecturer
Van Aken, Sam Installation Sculptor, Educator
Witkin, Jerome Painter, Draftsman

Tappan

Dell, Robert Christopher Environmental Artist, Educator

Tarrytown

Butler, Joseph Thomas Curator, Writer
Gursoy, Ahmet Painter
Holt, David John Painter, Educator
Price, Helen Burdon Painter, Printmaker

Troy

Adams, Hank M Craftsman

Trumansburg

Vann, Samuel LeRoy Painter

Tuxedo Park

Simon, Robert Barry Art Dealer, Historian

Ulster Park

Clarke, Bud (Warren) F Designer, Painter

Utica

Cimbalo, Robert W Painter, Printmaker
Schweizer, Paul Douglas Museum Director Emeritus, Art Historian

Valhalla

Lombardi, Don Dominick Artist

Valley Cottage

Heinzen, MaryAnn Painter, Assemblage Artist
Longo-Muth, Linda L Painter, Instructor

Valley Stream

Borg, Joseph Printmaker, Collage Artist
Jennerjahn, W P Educator, Painter
Wasserman, Muriel Painter

Vestal

Adour, Colleen Sculptor, Educator

Victor

Keyser, William Alphonse, Jr Painter, Sculptor

Voorheesville

O'Connor, Thom Printmaker

Wading River

Marlow, Audrey Swanson Painter, Designer

Wainscott

Ashbaugh, Dennis John Painter
Russo, Alexander Peter Painter, Educator
Zucker, Joseph I Painter

Wallkill

Koch, Edwin E Sculptor, Painter

Wantagh

Glaser, David Painter, Sculptor

Wappingers Falls

Di Fate, Vincent Illustrator, Painter

Warwick

Bridges, Marilyn Photographer
Mack, Daniel R Designer, Craftsman
Talbot, Jonathan Painter, Collage Artist

Water Mill

French, Christopher Charles Painter, Writer
Strassfield, Christina Mossaides Museum Director, Curator
Sultan, Terrie Frances Museum Director

Waverly

Miran, Patricia Marie Painter, Printmaker

Wells

Van Alstine, John Richard Sculptor

West Falls

Lindemann, Edna M Museum Director, Educator

West Hurley

Langdo, Bryan Richard Illustrator, Writer
Weyhe, Arthur Sculptor

West Nyack

Ramos, Julianne Administrator, Consultant
Yeiser, Charles William Painter, Art Dealer
Zansky, Michael Painter, Sculptor, Photographer

West Point

Reel, David Mark Museum Director, Curator

Westburg

Barboza, Anthony Photographer, Painter

Westbury

Haleman, Laura Rand Sculptor, Artist
Sherbell, Rhoda Sculptor, Painter

Westport

Owen, Frank (Franklin) Charles Painter
Schira, Cynthia Tapestry Artist

White Plains

Cove, Rosemary Sculptor, Painter
Fisher, Jerome Collector
Manes, Belle Painter

Willow

Goetz, Mary Anna Painter, Instructor
Taback, Simms Illustrator, Designer

Woodmere

Ginsburg, Estelle Painter, Sculptor
Greenfield, Joan Beatrice Painter, Enamelist
Winick, Bernyce Alpert Painter, Photographer

Woodside

Katz, Don Sculptor, Stained Glass Artist
Salgian, Mitzura Artist
Warren, Tom Photographer, Conceptual Artist

Woodstock

Currie, Bruce Painter, Printmaker
Dechar, Peter Painter
Epstein, Yale Painter, Printmaker
Jordan, John L Sculptor, Video Artist
Lazansky, Edward Painter, Educator
Mackintosh, Sandra Sculpture, Collage Artist
McGloughlin, Kate Printmaker, Painter
Morse, Mitchell Ian Dealer, Consultant
Niedzialek, Terry Sculptor, Environmental Artist

Worcester

Habenicht, Wenda Sculptor

Yonkers

Agee, William C Educator, Historian
Botwinick, Michael Museum Director
Chavooshian, Marge Painter, Educator
Civale, Biagio A Printmaker, Painter
Gioello, Debbie Painter, Designer
Segal, Barbara Jeanne Sculptor, Instructor

Yorktown Heights

Fairweather, Sally H Art Dealer, Consultant
Naumann, Francis M Historian, Curator
Witt, John Painter, Printmaker
Brown, Stephen Pat Painter, Sculptor

NORTH CAROLINA

Blunk, Joyce Elaine Assemblage Artist, Painter
Bora (Boraev), Vadim Makharbekovich Sculptor, Painter
Cooke, Samuel Tucker Painter, Educator
Hobgood, E Wade Administrator, Educator
Hough, Jennine Painter, Instructor
Krause, Bonnie Jean Museum Consultant
Loewer, Henry Peter Writer, Illustrator
Martin, Doris-Marie Constable Designer, Sculptor
McDaniel, William Harrison (Harry) Sculptor

NORTH DAKOTA

OHIO

OKLAHOMA

PENNSYLVANIA (cont)

Fort Washington

Schmidt, Charles Painter, Curator

Gibsonia

Zollweg, Aileen Boules Artist, Writer

Gladwyne

Wind, Dina Sculptor

Glen Mills

Crawford, Bill (Wilbur) Ogden Illustrator, Administrator
Turner, Janet Sullivan Painter, Sculptor

Glenmoore

De Guatemala, Joyce Bush Vourvoulias Sculptor

Glenside

Frudakis, Zenos Sculptor

Grantham

Forsythe, Donald John Printmaker, Educator

Greensburg

O'Toole, Judith Hansen Museum Director, Writer

Grove City

Myford, James C Sculptor, Educator

Harrisburg

Bottini, David William Painter, Educator

Haverford

Williams, William Earle Photographer, Curator

Havertown

Kindermann, Helmmo Photographer, Painter
Spicer, Jean (Doris) Uhl Painter, Instructor, Writer, Author
Wilson, Elizabeth (Jane) Painter, Educator

Hazleton

Klesh-Butkovsky, Jane Graphic Artist, Painter

Herndon

Wiseman, Deanna Lynn Painter, Instructor

Horsham

Toll, Bruce E Collector
Winokur, Paula Colton Ceramist, Craftsman
Winokur, Robert Ceramic Artist

Huntingdon Valley

Edelman, Janice Watercolor, Writer

Huntington

Lutz, Winifred Ann Environmental Artist, Installation Sculptor

Indiana

Gillham, Andrew graphic design artist, educator, administrator
Olson, Charles Painter, Instructor

Jenkintown

Goldfine, Beatrice Painter, Sculptor
Langman, Richard Theodore Gallery Director
Miller, Elaine Sandra Painter, Printmaker

Jim Thorpe

Nagano, Shozo Painter

Julian

Yarber, Robert Painter

Kennett Square

Jackson, Robert Coleman Painter

Kutztown

Carroll, James F L Painter, Sculptor
Malenda, James William Enamelist, Educator
Quirk, Thomas Charles, Jr Painter, Sculptor
Summer, Evan D Artist
Talley, Dan R Writer, Photographer

Lancaster

Grand, Stanley I Director, Curator
Hay, Ike Sculptor, Educator
Limont, Naomi Charles Printmaker, Painter

Langhorne

Burtt, Larice Annadel Roseman Painter, Sculptor

Lederach

Hallman, Ted, Jr Tapestry Artist, Educator

Lenhartsville

Daub, Matthew Forrest Painter, Graphic Artist

Lewisburg

Richards, Rosalyn A Director

Ligonier

Hoffman, William McKinley, Jr Painter, Educator

Mansfield

Hamwi, Richard Alexander Painter, Educator

McKean

Kemenyffy, Susan B Hale Artist

Mechanicsburg

Annis, Norman L Educator, Sculptor
Warren, Win (Winton) W Painter, Lecturer

Media

Crivelli, Elaine Environmental Artist, Sculptor
Lisk, Penelope E Tsaltas Painter, Printmaker
Reichel, Myra Tapestry Artist, Weaver
Vitale, Magda Painter

Merion Station

Gillman, Derek A Museum Director, Administrator

Merrittstown

Kenton, Mary Jean Painter, Environmental Artist

Middletown

Michels, Kathryn Painter, Photographer

Milford

Kaplan, Phyllis Painter, Computer Artist

Mohnton

Gore, Jefferson Anderson Curator

Narberth

Alten, Jerry Director, Designer
Atlee, Emilie Des Painter, Instructor
Donohoe, Victoria Historian, Critic
Tyng, Alexandra Stevens Painter, Instructor

New Freedom

Theofiles, George Historian, Dealer

New Hope

McGinniss, Jim Sculptor

Newtown

Bender, May Painter
Bove, Richard Painter, Educator
Jansen, Catherine Sandra Photographer, Environmental Artist

Newville

Dubiel, Carolyn McPeek Collage Artist

Norristown

Grimley, Oliver Fetterolf Painter, Sculptor

North Wales

Szabo, Joseph George Cartoonist, Editor

Oakdale

Mulcahy, Kathleen Glass Artist, Sculptor

Ottsville

Smith, Michael A Photographer, Publisher

Oxford

Holmes, Larry W Painter, Educator

Pennsburg

Hendershot, Ray Painter

Pennsylvania Furnace

Maddox, Jerrold Warren Educator, Painter

Philadelphia

Akers, Adela Weaver, Craftsman
Asman, Robert Joseph Photographer, Printmaker
Bach, Laurence Photographer, Educator
Bantel, Linda Museum Director
Batchelor, Betsey Ann Painter, Educator
Bateman, Ronald C Painter
Bell, Roberley A Sculptor, Educator
Bobrowicz, Yvonne Pacanovsky Instructor, Weaver
Bower, John Arnold, Jr Architect, Educator
Brady, Luther W Collector, Educator, Patron
Brantley, James Sherman Painter
Brigham, David R Museum Director, Administrator
Buffington, Sean T Administrator, Educator
Burke, Daniel Museum Director, Educator
Burko, Diane Painter, Photographer
Camp, Donald Eugene Photographer
Casadei, Giovanni Painter
Castagno, John Edward Art Dealer, Painter
Couch, Robert Painter, Architect
Craig, Morgan Painter
Dallmann, Daniel Forbes Painter, Printmaker
Dickerson, Brian S Painter
Dolan, Margo Foundation Director, Art Dealer
Drutt, Helen Williams Dealer, Lecturer
Edmunds, Allan Logan Printmaker, Administrator
Formicola, John Joseph Painter, Educator
Frudakis, Evangelos William Sculptor, Instructor
Fuller, Jeffrey P Dealer, Gallery Director
Garcia, Ofelia Art Administrator, Educator
Goodman, Gwen Ducat Museum Director
Gould, Claudia Museum Director
Gregory, Joseph F Director
Hahn, Roslyn Dealer
Hanes, James (Albert) Painter
Harrity, Gail M Museum Director
Hom, Mei-ling Sculptor
Horvitz, Suzanne Reese Painter, Sculptor
Hough, Melissa Ellen Museum Director, Curator
Hurwitz, Michael H Craftsman, Mosaic Artist
Irish, Jane Painter, Administrator
Kerrigan, Maurie Sculptor, Painter
Kettner, David Allen Artist, Educator
King, Ray Sculptor, Light Artist
Kocot & Hatton Painters, Conceptual Artists
La Pelle, Rodger Painter, Dealer
Lum, Ken (Kenneth) Robert Conceptual Artist, Photographer
Maksymowicz, Virginia Ann Sculptor, Writer
Marzano, Albert Painter, Designer
Maxwell, Peter Foundation Director, Designer
McClenney, Cheryl Ilene Administrator
McGinnis, Christine Painter, Printmaker
Meister, Michael William Historian, Educator
Millett, Caroline Dunlop Designer, Consultant
Miraglia, Peter F Artist, Photographer
Mosley, Joshua Animator
Moss-Vreeland, Patricia Painter, Draftsman
Newman, Libby Painter, Printmaker
Newman, Walter Andrews, Jr Art Dealer, Gallery Director
Nissen, Chris (John Christian Nissen), III Painter
Olin, Laurie Dewar Architect, Educator
Olivere, Raymond Painter, Illustrator
Osborne, Frederick S Educator, Administrator
Paone, Peter Painter, Printmaker
Percy, Ann Buchanan Curator, Historian
Putman, Mary T Painter
Reed, Jeffrey Painter
Rishel, Joseph John, Jr Curator
Rosenfeld, Richard Joel Dealer
Rub, Timothy F Museum Director
Rumford, Ronald Frank Printmaker, Painter
Sadao, Amy Museum Director
Sadeo, Amy Museum Director
Santoleri, Paul D Painter, Muralist
Schaff, Barbara Walley Artist
Sewell, Darrel L Curator, Historian
Sewell, Leo Assemblage Artist, Sculptor
Shoemaker, Innis Howe Curator
Shores, (James) Franklin Painter
Simkin, Phillips M Sculptor
Staffel, Doris Painter, Educator
Stein, Judith Ellen Historian, Curator
Stinnett, Hester A Printmaker
Stitt, Susan (Margaret) Museum Director, Administrator
Strauss, Zoe Photographer
Striker, Cecil L Historian, Educator
Stroker, Robert T Administrator, Educator
Taylor, Marilyn Jordan Administrator, Educator, Architect
Taylor, Michael R Curator
Tobia, Blaise Joseph Photographer, Educator
Venturi, Robert Architect
Visco, Anthony Salvatore Educator, Sculptor
Warner, Herbert Kelii, Jr Printmaker
Wint, Dennis Michael Museum Director
Yaros, Constance G Painter, Sculptor
Zynsky, Toots Sculptor

Phoenixville

Weidner, Marilyn Kemp Conservator, Lecturer

Pipersville

Gordley, Marilyn Classe Painter, Printmaker
Roseman, Susan Carol Printmaker, Painter

SOUTH CAROLINA (cont)
Fraser, Mary Edna Environmental Artist, Craftsman
Hull, John Painter
Johnson, Diane Chalmers Historian, Educator
Peacock, Cliffton Painter
Phillips, Michael Painter, Sculptor
Sloan, Mark Museum Director, Artist
Wyrick, Charles Lloyd, Jr Publisher, Editor

Clemson
Shelnutt, Greg W. sculptor, educator

Columbia
Blackwell, Elise Writer, Educator
Brosius, Karen Museum Director
Collins, Bradford R Educator, Administrator, Painter
Dunn, Phillip Charles Educator, Administrator
Dwyer, James Painter, Educator
Edwards, James F Painter, Educator
Elkins, Toni Marcus Painter
Hansen, Harold (Harry) John Educator, Painter
Lyon, Robert F Sculptor, Educator
Mack, Charles Randall Historian, Collector
Mullen, Philip Edward Painter
Robinson, Chris (Christopher) Thomas Conceptual Artist, Educator
Woody, (Thomas) Howard Sculptor, Environmental Artist

Easley
Cheek, Ronald Edward Painter, Instructor
Flowers, Thomas Earl Painter, Educator

Greenville
Coburn, Bette Lee Painter
Dreskin, Jeanet Steckler Painter, Educator
Paladino, Paul Photographer, Educator
Ritts, Edwin Earl, Jr Administrator, Museum Director

Hilton Head Island
Bowler, Joseph, Jr Painter, Illustrator
Calkins, Robert G Historian, Educator
Greer, Walter Marion Painter
Morris, Jack Austin, Jr Museum Director, Art Dealer

Honeapath
Van Osdell, Barrie (Calabrese) Smith Painter, Instructor

Johns Island
Machiorlete, Patricia Anne Painter, Craftsman

McCormick
Hofer, Ingrid (Ingeborg) Painter, Instructor

Myrtle Beach
Powers, W Alex Painter

North Augusta
Rice, Edward Painter

Orangeburg
Twiggs, Leo Franklin Painter, Educator

Pawleys Island
Tarbox, Gurdon Lucius, Jr Museum Director, Administrator

Rock Hill
Freeman, David L Painter, Graphic Artist

Spartanburg
Boggs, Mayo Mac Sculptor, Educator
Bramlett, Betty Jane Administrator, Painter, Collage Artist
Nodine, Jane Allen Painter, Sculptor

Sumter
Davenport, Ray Painter
McKoy, Victor Grainger Sculptor

Wadmalaw Island
Carter, Yvonne Pickering Painter, Educator

SOUTH DAKOTA

Burbank
Navrat, Den(nis) Edward Educator, Painter

Fulton
Sougstad, Mike Graphic Artist, Educator

Hill City
Broer, Roger L Printmaker, Painter

Rapid City
Clark, Lynda K Museum Director, Painter

Sioux Falls
Grupp, Carl Alf Painter, Printmaker

Spearfish
Termes, (Dick A) Painter, Sculptor

Vermillion
Knedler, Cory Printmaker, Educator, Administrator

TENNESSEE

Brentwood
Goad, Anne Laine Art Dealer, Publisher
Harmon, Paul Painter, Printmaker

Chattanooga
Cress, George Ayers Painter, Educator
Kret, Robert A Museum Director
Martin, Chester Young Painter, Sculptor
Scarbrough, Cleve Knox, Jr Museum Director, Historian
White, E Alan Administrator, Painter

Clarksville
Crouch, Ned Philbrick Sculptor, Curator
Hochstetler, T Max Painter, Educator

Cookeville
Lee-Sissom, E (Evelyn) Janelle Sissom Painter

Cosby
Beam, Mary Todd Painter

Cottontown
Bryant, Olen L Sculptor, Educator

Franklin
Sulkowski, Elizabeth Brandon Painter
Sulkowski, Joseph H Painter

Germantown
Allgood, Charles Henry Art Historian, Painter
Purtle, Carol Jean Historian, Educator

Greenfield
Engler, Sherrie Lee Painter, Illustrator

Hendersonville
Jones, Theodore Joseph Sculptor, Printmaker

Hixson
Townsend, Gavin Edward Historian, Educator

Jackson
Carmichael, Donald Ray Painter

Jamestown
Parisi, Martha Graphic Artist, Printmaker

Jefferson City
Cleveland, R. Earl Administrator, Art Restorer

Johnson City
Dyer, M Wayne Painter, Designer
Murray, Catherine sculptor, educator, administrator
Ropp, Ann L Painter, Gallery Director

Kingsport
Cassell, Robert E, Jr Photographer, Administrator
Williams, Raymond Lester Painter, Instructor

Kingston Springs
Nutt, Craig Craftsman, Sculptor

Knoxville
Butler, David Museum Director
Habel, Dorothy (Dottie) Metzger Educator, Administrator
Leland, Whitney Edward Painter, Educator
Lyons, Beauvais Printmaker, Educator
Magden, Norman E Filmmaker, Video Artist
Smith, Todd D Museum Director
Stewart, F Clark Draftsman, Painter

Livingston
Bishop, Budd Harris Painter, Museum Director

Madison
Vatandoost, Nossi Malek Educator, Painter

Memphis
Califf, Marilyn Iskiwitz Painter, Collage Artist
Carmean, E A, Jr Historian, Curator
Czestochowski, Joseph S Museum Director
Davila, Maritza Printmaker
Jasud, Lawrence Edward Photographer, Educator
Jones, Ronald Lee, Jr Administrator, Writer
Kitchin, Cameron Museum Director
Lou, Richard A Educator, Administrator
Lyons, Al Director
Myatt, Greely Sculptor
Riseling, Robert Lowell Educator, Painter
Riss, Murray Photographer, Educator
Roberson, William Tapestry Artist, Collage Artist
Rochat, Rana painter

Murfreesboro
Johnson, Erin (Stukey) Painter, Sculptor

Nashville
Aurbach, Michael Lawrence Sculptor, Educator
Baeder, John Painter
Dettwiller, Kathryn King Painter
Edwards, Susan Harris Director
Havens, Jan Sculptor, Printmaker
Hazlehurst, Franklin Hamilton Historian, Educator
Kaufman, Loretta Ana Sculptor, Painter, Instructor
King, Myron Lyzon Dealer
Knowles, Susan Williams Curator, Critic
Mode, Carol A Painter
Neal, Michael Shane Painter, Instructor
Saftel, Andrew P Painter, Sculptor
Webb, Sarah A Painter
Zimmerman, Alice A Collector, Art Dealer

Sewanee
Ende, Arlyn Studio Artist
Hastings, Jack Byron Sculptor, Author

TEXAS

Alpine
Fairlie, Carol Hunter Educator, Painter

Amarillo
Fraze, Denny T Collage Artist, Educator
Hyde, Scott Photographer, Printmaker

Arlington
Curry, Kevin Lee Curator, Director
Grandee, Joe Ruiz Painter, Gallery Director
Huerta, Benito Painter, Curator
Maroney, Dalton Sculptor
Spurlock, William Historian, Critic

Austin
Barnett, Helmut Painter, Printmaker
Bucknall, Malcolm Roderick Painter
Chesney, Lee Roy, III Printmaker, Educator
Clarke, John R Historian, Critic
Domjan, Evelyn Painter, Printmaker
Friis-Hansen, Dana Museum Director
Hatgil, Paul Educator, Painter
Hauft, Amy Sculptor
Henderson, Linda Dalrymple Historian, Educator
High, Timothy Griffin Printmaker, Sculptor
Hite, Jessie Otto Museum Director
Lansdon, Gay Brandt Printmaker, Jeweler
Lundberg, William Assemblage Artist, Filmmaker
Marshall, Bruce Painter, Illustrator
Mayer, Susan Martin Educator, Museologist
McFarland, Lawrence D Photographer
Miller, Melissa Wren Painter
Milliken, Gibbs Painter, Educator
Mogavero, Michael Painter
Navarro, Eduardo Installation Sculptor
Risley, Jack Administrator, Sculptor
Sawyer, Margo Sculptor, Environmental Artist, Installation Artist
Shiff, Richard Educator
Smith, Jeffrey Chipps Historian
Stratakos, Steve John Craftsman, Tapestry Artist
Vater, Regina Vater Lundberg Conceptual Artist, Lecturer
Wade, Robert Schrope Painter, Sculptor
Waldman, Louis A Educator
White, Jack Painter
Yeager, Sydney Philen Painter, Printmaker

TEXAS (cont)

TEXAS (cont)

Mission

McClendon, Maxine Nichols Painter
Nichols, Edward Edson Painter, Educator

Montgomery

Herring, Jan (Janet) Mantel Painter, Writer

Nacogdoches

Beason, Donald Ray Educator, Sculptor
McCleary, Mary Fielding Collage Artist, Educator
Talbot, Christopher Administrator, Educator, Photographer
Wink, Don (Jon Donnel) Painter, Educator

Odessa

Lee, Nelda S Dealer

Pantego

Ray, Donald Arvin Painter

Richardson

Stott, Deborah Historian

Rockport

Moroles, Jesús Bautista Sculptor

San Antonio

Amado, Jesse V Sculptor
Binks, Ronald C Photographer, Painter
Casas, Melesio (Mel) Painter, Educator
Drutt, Matthew J W Director, Curator
Elder, Gene Wesley Collage Artist, Writer
Elliott, Gregory Administrator, Educator
Embrey, Carl Rice Painter, Instructor
Funk, Charlotte M Tapestry Artist, Educator
Funk, Verne J Sculptor, Educator
Haynes, David Historian, Consultant
Herring, William Arthur Painter
Klein, Jeanne Collector
Little, Ken Dawson Sculptor
Luber, Katherine Museum Director
Notestine, Dorothy J Instructor, Painter
Oettinger, Marion, Jr Curator
Parsons, Merribell Maddux Museum Director, Curator
Prescott, Kenneth Wade Museum Director, Administrator
Rubin, David S Curator, Writer
Rush, Kent Thomas Photographer, Printmaker
Scott, Bill Earl Painter
Snyder, Hills Sculptor, Writer
Tiemann, Robert E Painter, Sculptor
West, E Gordon Painter

San Elizario

Enriquez, Gaspar Painter, Metalsmith

Seminole

Clark, Vicky Jo Painter

Smithville

Kohut, Lorene Painter

Southlake

Sherwood, Leona Painter, Instructor

Spring

Wethington, Wilma Painter, Instructor

Tyler

Gentry, Augustus Calahan, Jr Painter, Printmaker
Hatcher, Gary C Educator, Administrator, Ceramist
Ott, Wendell Lorenz Museum Director, Painter
Pace, James Robert Collage Artist, Printmaker
Stephens, William Blakely Educator, Painter

Waco

Chatmas, John T Painter, Sculptor
Kemp, Paul Zane Educator, Sculptor
McClanahan, John D Painter, Educator

Wichita Falls

Band, David Moshe Painter, Art Dealer

Wylie

Pototschnik, John Michael Painter, Instructor

UTAH

Castle Valley

Zavada, Barbara Johanna Painter, Printmaker

Draper

Moyer, Linda Lee Painter, Educator

Lindon

Speed, (Ulysses) Grant Sculptor

Logan

Gelfand, Laura D Educator, Administrator
Terry, Christopher T Painter, Draftsman
Van Suchtelen, Adrian Printmaker, Educator

Mendon

Morgan, James L Painter

Ogden

Kanatsiz, Suzanne L Sculptor, Educator

Pleasant Grove

Jarvis, John Brent Painter

Provo

Barsch, Wulf Erich Painter, Printmaker
Bronson, Clark Everice Sculptor
Coleman, Michael B Painter
Gray, Campbell Bruce Museum Director, Museologist
Marshall, Robert Leroy Educator, Painter
Myer, Peter Livingston Kinetic Artist, Painter
Whitaker, William Painter, Illustrator

Redmond

Pierce, Diane Jean Painter, Illustrator

Saint George

Lindstrom, Gaell Painter, Educator

Salt Lake City

Brest van Kempen, Catel Pieter Painter
Christensen, Larry R Painter, Instructor
Christensen, Sharlene Painter, Instructor
De Waal, Ronald Burt Collector, Patron
Ferrell, Heather A Museum Director
Frazer, James (Nisbet), Jr Assemblage Artist, Installation Sculptor
Lake, Randall Painter, Printmaker
Rasmussen, Anton Jesse Painter, Administrator
Rohovit, Marah Brown Painter
Snapp, Brian Educator, Administrator
Tierney, Patrick Lennox Historian, Educator, Lecturer

Sandy

Wanlass, Stanley Glen Sculptor, Painter

South Jordan

Fraughton, Edward James Sculptor

Springville

Swanson, Vern Grosvenor Museum Director, Historian

VERMONT

Arlington

Housman, Russell F Painter, Educator

Bennington

Adams, Pat Painter, Educator
Federhen, Deborah Anne Curator, Historian

Brandon

Bull, Fran Painter, Printmaker
Young, Janie Chester Museum Director, Educator

Brattleboro

Mason, Emily Painter

Brookfield

Koren, Edward B Cartoonist, Illustrator

Burlington

Davison, Bill Educator, Printmaker
Dwyer, Nancy Sculptor, Painter
Parris, Nina Gumpert Educator, Photographer
Seide, Paul A Glass Blower, Sculptor
Stone, Judith Elise Artist, Architectural Historian

Charlotte

Robinson, Sally W Printmaker, Painter

Dorset

Marron, Pamela Anne Painter
Pitcher, John Charles Painter

East Calais

de Gogorza, Patricia (Gahagan) Sculptor, Printmaker

East Dorset

Howe, Nancy Painter

Fairlee

Walker II, Herbert Brooks Sculptor, Designer

Groton

Sultan, Altoon Painter

Jericho

Chase, Jack S(paulding) Sculptor

Marlboro

Olitski, Eve Painter

Middlebury

Andres, Glenn Merle Historian, Educator
Bumbeck, David Printmaker, Educator
Perry, Edward (Ted) Samuel Administrator, Professor
Saunders, Richard Henry Museum Director, Historian

Montpelier

Greene, Thomas Christopher Administrator, Writer

Newark

Van Vliet, Claire Printmaker, Bookmaker

North Bennington

Boepple, Willard Sculptor, Educator
Pibal, Ann Painter

North Pomfret

Semple, John Paulus Painter

North Troy

Fisher, Joel Sculptor

Pawlet

Torak, Elizabeth Painter
Torak, Thomas Painter

Pownal

Gibson, Walter Samuel Writer, Lecturer

Putney

Sproat, Christopher Townsend Sculptor, Designer

Saint Albans

Prent, Mark Environmental Artist, Sculptor

Saxtons River

Wood, John August Writer, Historian

Shaftsbury

Bubriski, Kevin E Photographer

Springfield

Eldredge, Mary Agnes Sculptor

Thetford

Matteson, Ira Sculptor, Draftsman

Townshend

Robinson, Duncan (David) Director, Historian

West Danville

Roosevelt, Michael Armentrout Printmaker, Art Appraiser

Weston

Kasnowski, Chester N Painter, Instructor

Williamstown

Gaylord, Frank Chalfant, II Sculptor, Designer

Williamsville

Bowen, Paul Sculptor

Woodstock

Horrell, Jeffrey L Librarian

VIRGINIA

WASHINGTON

WASHINGTON (cont)
Schlanger, Gregg Administrator

Goldendale
Schafroth, Colleen Director

Issaquah
Pennington, Sally Painter

Kent
Gard, Suzanne E Painter
Pierce, Danny P Sculptor, Painter

Kingston
Maki, Robert Richard Sculptor, Painter

Kirkland
Ho, Francis T Photographer, Educator

Lopez
Perry, Kathryn Powers Painter, Graphic Artist

Maple Valley
Frugé-Brown, Kathleen Painter, Printmaker

Medina
Tse, Stephen Painter, Educator

Mercer Island
Glazer, Jay M & Marsha S Collectors, Patrons

Normandy Park
Herman, Lloyd Eldred Museum Director

Olympia
Johnston, Thomas Alix Painter, Printmaker
Randlett, Mary Willis Photographer

Port Orchard
Bower, Marilyn Kay Painter, Instructor

Port Townsend
Ainsworth, Diane Painter

Pullman
Coates, Ross Alexander Historian, Painter

Sammamish
Rushworth, Michele D Painter, Instructor

Seattle
Adkison, Kathleen (Gemberling) Painter
Allen, Judith S Photographer, Educator
Allen, Paul Collector
Angell, Tony Sculptor, Painter
Araluce, Rick Sculptor
Berger, Paul Eric Collage Artist, Photographer
Braseth, John E Art Dealer, Consultant
Bravmann, Rene A Art Historian, Educator
Brody, David Painter, Educator
Bruch, Chris Sculptor
Burns, Marsha Photographer
Cartwright, Derrick R Museum Director
Celentano, Francis Michael Painter, Educator
Chihuly, Dale Patrick Sculptor, Glass Artist
Coupe, James Digital Artist
De Lory, Peter Photographer
Gates, Mimi Gardner Retired Museum Director
Grade, John Installation Sculptor
Hansen, Gaylen Capener Painter, Educator
Hayes, Randy (Randolph) Alan Painter
Hedreen, Betty Collector
Hedreen, Elizabeth & Richard Collector
Herard, Marvin T Sculptor, Educator
Hu, Mary Lee Goldsmith, Educator
Huchthausen, David Richard Sculptor, Educator
Jones, Fay Printmaker, Painter
Jonsson, Ted (Wilbur) Sculptor
King, Douglas R Museum Director
Kirsten-Daiensai, Richard Charles Painter, Printmaker
Lundin, Norman K Painter, Educator
Lynch, Perri Installation Sculptor, Environmental Artist
Marioni, Dante Glass Blower
Marioni, Paul Sculptor, Glass Blower
McDonnell, Joseph Anthony Sculptor, Painter
Oliver, Marvin E Craftsman
Ozubko, Christopher Educator, Graphic Artist
Patha, Camille Painter
Ritchie, William (Bill) H, Jr Printmaker, Video Artist
Rood, Kay Painter, Printmaker
Ross, Joan Stuart Painter, Printmaker
Ross, Sueellen Painter, Printmaker
Ruffner, Ginny Martin Sculptor, Glassblower
Sato, Norie Environmental Artist, Sculptor
Siems, Anne Painter
Spafford, Michael Charles Educator, Painter
Theobald, Gillian Lee Painter, Lithographer
Thompson, Cappy (Catherine) Painter
True, Ruth & William L Collectors
Warashina, M Patricia Clay Sculptor, Educator
West, Richard Vincent Museum Director, Historian
Wolf, Sylvia Gallery Director, Curator
Wright, Bagley Collector
Wright, Virginia Collector, Curator
Wunderlich, Paul Painter, Printmaker
Yoder, Robert Edward Artist
Zeitlin, Harry Leon Photographer

Sequim
Guilmet, Glenda J Painter, Photographer

Shoreline
Holm, Bill Historian, Painter
Laico, Colette Collage Artist, Painter

Snohomish
Guzak, Karen W Painter, Printmaker, Public Artist
Jones, Thomas William Painter

Spokane
Eldredge, Bruce B Museum Director, Administrator
Flahavin, Marian Joan Painter, Sculptor
Fyfe, Jo Suzanne (Storch) Instructor, Painter
Mobley, Karen R Painter, Administrator
Patnode, J Scott Educator, Museum Director

Tacoma
Close, (John) Timothy Museum Director
Fear, Daniel E Consultant, Editor
Hallam, John S Historian, Administrator
Marshall, John Carl Craftsman
Rades, William L Painter, Sculptor
Stebich, Stephanie A Museum Director

Vashon
Cole, Donald Painter

Walla Walla
Hara, Keiko Painter, Printmaker
Sawada, Ikune Painter
Wharton, David W Printmaker, Painter

Washougal
Plous, Phyllis Curator

Wenatchee
Woolschlager, Laura Totten Painter, Printmaker

WEST VIRGINIA

Charleston
Ambrose, Richard Michael Director, Curator
Atkins, Rosalie Marks Painter
Toth, Caryl Photographer

Fairmont
Smigocki, Stephen Vincent Painter, Printmaker

Huntington
Anderson, Winslow Designer, Painter
Culligan, Jenine Elizabeth Curator, Administrator
Hage, Raymond Joseph Art Dealer, Lecturer
Layne, Margaret Mary Director

Morgantown
Helm, Alison Educator, Administrator
Schultz, John Bernard Educator, Historian

Shepherdstown
Suttenfield, Diana Painter

Wheeling
Peace, Bernie Kinzel Printmaker, Collage Artist

WISCONSIN

Algoma
Look, Dona Sculptor

Arena
Weege, William Printmaker, Educator

Beloit
Olson, Richard W Painter, Educator

Cedarburg
Geniusz, Robert Myles Printmaker, Filmmaker

Delafield
Hopkins, B(ernice) Elizabeth Painter

Hartland
Stamsta, Jean Painter, Woven Fiber

Hollandale
Colescott, Warrington W Printmaker, Painter

Kenosha
Simoneau, Daniel Robert Painter, Photographer

Madison
Anderson, Wilmer (Louis) Painter, Writer
Applebaum, Leon Glass Blower, Sculptor
Archbold, Ann M Educator, Administrator
Breckenridge, Bruce M Ceramist, Educator
Conniff, Gregory Photographer, Writer
Crumb, Robert Dennis Cartoonist, Illustrator
Daily-Birnbaum, Elaine Painter
Fleischman, Stephen Museum Director, Curator
Garver, Fanny Art Dealer
Garver, Thomas H Consultant, Curator
Handler, Audrey Glass Blower, Sculptor
Kreilick, Marjorie E Mosaic Artist, Educator
Lakes, Diana Mary Painter
Loeser, Thomas Sculptor
Myers, Frances J Printmaker
Nice, Don Painter
Nicholson, Natasha Assemblage Artist, Sculptor
Panczenko, Russell Museum Director
Stevens, Andrew Rich Curator, Historian
Tarrell, Robert Ray Educator, Painter
Tesfagiorgis, Freida Printmaker, Educator
Weiss, Lee (Elyse C) Painter

Marinette
La Malfa, James Thomas Sculptor, Educator

Marshfield
Waisbrot, Ann M Administrator, Curator

Milwaukee
Balsley, John Gerald Painter, Sculptor
Barnett, David J Art Dealer, Painter
Brite, Jane Fassett Curator, Director
Carter, Curtis Lloyd Museum Director, Educator
Cucullu, Santiago Painter
Dronzek, Laura Ann Painter
Farrell, Patrick Painter, Printmaker
Hirsh, Annette Marie Silversmith, Goldsmith
Jensen, Dean N Dealer, Critic
Kaganovich, Yevgeniya Administrator, Educator, Metalsmith
Keegan, Daniel T Museum Director
Kohl-Spiro, Barbara Printmaker, Painter
Mason, Wally Museum Director
Michaels-Paque, J Painter, Sculptor
Poehlmann, JoAnna Illustrator, Printmaker
Quirk, James Director
Rosenblatt, Adolph Painter, Sculptor
Rosenblatt, Suzanne Maris Painter, Writer
Travanti, Leon Emidio Painter, Designer
Yoder, Janica Photographer, Educator

Mineral Point
Ross, James Matthew Akiba Assemblage Artist, Photographer

Mount Horeb
Becker, David Painter, Educator
Haatoum Hamady, Walter Samuel Collage Artist, Publisher
Zalucha, Peggy Flora Painter

Neenah
Smith, Jan Director, Curator

Onalaska
Bartz, James Ross Painter

Oshkosh
Donhauser, Paul Stefan Sculptor, Painter
Pontynen, Arthur Educator, Administrator

Port Washington
Gruen, Shirley Schanen Painter

Racine
Holmes, David Valentine Sculptor, Painter
Johns, Christopher K(alman) Painter, Educator
Mathis, Emile Henry, II Dealer, Collector
Pepich, Bruce Walter W Museum Director, Curator

WYOMING

PUERTO RICO

CANADA

ALBERTA

BRITISH COLUMBIA

MANITOBA

NEW BRUNSWICK

NEWFOUNDLAND AND LABRADOR

NOVA SCOTIA

ONTARIO

ONTARIO (cont)

Durham

White, Norman Triplett Sculptor, Kinetic Artist

Georgian Bluffs

Hogbin, Stephen Sculptor

Grand Valley

Adams, Kim Hastings Sculptor

Grimsby

Reitzenstein, Reinhard Sculptor, Environmental Artist

Guelph

Betteridge, Lois Etherington Lecturer, Silversmith

Hamilton

Carter, Harriet (Estelle) Manore Painter

King City

Tahedl, Ernestine Stained Glass Artist, Painter

Kingston

Dorn, Peter Klaus Designer, Graphic Artist
Finley, Gerald Eric Historian
Swain, Robert Francis Gallery Director

Kitchener

Goetz, Peter Henry Painter, Lecturer

London

Ariss, Herbert Joshua Painter, Illustrator
Ariss, Margot Joan Phillips Painter, Sculptor
Atkinson, Eric Newton Painter, Educator
Dale, William Scott Abell Historian, Educator
Favro, Murray Sculptor
Fenwick, Roly (William Roland) Painter, Educator
Livick, Stephen Photographer
Pas, Gerard Peter Painter, Sculptor
Poole, Nancy Geddes Gallery Director

Markham

Maki, Sheila A Printmaker, Painter

Maynooth

Miezajs, Dainis Painter, Instructor

Mississauga

La Pierre, Thomas Painter, Printmaker

Mount Brydges

Thibert, Patrick A Sculptor, Educator

Niagara on the Lake

Scott, Campbell Printmaker, Sculptor

North York

Bieler, Ted Andre Educator, Sculptor

Oakville

Matsubara, Naoko Printmaker, Painter
Shemdin, Azhar H Painter, Assemblage Artist

Ottawa

Bell, Philip Michael Administrator, Historian
Bourdeau, Robert Charles Photographer
Cazort, Mimi Curator, Historian
De Kergommeaux, Duncan Painter, Educator
Dickson, Jennifer Joan Photographer, Lecturer
Durr, Pat (Patricia) (Beth) Painter, Printmaker
Mayer, Marc Museum Director
Reid, Leslie Painter, Photographer, Video Artist

Owen Sound

Willmott, Elizabeth Ann Sculptor, Photographer

Pickering

Semak, Michael Photographer, Educator

Port Hope

Blackwood, David (Lloyd) Painter, Printmaker

Shanty Bay

Bachinski, Walter Joseph Painter, Printmaker

Stratford

Green, Art Painter

Thornhill

Firer, Serge Printmaker, Graphic Artist

Thunderbay

Clarke, Ann Painter, Educator

Toronto

Andrews, Kim Painter
Aquino, Humberto Painter
Armstrong, Geoffrey Painter, Architect
Astman, Barbara Anne Photographer, Visual Artist
Belanger, Ron Painter
Beveridge, Karl J Photographer, Collage Artist
Blazeje, Zbigniew (Ziggy) Blazese Sculptor, Painter
Boigon, Brian Joseph Conceptual Artist, Writer
Bolliger, Therese Educator, Sculptor
Cetín, Anton Painter, Printmaker
Cliff, Denis Antony Painter, Instuctor
Cumming, Glen Edward Consultant
De Heusch, Lucio Painter
Dillow, Nancy Elizabeth Robertson Administrator, Historian
Doyle, Noel Francis Painter, Sculptor
Drapell, Joseph Painter, Filmmaker
Duff, Ann MacIntosh Painter, Printmaker
Elder, R Bruce Filmmaker, Critic
Feist, Harold E Painter, Sculptor
Fleisher, Pat Designer, Curator
Gale, Peggy Writer, Curator
Graham, K M Painter, Printmaker
Gurney, Janice Sigrid Conceptual Artist, Photographer
Heath, Dave (David) Martin Photographer
Hendeles, Ydessa Gallery Owner, Collector
Houle, Robert James Painter, Consultant
Jaworska, Tamara Fiber Artist, Tapestry Artist
Kaye, David Haigh Textile Artist, Art Dealer
Kramer, Burton Artist, Designer
Kravis, Janis Designer, Architect
Leshyk, Tonie Sculptor, Draftsman
Lexier, Micah Sculptor
Lochnan, Katharine A Curator, Writer
MacKenzie, Hugh Seaforth Painter, Etcher
Markle, Sam Dealer, Sculptor
Martin, Jane Painter, Draftsman
Massey, John Collage Artist, Conceptual Artist
Moos, Walter A Dealer
Murdock, Greg Painter
Murray, Ian Stewart Sculptor, Conceptual Artist
Nasgaard, Roald Curator, Historian
Partridge, David Gerry Painter, Sculptor
Patton, Andy (Andrew) John Painter
Reeves, John Alexander Photographer
Sassone, Marco Painter, Printmaker
Schwarz, Judith Sculptor, Draftsman
Selznick-Drutz, June Painter, Educator
Sewell, Richard George Printmaker, Painter
Shaw, Joseph Winterbotham Historian, Educator
Snow, Michael Sculptor, Filmmaker
Steele, Lisa Video Artist
Sutton, Carol (Lorraine) Painter
Tanenbaum, Joey Collector
Timmas, Osvald Painter, Lecturer
Tomcik, Andrew Michael Educator, Designer
Tuer, Dot (Dorothy) J Critic, Curator
Van Ginkel, Blanche Lemco Architect, Educator
Zeidler, Eberhard Heinrich Architect, Designer
Zemans, Joyce L Educator, Art Historian

Wasaga Beach

Kravjansky, Mikulas Painter, Printmaker, Designer

Welland

Tulumello, Peter M Consultant, Designer

West Lorne

Redinger, Walter Fred Sculptor, Muralist
Zelenak, Edward J Sculptor

Wiarton

Watson, Mary Anne Printmaker, Painter

Willowdale

Collyer, Robin Sculptor, Photographer
Robb, Charles Painter
Wiitasalo, Shirley Painter

Windsor

Hunkler, Dennis Painter, Draftsman

QUEBEC

Ayers Cliff

Beament, Tib (Thomas Harold) Painter

Beaconfield

Harder, Rolf Peter Graphic Designer, Painter

Chicoutimi

Seguin, Jean-Pierre Painter, Photographer

Gatineau

Ostiguy, Jean-Rene Painter, Art Historian

La Salle

DeAngelis, Joseph Rocco Sculptor, Painter

Laval

Bruni, Umberto Painter, Graphic Artist

Luskville

Hlavina, Rastislav Sculptor, Writer

Montreal

Briansky, Rita Prezament Painter, Instructor
Cardinal, Marcelin Painter, Collage Artist
Cohen, Sorel Conceptual Artist, Photographer
Daigneault, Gilles Curator, Critic
De Moura Sobral, Luis Historian, Critic
Falsetto, Mario Educator
Franklin, Hannah Sculptor, Painter
Gaucher, Yves Printmaker, Painter
Gaudard, Pierre Photographer, Graphic Artist
Hanks, David Allen Curator, Writer
Hartal, Paul Painter, Writer
Knudsen, Christian Painter, Photographer
Lambert, Phyllis Architect, Director
Lamoureux, Marie France Art Dealer, Gallery Director
Layne, Barbara J Instructor
Lerner, Loren Ruth Educator
Letendre, Rita Painter, Printmaker
London, Naomi Sculptor
Merola, Mario Sculptor, Painter
Molinari, Guido Painter, Sculptor
Paikowsky, Sandra R Curator, Historian
Palumbo, Jacques Painter, Sculptor
Schleeh, Hans Martin Sculptor
Schweitzer, John Andrew Collage Artist, Curator
Shaw, John Palmer Painter, Printmaker
Steinberg, Blema Collector
Steinberg, H Arnold Collector
Steinhouse, Tobie (Thelma) Painter, Printmaker
Sullivan, Francoise Painter, Sculptor
Swartzman, Roslyn Printmaker, Sculptor
Tousignant, Claude Painter, Sculptor
Tousignant, Serge Photographer, Conceptual Artist
Vaillancourt, Armand Sculptor, Painter
Wertheimer, Esther Sculptor

Montreal West

Missakian, Berge Artin Painter

Ogden

Whittome, Irene F Sculptor, Painter

Quebec

Martel, Richard Conceptual Artist, Editor
Schlitter, Helga Painter, Sculptor

Rosemere

Brunet-Weinmann, Monique Critic, Curator

Saint Bruno

Readman, Sylvie Photographer

Val-David

Baxter, Bonnie Jean Printmaker, Painter

Vaudreuil-Dorion

Braitstein, Marcel Sculptor, Educator

Westmount

Dyens, Georges Maurice Sculptor
Owens, Gwendolyn Jane Administrator, Curator

SASKATCHEWAN

Lumsden

Fafard, Joe (Joseph) Yvon Sculptor

Regina

Cowin, Jack Lee Printmaker, Painter

Saskatoon

Bornstein, Eli Painter, Sculptor
Hamilton, W Paul C Educator, Historian
Ringness, Charles Obert Educator, Printmaker

Other Countries

ARGENTINA

Costantini, Eduardo Collector

AUSTRALIA

Valier, Biron (Frank) Painter, Printmaker

AUSTRIA

Essl, Agnes & Karlheinz, Sr Collector

BELGIUM

Decelle, Philippe Collector, Curator
Jones, Kim Conceptual Artist
Libeert, Mimi & Filiep J Collector
Rabinowitch, Royden Leslie Sculptor
Torres, Mario Garcia Conceptual Artist
Ullens de Schooten, Myriam & Guy Francis Collectors, Administrators
Vanhaerents, Walter Collector
Vanmoerkerke, Edith and Mark Collectors

BRAZIL

Paz, Bernardo Collector
Joo, Eungie Curator
Zamora, Hector Installation Sculptor

BRUNEI DARUSSALAM

Hassanal Bolkiah, His Majesty Mu'izzaddin Waddaulah Collector

EGYPT

Hefuna, Susan Video Artist, Photographer

FRANCE

Adamo, David Installation Sculptor
Arnault, Helene & Bernard Jean Etienne Collector
Baltz, Lewis Photographer
Crotto, Paul Painter, Sculptor
De Galbert, Antoine Administrator, Collector
Edouard, Pierre Painter, Sculptor
Gutierrez, Yolanda Sculptor
Hicks, Sheila Sculptor
Jacobs, Harold Painter, Sculptor
Kurhajec, Joseph A Sculptor
Levee, John H Painter, Sculptor
Linn, Steven Allen Sculptor
Massey, Ann James Painter, Graphic Artist
Matisse, Jackie (Jacqueline) Matisse Monnier Painter, Sculptor
Noel, Jean Sculptor
Petlin, Irving Painter
Pinault, François-Henri Collector
Plossu, Bernard Photographer
Prado-Arai, Namiko Visual Artist
Prat, Louis-Antoine & Veronique Collector, Writer
Reid, Sheila Assemblage Artist, Writer
Renouf, Edda Painter, Printmaker
Rothschild, Eric de Collector
Saunders, Marr Painter
Wertheimer, Alain Collector

GERMANY

Anderson, Curtis Leslie Conceptual Artist, Painter
Boros, Christian Collector
Brandhorst, Udo Collector
Brenner, Birgit Installation Sculptor
Burda, Frieder Collector
Falckenberg, Harald Collector
Goetz, Ingvild Collector
Graydon, Andy Video Artist
Hoffmann, Erika Collector, Patron
Iannone, Dorothy Painter, Writer
Piper, Adrian Margaret Smith Conceptual Artist, Writer
Taschen, Benedikt Collector
Würth, Reinhold Collector
Yang, Haegue Installation Sculptor

GREECE

Daskalopoulos, Dimitris Collector
Joannou, Dakis Collector
Martinos, Dinos Collector

HONG KONG

Lau, Joseph Luen-Hung Collector

INDIA

Chopra, Nikhil Photographer

INDONESIA

Kaida, Tamarra Photographer

IRELAND

Magnier, Susan & John Collectors

ISRAEL

Shaman, Sanford Sivitz Museum Director, Curator

ITALY

Rebaudengo, Patrizia Sandretto Re Collector
Bertelli, Patrizio Collector
Cecil, Charles Harkless Painter, Educator
Cook, Robert Howard Sculptor, Medalist
D'Almeida, George Painter
Gori, Giuliano Collector
Hsiao, Chin Painter, Sculptor
Irwin, Lani Helena Painter
Prada, Miuccia Bianca Collector

JAPAN

Fukutake, Soichiro Collector
Honjo, Naoki Photographer
Yanai, Tadashi Collector

MEXICO

Aguilera, Alejandro Sculptor
Agustin, Hernandez Architect, Sculptor
Alonso, Eugenio Lopez Collector
Amaya, Armando Sculptor
Amoroso, Nicolas Alberto Amoroso Boelcke Painter, Filmmaker
Angulo, Chappie Painter, Illustrator
Aquino, Edmundo Painter, Sculptor
Beltran, Felix Painter, Printmaker
Biblos, Mahia Sculptor, Designer
Birbil, Paul Gregory Painter, Printmaker
Bragar, Philip Frank Painter, Sculptor
Cattan, Emilia Painter, Printmaker
Cauduro, Rafael Painter, Muralist
Clement, Kathleen Painter, Graphic Artist
Colina, Armando G Gallery Director, Editor
De la Vega, Gabriela Painter, Illustrator
Escobedo, Helen Environmental Artist
Felguerez, Manuel Painter, Sculptor
Flores, Carlos Marini Architect, Historian
Garcia Guerrero, Luis Painter
Garza Laguera, Eugenio Collector
Goldberg, Norma Sculptor
Guerra, Konrado Avina Painter, Sculptor
Hayes, Carolyn Hendrick Painter, Sculptor
Hijar, Alberto Serano Critic, Educator
Hooper, Jack Meredith Painter, Printmaker
Kassner, Lily Historian, Critic
Kempe, Richard Joseph Collector, Curator
Landau, Myra Painter, Muralist
Leyva, Alicia Painter
Lozoya, Agustin Portillo Painter
Luque, Jose Antonio Critic, Curator
Mayer, Monica P Writer, Conceptual Artist
Palau, Marta Environmental Artist, Sculptor
Parra, Carmen Painter, Printmaker
Pereznieto, Fernando Painter, Sculptor
Ruz, Thelma Sculptor
Slim Helú, Carlos Collector
Stavans, Isaac Painter
Tobler, Gisela Erna Maria Painter, Architect
Villarreal-Castelazo, Eduardo Architect, Painter
Wong, Lucille (Lucila) Guerra Wong Painter, Printmaker

NETHERLANDS

Krulik, Barbara S Director, Museologist
Sanders, Jeannette & Martijn Collector
Van Caldenborgh, Joop Collector

NORWAY

Astrup, Hans Rasmus Collector, Museum Founder

RUSSIA

Zhukova, Dasha Collector

SPAIN

Abello, Juan Collector
Andreason, Lee Sculpture
Arango, Placido G, Jr Collector
Koplowitz, Alicia Collector
Miller, Arthur Green Educator, Historian
Rocamora, Jaume Painter

SWAZILAND

Ringier, Ellen & Michael Collector

SWITZERLAND

Barbier-Mueller, Monique & Jean-Paul Collector, Museum Founder
Bechtler-Lanfranconi, Cristina & Thomas W Collector
Cytter, Keren Video Artist, Photographer
Gottschalk, Fritz Designer, Lecturer
Grether, Esther Collector
Hess, Donald Marc Contemporary Art Collector
Keller, Samuel Museum Director
Merzbacher, Gabrielle & Werner Collector
Mosset, Olivier Painter
Oeri, Maja Collector
Ortiz, George Collector
Sigg, Uli Collector

TAIWAN

Chen, Pierre TM Collector
Huang, Frank C Collector
Li-lan Painter

THAILAND

Weerasethakul, Apichatpong Filmmaker

TURKEY

Duben, Ipek Aksugur Painter, Sculptor
Kirac, Inan & Suna Collector

UKRAINE

Pinchuk, Victor Collector

UNITED KINGDOM

Cohen, Cherryl & Frank Collector
Abramovich, Roman Arkadyevich Collector
Aliki, Liacouras Brandenberg Illustrator, Writer
Altfest, Ellen Painter
Bartolini, Massimo Sculptor, Photographer
Blackburn, David Painter
Burns, Josephine Painter
Carswell, John Museum Director, Painter
Condo, George Painter, Sculptor
Dennison, Keith Elkins Consultant, Curator
Durham, Jimmie Sculptor, Essayist
Embiricos, Epaminondas George (Pandy Embiricos) Collector
Floyer, Ceal Sculptor
Gander, Ryan Filmmaker, Installation Sculptor
Gottesman, Geraldine & Noam Collector
Graff, Laurence Collector
Gyatso, Gonkar Printmaker
Hackenbroch, Yvonne Alix Curator, Writer
Hiller, Susan Conceptual Artist
Hirst, Damien Conceptual Artist, Collector
Hubbard, John Painter
Jones, Allen Christopher Painter, Printmaker, Sculptor
Khalili, Nasser David Collector
Lagrange, Pierre Collector
Laumann, Lars Video Artist
Lijn, Liliane Sculptor, Writer
Lubar, Katherine Painter
Nash, David Sculptor
Phillpot, Clive James Writer, Curator
Quentel, Holt Painter
Ramos, Theodore Painter, Muralist

OTHER COUNTRIES (cont)

Reeves, Daniel McDonough Video Artist, Installation Artist
Saatchi, Charles Collector
Said, Wafic Rida Collector
Sainsbury, David Collector
Salmon, Margaret Photographer, Video Artist
Shearer, Steven Collage Artist, Painter
Sherwood, James Blair Patron
Simon, Peter Collector
Stella, Frank Painter
Thompson, Paul Warwick Administrator
Warner, Marina Writer, Critic
Zabludowicz, Poju Collector

VENEZUELA

Cisneros, Patricia & Gustavo Alfredo Collector
Phelps de Cisneros, Patricia Collector

Address Not Published

Aadland, Dale Lynn Printmaker, Painter
Abbe, Elfriede Martha Sculptor, Printmaker
Abbott, Linda J Stained Glass Artist, Instructor
Abish, Cecile Environmental Artist, Photographer
Abou-Issa, Issa Painter, Sculptor
Abraham, Carol Jeanne Assemblage Artist, Ceramist
Abramovic, Marina Performance Artist
Abramson, Elaine Sandra Cartoonist, Designer, Art Licensor, Author, Speaker
Adams, Derrick Conceptual Artist
Adams, Lisa Kay Painter
Adams, Mac Sculptor, Photographer
Adibi, Elise Painter, Photographer
Adler, Tracy L Curator, Educator
Aho, Paul Richard Painter
Ahrendt, Mary E Conceptual Artist
Ahuja, Mequitta Painter
Aksel, Erdag Sculptor, Instructor
Albano, Patrick Louis Art Dealer
Alden, Richard Painter
Alejo, Mauricio Photographer
Alexander, Anthony K Sculptor
Alexander, Wick Painter
Alexander-Greene, Grace George Educator, Museum Director
Alexenberg, Mel Conceptual Artist, Educator
Alicea, Jose Printmaker
Allen, Constance Olleen Webb Painter, Jewelry Designer
Allen, Edda Lynne Painter, Art Dealer
Allen, Jonathan Painter, Collage Artist
Allen, Terry Multi-Media Artist
Alpert, George Photographer, Painter
Alvarez-Cervela, Jose Maria Educator, Historian
Anastasi, William (Joseph) Painter, Sculptor
Anderson, Bruce A Goldsmith, Sculptor
Anderson, Dawolu Jabari Illustrator
Anderson, Laura (Grant) Painter
Anderson-Staley, Keliy Photographer
Andrade, Bruno Painter
Angelo, Sandra McFall Writer, Instructor
Angeloch, Robert Painter, Printmaker
Antic, Miroslav Painter, Illustrator
App, Timothy Painter, Educator
Appel, Thelma Painter, Instructor
Aram, Kamrooz Painter
Arceneaux, Edgar Installation Sculptor
Argent, Philip Painter
Argue, Douglas Painter
Arias-Misson, Alain Visual Poet, Graphic Artist
Armstrong, Carol Painter
Arnold, Paul Beaver Educator, Printmaker
Arnold, Skip Video Artist, Performance Artist
Aron, Marlene Installation Sculptor
Arvidson, Betsy Printmaker
Asher, Frederick M Historian, Educator
Ashkin, Michael Sculptor
Askman, Tom K Painter, Educator
Atkins, Robert Critic, Educator, Editor
Attal, M George Art Dealer, Consultant
Attie, Shimon Photographer, Video Installation
Auerbach, Lisa Anne Photographer
Auerbach, Tauba Printmaker
Augustine, Seth Sculptor
Austin, Pat Painter, Printmaker
Ayers, Carol Lee Painter, Gallery Director
Baas, Jacquelynn Director, Writer
Bachert, Hildegard Gina Art Dealer
Bacot, Henry Parrott Museum Director, Educator
Badgett, Steven Artist
Baer, Adam Photographer, Video Artist
Bagget, William (Carter), Jr Printmaker, Muralist
Bai, Lisha Painter
Baibakov, Oleg Collector
Baibakova, Maria Collector
Bailey, Barry Stone Sculptor, Painter
Bailey, Clayton George Sculptor, Ceramist
Bailey, William Harrison Painter
Bakanowsky, Louis J Sculptor, Architect
Baker, Blanche Sculptor, Instructor
Baker, Cornelia Draves Printmaker, Painter
Baker, Nancy Schwartz Painter, Printmaker
Bakker, Gabrielle Painter
Balaban, Diane Painter
Balance, Jerrald Clark Painter
Balas-Whitfield, Susan Painter, Filmmaker
Baldwin, Gordon C Curator
Baldwin, Richard Wood Illustrator, Sculptor
Baldwin, Russell W Educator, Gallery Director
Balisle, Jenny Ella Painter, Educator
Ball, Ken Weston Artist
Ball, Lillian Sculptor
Ball, Susan L Administrator, Historian
Balmori, Diana Landscape Architect
Banks, Marcia Gillman Painter, Illustrator
Banning, Jack, Jr Art Dealer
Barbeau, Marcel (Christian) Painter, Sculptor
Barbee, Robert Thomas Painter, Graphic Artist
Bard, Joellen Instructor, Painter
Bard, Perry Video Artist, Installation Sculptor
Barletta, Emily Weaver, Fiber Artist
Barnes, Margo Painter
Barnett, Cheryl L Sculptor
Baron-Malkin, Phyllis Educator, Painter
Barone, Mark Painter
Barrell, Bill Painter, Collector
Barrett, Deborah Collage Artist
Barrett, Terry M Writer, Educator
Barrett, William O Administrator
Barrow, Thomas Francis Photographer, Educator
Barth, Uta Conceptual Artist, Photographer
Bartlett, Bo Painter
Bassin, Joan Historian, Educator
Bassler, Robert Covey Sculptor, Painter
Battenfield, Jackie Painter
Bautzmann, CA-OPA (Nancy Annette) Painter
Baxter, Paula Adell Educator, Writer
Beard, Mark Painter
Beardsley, Barbara H Conservator
Beaumont, Mona Painter, Graphic Artist
Beck, Lonnie Lee Painter, Educator
Beckwith, Mary Ann Painter, Educator
Bedrick, Jeffrey K Painter, Illustrator
Beech, John Installation Sculptor
Beerman, John Thorne Painter
Beerman, Miriam Painter, Printmaker
Belcher, Jaq Conceptual Artist
Bell, Mary Catherine Art Dealer
Bellospirito, Robyn Suzanne Painter, Writer
Belville, Scott Robert Painter, Educator
Beman, Lynn Susan Museum Director, Historian
Ben-Haim, Tsipi Critic, Executive Director
Benglis, Lynda Sculptor, Painter
Benjamin, Alice Painter, Educator
Benson, Martha J Jeweler, Assemblage Artist
Benton, Daniel C Patron
Ben Tre, Howard B Sculptor, Draftsman
Bercowetz, Jesse Installation Sculptor
Berg, Michael R Painter, Printmaker
Berge, Dorothy Alphena Sculptor, Instructor
Berger, Jerry Allen Director, Curator
Berger-Kraemer, Nancy Assemblage Artist
Berghash, Mark W Photographer, Painter
Berguson, Robert Jenkins Draftsman, Painter
Berio, Marina Draftsman, Printmaker
Berkenblit, Ellen Painter
Berkman, Lillian Collector
Berkowitz, Henry Painter, Designer
Berman, Michael P Photographer
Bermingham, John C Painter
Bernheim, Stephanie Hammerschlag Painter, Photographer
Berry, Glenn Painter, Educator
Bertoni, Christina Ceramist, Painter
Betsky, Aaron Museum Director
Beverland, Jack E Painter
Bhabha, Huma Sculptor
Biederman, James Mark Painter, Sculptor
Bigelow, Anita (Anne) (Edwige Lourie) Graphic Artist, Printmaker
Bills, Linda Sculptor
bin Mohammad bin Ali al-Thani, Sheikh Saud Collector
Birmelin, Robert Painter, Draftsman
Black, Debra & Leon David Collector
Black, Jappie King Sculptor, Textile Artist
Black, Mary McCune Curator, Painter
Blackburn, Ed M Painter
Blagden, Thomas P Painter
Blair, Dike Painter, Sculptor
Blair, Philippa Mary Painter, Educator
Blasco, Isidro M Sculptor, Architect
Blue, Patt Photographer, Writer
Blum, Eric Painter
Blumberg, Ron Painter
Blumrich, Stephen Designer
Boardman, Seymour Painter
Bobins, Norman R Patron
Bocchino, Serena Maria Painter, Educator
Bodenmann, Hans U Collector
Bodycomb, Rosalyn Painter
Bohen, Barbara E Historian, Museologist
Bolas, Gerald Douglas Museum Director, Consultant
Bolger, Doreen Retired Museum Director, Curator
Bolomey, Roger Henry Sculptor
Bolton, Robin Jean Painter, Graphic Artist
Bonner, Jonathan G Sculptor
Booth, Laurence Ogden Sculptor, Architect
Booth, Mark Painter
Bootz, Antoine H Photographer
Boretz, Naomi Painter, Educator
Born, James E Sculptor
Bornstein, Jennifer Printmaker
Borofsky, Jonathan Sculptor, Painter
Borshch, Dmitry Gennadievich Printmaker, Draftsman
Bostick, William Allison Painter, Calligrapher, Designer, Illustrator, Printmaker
Bott, H(arvey) J(ohn) Sculptor, Painter
Bowen-Forbes, Jorge C Painter
Bowers, Andrea Video and Installation Artist
Bowling, Katherine Painter
Bowlt, John Art Historian, Educator
Boyd, Karen White Educator, Fiber Artist
Boyd, Robert Sculptor, Video Artist
Boylan, John Lewis Painter, Printmaker
Bradley, Joe Painter
Bradley, Slater Photographer
Bradley, William Steven Museum Director, Educator
Bradshaw, Dove Painter, Sculptor
Brady, Charles Painter, Sculptor
Brainard, Barbara Printmaker, Painter
Brangoccio, Michael David Painter, Collage Artist
Bratt, Byron H Printmaker
Brauntuch, Troy Painter
Brazda, Bonizar Installation Sculptor, Conceptual Artist
Brearey, Susan Winfield Painter, Educator, Gallery Director
Breckenridge, Ethan Sculptor
Breiger, Elaine Printmaker, Painter
Brendel, Bettina Painter, Lecturer
Breslaw, Cathy L Painter, Educator
Bress, Brian Collage Artist
Breuer, Bradford R Patron, Museum Director
Breuning, Olaf Photographer, Sculptor
Brickner, Alice Painter, Printmaker
Bridenstine, James A Museum Director, Collector
Briggs, Alice Leora Draftsman, Installation Sculptor
Bright, Sheila Pree Photographer
Brilliant, Richard Educator, Writer
Broderick, Herbert Reginald, III Educator
Brodie, Regis Conrad Ceramist, Painter
Brooks, Kelly Gavin Painter
Brown, Aaron Morgan Painter
Brown, Anita Painter
Brown, Bruce Robert Painter, Sculptor
Brown, Carol K Painter, Sculptor
Brown, Constance George Gallery Director, Art Dealer
Brown, Gillian Conceptual Artist, Photographer
Brown, Iona Rozeal Painter
Brown, Peter C Sculptor, Painter
Brown, Petey Painter
Brown, Sarah M Painter, Instructor
Browning, Mark Daniel Painter, Sculptor
Bruguera, Tania Kinetic Artist, Video Artist
Brummel, Marilyn Reeder Collage Artist, Printmaker
Bruno, Santo M Painter
Bruno, Vincent J Historian, Administrator
Brust, Robert Gustave Painter, Writer
Bryans, John Armond Instructor, Painter
Bryant, Laura Militzer Weaver
Bryant, Tamara Thompson Painter, Sculptor
Bryson, Louise Henry Patron
Bucher, Karen Photographer
Buchman, James Wallace Sculptor, Educator
Bulka, Michael Critic
Burch, G. David Photographer, Sculptor
Burckhardt, Tom Painter
Burger-Calderon, Monique & Max Collector
Burgos, Joseph Agner, Jr Painter, Writer
Burk, A Darlene Dealer, Collector
Burke, Daniel V Painter, Educator
Burns, Mark A Ceramist
Burns, Sheila Painter, Lecturer
Burns, Stan Painter, Sculptor
Burnside, Chris Painter
Burr, Tom Artist
Burson, Nancy Photographer, Conceptual Artist
Burt, David Sill Sculptor
Butler, Connie Curator

ADDRESS NOT PUBLISHED (cont)

Butler, James D Printmaker, Painter
Butter, Tom Sculptor, Instructor
Byars, Donna Sculptor, Collage Artist
Byers, Fleur Painter
Caesar, Jedediah Sculptor
Cahana, Alice Lok Painter
Cain, David Paul Painter, Photographer
Cain, Sarah Collage Artist
Calabrese, Karen Ann Painter, Instructor
Calabro, Joanna Sondra Painter, Sculptor
Calabro, Richard Paul Sculptor, Painter
Callari, Emily Dolores Painter, Restorer
Camner, Anna Ingrid Painter
Campbell, Beth Painter, Installation Sculptor
Campbell, Crystal Z Sculptor
Campbell, Naomi Interdisciplinary Visual Artist, Public Artist
Campbell, Richard Horton Painter, Printmaker
Camper, Fred Educator
Campuzano, Anthony Collage Artist
Candioti, Beatriz A Painter
Canier, Caren Painter, Educator
Canniff, Bryan Gregory Designer, Director
Canright, Sarah Anne Painter
Cantone, Vic Cartoonist, Lecturer
Cantor, Fredrich Painter, Photographer
Cantwell, William Richard Painter, Printmaker
Cao, Gilda Photographer, Painter
Caplan Ciarrocchi, Sandra Painter, Educator
Carbone, David Painter, Critic
Carboni, Stefano Curator
Cardoso, Anthony Painter, Sculptor
Carlson, Mary Sculptor
Carter, Carol Painter
Carter, Warrick Livingston educator, composer
Casebere, James E Photographer, Sculptor
Casey, John Thayer Painter, Sculptor
Cassell, Beverly Painter
Cassullo, Joanne Leonhardt Patron
Castellanos, Laura Painter, Graphic Artist
Catchi Painter, Printmaker
Cate, Phillip Dennis Historian, Director
Caton, David Painter
Catterall, John Edward Painter, Educator
Celli, Paul Painter, Educator
Cenci, Silvana Sculptor
Chalmers, Kim Educator, Studio Artist
Chandra, Freddy Installation Sculptor
Chang, Lishan Installation Sculptor, Photographer
Chang-Il, Kim Collector, Gallery Owner
Chappelle, Jerry Leon Ceramist, Sculptor
Charkow-Hollander, Natalie Sculptor
Chase, Doris (Totten) Video Artist, Sculptor
Chase, W(illiam) Thomas Conservator
Chen, Hilo Painter
Chesley, Paul Alexander Photographer
Chi, Ke-Hsin (Jenny) Painter
Childers, Malcolm Graeme Photographer, Printmaker
Chiroussot-Chambeaux, Jane Curator, Critic
Christensen, Neil C Painter
Christison, Muriel B Educator, Museum Director, Art Historian
Christo and Jeanne-Claude Artists
Christopherson, Howard Martin Photographer, Art Dealer
Christy, Bonnie Beth Painter
Church, Maude Painter, Illustrator
Chusid, Evette Painter
Cicansky, Victor Sculptor
Ciezadlo, Janina A Critic, Educator
Cingillioglu, Halit Collector
Cipolla, Vin Administrator
Clark-Langager, Sarah Ann Gallery Director, Curator
Clark-Mendes, Cybele Photographer
Clarke, Kevin Photographer, Conceptual Artist
Clayton, Christian Painter
Clayton, Robert Painter
Cleary, Barbara B Painter, Instructor
Clifton, Michelle Gamm Sculptor, Filmmaker
Climo, Lindee Painter, Illustrator
Clinton, Paul Arthur Printmaker, Instructor
Clothier, Peter Dean Writer, Critic
Clymer, Albert Anderson Painter
Cobb, Virginia Horton Painter, Lecturer
Coburn, Ralph (M H) Painter
Coffey, Susanna Jean Painter
Cogger, Cassia Zamecki painter
Cohen, Alan Barry Photographer, Educator
Cohen, Cora Painter
Cohen, David Critic, Curator
Cohen, Lynne G Photographer, Educator
Coit, M B Painter, Sculptor
Cokendolpher, Eunice Loraine Painter, Instructor
Colarusso, Corrine Camille Painter, Instructor
Colby, Bill Printmaker, Painter
Cole, Grace V Painter, Instructor
Colen, Dan Artist
Collado, Lisa Collage Artist, Assemblage Artist, Painter
Collins, Jim Sculptor, Collage Artist
Colosi, David Installation Sculptor
Colp, Norman B Photographer, Curator
Condren, Stephen F Painter
Conelli, Maria Ann Administrator, Educator, Historian
Conneen, Jane W Printmaker, Book Artist
Connelly, Chuck Painter
Conner, Ann Printmaker
Conrad, Nancy R Painter
Continos, Anna Painter, Designer
Cook, Michael David Painter, Video Artist
Cook, R Scott & Soussan A E Art Dealer, Critic
Cooke, Judy Painter
Cooper, Wayne Painter, Sculptor
Cormier, Robert John Painter, Lecturer
Cornell, Henry Patron
Corona, Livia Photographer
Corriel, Eric Video Artist, Designer
Costa, Eduardo Conceptual Artist, Painter
Cote, Alan Painter
Couturier, Marion B Dealer, Collector
Couwenberg, Alexander Painter
Cowles, Charles Art Dealer, Collector
Cox, Renée Photographer
Cozad, Rachael Blackburn Museum Director, Art Appraiser
Craig, James Hicklin Consultant
Crandall, Dorris Instructor, Painter
Crane, Jean Painter
Crawford, Thom Cooney Painter, Sculptor
Crimmins, Jerry (Gerald) Garfield Painter, Sculptor
Crite, Allan Rohan Painter, Illustrator
Cronin, Patricia Sculptor
Crosby, Ranice W Illustrator, Educator
Crum, David Painter
Cuoghi, Roberto Video Artist, Conceptual Artist
Cutler, Ronnie Painter
Cyphers, Peggy K Painter, Printmaker
Czimbalmos, Szabo Kalman Painter, Educator
D'Agostino , Claudio A Sculptor, Painter
Dahl, Stephen M Photographer
Dailey, Victoria Keilus Writer, Art Dealer
Daley, Cathy Painter
D'Amico, Larry Painter, Printmaker
Danly, Susan Curator, Historian
Daou, Annabel Conceptual Artist, Draftsman
Daugherty, Michael F Educator, Sculptor
Davidovich, Jaime Painter, Video Artist
Davidow, Joan Carlin Director, Curator
Davidson, Herbert Laurence Painter, Printmaker
Davis, Brad (Bradley) Darius Painter
Davis, Christine Photographer
Davis, Ellen N Historian
Davis, Jerrold Painter
Davis, Stephen A Painter
Day, Burnis Calvin Painter, Instructor
Day, Gary Lewis Printmaker, Painter
Dayan, Amalia Collector
Dean, James Painter, Curator
De Backer, Katelijne Administrator
Debeers, Sue Photographer
DeBellevue, Lucky Sculptor
De Berardinis, Olivia Painter
Debonne, Jeannette Painter, Printmaker
DeBrincat, Alicia Painter
Debrosky, Christine A Painter
De Carvalho, Priscila Painter
Decil, Stella (Del) Walters Painter, Instructor
DeFazio, Teresa Galligan Painter, Gallery Director
DeGiulio, Lucas Artist
De Groat, Diane Illustrator, Designer, Writer
de Gunzburg, Charles Collector
de Gunzburg, Nathalie Collector
De La Torre, Einar Glass Blower
DeLauro, Joseph Nicola Sculptor, Educator
Deloney, Jack Clouse Painter, Illustrator
DeMatties, Nick Painter
Demsky, Hilda Green Painter, Environmental Artist
Dennett, Lissy W Painter, Printmaker
Dennis, Don W Painter, Instructor
Dentler, Anne Lillian Painter, Illustrator
De Ricco, Hank Sculptor
DeRosier, Deborah Rush Painter, Educator
De Rothschild, Eric Alain Robert David Collector
DeRoux, Daniel Edward Painter, Sculptor
DeSantis, Diana Painter
Deschamps, Francois Photographer
Desmett, Don Curator, Gallery Director
DeWitt, Edward Painter, Sculptor
de Zegher, Catherine Museum Director
Diamond, Cathy Painter, Conservator
Diamond, Paul Photographer
Diamond, Shari Photographer
Dias-Jorgensen, Aurora Abdias Painter
Dibert, Rita Jean Painter, Photographer
Dice, Elizabeth Jane Craftsman, Illustrator
Dickson, Mark Amos Painter, Printmaker
Diehl, Guy Painter, Instructor
Difronzo, Francis G Painter
Di Giacinto, Sharon Painter
Diker, Charles & Valerie Collector
Dill, Laddie John Painter, Sculptor
Dinkin, Larry Painter
Dirks, John Sculptor, Cartoonist
Di Suvero, Mark Painter, Sculptor
Dittmer, Frances R Collector
Dobkin, John Howard Administrator, Consultant
Dodge, Robert G Painter, Sculptor
Dodson, Donna Sculptor
Dodworth, Allen Stevens Art Appraiser, Curator
Dolmatch, Blanche Painter
Donahue, Thomas John Painter, Instructor
Donley, Robert Morris Painter, Educator
Donneson, Seena Sculptor, Graphics Artist
Doogan, Bailey Painter, Instructor
Dorosh, Daria Painter, Sculptor
Dorrien, Carlos Guillermo Sculptor
Douglas, Leah Gallery Director, Curator
Dove, Daniel Painter
Dowley, Jennifer Director
Downen, Jill Installation Sculptor
Doyle, Tom Sculptor, Educator
Draeger, Christoph Installation Sculptor
Drake, James Printmaker, Sculptor
Drew, Leonardo Sculptor
Driscoll, Ellen Sculptor, Instructor
Drucker, Zackary Video Artist, Photographer
Dubnau, Jenny Painter
Dunn, Amanda Gordon Sculptor, Painter
Dunning, Jeanne Photographer, Video Artist
Dunsky, Annie Painter
Dutta, Anindita Sculptor
Dyson, Torkwase Collage Artist, Video Artist
Eades, Luis Eric Painter, Educator
Eagen, Christopher T Director
Earls-Solari, Bonnie Curator
Eastcott, R. Wayne Printmaker, Painter
Eberle, Edward Samuel Ceramist, Draftsman
Echelman, Janet Sculptor, Painter
Edelson, Gilbert S Administrator, Lecturer
Edelstein, Teri J Museum Director, Historian
Eder, James Alvin Printmaker, Painter
Edmiston, Sara Joanne Educator, Designer
Edson, Gary F Museologist, Museum Director
Eidelberg, Martin Historian
Eisenstat, Jane Sperry Painter
Eisworth, Barry Architect, Educator
Elderfield, John Historian, Curator
Elkins, Lane Educator, Ceramist
Elliot, Catherine J Painter, Graphic Artist
Ellis, Andra Painter, Ceramist
Ellis, David Painter
Ellis, Robert M Painter
Ellison, Robert W Sculptor
Elowitch, Robert Jason Dealer, Patron
English, Simon Richard Bathurst Painter, Draftsman
Enos, Chris Photographer
Enwezor, Okwui Educator, Curator
Erbe, Chantell Van Graphic Artist, Painter
Erbe, Gary Thomas Painter
Erickson, Marsha A Director, Administrator
Eriksen, Gary Sculptor, Medalist
Ernstrom, Adele Mansfield Historian
Escalet, Frank Diaz Painter, Sculptor
Eshoo, Robert Painter
Estern, Neil Carl Sculptor
Esterow, Milton Editor, Publisher
Estes, Richard Painter
Etchison, Bruce Conservator, Painter
Ettl, Georg Painter, Sculptor
Etzold, Eckhard Painter
Evans, Nancy Painter
Fabiano, Diane Fabian Painter
Falconer, Marguerite Elizabeth Painter, Instructor
Fanara, Sirena Painter, Lecturer
Farrens, Juanita G Painter, Sculptor
Fast, Omer Filmmaker
Faulconer, Mary (Fullerton) Painter, Designer
Faulhaber, Patrick Painter
Feeney, Brendan Ben Educator, Visual Artist
Feher, Tony artist
Fein, Stanley Painter, Designer
Feingold, Ken Artist
Feldman, Roger Lawrence Sculptor, Educator
Feldman, Walter (Sidney) Painter, Printmaker
Felker, David Larry Sculptor, Gallery Director
Feller, Deborah Painter, Draftsman
Feltus, Alan Evan Painter, Educator
Fendrich, Laurie Painter
Ferber, Linda S Curator, Historian
Ferguson, Max Painter, Printmaker
Ferguson-Huntington, Kathleen E Painter
Fernandez, Jake Painter; Photographer
Fernie, John Chipman Sculptor
Ferrara , Annette Editor, Educator
Ferris, Michael Sculptor

ADDRESS NOT PUBLISHED (cont)

Fetchko, Peter J Museum Director
Fichera, Jeffrey Painter
Fiero, Gloria K Educator, Historian
Fine, Elsa Honig Art Historian, Editor
Fine, Sally S Sculptor, Painter
Finkelstein, Henry D Painter, Educator
Fiore, Rosemarie Painter
Fisher, Kim Painter
Fiss, Cinthea Photographer, Video Artist
Fitts, Michael Painter
Fitzgerald, Betty Jo Painter, Printmaker
Fleming, Mary Margaret Gallery Director
Fletcher, Harrell Educator, Filmmaker
Flick, Friedrich Christian Collector
Flower, Michael Lavin Art Dealer, Photographer
Floyd, Carl Leo Sculptor, Environmental Artist
Fluek, Toby Painter, Graphic Artist
Fogg, Rebecca Snider Printmaker, Painter
Foley, Timothy Albert Art Dealer
Foosaner, Judith Educator, Painter
Ford, Kianga K Installation Sculptor
Foresta, Merry A Curator
Forman, Seth Michael Painter
Fornas, Leander Printmaker, Instructor
Fort-Brescia, Bernardo M Architect
Foster, Steven Douglas Photographer
Fotopoulos, James Filmmaker
Foulkes, Llyn Painter
Fowler, Adam Collage Artist
Fowler, Frank Eison Art Dealer, Consultant
Fox, Catherine Writer, Critic
Fox, Lincoln H Sculptor
Frackman, Noel Critic, Historian
Frank, Charles William, Jr Wood Carver, Writer
Frank, Mary Sculptor, Painter
Frank, Rachel E Sculptor
Frankel, Stuart & Maxine Collector
Franklin, David Museum Director, Curator
Fratkin, Leslie Photographer
Freedman, Jacqueline Painter
Freeman, Tina Photographer, Consultant
Frehm, Lynne Painter
Frelin, Adam Sculptor, Video Artist
French, Stephanie Taylor Administrator
Freundlich, August L Administrator, Collector
Friedman, Bernard Harper Writer
Friedman, Charley Conceptual Artist
Friese, Nancy Marlene Painter, Printmaker
Froehlich, Anna & Josef Collector
Fromboluti, Sideo Painter
Fromentin, Christine Anne Painter, Graphic Artist
Fryberger, Betsy G Curator
Fuglie, Gordon Louis Gallery Director, Historian
Fuld, Richard Severin, Jr Collector, Patron
Fulton Ross, Gale Artist
Furnas, Barnaby Painter
Fusco, Laurie S Historian, Educator
Fusco, Yolanda Painter, Printmaker
Gable, John Oglesby Painter, Muralist
Gale , Ann Painter
Galindo, Regina Jose Visual Artist, Performance Artist
Gallagher, Carole Photographer, Writer
Gallagher, Cynthia Painter, Educator
Gallander, Cathleen S Art Dealer, Representative
Gallarda, Michael Artist
Gallo, Enzo D Sculptor
Gallo, Frank Sculptor, Educator
Galloway, Paul Painter
Gamache, Claudette Theresa Painter
Gamble, Sarah Painter
Ganek, Danielle & David Collector
Ganihar, Tomer Photographer
Garcia, Rupert (Marshall) R Painter, Educator
Garey, Patricia Martin Ceramist, Painter
Gartel, Laurence M Computer Artist, Photographer
Gates, Harry Irving Sculptor, Educator
Gates, Jay Rodney Museum Director
Gates, Jeff S Photographer, Designer
Gates, Theaster, Jr Ceramist, Sculptor
Gaucher-Thomas, Nancy A Painter, Instructor
Gauthier, Ninon Curator, Art Historian
Gauthier, Suzanne Anita Painter
Gauvreau, Robert George Photographer, Educator
Gay, Betsy (Elizabeth) Dershuck Painter, Instructor
Gaydos, Tim (Timothy) John Painter, Sculptor
Gedeon, Peter Ferenc Photographer, Curator
Gee, Helen Art Consultant, Curator
Geier, Philip Henry, Jr Patron
Geisert, Arthur Frederick Printmaker, Illustrator
Gentile, Gloria Irene Designer, Sculptor, Painter
George, Thomas Painter, Draftsman
Geran, Joseph, Jr Sculptor, Designer
Gerard, Celia Sculptor
Gerlovina & Gerlovin, Rimma & Valeriy Conceptual Artists, Photographers
Getler, Helen Art Dealer, Consultant
Ghent, Henri Critic, Writer
Giampietro, Isabel Antonia Sculptor, Designer
Gianlorenzi, Nona Elena Painter, Dealer
Gibb, Ann W Painter
Gibson, Sandra Painter, Filmmaker
Giddens, Kathleen Colette Painter, Educator
Gilbert, Aaron J Painter
Gillingwater, Denis Claude Sculptor, Educator
Gilmore, Kate Video Artist
Ginsberg, Elizabeth G Painter, Photographer
Ginzburg, Yankel (Jacob) Painter, Sculptor
Ginzel, Andrew H Artist, Educator
Gioia, Dana (Michael) Critic, Editor, Administrator
Gipe, Lawrence Painter
Gips, C L Terry Photographer, Educator
Giurgola, Romaldo Architect
Glorig, Ostor Painter, Craftsman
Goddard, Janet Sniffin Gallery Director, Educator
Godwin, Judith Painter
Goicolea, Anthony Photographer, Sculptor
Golbert, Sandra Artist, Writer
Gold, Leah Painter, Printmaker
Gold, Lois M Painter
Goldberg, Glenn Painter
Goldberger, Paul Jesse Critic, Writer, Educator, Editor
Golden, Judith Greene Photographer-Mixed Media
Goldman, Judith Writer, Curator
Goldner, Janet Sculptor
Goldstein, Gladys Painter, Collage Artist
Goldstein, Sheldon (Shelly) Painter
Golici, Ana Artist
Gomez, Mirta & Eduardo Delvalle Photographer
Goode, Joe Painter
Goodman, Cynthia Writer, Curator
Goodman, Mark Photographer
Gordley, Metz Tranbarger Painter
Gordon, David S Consultant
Goring, Trevor Painter, Writer
Gossel, Greg Painter
Gould, Karen Writer, Historian
Goulet, Lorrie Sculptor, Painter
Gowdy, Marjorie E Museum Director
Grabarsky, Sheila Painter
Graham, Bob Painter, Muralist
Graham, Paul Photographer
Grainger, Nessa Posner Painter, Collage Artist
Grandpré, Mary Illustrator
Grassl, Anton M Painter, Photographer
Gray, Jim Painter, Sculptor
Green, Jesse Aron Video Artist
Green, Jonathan Painter, Printmaker
Green, Roger J Critic, Historian
Greenhalgh, Paul Administrator, Curator
Greenwood, Norma Painter
Grelle, Martin Glen Painter
Gribbon, Deborah Museum Director
Gribbon, Jenna Painter, Video Artist
Grier, Margot Edmands Librarian, Administrator
Griesgraber, Michael Joseph Painter
Grieve, Markus Installation Sculptor
Griffin, Rashawn Sculptor, Painter
Griffith, Roberta Ceramist, Painter
Gronk Painter
Grooms, Red Painter, Sculptor
Gropper, Cathy Painter, Sculptor
Gross Brown, Linda J Painter, Juror
Grossman, Bonnie Gallery Director
Growdon, Marcia Cohn Administrator, Historian
Grunwaldt, Carmela C Painter
Guerrier, Adler Photographer
Gunn, Paul James Painter, Educator
Guralnick, Jody Painter, Collage Artist
Gurney, George Curator, Historian
Gusella, Ernest Video Artist
Guyton, Tyree Sculptor, Painter
Guzmán, Daniel Draftsman
Gyung Jin, Shin Sculptor, Video Artist
Ha, Hyoungsun Photographer
Haase, Cynthia Painter
Hackett, Theresa Painter, Printmaker
Haddock, Jon Cartoonist
Hagan, James Garrison Sculptor, Instructor
Halbrooks, Darryl Wayne Painter, Printmaker
Hale, Keith Painter
Halegua, Alfredo Sculptor
Hallenbeck, Pomona Juanita Painter, Instructor
Haller, Douglas Martin Curator, Historian
Halley, Peter Painter
Halligan, Roger Phillip Sculptor, Designer
Hamada, Hiroyuki Sculptor
Hamill, David Painter
Hammerbeck, Wanda Lee Photographer
Han, Debbie Photographer, Painter
Han, Moo Kwon Video Artist
Hanan, Laura Molen Painter, Graphic Artist
Hankey, Robert E Educator, Administrator
Hansalik, Konrad F Printmaker, Painter
Hanson, Chris Sculptor
Hapgood, Susan T Curator, Critic
Harabasz, Ewa Painter
Harder, Rodney Painter
Harding, Noel Robert Sculptor, Video Artist
Hari, Kenneth Painter, Sculptor, Printmaker
Harkness, John Cheesman Architect
Harmon, David Edward Painter, Educator
Harper, Michaele Ann Painter
Harris, Paul Sculptor
Harris, Robert George Painter, Illustrator
Harris, William Wadsworth, II Painter, Collage Artist
Hart, Heather Installation Sculptor
Hart, Kimberley Sculptor
Hartford, Jane Davis Textile Artist, Craftsman
Hartley, Katherine Ann Painter, Instructor
Harvest, Judith R Conceptual Artist, Painter
Harvey, Ellen Artist
Harvey, Peter Francis Painter, Designer
Hassenfeld, Kirsten Sculptor
Hatch, (Mr & Mrs) Marshall Collectors
Hausman, Fred S Sculptor, Designer
Hayes, Gerald Painter, Photographer
Hayes, Laura M Conserver, Art Appraiser
Hayes, Sharon Installation Sculptor
Hazlewood, Carl E Curator, Painter
Healy, Anne Laura Sculptor, Educator
Healy, Deborah Ann Illustrator, Educator
Healy, Julia Schmitt Painter, Educator
Hearn, M F (Millard Fillmore), Jr Administrator, Historian
Heartney, Eleanor Critic, Curator
Heath, Samuel K Museum Director
Hedden, Claire Sculptor
Heeks, Willy Painter
Heffernan, Julie Painter
Hegarty, Valerie Sculptor
Heginbotham, Jan Sturza Sculptor
Heiferman, Marvin Curator, Writer, Publisher
Heizer, Michael Environmental Artist, Sculptor
Heller, Susanna Painter, Instructor
Helsell, Charles Paul Curator
Hendon, Cham Painter
Hennessy, Richard Painter
Henry, Dale Painter
Henry, Robert Painter, Educator
Hepler, Anna Sculptor, Assemblage Artist
Herbert, Annick & Anton Collectors
Herdlick, Catherine Game Designer, Consultant
Herridge, Elizabeth Art Historian
Herritt, Linda S Sculptor
Herrmann, John J, Jr Curator
Hersch, Jeff Photographer
Hershey, Nona Printmaker, Painter
Herzog, Elana Sculptor
Hess, F Scott Painter, Instructor
Heusser, Eleanore Elizabeth Heusser Ferholt Painter
Hewitt, Leslie Photographer, Sculptor
Heyman, Daniel Printmaker, Educator
Heyman, Ira Michael Administrator, Educator
Hibel, Edna Painter, Printmaker
Higgins, Edward Koelling Ceramist, Jeweler
Hild, Nancy Painter
Hiler, Seth Ruggles Painter
Hill, Charles Christopher Collage Artist, Painter
Hill, Patrick Sculptor
Hill, Robyn Lesley Painter, Designer
Hiller, Betty R Consultant, Appraiser
Hillman, Arthur Stanley Graphic Artist, Educator
Hixon, Karen J Patron
Hobbs, Frank I, Jr Painter, Instructor
Hodgkin, Carter Painter, Printmaker
Hodgkins, Rosalind Selma Painter
Hoeber, Julian Video Artist
Hoffman, Eric Painter, Printmaker
Holden, Donald Painter, Writer
Holder, Kenneth Allen Painter, Educator
Holland, Hillman Randall Art Dealer
Hollen-Bolmgren, Donna Painter, Papermaker
Holloway, Evan Sculptor
Holsinger, Jayne Painter
Holstad, Christian Artist
Holtz, Itshak Jack Painter, Printmaker
Holtzman, Chuck Graphic Artist
Holvey, Samuel Boyer Sculptor, Designer
Honjo, Masako Painter
Hood, Graham Stanley Museum Director, Writer
Hooks, Earl J Educator, Sculptor
Hoover, George Schweke Architect
Horn, Alan F Collector
Horne, Ralph Albert Painter, Writer
Horvat, Vlatka Photographer, Sculptor
Horvath, Sharon Painter
Hotard, Susan F Painter
Hotchner, Holly Museum Director, Conservator, Curator
Hourian, Mohammad Painter, Art Dealer
Houser, Jim (James C) Painter, Educator
Howard, Dan F Painter, Educator
Howat, John Keith Historian
Hoy, Anna Sew Sculptor
Hricko, Richard Printmaker

ADDRESS NOT PUBLISHED (cont)

Littrell, Doris Marie Dealer
Litwin, Ruth Forbes Printmaker, Painter
Livingstone, Biganess Painter
Liz-N-Val Sculptor, Painter
Lloyd Webber, Andrew Collector
Lobdell, Frank Painter
Lockhart, Sharon Photographer, Filmmaker
London, Barbara Curator
Long, A Mitchell Painter
Long, Phillip C Museum Director
Longo, Vincent Painter, Printmaker
Longstreth, Jake Painter
Longval, Gloria Painter, Ceramist
Looney, Daniel Stephen Painter
Lorber, Richard Critic, Educator
Lorelli, Elvira Mae Sculptor, Painter
Lorenz, Marie Architect, Sculptor
Loving, Richard Maris Painter, Printmaker
Lowenthal, Constance Historian, Consultant
Lubell, Ellen Critic, Writer
Lucas, Christopher Conceptual Artist
Lucas, Georgetta Snell Painter
Lufkin, Martha BG Writer
Lukin, Sven Painter
Lumbers, James Richard Painter
Lumpkin, Libby Museum Director
Lumsden, Ian Gordon Director
Lunder, Peter & Paula H Collector
Luneau, Claude Sculptor
Lunney, Kevan Fiber Artist
Luz, Virginia Painter
Lynne, Ninah & Michael Collector
Lyon, Giles Andrew Painter
Lyons, Carol Painter, Printmaker
Macaulay, David Alexander Designer, Illustrator
MacDonald, William L Historian, Writer
Mac Whinnie, John Vincent Painter, Sculptor
Magid, Jill Conceptual Artist, Installation Sculptor, Video Artist
Magnotta, Frank Printmaker
Magsig, Stephen painter
Mahr, Erika Artist
Maidoff, Jules Painter, Printmaker
Majdrakoff, Ivan Painter, Assemblage Artist
Majore, Frank Photographer
Makanowitzky, Barbara Painter
Makler, Hope Welsh Art Dealer
Malamed, Lyanne Painter
Malen, Lenore Video Artist, Photographer
Maler, Leopoldo Mario Conceptual Artist, Educator
Maler, M Leopoldo Mario Sculptor
Mallin, Sherry & Joel Collectors
Mallory, Ronald Painter, Sculptor
Mangold, Sylvia Plimack Painter
Manhold, John Henry Sculptor
Manilow, Lewis Collector, Patron
Manship, John Paul Painter, Sculptor
Mansion, Gracie Art Dealer
Manter, Margaret C Painter
Manuella, Frank R Designer, Conceptual Artist
Marais Painter
Marasco, Rose Photographer, Educator
Marcus, Gerald R Painter, Printmaker
Maret, Russell Designer, Publisher
Marion, John Louis Collector
Markowitz, Marilyn Painter, Printmaker
Marlieb, William (Bill) Franklin Painter
Marquis, Richard Craftsman
Marrero, Marlo R Photographer, Sculptor
Marsh, Charlene Marie Artist, Painter
Marsh, David Foster Educator, Painter
Marsh, Fredrik Photographer
Marshall, James Duard Painter, Printmaker
Martin, Alexander Toedt Educator, Painter
Martin, Lucille Caiar Painter, Muralist
Martin, Walter Sculptor
Marton, Pier Video Artist, Educator
Martone, William Robert Painter, Instructor
Marx, Susan & Larry Collectors
Masih, Lalit K Painter
Masnyj, Yuri Painter, Sculptor
Masters, Deborah Sculptor
Mataranglo, Robert Patrick Video Artist, Muralist
Matsuda-Dunn, Pamela Painter
Matthews, Harriett Sculptor, Educator
Matthews, Robert Draftsman
Matthews, William (Cary) Painter
Mattingly, James Thomas Printmaker, Painter
Matzkin, Alice Rosalinda Painter, Writer
Maurer, Neil Photographer
Mavromatis, Dimitri collector
Mawdsley, Richard Silversmith, Goldsmith
May, Daniel Striger Dealer
Mayes, Elaine Photographer, Video Artist
Mayfield, Signe S Curator
Mayne, Thom Architect
Mayo, Marti Museum Director, Curator
Mazze, Irving Sculptor, Medalist
McCall, Ann Painter, Printmaker
McCallum, Corrie Parker Instructor, Painter
McCannel, Louise Walker Collector
McCorison, Marcus Allen Librarian
McCormick, Pam(ela) Ann Sculptor
McDean, Craig Photographer
McDonald, Susan Strong Painter, Printmaker
McDowell, Wayne Painter
McDuff, Fredrick H Painter, Printmaker
McGee, Winston Eugene Painter, Educator
McIlvain, Douglas Lee Educator, Sculptor
McKay, Renee Painter
McKean, Michael Jones Installation Sculptor, Educator
McKee, Hunter Painter
McLeod, Cheryl O'Halloran Painter, Instructor
McMillan, Constance Painter, Illustrator
McMillan, Stephen Walker Printmaker, Photographer
McNamara, John Painter
McNany, Tim Photographer
McNeil, Henry S, Jr Collector
McNett, Dennis Sculptor, Graphic Artist
McOwen, C Lynn Art Dealer, Collector
McPherson, Craig Painter, Printmaker
McPherson, Larry E Photographer, Educator
Meadows, Jason Sculptor
Medina, Juan Painter
Melamed, Dana Painter
Melamid, Alexander Painter
Menconi, Michael Angelo Glassblower, Sculptor
Menschel, Robert Benjamin Patron
Menses, Jan Painter, Printmaker
Meredith, Michael Architect
Merhi, Yucef Installation Sculptor, Video Artist
Merida, Margaret Braden Craftsman, Instructor
Meromi, Ohad Video Artist, Sculptor
Mew, Tommy Painter, Conceptual Artist
Meyer, Edward Henry Patron
Meyer, Joshua Painter
Meyer, Melissa Painter
Meyer, Milton E, Jr Painter
Miccoli, Arnaldo Painter, Collage Artist
Michod, Susan A Painter
Middleton, John S Collector
Mieczkowski, Edwin Painter
Mik, Aernout Video Artist, Installation Sculptor
Mikus, Eleanore Painter
Milan, Wardell, II Photographer
Miles, Ellen Gross Historian, Curator
Miller, Brad Craftsman, Ceramist
Miller, Harvey S Shipley Patron
Miller, Ruth Ann Painter
Milloff, Mark David Painter, Sculptor
Milton, Peter Winslow Printmaker
Mincemoyer, Carin Installation Sculptor
Mindich, Eric Patron
Minick, Roger Photographer, Writer
Miotte, Jean Painter
Mishler, John Milton Artist, Educator
Mitchell, Dianne Painter
Mitchell, Jeffry Painter, Sculptor
Mitchell, Maceo Painter
Mitchell, N Donald Administrator, Dealer
Mnuchin, Steven T Patron
Modi-Vitale, Lydia Museum Director, Curator
Moldroski, Al R Painter, Educator
Mollett, David Educator, Administrator
Momin, Shamim M Curator
Monaghan, Kathleen Mary Director
Mondini-Ruiz, Franco Artist
Monet, Diane L. Painter
Monforte, Ivan Performance Artist
Mongrain, Claude Sculptor
Mongrain, Jeffrey Sculptor
Monks, Alyssa Painter
Monroe, Gerald Painter, Educator
Montesinos, Vicky Painter, Printmaker
Montgomery, Steven Sculptor, Photographer
Montrose-Graem, Douglass J Museum Director, Painter, Poet, Music Maker
Moon, Jaye Sculptor
Moon, Marc Painter, Instructor
Moore, Anne F Museum Director, Educator
Moore, John J Painter, Educator
Moore, Robert James Painter, Photographer
Moores, Peter Collector
Moreno, David Painter
Morgan, Robert Coolidge Writer, Painter
Morgan, Susan Painter, Instructor
Morgin, Kristen Ceramist
Morimoto, Masao Sculptor
Morris, Rebecca Painter
Morris, Wendy Sue Painter
Morrissey, Leo Conceptual Artist
Moscatt, Paul N Painter, Instructor
Mosch, Deborah Cherry Educator, Painter
Moseman, M L (Mark) Painter, Curator
Moser, Jill Painter
Moser, Kenna J Painter
Mottram, Ronald Administrator, Historian
Moya, Robert Painter, Printmaker
Moyers, William Painter, Sculptor
Mozley, Anita Ventura Curator, Critic
Muchnic, Suzanne Critic, Instructor
Muirhead, Ross P Kinetic Artist, Photographer
Mulhern, Michael Painter
Mullen, James Martin Educator, Printmaker
Muller, Max Paul Painter, Instructor
Muñoz, Paloma Sculptor
Munro, Janet Andrea Painter
Munro, JP Artist
Munroe, Victoria Art Dealer
Murphy, Marilyn L Painter, Educator
Murphy, Mary Marguerite Painter, Instructor
Murtic, Edo Painter, Enamelist
Musco, Lydia Sculptor
Musgrave, Shirley Hudson Educator, Photographer
Myers, Dorothy Roatz Painter, Critic
Myers, Martin Sculptor, Painter
Myers, Rita Video Artist
Nadler, Arny Sculptor
Nardone, Vincent Joseph Painter, Juror
Narotzky, Norman David Painter, Printmaker
Nash, Alyce Louise (Sandy) Consultant
Natale, Marie Painter, Instructor
Nawabi, Kymia Painter
Nawrocki, Dennis Alan Educator, Curator
Neely, Anne painter
Neff, John Hallmark Art Historian, Museum Director
Negroponte, George Painter
Nelson, Jon Allen Curator, Historian
Nerburn, Kent Michael Sculptor, Critic
Neumann, Hubert Collector
Newbegin, Katherine Photographer
Newcomb, Lynn Sculptor, Printmaker
Newkirk, Kori Assemblage Artist
Newman, Elizabeth H Sculptor
Newman, Laura Painter
Newman, Richard Charles Sculptor, Collage Artist
Newsom, Barbara Ylvisaker Administrator, Writer
Newsome, Rashaad Germain Video Artist, Sculptor
Ng, Natty (Yuen Lee) Painter, Graphic Designer
Niarchos, Philip S Collector
Nicholson, Roni Sculptor
Nicosia, Nic Photographer
Niederer, Carl Painter
Niese, Henry Ernst Painter, Educator
Nimmer, Dean Educator, Painter
Nind, Jean Painter, Printmaker
Nipper, Kelly Photographer
Nisula, Larry Painter, Sculptor
Nix, Nelleke Writer, Visual Artist
Nix, Patricia (Lea) Sculptor, Painter
Nodiff, Jack Painter
Noguchi, Rika Photographer
Noland, William Sculptor, Photographer
Nordin, Phyllis E Sculptor, Painter
Nordstrom, Alison Devine Administrator, Curator
Northridge, Matthew Sculptor, Collage Artist
Norton, Mary Joyce Painter, Jeweler
Norwood, Malcolm Mark Painter, Educator
Nowytski, Sviatoslav Filmmaker, Photographer
Obringer, Patricia Mary Sculptor, Muralist
Ochoa, Ruben Sculptor, Environmental Sculptor
Ocvirk, Otto G Sculptor, Printmaker
O'Dell, Erin (Anne) Painter, Designer
Oginz, Richard Sculptor, Draftsman
Okoshi, E Sumiye Painter, Collage Artist
Okun, Jenny Photographer
Olbricht, Thomas Collector
Olea, Hector Curator
Olsen, Rune Sculptor
O'Neal, Roland Lenard Illustrator, Painter
O'Neil, Robyn Painter
Ono, Yoko Conceptual Artist
Oppenheimer, Sara Installation Sculptor
Orellana, Fernando Sculptor
Orth, Maggie Artist
Ortlip, Paul Daniel Painter
Oshiro, Kaz Installation Sculptor
Ostendarp, Carl Painter
Ostrow, Saul Critic, Educator
Ostrow, Stephen Edward Administrator, Curator
O'Sullivan, Judith Roberta Museum Director, Painter, Writer
Otani, June Illustrator, Printmaker
Overland, Carlton Edward Curator, Historian
Ovitz, Judy & Michael S Collector, Patron
Oxman, Katja Printmaker
Oxman, Mark Sculptor, Educator
Ozonoff, Ida Painter, Collage Artist
Pachter, Charles Painter, Printmaker
Padovano, Anthony John Sculptor, Draftsman
Page, Jean Jepson Collector, Historian
Paglen, Trevor Photographer
Paine, Roxy Sculptor, Conceptual Artist
Paisner, Claire Painter
Palmer, Laura Higgins Artist
Panas, Lydia Photographer

ADDRESS NOT PUBLISHED (cont)

Sheehan, Evelyn Painter
Sheller, G A Painter, Photographer
Shelley, Ward Sculptor, Painter
Sherman-Zinn, Ellen R Painter, Designer
Shin, Jean Installation Sculptor
Shirley, Jon Anthony Collector
Shirley, Mary Collector
Shkurpela, Dasha Painter, Sculptor
Shooster, Stephen Leon Conceptual Artist, Author
Shore, Stephen Photographer
Shotwell, Kenneth E Painter, Printmaker
Shrigley, David Draftsman
Sickler, Michael Allan Painter, Collage Artist
Sideman, Carol K Painter
Siegel, Fran Painter
Siena, James Painter
Sigal, Lisa Painter
Siguroardottir, Katrin Installation Sculptor
Silook, Susie Sculptor, Craftsman
Silver, Larry Arnold Curator, Historian
Simon, Amy Photographer
Simon, Michael A Photographer
Simon, Taryn Photographer
Simpson, Lorna Photographer, Filmmaker
Sindelir, Robert John Gallery Director, Administrator
Singer, Michael Sculptor
Sinner, Steve sculptor
Skelley, Robert Charles Educator, Printmaker
Skoler, Celia Rebecca Consultant, Gallery Director
Slade, George G Historian, Administrator
Slade, Roy Painter, Museum Director
Slatton, Ralph David Printmaker, Graphic Artist
Sligh, Clarissa T Photographer, Painter
Smalley, David Allan Sculptor, Educator
Smith, Albert E Painter
Smith, Cary Painter
Smith, Clifford Painter
Smith, Elizabeth Angele Curator
Smith, Elliot Dealer, Historian
Smith, Frank Anthony Painter
Smith, Gary Haven Sculptor
Smith, Greg Painter, Graphic Artist
Smith, Josh Collage Artist
Smith, Kiki Painter, Sculptor
Smith, Lawson Wentworth Sculptor, Educator
Smith, Rene Painter
Smith, Shinique Amie Assemblage Artist
Smith-Stewart, Amy Gallery Director, Curator
Sniffen, Frances Sculptor, Painter
Snodgrass-King, Jeanne Owen (Mrs M Eugene King) Consultant, Writer
Snow, Agathe Installation Sculptor
Snow, Maryly A Librarian, Printmaker
Snyder, Dean Sculptor
Snyder, Joan Painter
Soave, Sergio Educator, Printmaker
Sokolowski, Thomas Museum Director
Solberg, Morten Edward Painter
Solien, TL Painter
Sonday, Milton Franklin, Jr Curator
Song, Suzanne Painter
Sonnenberg, Frances Sculptor
Sonnenberg, Hendrika Sculptor
Sorkin, Emily Art Dealer, Gallery Director
Sottung, George (K) Painter, Sculptor
South, Jane Sculptor
Sowers, Russell Frederic Gallery Director, Museum Director
Spear, Laurinda Hope Architect
Spencer, Harold Edwin Historian, Painter
Spencer, Susan Elizabeth Painter, Instructor
Sperakis, Nicholas George Painter, Printmaker
Speyer, Nora Painter
Spindelman, Margot Painter
Spitz, Barbara S Printmaker, Photographer
Spitzer, Serge Installation Sculptor, Conceptual Artist
Spohn, Franz Frederick Printmaker, Illustrator
Spratt, Frederick R Gallery Director, Painter
Squires Ganz, Sylvia (Tykie) Painter
Staab, Roy Installation Sculptor
Stapen, Nancy Critic, Writer
Stark, Kathy Painter
Starr, Susanna Sculptor
Steiner, Paul Writer, Critic
Steiner, Sherry L Painter, Writer, Instructor, Gallery Director
Steinhardt, Alice Draftsman, Painter - Acrylic, Oil
Steinkamp, Jennifer Sculptor, Installation Artist
Steinman, Barbara Conceptual Artist, Photographer
Stephens, Thomas Michael Kinetic Artist, Designer
Stevanov, Zoran Painter, Sculptor
Stevenson, Harold Painter
Stewart, Lorelei Curator, Administrator
Stewart, William Painter, Educator
Stiebel, Gerald G Dealer
Stillman (Myers), Joyce L Painter, Lecturer
Stockman, Jennifer Blei Patron
Stokes, Leonard Collage Artist
Stone, Jim (James) J Photographer, Writer
Stones, Margaret Alison Educator, Historian
Storm, Larue Painter
Stout, Renee Sculptor, Photographer, Painter, Installation Artist
Strassberg, Roy I Ceramist, Sculptor
Strassheim, Angela Photographer
Stratton, Julia Sculptor
Streeter, Tal Sculptor, Writer
Streett, Tylden Westcott Sculptor, Instructor
Stronghilos, Carol Painter
Strunck, Juergen Printmaker, Professor
Stryk, Suzanne Painter
Sturgeon, Mary C Educator, Historian
Stutesman, Cezanne Slough Painter
Suba, Susanne (Mrs Bertam Bloch) Painter, Illustrator
Subotsky, Mikhael Photographer
Sujo, Clara Diament Gallery Director, Curator, Writer
Sullivan, Ruth Wilkins Curator, Lecturer
Sures, Jack Ceramist, Educator
Sussman, Eve Painter
Suzuki, Taro Sculptor, Painter
Swanson, J N Painter, Sculptor
Swanson, Ray V Painter
Syjuco, Stephanie Installation Sculptor
Szoke, John Dealer, Publisher
Taft, Frances Prindle Educator, Painter - Watercolor
Tahir, Abe M, Jr Consultant
Taira, Masa Morioka Gallery Director, Consultant
Takagi, Mayumi Painter, Sculptor, Printmaker
Takahashi, Ginger Brooks Photographer
Tallman, Ami Painter
Tan, Noelle Photographer
Tanenbaum, Toby Collector
Taradash, Meryl Environmental Artist, Kinetic Artist
Tarasiewicz, Tamara Painter
Tate, Gayle Blair Painter
Tatham, David Frederic Historian
Taubes, Timothy Evan Critic, Curator
Tay, Eng Painter
Taylor, Brie (Benjamin de Brie) Educator, Painter
Taylor, Christopher Glass Blower
Taylor, David J Photographer
Taylor, Davis Educator
Taylor, Henry Painter
Taylor, Janet R Tapestry Artist, Weaver
Taylor, Rosemary Ceramist, Sculptor
Tayou, Pascale Marthine Sculptor
Tegeder, Dannielle Painter
Teiger, David Collector
Terrassa, Jacqueline Museum Director
Thater, Diana Video Artist, Painter
Thomas, Cheryl Ann Sculptor, Ceramist
Thomas, Elaine Freeman Educator, Administrator
Thomas, Hank Willis Photographer
Thompson, Donald Roy Painter, Educator
Thompson, Mark L Sculptor
Thompson, Virginia Abbate Painter, Instructor
Thorne-Thomsen, Ruth T Photographer, Educator
Tice, George (Andrew) Photographer, Author
Tileston, Jackie Artist
Tobin, Steve Robert sculptor
Toda, Fumiko Painter, Printmaker
Toguo, Barthélémy Painter
Tompkins, Michael Painter
Tonelli, Edith Ann Museum Director, Historian
Toperzer, Thomas Raymond Museum Director, Painter
Toscano, Dolores A Painter, Sculptor
Toth, Georgina Gy Art Librarian
Trager, Philip Photographer
Travers-Smith, Brian John Painter, Instructor
Traynor, John C Painter
Tredennick, Dorothy W Educator, Lecturer
Tripp, Jan Peter Painter, Printmaker
Trippi, Peter Bruce Museum Director
Trop, Sandra Museum Director
Trueblood, L'Deane Sculptor, Painter
Trujillo, Marc Painter
Tsai, Hsiao Hsia Painter, Sculptor
Tsai, Winnie C Painter, Educator, Calligrapher
Tsarikovsky, Valery (Tsar) Painter, Muralist
Tuchman, Maurice Museum Curator
Tupitsyn, Margarita Critic, Curator
Turk, Rudy H Museum Director, Painter
Turnbull, Betty Curator
Turner, Evan Hopkins Museum Director
Turnure, James Harvey Educator, Historian
Tyler, Ron C Art Historian, Museum Director
Ullman, (Mrs) George W Collector
Ulrich, Brian Photographer
Upton, Richard Thomas Painter, Printmaker
Urso, Josette Painter
Urso, Leonard A Sculptor, Painter
Utterback, Camille Digital and Video Artist
Valadez, John Painter
Valenti, Thomas Painter, Instructor, Administrator
Valentin, Jean-Pierre Dealer
Valla, Teressa Marie Painter, Kinetic Sculptor
Van Buren, Richard Sculptor
Vanden Berge, Peter Willem Sculptor, Muralist
Vaness, Margaret Helen Photographer, Writer
Van Harlingen, Jean (Ann) Environmental Artist, Painter
Vanier, Jerre Lynn Art Dealer, Director
Van Schaack, Eric Historian, Educator
Vargas, Josephine Illustrator, Painter
Veca, Mark Dean Painter
Vegara, Camilo Jose Photographer
Vekris, Babis A Kinetic Artist, Sculptor
Velarde, Kukuli Ceramist
Velasquez, Oscar Painter, Illustrator
Velez, Edin Video Artist
Velick, Bruce Curator
Venable, Charles L Museum Director
Venegas, Haydee E Consultant
Venet, Bernar Sculptor, Conceptual Artist
Venezia, Michael Painter
Vergano, Lynn B Painter, Lecturer
Versteeg, Siebren Conceptual Artist
Vetrocq, Marcia E Editor
Vikan, Gary Kent Museum Director
Vine, Marlene Printmaker, Painter
Vinella, Ray (Raimondo) John Painter, Sculptor
Violet, Ultra Painter, Writer
Violette, Banks Painter, Sculptor
Virgona, Hank (Henry) P Painter, Printmaker
Vo-Dinh, Mai Painter, Printmaker
Vogel, (Mr & Mrs) Herbert Collectors
Vogelstein, Barbara Collector
Vogelstein, John L Collector
Voisine, Don Painter
Volicer, Nadya Sculptor
Vonbetzen, Valerie Painter
Von Brandenburg, Ulla Sculptor, Video Artist
von Habsburg, Francesca Collector
Von Mertens, Anna Textile Artist
von Recklinghausen, Marianne Bowles Painter, Sculptor
Von Rydingsvard, Ursula Sculptor
Vote, Melanie Painter
Wagner, Sarah Installation Sculptor
Wahl, Jonathan C Sculptor
Wainwright, Robert Barry Painter, Printmaker
Walker, John Seibels Painter
Walker, Larry Painter, Educator
Walker, Laurie Ann Sculptor, Conceptual Artist
Walker, Mary Carolyn Craftsman, Jeweler
Walker, Randy Sculptor
Wallace Patruziello, Sarah Painter
Walsh, Nan Painter, Sculptor
Walton, Alice Louise Collector
Walton, Lee Conceptual artist, Draftsman
Wambaugh, Michele Fine Art Photographer
Wands, Robert James Educator, Painter
Wang, Sam Photographer
Warck Meister, Lucia Installation Sculptor, Video Artist
Ward, John Lawrence Historian, Painter
Warnecke, John Carl Architect
Warren, Julianne Bussert Baker Photographer, Historian
Warren, Russ Painter
Warrior, Della C Administrator
Washington, James W, Jr Sculptor, Painter
Wastrom, Erika Painter
Watson, Aldren A Designer, Illustrator
Watson, Clarissa H Dealer, Writer
Watson, Ross Curator
Wattles, Virginia Artist
Wax, Jack Glass Artist, Eduactor
Wearing, Gillian Conceptual Artist
Weaver, Cheyenne Sculptor
Webb, Alex(ander) (Dwight) Photographer
Webb, Jeffrey R Painter, Educator
Webster, Sally (Sara) B Historian
Weglarz, Lorraine D Installation Sculptor, Environmental Artist
Weinbaum, Jean Painter, Sculptor
Weingarten, Hilde (Kevess) Painter, Printmaker
Weisberg, Ruth Ellen Painter, Educator
Weiss, Madeline Painter
Welch, James Edward Painter
Weld, Alison Gordon Painter, Assemblage Artist, Conceptual Artist
Weldon, Barbara Maltby Painter
Welitoff, Suara Video Artist
Wells, Charles Sculptor, Printmaker
Welty, Jennifer Roth Painter, Instructor
Wesley, John Painter
West, Christina A Ceramist
Westervelt, Robert F Historian, Ceramist
Wheadon, Nico Curator, Photographer
White, Brook Forrest, Jr Glass Blower
White, Deborah Dealer
White, Mary Bayard Sculptor, Educator

Professional Classifications Index

ADMINISTRATOR

ADMINISTRATOR (cont)
Melton, Terry R
Miles, Christine M
Miley, Randolph Benton
Miller, Joan Vita
Miller, John Franklin
Miller, Rodney E
Mitchell, N Donald
Mitchell, Shannon Dillard
Mobley, Karen R
Mollett, David
Moore, Fay
Morrin, Peter Patrick
Morrisey, Marena Grant
Moses, Jennifer
Mottram, Ronald
Moy, James S
Muhl, Erica
Mulfinger, Jane
Munitz, Barry
Murray, Catherine
Murray, Reuben
Nadarajan, Gunalan
Nestor, Lula B
Nordstrom, Alison Devine
Nunes, Grafton J
O'Connell, Daniel Moylan
O'Connell, Kenneth Robert
Okala, Chinedu
O'Keefe, Michael
O'Leary, Daniel
Olenick, David Charles
Orze, Joseph John
Osborne, Frederick S
Ostrow, Stephen Edward
O'Sullivan, Judith Roberta
Outterbridge, John Wilfred
Owens, Gwendolyn Jane
Packard, Sally
Pagani, Catherine
Parker, Ron
Parry, Pamela Jeffcott
Pasternak, Anne
Pease, David G
Perry, Edward (Ted) Samuel
Pettibone, John Wolcott
Piasecki, Jane B
Pierce, Charles Eliot, Jr
Pinnell, Peter J
Pirnat-Dressler, Nia
Platt, Melvin
Polcari, Stephen
Pollock, Lindsay
Polsky, Cynthia Hazen
Pontynen, Arthur
Prescott, Kenneth Wade
Pressly, Nancy Lee
Price, Barbara Gillette
Probst, Robert
Putterman, Susan Lynn
Quirarte, Jacinto
Radan, George Tivadar
Radecki, Martin John
Radice, Anne-Imelda Marino
Rafferty, Emily
Rahja, Virginia Helga
Ramos, Julianne
Rasmussen, Anton Jesse
Ray, Katerina Ruedi
Reese, Thomas Ford
Reeser, Robert D
Reeve, Deborah B
Relyea, Lane
Rhodes, David
Rico-Gutierrez, Luis
Rieth, Sheri Fleck
Risley, Jack
Ritts, Edwin Earl, Jr
Robertson, Charles J
Rogers, Richard L
Rose, Deedie Potter
Rosenberg, Herb
Roth, Michael S
Rubin, Patricia
Ruffo, Joseph Martin
Rust, Edwin C
Sabol, Frank Robert
Schar, Stuart
Schlanger, Gregg
Schutte, Thomas Frederick
Scoates, Christopher
Seeger, Matthew W
Seipel, Joseph H
Serenyi, Peter
Sevigny, Maurice Joseph, II
Seymour, Claudia Hultgren
Shaheen, Gary Edward
Sheon, Aaron
Simon, Leonard Ronald
Simonson, Anne
Sindelir, Robert John
Slade, George G
Smith, Gil R
Smith, John W
Snapp, Brian
Somerville, Romaine Stec
Sorell, Victor Alexander
Spink, Walter M
Sprouls, David
Spurgin, John Edwin
Stanley, John Slusarski
Stauffer, George B
Stebbins, Theodore Ellis, Jr
Steglich, David M
Stein, Claire A
Steiner, Rochelle
Stephens, Elisa
Stevens, Jane M
Stewart, Lorelei
Stitt, Susan (Margaret)
Stoppert, Mary Kay
Streetman, John William, III
Stroker, Robert T
Stuart, Nancy
Sumner, Stephen Charles
Svedlow, Andrew Jay
Tai, Jane S
Talbot, Christopher
Tarbox, Gurdon Lucius, Jr
Taylor, Marilyn Jordan
Tenenbaum, Ann
Tepper, Steven J
Thomas, Elaine Freeman
Thompson, Lydia
Thompson, Paul Warwick
Thompson, Wade S
Thorne, Martha
Tichich, Richard
Tió, Adrian R
Tomasini, Wallace J
Towner, Mark Andrew
Trecker, Stanley Matthew Matthew
Tuegel, Michele Beckman
Tullos, Mark A, Jr
Tuman, Donna
Tuski, Donald
Ullens de Schooten, Myriam & Guy Francis
Valenti, Thomas
Vandenburgh, Laura
VanderWeg, Phillip Dale
Vescolani, Bert
Voos, William John
Wahlman, Maude Southwell
Wahrhaftig, Claire Isaacs
Waisbrot, Ann M
Wallace, Paula S
Walsh, Janet Barbara
Warden, P Gregory
Warlick, M.E.
Warrior, Della C
Watson, Mary Jo
Weaver, AM
Weaver, Michael K
Weber, Susan
Weidell, Charleen
Weiler, Melody M
Weinberg, Ephraim
Westermann, Mariët
Westin, Robert H
Wexler, Alice
White, E Alan
White, Michael
Whyte, Bruce Lincoln
Wightman, William
Wilson, Charles
Wilson, John David
Wise, Suzanne Tanderup
Young, Charles E
Young, Richard Alan
Zauft, Richard
Zemans, Joyce L
Zivkovich, Kay Pick

ARCHITECT

Agustin, Hernandez
Allen, Stan
Armstrong, Geoffrey
Bakanowsky, Louis J
Ball, Ken Weston
Ballard, James A
Balmori, Diana
Blasco, Isidro M
Booth, Laurence Ogden
Bower, John Arnold, Jr
Brodsky, Alexander Ilya Utkin
Carlhian, Jean Paul
Carter, Jerry Williams
Cassell, Stephen
Cutler, Laurence S
Drezner, A L
Eiswerth, Barry
Flores, Carlos Marini
Forgey, Benjamin Franklin
Fort-Brescia, Bernardo M
Fowle, Bruce S
Friedberg, M. Paul
Gang, Jeanne
Gillman, Derek A
Giurgola, Romaldo
Graves, Michael
Haeg, Fritz
Hall, William A
Harkness, John Cheesman
Holl, Steven Myron
Hoover, George Schweke
Jacobsen, Hugh Newell
Johansen, John Maclane
Joseph, Wendy Evans
Kaskey, Raymond John
Khedoori, Rachel
Kinoshita, Gene
Kleinman, Kent
Krasnyansky, Anatole Lvovich
Kravis, Janis
Lamantia, James
Lambert, Phyllis
Libeskind, Daniel
Lichaw, Pessia
Lorenz, Marie
Martin, Margaret M
Mayne, Thom
Meier, Richard Alan
Meredith, Michael
Moe, Kiel K
Morrison, Boone M
Newick, Craig D
Olin, Laurie Dewar
Otero-Pailos, Jorge
Pailos, Jorge Otero
Pasquarelli, Gregg Andrew
Peckham, Nicholas
Polshek, James
Portman, John C, Jr
Potrc, Marjetica
Provisor, Janis
Quigley, Robert Wellington
Rico-Gutierrez, Luis
Riley, Terence
Robins, Joyce
Roche, (Eamonn) Kevin
Rolland, Peter George
Romney, Hervin A R
Rybczynski, Witold Marian
Sample, Hilary
Sanderson, Warren
Santos, Adele Naude
Schweder, Alex
Scogin, Mack
Scully, Vincent Joseph, Jr
Selldorf, Annabelle M
Shepard, Mark
Siegel, Barbara
Sorkin, Michael
Spear, Laurinda Hope
Talbert, Richard Harrison
Taylor, Marilyn Jordan
Tigerman, Stanley
Tobler, Gisela Erna Maria
Towers, Joel
Tschumi, Bernard
Tsien, Billie
Van Ginkel, Blanche Lemco
Van Valkenburgh, Michael
Venturi, Robert
Villarreal-Castelazo, Eduardo
Vinoly, Rafael
Voorsanger, Bartholomew
Warnecke, John Carl
White, Michael
Williams, Tod
Yarinsky, Adam
Yegul, Fikret Kutlu
Zeidler, Eberhard Heinrich
Zucker, Bob

ART APPRAISER

Cooper, Theodore A
Cozad, Rachael Blackburn
Dodworth, Allen Stevens
Gardiner, Henry Gilbert
Gorvy, Brett
Hayes, Laura M
Hermus, Lance Jay
Mayer, Sondra Elster
Mayo, Pamela Elizabeth
McCarron, Paul
Mohle, Brenda Simonson
Moore, Anne F
Moore Nicholson, Myreen
Rosenberg, Alex Jacob
Rotter, Alex
St Lifer, Jane
Schuster, Cita Fletcher (Sarah E)
Sherratt, Holly
Smither, Edward Murray

ART DEALER

Adamson, Jerome D
Albano, Patrick Louis
Alexander, Edmund Brooke
Allen, Edda Lynne
Allrich, M Louise Barco
Altermann, Tony
Arnold, Jack
Attal, M George
Bachert, Hildegard Gina
Band, David Moshe
Banks, Robert Harris
Banning, Jack, Jr
Barnes, Molly
Barnett, David J
Barrios, Benny Perez
Baum, Jayne H
Baxter, Douglas W
Beilin, Howard
Bell, Mary Catherine
Bergen, Jeffrey B
Berggruen, John Henry
Bernstein, Saralinda
Bolen, John E
Bolen, Lynne N
Boler, John Alfred
Bonino, Fernanda
Braseth, John E
Braunstein, Ruth
Brown, Alan M, Jr

ART DEALER (cont)
Brown, Constance George
Brown, Robert K
Bryant, Linda Goode
Burk, A Darlene
Carson, G B
Castagno, John Edward
Cawley, Joan Mae
Challis, Richard Bracebridge
Chambers, William McWillie
Chapline, Claudia Beechum
Chichura, Diane B
Christopherson, Howard Martin
Clark, Garth Reginald
Cohen, Mildred Thaler
Cohn, Frederick Donald
Cohn, Richard A
Cook, R Scott & Soussan A E
Cooper, Paula
Cooper, Theodore A
Couturier, Marion B
Cowles, Charles
Cuningham, Elizabeth Bayard (Mrs E W R Templeton)
Cutler, Bess
Cutler, Judy Goffman
Dailey, Victoria Keilus
Daniel, Kendra Cliver Krienke
Davidson, Maxwell, III
Davis, Kimberly Brooke
De Andino, Jean-Pierre M
Deats, (Margaret)
Degn, Katherine Kaplan
Dennison, Lisa
Deutschman, Louise Tolliver
De Wan-Carlson, Anna
Dolan, Margo
Donnangelo, David Michael
Dorfman, Fred
Driscoll, John Paul
Drutt, Helen Williams
Edwards, Gary Maxwell
Eisenberg, Jerome Martin
Ellis-Tracy, Jo
Elowitch, Annette
Elowitch, Robert Jason
Fairweather, Sally H
Feigen, Richard L
Feinman, Stephen E
Feld, Stuart P
Feldman, Arthur Mitchell
Felsen, Rosamund
Findlay, David B, Jr
Fink, Alan
Fink, Joanna Elizabeth
Fisher, Philip C
Flower, Michael Lavin
Foley, Timothy Albert
Folk, Tom C
Ford Nussbaum Drill, Sheila
Fowler, Frank Eison
Fraenkel, Jeffrey Andrew
Freudenheim, Nina
Friedman, Marvin Ross
Fritzler, Gerald J
Fuller, Jeffrey P
Gagosian, Larry Gilbert
Gallander, Cathleen S
Garver, Fanny
Gerst, Hilde W
Getler, Helen
Gillman, Barbara Seitlin
Gladstone, Barbara
Glick, Paula F
Goad, Anne Laine
Gobuzas, Aldona M
Goldstein, Charles Barry
Goodman, James Neil
Gordon, Albert F
Graham, Robert C, Jr
Gray, Richard
Greenberg, Howard
Greenberg, Ronald K
Hage, Raymond Joseph
Hahn, Roslyn
Hamilton, Patricia Rose
Hampson, Ferdinand Charles
Hansley, Lee
Harcus, Portia Gwen
Harris, Lily Marjorie
Haslem, Jane N
Haulenbeek, Nancy E
Heath, David C
Hedberg, Gregory Scott
Hermus, Lance Jay
Hill, James Berry
Hill, John Conner
Hobbs, Gerald S
Hoffman, Nancy
Holland, Hillman Randall
Hooks, Geri
Hourian, Mohammad
Howlett, D(onald) Roger
Hughes, Paul Lucien
Hutchins, Robin
Iannetti, Pasquale Francesco Paolo
Ingber, Barbara
Janis, Conrad
Jean, Beverly Strong
Jensen, Dean N
Johnson, Miani
Kabakov, Emilia
Kahan, Alexander
Kahan, Leonard
Kallir, Jane Katherine
Kanegis, Sidney S
Kaplan, Jacques
Katselas, Milton George
Katzen, Hal Zachery
Kaye, David Haigh
Kelley, Chapman
Kelso, David William
Kennedy, Marla Hamburg
Killeen, Melissa Helen
Kimmel-Cohn, Roberta
King, Myron Lyzon
Kornblatt, Barbara Rodbell
Kornetchuk, Elena
Krakow, Barbara L
Lally, James Joseph
Lamoureux, Marie France
Langman, Richard Theodore
La Pelle, Rodger
Law, Jan
Lawrence, Susan
Leach, Elizabeth Anne
Lee, Mack
Lee, Nelda S
Leeber, Sharon Corgan
Lehr, Janet
Levit, Héloïse (Ginger) Bertman
Levy, Bernard
Levy, S(tephen) Dean
Lewin, Bernard
Littrell, Doris Marie
Long, Meredith J
Long-Murphy, Jenny
Lord, Michael Harry
Ludman, Joan Hurwitz
Luntz, Irving
Lyons, Francis E, Jr
MacDougall, Anne
Makler, Hope Welsh
Mangel, Benjamin
Mangel, Deborah T
Mansion, Gracie
Marcus, Angelo P
Markel, Kathryn E
Markle, Sam
Marks, Matthew Stuart
Mason, Lauris Lapidos
Mathis, Emile Henry, II
May, Daniel Striger
Mayer, Sondra Elster
Mayo, Robert Bowers
McCarron, Paul
McKee, David Malcolm
McKee, Renee Conforte
McOwen, C Lynn
Meek, J William, III
Meisel, Louis Koenig
Melberg, Jerald Leigh
Merida, Frederick A
Michaux, Ronald Robert
Milant, Jean Robert
Missal, Joshua M
Mitchell, N Donald
Mitchell-Innes, Lucy
Mohle, Brenda Simonson
Moody, Elizabeth C
Moore, Anne F
Moore, Bridget
Moore, Sabra
Moos, Walter A
Morris, Florence Marie
Morris, Jack Austin, Jr
Morse, Mitchell Ian
Moss, Tobey C
Muller, Max Paul
Munroe, Victoria
Murphy, Susan Avis
Natzmer Valentine, Cheryl
Newman, Louis
Newman, Walter Andrews, Jr
Nielsen, Nina I M
O'Connor-Myer, Rose Ann
Olenick, David Charles
Oliver, Sandra (Sandi)
Owens, Tennys Bowers
Palmer, Meredith Ann
Parkerson, John E
Payson, John Whitney
Pence, John Gerald
Perlow, Katharina Rich
Pesner, Carole Manishin
Pierce, Patricia Jobe
Portnoy, Theodora Preiss
Posner, Judith L
Propersi, August J
Pucker, Bernard H
Rapp, M Yvonne
Riegle, Robert Mack
Robertson, Ruth
Robinson, Thomas V
Rolly, Ronald Joseph
Romero, Megan H
Rose, Peter Henry
Rosenberg, Carole Halsband
Rosenfeld, Samuel L
Rotenberg, Judi
Rothschild, John D
Rowand, Joseph Donn
Rubin, Lawrence
Sacks, Beverly
Sadik, Marvin Sherwood
Saphire, Lawrence M
Schab, Margo Pollins
Schneider, Lisa Dawn
Schneier, Donna Frances
Schusterman, Gerrie Marva
Segal, Tama & David
Segal, Thomas H
Shainman, Jack S
Shepard, Lewis Albert
Simon, Robert Barry
Smith, Elliot
Solomon, Gerald
Solomon, Richard H
Solway, Carl E
Sonnabend, Joan
Sorkin, Emily
Spitler, Clare Blackford
Stanton, Sylvia Doucet
Stern, Louis
Stevens, Thelma K
Stewart, John Stewart Houston
Stiebel, Gerald G
Stone, M Lee
Stux, Stefan Victor
Sussman, Bonnie Kaufman
Szoke, John
Tasende, Jose Maria
Thaw, Eugene Victor
Theofiles, George
Thompson, Michael
Toll, Barbara Elizabeth
Turnbull, Betty
Valentin, Jean-Pierre
Vanier, Jerre Lynn
Verzyl, June Carol
Vizner, Nikola
Volid, Ruth
Walker, Berta
Waltzer, Stewart Paul
Washburn, Joan T
Watkins, Ragland Tolk
Watson, Clarissa H
Waxter, Dorsey
Weissman, Julian Paul
Westlund, Harry E
Westwater, Angela King
Whitchurch, Charles A
White, Deborah
White, Stephen Leon
Whiteside, William Albert, II
Wiebe, Charles M
Wiggins, K Douglas
Williams, Melissa
Wilson, John David
Wise, Takouhy
Wolff, Robert W, Jr
Wooby, William Joseph
Wunderlich, Susan Clay
Yarotsky, Lori
Yeiser, Charles William
Zimmerman, Alice A
Zwirner, David

ASSEMBLAGE ARTIST

Abraham, Carol Jeanne
Aronson, Sanda
Aubin, Barbara
Baker, Dianne Angela
Bakke, Karen Lee
Behrens, Mary Snyder
Benson, Martha J
Block, Virginia Schaffer
Blunk, Joyce Elaine
Boghosian, Varujan
Bremer, Marlene
Buchman, Arles (Arlette) Buchman
Collado, Lisa
Cusick, Nancy Taylor
Deckert, Clinton A
Dezzany, Frances Jean
DiDomenico, Nikki
Dorfman, Bruce
Enos, Chris
Enstice, Wayne
Fincher, John H
Fisher, Carole Gorney
Foolery, Tom
Francis, Jean Thickens
Gilchriest, Lorenzo
Goell, Abby Jane
Hammer, Elizabeth B
Heinzen, MaryAnn
Hepler, Anna
Houston, Bruce
Howe, Nelson S
Hoyt, Ellen
Jackson, Matthew Day
Johnson, Martin Brian
Kane, Bill
Karametou, Maria
Katz, Leandro
Keller, Rhoda
Kelm, Bonnie G
Koller-Davies, Eva
Koo, Jeong-A
Kosta, Angela
Lanigan-Schmidt, Thomas
Levine, Barbara
Levinson, Mimi W
Lucas, Bonnie Lynn
Lundberg, William
Majdrakoff, Ivan

COLLAGE ARTIST (cont)
Hancock, Trenton Doyle
Harris, William Wadsworth, II
Harrison, Alice
Hill, Charles Christopher
Hoff, Margo
Horvat, Olga
Hutchins-Malkmus, Jessica Jackson
Irvin, Marianne Fanelli
Jones, Cynthia Clarke
Kadlec, Kristine
Kaiser, Diane
Kamys, Walter
Kikuchi-Yngojo, Alan
Kornbluth, Frances
Krause, Dorothy Simpson
Kroll, Lynne Francine
Kuczun, Ann-Marie
Kunsch, Louis
Laico, Colette
Lea, Stanley E
Lenker, Marlene N
Lerner, Sandra
Levering, Robert K
Livingston, Constance Kellner
Lunney, Kevan
Lynch, Mary Britten
Mac Innes, David Harold
Mackintosh, Sandra
Marks, Roberta Barbara
Massey, John
Maxwell, Jane Hoffman
McCabe, Maureen M
McCleary, Mary Fielding
Mead, Gerald C, Jr
Meeker, Barbara Miller
Miccoli, Arnaldo
Miller, Dolly (Ethel) B
Miller, Joan
Morrison, Edith Borax
Munk, Loren James
Mutu, Wangechi
Naves, Mario
Nessim, Barbara
Newman, Louis
Newman, Richard Charles
Nikkal, Nancy Egol
Noda, Takayo
Northridge, Matthew
Obler, Geri
Okoshi, E Sumiye
Ozonoff, Ida
Pace, James Robert
Palko Kolosvary, Paul
Patterson, Dane
Peace, Bernie Kinzel
Pedersen, Carolyn H
Perroni, Carol
Peters, Diane (Peck)
Peters, Larry Dean
Phillips, Harriet E
Phoenix, Kaola Allen
Pildes, Sara
Pizzat, Joseph
Price, Diane Miller
Promutico, Jean
Puckett, Richard Edward
Raab, Gail B
Rafferty, Joanne Miller
Reedy, Susan
Ritzer, Gail L
Rizzie, Dan
Robbins, Joan Nash
Roberson, William
Rose, Roslyn
Saar, Betye
Sakai, Kiyoko
Schaffer, Debra S
Schiavina, Laura M
Schmit, Randall
Schneider, Shellie
Scholder, Laurence
Schweitzer, John Andrew
Shaddle Baum, Alice
Shaheen, Gary Edward
Shapiro, Lois M
Shearer, Steven
Sickler, Michael Allan
Simonian, Judith
Smith, Alexis (Patricia Anne)
Smith, Josh
Smith, Rowena Marcus
Smith, Susan
Soppelsa, George
Sorokin, Janet
Stewart, Duncan E
Stokes, Leonard
Stoloff, Carolyn
Stone, Judith Elise
Stonehouse, Fred A
Sweet, Steve (Steven) Mark
Talbot, Jonathan
Taylor, Sandra Ortiz
Tomchuk, Marjorie
Urichta, Rey
Vierthaler, Bonnie
Wallenstein, Ellen
Warriner, Laura B
Weiss, Marilyn Ackerman
Wheeler, Janet B
White, Pae
Whitson, Peter Whitson Warren
Willoughby, Jane Baker
Wilmeth, Ernest, II
Wimberley, Frank Walden
Woodson, Shirley Ann
Yoder, Robert Edward
Yunich, Beverly B
Zucker, Murray Harvey

COLLECTOR

Abello, Juan
Abramovich, Roman Arkadyevich
Adrian, Barbara Tramutola
Allen, Paul
Alonso, Eugenio Lopez
Arango, Placido G, Jr
Arnault, Helene & Bernard Jean Etienne
Arnold, John Douglas
Astrup, Hans Rasmus
Baibakov, Oleg
Baibakova, Maria
Balzekas, Stanley, Jr
Barbier-Mueller, Monique & Jean-Paul
Barrell, Bill
Beatty, Frances Fielding Lewis
Bechtler-Lanfranconi, Cristina & Thomas W
Bell, Maria & William J, Jr
Berkman, Lillian
Berman, Bernard
Bertelli, Patrizio
bin Mohammad bin Ali al-Thani, Sheikh Saud
Black, Debra & Leon David
Blitz, Nelson, Jr
Bloch, Henry Wollman
Bluhm, Neil Gary
Bodenmann, Hans U
Bolen, John E
Bolen, Lynne N
Boler, John Alfred
Boros, Christian
Bowes, Frances
Brady, Luther W
Braman, Irma
Braman, Norman
Brandhorst, Udo
Bren, Donald L
Bridenstine, James A
Broad, Edythe & Eli
Bryant, Donald L, Jr
Bunnen, Lucinda Weil
Burda, Frieder
Burger-Calderon, Monique & Max
Burk, A Darlene
Burnet, Peggy & Ralph W
Cartin, Mickey
Chang-Il, Kim
Chen, Pierre TM
Cingillioglu, Halit
Cisneros, Ella Fontanals
Cisneros, Patricia & Gustavo Alfredo
Cohen, Cherryl & Frank
Cohen, Jean R
Cohen, Steven A
Conley, Zeb Bristol, Jr
Costantini, Eduardo
Courtright, Robert
Couturier, Marion B
Cowles, Charles
Cramer, Douglas S
Daskalopoulos, Dimitris
David-Weill, Helene & Michel Alexandre
Davidson, Ian J
De Andino, Jean-Pierre M
Decelle, Philippe
De Galbert, Antoine
de Gunzburg, Charles
de Gunzburg, Nathalie
De La Cruz, Carlos
De La Cruz, Rosa
De Rothschild, Eric Alain Robert David
De Waal, Ronald Burt
DeWoody, Beth Rudin
Diker, Charles & Valerie
Dittmer, Frances R
Dodds, Robert J, III
Dreyfus-Best, Ulla
Dubin, Glenn
Edlis, Stefan T
Ehrenkranz, Joel S & Anne
Eisenberg, Jerome Martin
Eisenstein, (Mr & Mrs) Julian
Embiricos, Epaminondas George (Pandy Embiricos)
Essl, Agnes & Karlheinz, Sr
Eurich, Judith
Falckenberg, Harald
Farley, Katherine G
Farver, Suzanne
Feigen, Richard L
Fertitta, Frank J, III
Fertitta, Lorenzo J
Fineberg, Gerald S
Fisher, Doris F
Fisher, Jerome
Fleischman, Aaron I
Flick, Friedrich Christian
Flick, Paul John
Ford, John Gilmore
Frankel, Stuart & Maxine
Freudenheim, Nina
Freundlich, August L
Froehlich, Anna & Josef
Fuhrman, Glenn R
Fukutake, Soichiro
Fuld, Richard Severin, Jr
Furman, (Dr & Mrs) Arthur F
Ganek, Danielle & David
Garza Laguera, Eugenio
Gildzen, Alex
Glazer, Jay M & Marsha S
Goetz, Ingvild
Goldberg, Carol
Goodman, James Neil
Gori, Giuliano
Gottesman, Geraldine & Noam
Gould, Philip
Graff, Laurence
Gray, Thomas Alexander
Greaves, James L
Greenberg, Ronald K
Grether, Esther
Griffin, Anne & Kenneth C
Gund, Agnes
Hack, Phillip S & Patricia Y
Haley, Gail E
Hall, Christine & Andrew J
Halle, Diane & Bruce T
Hampton, Ambrose Gonzales, Jr
Harnett, Lila
Hassanal Bolkiah, His Majesty Mu'izzaddin Waddaulah
Hatch, (Mr & Mrs) Marshall
Hedreen, Betty
Hedreen, Elizabeth & Richard
Heintz, Florent
Hembrey, Shea
Hendeles, Ydessa
Herbert, Annick & Anton
Hess, Donald Marc
Hessel, Marieluise
Heyman, Ronnie Feuerstein
Hill, J(ames) Tomilson
Hirst, Damien
Hoffman, Marguerite Steed
Hoffmann, Erika
Holdeman, Joshua
Holladay, Wilhelmina Cole
Hooks, Geri
Hort, Michael & Susan
Huang, Frank C
Hubert, Anne M
Hudson, Edward Randall
Iannetti, Pasquale Francesco Paolo
Irmas, Audrey Menein
Irwin, George M
Janis, Conrad
Joannou, Dakis
Johnson, Barbara Piasecka
Johnson, Edward C, III
Jung, Hugo & Ingrid
Kaplan, Jacques
Kaplan, Muriel S
Kelbaugh, Ross J
Kempe, Richard Joseph
Kemper, Rufus Crosby & Mary Barton Stripp
Kempner, Helen Hill
Khalili, Nasser David
Kinney, Gilbert Hart
Kinoshita, Gene
Kirac, Inan & Suna
Klein, Jeanne
Klein, Michael L
Knecht, Uli
Koplowitz, Alicia
Kramer, Linda Lewis
Kramlich, Richard & Pamela
Kraus, Jill Gansman
Kraus, Peter Steven
Kravis, Henry R
Kravis, Marie-Josee
Lagrange, Pierre
Landau, Barbara Downey
Landau, Emily Fisher
Landau, Jon
Larkin, John E, Jr MD
Lau, Joseph Luen-Hung
Lauder, Evelyn H
Lauder, Jo Carole
Lauder, Leonard Alan
Lauder, Ronald Stephen
Learsy, Raymond J
Lee, Barbara
Lewin, Bernard
Lewis, Joseph
Lewis, Peter Benjamin
Libeert, Mimi & Filiep J
Liechtenstein, Hans-Adam von und zu, II
Liechtenstein, Marie Aglae von und zu
Lindemann, Adam
Lloyd Webber, Andrew
Loeb, Margaret & Daniel S
London, Alexander
Lunder, Peter & Paula H
Lynne, Ninah & Michael
Mack, Charles Randall
Macklowe, Linda & Harry
Magnier, Susan & John
Mallin, Judith Young

COLLECTOR (cont)

Mallin, Sherry & Joel
Manilow, Lewis
Marcus, Angelo P
Marcus, Robert (Mrs) P
Margulies, Martin Z
Marion, Anne Windfohr
Marion, John Louis
Marlor, Clark Strang
Marron, Donald Baird
Martinez, David
Martinos, Dinos
Mathis, Emile Henry, II
Mavromatis, Dimitri
Mayo, Robert Bowers
McCannel, Louise Walker
McFadden, Mary
McOwen, C Lynn
Melberg, Jerald Leigh
Menil, Georges & Lois de
Merzbacher, Gabrielle & Werner
Meyerhoff, Robert E
Middleton, John S
Minskoff, Edward & Julie J
Moir, Alfred
Moores, Peter
Mulfinger, Jane
Muniot, Barbara King
Nardin, Mario
Neeson, H Gael
Newhouse, Victoria & Samuel I, Jr
Niarchos, Philip S
Norris, William A
Norton, Peter K
Oeri, Maja
Ortiz, George
Ovitz, Judy & Michael S
Page, Jean Jepson
Pappajohn, John & Mary
Payson, John Whitney
Paz, Bernardo
Penney, Charles Rand
Perelman, Jeffrey E
Perelman, Marsha Reines
Perelman, Ronald Owen
Phelan, Amy
Phelps de Cisneros, Patricia
Phillips, Gifford
Phillips, James M
Pinault, François-Henri
Pinchuk, Victor
Pizzuti, Ronald A
Plotnick, Elizabeth & Harvey Barry
Polsky, Cynthia Hazen
Porter, Richard James
Portman, John C, Jr
Powers, John & Kimiko
Prada, Miuccia Bianca
Prat, Louis-Antoine & Veronique
Price, Joe D & Etsuko
Pritzker, Lisa & John A
Pritzker, Penny S
Pritzlaff, (Mr & Mrs) John, Jr
Pulitzer, Emily Rauh
Rachofsky, Cindy & Howard
Rales, Emily and Mitchell P
Rales, Steven M
Rebaudengo, Patrizia Sandretto Re
Reeves, James Franklin
Rensch, Roslyn
Resnick, Stewart Allen
Revington Burdick, Elizabeth
Riegle, Robert Mack
Riggio, Louise & Leonard
Ringier, Ellen & Michael
Robinson, Thomas V
Rockefeller, John (Jay) D, IV
Rockefeller, Sharon Percy
Rodenstock, Inge
Rose, Deedie Potter
Rose, Edward W, III
Rosen, Aby J
Rosenfeld, Samuel L
Ross, Wilbur Louis, Jr
Rothschild, Eric de
Rubell, Donald
Rubell, Mera
Rubin, Lawrence
Rudman, Betty & Isaac
Rust, David E
Saatchi, Charles
Said, Wafic Rida
Sainsbury, David
Samuels, John Stockwell, III
Sanders, Ida
Sanders, Jeannette & Martijn
Sanders, Marieke
Sanders, Piet
Sanders, Pieter, Jr
Sandground, Mark Bernard, Sr
Sarofim, Fayez S
Sarofim, Louisa Stude
Saul, Andrew M
Saul, Denise
Schoen, (Mr & Mrs) Arthur Boyer
Schreyer, Chara
Schulte, Arthur D
Schwab, Charles R
Schwab, Helen O'Neill
Schwartz, Marianne & Alan E
Sender, Lenore & Adam D
Shack, Richard
Shirley, Jon Anthony
Shirley, Mary
Sigg, Uli
Silverman, Lila & Gilbert B
Simon, Peter
Slim Helú, Carlos
Smidt, Eric
Sneed, Patricia M
Sonnabend, Joan
Speiser, Stuart M
Speyer, Jerry I
Steczynski, John Myron
Steinberg, Blema
Steinberg, H Arnold
Steinhardt, Judy
Steinhardt, Michael H
Stent, Terry & Margaret
Stern, H Peter
Stoffel, Gayle & Paul T
Stone, Norah
Stone, Norman Clement
Strauss, Matthew & Iris
Stroud, Billy
Swofford, Beth
Tananbaum, Lisa & Steven Andrew
Tanenbaum, Joey
Tanenbaum, Toby
Taschen, Benedikt
Teiger, David
Tenenbaum, Ann
Tenzer, (Dr & Mrs) Jonathan A
Thaw, Eugene Victor
Thomson, David K R
Toll, Bruce E
Torf, Lois Beurman
True, Ruth & William L
Ullens de Schooten, Myriam & Guy Francis
Ullman, (Mrs) George W
Valentine, Dean
Van Caldenborgh, Joop
Vanhaerents, Walter
Vanmoerkerke, Edith and Mark
Verzyl, June Carol
Vogel, (Mr & Mrs) Herbert
Vogelstein, Barbara
Vogelstein, John L
von Habsburg, Francesca
Wachs, Ethel
Walton, Alice Louise
Warren, Tom
Weber, Susan
Wertheimer, Alain
Wexner, Abigail
Wexner, Leslie Herbert
White, Stephen Leon
Williams, Dave Harrell
Williams, Katherine
Williams, Reba White
Winter, Hope Melamed
Woolf-Pettyjohn, Nancy Anne
Wright, Bagley
Wright, Virginia
Würth, Reinhold
Wynn, Stephen A
Yanai, Tadashi
Zabludowicz, Anita
Zabludowicz, Poju
Zhukova, Dasha
Ziff, Jerrold
Zimmerman, Alice A

CONCEPTUAL ARTIST

Adams, Dennis Paul
Adams, Derrick
Ahrendt, Mary E
Alden, Todd
Aldrich, Lynn (Barron)
Alexander, Vikky M
Alexenberg, Mel
Allen, Roberta
Allyn, Jerri
Altman, Edith
Alys, Francis
Anderson, Curtis Leslie
Anderson, Laurie
Antin, Eleanor
Antol, Joseph (Jay) James
Aylon, Helène
Backström, Fia
Baer, Rod
Baldessari, John Anthony
Balkin, Amy
Bapst, Sarah
Barr, David John
Barth, Uta
Bauer, Will N
Beirne, Bill
Belcher, Jaq
Bell, Lilian A
Bidlo, Mike
Boardman, Deborah
Bob & Bob
Boigon, Brian Joseph
Brazda, Bonizar
Brodkin, Ed
Bronson, A A (Michael Wayne Tims)
Brown, Gillian
Buchanan, Nancy
Bull, Hank
Burkhardt, Ronald Robert
Burkhart, Kathe K
Burson, Nancy
Carducci, Vince
Chan, Gaye
Chiarlone, Rosemarie
Clarke, Kevin
Cohen, Sorel
Colson, Greg J
Corris, Michael
Costa, Eduardo
Coupe, James
Crown, Roberta Lila
Cumming, Robert H
Cuoghi, Roberto
Curmano, Billy X
Cutler-Shaw, Joyce
Daou, Annabel
Denes, Agnes
Diao, David
DiDomenico, Nikki
Donnelly, Trisha
Easterson, Sam Peter
Edelson, Mary Beth
Edwards, Jonmarc
Einarsson, Gardar Eide
Eins, Stefan
Ewald, Wendy T
Fenton, Julia Ann
Fisher, Vernon
Foreman, Laura
Fox, Terry Alan
Fraser, Andrea R
Frederick, Helen C
Friedman, Charley
Gaines, Charles
Ganahl, Rainer
Garoian, Charles Richard
Gerber, Gaylen
Gerlovina & Gerlovin, Rimma & Valeriy
Giorno, John
Goldman, Matt
Goldring, Nancy Deborah
Greenly, Colin
Gurney, Janice Sigrid
Haacke, Hans Christoph
Harrison, Helen (Mayer) & Newton
Harroff, William Charles Brent
Harvest, Judith R
Hashimoto, Kelly Ann
Higgins, Larkin Maureen
Hill, Christine
Hiller, Susan
Hirst, Damien
Holzer, Jenny
Horwitz, Channa
Huey, Michael CM
Hull, Cathy
Hutchinson, Peter Arthur
Ireland, Patrick
Jaquet, Louis
Johnson, Martin Brian
Johnstone, Mark
Jonas, Joan
Jones, Kim
Josten, Katherine Ann
Kariya, Hiroshi
Kavleski, Charleen Verena
Kelly, Mary
Kersels, Martin
Knerr, Erika Tilde
Kocot & Hatton
Kosuth, Joseph
Kramer, Margia
Kremers, David
Krims, Les
Kruger, Barbara
Krupp, Barbara D
Kunce, Samm
Lacy, Suzanne
Lamarre, Paul
Lamm, Leonid Izrail
Laramee, Eve Andree
Laster, Paul
Laxson, Ruth
Lemieux, Annette Rose
Leung, Simon
Levenson, Dan
Lowman, Nate
Lucas, Christopher
Luce, C(harles) Beardsley
Lum, Ken (Kenneth) Robert
Mac Innes, David Harold
Magid, Jill
Magno, Liz
Maler, Leopoldo Mario
Malpede, John
Mannor, Margalit
Manuella, Frank R
Martel, Richard
Martinez, Daniel Joseph
Massey, John
Mathias, Thelma
Mathis, Billie Fritz
Mayer, Monica P
McCall, Anthony
Michels, Ann Harrison
Minsky, Richard
Montano, Linda (Mary)
Morrissey, Leo
Mullican, Matt
Murray, Ian Stewart
Nemec, Vernita McClish
Neustein, Joshua

CONSERVATOR

CONSULTANT

CRAFTSMAN

CRITIC

CURATOR

CURATOR (cont)
Fitch, Blake
Fleisher, Pat
Fleming, Lee
Fletcher, Valerie J
Foresta, Merry A
Fox, Judith Hoos
Frank, Peter Solomon
Franklin, David
Frazier, LaToya Ruby
Fryberger, Betsy G
Fuller, Diana
Gabriel, Jeanette Hanisee
Gaddis, Eugene Richard
Galassi, Susan Grace
Gale, Peggy
Gallo, Ruben A
Gamwell, Lynn
Garrels, Gary
Garver, Thomas H
Gauthier, Ninon
Gear, Emily
Gedeon, Peter Ferenc
Gee, Helen
Gentele, Glen
Gerdts, Abigail Booth
Glanz, Andrea E
Glasgow, Vaughn Leslie
Goheen, Ellen Rozanne
Golden, Thelma
Goldman, Judith
Goldstein, Ann
Goodman, Cynthia
Gordon, Joy L
Gore, Jefferson Anderson
Gould, Philip
Grand, Stanley I
Greaves, James L
Green, Nancy Elizabeth
Greenhalgh, Paul
Greenough, Sarah
Griswold, William M
Gross, Jennifer R
Grossman, Sheldon
Grossman, Wendy A
Grundberg, Andy
Guo-Qiang, Cai
Gurney, George
Hackenbroch, Yvonne Alix
Hai, Willow Weilan
Hall, Michael David
Haller, Douglas Martin
Hampson, Ferdinand Charles
Hand, John Oliver
Hanks, David Allen
Hansley, Lee
Hapgood, Susan T
Harlow, Ann
Harper, Gregory Franklin
Harris, Paul Rogers
Hartigan, Lynda Roscoe
Hartz, Jill
Haskell, Barbara
Hazlewood, Carl E
Heartney, Eleanor
Heiferman, Marvin
Helsell, Charles Paul
Henderson, Robbin Legere
Hernandez, Jo Farb
Herrmann, John J, Jr
Hess, Stanley William
High, Steven S
Hills, Patricia
Hinson, Tom Everett
Hobbs, Robert
Hoge, Robert Wilson
Holverson, John
Hopkins, Terri
Hoptman, Laura
Hotchner, Holly
Hough, Melissa Ellen
Houk, Pamela P
Houle, Robert James
Huberman, Anthony
Hubert, Anne M
Huerta, Benito
Hughto, Margie A
Huldisch, Henriette
Hunt, David Curtis
Hunter-Stiebel, Penelope
Iles, Chrissie
Ingber, Barbara
Ives, Colta Feller
Jacobowitz, Ellen Sue
Jacobson, Heidi Zuckerman
Jashinsky, Judy
Jeffers, Wendy
Jenkens, Garlan F
Johnson, Carol M
Johnson, Diana L
Johnson, J Stewart
Johnson, Kaytie
Johnson, Robert Flynn
Johnston, William Ralph
Johnstone, Mark
Jones, Michael Butler
Jones, Patty Sue
Joo, Eungie
Kabakov, Emilia
Kampf, Avram S
Kaplan, Flora Edouwaye S
Kazor, Virginia Ernst
Kearney, Lynn Haigh
Kelly, Franklin Wood
Kempe, Richard Joseph
Kennedy, Marla Hamburg
Kertess, Klaus
Kessler, Jane Q
Ketchum, Robert Glenn
King, Elaine A
Kirshner, Judith Russi
Klausner, Betty
Kleeblatt, Norman L
Klein, Richard
Knode, Marilu
Knowles, Susan Williams
Knutsson, Anders
Koenig, Peter Laszlo
Kohler, Ruth DeYoung
Kolodzei, Natalia
Koob, Pamela Nabseth
Kornhauser, Elizabeth Mankin
Kotik, Charlotta
Kowal, Cal (Lee)
Kraft, Craig Allan
Krane, Susan
Krantz, Claire Wolf
Kropf, Joan R
Kuwayama, George
Lagoria, Georgianna Marie M
Landis, Ellen Jamie
Lapkus, Danas
Larsen, Susan C
Laskin, Myron, Jr
Lauf, Cornelia
Lawall, David Barnard
Lawrence, Annette
Lawson, Karol Ann
Lee, Ellen Wardwell
Leeds, Valerie Ann
Lehman, Arnold L
Lerner, Martin
Lesko, Diane
Levin, Kim
Levine, Barbara
Levkova-Lamm, Innessa
Lilyquist, Christine
Linhares, Philip E
Lippincott, Louise
Lippman, Sharon Rochelle
Lipton, Barbara B
Lipton, Leah
Lochnan, Katharine A
Locke, Michelle Wilson
London, Barbara
Lord, Michael Harry
Lovell, Margaretta Markle
Loving, Charles R
Lowe, Sarah
Luchs, Alison
Luckner, Kurt T
Lunsford, John (Crawford)
Luque, Jose Antonio
Maddox, Jerald Curtis
Madonia, Ann C
Magliozzi, Ron
Maklansky, Steven V
Manchanda, Catharina
Mangel, Deborah T
Manhart, Marcia Y
Mann, C Griffith
Mann, James Robert
Maria, Levya
Marshall, John
Martin, Lys
Martin, Younghee Choi
Mathews, Nancy Mowll
Mayfield, Signe S
Mayo, Margaret Ellen
Mayo, Marti
McFadden, David Revere
Meade, Fionn
Meadows, Patricia B
Mergel, Jen
Meslay, Olivier
Metzger, Robert Paul
Mhire, Herman P
Miles, Ellen Gross
Miller, Marc H
Mitchell, Shannon Dillard
Moakley, Paul
Mock, Martha L
Modi-Vitale, Lydia
Moir, Alfred
Moldenhauer, Susan
Molesworth, Helen
Momin, Shamim M
Monk, Robert Evan, Jr
Moore, John L
Morin, France
Moseman, M L (Mark)
Moser, Joann
Mozley, Anita Ventura
Muller, Priscilla Elkow
Munhall, Edgar
Murray, Richard Newton
Myers, Terry R
Nadarajan, Gunalan
Nasgaard, Roald
Nash, Steven Alan
Naumann, Francis M
Nawrocki, Dennis Alan
Nelson, Jane Gray
Nelson, Jon Allen
Nemec, Vernita McClish
Nemser, Cindy
Nickel, Douglas Robert
Nicoll, Jessica F
Nordan, Antoinette Spanos Johnson
Nordstrom, Alison Devine
Norelli, Martina Roudabush
Norfleet, Barbara Pugh
Norris, Merry
Oettinger, Marion, Jr
Olea, Hector
Olin, Ferris
Olson, Roberta Jeanne Marie
Orr-Cahall, Anona Christina
Ostiguy, Jean-Rene
Ostrow, Stephen Edward
Ottmann, Klaus
Overland, Carlton Edward
Owens, Gwendolyn Jane
Oyuela, Raul M
Paikowsky, Sandra R
Pal, Pratapaditya
Palladino-Craig, Allys
Parsons, Merribell Maddux
Pasternak, Anne
Patton, Tom
Payton, Cydney M
Pennington, Estill Curtis
Pepich, Bruce Walter W
Percy, Ann Buchanan
Pesanti, Heather
Peterson, Robyn G
Pettibone, John Wolcott
Phillips, Christopher
Phillips, Lisa
Platow, Raphaela
Platzker, David
Plous, Phyllis
Pohlman, Lynette
Pollei, Dane F
Posner, Helaine J
Pressly, Nancy Lee
Price, Marla
Prodger, Phillip
Putterman, Susan Lynn
Ralapati, Megha
Ramirez, Mari Carmen
Ramírez-Montagut, Mónica
Randall, Lilian M C
Rathbone, Eliza Euretta
Ravenal, John B
Raymond, Yasmil
Reed, Dennis James
Reid, Katharine Lee
Reilly, Bernard Francis
Reilly, Maura
Reynolds, Jock
Reynolds, Valrae
Ribas, Joao
Riccio, Louis Nicholas
Richardson, Trevor J
Rindfleisch, Jan
Rishel, Joseph John, Jr
Roberts, Mark Dennis
Robertson, E Bruce
Robison, Andrew
Rodriguez, Geno (Eugene)
Rogers, Sarah
Rooks, Michael
Rosenfield, John M
Rosensaft, Jean Bloch
Rosenthal, Mark L
Rosenzweig, Phyllis D
Roth, Moira
Rothkopf, Scott
Roy, Rajendra
Royce-Silk, Suzanne
Rubin, David S
Rubinstein, Charlotte Streifer
Rudenstine, Angelica Zander
Ruiz, Jose
Rust, David E
Rychlak, Bonnie L
St John, Terry N
Saltz, Jerry
Salvesen, Britt
San Chirico, Joanie
Sauer, Jane Gottlieb
Scalzo, Joyce Ann
Schaefer, Scott Jay
Schildkrout, Enid
Schmidt, Charles
Schneiderman, Richard S
Schwab, Judith A
Schwager, Michael R
Schwartz, David
Schweitzer, John Andrew
Scoates, Christopher
Scott, Deborah Emont
Segal, Tama & David
Self, Dana Rae
Selz, Peter H
Sewell, Darrel L
Sewell, Jack Vincent
Shackelford, George T M
Shaman, Sanford Sivitz
Shapiro, Michael Edward
Shaw, Karen
Shaw, Louise E
Shimizu, Yoshiaki
Shiner, Eric C
Shlien, Helen S
Shoemaker, Innis Howe
Sill, Gertrude Grace
Silver, Larry Arnold
Silverman, Lanny Harris

DESIGNER

DIRECTOR

DIRECTOR (cont)
Clarke, Bud (Warren) F
Collens, David R
Coolidge, Matthew
Curreri-Ermatinger, Dyana M
Curry, Kevin Lee
Dailey, John Revell
Danzker, Jo-Anne Birnie
Davidow, Joan Carlin
DeGette, Andrea M
DeGuzman, Nicole
DiTommaso, Francis
Divelbiss, Maggie
Dolan, Margo
Doll, Nancy
Dowley, Jennifer
Drutt, Matthew J W
Eagen, Christopher T
Edminston, Scott
Edwards, Susan Harris
Enyeart, James Lyle
Erickson, Marsha A
Faude, Wilson Hinsdale
Finkelpearl, Tom
Firstenberg, Jean Picker
Gentile, Gloria Irene
Gevas, Sophia
Goldstein, Ann
Goldston, Bill
Goley, Mary Anne
Gregory, Joseph F
Guerin, Charles
Hackett, Dwight Vernon
Hai, Willow Weilan
Hannum, Terence J
Harper, Gregory Franklin
Hartshorn, Willis E
Haskell, Heather
Hawley, Anne
Hennessy, Tricia
Herman, Bernard J
Hoffman, Marilyn Friedman
Holcomb, Grant
Hunt, Michael
Hurwitz, Adam
Jacobowitz, Ellen Sue
Josten, Katherine Ann
Joyner, John Brooks
Kardon, Janet
Kelsey, John
Keough, Jeffrey
Klein, Richard
Knight, Robert
Krulik, Barbara S
LaDouceur, Philip Alan
Lambert, Phyllis
Larson, Judy L
Lawrence, Annette
Layne, Margaret Mary
Lee, Katharine C
Leff, Cathy
Levinthal, Beth E
Liotta, Jeanne
Losier, Marie
Lumsden, Ian Gordon
Lyons, Al
MacDonald, Robert R
Malone, Peter
Malpede, John
Martinez, Carlos
Maxwell, Peter
Mayo, Marti
McCarthy, Christine M
McGee, J David
Melnick, Robert Z
Metzger, Robert Paul
Millard, Charles Warren, III
Miller, Anelle
Monaghan, Kathleen Mary
Morrisey, Marena Grant
Muno, Richard Carl
Nelson, Harold B
Palladino-Craig, Allys
Pavlova, Marina
Peterson, Robyn G
Pierce, Charles Eliot, Jr
Pietrzak, Ted
Prakapas, Dorothy
Quick, Edward Raymond
Quirk, James
Raintree, Shawn
Ralapati, Megha
Reilly, Richard
Reynolds, John (Jock) M
Rindfleisch, Jan
Saborsky, Teresa
Sadan, Mark
Saxton, Carolyn Virginia
Sbarge, Suzanne
Schaefer, Robert Arnold, Jr
Schafroth, Colleen
Schapp, Rebecca Maria
Schloder, John E
Schultz, Douglas George
Scott, Julie
Seligman, Thomas Knowles
Shooster, Stephen Leon
Sidner, Robert Brown
Silverman, Lanny Harris
Smith, Gregory Allgire
Smith, Jan
Smith, Lawry
Stewart, John Lincoln
Stewart, Sheila L
Strickler, Susan Elizabeth
Strokosch, Caitlin
Stux, Stefan Victor
Sundberg, Carl Gustave
Sundblad, Emily
Sussman, Gary Lawrence
Talbott, Susan Lubowsky
Trechsel, Gail Andrews
Tromeur, Robyn Lori
Valdes, Karen W
Vanier, Jerre Lynn
Vigtel, Gudmund
Warshaw, Elaine N
White, Deborah
Wilson, Kay E

DRAFTSMAN

Anderson, Robert Dale
Anthony, William Graham
Antrim, Craig Keith
Arcilesi, Vincent J
Bachardy, Don
Baroff, Jill (Emily)
Ben Tre, Howard B
Berguson, Robert Jenkins
Berio, Marina
Biel, Joe
Bilodeau, Daniel Alain
Birmelin, Robert
Bohlen, Nina (Celestine Eustis Bohlen)
Briggs, Alice Leora
Broker, Karin
Brown, Gary Hugh
Casas, Fernando R
Chevins, Christopher M
Cook, Stephen D
Cronin, Robert (Lawrence)
Daou, Annabel
Drake, Peter
Duncan, Richard (Hurley)
Duque, Adonay
Eberle, Edward Samuel
Eden, Glenn
Elloian, Peter
Elyashiv, Yizhak
English, Simon Richard Bathurst
Feller, Deborah
Finke, Leonda Froehlich
Gechtoff, Sonia
Geiger, Phillip Neil
George, Thomas
Gitlin, Michael
Glier, Mike
Goldsleger, Cheryl
Goodman, Janis G
Guzmán, Daniel
Hough, Winston
Howze, James Dean
Hunkler, Dennis
Isaacson, Marcia Jean
Jacobsen, Colter
Kelley, Heather Ryan
Kimball, Wilford Wayne, Jr
King, Clive
Kjok, Sol
Koch, Philip
Koscielny, Margaret
Kosta, Angela
Lasansky, Leonardo
Leshyk, Tonie
Leys, Dale Daniel
Lieberman, Louis (Karl)
Lima, Jacqueline (Dutton)
Martin, Jane
Martin, Younghee Choi
Matteson, Ira
Matthews, Robert
Mayhew, Timothy David
Morrow, Terry
Moss-Vreeland, Patricia
Munce, James Charles
Murphy, Hass
Newman, John
Nutt, Jim
Oginz, Richard
Padovano, Anthony John
Paige, Wayne Leo
Palevitz, Robert
Peterson, Ben
Pfaffman, William Scott
Phillips, Tony
Piene, Chloe
Pochmann, Virginia
Polan, Annette
Ramanauskas, Dalia Irena
Richards, Bill (William) A
Robinson, Duncan (David)
Ross, Janice Koenig
Routon, David F
Schmidt, Teresa Tempero
Schneider, Julie Saecker
Schulz, Charlotte
Schwalb, Susan
Schwarz, Judith
Shechter, Laura J
Shrigley, David
Smith, Gary Douglas
Steczynski, John Myron
Steinhardt, Alice
Stewart, F Clark
Terry, Christopher T
Torn, Jerry (Gerald J)
Twarogowski, Leroy Andrew
Wallin, Leland (Lee) Dean
Walton, Lee
Waugh, Michael
Weiss, Clemens
White, Franklin
Wingo, Michael B
Witkin, Jerome
Wojtyla, Haase (Walter) Joseph
Wroblewski, Jennifer

EDITOR

Adams, Laurie Schneider
Atkins, Robert
Baker, Elizabeth C
Baldridge, Mark S
Bandy, Mary Lea
Behrens, Roy R
Blake, Jane Salley
Blumrich, Stephen
Cembalest, Robin
Chiroussot-Chambeaux, Jane
Colina, Armando G
Cullum, Jerry
D'Andrea, Jeanne
Ebony, David
Esterow, Milton
Fear, Daniel E
Ferrara, Annette
Fine, Elsa Honig
Fortin, Sylvie
Fuller, Diana
Gilchrist, E. Brenda
Gioia, Dana (Michael)
Goddard, Donald
Goldberger, Paul Jesse
Harbutt, Charles
Hartman, Rose
Hochfield, Sylvia
Kennon, Arthur Bruce
Koplos, Janet
Kuchta, Ronald Andrew
Kusnerz, Peggy Ann F
Macadam, Barbara A
Martel, Richard
Martin, Floyd W
Mason, Francis, Jr
McPherson, Bruce Rice
McTwigan, Michael
Merkel, Jayne (Silverstein)
Meyer, Susan E
Morin, James Corcoran
Morton, Robert Alan
Nemser, Cindy
Noriega, Chon A
Rich, David
Rinehart, Michael
Robbins, Eugenia S
Rossen, Susan F
Santiago-Ibarra, Beatrice Mayte
Schjeldahl, Peter
Sward, Robert S
Szabo, Joseph George
Thorson, Alice R
Vetrocq, Marcia E
Wechsler, Susan
Weiss, John Joseph
Westwater, Angela King
Wyrick, Charles Lloyd, Jr

EDUCATOR
(COLLEGE/UNIVERSITY)

Ackerman, Gerald Martin
Ackerman, James S
Ackerman, Rudy Schlegel
Adams, Henry
Adams, Pat
Addison, Byron Kent
Adler, Tracy L
Adour, Colleen
Agee, William C
Aistars, John
Akawie, Thomas Frank
Albrecht, Donald
Alexander-Greene, Grace George
Alexenberg, Mel
Alexick, David Francis
Alfano, Edward C
Allara, Pamela Edwards
Allen, Bruce Wayne
Allen, Jere Hardy
Allen, Judith S
Allen, Stan
Allen, William J
Allumbaugh, James
Allyn, Jerri
Altmann, Henry S
Altshuler, Bruce J
Alvarez, Candida
Alvarez-Cervela, Jose Maria
Ambrose, Charles Edward
Ambrose, Kirk
Anderson, Daniel J
Anderson, Maxwell L
Andres, Glenn Merle
Annis, Norman L
Anreus, Alejandro
Antreasian, Garo Zareh
App, Timothy

EDUCATOR (cont)
Dluhy, Deborah Haigh
Dmytruk, Ihor R
Do, Kim V
Dodd, Lois
Dodd, M(ary) Irene
Dolkart, Andrew S
Donahue, Philip Richard
Donehoo, Jonathan
Donley, Robert Morris
Dooley, David I
Dorethy, Rex E
Doudera, Gerard
Dowell, John E, Jr
Doyle, Joe
Doyle, Tom
Drachnik (Cay), Catherine Meldyn
Dreskin, Jeanet Steckler
Driskell, David Clyde
Drohojowska-Philp, Hunter
Dunlap, William
Dunn, Phillip Charles
Dwyer, Eugene Joseph
Dwyer, James
Eades, Luis Eric
Edgerton, Debra
Edison, Diane
Edminston, Scott
Edmiston, Sara Joanne
Edwards, James F
Edwards-Tucker, Yvonne Leatrice
Eger, Marilyn Rae
Ehrlich, George
Eickhorst, William Sigurd
Eickmeier, Valerie
Eisenberg, Marvin
Eisner, Elliot Wayne
Eiswerth, Barry
Elkins, Lane
Ellinger, Ilona E
Elliott, Gregory
Emmert, Pauline Gore
Engeran, Whitney John, Jr
Enwezor, Okwui
Epting, Marion Austin
Erdle, Rob
Erikson, Christine
Erman, Bruce
Evans, Garth
Evans, Robert Graves
Even, Robert Lawrence
Ewald, Wendy T
Facey, Martin Kerr
Faimon, Peg
Fairfield, Richard Thomas
Fairlie, Carol Hunter
Falsetta, Vincent Mario
Falsetto, Mario
Fay, Ming G
Feeney, Brendan Ben
Feinberg, Jean
Feldman, Bella
Feldman, Edmund Burke
Feldman, Joel Benet
Feltus, Alan Evan
Feng, Z L
Fensch, Charles Everette
Fenwick, Roly (William Roland)
Ferguson, Russell
Ferrara, Annette
Ferreira, Armando Thomas
Fichter, Robert W
Fiero, Gloria K
Finch, Richard Dean
Fine, Jud
Finke, Leonda Froehlich
Finkelstein, Henry D
Finley, Gerald Eric
Fiorani, Francesca
Fisch, Arline Marie
Fischer, Thomas Jeffrey
Flam, Jack D
Fleischer, Roland Edward
Fleminger, Susan N
Fletcher, Harrell
Flick, Robbert
Flowers, Thomas Earl
Fogg, Monica
Foosaner, Judith
Formicola, John Joseph
Fornas, Leander
Forsyth, Ilene H(aering)
Forsythe, Donald John
Foster, April
Franceschini, Amy
Frankel, Dextra
Fraze, Denny T
Freedberg, David
Freund, Will Frederick
Frey, Barbara Louise
Friedberg, Richard S
Frinta, Mojmir Svatopluk
Frost, Stuart Homer
Funk, Verne J
Furman, David Stephen
Fusco, Laurie S
Gaines, Charles
Galassi, Susan Grace
Gallagher, Cynthia
Galles, Arie Alexander
Gallo, Frank
Galloway, Julia
Gammon, Juanita L
Ganis, Lucy
Ganis, William V
Garcia, Ofelia
Garcia, Rupert (Marshall) R
Garoian, Charles Richard
Garrard, Mary DuBose
Gates, Harry Irving
Gauvreau, Robert George
Gelber, Samuel
Gelfand, Laura D
Gelinas, Robert William
Gerdts, William H
Germano, Thomas
Geske, Norman Albert
Ghikas, Panos George
Gibbons, Arthur
Gibbons, Hugh (James)
Gibson, Benedict S
Gibson, Walter Samuel
Giddens, Kathleen Colette
Gilbert, Bill
Gillham, Andrew
Gillingwater, Denis Claude
Gilmor, Jane E
Gips, C L Terry
Girard, (Charles) Jack
Glaser, Bruce
Glasson, Lloyd
Gluck, Heidi
Goddard, Janet Sniffin
Godsey, Glenn
Goehlich, John Ronald
Goetzl, Thomas Maxwell
Goggin, Nan Elizabeth
Gold, Sharon Cecile
Goldberger, Paul Jesse
Goldring, Nancy Deborah
Gonzalez, Tony
Goodell, Rosemary W
Goodwin, Daniel
Gordley, Scott Matthew
Gordon, John S
Gore, Tom
Gorski, Richard Kenny
Gough, Georgia Belle Leach
Gourevitch, Jacqueline
Grabski, Joanna
Graves, Michael
Gray, Richard
Green, Art
Greenamyer, George Mossman
Greer, Wesley Dwaine
Gregor, Harold Laurence
Gregory, Joan
Griffiths, William Perry
Grigsby, Jefferson Eugene, Jr
Grimes, Margaret W
Griner, Ned H
Grippi, Salvatore William
Gron, Jack
Grossman, Barbara
Grossman, Maurice Kenneth
Gunasinghe, Siri
Gunn, Paul James
Gunter, Frank Elliott
Gussow, Sue Ferguson
Gutzeit, Fred
Guyer, Paul
Gyermek, Stephen A
Habel, Dorothy (Dottie) Metzger
Hackett, Mickey
Hafif, Marcia
Hageman, Charles Lee
Hahn, Betty
Hall, Michael David
Hallman, Ted, Jr
Hamann, Marilyn D
Hamblen, Karen A
Hamilton, George Earl
Hamilton, W Paul C
Hammett, Dan
Hammond, Gale Thomas
Hammond, Mary Sayer
Hampton, Anita
Hampton, Phillip Jewel
Hamwi, Richard Alexander
Hancock, Jory
Hankey, Robert E
Hannibal, Joseph Harry
Hannum, Gillian Greenhill
Hansen, Gaylen Capener
Hansen, Harold (Harry) John
Harden, Marvin
Harmon, David Edward
Harootunian, Claire M
Harries, Mags (Margaret) L
Harris, Ronna S
Harrison, Tony
Hart, Allen M
Hartley, Paul Jerome
Hartman, Joanne A
Hartman, Robert Leroy
Hatch, Connie
Hatch, W A S
Hatcher, Gary C
Hatfield, Donald Gene
Hatgil, Paul
Hatke, Walter Joseph
Hauer, Erwin Franz
Hausman, Jerome Joseph
Havelock, Christine Mitchell
Hawkins, Margaret
Hay, A John
Hay, Dick
Hay, Ike
Hayes, Cheryl
Haynes, Douglas H
Hazlehurst, Franklin Hamilton
Head, Robert William
Healy, Anne Laura
Healy, Deborah Ann
Heath, Dave (David) Martin
Hedrick (FKA Dietrich), Linnea S
Hein, Max
Heinicke, Janet L Hart
Heldt, Carl Randall
Helm, Alison
Hendershot, J L
Henderson, Linda Dalrymple
Hennessy, Tricia
Henry, Robert
Herard, Marvin T
Herbert, Frank Leonard
Herbert, Robert L
Hernandez, Sam
Hertz, Richard A
Herzberg, Thomas
Hethom, Janet
Hewitt, Duncan Adams
Heyman, Daniel
Heyman, Ira Michael
Hickman, Paul Addison
Hide, Peter Nicholas
Higgins, Larkin Maureen
Hijar, Alberto Serano
Hill, Peter
Hillman, Arthur Stanley
Hilson, Douglas
Hindes, Chuck (Charles) Austin
Hinman, Charles B
Hitchcock, Howard Gilbert
Hitner, Chuck
Ho, Francis T
Ho, Kong
Hobbs, Jack Arthur
Hobgood, E Wade
Hochhauser, Marilyn Helsenrott
Hochstetler, T Max
Hoffman, Neil James
Hoffman, William McKinley, Jr
Hoge, Robert Wilson
Hoi, Samuel Chuen-Tsung
Holcomb, Grant
Holder, Kenneth Allen
Holen, Norman Dean
Holmes, Larry W
Holownia, Thaddeus J
Holste, Thomas James
Holt, David John
Homer, William Innes
Hooks, Earl J
Horn, Bruce
Hourihan, Dorothy Dierks
House, John C
Houser, Jim (James C)
Housman, Russell F
Howard, Dan F
Hsu, Pang-Chieh
Hu, Mary Lee
Hubschmitt, William E
Huchthausen, David Richard
Hungerford, Constance Cain
Hunter, Debora
Hunter, Leonard LeGrande, III
Hupp, Frederick Duis
Hurewitz, Florence K
Hurlstone, Robert William
Hutchens, James William
Hyman, Isabelle
Ikeda, Yoshiro
Isaacson, Marcia Jean
Ishaq, Ashfaq
Iversen, Earl Harvey
Ives, Colta Feller
Iwamasa, Ken
Jachna, Joseph David
Jackson, Marion Elizabeth
Jacob, Wendy
Jacobs, David (Theodore)
Jacobs, Peter Alan
Jacobsen, Michael A
Jacobus, John M
Jaffe, Ira S
Jaffe, Irma B
Jasud, Lawrence Edward
Jennerjahn, W P
Jensen, Clay Easton
Jensen, Robert
Jergens, Robert Joseph
Jerry, Michael John
Jevbratt, Lisa
Johns, Christopher K(alman)
Johnson, Charles W
Johnson, Diane Chalmers
Johnson, Homer
Johnson, James Alan
Johnson, Lee
Johnson, Lester L
Johnson, Linda K
Johnson, Lois Marlene
Johnson, Ronald W
Johnson, Tillian
Johnston, Richard M
Jones, Arthur F
Jones, Charlott Ann
Jones, Dennis
Jones, Lois Swan

EDUCATOR (cont)

Olson, Linda A
Olson, Richard W
Olynyk, Patricia J
Omar, Margit
Ondish, Andrea
Onorato, Ronald Joseph
Orenstein, Gloria Feman
Ortiz, Raphael Montanez
Osborne, Cynthia A
Osborne, Frederick S
O'Sickey, Joseph Benjamin
Osterburg, Lothar
Osterman, William T
Ostrom, Gladys Snell
Ostrow, Saul
Oxman, Mark
Ozubko, Christopher
Packard, Sally
Pagani, Catherine
Pagel, David
Paladino, Paul
Papier, Maurice Anthony
Pardee, Hearne
Pardee, William Hearne
Parfenoff, Michael S
Parker, Ron
Parks, Carrie Anne
Parlin, James
Parris, Nina Gumpert
Parton, Ralf
Partridge, Loren Wayne
Paskewitz, Bill, Jr
Paterson, Anthony R
Patnode, J Scott
Patrick, Joseph Alexander
Patterson, Curtis Ray
Pavlova, Marina
Pearlstein, Philip
Pearson, John
Pecchenino, J Ronald
Peck, Lee Barnes
Peck, William Henry
Peckham, Nicholas
Pekarsky, Mel(vin) Hirsch
Pell, Richard
Penkoff, Ronald Peter
Pentak, Stephen
Pepe, Sheila
Perlin, Ruth Rudolph
Perlman, Joel Leonard
Perry, Donald Dean
Perry, Edward (Ted) Samuel
Peterson, Dorothy (Hawkins)
Peterson, Larry D
Peven, Michael David
Pfaff, Judy
Phelan, Andrew L
Piatek, Francis John
Piehl, Walter Jason, Jr
Pierce, Ann Trucksess
Pijanowski, Eugene M
Pincus-Witten, Robert A
Pindell, Howardena Doreen
Pirkl, James Joseph
Pizzat, Joseph
Place, Bradley Eugene
Plagens, Peter
Plumb, James Douglas
Plummer, Carlton B
Polli, Andrea
Pollitt, Jerome Jordan
Polonsky, Arthur
Ponsot, Claude F
Pontynen, Arthur
Poplawska, Anna
Porter, Jeanne Chenault
Porter, Katherine Pavlis
Postiglione, Corey M
Poulos, Basilios Nicholas
Povse, Matthew R
Powell, Dan T
Praczukowski, Edward Leon
Pressly, William Laurens
Preston, George Nelson
Price, Leslie Kenneth
Prince, Arnold
Prince, Richard Edmund
Pritikin, Renny
Probst, Robert
Pross, Lester Fred
Pujol, Elliott
Purtle, Carol Jean
Putterman, Florence Grace
Quiñones Keber, Eloise
Quiroz, Alfred James
Rainer, Yvonne
Raiselis, Richard
Ramos, (Mel) Melvin John
Rand, Harry
Rayen, James Wilson
Read, Dave (David) Dolloff
Redd, Richard James
Reddington, Charles Leonard
Reddix, Roscoe Chester
Reeser, Robert D
Reichert, Donald Karl
Reimann, William P
Reker, Les
Reynolds, Jock
Reynolds, Robert
Rhodes, David
Ribas, Joao
Richardson, Sam
Richardson, W C
Rico-Gutierrez, Luis
Rieth, Sheri Fleck
Riley, Barbra Bayne
Ringness, Charles Obert
Risbeck, Philip Edward
Riseling, Robert Lowell
Riss, Murray
Ristau, Jacob Robert
Roberson, Samuel Arndt
Roberts, William Edward
Robinson, Chris (Christopher) Thomas
Robinson, Lilien Filipovitch
Robinson, Mary Ann
Rode, Meredith Eagon
Rogers, Barbara
Rogers, Bryan Leigh
Rogers, Earl Leslie
Rogers, Michael
Rogers, Richard L
Roots, Garrison
Rorex, Robert Albright
Rosas, Mel
Rosenberg, Charles Michael
Rosenberg, Herb
Rosenfield, John M
Rosenthal, Deborah Maly
Ross, James Matthew Akiba
Roster, Fred Howard
Roth, Michael S
Roth, Moira
Roth, Richard
Rothenberg, Barbara
Rothenberg, Stephanie
Roussel, Claude Patrice
Rowan, Dennis Michael
Rowan, Herman
Rowe, Charles Alfred
Rozman, Joseph John
Ruggles, Joanne Beaule
Rush, Jean C
Rush, Jon N
Rush, Kent Thomas
Russo, Alexander Peter
Russotto, Paul
Ruyle, Lydia Miller
Rybczynski, Witold Marian
Sabol, Frank Robert
Saff, Donald Jay
St Florian, Friedrich Gartler
Sakaoka, Yasue
Salinger, Adrienne
Salmon, Raymond Merle
Saltzman, Marvin
Salvesen, Britt
Salvest, John
Sandoval, Arturo Alonzo
Sandusky, Billy Ray
Sangiamo, Albert
Santiago, Richard E
Sapp, William Rothwell
Saturen, Ben
Satz, Janet
Saunders, J Boyd
Saunders, Raymond Jennings
Savoy, Chyrl Lenore
Scalera, Michelle Ann
Scanga, Carrie
Schaad, Dee
Schaefer, Ronald H
Schar, Stuart
Schein, Eugenie
Scherer, Herbert Grover
Scherpereel, Richard Charles
Schietinger, James Frederick
Schildkrout, Enid
Schirm, David
Schmaltz, Roy Edgar
Schmidt, Randall Bernard
Schmutzhart, Berthold Josef
Schneider, Gary
Schneider, Kenny
Schneider, Richard Durbin
Schreffler, Michael
Schultz, John Bernard
Schultz, Stephen Warren
Schulz, Anne Markham
Schulz, Charlotte
Schwager, Michael R
Schwieger, C Robert
Scogin, Mack
Scott, John Beldon
Scucchi, Robie (Peter), Jr
Scully, Vincent Joseph, Jr
Sears, Elizabeth L
Seawright, James L, Jr
Seeger, Matthew W
Seipel, Joseph H
Selsor, Marcia Lorraine
Selznick-Drutz, June
Semak, Michael
Sensemann, Susan
Sevigny, Maurice Joseph, II
Shadrach, Jean H
Shankman, Gary Charles
Shannon, Joe
Shapiro, David Joel
Sharlin, Jonathan
Shaw, Joseph Winterbotham
Sheard, Wendy Stedman
Shelnutt, Greg W.
Shelton, Robert Lee
Shepard, Mark
Sherman, Claire Richter
Shiff, Richard
Shipley, Roger Douglas
Shuler, Thomas H, Jr
Sieg, Robert Lawrence
Siegesmund, Richard
Sigala, Stephanie Childs
Silberstein-Storfer, Muriel Rosoff
Silva, Jude Hutton
Silver, Rawley A
Silverman, Ronald H
Simmons, John Herbert
Simon, David L
Simonson, Anne
Simpson, William Kelly
Skelley, Robert Charles
Slavick, Susanne Mechtild
Slemmons, Rod
Slone, Sandi
Slotnick, Mortimer H
Slusky, Joseph
Smalley, David Allan
Smalley, Stephen Francis
Smedley, Geoffrey
Smith, Barbara Turner
Smith, David Loeffler
Smith, Gregory Allgire
Smith, Lawson Wentworth
Smith, Ralph Alexander
Smith, Robert Lewis
Smith, Sherri
Smith, Terry
Smuskiewicz, Ted
Snapp, Brian
Soave, Sergio
Sokolow, Isobel Folb
Sommese, Lanny Beal
Sougstad, Mike
Spaar, Lisa Russ
Spafford, Michael Charles
Spann, Susanna Evonne
Spear, Richard Edmund
Spector, Jack J
Speight, Jerry Brooks
Spink, Walter M
Spinka, William J
Spinski, Victor
Springer, Bethany
Sprout, Francis
Squier, Jack Leslie
Stack, Gael Z
Staffel, Doris
Stake, Peter
Stanczak, Julian
Stanforth, Melvin Sidney
Stankiewicz, Mary Ann
Starr, Sydney
Stauffer, George B
Steczynski, John Myron
Steele, Benjamin Charles
Stein, Ludwig
Stephens, Curtis
Stephens, William Blakely
Stephenson, John H
Stephenson, Susanne G
Sterritt, Coleen
Stevens, Thelma K
Steward, James
Stewart, Paul LeRoy
Stewart, Regina
Stewart, William
Stillman, Damie
Stokstad, Marilyn
Stomps, Walter E, Jr
Stoner, Joyce Hill
Stones, Margaret Alison
Storr, Robert
Strange, Georgia
Strawn, Martha (A)
Striker, Cecil L
Stroker, Robert T
Stroud, Peter Anthony
Stuler, Jack
Sturgeon, Mary C
Sturtz-Davis, Shirley Zampelli
Subramaniam, Radhika
Sullivan, Graeme
Sullivan, Scott A
Sumner, Stephen Charles
Sunderland, Nita Kathleen
Sures, Jack
Sutter, James Stewart
Sylvester, Robert
Szeitz, P Richard
Tacha, Athena
Taft, Frances Prindle
Talbot, Christopher
Tan, LiQin
Tarrell, Robert Ray
Tate, Blair
Tatham, David Frederic
Taylor, Brian David
Taylor, Brie (Benjamin de Brie)
Taylor, Davis
Taylor, Marilyn Jordan
Teczar, Steven W
Tefft, Elden Cecil
Tellier, Cassandra Lee
Tennant, Donna Kay
Tepfer, Diane
Tepper, Steven J
Tesfagiorgis, Freida

ENAMELIST

ENVIRONMENTAL ARTIST

ENVIRONMENTAL SCULPTOR

FILMMAKER

FILMMAKER (cont)
Green, Jonathan (William)
Greenfield, Amy
Greenfield-Sanders, Timothy
Haar, Tom
Haxton, David
Hay, (George) Austin
Henderson, Mike
Herbert, James Arthur
Hubbard, Teresa
Huot, Robert
Iimura, Takahiko
Jamie, Cameron
July, Miranda
Kagemoto, Haro
Katz, Leandro
Kelley, Lauren
Kentridge, William
Khedoori, Rachel
Kleckner, Susan
Knecht, John
Lee, Lara
Lee, Nikki S
Leslie, Alfred
Levitt, Helen
Lieber, Edvard
Liebling, Jerome
Linzy, Kalup
Lipzin, Janis Crystal
Lockhart, Sharon
Lundberg, William
Magden, Norman E
Mangolte, Babette M
McCall, Anthony
Niblock, Phill
Nowytski, Sviatoslav
O'Connell, Kenneth Robert
Padula, Fred David
Phillips, Robert J
Rabinovitch, William Avrum
Rainer, Yvonne
Ravett, Abraham
Rubinfien, Leo H
Schneemann, Carolee
Schneider, Kenny
Schwartz, Lillian (Feldman)
Silver, Shelly Andrea
Simpson, Lorna
Sipho, Ella
Snow, Michael
Stratman, Deborah
Thacher, Anita
Tilley, Lewis Lee
Torlakson, James Daniel
Trecartin, Ryan
Vasell, Chris
Waters, Jack
Wechsler, Judith Glatzer
Wilda, Steven A
Woods, Lauren
Zahedi, Caveh

GALLERY DIRECTOR

See also **Museum Director**

Adamson, Jerome D
Alinder, James Gilbert
Amalfitano, Lelia
Arnot, Andrew H
Ayers, Carol Lee
Baldwin, Russell W
Balka, Sigmund Ronell
Bartlett, Christopher E
Baruch, Barbara
Battis, Nicholas
Bekman, Jen
Bell, Anonda
Berggruen, John Henry
Brearey, Susan Winfield
Brown, Constance George
Brown, Eric L
Bryant, Linda Goode
Buecker, Robert
Bull, Fran
Burnett, Amy Louise
Butts, H Daniel, III
Cannuli, Richard Gerald
Chang-Il, Kim
Cheim, John
Chrismas, Douglas James
Christensen, Val Alan
Clark-Langager, Sarah Ann
Cocker, Barbara Joan
Cohan, James
Cohen, Mildred Thaler
Colina, Armando G
Collins, Thom
Collinson, Janice
Conley, Zeb Bristol, Jr
Cooper, Rhonda H
Crandall, Judith Ann
Cutler, Judy A Goffman
Cutler, Judy Goffman
Dahl, Sherri Ann
Davis, Kimberly Brooke
Dean, Kevin Lee
DeFazio, Teresa Galligan
Desmett, Don
Dorfman, Fred
Douglas, Leah
Drummer, William Richard
Evans, Steven
Feinman, Stephen E
Felker, David Larry
Felsen, Rosamund
Ferris, Daniel B
Findlay, Michael
Fink, Joanna Elizabeth
Fitzpatrick, Robert John
FitzSimonds, Carol Strause
Fleming, Mary Margaret
Fraser, Catriona Trafford
Fuglie, Gordon Louis
Fuller, Jeffrey P
Goddard, Janet Sniffin
Gonzalez, Mauricio Martinez
Gorney, Jay Philip
Grachos, Louis
Grandee, Joe Ruiz
Grossman, Bonnie
Hargis, Barbara Picasso
Hedberg, Gregory Scott
Hendeles, Ydessa
Henry, Steven P.
Higgins, Brian Alton
Hutchins, Robin
Johnson, Diana L
Karten, Nowell J
Kawecki, Jean Mary
Kelley, Donald Castell
Kennedy, Robyn L
Killeen, Melissa Helen
Klobe, Tom
Knight, David J
Korow-Bieber, Elinore Maria Vigh
Lamoureux, Marie France
Langman, Richard Theodore
Levy, S(tephen) Dean
Lewis, Louise Miller
Lieber, Lola
Lippman, Judith
Lippmann, Janet Gurian
Littman, Brett
Lotz, Steven Darryl
Lynch, Florence
Martin, Mary Finch
Mays, Peter
McAllister, Geraldine E
McManus, James William
Mellor, Mark Adams
Mew, Tommy
Michaux, Ronald Robert
Miller, Virginia Irene
Mineo, Jean
Moody, Elizabeth C
Newman, Walter Andrews, Jr
Nordland, Gerald John
Parker, Wilma
Parkerson, John E
Perelman, Isaac
Perlow, Katharina Rich
Poole, Nancy Geddes
Posner, Helaine J
Pritikin, Renny
Raby, Julian
Rebbeck, Lester James, Jr
Reynolds, Jock
Richardson, Trevor J
Roach, Stephanie
Rolly, Ronald Joseph
Ropp, Ann L
Rosen, Andrea
Rowand, Joseph Donn
Ruttinger, Jacquelyn
St George, William (M)
Schusterman, Gerrie Marva
Setford, David F
Shainman, Jack S
Simor, Suzanna B
Sindelir, Robert John
Skoler, Celia Rebecca
Smith, B J
Smith, Gary
Smith-Stewart, Amy
Sorkin, Emily
Sowers, Russell Frederic
Spratt, Frederick R
Steel, Virginia Oberlin
Steiner, Sherry L
Stirratt, Betsy (Elizabeth) Anne
Stoppert, Mary Kay
Sujo, Clara Diament
Sullivan, JuneAnn Margaret
Sussman, Bonnie Kaufman
Sussman, Jill
Swain, Robert Francis
Taira, Masa Morioka
Takayama, Martha Tepper
Tasende, Jose Maria
Thurmer, Robert
Tunis, Roslyn
Vizner, Nikola
Wade, Valerie
Waller, Susan
Waxter, Dorsey
Weinzapfel, Connie A
Wilson, Carrie Lois
Wirtz, Stephen Carl
Wise, Takouhy
Wolf, Sylvia
Wortz, Melinda Farris
Zwirner, David

GLASS BLOWER

Applebaum, Leon
Bernstein, William Joseph
Brejcha, Vernon Lee
Caldwell, Graham
Carlson, Robert Michael
Chihuly, Dale Patrick
Clark, Jon Frederic
De La Torre, Einar
De La Torre, Jamex
D'Onofrio, Bernard Michael
Fero, Shane
Handler, Audrey
Hurlstone, Robert William
Ichikawa, Etsuko
Ipsen, Kent Forrest
Levin, Robert Alan
Lipman, Beth
Marioni, Dante
Marioni, Paul
Menconi, Michael Angelo
Mulcahy, Kathleen
Ohno, Mitsugi
Ruffner, Ginny Martin
Seide, Paul A
Simpson, Josh (Josiah) J L Simpson
Strachan, Tavares
Taylor, Christopher
Van Cline, Mary
Warehall, William Donald
Wax, Jack
White, Brook Forrest, Jr

GOLDSMITH

Anderson, Bruce A
Baldridge, Mark S
De La Verriere, Jean Jacques
Enriquez, Gaspar
Floret, Evelyn
Flynn, Pat L
Getty, Nilda Fernandez
Grissom, Freda Gill
Hirsh, Annette Marie
Hu, Mary Lee
Kuehnl, Claudia Ann
Lechtzin, Stanley
Mawdsley, Richard
Renk, Merry
Smith, Jo-an
Van Duinwyk, George Paul
Wegner, Nadene R

GRAPHIC ARTIST

Anderson, Scott
Anderson, Warren Harold
Arcangel, Cory
Arday, Donald K
Arias-Misson, Alain
Avant, Tracy Wright
Barbee, Robert Thomas
Barkus, Mariona
Beachum, Sharon Garrison
Beaumont, Mona
Belag, Andrea
Bennett, John M
Bigelow, Anita (Anne) (Edwige Lourie)
Bolton, Robin Jean
Boyd, (David) Michael
Broderick, James Allen
Brower, Steven
Brown, James
Bruni, Umberto
Capes, Richard Edward
Carpenter, Joseph Allan
Castellanos, Laura
Chen, Hsin-Hsi
Church, Maude
Clement, Kathleen
Cohen, Reina Joyce
Colker, Edward
Daub, Matthew Forrest
Davis, Meredith J
des Rioux (de Messimy), Deena (Victoria Coty)
Donneson, Seena
Dorn, Peter Klaus
Dorst, Mary Crowe
Elliot, Catherine J
Erbe, Chantell Van
Essley, Roger Holmer
Firer, Serge
Fleming, Margaret Nielsen
Fluek, Toby
Freeman, David L
Fromentin, Christine Anne
Galinsky, Norman
Gammon, Juanita L
Gaudard, Pierre
Gialanella, Donald G
Gillham, Andrew
Giuffre, Hector
Glorig, Ostor
Gluhman, Margaret A
Goggin, Nan Elizabeth
Goldszer, Bath-Sheba
Gorski, Richard Kenny
Gough, Robert Alan
Graber, Steven Brian
Harroun, Dorothy Sumner
Hein, Max
Hennessy, Tricia

HISTORIAN

HISTORIAN (cont)
Jacobsen, Michael A
Jacobus, John M
Jaffe, Irma B
Jay, Bill
Johnson, Charles W
Johnson, Diane Chalmers
Johnson, Eugene Joseph
Johnson, Ronald W
Johnston, Roy
Jonaitis, Aldona
Joost-Gaugier, Christiane L
Jordan, George Edwin
Jordan, William B
Joyner, John Brooks
Kagan, Andrew Aaron
Kagle, Joseph L, Jr
Kahan, Mitchell Douglas
Kan, Michael
Kaplan, Julius David
Karlstrom, Paul Johnson
Kassner, Lily
Keeley, Shelagh
Kelbaugh, Ross J
Kelly, Franklin Wood
Kennon, Robert Brian
Kester, Grant
Kidwell, Michele Falik
King, Elaine A
Kirkpatrick, Diane
Kitao, T Kaori
Klein, Cecelia F
Klein, Michael Eugene
Kleinbauer, W Eugene
Klitzke, Theodore Elmer
Kloss, William
Knox, George
Koob, Pamela Nabseth
Kornetchuk, Elena
Korshak, Yvonne
Korzenik, Diana
Kotik, Charlotta
Kovinick, Philip Peter
Krinsky, Carol Herselle
Kusnerz, Peggy Ann F
Kuwayama, George
Landau, Ellen Gross
Landis, Ellen Jamie
Langer, Sandra Lois (Cassandra)
Larsen, Susan C
Laskin, Myron, Jr
Lauf, Cornelia
Lavin, Irving
Lavin, Marilyn Aronberg
Lawall, David Barnard
Lee, Briant Hamor
Lee, Eric McCauley
Lemon, Robert S, Jr
Lerner, Martin
Levin, Gail
Levy, David Corcos
Levy, Mark
Lewis, Douglas
Lewis, Samella Sanders
Li, Chu-Tsing
Lilyquist, Christine
Lindgren, Carl Edwin
Lippman, Sharon Rochelle
Lipton, Leah
Long, Rose-Carol Washton
Lorber, D Martin H B
Lovell, Margaretta Markle
Lowenthal, Constance
Luchs, Alison
Lunsford, John (Crawford)
Lyons, Lisa
MacDonald, Bruce K
MacDonald, Robert R
MacDonald, William L
Mack, Charles Randall
Madden-Work, Betty I
Maddox, Jerald Curtis
Mahoney, Michael R T
Marable, Darwin William
Markle, Greer (Walter Greer Markle)
Marlor, Clark Strang
Marrow, James Henry
Marter, Joan
Martin, Floyd W
Masheck, Joseph Daniel Cahill
Mathews, Nancy Mowll
McCauley, Elizabeth Anne
McKenzie, Allan Dean
McNally, Sheila John
McNamara, Mary Jo
McPhee, Sarah Collyer
Meisel, Louis Koenig
Meister, Mark J
Meister, Michael William
Meyer, James Sampson
Meyer, Jerry Don
Mezzatesta, Michael
Michaels, Barbara L
Michels, Eileen Manning
Mickenberg, David
Miles, Ellen Gross
Miller, Arthur Green
Moore, Alan Willard
Morganstern, Anne McGee
Morganstern, James
Morishita, Joyce Chizuko
Moser, Joann
Moss, Tobey C
Mottram, Ronald
Moulton, Susan Gene
Mount, Marshall Ward
Moxey, Patricio Keith Fleming
Muhlert, Jan Keene
Muller, Priscilla Elkow
Myron, Robert
Nagy, Rebecca Martin
Nasgaard, Roald
Nash, Steven Alan
Natzmer Valentine, Cheryl
Naumann, Francis M
Nees, Lawrence
Neff, John Hallmark
Nelson, Jon Allen
Nold, Carl R
Nordan, Antoinette Spanos Johnson
Norton, Paul Foote
Nyerges, Alexander Lee
O'Connor, Francis Valentine
O'Connor, Stanley James
Olin, Ferris
Olson, Roberta Jeanne Marie
Onorato, Ronald Joseph
Orenstein, Gloria Feman
Otero-Pailos, Jorge
Overland, Carlton Edward
Page, Jean Jepson
Paikowsky, Sandra R
Pal, Pratapaditya
Parry, Ellwood Comly, III
Partridge, Loren Wayne
Pasquine, Ruth
Patrick, Darryl L
Patton, Sharon Frances
Pearman, Sara Jane
Peck, William Henry
Péladeau, Marius Beaudoin
Pendergraft, Norman Elveis
Pennington, Estill Curtis
Percy, Ann Buchanan
Perkinson, Roy L
Perlin, Ruth Rudolph
Perloff, Marjorie G
Perry, Regenia Alfreda
Phillips, Christopher
Pierce, Patricia Jobe
Pilgrim, Dianne Hauserman
Polcari, Stephen
Pollitt, Jerome Jordan
Polzer, Joseph
Poor, Robert John
Porter, Jeanne Chenault
Porter, Richard James
Powell, Earl Alexander, III
Pressly, William Laurens
Preston, George Nelson
Preziosi, Donald A
Prodger, Phillip
Prown, Jules David
Pugh, Grace Huntley
Purtle, Carol Jean
Quiñones Keber, Eloise
Quirarte, Jacinto
Radan, George Tivadar
Raguin, Virginia C
Ragusa, Isa
Rand, Harry
Reed, Cleota
Reese, Thomas Ford
Reeves, James Franklin
Reff, Theodore
Regier, Randy J
Reilly, Bernard Francis
Reilly, Richard
Rensch, Roslyn
Rice, Anthony Hopkins
Rice, Shelley Enid
Rigby, Ida Katherine
Robb, David Metheny, Jr
Roberson, Samuel Arndt
Robertson, E Bruce
Robinson, Duncan (David)
Robinson, Franklin W
Robinson, Lilien Filipovitch
Rorex, Robert Albright
Rosenberg, Charles Michael
Rosenthal, Donald A
Rosenthal, Mark L
Rosenzweig, Daphne Lange
Rossen, Susan F
Roth, Leland M(artin)
Roth, Moira
Rubin, Patricia
Rudenstine, Angelica Zander
Sachs, Samuel, II
Sanderson, Warren
Sandler, Irving Harry
Saretzky, Gary Daniel
Saunders, Richard Henry
Scarbrough, Cleve Knox, Jr
Schaefer, Scott Jay
Schmandt-Besserat, Denise
Schneiderman, Richard S
Schreffler, Michael
Schultz, John Bernard
Schulz, Anne Markham
Schulze, Franz
Schwartz, Marvin D
Schweizer, Paul Douglas
Scott, John Beldon
Scribner, Charles, III
Seaberg, Libby W
Sears, Elizabeth L
Segger, Martin Joseph
Selz, Peter H
Semowich, Charles John
Senie, Harriet F
Serenyi, Peter
Sewell, Darrel L
Shaw, Joseph Winterbotham
Shaw, Nancy (Rivard)
Shaw, Paul Jefferson
Sheard, Wendy Stedman
Sheon, Aaron
Shepard, Lewis Albert
Sherman, Claire Richter
Shimizu, Yoshiaki
Silver, Larry Arnold
Simmons, John Herbert
Simon, David L
Simon, Robert Barry
Simpson, William Kelly
Sims, Lowery Stokes
Slade, George G
Slatkin, Wendy
Slive, Seymour
Smith, Elliot
Smith, Frances Kathleen
Smith, Gil R
Smith, Jeffrey Chipps
Smith, Terry
Sokol, David Martin
Sorell, Victor Alexander
Spangenberg, Kristin L
Spector, Jack J
Spencer, Harold Edwin
Sponenburgh, Mark
Spurlock, William
Stahl, Alan M
Stebbins, Theodore Ellis, Jr
Stein, Judith Ellen
Stevens, Andrew Rich
Stillman, Damie
Stokstad, Marilyn
Stone, Judith Elise
Stones, Margaret Alison
Stott, Deborah
Strickler, Susan Elizabeth
Striker, Cecil L
Stuckey, Charles F
Sturgeon, Mary C
Sturges, Hollister
Sullivan, Scott A
Sutton, Peter C
Swanson, Vern Grosvenor
Sweeney, J Gray
Tannenbaum, Barbara Lee
Tasse, M Jeanne
Tatham, David Frederic
Taylor, Michael D
Theofiles, George
Thistlethwaite, Mark Edward
Tierney, Patrick Lennox
Timpano, Anne
Toker, Franklin
Tolles, Bryant Franklin, Jr
Tomasini, Wallace J
Topper, David R
Townsend, Gavin Edward
Travis, David B
Trenton, Patricia Jean
Troy, Nancy J
Trutty-Coohill, Patricia
Turnure, James Harvey
Tyler, Ron C
Vandersall, Amy L
Van Schaack, Eric
Verostko, Roman Joseph
Viditz-Ward, Vera Louise
Vincent, Clare
Wahlman, Maude Southwell
Walford, E John
Wallace, William E
Wallach, Alan
Waller, Aaron Bret
Ward, John Lawrence
Warren, Julianne Bussert Baker
Watson, Katharine Johnson
Wayne, Cynthia M
Weaver, AM
Webster, Sally (Sara) B
Wechsler, Judith Glatzer
Weidman, Jeffrey
Weinberg, Jonathan Edman
Weisberg, Gabriel P
Werness, Hope B
West, Richard Vincent
Westervelt, Robert F
Westin, Robert H
Wharton, Annabel Jane
White, Robert Rankin
Wiebe, Charles M
Wilkins, David George
Williams, Benjamin Forrest
Williams, David Jon
Williams, John Alden
Williams, John Wesley
Wilmerding, John
Wilson, Jean S
Wise, Suzanne Tanderup
Withers, Josephine
Wolanin, Barbara A
Wood, John August
Worthen, Amy Namowitz
Wriston, Barbara
Yard, Sally Elizabeth

ILLUMINATOR

ILLUSTRATOR

Children's Books

INSTALLATION SCULPTOR

INSTALLATION SCULPTOR (cont)

Putnam, Adam
Putrih, Tobias
Ramirez (ERRE), Marcos
Riley, Duke
Robinson, Nadine Caroline
Robinson, Nathaniel
Rodriguez, Bert
Romano, Salvatore Michael
Rowe, Heather
Roysdon, Emily
Ruiz, Jose
Sarabia, Eduardo
Saraceno, Tomas
Sasamoto, Aki
Scanga, Carrie
Scanlan, Joe
Schiff, Jeffrey Allen
Shin, Jean
Siguroardottir, Katrin
Simmons, Xaviera Vincenta
Skogerson, Gretchen
Snow, Agathe
Spitzer, Serge
Staab, Roy
Syjuco, Stephanie
Sze, Sarah
Temple, Mary
Tsai, Charwei
Van Aken, Sam
Von Brandenburg, Ulla
Wagner, Sarah
Warck Meister, Lucia
Weglarz, Lorraine D
Weiss, Monika
Welch, Roger
Wischer, Wendy
Xiuzhen, Yin
Yamamoto, Nami
Yang, Haegue
Ybarra, Mario, Jr
Yordanov, Plamen
York, Susan
Zamora, Hector

INSTRUCTOR
(STUDIO/ART SCHOOL)

Abbott, Linda J
Ablow, Roselyn Karol (Roz Karol Ablow)
Abrams, Edith Lillian
Accetta, Suzanne Rusconi
Adato, Linda Joy
Aksel, Erdag
Akutsu, Shoichi
Albanese, Rose Ann
Amelchenko, Alison M
Amico, David Michael
Anastasia, Susanna
Andry, Keith Anthony
Angelo, Sandra McFall
Appel, Thelma
Atlee, Emilie Des
Atwood Pinardi, Brenda
Aunio, Irene
Avakian, John
Baker, Blanche
Baldassano, Vincent
Barnes, Curt (Curtis) Edward
Barta, Dorothy Woods Vadala
Berg, Siri
Berge, Dorothy Alphena
Besant, Derek Michael
Betts, Judi Polivka
Bieltvedt, Arnor G
Bobrowicz, Yvonne Pacanovsky
Bordes, Adrienne
Bower, Marilyn Kay
Branfman, Steven
Briansky, Rita Prezament
Brown, June Gottlieb
Brown, Peggy Ann
Brown, Sarah M
Brush, Leif
Bryans, John Armond
Burpee, James Stanley
Butter, Tom
Byers, Fleur
Cadillac, Louise Roman
Cady, Samuel Lincoln
Campbell, David Paul
Campbell, Rebecca
Capes, Richard Edward
Caplan Ciarrocchi, Sandra
Caporale-Greene, Wende
Caroompas, Carole J
Cattaneo, (Jacquelyn A) Kammerer
Chapin, Deborah Jane
Chavez, Joseph Arnold
Cheek, Ronald Edward
Christensen, Larry R
Christensen, Sharlene
Cleary, Barbara B
Cliff, Denis Antony
Clinton, Paul Arthur
Clutz, William
Cockrill, Sherna
Cogswell, Margaret Price
Cokendolpher, Eunice Loraine
Colarusso, Corrine Camille
Cole, Grace V
Coleman, M L (Michael Lee)
Colquhoun, Peter Lloyd
Condren, Stephen F
Cortese, Don F
Cottone-Kolthoff, Carol
Couper, Charles Alexander
Crandall, Dorris
Cunningham, Francis
Das, Ratindra
Davidson, David Isaac
Davies, Kenneth Southworth
Dawson, Doug
Day, Burnis Calvin
de Campos, Nuno
Decil, Stella (Del) Walters
De Donato, Louis
Dennis, Don W
Derby, Mark
Dickerson, Daniel Jay
Dickerson, Vera Mason
Diehl, Guy
DiPerna, Frank Paul
Donahue, Thomas John
Doogan, Bailey
Dorfman, Bruce
Douglas, Edwin Perry
Driesbach, Walter Clark, Jr
Dunlap, Loren Edward
Edelman, Janice
Egan, Laury Agnes
Egeli, Cedric Baldwin
Embrey, Carl Rice
Estabrook, Reed
Falconer, Marguerite Elizabeth
Faragasso, Jack
Federico, Frank
Fitch, Steve (Steven) Ralph
Flattmann, Alan Raymond
Fortunato, Nancy
Fox, Michael David
France-Vaz, Nanci
Frassinelli, Hannah
Frederick, Deloras Ann
Freeman, Kathryn
Friedman, Lynne
Frudakis, Evangelos William
Fyfe, Jo Suzanne (Storch)
Gabin, George Joseph
Gantz, Ann Cushing
Gatto, Paul Anthony
Gay, Betsy (Elizabeth) Dershuck
Gerbracht, Bob (Robert) Thomas
Godfrey, Winnie (Winifred) M
Goetz, Mary Anna
Golembeski, Beverly L
Goree, Gary Paul
Grado, Angelo John
Graff, Frederick C
Grastorf, Jean H
Green, Tom
Greene, Daniel E
Grippe, Florence (Berg)
Gross, Julie
Grosse, C(arolyn) Ann Gawarecki
Gruver, Mary Emmett
Guastella, C Dennis
Gunderson, Karen
Gutman, Bertha Steinhardt
Guzevich-Sommers, Kreszenz (Cynthia)
Halliday, Nancy R
Hammett, Polly Horton
Hanna, Annette Adrian
Hardy, David Whittaker, III
Hardy, (Clarion) Dewitt
Harrison, Myrna J
Hartley, Katherine Ann
Hartwig, Heinie
Harvey, Donald Gene
Hawkins, Thomas Wilson, Jr
Heidel, Theresa Troise
Heinemann, Peter
Heller, Susanna
Henry, Jean
Hess, F Scott
Heston, Joan
Hibbs, Barbara J E
Hobbs, Frank I, Jr
Hofer, Ingrid (Ingeborg)
Hollerbach, Serge
Hollingsworth, Alvin Carl
Huff, Laura Weaver
Humphrey, Nene
Hunt, Courtenay
Hunter, Robert Douglas
Indiviglia, Salvatore Joseph
Irvine, Betty Jo
Ivers, Christine D
Jackson, Charlotte
Jerdon, William Harlan
Jorgensen, Bob (Robert A)
Kam, Mei K
Kardon, Carol
Kasnowski, Chester N
Kaufman, Loretta Ana
Kaye, Mildred Elaine
Kellar, Martha Robbins
Kemp, Sue
Kilguss, Elsie Schaich
Kinstler, Everett Raymond
Kirstein, Janis Adrian
Kord, Victor George
Kraft, Yvette
Kruskamp, Janet
Kurlander, Honey W
Lampasona, Eydi
Lane, Marion Arrons
Lanigan-Schmidt, Thomas
Layne, Barbara J
Leaf, Ruth
Leites, Ara (Barbara) L
LeMay, Harry Adrian
LeMay, Nancy
Leslie, Jimmy
Lesnick, Stephen William
Levitz, Ilona S
Lewis, Marcia
Lewis, Nat Brush
Lewis, Ronald Walter
Lewis, William R
Liljegren, Frank
Lindenberg, Mary K
Lomahaftewa, Linda Joyce
Longo-Muth, Linda L
Lord, Carolyn Marie
Lucas, Bonnie Lynn
Luisi, Jerry
Lynch, Mary Britten
Madura, Jack Joseph
Mahaffey, Merrill Dean
Malta, Vincent
Mancuso, Leni
Martone, William Robert
McCallum, Corrie Parker
McCarthy, Christine M
McCarty, Lorraine Chambers
McCullough, Edward L
McLeod, Cheryl O'Halloran
McReynolds, (Joe) Cliff
McVicker, Charles Taggart
Mendenhall, Jack
Merida, Margaret Braden
Meyers, Dale (Mrs Mario Cooper)
Miezajs, Dainis
Molnar, Michael Joseph
Moment, Joan
Moon, Marc
Moore, Scott Martin
Morenon, Elise
Morgan, Susan
Morgenlander, Ella Kramer
Morisue, Glenn Takanori
Moscatt, Paul N
Muchnic, Suzanne
Murphy, Mary Marguerite
Natale, Marie
Neal, Michael Shane
Nelson, Rich
Notestine, Dorothy J
Nourse, Mike
Ohe, Katie
Oliver, Julie Ford
Olson, Bettye Johnson
Olson, Charles
Olson, Maxine
Osborne, John Phillip
Parker, June
Parmenter, Susan Elizabeth
Passantino, George Christopher
Patrick, Genie Hudson
Patterson, Shirley Abbott
Pearson, James Eugene
Pech, Arleta
Peluso, Marta E
Penney, Jacqueline
Peppard, Jacqueline Jean
Perez, Vincent
Perlmutter, Linda M
Perrotti, Barbara
Phillis, Marilyn Hughey
Piccirillo, Alexander C
Piet, John Frances
Pijoan, Irene Maria Elizabeth
Plaster, Alice Marie
Pollard, Herschel Newton
Pollard, Jann Lawrence
Pototschnik, John Michael
Prall, Barbara Jones
Pratt, Elizabeth Hayes
Price, Morgan Samuel
Provder, Carl
Ragland, Bob
Rankin, Don
Raskind, Philis
Reilly, John Joseph
Reimers, Gladys Esther
Relkin, Michele Weston
Reynard, Carolyn Cole
Richards, Rosalyn A
Rider Berry, Tarah J
Rippe, Dan (Christian)
Robb, Peggy Hight
Roberts, Donald
Robinson, Donald Warren
Rohrbacher, Patricia
Rooke, Fay Lorraine (Edwards)
Rorick, William Calvin
Rose, Leatrice
Rose, Peggy Jane
Ross, John T
Ross, Rhoda Honore
Rossman, Ruth Scharff
Rudman, Joan (Combs)
Rudy, Helen
Rupprecht, Elizabeth
Rushworth, Michele D

JEWELER

JUROR

KINETIC ARTIST

LECTURER

LIBRARIAN

MEDALIST

MOSAIC ARTIST

MOSAIC ARTIST (cont)

Mandel, Mike
Weber, John Pitman
Zweerts, Arnold

MURALIST

Arai, Tomie
Arnold, Joseph Patterson
Baca, Judith
Bagget, William (Carter), Jr
Beckmann, Robert Owen
Bender, Leslie Marilyn
Bransby, Eric James
Brothers, Barry A
Buonagurio, Edgar R
Callahan, Aileen Loughlin
Castillo, Mario Enrique
Charlot, Martin Day
Cocchiarelli-Berger, Maria Giovanna
Collins, Harvey Arnold
Connolly, Jerome Patrick
Czimbalmos, Szabo Kalman
DesJarlait, Robert D
Frankford, Shawna
Gable, John Oglesby
Graham, Bob
Griesedieck, Ellen
Groat, Hall Pierce, Sr
Haas, Richard John
Hanner, Jean Patricia
Healy, Julia Schmitt
Henderson, Victor
Hernandez, Ester
Ho, Kong
Imana, Jorge Garron
Incandela, Gerald Jean-Marie
Janjigian, Lucy Elizabeth
Jankowski, Theodore Andrew
Jenkins, Ulysses Samuel, Jr
Kaplan, Stanley
Kaprov, Susan
Kilb, Jenny
Knerr, Erika Tilde
Kouns, Marjorie
Kramer, Louise
Landau, Myra
Larson, Sidney
Lee, Mary Virginia
Legrand, Yolene
Leopold, Susan
Lynch, Thom
Macdonell, Cameron
Marchini, Claudia H
Martin, Lucille Caiar
Martinez, Ernesto Pedregon
Mataranglo, Robert Patrick
Merola, Mario
Nantandy
Naylon, Betsy Zimmermann
O'Connell, Daniel Moylan
Palaia, Franc (Dominic)
Parmenter, Susan Elizabeth
Peters, Diane (Peck)
Pisani, Joseph
Rakocy, William (Joseph)
Ramos, Theodore
Rand, Archie
Redinger, Walter Fred
Regat, Jean-Jacques Albert
Regat, Mary E
Richardson, Frank, Jr
Rippey, Clayton
Rodeiro, Jose Manuel
Romano, Antonio
Rose, Samuel
Santoleri, Paul D
Schlesinger, Christina
Slonem, Hunt
Sochynsky, Ilona
Sweitzer, Charles Leroy
Tacla, Jorge
Tsarikovsky, Valery (Tsar)
Valesco, Frances
Vanden Berge, Peter Willem
Webb, Patrick
Weber, John Pitman
Whitcomb, Kay
Woodward, William
Yasko, Caryl A(nne)
Young, Leslie (McClure)
Yu, Shan

MUSEOLOGIST

Atkinson, Tracy
Bohen, Barbara E
Bol, Marsha C
Brody, J(acob) J (erome)
Carter, David Giles
Dailey, Chuck (Charles) Andrew
Dellis, Arlene B
Edson, Gary F
Fraser, Andrea R
Graham, Lanier
Gray, Campbell Bruce
Greenwald, Alice (Alice Marian Greenwald-Ward)
Hall, Robert L
Hess, Stanley William
Holo, Selma R
Kelm, Bonnie G
Krulik, Barbara S
Mayer, Susan Martin
Rakocy, William (Joseph)
Sipiora, Leonard Paul
Sokol, David Martin
Streetman, John William, III
Wright, Vicki C

MUSEUM DIRECTOR

Ackerman, Andy
Adams, Celeste Marie
Adamson, Glenn
Ahern, Maureen J
Alexander-Greene, Grace George
Allen, Brian
Alswang, Hope
Ambrose, Andy
Andersen, Jeffrey W
Anderson, Gail Kana
Anderson, Maxwell L
Anderson, Ross Cornelius
Andrews, Gail
Appel, Eric A
Armstrong, Richard
Arteaga, Agustín
Bacigalupi, Don
Bacot, Henry Parrott
Bailey, Colin B
Bailin, David
Ballinger, James K
Balzekas, Stanley, Jr
Bandes, Susan Jane
Bantel, Linda
Barker, Elizabeth E
Barrie, Dennis Ray
Baumann, Caroline
Beam, Patrice K
Begley, J (John) Phillip
Beman, Lynn Susan
Benezra, Neal
Benjamin, Brent R
Berg, Mona Lea
Berreth, David Scott
Bessire, Mark HC
Betsky, Aaron
Biesenbach, Klaus
Bishop, Budd Harris
Blaugrund, Annette
Block, Holly
Bloomfield, Sara J
Blume, Peter F
Blumenthal, Arthur R
Bodine, William B, Jr
Bol, Marsha C
Bolas, Gerald Douglas
Bolge, George S
Bolger, Doreen
Bollerer, Fred L
Bomford, David
Botwinick, Michael
Bowman, Leslie Greene
Bradley, Betsy
Bradley, William Steven
Brand, Michael
Breuer, Bradford R
Bridenstine, James A
Brigham, David R
Brooke, David Stopford
Brosius, Karen
Brougher, Kerry
Broun, Elizabeth Gibson
Brown, Charlotte Vestal
Brownawell, Christopher J
Bruni, Stephen Thomas
Bullard, Edgar John, III
Burger, Gary C
Burke, Daniel
Burke, James Donald
Burnside, Madeleine Hilding
Bush, Martin H
Butler, Charles Thomas
Butler, David
Byrnes, James Bernard
Campbell, Thomas P
Carswell, John
Carter, Curtis Lloyd
Cartwright, Derrick R
Cash, Sarah
Castile, Rand
Chandler, Angelyn Sanders
Chepp, Mark
Chiu, Melissa
Christison, Muriel B
Clark, Lynda K
Clark, Michael
Cleave, Marcie Van
Close, (John) Timothy
Codding, Mitchell Allan
Conforti, Michael Peter
Conklin, Jo-Ann
Consey, Kevin E
Cook, Silas Baldwin
Coopersmith, Georgia A
Coraor, John E
Cormier, Cindy
Corrin, Lisa G
Cowart, Jack
Cozad, Rachael Blackburn
Crane, Michael Patrick
Crosman, Christopher Byron
Crum, Katherine B
Cubiñá, Silvia Karman
Culver, Michael L
Cuno, James
Cutler, Judy A Goffman
Cutler, Laurence S
Czarniecki, M J, III
Dalton-Meyer, Marie
Danko, Linda AK
Danoff, I Michael
Darling, Sharon Sandling
Davies, Hugh Marlais
Davis, Darwin R
Deitch, Jeffrey
De la Torre, David Joseph
Delehanty, Suzanne
Demetrion, James Thomas
Dempsey, Bruce Harvey
Desmarais, Charles Joseph
Dewitt, Katharine Cramer
de Zegher, Catherine
Dietrich, Bruce Leinbach
Dixon, Jenny (Jane) Hoadley
Doezema, Marianne
Doherty, Peggy M
Driesbach, Janice
Druick, Douglas Wesley
Duff, James H
Dursum, Brian A
Ebitz, David MacKinnon
Edelstein, Teri J
Edmonds, Tom
Edson, Gary F
Eiland, William U
Eldredge, Bruce B
Ellis, George Richard
Escallon, Ana Maria
Fabing, Suzannah J
Farver, Jane
Feinberg, Larry J
Feldman, Arthur Mitchell
Feldman, Kaywin
Ferguson, Charles B
Fern, Alan Maxwell
Ferrell, Heather A
Ferriso, Brian J
Fetchko, Peter J
Fillin-Yeh, Susan
Finkelpearl, Tom
Fitch, Blake
Fleischman, Stephen
Fleming, Jeff
Fogarty, Lori
Forbes, Donna Marie
Franklin, David
Freed, Douglass Lynn
Friedman, Martin
Friis-Hansen, Dana
Futter, Ellen V
Gaiber, Maxine Oliansky
Gaither, Edmund B
Galina, Brenda Moss
Gardiner, Henry Gilbert
Gates, Jay Rodney
Gaudieri, Alexander V J
Gealt, Adelheid Medicus
Gear, Emily
Gedeon, Lucinda Heyel
Geldin, Sherri
Gentele, Glen
Geske, Norman Albert
Gillman, Derek A
Glass, Brent D.
Glenn, Constance White
Golden, Thelma
Goodman, Gwen Ducat
Gordon, Joy L
Gould, Claudia
Govan, Michael
Gover, Kevin
Gowdy, Marjorie E
Grand, Stanley I
Gray, Campbell Bruce
Green, Jonathan (William)
Gribbon, Deborah
Griswold, William M
Grogan, Kevin
Grynsztejn, Madeleine
Gualtieri, Joseph P
Gumpert, Lynn
Halbreich, Kathy
Hallmark, Donald
Hardy, Saralyn Reece
Harleman, Kathleen Towe
Harlow, Ann
Harrison, Helen Amy
Harrity, Gail M
Hartz, Jill
Hawley, Anne
Heath, Samuel K
Heinrich, Christoph
Heiss, Alanna
Helfenstein, Josef
Hennessey, William John
Henrich, Sarah E
Henry, James Pepper
Henry, John B, III
Herman, Lloyd Eldred
Hernandez, Jo Farb
High, Steven S
Hirschel, Anthony G
Hite, Jessie Otto
Hogan, Felicity
Holmes, Willard
Holo, Selma R

PAINTER

PAINTER (cont)
Buecker, Robert
Buist, Kathy
Bujnowski, Joel A
Bulka, Douglas
Buonagurio, Edgar R
Burford, James E
Burgess, Joseph James, Jr
Burggraf, Ray Lowell
Burke, Daniel V
Burkhardt, Ronald Robert
Burko, Diane
Burleson, Charles Trentman
Burns, Josephine
Burns, Sheila
Burns, Stan
Burpee, James Stanley
Burr, Tricia
Burton, Judith Ann
Bush, Jill Lobdill
Bushnell, Kenneth Wayne
Bushnell, Kenneth Wayne
Buszko, Irene J
Butchkes, Sydney
Butler, James D
Butti, Linda
Byrd, Jerry
Caddell, Foster
Cade, Walter, III
Cady, Dennis Vern
Cady, Samuel Lincoln
Calabro, Joanna Sondra
Calabro, Richard Paul
Calamar, Gloria
Callahan, Aileen Loughlin
Callister, Jane
Cameron, Eric
Campbell, David Paul
Campbell, Richard Horton
Cannuli, Richard Gerald
Canright, Sarah Anne
Cantine, David
Caplan Ciarrocchi, Sandra
Caporale-Greene, Wende
Cardinal, Marcelin
Cardoso, Anthony
Carlson, Cynthia J
Carnwath, Squeak
Caroompas, Carole J
Carpenter, Earl L
Carrero, Jaime
Carroll, James F L
Carter, Carol
Carter, Gary
Carter, Nanette Carolyn
Carulla, Ramon
Casadei, Giovanni
Casas, Fernando R
Casas, Melesio (Mel)
Casellas, Joachim
Casey, Tim (Timothy) William
Cassara, Frank
Castrucci, Andrew
Caswell, Helen Rayburn
Catchi
Caton, David
Cattan, Emilia
Cattaneo, (Jacquelyn A) Kammerer
Catterall, John Edward
Cauduro, Rafael
Cecil, Charles Harkless
Cecil-Wishing, Devin
Celentano, Francis Michael
Cetín, Anton
Chaiklin, Amy
Chambers, William McWillie
Chambers, William Thomas
Chapin, Deborah Jane
Chaplin, George Edwin
Chapman, Gary Howard
Chappell, Berkley Warner
Charles, Larry
Charlot, Martin Day
Chase, Jeanne Norman
Chase, Louisa L
Chatmas, John T
Chemeche, George
Chen, Hilo
Cheng, Emily
Cheshire, Craig Gifford
Chesney, Lee R, Jr
Chevins, Christopher M
Chilton, Fred
Cho, Y(eou) J(ui)
Chodkowski, Henry, Jr
Christensen, Neil C
Christiansen, Diane
Christman, Reid August
Christy, Bonnie Beth
Christy, Bonnie Beth
Chu, Julia Nee
Church, Maude
Churchill, Diane
Ciarrocchi, Ray
Cicero, Carmen Louis
Cifolelli, Alberta
Cintron, Joseph M
Civitello, John Patrick
Civitico, Bruno
Clark, Michael Vinson
Clarke, John Clem
Cleary, Barbara B
Clement, Kathleen
Cliff, Denis Antony
Climo, Lindee
Close, Mary
Clymer, Albert Anderson
Cocker, Barbara Joan
Cockrill, Sherna
Coe, Anne Elizabeth
Coe, Henry
Cogan, John D(ennis)
Coheleach, Guy Joseph
Cohen, Cora
Cohen, Jean
Coit, M B
Coker, Carl David
Colao, Rudolph
Colarusso, Corrine Camille
Cole, Donald
Cole, Grace V
Cole, Max
Coleman, Constance Depler
Coleman, Donna Leslie
Coleman, M L (Michael Lee)
Coleman, Michael B
Collery, Paula
Collins, Dan (Daniel) McClellan
Colway, James R
Concannon, George Robert
Condren, Stephen F
Conger, William
Conn, David Edward
Connelly, Chuck
Connolly, Jerome Patrick
Conrad, Nancy R
Constantine, Greg John
Cook, Joseph Stewart
Cooke, Judy
Coover, Doris Gwendolyn
Copenhaver-Fellows, Deborah Lynne Fellows
Copt, Louis J
Cormier, Robert John
Costan, Chris
Cote, Alan
Cottingham, Robert
Cotton, Will
Couper, Charles Alexander
Courtney, Suzan
Courtright, Robert
Covington, Harrison Wall
Cowan, Ralph Wolfe
Coyne, John Michael
Craft, Douglas D
Craig, Nancy Ellen
Craven, David James
Crawford, Thom Cooney
Creecy, Herbert Lee
Cretara, Domenic Anthony
Criswell, Warren
Crooks, Roselyn J
Crotto, Paul
Crown, Roberta Lila
Crozier, Richard Lewis
Crum, David
Crump, Walter Moore, Jr
Culver, Michael L
Cummings, David William
Cunnick, Gloria Helen
Cunningham, Francis
Cuppaidge, Virginia
Currie, Bruce
Cutler, Ronnie
Cyphers, Peggy K
Dacey, Paul
Dailey, Chuck (Charles) Andrew
Daley, Cathy
Dallmann, Daniel Forbes
D'Almeida, George
Dal Poggetto, Sandra Hope
D'Amico, Larry
Dani
Dantzic, Cynthia Maris
Danziger, Fred Frank
Darton, Christopher
Daskaloff, Gyorgy
Davenport, Ray
Davenport, Rebecca Read
David, Ivo
Davidek, Stefan
Davidson, David Isaac
Davidson, Herbert Laurence
Davies, Kenneth Southworth
Davis, Brad (Bradley) Darius
Davis, Robert
Davis, Ronald
Davis, Thelma Ellen
Dawson, John Allan
Day, Burnis Calvin
Deaderick, Joseph
Dean, Nat
De Berardinis, Olivia
De Blasi, Anthony Armando
Debonne, Jeannette
Debrosky, Christine A
De Champlain, Vera Chopak
Dechar, Peter
Decil, Stella (Del) Walters
Deckert, Clinton A
De Donato, Louis
de Groot, Pat
De Kergommeaux, Duncan
de Lama, Alberto
De La Vega, Antonio
Della-Volpe, Ralph Eugene
Dellosso, Gabriela Gonzalez
DeLoyht-Arendt, Mary
DeMatties, Nick
De Monte, Claudia
Demsky, Hilda Green
Dennett, Lissy W
Dentler, Anne Lillian
Dernovich, Donald Frederick
DeSantis, Diana
De Santo, Stephen C
de Smet, Lorraine
Desmidt, Thomas H
Dettwiller, Kathryn King
Devereux, Mara
Devine, Nancy
DeWitt, Edward
Diamond, Cathy
Dias-Jorgensen, Aurora Abdias
Diaz, Lope (Max)
Dibert, Rita Jean
Di Cerbo, Michael
Dickerson, Brian S
Dickerson, Vera Mason
Dickson, Mark Amos
Diehl, Hans-Jurgen
Di Fate, Vincent
Di Giacinto, Sharon
Di Giacomo, Fran
Dill, Laddie John
Dingle, Kim
Dinkin, Larry
Dinnerstein, Harvey
Dinnerstein, Simon A
Dixon, Ken
Dixon, Willard
Do, Kim V
Dodd, Lois
Dodd, M(ary) Irene
Dodge, Robert G
Dolmatch, Blanche
Domjan, Evelyn
Donley, Ray
Donley, Robert Morris
Donmez, Yucel
Doo Da Post, Edward Ferdinand Higgins III
Doogan, Bailey
Dooley Waller, M L
Doray, Audrey Capel
Douglas, Edwin Perry
Douglas, Tom Howard
Dowell, James Thomas
Downer, Spelman Evans
Downes, Rackstraw
Doyle, Joe
Drapell, Joseph
Drasler, Gregory J
Dreiband, Laurence
Dreskin, Jeanet Steckler
Drummond, Sally Hazelet
DuBack, Charles S
Dubasky, Valentina
Dublac, Robert Revak
Dubrow, John
Duffy, Michael John
Du Jardin, Gussie
Dunkelman, Loretta
Dunlap, Loren Edward
Dunow, Esti
Duque, Adonay
Duren, Stephen D
Durham, Jeanette R
Durham, William
Durr, Pat (Patricia) (Beth)
Dutton, Allen A
Duval, Jeanne
Dverin, Anatoly
Dwyer, James
Dwyer, Nancy
Dyer, M Wayne
Dyyon, Mario
Eastcott, R. Wayne
Eastman, Gene M
Eberly, Vickie
Eckart, Christian
Ecker, Robert Rodgers
Eddy, Don
Edelman, Ann
Edelman, Rita
Edelson, Mary Beth
Eden, Glenn
Edge, Douglas Benjamin
Edison, Diane
Edouard, Pierre
Edwards, Benjamin
Edwards, Jonmarc
Egeli, Cedric Baldwin
Eger, Marilyn Rae
Egleston, Truman G
Eisenberg, Sonja Miriam
Eisentrager, James A
Eisinger, Harry
Eisner, Carole Swid
Eliot, Lucy Carter
Elkins, Toni Marcus
Elliot, John
Elliott, Anne
Ellis, Richard
Embrey, Carl Rice
Emmert, Pauline Gore
Encinias, John Orlando
Enders, Elizabeth
Engelson, Carol
Enright, Judy A

PAINTER (cont)
Howard, Dan F
Howe, Nancy
Howell, James
Howes, Royce Bucknam
Hsiao, Chin
Hubbard, John
Huggins, Victor, Jr
Hughes, Edward John
Hull, Gregory Stewart
Hunkler, Dennis
Hunt, Courtenay
Hunter, Robert Douglas
Hushlak, Gerald
Hynes, Frances M
Hyson, Jean
Impiglia, Giancarlo
Ingram, Michael Steven
Ipcar, Dahlov
Irvin, Marianne Fanelli
Irwin, Lani Helena
Isaacs, Ron
Isaacson, Lynn Judith
Iwamoto, Ralph Shigeto
Jacklin, Bill (William)
Jackson, Herb
Jackson, Jeanine Careri
Jackson, Oliver Lee
Jackson, Suzanne
Jacob, Ned
Jacobs, Harold
Jacobs, Ralph, Jr
Jacobs, Scott E
Jacobshagen, N Keith, II
Jacquemon, Pierre
Jacquette, Julia L
Jacquette, Yvonne Helene
Jaeger, Brenda Kay
Jaffe, Shirley
Jakob, Bruno
Janjigian, Lucy Elizabeth
Jankowski, Theodore Andrew
Janowich, Ronald
Janowitz, Joel
Jans, Candace
Jaque, Louis
Jaramillo, Virginia
Jaudon, Valerie
Jay, Norma Joyce
Jean, Beverly Strong
Jeffers, Wendy
Jennerjahn, W P
Jensen, Elisa
Jerins, Edgar
Jessen, Shirley Agnes
Jessup, Robert
Jilg, Michael Florian
Jimerson, Annette Princess
Joelson, Suzanne
Johanningmeier, Robert Alan
Johanson, George E
Johns, Christopher K(alman)
Johnson, Barbara Louise
Johnson, Brent
Johnson, Lee
Johnston, Roy
Johnston, Thomas Alix
Jolley, Donal Clark
Jones, Donald Glynn
Jones, Fay
Jones, Jane
Jones, Lou Mary Louise Humpton
Jones, Norma L
Jones, Patty Sue
Jones, Ruthe Blalock
Jorgensen, Bob (Robert A)
Joseph, Stefani A
Juarez, Roberto
Judd, De Forrest Hale
Jung, Kwan Yee
Jung, Yee Wah
Jurney, Donald (Benson)
Kagle, Joseph L, Jr
Kahan, Leonard
Kahn, Tobi Aaron
Kahn, Wolf
Kaiser, S(haron) Burkett
Kaish, Morton
Kalb, Marty Joel
Kalina, Richard
Kamys, Walter
Kapheim, Thom
Kaplan, Phyllis
Kaplan, Sandra
Kaplinski, Buffalo
Kapp, E Jeanne
Kardon, Carol
Karimi, Reza
Karnes, Mark
Karp, Aaron S
Kastner, Barbara H
Katano, Marc
Katayama, Toshihiro
Katselas, Milton George
Katz, Morris
Kaufman, Irving
Kaulitz, Garry Charles
Kay, Reed
Kearns, James Joseph
Keena, Janet L
Kelley, Chapman
Kelley, Heather Ryan
Kelley, Ramon
Kelly, Joe Ray
Kelly, Kevin T
Kelly, Robert James
Kemp, Arnold Joseph
Kennedy, James Edward
Kenney, Estelle Koval
Kennington, Dale
Kent, H Latham
Kenton, Mary Jean
Kepalas
Kepets, Hugh Michael
Kermes, Constantine John
Kerns, Ed (Johnson), Jr
Kessler, Alan
Kessler, Linda
Kessler, Margaret Jennings
Keveson, Florence
Kevorkian, Richard
Khachian, Elisa A
Kieferndorf, Frederick George
Kielkopf, James Robert
Kiland, Lance Edward
Kilb, Jenny
Kilian, Austin Farland
Kim, Po (Hyun)
Kimes, Don
King, Brian Jeffrey
King, Clive
King, Marcia Gygli
King, Vikki Killough Vranich
Kipniss, Robert
Kittredge, Nancy (Elizabeth)
Klamen, David
Klarin, Karla S
Klaven, Marvin L
Kleemann, Ron
Kleinberg, Susan
Klement, Vera
Knepper-Doyle, Virginia
Knock, Sarah
Knowles, Richard H
Knowlton, Jonathan
Knutsson, Anders
Kobayashi, Hisako
Kocar, George Frederick
Koch, Gerd Herman
Koch, Philip
Koehler, Henry
Kogan, Deborah
Kohut, Lorene
Koller-Davies, Eva
Komarin, Gary
Konopka, Joseph
Koppelman, Dorothy
Kopriva, Sharon
Korman, Sharon
Kossoff, Leon
Kostabi, Mark
Kotoske, Roger Allen
Kozmon, George
Kraal, Lies
Kraft, Yvette
Krashes, Barbara
Krasnyansky, Anatole Lvovich
Krate, Nat
Kreutz, Gregg
Kreznar, Richard J
Krieger, Ruth M
Kriegstein, Zara
Kroll, David
Kronsnoble, Jeffrey Michael
Krueger, Lothar David
Kuckei, Peter
Kuehn, Frances
Kuhlman, Walter Egel
Kuopus, Clinton
Kurlander, Honey W
Kurtz, Richard
Kurz, Diana
Kuwayama, Tadaaki
Kwak, Hoon
Labonte, Dick
Labrie, Christy
Lafleur, Laurette Carignan
Lahtinen, Silja (Liisa) Talikka
Lakes, Diana Mary
Lalin, Nina
Lamantia, Paul Christopher
Lamb, Matt
Lambert, Ed
LaMontagne, Armand M
LaMonte, Angela Mae
Lamuniere, Carolyn Parker
Landfield, Ronnie (Ronald) T
Lane, William
Lanyon, Ellen
LaPalombara, Constance
La Pelle, Rodger
La Pierre, Thomas
Lapin, Annie
Lapointe, Frank
La Porta, Elayne B
Larmer, Oscar Vance
Larraz, Julio F
LaRue, Joan Marron
Lasker, Joe (Joseph) L
Lau, Rex
Laurence, Geoffrey F
Lavadour, James
Law, Jan
Lawrence, Rodney Steven
Lawson, Thomas
Leavens, Evelyn
Lebejoara, Ovidiu
LeBey, Barbara
Lecky, Susan
Lee, Catherine
Lee, Li Lin
Lee, Mary Virginia
Leeson, Tom
Leete, William White
Legrand, Yolene
Lehr, Mira T(ager)
Leibowitz, Bernice
Leis, Marietta Patricia
Leites, Ara (Barbara) L
LeMay, Nancy
Lenaghan, Andrew
Lenker, Marlene N
Lerner, Sandra
Leslie, Jimmy
Lesnick, Stephen William
Letendre, Rita
Levee, John H
Levering, Robert K
Levine, Edward
Levine, Phyllis Jean
Levine, Tomar
Levitz, Ilona S
Levy, Tibbie
Lewis, Donald Sykes, Jr
Lewis, Michael H
Lewis, Nat Brush
Lewton, Val Edwin
Lhotka, Bonny Pierce
Li-lan
Liccione, Alexander
Lieber, Lola
Lieber, Thomas Alan
Lieberman, Meyer Frank
Liebman, Sarah
Liljegren, Frank
Lincoln, Jane Lockwood
Linhares, Judith
Link, Lawrence John
Link, Phyllida K
Linton, Harold
Lippmann, Janet Gurian
Lipsky, Pat
Lipton, Sondra
Lis, Janet
Lisaius, Fred A
Little, James
Livingstone, Biganess
Loehle, Betty Barnes
Loehle, Richard E
Loftus, Peter M
Logemann, Jane Marie
Lomahaftewa, Linda Joyce
Longo, Vincent
Longo-Muth, Linda L
Longobardi, Pam
Longval, Gloria
Lopina, Louise Carol
Lotz, Steven Darryl
Loving, Richard Maris
Loy, John Sheridan
Lozoya, Agustin Portillo
Lucas, Charlie
Luino, Bernardino
Lumbers, James Richard
Lundsfryd, Tine
Lusker, Ron
Lutes, Jim (James)
Luz, Virginia
Lynch, Thom
Lynds, Clyde
Lynn, Judith
Lyon, Giles Andrew
Lysun, Gregory
Maas, Marion Elizabeth
Macaray, Lawrence Richard
MacBird, Rosemary (Simpson)
MacDonald, Bruce K
Macdonald, Carroll
MacKillop, Rod
MacNeill, Frederick Douglas
Macpherson, Kevin
Maddox, Jerrold Warren
Magel, Catharine Anne
Mahaffey, Merrill Dean
Mai, James L
Maier, Maryanne E
Mailman, Cynthia
Mainardi, Patricia M
Maki, Countess Hope Marie
Malo, Teri (A)
Malone, James Hiram
Malone, Peter
Malta, Vincent
Mancini, John
Mandel, John
Manes, Belle
Mango, Robert J
Mangold, Sylvia Plimack
Mann, Frank
Manville, Elsie
Mapes, Doris Williamson
Marais
Marchini, Claudia H
Marcus, Gerald R
Marcus, Irving E
Marcus, Marcia
Mari, M
Mariner, Donna M
Markarian, Alexia (Mitrus)
Markman, Ronald

PAINTER (cont)

Rahja, Virginia Helga
Raiselis, Richard
Raissnia, Raha
Raleigh, Henry Patrick
Ramsey, Dorothy J
Rand, Archie
Randolph, Lynn Moore
Rasmussen, Anton Jesse
Rathle, Henri (Amin)
Ray, Donald Arvin
Rayen, James Wilson
Rector, Marge (Lee)
Reddington, Charles Leonard
Reddix, Roscoe Chester
Redgrave, Felicity
Reding, Barbara Endicott
Redmond, Catherine
Redmond, Rosemary
Reece, Maynard
Reed, David
Reed, Jeffrey
Reed, Paul Allen
Reeder, Scott
Reedy, Susan
Reeves, Esther May
Reichert, Donald Karl
Reid, Charles Clark
Reid, Leslie
Reid Jenkins, Debra L
Reilly, Jack
Reilly, John Joseph
Reilly, Nancy
Reininghaus, Ruth
Reinkraut, Ellen Susan
Reisman, Celia
Reker, Les
Remsen, John
Rendl, M(ildred) Marcus
Renouf, Edda
Resek, Kate Frances
Resnick, Don
Revri, Anil
Reynard, Carolyn Cole
Reynolds, James Elwood
Reynolds, Wade
Rich, David
Rich, Garry Lorence
Richard, Jack
Richards, Bill
Richards, David Patrick
Richardson, Jean
Richardson, W C
Richter, Hank
Rieber, Ruth B
Riess, Lore
Rifka, Judy
Riley, Enrico
Riley, Sarah A
Ripps, Rodney
Ripstein, Jacqueline
Rivera, Elias J
Rivera, George
Rivo, Shirley Winthrope
Rizzi, James
Robb, Charles
Robb, Laura Ann
Robb, Peggy Hight
Robbin, Tony
Roberts, Mark
Roberts, William Edward
Robertson, Lorna Dooling
Robinson, Charlotte
Robinson, Jay
Robinson, Margot Steigman
Rocamora, Jaume
Roche-Rabell, Arnaldo
Roda, Rhoda Lillian Sablow
Rodeiro, Jose Manuel
Rodriquez, Ernesto Angelo
Rogers, Muriel I
Rogers, Peter Wilfrid
Ropp, Ann L
Rose, Leatrice
Rose, Samuel
Rosenblatt, Adolph
Rosenblatt, Suzanne Maris
Rosenfeld, Sharon
Rosenthal, Deborah Maly
Ross, Janice Koenig
Ross, Rhoda Honore
Rossman, Ruth Scharff
Rotenberg, Judi
Roth, Frank
Rothafel, Sydell
Rothenberg, Susan
Routon, David F
Row, David
Rowan, Herman
Rowe, Charles Alfred
Rowe, Michael Duane
Royer, Mona Lee
Rubin, Sandra Mendelsohn
Ruda, Edwin
Rudinsky, Alexander (John)
Rudy, Helen
Ruehlicke, Cornelia Iris
Rupprecht, Elizabeth
Rusak, Halina R
Ruscha, Edward Joseph
Rush, Jean C
Russell, Christopher Ryan
Russell, Jeff
Russo, Alexander Peter
Russotto, Paul
Saar, Lezley
Sabo, Betty Jean
Sadowski, Carol (Louise) Johnson
Saftel, Andrew P
St Clair Miller, Frances
St George, William (M)
St John, Terry N
St Maur, Kirk
St Tamara
Sakuyama, Shunji
Salinas, Baruj
Salt, John
Salter, Richard Mackintire
Samburg, Grace (Blanche)
Samimi, Mehrdad
Sampson, Frank
Samson, Carl Joseph
Sanchez, Thorvald
Sanden, John Howard
Sanders, Joop A
Sandol, Maynard
Sandusky, Billy Ray
Sanin, Fanny
Sargent, Margaret Holland
Sarsony, Robert
Sato, Masaaki
Saturen, Ben
Saunders, Edith Dariel Chase
Saunders, Marr
Sauter, Gail E
Sawada, Ikune
Sax, (Steve G Sacks)
Sayles, Eva
Sazegar, Morteza
Schaechter, Judith
Schenck, William Clinton
Schepis, Anthony Joseph
Schiavina, Laura M
Schiebold, Hans
Schiff, Molly Jeanette
Schildknecht, Dorothy E
Schirm, David
Schlesinger, Christina
Schmidt, Charles
Schmidt, Edward William
Schmidt, Frederick Lee
Schnackenberg, Roy
Schneider, Janet M
Schneider, Jo Anne
Schnurr, Elinore
Schofield, Roberta
Schroeck, R D
Schrohenloher, Sally A
Schulson, Susan
Schultz, Stephen Warren
Schurr, Jerry M
Schutz, Dana
Schwarm, Harold Chambers
Schwartz, Ruth
Scott, B Nibbelink (Barbara Gae Scott)
Scott, Bill Earl
Searle, William Ross
Searles, Charles
Seidl, Claire
Seidler, Doris
Seitz-Elliott, Patricia Lynne
Seltzer, Joanne Lynn
Seltzer, Peter Lawrence
Seltzer, Phyllis
Semmel, Joan
Sensemann, Susan
Seslar, Patrick George
Sewell, Richard George
Sexton, Janice Louise
Seyler, Monique G
Seymour, Claudia Hultgren
Shadrach, Jean H
Shaffer, Fern
Shahly, Jehan
Shahn, Abby
Shankman, Gary Charles
Shannon, R Michael
Shap, Sylvia
Shapiro, Babe
Shapiro, David
Sharon, Russell
Sharp, Anne Catherine
Sharp, Susan S
Shaw, John Palmer
Sheirr, Olga (Krolik)
Shemdin, Azhar H
Shemesh, Lorraine R
Shepherd, William Fritz
Sherman, Z Charlotte
Sherman-Zinn, Ellen R
Sherr, Ronald Norman
Sherrod, Philip Lawrence
Sherwood, Leona
Shilson, Wayne Stuart
Shimomura, Roger
Shores, (James) Franklin
Shorr, Harriet
Shotwell, Kenneth E
Siberell, Anne Hicks
Sickler, Michael Allan
Siems, Anne
Siff, Marlene Ida
Sillman, Amy (Denison)
Silverberg, June Roselyn
Silverman, Ronald H
Simons, Dona
Simpson, David
Simpson, Marilyn Jean
Singer, Esther Forman
Singletary, Michael James
Sipho, Ella
Skalagard, Hans
Skupinski, Bogdan Kazimierz
Slavick, Susanne Mechtild
Slider, Dorla Dean
Sloan, Jeanette Pasin
Sloan, Ronald J
Slonem, Hunt
Slotnick, Mortimer H
Smith, Andrea B
Smith, B J
Smith, Clifford
Smith, David Loeffler
Smith, Dinah Maxwell
Smith, Frank Anthony
Smith, Jack Richard
Smith, Jo-an
Smith, Linda Kyser
Smith, Susan
Smuskiewicz, Ted
Solem, (Elmo) John
Somers, Frederick D(uane)
Sommer, Susan
Soppelsa, George
Sorokin, Janet
Sorokin, Maxine Ann
Southey, Trevor J T
Spelman, Jill Sullivan
Spence, Andrew
Spencer, Harold Edwin
Spiess-Ferris, Eleanor
Sprick, Daniel
Squadra, John
Squires, Gerald Leopold
Squires Ganz, Sylvia (Tykie)
Stach, Judy
Stack, Frank Huntington
Stack, Michael T
Stallwitz, Carolyn
Staloff, Fred
Stanbridge, Harry Andrew
Stanley, Robert A
Stanton, Harriet L
Stanton, Sylvia Doucet
Staprans, Raimonds
Starkweather-Nelson, Cynthia Louise
Stasack, Edward Armen
Statman, Jan B
Staub, Carol Anne
Stavans, Isaac
Staven, Leland Carroll
Steen, Carol J
Steinhardt, Alice
Steinhouse, Tobie (Thelma)
Stephanson, Loraine Ann
Stephens, William Blakely
Stevanov, Zoran
Steward, Aleta Rossi
Stewart, Dorothy S
Stewart, F Clark
Stewart, John P
Stewart, William
Steynovitz, Zamy
Sticker, Robert Edward
Stillman (Myers), Joyce L
Stirnweis, Shannon
Stirratt, Betsy (Elizabeth) Anne
Stoloff, Carolyn
Stomps, Walter E, Jr
Stonehouse, Fred A
Storey, David
Storm, Howard
Stout, Richard Gordon
Straus, Sandy
Strawn, Melvin Nicholas
Stroud, Billy
Stroud, Peter Anthony
Struck, Norma Johansen
Stuart, Joseph Martin
Stuart, Sherry Blanchard
Stutesman, Cezanne Slough
Sublett, Carl Cecil
Sudlow, Robert N
Suggs, Pat(ricia) Ann
Sullivan, Barbara Jean
Sullivan, David Francis
Sullivan, Francoise
Sullivan, Jim
Sultan, Altoon
Summer, (Emily) Eugenia
Sutton, Carol (Lorraine)
Swain, Robert
Swanson, J N
Swartz, Beth Ames
Sweet, Mary (French)
Sweitzer, Charles Leroy
Swetcharnik, Sara Morris
Tabak, Chaim
Tacla, Jorge
Tahedl, Ernestine
Takashima, Shizuye Violet
Talasnik, Stephen
Talbot, Jonathan
Taliaferro, Nancy Ellen Taylor
Tamburine, Jean Helen
Tanger, Susanna
Tanksley, Ann
Tansey, Mark

PAINTER (cont)

PAINTER (cont)
Gable, John Oglesby
Gallagher, Kathleen Ellen
Ganley, Betty
Gard, Suzanne E
Gardner, Sheila
Garro, Barbara
Gatto, Rose Marie
Gaucher-Thomas, Nancy A
Gay, Betsy (Elizabeth) Dershuck
Gentile, Gloria Irene
Gentry, Augustus Calahan, Jr
Gentry, Warren Miller
George, Thomas
Gill, Jean Kennedy
Gioello, Debbie
Glesmann, Sylvia Maria
Gnott, Jacqueline
Goetz, Peter Henry
Golden, Rolland Harve
Golembeski, Beverly L
Goodspeed, Barbara
Goodwin, Guy
Gorchov, Ron
Graese, Judy (Judith) Ann
Graff, Frederick C
Grafton, Rick (Frederick) Wellington
Grainger, Nessa Posner
Grastorf, Jean H
Grauer, Gladys Barker
Greaver, Harry
Gregory-Goodrum, Ellna Kay
Grimes, Margaret W
Grodsky, Sheila Taylor
Gross, Marilyn A
Grosse, C(arolyn) Ann Gawarecki
Guida, Dominick
Hagin, Nancy
Hallenbeck, Pomona Juanita
Hamilton, George Earl
Hammett, Polly Horton
Hamwi, Richard Alexander
Hanks, Steve
Hardy, (Clarion) Dewitt
Harkins, George C, Jr
Harmon, Barbara Sayre
Harmon, Cliff Franklin
Harris, Carolyn
Harte, John
Hasegawa, Noriko
Hatch, W A S
Hayes, Tua
Heidel, Theresa Troise
Heinzen, MaryAnn
Hensley, Jackson Morey
Hill, Peter
Hill, Robyn Lesley
Hodge, R Garey
Hofer, Ingrid (Ingeborg)
Hoie, Claus
Holabird, Jean
Holden, Donald
Hough, Jennine
Hough, Winston
Hovsepian, Leon
Huddy, Margaret Teresa
Hui, Pat
Hunter, Robert Howard
Hynes, Frances M
Jackson, Paul C
Jackson, Suzanne
Jacobsen, Michael A
Jaidinger, Judith Clarann Szesko
James, Christopher P
Jamison, Philip
Jessen, Shirley Agnes
Johnson, Brent
Johnson, Cecile Ryden
Johnson, Douglas Walter
Jolley, Donal Clark
Jones, Norma L
Jones, Thomas William
Jordan, Beth McAninch
Jung, Kwan Yee
Jung, Yee Wah
Kaiser, Vitus J
Kam, Mei K
Kamys, Walter
Kan, Kit-Keung
Kaplinski, Buffalo
Karimi, Reza
Keary, Geri
Keck, Jeanne Gentry
Keena, Janet L
Kelley, Ramon
Kemp, Arnold Joseph
Kemp, Sue
Khachian, Elisa A
Khalil, Claire Anne
Kieffer, Mary Jane
Kilguss, Elsie Schaich
Kiousis, Linda Weber
Kirsten-Daiensai, Richard Charles
Kleemann, Ron
Kolisnyk, Peter
Kuczun, Ann-Marie
LaCom, Wayne Carl
Laessig, Robert
Lafleur, Laurette Carignan
Lafon, Dee J
Lahr, J(ohn) Stephen
Lai, Waihang
Lakes, Diana Mary
Lalin, Nina
Lane, William
Langford-Stansbery, Sherry K
LaPalombara, Constance
Larraz, Julio F
Law, Jan
Lawrence, James A
Lawton, Florian Kenneth
Leavens, Evelyn
Lecky, Susan
Lee, David (Tzeh-Hsian)
Lee, Dora Fugh
Lee, Margaret F
Leesman, Beverly Jean
Leet, Richard (Eugene)
Lerner-Levine, Marion
Lew, Weyman
Lewis, William Arthur
Lewis, William R
Leyva, Alicia
Lhotka, Bonny Pierce
Liles, Catharine (Burns)
Lindenberg, Mary K
Lok, Joan M
Looney, Daniel Stephen
Lopina, Louise Carol
Lord, Carolyn Marie
Lutz, Marjorie Brunhoff
Luz, Virginia
Lyford, Cabot
Lynn, Judith
Lyons, Carol
Maas, Marion Elizabeth
MacBird, Rosemary (Simpson)
MacDougall, Anne
Machiorlete, Patricia Anne
MacKenzie, Hugh Seaforth
MacNeill, Frederick Douglas
Madan-Shotkin, Rhoda
Madden-Work, Betty I
Madura, Jack Joseph
Malone, Patricia Lynn
Manolakas, Stanton Peter
Manter, Margaret C
Mapes, Doris Williamson
Marsh, David Foster
Marshall, Bruce
Martin, Chester Young
Martin, Margaret M
Martino, Nina F
Masih, Lalit K
Massie, Anne Adams Robertson
Masterfield, Maxine
Mathis, Billie Fritz
Matthews, William (Cary)
Mays, Victor
Mazer, Mike
McGrew, Bruce Elwin
McIlvain, Frances H
McKay, Renee
McKie, Todd Stoddard
McLean, Richard
McNamara, William Patrick, Jr
Melikian, Mary
Mellor, Mark Adams
Meyer, Morris Albert
Meyers, Dale (Mrs Mario Cooper)
Michels, Kathryn
Michod, Susan A
Middleman, Raoul Fink
Miezajs, Dainis
Miller, Kathryn
Miller, Ruth Ann
Miotke, Anne E
Miran, Patricia Marie
Mitchell, Dean Lamont
Mitchell, Dianne
Moore, Ina May
Moore, Scott Martin
Morenon, Elise
Morgan, James L
Morrell, Wayne (Beam)
Mortensen, Gordon Louis
Moss, Karen Canner
Moyer, Linda Lee
Muccioli, Anna Maria
Mugar, Martin Gienandt
Murphy, Susan Avis
Murray, Robert (Gray)
Murrell, Carlton D
Nadolski, Stephanie Lucille
Naegle, Montana
Nagano, Paul Tatsumi
Natale, Marie
Nawara, Lucille Procter
Nechis, Barbara
Neff, John A
Neilson, Mary Ann
Nestor, Lula B
Nicholas, Thomas Andrew
Nichols, Edward Edson
Niederer, Carl
Nilsson, Gladys
Nilsson, Katherine Ellen
Nissen, Chris (John Christian Nissen), III
North, Judy K Rafael
Notestine, Dorothy J
Nyren, Edward A
Obuck, John Francis
O'Connell, Ann Brown
O'Dell, Erin (Anne)
O'Hagan, Desmond Brian
Orr, Joseph Charles
Osby, Larissa Geiss
Pachner, William
Parker, Robert Andrew
Paskewitz, Bill, Jr
Patterson, Patricia
Patton, Karen Ann
Paulsen, Brian Oliver
Payne Goodwin, Louis (Doc)
Pedersen, Carolyn H
Pellettieri, Michael Joseph
Pena, Amado Maurilio, Jr
Peppard, Jacqueline Jean
Perlmutter, Linda M
Pershan, Marion
Peters, Diane (Peck)
Petro, Joe, III
Phillis, Marilyn Hughey
Pierce, Ann Trucksess
Pinckney, Stanley
Pirnat-Dressler, Nia
Pisani, Joseph
Plott, Paula Plott Amos
Plummer, Carlton B
Pochmann, Virginia
Ponsot, Claude F
Poslitur, Inga
Potter, (George) Kenneth
Powers, W Alex
Prall, Barbara Jones
Preciado, Pamela
Preslan, Kris
Prewitt, Merle R(ainey)
Prey, Barbara Ernst
Price, Joe (Allen)
Prosia, DeAnn
Puelz, Susan P
Punia, Constance Edith
Rabkin, Leo
Ramanauskas, Dalia Irena
Rathle, Henri (Amin)
Rawlins, Sharon Elizabeth Roane
Reich, Olive B
Reininghaus, Ruth
Reis, Mario
Renk, Merry
Resnick, Don
Rizzolo, Louis (Lou) B M
Robb, Laura Ann
Robbins, Joan Nash
Robinson, Aviva
Robles-Galiano, Estela
Rogers, Muriel I
Roman, Shirley
Rosenfeld, Sharon
Ross, Conrad H
Ross, Joan M
Roth, Richard
Royer, Mona Lee
Rubin, Sandra Mendelsohn
Rudman, Joan (Combs)
Ruehlicke, Cornelia Iris
Ruffing, Anne Elizabeth
Rumford, Ronald Frank
Ruthven, John Aldrich
Rutland, Lilli Ida
Sakson, Robert (G)
Salminen, John Theodore
Salomon, Johanna
Salt, John
Sanders, Joop A
Sandol, Maynard
San Soucie, Patricia Molm
Sarsony, Robert
Savage, Roger
Sawada, Ikune
Sazegar, Morteza
Schwarm, Harold Chambers
Scott, Bill Earl
Seabourn, Connie
Searle, William Ross
Seiden, Arthur
Sexton, Janice Louise
Sheirr, Olga (Krolik)
Sherman, Z Charlotte
Sherwood, Leona
Shores, (James) Franklin
Shubin, Morris Jack
Siamis, Janet Neal
Sideman, Carol K
Sigal-Ibsen, Rose
Simmons, Julie Lutz
Simoneau, Daniel Robert
Sinclair, Robert (W)
Slider, Dorla Dean
Smigocki, Stephen Vincent
Smith, Andrea B
Smith, Donald C
Smith, Rowena Marcus
Sowinski, Stanislaus Joseph
Spencer, Susan Elizabeth
Spicer, Jean (Doris) Uhl
Spink, Frank Henry
Stallwitz, Carolyn
Staub, Carol Anne
Steel, Philip S
Stern, Louise G
Stewart, Dorothy S
Sticker, Robert Edward
Stoddard, Elizabeth Jane
Stone, Don
Stouffer, Daniel Henry, Jr
Sturtz-Davis, Shirley Zampelli
Suba, Susanne (Mrs Bertam Bloch)

PATRON

PHOTOGRAPHER

PHOTOGRAPHER (cont)

Parris, Nina Gumpert
Pascual, Marlo
Patton, Tom
Paul, William D, Jr
Peluso, Marta E
Peress, Gilles
Petracca, Antonio
Petrulis, Alan Joseph
Peven, Michael David
Phillips, Bertrand D
Phillips, Robert J
Pinkel, Sheila Mae
Plossu, Bernard
Plowden, David
Powell, Dan T
Price, Sara J
Prince, Richard
Printz, Bonnie Allen
Pronin, Anatoly
Ranalli, Daniel
Randlett, Mary Willis
Rankaitis, Susan
Ravett, Abraham
Raymond, Lilo
Read, Dave (David) Dolloff
Readman, Sylvie
Reagan, Rourk C
Redmond, Rosemary
Reeves, John Alexander
Reid, Leslie
Renner, Eric
Rentsch, Andreas
Resnick, Marcia
Rexroth, Nancy Louise
Reynolds, Hunter
Rhode, Robin
Richards, Eugene
Rider Berry, Tarah J
Riley, Barbra Bayne
Riss, Murray
Roberts, Mark Dennis
Rodriguez, Geno (Eugene)
Rogers, Art
Rokeach, Barrie
Rose, Roslyn
Rose, Thomas Albert
Rosser, Donna King
Rowland, Adele
Rowland, Anne
Rubello, David Jerome
Rubinfien, Leo H
Rugolo, Lawrence
Rupp, Sheron
Ruscha, Edward Joseph
Rush, Kent Thomas
Russell, Jeff
Sadan, Mark
Sager, Anne
Sahlstrand, James Michael
Sal, Jack
Salinger, Adrienne
Salmon, Margaret
Sanchez, John
Sandman, Jo
Sandrow, Hope
Saretzky, Gary Daniel
Sattler, Jill
Sawyer, Errol Francis
Scanlan, Joe
Schaefer, Robert Arnold, Jr
Scheer, Sherie (Hood)
Schenning, Matthew
Schiff, Melanie
Schneider, Gary
Schnitzer, Klaus A
Schulman, Arlene
Schultz, Michael
Schwartz, Sing-Si
Seawell, Thomas Robert
Seed, Suzanne Liddell
Seguin, Jean-Pierre
Seidl, Claire
Semak, Michael
Sexton, John (William)
Shaffer, Fern
Shambroom, Paul D
Shap, Sylvia
Sharlin, Jonathan
Shay, Art
Sheikh, Fazal
Sheirr, Olga (Krolik)
Sheller, G A
Sherman, Cindy
Shibata, Toshio
Shore, Stephen
Shuler, Thomas H, Jr
Simmons, Laurie
Simon, Amy
Simon, Michael A
Simon, Taryn
Simoneau, Daniel Robert
Simpson, Lorna
Singer, Jonathan M
Sira, Victor
Skoff, Gail Lynn
Skupinski, Bogdan Kazimierz
Sky, Carol Veth
Slaughter, Kwabena
Sligh, Clarissa T
Smith, Allison V
Smith, Dinah Maxwell
Smith, E E
Smith, Keith A
Smith, Luther A
Smith, Michael A
Smith, Raymond Walter
Soth, Alec
Sousa, John Philip
Spira, Bill
Spitz, Barbara S
Staller, Eric P
Stallwitz, Carolyn
Stanich, Nancy Jean
Stark, Robert
Stark, Ron
Stautberg, Ann
Steinman, Barbara
Stella, Harry
Stettner, Louis
Stevens, Jane Alden
Stevens, Jane M
Stone, Jim (James) J
Strassheim, Angela
Strauss, Zoe
Strawn, Martha (A)
Stuart, Nancy
Stuler, Jack
Stummer, Helen M
Subotsky, Mikhael
Suggs, Don
Sugimoto, Hiroshi
Sugiura, Kunie
SuZen, Susan R Rubinstein
Swigart, Lynn S
Tague, Dan
Takahashi, Ginger Brooks
Talley, Dan R
Tan, Noelle
Taylor, Brian David
Taylor, David J
Taylor, Maggie
Thomas, Hank Willis
Thomason, Michael Vincent
Thompson, Jean Danforth
Thompson, Lynn P
Thorne-Thomsen, Ruth T
Tice, George (Andrew)
Tillmans, Wolfgang
Tobia, Blaise Joseph
Torbert, Stephanie Birch
Torn, Jerry (Gerald J)
Toth, Caryl
Tousignant, Serge
Towner, Mark Andrew
Trager, Neil C
Trager, Philip
Traub, Charles H
Tress, Arthur
Truby, Betsy Kirby
Tuckerman, Jane Bayard
Turconi, Sue (Susan) Kinder
Turner, Judith Estelle
Twardowicz, Stanley Jan
Ulrich, Brian
Ulrich, David Alan
VanDelinder, Debra L
Vegara, Camilo Jose
Verene, Chris
Vestal, David
Viditz-Ward, Vera Louise
Vitali, Julius M
von zur Muehlen, Bernis Susan
Von zur Muehlen, Peter
Vos, Claudia
Waksberg, Nomi
Wall, Jeff
Wallenstein, Ellen
Wallin, Lawrence Bier
Walsh, Anne
Wambaugh, Michele
Wang, Sam
Warren, Julianne Bussert Baker
Warren, Tom
Wasow, Oliver
Webb, Alex(ander) (Dwight)
Weems, Carrie Mae
Wegman, William
Weida, Donna Lee
Weiler, Joseph Flack
Weiss, John Joseph
Weissman, Walter
Weller, Paul
Wenger, Jane (B)
Wessel, Henry
Wexler, Jerome LeRoy
Wexler, Peter J
Wheadon, Nico
White, Amos, IV
Widmer, Gwen Ellen
Williams, Christopher
Williams, William Earle
Willmott, Elizabeth Ann
Wilson, Helena Chapellin Wilson
Wilson, Wallace
Winick, Bernyce Alpert
Winokur, Neil
Winterberger, Suzanne
Wise, Kelly
Witkin, Joel-Peter
Xing, Danwen
Yager, David
Yamashiro, Tad
Yamrus, Frank
Yates, Steven A
Yoder, Janica
Yost, Leon C
Young, Barbara
Young, Tom (Thomas) William
Zanisnik, Bryan
Zansky, Michael
Zauft, Richard
Zeitlin, Harry Leon
Zucker, Bob

PRINTMAKER

Abramowicz, Janet
Abularach, Rodolfo Marco
Acebo, Davis Terry
Anderson, Robert Dale
Arvidson, Betsy
Asman, Robert Joseph
Auerbach, Tauba
Avakian, John
Ayres, Julia Spencer
Bachinski, Walter Joseph
Barker, Al C
Barron, Susan
Barsch, Wulf Erich
Bearce, Jeana Dale
Behnken, William Joseph
Bensignor, Paulette (Mrs Philip Steinberg)
Berio, Marina
Bloomfield, Suzanne
Booth, Dot
Bosman, Richard
Bostick, William Allison
Brainard, Barbara
Brannon, Matthew
Brendel, Bettina
Britton, Daniel Robert
Brody, Blanche
Broer, Roger L
Bryan, Sukey
Buhler, Ken
Bumbeck, David
Burdock, Harriet
Burleigh, Kimberly
Bynum, E (Esther Pearl) Anderson
Cabot, Mary A. Booth
Campbell, Naomi
Carter, Mary
Chappell, Kate Cheney
Chesney, Lee R, Jr
Clements, Dawn
Cochran, Dorothy Parcells
Colangelo, Carmon
Colby, Bill
Collins, David
Cottrell, Marsha
Crossgrove, Roger Lynn
Cummins, Maureen
Dacey, Paul
Danziger, Joan
Davison, Bill
Day, Gary Lewis
De Boschnek, Chris (Christian) Charles
de Gogorza, Patricia (Gahagan)
Dennis, Donna Frances
Dentz, Shoshana
De Vore, Sadie Davidson
DiBenedetto, Steve
Di Cosola, Lois Bock
Dowell, John E, Jr
Drum, Sydney Maria
Durr, Pat (Patricia) (Beth)
Ecker, Robert Rodgers
Eder, James Alvin
Elloian, Peter
Elyashiv, Yizhak
Ensrud, Wayne
Ettenberg, Franklin Joseph
Faden, Lawrence Steven
Fagan, Alanna
Fairey, Shepard
Fantazos, Henryk Michael
Farrell, Patrick
FeBland, Harriet
Feinstein, Rochelle H
Fidler, Spencer D
Firestein, Cecily Barth
Flexner, Roland
Fohr, Jenny
Folman, Liza
Frances, (Sherana) Harriette
Frank, Helen Goodzeit
Frederick, Helen C
Frugé-Brown, Kathleen
Ganesh, Chitra
Gill, Bryan Nash
Gillespie, Oscar Jay
Goldston, Bill
Gordley, Marilyn Classe
Graving, Brandon
Grupp, Carl Alf
Gyatso, Gonkar
Haack, Cynthia R
Hackett, Theresa
Hara, Keiko
Hari, Kenneth
Harris, Conley
Haseltine, James Lewis
Hershey, Nona
Heyman, Daniel
Hillis, Richard K
Hodgkin, Carter
Holbrook, Peter Greene

PRINTMAKER (cont)

Hussong, Randy
Hwang, Kay
Iglesias, Lisa
Jackson, Suzanne
Jacquette, Yvonne Helene
Jannetti, Tony
Jewell, Joyce
Jilg, Michael Florian
Johnston, Ynez
Jones, Allen Christopher
Jones, Frederick
Kalina, Richard
Katz, Cima
Kiland, Lance Edward
Kiley, Katie
Kinkade, Catherine
Klein, Sabina
Knedler, Cory
Knight, William
Knippers, Edward
Kornblum, Myrtle
Krieger, Ruth M
Kronzon, Ziva
La Duke, Betty
Lane, Miharu
Lane, Rosemary Louise
La Porta, Elayne B
Lathan-Stiefel, Caroline
Lau, Rex
Lawson, James Emmett
Lea, Stanley E
Leary, Daniel
Leggett, Ann Vaughan
Leitao, Catarina
Letendre, Rita
Liao, Shiou-Ping
Lieberman, Meyer Frank
Limont, Naomi Charles
Little, James
Litwin, Ruth Forbes
Luce, C(harles) Beardsley
Mac Innes, David Harold
Magnotta, Frank
Mari, M
Markowitz, Marilyn
Martin, Dianne L
Marx, Robert Ernst
McDonald, Susan Strong
McGinnis, Christine
McGloughlin, Kate
Mesibov, Hugh
Mitty, Lizbeth J
Morper, Daniel
Morse, Marcia Roberts
Moy, Seong
Moya, Robert
Mullen, James Martin
Murakami, Takashi
Nichols, Francis N, II
Nugent, Bob L
O'Connell, Ann Brown
Oda, Mayumi
Olshan, Bernard
Ortega, Tony (Anthony) David
Osterburg, Lothar
Pachter, Charles
Paschall, Jo Anne
Patterson, Dane
Perez, Enoc
Pheobus, Alyssa
Piskoti, James
Pletka, Paul
Plevin, Gloria Rosenthal
Porges, Maria Franziska
Potrc, Marjetica
Potter, (George) Kenneth
Pyzow, Susan Victoria
Quiller, Stephen Frederick
Quinlan, Eileen
Rackus, George (Keistus)
Raftery, Andrew Stein
Raviv, Ilana
Rawlins, Sharon Elizabeth Roane
Revitzky, Dennis L
Rhodes, Curtis A
Richards, Bruce Michael
Richards, Rosalyn A
Riley, Sarah A
Ritchie, Charles Morton, Jr
Roosevelt, Michael Armentrout
Roseman, Susan Carol
Rubio, Alex
Rugolo, Lawrence
Rush, John
Rush, Kent Thomas
Sampson, Frank
Sangram, Majumdar
Schiff, Molly Jeanette
Schrero, Ruth Lieberman
Seabourn, Bert Dail
Segal, Mary
Seltzer, Joanne Lynn
Semowich, Charles John
Sencial, Gabriel Jaime
Sexauer, Donald Richard
Shaffer, Richard
Shaw, John Palmer
Shives, Arnold Edward
Shukman, Solomon
Singer, Alan Daniel
Skupinski, Bogdan Kazimierz
Smolarek, Waldemar
Soave, Sergio
Softic, Tanja
Sommer, Susan
Sorman, Steven
Spandorfer, Merle Sue
Squires, Gerald Leopold
Stamaty, Clara Gee Kastner
Stanbridge, Harry Andrew
Stern, Louise G
Stevens, Elisabeth Goss
Strunck, Juergen
Sweet, Mary (French)
Takagi, Mayumi
Tanksley, Ann
Targan, Judy
Teichman, Mary Melinda
Thrall, Arthur
Toney, Anita Karen
Toulis, Vasilios (Apostolos)
Trombetta, Annamarie
Tullis, Garner H
Turner, Alan
Vena, Dante
Vine, Marlene
Walters, Ernest
Wasserman, Burton
Watson, Mary Anne
Wells, Charles
Wharton, David W
White, B J (Beverly)
Wisneski, Kurt
Wolpert, Etta
Wortzel, Adrianne
Xu, Bing
Younger, Dan Forrest
Yust, David E

All Media

Achepohl, Keith Anden
Adler, Myril
Aho, Paul Richard
Alicea, Jose
Amos, Emma
Appelson, Herbert J
Arai, Tomie
Asher, Lila Oliver
Askin, Walter Miller
Atkinson, Conrad
Barber, Philip Judd
Barooshian, Martin
Barth, Charles John
Bauer, Betsy (Elizabeth)
Baxter, Bonnie Jean
Beall, Dennis Ray
Beallor, Fran
Beltran, Felix
Berg, Michael R
Bertine, Dorothy W
Bilder, Dorothea A
Bills, Mitchell
Bleach, Bruce R
Borg, Joseph
Boutis, Tom
Boyd, Lakin
Brodsky, Judith Kapstein
Brooks, Wendell T
Bujnowski, Joel A
Calman, W(endy) L
Camarata, Martin L
Campbell, Richard Horton
Cardillo, Rimer Angel
Carson, Sol Kent
Carter, Patricia
Cassara, Frank
Castrillo, Rebecca
Caswell, Sally (Caswell-Linhares)
Chafetz, Sidney
Chappell, Berkley Warner
Chase, Jeanne Norman
Chernow, Ann
Chesney, Lee Roy, III
Childers, Malcolm Graeme
Christensen, Val Alan
Cimbalo, Robert W
Cottingham, Robert
Coughlin, Jack
Courtney, Suzan
Cowin, Jack Lee
Crispo, Dick
Criswell, Warren
Crouse, Michael Glenn
Cunningham, E C (Eldon) Lloyd
Dallmann, Daniel Forbes
D'Amico, Larry
Davila, Maritza
Davis, Ronald
de Lama, Alberto
Delgyer, Leslie
Dickson, Mark Amos
Doner, Michele Oka
Dorfman, Elissa
Drake, James
DuBack, Charles S
Duffy, Michael John
Duncan, Richard (Hurley)
Epstein, Yale
Epting, Marion Austin
Erenberg, Samuel Joseph
Evaul, William H, Jr
Fairfield, Richard Thomas
Feld, Augusta
Feldman, Franklin
Feldman, Walter (Sidney)
Felter, June Marie
Ferguson, Max
Field, Philip Sidney
Finch, Richard Dean
Fine, Ruth E
Fishman, Barbara (Ellen) Schwartz
Fitzgerald, Joe
Fornas, Leander
Fox, Carson
Francis, Madison Ke, Jr
Freed, David
Freimark, Bob (Robert)
Fricano, Tom S
Gaines, Alan Jay
Geniusz, Robert Myles
Ginzel, Roland
Giovanni
Greaver, Hanne
Greenbaum, Marty
Grillo, John
Gunn, Ellen
Guzak, Karen W
Hammerman, Pat Jo
Harmon, Paul
Hester, Nathaniel Christopher
Hibel, Edna
Hodes, Suzanne
Hooper, Jack Meredith
Hormuth, Jo
Ida, Shoichi
Jacklin, Bill (William)
Jackson, Herb
Jacobs, Jim
Jerviss, Joy
Johanson, George E
Jones, James Edward
Kamm, David Robert
Kaplan, Sandra
Karn, Gloria Stoll
Kaulitz, Garry Charles
Kennon, Robert Brian
Kipniss, Robert
Komar and Melamid
Koopalethes, Olivia Alberts
Kowalke, Ronald Leroy
Kozo
Krug, Harry Elno
Lahtinen, Silja (Liisa) Talikka
Lang, J T
Lansdon, Gay Brandt
La Pierre, Thomas
La Plant, Mimi
Lasansky, Leonardo
LeBey, Barbara
Leiber, Gerson August
Levin, Morton D
Lichaw, Pessia
Longo, Vincent
Loring, John
Lyons, Beauvais
Maidoff, Jules
Majeski, Thomas H
Malone, Robert R
Maltzman, Stanley
Martin, Doris-Marie Constable
Mauro, Robert F
McGough, Charles E
McLean, James Albert
McSheehy, Cornelia Marie
Meisel, Susan Pear
Melton, Terry R
Menses, Jan
Merida, Frederick A
Miller, Daniel Dawson
Mills, Agnes
Mills, Lev Timothy
Miyamoto, Wayne Akira
Morrow, Terry
Muranaka, Hideo
Nakazato, Hitoshi
Nama, George Allen
Nawrocki, Thomas Dennis
Newman, Libby
Nuchi, Natan
Obler, Geri
Olynyk, Patricia J
Ondish, Andrea
Osborn, Kevin Russell
Osborne, Cynthia A
Paone, Peter
Parra, Carmen
Parsons, Cynthia Massey
Paul, Ken (Hugh)
Pellettieri, Michael Joseph
Pergola, Linnea
Pogany, Miklos
Ponce de Leon, Michael
Powelson, Rosemary A
Pozzatti, Rudy O
Pozzi, Lucio
Price, Rita F
Rafferty, Andrew
Ragland, Jack Whitney
Rakovan, Lawrence Francis
Redd, Richard James
Red Star, Kevin (Running Rabbit)
Ries, Martin
Riess, Lore
Ritchie, William (Bill) H, Jr
Roberts, Donald
Romano, Clare
Ross, John T
Rotholz, Rina
Ruffo, Joseph Martin

PRINTMAKER (cont)

Debonne, Jeannette
De Guzman, Evelyn Lopez
Dennett, Lissy W
Edell, Nancy
Edmunds, Allan Logan
Esaki, Yasuhiro
Fitzgerald, Betty Jo
FitzSimonds, Carol Strause
Flanery, Gail
Forsythe, Donald John
Fuerst, Shirley Miller
Furr, Jim
Gagan, Jamie L.
Gaucher, Yves
Gaudieri, Alexander V J
Geller, Esther Geller Shapero
Gold, Leah
Gregory-Goodrum, Ellna Kay
Gross, Marilyn A
Gurlik, Philip John
Halbrooks, Darryl Wayne
Hamlin, Louise
Harjo, Benjamin, Jr
Hausrath, Joan W
Hendershot, J L
Hildebrand, June Marianne
Hildreth, Joseph Alan
Hoare, Tyler James
Hoffman, Eric
Hushlak, Gerald
Johnson, Barbara Louise
Johnson, Lois Marlene
Jones, Theodore Joseph
Kanter, Lorna J
Kaplan, Stanley
Kravjansky, Mikulas
Kriegstein, Zara
Leaf, Ruth
Lindroth, Linda
Lisk, Penelope E Tsaltas
Loving, Richard Maris
Lyons, Carol
Mandelbaum, Lyn
Marshall, James Duard
Mastrangelo, Bobbi
Matyas, Diane C
Maughelli, Mary L
McCue, Harry
Mehn, Jan (Jan Von der Golz)
Mendelson, Haim
Miller, Elaine Sandra
Moore, Pamela A
Munoz, Rie
Nadolski, Stephanie Lucille
Narotzky, Norman David
Neal, (Minor) Avon
Newberg, Deborah
Oxman, Katja
Parisi, Martha
Passuntino, Peter Zaccaria
Paulos, Daniel Thomas
Peruo, Marsha
Pierce, Constance Laundon
Pitts, Richard G
Prado-Arai, Namiko
Price, Helen Burdon
Reddy, Krishna N
Rizzi, James
Robbins, Michael Jed
Rogers, P J
Roman, Shirley
Rood, Kay
Ross, Joan Stuart
Rowan, Dennis Michael
Ruby, Laura
Rumford, Ronald Frank
Ruyle, Lydia Miller
Sahlstrand, Margaret Ahrens
Salinas, Baruj
Sarsony, Robert
Savenor, Betty Carmell
Schreiber, Eileen Sher
Scott, Campbell
Seltzer, Phyllis
Shotwell, Kenneth E
Spagnolo, Kathleen Mary
Stegman, Patricia
Steinhoff, Monika
Stoltenberg, Donald Hugo
Sullivan, Anne Dorothy Hevner
Swartzman, Roslyn
Sznajderman, Marius S
Valdez Gonzalez, Julio E
Valincius, Irene
Van Suchtelen, Adrian
Van Vliet, Claire
Vernon, Karen
Warner, Herbert Kelii, Jr
Weingarten, Hilde (Kevess)
Woolschlager, Laura Totten
Yager, David
Youkeles, Anne
Youngblood, Judy
Zirker, Joseph

Serigraphy, Silkscreen

Akins, Future Rene
Anderson, William Thomas
Angeloch, Robert
Baker, Cornelia Draves
Barnett, Helmut
Bartek, Tom
Berlyn, Sheldon
Campbell, Nancy B
Carvalho, Josely
Christ-Janer, Arland F
Coover, Doris Gwendolyn
Curran, Darryl Joseph
Davidek, Stefan
De Wan-Carlson, Anna
Duff, Ann MacIntosh
Eastcott, R. Wayne
Faegenburg, Bernice K
Fitzgerald, Astrid
Fumagalli, Barbara Merrill
Gill, Gene
Ginsburg, Estelle
Giorno, John
Goldberg, Arnold Herbert
Gradus, Ari
Green, Jonathan
Hallenbeck, Pomona Juanita
Hanna, Paul Dean, Jr
Harvey, Donald
Hernandez, Ester
High, Timothy Griffin
Huff, Laura Weaver
Igo, Peter Alexander
Kassoy, Hortense
Kaye, Mildred Elaine
Kimura, Riisaburo
Kirsten-Daiensai, Richard Charles
Klein, Beatrice (T)
Knowles, Alison
Kohl-Spiro, Barbara
Kozo
Kreneck, Lynwood
Lummus, Carol Travers
Maki, Sheila A
Massie, Lorna
McCall, Ann
McDuff, Fredrick H
McElroy, Jacquelyn Ann
McKnight, Thomas Frederick
Meader, Jonathan (Ascian)
Merkl, Elissa Frances
Moon, Jim (James) Monroe
Moore, Wayland D
Nind, Jean
Noda, Masaaki
Ocepek, Lou (Louis) David
Peterson, Gwen Entz
Petro, Joe, III
Phillips, Harriet E
Pletscher, Josephine Marie
Poleskie, Stephen Francis
Price, Joe (Allen)
Richards, Sabra
Robbins, Hulda D
Roberts, Steven K
Sassone, Marco
Schenck, William Clinton
Schurr, Jerry M
Schwieger, C Robert
Stewart, Norman
Stovall, Luther McKinley
Sullivan, David Francis
Tabor, Virginia S
Vaux, Richard
Wong, Lucille (Lucila) Guerra Wong

Woodcut

Abany, Albert Charles
Abbe, Elfriede Martha
Arnold, Paul Beaver
Barber, Cynthia
Bettinson, Brenda
Bigelow, Anita (Anne) (Edwige Lourie)
Brickner, Alice
Brody, Arthur William
Carter, (Charles) Bruce
Casida, Kati
Conner, Ann
Covey, Rosemary Feit
Currie, Bruce
Dallas, Dorothy B
Dance, Robert Bartlett
Davison, Nancy R
Domjan, Evelyn
Enright, Judy A
Feldman, Aline M
Feldman, Joel Benet
Gary, Jan (Mrs William D Gorman)
Hansalik, Konrad F
Hedman, Teri Jo
Herman, Roger
Jaidinger, Judith Clarann Szesko
Kapheim, Thom
Kermes, Constantine John
Koster, Marjory Jean
Kunc, Karen
Lincoln, Jane Lockwood
Malo, Teri (A)
Matsubara, Naoko
McNamara, William Patrick, Jr
Mogensen, Paul
Mortensen, Gordon Louis
Mosenthal, Charlotte (Dembo)
Nesbitt, Ilse Buchert
Noble, Helen (Harper)
Peace, Bernie Kinzel
Quackenbush, Robert
Rowan, Frances Physioc
Sadle, Amy Ann Brandon
Sawai, Noboru
Skelley, Robert Charles
Stinnett, Hester A
Summers, Carol
Tesfagiorgis, Freida
Trueblood, Emily Herrick
Vo-Dinh, Mai
Walters, Sylvia Solochek
Washmon, Gary Brent
Watia, Tarmo
Whitman, Karen
Williams, Idaherma

PUBLISHER

Alexander, Edmund Brooke
Arnold, Jack
Banks, Robert Harris
Blake, Jane Salley
Bratcher, Collen Dale
Cawley, Joan Mae
Czestochowski, Joseph S
Esterow, Milton
Feinman, Stephen E
Gladstone, M J
Goad, Anne Laine
Haatoum Hamady, Walter Samuel
Hackett, Dwight Vernon
Heiferman, Marvin
Hobbs, Gerald S
Johnson, Douglas Walter
King, Brian Jeffrey
King, Vikki Killough Vranich
Levin, Hugh Lauter
London, Alexander
Lupper, Edward
Mahlmann, John James
Maret, Russell
McGilvery, Laurence
McPherson, Bruce Rice
Navaretta, Cynthia
Neal, (Minor) Avon
Paternosto, Cesar Pedro
Perez-Zapata, Guilloume
Persky, Robert S
Posner, Judith L
Rosenberg, Bernard
Sadle, Amy Ann Brandon
Seckel, Cornelia
Smith, Michael A
Solomon, Richard H
Stewart, Norman
Szoke, John
Takayama, Martha Tepper
Torf, Lois Beurman
Tustian, Brenda Harris
Westlund, Harry E
Wyrick, Charles Lloyd, Jr
Zabel, Cynthia

RESTORER

See also **Conservator**

Callari, Emily Dolores
Fisher, Sarah Lisbeth
Flynn, John (Kevin)
Frankford, Shawna
Grassi, Marco
Gurbacs, John Joseph
Knowlton, Daniel Gibson
Levenson, Rustin S
Lysun, Gregory
Moore, Sabra
Pravda, Muriel
Richard, Jack
Simmons, Julie Lutz
Squadra, John
Zarand, Julius John

SCULPTOR

Abou-Issa, Issa
Adams, Phoebe
Adickes, David (Pryor)
Agee, Ann G
Ahearn, John
Ahrens, Hanno D
Aksel, Erdag
Alexander, Peter
Allen, Bruce Wayne
Allen, E Douglas
Amado, Jesse V
Amato, Michele (Micaela)
Ambe, Noriko
Anderson, Troy
Andreason, Lee
Andrews, Charleen Kohl
Angell, Tony
Anker, Suzanne C
Annis, Norman L
Antoni, Janine
Applebaum, Leon
Aquino, Edmundo
Arakawa, Ei
Araluce, Rick
Ariss, Margot Joan Phillips
Armajani, Siah
Ascalon, David
Ashkin, Michael
Averbuch, Ilan
Bachner, Barbara L
Bailey, Clayton George

SCULPTOR (cont)

SCULPTOR (cont)
Drumm, Don
Dunn, Amanda Gordon
Durham, William
Duval Carrie, Edouard
Dwyer, Nancy
Echelman, Janet
Edge, Douglas Benjamin
Eisner, Gail Leon
Elder, David Morton
Emery, Lin
Escalet, Frank Diaz
Ettl, Georg
Faust, James Wille
Favro, Murray
Felguerez, Manuel
Felker, David Larry
Fernie, John Chipman
Ferrara, Jackie
Fine, Jud
Finkelstein, Max
Fischer, John
Floyd, Carl Leo
Ford, John
Foreman, Laura
Fox, Carson
Fox, Terry Alan
Francis, Madison Ke, Jr
Frank, Mary
Fraughton, Edward James
Friedman, Alan
Gallo, Enzo D
Gallo, Frank
Gates, Harry Irving
Gaylord, Frank Chalfant, II
Gebhardt, Roland
Geller, Matthew
Geran, Joseph, Jr
Gialanella, Donald G
Giampietro, Isabel Antonia
Gianakos, Cris
Gilmor, Jane E
Gitlin, Michael
Gorbaty, Norman
Goreniuc, Mircea C Paul
Gray, Jim
Gresser, Seymour Gerald
Grey, Alex V
Griffin, Chris A
Grillo, Esther Angela
Grom, Bogdan
Grossman, Nancy
Grosvenor, Robert
Haacke, Hans Christoph
Haber, Ira Joel
Hamilton, Juan
Hansen, James Lee
Haozous, Bob
Harries, Mags (Margaret) L
Harrison, Jan
Harvey, Andre
Heizer, Michael
Helder, David Ernest
Hendricks, Edward Lee
Hepper, Carol
Hera
Herard, Marvin T
Heric, John F
Hernandez, Sam
Hewitt, Duncan Adams
Hogbin, Stephen
Holen, Norman Dean
Hom, Mei-ling
Hormuth, Jo
Hoy, Harold H
Hudson, Robert H
Hughes, Síocháin I
Hunter, Leonard LeGrande, III
Hurtig, Martin Russell
Hyams, Harriet
Irwin, Robert
Italiano, Joan
Jacquard, Jerald (Wayne)
Jellico, Nancy R
Jensen, Leo
Johnston, Randy James
Jones, Ben
Jones, Carter R, Jr
Jordan, John L
Kaiser, Benjamin
Kaish, Luise
Kallenberger, Kreg
Kang, Ik-Joong
Kaplan, Muriel S
Kassoy, Hortense
Kaufman, Mico
Kelley, Donald William
Kelly, Ellsworth
Kennedy, James Edward
Keough, Jeffrey
Kessler, Alan
King, Ray
King, William
Kirk, Jerome
Kleiman, Alan
Koch, Edwin E
Koss, Gene H
Kostabi, Mark
Kramer, Louise
Kravitz, Walter
Kreznar, Richard J
Krieger, Florence
Kunce, Samm
Kurhajec, Joseph A
Kusama, Yayoi
Lafon, Dee J
Lamarre, Paul
Lamb, Darlis Carol
Langager, Craig T
LaPlantz, David
Laramee, Eve Andree
Larsen, Patrick Heffner
Lawton, James L
Leeson, Tom
LeRoy, Hugh Alexander
Leshyk, Tonie
Levin, Carol Gellner
Levin, Robert Alan
Levine, Erik
Levine, Les
Lewis, Joseph S, III
Lieberman, Louis (Karl)
Liebowitz, Janet
Lijn, Liliane
Liles, Raeford Bailey
Linn, Steven Allen
Lintault, Roger Paul
Little, Ken Dawson
Liz-N-Val
Lobello, Peter
Loeser, Thomas
London, Naomi
Lorelli, Elvira Mae
Lucchesi, Bruno
Lyford, Cabot
Lyon, Robert F
Madsen, Loren Wakefield
Magnan, Oscar Gustav
Magno, Liz
Maki, Robert Richard
Maler, M Leopoldo Mario
Mallory, Ronald
Manera, Enrico Orlando
Mansfield, Robert Adams
Marioni, Paul
Marisol
Markle, Sam
Martin, Knox
Matteson, Ira
Matthews, Harriett
McCormick, Pam(ela) Ann
McCracken, Philip
McCullough, David William
McDaniel, William Harrison (Harry)
McDonnell, Joseph Anthony
McGowin, Ed (William Edward)
McManus, James William
Michaux, Henry Gaston
Miller, Daniel Dawson
Milloff, Mark David
Mills, Agnes
Milonas, Minos (Herodotos Milonas)
Mintich, Mary Ringelberg
Molinari, Guido
Monaghan, William Scott
Monk, Nancy
Moquin, Richard Attilio
Morrel, Owen
Moss, Joe (Francis)
Murphy, Hass
Murray, Ian Stewart
Murrill, Gwynn
Myers, Martin
Nardin, Mario
Nasisse, Andy S
Newman, John
Newman, Mari Alice Mae
Newman, Mary Alice Mae
Newsome, Rashaad Germain
Nix, Patricia (Lea)
Nordin, Phyllis E
Norgard, Karen-Sam
Ocvirk, Otto G
Padovano, Anthony John
Paine, Roxy
Parton, Ralf
Pas, Gerard Peter
Patterson, Clayton Ian
Pearson, James Eugene
Peck, Judith
Pekar, Ronald Walter
Peters, John D
Pethick, Jerry Thomas Bern
Pfaffman, William Scott
Phillips, Ellen T
Phillips, Michael
Pierce, Danny P
Pitynski, Andrzej P
Pondick, Rona
Post, Anne B
Prince, Richard Edmund
Pruitt, Lynn
Puryear, Martin
Quinn, Brian Grant
Quisgard, Liz Whitney
Rabinowitch, Royden Leslie
Raimondi, John
Rector, Marge (Lee)
Reiss, Roland
Remsing, Joseph Gary
Renee, Lisabeth
Ritchey, Rik
Roberts, Steven K
Robins, Joyce
Robinson, Aminah Brenda Lynn
Rogers, John H
Romans, Van Anthony
Ross, Charles
Roster, Fred Howard
Roux, Barbara Agnes
Ruby, Laura
Rust, Edwin C
Saar, Alison M
Saftel, Andrew P
St Maur, Kirk
Sakaoka, Yasue
Samuels (Joesam), Joe
Saxe, Henry, OC
Sayre, Roger L
Schaefer, Gail
Schmutzhart, Berthold Josef
Schneider, Kenny
Schultz, Saunders
Sebastian, Jill C
Sebelius, Helen
Segall-Marx, Madeleine (Maddy Marx)
Seplowin, Charles Joseph
Serra, Richard
Serra, Rudy
Shah, Ela
Shaw, Richard Blake
Sherbell, Rhoda
Sherrill, Milton Louis
Siler, Todd (Lael)
Simkin, Phillips M
Skurkis, Barry A
Sloan, Jennifer
Smith, Lawson Wentworth
Smith, Mimi
Sniffen, Frances
Sokov, Leonid
Sonnenberg, Frances
Soreff, Stephen
Sottung, George (K)
Spinka, William J
Squier, Jack Leslie
Stelzer, Michael Norman
Sterritt, Coleen
Stevanov, Zoran
Straight, Elsie H
Strawn, Melvin Nicholas
Sturman, Eugene
Sunderland, Nita Kathleen
Sussman, Gary Lawrence
Suzuki, Taro
Svenson, John Edward
Szold, Lauren G
Tayou, Pascale Marthine
Tinsley, Barry
Tobias, Robert Paul
Tolpo, Vincent Carl
Torres, Frances
Trakas, George
Trakis, Louis
Treister, Kenneth
Tsai, Hsiao Hsia
Urso, Leonard A
Vaillancourt, Armand
Valentine, DeWain
Vallance, Jeffrey K R
VanderWeg, Phillip Dale
Van Sant, Tom R
Van Winkle, Lester G
Villinski, Paul S
Visco, Anthony Salvatore
Volkersz, Willem
Wahling, Jon B
Walker II, Herbert Brooks
Walsh, Nan
Wanlass, Stanley Glen
Wasko-Flood, Sandra Jean
Weil, Marianne
Weiner, Lawrence Charles
Weiss, Clemens
Weyhe, Arthur
Wheelwright, Joseph Storer
Whiten, Tim (Timothy) Grover
Whittome, Irene F
Williams, Todd
Willis, Jay Stewart
Willmott, Elizabeth Ann
Wilson, Douglas Fenn
Winsor, Jackie
Witold, Kaczanowski
Woodham, Derrick James
Woody, (Thomas) Howard
Worth, Karen
Yanish, Elizabeth Shwayder
Yedidsion, Meira
Yes, Phyllis A
Yuen, Kee-ho
Zack, Badanna Bernice
Zahourek, Jon Gail
Zelenak, Edward J
Zimmerman, Elyn
Zito, Joseph (Phillip)
Zittel, Andrea
Zlatkoff, Charles

Clay
Adour, Colleen
Breen, Harry Frederick, Jr
Breschi, Karen Lee
Bronson, Clark Everice
Bryant, Olen L
Bugbee-Jackson, Joan (Mrs John M Jackson)
Buonagurio, Toby Lee
Butterly, Kathy

SCULPTOR (cont)
Caswell, Jim (James) Daniel Caswell-Davis
Chappelle, Jerry Leon
Chatterley, Mark D
Chavez, Joseph Arnold
Citron, Harvey Lewis
Cornell, David E
Costanza, John Joseph
Culbreth, Carl R
Dabbert, Patricia Ann
Dalglish, Meredith Rennels
De Castro, Lorraine
Dennett, Lissy W
Devereux, Mara
Donhauser, Paul Stefan
Dyyon, Mario
Eardley, Cynthia
Everhart, Don, II
Fafard, Joe (Joseph) Yvon
Fellows, Fred
Ferreira, Armando Thomas
Fleming, Frank
Fondaw, Ron
Fox, Judy (Judith) C
Funk, Verne J
Furman, David Stephen
Gaylord, Frank Chalfant, II
Genute, Christine Termini
Gerich, Betty A.
Gernhardt, Henry Kendall
Gilhooly, David James, III
Gill, John P
Girard, Bill
Glover, Robert
Goldfine, Beatrice
Grabel, Susan
Gray, Elise Norris
Grygutis, Barbara
Hammond, Phyllis Baker
Hanson, JB
Havens, Jan
Hay, Dick
Heginbotham, Jan Sturza
Higby, (Donald) Wayne
Huntoon, Abby E
Jimerson, Annette Princess
Jones, Michael Butler
Jonsson, Ted (Wilbur)
Kaufman, Loretta Ana
Keller, Rhoda
Kochman, Alexandra D
Kwong, Eva
Larsen, D Dane
Lay, Patricia Anne
Lebejoara, Ovidiu
Lee, Dora Fugh
Lewis, Carole
Lighton, Linda
London, Anna
Lord, Andrew
Luisi, Jerry
MacClintock, Dorcas
MacDougall, Peter Steven
Magel, Catharine Anne
Maior, Philip
Mann, Jean (Adah)
Mason, John
Mayer, Billy (William) Robert Mayer
Mayeri, Beverly
McGlynn, Mary Aspinwall
McRoberts, Sheryl Ann
Melchert, James Frederick
Mignosa, Santo
Milnes, Robert Winston
Moonelis, Judith C
Muir, Emily Lansingh
Muñoz, Paloma
Nicholas, Donna Lee
Nieto, John W
Notkin, Richard T
Olson, Linda A
Pendergrass, Christine C
Penny, Donald Charles
Perry, Lincoln Frederick
Prange, Sally Bowen
Rady, Elsa
Raskind, Philis
Rasmussen, Robert (Redd Ekks) Norman
Reinertson, Lisa
Rippon, Ruth Margaret
Rosenblatt, Adolph
Rosenfeld, Sarena
Rush, Andrew
Scala, Joseph A
Schietinger, James Frederick
Schlanger, Jeff
Scott, B Nibbelink (Barbara Gae Scott)
Selvin, Nancy
Sexton, Janice Louise
Shannonhouse, Sandra
Sherman, Sarai
Smith, Gary
Spinosa, Gary Paul
Spinski, Victor
Stewart, Bill
Strassberg, Roy I
Strawn, Bernice I
Strong, Leslie (Sutter)
Swanson, J N
Swetcharnik, Sara Morris
Taylor, Rosemary
Thomas, Cheryl Ann
Tornheim, Norman
Townsend, Storm D
Turlington, Patricia R
Unterseher, Chris Christian
Vanden Berge, Peter Willem
Wilmeth, Ernest, II
Wilson, Melissa Anne
Wood, Robert L
Young, Robert S W
Youngblood, Daisy
Zakin, Mikhail

Metal, Cast
Adams, Alice
Adelman, Bunny
Agid, Lucy Bradanovic
Amaya, Armando
Arnett, Joe Anna
Baker, Blanche
Ball, Ken Weston
Bannister, Pati (Patricia) Brown Bannister
Barnett, Cheryl L
Barrett, Bill
Beasley, Bruce
Beckner, Joy Kroeger
Blum, Helaine Dorothy
Boepple, Willard
Booth, Michael Gayle
Born, James E
Breitenbach, William John
Bronson, Clark Everice
Brookner, Jackie
Bruskin, Grisha
Burns, Stan
Carlson, George Arthur
Casida, Kati
Chase-Riboud, Barbara
Chemeche, George
Citron, Harvey Lewis
Copenhaver-Fellows, Deborah Lynne Fellows
Coughlin, Jack
Daly, Stephen Jeffrey
Dani
DeMartis, James Michael
Dhaemers, Robert August
DiPasquale, Paul Albert
Dorrien, Carlos Guillermo
Downs, Douglas Walker
Eardley, Cynthia
Engler, Kathleen Girdler
Eriksen, Gary
Ferrari, Virginio Luigi
Ferrell, Catherine (Klemann)
Fix, John Robert
Fleming, Frank
Fox, Lincoln H
Freeland, Bill
Frudakis, Anthony P
Fuhrman, Esther
Gibbs, Tom
Girard, Bill
Glasser, Norma Penchansky
Glasson, Lloyd
Goldberg, Norma
Goodacre, Glenna
Gore, Samuel Marshall
Greenamyer, George Mossman
Greer, John Sydney
Greeves, R V (Richard Vernon)
Gurevich, Grigory
Halahmy, Oded
Hampton, John Wade
Hansen, James Lee
Hansen, Robert
Harrington, Chestee Marie
Harris, Paul
Harrison, Carole
Harvey, Andre
Hastings, Jack Byron
Heginbotham, Jan Sturza
Hitchcock, Howard Gilbert
Hostetler, David L
Huntington, Jim
Jeynes, Paul
Johnston, Barry Woods
Kaskey, Raymond John
Kavanagh, Cornelia Kubler
Kepalas
Kimmelman, Harold
Koenig, Elizabeth
La Malfa, James Thomas
Langland, Tuck
Lekberg, Barbara
Lewis, Carole
Lindsay, Arturo
Linn, Steven Allen
Ludtke, Lawrence Monroe
Lundeen, George Wayne
Maior, Philip
Marsh, Thomas A
Martin, Bill
Mavroudis, Demetrios
Medenica, Branko
Mellon, Marc Richard
Meyer, Seymour W
Morcos, Maher N
Morin, Thomas Edward
Moyers, William
Muccioli, Anna Maria
Myford, James C
Nama, George Allen
Naranjo, Michael Alfred
Neri, Manuel
Newmark, Marilyn
Nuss, Joanne Ruth
Olson, Gene Russell
Orduno, Robert Daniel
Otterness, Tom
Oxman, Mark
Palumbo, Jacques
Paterson, Anthony R
Piet, John Frances
Pinsker, Essie
Porta, Siena Gillann
Prip, Janet
Recanati, Dina
Richter, Hank
Rubin, Donald Vincent
Sabo, Betty Jean
Sander, Sherry Salari
Saylors, Jo An
Schmidt, Julius
Schon, Nancy Quint
Schwebel, Renata Manasse
Scott, Sandy (Sandra) Lynn
Shapiro, Joel Elias
Shaw, Isabel
Sheppard, Joseph Sherly
Silvertooth, Dennis Carl
Slavin, Arlene
Snidow, Gordon E
Snyder, Ruth (Cozen)
Speed, (Ulysses) Grant
Strawn, Bernice I
Stubbs, Lu
Swergold, Marcelle M
Talaba, L (Linda) Talaba Cummens
Tamburine, Jean Helen
Tempest, Gerard Francis
Torcoletti, Enzo
Toscano, Dolores A
Trueblood, L'Deane
Tye, William Roy
Ullberg, Kent
Valdez, Vincent E
Ventimiglia, John Thomas
Vielehr, Bill
Wagoner, Robert B
Wardlaw, George Melvin
Webster, Meg
Weil, Marianne
Weimer, Dawn
Weisman, Gary Michael
Wertheimer, Esther
White, Bruce Hilding
Wilcox, Leslie
Williams, Chester Lee
Williford, Hollis R
Wilson, Melissa Anne
Wyatt, Greg Alan
Yaros, Constance G
Zaikine, Victor (Zak) Eugene
Zajac, Jack
Zivic, William Thomas
Zucker, Murray Harvey

Metal, Precious
Anderson, Bruce A
Boggs, Mayo Mac
De Guatemala, Joyce Bush Vourvoulias
Dial, Gail
Fuhrman, Esther
Handler, Audrey
Harvey, Andre
Herschler, David Elijah
Kavanagh, Cornelia Kubler
Lacktman, Michael
Manhold, John Henry
Manship, John Paul
Marton, Tutzi
Rubin, Donald Vincent
Stutesman, Cezanne Slough

Metal, Welded
Allain, Rene Pierre
Anderson, David Kimball
Baer, Rod
Balderacchi, Arthur Eugene
Balossi, John
Barrett, Bill
Beal, Mack
Benton, Suzanne E
Bloch, Babette
Bolomey, Roger Henry
Brooks, Jan
Brown, Carol K
Brown, David Lee
Brubaker, Jack
Buchanan, Sidney Arnold
Burt, David Sill
Capps, Kenneth P
Cariola, Robert J
Caudill, Dave
Censor, Therese
Chase, Jack S(paulding)
Crouch, Ned Philbrick
Davy, Woods
D'Innocenzo, Nick
Dirks, John
Dunbar, Michael Austin

SCULPTOR (cont)
Sadow, Harvey S, Jr
Saito, Seiji
Sanabria, Robert
Sato, Norie
Sauer, Jane Gottlieb
Savoy, Chyrl Lenore
Saxe, Henry, OC
Schlitter, Helga
Schmidt, Randall Bernard
Schule, Donald Kenneth
Schumacher, Judith Klein
Schwab, Judith A
Schwarz, Judith
Scott, Campbell
Seaberg, Libby W
Seamans, Beverly Benson
Seiden, Katie
Sewell, Leo
Shaddle Baum, Alice
Shaw, Donald Edward
Siff, Marlene Ida
Sloan, Jennifer
Smedley, Geoffrey
Snyder, Hills
Sperath, Albert Frank
Spira, Bill
Sproat, Christopher Townsend
Steinbach, Haim
Steinman, Barbara
Stephen, Francis B
Streeter, Tal
Streett, Tylden Westcott
Strong-Cuevas, Elizabeth
Stuart, Michelle
Swartzman, Roslyn
Therrien, Robert
Thomas, Kathleen K
Thurmer, Robert
Tiemann, Robert E
Tolle, Brian
Tousignant, Claude
Turrell, James Archie
Umlauf, Karl A
Valdez, Vincent E
Van Leunen, Alice Louise
Vega, Edward
Venable, Susan C
Vidal, Francisco
Volkin, Hilda Appel
Von Rydingsvard, Ursula
Waddell, John Henry
Wade, Robert Schrope
Wald, Sylvia
Wales, Kitty
Walker, Laurie Ann
Walker, Sharyne Elaine
Warburg, Stephanie Wenner
Weinbaum, Jean
Weitzman, Eileen
Welch, Charles D
White, James Richard
White, Karen J
Whiten, Colette
Willenbecher, John
Williams Whiting, Janice E
Wimmer, Gayle
Wint, Florence Edythe
Wong, Paul Kan
Wood, Nicholas Wheeler
Yamaguchi, Yuriko
Zaima, Stephen Gyo
Zeitlin, Harriet
Zeller, Frederic

Plastic
Breed, Charles Ayars
Coit, M B
Dignac, Geny (Eugenia) M Bermudez
Fafard, Joe (Joseph) Yvon
Fox, Michael David
Franklin, Hannah
Fuerst, Shirley Miller
Gilhooly, David James, III
Hausman, Fred S
Hayes, Carolyn Hendrick
Kern, Arthur (Edward)
Koscielny, Margaret
Kostyniuk, Ronald P
Levee, John H
Livingston, Constance Kellner
Porta, Siena Gillann
Redinger, Walter Fred
Setlow, Neva C (Delihas)
Shipley, Roger Douglas
Staprans, Raimonds
Swergold, Marcelle M
Termes, (Dick A)
Umlauf, Karl A
Van Buren, Richard
Vasa
Weedman, Kenneth Russell
White, Norman Triplett

Stone
Agid, Lucy Bradanovic
Allman, Margo
Allmond, Charles
Bailey, Richard H
Beasley, Bruce
Bloom, Alan David
Brown, Edith Rae
Caponi, Anthony
De Guatemala, Joyce Bush Vourvoulias
de Musée, Moran
Dennett, Lissy W
Dorrien, Carlos Guillermo
Dusenbery, Walter
Ferrell, Catherine (Klemann)
Fox, Lincoln H
Freeland, Bill
Gibbs, Tom
Goldberg, Norma
Goulet, Lorrie
Greer, John Sydney
Harvey, Andre
Henry, John Raymond
Hofmann, Kay
Huntington, Jim
Jackson, Oliver Lee
Jones, Carter R, Jr
Kavanagh, Cornelia Kubler
Koenig, Elizabeth
Longhurst, Robert E
Lutz, Marjorie Brunhoff
Manhold, John Henry
Mazze, Irving
Moroles, Jesús Bautista
Naranjo, Michael Alfred
Neri, Manuel
Perry, Frank
Pinardi, Enrico Vittorio
Pinsker, Essie
Polta, Voleen Jane
Reddy, Krishna N
Reese, Marcia Mitchell
Regat, Jean-Jacques Albert
Schleeh, Hans Martin
Segal, Barbara Jeanne
Shepp, Alan
Tabak, Chaim
Torcoletti, Enzo
Vaadia, Boaz
Van Alstine, John Richard
Varo, Marton Geza
Warshaw, Elaine N
Washington, James W, Jr
Watkins, Lewis
Zajac, Jack
Zelin, Elaine

Wood
Allmond, Charles
Altman, Edith
Andrus, Barbara
Arnoldi, Charles Arthur
Arum, Barbara
Azara, Nancy J
Beal, Mack
Bolomey, Roger Henry
Brady, Robert D
Bragar, Philip Frank
Brown, Peter C
Browning, Mark Daniel
Buchanan, Beverly
Butchkes, Sydney
Carroll, James F L
Castle, Wendell Keith
Colby, Victor E
Dale, Ron G
de Gogorza, Patricia (Gahagan)
De Kansky, Igor
De Ricco, Hank
Dowd, Jack
Doyle, Tom
Driesbach, Walter Clark, Jr
Feist, Harold E
Frank, Charles William, Jr
Freeland, Bill
Ganis, Lucy
Gillen, John
Gilson, Giles
Goode, Joe
Greer, Jane Ruth
Grimley, Oliver Fetterolf
Grooms, Red
Habenicht, Wenda
Hagan, James Garrison
Harris, Charney Anita
Hayes, Carolyn Hendrick
Helzer, Richard Brian
Hendricks, James (Powell)
Henkle, James Lee
Holden, Michael B
Holmes, David Valentine
Holoun, Harold Dean
Hostetler, David L
Hueter, James Warren
Impiglia, Giancarlo
Isaacs, Ron
Isaacson, Lynn Judith
Jacobs, Peter Alan
Jones, Theodore Joseph
Joseph, Tommy
Kahn, Tobi Aaron
Kamen, Rebecca
Katz, Don
Keister, Steve (Stephen) Lee
Kelmenson, Lita
Kerrigan, Maurie
Koehler, Ronald Gene
Kotoske, Roger Allen
LaMontagne, Armand M
Laub, Stephen
Leigh, Harry E
Lewis, Mary
Lindquist, Mark
Longhurst, Robert E
Lutz, Marjorie Brunhoff
Manspeizer, Susan R
Markowski, Eugene David
Maroney, Dalton
Marsh, Thomas A
McDaniel, William Harrison (Harry)
McIlvain, Douglas Lee
McKoy, Victor Grainger
Monteith, Clifton J
Mosley, Thaddeus
Nelson, Pamela Hudson
Nerburn, Kent Michael
Niemann, Edmund E
Noel, Jean
Nutt, Craig
Peters, Jim (James) Stephen
Pincus, Laurie Jane
Plott, Paula Plott Amos
Powell, Gordon
Rades, William L
Recanati, Dina
Regat, Mary E
Rogers, P J
Roussel, Claude Patrice
Saville, Ken
Schlanger, Jeff
Scott, Arden
Searles, Charles
Sharon, Russell
Shaw, Ernest Carl
Shaw, Reesey
Sieg, Robert Lawrence
Smith, Nan S(helley)
Stern, Arthur I
Stevens, Michael Keith
Storm, Howard
Stubbs, Lu
Sudlow, Robert N
Swick, Linda Ann
Tabak, Chaim
Taylor, Alison Elizabeth
Tornheim, Norman
Torreano, John Francis
Townsend, John F
Tucholke, Christel-Anthony
Umlauf, Karl A
Von Rydingsvard, Ursula
Webster, Meg
Wenzel, Joan Ellen
Werner, Howard
Whiteley, Elizabeth
Wirsum, Karl

SILVERSMITH

Betteridge, Lois Etherington
Butt, Harlan W
Coulter, Lane
De La Verriere, Jean Jacques
Fix, John Robert
Getty, Nilda Fernandez
Hirsh, Annette Marie
Krentzin, Earl
Mawdsley, Richard
Maxfield, Roberta Masur
Schulson, Susan
Thompson, Ernest Thorne, Jr
Van Duinwyk, George Paul
Vitali, Ubaldo
Weidell, Charleen
Yuen, Kee-ho

STAINED GLASS ARTIST

Abbott, Linda J
Anderson, Mark Robert
Ascalon, David
Boussard, Dana
Close, Frank
Corso, Samuel (Joseph)
Daniels, Astar Charlotte Louise Daniels
Hyams, Harriet
Katz, Don
Kehlmann, Robert
Kettlewood, Bea Card
King, Ray
Kuckei, Peter
Labrie, Christy
Mandelbaum, Ellen
McGuire, Maureen
McIlvane, Edward James
Mueller, OP, (Sister) Gerardine
Polta, Voleen Jane
Schaechter, Judith
Stern, Arthur I
Tahedl, Ernestine
Traylor, Angelika
Tyser, Patricia Ellen
Waletzky, Tsirl (Cecelia) Grobla
Wood, Ron
Zgoda, Larry

TAPESTRY ARTIST

Aber, Ita
Beck, Doreen

TAPESTRY ARTIST (cont)

Cook, Lia
De Amaral, Olga
Elliott, Lillian
Ende, Arlyn
Filomeno, Angelo
Funk, Charlotte M
Gillie, Phyllis I Danielson
Greene, Louise Weaver
Hallman, Ted, Jr
Hartford, Jane Davis
Jannicelli, Matteo
Jaworska, Tamara
Kaye, David Haigh
Kowalski, Libby R
Larzelere, Judith Ann
Lukasiewicz, Nancy Bechtold
Lundberg, Thomas Roy
Lynn, Judith
Marsh, Charlene Marie
Minear, Beth
Murashima, Kumiko
Nava, John
Newport, Mark
Orth, Maggie
Pinckney, Stanley
Reichel, Myra
Renee, Paula
Roberson, William
Roda, Rhoda Lillian Sablow
Scheuer, Ruth
Schira, Cynthia
Stratakos, Steve John
Tate, Blair
Taylor, Janet R
Tolpo, Carolyn Lee
Von Mertens, Anna
Westfall, Carol D

VIDEO ARTIST

Allen, Terry
Alpert, Richard Henry
Alvarado-Juárez, Francisco
Andrews, Lawrence
Arnold, Skip
Baer, Adam
Barber, Bruce Alistair
Bard, Perry
Barron, Ros
Bauer, Will N
Beirne, Bill
Bell-Smith, Michael
Birnbaum, Dara
Bouchet, Mark
Bowers, Andrea
Boyd, Robert
Boyer, Nathan P
Bratton, Christopher Alan
Breder, Hans Dieter
Bruguera, Tania
Buchanan, Nancy
Buckingham, Matthew
Buitron, Robert C
Bull, Hank
Carter, Jerry Williams
Chan, Paul
Chase, Doris (Totten)
Chernick, Myrel
Chong, Ping
Cook, Michael David
Corriel, Eric
Coupe, James
Cowin, Eileen
Crandall, Jordan
Cuoghi, Roberto
Cytter, Keren
Dalglish, Jamie
Davidovich, Jaime
Dickinson, Eleanor Creekmore
Djurberg, Nathalie
Drucker, Zackary
Duben, Ipek Aksugur
Dunning, Jeanne
Dyson, Torkwase
Easterson, Sam Peter
Eichel, Edward W
Esquivias, Patricia
Fessler, Ann Helene
Fiskin, Judy
Fiss, Cinthea
Frelin, Adam
Gartel, Laurence M
Gauntt, Jeff
Gilmore, Kate
Goin, Peter
Gordin, Misha
Grabill, Vin (E Vincent, Jr)
Graydon, Andy
Green, Jesse Aron
Greenfield, Amy
Gribbon, Jenna
Gromala, Diane
Gusella, Ernest
Gyung Jin, Shin
Hall, Douglas E
Han, Moo Kwon
Harding, Noel Robert
Hashimoto, Kelly Ann
Hefuna, Susan
Hendricks, David Charles
Hill, Gary
Hoeber, Julian
Honig, Ethelyn
Houghton, Barbara Jean
House, Suda Kay
Hsieh, Tehching
Iimura, Takahiko
Jenkins, Ulysses Samuel, Jr
Jevbratt, Lisa
Jonas, Joan
Jordan, John L
Joskowicz, Claudia
Jury, Sam
Kilimnik, Karen
Knecht, John
Kolasinski, Jacek J
Korot, Beryl
Kunin, Julia
La Bobgah, Robert Gordon
Laumann, Lars
Lee, Susie J
Levine, Les
Lewenz, Lisa
London, Naomi
Lukkas, Lynn C
Magden, Norman E
Magenta, Muriel
Magid, Jill
Malen, Lenore
Manual, Ed Hill & Suzanne Bloom
Marketou, Jenny
Marton, Pier
Mataranglo, Robert Patrick
Mayes, Elaine
McCafferty, Jay David
McCarthy, Paul
Meltzer, Julia
Merhi, Yucef
Meromi, Ohad
Metcalfe, Eric William
Mik, Aernout
Miller, Tracy A
Montano, Linda (Mary)
Mosley, Joshua
Muntadas, Antonio
Myers, Rita
Nauman, Bruce
Newsome, Rashaad Germain
Niblock, Phill
Nourse, Mike
O'Grady, Lorraine
Orentlicher, John
Parreno, Philippe
Patterson, Clayton Ian
Pearlstein, Alix
Peiperl, Adam
Pell, Richard
Pettibon, Raymond
Piene, Chloe
Poledna, Mathias
Porter, Liliana
Redgrave, Felicity
Reeves, Daniel McDonough
Reginato, Angela
Reilly, Jack
Ritchie, William (Bill) H, Jr
Roser, Ce (Cecilia)
Rothenberg, Stephanie
Rudelius, Julika
Ruilova, Aida
Salmon, Margaret
Scher, Julia
Schneider, Rosalind L
Schulnik, Allison
Sears, Kelly
Serra, Richard
Sher, Elizabeth
Silver, Shelly Andrea
Simanski, Claire Dvorak
Simons, Dona
Skogerson, Gretchen
Smith, Barbara Turner
Sonnier, Keith
Spiegel, Laurie
Steele, Lisa
Sturgeon, John Floyd
Sullivan, Catherine
Thater, Diana
Tilley, Lewis Lee
Torres, Frances
Tribe, Kerry
Tribe, Mark
Turner, Judith Estelle
Utterback, Camille
Valdovino, Luis Hector
Van Allen, Adrian
Velez, Edin
Viola, Bill
Vogt, Erika
Von Brandenburg, Ulla
Warck Meister, Lucia
Weintraub, Annette
Weiss, Monika
Welch, Roger
Welitoff, Suara
Will, John A
Zahedi, Caveh
Zanisnik, Bryan

WEAVER

Adamson, Linny J
Akers, Adela
Aspell, Amy Suzanne
Barletta, Emily
Black, Jappie King
Bobrowicz, Yvonne Pacanovsky
Boyd, Karen White
Bryant, Laura Militzer
Curtis, Dolly Powers
Dice, Elizabeth Jane
Elliott, Lillian
Funk, Charlotte M
Hanson, JB
Hausrath, Joan W
Hicks, Sheila
Hughes, Beverly
Kindahl, Connie
Minear, Beth
Reichel, Myra
Replinger, Dot (Dorothy Thiele)
Robinson, Sally W
Saldana, Zoe Sheehan
Sandoval, Arturo Alonzo
Schultz, Marilou
Smith, Sherri
Steel, Hillary
Taylor, Janet R
Wahling, Jon B
West, Virginia M
Yahoozer, Paul

WRITER

Abbett, Robert Kennedy
Abram, Ruth J
Abt, Jeffrey
Adams, Robert McCormick
Agar, Eunice Jane
Akers, Gary
Alf, Martha Joanne
Aliki, Liacouras Brandenberg
Alinder, Mary Street
Allen, E Douglas
Almond, Paul
Altshuler, Bruce J
Ames, Lee Judah
Anderson, Wilmer (Louis)
Anderson-Spivy, C Alexandra
Angelini, John Michael
Angelo, Sandra McFall
Antin, David A
Apple, Jacki
Ashton, Dore
Atlas, Nava
Baas, Jacquelynn
Baer, Jo
Baker, Jill Withrow
Baker, Kenneth
Bankowsky, Jack
Bannard, Walter Darby
Bansemer, Roger L
Barker, Walter William, Jr
Barrett, Terry M
Barta, Dorothy Woods Vadala
Bartlett, Jennifer Losch
Basquin, Kit (Mary Smyth)
Baxter, Paula Adell
Beall, Karen Friedmann
Beck, Doreen
Behr, Marion Ray
Belan, Kyra
Bellospirito, Robyn Suzanne
Bennett, John M
Benton, Suzanne E
Blackwell, Elise
Blue, Patt
Boccia, Edward Eugene
Boigon, Brian Joseph
Bowman, Bruce
Boyle, Richard J
Bratcher, Collen Dale
Braun, Emily
Brilliant, Richard
Brommer, Gerald F
Bronson, A A (Michael Wayne Tims)
Brown, Hilton
Brown, Robert K
Browning, Dixie Burrus
Brumfield, William Craft
Brust, Robert Gustave
Budny, Virginia
Burgos, Joseph Agner, Jr
Burnett, Amy Louise
Butler, Joseph Thomas
Caddell, Foster
Calle, Paul
Caswell, Helen Rayburn
Chapline, Claudia Beechum
Chase-Riboud, Barbara
Clothier, Peter Dean
Collings, Betty
Comini, Alessandra
Conniff, Gregory
Converse, Elizabeth
Corbin, George Allen
Corbino, Marcia Norcross
Corris, Michael
Cottingham, Laura Josephine
Cox, Richard William
Craig, Gerry
Crandall, Judith Ann
Craven, Wayne
Creevy, Bill
Crespo, Michael Lowe
Crosman, Christopher Byron
Crump, James

WRITER (cont)
Curran, Douglas Edward
Dadi, Iftikhar
Dailey, Victoria Keilus
Dantzic, Cynthia Maris
Danzker, Jo-Anne Birnie
Dater, Judy
David, Ivo
Davis, James Wesley
Dawdy, Doris Ostrander
Deats, (Margaret)
Decter, Betty Eva
D'Elaine
De Nike, Michael Nicholas
Denson, G Roger
DesJarlait, Robert D
Diamonstein-Spielvogel, Barbaralee
Digby, Lynne
Dinnerstein, Lois
Dodrill, Donald Lawrence
Dorfman, Geoffrey
Drohojowska-Philp, Hunter
Duben, Ipek Aksugur
Dusard, Jay
Eaton, Tom
Edelman, Janice
Edwards, Gary Maxwell
Elder, Gene Wesley
Ellenzweig, Allen Bruce
Elliot, Sheila
Enstice, Wayne
Escallon, Ana Maria
Ewald, Elin Lake
Farnham, Alexander
Fechter, Claudia Zieser
Feldman, Franklin
Fessler, Ann Helene
Firestein, Cecily Barth
Fisher, Joel
Fitzgerald, Astrid
Fitzgerald, Joan V
Flach, Victor H
Flax, Florence P (Roselin Polinsky)
Fleming, Lee
Folsom, Rose
Foster, Stephen C
Fox, Catherine
Frank, Charles William, Jr
Frazer, James (Nisbet), Jr
French, Christopher Charles
Freund, Will Frederick
Friedman, Bernard Harper
Fuller, Mary (Mary Fuller McChesney)
Gablik, Suzi
Gale, Peggy
Gallagher, Carole
Ganis, William V
Garbutt, Janice Lovoos
Garrison, Gene K
Garver, Walter Raymond
Geller, Bunny Zelda
Ghent, Henri
Gibson, Walter Samuel
Gildzen, Alex
Gillick, Liam
Gjertson, Stephen Arthur
Gleim-Jonas, Lisa
Glenn, Constance White
Glick, Paula F
Glines, Karen
Goddard, Donald
Goldberger, Paul Jesse
Goldin, Nan
Goldman, Judith
Goldring, Elizabeth
Goldsmith, Barbara
Goodman, Calvin Jerome
Goodman, Cynthia
Gordon, Coco
Goring, Trevor
Gould, Karen
Grant, Daniel Howard
Green, Nancy Elizabeth
Greene, Thomas Christopher
Gresser, Seymour Gerald
Gropper, Cathy
Gruen, John
GXI
Haber, Ira Joel
Hackenbroch, Yvonne Alix
Halaby, Samia A
Hale, Nathan Cabot
Hamblen, Karen A
Hammond, Leslie King
Hanks, David Allen
Harrell, Margaret Ann
Hartal, Paul
Hawkins, Margaret
Hawkins, Myrtle H
Held, (John) Jonathan, Jr
Herring, Jan (Janet) Mantel
Hersch, Jeff
Hethom, Janet
High, Kathryn
Hirsch, Gilah Yelin
Hlavina, Rastislav
Hobbs, Jack Arthur
Holden, Donald
Hood, Graham Stanley
Horne, Ralph Albert
Howze, James Dean
Huddy, Margaret Teresa
Iannone, Dorothy
Irving, Donald J
Isaacson, Philip Marshal
James, A Everette, Jr
Jennings, Jan Noreus
Johanningmeier, Robert Alan
Johnson, Joyce
Johnson, Linda K
Jones, Lois Swan
Jones, Ronald Lee, Jr
July, Miranda
Kadlec, Kristine
Kallir, Jane Katherine
Kamm, Dorothy Lila
Kangas, Gene
Karlen, Peter H
Karlstrom, Paul Johnson
Katchen, Carole Lee
Kaufman, Nancy
Kay, Reed
Keener, Polly Leonard
Kelsey, John
Kepner, Rita
Kertess, Klaus
Kessler, Jane Q
Kidwell, Michele Falik
Kimmel-Cohn, Roberta
Klausner, Betty
Klein, Michael Eugene
Kleinbauer, W Eugene
Klement, Vera
Kloss, William
Knoebel, David J
Knox, George
Koestenbaum, Wayne
Korn, Henry
Korzenik, Diana
Kostelanetz, Richard
Kovinick, Philip Peter
Kowal, Dennis J
Kozloff, Max
Kutner, Janet
Lacy, Suzanne
La Duke, Betty
Langdo, Bryan Richard
Larson, Kay L
Lavine, Steven David
Lawson, Thomas
Leach, Elizabeth Anne
LeBey, Barbara
Leeds, Valerie Ann
Leesman, Beverly Jean
Levit, Héloïse (Ginger) Bertman
Levy, Mark
Libby, Gary Russell
Lijn, Liliane
Lippard, Lucy Rowland
Lippman, Mandy
Lipsky, Pat
Lochnan, Katharine A
Loewer, Henry Peter
Lotringer, Sylvere
Lowe, Sarah
Lubell, Ellen
Ludman, Joan Hurwitz
Lufkin, Martha BG
MacClintock, Dorcas
MacDonald, William L
Madsen, Roy Paul
Mainardi, Patricia M
Maksymowicz, Virginia Ann
Mallin, Judith Young
Malone, James Hiram
Mariner, Donna M
Marker, Mariska Pugsley
Marshall, Bruce
Martin, Roger
Mason, Francis, Jr
Mason, Lauris Lapidos
Matzkin, Alice Rosalinda
Mayer, Monica P
McCauley, Elizabeth Anne
McCoy, Pat A
McCurdy, Michael Charles
Metcalf, Bruce B
Meyer, James Sampson
Meyer, Susan E
Michael, Gary
Michaels, Barbara L
Millard, Charles Warren, III
Miller, Marc H
Miller, Nicole
Minick, Roger
Mitchell, Margaretta K
Montrose-Graem, Douglass J
Morgan, Robert Coolidge
Morgan, Roberta Marie
Morgan, William
Morse, Marcia Roberts
Movalli, Charles Joseph
Mowry, Elizabeth M
Munro, Eleanor
Murchie, Donald John
Narkiewicz-Laine, Christian K
Nasisse, Andy S
Navaretta, Cynthia
Neher, Ross James
Neil, J M
Nelson, Aida Z
Nelson, Mary Carroll
Nigrosh, Leon Isaac
Nix, Nelleke
Norton, Paul Foote
O'Beil, Hedy
O'Gorman, James Francis
Orland, Ted N
Ostrom, Gladys Snell
O'Toole, Judith Hansen
Parker, Ann (Ann Parker Neal)
Parker, Nancy Winslow
Parry, Eugenia
Parsons, Cynthia Massey
Paulos, Daniel Thomas
Peck, Judith
Péladeau, Marius Beaudoin
Penney, Jacqueline
Perlman, Bennard B
Persky, Robert S
Peyton, Elizabeth Joy
Phelan, Andrew L
Phillips, Gifford
Phillpot, Clive James
Pike, Joyce Lee
Pincus-Witten, Robert A
Piper, Adrian Margaret Smith
Plowden, David
Prat, Louis-Antoine & Veronique
Raleigh, Henry Patrick
Ramsey, Dorothy J
Reep, Edward Arnold
Reid, Charles Clark
Reid, Sheila
Rendl, M(ildred) Marcus
Reuter, Laurel J
Reynolds, John (Jock) M
Richards, David Patrick
Ripstein, Jacqueline
Robbins, Eugenia S
Robison, Andrew
Robles-Galiano, Estela
Rogers, Peter Wilfrid
Rokeach, Barrie
Roosevelt, Michael Armentrout
Rosen, Diane
Rosenblatt, Suzanne Maris
Roth, Leland M(artin)
Rubin, David S
Rubinstein, Charlotte Streifer
Rush, Michael James
Rybczynski, Witold Marian
Sanabria, Robert
Sanders, Rhea
Sandground, Mark Bernard, Sr
Saphire, Lawrence M
Schulman, Arlene
Schulzke, Margot Seymour
Schupp, Ronald Irving
Schwartz, Lillian (Feldman)
Scott, John Beldon
Scully, Vincent Joseph, Jr
Seckel, Cornelia
Seed, Suzanne Liddell
Self, Dana Rae
Seslar, Patrick George
Sherrod, Philip Lawrence
Sill, Gertrude Grace
Silver, Rawley A
Silverman, Ronald H
Simon, Leonard Ronald
Slate, Joseph Frank
Smith, Ralph Alexander
Snodgrass-King, Jeanne Owen (Mrs M Eugene King)
Snowden, Gilda
Snyder, Hills
Sorensen, Lee Richard
Spaar, Lisa Russ
Spector, Naomi
Speight, Jerry Brooks
Spicer, Jean (Doris) Uhl
Squiers, Carol
Stapen, Nancy
Statman, Jan B
Stavitsky, Gail Beth
Steiner, Paul
Steiner, Raymond John
Steiner, Sherry L
Stevens, Elisabeth Goss
Stewart, John Lincoln
Stone, Jim (James) J
Streeter, Tal
Stummer, Helen M
Sujo, Clara Diament
Sullivan, Graeme
Sullivan, Ronald Dee
Sward, Robert S
Szilvasy, Linda Markuly
Talley, Dan R
Tarbet, Urania Christy
Tarshis, Jerome
Taylor, Robert
Temple, Leslie Alcott (Leslie Jane Atkinson)
Tennant, Donna Kay
Thenhaus, Paulette Ann
Thornton, Richard Samuel
Thurston, Jacqueline Beverly
Tice, George (Andrew)
Tillenius, Clarence Ingwall
Tomkins, Calvin
Toschik, Larry
Tully, Judd
Turner, Norman Huntington
VanDerpool, Karen
Van Haaften, Julia
Van Laar, Timothy
Vestal, David

Necrology
Cumulative 1953-2016

AACH, HERB Painter, Writer (1923-1985)
AARONS, GEORGE Sculptor (1896-1980)
ABBOTE, PAUL S Sculptor (1884-1972)
ABBOTT, EDITH Painter (-1964)
ABBOTT, JOHN EVANS Library Director (-1952)
ABEELL, SAMUEL Art Patron (1925-1969)
ABEL, MYER Lithographer, Painter (1904-)
ABEL, RAY Illustrator, Printmaker (1911-2008)
ABELL, WALTER HALSEY Educator (1897-1956)
ABLOW, JOSEPH Painter, Writer (1928-2012)
ABRACHEFF, IVAN Painter (1903-1960)
ABRAMS, HARRY N Publisher, Collector (1905-1979)
ABRAMS, HERBERT E Lecturer, Painter (1921-2003)
ABRAMS, RUTH (DAVIDSON) Painter, Critic (-1986)
ABRIL, BEN (BENJAMIN) Painter (1923-)
ACKERMAN, FRANK EDWARD Painter, Designer (1933-)
ACKERMANN, JOHN JOSEPH Painter, Designer (1889-1950)
ADAMS, (MOULTON) LEE Painter, Illustrator (1922-1971)
ADAMS, ANSEL EASTON Photographer (1902-1984)
ADAMS, CLINTON Painter, Historian (1918-2002)
ADAMS, JAY H Jeweler, Medalist (1937-)
ADAMS, MARGARET BOROUGHS Painter (-1965)
ADAMS, PAT Painter, Educator (1928-2001)
ADAMS, WAYMAN Painter (1885-1959)
ADAMY, GEORGE E Educator, Sculptor (1925-)
ADDAMS, CHARLES Cartoonist (1912-1988)
ADEN, ALONZO J Museum Director (1906-1963)
ADKINS, TERRY R Sculptor (1953-2014)
ADLER, SAMUEL (MARCUS) Painter, Educator (1898-1979)
ADLOW, DOROTHY Critic (-1964)
AGA-OGLU, MEHMET Educator, Lecturer, Writer (1896-1948)
AGOPOFF, AGOP MINASS Sculptor (-1983)
AGOSTINI, PETER Sculptor (1913-1993)
AHERN, EUGENE (GENE) Cartoonist (1896-1960)
AHLGREN, ROY B Painter, Printmaker (1927-)
AIDLEN, JEROME Sculptor, Instructor (1935-1986)
AIKEN, CHARLES Painter (1872-1965)
AIROLA, PAAVO Painter, Writer (-1983)
AJAY, ABE Painter, Sculptor (1919-1998)
AJOOTIAN, KHOSROV Educator (1891-1958)
AKE, JOHN Sculptor (-1998)
AKSTON, JAMES Collector, Patron
ALAN, JAY Cartoonist (1907-1965)
ALBEE, PERCY F Painter (1885-1959)
ALBERS, ANNI Textile Artist (1899-1994)
ALBERS, JOSE F Painter, Printmaker (1888-1976)
ALBERTAZZI, MARIO Painter, Art Critic (1920-1991)
ALBRECHT, MARY DICKSON Sculptor, Designer (1930-2008)
ALBRIGHT, ADAM EMORY Painter (1862-1957)
ALBRIGHT, HENRY J Educator, Painter (-1951)
ALBRIGHT, IVAN LE LORRAINE Painter (1897-1983)
ALBRIGHT, THOMAS Critic, Writer (1935-)
ALCOPLEY, L Painter, Graphic Artist (1910-1992)
ALDER, MARY ANN Painter, Art Restorer (-1952)
ALDRICH, LARRY Collector (1906-2001)
ALDWINCKLE, ERIC Designer, Painter (1909-1980)
ALEXANDER, CHRISTINE Curator (1893-1975)
ALEXANDER, DIANE DAVENPORT Painter (-1999)
ALEXANDER, JUDITH Art Dealer, Collector (1932-2004)
ALEXANDER, KENNETH LEWIS Cartoonist (1924-2012)
ALEXANDER, ROBERT SEYMOUR Educator, Designer (1923-1997)
ALFSEN, JOHN MARTIN Painter (-1972)
ALLEN, LORETTA B Painter, Designer (-2000)
ALLEN, (HARVEY) HAROLD Photographer, Writer (1912-)
ALLEN, ARTHUR D Painter, Lithographer (-1949)
ALLEN, CHARLES CURTIS Painter, Educator (1886-1950)
ALLEN, CLARENCE CANNING Painter, Instructor (1897-1989)
ALLEN, JANE MENGEL (MRS ARTHUR) Painter (1888-1952)
ALLEN, JUNIUS Painter (1898-1962)
ALLEN, MARGO (MRS HARRY SHAW) Sculptor, Painter (1894-1988)
ALLEN, MARY STOCKBRIDGE Painter, Sculptor (1869-1949)
ALLING, CLARENCE (EDGAR) Museum Director, Ceramist (1933-)
ALLOWAY, LAWRENCE Art Historian, Curator (1927-1990)
ALLWELL, STEPHEN S Sculptor (1906-)
ALMY, FRANK ATWOOD Museum Director (1900-1956)
ALPS, GLEN EARL Educator, Printmaker (1914-1996)
ALQUIST, LEWIS Sculptor, Educator (1946-2005)
ALSTON, CHARLES HENRY Painter, Educator (1907-1977)
ALTFELD, MERWIN RICHARD Painter, Educator, Art Juror (1913-2007)
ALTMAN, HAROLD Printmaker, Educator (1924-2003)
ALTMAYER, JAY P Collector (1915-1999)
ALTSCHUL, ARTHUR G Collector, Patron (1920-2002)
ALVORD, MURIEL Painter (-1960)
AMAROTICO, JOSEPH ANTHONY Painter, Conservator (1931-)
AMATEIS, EDMOND ROMULUS Sculptor (1897-1981)
AMATNIEK, SARA Printmaker, Graphic Artist (1922-1996)
AMBERSON, GRACE D (MRS WILLIAM R) Painter (1894-1957)
AMEN, IRVING Painter, Printmaker (1918-)
AMES, ARTHUR FORBES Painter, Educator (1906-1975)
AMFT, ROBERT Painter, Photographer (1916-2012)
AMINO, LEO Sculptor, Instructor (1911-1989)
AMISANO, JOSEPH Architect (1917-2008)
AMSDEN, FLOYD T Collector, Patron (1913-)
AMSTER, SALLY Painter (-1988)
ANARGYROS, SPERO Sculptor (1915-2004)

ANDERSEN, ANDREAS STORRS Educator, Painter (1908-1974)
ANDERSON, CARL THOMAS Cartoonist, Illustrator (1865-1948)
ANDERSON, DAVID Art Dealer, Collector (1935-2010)
ANDERSON, DAVID C Sculptor, Photographer (1931-)
ANDERSON, GUY IRVING Painter (1906-1998)
ANDERSON, HOWARD BENJAMIN Photographer (1903-)
ANDERSON, IVAN DELOS Painter, Printmaker (1915-1991)
ANDERSON, JEREMY RADCLIFFE Sculptor, Educator (1921-1982)
ANDERSON, JOHN S Sculptor (1928-)
ANDERSON, KENNETH L Administrator, Architect (1939-1990)
ANDERSON, LENNART Painter, Instructor (1928-2015)
ANDRADE, EDNA WRIGHT Painter, Educator (1917-2008)
ANDREJEVIC, MILET Painter (1925-1989)
ANDREWS, BENNY Painter, Lecturer (1930-)
ANDREWS, MARION Painter (-2011)
ANDREWS, SYBIL Printmaker (1898-1992)
ANGEL, JOHN Sculptor (1881-1960)
ANGELO, DOMENICK MICHAEL Sculptor (1925-1976)
ANGELO, EMIDIO Cartoonist, Painter (1903-)
ANKRUM, JOAN Art Dealer (1914-2001)
ANNENBERG, WALTER H Collector, Patron (1908-2002)
ANSBACHER, JESSIE Painter (-1964)
ANSPACH, ERNST Collector (1913-2002)
ANTONAKOS, STEPHEN Sculptor (1926-2013)
ANTONOVICI, CONSTANTIN Sculptor, Lecturer (1911-2002)
ARAKAWA, (SHUSAKU) Painter (1936-2010)
ARCHAMBAULT, LOUIS Sculptor (1915-2003)
ARCHER, DOROTHY BRYANT Painter, Instructor (1919-)
ARCHIPENKO, ALEXANDER Sculptor (1887-1964)
ARCOMANO, CATHRYN Painter (-2012)
ARD, SARADELL Educator, Painter (1920-2009)
ARDIZZONE, EDWARD Painter, Illustrator (1900-1979)
ARGALL, CHARLES G Painter
ARKUS, LEON A Museum Director, Consultant (1915-1999)
ARLT, WILLIAM H Designer, Teacher, Painter (1868-)
ARMSTRONG, ROGER JOSEPH Painter, Cartoonist (1917-2007)
ARMSTRONG, THOMAS NEWTON III Museum Director (1932-)
ARNASON, H HARVARD Art Historian, Writer (1909-1986)
ARNESON, ROBERT Sculptor (1930-)
ARNEST, BERNARD Painter, Educator (1917-1986)
ARNHEIM, RUDOLF Educator, Writer (1904-2007)
ARNO, PETER Cartoonist (1904-1968)
ARNOLD, RALPH MOFFETT Painter, Educator (1928-)
ARONSON, BORIS Designer, Painter (1900-1980)
ARONSON, DAVID Painter, Sculptor (1923-2015)
ARTIS, WILLIAM ELLISWORTH Educator, Ceramist (1914-1977)
ARTSCHWAGER, RICHARD ERNST Sculptor, Painter (1923-2013)
ARTZ, FREDERICK B Historian, Writer (1894-1983)
ARTZYBASHEFF, BORIS Illustrator (1899-1965)
ARYE, LEONORA E Sculptor (1931-2001)
ASAWA, RUTH (ASAWA LANIER) Sculptor, Painter (1926-2013)
ASCHER, MARY Painter, Printmaker
ASHBY, CARL Painter, Instructor (1914-2004)
ASHER, ELISE Painter, Poet (1914-2004)
ASHER, MICHAEL Conceptual Artist (1943-2012)
ASHTON, ETHEL V Artist (-1975)
ASHTON, MAL STANHOPE (MALONE) Artist (1878-1976)
ASIHENE, EMMANUEL V Educator, Painter (1937-)
ASKENAZY, MISCHA Painter (1888-1961)
ASKEVOLD, DAVID Conceptual Artist, Instructor (1940-2008)
ASKEW, PAMELA Educator, Writer
ASO, KAJI Painter, Educator (-2006)
ATHERTON, J CARLTON Craftsman (1900-1964)
ATHERTON, JOHN Painter, Illustrator (1900-1952)
ATIRNOMIS, (RITA SIMON) Painter, Printmaker (1938-)
ATKINS, ALBERT H Sculptor, Painter (-1951)
ATWELL, ALLEN Educator, Painter (1925-1993)
AUDETTE, ANNA HELD Painter (-2013)
AUER, JAMES MATTHEW Art Critic, Filmaker (1928-2004)
AUERBACH, RITA ARGEN Painter, Instructor (1933-2013)
AUERBACH-LEVY, WILLIAM Etcher (1889-1964)
AULT, GEORGE Artist
AULT, GEORGE COPELAND Painter (1891-1948)
AUSBY, ELLSWORTH AUGUSTUS Painter, Instructor (1942-2011)
AUSTIN, DARREL Painter (1907-1994)
AUSTIN, JO-ANNE Dealer (1925-)
AUSUBEL, SHEVA Painter (1896-1957)
AUTH, ROBERT R Printmaker, Painter (1926-)
AUTH, TONY, JR (WILLIAM ANTHONY) Editorial Cartoonist (1942-2014)
AUTIO, RUDY Ceramist, Educator (1926-2007)
AUTRY, CAROLYN Printmaker, Educator (1940-2011)
AUVIL, KENNETH WILLIAM Educator, Printmaker (1925-1999)
AVEDISIAN, EDWARD Painter, Sculptor (1936-2007)
AVEDON, RICHARD Photographer (1923-2004)
AVERY, FRANCES Painter, Photographer (1910-2006)
AVERY, MILTON Painter (1893-1965)
AVERY, MYRTILLA Museum Director (-1959)
AVERY, RALPH HILLYER Painter, Illustrator (1906-1976)
AVINOFF, ANDREY Painter, Illustrator (1884-1948)
AVISON, DAVID Photographer (1937-2004)
AYERS, HESTER MERWIN Portrait Painter (1902-1975)
AYLWARD, WILLIAM J Painter (1875-1958)
AZUMA, NORIO Painter (1928-2004)
BABER, ALICE Painter, Printmaker (1928-1982)
BACH, OTTO KARL Museum Director, Writer (1909-1990)
BACH, RICHARD F Educator (1887-1968)
BACIGALUPA, ANDREA Sculptor, Painter (1923-2015)
BACKUS, STANDISH, JR Painter, Muralist (1910-1989)
BACON, PEGGY Painter, Writer (1895-1987)
BADER, FRANZ Art Dealer, Bookseller (1903-1994)
BADNER, MINO Historian (1940-1978)
BAER, MORLEY Photographer (1916-)
BAILEY, CLARK T Sculptor, Educator (1932-1978)
BAILEY, WORTH Historian (1908-1980)
BAIN, LILIAN PHERNE Painter, Etcher (1873-)
BAIZERMAN, SAUL Sculptor (1889-1957)
BAKATY, MIKE Painter, Sculptor (1936-)
BAKER, CHARLES EDWIN Art Historian, Writer (1902-1971)
BAKER, EUGENE AMES Painter, Serigrapher (1928-)
BAKER, GEORGE P Educator, Kinetic Artist (1931-1997)
BAKER, RALPH BERNARD Painter, Educator (1932-)
BAKER, RICHARD BROWN Collector (1912-2002)

BALA, PAUL Painter, Architect (-1998)
BALDWIN, HAROLD FLETCHER Sculptor, Painter (1923-2005)
BALDWIN, HARRY II Painter
BALDWIN, JOHN Educator, Sculptor (1922-1987)
BALDWIN, MURIEL FRANCES Art Librarian
BALDWIN, ROGER N Critic, Curator (1950-2004)
BALES, J (JEAN) ELAINE Painter, Sculptor (1946-2004)
BALL, WALTER N Painter, Educator (1930-2005)
BALLIN, HUGO Painter (1879-1956)
BALOG, MICHAEL Painter, Sculptor (1946-)
BANDY, RON F Painter, Educator (1936-2001)
BANEY, RALPH RAMOUTAR Sculptor (1929-)
BANKS, VIRGINIA Painter (1920-1985)
BANNING, BEATRICE HARPER Etcher (1885-)
BANNISTER, EDWARD MITCHELL Painter (1828-1901)
BARAN, TRACEY Photographer (-2008)
BARANIK, RUDOLF Painter (1920-1998)
BARANOFF, MORT Printmaker, Painter (1923-1978)
BARBAROSSA, THEODORE C Sculptor (1906-1992)
BARBER MURIEL V Painter (-1971)
BARBER, JOHN Painter (1898-1965)
BARBERA, JOE Cartoonist
BARBERIS, DOROTHY WATKEYS Painter
BARBOUR, ARTHUR J Painter, Writer (1926-2006)
BAREISS, WALTER Patron (1919-2007)
BARINGER, RICHARD E Painter, Designer (1921-1980)
BARKER, ALBERT WINSLOW Lithographer, Teacher (1874-1947)
BARKER, VIRGIL Writer, Critic (1890-1964)
BARLQGA, VIOLA H Painter (1890-)
BARNES, EDWARD LARRABEE Architect (1915-2004)
BARNET, WILL Painter, Printmaker (1911-2012)
BARNETT, EARL D Painter, Portraitist (-2003)
BARNETT, EDWARD WILLIS Director, Designer (1922-1987)
BARNETT, HERBERT P Educator, Painter (1910-1972)
BARNEY, MAGINAL WRIGHT Craftsman (-1966)
BARR, ALFRED HAMILTON, JR Art Historian, Administrator (1902-1981)
BARR, ALLAN Painter (1890-1959)
BARR, ROGER Collage Artist, Sculptor (1921-1999)
BARRETT, H STANFORD Painter, Educator (1909-1970)
BARRETT, ROBERT DUMAS Painter (1903-)
BARRETT, THOMAS R Painter, Instructor (1927-2009)
BARRETT, THOMAS WEEKS Painter, Designer (1902-1947)
BARRIE, ERWIN S Painter (1886-1983)
BARRY, ANNE MEREDITH Printmaker, Painter (1932-)
BARSCHEL, HANS J Designer, Photographer (1912-1998)
BARTHE, RICHMOND Sculptor (1901-1989)
BARTLE, DOROTHY BUDD Curator, Lecturer (1924-2005)
BARTLETT, DANA Painter (1882-1957)
BARTLETT, FRED STEWART Administrator, Museum Director (1905-1988)
BARTLETT, ROBERT WEBSTER Painter, Designer (1922-1979)
BARTLETT, SCOTT Filmmaker (1943-1990)
BARTON, BILLIE JO Instructor, Painter (1926-)
BARTON, JOHN MURRAY Painter, Printmaker (1921-2000)
BARUCH, ANNE Art Dealer, Lecturer (-2007)
BARUCH, RUTH-MARION Photographer, Writer (1922-1997)
BARZUN, JACQUES MARTIN Writer, Art Critic (1907-2012)
BASHOR, JOHN W Educator, Painter (1926-2013)
BASKIN, LEONARD Sculptor, Graphic Artist (1922-2000)
BASQUIAT, JEAN MICHEL Painter (1961-1988)
BASS, JOHANNA (MRS JOHN) Collector, Patron (-1970)
BASS, JOHN Collector, Patron (1891-1978)
BATCHELOR, CLARENCE DANIEL Cartoonist (1888-1977)
BATE, NORMAN ARTHUR Educator, Printmaker (1916-1980)
BATES, CAROL Painter (1895-)
BATES, KENNETH FRANCIS Enamelist, Craftsman (1904-)
BATES, KENNETH Painter (1895-1973)
BATES, LEO JAMES Painter, Filmmaker (1944-2013)
BATES, MAXWELL BENNETT Painter, Lithographer (1906-1980)
BATT, MILES Girard, Painter, Instructor (1933-2015)
BATTAGLIA, PASQUALE M Painter (1905-1959)
BAUM, DON Sculptor, Curator (1922-2008)
BAUMBACH, HAROLD Painter, Printmaker (1905-2001)
BAUMGARTNER, WARREN W Illustrator (1894-1963)
BAVINGER, EUGENE ALLEN Painter, Educator (1919-)
BAXENDELL, JULIE Painter (1934-)
BAYEFSKY, ABA Painter, Printmaker (1923-2001)
BAYER, HERBERT Painter, Architect (1900-)
BAYER, JEFFREY JOSHUA Educator, Sculptor (1942-1983)
BAYLESS, RAYMOND GORDON Painter, Writer (1920-2004)
BAYLINSON, A S Painter, Teacher (1882-1950)
BAYLOS, ZELMA U Painter, Sculptor
BAZIOTES, WILLIAM Painter (1912-1963)
BEACH, WARREN Painter, Museum Director (1914-1999)
BEAL, JACK Painter (1931-2013)
BEAL, REYNOLDS Painter, Etcher (1867-1951)
BEALL, LESTER THOMAS Illustrator, Designer (1902-1969)
BEALMER, WILLIAM Consultant, Educator (1919-2001)
BEAMENT, HAROLD Painter (1898-)
BEAR, DONALD Museum Director (1905-1952)
BEARD, MARION L PATTERSON Lecturer, Painter
BEARD, RICHARD ELLIOTT Painter, Educator (1928-2012)
BEATTIE, GEORGE Painter, Art Administrator (1919-1997)
BECK, MARTHA ANN Museum Director, Curator (1938-2014)
BECK, STEPHEN R Painter, Educator (1937-2002)
BECKER, BETTIE (BETTIE GERALDINE WATHALL) Painter, Graphic Artist (1918-1997)
BECKER, JOHANNA LUCILLE Historian, Ceramist (1921-2012)
BECKER, NAOMI Sculptor (-1974)
BECKWITH, JAMES Painter, Craftsperson (1907-)
BEELKE, RALPH G Educator (1917-)
BEETZ, CARL HUGO Painter, Instructor (1911-1974)
BEGG, JOHN ALFRED Designer, Sculptor (1903-1974)
BEGGS, THOMAS MONTAGUE Consultant, Painter (1899-1990)
BEL GEDDES, NORMAN Designer (1893-1958)
BELCHER, HILDA Painter (1881-1963)
BELIAN, GARABED Dealer, Historian
BELKNAP, MORRIS B Painter (-1952)
BELL, ALISTAIR MACREADY Printmaker, Painter (1913-)
BELL, CHARLES A Sculptor (-1976)
BELL, R MURRAY Collector (-1998)
BELLAMY, RICHARD Art Dealer (1927-1998)
BELLIN, MILTON R Painter, Muralist

BELLINGER, LOUIS A Curator (-1968)
BELLMER, HANS Painter, Graphic Artist & Sculptor (1902-1975)
BELMONT, IRA JEAN Painter (1885-1964)
BEMELMANS, LUDWIG Painter (1898-1963)
BEMIS, WALDO EDMUND Designer, Illustrator (-1951)
BENDA, W T Designer, Illustrator (1891-1948)
BENDELL, MARILYN Painter, Instructor (1921-2003)
BENES, BARTON LIDICE Collage Artist, Sculptor (1942-2012)
BENESCH, OTTO Art Historian (1896-1964)
BENESON, EDWARD HARTLEY Collector, Patron (1914-2005)
BENGTZ, TURE Museum Director, Painter (1907-1973)
BENHAM, ROBERT CHARLES, Painter (1913-2002)
BENJAMIN, KARL STANLEY Painter, Educator (1925-2012)
BENN, BEN Painter (1884-1983)
BENNETT, RUTH M Craftsman (1899-1960)
BENNEY, ROBERT Painter, Illustrator (-2001)
BENSCO, CHARLES J Painter (1894-1960)
BENSON, ELAINE KG Art Dealer, Writer (1924-1998)
BENSON, ELIZABETH POLK Historian, Writer (1924-2005)
BENSON, EMANUEL M Art Administrator, Art Dealer (1904-1971)
BENSON, FRANK W Painter, Etcher (1862-1951)
BENSON, JOHN P Painter (1865-1947)
BENTON, MARGARET PEAKE Painter (-1975)
BENTON, THOMAS HART Painter, Writer (1889-1975)
BENTON, WILLIAM Collector (1900-1973)
BENTZ, JOHN Painter (-1951)
BENY, ROLOFF Photographer, Writer (1924-)
BENZ, LEER Printmaker, Painter (-1984)
BERD, MORRIS Painter, Educator (1914-2007)
BEREN, STANLEY O Patron (1920-2007)
BERENSON, BERNARD Art Authority (1865-1959)
BERG, PHIL Collector, Patron (1902-)
BERGMAN, ROBERT P Museum Director, Historian (1945-1999)
BERHARD, MRS RICHARD J Collector
BERKMAN, ARRON Painter, Gallery Director (1900-1991)
BERKO, FERENC Photographer (1916-2000)
BERMAN, AARON Art Dealer, Collector (1922-2013)
BERMAN, EUGENE Painter, Designer (1899-1972)
BERMAN, FRED J Painter, Photographer (1926-2011)
BERMAN, PHILIP I Collector, Patron (1915-1997)
BERMINGHAM, PETER Museum Director, Curator (1937-1999)
BERMUDEZ, JOSE YGNACIO Sculptor, Painter (1922-1998)
BERN HEIMER, RICHARD Educator (1907-1958)
BERNARD, DAVID EDWIN Printmaker, Educator (1913-2006)
BERNARDINI, ORESTES Designer (1880-1957)
BERNDT, WALTER Cartoonist (1900-1979)
BERNEY, BERTRAM S Painter (1884-)
BERNHARD, RUTH Photographer (1905-)
BERNINGHAUS, OSCAR E Painter, Designer (1874-1952)
BERNSTEIN, BENJAMIN D Collector (1907-2003)
BERNSTEIN, EDWARD I Collector (1917-2014)
BERNSTEIN, EVA Painter (1871-1958)
BERNSTEIN, GERALD Painter, Restorer (1917-)
BERNSTEIN, SYLVIA Painter, Sculptor (1914-1990)
BERNSTEIN, THERESA Painter, Printmaker (-2002)
BERRY, WILLIAM AUGUSTUS Educator, Graphic Artist (1933-2010)
BERRY, WILLIAM DAVID Illustrator, Sculptor (1926-1979)
BERRYMAN, CLIFFORD KENNEDY Cartoonist, Illustrator (1869-1949)
BERTHOT, JAKE Painter (1939-2014)
BERTOIA, HARRY Sculptor, Graphic Artist (1915-1978)
BERTOIA, (MR) VAL Designer, Sculptor (1949-)
BETENSKY, ROSE HART Painter, Art Administrator (1923-2007)
BETTISON, JAMES Painter (1957-1998)
BETTMANN, OTTO LUDWIG Historian (1903-1998)
BETTS, EDWARD HOWARD Painter (1920-2008)
BETTS, LOUIS Painter (1873-1961)
BEVLIN, MARJORIE ELLIOTT Painter, Writer (1917-2009)
BIBERMAN, EDWARD Painter, Graphic Artist (1904-1986)
BICE, CLARE Administrator, Painter (1909-1976)
BIDDLE, GEORGE Painter, Sculptor (1885-1973)
BIDDLE, JAMES Administrator, Collector (1929-2005)
BIDDLE, WATSON Painter (1904-)
BIEBER, MARGARETE Art Historian (1880-1978)
BIEDEL, FRANKLIN M Museum Director (1908-1966)
BIELER, ANDRE CHARLES Painter, Muralist (1896-1989)
BIERLY, EDWARD J Painter, Illustrator (1920-2004)
BIERMAN, SAMUEL Art Advisor (1902-1978)
BIGGER, MICHAEL D Sculptor (1928-2011)
BIGGERS, JOHN THOMAS Educator, Printmaker (1924-2001)
BILLECI, ANDRE GEORGE Sculptor, Educator (1933-2011)
BILLINGS, HENRY Painter, Illustrator (1901-1987)
BILOTTI, SALVATORE F Sculptor (1879-1953)
BIMROSE, ARTHUR SYLVANUS JR Cartoonist (1912-)
BING, ALEXANDER Painter (1878-1959)
BINNING, BERTRAM CHARLES Painter (1909-1976)
BIRCHANSKY, LEO Painter, Cartoonist (1887-1949)
BIRELINE, GEORGE LEE Painter, Educator (1923-2002)
BIRKIN, MORTON Painter (1919-)
BISCHOFF, ELMER Painter, Educator (1916-1991)
BISGARD, JAMES DEWEY Collector, Patron (1898-1975)
BISHOP, BARBARA LEE Educator, Printmaker (1938-)
BISHOP, MARJORIE CUTLER Painter (-1998)
BISHOP, RICHARD EVETT Printmaker (1897-19751)
BISHOP, ROBERT CHARLES Museum Director, Art Writer (1938-1991)
BISSETTE, SAMUEL DELK Painter, Photographer (1921-2006)
BITTLEMAN, ARNOLD I Painter, Educator (1933-)
BLACK, ELEANOR SIMMS (MRS ROBERT M) Painter (1872-1949)
BLACK, MARY CHILDS Curator, Writer (-1992)
BLACK, WENDELL H Educator (1919-1972)
BLACKBURN, MORRIS (ATKINSON) Painter, Printmaker (1902-1979)
BLACKBURN, ROBERT Printmaker, Educator (1920-2003)
BLAI, BORIS Sculptor, Educator (1898-1985)
BLAINE, NELL Painter, Printmaker (1922-1996)
BLAIR, ROBERT NOEL Painter, Sculptor (1912-2003)
BLAIR, STREETER Painter (-1966)
BLAKE, JEREMY Artist (1971-2007)
BLAKE, LEO B Illustrator (1887-1976)
BLAKE, PETER JOST Architect, Critic (1920-)
BLANCH, ARNOLD Painter (1896-1968)
BLANCHARD, CAROL Painter, Illustrator (1918-)

BLANCHFIELD, HOWARD JAMES Painter (1896-1957)
BLANDING, DON Author (1894-1957)
BLAUSTEIN, AL Painter, Printmaker (1924-2004)
BLEIBERG, GERTRUDE TIEFENBRUN Painter, Printmaker (-2001)
BLEIFELD, STANLEY Sculptor, Medalist (1924-2011)
BLISS, MRS ROBERT WOODS Collector (-1969)
BLISS, ROBERT WOODS Patron, Diplomat (1875-1962)
BLOCH, ALBERT Painter (1882-1961)
BLOCH, E MAURICE Art Historian, Educator (-1989)
BLOCH, JULIUS Painter (1888-1966)
BLOCH, MILTON JOSEPH Art Administrator, Museum Director (1937-2012)
BLOCK, ADOLPH Sculptor, Instructor (1906-1978)
BLOCK, AMANDA ROTH Painter, Printmaker (1912-2011)
BLODGETT, EDMUND WALTON Painter (1908-)
BLODGETT, GEORGE WINSLOW Sculptor (1888-)
BLOEDEL, LAWRENCE HOTCH KISS Collector (1902-1976)
BLOOM, HYMAN Painter (1913-2009)
BLOS, PETER W Painter, Instructor (1908-1986)
BLOWER, DAVID HARRISON Painter (1901-1976)
BLUMBERG, YULI Painter (1894-1964)
BLUME, PETER Painter, Sculptor (1906-1992)
BLUMENSCHEIN, ERNEST LEONARD Painter (1874-1960)
BLUMENSCHEIN, MARY GREEN Painter (1869-1958)
BLUMENTHAL, FRITZ Painter, Printmaker (1913-2002)
BLUMENTHAL, MARGARET M Designer (1905-)
BOAL, SARA METZNER Painter, Instructor (1896-1979)
BOBAK, BRUNO JOSEPH Painter, Printmaker (1923-2012)
BOBLETER, LOWELL STANLEY Educator, Painter (1902-1973)
BOCOUR, LEONARD Paint Manufacturer (1910-1993)
BODE, ROBERT WILLIAM Designer, Painter (1912-)
BODIN, PAUL Artist (1910-1994)
BODINE, HELEN Painter
BOE, ROY ASBJORN Historian, Educator (1919-)
BOEHLER, HANS Painter (1884-1961)
BOESCHENSTEIN, BERNICE (MRS C K) Painter (1906-1951)
BOESE, ALVIN WILLIAM Collector (1910-1986)
BOGART, GEORGE A Painter (1933-)
BOGDANOVIC, BOGOMIR Painter (1923-2011)
BOGGS, FRANKLIN Muralist, Sculptor (1914-)
BOGGS, JEAN SUTHERLAND Museum Director, Art Historian (1922-2014)
BOHLAND, GUSTAV Sculptor (1897-1959)
BOHNENKAMP, LESLIE GEORGE Sculptor, Instructor (1943-1997)
BOHNERT, HERBERT Portrait Painter (1890-1967)
BOHROD, AARON Painter, Educator (1907-1992)
BOLINSKY, JOSEPH ABRAHAM Sculptor, Educator (1917-2002)
BOLOTOWSKY, ILVA Painter, Educator (1907-1981)
BOND, ROLAND S Collector (1898-)
BONEVARDI, MARCELO Artist (1929-1994)
BONGART, SERGEI R Painter, Instructor (-1985)
BONGIORNO, LAURINE MACK Historian (1903-1988)
BONINO, ALFREDO Art Dealer (1925-1981)
BONNAR, JAMES KING Painter (1885-1961)
BONNEY, THERESE Photographer (1895-1978)
BONNYCASTLE, MURRAY C Painter
BOOGAR, WILLIAM F Sculptor (1893-1958)
BOOKATZ, SAMUEL Painter, Sculptor (1910-2009)
BOOKBINDER, JACK Painter, Printmaker (1911-1990)
BOORAEM, HENDRIK Painter (1886-1951)
BOOTH, CAMERON Painter (1892-1980)
BOOTH, NINA MASON Painter (1884-)
BOPP, EMERY Painter, Educator (1924-2008)
BORDEN, JAMES ERWIN Painter (1921-1990)
BORDUAS, PAUL EMILE Painter (-1960)
BORGATTA, ROBERT EDWARD Painter, Sculptor (1921-2009)
BORGENICHT, GRACE (GRACE BORGENICHT BRANDT) Art Dealer, Collector (1915-2001)
BORGHI, GUIDO RINALDO Painter (1903-1971)
BORGLUM, JAMES LINCOLN BE LA MOTHE Sculptor, Photographer (1912-1986)
BORIS, BESSIE Painter (-1993)
BORN, WOLFGANG Historian, Writer (1893-1949)
BORNE, MORTIMER Sculptor, Painter (1902-1987)
BOROCHOFF, (IDA) SLOAN Painter, Printmaker
BORSTEIN, YETTA Painter (-1968)
BOSA, LOUIS PAINTER (1905-1981)
BOSIN, BLACKBEAR Painter, Designer (1921-1980)
BOSSE, JANET C Painter, Ceramist (-2000)
BOSSERT, EDYTHE H Painter (1908-1997)
BOSWELL, PEYTON, JR Writer, Editor (1904-1950)
BOSZIN, ANDREW Painter, Sculptor (1923-2006)
BOTELLO, ANGEL Painter, Sculptor (1913-1986)
BOTHMER, BERNARD V Historian, Instructor (1912-1993)
BOTKIN, HENRY Painter, Writer (1896-1983)
BOTTIS, HUGH P Printmaker (-1964)
BOUCHARD, LORNE HOLLAND Painter, Illustrator (1913-1978)
BOUCHE, LOUIS Painter (1896-1969)
BOUCHE, RENE Portrait Painter (-1963)
BOUCHER, TANIA KUNSKY Painter, Sculptor (1927-2006)
BOULDIN, MARSHALL JONES III Painter (1923-2012)
BOURBON, DAVID Art Critic, Writer (1934-1998)
BOURDELL, PIERRE VAN PARYS Sculptor (-1966)
BOURGEOIS, LOUISE Sculptor (1911-2010)
BOVER, RUSS (RUSSELL WALTER) Graphic Artist, Painter (1928-)
BOWDOIN, HARRIETTE Painter (-1947)
BOWEN, GAZA Sculptor, Environmental Artist (1944-2005)
BOWER, ALEXANDER Museum Director (1875-1952)
BOWES, BETTY MILLER Painter, Consultant (-2007)
BOWLES, JANET PAYNE Craftsman (1882-1948)
BOWLING, JACK Silversmith, Printmaker (1903-1979)
BOWMAN, KEN Painter (1937-2014)
BOWMAN, RUTH Art Historian, Educator (1923-)
BOXER, STANLEY (ROBERT) Painter, Sculptor (1926-2000)
BOYCE, GERALD G Educator, Painter (1925-1999)
BOYCE, RICHARD Sculptor (1920-)
BOYCE, WILLIAM G Museum Director, Educator (1921-1992)
BOYD, E Art Administrator, Writer (1903-1974)
BOYD, JAMES HENDERSON Printmaker, Sculptor (1928-2002)
BOYD, JOHN DAVID Educator, Printmaker (1939-)
BOYD, RUTHERFORD Painter, Designer (-1951)
BOYER, MARIETTA P Librarian (1932-1997)
BOYER, RALPH LUDWIG Painter, Etcher (1879-1951)
BOYKO, FRED Painter, Educator (1894-1951)
BOYNTON, JACK (JAMES) W Painter, Printmaker (1928-)
BRACH, PAUL HENRY Painter (1924-2007)

BRACKMAN, ROBERT Painter, Educator (1898-1980)
BRADFORD, FRANCIS SCOTT Painter (1898-1961)
BRADFORD, HOWARD Printmaker, Painter (1919-2008)
BRADSHAW, GLENN RAYMOND Painter, Educator (1922-2013)
BRADSHAW, ROBERT GEORGE Painter, Educator (1915-2004)
BRAIDEN, ROSE MARGARET J Painter, Illustrator (1923-)
BRAIDER, DONALD Art Writer (1923-1977)
BRAINARD, JOE Graphic Artist, Designer (1942-1994)
BRAKHAGE, JAMES STANLEY Filmmaker, Lecturer (1933-2003)
BRAKKE, P(ERRY) MICHAEL Painter, Educator (1943-)
BRANDON, WARREN EUGENE Painter (1916-1977)
BRANDT, FREDERICK ROBERT Curator (1936-)
BRANDT, REX (REXFORD ELSON) Painter, Printmaker (1914-2000)
BRANNER, ROBERT Art Historian (1927-1973)
BRANSOM, (JOHN) PAUL Painter, Illustrator (1885-1979)
BRANSTETTER, GWENDOLYN H Painter (-2009)
BRAOLEY, MRS. HARRY LYNDE Collector
BRAWLEY, ROBERT JULIUS Painter, Educator (1937-2006)
BRAXTON, WILLIAM E Painter (1878-1932)
BRAY, JOHN Cartoonist (1879-1978)
BRAZEAU, WENDELL (PHILLIPS) Painter (1910-1974)
BRECHER, SAMUEL Painter (1897-1982)
BRECKENRIDGE, JAMES D Art Historian (1926-1982)
BREER, ROBERT C Sculptor, Filmmaker (1926-2011)
BREESKIN, ADELYN DOHME Administrator, Consultant (1896-1986)
BREGER, DAVE (DAVID) Cartoonist (1908-1970)
BREITENBACH, EDGAR Historian (1903-1977)
BRENDEL, OTTO J Art Historian (1901-1973)
BRENER, ROLAND Sculptor, Educator (1942-2006)
BRENNAN, FANNY (FRANCES) M Painter (-2001)
BRENNER, SHORE HODGE Weaver, Educator (1949-)
BRENSON, THEODORE Painter (1893-1959)
BREWER, BESSIE MARSH Etcher, Lithographer (1883-1952)
BREWINGTON, MARION VERNON Art Historian, Writer (1902-1974)
BREWSTER, MARGARET EMILIA Painter (1932-)
BRICE, WILLIAM Painter, Printmaker (1921-1997)
BRIGGS, ERNEST Painter, Instructor (1923-1984)
BRIGGS, LAMAR A Painter (1935-2015)
BRIGHTWELL, WALTER Painter (1919-2005)
BRIGOS, AUSTIN Illustrator, Collector (1808-1973)
BRIGOS, BERTA N Painter, Writer (1884-1976)
BRINLEY, DANIEL PUTNAM Painter (1879-1963)
BRISTAH, JAMES W Gallery Director (1918-)
BRITSKY, NICHOLAS Painter, Educator (1913-2005)
BRITT, NELSON CLARK Museum Director, Painter (1944-2004)
BRITTAIN, MILLER G Painter (-1968)
BRITTON, HARRY Painter (1879-1958)
BRITTON, JAMES II Critic, Illustrator (1915-1983)
BROADD, HARRY ANDREW Painter, Historian (1910-)
BROADLEY, HUGH T Historian, Administrator (1922-2005)
BROADMAN, NELL Painter (-1968)
BRODER, PATRICIA JANIS Historian, Writer (1935-2002)
BRODEUR, CATHERINE R Painter
BRODIE, AGNES HAHN Sculptor, Painter (1924-1992)
BRODIE, GANDY Painter, Designer (1924-1975)
BRODSKY, HARRY Printmaker, Painter (1908-)
BRODY, RUTH Painter, Graphic Artist (1917-2006)
BROMBERG, FAITH Painter (1919-1990)
BROMUND, CAL E Painter (1903-1979)
BRONER, MATHEW Painter, Printmaker (1924-2005)
BROOK, ALEXANDER Painter (1898-1980)
BROOKS, H(AROLD) ALLEN Historian, Lecturer (1925-2010)
BROOKS, HARRY A Gallery Director, Art Dealer (1913-2000)
BROOKS, JAMES Painter (1906-1992)
BROSEN, FREDERICK Painter, Printmaker (1954-)
BROSS, ALBERT L JR Painter (1921-2013)
BROUGH, RICHARD BURRELL Educator, Designer (1920-1996)
BROUILLETTE, AL(BERT) C Painter, Instructor (1924-2000)
BROUILLETTE, GILBERT T Art Dealer, Consultant-Research
BROUSSARD, JAY REMY Museum Director, Painter (1920-1976)
BROWN, BRIAN Director (1911-1958)
BROWN, CARLYLE Painter (-1964)
BROWN, GEORGE BYRON Painter (1907-1961)
BROWN, JAMES MONROE Museum Director (1917-1998)
BROWN, JOHN CARTER Museum Director, Administrator (1934-2002)
BROWN, JOSEPH Sculptor, Educator (1909-)
BROWN, JUDITH GWYN Illustrator, Painter (1933-1992)
BROWN, JUNE GOTTLIEB Painter, Instructor (1932-2015)
BROWN, MARBURY HILL Painter, Instructor (1925-1997)
BROWN, MARGARET Writer (1910-1952)
BROWN, MILTON WOLF Historian (1911-1998)
BROWN, PAUL Illustrator (1893-1958)
BROWN, RICHARD F Museum Director (1916-1979)
BROWN, RICHARD M Portrait Painter (-1964)
BROWN, ROGER Painter (1911-1997)
BROWN, ROY Painter (1879-1956)
BROWNE, VIVIAN E Painter, Educator (1929-1993)
BROWNHILL, HAROLD Painter, Illustrator
BROWNING, COLLEEN Painter (1929-)
BROWNING, G WESLEY Painter (1868-1951)
BRUN, THOMAS Sculptor, Instructor (1911-2003)
BRUNDAGE, AVERY Collector (1887-1975)
BRUNS, FREDERICK R, JR Curator (1913-1979)
BRUSCA, JACK Painter (1939-1993)
BRUSSEL-SMITH, BERNARD Printmaker (1914-1989)
BRY, EDITH Assemblage Artist, Collage Artist (1898-1992)
BRYANT, EDWARD ALBERT Writer, Consultant (1928-2003)
BUBA, JOY FLINSCH Sculptor, Illustrator (1904-)
BUCHANAN, JERRY Painter, Educator (1936-1992)
BUCHANAN, JOHN EDWARD JR Museum Director, Administrator (1953-2011)
BUCHER, FRANCOIS Historian, Educator (1927-)
BUCK, RICHARD D Conservator (1903-1977)
BUCKLEY, JOHN MICHAEL Painter (1891-1958)
BUCKNER, KAY LAMOREUX Painter, Draftsman (1935-)
BUCKSBAUM, MELVA JANE Collector (-2015)
BUECHNER, THOMAS SCHARMAN Painter, Writer (1926-2010)
BUFF, CONRAD Printmaker, Illustrator (1886-1975)
BUKI, ZOLTAN Curator, Administrator (1929-2003)
BULLIET,CJ Art Critic (1883-1952)
BULLOCK, JAMES BENBOW Sculptor (1929-)
BULLOCK, WYNN Photographer (1902-1975)
BULTMAN, FRITZ Sculptor, Painter (1919-1985)

BUMGARDNER, JAMES ARLISS Painter, Educator (1935-2016)
BUNCE, LOUIS DEMOTT Painter (1914-1983)
BUNKER, GEORGE Painter, Educator (1923-1991)
BUNTING, BAINBRIDGE Historian, Educator (1913-1981)
BURCH, CLAIRE R Painter, Writer, Filmmaker (1925-2009)
BURCHFIELD, CHARLES Painter (1893-1967)
BURCHFIELD, JERRY LEE Photographer, Educator, Author (1947-)
BURCK, JACOB Cartoonist, Painter (1904-1982)
BURCKHARDT, RUDY Painter, Filmmaker (1914-2001)
BURDEN, CHRIS Conceptual Artist, Sculptor (1946-2015)
BURFORD, BYRON LESLIE Painter, Printmaker (1920-2011)
BURGART, HERBERT JOSEPH Educator, Administrator (1932-2002)
BURGESS, JOSEPH E Painter (1891-1961)
BURKE, E AINSLIE Painter, Educator (1922-1991)
BURKE, MARY GRIGGS Collector (-2012)
BURKE, WILLIAM LOZIER MUNRO Historian (1906-1961)
BURKHARDT HANS GUSTAV Painter, Printmaker (1904-1994)
BURLEY, LINA Painter (1922-2005)
BURLIN, PAUL Painter (1886-1969)
BURLUIK, DAVID Painter (1882-1967)
BURNETT, BARBARA ANN Painter (1927-2003)
BURNETT, CALVIN Painter, Printmaker (1921-2007)
BURNEY, MINNA Educator (1891-1958)
BURNS, HARRISON D Painter, Instructor (1946-1991)
BURNS, JEROME Painter, Printmaker (1919-2003)
BURNS, SID Sculptor, Collector (1916-1979)
BURNSHIDE, KATHERINE TALBOTT Painter
BURNSIDE, CAMERON Painter, Educator (1887-1952)
BURRISS R (RILEY) HAL Painter, Illustrator (1892-1991)
BURROUGHS, MARGARET T G Lecturer, Painter (1917-)
BURROWS, PEARL Painter (1903-1960)
BURROWS, SELIG S Collector, Historian (1913-1997)
BURT, CLYDE EDWIN Ceramist, Educator (-1981)
BURTON, NETTA M Painter (-1960)
BURTON, SCOTT Sculptor, Conceptual Artist (1939-1989)
BUSA, PETER Painter, Sculptor (1914-1983)
BUSBEE, JULIANA ROYSTER Craftsman (1877-1962)
BUSCH, MICHAEL Artist
BUSH, BEVERLY Painter, Sculptor (-1969)
BUSH, ELLA SHEPART Painter (1863-)
BUSH, JACK Painter (1909-1977)
BUSH, WILLIAM BROUGHTON Painter (1911-)
BUSHMAN, DAVID FRANKLIN Painter, Educator (1945-2010)
BUSHMILLER, ERNIE PAUL Cartoonist (1905-)
BUSSABARGER, ROBERT FRANKLIN Sculptor, Painter, Ceramist (1922-)
BUTLER, EUGENIA P Conceptual Artist (-2008)
BUTLER, JOSEPH (GREEN) Administrator, Painter (1911-1981)
BUXBAUM, ROBERT Sculptor (1939-2006)
BUZZELLI, JOSEPH ANTHONY Painter, Sculptor (1907-)
BYARS, JAMES LEE Conceptual Artist
BYE, RANULPH Painter (1916-2003)
BYRON, CHARLES ANTHONY Dealer (1920-2013)
BYRUM, RUTHVEN HOLMES Educator (1896-)
CADGE, WILLIAM FLEMMING Designer, Photographer (1924-2003)
CADLE, RAY KENNETH Craftsman, Painter (1906-2002)
CADMUS, PAUL Painter, Printmaker (1904-1999)
CADORIN, ETTOR Sculptor (1876-1951)
CAGE, JOHN Printmaker (1912-1992)
CAHAN, SAMUEL G Artist (-1974)
CAHILL, HOLGER Art Authority (1893-1960)
CAHILL, JAMES FRANCIS Historian, Educator (1926-2014)
CAIN, JOSEPH ALEXANDER Painter, Educator (1920-1980)
CAJORI, CHARLES F Painter (1921-2013)
CALAPAI, LETTERIO Printmaker, Painter (1902-1993)
CALAS, NICHOLAS Critic (-1989)
CALCAGNO, LAWRENCE Painter (1913-1993)
CALDER, ALEXANDER Sculptor (1898-1976)
CALDWELL, JOHN Curator (1941-1993)
CALHOUN, LARRY DARRYL Painter, Ceramist (1937-2015)
CALKINS, KINGSLEY MARK Painter, Educator (1917-2004)
CALKINS, LORING GARY Designer (1887-1960)
CALLAHAN, HARRY M Photographer (1912-1999)
CALLAHAN, KENNETH Painter (1905-1986)
CALLERY, MARY Sculptor (1903-1977)
CALLICOTT, BURTON HARRY Painter, Calligrapher (1907-2003)
CALLISEN, STERLING A Historian, Lecturer (1899-1988)
CALROW, ROBERT F Instructor, Painter (1916-1998)
CALVERT, JENNIE C (MRS. FINLEY H) Painter (1878-)
CAMERON, DUNCAN F Museum Director (1930-2006)
CAMFFERMAN, PETER MARIENUS Painter (1890-1951)
CAMHI, MORRIE Photographer, Educator (1928-1999)
CAMINS, JACQUES JOSEPH Painter, Printmaker (1904-1988)
CAMLIN, JAMES A Painter (1918-1982)
CAMPANELLI, PAULINE Painter, Writer (-2001)
CAMPBELL, (JAMES) LAWRENCE Painter, Writer (1914-1998)
CAMPBELL, CHARLES MALCOLM Painter, Sculptor (1908-1985)
CAMPBELL, DOROTHY BOSTWICK Painter, Sculptor (1899-2001)
CAMPBELL, EDMUND S Painter, Architect (1884-1951)
CAMPBELL, ORLAND Portrait Painter (1890-1972)
CAMPBELL, SARA WENDELL Illustrator (1886-1960)
CAMPBELL, VIVIAN (VIVIAN CAMPBELL STOLL) Collector, Writer (1919-1986)
CAMPBELL, WILLIAM HENRY Painter (1915-2012)
CAMPBELL, WILLIAM PATRICK Art Historian, Curator (1914-1976)
CANADAY, JOHN EDWIN Critic (1907-1985)
CANDELL, VICTOR Painter, Educator (1903-1977)
CANFIELD, JANE (WHITE) Sculptor (1897-1984)
CANIFF, MILTON ARTHUR Cartoonist (1907-1988)
CANTEY, SAM BENTON III Collector (-1973)
CANTOR, ROBERT LLOYD Educator, Designer (1919-1986)
CANTOR, RUSTY Painter, Sculptor (1927-2012)
CAPA, CORNELL Photographer, Museum Director (1918-2008)
CAPLAN, JERRY L Sculptor, Educator (1922-2004)
CAPP, AL Cartoonist (1909-1979)
CAREWE, SYLVIA Painter, Tapestry Artist
CAREY, JOHN THOMAS Educator, Historian (1917-1990)
CARLES, ARTHUR B Painter (1882-1952)
CARLIN, ELECTRA MARSHALL Dealer
CARMACK, PAUL R Cartoonist (1895-1977)
CARO, ANTHONY Sculptor (1924-2013)
CARONE, NICOLAS Artist (1917-2010)

CARPENTER, GEORGE ROBERT Painter (1928-)
CARPENTER, GILBERT (BERT) FREDERICK Painter, Educator (1920-2003)
CARPENTER, JAMES MORTON Historian, Artist (1914-1992)
CARRICK, DONALD F Illustrator, Painter (1929-)
CARRILLO, LILIA Painter (1929-1974)
CARRINGTON, JOY HARRELL Painter, Illuminator (-1999)
CARRINGTON, OMAR RAYMOND Painter, Instructor (1904-1991)
CARROLL, JOHN Painter (1892-1959)
CARROLL, RICHARD S Museum Director (1929-2003)
CARRUTH, PAUL H Illustrator (1892-1961)
CARSTENSON, CECIL C Sculptor, Lecturer (1906-1991)
CARTER, DEAN Sculptor, Educator (1922-2013)
CARTER, DUDLEY CHRISTOPHER Sculptor (1911-1992)
CARTER, FREDERICK TIMMINS Painter, Illustrator (1925-)
CARTER, HELENE Illustrator (1887-1960)
CARTMELL, HELEN Painter, Designer (1923-2015)
CASANOVA, ALDO JOHN Sculptor, Educator (1929-2014)
CASARELLA, EDMOND Sculptor, Printmaker (1920-1996)
CASCIERI, ARCANGELO Sculptor, Instructor (1902-1997)
CASE, ELIZABETH Painter, Writer (1930-2006)
CASE, REGINALD Painter, Collage Artist (-2009)
CASEY, ELIZABETH TEMPLE Curator (1901-1990)
CASSEL, JOHN HARMON Cartoonist
CASSIDY, MARGARET CAROL (MRS JOHN MANSHIP) Sculptor (-2000)
CASSILL, HERBERT CARROLL Printmaker, Educator (1928-2008)
CASTANIS, MURIEL (JULIA BRUNNER) Sculptor (1926-)
CASTANO, GIOVANNI Art Dealer, Painter (1896-)
CASTELLI, LEO Dealer (1907-1999)
CASTLE, MRS ALFRED L Art Patron (1886-1970)
CATER, AUGUSTUS D (AD) Cartoonist (1895-1957)
CATHERS, JAMES O Sculptor, Educator (1934-1982)
CATLETT, ELIZABETH Sculptor, Printmaker (1919-2012)
CATLIN, STANTON LOOMIS Musicologist, Historian (1915-1997)
CAVAGLIERI, GIORGIO Architect (1911-2007)
CAVALLITO, ALBINO Sculptor (1905-1966)
CAVALLON, GIORGIO Painter
CAVANAUGH, JOHN W Sculptor (1921-)
CAVE, LEONARD EDWARD Sculptor, Educator (1944-2006)
CAVER, WILLIAM RALPH Sculptor, Printmaker (1932-2005)
CECERE, GAETANO Sculptor, Lecturer (1894-1985)
CEGLIA, VINCENT Painter (1923-)
CELIS, PEREZ Painter, Sculptor (1939-2008)
CELLINI, JOSEPH Illustrator (1924-)
CERNUDA, PALOMA Painter (1948-2003)
CERNUSCHI, ALBERTO C Dealer, Critic
CERVENE, RICHARD Painter, Curator
CHAET, BERNARD ROBERT Painter, Educator (1924-2012)
CHALIAPIN, BORIS Painter (1907-1979)
CHALKE, JOHN Ceramist, Sculptor (1940-2014)
CHAMBERLAIN, ANN Installation Sculptor, Environmental Sculptor (1951-2008)
CHAMBERLAIN, BETTY Art Administrator, Writer (1908-1983)
CHAMBERLAIN, JOHN ANGUS Sculptor (1927-2011)
CHAMBERLAIN, SAMUEL Printmaker, Writer (1895-1975)
CHAMBERS, JOHN Painter, Filmmaker (1911-1978)
CHAMBI, MARTIN Photographer (1891-1973)
CHANDLER, ELISABETH GORDON Sculptor, Instructor (1913-2006)
CHANDOR, DOUGLAS Portrait Painter (1897-1953)
CHANEY, ROBERT H Collector (-2008)
CHANIN, ABRAHAM L Lecturer
CHAPELLIER, GEORGE Art Dealer, Collector (1890-1978)
CHAPELLIER, ROBERT Art Dealer (-1974)
CHAPIN, (M) ANNE Sculptor, Educator (1930-1986)
CHAPIN, FRANCIS Painter (1899-1965)
CHAPIN, MYRON BUTMAN Painter (1887-1958)
CHAPMAN, CHARLES SHEPARD Painter (1879-1962)
CHAPMAN, HOWARD EUGENE Director, Cartoonist (1913-1977)
CHAPMAN, WALTER HOWARD Painter, Illustrator (1912-2015)
CHAPPELL, WALTER (LANDON) Photographer, Curator (1925-2000)
CHARLES, CLAYTON (HENRY) Sculptor, Educator (1913-1976)
CHARLESWORTH, SARAH E Photographer, Conceptual Artist (1947-2013)
CHARLOT, JEAN Painter, Historian (1898-1979)
CHARNEY, MELVIN Sculptor, Architect (1935-2012)
CHASE, ALLAN (SEAMANS) Sculptor, Muralist
CHASE, EDWARD Portrait Painter (1884-1965)
CHASE, FRANK SWIFT Painter (1886-1958)
CHASE, GEORGE H Educator, Writer (1874-1952)
CHASE, JOSEPH CUMMINGS Portrait Painter (1878-1965)
CHASE, SIDNEY M Painter (1877-1957)
CHATTERTON, CLARENCE KERR Painter (1880-1973)
CHEATHAM, FRANK REAGAN Painter, Designer (1936-2002)
CHEFFETZ, ASA Engraver (1897-1965)
CHENEY, SHELDON Writer, Historian (1886-1980)
CHERNEY, MARVIN Painter (-1966)
CHERRY, BERMAN Painter (1909-1992)
CHESTERTON, DAVID Educator, Graphic Artist (1930-)
CHETHLAHE (DAVID CHETHLAHE PALADIN) Painter, Designer (1926-1984)
CHEW, HARRY Painter, Educator (1925-)
CHEW, PAUL ALBERT Historian, Educator (1925-2004)
CHIAN-CHIU, CHOW Painter, Historian (1910-2004)
CHIAPELLA, EDWARD EMILE Painter (1889-1951)
CHILDERS, BETTY BIVINS Collector, Patron (1913-1982)
CHILDS, BERNARD Painter, Printmaker (1910-1985)
CHILLIDA, EDUARO Sculptor (1924-)
CHIMES, THOMAS JAMES Painter (1921-2009)
CHOATE, NATHANIEL Sculptor (1899-1965)
CHOUINARD, MRS NELBERT Educator (-1969)
CHOW LEUNG, CHEN-YING Painter, Calligrapher (1921-2005)
CHRISTENSEN, DAN Painter (1942-)
CHRISTENSEN, RALPH Painter (1897-1961)
CHRISTENSEN, RONALD JULIUS Painter, Printmaker (1923-)
CHRISTENSON, HANS-JORGEN THORVALD Designer, Silversmith (1924-1983)
CHRIST-JANER, ALBERT WILLIAM Painter, Printmaker (1910-1973)
CHRISTOPER, WILLIAM R Painter (1924-1973)
CHRISTY, HOWARD CHANDLER Painter (1872-1952)

CHUMLEY, JOHN WESLEY Painter (1928-)
CHURCH, FREDERICK E Painter (1826-1900)
CIAMPAGLIA, CARLO Muralist (1891-1975)
CIANCIO, JUNE (KIRKPATRICK) Painter, Instructor (1920-2008)
CIKOVSKY, NICOLAI Painter, Muralist (1894-1984)
CISNEROS, JOSE B Illustrator, Painter (1910-2009)
CITRON, MINNA WRIGHT Painter, Printmaker (1896-1991)
CLAGUE, JOHN ROGERS Sculptor (1928-2004)
CLANCY, JOHN Art Dealer (-1981)
CLAPP, MAUDE CAROLINE EDE Painter (1876-1960)
CLARE, STEWART Research Artist (1913-1992)
CLARK, ALLAN Sculptor (1896-1950)
CLARK, ALSON SKINNER Painter, Lithographer (1876-1949)
CLARK, ANTHONY MORRIS Curator, Collector (1923-1976)
CLARK, CLAUDE Instructor, Painter (1915-2001)
CLARK, ELIOT CANDEE Painter (1883-1980)
CLARK, G FLETCHER Sculptor (1899-1982)
CLARK, MABEL BEATRICE SMITH Painter (-1957)
CLARK, ROLAND Painter (1874-1957)
CLEAR, CHARLES V Museum Consultant
CLEARY, MANON CATHERINE Painter, Draftsman (1942-2011)
CLEAVER, DALE GORDON Historian, Educator (1928-2000)
CLEAVES, MURIEL MATTOCK (MRS H) Illustrator, Painter (-1947)
CLELAND, THOMAS MAITLAND Illustrator (1880-1964)
CLEVELAND, HELEN BARTH Administrator, Instructor
CLIME, WINFIELD SCOTT Painter (1881-1958)
CLINEDINST, MAY SPEAR Painter (1887-)
CLISBY, ROGER Curator, Historian (1939-1994)
CLOSE, MARJORIE (PERRY) Painter, Lecturer (1899-1978)
CLYMER, JOHN F Painter, Illustrator (1907-1989)
COATES, ROBERT M Writer, Art Critic (1897-1973)
COBB, RUTH Painter (1914-2008)
COBER, ALAN E Illustrator, Printmaker (1935-1998)
COCHRAN, GEORGE MCKEE (REDBIRD) Painter, Writer (1908-1990)
COE, LLOYD Painter, Illustrator (1899-1977)
COE, MATCHETT HERRING Sculptor (1907-1999)
COE, RALPH TRACY Consultant, Historian (1929-2010)
COE, ROLAND Cartoonist
COFFEY, MABEL Painter, (1874-1949)
COFFMAN HAL Cartoonist (1883-1958)
COHEN, ARTHUR MORRIS Painter, Graphic Artist (1928-2012)
COHEN, BRUCE JOEL Painter (1953-)
COHEN, H GEORGE Painter, Educator (1913-1980)
COHN, MAX ARTHUR Painter, Printmaker (1903-1998)
COHOE, GREY Printmaker, Painter (1944-)
COINER, CHARLES T Painter (1897-1989)
COKE, VAN DEREN Photographer, Historian (1921-)
COLBORN, JANE TAYLOR Sculptor, Educator (1913-1983)
COLBURN, FRANCIS PEABODY Painter (1909-1984)
COLBY, HOMER WAYLAND Illustrator, Etcher (1874-1950)
COLEMAN, RALPH P Painter (1892-1968)
COLESCOTT, ROBERTH Painter, Educator (1925-2009)
COLETTI, JOSEPH ARTHUR Sculptor, Writer (1898-1973)
COLIN, RALPH FREDERICK Collector (1900-)
COLLAZO, CARLOS ERICK Painter, Graphic Artist (1956-1990)
COLLES, GERTRUDE Painter (1869-1957)
COLLETT, FARRELL REUBEN Painter, Educator (1907-2000)
COLLEY, WILLIAM, JR Collector, Patron (1910-1984)
COLLIER, ALAN CASWELL Painter (1911-1990)
COLLIER, ALBERTA Critic, Consultant (1911-1987)
COLLIER, LEO NATHAN (NATE) Cartoonist (-1961)
COLLINS, GEORGE R, Historian, Educator (1917-1993)
COLLINS, JOHN IRELAND Painter (1926-1982)
COLLINS, KREIGH Illustrator (1908-1974)
COLLINS, LOWELL DAUNT Painter, Dealer (1924-2003)
COLLINS, ROY H Illustrator (-1949)
COLMAN, VIRGINIA O'CONNELL Sculptor, Graphic Artist (-1999)
COLSON, CHESTER E Painter, Educator (1917-1985)
COLT, JOHN NICHOLSON Painter, Educator (1925-1998)
COLVILLE, ALEXANDER Painter, Printmaker (1920-2013)
CONE, GERRIT CRAIG Art Administrator (1947-1997)
CONE, MARVIN Painter (1891-1964)
CONGDON, WILLIAM (GROSVENOR) Painter, Writer (1912-1998)
CONGER, CLEMENT E Curator (1912-2004)
CONKLIN, GLORIA ZAMKO Painter (1925-2000)
CONNAWAY, JAY HALL Painter (1893-1970)
CONNER, BRUCE Graphic Artist, Collage Artist, Filmmaker (1933-2008)
CONNER, JOHN RAMSEY Painter (1869-1952)
CONOVER, ROBERT FREMONT Printmaker, Painter (1920-1998)
CONRAD, PAUL FRANCIS Cartoonist, Sculptor (1924-2010)
CONROW, WILFORD SEYMOUR Painter (1880-)
CONSTABLE, WILLIAM GEORGE Art Historian, Writer (1887-1976)
CONSTANT, GEORGE Painter (1892-1978)
COOK, GLADYS EMERSON Illustrator, Painter (1899-)
COOK, HOWARD NORTON Painter, Lecturer (1911-1980)
COOK, PETER (GEOFFREY) Painter (1915-1992)
COOK, WALTER WILLIAM SPENCER Educator (1888-1962)
COOKE, HEREWARD LESTER Art Historian, Painter (1916-1973)
COOKE, KATHLEEN MCKEITH Painter, Sculptor (1908-1978)
COOLEY, DIXIE (MRS JOHN L) Painter (1896-)
COOPER, ANTHONY J Painter (1907-1992)
COOPER, FRED G Cartoonist (1883-1962)
COOPER, MARVE H Painter Curator (1939-)
COOPER, RICHARD Painter (1945-1979)
COORMARASWAMY, ANADA K Museum Curator (1877-1947)
COOTES, FRANK GRAHAM Painter (1879-1960)
COPPEDGE, ARTHUR L Painter, Educator (1938-)
COPPINI, POMPEO LUIGI Sculptor (1870-1957)
COPPOLA, ANDREW Sculptor, Draftsman (1941-1990)
CORBETT, EDWARD M Educator, Painter (1919-1971)
CORBETT, GAIL SHERMAN (MRS HARVEY WILEY CORBETT) Sculptor (1871-1951)
CORBINO, JOHN Painter (1905-1964)
CORCOS, LUCILLE Painter, Illustrator (1908-1973)
CORISH, JOSEPH RYAN Painter (1909-1988)
CORNELIUS, MARTY Painter, Illustrator (1913-1979)
CORNELL, JOSEPH Sculptor (1903-1972)
CORNELL, THOMAS BROWNE Sculptor (1937-2012)
CORNETTE, MARY ELIZABETH Dealer, Painter (1909-2005)

CORNWELL, DEAN Illustrator (1892-1960)
CORPRON, CARLOTTA M Educator, Photographer (1911-1988)
CORREA, FLORA HORST Painter (1908-2007)
CORTIGLIA, NICCOLO Painter, Restorer (1893-)
CORTOR, ELDZIER Painter, Printmaker (1916-2015)
COSGROVE, J O'HARA II Illustrator (1908-1968)
COSLA, OK Collector
COST, JAMES PETER Painter (1923-)
COSTIGAN, JOHN EDWARD Painter (1888-1972)
COTSWORTH, STAATS Painter (1908-1979)
COTT, JEAN CAHAN Painter
COTTON, LILLIAN Painter (1901-1962)
COTTON, WILLIAM HENRY Painter (1880-1951)
COUCH, URBAN Consultant, Educator (1927-)
COURT, LEE WINSLOW Painter (1903-1992)
COURTICE, RODY KENNY Painter (-1973)
COVERT, JOHN Painter (1882-1960)
COVEY, ARTHUR Painter (1878-1960)
COVEY, VICTOR CHARLES B Conservator, Consultant (1928-1989)
COWAN, WOODSON MESSICK Cartoonist, Painter (1886-1977)
COWDREY, MARY BARTLETT Art Historian, Art Critic (1910-1974)
COWLES, RUSSELL Painter (1887-1979)
COX, ALLYN Painter (1896-1982)
COX, E MORRIS Collector (1903-2003)
COX, J HALLEY Painter (1910-)
COX, PAT Assemblage Artist, Sculptor (-2014)
COYER, MAX R Painter (1954-1988)
COZE-DABIJA, PAUL Painter, Writer (1903-1975)
CRAFT, DAVID RALPH Painter, Photographer (1945-2013)
CRAMPTON, ROLLIN Painter (1886-1970)
CRANDELL, BRADSHAW Painter (-1966)
CRANE, ROY (CAMPBELL) Cartoonist, Writer (1901-1977)
CRASKE, LEONARD Sculptor, Lithographer (-1950)
CRATZ, BENJIMIN ARTHUR Painter, Cartoonist (1888-)
CRAVATH, GLENN Cartoonist (-1964)
CRAWFORD, CATHERINE BETTY Painter (1910-2002)
CRAWFORD, EARL Painter (1890-1960)
CRAWFORD, RALSTON Painter, Lithographer (1906-1977)
CRAWFORD, WILLIAM H Cartoonist, Sculptor (1913-)
CREAN, HUGH R Administrator, Lecturer (-2008)
CREECH, FRANKLIN UNDERWOOD Sculptor, Graphic Artist (1941-2006)
CRESPI, PACHITA Painter (1900-1971)
CRESPIN, LESLIE A Painter, Assemblage Artist (1947-2001)
CRESSON, MARGARET Sculptor, Writer (1889-1973)
CRILLEY, JOSEPH JAMES Painter (1920-2008)
CRIQUETTE (RUTH DUBARRY MONTAGUE) Painter, Writer (-1991)
CRISP-ELLERT, JOANN Painter, Writer (1924-2007)
CRISS, FRANCIS H Painter (1911-1973)
CROCKETT, GIB (GIBSON M) Cartoonist, Painter (1912-2001)
CROCKWELL, DOUGLAS Commercial Artist (1904-1968)
CRONIN, TONY Gallery Director (-1979)
CROOKS, W SPENCER Painter, Lecturer (1917-2004)
CROSBY, SUMNER MCKNIGHT Art Historian (1909-1982)
CROSS, WATSON JR Painter, Video Artist (1918-1997)
CROUGHTON, AMY H Critic (1880-1911)
CROW, CAROL (WILSON) Sculptor, Photographer (1915-1997)
CROWELL, LUCIUS Painter, Sculptor (1911-1988)
CROWN, KEITH ALLEN Painter (1918-2010)
CRUMP, KATHLEEN (WHEELER) Sculptor (1884-1977)
CRUMP, W LESLIE Painter (1894-1962)
CRUZ, EMILIO ANTONIO Painter (1938-2004)
CSOKA, STEPHEN Painter (-1989)
CULHANE, SHAMUS H Filmmaker, Writer (1908-1996)
CUMING, BEATRICE Painter (1903-1975)
CUMMINGS, FREDERICK JAMES Administrator, Historian (1933-1990)
CUMMINGS, PAUL Writer, Historian (-1997)
CUNNINGHAM, BENJAMIN FRAZIER Painter, Educator (1904-1975)
CUNNINGHAM, CHARLES CREHORE Curator, Lecturer (1910-1979)
CUNNINGHAM, IMOGEN Photographer (1883-1976)
CUNNINGHAM, JEAN HIMROD STULL Painter (1929-)
CUNNINGHAM, MARION Serigrapher, Lithographer (1911-)
CUNNINGHAM, MERCE Conceptual Artist (-2009)
CUPRIEN, FRANK W Painter (1871-1948)
CURLEY, DONALD HOUSTON Painter, Lecturer (1940-2009)
CURRIER, CYRUS BATES Painter, Designer (1868-)
CURTIS, CONSTANCE Painter (-1959)
CURTIS, DAVID Painter, Printmaker (1949-2002)
CURTIS, PHILIP Painter (1907-2000)
CURTIS, ROGER WILLIAM Painter, Dealer (1910-2000)
CUSUMANO, STEFANO Painter, Educator (1912-1975)
CUTHBERT, VIRGINIA Painter (1908-2002)
CUTLER, ETHEL ROSE Painter, Designer, Educator (1915-)
CUTRONE, RONNIE BLAISE Painter (1948-2013)
CZUFIN, RUDOLF Director (1901-1979)
D'ANDREA ALBERT PHILIP Educator, Sculptor (1897-1983)
D'AULAIRE EDGAR PARIN Illustrator, Painter (1898-1986)
DA COSTA, BEATRIZ Environmental Artist, Educator
DABO, LEON Painter (1868-1960)
DAGYS, JACOB Sculptor (1905-1989)
DAHL, FRANCIS W Cartoonist (1907-1973)
DAHLBERG, EDWIN LENNART Painter (1901-1984)
DAHLER, WARREN Painter (1897-1961)
DAILEY, MICHAEL DENNIS Painter, Educator (1938-2009)
DAILY, EVELYNNE MESS Painter, Etcher (1903-2003)
DAINGERFIELD, MARJORIE JAY Sculptor (-1977)
DALE, BENJAMIN MORAN Illustrator (1889-1951)
DALI, SALVADOR Designer, Painter (1904-1989)
DALY, NORMAN Painter, Sculptor (1911-2008)
DAMAZ, PAUL F Writer, Architect (1917-2008)
DANBY, KENNETH EDISON Painter, Printmaker (1940-2007)
DANHAUSEN, ELDON Sculptor, Educator
DANIEL, LEWIS C Painter, Illustrator (1901-1952)
DANIELS, DAVID M Collector, Patron (1927-2002)
DANTO, ARTHUR COLEMAN Critic (1924-2013)
DAPHNIS, NASSOS Painter, Sculptor (1914-2010)
D'ARCANGELO, ALLAN M Painter (1930-1998)
DARIUS, DENYLL (DENNIS MITCHELL) Painter (1942-1976)
DARLING, JAY NORWOOD (DING) Cartoonist (1876-1962)
DARROW, WHITNEY Cartoonist (1909-1999)
DASBURG, ANDREW MICHAEL Painter (1887-1979)

DASH, HARVEY DWIGHT Administrator, Painter (1924-2002)
DATUS, JAY Painter, Art Administrator (1914-1974)
DATZ, A MARK Painter (1889-)
DAUDELIN, CHARLES Sculptor (1920-2001)
DAUGHERTY, JAMES HENRY Painter, Writer (1898-1974)
DAUGHERTY, MARSHALL HARRISON Sculptor, Medalist (1915-1991)
DAVENPORT, EDITH FAIRFAX Painter (1880-1957)
DAVEY, RANDALL Painter (1887-1964)
DAVIDSON, ABRAHAM A Art Historian, Photographer (1935-)
DAVIDSON, ALLAN ALBERT Painter, Sculptor (1913-1988)
DAVIDSON, JO Sculptor (1883-1952)
DAVIDSON, MORRIS Painter (1898-1979)
DAVIES, HAYDN LLEWELLYN Sculptor, Painter (1921-2008)
DAVIS, (MR & MRS) WALTER Collectors, Patrons (-1991)
DAVIS, DAVID E Sculptor (1920-2002)
DAVIS, DONALD ROBERT Painter, Dealer (1909-1990)
DAVIS, DOUGLAS MATTHEW Artist, Critic (1933-2014)
DAVIS, ESTHER M Sculptor, Painter (1893-1974)
DAVIS, GENE B Painter (1920-1985)
DAVIS, HARRY ALLEN Painter, Muralist (1914-2006)
DAVIS, JACK R Painter, Educator
DAVIS, JAMES Abstract Artist (1901-1974)
DAVIS, JOHN SHERWOOD Potter, Administrator (1942-2003)
DAVIS, LEW E Painter (1910-1979)
DAVIS, MARIAN B Historian, Curator (1911-)
DAVIS, PHIL Cartoonist (-1964)
DAVIS, ROBERT TYLER Administrator, Historian (1904-)
DAVIS, STUART Painter (1894-1964)
DAVIS, WAYNE LAMBERT Painter, Illustrator (1914-1988)
DAVIS, WILLIAM D Educator, Printmaker (1936-2003)
DAVIS, WILLIAM STEEPLE Painter (1884-1961)
DAVISSON, HOMERG Painter (1866-)
DAWSON, EVE Painter
DAY, CHON (CHAUNCEY ADDISON) Cartoonist (1907-2000)
DAY, HORACE TALMAGE Painter, Director (1909-)
DAY, JOHN Painter, Educator (1932-1984)
DAY, LARRY (LAWRENCE JAMES) Painter, Educator (1921-)
DAY, MABEL K Painter (1884-)
DAY, WORDEN Sculptor, Printmaker (1916-1986)
DE ARMOND, DALE BURLISON Printmaker, Illustrator (1914-2006)
DE BORHEGYI STEPHEN Museum Director, Writer (1911-1969)
DE BOTTON, JEAN PHILIPPE Painter, Sculptor (-1978)
DE COUX, JANET Sculptor (-2002)
DE CREEFT, JOSE Sculptor, Educator (1884-1982)
DE DIEGO, JULIO Painter, Illustrator (1900-1979)
DE ERDELY, FRANCIS Painter, Educator (1904-1959)
DE FOREST, ROY DEAN Painter, Sculptor (1930-2007)
DE FRANCISCI, ANTHONY Sculptor (1887-1964)
DE GRAZIA, ETTORE TED Painter (1909-1982)
DE JONG, GERRIT, JR Lecturer, Writer (1892-1979)
DE KOONING, ELAINE MARIE CATHERINE Painter, Writer (1920-1989)
DE LESSEPS, TAUNI Sculptor, Painter (1920-)
DE LISIO, MICHAEL Sculptor (-2003)
DE MARCO, JEAN ANTOINE Sculptor (1898-1990)
DE MARIA, WALTER Sculptor (1935-2013)
DE MARTELLY, JOHN STOCKTON Painter, Printmaker (1903-1980)
DE MARTINI, JOSEPH Painter (1896-)
DE MENIL, JOHN Collector (1904-1973)
DE MISKEY, JULIAN Sculptor, Printmaker (-1986)
DE NAGY, TIBOR J Dealer, Collector (1910-1993)
DE POL, JOHN H Printer, Designer (1913-2004)
DE PREY, JUAN Painter (-1962)
DE RIVERA, JOSE Sculptor (1904-1985)
DE ROTHSCHILD, ELIE ROBERT Collector (1917-2007)
DE RUTH, JAN Printer, Paintmaker (1922-1911)
DE TORE, JOHN E Painter (1902-1975)
DEAL, JOE Photographer, Educator (1947-2010)
DEAN, ERNEST WILFRID Painter
DEAN, NICHOLAS BRICE Printmaker, Photographer (1933-2005)
DEAN, PETER Painter (1939-1993)
DECARAVA, ROY RUDOLPH Photographer, Educator (1919-2009)
DECKER, JOHN Painter (1895-)
DEDINI, ELDON LAWRENCE (1921-2000)
DEE, LEO JOSEPH Graphic Artist, Painter (1931-2004)
DEEM, GEORGE Painter (1932-2008)
DEFRANCESCO, ITALO I Educator (1901-1967)
DEHN, ADOLF Graphic Artist (1895-1968)
DEHNER, DOROTHY Sculptor, Printmaker (1901-1994)
DEINES, E HUBERT Engraver (1894-1967)
DEKNATEL, FREDERICK BROACKWAY Art Historian, Educator (1905-1973)
DEL CASTILLO, MARY VIRGINIA Painter (1865-)
DELANEY, BEAUFORD Painter (1902-1979)
DELONGA, LEONARD ANTHONY Sculptor, Educator (1925-1990)
DELSON, ELIZABETH Painter, Printmaker (1932-2005)
DEMANCE, HENRI Painter (1871-1948)
DEMETROIS, GEORGE Sculptor (1896-1974)
DEMIANOFF, RENEE LOCKHART Director (1910-1962)
DEMPSEY, RICHARD W Painter, Lecturer (1909-)
DENNIS, BURT MORGAN Etcher (1892-1960)
DENNIS, CHARLES HOUSTON Cartoonist (1921-2002)
DENNIS, GERTRUDE WEYHE Art Dealer
DENNISTON, DOUGLAS Painter, Educator (1921-2004)
DENSLOW, DOROTHEA HENRIETTA Sculptor (1900-1971)
DENTZEL, CARL SCHAEFER Museum Director, Writer (1913-1980)
DENZLER, NANCY J Sculptor, Painter (1936-2013)
DEO, MARJORIE NEE, Painter (1907-1996)
DEPILLARS, MURRY N Administrator, Illustrator (1938-2008)
DEPINNA, VIVIAN Painter (1883-1978)
DERGALIS, GEORGE Painter, Sculptor (1928-2012)
DERUJINSKY, GLEB W Sculptor, Craftsman (1888-1975)
DESSAR, LOUIS PAUL Painter (1867-1952)
DESSNER, MURRAY Painter (1934-)
DEVLIN, HARRY Painter, Cartoonist (1918-2001)
DEVLIN, WENDE Painter (1918-2002)
DEVREE, HOWARD Critic (1890-1966)
D'HARNONCOURT, ANNE Historian, Museum Director (1943-2008)
DIBBLE, GEORGE Painter, Writer (1904-2001)
DIBONA, ANTHONY Sculptor, Lithographer (1896-)
DICKERSON, WILLIAM JUDSON Painter (1904-)
DICKINSON, EDWIN W Painter (1891-1979)

DIEBENKORN, RICHARD Painter (1922-1993)
DIENES, SARI Assemblage Artist, Printmaker (1898-1992)
DIETSCH, C PERCIVAL Sculptor (1881-1961)
DIETZ, CHARLES LEMOYNE Museum Director, Painter (1910-2002)
DIFRANZA, AMERICO M Painter (1919-2004)
DIGIORGIO, JOSEPH J Painter (1931-2000)
DIGIUSTO, GERALD N Sculptor (1929-1987)
DILLER, BURGOYNE Painter (1906-1965)
DILLON, C DOUGLAS Patron, Collector (1909-2003)
DIMAN, HOMER Painter (1914-1974)
DIMONDSTEIN, MORTON Sculptor, Painter (1920-)
DIMSON, THEO Designer, Illustrator (1930-2012)
DINGER, CHARLOTTE Collector, Writer (-1996)
DIODA, ADOLPH T Sculptor, Assemblage Artist (1915-1991)
DIRK, NATHANIEL Painter (1896-1961)
DIRKS, RUDOLPH Cartoonist (-1968)
DIRUBE, ROLANBO LOPEZ Painter, Sculptor (1928-1997)
DISMUKES, MARY ETHEL Painter (-1951)
DISTEFANO, DOMENIC Painter, Instructor (1924-)
DIXON, FRANCIS S Painter (1879-1967)
DOBBS, ELLA VICTORIA Educator (1866-1952)
DOBBS, JOHN BARNES Painter (1931-)
DOBKIN, ALEXANDER Painter (1908-1975)
DOBSON, DAVID IRVING (DIAMONOSTEIN) Painter (1883-1957)
DOCKSTADER, FREDERICK J Consultant, Historian (1912-1998)
DOCKTOR, IRV Painter, Illustrator (1918-2008)
DODD, H(ELEN) C(AROLYN) Painter (1924-2014)
DODGE, HAZEL (MRS WILLIAM TURMAN) Curator (1903-1957)
DODGE, JOSEPH JEFFERS Painter, Lecturer (1917-)
D'OENCH, ELLEN GATES Curator, Educator (1930-2009)
DOGANCAY, BURHAN Painter, Sculptor, Photographer (1929-2013)
DOHANOS, STEVAN Illustrator, Painter (1907-1994)
DOHERTY, MICHAEL STEPHEN Editor, Printmaker (1948-2001)
DOI, ISAMI Painter (1903-1965)
DOLE, WILLIAM Painter, Educator (1917-1983)
DOMBEK, BLANCHE M Painter, Sculptor (-1987)
DOMJAN, JOSEPH (SPIRI) Painter, Printmaker (1907-)
DONAHEY, JAMES HARRISON Cartoonist (1875-1949)
DONAHUE, BENEDICT SR Educator
DONATI, ENRICO Painter, Sculptor (1909-2008)
DONATO, GIUSEPPE Sculptor (1881-1965)
DONNELLY, MARIAN CARD Historian, Educator (1923-)
DONNELLY, MARY E Painter (1898-1963)
DOOLIN, JAMES LAWRENCE Painter, Educator (1932-2002)
DOREN, ARNOLD T Photographer, Educator (1935-2003)
DOREN, HENRY J T Painter, Educator (1929-)
DORN, RUTH (DORNBUSH) Painter (1925-2004)
DORNER, ALEXANDER Historian (1893-)
DORR, (VIRGINIA) NELL Photographer (1893-)
DORRA, HENRI Historian, Educator (1924-2002)
DORSKY, MORRIS Historian, Educator (1918-2000)
DORST, CLAIRE V Painter, Printmaker (1922-)
DOUGLAS, AARON Painter (1900-1979)
DOUGLAS, FREDERIC HUNTINGTON Curator (1897-1951)
DOUGLAS, LESTER Designer (1894-1961)
DOUGLAS, ROBERT LANGTON Critic (-1951)
DOVE, ARTHUR GARFIELD Painter (1880-1946)
DOW, HELEN JEANNETTE Historian, Educator (1926-1993)
DOWDEN, ANNE OPHELIA TODD Painter, Writer (1907-)
DOWLING, ROBERT W Patron (1895-1973)
DOWNEY, JUAN Video Artist, Architect (1940-1993)
DOWNS, STUART CLIFTON Administrator, Educator (1950-2013)
DOYLE, JOHN LAWRENCE Printmaker, Painter (1939-)
DOYON, GERARD MAURICE Educator, Historian (1923-1990)
DRABKIN, STELLA Painter, Designer (1900-1976)
DRAPALIK, BETTY R Painter, Consultant (-2007)
DRAPER, WILLIAM FRANKLIN Painter, Instructor (1912-2003)
DREIER, KATHERINE S Painter, Lecturer (1877-1952)
DREIKAUSEN, MARGRET Painter (1937-2007)
DREITZER, ALBERT J Collector, Patron (1902-1985)
DRESSER, LOUISA (LOUISA DRESSER CAMPBELL) Administrator, Historian (1907-1988)
DREWES, WERNER Painter, Printmaker (1899-1985)
DREWLOWE, EVE Painter, Sculptor (1924-1988)
DREXLER, ARTHUR JUSTIN Director, Curator (1925-1987)
DREXLER, LYNNE Painter (-1999)
DRIGGS, ELSIE Painter (1898-1992)
DROGKAMP, CHARLES Painter (-1958)
DRUMMOND, ARTHUR A Painter, Illustrator (1891-)
DRURY, WILLIAM H Painter (1888-1960)
DRYER, MOIRA JANE Painter, Sculptor (1957-1992)
DRYFOOS, NANCY Sculptor (1918-1991)
DRYSDALE, NANCY MCINTOSH Patron, Dealer (1931-2003)
DU BOIS, GUY PENE Painter (1884-1951)
DU MONO, FRANK V Painter (1865-1951)
DU PEN, EVERETT GEORGE Sculptor, Educator (1912-2005)
DUANE, TANYA Painter, Collage Artist
DUBANIEWICZ, PETER PAUL, Painter (1913-2003)
DUBLE, LU Sculptor (1896-1970)
DUBOIS, MACY Architect, Designer (1929-2007)
DUCA, ALFRED MILTON Painter, Sculptor (1920-1997)
DUCKWORTH, RUTH Sculptor, Ceramist (1919-2009)
DUFFY, EDMUND Cartoonist (1899-1962)
DUFNER, EDWARD Painter (1871-1957)
DUHME, H RICHARD JR Sculptor, Educator (1914-2005)
DUKES, CAROLINE Painter, Printmaker (1929-2003)
DUNCAN, HARRY ALVIN Printer, Designer (1916-1997)
DUNCAN, RUTH S Painter (1908-)
DUNCANSON, ROBERT Painter (1817-1872)
DUNN, ALAN (CANTWELL) Cartoonist, Writer (1900-1974)
DUNN, CAL Painter, Filmmaker (1915-2000)
DUNN, HARVEY T Illustrator, Painter (1884-1952)
DUPONT, HENRY F Museum Curator (1880-1969)
DURLACH, MARCUS RUSSELL Painter (1911-1991)
DUVEEN, ANNETA Sculptor, Designer (1924-2007)
DUVOISIN, ROGER Writer, Illustrator (1904-1980)
DWIGGINS, CLARE Cartoonist (1874-1958)
DWIGGINS, WILLIAM ADDISON Designer (1880-1956)
DWIGHT, EDWARD HAROLD Museum Director (1919-1981)
EAMES, JOHN HEAGAN Etcher, Painter (1900-2002)
EARLS, PAUL Environmental Artist (1934-1998)
EASBY, DUDLEY T JR Art Administrator, Art Historian (1905-1973)

EASTERWOOD, HENRY LEWIS Educator, Tapestry Artist (1934-2002)
EASTMAN, ALVIN CLARK Orientalist (1894-1959)
EASTMAN, WILLIAM JOSEPH Painter (1881-1950)
EASTON, FRANK LORENCE Painter (1884-)
EASTON, ROGER DAVID Painter, Jeweler (1923-2005)
EBERLE, MERAB Critic (-1959)
EBERMAN, EDWIN Administrator, Educator (1905-1988)
ECKE, GUSTAV Museum Curator (-1971)
ECKELBERRY, DON RICHARD Painter (1921-)
ED, CARL Cartoonist (1890-1959)
EDMONDSON, LEONARD Printmaker (1916-2002)
EDMONSTON, PAUL Educator, Editor (1922-2011)
EDWARDS, EMMET Painter (1907-)
EDWARDS, GEORGE WHARTON Painter, Illustrator (1869-1950)
EDWARDS, PAUL BURGESS Painter, Educator (1935-2005)
EDWARDS, ROBERT Painter, Engraver (1879-1948)
EGAS, CAMILO Educator (1897-1962)
EGBERT, ELIZABETH FRANCES Sculptor, Educator (1945-2014)
EGE, OTTO F Educator, Writer (1888-1911)
EGGERS, GEORGE WILLIAM Educator (1883-1958)
EGGERS, RICHARD Architect (1918-1979)
EGLESON, JIM (JAMES DOWNEY) Printmaker, Painter (1907-)
EGLITIS, LAIMONS Painter, Educator (1929-2007)
EGRI, TED Sculptor, Painter (1913-2011)
EHRMAN, FREDERICK L Collector (1906-1973)
EICHENBERG, FRITZ Graphic Artist, Illustrator (1911-1990)
EIDE, PALMER Sculptor, Designer (1906-1991)
EISENLOP, EDWARD G Painter (1873-1961)
EISENSTAT, BENJAMIN Painter, Illustrator (1915-)
EISNER, DOROTHY (DOROTHY EISNER MCDONALD) Painter, Collage Artist (1906-)
EITEL, CLIFFE DEAN Painter, Etcher (1909-)
EITNER, LORENZ E A Historian, Museum Director (1919-2009)
ELDER, ARTHUR JOHN Painter, Etcher (1874-)
ELDLITZ, DOROTH MEIGS Patron, Photographer (1891-1976)
ELDREDGE, STUART EDSON Painter (1902-1992)
ELIASH, ZARA Sculptor (1914-2002)
ELIASON, BIRDELL Painter, Illustrator
ELIASOPH, PAULA Painter, Writer (1895-)
ELISOFON, ELIOT Painter, Photographer (1911-1973)
ELKON, ROBERT Art Dealer, Collector (1928-1983)
ELLERHUSEN, FLORENCE COONEY Painter (-1950)
ELLERHUSEN, ULRIC H Sculptor (1879-1951)
ELLIOTT, BETTE G Painter, Instructor (1920-2011)
ELLIOTT, DOROTHY BADEN Conservator (1914-)
ELLIOTT, JAMES HEYER Administrator, Consultant (1924-2000)
ELLIOTT, PHILIP CLARKSON Painter (1903-1985)
ELLIS, CARL EUGENE Art Administrator, Instructor (1932-1977)
ELLIS, FREMONT Painter (1897-1985)
ELLIS, JOSEPH BAILEY Educator, Sculptor (1890-)
ELLIS, RAY Painter, Lecturer (1921-2013)
ELLIS, ROBERT CARROLL Painter, (1923-1979)
ELLISON, SHIRLEY (SHIRLEY ELIASON HAUPT) Painter, Educator (1926-1988)
ELLSWORTH Illustrator (1885-1961)
ELOUL, KOSSO Sculptor (1920-1998)
ELSNER, LARRY EDWARD Sculptor, Educator (1930-)
ELY, FANNY G Painter (1879-1961)
EMBRY, NORRIS Painter (1921-1981)
EMERSON, ROBERTA SHINN Museum Director (1922-1998)
EMERSON, WALTER CARUTH Painter, Educator (1912-2002)
EMIL, ALLAN D Collector, Patron (1898-1976)
EMIL, ARTHUR D Collector (1924-2010)
EMMERICH, ANDRE Art Dealer, Writer (1924-2007)
EMMERICH, IRENE HILLEBRAND Painter
EMMET, LYDIA FIELD Painter (1886-1952)
ENFIELD, HARRY Illustrator (1906-1958)
ENGEL, HARRY Painter (1901-1970)
ENGEL, MICHAEL M Art Publicist (1896-1969)
ENGGASS, ROBERT Historian, Educator (1921-2003)
ENGLISH, HAL (HAROLD) J Painter (1910-2008)
ENGLISH, JOHN ARBOGAST Painter (1913-2013)
ENO, JAMES LORNE Painter, Educator (1887-1952)
ENSER, GEORGE Designer (1890-1911)
EPSTEIN, BETTY O Sculptor, Painter (1920-1999)
EPSTEIN, ETHEL S Collector
ERDELAC, JOSEPH MARK Collector, Patron
ERICKSON, JOY M Painter, Graphic Artist (1932-2008)
ERICSON, BEATRICE Painter (-1997)
ERICSON, ERNEST Illustrator, Instructor (-1981)
ERLANGER, ELIZABETH N Painter, Lecturer (1901-1975)
ERNST, JIMMY Painter, Educator (1920-)
ERNST, MAX Painter, Sculptor (1911-1976)
ERSKINE, HAROLD PERRY Sculptor (1879-1951)
ERWIN, FRAN (FRANCES) SUZANNE Painter, Sculptor (-2003)
ESCHMANN, JEAN CHARLES Craftsman (1896-1961)
ESHERICK, W HARTON Sculptor, Designer (1887-1970)
ESLER, JOHN KENNETH Printmaker, Painter (1933-2001)
ETNER, STEPHEN MORGAN Painter (1903-)
ETON, ALLEN HENDERSHOTT Writer (1878-1962)
ETROG, SOREL Sculptor, Painter (1933-2014)
ETTINOHAUSEN, RICHARD Administrator (1906-1979)
ETTLING, RUTH (DROITCOUR) Painter, Printmaker (1910-2003)
EVANS, DONALD Painter (1946-1977)
EVANS, GROSE Historian, Educator (1916-2003)
EVANS, JOHN Collage Artist, Painter (1932-2012)
EVANS, MINNIE Painter (1892-1987)
EVANS, RICHARD Painter, Educator (1923-2013)
EVANS, RUDULPH Sculptor (1879-1960)
EVERETT, LEN G Painter
EVERETT, MARY O (MRS HG) Painter (1876-1948)
EVERGOOD, PHILIP Painter, Graphic Artist (1901-1973)
EVERINGHAM, MILLARD Painter, Etcher (1912-)
EVETT, KENNETH WARNOCK Painter, Critic (1913-2005)
EWEN, PATERSON Painter, Educator (1925-)
EWING, BAYARD Administrator, Collector (1916-1991)
FABE, ROBERT Painter, Educator (1917-2004)
FABRES, OSCAR Cartoonist (1895-1961)
FABRI, RALPH Painter, Writer (1894-1975)
FAHLSTROM, OYVIND Painter (1928-1976)
FAIERS, TED (EDWARD SPENCER) Painter, Printmaker (1908-1985)
FAINTER, ROBERT A Educator, Painter (1942-1978)

FAIRCHILD, MAY Painter (1872-1959)
FAISON, SAMSON LANE JR Historian, Museum Director (1907-)
FALKENSTEIN, CLAIRE Sculptor (-1997)
FALLS, CHARLES BUCKLES Illustrator (1874-1959)
FALTER, JOHN Illustrator (1910-1982)
FANE, LAWRENCE Sculptor (1933-2008)
FANGOR, VOY Painter (1922-2015)
FARIAN, BABETTE S Painter, Graphic Artist (1916-)
FARIS, BRUNEL DE BOST Painter, Educator (1937-2005)
FARLOW, HARRY Painter (1882-1956)
FARMER, MABEL McKIBBIN Engraver (1903-)
FARNHAM, EMILY Painter, Writer (1912-2004)
FARNSWORTH, HELEN SAWYER Painter, Writer (-1999)
FARR, FRED Sculptor (1914-1973)
FARRELL, KATHERINE L Painter, Etcher (1857-)
FARRIS, JOSEPH Cartoonist, Painter, Author (1924-2015)
FARROW, PATRICK VILLIERS Sculptor (1942-2009)
FARWELL, BEATRICE Historian, Educator (1920-2009)
FASANO, CLARA Sculptor (-1990)
FASTOVE, AARON (AARON FASTOVSKY) Painter (1898-1979)
FAULKNER, BARRY Painter (1911-1966)
FAULKNER, KADY B Painter, Educator (1901-1977)
FAULKNER, RAY N Educator, Writer (1906-1975)
FAUSETT, LYNN Painter (1894-1977)
FAWCETT, ROBERT Illustrator (1903-1967)
FAY, WILBUR M Designer (1904-1959)
FEARING, WILLIAM KELLY Educator, Painter (1918-)
FEDELLE, ESTELLE, Painter, Lecturer (1914-2001)
FEELEY, PAUL Painter (1913-1966)
FEHER, JOSEPH Curator, Painter (1908-1987)
FEIGIN, DOROTHY L Painter (1904-1969)
FEIGL, HUGO Art Dealer (1890-1961)
FEINBLATT, EBRIA Historian
FEININGER, ANDREAS B L Photographer, Writer (1906-1999)
FEININGER, T LUX Painter, Writer (1910-2011)
FEITELSON, LORSER Painter (1898-1978)
FEJES, CLAIRE Painter, Writer (1920-)
FELDHAUS, PAUL A Educator, Printmaker (1926-2005)
FELS, C P Painter, Writer (1912-1991)
FENCI, RENZO Sculptor (1914-1999)
FENICAL, MARLIN E Painter, Photographer (1907-1983)
FENTON, ALAN Painter, Instructor (1927-2000)
FENTON, BEATRICE Sculptor (1887-1983)
FENTON, HOWARD CARTER Painter, Educator (1910-2006)
FENTON, JOHN NATHANIEL Painter, Etcher (1912-1977)
FERBER, HERBERT Sculptor, Painter (1906-1991)
FERGUSON, BARCLAY (VISCOUNT OF LAMOND) Painter, Muralist (1924-1991)
FERGUSON, GERALD Painter (1937-2009)
FERNALD, HELEN ELIZABETH Educator (1891-1964)
FERRARI, FEBO Sculptor (1865-)
FERREN, JOHN Painter (1905-1970)
FETT, WILLIAM F Instructor, Painter (1918-2006)
FICKLEN, JACK HOWELLS Cartoonist (1911-1980)
FIELD, SAUL Printmaker, Lecturer (1912-1987)
FIELDS, MITCHELL Sculptor (1901-1966)
FIENE, ALICIA W Painter (1919-1961)
FIENE, ERNEST Painter (1894-1965)
FIERO, EMILIE L Sculptor (1889-1974)
FILECKENSTEIN, OPAL R Painter, Ceramist (1911-1996)
FILIPOWSKI, RICHARD E Sculptor, Educator (1923-)
FILMUS, TULLY Painter, Lecturer (1903-1995)
FILTZER, HYMAN Sculptor, Restorer (1911-1967)
FINCH, RUTH WOODWARD Writer, Photographer (1916-2004)
FINCK, FURMAN J Painter, Instructor (1900-)
FINDLAY, HELEN T Dealer (1909-1992)
FINDLING, SIDNEY Painter, Instructor (1922-2004)
FINE, PERLE Painter (1905-1988)
FINK, HERBERT LEWIS Painter, Educator (1921-)
FINK, LOUIS R Painter (1925-l980)
FINK, RAY Sculptor, Educator (1922-1998)
FINKELSTEIN, LOUIS Educator, Painter (1923-2000)
FINLAYSON, DONALD LORD Educator (1897-1960)
FINLEY, DAVID EDWARD Art Administrator (1890-1977)
FINLEY, MARY L Painter (-1964)
FINTA, ALEXANDER Sculptor (1881-1951)
FIORE, JOSEPH ALBERT Painter, Instructor (1925-2008)
FISCHER, MILDRED (GERTRUDE) Designer, Craftsman (1907-2000)
FISCHETTI, JOHN Cartoonist (1916-1980)
FISH, DOROTHY S Ceramist (1906-1958)
FISH, RICHARD G Designer, Painter (1925-2008)
FISHER REGINALD Writer (1906-1966)
FISHER, ROB (ROBERT) NORMAN Sculptor, Lecturer (1939-2009)
FISHER, SANDRA Painter (1947-1994)
FISKE, GERTRUDE Painter (1879-1961)
FITCH, GEORGE HOPPER Collector, Patron (1909-2004)
FITE, FIARVEY Sculptor (1903-1976)
FITZGERALD, EDMUND J Painter, Lecturer (1912-1989)
FITZGERALD, HARRIET Painter, Lecturer (1904-1984)
FITZGERALD, J EDWARD Photographer (1923-1977)
FITZSIMMONS, JAMES JOSEPH Painter, Architect (1908-)
FLAGG, JAMES MONTGOMERY Illustrator (1977-1960)
FLANAGAN, BARRY Sculptor (1941-2009)
FLANAGAN, JOHN F Sculptor (1898-1952)
FLAVIN,. DAN Artist, Writer (1933-1996)
FLECK, PAUL DUNCAN Director (1934-1992)
FLECKER, MAURICE NATHAN Painter, Educator (1940-)
FLEISCHMANN, ADOLF R Painter (-1969)
FLEISCHMANN, JULIUS Collector
FLEISHMAN, LAWRENCE ARTHUR Art Dealer, Publisher (1925-1997)
FLEMING, ALLAN ROBB Designer, Calligrapher (1929-1977)
FLEXNER, JAMES THOMAS Writer, Historian (1908-2003)
FLIEGEL, LESLIE Painter (1912-1968)
FLINT, JANET ALTIC Curator, Historian (1935-2005)
FLOCH, JOSEPH Painter (1895-1977)
FLOETER, KENT Painter, Sculptor (1937-2004)
FLOETHE, RICHARD Illustrator, Designer (1901-1988)
FLOOD, EDWARD C Sculptor, Painter (1944-1985)
FLORSHEIM, RICHARD A Painter, Printmaker (1916-1979)
FLORY, ARTHUR L Graphic Artist, Painter (1914-1972)
FLUME, VIOLET SIGOLOFF Dealer, Restorer (1920-2007)
FOGEL, SEYMOUR Painter, Sculptor (1911-1984)
FOLEY, DOROTHY SWARTZ Painter, Printmaker (1922-2004)
FOLLETT, JEAN FRANCES Sculptor, Painter (1917-1991)
FONDREN, HAROLD M Art Dealer (1922-1999)
FONTAINE, E JOSEPH Painter (-2004)
FONTANNINI, CLARE Educator, Sculptor (-1984)

FOOTE, JOHN JR Painter (-1968)
FOOTE, WILL HOWE Painter (1874-1965)
FORBES, EDWARD W Museum Director (1873-1969)
FORCE, JULIANA R Museum Director (-1948)
FORD, CHARLES HENRI Painter, Photographer (1913-   )
FORD, ELEANOR CLAY Patron (1896-1976)
FORESTER, RUSSELL Painter, Sculptor (1920-2002)
FORGE, ANDREW MURRAY Writer, Painter (1923-   )
FORREST, JAMES TAYLOR Museum Director, Educator (1919-2005)
FORRESTER, CHARLES HOWARD Sculptor (1928-2010)
FORRESTER, PATRICIA TOBACCO Painter, Printmaker (1940-2011)
FORST, MILES Sculptor, Educator (1923-2006)
FORSYTH, CONSTANCE Painter, Printmaker (1903-1987)
FOSBURGH, JAMES WHITNEY Painter, Writer (1910-1978)
FOSOICK, SINA G Art Administrator, Collector (-1983)
FOSTER, GENEVIEVE Writer, Illustrator (1893-1979)
FOSTER, HAL Cartoonist, Painter (1892-1982)
FOSTER, JAMES W SR Museum Director
FOSTER, KENNETH E Museum Director (-1964)
FOURNIER, ALEXIS JEAN Painter (1865-1948)
FOUSEK, FRANK DANIEL Printmaker, Painter (1913-1979)
FOWLER, ALFRED Writer (1889-   )
FOWLER, MEL (WALTER) Sculptor (1921-   )
FOWLER, MEL Printmaker, Painter (1922-   )
FOX, CHARLES HAROLD Craftsman (1905-1979)
FOX, MILTON S Painter (1904-1971)
FRACE, CHARLES LEWIS Painter (1926-2005)
FRALEY, DAVID K Painter (1952-   )
FRAMPTON, HOLLIS Filmmaker (1936-1984)
FRANCIS, BILL DEAN Designer, Administrator (1929-   )
FRANCO, ROBERT JOHN Painter, Educator (1932-   )
FRANGELLA, LUIS Painter (1944   )
FRANKENSTEIN, ALFRED VICTOR Art Critic, Art Historian (1906-1981)
FRANKENTHALER, HELEN Painter, Printmaker (1928-2011)
FRANKFURTER, ALFRED Art Editor (-1965)
FRANKL, PAUL THEODORE Designer (1876-1958)
FRANKLE, PHILIP Painter (1913-1968)
FRANKLIN, CLARENCE Collector (-1967)
FRANKLIN, DOUGLAS (FERRAR) Art Historian, Educator (1929-1982)
FRANKLIN, GILBERT ALFRED Sculptor, Educator (1919-2004)
FRASCONI, ANTONIO Graphic Artist, Painter (1919-2013)
FRASER, LAURA G Sculptor (1889-1966)
FRASER, MALCOLM Painter (1869-1949)
FRAZIER, KENNETH Painter (1867-1949)
FRAZIER, RICHARD WILLIAMS Sculptor (1922-1983)
FREDENTHAL, DAVID Painter (1914-1958)
FREDERICK, EUGENE WALLACE Printmaker, Educator (1927-   )
FREDERICKS, BEVERLY MAGNUSON Painter, Restorer (1928-2007)
FREDERICKS, MARSHALL MAYNARD Sculptor (1908-1998)
FREED, ERNEST BRADEIELD Printmaker, Painter (1908-   )
FREED, HERMINE Video Artist, Photographer (1940-1998)
FREED, WILLIAM Painter (1902-1984)
FREEDBERG, SYDNEY JOSEPH Historian, Educator (1914-1997)
FREEDMAN, DON Author, Illustrator (1909-1978)
FREEDMAN, MAURICE Painter (1904-   )
FREEMAN, GERTRUDE Collector (1927-   )
FREEMAN, JANE Painter (1885-1963)
FREER, HOWARD MORTIMER Painter (1904-1960)
FREIFELD, ERIC Painter, Educator (1919-   )
FREILICH, MICHAEL L Art Dealer, Collector (1912-1975)
FREIMAN, ROBERT J Painter (1917-1991)
FRENCH, RAY H Printmaker, Painter (1919-2000)
FRENCH, STEPHEN WARREN Painter, Sculptor (1934-2014)
FREUD, LUCIAN MICHAEL Painter (1922-2011)
FREUND, TIBOR Painter, Muralist (1910-2007)
FREY, ERWIN F Sculptor (1892-1967)
FREY, VIOLA Sculptor, Painter (1933-2004)
FRIBERG, ARNOLD Painter, Publisher (1913-2010)
FRICK, JOAN Painter, Conceptual Artist (1942-2011)
FRICK, ROBERT OLIVER Painter, Instructor (1920-1997)
FRID, TAGE P Designer (1915-   )
FRIEDENSOHN, ELIAS Painter, Sculptor (1924-1991)
FRIEDLAENDER, WALTER Art Historian (-1966)
FRIEDLANDER, ISAC Engraver (1890-1968)
FRIEND, DAVID Painter, Educator (1899-1978)
FRINK, ELISABETH Sculptor (-1993)
FRISHMUTH, HARRIET WHITNEY Sculptor (1880-1979)
FROELICH, PAUL Painter (1897-   )
FROMAN, RAMON MITCHELL Painter (1908-1980)
FROMBERG, GERALD Educator, Filmmaker (1925-1977)
FRONCKOWIAK, ARTHUR Painter (1949-2009)
FROUCHTBEN, BERNARD Painter (1878-1956)
FRUHAUF, ALINE Printmaker (1907-1978)
FRUMKIN, ALLAN Dealer (1926-2002)
FRY, EDWARD F Educator, Critic (1935-1992)
FRY, JUDY ARLINE Painter, Jeweler (1938-2007)
FUERSTENBURO, PAUL W Commercial Artist (1875-1953)
FUKUHARA, HENRY Painter, Instructor (1913-2010)
FULLER, META VAUX WARRICK Sculptor (1877-1968)
FULLER, R BUCKMINSTER Design Scientist (1895-1983)
FULLER, RICHARD EUGENE Museum Director (1897-1976)
FULTON, CYRUS JAMES Painter (1873-1949)
FULTON, FRED FRANKLIN Painter, Historian (1920-2003)
FUMAGALLI, ORAZIO Educator, Sculptor (1921-2004)
FUSSINER, HOWARD Painter, Educator (1923-2006)
GABO, NAUM Sculptor (1890-1977)
GABRIELSON, WALTER OSCAR Painter (1935-2008)
GAGNON, CHARLES EUGENE Sculptor (1934-2012)
GAHAGAN, JAMES (EDWARD) Painter, Educator (1919-2000)
GAILIS, JANIS Painter (1909-1975)
GALE, WALTER RASIN Educator (1878-1959)
GALLATIN, ALBERT EUGENE Painter (1882-1952)
GALLI, STANLEY WALTER Painter (1912-2009)
GALLI, WARREN J Painter, Writer (1923-2001)
GALLO, WILLIAM VICTOR Cartoonist, Illustrator (1922   -)
GALOS, BEN Painter (-1963)
GALVAN, JESUS GERRERO Painter
GANNAM, JOHN Painter (1907-1965)
GARBATY, EUGENE L Collector (-1966)
GARBE, WILLIAM Painter, Editor (1948-1989)
GARBER, DANIEL Painter (1880-1958)
GARBISCH, BERNICE CHRYSLER Collector
GARBISCH, EDGAR WILLIAM Collector (1899-1979)

GARCHIK, MORTON LLOYD Painter, Printmaker (1929-2009)
GARDNER, JOAN A Painter, Book Artist (1933-1982)
GARMAN, ED Painter, Writer (1914-2004)
GARNER, ARCHIBALD Sculptor, Designer (1904-1970)
GARNETT, WILLIAM ASHFORD Photographer, Educator (1916-2006)
GARNSEY, CLARKE HENDERSON Historian, Educator (1913-2012)
GARRETT, STUART GRAYSON Painter, Educator (1922-1996)
GARRISON, JESSE JANES Educator (1901-)
GARTH, JOHN Painter, Writer (1894-1971)
GASPARRO, FRANK Sculptor, Instructor (1909-2001)
GASSER, HENRY MARTIN Painter, Writer (1909-1981)
GATCH, LEE Painter (1909-1968)
GATEWOOD, MAUD Painter (1934-2004)
GATLING, EVA INGERSOLL Consultant, Historian (1912-2000)
GATRELL, MARION THOMPSON Educator, Painter (1909-)
GATRELL, ROBERT MORRIS Educator, Painter (1906-1982)
GAUDIN, MARGUERITE Designer (1909-)
GAUGH, HARRY E Educator, Critic (-1992)
GAYNE, CLIFTON ALEXANDER, JR Educator (1912-1971)
GEARHART, MAY Etcher
GEBER, HANA Sculptor, Instructor (1910-)
GEE, YUN Painter (1906-1963)
GEESEY, TITUS CORNELIUS Collector, Patron (1893-1969)
GEHR, MARY (RAY) Printmaker, Painter (-1997)
GEIGER, EDITH R Painter (1912-2004)
GEIGER, ELIZABETH DE CHAMISSO Sculptor
GEIS, MILTON ARTHUR Painter, Designer (1926-2005)
GEISEL, THEDOR SEUSS (Dr Seuss) Illustrator, Writer (1904-1991)
GELD, JAN Painter, Printmaker (1906-1978)
GELMAN, MILTON Collector (1914-1991)
GELOZADLER, HENRY Curator, Historian (1935-1994)
GELTMAN, LILY Collage Artist, Painter (1903-2001)
GENTRY, HERBERT Painter, Graphic Artist (1919-2003)
GEORGE, RAYMOND ELLIS Printmaker, Educator (1933-2005)
GEORGES, PAUL G Painter (1923-2002)
GEPPONI, ANGELO Painter, Educator (1911-2001)
GERACI, LUCIAN ARTHUR Painter, Dealer (1923-2005)
GERARD, PAULA (RENISON) Painter, Draftsman (1907-1991)
GERARDIA, HELEN Painter, Printmaker
GERENDAY, LACI ANTHONY DE Sculptor (1911-)
GERSHOY, EUGENE Sculptor, Painter (1901-1983)
GERSOVITZ, SARAH VALERIE Painter, Printmaker
GERTH, RUTH Illustrator (-1952)
GERZSO, GUNTHER Painter, Graphic Artist (1915-2000)
GETTY, J PAUL Collector, Writer (1892-1976)
GFISSDUHLER, ARNOLD Sculptor (1897-1993)
GIAMBRUNI, TIO Sculptor (1925-1971)
GIBBERED, ERIC WATERS Painter (1897-1972)
GIBRAN, KAHLIL GEORGE Sculptor (1922-2008)
GIBSON, JAMES D Video Artist, Painter (1938-2003)
GIBSON, ROLAND Collector, Curator (1902-)
GIBSON, SYBIL (SYBIL GIBSON DEYARMON) Painter (1908-1995)
GIESCHEN, MARTIN JOHN Educator, Painter (1918-1991)
GIFFUNI, FLORA BALDINI Painter, Lecturer (1919-2009)
GIKOW, RUTH (RUTH GIKOW LEVINE) Painter, Printmaker (1913-1982)
GILBERT, ARNOLD MARTIN Collector, Photographer (1921-)
GILBERT, CLYDE LINGLE Painter (1898-1986)
GILBERT, LIONEL Painter, Instructor (1912-2005)
GILBERT, SHARON Collage Artist, Conceptual Artist (1944-2005)
GILCHRIST, AGNES ADDISON Art & Architectural Historian (1907-1976)
GILES, NEWELL WALTON, JR Painter (1928-2004)
GILKEY, GORDON WAVERLY Curator, Educator (1912-2000)
GILKEY, RICHARD CHARLES Painter, Sculptor (1925-1997)
GILL, FREDERICK JAMES Painter, Instructor (1906-1974)
GILLESPIE, DOROTHY MURIEL Painter, Sculptor (1920-)
GILLESPIE, GREGORY JOSEPH Painter (1936-2000)
GILLIES, MARY ANN Artist
GILMARTIN, F THOMAS Administrator, Consultant (1940-)
GILPIN, HENRY EDMUND Photographer, Educator (1922-2012)
GILPIN, LAURA Photographer, Writer (1891-1979)
GILRLN, THEODORE H Painter (-1967)
GIUSTI, GEORGE Designer, Sculptor (- 1990)
GLAMAN, EUGENIE FISH Etcher (1872-1956)
GLARNER, FRITZ Painter (1899-1972)
GLASGOW, LUKMAN Ceramist Administrator (1935-1988)
GLASHAUSSER, SUELLEN Sculptor (1945-2000)
GLASS, WENDY D Dealer, Collector (1925-2006)
GLASSMAN, RONALD Painter, Printmaker (1940-2005)
GLEASON, JOE DUNCAN Painter (1879-1951)
GLICKMAN, ARTHUR Sculptor (1923-2011)
GLICKMAN, MAURICE Sculptor, Writer (1906-)
GLINES, ELLEN (MRS WALTER A) Painter (-1951)
GLINSKKY, VINCENT Sculptor, Educator (1895-1975)
GLOVSKY, ALAN Sculptor, Environmental Artist (1951-2000)
GLUHMAN, JOSEPH WALTER Historian, Graphic Artist (1934-2002)
GLYDE, HENRY GEORGE Painter, Educator (1906-1998)
GODDARD, VIVIAN Painter
GODWIN, FRANCES GRAY Historian (1908-1979)
GOETZ, EDITH JEAN Painter, Instructor (1918-1986)
GOETZ, OSWALD H Lecturer (1896-1960)
GOETZ, RICHARD VERNON Painter, Instructor (1915-1991)
GOLDBERG, CHAIM Painter, Sculptor (1917-2004)
GOLDBERG, ELIAS Painter (1887-1975)
GOLDBERG, JUDITH Art Dealer (1947-)
GOLDBERG, MICHAEL Painter (1924-2007)
GOLDBERG, NORMAN LEWIS Writer, Lecturer (1906-1982)
GOLDIN, AMY Art Critic (1926-1978)
GOLDIN, LEON Painter (1923-)
GOLDOWSKY, NOAH Art Dealer (1909-)
GOLDSMITH, ELSA M Painter, Graphic Artist (1920-)
GOLDSMITH, LAWRENCE CHARLES Painter, Instructor (1916-2004)
GOLDSMITH, MORTON RALPH Collector, Patron (1882-1971)
GOLDSTEIN, HOWARD Painter, Educator (1933-2013)
GOLDSTEIN, MILTON Printmaker, Painter (1914-2004)
GOLDSTEIN, NATHAN Painter, Writer (1927-2013)

GOLDWATER, ROBERT Art Historian (1907-1973)
GOLINKIN, JOSEPH WEBSTER Painter, Printmaker (1896-1977)
GOLLIN, JOSHUA A Collector, Patron (1905-)
GOLUB, LEON Painter (1922-2004)
GOLUBIC, THEODORE Sculptor, Designer (1928-1998)
GOMEZ-SICRE, JOSE Administrator, Critic (1916-1991)
GONZALEZ, JUAN J Painter (1945-1993)
GONZALEZ-TORRES, FELIX Painter (1957-1996)
GOOCH, DONALD BURNETTE Painter (1907-1985)
GOODBRED, RAY EDWARD Painter, Educator (1929-)
GOODELMAN, AARON J Sculptor (1891-1978)
GOODMAN, BERTRAM Painter (1904-1988)
GOODMAN, FLORENCE JEANNE Writer, Collector (1922-2006)
GOODMAN, SIDNEY Painter (1936-2013)
GOODNOUGH, ROBERT ARTHUR Painter (1917-2010)
GOODNOW, FRANK A Painter, Educator (1923-2004)
GOODRICH, JAMES W Administrator, Collector (1939-2007)
GOODRICH, SUSAN Painter (1933-2002)
GOODWIN, BETTY Graphic Artist, Printmaker (1923-2008)
GOOSSEN, EUGENE COONS Writer, Educator (1920-1997)
GORDER, CLAYTON J Painter, Educator (1936-1987)
GORDON, DONALD EDWARD Historian, Educator (1931-)
GORDON, JOHN Administrator, Historian (1912-1978)
GORDON, MAXWELL Painter (1910-1982)
GORDON, VIOLET Illustrator, Writer (1907-2005)
GORDY, ROBERT P Painter, Printmaker (1933-1986)
GORELICK, SHIRLEY Painter, Printmaker (1924-2000)
GORHAM, SIDNEY Painter (1870-1947)
GORMAN, WILLIAM D Painter, Graphic Artist (1925-2005)
GORSLINE, DOUGLAS WARNER Painter, Illustrator (1913-1985)
GOSS, JOHN Illustrator (1886-)
GOTO, JOSEPH Sculptor (1920-1994)
GOTTLIEB, ADOLPH Painter (1903-1974)
GOTTLIEB, CARLA Educator, Art Historian (1912-2004)
GOTTSCHALK, MAX JULES Designer, Instructor (1909-2005)
GOULD, NADIA D Painter, Writer (-2007)
GOUMA-PETERSON Educator, Historian (1933-2001)
GOVAN, FRANCIS HAWKS Educator, Painter (1916-)
GOWANS, ALAN, Historian, Lecturer (1923-2001)
GRABACH, JOHN R Painter, Instructor (1880-1981)
GRAHAM, JOHN D Painter (1881-1961)
GRAHAM, LOIS (M GORD) Painter (1930-)
GRAHAM, RICHARD MARTSON Sculptor, Educator (1939-)
GRAHAM, ROBERT Sculptor (1938-2008)
GRAHAM, WALTER Painter, Sculptor (1903-2000)
GRAMATKY, HARDIE Painter, Writer (1907-1979)
GRANLUND, PAUL THEODORE Sculptor (1925-2003)
GRANT, ART Conceptual Artist, Educator (1927-)
GRANT, GORDON HOPE Etcher (1875-1962)
GRANT, J JEFFREY Painter (1883-1960)
GRASSO, JACK Painter (1927-)
GRAVES, BRADFORD Sculptor, Educator (1939-1998)
GRAVES, JOHN W Collector (-1975)
GRAVES, MAITLAND Writer, Painter (1902-)
GRAVES, MORRIS Painter (1910-2001)
GRAY, CLEVE Painter, Sculptor (1918-2004)
GRAY, DON Painter, Critic (1935-2005)
GRAY, HAROLD Cartoonist (1894-1968)
GRAY, JABEZ Painter (-1950)
GRAY, MARIE ELISE Painter (1914-2010)
GRAY, ROBERT HUGH Painter, Educator (1931-1999)
GRAY, ROBERT WARD Administrator (1916-2007)
GRAY, WELLINGTON BURBANK Educator, Designer (1919-1977)
GRAYSON, CLIFFORD PREVOST Painter (1857-1951)
GRAZIANI, SANTE Painter, Educator (1920-2005)
GREACEN, EDMUND Painter (1877-1949)
GREATHOUSE, WALSER S Museum Director (-1966)
GRECO, ROBERT Painter (-1965)
GREEN, BERNARD Painter (1887-1951)
GREEN, DAVID OLIVER Sculptor, Educator (1908-2000)
GREEN, WILDER Administrator, Architect (1927-2005)
GREENBAUM, DOROTHEA SCHWARCZ Sculptor, Graphic Artist (1913-1986)
GREENBERG, ELENOR SIMINOW Painter, Printmaker (1914-2002)
GREENBERG, IRWIN Painter, Instructor (1922-2009)
GREENE, BALCOMB Painter (1904-1990)
GREENE, ELMER WESTLEY, JR Painter (1907-1964)
GREENE, ETHEL MAUD Painter (1912-)
GREENE, GERTRUDE (MRS BALCOMB GREENE) Painter (1904-1956)
GREENE, J BARRY Painter (1895-1966)
GREENE, STEPHEN Painter (1918-1999)
GREENE, VERNON VAN ATTA Cartoonist (-1965)
GREENE-MERCIER, MARIE ZOE Sculptor, Draftsman (1911-2001)
GREENES, RHODA Sculptor (1926-1979)
GREEN-FIELD, ALBERT Art Publicist
GREENLEAF, ESTHER (HARGRAVE) Painter, Printmaker (1905-1981)
GREENLEAF, RAY Illustrator (-1950)
GREENSPAN, GLADYS Painter (1923-2010)
GREENSTEIN, ILISE Painter, Conceptual Artist (1928-)
GREENSTONE, MARION Painter (1925-2005)
GREENWOOD, MARION Painter, Lithographer (1909-1970)
GREGG, RICHARD NELSON Museum Director (1926-1986)
GREGORY, (ELEANOR) ANNE Educator, Calligrapher (-1997)
GREGORY, ANGELA Sculptor, Educator (1903-1990)
GREGORY, JOHN Sculptor (1879-1951)
GREGORY, WAYLANDE Sculptor, Designer (1905-1971)
GREISSLE HERMANN A Printmaker, Painter (1925-1991)
GRENELL, BARBARA Tapestry Artist, Weaver (1944-2001)
GRIER, BARRY DOBSON MILLER Museum Director (1914-1972)
GRIESSLER, FRANZ ANTON Painter (1897-1974)
GRIFFIN, RACHAEL S Art Administrator, Writer (-1983)
GRIFFIN, SALLIE THOMPSON Painter, Photographer (1940-)
GRIFFITH, LOUIS OSCAR Painter (1875-1956)
GRIGAUT, PAUL L Museum Curator (-1969)
GRIGGS, MAITLAND LEE Collector (1902-1989)
GRIGOR, MARGARET CHRISTIAN Sculptor (1912-1981)
GRIMALDI, VINCE Painter, Collage Artist (1929-2011)
GRIMES, FRANCES T Sculptor (1869-1963)
GRIMM, LUCILLE DAVIS Painter (1929-2002)
GRIMM, RAYMOND MAX Sculptor, Potter (1924-2012)
GRINAGER, ALEXANDER Painter (1865-1949)
GRISSOM, EUGENE EDWARD Historian, Writer (1922-2009)

GRODENSKY, SAMUEL Painter (1894-1974)
GROOVE, MARGARET JOAN Administrator, Educator (1935-)
GROPPER, WILLIAM Painter, Lithographer (1897-1977)
GROSHANS, WERNER Painter (1913-1986)
GROSS, CHAIM SCULPTOR Instructor (1904-1991)
GROSS, CHARLES MERRILL Sculptor, Painter (1935-2002)
GROSS, ESTELLE SHANE Dealer (-1992)
GROSSMAN, MORTON Painter (1926-1998)
GROSZ, GEORGE Painter (1893-1959)
GROTELL, MAIJA Ceramist, Educator (1899-1973)
GROTENRATH, RUTH Painter, Printmaker (1912-1985)
GROTH, BRUNO Sculptor (1905-1991)
GROVES, HANNAH CUTIER Painter, Etcher (1868-1952)
GRUBAR, FRANCIS STANLEY Historian, Lecturer (1924-1991)
GRUBB, PAT PINCOMBE Painter, Writer (1922-1977)
GRUBER, AARONEL DEROY Painter, Sculptor, Photographer (-2011)
GRUBERT, CARL ALFRED Cartoonist (1911-1979)
GRUCZA, LEO (VICTOR) Painter, Educator (1935-2010)
GRUENTHER, SUE CORY (MRS RUDOLPH) Painter (-1948)
GRUERRERO, JOSE Painter, Printmaker (1914-)
GRUGER, FREDERICK R Illustrator (1871-1953)
GRUMMANN, PAUL H Museum Director (-1950)
GRUNDY, J(OHN OWEN) Patron, Writer (1911-1985)
GRUPPE, EMIL ALBERT Painter (1896-1978)
GRUPPE, KARL HEINRICH Sculptor (1893-1982)
GRUSHKIN, PHILIP Designer, Calligrapher (1911-1998)
GUADAGNOLI, NELLO T Dealer (1929-2005)
GUCCIONE, JUANITA Painter (-1999)
GUENTHER, PETER W Historian, Educator (1920-2005)
GUERIN, JOHN WILLIAM Painter, Educator (1920-)
GUGGENHEIM, HARRY FRANK Collector, Publisher, Writer (1890-1971)
GUGGENHEIM, PEGGY Collector, Patron (1898-1979)
GUGGENHEIMER, RICHARD HENRY Painter, Writer (1906-1977)
GUGLIELMI, LOUIS O Painter (1906-1956)
GUINZBURG, FREDERICK Sculptor (1897-1978)
GUMBERTS, WILLIAM A Collector, Patron (1912-)
GUMPEL, HUGH Painter, Instructor (1926-2011)
GUNDLACH, HELEN FUCHS Painter (1892-1959)
GUSSOW, ALAN Painter, Sculptor (1931-1997)
GUSSOW, ROY Sculptor, Environmental Artist (1918-2011)
GUSTAVSON, LELAND Illustrator (-1966)
GUSTON, PHILIP Painter (1913-1980)
GUTMANN, JOHN Educator, Photographer (1905-1998)
GUTMANN, JOSEPH Historian, Lecturer (1923-2004)
GUY, JAMES M Painter, Educator (1910-1983)
GUZMAN-FORBES, ROBERT Painter, Illustrator (1929-2004)
GWATHMEY, ROBERT Painter (1903- 1988)
GWATHMEY, CHARLES Architect (1938-2009)
GYRA, FRANCIS JOSEPH JR Instructor, Painter (1914-)
HADER, ELMER (STANLEY) Illustrator, Writer (1889-1973)
HADLEY, ROLLIN VAN NOSTRAND Museum Director (1927-1992)
HADLOCK, WENDELL STANWOOD Museum Director (1911-1978)
HAERER, CAROL Painter (1933-2002)
HAGAN, FREDERICK Printmaker, Painter (1918-2003)
HAGERSTRAND, MARTIN ALLAN Museum Director, Administrator (1911-1999)
HAGGIN, BEN ALL Painter, Designer (1882-1951)
HAGUE, RAOUL Sculptor (1905-1993)
HAHN, EMANUEL OTTO Sculptor (1911-1957)
HAHN, PATIGIAN Sculptor (1876-1950)
HAINES, RICHARD Painter, Muralist (1906-1984)
HALE, LILLIAN WESTCOTT Painter (1881-1963)
HALE, ROBERT BEVERLY Administrator, Instructor (1901-)
HALEY, JOHN CHARLES Painter, Sculptor (1905-1991)
HALEY, ROBERT D Painter (1893-1959)
HALEY, SALLY Painter (1908-2007)
HALFF, ROBERT H Collector (1908-2004)
HALL, REX EARL Painter, Educator (1924-2004)
HALLAM, BEVERLY (LINNEY) Painter, Photographer (1923-2013)
HALPRIN, LAWRENCE Architect (1916-2010)
HALSEY, WILLIAM MELTON Painter, Sculptor (1915-2002)
HALSMAN, PHILIPPE Photographer (1906-1979)
HAMBLETON, MARY Artist (-2009)
HAMBLETT, THEORA Painter, Illustrator (1895-)
HAMES, CARL MARTIN Dealer (1938-2002)
HAMLETT, DALE EDWARD Painter, Educator (1921-2011)
HAMM, BETH CREEVY Painter (1885-1958)
HAMMER, ALFRED EMIL Painter, Educator (1925-2009)
HAMMER, ARMAND Collector, Dealer (1898-1990)
HAMMER, VICTOR KARL Painter (-1967)
HAMMERSLEY, FREDERICK Painter (1919-2009)
HAMMOND, NATALIE HAYS Painter, Museum Director (1904-)
HAMPTON, BILL Painter (1925-1977)
HANCOCK, WALKER (KIRTLAND) Sculptor (1901-1998)
HAND, MOLLY WILLIAMS Teacher, Painter (1892-1951)
HANDFORTH, THOMAS S Lithographer (1897-1948)
HANFMANN, GEORGE M A Educator, Historian (1911-1986)
HANKS, NANCY Administrator (1927-1983)
HANLEN, JOHN (GARRETT) Painter, Instructor (1922-2003)
HANLEY, T EDWARD Collector (-1969)
HANNA, KATHERINE Museum Director (1913-1988)
HANNA, THOMAS KING Painter (-1951)
HANNAH, JOHN JUNIOR Printmaker, Educator (1923-2009)
HANSEN, ARMIN CARL Painter (1886-1957)
HANSEN, ARNE RAE Art Dealer, Historian (1940-1992)
HANSEN, SARAH EVELETH CAMPBELL Art Dealer, Gallery Director (1917-2013)
HANSON, ANNE COFFIN Historian (1921-2004)
HANSON, JO Sculptor, Environmental Artist (-2007)
HANSON, LAWRENCE Sculptor, Educator (1936-1992)
HANVILLE, ROBERT T Painter, Illustrator (1924-1993)
HAPKE, PAUL FREDERICK Painter, Educator (1922-1984)
HARARI, HANANIAH Painter (1912-2000)
HARBART, GERTRUDE FELTON Educator, Instructor (-1999)
HARDER, CHARLES MADRY Craftsman (1899-1951)
HARDIN, ADLAIS Sculptor (1901-1989)
HARDY, GEORGE Painter (-1959)
HARDY, HOWARD (COLLINS) Painter, Instructor (1900-1988)
HARDY, ROBERT Educator, Ceramist (1938-2006)

HARE, DAVID Sculptor (1917-1992)
HARE, MICHAEL MEREDITH Scholar (1909-1968)
HARER, FREDERICK W Painter, Sculptor (1879-1949)
HARING, KEITH Painter (1958-1990)
HARLAN, ROMA CHRISTINE Painter (1912-2003)
HARLEY, RALPH LEROY, JR Photographer, Educator (1934-2005)
HARMON, LILY Painter, Writer (1912-1998)
HARPER, GEORGE COBURN Etcher (1887-1962)
HARPER, JOHN RUSSELL Art Historian (1914-1983)
HARRINGTON, LAMAR Curator, Director (1917-2005)
HARRIS, BEN JORJ Illustrator (1904-1957)
HARRIS, HARVEY SHERMAN Painter, Educator (1915-1999)
HARRIS, JULLIAN HOKE Sculptor, Architect (1906-1987)
HARRIS, LUCILLE S Painter, Printmaker (1914-1984)
HARRIS, MARGIE COLEMAN Painter (1891-)
HARRISON, (WILLIAM) ALLEN Painter (1911-)
HARRITON, ABRAHAM Painter (1893-1986)
HARSANYL, CHARLES Painter (1905-1973)
HART MORGAN DRAKE Painter (1899-)
HART, AGNES Painter, Instructor (-1979)
HART, JOHN FRANCIS Cartoonist, Engraver (1868-)
HART, JOHN LEWIS Cartoonist (1931-2007)
HARTGEN, VINCENT ANDREW Educator, Painter (1914-2002)
HARTIGAN, GRACE Painter (1922-2008)
HARTL, LEON Painter (1889-)
HARTLEY, W DOUGLAS Sculptor, Educator (1921-2006)
HARTMAN, BERTRAM Painter (1882-)
HARTMANN, GEORGE THEO Painter, Etcher (1894-1976)
HARTT, FREDERICK Historian, Educator (1914-1991)
HARTWELL, GEORGE KENNETH Lithographer (1891-1949)
HARVEY JAMES V Painter (-1965)
HARVEY, ROBERT MARTIN Painter (1924-2004)
HASELTINE, MAURY (MARGARET WILSON) Painter, Consultant (1925-1998)
HASELTINE, HERBERT Sculptor (1877-1962)
HASEN, BURTON STANLEY Painter, Printmaker (1947-)
HASKELL, WILLIAM H Educator (1875-1951)
HASKINS, JOHN FRANKLIN Historian, Educator (1919-1991)
HASTIE, REID Educator, Writer (1916-1997)
HASWELL, ERNEST BRUCE Sculptor (1889-1965)
HATCH, EMILY NICHOLS Painter (1871-1959)
HATCH, JOHN W Painter, Lecturer (1919-1998)
HATHAWAY, CALVIN S Curator (-1974)
HATHAWAY, LOVERING Painter (1898-1949)
HATLO, JAMES Cartoonist (1898-1963)
HAUG, DONALD RAYMOND Painter (1925-1999)
HAUGHEY, JAMES M Painter, Calligrapher (1914-2007)
HAUSCHKA, CAROL SPAETH Painter (1883-1948)
HAUSEY, ROBERT MICHAEL Painter (1949-2009)
HAUSMANN, MARIANNE PISKO Painter
HAVENS, JAMES DEXTER Graphic Artist (1900-1960)
HAVENS, MURRY P Designer
HAWES, LOUIS Historian (1931-)
HAWKES, ELIZABETH H Curator, Consultant (1943-)
HAWLEY, MARARET FOOTE Portrait Painter (1880-1963)
HAWORTH, B COQUILL Painter (1904-)
HAWORTH, PETER Painter, Stained Glass Artist (1889-)
HAWTHORNE, JACK GARDNER Educator, Painter (1921-2003)
HAYDEN, PALMER C Painter (1893-1973)
HAYES, DAVID VINCENT Sculptor (1931-2013)
HAYES, WILLIAM CHRISTOPHER Museum Curator (-1963)
HAYNES, GEORGE EDWARD Painter, Illustrator (1910-)
HAYNIE, HUGH Cartoonist (1927-1999)
HAYNIE, RON Painter, Educator (1945-2008)
HAYWARD, PETER Painter, Sculptor (1905-1994)
HAZELL, FRANK Painter (1883-)
HEAD, GEORGE BRUCE Painter, Designer (1931-2009)
HEALY, ARTHUR K D Painter, Lecturer (1902-1978)
HEBALD, MILTON ELTING Sculptor, Printmaker (1917-2015)
HEBER, CARL A Sculptor (1885-1956)
HEBERLING, GLEN AUSTIN Painter, Illustrator (1915-2002)
HECHT, ZOLTAN Painter (1890-1968)
HECKSCHER, WILLIAM SEBASTIAN Historian, Painter (1904-1999)
HEDRICK, WALLY BILL Painter, Sculptor (1928-2003)
HEERAMANECK, NASIL M Collector, Patron, Art Dealer (1902-1971)
HEFNER, HARRY SIMON Painter, Educator (1911-2006)
HEINTZELMAN, ARTHUR W Etcher (1890-1965)
HEISKELL, DIANA Painter
HELCK, PETER Painter, Printmaker (1893-1988)
HELD, ALMA M Painter (-1988)
HELD, JOHN, JR Cartoonist (1889-1958)
HELD, JULIUS S Educator, Writer (1905-2002)
HELD, PHILIP Photographer, Painter (1920-1999)
HELIKER, JOHN EDWARD Painter, Educator (1909-2000)
HELLER, DOROTHY Painter
HELLER, MAXWELL Painter (1881-1963)
HELM, JOHN F JR Educator, Painter (1900-1972)
HELMAN, PHOEBE Sculptor, Painter (1929-1994)
HELWIG, ARTHUR LOUIS Painter, Instructor (1899-1976)
HEMPHILL, HERBERT WAIDE JR Curator, Lecturer (1929-1998)
HENDERSON, LESTER KLERSTEAD Photographer (1906-)
HENISCH, HEINZ K Historian, Photographer (1922-2006)
HENNING, EDWARD BURK Curator, Historian (1922-1993)
HENRICKSEN, RALF CHRISTIAN Educator, Painter (1907-1975)
HENRY, GERRIT VAN KEUREN Critic (1950-2003)
HERBERT, APRIL H Sculptor (1934-2005)
HERBERT, MARIAN Painter (1899-1960)
HERING, HARRY Painter (1887-1967)
HERING, HENRY Sculptor (1874-1949)
HERMAN, VIC Painter, Writer (-1999)
HERO, PETER DECOURCY Administrator, Historian (1942-2009)
HERPST, MARTHA JANE Painter (1911-)
HERR, RICHARD JOSEPH Sculptor, Instructor (1937-2009)
HERRINGTON, ARTHUR W Collector, Patron (1891-1970)
HERRINGTON, NELL RAY Collector, Patron
HERSEY, GEORGE LEONARD Historian (1927-2007)
HERSHFIELD, LEO Illustrator (1904-1979)
HERSTAND, ARNOLD Director
HERTER, ALBERT Painter (1871-1950)
HERVES, MADELINE Painter (-1969)
HERZBRUN, HELENE McKINSEY Painter, Educator (-1984)
HERZOG, PRISCILLA JENNE Painter, Instructor (1922-2008)
HESKETH Sculptor (-1987)

HESS, THOMAS B Critic, Writer (1920-1978)
HESSE, EVA Sculptor (1936-1972)
HEUERMANN, MAGDA Painter (1868-)
HEWITT, FRANCIS RAY Painter, Educator (1936-1992)
HEWITT, THURMAN H Painter, Designer (1919-2001)
HEYL, BERNARD CHAPMAN Scholar (1905-1966)
HEYMAN, SAMUEL J Collector (1939-2009)
HIBBARD, ALDRO THOMPSON Painter (1886-1972)
HIBBARD, HOWARD Historian, Writer (1928-1984)
HICKEN, PHILIP BURNHAM Painter, Printmaker (1910-1985)
HIGGINS, (GEORGE) EDWARD Sculptor (1930-2006)
HIGGINS, DICK Painter, Printmaker (1938-1998)
HIGGINS, EUGENE Painter (1875-1958)
HIGGINS, VICTOR Painter (1884-1949)
HIGHTOWER, JOHN B Administrator, Museum Director (1933-2013)
HILDERBRANDT, HOWARD LOGAN Painter (1874-1958)
HILER, HILAIRE Painter (1898-1966)
HILL, (JAMES) JEROME I Painter (1905-)
HILL, CLINTON J Painter, Sculptor (1922-2003)
HILL, DOROTHY KENT Museum Curator (1907-)
HILL, GEORGE SNOW Painter (1898-1969)
HILL, HAROLD WAYNE Painter, Sculptor (1933-1989)
HILL, HOMER Illustrator
HILL, JOHN HENRY Painter (1839-1922)
HILL, JOHN WILLIAM Painter (1812-1879)
HILL, POLLY KNIPP Etcher, Painter (1900-1990)
HILLIGOSS, MARTHA M Librarian (1928-1987)
HILLS, LAURA COOMBS Painter (1859-1952)
HILLSMITH, FANNIE Painter (1911-2007)
HINES, JOHN M Painter (-1982)
HINKHOUSE, FOREST MELICK Writer, Consultant (1925-2004)
HINKLE, CLARENCE Painter (1890-1960)
HINTON, CHARLES LOUIS Painter (1869-1950)
HIOS, THEO Painter, Graphic Artist (1910-1999)
HIRSCH, JOSEPH Painter (1910-1981)
HIRSCH, STEFAN Educator (1899-1964)
HIRSCHFELD, ALBERT Graphic Artist (1903-2003)
HIRSCHHORN, JOSEPH H Collector (1889-1981)
HITCHCOCK, HENRY RUSSELL Historian, Critic (1903-1986)
HIXSON, KATHRYN Critic (-2010)
HLLLMAN, ALEX L Collector (1900-1968)
HNIZDOVSKY, JACQUES Painter, Printmaker (1915-1985)
HOBBS, ROBERT DEAN Printmaker, Consultant (1928-)
HOBSON, KATHERINE THAYER Sculptor (1889-1992)
HOCKADAY, HUGH Painter (1892-1968)
HODGELL, ROBERT OVERMAN Printmaker, Sculptor (1922-2000)
HODGES, ELAINE R(ITA) S(NYDER) Illustrator, Instructor (1937-2006)
HOEHN, HARRY Painter, Printmaker (1819-1974)
HOFER, EVELYN Photographer (-2009)
HOFFBERG, JUDITH A Publisher, Curator (1934-2009)
HOFFMAN, ARNOLD JR Painter, Director (1915-1991)
HOFFMAN, ARNOLD Painter (-1966)
HOFFMAN, EDWARD FENNO III Sculptor (1916-1991)
HOFFMAN, ELAINE JANET Painter, Lecturer (-2005)
HOFFMAN, HARRY Z Painter, Cartoonist (1908-1990)
HOFFMAN, LARRY GENE Museum Director, Consultant (1933-1991)
HOFFMAN, MALVINA Sculptor (1887-1966)
HOFFMAN, MICHAEL E Editor, Curator (1942-2001)
HOFFMAN, RICHARD PETER Painter, Photographer (1911-1997)
HOFFMAN, WILLIAM A Ceramist, Sculptor (1920-)
HOFMANN, HANS Painter, Educator (1880-1961)
HOFSTED, JOLYON GENE Sculptor, Educator (-2004)
HOIE, HELEN HUNT Painter, Collage Artist (-2000)
HOKANSON, HANS Sculptor, Collage Artist (1925-1997)
HOLBROOK, HOLLIS HOWARD Muralist, Painter (1909-1984)
HOLCOMB, ALICE (MCCAFFERY) Painter (1906-1977)
HOLCOMBE, BLANCHE KEATON Painter, Educator (1912-)
HOLCOMBE, R GORDON, JR Collector, Patron (1913-2005)
HOLDEN, RUTH EGRI Painter (1911-1996)
HOLGATE, EDWIN HEADLEY Painter (1882-1977)
HOLLAND, JANICE Illustrator (1913-1962)
HOLLISTER, PAUL Writer, Painter (1918-2004)
HOLLOWAY, H MAXSON Museum Director (-1966)
HOLM, MILTON W Painter (-1999)
HOLMGREN, R JOHN Illustrator (1997-1963)
HOLT, CHARLOTTE SINCLAIR Medical Illustrator, Sculptor (1914-1990)
HOLT, NANCY LOUISE Sculptor, Filmmaker (1938-2014)
HOLTY, CARL ROBERT Painter, Writer (1900-1973)
HOMAR, LORENZO Painter, Printmaker (1913-2004)
HONIG, ELEANOR D Painter, Printmaker
HONIG, MERVIN Painter, Painting Conservator (1920-1990)
HOOD, DORTHY Painter (1919-2000)
HOOD, ETHEL Painter, Sculptor (1908-1982)
HOOD, GEORGE W Painter (1869-1949)
HOOK, FRANCES A Painter (1912-1981)
HOOVER, JOHN JAY Sculptor (1919-2011)
HOOVER, MARIE LOUISE (ROCHON) Artist (1895-1976)
HOPKINS, BUDD Painter, Sculptor (1931-2011)
HOPKINS, HENRY TYLER Museum Director, Educator (1928-2009)
HOPKINS, KENDAL COLES Painter (1909-1991)
HOPKINS, KENNETH R Museum Director, Restorer (1922-2006)
HOPKINS, PETER Painter, Writer (1911-1999)
HOPKINSON, CHARLES Painter (1869-1962)
HOPPER, CHARLES Painter (1882-1967)
HOPPER, MARIANNE SEWARD Painter (1904-)
HOPPER, JON Painter (-1968)
HOPPES, LOWELL E Cartoonist (1913-2002)
HOPTNER, RICHARD Sculptor (1921-2002)
HORCH, LOUIS L Collector (1899-1979)
HORD, DONAL Sculptor (1902-1966)
HORNADAY, RICHARD HOYT Painter, Educator (1927-2013)
HORNE, (ARTHUR EDWARD) CLEEVE Painter, Sculptor (1912-)
HORNUNG, CLARENCE PEARSON Designer, Writer (1899-1997)
HORNUNG, GERTRUDE SEYMOUR Lecturer, Collector (1908-2000)
HORNYANSKY, NICHOLAS Etcher (1896-1965)
HOROSHAK, RICHARD J Art Dealer, Consultant (1940-)
HOROWITZ, (MR & MRS) RAYMOND J Collectors
HOROWITZ, BENJAMIN Administrator, Art Dealer (1912-2004)

HORWITT, WILL Sculptor (1934-1995)
HOUGHTON, ARTHUR A JR Administrator (1906-1990)
HOUSE, JAMES CHARLES, JR Sculptor (1902-)
HOUSER, ALLAN Sculptor, Painter (1914-1994)
HOUSTON, JAMES A Designer, Painter (1921-2005)
HOVANNES, JOHN Painter (1904-1973)
HOVEY, WALTER READ Historian, Educator (1949-1992)
HOVING, THOMAS Consultant, Museum Director (1931-2009)
HOWARD, (HELEN) BARBARA Painter, Printmaker (1926-2002)
HOWARD, EDWARD Sculptor (1888-1956)
HOWARD, ROBERT A Sculptor, Educator (1922-1999)
HOWARD, ROBERT BOARDMAN Sculptor (1896-1983)
HOWE, KATHERINE L MALLET Painter (-1957)
HOWE, OSCAR Painter, Educator (1915-1983)
HOWELL, HANNAH JOHNSON Librarian (1905-1988)
HOWETT, JOHN Historian, Critic (1926-)
HOWITT, JOHN NEWTON Illustrator (1885-1958)
HOWLAND, EDITH Sculptor (-1949)
HOWLAND, GARTH Educator, Painter (1897-1950)
HOWLAND, RICHARD HUBBARD Architectural Historian (1910-)
HOYT, FRANCES WESTON Painter (1908-2005)
HOYT, WHITNEY F Painter Collector (1910-1990)
HUBBARD, CHARLES D Painter (1876-1950)
HUBBELL, HENRY SALEM Painter (1870-1949)
HUBENTHAL, KARL SAMUEL Cartoonist, Painter (1917-1998)
HUBLER, JULIUS Printmaker, Painter (1919-2003)
HUCK, ROBERTO Educator (1923-1960)
HUDSON, JACQUELINE Painter, Graphic Artist (-2001)
HUEBLER, DOUGLAS Conceptual Artist (1924-1997)
HUEY, FLORENCE GREENE Painter (1872-1960)
HUGHES, ROBERT S F Critic, Lecturer (1938-2012)
HUGO, JOAN (DOWEY) Critic, Administrator (1930-2006)
HULL, MARIE (ATKINSON) Painter (-1980)
HULMER, ERIC CLAUS Curator, Conservator (1915-1988)
HULTBERG, JOHN P Painter, Printmaker (1922-2005)
HUMES, RALPH H Sculptor (1902-1981)
HUMPHROY, JACK WELDON Painter (-1967)
HUNT, LYNN Fainter (1878-1960)
HUNT, WAYNE WOLF ROBE (KEWA-TSE-SHE) Silversmith, Painter (1905-1977)
HUNTER, FRANCIS TIPTON Illustrator (1896-)
HUNTER, JOHN H Painter, Printmaker (1934-)
HUNTER, MEL Printmaker, Painter (1927-2004)
HUNTER, SAM Historian (1923-2014)
HUNTINGTON, A MONTOOMERY Designer (-1967)
HUNTINGTON, ANNA V HYATT Sculptor (1876-1973)
HUNTINGTON, MARGARET WENDELL Painter (1867-1951)
HUNTLEY, DAVID C Painter, Administrator (1930-2004)
HUNTLEY, VICTORIA HUTSON Lithographer (1900-1970)
HUPY, ART Curator, Photographer (1924-2003)
HURD, PETER Painter, Writer (1904-)
HURLEY, EDWARD TIMOTHY Etcher, Painter (1869-1950)
HURLEY, WILSON Painter (1924-2008)
HURSON, MICHAEL Draftsman, Painter (1941-)
HURST, RALPH N Sculptor, Educator (1918-2003)
HUSEBOE, ARTHUR ROBERT Writer, Collector (1931-2010)
HUTCHINSON, JANETL Collector, Curator (1917-2006)
HUTCHINSON, MAX Art Dealer, Gallery Director (1925-1999)
HUTCHISON, MARY ELIZABETH Painter (1904-1970)
HUTINGTON, JOHN W Collector, Patron (1910-1976)
HUTTON, DOROTHY WACKERMAN Designer, Printmaker (1899-2001)
HUTTON, HUGH MCMILLEN Cartoonist (1897-1976)
HUTTON, WILLIAM Museum Curator (1926-2000)
HUXTABLE, ADA LOUISE Critic, Historian (-2013)
IACURTO, FRANCESCO Painter (1908-2001)
IHLE, JOHN LIVINGSTON Printmaker, Educator (1925-2002)
ILIGAN, RALPH W Painter (1994-1960)
INGLE, TOM Painter, Lecturer (1920-1973)
INMAN, PAULINE WINCHESTER Printmaker, Illustrator (1904-1990)
INSLEY, WILL Painter, Draftsman (1929-2011)
INVERARITY, ROBERT BRUCE Museum Director, Painter (1908-1999)
IORIO, ADRIAN J Illustrator (1879-1957)
IPPOLITO, ANGELO Painter, Educator (1922-2001)
IPSEN, ERNEST L Portrait Painter (1869-1950)
IREDELL, RUSSELL Painter (1889-1959)
IRELAND, DAVID Printmaker (1930-2009)
IRVIN, REA Painter (1881-1972)
IRVING, ANNA DUER Painter (1873-1957)
ISAACS, BETTY LEWIS Sculptor (1894-1971)
ISAACS, CAROLE SCHAEFER Collector, Patron (1931-1980)
ISKOWITZ, GERSHON Painter (1921-1988)
ISRAEL, MARVIN Designer, Painter (1924-1985)
ISROFF, LOLA K Painter (-2000)
ITTLESON, HENRY, JR Collector (1900-1973)
IVES, NORMAN S Painter, Printmaker, Graphic Designer (1924-1978)
IVINS, WILLIAM M, JR Curator (1881-1961)
IZUMI, KIYOSHI Architect, Educator (1921-1996)
JACK, RICHARD Painter (-1952)
JACKSON, A B Educator, Painter (1925-1981)
JACKSON, ALEXANDER YOUNG Painter (1882-1974)
JACKSON, ANN Painter (-1956)
JACKSON, ANNIE HURLBURT Painter (1877-)
JACKSON, BILLY MORROW Painter, Educator (1926-2006)
JACKSON, HARRY ANDREW Painter, Sculptor (1924-2011)
JACKSON, HAZEL BRILL Sculptor (-1991)
JACKSON, HENRY ALDEN Textile Designer (-1952)
JACKSON, JOHN EDWIN Painter, Designer (1875-)
JACKSON, LESLEY Painter (1866-1958)
JACKSON, MARTHA Gallery Director (-1969)
JACKSON, SARAH Sculptor, Graphic Artist (1924-)
JACOBS, HELEN NICHOLS Painter (1924-2013)
JACOBS, MICHEL Painter (1877-1951)
JACOBSON, ARTHUR Painter, Printmaker (1924-)
JACOBSSON, STEN WILHELM JOHN Painter, Sculptor (1899-1983)
JAFFE, WILLIAM B Collector (-1972)
JAMES, ALFRED EVERETT Painter, Photographer
JAMES, CATTI Sculptor, Consultant (1940-2009)
JANELSINS, VERONICA Painter, Illustrator (1910-2001)
JANICKI, HAZEL (MRS WILLIAM SCHOCK) Painter, Instructor (1918-1976)
JANIS, SIDNEY Dealer, Writer (1896-1989)
JANKO, MAY Printmaker, Painter (1926-2003)
JANSON, HORST WOLDEMAR Art Historian (1913-1982)

JANSSEN, HANS Educator, Museum Curator
JARMAN, WALTON MAXEY Collector (1904-1980)
JARRELL, RANDALL Critic, Poet (1914-1965)
JAUSS, ANNE MARIE Painter, Illustrator (1907-)
JECT-KEY, DAVID Painter
JEFFE, HULDAH C Painter (1906-2001)
JEFFERSON, JACK ANDREW Painter, Printmaker (1920-2000)
JEFFERYS, CHARLES WILLIAM Illustrator (1869-1951)
JELINEK, HANS Printmaker, Educator (-1992)
JELLICO, JOHN ANTHONY Director, Painter (1914-2004)
JENKINS, DURPIS Cartoonist (1897-1966)
JENKINS, PAUL Painter (1923-2012)
JENKINS, PAUL RIPLEY Sculptor, Painter (1904-1974)
JENNEWEIN, C PAUL Sculptor (1890-1978)
JENSEN, ALFRED Painter (1903-1991)
JENSEN, CECIL LEON Cartoonist (1902-1976)
JENSEN, JOHN EDWARD Painter, Designer (1921-1982)
JENSEN, MARIT Painter, Sculptor
JESWALD, JOSEPH Painter (1927-2009)
JETER, RANDY JOE Drawer, Educator (1937-1997)
JEWELI, WILLIAM M Educator, Painter (1905-1990)
JOFFE, BERTHA Designer (1912-2010)
JOHANSEN, JOHN C Portrait Painter (1876-1964)
JOHN, GRACE SPAULDING Painter Writer (1890-1972)
JOHNSON, AVERY FISCHER Painter, Illustrator (1906-1990)
JOHNSON, BEN Painter (1902-1967)
JOHNSON, BRUCE Museum Director (1949-1976)
JOHNSON, CONTENT Portrait Painter (-1949)
JOHNSON, CROCKOT Painter, Writer (1906-1976)
JOHNSON, DORRIS MILLER Painter (1909-2001)
JOHNSON, ELLEN HULDA Historian, Critic (1910-1992)
JOHNSON, ERNEST (MELVIN) Painter, Inatmetor (1924-1996)
JOHNSON, FRIDOLE LESTER Designer, Writer (1905-1988)
JOHNSON, HERBERT FISK Patron (1901-1980)
JOHNSON, IVAN EARL Educator, Craftsman (1911-2003)
JOHNSON, JAMES RALPH Painter, Writer (1922-)
JOHNSON, JEANNE PAYNE (MRS LOUIS C) Painter (1887-1958)
JOHNSON, KATHERINE KING Administrator, Painter (1906-)
JOHNSON, LESTER F Painter, Educator (1919-2010)
JOHNSON, MALVIN GRAY Painter (1896-1934)
JOHNSON, MARIAN WILLARD Dealer (1904-)
JOHNSON, RAY Painter (1927-1995)
JOHNSON, ROBERT JAY Dealer, Collector (1951-1990)
JOHNSON, SARGENT Sculptor (1888-1967)
JOHNSON, UNA E Curator, Writer (-1997)
JOHNSTON, HELEN HEAD Book Dealer
JOHNSTON, ROBERT HAROLD Administrator, Craftsman (1928-2005)
JOLLEY, GERALDINE FI(RIORRY) Painter, Sculptor (1910-)
JONES, ALBERTUS EUGENE Painter (1882-1951)
JONES, DEXTER CHARLES WEATHERBEE Sculptor, Designer (1926-)
JONES, FRANKLIN REED Painter, Writer (1920-2007)
JONES, HENRY WANTON Painter, Sculptor (1925-2003)
JONES, JACOBINE Sculptor
JONES, JOSEPH JOHN (JOE) Painter (1909-1963)
JONES, JUDY VOSS Printmaker, Painter (1949-2004)
JONES, LOIS MAILOU (MRS V PIERRE-NOEL) Painter, Designer (1905-1998)
JONES, LOUIS C Museum Director (1908-1990)
JONES, MURRAY Painter
JONSON, JON M Sculptor (1893-1947)
JONSON, RAYMOND Painter, Gallery Director (1891-1982)
JORDAN, BARBARA SCHWINN Painter (1907-2005)
JORDAN, LENA E Painter
JORGENSEN, FLEMMING Painter (1934-)
JORGENSEN, SANDRA Painter, Educator (1934-1999)
JORN, ASGER Painter, Writer (1904-1973)
JORNS, BYRON CHARLES Painter (1989-1958)
JOSIMOVICH, GEORGE Painter Designer (1894-)
JOSSET, RAOUL Sculptor (1900-1951)
JOVINE, MARCEL Medalist, Designer (1921-2003)
JOYCE, J DAVID Photographer, Sculptor (1946-2003)
JUDD, DONALD CLARENCE Sculptor, Architect (1928-1994)
JUDSON, ALICE Painter (-1948)
JUDSON, JEANNETTE ALEXANDER Painter, Collage Artist (1912-2002)
JUHAROS, STEPHEN Painter (1913-2010)
JULES, MERVIN M Painter, Educator (1912-1994)
JUNGWIRTH, LEONARD D Sculptor (1903-1964)
JUNKIN, MARION MONTAGUE Painter, Educator (1905-1977)
JUOSON, SYLVIA SHAW Sculptor (1897-1979)
JURECKA, CYRIL Educator (1884-)
JURINKO, ANDY (ANDREW) FLOYD Painter (1939-2011)
JUSTUS, ROY BRAXTON Cartoonist (1901-1983)
KACERE, JOHN C Painter (1920-1999)
KACHADOORIAN, ZUBEL Painter, Educator (1924-2002)
KACHINSKY, ALEXANDER Painter (1888-1958)
KACHORGIS, GEORGE JOSEPH Painter, Educator (1907-1974)
KAD, RUTH (YU-HSIN) LEE Fiber Artist, Educator (-1985)
KAEP, LOUIS JOSEPH Painter (1903-1991)
KAGY, SHEFFIELD HAROLD Painter, Printmaker (1907-1989)
KAHILL, JOSEPH B Painter (1882-1957)
KAHN, A MICHAEL Painter, Designer (1917-2000)
KAHN, GARY Sculptor (1947-1974)
KAHN, PETER Painter, Graphic Designer (1921-)
KAHN, RALPH Dealer, Lecturer (1920-1987)
KAHN, SUSAN B Painter (1924-2010)
KAINEN, JACOB Painter, Printmaker (1909-2001)
KAISER, CHARLES JAMES Painter, Graphic Artist (1939-2011)
KAJIWARA, TAKUMA Painter (1877-1960)
KALLEM, HENRY Painter (1912-)
KALLER, ROBERT JAMESON Dealer (-1959)
KALLIR, OTTO Art Dealer, Historian (1894-1978)
KAMIHIRA, BEN Painter (1925-2004)
KAMROWSKI, GEROME Painter, Sculptor (1914-2004)
KAN, DIANA Painter, Lecturer (1926-2010)
KANAGA, CONSEULO Photographer (1894-1978)
KANE, BOB PAUL Painter (1937-)
KANE, MARGARET BRASSLER Sculptor (1909-2006)
KANEMITSU, MATSUMI Painter, Lecturer (1922-1992)
KANOVITZ, HOWARD Painter (1929-2009)
KANTACK, WALTER W Industrial Artist (1889-1953)
KANTOR, MORRIS Painter (1896-1974)

KAPLAN, GEORGE Printmaker (1920-1997)
KAPLAN, JOSEPH Painter (1900-1980)
KAPLAN, LEO Assemblage Artist, Collage Artist (1912-)
KAPPEL, PHILIP Writer, Etcher (1901-1981)
KARASZ, MARISKA Craftsman (1898-1960)
KARFIOL, BERNARD Painter (1886-1952)
KARP, LEON Painter (-1951)
KARPEL, ELI Sculptor (1916-1998)
KARPICK, JOHN Painter (1884-1960)
KARSH, YOUSUF Photographer (1908-2002)
KARWELIS, DONALD CHARLES Painter, Instructor (1934-2003)
KASS, JACOB JAMES Painter (1910-2000)
KASSOY, BERNARD Painter, Printmaker (1914-2008)
KASTEN, KARL ALBERT Painter, Printmaker (1916-2010)
KASTOR, HUGO Painter
KATSOULIDIS, PANAGIOTIS Graphic Artist (1933-2002)
KATZ, (ALEXANDER) RAYMOND Painter (1895-1974)
KATZ, HILDA (HULDER WEBER) Painter, Writer (1909-1997)
KATZ, JOSEPH M Collector, Patron (1903-)
KATZ, SIDNEY L Architect (1915-1978)
KATZENBACH, WILLIAM E Designer, Lecturer (1904-1975)
KATZENBERG, DENA S Consultant, Curator
KATZENELLENBOGEN, ADOLF EM Educator (1901-1964)
KATZENSTEIN, IRVING Painter (1902-)
KATZFN, LILA (PELL) Sculptor, Educator (1937-1998)
KATZMAN, HERBERT Painter, Instructor (1923-2004)
KAUFMAN, ENIT Painter (1898-1961)
KAUFMAN, STUART MARTIN Painter, Illustrator (1926-1977)
KAUFMANN, ROBERT Painter (1914-1959)
KAUPELIS, ROBERT JOHN Painter, Educator (1928-2009)
KAYE, GEORGE Painter, Educator (1911-2000)
KAYN, HILDE B Painter (1903-1950)
KAZ, JOYCE ZICKERMAN Painter (1936-1979)
KAZ, NATHANIEL Sculptor, Instructor (1917-2010)
KEALLY, FRANCIS Architect, Sculptor (1889-1978)
KEANE, BIL Cartoonist (1922-2011)
KEATS, EZRA JACK Illustrator, Writer (1916-1983)
KECK, CHARLES Sculptor (1875-1951)
KECK, HARDU Painter, Administrator (1940-2003)
KECK, SHELDON WAUGH Educator, Conservator (1910-1993)
KEENE, PAUL FARWELL Painter (1920-2009)
KEFAUVER, NANCY Art Advisor (-1967)
KELLEHER, PATRICK JOSEPH Historian, Musicologist (1917-1985)
KELLER, DEANE Educator, Painter (1901-1992)
KELLER, HENRY G Painter, Etcher (1870-1949)
KELLEY, MIKE Painter (1954-2012)
KELLOGG, MAURICE DALE Painter, Lecturer (1919-1984)
KELLY, ELLSWORTH Painter, Sculptor (1923-2015)
KELPE, PAUL Painter (1902-1985)
KEMBLE, RICHARD Printmaker, Sculptor (1932-)
KEMPER, JOHN GARNER Painter, Graphic Artist (1909-1991)
KEMPTON, GRETA Painter (1903-1991)
KENDA, JUANITA ECHEVERRIA Painter, Writer (1923-)
KENDERDINE, AUGUSTUS FREDERICK Painter (-1947)
KENNEDY, J WILLIAM Painter (1903-)
KENNEDY, JANET ROBSON Painter, Illustrator (1902-1974)
KENT, FRANK WARD Painter (1912-1977)
KENT, JACK Illustrator (1920-1985)
KENT, NORMAN Engraver, Book Designer (1903-1972)
KENT, ROCKWELL Painter (1882-1971)
KEPES, GYORGY Painter, Educator (1906-2001)
KERKAM, EARL Painter (1890-1965)
KERR, ARTHUR Director (1926-1979)
KERR, E COE Art Dealer (1914-1973)
KERSLAKE, KENNETH ALVIN Printmaker, Educator (1930-2007)
KERSWILL, J W ROY Painter (1925-2002)
KESTNBAUM, GERTRUDE DANA Collector (-1982)
KETCHAM, HENRY KING (HANK) Cartoonist (1920-2001)
KETCHAM, RAY WINFRED JR Dealer, Designer (1922-2009)
KEVE, FLORENCE Educator
KEY, TED Cartoonist, Illustrator (1912-2008)
KEYES, BERNARD M Painter (1898-1973)
KEY-OBERB, ELLEN BURKE Sculptor (1905-)
KEY-OBERB, ROLF Ceramist (1900-1959)
KEYSER, ERNEST WISE Sculptor (1876-1959)
KHOURI, ALFRED Painter (-1962)
KIAH, VIRGINIA JACKSON Painter, Museum Director (1911-2001)
KIBBEY, ILAH MARIAN Painter (1883-1958)
KIENBUSCH, WILLIAM AUSTIN Painter (1914-1979)
KIESLER, FREDERICK J Architect (1892-1966)
KIHN, WILLIAM LANGDON Painter (1898-1957)
KIJANKA, STANLEY JOSEPH Painter (1937-1981)
KIKER, EVELYN COALSON Painter, Instructor (1932-)
KILENYI, JULIO Sculptor (1886-1959)
KILGORE, AL Cartoonist (1927-1983)
KILGORE, RUPERT Educator (1910-1971)
KILHAM, WALTER H Painter, Architect (1868-1948)
KILLAM, WALT Painter, Art Dealer (1907-1979)
KILLEBREW, BETTY RACKLEY Educator (1931-2002)
KILPATRICK, ADA ARILLA Painter (-1951)
KILPATRICK, ELLEN PERKINS Painter (1877-1951)
KIMAK, GEORGE Painter (1921-1972)
KIMBALL, YEFFE Painter (1914-1978)
KIMBROUGH, SARA DODGE Painter (-1990)
KING, CLINTON BLAIR Painter, Printmaker (1901-1979)
KING, ELEANOR (ELEANOR KING HOOKHAM) Painter, Patron (1909-2003)
KING, FRANK O Cartoonist (1883-1969)
KING, HAMILTON Illustrator (1871-1952)
KING, MABEL DEBRA Painter (1895-1950)
KING, PAUL Painter (1867-1947)
KING, WARREN THOMAS Cartoonist (1916-1978)
KING, WILLIAM Sculptor (1925-)
KINGHAN, CHARLES ROSS Painter (1895-1984)
KINGMAN, DONG Painter, Illustrator (1911-2000)
KINGMAN, EUGENE Painter, Art Administrator (1909-1975)
KIPPENBERGER, MARTIN Painter (1953-1997)
KIRBY, KENT BRUCE Printmaker, Photographer (-2005)
KIRK, FRANK C Painter (1889-1963)
KIRKBRIDE, EARLE R Painter (1891-1968)
KIRKLAND, VANCE HALL Painter (1904-1981)
KIRKWOOO, MARY BURNETTE Painter (1904-1995)
KIRSCHENBAUM, JULES Painter, Educator (1920-2000)
KISELEWSKI, JOSEPH Sculptor (1901-1986)

KISKADDEN, ROBERT MORGAN Painter (1918-2004)
KITAJ, R B Painter, Printmaker (1932-2007)
KITNER, HAROLD Educator, Painter (1921-2004)
KITZINGER, ERNST Historian (1912-2003)
KLEBE, GENE (CHARLES EUGENE) Painter, Writer (1918-)
KLEINBARDT, ERNEST Painter (1875-1962)
KLETT, WALTER CHARLES Illustrator (1897-1966)
KLEY, ALFRED JULIUS Craftsman (1895-1957)
KLINE, ALMA Sculptor
KLINE, FRANZ Painter (1910-1962)
KLINE, GEORGE T Illustrator (1874-1956)
KLINE, HARRIET Painter, Papermaker (1916-)
KLINE, RONALD WAYNE Printmaker, Publisher (1949-2005)
KLINKER, ORPHA Etcher (-1964)
KLONIS, BERNARD Painter (1906-1957)
KNAPP, SADIE MAGNET Painter, Sculptor (1909-2004)
KNATHS, (OTTO) KARL Painter (1891-1971)
KNIGHT, FREDERIC CHARLES Painter (1898-1979)
KNIGHT, TACK (BENJAMIN THACKSTON) Cartoonist (1895-1976)
KNIPSCHILD, ROBERT Painter, (1927-2004)
KNOWLTON, MAUDE BRIGGS Painter (1876-1956)
KO, ANTHONY Printmaker, Educator (1934-)
KOCH, BERTHA COUCH Painter (1899-1975)
KOCH, JOHN Painter, Collector (1909-1978)
KOCH, ROBERT Historian, Writer (1918-2003)
KOCH, WILLIAM EMERY Dealer, Collector (1922-1987)
KOCHTA, RUTH MARTHA Art Dealer, Painter (1924-2003)
KODNER, MARTIN Art Dealer, Consultant (1934-)
KOENIG, CATHERINE CATANZARO Painter (1921-2004)
KOENIG, JOHN FRANKLIN Painter, Photographer (1924-)
KOERNER, HENRY Painter, Lecturer (1915-1991)
KOESTNER, DON Painter (1923-2009)
KOGA, MARY Photographer (1920-)
KOGELNIK, KIKI Painter, Sculptor (1935-1997)
KOGER, IRA MCKISSICK Collector, Patron (1912-2004)
KOHLER, ROSE Sculptor, Painter (1873-1947)
KOHLHEPP, DOROTHY IRENE Painter (-1964)
KOHLHEPP, NORMAN Painter, Conservator (-1986)
KOHLMEYER, IDA (R) Painter, Sculptor (1912-1997)
KOHN, GABRIEL Sculptor (1910-1975)
KOHN, MISCH Painter, Printmaker (1916-2003)
KOHN, WILLIAM ROTH Painter, Educator (1931-2004)
KOLDE, FREDERICK WILLIAM Painter (1870-)
KOLDORF, IRENE JANET Sculptor (1925-2013)
KOLIN, SACHA Sculptor, Painter (1911-1975)
KOLODNER, NATHAN K Dealer (1950-)
KOLTUN, FRANCES LANG Collector, Lecturer (-2010)
KOMAR, MATHIAS Dealer (1909-)
KONI, NICOLAUS Sculptor, Lecturer (1911-2000)
KONRAD, ADOLF FERDINAND Painter
KOOPMAN, JOHN R Painter (1881-1949)
KOPLOWITZ, BENJAMIN (BEN KOPEL) Painter (1893-)
KOPMAN, BENJAMIN Painter (1887-1965)
KOPPE, RICHARD Painter, Educator (1916-)
KOPPELMAN, CHAIM Printmaker, Educator (1920-2009)
KORDA, VINCENT Director, Painter
KORMENDI, EUGENE Sculptor (1889-1959)
KORN, ELIZABETH P Painter, Illustrator (1900-)
KOSA, EMIL J, JR Painter (1903-1968)
KOTIN, ALBERT Painter, Educator (1907-1980)
KOTTLER, HOWARD WILLIAM Sculptor, Educator (1930-)
KOURSAROS, HARRY G Painter (1928-1986)
KOUWENHOVEN, JOHN A Writer, Educator (1909-1990)
KOWALEK, JON W Museum Director, Lecturer (1934-)
KOWALSKI, DENNIS ALLEN Conceptual Artist (1938-)
KOZLOW, RICHARD Painter, Sculptor (1926-2008)
KRAMER, JACK N Painter, Educator (1923-1984)
KRAMRISCH, STELLA Curator, Educator (1896-1993)
KRANER, FLORIAN G Painter, Educator (1908-)
KRASNER, LEE Painter (1908-1984)
KRAUSZ, LASZLO Painter (1903-1979)
KRAUTH, HARALD Painter (1923-1997)
KREBS, ROCKNE Sculptor (1938-2011)
KREINDLER, DORIS BARSKY Painter, Lithographer (1901-1974)
KREMPEL, RALF Painter, Assemblage Artist (1935-2005)
KRIENSKY (MORRIS E) Painter, Writer (1917-1998)
KRIES, HENRY Sculptor (-1963)
KRIESBERG, IRVING Painter (1919-2009)
KROLL, LEON Painter, Lithographer (1884-1974)
KRONBERG, LOUIS Painter (1872-1965)
KRUSHENICK, JOHN Painter, Consultant (1927-1998)
KRUSHENICK, NICHOLAS Painter (1929-1999)
KUEHN, EDMUND KARL Painter, Lecturer (1916-2011)
KUEKES, EDWARD D Cartoonist (1901-1987)
KUH, KATHERINE Critic, Consultant (1904-1994)
KUHLER, OTTO AUGUST Etcher, Painter (1894-1977)
KUHN, BOB Draftsman, Painter (1920-2007)
KUHN, MARYLOU Educator, Painter (1923-1999)
KUHN, WALT Painter (1880-1949)
KUJUNDZIC, ZELJKO D Ceramist, Sculptor (1920-2003)
KULICKE, ROBERT M Craftsman, Painter (1924-2007)
KULTERMANN, UDO Art Historian, Architectural Historian (1927-2013)
KUMM, MARGUERITE ELIZABETH Painter, Printmaker (-1992)
KUNIYOSHI, YASUO Painter (1893-1953)
KUNTZ, ROGER EDWARD Painter, Sculptor (1926-1975)
KUPFERMAN, LAWRENCE Painter, Printmaker (1909-1982)
KUPFERMAN, MURRY Painter, Sculptor (1897-2002)
KURELEK, WILLIAM Painter (1927-1977)
KURTZ, BRUCE D Historian, Curator (1943-2003)
KURTZ, ELAINE Painter (1928-2003)
KURZ, GERTRUDE ALICE Craftsman (-1951)
KUSHNER, DOROTHY BROWDY Painter, Printmaker (1909-2000)
KUVSHINOFF, NICOLAI Sculptor, Painter (1910-1997)
L'ENGLE, WILLIAM JOHNSON Painter (1884-1957)
LA FON, JULIA ANNA Painter, Craftsman (1919-1981)
LA HOTAN, ROBERT Painter (1927-2002)
LA MORE, CHET HARMON Painter, Sculptor (1908-1980)
LAATSCH, GARY Sculptor (1956-)
LABICHE, WALTER ANTHONY Administrator, Instructor (1924-1979)
LABRIE, ROSE Painter, Writer (1916-1986)
LACK, RICHARD FREDERICK Painter, Instructor (1928-2009)
LADER, MELVIN PAUL Historian, Educator (1947-)
LADERMAN, GABRIEL Painter, Educator (1929-2011)
LAFAYE, NELL MURRAY Painter, Educator (1937-1990)

LAFFOLEY, PAUL (GEORGE), JR Painter, Architect (1935-2015)
LAGATTA, JOHN Illustrator (1894-1976)
LAGER, FANNIE Sculptor, Painter, Collector (1911-2004)
LAHEY, MARGUERITE DUPREZ Rare Book Binder (1880-1958)
LAHEY, RICHARD (FRANCIS) Painter, Lecturer (1893-1979)
LAING, RICHARD HARLOW Administrator, Artist (1932-2012)
LAKE, FREDERIC Art Dealer
LAM, JENNETTE (BRINSMADE) Painter, Educator (1911-1985)
LAMANNA, CARMEN Art Dealer, Gallery Director (1927-1991)
LAMB, ADRIAN S Painter (-1989)
LAMMEL, ROBERT C Painter, Architect (1913-2003)
LAMONT, FRANCES K Sculptor (-1975)
LAMPITOC, ROL PONCE Painter, Printmaker
LANDACRE, PAUL Engraver (1893-1963)
LANDAU, JACOB Painter, Printmaker (1917-2001)
LANDECK, ARMIN Painter, Engraver (1905-)
LANDON, EDWARD AUGUST Printmaker, Painter (1910-1984)
LANDSMAN, STANLEY Sculptor (1930-)
LANE, ALVIN S Collector (1918-2007)
LANG, RODGER ALAN Sculptor, Educator (1942-2000)
LANGE, DOROTHEA Photographer (1895-1965)
LANGLAIS, BERNARD Sculptor, Painter (1921-1977)
LANGSNER, JULES Art Writer (-1967)
LANGSTON, MILDRED Art Dealer, Collector (1902-1976)
LANGTON, BERENICE Sculptor (1878-1959)
LANKES, JULIUS J Engraver (1884-1960)
LANSDOWNE, JAMES FENWICK Painter (1937-2008)
LANSNER, FAY Painter
LANTZY, DONALD MICHAEL Administrator, Printmaker (1942-2009)
LAPLANTZ, SHEREEN Book Artist, Writer (1947-2003)
LAPOSKY, BEN FRANCIS Designer, Video Artist (1914-2000)
LARCADA, RICHARD KENNETH Art Dealer (1935-)
LARK, RAYMOND Draftsman, Painter (1939-2004)
LARK, SYLVIA Painter, Printmaker (1847-)
LARKIN, OLIVER Educator (1896-1970)
LARKIN, WILLIAM Painter, Printmaker (1902-1969)
LARSEN, ERIK Consultant, Educator (1911-2006)
LARSEN, OLE Painter, Illustrator (-1984)
LARSEN, ROBERT WESLEY Painter (1923-2002)
LARSON, JANE (WARREN) Ceramist, Writer (1922-)
LASANSKY, MAURICIO L Printmaker, Draftsman (1914-2012)
LASH, KENNETH Educator, Writer (1908-1985)
LASKA, DAVID Designer, Painter (1910-2003)
LASSAW, IBRAM Sculptor, Painter (1913-2003)
LASSEN, BEN Painter (-1968)
LASSNIG, MARIA Painter, Filmmaker (-2014)
LASUCHIN, MICHAEL Printmaker, Painter (1923-)
LATHROP, GERTRUDE K Sculptor (1896-1986)
LATOUR, IRA HINSDALE, JR Photographer, Historian (1919-2015)
LAUB-NOVAK, KAREN Sculptor, Painter, Printmaker, Writer (1937-2009)
LAUCK, ANTHONY JOSEPH Sculptor, Educator (1908-2001)
LAUFMAN, SIDNEY Painter (1911-1985)
LAUGHLIN, ALICE D Painter (1895-1952)
LAUGHLIN, MORTIMER Painter (1918-2008)
LAUGHLIN, THOMAS Painter, Publisher (-1965)
LAUNOIS, JOHN RENE Photographer
LAURENT, JOHN LOUIS Painter, Educator (1921-2005)
LAURENT, ROBERT Sculptor, Collector (1890-1970)
LAURITZ, PAUL Painter (1899-1975)
LAUTERER, ARCH Designer (1904-)
LAVANOUX, MAURICE Art Editor (-1974)
LAVENTHOL, HANK Painter, Printmaker (1927-2001)
LAW, MARGARET Painter
LAWRENCE, HELEN HUMPHREYS Painter (1879-)
LAWRENCE, JACOB Painter, Mosaic Artist (1917-2000)
LAWRIE, LEE Sculptor (1877-1963)
LAWSON, ROBERT Illustrator (1892-1957)
LAWTON, NANCY Painter, Graphic Artist (1950-2007)
LAX, DAVID Painter (1910-1990)
LAYNOR, HAROLD ARTHUR Painter (1922-1991)
LAYTON, GLORIA (MRS HARRY GEWISS) Painter (1914-)
LAZARUS, MARVIN P Photographer (1918-1992)
LAZZARI, PIETRO Sculptor, Painter (1888-1979)
LAZZELL, BLANCHE Painter (1878-1956)
LE CLAIR, CHARLES Painter, Educator (1914-2007)
LE PRINCE, GABRIELLA Ceramist (-1953)
LE ROY, HAROLD M Painter, Graphic Artist (1905-)
LEA, TOM Painter, Writer (1907-2001)
LEACH, LOUIS LAWRENCE Sculptor (1885-1957)
LEADER, GARNET ROSAMONDE Administrator, Painter (-2002)
LEAF, MUNRO Illustrator (1906-1977)
LEAKE, EUGENE W Painter (1911-2005)
LEAKE, GERALD Painter (1885-1975)
LEAR, GEORGE Engraver (1879-1956)
LEATHERS, WINSTON LYLE Painter, Printmaker (1932-2004)
LEBECK, CAROL E Ceramist, Painter, Educator (1931-)
LEBRUN, RICO (FREDERICO) Painter (1900-1964)
LECHAY, JAMES Painter (1907-2001)
LECOQUE Painter, Writer (1891-1981)
LEDGERWOOD, ELLA RAY Painter (-1951)
LEE, AMY FREEMAN Painter, Lecturer (1914-2004)
LEE, ARTHUR Sculptor (1880-1961)
LEE, CAROLINE D Fine Art Appraiser (1934-2003)
LEE, GEORGE J Art Administrator, Photographer (1919-1976)
LEE, RENSSELAER WRIGHT Historian, Educator (1888-1984)
LEE, RUSSELL W Photographer, Educator (1903-1986)
LEECH, HILTON Painter, Instructor (1906-1969)
LEEDS, ANNETTE Painter (1916-1998)
LEEPER, DORIS MARIE Sculptor, Painter (1929-2000)
LEES, HARRY HANSON Illustrator
LEE-SMITH, HUGHIE Painter, Instructor (1915-1999)
LEFCOURT, IRWIN Dealer (1910-2004)
LEFEBRE, JOHN Art Dealer (1905-1986)
LEFEBVRE D'ARGENCE, RENE-YVON Museum Director, Writer (1928-1997)
LEFEVRE, LAWRENCE E Painter (1904-1960)
LEFEVRE, RICHARD JOHN Painter, Illustrator (1931-)
LEFF, JULIETTE Painter, Educator (1939-1987)
LEFRANC, MARGARET (MARGARET LEFRANC SCHOONOVER) Painter, Illustrator (-1998)
LEHMAN, IRVING Painter, Sculptor (1900-1983)
LEHMAN, ROBERT Collector (-1969)

LEIGHTON, A C Painter (-1965)
LEIGHTON, THOMAS CHARLES Painter, Instructor (1913-1976)
LEIN, MALCOLM EMIL Administrator, Designer (1913-2003)
LEIPZIG, ARTHUR Photographer, Educator (1918-2014)
LEITES, SUSAN Painter, Educator (-1996)
LEITH-ROSS, HARRY Painter (1896-)
LEITMAN, SAMUEL Painter (1908-1981)
LEM, RICHARD DOUGLAS Painter (1933-2004)
LEMIEUX, JEAN PAUL Painter (1904 -)
LENHARDT, SHIRLEY M Painter (1934-)
LENNEY, ANNIE Painter (1900-)
LENSKI, LOIS Writer, Illustrator (1893-)
LENSON, MICHAEL Painter (1903-1971)
LENTELLI, LEO Sculptor (1892-1962)
LENTINE, JOHN Painter
LEON, DENNIS Sculptor, Educator (1933-)
LEON, RALPH BERNARD Painter, Illustrator (1932-2000)
LEONID (LEONID BERMAN) Painter (1886-1976)
LEOPOLD, RUDOLF Collector (1925-2010)
LERMAN, DORIS (HARRIET) Painter, Sculptor (-2001)
LERMAN, ORA Painter, Sculptor (1938-1998)
LERNER, ABRAM Museum Director, Painter (1913-2007)
LERNER, LESLIE ALLEN Painter (1949-2005)
LERNER, NATHAN BERNARD Photographer, Painter (1913-1997)
LERNER, RICHARD J Art Dealer (1929-1982)
LESH, RICHARD D Painter, Instructor (1927-2007)
LESHER, MARIE PALMISANO Sculptor (1919-2005)
LESLIE, JOHN Painter, Fine Art Photographer, Sculptor, Designer (1923-)
LESTER, MICHELLE Illustrator, Tapestry Artist (1942-2002)
LEVENTHAL, RUTH LEE Sculptor, Painter (1923-1989)
LEVER, R HAYLEY Painter (1876-1968)
LEVI, CARLO Painter, Writer (1902-1975)
LEVI, JULIAN E Painter, Educator (1900-1982)
LEVINE, DAVID Cartoonist, Painter (1926-2009)
LEVINE, JACK Painter (1915-2010)
LEVINE, MELINDA (ESTHER) Critic, Editor (1947-2004)
LEVINSON, MON Sculptor, Painter (1926-2014)
LEVIT, HERSCHEL Photographer, Historian (1912-1986)
LEVITINE, GEORGE Historian (1916-)
LEVITT, ALFRED Painter, Prehistorian (1894-2000)
LEV-LANDAU (SAMUEL DAVID LANDAU) Painter (1895-1979)
LEVY, BEATRICE S Painter (1892-1974)
LEVY, FLORENCE N Writer, Editor (1870-1947)
LEVY, HILDA Painter, Sculptor
LEVY, JULIEN Educator, Writer (1906-1981)
LEVY, LEON Administrator, Collector (1925-2003)
LEWANDOWSKI, EDMUND D Painter, Administrator (1914-1998)
LEWIN, MILTON J Historian (1929-1979)
LEWIS, ALLEN Etcher (1873-1957)
LEWIS, DON S, SR Art Dealer, Painter (1919-2004)
LEWIS, GOLDA Assemblage Artist, Papermaker (1914-2005)
LEWIS, MARTIN Printmaker (1883-1962)
LEWIS, NORMAN WILFRED Painter, Instructor (-1979)
LEWIS, STANLEY Sculptor, Printmaker (1930-2006)
LEWITIN, LANDES Painter (-1966)
LEWITT, SOL Painter (1928-2007)
LEYDENFROST, ALEXANDER Illustrator (1889-1961)
LEYENDECKER, JOSEPH C Painter (1874-1951)
LIAS, THOMAS R Painter
LIBBY, WILLIAM C Painter, Writer (1919-)
LIBERI, DANTE Painter, Sculptor (1919-2004)
LIBERMAN, ALEXANDER Painter, Sculptor (1912-1999)
LIBERTE, JEAN Painter (1896-1965)
LIBERTS, LUDOLFS Painter (1895-1951)
LIBHART, MYLES LAROY Administrator, Writer (1931-1990)
LICHTEN, FRANCES Writer (1889-1961)
LICHTENBERG, MANES Painter (-2009)
LICHTENSTEIN, ROY Painter, Sculptor (1923-1987)
LICHTENSTEIN, SARA Art Historian (1929-)
LICHTY, GEORGE M Cartoonist (1905-)
LIDDLE, NANCY HYATT Museum Director, Consultant (1931-2004)
LIEBER, FRANCE Printmaker, Painter
LIEBERMAN, HARRY Painter, Sculptor (1876-1983)
LIEBES, DOROTHY (MRS RELMAN MORIN) Textile Designer (1899-1972)
LILIENFIELD, KARL Scholar (-1966)
LINCOLN, DIANE THOMAS Painter, Curator (1948-2012)
LINCOLN, RICHARD MATHER Ceramist, Educator (1929-)
LINDENFELD, LORE Craftsman (1921-2010)
LINDNER, RICHARD Painter (1911-1978)
LINDSAY, KENNETH C Historian, Writer (1919-2009)
LINN, JOHN WILLIAM Administrator, Writer (1936-2002)
LINTOTT, EDWARD BARNARD Painter (1875-1951)
LIPCHITZ, JACQUES Sculptor (1891-1973)
LIPMAN, HOWARD W Collector (1905-1992)
LIPMAN-WULF, PETER Sculptor, Printmaker (1905-1993)
LIPOFSKY, MARVIN BENTLEY Sculptor, Glass Artist (1938-2016)
LIPPERT, LEON Painter
LIPPINCOTT, JANET Painter, Printmaker (1918-)
LIPPOLD, RICHARD Sculptor (1915-2002)
LIPSCOMB, GUY FLEMING JR Painter, Instructor (1917-)
LISSIM, SIMON Painter, Designer (1900-1981)
LIST, VERA G Patron, Collector (1908-2002)
LISTON, MRS FLORENCE CARY Portraitist (-1964)
LITAKER, THOMAS (FRANKLIN) Painter (1904-1976)
LITTLE, JOHN Painter, Sculptor (1907-)
LITTLETON, HARVEY K Educator, Glass Blower (1922-2013)
LITZ, JAMES C Painter (1948-)
LIZER, HARLAN DE LOS Painter (1910-2003)
LO MEDICO, THOMAS GAETANO Sculptor, Designer (1904-1985)
LOBER, GEORGE J Sculptor (1892-1961)
LOCHRIE, ELIZABETH DAVEY Painter, Sculptor (1890-1981)
LOCKS, MARIAN Art Dealer, Collector (1915-)
LOCKWOOD, WARD Painter (1894-1963)
LOEHR, MAX Curator, Educator (1903-1988)
LOEWY, RAYMOND Designer, Graphic Artist (1893-1986)
LOGAN, DAVID GEORGE Metalsmith, Educator (1937-)
LOGAN, MAURICE Painter, Illustrator (1856-1977)
LOGGIE, HELEN A Printmaker, Painter (-1976)
LOLOMA, CHARLES Jeweler, Silversmith (1921-1991)
LOMBARD, ANNETTE Painter, Instructor (1929-2002)
LOMBARDO, JOSEF VINCENT Art Historian, Writer (1908-1992)

LOMONACO, STEPHEN Painter, Instructor (1931-2014)
LONDON, ELCA Dealer (1930-1990)
LONG, C CHEE Craftsman, Goldsmith (1942-)
LONG, HUBERT Sculptor (1907-1992)
LONG, SCOTT Cartoonist (1907-1991)
LONG, STANLEY M Painter (1892-1972)
LONG, WALTER KINSCELLA Museum Director, Painter (1904-1986)
LONGACRE, LYDIA E Miniature Painter (1870-1951)
LONGACRE, MARGARET GRUEN Printmaker, Lecturer (1910-1976)
LONGAKER, JON DASU Educator, Writer (1920-2002)
LONGLEY, BERNIQUE Painter, Sculptor (1923-1999)
LONGLEY, EVELYN LOUISE Painter (1911-1959)
LONGSTAFFE, JOHN RONALD Collector (1934-)
LOONEY, ROBERT FAIN Curator, Librarian (1925-)
LOPEZ, MICHAEL JOHN Ceramist (1937-2003)
LORAN, ERLE Painter, Writer (1905-1999)
LORD, HARRIET Painter (1879-1958)
LORENZANI, ARTHUR EMANUELE Sculptor (1886-1986)
LORFANO, PAULINE DAVIS Painter (1928-2014)
LORIMER, AMY MCCLELLAN Painter
LOSCH, TILLY Painter (1904-1975)
LOTHROP, KRISTIN CURTIS Sculptor (1930-2004)
LOTTES, JOHN WILLIAM Educator, Administrator (1934-1996)
LOUGHLIN, JOHN LEO Painter (1931-2004)
LOUIS, MORRIS Painter (1912-1963)
LOURIE, HEBERT S Painter, Educator (1923-1981)
LOVATO, CHARLES FREDERIC Printmaker, Craftsperson (1937-1988)
LOVE, FRANCES TAYLOR Writer, Publisher (1926-2010)
LOVELL, TOM Painter, Illustrator (1909-1997)
LOVET-LORSKI, BORIS Sculptor (1894-1973)
LOW, SANFORD Museum Director, Painter (1905-1964)
LOWE, EMILY Painter (-1966)
LOWE, MARVIN Painter, Printmaker (1927-)
LOWELL, ORSON BYRON Illustrator (1871-1956)
LOWENFELD, VIKTOR Educator (1903-1960)
LOWENGRUND, MARGARET Painter (1905-1957)
LOWRY, BATES Historian, Museum Director (1923-2004)
LOZOWICK, LOUIS Painter, Printmaker (1892-1973)
LUCA, MARK Printmaker (1918-2005)
LUDGIN, EARLE Collector (1898-1981)
LUDLAM, EUGENIE SHONNARD Sculptor (1936-1978)
LUDWIG, EVA Sculptor (1923-2010)
LUKE, ALEXANDRA Painter (1901-)
LUKOSIUS, RICHARD BENEDICT Painter, Craftsman (1918-)
LUNA (ANTONIO RODRIGUEZ) Painter (1910-1984)
LUNDBORG, FLORENCE Painter (-1949)
LUNDEBERG, HELEN Painter (1908-1999)
LUNDIE, EDWIN HUGH Architect (1886-1972)
LUQUIENS, HUC-MAZELET Etcher (1882-1961)
LURIE, BORIS Painter, Sculptor (1924-2008)
LUTZ, DAN S Painter (1906-1979)
LYE, LEN Painter, Kinetic Artist (1901-1981)
LYMAN, JOHN Painter (-1967)
LYNCH, GERALD Sculptor (1944-2000)
LYNES, RUSSELL Writer, Critic (1910-1992)
LYTTON, BART Collector (-1968)
LYTTON, CONSTANCE B Printmaker, Painter
MABE, MANABU Painter (1924-1998)
MACAGY, DOUGLAS GUERNSEY Art Administrator (1913-1973)
MACAGY, JERMAYNE Educator
MACALISTER, PAUL RITTER Designer, Collector (1911-1990)
MACDONALD, COLIN SOMERLED Writer, Publisher, Painter (1925-2012)
MACDONALD, GRANT Painter, Illustrator (1909-1987)
MACDONALD, HERBERT Painter (1898-1972)
MACDONALD, JAMES W A Painter (1824-1908)
MACDONALD, THOMAS REID Painter (1908-)
MACDONALD-WRIGHT, STANTON Painter (1890-1973)
MACEK, M D (MILA D) Painter
MACGILLIS, ROBERT DONALD Painter, Printmaker (1936-2002)
MACGILVARY, NORWOOD Painter, Educator (1874-1949)
MACHAMER, JEFFERSON Cartoonist (1900-1960)
MACHETANZ, FRED Painter, Lithographer (1908-2002)
MACHLIN, SHELDON M Sculptor, Printmaker (1908-1975)
MACIUNAS, GEORGE Designer (1931-1979)
MACIVER, LOREN Painter (1909-1989)
MACK, RODGER ALLEN Sculptor, Educator (1938-2002)
MACKAY, DONALD CAMERON Painter, Historian (1906-1978)
MACKEOWN, IDA C Portrait Painter (-1952)
MACKY, SPENCER Educator (1880-1958)
MACLAGGER, RICHARD JOSEPH Dealer, Collector (1947-1989)
MACLANE, JEAN Painter (1878-1964)
MACLEAD, YAN Sculptor (1899-1978)
MACLEOD, PEGI NICHOL Painter, Teacher
MACNELLY, JEFFREY KENNETH Cartoonist, Sculptor (1947-2000)
MACNUTT, GLENN GORDON Painter, Illustrator (1906-1997)
MACOMBER, ALLISON Painter, Sculptor (1916-1979)
MACOMBER, WILLIAM B Administrator (1921-2003)
MADSEN, VIGGO HOLM Printmaker, Craftsman (1925-1999)
MAGAFAN, ETHEL Painter, Muralist (1906-1983)
MAGAFAN, JENNE Painter, Lithographer (1916-1952)
MAHEY, JOHN A Museum Director (1932-)
MAHMOUD, BEN Painter, Educator (1935-2009)
MALBIN, LYDIA W Collector (1897-1999)
MALDARELLI, ORONZIO Sculptor (1892-1963)
MALICOAT, PHILIP CECIL Painter (1908-1981)
MALINA, FRANK JOSEPH Painter, Editor (1912-1981)
MALLARY, ROBERY W Sculptor, Educator (1917-1997)
MALLORY, MARGARET Collector, Filmmaker (1911-)
MALMAN, CHRISTINA Magazine Cover Artist (1902-1958)
MALONE, LEE H B Museum Director (1903-1989)
MALONE, NOLA LANGER Illustrator, Writer (1930-2003)
MALOOF, SAM Sculptor (1916-2009)
MALPASS, MICHAEL ALLEN Sculptor (1946-1992)
MALRAUX, ANDRE Writer (1900-1976)
MALSCH, ELLEN L Painter, Instructor (-1988)
MALVERN, CORINNE Illustrator (-1956)
MANARAY, THELMA ALBERTA Printmaker, Painter (1913-)
MANDEL, HOWARD Painter, Sculptor (1917-1999)
MANGRAVITE, PEPPINO GINO Painter, Lecturer (1896-1978)
MANKOWSKI, BRUNO Sculptor (1902-1990)

MANN, MARGERY (MARGARET MANN VASEY) Photographer, Curator (1919-1977)
MANN, MAYBELLE Historian, Writer (1915-2007)
MANN, WARD PALMER Painter (-2005)
MANNING, HILDA SCUDDER Sculptor (-1988)
MANNING, REG (REGINALD WEST) Designer (1905-1986)
MANO, TORU Curator (1945-2001)
MANRAY Artist, Photographer (1890-1976)
MANSHIP, PAUL Sculptor (1885-1966)
MANSO, LEO Painter, Educator (1914-1993)
MANUEL, K(ATHRYN) LEE Craftsman (-2003)
MANVILLE, ELLA VIOLA GRAINGER Painter (1889-1979)
MAPPLETHORPE, ROBERT Photographer (1946-1989)
MARADIAGA, RALPH Director, Designer (1934-1985)
MARAGIRIOTTI, VINCENT Muralist (1888-1978)
MARANS, MOISSAYE Sculptor, Instructor (1902-1977)
MARANTZ, IRVING Painter (1912-1972)
MARBERGER, A ALDAR Dealer, Museum Director (1947-1988)
MARCA-RELLI, CONRAD Painter, Collage Artist (1913-2000)
MARCUS, EDWARD S Collector (1910-1972)
MARCUS, STANLEY Collector (1905-2002)
MAREE, WENDY P Painter, Sculptor (1938-2002)
MAREMONT, ARNOLD H Collector (1904-1978)
MARGULES, DEHIRSH Painter (1899-1965)
MARGULIES, HERMAN Painter (1922-2004)
MARGULIES, ISIDORE Sculptor, Kinetic Artist (1921-2008)
MARGULIES, JOSEPH Painter, Printmaker (1896-1986)
MARGULIS, MARTHA (BOYER) Painter, Printmaker (1928-2003)
MARIL, HERMAN Painter, Printmaker (1908-1986)
MARIN, JOHN Painter (1870-1951)
MARINO, ALBERT JOSEPH Collector (1899-1975)
MARINO-MERLO, JOSEPH Painter (1906-1956)
MARINSKY, HARRY Sculptor, Painter (1909-2008)
MARION, HARRIET REGINA Painter, Educator (-2010)
MARK, ENID EPSTEIN Printmaker, Photographer (1932-2008)
MARK, MARY ELLEN Photographer (1940-2015)
MARKLEY, DORIS YOCUM Photographer, Printmaker (1921-)
MARKMAN, SIDNEY DAVID Administrator, Historian (1911-)
MARKOW, JACK Cartoonist, Painter (1905-1993)
MARKS, CEDRIC H Collector, Patron (-2000)
MARKS, CLAUDE Painter, Writer (1915-1991)
MARKS, GEORGE B Painter, Sculptor (1923-1983)
MARKS, ROYAL S Dealer, Collector (1927-1987)
MARKUS, HENRY A Collector
MARRIOTT, WILLIAM ALLEN Painter, Educator (1942-)
MARSH, (EDWIN) THOMAS Potter, Educator (1934-1991)
MARSH, FRED DANA Painter (1872-1911)
MARSH, REGINALD Painter (1898-1954)
MARSHAK, ARTHUR Sculptor, Ceramist (1927-2004)
MARSHALL, EDMUND Photographer (1938-1979)
MARSHALL, RALPH Educator, Photographer (1923-1984)
MARSTELLER, WILLIAM A Collector (1914-1987)
MARTELL, BARBARA BENTLEY Painter
MARTIN, FLETCHER Painter (1904-1979)
MARTIN, JOHN RUPERT Historian, Lecturer (1916-2000)
MARTIN, KEITH MORROW Painter (1911-1983)
MARTIN, RICHARD (HARRISON) Historian, Curator (1946-1999)
MARTIN, THOMAS Painter, Educator (1943-2000)
MARTINELLO, EZIO Sculptor (1913-)
MARTINET, MARJORIED Painter (1886-1981)
MARTINO, BABETTE Painter (-2011)
MARTINO, EVA Painter, Sculptor (-2012)
MARTINO, GIOVANNI Painter (1908-1998)
MARTMER, WILLIAM PHILIP Painter (1939-1982)
MARTZ, KARL Ceramist, Educator (1912-1987)
MARYAN, MARYAN S Painter (1927-1977)
MARZIO, PETER CORT Museum Director, Historian (1943-2010)
MASER, EDWARD ANDREW Historian, Museum (1923-1988)
MASON, ALDEN C Painter, Educator (1919-2013)
MASON, ALICE FRANCES Lithographer, Painter (1895-)
MASON, ALICE TRUMBALL Painter (1904-1971)
MASON, FRANK HERBERT Painter, Instructor (1921-2009)
MASON, MAUDE M Painter (1867-1951)
MASON, ROY MARTELL Painter (1886-1972)
MASSEY, ROBERT JOSEPH Painter, Educator (1911-1993)
MAST, GERALD Painter (1908-1971)
MATASSA, JOHN P Painter, Educator (1945-2004)
MATEO, JULIO Painter, Printmaker (1951-2013)
MATISSE, PIERRE Dealer (1900-1989)
MATLICK, GERALD ALLEN Painter, Historian (1947-1988)
MATTA-CLARK, GORDON Sculptor (1945-1978)
MATTERN, KARL Painter (1882-1969)
MATTHEWS, WANDA MILLER Printmaker (1930-2001)
MATTISON, DONALD MANGUS Painter (1905-1975)
MATTISON, HENRY (ELIS) Painter (1887-1971)
MATULKA, JAN Painter (1890-1972)
MAULDIN, WILLIAM HENRY Cartoonist, Writer (1921-2003)
MAUNSBACH, GEORGE ERIC Painter (1890-)
MAURER, SASCHA Painter (1897-1961)
MAVROS, DONALD ODYSSEUS Ceramist, Sculptor (1927-2010)
MAXON, JOHN Museum Director (1916-1977)
MAXWELL, JOHN Painter (-1997)
MAXWELL, WILLIAM JACKSON Sculptor, Environmental Artist (-2000)
MAYEN, PAUL Designer (1918-2000)
MAYER, BENA FRANK Painter (1898-1991)
MAYER, GRACE M Curator, Collector (-1996)
MAYER, RALPH Painter, Writer (1895-1979)
MAYER, ROBERT ANTHONY Administrator, Photographer (1933-2008)
MAYHEW, EDGAR DE NOAILLES Educator, Museum Director (1913-1990)
MAYHEW, ELZA Sculptor (1916-2004)
MAYOR, A HYATT Curator (1901-1980)
MAYS, PAUL KIRTLAND Painter (1887-1961)
MAZUR, MICHAEL Painter, Printmaker (1935-2009)
MAZZONE, DOMENICO Sculptor, Painter (1927-)
MCBEY, JAMES Painter (1884-1951)
MCBRIDE, HENRY Critic (1867-1962)
MCCALL, ROBERT THEODORE Illustrator, Painter (1919-2010)

MCCANDLESS, BARBARA ANN Curator, Historian (1949-2005)
MCCARTHY, DENNIS Sculptor, Educator (1921-2006)
MCCARTHY, DORIS JEAN Painter, Instructor (1910-)
MCCARTHY, JUSTIN Painter (1892-)
MCCARTIN, WILLIAM FRANCIS (1905-2003)
MCCASLIN, WALTER WRIGHT Art Critic, Writer (1924-)
MCCAUSLAND, ELIZABETH Writer (1889-1965)
MCCHESNEY, CLIFTON Painter, Educator (1929-2011)
MCCHESNEY, ROBERT PEARSON Painter, Muralist (1913-2008)
MCCLOSKEY, ROBERT Painter, Illustrator (1914-2003)
MCCORMICK, KATHARINE H Painter (1882-1960)
MCCOSH, DAVID J Painter (1903-1980)
MCCOUCH, GORDON MALLET Painter (1885-1962)
MCCOY, JOHN W Painter (1910-1999)
MCCRACKEN, JOHN HARVEY Sculptor, Painter (1934-2011)
MCCREADY, KAREN (KAREN MCCREADY NOBLET) Art Dealer (1946-2000)
MCCREERY, FRANC ROOT (MRS) Painter (-1957)
MCCULLOUGH, JOSEPH Administrator, Painter (1922-2012)
MCCURRY, HARR ORR Museum Director (1889-1964)
MCDARRAH, FRED WILLIAM Photographer, Editor (1926-2007)
MCDONALD, JOHN STANLEY Art Dealer (1943-1981)
MCDOO, DONALD ELDRIDGE Painter, Printer (1929-)
MCDOUGAL, IVAN ELLIS Painter, Instructor (1927-2005)
MCEACHRON, (GENEVIEVE) ANN Painter, Instructor (1926-2015)
MCEVILLEY, THOMAS Writer, Critic (1939-2013)
MCEWEN, JEAN Painter (1923-1999)
MCFARREN, GRACE Painter (1914-2012)
MCFEE, HENRY LEE Painter (1896-1953)
MCFEE, JUNE KING Educator (1917-2008)
MCGEE, OLIVIA JACKSON Painter, Illustrator (1915-1987)
MCGILL, HAROLD A Cartoonist (-1952)
MCGLYNN, THOMAS Sculptor (1906-)
MCGOVERN, ROBERT F Painter, Sculptor (1933-2011)
MCGREW, R BROWNELL Painter (1916-1994)
MCHUGH, ADELIZA SORENSON Dealer, Collector (1912-2003)
MCHUGH, JAMES FRANCIS Collector (-1969)
MCINTOSH, HAROLD Painter (1916-1996)
MCKAY, JOHN SANGSTER Administrator, Educator (1921-2003)
MCKEE, FRANCES BARRETT Illustrator (1909-1975)
MCKEEBY, BYRON GORDON Printmaker, Educator (1936-1984)
MCKENDRY, JOHN Curator (1933-1975)
MCKENNA, GEORGE LAVERNE Curator (1924-2007)
MCKENZIE, VINNORMA SHAW Painter (1890-1952)
MCKESSON, MALCOLM FORBES Painter, Sculptor (1909-)
MCKIM, WILLIAM WIND Lithographer, Painter (1916-1895)
MCKININ, LAWRENCE Educator, Painter (1917-)
MCKINLEY, RUTH GOWDY Ceramist, Designer (1911-1981)
MCKINNEY, TATIANA LADYGINA Painter, Instructor (1909-2008)
MCLAUGHLIN, DONAL Architect (1875-1978)
MCLAUGHLIN, JOHN Artist (1899-1976)
MCMAHON, A PHILIP Writer, Educator (1890-)
MCMANUS, JAMES Painter (1882-1955)
MCMEIN, NEYSA Painter, Designer (1890-)
MCMILLAN, ROBERT W Painter, Educator (1915-1991)
MCMILLLAN, MARY Painter (1885-)
MCMULLEN, E ORMOND Painter (1888-)
MCMURTRIE, EDITH Painter (1883-)
MCNEAR, EVERETT C Painter, Designer (1904-1984)
MCNETT, WILLIAM BROWN Illustrator (1896-1969)
MCNULTY, KNEELAND Curator, Writer (1921-1991)
MCNULTY, WILLIAM CHARLES Painter (1884-1963)
MCPHARLIN, PAUL Writer, Illustrator (1903-1948)
MCQUILLAN, FRANCES Painter, Instructor (-1996)
MCVEY, LEZA Ceramist, Weaver (1907-1984)
MCWHINNIE, HAROLD JAMES Printmaker, Collage Artist (1929-2004)
MCWHORTER, ELSIE JEAN Painter, Sculptor (1932-)
MEAD, KATHERINE HARPER Curator, Historian (1929-)
MEADMORE, CLEMENT L Sculptor (1929-2005)
MEADOWS, ALGUR H Patron (1899-1980)
MEANS, ELLIOTT Painter (1905-1962)
MECHLIN, LEILA Critic, Writer (1894-1949)
MECKLEM, AUSTIN MERRILL Painter (1894-1951)
MEDEARIS, ROGER Painter, Printmaker (1920-2001)
MEDRICH, LIBBY E Sculptor (-2006)
MEEHAN, WILLIAM DALE Painter, Educator (1930-1997)
MEEKER, DEAN JACKSON Printmaker, Sculptor (1920-2002)
MEGGS, PHILIP B Designer, Historian (1942-2002)
MEGIS, JOHN LIGGET Painter, Collector (1916-)
MEHRING, HOWARD WILLIAM Painter (1931-1978)
MEIERE, HILDRETH Painter (-1960)
MEIGS, JOHN LIGGETT Painter, Collector (1916-2003)
MEIGS, WALTER Painter (1918-1988)
MEISS, MILLARD Art Historian, Writer (1904-1975)
MEITZLER, NEIL (HERBERT) Painter (1930-2009)
MEIXNER, MARY LOUISE Painter, Educator (1916-2004)
MELAMED, ABRAHAM Collector, Patron (1914-)
MELCARTH, EDWARD Painter, Sculptor
MELCHER, BETSY FLAGG Painter (1900-1991)
MELLON, PAUL Collector (1907-)
MELLOR, GEORGE EDWARD Educator, Sculptor (1928-1987)
MELVIN, GRACE WILSON Painter, Illustrator (-1977)
MELVIN, RONALD MCKNIGHT Museum Director (1927-2006)
MENCONI, RALPH JOSEPH Sculptor (1915-1972)
MENDELOWITZ, DANIEL MARCUS Painter, Writer (1905-1980)
MENKES, SIGMUND J Painter (1896-1986)
MEOSSNER, LEO J Painter, Engraver (1885-1977)
MEREDITH, DOROTHY LAVERNE Weaver, Educator (1906-1986)
MERKIN, RICHARD MARSHALL Painter, Printmaker (1938-2009)
MERMIN, MILDRED (SHIRE) Painter (-1985)
MERRICK, JAMES KIRK Painter, Educator (1905-1985)
MERRITT, FRANCIS SUMNER Painter, Printmaker (1913-2000)
MERTIN, ROGER Photographer (1942-2001)
MERYMAN, HOPE Artist, Illustrator (-1975)
MESS, GEORGE JO Painter (1898-1962)

MESS, GORDON BENJAMIN Painter (1900-1959)
MESSEGUER, VILLORO BENITO Painter, Sculptor (1930-1982)
MESSER, THOMAS MARIA Museum Director, Historian (1920-2013)
MESSERSMITH, FRED LAWRENCE Painter, Educator (1924-2009)
MESSICK, BEN (NEWTON) Painter, Instructor (1911-)
MESTROVIC, IVAN Sculptor (1884-1962)
METZKER, RAY K Photographer, Educator (1931-2014)
MEYER, EL(MER) FREDERICK Painter, Writer (1910-2001)
MEYER, FRANK HILDBRIDGE Painter, Printmaker (1923-1996)
MEYER, FRED (ROBERT) Sculptor, Painter (-1986)
MEYER, FREDERICK H Educator (1873-1961)
MEYER, HERBERT Painter (1882-1960)
MEYEROWITZ, WILLIAM Painter (1896-1981)
MEYERS, LEONARD H Computer Art (1932-1979)
MEYERS, ROBERT WILLIAM Illustrator (1919-1970)
MICALE, ALBERT Painter, Sculptor (-1993)
MICHAJLOW, EUSTACHY Painter (1930-2008)
MIDENER, WALTER Sculptor, Instructor (1912-1998)
MIDGETTE, WILLARD FRANKLIN Painter, Printmaker (1937-1978)
MIELZINER, JO Designer, Lecturer (1901-1976)
MIES VAN DER ROHE, LUDWIG Architect (1886-1969)
MILCH, HAROLD CARLTON Art Dealer (1908-)
MILES, JEANNE PATTERSON Painter, Sculptor (1908-1999)
MILHOLLAND, RICHARD ALEXANDER Painter, Instructor (1946-2004)
MILHOUS, KATHERINE Illustrator, Writer (1894-1977)
MILLER, BARSE Painter, Educator (1924-1973)
MILLER, BURR Sculptor (1904-1958)
MILLER, DONALD Critic, Writer (1934-2003)
MILLER, DONALD LLOYD Painter, Muralist (1923-1993)
MILLER, DONALD RICHARD Sculptor, Medallist (1925-1989)
MILLER, F JOHN Painter, Mosaic Artist (1929-2015)
MILLER, HELEN PENDELTON Etcher (1888-1957)
MILLER, JEAN JOHNSON Librarian, Historian (1918-)
MILLER, JOHN PAUL Jeweler (1918-)
MILLER, KENNETH HAYES Painter, Teacher (1876-1952)
MILLER, MELVIN ORVILLE JR Painter (1937-)
MILLER, NANCY TOKAR Painter (1941-2014)
MILLER, RICHARD KIDWELL Painter (1930-2012)
MILLER, ROBERT PETER Art Dealer (1939-2011)
MILLET, CLARENCE Painter (1897-1959)
MILLIKEN, WILLIAM M Museum Director, Curator (1889-1978)
MILLMAN, EDWARD Painter (1907-1964)
MILLS, FREDERICK VAN FLEET Designer, Educator (1925-2008)
MILLS, PAUL CHADBOURNE Museum Director, Consultant (1924-2004)
MINA-MORA, DORISE OLSON Painter (1932-1991)
MINER, DOROTHY EUGENIA Museum Curator, Art Historian (1906-1973)
MINEWSKI, ALEX Painter, Educator (1917-1979)
MINNEGERODE, CUTHBERT POWELL Museum Director (1876-1951)
MINNICK, ESTHER TRESS Painter (-1999)
MISSAL, PEGGE Art Dealer, Consultant (1923-2001)
MITCHELL, ALFRED R Painter (1888-1972)
MITCHELL, ANN Printmaker, Painter (1927-2013)
MITCHELL, BRUCE HANDISIDE Painter (1908-1963)
MITCHELL, CLIFFORD Architect, Painter (1925-2005)
MITCHELL, DANA COVINGTON Collector (1918-)
MITCHELL, ELEANOR Consultant, Librarian (1907-)
MITCHELL, GLEN Painter (1894-1972)
MITCHELL, HENRY (WEBER) Sculptor (1915-1990)
MITCHELL, JOAN Painter (1926-)
MITCHELL, THOMAS W Painter
MITCHELL, WALLACE (MACMAHON) Museum Director, Painter (1911-1977)
MITRA, GOPAL C Painter, Printmaker (1928-1992)
MIYASHITA, TAD Painter (1922-1979)
MOCHI, UGO Sculptor (1894-1977)
MOCHON, DONALD Graphic Artist, Educator (1916-)
MOCK, GEORGE ANDREW Painter (1886-)
MODEL, EVSA Artist (1900-1976)
MOE, HENRY ALLEN Art Administrator (1894-1975)
MOEHL, KARL J Painter, Writer (1925-2009)
MOFFETT, ROSS E Painter (1888-1971)
MOFFITT, JOHN FRANCIS Historian, Painter (1940-2008)
MOGGRIDGE, BILL Designer, Museum Director (-2012)
MOHN, CHERI (ANN) Painter, Instructor (1936-2005)
MOLARSKY, MAURICE Painter, Educator (1885-1950)
MOLLER, HANS Painter (1905-2000)
MONAGHAN, KEITH Painter, Educator (1921-2001)
MONES, ARTHUR Photographer (1919-1998)
MONONGYE, PRESTON LEE Silversmith, Printmaker (1927-1988)
MONTAGUE, JAMES L Painter, Printmaker (1906-)
MONTANA, BOB Cartoonist (1920-1975)
MONTANA, PIETRO Sculptor, Painter (1890-1978)
MONTGOMERY, CHARLES FRANKLIN Art Administrator, Educator (1910-1978)
MONTGOMERY, CLAUDE Painter, Etcher (1912-1990)
MONTHAN, GUY Photographer, Educator (1925-2006)
MONTLACK, EDITH Painter (-2003)
MOON, CARL Illustrator (1879-1948)
MOORE, ROBERT ERIC Painter (1927-)
MOOSE, PHILIP ANTHONY Painter, Illustrator (1921-2001)
MOOSE, TALMADGE BOWERS Painter, Illustrator (1933-2003)
MORA, FRANCISCO Painter (1922-2002)
MORALES, ARMANDO Painter, Printmaker (1927-2011)
MORANG, ALFRED GWYNNE Painter (1901-1951)
MORATH, INGE (INGE MORATH MILLER) Photographer (1923-2002)
MORDVINOFF, NICOLAS Painter, Illustrator (1911-1973)
MORE, HERMON Museum Director (1887-1968)
MORGAN, GLADYS B Painter, Lithographer (1899-1981)
MORGAN, MARITZA LESKOVAR Painter, Illustrator (1921-)
MORGAN, MYRA J Art Dealer (1938-2005)
MORGAN, NORMA GLORIA Painter, Engraver
MORGAN, WALLACE Illustrator (1873-1948)
MORIN-MILLER, CARMEN A Author, Curator (-2007)
MORISSET, GERARD Educator (1898-1970)
MORITA, JOHN TAKAMI Printmaker, Video Artist (1943-)
MORRIS, CARL Painter (1911-1993)
MORRIS, DONALD FISCHER Dealer (1925-2004)
MORRIS, DUDLEY H, JR Painter (1912-1966)
MORRIS, GEORGE FORD Painter (-1860)
MORRIS, GEORGE L K Painter, Sculptor (1905-1975)

MORRIS, HILDA Sculptor (-1990)
MORRIS, KYLE RANDOLPH Painter (1918-1979)
MORRIS, ROGER DALE Painter (1947-2011)
MORRISON, FRITZI MOHRENSTECHER Painter, Lecturer (-2008)
MORRISON, GEORGE Painter, Sculptor (1919-)
MORROW, BENJAMIN FRANCIS Painter (1891-1958)
MORROW, ROBERT EARL Designer, Muralist (1917-2004)
MORSE, DOROTHY B Illustrator, Educator (1906-1979)
MORSE, GLENN TILLEY Painter (1870-1950)
MORSE, ROSABELLE (JACQUELINE) Painter (-2002)
MORTON, REE Sculptor, Painter (1936-1977)
MORTON, RICHARD H Painter, Graphic Artist (1921-2003)
MOSBY, DEWEY FRANKLIN Museum Director, Historian (1942-2012)
MOSBY, WILLIAM HARRY Painter (1898-1964)
MOSCA, AUGUST Painter, Printmaker (1907-2003)
MOSE, CARL C Sculptor, Lecturer (1903-1973)
MOSELSIO, SIMON Sculptor (1880-)
MOSER, FRANK H Painter (1886-1964)
MOSES, ANNA MARY ROBERTSON (GRANDMA) Painter (1860-1961)
MOSES, BETTE J Painter (-2006)
MOSES, FORREST KING Painter (1893-1974)
MOSKOWITZ, IRA Painter, Printmaker (1912-2001)
MOSLEY, ZACK T Illustrator, Cartoonist (1906-1993)
MOTHERWELL, ROBERT Painter, Printmaker (1915-1991)
MOTT-SMITH, MAY Medallist, Painter (1879-1952)
MOUFARREGE, NICHOLAS A Painter, Critic (1947-)
MOY, MAY (WONG) Painter, Instructor (1913-2003)
MOYER, ROY Painter, Administrator (1921-2007)
MUEHSAM, GERD Librarian, Writer (1913-1979)
MUELLER, STEPHEN Painter (1947-2011)
MUIR, WILLIAM HORACE Sculptor (1902-1965)
MULLER, GEORGE F Painter (1866-1958)
MULLER, HELEN B Painter, Gallery Director (1922-1999)
MULLER, JAN Painter (1922-1958)
MULLICAN, LEE Painter, Educator (1919-1978)
MULLIN, WILLARD Cartoonist (1902-1979)
MUNDY, ETHEL FRANCES Sculptor (-1964)
MUNDY, LOUISE EASTERDAY Painter (1870-1952)
MUNFORD, ROBERT WATSON Painter, Educator (1925-1991)
MUNOWOTZ, KEN Illustrator (1936-1978)
MUNRO, THOMAS Art Scholar (1897-1974)
MUOGE, EDMOND WEBSTER, JR Collector (1904-1984)
MURANYI, GUSTAVE Painter (1872-1961)
MURCH, ANNA VALENTINA Conceptual Artist, Environmental Artist (1948-2014)
MURCH, WALTER Painter (1907-1967)
MURCHOSON, JOHN D Collector (1921-1978)
MURDOCK, ROBERT MEAD Curator (1941-2009)
MURPHY, CHESTER GLENN Painter (1907-1997)
MURPHY, GLADYS WILKINS Painter, Craftsman (1907-1985)
MURPHY, ROWLEY WALTER Painter, Designer (1891-1975)
MURRAY, ALBERT (KETCHAM) Painter (1906-1992)
MURRAY, ELIZABETH Painter (1940-2007)
MURRAY, FLORETTA MAY Administrator, Painter (-2001)
MURRAY, FRANK WALDO Painter (1884-1956)
MURRAY, WILLIAM COLMAN Collector, Patron (1899-1977)
MUSGROVE, A J Museum Director
MUSSELMAN, DARWIN B Painter (1916-2001)
MYERS, ETHEL K Sculptor (1881-1960)
MYERS, FRANK HARMON Painter (1899-1951)
MYERS, FRED A Museum Director (1937-)
MYERS, GEORGE HEWITT Museum President (1865-1957)
MYRICK, KATHERINE S Painter
NADEL, ANN HONIG Sculptor, Ceramist (1940-2008)
NADLER, HARRY Painter, Educator (1930-1990)
NAEGLE, STEPHEN HOWARD Painter, Sculptor (1938-1981)
NAEVE, MILOM Curator, Historian (1931-2009)
NAGEL, STINA Painter (1918-1969)
NAGLER, EDITH KROGER Painter (1895-1986)
NAGLER, FRED Printmaker, Sculptor (1890-1983)
NAHA, RAYMOND Painter (-1975)
NAILOR, GERALD LLOYDE Painter, Illustrator (1917-1952)
NAIMAN, LEE Consultant (1926-1986)
NAKAMIZO, FUJI Painter (1889-)
NAKAMURA, KAZUO Painter (1926-)
NAMUTH, HANS Photographer, Filmmaker (1915-1990)
NASH, RAY Art Historian (1905-1982)
NASHER, RAYMOND DONALD Collector (1921-)
NASON, GERTRUDE Painter (1890-)
NASON, THOMAS W Engraver (1888-1971)
NATHAN, HELMUTH MAX Educator, Painter (1901-1979)
NATHANS, RHODA R Photographer (1940-1998)
NATKIN, ROBERT Painter (1930-2010)
NATZLER, GERTRUD Ceramic Craftsman (1908-1971)
NATZLER, OTTO Ceramist, Sculptor (1908-2007)
NAVAS, ELIZABETH S Collector, Patron (1895-)
NAY, MARY SPENCER Painter, Educator (1913-1993)
NEAL, REGINALD H Painter, Printmaker (1909-1992)
NEANDROSS, SIGURD Sculptor (1869-1958)
NEBEL, BERTHOLD Sculptor (1889-1964)
NEDDEAU, DONALD FREDERICK PRICE Painter, Designer (1913-1998)
NEEL, ALICE Painter (1900-1984)
NEFF, JOSEPH Collector (1900-1969)
NEIDHARDT, (CARL) RICHARD Painter, Sculptor (1921-2009)
NEILL, BEN E Painter (1914-2001)
NEILSON, KATHERINE B Art Historian (1902-1977)
NEILSON, RAYMOND P R Painter (1891-1964)
NEIMAN, LEROY Painter, Printmaker (1926-2012)
NELSON, GEORGE LAURENCE Painter (1887-1975)
NELSON, JACK D Sculptor, Graphic Artist (1929-1997)
NEMEC, NANCY Printmaker, Painter (1923-2003)
NEMEROV, DAVID Painter (-1963)
NEPOTE, ALEXANDER Painter (1913-1986)
NESBERT, VINCENT Miniature Painter (-1976)
NESBITT, ALEXANDER JOHN Educator, Calligrapher (1901-1995)
NESBITT, JACKSON LEE Printmaker (1913-2008)
NESBITT, LOWELL BLAIR Painter, Sculptor (1933-1993)
NESEMANN, ENNO Painter (1861-1949)
NESS, (ALBERT) KENNETH Painter, Designer (1903-2001)
NESS, EVALINE (MRS ARNOLD A BAYARD) Illustrator, Writer (1910-)
NEUBERGER, ROY R Collector, Patron (1903-)
NEUGEBERGER, MARGOT Designer, Craftsman (1929-1996)
NEUHAUS, MAX Sculptor, Lecturer (1939-2009)

NEUMANN, J B Art Dealer, Critic (1887-1961)
NEUMANN, WILLIAM A Educator, Goldsmith (1924-1995)
NEUMEYER, ALFRED Art Historian (1901-1973)
NEUTRA, RICHARD Architect (1892-1970)
NEW, LLOYD H KIVA Educator (-2002)
NEWBERRY, CLARE TURLAY Illustrator (1903-1970)
NEWBERRY, JOHN S Museum Curator (-1964)
NEWHALL, ADELAIDE MAY Painter (1894-1960)
NEWHALL, BEAUMONT Photographer, Educator (1908-)
NEWHOUSE, BERTRAM MAURICE Art Dealer (1888-1982)
NEWHOUSE, CLYDE MORTIMER Dealer, Historian (1920-1990)
NEWMAN, BARNETT Painter (1905-1970)
NEWMAN, ELIAS Painter (1903-1999)
NEWTON, DOUGLAS Administrator, Museum Director (1920-2001)
NEWTON, GRACE HAMILTON (MRS ARTHUR NEWTON) Painter (-1958)
NEWTON, MARGARET, Painter (1893-1960)
NICHOLS, DONALD EDWARD Designer, Educator (1922-1987)
NICHOLS, ELEANOR CARY Designer, Mettalsmith (1903-1988)
NICHOLS, HOBART Painter (1869-1962)
NICHOLS, JAMES WILLIAM Painter (1928-2004)
NICHOLS, SPENCER B Painter (1875-1950)
NICHOLSON, BEN Painter (1894-1952)
NICHOLSON, THOMAS D Director (1922-)
NICKLE, ROBERT W Painter, Educator (1919-1980)
NICOLOSI, JOSEPH Sculptor (1893-1961)
NIEMEYER, ARNOLD MATTHEW Collector, Patron (1913-1990)
NILES, ROSAMOND Painter (1891-)
NISBET, ROBERT H Painter (1879-1961)
NITZSCHE, ELSA KOENIG Portrait Painter (1880-1952)
NOA, FLORENCE Printmaker, Educator (1941-1989)
NOBLE, JOHN A Fainter, Lithographer (1903-1983)
NODEL, SOL Illuminator Designer (1912-1976)
NOEL, DONALD CLAUDE Sculptor, Mosaic Artist (1930-2008)
NOFER, FRANK Painter, Graphic Artist (1929-2002)
NOGGLE, ANNE Photographer, Educator (1922-2005)
NOGUCHI, ISAMU Sculptor (1904-1989)
NOLAND, KENNETH Painter, Printmaker (1924-2010)
NOLTE, GUNTER Sculptor, Draftsman (1938-2000)
NOORDHOEK, HARRY CECIL Sculptor, Painter (1909-1992)
NORBURY, LOUISE H Painter (1878-1952)
NORDELL, EMMA PARKER (POLLY) Painter
NORTARO, ANTHONY Sculptor (1905-1984)
NORTON, ANN W Sculptor (-1982)
NOTARBARTOLO, ALBERT Painter, Environmental Artist (1934-2008)
NOVOTNY, ELMER LADISLAW Painter, Educator (1909-1987)
NOWACK, WAYNE KENYON Painter, Graphic Artist (1923-2004)
NOWAK, LEO Illustrator, Cartoonist (1924-2001)
NOYES, ELIOT Architect, Designer (1910-1977)
NUDERSCHER, FRANK BERNARD Painter (1881-1951)
NUGENT, ARTHUR WILLIAM Cartoonist, Illustrator (1891-1975)
NUKI, (DANIEL MILLSAPS) Painter, Writer (1918-1984)
NUNN, FREDERIC Painter (1879-)
O'HANLON, RICHARD E Sculptor, Painter (1906-1985)
O'HARA, (JAMES) FREDERICK Printmaker (1904-1980)
O'HARA, ELIOT Painter (1890-1969)
O'KEEFFE, GEORGIA Painter (1887-1986)
OAKES, WILLIAM LARRY Painter, Sculptor (1944-)
OAKLEY, VIOLET Painter (1874-1960)
OBERHARDT, WILLIAM Illustrator (1892-1955)
OBRIEN, WILLIAM VINCENT Art Dealer (1902-)
OCHIKUBO, TETSUO Painter, Designer (1923-1975)
OCHS, RICHARD WAYNE Painter, Instructor (1938-2006)
OCHTMAN, DOROTHY (MRS WA DEL MAR) Painter (1892-1971)
OENSLAGER, DONALD MITCHELL Stage Designer (1902-1975)
OERI, GEORGINE Critic (-1968)
OFFIN, CHARLES Z Collector, Critic (1899-1989)
OFFNER, ELLIOT Sculptor, Printmaker (1931-2010)
OGDEN, RALPH E Collector, Patron (-1974)
OGG, OSCAR Designer, Writer (1908-1971)
OGILVIE, WILL (WILLIAM ABERNETHY) Painter (1901-1989)
OHLSON, DOUGLAS DEAN Painter, Educator (1936-2010)
OKADA, KENZO Painter (1902-1982)
OKUN, BARBARA-ROSE Art Dealer, Gallery Director (1932-2007)
OLINSKY, IVAN G Painter (1878-1962)
OLITSKI, JULES Painter, Sculptor (1922-)
OLIVEIRA, NATHAN Painter (1928-2010)
OLIVER, RICHARD BRUCE Architect (1942-1993)
OLMER, HENRY Sculptor (1887-1950)
OLPIN, ROBERT SPENCER Historian, Administrator (1940-2005)
OLSEN, HERB Painter, Writer (1905-1973)
O'NEIL, JOHN JOSEPH Administrator, Designer (1932-2004)
O'NEIL, JOHN Painter, Educator (1915-2004)
ONLEY, TONI Painter, Printmaker (1928-2004)
OPDYCKE, LEONARD Educator (1895-1977)
OPPENHEIM, DENNIS A Sculptor (1938-2011)
OPPENHEIM, SAMUEL EDMUND Painter (1901-1992)
OPPENHEIMER, SELMA L Painter (1898-)
ORDER, TRUDY Painter (1944-)
ORKIN, RUTH (MRS MORRIS ENGEL) Photographer, Filmmaker (1921-1985)
ORLING, ANNE Consultant, Painter (-1989)
ORLOFF, LILY Painter (1908-1957)
ORLOWSKY, LILLIAN Painter, Collage Artist (1914-2004)
ORME, LYDIA GARDNER Painter (-1963)
ORR, ARTHUR (Leslie) Painter, Graphic Artist (1938-2005)
ORR, ELLIOT Painter (1904-1997)
ORTLIP, MARY KRUEGER Painter (-2001)
ORTMAN, GEORGE EARL Painter, Sculptor (1926-2015)
OSBORNE, ROBERT LEE Painter, Educator (1928-2004)
OSGOOD, RUTH Painter (-1977)
O'SHEA, TERRENCE PATRICK Painter, Sculptor (1941-)
OSSORIO, ALFONSO Painter, Sculptor (1916-1980)
OSTENDORF, (ARTHUR) LLOYD JR Painter, Instructor (1921-2000)
OSTER, GERALD Painter, Kinetic Artist (1918-1993)
OSTUNI, PETER W Painter (1909-1992)
OSVER, ARTHUR Painter (1912-2006)
OSYCZKA, BOHDAN DANNY Painter (1921-2010)
OTTIANO, JOHN WILLIAM Jeweler, Sculptor (1926-)
OUBRE, HAYWARD LOUIS Sculptor, Painter (-2006)

OWEN, FREDERICK Painter (1869-1959)
OZENFANT, AMEDEE J Painter (1886-1966)
PABLO Painter, Educator (1934-)
PACE, STEPHEN S Painter, Printmaker (1918-2010)
PACH, MAGDA F Painter (1884-1950)
PACH, WALTER Writer (1883-1951)
PACKER, CLAIR LANGE Painter, Writer (1901-1978)
PACKER, FRANCIS H Sculptor (1873-1957)
PACKER, FRED L Cartoonist (1886-1956)
PADDOCK, WILLARD DRYDEN Painter (1873-1956)
PAEFF, BASHKA (BASHKA PAEFF WAXMAN) Sculptor (1893-1979)
PAGAN, RICHARD Painter, Sculptor (1954-1999)
PAGE, GROVER Cartoonist (1893-1958)
PAGENT-FREDERICKS, J ROUS-MARTEN Illustrator (1905-1963)
PAGES, JEAN Illustrator, Muralist (1907-1977)
PAINE, ROBERT T Museum Curator (1900-1965)
PALAZZOLA, GUY Administrator Educator (1919-1978)
PALEY, WILLIAM S (MRS) Collector
PALEY, WILLIAMS (MR) Collector (1901-1990)
PALLASCH, MAGDALENA HELENA Artist (1908-2011)
PALMER, ALLEN INGELS Painter (1910-1950)
PALMER, DELOS Painter (1891-1961)
PANZA DI BIUMO, GIUSEPPE Collector (1923-2010)
PAPASHVILY, GEORGE Sculptor, Writer (1898-1978)
PAPASIAN, JACK C Sculptor (1878-1957)
PARADISE, PHIL (HERSCHEL) Painter, Sculptor (1905-1997)
PARDI, JUSTIN A Painter (1898-1951)
PARDON, EARL B Craftsman, Educator (1926-1991)
PAREDES, LIMON MARIANO Engraver, Painter (1912-1878)
PARELLA, ALBERT LUCIAN Painter, Instructor (1909-1999)
PARIS, HAROLD PERSICO Sculptor (1925-1979)
PARIS, JEANNE C Critic, Consultant (-2002)
PARISH, NORMAN Gallery Director (1937-2013)
PARK, MADELEINE F Sculptor (1891-1960)
PARKER, ALFRED Illustrator (1906-1985)
PARKER, GEORGE WALLER Painter (1888-1957)
PARKER, JONI Y Painter, Instructor (-2014)
PARKER, RAYMOND Painter (1922-1990)
PARKER, THOMAS Administrator (1904-1967)
PARKHURST, CHARLES Educator, Curator (1913-2008)
PARKHURST, VIOLET KINNEY Painter, Writer (1926-)
PARRINO, GEORGE Painter, Educator (1942-2011)
PARRISH, MAXFIELD Painter (1870-1966)
PARSHALL, DEWITT Painter (1864-1956)
PARSONS, BETTY BIERNE Painter, Art Dealer (1900-1982)
PARSONS, DAVID GOODE Sculptor, Educator (1911-2005)
PARSONS, EDITH BARRETTO Sculptor (1878-1956)
PARSONS, ERNESTINE Painter (1884-1967)
PARSONS, LLOYD HOLMAN Painter (1883-1968)
PARTCH, VIRGIL FRANKLIN Cartoonist, Illustrator (1906-)
PARTON, NIKE Painter, Environmental Artist (1922-2005)
PARTRIDGE, ROI Printmaker (1889-1984)
PARTZ, FELIX (RON GABE) Painter (1945-1994)
PASCAL, DAVID Painter, Cartoonist (1918-2003)
PASCHKE, EDWARD Painter (1939-2004)
PASINSKI, IRENE Painter, Sculptor (1923-2002)
PASSLOF, PAT Painter, Educator (1928-2011)
PATRICK, RANSOM R Educator (1906-1971)
PATTERSON, CHARLES ROBERT Painter (1875-1958)
PATTISON, ABBOTT Sculptor, Painter (1916-1999)
PATTY, WILLIAM A Painter (1898-1961)
PAUL, BORIS DUPONT Painter (1900-)
PAUL, SUZANNE Photographer (1945-2005)
PAULIN, RICHARD CALKINS Museum Director (1928-2004)
PAULSON, MICHAEL Artist
PAYNE, JOHN D Sculptor, Educator (1934-)
PEABODY, AMELIA Sculptor (1890-1984)
PEAK, CHANNING Painter, Muralist (1910-1991)
PEAK, ROBERT Painter, Illustrator (-1992)
PEARLMAN, E(TTA) S Painter (1939-2006)
PEARLMAN, HENRY Collector (1895-1974)
PEARLSTEIN, SEYMOUR Painter, Educator (1923-)
PEARMAN, KATHARINE K Painter (1893-1961)
PEARSON, HENRY C Painter, Instructor (1914-)
PEARSON, JOSEPH T, JR Painter (1876-1951)
PEARSON, RALPH M Etcher (1883-1958)
PECK, EDWARD Gallery Director (-1970)
PECK, JAMES EDWARD Painter, Designer (1907-2002)
PEEBLES, ROY B Painter (1899-1951)
PEETS, ORVILLE Painter (1884-1968)
PEIRCE, WALDO Painter (1894-1970)
PELLICONE, WILLIAM Painter, Sculptor (1915-2004)
PENA, TONITA Painter (1895-1949)
PENCZNER, PAUL JOSEPH Painter (1916-2010)
PENNEY, JAMES Painter, Educator (1910-1982)
PENNOYER, A SHELDON Painter (1889-1957)
PENNY, AUBREY JOHN ROBERT Painter, Sculptor (1917-2000)
PEPPER, CHARLES HOVEY Painter (1864-1950)
PERARD, VICTOR S Etcher (1867-1957)
PEREHUDOFF, WILLIAM W Painter, Muralist (1918-2013)
PEREIRA, I RICE Painter (1901-1971)
PERINE, ROBERT HEATH Painter, Writer (1922-2004)
PERKINS, ANN Historian, Educator (1915-2006)
PERKINS, CONSTANCE M Educator, Critic (1903-)
PERKINS, G HOLMES Architect, Educator (1904-2004)
PERKINS, MABLE H Collector (1880-1974)
PERKINS, MARION Sculptor (1908-1961)
PERKINS, PHILIP R Painter (-1968)
PERKINS, ROBERT EUGENE Administrator (1931-1997)
PERKINS-RIPLEY, LUCY FAIRFIELD O Painter
PERLIN, BERNARD Painter, Illustrator (1918-2014)
PERLS, FRANK (RICHARD) Art Dealer, Collector (1910-1975)
PERLS, KLAUS G Dealer (1912-2008)
PERRET, FERDINAND Historian (1888-1960)
PERRET, NELL FOSTER Painter, Printmaker (1916-1986)
PERRETT, GALEN J Painter (1875-1949)
PERRIN, C ROBERT Painter, Illustrator (1915-1999)
PERRY, CHARLES OWEN Sculptor (1929-2011)
PERRY, RAYMOND Painter (1876-1960)
PETERDI, GABOR F Painter, Printmaker (1915-)
PETERS, CARL W Painter (1897-1980)
PETERS, FRANCIS C Painter (1902-1977)
PETERSHAM, MISKA Illustrator (1888-1959)
PETERSON, A E S Painter, Printmaker (1908-1984)
PETERSON, HAROLD PATRICK Librarian (1935-1994)
PETERSON, JANE Painter (1876-1965)
PETERSON, JOHN P Craftsman (-1949)
PETERSON, PERRY Illustrator (1908-1958)
PETITTO, BARBARA BUSCHELL Painter, Curator (-2003)

PETREMONT, CLARICE M Painter (-1949)
PETRIE, FERDINAND RALPH Painter, Illustrator (1925-2007)
PETRO, JOSEPH (VICTOR) JR Painter, Illustrator (1932-)
PETTUS, JANE M Painter (1908-)
PEYTON, BERTHA MENZLER Painter (1871-1947)
PFEIFFER, FRITZ Painter (1889-1960)
PFEIFFER, HEINRICH H Painter (1874-)
PFISTER, JEAN JACQUES Painter (1878-1949)
PHELAN, LINN LOVEJOY Designer (1906-1992)
PHELPS, EDITH CATLIN Painter (1875-1961)
PHELPS, NAN Painter (-1990)
PHILBRICK, OTIS Painter, Printmaker (1888-1973)
PHILIP, LOTTE BRAND Historian (1910-)
PHILIPP, ROBERT Painter (1895-1981)
PHILLIPS, ARTHUR BYRON Painter, Sculptor (1930-2008)
PHILLIPS, DICK (RICHARD) CORTEZ Painter, Instructor (1933-2011)
PHILLIPS, DOROTHY W Art Administrator, Writer (1906-1977)
PHILLIPS, DUNCAN Museum Director (1886-1966)
PHILLIPS, DUTCH (JAMES) O JR Gallery Director, Dealer (1944-)
PHILLIPS, J CAMPBELL Painter (1873-1949)
PHILLIPS, JAMES Historian, Painter (1929-)
PHILLIPS, LAUGHLIN Museum Chairman, Director (1924-)
PHILLIPS, MARJORIE Painter (1894-1995)
PHIPPS, DARLEEN (MARIE) Painter (1929-1999)
PICKEN, GEORGE Painter, Printmaker (1898-1971)
PICKENS, ALTON Painter, Instructor (1917-1991)
PICKFORD, ROLLIN JR Painter (-2010)
PICKHARDT, CARL Painter, Printmaker (1908-2004)
PIENE, OTTO Sculptor, Painter (1928-2014)
PIERCE, DELILAH W Painter, Educator (1904-1992)
PIERCE, GARY Painter (-1969)
PILGRIM, JAMES F Curator, Administrator (1941-2002)
PILLIN, POLIA Painter, Ceramist (1909-1992)
PIMENTEL, DAVID DELBERT Goldsmith, Educator (1943-2004)
PINCHBECK, PETER G Painter (1940-2000)
PINCUS, DAVID N Collector (-2011)
PINEDA, MARIANNA Sculptor (1925-1996)
PINTO, ANGELO RAPHAEL Painter, Printmaker (1908-1994)
PINTO, BIAGIO Painter (1911-1989)
PIONK, RICHARD C Painter (1938-2007)
PIPER, JANE Painter (1916-1991)
PISANO, RONALD GEORGE Historian, Consultant (1948-2000)
PITTMAN, HOBSON Painter (1900-1972)
PITTMAN, KATHRYN Painter, Instructor (1915-1979)
PITZ, HENRY CLARENCE Painter, Writer (1895-1976)
PLATE, WALTER Painter, Educator (1925-1972)
PLATT, ELEANOR Sculptor (1910-1974)
PLAVCAN, JOSEPH MICHAEL Painter, Sculptor (1908-1981)
PLEASANTS, FREDERICK R Collector, Patron (1906-)
PLEISSNER, OGDEN MINTON Painter (1905-1983)
PLUNGUIAN, GINA Painter (-1962)
POCCIRILLO, FURID Sculptor (1868-1949)
POGACH, GERALD Painter, Sculptor (-1996)
POHL, HUGO DAVID Painter (1878-1960)
POINIER, ARTHUR BEST Editorial Cartoonist (1911-)
POKE, JOHN Illustrator, Painter (1900-1979)
POLAN, LINCOLN M Collector, Patron (1909-1999)
POLAN, NANCY MOORE Painter, Printmaker
POLANSKY, LOIS B Printmaker, Painter (1939-2003)
POLKE, SIGMAR Photographer (1941-2010)
POLKES, ALAN H Collector, Patron (1931-)
POLLACK, LOUIS Art Dealer (1921-1970)
POLLACK, PETER Photographer, Writer (1911-1978)
POLLACK, REGINALD MURRAY Painter, Sculptor (1924-2001)
POLLACK, VIRGINIA MORRIS Sculptor
POLLAND, DONALD JACK Sculptor (1932-2003)
POLLET, JOSEPH Painter (1898-1979)
POLLEY, FREDERICK Painter (1875-)
POLLOCK, JACKSON Painter (1912-1956)
POLLOCK, JAMES ARLIN Painter (1898-1949)
POMEROY, FREDERICK GEORGE Painter, Restorer (1924-2011)
POMEROY, JAMES CALOWELL Performance Artist, Photographer (1945-1992)
POMEROY, MARY BARNAS (MRS F G POMEROY) Painter, Illustrator (1921-2010)
POMMER, RICHARD Educator, Historian (1930-1992)
POND, DANA Painter (1880-1962)
POND, WILLI BAZE (MRS CHARLES E) Painter (1896-1947)
POOLE, ABRAM Painter (1882-1961)
POOLE, EARL LINCOLN Illustrator, Art Administrator (1891-1972)
POOR, ANNE Painter (1918-2002)
POOR, HENRY VARNUM Painter (1888-1970)
POPE, JOHN ALEXANDER Historian, Museum Director (1906-1992)
POPE, MARION HOLDEN Painter (-1958)
POPESCU, CARA Sculptor, Printmaker (-1991)
POPINSKY, ARNOLD DAVE Sculptor, Ceramist (1930-2010)
POPKIN, ELSIE DINSMORE Graphic Artist (1937-2005)
PORADA, EDITH Historian (1912-1994)
PORAY, STAN P Painter, Designer (1888-1948)
PORSMAN, FRANK O Painter (1905-)
PORTANOVA, JOSEPH DOMENICO Sculptor, Designer (1909-1979)
PORTER, ALBERT WRIGHT Educator, Painter (1923-2008)
PORTER, ELIOT FURNESS Photographer, Writer (1901-1990)
PORTER, FAIRFIELD Painter, Lecturer (1907-1975)
PORTNOFF, ALEXANDER Sculptor (1887-1949)
POST, GEORGE BOOTH Painter (1906-1997)
POST, MARION (MARION POST WOLCOTT) Photographer (1910-1990)
POTTER, TED Painter, Administrator (1933-)
POTTER, WILLIAM J Painter (1883-1964)
POTTS, CHARLES A Administrator (-1986)
POUNIAN, ALBERT KACHOUNI Painter, Curator (1924-2000)
POUPENEY, MOLLIE Ceramist, Writer (1926-2002)
POUSETTE-DART, NATHANIEL J Painter (1886-1965)
POUSETTE-DART, RICHARD Painter, Sculptor (1916-1992)
POWELL, DOANE Craftsman (1881-1951)
POWELL, LYDIA BOND Art Administrator, Consultant (1892-1978)
POWERS, MARILYN Painter (1925-1976)

POWERS, MARY SWIFT Painter (1885-1959)
POZITZ, SILVIA Collector, Patron (-1991)
PRAGER, DAVID A Collector (1913-1997)
PRAKAPAS, EUGENE JOSEPH Art Dealer, Editor (1932-2011)
PRATT, DUDLEY Sculptor (1897-1975)
PRATT, ELIZABETH SOUTHWOCK Painter (-1964)
PRATT, VERNON GAITHER Painter, Educator (1940-2000)
PREDERGAST, CHARLES E Painter (1868-1948)
PRESSER, JOSEF Painter (1907-1967)
PRESTINI, JAMES LIBERO Sculptor, Designer (1908-1993)
PRESTON, ALICE BOLAM (MRS FRANK I) Illustrator (1889-1958)
PRESTON, HARRIET BROWN Painter (1892-1961)
PRESTON, JAMES M Painter (1874-1961)
PRESTOPINO, GREGORIO Painter (1907-)
PREZZI, WILMA M Painter (1915-)
PRICE, CHESTER B Illustrator (1885-1962)
PRICE, CLAYTON S Painter (1874-1950)
PRICE, FREDERIC NEWLIN Museum Director (1884-1963)
PRICE, GARRETT Cartoonist (1897-1979)
PRICE, KENNETH Printmaker, Sculptor (1935-2012)
PRICE, MARGARET E Illustrator, Painter (1888-)
PRICE, MICHAEL BENJAMIN Sculptor, Educator (1940-2001)
PRICE, MINNIE Painter (1877-1951)
PRICE, NORMAN MILLS Illustrator (1877-1951)
PRICE, ROSALIE PETTUS Painter
PRICE, VINCENT Collector, Dealer (1927-1993)
PRIEBE, KARL Painter (1914-1976)
PRIEST, ALAN Museum Curator (1898-1969)
PRIEST, HARTWELL WYSE Painter, Printmaker (1901-2004)
PRINCE, WILLIAM MEADE Illustrator (1893-1951)
PRIOR, HARRIS KING Art Administrator, Educator (1911-1975)
PROCHOWNIK, WALTER A Educator, Painter (1923-2000)
PROCTOR, A PHIMISTER Sculptor (1862-1950)
PROHASKA, RAY Painter, Illustrator (1901-1981)
PROKOPOFF, STEPHEN Museum Director, Historian (1929-2001)
PUCCINELLI, RAIMONDO Sculptor, Graphic Artist (1904-1986)
PUFAHL, JOHN K Educator, Printmaker (1942-1998)
PULOS, ARTHUR JON Designer, Educator (1917-)
PURSER, STUART ROBERT Painter, Educator (1907-1986)
PUSHMAN, HOVSEP Painter (1877-1966)
PUTMAN, BRENDA Sculptor (1890-1975)
PUTMAN, JOHN B (MRS) Collector (1903-)
QUANDT, RUSSELL JEROME Museum Art Restorer (1919-1970)
QUATTROCCHI, EDMONDO Sculptor (1889-1966)
QUINN, NOEL JOSEPH Painter, Instructor (1915-1993)
QUINN, ROBERT HAYES Illustrator (1902-1962)
QUIRK, FRANCIS JOSEPH Painter, Museum Director (1907-1974)
QUIRT, WALTER Painter, Educator (1902-1868)
QUISTGAARD, JOHAN WALDEMAR DE REHLING Portrait Painter (1877-1962)
RAAB, ADA DENNETT (MRS S V) Painter (-1950)
RADOCZY, ALBERT Painter (1914-2008)
RAGGIO, OLGA Historian, Curator (1926-2009)
RAHILL, MARGARET FISH Curator, Critic (1919-1998)
RAHMING, NORRIS Painter (1886-1959)
RAINS, BAXTER Sculptor, Consultant (1938-2009)
RAINVILLE, PAUL Museum Director (-1952)
RALSTON, JAMES KENNETH Painter, Illustrator (1896-1987)
RANDALL, (LILLIAN) PAULA Sculptor, Designer (1885-1985)
RANDALL, RICHARD HARDING JR Curator, Historian (1926-1997)
RANES, CHRIS Painter, Designer (1929-2002)
RANEY, SUZANNE BRYANT Printmaker (-1967)
RANN, VOLLIAN BURR Painter (1897-1956)
RANNEY, GLEN ALLISON Painter (1896-1959)
RANSON, NANCY SUSSMAN Painter, Printmaker (1905-)
RASCOE, STEPHEN THOMAS Painter, Educator (1924-2008)
RASKO, MAXIMILIAN A Painter (1884-1961)
RATHBONE, PERRY TOWNSHEND Museum Director (1911-2000)
RATKAI, GEORGE Painter, Sculptor (1907-1999)
RATTNER, ABRAHAM Painter (1895-1978)
RATZKA, ARTHUR L Painter (1869-)
RAU, WILLIAM R Artist (1874-)
RAUCH, JOHN G Collector, Patron (1890-1976)
RAUSCHENBERG, ROBERT Painter, Photographer (1925-2008)
RAVENSCROFT, ELLEN Painter (1876-1949)
RAVESON, SHERMAN HAROLD Painter, Writer (1907-1974)
RAY, CHRISTOPHER T Sculptor, Craftsman (1937-)
RAY, ROBERT (DONALD) Painter, Photographer (1924-2002)
RAY, RUTH (MRS JOHN REGINALD GRAHAM) Painter (1919-1977)
RAY, TIMOTHY L Painter, Educator (1940-2013)
RAYMOND, ALEXANDER Cartoonist (1909-1956)
RAYNER, GORDON Painter (1935-)
READ, HELEN APPLETON Art Historian, Art Critic (1887-1974)
READE, ROMA (MABEL KELLEY AUBREY) Painter (1877-1958)
READIO, WILFRED A Painter (1895-1961)
REALE, NICHOLAS ALBERT Painter, Instructor (1922-)
REASON, PATRICK Engraver (1817-1852)
REBAY, HILLA Painter (1885-1983)
RECCHIA RICHARD (HENRY) Sculptor (1885-1983)
REDEIN, ALEX S Painter, Instructor (1912-)
REDER, BERNARD Sculptor (1897-1963)
REDFIELD, EDWARD W Painter (1869-1965)
REED, DOEL Painter, Printmaker (1894-)
REED, JESSE FLOYD Painter, Printmaker (1920-2011)
REED, WALT ARNOLD Historian, Dealer (1917-2015)
REESE, WILLIAM FOSTER Painter (1938-2010)
REEVES, J MASON Painter (1898-1973)
REFREGIER, ANTON Painter (1905-1979)
REGENSBURG, SOPHY P Painter, Collector (1885-1974)
REGENSTEINER, ELSE (FRIEDSAM) Designer, Weaver (1906-2003)
REGESTER, CHARLOTTE Painter
REICH, NATHANIEL E Painter, Collage Artist (1907-2004)
REICH, SHELDON Historian, Lecturer (1931-2002)
REICHARD, STEPHEN BRANTLEY Administrator (1949-)
REICHEK, JESSE Painter, Educator (1916-2005)
REICHMAN, FRED Painter (-2005)
REID, GEORGE AGNEW Painter (-1947)
REIF, (F) DAVID Sculptor, Educator, Painter (1941-2009)
REIFF, ROBERT FRANK Art Historian, Painter (1918-1982)

REILLY, ELVIRA Painter (1899-1958)
REINDEL, WILLIAM GEORGE Painter (1871-1948)
REINDORF, SAMUEL Painter (1914-1988)
REINHARDT, AD F Painter (1913-1967)
REISE, BARBARA Art Critic (-1978)
REISMAN, PHILIP Painter (1904-1992)
REISS, LIONEL S Painter, Writer (1929-)
REMBERT (LILES), VIRGINIA PITTS Art Historian, Educator (1921-2013)
REMENICK, SEYMOUR Painter, Instructor (1923-1999)
REMINGTON, DEBORAH WILLIAMS Painter (1935-2010)
REMMEY, PAUL B Illustrator
RENIER, JOSEPH EMILE Sculptor (-1966)
RENNINGER, KATHARINE STEELE Painter (1925-2004)
RENOUF, EDWARD Painter, Sculptor (1906-1999)
RESNICK, MILTON Painter (1917-2004)
RETTEGI, STEVEN Painter (1932-)
REUMAN, SCOTT CAMPBELL Sculptor, Writer (1949-)
REVINGTON, GEORGE D, III Collector
REWALD, JOHN Curator, Writer (1912-1994)
REY, H A Illustrator, Writer (1898-1977)
REYNARD, GRANT T Painter (1887-1967)
REYNOLDS, LLOYD J Calligrapher (1887-1978)
REYNOLDS, PATRICIA ELLEN Painter (1934-2015)
REYNOLDS, RALPH WILLIAM Painter, Educator (1905-1991)
RHYNE, CHARLES SYLVANUS Historian (1932-)
RIBA, PAUL F Painter (1912-1977)
RIBAK, LOUIS Painter (1902-1980)
RICCI, ULYSSES Sculptor (1888-1960)
RICCIO, LOUIS NICHOLAS Painter, Curator (1931-)
RICE, HAROLD RANDOLPH Educator, Writer (1912-1987)
RICE, NORMAN LEWIS Painter, Educator (1905-1994)
RICH, DANIEL CATTON Art Administrator, Lecturer (1904-1976)
RICH, LORIMER Architect (1892-1978)
RICHARDS, GLENORA Painter (1909-2009)
RICHARDSON, EDGAR PRESTON Historian (1902-1995)
RICHARDSON, JAMES LEWIS Educator, Printmaker (1927-)
RICHARDSON, JOHN ADKINS Historian, Educator (1929-)
RICHENBURG, ROBERT BARTLETT Painter, Sculptor (1917-)
RICHMOND, LAWRENCE Collector (1909-1978)
RICHTER, GISELA MARIE AUGUSTA Museum Curator, Writer (1882-1972)
RICHTER, HANS Artist, Filmmaker (1888-1976)
RICKEY, GEORGE W Kinetic Artist, Sculptor (1907-2002)
RIDABOCK, RAY (BUDD) Painter, Instructor (1904-1970)
RIDLEY, GREGORY D, JR Painter, Sculptor (1925-2004)
RIEKER, ALBERT GEORGE Sculptor (1889-1959)
RIEPPEL, LUDWIG Sculptor (1861-1960)
RIGGS, GERRY Museum Director, Educator (1950-)
RIGGS, ROBERT Lithographer (1896-1970)
RIGLEY, FREDERICK WILDERMUTH Painter, Instructor (1914-2009)
RILEY, BERNARD JOSEPH Painter (1911-1984)
RINGIUS, CARL Painter (1879-1950)
RIPLEY, ALDEN LASSELL Painter (1896-1969)
RIPLEY, ROBERT L Illustrator (1893-1949)
RIPPEL, M (MORRIS) CONRAD Painter (1930-2009)
RIPPON, THOMAS MICHEAL Sculptor, Collector (1954-)
RISHELL, ROBERT CLIFFORD Painter, Sculptor (1917-1976)
RISLEY, JOHN HOLLISTER Sculptor (1919-2002)
RIST, LOUIS G Printmaker (1888-1959)
RITCHIE, ANDREW C Administrator, Historian (1907-1978)
RITMAN, LOUIS Painter (1889-1963)
RITSCHEL, WILLIAM Painter (1864-1949)
RIU, VICTOR Sculptor (1887-1974)
RIVERON, ENRIQUE Painter, Sculptor (1902-1998)
RIVERS, LARRY Painter (1923-2002)
ROBBINS, FRANK Cartoonist, Illustrator (1907-)
ROBBINS, WARREN M Museum Director, Educator (1923-2008)
ROBERTS, BILL Cartoonist (1914-1978)
ROBERTS, CLYDE HARRY Painter, Instructor (1923-2011)
ROBERTS, COLETTE (JACQUELINE) Critic, Administrator (1910-1971)
ROBERTS, HELENE EMYLOU Historian, Editor (1931-2008)
ROBERTS, MORTON Painter (1927-1964)
ROBERTS, PERCIVAL R Educator (1935-)
ROBERTS, TOM (THOMAS KEITH) Painter (1908-)
ROBERTS, VIOLET KENT Painter (1880-)
ROBERTSON, PAUL CHANDLER Painter (1902-1961)
ROBERTSON, SARAH M Painter (-1948)
ROBERTSON, TED WALTER Painter, Instructor (1942-2002)
ROBINSON, ARTHUR GROVE Painter, Printmaker (1935-2002)
ROBINSON, BOARDMAN Painter, Educator (1876-1952)
ROBINSON, MARIE RACHELLE Dealer, Painter (1919-1988)
ROBINSON, THEODORE Painter (1852-1896)
ROBUS, HUGO Sculptor (1885-1964)
ROCH, ERNST Graphic Designer (1928-2003)
ROCHÉ, ROBERT (RICHARD) Painter (1921-2004)
ROCKEFELLER, JOHN DAVISON III Collector, Patron (1906-1978)
ROCKEFELLER, LAWRENCE S (MRS) Collector (1910-1997)
ROCKEFELLER, NELSON ALDRICH Collector, Patron (1908-1979)
ROCKEFELLER, WINTHROP Collector (1912-1973)
ROCKWELL, NORMAN Illustrator (1894-1978)
RODMAN, SELDEN Writer, Critic (1909-2002)
ROEDIGER, JANICE ANNE Artist (-2010)
ROESCH, KURT (FERDINAND) Painter (1905-)
ROESLER, NORBERT LEONHARD HUGO Collector (1901-)
ROGALSKI, WALTER Printmaker, Lecturer (1923-1996)
ROGERS, BRUCE Designer (1870-1957)
ROGERS, CHARLES B Painter, Museum Director (1911-1987)
ROGERS, JOHN Painter (1906-1985)
ROGERS, MARGARET ESTHER Painter (1873-1961)
ROGERS, MEYRIC REYNOLD Museum Curator (1893-1972)
ROGERS, ROBERT STOCKTON Painter (1896-)
ROGNAN, LLOYD NORMAN Illustrator, Painter (1923-2005)
ROGOVIN, MILTON Photographer (1909-2011)
ROHLAND, PAUL Painter, Serigrapher (1884-1953)
ROHLFING, CHRISTIAN Administrator, Curator (1916-2004)
ROJAN, KOVSKY FEODOR STEPANOVICH Illustrator (1891-1970)
ROLAND, JAY Painter (1905-1960)
ROLLER, MARION BENDER Sculptor, Painter (-2012)
ROLLINS, JO LUTZ Dealer, Painter (1896-1989)
ROMANO, EMANUEL GLICEN Painter, Illustrator (1897-)
ROMANS, CHARLES JOHN Painter (1891-1973)

ROMBOUT, LUKE Consultant (1933-2000)
RONALD, WILLIAM Painter (1926-1998)
RONEY, HAROLD ARTHUR Painter, Lecturer (1899-1986)
RONNEBECK, ARNOLD H Sculptor (1885-1947)
ROOD, JOHN Sculptor, Painter (1906-1974)
ROODY, EDITH JEANNETTE Painter
ROOK, EDWARD F Painter (1870-1960)
ROOT, EDWARD WALES Art Authority, Collector (1884-1956)
ROOT, MRS EDWARD W Collector
RORIMER, JAMES J Museum Director (1905-1966)
ROSAND, DAVID Historian, Critic (1938-2014)
ROSE, HANNA TOBY Art Administrator (1909-1976)
ROSE, HERMAN Painter, Printmaker (1909-2007)
ROSE, IVER Painter (1899-1972)
ROSELAND, HARRY HERMAN Painter (1866-1950)
ROSEN, CAROL M Sculptor, Printmaker (-2014)
ROSEN, CHARLES Painter, Illustrator (1878-1950)
ROSEN, DAVID Restorer (1880-1960)
ROSEN, ESTHER YOVITS Painter, Sculptor (1916-1999)
ROSENBERG, HAROLD Writer, Educator (1906-1978)
ROSENBERG, JAKOB Writer (1893-1990)
ROSENBERG, SAEMY Art Dealer
ROSENBERG, SAMUEL Painter (1896-1972)
ROSENBLUM, JAY Painter, Printmaker (1933-1989)
ROSENBLUM, RICHARD STEPHEN Printmaker, Sculptor (1940-2000)
ROSENBLUM, ROBERT Historian (1927-)
ROSENQUIT, BERNARD Painter, Printmaker (1923-1991)
ROSENTHAL, (MRS) ALAN H Collector (-1990)
ROSENTHAL, DAVID Painter, Restorer (1876-1949)
ROSENTHAL, DORIS Painter, Lithographer (-1971)
ROSENTHAL, EARL EDGAR Educator, Historian (1921-2007)
ROSENTHAL, GERTRUDE Historian, Administrator (1903-1989)
ROSENTHAL, LESSING JULIUS Collector, Patron (1891-1979)
ROSENTHAL, RACHEL Performance Artist (1926-2015)
ROSENTHAL, SEYMOUR Painter, Lithographer (1921-2007)
ROSIN, HARRY Sculptor, Educator (1897-1973)
ROSKILL, MARK WENTWORTH Historian, Critic (1933-2000)
ROSOFSKY, SEYMOUR Painter, Printmaker (1924-)
ROSS, ALEXANDER Painter (1908-1990)
ROSS, ALVIN Painter, Educator (1920-1975)
ROSS, C CHANDLER Portrait Painter (-1952)
ROSS, LOUIS Mural Painter (1901-1963)
ROST, MILES ERNEST Painter (1891-1961)
ROSTAND, MICHEL Painter (1895-)
ROSZAK, THEODORE Painter, Sculptor (1907-1981)
ROTAN, WALTER Sculptor (1912-2001)
ROTH, BEN Cartoonist (1910-1960)
ROTH, JACK (RODNEY) Painter (1927-)
ROTHKO, MARK Painter (1903-1970)
ROTHMAN, SIDNEY Gallery Director, Critic (-1995)
ROTHROCK, ILSE SKOPSNA Librarian (1928-1981)
ROTHSCHILD, AMALIE (ROSENFELD) Sculptor, Painter (1916-2001)
ROTHSCHILD, HERBERT Art Collector (1892-1976)
ROTHSCHILD, JUDITH Painter, Collage Artist (-1993)
ROTHSCHILD, LINCOLN Sculptor, Writer (1902-1983)
ROTHSTEIN, ARTHUR Photographer (1915-1985)
ROTIER, PETER Painter (1888-)
ROUSSEAU, THEODORE, JR Museum Curator (1912-1974)
ROUSSEAU-VERMETTE, MARIETTE Tapestry Artist, Educator (1926-2006)
ROVELSTAD, TRYGUE A Sculptor (-1990)
ROVIN, BELL Painter, Sculptor (1911-1980)
ROWAN, EDWARD BEATTY Painter (1898-1946)
ROWE, CORINNE Painter (-1965)
ROWE, GUY Painter (1894-1969)
ROWE, REGINALD M Painter, Sculptor (1920-2007)
ROWLAND, BENJAMIN J R Educator (1904-1972)
ROWLAND, ELDEN HART Painter (1915-1982)
ROZZI, JAMES A Painter, Sculptor (1921-)
RUBEL, C ADRAIN Collector (1904-1978)
RUBEN, LEONARD Designer, Educator (1921-2004)
RUBEN, RICHARDS Painter, Educator (1925-1998)
RUBENSTEIN, LEWIS W Painter, Printmaker (1908-2003)
RUBIN, ARNOLD GARY Historian (1937-1988)
RUBIN, HY Illustrator (1905-1960)
RUBIN, IRWIN Painter, Designer (1930-)
RUBIN, SAMUEL Patrons (1901-1978)
RUBINS, DAVID KRESZ Sculptor (1902-1985)
RUDQUIST, JERRY JACOB Painter, Educator (1934-)
RUELLAN, ANDRÉE Painter (1905-2006)
RUEPPEL, MERRILL C Museum Director (1925-)
RUNGIUS, CARL, Painter (1869-1959)
RUSKIN, LEWIS Collector, Patron (1905-1981)
RUSSELL, BRUCE ALEXANDER Cartoonist (1903-1963)
RUSSELL, HELEN CROCKER Collector (1896-1966)
RUSSELL, HELEN DIANE Historian (1936-2004)
RUSSELL, MORGAN Painter (1886-1953)
RUSSIN, ROBERT I Sculptor, Educator (1914-2007)
RUSSO, MICHELE Painter (1909-2004)
RUSSOLI, FRANCO Art Critic (1923-1977)
RUTSCH, ALEXANDER Sculptor, Painter (-1997)
RUZICKA, RUDOLPH Illustrator, Designer (1883-1978)
RYAN, ELIZABETH Painter (1908-)
RYDER, CHAUNCEY FOSTER Painter (1868-1949)
RYDER, MAHLER BESSINGER Collage Artist, Illustrator (1937-1991)
RYLAND, ROBERT KNIGHT Painter (1873-1951)
SAARJNEN, EERO Architect, Designer (1910-1961)
SABATINI, RAPHAEL Painter, Sculptor (1896-1985)
SABLER, HELEN GERTRUDE Painter (-1950)
SACHS, JAMES H Collector, Patron (1907-1971)
SACHS, PAUL J Educator (1878-1965)
SACHSE, JANICE R Painter, Printmaker (1908-1998)
SACKLER, MORTIMER DAVID Patron (-2010)
SACKS, RAY Art Dealer, Consultant (-2001)
SADEK, GEORGE Educator, Designer (1928-)
SAGE, BILL B Ceramist, Instructor (-1990)
SAGE, KAY (TANGUY) Painter (1898-1963)
SAIDENBERG, DANIEL Dealer (1906-1997)
SAINT, LAWRENCE Painter (1855-1961)
SALEMME, LUCIA AUTORINO Painter, Writer (1919-)
SALEMME, MARTHA Painter (1912-2004)
SALERNO, CHARLES Sculptor, Educator (1916-1999)
SALTER, GEORGE Book Designer (1907-1967)
SALTER, JOHN RANDALL Sculptor, Painter (1898-1978)
SALTONSTALL, ELIZABETH Painter (1900-1990)
SALVATORE, VICTOR Sculptor (1885-1965)
SAMERJAN, GEORGE E Designer, Painter (1915-2005)
SAMPLE, PAUL Painter (1896-1974)

SAMSTAG, GORDON Painter, Sculptor (1906-)
SAMUELS, GERALD Painter, Sculptor (1927-2004)
SANABRIA, SHERRY ZVARES Painter (1937-2014)
SANDER, LUDWIG Painter (1906-1975)
SANDERS, HERBERT HARVEY Ceramist, Writer (1909-)
SANDERSON, CHARLES HOWARD Painter, Educator (1925-1999)
SANDESON, WILLIAM SEYMOUR Cartoonist (1913-2003)
SANDMAN, ALAN Sculptor, Publisher (1947-2007)
SANGUINETTI, EUGENE F Administrator, Lecturer (1917-2002)
SANKOWSKY, ITZHAK Painter, Sculptor (1908-1994)
SARASON, HENRY Photographer (1896-1979)
SARDEAU, HELENE Sculptor (1889-1968)
SARGENT, RICHARD Photographer, Curator (1932-2012)
SARKIS (SARKIS SARKISIAN) Painter (1909-1977)
SARNOFF, ARTHUR SARON Painter, Illustrator (1912-2000)
SASAKI, TOSHIO Sculptor, Environmental Artist (1946-2007)
SATO, TADASHI Painter, Designer (1923-2005)
SAUGSTAD, OLAF Craftsman, Educator (-1950)
SAUNDERS, AULUS WARD Painter, Educator (1904-1991)
SAUNDERS, CLARA ROSMAN Painter, Educator (-1951)
SAVAGE, AUGUSTA Sculptor (1900-1962)
SAVAGE, NAOMI Photographer (1927-2005)
SAVAGE, TOM ALLEN Painter (-2012)
SAVAS, JO-ANN Painter, Instructor (1934-)
SAVITT, SAM Painter, Illustrator
SAVITZ, FRIEDA Painter, Instructor (1931-1985)
SAWKA, JAN A Painter, Printmaker (1946-2012)
SAWYER, CHARLES HENRY Museum Director (1906-2005)
SAWYER, PHILIP AYER Painter (-1949)
SAWYER, WELLS M Painter (1863-)
SAXON, CHARLES DAVID Cartoonist, Illustrator (1920-1988)
SCALISE, NICHOLAS PETER Painter (1932-2009)
SCANGA, ITALO Sculptor, Educator (1932-2001)
SCARAVAGLIONE, CONCETTA MARIA Sculptor (1900-1975)
SCARPA, DOROTHEA Painter, Educator (1926-)
SCARPITTA, SALVATORE Sculptor, Painter (1919-2007)
SCHACTMAN, BARRY ROBERT Painter, Educator (1930-2015)
SCHAFER, ALICE PAULINE Printmaker (1899-1980)
SCHAFFER, ROSE Painter, Lecturer (-1989)
SCHAN, BERNARDA BRYSON Painter (1903-2004)
SCHANKER, LOUIS Printmaker, Painter (1903-1981)
SCHAPIRO, MIRIAM Painter, Sculptor (1923-2015)
SCHARY, SAUL Illustrator, Painter (1904-1978)
SCHAUMBURG, DONALD ROLAND Educator, Ceramist (1919-2003)
SCHEIRER, GEORGE A Hand Bookbinder (1895-1959)
SCHELLIN, ROBERT WILLIAM Painter, Craftsman (1910-1985)
SCHELLSTEDE, RICHARD LEE Art Dealer (1948-2004)
SCHEYER, ERNST Historian, Lecturer (1900-1985)
SCHIEFER, JOHANNES Painter, Curator
SCHIFF, GERT K A Historian (1926-1990)
SCHINDLER, R M Architect (1887-1953)
SCHLAIKJER, JES (WILHELM) Painter, Illustrator (1897-1982)
SCHLICHER, KARL THEODORE Painter, Historian (1905-1989)
SCHMALZ, CARL (NELSON) JR Painter, Educator (1926-2013)
SCHMECKEBIER, LAURENCE E Historian, Sculptor (1906-)
SCHMEIDLER, BLANCHE J Painter
SCHMIDT, FREDERICK LOUIS Painter, Illustrator (1922-2004)
SCHMIDT, KATHERINE (KATHERINE SCHMIDT SHUBERT) Painter (1898-1978)
SCHMITZ, CARL LUDWIG Sculptor (1900-1967)
SCHNAKENBERG, HENRY Painter (1892-1970)
SCHNEEBAUM, TOBIAS Painter (1921-2005)
SCHNEIDER, JANE HARRIS Sculptor (1932-)
SCHNIEWIND, CARL O Curator (1900-1957)
SCHNITTMANN, SASCHA S Sculptor (1913-)
SCHOELKOPF, ROBERT J JR Dealer (1927-1991)
SCHOEN, EUGENE Designer (1880-1957)
SCHOENER, JASON Painter, Lecturer (1919-1997)
SCHOENHERR, JOHN (CARL) Painter, Illustrator (1935-2010)
SCHOLDER, FRITZ Painter, Sculptor (1937-2005)
SCHOLLE, HARDINGE Museum Director (-1969)
SCHONWALTER, JEAN FRANCES Sculptor, Painter
SCHOOLEY, ELMER WAYNE Painter, Educator (1916-)
SCHORR, JUSTIN Painter, Educator (1928-2005)
SCHRACK, JOSEPH EARL Painter (1890-1973)
SCHRECKENGOST, VIKTOR Designer, Sculptor (1906-2008)
SCHREIBER, GEORGES Painter (1904-1977)
SCHREIBER, MARTIN Sculptor, Painter (1923-2005)
SCHREIVER, GEORGE AUGUST Curator, Art Historian (-1977)
SCHREYER, GRETA L Painter, Printmaker (1917-2005)
SCHROEDER, ERIC Museum Curator, Writer (1904-)
SCHUCKER, CHARLES Painter, Educator (1908-1998)
SCHUELER, JON R Painter (1916-1992)
SCHULE, CLIFFORD HAMILTON Painter, Sculptor (1918-2000)
SCHULLER, GRETE Sculptor
SCHULLER, NANCY SHELBY Librarian, Historian (1942-2011)
SCHULMAN, JACOB Collector (1915-1987)
SCHULMAN, ROBERT Painter, Director (1924-2004)
SCHULTZ, CAROLINE REEL Painter, Lecturer (1936-2004)
SCHULTZ, HAROLD A Painter, Educator (1907-2004)
SCHULZ, ROBERT EMIL Illustrator, Painter (1929-1978)
SCHULZ, CHARLES MONROE Cartoonist (1922-2000)
SCHULZ, JUERGEN Educator, Historian (1927-2014)
SCHUPLINSKY, WALTER Painter (1921-1990)
SCHUSTER, DONNA NORINE Painter (1883-1953)
SCHUSTER, CARL Art Historian, Art Writer (1904-)
SCHUTZ, ANTON Restorer, Writer (1894-1977)
SCHUTZ, ESTELLE Painter, Printmaker (1907-2005)
SCHUTZ, PRESCOTT DIETROCH Dealer (1948-1990)
SCHUYLER, PHILIP (GRIFFIN) Painter, Educator (1913-)
SCHWABACHER, ETHEL K Painter (1903-1984)
SCHWACHA, GEORGE Painter (1908-1986)
SCHWARTZ, HENRY Painter, Instructor (1927-2009)
SCHWARTZ, MANFRED Painter (1909-1970)
SCHWARTZ, MARJORIE WATSON Painter (1905-)
SCHWARTZ, THERESE Painter, Writer (1928-2005)
SCHWARTZMAN, DANIEL Architect (1909-1977)
SCHWARZ, FELIX CONRAD Painter, Educator (1906-1990)
SCHWARZ, FRANK HENRY Painter (1894-1951)

SCHWARZ, HEINRICH Curator, Educator (1894-1974)
SCHWEDLER, WILLIAM A Painter (1942-1982)
SCHWEISS, RUTH KELLER Sculptor, Designer (-1995)
SCHWEITZER, M R Dealer, Gallery Director (1911-)
SCHWIDDER, ERNST Sculptor, Designer (1931-1998)
SCHWIERING, CONRAD Painter (1916-)
SCOTT, BERTHA Portrait Painter (1884-1965)
SCOTT, C(HARLES) A(RTHUR) Sculptor (1940-2004)
SCOTT, CLYDE EUGENE Painter (1884-1959)
SCOTT, HENRY E Painter, Educator (1900-1990)
SCOTT, JOHN TARRELL Printmaker, Sculptor (1940-2007)
SCOTT, MARTHA F Printmaker, Sculptor (1916-1996)
SCOTT-GIBSON, HERBERT NATHANIEL Art Administrator, Educator (1928-1981)
SCRIVNER, (BOB) ROBERT MACFIE Sculptor, Curator (1914-1999)
SCULTHORPE, PETER Painter, Printmaker (1948-2014)
SEAMAN, DRAKE F Painter (-2000)
SEAMES, CLARANN Painter, Illustrator (-1992)
SEARLES, STEPHEN Sculptor, Painter
SEAVER, ESTHER Educator (-1965)
SEGAL, GEORGE Sculptor (1924-2000)
SEGY, LADISLAS Dealer, Collector (1904-1998)
SEIBEL, FRED O Cartoonist (1886-1968)
SEIDE, CHARLES Painter, Educator (1915-1980)
SEIDEL, ALEXANDER CARL-VICTOR Painter, Designer (1897-1979)
SEITZ, WILLIAM CHAPIN Educator, Art Historian (1914-1974)
SELDIS, HENRY J Art Critic (1925-1978)
SELEY, JASON Sculptor (1919-1983)
SELIG, J DANIEL Museum Director, Curator (1938-)
SELIGER, CHARLES Painter (1926-2009)
SELIGMAN, CHARLES Art Dealer (1893-1978)
SELIGMANN, HERBERT J Writer (1891-1984)
SELIGMANN, KURT Painter, Printmaker (1900-1962)
SELLECK, MARGARET Painter (1892-)
SELLERS, JOHN LEWIS Educator, Designer (1934-2000)
SELLIN, DAVID Lecturer, Curator (1930-2006)
SELONKE, IRENE A Painter (-1981)
SELVIG, FORREST HALL Historian, Writer (1924-2008)
SEMANS, JAMES HUSTEAD Patron (1932-2004)
SENNHAUSER, JOHN Painter, Designer (-1978)
SERGER, FREDERICK B Painter (1889-1965)
SERGER, HELEN Art Dealer (1901-1989)
SERISAWA, SUEO Painter (1910-2004)
SESSLER, ALFRED A Painter (1909-1963)
SETTERBERG, CARL GEORG Painter, Illustrator (1897-)
SEVERSON, WILLIAM CONRAD Sculptor (1924-1999)
SEWELL, HELEN MOORE Illustrator (1897-1957)
SEXTON, EMILY STRYKER Painter (1880-1948)
SEYFERT, RICHARD LEOPOLD Painter, Instructor (1915-1979)
SEYMOUR, CHARLES JR Art Historian, Curator (1912-1977)
SHACKELFORD, SHELBY Painter (1899-1987)
SHADBOLT, JACK LEONARD Painter (1909-1998)
SHAFER, BURR Cartoonist (-1965)
SHAFER, MARGUERITE (PHILLIPS) NEUHAUSER Artist (1888-1976)
SHAHN, BEN Painter (1898-1969)
SHANER, (GEORGE) DAVID Ceramist, Craftsman (1934-2002)
SHANGRAW, CLARENCE FRANK Historian, Curator (1935-2004)
SHANGRAW, SYLVIA CHEN Historian, Curator (1937-)
SHAPIRO, DAVID Painter, Printmaker (1916-2005)
SHAPLEY, JOHN Historian (1890-1969)
SHAPSHAK, RENE Sculptor (-1985)
SHARON, MARY B Painter (1891-1961)
SHARP, WILLIAM Painter (1900-1961)
SHARP, WILLOUGHBY Video Artist, Consultant (1936-2008)
SHATTER, SUSAN LOUISE Painter (1943-2011)
SHAVER, JAMES ROBERT Painter (1867-1949)
SHAW, CHARLES GREEN Painter, Writer (1892-1974)
SHAW, WILFRED B Painter (1881-)
SHEAKS, BARCLAY Painter, Writer
SHEELER, CHARLES Painter (1883-1965)
SHEETS, MILLARD Designer, Painter (1907-1989)
SHEFFER, GLENN C Painter, Illustrator (1881-1948)
SHEFFERS, PETER WINTHROP Painter (1893-1949)
SHEPHERD, REGINALD Painter, Printmaker (1924-)
SHEPLER, DWIGHT (CLARK) Painter, Writer (1905-)
SHEPPARD, CARL DUNKLE Historian (1916-1998)
SHEPPARD, JOHN CRAIG Painter, Educator (1913-1978)
SHERIDAN, HELEN ADLER Curator (-2008)
SHERMAN, JOHN K (URTZ) Critic (1898-1969)
SHERWOOD, ROSINA EMMET Painter (1854-1948)
SHERWOOD, SHERRY Designer (1902-)
SHERWOOD, WILLIAM ANDERSON Painter, Etcher (1875-1951)
SHIBLEY, GERTRUDE Painter (1916-2006)
SHIH, JOAN FAI Painter, Instructor (-2007)
SHIKLER, AARON Painter (1922-2015)
SHINN, EVERETT Painter (1876-1953)
SHIPLEY, JAMES R Educator, Designer (1910-1990)
SHIRAI, AKIKO Painter, Printmaker (-2001)
SHOEMAKER, PETER Painter (1920-1998)
SHOENFELT, JOSEPH FRANKLIN Painter (1918-1968)
SHOKLER, HARRY Painter, Serigrapher (1896-)
SHOOTER, TOM Painter (1941-2004)
SHOPE, IRVIN (SHORTY) Painter (1900-1977)
SHOPEN, KENNETH Painter (1902-1967)
SHORE, ROBERT Painter, Illustrator (1924-)
SHORNEY, MARGO KAY (MCIVER) Art Dealer, Sculptor (1930-1996)
SHORTER, EDWARD SWIFT Painter, Collector (1902-)
SHOWELL, KENNETH L Painter (1939-1997)
SHRADY, FREDERICK Sculptor (1907-1990)
SHRYOCK, BURNETT HENRY, SR Painter (1904-1971)
SHUCK, KENNETH MENAUGH Museum Director, Painter (1921-1992)
SHULKIN, ANATOL Painter (1901-1961)
SHULL, JAMES MARION Painter (1872-1948)
SHUNNEY, ANDREW Painter (1921-)
SHUTE, BEN E Painter (1905-1986)
SIBLEY, CHARLES KENNETH Painter, Educator (1921-2005)
SICA Printmaker, Sculptor (1932-)
SIDERIS, ALEXANDER Painter (1898-1978)
SIEBER, ROY Educator, Historian (1923-2001)
SIEGEL, (LEO) DINK Illustrator, Cartoonist (-2003)
SIEGEL, ADRIAN Photographer, Painter (1898-1978)
SIEGL, THEODOR Conservator, Lecturer (-1976)
SIEGRIST, LUNDY Painter (1925-1985)

SIEVAN, MAURICE Painter (1898-1981)
SIGISMUND, VIOLET M Painter, Printmaker (-2003)
SIGLER, HOLLIS Painter (1948-2001)
SIHVONEN, OLI Painter (1921-1991)
SILKOTCH, MARY ELLEN Painter (1911-)
SILVA, WILLIAM POSEY Painter (1859-1948)
SILVER, PAT Graphic Artist, Painter (1922-1992)
SILVERCRUYS, SUSANNE (MRS EDWARD FORD STEVENSON) Sculptor, Lecturer (1899-1973)
SILVERMAN, MEL Painter (-1966)
SIMMONS, CLEDA-MARIE Painter, Muralist (1927-2005)
SIMMONS, WILLIAM Etcher (1884-1949)
SIMON, BERNARD Sculptor, Instructor (1896-1980)
SIMON, C M Museum Director (1936-2006)
SIMON, ERIC M Illustrator, Designer (1892-1978)
SIMON, HELENE Sculptor (-2010)
SIMON, HOWARD Illustrator, Painter (1903-1979)
SIMON, NORTON Collector (1907-1993)
SIMON, SYDNEY Sculptor, Painter (1917-1997)
SIMONDS, JOHN ORMSBEE Architect (1913-2005)
SIMONET, SEBASTIAN Illustrator, Painter (1898-1948)
SIMONI, JOHN PETER Painter, Educator (1911-2003)
SIMONS, LOUIS BEDELL Painter (1912-1977)
SIMPER, FREDERICK Painter (1914-2002)
SIMPSON, MARSHALL Painter (1900-1958)
SIMPSON, MERTON DANIEL Painter, Dealer (1928-2013)
SIMPSON, WILLIAM Painter (1818-1872)
SIMSON, BEVLYN A Painter, Printmaker (1917-2008)
SINAIKO, ARLIE Sculptor, Collector (1902-)
SINGER, ARTHUR B Illustrator, Painter (1917-1990)
SINGER, NANCY BARKHOUSE Dealer (1912-2003)
SINNARD, ELAINE (JANICE) Painter, Sculptor (1926-2012)
SINSABAUGH, ART Photographer, Educator (1924-1983)
SINTON, NELL (WALTER) Painter, Instructor (-1997)
SIPORIN, MITCHELL Painter, Educator (1910-1976)
SIQUEIROS, DAVID ALFARO Painter (1896-1974)
SIRUGO, SAL (SALVATORE) Painter (-2013)
SISCHY, INGRID BARBARA Editor, Curator (1952-2015)
SISSON, JACQUELINE D Librarian, Educator (1925-1980)
SISSON, LAURENCE P Painter (1928-2015)
SIUMMERS, DUDLEY GLOYNE Painter, Illustrator (1892-1975)
SIVARD, ROBERT PAUL Painter (1914-1990)
SKEGGS, DAVID POTTER Designer, Painter (1924-1973)
SKEMP, ROBERT OLIVER Painter (1910-1984)
SKILES, CHARLES Cartoonist (-1969)
SKINAS, JOHN CONSTANTINE Painter (-1966)
SKLAR, DOROTHY Painter
SKLAR, GEORGE Painter (1905-1968)
SKOOGFORS, OLAF Silversmith (-1975)
SLATER, FRANK Portrait Painter (-1965)
SLATKES, LEONARD J Historian (1930-2003)
SLATKIN, CHARLES E Art Dealer (1908-1977)
SLATKIN, YEFFE KIMBALL Painter (1914-1978)
SLAUGHTER, HAZEL BURNHAM Painter (1888-1979)
SLAUGHTER, LURLINE EDDY Painter (1919-1991)
SLEIGH, SYLVIA Painter, Educator (1916-2010)
SLICK, JAMES NELSON Painter, Sculptor (1901-1979)
SLIVKA, DAVID Sculptor (-2010)
SLOAN, JOHN Painter, Educator (1871-1951)
SLOAN, ROBERT SMULLYAN Painter (1915-2013)
SLOANE, ERIC Painter (1910-1985)
SLOANE, JOSEPH CURTIS Historian (1909-)
SLOANE, PHYLLIS LESTER Painter, Printmaker (-2009)
SLOBODKIN, LOUIS Sculptor, Illustrator (1903-1975)
SMALLEY, JANET Illustrator (1893-)
SMEDLEY, WILL LARYMORE Painter (1871-)
SMITH, ALBERT DELMONT Portrait Painter (1886-1962)
SMITH, ANDRE Painter (1880-1959)
SMITH, BARBARA NEFF Patron (1908-1977)
SMITH, CECIL ALDEN Painter, Sculptor (1910-1984)
SMITH, CLYDE Painter (1932-)
SMITH, DAVID Sculptor (1906-1965)
SMITH, EMILY GUTHRIE Painter (1909-1987)
SMITH, GORDON MACKINTOSH Museum Director (1906-1979)
SMITH, GREGORY Painter
SMITH, HELEN M Illustrator, Painter (1917-2005)
SMITH, HENRY HOLMES Photographer, Educator (1909-1986)
SMITH, HOWARD ROSS Curator (1910-)
SMITH, JACOB GETLAR Painter (1898-1958)
SMITH, JUDSON Painter (1880-1962)
SMITH, JUSTIN V Collector (1903-)
SMITH, LAWRENCE M C Collector, Patron (1902-1975)
SMITH, LEON POLK Painter, Cottage Artist (1906-1996)
SMITH, LYN WALL Writer, Painter (1909-1979)
SMITH, ROBERT C Educator (1912-1975)
SMITH, SAM Painter, Educator (1918-1999)
SMITH, TONY Sculptor (1902-)
SMITH, VINCENT D Painter, Printmaker (1929-2003)
SMITH, W HARRY Painter, Restorer (1875-1951)
SMITH, WALT ALLEN Sculptor, Designer (1910-1971)
SMITH, WILLIAM ARTHUR Painter, Printer (1918-)
SMITHSON, ROBERT Sculptor, Lecturer (1938-1974)
SMOLIN, NAT Sculptor, Painter (1890-1950)
SMONGESLI, JOSEPH LEON Painter, Designer (1914-2001)
SMYTH, ED Illustrator, Painter (1916-1996)
SNELOROVE, GORDON WILLIAM Educator
SNOW, DASH Photographer (1981-2009)
SNOW, LEE ERLIN Painter, Instructor (1924-2007)
SOBY, JAMES THRALL Writer, Critic (1906-1979)
SOGLOW, OTTO Cartoonist (1900-1975)
SOLDNER, PAUL EDMUND Sculptor, Ceramist (1921-2011)
SOLES, WILLIAM Sculptor (-1967)
SOLINGER, DAVID M Collector, Patron
SOLLINS, SUSAN Curator (-2014)
SOLMAN, JOSEPH Painter (1909-2008)
SOLOMON, (MRS) SIDNEY L Collector (1909-2006)
SOLOMON, HOLLY Art Dealer, Collector (-2002)
SOLOMON, HYDE Painter (1911-)
SOLON, HARRY Painter (1873-1958)
SOLOWEY, BEN Cartoonist (1901-1978)
SOLTESZ, FRANK JOSEPH Painter (1912-1986)
SOMBERG, EMILIJA O K Painter (1924-)
SOMBERG, HERMAN Painter (1917-1991)
SOMMA, THOMAS P Historian, Museum Director (1949-)
SOMMER, WASSILY Painter, Educator (1912-1979)
SOMMERBURG, MIRIAM Mosaic Artist, Sculptor (-1980)
SONED, WARREN Painter (1911-1966)
SONNENSCHEIN Patron, Historian (1917-1981)
SOPHER, AARON Painter, Illustrator (1905-1972)
SOPHER, BERNHARD D Sculptor (1879-1949)
SORBY, J RICHARD Painter, Designer (1911-2001)
SOREFF, HELEN Painter (1937-1998)

SORENSEN, JEAN Painter
SORENSEN, JOHN HJELMHOF Cartoonist (1923-1969)
SORIA, MARTIN SEBASTIAN Educator (1911-1961)
SOROKIN, DAVIS Art Dealer, Painter (1908-1977)
SOUTHWELL, WILLIAM JOSEPH Painter, Writer (1914-2002)
SOVIAK, HARRY Painter, Sculptor (1935-)
SOYER, ISAAC Painter, Instructor (1902-1981)
SOYER, MOSES Painter (1899-1974)
SOZID, ARMANDO Painter (-1966)
SPAETH, OTTO Collector (1897-1966)
SPANDORF, LILY GABRIELLA Painter, Muralist (-2000)
SPARK, VICTOR DAVID Dealer (1898-1991)
SPAVENTA, GEORGE Sculptor (1918-1978)
SPAYREGEN, MORRIS Collector
SPEAR, ARTHUR P Painter (1879-1959)
SPEICHER, EUGENE E Painter (1883-1962)
SPEIGHT, FRANCIS Painter, Educator (1896-1989)
SPENCER, HUGH Illustrator, Photographer (1887-1975)
SPENCER, LEONTINE G Painter (1882-1964)
SPENCER, NILES Painter (1893-1952)
SPERO, NANCY Painter, Collage Artist (1926-2009)
SPERRY, ROBERT Ceramist (1927-1998)
SPICER-SIMPSON, THEODORE Sculptor (1871-1959)
SPIEGEL, EMILY JOY Collector
SPIEGEL, JERRY Collector
SPIEGELMAN, LON HOWARD Painter, Publisher (1941-2002)
SPOHN, CLAY (EDGAR) Painter, Instructor (1898-1977)
SPRADLING, FRANK L Painter (1885-1972)
SPRAGUE-SMITH, ISABELLE DWIGHT (MRS CHARLES) (1861-1951)
SPRANG, ELIZABETH Painter, Sculptor (-1993)
SPRINGHORN, CARL Painter (1897-1971)
SPRINGWEILER, ERWIN FREDERICK Sculptor (1896-1968)
SPRUANCE, BENTON Lithographer (1904-1967)
SPURGEON, SARAH (EDNA M) Painter, Educator (1903-1985)
SQUIRE, ALLAN TAFT Designer
SQUIRES, NORMA JEAN Painter, Writer
ST AMAND, JOSEPH Painter (1925-1992)
ST CLAIR, MICHAEL Art Dealer (1912-1999)
ST GAUDENS, HOMER Educator (1879-1958)
ST JOHN, BRUCE Administrator, Historian (1916-)
STACHELBERG, CHARLES G Collector, Patron
STACKS, WILLIAM LEON Painter, Restorer (1928-1991)
STACY, DONALD L Painter, Educator (1925-2008)
STADLER, ALBERT Painter (1923-2000)
STAEMPFLI, GEORGE W Dealer, Painter (1910-1999)
STAFFEL, RUDOLF HARRY Ceramist, Instructor (1911-2002)
STAGG, MRS JESSIE A Sculptor (1891-1958)
STALLMAN, EMMA S Craftsman (1888-1959)
STAMATS, PETER OWEN Collector, Patron (1929-2003)
STAMATY, STANLEY Cartoonist, Illustrator (1916-1979)
STAMELOS, ELECTRA GEORGIA MOUSMOULES Painter, Educator (-2007)
STAMOS, THEODOROS (S) Painter (1922-1997)
STAMPER, WILSON YOUNG Painter (1912-1988)
STAMPFLE, FELICE Curator, Writer (1912-2000)
STANDEN, EDITH APPLETON Historian (1905-1998)
STANKIEWICZ, RICHARD PETER Sculptor, Educator (1922-1983)
STANLEY, BOB Painter (1932-)
STAPLES, ROY HARVARD Painter (1905-1958)
STAPP, RAY VERYL Painter, Printmaker (1913-2000)
STARK, GEORGE KING Educator, Sculptor (1923-1992)
STARK, JACK GAGE Painter (1882-1950)
STARKWEATHER, WILLIAM E B Painter (1878-1969)
STARRS, MILDRED Painter
STARS, WILLIAM KENNETH Educator, Museum Director (1921-1985)
STAUFFER, EDNA PENNYPACKER Painter (1887-1956)
STAUFFER, RICHARD L Sculptor, Educator (1932-2005)
STAVENITZ, ALEXANDER RAQUL Etcher (1901-1960)
STEA, CESARE Sculptor (1893-1960)
STEAD, REXEORD ARTHUR Administrator, Historian (1923-)
STEARNS, ROBERT Curator, Administrator (1947-2014)
STECHER, RUTH (RUSTY) L Painter, Instructor (1924-2008)
STECHOW, WOLFGANG Art Historian (1896-1975)
STECKEL, ANITA Collage Artist, Painter (-2012)
STEDMAN, WILFRED HENRY Sculptor (1882-1950)
STEEGMULLER, BEATRICE STEIN Painter (-1961)
STEENE, WILLIAM Painter (1888-1965)
STEFAN, ROSS Painter (1934-1999)
STEG, JAMES LOUIS Printmaker, Sculptor (-2002)
STEGEMAN, CHARLES Painter, Educator (1924-)
STEICHEN, EDWARD Photographer (1879-1979)
STEIG, WILLIAM Cartoonist, Sculptor (1907-2003)
STEIGER, FREDERIC Painter, Instructor (-1990)
STEIN, ROGER BREED Historian, Educator (1932-2010)
STEIN, RONALD JAY Painter, Sculptor (1930-2000)
STEINBERG, LEO Educator, Historian (1920-2011)
STEINBERG, MRS MILTON (EDITH) Art Director (1910-1970)
STEINBERG, RUBIN Collage Artist, Painter (1934-)
STEINBERG, SAUL Cartoonist (1914-1999)
STEINER, JEFFREY JOSEF Administrator, Collector (1937-2008)
STEINER, RALPH Photographer (1899-1986)
STEINITZ, KATE TRAUMAN Writer, Historian (1893-)
STEINMETZ, GRACE ERNST TITUS Painter (1911-2004)
STELL, H KENYON Printmaker, Historian (1910-1990)
STEPHANY, JAROMIR Photographer, Educator (1930-2010)
STEPPAT, LEO LUDWIG Sculptor, Educator (1910-1964)
STERMER, DUGALD ROBERT Illustrator, Writer (1936-2011)
STERN, ARTHUR LEWIS (MR) Collector (1911-)
STERN, ARTHUR LEWIS (MRS) Collector (1913-)
STERN, HAROLD PHILLIP Museum Director, Writer (1922-1977)
STERN, JAN PETER Sculpture (1926-2004)
STERNBERG, HARRY Graphic Artist, Painter (1904-2001)
STERNBERG, PAUL Collector (1917-2004)
STERNBERG, PAUL EDWARD, SR Curator, Consultant (1934-2003)
STERNE, HEDDA Painter (1916-2011)
STERNE, MAURICE Painter (1878-1957)
STERRETT, CLIFF Cartoonist (1883-1964)
STEVENS, EDWARD JOHN JR Painter, Director (1923-1988)
STEVENS, LAWRENCE TENNY Sculptor, Educator (1896-1972)
STEVENS, WALTER HOLLIS Painter, Educator (1927-1980)
STEVENS, WILLIAM ANSEL Painter, Cartoonist (1919-)

STEVENSON, ABROCKIE Painter, Educator (1919-2009)
STEVENSON, BEULAH Painter (-1965)
STEVENSON, RUTH CARTER Collector, Patron (1923-2013)
STEWARD, DONN HORATIO Printmaker, Publisher (1921-1986)
STEWARD, JARVIS ANTHONY Educator, Painter (1914-1981)
STEWART, J(OHN) DOUGLAS Historian (1934-2008)
STEWART, JACK Painter, Educator (1926-)
STIEGELMEYER, NORMAN EARL Painter, Sculptor (1937-)
STILES, HELEN Painter, Printmaker (-1992)
STILL, CLYFFORD Painter (1904-1981)
STILLMAN, GEORGE Painter (1921-)
STILWELL, WILBUR MOORE Educator, Writer (1908-1974)
STITES, RAYMOND SOMMERS Historian, Writer (1899-1974)
STOESSEL, HENRY KURT Painter, Designer (1909-)
STOEVEKEN, ANTHONY CHARLES Printmaker, Educator (1938-)
STOFFA, MICHAEL Instructor, Painter (-2001)
STOIANOVICH, MARCELLE Painter, Printmaker (-2015)
STONE, ANNA B Painter (1874-1949)
STONE, BEATRICE Sculptor (1900-1962)
STONE, EDWARD DURELL Architect (1902-1978)
STONE, FRED J Art Dealer, Consultant (1919-2003)
STONEHILL, MARY (MRS GEORGE) Painter (1900-1951)
STOOPS, HERBERT M Illustrator (1887-1948)
STORM, MARK (KENNEDY) Painter, Sculptor (1911-2002)
STORRS, JOHN Sculptor (1885-1956)
STORY, WILLIAM EASTON Painter, Museum Director (1925-1998)
STOUMEN, LOU Filmmaker, Photographer (1916-1991)
STOUT, FRANK J Painter, Sculptor (1926-)
STOUT, GEORGE LESLIE Consultant (1897-1978)
STRALEM, DONALD S Collector, Patron (1903-1976)
STRATER, HENRY Painter (1896-1987)
STRATTON, DOROTHY Painter, Printmaker (1908-)
STRAUSER, STERLING BOYD Painter (1907-)
STRAUSS, WALTER LEOPOLD Historian, Publisher (1932-1988)
STRAUTMANIS, EDVINS Painter, Sculptor (1933-1992)
STRICKLAND, THOMAS J Painter (1932-1999)
STRIDER, MARJORIE VIRGINIA Sculptor, Painter (-2014)
STRINGER, MARY EVELYN Educator, Art Historian (1921-2005)
STRISIK, PAUL Painter (1918-1998)
STROESSNER, ROBERT JOSEPH Curator, Historian (1942-1991)
STROSAHL, WILLIAM Painter (1910-2002)
STROTHMANN, FRED Illustrator (1880-1958)
STRUNK, HERBERT JULOAN Sculptor (1891-)
STUART, DAVID Dealer (-1984)
STUBBLEDINE, JAMES HARVEY Historian (1920-1987)
STUIDA, WILLIAM Art Authority (1877-1959)
STULL, CUNNINGHAM, JEAN HIMROD Painter (1929-)
STUMP, M PAMELA Sculptor (1928-2007)
STURTEVANT, ELAINE Video Artist (1930-2014)
STYKA, ADAM Painter (1890-1959)
STYLES, GEORGE WILLIAM Painter (1887-1949)
SUGARMAN, GEORGE Sculptor, Painter (1912-1999)
SULLINS, ROBERT M Painter (1926-1991)
SULLIVAN, BILL Painter, Printmaker (1942-)
SULTAN, LARRY A Photographer, Educator (1946-2009)
SUMMY, ANNE TUNIS Painter, Printmaker (1912-1986)
SUNDIN, ADELAIDE TOOMBS Ceramist, Sculptor (1915-2010)
SURREY, MILT Painter (1922-2004)
SURREY, PHILIP HENRY Painter (1910-1990)
SUSSMAN, ARTHUR Painter (1927-2008)
SUSSMAN, RICHARD N Painter, Graphic Artist (1909-1971)
SUSSMAN, WENDY Painter (1949-2001)
SUTHERLAND, SANDY Painter (1902-)
SUTTON, GEORGE MIKSCH Painter, Illustrator (1898-1982)
SUTTON, RUTH HAVILAND Painter (1898-1960)
SVENDSEN, LOUISE AVERILL Curator (1915-1994)
SVERDLOVE, ZOLITA Painter, Printmaker (1936-)
SVOBODA, VINCENT A Painter (1877-1961)
SWAN, BARBARA Painter (1922-)
SWAN, BRADFORD F Art Critic, Painter (1907-1976)
SWANN, ERWIN Collector, Patron (1906-1973)
SWARTBURG, B ROBERT Architect (1895-1975)
SWARTZ, PHILIP SCOTT Painter, Collector (1936-1990)
SWARZENSKI, GEORG Research Fellow (1876-1957)
SWAY, ALBERT Painter, Etcher (1913-2003)
SWAZO, (PATRICK SWAZO HINDS) Painter, Illustrator (1924-1974)
SWENEY, FRED Illustrator, Painter (1912-1995)
SWENSON, HOWARD WILLIAM Sculptor (1901-1960)
SWIGGETT, JEAN DONALD Graphic Artist, Painter (1910-)
SWINDELL, BERTHA Painter (1874-1951)
SWINNERTON, EDNA HUESTIS Miniature Painter (-1964)
SWINNERTON, JAMES Cartoonist, Painter (1875-1974)
SYLVESTER, LUCILLE Painter, Writer (1909-)
SYLVESTRE, GUY Critic, Writer (1918-)
SZABO, STEPHEN LEE Photographer (1940-2000)
SZABO, ZOLTAN Painter, Writer (1928-2003)
SZANTO, LOUIS P Painter (1889-1965)
SZARKOWSKI, T(HADDEUS) JOHN Administrator (1925-2007)
SZASZ, FRANK V Painter, Printmaker (1925-1995)
SZYK, ARTHUR Illustrator (1894-1951)
TAFEL, EDGAR Architect (1912-2011)
TAGGART, WILLIAM JOHN Painter, Sculptor (1940-2007)
TAIT, KATHARINE LAMB Painter, Designer (1895-1981)
TAKACH, MARY H Museum Director, Historian (1932-1997)
TAKEMOTO, HENRY TADAAKI Craftsman, Sculptor (1930-2015)
TAKIS, NICHOLAS Painter (1903-1965)
TALBOT, JAROLD DEAN Painter, Director (1907-1997)
TALBOT, WILLIAM (H M) Kinetic Artist, Sculptor (1918-1980)
TAM, REUBEN Painter, Poet (1916-1992)
TAMAYO, RUFINO Painter (1899-1991)
TAMOTZU, CHUZO Artist
TANGUY, YVES Painter (1900-1955)
TANNER, HENRY OSSAWA Painter (1859-1937)
TANNER, WARREN Painter, Administrator (1942-)
TAPER, GERI Painter, Environmental Artist (1929-2006)
TAPIES, ANTONI Painter, Sculptor (1923-2012)
TARDO, RODULFO Sculptor, Educator (1919-1998)

TARNOPOL, GREGOIRE Painter, Collector (1891-1979)
TASCONA, ANTONIO TONY Painter, Printmaker (1926-2006)
TATISTCHEFF, PETER ALEXIS Dealer, Gallery Director (1938-)
TATTI, BENEDICT MICHAEL Sculptor, Painter (1917-1993)
TAUBES, FREDERIC Painter, Writer (1900-1981)
TAUCH, WALDINE AMANDA Sculptor, Collector (1892-1986)
TAWNEY, LENORE Weaver, Assemblage Artist (-2007)
TAYLOR, AL C Sculptor, Printmaker (1948-1999)
TAYLOR, ANNA HEYWARD Painter (1879-1956)
TAYLOR, DAVIDSON Director (1907-1979)
TAYLOR, EMILY (MRS J MADISON TAYLOR) Miniature Painter (1860-1952)
TAYLOR, FRANCIS HENRY Museum Director (1903-1857)
TAYLOR, FREDERICK BOURCHIER Painter, Sculptor (1906-)
TAYLOR, GAGE Painter, Illustrator (1942-2000)
TAYLOR, HARRY GEORGE Printmaker (1918-2002)
TAYLOR, HUGH HOLLOWAY Historian, Educator (1941-2000)
TAYLOR, JOHN (WILLIAMS) Painter, Printmaker (1897-1983)
TAYLOR, JOHN CE Painter, Educator (1902-1985)
TAYLOR, JOHN LLOYD Director, Consultant (1935-)
TAYLOR, JOSHUA CHARLES Museum Director, Historian (1917-1981)
TAYLOR, LISA Museums Director (1933-1991)
TAYLOR, PAUL Writer, Critic (1958-1992)
TAYLOR, PRENTISS (HOTTEL) Painter, Lithographer (1907-1991)
TAYLOR, RENE CLAUDE Museum Director, Historian (1916-1997)
TEAGUE, DONALD Painter (1897-1991)
TEAGUE, WALTER DORWIN Designer (1884-1960)
TEE-VAN, HELEN DAMROSCH Painter, Illustrator (1893-1976)
TEFET, CHARLES EUGENE Sculptor (1874-)
TEICHMAN, SABINA Painter, Sculptor (-1983)
TEILHET-FISK, JEHANNE HILDEGARDE Historian, Educator (1939-)
TELLER, JANE (SIMON) Sculptor
TEMPLETON, ROBERT CLARK Painter (1929-1991)
TENGGREN, GUSTAV ADOLF Painter (1896-1970)
TEPPER, NATALIE ARRAS Painter (1895-1950)
TERRIS, ALBERT Sculptor, Educator (1916-)
TERRY, DUNCAN NILES Stained Glass Artist, Craftsman (1909-1989)
TERRY, HILDA Cartoonist, Writer (1914-2006)
TETHEROW, MICHAEL Painter (1942-2007)
TETTLETON, ROBERT LYNN Painter, Educator (1929-2013)
THAL, SAMUEL Etcher (1903-)
THALACKER, DONALD WILLIAM Administrator, Architect (1939-1987)
THEODORE, ION PAN Sculptor, Instructor (-1997)
THIELEN, GREG GLEN Curator (1940-1994)
THOLLANDER, EARL Illustrator, Graphic Artist (1922-2001)
THOMAS, ALMA WOODSEY Painter (1891-1978)
THOMAS, BYRON Painter (1902-1978)
THOMAS, H REYNOLDS Painter, Illustrator (1927-1991)
THOMAS, HELEN (DOANE) Writer, Painter (-2003)
THOMAS, JOHN Painter, Printmaker (1927-2001)
THOMAS, MARY LEATH Painter (1905-1959)
THOMAS, ROBERT CHESTER Sculptor (1924-1987)
THOMAS, STEFFEN WOLFGANG Sculptor, Painter (1906-1990)
THOMAS, THALIA ANN MARIE Painter, Educator (1935-2002)
THOMAS, YVONNE Painter (-2009)
THOMASOS, DENYSE Painter, Sculptor (1964-)
THOMPSON, BOB Painter (-1966)
THOMPSON, ERNEST THORNE Educator, Painter (-1992)
THOMPSON, FREDERICK Painter (1904-1956)
THOMPSON, GEORGE LOUIS Designer (1913-1981)
THOMPSON, JULIET H Painter (-1956)
THOMPSON, KENNETH WEBSTER Illustrator, Painter (1907-)
THOMPSON, LESLIE P Painter (1880-1963)
THOMPSON, RICHARD EARL SR Painter (1914-1991)
THOMPSON, WALTER WHITCOMB Painter (1892-1948)
THOMSON, CARL L Painter, Art Appraiser (1913-)
THORP, EARL NORWELL Sculptor (-1951)
THORPE, HILDA (SHAPIRO) Painter, Sculptor (1919-2000)
THURLOW, FEARN CUTLER Curator (1924-1982)
THWAITES, CHARLES WINSTANLEY Painter, Muralist (1904-2002)
TIBBS, THURLOW EVANS JR Writer, Collector (-1997)
TILLIM, SIDNEY Painter, Instructor (1925-2001)
TILLMAN, PATRICIA ANN Sculptor (-2012)
TISCHLER, VICTOR Painter, Lithographer (1890-1951)
TISHMAN, JACK A Collector (-1966)
TOBEY, ALTON S Painter, Sculptor (1914-2005)
TOBEY, MARK Painter (1890-1976)
TOBIAS, JULIUS Sculptor, Painter (1915-1999)
TOBIAS, THOMAS J Collector, Museum Trustee (1906-1970)
TOFEL, JENNINGS Painter (1892-1959)
TOIGO, DANIEL JOSEPH Painter (1912-1992)
TOLGESY, VICTOR Sculptor, Writer (1928-1980)
TOLLIVER, MOSE Painter (1915-)
TOMLIN, BRADLEY WALKER Painter (1899-1953)
TOMPKINS, ALAN Painter, Educator (1907-2008)
TONEY, ANTHONY Painter, Educator (1913-2004)
TOO, OSMA GALLINGER Writer, Weaver (-1983)
TOOKER, GEORGE Painter, Printmaker (1920-2011)
TOPCHEVSKY, MORRIS Painter, Etcher (1899-)
TOPPING, JAMES Painter (1879-1949)
TORBERT, DONALD ROBERT Educator, Historian (1910-1985)
TORRES, HORACIO Painter (1924-1976)
TORREY, ELLA KING Administrator (1957-)
TOVISH, HAROLD Sculptor (1921-)
TOWN, HAROLD BARLING Painter, Writer (1924-1990)
TOWNLEY, HUGH Sculptor, Printmaker (1923-2008)
TOWNSEND, (ALVIN) NEAL Ceramist, Painter (1934-2002)
TOWNSEND, LEE Painter (1895-1965)
TRACY, BERRY BRYSON Curator, Administrator (1933-1984)
TRANK, LYNN EDGAR Educator, Painter (1918-2004)
TRAPHAGEN, ETHEL Designer (1882-1963)
TRAPIER, PIERRE PINCKNEY ALSTON Painter (1897-1957)
TRAPP, FRANK ANDERSON Museum Director, Historian (1922-2005)

TRAUERMAN, MARGY ANN Painter, Instructor
TRAVERS, GWYNETH MABEL Printmaker (1911-1982)
TRAVIS, KATHRYNE HAIL Painter (1894-1972)
TRAVIS, OLIN (HERMAN) Painter (1888-1975)
TREASTER, RICHARD A Painter, Educator (1932-2002)
TREES, CLYDE C Numismatist (1885-1960)
TREIMAN, JOYCE WAHL Painter, Sculptor (1922-1991)
TRIMM, ADON Painter (1895-1959)
TROCHE, E GUNTER Museum Director (1909-1971)
TROFON, HARRIETTE Painter, Sculptor
TROVA, ERNEST TINO Sculptor, Painter (1927-2009)
TRUBNER, HENRY Curator, Museologist (1920-1999)
TRUEX, VAN DAY Painter, Designer (1904-)
TSCHACBASOV, NAHUM Painter, Printmaker (1899-1984)
TSEU, ROSITA HSU Administrator, Instructor (1916-2003)
TSUTAKAWA, GEORGE Sculptor, Painter (1910-1997)
TUBBY, JOSIAH THOMAS Painter (1875-1958)
TUCKER, CHARLES CLEMENT Painter (1913-1996)
TUCKER, CURTIS (DEE) Ceramist, Lecturer (1938-1992)
TUCKER, JAMES EWING Curator, Painter (1930-2010)
TUCKER, MARCIA Museum Director, Curator (1940-)
TUDOR, ROSAMOND Painter, Etcher (1878-1949)
TUFTS, ELEANOR M Historian, Educator (-1991)
TULLSEN, REX Painter, Instructor (1907-1991)
TULVING, RUTH Painter, Printmaker (-2012)
TUNIS, EDWIN Writer, Illustrator (1897-1973)
TUPPER, ALEXANDER GARFIELD Painter
TURANO, DON Sculptor, Medalist (1930-2002)
TURNBULL, GRACE HJLL Sculptor, Painter (1880-1976)
TURNBULL, JAMES B Painter (1906-1976)
TURNER SR, JAMES THOMAS Sculptor, Painter (1933-2001)
TURNER, A RICHARD Historian, Educator (1932-2011)
TURNER, HARRIET FRENCH Painter (-1967)
TURNER, HERBERT B Painter (1925-2010)
TURNER, JANET E Printmaker, Educator (1914-1988)
TURNER, JOSEPH Patron (1892-1973)
TURNER, RAYMOND Sculptor (1903-1985)
TURNER, ROBERT CHAPMAN Ceramist, Educator (1913-2005)
TURNER, THEODORE ROY Educator, Painter (1922-2002)
TWIGGS, RUSSELL GOULD Painter (1898-1991)
TWIGG-SMITH, LAILA Collector (1944-)
TWOMBLY, CY Painter (1928-2011)
TWORKOV, JACK Painter (1900-1982)
TYNG, ANNE GRISWOLD Architect (1920-2011)
TYSON, MARY (MRS KENNETH THOMPSON) Painter (1909-2001)
TYTELL, LOUIS Painter (1913-2001)
UCELLO, VINCENZA AGATHA Painter, Director (-2004)
UCHIMA, ANSEI Printmaker, Painter (1921-2000)
UCHIMA, TOSHIKO Painter, Assemblage Artist (1918-2000)
UGLOW, ALAN Painter (1941-2011)
UHLER, RUTH PERSHING Painter (1898-)
UHRMAN, CELIA Painter, Writer (1927-1998)
UHRMAN, ESTHER Painter, Writer (1921-2004)
ULLMAN, HAROLD P Collector (1899-)
ULP, CLIFFORD McCORMICK Painter (1885-1957)
ULREOCH, NURA WOODSON Painter (-1950)
UNDERWOOD, ELISABETH (KENDALL) Artist (1896-1976)
UNDERWOOD, EVELYN NOTMAN Painter (1898-1983)
UNGER, MARY ANN Sculptor (1945-1999)
UNWIN, NORA SPICER Illustrator, Printmaker (-1982)
UPJOHN, EVERARD MILLER Historian (1903-1978)
URBACH, LES Sculptor (-1997)
URBAITIS, ELENA Painter, Sculptor (-2006)
URBAN, ALBERT Painter (1909-1959)
URBAN, REVA Painter, Sculptor (1925-1987)
USHER, DAVID Publisher, Art Dealer (1939-1997)
USHER, ELIZABETH REUTER (MRS WILLIAM ARTHUR SCAR) Librarian, Lecturer (-2009)
USHER, RUBY WALKER Painter (1889-1957)
USUI, KIICHI Curator (1931-2001)
VACCARO, NICK DANTE Educator, Painter (1931-2002)
VACCARO, PATRICK FRANK Printmaker, Painter
VAIL, LAURENCE Collegiate (1857-1968)
VALENCIA, CESAR Painter, Muralist (1918-2007)
VALENSTEIN, ALICE Painter, Collector (1904-2002)
VALENTINER, WILLIAM REINHOLD Museum Director (1880-1958)
VALINSKI, DENNIS JOHN Sculptor, Lecturer (1946-1979)
VALTMAN, EDMUND Cartoonist, Editor (1914-2005)
VAN BRUGGEN, COOSJE Artist, Author (1942-2009)
VAN BUREN, RAEBURN Illustrator, Cartoonist (1891-1987)
VAN DER BEEK, EDWARD STANLEY Filmmaker, Video Artist (1927-1984)
VAN DER MARCK, JAN Historian, Critic (1929-2010)
VAN DER POOL, JAMES GROTE Historian (1903-1979)
VAN DER ROHE, LUDWIG M Architect (-1969)
VAN DER VOORT, AMANDA VENELIA Painter (-1980)
VAN DOMMELEN, DAVID B Writer, Fiber Artist (1929-2010)
VAN DOREN, HAROLD LIVINGSTON Designer (1896-1957)
VAN DRESSER, WILLIAM Portrait Painter (1871-1950)
VAN HOESEN, BETH Printmaker (1926-2010)
VAN HOOK, DAVID H Painter, Administrator (1923-1986)
VAN LEER, W LEICESTER Collector (1905-)
VAN OORDT, PETER Painter, Graphic Artist (1903-1988)
VAN RIPER, PETER Printmaker, Conceptual Artist (1942-)
VAN ROSEN, ROBERT E Industrial Designer (1904-1966)
VAN SOELEN, THEODORE Painter (1880-1964)
VAN TONGEREN, HERK Sculptor (1943-1988)
VAN WOLF, HENRY Sculptor (1898-1982)
VANDER SLUIS, GEORGE J Painter, Educator (1915-1984)
VANN, LOLI (MRS LILIAN VAN YOUNG) Painter (1913-1999)
VARGA, FERENC Sculptor (-1989)
VARGA, MARGIT Painter, Writer (1908-2005)
VARGIS, POLYGNOTIS Sculptor (1894-1965)
VARGO, JOHN Educator, Painter (1929-)
VARLEY, FREDERICK H Painter (-1969)
VASILIEFF, NICHOLAS Painter (1892-1970)
VASILS, ALBERT Painter, Illustrator (1915-)
VAWTER, MARY H MURRAY Painter (1871-)
VELSEY, SETH M Sculptor (1903-1967)
VERNER, ELIZABETH O'NEILL Etcher, Writer (1883-1979)
VERTES, MARCEL Painter (1895-1961)
VERZYL, KENNETH H Dealer, Draftsman (1922-1987)
VEVERS, TONY Assemblage Artist, Educator (1926-2008)
VIAN, ORFEO Educator, Printmaker (1924-1989)
VICENTE, ESTEBAN Painter (1903-2001)
VICKERS, RUSS(ELL GERON) Painter, Conceptual Artist (1923-1997)
VICKREY, ROBERT REMSEN Painter (1926-2011)

VIESULAS, ROMAS Printmaker, Educator (1918-)
VIGIL, VELOY JOSEPH Painter, Printmaker (1931-1997)
VILLA, CARLOS Painter (1936-2013)
VILLON, VLADIMAR Exhibition Director (1905-1976)
VOELKER, ELIZABETH Painter, Collage Artist (1931-)
VOGEL, EDWIN CHESTER Collector (1883-1973)
VOLKMAR, LEON Ceramist (1879-1959)
VOLLMER, RUTH Sculptor (-1982)
VON BOTHMER, DIETRICH FELIX Curator, Educator (1918-2009)
VON DER LANCKEN, FRANK Painter (1872-1950)
VON FUEHRER, OTTMAR F Painter (-1967)
VON JOST, ALEXANDER Painter (1889-1968)
VON SCHLEGELL, DAVID Sculptor (1920-1992)
VON WEISE, WENDA FRAKER Printmaker, Tapestry Artist (1941-)
VON WICHT, JOHN Painter, Graphic Designer (1888-1970)
VON WIEGAND, CHARMION Painter, Writer (1898-1993)
VORIS, MARK Educator, Painter (1907- 974)
VORWERK, E CHARLSIE Painter, Illustrator (1934-2003)
VOSE, ROBERT C Art Dealer (1873-1965)
VOULKOS, PETER Sculptor, Educator (1924-2002)
VUILLEMENOT FRED A Designer, Sculptor (1890-1952)
VYTLACIL, VACLAV Painter, Educator (1892-)
WAALAND, JAMES BREARLEY, II Dealer, Gallery Director (1953-2005)
WAANO-GANO, JOE Painter, Lecturer (1906-1982)
WACHS, ETHEL Educator, Collector (1923-2011)
WACHSTETER, GEORGE Illustrator (1911-2004)
WADDELL, RICHARD H Art Dealer (-1974)
WADDINGHAM, JOHN ALFRED Painter, Printmaker (1915-2002)
WAGNER, BLANCHE COLLET Lecturer (1873-)
WAGNER, GLADYS NOBLE Painter, Sculptor (1907-)
WAGNER, GORDON PARSONS Assemblage Artist, Environmental Artist (1915-1987)
WAGNER, RICHARD ELLIS Painter (1923-2009)
WAITZKIN, STELLA Sculptor, Painter (-2004)
WALCH, JOHN LEO Painter, Sculptor (1918-2003)
WALD, CAROL Painter (1935-2000)
WALD, PALMER B Administrator (1930-1988)
WALDRON, JAMES MACKEILAR Painter (1909-1974)
WALINSKA, ANNA Painter, Lecturer (1916-1997)
WALKER, EVERETT Educator (-1968)
WALKER, HENRY BABCOCK JR Collector (1885-1966)
WALKER, HERSCHEL CAREY Collector
WALKER, HUDSON D Collector, Art Administrator (1907-1976)
WALKER, JAMES ADAMS Painter, Printmaker (1921-1987)
WALKER, LYDIA LE BARON Designer (1869-1958)
WALKEY, FREDERICK P Consultant (1922-2001)
WALKOWITZ, ABRAHAM Painter (1890-1965)
WALL, MARGARET V Museum Director (1895-1958)
WALL, RALPH ALAN Painter (1932-2009)
WALLACE, FREDERICK E Painter (1893-1958)
WALLACE, JOHN Painter (1929-)
WALLEEN, HANS AXEL Illustrator (1902-1978)
WALLEN, BURR Historian, Curator (1941-)
WALMSLEY, WILLIAM AUBREY Printmaker, Collector (1923-2003)
WALTER, MARTHA Painter (1875-1976)
WALTER, WILLIAM F Artist (1904-1977)
WALTMANN, HARRY FRANKLIN Painter (1871-1951)
WALTON, HARRY A JR Collector (1918-)
WANDS, ALFRED JAMES Painter, Graphic Artist (1904-1998)
WARD, EVELYN SVEC Tapestry Artist, Collage Artist (-1989)
WARD, LAURISTON Curator (1883-1960)
WARD, LYND (KENDALL) Illustrator, Writer (1905-1985)
WARD, PHILLIP A Ceramist, Educator (1927-)
WARD, WILLIAM EDWARD Designer, Painter (1922-2004)
WARDELL, ALLEN Museum Director, Consultant (1935-1999)
WARDER, WILLIAM Painter, Writer
WARING, LAURA WHEELER Portrait Painter (-1949)
WARK, ROBERT RODGER Administrator, Historian (1924-2007)
WARNEKE, HEINZ Sculptor (1895-1983)
WARNER, EVERETT LONGLEY Painter (1877-1963)
WARNER, JO Painter (1931-1999)
WARREN, CALLIE Administrator (-1984)
WARREN, FERDINAND EARL Painter, Administrator (1899-1981)
WARREN, L D Cartoonist (1906-1992)
WARREN, MRS GEORGE HENRY Collector (1897-1976)
WARSHAW, HOWARD Painter (1920-)
WARSHAW, LARRY Painter, Photographer (1936-)
WARSHAWSKY, ABEL GEORGE Painter (1884-1962)
WARSINSKE, NORMAN GEORGE Sculptor, Painter (1929-2007)
WASEY, JANE Sculptor (1912-)
WASHBURN, CADWALLADER Painter (1866-1965)
WASHBURN, GORDON BAILEY Museum Director (1904-)
WASHBURN, LOUESE B Painter (1875-1959)
WASSERMAN, JACK Educator (1921-1980)
WATERHOUSE, CHARLES Illustrator, Painter (1924-2013)
WATERMAN, DONALD CALVIN Designer, Educator (1928-1979)
WATERS, GEORGE FITE Sculptor (1894-1961)
WATERS, TERRANCE Architect (1920-2004)
WATKINS, FRANKLIN CHENAULT Painter (1894-1972)
WATROUS, JAMES SCALES Painter, Historian (1908-1999)
WATSON, DARLIENE KEENEY Painter (1929-)
WATSON, HILDEGARDE LASELL Artist, Patron (-1976)
WATTS, DOROTHY BURT (TROUT) Artist (1892-1977)
WAUGH, COULTON Painter, Writer (1886-1973)
WAUGH, SIDNEY B Sculptor (1904-1963)
WAYNE, JUNE Painter, Printmaker (1918-2011)
WEALE, MARY JO Painter, Educator (1924-)
WEAVER, JOHN BARNEY Sculptor (1920-2012)
WEBB, AILEEN OSBORN Painter, Enamelist (1892-1979)
WEBB, TODD Photographer, Historian (1905-2000)
WEBER, ALBERT JACOB Painter, Educator (1919-2004)
WEBER, FREDERICK THEODORE Painter (1883-1956)
WEBER, HUGO Painter (1918-1971)
WEBER, JANET RUTH Painter (1925-)
WEBER, MAX Painter, Sculptor (1881-1961)
WEBER, SYBILLA MITTELL Painter (1892-1957)
WEBSTER, H T Cartoonist (1885-1952)
WEBSTER, STOKELY Painter, Printmaker (1912-2002)
WECHSIER, HERMAN J Art Consultant, Writer (1904-1976)
WECHTER, VIVIENNE THAUL Educator, Painter (-2001)
WEDDIGE, EMIL A Printmaker, Painter (1907-2001)

WEDOW, RUDY Sculptor (1906-1965)
WEEBER, GRETCHEN Painter
WEEKS, JAMES (DARRELL NORTHRUP) Painter, Art Dealer (1922-1998)
WEEKS, LEO ROSCO Painter, Illustrator (1903-1977)
WEEMS, KATHERINE LANE Sculptor (1899-)
WEHR, PAUL ADAM Illustrator, Designer (1914-1973)
WEHR, WESLEY CONRAD Painter, Paleontologist (1929-2004)
WEIDENAAR, REYNOLD HENRY Etcher, Painter (1915-1985)
WEIDNER, ROSWELL THEODORE Painter, Instructor (1911-1999)
WEIHS, ERIKA Painter, Illustrator-Children's Books (1917-)
WEIL, LISL Illustrator, Writer
WEIL-GARRIS BRANDT, KATHLEEN Historian, Educator
WEILL, ERNA Sculptor, Instructor (1904-1996)
WEIN, ALBERT W Sculptor, Painter (1915-1991)
WEINBERG, BELLA Painter, Writer (1912-2002)
WEINBERG, LOUIS Sculptor (1918-)
WEINBERGER, MARTIN Educator, Scholar (-1965)
WEINER, ABE Painter, Instructor (1917-1993)
WEINER, TED Collector, Patron (1911-1979)
WEINGAERTNER, HANS Painter (1896-1970)
WEINHARDT, CARL Museum Director, Historian (1922-)
WEINMAN, ADOLPH ALEXANDER Sculptor (1870-1952)
WEINMAN, ROBERT ALEXANDER Sculptor (1915-2003)
WEISBECKER, CLEMENT Painter
WEISEL, DEBORAH DELP Painter (-1951)
WEISS, DAVID Sculptor, Photographer, Installation Sculptor (1946-2012)
WEISS, HARVEY Sculptor, Writer (1922-)
WEISSBUCH, OSCAR Painter (-1948)
WEITZMANN, KURT Educator, Historian (1904-1993)
WELCH, JAMES WYMORE Painter, Muralist (1928-2008)
WELCH, LIVINGSTON Sculptor, Painter (1901-1976)
WELCH, MABEL R Painter (-1959)
WELCH, ROBERT G Collector (1915-)
WELCH, STUART CARY Curator, Historian (1928-)
WELLBORN, J(EANETTE) D(ARLEEN) Painter (1943-)
WELLER, ALLEN STUART Educator, Historian (1907-1997)
WELLER, JOHN SIDNEY Painter, Printmaker (1928-1981)
WELLINGTON, DUKE Painter (1896-1987)
WELLIVER, NEIL G Painter (1929-2005)
WELLS, CADY Painter (1904-1954)
WELLS, MAC Painter, Educator (1925-2009)
WELLS, THOMAS (WINCHESTER) Painter (1916-2004)
WELPOTT, JACK WARREN Photographer, Educator (1923-)
WENGENROTH, STOW Lithographer (1906-1978)
WENGER, MURIEL Dealer, Collector (1915-1989)
WENLEY, ARCHIBALD GIBSON Museum Director (1898-1962)
WENSLEY, WILLIAM CHARLES Painter, Instructor (-1984)
WENTWORTH, MURRAY JACKSON Painter, Instructor (1927-2008)
WERNER, (CHARLES GEORGE) Cartoonist (1909-1997)
WERNER, ALFRED Critic, Writer (1911-1979)
WERNER, DONALD (LEWIS) Collage Artist, Painter (1929-2010)
WERNER, NAT Sculptor (1907-1991)
WERTHEIM, MRS MAURICE Collector (-1974)
WESCHLER, ANITA Sculptor, Painter
WESCOTT, PAUL Painter (1904-1970)
WESSELS, GLENN ANTHONY Painter (1895-1982)
WEST, PENNERTON Painter (-1965)
WESTERMANN, HORACE CLIFFORD Sculptor, Painter (1922-1981)
WESTON, HAROLD Painter (1894-1972)
WETHEY, HAROLD EDWIN Historian (1902-1984)
WETMORE, GORDON (STANLEY GORDON) Painter, Writer (1938-2011)
WHARTON, CAROL FORBES (MRS JAMES P) Painter (1907-1958)
WHARTON, JAMES PEARCE Educator (1893-1963)
WHEELER, ORSON SHOREY Sculptor, Lecturer (1902-)
WHEELOCK, WARREN F Painter (1880-1960)
WHIPPLE, BARBARA Graphic Artist, Gallery Director (-1989)
WHITAKER, FREDERIC Painter (1891-1980)
WHITE, ALBERT Dealer, Collector (-1991)
WHITE, CHARLES WILBERT Painter, Educator (1918-1979)
WHITE, EUGENE B Painter (-1966)
WHITE, MINOR Photographer (1908-1976)
WHITE, PHILIP BUTLER Painter, Collector (1935-2001)
WHITE, RALPH Painter, Educator
WHITE, ROBERT (WINTHROP) Sculptor, Educator (1921-2002)
WHITE, WALTER L Painter (-1963)
WHITEHILL, WALTER MUIR Writer, Historian (1905-1978)
WHITEHOUSE, DAVID BRYN Historian (1941-2013)
WHITENER, PAUL A W Museum Director (1911-1959)
WHITNEY, CHARLES E Interior Designer, Publisher (1903-1977)
WHITNEY, EDGAR ALBERT Painter, Instructor (1891-)
WHITNEY, ISABEL LYDIA Painter (-1962)
WHITNEY, JOHN HAY Administrator, Collector (1904-1982)
WHITNEY, MAYNARD MERLE Sculptor, Educator (1931-2012)
WHITNEY, PHILIP RICHARDSON Painter (1878-)
WHITNEY, WILLIAM KUEBLER Painter, Historian (1921-1985)
WHITTEMORE, HELEN SIMPSON Painter
WHORF, JOHN Painter (1903-1959)
WHYTE, RAYMOND A Painter (1923-2003)
WIBSTROM, EDWARD FREDERICK Sculptor (1903-1989)
WICKISER, RALPH LEWANDA Administrator, Painter (1910-1998)
WICKS, EUGENE CLAUDE Painter, Educator (1931-2005)
WIEGAND, ROBERT Painter (1934-1994)
WIEGHARDT, PAUL Painter, Educator (1897-1969)
WIELAND, JOYCE Painter, Filmmaker (1931-1998)
WIENER, GEORGE Art Dealer
WIENER, PHYLLIS Painter, Sculptor (1921-2013)
WIESENFELD, PAUL Painter (1942-1990)
WIGGINS, BILL Painter (1917-2013)
WIGGINS, GUY C Painter (1883-1962)
WIGGINS, MYRA ALBERT Painter (1869-1956)
WIGGINS, WALTON WRAY Writer, Photographer (1924-1992)
WIGHT, FREDERICK S Painter, Administrator (1902-1986)
WILBUR, LAWRENCE NELSON Painter, Printmaker (1897-1988)
WILCOX, LUCIA Painter
WILCOX, RUTH Librarian (1889-1958)

WILDENHAIN, FRANS Potter (1905-1980)
WILDENSTEIN, FELIX Gallery Director (-1952)
WILDENSTEIN, GEORGES Art Editor (1892-1963)
WILDER, MITCHELL ARMITAGE Administrator (1913-1979)
WILDER, NICHOLAS Artist
WILDMAN, CAROLINE LAX Painter (-1949)
WILE, ANDREW JEFFREY Painter (1949-1982)
WILES, IRVING R Portrait Painter (1861-1948)
WILFORD, LORAN Painter, Educator (1892-1972)
WILFRED, THOMAS Sculptor (1889-1968)
WILKE, HANNAH Sculptor, Instructor (1940-1993)
WILKE, ULFERT S Painter, Administrator (1907-1988)
WILKINSON, JOHN Painter (1913-1973)
WILLARD, FRANK H Cartoonist (1893-1958)
WILLARD, HELEN Curator (-1979)
WILLET, HENRY LEE Craftsman (1899-1983)
WILLETT, JACQUES Painter (1882-1958)
WILLIAMS, EDWARD K Painter (1870-)
WILLIAMS, FREDERIC ALLEN Sculptor (1899-1958)
WILLIAMS, FREDERICK BALLARD Painter (1871-1956)
WILLIAMS, HERMANN WARNER JR Art Administrator, Writer (1908-1975)
WILLIAMS, HIRAM DRAPER Painter (1917-2003)
WILLIAMS, JULIA TOCHIE Painter (1887-1948)
WILLIAMS, KEITH SHAW Painter, Etcher (1905-1951)
WILLIAMS, LEWIS W II Historian, Educator (1918-1990)
WILLIAMS, NEIL Artist
WILLIAMS, WARNER Sculptor, Designer (1903-1982)
WILLIAMS, WAYNE FRANCIS Sculptor (1937-)
WILLIAMS, WHEELER Sculptor (1897-1972)
WILLIAMSON, ADA C Painter (1883-1958)
WILLIAMSON, CLARA McDONALD Painter (-1976)
WILLIAMSON, JASON H Painter (1926-2011)
WILLIS, ELIZABETH BAYLEY, Historian, Collector (-2003)
WILLIS, ROBERT E Painter, Printmaker (1922-)
WILSON, BEN Painter, Lecturer (1913-2001)
WILSON, CHARLES BANKS Painter, Printmaker (1918-2013)
WILSON, EDWARD N (ED) Sculptor, Educator (1925-1997)
WILSON, GEORGE LEWIS Painter (1930-1987)
WILSON, HELEN Sculptor (1884-1974)
WILSON, JANE Painter (1924-2015)
WILSON, JOHN Sculptor, Printmaker (1922-2001)
WILSON, ORME Patron (1885-1966)
WILSON, RICHARD BRIAN Painter (1944-2002)
WILSON, SOL Painter (1896-1974)
WILSON, TOM Cartoonist (1931-2011)
WILTON, ANNA KEENER Painter Educator (1895-)
WILWERS, EDWARD M (1918-2002)
WINCHESTER, ALICE Editor, Writer (1907-)
WINDEKNECHT, MARGARET BLAKE Fiber Artist, Writer (1936-)
WINDELL, VIOLET BRUNER Graphic Artist, Cartoonist (1922-2005)
WINGERT, PAUL STOVER Writer, Art Historian (1900-1974)
WINGERTER, JOHN PARKER Painter (1940-2004)
WINKEL, NINA Sculptor, Lecturer (1905-1990)
WINOGRAND, GARRY Photographer, Lecturer (1928-1984)
WINOKUR, JAMES L Collector, Critic (1922-2009)
WINSLOW, HELEN Painter (1916-)
WINSLOW, RALPH E Architect (1902-1978)
WINSTANLEY, JOHN BREYFOGLE Painter (1874-1947)
WINTER, ANDREW Painter (1892-1958)
WINTER, EZRA Painter (1886-1949)
WINTER, RUTH Painter (1913-2010)
WIRTSCHAFTER, BUD Filmmaker, Instructor (1924-1988)
WISA, LOUIS SR Cartoonist (-1953)
WISE, HOWARD Administrator (1903-1989)
WISE, LOUISE WATERMAN (MRS STEPHENS) Painter (-1947)
WISNOSKY, JOHN G Painter, Educator (1940-2006)
WITAKER, EILEEN MONAGHAN Painter (1911-2005)
WITTEN BORN, GEORGE Collector, Art Dealer (1905-1974)
WITTMACK, EDGAR FRANKLIN Illustrator (1894-1956)
WOELFFER, EMERSON Painter (1914-2003)
WOHLENHAUS, GRACE FORCIER Painter (1919-2010)
WOIDE, ROBERT E Painter, Photographer (1927-)
WOJNAROWICZ, DAVID Painter, Sculptor (1954-1992)
WOLFE, ANN (ANN WOLFE GRAUBARD) Sculptor
WOLFE, MILDRED NUNGESTER Painter, Designer (1912-2009)
WOLFF, ROBERT J Painter, Writer (1905-1978)
WOLFF, WILLIAM H Dealer (1906-1991)
WOLFSON, SIDNEY Painter, Sculptor (1911-1973)
WOLINS, JOSEPH Painter (1915-)
WOLLE, MURIEL SIBELL Painter, Writer (1898-1977)
WONG, JASON Museum Director, Designer (1934-2002)
WONNER, PAUL JOHN Painter (1920-)
WONTERSTEEN, BERNICE MCILHENNY Administrator, Collector (1903-1986)
WOOD, BEATRICE Ceramist, Educator (-1998)
WOOD, JAMES NOWELL Historian, Administrator (1941-2010)
WOOD, MARCIA JOAN Sculptor (1933-2001)
WOOD, ROBERT E Painter, Instructor (1926-1999)
WOODLOCK, ETHELYN HURD Painter (1907-2001)
WOODRUFF, HALE A Painter, Educator (1900-1980)
WOODS, ROOSEVELT (RIP) Painter, Printmaker (1933-2000)
WOODS, SARAH LADD Collector, Patron (1895-1980)
WOODS, WILLIS FRANKLIN Consultant (1920-1988)
WOODSIDE, GORDON WILLIAM Dealer, Collector
WOODWARD, ROBERT STRONG Painter (1885-1957)
WOODWARD, STANLEY Painter (1890-1970)
WOOLF, SAMUEL J Painter (1880-1948)
WORCESTER, EVA Painter (1892-1970)
WORTH, PETER JOHN Sculptor, Historian (1917-)
WORTHAM, HAROLD Painter, Art Consultant (1909-1974)
WORTHMAN, DENYS Cartoonist (1886-1958)
WOSK, MIRIAM Collage Artist, Painter (1947-2010)
WOSTREL, NANCY J Painter, Illustrator (-2012)
WRAY, MARGARET MASLE Painter (-1988)
WRIGHT, BERNARD Painter, Graphic Artist (1938-1999)
WRIGHT, CATHARINE MORRIS Painter, Writer (1899-1988)
WRIGHT, G ALAN Sculptor (1927-)
WRIGHT, GEORGE HAND Etcher, Painter (1872-1951)
WRIGHT, LLOYD Architect (1890-1978)
WRIGHT, MILTON Painter, Educator (1920-2005)
WRIGHT, ROBERT A Cartoonist (1900-1958)
WRIGHT, RUSSEL Designer, Sculptor (1904-1976)
WRIGHT, STANLEY MARC Painter, Instructor (1911-)
WU, LINDA YEE CHAU Sculptor (1919-2004)
WUERPEL, EDMUND HENRY Painter (1886-1958)
WUNDER, RICHARD PAUL Historian, Administrator (1926-2002)

WUNDERLICH, RUDOLF G Dealer (1920-2004)
WURDEMANN, HELEN (BARONESS ELENA GUZZARDO) Administrator, Collector
WURTZBURGER, JANET E C Collector, Patron (1908-)
WYETH, ANDREW NEWELL Painter (1917-2009)
WYETH, HENRIETTE (MRS PETER HURD) Painter (1907-)
WYMAN, WILLIAM Sculptor (1922-1980)
WYNNE, ALBERT GIVENS Painter, Calligrapher (1922-)
XCERON, JEAN Painter (1890-1967)
YAEGER, EDGAR LOUIS Painter, Muralist (1904-1997)
YAFFEE, EDITH WIDING Painter (1895-1961)
YAGHJIAN, EDMUND Painter, Instructor (1903-1997)
YARDE, RICHARD Painter, Educator (1939-2011)
YARDLEY, RICHARD QUINCY Cartoonist (1903-1979)
YEE, CHIANG Painter, Calligrapher (1903-1977)
YERBYSMITH, ERNEST ALFRED Sculptor (-1952)
YOORS, JAN Tapestry Artist, Photographer (1922-1977)
YORK, RICHARD TRAVIS Art Dealer, Gallery Director (1950-2003)
YORK, ROBERT Cartoonist (1919-1975)
YOSHIDA, RAY KAKUO Painter, Educator (1930-2009)
YOSHIMURA, FUMIO Sculptor (1926-2002)
YOST, FRED J Painter (1888-1968)
YOUNG, CHARLES ALEXANDER Painter; Educator (1930-2005)
YOUNG, CHIC (MURAT BERNARD YOUNG) Cartoonist (1901-1973)
YOUNG, CLIFF Painter, Muralist (1905-1985)
YOUNG, JOSEPH LOUIS Sculptor, Muralist (1919-2007)
YOUNG, MAHONRI M Sculptor (1877-1957)
YUNKERS, ADJA Painter, Educator (1900-1983)
ZAAGE, HERMAN H Printmaker, Educator (1927-)
ZACHA, WILLIAM Painter, Sculptor (1920-1998)
ZACKS, SAMUEL JACOB Collector, Patron (1904-1970)
ZALESKI, JEAN Painter, Lecturer (-2010)
ZALLINGER, RUDOLPH FRANZ Painter, Educator (1919-1995)
ZAMMITT, NORMAN Painter, Sculptor (1931-2007)
ZEIDENBERGS, OLAFS Sculptor (1936-2006)
ZEIGLER, LEE WOODWARD Illustrator (1896-1952)
ZEISLER, CLAIRE (BLOCK) Sculptor, Collector (1903-1991)
ZELLERBACH, HAROLD L Patron, Director (1895-1978)
ZERBE, KARL Painter, Educator (1903-1972)
ZILZER, GYULA Printmaker, Painter (1898-1969)
ZIMMER, FRITZ Sculptor
ZIMMER, WILLIAM Critic (-2007)
ZIMMERMAN, FREDERICK A Painter, Instructor (1886-1974)
ZIMMERMAN, KATHLEEN MARIE Collage Artist, Painter (1923-)
ZIOLKOWSKI, KORCZAK Sculptor (1908-1982)
ZOGBAUM, WILFRED Painter (-1965)
ZOGROSSER, CARL Writer (1891-1975)
ZORACH, MARGUERITE T Painter (1887-1968)
ZORACH, WILLIAM Sculptor (1887-1966)
ZOROLI, ANGELO GERARDO Sculptor (1899-1948)
ZOX, LARRY Painter (1937-)
ZUCKER, JACQUES Painter (1900-1981)
ZUCKERMAN, RUTH VICTOR Sculptor, Photographer (1933-)
ZUEHLKE, CLARENCE EDGAR Painter (-1963)
ZUNIGA, FRANCISCO Sculptor, Graphic Artist (1912-1998)
ZWICK, ROSEMARY G Sculptor, Printmaker (1925-1995)